Footsteps In The Dark

Also available by Georgette Heyer

Classic Novels
Black Moth
These Old Shades
Devil's Club

Georgian Classics
Masqueraders
The Convenient Marriage
Faro's Daughter
Powder and Patch

Classic Heroines
Arabella
Venetia
Frederica

Classic Heroes
Sylvester
The Unknown Ajax
False Colours
The Nonesuch

Classic Adventures
Beauvallet
Royal Escape
An Infamous Army
The Spanish Bride

Mystery and Murder Novels
The Talisman Ring
The Reluctant Widow
The Quiet Gentleman
The Toll-Gate
Cousin Kate

London Novels
Regency Buck
The Grand Sophy
Cotillion
April Lady

Bath Novels
Friday's Child
Bath Tangle
Black Sheep
Lady of Quality

Regency Travels
The Corinthian
The Foundling
Sprig Muslin
Charity Girl

Medieval Classics
Simon the Coldheart
The Conqueror
My Lord John

Classic Crime
Footsteps in the Dark
Why Shoot a Butler?
The Unfinished Clue
Death in the Stocks
Behold, Here's Poison
They Found Him Dead
A Blunt Instrument
No Wind of Blame
Envious Casca / A Christmas Party
Penhallow
Duplicate Death
Detection Unlimited

Georgette Heyer

Footsteps In The Dark

WILLIAM HEINEMANN: LONDON

1 3 5 7 9 10 8 6 4 2

William Heinemann
20 Vauxhall Bridge Road
London SW1V 2SA

William Heinemann is part of the Penguin Random House group of companies whose addresses can be found at global.penguinrandomhouse.com.

First published in the United Kingdom by Longmans, Green & Co, Ltd in 1932
First published by Arrow Books in 2007
This edition published in 2018

www.penguin.co.uk

A CIP catalogue record for this book is available from the British Library.

ISBN 9781785152139

Printed and bound in Great Britain by Clays Ltd, Elcograf S.p.A.

Penguin Random House is committed to a sustainable future for our business, our readers and our planet. This book is made from Forest Stewardship Council® certified paper.

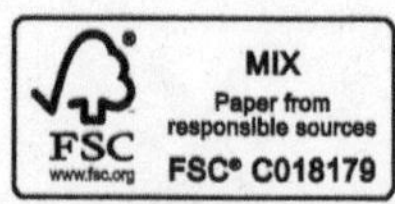

Footsteps In The Dark

One

'And I suppose this is the approach-course,' said Charles Malcolm. 'Full of natural hazards.'

His wife, Celia, replied with dignity: 'That is the tennis-court.' Charles made a derisive noise. 'All it needs,' she said, eyeing him, 'is a little levelling.'

'All it needs,' said Charles rudely, 'is a hay-cutter and a steam-roller. And this is the place you wouldn't sell!'

His sister-in-law took up the cudgels. 'It's perfectly lovely, and you know it. As soon as Celia and I set eyes on it we fell for it.'

'That I can believe,' said Charles. 'A mullioned window or two, and a ruined chapel, and I'd expect you two to go over at the knees. But Peter was with you. What did he fall for? Beer at the local pub?'

'There's a trout-stream at the bottom of the garden,' Margaret pointed out.

'So there is,' Charles agreed. 'And another in the servants' hall for wet days. Bowers showed it to me.'

'Simply because there was a pane of glass out of one of the windows!' Celia said hotly. 'Of course the rain came in!'

Margaret tucked her hand in Charles' arm. 'Wait till

you've seen your bedroom. It's got linen-fold panelling, and there's a cupboard which is all part of it, and which takes you ages to find.'

'That really is jolly,' Charles said. 'Then if anyone burgles our room he won't be able to find my dress-coat. I suppose I can mark the place with a cross.'

'No, you have a compass, and take bearings,' retorted his wife. 'Come on in, and we'll show you.'

They turned away from the tennis-court and began to walk back towards the house down one of the neglected paths that wound between flower-beds to the terrace on the south side of the building.

'Chas, can you look at it with the sun on that heavenly grey stone, and blame us for refusing to part with it?' Margaret exclaimed.

'I'll wait till I've seen my room,' Charles replied.

But he had to admit that this house, which had been left to his wife and her brother and sister, was artistically all that could be desired. Built originally many hundreds of years before of grey stone, much of it was now ruined, and much had been added at different periods, so that the present house was a rambling structure, set in wooded grounds where oaks, which had been there when the Conqueror landed, reared up huge gnarled trunks from out of a tangle of undergrowth. A drive of about a quarter of a mile in length twisted through the trees to the gates that opened on to the road which led to the village of Framley, a mile away if you went by road, but much less if you walked across the fields at the back of the house.

Down the road towards the village, but set back inside the Priory grounds, were the ruins of the chapel which had so captivated Celia's fancy. Dismantled during the Reformation, and later battered by Cromwell's cannon, not much of it now remained, but fragments of the walls rose up crumbling out of the grass. Here and there part of the walls remained to show the Gothic windows, but for the most part they were no more than a few feet in height.

The Priory itself had been restored so that the many rebuildings and additions had left little outward appearance of the old home of the monks. Celia, who had acquired a book on Old Abbeys, declared that the library, a big room giving on to the terrace, was the original refectory, but she admitted that the panelling was probably of later date.

The place had come to her quite unexpectedly. An uncle whom she, in company with Peter and Margaret, had visited at dutiful intervals during his lifetime, had bequeathed the Priory to his nephew and his two nieces. No lover of rural solitudes, he himself had never occupied the house. In his turn he had inherited it some five years before from his sister, who had lived there through marriage and widowhood. As she left it so it now stood, and no sooner had Celia Malcolm, and Peter and Margaret Fortescue seen it, than they declared it was just the place they had dreamed of for years. At least, the two sisters said so. Peter was less enthusiastic, but agreed it would be a pity to sell it.

It had been to let for quite a long time, but ever since the first tenants who rented the house two years after the death of its original owner, had left, no one had made even the smallest offer for it.

'Your uncle had a good deal of trouble over the

house,' had said Mr Milbank, the solicitor. 'When she lived in it his sister never made any complaint, but she was an eccentric old lady, and it's conceivable she wouldn't have cared. But the fact of the matter is, Mrs Malcolm, the house has got rather a bad name. The people your uncle let it to took it for three years – and they left at the end of one. They said the place was haunted.'

'Oo!' said Margaret. 'What a thrill for us!'

The lawyer smiled. 'I shouldn't build on it, Miss Fortescue. I think you'll find that it's nothing more thrilling than rats. But I thought I'd warn you. So that if you feel you'd rather not take possession of a reputedly haunted house you might like me to follow up this offer.' He lifted up a sheet of note-paper that lay on his desk, and looked inquiringly at Peter.

'Is that the offer you wrote to us about?' Peter asked. 'Some fellow who saw the board up when he was motoring in that part of the world, and wanted to know particulars?'

Mr Milbank nodded. Celia and Margaret turned anxiously to their brother, and began to urge the desirability of owning a country house so near to town, and yet so ideal in situation and character.

The trout stream won Peter over. Charles, a young barrister with a growing practice, had no time to waste, so he said, in going to look at a house which his wife was apparently set on inhabiting whether he liked it or not. He placed his trust in Peter.

'And nicely you've abused it,' he said, over tea in the library. 'For two months you three have dashed to and fro, doing what you called "getting it ready to live in."

Incidentally you lulled my suspicions with lying stories about the house, till I almost believed it was something like your description. You' – he pointed an accusing finger at Margaret – 'said it was the ideal home. The fact that there was only one bathroom and a system of heating water that won't do more than one hot bath at a time, you carefully concealed.'

'Do you good to have a few cold baths,' remarked Peter, spreading jam on a slice of bread and butter. 'It isn't as though we propose to live here through the winter. Moreover, I don't see why we shouldn't convert one of the bedrooms into a second bathroom, and put in a better heating arrangement. Not immediately, of course, but at some future date.'

Charles eyed him coldly. 'And what about light? Oh, and a telephone! I suppose we can wire the house while we're about it. This must be what Celia called "getting a country-house for nothing." I might have known.'

'Personally,' said Celia, 'I prefer lamps and candles. Electric light would be out of place in a house like this, and as for a telephone, that's the one thing I've been wanting to escape from.' She nodded briskly at her husband. 'You're going to have a real holiday this year, my man, quite cut off from town.'

'Thanks very much,' said Charles. 'And what was it you said just before tea? Something about going to the village to order bacon for breakfast?'

'Well, you can take the car,' Celia pointed out. 'And you might try and get hold of a gardener in the village. I think the garden is rather more than you and Peter can manage.'

'It is,' said Charles, with conviction. 'Much more.'

The door opened at that moment to admit a middle-aged lady of comfortable proportions, and placid demeanour. This was Mrs Bosanquet, the Fortescues' aunt. She accepted a chair, and some tea, condemned a solid-looking cake, and embarked on bread and butter.

'I have unpacked my boxes,' she announced, 'but I twice lost the wardrobe.'

'What, have you got one of those little practical jokes?' Charles demanded.

Mrs Bosanquet turned an amiable and inquiring countenance towards him. She was deaf. When Charles had repeated his question, she nodded. 'Yes, dear, but I have stuck a piece of stamp-paper on the catch. A very quaint old house. I was talking to Mrs Bowers, and she tells me you could lose yourself in the cellars.'

'That's nothing,' said Charles, getting up. 'I lost myself getting from our room to my dressing-room. Of course it would simplify matters if we locked a few of the empty rooms, but I agree it would take away from the sporting element. Are you coming to the village, Peter?'

'I am,' Peter replied. 'I will introduce you to some very fine draught beer there.'

'Lead on!' Charles said, brightening.

The lane that led to Framley was wooded, and picturesque enough to draw a grudging word of approval from Charles. Peter, negotiating a hairpin bend, said: 'Seriously, Chas, the place has possibilities.'

'I don't deny it. But what's all this bilge about noises and hauntings, and footsteps in the dark?'

'God knows. In the village they all but cross themselves if you mention the Priory. I daresay there are rats. Milbank said . . .'

'Look here, do you mean to say you knew about this haunting before you came down here? And not one word to me?'

Peter said in some surprise: 'I didn't think anything of it. You aren't going to tell me you'd have refused to live in the place if you'd known?'

'Aren't I?' said Charles grimly. 'If you'd left as many desirable residences and hotels at a moment's notice as I have, all because Celia "felt something queer" about them, you'd never have come near the place.'

'She says she doesn't believe there's anything wrong with the house. All village superstition.'

'Does she? Well, I'll lay you six to one in sovereigns that the first rat heard scuttling overhead will spell our departure. Especially with Bowers shivering round the house.'

'What's the matter with him? Been listening to village gossip?'

'That, and natural palsy of spirit. He unpacked my things and gave a life-like imitation of the mysterious butler of fiction while he did so. "All I know is, sir, I wouldn't go down those cellar stairs after dark, not if I were paid to." Oh yes, and I need hardly say that the first night he and Mrs Bowers spent alone in the house before you came down, he heard footsteps outside his door, and a hand feeling over the panels.'

'Silly ass!' Peter said. 'You can console yourself with the thought that it would take more than a ghost to upset the redoubtable Mrs Bowers. Allow me to tell you that we are now approaching the Bell Inn. Genuine fourteenth century – in parts.'

The car had emerged from the tree-shadowed lane

into the outskirts of the village, which stretched aimlessly along one narrow main street. The Bell Inn, a picturesque and rambling old hostelry built round a courtyard, was one of the first buildings on the street. Peter Fortescue ran the car up to the door and switched off the engine. 'Opening time,' he grinned. 'Take heart, Chas, I can vouch for the beer.'

They entered into a long, low-pitched taproom, with a beamed ceiling, and little latticed windows that gave on to the street. Oak settles formed various secluded nooks in the room, and behind the bar stood a landlord of such comfortable proportions and such benevolent mien that he might well have stepped from the pages of Dickens.

Leaning against the bar, and apparently engaging Mr Wilkes in desultory conversation, was his very antithesis, a thin, wiry little man, with a very sharp face and pale eyes that darted from object to object with a quickness that gave a disagreeable impression of shiftiness. He glanced at Peter as Peter crossed the threshold, and at once looked away again.

'Evening, Wilkes,' Peter said. 'I've brought my brother-in-law along to try that draught bitter of yours.'

Mr Wilkes beamed upon them both. 'Very glad to see any friend of yours here, sir. Two half-cans, sir? You shall have it.' He took down a couple of pewter tankards from a shelf behind him, and drew two half-pints of frothing beer. Having supplied his patrons with this, he wiped down the bar with a mechanical action, and said affably: 'And how are you getting on up at the Priory, sir, if I may ask?'

'All right, thanks. We haven't seen your ghost yet. When does he usually show up?'

The smile faded. Mr Wilkes looked at Peter rather queerly, and said in an altered voice: 'I wouldn't joke about it, sir, not if I was you.'

Charles emerged from his tankard. 'Has my man Bowers been in here at all?' he demanded.

The landlord looked surprised; the small stranger, who had edged away a little when the newcomers first entered, shot a quick look at Charles.

'Yes, sir, several times,' Wilkes answered.

'I thought so,' said Charles. 'And did you tell him that the ghost prowled round the passages, and pawed all the doors?'

Wilkes seemed to draw back. 'Has he heard it again?' he asked.

'Heard my eye!' Charles retorted. 'All he heard was what you told him, and his own imagination.'

'Joking apart, Wilkes, you don't really believe in the thing, do you?' Peter asked.

The small man, who had looked for a moment as though he were going to say something, moved unobtrusively away to a seat by one of the windows, and fishing a crumpled newspaper from his pocket began to read it.

For a moment Wilkes did not reply; then he said quite simply: 'I've seen it, sir.' Peter's brows lifted incredulously, and Wilkes added: 'And what's more, I've seen as reasonable a man as what you are yourself pack up and leave that place with two years of his lease still to run. A little over five years it is since I took over this house, and when I first come here the Priory was standing as empty as when you first saw it. I suppose old Mrs Matthews, that used to own it, had been dead a matter of a year or fifteen months. From all accounts she was a queer one. Well, there was the Priory, going to ruin, as you might say, and never a soul would go near the place after dark, not if they was paid to. Now, I daresay you'll agree I don't look one of the fanciful ones myself, sir, and nor I'm not, and the first thing I did when I heard what folk said of the place, was to make a joke of it, like what you're doing now. Then Ben Tillman, that keeps the mill up to Crawshays, he laid me I wouldn't go up to the old ruin after dark one night.' He paused, and again wiped down the bar with that odd air of abstraction. He drew a long breath, as though some horror still lingered in his memory. 'Well, I went, sir. Nor I wasn't afraid – not then. It was a moonlit night, and besides that I had my torch if I'd needed it. But I didn't. I sat down on one of those old tombs you'll find in the chapel, half covered by grass and weeds. I didn't think anything out of the ordinary for some while. If I remember rightly, I whistled a bit, by way of passing the time. I couldn't say how long it was before I noticed the change. I think it must have come gradual.'

'What change?' asked Charles, unimpressed.

Again the landlord paused. 'It's very hard to tell you, sir. It wasn't anything you could take hold of, as you might say. Things looked the same, and there wasn't more than a breath of wind, yet it got much colder all at once. And it was as fine a June night as you could hope for. I don't know how I can explain it so as you'd understand, but it was as though the cold was spreading right over me, and into me. And instead of whistling tunes to myself, and thinking how I'd have the laugh over Ben Tillman, I found I was sitting still – still as death. It had sort of crept on me without my noticing, that fear of moving. I couldn't have told you why *then*, but I knew I daren't stir a finger, nor make a sound. I can tell you, with that fear in my very bones I'd have given all I had to get up and run, and let Ben say what he would. But I couldn't. Something had got me. No, I don't know what it was, sir, and I can't explain it anyhow else, but it was no laughing matter. Do you know how it is when you've got the wind up, and you sit listening like as if your ear-drums 'ud burst with the strain? Well, that's how I was, listening and watching. Whenever a leaf rustled I strained my eyes to see what was there. But there was nothing. Then it stole over me that there was something behind me.' He stopped, and passed the back of his hand across his forehead. 'Well, that's a feeling anyone can get if he's properly scared, but this was more than a feeling. I *knew* it. I'd still got some of my wits left and I knew there was only one thing to be done, and that was turn round, and look. Yes, it sounds easy, but I swear to you, sir, it took every ounce of courage in me. I did it. I fair wrenched myself round, with the blood hammering in my head. And I saw it, plain as I see you, standing right behind me, looking down at me.'

'Saw *what*?' demanded Peter, quite worked up.

The landlord gave a shiver. 'They call it the Monk round here,' he answered. 'I suppose it was that. But I only saw a tall black figure, and no face, but just two eyes looking out of blackness straight at me.'

'Your pal Tillman dressed up to give you a fright,' said Charles.

Wilkes looked at him. 'Ben Tillman couldn't have vanished, sir. And that's what the Monk did. Just disappeared. You may say I imagined it, but all I know is I wouldn't do what I did that night again, not for a thousand pounds.'

There was a slight pause. The man by the window got up and strolled out of the taproom. Peter set his tankard down. 'Well, thanks very much,' he said. 'Cheery little story.'

Charles had been watching the thin stranger. 'Who's our departed friend?' he inquired.

'Commercial, sir. He's working the places round here with some sort of a vacuum-cleaner, so I understand, and doing a bit of fishing in between-whiles.'

'Seemed to be interested in ghosts,' was all Charles said.

But when he and Peter had left the Bell Inn, Peter asked abruptly: 'What did you mean by that, Chas? Did you think the fellow was listening to us?'

'Didn't you?' Charles said.

'Well, yes, but I don't know that that was altogether surprising.'

'No. But he didn't seem to want us to notice his interest, did he? Where's this grocer we're looking for?'

At the grocer's, which turned out to be also the post-office and linen-draper, after the manner of village shops, the two men were accosted by a gentleman in clerical attire, who was buying stamps. He introduced himself as the Vicar, and told them that he and his wife were only waiting until the newcomers had had time to settle into the Priory before they paid a call on them.

'One is glad to see the Priory occupied once more,' he said. 'Alas, too many of our old houses are spurned nowadays for lack of "modern conveniences."'

'We were rather under the impression, sir, that this particular house has been spurned on account of ghosts,' Peter said.

The Vicar smiled. 'Ah, I fear you must seek confirmation of that story from one more credulous than my poor self,' he announced. 'Such tales, I find, invariably spring up round deserted houses. I venture to prophesy that the Priory ghost proves itself to be nothing more harmful than a mouse, or perhaps a rat.'

'Oh, so we think,' Charles answered. 'But it's really rather a nuisance, for my wife had banked on getting a local housemaid, and the best she can manage is a daily girl, who takes precious good care she's out of the place before sundown.'

Mr Pennythorne listened to this with an air of smiling tolerance. 'Strange how tenacious these simple country-folk are of superstitions,' he said musingly. 'But you are not without domestic help, one trusts?'

'No, no, we have our butler and his wife.' Charles gathered up his change from the counter, and thrust an unwieldy package into Peter's hands. 'Are you going our way, sir? Can we drop you anywhere?'

'No, I thank you. Is it your car that stands outside the Bell Inn? I will accompany you as far as that if I may.'

They strolled out of the shop, and down the street. The Vicar pointed out various tumbledown old buildings of architectural interest, and promised to conduct them personally round the church some day. 'It is not, I fear, of such antiquity as the ruins of your chapel,' he sighed, 'but we pride ourselves upon our east window. Within the last few years we have been fortunate enough to procure a sufficient sum of money to pay for the cleaning of it – no light expense, my dear Mr Malcolm – but we were greatly indebted to Colonel Ackerley, who showed himself, as indeed he always does, most generous.' This seemed to produce a train of thought. 'No doubt you have already made his acquaintance? One of our churchwardens; and an estimable fellow – a *pukka sahib*, as he would himself say.'

'Is he the man who lives in the white house beyond ours?' asked Peter. 'No, we haven't met him yet, but I think I saw him at the Bell one evening. Cheery-looking man, going grey, with regular features, and a short moustache? Drives a Vauxhall tourer?'

The Vicar, while disclaiming any knowledge of cars, thought that this description fitted Colonel Ackerley. They had reached the Bell Inn by this time, and again refusing the offer of a lift the Vicar took his leave, and walked off briskly down the street.

When Charles and Peter reached the Priory it was nearly time for dinner, and long shadows lay on the ground. They found the girls in the library with Mrs Bosanquet, and were greeted by a cry of: 'Oh, here you are! We quite forgot to tell you to buy a couple of ordinary lamps to fix on to the wall.'

'What, more lamps?' demanded Peter, who had a lively recollection of unpacking a positive crate of them. 'Why on earth?'

'Well, we haven't got any for the landing upstairs,' explained Celia, 'and Bowers says he'd rather not go up without a light. Did you ever hear such rot? I told him to take a candle.'

'To tell you the honest truth,' confessed Margaret, 'I don't awfully like going up in the dark myself.'

Charles cast up his eyes. 'Already!' he said.

'It isn't that at all,' Margaret said defiantly. 'I mean, I'm not imagining ghosts or anything so idiotic, but it is a rambling place, and of course one does hear odd sorts of noises – yes, I know it's only rats, but at night one gets stupid, and fanciful, and anyway, there is a sort of feeling that – that one's being watched. I've had it before, in old houses.'

'Have you really felt it here?' asked Celia, wide-eyed.

'Oh, it's nothing, Celia, but you know how it is when you go to Holyrood, or Hampton Court, or somewhere. There's a sort of atmosphere. I can't explain, but *you* know.'

'Damp?' suggested Peter helpfully.

His sisters looked their scorn. 'No, silly,' said Margaret. 'As though the spirits of all those dead and gone people were looking at one from the walls. That's a bit what I feel here.'

Mrs Bosanquet put down her needlework and said mildly: 'You feel someone in the wall, my dear? I do hope to goodness there isn't a skeleton anywhere. I never could bear the thought of them, for they seem to me most unnatural.'

'Aunt!' shrieked Celia. 'A skeleton in the wall? Don't be so awful! Why should there be?'

'I daresay there's no such thing, my dear, but I always remember reading a most unpleasant story about someone who was walled up in a monastery, or a convent – I forget which, but it was something to do with monks, I know.'

'Oh Aunt Lilian, Aunt Lilian!' groaned Charles. '*Et tu, Brute!*'

‘If I thought for one moment,’ said Celia emphatically, ‘that anyone had been walled up inside this house, I’d walk out here and now.’

‘Quite right, my dear,’ agreed Mrs Bosanquet. ‘One can’t be too careful. I always remember how there was an outbreak of the plague when they disturbed the old burial place somewhere in London.’

‘On which cheerful thought,’ said Charles, as a gong sounded in the hall, ‘we go in to dinner. Anyone any appetite?’

In spite of Mrs Bosanquet’s gloomy recollections it seemed that no one’s appetite had failed. Dinner was served in the square dining-room at the side of the house, and though the undrawn curtains let in the soft evening light, Celia had placed shaded candles on the table, so that the room had a warm, inviting appearance. By common consent there was no more talk of ghosts or skeletons. They went back to the library after dinner, and while Mrs Bosanquet proceeded to lay out a complicated Patience, the others sat down to the Bridge-table. Even when a scutter somewhere in the wainscoting startled them all it did not need the men’s assurances to convince the girls that the place was rat-ridden.

‘I know,’ said Celia, gathering up her cards. ‘Mrs Bowers is going to set a trap.’

‘I am not fond of rats,’ remarked her aunt. ‘Mice I don’t mind at all. Poor little things. Ah, if that had been a red queen I might have brought it out. I once stayed in a farmhouse where they used to run about in the lofts over our heads like a pack of terriers.’

Margaret, who was Dummy, got up from the table and wandered over to the window. The moon had risen, and now bathed the whole garden in silver light. She gave an exclamation: 'Oh, look how beautiful! I wish we could see the chapel from here.' She stepped out on to the terrace, and stood leaning her hands on the low parapet. The night was very still and cloudless, and the trees threw shadows like pools of darkness. The shrubbery hid the ruins of the chapel from sight.

'You can see it from your bedroom, I should think,' called Peter. 'Come on in: we're two down, all due to your reckless bidding.'

She came in reluctantly and took her place at the table. 'It seems a pity to be playing bridge on a night like this. Does anyone feel inclined to wander up to the chapel with me?'

'Don't all speak at once,' Charles advised them unnecessarily.

'Personally,' said Celia, 'I'm going to bed after this rubber. We'll all go some other night.'

Half an hour later only the two men remained downstairs. Charles went over to the windows, and shut and bolted them. 'Think it's necessary to make a tour of the back premises?' he asked, yawning.

'Lord, no! Bowers'll have taken precious good care to see that it's all locked up. I'll go and put the chain on the front door.' Peter went out, and Charles bolted the last window, and turned to put out the big oil-lamp that hung on chains from the ceiling. The moonlight shone in at the uncurtained window, and as Charles turned towards the door he heard what sounded like the rustling of a skirt against the wall behind him. He looked quickly over his shoulder. There was no one but himself in the room, but he could have sworn that he heard faint footsteps.

Peter's voice called from the hall. 'Coming, Chas?'

'Just a moment.' Charles felt in his pocket for matches and presently struck one, and walked forward so that its tiny light showed up the shadowed corner of the room.

Peter appeared in the doorway, candle in hand. 'What's up? Lost something?'

The match burned out. 'No, I thought I heard something – a rat,' Charles said.

Two

The Vicar and his wife came to call at the Priory two days later. Mrs Pennythorne wore pince-nez and white kid gloves, and she told Celia that there was little society in the neighbourhood. There were the Mastermans, at the Manor House, but they never called on anyone, and there was Mr Titmarsh, at Crossways, but he was so very odd in his habits that Mrs Pennythorne could hardly recommend him as an acquaintance. Further questioning elicited the explanation that the oddness of Mr Titmarsh's habits was due to his hobby, which was collecting moths. Mrs Pennythorne said that his manners were sadly brusque, and he wandered about at night, presumably in search of specimens for his collection. Then there was Dr Roote, and his wife, and although Mrs Pennythorne was loth to speak ill of anyone really she ought to warn Celia that it was all too certain that the doctor drank. Finally there was Colonel Ackerley, at the White House, who neither drank nor collected moths, but who was a bachelor, which was a pity. Mrs Pennythorne went on to enumerate the failings of various farmers and villagers, and Charles, who, his wife was wont to say, was never backward in devising methods of escape for himself, suggested to the Vicar that he might like to stroll out to look at the ruins of the chapel.

The Vicar was nothing loth, and ignoring a look of mingled threat and appeal from his wife, Charles led him out.

The Vicar discoursed on Norman and Early English architecture in the chapel, and strove to decipher long obliterated inscriptions upon the few tombs that thrust up through the grass and weeds that had grown over the floor of the building.

They returned presently to the house to find that another caller had arrived. This was Colonel Ackerley, and he proved to be a more congenial guest than either of the Pennythornes, who soon took their leave.

The Colonel was a man of some forty-five years, or more, with a manner rather typical of the army, but otherwise inoffensive. He shook hands with great heartiness, and said that had he known of the presence of Mrs Pennythorne in the house he should have turned tail and run.

The girls promptly warmed to him. 'You must stay and have tea with us,' Celia said. 'And does the doctor really drink, or is it drugs?'

'Ah, poor old Roote!' said the Colonel charitably. 'Mustn't be unchristian, I suppose. Leave that to the Vicar's wife, what?' His ready laugh broke from him. 'Still, I must admit poor Roote is rather too fond of the bottle. A good doctor, mind you, and whatever they say I'll not believe he was ever the worse for wear except in his off-hours. Wife's a bit of a tartar, I believe.'

'What about the eccentric Mr Titmarsh?' inquired Margaret.

'Not an ounce of harm in him, my dear young lady,' the Colonel assured her. 'Queer old bird: not much in my line, I'm afraid. Very clever, and all that sort of thing, so they say. Don't be surprised if you run up against him in the dark one night. Gave me the shock of my life when I first found him in my garden. Thought he was a burglar.' He burst out laughing again. 'Told me he was putting lime on a tree, or some such flum-diddle. He's a – what d'ye call it? – entomologist.'

Peter handed him his cup and saucer. 'Well, I'm glad you warned us, Colonel. Otherwise we might have mistaken him for our ghost.'

'You don't mean to tell me you believe in that story?' demanded Colonel Ackerley.

'Of course we don't!' said Celia. 'But our butler does, and so does the housemaid. Bowers swears he's heard ghostly hands feeling over his door at night.'

The Colonel set down his cup. 'Has he, by Gad?' he said. 'But you haven't heard anything yourselves, have you?'

Celia hesitated. It was Margaret who answered. 'Yes, I think we all have, but we put it down to rats.'

The Colonel looked from one to the other. 'Footsteps, do you mean?'

'That and other odd sounds. It's nothing.'

The Colonel drank the rest of his tea in two gulps. 'Well, it's not often one comes across two such sensible ladies,' he said. 'I don't mind admitting to you that if I were in a house and heard what you call odd sounds I don't believe I could stand it. Bullets I can put up with at a pinch, but I draw the line at spooks. Yes, I draw the line at spooks, and I'm not ashamed to say so.'

'I quite agree with you,' Mrs Bosanquet said, bestowing her placid smile upon him. 'I can't approve of this modern craze for the supernatural. I once spent a whole hour with a ouija board, and the only thing it wrote was M about a hundred times, and then something that looked like Mother's Marmalade, which seemed to me absurd.'

'You ought to try again here, Aunt,' said Margaret. 'Then, if there's anything in it, perhaps our ghost will tell you the story of his life.'

'Who knows?' said Peter flippantly, 'he might even lead you to some hidden treasure.'

Mrs Bosanquet merely shook her head, but the idea seemed to take root in her mind, for when Charles and Peter came back from seeing the Colonel out, she suddenly said: 'Though mind you, Peter, if there were a ghost here I know just what I should do.'

'Of course you do, darling,' said Charles. 'You'd put your head under the clothes, and say your prayers, same as you did when your flat was burgled.'

Mrs Bosanquet was quite unabashed. 'I should instantly summon the Vicar to exorcise it,' she said with dignity.

Charles' shout of laughter was broken off sharply. A sound, like a groan, muffled as though by stone walls, startled him into silence. 'Good God, what's that?' he rapped out.

Celia had grown suddenly white, and instinctively Margaret drew closer to her brother. The groan had held a note almost like a wail, long-drawn-out and slowly dying.

No one answered Charles for a moment. Only Celia

gave a little shiver, and glanced round fearfully. Mrs Bosanquet broke the awed silence. 'What is what, my dear?' she asked calmly.

'Didn't you hear it?' Margaret said. 'As though – as though – someone – gave an awful – groan.'

'No, my dear, but you know I don't hear very well. Probably a creaking door.'

Charles recovered himself. 'Not only probably, but undoubtedly,' he said. 'It startled me for the moment. Comes of talking about ghosts. I'm going round with an oil-can.' He left the room, ignoring an involuntary cry from his wife.

'Do you really think it was that?' Margaret said. 'I'm not being spooky, but – but it seemed to come from underneath somewhere.'

'Don't be an ass, Peg,' her brother advised her. 'If you ask me it came from outside. I'll bet it's the door leading out of the garden-hall. I meant to oil the hinge before, and it's got worse after the rain we had last night.'

'If you're going to look, I'm coming with you,' Margaret said firmly.

Celia half-rose from her chair, and then sat down again.

'I shall stay and keep Aunt Lilian company,' she announced in the voice of a heroine. 'Whoever heard of a daylight ghost? We're all getting nervy. I shall bar ghost-talk for the future.'

In the garden-hall, where Celia was in the habit of filling the flower-vases, Peter and Margaret found Charles with Bowers beside him, holding an oil-can in a shaking hand.

'Oh, so you thought it was this door too, did you?' Peter said. 'What's the matter with you, Bowers?'

Bowers cast him a look of reproach. 'We heard it, sir, Mrs Bowers and me. Seemed to come from somewhere quite close. It gave Mrs Bowers such a turn she nearly dropped her frying-pan. "Good gracious alive!" she said. "Who's being murdered?" And she's not one to fancy things, sir, as you well know.' Gloomily he watched Charles open the door into the garden. It squeaked dismally, but the sound was not the groan they had heard before. 'No, sir, it's not that, and nor it's not any other door in the house, though they do squeak, I won't deny. There's something uncanny about this place. I said it as soon as I set eyes on it, and I can tell you, sir, it's taking years off my life, living here.'

'Is there any other door leading out on this side of the house?' Peter said. 'I could swear it came from this direction.'

'There's only the long window in the drawing-room,' said Margaret. She stepped out on to the gravel-path, and looked along the side of the house. 'I can't see any other. I say, it is rather beastly, isn't it? Of course I know things do echo in these places, but . . . Why, who's that?'

Charles came quickly out to her side. 'Where?' he said sharply. 'Hullo, there's a chap walking past the shrubbery!' He started forward, Peter at his heels, and hailed the stranger rather sharply.

A man in fisherman's attire, and carrying a creel and a rod, was walking through the trees beyond the shrubs that ran close up to the wall of the house. He stopped as Charles hailed him, and came to meet him. He was a dark young man of about thirty, with very black brows that grew close over the bridge of his nose, and a mouth that was rather grim in repose. 'I beg your pardon,' he said, 'I'm afraid I'm trespassing.' He spoke in a curt way, as though he were either shy or slightly annoyed. 'I've been fishing the Crewel, and a man told me I could get back to the village by a short cut through your grounds. Only I don't seem able to find it.'

Charles said: 'There is a right-of-way, but you are some distance from it. In fact, your guide seems to have directed you to the wrong side of the house.'

The stranger reddened. 'I'm sorry,' he said stiffly. 'Could you point out the way to it?'

Margaret who had come up, and had been listening curiously, said suddenly: 'Why you're the man who changed the wheel for me yesterday!'

The stranger raised his hat, slightly bowing.

'Are you staying at the Bell?' Margaret inquired.

'Yes. I've come down for some trout-fishing,' he answered.

'There seems to be some quite good fishing here,' Peter said, bridging yet another gap in the conversation.

'Quite good,' agreed the dark young man. He shifted his rod from one hand to the other. 'Er – can I reach the right-of-way from here, or must I get back to the road?'

'Oh no, I'll show you the way,' Margaret said, with her friendly smile. 'It's only just across the drive.'

'It's very good of you, but really you must not trouble . . .'

'It's no trouble. And this place is so overgrown with trees and bushes you can easily miss the way. Peter, you'd better go back and tell Celia it's all right. Come on, Mr – I don't think I know your name?'

'Strange,' said the young man. 'Michael Strange.'

'I'm Margaret Fortescue,' she told him. 'This is my brother, and this is my brother-in-law, Mr Malcolm.'

Again the young man bowed. 'Are you staying long in this part of the world?' asked Charles.

'Just for a week or two,' Strange replied. 'I'm on my holiday.'

'Er – won't you come into the house?' Peter suggested. 'And have a cocktail or something?'

'Thanks, but I think I must be getting along. If Miss Fortescue will really be so kind as to show me the short cut to the village . . .'

'Yes, rather,' Margaret said. 'Perhaps you'll look us up some other time. Come on.'

They set off together, leaving the two others to watch them out of sight.

'Well, there you are,' said Charles. 'Apparently she's got off again. And would you explain to me how a man making for a perfectly well-known right-of-way fetches up under our drawing-room windows?'

Peter was frowning. 'He doesn't – if he *is* looking for the right-of-way. Common sense must tell him that it can't run this side of the house. To tell you the truth, Chas, I don't like your black-browed friend. Just what was he doing, snooping around here?'

'He wasn't exactly communicative, so I can't say. Might have wanted to take a look at the Priory, of course. Lots of people can't keep off a ruin.'

'He didn't look to me that sort,' Peter said, still frowning.

Charles yawned. 'Probably a mere ass without any bump of locality.'

'And he didn't look like that either.'

'Oh, all right, then, no doubt he came to abduct Margaret. Now what about this groaning door?'

But Michael Strange made no attempt to abduct Margaret. She led him round the corner of the house on to the avenue that ran down to the gates, and cut across this into the wood that lay between the house and the road.

'I'm taking you past the chapel,' she said. 'The footpath is beyond that, you know. You must have asked the way of one of the yokels. Isn't it odd that they never can direct one intelligibly?'

'They always assume too much local knowledge on one's part,' he nodded. A smile, which showed a row of very white teeth, put his rather grim expression to flight. 'There's altogether too much of the "past-Parson-Gregory's-and-turn-right-handed-when-you-get-to-Jackson's-farm" about their directions.'

'I know,' she said, laughing. 'I'm one of those unfortunate people who never know which way I ought to go, too. Tell me, do you know many of the people down here, or is it your first visit?'

'My first,' he answered. 'I was told the fishing was good, and the inn comfortable, so I thought I'd give it a trial. You're new to the place yourself, aren't you?'

'Yes, we only moved in a week ago.' Her dimple peeped out. 'I must tell you, because it's really rather funny: when we saw you just now we thought you were our ghost.'

He glanced down at her. 'Have you got a ghost?' he asked. 'How exciting! What sort of a ghost?'

'Well, we're not sure about that. A squeaking one, anyway.'

'That doesn't sound very awful. Haven't you seen it?'

'No, thank goodness. Of course I don't suppose it's a ghost at all, really, but when we came out we'd just heard the most gruesome sort of a groan. Honestly, it made one's blood run cold. So Chas – my brother-in-law – is going round oiling all the door-hinges. Look, that's the chapel. Doesn't it look eerie and romantic?'

'Yes, I don't think I should care to spend the night up there alone,' Strange admitted.

They stood still for a moment, surveying the ruin. Strange glanced back towards the house. 'H'm. It's rather cut off by the trees, isn't it? Can you see it from the house at all?'

'No, not from downstairs. You can from my window, and the landing window. Why?'

'I only thought it was rather a pity anything so picturesque should be out of sight.'

They walked on slowly. 'If the place is haunted at all, I'm sure the ghost lives in the chapel,' Margaret said lightly. 'If I had the courage of a mouse, which I haven't, I'd get my brother to sit up with me and watch.'

'I think it's just as well you haven't,' said Strange, with another of his swift transforming smiles. 'You never know, and – I should hate you to get a fright.'

'Oh, nothing would induce Peter to forsake his bed,' she said. 'Besides, he doesn't believe in ghosts. Here's your path. You can't miss the way now.' She stopped and held out her hand.

Michael Strange took it in his. 'Thank you very much,' he said. 'It was awfully good of you to bother. I – hope you get another puncture when I'm in the offing.'

'How nice of you.' She smiled, and withdrew her

hand. 'Do come and see us if ever you feel like it. Good-bye!'

She watched him stride away down the footpath, and turned, and went slowly back to the house.

'Well, did you find out anything about the fellow?' her brother asked when she entered the library.

'Oh, he's just on his holiday,' she replied.

'So we gathered,' said Charles. 'What's his job?'

'I didn't ask. Why were you two so stuffy? You don't think he was responsible for the noise we heard, do you?'

'That solution hadn't occurred to me,' said Charles. 'I admit he didn't give me the impression of one who would stand under someone else's window and groan at them. Still, you never know.'

Celia held up her finger. 'I protest. We are not going to talk about groans or ghosts any more. Carried?'

'Carried unanimously,' said Peter.

That resolution might have been kept longer had it not been for the happenings of the next night.

It was about half-past ten when a crash that resounded through the house penetrated even to Mrs Bosanquet's ears, and made Celia, who was improvising idly on the piano, strike a jangling discord. The crash seemed to come from the upper landing, and it was followed by a bump-bump-bump, as though some hard object were rolling down the stairs.

'Good Lord, who's smashing up the place now?' said Charles, getting out of his chair. He went to the door, and opened it. 'That you, Peter?' he called.

The study door opposite opened. 'No. What on earth's happened?' Peter asked.

'Dunno. Without wishing to leap to conclusions I

should hazard a guess that something has fallen over.' Charles picked up the lamp that stood on the hall table, and walked to the foot of the stairs.

'I believe it was a picture,' Celia said, at his side. 'It sounded to me like glass breaking.'

She ran up ahead of him, and rounded the half-landing. A little exclamation broke from her. 'Oh, there's something on the stairs! Do hurry up with the lamp, Charles.' She bent and groped for the thing her foot had kicked against. 'Whatever can it be?' she wondered. Then Charles reached the half-landing, and the light he carried showed Celia what she held between her hands.

It was a human skull and the hollow eye-sockets glared up at her, while the teeth of the fleshless upper jaw grinned as though in macabre mockery.

Celia gave a shuddering cry, and dropped the hideous thing, shrinking back against the wall. 'Oh Charles! Oh Charles!' she whispered, like a frightened child.

He was beside her in a moment, holding her in the circle of his arm, himself staring down at the skull at their feet. For a moment words apparently failed him.

Peter came up the stairs two at a time. 'What is it?' he asked impatiently. Then he too saw, and stopped dead. 'Gosh!' he gasped. Over his shoulder he jerked: 'Don't come up, Margaret.'

'But what *is* it?' she called. 'Why did Celia scream?'

'Oh, it's nothing!' said Charles, recovering his sangfroid. 'Just a skull rolling about the place. You trot off downstairs, Celia, while I investigate.'

'I – I think I will,' she said, and went past the skull with her eyes steadily averted.

'Take her into the library, Peg,' Charles ordered. He

watched her go shakily downstairs, and turned to Peter. 'Look here, this is a bit thick,' he said. 'I don't know about you, but I'm all of a sweat. Footsteps and groans I can put up with, but when it comes to finding people's remains lying about the place I've had enough.'

Peter bent and picked up the skull, and placed it on the window-seat. 'Question is, where did it come from?' he said. 'Bring that lamp upstairs.'

They went on up to the landing, holding the lamp high so that the light was thrown before them. At the head of the stairs a big picture had fallen to the ground, and pieces of glass winked at them from the carpet. The lamplight showed a dark aperture where the picture had hung, and when the two men went closer they saw that part of the panelling was apparently missing. Peter felt in his pocket for the torch he carried, and switched it on, flashing the light into the hidden cupboard. It revealed a small chamber in the wall, and something else besides. A heap of bones were huddled on the floor of the chamber.

'Good Lord! A priest's hole!' Peter said. 'And some poor devil got in and couldn't get out. I say – pretty beastly, what?'

Charles set the lamp down on the table against the wall, and in silence looked at the dreadful remains. After a moment Peter cleared his throat, and said: 'Well – that's that. How did it all happen? I mean – there must have been something besides the picture hiding this hole.' He began to inspect the moulding all round the cavity. One of the rosettes was out of place. He put his hand on it, trying to see whether it would move, and found that it twisted stiffly between his fingers. The missing panel at once slid back into place. He opened it again, frowning. 'Odd. It looks as though the corner of the picture must have knocked it as it fell, yet I don't quite see how it can have forced the rosette round like that. Obviously the – the skeleton was huddled against the panel, and when it opened the skull fell out. You know, Chas, the idea of that poor beggar shut up there, dying of thirst . . .'

'Just a moment,' Charles said. 'Give me the torch, will you? Thanks.' He directed its light into the hole again and closely scrutinised the bones that lay there. 'Take a look, Peter. Does it strike you the bones are in rather a funny position?'

'What do you mean?' Peter peered at them. 'I don't know. There are the leg-bones, and the arms, all right. Difficult to say how they'd fall once the flesh had rotted away.'

'They look wrong to me,' Charles said. 'Almost as though they'd been put there by someone who wasn't an expert. Give me a hand up: I'm going to see if there isn't an answering catch on the inside of the panelling.'

Peter helped him to climb into the hole. 'What are you driving at? D'you mean that the fellow was murdered and his bones thrown in months later?'

'I don't know. No, there's no fastening on this side. Faugh! what a smell of must!' He clambered out again. 'Let's take another look at the catch.' He tested it several times. It moved very stiffly. 'I shouldn't have said that it was possible for the picture to have pushed it out of place,' he said. He went across to where the picture lay and closely inspected the broken wire. It was old and rusty, and if it had been cut the operation had been performed too skilfully for it to be apparent.

‘I agree with you,’ Peter said. ‘But that’s how it must have happened. Hang it all, who could have faked this, and why? Not quite the sort of practical joke any of us would stage.’

‘If it was faked,’ said Charles slowly, ‘I’ve an idea it wasn’t done for a joke. Mind you, I’m not saying it was faked. It may have happened as we think it did. But I’m not entirely satisfied.’

‘But who would . . . ?’

‘Damn it, I don’t know! Put the skull back, and close it up for to-night. To-morrow we shall have to bury the bones.’

‘To-morrow,’ said Peter, ‘Celia and Margaret will pack their trunks and we shall depart.’

Charles looked at him. ‘I’m staying. No ghost, or pseudo-ghost is going to frighten me out of this place. What about you?’

Peter grinned. ‘Righto, I’m with you. But if you think this is part of a campaign to scare us away I’m going to town to fetch my old service revolver. Not that I think you’re right. If the picture caught the rosette a pretty hard knock it might quite well have done the trick. Do you want to search the house?’

‘Too late,’ Charles said. ‘Whoever was here – if anyone was here at all – has had loads of time to make a get-away.’ He placed the skull back in the cavity, and closed the panel. ‘Bowers had better come and clear away these bits of glass. I think we won’t mention the priest’s hole to him.’ He started to go downstairs, and as he reached the half-landing the door leading into the servants’ wing below was burst open, and Bowers himself came into the hall with a very white face, and starting eyes. Charles called to him before he could reach the library door, and the butler jumped as though he had been shot.

A scared face was turned upward. 'Oh, it's you, sir!' Bowers gasped. 'Sir, I've seen it – I've seen the Monk! Oh Gawd, sir, we oughtn't ever to have come here!'

'Rubbish!' said Charles testily. 'What do you mean, you've seen the Monk? Where?'

'Out there in the moonlight, sir, plain as I see you. Gliding over the lawn it was, in a long black cloak. It's more than flesh and blood can bear, sir, and stay in this place I daren't, not for a thousand pounds!'

'Steady, you ass!' Peter interposed. 'Just you show us where you think you saw this Monk of yours.'

'Out of the pantry window, when I was bolting it for the night. Making for the trees at the end of the lawn it was, and it vanished amongst them, sir. You won't see it now: it's gone, but we've had our warning all right.'

'We'll see about that,' said Charles. 'Not a word of this to your mistress, Bowers.' He ran down the remaining stairs into the hall, and selected a stout walking-stick from the stand by the front-door. 'Bring your torch along, Peter. We'll go out through the garden-hall.'

'It's tempting Providence, sir,' Bowers moaned, following at their heels.

Charles was drawing back the bolts from the door leading into the garden. 'Console yourself, Bowers. If it's a ghost it can't hurt you.'

'Don't you be so sure of that, sir!' Bowers said forebodingly.

The door swung open. The gardens on that side of the house were flooded by moonlight, but where the spinney flanked the lawn it was very dark. The stillness seemed to wrap them round; not even a breath of wind stirred the leaves on the branches.

'Better take a look amongst the trees,' Peter said in a low voice.

'Don't you go, sir, you don't know what might happen to you!'

'Well, I'm not asking you to come,' Peter said. 'Do pull yourself together!'

Together he and Charles stepped out on to the gravel-path, and began to cross the lawn towards the belt of trees.

'Bit of imagination, if you ask me,' Peter growled. 'Good job he didn't see that skeleton.' Then he grabbed at Charles' arm, and gripped it hard. Some shadow had moved among the still shadows of the trees. 'There is something there!' Peter breathed. 'Go carefully!'

They stole forward in the lee of the overgrown hedge, and as they drew nearer to the trees a figure seemed to slide out of the darkness before them. They saw a form standing motionless on the edge of the lawn. Its face was in shadow, but it looked their way, and seemed to be awaiting them. Involuntarily they checked, for there was something strangely eerie about the waiting form, nor could they distinguish more than the outline of the figure, which seemed to be draped in some long garment that looked rather like a cassock. Then the figure moved and the spell was broken.

'I fear I am committing an act of trespass,' a mild voice announced. 'I am in pursuit of a specimen rare indeed in this country. Permit me to make myself known to you; I fear you thought me a thief in the night.' As it spoke the figure removed a slouch hat, and revealed a countenance adorned with steel-rimmed spectacles, and surmounted by sparse grey hair. 'I am an entomologist: my name is Ernest Titmarsh,' it said.

Three

For a moment they stared at one another; then Peter began to laugh. Mr Ernest Titmarsh, far from being offended, beamed affably upon him. Peter pulled himself together as soon as he could, and said with a quiver in his voice: 'I beg your pardon, but really it's rather funny. You see, whenever we catch sight of anyone wandering about in our grounds we think he's a ghost.'

Mr Titmarsh blinked at him. 'Dear me, is that so indeed? A ghost, did you say?'

'Yes,' Charles said gravely. 'It's – it's an idiosyncrasy of ours.'

Mr Titmarsh replaced his hat upon his head, and seemed to give the matter some thought. Light broke upon him. 'Of course, of course!' he said. 'This is the Priory!'

'Didn't you know?' asked Peter, somewhat surprised.

'Now I come to look about me, yes,' replied their eccentric visitor. 'But I fear I am very absent-minded. Yes, yes, indeed, I owe you an apology. You are not, I suppose, interested in entomology?'

'I'm afraid I know very little about it,' confessed Peter.

'An absorbing study,' Mr Titmarsh said with enthusiasm. 'But it leads one into committing acts of trespass, as you perceive. Yes, I am much to blame. I will at once depart.'

'Oh, don't do that!' Charles interposed. 'We haven't the smallest objection to you – er – catching moths in our grounds. Now we know who you are we shan't take you for a ghost again.'

'Really,' said Mr Titmarsh, 'this is most kind. I repeat, *most* kind. Am I to understand that I have your permission to pursue my studies in your grounds? Tut-tut, this puts me under quite an obligation. Two evenings since, I observed what I believe to be an oleander hawk-moth. Yes, my dear sir, actually that rarest of specimens. I have great hopes of adding it to my collection. That will be indeed a triumph.'

'Well, in that case, we won't interrupt you any longer,' Charles said. 'We'll just wish you luck, and retire.'

Mr Titmarsh bowed with old-world courtesy, and as though his hobby suddenly called him, turned, and darted back amongst the trees.

'And there we are,' said Charles. 'Might as well live in a public park, as far as I can see. I wish I'd remembered to ask him if he was interested in skeletons.'

'I admit it looked a bit fishy, finding him snooping about just at this moment,' said Peter, 'but somehow I don't see him in the rôle of house-breaker. We'd better go in and reassure the girls.'

In the garden-hall they found Bowers, who had watched their proceedings with a gradual return to calm. He looked slightly sheepish when he learned who was the visitor, but he advanced the opinion that they had not heard the last of the Monk yet. This they were inclined to believe, but when they rejoined the girls they assumed the manner of those who had successfully laid a ghost.

Celia was not convinced, however. The discovery of the skeleton, she said, accounted for every strange noise they had heard, since its unquiet spirit was obviously haunting the scene of its ghastly end.

'I don't know about that,' said Mrs Bosanquet firmly, 'but I do know that it is most unhygienic to have dead bodies walled up in the house, and unless it is at once removed, and the place thoroughly fumigated, I shall return to town to-morrow.'

'Oh!' said Celia, shuddering, 'you don't suppose I'm going to stay here any longer do you, Aunt? We shall all go home to-morrow. I only wish we'd sold the place when we had the offer.'

'Look here, Celia,' Peter said. 'If the ghost of that poor devil really has been haunting the place it's ten to one it'll stop bothering us once we've buried the remains. Don't fuss, Aunt Lilian. Of course we're going to bury the skeleton, and you can fumigate as much as you like. But I do think we oughtn't to throw up the sponge quite so easily.'

'Easily!' said Celia. 'I don't know what more you're waiting for! I shan't know a quiet moment if I have to stay in this place another day.'

Margaret was looking from Charles to her brother. 'Go on, Peter. You think we ought to give the place another chance?'

'I do. Hang it all, we shall look a pretty good set of asses if we bunk back to town simply because we've heard a few odd noises, and discovered a skeleton in a priest's hole.'

'Shall we?' said Celia, with awful irony. 'I suppose we ought to have expected an ordinary little thing like a skeleton?'

'Not the skeleton, but we might have guessed there'd be a priest's hole. Be a sport, Celia! If you actually see a ghost, or if any more skulls fall out of cupboards I'll give in, and take you back to town myself.'

Celia looked imploringly at her husband. 'I can't, Chas. You know what I am, and I can't help it if I'm stupid about these things, but every time I open my wardrobe I shall be terrified of what may be inside.'

'All right, darling,' Charles replied. 'You shan't be martyred. I suggest you and Margaret and Aunt Lilian clear out to-morrow. I'll run you up to town, and . . .'

Celia sat bolt upright. 'Do you mean you'll stay here?'

'That's rather the idea,' he admitted.

'Charles, you can't!' she said, agitated. 'I won't let you!'

'I shan't be alone. Peter's staying too.'

Celia clasped his arm. 'No, don't, Charles. You don't *know* what might happen, and how on earth could I go away like that, and leave you here?'

Margaret's clear voice made itself heard. 'Why are you so keen to stay?' she asked.

'Pride, my dear,' Charles said. 'Of course, with me it's natural heroism. Peter's trying to live up to me.'

She shook her head. 'You've got something up your sleeve. Neither of you would be so silly as to stay on here, mucking up your holiday, just to prove you weren't afraid of ghosts.'

'But it's getting worse!' Celia cried. '*What* have you got up your sleeve? I insist on knowing! Chas! Peter!'

Peter hesitated. 'To tell you the truth, Sis, I don't quite know. As far as I can make out, Chas has got an idea someone's at the root of all this ghost business.'

With great deliberation Mrs Bosanquet put down her Patience pack. 'I may be stupid,' she said, 'but I don't understand what you're talking about. Who is at the back of what you call this "ghost business," and why?'

'Dear Aunt,' said Charles, 'that is precisely the problem we hope to solve by staying here.'

'All those noises? The picture falling down?' Margaret said eagerly. 'You think someone did it all? Someone real?'

'I don't know, but I think it's possible. I may be wrong, in which case I'll eat my disbelief, and go about henceforward swearing there are such things as ghosts.'

'Yes, that's all very well,' objected Celia, 'but why on earth should anyone want to make ghost-noises and things at us? And who could have done it? Neither of the Bowers would, and how could anyone else get into the house without us knowing?'

'Easily,' said Charles. 'There's more than one way in, besides windows.'

'That quite decides me,' Mrs Bosanquet announced. 'No one is a greater believer in fresh air than I am, but if I am to remain in this house, I shall sleep with my windows securely bolted.'

'I still don't quite see it,' Margaret said. 'I suppose it would be fairly easy to get into the house, but you haven't explained why anyone should want to.'

'Don't run away with the idea that I'm wedded to this

notion!' Charles warned her. 'I admit it sounds far-fetched, but it has occurred to me that someone – for reasons which I can't explain – may be trying to scare us out of this place.'

There was a short silence. Celia broke it. 'That's just like you!' she said indignantly. 'Sooner than own you've been wrong all these years about ghosts you make up a much more improbable story to account for the manifestations. I never heard such rot in all my life!'

'Thank you, darling, thank you,' Charles said gravely.

'Hold on a minute!' interrupted Margaret. 'Perhaps Chas is right.'

Celia almost snorted. 'Don't you pay any attention to him, my dear. He'll tell us next it's the man who wanted to buy the Priory from us trying to get us out of it.'

'Well, while we're on the improbable lay, what about that for a theory?' demanded Peter. 'Resourceful sort of bloke, what?'

Mrs Bosanquet resumed her Patience. 'Whoever it may be, it's a piece of gross impertinence,' she said. 'You are quite right, Charles. *I* am certainly not going to leave the place because some ill-bred person is trying to frighten me away. The proper course is to inform the police at once.'

'From my small experience of local constabulary I don't think that'd be much use," said Charles. 'Moreover what with Margaret's sinister pal and the egregious Mr Titmarsh, we've got quite enough people littered about the grounds without adding a flat-footed bobby to the collection.'

'Further,' added Peter, 'I for one have little or no desire to figure as the laughing-stock of the village. I move that we keep this thing quiet, and do a little sleuthing on our own.'

Margaret waved a hand aloft at once. 'Rather! I say, this is getting really thrilling. Come on, Celia, don't be snitchy!'

'All right,' Celia said reluctantly. 'I can't go away and leave you here, so I suppose I've got to give in. But I won't go upstairs alone after dark, and I won't be left for one moment by myself in this house, day or night, and Charles isn't to do anything foolhardy, and if anything awful happens we all of us clear out without any further argument.'

'Agreed,' Peter said. 'What about you, Aunt Lilian?'

'Provided the dead body is decently interred, and a secure bolt fixed to my door, I shall certainly remain,' answered Mrs Bosanquet.

'What could be fairer than that?' said Charles. 'If you like you can even superintend the burial.'

'No, thank you, my dear,' she replied. 'I have never yet attended a funeral, and I don't propose to start with this body in which I have not the smallest interest. Not but what I am very sorry that whoever it was died in such unpleasant circumstances, but I do not feel that it has anything to do with me, and I could wish it had happened elsewhere.'

'Well, since we're all making stipulations,' Margaret put in, 'I can't help feeling that I should rather like to have the door between Peter's room and mine open. D'you mind, Peter?'

'I can bear it,' he answered. 'As for the bones, Chas and I will bury them to-morrow, and we'll say nothing about them, any of us. See?'

'Just as you please, my dear,' Mrs Bosanquet replied. 'But I cannot help feeling that the police should be told. However, that is for you to decide. Celia, you had better come up to bed. I am coming too, so there is nothing to be alarmed about.'

'I hate the idea of going up those stairs,' Celia shuddered.

'Nonsense!' said Mrs Bosanquet, and bore her inexorably away.

The two men's task next morning was sufficiently gruesome to throw a cloud of depression over their spirits. Not even the sight of Mrs Bosanquet sprinkling Lysol in the priest's hole could lighten the general gloom, and when, after lunch, Charles suggested that he and Peter might go out fishing it was with somewhat forced cheerfulness that Peter agreed.

But an afternoon spent by the trout stream did much to restore their spirits. The fish were rising well, and the weather conditions were ideal.

They worked some way down the stream, and when they at last set out to return to the Priory they found themselves a considerable distance away from it. Charles' bump of locality, however, served them well, and he was able to lead the way home across country, by a route that brought them eventually to the footpath Michael Strange had so unaccountably failed to find.

It was already nearly time for dinner, and the two men quickened their steps. They had left the footpath, and were just skirting the ruined chapel when the sound of footsteps made them glance back towards the right-of-way. Where they stood they were more or less hidden from the path by a portion of the chapel wall.

Thinking the pedestrian one of the villagers on his way home, they were about to continue on their way when the man came into sight round a bend in the path, and they saw that it was none other than the commercial gentleman they had first seen in the taproom of the Bell Inn. This in itself was not very surprising, but the stranger's behaviour caused both men, as though by tacit consent, to draw farther into the lee of the chapel wall. The small stranger was proceeding rather cautiously, and looking about him as though he expected to meet someone. He paused as he came abreast of the chapel, and peeped into the ruins. Then, after hesitating for a moment he gave a surprisingly sweet whistle, rather like the notes of a thrush. This was answered almost at once from somewhere near at hand; there came a rustling amongst the bushes, and Michael Strange stepped out on to the path from the direction of the Priory gardens.

Charles placed a warning hand on Peter's arm; Peter nodded, and stayed very still.

'Any luck?' inquired the small man, in a low voice.

Strange shook his head. 'No. We shall have to try the other way again.'

'Ah!' said the other gloomily. 'I don't half like it, guv'nor, and that's the truth. Supposing we was to be seen? It would look a bit unnatural, wouldn't it? It's risky, that's what it is. One of them might wake up, and I don't see myself doing no spook stunts. Clean out of my line, that is. I done some jobs in my time, as you know, but I don't like this one. It's one thing to crack a crib, but this job ain't what I'd call straightforward.'

'You'll be all right,' Strange said rather impatiently. 'If

you'd remember not to waylay me where we might easily be seen together. Go on ahead. I'll follow.'

'All right, guv'nor: just as you say,' the small man replied, unabashed, and moved off down the path.

When Strange had gone Charles looked at Peter. 'Very interesting,' he said. 'What did you make of it?'

'God knows. It sounded as though they were going to burgle the place, but I suppose it's not that. It looks very much as though one or both of them were responsible for last night's picnic.'

'And they'll have to "try the other way again,"' mused Charles. 'Look here, Peter, are you game to sit up to-night with me, and see what happens?'

'Of course, but Celia'll throw a fit.'

'I'll join you as soon as she's asleep. If nothing happens we've simply got to repeat the performance till something does. I wish I knew what they were after.'

'Meanwhile,' said Peter, consulting his wrist-watch, 'it's already half-past seven, and we're dining with old Ackerley at eight.' He stopped suddenly. 'By Jove! Think that mysterious pair will get going in the house while we're out? I hadn't thought of that.'

'No,' said Charles. 'The little chap spoke of one of us "waking up."'

'All the same,' Peter said, 'I move that we don't stay late at the White House.'

In spite of what Charles said, Peter felt ill at ease about leaving the Priory in the sole charge of the Bowers. Clever crooks, he was sure, would know the movements of their prospective victims. Yet if burglary were meditated surely these particular crooks would find it an easy enough task to break into the Priory without shadowing the place at all hours, and searching for – what? There he found himself up against a blank wall again. Strange and his odd companion had certainly been looking for something, but what it was, or what connexion it could have with a possible burglary he had no idea.

He realised that his mind harped all the time on burglary, and was forced to admit to himself that it was an improbable solution. There was very little of value in the house, and if anything so unlikely as hidden treasure were being sought for it was incredible that the thieves should have waited until the house was tenanted before they made an attempt to find it.

Charles obviously connected the affair of the previous evening with Strange, in which case it looked as though Strange's primary object was to frighten the tenants out of the house. He wondered whether he would seize the opportunity this dinner-party afforded to stage another, and even more nerve-racking, booby-trap.

Peter arrived at the White House with the rest of his family just as eight o'clock struck. His sisters, who had reviled both him and Charles for staying out so late, drew two sighs of relief.

'Scaremongers,' said Charles. 'I told you it wouldn't take us ten minutes to get here.'

They had walked to the White House across their own grounds, a proceeding which Celia had condemned, dreading the return late at night, but which had been forced on them, not only on account of its convenience, but on account also of the car, which had developed slight magneto trouble, and refused to start.

They entered the drawing-room to find that Mr

Titmarsh, and Dr Roote and his wife, fellow-guests, had already arrived, and Celia was just telling her host laughingly that if they were late he must blame her menfolk, when the Colonel's butler opened the door to announce yet another guest. To Peter's amazement Michael Strange walked into the room.

'I don't think you know Strange, do you?' the Colonel said, to the room at large. He began to introduce the dark young man.

'Yes, we've met twice,' Margaret said, when it came to her turn. She smiled at Strange. 'How do you do? How's the fishing?'

'Splendid!' he said. He turned to Charles. 'Have you tried the streams here yet?'

Seen in such civilised surroundings it was hard to believe that this young man was the same who had, not an hour ago, held a furtive conversation with a character whose own words proclaimed him to be a member of the criminal classes. Feeling more completely at sea than ever, Charles answered his question with a description of the afternoon's sport. Dinner was announced almost immediately, and the Colonel began to marshal his guests.

'I must apologise for our uneven numbers,' he said breezily. 'Four ladies to six men! Well, I think we'd better go in all together. Mrs Bosanquet, let me show you the way.'

'Too many men is a fault on the good side, anyway, isn't it?' Mrs Roote said. She was a good-looking blonde, grown a little haggard, and with a rather harsh voice. Her husband was an untidy individual of some forty years, whose huskiness of speech and rather hazy eye betrayed his weakness. His address, however, was pleasant, and he seemed to be getting on well with Celia, whom he took in to dinner behind the Colonel and Mrs Bosanquet.

The White House was a solid Victorian building, with large airy rooms, and the boon of electric light. It was furnished in good if rather characterless style, but evidence of the Colonel's ownership existed in the various trophies that adorned the dining-room walls. Mrs Bosanquet remarked as she took her seat at the round table that it was pleasant to find herself in an up-to-date house again.

'Oh, I'm afraid the White House is a very dull affair after the Priory,' Colonel Ackerley replied. 'Suits me, you know; never had much use for old buildings. Full of draughts and inconvenience, *I* always say, but I'm afraid I'm a regular vandal. I can see Mrs Malcolm shaking her head at me.'

Celia laughed. 'I wasn't,' she assured him. 'I was shaking it at Mr Titmarsh.' She turned to her other neighbour again. 'No, I'm absolutely ignorant about butterflies and things, but it sounds *most* interesting. Do . . .'

Mr Titmarsh eyed her severely. 'Moths, madam!' he said.

'Yes, moths. I meant moths. I've noticed quite a number here. They will fly into our candles.'

Margaret, who was seated between her brother and Strange, said softly: 'Do listen to my sister floundering hopelessly!' She shook out her table-napkin, and began to drink her soup. 'You know, you're a fraud,' she said. 'You told me you didn't know anyone in Framley.'

'Honestly, it was quite true,' Michael replied. 'I only met the Colonel last night. He blew into the Bell, and we got talking, and he very kindly asked me to dine with him. In fact' – his eyes twinkled – 'he wouldn't take No for an answer.'

'I think you must be a recluse, or something,' Margaret teased him. 'Why should you want him to take No for an answer?'

'I didn't,' said Strange, looking down at her, with a smile. 'He told me you were coming.'

Margaret blushed at that, but laughed. 'I feel I ought to get up and bow,' she said.

Peter, who had heard, leaned forward to speak to Strange across his sister. 'Were you on the right-of-way late this afternoon?' he asked. 'I thought I caught a glimpse of you.'

If he hoped that Michael Strange would betray uneasiness he was disappointed. 'Yes,' Strange said tranquilly. 'I was fishing the Crewel again to-day. I didn't see you.'

'Oh, I was some way off,' Peter answered.

In a momentary lull in the general conversation Celia's voice was heard. 'And you saw this rare moth in our grounds? How exciting! Tell me what it looks like.'

'Ah, that oleander hawk-moth,' said Charles. 'Did you have any luck, sir?'

'Not yet,' Mr Titmarsh said. 'Not yet, but I do not despair.'

The Colonel broke off in the middle of what he was saying to Mrs Bosanquet to exclaim: 'Hullo, have you been chasing moths at the Priory, Titmarsh? Never shall forget how I took you for a burglar when I first found you in my garden.'

His hearty laugh was echoed more mildly by the entomologist, who said: 'I fear I am somewhat remiss in asking the permission of my good neighbours if I may trespass harmlessly on their land. Your husband,' he added, looking at Celia, 'mistook me for a ghost.'

'Oh, have you seen the Priory ghost yet?' Mrs Roote inquired. 'Do harrow us! I adore having my flesh made to creep.'

Strange, who had looked directly across the table at Mr Titmarsh from under his black brows, said quietly to Margaret: 'Is that really true? Does he prowl round the countryside looking for moths?'

'Yes, so they all say. Charles and Peter saw him in our garden last night. He's rather eccentric, I think.'

'What with myself and – what's his name? Titmarsh? – you seem to be beset by people who roam about your grounds at will,' Strange remarked. 'If I remember rightly you said you took me for the ghost as well.'

'Ah, that was just a joke,' Margaret answered. 'I didn't really. And of course Charles and Peter wouldn't have taken Mr Titmarsh for one in the ordinary course of events.'

'You mean that you all rather expect to see the famous Monk?'

'No, but that was the night . . .' She broke off.

Strange looked inquiringly down at her. 'Yes?'

'Nothing,' Margaret said rather lamely.

'That sounds very mysterious,' Strange said. 'Have you been having trouble with the Monk?'

She shook her head. Colonel Ackerley called across the table: 'What's that? Talking about the Priory ghost? These fair ladies are much too stout-hearted to believe in it, Strange. It would take more than the Monk to shake your nerve, Mrs Bosanquet, wouldn't it?'

'I am thankful to say I have never suffered from nerves,' Mrs Bosanquet responded. 'But it is certainly very disturbing when . . .' She encountered Charles' eye and blinked. 'When the servants are afraid to stay in the house after dark,' she concluded placidly.

'I'm sure you've seen something!' chattered Mrs Roote. 'Or at least heard awful noises. Now haven't you, Mrs Bosanquet?'

'Unfortunately,' replied Mrs Bosanquet, 'I suffer from slight deafness.'

'I see you're all of you determined not to satisfy our morbid curiosity,' said Strange.

Mr Titmarsh took off his spectacles and polished them. 'On the subject of ghosts,' he said, 'I am a confirmed sceptic. I am devoid of curiosity.'

'Well, I don't know so much about that,' said Dr Roote. 'I remember a very queer experience that happened to a friend of mine once. Now, he was one of the most matter-of-fact people I know . . .' He embarked on a long and rather involved ghost story, interrupted and prompted at intervals by his wife, and it only ended with the departure of the ladies from the dining-room.

Two bridge tables were formed presently, but the party broke up shortly before eleven. The Rootes were the first to leave, and they were soon followed by the Priory party and Strange. Strange's two-seater stood at the door, and when he found that the others were walking back across the park he promptly offered to take the three women in his car.

Celia, who had already begun to peer fearfully into the

darkness, jumped at the offer, but stipulated that Strange should not leave them until Charles and Peter had reached the house. 'You'll think me a fool,' she said, 'but the Priory after dark is more than I can bear. Can we really all get into your car?'

'If one of you doesn't mind sitting in the dickey I think it can be managed,' Strange replied. 'And of course I'll wait till your husband gets back. I'm only sorry I can't take you all.'

'Well, really, this is most opportune,' said Mrs Bosanquet, getting into the little car. 'I notice that there is quite a heavy dew on the ground.'

Whatever Strange's wishes may have been it was Margaret who sat in the dickey, while Celia managed to insert her slim person between Mrs Bosanquet and the door.

'We've no business to impose on you like this, of course,' Celia said, as the car slid out of the White House gates. 'It's only a step, across the park, but I do so hate the dark.'

'It's not an imposition at all,' Michael answered. He drove down the road for the short distance that separated the White House from the Priory, and turned carefully in at the rather awkward entrance to the long avenue. The headlights showed the drive winding ahead, and made the tall trees on either side look like walls of darkness. The house came presently into sight, and in a few moments they were all inside the softly-lighted hall.

Celia stood for an instant as though listening. The house seemed to be wrapped in stillness. 'I love it by day,' she said abruptly. 'It's only at night it gets different. Like this. Can't you feel it? A sort of boding.'

'Why are you so afraid of it?' Strange asked her. 'You must have some reason other than village-gossip. Has anything happened to alarm you?'

She gave a tiny shiver. 'I'm a fool, that's all,' she answered. 'Let's go into the library.' A tray with drinks had been set out there. 'Do help yourself,' she said. 'There's whisky, or a soft drink, whichever you prefer.'

'Can I bring you anything?'

'I'd like some lemonade, please.'

Mrs Bosanquet emerged from the cloud of tulle she had swathed round her head. 'My own opinion is, and always will be,' she said firmly, 'that there are no such things as ghosts. And if – mind you, I only say *if* – I thought there was anything odd about a house, I, personally, should inform the police.'

Strange carried a glass over to where Celia was sitting. 'Is that what you've done?' he asked.

'Not at all,' she replied. 'I said "if." '

'Would you do that, Mr Strange?' Margaret inquired. 'Just supposing you heard weird sounds and things?'

'No, I don't think I should,' he said. 'I'm afraid I haven't much opinion of village policemen.'

'My husband hasn't either,' Celia said. She heard a latchkey grate in the lock. 'Here he is!' she said. 'Is that you, Charles?'

'I'm not quite sure,' came the answer. 'It used to be, but since the experiences of the last ten minutes . . .'

'Good heavens, you haven't seen the ghost, have you?' cried Margaret.

Charles appeared in the doorway, minus his shoes. Over his shoulder Peter said, grinning: 'He encountered a little mud, that's all.'

'If you want to know the truth,' said Charles, 'I have narrowly escaped death by drowning in quicksands. Thank you, yes, and don't overdo the soda! Too much of water hast thou, poor Charles Malcolm.'

'Oh, I know! You must have found that boggy patch,' said Margaret.

'I trust it was not the cesspool,' Mrs Bosanquet said, in mild concern.

'So do I,' Charles said. 'That thought had not so far occurred to me, but – but I do hope it wasn't.'

'Take heart,' said Strange, setting down his glass. 'I think your cesspool is more likely to be down near the river.' He went up to Celia, and held out his hand. 'I'm sure you're longing to get to bed, Mrs Malcolm, so I'll say good-night.'

He took his leave of them all. Peter escorted him to the front door, and when the two of them had left the room Charles said: 'Well, of all the miserable conspirators commend me to you three! I should think by to-morrow the whole countryside will know that something has happened here.'

'Really, Charles!' Mrs Bosanquet expostulated. 'It is true that I was about to make a reference to what happened last night, but I am sure I covered it up most naturally.'

'Dear Aunt,' said Charles frankly, 'not one of you would have deceived an oyster.'

Peter came back into the room. 'You seem to be getting very thick with Strange,' he said to his sister. 'Did you happen to find out what he is, or anything about him?'

'He's a surveyor,' said Charles, finishing what was left of his whisky and soda.

'A surveyor?' echoed Margaret. 'How do you know? Did he tell you so?'

'To the deductive mind,' said Charles airily, 'his profession was obvious from his knowledge of the probable whereabouts of our cesspool.'

'Ass!' said Celia. 'Come on up to bed. What does it matter what he is? He's nice, that's all I know.'

It was two hours later when Charles came downstairs again, and he had changed into a tweed suit, and was wearing rubber-soled shoes. Peter was already in the library, reading by the light of one lamp. He looked up as Charles came in. 'Celia asleep?' he asked.

'She was when I left her, but I've trod on nineteen creaking boards since then. Have you been round the house?'

'I have, and I defy anyone to get in without us hearing.'

Charles went across to draw the heavy curtains still more closely together over the windows. 'If Strange really means to try and get in to-night, he won't risk it for another hour or two,' he prophesied. 'Hanged if I can make that fellow out!'

'From what I could gather,' Peter said, 'he did his best to pump Margaret. Seemed to want to find out how we were getting on here.'

Charles grunted, and drew a chair up to the desk and proceeded to study a brief which had been sent on from town that morning. Peter retired into his book again, and for a long while no sound broke the silence save the crackle of the papers under Charles' hand, and the measured tick of the old grandfather clock in the hall. At last Peter came to the end of his novel, and closed it. He yawned, and looked at his wrist-watch. 'Good Lord! two o'clock already! Do we sit here till breakfast-time? I've an idea I shan't feel quite so fresh to-morrow night.'

Charles pushed his papers from him with a short sigh of exasperation. 'I don't know why people go to law,' he said gloomily. 'More money than sense.'

'Got a difficult case?' inquired Peter.

'I haven't got a case at all,' was the withering retort. 'And that's counsel's learned opinion. Would you like to go and fetch me something to eat from the larder?'

'No,' said Peter, 'since you put it like that, I shouldn't.'

'Then I shall have to go myself,' said Charles, getting up. 'There was a peculiarly succulent pie if I remember rightly.'

'Well, bring it in here, and I'll help you eat it,' Peter offered. 'And don't forget the bread!'

Before Charles could open his mouth to deliver a suitable reply a sound broke the quiet of the house, and brought Peter to his feet in one startled bound. For the sound was that same eerie groan which they had heard before, and which seemed to rise shuddering from somewhere beneath their feet.

Four

The weird sound died, and again silence settled down on the house. Yet somehow the silence seemed now to be worse than that hair-raising groan. Something besides themselves was in the house.

Peter passed his tongue between lips that had grown suddenly dry. He looked at Charles, standing motionless in the doorway. Charles was listening intently; he held up a warning finger.

Softly Peter went across to his side. Charles said under his breath:

'Wait. No use plunging round the house haphazard. Turn the lamp down.'

Peter went back, and in a moment only a glimmer of light illumined the room. He drew his torch out of his pocket and stood waiting by the table.

It seemed to him that the minutes dragged past. Straining his ears he thought he could hear little sounds, tiny creaks of furniture, perhaps the scutter of a mouse somewhere in the wainscoting. The ticking of the clock seemed unusually loud, and when an owl hooted outside it made him jump.

A stair creaked; Charles' torch flashed a white beam of

light across the empty hall, and went out again. He slightly shook his head in answer to Peter's quick look of inquiry.

Peter found himself glancing over his shoulder towards the window. He half thought that one of the curtains moved slightly, but when he moved cautiously forward to draw it back there was nothing there. He let it fall into position again, and stood still, wishing that something, anything, would happen to break this nerve-racking silence.

He saw Charles stiffen suddenly, and incline his head as though to hear more distinctly. He stole to his side. 'What?' he whispered.

'Listen!'

Again the silence fell. Peter broke it. 'What did you hear?'

'A thud. There it is again!'

A muffled knock reached Peter's ears. It seemed to come from underneath. In a moment it was repeated, a dull thud, drawing nearer, as though something was striking against a stone wall.

'The cellars!' Peter hissed. 'There must be a way in that we haven't found!'

Again the knocking, deadened by the solid floor, was repeated. It was moving nearer still, and seemed now to sound directly beneath their feet.

'Come on!' Charles said, and slipped the torch into his left hand. He picked up the stout ash-plant which he had placed ready for use, and stole out, and across the hall to the door that shut off the servants' wing from the rest of the house.

The stairs leading down to the cellars were reached at

the end of the passage. They were stone, and the two men crept down them without a sound to betray their presence. At the foot Charles said in Peter's ear: 'Know your way about?'

'No,' Peter whispered. 'We don't use the cellars.'

'Damn!' Charles switched on his torch again.

The place felt dank and very cold. Grey walls of stone flanked the passage; the roof was of stone also, and vaulted. Charles moved forward, down the arched corridor, in the direction of the library. Various cellars led out of the main passage; in the first was a great mound of coal, but the rest were empty.

The passage seemed to run down one side of the building, but the vaults that gave on to it led each one into another, so that the place was something of a labyrinth. The knocking sounded distinctly now, echoing through the empty cellars. Charles held his torch lowered, so that the circle of light was thrown barely a yard in front of him.

Suddenly the knocking ceased, and at once both men stood still, waiting for some sound to guide them.

Ahead of them, where the passage ended, something moved. Charles flashed his torch upwards, and for a brief instant he and Peter caught a glimpse of a vague figure. Then, as though it had melted into the wall, it was gone, and a wail as of a soul in torment seemed to fill the entire place.

The sweat broke out on both men's foreheads, and for a second neither could move for sheer horror. Then Charles pulled himself together and dashed forward, shouting to Peter to follow.

'My God, what was it?' Peter gasped.

'The groan we've all heard, of course. Damn it, he can't have got away!'

But the place where the figure had stood was quite empty. An embrasure in the wall seemed to mark the spot where they had seen it, yet if the apparent melting into the wall had been no more than a drawing back into this niche that could not solve the complete disappearance of the figure.

The two men stared at one another. Charles passed the back of his hand across his forehead. 'But – but I saw it!' he stammered.

'So did I,' Peter said roughly. 'Good God, it *can't* be . . . This is getting a bit too weird to be pleasant. Look here . . . Damn it, that was no ghost. There must be a secret way through the wall.' His torch played over the wall. It was built of great stone slabs each about four foot square. He began to feel them in turn. 'We must be under the terrace,' he said. 'Gosh, don't you see? We're standing on the level of the ground here!' One of the blocks gave slightly under the thrust of his hand. 'Got it!' he panted, and set his shoulder to it. It swung slowly outward, turning on some hidden pivot, and as it moved that hideous wail once more rent the stillness.

'So that's it, is it?' Charles said grimly. 'Well, I don't mind telling you that I'm damned glad we've solved the origin of that ghastly noise.' He squeezed through the opening in Peter's wake, and found himself, as Peter had prophesied, in the garden directly beneath the terrace. There was no sign of anyone amongst the shrubs near at hand, and it was obviously useless to search the grounds. After a moment both men slipped back into the cellar, and pushed the stone into place again.

'Might as well have a look round to see what that chap was after,' Peter said. 'Why the banging? Is he looking for a hollow wall, do you suppose? Dash it, I rejected hidden treasure as altogether too far-fetched, but it begins to look remarkably like it!'

'Personally I don't think we shall find anything,' Charles answered. 'Still, we can try. What a maze the place is!'

Together they explored all the cellars, but Charles was right, and there was nothing to be seen. Deciding that their nocturnal visitor would hardly attempt another entrance now that his way of ingress had been discovered, they made their way up the stairs again.

As they crossed the hall towards the library door a glimmer of light shone on the landing above, and Margaret's voice called softly: 'Peter.'

'Hullo!' Peter responded.

'Thank goodness!' breathed his sister, and came cautiously down to join him. In the lamplight her face looked rather pale, and her eyes very big and scared. 'That awful groan woke me,' she said. 'I heard it twice, and called to you, Peter. Then when you didn't answer I went into your room and saw the bed hadn't been slept in. I got the most horrible fright.'

'Don't make a row. Come into the library,' Peter commanded. 'You didn't wake Celia, did you?'

'No, I guessed you and Charles had staged something. Did you hear the groan? What have you been doing?'

'We not only heard it, but on two occasions we caused it,' Peter said, and proceeded to tell her briefly all that had happened.

She listened in wondering silence, but when he spoke

of the part he believed Strange to be playing, she broke in with an emphatic and somewhat indignant headshake. 'I'm sure he isn't a crook! And I'm perfectly certain he'd never make awful noises to frighten us, or put skeletons where we should find them. Besides, why should he?'

'I'm not prepared to answer that question without due warning,' Charles said cautiously. 'All I know about him at present is that he's a rather mysterious fellow who holds distinctly fishy conversations with a palpable old lag, and who – apparently – knows how to get round persons of your sex.'

'That's all rot,' Margaret said without hesitation. 'There's nothing in the least mysterious about him, and I expect if you'd heard more of it you'd have found that the fishy conversation was quite innocent really. You know how you can say things that sound odd in themselves, and yet don't mean anything.'

'I hotly resent this reflection upon my conversation,' Charles said.

'You've got to remember too, Peg, that when we heard that groan before, we found Strange close up to the house, and on the same side as the secret entrance,' Peter interposed. 'I don't say that that proves anything, but it ought to be borne in mind. I certainly think that Mr Michael Strange's proceedings want explaining.'

'I think it's utterly absurd!' Margaret said. 'Why, you might as well suspect Mr Titmarsh!' Having delivered herself of which scornful utterance, she rose, and announced her intention of going back to bed.

To be on the safe side, Charles and Peter spent the following morning in sealing up the hidden entrance. An account of the night's happenings did much to reconcile

Celia to her enforced stay at the Priory. Human beings, she said, she wasn't in the least afraid of.

'I only hope,' said Mrs Bosanquet pessimistically, 'that we are not all murdered in our beds.'

Both she and Celia were agreed that the latest development made the calling in of police aid imperative. The men were still loth to do this, but they had to admit that Celia had reason on her side.

'There's no longer any question of being laughed at,' she argued. 'Someone broke into this house last night, and it's for the police to take the matter in hand. It's all very well for you two to fancy yourselves in the rôle of amateur detectives, but I should feel a lot easier in my mind if some real detectives got going.'

'How can you?' said Charles unctuously. 'When you lost your diamond brooch, who found it?'

'I did,' Celia replied. 'Wedged between the bristles of my hair-brush. That was after you'd had the waste up in the bath, and two of the floor-boards in our room.'

'That wasn't the time I meant,' said Charles hastily.

Celia wrinkled her brow. 'The only other time I lost it was at that hotel in Edinburgh, and then you stepped on it getting out of bed. If that's what you mean . . .'

'Well, wasn't that finding it?' demanded Charles. 'Guided by a rare intuition, I rose from my couch, and straightway put my – er – foot on the thing.'

'You did. But that wasn't quite how you phrased it at the time,' said Celia. 'If I remember rightly . . .'

'You needn't go on,' Charles told her. 'When it comes to recounting incidents in which I played a prominent part you never do remember rightly. To put it bluntly, for gross misrepresentation of fact you're hard to beat.'

'Time!' called Peter. 'Let's put it to the vote. Who is for calling in the police, or who is not? Margaret, you've got the casting vote. What do you say?'

She hesitated. 'I think I rather agree with Celia. You both suspect Mr Strange. Well, I'm sure you're wrong. Let the police take over before you go and make fools of yourselves.' She added apologetically: 'I don't mean to be rude about it, but . . .'

'I'm glad to know that,' said Charles. 'I mean, we might easily have misunderstood you. But what a field of conjecture this opens out! I shall always wonder what you'd have said if you had meant to be rude.'

'Well, you'll know in a minute,' retorted Margaret. 'And it's no good blinking facts: once you and Peter get an idea into your heads, nothing on God's earth will get it out again. You will make fools of yourselves if you go sleuthing after the unfortunate Mr Strange. If he is at the root of it the police'll find him out, and if he isn't they'll find *that* out weeks before you would.'

After that, as Peter said, there was nothing to be done but to go and interview the village constable at once. Accordingly he and Charles set out for Framley after lunch, and found the constable, a bucolic person of the name of Flinders, digging his garden.

He received them hopefully, but no sooner had they explained their errand than his face fell somewhat, and he scratched his chin with a puzzled air.

'You'd better come inside, sir,' he said, after profound thought. He led them up the narrow path to his front door, and ushered them into the living-room of his cottage. He asked them to sit down and to excuse him for a moment, and vanished into the kitchen at the back of the cottage. Sounds of splashing followed, and in a few moments Constable Flinders reappeared, having washed his earth-caked hands, and put on his uniform coat. With this he had assumed an imposing air of officialdom, and he held in his hand the usual grimy little notebook. 'Now, sir!' he said importantly, and took a chair at the table opposite his visitors. He licked the stub of a pencil. 'You say you found some person or persons breaking into your house with intent to commit a robbery?'

'I don't think I said that at all,' Charles replied. 'I found the person in my cellars. What he came for I've no idea.'

'Ah!' said Mr Flinders. 'That's very different, that is.' He licked the pencil again, reflectively. 'Did you reckernise this person?'

Charles hesitated. 'No,' he answered at last. 'There wasn't time. He escaped by this secret way I told you about.'

'Escaped by secret way,' repeated Mr Flinders, laboriously writing it down. 'I shall have to see that, sir.'

'I can show you the spot, but I'm afraid we've already cemented it up.'

Mr Flinders shook his head reproachfully. 'You shouldn't have done that,' he pronounced. 'That'll make it difficult for me to act, that will.'

'Why?' asked Peter.

Mr Flinders looked coldly at him. 'I ought to have been called in before any evidence of the crime had been disturbed,' he said.

'There wasn't a crime,' Peter pointed out.

This threw the constable momentarily out of his stride. He thought again for some time, and presently asked:

'And you don't suspect no one in particular?'

Peter glanced at Charles, who said: 'Rather difficult to say. I haven't any good reason to suspect anyone, but various people have been seen hanging about the Priory at different times.'

'Ah!' said Mr Flinders. 'Now we are getting at something, sir. I thought we should. You'll have to tell me who you've seen hanging round, and then I shall know where I am.'

'Well,' said Charles. 'There's Mr Titmarsh to start with.'

The constable's official cloak slipped from his shoulders. 'Lor', sir, he wouldn't hurt a fly!' he said.

'I don't know what he does to flies,' retorted Charles, 'but he's death on moths.'

Mr Flinders shook his head. 'Of course I shall have to follow it up,' he said darkly. 'That's what my duty is, but Mr Titmarsh don't mean no harm. He was catching moths, that's what he was doing.'

'So he told us, and for all I know it may be perfectly true. But I feel I should like to know something about the eccentric gentleman. You say he's above suspicion . . .'

He was stopped by a large hand raised warningly. 'No, sir, that I never said, nor wouldn't. It'll have to be *sifted.* That's what I said.'

'. . . and,' continued Charles, disregarding the interruption, 'I can't say that I myself think he's likely to be the guilty party. How long has he lived here?'

Mr Flinders thought for a moment. 'Matter of three years,' he answered.

'Anything known about him?'

'There isn't nothing known *against* him, sir,' said the

constable. 'Barring his habits, which is queer to some folk's way of thinking, but which others who has such hobbies can understand, he's what I'd call a very ordinary gentleman. Keeps himself to himself, as the saying is. He's not married, but Mrs Fellowes from High Barn, who is his housekeeper, hasn't never spoken a word against him, and she's a very respectable woman that wouldn't stop a day in a place where there was any goings-on that oughtn't to be.'

'She might not know,' Peter suggested.

'There's precious little happens in Framley that Mrs Fellowes don't know about, sir,' said Mr Flinders. '*And* knows more than what the people do themselves,' he added obscurely, but with considerable feeling.

'Putting Mr Titmarsh aside for the moment,' said Charles. 'The other two men we've encountered in our grounds are a Mr Strange, who is staying at the Bell, and a smallish chap, giving himself out to be a commercial traveller, who's also at the Bell.' He recounted under what circumstances he had met Michael Strange, and the constable brightened considerably. 'That's more like it, that is,' he said. 'Hanging about on the same side of the house as that secret entrance, was he?'

'Mind you, he may have been speaking the truth when he said he had missed his way,' Charles warned him.

'That's what I shall have to find out,' said Mr Flinders. 'I shall have to keep a watch on those two.'

'You might make a few inquiries about them,' Peter suggested. 'Discover where they come from, and what Strange's occupation is.'

'You don't need to tell *me* how to act, sir,' said Mr

Flinders with dignity. 'Now that I've got a line to follow I know my duty.'

'There's just one other thing,' Charles said slowly. 'You'd probably better know about it.'

'Certainly I had,' said Mr Flinders. 'If you was to keep anything from me I couldn't act.'

'I suspect,' said Charles, 'that whoever got into the Priory has some reason for wishing to frighten us out of it.'

Mr Flinders blinked at him. 'What would they want to do that for?' he asked practically.

'That's what we thought you might find out,' Charles said.

'If there's anything to find you may be sure I shall get on to it,' Mr Flinders assured him. 'But you'll have to tell me some more.'

'I'm going to. A few nights ago a picture fell down at the top of the stairs, and when we went up to investigate my wife found the upper half of a human skull on the stairs. My brother-in-law and I then discovered a priest's hole in the panelling where the picture had hung, and in it a collection of human bones.'

The effect of this on the constable was not quite what they had hoped. His jaw dropped, and he sat staring at them in round-eyed horror. 'My Gawd, sir, it's the Monk!' he gasped. 'You don't suppose I can go making inquiries about a ghost, do you? I wouldn't touch it – not for a thousand pounds! And here's me taking down in me notebook what you told me about Mr Titmarsh and them two up at the Inn, and all the time you've seen the Monk!' He drew a large handkerchief from his pocket, and wiped his brow with it. 'If I was you, sir, I'd get out of that house,' he said earnestly. 'It ain't healthy.'

'Thanks very much,' said Charles. 'But it is my firm belief that someone is behind all this Monk business. And I suspect that that skeleton was put there for our benefit by the same person who got into the cellars.'

'Hold hard!' said Peter suddenly. 'It's just occurred to me that we didn't hear the groan of that stone-slab being opened on the night the picture fell.'

They stared at one another for a moment. 'That's one up to you,' Charles said at length. 'Funny I never thought of that. We couldn't have missed hearing it, either. Then . . .' he stopped, frowning.

The constable shut his notebook. 'I'd get out of the Priory, sir, if I was you,' he repeated. 'The police can't act against ghosts. What you saw that night was the Monk, and the noise you heard . . .'

'Was caused by the stone-block opening,' finished Charles. 'We proved that.'

Mr Flinders scratched his chin again. A solution dawned upon him. 'I'll tell you what it is, sir. Maybe you're right, and what you saw in the cellars was flesh and blood. I shall get on to that, following up the line you've given me. But there wasn't any flesh and blood about that skeleton.'

'I'm thankful to say that there wasn't,' said Charles. 'Dry bones were quite enough for us.'

'What I meant,' said Mr Flinders, with a return to his official manner, 'was that no human being caused that skeleton to be put into this hole you speak about. What you've done, sir, is you've found out the secret of the Priory. That's what you've done. Now we know why it's haunted, and my advice to you is, "Pull it down."'

'You won't mind if we don't follow it, will you?' Charles said, sarcastically.

'That's for you to decide,' said Mr Flinders. 'But how you've got to look at it is like this: When this stone, which you have improperly sealed up, opened, it made a noise which could be heard all over the house. Following on that, the person or persons that nefariously broke into the Priory by that way couldn't do it without you knowing. That's fact, that is. The police have to work on facts, sir, and nothing else. Now you say that when this picture fell down you hadn't heard that stone open. From which it follows that no person or persons did open it that night. That's logic, isn't it, sir?'

'I'll take your word for it,' said Charles. 'And here's a second way for you to look at it: It is just possible that there is another entrance to the Priory which we don't know anything about.'

Five

The immediate effect of the visit to Constable Flinders was a visit to the Priory paid by that worthy individual the very next day. Celia received him with a flattering display of relief, and the constable, a shy man, flushed very red indeed when she told him she was sure everything would be cleared up now that he had taken the matter in hand. However, he knew that she spoke no less than the truth, and said as much. He then requested her to show him the priest's hole.

'I will, of course,' she said, 'but I wish my husband or my brother were in, because I can hardly bear to open that ghastly panel.'

Following her delicately up the stairs Mr Flinders said that he could quite understand that. When she had succeeded in locating the rosette which worked the panel, and had twisted it round, he peered inside the dark recess almost as fearfully as Celia herself. There was nothing there, but it smelted strongly of Lysol. After deliberating for a while, the constable announced his intention of climbing into the hole. He succeeded in doing this, not without inflicting several scratches on the panelling, and once inside he very carefully inspected the walls. Celia watched him hopefully, and wondered whether the scratches could be got rid of.

Mr Flinders climbed out again, and picked up his helmet from the floor where he had placed it. 'Nothing there, madam,' he said.

'What were you looking for?' inquired Celia.

'There might have been a way in,' explained Mr Flinders. 'Not that I think so meself,' he added, 'but the police have to follow everything up, you see.'

'Oh!' said Celia, a little doubtfully. She closed the panel again. 'Is there anything else you'd like to see upstairs?'

Mr Flinders thought that he ought to make a reconnaissance of the whole house. He seemed depressed at being unable to explore Mrs Bosanquet's room, but when he learned that that lady was enjoying her afternoon rest he said that he quite understood.

A thorough examination of the other rooms took considerable time, and Celia grew frankly bored. Beyond remarking that the wall-cupboards were a queer set-out, and no mistake; that a thin man might conceivably get down the great chimney in the chief bedroom; and that a burglar wouldn't make much trouble over getting in at any one of the windows, Mr Flinders produced no theories. On the way downstairs, however, he volunteered the information that he wouldn't sleep a night in the house, not if he was paid to. This was not reassuring, and Celia at once asked him whether he knew anything about the Priory hauntings. Mr Flinders drew a deep breath, and told her various stories of things heard on the premises after dark. After this he went all over the sitting-rooms, and asked to be conducted to the secret entrance to the cellars.

'I'll tell Bowers to take you down,' said Celia. 'He knows, because he helped seal it up.'

In the kitchen she left him in charge of Mrs Bowers, a formidable woman who eyed him with complete disfavour. An attempt on his part to submit her kitchen to an exhaustive search was grimly frustrated. 'I don't hold with bobbies poking their noses where they're not wanted, and never did,' she said. 'It 'ud take a better burglar than any I ever heard of to get into my kitchen, and if I find one here I shall know what to do without sending for you.'

Mr Flinders, again very red about the ears, said huskily that he had to do his duty, and meant no offence.

'That's right,' said Mrs Bowers, 'you get on and do your duty, and I'll do mine, only don't you go opening my cupboards and turning things over with your great clumsy hands, or out you go, double-quick. Nice time I should have clearing up after you'd pulled everything about.'

'I'm sure the place does you credit,' said Mr Flinders feebly, with a vague idea of propitiating her. 'What I thought was, there might be a way in at the back of that great dresser.'

'Well, there isn't,' she replied uncompromisingly, and began to roll and bang a lump of pastry with an energy that spoke well for her muscular powers.

'I suppose,' said Mr Flinders, shifting his feet uneasily, 'I suppose you wouldn't mind me taking a look inside the copper? I *have* heard of a man hiding in one of them things.'

'Not in this house, you haven't,' responded Mrs Bowers. 'And if you think I'm going to have you prying into the week's washing you're mistaken. The idea!'

'I didn't know you'd got the washing in it,' apologised Mr Flinders.

'No, I expect you thought I kept goldfish there,' retorted the lady.

This crushing rejoinder quite cowed the constable. He coughed, and after waiting a minute asked whether she would show him the cellars. 'Which I've been asked to inspect,' he added boldly.

'I've got something better to do than to waste my time trapesing round nasty damp cellars at this hour,' she said. 'If you want to go down I'm sure I've no objection. You won't find anything except rats, and if you can put those great muddy boots of yours on one instead of dirtying my clean floor with them you'll be more use than ever I expected. Bowers!'

In reply to this shrill call her husband emerged presently from the pantry, where it seemed probable that he had been enjoying a brief siesta. Mrs Bowers pointed the rolling-pin at Mr Flinders. 'You've got to take this young fellow down to the cellars and show him the place where the master made all that mess with the cement yesterday,' she said. 'And don't bring him back here. I've never been in the habit of having bobbies in my kitchen and I'm not going to start at my time of life.'

Both men withdrew rather hastily. 'You mustn't mind my missus,' Bowers said. 'It's only her way. She doesn't hold with ghosts, and things, but I can tell you I'm glad to see you here. Awful, this place is. You wouldn't believe the things I've heard.'

By the time they had explored the dank, tomb-like cellars, and twice scared themselves by holding the lamp in such a way that their own shadows were cast in weird elongated shapes on the wall, Bowers and the constable were more than ready to confirm a sudden but deep friendship in a suitable quantity of beer. They retired to the pantry, and regaled themselves with this comforting beverage until Bowers found that it was time for him to carry the tea-tray into the library. Upon which Constable Flinders bethought himself of his duty, and took his departure by the garden-door, thus avoiding any fresh encounter with the dragon in the kitchen.

It was at about the same moment that Margaret, returning from a brisk tramp over the fields, emerged on to the right-of-way, and made her way past the ruined chapel towards the house. The sight of someone kneeling by one of the half-buried tombs apparently engaged in trying to decipher the inscription, made her stop and look more closely. Her feet had made no sound on the turf, but the kneeling figure looked round quickly, and she saw that it was Michael Strange.

She came slowly towards him, an eyebrow raised in rather puzzled inquiry. 'Hullo!' she said. 'Are you interested in old monuments?'

Strange rose, brushing a cake of half-dry mud from his ancient flannel trousers. 'I am rather,' he said. 'Do you mind my having a look round?'

'Not at all,' Margaret said. 'But I'm afraid you won't find much of interest.' She sat down on the tomb, and dug her hands into the pockets of her Burberry. 'I didn't know you were keen on this sort of thing.'

'I know very little about it,' he said, 'but I've always

been interested in ruins. It's a pity this has been allowed to go. There's some fine Norman work.'

She agreed, but seemed to be more interested in the contemplation of one of her own shoes. 'Are you staying here long?' she asked.

'Only for another week or so,' he replied. 'I'm on holiday, you know.'

'Yes, you told me so.' She looked up, smiling. 'By the way, what do you do, if it isn't a rude question?'

'I fish mostly.'

'I meant in town.'

'Oh, I see. I have my work, and I manage to get some golf over the week-ends. Do you play?'

'Very badly,' Margaret answered, feeling baulked. She tried again. 'What sort of work do you do?'

'Mostly office-stuff, and very dull,' he said.

Margaret decided that further questioning would sound impertinent, and started a fresh topic. 'If you're interested in old buildings,' she said, 'you ought to go over the Priory itself. It's the most weird place, full of nooks and crannies, and rooms leading out of one another.'

'I noticed some very fine panelling when I took you home the other night,' he said. 'Have you any records of the place, I wonder?'

'No, funnily enough we haven't,' she answered. 'You'd think there ought to be something, and as far as I know my uncle didn't take anything out of the house when Aunt Flora died, but we can't find anything.'

'Nothing amongst the books?'

'There aren't many, you know. No, nothing. Celia was awfully disappointed, because she thought there was bound to be a history, or something. And we should rather like to find out whether there's any foundation for the story of the haunting.'

Strange sat down beside her on the tomb. 'How much store do you set by that tale?' he asked. 'Do you really believe in it?'

'I don't really know,' she said, wrinkling her brow. 'I haven't seen the famous Monk, and until I do – I'll reserve judgment.'

'Very wise,' he approved. 'And if you *do* see it I wish you'd tell me. I should like to have first-hand evidence of a real ghost.' He chanced to glance up as he spoke, and his eyes narrowed. 'Oh!' he said, in rather a curt voice. 'So you did call in the police after all?'

Margaret looked quickly in the same direction. Mr Flinders was tramping down one of the paths, very obviously on his way from the house back to the village. Without quite knowing why, she felt slightly guilty. 'Yes. We – we thought we'd try and get to the bottom of our ghost.'

He turned his head, and looked directly at her. 'You've made up your minds to keep whatever you've seen, or heard, to yourselves,' he said abruptly. 'You're scared of this place, aren't you?'

She was startled. 'Well, really, I – yes, a bit, perhaps. It's not surprising considering what tales they tell about it round here.'

'You'll think me impertinent,' he said, 'but I wish you'd leave it.'

It was her turn now to look at him, surprised, rather grave. 'Why?' she said quietly.

'Because if the place is haunted, and you saw

anything, it might give you a really bad fright. Where's the sense in staying in a house that gives you the creeps?'

'You're very solicitous about me, Mr Strange. I don't quite see why.'

'I don't suppose you do,' he said, prodding the ground between his feet with his walking stick. 'And I daresay I've no right to be – solicitous about you. All the same, I am.'

She found it hard to say anything after this, but managed after a short pause to remark that a ghost couldn't hurt her.

He made no answer, but continued to prod the ground, and with a nervous little laugh, she said: 'You look as though you thought it could.'

'No, I'm not as foolish as that,' he replied. 'But it could scare you badly.'

'I didn't think you believed in the Monk. You know, you're being rather mysterious.'

'I believe in quite a number of odd things,' he said. 'Sorry if I sounded mysterious.'

She pulled up a blade of grass, and began to play with it. 'Mr Strange.'

He smiled. 'Miss Fortescue?'

'It isn't what you sound,' she said, carefully inspecting her blade of grass. 'It's – things you do.'

There was an infinitesimal pause. 'What have I done?' Strange asked lightly.

She abandoned the grass, and turned towards him. 'Last night, at about one o'clock when we had summer lightning, I – it woke me.'

'Did it? But what has that got to do with my mysterious behaviour?'

She looked into his eyes, and saw them faintly amused. 'Mr Strange, I got up to close my window, in case it came on to rain. I saw you in one of the flashes.'

'You saw *me*?' he repeated.

'Yes, by the big rose bush just under my window. I saw you quite clearly. I didn't say anything about it to the others.'

'Why not?' he said.

She flushed. 'I don't quite know. Partly because I didn't want to frighten Celia.'

'Is that the only reason?'

She was silent.

'I was in the Priory garden last night,' he said. 'I can't tell you why, but I hope you'll believe that whatever I was doing there – I'd – I'd chuck it up sooner than harm you in any way, or – or even give you a fright.' He paused, but she still said nothing. 'I don't know why you should trust me, but you seem to have done so, and I'm — jolly grateful. Can you go on trusting me enough to keep this to yourself?'

She raised troubled eyes. 'I ought not to. I ought to tell my brother. You see, I – I don't really know anything about you, and – you must admit – it's rather odd of you to be in our grounds at that hour. I suppose you can't tell me anything more?'

'No,' he said. 'I can't. I wish I could.'

She got up. 'I shan't say anything about having seen you. But I warn you – you may be found out, another time. You want to get us out of the Priory – and we aren't going. So – so it's no use trying to frighten us away. I – I expect you know what I mean.'

He did not answer, but continued to watch her rather

closely. She held out her hand. 'I must go, or I shall be too late for tea. Good-bye.'

'Good-bye,' Strange said, taking her hand for a moment in his strong clasp. 'And thank you.'

The rest of the family noticed that Margaret was rather silent at tea-time, and Mrs Bosanquet asked her if she were tired. She roused herself at that, disclaimed, and, banishing Strange from her thoughts for a while, gave her attention to Celia, who was recounting the proceedings of Constable Henry Flinders.

'And as far as I can see,' Celia said, 'there those scratches will remain.'

'You would have him,' Charles reminded her. 'You despised our efforts, and now that you've got a trained sleuth on to the job you're no better pleased.'

'What I'd really like,' Celia said, 'and what I always had in mind was a detective, not an ordinary policeman.'

'You don't appreciate friend Flinders,' Peter told her. 'He may not be quick, but he's thorough. Why, he even inspected the bathroom, didn't he?'

'That's right,' said Charles. 'Dogged does it is Henry's watchword. He won't leave a mouse-hole undisturbed. You wait till he comes down our chimney one night to see if it can be done, before you judge him.'

But during the next two days, as fresh evidence of the constable's devotion to duty was continually forthcoming, he became even less popular. On the first day of his watch, Jane, the housemaid, was with difficulty persuaded to rescind her 'notice,' which she promptly gave on discerning the constable crouched under a rhododendron bush. She was on her way home, soon after sundown, and this unnerving sight induced her to give way to a strong fit of hysterics under the drawing-room window. Celia and Peter rushed out in time to witness the aghast constable endeavouring to reassure Jane, while Mrs Bowers, first upon the scene, divided her attention between scolding the distraught damsel, and predicting the future that awaited those who could find nothing better to do than to frighten silly girls out of their wits.

When Constable Flinders had stumbled over a cucumber-frame in the dark, and smashed two panes of glass with the maximum noise, got himself locked in the gardener's shed by mistake, and arrested Charles on his return from a game of billiards with Colonel Ackerley, it was unanimously agreed that his energy should be gently but firmly diverted. In spite of his incorrigible habit of doing the wrong thing they had all of them developed quite an affection for the constable, and it was with great tact that Peter suggested that a watch on the Priory was useless, and that Mr Flinders would do well to turn his attention to the possible suspects.

The constable, whom only the strongest sense of duty induced to patrol the dread Priory after dark, was not at all hurt, but on the contrary much relieved at being dismissed from his heroic task, and thereafter the Priory saw him no more. Celia, who had been the bitterest in denunciation of his folly, even confessed to missing him. During his guard he had been quite useful in giving her horticultural advice and he had very kindly weeded three of the flower-beds for her, incidentally rooting up a cherished cutting of hydrangea, which he assured her would never flourish in such a spot.

It was not long, however, before they heard of Mr

Flinders' new activities, for Charles encountered Mr Titmarsh in the village street, and Mr Titmarsh, catching sight of the constable some way off, remarked fretfully that he did not know what had come over the fellow.

With a wonderful air of blandness Charles inquired the reason of this sudden remark. Mr Titmarsh said with asperity that the constable was apparently running after his parlour-maid, since he was forever stumbling over him, either waiting by the gate or prowling round the house. 'And apparently,' said Mr Titmarsh, 'he thinks it necessary to enlist my sympathy by exhibiting a wholly untutored interest in my hobby. He has taken to bringing me common specimens for my opinion, and last night when I was out with my net I found the man following me. Most irritating performance, and I fear I spoke a little roughly to him. However, it seems he is genuinely anxious to observe the methods I employ, and really it is of no use to lose one's temper with such a simple fellow.'

When this was recounted to the others it afforded them considerable amusement, but when Peter said: 'I never met such an ass in my life,' Charles reproved him. 'He's doing well,' he said, selecting a walnut from the dish. 'Much better than I expected. I admit his Boy Scout stunts are a little obvious, but look at his ready wit! When old Titmarsh discovered him in ambush, did his presence of mind desert him? Not at all. He said he wanted to look for moths too. That's what I call masterly.'

'I think myself,' said Mrs Bosanquet, carefully rolling up her table-napkin, 'that we were very wise to call him in. Not that I consider him efficient, for I do not, but ever since he took the matter in hand we have heard nothing out of the way in the house. No doubt whoever it was who caused us all the annoyance knows he is on the watch and will trouble us no more.'

'No one could fail to know it,' said Peter. 'During the three days when he sojourned with us he so closely tracked and interrogated everyone who came to the house that the whole countryside must have known that we'd called him in. I'm beginning to feel positively sheepish about it. The villagers are all on the broad grin.'

'I don't care what the villagers think,' Celia said. 'We did the only sensible thing. Other people don't grin. The Colonel told me he thought it was a very wise precaution.'

'You didn't tell him why we did it, I hope?' Peter said.

'No, but I don't really see why we should keep it so dark. I merely said we'd heard noises, and Bowers was getting the wind-up so much that something had to be done.'

'The reason why we should keep it dark,' explained her brother patiently, 'is, as I've told you at least six times . . .'

'Seven,' said Charles. 'This makes the eighth. And I've told her three – no, let me see . . .'

'Shut up!' said Celia. 'I know what you're going to say. If we tell one person he or she will repeat it, and it'll get round to the person who did it all. Well, why not?'

'I should be guided by what your husband says, my dear,' said Mrs Bosanquet. 'The least said the better, I am sure. And if the Colonel's coming in to coffee and bridge with you this evening we had better move into the drawing-room, for he may arrive at any moment.'

The party accordingly adjourned, and in a few minutes Bowers announced Colonel Ackerley.

'Upon my soul,' the Colonel said, accepting the coffee Peter handed him, and a glass of old brandy, 'I must say I hope you people won't allow yourselves to be scared away from the Priory. I had almost forgotten what it was like to have any neighbours.' He bowed gallantly to Celia. 'And such charming ones too.' He sipped his liqueur. 'It's a great boon to a lonely old bachelor like myself to be able to pop in for a quiet rubber in the evenings.'

'Think how nice it is for us to have such a friendly neighbour,' Celia smiled. 'So often people who live in the country get stuffy, and won't call on newcomers till they've been in the place for years.'

'Well, when one has knocked about the world as I have, one gets over all that sort of rubbish!' replied the Colonel. 'Never had any use for stand-offishness. Aha, Miss Fortescue, I see you are preparing for the engagement. What do you say? Shall we two join forces and have our revenge on Mr and Mrs Malcolm?'

Margaret had swept the cards round in a semi-circle. 'Yes, do let's!' she agreed. 'We owe them one for our awful defeat last time we played. Shall we cut for seats?'

They took their places at the table, and as the cards were dealt the Colonel bethought himself of something, and said with his ready laugh: 'By the way, what have you done with your watch-dog? Give you my word I was expecting him to pounce out on me at any moment, for I strolled across the park to get here.'

'Oh, we've diverted him,' Charles answered. 'Our nerves wouldn't stand it any longer.'

'Besides, he's done the trick,' Celia said. 'Bowers,

whose faith in him is really touching, seems to be settling down quite happily. If I did this, I shall say a spade.'

The game proceeded in silence for some time, but at the end of the rubber the Colonel reverted to the subject, and cocking a quizzical eyebrow in Charles' direction said: 'By the by, Malcolm, have you been setting your sleuth on to old Titmarsh? Oh, you needn't mind telling me! *I* shan't give you away!'

'We had to get rid of him somehow,' Peter said. 'So we thought Titmarsh would keep him well occupied.'

This seemed to amuse the Colonel considerably, but after his first outburst of laughter he said: 'But you don't think old Titmarsh has been playing jokes on you, do you?'

'Not at all,' said Peter. 'It was our Mr Flinders who thought he ought to be watched. All very providential.'

'Well, if he discovers anything against the old boy, I'll eat my hat,' the Colonel declared.

Shortly after eleven he took his leave of them, and in a little while the girls and Mrs Bosanquet went up to bed. Having bolted the drawing-room windows, the men prepared to follow them, and in another hour the house was dark and silent.

Mrs Bosanquet, who had been troubled lately with slight insomnia, was the only one of the party who failed to go to sleep. After lying awake for what seemed to her an interminable time she decided that the room was stuffy, and got up to open the window, which she still kept shut in case anyone should attempt to effect an entrance by that way. 'But that is all put a stop to now,' she told herself, as she climbed back into bed.

The opening of the window seemed to make matters worse. At the end of another twenty minutes sleep seemed farther off than ever. Mrs Bosanquet felt for the matches on the table beside her bed, and lit her candle. She looked round for something to read, but since she was not in the habit of reading in bed there were no books in the room. It at once seemed to her imperative that she should read for a while, and she sat up, debating whether she should venture down to the library in search of a suitable book, or whether this simple act demanded more courage than she possessed. There was a tin of sweet biscuits in the library, she remembered, and the recollection made her realise that she was quite hungry. 'Now I come to think of it,' Mrs Bosanquet informed the bedpost, 'my dear mother used always to say that if one could not sleep it was a good plan to eat a biscuit. Though,' she added conscientiously, 'she did not in general approve of eating anything once one had brushed one's teeth for the night.'

The tin of biscuits began to seem more and more desirable. Mrs Bosanquet lay down again, sternly resolved to think of something else. But it was no use. Biscuits, very crisp and sweet, would not be banished from her mind, and at the end of another ten minutes Mrs Bosanquet would have faced untold dangers to get one.

She got out of bed and put on her dressing-gown. It occurred to her that she might wake Peter, whose room was opposite hers, and ask him to go down to the library for her, but she dismissed this pusillanimous idea at once. Mrs Bosanquet was a lady who prided herself upon her level-headedness; she did not believe in ghosts; and she would feel very much ashamed to think that anyone should suspect her of being too nervous to walk downstairs alone in the middle of the night.

'Nerves,' Mrs Bosanquet was in the habit of saying severely, 'were never encouraged when I was young.'

'I shall go quietly downstairs, get a biscuit to eat, and select a book from the shelves without disturbing anyone,' she said firmly, and picked up her candle.

The lamp had been turned out in the passage, and since there was no moon the darkness seemed intense. Another woman might have paused, but Mrs Bosanquet was not afraid of the dark. 'What would alarm me,' she reflected, 'would be a light burning; for then I should know that someone was in the house.'

But the ground-floor was as dark as the upper storey. Mrs Bosanquet went cautiously downstairs with one hand on the baluster-rail, and the other holding her candle up. The stairs creaked annoyingly, and in the stillness each creak sounded abnormally loud. Mrs Bosanquet murmured: 'Tut-tut!' to herself, and hoped that Celia would not be awakened by the noise.

The library door was ajar; she pushed it open, and went in. The biscuit-tin, she remembered, stood on a small table by the door, and she peered for it, blinking. Yes, there it was. She set the candle down and opened it, and slipped two of the biscuits into the pocket of her dressing-gown. She had quite recovered from her rather shame-faced feeling of trepidation, for no skulls had bounced at her feet, or anything else of such a disturbing nature. She picked up the candle again, and turned to the bookshelves that ran along the wall opposite the fireplace. It was very hard to see far by the light of one candle, and she knocked her shin on a chair as she moved across the room.

The difficulty was to find anything one wanted to read. She held the candle close up to the row of books, and slowly edged along in front of the shelves, surveying a most unpromising selection of titles. '*Meditations on Mortality*,' read Mrs Bosanquet. 'Dear me, how gloomy. *The Sermons of Dr Brimley*. That might send me to sleep, but I really don't think . . . *Tyndall on Light* . . . Ah, this is better!' She came opposite a collection of novels, and reached up a hand to pull one down from the shelf. Then, just as her fingers had half-pulled the volume from its place an unaccountable feeling of dread seized her, and she stayed quite still, straining her ears to catch the least sound. All she could hear was the beating of her own heart, but it did not reassure her. Mrs Bosanquet, who did not believe in nerves, knew that something was in the room with her.

'It's nonsense,' she told herself. 'Of course there isn't. Of *course* there isn't!' She forced herself to draw the book out from its place, but her unreasoning conviction grew. It seemed as though she dared not move or look round, but she knew that was absurd. 'I've *got* to turn round,' she thought. 'It's all nonsense. There's nothing here. I can't stand like this all night. I *must* turn round.'

Fearfully she began to edge towards the door. She found that it had become almost impossible to breathe, and realised that her terror was growing.

'It's always worse if one turns one's back on things,' Mrs Bosanquet thought. 'Suppose it crept up behind me? Suppose I felt a hand touching me?'

The leap of her heart was choking her; she felt as

though she might faint if she went on like this. She stopped, and very cautiously peered over her shoulder. There was nothing. Yet what was that vague, dark figure by the fireplace? Only the tall-backed arm-chair, of course. She was so sure of it that she took a step towards it, and lifted her candle to see more clearly.

The dark shape grew distinct in the tiny light. A cowled figure was standing motionless by the fireplace, and through the slits in the cowl two glittering eyes were fixed upon Mrs Bosanquet. She stood as though paralysed, and even as she stared at it the figure moved, and glided towards her with one menacing hand stretched out like the talon of a bird of prey.

The spell broke. For the first time in her life Mrs Bosanquet gave a wild, shrill scream, and crumpled up in a dead faint on the floor.

Six

Mrs Bosanquet groped her way back to consciousness to find the room full of lamplight, and the rest of the family gathered solicitously about her. Someone had laid her upon the sofa, someone else was bathing her forehead with water, while a third held a bottle of smelling-salts to her nose. She opened her eyes, and looked up, blankly at first, into Celia's concerned face. She heard a voice saying: 'It's all right: she's coming round,' and by degrees her recollection came back to her. She opened her eyes again, and struggled up into a sitting posture, unceremoniously thrusting aside the smelling bottle and the brandy that Margaret was trying to give her. 'Where is it?' she demanded, looking round her suspiciously.

'Where is what, Aunt Lilian?' Celia said soothingly. 'Are you feeling better now?'

'I am perfectly well. No, my dear child, I never touch spirits. Where did it go? Did you see it?'

Celia patted her hand. 'No, dear, we didn't see anything. I woke up, hearing you scream, and when we got downstairs we found you had fainted. Did you feel ill in the night, Aunt, or what?'

'I came to get a book and a biscuit,' Mrs Bosanquet replied. 'Was there no one but myself in the room?'

'Why no, darling, how should there be? Did you think you saw someone?'

'Think!' said Mrs Bosanquet indignantly. 'Do you suppose I should scream for help merely because I thought I saw someone? I did see it, as plainly as I can see you.'

Charles came forward, ousting his wife from her place by the invalid's side. 'What did you see, Aunt Lilian?' he asked. 'Do you feel well enough to tell us about it?'

'Certainly I am well enough to tell you,' she said. 'My dears, it is all perfectly true, and I am not ashamed to own that I have been wrong. The house *is* haunted, and the first thing to be done in the morning is to summon the Vicar.'

Celia gave a gasp of horror, and clasped her brother's arm nervously. 'Oh, what have you seen?' she cried.

Mrs Bosanquet took the glass of water from Margaret, and drank some. 'I have seen the Monk!' she said dramatically.

'Good Lord!' Peter exclaimed. 'You haven't really, have you? Are you sure you didn't imagine it?'

A withering glance was cast at him. 'It is true that I so far forgot myself as to scream, and faint, but I can assure you, my dear Peter, that I am not such a fool that I would imagine such a thing. It was standing almost exactly where you are now, and it began to move towards me, with its arm stretched out as though it were pointing at me.'

Celia shuddered, and looked round fearfully.

'Just what did it look like?' Charles asked quietly.

'Like a monk,' said Mrs Bosanquet. 'It had a cowl over its face, and I trust I am not a fanciful woman, but there was something indescribably menacing and horrible about it. I can see its eyes now.'

'Where?' shrieked Celia, clutching Peter again.

'In my mind's eye. Don't be foolish, my dear, it is not here now. Its robe was black, and so were its hands – at least the one that pointed at me was. I daresay I am stupid, but that seemed to me to make it even more unnerving.'

Charles turned quickly towards Peter. 'That settles it! Gloves! Now how did he make his get-away?'

'Almost any way,' Peter said. 'He'd have had plenty of time to get across the hall before any of us reached the stairs.'

'It is no use being obstinate about it,' Mrs Bosanquet said. 'It was no man, but an apparition. I am now convinced of the existence of such things. Perhaps it was sent to open my eyes.'

'All dressed up in a Dominican habit and black gloves,' said Charles. 'I hardly think so. Take a look at the front door, Peter.'

'Bolted, and the chain in position. I happened to notice. What about this window?'

Charles strode across to it, and flung back the curtains. 'It's bolted – no, by Jove, it's not!' He turned to Bowers, who up till now had been a scared auditor. 'Bowers, do you remember if you bolted this to-night?'

Bowers shook his head. 'No, sir. At least, I don't think so. Begging your pardon, sir, but the mistress always likes it left open till you go up to bed. I thought you bolted it.'

'That's right,' Peter said. 'And to-night we sat in the

drawing-room. That's how it got forgotten. Cheer up, Aunt Lilian! What you saw was someone dressed up to give you a fright, and that's how he got in.'

'No, my dear, you are wrong,' Mrs Bosanquet said firmly. 'It had no need of doors or windows. For all we know it is still present, though now invisible.'

Celia gave one moan of horror, and implored Charles to take her back to town at once.

'I think we'd all better go back to bed for the rest of the night, and discuss it in the morning,' Charles said. 'I don't see that we shall do much good trying to search the garden now. We'll bolt this window, though. And what about having Margaret to sleep in your room, Aunt? Would you prefer it?'

'Not at all,' she replied. 'If it re-appeared, Margaret would be of no assistance to me, or any of you. I shall go quietly up, and to sleep, for I feel I shall not see it again to-night.'

On account of the night's disturbance breakfast was put back next morning for an hour, but contrary to everyone's expectations Mrs Bosanquet was the first down. When Celia, Margaret, and Peter appeared they found her looking as placid as ever, and reading the morning paper. 'Good morning, my dears,' she said, laying the paper down. 'I see there has been fresh trouble in China. I feel one has so much to be thankful for in not being Chinese.'

'Darling Aunt Lilian!' said Margaret, twinkling. 'You really are a marvellous person!'

'On the contrary I fear I am a very ordinary one. And why you should think so merely because I remarked . . .'

'Oh, I didn't! But after what you went through last night I wonder you can be so calm.'

'I lay awake and thought about that for some time after you had left me,' said Mrs Bosanquet. 'Do you know, I have come to the conclusion that I behaved very foolishly?'

Celia looked up hopefully. 'Do you mean you may have imagined it after all?'

'No, my dear, certainly not. I am not at all imaginative. In fact, your uncle used very often to say I was too mundane. But then he was extremely imaginative himself, and could tell the most entertaining stories, as I daresay you remember.'

'Then how did you behave foolishly?' asked Peter, helping himself from one of the dishes on the sideboard.

'In screaming in that uncontrolled manner. I realise now that my proper course would have been to have challenged the apparition, and commanded it to tell me what it wanted. For, on thinking it over, I am convinced it manifested itself for some good purpose. Thank you, Peter, yes, I will have an egg.' She began to tap the shell briskly. 'It is obviously an unquiet spirit, and when you consider that it no doubt belongs to the remains you discovered in that very nasty, airless little cupboard, one can hardly wonder at it.'

'I do wish you wouldn't, Aunt!' begged Celia. 'Even in broad daylight you give me the creeps.'

'Then you are being very silly, dear child. Good morning, Charles. I hope you slept well to make up for your loss of sleep earlier in the night.'

Charles took his seat at the head of the table. 'I am grateful for the inquiry, Aunt, but no, I didn't. I might have, but for the fact that I was constrained to get up three times; once to look under the bed, once to open the wardrobe, once to demonstrate to your niece that the noise she persistently heard was the wind rustling the creeper outside the window.'

'Well, I'm sorry, darling,' Celia said, 'but after what happened you can't be surprised that I was nervous.'

'Surprise, my love,' responded her husband, 'was not the emotion I found myself a prey to.'

'Perhaps it'll convince you that the only thing to do is to go back to town this very day,' Celia said pleadingly.

'I confess that a prospect of any more such nights doesn't attract me,' said Charles. 'But what's the opinion of Aunt Lilian?'

'I was about to say, when you came in,' answered Mrs Bosanquet, 'that I have considered the matter very carefully, and come to the conclusion that we should be doing wrong to leave the Priory.'

Charles paused in the act of conveying a piece of toast from his plate to his mouth, and stared at her. 'Well, I'm damned!' he said inelegantly. 'Give me some coffee, Celia: I must drink Aunt Lilian's health.'

'Very wrong indeed,' nodded Mrs Bosanquet. 'Perhaps we have it in our power to set the ghost free. It probably wants us to do something, and to that end it has been endeavouring to attract our notice.'

'I see,' said Charles gravely. 'And probably it can't make out why we all seem so shy of it. I wonder how it'll try to – er – attract our notice next? It's already knocked a picture down, and thrown a skull at our feet, and made you faint. It must be getting quite disheartened at our failure to appreciate the true meaning of these little attentions.'

'It is all very well for you to make a mock of such things, Charles,' Mrs Bosanquet said with dignity, 'but I am perfectly serious. So much so that I am determined to do my best to get into communication with it. And since Margaret is going to town on Thursday to see her dentist I shall ask her to call at my flat, and request Parker to give her my planchette board, which is in the old brown trunk in the lobby.'

Celia was regarding her in fascinated horror. 'Are you really proposing to sit with a planchette in this house?' she asked faintly.

'Not only I, my dear, but all of us. We sit round in a circle, laying the tips of our fingers on the board, and wait for some message to be transcribed.'

'Nothing,' said Celia vehemently, 'would induce me to take part in any such proceeding! The whole thing's bad enough as it is without us trying to invoke the Monk.'

'Very well,' said Mrs Bosanquet, not in the least ruffled, 'if that is how you feel about it it would be no good your attempting to sit with us. But I for one shall certainly make the attempt.'

'This means you won't go back to town!' Celia said unhappily. 'I knew what it would be! No, don't tell me I can go without you, Charles. I may be a bad wife, and wake you up to look in the wardrobe in the small hours, but I am not such a bad wife that I'd go away and leave you with a ghost and a planchette.'

'I wish you would go back to town, old lady,' Charles said. 'I don't mean that I don't appreciate this self-immolating heroism, but it's no use scaring yourself, and nothing dire is at all likely to happen to me. If I thought there was any danger,' he added handsomely, 'you should stay and share it with me.'

'Thanks,' said Celia. 'I might have known you'd joke about it. I don't know whether there's what you call danger, but if you're going to ask for trouble by putting your hands on Aunt's horrible planchette I shan't leave your side for one moment.'

'Cheer up!' Charles said. 'I don't mind giving the board a shove to please Aunt Lilian, but last night has completely convinced me that the Monk is as real as you are. In fact, if Margaret is going to town on Thursday she can rout out my service revolver, and the cartridges she'll find with it, and bring them back with her.'

'If you think that I should be pleased by you deliberately pushing the board, you are sadly mistaken,' said Mrs Bosanquet severely. 'Moreover, I have the greatest objection to fire-arms, and if you propose to let off guns at all hours of the day I shall be obliged to go back to London.'

She was with difficulty appeased, and only a promise extracted from Charles not to fire any lethal weapon without due warning soothed her indignation. Breakfast came to an end, and after Celia had had a heart-to-heart talk with her husband, and Margaret had begged Peter not to do anything rash, such as shooting at vague figures seen in the dark, the two men left the house, ostensibly to fish.

'What we are going to do now,' said Charles, 'is to carry on some investigations on our own.'

'Then we'd better drift along to the Bell,' said Peter. 'We may as well put in some fishing till opening time, though. If you want to pump old Wilkes you won't find him up yet.'

Charles consulted his watch. 'I make it half-past ten.'

'I daresay you do, but friend Wilkes takes life easy. He's never visible at this hour. Not one of our early risers.'

'All right then,' Charles said. 'We might fish the near stream for a bit.'

Sport, however, proved poor that morning, and shortly before twelve they decided to give up, and stroll on towards the inn. They were already within a few minutes' walk of it, and they arrived before the bar was open.

'Have you been into the courtyard yet?' Peter asked. 'You ought to see that. Real Elizabethan work; you can almost imagine miracles and moralities being played there. Come on.' He led the way through an arch in the middle of the building, and they found themselves in a cobbled yard, enclosed by the house. A balcony ran all round the first storey, and various bedroom windows opened on to this. A modern garage occupied the end of the building opposite the archway into the street, but Mr Wilkes had had this built in keeping with the rest of the inn, and had placed his petrol pump as inconspicuously as possible. Some clipped yews in wooden tubs stood in the yard, and the whole effect was most picturesque. Having inspected the older part of the house, and ascertained that the original structure did indeed date from the fourteenth century, they wandered into the garage, which they found stood where the old stables had once been. Michael Strange's two-seater was standing just inside the entrance and one of the garage hands was washing it down. Charles, under pretext of examining the car, soon fell into easy conversation with the man, and leaving him to extract what information he could, Peter strolled off to where he could hear the throb of an engine at work. He had some knowledge of such machines, and a great deal of interest. He easily located the engine-room, went in, leaving the door open behind him, and found, as he had thought, that the engine drove the electric light plant. No one was there, and the first thing that struck him was the size of the plant. Puzzled, he stood looking at it, wondering why such a powerful machine and such a large plant had been installed for the mere purpose of supplying light for the inn. He was just about to inspect it more closely when someone came hurriedly into the room behind him.

'Oo's in 'ere?' demanded a sharp voice.

Peter turned to find Spindle, the barman, at his elbow. The man looked annoyed, but when he saw whom he was addressing he curbed his testiness, and said more mildly: 'Beg pardon, sir, but no one's allowed inside this 'ere engine-room.'

'That's all right,' said Peter. 'I shan't meddle with it. I was just wondering why . . .'

'I'm sorry, sir, but orders is orders, and I shall 'ave to ask you to come out. If the boss was to 'ear about me leaving the door unlocked I should get into trouble.' He had edged himself round Peter, obscuring his view of the plant, and now tried to crowd him out. Somewhat surprised Peter gave way, and backed into the yard again.

'You seem to be afraid I shall upset it. What's the matter?' he said.

Spindle was locking the door of the place, and until he had pocketed the key he did not answer. Then he said: 'It's not that, sir, but we 'ave to be careful. You wouldn't believe the number of young fellers we've 'ad go in and start messin' about with the plant, to see 'ow it worked. Cost Mr Wilkes I wouldn't like to say 'ow much money to 'ave it put right once, sir. Not that I mean you'd go for to 'urt it, but I've 'ad me orders, and it's as much as my place is worth to let anyone in.'

'Oh, all right,' said Peter, still surprised at the man's evident perturbation. 'But why has Wilkes installed such a large plant? Surely it's generating far more electricity than you can possibly use?'

'I couldn't say, sir, I'm sure. And begging your pardon, sir, it's opening time, and I've got to get back to me work.' He touched his forehead as he spoke and scuttled off into the inn again, leaving Peter to stare after him in still greater bewilderment.

Charles came across the yard from the garage. 'Did I hear certain magic words? I move that we repair to the bar forthwith. What have you been up to?'

'I went to look at the electric-light plant, only that ass, Spindle, hustled me out before I'd had time to see much. I must ask Wilkes about it.'

Charles groaned. 'Must you? I mean, we didn't come to talk about amps and dynamos, and I know from bitter experience that once you get going on that soul-killing topic . . .'

'I want to know why Wilkes has got such a powerful plant. I hadn't time to look closely, but from what I could see of it it was generating enough electricity to light the whole village.'

'Well, perhaps it does,' Charles suggested. 'Can we get into the bar without going back into the street?'

'Yes, through the coffee-room.' Peter opened a door which led into a dark little passage, with kitchens giving on to it. At the end of the passage was the coffee-room, and they walked through this to the frosted glass door that opened into the taproom itself.

There was no one but Spindle in the taproom when they entered, but they had hardly given their orders when Wilkes came in from his private sanctum, and bade them a cheery good morning.

'Hullo, Wilkes! Just up?' Peter twitted him.

The landlord smiled good humouredly. 'Now, sir, now! You will have your joke. Two half-cans was it? Come on, Spindle, look alive! There you are, sir!' He seized the tankards from his henchman, and planked them down in front of his guests.

'Very quiet this morning, aren't you?' Charles said.

'Well, we're only just open, sir. They'll start coming in presently. I see you've been fishing. Bad weather for it today.'

'Rotten. No luck at all.' Charles took a draught of beer. 'How's business with you?'

'So-so, sir, so-so. We get a fair sprinkling of car people in to lunch, but there's not many as stays the night.'

'I see Mr Strange is still here.'

'Yes, sir, he's here. And there's Miss Crowslay and Miss Williams, down for their usual fortnight, and Mr Ffolliot. Artists, sir, great place for artists and such-like, this is.'

'Still got your commercial?'

'In a manner of speaking I suppose I have, but he's one

of them as is here to-day and gone to-morrow, if you know what I mean. Well, it's the nature of his business, I daresay, but I'd rather have someone more regular, so to speak. That Mr Fripp, well, you never know where you are with him because some days he has to go off and spend the night away, and others he's back to supper when you wasn't expecting him. However, as my missus was saying only this morning, it's all in the way of business, and I'm sure times are that bad I'm glad to get anyone staying in the house.'

Peter put down his tankard. 'I say, Wilkes, what's the meaning of that monstrous electric plant you've got outside? You can't need a thing that size, surely?'

The landlord coughed, and looked rather sheepish. 'I'm sorry you've seen that, Mr Fortescue, sir.'

'Yes, but why? Spindle pushed me out before I'd time to do more than glance at the thing. He seemed in a great way about it.'

Spindle looked deprecatingly at the landlord, and withdrew to the other end of the bar.

'Spindle's a fool, sir,' said Mr Wilkes, not mincing matters. 'Though mind you, you wouldn't hardly believe the number of people there are that ain't to be trusted anywhere near a delicate bit of machinery. I do have to be strict, and that's a fact. Of course, I know you're different, sir, and that's why I'm sorry you saw it.' He went through the form of wiping down the bar, which seemed to be a habit with him. 'You see, sir, in a manner of speaking I was a bit had over that plant.'

'I should think you were,' Peter said. 'You could supply the whole village with it.'

'Well, I don't know about that, sir,' Mr Wilkes said

cautiously. 'It ain't such a powerful machine as what it looks. Still, I don't deny it's bigger nor what I want. Not but what we use a lot of power here. Because, mind you, I had the whole place wired for heating as well, there not being any gas laid on, and then there's the refrigerators, and vacuum cleaners and what not.'

'Rot!' Peter said, 'you don't need a plant that size for the amount of electricity you use in heating.'

Mr Wilkes once more wiped down the bar. 'True enough, sir, I don't. But when I took over this house I don't mind telling you I hadn't ever had anything to do with electric plants, me having always lived in a town. I didn't know no more about it than what half the young gentlemen do, who try and meddle with it. And I did have a notion to run a laundry off it, just by way of a side-business, as you might call it. So what with one thing and another I let myself be talked into putting up a plant that cost me a mint of money, and ain't, between ourselves, as cheap to run as what the smooth-tongued fellow that sold it me said it would be. Excuse me, sir, half a moment!' He hurried away to attend to a farmer who had come in, and Charles and Peter went to sit down at a table in the window.

The taproom began to fill up, and soon there were quite a number of people in it. They were mostly villagers, and there was no sign of Strange, or his odd associate. But a few minutes before one o'clock a man came in who was obviously no farm-hand. He attracted Peter's attention at once, but this was not surprising, since his appearance and conduct were alike out of the ordinary. Artist was stamped unmistakably upon him. His black hair was worn exceedingly long; he had a carelessly tied, very flowing piece of silk round his neck; his fingers were stained with paint; he had a broad-brimmed hat crammed on to his head; and was the owner of a pointed beard.

'Good Lord, I thought that type went out with the 'Nineties!' murmured Peter.

The artist walked rather unsteadily up to the bar, and leaning sideways across it, said with a distinct foreign accent: 'Whisky. Double.'

Wilkes had watched his approach frowningly, and he now hesitated, and said something in a low voice. The artist smote his open hand down on the bar, and said loudly: 'My friend, you give me what I say. You think I am drunk, *hein*? Well, I am not drunk. You see? You give me . . .'

'All right, Mr Dooval,' Wilkes said hastily. 'No offence I hope.'

'You give me what I say,' insisted M. Duval. 'I paint a great picture. So great a picture the world will say, why do we not hear of this Louis Duval?' He took the glass Wilkes handed him, and drained it at one gulp. 'Another. And when I have painted this picture, then I tell you I have finished with everything but my art.' He stretched out a hand that shook slightly towards his glass. His eye wandered round the room: his voice sank to the grumbling tone of the partially intoxicated. 'I will be at no man's call. No, no: that is over when I have paint my picture. You hear?'

Mr Wilkes seemed to be trying to quieten him by asking some questions about the picture he was painting.

'It is not for such as you,' M. Duval said. 'What have the English to do with art? Bah, you do not know what feelings I have in me, *here* . . .' He struck his chest. 'To think I must be with you, and those others – *canaille*!'

'Gentleman seems a little peevish,' remarked Charles, *sotto voce.*

His voice, though not his words, seemed to reach M. Duval's ears, for he turned, and stared hazily across the room. A smile that closely resembled a leer curled his mouth, and picking up his glass he made his way between the tables to the window, and stood leaning his hand on the back of a chair, and looking down at Charles. 'So! The gentleman who dares to live in the haunted house, not?' He shook with laughter, and raising his glass unsteadily, said: '*Voyons*! a toast! *Le Moine!*'

Charles was watching him under frowning brows. He went on chuckling to himself, and his eyes travelled from Charles' face to Peter's. 'You do not drink? You do not love him, our Monk?' He pulled the chair he held out from the table, and collapsed into it. '*Eh bien!* You do not speak then? You do not wish to talk of *Le Moine*? Perhaps you have seen him, no?' He paused; he was sprawling half-way across the table, and the foolish look in his eyes was replaced by a keener more searching gleam. 'But you have not seen his face,' he said with a strange air of quite sudden seriousness. 'There is no one has ever seen his face, not even I, Louis Duval!'

'Quite so,' said Charles. 'I haven't. Do you want to?'

A look of cunning crept into the artist's face. He smiled again, a slow, evil smile that showed his discoloured teeth. 'I do not tell you that. Oh, no! I do not tell you that, my friend. But this I tell you: you will never see his face, but you will go away from that house which is his, that house where he goes, *glissant*, up and down the stairs, though you do not see, where he watches you, though you do not know. Yes, you will go. You will go.' He fell to chuckling again.

'Why should we go?' Peter asked calmly. 'We're not afraid of ghosts, you know!'

The artist swayed with his insane giggling. 'But *Le Moine* is not like other ghosts, my friend. *Ah non*, he is not – like – other ghosts!'

The landlord had crossed the room, and now threw an apologetic glance at Peter. But he spoke to the artist. 'You'd like your usual table, moossoo, wouldn't you? You'll take your lunch in the coffee-room, I daresay, and there's as nice a leg of lamb waiting as ever I saw.'

The artist turned on him with something of a snarl. 'Away, cattle! You think you can tell me what I shall do and what I shall not do, but it is not so!'

'I'm sure, sir, I never had no such idea, but your lunch'll be spoiled if you don't come to eat it, and I've got some of the green peas cooked the French way you like.'

'I do not eat in this place, where you cook food fit for pigs. Yes, you wish that I go, but I do not go till I choose, and you dare not speak, my gross one, for me. I am Louis Duval, and there is not another in the world can do what I do! Is it not so? *Hein?* Is it not so?'

The landlord had an ugly look in his eye, but to Charles' and Peter's surprise he said soothingly: 'That's right, sir. Wonderful your pictures are.'

M. Duval looked at him through half-shut eyes; his voice sank; he said almost in a whisper: 'Sometimes I have thoughts in my head, gross pig, which you do not dream. Sometimes I think to myself, has no one seen the face of *Le Moine*? Has not Wilkes seen it? Eh? You do not like that, perhaps. Perhaps, too, you are afraid, just a little afraid of poor Louis Duval.'

'Me seen it?' echoed the landlord. 'Lor', Mr Dooval, I'm thankful I haven't, and that's a fact. Now you give over talking of spooks, sir, do. You've got half the room listening to you, like silly fools, and these gentlemen don't want to hear them sort of stories.'

Contrary to Peter's expectations the drunken artist allowed himself to be helped out of his chair, and gently propelled across the bar to the coffee-room door. Those villagers who still remained in the bar watched his exit with grins and nudges. When he had disappeared, and Wilkes with him, Peter addressed a solid-looking farmer who was seated near to him. 'Who's that chap?' he asked.

'He's a furriner, sir,' the farmer answered. 'An artist. I daresay you've seen his cottage, for it ain't far from the Priory.'

'Oh, he lives here, does he? Which is his cottage?'

'Why, sir, it's that white cottage with the garden in front that's a sin and shame to look at, it's that covered in weeds.' He began to sketch with a stubby finger on the table before him. 'Supposing the Priory's here, sir, where I've put my thumb. Well, you go on down the road, like as if you was coming to the village, and there's a bit of a lane leading off a matter of a quarter of a mile from this inn. You go up there not more'n a hundred yards, and you come right on the cottage. That's where he lives.'

'I see. Yes, I know the place. Has he lived there long?'

The farmer rubbed his ear. 'I don't know as I could rightly say how long he's been here. Not more'n five years, I reckon. We've kind of got used to him and his ways, and I never heard he did anyone any harm, bar walking over fields while the hay is standing. Mind you, it ain't so often you see him like he is to-day. He gets fits of it, so to speak. Now I come to think on it, it hasn't had a bout on him for a matter of three months. But whenever he gets like this he goes round maundering that silly stuff you heard. Enough to get on your nerves it is, but he's fair got the Priory ghost on the brain.' He got up as he spoke, and wishing them a polite good-day, made his way out.

'Quite interesting,' Charles said. 'I think it's time we made a move.'

On their way home down the right-of-way they talked long and earnestly over all that the drunken artist had said.

'It is well known,' Charles said at last, 'that you can't set much store by what a drunken man may say, but on the other hand it's always on the cards that he'll let out something he didn't mean to. I feel that M. Louis Duval may be worth a little close investigation.'

'What surprised me,' Peter remarked, 'was the way Wilkes bore with him. I expected to see Duval kicked out.'

'If he's in the habit of eating his meals at the Bell you can understand Wilkes humouring him. And apparently he's not always tight by any means. The most intriguing thing about him was his interest in the Monk. I don't know what you feel about it, but I should say he knew a bit about monks.'

'I'm all for getting on his tracks,' Peter answered. 'At the same time, he was so dam' fishy and mysterious that I'm inclined to think it was a bit too sinister to mean anything. Think he is the Monk?'

'Can't say. If I knew what the Monk was after I should find this problem easier to solve.'

They walked on for some time in silence. Peter broke it by saying suddenly: 'I don't know. It was typical drunken rot when you come to think of it. All that stuff about the Monk walking up and downstairs though we don't see him, and watching us though we don't know it. You can't get much sense out of that. Ghost-twaddle.'

'I was thinking of something else he said,' Charles said slowly. 'I'd rather like to know what he meant by no one ever having seen the Monk's face, not even himself. That wasn't quite the usual ghost-talk we hear in this place.'

'N-no. But I'm not sure that it's likely to lead anywhere. Still, I agree he wants looking into.'

They had reached the Priory by this time, and agreeing to say nothing of the morning's encounter to the others they went in, and found the three women already seated at the lunch-table.

'Did you have any luck?' Margaret asked.

'No, there's too much sun,' Peter answered. He paused in the act of helping himself to salad, and lifted his head. 'What's the strange noise?'

There was a distinct and rather unpleasant sound of humming that seemed to proceed from somewhere above. Margaret laughed. 'Ask Celia. She let us in for it.'

They looked inquiringly at her. 'Sounds like a vacuum cleaner or something,' said Charles.

'It is,' Celia confessed. 'I couldn't help it, though. Really, he was so persistent I hadn't the heart to go on saying no.'

'I think it's a very good plan,' said Mrs Bosanquet. 'I'm sure there must be a great deal of dust in all the carpets, and this will save having them taken up, which I was going to suggest.'

'But what do you mean?' Peter demanded. 'We've no electricity here, so how can you . . .'

'Oh, it isn't an electric one! It's some new sort of patent affair, but I really didn't pay much attention, because I've no intention of buying it. Only the man was so anxious to show me the amount of dust it would draw out of the carpets and chairs that I let him demonstrate. After all, it's costing us nothing, and it seems to please him.'

'A man, with a vacuum-cleaner for sale,' Charles repeated. 'A man . . .' He looked at Peter, and as though by common consent they both got up.

'Well, what on earth's the matter?' Celia asked. 'You don't mind, do you?'

'I'm not at all sure,' said Charles. 'I'll tell you when I've seen this clever salesman.' He threw down his table-napkin, and went quickly out of the room, and up the stairs. The droning noise came from Mrs Bosanquet's room, and he went in. Busily engaged in running a cleaner over the floor was the shifty-eyed commercial staying at the Bell Inn.

Seven

For a moment they eyed one another in silence. Then the man with the vacuum-cleaner said: 'Good morning, sir. I wonder whether I can interest *you* in this here cleaner? No electric power required. Practically works itself, needing only the 'and to guide it. Like this, sir, if you will kindly watch what I do.' He began to run it over the carpet, still talking volubly. 'You can see for yourself, sir, 'ow easy to work this here cleaner is. Sucks up every speck of dust, *but* does *not* take off the nap of the carpet, which is a thing as can't be said of every cleaner on the market. We claim that with this here cleaner we 'ave done away with all servant trouble. Cheap to buy, and costs nothing to run. I will now demonstrate to you, sir, what it has done, by turning out the dust at present contained in this bag, which you see attached to the cleaner. All of which dust, sir, 'as been sucked out of this very carpet.'

'Don't trouble,' said Charles. 'I'm not buying it.'

The little man smiled tolerantly. 'No, sir? Well I don't know as how I should expect a gentleman to be interested in this here cleaner, not but what I '*ave* sold to bachelors many a time. But I hope when your good lady sees the dust and dirt which this here cleaner has extracted from all carpets, upholstered chairs, curtains, and etcetera, she'll be tempted to give me an order, which the firm which I 'ave the honour to represent will execute with their custom'ry dispatch.'

'And what is the name of the firm you have the honour to represent?' Charles inquired blandly.

If he expected the invader to be embarrassed he was disappointed.

'Allow me, sir!' beamed the little man, and inserting a finger and thumb into his waistcoat pocket he drew out a card, which he handed to Charles.

It was an ordinary trade-card, bearing the name and address of a firm in the city, and purporting to belong to a Mr James Fripp.

'That's me name, sir,' explained Mr Fripp, pointing it out. 'And I 'ope that when ordering you will 'ave the goodness to mention it, supposing I can't tempt you to give me an order now, which I 'ope I shall do when you 'ave seen for yourself that this here cleaner is all that we claim it to be.'

Charles put the card carefully into his pocket-book. 'We'll see,' he said. 'Do I understand that you propose to clean all the rooms of the house for us?'

'I'm sure I shall be pleased to, sir, but if you're satisfied, 'aving seen what 'as been effected under your own eye . . .'

'Oh no!' Charles said pleasantly. 'For all I know it might break down before it had gone over half the house.' Mr Fripp looked reproachful. 'This here cleaner,' he said, 'is constructed in such a way that it can't go wrong. I should mention that we give a year's guarantee with it, as is usual. But I shall be pleased to take it over every room in the 'ouse, to convince you, sir, of the truth of all I say.'

'Excellent,' said Charles. 'And in case I make up my mind to buy it I'll send my man up to watch you, so that he will know in future how to manipulate it.'

'That,' said Mr Fripp, 'is as you like, sir, but I should like to assure you that a child could work this here cleaner.'

'Nevertheless,' said Charles, stepping to the bell-rope, and jerking it sharply, 'I should like Bowers to – observe what you do.'

Those quick-glancing eyes darted to his face for an instant. 'I'm sure I shall be pleased to show him all I can, sir,' Mr Fripp said, not quite so enthusiastically.

Charles' smile was a little grim. When Bowers appeared in answer to the bell, he told him that he was to accompany Mr Fripp from room to room, and closely to watch all he did. Mr Fripp looked at him sideways.

'Yes, sir,' Bowers said, a trifle perplexed. 'But I haven't served the sweet yet, sir.'

'Never mind,' said Charles. 'We'll manage on our own. You stay with Mr Fripp – in case his cleaner goes out of action. And just see that he doesn't knock the panelling with it. We don't want any scratches.'

'No, sir, very good,' Bowers said, and resigned himself to his fate.

But the look that Mr Fripp cast on Charles' vanishing form was one of something bordering on acute dislike.

In the dining-room Charles was greeted by a demand from his wife to explain what on earth was the matter with him.

'If,' said Charles, resuming his seat, 'you would occasionally employ your brain, dear love, you might realise that the last thing we desire is a stranger let loose in the house. Oh, and if anyone wants any pudding he or she will have to get it for themselves, as Bowers is otherwise engaged.'

'It's on the sideboard,' Celia said. 'But really, Chas, I don't quite see what harm a man selling a vacuum-cleaner can do. And I asked him for his card, just to be on the safe side.'

'Was it our friend at the Bell?' Peter asked.

'It was. I am happy to think that I've given him a nice, solid afternoon's work.' He inspected Mr Fripp's card again. 'Yes. I think this is where one calls for a little outside assistance.'

Celia pricked up her ears. '*Not* Flinders again!' she begged.

'No, not Flinders,' Charles said. 'I should be loth to interrupt his entomological studies. But I feel a few discreet inquiries might be put through.'

'If you're going to call in Scotland Yard, I for one object,' Peter said. 'We've no data for them, and they'll merely think us credulous asses.'

Charles slipped his table-napkin into its ring, and got up. 'I can hardly improve on the favourite dictum of Mr Flinders,' he said with dignity. 'You don't need to tell *me* how to act.'

'Well, what are you going to do?' Margaret asked.

'Write a letter,' Charles answered, and went out.

Peter presently ran him to earth in the small study at the front of the house. 'Why the mystery?' he inquired. 'Are you getting an inquiry agent on to James Fripp?'

'I am,' Charles said, directing the envelope. 'There's a chap I've once or twice had dealings with who'll do the job very well.'

'What about Strange? Think it's worth while setting your sleuth on him?'

'I did consider it, but I think not. As far as Fripp's concerned it ought to be fairly easy, since I've got his card. Brown can get on to this firm he apparently works for. But regarding Strange we've nothing to give Brown to start on. If he's a wrong 'un it's highly unlikely that Strange is his real name. The man we want now is friend Flinders.'

Peter groaned. 'Do we? Why?'

'To find out a little more concerning M. Louis Duval. I'm rather surprised Flinders hasn't mentioned him.'

But the reason for this omission was soon forthcoming. Flinders, when they visited him in his cottage later that afternoon, said with considerable hauteur that they had only asked him questions about the gentry. 'And that Dooval,' he added, 'ain't gentry, besides being a furriner. You've only got to look at the place he lives in. Pig-sty ain't in it. What's more, he does for himself. Ah, *and* in more ways than one!' He permitted himself to give vent to a hoarse crack of laughter at his own wit. 'But what I *meant* was, he doesn't have no one up to clean the place for him, nor cook his breakfast.' He shook his head. 'He's a disgrace to the neighbourhood, that's what he is. He goes round painting them pictures what no one can make 'ead nor tail of as I ever heard on, and half the time he's drunk as a lord. Getting worse, he is. Why, I remember when he first come here, barring the fact of his being a furriner, there wasn't really much you could take exception to about him. Very quiet, he used to be, and you never saw him in drink more'n was respectable, though there *are* some as say that it ain't only drink as is *his* trouble.'

'Drugs?' Charles said. 'I rather suspected as much.'

'Mind you, I never said so,' Mr Flinders warned him, 'nor I wouldn't, me knowing my duty too well. But Mrs Fellowes, what I told you about before – her as is housekeeper to Mr Titmarsh – she spread it about that Dooval was one of those dope-fiends you read about in the *News of the World*. And the reason she had for saying it was on account of her working for a gentleman in London once, what was in the 'abit of taking drugs, which she said made her reckernise it right off.'

'By the way,' Peter interrupted, 'how is Mr Titmarsh getting on?'

The constable shook his head. 'Ah, now you're asking, sir. Well, I don't mind telling you that when you first came here asking me questions about him, I didn't set much store by it. But I been keeping a close watch on him, sir, like I said I would, and I'm bound to say he's fishy.'

'What's he done?'

'That,' said Mr Flinders cautiously, 'I couldn't go so far as to say, him having got into the habit of giving me the slip. Behaves like as if he knew he was being followed, and didn't wish for anyone to see what he was up to.' An odd sound proceeding from Charles made him turn his head inquiringly. 'You was saying, sir?'

'Nothing,' Charles replied hastily. 'At the moment I'm more interested in Duval than in Titmarsh. Does Duval go down to the inn every morning?'

‘He eats his dinner there most days,’ Flinders answered. ‘Though when he’s got one of his fits on him I don’t believe he touches a bite. You’ll see him at the Bell most evenings, but he’s painting one of these ’orrible pictures of his now, and he’s out most of the day.’

‘What’s he painting?’ Charles asked.

‘Pink rats, I should think, sir, judging from what I see of him last night,’ said the constable facetiously. ‘What’s more, if he told me he was painting pink rats I’d believe him a lot easier than what I do when he says he’s painting the mill-stream. Because anything more unnatural I never did see. Looks like a nightmare, if you ask me.’

‘The mill-stream. That’s past the village, isn’t it?’

‘That’s right, sir. If you was to think of taking a look at the picture you’ll find him painting it on the near bank, just below the mill.’

‘I rather think I’ll wander along that way,’ Charles said.

‘I take it you don’t want me?’ Peter asked him.

‘N-no. Might perturb him if two of us rolled up. I’ll see what I can find out.’

They took their leave of the constable, and drove on to the village. At the Bell, Charles got out of the car and proceeded on foot down the street to the fields that lay beyond.

It was no more than a ten minutes’ walk to the mill, and as Flinders had predicted, Charles was rewarded by the sight of M. Duval at work on his sketch.

Charles approached from behind him, and thus had leisure to observe the artist before his own presence was detected. The man looked more of a scarecrow than ever, but if he was under the influence of drink or drugs this was not immediately apparent. He seemed to be absorbed in his work, and it was not until Charles stopped at his elbow that he looked round.

There was suspicion in his nervous start, and he glared up at Charles out of his bloodshot eyes.

'Good afternoon,' Charles said pleasantly. 'I apologise for being so inquisitive. If I may say so, you are painting a very remarkable picture.'

This was no less than the truth. Privately Charles thought that Flinders' strictures were not without reason. The sketch before him was weird in the extreme, yet although it could hardly be said to represent the old mill, even Charles, no connoisseur, could see that it was executed with a certain perverted skill.

The artist sneered, and said disagreeably: 'What do you English know of art? Nothing, I tell you!'

'I'm afraid you're right,' Charles agreed. 'But this, I take it, is not destined for our Academy? You exhibit in the Salon, no doubt?'

This piece of flattery found its mark. 'It is true,' M. Duval said. 'With this picture, my *chef-d'oeuvre*, I make my name. The world will know me at last.' The momentary fire died out of his face. He shrugged, and said with a return to his sullen manner: 'But how should you appreciate a work of genius?'

'What strikes me particularly,' Charles persevered, 'is your treatment of shadows. In fact . . .'

'I see them red,' M. Duval said sombrely. 'Dull red.'

'Very few people have the eye to see them like that,' said Charles truthfully.

He soon found that no flattery was too gross to please M. Duval, and he proceeded, as he afterwards told Peter, to spread himself. At the end of twenty minutes the artist had mellowed considerably, and when Charles said solemnly that Framley was fortunate indeed to have attracted one who was so obviously a genius, he threw down his brush with a gesture of bitter loathing, and cried out: 'You think I live here because I choose? Ah, *mon Dieu*!' He leaned forward on his camp-stool, and the hand which held his palette shook with some overpowering emotion. 'I think all the time how I shall get away!' he said tensely. 'Five years I have lived here, five years, m'sieur! Figure to yourself! But the day comes when I see it no more. Then – pouf! I am gone, I am free!' He seemed to recollect himself, and a smile of weak cunning showed his discoloured teeth. 'You think I talk strangely, *hein*? Not like you English, who are always cold, like ice. To those others I am nothing but a mad Frenchman, but you, my friend, you have seen that I have a genius in me!' He slapped his chest as he spoke. 'Here, in my soul! You have admired my picture; you have not laughed behind my back. And because you have sympathised, because you have recognised the true art, I will tell you something.' He plucked at Charles' sleeve with fingers like talons, and his voice sank. 'Take care, m'sieur, you who think to live in that house which is the home of *Le Moine*. I warn you, take care, and do not try to interfere with him. I tell you, it is not safe. You hear me? There is danger, much, much danger.'

'Thanks for the warning,' Charles said calmly. 'But I don't really think a ghost could do me much harm, do you?'

The artist looked at him queerly. 'I say only, take care. You have tried to find *Le Moine*, I think, because you do not believe in ghosts. But I tell you there is great danger.'

'I see. You think I should be unwise to try and find out who he is?'

'There is no one who knows that,' M. Duval said slowly. 'No one! But maybe this poor Duval, who paints pictures that the world laughs at, maybe he might – one day – know – who is – *Le Moine.*' He was smiling as he said it, and his eyes were clouded and far away. His voice sank still lower till it was little more than a whisper. 'And if I know, then, then at last I will be free, and I will have revenge! Ah, but that will be sweet!' His claw-like hands curled as though they strangled some unseen thing.

'Forgive me,' said Charles, 'but has the Monk done you some injury?'

His words jerked Duval back from that dreamy, half-drugged state. He picked up his brush again. 'It is a ghost,' he muttered. 'You have said it yourself.'

Seeing that for the present at least there was little hope of getting anything more out of the artist, Charles prepared to take his departure. 'Ghost or no ghost,' he said deliberately, 'I intend to find out – what I can. You seem to have some idea of doing the same thing. If you want my assistance I suggest you come and call on me at the Priory.'

'I do not want assistance,' Duval said, hunching his shoulders rather like a pettish child.

'No? Yet if I were to say one day that I had seen the face of the Monk . . .?' Charles left the end of the sentence unfinished, but its effect was even more than he had hoped.

Duval swung round eagerly. 'You have seen – but no! You have seen nothing. He does not show his face, the

Monk, and it is better if you do not try to see it.' He fixed his eyes on Charles' face, and said in a low voice: 'One man – saw – just once in his life. One man alone, m'sieur!'

'Oh? Who is he?'

'It does not matter now, m'sieur, who he is, for he is dead.'

Charles was half-startled, and half-scornful. 'What did he die of? Fright?'

The artist bent his gaze on his sketch again. 'Perhaps,' he said. 'Yet me, I do not think he died of fright.' He began to squeeze paint from one of his tubes. 'You will go back to your Priory, m'sieur, but you will remember what I say, is it not?'

'Certainly,' Charles said. '*And* I shall hope to see your picture again when it is more finished, if you will let me.'

There was something rather pathetic about the way Duval looked up at that, unpleasant though the man's personality might be. 'You like it enough to wish to see more? But I have many pictures in my cottage, perhaps not so fine as this, but all, all full of my genius! One day perhaps you come to see me, and I show you. Perhaps you will see something you like enough to buy from me, *hein*?'

'That was what I was thinking,' lied Charles.

The Monk was forgotten; avarice gleamed in the artist's eye. He said swiftly: '*Bon*! You come very soon, and I show you the best that I have painted. Perhaps you come to-morrow? Or the day after?'

'Thanks, I'd like to come to-morrow if I may. Shall we say about this time?' He consulted his wrist-watch. 'Half-past three? Or does that break into your working hours?'

'But no! I am quite at your service,' M. Duval assured him.

'Then *au revoir*,' Charles said. 'I'll see you to-morrow.'

M. Duval's farewell was as cordial as his greeting had been surly. Charles walked briskly back to the village, trying as he went to separate the grain of his talk from the chaff.

One thing seemed clear enough: unless the man were a consummate actor, he was not the Monk. It seemed improbable that, in his half-drugged condition, he could be acting a part, but on the other hand that very condition made it dangerous to set too much store by what he said. Much of it sounded suspiciously like the waking dreams experienced by drug-addicts, yet when he had spoken of the Monk, Charles thought that he had detected a look of perfectly sane hatred in his eyes. He had not been talking of a ghost: that much was certain. To Duval, the Monk was real, and, apparently, terrible. It was possible, of course, that in a state that resembled delirium his mind had seized on the idea of the ghostly inmate of the Priory, and woven a story about it. Possible, Charles admitted, but hardly probable.

If one accepted the provisional hypothesis that the Monk was no ghost, one was immediately faced with two problems. The first, Charles thought, was the reason he could have for what seemed a senseless masquerade; the second, which might perhaps be easier to solve if the first were discovered, was his identity.

Since they had had, so far, no means of identifying any single thing about him, he might be any one of the people with whom they had become acquainted, or, which was quite possible, someone whom they had never seen.

The artist apparently knew something, but how much it was hard to decide. Charles hoped that on the following day he might, by buying one of his pictures, induce him to disclose more. If he was weaving a fanciful tale out of his own clouded mind it would be merely misleading, of course, but Charles felt that for the sake of the remote chance of discovering the Monk's object in haunting the Priory, this must be faced.

He had reached the Bell Inn by this time. The bar was not open, but on the other side of the archway into the yard there was a draughty apartment known as the lounge. Here he found his brother-in-law seated in an uncomfortable leather chair, and chatting to Colonel Ackerley. The Colonel's golf clubs were propped against one of the tables, and he was wearing a suit of immensely baggy plus-fours.

'Aha, here's Malcolm!' he said, as Charles entered the room. 'Sit down, my dear fellow! Been fishing? I'm on my way back from my day's golf! Noticed your car outside and looked in to see which of you was trying to get a drink out of hours. Found you out, eh?'

'It cannot be too widely known,' said Charles, 'that I am more or less of a teetotaller.'

'But mostly less,' Peter interpolated.

The Colonel was much amused by this, and repeated it. 'More or less – that's very good, Malcolm. I must remember that. Might mean either, what? But what have you been doing? Calling on the Vicar's wife?'

'I regard that as a reflection on my sobriety, sir,' Charles said gravely. 'No. I've been watching a very odd specimen paint a still odder picture.'

The Colonel lifted his brows. 'That French johnny?

Can't say I understand much about art, but I've always thought his pictures were dam' bad. I'm a plain man, and if I look at a picture I like to be able to see what it's meant to be. But I daresay I'm old-fashioned.'

'I should rather like to know,' said Charles, 'what he's doing here. Know anything about him, sir?'

The Colonel shook his head. 'No, afraid I don't. Never really thought about it, to tell you the truth.'

'He's not exactly prepossessing,' Peter remarked. 'He may be a bit of a wrong 'un who finds it wiser not to return to his native shores.'

''Pon my soul, you people have got mysteries on the brain!' exclaimed the Colonel. 'First it's poor old Titmarsh, and now it's what's-his-name? – Duval. What's he been up to, I should like to know?'

'Intriguing us by his conversation,' said Charles lightly. 'Making our blood run cold by his sinister references to our Monk.'

The Colonel threw up his hands. 'No, no, once you get on to that Monk of yours I can't cope with you, Malcolm. Now really, really, my dear fellow, you don't seriously mean to tell me you've been listening to that sodden dope-fiend?'

Charles looked up quickly. 'Ah! So you think he's a dope-fiend too, do you?'

The Colonel caught himself up. 'Daresay one oughtn't to say so,' he apologised. 'Slander, eh? But it's common talk round here.'

He glanced over his shoulder as someone opened the door. Wilkes had put his head into the room to see who was there. He bade them good afternoon, and wanted to know whether he might tell John, the waiter, to serve them with tea. They all refused, but the Colonel detained Wilkes. 'I say, Wilkes,' he called, 'here's that artist fellow been maundering to Mr Malcolm about the Priory ghost. Is he drunk again?'

Wilkes came farther into the room, shaking his head. 'I'm afraid so, sir. Been carrying on something chronic these last three days. First it's the Monk, then it's eyes watching him in the dark, till he fair gives me the creeps, and yesterday nothing would do but he must tell me how there was a plot about to keep him from being reckernised. If you ask me, sir, he's gone clean potty.'

'Dear, dear, something will have to be done about it if that's so,' Colonel Ackerley said. 'You never know with these drug fiends. He may turn dangerous.'

'Yes, sir, that's what I've been thinking,' Wilkes said. 'He's got a nasty look in his eye some days.'

'Better keep your carving-knife out of reach,' the Colonel said laughingly.

At that moment Peter chanced to look at the window. 'Hullo!' he said. 'There's your pal, Fripp, Chas. Looks a trifle jaded.'

Charles glanced round, but Fripp had passed the window. 'I daresay. There are quite a lot of rooms at the Priory,' he remarked.

The Colonel pricked up his ears. 'Fripp? Fripp? Seem to know that name. Wait a bit! Is he a fellow with some sort of a vacuum-cleaner?'

'He is,' said Charles. 'He has been spending the afternoon demonstrating it at the Priory. In fact, all over the Priory.'

'Perfect pest, these house-to-house salesmen,' fumed

the Colonel. 'Came to my place the other day, but my man sent him about his business.'

'I told him he wouldn't do no good in these parts,' Wilkes said. 'What I can't make out is how he comes to be making this place his headquarters, so to speak. Don't seem reasonable, somehow, but I suppose he knows his business. You're sure you wouldn't like tea, sir?'

'We must be getting along at any rate,' Peter said, rising. 'When are you coming in for another game of bridge, Colonel? Why not come home with us now, and have some tea, and a game?'

The Colonel said that nothing would please him more, and accordingly they all went out together, and drove back to the Priory to find Celia in ecstasies over the dustless condition of the house, and quite anxious to send an order for a cleaner at once.

Eight

On the following afternoon Peter went off with Colonel Ackerley to play golf on the nearest course, some four miles away on the other side of the village. Margaret, whose appointment with the dentist fell on this day, had taken the car up to London, so that Charles, no believer in such forms of exercise, was compelled to walk to M. Duval's cottage.

He found it easily enough, but even the farmer's disparaging remarks upon it had not quite prepared him for anything so tumbledown and dreary. It had an air of depressing neglect; the garden was overgrown with docks and nettles, every window wanted cleaning, and in places the original white plaster had peeled off the walls, leaving the dirty brown brick exposed.

The hinges of the gate were broken, and it stood open. Charles made his way up the path to the door of the cottage, and knocked on the blistered panels with his walking stick. After a few moments footsteps approached, Charles heard a bolt drawn, and the door was opened by M. Duval.

It was plain that he had made an effort to tidy not only the living-room of his abode, but also his own person. His shirt was clean, and he had evidently done his best to remove some of the stains from his coat. Also he was sober, but he betrayed by his nervousness, and his unsteady hand, what a hold over him drugs had obtained.

He was almost effusive in his welcome, and insisted that Charles should take tea with him as a preliminary to any negotiations they might enter into. The kettle, he said, was already on the stove. He seemed so anxious to play the host to the best of his ability that Charles accepted his offer.

'I will make it on the instant,' Duval told him. 'I do not keep a servant, m'sieur. You will excuse me?'

'Of course,' Charles said. 'And while you're getting tea perhaps I may take a look at your work?'

Duval made a gesture that swept the little room. 'You see my work, m'sieur, before you.'

All manner of canvases were propped against the walls, some so weird that they looked to be no more than irrelevant splashes of colour, some a riot of cubes, one or two moderately understandable.

'Look your fill!' Duval said dramatically. 'You look into my soul.'

For the sake of M. Duval's soul Charles hoped that this was an exaggeration. However, he bowed politely, and begged his host not to mind leaving him. Thus adjured, the artist disappeared into the lean-to kitchen that was built out at the back of the cottage, and Charles was left to take stock of his surroundings.

These were miserable enough. The cottage, which bore signs of considerable antiquity, had but the one living-room, from which a precipitous staircase led up between two walls to the upper storey. At the back a door led into the kitchen; at the front were lattice windows and the principal door of the house, and on one side a huge fireplace occupied almost the entire wall. The ceiling was low, and a wealth of old oak formed worm-eaten beams, in between which the cobwebs of years had formed. Charles judged that originally the room had served as kitchen and living-room combined, for from the great central beam one or two big hooks still protruded, from which, doubtless, flitches of bacon had hung in olden days.

The furniture was in keeping with the dilapidated building itself. A strip of dusty carpet lay across the floor; there were two sound chairs, and one with a broken leg that sagged against the wall; a table, an easel, a cupboard, and a deal chest that stood under the window, and which was covered with a litter of tubes, brushes, rags, and bits of charcoal.

There remained the pictures, and until Duval came back with the tea-pot Charles occupied himself in trying to make up his mind which he could best bring himself to buy.

Duval reappeared shortly, and set the tea-pot down on the table. He suggested, not without a hopeful note in his voice, that perhaps his guest would prefer a whisky and soda, but this Charles firmly declined.

'Eh *bien*, then I give you sugar and milk, yes? So? You have looked at my pictures? Presently I will explain to you what I have tried to express in them.'

'I wish you would,' Charles said. 'I can see that they are full of ideas.'

No further encouragement was needed to start the

artist off on his topic. He talked volubly, but rather incoherently, for over half an hour, until Charles' head reeled, and he felt somewhat as though he had stepped into a nightmare. But his polite questions and apparently rapt interest had the effect of banishing whatever guard the artist had set upon his tongue and he became expansive, though mysterious on the subject of his own enforced sojourn at Framley.

Realising that in all probability any attempt to question Duval as to his obscure meaning would drive him into his shell, Charles contented himself with sympathising.

'Whoever is to blame for keeping you here,' he said solemnly, 'is a criminal of the deepest dye.'

This pleased. 'Yes he is wicked. You do not know, m'sieur! But I shall have my revenge on him, perhaps soon. I tell you, I will make him suffer! He shall pay. Yes, he shall pay and pay for the years which I have spent in exile.' A little saliva dribbled from the corner of his mouth; he looked unpleasantly like a dog drooling at the sight of a bone.

With a feeling of disgust, and more than half convinced that he was wasting his time on a madman, Charles turned to the pictures, and soon made his choice. M. Duval seemed disappointed when he fixed on the least Futuristic of his works, but after an attempt to induce Charles to buy 'Sunset in Hades' he consented to roll up the more innocuous 'Reapers.'

Outside the sky had for some time been growing steadily more overcast, and as Charles prepared to take his leave, a flash of lightning lit up the darkening room, to be followed in a very few moments by an ominous rumble of thunder. The rain did not seem to be far off, and since he had no overcoat Charles was reluctantly compelled to postpone his departure.

The artist seemed to become more restless with the approach of the storm, and as the light went he took to glancing over his shoulder as though he expected to see someone. When a second and much louder clap of thunder came he jumped uncontrollably, and muttered something about fetching a lamp. He went through into the kitchen, and came back presently with a cheap oil-lamp which he set down on the table.

'I do not like the darkness,' he said. 'Perhaps you think I am strange to say that, but when one lives always alone, m'sieur, one has fancies.' He gave a little shiver, and his eyes stared into Charles' for a moment. 'But there are things which are not fancies.' Again he looked round, then leaning towards Charles he said hardly above a whisper: 'I know that there is one who watches. I have felt his eyes through my window, I bolt my door, but when I go out he follows. I have heard his footsteps, but when I look there is no one there. Sometimes I think I cannot bear it, for at night, m'sieur, it is so still, and I am alone. Sometimes I think maybe I shall go mad one day. But I am not mad. No, I am not mad yet.'

'Who watches you?' Charles said quietly. 'Have you any idea?'

Duval shook his head. 'I do not know. Sometimes I think – but I do not say.'

'I hope,' said Charles, 'that it is not our Monk?'

The artist gave a start, and grew sickly pale all at once. 'No, no!' he said. 'But do not speak so loud, m'sieur! You do not know who may be listening.'

Since a heavy rain was now beating against the windows it seemed absurd to suppose that anyone could be lurking outside, but Charles saw that it was useless to reason with one whose nerves were so little under control. To humour the artist, he lowered his voice. 'It is unwise, then, even to mention the Monk?' he asked.

Duval nodded vigorously. 'For me, yes. There are those who listen to what I say though they seem to be deaf. M'sieur, I tell you it is too much! Sometimes when I am alone in this house I think it would be better to give it all up, not to attempt – I have not the courage, he is clever, ah, but clever!'

'My friend,' Charles said, 'I think someone has some sort of a hold over you. Don't be alarmed: I'm not asking what it is.'

The thunder crashed above their heads, and involuntarily Duval winced. 'Yes, he has what you call a hold, but what if I get a hold over him? What then, *hein*?' His fingers curled and uncurled; he looked so haggard that once more Charles found himself pitying him against his will.

'Forgive me if I say that I think you would do well to get away from this lonely life of yours. It has preyed too much on your mind.'

The artist's eyes stared wildly at him. 'I cannot get away!' he burst out. 'I am tied, tied! I dare not speak, even! What I could tell! Ah, m'sieur, there are things I know that you would give all to learn. Yes, I am not a fool; I know what you are seeking, you and that other. You will not find it, but I – I might! You do not believe? You think I talk so because perhaps I am drunk? You are wrong. It is true that sometimes I have drunk too much.

To-day, no! What is it you desire to see? You will not answer? But I know, m'sieur! You desire to see the face of the Monk.'

Charles would have spoken, but he swept on, as though a spate of words had been loosed in him. 'You will not. But I desire it also, and I tell you the day comes when I shall see it. And if I see it, only for one little minute! one little, little minute, what shall I do? Shall I tell you? Ah no, m'sieur! No, no, no, I tell no one, but I am free! And it will be for me then to revenge myself, for me to be master!'

A flash of lightning made Charles blink. There was the scrape of a chair. Duval had sprung up, and was staring towards the window. 'What was that,' he gasped. 'What was that, m'sieur? A face? A face pressed to the glass?'

'Nonsense,' Charles said calmly. 'It was nothing but that sunflower blown against the window. Look!'

The sweat stood on Duval's forehead. 'Truly? Yes, yes, I see. It was nothing. Yet for a moment I could have sworn I saw – something. It is this accursed storm. I do not like the lightning. It makes me what you call on edge. Sometimes I fear I have not the courage to go on with what I have made up my mind I must do to be free. For when I am here with the darkness I remember that other who died.' He went to the cupboard and opened it, and pulled out a whisky bottle, half-full, and two thick glasses, 'You will take a little drink with me? This storm – one's nerves demand it.'

'Not for me, thanks,' Charles answered. 'May I suggest that if you've reason to think someone is watching you your best course is to inform the police.'

Duval cast a quick, furtive look at him. The whisky spilled into his glass. He tossed it off, neat, and seemed to regain what little composure he possessed. 'No, I do not do that. You will not listen to me: I talk folly, *hein*? Me, I am Louis Duval, and I am not afraid.'

The rain had practically ceased by now, and Charles got up. 'Then since the storm seems to be passing over you won't mind if I say good-bye, will you?' He picked up the picture he had bought. 'I shall – er – value this, I assure you. And if at any time you'd like to take me rather more into your confidence you know where I'm to be found, don't you?'

'I thank you. And for this' – he held up Charles' cheque – 'I thank you also.' With his self-command his arrogance too was creeping back. 'The day comes when you will congratulate yourself that you were once able to buy a picture of Louis Duval's for so small a price.'

That view was not shared either by Charles, or by any of his relatives. When he exhibited the painting at the Priory an astonished silence greeted it.

'Yes,' he said blandly, 'I thought you'd be hard put to it to find words to express your emotions.'

Peter breathed audibly through his nose. 'You were right,' he said.

'Nice piece of work, isn't it? I particularly like the woman's splay feet. Where shall we hang it?'

'I suggest the coal-cellar,' said Peter.

Mrs Bosanquet was regarding the picture through her lorgnette. 'What an exceedingly ill-favoured young person!' she remarked. 'Really, almost disgusting. And what is she waving in her hand, pray?'

'Since I am informed that the title of this masterpiece

is "Reapers" I should hazard a guess that it must be a sickle,' Charles replied.

Celia found her tongue. 'Charles, how *could* you?' she demanded. 'Have you gone mad, or something?'

'Not at all. I'm supporting modern art.'

'You don't know anything about art, ancient or modern. I can't get over you going out and wasting your money on an awful thing like this! You don't suppose that I could live with it on my walls, do you?'

'Shove it up on the stairs,' suggested Peter. 'Then the next time the Monk goes *glissant* up and down, though we do not see, it'll give him something to think about. After all we owe him one for that skull.'

'My dear,' said Mrs Bosanquet gravely, 'you should not make a jest of these things. When Margaret returns from London with my planchette board I shall hope to convince you as I myself have been convinced.'

'Aunt, you promised you wouldn't talk about the Monk!' Celia said uneasily. 'Just when I was beginning to forget about it too!'

'It was not I who started it, dear child,' Mrs Bosanquet pointed out. 'But by all means let us talk of something else. I do trust, Peter, that you are not serious in wishing to hang that very unpleasant picture on the stairs.'

'Well, we shall have to hang it somewhere,' Peter said. 'Old Ackerley will want to see it. When he asked me where you were, Chas, and I told him you'd gone to buy one of Duval's pictures, I thought he'd throw a fit.'

'You can jolly well tell him then that you didn't buy a picture after all,' Celia said. 'I won't have you making yourself a laughing-stock. It'll be all over Framley that you've been had.'

Charles listened to this with a suspicious air of interest. 'Do I understand you all to mean that you feel these walls are unworthy to bear the masterpiece?' he inquired.

'You can put it like that, if you choose,' Celia said.

'Very well,' he replied, and began carefully to roll it up again. 'I've always wanted to see my name in the papers as one who has presented a work of art to the nation. I wonder where they'll hang it? It would go rather well amongst the Turners.'

'And the worst of it is,' Celia said later to her brother, 'he's quite capable of sending it to the National Gallery, if only to tease me.'

Peter was more interested in the result of Charles' visit than in the fate of the picture, but it was not until he was dressing for dinner that he had an opportunity of speaking to him alone. Charles came in while he was wrestling with a refractory stud, and sat down on the edge of the bed.

'Good. I hoped you'd come in,' Peter said. 'God damn this blasted laundry! They starch the thing so that . . . Ah, that's got it! Well, did you discover anything, or is he merely potty?'

'A bit of both,' Charles said. He selected a cigarette from his case, and lit it. 'From a welter of drivel just one or two facts emerge. The most important of these is that unless Duval is completely out of his mind, which I doubt, the Monk is a very real personage. Further, it would appear that he has some hold over Duval, who, with or without reason, fears him like the devil. It seems fairly obvious that the Monk – and very likely Duval too – is engaged in some nefarious pursuit, and I rather gathered from what our friend said that he – I'm talking now of Duval – is only waiting for the chance to blackmail him.'

'What about?' Peter asked, busy with his tie.

'God knows. I couldn't arrive at it. It sounds absurd, but everything seemed to hinge on the Monk's face.'

'Talk sense,'said Peter shortly.

'Quite impossible,' Charles replied, flicking the ash off his cigarette. 'I'm giving you the gist of Duval's conversation. Put plainly, the Monk is strictly incognito. According to Duval the only man who ever saw his face immediately died. Manner not specified, but all very sinister.'

'Doesn't say much for the Monk's face,' Peter commented. His eyes met Charles' in the mirror, and he saw that Charles was frowning slightly. He turned. 'Look here, how much faith do you place in this rigmarole?'

Charles shrugged. 'Can't say. After all we had ourselves decided that the Monk was no ghost.'

Peter picked up his waistcoat and put it on. 'Neither you nor I have so far set eyes on this precious Monk,' he reminded Charles. 'We know there's a legend about a monk haunting this place; we've had a skull drop at our feet, and we suspect – suspect, mind you – human agency. Not necessarily the Monk. The only person to see it is Aunt Lilian. I admit she's not the sort of person likely to imagine things, but you've got to bear in mind that it was late at night, and she, in common with the rest of us, had probably got the Monk slightly on the brain. She got the wind up – admits that herself. Started to "feel" things. Works herself into a state in which she's ripe for seeing anything. She has a candle only, and by its light she sees, or thinks she sees, a cowled figure.'

'Which according to her account, moved towards her,' Charles interpolated.

'True, and as I say, she's not nervous or given to imaginative flights. I don't say she didn't see all that. But I do say that some trick of the shadows cast by a feeble light held in her probably not very steady hand, coupled with her own quite natural fears, may have deceived her. The only other thing we've got to go on is the ravings of this artist-bloke, in whom you can't place much reliance.'

'Not quite,' Charles said. 'We know that there is something queer about this house. I don't want to lay undue stress on all that has happened, but on the other hand I don't want to run to the other extreme of pooh-poohing undoubtedly odd proceedings. There was the episode of the groaning stone; there was the exceedingly fishy conversation we overheard between Strange and Fripp. Without that proof that someone is taking an extraordinary interest in the Priory I might easily discount everything Duval said. But we *know* that someone broke into the place by a secret entrance; we know that Strange had something to do with it. What he's after I don't pretend to say, but it's fairly obvious that he is after something. Given those facts I don't feel justified in brushing Duval aside as irrelevant. In fact, I'll go so far as to say that I have a strong conviction that he is perhaps the most relevant thing we've struck yet.'

Peter tucked a clean handkerchief into the breast-pocket of his dinner-jacket. 'But the whole thing seems so utterly fantastic,' he complained. 'I daresay Duval is in someone's power: I always said he looked a wrong 'un. But what the hell has it got to do with the Priory?'

'That,' said Charles, 'is what we've got to find out.'

'Thanks very much. And just where do we start? The most likely explanation advanced so far is hidden treasure. Well, if you want to spend the rest of our stay prising up solid stone slabs in the cellar, you've more energy than I've ever yet seen you display.'

Charles threw the end of his cigarette out of the open window. 'If it's buried treasure the field isn't as narrow as that. Fripp, to my mind, wanted a chance to explore the rest of the house.'

'Well, that settles it. You can't take up the floorboards in every room, and go twisting every bit of moulding in the panelling in the hope of discovering another priest's hole. If we'd a history of the place no doubt we should find out all about it. But we haven't.'

'No,' said Charles. '*We* haven't. And, do you know, I find that rather surprising.'

Peter stared. 'Do you mean someone may have pinched it?'

'Hasn't that occurred to you? This place obviously has a history – must have had. You'd expect to find some record in the library.'

'Well, yes, you might, but on the other hand the house has changed hands a lot since the place was a monastery. It may have got lost, or bought by a collector or something like that.'

'Quite so. But there's something more to it than that. When the point was first raised it struck me as being curious. I thought it worth while to drop a line to Tim Baker, and ask him to see whether a history of this place existed in the British Museum library. To-night I had his answer.' He drew a letter from his pocket, and opened it. 'There is a history, and a copy of it is in the Museum.

And two pages have been torn out. What do you make of that?'

'Good Lord!' Peter said blankly. 'I say, things do begin to look a bit sinister, don't they? What do you propose we do about it? Call in Scotland Yard?'

'I've been playing with that idea for some days, but I'm not in love with it. I don't quite see myself spinning this yarn to some disillusioned official. If we'd any real data to give the Yard, well and good. But I ask you, what does our tale sound like, in cold blood? A hotch-potch without one solid fact to go on. We hear noises, we discover a skeleton, we listen to what a drunken Frenchman has to say, and see various people wandering about the grounds. The only fact we've got is that someone broke into the cellars, and that's a matter for the local police to deal with. It's not good enough.'

Peter nodded. 'That's what I feel myself, I must say. At the same time we're not getting anywhere – principally because we don't know where to start. If this inquiry agent of yours throws any discreditable light on Fripp's past, what do you say to running over to Manfield, and having a chat with the District Inspector?'

A gong chimed in the hall below them. Charles got up. 'We can do that, of course. Personally, I'm rather pinning my faith to Duval. I rather think he'll let something out sooner or later which may give us a line on it.'

They went slowly down to the library, where Celia and Mrs Bosanquet were awaiting them.

'Margaret not back yet?' Charles said.

Celia prepared to go in to dinner. 'No, but I was hardly expecting her. She said if Peggy Mason was free she might have an early dinner with her in town, and get back here about nine-thirty, before it's quite dark.'

'I hope,' said Mrs Bosanquet, 'that she will not have forgotten to call at my flat for the planchette.'

Nine

Margaret spent a successful day in London. The dentist did not keep her waiting more than a quarter of an hour, and his excavations were not too painful. In the afternoon she visited the flat Peter and she owned in Knightsbridge, and unearthed his service revolver from a trunk in the box-room. Next she drove to Celia's house in Kensington, and after prolonged search located Charles' revolver. There remained only Mrs Bosanquet's planchette, and this the maid she had left in charge of her flat was easily able to find. By the time all these commissions had been executed Margaret was feeling ready for tea, and after that she had some shopping of her own to do. This occupied her till six o'clock, and then, somewhat weary, but with the consciousness of having left nothing undone, she drove to her club, and sat down to await the arrival of her friend, Peggy Mason.

She did not expect Mrs Mason before seven o'clock, so that she had almost an hour to while away. Under the disapproving glare of one of the more elderly members of the club she ordered a cocktail, and curled herself up in a large arm-chair with an illustrated journal, a cigarette, and her Bronx.

The journal was, as usual, full of pictures of sunburnt people snapped on the Lido, but the odd thing about it was that though the legend under the snapshots might read: 'Lord So-and-so and Miss Something-else in a happy mood,' Lord So-and-so's face became unaccountably the face of Michael Strange. Information concerning the doings of all these leisured people changed to such irrelevant scraps as: 'But what was he doing in the garden at that hour?' and: 'Could he really have been in our cellars that day we tried to locate the groan and saw him by the drawing-room windows?'

Margaret told herself severely that she was thinking a great deal too much about Michael Strange, and applied herself to the *Tatler* with a firm resolve to think about him no more.

But excellent though the resolve might be it was impossible to keep to it. Margaret gave up all pretence of doing so after five minutes, and permitted her refractory mind to do as it pleased.

Except for a brief infatuation for her drawing-master which attacked her at the age of sixteen she had never been in love. Her mother had died when she was still at school, her father three years later, and since that time she and Peter had kept house together. They were a very devoted couple, and so far Margaret had not felt in the least tempted to leave him for any one of the several suitors who had wished her to marry them. In the nicest possible way she had refused all offers, and it said much for her that these rejections never interfered with her friendship with the young man in question, nor, which was more important, with his friendship with her brother. One or two continued to cherish hopes, but when the most importunate of her suitors consoled himself eventually elsewhere, Margaret, no dog-in-the-manger, was unaffectedly glad and promptly made a friend of his bride, the very lady who was to dine with her this evening.

Until she met Michael Strange she was almost sure that she was not the sort of girl who fell in love. She wasn't at all cast down by this conviction; she didn't want to fall in love. People in love became sloppy, she thought, and they were a nuisance to all their friends, which was a pity. A girl had once told her raptly that she had known as soon as she had set eyes on the young man of her affections, that she would either marry him or no one. Margaret had considered this not only absurd, but sickly.

But during the past week she had somewhat modified her judgment. Not that she would ever be such a ninny as to fall flat in front of a man in that nauseating fashion, she told herself. Still, without going to such extremes she was bound to acknowledge that Mr Michael Strange had done something very queer indeed to her.

As to falling in love, that was rot, of course. One didn't fall in love with complete strangers, and certainly not with strangers who behaved as oddly as he was behaving. But the fact remained that from that very first meeting, when he had changed one of the wheels of the car for her she had, in her own words, 'taken to him,' as she could not remember ever having 'taken to' anyone before. There was something about his smile, which lost nothing by being rather rarely seen, that attracted her. He was good-looking too, but she didn't think that had much to do with it, for she knew men far better-looking, and she hadn't 'taken to' them in the least. No, it wasn't anything she could explain, but she just liked him very much.

She was in the habit of being as honest with herself as she could, and at this point she paused. There was rather more to it than just liking him very much. She had a suspicion that the same romantically-minded girl who had rhapsodised over her own emotions, would have described the effect of Mr Michael Strange on her friend as 'thrilling.' Margaret was not in the habit of being thrilled by young men, however personable, and she felt slightly affronted to think that such an idea had even crossed her mind. Then a really shocking thought reared up its head: she wouldn't mind if Mr Michael Strange tried to kiss her. Quite disgusted with herself, she realised that so far from minding she would rather like it. For one who had the greatest objection to stray embraces, this was unheard of. Margaret put the thought hurriedly aside: in every other way she prided herself on her modernity, but when it came to letting men maul you about – no!

But leaving that out of the question, there was no denying that Michael Strange had made her feel that she would like to see more of him.

Then had come the surprise of finding him in the Priory garden. When she had seen who he was she had instantly acquitted him, in her mind, of having had anything to do with the groan they had heard. But Charles and Peter, both likely, she realised, to be more impartial than herself, had thought his presence suspicious. They had not been reassured either by his explanation or the manner in which he gave it. Thinking it over she was bound to admit that he had sounded mysterious. At Colonel Ackerley's dinner-party, moreover, she had tried to find out more about him, and he had evaded her questions. Then there was the occasion when she had discovered him apparently studying half-obliterated inscriptions on the tombs in the ruined chapel. She had taxed him openly that time with having been in the Priory garden one night. She had known, with an unaccountable feeling of disillusionment, that he was going to deny it, and unreasonably, just because somehow she could not bear that he should lie to her, she had said quickly that she had recognised him. It would have been useless for him to deny it after that, and he had not done so. But neither had he given her any explanation of his conduct.

Margaret was no fool, and her reason told her that had there been an innocent explanation he must have given it. Since he had not done so she was forced to face the probability of his being engaged upon some discreditable business. What it could be she had no idea, but she had the impression that her presence at the Priory discomposed him. He did not want her there; he had tried to persuade her to go away. Just as though he did not want her to find out what he was doing; as though her presence made him regret what he meant to do.

He had asked her to trust him, saying frankly that there was no reason why she should. And against her reason she had trusted him, even to the extent of never mentioning his presence by night in the garden to her brother or to Charles.

Was he a crook? one of those master-crooks of fiction, who had such address and charm that no one ever suspected them? Was it possible that he was some sort of a cat-burglar who had used the empty and reputedly haunted Priory as a *cache* for his hauls? Had he hidden jewels or bank-notes in some secret hiding-place at the Priory, pending their disposal? Or was he the head of some large criminal organisation who had made a haunted house their headquarters? That might account for the attempts it seemed fairly certain he had made to frighten the new tenants away, but she could not help feeling that a less risky proceeding would have been to have changed his headquarters.

An idea flashed into her mind. She glanced at her wristwatch: ten minutes to seven. It was too late to catch Mr Milbank at his office, but he would not mind if she rang him up at his home. She got up, hesitating. It might be better if she went round to see him after dinner; he lived in town, and she knew that both he and his wife would be delighted to see her, for both had known her almost from the cradle.

She picked up her gloves and her handbag and left the lounge. She found a telephone-box disengaged, and after painstakingly reading all the alarming information about pressing buttons A and B, dropped two pennies into the slot, and gave the number she wanted. She was soon connected, remembered to press the right button, and asked whether she might speak to Mr Milbank.

'Speaking,' Mr Milbank's voice replied.

'Oh, is that you?' Margaret said. 'This is Margaret Fortescue . . . Yes, I've been up for the day. I'm speaking from the club . . . I say, I'm awfully sorry to be a pest, and I know I ought to have thought of it earlier, but would it be a ghastly nuisance if I came round to see you after dinner just for a few moments? . . . What? . . . It's frightfully sweet of you both, but I can't. You see, I've got a friend dining with me here. Could I blow in about half-past eight or nine? . . . Well, I shall try and make it as early as I can, because I don't want to be late getting home, but you know what it is when you have anyone to dinner . . . Righto, then, I'll come along as soon after dinner as I can. Thanks awfully! *Au revoir!*' She hung up the receiver, and went back to the lounge, where she found Peggy Mason awaiting her, and a diminutive page loudly chanting her name.

Margaret kissed her friend. 'Hullo! I say, wait a minute till I stop that youth howling for me. Do you ever recognise your own name when you hear it shouted like that?' She darted off to intercept the page, who having failed to obtain response to his call, was on the point of passing on to the dining-room. When she came back Peggy greeted her with a great many questions, and items of news, and these proved so absorbing that Michael Strange was forgotten for a while.

It was nearly ten minutes to nine when Margaret remembered to look at the time. 'Peggy, you brute, you've kept me talking twenty minutes longer than I meant to. Look here, I've got to go.'

'That's right,' said Mrs Mason, 'throw your guest out. Where were you brought up?' She pulled on her gloves. 'You are a mutt not to come and spend the night with me as I suggested. Sure you won't change your mind? You can ring the Priory up, can't you?'

'Not on the telephone. No, really I can't, Peggy. I've got to go and see our solicitor too: that's why I'm pushing you off.'

'Solicitor be blowed,' said Mrs Mason inelegantly.

'Who ever goes to see solicitors at this hour? All right, my girl, I'm going. I shall tell Bill when he gets back from France that you had an assignation with some man you kept very dark.' Her sharp eyes detected a rising blush in Margaret's cheeks. 'Hul-*lo*!' she said, surprised. 'Don't say I've hit the nail on the head? Is there someone?'

'No, of course not, you idiot. I'm going to see my solicitor and his wife at their house in Chelsea. Can I drop you?'

'As I live in the wilds of Hampstead, which fact you are well aware of, I regard that offer as a clear proof that you are dithering. And the only explanation for that . . .'

'Will you shut up?' said Margaret, and dragged her forth.

A quarter of an hour later her car drew up outside the Milbanks' house on the Embankment. She was ushered at once into the drawing-room on the first floor, and found both Mr and Mrs Milbank there. They both gave her a warm welcome, and for a little while they were all engaged in the usual conversation of old friends. But when Margaret had set down her coffee-cup, Mr Milbank said: 'Well, what is it you want to see me about, Margaret? Have you been run in for furious driving?'

'Certainly not!' said Margaret indignantly. 'I may not be one of the world's best drivers, but at least I've never been had up. It really isn't anything frightfully important, but I thought that since I happened to be in town I might as well drop in and ask you about it.'

Mrs Milbank began to fold up the work she had started to embroider. 'Is it private, Margaret? Would you like me to vanish, with a plausible excuse?'

'No, not a bit! Please don't go! I wanted to ask you, Mr Milbank, whether you can remember the name of the man who wanted to know if the Priory was for sale.'

The solicitor wrinkled his brow. 'I'm not sure that I can. The file is at the office, of course, and I can let you know to-morrow. Rather an ordinary name, as far as I remember. I think it was Robinson.' He gazed up at the ceiling. 'Yes, I'm nearly certain it was. George Robinson. But I won't swear to it.'

'I see. You didn't actually meet him, did you?'

'No, he wrote, and I distinctly remember that I sent your answer to a poste-restante address, as he explained that he was on a motor tour. Why? Have you reconsidered your decision?'

'No, but we – we rather wanted to know who it was. We don't mean to sell the Priory yet.'

'I'm rather relieved to hear you say that,' smiled the lawyer, 'for I had another man in making inquiries, and turned him down.'

Margaret looked quickly towards him. 'Another man? Wanting to buy the place?'

'I imagine he must have had some such idea, though he didn't actually say so. I told him that you had no intention of selling.'

'Who was he?' Margaret asked. 'Anyone we know?'

'I shouldn't think so. He never told me his name, because, as I say, things never got as far as that. He was a youngish man – between thirty and thirty-five, I should say. Nice looking, very dark, fairly . . .'

'Dark?' Margaret faltered.

'Yes, very dark. Black hair and eyebrows, rather a tanned complexion, fairly tall. My dear, what *is* all this about? Why are you so anxious to know what he looked like?'

'Well! – well, we – we met someone at a party who – who seemed rather interested in the Priory, and we suspected he wanted to buy it,' Margaret explained. 'Did he seem keen to when you saw him?'

'Not to the extent of badgering me to forward an offer. He didn't even make one.'

'I wish you'd tell me just what he did say,' Margaret begged.

'I'll try, since you make such a point of it,' Mr Milbank said, still rather surprised. 'He said he had been asked to make some inquiries about a house which he understood had been standing empty for several years. I assumed he was acting for someone else, but of course he may have merely put it that way. Lots of people do, if they don't want you to think they're set on buying a thing. He said he hoped he was not too late in coming to see me, as he had heard that someone else had been after the house.'

Margaret's eyes were fixed intently on the solicitor's face. 'Oh! He'd heard that, had he? Did he say how?'

'No, and I'm afraid I didn't ask him. I told him that you had no thought of selling. Let me see: what did he say next? Yes, I think he said: "Then there's no truth in what I heard – that the present owners are considering an offer they have received?" I assured him that you were entertaining no such idea, that you had, in fact, definitely refused to sell. After that I think he chatted for a few minutes about the place. Something he said about having seen the house from his car made me suspect that he might be this man, Robinson, or whatever his name is, trying a new way of getting the Priory. I asked him whether I was not right in supposing he had written to me before concerning this matter. Whether it was he, or someone behind him who wrote I really don't know, but I distinctly remember that he did not answer for a moment. Which made me all the more certain, as you can imagine. However, I wasn't particularly interested, so I didn't go into it. He said it was quite possible that his friend had written to me, but no doubt I'd had a great many such letters, or something of the sort. I'm a busy man, as you know, and I thought I'd wasted enough time on the matter. So when he said that in the event of your wishing to sell after all, he hoped I'd let him know before you accepted any other offer, I fear I rather cut him short, and told him that I did not think he need worry himself, as for one thing you had no wish to sell the Priory, and for another the only other offer I had received on your behalf was entirely tentative. He still didn't seem satisfied, and even went so far as to request me not to advise my other client of any change in your decision before letting him know. So I told him that in any case it would be quite out of my power to do so since I had only an old poste-restante address to write to. That did seem to settle him, and he went off – quite forgetting, by the way, to leave me his address!'

'I see,' Margaret said slowly. 'Yes – I think that sounds like the man we thought was after the place. Thanks awfully for telling me.'

'I may be very inquisitive,' Mr Milbank said, 'but I do wish you'd tell me why you're so anxious to hear all this.'

She smiled. 'Sheer curiosity, Mr Milbank. I – I wondered whether he'd have the cheek to come and interview you about it. Apparently he had.' She glanced at the clock, and started up. 'Oh, Lord, I shall be hideously late if I don't start.'

She took her leave of them both and went down to her car. Mr Milbank accompanied her to the front door, wondering what lay behind her visit, and waved farewell to her from the top of his steps. She let in the clutch, and the car slid forward.

Her suspicion had been a true one, but this afforded her very little satisfaction. It seemed to be just one more link in the chain of evidence against Strange.

'And I ought to tell Peter,' she said to herself, slipping past a tram. 'It's absolutely wrong of me not to. Michael Strange is nothing to me, nor ever likely to be, and for all I know he may be planning something perfectly dreadful. And it's no good getting sloppy and sentimental, and thinking how a Good Woman's Love might reclaim him, because that's the sort of rot that makes me sick. Besides, I'm not in love with him.'

'Aren't you?' Conscience inquired. 'Then are you going to tell Peter all you know?'

'I promised I'd say nothing,' Margaret argued. 'I may have been wrong to do so, but I did, and that's that.'

'You didn't promise not to say anything about this visit to Milbank,' Conscience pointed out.

'If I see any reason to of course I shall tell Peter,' Margaret decided. 'But for the present I mean to tackle Strange myself. And it's no good thinking he's the Monk because I don't believe it, and what's more I won't believe it.'

'What about him saying that you might get a bad fright?'

'That doesn't prove anything at all. Anyway, I don't believe he'd be the one to frighten me.'

'Doesn't it throw a little light on the fact that he seemed so anxious to get you away from the Priory?'

'No, it does not,' Margaret muttered crossly, and took a corner recklessly wide.

The interminable argument went on throughout her drive back to the Priory. Only one clear point emerged from it, and that was that she didn't want to give Charles and Peter any fresh grounds for suspecting Strange unless she were absolutely forced to. Whereat Conscience said very nastily: 'What price Loyalty, eh?'

Since she had not left the Milbanks' house until a few minutes before ten there was no hope of reaching the Priory till after eleven. Margaret knew that Celia, remembering her dinner engagement, would not be likely to worry over her lateness, but she was not quite at ease about it herself. It was true there was a moon, but all the same she did not relish the prospect of that drive up from the gates to the house. Even in daylight there was something rather eerie about woods, and the avenue led through unmistakable woodland. She and Celia had gone into ecstasies over it, for they had seen it first in bluebell time, but they had not then known that it had a reputation for being haunted.

The nearer she got to Framley the less inclined she was for the drive up the avenue, but by dint of telling herself she was not at all afraid, and thinking very hard of all sorts of things not even remotely connected with ghosts, she achieved a certain stoicism about it, and turned in at the iron gates quite determined to drive boldly and quickly up to the house, and not to peer furtively ahead.

And then the worst happened. The entrance to the drive was an awkward one, and the gates rather narrow. The avenue curved sharply just inside them, and was flanked on either side by a ditch that kept it drained. Margaret turned in at the gates much too boldly, and jammed the car. She said: 'Damn!' under her breath, and proceeded to back. After some not very skilful manoeuvring she succeeded in clearing the gates. In she swept, misjudged the bend in the avenue, swung the wheel round too late and too hard, and skidded gently into the ditch.

She was too much annoyed with herself to think about ghosts. Feeling glad that Peter was not present to mock at her bad driving, she changed down into first and tried to get the car back on to the avenue. But the heavy storm of the day before had made the surface rather slimy, and the ditch, judging from the squelch which her back wheel made as it descended into it, was full of mud. The engine roared fruitlessly, and after several more attempts Margaret was forced to give it up. The car would have to be pulled out; and meanwhile she was faced with a lonely walk up to the house.

It serves me right for being such a fool, she thought. And it's no use sitting here getting cold feet about it. Out you get, you idiot!

She stepped out, and collected her handbag and coat. She eyed the planchette board dubiously, but decided to leave it, in company with her own purchases, and the two revolvers, which she had hidden under the back seat. She slipped on the coat to save having to carry it, and digging her hands into its capacious pockets, set off up the avenue.

She had rounded the second bend, and only one more separated her from the sight of the house when she saw the Monk. Straight ahead of her, gliding across the avenue in the cold silver light, was that sinister, hooded figure. She stopped dead in her tracks with a gasp of horror. She saw it plainly, caught a glimpse of a cowled face that was somehow more terrifying than all the rest, and then it melted into the shadows on the other side of the avenue.

Her instinct was to turn and run back the way she had come. The figure had vanished, but it might be there, in the shadows, waiting for her to come up to it. She stood as though chained to the spot, her knees shaking under her.

I can't go on! she thought. Where am I to go to if I run back? What shall I do? What *shall* I do?

It might be anywhere amongst the dark trees that surrounded her. It had come towards Mrs Bosanquet, menacing her with an outstretched hand. If it had seen her it might even now be flitting up to her unseen in the shadows. It would be better to dart on to the house than to turn back. Perhaps someone would hear her if she screamed for help; no one would hear if she ran the other way.

A little rustle behind her decided the matter. Not daring to look round, or to shout for help, she ran as though for her life down the avenue towards the house. As she sped past the place where she had seen the Monk disappear she had an awful feeling that the cowled figure was following her. Sobbing dryly from sheer fright she gained the last bend and saw the house ahead of her.

Then immediately ahead of her a form stepped out

from the shadow of a great rhododendron bush. She was breathless, and panting, but she gave one faint, desperate cry of 'Peter!'

The figure seemed to leap towards her, she tried to call again, but a hand was clapped over her mouth, and a strong arm thrown round her shoulders. 'Don't scream!' an urgent whisper commanded, and almost fainting from shock she stared wildly up into the face of Michael Strange.

Ten

For a moment he continued to hold her, then he removed his hand from her mouth, and said coolly, under his breath: 'Sorry, but I couldn't let you give the alarm. Tell me quickly, what did you see?'

Irrationally, her fright had left her the instant she had recognised him. But her head whirled. What was he doing there? Was it possible that his had been the figure she had seen? And if so what had he done with his disguise?

His hand grasped her wrist, not roughly, but compellingly. 'What did you see? You must tell me.'

She looked at him, trying to read his face in the moonlight. 'The Monk,' she answered, in a low voice.

'Damnation!' Michael muttered. 'Where?'

She pointed the way she had come, and as though by doing it she conjured up a presence, footsteps came to their ears.

Without ceremony Michael pulled her quickly into the shadow of the rhododendron bush. She glanced at him, and saw that his eyes were fixed on the bend in the avenue. A moment later a figure in a large ulster came into sight, peering about.

'Miss Fortescue!' called Mr Ernest Titmarsh. 'Miss Fortescue! Is there anything the matter? Tut, tut, I made sure I saw her!'

The grip on Margaret's wrist was removed; there was a movement beside her, she looked quickly round, and found that she was alone. As silently and as unexpectedly as he had appeared, Mr Michael Strange had vanished.

Feeling utterly bewildered, and not a little shaken, Margaret stepped out into the moonlight, and waited for Mr Titmarsh to come up with her. 'I'm here,' she said, with the calm of reaction.

He hurried up, butterfly net in hand. 'Dear, dear, I did not at once perceive you. But what is the matter? I heard you call out, and saw you running. I do trust you did not catch sight of me, and take me for a ghost?'

'Mr Titmarsh, did you cross the avenue down there a moment ago?' she asked. 'Going towards the chapel?'

'By no means,' he answered. 'I was pursuing an oak-eggar just by that swampy patch of ground on the other side of the avenue. Surely you have not seen someone unauthorised prowling about the park?'

'Yes. That is – it was the Monk. I knew I couldn't be mistaken. That horrible cowl . . .! I'm sorry, but really I feel rather groggy. Would you mind coming with me as far as the house?'

'My dear young lady! Of course, of course, but your eyes must have deceived you. Pray take my arm! Quite impossible, Miss Fortescue. I saw no monk, and surely I must have done so had there been one.'

She shook her head. 'You might not. There are so many bushes. I couldn't have been deceived. I saw it plainly.'

'Nerves, my dear Miss Fortescue, nothing but nerves. You must not let yourself believe in these silly ghost-tales. Why, you are quite upset by it! This will not do at all! Now I will pull the bell, and in a moment you will be inside, and quite safe.'

The bell clanged noisily in answer to Mr Titmarsh's vigorous tug, and almost at once quick steps sounded within, and Peter himself opened the door. 'That you, Margaret? I began to think you must have had a – good Lord, what's the matter?'

She grasped his coat weakly, and gave a small uncertain laugh. 'Oh Peter, I've seen the Monk! For goodness sake let me sit down; I feel like a piece of chewed string.'

Mr Titmarsh clucked rather like an old hen. 'I saw Miss Fortescue running up the avenue, and went at once to her assistance. I am afraid she is a little over-wrought: she seems to have caught sight of something which she took for the Monk. Possibly a shrub, or even, though I should be grieved indeed to think so, myself.'

Peter slipped his arm round Margaret. 'Come in, sir. Very good of you to escort her. Buck up, old lady: it's all right now.' He half-led, half-carried her into the library, and put her down into the nearest chair. 'Like a drink, Sis? Feeling all right?'

Celia sprang up. 'Margaret! What's the matter, darling? Oh, good heavens, don't say *you've* seen it!'

The colour was coming back to Margaret's face. She sat up. 'Sorry, all of you. No, I'm perfectly all right now, Peter. Truly. Yes, I have, Celia. The Monk. And I made a dash for the house, and – and then – Mr Titmarsh came up.'

'And I am much distressed to think that I may have been the innocent cause of your alarm,' Mr Titmarsh put in. 'If I had not obtained permission from your good brother-in-law to pursue my search in his grounds, I should be even *more* distressed.'

'No, it wasn't you,' Margaret said. 'It was a cowled monk, just as Aunt Lilian described.' She looked round. 'Where is Aunt Lilian?'

'She had a headache, and went up to bed early,' Celia replied. 'But darling, how awful for you! Oh, we *can't* stay any longer in this beastly, hateful house!

'But Margaret, where's the car?' Charles asked. 'Why were you on foot?'

'I ditched it,' said Margaret fatalistically.

'Oh!' said Charles. 'I suppose it seemed to you to be the only thing to do, but – don't think I'm criticising – why?'

This had the effect of making her laugh, and a great deal of her self-possession was restored. 'I didn't do it on purpose. I made a muck of the turn at the gates, and one of the back wheels skidded into the ditch. It'll have to be pulled out. So then I had to walk up to the house. And all this happened.' She got up. 'I say – do you mind if I don't talk about it any more to-night? I feel a bit queer still, and I think I'd like to go up to bed.'

'Of course you shall,' Celia said instantly. 'Don't worry her with questions, you two. Come along, darling.'

At the door Margaret looked back. 'Oh, I got the revolvers. They're under the back seat. I thought I'd better tell you.'

'Revolvers?' said Mr Titmarsh blinking. 'Dear me, sounds very bloodthirsty. Really I do not think I should advise you to use them, Mr Malcolm. Tut, tut, there is no knowing whom you might not shoot by mistake.'

'Well I can safely promise not to shoot you by mistake,' said Charles.

However, this assurance did not relieve Mr Titmarsh's alarms. He seemed genuinely perturbed, and tried once more to convince the two men that Margaret had been the victim of a hallucination. Neither of them attempted to argue the point, and at last, after refusing the offer of a drink, Mr Titmarsh took his leave, and made off again down the avenue.

As he shot the bolts of the front door home, Peter looked at Charles. 'I think this is where we talk to the District Inspector,' he said. 'I still don't believe that Titmarsh is the man we're after, but his presence in the grounds at just that moment is a little too significant to be brushed aside.'

Charles nodded. 'All right, we'll go over to Manfield to-morrow.'

It was long before Margaret fell asleep that night. She had omitted any reference to Michael Strange in her account of what happened. Until she started to tell the others all about it she had meant to keep nothing back. And then somehow or other she had left that gap, and at once had been horrified at herself for not telling the whole truth. Only the moment the words 'and then Mr Titmarsh came up' had passed her lips, it had seemed impossible to add, 'but before that Michael Strange appeared, and clapped his hand over my mouth.' It would look so odd not to have told that first of all. She asked instead to be allowed to go to bed, with a vague idea of thinking the whole situation over. She now realised that it would be far more impossible to say at breakfast next day: 'By the way I quite forgot to tell you that Michael Strange was there too.'

But on one point her mind was made up. Unless he gave some explanation of his conduct he could not expect her to go on blindly trusting him. She would see him without fail next day, and demand to know what he was doing in the Priory grounds at that hour.

On this resolve she at last fell asleep. When she awoke next morning she did not feel quite as guilty as she had the night before. After all, she thought, if Strange refused to explain himself, it would not be too late to inform the others, and she had no doubt she would be able to think out some plausible reason for not having done so before.

To the questions that Charles and Peter put to her during breakfast she returned perfectly composed replies, but when she learned that they intended to put the matter now into the hands of the County Police she rather changed colour. If a police-inspector were to question her it would be very difficult to know how to answer him. Like most people who have never had any dealings with it she had a somewhat nervous dread of the Law, and a hazy idea that you got had up for not telling the police all you knew. However, it was no good meeting your troubles half-way, and the main thing now was to tackle Michael Strange.

Mrs Bosanquet, in spite of her own terrifying experience, was quite annoyed to think that Margaret and not she had encountered the Monk. She told Margaret she had missed a great opportunity, and when Charles made a dry reference to the manner in which she had greeted the opportunity when it came to her, she said severely that there were some things that were better forgotten. She was happy in the possession of her planchette, and she proposed that they should have a sitting that very evening.

'In the evening?' Celia said. 'Not for worlds! I might summon up enough courage to sit in daylight, but not after dark, thank you!'

'I doubt very much whether we should get any results by day,' Mrs Bosanquet said dubiously. 'I know that for some reason or other which I never fathomed spirits seem to find it easier to manifest themselves in the dark.'

'Look here!' said Peter, 'are we expected to sit round in the dark like a lot of lunatics with our hands on that board?'

'Not, I trust, like a lot of lunatics,' Mrs Bosanquet said coldly.

'I won't do it,' Celia announced. 'I know what it'll be. Either Chas or Peter will start pushing just to frighten us.'

'What I was really thinking of,' said Charles meditatively, 'was appearing in a false nose and some luminous paint. But I won't if you don't care for the idea.'

'Charles,' said Celia quite seriously, 'unless you swear to me you won't play the fool I'll walk out of this house here and now.'

'My dear child,' Mrs Bosanquet said reassuringly, 'if you feel any alarm it would be much better if you didn't attempt to sit at all. And of course Charles is only making fun of you.'

'But if you're all going to sit I shall *have* to,' Celia said. 'I couldn't stay by myself while you conjured up ghosts. I should die of fright.'

'I have been told,' remarked Mrs Bosanquet, 'though

I must say I never experienced anything of the sort myself, that sometimes the spirits actually lift tables off their legs, and give one quite hard knocks to manifest their presence.'

'In that case,' said Charles, 'you can count me out. I'm not going to sit and allow myself to be buffeted about in this or any other cause.'

'I think,' Mrs Bosanquet replied, 'that we are unlikely to get any results at all if you approach the subject in a spirit of levity.'

When breakfast was over Charles and Peter went off to see what could be done about hauling the car out of the ditch. They had no sooner gone than Margaret announced her intention of cycling into the village to buy darning-silk. Celia seemed inclined to accompany her, but since she had promised to go for a sedate walk with Mrs Bosanquet, she had to give up the idea. She wrote out a list of groceries to be ordered at the village store, and said that she and Mrs Bosanquet might stroll to meet Margaret on her way home.

Margaret's first house of call was not the village store, but the Bell Inn. She inquired of the porter whether Mr Strange was in, and while he went to find out, she sat down in the lounge, and watched two rather nondescript females collect their sketching paraphernalia preparatory to setting out. They eyed her with the usual faint air of hostility displayed to one another by most English people, and after ascertaining that they had not forgotten the sandwiches or the camp-stools, or the thermos, soon left her in sole possession of the lounge.

She had not long to wait before the door at one end of the lounge was opened, and Michael Strange came briskly into the room. He did not seem surprised to see her, but said without preamble: 'I'm sorry to have been so long, Miss Fortescue: I was just finishing my breakfast. Won't you sit down?'

'I hope I didn't interrupt you,' she said stiffly.

'Not at all. It's a disgraceful hour at which to be breakfasting in any case. But I had a very late night.'

Margaret fairly gasped. Of all the cool, calm cheek! she thought. She remained standing, and looking him squarely in the face, said: 'Mr Strange, I think you must know why I've come to see you this morning.'

The hint of a smile touched his mouth. 'I can guess,' he said. 'I wish you hadn't seen me last night, but you did, and the mischief's done.'

Her heart sank. 'Then you are the Monk!' she cried sharply.

His brows seemed to snap together over the bridge of his nose. He looked quickly round, and said quietly: 'Please don't raise your voice. You don't know who may be listening.'

'I don't care,' she said.

'But I do,' he answered, and moved softly to the door and opened it.

She watched him look down the passage and go to the other door and open that too. 'You probably have good reason to care,' she shot at him.

'I have,' he said imperturbably. He shut the door and came back into the room. 'I wish you would sit down,' he said. 'And just remember to keep your voice lowered.' He pulled a chair forward, and reluctantly she did sit down. 'Now then! I suppose if I say I am certainly not the Monk you won't believe me?'

'How can I?' she said. 'I saw it last night, and it disappeared into the shadows on the same side of the avenue as you emerged from two minutes later.'

He nodded. 'It does look black, doesn't it? I don't think I'll waste time in trying to prove my innocence. What I do want to say is this: get out of the Priory, and get out quickly! Never mind why, but just go. I say this as one who – thinks a great deal of your safety. You saw something last night: if you stay you may see much more, and Marg – Miss Fortescue, believe me, I don't want you to run even the slightest chance of getting hurt or frightened.'

He spoke with such evident sincerity that she found herself saying in a much friendlier tone: 'Mr Strange, can't you explain yourself? You must see that I can't possibly believe you when you won't – give me any reason for your conduct.'

'I can't!' he said. His hand opened and shut. 'You mustn't ask me, Miss Fortescue. I'd give anything to be able to take you into my confidence, but it's impossible. For one thing I – well, it's no good: I daren't tell you.'

'Daren't?' she repeated. 'You are afraid that I should give you away?'

He did not answer for a moment. Then he laid his hand on hers, and clasped it. 'Look here, I've undertaken something, and come what may I must carry it through,' he said. 'When I took it on I didn't bargain for *you*, but I can't let you make any difference. Only I wish to God you'd clear out of the Priory!'

She withdrew her hand. 'Then I am right in thinking that all along you've wanted to get us out of the house?'

'Yes, I have wanted to.'

'Why?' she said directly.

'I've told you. It's not safe, and I can't be answerable for what may happen.'

'It is not by any chance because our presence interferes with what you are doing?'

'It does interfere, but that is not why I'm so anxious you should go. Miss Fortescue, I don't think there's much I wouldn't do for you, but if you persist in remaining at the Priory I can't guarantee your safety. Do you understand? You'll be running a risk of – danger, and I can't stop it, and I might not be able to help you. And God knows if anything were to happen to you . . .' He broke off.

She found herself saying: 'Well?'

He looked quickly towards her. 'I think you must know what I – what I feel about you,' he said.

Her eyes fell. 'I only know that you don't trust me, though you expect me to trust you,' she answered, almost inaudibly.

'It isn't that I don't trust you, but I *can't* tell you – Oh, damn it all, why did I ever take this on?' He got up abruptly, and began to pace up and down the room.

She watched him in silence for a moment. He was frowning, and when he frowned he did look rather sinister, she thought. 'Have you considered that if – that if you think . . . Have you considered that you might give it up?' she said, stumbling badly.

'No!' he threw over his shoulder. 'Not that it would be any good if I did.'

There was another short silence. Margaret tried again. 'Is what you're doing of such vital importance?' she asked.

'Yes, of vital importance.' He came back to her side. 'Margaret, if I were at liberty to take you into my confidence I would, but too much hangs on it. I can't do it. I know things look black: they *are* black, but will you believe that it's not what you think?'

'I don't know quite *what* to think,' she said.

'You've seen me in some odd circumstances, you've seen me do things that look more than suspicious. I don't deny it, and I may have to do things that will seem far more suspicious. But I swear to you I've a good reason for all I do, even though I can't tell you what it is. Margaret, I've no right to ask you, as things are, but will you try and trust me a little longer? Will you trust me sufficiently to do as I beg of you, and leave the Priory till I've finished the job I've undertaken?'

She found it hard to meet his eyes, and felt a wave of colour rise in her cheeks. 'Even though I – said yes, my brother and brother-in-law wouldn't go.'

'If you can't persuade them they can take their chance,' he said. 'But will you go? You and your sister, and your aunt?'

She shook her head. 'No, I can't do that. You couldn't expect me to go away and leave my brother in danger. And nothing would induce Celia to leave Charles.'

He said impatiently: 'Good God, haven't you had enough happen in that house to make you see the only thing to do is to clear out?'

At that she looked up. 'What do you know about anything that has happened at the Priory?' she asked gravely.

He bit his lip. After a moment she said: 'Were you responsible for – things that have happened?'

'I can't answer you, and I don't want to lie to you,' he said curtly. 'I can only tell you that from me you stand in no danger whatsoever. But I'm not the only one mixed up in this.' He made a little gesture of despair. 'It's no good going on like this. If you won't go, you won't. But I have warned you, and you can believe that I know what I'm talking about.'

She began to twist the strap of her handbag round her finger. 'I do believe that you – wouldn't hurt me, or any of us,' she began.

He interrupted her. 'Hurt you! My God, no! Can't you understand, Margaret? I – I *love* you!"

She bent her head still lower over the absorbing strap. 'Please – you mustn't . . .!' she said inarticulately.

'I know I mustn't. But you don't know what it's like for me to see you here . . . I wish to God I'd met you under other circumstances!' He ran his fingers up through his crisp black hair. 'And yet I don't know that I'd have had a better chance,' he said despondently. 'The whole thing seems hopeless, and it's no good for anyone in my – line of business – to think of a girl like you.'

In a very muffled voice Margaret said: 'If I – if I knew it was honest – I – I shouldn't care – what your line of business was.' She tried to achieve a lighter note. 'As long as it isn't keeping a butcher's shop, or – or anything like that,' she added with a wavering smile.

He made a movement as though he would take her hand again, but checked it. 'I've no right to speak at all till I can – clear up all this mess,' he said. 'But to know that you – well, one day I hope I shall be able to say all the things I want to say now. One thing I must ask you though: Will you trust me enough not to mention to anyone that you saw me in your grounds last night?'

All the reason she possessed told her to say 'No,' but something far stronger than reason made her say instead: 'All right, I – I will.'

'My God, you are a wonderful girl,' he said unsteadily.

She got up. 'I must go. But I'd like to warn you of something. I didn't tell my people that you were there last night. You guessed I hadn't, didn't you? But Peter and Charles have motored into Manfield to-day, to tell the County Police what has been happening at the Priory. And – I think they'll tell the inspector to keep an eye on you.'

'Thank-you,' he said. His smile flashed out. 'Don't worry your head over me,' he said. 'The police aren't going to get me.'

She held out her hand. 'I should be – very sorry if they did,' she said. 'Good-bye.'

He took her hand, looked at it for a moment as it lay in his, and then bent his head and kissed it.

Eleven

Having extricated the car from the ditch with the aid of a farm-horse, Charles and Peter drove it into Manfield, the market town that lay some six miles to the east of Framley. Here was the headquarters of the County Police, and in the red-brick police-station they found the District Inspector.

This individual was of a different type from Constable Flinders. He was a wiry man of medium height, with foxy hair and a moustache meticulously waxed at the ends. He had a cold blue eye and a brisk manner, and his air of business-like competence promised well.

He listened without comment to the story Charles unfolded, only occasionally interrupting to put a brief question. His face betrayed neither surprise nor interest, and not even the episode of the discovered skeleton caused him to do more than nod.

'One had the impression,' Charles said afterwards, 'that such occurrences were everyday matters in this part of the world.'

'You say the picture fell,' the inspector recapitulated. 'You have a suspicion someone was responsible. Any grounds for that, sir?'

'None,' said Charles.

'Except,' Peter put in, 'that we can neither of us see how the falling picture could have knocked the rosette in the panelling out of place.'

The inspector made dots on his blotting-pad with the point of a pencil he held. 'Very hard to say that it could not, sir, from all you tell me. You haven't tested it?'

'No,' said Charles, 'funnily enough we haven't. Though there are quite a lot of pictures in the house, and if we'd smashed one in the test we could always have tried another.'

The first sign of emotion crept into the inspector's face. The cold blue eyes twinkled. 'Very true, sir,' he said gravely. 'Now there is the entrance into the cellars. You say you heard this move on several occasions, and on the last you went down and saw someone make his escape that way. Did you recognise this person?'

'No,' Charles said. 'There was hardly time for that.'

'Very good, sir. And since you have sealed up that entrance no further attempt has been made to break into the house?'

'On the contrary. My aunt encountered the Monk in the library.'

The inspector made more dots. 'The lady being, I take it, a reliable witness?'

'Most reliable. Moreover, up till then she had no belief in the story that the Priory is haunted.'

'Quite so, sir. And on that occasion you discovered the window into the library to have been open?'

'Unbolted. It was shut, however.'

'But I understand it could be opened from outside?'

'Yes, certainly it could.'

'And this – Monk – would have had plenty of time to escape by that way, pausing to shut the window behind him, in between the time of the lady's falling into a faint, and your arrival on the scene?'

'Plenty of time. So much so that neither my brother-in-law nor I thought it would be of any use to search the grounds.'

'I see, sir. And since that occasion no one has, to your knowledge, been in the house?'

'Not to my knowledge. But last night, as I told you, my sister-in-law distinctly saw the Monk in the grounds. A moment later Mr Ernest Titmarsh ran up to her.'

The inspector nodded. 'If you don't mind, sir, we'll take the people who have acted suspiciously in your opinion, one by one. Ernest Titmarsh: that's the first?'

'No. The first was a fellow who's staying at the Bell Inn, in the village.'

'Name, sir?'

'Strange, Michael Strange. He is the man whom we found wandering close to the house when we first heard the stone move. He's a man I'd like you to get on to.'

'Inquiries will be made, sir.'

'He is also the man whom we overheard talking in an exceedingly suspicious manner to James Fripp, traveller for Suck-All Cleaners. About whom I have received the following information.' He took a letter from his pocket-book, and handed it to the inspector.

The inspector read the letter through. The inquiry agent had not been able to discover very much about James Fripp, for the firm for which he worked had engaged him only a month previously, and knew nothing about his former occupation. But the agent gave, for what it was worth, the information that before the war a man going under the name of Jimmy Fripp, and corresponding more or less with Charles' description of the commercial traveller, had been on two occasions imprisoned for burglary. His last incarceration took place in 1914; he had been released shortly after war broke out, and had joined the army. Since the end of the war he had been lost trace of, nor could the agent discover what type of work, honest or otherwise, he had been employed in. It seemed possible that the Fripp in question might be the same man, but no proof of this was forthcoming.

The inspector folded the letter, and gave it back to Charles. 'Thank you, sir. You don't need to worry about him; we've got our eye on him all right.'

'The man I'm really worrying about,' Charles answered, 'is Strange. We know he's in collusion with Fripp, and that being so there can be little doubt that Fripp is working under his orders.'

The inspector nodded, but again repeated: 'You don't need to worry. We'll look after Mr Strange too.'

Peter was not quite satisfied with this. 'Yes, I know, but what do you propose to do? We're getting a little tired of this mystery, and we'd like a stop put to it.'

'Well, sir, I'm sure I can understand that, and you may depend upon it we shall do our best. And if I might suggest something, I wouldn't advise either of you gentlemen to mention to anyone that you've been to see me about this. Whoever it is that has been annoying you, we don't want to put him on his guard, and once you tell one person a bit of news it has a way of spreading.'

'Quite so,' Peter said. 'We have been rather careful all

through not to talk of what has happened. But you still haven't told us what you mean to do. Are you going to put a man on to watch the Priory?'

'Yes,' Charles said, flicking a speck of cigarette ash off his sleeve, 'and if you do, need he smash the cucumber frames? It isn't that they contain any cucumbers, but . . .'

The inspector's lips twitched. 'I quite understand, sir. But . . .'

'And he's not to frighten the housemaid,' Charles continued. 'Also, I may be unreasonable, but I have a constitutional dislike for being arrested in my own grounds. If I can't come and go unchallenged I shall become unnerved, and the consequences may be hideous.'

'My brother-in-law,' said Peter, thinking it time to intervene, 'is referring to the well-meaning efforts of Constable Flinders.'

'Yes, sir. Very annoying, I'm sure. But you won't be worried in that way again. If you will leave the matter in our hands, I think I can promise we shall be able to clear it all up in a very short while.'

'Well, I must say I hope so,' Peter remarked, gathering up his hat and stick. 'We came down to Framley for a quiet holiday, and so far we've had no peace at all.'

'Just a moment,' Charles said. 'What about Duval?'

The inspector fingered the tips of his moustache. 'I've made a note of all you told me about him, sir.'

'Yes, I know: I saw you. But doesn't it strike you that he might, if interrogated skilfully, throw a good deal more light on the matter?'

'He might, sir, and of course we shall have to consider that. But on the other hand you never know with these dope-maniacs. Still, I shall go into it. You can safely leave it to me.'

Peter looked at Charles. 'I think that's all, isn't it? There's nothing else we wanted to ask the inspector?'

Charles' expression of rather sleepy boredom had been growing steadily more marked. 'I can't remember anything else,' he replied. 'Unless you think we might invite him to come and take part in our seance to-night? Or do you think the presence of a stranger might make the Monk shy?'

'Yes, I do,' said Peter hastily, and edged him towards the door.

The inspector held it open for them, and they went through into the charge room. A man in a felt hat and a light raincoat was standing by the counter that ran across the end of the room, and as the door opened he glanced over his shoulder. For a fleeting instant his eyes encountered Charles', then he turned his back again, and bent over some form he appeared to be filling in. But quickly though he moved Charles had had time to recognise him. It was Michael Strange.

'Oh, half a minute!' Charles said. 'I think I've left my gloves on your table, inspector.'

'Gloves? You didn't have any, did you?' Peter asked.

'Yes, I did,' Charles said, and went past him, back into the room. He motioned to the inspector to close the door, and as soon as this had been done, he said softly: 'No gloves at all, but I've just seen the very man we've been discussing. Strange.'

'Have you, sir? Here?' the inspector asked.

'Outside, filling up some form. He didn't want me to recognise him, for he turned his back at once. I should like very much to know what he's doing. It looks to me as though he followed us here, to find out what we were up to.'

The inspector nodded. 'Good job you saw him, sir. Now you go out, will you, quite naturally, and I'll have a word with this Mr Strange, just casually, you understand. I shall soon find out what he came for.' He pulled the door open again. 'That's right, sir. And you'd be surprised the number of pairs of gentlemen's gloves that get lost. Not but what you could hardly leave them in a better place than the station-house, could you? Good morning to you, sir.'

Outside Charles looked round for Strange's car, but it was not visible. Since it seemed improbable that he had walked to Manfield it was clear that he had parked it somewhere where it would not be seen. Charles got into his own car, and waited for Peter to take his place beside him. As he let in the clutch Peter said: 'Well, where are the gloves?'

'In the top right-hand drawer of my dressing-table so far as I know,' Charles answered. 'That, my boy, was a blind.'

'Was it indeed? Why?'

'Did you see that fellow who was waiting in the charge room?'

'No – that is, yes, I believe I did notice someone, now you come to mention it. I can't say I paid much attention to him, though. What about him?'

'Michael Strange.'

'No!' Peter said. 'Are you sure?'

'Positive. He turned his head as I came out of the inspector's room. That inspector-fellow is going to ask what his business is. With all due deference to Inspector Tomlinson I could have told him the answer. He'll dish up some cock-and-bull story of having lost something, but if he didn't follow us to try and find out just what we were going to tell the police, I'm a Dutchman.' He hooted violently at an Austin Seven which was wavering undecidedly in the middle of the road. 'And I wouldn't mind betting that he overheard every word we said in that room.'

'It does look like it, but wasn't there a bobby in the charge room?'

'There was when we came out, but do you suppose a clever fellow couldn't have got rid of him for quite as long as he wanted?'

'Might, of course. But how the devil did Strange know we were coming here to-day?'

'Well, we've talked about it pretty freely, haven't we?'

'In our own house, Chas!'

'Also while we were getting the car out of the ditch. You said: "If they don't buck up with that horse we shan't have time to get to Manfield and back before lunch." '

'I didn't say anything about the police-station, did I?'

'I don't remember. But whatever you said it looks as though you were overheard, and Mr Michael Strange thought it worth his while to follow us.'

Peter sat pondering it for a while. 'Of course he might have been concealed in the wood, but, dash it! he must be pretty acute if he connected a visit to Manfield with the police! Why, half the countryside goes to shop there! No, it looks to me as though someone told him.'

'Who?'

'The housemaid! She could have heard us talking at breakfast.'

'My dear Peter, she's no crook's accomplice!'

'She's a dam' silly girl though, and if Strange wanted to pump her he could.'

They had emerged from the outskirts of the town into the open country, and Charles put his foot on the accelerator. 'Yes, that's possible, of course. One thing that seems to me quite obvious is that Strange is going to be more than a match for Inspector Tomlinson.'

Peter waited until the car had swung round a bend in the road before he spoke. Charles' driving, skilful though it might be, kept his passengers in a constant state of breathlessness. 'Do you think Tomlinson means to do anything, or does he discount all we say in favour of the ghost theory?'

'The impression I got was that he gave us the benefit of the doubt, but privately considered us a fanciful pair who'd got the wind up. He'll send a man over to lurk about the place for a couple of days, and that'll be the end of it.'

'Give him a trial,' Peter said. 'I must say he didn't seem to be overburdened with ideas, but he may have kept them to himself.'

They reached the Priory to find the others just getting up from lunch. 'Oh, Charles!' Celia exclaimed, 'the tennis-net has arrived, and Bowers and Coggin have been putting up the stop-netting all the morning. And if you'll come and do the measuring I'll mark the court out, and we can play after tea.'

This programme was faithfully carried out, and not even the depressions and the bumps in the court damped

Celia's enthusiasm. 'It adds to the fun,' she said, when Charles failed to reach a ball that bounced unaccountably to the right.

When they came off the court after a couple of hours play they were pleasantly weary, and, as Margaret said, were beginning to get to know the peculiarities of the ground. It was just as Charles had announced his intention of spending a lazy evening that Celia remembered to break a piece of news to them all which put an end to such dreams.

'I forgot to tell you,' she said guiltily, 'that I've given Bowers leave off, and I said they could have the car. They're going to the cinema in Manfield, and I said it would be all right if they just put a cold supper on the table – and – and we'd clear it away, and wash up.'

'Did you indeed?' said Charles instantly. 'Now isn't that a pity? Because I've just remembered that I shall have to go out directly after supper, so I shan't be able to . . .'

'Liar,' said Celia, without heat.

'Besides,' Margaret put in, 'you can't go and desert us. We've promised Aunt Lilian we'll try out her planchette.'

Celia's face clouded. 'Margaret, if we talk hard about something else, don't you think she might forget about it?'

'No,' said Margaret, considering this. 'It would only be a case of putting off the evil hour. I think we'd better do it once, just to please her, and then when nothing happens she'll probably get bored with it.'

'But supposing something *did* happen?' Celia pointed out.

'Well, it 'ud be rather interesting, I think,' Margaret said coolly.

Celia was so far from agreeing with her that she did her best to keep Mrs Bosanquet's mind off the subject all through supper. But it was to no avail. When the meal had been cleared away, and the family had repaired to the library, Mrs Bosanquet produced her board, and said: 'Well, my dears, shall we have our sitting?'

'I wish you wouldn't talk as though we were a collection of fowls,' Charles complained. 'Provided I am supplied with a comfortable chair I don't mind lending what I feel sure will be powerful assistance.'

Celia looked at him suspiciously. 'If that means that you're going to fool about . . .'

'Hush!' said her husband reprovingly. 'For all you know I may be a strong medium. In fact I shouldn't be surprised if I went into a trance. Time will be as nothing to me. All the secrets of the future will be revealed to me.'

'Yes, dear, quite possibly you are a natural medium,' Mrs Bosanquet said. 'But when people come out of trances they don't remember anything that happened to them while they were in the trance. At least, so I have always understood.'

'In that case,' said Charles, 'I charge you all the instant you see me fall into a trance to ask me what's going to win the 3.20 to-morrow. And see you write down the answer.'

'If you go into a trance,' said Peter, 'that isn't the only thing we'll ask you. There are lots of things about your past I've long wanted to know.'

Mrs Bosanquet was arranging chairs round a small table. 'That will do, my dear,' she said. 'You know it is no use approaching this in a spirit of levity. Now let us all take our places round the table, and then I'll turn the light down.'

Celia was already showing a tendency to cling to Charles' hand. 'Not right out, Aunt!' she implored.

'No, I will leave just a glimmer. I don't think we need draw the curtains, do you, Margaret? There doesn't seem to be any moon to-night. And it will make the room so stuffy. Now, are you all ready?'

'Wait a moment!' Celia begged. 'Charles, you've got to sit by me!'

'Celia, you goose!' Margaret said softly. 'You don't really expect anything to happen do you?' She took the seat on her sister's left, and Peter sat down beside her.

Mrs Bosanquet turned the central lamp out, and lowered the wick of the one that stood on a table by the fireplace, until only a tiny flame showed. Then she groped her way to the empty chair between her nephews and sat down.

'Oh, isn't it dark and horrible?' shuddered Celia.

'You'll get used to it,' Margaret said soothingly. 'Already I can just see, vaguely. What do we have to do, Aunt Lilian?'

Mrs Bosanquet, happy in having induced them to take part in the séance, at once assumed the rôle of preceptress. 'First, you must be quite comfortable in your chairs,' she said.

'That knocks me out,' Charles interrupted. 'No one could be comfortable in a chair like this. There are already three knobs pressing into my spine.'

By the time he had solemnly tested three other chairs, and decided in favour of a Queen Anne upholstered chair with slim wooden arms, even Celia had begun to giggle.

With unimpaired patience Mrs Bosanquet started again. 'Now, are you all settled?'

'Yes,' Margaret said, before Charles had time to speak. 'Go on, Aunt, what next?'

'We all lay just the tips of our fingers on the board, taking care not to press or lean on it.'

'Here, who's going to hold my arms up?' demanded Charles, having tried the effect of obeying these instructions.

'No one, my dear. You just sit with them extended. Now you must all of you try to make your minds a blank . . .'

'That oughtn't to be difficult for some of us,' said Peter.

'True,' agreed Charles, 'but to think this was the one occasion when Flinders would have been really useful, and we weren't warned in time to call him in!'

'Shut up, Chas!' Margaret said severely. 'All right, Aunt. Anything else?'

'No, dear. Only when the board begins to move you must on no account push it, or in any way seek to influence it. Think of something else, and just keep your hands perfectly steady. Have you all got your fingers on the board? Then we will be quite quiet now, and wait.'

Dead silence fell. In the dim light they could just perceive one another, but Celia could not keep her eyes from peering fearfully into the darkness beyond. After perhaps three minutes, Charles said suddenly: 'What happens if I sneeze?'

''Sh!' said Mrs Bosanquet.

Another silence fell. This time it was Peter who broke it. 'I say, are you sure this is right?' he asked. 'Isn't it only one person who manipulates a planchette? Or am I thinking of a ouija board?'

''Sh!' said Mrs Bosanquet again.

Time crept by. Margaret's arms began to feel rather numb, and still the board did nothing but tremble slightly with the involuntary muscular twitches of all their hands. She became aware of a sound, and listening intently, identified it as somewhat stertorous breathing. She tried to see the faces of her companions, and at that moment Mrs Bosanquet herself spoke: 'My dears!' she said impressively, 'I do believe Charles was right, and he's gone into a trance. His hands are no longer on the board, and he is breathing just like a medium did whom I once visited. Charles! Can you hear me?'

A slight, but unmistakable snore answered her. 'Kick him, Celia!' said Peter. 'The blighter's gone to sleep.'

Celia promptly shook her husband, who grunted, yawned, and sat up. 'Charles, you're not to go to sleep! It's too bad of you!' she scolded.

'Asleep?' said Charles. 'Did I seem to you to be asleep?'

'You did,' said Peter grimly. 'Snoring like a pig.'

'Nonsense,' Charles replied. 'And I warned you what might happen! You've gone and roused me out of what might have proved to be a valuable trance.'

Mrs Bosanquet said worriedly: 'We shall never get any results like this!'

'It's all right, Aunt Lilian,' Celia reassured her. 'I'll see he stays awake.'

'Well, I do trust there will be no more interruptions,' Mrs Bosanquet sighed.

Under her breath Celia said: 'It isn't fair to tease her, Chas. Do behave decently!'

Thus adjured Charles again placed his hands on the board, and they sat in another hopeful silence.

This time the silence was of such long duration that even Mrs Bosanquet began to feel sleepy. But just as she had decided that her arms were aching too much, and she had better suggest a postponement of the séance, the board moved quite an inch across the paper underneath it.

'Peter, you pushed!' Margaret said.

'I swear I didn't!'

''Sh!' Mrs Bosanquet begged.

Once it had started the board seemed to grow quite energetic, and began to describe circles, and make jerky darts in every direction.

'It keeps on leaving me behind,' Charles complained. 'There it goes again! Now I've lost it.'

'Charles, you must keep your hands on it!' Mrs Bosanquet told him.

'I can't; it doesn't seem to like me.'

'It's all jolly fine,' Peter remarked, as the board made a dash to one side, 'but it can't be writing! It keeps going backwards.'

'It's drawing a plan of the Priory,' Charles prophesied. 'Yes, I thought so; that's that corner by the garden-hall, I'll bet.'

'It often starts like this,' Mrs Bosanquet said. 'It will settle down, if we are patient.'

'I hope you may be right,' Charles answered. 'I've taken enough exercise to-day without having to chase this blinking board all over the table now. Ah, the beggar nearly got away from me that time!'

'You know, if no one is pushing it, it really is rather wonderful,' Margaret said.

'Listen! What was that?' Mrs Bosanquet exclaimed. 'Did you hear a sharp sound rather like a rap?'

'Sorry,' Celia said. 'It was me. One of my earrings has dropped on to the floor.'

At that moment Peter cried: 'Ouch!' and Mrs Bosanquet said quite excitedly: 'There! I knew something would happen! Did you feel anything, Peter?'

'*Feel* anything?' he exploded. 'That brute . . .'

'Fancy Peter being singled out!' marvelled his brother-in-law. 'Sit still, Peter: the Monk is probably trying to attract your attention. You may feel something else if you wait.'

'If I feel anything else,' said Peter savagely, 'I'll scrag you!'

'But my dear, what has it got to do with Charles?' Mrs Bosanquet asked. 'You really *must* try and keep calm.'

'You don't suppose any spirit was responsible, do you?' Peter said. 'That brute Charles kicked me on the shin.'

'If you did do anything so inconsiderate, Charles, I must beg you not to repeat it. And *please* don't talk any more!'

She sounded so hurt that Charles repented, and relapsed once more into silence.

The board continued to move jerkily over the paper. Celia began to yawn. Then, startling them all into rigidity, two sharp raps sounded somewhere in the room.

Celia drew in her breath sharply, and shrank against Charles.

'Quiet, all of you!' whispered Mrs Bosanquet. 'I will speak to it!'

Two more raps sounded: Peter's chair slid softly backwards.

Mrs Bosanquet uplifted her voice. 'Whoever you may be, I charge you, answer me! Rap once for Yes, and twice for No, and then we shall understand you. Do you wish to communicate with us?'

'Oh don't! Please stop!' Celia gasped.

An apologetic voice spoke out of the darkness, and both Charles and Peter sprang up. 'Well yes, Mum, in a manner of speaking I do,' it said. 'But if I got to stand rapping on this 'ere window, I don't see as how I shall ever get much forrader, as they say.'

A shout of laughter broke from Charles. 'Flinders!' he cried. 'I might have known it!'

Twelve

He stepped to the lamp and turned it up. Standing just outside the open French window was Constable Flinders.

'How very disappointing!' said Mrs Bosanquet. 'I'm afraid that has broken the thread.'

Celia, whose cheeks were still ashen with fright, began to laugh.

'Come in, Flinders,' Charles said. 'And what on earth are you doing, creeping round the house?'

The constable removed his helmet, and having looked round to be quite sure there was no mat on which he ought to wipe his feet, stepped into the room. 'I'm sure I beg your pardon, sir, if I gave you a start, but when I went and knocked on the back door there wasn't no one there, and I see the kitchen all dark. So I come round to the front and happening to see this here window open, and a bit of a light burning, I thought as how I would take the liberty of seeing if you was in here. Because,' he added, with a touch of severity, 'if you wasn't I should have had to warn you not to go leaving windows open on the ground floor.'

'But what do you want?' Peter demanded. 'And how

did you manage to come right up to the window without us hearing you?'

The constable looked gratified. 'I do move quietly, sir, don't I? I've had rubbers put on my boots, that's what I've done. Just to be on the safe side, so to speak.'

'They'll be asking you to join the C.I.D. soon,' Charles said admiringly. 'Sit down, and tell us what you came about.'

'Thank you, sir.' Mr Flinders selected the straightest chair he could see, and sat down on the edge of it. 'Well, sir, it's like this. After what you told me about that furrin chap – that Dooval – I give the matter a lot of thought, and I come to the conclusion the best thing I could do was to watch him as much as I could, without losing sight of Mr Titmarsh. And I can tell you, sir, he's one man's work, he is. I lorst him again the other night, and it's my belief he gave me the slip on purpose. Well, sir, this very evening when I was trailing Mr Titmarsh, who should I see but this Dooval?'

'Where?' Charles said.

'Right here, sir. That is, up by the ruin, me being on the right-of-way at the time, wondering where that old – where Mr Titmarsh had got to. I don't mind telling you, sir, that it gave me quite a turn, seeing him. "My Gawd!" I says to myself. "Is that the Monk?" Then I got my lamp on to him, and I see who it was. I called out to him, but before you could say "knife" he'd done a bunk, sir. Scared out of his life, he was. So I thought the best thing I could do, seeing as I was so handy, was to come right up on to the house and tell you.'

'Quite right,' Charles said. He turned, as Margaret, who had slipped out of the room a minute or two before, came back with a tray. 'Good idea, Margaret,' he approved. 'You'll have a glass of beer, after your labours, Flinders?' He got up and unscrewed the top of the bottle. It made a pleasant hissing sound. The constable watched the golden liquid froth into the glass, and his eye glistened. Charles held out the glass.

'Not supposed to take anything when we're on duty, you know, sir,' the constable said, accepting it.

Charles poured out two more glasses. 'You can't be on duty at this time of night,' he said.

'Well, sir, since you make a *point* of it,' said Mr Flinders, and raised the glass. 'Here's your very good health, sir.'

'Same to you,' said Charles.

Celia spoke. 'Charles, you must tell this French person you will *not* have him wandering about in our grounds. Really, it's a bit too thick! Apparently the whole countryside regards this place as common land. I won't put up with it any longer!'

'What can he be doing here, anyway?' Margaret wondered.

'Looking for the Monk, like the rest of us,' answered Charles. 'Let's form a society, shall we?'

'No,' said Celia crossly. 'We shan't. I'm sick to death of the Monk!'

'Well, I'll go and have a chat with Duval to-morrow,' Charles promised.

He had no particular desire to set foot inside the artist's dreary little cottage again, so on the following morning he cut short his fishing, and strolled on to the Bell Inn in the hope of meeting Duval there. He was rewarded by the sight of the artist seated alone in the taproom at a table in the corner. He had a glass of whisky before him, and he was sitting in a slack attitude, with his hands clasped between his knees, and his eyes staring moodily at the ground. He looked up as Charles came across the room, and a furtive expression crept into his face.

Charles sat down on the settle beside him, and having ascertained that the only two people within earshot were busily discussing fat stock, he said: 'Good morning. I was looking for you.'

'I do not know why,' Duval said sullenly. 'I will not tell you anything. It is better that you go away and leave me alone.'

'Oh yes, I think you do know,' Charles replied. 'Last night you were seen in our grounds.'

The artist gave a shiver, and one of his claw-like hands grasped Charles' knee under cover of the table. 'Be quiet!' he muttered. 'Have I not said even the walls have ears?'

'It is not a very original observation,' Charles remarked. 'Moreover, no one is listening to us. What I want to say is this: I can't have you pursuing your search for the Monk in my grounds. Sorry if I seem obstructive, but there are too many people already in the habit of treating the place as though it were their own.'

'Speak that name again, and I leave you!' Duval said. His hands were shaking. 'If it were known – if someone saw me with you, I do not know what might happen. If you must talk with me, talk of my art.'

He raised his voice to an unnatural pitch, and said boisterously: 'Yes, my friend, it is true I have the eye for colour, even as you say. I see colour like no one else has ever seen it.'

Two people had come into the taproom together, and both looked round. They were Wilkes and Michael Strange. Strange, after one glance, turned away, but Wilkes kept his eyes on the pair in the corner for a moment or two, and made an involuntary grimace of annoyance.

Again the artist's fingers closed on Charles' knee. 'Be careful!' he said, so softly that Charles only just caught the words. 'Look who has entered! For the love of God, m'sieur, guard your tongue! If that one knew that I had spoken with you of – of the things we both know of . . . !' He broke off, passing his tongue between his lips.

Michael Strange, a tankard in his hand, was making his way towards a seat by the window. He bestowed a curt nod on Charles, and sitting down began to scan the columns of a newspaper. The length of room separated him from the corner table, and Charles said: 'I've no wish to upset you, but do you understand that I cannot permit you to haunt my grounds?'

The artist got up. 'I go. I speak with you another time. Here, it is not safe. I come up to speak with you to-night perhaps, when no one can see.' Once more he raised his voice, in unconvincing joviality: 'Ah, you are too good, m'sieur! But it is true: I have revolutionised the art of painting.'

The landlord came up to them. ''Morning, sir. 'Morning, moossoo. Got everything you want, sir? What, you off, moossoo? Well, this is a short visit you've paid the Bell to-day, and no mistake.'

The artist clapped him on the shoulder. 'My friend, this gentleman has bought from me a picture! He is not an artist, no, but he is a connoisseur!'

That's very nice, sir, I'm sure,' Wilkes said, and passed on.

Duval picked up his hat, and without another word to Charles went out of the bar. After a few moments Charles followed him, and went rather thoughtfully home.

So far Inspector Tomlinson had been as good as his word: they were not worried by any apparent supervision. As far as Charles could make out no one had come over to Framley either to watch or to make inquiries, and his suspicions that the inspector had not taken the matter very seriously began to grow stronger.

At lunch-time Celia asked whether he had seen Duval and forbidden him to come any more to the Priory. When she heard that the artist proposed to pay them a visit that night she was anything but pleased. 'He can't come tonight!' she said. 'You know we've got the Rootes and Colonel Ackerley dining with us.'

'I can't help it,' Charles replied. 'I don't propose to ask him to dinner. If he does turn up I'll tell Bowers to push him into the study. I shall soon be able to get rid of him.'

Margaret said, without raising her eyes from her plate: 'You didn't ask Mr Strange to dinner too?'

'I did not,' said Charles with emphasis.

'I wondered,' Margaret explained off-handedly, 'because I thought Celia wanted him invited.'

Her brother regarded her intently. 'Celia? I was under the impression that it was you who seemed keenest about it.' He waited to hear what she would say, but she said nothing at all. 'Look here, Sis, I know you've got rather a soft corner for that fellow, but you can take it from me that there's something very fishy about him. And if you happen to meet him at any time, I'd like you to be very much on your guard. See?'

Margaret flushed scarlet. 'What do you mean? Why should I meet him? And I don't know why you should think I have a soft corner for him simply because I won't leap to conclusions as you're doing.'

'All right, keep your hair on,' Peter recommended. 'But I don't mind telling you that yesterday this precious Mr Strange of yours somehow or other got wind of our visit to the police, and followed us. I just mention it so that you shall see there is a real need for you to be on your guard when talking to him.'

Startled grey eyes flew to his face. 'Followed you?' Margaret said. 'To – to Manfield?'

Peter nodded. 'How he got wind of it we don't know, but it seems fairly certain that he did.'

She knew only too well from what source Michael Strange had obtained his information. She felt guilty and unhappy, knowing that she was doing wrong to withhold her own discoveries from her relations. She finished the meal in silence, aware of her brother's scrutiny, and took care to avoid a tête-à-tête conversation with him afterwards. This was an easy matter, as they all played tennis again during the afternoon, and there was no opportunity for him to speak to her alone in between the last set and the arrival of their guests.

She lingered over her dressing, and did not go down to the drawing-room until she had heard one of the visitors arrive. She entered the room at length to find Colonel Ackerley apparently discussing whooping-cough with the doctor.

'I'm afraid there's no doubt about it,' Roote was

saying. 'But it oughtn't to interfere with you, Colonel.'

Celia turned as Margaret came in. 'Oh, Margaret, isn't it a nuisance for the Colonel? His butler's little boy has developed whooping-cough!'

'All the fault of these cinemas,' grumbled the Colonel, shaking hands with Margaret. 'Time and again I've said people had no business to let their children go to those germ-ridden holes. But you might as well talk to a brick wall as to that housekeeper of mine. Silly fools, both she and her husband.'

Dr Roote drank his cocktail in a gulp. 'Well, I don't see what you're worrying about,' he said. 'All kids go through it, and it isn't as though this one lives in your house.'

'No, but I shall have him whooping all over the garden if I know anything about it. Never wanted a couple with a child, but like a fool I gave way and let 'em live over the garage. Ought to have stuck to my original intention, and barred children.' He put down his glass, and seemed to make an effort to throw off his annoyance. 'Well, well, you'll say I'm a crotchetty old bachelor, eh, Mrs Malcolm?'

'Not a bit,' Celia assured him. 'I say instead that you'll take a brighter view after dinner.'

It was not until shortly before ten o'clock that Bowers came in to announce the arrival of M. Duval. Charles had cut out of the bridge four, and was standing behind the Colonel, watching him play, with considerable skill, a difficult hand. Bowers came up to him, and said softly: 'M. Duval, sir. I've shown him into the study.'

'No spade, Colonel?' Celia asked quickly.

The Colonel, frowning over the dummy she had laid

down for him, glanced at his own cards again. 'Bless my soul, did I pull out that club? Thanks, partner.' He picked the club up again and followed suit. The third player seemed to be wool-gathering. The Colonel said impatiently: 'Come on, Roote!'

The doctor, who had been looking at Charles, started. 'Sorry, sorry! What's led?' He played, and again looked at Charles. 'Didn't know you'd struck up a friendship with Duval, Malcolm.'

'I shouldn't describe my dealings with him exactly as a friendship,' Charles answered. 'I allowed myself to be inveigled into buying one of his pictures, and since then he's been trying hard to make me buy another. All right, Bowers, I'll come.'

He followed the butler out, and went across the hall to the study.

The artist was standing peering out of the window into the darkness. He started round as the door opened, and Charles saw that he was in one of his most nervous moods. No sooner was the door shut than he said hurriedly: 'M'sieur, you permit that I draw the curtains?'

'Certainly, if you like,' Charles replied.

'I must not be seen here,' Duval said, pulling the curtains across the window. 'Once I thought I heard a step behind me, but when I looked there was no one. I do not think I am followed here, but I am not sure. Sometimes I hear noises, but perhaps they are in my head. For it is very bad, m'sieur, ah, but very bad!'

'I'm sorry,' Charles said. 'Now what is it you want to see me about?'

The artist drew closer to him. 'There is no one outside? You are sure? No one can hear?'

'No, no one.'

Duval cast a glance round the room. 'I do not like this house. I do not know where the stairs are, but he goes up them like a ghost, m'sieur, and he can hear.'

'The stairs,' said Charles patiently, 'are at the other end of the hall, and since each step has its own creaking board I defy anyone to go up like a ghost. The only people in the house are ourselves, my family, my servant and his wife, and three guests, who are playing bridge in the library.'

Duval said suspiciously. 'Those three? Who are they?'

'Dr and Mrs Roote, and Colonel Ackerley.'

Duval seemed satisfied, but he sank his voice even lower. 'M'sieur, I will be quick. I come to say to you that you must not set your *gendarme* to watch me. You must tell him there is no harm in poor Duval. M'sieur, it is true! I do not do you any evil when I am in your garden, and I must go there, though I fear greatly, yes greatly! It is there I think I find the Monk. Something I have discovered. But your *gendarme* he challenge me, and I go away before I have discovered the great mystery. M'sieur, I implore you permit that I search here.'

'My dear fellow,' Charles said, 'I really can't have you prowling about the grounds. My wife doesn't like it, and I warn you I've got a revolver, and I'm liable to shoot if I see anyone suspicious lurking near the house.'

This threat did not have much effect. 'But me you know, and you would not shoot me after all your so great kindness. No, no, I know better. And I tell you it is of importance – of importance unheard of that you do not let that *gendarme* follow me. If I am watched what can I do? And he, that imbecile, he goes so clumsily he can be heard, and it is not only Duval who hears him.'

'You mean – you think you're on the track of the Monk.'

The guarded look came creeping back into the artist's wild eyes. 'I do not say.'

'Then in that case I fear *I* do not call off my watchdog.'

'But, m'sieur, I have told you I do no harm! I would not hurt you, or those others. What do I care for them? But nothing!'

'Look here,' Charles said, 'why all this mystery? You've already said you expect to find the Monk in these grounds.'

The artist passed his hand across his brow. 'Sometimes I do not know quite what I say. I do not wish to tell you that, for you understand it is no use if someone else finds him. I must be that one. M'sieur, think! For years I have waited. At first I did not care: I was content. But now I am not any longer content, and I think that it is better to have courage than to go on like this. For me, I have genius, and I will not be what you call underdog all my life. Better dead, m'sieur! Yes, I have thought that. Better dead! But I do not mean to die. Not like that other. For see, m'sieur! I am armed.' He showed Charles a wicked-looking knife, and grinned fiendishly. 'That would slip between the ribs, *hein*! Softly, oh but softly! When I hear footsteps in the dark, I take hold of him, my little knife, and courage comes to me.'

'Indeed? said Charles, beginning to think that the man was really mad. 'And do I understand that that is meant for the Monk?'

Duval nodded. 'Yes, but I do not wish to kill him. No, that is not good. I wish only to see his face, for once I have seen it, m'sieur, he is in my power, and I hold him like that.' He closed his fingers tightly.

'Well, when he's in your power,' Charles said, 'perhaps you'll be so good as to tell him to cease haunting this house.'

'Yes, perhaps I do that for you, m'sieur, if you let me search as I please. For I have made up my mind that even if I must go down amongst the dead to do it I will find him.'

'Let's hope no such journey will be necessary,' Charles suggested, and was surprised to see that leering secret smile twist the artist's mouth again. 'In the meantime, I don't think you need worry about Constable Flinders.'

'And I may search? You will not forbid me?'

'Well, we'll see about that,' Charles said, bent only on getting rid of him. 'And now I'm afraid I shall have to ask you to go, because I can't leave my guests any longer.'

The artist clutched his wrist. 'You will not tell the *gendarme* to arrest poor Duval?'

'No, I won't do anything like that,' Charles promised, and opened the door. He saw Duval out into the porch, and watched him dart out of the beam of light thrown through the open door. With a shrug of the shoulders he shut the door again, and went back to the library.

As he entered the room Celia looked up as though she were about to say something, but encountering a warning frown changed her mind.

'Well, Malcolm, bought another picture?' the Colonel chaffed him. 'You know, you haven't yet shown us the first one you bought.'

Charles shook his head. 'I never show it to people after

dark,' he said. 'It upsets them. Did you make your contract, by the way? That four spade one you were playing when I left you?'

'Yes, we made it,' Ackerley replied. 'Oughtn't to have, but Roote discarded a diamond. Aha, Roote, caught you napping that time, didn't I? Can't think why you held on to the heart.'

Dr Roote merely grunted. He had embarked on his third whisky since dinner, and though still perfectly sensible was looking slightly hazy. In a little while his wife, seeing him look round for the decanter again, gave the signal for the party to break up. Colonel Ackerley stayed on for about twenty minutes after the Rootes had gone, and then he too took his departure.

Gathering up the scattered cards, Celia said: 'I'm sorry for that little woman. I should divorce you, Charles, if you got fuddled every evening.'

'I do not at any time approve of drunkenness,' announced Mrs Bosanquet, 'and when a doctor falls into the habit of taking rather too much, I consider it most reprehensible. Now, if one of us was attacked by appendicitis in the middle of the night, what would be the use of sending for Dr Roote? Mrs Bowers was telling me that they say in the village that he can't be got out of bed at night to attend to anyone, and we all know what that means.'

'If you get attacked by appendicitis, Aunt, we'll send for Ponsonby, from Manfield,' Peter promised.

'Yes, my dear, I hope that you would. But my appendix was removed some years ago,' said Mrs Bosanquet with mild triumph.

An hour later, as Peter was about to blow out his

candle, and go to sleep, his door opened softly, and Charles came in, fully dressed.

'Hullo!' Peter said. 'Anything wrong?'

'No, but I've got a fancy to do a little sleuthing myself. Do you feel like accompanying me?'

Peter raised himself on his elbow. 'Who are you going to track?'

'Friend Duval. Unless he's clean cracked, he thinks he's on to the Monk's trail, and I can't help feeling it might be worth our while to follow him.'

The bed creaked in the adjoining room, and in a moment Margaret appeared in the open doorway with her dressing-gown caught hastily round her. 'If you don't want to be overheard you'd better see that the door's shut in future,' she said. 'Go on. What did Duval say to-night?'

Charles gave them a brief résumé of the artist's conversation. Peter sat up when he had finished. 'The knife business makes it look as though he's mad,' he said, 'but if we don't try and find out what he's up to we're a couple of fools. If you'd like to clear out, Sis, I propose to dress.'

'You can take your clothes into my room,' said his sister disobligingly. 'I want to hear some more. Who did he think was following him, Charles?'

'I don't know. The Monk, presumably. I have an idea he's afraid of Strange.'

Conscious of her brother's sidelong scrutiny Margaret said calmly: 'Why?'

Charles told her what Duval had said that morning when Strange had entered the taproom with the landlord. She nodded. 'I see.' She watched Peter swing his legs out of bed, and sat down, folding her dressing-gown more tightly round her.

Peter collected his clothes, and disappeared into her room. Through the open doorway his voice reached them: 'What about Celia?'

'She doesn't like it, but she says if Margaret will go and keep her company and I promise to run no risks I may go just this once.'

Margaret raised her eyes. 'What are you going to do, Charles?'

'It all depends,' he answered. 'I don't propose to run any unnecessary risks, and from Duval's account the Monk is a dangerous customer. But if by following Duval we can get a sight of the Monk it's worth doing.'

'You mean, you'd follow the Monk, and see where he went to?'

'That's the general idea.'

Margaret looked straight ahead of her for a moment, as though she were considering. 'Yes,' she said at last. 'I think perhaps you ought to. But don't shoot, Charles. Either of you. You don't want to land yourselves in a mess, and you mustn't forget that you don't know what the Monk is after. He may not be doing anything criminal.'

'The only shooting I'm likely to do will be in self-defence,' Charles replied.

Peter came back into the room in his shirt-sleeves. 'Don't you worry, Sis. We shan't get into trouble.'

'You might get excited, and do something you wouldn't do in cold blood,' she insisted. 'And I've got a sort of idea that the Monk doesn't want to hurt any of us.'

Peter got into his coat, and buttoned it. 'Where did

you get that idea from, if I may ask?'

'I don't know. But I do feel that you oughtn't to leap to conclusions.' She got up. 'Well, I'll go along to Celia now. Good luck, you two.' She went out, leaving her brother to frown after her.

'Strike you that Margaret takes an unduly sympathetic interest in the Monk?' he said. 'I don't quite like it. That fellow, Strange, has been getting at her, if you ask me.'

'She's too sensible,' Charles said. 'Are you ready?'

Together they went downstairs, and let themselves out by the front door. The night was rather overcast, but the waning moon shone fitfully through the clouds.

'Good: shan't need our torches,' Charles said, slipping his into the pocket of his tweed coat. 'The chapel is our goal, I think. That's where Flinders saw Duval.'

They made their way to the ruin, and cautiously inspected it. No one was there, and a deep silence brooded over the place. They searched the ground all about it without success, and at last Peter said: 'Look here, it's no use wandering aimlessly through the woods. It 'ud be more sensible if we walked down to Duval's cottage to see whether he's there or not. If he's tucked up in bed I think we can safely write him down a lunatic. If he's not there – well, he may still be a lunatic, but we can lie in wait for him on the road and see which direction he comes from. That'll narrow the field for us to-morrow night.'

'All right,' Charles said reluctantly. 'Not that I think it helps much, but I agree we shan't do much good going on like this.'

They started to walk down the right-of-way. 'What's more,' Peter pointed out, 'it's just possible that he may not have ventured out yet. After all, he knew we had a dinner-party, and since he seems very loth to let anyone catch sight of him he'd be bound to give the party some time to break up.' He flashed his torch on to his wristwatch. 'It's only just on midnight. Duval might well think we should still be up.'

'True,' Charles agreed. 'Anyway, we can but try your idea.'

They walked on in silence, until they came to the place where the right-of-way joined the main road into Framley. A few yards up the road the lane that ran past Duval's cottage branched off. They turned into this, and went softly up it till they saw the broken gate that led into the cottage garden. They paused in the lee of the untrimmed hedge, and craned their necks to obtain a glimpse of the tumble-down building. No light shone from either of the upper windows, but they thought they could see a dim glow in the ground floor.

'How many rooms?' Peter whispered.

'One downstairs, besides the kitchen.'

Peter stole to the gate, from where he could get a clear view of the cottage. He rejoined Charles in a minute or two. 'There is a light burning downstairs,' he whispered. 'But I think the curtains are drawn. I move that we walk up past the place and wait under the hedge to see whether he comes out or not. If he does he's bound to come this way, and he won't see us if we're the other side of the gate.'

Charles nodded, and followed him to a distance of a few yards beyond the gate. A ditch, with a bank surmounted by a hedge, flanked the lane, and they sat down on this bank in silence.

No sound came from the house on the other side of the ditch. After perhaps twenty minutes Charles yawned.

'We must look uncommonly silly,' he remarked. 'I don't believe he's in. Or else he's gone to bed, and left a light burning.'

Peter stood up. 'I'm going to try and have a look inside,' he said.

'You can't go spying in at a man's windows,' Charles objected.

'Can't I?' Peter retorted. 'Well, you watch me, and see. I've no compunction about spying on Duval whatsoever. The trouble with you is that you've got a legal mind. I don't somehow see Duval & Co. displaying a like punctiliousness where we're concerned.'

He carefully lifted the sagging gate out of position, and stole up the tangled path to the house. Charles saw him apparently listening at the window; then he crept round to the back, and was gone for some time.

He rejoined Charles presently. 'Can't hear a sound,' he said. 'But there's certainly a light. Just you come up, will you?'

Charles sacrificed his principles, and followed Peter up to the front door. He stood listening intently. It was just as Peter had said: not the smallest sound came from the room on the other side of the door.

'I believe you're right,' Charles whispered. 'He's either out, or asleep. If he's asleep I propose to wake him.'

Before Peter could stop him he had raised his hand and knocked smartly on the door.

'You ass!' Peter hissed. 'If he's there we don't want to disturb him!'

'If he's there his talk was all moonshine, and it doesn't matter whether we disturb him or not,' Charles replied. He knocked again.

The answering silence was a little uncanny. They waited, then Charles knocked louder than ever.

'By Jove, I believe he is out!' Peter said. 'Take care he doesn't come back suddenly and see you.' He moved boldly towards the window, and set his eye to the dirty glass where the curtains inside just failed to meet. Suddenly he spoke in a sharp, uneasy voice. 'Charles, just come here a moment. There's something . . . Here, take a look. What's that thing you can just see?'

All his scruples forgotten Charles pressed his face up against the glass. 'I can't quite – it looks like an arm. Yes, it is. Then someone must be standing there! But – damn this curtain!' He pressed closer, staring between the narrow gap in the curtain. The thing that was just discernible was unmistakably an arm in an old tweed sleeve, and below the edge of the frayed cuff a hand hung slackly. Charles stood still, trying to see more, but the gap was too small. But all the time he watched the hand never moved, and no sound broke the silence.

He turned. 'There's something wrong here,' he said. 'We've got to get in. Try the door.'

Peter put his hand on the latch. 'Bound to be bolted – unless he's out.'

But the latch lifted, and no bolt held the door in place. He pushed it cautiously open and peered in. Then a startled exclamation brought Charles up quickly to look over his shoulder. 'Oh, my God,' Peter cried on a note of horror.

For there, in the centre of the squalid little room was Louis Duval, quite dead, and hanging from one of the hooks in the beam that Charles had noticed.

Thirteen

The body hung horribly limply, and the face which was turned towards them was slightly discoloured as though death had resulted from strangulation rather than dislocation. The mouth hung open, and between lids that were almost shut the whites of the eyes gleamed in the lamplight.

Peter's hand fell from the latch of the door which he was still holding. He felt sick, but conquering the rising nausea he went up to that still figure, and touched one of the drooping hands. It felt chilly, and with a feeling of loathing he let it fall. The arm swung for a moment and then was still.

'Dead . . .' Charles said. 'Poor chap!'

Peter was looking round the room; it was untidy, and a dirty plate with a knife and fork stood on the table, but there were no signs of any struggle having taken place. The only thing that seemed significant was a fallen chair, and from its position it looked as though Duval had kicked it from under his feet when the rope was round his neck. 'Think the whole affair got on his nerves so badly that he – did himself in?' Peter said, instinctively lowering his voice.

Charles shook his head. 'I don't know. It's possible; he was pretty distraught to-night. But I can't help thinking of what he said about the other man who died.'

Peter jumped and looked round. 'You don't think – the Monk did this?'

Charles did not answer immediately. 'He was trying to find out who the Monk is,' he said after a short pause. 'He was scared out of his life; he was afraid he was being followed. So much was he afraid that he carried a fairly murderous knife on him. Now we find this.' He made a gesture towards the hanging corpse.

'No sign of a struggle,' Peter said, again scanning the room. 'And his hands are free, and there's that chair which he obviously stood on.'

'His hands might have been bound,' Charles said. 'No, don't touch them. This is a matter for the police. Come on, let's get out of this: we can't do anything here. We'd better go on to the Inn, and ring up the police-station at Manfield.'

'Charles, we can't leave him hanging there!' Peter said, impelled by his horror of that dangling corpse.

'He's been dead for at least an hour from the look of it,' Charles said. 'We can't do any good by cutting him down, and the police won't thank us for interfering. Come on: let's get out, for God's sake!'

Peter followed him into the garden. As Charles shut the door he said: 'Door was unbolted. It looks damned black to me.'

'Why should he bolt the door if he meant to kill himself?' was Peter's answer.

Charles did not say anything. Both he and Peter were glad to be out of that dreadful room, and they set off at a brisk pace towards the village.

The Inn was only some ten minutes' walk distant from the cottage, and they soon reached it. The place was in darkness, but they pressed the electric bell, and heard it ring somewhere inside. After a short interval the door was opened, and the barman's startled face looked out.

'I want to use your telephone,' Charles said curtly. 'It's urgent, so let me in, will you?'

Spindle seemed reluctant to let him pass, but Charles pushed by him without ceremony. 'Where is it?' he asked impatiently.

'What – what's happened, sir?' Spindle said. 'I 'ope – no one's taken ill?'

'Never you mind,' Charles said. 'Where's the telephone?'

'There's a box outside the coffee-room, sir. But I don't know as – I don't know as Mr Wilkes . . .'

'Rubbish! Wilkes can't possibly object to having his telephone used. Where is he?'

'He's gorn to bed, sir. I'll show you where the 'phone is, and call 'im.'

He led the way down the passage to a telephone box, and casting another wondering look at them made off in the direction of the back premises.

Charles found the number he wanted, and stepped into the box. Peter remained at his elbow, listening. He supposed the landlord's room must be reached by way of the back stairs since Spindle had gone in that direction, but a moment later Spindle reappeared, and saying that he would rouse Mr Wilkes at once, went quickly up the stairs that ran up at the front of the house.

Charles had at last got himself connected with the

police-station, and was endeavouring to make an apparently sleepy constable understand. 'Hullo! Hullo, is that Manfield Police Station? . . . Yes? This is Malcolm speaking – *Malcolm* . . . M.A.L.C.O.L.M. – yes, *Malcolm*, from Framley . . . No, *Framley*. Is Inspector Tomlinson there? . . . Damn! Look here, you'd better send a man over at once. There's been an accident . . . No, I said there's been an accident . . . Yes, that's right . . . What? . . . Well, it's either suicide, or murder, and the sooner you get a man over here the better . . . You'll what? . . . Oh good, yes! . . . I'm speaking from the Bell Inn, and if you call for me here I'll take you to the place. Right, good-bye.' He hung up the receiver, and turned to tell Peter what the constable had said. 'He's going to get hold of Tomlin . . .' He broke off, staring past Peter. The front door was open, and on the threshold, his hand on the latchkey which he had not yet withdrawn from the lock, was Michael Strange, standing as though arrested by what he had heard, and looking directly at him.

Peter turned quickly, following the direction of Charles' gaze. 'Strange!' he ejaculated. 'What the hell are you doing?'

Strange drew the key out of the lock, and shut the door. 'I might echo that question,' he said coolly. He came towards them, and they saw that he was looking decidedly unpleasant. 'What have you found?' he said.

Charles laid a restraining hand on Peter's arm. 'Do you know, that is something we propose to tell the police,' he said. 'I don't immediately perceive what it has to do with you.'

Strange looked at him under frowning brows. 'Look

here,' he said harshly, 'if you're wise you'll stop poking your nose in where it's not wanted.'

Charles' brows rose in polite surprise. 'Is that a threat?' he inquired.

'No, it's not a threat. It's a warning, and one which you'd do well to follow.' He swung around on his heel as he spoke and went up the stairs without another word.

Peter had started forward as though to pursue him, but again Charles checked him. 'Leave it,' he said. 'We've no right to detain him. All we can do is to tell the police.'

'While you stand on ceremony he'll get clean away!' Peter said hotly.

'I don't think it,' Charles answered, 'if he had anything to do with what we found to-night I'm pretty sure we've discovered who the Monk is. And he's a damned cool customer – much too cool to give himself away by bolting.' He glanced up the staircase. 'I don't know about you, but I feel as though I could do with a stiff peg. What on earth's Wilkes up to all this time?'

As though in answer to his question the landlord came into sight at the top of the stairs. 'Sorry to keep you waiting, sir,' he said, 'but I stayed to pop on my clothes. Spindle says you wanted to use the telephone, urgent, sir. I do hope nothing's wrong up at the Priory?' He came down as quickly as a man of his bulk might, and they saw that he was fully clothed and that his placid countenance had taken on a look of anxiety.

'No, there's nothing wrong at the Priory,' Charles answered. 'It's that fellow, Duval. We've just been up to his place, and – he's dead.'

The landlord fell back a pace. '*Dead?*' he echoed.

'Dooval? So that's . . .' A cough broke off what he was about to say. He went on again when the spasm was at an end: 'So that's why he never turned up to-night like he generally does,' he said. 'How – what happened, sir? Was it the drugs he takes, do you think? Perhaps he ain't actually dead. I have heard as how they often goes into a kind of a stupor.'

'He's dead right enough,' Charles said grimly. 'We found him hanging from his own ceiling.'

The landlord's rosy cheeks turned suddenly pale. 'Hanging?' he whispered. 'You mean – someone – did him in?'

'No, it looks like suicide on the whole. I say, can you get us a drink? We feel we need one after this.'

Wilkes turned mechanically towards the bar. 'Yes, sir. That is, it's after hours, you know, sir, but I can stretch a point seeing what the reason is. I – I take it you wanted to ring up the police?'

'Naturally. They'll be over in about half an hour, I should imagine. Can we sit and wait here till they come?'

'Yes, sir, certainly. Will you have a whisky? And I'd be glad if you'd keep it quiet that I served you after hours, if you don't mind, sir.' He measured out two tots, still looking rather pale about the gills. Charles told him to pour a third for himself, and he did so. 'Hanged!' he repeated. 'My Gawd, sir, I can't get over it! Regular shock it is, when I think how he took his dinner here this morning same as usual. He did seem a bit queerer than usual now I come to think of it, but there, he was always such a one for going off into one of them silly fits that I didn't set any store by it.'

'What about the soda, Wilkes?' Peter interrupted.

The landlord started. 'I'm sure I beg your pardon, sir.' He produced a siphon, and squirted the soda-water into the glasses. 'It's given me such a turn I don't hardly know what I'm doing.' He sat down limply. 'To think of him – dead! And like that too. It must have upset you, finding him,' he shuddered.

'Yes, not a pretty sight,' Charles said.

They remained seated in the bar, until the noise of a car approaching roused Wilkes from his awe-struck meditations. The car drew up outside, and he hurriedly concealed the tell-tale glasses. 'I'll go and let 'em in, sir,' he said, and went out to the main door.

Charles and Peter followed him. Inspector Tomlinson was standing in the entrance, and at sight of Charles he said briskly: 'Very good of you to wait, sir. Hope we haven't kept you. If you'll come out I've got a car here, and you can tell me what has happened while we go along to this place. Where is it, sir?'

'Only a stone's throw. I'll direct you.'

'Who's the dead man, sir? Do you know him?'

'Duval. The artist I spoke to you about.'

'I remember, sir,' the inspector said. As usual he displayed nothing but a business-like and detached interest in the occurrence. 'Will you get in beside Sergeant Matthews in the front, sir, and tell him the way? This is Dr Puttock, the Divisional Surgeon. Can you find room behind, Mr Fortescue? I'm afraid it's a tight fit.'

Peter managed to wedge himself between Dr Puttock and the inspector, and the car started forward. In a few minutes it turned into the rough lane, and drew up outside the cottage.

'I shall have to ask you gentlemen to come in with me,' the inspector said. 'Hope you don't mind, sir.'

'No, it's all right,' Charles said, and got out of the car.

They went into the cottage, and the sergeant, producing a note-book began to write in it, his eyes lifting from it from time to time to observe everything in the room. None of the three men paid any attention to Charles or Peter for some time, but when the body had been taken down and laid on the floor, the inspector seemed to become aware of them again, and said kindly: 'Not very pleasant for you two gentlemen, but we shan't keep you very long, I hope . . . Note the position of that chair, Matthews. Looks as though deceased must have stood upon it, doesn't it?' He glanced down at the doctor who was kneeling beside the body, making some sort of an inspection. 'Clear case of suicide, eh, doctor? As soon as the ambulance comes we'll get the body away.'

The doctor spoke over his shoulder. 'Hand me my bag, will you, inspector?' He opened it, and took out a pair of forceps. As far as Peter could see, from his place by the door, he was doing something inside the dead man's mouth. Then the doctor shifted his position slightly, and Peter could see only his back. At length he got up, and closely scrutinised something that his forceps had found. He took a test-tube from his case, and carefully dropped the infinitesimal thing the forceps held into it. Then he corked it tightly.

The inspector watched him with the air of an inquisitive terrier. 'Got something, doctor?'

'I shall want to do a more thorough examination,' the doctor replied. He glanced down at the body. 'You can cover it, sergeant. I've finished for the present.' He replaced the test tube in his case. 'I'm not satisfied that this is a case of suicide,' he said. 'I found a scrap of cotton wool in the deceased's nostrils, very far back.'

The inspector pursed his lips into a soundless whistle. 'Nothing in the mouth, doctor?'

'Nothing now,' said the doctor significantly.

'Better go over the place for finger-prints,' the inspector said. 'Now, Mr Malcolm, if you please, I'd like to hear just how you happened to find the body.'

Charles gave him a clear and concise account of all that had passed that evening, up to the time of the discovery of the corpse. He neither omitted any relevant point nor became discursive, and at the end of his statement Sergeant Matthews, who had taken it down, looked up gratefully.

'Thank you, sir,' the inspector said. 'If more witnesses were as clear as you are the police would have an easier time.'

Charles smiled. 'I'm not exactly new to this sort of thing,' he said.

The inspector cast him a shrewd glance. 'I thought I'd spotted you, sir. I saw you at the Norchester Assizes about six months ago, didn't I?'

'Quite possibly,' Charles said. 'Now there's one other thing I'd like to mention. When my brother-in-law and I reached the Bell Inn, the barman went to rouse Wilkes, the landlord, while I was ringing you up. As soon as I had finished speaking to the station, I turned round to find that Strange had come in with his own latchkey, and had been listening to all I'd said.'

The doctor looked up sharply. 'Strange?' he repeated.

'Yes, doctor, we've got a note about him,' the inspector said. 'Go on, sir.'

'He asked us what we had found, and upon my refusing to tell him, he seemed distinctly annoyed, and said, as near as I can remember, that he advised us to stop poking our noses where they weren't wanted. I asked whether that was a threat, and he replied that it was a warning which he advised us to take.'

'That's very interesting, sir,' the inspector said. 'You say he came in from the street?'

'Yes, using his own key.'

'Then Strange was not in the Inn when this happened,' the inspector said. 'I think I'll be having a word with him.' He nodded to the sergeant. 'You'd better run these gentlemen back to their home, Matthews. I take it they know at the Inn where we are, sir?'

'Wilkes knows, yes.'

'Then he'll direct the ambulance on. Now, sir, I don't think there's any need for me to keep you standing about here any longer, but if you could make it convenient to come over to the station to-morrow we may have something more to ask you. And we'd like you to read through your statement, which we'll have put into longhand by then, and sign it. Sergeant Matthews will drive you home now. I hope what you've seen won't keep you awake.' He went out with them to the car, and saw them off. The police car backed down the lane to the main road, and in a very short time deposited them at their own front door.

Celia and Margaret were both awake, and no sooner had the two men entered the house than Margaret leaned over the banisters, and asked them to come up at once and tell them what had happened.

Celia was sitting up in bed with a shawl round her shoulders. 'Thank goodness you're back!' she sighed. 'You've been away such ages we've imagined all sorts of horrors. Did you discover anything?'

Charles and Peter exchanged glances. 'They're bound to know when the inquest comes on,' Peter said. 'Tell them.'

'Inquest?' Margaret said sharply. 'Who's dead? You haven't – no, of course you haven't.'

'It's Duval,' Charles explained. 'We didn't find him in our grounds, so Peter suggested we should go down to his cottage. And we found him there, dead.'

'Murdered?' Celia quavered, gripping her shawl with both hands.

'We don't know,' Charles answered, sitting down on the edge of the bed. 'Apparently he hanged himself, but we shan't know definitely whether it was suicide or not till the inquest, I imagine.'

'But what a ghastly thing!' Margaret said. 'Who can – oh, surely it wasn't murder? Why should anyone think so?'

'Well, perhaps it isn't,' Charles said consolingly. 'Peter and I have got to go over to the police-station to-morrow, and we may hear something fresh then. At present we only know that the doctor wasn't satisfied, and is going to conduct a post mortem.'

'Please tell us just what happened!' Margaret begged.

Charles made the story as short as possible, and he did not mention the doctor's discovery. At the end of his tale Celia said: 'If anyone killed him it was the Monk, and now we know for certain he's not a ghost. Well, I always said I wasn't scared of flesh and blood, but do you think it's safe for us here?'

'Yes, I think so,' her brother replied. 'If the Monk did murder Duval it's fairly certain he did it because Duval had discovered his identity. Or even because he knew Duval had been talking to us. He isn't likely to try to do any of us in. Too risky, for one thing, and for another, no motive.'

'How could he have known that Duval had talked to us?' Margaret asked. 'Do you think he followed him here this evening?'

'Duval undoubtedly thought that possible. It would be easy for him to find out that we'd had dealings with Duval without that, though. I never made any secret of the fact that I visited him, and all sorts of people have seen me talking to him at various times,' Charles said. 'Wilkes, Ackerley, the Rootes – they all knew, not to mention various locals who've seen Duval and me together at the Bell.'

'And, from what you told us to-day, Mr Strange as well,' Margaret said, meeting her brother's eye.

'Yes, Strange, too.' Charles glanced at his watch. 'Well, I don't know how the rest of you feel, but I'm all for bed.'

Margaret got up rather reluctantly. 'Yes, I suppose we'd better try and get some sleep,' she agreed. 'But I do wish we weren't so much in the dark still. Well, good night, you two. Coming, Peter?'

Brother and sister went out together, and soon quiet descended on the house.

The two men drove over to Manfield on the following

morning. It was a Sunday, and the market-town had a forlorn appearance. Even the police-station seemed rather deserted, and the constable in charge ushered them immediately into the inspector's office. Here in a short time the inspector joined them.

He bade them good morning, thanked them for coming over in such good time, and sat down behind his desk.

'Discovered anything fresh?' Charles asked, drawing up his chair.

The inspector shook his head. 'Looks like a nasty case against someone, sir,' he said. 'The inquest will be held on Tuesday, and I'm afraid both you gentlemen will have to give evidence.'

'Of course,' Charles said. 'We were quite prepared for that. Can you tell us anything more?'

'Well, sir, strictly speaking I ought not to, but seeing how much you know already, I don't mind telling you that the Divisional Surgeon has just finished his post mortem, and there doesn't seem to be much doubt that it's murder. I needn't ask you not to repeat this, sir, I know.'

'Of course not. What did he discover?'

'It's that piece of cotton wool, sir. Looks as though Duval was chloroformed, and then strung up. Dr Puttock found traces of chloroform still lingering. And during his examination he found various abrasions on the deceased's body as though there had been a bit of a struggle, and in it Duval had knocked against things – the table, maybe, or something like that. Then, sir, the doctor found a bit of skin in one of his finger-nails, as though he might have clawed at someone's face, or hand, or whatever it may have been.'

'Any finger-prints?' Charles asked.

'No, sir. Only the deceased's on that plate you saw, and the glass, and such-like. Whoever did this job took care to wear gloves.' He unlocked a drawer in his desk, and took out an envelope. From this he shook a black bone button. 'After you'd gone, I had a good look round and I found this lying under the coal-box. Must have rolled there.'

Charles and Peter inspected it. It was about the size of a farthing, a cheap-looking button with a pattern stamped on it. 'Looks like an ordinary glove-button,' Peter said.

'Just so, sir. Made in France, too, but that doesn't tell us much. But I went through all the deceased's belongings, and there wasn't a single pair of gloves in the house, let alone one lacking a button. It doesn't prove anything, but it's something to go on.' He put it back into the envelope.

'You're not producing that at the inquest, are you?' Charles asked.

'Oh no, sir,' the inspector replied, smiling. 'The police aren't as thick-headed as that, you know. Our course is to ask for an adjournment. You've never seen anyone wearing gloves with this type of button, I suppose?' They shook their heads. 'No, well, I didn't expect you would have, but there was just a chance of it.' He locked it away again. 'You won't mention that to anyone, if you please, sir.'

'Certainly not.' Charles looked round as the door opened. A man came in with a typewritten document, which he laid before the inspector.

'That's right, Jenkins,' the inspector said. 'That'll be

all. Now, sir, would you please read through what you said last night, and see that we've got it down right? And if you'd just tell me your part of the story, Mr Fortescue, I'll take it down, and we shall have everything shipshape.'

Peter briefly recounted his share in the night's happenings. When he had done Charles put down the typewritten sheets. 'Yes, that's right,' he said. 'Want me to sign it?' He drew out his fountain pen, and scrawled his name at the bottom of the statement. As he screwed the cap on again, he said: 'I don't think, inspector, that when we came to see you the other day you set much store by our tale, but has it occurred to you just where all this points?'

'Yes, sir, it has,' the inspector replied at once. 'And you'll pardon me, but I did set considerable store by what you told me. If I hadn't I wouldn't have been quite so open with you this morning. But you see, what you told me wasn't the first thing I'd heard about the Priory Monk. I've been remarkably interested in him for some time.'

'No good asking you what your previous information was, I suppose?' Charles asked.

'No, sir, I'm afraid it's not. But you can be quite sure I'm not taking the matter lightly. I know what you think. You think that it was the Monk who murdered Duval. Well, it's not for me to give my opinion, lacking any proof, but I would like you, if you will, sir, to try and remember just what Duval said to you about the Monk.'

As well as he could Charles gave the gist of Duval's remarks, but as he warned the inspector, Duval had made so many vague references to that mysterious figure that he found it hard to recollect them all. But on one point his memory was perfectly clear: Duval believed that the only man who had ever seen the Monk's face had been murdered, and he knew that in trying to discover the Monk's identity he was running a great risk. 'So much so,' Charles said, 'that he had taken to carrying a businesslike looking knife about with him.'

'Yes, and that raises a question,' Peter put in. 'If he was murdered last night, there must have been a bit of a struggle. The fragment of skin proves that. And you can't chloroform a man without overpowering him first. If the Monk did it, why didn't Duval draw his knife? He must have had time, because as soon as he set eyes on the Monk he'd have been on his guard. The Monk can't have taken him unawares in his own house. Was the knife on him?'

'Yes, sir, it was. But you can look at it in another way. We know from what Duval said to Mr Malcolm here the very night he died that he hadn't seen the Monk's face then. He'd discovered something, but it seems fairly plain it wasn't the Monk. If you think it over, he had precious little time to discover who the Monk was in between the time when Mr Malcolm says he left the Priory, and you found him hanging in his cottage. From the fact of his evidently having been taken by surprise, since he never got the chance to draw his knife, doesn't it look as though whoever it was who went to his cottage didn't go in his disguise of a Monk? Looked at in that light, my reading of the thing is that the person who visited Duval didn't rouse any suspicion in him. He didn't know who the Monk was; some man whom he didn't suspect at all came to his house, possibly with a plausible excuse. He let him in, and before he knew where he was this person had clapped the pad over his face. We'll say there was a struggle: it looks as though the murderer was a pretty strong man. Duval was a bit of a weed, besides being weakened by the dope he took, but you try holding a handkerchief over a man's face when that man's struggling. It's not easy, and a struggle there must have been. But you can understand Duval trying too hard to wrench his assailant's hand away from his mouth to have time to try and get at his knife. For what it's worth, I found a broken plate in the kitchen, but the place was such a pig-sty there's no saying it was put there by the murderer. Still, it might have been, and we know he set the room to rights when he'd finished Duval. One of the cold-blooded ones, he is: you do find 'em sometimes. He staged the whole thing to look like a suicide, and it's the doctor's opinion he was cute enough to remove any of the pad that may have got into Duval's mouth. But that scrap you saw the doctor extract from Duval's right nostril he missed. The doctor only found it with his forceps. If it hadn't been for that it *would* have looked like a clear case of suicide, especially with a man of Duval's temperament. But a man don't chloroform himself when he sets out to commit suicide by hanging, and even if he did, that's ruled out by the fact that there was no trace of the bottle, nor the pad either. No, it's murder right enough, and if you ask me, murder by some person whom Duval didn't dream was likely to attack him.'

Both men had listened to him in attentive silence. 'If that is so,' Charles said slowly, 'it seems to exonerate Strange. For if I'm not very much mistaken Duval was afraid of Strange.'

'But did he suspect him of being the Monk?' Peter asked.

'No, I don't know that he did, but he thought Strange had something to do with the Monk. At least, so I infer from what he said when he saw Strange come into the bar yesterday morning.'

The inspector was fingering the typewritten statement. 'I wouldn't go about saying Strange did this, sir,' he said slowly.

'Well, naturally not, but you must admit things look pretty black against him. Did you see him after we'd left you last night?'

'Yes, sir, I saw him. You'll understand I can't tell you anything about him, but you can set your mind at rest on one point: there's nothing Strange can do that we shan't know about. So in case you were feeling that we are leaving any dangerous person at large you can be sure that his doings are known to us, and you don't stand in danger from him.'

'I must say, I'm glad to hear you're keeping a watch on him,' Charles said, preparing to get up. 'Well, we mustn't waste your time. If there's nothing else you want me to tell you I think we'd better be pushing off.'

'No, sir, nothing else, only to remind you again not to talk of this. The inquest will be held here at eleven-thirty on Tuesday.'

Charles nodded. 'We'll be here. I take it I shan't be wanted to speak about Duval's fears of the Monk?'

The inspector came as near to a wink as so staid an individual could. 'The coroner won't want to hear any ghost stories, sir,' he said meaningly.

Fourteen

The news of Duval's death had spread round the neighbourhood as such news does spread, and when it was known that the people to discover the corpse were Charles Malcolm and Peter Fortescue, not only Roote and Colonel Ackerley, but Mr Titmarsh as well, all found excuses to call at the Priory on the chance of picking up some fresh news. The Colonel, who knew the family best, was entirely frank. 'Sheer curiosity, Mrs Malcolm,' he twinkled. 'That's what's brought me up to see you.' But even he could extract nothing more from Charles and Peter than was already known.

Mr Titmarsh said that he had come to inquire how Margaret was after her experience on Thursday; Dr Roote thought that he had left his scarf at the Priory on Saturday evening. And both gentlemen tried their hardest to pump Charles, and went away dissatisfied. On Monday morning Celia met Mrs Pennythorne, the Vicar's wife, in the village shop. Mrs Pennythorne was far too adroit to ask questions, but she greeted Celia most effusively, and said that she had been meaning for some days to ask the whole Priory party over to dinner. As Celia was perfectly well aware of the fact that Mrs

Pennythorne did not like her, she was not taken in by this, and she declined the invitation to dine at the Vicarage on the following evening on the score of the inquest, which might last till late. Not to be baulked, Mrs Pennythorne begged her to choose her own day, and she was so persistent that Celia was forced to accept an invitation for Wednesday.

When she broke the news to the family there was an outcry from all but Mrs Bosanquet, who said reprovingly that the Vicar was a most interesting man, and she should be glad of an opportunity of consulting him as to the best method of exorcising unquiet spirits.

'All right,' Charles said. 'You go, and say the rest of us have developed smallpox.'

'You and I have simply got to go,' Celia said. 'I'd have got out of it if I could, but she just wouldn't take no for an answer. But I really didn't see that it was fair to let you all in for it, so I said I couldn't speak for the rest of you. If Aunt Lilian wants to go surely three of us'll be enough. You don't want to, do you, Margaret?'

'Not much!' Margaret said. 'You're a true friend and sister, Celia. Peter and I will spend a tête-à-tête evening.'

'She may be a true sister, but as a wife she's a stumer,' Charles announced. 'Anyone with a grain of resource would have said that I was so unnerved by finding Duval's body that only complete quiet could restore me.'

'I hardly think she'd have been convinced,' Celia replied. 'By the way, Margaret and I can come to the inquest, can't we?'

'If you like,' Charles answered. 'But it won't be at all interesting.'

Mrs Bosanquet assumed her most disapproving

expression. 'If you take my advice, my dears, you will stay quietly at home with me. You do not want people to think you are some of these sensation-hunters we hear so much about nowadays. In my opinion, inquests and murder trials are not things that can interest women of breeding.'

'But this is different, because Chas and Peter are mixed up in it,' Celia objected. 'Besides, everyone's going, even Mr Titmarsh. Colonel Ackerley said that though he didn't want to seem heartless, Framley hasn't had anything so thrilling happen since he came to live here.'

'That may be, my dear, but the Colonel is not a female. Quite the reverse, in fact, for being a soldier I've no doubt he holds human life very cheaply.'

Later in the day Constable Flinders paid them a visit, and shook his head broodingly. 'You ought to have sent for me, sir,' he said reproachfully. 'It would have been a nice case for me to handle, and there's no denying there's precious little scope in Framley for a man who has ambition.'

'Sorry,' Charles said. 'But I thought you were watching him.'

'I can't be everywhere at once, sir, can I? I go and take my eye off him for half a moment, just to make sure that Mr Titmarsh wasn't getting up to mischief, and I'm blessed if he don't go and hang himself. I suppose the next thing'll be I'll find while I been about my ordinary duties that tiresome old bug-hunter – Mr Titmarsh, I should say – has gone and done himself in with his own killing-bottle.'

'Well, that'll give you a case anyhow,' Charles consoled him.

The constable said austerely: 'You mustn't get it into your head, sir, that the police want people to go about killing themselves. All I said was, it's a bit hard that when a Framley man commits sooicide them chaps from Manfield get called in before I hear anything about it. Not that I'm blaming you, sir,' he added handsomely. 'No doubt you done as you see fit, and it isn't everyone who keeps his head on his shoulders when he goes and finds a thing like a corpse.'

The inquest, as Charles had predicted, was not particularly interesting to Celia and Margaret, but those outside the family who had not imagined that any other verdict than suicide would be forthcoming, were in a positive buzz of speculation and wonderment.

Charles and Peter recounted all that they had done, both citing as their reason for visiting Duval's cottage his suspicious presence in their grounds on the night before. The inspector was called, and also Dr Puttock, and the inspector then asked for an adjournment, pending further police inquiries. This was granted, and for the time being the case was over.

'And I vote,' said Peter, 'that we ask old Ackerley in for some tennis this afternoon, and try to get the taste of all this out of our mouths.'

They waited for the Colonel outside the court-room, and when he appeared he readily accepted the invitation. 'I won't ask questions now,' he said, 'but I warn you, I'm all agog to hear a bit more. If you don't want to fall into Mrs Pennythorne's clutches, you'd better get away before she catches you. I saw her making for the door fairly bursting with curiosity.'

'Then let's clear out at once,' Peter said. 'Half-past

three suit you, Colonel? We ought to tell you that the court's a terror, and full of docks.'

'Be able to blame it then for my bad shots,' the Colonel said.

They escaped just as the Vicar's wife emerged from the court-room, and drove back to the Priory in time for a late lunch. The Colonel arrived punctually at half-past three, and proved to be a player of considerable standing.

'What a pity we couldn't have got another man!' Celia said when they repaired to the terrace for tea. 'But Dr Roote doesn't look as though he'd be any good, and I can't see Mr Titmarsh standing up to you, Colonel.'

'Give me a mixed double every time,' the Colonel said. 'Much better fun! But I'm out of practice. When I was in India I used to play a lot. I've rather given up of late years.'

'What part of India were you stationed in?' Peter asked. 'I've got a cousin who's just had the luck to be sent to Wellington.'

'Oh, I've been all over the place,' the Colonel answered. 'But I didn't come here to talk about India, young man. Out with it! Did you know the police thought it was murder?'

'Now then, sir, you ought to know better than to try and drag information out of us,' Charles said. 'Of course I need hardly say that the police perceiving at once that we had missed our vocations, entrusted us with all their secrets. In fact, we're considering entering the force on the strength of it.'

'Yes, yes, but you needn't be so close,' the Colonel said. 'What I can't understand is, who in the world should want to murder that French fellow? Seemed harmless enough, I always thought.'

'I've got a theory about it,' said Charles, helping himself to a cucumber sandwich. 'Who knows but what he may have possessed an oleander hawk-moth? We are all aware that Mr Titmarsh is expending untold energy in his pursuit of this elusive specimen. Very well, then. He found that Duval had one, and so . . .'

'Really, Chas, I don't think you ought to joke about it,' Celia said. 'It's not exactly decent.'

'Well, why was he in your grounds?' the Colonel asked, not to be put off. 'Was that what he came up to see you about Saturday evening? You know, you're being quite maddening, and it's my belief you know a lot more than you pretend.'

'Of course I do,' said Charles. 'Didn't I say so?'

'Oh, I give you up!' the Colonel said hopelessly. 'All I can say is, I hope it hasn't given you a distaste for the Priory.'

'Not at all,' Charles said, demolishing another sandwich. 'Why should it?'

'I don't know, but after all the business about the ghost which you spoke of some time ago, I was afraid finding a corpse – must have been a bit of a shock, eh? Glad I didn't stumble on it – might rather put the lid on it.'

'A new theory,' Peter remarked. 'The Priory ghost killed Duval. You'll be making my sister nervous, if you're not careful, sir.'

'Well, I wouldn't do that for the world,' said the Colonel gallantly, and began at once to talk of something else.

But it seemed as though no conversation could for

long steer clear of the problems besetting the owners of the Priory. The Colonel's talk led to a description of a round of golf he had played the day before, and since his partner had been Michael Strange it was not surprising that he began to talk about him. 'Seems a nice chap,' he said. 'How do you get on with him?'

'We hardly know him,' Celia replied.

'He's played golf with me once or twice,' the Colonel said. 'Retiring sort of fellow, but I always feel sorry for people taking a holiday by themselves. Dull work, what? What's his job by the way? Haven't liked to ask him outright since he seemed so uncommunicative. Wondered whether, like so many poor fellows since the war, he's had to take up some rotten thing like selling from house to house. Distressing, the number of sahibs who are doing jobs they wouldn't have touched in 1914.'

'I'm afraid we can't tell you anything about him,' Celia said. 'We've really only met him to talk to once, and that was at your party.' She looked round. 'Will anyone have any more tea? No? Then what about another set?'

The next day passed quietly enough, and was only marred, Charles said, by the prospect of having to go to dinner with the Pennythornes. He spoke bitterly on the subject of people who shirked their clear duty, but his words made not the slightest impression on either Peter or Margaret.

'We shall be with you in spirit,' Peter told him, but so far from consoling Charles this assurance provoked him to embark on a denunciation of his brother-in-law's character, which was only stopped by Celia hustling him upstairs to change into his dress clothes.

Peter and Margaret enjoyed a tête-à-téte meal, and sat down afterwards in the library to play piquet together. After three hard-fought rubbers they gave it up, and to Margaret's dismay Peter, instead of retiring as he usually did, into a book, showed a disposition to talk. She had a shrewd idea whither his conversation would lead, and she was not mistaken. In a very short time Peter, busy with the filling of a pipe, tackled her bluntly. 'I say, Sis, mind if I ask you a question?'

She minded very much indeed, but she had to say No.

'We've always been pretty frank with each other,' Peter said, 'or I wouldn't ask. But aren't you a bit more interested in that fellow Strange than you pretend to be?'

Margaret reflected gloomily on the manifold failings of the male sex, and decided that the worst of these was the appallingly blunt questions men asked. 'I don't think so,' she replied. 'I must say I do rather like him. I'm sorry you've got such a down on him. Does he wear the wrong kind of tie?'

Peter refused to be put off by such flippancy. 'I don't want to be officious,' he explained painstakingly, 'and I don't say for a moment that you aren't quite capable of looking after yourself, but I have got a distinct impression that Strange has got on your soft side. Am I right?'

'Very seldom,' Margaret retorted. 'But I've already said I like the man. Perhaps that's partly your fault, because you and Chas run him down so much.'

'Rot!' Peter said sweepingly. 'All Charles and I have said is that Strange behaves in a way that can't be described as anything but fishy. You must admit that he does.'

Margaret was silent. Peter struck a match and said

between puffs: 'I've a suspicion you've seen rather more of the fellow than I have. Has he ever told you anything about himself?'

She could answer that quite truthfully. 'No.'

'Well, has he ever said anything to make you think that we're on the wrong track about him?'

She thought for a moment, wondering how much she could divulge without breaking her word to Strange. Peter had always been her confidant, more so than Celia, who was older, and who no longer lived with them, and never till now had she kept anything from him. It was uncomfortable to be so torn between two feelings, uncomfortable and unaccustomed. Yet something deeper than her friendship with her brother now had her in its hold, and even while one part of her longed to tell him everything, the other prompted her to keep silence. She looked up to find that Peter was regarding her steadily. She coloured, and said: 'It's very hard to say. But from – things he has said to me I do feel perfectly sure that whatever he may be doing he doesn't want to hurt or alarm us in any way.'

Peter's brows rose. 'Really? Then he admits he's at the bottom of our mystery?'

'No. He never said that. But he did say that he wished we would leave the Priory. I think I can safely tell you that.'

'Did he, indeed? Any reason?'

She hesitated. 'N-no. Only that – he didn't want us to be in any danger.'

'Think he was responsible for that skeleton?'

'I don't know, Peter,' she said honestly.

He smoked in silence for a while. At last he said:

'Don't you see, Sis, that what you've told me practically proves that my suspicions aren't by any means groundless?'

'In a way I do, but . . . Look here, Peter, you know I'm not the sort of silly fool who gasses about intuition and all that sort of rot, don't you?'

He grinned. 'Yes, thank God!'

'Well, I'm not, but I don't mind admitting that about Strange I have got an absolute conviction that he isn't out to harm any of us. I agree he's being mysterious, and I agree that for some reason or other he may want to get us out of this place. But I don't believe the reason is a bit what you think.'

'My dear girl, I don't know what to think!'

'No, but you've got an idea that he's a wrong 'un. And that's where I think you're mistaken. If he wants to get possession of this house it's for some purpose we've none of us guessed.'

He hunched his shoulders lower in his chair. 'Quite sure you aren't being a bit led away by a personable exterior?'

'Ever known me fall for a handsome face?'

'I haven't, but I shouldn't like to swear that you never would. And I grant you Strange is a nice-looking chap, and a powerful-looking one too, which as far as I can make out is what most women like in a man.'

'Well, if that's the line you mean to stick to it's not much good my arguing,' Margaret said with some asperity.

Conversation showed a tendency to flag after that. Presently Peter said: 'One thing that seems to me to stand out a mile is that you're keeping something up your sleeve. Not cricket, Sis.'

'Oh, shut up!' Margaret said crossly. 'Even supposing I were I don't see that it makes much odds now that you've told the police the whole story.'

'If you know anything about Strange that we don't, it might help the police considerably.'

'I haven't the smallest desire to help the police,' Margaret replied. 'I hate policemen: they come nosing round after wireless licences, and tell you you don't know how to drive your car just because you misunderstand their silly signals. Anyway, I don't want to talk about Michael Strange any more.' She gave a little shiver. 'I say, don't you think it's beastly cold?'

'It is chilly,' he agreed. 'Wind's in the north. Like me to shut the window?'

'You might push it to just a bit. It'll get airless if we have it completely shut. I've half a mind to put a match to the fire. Look and see if there's any coal in the scuttle.'

He lifted the lid. 'Empty. We can soon get some though, if you really want a fire. Seems ridiculous in July, I must say.'

'Nothing's ridiculous with the English climate. Honestly, wouldn't you rather like a fire?'

'I don't mind one way or the other. If you're cold, have one.' He reached out a hand to the bell-pull, and tugged it.

'It's broken,' Margaret informed him. 'Celia didn't think it was worth while having it mended. If you take the scuttle out to the kitchen Bowers'll fill it, and bring it back.'

'All right,' he said obligingly. 'Though you're a pest, you know.' He dragged himself out of his chair and picked up the scuttle. 'This is where an electric heater would come in handy.'

'Oh no, think how cheery it'll be to see a blaze!' Margaret encouraged him.

He went out, and she picked up the matches and knelt down before the wide grate. A fire had already been laid, and enough coal to start it had been arranged on top of the wood. Margaret lit the edges of the newspaper, and had the satisfaction of hearing, in a few seconds, a promising crackle. The wood was dry, and caught easily, and Margaret, seeing that no frenzied fanning was going to be necessary, got up from her knees. She put out her hand to help herself up by one of the projecting bits of the moulding that ran round the fireplace, and to her surprise the carved wooden apple that her fingers had grasped twisted right round. She stared at it, and then quickly looked round the room, remembering the rosette that had moved to slide back the panel of the priest's hole.

Beside the fireplace a dark cavity yawned in the panelling.

She scrambled up, and forgetting that Peter had gone through the door that led to the servants' quarters, called to him. 'Peter, come here quickly!'

Then she remembered that he could not hear her, and she stood for a minute, looking at the gap in the panels. Not for worlds, she thought, would she venture inside until Peter came back, but sheer curiosity impelled her to tiptoe towards it, and try to peep in.

It was so dark that she could only see that it seemed to be a narrow stone stairway, leading up in the thickness of the wall. The central lamp threw its light so that it only illumined the step immediately in a line with the opening, and the stone wall beyond. Margaret could not see more than the dim outline of another step leading downwards. She was half afraid that some horrible skeleton might be inside, but she could not perceive anything of that nature. Holding with one hand to the edge of the panel, she ventured to step just inside, in the hope of being able to see where the stairs led. Leaning her other hand against the wall she craned forward trying to pierce the darkness below her. She moved her right hand from the wall to feel ahead of her, wondering whether she was really standing on a staircase, or whether it was only another priest's hole. Her hand did not, as she had half expected, encounter another wall, but to her annoyance a gold bangle that she wore and whose clasp she had been meaning to have strengthened, came undone, and fell with a tinkle on to the second step, which she could just perceive. Involuntarily she stooped to pick it up, but to reach it she had to let go of the panel she still held, and take one step down on to the second stair. Her fingers had closed on the bangle and she was about to step back on to the level of the library floor when she was startled to see the shaft of light cast by the lamp in the room disappearing. She turned like a flash, and saw to her horror that the panel was sliding noiselessly back into place.

She flung herself forward, but she was too late. The panel had closed, and she was in utter darkness.

In the terror of finding herself a prisoner she lost her head, and shrieked for her brother, beating wildly on the back of the panel, trying to tear it open. She only succeeded in breaking a finger-nail, and her panic grew. She screamed, 'Help! help! Peter, Peter, Peter!'

Somewhere below her she heard a soft, padding step,

and the hush of a robe brushing against the wall. Like a mad woman she clawed at the panel. 'Quick! oh quick! Peter, *help*!'

Then in the darkness a gloved hand stole across her mouth, and an arm in a wide sleeve was round her, holding her in a vice.

She tried to break free, to jerk her head away, but her arms were clamped to her sides and that horrible, gloved hand was like a gag over her mouth.

She felt herself slipping into unconsciousness, and through the sudden roaring in her ears she heard as though from a great distance Peter's voice calling: 'Margaret, what is it? Where are you?'

A low, inhuman chuckle sounded immediately above her head, and there was something so gloating and fiendish in that soft sound that terror such as she had never known seized her. Then the waves met over her head and she fainted.

Fifteen

As he came into the hall from the servants' wing Peter heard Margaret's scream. It sounded muffled, but he heard her shriek his name, and crossed the hall in three bounds.

'Margaret, what is it?' he cried. 'Where are you? Margaret! Margaret!'

The room was empty, and no answering call came to him. He stared round, then sprang instinctively to the window, only to find that the falling bolt was as he had left it, just holding the double windows together. She could not have gone that way, and hardly knowing what he did he tore the curtains apart and dragged the big leather screen aside. But she was not in the room. Yet a moment before he had heard her voice coming from this direction: she could not have gone far!

'Think! think!' drummed his brain. 'Don't lose your head! Think!'

He came back into the middle of the room, and as he once more glared round for some clue to her whereabouts his eye caught sight of a crumpled handkerchief lying near the wall beside the fireplace. Quickly he crossed to where it lay, and picked it up. It was one of the flimsy scraps of crêpe-de-chine she always used; he had returned it to her twice already this evening, for she invariably dropped it about.

His thoughts raced. She had been sitting on the other side of the fireplace all the evening; if she had dropped her handkerchief here she must for some reason or other have moved to this spot after he had left the room. What could have taken her there? His eyes ran swiftly over that side of the room. Not a book, for the shelves were on the opposite wall; nor the coal-scuttle, for he had taken that away. She must have stepped close up to the wall, too, for the handkerchief had been touching the wainscoting. Light began to break on Peter. She hadn't gone out by the window; she hadn't gone by the door, since when she screamed he had just come back into the hall, and must have seen her had she left the room by that exit. There remained only one solution: somewhere in the room was a secret entrance that they had none of them discovered.

He at once inspected the panelling, and went to the place where the handkerchief had lain, and sounded the panels all along that side of the fireplace. It was hard at first to detect a difference, but by dint of repeated banging on two panels he was almost sure that one had a different, and more hollow note. It was probably padded on the inside to disguise it, he guessed, and he began to feel all round the beading for any catch there might be. Some echo of Margaret's frantic cry still seemed to sound in his ears, and his hands moved with feverish haste over the woodwork. She must have accidentally discovered the moving panel, and then – what had happened? A rather sickening fear stole into him; his fingers tore fruitlessly at the beading; he even set his shoulder to the panel in a vain attempt to break it down. His reason checked him once more. It was no use getting desperate: he must think, and think quickly. How had she discovered the panel? Not by design, that much was certain. By accident it must have been, and what could she have been doing that led her to put her hand on the spring that worked it?

His gaze, searching the room, fell on the fire, which was now burning brightly. Of course! She had been lighting the fire! What a fool he was not to have remembered that earlier! He strode up to the grate, and as he bent to scrutinise it there flashed into his mind the recollection of the rosette that had moved to slide back the panel into the priest's hole at the top of the stairs. If another such hole existed it was almost certain that it was worked by the same sort of device.

He fell on his knees, wrenching and twisting at the carved surround of the grate. It was a garland in a design of apples and pomegranates and leaves. Inch by inch he went over it, his heart sinking as leaf after leaf, fruit after fruit remained immovable under his probing fingers. Then, when only one more cluster remained untested he found the wooden apple that turned, and almost let out a yell of triumph as it slid in his hold.

His eyes were fixed on the panel he suspected, and even as he turned the apple, he saw it glide back to reveal the same dark cavity that had startled Margaret.

He sprang to his feet. His only thought was to get to his sister; even had it entered his head in that moment of anxiety he would not have paused to fetch his revolver, upstairs, locked in a drawer of his dressing-table. Without stopping to consider he was through the aperture, and standing on the first step. 'Margaret!' he shouted. 'Margaret, Margaret! Where are you?'

There was a faint movement behind him, he started round, but just a second too late. Something struck him a stunning blow on the head, and he fell without a sound, sprawling down the narrow stairs. A moment later a cowled figure moved across the aperture, and then once more the panel slid back into place, and the library was empty and silent.

Five minutes afterwards Bowers came into the room with the coal-scuttle. He looked round, rather surprised to see no one, but concluded that Peter and Margaret had either strolled out into the moonlight, or were in some other room. He made up the fire, and then went over to draw the curtains. He wondered why they had been pulled aside, for he distinctly remembered drawing them while his young master and mistress were still in the dining-room. As he pulled them together he noticed the position of the double French windows, which though open, had been set so that the falling-bolt just held them together, and prevented them swinging wide into the room. If Peter and Margaret had gone out, it was not by that way. He supposed they must have gone by the front door, perhaps meaning to stroll down the avenue to meet the rest of their party who would soon be returning from their dinner engagement. Funny tastes people had, Bowers reflected. As for him he'd do anything sooner than walk down that avenue after dark.

He began to tidy the room, shaking up cushions, and emptying the ash trays. The screen seemed to be out of place; he adjusted it carefully, and straightened the position of one of the chairs. Glancing at the clock he saw that it was already after ten, and time for him to bring in the usual tray of glasses, whisky decanter, soda-siphon and lemonade. With a final look round the room he went away to the pantry to prepare the tray. By the time he had collected the decanter from the dining-room, and returned to the library, ten minutes had gone by. Since there was still no sign of Peter or Margaret it seemed certain that they must have gone out. In which case, Bowers thought, remembering his friend Flinders' warning, it was very unwise of them to have left the window open. He moved across to it, and not only shut it, but bolted it as well. Then he went back again to the kitchen, where Mrs Bowers was folding up her crochet-work preparatory to going to bed.

'Locked everything up, Bowers?' inquired that martial woman.

'All but the front door,' he replied. 'Lot of use it was me having to go down those cellar stairs for a scuttle-full of coal! They've gone out.'

'Gone out?' Mrs Bowers echoed. 'At this time of night?'

'Must have. Neither of them was in the library when I went in with the scuttle, nor when I took the tray in.'

'Well, that's not like Miss Margaret to want a fire one moment and then go trapesing out in the garden the next,' remarked Mrs Bowers. 'They're probably in the study.'

'What would they go and sit there for, when they've lit a fire in the library?' Bowers demanded.

'Don't ask *me*!' his wife abjured him. 'But if that's what they are doing all I can say is Miss Margaret'll catch her death, and start one of her coughs, for it's the coldest room in the house. I think I'll go along and see what she is up to.' She got out of her chair, not without effort, for she was a lady of ample proportions, and sailed away to scold Margaret for her imprudence.

But the study was in darkness, and Mrs Bowers' opening gambit of 'Now, Miss Margaret, you know you didn't ought to sit in this cold room,' was cut off short. Mrs Bowers went across to the library; that was empty too, and so were both the drawing and dining-rooms.

Bowers had followed his wife into the front part of the house by this time, and he again repeated his own conviction that they had strolled out.

'What, after Mr Peter saying Miss Margaret was feeling shivery, and would like a fire? Stuff and nonsense!'

'Well, if they haven't gone out, where are they?' Bowers asked reasonably. 'Perhaps Mr Peter thought a walk would warm his sister up.'

'If he thought anything so silly he'll have a few straight words with me when he comes in, grown up or not!' declared Mrs Bowers with a look in her eye that all the Fortescues had been familiar with since babyhood. 'Bowers, my man, just you pop up and knock on their bedroom doors to make sure they're not there.'

'Well, they aren't, because they haven't taken their candles,' said Bowers, pointing to the array on the hall table.

'Never you mind whether they've taken candles or not, you go up and see,' commanded his wife.

Sighing, Bowers obeyed, but he soon reappeared with the intelligence that it was just as he had said: no one was upstairs. 'I tell you what,' he said. 'They've gone to meet the others, and they wanted the fire lit for when they come in.'

'It does look like it,' Mrs Bowers admitted. 'And if that's what they have done, I'm not going up myself till they're in. I know Miss Margaret, none better! Never was there a child like her for catching colds, and the first thing she'll do when she gets in is to pop right into bed with a hot bottle, or my name's not Emma Bowers.' With that she proceeded majestically back to the kitchen, and resumed her seat by the fire. She picked up her crochet again, but her eyes kept lifting to the clock on the mantelpiece, and when the hands pointed to eleven, she could no longer contain herself. 'I'll give Mr Peter a piece of my mind when he comes in!' she said wrathfully. 'When did you take that scuttle to the library, Bowers?'

'I dunno. Bit after ten, I think,' Bowers answered, deep in the racing columns of a newspaper.

'Then they've been out a full hour! I never did in all my life! Hark, was that the front door? For the love of goodness, stop reading that nasty trash!'

Bowers put the paper down meekly, and listened. Voices sounded in the hall. 'That's the master I can hear,' he said.

Mrs Bowers once more arose and sallied forth. In the hall Mrs Bosanquet was unwinding the inevitable tulle from her head. As Mrs Bowers came into the hall Charles said: 'Ten o'clock would have been a godly hour at which to have taken our leave. I shall never forgive you, Aunt Lilian. Never.'

'I'm sorry if you were anxious to go, my dear,' was the placid reply, 'but I was in the middle of a very interesting discussion with the Vicar. I found him most enlightened:

not in the least hide-bound, as I had feared might be the case.'

Celia saw Mrs Bowers. 'Hullo, still up, Emma?' she said.

'Miss Celia, where's Miss Margaret and Mr Peter? Didn't you meet them?'

'Meet them? No, did they set out to look for us?'

'That's what we don't know, madam. Bowers thought so, but I said all along they wouldn't do a thing like that on a night as cold as this is. All I do know is, they aren't in the house.'

'What's that?' Charles stopped arguing with Mrs Bosanquet, and stepped to his wife's side. 'When did they go out?'

'It must have been about ten o'clock, sir, from what Bowers tells me.'

'But how funny!' said Celia. 'What in the world can have possessed them? Do you suppose they got bored, and went to look up the Colonel?'

'Well, Miss Celia, they may have done so, but all I can say is it's not like Miss Margaret to go ordering a fire to be lit if she means to go out the moment it's done.'

'A fire? Did she order a fire?' Charles asked.

'Yes, sir, she did. Mr Peter came out to the kitchen with the library scuttle, which was empty.' She looked over her shoulder at Bowers. 'Round about ten o'clock that would have been, wouldn't it, Bowers?'

'Just about then, or maybe a minute or two after,' Bowers agreed.

'But you say they went out at ten,' frowned Charles.

'So they must have, sir,' Bowers replied. 'Because it didn't take me more than five minutes to fill the scuttle, and when I took it back to the library, which I did straight away, there wasn't a sign of either of them. I didn't set much store by it, but when I came back with the tray ten minutes after that, and they still weren't there, I did think it was a bit funny, and I mentioned it to Mrs Bowers, just in a casual way.'

'Perhaps Margaret has induced her brother to walk up to the ruin by moonlight,' suggested Mrs Bosanquet, who had caught perhaps half of what had been said. 'It is a very clear night, but I must say I think it was imprudent of the dear child to go out with the wind in the north as it is.'

'My dear Aunt Lilian, they wouldn't spend an hour at the chapel!' Charles said.

'An hour! No, certainly not. But have they been gone for so long as that?'

Celia was looking at her husband. 'Charles, you're worried?'

'I am bit,' he confessed. 'I can't see why they should want to go out like that. No one came to the house during the evening, I suppose?'

'No, sir, no one to my knowledge. That is, no one rang the front-door bell, nor yet the back either.'

'They *must* have gone to the Colonel's!' Celia said.

'Then what did they want a fire for, Miss Celia?' struck in Mrs Bowers.

'Perhaps they thought it was such a sudden change in the weather that we might be cold after our drive,' Celia suggested.

'No, madam, they never thought that, for as I was just saying to Bowers, Mr Peter brought that scuttle out, and said Miss Margaret was feeling shivery, and was going to light the fire. Which she must have done – unless you did, Bowers?'

'No, I never lit it,' Bowers answered. 'It was burning up fine when I brought the scuttle in.'

Charles strode over to the library, and went in. 'Windows been shut all the evening?' he asked.

'No, sir. When I came in I found them just held together. I'll show you, sir.' He drew back the bolts, and placed the windows as Peter had left them. 'Like that, sir.'

'I see. With the bolt holding them together?'

'Yes, sir. I particularly noticed that, because I saw by it that they couldn't have gone out on to the terrace.'

'You didn't notice anything else out of the ordinary? Nothing was disturbed?'

'Well, sir, things were a bit untidy, but only in a natural way, if you understand me. Ash trays full, and the paper on the floor, and the cushions a bit squashed. Nothing else, sir.'

Celia laid her hand on Charles' arm. 'Charles, you don't think anything can have happened to them, do you?' she asked anxiously.

'I hope not, but I don't quite like the sound of it. Can you think of any reason for them wanting to go out at ten o'clock?'

'No, I can't. Unless Aunt Lilian's solution is the right one. After all, we never did go up to the chapel by moonlight, and Margaret more than once said she'd like to.'

'I'd better go up and take a look,' Charles decided. 'You others might search the house – though why they should conceal themselves I can't imagine.'

'Charles, take your revolver!' Celia called after him, as he left the room.

'I'm going to,' he said over his shoulder.

It was quite a little walk to the chapel from the house, and he did not come back for nearly twenty minutes. They had heard his voice occasionally, shouting the names of the missing couple, but no answering call had come to their ears. Both Celia and Mrs Bosanquet were feeling very anxious by the time he returned, and when he shook his head in answer to their eager inquiries they began to look rather scared.

'But it is quite ridiculous!' Mrs Bosanquet said. 'They must be somewhere!'

'Undoubtedly,' said Charles. 'But where? You've been all over the house?'

'Yes, there's no sign of them,' Celia replied. 'You – don't think they can have gone up to the ruin, and – and found the Monk, and he – did something to them?'

'I should hope it would take more than that dratted Monk to tackle the pair of them!' snorted Mrs Bowers.

But the idea was taking hold of Celia. 'Supposing he had a gun?'

'If Peter had any sense he wouldn't take Margaret up to the chapel at night without his revolver,' Charles said. 'I'll go and look in his room, and see if it's in his dressing-table. That's where he keeps it.' He went out, but this time he was soon back again, and in his hand he carried Peter's revolver. Looking distinctly grim he laid it down on the table.

Celia's fingers gripped the arms of the chair she had sunk into. 'Then they were unarmed! Charles, it's the

Monk! I know it's the Monk! Oh, fool, *fool* that I was to suggest they should stay here alone this evening.'

'Steady!' Charles said. 'Don't leap to conclusions, Celia. For all we know they had a perfectly good reason for going out, and they'll walk in any moment. They may even have walked down the road to meet us, as Bowers suggested, and we missed them.'

'How could we miss them?'

'Easily. We were all talking, and I for one never scrutinise pedestrians.'

'But they'd have stopped us!' Celia pointed out.

'Not necessarily. You must remember that our headlights were on, and the glare would prevent them recognising the car till it was abreast of them. And I was driving pretty fast, too. They may have called to us, and failed to make us hear.'

Celia looked at the time. 'But, darling, it's a quarter to twelve, and we've been in three-quarters of an hour! They must have got back by now. Why, if they set out at ten they've had time to get as far as the Vicarage and back again by now!'

'No, not quite,' Charles said. 'Not that I see either of them walking all that distance just to meet us. I'll tell you what: I think I'd better get the car out of the garage again, and run back as far as the Vicarage, just in case they were cracked enough to walk as far as that, and have met with some accident. Sprained ankle, or something of that sort. Then if I don't find them I'll go in to Ackerley's place, and ring up the police-station from there, and bring Ackerley himself along to help me search.' He picked up Peter's revolver. 'Bowers, you know how to handle this, don't you?'

'Yes, sir,' Bowers answered, taking it.

'I want you to stay in this room with Mrs Malcolm and Mrs Bosanquet, and on no account to leave them. Quite understand?'

'Don't you worry, sir!' Mrs Bowers said, picking up the poker. 'I just wish that Monk *would* come in, that's all! I'd Monk him!'

Celia nodded bravely. 'Yes, that will be best. Don't waste any time, Charles: we shall be all right. There's nothing we can do while you're gone, is there? It's so awful to have to sit here so helplessly.'

Charles was buttoning up his overcoat again. 'I'd rather you stayed all together in this room,' he said. 'I daresay there's no reason for me to be alarmed about you, but I'm not taking any more risks. I'll be back as soon as I possibly can.' He bent and kissed Celia's pale lips. 'Keep your pecker up, old lady. I shall probably meet them in the avenue.' He hurried away as he spoke, and the next instant they heard the front door bang behind him.

Charles went quickly round to the garage, and got the car out. He laid his revolver on the seat beside him, and after backing and turning the car, drove off down the avenue to the gates.

The Vicarage lay on the other side of the village, and Charles drove through the narrow, deserted street at a pace that made a solitary pedestrian leap out of harm's way. There was no sign of Peter and Margaret anywhere along the road, and since they had pleaded a previous engagement as their excuse for not joining the dinner-party that evening, they would certainly not have gone into the Vicarage. Moreover the house was in darkness, and seeing this, Charles turned the car, and started to drive back the way he had come.

In the village street he overtook a bicyclist, and his powerful headlights showed this late plodder to be Constable Flinders. Charles drew up beside him. 'I've got your case for you, Flinders,' he said. 'Can you leave that bicycle, and come up to the Priory?'

Mr Flinders stared at him. 'Lor', sir, what's happened?'

'Mr and Miss Fortescue have disappeared, and I'd like you to go up and stand guard over my wife and aunt. Leave – no, shove it on the back seat. Can you?'

'Me bike, sir? It'll dirty your cushions, won't it?' the constable said dubiously.

'What the hell does that matter? Lift it in.'

'Well, if you say so, sir, I will,' the constable said, and hoisted his bicycle into the back of the car. He then got in beside Charles, and instinctively grasped the seat with both hands as the car shot forward. 'Sir,' he said solemnly, 'if I was on dooty and saw you driving like this I should have to run you in. I should really, sir.'

'No doubt, but I happen to be in a hurry. Now look here, this is what has happened.' Briefly he told Flinders of his brother's and sister-in-law's unaccountable disappearance.

The constable listened in open-mouthed astonishment, and at the end of it collected his wits sufficiently to say: 'Well, one thing I can tell you, sir. It ain't Mr Titmarsh, for he's not been out of his house the whole evening.'

'I didn't suppose it was,' said Charles impatiently.

'No, sir,' said the constable, rather hurt, 'but it

narrows it down, so to speak, don't it, when we know for certain it wasn't him?'

'When we get to the Priory,' Charles said, paying no heed to this, 'I'll put you down, and you can cycle up to the house and wait for me there. I'm going on to Colonel Ackerley's house to telephone to Manfield, and I hope to bring the Colonel back with me to help search the grounds.'

'Do I understand you to mean, sir, that you mean to call in them chaps at the police-station?'

'You do.'

The constable coughed. 'In a manner of speaking, sir, that should have been left for me to do, if I see fit.'

'I'm afraid you'll have to overlook the irregularity for once,' Charles replied, pulling up at the Priory gates.

The constable got out, and extricated his bicycle from the back of the car. 'Very irregular, sir, that's what it is,' he said. 'I don't hardly know what to say about it.'

'Think it out on your way up to the house,' Charles advised him, and drove on while this retort was slowly filtering through to the constable's brain.

No light shone from any window in the White House, but since it was now some time past midnight Charles had hardly expected the Colonel to be still up. He drove to the front door, switched off his engine, and got out, thrusting his unwieldy gun into the deep pocket of his overcoat. He found the electric bell, and pressed it. He heard it ring somewhere inside the house, and kept his finger on it for some time.

Nothing happened. Charles rang again, and beat a loud tattoo on the door with the rather ornate knocker. There was still no answer. The Colonel must be a heavy sleeper, Charles thought, and remembered that Ackerley's butler and cook slept over the garage, a few yards from the house. He stepped back into the drive, and scanned the upper windows, wondering which was the Colonel's room. Setting his hands to form a funnel round his mouth he shouted: 'Colonel! Colonel Ackerley!'

No answer came from the house, but a light showed above the garage, and presently a window was thrown up there, and a voice called: 'Who is it? What do you want?'

Charles walked along till he stood under this window. The Colonel's butler was leaning out. 'I want to use the Colonel's telephone,' Charles said. 'It's very urgent. Is he in?'

'I'm sure I don't know, sir,' the butler answered rather sulkily. 'Who *are* you?'

'Charles Malcolm, from the Priory. I can't make the Colonel hear at the house. Think you could come down and let me in?'

The butler's voice changed. 'Mr Malcolm! I beg your pardon, sir: I didn't recognise you. Yes, sir, I'll be down in just a moment if you wouldn't mind waiting.'

He drew in his head, and Charles paced up and down in front of the house in a fret of impatience. Presently the butler came down, having pulled on a pair of trousers and a coat. 'Sorry to keep you, sir. You wish to use the telephone? I hope nothing serious, sir?'

'It is rather. Is the Colonel out, or just a heavy sleeper?'

'I expect he's out, sir. He very often goes out after dinner. I believe he plays bridge at the County Club at Manfield, sir.'

'Very late to be still at the club, surely?'

'The Colonel never goes to bed much before midnight, sir. And, of course, I don't know when he comes in, as I don't sleep in the house.' He inserted a key into the Yale lock of the front door, and turned it. 'If you'll excuse me, sir, I'll go first and switch on the light. The telephone is in the study, sir. This way, please.'

He ushered Charles into the Colonel's sanctum, and discreetly left him there, shutting the door as he went out.

It did not take Charles long to get connected with the police-station and he was lucky enough to find someone intelligent on duty. This officer said that he would get on to the inspector at once, and he promised that a couple of men should be sent off to the Priory as soon as the inspector was informed of what had occurred.

Charles hung up the receiver, and was just about to leave the room when an idea struck him, and he lifted the receiver off its hook again. When the exchange spoke he gave the number of the Bell Inn, and waited.

After a considerable pause, he heard Spindle's unmistakable voice. ''Ullo! Bell Inn. 'Oo is it?'

'Malcolm speaking, from the Priory. Would you please ask Mr Strange to come to the telephone?'

''Old on, please,' said the voice.

Another, and longer pause, followed. Then Spindle spoke again. ''Ullo, are you there? Mr Strange is not in his room, sir. Can I take a message?'

'Are you sure he's not in the lounge?' Charles asked.

'No, sir, I've bin to see. Mr Strange is out.'

'Where's he gone?'

'I couldn't say, sir. 'E 'as 'is own key, you see, because 'e told Mr Wilkes 'e'd got friends in Manfield, and 'e'd be visiting them a good deal, and staying late. Lots of gentlemen prefers to 'ave a key, because I go off duty at one o'clock, sir, you see.'

'I see,' Charles said. 'No, there's no message, thanks. Sorry to have bothered you. Good-bye.' He hung up the receiver again, and went out into the hall, where the butler was waiting.

'That's all,' Charles said. 'Will you explain to the Colonel that I had to telephone very urgently? I'm sure he'll understand. And thanks very much for coming down to let me in.'

'Thank *you*, sir,' the butler said, pocketing the douceur. 'The Colonel will be sorry he wasn't in, I know.' He accompanied Charles out into the drive again, and watched him get into the car. Charles bade him good night, and set off again for home.

He did not put the car in the garage this time, but left it standing outside the front door. In the library Constable Flinders was trying to avoid Mrs Bowers' indignant glare, and at the same time to prove himself master of the situation.

Celia looked up anxiously. 'No luck?'

'None. I got on to Manfield, and they're sending over at once. Then I rang up the Bell Inn, and asked to speak to Strange.' He took off his overcoat, and Celia saw that his good-humoured countenance was looking decidedly grim. 'And Strange,' he said, 'is not there.'

Sixteen

Someone was calling him. Peter could hear his name being spoken, but the voice was very far away. He became aware of a dull ache in his head, and opened his eyes with a groan. The voice sounded nearer; he identified it gradually as his sister's, and as the mist cleared from before his eyes he saw her face above him. Puzzled, he stared up at her. She was stroking his cheek. 'Darling, you're better now, aren't you? Peter, speak to me, please speak to me!'

He blinked; his head was splitting, he thought. He said thickly: 'Hullo . . . Margaret! What – what's happened?'

She appeared to be crying. 'Oh, thank God!' she said. 'I thought you were dead. Oh, my dear, how did he get you?'

He moved his head, staring round him. He was lying on a bare stone floor, in a queer cell-like room which he never remembered to have seen before. His brain felt clogged, but bit by bit his memory was returning. He struggled up on his elbow, grasping Margaret's wrist. 'You called me!' he said. 'I couldn't find you. Then I . . .' He broke off, as the whole scene came rushing back to him. 'My God, where are we?' he said. 'What happened to you?' He put his hand to his head feeling it tenderly. 'Lord, my head! Something must have knocked me out. How did I get here? How did you get here?'

She helped him to his feet. He was still feeling sick and dizzy, and was glad to sink down on to a chair by the plain deal table, and to rest his head in his hands. Margaret knelt beside him. 'It was the Monk,' she said.

'I heard you call,' he said. 'Couldn't find you. Then I saw your handkerchief.'

'Where?' she asked.

'By the panel. Made me think. Realised there must be a way we hadn't found. Got on to the moulding. An apple. Did you twist it?'

'Yes, yes. By the fireplace. And then?'

'Saw the panel move. So anxious about you, like a fool never stopped to think. Dashed in. Shouted to you. Then . . .' He stopped, frowning. 'Yes, I heard something behind me. I think I turned round. I don't remember anything else. What happened to you? How did you get here? Who brought me here?'

She glanced fearfully over her shoulder at the door of their prison. It was shut, but a steel grille at the height of a man's head was let into it. A sort of shutter with round holes cut in it was drawn across the grille on the outside. She turned back to Peter, and slid her hand into his. 'When you'd gone I knelt down and lit the fire. Then I started to get up, and you know how you put out your hand to steady yourself? Well, I did that, and caught on to the apple in the carving. It moved, and I saw the opening in the wall, just as you did. I called you, but you'd gone. I never meant to go in, but there didn't seem to be anything there, and I did just step inside, holding on to the panel all the time. Peter, it was a staircase! Did you realise that?'

'Yes, I remember thinking in a flash how that was what Duval must have meant when he said the Monk went up and down the stairs though we didn't see. Go on: what happened next?'

She shuddered. 'It was so awful . . . my bangle – you know the one – came undone, and fell on to the second step. I didn't stop to think: I never dreamed – anyone was there. I let go the panel and just stepped down one stair to pick it up.' Her fingers clung suddenly to his hand. 'Peter, I saw the light going, and I turned round, and the panel was closing! Peter! I nearly went mad! I couldn't stop it, and that's when I screamed. I tried to tear it open; it was pitch dark, and I couldn't see any catch, or feel anything. I shrieked for you again and again. Then – then I heard something moving.' She was shaking like a leaf. He put his arm round her, clumsily patting her shoulder. 'A sort of padding footstep, coming nearer and nearer. And I couldn't see, couldn't move that awful panel. Then – I felt something creep over my mouth. It felt horrible, horrible! Then I knew it was a hand in a glove. It gripped my face so that I could hardly breathe, and an arm grasped me round above the elbows. I couldn't move, I heard you call out to me from the library, and then – then, there was a fiendish sort of chuckle, quite soft, but so utterly wicked, and cruel, that it just finished me, and I fainted. When I came to I was in this place, quite alone. I didn't know how I got here, or who that hand belonged to – or – or how long I'd been here till the door opened, and I saw the Monk standing there. He didn't speak; he looked at me for a moment through those slits in his cowl, then he turned and bent down and started to drag something in. It was you, Peter, and oh, I thought you were dead, I thought you were dead! He just let you fall on the floor, and went out. I hadn't any water or anything to bring you to. I undid your collar, and when you didn't move, I was so desperate I shrieked for someone to come and at least let me have some water. But no one did and no one answered. Only this awful roaring noise went on.'

He lifted his head. 'Then there is a noise? It's not just in my head?'

'No, it's never stopped all the time I've been here.'

He sat for a few minutes trying to collect his thoughts. 'Poor kid!' he said. 'Ghastly for you. And a fat lot of good I've been to you!'

She laid her cheek against his arm. 'You're here, and that's all I care about. You don't know what it was like to be alone. At least we're together now.'

'If only my head didn't ache so much I might be able to think,' he said. He looked round, and blinked. 'Where the hell are we?' he said. 'Electric light?'

She glanced up at the bulb that had caught his attention. 'So it is. I haven't had time to notice it till now. Then we can't be in the Priory, can we?'

He got up, and began to move round the small room. It was like a square cave cut out of solid stone, all except the door which was made of thick wood. 'No window,' he said. 'We must be underground.' He went to the door, and slipping his hand sideways between two of the bars of the grille, tried to push back the shutter by inserting a finger into one of the ventilation holes. He could not move it, nor could he manage to see anything through the holes.

'If we're underground that accounts for the coldness and the smell of damp,' Margaret said. 'Peter – you don't think – they're going to leave us here – to starve?'

'Of course not,' he said instantly. He stood by the door, listening. 'That noise,' he said. 'That's a machine and an electric one, or I've never heard one!' He stared across at his sister, dawning suspicion in his eyes. He seemed about to speak, then checked himself, and went up to one of the walls, and closely inspected the stone blocks that formed it. 'I believe we're under the cellars,' he said. 'I'm no geologist, but this looks to me exactly the same sort of stone as that one that moved and we sealed up. We are in the Priory!'

'Right under the ground?' she asked. 'Below the cellars even?'

'I'm not sure, but I think we must be. The place feels like a tomb, much more so than the cellars did.' He looked round again. 'Why, what fools we've been not to think of it! Didn't those old monks often have underground passages leading from the monastery to the chapel?'

'Yes, I believe they did,' she said. 'You think that's where we are? But this is a room!'

'Cut, if I'm not much mistaken, in the foundations of the house. I don't know much about monasteries, but I suppose the monks must have had a use for an underground room or so. Storing valuables in times of stress, and all that sort of thing.'

'But the light!' she objected. 'There's no electricity at the Priory.'

'It must be worked by a plant. Good God!'

'What?' she said quickly.

'At the Bell! That big plant I saw there! But it can't possibly . . .' He broke off, utterly bewildered.

'Did you see a plant there? You never told me.'

'I forgot about it. It was one day when Charles and I were there. I got into the engine-room, and I was just thinking what a ridiculously big machine it was for the work it had to do when Spindle hustled me out. Yes, by Jove, and I wondered at the time why he seemed so upset at finding me there. But Wilkes gave a plausible sort of explanation, and I never thought any more about it. Why, good Lord, do you realise that if I'm right, and it's that plant that produces this light, and works the machine we can hear, Wilkes must be in this, up to the eyes?'

'Wilkes?' she repeated incredulously. 'That fat, smiling landlord? He couldn't be!'

'I don't know so much. And that throws a fresh light on it. Strange! He's staying at the Bell. For all we know he and Wilkes are hand in glove over this.'

'Oh, no!' she said. 'It isn't Michael Strange! It can't be! Not after what he said to me! No, no, I won't believe that!'

He did not press the point. He stood still, listening to the throb and the muffled roar of the machine, trying to think what it could be. The noise it made stirred some chord of memory in his brain. Margaret started to speak, and he signed to her to be quiet, with a quick frown and a finger held up.

Suddenly he remembered. Once, a couple of years before, he had been shown over a model printing works. He swung round, and exclaimed beneath his breath: 'Margaret! I believe it's a printing press!'

She waited, searching his face. He seemed to be listening more intently than ever. 'I don't see . . .' she began.

'Forgers!' he said. 'I can't see what else it can possibly be – if it is a press.'

'Forgers?'

'Probably forgers of bank-notes. I don't know.' He came back to the table and sat down on the edge of it. 'Let's get this straight. I believe we've hit on the secret of the Priory. If there's a gang of forgers at work here that would account for the efforts to get us out of the house. Jove, yes, and what a god-sent place for a press! Empty house, reputation for being haunted, only needed a little ghost-business to scare the countryside stiff, *and* to scare the former tenants out! I can't think why we never even suspected it.'

'But Peter, it's fantastic! How could a gang of forgers know of this underground passage, and that sliding-panel?'

'Not the gang, but the man at the head of it. The man who stole the book from the library, and tore the missing pages from the copy at the British Museum. The Monk, in fact.'

'You mean Michael Strange, don't you?'

'I don't know whether I mean him or not, but it's clear that the Monk's no ordinary forger. He's someone who knew something about the Priory, someone who's devilish thorough and devilish clever.'

She caught his hand, pressing it warningly. The bolts were being drawn back from the door of their cell. Peter thrust her behind him, and turned to face the door.

It opened, and the first thing they saw was the blunt

nose of an automatic. A rough voice said: 'Keep back, both of you.'

They obeyed; there was nothing else to do. The door opened farther, and they saw a man standing there in the rough clothes of a country labourer. A handkerchief was tied round the lower half of his face, and a cloth cap was on his head. He had a bottle of water in his left hand, and this he set down on the floor. 'Keep as you are!' he warned them, and took a step backwards, feeling behind him. He pulled a second chair in, and thrust it into the cell. 'You can have that, and the water,' he said. 'And I wouldn't waste my breath shouting for help, if I was you. No one'll hear you, not if you shout till you're black in the face.'

'Where are we?' Peter said, not that he had much hope of getting an answer.

'You're where no one'll ever think to look for you,' the man replied.

Margaret said: 'But you can't keep us here! Oh please, don't go! You couldn't leave us here to starve!'

'It's none of my business,' was the callous answer. 'And there's precious little the Monk stops at, I can tell you. You've interfered with him. *That's* what happens to people as cross the Monk's path.' He drew his thumb across his throat in a crude descriptive gesture.

'Look here,' Peter said, 'I'm a pretty rich man, and if you get us out of this there's a fat reward waiting for you, and no awkward questions asked.'

The man laughed. 'Me? No bloody fear! Know what happened to Dooval? I've got no wish to go the same road, thank you kindly.'

'I'll see nothing happens to you.'

'Oh, you will, will you? Think you could stop the Monk? Well, there ain't a soul that knows him, and if you had a guard of fifty policemen he'd still get you. You wouldn't clear out of the Priory, you kept on nosing round after the Monk. And he's got you, and you talk about escaping! You won't do that, my fine gentleman, don't you fret. Nor no one won't recognise you if ever they finds you, for you'll be no more'n a skeleton. You crossed the Monk's path.' With that he gave another of his brutal laughs, and went out, and shot the bolts home again.

Margaret sat down limply. 'Peter, he can't mean that! No one could be as awful as that!'

'Of course they couldn't, Sis. Keep a stiff upper lip. Even supposing they do mean to clear out and leave us to rot, do you suppose Charles is going to do nothing?'

'But he said – no one would ever think to look for us here. Oh, Peter, why ever didn't we leave the Priory as Celia wanted?'

'Nonsense!' he said bracingly. 'When Charles finds we've disappeared he'll pull the Priory down stone by stone. Listen, Sis! Don't give way! Already Charles knows there's something odd about the place. You don't suppose he and Celia would calmly give us up for lost when they must guess we're somewhere in the house? They'll have Scotland Yard on to it, and the whole countryside will be up. There isn't the slightest doubt that they'll find us.'

She pointed out the water-bottle. 'And we've got that – to last us till they do find us. It might take them weeks. Or perhaps the Monk will do as that man meant, and kill us.'

'If he were going to kill us he'd hardly have bothered to let us have any water, or a second chair,' Peter pointed out. 'Sis, if you let go of yourself, you're not the girl I take you for. We may even find a way out ourselves. My dear kid, people don't get buried alive in the twentieth century!'

She knew that he was talking more to reassure her than from any real conviction, but she pulled herself together. 'Yes. Of course. Sorry. Do you suppose this machine goes on all day, or will they all go away?'

'Go away, I should think. Too risky to work by day. When they've cleared off we can try and force that shutter back. I might be able to reach the top bolt, and that would give us a better chance of breaking the door down. Or I might be able to drive the wood in with the help of one of the chairs. What we've got to do is to keep our spirits up and talk of something else till the gang has gone. Wonder how they ventilate this place?'

She tried to follow his lead. 'Yes, they must have some sort of ventilation, mustn't they? And though it's musty, and sort of close, it isn't airless, is it? How would they do it?'

'Don't quite know. If they've got power enough to work a machine they've probably rigged up some system of fans, same as they have in mines. But there must be an outlet somewhere, and that's what I can't make out.'

They speculated on this for some time in rather a half-hearted fashion. Then Peter produced his cigarette-case, and they lit up, and smoked for a while, trying to think of something cheerful to talk about.

It was not only damp, but also cold, in the stone room, and Margaret had no coat. Peter saw her shiver, and began to take off his coat. 'Sis, why didn't you sing out? You must be frozen in that thin dress. Here, put this on.'

She demurred, but he insisted, and at last she put it on gratefully: Peter looked at his watch. 'Nearly one o'clock. I'd give something to know what old Chas is doing.'

'Celia will be dreadfully worried,' Margaret said. 'I wonder what they thought when they found us gone? Oh, Peter, suppose they were late, and just jumped to the conclusion we'd gone to bed, and didn't bother to look?'

'You're forgetting Bowers,' he reminded her. 'He went to get the coal, and when he got back to the library and found no trace of us, he must have thought it a trifle odd. I'll tell you what, Sis, that fire of yours was a stroke of genius. Because when the others hear how we took the trouble to light it they're bound to smell a rat. They can't think we went to bed, or strolled out for a walk, or anything like that.'

These cheerful surmises occupied them for another half-hour, each one producing fresh reasons why Charles and Celia must guess what had happened. But they could not keep it up for ever, and again silence fell between them, and they sat busy with their much less cheerful thoughts.

Peter was chiefly anxious on the score of time. Though he spoke optimistically to Margaret he was less certain in his own mind that the Monk would not leave them to starve. He could not but remember Duval's fate, and the cold-blooded way in which that murder had been carried out. He did not doubt that before he gave up hope of finding the missing pair Charles really would demolish the Priory, but it might be too late by then. They could hardly hope that Charles too would hit on the panel in the library, for thinking it over, Peter realised that no one could guess that they had been kidnapped there. It would be much more likely that Charles would think they had gone out into the grounds. One thing Peter felt sure about: Charles would connect Michael Strange with this. Therein lay the greatest hope of a swift deliverance, for Strange might be made to talk.

Margaret's thoughts were by no means so reasoned or consecutive; she was still shaken by the terrifying experience she had gone through, and it seemed as though her brain could do nothing but repeat scraps of what Strange had said to her that day at the Inn. He had said it was no use supposing that she would ever look at a man in his 'line of business.' But he had said that from him she stood in no danger. Yes, but had he not added that he was not the only person mixed up in this? He had said too that there was danger, and that he might be powerless to help her. Unless he was the most accomplished and heartless liar he could not, on the face of it, be the Monk. It was possible that he was working under the Monk's orders, and if that were so Margaret felt convinced that the Monk had some unbreakable hold over him. He had told her that he *must* go on with the job he had undertaken. What else could that mean?

Peter's voice broke into her thoughts. 'Margaret, you say the Monk lugged me in here. What did he look like?'

She gave a shiver. 'You've seen pictures of those Inquisition people? Well, like that. He's got a long black robe on, with a cord round the waist, and a cowled hood drawn right down over his head and face. And do you remember what Aunt Lilian said about the black hand that pointed at her? Well, that was true. He wears black gloves, sort of cotton ones, with buttons, only he doesn't do them up. That was the only bit of him you could see for the disguise – his wrists. I particularly noticed, because it was the only thing about him that looked human. There was a button off one glove, too. Isn't it funny what stupid little things one fixes on?'

'A button off,' Peter said. 'Well, I thought as much.'

'Why? What did you think?'

'Nothing. Something the police told us, and we weren't to repeat. Could you see what sort of build he was?'

'No, not very well with that loose robe on. Fairly tall, but not out of the way. A powerful man, because he managed to drag you to this place, and I couldn't see anyone else helping him. And his arm felt like steel when he held me.'

'And he didn't say anything?'

'No. That seemed to make him even more sinister. That, and the dreadful chuckle.'

'Doesn't really help us much,' Peter said. He looked at his watch again. 'Half past two. Look here, Sis, I think you'd better try and get some sleep. You've had a very strenuous time, and you're looking fagged out. And you mustn't forget we shall have a busy time ahead of us when this crowd clears off. Suppose you were to sit on my knee. Think you could snooze a bit with your head on my shoulder?'

She shook her head. 'I couldn't, Peter. And I'm not a light weight, you know. I should wear you out.'

'Oh no, you wouldn't!'

'Really, I'd rather not. I'm not sleepy. Anything but. Let's play some guessing game to keep ourselves occupied. Animal, vegetable, or mineral. You start.'

'All right,' he said. There was a pause. 'I've thought. Go ahead.'

The game seemed dreary beyond relief, but they kept on at it valiantly for nearly an hour. Then Margaret gave it up, and they began to wonder again what Charles and Celia were doing.

It was nearly four o'clock when the noise of the engine suddenly ceased. Margaret instinctively felt for Peter's hand. They sat in silence, listening, and presently they heard a door open and a murmur of voices. They could distinguish no voice they knew, nor could they catch what was said. Footsteps sounded retreating in the distance, and when these had died away they heard a key grate in a lock. Someone had remained behind, and there could be little doubt who that someone was.

Peter gently pulled Margaret to her feet, and led her to the wall alongside the door, so that she should be out of range of a shot fired through the grille. He placed himself as near to the door as he dared, determined to make a fight for it if the Monk came into the room.

But no one came. They heard the padding footstep which Margaret had described, and it died away as the others had done.

After the noise of the machine the silence that now hung over the tomb-like place was so profound that Margaret felt that she knew at last what was meant by 'hearing a silence.' Nothing broke it, and she realised with a feeling of panic how completely buried alive they were. She felt she dared not speak, but presently Peter turned and said; 'Gone. We'd better wait a bit before we get to work.'

She nodded. The palms of her hands felt cold and

sticky. She had an awful fear that the Monk might be still there, listening to them, waiting.

The minutes crept by. Peter whispered: 'I'm going to give him half an hour's grace, just in case he hasn't gone. We've got loads of time. Let's sit down again. But if I say "move" get back to this wall again. See?'

'Yes,' she replied. 'We'd – we'd better go on talking, hadn't we?'

'That's the idea. Let's play *I love my love with an A*, as we used to when we were kids.'

This programme was faithfully carried out, and since neither of them seemed to be able to think of drinks beginning with D, or attributes beginning with Q it took them more than half an hour to struggle through the alphabet. When they had at last come to the end, Peter got up. 'I think it's safe enough now,' he said. 'If he were coming to do us in he wouldn't wait all this time. You sit still. I'm going to try and move that shutter.'

For perhaps twenty minutes he tried by every means he could think of to force it open, but it was of no avail. He banged on the door, to test the thickness of the wood. It sounded very solid, but he could at least try to break through. He picked up one of the chairs, and drove it with all his might against the door until one of its legs broke, and he was forced to pause for a while to get his breath. He sat down on the table, wiping the sweat from his face. 'Well – I'm warm enough now, anyway,' he said, trying to coax a smile into Margaret's wan countenance.

She did smile, but it was a pathetic effort. He patted her hand. 'Cheer up, Sis: we'll get out all right.'

He sat still for a few minutes, trying to think what

other implements he could use against the door. He felt Margaret's hand gripping his arm, and glanced down at her. Her eyes were fixed on the door, and she was white as death. He looked quickly in the same direction, and saw what had attracted her attention. Inch by inch the shutter was sliding back.

'Move!' Peter said under his breath, but it seemed as though she either did not hear him, or dared not stir. He slipped in front of her, shielding her; there was no time to force her over to the wall.

The panel slid still farther; they saw a cowled face behind the grille, and through the slits in the cowl eyes glittered as the light caught them.

Peter stood perfectly still, and his mouth felt unpleasantly dry all at once.

The sinister face disappeared; there was a sound of bolts being drawn, and the door was opened. On the threshold stood the Monk, an automatic in his right hand. He put up his other hand, and pulled the cowl back from his head.

A bitter cry broke from Margaret. 'My God! *You*!' she gasped.

For the Monk was none other than Michael Strange.

Seventeen

For an instant they all three stared at one another. Then Strange said in a voice of blank surprise: 'How the devil did you get here?' His eyes travelled to Margaret's tense face, and he took a quick step towards her. 'Please don't look like that! It's all right, Miss Fortescue.'

Peter decided that he could not have recovered from the blow on his head so completely as he had thought. 'How did we get here?' he repeated. 'That won't quite do, Master Monk! I don't know what your little game is, but . . .'

Strange said impatiently: 'I'm not the Monk. Oh, I know I'm togged up in the same disguise, but you can't really think I'm he!'

Margaret leaned forward eagerly. 'You're not? Oh, I said you couldn't be!'

His eyes softened. 'You believe me, Miss Fortescue? Without proof? In spite of appearances?'

She nodded. 'If you tell me so,' she said quite simply.

It seemed as though he was going to take her hand, but he did not. He said only: 'Thank you.' Then he turned to Peter. 'I told you you'd get yourself into a mess if you didn't stop poking your nose into my affairs,' he remarked cheerfully. 'I'm not the Monk, and my name isn't Strange. I'm Inspector Draycott, of the C.I.D.' He thrust his hand into the front of his robe. 'I've got a card somewhere, in case you still don't believe me.'

'Draycott!' Peter said. 'You don't mean you're the man who handled that big case against Williams last year?'

'I did, yes. Who told you? Malcolm? I was always afraid he might spot me.'

'I don't think he ever saw you till we came down here,' Peter said, feeling rather limp. 'Then are you after the Monk?'

'Of course. I've been after him for months.'

'And you've known about this place all the time?'

'I've suspected it, but I only found the way in to-night. Look here, I think we'd better reserve my story till we're out of this, don't you? Miss Fortescue must be worn out. How did you get here?'

'Through the panel in the library!' Margaret said. 'I found it by accident.'

'Then there is an entrance from the Priory!' Michael exclaimed. 'But you didn't come down here just for fun, did you?'

'No, no!' Margaret said, and quickly told him all that had happened to them.

He listened frowningly. His comment, which made Margaret laugh, was: 'Damn. From my point of view this is the worst thing that could possibly have happened.'

He saw her eyes dancing, and smiled ruefully. 'Yes, I know, but don't you see that when the Monk finds you're gone to-morrow night he'll know this place is discovered, and clear out. And the devil's in it that I don't know where his get-away is.' He shrugged. 'Well, I shall have to find it during the next twelve hours, that's all. The first thing to do is to get you out of here.'

'By the way, where are we?' Peter asked.

'You're under the Priory.'

'I thought as much! But did you get in by the panel in the library?'

'No, I never knew of that. I got in through the cellars of the Bell Inn. The passage leads right under your grounds. I suppose neither of you have the faintest idea how you came here, after the Monk caught you?' They shook their heads. 'Then we shall just have to search till we find the way. I can take you back to the Bell easily enough, but it'll mean walking home from there, as I daren't get my car out of the garage for fear of rousing Wilkes or Spindle. And I should say you've had about enough for one night.'

'No, we haven't, have we, Peter?' Margaret said. 'I agree that we ought to find the way back to the library, but we're quite game to do what you want us to. You didn't come down here just to look for us, did you?'

'I didn't. I came to reconnoitre, and to find where the press is.'

'Then before we try and find the way out let's get on with the reconnoitring,' Margaret said briskly. 'I don't feel done-up at all now.'

Michael looked at her uncertainly, but Peter clinched the matter. 'I'm damned if I'll go meekly home at this stage!' he said. 'I was right then? It is a printing press?'

'Yes, it's a press all right. I want to locate it first, and make sure how many ways there are of getting into it. I've found one, I think.' He led the way out of the square cell, and they found themselves in a low, vaulted passage in which Peter could not stand fully upright.

Turning to the right Michael stopped in front of a stout door similar to the one they had come through, except that it boasted a lock. He tried it, but it did not open. 'I think I'll go and get Jimmy Fripp,' he said. 'He's much cleverer at opening doors than I am, and we shall waste less time in the long run. You'd better come along too, just in case of accidents. Mind your heads.' He went before them up the passage, his torch showing them the way. Once a rat scuttered off almost under their feet, but Margaret had gone through too much to be discomposed by a mere rodent.

As they proceeded down the passage the air became noticeably fresher, and the reason for this was soon made apparent, for they saw a square opening in the side of the passage. No light could be seen through it, but it was obviously a window. Peter stopped Michael to point to it. 'Ventilation? But aren't we underground?'

'Yes, and that was one of my main difficulties – to find how this place, if it really did exist – was ventilated. Not very easy with all you suspicious people on the watch. Remember that night you saw me, Marg – Miss Fortescue?'

'Margaret will do,' she said. 'Yes. Were you looking for it then?'

'I was, but I didn't find it till later. Have you ever looked down the well in that bit of the garden that looks as though it were once a sort of pleasaunce?'

'The well? Oh, I know! No, I hate looking down wells.

I don't think any of us found it for quite a long time, did we, Peter?'

'I don't think we did. But I'm afraid I never even thought about it.'

'You might easily fail to see it unless you happened to stumble on it as I did,' Michael said. 'The weeds have grown up all round it, and it only sticks up a couple of feet out of the ground. That's it.' He pointed to the opening. 'Cut right down in the side of the well. Clever, isn't it? Come along; we'll get hold of Jimmy before we start talking.'

'Fripp?' Peter said, following at his heels down the passage. 'Do you know Charles and I once heard you holding a most suspicious conversation with that fellow?'

'Did you? Yes, it's his one fault, and I can't break him of it. He will talk where he can be overheard.'

'Charles set an inquiry agent on to him. Look here, is he an ex-burglar or not?'

'Yes, he's an old lag,' Michael answered. 'He was my batman during the war, and I took a fancy to him, and kept him on as my servant when we were both demobilised. He's a useful sort of chap on a job like this. Pick any lock under the sun.'

Margaret chuckled. 'Aren't you afraid to leave anything about?'

'Not a bit. He's one of the very few who do really turn over new leaves. Sorry he upset you. How much did your inquiry agent get hold of?'

'Precious little. But if he's your servant how does he find the time to travel for Suck-All Cleaners?'

'He doesn't. That's a put-up job. The head of the firm

is a pal of mine, and he employed Jimmy to oblige me. It's answered fairly well on the whole, though Marson – that's the head of Suck-All Cleaners – was very dubious. Said Jimmy wasn't the right type at all.'

'I don't know about that,' Peter said. 'He very nearly sold a cleaner to my elder sister.'

Michael looked over his shoulder, grinning. 'I know. I don't think he'll ever forgive Malcolm. You know, I'm sorry to have to say so, but you people have been the most ungodly nuisances I ever came across. If you had let Jimmy alone in the house he'd probably have found that sliding panel.'

'If it comes to that,' Margaret retorted from the rear, 'if only you'd told us who you were we shouldn't have got in your way.'

'You don't know how much I wanted to. But I couldn't. I was acting in absolute secrecy. I didn't even know at first that you mightn't be mixed up in this. And you must see that for me to have told you all about myself would have been most dangerous. You might have talked, or let something slip out unwittingly.' He paused, and signed to them to stand still. They saw that they had reached the end of the passage, and were confronted by a flight of worn stone steps. 'Will you stay here?' Michael said. 'And don't talk, because I'm going to open the trap.' He went softly up the steps, and they waited in silence for him to reappear.

Presently they saw the torch-light approaching again; Michael came into view, and behind him was James Fripp. This individual greeted them with a headshake. 'Well, this is a fine set-out, and no mistake,' he remarked, with an entire disregard of the manners usually required of a gentleman's servant. 'Some people don't seem able to keep out of trouble, and that's a fact.'

'Shut up,' said Michael. 'Some people can't keep their mouths shut, and you're one of them. Do you know, Mr Fortescue heard you talking once, and set an inquiry agent on to you?'

'That's a nice thing!' exclaimed Mr Fripp indignantly. 'Set one of them busies on to me? Why, I'm as innocent as a babe unborn! And if anyone told you different they're a liar. Most of the police are, barring Mr Draycott, who ain't as bad as some,' he added gloomily.

'Come and see if you can open a door without damaging the lock,' Michael interrupted, and began to lead the way back.

Mr Fripp said, with an air of unconvincing virtue: 'I'll do what I *can*, just to oblige, but you needn't talk as though I was in the 'abit of picking locks, sir.'

'Don't be an ass,' Michael said. 'Mr and Miss Fortescue know all about you.'

'No one don't know all about me,' Mr Fripp announced firmly. 'There's always people ready to swear a man's life away, and I've come across more than most in my time. You didn't ought to pay attention to everything you 'ear, miss.'

Margaret assured him that she never paid attention to malicious reports. Mr Fripp said that it did her credit.

They walked on in single file until they reached the locked door. Peter judged the distance to be about a quarter of a mile, and realised that the passage must run straight beneath the Priory grounds to the Inn.

Mr Fripp bent down, and turned his torch on to the lock. Then he felt in his pockets for some slim-looking tools, which he laid on the ground. One of these he inserted gently into the lock.

'Can you do it without any damage?' Michael asked.

Mr Fripp forgot his role of injured innocence. 'Lor' yes, sir! If you'd seen some of the locks I've picked you wouldn't ask me whether I could open this one. It ain't worthy of me, this ain't.' He worked in silence for a short while, and then, turning the instrument he held, he pushed the door. It opened without a sound, for it had no other fastening than the lock.

Michael flashed his torch into the room. They saw a press in the centre, and some smaller machines round it. The room was a fair size, and contained only the machines, a few wooden stools, and a safe.

'Electric light and all!' said Mr Fripp admiringly, and switched it on. 'Do themselves proud, don't they? There's no denying it don't pay to be honest, no matter what they say.'

Peter and Michael were both inspecting the press. Margaret sat down on one of the high stools, and listened to their highly technical comments. Mr Fripp stood beside her, and seemed to take as little interest in the press as she did. 'Wonderful how they can make it out, ain't it, miss?' he said affably.

She agreed. 'Is it all printed by that big machine in the middle?' she inquired.

Michael heard her. 'No, this is where they roll it off. Come and look.'

She went up to him, and he showed her an engraved plate. 'See? That's the plate. The paper goes between those rollers and when the current's turned on, that plate slides backwards and forwards, while the rollers press the paper on to it, and shoot it out this end, roughly speaking.'

'I see. It's like looking-glass writing, isn't it? What are the other machines?'

'One of them cuts the paper. This one. I don't understand all of them.'

'Neat little affair,' Peter said. 'I suppose this is the engraver's corner. Wonder who does it?'

'Unless I'm much mistaken, Duval was the engraver,' Michael answered. He looked round the room. 'Only the one door. Better test the walls, though. Where you find one moving stone-block you're likely to find another.'

Peter looked up quickly. 'Oh, so it was you, then?'

'Yes. Sorry if I gave you all a scare. It wasn't me you saw in the cellars, though. That was Fripp. He was trying to find a way into this place from there.'

'Look here!' Peter said. 'Have we also to thank you for our skeleton? Because if so . . .'

'What skeleton?' Michael asked, moving along one wall, testing as he went.

'That one we found in the priest's hole.'

'I never knew you did. No, that must have been one of the Monk's attentions.'

'But, Michael, you said that day at the Inn that you were responsible for what had happened at the Priory!' Margaret objected.

'I don't think I said that, did I? If I did I thought you were referring to the groaning stone. Anything that side, Jimmy?'

'Not that I can find, sir. Nothing there, Mr Fortescue?'

'Nothing,' Peter said, dusting his hands.

'Well, that's something, anyway,' Michael said. 'They

can't get out of this room by any other way than the door. If I can only find the Monk's own entrance I may get him yet.'

Margaret was puzzled. 'But doesn't he come in through the Inn? What's that entrance for, then?'

'The rest of his gang. I watched them go down this evening, and I watched them come up. At neither time was the Monk with them, and from what I heard they none of them, with the possible exception of Wilkes, know his way in or who he is.'

'By Jove!' Peter said. 'Then I'll bet that's what Duval had discovered! You know, he came up to see Charles the very night he was murdered, and he told him that though he hadn't found out who the Monk was – "seen his face," was the way he put it – he had found out something.'

'I think there's no doubt he did find the Monk's way, and that's why the Monk murdered him. What's more, I still believe it comes out at the chapel.'

Margaret remembered something. 'Peter, didn't Charles say Duval talked about finding the Monk if he had to go down amongst the dead to do it?'

'Yes, I believe he did. We thought he was cracked. Have you tried to find an entrance in the chapel, Strange – I mean Draycott?'

'Till I'm sick of the sight of masonry,' Michael replied. 'And unless I find it I can't be sure that is his way in, so that I daren't make a raid in case he gets away by some passage we don't know of. The rest of the gang's no use unless I can get the Monk. No, there's no other entrance here. We'd better try and find the secret stairway. If we can't, I'll nip back to the Inn, and go to the Priory, and attack it from that side. Come along, Jimmy, and take care how you lock the door.'

They went out again into the passage, switching off the light. While Fripp locked the door, Michael bolted the one into the Fortescues' late prison, and fixed the shutter in position again.

'Now as far as I can make out,' he said, 'we must be standing at the moment either on the level of the cellars, or below them. Probably below, judging from the depth of that opening into the well. And we mustn't forget that on the library side of the Priory the cellars are on the level of the ground. Moreover, if that machine was only just below the sitting-room you must have heard it. The question is what part of the house are we under? If the Inn is there' – he pointed up the passage – 'then the chapel ought to be more or less in *that* direction. Well, we'll see where the passage leads this way.' He led them on, flashing his torch ahead. The passage ended in an archway and through this they went, finding themselves in another of the cell-like apartments. It was bare of furniture, and out of it led yet one more.

'Talk about the 'Astings Caves!' said Mr Fripp. 'They aren't in it with this.'

'Try for a moving block,' Michael said. 'Time's getting on, and I must be back at the Inn before anyone's up. Fortescue, you take that wall, will you? Just run along it: never mind about the upper blocks. Get on with it, Fripp! Don't stand mooning about!'

They started once more to try and move one of the stone blocks that made up the wall. 'The things the perlice get up to!' Mr Fripp remarked. 'Give me an honest job of burglary, that's what I say! Well, it ain't 'ere, sir. If we've got many more of these rooms to go over you'll have to send me to one of them sanatoriums where you lay out on a nice balcony the whole blooming day.'

But only one other room led out of the one they were in, and it was comparatively small. They started to test its walls, but before Peter had got more than half-way along his side of the room Michael said: 'Got it!'

He set his shoulder to the block, and it swung easily and silently on its hidden pivot.

'Took the trouble to oil this one,' commented Mr Fripp. 'Now mind what you're about, sir. Let me 'ave a look!'

'It's all right,' Michael said, drawing his head and shoulders back into the room. 'Only be careful how you step, Margaret. We're right on the staircase. Can you get through if I go first, and give you a hand?'

'Good Lord, yes!' she said. As soon as he had climbed through the gap, she scrambled after him, and found herself standing on the narrow stone stairway. They seemed to be somewhere in the middle of it, for the stairs went down as well as up.

The other two squeezed through the opening, and Michael pressed the block back into position. The light of his torch showed nothing to distinguish this block from any of the others.

'We shall have to count the stairs,' Michael said. 'I propose to explore downstairs after I've deposited you two at the Priory. Mind how you step, Margaret: the stairs are very steep and narrow.'

They climbed in silence, each of them counting to themselves as they went. Margaret's legs were aching badly by the time they came to a halt; and she was thankful to get even a short rest.

Michael's torch was playing over the wall that flanked the staircase on the right, and they saw that the stone had ended, and they were standing behind rough brick. Michael moved on again.

'There! If I haven't lorst count!' said Mr Fripp disgustedly.

The brick gave place to what looked like a wooden partition of thick deal.

'Clever,' Michael said. 'Nailed the deal on behind the oak panel to deaden the hollow sound. Here we are!' His torch showed a plain round knob past the panel. He went on up two more stairs, and twisted it. Nothing happened. 'That's odd!' Michael said. 'It surely must be this knob that corresponds to the apple in the carving the other side. You didn't do anything but turn it, did you, Margaret?'

'No, nothing.'

He asked abruptly: 'Did the Monk come up or down?'

'Up. I was standing on the second stair, where Peter is now, when the panel closed.'

'There's no knob farther down,' Michael said. An idea occurred to him. 'I wonder – get off that stair, will you, Fortescue?'

Peter moved, and as Michael once more turned the knob the panel slid back.

'Clever little dodge,' Michael remarked.

He was interrupted by a strangled shriek from within the library. 'Charles, look! look!' Celia cried.

'Seventy-three, counting this one,' Peter said. 'It's all right, Celia: it's us!'

Eighteen

He stepped through the opening into the library, as he spoke, and found himself confronting Charles' levelled revolver. Celia and Mrs Bosanquet were gazing with startled fixity at him, and Inspector Tomlinson had just lowered a Colt automatic.

Charles put down his revolver, and swallowed twice before he spoke. Then he said: 'Oh, hullo! Just back?' His flippancy deserted him. 'Gosh, you have given us a fright! Where's Margaret? What happened?'

Margaret came through the aperture, and at sight of her Celia jumped up and flew to embrace her. 'Oh, darling, I've been thinking you dead ever since ten o'clock!' she said, half-crying. 'Who found you? Did you escape by yourselves?'

By this time both Michael and Fripp had come into the room. Charles wrung Michael's hand. 'Good man! Yes, we know all about you. The inspector had to split on you.'

There was a positive babel of talk. After a while Mrs Bosanquet made herself heard above it. 'But surely that is the man who cleaned all the rooms so thoroughly?' she said in a bewildered voice, and pointed at Fripp.

'Yes, ma'am,' said Fripp with feeling, 'and if I was you I wouldn't have one of them cleaners in the house, not if I was paid to. They're enough to break your heart.'

Michael, who had been speaking to Inspector Tomlinson, now glanced at his watch. 'Good Lord, it's almost five o'clock! Fripp and I had better hurry, or we shall run into one of the servants at the Inn. Look here, you people, the best thing you can do is to go to bed, and get what sleep you can. I'll come back after breakfast, tell you some of the things you're all dying to know, and set about the job of finding that other entrance. Now that you've discovered this panel it ought to be easy. There's only one other thing: Fortescue and his sister have got to keep themselves hidden. No one must know that they've been found. See? No one. In fact you must give the impression to anyone you happen to see that you're worried to death, and are sure that they must have gone out, and got kidnapped in the grounds, or something of that sort.' He looked at Mrs Bowers rather dubiously, but she nodded. 'Sure you understand? And don't let that housemaid of yours find them here.'

'It's her half-day,' said Mrs Bowers. 'Nor she don't turn up till nine in the mornings, and mostly late. I'll nip up and make Miss Margaret's and Mr Peter's beds before she gets here, and she don't ever go into any of the sitting-rooms.'

'Better not have her at all to-morrow,' Charles said. 'Can you get rid of her without her smelling a rat, Emma?'

She thought for a moment. 'Yes, sir. If Miss Margaret and Mr Peter aren't supposed to be here there'll only be the two bedrooms to do. I'll say she can have the whole day, since we're all at sixes and sevens. You leave it to me.'

Mrs Bosanquet had been scrutinising Michael through her lorgnette. She now turned to Charles, and said in the perfectly audible voice deaf people imagine to be a whisper: 'My dear, you may say what you please about that young man being a detective, but it appears to me that he is the same malicious person who pointed at me in the dark.'

Michael laughed. 'I've never pointed at you, Mrs Bosanquet. I'll explain it all to you later. Come on, Fripp: we'll go back the way we came. You'll turn up again later in the morning, inspector. You understand what I want you to do?'

'Yes. Send a man over to make a lot of inquiries, and make it seem we're on the wrong track. Well, Flinders will do a bit of searching all the morning, I don't doubt, and so long as he doesn't know the truth he'll put every one off the scent. I'll get back to the station now, and be with you again about ten.'

Margaret said worriedly: 'Must you go back that way? I suppose it's safe, but I don't like to think of you down there.'

Charles opened his eyes at that, but Margaret did not notice his surprise.

'I shall be all right,' Michael said. 'You go and get some sleep. So long!' He went through on to the stair, Fripp followed him, and as Michael set his foot on the second step the panel slid into place again.

Charles went to see the inspector off the premises. When he came back Margaret was telling her story to her sister and aunt. Charles listened to it in silence, but when she had finished he drew a long breath. 'Talk about halfwits!' he said. 'Why did you want to go and step into the cavity?'

'I know it was silly, but . . .'

'Silly?' said Charles. 'Call a spade a spade for once. You go through the opening, drop bracelets about, shout to Peter to come and have a look at what you've found, as though it were a sovereign left over from before the war, and then you're surprised the Monk grabs you. I don't blame him, poor chap. As for Peter – can you beat it? If his face was different he'd be cut out for the hero in a popular thriller. He knew Margaret had been pinched, but did he get his revolver? Not a bit of it! After making enough noise on the panel to bring up half a hundred monks, he bursts in, all full of heroism, and very properly gets knocked on the head.'

'Well, I'd like to know what you'd have done in my place,' Peter said.

'I should at least have remembered the planchette,' Charles said.

Celia interposed as Peter was about to retort. 'No, don't bother to answer him, Peter. Come up to bed. You must both be worn out.'

Accordingly they all went upstairs, and in spite of the fact that Margaret felt she would not be able to close her eyes, so wide-awake did she feel, she dropped into a dreamless sleep almost as soon as her head had touched the pillow.

She awoke four hours later, feeling rather heavy-eyed, but not in the least inclined to stay in bed. She wondered whether it would be safe to venture out of her room, and at that moment Celia cautiously looked in.

'Oh, you're awake! Darling, will you have breakfast in bed?'

'No, rather not!' Margaret said, getting up. 'Where's Jane? Is it all right for me to go and have a bath?'

'My dear, it's absolutely providential! She's apparently so scared by the news of your disappearance, which Flinders seems to be zealously spreading round the village, that she hasn't come at all! Her father turned up at eight with a feeble excuse, and we're quite safe. I told Mrs Bowers we'd have breakfast at half-past nine. I'll go and see if Charles is out of the bathroom yet.' She withdrew, and Margaret collected her towels and sponges, and prepared to follow her.

They had just started breakfast when Michael came in.

'Hullo!' Peter said. 'Had breakfast?'

'Yes thanks, I had some at the Bell. How are you both feeling?'

'I've got a whacking great bump on my head, but otherwise we're all right. Sit down and have a second breakfast. Did you get back safely last night?'

'Yes, but only just in time,' Michael answered, sitting beside Margaret. 'Thanks, Mrs Malcolm.' He took the coffee-cup she had handed him. 'Look here, the first thing I want to know . . .'

Charles, who had got up to carve some ham for him, turned. 'I beg your pardon? I admit I'm not feeling at my best this morning, but it seemed to me that you said *you* wanted to know something.'

'I do,' Michael said brazenly.

Charles returned to his chair and sat down. 'Someone else can go on carving,' he said. 'I'm not strong enough.

Moreover, I don't want to give him any of that peculiarly succulent ham now. A remark more calculated to provoke a peaceful man to homicide I've never yet heard.'

'Sorry,' Michael grinned. 'But it's important. Did either you or your sister, Fortescue, get any idea of the Monk's identity?'

'What, don't you know who he is?' Charles demanded.

'Not yet.'

Charles looked round at the others. 'I don't believe he's a detective at all. Let's exorcise him. Anyone got any wolfbane, or is that only good against vampires?'

'You needn't pay any attention to Charles,' Margaret said. 'We never do. Peter didn't see the monk, and I didn't recognise him at all. He never spoke, and the disguise absolutely covered him.'

'Just one thing!' Peter said. 'There was a button missing from one glove.'

Michael's eyes brightened. 'So even the Monk slips up occasionally! That's going to be very valuable. You can't tell me anything more about him?'

'No, except that he's about your height,' Margaret said, 'and very strong.'

'I see. I hoped he might have given you some clue to his identity.'

'Haven't you got any idea who he is?' Margaret asked.

'I've got a strong suspicion, but that's not quite enough.'

'Oh, do tell us,' Celia begged.

He shook his head. 'I'm afraid I can't do that.'

Charles reached out a hand for the marmalade. 'Let it be clearly understood,' he said, 'that if you don't propose to gratify our curiosity, you've obtained that ham under false pretences. Kindly let us have the whole story.'

'All right,' Michael said. 'How much did Tomlinson tell you?'

'Practically nothing. When he turned up last night I told him that I'd rung you up at the Bell, and found you out. Where were you, by the way?'

'Hidden in the cellar. Where did you ring up from?'

'Ackerley's place. He was out, but the butler let me in.'

'I see,' said Michael. 'What time was it?'

'About midnight. Well, considering everything you'll hardly be surprised when I say that I regarded your absence as fishy in the extreme. The inspector seemed extraordinarily loth to do anything, and I rather lost patience. I threatened to go to the Bell, knock them up, and lie in wait for you. That upset old Tomlinson, and after a bit he took me aside and after swearing me to secrecy, told me who you were. That rather changed the complexion of things, of course. His point was that if you weren't at the Bell you were on the Monk's tracks. Who the Monk was, or what he was up to, he wouldn't tell me. The only thing he was worrying about was to keep me from giving the alarm and thus spoiling your game. He held that nothing could be done till you turned up. I agreed to give you till this morning to put in an appearance, and then you turned up. Now let's have your story.'

'It's rather long,' Michael said, 'but I'll make it as brief as I can. It began four years ago. I wasn't on it then, of course, but about that time the French police discovered that there were a number of forged Banque de France notes circulating through the country. These notes were obviously the work of an absolute master, and it takes an expert all his time to detect them. Well, I won't go into all the early details, but it soon became apparent that whoever was responsible for the notes was a pretty cunning rogue who knew not only how to hide his tracks, but how to keep his staff in such dread of him that they'd go to gaol sooner than speak. About three years ago the French police got hold of one of the Monk's agents, but nothing they could threaten or promise had the slightest effect on him. He's serving his term now. The only thing he said from start to finish was that prison was better than what would certainly happen if he spoke.'

'Poor thing!' said Mrs Bosanquet charitably. 'Let us hope that he will see the error of his ways and reform. Though I believe the French prisons are not so good as ours in that respect. But do go on, Mr . . . Do you mind telling me what your name is?'

'Draycott,' he replied.

'A much better name than Strange,' she approved.

'Thank you,' he said gravely. 'Where was I? Oh yes! Well, these notes went on circulating, and to make it more difficult they were not all of one denomination, as is generally the case. The Sûreté is pretty good at its job, you know, but it was completely baffled. Whenever the police thought they were on the right track it led them to a blank wall. The man who eventually discovered the key to the mystery was a Customs official at Boulogne, who knew nothing whatever about it. There was a man called Alphonse Martin who was employed by a firm of manufacturers of cheap goods outside Paris. They turn out quantities of so-called Parisian novelties, such as you'll see in any second-class linen-draper's. Pocket combs, studded with paste, puff-boxes, and all that sort of meretricious junk that's designed to catch the eyes of city typists, and domestic servants. As you probably know, one of the chief markets for that particular class of goods is England. Most firms deal through an agent – a middleman – or rather, they used to before the war. But the middleman, though he still exists, had been getting more and more squeezed out of late years, since manufacturers have discovered that he isn't necessary, and it pays them far better to sell direct to the various stores. One of the foreign firms who had tried this, and found it was a success, was this firm for which Martin worked. Martin was a man of about thirty-five, and had been employed by the firm for years. Married man, with children, who lived at Neuilly, led a very respectable sort of life, was well known to any number of people, and was altogether above suspicion. He was a man of fair education, and he had the advantage of being able to speak English through having lived over here for some years when he was in his early twenties. This qualification, coupled with his good record, and the fact that he was apparently a very capable salesman, got him promoted to the job of acting as the firm's chief agent for England. He was known to most of the buyers of London and provincial stores, and he used to come over from time to time with suitcases full of samples. The Customs officials all got to know him, he never tried to smuggle anything through, and after a bit his baggage was never searched except in a perfunctory way.

'This might have gone on for ever if a new Customs officer hadn't been sent to the Douane at Boulogne to take the place of someone who was leaving. The fellow was a young chap, very keen to show himself smart at the job, and he didn't know Martin from Adam. Unfortunately for him Martin fell into his hands on the last of his journeys from London back to Paris. Whether the new official found anything irregular amongst the goods Martin was carrying, or whether he was merely being officious, I don't know, but at all events, he took exception to something or other, and made Martin unpack the whole of one suitcase. This is where the *douanier* really did show that he was a smart fellow, for in the course of his suspicious search through the suitcase, he noticed that the cubic content of the inside didn't correspond with the size of the case on the outside. In fact, he discovered that the suitcase had a false bottom and false sides. Martin put up some story of a specially strengthened frame; it didn't entirely satisfy the *douanier* and he talked of making further investigations. Then Martin lost his head, and tried to bolt. After that the game was up, of course. He was caught, the suitcase was examined, and a whole consignment of Banque de France notes was found to be lining the bottom and the sides. Same with the two other cases he had.

'That put the Sûreté on to the right track at last. Martin, like the other man, refused to talk, and there was nothing found on him to give the police any further clue. Or so they thought. They sent a man over to London, and this is where the C.I.D. steps in.'

'Did you take it on then?' Margaret inquired.

'No, another man was put on to it at first, but after a bit they had to transfer him to another job, and I took over.'

'You mean,' Celia said shrewdly, 'the other man failed to solve it, don't you?'

He reddened. 'I expect he'd have solved it if he'd had more time, Mrs Malcolm.'

'That's all right, Celia,' her husband said. 'This is the man behind the scenes in that big murder case you used to read religiously in all the evening papers about six months ago. He's only being bashful. Go on, Draycott: how did you get on to this place?'

'Oh, that was really a slice of luck!' Michael assured them. 'When I went through everything Martin had had on him at the time of his capture, I found just one thing that looked as though it might be worth following up. He had his order-book, his passport, and licence, and various papers connected with his business. They didn't help. The only other things he had were a London hotel bill, a letter from his wife, a local time-table, and a small account-book in which he kept a check of his running expenses. I had a look at the time-table first. It was one of those rotten little paper books you buy for twopence at the railway station. It was a time-table of trains on the line that runs through Manfield to Norchester. Now Norchester's not a very likely spot for a traveller in Parisian novelties, and as you know, it's the only place of any size on this line. Still, it was quite possible that there was some shop there that stocked these goods.

'The next thing I got on to was the account-book. Martin was a very methodical man, and he didn't just jot down his expenses roughly. Obviously his instinct was to write down exactly what he'd spent every penny on, and the book was full of items such as "'Bus to Shepherds Bush, so much," and "Cigarettes, so much." Also he kept a strict account of his railway fares. Usually he put down the town he went to, but sometimes it was just: "Train fare, so much." At first this didn't seem to lead anywhere, but I studied the book very closely, and I found after wading through pages of that sort of stuff that though he sometimes put down "Fare to Birmingham," and sometimes only "Fare to B," or even just "train fare, so much," there was one train fare that kept on recurring and never had anything more against it than the words "train fare." The sum was six and eightpence, and by good luck it was the only six and eightpenny fare he ever had. I tabulated all his various journeys, and found that there was no mention in his accounts of any town on this particular line. So then I got down to it, and studied his time-table. It took in the Tillingford Junction areas as well, so there was a fair field. I noted the names of all the stations you could get to for six and eightpence, and those that had cheap day returns at that price. In the end I got it down to five, of which Manfield was one.'

'I call that most ingenious!' said Mrs Bosanquet, who had been listening enthralled. 'But wasn't it still very difficult?'

'It wasn't so much difficult as boring,' Michael replied. 'It was a case of nosing about at pubs, and such-like places, and trying to find out whether there were any suspicious people in any of these places. When I worked round to Manfield it was just at the time that you were moving into this house, and there was a fair amount of talk about it. When I learned that the house had been empty for years, and was supposed to be haunted, I thought I was getting warm, and I moved on to Framley. Fripp followed me, and between us we soon found out enough to make us feel we'd hit on the place we were looking for. Only' – he smiled – 'you'd taken possession of the house, your servants were already here, and it was very difficult for me to do much. But I managed to pick up a good deal of information one way and another, and when I heard of previous tenants being frightened away, and of a cowled figure being seen, I was as sure as a man can be that the Priory was the source of the false banknotes.'

'Not happening to believe in ghosts,' said Charles, with an eye on his aunt.

She was quite equal to it, and answered with complete composure: 'This has been a lesson to all of us not to be credulous, I am sure. If you remember, Charles, from the very first I said that you were imagining things. Pray continue, Mr Draycott.'

Charles seemed incapable of speech. Michael went on: 'I got on to Inspector Tomlinson at Manfield, and he was exceedingly helpful. Through him I learned what there was to know about most of the people here. Naturally Duval was the most suspicious character. I won't bore you with the stages at which I arrived at the conclusion that there was an underground passage. Suffice it that I did arrive at it. Finding that opening into the well clinched the matter. And I hit on the moving stone. That didn't lead to much, but a visit, on the off-chance, to the British Museum library disclosed one significant fact.'

'We know!' Peter interrupted. 'Two pages torn out of the history of this house!'

'Oh, did you get on to that too? Yes, that was it. That same day I went to visit your solicitor, to find out whether anyone had tried to get you to sell the house, and if so, who he was, and where he came from.'

'I found that out,' Margaret said. 'You don't know how it worried me.'

'Did it? I'm sorry.' He smiled down at her, and Celia caught her husband's eye significantly. 'I drew a blank, except that I found someone had tried to buy the place. I next got on to Wilkes.'

'Yes, what made you suspect him?' Peter asked. 'Was it that electric-plant of his?'

'Not at first. It was just one little thing after another. I found that when you traced all the Priory ghost stories back they generally came from the same source: Wilkes. The very day you arrived' – he nodded at Charles – 'Wilkes spun a very fine yarn about having seen the Monk. I don't know if you remember, but Fripp was in the bar at the time, and he recounted the whole story to me. It was a good story I thought, and there was only one flaw. Wilkes couldn't be content to confine himself to eerie feelings and shadowy figures: he had to strain after an effect, which he doubtless thought very terrifying, and say he saw the Monk standing behind him. And he then committed the crowning error of saying the Monk just vanished into thin air. That was going a bit too far, and it set me on to his tracks. Then there was Duval. He used to come every day to the Bell, and he wasn't exactly the sort of customer a landlord of Wilkes' type encourages as a general rule. When he was drunk he got talkative, and rather abusive, but so far from throwing him out Wilkes always seemed anxious to humour him. The electric light plant I couldn't get a glimpse of for quite some time, but one thing I did see: Nearly every night, at opening-time, most of the village turns up at the Bell, as you probably know. They're in and out the whole evening, and the bar's usually pretty full. I kept a watch on the various *habitués*, and I noticed that two of the men who went in I never saw come out again. Moreover, Wilkes was never visible in the early morning, and it looked very much as though he was in the habit of keeping remarkably late hours. That gave me the idea that there might be a way down to the underground passage from the Inn. As you know, the Bell is very old, and it may well have been some sort of an annexe to the original monastery. The difficulty was to locate this possible entrance, and that's not an easy matter in a public inn. You never know whom you'll run into if you start prowling about. However, I got a chance to go down into the cellars unperceived yesterday, and I seized it. It's full of bins, and I managed to hide myself successfully. It was one of the most uncomfortable evenings I ever spent, for once down I didn't dare come up again till I'd discovered all I hoped to. I saw Wilkes, Spindle and two other men come down soon after closing time, and I watched them shift a big cask that stood on top of the trap-door. All but Spindle went down, and when he had replaced the cask over the trap, Spindle went off again. He's obviously the look-out man. The night Duval was murdered, and you came to the Bell, Malcolm – do you remember what a time it took for Wilkes to materialise?'

'I do indeed,' Charles said.

'Spindle, didn't go upstairs to wake him. He nipped down the back stairs, gave the signal that would summon Wilkes – there's an electric bell just inside the trap door, by the way – and nipped up again. Wilkes came hurrying back, went up the back stairs, and came down the front fully dressed. You thought that was what had taken him so long.

'But I'm wandering from the point. Where was I?'

'Behind a beer-barrel,' said Charles. 'Come to think of it, you might have chosen a worse hiding-place. Go on.'

'I wish I'd thought of that earlier,' Michael said. 'I thought it a rotten spot. I stayed there till about four o'clock when Wilkes and Co returned. Still, I was repaid, for the two strangers were full of something that had happened. Evidently they hadn't been able to give vent to their feelings down below, and they meant to talk it all over with Wilkes before they left the Inn. Duval was mentioned, and apparently neither of them had the smallest doubt that the Monk had done him in. They were in a great way about that, partly out of fear of the Monk, partly because they thought Duval's death would bring the police down on them. Then one of them said that it wasn't that so much as "what's happened to-night." They both agreed about that, and the other one said that it was too thick, and he wouldn't be a party to murder. Wilkes tried to soothe him by saying there'd be no murder, but it was plain that the milder one of the pair wasn't satisfied. He kept on saying that he wouldn't stand for it, until the other one turned on him and told him to go and tell the Monk so if he dared. He replied if he knew who the Monk was, he would, and be damned to the lot of them, and then they both rounded on Wilkes, and accused him of knowing the Monk's identity. The ferocious one said that it was his belief Duval had found "where the Monk goes," and he'd half a mind to have a shot at doing the same thing. Wilkes managed to pacify him, and I learned from what he said that the Monk meant to clear out as "soon as the run's finished," things having got suddenly dangerous. That was you, of course, but I didn't know that at the time. After a bit more palaver they all cleared out, and as soon as I dared I went up to my room, ascertained that Wilkes had gone to bed, got hold of Fripp and a perfectly good disguise – hired from Clarkson's, by the way – and went down to see what I could discover. The rest you know.' He glanced at the clock on the mantelpiece. 'Tomlinson ought to be arriving at any moment now, and as soon as he comes I want to investigate the rest of that staircase.'

'I never heard such a thrilling tale in my life!' Celia said. 'And you can say what you please, but I think you're a pretty clever detective!'

'Hear, hear!' Peter said. 'By the way, what if the Monk takes it into his head to go down some time to-day to have a look at us?'

'I thought of that,' Michael said, 'but I can't see any reason why he should. Neither Wilkes nor Spindle will: it's far too risky, besides which I've left Fripp to make himself a nuisance to Wilkes. The Monk can't go, because to be seen in daylight might give him away, and now of all times he won't take any chances.'

Bowers came into the room, and went to Charles. 'Colonel Ackerley has called, sir, and he says if you could spare a moment he would like to speak to either you or the mistress. I've shown him into the library.'

'All right, I'll come,' Charles said. 'I take it I'd better keep your presence here a secret even from him, Draycott?'

'Yes, don't tell anyone,' Michael answered.

When Charles entered the library the Colonel rose from a chair by the window. 'My dear fellow, I hope I haven't disturbed you, but I felt I must come up to inquire. My man told me about you coming up to my place to telephone last night, and this morning the milkman told him what had happened. Now is there any mortal thing I can do? Is my car any use to you? I never was more shocked in my life. Have you any idea what can have become of them?'

'None,' Charles said. 'We're worried to death about it. As far as we can make out they must have strolled out, possibly to meet us – we were dining with the Pennythornes, you know – and what happened then, or who spirited them away, we haven't the foggiest notion. The police are on to it, of course. The whole thing's a mystery. It seems certain somebody must have kidnapped them, but who, or why, we simply don't know. My wife's in a dreadful state: expects to hear of their bodies being discovered in some wood. I can't think it's as bad as that, though. It's awfully good of you to offer to help: I hoped I'd be able to get hold of you last night.'

'I was over at Manfield. I'd have come like a shot if I'd been in. But can I do anything to-day?'

'Thanks very much, sir, but I don't think you can. Now the police have taken over, there's really nothing any of us can do. Of course we're getting on to the hospitals, and circulating a description. But it's awfully good of you to offer.'

'Good of me be damned! I'm only sorry there's nothing I *can* do. But I needn't keep you here at any rate. I know you must be wishing me at Jericho. Don't forget to call me up if you want anything at any time. I may have to run over to Norchester this afternoon, and I might be late back. But my man will let you in if you should want to telephone again. You'll convey my deepest sympathy to your wife, won't you?'

He had hardly been gone five minutes when the police-car arrived, and the inspector got out. He was shown into the dining-room at once.

'I'm afraid I'm a bit late,' he said. 'I got detained. Now, what are the plans, inspector? We're all of us pretty well in your hands.'

'It'll have to be to-night,' Michael said. 'Can you manage it?'

'Yes, I've arranged for the Flying Squad from Norchester to be here. That's all right,' the inspector answered. 'I take it we've got to try and find this other entrance?'

'We're only waiting for you, to start,' Michael answered. He looked inquiringly at Peter and Charles. 'Are you game to come and help us?'

'Not only game to, but all bursting with enthusiasm,' Charles said. 'You don't mind, do you, Celia?'

'Not if Mr Draycott is going to be with you,' she said. 'If anyone else comes to inquire, what shall I tell them?'

Charles repeated what he had said to the Colonel. 'And I think Margaret ought to retire to her room,' he added. 'If anyone happened to look in at the window and see her the game would be up.'

'All right,' Margaret agreed. 'I'll stay upstairs till you get back. You'll return here, won't you, Michael?'

'Yes, if I may,' he said. 'Sorry you've got such a dull morning ahead of you, but it'll be all over by to-night.'

Five minutes later the four men were once more on the secret stair.

'We'd better go up first, and make sure where it leads to,' Michael said. 'There's obviously a way into it from the first floor.'

They followed him up the stairs until they came to a blank wooden partition. The usual knob was found, and as they expected the partition opened. Something that looked at first like a curtain was hanging just inside, but when Michael flashed the light on to it they saw that it was a dressing-gown.

'One of the cupboards,' Michael said.

A sharp voice called: 'Who's there? Come out at once!'

'Great Jupiter!' said Charles. 'It's Aunt Lilian!'

'In that case, you can go first,' said Michael, and made way for him to pass.

Mrs Bosanquet, on the other side of the cupboard-door, said quaveringly: 'I am not afraid of you, and I warn you the police are in the house, and I have rung my bell!'

'Well, stop ringing it, Aunt,' said Charles, emerging.

She was backed against the wall, but at sight of him wrath took the place of the alarm in her face. 'Well really, Charles!' she said. 'How dare you hide yourself in my wardrobe?'

'I didn't. We're all here . . .'

'All? Do you mean two strange men are mixed up with my clothes?'

'No, but there's a way on to the secret stair at the back of your wardrobe. Come and look.'

Mrs Bosanquet clutched at the bed-post. 'Are you

telling me that I have been sleeping in this room and the whole while that Monk-person has been able to get in?' she asked faintly. 'No, I don't want to see it. And I don't want those men pushing their way through my dresses. Go away, please. I am about to transfer all my belongings into Margaret's room.'

Charles retreated, and closed the panel behind him. 'Very unpleasant shock for the lady,' the inspector said gravely.

'All things considered,' Charles said, 'I think we'd better go *down* stairs.'

'Yes, sir, I think we had. I'll post a man in that room to-night, inspector.'

'It would be as well,' Michael agreed. 'That seems to be the only entrance up here. Will you go ahead?'

'You take the lead,' Tomlinson replied, and made room for him to squeeze past,

'Take care how you tread,' Michael warned them, and began to descend.

They went down, and down, past the library, past the moving stone, which Michael pointed out to them. At every step the atmosphere grew colder and danker. 'I'm glad I'm not alone,' said Charles. 'I don't like it one little bit.'

'Nor do I,' confessed the inspector. 'Like going into a grave. My word, it's damp, isn't it?'

'I think in all probability we are going into a grave,' Michael said. 'Something very like it, anyway.'

'Smells filthy,' said Peter. 'I can't stand must.'

'We're at the bottom now, anyway. Look out for your heads.'

'I shall have to have someone to hold my hand soon,'

Charles remarked. 'Do I understand we're likely to come out at the chapel?'

'That's what we're hoping,' Michael answered.

'Speak for yourself,' Charles recommended. 'I'm not hoping anything of the kind.'

The inspector gave a chuckle, which echoed rather eerily.

'Please don't do that again!' said Charles. 'It unnerves me. Of course we only want a few bats to complete the picture.'

'What's that ahead?' Peter asked suddenly, peering over Michael's shoulder. 'By Jove, you're right, Draycott! We've got to the crypt! Well, we always knew there must be one under the ruins.'

In a moment they were all standing in a low vaulted space. The vaults were supported by stone pillars, and as Michael's torch slowly swept the place they saw grim relics on the flagged floor. There were old worm-eaten coffins; one or two had rotted away, and a few bones, crumbling to dust, lay amongst the remains of the wooden shells. The lid of one coffin had been prised open, and when they looked into it they saw that it was empty.

'You bet that's where our skeleton came from!' Peter said. 'Gosh, what a gruesome place!'

Charles wiped his brow: 'Yes, not my idea of the ideal entrance-hall,' he agreed. 'I'm shortly going to develop the horrors.'

'Postpone them for a bit,' begged Michael. 'We've got to discover the way out. You've got torches, haven't you? Then let's get on to it.'

They set to work to explore the crypt. The first thing

to attract their attention was a flight of stone steps, that had once obviously led up to the floor of the chapel, but these only mounted for a few feet before they were blocked by fallen masonry, and the earth that had accumulated on top with the passing of years. Michael tested them in vain, and sprang down again.

'Hi!' Charles called from the other end of the crypt. 'Come over here! I always said I'd missed my vocation. I've found the gentleman's front-steps.'

With one accord they all hastened to where he was standing. He played his torch up the wall where the vaulting had broken away. A set of iron rails ran up, like a ladder.

'That's it!' Michael said. He inspected the dust and the jagged bits of stone at his feet. 'What's more, that vaulting has been deliberately broken down. What do you think, inspector?'

'It looks like it,' the inspector answered. 'Especially as the roof's good nearly everywhere else.' He stood directly beneath the broken roof and turned his torch upwards. 'That's queer. There's a sort of square place forming what looks like a second roof. Can you see, Draycott?' He stepped back to make room for Michael. 'It's a good bit higher than the rest of the vaulting too. What do you suppose it can be?'

'Unless I'm much mistaken it's one of the tombs,' Michael answered. 'The whole of the bottom has been taken away, and the floor of the chapel. Good Lord, I hand it to the Monk! He's thorough. I'm going up. You might keep your torch on it, to show me the way, one of you.' He pocketed his own, and started to climb the vertical ladder. They waited anxiously for the result. 'To think of the hours I've spent examining all those beastly tombs!' Michael said from above their heads. 'I suspected them right off, but I couldn't get one of them to open. Hullo!'

'What?' came from three pairs of lips at once.

'A sort of handle. Wait a bit.' He removed his right hand from the rail above him and reached up to turn the handle. 'It seems to be something on the same sort of principle as a Yale lock,' he said, and pressed upwards. 'Yes, by Jove, it moves! Throw the light more to the side, will you? I thought so! It's hinged. That accounts for my being able to lift it. Take the light away now; I'm going to open it.'

They switched off their torches, but they were not long in darkness, for the solid stone slab that Michael was pressing, opened slowly upwards, and a shaft of daylight filtered into the crypt.

Michael climbed carefully higher, until he could see over the top of the tomb. 'It's all right. There's no one here. I just want to see how this works from outside.' He swung the slab right back, and climbed out. He was gone for perhaps five minutes, and they saw him swing a leg over the side of the tomb again, and pull the slab to after him. They heard the lock click as it shut.

He came quickly down the ladder again. 'No wonder I couldn't find it. Unless you knew exactly where to look you never would. There's a slit in the carving on the side of the tomb. Beautiful bit of work. It's just wide enough to take a very thin flat key. The Monk's put a complete lock on the lid of the tomb, and a couple of hinges. Well, I think that's settled his little hash once and for all. We've got him, inspector.'

Nineteen

When they got back to the library, after a thorough examination of the secret cellar, it was nearly one o'clock, and Celia had received several callers. Even Mrs Pennythorne had bicycled over to inquire after the missing couple, and Mrs Roote, and Mr Titmarsh had also come to offer their sympathy.

Since Charles had seen the underground passage and the rooms that led out of it he and Peter had had a quiet consultation. As a result of this Peter took Michael Draycott aside just before they all went in to lunch, and tackled him frankly.

'Look here, Draycott,' he said, 'I'm going to ask you a plain question, and I want you to answer quite honestly: isn't Margaret's and my escape from that cell going to make your job to-night rather ticklish?'

Michael hesitated. 'Well, of course, it does complicate things, I admit,' he said. 'Still, it can't be helped.'

'It might be helped,' Peter said. 'If we went back.'

'No, that wouldn't do at all, sporting of you though it is to suggest it. I couldn't allow it.'

'Don't you run a risk of failing to bring off your *coup* if we're discovered to have escaped?'

'I'm hoping for the best,' Michael answered lightly. 'If it were only you I'd ask you to go back, but to let Miss Fortescue go down again is out of the question.'

'Go down where?' Margaret had come up to them, and caught the last words.

Michael turned to her with the special smile he seemed to keep for her. 'Nowhere,' he said.

She laughed. 'What a snub! But do tell me what's out of the question?'

It was Peter who answered. 'Margaret, it has occurred to me, and to Chas as well, that us not being in that cell to-night may ruin Draycott's plans. He won't say so, but . . .'

'You're exaggerating,' Michael said. 'And in any case what you suggest can't be considered for a moment.'

'Inspector Tomlinson doesn't agree with you. He thinks it can.' Peter looked down at his sister. 'What we've been thinking is this, Margaret: if Wilkes and those others happened to go down to-night before the Monk and found us gone, they'd give the alarm. If the Monk goes first, which is even more likely, Draycott will have to close in on him, and let the rest of the crowd go hang. Do you see?'

Margaret looked from him to Michael. 'I hadn't thought of that. You think we ought to go back?'

'No, I don't,' Michael said.

'I leave it to you, Sis,' Peter told her. 'I know it won't be nice for you, but do you think you could screw up your courage enough to do it?'

She seemed to consider. 'Could you get hold of an automatic for me, Michael? I could hide it in my dress. If I had a gun I'd do it.'

Peter nodded. 'She's a pretty good shot, Draycott. You can trust her with a gun.'

'I can't manage the double pull of a service revolver, or I'd borrow Charles',' Margaret said.

The inspector, who had come up, and had been listening, said: 'If you'll consent to be shut up down there again, miss – and if you do I'd like to say that there's very few ladies who've got your pluck – you'll both be fitted with a couple of Colts. Not that I think you'll have any need to use them. All we want you to do is to sit in that cell, as if you'd been there all day, and *keep* there till Mr Draycott gives the word for you to come out. We'll draw the bolts back as we come down the passage, but don't come out, either of you. There may be a bit of shooting, you see. While you're behind that stone wall you're safe enough, but we don't want you mixed up with the scuffle there's bound to be outside.'

Margaret smiled at Michael, who was frowning. 'At that rate I don't see that we shall be in any danger at all. It'll just be rather boring, having to wait. I'm game.'

The inspector turned to Michael. 'You're in charge, Draycott, I know, and it's for you to give the orders, but if you'll allow me to make the suggestion, the lady won't come to any harm, and it's taking a big chance if she stays up here.'

'I know,' Michael said. He hesitated. Then he laughed ruefully: 'Oh, Margaret, you *are* a nuisance!'

'No, I'm not. Peter's quite capable of looking after me – and after all, the last thing the Monk would do would be to waste time in shooting us for no reason at all. Consider it settled. When ought we to go down again?'

'Good girl!' Peter said, and went off to tell Charles.

The inspector saw Michael take Margaret's hand, and opened his eyes very wide indeed. He murmured something about going to speak to the sergeant, and withdrew.

'Margaret – I can't tell you what I think of your pluck, and your sportsmanship,' Michael said.

She blushed charmingly. 'If you're going down there – do you think I wouldn't want to – to be there too?' she asked.

For a moment he looked at her; then, without quite knowing how she got there, she found herself in his arms.

There was a loud cough in the doorway. 'Don't mind me,' Charles said. 'Of course if I were tactful I should go silently away. But I want my lunch, and Celia won't start till you come.'

Both scarlet in the face, they fell apart. 'Oh – oh is it ready?' Margaret asked. 'We're just coming. And – er – Chas!'

'Yes?'

'We – Michael and I – we're going to be married.'

'What a surprise!' Charles said. 'I ought to have had warning of this.' He grasped Michael's hand. 'Congratulations! And do you mind coming in to lunch?'

Over lunch they discussed their plans, and it was decided that Peter and Margaret should descend into their prison again not later than eight o'clock, to be on the safe side. Michael, Tomlinson, Charles, and three of the Flying Squad from Norchester would take up their positions in the house. It would be Charles' duty, aided by the ubiquitous Flinders, to stand by the panel in the library, in case the Monk managed to reach it. Sergeant Matthews had already blocked up the entrance into Mrs

Bosanquet's room, since they were too short of men to spare a couple to stand guard there. The sergeant and one other man were to lie in wait in the chapel, concealed amongst the ruins, and when they saw the Monk go down through the tomb they were to signal with a torch to the house, where a man would be on the look-out from one of the upper windows. Their task was then to stand by the tomb, and hold the stone slab down in case the Monk doubled back to make an escape that way. There was no hiding place in the crypt, and Michael had judged that it would be safer not to attempt to post any men inside the secret entrance. At the Inn, Fripp was to keep a lookout, and as soon as he had seen Wilkes and the two other men descend into the cellars he was to signal from his window to the police lying in wait outside. One of them would speed off at once to the Priory on his motorbicycle to tell Michael that all was well; the other three would enter the Inn, arrest Spindle before he could give the alarm, and bottle up the second entrance.

'Do you still suspect anyone in particular?' Margaret asked Michael when he returned to the Priory shortly after six.

'I'm sure of it,' he answered. 'I found out one thing that settles it – or so I think.'

'I do think you're a tantalising person!' complained Celia.

'I don't like him,' Charles announced. 'Don't marry him, Margaret. We can't have a policeman in the family. What about our wireless licence? He's bound to find out that it's expired.'

They dined early, and as soon as the meal was over

Margaret went up to change into the frock she had worn on the previous evening. With a praiseworthy attention to detail she made her hair look tousled, and wiped all the powder off her face. As Charles remarked, in a newly engaged girl this deed almost amounted to heroism.

At eight o'clock they opened the panel and went down those cold, damp stairs, Michael leading the way. It was nervous work, for the Monk might already have entered, unlikely though this was. However, Margaret felt the butt of the Colt she carried in the pocket of Peter's coat, which she had put on, and took heart. If there was going to be any shooting, she thought, someone would get a surprise.

They climbed through the moving stone, and made their way cautiously through the two vaults to the passage. The place was eerily silent, and it was evident that no one had yet come down into it. The light was still on in their cell, and they entered. Then Michael shut them in, and bolted the door, and returned to the library.

'Ugh!' said Margaret cheerfully. 'Well, who says the age of adventure is dead? I hope we don't have to wait long.'

'Careful!' Peter said. 'The Monk moves pretty softly, and we don't want to be overheard. We'd better talk of something else.'

This they did while the slow hours dragged past. In spite of the gun in her pocket the long wait began to get on Margaret's nerves, and by eleven o'clock she had no need to assume an expression of anxiety. Her eyes had begun to look a little strained, and she was very pale.

Then they heard that padding footstep, and Margaret instinctively grasped Peter's arm. It came nearer, and then stopped. The shutter slid back, and once more they saw the cowled face at the grille. For perhaps fifteen tense seconds the eyes they could see through the slits observed them. Then, just as Peter had thumbed down the safety catch of the pistol behind him, the shutter closed again, and the footsteps passed on.

Margaret was shaking. 'I don't think I can bear it for much longer,' she whispered.

They heard the grate of a key, and knew that the Monk had unlocked the door into the printing-room. There was a long, long pause. Once they thought they heard the soft footfall again, but they could not be certain.

Another hour crept by. Margaret felt cold, and rather sick. 'It's – it's like waiting at the dentist's when you're going to have a tooth out,' she whispered, trying to smile.

Even as she said it they heard footsteps approaching, and the murmur of voices.

'The rest of the gang,' Peter said. 'Feeling all right, Sis?'

She grimaced, but nodded.

The voices drew closer: they heard the same man who had brought the water on the night previous, say: 'Well, this is my last night, and I don't care who hears me say it. Things are getting a sight too hot for me.'

Someone, probably Wilkes, Peter guessed, said something in a low voice. 'Let 'em hear!' the other replied. 'They won't hear much after to-night.' Then the voices ceased, and in a few minutes the roar of the engine started.

It seemed to the two who waited in their cell that hours passed. Margaret looked at Peter with a scared question in her eyes. He put his lips to her ear. 'Don't forget they had to wait for the signal. 'Tisn't as long as we think, Sis. Don't fuss!'

They relapsed into listening silence again. 'Difficult to hear above the row of the engine,' Peter said.

But he too was beginning to wonder whether any hitch had occurred. Then the shutter slid back, and they saw Michael's face for a moment. Peter went to the door, and Michael whispered: 'I'm going to draw back the bolts, but whatever you do, don't come out till you're given the word.' He disappeared as he spoke; they heard the bolts drawn cautiously back, and then Peter beckoned Margaret to come and stand out of range of the grille.

Outside in the passage, the four other men had halted behind Michael. A stream of light came from the room beyond Peter and Margaret's cell, and they knew that the men were working with the door open, probably for the sake of air.

Michael gave the signal, and they crept forward.

Michael and Tomlinson reached the door together. 'Hands up!' Michael said. 'The first man who moves I shoot!'

Even as the words left his mouth there was a report, and the light went out; someone had fired at the electric bulb, and the place was plunged into sudden darkness.

But in that brief moment Michael had had time to see the whole room in one lightning glance. Wilkes was there, working the central machine; the two other men were there, but there was no sign of the Monk.

In a moment there was turmoil. A gun cracked, and the inspector's revolver answered it. Someone's torch lit up a corner of the room for a brief instant, then there was a scuffle in the doorway, another shot, and a wild struggle in the passage. Above the noise of the engine and the fight, Michael shouted: 'He's not here! Collar those men!' He felt a shot whistle past his head, ducked, and ran back down the passage, a gun in one hand, his torch in the other.

Behind him the noise grew fainter and fainter; he could safely leave Inspector Tomlinson to deal with the three others but something far more important remained to be done. The Monk had not been in the printing-room. Michael had a sickening fear that there was some other entrance he had failed to discover, but the first thing to do was to race for the crypt, in case the Monk had gone that way. As he ran he cursed himself for not having taken the precaution to go up the stairs past the library before he led the police down. The Monk must have been on the stairs when they came through the panel; he might have been listening to what had been said in the library, waited for them to get through the moving stone, and then gone on down to the crypt. Well, he couldn't get out through the tomb, in any case, Michael reflected.

He reached the stone, and set his shoulders to it. It was dangerous work, for the Monk might even then be lying in wait to shoot down his pursuers. He stayed for a moment, with a leg over the barrier, and his torch lighting up the stairs. He could see nothing, but below him he thought he heard a rustle. He sprang through and went on down. There was no sign of life in the low passage that led at the foot of the stairs to the crypt, and no glimmer of light shone in the crypt itself. He reached it, and his torch flashed round, searching every corner.

The crypt was empty. He sprang for the iron ladder, scrambled up, and shouted: 'All right there? No one tried to get out?'

The men outside answered: 'All right here, sir.'

He climbed down again. There must be another way out, and like a blundering fool he had allowed the Monk to escape.

He heard Sergeant Matthews' voice echoing down the passage: 'Where are you, sir? Mr Draycott! Where are you?'

'Here!' Michael called, and in a few minutes the sergeant came hurrying into the crypt.

'Has he got away, sir? We got the others. The inspector's gorn up to be sure he hasn't forced that panel at the top of the stairs. Lord, this is bad luck, ain't it, sir?'

Michael was searching the crypt for any sign of an entrance. Suddenly he stopped, his torch-light turned full on to one of the coffins. It was the coffin they had looked into that morning. Then the lid had lain beside it. But now the lid covered it.

The light swept on. Michael said: 'He's not here. We'd better get back to the library. Just a moment though: I'll make sure there's nothing behind these stairs.'

To the sergeant's astonishment instead of going to the block staircase he pulled a note-book and a pencil from his pocket, scrawled rapidly, and then said: 'Come over here and look, sergeant.'

The sergeant opened his mouth, saw Michael scowl at him, and shut it again. He went to him, and Michael thrust the open book into his hands. 'Just sound this wall,' he said, proceeding to do so.

The sergeant's puzzled eyes read: 'He's in the coffin. If

we lift the lid one of us'll get shot. Pretend to go away; take shoes off in passage, creep back, crouch down at head and foot of coffin, and wait for lid to lift. Then collar him as he gets out.'

'No, there's nothing here,' Michael said loudly. 'He's gone the other way. No use keeping those two up there by the tomb. I'll send them off to search the grounds.'

The sergeant's wits worked slowly but surely. 'Right, sir: I'll give the word to them.' He stepped under the hollow tomb, and setting his hands to his mouth shouted: 'He's got away. Search the grounds!'

'Come on then!' Michael said. 'We've no time to lose.'

Together they went back into the passage, and along it for some yards. At a sign from Michael the sergeant stopped and began to take off his boots. In another moment they stood up in their stockinged feet, and began to creep back to the crypt.

Michael had to take the risk of a light being seen inside the coffin; he turned his torch on for just long enough to locate the coffin. Then the light disappeared again, and in the dense darkness they went up to the coffin, and crouched down at each end.

Not a sound broke the stillness. Michael set his teeth, and tried to think what he would do if no one were in this coffin.

A creak almost made him start. The coffin lid was lifting. He stayed, ready to spring. The sound of a scrape and a thud told him that the lid had been lowered to the floor of the crypt. He heard a noise as of a body moving in the coffin; he rose stealthily. He was so near the coffin that he felt some rough material brush his cheek as he got up. It gave him the position of the Monk, and he made his spring. 'Light, sergeant!' he shouted.

A pistol shot sounded; Michael had his arms clamped round a struggling form. The sergeant's torch flashed on, and the sergeant came dashing to help.

'The gun! The gun!' Michael cried. The sergeant seized the Monk's pistol arm, and wrenched it round. The gun fell clattering to the ground and the sergeant quickly picked it up.

To and fro the struggling men swayed, and before the sergeant had time to reach them they were down on the floor, Michael uppermost.

The sergeant called: 'All right, sir!' and launched his bulk into the fray.

'Got him!' Michael panted, and there was a click as the handcuffs snapped together. 'Take him, sergeant, and be careful; he's damned strong.'

The sergeant had blown long and loud on his whistle, and they could hear men hurrying down the passage. The Monk, once the handcuffs were on, had ceased to struggle, but stood passive in the sergeant's grip. From first to last he had not uttered a word.

The inspector dashed in, followed by a sturdy constable. 'You've got him?' he cried. 'Well done, sir! Well done! Hullo, are you hurt?'

'Only a scratch,' Michael said. 'Flesh wound. Couldn't grab his pistol hand in time. Take him up to the house.'

In the library were by this time not only Charles and Flinders, but Celia and Mrs Bosanquet as well, and the two prisoners from below, who had been escorted up, after the capture of the gang, by a solicitous policeman.

When the Monk came through the open panel Mrs

Bosanquet gave a small shriek of dismay, and not even the sight of the guard about the cowled figure reassured her. She got behind a table, and commanded Charles not to take his gun off the Monk for one moment.

Michael came through the panel. 'Now then!' he said. 'Let us have a look at you.' He went up to the still figure, and pulled the cowl back from the Monk's head.

There was a gasp of utter astonishment from Celia. For the man who stood revealed was none other than Colonel Ackerley.

He made no movement to resist, and the expression on his face as he looked at the assembled company was one of sardonic scorn.

'But – but I don't understand!' Mrs Bosanquet said in a voice of complete bewilderment. 'That's the Colonel!'

Michael had taken the handcuffed wrists and jerked them up to look at the gloves the Colonel wore. As Margaret had described, they were buttoned gloves of some cotton fabric, and one button was missing. 'That was a little mistake of yours, Colonel,' he said. 'I shouldn't have expected you to slip up on a detail like that.'

It was plain the Colonel, not in the habit of buttoning his gloves, had not until now noticed the loss of one significant button. His eyes searched Michael's face for a moment, and a shade of uneasiness crept into his own.

None of this was betrayed by his voice, however. 'Well, Mr Strange,' he said, quite in his own manner. 'I congratulate you. You are cleverer than the others who have tried to find me out.' He looked at Charles, and his sneer returned. 'Your efforts were not quite so brilliant.' His glance went back to Michael; it was as though he felt everyone else in the room to be beneath contempt. 'As a matter of interest, how did you guess my identity?'

'When a man of your stamp is seen to be on terms of apparent intimacy with the local publican,' Michael answered, 'one is apt to draw unwelcome conclusions.'

The Colonel raised his brows. 'Indeed, Mr Strange? Or to leap to conclusions, shall we say? If you had no other reason than that for suspecting me you made a lucky guess.'

Michael smiled. 'Oh, not quite!' he said. 'When a man gives out that he is going to play bridge at the County Club in Manfield, and I discover his car to be still in the locked garage, I feel that requires a little explanation. I'm sorry I can't give you a more detailed account of all the things that led me to be sure you were the man I was after, but time is getting on. You will no doubt hear all you want to know at your trial.' He made a sign to Inspector Tomlinson, and the two attendant policemen grasped the Colonel's arms again to march him away.

He resisted, but it was only to bow to Gelia. '*Au revoir*, my dear Mrs Malcolm,' he said. He turned to Margaret, who had been standing like a statue, listening. 'As for you, Miss Fortescue, I am sure that you will be relieved to know that in spite of your damnably annoying behaviour, I had very little intention of leaving you to starve as you so palpably feared. And may I give you a word of advice? When next you escape from prison, and return to it with the idea of bluffing your captor, drink some of the water you have been supplied with. Had you thought of that you would have given your clever Mr Strange less trouble, for I might then have been in the printing-room when he surprised my staff.'

She did not answer him; he laughed shortly, and turned to Mrs Bosanquet. 'I was amused at your efforts to conjure up my wraith, madam,' he said. 'I was behind the panel at the time, and really I was almost tempted to appear. I always hate to disoblige the ladies.' He bowed again, and without so much as glancing at the men of the party, went out under escort.

There was a long silence. Then Charles sat down weakly. 'Let no one speak to me,' he said. 'I shall no doubt recover in time.'

'But *Ackerley*!' Peter stammered. 'Draycott, how the devil did you arrive at it?'

'Well, you heard some of my reasons,' Michael said. 'But the first clue I had was Time. You see these forgeries have been going on for five years, and it seemed probable that they were from the beginning carried out from this place. That ruled out Titmarsh: he only came here three years ago. Roote has been here an even shorter time; various other inhabitants round about have been here too long a time. It was only Ackerley who came to live at the White House five years ago, and I thought it significant that his arrival was shortly followed by the arrival not only of Duval, but of Wilkes also to take over the Bell Inn. Now Wilkes paid a very large sum for the Bell: too large a sum for an inn so little frequented. And by lying up in odd corners I found that a pretty close intimacy seemed to exist between the two men. Wilkes was the only one who knew who the Monk was; you might call him the Monk's chief of staff. That set me on to Ackerley, and that's where Fripp came in handy. After the murder of Duval I let Fripp break into the Colonel's house one night when the servants had gone to bed. You know that they slept over the garage. And of course the Colonel was out on his secret business. I told you Fripp was clever with locks. And he's not burdened with any scruples. He found a bottle of chloroform, which is now in my possession . . .'

'But didn't the Colonel miss it?' Charles demanded.

'No; for the very good reason that Fripp exchanged it for one almost identical. He also found the missing book. I'll let you have that when the trial's over; those two pages cut from the copy at the British Museum are most interesting.'

'House-breaking!' Charles said, casting up his eyes. 'Our incorruptible police!'

'Oh no!' Michael grinned. 'Jimmy's not a policeman. He would be insulted to hear you say so.'

Peter struck in: 'But an officer in the army – I suppose he wasn't, though?'

'On the contrary, he was. But he left the army under rather odd circumstances. It was hushed up, but I discovered on inquiry that his reputation was not exactly savoury. I wondered when he seemed loth to tell me where exactly he had been stationed.'

'I can't get over it!' Celia burst out. 'That cheery, sporting Colonel! He must be a *monster*!' She got up. 'I'm going to bed. My head's in a positive whirl. And Charles! All these horrible secret passages have got to be blocked up.'

'Leave it to Draycott,' said Charles. 'I'm going away for a rest-cure. And I suppose he's going to be as much an owner as I am. Not that I approve, but there! when are my wishes ever considered?' He rose and prepared to follow his wife out. Over his shoulder he said: 'And don't be more than half an hour saying good night, you two.'

But they were almost as long as that over it. Safe in Michael's arms Margaret said: 'But why did you say I'd never look at anyone in your "line of business"?'

'Well, I was afraid you wouldn't,' he explained. 'After all, I'm only what Jimmy calls a "beastly busy." How could I dream you'd ever even think of marrying me?'

She buried her face in his shoulder. 'I said I shouldn't care as long as it was honest,' she said, muffled.

He laughed softly as he bent to kiss her, 'Or a butcher's shop!' he reminded her.

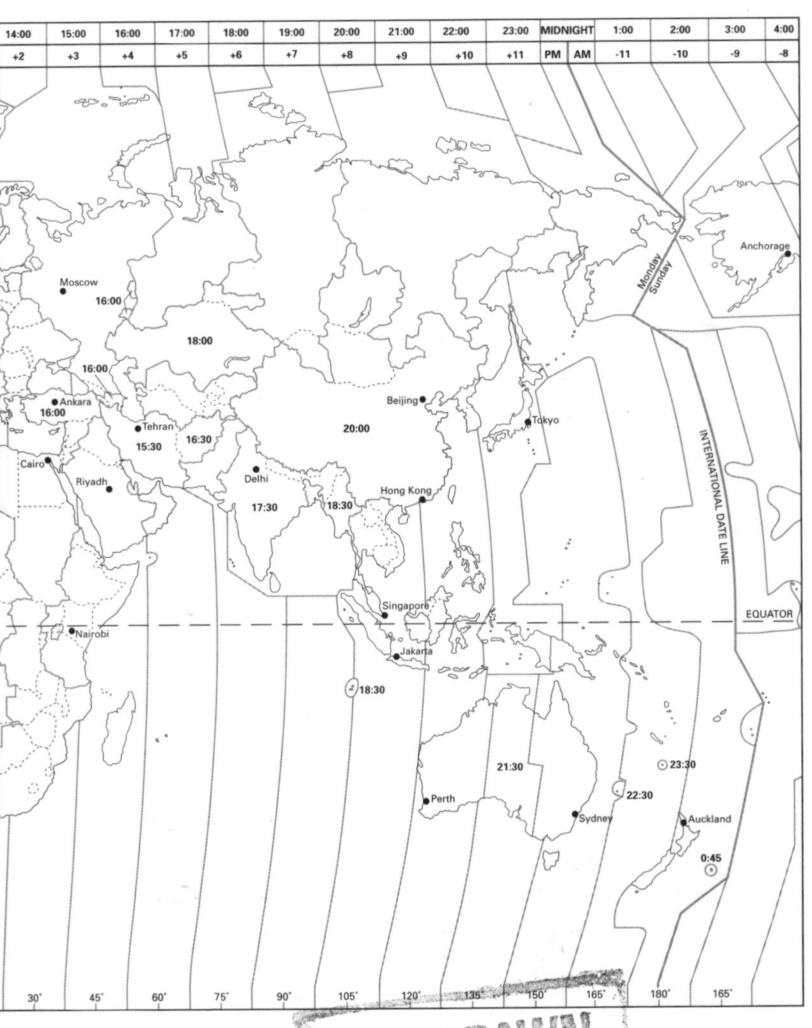

14:00
15:00
16:00
17:00
18:00
19:00
20:00
21:00
22:00
23:00
MIDNIGHT
1:00
2:00
3:00
4:00
+2
+3
+4
+5
+6
+7
+8
+9
+10
+11
PM
AM
-11
-10
-9
-8
Moscow
16:00
18:00
16:00
Ankara
16:00
Tehran
15:30
16:30
Cairo
Riyadh
Delhi
17:30
18:30
Beijing
20:00
Tokyo
Hong Kong
Singapore
Jakarta
Nairobi
18:30
Perth
21:30
Sydney
22:30
23:30
Auckland
0:45
Anchorage
Monday
Sunday
INTERNATIONAL DATE LINE
EQUATOR
30°
45°
60°
75°
90°
105°
120°
135°
150°
165°
180°
165°

THE STATESMAN'S YEARBOOK
2006

'I would advise all in general that they would take into serious consideration the true and genuine ends of knowledge; that they seek it neither for pleasure, or contention, or contempt of others or for profit or fame, or for honour and promotion; or suchlike adulterate or inferior ends: but for the merit and emolument of life, and that they regulate and perfect the same in charity: for the desire of power was the fall of angels; the desire of knowledge the fall of man; but in charity there is no excess, neither men nor angels ever incurred danger by it.'

Francis Bacon, 1561–1626.

Editors

Frederick Martin	1864–1883
Sir John Scott-Keltie	1883–1926
Mortimer Epstein	1927–1946
S. H. Steinberg	1946–1969
John Paxton	1969–1990
Brian Hunter	1990–1997
Barry Turner	1997–

Credits

Publisher	Alison Jones (London) Garrett Kiely (New York)
Editor	Barry Turner
Editorial Assistant	Jill Fenner
Senior Research Editor	Nicholas Heath-Brown
Research	James Matthews Helen Warren Daniel Smith Reena Badiani Richard German Robert McGowan Nicola Varns Andrew Clarke Martha Nyman
Index	Richard German
Production	Phillipa Davidson-Blake Michael Card Shirley Card
Marketing	Sanphy Thomas (London) Erin Igoe (New York)

email: sybcomments@palgrave.com

THE STATESMAN'S YEARBOOK

THE POLITICS, CULTURES AND ECONOMIES OF THE WORLD

2006

EDITED BY

BARRY TURNER

palgrave
macmillan

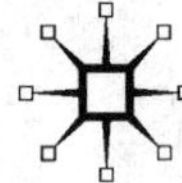

Published annually since 1864

This edition published 2005 by
PALGRAVE MACMILLAN
Houndmills, Basingstoke, Hampshire RG21 6XS and
175 Fifth Avenue, New York, N.Y.10010
Companies and representatives throughout the world

PALGRAVE MACMILLAN is the global academic imprint of the Palgrave Macmillan division of St. Martin's Press, LLC and of Palgrave Macmillan Ltd. Macmillan® is a registered trademark in the United States, United Kingdom and other countries. Palgrave is a registered trademark in the European Union and other countries.

ISBN-10 1–4039–1482–6
ISBN-13 978–1–4039–1482–8
ISSN 0081–4601

This book is printed on paper suitable for recycling and made from fully managed and sustained forest sources.

A catalogue record for this book is available from the British Library.

Library of Congress Cataloging-in-Publication Data

Data available

10 9 8 7 6 5 4 3 2 1
14 13 12 11 10 09 08 07 06 05

Printed in Malaysia

CONTENTS

Part I: International Organizations

CONTENTS

Part II: Countries of the World A–Z

CONTENTS

CONTENTS

KEY WORLD FACTS

• World population in 2005	6,454 million (3,245 million males and 3,209 million females)
• World population under 30 in 2005	3,485 million
• World population over 60 in 2005	668 million
• World population over 100 in 2005	241,000
• World economic growth rate in 2004	4%
• Number of illiterate people	960 million
• Number of unemployed people	185 million
• Average world life expectancy	69·1 years for females; 64·9 years for males
• Annual world population increase	76·61 million people
• Number of people living outside country of birth	185 million, or nearly 3% of the world's population
• Fertility rate	2·7 births per woman
• Urban population	47·8% of total population
• World defence expenditure	US$997·2 billion
• Number of TV sets	1·36 billion
• Number of radio receivers	2·18 billion
• Number of cigarettes smoked	5,600 billion a year
• Number of Internet users	665 million
• Number of mobile phone users	1·3 billion
• Number of motor vehicles on the road	647 million
• Number of people who cross international borders every day	2 million
• Number of people living in extreme poverty	1·1 billion
• Number of people living in urban slums	924 million
• Number of malnourished people	852 million
• Number of overweight people	1·1 billion
• Number of obese adults	300 million
• Number of people dying of starvation	24,000 every day
• Number of people lacking clean drinking water	1 billion
• Number of people lacking adequate sanitation	3 billion
• Number of reported executions in 2004	3,797
• Number of people worldwide exposed to indoor air pollution that exceeds WHO guidelines	1 billion
• Annual carbon dioxide emissions	6·7 billion tonnes of carbon

CHRONOLOGY

CHRONOLOGY

April 2004–March 2005

Week beginning 4 April 2004

Dr Edward Fenech Adami, prime minister of Malta from 1987–96 and 1998–March 2004, took office as president.

In the elections to Indonesia's House of People's Representatives the Party of the Functional Groups (Golkar) came first, winning 128 seats, followed by the Indonesian Democratic Party of Struggle (PDIP) with 109 seats.

Rolandas Paksas, the president of Lithuania, was impeached. Artûras Paulauskas took over as acting president.

Mahinda Rajapaksa took office as prime minister of Sri Lanka.

In Algeria's presidential elections the incumbent Abdelaziz Bouteflika (National Democratic Rally) won a second term of office, gaining 85·0% of the votes cast. Ali Benflis (National Liberation Front) won 6·4% and Abdallah Djaballah (el-Islah) 5·0%.

Week beginning 11 April 2004

Alfred Maseng was elected president of Vanuatu by an electoral college in the fourth round of voting, receiving 40 votes against 16 for the government-backed candidate Kalkot Mataskelekele.

In South Africa's parliamentary elections, the African National Congress won the largest share of the vote with 69·7% and 279 seats in the National Assembly. The Democratic Alliance came second with 50 seats, and the Inkatha Freedom Party third with 28.

France-Albert René stepped down and was succeeded as president of the Seychelles by vice-president James Alix Michel.

Elections to the National Assembly were held in South Korea. The Uri Party won 152 seats, ahead of the Grand National Party with 121.

José Luis Rodríguez Zapatero took office as prime minister of Spain.

In presidential elections in Slovakia, Ivan Gašparovič (Movement for Democracy) defeated former prime minister Vladimir Mečiar of the LS-HZDS.

Week beginning 18 April 2004

Senegal's prime minister, Idrissa Seck, was dismissed by president Abdoulaye Wade and replaced by Macky Sall.

Thabo Mbeki was re-elected as president of South Africa by parliament.

Week beginning 25 April 2004

Elections were held to the Federal Assembly of the Comoros. Supporters of the three regional presidents won 12 of the 18 elected seats; supporters of federal president Azaly Assoumani won six. Holding a majority, the regional presidents each appointed an additional five legislators.

In the Austrian presidential election Heinz Fischer (Social Democratic Party) won 52·4% of the vote against 47·6% for minister for foreign affairs Benita Ferrero-Waldner (Austrian People's Party).

The National Assembly elections in Equatorial Guinea were boycotted by most opposition parties. The ruling Democratic Party of Equatorial Guinea (PDGE) won 68 of the 100 seats, its allies (the so-called 'democratic opposition') won 30 seats and the Convergence for Social Democracy won 2.

In Macedonia, the second round of presidential elections resulted in victory for Branko Crvenkovski (Social Democratic League of Macedonia), the incumbent prime minister, with 60·6% of votes cast against 39·4% for Saško Kedev (Internal Macedonian Revolutionary Organization–Democratic Party for Macedonian National Unity).

After the resignation of prime minister Ahmed Mohamed Ag Hamani, Ousmane Issoufi Maïga took office as prime minister of Mali.

Guinea's prime minister François Lonseny Fall resigned.

Ten countries became the latest members of the European Union—Cyprus (Greek-Cypriot part only), Czech Republic, Estonia, Hungary, Latvia, Lithuania, Malta, Poland, Slovakia and Slovenia.

Week beginning 2 May 2004

Leszek Miller resigned as prime minister of Poland. President Aleksander Kwaśniewski designated Marek Belka, the finance minister, as Miller's successor.

In Panama's presidential election, Martín Torrijos Espino of the Revolutionary Democratic Party won 47·5% of votes cast, followed by Guillermo Endara Galimany (Solidarity Party) with 30·6%. In the concurrent Legislative Assembly elections, the Revolutionary Democratic Party won 41 seats, ahead of the Arnulfist Party with 17.

Rodrigo Rato of Spain was named managing director of the International Monetary Fund.

Prime minister Surya Bahadur Thapa of Nepal resigned.

Week beginning 9 May 2004

The fourth and final phase of India's parliamentary elections took place. The Indian National Congress (INC) and its allies gained 217 seats; the National Democratic Alliance gained 185 seats (with the Bharatiya Janata Party winning 138 seats); and the Left Front won 59 seats. Prime minister Atal Bihari Vajpayee of the BJP resigned, remaining in a caretaker capacity while the INC organized a new government.

Carlos Gomes Júnior, of the African Party for the Independence of Guinea and Cape Verde (PAIGC), took office as prime minister of Guinea-Bissau.

Presidential elections in the Philippines were won by president Gloria Macapagal-Arroyo, although results were not released until 20 June.

President Alfred Maseng of Vanuatu was removed from office by the Supreme Court.

Roh Moo-hyun was reinstated president of South Korea by the Constitutional Court, which rejected Roh's parliamentary impeachment. Prime minister Goh Kun offered his resignation but was persuaded by Roh to remain until a new cabinet could be formed. Goh Kun officially resigned two weeks later.

Week beginning 16 May 2004

In presidential elections in the Dominican Republic, ex-president Leonel Antonio Fernández Reyna of the Dominican Liberation Party won 57·1% of the vote, ahead of incumbent Rafael Hipólito Mejía Domínguez of the Dominican Revolutionary Party with 33·6%.

Sonia Gandhi declined the premiership of India, despite emotional appeals from her supporters. Manmohan Singh, of the Indian National Congress, became India's first Sikh prime minister, forming a coalition government with eleven other parties.

In Malaŵi's parliamentary elections the Malaŵi Congress Party (MCP—formerly the only legal party) came first with 59 seats, followed by the United Democratic Front (UDF) with 49. At the concurrent presidential elections Bingu wa Mutharika (UDF) won with 35·9% of the vote, ahead of John Tembo (MCP) with 27·1%, and Gwanda Chakuamba (Mgwirizano) with 25·7%. There were two other candidates. Both the second and the third-placed candidates challenged the results and the fairness of the elections.

Week beginning 23 May 2004

Horst Köhler, formerly managing director of the International Monetary Fund, was elected president of Germany by the Federal Convention.

Iyad Allawi was named interim prime minister of Iraq.

Week beginning 30 May 2004

Sheikh Ghazi al-Yawer was named interim president of Iraq. Iyad Allawi took office as prime minister and an interim government was sworn in one month ahead of schedule.

Antonio Saca took office as president of El Salvador.

King Gyanendra reappointed Sher Bahadu Deuba as prime minister of Nepal.

Hari Kostov was approved as prime minister by the Assembly of Macedonia.

Week beginning 6 June 2004

Prime minister Cándido Muatetema Rivas and the government of Equatorial Guinea resigned.

Elections were held to the European Parliament. The European People's Party–European Democrats became the largest group with 268 seats. The Party of European Socialists totalled 200 seats.

Week beginning 13 June 2004

Elections took place to Luxembourg's Chamber of Deputies. The Christian Social Party (CSV) won 24 seats, ahead of the Socialist Workers' Party (LSAP) with 14.

Ivan Gašparovič took office as president of Slovakia.

Week beginning 20 June 2004

Nauru's president René Harris was ousted by a parliamentary motion of no-confidence. He was succeeded by his predecessor, Ludwig Scotty.

Marek Belka was confirmed as prime minister of Poland, winning a parliamentary motion of confidence.

A presidential election was held in Iceland. Incumbent Ólafur Ragnar Grímsson was re-elected with 85·6% of the vote, ahead of Baldur Ágústsson with 12·5%.

Week beginning 27 June 2004

Elections were held to Mongolia's parliament. Following a second ballot for two undecided seats the final results gave the ruling Revolutionary People's Party (MAKN) 37 seats against 34 for the Motherland Democracy Coalition (EOA).

The ruling Liberal Party of prime minister Paul Martin won elections in Canada with 135 seats ahead of the Conservative Party with 99.

Portuguese prime minister José Durão Barroso was chosen to succeed Romano Prodi as president of the European Commission.

Lee Hai-chan was approved as prime minister by South Korea's National Assembly.

Chaudhry Shujaat Hussain took office as prime minister of Pakistan following the resignation of Mir Zafarullah Khan Jamali.

Vladimír Špidla resigned as prime minister of the Czech Republic.

Horst Köhler took office as federal president of Germany.

Week beginning 4 July 2004

Portuguese prime minister José Manuel Durão Barroso resigned to assume the presidency of the European Commission. President Jorge Sampaio asked Pedro Santana Lopes to form a government.

President Thomas Klestil of Austria died. As a result his successor, Heinz Fischer, was sworn in two days earlier than he was due to take office.

Parliamentary elections in Vanuatu were won by the National United Party, with 10 out of 52 seats, ahead of the Union of Moderate Parties, the Vanua'aku Pati and independents, each of which won 8 seats.

Egypt's prime minister Atef Ebeid resigned. He was succeeded by Ahmad Nazif.

Week beginning 11 July 2004

In Lithuania, Valdas Adamkus took office as president for a second time having previously served from 1998 to 2003.

In Cambodia, the coalition government was revived between the Cambodian People's Party and the royalist FUNCINPEC Party following a deadlock that had lasted nearly a year since the parliamentary election.

Palestinian prime minister Ahmed Qureia resigned, but president Yasser Arafat rejected the resignation and Qureia agreed to stay on.

Week beginning 18 July 2004

In Belgium, a new government included Karel De Gucht as foreign minister.

A new cabinet in Canada included Pierre Pettigrew as foreign minister and William Graham as defence minister.

Josep Borrell of Spain was elected president of the European Parliament.

Week beginning 25 July 2004

Vanuatu's Parliament elected Josias Moli as speaker and thus as acting president. Serge Vohor was elected prime minister and Barak Sopé named foreign minister.

Week beginning 1 August 2004

Following the earlier resignation of the Czech prime minister, Vladimír Špidla, the cabinet of his successor, Stanislav Gross, was appointed.

Week beginning 8 August 2004

Singapore's prime minister Goh Chok Tong stepped down; Lee Hsien Loong was sworn in as his successor.

In Vanuatu, the electoral college failed to elect a president after the removal of the previous president. The college later reconvened for a second round, and several votes were again inconclusive before Kalkot Mataskelekele was elected with 49 votes against 7 for Willie David Saul.

Week beginning 15 August 2004

In Bhutan, Lyonpo Yeshey Zimba took office as prime minister.

Tsakhiagiyn Elbegdorj was chosen by parliament to be Mongolia's new prime minister.

Week beginning 22 August 2004

Pakistan's prime minister, Chaudhry Shujaat Hussain, resigned to allow finance minister Shaukat Aziz to take over the post.

Following the resignation of Hungarian prime minister Péter Medgyessy, the ruling Socialist Party chose Ferenc Gyurcsány as his successor.

In Tuvalu, prime minister Saufatu Sopoanga's government was toppled in a vote of no confidence. Deputy prime minister Maatia Toafa became acting prime minister.

Week beginning 29 August 2004

A new Somali Transitional Federal Parliament, based in the Kenyan capital Nairobi, was inaugurated.

Martín Torrijos took office as president of Panama, with Samuel Lewis Navarro becoming first vice-president and foreign minister.

A group of hostage takers seized a school in Beslan, in the Russian republic of North Ossetia. A three-day stand-off ended with more than 350 people killed, nearly half of them children.

The Lebanese parliament voted to extend president Émile Lahoud's six-year term by three further years.

Week beginning 5 September 2004

The foreign ministers of India and Pakistan met in the first formal ministerial talks since the two countries nearly went to war following an attack on the Indian parliament in late 2001.

Week beginning 12 September 2004

The Icelandic prime minister Davíð Oddsson swapped positions with foreign minister Halldór Ásgrímsson.

President Fradique Bandeira Melo de Menezes of São Tomé e Príncipe dismissed prime minister Maria das Neves and appointed Damião Vaz de Almeida as her successor.

Week beginning 19 September 2004

In the parliamentary elections in Kazakhstan, president Nursultan Nazarbaev's Otan (Fatherland) party won 42 seats in the 77-seat assembly, with the pro-presidential Aist (Agrarian and Industrial Union of Workers Block) second with 11 seats. Observers said that the election fell short of acceptable standards. A second round run-off was required in several constituencies where no single candidate won a majority.

In Indonesia, Susilo Bambang Yudhoyono won the presidential election run-off with 60·9% of the vote, defeating incumbent Megawati Sukarnoputri with 39·1%.

Brunei's parliament was reopened for the first time in 20 years.

Week beginning 26 September 2004

In a cabinet reshuffle in Japan, Nobutaka Machimura was appointed foreign minister.

In Chile, a cabinet reshuffle saw Ignacio Walker Prieto become foreign minister and Jaime Ravinet defence minister.

In a cabinet reshuffle in Ireland, Dermot Ahern replaced Brian Cowen as foreign minister with Cowen moving to finance while Willie O'Dea became defence minister. Irish president Mary McAleese was confirmed for a second term.

Week beginning 3 October 2004

In parliamentary elections in Slovenia the Slovenian Democratic Party won 29 seats with 29·1% of votes cast, ahead of the ruling Liberal Democracy of Slovenia in second place, with 23 seats and 22·8% of the vote.

President Levy Patrick Mwanawasa of Zambia dismissed vice-president Nevers Mumba and appointed Lupando Mwape his successor.

King Norodom Sihanouk of Cambodia abdicated on health grounds.

Wangari Maathai, a Kenyan environmentalist and human rights campaigner, was awarded the Nobel Peace Prize.

In Australia's general election the governing coalition was returned to power with the Liberal Party taking 74 of 150 seats in the House of Representatives and its partner the National Party 12. The opposition Labor Party won 60 seats and independents 3.

Afghanistan's first-ever presidential election was won by head of the transitional government, Hamid Karzai, with 55·4% of votes cast, defeating Yunus Qanooni, with 16·3% of the vote, and 16 other candidates.

Week beginning 10 October 2004

In the first round of parliamentary elections in Lithuania, the Labour Party won 23 of 75 seats, ahead of prime minister Algirdas Brazauskas' coalition 'For a Working

Lithuania' with 19 and the Homeland Union with 11. The remaining 66 seats were allocated in the second round, giving the Labour Party a total of 38 seats, 'Working for Lithuania' 32 and the Homeland Union 25.

Somalia's Transitional Federal Parliament chose a new president. Abdullahi Yusuf Ahmed was elected in a third round run-off with 189 votes, against 79 for Abdullahi Ahmed Addou. There were 26 candidates in the first round.

In presidential elections in Cameroon incumbent Paul Biya was re-elected with 70·9% of the vote ahead of John Fru Ndi with 17·4% and Adamou Ndam Njoya with 4·5%.

Maatia Toafa, Tuvalu's acting prime minister for the previous six weeks, was confirmed by parliament by eight votes to seven against Elisala Pita.

Week beginning 17 October 2004

In a referendum held in Belarus 86·2% of votes cast were in favour of the abolition of the two-term limit on the presidency. The vote was widely regarded as fraudulent. Likewise, parliamentary elections, which gave an overwhelming majority to the government, were said to be corrupt.

Gen. Khin Nyunt was replaced as prime minister of Myanmar by Lt. Gen. Soe Win.

Ursula Plassnik was named Austria's new foreign minister.

Prime minister Rafiq al-Hariri of Lebanon resigned. President Émile Lahoud named Omar Karami his successor.

In Nauru, followers of president Ludwig Scotty won a majority in parliamentary elections. He was elected president unopposed.

Week beginning 24 October 2004

In presidential elections in Tunisia, incumbent Zine El Abidine Ben Ali (Constitutional Democratic Assembly) was re-elected with 94·4% of the votes cast, ahead of Mohamed Bouchiha (Popular Unity Party) with 3·8% and two other candidates. In parliamentary elections, the Constitutional Democratic Assembly won 152 of 189 seats, the Movement of Democratic Socialists 14 and the Popular Unity Party 11.

In parliamentary elections in St Kitts and Nevis, the ruling Labour Party won 7 of 11 seats, ahead of the Concerned Citizens Movement with 2 seats.

In Bosnia-Herzegovina, Borislav Paravac took over as chairman of the presidency.

In Latvia, the government of prime minister Indulis Emsis resigned.

The European Union's new constitution was signed by leaders of the 25 member states.

Parliamentary elections in Botswana were won by the ruling Botswana Democratic Front, with 44 of 57 seats, ahead of the Botswana National Front with 12 seats.

Week beginning 31 October 2004

In presidential elections in Uruguay, Tabaré Vázquez (Progressive Encounter-Broad Front-New Majority) received 50·4% of the vote, beating Jorge Larrañaga (National Party) into second place with 34·3%. Elections to the Chamber of Deputies were won by the Progressive Encounter-Broad Front-New Majority with 53 seats, ahead of the National Party in second place with 34 seats and the Colorado Party third with 10 seats.

Ferenc Somogyi was sworn in as Hungary's new foreign minister.

In presidential elections in Palau, incumbent Tommy Remengesau won with 66·5% of votes cast against 33·5% for Polycarp Basilius.

President Sheikh Zayed bin Sultan al-Nahyan of the United Arab Emirates died. The Federal Council elected his oldest son, Sheikh Khalifa bin Zayed al-Nahyan, his successor.

In the US presidential elections incumbent George W. Bush (Republican) won 286 electoral college votes, receiving 50·73% of the poplar vote. John Kerry (Democrat) won 251 electoral college votes, receiving 48·27% of the popular vote. The Republicans also kept control of both the House of Representatives and the Senate, in the former increasing their representation to 232 of 435 members and in the latter to 55 of 100 members.

Somalian president Abdullahi Yusuf Ahmed named Ali Muhammad Ghedi prime minister.

Week beginning 7 November 2004

Burundi's president Domitien Ndayizeye dismissed his vice-president, Alphonse Marie Kadege, replacing him with Frédéric Ngenzebuhoro.

President Yasser Arafat of the Palestinian-Administered Territories died. Parliament Speaker Rauhi Fattouh succeeded him as acting president.

Week beginning 14 November 2004

Macedonian prime minister Hari Kostov resigned.

Presidential elections in Namibia were won by Hifikepunye Pohamba (South West Africa People's Organization/SWAPO) with 76·4% of votes cast, ahead of Ben Ulenga (Congress of Democrats) with 7·3%. In parliamentary elections SWAPO won 55 of the available 72 seats, with 75·1% of the vote.

The European Parliament approved the new European Commission headed by José Manuel Durão Barroso.

In Italy, deputy prime minister Gianfranco Fini was appointed foreign minister.

Week beginning 21 November 2004

Following the second round of presidential elections in Ukraine, deemed by western observers to be flawed, protesters gathered in central Kyiv after the election commission indicated that Viktor Yanukovich had won. In the first round, reformist former prime minister Viktor Yushchenko had won 39·9% of the vote with incumbent prime minister Viktor Yanukovich in second place with 39·3%. The official second round results gave victory to Yanukovich, with 49·5% of the vote, against 46·6% for Yushchenko. However, parliament declared the poll invalid and the Supreme Court annulled the second round of the election. When it was held again Viktor Yushchenko received 52·0% of the vote and Viktor Yanukovich 44·2%.

Latvian president Vaira Vīķe-Freiberga nominated Aigars Kalvitis as prime minister.

Week beginning 28 November 2004

In presidential elections in Romania prime minister Adrian Năstase of the National Union received 40·9% of the vote, with Traian Băsescu of the Justice and Truth Alliance second with 33·9% and Corneliu Vadim Tudor of the Greater Romania Party third with 12·6%. As a result a second-round run-off was required in which Traian Băsescu was elected president with 51·2% of the vote against 48·8% for Adrian Năstase. In parliamentary elections the National Union won 132 of 332 seats with 36·8% of the vote, ahead of the Justice and Truth Alliance with 113 (31·5%).

The Slovenian parliament approved the cabinet of the new prime minister, Janez Janša.

In the second round of presidential elections in Niger incumbent Tandja Mamadou won 65·5% of the votes against former prime minister Mahamadou Issoufou with 34·5%. In the first round of elections Tandja Mamadou had won 40·7% of the vote, Mahamadou Issoufou 24·6% and former president Mahamane Ousmane 17·4%.

Week beginning 5 December 2004

In presidential elections in Ghana, incumbent John Agyekum Kufuor of the New Patriotic Party (NPP) won 52·5% of the vote with John Atta Mills of the National Democratic Congress (NDC) taking 44·6%. Parliamentary elections were won by the New Patriotic Party, with 128 of 230 seats.

President Paul Biya of Cameroon appointed a new government with Ephraïm Inoni as prime minister.

The Swiss parliament elected Samuel Schmid president for 2005.

Cellou Dalein Diallo was appointed prime minister of Guinea eight months after his predecessor's resignation.

In Portugal, the government of prime minister Pedro Santana Lopes resigned.

In parliamentary elections in Taiwan the Democratic Progressive Party took 89 of 225 seats with 35·7% of the vote, against 79 seats and 32·8% for the Nationalist Party.

Vanuatu's prime minister Serge Vohor was removed from office following a no-confidence motion vote. Deputy prime minister Ham Lini was elected his successor.

Week beginning 12 December 2004

In the UK, Home Secretary David Blunkett resigned. Charles Clarke was appointed his successor.

The European Union agreed to begin membership negotiations with Turkey in Oct. 2005.

Week beginning 19 December 2004

In parliamentary elections in Turkmenistan, all 50 seats were filled by supporters of president Saparmurad Niyazov and his Democratic Party, no other parties being allowed to stand.

Week beginning 26 December 2004

An earthquake under the Indian Ocean triggered off a tsunami that resulted in more than 290,000 deaths, notably in Indonesia—where 237,000 people lost their lives—Sri Lanka, India and Thailand.

Samuel Schmid took office as president of Switzerland.

The new Turkish lira replaced the Turkish lira as the national currency at a rate of one new Turkish lira to one million Turkish lira.

Week beginning 2 January 2005

Polish foreign affairs minister Włodzimierz Cimoszewicz announced his resignation. Adam Rotfeld was named his successor.

Week beginning 9 January 2005

In the election for president of the Palestinian Authority, Mahmoud Abbas won with 67·4% of votes cast, ahead of Mustafa Barghouti with 21·0%.

As a result of the second round of elections in Uzbekistan the Liberal-Democratic Party held 41 of the 120 seats, followed by the People's Democratic Party with 28. In the first round of elections, criticized for electoral abuses, the Liberal-Democratic Party had won 21 of 62 seats, ahead of the People's Democratic Party in second place and the Self-Sacrifice National Democratic Party third. All parties taking part in the election were loyal to President Islam Karimov—opposition parties were barred from participating.

A new government was formed in Israel, including Shimon Peres as deputy prime minister.

Week beginning 16 January 2005

In the second round of presidential elections in Croatia incumbent president Stipe Mesić won a second term with 65·9% of votes cast, against 34·1% for Jadranka Kosor. In the first round Stipe Mesić had received 48·9% of the vote, ahead of Jadranka Kosor with 20·3% and Boris Mikšić 17·8%.

George W. Bush was sworn in for a second term as US president.

In parliamentary elections in the Maldives all candidates for the 42 seats ran officially as independents, but both the government and the opposition Maldives Democratic Party—which operates in self-imposed exile out of Sri Lanka—claimed victory.

Week beginning 23 January 2005

Viktor Yushchenko was sworn in as president of Ukraine. He named Yuliya Tymoshenko acting prime minister.

In Taiwan, prime minister Yu Shyi-kun and his cabinet resigned. President Chen Shui-bian appointed Frank Hsieh his successor.

Week beginning 30 January 2005

In parliamentary elections in Iraq the Shia-backed United Iraqi Alliance won 140 of 275 seats with 48·2% of the vote, ahead of the Kurdish Unity List with 75 seats and 25·7% and prime minister Iyad Allawi's Iraqi List with 40 and 13·8%.

King Gyanendra of Nepal dismissed the government of prime minister Sher Bahadur Deuba and assumed power.

Armando Guebuza was sworn in as president of Mozambique.

Chad's prime minister Moussa Faki resigned. He was succeeded by Pascal Yoadimnadji.

Zurab Zhvania, prime minister of the former Soviet republic of Georgia, died. Finance minister Zurab Nogaideli succeeded him as prime minister.

Togo's president Gnassingbé Eyadéma died. The military installed his son, Faure Gnassingbé, as his successor.

Week beginning 6 February 2005

In parliamentary elections in Thailand the ruling Thai Rak Thai party won 375 of 500 seats, ahead of the Democrat Party with 96 and the Thai Nation with 27.

In parliamentary elections in Denmark, the ruling Liberal Party took 52 seats with 29·1% of the vote, against 47 seats for the Social Democrats and 24 seats for the Danish People's Party.

Karolos Papoulias was elected president of Greece, receiving 279 votes in the 300-member parliament.

Week beginning 13 February 2005

Lebanon's former prime minister Rafiq al-Hariri was killed in a bomb attack.

The Kyoto Protocol, aiming to reduce total greenhouse gas emissions of developed countries, came into force.

Michael Chertoff was confirmed as US Secretary of Homeland Security, thereby filling the last vacancy in President George W. Bush's second-term cabinet. Major changes from his first-term cabinet included Condoleezza Rice as Secretary of State and Alberto 'Al' Gonzales as Attorney General.

Week beginning 20 February 2005

In parliamentary elections in Portugal, the Socialist Party won 120 seats with 45·1% of votes cast, the Social Democratic Party 72 with 28·7% and the Communist Party/Green Party coalition 14 with 7·6%.

The UN High Commissioner for Refugees, Ruud Lubbers, resigned. His deputy Wendy Chamberlin took over as acting high commissioner.

Week beginning 27 February 2005

In the first round of parliamentary elections in Kyrgyzstan, 35 of the 75 seats were allocated, thereby triggering a second round. However, following protests the Supreme Court annulled the results and the Upper House of parliament named Kurmanbek Bakiyev acting prime minister and acting president. The new parliament later confirmed Bakiyev as interim prime minister and the Upper House was dissolved.

In legislative elections in Tajikistan the People's Democratic Party of Tajikistan won 52 of 63 seats ahead of the Communist Party with 4 and the Islamic Renaissance Party of Tajikistan with 2.

The Lebanese government, led by prime minister Omar Karami, resigned.

In Uruguay, Tabaré Vázquez was sworn in as president. Rodolfo Nin Novoa became vice-president.

Week beginning 6 March 2005

In parliamentary elections in Moldova the Party of Communists of the Republic of Moldova won 56 seats with 46·0% of votes cast, the Democratic Moldova bloc 34 with 28·5% and the Christian Democratic People's Party 11 with 9·1%.

Hong Kong's chief executive Tung Chee-hwa resigned. Chief Secretary for Administration Donald Tsang became the acting chief executive.

Karolos Papoulias was sworn in as president of Greece.

In Portugal, José Sócrates was sworn in as prime minister. The new cabinet included Diogo Freitas do Amaral as foreign minister and Luís Amado as defence minister.

Week beginning 13 March 2005

In the first round of presidential elections in the Central African Republic, incumbent president Gen. François Bozizé received 42·9% of the vote, ahead of former prime minister Martin Ziguélé (Liberation Movement of the Central African People) with 23·5% and former president André Kolingba (Democratic Rally of Central Africa) 16·4%.

Parliamentary elections in Liechtenstein were won by the Progressive Citizens' Party with 12 out of 25 seats and 48·7% of the vote, ahead of the Patriotic Union with 10 and 38·2% and the Free List with 3 and 13%.

In parliamentary elections in Tonga the Human Rights and Democracy Movement won seven out of nine seats with 38·9% of votes cast.

Week beginning 20 March 2005

Estonian Prime Minister Juhan Parts resigned. President Arnold Rüütel subsequently asked Andrus Ansip to form a new government.

In Namibia, Hifikepunye Pohamba was sworn in as president and appointed Nahas Angula prime minister.

Week beginning 27 March 2005

In Bosnia-Herzegovina, Dragan Čović was dismissed as the Croat member of the presidency by UN High Representative, Paddy Ashdown.

In the Czech Republic, members of the KDU-ČSL resigned from the cabinet. Prime Minister Stanislav Gross subsequently resigned and was replaced by Jiří Paroubek.

Paul Wolfowitz was approved as president of the World Bank.

In parliamentary elections in Zimbabwe, the Zimbabwe African National Union-Patriotic Front won 78 of the 150 seats with 58·8% of votes cast and the Movement for Democtartic Change won 41 seats with 37·5%.

Pope John Paul II died.

ADDENDA

ADDENDA

All dates are 2005

ALGERIA. In a cabinet reshuffle announced on 1 May Mohammed Bedjaoui became *Foreign Minister* and Mourad Medelci *Finance Minister*.

AUSTRIA. On 11 May the *Nationalrat* (Lower House) voted in favour of the new EU Constitution by 182 votes to 1. The *Bundesrat* (Upper House) ratified the constitution on 25 May by 59 votes to 3.

BELGIUM. On 13 May Guy Verhofstadt's government won a vote of confidence by 97 votes to 50.

BURUNDI. Jean-Marie Ngendahayo was appointed *Interior Minister* on 11 May.

CANADA. Paul Martin's government won a vote of confidence in the House of Commons on 19 May by 153 votes to 152.

In British Columbia's Legislative Assembly elections on 17 May the Liberal Party won 46·0% of the vote and 46 of the 79 available seats, the New Democratic Party won 41·3% and 33 seats, and the Green Party 9·1%. Turn-out was 53%.

CAYMAN ISLANDS. On 11 May Legislative elections were held in which the People's Progressive Movement won 9 of the 15 available seats, the United Democratic Party 5, and ind. 1. Turn-out was 78%.

CHILE. On 9 May Adriana Delpiano replaced José Miguel Insulza Salinas as *Interior Minister*.

CONGO, DEMOCRATIC REPUBLIC OF. A new constitution was adopted on 16 May.

CZECH REPUBLIC. Jiří Paroubek's coalition government won a confidence vote on 13 May by 101 votes to 99.

DENMARK. Prince Joachim and Princess Alexandra finalized their divorce on 9 April.

DJIBOUTI. On 22 May a new government was formed which included Mahamoud Ali Youssouf as *Foreign Minister*, Ali Farah Assoweh as *Finance Minister* and Yacin Elmi Bouh as *Interior Minister*. Ougoureh Kifleh Ahmed was reappointed *Defence Minister*.

ETHIOPIA. Parliamentary elections were held on 15 May. Provisional results suggested that the Ethiopian People's Revolutionary Democratic Front (EPRDF) had won 165 of the 270 seats announced, followed by the Coalition for Unity and Democracy (CUD) with 85 seats, United Ethiopian Democratic Front (UEDF) 14, Afar National Democratic Party (ANDP) 2, Oromo Fedaralist Democratic Movement (OFDM) 2, Sheko and Mezenger People's Democratic Unity Organization (SMPDUO) 1 and the Somali People's Democratic Party (SPDP) 1. Final results were scheduled to be announced on 8 June.

GERMANY. On 12 May the *Bundestag* (Lower House) approved the new EU Constitution by 569 votes to 23, with two abstentions. The *Bundesrat* (Upper House) was scheduled vote on 27 May.

In North Rhine-Westphalia the Diet was elected on 22 May. The Christian Democrats won 89 of the 187 available seats with 44·8% of the votes cast, the Social Democrats won 74 seats with 37·1%, the Free Democrats 12 with 6·2% and the Greens 12 with 6·2%. Turn-out was 63%.

MONGOLIA. In presidential elections on 22 May, Nambaryn Enkhbayar (Revolutionary People's Party of Mongolia) won with 53% of the vote against Mendsaikhany Enkhsaikhan (Democratic Party) with 20%. Turn-out was 75%.

NEPAL. On 29 April King Gyanendra lifted the state of emergency imposed on 1 Feb.

NETHERLANDS ANTILLES. At a non-binding referendum in Curaçao on 8 April, 68% of votes cast favoured Curaçao seceding from the Netherlands Antilles and becoming a territory of the Netherlands in its own right. At a contemporaneous referendum in Sint Eustatius, 76% voted to remain within the Netherlands Antilles but subject to a federal restructure.

ST VINCENT AND THE GRENADINES. In a cabinet reshuffle announced on 5 May, Mike Browne was appointed the *Foreign Affairs and Trade Minister*, Louis Straker the *Transport, Works and Housing Minister* and Clayton Burgin the *Education, Youth and Sport Minister*.

SLOVAKIA. On 11 May Slovakia ratified the new EU constitution. The parliament approved the treaty by 116 votes to 27, with four abstentions.

SPAIN. The EU Constitution, approved in a referendum on 20 Feb., was ratified by Parliament on 28 April with 311 votes to 19 and by the Senate on 18 May with 225 votes to 6.

ZIMBABWE. The currency was devalued by 45% on 19 May. Z$9,000 became equal to US$1, compared to Z$6,200 previously.

INTERNATIONAL RELATIONS

CASPIAN OIL PIPELINE. On 25 May an oil pipeline connecting the Caspian and Mediterranean seas opened. The pipeline flows from Baku, Azerbaijan to Ceyhan, Turkey via Georgia.

PART I

INTERNATIONAL ORGANIZATIONS

HOW WELL DO WE KNOW OURSELVES?

Barry Turner explores the contradictions inherent in nationalist dogma

Nationalism is back in fashion. It is almost too easy to blame 9/11 but it is in the wake of that most notorious of terrorist outrages that countries boasting their international credentials have started looking in on themselves. From America to Japan and across Europe, there is talk of defining national identity in a way that excludes outsiders, the very opposite of that once praised internationalism that celebrates tolerance, diversity and freedom. Causes that used to be the preserve of eccentric fringe parties—discrimination against immigrants of a particular race or religion, for example—are now part of mainstream politics.

For the western democracies this must create a sense of déjà vu, because, as we may need to remind ourselves, nationalism in its rawest form is entirely a European invention, one that was adopted and refined by the United States before it became the guiding principle of emerging states and the rallying cry of modern demagogues.

The doctrine of nation being something more than a collection of individuals (to use Hume's definition) is a product of the French Revolution. Presented as an alternative to royal absolution, nationalism was equated with the collective will, an abstraction that was brought into play to justify strong government. Then, as now, nationalism was linked to extremism. As Elie Kedourie has pointed out in a powerful critique, nationalism 'represented politics as a fight for principles … but since principles do not abolish interests, a pernicious confusion resulted'. Conflicting claims to represent the true spirit of nationalism could only be settled by violence. 'Terrorism became the hallmark of purity.' In one of the more terrifying expositions of nationalism, St Just was able to profess 'something terrible in the sacred love of fatherland; it is so exclusive as to sacrifice everything to the public interest, without pity, without fear, without respect for humanity … What produces the general good is always terrible'.

This concept of nation as a higher reality and, as such, a justification for often ruthless discrimination against those who for political, linguistic, racial or religious reasons, stood apart from the majority, featured strongly in the affairs of nineteenth century Europe. At the same time, a more liberal interpretation of nationalism found favour with those on the political left who saw it as a means of giving freedom to minorities under alien domination. This had particular force in the United States which, having forced an exit from the British Empire and not lived to regret it, was only too keen for other subject peoples to break the imperial chain. Nationalism as a promoter of freedom hit its highest note of idealism after the Great War when President Woodrow Wilson promoted self-rule as the recipe for a lasting peace.

Nationalism continued to flavour international relations between the world wars, deployed by left and right as it suited their territorial ambitions. Hitler was proud to call himself a nationalist—it was his excuse for occupying countries with sizeable German communities or citizens who spoke German or, in the case of Holland, an approximate language. But by no stretch of semantics was Hitler in the same category as Woodrow Wilson. Stalin had it both ways, promoting nationalism in countries where Marxism had no hold while ruthlessly repressing such sentiment when it seemed to threaten Soviet interests.

Despite the confusion, in the popular mind nationalism was a virtue while internationalism, epitomized by an ineffectual League of Nations, was branded as a surrender of inalienable rights. Nationalism was said to be the only basis on which a people could enjoy a government exclusively its own and empower that government to exercise legitimate authority. Various permutations of history and culture were cited to justify preconceived notions of association and mutual loyalty. Emotion easily outweighed rational analysis. To follow Kedourie, there was no logical reason to assume that European boundaries were determined by a natural pattern. 'France is a state not because the French constitute a nation; rather the French state is the outcome of dynastic ambitions, of circumstances, of lucky wars, of administrative and diplomatic skills. It is these which maintained order, enforced laws and carried out policies; these which made possible at last the cohesive existence of Frenchmen within the French state.'

If nationalism cannot provide an explanation for past political developments, neither can it offer a rule of thumb for the parcelling out of communities into sovereign states.

> 'The world is indeed diverse, much too diverse, for the classifications of nationalist anthropology. Races, languages, religions, political traditions and loyalties are so inextricably intermixed that there can be no clear convincing reason why people who speak the same language, but whose history and circumstances otherwise widely diverge, should form one state, or why people who speak two different languages and whom circumstances have thrown together should not form one state. On nationalist logic, the separate existence of Britain and America, and the union of English and French Canadians within the Canadian state, are both monstrosities of nature; and a consistent nationalist interpretation of history would reduce large parts of it to inexplicable and irritating anomalies.'

Just how far nationalist certainty is dependent on myth was illustrated recently in a documentary called, 'Whose is this Song?' by the Bulgarian filmmaker Adela Peeva. The idea for the movie was born at a restaurant in Istanbul where the director and a group of friends—a Serb, a Turk, an Arab and two Bulgarians fell to arguing about the origins of a familiar tune, each asserting exclusive possession as a famous national song. The movie develops this theme with interviewees from each country displaying shocked anger or disbelief when Peeva suggests the same tune is also claimed by their neighbours. She concludes that however many versions there are, 'they all point to the fact that most Balkan nations share a tradition passed down to them by what was once the Ottoman Empire and the Byzantine Empire before that'. This goes against the common belief that the Turks were oppressors who sought to crush national identities. In reality, nineteenth century nationalism redefined popular culture in national terms, exacerbating differences that led eventually to the inter-ethnic conflicts of the 1990s in the former Yugoslavia.

Yet, for the most part, national illusions are allowed to go unchallenged. Even in Europe where economic union has overcome some of the more obvious prejudices, there are revived fears of what 'others' may do to damage national self-interest, another of those notoriously ambiguous concepts that have more to do with an aversion to change of any sort than with problems of substance. Witness the widespread opposition to the proposed European constitution notwithstanding the assiduous efforts of its framers to avoid controversy. Meanwhile, the real achievements of the EU are underplayed. Start with the fact, as Jeremy Rifkin reminds us, that the EU is 'the first multinational political institution in history with the power to compel compliance to universal human rights statutes among its member countries and the 455 million people living within its jurisdiction'. To the proverbial visitor from outer space it would seem incredible that the gains need to be spelled out, as they were recently in *The Economist*.

> 'In 2004, a continent that had been wracked by war for centuries can look back on almost 60 years spent largely at peace. A continent that lay in economic ruins in 1945 is now prosperous as never before. A continent that in 1942 could list only four proper democracies is almost entirely democratic. A continent that was divided by the iron

> curtain until 1989 now enjoys free movement of people and common political institutions for 25 countries, stretching from the Atlantic coast of Portugal to the borders of Russia.'

The nationalist resurgence is unlikely to destroy the EU but it most certainly exacerbates the risks of conflict between and within nations. As already noted, nationalism by any definition is intolerant of minorities. As such it leans towards majority rule, a widely accepted form of democracy which is not democracy at all but simply dictatorship in disguise. The only true democracy is one that tries, however imperfectly, to reconcile conflicting claims, one that must entail a broadminded respect for different or opposing views.

Just how far we are departing from the ideal can be seen in the worldwide tendency of developed nations to tighten, almost to strangling point, the restrictions on immigration. The rules are invariably discriminating. It is only those who are 'not like us' who are told to stay away. As for the strangers already in our midst, according to nationalist doctrine, they must be made to conform by following established customs even to the extent of dressing in ways that do not seem strange to the majority. It is a sad irony that it is in the land of 'liberty, equality and fraternity' that a ban has been imposed on displays of religious symbols in schools. It is even more shocking to observe the cavalier manner in which the United States and Britain can use the terrorist threat to justify bending the rule of law. Innocent until proved guilty no longer has common application. When it comes to those suspected of terrorist links, it is the reverse that seems to hold true.

While the war on terrorism is fought (can it ever be won?) the internationalists among us can expect a bumpy ride. But there is some comfort in knowing that there is a counter-movement which gives hope to those who dread a return to the excesses of nationalism. It used to be said that tourism was the best antidote to chauvinism; the greater the interchange between countries, the easier it is to understand that people are much the same the world over, with the same hopes and fears. If there is any truth in this, how much more powerful must be the effects of the IT revolution with its communication channels flowing freely across territorial borders. If the small-minded ignorance of nationalist rhetoric is vulnerable to anything, it is to the free expression contained in a worldwide information system. It was Einstein who described nationalism as an infantile disease—'the measles of mankind'. It could be, that despite superficial appearances, we are close to finding a cure.

References:

Elie Kedourie, *Nationalism*. Hutchinson, 1961

Jeremy Rifkin, *The European Dream*. Polity, 2004

Anatol Lieven, *America Right or Wrong. An Anatomy of American Nationalism*. HarperCollins, 2004

Samuel P. Huntington, *Who Are We? America's Great Debate*. Simon & Schuster, 2004

Nicholas Wood, *The Strains of a Balkan Ballad*. International Herald Tribune, 16 Nov. 2004

*Outgrowing the Unions. A Survey of the European Unio*n. The Economist, 25 Sept. 2004

UNITED NATIONS (UN)

Origin and Aims. The United Nations is an association of states which have pledged themselves to maintain international peace and security and co-operate in solving international political, economic, social, cultural and humanitarian problems towards achieving this end. The name 'United Nations' was devised by United States President Franklin D. Roosevelt and was first used in the Declaration by United Nations of 1 Jan. 1942, during the Second World War, when representatives of 26 nations pledged their Governments to continue fighting together against the Axis Powers.

The United Nations Charter, the constituting instrument of the UN, was drawn up by the representatives of 50 countries at the United Nations Conference on International Organization, which met in San Francisco from 25 April to 26 June 1945. Those delegates deliberated on the basis of proposals worked out by the representatives of China, the Soviet Union, the United Kingdom and the United States at Dumbarton Oaks (Washington, D.C.) from 21 Aug. to 28 Sept. 1944. The Charter was signed on 26 June 1945 by the representatives of the 50 countries. Poland, which was not represented at the Conference, signed it later and became one of the original 51 member states. Nothing contained in the Charter authorizes the organization to intervene in matters which are essentially within the domestic jurisdiction of any state.

The United Nations officially came into existence on 24 Oct. 1945, with the deposit of the requisite number of ratifications of the Charter with the US Department of State. United Nations Day is celebrated on 24 Oct. each year.

Today, 80% of the UN's work is devoted to helping developing countries build the capacity to help themselves. This includes promoting the creation of independent and democratic societies, which it is hoped will offer vital support for the Charter's goals in the 21st century; the protection of human rights; saving children from starvation and disease; providing relief assistance to refugees and disaster victims; countering global crime, drugs and disease; and assisting countries devastated by war and the long-term threat of landmines.

Members. New member states are admitted by the General Assembly on the recommendation of the Security Council. The Charter provides for the suspension or expulsion of a member for violation of its principles, but no such action has ever been taken. It has 191 member states. (For a list of these, see below.)

Finance. Assessments on member states constitute the main source of funds. These are in accordance with a scale specified by the Assembly, and determined primarily by the country's share of the world economy and ability to pay, in the range 22%–0·001%. The Organization is prohibited by law from borrowing from commercial institutions.

A Working Group on the Financial Situation of the United Nations was established in 1994 to address the long-standing financial crisis which has come about because of the non-payment of assessed dues by many member states, severely threatening the Organization's ability to fulfil its mandates. As of 31 Dec. 2004 member states owed the UN a total of US$2,965m., of which the USA owed US$975m. (33%). Total debts outstanding to the UN regular budget as of 31 Dec. 2004 were US$357m., of which the USA's share was US$241m. (68%).

Official languages: Arabic, Chinese, English, French, Russian and Spanish.

Structure. The UN has six principal organs established by the founding Charter. All have their headquarters in New York except the International Court of Justice, which has its seat in The Hague. These core bodies work through dozens of related agencies, operational programmes and funds, and through special agreements with separate, autonomous, intergovernmental agencies, known as Specialized Agencies, in order to provide an increasingly cohesive programme of action in the fields of peace and security, justice and human rights, humanitarian assistance, and social and economic development. The six principal UN organs are as follows:

1. **The General Assembly**, composed of all members, is the main deliberative body; each member has one vote. It meets once a year, commencing on the first Tuesday following 1 Sept., and the general debate is organized over a period of two weeks, beginning the 3rd week of Sept. (The 59th Session opened on 14 Sept. 2004.)

At the start of each session, the Assembly elects a new President, 21 vice-presidents and the chairmen of its six main committees, listed below. To ensure equitable geographical representation, the presidency of the Assembly rotates each year among the five geographical groups of states: African, Asian, Eastern European, Latin American and the Caribbean, and Western European and other States. Special sessions may be convoked by the Secretary-General if requested by the Security Council, by a majority of members, or by one member if the majority of the members concur. Emergency sessions may be called within 24 hours at the request of the Security Council on the vote of any nine Council members, or a majority of United Nations members, or one member if the majority of members concur. Decisions on important questions, such as peace and security, new membership and budgetary matters, require a two-thirds majority; other questions require a simple majority of members present and voting.

The work of the General Assembly is divided between six Main Committees, on which every member state is represented. These are: Disarmament and International Security Committee (First Committee); Economic and Financial Committee (Second Committee); Social, Humanitarian and Cultural Committee (Third Committee); Special Political and Decolonization Committee (Fourth Committee); Administrative and Budgetary Committee (Fifth Committee); Legal Committee (Sixth Committee).

There is also a General Committee charged with the task of co-ordinating the proceedings of the Assembly and its Committees, and a Credentials Committee. The General Committee consists of 28 members: the president and 21 vice-presidents of the General Assembly and the chairmen of the six main committees. The Credentials Committee consists of nine members appointed by the Assembly on the proposal of the President at each session. In addition, the Assembly has two standing committees—an Advisory Committee on Administrative and Budgetary Questions, and a Committee on Contributions; and may establish subsidiary and ad hoc bodies when necessary to deal with specific matters. These include: Special Committee on Peacekeeping Operations (100 members), Human Rights Committee (18 members), Committee on the Peaceful Uses of Outer Space (67 members), Conciliation Commission for Palestine (3 members), Conference on Disarmament (65 members), International Law Commission (34 members), Scientific Committee on the Effects of Atomic Radiation (21 members), Special Committee on the Situation with Regard to the Implementation of the Declaration on the Granting of Independence to Colonial Countries and Peoples (24 members), and Commission on International Trade Law (36 members).

The General Assembly has the right to discuss any matters within the scope of the Charter and, with the exception of any situation or dispute on the agenda of the Security Council, may make recommendations on any such questions or matters. Occupying a central position in the UN, the Assembly receives reports from other organs, admits new members, directs activities for development, sets policies and determines programmes for the Secretariat, appoints the Secretary-General, who reports annually to it on the work of the Organization, and approves the UN budget.

Under the 'Uniting For Peace' resolution adopted by the General Assembly in Nov. 1950, the Assembly is also empowered to take action if the Security Council, because of a lack of unanimity of its permanent members, fails to exercise its primary responsibility for the maintenance of international peace and security in any case where there appears to be a threat to the peace, breach of the peace or act of aggression. In this event, the General Assembly may consider the matter immediately with a view to making appropriate recommendations to members for collective measures, including, in the case of a breach of the peace or act of aggression, the use of armed force when necessary, to maintain or restore international peace and security.

2. **The Security Council** has primary responsibility, under the Charter, for the maintenance of international peace and security. It is so organized as to be able to function continuously. A representative of each of its members must be present at all times at UN Headquarters, but it may meet elsewhere as best facilitates its work.

The Presidency of the Council rotates monthly, according to the English alphabetical order of members' names. The Council consists of 15 members: five permanent and ten non-permanent elected for a two-year term by a two-thirds majority of the General Assembly. Each member has one vote. Retiring members are not eligible for immediate re-election. Any other member of the United Nations may participate without a vote in the discussion of questions specially affecting its interests.

Decisions on procedural questions are made by an affirmative vote of at least nine members. On all other matters, the affirmative vote of nine members must include the concurring votes of all permanent members (subject to the provision that when the Council is considering methods for the peaceful settlement of a dispute, parties to the dispute abstain from voting). Consequently, a negative vote from a permanent member has the power of veto, and all five permanent members have exercised this right at one time or other. If a permanent member does not support a decision but does not wish to veto it, it may abstain. Under the Charter, the Security Council alone has the power to take decisions which member states are obligated to carry out.

The Council has two standing committees—the Committee of Experts on Rules of Procedure and the Committee on the Admission of New Members. It may establish ad hoc committees and commissions, such as the Committee on Council Meetings away from Headquarters.

When a threat to peace is brought before the Council, it may undertake mediation and set out principles for a settlement, and may take measures to enforce its decisions by ceasefire directives, economic sanctions, peacekeeping missions, or in some cases, by collective military action. For the maintenance of international peace and security, the Council can, in accordance with special agreements to be concluded, call on the armed forces, assistance and facilities of the member states. It is assisted by a Military Staff Committee consisting of the Chiefs of Staff of the permanent members of the Council or their representatives.

The Council also makes recommendations to the Assembly on the appointment of the Secretary-General and, with the Assembly, elects the judges of the International Court.

In Nov. 2002 the Security Council adopted Resolution 1441, holding Iraq in 'material breach' of disarmament obligations. Weapons inspectors under the leadership of Hans Blix (Sweden) returned to Iraq four years after their last inspections, but US and British suspicion that the Iraq regime was failing to comply led to increasing tension, resulting in the USA, the UK and Spain declaring that they reserved the right to disarm Iraq without the need for a further Security Council resolution. Other Security Council members, notably China, France, Germany and Russia, opposed the proposed action, resulting in a major split in the Security Council. On 20 March 2003 US forces, supported by the UK, launched attacks on Iraq, and initiated a war aimed at bringing an end to Saddam Hussein's rule.

Permanent Members. China, France, Russian Federation, UK, USA (Russian Federation took over the seat of the former USSR in Dec. 1991).

Non-Permanent Members. Algeria, Benin, Brazil, Philippines and Romania (until 31 Dec. 2005); Argentina, Denmark, Greece, Japan, Tanzania (until 31 Dec. 2006).

Finance. The budget for UN peacekeeping operations in 2004–05 was US$3·9bn. The estimated total cost of operations between 1948 and mid-2004 was US$31·5bn. In Jan. 2005 outstanding contributions to peacekeeping totalled US$2·3bn.

3. **The Economic and Social Council (ECOSOC)** is responsible under the General Assembly for co-ordinating the functions of the UN with regard to international economic, social, cultural, educational, health and related matters. The year-round work of the Council is carried out by related organizations, specialized agencies, and subsidiary bodies, commissions and committees, which meet regularly and report back to it.

It consists of 54 member states elected by a two-thirds majority of the General Assembly for a three-year term. Members are elected according to the following geographic distribution: Africa, 14 members; Asia, 11; Eastern Europe, 6; Latin America and Caribbean, 10; Western Europe and other States, 13. A third of the members retire each year. Retiring members are eligible for immediate re-election. Each member has one vote. Decisions are made by a majority of the members present and voting.

The Council holds one five-week substantive session a year, alternating between New York and Geneva, and one organizational session in New York. The substantive session includes a high-level meeting attended by Ministers, to discuss economic and social issues. Special sessions may be held if required. The President is elected for one year and is eligible for immediate re-election.

The subsidiary machinery of ECOSOC is as follows:

Nine Functional Commissions. Statistical Commission; Commission on Population and Development; Commission for Social Development; Commission on Human Rights (and Subcommission on Prevention of Discrimination and Protection of Minorities); Commission on the Status of Women; Commission on Narcotic Drugs (and Subcommission on Illicit Drug Traffic and Related Matters in the Near and Middle East); Commission on Science and Technology for Development; Commission on Crime Prevention and Criminal Justice; Commission on Sustainable Development.

Five Regional Economic Commissions. ECA (Economic Commission for Africa, Addis Ababa, Ethiopia); ESCAP (Economic and Social Commission for Asia and the Pacific, Bangkok, Thailand); ECE (Economic Commission for Europe, Geneva, Switzerland); ECLAC (Economic Commission for Latin America and the Caribbean, Santiago, Chile); ESCWA (Economic Commission for Western Asia, Beirut, Lebanon).

Nine Standing Committees and Subsidiary Expert Bodies. Committee for Programme and Co-ordination; Commission on Human Settlements; Committee on Non-Governmental Organizations; Committee on Natural Resources; Committee for Development Planning; Committee on Economic, Social and Cultural Rights; Committee on New and Renewable Sources of Energy and on Energy for Development; Ad Hoc Group of Experts on International Co-operation in Tax Matters; Committee of Experts on the Transport of Dangerous Goods.

Other related operational programmes, funds and special bodies, which report to ECOSOC (and/or the General Assembly) include: the United Nations Children's Fund (UNICEF); Office of the United Nations High Commissioner for Refugees (UNHCR); United Nations Conference on Trade and Development (UNCTAD); United Nations Development Programme (UNDP) and Population Fund (UNFPA); United Nations Environment Programme (UNEP); World Food Programme (WFP); International Research and Training Institute for the Advancement of Women (INSTRAW); United Nations Office on Drugs and Crime (ODC).

In addition, the Council may make arrangements for consultation with international non-governmental organizations (NGOs) and, after consultation with the member concerned, with national organizations. There are over 1,600 non-governmental organizations which have consultative status with the Council. Non-governmental organizations may send observers to the Council's public meetings and those of its subsidiary bodies, and may submit written statements relevant to its work. They may also consult with the UN Secretariat on matters of mutual concern. The term of office of the members listed below expires on 31 Dec. of the year mentioned after the country.

Members. Albania (2007), Armenia (2006), Australia (2007), Azerbaijan (2005), Bangladesh (2006), Belgium (2006), Belize (2006), Benin (2005), Brazil (2007), Canada (2006), Chad (2007), China (2007), Colombia (2006), Congo, Democratic Republic of the (2007), Congo, Republic of the (2005), Costa Rica (2007), Cuba (2005), Denmark (2007), Ecuador (2005), France (2005), Germany (2005), Greece (2005), Guinea (2007), Iceland (2007), India (2007), Indonesia (2006), Ireland (2005), Italy (2006), Jamaica (2005), Japan (2005), Kenya (2005), Lithuania (2007), Malaysia (2005), Mauritius (2006), Mexico (2007), Mozambique (2005), Namibia (2006), Nicaragua (2005), Nigeria (2006), Pakistan (2007), Panama

(2006), Poland (2006), Portugal (2005), Russia (2007), Saudi Arabia (2005), Senegal (2005), South Africa (2007), South Korea (2006), Tanzania (2006), Thailand (2007), Tunisia (2006), United Arab Emirates (2006), United Kingdom (2007), USA (2006).

Finance. In 2002, US$7,338m. in socio-economic development assistance grants was provided through the organizations of the UN system.

4. **The Trusteeship Council** was established to ensure that Governments responsible for administering Trust Territories take adequate steps to prepare them for self-government or independence. It consists of five permanent members of the Security Council. The task of decolonization was completed in 1994, when the Security Council terminated the Trusteeship Agreement for the last of the original UN Trusteeships (Palau), administered by the USA. All Trust Territories attained self-government or independence either as separate States or by joining neighbouring independent countries. The Council formally suspended operations on 1 Nov. 1994 following Palau's independence. By a resolution adopted on 25 May 1994 the Council amended its rules of procedure to drop the obligation to meet annually and agreed to meet as occasion required.

The proposal from UN Secretary-General Kofi Annan, in the second part of his reform programme, in July 1997, is that it should be used as a forum to exercise their 'trusteeship' for the global commons, environment and resource systems.

Members. China, France, Russia, UK, USA.

5. **The International Court of Justice** is the principal judicial organ of the UN. It has a dual role: to settle in accordance with international law the legal disputes submitted to it by States; and to give advisory opinion on legal questions referred to it by duly authorized international organs and agencies.

It operates under a Statute, which is an integral part of the United Nations Charter. Only States may apply to and appear before the Court. The member states of the United Nations (at present numbering 191) are so entitled. The Court is composed of 15 judges, each of a different nationality elected with an absolute majority to nine-year terms of office by both the General Assembly and the Security Council. The composition of the Court must also reflect the main forms of civilization and principal legal systems of the world. Elections are held every three years for one-third of the seats, and retiring judges may be re-elected. Members do not represent their respective governments but sit as independent magistrates in the Court, and must possess the qualifications required in their respective countries for appointment to the highest judicial offices, or be jurists of recognized competence in international law.

Candidates are nominated by the national panels of jurists in the Permanent Court of Arbitration established by the Hague Conventions of 1899 and 1907. The Court elects its own President and Vice-President for a three-year term, and is permanently in session.

Decisions are taken by a majority of judges present, subject to a quorum of nine members, with the President having a casting vote. Judgment is final and without appeal, but a revision may be applied for within ten years from the date of the judgment on the ground of a new decisive factor. When the Court does not include a judge possessing the nationality of a State party to a case, that State has the right to appoint a person to sit as judge *ad hoc* for that case, on equal terms with Members.

While the Court normally sits in plenary session, it can form chambers of three or more judges to deal with specific matters. Judgments by chambers are considered as rendered by the full Court. In 1993, in view of the global expansion of environmental law and protection, the Court formed a seven-member Chamber for Environmental Matters.

Judges. The nine-year terms of office of the judges currently serving end on 5 Feb. of the year indicated next to their name: Shi Jiuyong, President (China) (2012), Raymond Ranjeva, Vice-President (Madagascar) (2009), Abdul G. Koroma (Sierra Leone) (2012), Vladlen S. Vereshchetin (Russian Federation) (2006), Rosalyn Higgins (UK) (2009), Gonzalo Parra-Aranguren (Venezuela) (2009), Pieter H. Kooijmans (Netherlands) (2006), José F. Rezek (Brazil) (2006), Awn Shawkat Al-Khasawneh (Jordan) (2009), Thomas Buergenthal (USA) (2006), Nabil Elaraby

(Egypt) (2006), Hishashi Owada (Japan) (2012), Bruno Simma (Germany) (2012), Peter Tomka (Slovakia) (2012), Ronny Abraham (France) (2009).

Competence and Jurisdiction. In contentious cases, only States may apply to or appear before the Court, which is open only to parties to its Statute, which automatically includes all Members of the UN. The conditions under which the Court will be open to other states are laid down by the Security Council. The jurisdiction of the Court covers all matters which parties refer to it, and all matters provided for in the Charter or in treaties and conventions in force. Disputes concerning the jurisdiction of the Court are settled by the Court's own decision. The Court may apply in its decision:

(a) international conventions;
(b) international custom;
(c) the general principles of law recognized by civilized nations;
(d) as subsidiary means for the determination of the rules of law, judicial decisions and the teachings of highly qualified publicists. If the parties agree, the Court may decide a case *ex aequo et bono*.

Since 1946 the Court has delivered 88 judgments on disputes concerning *inter alia* land frontiers and maritime boundaries, territorial sovereignty, the non-use of force, non-interference in the internal affairs of States, diplomatic relations, hostage-taking, the right of asylum, nationality, guardianship, rights of passage and economic rights.

The Court may also give advisory opinions on legal questions to the General Assembly, the Security Council, certain other organs of the UN and 16 specialized agencies of the UN family.

Since 1946 the Court has given 25 advisory opinions, concerning *inter alia* admission to United Nations membership, reparation for injuries suffered in the service of the United Nations, territorial status of South-West Africa (Namibia) and Western Sahara, expenses of certain United Nations operations, the status of human rights informers, the threat or use of nuclear weapons and legal consequences of the construction of a wall in the Occupied Palestinian Territory.

Finance. The expenses of the Court are borne by the UN. No court fees are paid by parties to the Statute.

Official languages: English, French.
Headquarters: The Peace Palace, 2517 KJ The Hague, Netherlands.
Website: http://www.icj-cij.org
Registrar: Philippe Couvreur (Belgium).

6. **The Secretariat** services the other five organs of the UN, administering their programmes and carrying out the Organization's day-to-day work with its increasingly streamlined staff of some 8,900 at the UN Headquarters in New York and all over the world.

At its head is the Secretary-General, appointed by the General Assembly on the recommendation of the Security Council for a five-year, renewable term. The Secretary-General acts as chief administrative officer in all meetings of the General Assembly, Security Council, Economic and Social Council and Trusteeship Council. An Office of Internal Oversight, established in 1994 under the tenure of former Secretary-General Boutros Boutros-Ghali (Egypt), pursues a cost-saving mandate to investigate and eliminate waste, fraud and mismanagement within the system.

The Secretary-General is assisted by Under-Secretaries-General and Assistant Secretaries-General. A new appointment of Deputy Secretary-General was agreed in principle by the General Assembly in 1997 and was announced in Jan. 1998.

Finance. The financial year coincides with the calendar year. The budget for the two-year period 2004–05 is US$3,160,860,300, compared to US$2,890,818,700 in 2002–03.

Headquarters: United Nations Plaza, New York, NY 10017, USA.
Website: http://www.un.org
Secretary-General: Kofi Annan (appointed 1 Jan. 1997 and re-elected 29 June 2001, Ghana). Deputy Secretary-General: Louise Fréchette (appointed 12 Jan. 1998, Canada).

MEMBER STATES OF THE UN

The 191 member states, with percentage scale of contributions to the Regular Budget in 2004 and year of admission:

	% contribution	*Year of admission*
Afghanistan	0·002	1946
Albania	0·005	1955
Algeria	0·076	1962
Andorra	0·005	1993
Angola	0·001	1976
Antigua and Barbuda	0·003	1981
Argentina[1]	0·956	1945
Armenia	0·002	1992
Australia[1]	1·592	1945
Austria	0·859	1955
Azerbaijan	0·005	1992
Bahamas	0·013	1973
Bahrain	0·030	1971
Bangladesh	0·010	1974
Barbados	0·010	1966
Belarus[1, 3]	0·018	1945
Belgium[1]	1·069	1945
Belize	0·001	1981
Benin	0·002	1960
Bhutan	0·001	1971
Bolivia[1]	0·009	1945
Bosnia-Herzegovina	0·003	1992
Botswana	0·012	1966
Brazil[1]	1·523	1945
Brunei	0·034	1984
Bulgaria	0·017	1955
Burkina Faso	0·002	1960
Burundi	0·001	1962
Cambodia	0·002	1955
Cameroon	0·008	1960
Canada[1]	2·813	1945
Cape Verde	0·001	1975
Central African Rep.	0·001	1960
Chad	0·001	1960
Chile[1]	0·223	1945
China[1]	2·053	1945
Colombia[1]	0·155	1945
Comoros	0·001	1975
Congo, Dem. Rep. of the[5]	0·003	1960
Congo, Rep. of the	0·001	1960
Costa Rica[1]	0·030	1945
Côte d'Ivoire	0·010	1960
Croatia	0·037	1992
Cuba[1]	0·043	1945
Cyprus	0·039	1960
Czech Republic[8]	0·183	1993
Denmark[1]	0·718	1945
Djibouti	0·001	1977
Dominica	0·001	1978
Dominican Republic[1]	0·035	1945
East Timor	0·001	2002
Ecuador[1]	0·019	1945
Egypt[1, 9]	0·120	1945
El Salvador[1]	0·022	1945
Equatorial Guinea	0·002	1968
Eritrea	0·001	1993
Estonia	0·012	1991
Ethiopia[1]	0·004	1945
Fiji Islands	0·004	1970
Finland	0·533	1955
France[1]	6·030	1945
Gabon	0·009	1960
Gambia	0·001	1965
Georgia	0·003	1992
Germany[2]	8·662	1973
Ghana	0·004	1957
Greece[1]	0·530	1945
Grenada	0·001	1974
Guatemala[1]	0·030	1945
Guinea	0·003	1958
Guinea-Bissau	0·001	1974
Guyana	0·001	1966
Haiti[1]	0·003	1945
Honduras[1]	0·005	1945
Hungary	0·126	1955
Iceland	0·034	1946
India[1]	0·421	1945
Indonesia[4]	0·142	1950
Iran[1]	0·157	1945
Iraq[1]	0·016	1945
Ireland, Rep. of	0·350	1955
Israel	0·467	1949
Italy	4·885	1955
Jamaica	0·008	1962
Japan	19·468	1956
Jordan	0·011	1955
Kazakhstan	0·025	1992
Kenya	0·009	1963
Kiribati	0·001	1999
Korea (North)	0·010	1991
Korea (South)	1·796	1991
Kuwait	0·162	1963
Kyrgyzstan	0·001	1992
Laos	0·001	1955
Latvia	0·015	1991
Lebanon[1]	0·024	1945
Lesotho	0·001	1966
Liberia[1]	0·001	1945
Libya	0·132	1955
Liechtenstein	0·005	1990
Lithuania	0·024	1991
Luxembourg[1]	0·077	1945
Macedonia[6]	0·006	1993
Madagascar	0·003	1960
Malaŵi	0·001	1964
Malaysia[7]	0·203	1957
Maldives	0·001	1965
Mali	0·002	1960
Malta	0·014	1964
Marshall Islands	0·001	1991
Mauritania	0·001	1961
Mauritius	0·011	1968
Mexico[1]	1·883	1945
Micronesia	0·001	1991
Moldova	0·001	1992
Monaco	0·003	1993
Mongolia	0·001	1961
Morocco	0·047	1956
Mozambique	0·001	1975
Myanmar[10]	0·010	1948
Namibia	0·006	1990

	% contribution	Year of admission		% contribution	Year of admission
Nauru	0·001	1999	Slovakia[8]	0·051	1993
Nepal	0·004	1955	Slovenia	0·082	1992
Netherlands[1]	1·690	1945	Solomon Islands	0·001	1978
New Zealand[1]	0·221	1945	Somalia	0·001	1960
Nicaragua[1]	0·001	1945	South Africa[1]	0·292	1945
Niger	0·001	1960	Spain	2·520	1955
Nigeria	0·042	1960	Sri Lanka	0·017	1955
Norway[1]	0·679	1945	Sudan	0·008	1956
Oman	0·070	1971	Suriname	0·001	1975
Pakistan	0·055	1947	Swaziland	0·002	1968
Palau	0·001	1994	Sweden	0·998	1946
Panama[1]	0·019	1945	Switzerland	1·197	2002
Papua New Guinea	0·003	1975	Syria[1, 11]	0·038	1945
Paraguay[1]	0·012	1945	Tajikistan	0·001	1992
Peru[1]	0·092	1945	Tanzania[12]	0·006	1961
Philippines[1]	0·095	1945	Thailand	0·209	1946
Poland[1]	0·461	1945	Togo	0·001	1960
Portugal	0·470	1955	Tonga	0·001	1999
Qatar	0·064	1971	Trinidad and Tobago	0·022	1962
Romania	0·060	1955	Tunisia	0·032	1956
Russia[1, 13]	1·100	1945	Turkey[1]	0·372	1945
Rwanda	0·001	1962	Turkmenistan	0·005	1992
St Kitts and Nevis	0·001	1983	Tuvalu	0·001	2000
St Lucia	0·002	1979	Uganda	0·006	1962
St Vincent and the Grenadines	0·001	1980	Ukraine[1]	0·039	1945
Samoa	0·001	1976	United Arab Emirates	0·235	1971
San Marino	0·003	1992	UK[1]	6·127	1945
São Tomé e Príncipe	0·001	1975	USA[1]	22·000	1945
Saudi Arabia[1]	0·713	1945	Uruguay[1]	0·048	1945
Senegal	0·005	1960	Uzbekistan	0·014	1992
Serbia and Montenegro[1, 14, 15]	0·019	1945	Vanuatu	0·001	1981
Seychelles	0·002	1976	Venezuela[1]	0·171	1945
Sierra Leone	0·001	1961	Vietnam	0·021	1977
Singapore[17]	0·388	1965	Yemen[16]	0·006	1947
			Zambia	0·002	1964
			Zimbabwe	0·007	1980

[1]Original member. [2]Pre-unification (1990) as two states: the Federal Republic of Germany and the German Democratic Republic. [3]As Byelorussia, 1945–91. [4]Withdrew temporarily, 1965–66. [5]As Zaïre, 1960–97. [6]Pre-independence (1992), as part of Yugoslavia, which was an original member. [7]As the Federation of Malaya till 1963, when the new federation of Malaysia (including Singapore, Sarawak and Sabah) was formed. [8]Pre-partition Czechoslovakia (1945–92) was an original member. [9]As United Arab Republic, 1958–71, following union with Syria (1958–61). [10]As Burma, 1948–89. [11]As United Arab Republic, by union with Egypt, 1958–61. [12]As two states: Tanganyika, 1961–64, and Zanzibar, 1963–64, prior to union as one republic under new name. [13]As USSR, 1945–91. [14]As Yugoslavia, 1945–2003. [15]Excluded from the General Assembly in 1992; re-admitted in Nov. 2000. [16]As Yemen, 1947–90, and Democratic Yemen, 1967–90, prior to merger of the two. [17]As part of Malaysia, 1963–65.

The USA is the leading contributor to the Peacekeeping Operations Budget, with 26·6752% of the total at July 2004, followed by Japan (19·4680%), Germany (8·6620%), UK (7·4290%), France (7·3114%), Italy (4·8850%), Canada (2·8130%), Spain (2·5200%) and China (2·4893%). All other countries contribute less than 2%.

Publications. Yearbook of the United Nations. New York, 1947 ff.—*United Nations Chronicle. Quarterly.—Monthly Bulletin of Statistics.—General Assembly: Official Records: Resolutions.—Reports of the Secretary-General of the United Nations on the Work of the Organization.* 1946 ff.—*Charter of the United Nations and Statute of the International Court of Justice.—Official Records of the Security Council, the Economic and Social Council, Trusteeship Council and the Disarmament Commission.—Demographic Yearbook.* New York.—*Basic Facts About the United Nations.* New York, 2002.—*Statistical Yearbook.* New York, 1947 ff.—*Yearbook of International Statistics.* New York, 1950 ff.—*World Economic Survey.* New York, 1947 ff.—*Economic Survey of Asia and the Far East.* New York, 1946 ff.—*Economic Survey of Latin America.* New York, 1948 ff.—*Economic Survey of Europe.* New York, 1948 ff.—*Economic Survey of Africa.* New York, 1960 ff.—*United Nations Reference Guide in the Field of Human Rights.* UN Centre for Human Rights, 1993.

Further Reading

Arnold, G., *World Government by Stealth: The Future of the United Nations.* Macmillan, 1998
Baehr, P. R. and Gordenker, L., *The United Nations in the 1990s.* 2nd ed. London, 1994
Bailey, S. D. and Daws, S., *The United Nations: a Concise Political Guide.* 3rd ed. London, 1994
Baratta, J. P., *United Nations System* [Bibliography]. Oxford and New Brunswick (NJ), 1995
Beigbeder, Y., *The Internal Management of United Nations Organizations: the Long Quest for Reform.* London, 1996
Butler, R., *The Greatest Threat: Iraq, Weapons of Mass Destruction and the Crisis of Global Security.* Public Affairs, New York, 2000
Carnegie Commission on Preventing Deadly Conflict, Preventing Deadly Conflict: Final Report. New York, 1997
Cortright, D. and Lopez, G. A., *The Sanctions Decade: Assessing UN Strategies in the 1990s.* Lynne Rienner Publishers, Boulder, 2000
Durch, W. J., *The Evolution of UN Peacekeeping: Case Studies and Comparative Analysis.* New York, 1993
Gareis, S. B. and Varwick, J., *The United Nations: An Introduction.* Basingstoke and New York, 2005
Ginifer, J. (ed.) *Development Within UN Peace Missions.* London, 1997
Hoopes, T., and Brinkley, D., *FDR and the Creation of the UN.* Yale Univ. Press, 1998
Luard, E., *The United Nations: How It Works and What It Does.* 2nd ed. London, 1994
Meisler, S., *United Nations: The First Fifty Years.* Atlantic Monthly Press, 1998
New Zealand Ministry of Foreign Affairs, *UN Handbook.* 1997
Osmanczyk, E., *Encyclopaedia of the United Nations.* London, 1985
Parsons, A., *From Cold War to Hot Peace: UN Interventions, 1947–94.* London, 1995
Pugh, M., *The UN, Peace and Force.* London, 1997
Ratner, S. R., *The New UN Peacekeeping: Building Peace in Lands of Conflict after the Cold War.* London, 1995
Righter, R., *Utopia Lost: the United Nations and World Order.* New York, 1995
Roberts, A. and Kingsbury, B. (eds.) *United Nations, Divided World: the UN's Roles in International Relations.* 2nd ed. Oxford, 1993
Simma, B. (ed.) *The Charter of the United Nations: a Commentary.* OUP, 1995
Williams, D., *The Specialized Agencies of the United Nations.* London, 1987

UNIVERSAL DECLARATION OF HUMAN RIGHTS

On 10 Dec. 1948 the General Assembly of the United Nations adopted and proclaimed the Universal Declaration of Human Rights.

Preamble

Whereas recognition of the inherent dignity and of the equal and inalienable rights of all members of the human family is the foundation of freedom, justice and peace in the world,

Whereas disregard and contempt for human rights have resulted in barbarous acts which have outraged the conscience of mankind, and the advent of a world in which human beings shall enjoy freedom of speech and belief and freedom from fear and want has been proclaimed as the highest aspiration of the common people,

Whereas it is essential, if man is not to be compelled to have recourse, as a last resort, to rebellion against tyranny and oppression, that human rights should be protected by the rule of law,

Whereas it is essential to promote the development of friendly relations between nations,

Whereas the peoples of the United Nations have in the Charter reaffirmed their faith in fundamental human rights, in the dignity and worth of the human person and in the equal rights of men and women and have determined to promote social progress and better standards of life in larger freedom,

Whereas Member States have pledged themselves to achieve, in co-operation with the United Nations, the promotion of universal respect for and observance of human rights and fundamental freedoms,

Whereas a common understanding of these rights and freedoms is of the greatest importance for the full realization of this pledge,

Now, Therefore THE GENERAL ASSEMBLY proclaims THIS UNIVERSAL DECLARATION OF HUMAN RIGHTS as a common standard of achievement for all peoples and all nations, to the end that every individual and every organ of society, keeping this Declaration constantly in mind, shall strive by teaching and education to promote respect for these rights and freedoms and by progressive measures, national and international, to secure their universal and effective recognition and observance, both among the peoples of Member States themselves and among the peoples of territories under their jurisdiction.

Article 1. All human beings are born free and equal in dignity and rights. They are endowed with reason and conscience and should act towards one another in a spirit of brotherhood.

Article 2. Everyone is entitled to all the rights and freedoms set forth in this Declaration, without distinction of any kind, such as race, colour, sex, language, religion, political or other opinion, national or social origin, property, birth or other status. Furthermore, no distinction shall be made on the basis of the political, jurisdictional or international status of the country or territory to which a person belongs, whether it be independent, trust, non-self-governing or under any other limitation of sovereignty.

Article 3. Everyone has the right to life, liberty and security of person.

Article 4. No one shall be held in slavery or servitude; slavery and the slave trade shall be prohibited in all their forms.

Article 5. No one shall be subjected to torture or to cruel, inhuman or degrading treatment or punishment.

Article 6. Everyone has the right to recognition everywhere as a person before the law.

Article 7. All are equal before the law and are entitled without any discrimination to equal protection of the law. All are entitled to equal protection against any discrimination in violation of this Declaration and against any incitement to such discrimination.

Article 8. Everyone has the right to an effective remedy by the competent national tribunals for acts violating the fundamental rights granted him by the constitution or by law.

Article 9. No one shall be subjected to arbitrary arrest, detention or exile.

Article 10. Everyone is entitled in full equality to a fair and public hearing by an independent and impartial tribunal, in the determination of his rights and obligations and of any criminal charge against him.

Article 11. (1) Everyone charged with a penal offence has the right to be presumed innocent until proved guilty according to law in a public trial at which he has had all the guarantees necessary for his defence.

(2) No one shall be held guilty of any penal offence on account of any act or omission which did not constitute a penal offence, under national or international law, at the time when it was committed. Nor shall a heavier penalty be imposed than the one that was applicable at the time the penal offence was committed.

Article 12. No one shall be subjected to arbitrary interference with his privacy, family, home or correspondence, nor to attacks upon his honour and reputation. Everyone has the right to the protection of the law against such interference or attacks.

Article 13. (1) Everyone has the right to freedom of movement and residence within the borders of each state.

(2) Everyone has the right to leave any country, including his own, and to return to his country.

Article 14. (1) Everyone has the right to seek and enjoy in other countries asylum from persecution.

(2) This right may not be invoked in the case of prosecutions genuinely arising from non-political crimes or from acts contrary to the purposes and principles of the United Nations.

Article 15. (1) Everyone has the right to a nationality.

(2) No one shall be arbitrarily deprived of his nationality nor denied the right to change his nationality.

Article 16. (1) Men and women of full age, without any limitation due to race, nationality or religion, have the right to marry and to found a family. They are entitled to equal rights as to marriage, during marriage and at its dissolution.

(2) Marriage shall be entered into only with the free and full consent of the intending spouses.

(3) The family is the natural and fundamental group unit of society and is entitled to protection by society and the State.

Article 17. (1) Everyone has the right to own property alone as well as in association with others.

(2) No one shall be arbitrarily deprived of his property.

Article 18. Everyone has the right to freedom of thought, conscience and religion; this right includes freedom to change his religion or belief, and freedom, either alone or in community with others and in public or private, to manifest his religion or belief in teaching, practice, worship and observance.

Article 19. Everyone has the right to freedom of opinion and expression; this right includes freedom to hold opinions without interference and to seek, receive and impart information and ideas through any media and regardless of frontiers.

Article 20. (1) Everyone has the right to freedom of peaceful assembly and association.

(2) No one may be compelled to belong to an association.

Article 21. (1) Everyone has the right to take part in the government of his country, directly or through freely chosen representatives.

(2) Everyone has the right of equal access to public service in his country.

(3) The will of the people shall be the basis of the authority of government; this will shall be expressed in periodic and genuine elections which shall be by universal and equal suffrage and shall be held by secret vote or by equivalent free voting procedures.

Article 22. Everyone, as a member of society, has the right to social security and is entitled to realization, through national effort and international co-operation and in accordance with the organization and resources of the State, of the economic, social and cultural rights indispensable for his dignity and the free development of his personality.

Article 23. (1) Everyone has the right to work, to free choice of employment, to just and favourable conditions of and to protection against unemployment.

(2) Everyone, without any discrimination, has the right to equal pay for equal work.

(3) Everyone who works has the right to just and favourable remuneration ensuring for himself and his family an existence worthy of human dignity, and supplemented, if necessary, by other means of social protection.

(4) Everyone has the right to form and to join trade unions for the protection of his interests.

Article 24. Everyone has the right to rest and leisure, including reasonable limitation of working hours and periodic holidays with pay.

Article 25. (1) Everyone has the right to a standard of living adequate for the health and well-being of himself and his family, including food, clothing, housing and medical care and necessary social services, and the right to security in the event of unemployment, sickness, disability, widowhood, old age or other lack of livelihood in circumstances beyond his control.

(2) Motherhood and childhood are entitled to special care and assistance. All children, whether born in or out of wedlock, shall enjoy the same social protection.

Article 26. (1) Everyone has the right to education. Education shall be free, at least in the elementary and fundamental stages. Elementary education shall be compulsory. Technical and professional education shall be made generally available and higher education shall be equally accessible to all on the basis of merit.

(2) Education shall be directed to the full development of the human personality and to the strengthening of respect for human rights and fundamental freedoms. It shall promote understanding, tolerance and friendship among all nations, racial or religious groups, and shall further the activities of the United Nations for the maintenance of peace.

(3) Parents have a prior right to choose the kind of education that shall be given to their children.

Article 27. (1) Everyone has the right freely to participate in the cultural life of the community, to enjoy the arts and to share in scientific advancement and its benefits.

(2) Everyone has the right to the protection of the moral and material interests resulting from any scientific, literary or artistic production of which he is the author.

Article 28. Everyone is entitled to a social and international order in which the rights and freedoms set forth in this Declaration can be fully realized.

Article 29. (1) Everyone has duties to the community in which alone the free and full development of his personality is possible.

(2) In the exercise of his rights and freedoms, everyone shall be subject only to such limitations as are determined by law solely for the purpose of securing due recognition and respect for the rights and freedoms of others and of meeting the just requirements of morality, public order and the general welfare in a democratic society.

(3) These rights and freedoms may in no case be exercised contrary to the purposes and principles of the United Nations.

Article 30. Nothing in this Declaration may be interpreted as implying for any State, group or person any right to engage in any activity or to perform any act aimed at the destruction of any of the rights and freedoms set forth herein.

NOBEL PEACE PRIZE WINNERS: 1980–2004

When the scientist, industrialist and inventor Alfred Nobel died in 1896, he made provision in his will for his fortune to be used for prizes in Physics, Chemistry, Physiology or Medicine, Literature and Peace. A prize for Economics was added later. The Norwegian Nobel Committee awards the Nobel Peace Prize, and the Nobel Foundation in Stockholm (founded 1900; Mailing address: Box 5232, SE-10245, Stockholm, Sweden) awards the other five prizes. The Prize Awarding Ceremony takes place on 10 Dec., the anniversary of Nobel's death. The last 25 recipients of the Nobel Peace Prize, worth 10m. Sw. kr. in 2004, are:

2004 – Wangari Maathai (Kenya) for her contribution to sustainable development, democracy and peace.

2003 – Shirin Ebadi (Iran) for her work fighting for democracy and the rights of women and children.

2002 – Jimmy Carter (USA) for his decades of untiring effort to find peaceful solutions to international conflicts, to advance democracy and human rights, and to promote economic and social development.

2001 – the United Nations and Kofi Annan for a better organized and more peaceful world.

2000 – Kim Dae-jung for his work for democracy and human rights in South Korea and in East Asia in general, and for peace and reconciliation with North Korea in particular.

1999 – *Médecins Sans Frontières* (Doctors Without Borders) in recognition of the organization's pioneering humanitarian work on several continents.

1998 – John Hume and David Trimble for their efforts to find a peaceful solution to the conflict in Northern Ireland.

1997 – ICBL (*International Campaign to Ban Landmines*) and Jody Williams for their work for the banning and clearing of anti-personnel mines.

1996 – Carlos Felipe Ximenes Belo and José Ramos-Horta for their work towards a just and peaceful solution to the conflict in East Timor.

1995 – Joseph Rotblat and the *Pugwash Conferences on Science and World Affairs* for their efforts to diminish the part played by nuclear arms in international politics and eventually to eliminate such arms.

1994 – Yasser Arafat (Chairman of the Executive Committee of the PLO, President of the Palestinian National Authority), Shimon Peres (Foreign Minister of

Israel) and Yitzhak Rabin (Prime Minister of Israel) for their efforts to create peace in the Middle East.

1993 – Nelson Mandela (Leader of the ANC) and Fredrik Willem De Klerk (President of the Republic of South Africa).

1992 – Rigoberta Menchú Tum (Guatemala) for his campaign work for human rights, especially for indigenous peoples.

1991 – Aung San Suu Kyi (Myanmar), opposition leader and human rights advocate.

1990 – Mikhail Sergeyevich Gorbachev (president of the USSR) for helping bring the Cold War to an end.

1989 – The 14th Dalai Lama (Tenzin Gyatso) for his religious and political leadership of the Tibetan people.

1988 – *The United Nations Peace-Keeping Forces*.

1987 – Oscar Arias Sánchez (President of Costa Rica) for initiating peace negotiations in Central America.

1986 – Elie Wiesel (USA), author and humanitarian.

1985 – *International Physicians for the Prevention of Nuclear War*, Boston, USA.

1984 – Desmond Mpilo Tutu (South Africa, Bishop of Johannesburg) for his work against apartheid.

1983 – Lech Wałęsa (Poland), founder of Solidarity and human rights campaigner.

1982 – Alva Myrdal (Sweden) and Alfonso García Robles (Mexico) for their work as delegates to the United Nations General Assembly on Disarmament.

1981 – *Office of the United Nations High Commissioner for Refugees*, Geneva, Switzerland.

1980 – Adolfo Pérez Esquivel (Argentina), human rights leader.

Norwegian Nobel Committee Headquarters: Det Norske Nobelinstitutt, Drammensveien 19, N-0255 Oslo, Norway.
Website: http://www.nobel.no/

UNITED NATIONS SYSTEM

Operational Programmes and Funds. The total operating expenses for the entire UN system, including the World Bank, IMF and all the UN funds, programmes and specialized agencies, come to US$18,200m. a year. Some 53,300 people work in the UN system, which includes the Secretariat and 28 other organizations.

Social and economic development, aimed at achieving a better life for people everywhere, is a major part of the UN system of organizations. In the forefront of efforts to bring about such progress is the United Nations Development Programme (UNDP), the world's largest agency for multilateral technical and pre-investment co-operation. It is the funding source for most of the technical assistance provided for sustainable human development by the UN system, and in 2000 helped people in 174 countries and territories, supporting some 5,000 projects, which focus on poverty elimination, environmental regeneration, job creation and the advancement of women.

UNDP assistance is provided only at the request of governments and in response to their priority needs, integrated into overall national and regional plans. Its activities are funded mainly by voluntary contributions outside the regular UN budget. 87% of the UNDP's core programme funds go to countries with an annual per capita GNP of US$750 or less, which are home to 90% of the world's poorest peoples. Headquartered in New York, the UNDP is governed by a 36-member Executive Board, representing both developing and developed countries.

Administrator: Mark Malloch Brown (UK).

United Nations development agencies include the *United Nations Children's Fund (UNICEF)*. It was established in 1946 by the United Nations General Assembly as the United Nations International Children's Emergency Fund, to meet the emergency needs of children of post-war Europe. In 1953 the organization became a permanent part of the UN and its mandate was expanded to carry out long-term programmes to benefit children worldwide. Guided by the Convention on the Rights of the Child and its Optional Protocols, UNICEF supports low-cost community-based programmes in immunization, nutrition, education, HIV/AIDS, water supply, environmental sanitation, gender issues and development, and child protection in more than 158 countries and territories. In 2001, with the assistance of UNICEF, WHO and other key partners, a record 575m. children were vaccinated against polio. UNICEF is the largest supplier of vaccines to developing countries, providing 40% of the world's doses of vaccine for children. UNICEF also provides relief and rehabilitation assistance in emergencies.

UNICEF served as the substantive secretariat for the UN General Assembly Special Session on Children held in New York from 8–10 May 2002, and supported a wide range of consultations and events around the world to ensure that children and young people had a voice in the process and in the Session itself. The Special Session adopted the outcome document, 'A World Fit For Children', setting 21 concrete time-bound goals for children on four key priorities: promoting healthy lives; providing quality education for all; protecting children against abuse, exploitation and violence; and combating HIV/AIDS.

In 2003 UNICEF intensified its '25 by 2005' campaign to accelerate progress in 25 countries where girls fall behind boys in enrolment, and where intensified actions would make the greatest impact.

UNICEF works towards eliminating the worst forms of child labour, protecting children affected by armed conflict and, in 2003, also supported programmes for children orphaned by HIV/AIDS in 38 countries in sub-Saharan Africa.

Executive Director: Ann Veneman (USA).

The United Nations Population Fund (UNFPA) was established in 1969 and is the world's largest multilateral source of population assistance. About a quarter of all population assistance from donor nations to developing countries is channeled through UNFPA. The fund extends assistance to developing countries at their request to help them address reproductive health and population issues, and raises awareness of these issues in all countries.

In 2000 UNFPA provided assistance to 142 developing nations, with special emphasis on increasing the quality of reproductive health services, ending the gender discriminations and violence, formulating effective population policies and reducing the spread of HIV/AIDS.

UNFPA's three main areas of work are: to help ensure universal access to reproductive health, including family planning and sexual health, to all couples and individuals on or before the year 2015; to support population and development strategies that enable capacity-building in population programming; to promote awareness of population and development issues, and to advocate for the mobilization of the resources and political will necessary to accomplish its area of work. UNFPA's *The State of World Population* report is published annually.

Executive Director: Thoraya Obaid (Saudi Arabia).

The UN Environment Programme (UNEP), established in 1972, works to encourage sustainable development through sound environmental practices everywhere. UNEP has its headquarters in Nairobi, Kenya and other offices in Paris, Geneva, Bangkok, Washington, D.C., New York, Osaka, Manama and Mexico City. Its activities cover a wide range of issues, from atmosphere and terrestrial ecosystems, to the promotion of environmental science and information, to an early warning and emergency response capacity to deal with environmental disasters and emergencies. UNEP's present priorities include: environmental information, assessment and research; enhanced co-ordination of environmental conventions and development of policy instruments; fresh water; technology transfer and industry; and support to Africa. Information networks and monitoring systems established by the UNEP include: the Global Environment Information Exchange Network (INFOTERRA); Global Resource Information Database (GRID); the International Register of Potentially Toxic Chemicals (IRPTC); and the recent UNEP.net, a web-based interactive catalogue and multifaceted portal that offers access to environmentally relevant geographic, textual and pictoral information. In June 2000 the World Conservation and Monitoring Centre (WCMC) based in Cambridge, UK became UNEP's key biodiversity assessment centre. UNEP's latest state-of-the-environment report is the *GEO Year Book,* 2004–05.

Executive Director: Klaus Töpfer (Germany).

Other UN programmes working for development include: the *UN Conference on Trade and Development (UNCTAD)*, which promotes international trade, particularly by developing countries, in an attempt to increase their participation in the global economy; and the *World Food Programme (WFP)*, the world's largest international food aid organization, which is dedicated to both emergency relief and development programmes.

The *UN Centre for Human Settlements (Habitat)*, which assists over 600m. people living in health-threatening housing conditions, was established in 1978. The 58-member *UN Commission on Human Settlements (UNCHS)*, Habitat's governing body, meets every two years. The Centre serves as the focal point for human settlements action and the co-ordination of activities within the UN system.

In addition to its regular programmes, the UNDP administers various special-purpose funds, such as the *UN Capital Development Fund (UNCDP)*, a multilateral donor agency working to develop new solutions for poverty reduction in the least developed countries, the *United Nations Volunteers (UNV)* and the *UN Development Fund for Women (UNIFEM)*, whose mission is the empowerment of women and gender equality in all levels of development planning and practice. Its three areas of immediate concern are: strengthening women's economic capacity; engendering governance and leadership; and promoting women's rights. Together with the World Bank and UNEP, the UNDP is one of the managing partners of the Global Environment Facility (GEF), a US$2,000m. fund to help countries translate global concerns into national action so as to help fight ozone depletion, global warming, loss of biodiversity and pollution of international waters.

The United Nations Development Programme is active in 166 countries. At country level, it is responsible for all UN development activity. The head of each country office acts as Resident Co-ordinator for UNDP.

The United Nations Office on Drugs and Crime (UNODC) educates the world about the dangers of drug abuse; strengthens international action against drug production, trafficking and drug related crime; promotes efforts to reduce drug abuse, particularly among the young and vulnerable; builds local, national and international partnership to address drug issues; provides information, analysis and expertise on the drug issue; promotes international co-operation in crime prevention and control; supports the development of criminal justice systems; and assists member states in addressing the challenges and threats posed by the changing nature of transnational organized crime.

Executive Director: Antonio Maria Costa (Italy).

The UN work in crime prevention and criminal justice aims to lessen the human and material costs of crime and its impact on socio-economic development. The UN Congress on the Prevention of Crime and Treatment of Offenders has convened every five years since 1955 and provides a forum for the presentation of policies and progress. The Tenth Crime Congress (Vienna, 2000) discussed how to promote the rule of law and to strengthen the criminal justice system and also international co-operation in combating transnational organized crime. The *Commission on Crime Prevention and Criminal Justice*, a functional body of ECOSOC, established in 1992, seeks to strengthen UN activities in the field, and meets annually in Vienna. The interregional research and training arm of the UN crime and criminal justice programme is the *United Nations Interregional Crime and Justice Research Institute (UNICRI)* in Rome. An autonomous body, it seeks through action-oriented research to contribute to the formulation of improved policies in crime prevention and control.

Humanitarian assistance to refugees and victims of natural and man-made disasters is also an important function of the UN system. The main refugee organizations within the system are the *Office of the United Nations High Commissioner for Refugees (UNHCR)* and the *United Nations Relief and Works Agency for Palestine Refugees in the Near East (UNRWA)*.

UNHCR was created in 1951 to resettle 1·2m. European refugees left homeless in the aftermath of the Second World War. It was initially envisioned as a temporary office with a projected lifespan of three years. However, in 2003, in a move to strengthen UNHCR's capacity to carry out its work more effectively, the General Assembly removed the time limitation on the organization's mandate and extended it indefinitely, until 'the refugee problem is solved'. Today, with some 17m. persons of concern across the globe, UNHCR has become one of the world's principal humanitarian agencies. Its Executive Committee currently comprises 66 member states. With its Headquarters in Geneva, UNHCR has some 6,300 staff, 83% of whom work in field locations in 115 countries across the globe, and has twice been awarded the Nobel Peace Prize. UNHCR is a subsidiary organ of the United Nations General Assembly.

The work of UNHCR is humanitarian and non-political. International protection is its primary function. Its main objective is to promote and safeguard the rights and interests of refugees. In so doing UNHCR devotes special attention to promoting access to asylum and seeks to improve the legal, material and physical safety of refugees in their country of residence. Crucial to this status is the principle of *non-refoulement*, which prohibits the expulsion from or forcible return of refugees to a country where they may have reason to fear persecution. UNHCR pursues its objectives in the field of protection by encouraging the conclusion of intergovernmental legal instruments in favour of refugees, by supervising the implementation of their provisions and by encouraging Governments to adopt legislation and administrative procedures for the benefit of refugees. UNHCR is often called upon to provide material assistance (e.g. the provision of food, shelter, medical care and essential supplies) while durable solutions are being sought. Durable solutions generally take one of three forms: voluntary repatriation, local integration or resettlement in another country.

UNHCR works in tandem with governmental and non-governmental organizations, and within the UN framework one of its closest partnerships is with the World Food Programme (WFP). Other bodies with which significant collaborative work is undertaken include UNICEF, WHO, UNDP, ILO, the UN Centre for Human Settlements (UN-Habitat), the Joint UN Programme on HIV/AIDS (UNAIDS), the UN Department of Peacekeeping Operations (DPKO), the Office for the Coordination of Humanitarian Affairs (OCHA), the Office of the High Commissioner for Human Rights (OHCHR), the International Organization for Migration (IOM), the Red Cross/Red Crescent Movement Institutions (ICRC and IFRC) and many non-governmental organizations (NGOs). The Office also liaises closely with the World Bank and affiliated institutions, particularly in helping refugees to rebuild their lives and communities once they have returned home. At present, UNHCR is funded almost entirely by voluntary contributions. In 2004 UNHCR's expenditure amounted to approximately US$1bn.

High Commissioner (acting): Wendy Chamberlin (USA).

UNRWA was created by the General Assembly in 1949 as a temporary, non-political agency to provide relief to the nearly 750,000 people who became refugees as a result of the disturbances during and after the creation of the State of Israel in the former British Mandate territory of Palestine. 'Palestine refugees', as defined by UNRWA's mandate, are persons or descendants of persons whose normal residence was Palestine for at least two years prior to the 1948 conflict and who, as a result of the conflict, lost their homes and means of livelihood. UNRWA has also been called upon to help persons displaced by renewed hostilities in the Middle East in 1967. The situation of Palestine refugees in south Lebanon, affected in the aftermath of the 1982 Israeli invasion of Lebanon, was of special concern to the Agency in 1984. UNRWA provides education, health, relief and social services to eligible refugees among the 3·7m. registered Palestine refugees in its five fields of operation: Jordan, Lebanon, Syria, the West Bank and the Gaza Strip. Its mandate is renewed at intervals by the UN General Assembly, and has most recently been extended until 30 June 2008. The projected budget for 2002 was US$279·3m., funded entirely by donor countries.

Commissioner-General: Peter Hansen (Denmark).

The UN's activities in the field of human rights are the primary responsibility of the *High Commissioner for Human Rights*, a post established in 1993 under the direction and authority of the Secretary-General. The High Commissioner is nominated by the Secretary-General for a four-year term, renewable once. The principal co-ordinating human rights organ of the UN is the *Commission on Human Rights*, set up by ECOSOC in 1946. It has 53 members elected for three-year terms, meets for six weeks in Geneva each year, and is aided in its task by a Subcommission on Prevention of Discrimination and Protection of Minorities, composed of 26 experts from all over the world. The implementation of international human rights treaties is monitored by six committees (also called treaty bodies): the Human Rights Committee; the Committee against Torture; Committee on the Rights of the Child; Committee on Economic, Cultural and Social Rights; Committee on the Elimination of Racial Discrimination; Committee on Elimination of Discrimination against Women.

Training and Research Institutes. There are six training and research institutes within the UN, all of them autonomous.

United Nations Institute for Training and Research (UNITAR). The Institute was established in 1965 with a mandate to enhance the effectiveness of the UN in achieving its major objectives. Recently, its focus has shifted to training, with basic research being conducted only if extra-budgetary funds can be made available. Training is provided at various levels for agencies and institutions of UN member states, diplomatic personnel, universities, public interest groups and the private sector. By the end of 2003 some 65,000 participants from 200 countries had attended UNITAR courses, seminars or workshops.

Address: Palais des Nations, 1211 Geneva 10, Switzerland.

United Nations Institute for Disarmament Research (UNIDIR). Established in 1980 to undertake research on disarmament and security with the aim of assisting the international community in their disarmament thinking, decisions and efforts. Through its research projects, publications, small meetings and expert networks, UNIDIR promotes creative thinking and dialogue on both current and future security issues, through examination of topics as varied as tactical nuclear weapons, refugee security, computer warfare, regional confidence-building measures and small arms.

Address: Palais des Nations, 1211 Geneva 10, Switzerland.

United Nations Research Institute for Social Development (UNRISD). Established in 1963 to conduct multidisciplinary research into the social dimensions of contemporary problems affecting development, it aims to provide governments, development agencies, grassroots organizations and scholars with a better understanding of how development policies and processes of economic, social and environmental change affect different social groups.

Address: Palais des Nations, 1211 Geneva 10, Switzerland.

United Nations International Research and Training Institute for the Advancement of Women (INSTRAW). Established by ECOSOC and endorsed by the General Assembly in 1976, INSTRAW provides training, conducts research, and collects and disseminates information to promote gender equality and stimulate and assist women's advancement. Its 11-member Board of Trustees, which reports to ECOSOC, meets annually to review its programme and to formulate the principles and guidelines for INSTRAW's activities.

Address: POB 21747, Santo Domingo, Dominican Republic.

United Nations University (UNU). Sponsored jointly by the UN and UNESCO, UNU is guaranteed academic freedom by a charter approved by the General Assembly in 1973. It is governed by a 28-member Council of scholars and scientists, of whom 24 are appointed by the Secretary-General of the UN and the Director-General of UNESCO. Unlike a traditional university with a campus, students and faculty, it works through networks of collaborating institutions and individuals to undertake multidisciplinary research on problems of human survival, development and welfare; and to strengthen research and training capabilities in developing countries. It also provides postgraduate fellowships and PhD internships to scholars and scientists from developing countries. The University focuses its work within two programme areas: peace and governance, and environment and development.

Address: 53–70 Jingumae 5-chome, Shibuya-ku, Tokyo 150-8925, Japan.

University for Peace. Founded in 1980 to conduct research on, *inter alia*, disarmament, mediation, the resolution of conflicts, preservation of the environment, international relations, peace education and human rights. It organizes graduate degree programmes, undergraduate certificate programmes, and seminars and training for mid-career professionals.

Address: POB 138, Ciudad Colon, Costa Rica.
Website: http://www.upeace.org/

Information. *The UN Statistics Division* in New York provides a wide range of statistical outputs and services for producers and users of statistics worldwide, facilitating national and international policy formulation, implementation and monitoring. It produces printed publications of statistics and statistical methods in the fields of international merchandise trade, national accounts, demography and population, gender, industry, energy, environment, human settlements and disability, as well as general statistics compendiums including the *Statistical Yearbook* and *World Statistics Pocketbook*. Many of its databases are available on CD-ROM, diskette, magnetic tape and the Internet.

Website: http://unstats.un.org

UN Information Centre. Public Inquiries Unit, Department of Public Information, Room GA-57, United Nations Plaza, New York, NY 10017. There are also 33 UN Information Centres in other parts of the world.

Website: http://www.un.org

SPECIALIZED AGENCIES OF THE UN

The intergovernmental agencies related to the UN by special agreements are separate autonomous organizations which work with the UN and each other through the co-ordinating machinery of the Economic and Social Council. 19 of them are 'Specialized Agencies' within the terms of the UN Charter, and report annually to ECOSOC.

FOOD AND AGRICULTURE ORGANIZATION OF THE UNITED NATIONS (FAO)

Origin. In 1943 the International Conference on Food and Agriculture, at Hot Springs, Virginia, set up an Interim Commission, based in Washington, with a remit to establish an organization. Its Constitution was signed on 16 Oct. 1945 in Quebec City. Today, membership totals 187 countries. The European Union was made a member as a 'regional economic integration organization' in 1991.

Aims and Activities. The aims of FAO are to raise levels of nutrition and standards of living; to improve the production and distribution of all food and agricultural products from farms, forests and fisheries; to improve the living conditions of rural populations; and, by these means, to eliminate hunger. Its priority objectives are to encourage sustainable agriculture and rural development as part of a long-term strategy for the conservation and management of natural resources; and to ensure the availability of adequate food supplies, by maximizing stability in the flow of supplies and securing access to food by the poor.

In carrying out these aims, FAO promotes investment in agriculture, better soil and water management, improved yields of crops and livestock, agricultural research and the transfer of technology to developing countries; and encourages the conservation of natural resources and rational use of fertilizers and pesticides; the development and sustainable utilization of marine and inland fisheries; the sustainable management of forest resources and the combating of animal disease. Technical assistance is provided in all of these fields, and in nutrition, agricultural engineering, agrarian reform, development communications, remote sensing for climate and vegetation, and the prevention of post-harvest food losses. In addition, FAO works to maintain global biodiversity with the emphasis on the genetic diversity of crop plants and domesticated animals; and plays a major role in the collection, analysis and dissemination of information on agricultural production and commodities. Finally, FAO acts as a neutral forum for the discussion of issues, and advises governments on policy, through international conferences like the 1996 World Food Summit in Rome and the World Food Summit: five years later, held in Rome in 2002.

Special FAO programmes help countries prepare for, and provide relief in the event of, emergency food situations, in particular through the rehabilitation of agriculture after disasters. The *Special Programme for Food Security*, launched in 1994, is designed to assist target countries to increase food production and productivity as rapidly as possible, primarily through the widespread adoption by farmers of available improved production technologies, with the emphasis on high-potential areas. FAO provides support for the global co-ordination of the programme and helps attract funds. The *Emergency Prevention System for Transboundary Animal and Plant Pests and Diseases (EMPRES)*, established in 1994, strengthens FAO's existing contribution to the prevention, control and eradication of diseases and pests before they compromise food security, with locusts and rinderpest among its priorities. *The Global Information and Early Warning System (GIEWS)* provides current information on the world food situation and identifies countries threatened by shortages to guide potential donors. The interagency Food Insecurity and Vulnerability Information and Mapping System initiative (FIVIMS) was established in 1997, with FAO as its secretariat. More than 60 countries have nominated national focal points to co-ordinate efforts to collect and use statistics related to food insecurity more efficiently. Together with the UN, FAO sponsors the *World Food Programme (WFP)*.

Finance. The budget for the 2004–05 biennium was US$749·1m. FAO's Regular Programme budget, financed by contributions from member governments, covers the cost of its secretariat and Technical Co-operation Programme (TCP), and part of the costs of several special programmes.

FAO continues to provide technical advice and support through its field programmes in all areas of food and agriculture, fisheries, forestry and rural development. In 2003 expenditures in the field totalled US$405m., which paid for 1,600 field programme projects, about 380 of which were emergency operations. The programme was funded from FAO's regular budget, trust funds and the UN Development Programme. In addition, since 1964, over 1,470 projects prepared with the FAO Investment Centre's assistance have been approved for financing for total investments of US$76bn., including support loans from financing institutions of US$44bn.

Organization. The FAO Conference, composed of all members, meets every other year to determine policy and approve the FAO's budget and programme. The 49-member Council, elected by the Conference, serves as FAO's governing body between conference sessions. Much of its work is carried out by dozens of regional or specialist commissions, such as the Asia-Pacific Fishery Commission, the European Commission on Agriculture and the Commission on Plant Genetic Resources. The Director-General is elected for a renewable six-year term.

Headquarters: Viale delle Terme di Caracalla, 00100 Rome, Italy.
Website: http://www.fao.org
Director-General: Jacques Diouf (Senegal).

Publications. Unasylva (quarterly), 1947 ff.; *The State of Food and Agriculture* (annual), 1947 ff.; *Animal Health Yearbook* (annual), 1957 ff.; *Production Yearbook* (annual), 1947 ff.; *Trade Yearbook* (annual), 1947 ff.; *FAO Commodity Review* (annual), 1961 ff.; *Yearbook of Forest Products* (annual), 1947 ff.; *Yearbook of Fishery Statistics* (in two volumes); *FAO Fertilizer Yearbook; FAO Plant Protection Bulletin* (quarterly); *Environment and Energy Bulletin; Food Outlook* (monthly); *The State of World Fisheries and Aquaculture* (annual); *The State of the World's Forests; World Watch List for Domestic Animal Diversity; The State of Food Insecurity in the World.*

INTERNATIONAL BANK FOR RECONSTRUCTION AND DEVELOPMENT (IBRD) — THE WORLD BANK

Origin. Conceived at the UN Monetary and Financial Conference at Bretton Woods (New Hampshire, USA) in July 1944, the IBRD, frequently called the World Bank, began operations in June 1946, its purpose being to provide funds, policy guidance and technical assistance to facilitate economic development in its poorer member countries. The Group comprises four other organizations (see below).

Activities. The Bank obtains its funds from the following sources: capital paid in by member countries; sales of its own securities; sales of parts of its loans; repayments; and net earnings. A resolution of the Board of Governors of 27 April 1988 provides that the paid-in portion of the shares authorized to be subscribed under it will be 3%.

The Bank is self-supporting, raising most of its money on the world's financial markets. In the fiscal year ending 30 June 2002 it achieved a net income of US$2,778m. Income totalled US$7,876m. and expenditure US$5,952m.

In the fiscal year 2002 the Bank lent US$11·5bn. for 96 new operations in 40 countries. Cumulative lending had totalled US$371bn. by March 2003. 89% of borrowers took advantage of the new single-currency loans which became available in June 1996 to provide borrowers with the flexibility to select IBRD loan terms that are consistent with their debt-managing strategy and suited to their debt-servicing capacity. In order to eliminate wasteful overlapping of development assistance and to ensure that the funds available are used to the best possible effect, the Bank has organized consortia or consultative groups of aid-giving nations for many countries. These include Bangladesh, Belarus, Bolivia, Bulgaria, Egypt, Ethiopia, Jordan, Kazakhstan, Kenya, Kyrgyzstan, Macedonia, Malaŵi, Mauritania, Moldova, Mozambique, Nicaragua, Pakistan, Peru, Romania, Sierra Leone, Tanzania, the [Palestinian] West Bank and Gaza Strip, Zambia, Zimbabwe and the Caribbean Group for Co-operation in Economic Development.

For the purposes of its analytical and operational work, in 2003 the IBRD characterized economies as follows: low income (average annual *per capita* gross national income of $765 or less); lower middle income (between $766 and $3,035); upper middle income (between $3,036 and $9,385); and high income ($9,386 or more).

A wide variety of technical assistance is at the core of IBRD's activities. It acts as executing agency for a number of pre-investment surveys financed by the UN Development Programme. Resident missions have been established in 64 developing member countries and there are regional offices for East and West Africa, the Baltic States and South-East Asia which assist in the preparation and implementation of projects. The Bank maintains a staff college, the *Economic Development Institute* in Washington, D.C., for senior officials of member countries.

The Strategic Compact. Unanimously approved by the Executive Board in March 1997, the Strategic Compact set out a plan for fundamental reform to make the Bank more effective in delivering its regional programme and in achieving its basic mission of reducing poverty. Decentralizing the Bank's relationships with borrower countries is central to the reforms. The effectiveness of devolved country management and the bank's promotion of good governance and anti-corruption measures to developing countries are likely to be key policies of the new strategy.

Organization. As of March 2005 the Bank had 184 members, each with voting power in the institution, based on shareholding which in turn is based on a country's economic growth. The president is selected by the Bank's Board of Executive Directors. The Articles of Agreement do not specify the nationality of the president but by custom the US Executive Director makes a nomination, and by a long-standing, informal agreement, the president is a US national (while the managing director of the IMF is European). The initial term is five years, with a second of five years or less.

European office: 66 avenue d'Iéna, 75116 Paris, France. *London office:* New Zealand House, Haymarket, London SW1Y 4TE, England. *Tokyo office:* Kokusai Building, 1–1, Marunouchi 3-chome, Chiyoda-ku, Tokyo 100, Japan.

Headquarters: 1818 H St., NW, Washington, D.C., 20433, USA.
Website: http://www.worldbank.org
President: Paul Wolfowitz (USA).

Publications. World Bank Annual Report; Summary Proceedings of Annual Meetings; The World Bank and International Finance Company, 1986; *The World Bank Atlas* (annual); *Catalog of Publications,* 1986 ff.; *World Development Report* (annual); *World Bank Economic Review* (thrice yearly); *World Bank and the Environment* (annual); *World Bank News* (weekly); *World Bank Research Observer; World Tables* (annual); *Social Indicators of Development* (annual); *ICSID Annual Report; ICSID Review: Foreign Investment Law Journal* (twice yearly); *Research News* (quarterly).

INTERNATIONAL DEVELOPMENT ASSOCIATION (IDA)

A lending agency established in 1960 and administered by the IBRD to provide assistance on concessional terms to the poorest developing countries. Its resources consist of subscriptions and general replenishments from its more industrialized and developed members, special contributions, and transfers from the net earnings of IBRD. Officers and staff of the IBRD serve concurrently as officers and staff of the IDA at the World Bank headquarters.

In fiscal year 2002 disbursements totalled US$6,603m. for 813 operations. Pakistan was the single largest recipient of disbursements from adjustment lending.

INTERNATIONAL FINANCE CORPORATION (IFC)

Established in 1956 to help strengthen the private sector in developing countries, through the provision of long-term loans, equity investments, quasi-equity instruments, standby financing, and structured finance and risk management products. It helps to finance new ventures and assist established enterprises as they expand, upgrade or diversify. In partnership with other donors, it provides a variety of technical assistance and advisory services to public and private sector clients. To be eligible for financing, projects must be profitable for investors, must benefit the economy of the country concerned, and must comply with IFC's environmental and social guidelines.

The majority of its funds are borrowed from the international financial markets through public bond issues or private placements. Its authorized capital is US$2,361m.; total capital at 30 June 2004 was US$7,782m. IFC committed US$5,633m. in total financing in fiscal year 2004 and committed 217 projects in 65 developing countries. It has 177 members.

Headquarters: 2121 Pennsylvania Ave., NW, Washington, D.C., 20433, USA.
Website: http://www.ifc.org
President: Paul Wolfowitz (USA).

Publications. Annual Reports; Lessons of Experience (series); *Paths Out of Poverty.*

MULTILATERAL INVESTMENT GUARANTEE AGENCY (MIGA)

Established in 1988 to encourage the flow of foreign direct investment to, and among, developing member countries, MIGA is the insurance arm of the World Bank. It provides investors with investment guarantees against non-commercial risk, such as expropriation and war, and gives advice to governments on improving climate for foreign investment. It may insure up to 90% of an investment, with a current limit of US$50m. per project. In March 1999 the Council of Governors adopted a resolution for a capital increase for the Agency of approximately US$850m. In addition US$150m. was transferred to MIGA by the World Bank as operating capital. In March 2005 it had 164 member countries. It is located at the World Bank headquarters (see above).

Headquarters: 1818 H Street, NW, Washington, D.C., 20433, USA.
Website: http://www.miga.org

INTERNATIONAL CENTRE FOR SETTLEMENT OF INVESTMENT DISPUTES (ICSID)

Founded in 1966 to promote increased flows of international investment by providing facilities for the conciliation and arbitration of disputes between governments and foreign investors. The Centre does not engage in such conciliation or arbitration. This is the task of conciliators and arbitrators appointed by the contracting parties, or as otherwise provided for in the Convention. Recourse to conciliation and arbitration by members is entirely voluntary.

In March 2005 its Convention had been signed by 154 countries. 84 cases had been concluded by it and 72 were pending. Disputes involved a variety of investment sectors: agriculture, banking, construction, energy, health, industrial, mining and tourism.

ICSID also undertakes research, publishing and advisory activities in the field of foreign investment law. Like IDA, IFC and MIGA, it is located at the World Bank headquarters in Washington (see above).

Secretary-General: Roberto Dañino (Peru).
Website: http://www.worldbank.org/icsid

Publications. ICSID Annual Report; News from ICSID; ICSID Review: Foreign Investment Law Journal; Investment Laws of the World; Investment Treaties.

Further Reading

Caufield, C., *Masters of Illusion: The World Bank and the Poverty of Nations.* London, 1997
Nelson, P. J., *The World Bank and Non-Government Organizations: The Limits of Apolitical Development.* London, 1995
Salda, A. C. M., *World Bank* [Bibliography]. Oxford and New Brunswick (NJ), 1994
Wilson, C. R., *The World Bank Group: A Guide to Information Sources.* New York, 1991

INTERNATIONAL CIVIL AVIATION ORGANIZATION (ICAO)

Origin. The Convention providing for the establishment of the ICAO was drawn up by the International Civil Aviation Conference held in Chicago in 1944. A Provisional International Civil Aviation Organization (PICAO) operated for 20 months until the formal establishment of ICAO on 4 April 1947. The Convention on International Civil Aviation superseded the provisions of the Paris Convention of 1919 and the Pan American Convention on Air Navigation of 1928.

Functions. It assists international civil aviation by establishing technical standards for safety and efficiency of air navigation and promoting simpler procedures at borders; develops regional plans for ground facilities and services needed for international flying; disseminates air-transport statistics and prepares studies on aviation economics; fosters the development of air law conventions and provides technical assistance to states in developing civil aviation programmes.

Organization. The principal organs of ICAO are an Assembly, consisting of all members of the Organization, and a Council, which is composed of 33 states elected by the Assembly for three years, which meets in virtually continuous session. In electing these states, the Assembly must give adequate representation to: (1) states of major importance in air transport; (2) states which make the largest contribution to the provision of facilities for the international civil air navigation; and (3) those states not otherwise included whose election would ensure that all major geographical areas of the world were represented. The budget approved for 2002 was US$57·5m.

Headquarters: 999 University St., Montreal, PQ, Canada H3C 5H7.
Website: http://www.icao.int
President of the Council: Dr Assad Kotaite (Lebanon).
Secretary-General: Taïeb Chérif (Algeria).

Publications. Annual Report of the Council; ICAO Journal (nine yearly; quarterly in Russian); *ICAO Training Manual; Aircraft Accident Digest; Procedures for Air Navigation Services.*

INTERNATIONAL FUND FOR AGRICULTURAL DEVELOPMENT (IFAD)

The idea for an International Fund for Agricultural Development arose at the 1974 World Food Conference. An agreement to establish IFAD entered into force on 30 Nov. 1977, and the agency began its operations the following month. IFAD's purpose is to mobilize additional funds for improved food production and better nutrition among low-income groups in developing countries through projects and programmes directly benefiting the poorest rural populations while preserving their natural resource base. In line with the Fund's focus on the rural poor, its resources are made available in highly concessional loans and grants. By March 2003 the Fund had invested US$7·7bn. in loans and US$35·4m. in grants financing 628 projects in 115 developing countries.

Organization. The highest body is the Governing Council, on which all 164 member countries are represented. Operations are overseen by an 18-member Executive Board (with 17 alternate members), which is responsible to the Governing Council. The Fund works with many co-operating institutions, including the World Bank, regional development banks and financial agencies, and other UN agencies; many of these co-finance IFAD projects.

Headquarters: 107 Via del Serafico, Rome 00142, Italy.
Website: http://www.ifad.org
President: Lennart Båge (Sweden).

Publications. Annual Report; IFAD Update (thrice yearly); *Staff Working Papers* (series); *The State of World Rural Poverty.*

INTERNATIONAL LABOUR ORGANIZATION (ILO)

Origin. The ILO was established in 1919 under the Treaty of Versailles as an autonomous institution associated with the League of Nations. An agreement establishing its relationship with the UN was approved in 1946, making the ILO the first Specialized Agency to be associated with the UN. An intergovernmental agency with a tripartite structure, in which representatives of governments, employers and workers participate, it seeks through international action to improve labour and living conditions, to promote productive employment and social justice for working people everywhere. On its fiftieth anniversary in 1969 it was awarded the Nobel Peace Prize. In March 2005 it numbered 177 members.

Functions. One of the ILO's principal functions is the formulation of international standards in the form of International Labour Conventions and Recommendations. Member countries are required to submit Conventions to their competent national authorities with a view to ratification. If a country ratifies a Convention it agrees to bring its laws into line with its terms and to report periodically how these regulations are being applied. More than 7,000 ratifications of 185 Conventions had been deposited by 30 Sept. 2003. Procedures are in place to ascertain whether Conventions thus ratified are effectively applied. Recommendations do not require ratification, but member states are obliged to consider them with a view to giving effect to their provisions by legislation or other action. By 30 Sept. 2003 the International Labour Conference had adopted 194 Recommendations.

The ILO's programme and budget set out four strategic objectives for the Organization at the turn of the century: i) to promote and realize fundamental principles and rights at work; ii) to create greater opportunities for women and men to secure decent employment and income; iii) to enhance the coverage and effectiveness of social protection for all; iv) to strengthen tripartism and social dialogue.

Activities. In addition to its research and advisory activities, the ILO extends technical co-operation to governments under its regular budget and under the UN Development Programme and Funds-in-Trust in the fields of employment promotion, human resources development (including vocational and management training), development of social institutions, small-scale industries, rural development, social security, industrial safety and hygiene, productivity, etc. Technical co-operation also includes expert missions and a fellowship programme.

In 1994 the technical services offered by the ILO to its tripartite constituents came under scrutiny leading to a re-affirmation of technical co-operation as one of the principal means of ILO action. Since 1994 the process of implementing the new Active Partnership Policy made significant progress and today 16 multidisciplinary advisory teams are engaged in a dialogue with ILO constituents centred on the identification of Country Objectives to form the basis of the ILO's contribution.

In June 1998 delegates to the 86th International Labour Conference adopted a solemn ILO Declaration in Fundamental Principles and Rights at Work, committing the Organization's member states to respect the principles inherent in a number of core labour standards: the right of workers and employers to freedom of association and the effective right to collective bargaining, and to work toward the elimination of all forms of forced or compulsory labour, the effective abolition of child labour and the elimination of discrimination in respect of employment and occupation.

In June 1999 delegates to the 87th International Labour Conference adopted a new Convention banning the worst forms of child labour. The International Labour Conference 2003 adopted a budget of US$529·6m. for the 2004–05 biennium.

Field Activities. The ILO's *International Institute for Labour Studies* promotes the study and discussion of policy issues. The core theme of its activities is the interaction between labour institutions, development and civil society in a global economy. It identifies emerging social and labour issues by opening up new areas for research and action; and encourages systematic dialogue on social policy between the tripartite constituency of the ILO and the international academic community, and other public opinion-makers.

The *International Training Centre* of the ILO, in Turin, was set up in 1965 to lead the training programmes implemented by the ILO as part of its technical co-operation activities. Member states and the UN system also call on its resources and experience, and a UN Staff College was established on the Turin Campus in 1996.

Organization. The International Labour Conference is the supreme deliberative organ of the ILO; it meets annually in Geneva. National delegations are composed of two government delegates, one employers' delegate and one workers' delegate. The Governing Body, elected by the Conference, is the Executive Council. It is composed of 28 government members, 14 workers' members and 14 employers' members. Ten governments of countries of industrial importance hold permanent seats on the Governing Body. These are: Brazil, China, Germany, France, India, Italy, Japan, Russia, UK and USA. The remaining 18 government members are elected every three years. Workers' and employers' representatives are elected as individuals, not as national candidates. The ILO has a branch office in London (for UK and Republic of Ireland), and regional offices in Abidjan (for Africa), Bangkok (for Asia and the Pacific), Lima (for Latin America and the Caribbean) and Beirut (for Arab States).

Headquarters: International Labour Office, CH-1211 Geneva 22, Switzerland.
London Office: Vincent House, Vincent Square, London SW1P 2NB, UK.
Website: http://www.ilo.org
Director-General: Juan Somavia (Chile).
Governing Body Chairman: Philippe Séguin (France).

Publications (available in English, French and Spanish) include: *International Labour Review; Bulletin of Labour Statistics; Official Bulletin* and *Labour Education; Yearbook of Labour Statistics* (annual); *World Labour Report* (annual); *World Employment Report* (annual); *Encyclopaedia of Occupational Health and Safety; Key Indicators of the Labour Market* (*KILM*); *World of Work* (four a year).

INTERNATIONAL MARITIME ORGANIZATION (IMO)

Origin. The International Maritime Organization (formerly the InterGovernmental Maritime Consultative Organization) was established as a specialized agency of the UN by a convention drafted in 1948 at a UN maritime conference in Geneva. The Convention became effective on 17 March 1958 when it had been ratified by 21 countries, including seven with at least 1m. gross tons of shipping each. The IMCO started operations in 1959 and changed its name to the IMO in 1982.

Functions. To facilitate co-operation among governments on technical matters affecting merchant shipping, especially concerning safety and security at sea; to prevent and control marine pollution caused by ships; to facilitate international maritime traffic. The IMO is responsible for convening international maritime conferences and for drafting international maritime conventions. It also provides technical assistance to countries wishing to develop their maritime activities, and acts as a depositary authority for international conventions regulating maritime affairs. *The World Maritime University (WMU)*, at Malmö, Sweden, was established in 1983; the *IMO International Maritime Law Institute (IMLI)*, at Valletta, Malta and the *IMO International Maritime Academy*, at Trieste, Italy, both in 1989.

Organization. The IMO has 164 members and three associate members. The Assembly, composed of all member states, normally meets every two years. The 40-member Council acts as governing body between sessions. There are four principal committees (on maritime safety, legal matters, marine environment protection and technical co-operation), which submit reports or recommendations to the Assembly through the Council, and a Secretariat. The budget for 2004–05 amounted to £46,194,900.

Headquarters: 4 Albert Embankment, London SE1 7SR, UK.
Website: http://www.imo.org

e-mail: info@imo.org
Secretary-General: Efthimios Mitropoulos (Greece).
Publication. *IMO News.*

INTERNATIONAL MONETARY FUND (IMF)

The International Monetary Fund was established on 27 Dec. 1945 as an independent international organization and began financial operations on 1 March 1947; its relationship with the UN is defined in an agreement of mutual co-operation which came into force on 15 Nov. 1947. The first amendment to the IMF's Articles creating the special drawing right (SDR) took effect on 28 July 1969. The second amendment took effect on 1 April 1978. The third amendment came into force on 11 Nov. 1992; it allows for the suspension of voting and related rights of a member which persists in its failure to settle its outstanding obligations to the IMF.

Aims. To promote international monetary co-operation, the expansion of international trade and exchange rate stability; to assist in the removal of exchange restrictions and the establishment of a multilateral system of payments; and to alleviate any serious disequilibrium in members' international balance of payments by making the financial resources of the IMF available to them, usually subject to economic policy conditions to ensure the revolving nature of IMF resources.

Activities. Each member of the IMF undertakes a broad obligation to collaborate with the IMF and other members to ensure orderly exchange arrangements and to promote a system of stable exchange rates. In addition, members are subject to certain obligations relating to domestic and external policies that can affect the balance of payments and the exchange rate. The IMF makes its resources available, under proper safeguards, to its members to meet short-term or medium-term payment difficulties. The first allocation of SDRs was made on 1 Jan. 1970. A total of SDR 21·4bn. has been allocated to members in two allocations, completed in 1981.

To enhance its balance of payments assistance to its members, the IMF established a Compensatory Financing Facility on 27 Feb. 1963; temporary oil facilities in 1974 and 1975; a Trust Fund in 1976; and an Extended Fund Facility (EFF) for medium-term assistance to members with special balance of payments problems on 13 Sept. 1974. In March 1986 it established the Structural Adjustment Facility (SAF) to provide assistance to low-income countries. In Dec. 1987 it established the Enhanced Structural Adjustment Facility (ESAF) to provide further assistance to low-income countries facing high levels of indebtedness. In Oct. 1999 the ESAF was renamed as the Poverty Reduction and Growth Facility (PRGF) to reflect the increased focus on poverty reduction. In Dec. 1997 the Supplemental Reserve Facility (SRF) was established to provide short-term assistance to countries experiencing exceptional balance of payments problems owing to a large short-term financing need resulting from a sudden disruptive loss of market confidence, reflected in pressure on the capital account and the member's reserves.

Capital Resources. The capital resources of the IMF comprise SDRs and currencies that the members pay under quotas calculated for them when they join the IMF. A member's quota is largely determined by its economic position relative to other members; it is also linked to their drawing rights on the IMF under both regular and special facilities, their voting power, and their share of SDR allocations. Every IMF member is required to subscribe to the IMF an amount equal to its quota. An amount not exceeding 25% of the quota has to be paid in reserve assets, the balance in the member's own currency. The members with the largest quotas are: 1st, the USA; joint 2nd, Germany and Japan; joint 4th, France and the UK.

An increase of almost 60% in IMF quotas became effective in Nov. 1992 as a result of the 9th General Review of Quotas. Quotas were not increased under the 10th General Review. In the 11th General Review, the IMF's Executive Board adopted a resolution at its 1997 annual meeting, approving a one-time equity allocation of SDRs of SDR 21,400m., which would equalize all members' ratio of SDRs to quota at 29·3%. The Board also agreed to recommend a 45% increase in IMF quotas, which would raise total quotas from SDR 145,300m., in Sept. 1997, to SDR 209,500m.; an 85% majority of member countries is required for the quota increase to take effect. In Jan. 1999 the 85% majority had been met. As of Feb.

2003, on the conclusion of the 12th General Review, total quotas were SDR 213,000m.

Borrowing Resources. The IMF is authorized under its Articles of Agreement to supplement its resources by borrowing. In Jan. 1962 a four-year agreement was concluded with ten industrial members (Belgium, Canada, France, Germany, Italy, Japan, Netherlands, Sweden, UK, USA) who undertook to lend the IMF up to US$6,000m. in their own currencies, if this should be needed to forestall or cope with an impairment of the international monetary system. Switzerland subsequently joined the group. These arrangements, known as the General Arrangements to Borrow (GAB), have been extended several times. In early 1983 agreement was reached to increase the credit arrangements under the GAB to SDR 17,000m.; to permit use of GAB resources in transactions with IMF members that are not GAB participants; to authorize Swiss participation; and to permit borrowing arrangements with non-participating members to be associated with the GAB. Saudi Arabia and the IMF have entered into such an arrangement under which the IMF will be able to borrow up to SDR 1,500m. to assist in financing purchases by any member for the same purpose and under the same circumstances as in the GAB. The changes became effective by 26 Dec. 1983.

Surveillance. In order to oversee the compliance of members with their obligations under the Articles of Agreement, the IMF is required to exercise firm surveillance over members' exchange rate policies. In April 1996 the IMF established the Special Data Dissemination Standard (SDDS) to improve access to reliable economic statistical information for member countries that have, or are seeking, access to international capital markets. In Dec. 1997 it established the General Data Dissemination Standard (GDDS), which applies to all member countries and focuses on improved production and dissemination of core economic data. Information on both are available on the IMF's website.

The IMF works with the IBRD (World Bank) to address the problems of the most heavily indebted poor countries (most in Sub-Saharan Africa) through their Initiative for the Heavily Indebted Poor Countries (HIPCs). The HIPC Initiative is designed to ensure that HIPCs with a sound track record of economic adjustment receive debt relief sufficient to help them attain a sustainable debt situation over the medium term. The HIPC Initiative was enhanced in late 1999 to provide deeper and more rapid debt relief to a larger number of countries. The Poverty Reduction and Growth Facility (PRGF) is a concessional facility that helps low-income member countries with loans at a 0·5% annual interest rate with biannual repayments over five and a half to ten years. Members qualifying for PRGF funding may borrow up to 140% (under exceptional circumstances, 185%) of their quota under a three-year arrangement.

Organization. The highest authority is the Board of Governors, on which each member government is represented. Normally the Governors meet once a year, and may take votes by mail or other means between meetings. The Board of Governors has delegated many of its powers to the 24 executive directors in Washington, who are appointed or elected by individual member countries or groups of countries. The managing director is selected by the executive directors and serves as chairman of the Executive Board, but may not vote except in case of a tie. The term of office is for five years, but may be extended or terminated at the discretion of the executive directors. The managing director is responsible for the ordinary business of the IMF, under the direction of the executive directors, and supervises a staff of about 2,600. Under a long-standing, informal agreement, the managing director is European (while the President of the World Bank is a US national). There are three deputy managing directors. As of Dec. 2004 the IMF had 184 members.

The *IMF Institute* is a specialized department of the IMF providing training in macroeconomic analysis and policy, and related subjects, for officials of member countries, at the Fund's headquarters in Washington, the Joint Vienna Institute, the Joint Africa Institute, the Singapore Regional Training Institute, the IMF-Arab Monetary Fund Regional Training Program, the Joint China-IMF Training Program and the Joint Regional Training Center for Latin America. In addition, the IMF operates regional training centres: the Pacific Financial Technical Assistance Center (PFTAC), the Caribbean Regional Technical Assistance Center (CARTAC) and two

Regional Technical Assistance Centers in Africa (AFRITAC). Since its establishment in 1964 the Institute has trained more than 10,900 officials from 181 countries.

Headquarters: 700 19th St. NW, Washington, D.C., 20431, USA. Offices in Paris and Geneva and a regional office for Asia and the Pacific in Tokyo.
Website: http://www.imf.org
Managing Director: Rodrigo Rato (Spain).

Publications. Annual Report; Annual Report on Exchange Arrangements and Exchange Restrictions; International Financial Statistics (monthly); *IMF Survey* (2 a month); *Balance of Payments Statistics Yearbook; Staff Papers* (4 a year); *IMF Economic Issues pamphlets; IMF Occasional Paper series; Direction of Trade Statistics* (quarterly); *Government Finance Statistics Yearbook; World Economic Outlook* (2 a year); *The International Monetary Fund, 1945–65: Twenty Years of International Monetary Co-operation*, 3 vols. Washington, 1969; de Vries, M. G., *The International Monetary Fund, 1966–1971: The System Under Stress*, 2 vols. Washington, 1976; *The International Monetary Fund 1972–1978: Co-operation on Trial.* 3 vols. Washington, 1985; *Silent Witness, International Monetary Fund 1979–89.* Washington, 2001.

Further Reading

Humphreys, N. K., *Historical Dictionary of the International Monetary Fund.* Metuchen (NJ), 1994
James, H., *International Monetary Cooperation since Bretton Woods*. OUP, 1996
Salda, A. C. M., *The International Monetary Fund.* [Bibliography] Oxford and New Brunswick (NJ), 1993

INTERNATIONAL TELECOMMUNICATION UNION (ITU)

Origin. Founded in Paris in 1865 as the International Telegraph Union, the International Telecommunication Union took its present name in 1934 and became a specialized agency of the United Nations in 1947. Therefore, the ITU is the world's oldest intergovernmental body.

Functions. To maintain and extend international co-operation for the improvement and rational use of telecommunications of all kinds, and promote and offer technical assistance to developing countries in the field of telecommunications; to promote the development of technical facilities and their most efficient operation to improve the efficiency of telecommunication services, increasing their usefulness and making them, so far as possible, generally available to the public; to harmonize the actions of nations in the attainment of these ends.

Organization. The supreme organ of the ITU is the Plenipotentiary Conference, which normally meets every four years. A 46-member Council, elected by the Conference, meets annually in Geneva and is responsible for ensuring the co-ordination of the four permanent organs at ITU headquarters: the General Secretariat; Radiocommunication Sector; Telecommunication Standardization Sector; and Telecommunication Development Sector. The Secretary-General is also elected by the Conference. ITU has 189 member countries; a further 576 scientific and technical companies, public and private operators, broadcasters and other organizations are also ITU members.

Headquarters: Place des Nations, CH-1211 Geneva 20, Switzerland.
Website: http://www.itu.int
Secretary-General: Yoshio Utsumi (Japan).

UNITED NATIONS EDUCATIONAL, SCIENTIFIC AND CULTURAL ORGANIZATION (UNESCO)

Origin. UNESCO's Constitution was signed in London on 16 Nov. 1945 by 37 countries and the Organization came into being in Nov. 1946 on the premise that: 'Since wars begin in the minds of men, it is in the minds of men that the defences of peace must be constructed'. In Dec. 2004 UNESCO had 190 members including the UK, which rejoined in 1997 having left in 1985, and the USA, which rejoined in 2003 having left in 1984. They include six associate members which are not members of the UN (Aruba; British Virgin Islands; Cayman Islands; Macao; Netherlands Antilles; Tokelau).

Aims and Activities. UNESCO's primary objective is to contribute to peace and security in the world by promoting collaboration among the nations through education, science, communication, culture, and the social and human sciences in order to further universal respect for justice, democracy, the rule of the law, human rights and fundamental freedoms, affirmed for all peoples by the UN Charter.

Education. Various activities support and foster national projects to renovate education systems and develop alternative educational strategies towards a goal of lifelong education for all. The World Development Forum in Dakar in 2000 set an agenda for progress towards this aim expressed as six goals. Two of these, attaining universal primary education by 2015 and gender parity in schooling by 2005, are also UN Millennium Development Goals. Three elements define the context for pursuing this purpose: promoting education as a fundamental right, improving the quality of education and stimulating experimentation, innovation and policy dialogue. There are regional and sub-regional offices for education in 57 countries.

Science. UNESCO seeks to promote international scientific co-operation and encourages scientific research designed to improve living conditions and to protect ecosystems. Several international programmes to better understand the Earth's resources towards the advancement of sustainable development have been initiated, including the Man and the Biosphere (MAB) programme, the International Hydrological Programme (IHP), the Intergovernmental Oceanographic Commission (IOC) and the International Geoscience Programme (IGCP).

Culture. Promoting cultural diversity and intercultural dialogue is the principal priority of UNESCO's cultural programmes. The World Heritage Centre, with its World Heritage List now covering 788 sites around the world, promotes the preservation of monuments and natural sites.

Communication. Activities are geared to promoting the free flow of information, freedom of expression, press freedom, media independence and pluralism. Another priority is to bridge the digital divide and help disadvantaged groups in North and South participate in the knowledge societies created through the information and communication technologies. To this end, UNESCO promotes access to public domain information and free software, as well as encouraging the creation of local content.

Social and Human Sciences. UNESCO works to advance knowledge and intellectual co-operation in order to facilitate social transformations conducive to justice, freedom, peace and human dignity. It seeks to identify evolving social trends and develops and promotes principles and standards based on universal values and ethics, such as the *Universal Declaration on the Human Genome and Human Rights* (1997) and the *International Declaration on Human Genetic Data* (2003).

Organization. The General Conference, composed of representatives from each member state, meets biennially to decide policy, programme and budget. A 58-member Executive Board elected by the Conference meets twice a year and there is a Secretariat. In addition, national commissions act as liaison groups between UNESCO and the educational, scientific and cultural life of their own countries. The budget for the biennium 2004–05 was US$610m.

There are also twelve separate UNESCO institutes: the International Bureau of Education (IBE), in Geneva; the UNESCO Institute for Education (UIE), in Hamburg; the International Institute for Educational Planning (IIEP), in Paris; the International Institute for Capacity Building in Africa (IICBA), in Addis Ababa; the International Institute for Higher Education in Latin America and the Caribbean (IESALC), in Caracas; the Institute for Information Technologies in Education (IITE), in Moscow; the UNESCO Institute for Statistics (UIS), in Montreal; the Institute for Water Education (UNESCO-IHE), in Delft; the UNESCO International Centre for Technical and Vocational Education and Training (UNEVOC), in Bonn; the International Centre for Theoretical Physics (ICTP) and the Third World Academy of Sciences (TWAS), both in Trieste; and the European Centre for Higher Education (CEPES), in Bucharest.

Headquarters: UNESCO House, 7 Place de Fontenoy, 75352 Paris 07 SP, France.
Website: http://www.unesco.org
Director-General: Koïchiro Matsuura (Japan).

Periodicals (published quarterly). *Museum International; International Social Science Journal; The New Courier; Prospects; Copyright Bulletin; World Heritage Review.*

UNITED NATIONS INDUSTRIAL DEVELOPMENT ORGANIZATION (UNIDO)

Origin. UNIDO was established by the UN General Assembly in 1966 and became a UN specialized agency in 1985.

Aims. UNIDO helps developing countries, and countries with economies in transition, in their fight against marginalization and poverty in today's globalized world. It mobilizes knowledge, skills, information and technology to promote productive employment, a competitive economy and a sound environment. UNIDO focuses its efforts on relieving poverty by fostering productivity growth and economic development.

Activities. As a global forum, UNIDO generates and disseminates knowledge relating to industrial matters and provides a platform for the various actors—decision makers in the public and private sectors, civil society organizations and the policy-making community in general—to enhance co-operation, establish dialogue and develop partnerships in order to address the challenges ahead. As a technical co-operation agency, UNIDO designs and implements programmes to support the industrial development efforts of its clients. It also offers tailor-made specialized support for programme development. The two core functions are both complementary and mutually supportive. On the one hand, experience gained in the technical co-operation work of UNIDO can be shared with policy makers; on the other, the Organization's analytical work shows where technical co-operation will have the greatest impact by helping to define priorities.

Organization. As part of the United Nations common system, UNIDO has the responsibility for promoting industrialization throughout the developing world, in co-operation with its 171 member states. Its headquarters are in Vienna, Austria, and with 28 smaller country and regional offices, 13 investment and technology promotion offices and a number of offices related to specific aspects of its work, UNIDO maintains an active presence in the field. The General Conference meets every two years to determine policy and approve the budget. The 53-member Industrial Development Board (membership according to constitutional lists) is elected by the General Conference. The General Conference also elects a 27-member Programme and Budget Committee for two years and appoints a Director-General for four years.

Finance. UNIDO's financial resources come from the regular and operational budgets, as well as contributions for technical co-operation activities, budgeted at US$133·7m., US$22·0m. and US$193·6m. respectively, totalling US$349·3m. for 2002–03. Administrative costs represent 7·6% of the total budget estimates. The regular budget derives from assessed contributions from member states.

Technical co-operation is funded mainly from voluntary contributions from donor countries and institutions as well as UNDP, the Multilateral Fund for the Implementation of the Montreal Protocol, the Global Environment Facility, and the Common Fund for Communities.

Headquarters: Vienna International Centre, POB 300, A-1400 Vienna, Austria.
Website: http://www.unido.org
Director-General: Carlos Alfredo Magariños (Argentina).

Publications. *UNIDOScope* (weekly Internet newspaper); *UNIDO Annual Report; Industry for Growth into the New Millennium, African Industry 2000: The Challenge of Going Global; Using Statistics for Process Control and Improvement: An Introduction to Basic Concepts and Techniques; Guidelines for Project Evaluation; Practical Appraisal for Industrial Project Applications—Application of Social Cost-Benefit Analysis in Pakistan; Manual for the Evaluation of Industrial Projects; Guide to Practical Project Appraisal—Social Benefit-Cost Analysis in Developing Countries; Manual for Small Industrial Businesses: Project Design and Appraisal; Manual for the Preparation of Industrial Feasibility Studies; Manual on Technology Transfer Negotiations; Guidelines for Infrastructure Development Through Build-Operate-Transfer (BOT) Projects; Gearing up for a New Development Agenda; Reforming the UN System: UNIDO's Need-Driven Model; World Directory of Industrial Information Sources; Woodworking Machinery: A Manual on Selection Options; Competition and the World Economy; The International Yearbook of Industrial Statistics 2003; Industrial Development Report 2002/2003.*

UNIVERSAL POSTAL UNION (UPU)

Origin. The UPU was established in 1875, when the Universal Postal Convention adopted by the Postal Congress of Berne on 9 Oct. 1874 came into force. It has 190 member countries.

Functions. The UPU provides co-operation between postal services and helps to ensure a universal network of up-to-date products and services. To this end, UPU members are united in a single postal territory for the reciprocal exchange of correspondence. A Specialized Agency of the UN since 1948, the UPU is governed by its Constitution, adopted in 1964 (Vienna), and subsequent protocol amendments (1969, Tokyo; 1974, Lausanne; 1979, Rio de Janeiro; 1984, Hamburg; 1989, Washington; 1994, Seoul; 1999, Beijing; 2004, Bucharest).

Organization. It is composed of a Universal Postal Congress which meets every four years; a 41-member Council of Administration, which meets annually and is responsible for supervising the affairs of the UPU between Congresses; a 40-member Postal Operations Council; and an International Bureau which functions as the permanent secretariat, responsible for strategic planning and programme budgeting. A new UPU body, the Consultative Committee, was created at the Bucharest Congress. This committee represents the external shareholders of the postal sector as well as UPU member countries. The budget for the biennial period 2003–04 was 71·4m. Swiss francs.

Headquarters: Weltpoststrasse 4, 3000 Berne 15, Switzerland.
Website: http://www.upu.int
Director-General: Edouard Dayan (France).

Publications. Bucharest World Postal Strategy (2004), Postal Statistics (annual), *Postal Market 2004: Review and Outlook, Post 2005—Follow-up and Trends (2000), Union Postale* (quarterly), *POST*Code* (also in CD-ROM).

WORLD HEALTH ORGANIZATION (WHO)

Origin. An International Conference convened by the UN Economic and Social Council to consider a single health organization resulted in the adoption on 22 July 1946 of the Constitution of the World Health Organization, which came into force on 7 April 1948.

Functions. WHO's objective, as stated in the first article of the Constitution, is 'the attainment by all peoples of the highest possible level of health'. As the directing and co-ordinating authority on international health, it establishes and maintains collaboration with the UN, specialized agencies, government health administrations, professional and other groups concerned with health. The Constitution also directs WHO to assist governments to strengthen their health services; to stimulate and advance work to eradicate diseases; to promote maternal and child health, mental health, medical research and the prevention of accidents; to improve standards of teaching and training in the health professions, and of nutrition, housing, sanitation, working conditions and other aspects of environmental health. The Organization is also empowered to propose conventions, agreements and regulations, and make recommendations about international health matters; to revise the international nomenclature of diseases, causes of death and public health practices; to develop, establish and promote international standards concerning foods, biological, pharmaceutical and similar substances.

Methods of work. Co-operation in country projects is undertaken only on the request of the government concerned, through the six regional offices of the Organization. Worldwide technical services are made available by headquarters. Expert committees, chosen from the 55 advisory panels of experts, meet to advise the Director-General on a given subject. Scientific groups and consultative meetings are called for similar purposes. To further the education of health personnel of all categories, seminars, technical conferences and training courses are organized, and advisors, consultants and lecturers are provided. WHO awards fellowships for study to nationals of member countries.

Activities. The main thrust of WHO's activities in recent years has been towards promoting national, regional and global strategies for the attainment of the main social target of the member states: 'Health for All in the 21st Century', or the attainment by all citizens of the world of a level of health that will permit them to lead a socially and economically productive life. Almost all countries indicated a high level of political commitment to this goal; and guiding principles for formulating corresponding strategies and plans of action were subsequently prepared.

World Health Day is observed on 7 April every year. The 2005 theme for World Health Day was Make Every Mother and Child Count; the theme for 2004 was Road Safety. World No-Tobacco Day is held on 31 May each year; International Day Against Drug Abuse on 26 June; World AIDS Day on 1 Dec.

The 50th World Health Assembly which met in 1997 adopted numerous resolutions on public health issues. *The World Health Report, 1997: Conquering suffering, enriching humanity* focused on 'non-communicable diseases'. It warned that the human and social costs of cancer, heart disease and other chronic diseases will rise unless confronted now.

The number of cancer cases was expected to double in most countries by 2020. The incidence of lung cancers in women and prostate cancers in men in the Western world is becoming far more prevalent. The incidence of other cancers is also rising rapidly, especially in developing countries. Heart disease and stroke, the leading causes of death in richer nations, will become more common in poorer countries. Globally, diabetes will more than double by 2025, with the number of people affected rising from about 135m. to 300m., and there is likely to be a huge rise in some mental disorders, especially dementias and particularly Alzheimer's disease. Already an estimated 29m. people suffer from dementia, and at least 400m. suffer from other mental disorders ranging from mood and personality disorders to neurological conditions like epilepsy, which affects some 40m. worldwide.

These projected increases are reported to be owing to a combination of factors, not least population ageing and the rising prevalence of unhealthy lifestyles. Average life expectancy at birth globally reached 65 years in 1996. It is now well over 70 years in many countries and exceeds 80 years in some. In 1997 there were an estimated 380m. people over 65 years. By 2020 that number is expected to rise to more than 690m.

The ten leading killer diseases in the world are: coronary heart disease, 7·2m. deaths annually; cancer (all sites), 6·2m.; cerebrovascular disease, 4·6m.; acute lower respiratory infection, 3·7m.; perinatal conditions, 3·6m.; tuberculosis, 2·9m.; chronic obstructive pulmonary disease, 2·9m.; diarrhoea and dysentery, 2·5m.; HIV/AIDS, 2·3m.; malaria, 2·1m. Tobacco-related deaths, primarily from lung cancer and circulatory disease, amount to 3m. a year. Smoking accounts for one in seven cancer cases worldwide, and if the trend of increasing consumption in many countries continues, the epidemic has many more decades to run.

In response, WHO has called for an intensified and sustained global campaign to encourage healthy lifestyles and attack the main risk factors responsible for many of these diseases: unhealthy diet, inadequate physical activity, smoking and obesity.

World Health Report, 2004: Changing History had as its theme the fight against HIV/AIDS and called on the international community to formulate a comprehensive HIV/AIDS strategy, linking prevention, treatment, care and long-term support. It stated that HIV/AIDS was the leading cause of death among adults aged 15–59 worldwide and had been responsible for 20m. deaths. The number of people living with the disease was estimated at 34–46m. In 2003 two-thirds of people with HIV/AIDS were resident in Africa.

The report also detailed the economic impact of HIV/AIDS, stating that 'some countries in sub-Saharan Africa may be brought to the brink of economic collapse'. Key to meeting the challenge of the epidemic was implementing better systems for providing antiretroviral therapy. It was estimated that of 6m. people requiring antiretroviral therapy, 400,000 received it in 2003 with half of global treatment needs located in seven countries (South Africa, India, Kenya, Zimbabwe, Nigeria, Ethiopia and Tanzania). To this end the WHO launched the '3 by 5' initiative with the aim of providing antiretroviral therapy to 3m. people by the end of 2005.

Cloning in human reproduction. The 1997 Assembly adopted a resolution affirming that the use of cloning for the replication of human individuals is ethically unacceptable and contrary to human integrity and morality. In accepting the resolution delegates recognized the need to respect the freedom of ethically acceptable scientific activity and to ensure access to the benefits of its applications.

Joint UN Programme on HIV/AIDS (UNAIDS). In 1996 the Assembly reviewed implementation of the global strategy for the prevention and control of AIDS, and progress of the Joint UN Programme on HIV/AIDS (UNAIDS), which became operational in 1996. The impact of the HIV/AIDS epidemic is seen to be expanding and intensifying, particularly in developing countries, and new resource mobilization mechanisms were called for to support countries in combating HIV/AIDS. The Assembly requested WHO to facilitate the incorporation of UNAIDS-specific policies, norms and strategies into the activities of WHO at global, regional and country levels, and to collaborate in all aspects of resource mobilization for HIV/AIDS activities.

Organization. The principal organs of WHO are the World Health Assembly, the Executive Board and the Secretariat. Each of the 192 member states has the right to be represented at the Assembly, which meets annually in Geneva. The 32-member Executive Board is composed of technically qualified health experts designated by as many member states as elected by the Assembly. The Secretariat consists of technical and administrative staff headed by a Director-General, who is appointed for not more than two five-year terms. Health activities in member countries are carried out through regional organizations which have been established in Africa (Brazzaville), South-East Asia (New Delhi), Europe (Copenhagen), Eastern Mediterranean (Alexandria) and Western Pacific (Manila). The Pan American Sanitary Bureau in Washington serves as the regional office of WHO for the Americas. It is the oldest international health agency in the world and is the secretariat of the Pan American Health Organization (PAHO).

Finance. The global programme budget for 2002–03 submitted to the Executive Board in Jan. 2001 was US$2,222·7m.

Headquarters: Avenue Appia, CH-1211 Geneva 27, Switzerland.
Website: http://www.who.int
Director-General: Dr Lee Jong-wook (South Korea).

Publications. Annual Report on World Health; Bulletin of WHO (6 issues a year); *International Digest of Health Legislation* (quarterly); *Health and Safety Guides; International Statistical Classification of Diseases and Related Health Problems; WHO Technical Report Series; WHO AIDS Series; Public Health Papers; World Health Statistics Annual; Weekly Epidemiological Record; WHO Drug Information* (quarterly).

WORLD INTELLECTUAL PROPERTY ORGANIZATION (WIPO)

Origin. The roots of the World Intellectual Property Organization go back to the Paris Convention for the Protection of Industrial Property, adopted in 1883, and the Berne Convention for the Protection of Literary and Artistic Works (adopted 1886). The Convention establishing WIPO was signed at Stockholm in 1967 by 51 countries, and entered into force in April 1970. WIPO became a UN specialized agency in 1974.

Aims. To promote the protection of intellectual property throughout the world through co-operation among member states; and to ensure administrative co-operation among the intellectual property unions created by the Paris and Berne Conventions.

Intellectual property comprises two main branches: industrial property (inventions, trademarks and industrial designs) and copyright and neighbouring rights (literary, musical, artistic, photographic and audiovisual works).

Activities. There are three principal areas of activity: the progressive development of international intellectual property law; global protection systems and services; and co-operation for development. WIPO seeks to harmonize national intellectual property legislation and procedures; provide services for international applications for industrial property rights; exchange intellectual property information; provide training and legal and technical assistance to developing and other countries; facilitate the resolution of private intellectual property disputes; and marshal information technology as a tool for storing, accessing and using valuable intellectual property information.

New approaches to the progressive development of international intellectual property law. The development and application of international norms and standards is a fundamental part of WIPO's activities. It administers 21 treaties (15 on industrial property, six on copyright). The Organization plays an increasing role in making national and regional systems for the registration of intellectual property more user-friendly by harmonizing and simplifying procedures.

Global protection systems and services. The most successful and widely used treaty is the Patent Co-operation Treaty (PCT), which implements the concept of a single international patent application that is valid in many countries. Once such application is filed, an applicant has time to decide in which countries to pursue the application, thereby streamlining procedures and reducing costs. In 2001 the PCT system recorded 103,947 applications.

The treaties dealing with the international registration of marks and industrial designs are, respectively, the Madrid Agreement (and its Protocol) and the Hague Agreement. In 1999 there were more than 20,000 registrations of marks under the Madrid System, an equivalent of over 264,000 national trademark registrations. In 1999 WIPO registered 4,093 international deposits of industrial designs.

Co-operation for development. On 1 Jan. 2000 many developing and other countries, as members of the World Trade Organization, brought their national legislative and administrative structures into conformity with the Agreement on Trade-Related Aspects of Intellectual Property Rights (TRIPS). WIPO and WTO agreed, in the framework of a Co-operation Agreement which entered into force on 1 Jan. 1996, and a Joint Initiative launched in July 1998, on a joint technical co-operation initiative to provide assistance to developing countries to meet their obligations to comply with the TRIPS Agreement. This represented a major step in the international harmonization of the scope, standards and enforcement of Intellectual Property rights.

The newly created WIPO Worldwide Academy co-ordinates training activities, originates new approaches and methods to expand the scope, impact and accessibility of WIPO programmes, and creates more effective training tailored for diverse-user groups. The Academy has also launched an Internet-based distance-learning programme.

Impact of digital technology on intellectual property law. WIPO takes a range of initiatives to tackle the implications of modern digital and communications technology for copyright and industrial property law, and in electronic commerce transcending national jurisdictions. The WIPO Arbitration and Mediation Centre was established in 1994 to provide online dispute-resolution services. The Centre developed an operational and legal framework for the administration of disputes, including those relating to new technologies such as Internet Domain Name Disputes.

Organization. WIPO has three governing bodies: the General Assembly, the Conference and the Co-ordination Committee. Each treaty administered by WIPO has one or more Governing Bodies of its own, composed of representatives of the respective member states. In addition, the Paris and Berne Unions have Assemblies and Executive Committees. The executive head of WIPO is the Director-General, who is elected by the General Assembly. In March 2005 WIPO had 182 member states, with an international staff of around 850 from 86 countries. The budget for 2002–03 was 678m. Swiss francs, the majority of which was covered by revenue earned by the Organization's international registration and publication activities.

Official languages: Arabic, Chinese, English, French, Russian and Spanish.
Headquarters: 34 chemin des Colombettes, 1211 Geneva 20, Switzerland.
Website: http://www.wipo.int
Director-General: Dr Kamil Idris (Sudan).

Periodicals. Industrial Property and Copyright (monthly, bi-monthly, in Spanish); *PCT Gazette* (weekly); *PCT Newsletter* (monthly); *International Designs Bulletin* (monthly); *WIPO Gazette of International Marks* (fortnightly); *Intellectual Property in Asia and the Pacific* (quarterly).

WORLD METEOROLOGICAL ORGANIZATION (WMO)

Origin. A 1947 (Washington) Conference of Directors of the International Meteorological Organization (est. 1873) adopted a Convention creating the World

Meteorological Organization. The WMO Convention became effective on 23 March 1950 and WMO was formally established. It was recognized as a Specialized Agency of the UN in 1951.

Functions. (1) To facilitate worldwide co-operation in the establishment of networks of stations for the making of meteorological observations as well as hydrological or other geophysical observations related to meteorology, and to promote the establishment and maintenance of meteorological centres charged with the provision of meteorological and related services; (2) to promote the establishment and maintenance of systems for the rapid exchange of meteorological and related information; (3) to promote standardization of meteorological and related observations and ensure the uniform publication of observations and statistics; (4) to further the application of meteorology to aviation, shipping, water problems, agriculture and other human activities; (5) to promote activities in operational hydrology and to further close co-operation between meteorological and hydrological services; and (6) to encourage research and training in meteorology and, as appropriate, to assist in co-ordinating the international aspects of such research and training.

Organization. WMO has 181 member states and six member territories responsible for the operation of their own meteorological services. Congress, which is its supreme body, meets every four years to approve policy, programme and budget, and adopt regulations. The Executive Council meets at least once a year to prepare studies and recommendations for Congress, and supervises the implementation of Congress resolutions and regulations. It has 37 members, comprising the President and three Vice-Presidents, as well as the Presidents of the six Regional Associations (Africa, Asia, South America, North America, Central America and the Caribbean, South-West Pacific, Europe), whose task is to co-ordinate meteorological activity within their regions, and 27 members elected in their personal capacity. There are eight Technical Commissions composed of experts nominated by members of WMO, whose remit includes the following areas: basic systems, climatology, instruments and methods of observation, atmospheric sciences, aeronautical meteorology, agricultural meteorology, hydrology, oceanography and marine meteorology. A permanent Secretariat is maintained in Geneva. There are three regional offices for Africa, Asia and the Pacific, and the Americas. The budget for 2004–07 was 253·8m. Swiss francs.

Headquarters: 7 bis, avenue de la Paix, Case Postale 2300, CH-1211 Geneva 2, Switzerland.
Website: http://www.wmo.int
e-mail: wmo@wmo.int
Secretary-General: Michel Jarraud (France).

Publications. WMO Bulletin (quarterly); *WMO Annual Report.*

WORLD TOURISM ORGANIZATION (WTO)

Origin. Established in 1925 in The Hague as the International Congress of Official Tourist Traffic Associations. Renamed the International Union for Official Tourism Organizations after the Second World War when it moved to Geneva, it was renamed the World Tourism Organization in 1975 and moved its headquarters to Madrid the following year.

The World Tourism Organization became an executing agency of the United Nations Development Programme in 1976 and in 1977 a formal co-operation agreement was signed with the UN itself. With a UN resolution on 23 Dec. 2003 the World Tourism Organization became a specialized agency of the United Nations.

Aims. The World Tourism Organization exists to help nations throughout the world maximize the positive impacts of tourism, such as job creation, new infrastructure and foreign exchange earnings, while at the same time minimizing negative environmental or social impacts.

Membership. The World Tourism Organization has three categories of membership: full membership which is open to all sovereign states; associate membership which is open to all territories not responsible for their external relations; and affiliate membership which comprises a wide range of organizations and companies working either directly in travel and tourism or in related sectors. In Jan. 2005 the World Tourism Organization had 145 full members, seven associate members and almost 350 affiliate members.

Organization. The General Assembly meets every two years to approve the budget and programme of work and to debate topics of vital importance to the tourism sector. The Executive Council is the governing board, responsible for ensuring that the organization carries out its work and keeps within its budget. The World Tourism Organization has six regional commissions—Africa, the Americas, East Asia and the Pacific, Europe, the Middle East and South Asia—which meet at least once a year. Specialized committees of World Tourism Organization members advise on management and programme content.

Headquarters: Capitán Haya 42, 28020 Madrid, Spain.
Website: http://www.world-tourism.org
Secretary-General: Francesco Frangialli (France).

Publications. Yearbook of Tourism Statistics (annual); *Compendium of Tourism Statistics* (annual); *Travel and Tourism Barometer* (3 per year); *WTO News* (4 per year); *various others* (about 100 a year).

OTHER ORGANS RELATED TO THE UN

INTERNATIONAL ATOMIC ENERGY AGENCY (IAEA)

Origin. An intergovernmental agency, the IAEA was established in 1957 under the aegis of the UN and reports annually to the General Assembly. Its Statute was approved on 26 Oct. 1956 at a conference at UN Headquarters.

Functions. To accelerate and enlarge the contribution of atomic energy to peace, health and prosperity throughout the world; and to ensure that assistance provided by it or at its request or under its supervision or control is not used in such a way as to further any military purpose. In addition, under the terms of the Non-Proliferation Treaty, the Treaty of Tlatelolco, the Treaty of Rarotonga, the Pelindaba Treaty and the Bangkok Treaty: to verify states' obligation to prevent diversion of nuclear fissionable material from peaceful uses to nuclear weapons or other nuclear explosive devices.

Activities. The IAEA gives advice and technical assistance to developing countries on nuclear power development, nuclear safety and security, radioactive waste management, legal aspects of atomic energy use, and prospecting for and exploiting nuclear raw materials. In addition, it promotes the use of radiation and isotopes in agriculture, industry, medicine and hydrology through expert services, training courses and fellowships, grants of equipment and supplies, research contracts, scientific meetings and publications. During 2003 support for operational projects for technical co-operation involved 3,121 expert and lecturer assignments, 2,848 meeting and workshop participants, 2,107 participants in training courses and 1,411 fellows and visiting scientists.

Safeguards are the technical means applied by the IAEA to verify that nuclear equipment or materials are used exclusively for peaceful purposes. IAEA safeguards cover more than 95% of civilian nuclear installations outside the five nuclear-weapon states (China, France, Russia, UK and USA). These five nuclear-weapon states have concluded agreements with the Agency which permit the application of IAEA safeguards to all their civil nuclear activities. A total of 232 safeguards agreements in force in 148 states involved 2,363 safeguard inspections performed in 2003. Safeguards activities are applied routinely at over 900 facilities in 71 countries. A programme designed to prevent and combat illicit trafficking of nuclear weapons came into force in April 1996.

Organization. The Statute provides for an annual General Conference, a 35-member Board of Governors and a Secretariat headed by a Director-General. The IAEA had 138 member states in March 2005.

There are also research laboratories in Austria and Monaco. *The International Centre for Theoretical Physics* was established in Trieste, in 1964, and is operated jointly by UNESCO and the IAEA.

Headquarters: Vienna International Centre, PO Box 100, A-1400 Vienna, Austria.
Website: http://www.iaea.org
Director-General: Dr Mohamed ElBaradei (Egypt).

Publications. Annual Report; IAEA Bulletin (quarterly); *IAEA Yearbook; INIS Reference Series; Legal Series; Nuclear Fusion* (monthly); *Nuclear Safety Review* (annual); *INIS Atomindex* (CD-Rom); *Technical Directories; Technical Reports Series.*

WORLD TRADE ORGANIZATION (WTO)

Origin. The WTO is founded on the General Agreement on Tariffs and Trade (GATT), which entered into force on 1 Jan. 1948. Its 23 original signatories were members of a Preparatory Committee appointed by the UN Economic and Social Council to draft the charter for a proposed International Trade Organization. Since this charter was never ratified, the General Agreement remained the only international instrument laying down trade rules. In Dec. 1993 there were 111 contracting parties, and a further 22 countries applying GATT rules on a *de facto* basis. On 15 April 1994 trade ministers of 123 countries signed the Final Act of the GATT Uruguay Round of negotiations at Marrakesh, bringing the WTO into being on 1 Jan. 1995. As of March 2005 the WTO had 148 members.

The object of the Act is the liberalization of world trade. By it, member countries undertake to apply fair trade rules covering commodities, services and intellectual property. It provides for the lowering of tariffs on industrial goods and tropical products; the abolition of import duties on a variety of items; the progressive abolition of quotas on garments and textiles; the gradual reduction of trade-distorting subsidies and import barriers; and agreements on intellectual property and trade in services. Members are required to accept the results of the Uruguay Round talks in their entirety, and subscribe to all the WTO's agreements and disciplines. There are no enforcement procedures, however; decisions are ultimately reached by consensus.

Functions. The WTO is the legal and institutional foundation of the multilateral trading system. Surveillance of national trade policies is an important part of its work. At the centre of this is the *Trade Policy Review Mechanism (TPRM)*, agreed by Ministers in 1994 (Article III of the Marrakesh Agreement). The TPRM was broadened in 1995 when the WTO came into being, to cover services trade and intellectual property. Its principal objective is to facilitate the smooth functioning of the multilateral trading system by enhancing the transparency of members' trade policies. All members are subject to review under the TPRM, which mandates that four members with the largest share of world trade (European Union, USA, Japan, Canada) be reviewed every two years; the next 16, every four years; and others every six, with a longer period able to be fixed for the least-developed members. Also, in 1994, flexibility of up to six months was introduced into the review cycles, and in 1996, it was agreed that every second review of each of the first four trading entities should be an interim review. Reviews are conducted by the Trade Policy Review Body (TPRB) on the basis of a policy statement by the member under review and a report by economists in the Secretariat's Trade Policy Review Division.

The *International Trade Centre* (since 1968 operated jointly with the United Nations through UNCTAD) was established by GATT in 1964 to provide information and training on export markets and marketing techniques, and thereby to assist the trade of developing countries. In 1984 the Centre became an executing agency of the UN Development Programme, responsible for carrying out UNDP-financed projects related to trade promotion.

Organization. A two-yearly ministerial meeting is the ultimate policy-making body. The 144-member General Council has some 30 subordinate councils and committees. The *Dispute Settlement Body* was set up to deal with disputes between countries. Appeals against its verdicts are heard by a seven-member *Appellate Body*. In 2003 it was composed of representatives of Egypt, the European Union, Japan, Brazil, Australia, USA and India. Dispute panels may be set up *ad hoc*, and objectors to their ruling may appeal to the Appellate Body whose decision is binding. Refusal to comply at this stage can result in the application of trade sanctions. Each appeal is heard by three of the Appellate Body members. Before cases are heard by dispute panels, there is a 60-day consultation period. The previous GATT Secretariat now serves the WTO, which has no resources of its own other than its operating budget. The budget for 2004 was 161,776,500 Swiss francs.

Headquarters: Centre William Rappard, 154 rue de Lausanne, CH-1211 Geneva 21, Switzerland.
Website: http://www.wto.org
e-mail: enquiries@wto.org
Director-General: Supachai Panitchpakdi (Thailand).

Publications. Annual Report; International Trade: Trends and Statistics (annual); *WTO Focus* (ten a year).

Further Reading

Croome, J., *Reshaping the World Trading System.* WTO, 1996
Preeg, E., *Traders in a Brave New World.* Chicago Univ. Press, 1996

PREPARATORY COMMISSION FOR THE COMPREHENSIVE NUCLEAR-TEST-BAN TREATY ORGANIZATION (CTBTO)

The Preparatory Commission for the Comprehensive Nuclear-Test-Ban Treaty Organization (CTBTO Preparatory Commission) is an international organization established by the States Signatories to the Treaty on 19 Nov. 1996. It carries out the necessary preparations for the effective implementation of the Treaty, and prepares for the first session of the Conference of the States Parties to the Treaty.

The Preparatory Commission consists of a plenary body composed of all the States Signatories, and the Provisional Technical Secretariat (PTS). Upon signing the Treaty a state becomes a member of the Commission. Member states oversee the work of the Preparatory Commission and fund its activities. The Commission's main task is the establishment of the 337 facility International Monitoring System and the International Data Centre, its provisional operation and the development of operational manuals. The Comprehensive Nuclear-Test-Ban Treaty prohibits any nuclear weapon test explosion or any other nuclear explosion anywhere in the world. As of March 2005 the Treaty had 175 States Signatories and 120 ratifications.

Headquarters: Vienna International Centre, PO Box 1200, A-1400 Vienna, Austria.
Website: http://www.ctbto.org
Executive Secretary: Wolfgang Hoffmann (Germany).

ORGANIZATION FOR THE PROHIBITION OF CHEMICAL WEAPONS (OPCW)

The OPCW is responsible for the implementation of the Chemical Weapons Convention (CWC), which became effective on 29 April 1997. The principal organ of the OPCW is the Conference of the States Parties, composed of all the members of the Organization.

Given the relative simplicity of producing chemical warfare agents, the verification provisions of the CWC are far-reaching. The routine monitoring regime involves submission by States Parties of initial and annual declarations to the OPCW and initial visits and systematic inspections of declared weapons storage, production and destruction facilities. Verification is also applied to chemical industry facilities which produce, process or consume dual-use chemicals listed in the convention. The OPCW also when requested by any State Party conducts short-notice challenge inspections at any location under its jurisdiction or control of any other State Party.

The OPCW also co-ordinates assistance to any State Party that falls victim of chemical warfare as it fosters international co-operation in the peaceful application of chemistry.

By Nov. 2004 a total of 167 countries were States Parties to the Chemical Weapons Convention.

Headquarters: Johan de Wittlaan 32, 2517 JR The Hague, Netherlands.
Website: http://www.opcw.org
Director General: Rogelio Pfirter (Argentina).

EUROPEAN UNION (EU)

Origin. The Union is founded on the existing European communities set up by the Treaties of Paris (1951) and Rome (1957), supplemented by revisions, the Single European Act in 1986, the Maastricht Treaty on European Union in 1992, the Treaty of Amsterdam in 1997 and the draft Treaty of Nice in 2000.

Members. (25). As at May 2004: Austria, Belgium, Cyprus (Greek-Cypriot part only), Czech Republic, Denmark, Estonia, Finland, France, Germany, Greece, Hungary, Ireland, Italy, Latvia, Lithuania, Luxembourg, Malta, the Netherlands, Poland, Portugal, Slovakia, Slovenia, Spain, Sweden and the UK.

History. On 19 Sept. 1946, in Zürich, Winston Churchill called for a 'united states of Europe', but neither he nor his successor pressed for British involvement. Two years later, the Congress of Europe (the meeting in The Hague of nearly 1,000 Europeans from 26 countries calling for a united Europe) resulted in the birth in 1949 of the Council of Europe, a European assembly of nations whose aim (Art. 1 of the Statute) was: 'to achieve a greater unity between its members for the purpose of safeguarding and realizing the ideals and principles which are their common heritage'.

On 18 April 1951, subsequent to a proposal by the French foreign minister Robert Schuman (Schuman Declaration), Belgium, France, the Federal Republic of Germany, Italy, Luxembourg and the Netherlands signed the Treaty of Paris establishing the *European Coal and Steel Community (ECSC)*. The treaty provided for the pooling of coal and steel production and was regarded as a first step towards a united Europe. Encouraged by the success of the ECSC, plans were laid down for the establishment of two more communities. *The European Economic Community (EEC)* and *the European Atomic Energy Community (EAEC or Euratom)* were subsequently created under separate treaties signed in Rome on 25 March 1957. The treaties provided for the establishment by stages of a common market with a customs union at its core, the approximation of economic policies, and the promotion of growth in the nuclear industries for peaceful purposes.

To this end, Euratom was awarded monopoly powers of acquisition of fissile materials for civil purposes (it is not concerned with the military uses of nuclear power). Subsequently, the various powers of the three communities (ECSC, EAEC, EEC, sometimes referred to collectively as the European Community or EC) were transferred by a treaty signed in Brussels in 1965 to a single Council and single Commission of the European Communities, today the core of the EU. The Commission is advised on matters relating to EAEC by a Scientific and Technical Committee.

Enlargement. On 30 June 1970 membership negotiations began between the European Community and the UK, Denmark, Ireland and Norway. On 22 Jan. 1972 all four countries signed a Treaty of Accession, and with the exception of Norway which later rejected membership in a referendum in Nov. that year, the UK, Denmark and Ireland became full members on 1 Jan. 1973 (though Greenland exercised its autonomy under the Danish Crown to secede in 1985). Greece joined on 1 Jan. 1981; Spain and Portugal on 1 Jan. 1986. The former German Democratic Republic entered into full membership on reunification with Federal Germany in Oct. 1990, and following referenda in favour, Austria, Finland and Sweden became members on 1 Jan. 1995. In a referendum in Nov. 1994 Norway again rejected membership. On 1 May 2004 a further ten countries became members—Cyprus, Czech Republic, Estonia, Hungary, Latvia, Lithuania, Malta, Poland, Slovakia and Slovenia.

Single European Act. The enlarging of the Community resulted in renewed efforts to promote European integration, culminating in the signing in Dec. 1985 of the Single European Act. The SEA represented the first major revision of the Treaties of Rome and provided for greater involvement of the European Parliament in the decision-making process.

Maastricht Treaty on European Union. Further amendments were agreed at the Maastricht Summit of Dec. 1991 in the draft Treaty on European Union whereby moves to a common currency were agreed subject to specific conditions (including an opt-out clause for the UK) and the social dimension was recognized in a protocol (not applicable to the UK) allowing member states to use EC institutions for this purpose. Ratification by member states of the Maastricht Treaty proved unexpectedly controversial. In June 1992 the Danish electorate in a referendum voted against it, then reversed the decision in a second referendum in May 1993. Ratification was finally completed during 1993, with the UK ratifying on 2 Aug., and the European Union (EU) officially came into being on 1 Nov. that year.

Recent and Future Enlargement. On 16 July 1997 Jacques Santer presented *Agenda 2000*, the European Commission's detailed strategy for consolidating the Union through enlargement as far eastwards as Ukraine, Belarus and Moldova. It recommended the early start of accession negotiations with Hungary, Poland, Estonia, the Czech Republic and Slovenia under the provision of Article O of the Maastricht Treaty whereby 'any European State may apply to become a member of the Union' (subject to the Copenhagen Criteria set by the European Council at its summit in 1993).

In 2002 it was announced that ten countries would be ready to join in 2004, namely: Poland, Hungary, the Czech Republic, Slovakia, Lithuania, Latvia, Estonia, Slovenia, Cyprus and Malta. Following a series of referenda held in 2003 they all became members on 1 May 2004. A target date of 2007 is proposed for Bulgaria, Croatia and Romania to join. Turkey is also hoping to join, but talks on membership which are set to begin in Oct. 2005 may take up to 15 years. The Prince of Liechtenstein has made it known that he wishes his government to apply.

Objectives. The ultimate goal of the EU is 'an ever closer union among the peoples of Europe, in which decisions are taken as closely as possible to the citizen'. Priorities include the implementation of the Treaty of Amsterdam (new rights for citizens, freedom of movement, strengthening the institutions of the EU, employment); economic and monetary union; further expansion of the scope of the Communities; implementation of a common foreign and security policy; and development in the fields of justice and home affairs. At the European Summit held in Nice, France in Dec. 2000 it was agreed to concentrate on four main areas—the charter of fundamental rights, simplifying EU treaties, clarifying the balance of power between the EU and member states, and the possibility of a second chamber of parliament. In Dec. 2001 the Laeken European Conference adopted the Declaration on the Future of the European Union, committing the EU to becoming more democratic, transparent and effective, opening the way to a constitution for the people of Europe. The European Council set up a convention, comprising 105 members, under the chairmanship of former French president Valéry Giscard d'Estaing, to draft an EU constitution which must be ratified by all 25 states. The constitution includes provision for a President of the European Council, to replace the current six-month rotating presidency, to be elected by member states for 2½-year terms. There would also be an EU foreign minister and a charter of fundamental rights. Member states would have reduced powers of veto, although the veto would remain in key areas including taxation, defence and foreign policy. Plans for the new constitution to be ready for EU governments to sign after the ten new members joined on 1 May 2004 were disappointed when the Brussels summit of Dec. 2003 ended in stalemate over the weighting of voting rights for individual nations within the Council of Ministers. The constitution was signed on 29 Oct. 2004, but the 25 member countries have to ratify it, either by referendum or parliamentary vote, before it comes into force.

Structure. The institutional arrangements of the EU provide for an independent policy-making executive with powers of proposal (European Commission), various consultative and advisory bodies, and a decision-making body drawn from the Governments (Council of Ministers).

Defence. In Nov. 2000 European Union defence ministers agreed to commit personnel and equipment to a rapid reaction force that could be deployed in tackling crises in an area up to 4,000 km from Brussels at short notice. The first elements of the rapid reaction force are expected to become operational in the course of 2005. There will ultimately be a pool of approximately 100,000 personnel, 400 combat aircraft and 100 warships, but a maximum of 60,000 personnel will be serving at any one time to allow for the rotation of forces in the event of a lengthy operation. Although final numbers have not yet been agreed, Britain, France and Germany are likely to provide the largest number of troops, at around 12,000 to 13,000 each out of the total of 60,000. Denmark has decided to opt out. The European Union's first ever peacekeeping force (EUFOR) officially started work in Macedonia on 1 April 2003.

The European Union Institute for Security Studies (EUISS) was created by a Council Joint Action in July 2001 with the status of an autonomous agency. It contributes to the development of the Common Foreign and Security Policy (CFSP) through research and debate on major security and defence issues.

Major Policy Areas. The major policy areas of the EU were laid down in the Treaty of Rome of 25 March 1957 which guaranteed certain rights to the citizens of all member states, including the outlawing of economic discrimination by nationality, and equal pay for equal work as between men and women.

The single internal market. The single internal market represents the core of the process of economic integration and is characterized by the removal of obstacles to the four fundamental freedoms of movement for persons, goods, capital and services. Under the Treaty, individuals or companies from one member state may establish themselves in another country (for the purposes of economic activity) or sell goods or services there on the same basis as nationals of that country. With a few exceptions, restrictions on the movement of capital have also been ended. Under the Single European Act the member states bound themselves to achieve the suppression of all barriers to free movement of persons, goods and services by 31 Dec. 1992.

The *Schengen Accord* abolished border controls on persons and goods between certain EU states plus Norway and Iceland. It came into effect on 26 March 1995 and was signed by Austria, Belgium, Denmark, Finland, France, Germany, Greece, Iceland, Italy, Luxembourg, Netherlands, Norway, Portugal, Spain and Sweden.

Economic and Monetary Union. The establishment of the single market provided for the next phase of integration: economic and monetary union. The *European Monetary System (EMS)* was founded in March 1979 to control inflation, protect European trade from international disturbances and ultimately promote convergence between the European economies. At its heart was the *Exchange Rate Mechanism (ERM)*. The ERM is run by the finance ministries and central banks of the EU countries on a day-to-day basis; monthly reviews are carried out by the EU Monetary Committee (finance ministries) and the EU Committee of Central Bankers. Sweden is not in the ERM; the UK suspended its membership on 17 Sept. 1992. In Jan. 1995 Austria joined the ERM. Finland followed in 1996, and in Nov. that year the Italian lira, which had been temporarily suspended, was re-admitted.

With the introduction of the euro, exchange rates have been fixed for all member countries. The member countries are Austria, Belgium, Finland, France, Germany, Greece, Ireland, Italy, Luxembourg, Netherlands, Portugal and Spain. The euro became legal tender from 1 Jan. 2002 across the region. National currencies ran in parallel for certain periods depending on the country but were phased out by the end of Feb. 2002.

European Monetary Union (EMU). The single European currency with 11 member states came into operation in Jan. 1999 although it was not until 2002 that the currency came into general circulation. Greece subsequently joined in Jan. 2001. The euro-zone is the world's second largest economy after the USA in terms of output and the largest in terms of trade. EMU currency consists of the euro of 100 cents, with coins of 1, 2, 5, 10, 20 and 50 cents and 1 and 2 euros and notes of 5, 10, 20, 50, 100, 200 and 500 euros. EU member countries not in EMU will select a central rate for their currency in consultation with members of the euro bloc and the European Central Bank. The rate is set according to an assessment of each country's chances of joining the euro zone.

An agreement on the legal status of the euro and currency discipline, the Stability and Growth Pact, was reached by all member states at the Dublin summit on 13 Dec. 1996. Financial penalties will be applied to member states running a GDP deficit (negative growth) of up to 0·75%. If GDP falls between 0·75% and 2%, EU finance ministers will have discretion as to whether to apply penalties. Members running an excessive deficit will be automatically exempt from penalties in the event of a natural disaster or if the fall in GDP is at least 2% over one year.

Environment. The Single European Act made the protection of the environment an integral part of economic and social policies. Community policy aims at preventing pollution (the Prevention Principle), rectifying pollution at source, and imposing the costs of prevention or rectification upon the polluters themselves (the Polluter Pays Principle). The European Environment Agency (see below) was established to ensure that policy was based on reliable scientific data.

In March 2002 the 15 European Union member states agreed to be bound by the 1997 Kyoto Protocol to the United Nations Framework on Climate Change, which commits the EU to reduce its emissions of greenhouse gases by 8% from the 1990 levels between 2008 and 2012.

The Common Agricultural Policy (CAP). The objectives set out in the Treaty are to increase agricultural productivity, to ensure a fair standard of living for the agricultural community, to stabilize markets, to assure supplies, and to ensure reasonable consumer prices. In Dec. 1960 the Council laid down the fundamental principles on which the CAP is based: a single market, which calls for common prices, stable currency parities and the harmonizing of health and veterinary legislation; Community preference, which protects the single Community market from imports; common financing, through the European Agricultural Guidance and Guarantee Fund (EAGGF), which seeks to improve agriculture through its Guidance section, and to stabilize markets against world price fluctuations through market intervention, with levies and refunds on exports.

Following the disappearance of stable currency parities, artificial currency levels have been applied in the CAP. This factor, together with over-production owing to high producer prices, meant that the CAP consumed about two-thirds of the Community budget. In May 1992 it was agreed to reform CAP and to control over-production by reducing the price supports to farmers by 29% for cereals, 15% for beef and 5% for dairy products. In June 1995 the guaranteed intervention price for beef was decreased by 5%. In July 1996 agriculture ministers agreed a reduction in the set-aside rate for cereals from 10% to 5%. Fruit and vegetable production subsidies were fixed at no more than 4% of the value of total marketed production, rising to 4·5% in 1999. Compensatory grants are made available to farmers who remove land from production or take early retirement. The CAP reform aims to make the agricultural sector more responsive to supply and demand. Farm spending currently absorbs 46% of the EU budget but accounts for only 1·8% of Europe's GDP.

Customs Union and External Trade Relations. Goods or Services originating in one member state have free circulation within the EU, which implies common arrangements for trade with the rest of the world. Member states can no longer make bilateral trade agreements with third countries; this power has been ceded to the EU. The Customs Union was achieved in July 1968.

In Oct. 1991 a treaty forming the *European Economic Area (EEA)* was approved by the member states of the then EC and European Free Trade Association (EFTA). The EEA consists of the 25 EU members plus Iceland, Liechtenstein and Norway. Association agreements which could lead to accession or customs union have been made with Israel, Morocco and Turkey. The customs union with Turkey came into force on 1 Jan. 1996. Commercial, industrial, technical and financial aid agreements have been made with Algeria, Egypt, Jordan, Lebanon, Morocco, Russia, Serbia and Montenegro, Syria and Tunisia. In 1976 Canada signed a framework agreement for co-operation in industrial trade, science and natural resources, and a transatlantic pact was signed with the USA in Dec. 1995. Co-operation agreements also exist with a number of Latin American countries and groupings, and with Arab and Asian countries, and an economic and commercial agreement has been signed with the Association of South East Asian Nations (ASEAN). Partnership and co-operation agreements were signed with Ukraine in June 1994, Kazakhstan in Jan. 1995, Kyrgyzstan in Feb. 1995 and with Uzbekistan in June 1996. In the Development Aid sector, the EU has an agreement (the Cotonou Agreement, signed in 2000, the successor of the Lomé Convention, originally signed in 1975 but renewed and enlarged in 1979, 1984 and 1989) with some 60 African, Caribbean and Pacific (ACP) countries which removes customs duties without reciprocal arrangements for most of their imports to the Community.

The application of common duties has been conducted mainly within the framework of the *General Agreement on Tariffs and Trade (GATT)*, which was succeeded in 1995 by the establishment of the World Trade Organization.

Fisheries. The Common Fisheries Policy (CFP) came into effect in Jan. 1983, according to which all EU fishermen have equal access to the waters of member countries (a zone extending up to 200 nautical miles from the shore around all its coastlines), with the total allowable catch for each species being set and shared out between member countries according to pre-established quotas, with in some cases 'historic rights' applying, as well as special rules to conserve stock, preserve marine biodiversity, and the sustainable pursuit of fishing.

A number of agreements are in place with other countries (Canada, Norway, USA and some African countries) allowing reciprocal fishing rights. When Greenland withdrew from the Community in 1985 EU boats retained their fishing rights subject to quotas and limits, which were revised in 1995 owing to concern about overfishing of Greenland halibut. An agreement was initialled with Argentina in 1992.

Transport. Under the Maastricht Treaty, the Community must contribute to the establishment and development of trans-European networks in the areas of transport, telecommunications and energy infrastructures.

Competition. The Competition (anti-trust) law of the EU is based on two principles: that businesses should not seek to nullify the creation of the common market by the erection of artificial national (or other) barriers to the free movement of goods; and against the abuse of dominant positions in any market. These two principles have led among other things to the outlawing of prohibitions on exports to other member states, of price-fixing agreements and of refusal to supply; and to the refusal by the Commission to allow mergers or takeovers by dominant undertakings in specific cases. Increasingly heavy fines are imposed on offenders.

A number of structural funds have been established in an attempt to counter specific problems within and across the Community. These include:

European Social Fund. Provides resources with the aim of combating long-term unemployment and facilitating integration into the labour market of young people and the socially disadvantaged. The 2003 budget included an allocation of around €9,577m. for the Fund's commitments.

European Regional Development Fund. Intended to compensate for the unequal rate of development among different regions of the EU by encouraging investment and improving infrastructure in 'problem regions'.

Finances. The general budget of the EU covers all EEC and Euratom expenditure, and the administrative expenditure of the ECSC.

EU revenue in €1m.:

	Financial year 2003
Agricultural duties	1,395·0
Customs duties	9,462·1
VAT-based resource	21,260·1
GNI-based resource	51,515·3
Miscellaneous revenue	9,836·1
Total	93,468·6

Expenditure for the financial year 2003 was €91,974·7m., of which the European Agricultural Guidance and Guarantee Fund Guarantee Section accounted for €44,419·3m.

The resources of the Community (the levies and duties mentioned above, and up to a 1·4% VAT charge) have been surrendered to it by Treaty. The Budget is made by the Council and the Parliament acting jointly as the Budgetary Authority. The Parliament has control, within a certain margin, of non-obligatory expenditure (where the amount to be spent is not set out in the legislation concerned), and can also reject the Budget. Otherwise, the Council decides.

Official languages: Czech, Danish, Dutch, English, Estonian, Finnish, French, German, Greek, Hungarian, Italian, Latvian, Lithuanian, Maltese, Polish, Portuguese, Slovak, Slovenian, Spanish and Swedish.
Website: http://www.europa.eu.int

EU INSTITUTIONS

EUROPEAN COMMISSION

The European Commission consists of 25 members appointed by the member states to serve for five years. The Commission President is selected by a consensus of member state heads of government and serves a five-year term. The Commission acts as the EU executive body and as guardian of the Treaties. In this it has the right of initiative (putting proposals to the Council of Ministers for action) and of execution (once the Council has decided). It can take the other institutions or individual countries before the European Court of Justice should any of these fail to comply with European Law. Decisions on legislative proposals made by the Commission are taken in the Council of the European Union. Members of the Commission swear an oath of independence, distancing themselves from partisan influence from any source. The Commission operates through 37 Directorates-General and services.

At the European Summit held in Nice in Dec. 2000 it was decided that from 2005 each EU member state would have one commissioner until there are 27 members. A permanent limit of fewer than 27 will then be set, with the seats being rotated among member states.

The current Commission took office in Nov. 2004. Members, their nationality and political affiliation (S-Socialist/Social Democrat; C-Christian Democrat/Conservative; L-Liberal; G-Green; Ind-Independent) in Nov. 2004 were as follows.

President: José Manuel Barroso (Portugal, S).

The commissioners are:

Vice-president: Margot Wallström (Sweden, S); responsible for institutional relations and communication strategy.

Vice-president: Jacques Barrot (France, C); responsible for transport.

Vice-president: Siim Kallas (Estonia, L); responsible for administrative affairs, audit and anti-fraud.

Vice-president: Günter Verheugen (Germany, S); responsible for enterprise and industry.

Vice-president: Franco Frattini (Italy, C); responsible for justice, freedom and security.

Agriculture and Rural Development and Fisheries: Mariann Fischer Boel (Denmark, L).

Competition: Neelie Kroes (Netherlands, L).

Development and Humanitarian Aid: Louis Michel (Belgium, L).

Economic and Monetary Affairs: Joaquín Almunia (Spain, S).

Education, Training, Culture and Multilingualism: Ján Figeľ (Slovakia, C).

Employment, Social Affairs and Equal Opportunities: Vladimír Špidla (Czech Republic, S).

Energy: Andris Piebalgs (Latvia, L).

Enlargement: Olli Rehn (Finland, L).

Environment: Stavros Dimas (Greece, C).

External Relations and European Neighbourhood Policy: Benita Ferrero-Waldner (Austria, C).

Financial Programming and Budget: Dalia Grybauskaitė (Lithuania, Ind).

Fisheries and Maritime Affairs: Joe Borg (Malta, C).

Health and Consumer Protection: Markos Kyprianou (Cyprus, S).

Information Society and Media: Viviane Reding (Luxembourg, C).

Internal Market and Services: Charlie McCreevy (Ireland, C).

Justice, Freedom and Security: Franco Frattini (Italy, C).

Regional Policy: Danuta Hübner (Poland, Ind).

Science and Research: Janez Potočnik (Slovenia, Ind).

Taxation and Customs Union: László Kovács (Hungary, S).

Trade: Peter Mandelson (UK, S).

Headquarters: 200 rue de la Loi/Wetstraat, B-1049 Brussels, Belgium.

Secretary-General: David O'Sullivan (Ireland).

COUNCIL OF THE EUROPEAN UNION (COUNCIL OF MINISTERS)

The Council of Ministers consists of ministers from the 25 national governments and is the only institution which directly represents the member states' national interests. It is the Union's principal decision-making body. Here, members legislate for the Union, set its political objectives, co-ordinate their national policies and resolve differences between themselves and other institutions. The presidency rotates every six months. Luxembourg had the presidency during the first half of 2005, the UK has the presidency during the second half of 2005, Austria will have it during the first half of 2006 and Finland during the second half of 2006. There is only one Council, but it meets in different configurations depending on the items on the agenda. The meetings are held in Brussels, except in April, June and Oct. when all meetings are in Luxembourg. Around 100 formal ministerial sessions are held each year.

Decisions are taken either by qualified majority vote or by unanimity. Since the entry into force of the Single European Act in 1987 an increasing number of decisions are by majority vote, although some areas such as taxation and social security, immigration and border controls are reserved to unanimity. At the Nice Summit in Dec. 2000 agreement was reached that a further 39 articles of the EU's treaties would move to qualified majority voting. 26 votes were then needed to veto a decision (blocking minority), and member states were allocated the following number of votes: France, Germany, Italy and the UK, 10; Spain, 8; Belgium, Greece, the Netherlands and Portugal, 5; Austria and Sweden, 4; Denmark, Finland and the Republic of Ireland, 3; Luxembourg, 2. During a six-month transitional period that followed the accession of the ten new member states on 1 May 2004 these vote weightings remained unchanged, while the new members were allocated the following number of votes: Poland, 8; Czech Republic and Hungary, 5; Estonia, Latvia, Lithuania, Slovakia and Slovenia, 3; Cyprus and Malta, 2. As from 1 Nov. 2004 the allocation of vote weightings is: France, Germany, Italy and the UK, 29; Poland and Spain, 27; the Netherlands, 13; Belgium, the Czech Republic, Greece, Hungary and Portugal, 12; Austria and Sweden, 10; Denmark, Finland, the Republic of Ireland, Lithuania and Slovakia, 7; Cyprus, Estonia, Latvia, Luxembourg and Slovenia, 4; Malta 3. A qualified majority will be reached if a majority of member states approve a proposal and a minimum of 232 votes is cast in favour of the proposal. Each member state has a national delegation in Brussels known as the Permanent Representation, headed by Permanent Representatives, senior diplomats whose committee (Coreper) prepares ministerial sessions. Coreper meets weekly and its main task is to ensure that only the most difficult and sensitive issues are dealt with at ministerial level.

The General Secretariat of the Council provides the practical infrastructure of the Council at all levels and prepares the meetings of the Council and the European Council by advising the Presidency and assisting the Coreper and the various committees and working groups of the Council.

Legislation. The Community's legislative process starts with a proposal from the Commission (either at the suggestion of its services or in pursuit of its declared political aims) to the Council, or in the case of co-decision, to both the Council and the European Parliament. The Council generally seeks the views of the European Parliament on the proposal, and the Parliament adopts a formal Opinion after consideration of the matter by its specialist Committees. The Council may also (and in some cases is obliged to) consult the Economic and Social Committee and the Committee of the Regions which similarly deliver an opinion. When these opinions have been received, the Council will decide. Most decisions are taken on a majority basis, but will take account of reservations expressed by individual member states. The text eventually approved may differ substantially from the original Commission proposal.

Provisions of the Treaties and secondary legislation may be either directly applicable in member states or only applicable after member states have enacted their own implementing legislation. Community law, adopted by the Council (or by Parliament and the Council in the framework of the co-decision procedure) may take the following forms: (1) *Regulations*, which are of general application and binding in their entirety and directly applicable in all member states; (2) *Directives*, which are binding upon each member state as to the result to be achieved within a given time, but leave to the national authorities the choice of form and method of achieving this result; and (3) *Decisions*, which are binding in their entirety on their addressees. In addition the Council and Commission can issue recommendations, opinions, resolutions and conclusions which are essentially political acts and not legally binding.

Transparency. In order to make its decision-making process more transparent to the European citizens, the Council has, together with the European Parliament and the Commission, introduced a set of rules concerning public access to the documents of the three institutions. A considerable number of Council documents can be accessed electronically via the Council's public register of documents, whereas other documents which may not be directly accessible can be released to the public upon request. With a view to ensure the widest possible access to its decision-making process, some Council debates and deliberations are open to the public. The Council systematically publishes votes and explanations of votes and minutes of its meetings when it is acting as legislator.

Headquarters: 175 rue de la Loi, B-1048 Brussels, Belgium.
Secretary-General and High Representative for the Common Foreign and Security Policy of the European Union: Javier Solana (Spain).
Website: http://www.consilium.eu.int; http://ue.eu.int
e-mail: public.info@consilium.eu.int

THE EUROPEAN COUNCIL

Since 1974 Heads of State or Government have met at least twice a year (until the end of 2002 in the capital of the member state currently exercising the presidency of the Council of European Union, since 2003 primarily in Brussels) in the form of the European Council or European Summit as it is commonly known. Its membership includes the President of the European Commission, and the President of the European Parliament is invited to make a presentation at the opening session. The European Council has become an increasingly important element of the Union, setting priorities, giving political direction, providing the impetus for its development and resolving contentious issues that prove too difficult for the Council of the European Union. It has a direct role to play in the context of the Common Foreign and Security Policy (CFSP) when deciding upon common strategies, and at a more general level, when deciding upon the establishing of closer co-operation between member states within certain policy areas covered by the EU-treaties. Moreover, during recent years, the European Council has played a preponderant role in defining the general political guidelines within key policy areas with a bearing on growth and employment and in the context of the strengthening of the EU as an area of freedom, security and justice.

EUROPEAN PARLIAMENT

The European Parliament consists of 732 members, elected in all 25 EU member states for five-year terms between 10–13 June 2004. For the five-year term from 1999–2004 there had been 626 members elected in what were then the 15 member countries, but in June 2004 voting also took place in the ten countries that had joined the EU on 1 May 2004.

All EU citizens may stand or vote in their adoptive country of residence. Germany returned 99 members (99 in 1999), France, Italy and the UK 78 each (87 each in 1999), Poland and Spain 54 each (Spain 64 in 1999), the Netherlands 27 (31 in 1999), Belgium, Czech Republic, Greece, Hungary and Portugal 24 each (Belgium, Greece and Portugal 25 each in 1999), Sweden 19 (22 in 1999), Austria 18 (21 in 1999), Denmark, Finland and Slovakia 14 each (Denmark and Finland 16 each in 1999), Ireland and Lithuania 13 each (Ireland 15 in 1999), Latvia 9, Slovenia 7, Cyprus, Estonia and Luxembourg 6 each (Luxembourg 6 in 1999), and Malta 5.

Political groupings. Following the 2004 elections to the European Parliament the European People's Party–European Democrats (EPP–ED) had 268 seats, Party of European Socialists (PES) 200, Alliance of Liberals and Democrats for Europe (ALDE) 88, Greens/European Free Alliance (Greens/EFA) 42, European Unitary Left/Nordic Green Left (EUL/NGL) 41, Independence and Democracy Group

(IND/DEM) 37, Union for a Europe of Nations (UEN) 27, Non-attached members (NI) 29.

The Parliament has a right to be consulted on a wide range of legislative proposals and forms one arm of the Community's Budgetary Authority. Under the Single European Act, it gained greater authority in legislation through the 'concertation' procedure under which it can reject certain Council drafts in a second reading procedure. Under the Maastricht Treaty, it gained the right of 'co-decision' on legislation with the Council of Ministers on a restricted range of domestic matters. The President of the European Council must report to the Parliament on progress in the development of foreign and security policy. It also plays an important role in appointing the President and members of the Commission. It can hold individual commissioners to account and can pass a motion of censure on the entire Commission, a prospect that was realized in March 1999 when the Commission, including the President, Jacques Santer, was forced to resign following an investigation into mismanagement and corruption. Parliament's seat is in Strasbourg where the one-week plenary sessions are held each month. In the Chamber, members sit in political groups, not as national delegations. All the activities of the Parliament and its bodies are the responsibility of the Bureau, consisting of the President and 14 Vice-Presidents elected for a two-and-a-half year period.

Location: Brussels, but meets at least once a month in Strasbourg.
President: Josep Borrell (Spain; PES).

COURT OF JUSTICE OF THE EUROPEAN COMMUNITIES

The Court of Justice of the European Communities is composed of 25 judges and eight advocates general. It is responsible for the adjudication of disputes arising out of the application of the treaties, and its findings are enforceable in all member countries. A Court of First Instance (est. 1989) handles certain categories of cases, including cases arising under the competition rules of the EC and cases brought by Community officials.

Address: Court of Justice of the European Communities, L-2925 Luxembourg.
President of the Court of Justice: Vassilios Skouris (Greece).
President of the Court of First Instance: Bo Vesterdorf (Denmark).

EUROPEAN COURT OF AUDITORS

The European Court of Auditors was established by a treaty of 22 July 1975 which took effect on 1 June 1977. It consists of 25 members (one from each member state) and was raised to the status of a full EU institution by the 1993 Maastricht Treaty. It audits the accounts and verifies the implementation of the budget of the EU.

Address: 12, rue Alcide De Gasperi, L-1615 Luxembourg.
Website: http://www.eca.eu.int
e-mail: euraud@eca.eu.int
President: Hubert Weber (Austria).

EUROPEAN OMBUDSMAN

The Ombudsman was inaugurated in 1995 and deals with complaints from citizens, companies and organizations concerning maladministration in the activities of the institutions and bodies of the European Union. The present incumbent is P. Nikiforos Diamandouros (Greece).

Address: 1 avenue du Président Robert Schuman, B.P. 403, F-67001 Strasbourg Cedex, France.
Website: http://www.euro-ombudsman.eu.int
e-mail: euro-ombudsman@europarl.eu.int

EUROPEAN INVESTMENT BANK (EIB)

The EIB is the financing institution of the European Union, created by the Treaty of Rome in 1958 as an autonomous body set up to finance capital investment furthering European integration. To this end, the Bank raises its resources on the world's capital markets where it mobilizes significant volumes of funds on favourable terms. It directs these funds towards capital projects promoting EU economic policies. Outside the Union the EIB implements the financial components of agreements concluded under European Union development aid and co-operation policies. The members of the EIB are the member states of the European Union, who have all subscribed to the Bank's capital. Its governing body is its Board of Governors consisting of the ministers designated by each of the member states, usually the finance ministers.

Address: 100 Bd Konrad Adenauer, L-2950 Luxembourg.
Website: http://www.eib.org
President and Chairman of the Board: Philippe Maystadt (Belgium).

EUROPEAN SYSTEM OF CENTRAL BANKS (ESCB)
The ESCB is composed of the European Central Bank (ECB) and 25 National Central Banks (NCBs). The NCBs of the member states not participating in the euro area are members with special status; while they are allowed to conduct their respective national monetary policies, they do not take part in decision-making regarding the single monetary policy for the euro area and the implementation of these policies. The Governing Council of the ECB makes a distinction between the ESCB and the 'Eurosystem' which is composed of the ECB and the 12 fully participating NCBs.

Members. The 12 fully participating National Central Banks are from: Austria, Belgium, Finland, France, Germany, Greece, Ireland, Italy, Luxembourg, Netherlands, Portugal and Spain. The other 13 EU members (those which do not use the euro as their currency) have special status.

Functions. The primary objective of the ESCB is to maintain price stability. Without prejudice to this, the ESCB supports general economic policies in the Community with a view to contributing to the achievement of the objectives of the Community. Tasks to be carried out include: i) defining and implementing the monetary policy of the Community; ii) conducting foreign exchange operations; iii) holding and managing the official foreign reserves of the participating member states; iv) promoting the smooth operation of payment systems; v) supporting the policies of the competent authorities relating to the prudential supervision of credit institutions and the stability of the financial system.

The ECB has the exclusive right to issue banknotes within the Community.

Organization. The ESCB is governed by the decision-making bodies of the ECB: the Governing Council and the Executive Board. The Governing Council is the supreme decision-making body and comprises all members of the Executive Board plus the governors of the NCBs forming the Eurosystem. The Executive Board comprises the president, vice-president and four other members, appointed by common accord of the heads of state and government of the participating member states. There is also a General Council which will exist while there remain members with special status.

Address: Kaiserstrasse 29, 60311 Frankfurt am Main, Germany.
President: Jean-Claude Trichet (France).

The Consultative Bodies There are two main consultative committees whose members are appointed in a personal capacity and are not bound by any mandatory instruction.

1. *Economic and Social Committee.* The 222-member committee is consulted by the Council of Ministers or by the European Commission, particularly with regard to agriculture, free movement of workers, harmonization of laws and transport. It is served by a permanent and independent General Secretariat, headed by a Secretary-General.

Secretary-General: Patrick Venturini (France).

2. *Committee of the Regions.* A political assembly which provides representatives of local, regional and city authorities with a voice at the heart of the European Union. Established by the Maastricht Treaty, the Committee consists of 317 full members and an equal number of alternates appointed for a four-year term. It must be consulted by the European Commission and Council of Ministers whenever legislative proposals are made in areas which have repercussions at the regional or local level. The Committee can also draw up opinions on its own initiative, which enables it to put issues on the EU agenda.

President: Peter Straub (Germany).

STATISTICAL OFFICE OF THE EUROPEAN COMMUNITIES (EUROSTAT)
Eurostat's mission is to provide the EU with a high-quality statistical service. It receives statistical data collected according to uniform rules from the national statistical institutes of member states, then consolidates and harmonizes the data, before making them available to the public as printed or electronic publications. The data are directly available from the Eurostat website.

Address: Jean Monnet Building, L-2920 Luxembourg.
Website: http://www.europa.eu.int/comm/eurostat

EU general information. The Office for Official Publications of the European Communities is the publishing house of the institutions and other bodies of the European Union. It is responsible for producing and distributing EU publications on all media and by all means.

Address: 2 rue Mercier, L-2985 Luxembourg.
Website: http://publications.eu.int

EU AGENCIES AND OTHER BODIES

COMMUNITY PLANT VARIETY OFFICE Launched in 1995 to administer a system of plant variety rights. The system allows Community Plant Variety Rights (CPVRs), valid throughout the European Union, to be granted for new plant varieties as sole and exclusive form of Community intellectual property rights.

Address: P.O Box 2141-3, Boulevard Maréchal Foch, F-49021 Angers Cédex 02, France.

EUROPEAN MEDICINES AGENCY Founded in 1995 (as European Agency for the Evaluation of Medicinal Products) to evaluate the quality and effectiveness of health products for human and veterinary use.

Address: 7 Westferry Circus, Canary Wharf, London E14 4HB, UK.

EUROPEAN AGENCY FOR RECONSTRUCTION Founded in 2000, with responsibility for the management of the main EU assistance programmes in Serbia and Montenegro and the former Yugoslav Republic of Macedonia.

Address: Egnatia 4, Thessaloniki 54626, Greece.

EUROPEAN AGENCY FOR SAFETY AND HEALTH AT WORK Founded in 1996 in order to serve the information needs of people with an interest in occupational safety and health.

Address: Gran Via 33, E-48009 Bilbao, Spain.

EUROPEAN CENTRE FOR THE DEVELOPMENT OF VOCATIONAL TRAINING Generally known as Cedefop (Centre Européen pour le Développement de la Formation Professionnelle), it was set up to help policy-makers and practitioners of the European Commission, the member states and social partner organizations across Europe make informed choices about vocational training policy.

Address: PO Box 22427, Thessaloniki 55102, Greece.

EUROPEAN ENVIRONMENT AGENCY Launched by the EU in 1993 with a mandate to orchestrate, cross-check and put to strategic use information of relevance to the protection and improvement of Europe's environment. Based in Copenhagen, it has a mandate to ensure objective, reliable and comprehensive information on the environment at European level to enable its members to take the requisite measures to protect it. The Agency carries out its tasks through the European Information and Observation Network (EIONET). Membership is open to countries outside the EU that share the Agency's concerns. Current membership includes all EU countries, Bulgaria, Iceland, Liechtenstein, Norway, Romania and Turkey.

Address: Kongens Nytorv 6, 1050 Copenhagen K, Denmark.

EUROPEAN FOUNDATION FOR THE IMPROVEMENT OF LIVING AND WORKING CONDITIONS Launched in 1975 to contribute to the planning and establishment of better living and working conditions. The Foundation's role is to provide findings, knowledge and advice from comparative research managed in a European perspective, which respond to the needs of the key parties at the EU level.

Address: Wyatville Road, Loughlinstown, Dublin 18, Ireland.

EUROPEAN INVESTMENT FUND Founded in 1994 as a subsidiary of the European Investment Bank and the European Union's specialized financial institution. It has a dual mission that combines the pursuit of objectives such as innovation, the creation of employment and regional development with maintaining a commercial approach to investments. It particularly provides venture capital and guarantee instruments for the growth of small and medium-sized enterprises (SMEs). In 2002 it began advising entities in the setting up of financial enterprise and venture capital and SME guarantee schemes. A team has been created to structure and expand its advisory services.

Address: 43 avenue J. F. Kennedy, L-2968 Luxembourg.

EUROPEAN MONITORING CENTRE FOR DRUGS AND DRUG ADDICTION Established in 1993 to provide the European Union and its member states with objective, reliable and comparable information on a European level concerning drugs and drug addiction and their consequences.

Address: Rua da Cruz de Santa Apolónia 23–25, PT-1149-045 Lisbon, Portugal.

EUROPEAN MONITORING CENTRE ON RACISM AND XENOPHOBIA Established in 1997 as an independent body to contribute towards the combat against racism, xenophobia and anti-semitism throughout Europe. It has the task of reviewing the extent and development of the racist, xenophobic and anti-semitic phenomena in the European Union and promoting 'best practice' among the member states.

Address: Rahlgasse 3, A-1060 Vienna, Austria.

EUROPEAN TRAINING FOUNDATION Launched in 1995 to contribute to the process of vocational education and training reform that is currently taking place within the EU's partner countries and territories.

Address: Villa Gualino, viale Settimio Severo 65, I-10133 Turin, Italy.

EUROPOL Founded on 3 Jan. 1994 to exchange criminal intelligence between EU countries. Its precursor was the Europol Drug Unit, which initially dealt with the fight against drugs, progressively adding other areas. Europol took up its full activities on 1 July 1999. Europol's current mandate includes the prevention and combat of illicit drug trafficking, crimes involving illegal immigration networks, illicit vehicle trafficking, trafficking in human beings including child pornography, forgery of money and means of payment, illicit trafficking in nuclear and radioactive substances, terrorism and associated money laundering activities. There are about 300 staff members from all member states. Of these, 44 are ELOs (Europol Liaison Officers) working for their national police, gendarmerie or customs services. The 2001 budget was €35·4m. Member countries subscribe in proportion to their GNP.

Address: Raamweg 47, The Hague, Netherlands.
Website: http://www.europol.eu.int
e-mail: info@europol.eu.int
Director: Max-Peter Ratzel (Germany).

OFFICE FOR HARMONIZATION IN THE INTERNAL MARKET The Office was established in 1994, and is responsible for registering Community trade marks and designs. Both Community trade marks and Community designs confer their proprietors a uniform right, which confers all member states of the EU by means of one single application and one single registration procedure.

Address: Avenida de Europa 4, Apartado de Correos 77, E-03080 Alicante, Spain.

TRANSLATION CENTRE FOR BODIES OF THE EUROPEAN UNION Established in 1994, the Translation Centre's mission is to meet the translation needs of the other decentralized Community agencies. It also participates in the Interinstitutional Committee for Translation and Interpretation.

Address: Bâtiment Nouvel Hémicycle 1, rue du Fort Thüngen, L-1499 Luxembourg Kirchberg, Luxembourg.

EUROPEAN FOOD SAFETY AGENCY Founded in 2002 to provide independent scientific advice on all matters with a direct or indirect impact on food safety.

Address: Rue de Genève 1, B-1140 Brussels, Belgium.

Further Reading

Official Journal of the European Communities.—General Report on the Activities of the European Communities (annual, from 1967).—*The Agricultural Situation in the Community* (annual).—*The Social Situation in the Community* (annual).—*Report on Competition Policy in the European Community* (annual).—*Bulletin of the European Community* (monthly).—*Register of Current Community Legal Instruments* (biannual).

Brittan, L., *The Europe We Need.* London, 1994.— *A Diet of Brussels: The Changing Face of Europe.* London, 2000

Burca, de, Gràinne and Scott, Joanne, *Constitutional Change in the EU: From Uniformity to Flexibility?* Hart, Oxford, 2000

Cowles, M. G. and Dinan, D., *Developments in the European Union 2.* Palgrave Macmillan, Basingstoke and New York, 2004

Davies, N., *Europe: A History.* London, 1997

Dinan, D., *The Encyclopaedia of the European Union.* Boulder (CO) and Basingstoke, 2000.—*Europe Recast: A History of European Union.* Boulder (CO) and Basingstoke, 2004.—*Ever Closer Union? An Introduction to the European Union.* 3rd ed. Boulder (CO) and Basingstoke, 2005

Dod's European Companion. Hurst Green, East Sussex. Occasional

Greenwood, J., *Interest Representation in the European Union.* Palgrave Macmillan, Basingstoke and New York, 2003

Judge, D. and Earnshaw, D., *The European Parliament.* Palgrave Macmillan, Basingstoke and New York, 2003

Lea, Ruth, *The Essential Guide to the European Union.* Centre for Policy Studies, London, 2004

Lewis, D. W. P., *The Road to Europe: History, Institutions and Prospects of European Integration, 1945–1993.* Berne, 1994

Mancini, Judge G. F., *Democracy and Constitutionalism in the European Union.* Hart, Oxford, 2000

Mazower, M., *Dark Continent: Europe's 20th Century.* London, 1998

McCormick, J., *Understanding the European Union.* 3rd ed. Palgrave Macmillan, Basingstoke and New York, 2005

Nugent, N., *The European Commission.* Palgrave, Basingstoke and New York, 2001.—*The Government and Politics of the European Union.* 5th ed. Basingstoke and Durham (NC), 2003.—*European Union Enlargement.* Palgrave Macmillan, Basingstoke and New York, 2004

Wallace, Helen, Wallace, William and Pollack, Mark, (eds.) *Policy-Making in the European Union.* 5th ed. OUP, 2005

COUNCIL OF EUROPE

Origin and Membership. In 1948 the Congress of Europe, bringing together at The Hague nearly 1,000 influential Europeans from 26 countries, called for the creation of a united Europe, including a European Assembly. This proposal, examined first by the Ministerial Council of the Brussels Treaty Organization, then by a conference of ambassadors, was at the origin of the Council of Europe, which is, with its 46 member States, the widest organization bringing together all European democracies. The Statute of the Council was signed at London on 5 May 1949 and came into force two months later.

The founder members were Belgium, Denmark, France, Ireland, Italy, Luxembourg, the Netherlands, Norway, Sweden and the UK. Turkey and Greece joined in 1949, Iceland in 1950, the Federal Republic of Germany in 1951 (having been an associate since 1950), Austria in 1956, Cyprus in 1961, Switzerland in 1963, Malta in 1965, Portugal in 1976, Spain in 1977, Liechtenstein in 1978, San Marino in 1988, Finland in 1989, Hungary in 1990, Czechoslovakia (after partitioning, the Czech Republic and Slovakia rejoined in 1993) and Poland in 1991, Bulgaria in 1992, Estonia, Lithuania, Romania and Slovenia in 1993, Andorra in 1994, Albania, Latvia, Macedonia, Moldova and Ukraine in 1995, Croatia and Russia in 1996,

Georgia in 1999, Armenia and Azerbaijan in 2001, Bosnia-Herzegovina in 2002, Serbia and Montenegro in 2003 and Monaco in 2004.

Membership is limited to European states which 'accept the principles of the rule of law and of the enjoyment by all persons within [their] jurisdiction of human rights and fundamental freedoms'. The Statute provides for both withdrawal (Article 7) and suspension (Articles 8 and 9). Greece withdrew during 1969–74.

Aims and Achievements. Article 1 of the Statute states that the Council's aim is 'to achieve a greater unity between its members for the purpose of safeguarding and realizing the ideals and principles which are their common heritage and facilitating their economic and social progress'; 'this aim shall be pursued ... by discussion of questions of common concern and by agreements and common action'. The only limitation is provided by Article 1 (d), which excludes 'matters relating to national defence'.

The main areas of the Council's activity are: human rights, the media, social and socio-economic questions, education, culture and sport, youth, public health, heritage and environment, local and regional government, and legal co-operation. 198 Conventions and Agreements have been concluded covering such matters as social security, cultural affairs, conservation of European wildlife and natural habitats, protection of archaeological heritage, extradition, medical treatment, equivalence of degrees and diplomas, the protection of television broadcasts, adoption of children and transportation of animals.

Treaties in the legal field include the adoption of the European Convention on the Suppression of Terrorism, the European Convention on the Legal Status of Migrant Workers and the Transfer of Sentenced Persons. The Committee of Ministers adopted a European Convention for the protection of individuals with regard to the automatic processing of personal data (1981), a Convention on the compensation of victims of violent crimes (1983), a Convention on spectator violence and misbehaviour at sport events and in particular at football matches (1985), the European Charter of Local Government (1985), and a Convention for the Prevention of Torture and Inhuman or Degrading Treatment or Punishment (1987). The European Social Charter of 1961 sets out the social and economic rights which all member governments agree to guarantee to their citizens.

European Social Charter. The Charter defines the rights and principles which are the basis of the Council's social policy, and guarantees a number of social and economic rights to the citizen, including the right to work, the right to form workers' organizations, the right to social security and assistance, the right of the family to protection and the right of migrant workers to protection and assistance. Two committees, comprising independent and government experts, supervise the parties' compliance with their obligations under the Charter. A revised charter, incorporating new rights such as protection for those without jobs and opportunities for workers with family responsibilities, was opened for signature on 3 May 1996 and entered into force on 1 July 1999.

Human rights. The promotion and development of human rights is one of the major tasks of the Council of Europe. The European Convention on Human Rights, signed in 1950, set up special machinery to guarantee internationally fundamental rights and freedoms. The European Commission of Human Rights which was set up has now been abolished and has been replaced by the new European Court of Human Rights, which came into operation on 1 Nov. 1998. The European Court of Human Rights in Strasbourg, set up under the European Convention on Human Rights as amended, is composed of a number of judges equal to that of the Contracting States (currently 46). There is no restriction on the number of judges of the same nationality. Judges are elected by the Parliamentary Assembly of the Council of Europe for a term of six years. The terms of office of one half of the judges elected at the first election expired after three years, so as to ensure that the terms of office of one half of the judges are renewed every three years. Any Contracting State (State application) or individual claiming to be a victim of a violation of the Convention (individual application) may lodge directly with the Court in Strasbourg an application alleging a breach by a Contracting State of one of the Convention rights.

President of the European Court of Human Rights: Luzius Wildhaber (Switzerland).

The Development Bank, formerly the Social Development Fund, was created in 1956. The main purpose of the Bank is to give financial aid in the spheres of housing, vocational training, regional planning and development.

The *European Youth Foundation* provides money to subsidize activities by European youth organizations in their own countries.

Structure. Under the Statute, two organs were set up: an intergovernmental *Committee of [Foreign] Ministers* with powers of decision and recommendation to governments, and an interparliamentary deliberative body, the *Parliamentary Assembly* (referred to in the Statute as the Consultative Assembly)—both served by the Secretariat. A Joint Committee acts as an organ of co-ordination and liaison between the two and gives members an opportunity to exchange views on matters of important European interest. In addition, a number of committees of experts have been established. On municipal matters the Committee of Ministers receives recommendations from the Congress of Local and Regional Authorities of Europe. The Committee usually meets twice a year and has a rotatory chair; their deputies meet once a week.

The *Parliamentary Assembly* consists of 315 parliamentarians elected or appointed by their national parliaments (Albania 4, Andorra 2, Armenia 4, Austria 6, Azerbaijan 6, Belgium 7, Bosnia-Herzegovina 5, Bulgaria 6, Croatia 5, Cyprus 3, the Czech Republic 7, Denmark 5, Estonia 3, Finland 5, France 18, Georgia 5, Germany 18, Greece 7, Hungary 7, Iceland 3, Ireland 4, Italy 18, Latvia 3, Liechtenstein 2, Lithuania 4, Luxembourg 3, Macedonia 3, Malta 3, Moldova 5, Monaco 2, Netherlands 7, Norway 5, Poland 12, Portugal 7, Romania 10, Russia 18, San Marino 2, Serbia and Montenegro 7, Slovakia 5, Slovenia 3, Spain 12, Sweden 6, Switzerland 6, Turkey 12, Ukraine 12, UK 18). It meets three times a year for approximately a week. The work of the Assembly is prepared by parliamentary committees. Since June 1989 representatives of a number of central and East European countries have been permitted to attend as non-voting members ('special guests'). Armenia and Azerbaijan have subsequently become full members.

Although without legislative powers, the Assembly acts as the powerhouse of the Council, initiating European action in key areas by making recommendations to the Committee of Ministers. As the widest parliamentary forum in Western Europe, the Assembly also acts as the conscience of the area by voicing its opinions on important current issues. These are embodied in Resolutions. The Ministers' role is to translate the Assembly's recommendations into action, particularly as regards lowering the barriers between the European countries, harmonizing their legislation or introducing, where possible, common European laws, abolishing discrimination on grounds of nationality, and undertaking certain tasks on a joint European basis.

Official languages: English and French.
Headquarters: Council of Europe, F-67075 Strasbourg Cedex, France.
Website: http://www.coe.int
e-mail: infopoint@coe.int
Secretary-General: Terry Davis (UK).

Publications. European Yearbook, The Hague; *Yearbook on the Convention on Human Rights,* Strasbourg; *Catalogue of Publications* (annual); *Activities Report* (annual). Information on other bulletins and documents is available on the Council of Europe's website.

Further Reading

Cook, C. and Paxton, J., *European Political Facts of the Twentieth Century.* Macmillan, London, 2000

WESTERN EUROPEAN UNION (WEU)

Origin. In March 1948 the signing of the Brussels Treaty of Economic, Social and Cultural Collaboration and Collective Defence by Belgium, France, Luxembourg, the Netherlands and the UK opened the way for the establishment of Western European Union. Six years later, the Paris Agreements, signed in Oct. 1954, which amended the Brussels Treaty, gave birth to WEU as a new international organization and provided for the Federal Republic of Germany and Italy to join. WEU came into being in 1955. Today, as an international defence and security organization, it brings together 28 nations encompassing four types of status: member state, associate member, observer and associate partner. Only the ten member states are signatories to the modified Brussels Treaty and have full decision making rights in WEU. The other 18 countries have been increasingly associated with WEU's activities. WEU's role and operational capabilities developed considerably after 1991. This development was based on close co-operation with the European Union and NATO. WEU acquired the necessary instruments to undertake any European-led crisis management operations and worked to develop them further as preparation for the establishment within the European Union of a crisis management capability in accordance with the decisions taken at the Cologne European Council in June 1999. Following decisions taken by the European Council since its meeting in Cologne to strengthen the European Security and Defence Policy within the EU, WEU relinquished its crisis management functions to the EU on 1 July 2001.

Member states. Belgium, France, Germany, Greece, Italy, Luxembourg, the Netherlands, Portugal, Spain and the UK. Associate members: Czech Republic, Hungary, Iceland, Norway, Poland and Turkey. Observers: Austria, Denmark, Finland, Ireland and Sweden. Associate partners: Bulgaria, Estonia, Latvia, Lithuania, Romania, Slovakia and Slovenia.

Reform. A joint meeting of the foreign and defence ministers within the WEU framework, held in Rome on 26–27 Oct. 1984, was marked by the adoption of the founding text of WEU's reactivation: the *Rome Declaration*. Work on the definition of a European security identity and the gradual harmonization of its members' defence policies were among the stated objectives. Ministers recognized the 'continuing necessity to strengthen western security, and that better utilization of WEU would not only contribute to the security of Western Europe but also to an improvement in the common defence of all the countries of the Atlantic Alliance'.

In 1987 WEU foreign and defence ministers adopted the *Hague Platform on European Security Interests*, defining the conditions and criteria for European security, and the responsibilities of WEU members to provide an integrated Europe with a security and defence dimension. In 1987 and 1988, following the laying of mines in the Persian Gulf during the Iran–Iraq war, minesweepers dispatched by WEU countries helped secure free movement in international waters. Operation Cleansweep helped to complete the clearance of a 480-km sea lane from the Strait of Hormuz, and was the first instance of a concerted action in WEU. During the Gulf Crisis, at the end of 1990 and early 1991, co-ordinated action took place among WEU nations contributing forces and other forms of support to the coalition forces involved in the liberation of Kuwait.

At the Alliance Summit of Jan. 1994 NATO leaders gave their full support to the development of a European Security and Defence Identity (ESDI) and to the strengthening of WEU. They declared their readiness to make collective assets of the Alliance available for WEU operations. The Alliance leaders also endorsed the concept of Combined Joint Task Forces (CJTFs) with the objective not only of adapting Alliance structures to NATO's new missions but also of improving co-operation with WEU, and in order to reflect the emerging ESDI. Work on the CJTF concept came to fruition at the NATO Ministerial meeting in Berlin in June 1996. One of the fundamental objectives of the Alliance adaptation process identified by NATO Ministers in Berlin was the development of the European Security and Defence Identity within the Alliance.

With the agreement on the Treaty of Amsterdam revising the Treaty on European Union, WEU has drawn closer to the EU. In particular, the European Council's guidelines for the Common Foreign Security Policy (CFSP) 'shall obtain in respect of WEU for those matters for which the Union avails itself of the WEU'; and the Petersberg tasks have been incorporated into the EU Treaty. It is stated that WEU is an integral part of the development of the European Union, giving the Union access to an operational capability, notably in the context of the Petersberg tasks. In the WEU Ministerial Declaration of 22 July 1997 responding to the Treaty of Amsterdam, WEU confirmed its readiness to develop WEU's relations with the EU and work out arrangements for enhanced co-operation.

Operations. In the context of the Yugoslav conflict, WEU has undertaken three operations, two of them to help in the enforcement of sanctions imposed by the UN

Security Council (the WEU/NATO operation SHARP GUARD in the Adriatic and the WEU Danube operation) and one to assist in the European Union administration of the town of Mostar. From 1997 to 2001 WEU deployed a Multinational Advisory Police Element (MAPE) in Albania to assist in the reorganization of the Albanian Police. A WEU Demining Assistance Mission to Croatia (WEUDAM), operating from May 1999 to Nov. 2001, provided advice, technical expertise and training support to the Croatian Mine Action Centre.

Organization. WEU comprises an intergovernmental policy-making council and an assembly of parliamentary representatives, together with a number of subsidiary bodies set up by the council to facilitate its work. Since the 1984 reforms, the Council, supreme authority of the WEU, meets twice a year at ministerial level (foreign and defence) in the capital of the presiding country. The presidency rotates biannually. The Permanent Council, chaired by the Secretary-General, meets whenever necessary at ambassadorial level, at the WEU headquarters in Brussels. The WEU Assembly, located in Paris, comprises 115 parliamentarians of member states and meets twice a year, in plenary sessions in Paris. There are Permanent Committees on: defence questions and armaments; political affairs; technological and aerospace questions; budgetary affairs and administration; rules of procedure and privileges; and parliamentary and public relations.

Headquarters: WEU, B-1000 Brussels, Belgium.
Websites: http://www.weu.int; http://www.assembly-weu.org
Secretary-General: Dr Javier Solana Madariaga (Spain).

ORGANIZATION FOR SECURITY AND CO-OPERATION IN EUROPE (OSCE)

The OSCE is a pan-European security organization of 55 participating states. It has been recognized under the UN Charter as a primary instrument in its region for early warning, conflict prevention, crisis management and post-conflict rehabilitation.

Origin. Initiatives from both NATO and the Warsaw Pact culminated in the first summit Conference on Security and Co-operation in Europe (CSCE) attended by heads of state and government in Helsinki on 30 July–1 Aug. 1975. It adopted the *Helsinki Final Act* laying down ten principles governing the behaviour of States towards their citizens and each other, concerning human rights, self-determination and the interrelations of the participant states. The CSCE was to serve as a multilateral forum for dialogue and negotiations between East and West.

The Helsinki Final Act comprised three main sections: 1) politico-military aspects of security: principles guiding relations between and among participating States and military confidence-building measures; 2) co-operation in the fields of economics, science and technology and the environment; 3) co-operation in humanitarian and other fields.

From CSCE to OSCE. The Paris Summit of Nov. 1990 set the CSCE on a new course. In the Charter of Paris for a New Europe, the CSCE was called upon to contribute to managing the historic change in Europe and respond to the new challenges of the post-Cold War period. At the meeting, members of NATO and the Warsaw Pact signed an important Treaty on Conventional Armed Forces in Europe (CFE) and a declaration that they were 'no longer adversaries' and did not intend to 'use force against the territorial integrity or political independence of any state'. All 34 participants adopted the Vienna Document comprising Confidence and Security-Building Measures (CSBMs), which pertain to the exchange of military information, verification of military installations, objection to unusual military activities etc., and signed the Charter of Paris. The Charter sets out principles of human rights, democracy and the rule of law to which all the signatories undertake to adhere, and lays down the basis for East-West co-operation and other future action. The 1994 Budapest Summit recognized that the CSCE was no longer a conference and on 1 Jan. 1995 the CSCE changed its name to the Organization for Security and Co-operation in Europe (OSCE). The 1996 Lisbon Summit elaborated the OSCE's key role in fostering security and stability in all their dimensions. It also stimulated the development of an OSCE Document-Charter on European Security.

Members. Albania, Andorra, Armenia, Austria, Azerbaijan, Belarus, Belgium, Bosnia-Herzegovina, Bulgaria, Canada, Croatia, Cyprus, the Czech Republic, Denmark, Estonia, Finland, France, Georgia, Germany, Greece, Holy See, Hungary, Iceland, Ireland, Italy, Kazakhstan, Kyrgyzstan, Latvia, Liechtenstein, Lithuania, Luxembourg, Macedonia, Malta, Moldova, Monaco, Netherlands, Norway, Poland, Portugal, Romania, Russian Federation, San Marino, Serbia and Montenegro, Slovak Republic, Slovenia, Spain, Sweden, Switzerland, Tajikistan, Turkey, Turkmenistan, Ukraine, UK, USA and Uzbekistan. *Partners for co-operation:* Afghanistan, Japan, Mongolia, South Korea and Thailand. *Mediterranean partners for co-operation:* Algeria, Egypt, Israel, Jordan, Morocco, Tunisia.

Organization. The OSCE's regular body for political consultation and decision-making is the Permanent Council. Its members, the Permanent Representatives of the OSCE participating States, meet weekly in the Hofburg Congress Center in Vienna to discuss and take decisions on all issues pertinent to the OSCE. The Forum for Security Co-operation (FSC), which deals with arms control and confidence- and security-building measures, also meets weekly in Vienna. Summits—periodic meetings of Heads of State or Government of OSCE participating States—set priorities and provide orientation at the highest political level. In the years between these summits, decision-making and governing power lies with the *Ministerial Council*, which is made up of the Foreign Ministers of the OSCE participating States. In addition, a Senior Council also meets once a year in special session as the Economic Forum. The Chairman-in-Office has overall responsibility for executive action and agenda-setting. The Chair rotates annually. The Secretary-General acts as representative of the Chairman-in-Office and manages OSCE structures and operations.

The Secretariat is based in Vienna and includes a *Conflict Prevention Centre* which provides operational support for OSCE field missions. There are some 400 staff employed in OSCE institutions, and about 1,000 professionals, seconded by OSCE-participating states, work at OSCE missions and other field operations, together with another 2,500 local staff.

The *Office for Democratic Institutions and Human Rights* is located in Warsaw. It is active in monitoring elections and developing national electoral and human rights institutions, providing technical assistance to national legal institutions, and promoting the development of the rule of law and civil society.

The *Office of the Representative on Freedom of the Media* is located in Vienna. Its main function is to observe relevant media developments in OSCE participating States with a view to providing an early warning on violations of freedom of expression.

The *Office of the High Commissioner on National Minorities* is located in The Hague. Its function is to identify and seek early resolution of ethnic tensions that might endanger peace, stability or friendly relations between the participating States of the OSCE.

The budget for 2004 was €181m.

Headquarters: Kärntner Ring 5–7, A-1010 Vienna, Austria.
Website: http://www.osce.org
Chairman-in-Office: Dimitrij Rupel (Slovenia).
Secretary-General: Ján Kubiš (Slovakia).

Further Reading

Freeman, J., *Security and the CSCE Process: the Stockholm Conference and Beyond.* London, 1991

EUROPEAN BANK FOR RECONSTRUCTION AND DEVELOPMENT (EBRD)

History. The European Bank for Reconstruction and Development was established in 1991 when communism was collapsing in central and eastern Europe and ex-Soviet countries needed support to nurture a new private sector in a democratic environment.

Activities. The EBRD is the largest single investor in the region and mobilizes significant foreign direct investment beyond its own financing. It is owned by 60 countries and two intergovernmental institutions. But despite its public sector shareholders, it invests mainly in private enterprises, usually together with commercial partners. Today the EBRD uses the tools of investment to help build market economies and democracies in 27 countries from Central Europe to Central Asia.

It provides project financing for banks, industries and businesses, for both new ventures and investments in existing companies. It also works with publicly-owned companies, to support privatization, restructuring of state-owned firms and improvement of municipal services. The EBRD uses its close relationship with governments in the region to promote policies that will bolster the business environment.

The mandate of the EBRD stipulates that it must only work in countries that are committed to democratic principles. Respect for the environment is part of the strong corporate governance attached to all EBRD investments.

Organization. All the powers of the EBRD are vested in a Board of Governors, to which each member appoints a governor, generally the minister of finance or an equivalent. The Board of Governors delegates powers to the Board of Directors, which is responsible for the direction of the EBRD's general operations and policies. The President is elected by the Board of Governors and is the legal representative of the EBRD. The President conducts the current business of the Bank under the guidance of the Board of Directors.

Headquarters: 1 Exchange Square, London EC2A 2JN, UK.
Website: http://www.ebrd.com
President: Jean Lemierre (France).
Secretary-General (acting): Nigel Carter (UK).

EUROPEAN FREE TRADE ASSOCIATION (EFTA)

History and Membership. The Stockholm Convention establishing the Association entered into force on 3 May 1960. Founder members were Austria, Denmark, Norway, Portugal, Sweden, Switzerland and the UK. With the accession of Austria, Denmark, Finland, Portugal, Sweden and the UK to the EU, EFTA was reduced to four member countries: Iceland, Liechtenstein, Norway and Switzerland. In June 2001 the Vaduz Convention was signed. It liberalizes trade further among the four EFTA States in order to reflect the Swiss–EU bilateral agreements.

Activities. Free trade in industrial goods among EFTA members was achieved by 1966. Co-operation with the EU began in 1972 with the signing of free trade agreements and culminated in the establishment of a *European Economic Area (EEA)*, encompassing the free movement of goods, services, capital and labour throughout EFTA and the EU member countries. The Agreement was signed by all members of the EU and EFTA on 2 May 1992, but was rejected by Switzerland in a referendum on 6 Dec. 1992. The agreement came into force on 1 Jan. 1994.

The main provisions of the EEA Agreement are: free movement of products within the EEA from 1993 (with special arrangements to cover food, energy, coal and steel); EFTA to assume EU rules on company law, consumer protection, education, the environment, research and development, and social policy; EFTA to adopt EU competition rules on anti-trust matters, abuse of a dominant position, public procurement, mergers and state aid; EFTA to create an EFTA Surveillance Authority and an EFTA Court; individuals to be free to live, work and offer services throughout the EEA, with mutual recognition of professional qualifications; capital movements to be free with some restrictions on investments; EFTA countries not to be bound by the Common Agricultural Policy (CAP) or Common Fisheries Policy (CFP).

The EEA-EFTA states have established a Surveillance Authority and a Court to ensure implementation of the Agreement among the EFTA-EEA states. Political direction is given by the EEA Council which meets twice a year at ministerial level, while ongoing operation of the Agreement is overseen by the EEA Joint Committee. Legislative power remains with national governments and parliaments.

EFTA has formal relations with several other states. Declarations on co-operation were signed with Hungary, former Czechoslovakia and Poland (1990), Bulgaria, Estonia, Latvia, Lithuania and Romania (1991), Slovenia and Albania (1992), Egypt, Morocco and Tunisia (1995), the former Yugoslav Republic of Macedonia and the Palestine Liberation Organization (1996), Jordan and Lebanon (1997), Croatia, the Gulf Co-operation Council, Serbia and Montenegro and Mercosur (2000) and Algeria (2002). Free trade agreements have been signed with Turkey (1991), Israel and Czechoslovakia (1992, with protocols on succession with the Czech Republic and Slovakia in 1993), Poland and Romania (1992), Bulgaria and Hungary (1993), Estonia, Latvia, Lithuania and Slovenia (1995), Morocco (1997), the Former Yugoslav Republic of Macedonia and Mexico (2000), Jordan and Croatia (2001), Singapore (2002), Chile (2003) and Lebanon and Tunisia (2004). In Dec. 1998 an interim free trade agreement was signed with the Palestinian Authority and talks on an agreement began with Egypt. Negotiations on free trade agreements are ongoing with Canada, Egypt and Cyprus.

Organization. The operation of the free trade area among the EFTA states is the responsibility of the EFTA Council which meets regularly at ambassadorial level in Geneva. The Council is assisted by a Secretariat and standing committees. Each EFTA country holds the chairmanship of the Council for six months. For EEA matters there is a separate committee structure.

Brussels Office (EEA matters, press and information): 74 rue de Trèves, B-1040 Brussels.

Headquarters: 9–11 rue de Varembé, 1211 Geneva 20, Switzerland.
Website: http://www.efta.int
e-mail: efta-mailbox@secrbru.efta.be
Secretary-General: William Rossier (Switzerland).

Publications. Convention Establishing the European Free Trade Association; EFTA Annual Report; EFTA Fact Sheets: Information Papers on Aspects of the EEA; EFTA Bulletin.

EUROPEAN SPACE AGENCY (ESA)

History. Established in 1975, replacing the European Space Research Organization (ESRO) and the European Launcher Development Organization (ELDO).

Members. Austria, Belgium, Denmark, Finland, France, Germany, Ireland, Italy, the Netherlands, Norway, Portugal, Spain, Sweden, Switzerland, United Kingdom. Canada takes part in some projects under a co-operation agreement. Greece and Luxembourg will become members during 2005.

Activities. ESA is the intergovernmental agency in Europe responsible for the exploitation of space science, research and technology for exclusively peaceful purposes. Its aim is to define and put into effect a long-term European space policy that allows Europe to remain competitive in the field of space technology. It has a policy of co-operation with various partners on the basis that pooling resources and sharing work will boost the effectiveness of its programmes. Its space plan covers the fields of science, Earth observation, telecommunications, navigation, space segment technologies, ground infrastructures, space transport systems and microgravity research.

Headquarters: 8–10 rue Mario Nikis, 75738 Paris Cedex 15, France.
Website: http://www.esa.int
Director-General: Jean-Jacques Dordain (France).

CERN – THE EUROPEAN ORGANISATION FOR NUCLEAR RESEARCH

Founded in 1954, CERN is the world's leading particle physics research centre. By studying the behaviour of nature's fundamental particles, CERN aims to find out what our Universe is made of and how it works. CERN's biggest accelerator, the Large Electron Positron Collider (LEP), recreates conditions at the birth of the Universe. A yet more powerful accelerator, the Large Hadron Collider (LHC), is scheduled for completion during 2005. One of the beneficial byproducts of CERN activity is the Worldwide Web, developed at CERN to give particle physicists easy access to shared data. One of Europe's first joint ventures, CERN now has a membership of 20 member states: Austria, Belgium, Bulgaria, Czech Republic, Denmark, Finland, France, Germany, Greece, Hungary, Italy, the Netherlands, Norway, Poland, Portugal, Slovak Republic, Spain, Sweden, Switzerland, United Kingdom. Some 6,500 scientists, half of the world's particle physicists, use CERN's facilities.

Address: CH-1211 Geneva 23, Switzerland.
Website: http://www.cern.ch
Director-General: Dr Robert Aymar (France).

CENTRAL EUROPEAN INITIATIVE (CEI)

In Nov. 1989 Austria, Hungary, Italy and Yugoslavia met on Italy's initiative to form an economic and political co-operation group in the region.

Members. Albania, Austria, Belarus, Bosnia-Herzegovina, Bulgaria, Croatia, Czech Republic, Hungary, Italy, Macedonia, Moldova, Poland, Romania, Serbia and Montenegro, Slovakia, Slovenia, Ukraine.

Address: Executive Secretariat, Via Genova 9, 34132 Trieste, Italy.
Website: http://www.ceinet.org
e-mail: cei-es@cei-es.org

NORDIC COUNCIL

Founded in 1952 as a co-operative link between the parliaments and governments of the Nordic states. The co-operation focuses on Intra-Nordic co-operation, co-operation with Europe/EU/EEA and co-operation with the adjacent areas. The Council consists of 87 elected MPs and the committees meet several times a year, as required. Every year the Nordic Council grants prizes for literature, music, nature and environment.

Members. Denmark (including the Faroe Islands and Greenland), Finland (including Åland), Iceland, Norway, Sweden.

Address: Store Strandstræde 18, DK-1255 Copenhagen K, Denmark.
Website: http://www.norden.org/
e-mail: nordisk-rad@norden.org
President: Rannveig Guðmundsdóttir (Iceland).

NORDIC DEVELOPMENT FUND (NDF)

Established in 1989, the NDF is a development aid organization of the five Nordic countries, Denmark, Finland, Iceland, Norway and Sweden. NDF capital totals SDR 515m. and €330m. Credits are offered to developing countries, with poorer African, Asian and Latin American countries taking priority.

Address: Fabianinkatu 34, PO Box 185, FIN-00171 Helsinki, Finland.
Website: http://www.ndf.fi
e-mail: info.ndf@ndf.fi
President: Jens Lund Sørensen (Denmark).

NORDIC INVESTMENT BANK (NIB)

The Nordic Investment Bank, which commenced operations in Aug. 1976, is a multilateral financial institution owned by Denmark, Estonia, Finland, Iceland, Latvia, Lithuania, Norway and Sweden. It finances public and private projects both within and outside the Nordic area. Priority is given to projects furthering economic co-operation between the member countries or improving the environment. Focal points include the neighbouring areas of the member countries.

Address: Fabianinkatu 34, PO Box 249, FI-00171 Helsinki, Finland.
Website: http://www.nib.int
e-mail: info@nib.int
President: Johnny Åkerholm (Finland).

COUNCIL OF THE BALTIC SEA STATES

Established in 1992 in Copenhagen following a conference of ministers of foreign affairs.

Members. Denmark, Estonia, Finland, Germany, Iceland, Latvia, Lithuania, Norway, Poland, Russia, Sweden and the European Commission.

Aims. To promote co-operation in the Baltic Sea region in the field of trade, investment and economic exchanges, combating organized crime, civil security, culture and education, transport and communication, energy and environment, human rights and assistance to democratic institutions.

The Council meets at ministerial level once a year, chaired by rotating foreign ministers; it is the supreme decision-making body. Between annual sessions the Committee of Senior Officials and three working groups meet at regular intervals. In Oct. 1999 ministers of energy of the CBSS member states agreed to achieve the goal of creating effective, economically and environmentally sound and more integrated energy systems in the Baltic Sea region. Five summits at the level of heads of government of CBSS member states and the President of the European Commission have taken place; in 1996, 1998, 2000, 2002 and 2004. The Baltic Sea Region Energy Cooperation (BASREC) is made up of energy ministers from the region and is chaired by the energy minister from the chair country of the CBSS.

Official language: English.
CBSS Secretariat: Strömsborg, PO Box 2010, S-103 11 Stockholm, Sweden.
Website: http://www.cbss.st
Director of the Secretariat: Hannu Halinen (Finland).

EUROPEAN BROADCASTING UNION (EBU)

Founded in 1950 by western European radio and television broadcasters the EBU is the world's largest professional association of national broadcasters, with 72 active members in 52 countries of Europe, North Africa and the Middle East, and 50 associate members in 30 countries elsewhere in Africa, the Americas and Asia.

The EBU merged with the OIRT, its counterpart in eastern Europe, in 1993. The EBU's Eurovision Operations Department has a permanent network offering 50 digital channels on five satellites. Two satellite channels also relay radio concerts, operas, sports fixtures and major news events for Euroradio.

Headquarters: Ancienne Route 17, CH-1218 Grand-Saconnex, Geneva, Switzerland.
Websites: www.ebu.ch; www.eurovision.net
e-mail: ebu@ebu.ch

BLACK SEA ECONOMIC CO-OPERATION GROUP (BSEC)

Founded in 1992 to promote economic co-operation in the Black Sea region. Priority areas of interest include: trade and economic development; banking and finance; communications; energy; transport; agriculture and agro-industry; healthcare and pharmaceutics; environmental protection; tourism; science and technology; exchange of statistical data and economic information; combating organized crime, illicit trafficking of drugs, weapons and radioactive materials, all acts of terrorism and illegal immigration.

Members. Albania, Armenia, Azerbaijan, Bulgaria, Georgia, Greece, Moldova, Romania, Russia, Turkey, Ukraine.

Observers. Austria, Egypt, France, Germany, Israel, Italy, Poland, Slovakia, Tunisia.

The *Parliamentary Assembly of the Black Sea Economic Co-operation* is the BSEC parliamentary dimension. The *BSEC Business Council* is composed of representatives from the business circles of the member states. The *Black Sea Trade and Development Bank* is considered as the financial pillar of the BSEC. There is also an *International Center for Black Sea Studies* and a *Coordination Center for the Exchange of Statistical Data and Economic Information.*

Headquarters: İstinye Cad., Müşir Fuad Paşa Yalısı, Eski Tersane 80860, İstinye, İstanbul, Turkey.
Website: http://www.bsec.gov.tr
Secretary-General: Tedo Japaridze (Georgia).

DANUBE COMMISSION

History and Membership. The Danube Commission was constituted in 1949 according to the Convention regarding the regime of navigation on the Danube signed in Belgrade on 18 Aug. 1948. The Belgrade Convention, amended by the Additional Protocol of 26 March 1998, declares that navigation on the Danube from Kelheim to the Black Sea (with access to the sea through the Sulina arm and the Sulina Canal) is equally free and open to the nationals, merchant shipping and merchandise of all states as to harbour and navigation fees as well as conditions of merchant navigation. The Commission holds annual sessions and is composed of one representative from each of its 11 member countries: Austria, Bulgaria, Croatia, Germany, Hungary, Moldova, Romania, Russia, Serbia and Montenegro, Slovakia and Ukraine.

Functions. To ensure that the provisions of the Belgrade Convention are carried out; to establish a uniform buoying system on all navigable waterways; to establish the basic regulations for navigation on the river and ensure facilities for shipping; to co-ordinate the regulations for river, customs and sanitation control as well as the hydrometeorological service; to collect relevant statistical data concerning navigation on the Danube; to propose measures for the prevention of pollution of the Danube caused by navigation; and to update its recommendations regularly with a view to bringing them in line with European Union regulations on inland waterway navigation.

Official languages: German, French, Russian.
Headquarters: Benczúr utca 25, H-1068 Budapest, Hungary.
Website: http://www.danubecom-intern.org
e-mail: secretariat@danubecom-intern.org
President: Dr Stanko Nick (Croatia).
Director-General: Capt. Danail Nedialkov (Bulgaria).

EUROPEAN TRADE UNION CONFEDERATION (ETUC)

Established in 1973, the ETUC is recognized by the EU, the Council of Europe and EFTA as the only representative cross-sectoral trade union organization at a European level. It has grown steadily with a membership of 76 National Trade Union Confederations from 35 countries and 11 European Industry Federations with a total of 60m. members. The Congress meets every four years; the 10th Statutory Congress took place in Prague in May 2003.

Address: 5 Boulevard Roi Albert II, B-1210 Brussels, Belgium.
Website: http://www.etuc.org
e-mail: etuc@etuc.org
General Secretary: John Monks (UK).

AMNESTY INTERNATIONAL (AI)

Origin. Founded in 1961 by British lawyer Peter Benenson as a one-year campaign for the release of prisoners of conscience, Amnesty International has grown to become a worldwide organization, winning the Nobel Peace Prize in 1977.

Activities. AI is a worldwide movement of people who campaign for human rights. It works independently and impartially to promote respect for all the human rights set out in the Universal Declaration of Human Rights.

Historically, the main focus of AI's campaigning has been: to free all prisoners of conscience; to ensure a prompt and fair trial for all political prisoners; to abolish the death penalty, torture and other cruel, inhuman or degrading treatment or punishment; to end extrajudicial executions and 'disappearances'; to fight impunity by working to ensure perpetrators of such abuses are brought to justice in accordance with international standards.

AI has over 1·5m. members, subscribers and regular donors in more than 150 countries. The organization is a democratic, self-governing movement. Major policy decisions are taken by an International Council made up of representatives from all national sections. AI's national sections and local volunteer groups are primarily responsible for funding the movement. During the financial year 1 April 2002–31 March 2003 the international budget adopted by AI was £23,728,000 (including contingency).

Every year AI produces a global report detailing human rights violations in all regions of the world.

International Secretariat: Peter Benenson House, 1 Easton Street, London WC1X 0DW, UK.
Website: http://www.amnesty.org
Secretary-General: Irene Khan (Bangladesh).

BANK FOR INTERNATIONAL SETTLEMENTS (BIS)

Origin. Founded on 17 May 1930, the Bank for International Settlements fosters international monetary and financial co-operation and serves as a bank for central banks.

Aims. The BIS fulfils its mandate by acting as: a forum to promote discussion and facilitate decision-making processes among central banks and within the international financial community; a centre for economic and monetary research; a prime counterparty for central banks in their financial transactions; and an agent or trustee in connection with international financial operations.

Finance. Around 140 central banks and international financial institutions place deposits with the BIS. The total of currency deposits placed with the BIS amounted to SDR200bn. at the end of March 2004, representing 6·5% of world foreign exchange reserves.

Organization and Membership. There are 55 member central banks. These are the central banks or monetary authorities of Algeria, Argentina, Australia, Austria, Belgium, Bosnia-Herzegovina, Brazil, Bulgaria, Canada, Chile, China, Croatia, the Czech Republic, Denmark, Estonia, Finland, France, Germany, Greece, Hong Kong, Hungary, Iceland, India, Indonesia, Ireland, Israel, Italy, Japan, South Korea, Latvia, Lithuania, Macedonia, Malaysia, Mexico, the Netherlands, New Zealand, Norway, Philippines, Poland, Portugal, Romania, Russia, Saudi Arabia, Singapore, Slovakia, Slovenia, South Africa, Spain, Sweden, Switzerland, Thailand, Turkey, UK and USA, as well as the European Central Bank.

The BIS is administered by a Board of Directors, which is comprised of the governors of the central banks of Belgium, France, Germany, Italy and the UK and the Chairman of the Board of Governors of the US Federal Reserve System as *ex officio* members, each of whom appoints another member of the same nationality. The Statutes also provide for the election to the Board of not more than nine Governors of other member central banks. The Governors of the central banks of Canada, Japan, the Netherlands, Sweden and Switzerland are currently elected members of the Board.

Headquarters: Centralbahnplatz 2 and Aeschenplatz 1, CH-Basle, Switzerland.
Website: http://www.bis.org
e-mail: email@bis.org
Chairman: Nout Wellink (Netherlands).
Representative Office for Asia and the Pacific: 78th Floor, Two International Finance Centre, 8 Finance Street, Central, Hong Kong SAR, People's Republic of China.
Representative Office for the Americas: Torre Chapultepec, Rubén Dario 281, Col. Bosque de Chapultepec, 11580 México, D. F., Mexico.

Further Reading

Deane, M. and Pringle, R., *The Central Banks.* London and New York, 1995
Fleming's Who's Who in Central Banking. London, 1997
Goodhart, C. A. E., *The Central Bank and the Financial System.* London, 1995

COMMONWEALTH

The Commonwealth is a free association of sovereign independent states. It numbered 53 members in 2004. With a membership of 1·7bn. people, it represents over 30% of the world's population. There is no charter, treaty or constitution; the association is expressed in co-operation, consultation and mutual assistance for which the Commonwealth Secretariat is the central co-ordinating body.

Origin. The Commonwealth was first defined by the Imperial Conference of 1926 as a group of 'autonomous Communities within the British Empire, equal in status, in no way subordinate one to another in any aspect of their domestic or external affairs, though united by a common allegiance to the Crown, and freely associated as members of the British Commonwealth of Nations'. The basis of the association changed from one owing allegiance to a common Crown, and the modern Commonwealth was born in 1949 when the member countries accepted India's intention of becoming a republic at the same time as continuing 'her full membership of the Commonwealth of Nations and her acceptance of the King as the symbol of the free association of its independent member nations and as such the Head of the Commonwealth'. In 2004 the Commonwealth consisted of 32 republics and 21 monarchies, of which 16 are Queen's realms. All acknowledge the Queen symbolically as Head of the Commonwealth. The Queen's legal title rests on the statute of 12 and 13 Will. III, c. 3, by which the succession to the Crown of Great Britain and Ireland was settled on the Princess Sophia of Hanover and the 'heirs of her body being Protestants'.

A number of territories, formerly under British jurisdiction or mandate, did not join the Commonwealth: Egypt, Iraq, Transjordan, Burma (now Myanmar), Palestine, Sudan, British Somaliland and Aden. Five countries, Ireland in 1948, South Africa in 1961, Pakistan in 1972, Fiji (now Fiji Islands) in 1987 and Zimbabwe in 2003 have left the Commonwealth. Pakistan was re-admitted to the Commonwealth in 1989, South Africa in 1994, Fiji Islands in 1997. Nigeria was suspended in 1995 for violation of human rights but was fully reinstated on 29 May 1999. Pakistan was suspended from the Commonwealth's councils following a coup in Oct. 1999 but was readmitted in May 2004. Fiji Islands was also suspended from the Commonwealth's councils in May 2000 following a coup there but was re-admitted in Dec. 2001 following the restoration of democracy. Zimbabwe was suspended from the Commonwealth's councils for a year on 19 March 2002 for a 'high level of politically motivated violence' during the vote that saw President Robert Mugabe re-elected. In March 2003 it was suspended for a further nine months. The suspension was extended at the Abuja meeting in Dec. 2003. Mugabe responded by withdrawing Zimbabwe from the Commonwealth. Mozambique, admitted in Nov. 1995, is the first member state not to have been a member of the former British Commonwealth or Empire. Tuvalu is a special member, with the right to participate in all functional Commonwealth meetings and activities but not to attend meetings of Commonwealth Heads of Government.

MEMBER STATES OF THE COMMONWEALTH

The 53 member states, with year of admission:

	Year of admission		*Year of admission*
Antigua and Barbuda	1981	Kenya	1963
Australia[1]	1931	Kiribati	1979
Bahamas	1973	Lesotho	1966
Bangladesh	1972	Malaŵi	1964
Barbados	1966	Malaysia	1957
Belize	1981	Maldives	1982
Botswana	1966	Malta	1964
Brunei[2]	1984	Mauritius	1968
Cameroon	1995	Mozambique	1995
Canada[1]	1931	Namibia	1990
Cyprus	1961	Nauru[3]	1968
Dominica	1978	New Zealand[1]	1931
Fiji Islands[4]	1997	Nigeria[5]	1960
Gambia	1965	Pakistan[6]	1989
Ghana	1957	Papua New Guinea	1975
Grenada	1974	St Kitts and Nevis	1983
Guyana	1966	St Lucia	1979
India	1947	St Vincent and Grenadines	1979
Jamaica	1962	Samoa	1970

	Year of admission		*Year of admission*
Seychelles	1976	Tonga[2]	1970
Sierra Leone	1961	Trinidad and Tobago	1962
Singapore	1965	Tuvalu	1978
Solomon Islands	1978	Uganda	1982
South Africa[7]	1994	United Kingdom	1931
Sri Lanka	1948	Vanuatu	1980
Swaziland	1968	Zambia	1964
Tanzania	1961		

[1]Independence given legal effect by the Statute of Westminster 1931.
[2]Brunei and Tonga had been sovereign states in treaty relationship with Britain.
[3]Nauru was first a Mandate, then a Trust territory. It became a full member in 1999.
[4]Fiji left 1987; but rejoined in 1997. It changed its name to Fiji Islands in 1998.
[5]Nigeria was suspended in 1995 but re-admitted as a full member in 1999.
[6]Left 1972, rejoined 1989. [7]Left 1961, rejoined 1994.

Aims and Conditions of Membership. Membership involves acceptance of certain core principles, as set out in the Harare Declaration of 1991, and is subject to the approval of other member states. The Harare Declaration charts a course to take the Commonwealth into the 21st century and affirms members' continued commitment to the Singapore Declarations of 1971, by which members committed themselves to the pursuit of world peace and support of the UN.

The core principles defined by the Harare Declaration are: political democracy, human rights, good governance and the rule of law, and the protection of the environment through sustainable development. Commitment to these principles was made binding as a condition of membership at the 1993 Heads of Government meeting in Cyprus.

The Millbrook Action Programme of 1995 aims to support countries in implementing the Harare Declaration, providing assistance in constitutional and judicial matters, running elections, training and technical advice. Violations of the Harare Declaration will provoke a series of measures by the Commonwealth Secretariat, including: expression of disapproval, encouragement of bilateral actions by member states, appointment of fact-finders and mediators, stipulation of a period for the restoration of democracy, exclusion from ministerial meetings, suspension of all participation and aid and finally punitive measures including trade sanctions. An eight-member *Commonwealth Ministerial Action Group on the Harare Declaration* (*CMAG*) may be convened by the Secretary-General as and when necessary to deal with violations. The Group held its first meeting in Dec. 1995. Its terms of reference are as set out in the Millbrook Action Programme.

The *Commonwealth Parliamentary Association* was founded in 1911. As defined by its constitution, its objectives are to 'promote knowledge of the constitutional, legislative, economic, social and cultural aspects of parliamentary democracy'. It meets these objectives by organizing conferences, meetings and seminars for members, arranging exchange visits between members, publishing books, newsletters, reports, studies and a quarterly journal and providing an information service. Its principal governing body is the General Assembly, which meets annually during the Commonwealth Parliamentary Conference and is composed of members attending that Conference as delegates. The Association elects an Executive Committee comprising a Chair, President, Vice-President, Treasurer and 27 regional representatives, which meets twice a year. The Chair is elected for three-year terms.

Commonwealth Secretariat. The Commonwealth Secretariat is an international body at the service of all 53 member countries. It provides the central organization for joint consultation and co-operation in many fields. It was established in 1965 by Commonwealth Heads of Government as a 'visible symbol of the spirit of co-operation which animates the Commonwealth', and has observer status at the UN General Assembly.

The Secretariat disseminates information on matters of common concern, organizes and services meetings and conferences, co-ordinates many Commonwealth activities, and provides expert technical assistance for economic and social development through the multilateral Commonwealth Fund for Technical Co-operation. The Secretariat is organized in divisions and sections which correspond to its main areas of operation: international affairs, economic affairs, food production and rural development, youth, education, information, applied studies in government, science and technology, law and health. Within this structure the Secretariat organizes the biennial meetings of Commonwealth Heads of Government (CHOGMs), annual meetings of Finance Ministers of member countries, and regular meetings of Ministers of Education, Law, Health, and others as appropriate. To emphasize the multilateral nature of the association, meetings are held in different cities and regions within the Commonwealth. Heads of Government decided that the Secretariat should work from London as it has the widest range of communications of any Commonwealth city, as well as the largest assembly of diplomatic missions.

Commonwealth Heads of Government Meetings (CHOGMs). Outside the UN, the CHOGM remains the largest intergovernmental conference in the world. Meetings are held every two years. The 2002 CHOGM in Coolum, Australia, scheduled for Oct. 2001 but postponed following the attacks on the United States of 11 Sept. 2001, was dominated by the Zimbabwe issue, as was the meeting held in Abuja, Nigeria in Dec. 2003. The next meeting will be held in Nov. 2005 in Malta. A host of Commonwealth organizations and agencies are dedicated to enhancing interCommonwealth relations and the development of the potential of Commonwealth citizens. A list of these can be obtained from the *Commonwealth Institute* in London.

Commonwealth Day is celebrated on the second Monday in March each year. The theme for 2005 was 'Education—Creating Opportunity, Realising Potential'.

Overseas Territories and Associated States. There are 14 United Kingdom overseas territories (see pages 1735–61), six Australian external territories (see pages 225–9), two New Zealand dependent territories and two New Zealand associated states (see pages 1230–5). A dependent territory is a territory belonging by settlement, conquest or annexation to the British, Australian or New Zealand Crown.

United Kingdom Overseas Territories administered through the Foreign and Commonwealth Office comprise, in the Indian Ocean: British Indian Ocean Territory; in the Mediterranean: Gibraltar, the Sovereign Base Areas of Akrotiri and Dhekelia in Cyprus; in the Atlantic Ocean: Bermuda, Falkland Islands, South Georgia and South Sandwich Islands, British Antarctic Territory, St Helena and Dependencies (Ascension and Tristan da Cunha); in the Caribbean: Montserrat, British Virgin Islands, Cayman Islands, Turks and Caicos Islands, Anguilla; in the Western Pacific: Pitcairn Group of Islands.

The Australian external territories are: Ashmore and Cartier Islands, Australian Antarctic Territory, Christmas Island, Cocos (Keeling) Islands, Coral Sea Islands, Heard and McDonald Islands and Norfolk Island. The New Zealand external territories are: Tokelau Islands and the Ross Dependency. The New Zealand associated states are: Cook Islands and Niue.

Headquarters: Marlborough House, Pall Mall, London SW1Y 5HX, UK.
Websites: http://www.thecommonwealth.org; www.youngcommonwealth.org
Secretary-General: Don McKinnon (New Zealand).

Selected publications. Commonwealth Yearbook; Commonwealth Currents (quarterly); *The Commonwealth at the Summit: Communiqués of Commonwealth Heads of Government Meetings.*

Further Reading

The Cambridge History of the British Empire. 8 vols. CUP, 1929 ff.
Austin, D., *The Commonwealth and Britain.* London, 1988
Ball, M., *The 'Open' Commonwealth.* Duke University Press, Durham (North Carolina), 1971
Chan, S., *Twelve Years of Commonwealth Diplomatic History: Summit Meetings, 1979–1991.* Lampeter, 1992
Hall, H. D., *Commonwealth: A History of the British Commonwealth.* London and New York, 1971
Judd, D. and Slinn, P., *The Evolution of the Modern Commonwealth.* London, 1982
Keeton, G. W. (ed.) *The British Commonwealth: Its Laws and Constitutions.* 9 vols. London, 1951 ff.
Larby, P. and Hannam, H., *The Commonwealth* [Bibliography]. Oxford and New Brunswick (NJ), 1993

Madden, F. and Fieldhouse, D., (eds.) *Selected Documents on the Constitutional History of the British Empire and Commonwealth.* Greenwood Press, New York, 1994
Mansergh, N., *The Commonwealth Experience.* Macmillan, London, 1982
McIntyre, W. D., *The Significance of the Commonwealth, 1965–90.* Macmillan, London, 1991
Moore, R. J., *Making the New Commonwealth.* Oxford, 1987

COMMONWEALTH OF INDEPENDENT STATES (CIS)

The Commonwealth of Independent States, founded on 8 Dec. 1991 in Viskuli, a government villa in Belarus, is a community of independent states which proclaimed itself the successor to the Union of Soviet Socialist Republics in some aspects of international law and affairs. The member states are the founders, Russia, Belarus and Ukraine, and nine subsequent adherents: Armenia, Azerbaijan, Georgia, Kazakhstan, Kyrgyzstan, Moldova, Tajikistan, Turkmenistan and Uzbekistan.

History. Extended negotiations in the Union of Soviet Socialist Republics (USSR) in 1990 and 1991, under the direction of President Gorbachev, sought to establish a 'renewed federation' or, subsequently, to conclude a new union treaty that would embrace all the 15 constituent republics of the USSR at that date. According to a referendum conducted in March 1991, 76% of the population (on an 80% turn-out) wished to maintain the USSR as a 'renewed federation of equal sovereign republics in which the human rights and freedoms of any nationality would be fully guaranteed'. In Sept. 1991 the three Baltic republics—Estonia, Latvia and Lithuania—were nonetheless recognized as independent states by the USSR State Council, and subsequently by the international community. Most of the remaining republics reached agreement on the broad outlines of a new 'union of sovereign states' in Nov. 1991, which would have retained a directly elected President and an all-union legislature, but which would have limited central authority to those powers specifically delegated to it by the members of the union.

A referendum in Ukraine in Dec. 1991, however, showed overwhelming support for full independence, and following this the three Slav republics (Russia, Belarus and Ukraine) concluded the Minsk Agreement on 8 Dec. 1991, establishing a Commonwealth of Independent States (CIS), headquartered in Minsk. The USSR, as a subject of international law and a geopolitical reality, was declared no longer in existence, and each of the three republics individually renounced the 1922 treaty through which the USSR had been established.

The CIS declared itself open to other former Soviet republics, and to states elsewhere that shared its objectives, and on 21 Dec. 1991 in Alma-Ata, a further declaration was signed with eight other republics: Armenia, Azerbaijan, Kazakhstan, Kyrgyzstan, Moldova, Tajikistan, Turkmenistan and Uzbekistan. The declaration committed signatories to recognize the independence and sovereignty of other members, to respect human rights including those of national minorities, and to the observance of existing boundaries. Relations among the members of the CIS were to be conducted on an equal, multilateral, interstate basis, but it was agreed to endorse the principle of unitary control of strategic nuclear arms and the concept of a 'single economic space'. In a separate agreement the heads of member states agreed that Russia should take up the seat at the United Nations formerly occupied by the USSR, and a framework of interstate and intergovernment consultation was established. Following these developments Mikhail Gorbachev resigned as USSR President on 25 Dec. 1991, and on 26 Dec. the USSR Supreme Soviet voted a formal end to the 1922 Treaty of Union, and dissolved itself. Georgia decided to join on 9 Dec. 1993 and on 1 March 1994 the national parliament ratified the act.

The Charter, adopted on 22 Jan. 1993 in Minsk, proclaims that the Commonwealth is based on the principles of the sovereign equality of all members. It is not a state and does not have supranational authority.

Activities and Institutions. The principal organs of the CIS, according to the agreement concluded in Alma-Ata on 21 Dec. 1991, are the *Council of Heads of States*, which meets twice a year, and the *Council of Heads of Government*, which meets every three months. Both councils may convene extraordinary sessions, and may hold joint sittings. There is also a *Council of Defence Ministers*, established Feb. 1992, and a *Council of Foreign Ministers* (Dec. 1993). The Secretariat is the standing working organ.

At a summit meeting of heads of states (with the exception of Azerbaijan) in July 1992, agreements were reached on a way to divide former USSR assets abroad; on the legal cessionary of state archives of former Soviet states; on the status of an Economic Court; and on collective security. In 1992 an *Inter-Parliamentary Assembly* was established by seven member states (Armenia, Belarus, Kazakhstan, Kyrgyzstan, Russia, Tajikistan and Uzbekistan).

At a subsequent meeting in Jan. 1993 Armenia, Belarus, Kazakhstan, Kyrgyzstan, Russia, Tajikistan and Uzbekistan agreed on a charter to implement co-operation in political, economic, ecological, humanitarian, cultural and other spheres; thorough and balanced economic and social development within the common economic space; interstate co-operation and integration; and to ensure human rights and freedoms. Three participants (Ukraine, Moldova and Turkmenistan) agreed only to a declaration that the decision would be open for signing in the future. For the purpose of the maintenance and development of multilateral industrial, trade and financial relations, Heads of State established an *Inter-State Bank* and adopted a Provision on it. Its charter was signed by ten Heads of State (Armenia, Belarus, Kazakhstan, Kyrgyzstan, Moldova, Russia, Tajikistan, Turkmenistan, Ukraine, Uzbekistan) on 22 Dec. 1993.

The *CIS Inter-State Bank* was set up with a starting capital of 5,000m. roubles, to facilitate multilateral clearing of CIS interstate transactions. Members' contributions (by %), based on their share of foreign trade turnover in 1990, were as follows: Russia, 50%; Ukraine, 20·7%; Belarus, 8·4%; Kazakhstan, 6·1%; Uzbekistan, 5·5%; Moldova, 2·9%; Armenia, 1·8%; Tajikistan, 1·6%; Kyrgyzstan, 1·5%; Turkmenistan, 1·5%. The bank is an international settlement and financial-credit institution, established in accordance with the rules of international public law. The authorized capital on 1 Jan. 1999 was 20,000m. roubles.

In accordance with the Agreement on Armed Forces and Border Troops, concluded on 30 Dec. 1991, it was decided to consider and solve the issue on the transference of the management of the General-Purpose Armed Forces in accordance with the national legislation of member states. On 14 Feb. 1992 the *Council of Defence Ministers* was established. In 1993 the Office of Commander-in-Chief of CIS Joint Armed Forces was reorganized in a Staff for Co-ordinating Military Co-operation. Its Chief of Staff is appointed by the Council of Heads of State.

On 24 Sept. 1993 Armenia, Azerbaijan, Belarus, Kazakhstan, Kyrgyzstan, Moldova, Russia, Tajikistan and Uzbekistan signed an agreement to form an *Economic Union*. Georgia and Turkmenistan signed later (14 and 23 Jan. 1994). Ukraine became an associated member on 15 April 1994. In Oct. 1994 a summit meeting established the *Inter-State Economic Committee (MEK)* to be based in Moscow. Members include all CIS states except Turkmenistan. The Committee's decisions are binding if voted by 80% of the membership. Russia commands 50% of the voting power; Ukraine 14%. The Committee's remit is to co-ordinate energy, transport and communications policies. A *Customs Union* to regulate payments between member states with non-convertible independent currencies and a regulatory *Economic Court* have also been established.

On 29 March 1996 Belarus, Kazakhstan, Kyrgyzstan and Russia signed an agreement increasing their mutual economic and social integration by creating a *Community of Integrated States* (Tajikistan signed in 1998). The agreement established a Supreme Inter-Governmental Council comprising heads of state and government and foreign ministers, with a rotatory Chair, an integration committee of Ministers and an Inter-Parliamentary Committee.

On 2 April 1996 the Presidents of Belarus and Russia signed a treaty providing for political, economic and military integration, creating the nucleus of a *Community of Russia and Belarus*. The agreement establishes a Supreme Council comprising the Presidents, Prime Ministers and Speakers of both countries and the Chairman of the Executive Committee. A further treaty was signed on 22 May 1997, instituting common citizenship, common deployment of military forces and the harmonization of the two economies with a view to the creation of a common currency. The

Community was later renamed the *Union of Belarus and Russia* and signed subsequent agreements on equal rights for its citizens and equal conditions for state and private entrepreneurship.

In March 1994 the CIS was accorded observer status in the UN.

Headquarters: 220000 Minsk, Kirava 17, Belarus.
Website: http://www.cis.minsk.by
Executive Secretary: Yurii Yarov (Russia).

Further Reading

Brzezinski, Z. and Sullivan, P. (eds.) *Russia and the Commonwealth of Independent States: Documents, Data and Analysis.* Armonk (NY), 1996

INTERNATIONAL AIR TRANSPORT ASSOCIATION (IATA)

Founded in 1945 for inter-airline co-operation in promoting safe, reliable, secure and economical air services, IATA has over 230 members from more than 130 nations worldwide. IATA is the successor to the International Air Traffic Association, founded in the Hague in 1919, the year of the world's first international scheduled services.

Main offices: IATA Centre, Route de l'Aéroport 33, PO Box 416, CH-1215 Geneva, Switzerland. 800 Place Victoria, PO Box 113, Montreal, Quebec, Canada H4Z 1M1. 77 Robinson Road, #05-00 SIA Building, Singapore 068896.
Website: http://www.iata.org
Director-General: Giovanni Bisignani (Italy).

INTERNATIONAL COMMITTEE OF THE RED CROSS (ICRC)

The ICRC was founded in Geneva in Feb. 1863. Its mission is to lay down rules governing the use of force in war and to safeguard the weak. The ICRC's activities are aimed at protecting and assisting the victims of armed conflict and internal violence and enabling them to regain their autonomy. The main treaties governing international law are the Geneva Conventions (1949) and the Additional Protocols (1977).

The ICRC is independent of all governments and international organizations, is neutral and remains detached from all political issues related to conflict. It is, therefore, able to act as an intermediary between the parties to armed conflict and to promote dialogue in situations of internal violence. It helps to prevent the worsening of crises and helps to resolve them. It systematically reminds all military and civilian authorities directly involved in armed conflict or internal violence of their obligations under international humanitarian law and the other humanitarian rules by which they are bound.

The ICRC endeavours to promote international humanitarian law and the fundamental values underlying the law. As the founding member of the International Red Cross and Red Crescent Movement, the ICRC directs and co-ordinates the international work of the Movement's components. It acts in consultation with all other organizations involved in humanitarian work.

The ICRC relies for its financing on voluntary contributions from signatories to the Geneva Conventions, organizations such as the European Union, and public and private sources.

In 2001 the ICRC maintained a permanent presence in 69 countries with a total staff of around 11,000, and conducted operations in around 80 countries. The 27th

International Conference of the Red Cross and Red Crescent was held in Geneva in Nov. 1999 and adopted a Plan of Action for 2000–03.

Headquarters: 19 Avenue de la Paix, 1202 Geneva, Switzerland.
Website: http://www.icrc.org
President: Jakob Kellenberger (Switzerland).

Further Reading

Moorehead, Caroline, *Dunant's Dream: War, Switzerland and the History of the Red Cross.* HarperCollins, London, 1998

INTERNATIONAL CONFEDERATION OF FREE TRADE UNIONS (ICFTU)

Origin. The founding congress of the ICFTU was held in London in Dec. 1949 following the withdrawal of some Western trade unions from the World Federation of Trade Unions (WFTU), which had come under Communist control. The constitution, as amended, provides for co-operation with the UN and the ILO, and for regional organizations to promote free trade unionism, especially in developing countries. By Jan. 2005 the ICFTU represented 145m. workers across 233 national trade union centres in 154 countries and territories.

Aims. The ICFTU aims to promote the interests of working people and to secure recognition of workers' organizations as free bargaining agents; to reduce the gap between rich and poor; and to defend fundamental human and trade union rights. In 1996 it campaigned for the adoption by the WTO of a social clause, with legally binding minimum labour standards.

Organization. The Congress meets every four years. The 18th Annual World Congress was held in Miyazaki, Japan in Dec. 2004. It elects the General Secretary and an Executive Board of 53 members nominated on an area basis for a four-year period. Five seats are reserved for women, nominated by the Women's Committee, and one reserved for a representative of young workers. The Board meets at least once a year. Various committees cover economic and social policy, violation of trade union and other human rights, trade union co-operation projects and also the administration of the International Solidarity Fund. There are joint ICFTU–Global Union Federations for co-ordinating activities.

The ICFTU has branch offices in Geneva, New York and Washington, and regional organizations in Latin America (Caracas), Asia (Singapore) and Africa (Nairobi).

Headquarters: Bd. du Roi Albert II, N° 5, bte 1, Brussels 1210, Belgium.
Website: http://www.icftu.org
General Secretary: Guy Ryder (UK).
President: Sharan Burrow (Australia).

Publications. Trade Union World (monthly); *Annual Survey of Violations of Trade Union Rights* (annual); *ICFTU On-Line* (daily electronic news bulletin). Other publications available; contact the press department.

INTERNATIONAL CRIMINAL COURT (ICC)

Origin. As far back as 1946 an international congress called for the adoption of an international criminal code prohibiting crimes against humanity and the prompt establishment of an international criminal court, but for more than 40 years little progress was made. In 1989 the end of the Cold War brought a dramatic increase in the number of UN peacekeeping operations and a world where the idea of establishing an International Criminal Court became more viable. The United

Nations Conference of Plenipotentiaries on the Establishment of an International Criminal Court took place from 15 June–17 July 1998 in Rome, Italy.

Aims and Activities. The International Criminal Court is a permanent court for trying individuals who have been accused of committing genocide, war crimes and crimes against humanity, and is thus a successor to the *ad hoc* tribunals set up by the UN Security Council to try those responsible for atrocities in the former Yugoslavia and Rwanda. Ratification by 60 countries was required to bring the statute into effect. The court began operations on 1 July 2002 with 139 signatories and after ratification by 76 countries. By Oct. 2004 the number of ratifications had increased to 97.

Judges. The International Criminal Court's first 18 judges were elected in Feb. 2003, with six serving for three years, six for six years and six for nine years. Every three years six new judges will be elected. The 18 judges elected in 2003, with the year in which their term of office is scheduled to end, were: René Blattmann (Bolivia, 2009); Maureen Harding Clark (Ireland, 2012); Fatoumata Dembele Diarra (Mali, 2012); Adrian Fulford (United Kingdom, 2012); Karl Hudson-Phillips (Trinidad and Tobago, 2012); Claude Jorda (France, 2009); Hans-Peter Kaul (Germany, 2006); Philippe Kirsch (Canada, 2009); Erkki Kourula (Finland, 2006); Akua Kuenyehia (Ghana, 2006); Elizabeth Odio Benito (Costa Rica, 2012); Georghios Pikis (Cyprus, 2009); Navanethem Pillay (South Africa, 2009); Mauro Politi (Italy, 2009); Tuiloma Neroni Slade (Samoa, 2006); Song Sang-hyun (South Korea, 2006); Sylvia Helena de Figueiredo Steiner (Brazil, 2012); Anita Usacka (Latvia, 2006).

Prosecutor. Luis Moreno-Ocampo (Argentina) was elected the first prosecutor of the Court on 21 April 2003.

Headquarters: Maanweg 174, 2516 AB The Hague, Netherlands.
Website: http://www.icc-cpi.int

Further Reading

Macedo, Stephen (ed.), *Universal Jurisdiction: National Courts and the Prosecution of Serious Crimes Under International Law.* Univ. of Pennsylvania Press, 2003
Reydams, Luc, *Universal Jurisdiction: International and Municipal Perspectives.* OUP, 2003

INTERNATIONAL INSTITUTE FOR DEMOCRACY AND ELECTORAL ASSISTANCE (IDEA)

Created in 1995, International IDEA is an intergovernmental organization that seeks to promote and develop sustainable democracy worldwide. Global in membership and independent of specific national interests, IDEA works with both new and long-established democracies, helping to develop the institutions and culture of democracy. It operates at international, regional and national levels, working in partnership with a range of institutions.

Aims and Activities. IDEA aims to: help countries build capacity to develop democratic institutions; provide a meeting-place for and facilitate dialogue between democracy practitioners around the world; increase knowledge and expertise about elections and election observation; promote transparency, accountability, professionalism and efficiency in elections in the context of democratic development; develop and promote norms, rules and guidelines relating to multi-party pluralism and broader democratic processes. The principal areas of activity include: electoral systems and management; political participation, including women in politics; political parties, management and financing; post-conflict democracy building and reconciliation; democracy at local level; democracy indicators and assessment.

Membership. The International IDEA had 23 full member states and two observer states in March 2005.

Headquarters: Strömsberg, 103 34 Stockholm, Sweden.
Website: http://www.idea.int
Secretary-General: Karen Fogg (UK).

INTERNATIONAL MOBILE SATELLITE ORGANIZATION (IMSO)

Founded in 1979 as the International Maritime Satellite Organization (Inmarsat) to establish a satellite system to improve maritime communications for distress and safety and commercial applications. Its competence was subsequently expanded to include aeronautical and land mobile communications. Privatization, which was completed in April 1999, transferred the business to a newly created company and the Organization remains as a regulator to ensure that the company fulfils its public services obligations. The company has taken the Inmarsat name and the Organization uses the acronym IMSO. In Oct. 1999 the Organization had 86 member parties.

Organization. The Assembly of all Parties to the Convention meets every two years. There is also a 22-member Council of representatives of national telecommunications administrations as well as an executive Directorate.

Headquarters: 99 City Road, London EC1Y 1AX, UK.
Website: www.inmarsat.com
Director of the Secretariat, IMSO: Jerzy Vonau.
Chief Executive, Inmarsat Ltd: Andrew Sukawaty.

INTERNATIONAL OLYMPIC COMMITTEE (IOC)

Founded in 1894 by French educator Baron Pierre de Coubertin, the International Olympic Committee is an international non-governmental, non-profit organization whose members act as the IOC's representatives in their respective countries, not as delegates of their countries within the IOC. The Committee's main responsibility is to supervise the organization of the summer and winter Olympic Games. It owns all rights to the Olympic symbols, flag, motto, anthem and Olympic Games.

Aims. 'To contribute to building a peaceful and better world by educating youth through sport, practised without discrimination of any kind and in the Olympic Spirit, which requires mutual understanding with a spirit of friendship, solidarity and fair play.'

Finances. The IOC receives no public funding. Its only source of funding is from private sectors, with the substantial part of these revenues coming from television broadcasters and sponsors.

Address: Château de Vidy, Case Postale 356, CH–1007 Lausanne, Switzerland.
Website: http://www.olympic.org
President: Jacques Rogge (Belgium).

INTERNATIONAL ORGANIZATION FOR MIGRATION (IOM)

Established in Brussels in 1951 to help solve European population and refugee problems through migration, and to stimulate the creation of new economic opportunities in countries lacking certain manpower. IOM is committed to the principle that humane and orderly migration benefits migrants and society.

Members (109 as of Nov. 2004). Afghanistan, Albania, Algeria, Angola, Argentina, Armenia, Australia, Austria, Azerbaijan, Bahamas, Bangladesh, Belgium, Belize, Benin, Bolivia, Brazil, Bulgaria, Burkina Faso, Cambodia, Canada, Cape Verde,

Chile, Colombia, Congo (Democratic Republic of), Congo (Republic of), Costa Rica, Côte d'Ivoire, Croatia, Cyprus, Czech Republic, Denmark, Dominican Republic, Ecuador, Egypt, El Salvador, Estonia, Finland, France, Gambia, Georgia, Germany, Greece, Guatemala, Guinea, Guinea-Bissau, Haiti, Honduras, Hungary, Iran, Ireland, Israel, Italy, Japan, Jordan, Kazakhstan, Kenya, South Korea, Kyrgyzstan, Latvia, Liberia, Libya, Lithuania, Luxembourg, Madagascar, Mali, Malta, Mauritania, Mexico, Moldova, Morocco, Netherlands, New Zealand, Nicaragua, Niger, Nigeria, Norway, Pakistan, Panama, Paraguay, Peru, Philippines, Poland, Portugal, Romania, Rwanda, Senegal, Serbia and Montenegro, Sierra Leone, Slovakia, Slovenia, South Africa, Sri Lanka, Sudan, Sweden, Switzerland, Tajikistan, United Republic of Tanzania, Thailand, Tunisia, Turkey, Uganda, Ukraine, UK, USA, Uruguay, Venezuela, Yemen, Zambia and Zimbabwe. 24 governments and a large number of government agencies and NGOs have observer status.

Activities. As an intergovernmental body, IOM acts with its partners in the international community to: assist in meeting the operational challenges of migration; advance understanding of migration issues; encourage social and economic development through migration; work towards effective respect of human dignity and the well-being of migrants. Since 1952 the IOM has assisted some 11m. refugees and migrants to settle in over 125 countries. Throughout 2001 the organization assisted in the humanitarian emergency unfolding in Afghanistan by way of shelter programmes and the registration of IDPs (internally displaced persons), and by meeting the needs of the displaced brought on by drought and conflict. Those elsewhere supported by the IOM in 2001 included: India, following the earthquake affecting large areas in the west of the country; and Africa, in particular the collection and destruction of arms in the Democratic Republic of the Congo and the relocation of IDPs following continued fighting in the border region between Guinea and Sierra Leone. In 2001 IOM launched a 'Migration and Development in Africa Programme' and a 'Migration Policy and Research Programme'. IOM's operational budget in 2004 was US$641m.

Official languages: English, French, Spanish.
Headquarters: Route des Morillons 17, POB 71, 1211 Geneva 19, Switzerland.
Website: http://www.iom.int
Director-General: Brunson McKinley (USA).

INTERNATIONAL ORGANIZATION FOR STANDARDIZATION (ISO)

Established in 1947, the International Organization for Standardization is a non-governmental federation of national standards bodies from some 145 countries worldwide, one from each country. ISO's work results in international agreements which are published as International Standards. The first ISO standard was published in 1951 with the title 'Standard reference temperature for industrial length measurement'.

Some 15,400 ISO International Standards are available on subjects in such diverse fields as information technology, textiles, packaging, distribution of goods, energy production and utilization, building, banking and financial services. ISO standardization activities include the widely recognized ISO 9000 family of quality management system and standards and the ISO 14000 series of environmental management system standards. Standardization programmes are now being developed in completely new fields, such as food safety, security, social responsibility and the service sector.

Mission. To promote the development of standardization and related activities in the world with a view to facilitating the international exchange of goods and services, and to developing co-operation in the spheres of intellectual, scientific, technological and economic activity.

Headquarters: 1 rue de Varembé, Case postale 56, CH-1211 Geneva 20, Switzerland.
Website: http://www.iso.org
e-mail: central@iso.org
Secretary-General: Alan Bryden.

INTERNATIONAL ORGANIZATION OF THE FRANCOPHONIE

The International Organization of the Francophonie represents 63 countries and provinces/regions (including ten with observer status) using French as an official language. Objectives include the promotion of peace, democracy, and economic and social development, through political and technical co-operation. The Secretary-General is based in Paris.

Members. Albania, Andorra, Belgium, Benin, Bulgaria, Burkina Faso, Burundi, Cambodia, Cameroon, Canada, Canada–New Brunswick, Canada–Quebec, Cape Verde, Central African Republic, Chad, Comoros, Republic of the Congo, Democratic Republic of the Congo, Côte d'Ivoire, Djibouti, Dominica, Egypt, Equatorial Guinea, France, French Community of Belgium, Gabon, Greece, Guinea, Guinea-Bissau, Haiti, Laos, Lebanon, Luxembourg, Macedonia, Madagascar, Mali, Mauritania, Mauritius, Moldova, Monaco, Morocco, Niger, Romania, Rwanda, St Lucia, São Tomé e Príncipe, Senegal, Seychelles, Switzerland, Togo, Tunisia, Vanuatu, Vietnam. *Observers.* Armenia, Austria, Croatia, Czech Republic, Georgia, Hungary, Lithuania, Poland, Slovakia, Slovenia.

Headquarters: 28 rue de Bourgogne, 75007 Paris, France.
Website: http://www.francophonie.org
Secretary-General: Abdou Diouf (Senegal).

INTERNATIONAL ROAD FEDERATION (IRF)

The IRF is a non-profit, non-political service organization whose purpose is to encourage better road and transportation systems worldwide and to help apply technology and management practices to give maximum economic and social returns from national road investments.

Founded following the Second World War, over the years the IRF has led major global road infrastructure developments, including achieving 1,000 km of new roads in Mexico in the 1950s, and promoting the Pan-American Highway linking North and South America. It publishes *World Road Statistics*, as well as road research studies, including a 140-country inventory of road and transport research in co-operation with the US Bureau of Public Roads.

Headquarters: 2 chemin de Blandonnet, CH-1214 Vernier/GE, Switzerland.
Website: http://www.irfnet.org
Director-General (Geneva/Brussels): Tony Pearce (UK).
Director-General (Washington, D.C.): C. Patrick Sankey (USA).

INTERNATIONAL SEABED AUTHORITY (ISA)

The ISA is an autonomous international organization established under the UN Convention on the Law of the Sea (UNCLOS) of 1982 and the 1994 Agreement relating to the implementation of Part XI of the above Convention. It came into existence on 16 Nov. 1994 and became fully operational in June 1996.

The administrative expenses are met from assessed contributions from its members. Membership numbered 145 in Jan. 2004; the budget for the biennium 2003–04 was US$10,509,700.

The Convention on the Law of the Sea covers almost all ocean space and its uses: navigation and overflight, resource exploration and exploitation, conservation and pollution, fishing and shipping. It entitles coastal states and inhabited islands to proclaim a 200-mile exclusive economic zone or continental shelf (which may be larger). Its 320 Articles and nine Annexes constitute a guide for behaviour by states in the world's oceans, defining maritime zones, laying down rules for drawing sea boundaries, assigning legal rights, duties and responsibilities to States, and providing machinery for the settlement of disputes.

Organization. The Assembly, consisting of representatives from all member states, is the supreme organ. The 36-member Council, elected by the Assembly, includes the four largest importers or consumers of seabed minerals, four largest investors in seabed minerals, four major exporters of the same, six developing countries representing special interests and 18 members from all the geographical regions. The Council is the executive organ of the Authority. There are also two subsidiary bodies: the Legal and Technical Commission (currently 24 experts) and the Finance Committee (currently 15 experts). The Secretariat serves all the bodies of the Authority and under the 1994 Agreement is performing functions of the Enterprise (until such time as it starts to operate independently of the Secretariat). The Enterprise is the organ through which the ISA carries out deep seabed activities directly or through joint ventures.

Activities. In July 2000 the ISA adopted the Regulations for Prospecting and Exploration for Polymetallic Nodules in the Area. Pursuant thereto, it signed exploration contracts with seven contractors who have submitted plans of work for deep seabed exploration. These are: Institut Français de Recherche pour l'Exploitation de la Mer (IFREMER) and Association Française pour l'Etude de la Recherche des Nodules (AFERNOD), France; Deep Ocean Resources Development Co. Ltd (DORD), Japan; State Enterprise Yuzhmorgeologiya, Russian Federation; China Ocean Minerals Research and Development Association (COMRA); Interoceanmetal Joint Organization (IOM), a consortium sponsored by Bulgaria, Cuba, Czech Republic, Poland, Russian Federation and Slovakia; the government of South Korea; and the government of India.

Between 1998 and 2002 the ISA organized five workshops: the development of guidelines for the assessment of the possible environmental impacts arising from exploration for polymetallic nodules; proposed technologies for deep seabed mining of polymetallic nodules; the available knowledge on mineral resources other than polymetallic nodules in the deep seabed; a standardized system of data interpretation; prospects for international collaboration in marine environmental research. While continuing to develop a database on polymetallic nodules (POLYDAT), the Authority has also made significant progress towards the establishment of a central data repository for all marine minerals in the deep seabed.

Headquarters: 14–20 Port Royal St., Kingston, Jamaica.
Website: http://www.isa.org.jm
Secretary-General: Satya N. Nandan (Fiji Islands).

Publications. Handbook 2004; plus selected decisions and documents from the Authority's sessions; various others.

INTERNATIONAL TELECOMMUNICATIONS SATELLITE ORGANIZATION (ITSO)

Founded in 1964 as Intelsat, the organization was the world's first commercial communications satellite operator. Today, with capacity on a fleet of geostationary satellites and expanding terrestrial network assets, Intelsat continues to provide connectivity for telephony, corporate network, broadcast and Internet services.

Organization. In 2001 the member states of the organization implemented restructuring by transferring certain assets to Intelsat Ltd, a new Bermuda-based commercial company under the supervision of the International Telecommunications Satellite Organization, now known as ITSO. The Intelsat Global Service Corporation is located in Washington, D.C., and Intelsat Global Services & Marketing Ltd, the sales arm of the international firm, has its headquarters in London. Intelsat also has offices in Australia, Brazil, China, France, Germany, Hawaii, India, Peru and South Africa. There were 148 member countries in March 2005.

Headquarters: 3400 International Drive, NW, Washington, D.C., 20008–3006, USA.
Website: http://www.itso.int
Director-General: Ahmed Toumi (Morocco).

INTERNATIONAL TRIBUNAL FOR THE LAW OF THE SEA (ITLOS)

The International Tribunal for the Law of the Sea (ITLOS), founded in Oct. 1996 and based in Hamburg, adjudicates on disputes relating to the interpretation and application of the United Nations Convention on the Law of the Sea. The Convention gives the Tribunal jurisdiction to resolve a variety of international law of the sea disputes such as the delimitation of maritime zones, fisheries, navigation and the protection of the marine environment. Its Seabed Disputes Chamber has compulsory jurisdiction to resolve disputes amongst States, the International Seabed Authority, companies and private individuals, arising out of the exploitation of the deep seabed. The Tribunal also has compulsory jurisdiction in certain instances to protect the rights of parties to a dispute or to prevent serious harm to the marine environment, and over the prompt release of arrested vessels and their crews upon the deposit of a security. The jurisdiction of the Tribunal also extends to all matters specifically provided for in any other agreement which confers jurisdiction on the Tribunal. The Tribunal is composed of 21 judges, elected by signatories from five world regional blocs: five each from Africa and Asia; four from Western Europe and other States; four from Latin America and the Caribbean; and three from Eastern Europe. The judges serve a term of nine years, with one third of the judges' terms expiring every three years.

Headquarters: Am Internationalen Seegerichtshof 1, D-22609 Hamburg, Germany.
Website: http://www.itlos.org
Registrar: Philippe Gautier (Belgium).

INTERNATIONAL UNION AGAINST CANCER (UICC)

Founded in 1933, the UICC is an international non-governmental association of 263 member organizations in 84 countries.

Objectives. The UICC is the only non-governmental organization dedicated exclusively to the global control of cancer. Its objectives are to advance scientific and medical knowledge in research, diagnosis, treatment and prevention of cancer, and to promote all other aspects of the campaign against cancer throughout the world. Particular emphasis is placed on professional and public education.

Membership. The UICC is made up of voluntary cancer leagues, patient organizations, associations and societies as well as cancer research and treatment centres and, in some countries, ministries of health.

Activities. The UICC creates and carries out programmes around the world in collaboration with several hundred volunteer experts, most of whom are professionally active in UICC member organizations. It promotes co-operation between cancer organizations, researchers, scientists, health professionals and cancer experts, with a focus in four key areas: building and enhancing cancer control capacity, tobacco control, population-based cancer prevention and control, and transfer of cancer knowledge and dissemination. The last UICC World Cancer Congress was held in 2002 in Oslo and the next is scheduled to take place in Washington, D.C. in 2006. Thereafter the congress will takes place every two years.

Address: 3 rue du Conseil-Général, 1205-Geneva, Switzerland.
Website: http://www.uicc.org
President: Dr John Seffrin (USA).
Executive Director: Isabel Mortara (Switzerland).
Secretary-General: Dr Stener Kvinnsland (Norway).

INTER-PARLIAMENTARY UNION (IPU)

Founded in 1889 by William Randal Cremer (UK) and Frédéric Passy (France), the Inter-Parliamentary Union was the first permanent forum for political multilateral negotiations. The Union is a centre for dialogue and parliamentary diplomacy among legislators representing every political system and all the main political leanings in the world. It was instrumental in setting up what is now the Permanent Court of Arbitration in The Hague.

Activities. The IPU fosters contacts, co-ordination and the exchange of experience among parliaments and parliamentarians of all countries; considers questions of international interest and concern, and expresses its views on such issues in order to bring about action by parliaments and parliamentarians; contributes to the defence and promotion of human rights—an essential factor of parliamentary democracy and development; contributes to better knowledge of the working and development of representative institutions and to the strengthening of representative democracy.

Membership. The IPU had 140 members and seven associate members in March 2005.

Headquarters: Chemin du Pommier 5, C.P. 330, 1218 Le Grand Saconnex, Geneva 19, Switzerland.
Website: http://www.ipu.org
President: Sergio Páez Verdugo (Chile).
Secretary-General: Anders B. Johnsson (Sweden).

INTERPOL (INTERNATIONAL CRIMINAL POLICE ORGANIZATION)

Organization. Interpol was founded in 1923, disbanded in 1938 and reconstituted in 1946. The International Criminal Police Organization—Interpol was founded to ensure and promote the widest possible mutual assistance between all criminal police authorities within the limits of the law existing in the different countries worldwide and the spirit of the Universal Declaration of Human Rights, and to establish and develop all institutions likely to contribute effectively to the prevention and suppression of ordinary law crimes.

Aims. Interpol provides a co-ordination centre (General Secretariat) for its 181 member countries. Its priority areas of activity concern criminal organizations, public safety and terrorism, drug-related crimes, financial crime and high-tech crime, trafficking in human beings, and tracking fugitives from justice. Interpol centralizes records and information on international offenders; it operates a worldwide communication network.

Interpol's General Assembly is held annually. The General Assembly is the body of supreme authority in the organization. It is composed of delegates appointed by the members of the organization.

Interpol's Executive Committee, which meets four times a year, supervises the execution of the decisions of the General Assembly. The Executive Committee is composed of the president of the organization, the three vice-presidents and nine delegates.

Interpol's General Secretariat is the centre for co-ordinating the fight against international crime. Its activities, undertaken in response to requests from the police services and judicial authorities in its member countries, focus on crime prevention and law enforcement.

As of March 2005 Interpol's Sub-Regional Bureaus were located in Abidjan, Buenos Aires, El Salvador, Harare and Nairobi. The Interpol's Liaison Office for Asia is located in Bangkok.

Headquarters: 200 Quai Charles de Gaulle, 69006 Lyon, France.
Website: http://www.interpol.int
e-mail: cp@interpol.int
President: Jackie Selebi (South Africa).

ISLAMIC DEVELOPMENT BANK

The Agreement establishing the IDB (Banque islamique de développement) was adopted at the Second Islamic Finance Ministers' Conference held in Jeddah, Saudi Arabia in Aug. 1974. The Bank, which is open to all member countries of the Organization of the Islamic Conference, commenced operations in 1975. Its main objective is to foster economic development and social progress of member countries and Muslim communities individually as well as jointly in accordance with the principles of the Sharia. It is active in the promotion of trade and the flow of investments among member countries, and maintains a Special Assistance Fund for member countries suffering natural calamities. The Fund is also used to finance health and educational projects aimed at improving the socio-economic conditions of Muslim communities in non-member countries. A US$1·5bn. IDB Infrastructure Fund was launched in 1998 to invest in projects such as power, telecommunications, transportation, energy, natural resources, petro-chemical and other infrastructure-related sectors in member countries.

Members (55 as of Feb. 2005). Afghanistan, Albania, Algeria, Azerbaijan, Bahrain, Bangladesh, Benin, Brunei, Burkina Faso, Cameroon, Chad, Comoros, Côte d'Ivoire, Djibouti, Egypt, Gabon, The Gambia, Guinea, Guinea-Bissau, Indonesia, Iran, Iraq, Jordan, Kazakhstan, Kuwait, Kyrgyzstan, Lebanon, Libya, Malaysia, Maldives, Mali, Mauritania, Morocco, Mozambique, Niger, Oman, Pakistan, Palestine, Qatar, Saudi Arabia, Senegal, Sierra Leone, Somalia, Sudan, Suriname, Syria, Tajikistan, Togo, Tunisia, Turkey, Turkmenistan, Uganda, United Arab Emirates, Uzbekistan, Yemen.

Official language: Arabic. *Working languages:* English, French.
Headquarters: PO Box 5925, Jeddah 21432, Saudi Arabia.
Website: http://www.isdb.org
e-mail: idbarchives@isdb.org
President: Ahmed Mohamed Ali (Saudi Arabia).

MÉDECINS SANS FRONTIÈRES (MSF)

Origin. Médecins sans Frontières was founded in 1971 by a small group of doctors and journalists who believed that all people have a right to emergency relief.

Functions. MSF was one of the first non-governmental organizations to provide both urgently needed medical assistance and to publicly bear witness to the plight of the people it helps. Today MSF is an international medical humanitarian movement with branch offices in 18 countries. In 2003 MSF volunteer doctors, nurses, other medical professionals, logistical experts, water-and-sanitation engineers, and administrators departed on more than 3,400 missions and joined more than 16,000 locally hired staff to provide medical aid in nearly 80 countries. MSF was awarded the 1999 Nobel Peace Prize.

Headquarters: MSF International Office, Rue de Lausanne 78, CH-1211 Geneva 21, Switzerland.
Website: http://www.msf.org
Secretary-General: Marine Buissonnière.
President: Dr Rowan Gillies (Australia).

NORTH ATLANTIC TREATY ORGANIZATION (NATO)

Origin and History. On 4 April 1949 the foreign ministers of Belgium, Canada, Denmark, France, Iceland, Italy, Luxembourg, the Netherlands, Norway, Portugal, the UK and the USA signed the North Atlantic Treaty, establishing the *North Atlantic Alliance*. In 1952 Greece and Turkey acceded to the Treaty; in 1955 the Federal Republic of Germany; in 1982 Spain; in 1999 the Czech Republic, Hungary and Poland; and in 2004 Bulgaria, Estonia, Latvia, Lithuania, Romania, Slovakia and Slovenia, bringing the total to 26 member nations.

Functions. The Alliance was established as a defensive political and military alliance of independent countries in accordance with the terms of the UN Charter. It provides common security for its members through co-operation and consultation in political, military and economic as well as scientific and other non-military fields. The Alliance links the security of North America to that of Europe. NATO is the organization which enables the goals of the Alliance to be implemented.

Reform and Transformation of the Alliance. Following the demise of the Warsaw Pact in 1991, and the improved relations with Russia, NATO has undertaken a fundamental transformation of structures and policies to meet the new security challenges in Europe. Attention has focused in particular on the need to reinforce the political role of the Alliance.

An essential component of this transformation has been the establishment of close security links with the states of Central and Eastern Europe and those of the former USSR through the North Atlantic Co-operation Council (NACC), established in Dec. 1991 as an integral part of NATO's new Strategic Concept, which was adopted by heads of state and government at a summit in Rome earlier that year. The NACC was replaced by the Euro-Atlantic Partnership Council (EAPC) in 1997. The EAPC brings together NATO's member countries and its partner countries (the members of Partnership for Peace).

The Partnership for Peace (PfP) programme. The PfP builds on the momentum of co-operation created by the North Atlantic Co-operation Council. It was launched at the 1994 Brussels Summit and is expanding and intensifying political and military co-operation throughout Europe. In 1997 Allied Foreign and Defence Ministers launched a wide range of enhancement measures to PfP, which have strengthened it in political, security, military and institutional fields. Its core objectives are: the facilitation of transparency in national defence planning and budgeting processes; democratic control of defence forces; members' maintenance of capability and readiness to contribute to operations under the authority of the UN; development of co-operative military relations with NATO (joint planning, training and exercises) in order to strengthen participants' ability to undertake missions in the fields of peacekeeping, search and rescue, and humanitarian operations; development, over the longer term, of forces better able to operate with those of NATO member forces. NATO will consult with any active Partner which perceives a direct threat to its territorial integrity, political independence or security; and active participation in the Partnership is to play an important role in the process of NATO's expansion.

One of the most tangible aspects of co-operation between partner countries and NATO has been their individual participation in NATO-led peace-support operations, especially in the Balkans. PfP has done much to facilitate this and has also been a key factor in promoting a spirit of practical co-operation and commitment to the democratic principles that underpin the Alliance. Joint peacekeeping exercises take place on a regular basis in the PfP framework in both NATO and partner countries. A large number of nationally sponsored exercises in the spirit of PfP have also been set up. In March 2004 following the accession of the seven new members NATO had 20 PfP partners: Albania, Armenia, Austria, Azerbaijan, Belarus, Croatia, Finland, Georgia, Ireland, Kazakhstan, Kyrgyzstan, Macedonia, Moldova, Russia, Sweden, Switzerland, Tajikistan, Turkmenistan, Ukraine and Uzbekistan. Many of these countries have accepted the Alliance's invitation to send liaison officers to permanent facilities at NATO Headquarters in Brussels and to the Partnership Co-ordination Cell in Mons, Belgium, where the Supreme Headquarters Allied Powers Europe (SHAPE) is located.

Other key reforms undertaken include a reduced and more flexible force structure, development of increased co-ordination and co-operation with other international institutions (EU, UN, OSCE), development of the European Security and Defence Identity (ESDI), and the agreement to make NATO's assets and experience available to support international peace enforcement operations.

Efforts to strengthen the security and defence role of NATO's European Allies (the European Security and Defence Identity) were initially organized through the Western European Union (WEU). In 2000 the crisis management responsibilities of the WEU were increasingly assumed by the European Union (EU). A number of milestones can be identified in the development of ESDI between NATO, the WEU and the EU; the signing of the Maastricht Treaty in 1992, which allowed for the development of a common European security and defence policy; the endorsement of the concept of Combined Joint Task Forces in 1994 and of 'separable but not separate forces' that could be made available for European-led crisis response operations other than collective defence; the Berlin decisions in 1996, which included the building up of ESDI within the alliance; the EU Summits in Cologne and Helsinki in 1999, which led to important decisions on strengthening the ESDP and the development of an EU rapid reaction capability, and further developments in NATO-EU co-operation culminating in a joint declaration issued in Dec. 2002, which provided a formal basis for co-operation between the two organizations, outlining the political principles defining co-operation and giving the EU assured access to NATO planning capabilities for its own military operations.

NATO's military capabilities and its adaptability to include forces of non-NATO countries were decisive factors in the Alliance's role in implementing the Bosnian Peace Agreement. Following the signing of the Agreement in Paris on 14 Dec. 1995, and on the basis of the UN Security Council's Resolution 1031, NATO commenced implementation of the military aspects of the accord through the NATO-led multinational force, the Implementation Force (IFOR), under an operation code-named Joint Endeavour. Its task was to help the parties implement the peace accord to which they had freely agreed and create a secure environment for civil and economic reconstruction. IFOR was the largest-ever military operation undertaken by the Alliance. In Dec. 1996 it was replaced by a Stabilisation Force (SFOR), again under NATO leadership and committed to contributing to peace and stability in Bosnia-Herzegovina. The SFOR operation was concluded in Dec. 2004 and is being replaced by a new EU-led force drawing on NATO support in accordance with the agreement reached between the two organizations. NATO will maintain a military presence in the country to assist in specific areas such as defence reform, counter-terrorism and the apprehension of those indicted for war crimes.

In March 1999, following the collapse of negotiations with President Milošević of Yugoslavia on a settlement to the Kosovo crisis, NATO forces launched a series of attacks on Serb military targets. After an air campaign lasting 78 days these attacks were suspended and in accordance with the Military-Technical Agreement the full withdrawal of Yugoslav forces began. The deployment in Kosovo of a multinational security force, with substantial NATO participation, was synchronized with the Serb withdrawal before the end of June. The formal cessation of the air campaign was then announced by the Secretary General of NATO. Since June 1999 a NATO-led peacekeeping force (KFOR) has been deployed in Kosovo under a United Nations mandate.

Enlargement. In Dec. 1994 NATO foreign ministers initiated a study on enlargement, which was followed by intensified individual dialogues with interested partner countries and by an analysis of the relevant factors associated with the admission of new members. The conclusion was that, subject to agreed criteria, the accession of new members would enhance security and extend stability throughout the Euro-Atlantic area.

At the July 1997 meeting of Heads of State and Government in Madrid it was decided to invite three countries (Czech Republic, Hungary and Poland) to begin accession negotiations. By Dec. 1997 the three had signed accession agreements, and subsequently joined NATO in March 1999.

In April 1999 the Alliance adopted the Membership Action Plan (MAP) which is specifically designed to provide concrete advice and assistance to aspiring members with their own preparations for possible future membership. Nine partner countries were involved in this initiative: Albania, Bulgaria, Estonia, Latvia, Lithuania, Romania, Slovakia, Slovenia and the Former Yugoslavian Republic of Macedonia. At the Prague Summit in Nov. 2002 Bulgaria, Estonia, Latvia, Lithuania, Romania, Slovakia and Slovenia were invited to accession talks with NATO. They joined NATO officially on 29 March 2004.

On 27 May 1997, in Paris, NATO and Russia signed the Founding Act on Mutual Relations, Co-operation and Security, committing them to build together a lasting peace in the Euro-Atlantic area, and establishing a new forum for consultations and co-operation called the NATO-Russia Permanent Joint Council. NATO-Russia co-operation has since developed and a new level of partnership is being explored. In May 2002 the Permanent Joint Council was replaced by a new NATO-Russia Council which brings together the 26 NATO member countries and Russia in a forum in which they work as equal partners, identifying and pursuing opportunities for joint action in areas of common concern.

At the meeting in Sintra, Portugal, on 29 May 1997, a NATO-Ukraine charter was drawn up and initialled, to be signed in Madrid the following July. At the same time, Foreign Ministers agreed to enhance their dialogue, begun in 1995, with six countries of the Mediterranean (Egypt, Israel, Jordan, Mauritania, Morocco, Tunisia), and a new committee, the Mediterranean Co-operation Group was established to take the Mediterranean Dialogue forward. Algeria joined the Mediterranean Dialogue in March 2000.

On 12 Sept. 2001, following the attacks on New York and Washington on 11 Sept., for the first time in its history, NATO invoked articles of the Washington Treaty, declaring it considered the attack on the USA as an attack against all members of the Alliance. Actions were subsequently taken by NATO and by individual member countries in support of the US-led campaign against terrorism, in response to requests made by the USA.

Organization. The North Atlantic Council (NAC) is the highest decision-making body and forum for consultation within the Atlantic Alliance. It is composed of Permanent Representatives of all the member countries meeting together at least once a week. The NAC also meets at higher levels involving foreign ministers or heads of state or government, but it has the same authority and powers of decision-making, and its decisions have the same status and validity at whatever level it meets. All decisions are taken on the basis of consensus, reflecting the collective will of all member governments. The NAC is the only body within the Atlantic Alliance which derives its authority explicitly from the North Atlantic Treaty. The NAC has responsibility under the Treaty for setting up subsidiary bodies.

Committees and planning groups have since been created to support the work of the NAC or to assume responsibility in specific fields such as defence planning, nuclear planning and military matters.

The *Military Committee* is responsible for making recommendations to the Council and the Defence Planning Committee on military matters and for supplying guidance to the Allied Commanders. Composed of the Chiefs-of-Staff of member countries (Iceland, which has no military forces, may be represented by a civilian), the Committee is assisted by an International Military Staff. It meets at Chiefs-of-Staff level at least twice a year but remains in permanent session at the level of national military representatives. The military command structure of the Alliance is divided into two strategic commands, one based in Europe, responsible for operations (Allied Command Operations) and the other based in the USA, responsible for the continuous transformation of allied military capabilities to enable them to undertake new challenges and to respond to changing military requirements (Allied Command Transformation).

Finance. The greater part of each member country's contribution to NATO, in terms of resources, comes indirectly through its expenditure on its own national armed forces and on its efforts to make them interoperable with those of other members so that they can participate in multinational operations. Member countries also incur the deployment costs involved whenever they volunteer forces to participate in NATO-led operations.

Member countries make direct contributions to three budgets managed directly by NATO: namely the Civil Budget, the Military Budget and the Security Investment Programme. Member countries pay contributions to each of these budgets in accordance with agreed cost-sharing formulae broadly calculated in relation to their ability to pay. The contributions represent a small percentage of each member's overall defence budget.

Under the terms of the Partnership for Peace strategy, partner countries undertake to make available the necessary personnel, assets, facilities and capabilities to participate in the programme, and share the financial cost of any military exercises in which they participate.

Headquarters: NATO, 1110 Brussels, Belgium.
Website: http://www.nato.int
Secretary General: Jaap de Hoop Scheffer (Netherlands).

Publications. NATO publishes a series of printed and/or on-line publications, reference and audio-visual materials including the *NATO Review* (periodical); *NATO Update; NATO Briefings; the NATO Handbook; NATO in the 21st Century;* and *NATO Transformed.* Further details are available on the NATO website.

Further Reading

Carr, F. and Infantis, K., *NATO in the New European Order.* London, 1996
Cook, D., *The Forging of an Alliance.* London, 1989
Heller, F. H. and Gillingham, J. R. (eds.) *NATO: the Founding of the Atlantic Alliance and the Integration of Europe.* London, 1992
Smith, J. (ed.) *The Origins of NATO.* Exeter Univ. Press, 1990
Williams, P., *North Atlantic Treaty Organization* [Bibliography]. Oxford and New Brunswick (NJ), 1994
Yost, David S., *NATO Transformed: The Alliance's New Roles in International Security.* United States Institute for Peace, Washington, D.C., 1999

ORGANISATION FOR ECONOMIC CO-OPERATION AND DEVELOPMENT (OECD)

Origin. Founded in 1961 to replace the Organisation for European Economic Co-operation (OEEC), which was linked to the Marshall Plan and was established in 1948. The change of title marks the Organisation's altered status and functions: with the accession of Canada and USA as full members, it ceased to be a purely European body, and at the same time added development aid to the list of its priorities. The aims of the organization are to promote policies designed to achieve the highest sustainable economic growth and employment and a rising standard of living in member countries, while maintaining financial stability, and thus to contribute to the development of the world economy; to contribute to sound economic expansion in member as well as non-member countries in the process of economic development; and to contribute to the expansion of world trade on a multilateral, non-discriminatory basis in accordance with international obligations.

Members. Australia, Austria, Belgium, Canada, Czech Republic, Denmark, Finland, France, Germany, Greece, Hungary, Iceland, Ireland, Italy, Japan, South Korea, Luxembourg, Mexico, Netherlands, New Zealand, Norway, Poland, Portugal, Slovakia, Spain, Sweden, Switzerland, Turkey, UK and USA.

Activities. The OECD's main fields of programming are: economic policy; statistics; energy; development co-operation; sustainable development; public management; international trade; financial, fiscal and enterprise affairs; food, agriculture and fisheries; territorial development; environment; science, technology and industry; biotechnology and biodiversity; electronic commerce; initiatives to fight corruption; regulatory reform; ageing society; education, employment, labour and social affairs. Some short-term priority projects in 2004–05 included corporate governance, education, development issues and structural adjustment.

Relations with non-member countries. Through its *Centre for Co-operation with Non-Members (CCNM)* the OECD maintains co-operative relations with a wide range of transition and emerging market economies covering topics of mutual interest. OECD member country officials and experts engage their non-member counterparts in policy dialogue and conduct peer assessments while sharing each other's policy experiences. Activities with non-OECD economies are grouped around Global Forums in eight policy areas where the OECD has particular expertise and where global dialogue can have an important impact on policy-making. The Global Forums aim to achieve sustained results and to develop stable active networks of policy-makers in OECD member and non-member economies in eight key areas: sustainable development, the knowledge economy, governance, trade, agriculture, taxation, international investment and competition. The regional and country programmes provide for more targeted co-operation with non-OECD economies in Europe and Central Asia; Asia; and South America. There is a general programme for each region, as well as a specific programme for three countries (Russia, China and Brazil). There are also sub-regional programmes for South Eastern Europe and the Baltic region. OECD co-operation with Africa is being strengthened with the New Partnership for Africa's Development (NEPAD). Acting upon the initiative of Middle-Eastern and North African countries (MENA), the OECD has also launched the MENA-OECD Initiative.

Relations with developing countries. The OECD's Development Assistance Committee (DAC) is the principal body through which the Organisation deals with issues related to co-operation with developing countries. OECD member countries are major aid donors, and collectively they account for some 95% of total official development assistance (ODA), which amounted to US$69bn. in 2003. Much of the Organisation's development work is focused on how to spend and invest this aid in the most effective manner, so as to reduce poverty and ensure sustainable development in developing countries. Major developments in 2004 included work on aid effectiveness, security system reform, and preparations for the 2005 'Mutual Review of Development Effectiveness in the context of NEPAD', a consultation arrangement promoting mutual accountability among African nations and their development partners. The Sahel and West Africa Club is an informal forum for analysis, informed debate and action supporting the efforts of West Africans in defining medium and long-term development strategies for the region and advocating and promoting their implementation. It encourages and facilitates analysis, exchanges of views and decisions, both south-south and north-south, in four main areas: medium and long-term development perspectives of the region and new partnerships; agricultural transformation and sustainable development; local development and regional integration; governance, conflict dynamics, peace and security.

Relations with other international organizations. Under a protocol signed at the same time as the OECD Convention, the European Commission takes part in the work of the OECD. EFTA may also send representatives to attend OECD meetings. Formal relations exist with a number of other international organizations, including the ILO, FAO, IMF, IBRD, UNCTAD, IAEA and the Parliamentary Assemblies of the Council of Europe and NATO.

Relations with civil society. A few non-governmental organizations have been granted consultative status enabling them to discuss subjects of common interest and be consulted in a particular field by the relevant OECD Committee or its officers, notably the Business and Industry Advisory Committee to the OECD (BIAC) and the Trade Union Advisory Committee to the OECD (TUAC). Since 2000 the OECD has organized, annually, the OECD Forum, an international public conference, offering business, labour and civil society the opportunity to discuss key issues of the 21st century with government ministers and leaders of international organizations.

Organization. The governing body of OECD is the Council, made up of representatives of each member country and the European Commission. It meets from time to time (usually once a year) at the level of government ministers, with the chairmanship at ministerial level being rotated among member governments. The Council also meets regularly at official level, when it comprises the Secretary-General (chairman) and the Permanent Representatives to OECD (ambassadors who head resident diplomatic missions). It is responsible for all questions of general policy and may establish subsidiary bodies as required to achieve the aims of the organization. Decisions and recommendations of the Council are adopted by consensus of all its members.

The Council is assisted by an Executive Committee which prepares its work and is also called upon to carry out specific tasks where necessary. Apart from its regular meetings, the Executive Committee meets occasionally in special sessions attended by senior governments officials. The greater part of the work of the OECD is prepared and carried out by about 200 specialized bodies (Committees, Working Parties, etc). All members are normally represented on these bodies, except those of a restricted nature. Delegates are usually officials coming either from the capitals of member states or from the Permanent Delegations to the OECD. They are serviced by an international secretariat headed by the OECD Secretary-General. Funding is by contributions from member states, based on a formula related to their size and economy.

The International Energy Agency (IEA), and the Nuclear Energy Agency (NEA) are also part of the OECD system.

Headquarters: 2 rue André Pascal, 75775 Paris Cedex 16, France.
Website: http://www.oecd.org
Secretary-General: Donald J. Johnston (Canada).
Deputy Secretaries-General: Herwig Schlögl (Germany), Richard E. Hecklinger (USA), Berglind Asgeirsdottir (Iceland), Kiyotaka Akasaka (Japan).

Publications include: *OECD Policy Briefs* (20 a year); *OECD Economic Surveys* (by country, 18 titles a year); *Environmental Performance Reviews* (by country); *OECD Economic Outlook* (twice a year); *OECD Agricultural Outlook* (annual); *Education at a Glance* (annual); *OECD Employment Outlook* (annual); *OECD Science, Technology and Industry Outlook* (biennial); *Trends in International Migration* (annual); *OECD Health Data* (CD-ROM; annual); *Financial Market Trends* (twice a year); *Statistics of International Trade* (monthly); *International Trade by Commodity Statistics* (annual); *Main Economic Indicators* (monthly); *Energy Balances* (annual); *World Energy Outlook* (annual); *National Accounts* (quarterly and annual); *Quarterly Labour Force Statistics; Model Tax Convention; African Economic Outlook; Development Centre Policy Briefs.* For a full list of OECD publications, visit the website: http://www.oecd.org/bookshop.

Further Reading

Blair, D. J., *Trade Negotiations in the OECD: Structures, Institutions and States.* London, 1993

ORGANIZATION OF THE ISLAMIC CONFERENCE (OIC)

Founded in 1969, the objectives of the OIC are to promote Islamic solidarity among member states; to consolidate co-operation among member states in the economic, social, cultural, scientific and other vital fields of activities, and to carry out consultations among member states in international organizations; to endeavour to eliminate racial segregation, discrimination and to eradicate colonialism in all its forms; to take the necessary measures to support international peace and security founded on justice; to strengthen the struggle of all Muslim peoples with a view to safeguarding their dignity, independence and national rights; to create a suitable atmosphere for the promotion of co-operation and understanding among member states and other countries.

Members (57 as of March 2005). Afghanistan, Albania, Algeria, Azerbaijan, Bahrain, Bangladesh, Benin, Brunei, Burkina Faso, Cameroon, Chad, Comoros, Côte d'Ivoire, Djibouti, Egypt, Gabon, The Gambia, Guinea, Guinea-Bissau, Guyana, Indonesia, Iran, Iraq, Jordan, Kazakhstan, Kuwait, Kyrgyzstan, Lebanon, Libya, Malaysia, Maldives, Mali, Mauritania, Morocco, Mozambique, Niger, Nigeria, Oman, Pakistan, Palestine, Qatar, Saudi Arabia, Senegal, Sierra Leone, Somalia, Sudan, Suriname, Syria, Tajikistan, Togo, Tunisia, Turkey, Turkmenistan, Uganda, United Arab Emirates, Uzbekistan, Yemen. *Observer states:* Bosnia-Herzegovina, Central African Republic, Thailand.

Headquarters: PO Box 5925, Jeddah, Saudi Arabia.
Website: http://www.oic-un.org
Secretary-General: Dr Ekmeleddin İhsanoğlu (Turkey).

UNREPRESENTED NATIONS AND PEOPLES ORGANIZATION (UNPO)

UNPO is an international organization created by nations and peoples around the world who are not represented in the world's principal international organizations, such as the UN. Founded in 1991, UNPO now has 53 members representing over 100m. people worldwide.

Membership. Open to all nations and peoples unrepresented, subject to adherence to the five principles which form the basis of UNPO's charter: equal right to self-determination of all nations and peoples; adherence to internationally accepted human rights standards; to the principles of democracy; promotion of non-violence; and protection of the environment. Applicants must show that they constitute a 'nation or people' as defined in the Covenant.

Functions and Activities. UNPO offers an international forum for occupied nations, indigenous peoples, minorities and oppressed majorities, who struggle to regain their lost countries, preserve their cultural identities, protect their basic human and economic rights, and safeguard their environment.

It does not represent those peoples; rather it assists and empowers them to represent themselves more effectively. To this end, it provides professional services and facilities as well as education and training in the fields of diplomacy, human rights law, democratic processes, conflict resolution, and environmental protection. Members, private foundations and voluntary contributions fund the Organization.

In total six former members of UNPO (Armenia, Belau, East Timor, Estonia, Georgia and Latvia) subsequently achieved full independence and gained representation in the UN. Belau is now called Palau. Current members Bougainville and Kosovo are progressively achieving self-determination.

Headquarters: 40A Javastraat, NL-2585 AP The Hague, Netherlands.
Website: http://www.unpo.org
General Secretary: Marino Busdachin.

Publication. UNPO News (quarterly).

WORLD CONFEDERATION OF LABOUR (WCL)

Founded in 1920 as the International Federation of Christian Trade Unions, it went out of existence in 1940 as a large proportion of its 3·4m. members were in Italy and Germany, where affiliated unions were suppressed by the Fascist and Nazi regimes. Reconstituted in 1945 and declining to merge with the WFTU or ICFTU, its policy was based on the papal encyclicals *Rerum novarum* (1891) and *Quadragesimo anno* (1931), and in 1968 it became the WCL and dropped its openly confessional approach.

Today, it has Christian, Buddhist and Muslim member confederations, as well as organizations without religious reference. The WCL defines itself as pluralist and humanist. In its concern to defend trade union freedoms and assist trade union development, the WCL differs little in policy from the ICFTU above. A membership of 26m. in 116 countries is claimed. The biggest group is the Confederation of Christian Trade Unions (CSC) of Belgium (1·6m.).

Organization. The WCL is organized on a federative basis which leaves wide discretion to its autonomous constituent unions. Its governing body is the Congress, which meets every four years. The Congress appoints (or re-appoints) the Secretary-General at each four-yearly meeting. The General Council which meets at least once a year, is composed of the members of the Confederal Board (at least 22 members, elected by the Congress) and representatives of national confederations, international trade federations, and trade union organizations where there is no confederation affiliated to the WCL. The Confederal Board is responsible for the general leadership of the WCL, in accordance with the decisions and directives of the Council and Congress. There are regional organizations in Latin America (Caracas), Africa (Lomé) and Asia (Manila), and three liaison offices (Bucharest, Geneva and Washington).

Headquarters: 33 rue de Trèves, Brussels 1040, Belgium.
Website: http://www.cmt-wcl.org
Secretary-General: Willy Thys (Belgium).
President: Basile Mahan Gahé (Côte d'Ivoire).

Publications. Annual Report on Workers Rights; Teleflash (20 a year), *Labor Magazine* (4 a year).

WORLD COUNCIL OF CHURCHES

The World Council of Churches was formally constituted on 23 Aug. 1948 in Amsterdam. Today, member churches number over 340 from more than 120 countries.

Origin. The World Council was founded by the coming together of Christian movements, including the overseas mission groups gathered from 1921 in the International Missionary Council, the Faith and Order Movement, and the Life and Work Movement. On 13 May 1938, at Utrecht, a provisional committee was appointed to prepare for the formation of a World Council of Churches.

Membership. The basis of membership (1975) states: 'The World Council of Churches is a fellowship of Churches which confess the Lord Jesus Christ as God and Saviour according to the Scriptures and therefore seek to fulfil together their common calling to the glory of the one God, Father, Son and Holy Spirit.' Membership is open to Churches which express their agreement with this basis and satisfy such criteria as the Assembly or Central Committee may prescribe. Today, more than 340 Churches of Protestant, Anglican, Orthodox, Old Catholic and Pentecostal confessions belong to this fellowship.

Activities. The WCC's Central Committee comprises the Programme Committee and the Finance Committee. Within the Programme Committee there are advisory groups on issues relating to communication, women, justice, peace and creation, youth, ecumenical relations and inter-religious relations. Following the WCC's 8th General Assembly in Harare, Zimbabwe in 1998 the work of the WCC was restructured. Activities were grouped into four 'clusters'—Relationships; Issues and Themes; Communication; and Finance, Services and Administration. The Relationships cluster comprises four teams (Church and Ecumenical Relations, Regional Relations and Ecumenical Sharing, Inter-Religious Relations and International Relations), as well as two programmes (Action by Churches Together and the Ecumenical Church Loan Fund). The Issues and Themes cluster comprises four teams (Faith and Order; Mission and Evangelism; Justice, Peace and Creation; and Education and Ecumenical Formation).

In Aug. 1997 the WCC launched a Peace to the City campaign, as the initial focus of a programme to overcome violence in troubled cities. The Decade to Overcome Violence was launched in Feb. 2001 during the meeting of the WCC Central Committee in Berlin.

Organization. The governing body of the World Council, consisting of delegates specially appointed by the member Churches, is the Assembly, which meets every seven or eight years to frame policy. It has no legislative powers and depends for the implementation of its decisions upon the action of member Churches. The 9th General Assembly, to be held in Porto Alegre, Brazil in Feb. 2006, will have as its theme 'God, in your grace, transform the world'. A 154-member Central Committee meets annually to carry out the Assembly mandate, with a smaller 25-member Executive Committee meeting twice a year.

Headquarters: PO Box 2100, 150 route de Ferney, 1211 Geneva 2, Switzerland.
Website: http://www.wcc-coe.org
General Secretary: Rev. Dr Samuel Kobia (Kenya).

Publications. Annual Reports; Dictionary of the Ecumenical Movement, Geneva, 1991; *Directory of Christian Councils*, 1985; *A History of the Ecumenical Movement,* Geneva, 1993; *Ecumenical Review* (quarterly); *Ecumenical News International* (weekly); *International Review of Mission* (quarterly).

Further Reading

Castro, E., *A Passion for Unity.* Geneva, 1992
Raiser, K., *Ecumenism in Transition.* Geneva, 1994
Van Elderen, M. and Conway, M., *Introducing the World Council of Churches revised and enlarged edition.* Geneva, 1991

WORLD CUSTOMS ORGANIZATION

Established in 1952 as the Customs Co-operation Council, the World Customs Organization is an intergovernmental body with worldwide membership, whose mission it is to enhance the effectiveness and efficiency of customs administrations throughout the world. It has 164 member countries or territories.

Headquarters: Rue de l'Industrie 26–38, B-1040 Brussels, Belgium.
Website: http://www.wcoomd.org
Secretary-General: Michel Danet (France).

WORLD FEDERATION OF TRADE UNIONS (WFTU)

Origin and History. The WFTU was founded on a worldwide basis in 1945 at the international trade union conferences held in London and Paris, with the participation of all the trade union centres in the countries of the anti-Hitler coalition. The aim was to reunite the world trade union movement at the end of the Second World War. The acute political differences among affiliates, especially the east–west confrontation in Europe on ideological lines, led to a split. A number of affiliated organizations withdrew in 1949 and established the ICFTU. The WFTU now draws its membership from the industrially developing countries like India, Vietnam and other Asian countries, Brazil, Peru, Cuba and other Latin American countries, Syria, Lebanon, Kuwait and other Arab countries, and it has affiliates and associates in more than 20 European countries. It has close relations with the International Confederation of Arab Trade Unions, the Organization of African Trade Union Unity as well as the All-China Federation of Trade Unions, all of which participated at its Congress in New Delhi, India in 2000. Its Trade Unions Internationals (TUIs) have affiliates in Russia, the Czech Republic, Poland and other East European countries, Portugal, France, Spain, Japan and other OECD countries.

The headquarters of the TUIs are situated in Helsinki, New Delhi, Budapest, Mexico, Paris and Moscow. The WFTU and its TUIs have 130m. members, organized in 92 affiliated or associated national federations and six Trade Unions Internationals, in 130 countries. It has regional offices in Athens, New Delhi, Havana, Dakar, Damascus and Moscow and Permanent Representatives accredited to the UN in New York, Geneva, Paris and Rome.

Headquarters: POB 80, Posta 411, 14200 Prague 4, Czech Republic.
Website: http://www.wftu.cz
e-mail: wftu@login.cz
President: K. L. Mahendra (India).
General Secretary: Aleksander Zharikov (Russia).

Publications. Flashes From the Trade Unions (fortnightly, published in English, French, Spanish and Arabic), reports of Congresses, etc.

WORLD WIDE FUND FOR NATURE (WWF)

Origin. WWF was officially formed and registered as a charity on 11 Sept. 1961. The first National Appeal was launched in the United Kingdom on 23 Nov. 1961, shortly followed by the United States and Switzerland.

Organization. WWF is the world's largest and most experienced independent conservation organization with over 4·7m. supporters and a global network of 27 National Organizations, five Associates and 24 Programme Offices.

The National Organizations carry out conservation activities in their own countries and contribute technical expertise and funding to WWF's international conservation programme. The Programme Offices implement WWF's fieldwork, advise national and local governments, and raise public understanding of conservation issues.

Mission. WWF has as its mission preserving genetic, species and ecosystem diversity; ensuring that the use of renewable natural resources is sustainable now and in the longer term, for the benefit of all life on Earth; promoting actions to reduce to a minimum pollution and the wasteful exploitation and consumption of resources and energy. WWF's ultimate goal is to stop, and eventually reverse, the accelerating degradation of our planet's natural environment, and to help build a future in which humans live in harmony with nature.

Address: Avenue du Mont-Blanc, CH–1196 Gland, Switzerland.
Website: http://www.panda.org
Director General: Dr Claude Martin (Switzerland).
President Emeritus: HRH The Prince Philip, Duke of Edinburgh.
President: Chief Emeka Anyaoku (Nigeria).

AFRICAN DEVELOPMENT BANK

Established in 1964 to promote economic and social development in Africa.

Regional Members. (53) Algeria, Angola, Benin, Botswana, Burkina Faso, Burundi, Cameroon, Cape Verde, Central African Republic, Chad, Comoros, Congo (Dem. Rep. of), Congo (Rep. of), Côte d'Ivoire, Djibouti, Egypt, Equatorial Guinea, Eritrea, Ethiopia, Gabon, The Gambia, Ghana, Guinea, Guinea-Bissau, Kenya, Lesotho, Liberia, Libya, Madagascar, Malaŵi, Mali, Mauritania, Mauritius, Morocco, Mozambique, Namibia, Niger, Nigeria, Rwanda, São Tomé e Príncipe, Senegal, Seychelles, Sierra Leone, Somalia, South Africa (Rep. of), Sudan, Swaziland, Tanzania, Togo, Tunisia, Uganda, Zambia, Zimbabwe.

Non-regional Members. (24) Argentina, Austria, Belgium, Brazil, Canada, China, Denmark, Finland, France, Germany, India, Italy, Japan, South Korea, Kuwait, Netherlands, Norway, Portugal, Saudi Arabia, Spain, Sweden, Switzerland, UK, USA.

Within the ADB Group is the African Development Fund, established in 1972, which provides development finance on concessional terms to low-income Regional Member Countries which are unable to borrow on the non-concessional terms of the African Development Bank. Membership of the Fund is made up of 25 non-African State Participants, the African Development Bank and the Nigerian Trust Fund.

Official languages: English, French.
Headquarters: 01 BP 1387, Abidjan 01, Côte d'Ivoire.
Website: http://www.afdb.org
e-mail: afdb@afdb.org
President: Omar Kabbaj (Morocco).

AFRICAN EXPORT–IMPORT BANK (AFREXIMBANK)

Established in 1987 under the auspices of the African Development Bank to facilitate, promote and expand intra-African and extra-African trade. Membership is made up of three categories of shareholders: Class 'A' Shareholders consisting of African governments, African central banks and sub-regional and regional financial institutions and economic organizations; Class 'B' Shareholders consisting of African public and private financial institutions; and Class 'C' Shareholders consisting of international financial institutions, economic organizations and non-African states, banks, financial institutions and public and private investors.

Official languages: English, French, Arabic, Portuguese.
Headquarters: World Trade Center, 1191 Corniche El-Nil, Cairo 11221, Egypt.
Website: http//www.afreximbank.com
President and Chairman to the Board: Christopher C. Edordu.

AFRICAN UNION (AU)

History. The Fourth Extraordinary Session of the Assembly of the Heads of State and Government of the Organization of African Unity (OAU) held in Sirté, Libya on 9 Sept. 1999 decided to establish an African Union. At Lomé, Togo on 11 July 2000 the OAU Assembly of the Heads of State and Government adopted the Constitutive Act of the African Union, which was later ratified by the required two-thirds of the member states of the Organization of African Unity (OAU); it came into force on 26 May 2001. The Lusaka Summit, in July 2001, gave a mandate to translate the transformation of the Organization of African Unity into the African Union, and on 9 July 2002 the Durban Summit, in South Africa, formally launched the African Union.

Aims. The African Union aims to promote unity, solidarity, cohesion and co-operation among the peoples of Africa and African states, and at the same time to co-ordinate efforts by African people to realize their goals of achieving economic, political and social integration.

Activities. The African Union became fully operational in July 2002, and is working towards establishing 17 organs among which are a Pan-African parliament and a Peace and Security Council (both of which have now been inaugurated), the Economic, Social and Cultural Council (ECOSOC), a Central Bank and a Court of Justice.

Official languages: Arabic, English, French, Ki-Swahili, Portuguese and Spanish.
Headquarters: POB 3243, Addis Ababa, Ethiopia.
Website: http://www.africa-union.org
Chairman: Alpha Oumar Konane (Mali).

BANK OF CENTRAL AFRICAN STATES (BEAC)

The Bank of Central African States (Banque des Etats de l'Afrique Centrale) was established in 1973 when a new Convention of Monetary Co-operation with France was signed. The five original members, Cameroon, Central African Republic, Chad, Republic of the Congo and Gabon, were joined by Equatorial Guinea in 1985. Under its Convention and statutes, the BEAC is declared a 'Multinational African institution in the management and control of which France participates in return for the guarantee she provides for its currency'.

Official language: French.
Headquarters: Avenue Monseigneur Vogt, Yaoundé, Cameroon.
Website: http://www.beac.int
Governor: Jean-Félix Mamalepot.

Publications. Etudes et Statistiques (monthly bulletins); *Annual Report*; *Directory of Banks and Financial Establishments of BEAC Monetary Area* (annual); *Bulletin du Marché Monétaire* (monthly bulletins); *Annual Report of the Banking Commission.*

CENTRAL BANK OF WEST AFRICAN STATES (BCEAO)

Established in 1962, the Central Bank of West African States (Banque Centrale des Etats de l'Afrique de l'Ouest) is the common central bank of the eight member states which form the West African Monetary Union (WAMU). It has the sole right of currency issue throughout the Union territory and is responsible for the pooling of the Union's foreign exchange reserve; the management of the monetary policy of the member states; the keeping of the accounts of the member states treasury; and the definition of the banking law applicable to banks and financial establishments.

Members. Benin, Burkina Faso, Côte d'Ivoire, Guinea-Bissau, Mali, Niger, Senegal, Togo.

Official language: French.
Headquarters: Avenue Abdoulaye Fadiga, Dakar, Senegal.
Website: http://www.bceao.int
Governor: Charles Konan Banny.

Publications. Rapport annuel (annual); *Annuaire des Banques* (annual); *Bilan des Banques U.M.O.A.* (annual); *Notes d'information et statistiques* (monthly bulletin).

COMMON MARKET FOR EASTERN AND SOUTHERN AFRICA (COMESA)

COMESA is an African economic grouping of 19 member states who are committed to the creation of a Common Market for Eastern and Southern Africa. It was established in 1994 as a building block for the African Economic Community and replaced the Preferential Trade Area for Eastern and Southern Africa, which had been in existence since 1981.

Members. Angola, Burundi, Comoros, Democratic Republic of Congo, Djibouti, Egypt, Eritrea, Ethiopia, Kenya, Madagascar, Malaŵi, Mauritius, Rwanda, Seychelles, Sudan, Swaziland, Uganda, Zambia and Zimbabwe.

Objectives. To facilitate the removal of the structural and institutional weaknesses of member states so that they are able to attain collective and sustainable development.

Activities. COMESA's Free Trade Area (FTA) was launched on 31 Oct. 2000 at a Summit of Heads of States and Government in Lusaka, Zambia. The FTA participating states have zero tariff on goods and services produced in these countries.

In addition to creating the policy environment for freeing trade, COMESA has also created specialized institutions like the Eastern and Southern African Trade and Development Bank (PTA Bank), the PTA Reinsurance Company (ZEP-RE), the Clearing House and the COMESA Court of Justice, to provide the required financial infrastructure and service support. COMESA has also promoted a political risk guarantee scheme, the Africa Trade Insurance Agency (ATI), a Leather and Leather Products Institute (LLPI), as well as a cross-border insurance scheme, the COMESA Yellow Card.

Official languages: English, French, Portuguese.
Headquarters: COMESA Secretariat, COMESA Centre, Ben Bella Road, PO Box 30051, 10101 Lusaka, Zambia.
Website: http://www.comesa.int
Secretary General: Erastus Mwencha (Kenya).

EAST AFRICAN COMMUNITY

The East African Community (EAC) was formally established on 30 Nov. 1999 with the signing in Arusha, Tanzania of the Treaty for the Establishment of the East African Community. The Treaty envisages the establishment of a Customs Union, as the entry point of the Community, a Common Market, subsequently a Monetary Union and ultimately a Political Federation of the East African States. In Nov. 2003 the EAC partner states signed a Protocol on the Establishment of the East African Customs Union, which came into force on 1 Jan. 2005.

Members. Kenya, Tanzania, Uganda.

Website: http://www.eac.int
Headquarters: PO Box 1096, Arusha, Tanzania.
Secretary General: Nuwe Amanya-Mushega (Uganda).

EAST AFRICAN DEVELOPMENT BANK (EADB)

Established originally under the Treaty for East African Co-operation in 1967 with Kenya, Tanzania and Uganda as signatories, a new Charter for the Bank (with the same signatories) came into force in 1980. Under the original Treaty the Bank was confined to the provision of financial and technical assistance for the promotion of industrial development in member states but with the new Charter its remit was broadened to include involvement in agriculture, forestry, tourism, transport and the development of infrastructure, with preference for projects which promote regional co-operation.

Official language: English.
Headquarters: 4 Nile Avenue, Kampala, Uganda.
Website: http://www.eadb.org
Chairman of the Board: Christopher Kassami (Uganda).

ECONOMIC COMMUNITY OF CENTRAL AFRICAN STATES (CEEAC)

The Economic Community of Central African States (Communauté Economique des Etats de l'Afrique Centrale) was established in 1983 to promote regional economic co-operation and to establish a Central African Common Market. Plans were announced in Jan. 2004 for a free trade zone to be set up by the end of 2007.

Members. Angola, Burundi, Cameroon, Central African Republic, Chad, Democratic Republic of the Congo, Republic of the Congo, Equatorial Guinea, Gabon, Rwanda, São Tomé e Príncipe.

Headquarters: BP 2112, Libreville, Gabon.
Website: http://www.ceeac.eccas.org
President: Denis Sassou-Nguesso (Republic of the Congo).
Secretary-General: Louis Sylvain-Goma (Republic of the Congo).

ECONOMIC COMMUNITY OF WEST AFRICAN STATES (ECOWAS)

Founded in 1975 as a regional common market, and now aiming to operate a single currency zone by the end of 2005, ECOWAS later also became a political forum involved in the promotion of a democratic environment and the pursuit of fundamental human rights. In July 1993 it revised its treaty to assume responsibility for the regulation of regional armed conflicts, acknowledging the inextricable link between development and peace and security. Thus it now has a new role in conflict management and prevention through its Mediation and Security Council, which monitors the moratorium on the export, import and manufacture of light weapons and ammunition. However, it still retains a military arm, ECOMOG. It is also involved in the war against drug abuse and illicit drug trafficking.

Members. Benin, Burkina Faso, Cape Verde, Côte d'Ivoire, The Gambia, Ghana, Guinea, Guinea-Bissau, Liberia, Mali, Niger, Nigeria, Senegal, Sierra Leone, Togo.

Organization. It meets at yearly summits which rotate in the different capitals of member states. The institution is governed by the Council of Ministers, and has a secretariat in Abuja which is run by an Executive Secretary.

Official languages: English, French, Portuguese.
Headquarters: 60 Yakubu Gowon Crescent, Asokoro, Abuja, Nigeria.
Website: http://www.ecowas.int
e-mail: info@ecowasmail.net
Executive Secretary: Mohamed Ibn Chambas (Ghana).

INTERGOVERNMENTAL AUTHORITY ON DEVELOPMENT

The Intergovernmental Authority on Development was created on 21 March 1996 and has its origins in the Intergovernmental Authority on Drought and Development, which had been established in 1986. It has three priority areas of co-operation: conflict prevention, management and humanitarian affairs; infrastructure development; food security and environment protection.

Members. Djibouti, Eritrea, Ethiopia, Kenya, Somalia, Sudan, Uganda.

Website: http://www.igad.org
Headquarters: PO Box 2653, Djibouti, Republic of Djibouti.
Executive Secretary: Dr Attalla Hamad Bashir (Sudan).

LAKE CHAD BASIN COMMISSION

Established by a Convention and Statute signed on 22 May 1964 by Cameroon, Chad, Niger and Nigeria, and later by the Central African Republic, to regulate and control utilization of the water and other natural resources in the Basin (Sudan has also been admitted as an observer); to initiate, promote and co-ordinate natural resources development projects and research within the Basin area; and to examine complaints and promote settlement of disputes, with a view to promoting regional co-operation.

In Dec. 1977, at Enugu in Nigeria, the 3rd summit of heads of state of the commission signed the protocol for the Harmonization of the Regulations Relating to Fauna and Flora in member countries, and adopted plans for the multi-donor approach towards major integrated development for the conventional basin. An international campaign to save Lake Chad following a report on the environmental degradation of the conventional basin was launched by heads of state at the 8th summit of the Commission in Abuja in March 1994. The 10th summit, held in N'Djaména in 2000, saw agreement on a US$1m. inter-basin water transfer project.

The Commission operates an annual budget of 1bn. Francs CFA, and receives assistance from various international and donor agencies including the FAO, and UN Development and Environment Programmes.

Official languages: English, French.
Headquarters: BP 727, N'Djaména, Chad.
Website: http://www.cblt.org
e-mail: lcbc@intnet.td
Executive Secretary: Engr. Muhammad Sani Adamu.

NIGER BASIN AUTHORITY

As a result of a special meeting of the Niger River Commission (established in 1964), to discuss the revitalizing and restructuring of the organization to improve its efficiency, the Niger Basin Authority was established in 1980. Its responsibilities cover the harmonization and co-ordination of national development policies; the formulation of the general development policy of the Basin; the elaboration and implementation of an integrated development plan of the Basin; the initiation and monitoring of an orderly and rational regional policy for the utilization of the waters of the Niger River; the design and conduct of studies, researches and surveys; the formulation of plans, the construction, exploitation and maintenance of structure, and the elaboration of projects.

Members. Benin, Burkina Faso, Cameroon, Chad, Côte d'Ivoire, Guinea, Mali, Niger, Nigeria.

Official languages: English, French.
Website: http://www.abn.ne
Headquarters: BP 729, Niamey, Niger.
Executive Secretary: Muhammad Bello Tuga.

SOUTHERN AFRICAN DEVELOPMENT COMMUNITY (SADC)

The Southern African Development Co-ordination Conference (SADCC), the precursor of the Southern African Development Community (SADC), was formed in Lusaka, Zambia on 1 April 1980, following the adoption of the Lusaka Declaration—*Southern Africa: Towards Economic Liberation*—by the nine founding member states.

Members. The nine founder member countries were Angola, Botswana, Lesotho, Malaŵi, Mozambique, Swaziland, Tanzania, Zambia and Zimbabwe. The Democratic Republic of the Congo, Mauritius, Namibia, the Seychelles and South Africa have since joined. However, the Seychelles left in July 2004. As a result there are now 13 members.

Aims and Activities. SADC's Common Agenda includes the following: the promotion of sustainable and equitable economic growth and socio-economic development that will ensure poverty alleviation with the ultimate objective of its eradication; the promotion of common political values, systems and other shared values that are transmitted through institutions that are democratic, legitimate and effective; and the consolidation and maintenance of democracy, peace and security.

In contrast to the country-based co-ordination of sectoral activities and programmes, SADC has now adopted a more centralized approach through which the 21 sectoral programmes are grouped into four clusters; namely: Trade, Industry, Finance and Investment; Infrastructure and Services; Food, Agriculture, and Natural Resources; Social and Human Development and Special Programmes.

SADC has made significant progress in implementing its integration agenda since the 1992 Treaty came into force. Since then, 23 Protocols to spearhead the sectoral programmes and activities have been signed. The following protocols have entered into force: Immunities and Privileges; Combating Illicit Drug Trafficking; Energy; Transport, Communications and Meteorology; Shared Watercourse Systems; Mining; Trade; Education and Training; Development of Tourism; Health, Wildlife Conservation and Law Enforcement; Tribunal and the Rules of Procedure; Revised Protocol on Shared Watercourses; Amendment Protocol on Trade; Politics, Defense and Security Co-operation; Control of Firearms, Ammunition and Other Related Materials in SADC; Fisheries.

Official languages: English, French, Portuguese.

Headquarters: Private Bag 0095, Gaborone, Botswana.
Website: http://www.sadc.int
e-mail: registry@sadc.int
Executive Secretary: Dr Prega Ramsamy (Mauritius).

WEST AFRICAN DEVELOPMENT BANK (BOAD)

The West African Development Bank (Banque Ouest Africaine de Développement) was established in Nov. 1973 by an Agreement signed by the member states of the West African Monetary Union (UMOA), now the West African Economic and Monetary Union (UEMOA).

Aims. To promote balanced development of the States of the Union and to achieve West African economic integration.

Members. Benin, Burkina Faso, Côte d'Ivoire, Guinea-Bissau, Mali, Niger, Senegal, Togo.

Official language: French.
Headquarters: 68 Avenue de la Libération, Lomé, Togo.
Website: http://www.boad.org
e-mail: boadsiege@boad.org
President: Boni Yayi (Benin).

WEST AFRICAN ECONOMIC AND MONETARY UNION (UEMOA)

Founded in 1994, the UEMOA (Union Economique et Monétaire Ouest Africaine) aims to reinforce the competitiveness of the economic and financial activities of member states in the context of an open and rival market and a rationalized and harmonized juridical environment; to ensure the convergence of the macro-economic performances and policies of member states; to create a common market among member states; to institute a co-ordination for the national sector-based policies; and to harmonize the legislation, especially the fiscal system, of the member states.

Members. Benin, Burkina Faso, Côte d'Ivoire, Guinea-Bissau, Mali, Niger, Senegal, Togo.

Headquarters: 01 B.P. 543, Ouagadougou 01, Burkina Faso.
Website: http://www.uemoa.int
President: Soumaïla Cisse (Mali).

AGENCY FOR THE PROHIBITION OF NUCLEAR WEAPONS IN LATIN AMERICA AND THE CARIBBEAN (OPANAL)

The Agency (Organismo para la Proscripción de las Armas Nucleares en la América Latina y el Caribe) was established following the Cuban missile crisis to guarantee implementation of the world's first Nuclear-Weapon-Free-Zone (NWFZ) in the region. Created by the Treaty of Tlatelolco (1967), OPANAL is an inter-governmental agency responsible for ensuring that the requirements of the Treaty are enforced. OPANAL has played a major role in establishing other NWFZs throughout the world.

Organization. The Agency consists of three main bodies: the General Conference which meets for biennial sessions and special sessions when deemed necessary; the Council of OPANAL consisting of five member states which meet every two months plus special meetings when necessary; and the Secretariat General.

Members of the Treaty. Antigua and Barbuda, Argentina, Bahamas, Barbados, Belize, Bolivia, Brazil, Chile, Colombia, Costa Rica, Cuba, Dominica, Dominican Republic, Ecuador, El Salvador, Grenada, Guatemala, Guyana, Haiti, Honduras, Jamaica, Mexico, Nicaragua, Panama, Paraguay, Peru, St Kitts and Nevis, St Lucia, St Vincent and the Grenadines, Suriname, Trinidad and Tobago, Uruguay, Venezuela.

Headquarters: Schiller No. 326, 5th Floor, Col. Chapultepec Morales, México, D. F. 11570, Mexico.
Website: http://www.opanal.org
e-mail: info@opanal.org
Secretary-General: Edmundo Vargas Carreño (Chile).

ANDEAN COMMUNITY

On 26 May 1969 an agreement was signed by Bolivia, Chile, Colombia, Ecuador and Peru establishing the Cartagena Agreement (also referred to as the Andean Pact or the Andean Group). Chile withdrew from the Group in 1976. Venezuela, which was actively involved, did not sign the agreement until 1973. In 1997 Peru announced its withdrawal for five years.

The Andean Free Trade Area came into effect on 1 Feb. 1993 as the first step towards the creation of a common market. Bolivia, Colombia, Ecuador and Venezuela have fully liberalized their trade, while Peru aims at liberalization by the end of 2005. A Common External Tariff for imports from third countries has been in effect since 1 Feb. 1995.

In March 1996 at the Group's 8th summit in Trujillo in Peru, member countries (Bolivia, Colombia, Ecuador, Peru, Venezuela) set up the Andean Community, to promote greater economic, commercial and political integration between member countries under a new Andean Integration System (SAI).

The member countries and bodies of the Andean Integration System are now working to establish an Andean Common Market by Dec. 2005 and to implement a Common Foreign Policy, a social agenda, a Community policy on border integration, and policies for achieving joint macroeconomic targets.

Organization. The Andean Presidential Council, composed of the presidents of the member states, is the highest-level body of the Andean Integration System (SAI). The Commission and the Andean Council of Foreign Ministers are legislative bodies. The General Secretariat is the executive body and the Andean Parliament is the deliberative body of the SAI. The Court of Justice, which began operating in 1984, resolves disputes between members and interprets legislation. The SAI has other institutions: Andean Development Corporation (CAF), Latin American Reserve Fund (FLAR), Simon Bolivar Andean University, Andean Business Advisory Council, Andean Labour Advisory Council and various Social Agreements.

Further to the treaty signed by 12 South American countries in Dec. 2004, the Andean Community will gradually be integrated into the new South American Community of Nations.

Official language: Spanish.
Headquarters: Avda Paseo de la República 3895, San Isidro, Lima 17, Peru.
Website: http://www.comunidadandina.org
e-mail: contacto@comunidadandina.org
Secretary-General: Allan Wagner Tizón (Peru).

ASSOCIATION OF CARIBBEAN STATES (ACS)

The Convention establishing the ACS was signed on 24 July 1994 in Cartagena de Indias, Colombia, with the aim of promoting consultation, co-operation and concerted action among all the countries of the Caribbean, comprising 25 full member states and three associate members. A total of eight other non-independent Caribbean countries are eligible for associate membership.

Members. Antigua and Barbuda, Bahamas, Barbados, Belize, Colombia, Costa Rica, Cuba, Dominica, Dominican Republic, El Salvador, Grenada, Guatemala, Guyana, Haiti, Honduras, Jamaica, Mexico, Nicaragua, Panama, St Kitts and Nevis, St Lucia, St Vincent and the Grenadines, Suriname, Trinidad and Tobago, Venezuela.

Associate members. Aruba, France (on behalf of French Guiana, Guadeloupe and Martinique) and the Netherlands Antilles.

The CARICOM Secretariat, the Latin American Economic System (SELA), the Central American Integration System (SICA) and the Permanent Secretariat of the General Agreement on Central American Economic Integration (SIECA) were declared Founding Observers of the ACS in 1996. The United Nations Economic Commission for Latin America and the Caribbean (ECLAC) and the Caribbean Tourism Organization (CTO) were admitted as Founding Observers in 2000 and 2001 respectively.

Functions. The objectives of the ACS are enshrined in the Convention and are based on the following: the strengthening of the regional co-operation and integration process, with a view to creating an enhanced economic space in the region; preserving the environmental integrity of the Caribbean Sea which is regarded as the common patrimony of the peoples of the region; and promoting the sustainable development of the Greater Caribbean. Its current focal areas are trade, transport, sustainable tourism and natural disasters.

Organization. The main organs of the Association are the Ministerial Council and the Secretariat. There are Special Committees on: Trade Development and External Economic Relations; Sustainable Tourism; Transport; Natural Disasters; Budget and Administration. There is also a Council of National Representatives of the Special Fund responsible for overseeing resource mobilization efforts and project development.

Headquarters: ACS Secretariat, 5–7 Sweet Briar Road, St Clair, PO Box 660, Port of Spain, Trinidad and Tobago.
Website: http://www.acs-aec.org
e-mail: mail@acs-aec.org
Secretary-General: Dr Rubén Arturo Silié Valdez (Dominican Republic).

CARIBBEAN COMMUNITY (CARICOM)

Origin. The Treaty of Chaguaramas establishing the Caribbean Community and Common Market was signed by the prime ministers of Barbados, Guyana, Jamaica and Trinidad and Tobago at Chaguaramas, Trinidad, on 4 July 1973.

Six additional countries and territories (Belize, Dominica, Grenada, St Lucia, St Vincent and the Grenadines, Montserrat) signed the Treaty on 17 April 1974, and the Treaty came into effect for those countries on 1 May 1974. Antigua acceded to membership on 4 July that year; St Kitts and Nevis on 26 July; the Bahamas on 4 July 1983 (not Common Market); Suriname on 4 July 1995.

Members. Antigua and Barbuda, Bahamas, Barbados, Belize, Dominica, Grenada, Guyana, Haiti, Jamaica, Montserrat, St Kitts and Nevis, St Lucia, St Vincent and the Grenadines, Suriname, and Trinidad and Tobago. Anguilla, Bermuda, the British Virgin Islands, Cayman Islands and Turks and Caicos Islands are associate members.

Objectives. The Caribbean Community has the following objectives: improved standards of living and work; full employment of labour and other factors of production; accelerated, co-ordinated and sustained economic development and convergence; expansion of trade and economic relations with third States; enhanced levels of international competitiveness; organization for increased production and productivity; the achievement of a greater measure of economic leverage and effectiveness of member states in dealing with third States, groups of States and entities of any description; enhanced co-ordination of member states' foreign and foreign economic policies; enhanced functional co-operation.

At its 20th Meeting in July 1999 the Conference of Heads of Government of the Caribbean Community approved for signature the agreement establishing the Caribbean Court of Justice. They mandated the establishment of a Preparatory Committee comprising the Attorneys General of Barbados, Guyana, Jamaica, St Kitts and Nevis, St Lucia and Trinidad and Tobago assisted by other officials, to develop and implement a programme of public education within the Caribbean Community and to make appropriate arrangements for the inauguration of the Caribbean Court of Justice prior to the establishment of the CARICOM Single Market and Economy. To this end at its 23rd Meeting in July 2002 the Heads of Government agreed on immediate measures to inaugurate the Court by the second half of 2003, although delays meant it was not inaugurated until April 2005. Among the measures adopted was the establishment of a Trust Fund with a one-time settlement of US$100m. to finance the Court. The President of the Caribbean Development Bank was authorized to raise the funds on international capital markets, so that member states could access these funds to meet their assessed contributions towards the financing of the Court. The agreement establishing the Regional Justice Protection Programme was also approved for signature. The agreement establishes a framework for regional co-operation in the protection of witnesses, jurors, judicial and legal officers, law enforcement personnel and their associates.

Structure. The Conference of Heads of Government is the principal organ of the Community, and its primary responsibility is to determine and provide the policy direction for the Community. It is the final authority on behalf of the Community for the conclusion of treaties and for entering into relationships between the Community and international organizations and States. It is responsible for financial arrangements to meet the expenses of the Community.

The Community Council of Ministers is the second highest organ of the Community and consists of Ministers of Government responsible for Community Affairs. The Community Council has primary responsibility for the development of Community strategic planning and co-ordination in the areas of economic integration, functional co-operation and external relations.

The Secretariat is the principal administrative organ of the Community. The Secretary-General is appointed by the Conference (on the recommendation of the Community Council) for a term not exceeding five years, and may be re-appointed. The Secretary-General is the Chief Executive Officer of the Community and acts in that capacity at all meetings of the Community Organs.

Associate Institutions. Caribbean Development Bank (CDB); University of Guyana (UG); University of the West Indies (UWI); Caribbean Law Institute (CLI)/ Caribbean Law Institute Centre (CLIC); Secretariat of the Organisation of Eastern Caribbean States.

Official language: English.
Headquarters: Bank of Guyana Building, PO Box 10827, Georgetown, Guyana.
Website: http://www.caricom.org
Secretary-General: Edwin W. Carrington (Trinidad and Tobago).

Publications. CARICOM Perspective (1 a year); *Annual Report; Treaty Establishing the Caribbean Community; Caribbean Trade and Investment Report 2000.*

Further Reading

Parry, J. H., *et. al. A Short History of the West Indies.* Rev. ed. London, 1987

CARIBBEAN DEVELOPMENT BANK (CDB)

Established in 1969 by 16 regional and two non-regional members. Membership is open to all states and territories of the region and to non-regional states which are members of the UN or its Specialized Agencies or of the International Atomic Energy Agency.

Members—regional countries and territories: Anguilla, Antigua and Barbuda, Bahamas, Barbados, Belize, British Virgin Islands, Cayman Islands, Colombia, Dominica, Grenada, Guyana, Jamaica, Mexico, Montserrat, St Kitts and Nevis, St Lucia, St Vincent and the Grenadines, Trinidad and Tobago, Turks and Caicos Islands, Venezuela. *Non-regional countries:* Canada, China, Germany, Italy, United Kingdom.

Function. To contribute to the economic growth and development of the member countries of the Caribbean and promote economic co-operation and integration among them, with particular regard to the needs of the less developed countries.

Headquarters: PO Box 408, Wildey, St Michael, Barbados.
Website: http://www.caribank.org
e-mail: info@caribank.org
President: Dr Compton Bourne (Guyana).

Publications. Annual Report; Basic Information; Caribbean Development Bank: Its Purpose, Role and Functions; Summary of Proceedings of Annual Meetings of Board of Governors; Statements by the President; Financial Policies; Guidelines for Procurement; Procedures for the Selection and Engagement of Consultants by Recipients of CDB Financing; Special Development Fund Rules; Sector Policy Papers; CDB News (newsletter).

CENTRAL AMERICAN BANK FOR ECONOMIC INTEGRATION (BCIE)

Established in 1960, the Bank is the financial institution of the Central American Economic Integration and aims to implement the economic integration and balanced economic growth of the member states.

Members. (Regional) Costa Rica, El Salvador, Guatemala, Honduras, Nicaragua. (Non-regional) Argentina, China, Colombia, Mexico, Spain.

Official languages: Spanish, English.
Headquarters: Apartado Postal 772, Tegucigalpa, DC, Honduras.
Website: http://www.bcie.org
President: Dr Harry Brautigam (Nicaragua).

CENTRAL AMERICAN COMMON MARKET (CACM)

In Dec. 1960 El Salvador, Guatemala, Honduras and Nicaragua concluded the General Treaty of Central American Economic Integration under the auspices of the Organization of Central American States (ODECA) in Managua. Long-standing political and social conflicts in the area have repeatedly dogged efforts to establish integration towards the establishment of a common market.

Members. Costa Rica, El Salvador, Guatemala, Honduras and Nicaragua.

A protocol to the 1960 General Treaty signed by all five members and Panama in Oct. 1993 reaffirmed an eventual commitment to full economic integration with a common external tariff of 20% to be introduced only voluntarily and gradually.

A Treaty on Democratic Security in Central America was signed by all six members at San Pedro Sula, Honduras in Dec. 1995, with a view to achieving a proper 'balance of forces' in the region, intensifying the fight against trafficking of drugs and arms, and reintegrating refugees and displaced persons.

In addition, the CACM countries signed a new framework co-operation agreement with the EC in Feb. 1993, revising the previous (1985) failing agreement between them, to provide support to CACM's integration plans.

Headquarters: 4a Avenida 10–25, Zona 14, Ciudad de Guatemala, Guatemala.
Secretary-General: Haroldo Rodas Melgar (Guatemala).

EASTERN CARIBBEAN CENTRAL BANK (ECCB)

The Eastern Caribbean Central Bank was established in 1983, replacing the East Caribbean Currency Authority (ECCA). Its purpose is to regulate the availability of money and credit; to promote and maintain monetary stability; to promote credit and exchange conditions and a sound financial structure conducive to the balanced growth and development of the economies of the territories of the participating Governments; and to actively promote, through means consistent with its other objectives, the economic development of the territories of the participating Governments.

Members. Anguilla, Antigua and Barbuda, Dominica, Grenada, Montserrat, St Kitts and Nevis, St Lucia, St Vincent and the Grenadines.

Official language: English.
Headquarters: PO Box 89, Bird Rock, Basseterre, St Kitts and Nevis.
Website: http://www.eccb-centralbank.org/
e-mail: eccbinfo@caribsurf.com
Governor: Sir Dwight Venner (St Vincent and the Grenadines).

INTER-AMERICAN DEVELOPMENT BANK (IDB)

The IDB, the oldest and largest regional multilateral development institution, was established in 1959 to help accelerate economic and social development in Latin America and the Caribbean. The Bank's original membership included 19 Latin American and Caribbean countries and the USA. Today, membership totals 46 nations, including non-regional members.

Members. Argentina, Austria, Bahamas, Barbados, Belgium, Belize, Bolivia, Brazil, Canada, Chile, Colombia, Costa Rica, Croatia, Denmark, Dominican Republic, Ecuador, El Salvador, Finland, France, Germany, Guatemala, Guyana, Haiti, Honduras, Israel, Italy, Jamaica, Japan, Mexico, the Netherlands, Nicaragua, Norway, Panama, Paraguay, Peru, Portugal, Slovenia, Spain, Suriname, Sweden, Switzerland, Trinidad and Tobago, UK, USA, Uruguay, Venezuela.

The Bank's total lending up to 2000 has been US$106bn. for projects with a total cost of over US$263bn. Its lending has increased dramatically from the US$294m. approved in 1961 to US$6,311m. in 2002.

Current lending priorities include poverty reduction and social equity, modernization and integration, and the environment. The Bank has a Fund for Special Operations for lending on concessional terms for projects in countries classified as economically less developed. An additional facility, the Multilateral Investment Fund (MIF), was created in 1992 to help promote and accelerate investment reforms and private-sector development throughout the region.

The Board of Governors is the Bank's highest authority. Governors are usually Ministers of Finance, Presidents of Central Banks or officers of comparable rank. The IDB has country offices in each of its borrowing countries, and in Paris and Tokyo.

Official languages: English, French, Portuguese, Spanish.
Headquarters: 1300 New York Avenue, NW, Washington, D.C., 20577, USA.
Website: http://www.iadb.org
President: Enrique V. Iglesias (Uruguay).

LATIN AMERICAN ECONOMIC SYSTEM (SELA)

Established in 1975 by the Panama Convention, SELA (Sistema Económico Latinoamericano) promotes co-ordination on economic issues and social development among the countries of Latin America and the Caribbean.

Members. Argentina, Bahamas, Barbados, Belize, Bolivia, Brazil, Chile, Colombia, Costa Rica, Cuba, Dominican Republic, Ecuador, El Salvador, Grenada, Guatemala, Guyana, Haiti, Honduras, Jamaica, Mexico, Nicaragua, Panama, Paraguay, Peru, Suriname, Trinidad and Tobago, Uruguay, Venezuela.

Official languages: English, French, Portuguese, Spanish.
Headquarters: Apartado 17035, Caracas 1010–4, Venezuela.
Website: http://www.sela.org
e-mail: difusion@sela.org
Permanent Secretary: Roberto Guarnieri (Venezuela).

Publications. Capitulos (in Spanish and English, published thrice yearly); *SELA Antenna in the United States* (quarterly bulletin); *Integration Bulletin on Latin America and the Caribbean* (monthly).

LATIN AMERICAN INTEGRATION ASSOCIATION (ALADI/LAIA)

The ALADI was established to promote freer trade among member countries in the region.

Members. (12) Argentina, Bolivia, Brazil, Chile, Colombia, Cuba, Ecuador, Mexico, Paraguay, Peru, Uruguay and Venezuela.

Observers. (22) Andean Development Corporation (CAF), China, Commission of the European Communities, Costa Rica, Dominican Republic, El Salvador, Guatemala, Honduras, Inter-American Development Bank, Inter-American Institute for Cooperation on Agriculture (IICA), Italy, Latin American Economic System (SELA), Nicaragua, Organization of American States, Panama, Portugal, Romania, Russia, Spain, Switzerland, UN Development Programme, UN Economic Commission for Latin America and the Caribbean (ECLAC).

Official languages: Portuguese, Spanish.
Headquarters: Calle Cebollatí 1461, Casilla de Correos 20005, 11200 Montevideo, Uruguay.
Website: http://www.aladi.org
Secretary-General: Juan Francisco Rojas Penso (Venezuela).

LATIN AMERICAN RESERVE FUND

Established in 1991 as successor to the Andean Reserve Fund, the Latin American Reserve Fund assists in correcting payment imbalances through loans with terms of up to four years and guarantees extended to members, to co-ordinate their monetary, exchange and financial policies and to promote the liberalization of trade and payments in the Andean sub-region.

Members. Bolivia, Colombia, Costa Rica, Ecuador, Peru, Venezuela.

Official language: Spanish.
Headquarters: Edificio Banco de Occidente, Carrera 13, No. 27–47, Piso 10, Santafe de Bogota, DC, Colombia.
Website: http://www.flar.net
Executive President: Julio Velarde (Peru).

ORGANIZATION OF AMERICAN STATES (OAS)

Origin. On 14 April 1890 representatives of the American republics, meeting in Washington at the First International Conference of American States, established an International Union of American Republics and, as its central office, a Commercial Bureau of American Republics, which later became the Pan-American Union. This international organization's object was to foster mutual understanding and co-operation among the nations of the western hemisphere. This led to the adoption on 30 April 1948 by the Ninth International Conference of American States, at Bogotá, Colombia, of the Charter of the Organization of American States. This co-ordinated the work of all the former independent official entities in the inter-American system and defined their mutual relationships. The Charter of 1948 was subsequently amended by the Protocol of Buenos Aires (1967) and the Protocol of Cartagena de Indias (1985).

Members. This is on a basis of absolute equality, with each country having one vote and there being no veto power. Members (2004): Antigua and Barbuda, Argentina, Bahamas, Barbados, Belize, Bolivia, Brazil, Canada, Chile, Colombia, Costa Rica, Cuba (suspended 1962), Dominica, Dominican Republic, Ecuador, El Salvador, Grenada, Guatemala, Guyana, Haiti, Honduras, Jamaica, Mexico, Nicaragua, Panama, Paraguay, Peru, St Kitts and Nevis, St Lucia, St Vincent and the Grenadines, Suriname, Trinidad and Tobago, USA, Uruguay, Venezuela.

Permanent Observers. Algeria, Angola, Armenia, Austria, Azerbaijan, Belgium, Bosnia-Herzegovina, Bulgaria, Croatia, Cyprus, Czech Republic, Denmark, Egypt, Equatorial Guinea, Estonia, EU, Finland, France, Georgia, Germany, Ghana, Greece,

Holy See, Hungary, India, Ireland, Israel, Italy, Japan, Kazakhstan, South Korea, Latvia, Lebanon, Morocco, the Netherlands, Norway, Pakistan, Philippines, Poland, Portugal, Qatar, Romania, Russia, Saudi Arabia, Serbia and Montenegro, Slovakia, Spain, Sri Lanka, Sweden, Switzerland, Thailand, Tunisia, Turkey, UK, Ukraine, Yemen.

Aims and Activities. To strengthen the peace and security of the continent; promote and consolidate representative democracy, with due respect for the principle of non-intervention; prevent possible causes of difficulties and ensure the peaceful settlement of disputes among member states; provide for common action in the event of aggression; seek the solution of political, juridical and economic problems; promote by co-operative action economic, social and cultural development; and achieve an effective limitation of conventional weapons.

The Santiago Commitment to Democracy and the Renewal of the Inter-American System. With the emergence of democratically elected governments throughout the continent, the OAS has been increasingly concerned with the preservation, protection and promotion of democracy. At its 21st Regular Session (Santiago, Chile, 1991) the OAS General Assembly adopted the Santiago Commitment to Democracy and the Renewal of the Inter-American System as well as the Protocol of Washington (1992) to amend the Charter by provisions of the Resolution 1080 on representative democracy.

Declaration of Belém do Pará. At its 24th Regular Session (June 1994, Belém do Pará), the General Assembly adopted the Declaration of Belém do Pará, in which the ministers of foreign affairs and heads of delegation of member states declared their commitment to strengthening the OAS as the main hemispheric forum of political consensus, so that it may support: the realization of the aspirations of member states in promoting and consolidating peace, democracy, social justice, and development; their decision to promote and deepen co-operative relations in the economic, social, educational, cultural, scientific, technological and political fields; their commitment to continue and further the dialogue on hemispheric security; their determination to continue to contribute to the objective of general and complete disarmament; their determination to strengthen regional co-operation to increase the effectiveness of efforts to combat the illicit use of narcotic drugs and traffic therein; their decision to co-operate in a reciprocal effort towards preventing and punishing terrorist acts, methods and practices, and the development of international law in this matter; and their commitment to promote economic and social development for the indigenous populations of their countries.

Organization. Under its Charter the OAS accomplishes its purposes by means of:

(a) The General Assembly, which meets annually.

(b) The Meeting of Consultation of Ministers of Foreign Affairs, held to consider problems of an urgent nature and of common interest.

(c) The Councils: The Permanent Council, which meets on a permanent basis at OAS headquarters and carries out decisions of the General Assembly, assists the member states in the peaceful settlement of disputes, acts as the Preparatory Committee of that Assembly, submits recommendations with regard to the functioning of the Organization, and considers the reports to the Assembly of the other organs. The Inter-American Council for Integral Development (CIDI) directs and monitors OAS technical co-operation programmes.

(d) The Inter-American Juridical Committee which acts as an advisory body to the OAS on juridical matters and promotes the development and codification of international law. 11 jurists, elected for four-year terms by the General Assembly, represent all the American States.

(e) The Inter-American Commission on Human Rights which oversees the observance and protection of human rights. Seven members elected for four-year terms by the General Assembly represent all the OAS member states.

(f) The General Secretariat, which is the central and permanent organ of the OAS.

(g) The Specialized Conferences, meeting to deal with special technical matters or to develop specific aspects of inter-American co-operation.

(h) The Specialized Organizations, intergovernmental organizations established by multilateral agreements to discharge specific functions in their respective fields of action, such as women's affairs, agriculture, child welfare, Indian affairs, geography and history, and health.

In Sept. 2001 an Inter-American Democratic Charter was adopted. It sets out a simple, clear declaration: 'The peoples of the Americas have a right to democracy and their governments have an obligation to promote and defend it.' The Charter compels the OAS to take action against any member state that disrupts its own democratic institutions.

The Secretary-General is elected by the General Assembly for five-year terms. The General Assembly approves the annual budget which is financed by quotas contributed by the member governments. The budget in 2003 amounted to US$83·17m.

Headquarters: 17th Street and Constitution Avenue, NW, Washington, D.C., 20006, USA.
Website: http://www.oas.org
Secretary-General: José Miguel Insulza (Chile).

Publications. Charter of the Organization of American States. 1948.—*As Amended by the Protocol of Buenos Aires in 1967 and the Protocol of Cartagena de Indias in 1985; The OAS and the Evolution of the Inter-American System; Annual Report of the Secretary-General; Status of Inter-American Treaties and Conventions* (annual).

Further Reading

Sheinin, D., *The Organization of American States* [Bibliography]. Oxford and Metuchen (NJ), 1995

ORGANIZATION OF EASTERN CARIBBEAN STATES (OECS)

Founded in 1981 when seven eastern Caribbean states signed the Treaty of Basseterre agreeing to co-operate with each other to promote unity and solidarity among the members.

Members. Antigua and Barbuda, Dominica, Grenada, Montserrat, St Kitts and Nevis, St Lucia, St Vincent and the Grenadines. The British Virgin Islands and Anguilla have associate membership.

Functions. As set out in the Treaty of Basseterre: to promote co-operation among the member states and to defend their sovereignty and independence; to assist member states in the realization of their obligations and responsibilities to the international community with due regard to the role of international law as a standard of conduct in their relationships; to assist member states in the realization of their obligations and responsibilities to the international community with due regard to the role of international issues; to establish and maintain, where possible, arrangements for joint overseas representation and common services; to pursue these through its respective institutions by discussion of questions of common concern and by agreement on common action.

OECS's work is carried out through the office of the Director General which encompasses: the Legal Unit, Research and Communication Information Services, Functional Co-operation Services, Overseas Diplomatic Mission, Social and Sustainable Development Division, Economic Affairs Division and Corporate Service Division. These oversee the work of a number of specialized institutions, work units and projects in four countries. There is an OECS secretariat in St Lucia, which is comprised of several operating units, responsible for the following functions: Education and Human Resource Development, Export Development Unit, Legal Unit, Environment and Sustainable Development Unit, Pharmaceutical Procurement Service, Social Development Unit and OECS Sports Desk.

Official language: English.
Headquarters: Morne Fortune, PO Box 179, Castries, St Lucia.
Website: http://www.oecs.org
e-mail: oecs@oecs.org
Director-General: Dr Len Ishmael (St Lucia).

SECRETARIAT FOR CENTRAL AMERICAN ECONOMIC INTEGRATION (SIECA)

SIECA (Secretaría de Integración Económica Centroamericana) was created by the General Treaty of Central American Economic Integration in Dec. 1960. The General Treaty incorporates the Agreement on the Regime for Central American Integration Industries. In Oct. 1993 the Protocol to the General Treaty on Central Economic Integration, known as the Guatemala Protocol, was signed.

Members. Costa Rica, El Salvador, Guatemala, Honduras, Nicaragua. *Observer:* Panama.

Official language: Spanish.
Headquarters: 4a Avenida 10–25, Zona 14, Ciudad de Guatemala, Guatemala.
Website: http://www.sieca.org.gt
Secretary-General: Haroldo Rodas Melgar (Guatemala).

SOUTH AMERICAN COMMUNITY OF NATIONS (CSN/SACN)

In Dec. 2004 representatives of 12 South American countries signed the 'Cuzco Declaration' thereby founding a political and economic bloc modelled on the European Union. The aim is to establish a single currency, passport and parliament. The South American Community of Nations (SACN) will be created by the merger of the two existing major South American trade blocs: the Andean Community (Bolivia, Colombia, Ecuador, Peru and Venezuela) and the Southern Common Market or MERCOSUR (Argentina, Brazil, Paraguay and Uruguay), in addition to the market of Chile, and eventually those of Suriname and Guyana. The agreement paves the way for much-needed improvements in transport, energy and other infrastructure, thus facilitating intra-continental trade. The SACN aims to eliminate tariffs on non-sensitive products by 2014 and those on sensitive products by 2019. The bloc will create a single market of 361m. people with a combined GDP of US$973bn. However, insufficiently defined goals and ongoing disputes between members of the already-existing blocs may hamper development, as may future bilateral trade negotiations with the USA.

SOUTHERN COMMON MARKET (MERCOSUR)

Founded in March 1991 by the Treaty of Asunción between Argentina, Brazil, Paraguay and Uruguay, Mercosur committed the signatories to the progressive reduction of tariffs culminating in the formation of a common market on 1 Jan. 1995. This duly came into effect as a free trade zone affecting 90% of commodities.

A common external tariff averaging 14% applies to 80% of trade with countries outside Mercosur. Details were agreed at foreign minister level by the Protocol of Ouro Preto signed on 17 Dec. 1994.

In 1996 Chile negotiated a free-trade agreement with Mercosur which came into effect on 1 Oct. Two weeks later, Bolivia signed the same. In Dec. that year, an agreement conferring associate membership on Bolivia was also endorsed.

Organization. The member states' foreign ministers form a Council responsible for leading the integration process, the chairmanship of which rotates every six months. The permanent executive body is the Common Market Group of member states, which takes decisions by consensus. There is a Trade Commission and Joint Parliamentary Commission, an arbitration tribunal whose decisions are binding on member countries, and a secretariat in Montevideo.

Further to the treaty signed by 12 South American countries in Dec. 2004, MERCOSUR will gradually be integrated into the new South American Community of Nations.

Headquarters: Rincón 575 P12, 11000 Montevideo, Uruguay.
Website: http://www.mercosur.org.uy (Spanish and Portuguese only)
Administrative Secretary: Reginaldo Braga Arcuri (Brazil).

ASIAN DEVELOPMENT BANK

A multilateral development finance institution established in 1966 to promote economic and social progress in the Asian and Pacific region, the Bank's strategic objectives in the medium term are to foster economic growth, reduce poverty, improve the status of women, support human development (including population planning) and protect the environment.

The bank's capital stock is owned by 63 member countries, 45 regional and 18 non-regional. The bank makes loans and equity investments, and provides technical assistance grants for the preparation and execution of development projects and programmes; promotes investment of public and private capital for development purposes; and assists in co-ordinating development policies and plans in its developing member countries (DMCs).

The bank gives special attention to the needs of smaller or less developed countries, giving priority to regional, sub-regional and national projects which contribute to the economic growth of the region and promote regional co-operation. Loans from ordinary capital resources on non-concessional terms account for about 80% of cumulative lending. Loans from the bank's principal special fund, the Asian Development Fund, are made on highly concessional terms almost exclusively to the poorest borrowing countries.

Regional members. Afghanistan, Australia, Azerbaijan, Bangladesh, Bhutan, Cambodia, China, Cook Islands, East Timor, Fiji Islands, Hong Kong, India, Indonesia, Japan, Kazakhstan, Kiribati, South Korea, Kyrgyzstan, Laos, Malaysia, Maldives, Marshall Islands, Micronesia, Mongolia, Myanmar, Nauru, Nepal, New Zealand, Pakistan, Palau, Papua New Guinea, Philippines, Samoa, Singapore, Solomon Islands, Sri Lanka, Taiwan, Tajikistan, Thailand, Tonga, Turkmenistan, Tuvalu, Uzbekistan, Vanuatu and Vietnam.

Non-regional members. Austria, Belgium, Canada, Denmark, Finland, France, Germany, Italy, Luxembourg, Netherlands, Norway, Portugal, Spain, Sweden, Switzerland, Turkey, UK, USA.

Organization. The bank's highest policy-making body is its Board of Governors, which meets annually. Its executive body is the 12-member Board of Directors (each with an alternate), eight from the regional members and four non-regional.

The ADB also has resident missions: in Bangladesh; Cambodia; China; India; Indonesia; Kazakhstan; Kyrgyzstan; Laos; Nepal; Pakistan; the Philippines; Sri Lanka; Uzbekistan; Vietnam; and a regional mission in Port Vila, Vanuatu. There are also three representative offices: in Tokyo, Frankfurt and Washington, D.C.

Official language: English.
Headquarters: 6 ADB Avenue, Mandaluyong, Metro Manila, Philippines.
Website: http://www.adb.org
President: Haruhiko Kuroda (Japan).

ASIA-PACIFIC ECONOMIC CO-OPERATION (APEC)

Origin and Aims. APEC was originally established in 1989 to take advantage of the interdependence among Asia-Pacific economies, by facilitating economic growth for all participants and enhancing a sense of community in the region. Begun as an informal dialogue group, APEC is the premier forum for facilitating economic growth, co-operation, trade and investment in the Asia-Pacific region. APEC has a membership of 21 economic jurisdictions, a population of over 2·5bn. and a combined GDP of US$19trn. accounting for 47% of world trade.

APEC is working to achieve what are referred to as the 'Bogor Goals' of free and open trade and investment in the Asia-Pacific by 2010 for developed economies and 2020 for developing economies.

Members. Australia, Brunei, Canada, Chile, China, Hong Kong, Indonesia, Japan, South Korea, Malaysia, Mexico, New Zealand, Papua New Guinea, Peru, Philippines, Russia, Singapore, Taiwan, Thailand, USA and Vietnam.

Activities. APEC works in three broad areas to meet the Bogor Goals. These three broad work areas, known as APEC's 'Three Pillars', are: Trade and Investment Liberalization—reducing and eliminating tariff and non-tariff barriers to trade and investment, and opening markets; Business Facilitation—reducing the costs of business transactions, improving access to trade information and bringing into line policy and business strategies to facilitate growth, and free and open trade; Economic and Technical Co-operation—assisting member economies build the necessary capacities to take advantage of global trade and the new economy. The 15th APEC Ministerial Meeting, held in Bangkok, Thailand in Oct. 2003, called for increased measures to stop the spread of terrorism and weapons of mass destruction.

Official language: English.
Headquarters: 35 Heng Mui Keng Terrace, Singapore 119616.
Website: http://www.apecsec.org.sg
Executive Director: Ambassador Choi Seok-young (South Korea).

ASSOCIATION OF SOUTH EAST ASIAN NATIONS (ASEAN)

History and Membership. ASEAN is a regional intergovernmental organization formed by the governments of Indonesia, Malaysia, the Philippines, Singapore and Thailand through the Bangkok Declaration which was signed by their foreign ministers on 8 Aug. 1967. Brunei joined in 1984, Vietnam in 1995, Laos and Myanmar in 1997 and Cambodia in 1999. Papua New Guinea also has observer status.

Objectives. The main objectives are to accelerate economic growth, social progress and cultural development, to promote active collaboration and mutual assistance in matters of common interest, to ensure the political and economic stability of the South East Asian region, and to maintain close co-operation with existing international and regional organizations with similar aims.

Activities. Principal projects concern economic co-operation and development, with the intensification of intra-ASEAN trade, and trade between the region and the rest of the world; joint research and technological programmes; co-operation in transportation and communications; promotion of tourism, South East Asian studies, cultural, scientific, educational and administrative exchanges. The decision to set up an *ASEAN Free Trade Area (AFTA)* was taken at the Fourth Summit meeting, in Singapore in 1992, with the aim of creating a common market in 15 years, subsequently brought forward to 2002. AFTA applies to its first six signatories, namely Brunei, Indonesia, Malaysia, Philippines, Singapore and Thailand. In 2003 ASEAN leaders signed a declaration to establish a free trade area by 2020.

In Dec. 1995 heads of government meeting in Bangkok established a South-East Asia Nuclear-Free Zone, which was extended to cover offshore economic exclusion zones. Individual signatories were to decide whether to allow port visits or transportation of nuclear weapons by foreign powers through territorial waters. The *ASEAN Regional Forum (ARF)* was proposed at a meeting of foreign ministers in July 1993 to discuss security issues in the region. Its first formal meeting took place in July 1994 attended by all seven members and its dialogue partners (Australia, Canada, the EU, Japan, South Korea, New Zealand and the USA) and observers (China, Laos, Papua New Guinea, Russia and Vietnam).

ASEAN is committed to resolving the dispute over sovereignty of the Spratly Islands, a group of more than 100 small islands and reefs in the South China Sea. Some or all of the largely uninhabited islands have been claimed by Brunei, China, Malaysia, the Philippines, Taiwan and Vietnam. The disputed areas have oil and gas resources.

Organization. The highest authority is the meeting of Heads of Government, which takes place annually. The highest policy-making body is the annual Meeting of Foreign Ministers, commonly known as AMM, the ASEAN Ministerial Meeting, which convenes in each of the member countries on a rotational basis in alphabetical order. The AEM (ASEAN Economic Meeting) meets each year to direct ASEAN economic co-operation. The AEM and AMM report jointly to the heads of government at summit meetings. Each capital has its own national secretariat. The central secretariat in Jakarta is headed by the Secretary-General, a post that revolves among the member states in alphabetical order every five years.

Official language: English.
Headquarters: POB 2072, Jakarta 12110, Indonesia.
Website: http://www.aseansec.org
Secretary-General: Ong Keng Yong (Singapore).

ASEAN MEKONG BASIN DEVELOPMENT CO-OPERATION (MEKONG GROUP)

The ministers and representatives of Brunei, Cambodia, China, Indonesia, Laos, Malaysia, Myanmar, Philippines, Singapore, Thailand and Vietnam met in Kuala Lumpur on 17 June 1996 and agreed the following basic objectives for the Group: to co-operate in the economic and social development of the Mekong Basin area and strengthen the link between it and ASEAN member countries, through a process of dialogue and common project identification.

Priorities include: development of infrastructure capacities in the fields of transport, telecommunications, irrigation and energy; development of trade and investment-generating activities; development of the agricultural sector to enhance production for domestic consumption and export; sustainable development of forestry resources and development of mineral resources; development of the industrial sector, especially small to medium enterprises; development of tourism; human resource development and support for training; co-operation in the fields of science and technology.

Further Reading

Broinowski, A., *Understanding ASEAN.* London, 1982.—(ed.) *ASEAN into the 1990s.* London, 1990

Van Hoa, Tran, (ed.) *Economic Developments and Prospects in the ASEAN.* London, 1997

Wawn, B., *The Economics of the ASEAN Countries.* London, 1982

COLOMBO PLAN

History. Founded in 1950 to promote the development of newly independent Asian member countries, the Colombo Plan has grown from a group of seven Commonwealth nations into an organization of 24 countries. Originally the Plan was conceived for a period of six years. This was renewed from time to time until the Consultative Committee gave the Plan an indefinite life span in 1980.

Members. (Permanent Member Countries) Afghanistan, Australia, Bangladesh, Bhutan, Fiji Islands, India, Indonesia, Islamic Republic of Iran, Japan, South Korea, Lao People's Democratic Republic, Malaysia, Maldives, Myanmar, Nepal, New Zealand, Pakistan, Papua New Guinea, Philippines, Singapore, Sri Lanka, Thailand, USA and Vietnam. *(Provisional member country)* Mongolia.

Aims. The aims of the Colombo Plan are: (1) to provide a forum for discussion, at local level, of development needs; (2) to facilitate development assistance by encouraging members to participate as donors and recipients of technical co-operation; and (3) to execute programmes to advance development within member countries. The Plan currently has the following programmes: Programme for Public Administration (PPA); South-South Technical Co-operation Data Bank Programme (SSTC/DB); Drug Advisory Programme (DAP); Programme for Private Sector Development (PPSD); Colombo Plan Staff College for Technician Education (CPSC).

Structure. The Consultative Committee is the principal policy-making body of the Colombo Plan. Consisting of all member countries, it meets every two years to review the economic and social progress of members, exchange views on technical co-operation programmes and generally review the activities of the Plan. The Colombo Plan Council represents each member government and meets several times a year to identify development issues, recommend measures to be taken and ensure implementation.

Headquarters: 12 Melbourne Avenue, PO Box 596, Colombo 4, Sri Lanka.
Website: www.colombo-plan.org
e-mail: cplan@slt.lk
Secretary-General: Kittipan Kanjanapipatkul (Thailand).

Publications. Consultative Committee Meeting—Proceedings and Conclusions (biennial); *Report of the Colombo Plan Council* (annual); *The Colombo Plan Brochure* (annual); *The Colombo Plan Focus* (quarterly newsletter); *South-South Technical Co-operation in Selected Member Countries.*

ECONOMIC CO-OPERATION ORGANIZATION (ECO)

The Economic Co-operation Organization (ECO) is an intergovernmental regional organization established in 1985 by Iran, Pakistan and Turkey. ECO is the successor of the Regional Co-operation for Development (RCD). ECO was later expanded in 1992 to include seven new members: Afghanistan, Azerbaijan, Kazakhstan, Kyrgyzstan, Tajikistan, Turkmenistan and Uzbekistan. The objectives of the organization, stipulated in its Charter, the Treaty of Izmir, include the promotion of conditions for sustained economic growth in the region. While transport and communications, trade and investment, and energy are the high priority areas in ECO's scheme of work, other fields of co-operation such as industry, agriculture, health, science and education, drug control and human development are also on the agenda.

While summit meetings lend reaffirmation of the high level commitment of ECO member states to the goals and objectives of the organization, the Council of Ministers (COM) remains the highest policy and decision-making body of the organization, which meets at least once a year and is chaired by rotation among the member states.

ECO Summits were instituted with the First Summit held in Tehran in 1992; the Second Summit was held in Istanbul in 1993, the Third in Islamabad in 1995, the Fourth in Ashgabat in 1996, the Fifth in Almaty in May 1999, the Sixth in Tehran in 2000, the Seventh in Istanbul in 2002 and the Eighth in Dushanbe in 2004.

The long-term perspectives and priorities of ECO are defined in the form of two Action Plans: the Quetta Plan of Action and the Istanbul Declaration and Economic Co-operation Strategy.

ECO enjoys observer status with the United Nations, World Trade Organization and the Organization of Islamic Conference. A number of resolutions have been adopted in the UN General Assembly in the context of expansion of co-operation with ECO in the 1990s, most recently in Dec. 2001.

Headquarters: 1 Goulbou Alley, Kamranieh, PO Box 14155-6176, Tehran, Islamic Republic of Iran.
Website: http://www.ecosecretariat.org
e-mail: registry@ecosecretariat.org
Secretary-General: Askhat Orazbay (Kazakhstan).

PACIFIC ISLANDS FORUM (PIF)

In Oct. 2000 the South Pacific Forum changed its name to the Pacific Islands Forum. As the South Pacific Forum it held its first meeting of Heads of Government in New Zealand in 1971. The Agreement Establishing the Forum Secretariat defines the membership of the Forum and the Secretariat. Decisions are reached by consensus. The administrative arm of the Forum, known officially as the Pacific Islands Forum Secretariat, is based in Suva, Fiji. In Oct. 1994 the Forum was granted observer status to the UN.

Members. (2005) Australia, Cook Islands, Fiji Islands, Kiribati, Marshall Islands, Micronesia, Nauru, New Zealand, Niue, Palau, Papua New Guinea, Samoa, Solomon Islands, Tonga, Tuvalu and Vanuatu. In 1999 the French territory of New Caledonia was admitted to the Forum as an observer. In 2002 East Timor was admitted to the Forum as a Special Observer.

Functions. The Secretariat's mission is to provide policy options to the Pacific Islands Forum, and to promote Forum decisions and regional and international co-operation. The organization seeks to promote political stability and regional security; enhance the management of economies and the development process; improve trade and investment performance; and efficiently manage the resources of the Secretariat.

Activities. The Secretariat has four core divisions: Trade and Investment; Political and International Affairs; Development and Economic Policy; Corporate Services. The Secretariat provides policy advice to members on a wide range of social, economic and political issues. Since 1989 the Forum has held Post Forum Dialogues with key dialogue partners at ministerial level. There are currently twelve partners: Canada, China, EU, France, India, Indonesia, Japan, South Korea, Malaysia, the Philippines, the United Kingdom and the United States.

Organization. The South Pacific Bureau for Economic Cooperation (SPEC) began as a trade bureau and was established in 1972, before being re-organized as the South Pacific Forum Secretariat in 1988. It changed its name to the Pacific Islands Forum Secretariat in 2000. The Secretariat is headed by a Secretary General and Deputy Secretary General who form the Executive. The governing body is the Forum Officials Committee, which acts as an intermediary between the Secretariat and the Forum. The Secretariat operates four Trade Offices in Auckland, Beijing, Sydney and Tokyo.

The Secretary General is the permanent Chair of the Council of Regional Organisations in the Pacific (CROP), which brings together ten main regional organizations in the Pacific region: Fiji School of Medicine (FSM); Forum Fisheries Agency (FFA); Pacific Islands Development Programme (PIDP); Pacific Islands Forum Secretariat (PIFS); Secretariat for the Pacific Community (SPC); South Pacific Applied Geoscience Commission (SOPAC); South Pacific Board for Educational Assessment (SPBEA); South Pacific Regional Environment Programme (SPREP); South Pacific Tourism Organisation (SPTO); and the University of the South Pacific (USP).

Official language: English.
Headquarters: Ratu Sukuna Road, Suva, Fiji Islands.
Website: http://www.forumsec.org.fj
Secretary-General: Gregory Urwin (Australia).

SECRETARIAT OF THE PACIFIC COMMUNITY (SPC)

Until Feb. 1998 known as the South Pacific Commission, this is a regional intergovernmental organization founded in 1947 under an Agreement commonly referred to as the Canberra Agreement. It is funded by assessed contributions from its 27 members and by voluntary contributions from member and non-member countries, international organizations and other sources.

Members. American Samoa, Australia, Cook Islands, Fiji Islands, France, French Polynesia, Guam, Kiribati, Marshall Islands, Federated States of Micronesia, Nauru, New Caledonia, New Zealand, Niue, Northern Mariana Islands, Palau, Papua New Guinea, Pitcairn Islands, Samoa, Solomon Islands, Tokelau, Tonga, Tuvalu, UK, USA, Vanuatu, and Wallis and Futuna.

Functions. The SPC has three main areas of work: land resources, marine resources and social resources. It conducts research and provides technical assistance and training in these areas to member Pacific Island countries and territories of the Pacific.

Organization. The Conference of the Pacific Community is the governing body of the Community. Its key focus is to appoint the Director-General, to consider major national or regional policy issues and to note changes to the Financial and Staff Regulations approved by the CRGA, the Committee of Representatives of Governments and Administrations. It meets every two years. The CRGA meets once a year and is the principal decision-making organ of the Community. There is also a regional office in Fiji Islands.

Headquarters: BP D5, 98848 Nouméa Cedex, New Caledonia.
Website: http://www.spc.int
e-mail: spc@spc.int
Director-General: Lourdes Pangelinan (Guam).

SOUTH ASIAN ASSOCIATION FOR REGIONAL CO-OPERATION (SAARC)

SAARC was established to accelerate the process of economic and social development in member states through joint action in agreed areas of co-operation. The foreign ministers of the seven member countries met for the first time in New Delhi in Aug. 1983 and adopted the Declaration on South Asian Regional

Co-operation whereby an Integrated Programme of Action (IPA) was launched. The charter establishing SAARC was adopted at the first summit meeting in Dhaka in Dec. 1985.

Members. Bangladesh, Bhutan, India, Maldives, Nepal, Pakistan, Sri Lanka.

Objectives. To promote the welfare of the peoples of South Asia; to accelerate economic growth, social progress and cultural development; to promote and strengthen collective self-reliance among members; to promote active collaboration and mutual assistance in the economic, social, cultural, technical and scientific fields; to strengthen co-operation with other developing countries and among themselves. Co-operation within the framework is based on respect for the principles of sovereign equality, territorial integrity, political independence, non-interference in the internal affairs of other states, and mutual benefit. Agreed areas of co-operation under the *Integrated Programme of Action (IPA)* include agriculture and rural development; human resource development; environment, meteorology and forestry; science and technology; transport and communications; energy; and social development.

A SAARC Preferential Trading Arrangement (SAPTA) designed to reduce tariffs on trade between SAARC member states was signed in April 1993 and entered into force in Dec. 1995. In 1998 at the Tenth Summit in Colombo, the importance of achieving a South Asian Free Trade Area (SAFTA) as mandated by the Malé Summit in 1997 was reiterated and it was decided to set up a Committee of Experts to work on drafting a comprehensive treaty regime for creating a free trade area. The Colombo Summit agreed that the text of this regulatory framework would be finalized by 2001.

Organization. The highest authority of the Association rests with the heads of state or government, who meet annually at Summit level. The Council of Foreign Ministers, which meets twice a year, is responsible for formulating policy, reviewing progress and deciding on new areas of co-operation and the mechanisms deemed necessary for that. The Council is supported by a Standing Committee of Foreign Secretaries, by the Programming Committee and by 11 Technical Committees which are responsible for individual areas of SAARC's activities. There is a secretariat in Kathmandu, headed by a Secretary-General, who is assisted in his work by seven Directors, appointed by the Secretary-General upon nomination by member states for a period of three years which may in special circumstances be extended.

Official language: English.
Headquarters: PO Box 4222, Kathmandu, Nepal.
Website: http://www.saarc-sec.org
Secretary-General: Lyonpo Chenkyab Dorji (Bhutan).

ARAB FUND FOR ECONOMIC AND SOCIAL DEVELOPMENT (AFESD)

Established in 1968, the Fund commenced operations in 1974.

Aims. To contribute to the financing of economic and social development in Arabic states through: financing economic and social development projects by making loans on concessionary terms to governments and public enterprises and corporations, giving preference to projects which are vital to the Arab world and to inter-Arab projects; and financing private sector projects in member states by providing all forms and loans and guarantees to corporations and enterprises processing juridical personality.

Members. Algeria, Bahrain, Djibouti, Egypt, Iraq*, Jordan, Kuwait, Lebanon, Libya, Mauritania, Morocco, Oman, Palestine, Qatar, Saudi Arabia, Somalia*, Sudan,

Syria, Tunisia, United Arab Emirates, Republic of Yemen. *Membership suspended since 1993.

Headquarters: PO Box 21923, Safat 13080, Kuwait.
Website: http://www.arabfund.org
Director General and Chairman of the Board of Directors: Abdulatif Y. Al Hamad.

Publications. Annual Report; Joint Arab Economic Report.

ARAB MAGHREB UNION

The Arab Maghreb Union was founded in 1989 to promote political co-ordination, co-operation and 'complementarity' across various fields, with integration wherever and whenever possible.

Members. Algeria, Libya, Mauritania, Morocco, Tunisia.

By late 1996 joint policies and projects under way or under consideration included: the establishment of the Maghreb Investment and Foreign Trade Bank to fund joint agricultural and industrial projects; free movement of citizens within the region; joint transport undertakings, including railway improvements and a Maghreb highway; creation of a customs union; and establishment of a common market.

A Declaration committing members to the establishment of a free trade zone was adopted at the AMU's last summit in Tunis (April 1994). In Nov. 1992 members adopted a charter on protection of the environment.

Official language: Arabic.
Headquarters: 14 Rue Zalagh, Agdal, Rabat, Morocco.
Website: http://www.maghrebarabe.org
Secretary-General: Habib Boularès (Tunisia).

ARAB MONETARY FUND (AMF)

Origin. The Agreement establishing the Arab Monetary Fund was approved by the Economic Council of the League of Arab States in April 1976 and the first meeting of the Board of Governors was held on 19 April 1977.

Aims. To assist member countries in eliminating payments and trade restrictions, in achieving exchange rate stability, in developing capital markets and in correcting payments imbalances through the extension of short- and medium-term loans; the co-ordination of monetary policies of member countries; and the liberalization and promotion of trade and payments, as well as the encouragement of capital flows among member countries.

Members. Algeria, Bahrain, Comoros, Djibouti, Egypt, Iraq, Jordan, Kuwait, Lebanon, Libya, Mauritania, Morocco, Oman, Palestine, Qatar, Saudi Arabia, Somalia, Sudan, Syria, Tunisia, United Arab Emirates, Republic of Yemen.

Headquarters: PO Box 2818, Abu Dhabi, United Arab Emirates.
Website: http://www.amf.org.ae
Director General and Chairman of the Board of Directors: Jassim A. Al-Mannai.

Publications (in English and Arabic): *Annual Report; The Articles of Agreement of the Arab Monetary Fund; Money and Credit in Arab Countries* (annual); *National Accounts of Arab Countries* (annual); *Foreign Trade of Arab Countries* (annual); *Cross Exchange Rates of Arab Currencies* (annual); *Arab Countries: Economic Indicators* (annual); *Balance of Payments and External Public Debt of Arab Countries* (annual); *AMF Publications Catalogue* (annual); *Arab Monetary Fund: Structure and Activities (1977–83).* (In Arabic only): *The Joint Arabic Economic Report* (annual); *AMF Economic Bulletin; Developments in Arab Capital Markets* (quarterly).

ARAB ORGANIZATION FOR AGRICULTURAL DEVELOPMENT (AOAD)

The AOAD was established in 1970 and commenced operations in 1972. Its aims are to develop natural and human resources in the agricultural sector and improve the means and methods of exploiting these resources on scientific bases; to increase agricultural productive efficiency and achieve agricultural integration between the Arab States and countries; to increase agricultural production with a view to achieving a higher degree of self-sufficiency; to facilitate the exchange of agricultural products between the Arab States and countries; to enhance the establishment of agricultural ventures and industries; and to increase the standards of living of the labour force engaged in the agricultural sector.

Organization. The structure comprises a General Assembly consisting of ministers of agriculture of the member states, an Executive Council, a Secretariat General, seven technical departments—Food Security, Human Resources Development, Water Resources, Studies and Research, Projects Execution, Technical Scientific Co-operation, and Financial Administrative Department—and two centres—the Arab Center for Agricultural Information and Documentation, and the Arab Bureau for Consultation and Implementation of Agricultural Projects.

Members. Algeria, Bahrain, Djibouti, Egypt, Iraq, Jordan, Kuwait, Lebanon, Libya, Mauritania, Morocco, Oman, Palestine, Qatar, Saudi Arabia, Somalia, Sudan, Syria, Tunisia, United Arab Emirates, Republic of Yemen.

Official languages: Arabic (English and French used in translated documents and correspondence).
Headquarters: Street No. 7, Al-Amarat, Khartoum, Sudan.
Website: http://www.aoad.org
Director General: Dr Salem Al-Lozi.

GULF CO-OPERATION COUNCIL (GCC)

Origin. Also referred to as the Co-operation Council for the Arab States of the Gulf (CCASG), the Council was established on 25 May 1981 on signature of the Charter by Bahrain, Kuwait, Oman, Qatar, Saudi Arabia and the United Arab Emirates.

Aims. To assure security and stability of the region through economic and political co-operation; promote, expand and enhance economic ties on solid foundations, in the best interests of the people; co-ordinate and unify economic, financial and monetary policies, as well as commercial and industrial legislation and customs regulations; achieve self-sufficiency in basic foodstuffs.

Organization. The Supreme Council is formed by the heads of member states and is the highest authority. Its presidency rotates, based on the alphabetical order of the names of the member states. It holds one regular session every year, in addition to a mid-year consultation session. The Co-operation Council has a commission, called 'Commission for the Settlement of Disputes', which is attached to the Supreme Council. Also attached to the Supreme Council is the Consultative Commission. The Ministerial Council is formed of the Foreign Ministers of the member states or other delegated ministers and meets quarterly. The Secretariat-General is composed of Secretary-General, Assistant Secretaries-General and a number of staff as required. The Secretariat consists of the following sectors: Political Affairs, Military Affairs, Legal Affairs, Human and Environment Affairs, Information Centre, Media Department, Gulf Standardization Organization (GSO), GCC Patent Office, Secretary-General's Office, GCC Delegation in Brussels, Technical Telecommunications Bureau in Bahrain. In Jan. 2003 it launched a customs union, introducing a 5% duty on foreign imports across the trade bloc.

Finance. The annual budget of the GCC Secretariat is shared equally by the six member states.

Headquarters: PO Box 7153, Riyadh-11462, Saudi Arabia.
Website: http://www.GCC-SG.org
Secretary-General: Abdul Rahman bin Hamad Al-Attiyah.

Publications. Attaawun (quarterly, in Arabic); *GCC Economic Bulletin* (annual); *Statistical Bulletin* (annual); *Legal Bulletin* (quarterly, in Arabic).

Further Reading

Twinam, J. W., *The Gulf, Co-operation and the Council: an American Perspective.* Washington, 1992

LEAGUE OF ARAB STATES

Origin. The League of Arab States is a voluntary association of sovereign Arab states, established by a Pact signed in Cairo on 22 March 1945 by the representatives of Egypt, Iraq, Saudi Arabia, Syria, Lebanon, Jordan and Yemen. It seeks to promote closer ties among member states and to co-ordinate their economic, cultural and security policies with a view to developing collective co-operation, protecting national security and maintaining the independence and sovereignty of member states, in order to enhance the potential for joint Arab action across all fields.

Members. Algeria, Bahrain, Comoros, Djibouti, Egypt, Iraq, Jordan, Kuwait, Lebanon, Mauritania, Morocco, Oman, Palestine, Qatar, Saudi Arabia, Somalia, Sudan, Syria, Tunisia, United Arab Emirates and Republic of Yemen. Libya left the League of Arab States in Oct. 2002, citing its 'inefficiency' in dealing with the stand-off between Iraq and the USA and the Israeli–Palestinian conflict.

Joint Action. In the political field, the League is entrusted with defending the supreme interests and national causes of the Arab world through the implementation of joint action plans at regional and international levels, and with examining any disputes that may arise between member states with a view to settling them by peaceful means. The Joint Defence and Economic Co-operation Treaty signed in 1950 provided for the establishment of a Joint Defence Council as well as an Economic Council (renamed the Economic and Social Council in 1977). Economic, social and cultural activities constitute principal and vital elements of the joint action initiative.

Arab Common Market. An Arab Common Market came into operation on 1 Jan. 1965. The agreement, reached on 13 Aug. 1964, provided for the abolition of customs duties on agricultural products and natural resources within five years, by reducing tariffs at an annual rate of 20%. Customs duties on industrial products were to be reduced by 10% annually. However, it never became reality although it has remained the ambition of many people throughout the Arab world for many years since.

Organization. The machinery of the League consists of a Council, 11 specialized ministerial committees entrusted with drawing up common policies for the regulation and advancement of co-operation in their fields (information, internal affairs, justice, housing, transport, social affairs, youth and sports, health, environment, telecommunications and electricity), and a permanent secretariat.

The League is considered to be a regional organization within the framework of the United Nations at which its Secretary-General is an observer. It has permanent delegations in New York and Geneva for the UN, in Addis Ababa for the Organization of African Unity (OAU), as well as offices in Athens, Beijing, Berlin, Brussels, London, Madrid, Moscow, New Delhi, Paris, Rome, Vienna and Washington, D.C.

Headquarters: Al Tahrir Square, Cairo, Egypt.
Website: http://www.arableagueonline.org
Secretary-General: Amre Moussa (Egypt).

Further Reading

Clements, F. A., *Arab Regional Organizations* [Bibliography]. Oxford and New Brunswick (NJ), 1992
Gomaa, A. M., *The Foundation of the League of Arab States.* London, 1977

ORGANIZATION OF ARAB PETROLEUM EXPORTING COUNTRIES (OAPEC)

Established in 1968 to promote co-operation and close ties between member states in economic activities related to the oil industry; to determine ways of safeguarding their legitimate interests, both individual and collective, in the oil industry; to unite their efforts so as to ensure the flow of oil to consumer markets on equitable and reasonable terms; and to create a favourable climate for the investment of capital and expertise in their petroleum industries.

Members. Algeria, Bahrain, Egypt, Iraq, Kuwait, Libya, Qatar, Saudi Arabia, Syria, Tunisia*, United Arab Emirates. *Tunisia's membership was made inactive in 1986.

Headquarters: PO Box 20501, Safat 13066, Kuwait.
Website: http://www.oapecorg.org
Secretary-General: Abdulaziz A. Al-Turki.

Publications. Secretary General's Annual Report (Arabic and English editions); *Oil and Arab Co-operation* (quarterly; Arabic with English abstracts and bibliography); *OAPEC Monthly Bulletin* (Arabic and English editions); *Energy Resources Monitor* (Arabic); *OAPEC Annual Statistical Report* (Arabic/English).

ORGANIZATION OF THE PETROLEUM EXPORTING COUNTRIES (OPEC)

Origin and Aims. Founded in Baghdad in 1960 by Iran, Iraq, Kuwait, Saudi Arabia and Venezuela. The principal aims are: to unify the petroleum policies of member countries and determine the best means for safeguarding their interests, individually and collectively; to devise ways and means of ensuring the stabilization of prices in international oil markets with a view to eliminating harmful and unnecessary fluctuations; and to secure a steady income for the producing countries, an efficient, economic and regular supply of petroleum to consuming nations, and a fair return on their capital to those investing in the petroleum industry. It is estimated that OPEC members possess 75% of the world's known reserves of crude petroleum, of which about two-thirds are in the Middle East.

Members. (2004) Algeria, Indonesia, Iran, Iraq, Kuwait, Libya, Nigeria, Qatar, Saudi Arabia, United Arab Emirates and Venezuela. Membership applications may be made by any other country having substantial net exports of crude petroleum, which has fundamentally similar interests to those of member countries. Gabon became an associated member in 1973 and a full member in 1975, but in 1996 withdrew owing to difficulty in meeting its percentage contribution. Ecuador joined the Organization in 1973 but left in 1992.

Organization. The main organs are the Conference, the Board of Governors and the Secretariat. The Conference, which is the supreme authority meeting at least twice a year, consists of delegations from each member country, normally headed by the respective minister of oil, mines or energy. All decisions, other than those concerning procedural matters, must be adopted unanimously.

Headquarters: Obere Donaustrasse 93, A-1020 Vienna, Austria.
Website: http://www.opec.org
e-mail: prid@opec.org
Secretary-General (acting): Sheikh Ahmad Fahad Al Ahmad Al-Sabah (Kuwait).

Publications. Annual Statistical Bulletin; Annual Report; OPEC Bulletin (monthly); *OPEC Review* (quarterly); *OPEC General Information; Monthly Oil Market Report*; OPEC Statute.

Further Reading

Al-Chalabi, F., *OPEC at the Crossroads.* Oxford, 1989
Skeet, I., *OPEC: 25 Years of Prices and Policies.* CUP, 1988

OPEC FUND FOR INTERNATIONAL DEVELOPMENT

The OPEC Fund for International Development was established in 1976 to provide financial aid on advantageous terms to developing countries (other than OPEC members) and international development agencies whose beneficiaries are developing countries. In 1980 the Fund was transformed into a permanent autonomous international agency and renamed the OPEC Fund for International Development. It is administered by a Ministerial Council and a Governing Board. Each member country is represented on the Council by its finance minister.

The initial endowment of the fund amounted to US$800m. At the start of 2003 pledged contributions totalled US$3,435m., and the Fund had extended 953 loans totalling US$5,146·1m. of which US$3,952·5m. was for project financing, US$724·2m. for balance-of-payments support, US$305·3m. for programme funding and US$164·0m. for debt relief within the context of the Highly Indebted Poor Countries Initiative. In addition, and through its private sector window, the Fund had approved financing worth a total of US$189·3m. in 40 operations in support of private sector entities in Africa, Asia, Latin America, the Caribbean and Europe. Through its grant programme the Fund had also committed a total of US$272·3m. in support of a wide range of initiatives.

Headquarters: POB 995, A-1011 Vienna, Austria.
Website: http://www.opecfund.org
e-mail: info@opecfund.org
Director-General: Suleiman Jasir al-Herbish (Saudi Arabia).

ANTARCTIC TREATY

Antarctica is an island continent some 15·5m. sq. km in area which lies almost entirely within the Antarctic Circle. Its surface is composed of an ice sheet over rock, and it is uninhabited except for research and other workers in the course of duty. It is in general ownerless: for countries with territorial claims, *see* ARGENTINA; AUSTRALIA: Australian Antarctic Territory; CHILE; FRANCE: Southern and Antarctic Territories; NEW ZEALAND: Ross Dependency; NORWAY: Queen Maud Land; UNITED KINGDOM: British Antarctic Territory.

12 countries which had maintained research stations in Antarctica during International Geophysical Year, 1957–58 (Argentina, Australia, Belgium, Chile, France, Japan, New Zealand, Norway, South Africa, the USSR, the UK and the USA) signed the Antarctic Treaty (Washington Treaty) on 1 Dec. 1959. Austria, Brazil, Bulgaria, Canada, China, Colombia, Cuba, Czech Republic, Denmark, Ecuador, Estonia, Finland, Germany, Greece, Guatemala, Hungary, India, Italy, South Korea, North Korea, the Netherlands, Papua New Guinea, Peru, Poland, Romania, Slovakia, Spain, Sweden, Switzerland, Turkey, Ukraine, Uruguay and Venezuela subsequently acceded to the Treaty. The Treaty reserves the Antarctic area south of 60° S. lat. for peaceful purposes, provides for international co-operation in scientific investigation and research, and preserves, for the duration of the Treaty, the *status quo* with regard to territorial sovereignty, rights and claims. The Treaty entered into force on 23 June 1961. The 45 nations party to the Treaty (27 full voting signatories and 18 adherents) meet biennially.

An agreement reached in Madrid in April 1991 and signed by all 39 parties in Oct. imposes a ban on mineral exploitation in Antarctica for 50 years, at the end of which any one of the 27 voting parties may request a review conference. After this the ban may be lifted by agreement of three quarters of the nations then voting, which must include the present 27.

Headquarters: Av. Leandro Alem 884–4° Piso, C1001AAQ, Buenos Aires, Argentina.
Website: http://www.nsf.gov/od/opp/antarct/anttrty.jsp
e-mail: secret@ats.org.ar
Executive Secretary: Johannes Huber (Netherlands).

Further Reading

Elliott, L. M., *International Environmental Politics: Protecting the Antarctic*. London, 1994
Jørgensen-Dahl, A. and Østreng, W., *The Antarctic Treaty System in World Politics*. London, 1991
Meadows, J. *et al.*, *The Antarctic* [Bibliography]. Oxford and New Brunswick (NJ), 1994

KYOTO PROTOCOL

The protocol is an international environmental agreement signed by 84 countries under the UN Framework Convention on Climate Change. The agreement, adopted on 11 Dec. 1997, is based on principles set out in a framework convention signed at the Rio Summit in 1992, but did not become a legally binding treaty until 16 Feb. 2005.

Under the Kyoto Protocol governments must gather and share information on greenhouse gas emissions, launch national strategies for reducing greenhouse emissions and co-operate in preparing to adapt to the impacts of climate change.

The developed countries have committed themselves to reducing their collective emissions of six greenhouse gases to at least 5% below 1990 levels. These targets are scheduled to be met by the period 2008–12 with final reductions to be calculated as an average over this five-year period.

Actual emission reductions are expected to exceed substantially the minimum 5%. In particular, the richest industrialized countries will need to reduce their collective output by about 10%. This especially applies to the three most important gases—carbon dioxide, methane and nitrous oxide. The USA, the largest producer of greenhouse gas, has not ratified the protocol.

Headquarters: United Nations Framework Convention on Climate Change, Haus Carstanjen, Martin-Luther-King-Strasse 8, D-53175 Bonn, Germany.
Website: http://unfccc.int
e-mail: secretariat@unfccc.int
Executive Secretary: Joke Waller-Hunter (Netherlands).

PART II

COUNTRIES OF THE WORLD
A—Z

AFGHANISTAN

Islamic Republic of Afghanistan

Capital: Kabul
Population projection, 2010: 31·23m.
GDP per capita: not available

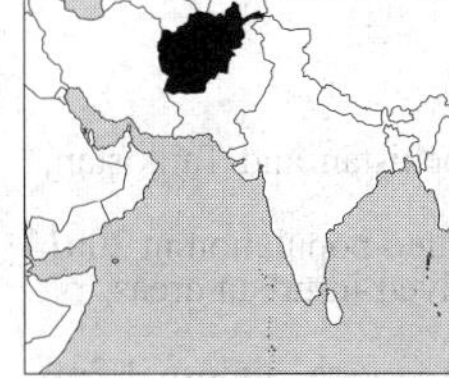

KEY HISTORICAL EVENTS

For much of the 19th century Afghanistan was part of the power struggle between Britain, the dominant power in India, and the Russian empire. While the country achieved independence after the First World War, tribal wars and banditry restricted economic and social development. Stability came in the period of Záhir Shah who ruled for 40 years. In 1964 he was able to overcome opposition and established parliamentary democracy. In 1973 there was a military coup led by his cousin and brother-in-law, and a former prime minister, Mohammed Daoud, who abolished the 1964 constitution and declared a republic. Záhir Shah abdicated on 24 Aug. 1973.

In April 1978 President Daoud was killed in a further coup which installed a pro-Soviet government. The new president, Noor Mohammad Taraki, was overthrown in Sept. 1979, whereupon the Soviet Union invaded Afghanistan in Dec., deposed his successor and placed Babrak Karmal at the head of government.

In Dec. 1986 Sayid Mohammed Najibullah became president amid continuing civil war between government and rebel Muslim forces. The USSR provided military support and development aid to the pro-Soviet administration while the USA extended limited support to the rebels. In the mid-1980s the UN began negotiations on the withdrawal of Soviet troops and the establishment of a government of national unity. Soviet troops began withdrawing from Afghanistan in early 1988.

After talks in Nov. 1991 with Afghan opposition movements ('mujahideen'), the Soviet government transferred its support from the Najibullah regime to an 'Islamic Interim Government'. As mujahideen insurgents closed in on Kabul, President Najibullah stepped down on 16 April 1992 but fighting continued.

In 1994 a newly formed militant Islamic movement, 'Taliban' (i.e. 'students of religion'), took Kabul, apparently with Pakistani support. The Taliban, most of whose leaders were Pashtuns, were in turn defeated by the troops of President Rabbani but in Sept. 1996 Taliban forces recaptured Kabul and set up an interim government under Mohamed Rabbani. Afghanistan was declared a complete Islamic state under Sharia law.

Government forces which had retreated to the north of Kabul counter-attacked but a new Taliban offensive, launched on 27 Dec. 1996, gave Taliban control of most of the country. The opposition Northern Alliance controlled the northeast of the country. Under the Taliban, irregular forces were disarmed and roads cleared of bandits. Rebuilding of towns and villages started. But the strict application of Islamic law ran counter to western sensitivities with the result that only three countries—Pakistan, Saudi Arabia and the United Arab Emirates—recognized the Taliban as the legal government.

In March 2001 Afghanistan was widely condemned for the destruction of ancient monuments that the Taliban deemed un-Islamic, including the world's tallest Buddhas. In May 2001 the ruling Taliban refused to extradite Osama bin Laden, a Saudi militant, to the USA to face charges connected to the bombing of American embassies in Kenya and Tanzania in 1998. In Sept. 2001 Ahmed Shah Masood, leader of the Northern Alliance, was killed by two suicide bombers.

Following the attacks on the USA on 11 Sept. 2001 Saudi Arabia and the United Arab Emirates broke off diplomatic relations with Afghanistan. The USA put pressure on the ruling Taliban to hand over Osama bin Laden, but without success. Consequently the USA launched air strikes on Afghanistan on 7 Oct. On 13 Nov. the Northern Alliance took the capital Kabul, effectively bringing an end to Taliban rule, and with the surrender of Kandahar the Taliban lost control of their last stronghold. On 27 Nov. representatives of rival factions, but excluding the Taliban, joined United Nations-sponsored talks in Germany on the future of their country.

Hamid Karzai, a Pashtun tribal leader, was chosen to head an interim power-sharing council, which took office in Kabul from 22 Dec. He was subsequently appointed president of the transitional government in June 2002. In Sept. 2002 he survived an assassination attempt.

'Whether or not Afghanistan can survive comes down, in part, to one simple question: are the forces of national integration there greater than the forces of local disintegration? Optimists say yes. They think Afghanistan is more stable than at any time in the past 24 years.' (*The Economist*, 16 Aug. 2003).

TERRITORY AND POPULATION

Afghanistan is bounded in the north by Turkmenistan, Uzbekistan and Tajikistan, east by China, east and south by Pakistan and west by Iran.

The area is 249,346 sq. miles (645,807 sq. km). The estimated population in 2001 was 26·8m. In 1995 an estimated 19·9% of the population lived in urban areas.

The UN gives a projected population for 2010 of 31·23m.

According to humanitarian agencies in Jan. 2002 there were almost 1·2m. internally displaced persons in Afghanistan. An estimated 4m. sought asylum outside Afghanistan including 2m. in Pakistan, 1·5m. in Iran, 26,000 in Turkmenistan, Tajikistan and Uzbekistan, and several hundred thousand in western European countries, Australia and North America. Approximately half of the internally displaced persons in Afghanistan moved prior to the events of Sept. 2001, for reasons such as drought and food scarcity. As a consequence of the US war in Afghanistan, numbers of refugees to Pakistan and Iran increased dramatically. Pakistan took more than 70,000 Afghan refugees in the months following 11 Sept. 2001 while Iran admitted some 60,000. In the meantime more than 1·6m. Afghans have returned to their country since a UN-sponsored programme began in early 2002, and in Dec. 2002 Pakistan and Afghanistan agreed to repatriate the remaining refugees, lodged in various camps in Pakistan, within three years.

The country is divided into 32 regions *(velayat)*. Area and estimated population in 2000:

Region	*Area (sq. km)*	*Population (1,000)*	Region	*Area (sq. km)*	*Population (1,000)*
Badakhshan	44,059	923	Kunar	4,941	494
Badghis	20,591	413	Kunduz	8,040	1,254
Baghlan	21,118	944	Laghman	3,843	627
Balkh	17,248	1,114	Logar	3,880	425
Bamyan	14,175	476	Nangarhar	7,727	1,452
Farah	48,471	484	Nimroz	41,005	200
Faryab	20,293	1,070	Nurestan[1]	9,225	–
Ghazni	22,915	1,246	Paktika	19,482	494
Ghowr	36,479	810	Paktiya	6,432	931
Helmand	58,584	1,035	Parwan	9,584	919
Herat	54,778	1,520	Samangan	11,262	595
Jawzjan	11,798	1,194	Saripul[1]	15,999	–
Kabul	4,462	2,839	Takhar	12,333	845
Kandahar	54,022	1,159	Uruzgan	30,784	737
Kapisa	1,842	530	Vardak	8,938	730
Khost[1]	4,151	–	Zabul	17,343	350

[1]Khost, Nurestan and Saripul did not exist at the time of the 2000 population estimates.

The capital, Kabul, had a population of 2·45m. in 1999. Other towns (with UN population estimates, 1988): Kandahar (225,500), Herat (177,300), Mazar i Sharif, (130,600), Jalalabad (55,000).

Main ethnic groups: Pashtuns, 38%; Tajiks, 25%; Hazaras, 19%; Uzbeks, 6%; Others, 12%. The official languages are Pashto and Dari.

SOCIAL STATISTICS

Based on 2001 estimates: birth rate, 41 per 1,000 population; death rate, 18 per 1,000; infant mortality, 147 per 1,000 live births; annual population growth rate, 3·5%. Life expectancy at birth, 47 years for men and 45 for women. Fertility rate, 2001, 6·8 births per woman.

The maternal mortality rate is among the highest in the world with some 16,000 pregnancy-related deaths every year.

CLIMATE

The climate is arid, with a big annual range of temperature and very little rain, apart from the period Jan. to April. Winters are very cold, with considerable snowfall, which may last the year round on mountain summits. Kabul, Jan. 27°F (–2·8°C), July 76°F (24·4°C). Annual rainfall 13" (338 mm).

CONSTITUTION AND GOVERNMENT

Following UN-sponsored talks in Bonn, Germany in Nov. 2001, on 22 Dec. 2001 power was handed over to an Afghan Interim Authority, designed to oversee the restructuring of the country until a second stage of government, the Transitional Authority, could be put into power. This second stage resulted from a *Loya Jirga* (Grand Council), which convened between 10–16 June 2002. The Loya Jirga established the Transitional Islamic State of Afghanistan. A Constitutional Commission was established, with UN assistance, to help the Constitutional Loya Jirga prepare a new constitution. A draft constitution was produced for public scrutiny in Nov. 2003 and was approved by Afghanistan's *Loya Jirga* on 4 Jan. 2004. The new constitution creates a strong presidential system, providing for a *President* and two *Vice-Presidents*, and a bicameral parliament. The lower house is the House of the People (*Wolesi Jirga*), directly elected for a five-year term, and the upper house the House of the Elder (*Meshrano Jirga*). The upper house is elected in three divisions. The provincial councils elect one third of its members for a four-year term. The district councils elect the second third of the members for a three-year term. The President appoints the remaining third for a five-year term. At least one woman is elected to the *Wolesi Jirga* from each of the country's 32 provinces, and half of the president's appointments to the *Meshrano Jirga* must be women. The president appoints ministers, the attorney general and central bank governor with the approval of the *Wolesi Jirga.* Cabinet ministers must be university graduates. Presidential and parliamentary elections, the first in 25 years, were scheduled for June 2004 but were put back to Oct. 2004. The parliamentary elections were subsequently delayed again and were set to be held in April 2005, but were postponed a further time until Sept. 2005.

RECENT ELECTIONS

Elections were held by the *Loya Jirga* on 13 June 2002. Hamid Karzai was elected president with 1,295 out of 1,575 votes cast, against 171 for Masooda Jalal and 89 for Mir Mohammad Mahfoz Nadai.

Afghanistan's first-ever presidential election, held on 9 Oct. 2004, was won by head of the transitional government Hamid Karzai, with 55·4% of votes cast, defeating Yunus Qanooni, with 16·3% of the vote, Haji Mohammad Mohaqiq with 11·6% and Abdul Rashid Dostum with 10·0%. There were 18 candidates in total. Turn-out was 70%. Parliamentary elections are set to take place in Sept. 2005.

CURRENT ADMINISTRATION

In March 2005 the government was composed as follows:

President: Hamid Karzai; b. 1957 (Pashtun; sworn in 19 June 2002).

Vice Presidents: Ahmad Zia Masood (Tajik); Karim Khalili (Hazara Shia).

Minister of Agriculture: Abdullah Ramin. *Anti-Narcotics:* Habibollah Qaderi. *Border and Tribal Affairs:* Abdolkarim Brahwi. *Commerce:* Hedayat Amin Arsala. *Communications:* Amirzai Senguin. *Defence:* Abdul Rahim Wardak. *Economy:* Mir-Mohammad Amin Farhang. *Education:* Nour Mohammad Qarqin. *Finance:* Anwar ul-Haq Ahady. *Foreign Affairs:* Dr Abdullah Abdullah. *Hajj (Pilgrimage) and Awqaf:* Nematollah Chahrani. *Higher Education:* Seyyed Amir-Shah Hasanyar. *Information and Culture:* Seyyed Rahin Makhdoom. *Interior:* Ali Ahmed Jalali. *Justice:* Sarwar Danesh. *Labour and Social Affairs:* Seyyed Ekramoddin Makroumi. *Martyrs and Disabled:* Sediqa Balkhi. *Mines and Industries:* Mir-Mohammad Sediq. *Public Health:* Seyyed Mohammad-Amin Fatemi. *Public Works:* Sohrab Ali Safari. *Return of Refugees:* Azam Dadfar. *Rural Development:* Mohammad Hanif Atmar. *Transport:* Enayatullah Qasemi. *Urban Development and Housing:* Mohammad Yousof Pashtun. *Water and Power:* Ismail Khan. *Women's Affairs:* Masouda Djalal. *Youth:* Amina Afzali.

Government Website: http://www.afghangovernment.com

DEFENCE

In 2001 military expenditure totalled US$245m. (US$11 per capita), representing 12·2% of GDP.

Casualties from landmines and unexploded munitions total 150–300 per month, a figure exacerbated by the crisis of late 2001.

A UN-mandated international force, ISAF, assists the government in the maintenance of security. It has been led by NATO since Aug. 2003 and comprises 8,000 peacekeepers, mostly from Europe

Army. The decimation of the Taliban's armed forces left Afghanistan without an army. A multi-ethnic Afghan National Army, under the command of President Hamid Karzai, has been established, currently numbering 15,000 but ultimately with a strength of 70,000. Border guards number around 12,000.

Air Force. Afghanistan's air forces have been severely damaged, but there are now plans for a new air force with a strength of 8,000.

INTERNATIONAL RELATIONS

UN sanctions were imposed in 1999 but were withdrawn following the collapse of the Taliban regime.

Afghanistan is a member of the UN, Asian Development Bank, ECO, Colombo Plan, OIC, IOM and Islamic Development Bank. In April 2003 the transitional government applied for membership of the WTO although membership negotiations are expected to take several years.

ECONOMY

In 2002 agriculture accounted for 49·1% of GDP, industry 19·8% and services 29·7%.

Overview. Reconstruction in Afghanistan started at the end of 2001, when the economy was in an impoverished state after more than 20 years of conflict, earthquakes and drought. Problems included largely defunct government and financial institutions, weak administrative capacity and a devastated infrastructure. Social indicators were among the worst in the world. Progress has been made in rebuilding institutions and in the implementation of sound economic policies. There has been a strong commitment to fiscal discipline. A new currency was launched in late 2002 and monetary policy has been restrained since then. Economic recovery has been high, real GDP, excluding opium production, is estimated to have grown by almost 30% in 2002–03. GDP growth was largely driven by the end of a prolonged drought and by donor assistance. Following the military campaign in Afghanistan pledges of economic aid came from many countries, totalling more than US$4·5bn, of which the USA pledged US$1·8bn. The informal sector seems to be growing alongside the formal—opium production is estimated by the UN to have reached 3,400 tonnes and the sector accounts for about half of overall GDP.

Currency. A new currency was introduced in Oct. 2002. Called the *afghani* (as was its predecessor), one of the new notes is worth 1,000 of the old ones. The old *afghani* had been trading at around 46,000 to the US$.

Budget. Revenues in 2002–03 were US$600m. and expenditures US$150m.

Performance. Real GDP growth (excluding opium production) was estimated at 29% in 2002–03.

Banking and Finance. Da Afghanistan Bank undertakes the functions of a central bank, holding the exclusive right of note issue. Founded in 1939, its *Governor* is Anwarulhaq Ahadi. The banking sector has undergone major reconstruction since the removal of the Taliban government in 2001.

Weights and Measures. The metric system is in increasingly common use. Local units include: one *khurd* = 0·11 kg; one *pao* = four khurds; one *charak* = four paos; one *sere* = four charaks; one *kharwar* = 580 kg or 16 maunds of 36·25 kg each; one *gaz* = 101·6 cm; one *jarib* = 60 x 60 kabuli yd or 0·202 ha; one *kulba* = 40 jaribs (area in which 2½ kharwars of seed can be sown); one jarib yd = 73·66 cm.

ENERGY AND NATURAL RESOURCES

Electricity. In 2000 there were six generating plants, four of which were hydroelectric. Installed capacity was 0·5m. kW in 2000. Production was estimated at 480m. kWh in 2000 with consumption an estimated 575m. kWh.

Oil and Gas. Natural gas reserves were 99bn. cu. metres in 2002. Production in 1998 was 137m. cu. metres. A consortium of oil and gas companies ('CentGas') was planning a US$2bn. natural gas pipeline from Turkmenistan through Afghanistan to Pakistan, although the withdrawal from the project of the US oil company Unocal in April 1998 led to doubts over the viability of the project. Since the installation of the Interim Authority, and with the developments of the past two years, both the CentGas project and other major oil and gas ventures within the region from US, Chinese and Iranian companies seem likely to proceed.

Minerals. There are deposits of coal, copper, barite, lapis lazuli, emerald, talc and salt.

Agriculture. The greater part of Afghanistan is mountainous but there are many fertile plains and valleys. In 2001 there were 7·91m. ha of arable land and 0·14m. ha of permanent cropland; 2·39m. ha were irrigated in 2001. 69·2% of the economically active population were engaged in agriculture in 1995. Principal crops include grains, rice, fresh and dried fruits, vegetables, cottonseed and potatoes.

Production, 2000, in 1,000 tonnes: wheat, 1,469; grapes, 330; potatoes, 235; rice, 233; maize, 115. Opium production in 2001 was just 200 tonnes (down from 4,581 tonnes in 1999), but in 2002 it rose again to 3,400 tonnes, and further to 3,600 tonnes in 2003. In 1998 the harvest was worth an estimated US$69m. The area under cultivation in 2003 was 80,000 ha, up from 7,606 ha in 2001 but down from 90,983 ha in 1999. For several years Afghanistan's annual narcotics production was more than twice that of the second largest producer, Myanmar. In Feb. 2001 the United Nations Drug Control Programme reported that opium production had been almost totally eradicated after the Taliban outlawed the cultivation of poppies. As a result in 2001 Myanmar became the largest producer of opium, but in 2002 and 2003 Afghanistan was again the leading producer. Despite a renewed clampdown on opium production and trafficking since the fall of the Taliban Afghanistan's farmers are being forced by poverty to revive the industry.

Livestock (2000): cattle, 3·5m.; sheep, 18·0m.; goats, 7·4m.; asses, 920,000; camels, 290,000; horses, 104,000; chickens, 7m.

Forestry. In 2000 forests covered 1·35m. ha, or 2·1% of the total land area. Timber production in 2001 was 3·07m. cu. metres.

Fisheries. In 2001 the total catch was estimated to be 800 tonnes, exclusively from inland waters.

INDUSTRY

Major industries include natural gas, fertilizers, cement, coalmining, small vehicle assembly plants, building, carpet weaving, cotton textiles, clothing and footwear, leather tanning and fruit canning.

Labour. The workforce was 8,851,000 in 1996 (65% males). In 1995 the unemployment rate was estimated at 8%.

INTERNATIONAL TRADE

Imports and Exports. Total exports (1999), US$150m.; imports US$600m. Main exported products: opium (illegal trade), non-edible crude materials (excluding fuels), manufactured goods (raw material intensive), machinery and transport equipment, fruits, nuts, hand-woven carpets, wool, hides, precious and semi-precious gems. The illegal trade in opium is the largest source of export earnings and accounts for half of Afghanistan's GDP. Main imports: foodstuffs and live animals, beverages and tobacco, mineral fuels, manufactured goods, chemicals and related products, machinery and transport equipment. Main import sources in 1997 were Singapore (19·2%), Japan (18·5%), China (6·9%) and India (4·8%). Leading export destinations were Pakistan (20·1%), Belgium-Luxembourg (8·7%), France (7·4%) and USA (6·7%).

Imports and exports were largely unaffected by the sanctions imposed during the Taliban regime.

COMMUNICATIONS

Roads. There were 20,720 km of roads in 2001, of which 3,120 km were paved. Approximately half of all road surfaces are in a poor state of repair as a result of military action, but rebuilding is underway. In Jan. 2003 women regained the right to drive after a ten-year ban. Approximately 31,000 passenger cars (1·4 per 1,000 inhabitants) and 25,000 trucks and vans were in use in 1996.

Rail. There are two short stretches of railway in the country, extensions of the Uzbek and Turkmen networks. A Trans-Afghan Railway was proposed in an Afghan-Pakistan-Turkmen agreement of 1994.

Civil Aviation. There is an international airport at Kabul (Khwaja Rawash Airport). The national carrier is Ariana Afghan Airlines, which in 2003 operated direct flights from Kabul to Amritsar, Delhi, Dubai, Frankfurt, Islamabad, İstanbul, Sharjah and Tehran. In 1999 scheduled airline traffic of Afghanistan-based carriers flew 2·7m. km, carrying 140,000 passengers (36,000 on international flights). The UN sanctions imposed on 14 Nov. 1999 included the cutting off of Afghanistan's air links to the outside world. In Jan. 2002 Ariana Afghan Airlines resumed services and Kabul airport was reopened. The airport was heavily bombed during the US campaign and is still under repair. Afghanistan's first private airline, Kam Air, was launched in Nov. 2003.

Shipping. There are practically no navigable rivers. A port has been built at Qizil Qala on the Oxus and there are three river ports on the Amu Darya, linked by road to Kabul. The container port at Kheyrabad on the Amu Darya river has rail connections to Uzbekistan.

Telecommunications. In 2002 there were 33,100 telephone main lines, or 1·4 per 1,000 inhabitants—the lowest penetration rate of any country outside Africa. There were 12,000 mobile phone subscribers in 2002 and 1,000 Internet users.

Postal Services. In 1998 there were 373 post offices.

SOCIAL INSTITUTIONS

Justice. A Supreme Court was established in June 1978. It retained its authority under the Taliban regime.

Under the Taliban, a strict form of Sharia law was followed. This law, which was enforced by armed police, included prohibitions on alcohol, television broadcasts, internet use and photography, yet received its widest condemnation for its treatment of women. Public executions and amputations were widely used as punishment under the regime.

A Judicial Commission will create a civil justice system in accordance with Islamic principles, international standards, the rule of law and Afghan legal traditions. In April 2004 Afghanistan carried out its first execution since the fall of the Taliban.

Religion. The predominant religion is Islam. An estimated 86% of the population are Sunni Muslims, and 9% Shias.

The Taliban provoked international censure in May 2001 by forcing the minority population of Afghan Hindus and Sikhs to wear yellow identification badges.

Education. Adult literacy was 31·5% in 1995 (male, 46·2%; female, 16·1%).

The primary enrolment ratio in 1999 was 38% for boys and 3% for girls. Enrolment at secondary and tertiary levels was even lower. In Jan. 2002 there were an estimated 3,600 primary schools, two-thirds of which were government-supported.

In 1995–96 there were five universities, one university of Islamic studies, one state medical institute and one polytechnic. Kabul University had 9,500 students and 500 academic staff. Formerly one of Asia's finest educational institutes, Kabul University lost many of its staff during the Taliban regime, and following the US bombing attacks it was closed down.

In areas controlled by the Taliban education was forbidden for girls. Boys' schools taught only religious education and military training. Female teachers and pupils have now returned to education after five years of exclusion.

Health. Afghanistan is one of the least successful countries in the battle against undernourishment. Between 1980 and 1996 the proportion of undernourished people rose from 33% of the population to 62%. Half of all Afghan children suffer from chronic malnutrition. One in four children die before reaching the age of five, largely as a result of diarrhoea, pneumonia, measles and other similar illnesses.

The bombing of Afghanistan beginning in Oct. 2001 severely disrupted the supply of aid to the country and left much of the population exposed to starvation.

In 1997 there were 2,556 physicians, 232 dentists, 4,182 nurses and 464 pharmacists in Afghanistan.

In the period 1990–98 only 6% of the population had access to safe drinking water (the lowest percentage of any country).

CULTURE

World Heritage Sites. There are two UNESCO sites in Afghanistan: the Minaret and Archaeological Remains of Jam (inscribed in 2002), a 12th century minaret; the Cultural Landscape and archaeological Remains of the Bamiyan Valley (2003), including the monumental Buddha statues destroyed by the Taliban in 2001.

Broadcasting. In 2000 there were 2·95m. radio receivers and 362,000 television receivers (colour by PAL).

Under the Taliban television stations were closed down—only one remained in operation, in a Northern Alliance-controlled area. Television sets were smashed or even publicly hanged. The single radio broadcasting station to remain in operation, Radio Afghanistan, was renamed Voice of Shariah and was used to broadcast official propaganda and religious sermons. It proclaimed itself as the only radio station in the world where music of any kind was banned. Since the collapse of the regime Radio Afghanistan has resumed services, as have Kabul TV and a number of other broadcasters.

Cinema. Cinemas were banned under the Taliban but have since reopened. The Afghan Film Institute is responsible for censorship.

Press. In 1996 there were 12 daily newspapers with a combined circulation of 113,000, at a rate of 5·6 per 1,000 inhabitants.

Under Taliban control there was only one, tightly-controlled, newspaper named *Shariat*. Other newspapers in circulation in Jan. 2002 were *Hewad*, *Anis* and the English-language *Kabul Times*.

Tourism. In 1998 there were 4,000 foreign tourists bringing in receipts of US$1m.

Calendar. The Afghan Interim Authority replaced the lunar calendar with the traditional Afghan solar calendar. The solar calendar was used in Afghanistan until 1999 when it was changed by the Taliban authorities who wanted the country to adopt the system used in Saudi Arabia. The change means the current year is 1384.

DIPLOMATIC REPRESENTATIVES

Of Afghanistan in the United Kingdom (31 Prince's Gate, London, SW7 1QQ)
Ambassador: Ahmad Wali Masoud.

Of the United Kingdom in Afghanistan (15th Street, Roundabout Wazir Akbar Khan, PO Box 334, Kabul)
Ambassador: Dr Rosalind Marsden, CMG.

Of Afghanistan in the USA (2341 Wyoming Avenue, NW, Washington, D.C., 20008)
Ambassador: Said Tayeb Jawad.

Of the USA in Afghanistan (Great Masood Road between Radio Afghanistan and Ministry of Public Health, Kabul)
Ambassador: Zalmay Khalilzad.

Of Afghanistan to the United Nations
Ambassador: Ravan Farhadi.

Of Afghanistan to the European Union
Ambassador: Humayun Tandar.

FURTHER READING

Amin, S. H., *Law, Reform and Revolution in Afghanistan.* London, 1991

Arney, G., *Afghanistan.* London, 1990

Edwards, David B., *Before Taliban: Genealogies of the Afghan Jihad.* Unv. of California Press, Berkeley, 2002

Ewans, Martin, *Afghanistan, A New History*. Curzon Press, Richmond, 2001

Goodson, Larry, *Afghanistan's Endless War: State Failure, Regional Politics and the Rise of the Taliban.* University of Washington Press, 2001

Griffiths, John, *Afghanistan: A History of Conflict.* Andre Deutsch, London, 2001

Hyman, A., *Afghanistan under Soviet Domination, 1964–1991.* 3rd ed. London, 1992

Jones, Schuyler, *Afghanistan.* [Bibliography] ABC-Clio, Oxford and Santa Barbara (CA), 1992

Magnus, Ralph H. and Naby, Eden, *Afghanistan: Mullah, Marx and Mujahid.* Revised ed. Westview Press, Boulder, 2002

Margolis, Eric, *War at the Top of the World: The Struggle for Afghanistan, Kashmir and Tibet.* Routledge, New York, 2001

Montgomery, John Dickey D. and Rondinelli, Dennis A., (eds.) *Beyond Reconstruction in Afghanistan: Lessons from Development Experience.* Palgrave Macmillan, Basingstoke, 2004

Nojumi, Neamatollah, *The Rise of the Taliban in Afghanistan.* Palgrave Macmillan, Basingstoke, 2001

Roy, O., *Islam and Resistance in Afghanistan.* 2nd ed. CUP, 1990

Rubin, B. R., *The Fragmentation of Afghanistan: State Formation and Collapse in the International System.* Yale Univ. Press, 1995.—*The Search for Peace in Afghanistan: from Buffer State to Failed State.* Yale Univ. Press, 1996

Smith, Mary, *Before the Taliban: Living with War, Hoping for Peace.* Iynx Publishing, Aberdour, 2002

Vogelsang, Willem, *The Afghans.* Blackwell, Oxford, 2002

National statistical office: Central Statistics Office, Ansar-i-Watt, Kabul.
Website: http://www.aims.org.af/cso

ALBANIA

Republika e Shqipërisë

Capital: Tirana
Population projection, 2010: 3·34m.
GDP per capita, 2002: (PPP$) 4,830
HDI/world rank: 0·781/65

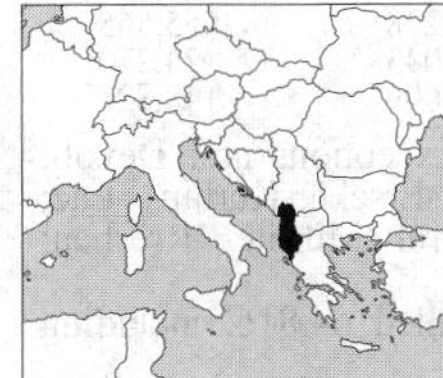

KEY HISTORICAL EVENTS

After the defeat of Turkey in the Balkan war of 1912, Albanian nationalists proclaimed Albania's independence and set up a provisional government.

During the First World War Albania was a battlefield between warring occupation forces. Albania was admitted to the League of Nations on 20 Dec. 1920. In Nov. 1921 her 1913 frontiers were confirmed with minor alterations. Italian influence grew from the mid-1920s. A friendship pact was signed with Italy in 1926 and a defence treaty in 1927. In April 1939 Mussolini invaded Albania and set up a puppet state. During the Second World War Albania suffered first Italian and then German occupation. Resistance was by royalist, nationalist republican and communist movements, often at odds with each other. The latter enjoyed the support of Tito's partisans, who were instrumental in forming the Albanian Communist Party on 8 Nov. 1941. Communists dominated the Anti-Fascist National Liberation Committee which became the Provisional Democratic Government on 22 Oct. 1944 after the German withdrawal, with Enver Hoxha, a French-educated school teacher and member of the Communist Party Central Committee, at its head. Large estates were broken up and the land distributed, though full collectivization was not brought in until 1955–59. Close ties were forged with the USSR but following Khrushchev's reconciliation with Tito in 1956 China replaced the Soviet Union as Albania's patron from 1961 until the end of the Maoist phase in 1977. The regime then adopted a policy of 'revolutionary self-sufficiency'. Following the collapse of the Soviet empire the People's Assembly adopted a decree legalizing opposition parties. A non-Communist government was elected in March 1992.

In 1997 Albania was disrupted by financial crises caused by the collapse of fraudulent pyramid finance schemes. A period of anarchy led to the fall of the administration and to fresh elections which returned a Socialist-led government. A UN peacekeeping force withdrew in Aug. 1997 but sporadic violence continued. In April 1999 the Kosovo crisis which led to NATO air attacks on Yugoslavian military targets set off a flood of refugees into Albania.

TERRITORY AND POPULATION

Albania is bounded in the north by Serbia and Montenegro, east by Macedonia, south by Greece and west by the Adriatic. The area is 28,748 sq. km (11,100 sq. miles). At the census of April 2001 the population was 3,126,163; density, 109 per sq. km.

The UN gives a projected population for 2010 of 3·34m.

In 2001, 57·9% of the population lived in rural areas. The capital is Tirana (population in 2003, 555,565); other large towns (population in 2003) are Elbasan (226,670), Durrës (209,289), Fier (201,397), Shkodër (184,989), Vlorë (148,821), Lushnjë (145,762), Korçë (144,439), Berat (126,608), Kavajë (81,145) and Gjirokastër (Argyrocastro) (56,664).

The country is administratively divided into 12 prefectures, 36 districts, 306 communes and 65 municipalities.

Districts	*Area (sq. km)*	*Population (2003)*	*Districts*	*Area (sq. km)*	*Population (2003)*
Berat	939	126,608	Gramsh	695	31,852
Bulqizë	469	38,105	Has	393	19,360
Delvinë	348	11,628	Kavajë	414	81,145
Devoll	429	34,951	Kolonjë	805	16,316
Dibër	1,088	79,582	Korçë	1,752	144,439
Durrës	433	209,989	Krujë	333	66,084
Elbasan	1,372	226,670	Kuçovë	84	35,557
Fier	785	201,397	Kukës	938	62,778
Gjirokastër	1,137	56,6641	Kurbin	273	54,886

Districts	Area (sq. km)	Population (2003)	Districts	Area (sq. km)	Population (2003)
Lezhë	479	72,001	Pogradec	725	71,738
Librazhd	1,023	70,045	Pukë	1,034	33,444
Lushnjë	712	145,762	Sarandë	749	40,398
Malësi e Madhe	555	37,232	Shkodër	1,973	184,989
Mallakastër	393	38,458	Skrapar	775	25,093
Mat	1,029	58,391	Tepelenë	817	30,189
Mirditë	867	34,202	Tirana	1,238	555,565
Peqin	109	32,777	Tropojë	1,043	24,270
Përmet	930	23,777	Vlorë	1,609	148,821

In most cases districts are named after their capitals. Exceptions are: Devoll, capital—Bilisht; Dibër—Peshkopi; Has—Krumë; Kolonjë—Ersekë; Kurbin—Laç; Mallakastër—Ballsh; Malësi e Madhe—Koplik; Mat—Burrel; Mirditë—Rrëshen; Skrapar—Çorovodë; Tropojë—Bajram Curri.

At the 1989 census, members of ethnic minorities totalled 64,816, including 58,758 Greeks and 4,697 Macedonians.

The official language is Albanian.

SOCIAL STATISTICS

2003: births, 47,012; deaths, 17,967. Rates in 2003 (per 1,000): births, 14·8; deaths, 5·7. Infant mortality, 2001, was 26 per 1,000 live births. Fertility rate (number of births per woman), 2·1 in 2000. Annual population growth rate, 1992–2002, –0·4%. Life expectancy at birth, 2003, 75·4 years for both males and females. Abortion was legalized in 1991.

CLIMATE

Mediterranean-type, with rainfall mainly in winter, but thunderstorms are frequent and severe in the great heat of the plains in summer. Winters in the highlands can be severe, with much snow. Tirana, Jan. 44°F (6·8°C), July 75°F (23·9°C). Annual rainfall 54" (1,353 mm). Shkodër, Jan. 39°F (3·9°C), July 77°F (25°C). Annual rainfall 57" (1,425 mm).

CONSTITUTION AND GOVERNMENT

A new constitution was adopted on 28 Nov. 1998. The supreme legislative body is the single-chamber *People's Assembly* of 140 deputies, 100 directly elected and 40 elected by proportional representation, for four-year terms. Where no candidate wins an absolute majority, a run-off election is held. The *President* is elected by Parliament for a five-year term.

National Anthem. 'Rreth Flamurit të përbashkuar' ('The flag that united us in the struggle'); words by A. S. Drenova, tune by C. Porumbescu.

RECENT ELECTIONS

Parliamentary elections took place on 24 June and 8 July 2001. The ruling Socialist Party of Albania (PSS) won 73 of the 140 seats with 42·0% of votes cast, the Union for Victory coalition 46 with 37·1%, the Democratic Party 6 with 5·1%, and the Social Democratic Party 4 with 3·6%. Other parties won three seats or fewer.

Parliament chose Alfred Moisiu (ind.) as president on 24 June 2002.

CURRENT ADMINISTRATION

President: Alfred Moisiu; b. 1929 (in office since 24 July 2002).

In March 2005 the government comprised:

Prime Minister: Fatos Nano (PSS; sworn in 31 July 2002, having previously held office from Feb.–June 1991 and July 1997–Oct. 1998).

Deputy Prime Minister: Namik Dokle. *Minister for Labour and Social Affairs:* Engjell Bejtja. *Foreign Affairs:* Kastriot Islami. *Public Order:* Igli Toska. *Defence:* Pandeli Majko. *Justice:* Fatmir Xhafa. *Local Government and Decentralization:* Ben Blushi. *Finance:* Arben Malaj. *Economy:* Anastas Angjeli. *Transport and Telecommunications:* Spartak Poçi. *Education and Science:* Luan Memushi. *Health:* Leonard Solis. *Culture, Youth and Sports:* Blendi Kosi. *Environment:* Ethem Ruka. *Integration:* Ermelinda Meksi. *Industry and Energy:* Viktor Doda. *Agriculture:* Agron Duka. *Territory Regulations and Tourism:* Bashkim Fino. *Minister of State and Co-ordination:* Marko Bello.

Albanian Parliament: http://www.parlament.al

DEFENCE

Conscription is for 12 months. Albania's armed forces are being reconstituted, a process that should be completed by 2010. In 2003 defence expenditure totalled US$76m. (US$24 per capita), representing 1·2% of GDP.

Army. Strength in 2002 was 20,000. There is an internal security force, and frontier guards number 500.

Navy. Navy personnel in 2002 totalled 2,500 officers and ratings. Of the 24 vessels in the navy there were 11 torpedo craft. There are naval bases at Durrës, Sarandë, Shëngjin and Vlorë.

Air Force. The Air Force had (2002) about 4,500 personnel, and operated 98 combat aircraft including MiG-15s, MiG-17s and MiG-19s.

INTERNATIONAL RELATIONS

Albania is a member of the UN, WTO, the Council of Europe, OSCE, the Central European Initiative, BSEC, IOM, OIC, Islamic Development Bank and the NATO Partnership for Peace.

ECONOMY

In 2002 agriculture accounted for 25·3% of GDP, industry 18·9% and services 55·7%.

Overview. The Albanian economy collapsed during the political turmoil of 1990. Unemployment rose to 30% and industrial production fell by nearly half by 1992. The government embarked on a reform programme of privatization and economic liberalization with the help of the World Bank and the IMF. The Tirana Stock Exchange was established in 1996 during a period of strong economic growth. GDP annual growth averaged 9% between 1993–95. Privatization of land, small businesses and housing was achieved in 1991–93. A privatization programme for large enterprises was initiated in 1995 under the aegis of the National Privatization Agency. However, the lack of banking sector reform led to informal credit arrangements such as pyramid schemes that grew enormously and collapsed in 1997. This sparked widespread social unrest and the downfall of the government.

The agricultural sector is the mainstay of the Albanian economy, experiencing a revival under private ownership and representing 54% of GDP in 1999. The industrial sector shrank from 44% to 25% of GDP (1990–98). Privatization of the state telecommunications company, Albtelecom, failed in 2002, hindered by a weak international market.

Currency. The monetary unit is the *lek* (ALL), notionally of 100 *qindars*. In Sept. 1991 the lek (plural, *lekë* or leks) was pegged to the ecu at a rate of 30 leks = one ecu. In June 1992 it was devalued from 50 to 110 to US$1. After several years of high inflation (225% in 1992), there was inflation of 5·3% in 2002 and 2·3% in 2003. Foreign exchange reserves were US$319m. in June 2002, total money supply was 156,469m. leks and gold reserves totalled 111,000 troy oz.

Budget. The fiscal year is the calendar year. Government revenues in 2000 totalled 130,642m. leks (tax revenue, 79·7%; non-tax revenue, 20·3%) and expenditures 170,621m. leks (current expenditure, 78·7%; capital expenditure, 21·3%).

Performance. Total GDP in 2003 was US$6·1bn. After the economy contracted by 10·5% in 1997 following the collapse of pyramid finance schemes, real GDP growth averaged 8·2% from 1998 to 2002, albeit with growth in 2002 of 3·4%.

Banking and Finance. The central bank and bank of issue is the Bank of Albania, founded in 1925 with Italian aid as the Albanian State Bank and renamed in 1993. Its *Governor* is Ardian Fullani. The Savings Bank of Albania, which serves around 75% of the Albanian market, was sold by the government to Raiffeisen Zentralbank Österreich AG in Dec. 2003. In 2002 it had total assets of US$1·4bn., approximately 60% of the total assets of the Albanian banking sector. In 2002 there were six other banks: American Bank of Albania; Arab-Albanian Islamic Bank; Fefad Bank; Italian-Albanian Bank; National Commercial Bank of Albania; and Tirana Bank SA.

A stock exchange opened in Tirana in 1996.

ENERGY AND NATURAL RESOURCES

Environment. Albania's carbon dioxide emissions from the consumption and flaring of fossil fuels in 2002 were the equivalent of 1·2 tonnes per capita.

Electricity. Albania is rich in hydro-electric potential. Although virtually all of the electricity is generated by hydro-electric power plants only 30% of potential hydro-electric sources are currently being used. Electricity capacity was 1·67m. kW in 2001. Production was 3·69bn. kWh in 2001 and consumption per capita 1,181 kWh.

Oil and Gas. Offshore exploration began in 1991. Oil has been produced onshore since 1920. Oil reserves in 2002 were 206m. bbls. Crude oil production in 2003, 359,253 tonnes. Natural gas is extracted. Reserves in 2002 totalled 4bn. cu. metres; output in 2000 was 17m. cu. metres.

Minerals. Mineral wealth is considerable and includes lignite, chromium, copper and nickel. Production, in 1999 (in 1,000 tonnes): chromium ore, 79; lignite (2000), 42; copper ore, 34. Nickel reserves are 60m. tonnes of iron containing 1m. tonnes of nickel, but extraction had virtually ceased by 1996. A consortium of British and Italian companies is modernizing the chrome industry with the aim of making Albania the leading supplier of ferrochrome to European stainless steel producers.

Agriculture. In 2001 the agricultural population was 1·78m., of whom 748,000 were economically active. The country is mountainous, except for the Adriatic littoral and the Korçë Basin, which are fertile. Only 24% of the land area is suitable for cultivation; 15% of Albania is used for pasture. In 2001 there were 578,000 ha of arable land and 121,000 ha of permanent cropland. 129,000 ha were irrigated in 2000.

A law of Aug. 1991 privatized co-operatives' land. Families received allocations, according to their size, from village committees. In 1998 there were 466,659 private agricultural holdings with a total area of 451,917 ha; average 0·96 ha. Since 1995 owners have been permitted to buy and sell agricultural land. In 2003 there were 7,774 tractors in use and 875 harvester-threshers.

Production (in 1,000 tonnes), 2003: total grains, 489 (including wheat 260 and maize 207); potatoes, 458; tomatoes, 203; grapes (2000), 79; sugarbeet (2000), 42; wine (2000), 7,413 hectolitres.

Livestock, 2003: sheep, 1,903,000; goats, 1,101,000; cattle, 684,000; asses, 170,000; pigs, 132,000; horses, 48,000; chickens, 4,087,000. Livestock products, 2001 (in 1,000 tonnes): beef, 59; mutton, lamb and goat, 32; pork, 10; poultry, 5; cheese (2000), 12; milk, 831; eggs, 608m. units.

Forestry. Forests covered 1,455,000 ha in 2003 (36·9% of the total land area), mainly oak, elm, pine and birch. Timber production in 2003 was 573,000 cu. metres.

Fisheries. The total catch in 2003 amounted to 3,703 tonnes (1,921 tonnes from sea fishing).

INDUSTRY

Output is small, and the principal industries are agricultural product processing, textiles, oil products and cement. Closures of loss-making plants in the chemical and engineering industries built up in the Communist era led to a 60% decline in production by 1993. Output in 2000 (in 1,000 tonnes): distillate fuel oil, 72; residual fuel oil, 63; kerosene, 58; cement (2001), 30; petrol, 24; rolled steel (1994), 17; beer (2003), 39·0m. litres; wine (2001), 1·4m. litres; 40m. bricks (1994); 126m. cigarettes (2001).

Labour. In 2003 the workforce was 1,089,000, of which 926,000 were employed (745,000 in the private sector). Unemployment was 15·0% at the end of 2003.

The average monthly wage in 2002 was 16,390 leks; the official minimum wage in 2003 was 10,060 leks. Minimum wages may not fall below one-third of maximum. Retirement age is 60 for men and 55 for women.

Trade Unions. Independent trade unions became legal in Feb. 1991.

INTERNATIONAL TRADE

Foreign investment was legalized in Nov. 1990. Foreign debt was US$1,312m. in 2002.

Imports and Exports. Exports in 2002 totalled US$330m.; imports, US$1,485m. Leading exports in 2001: textiles and clothing, 37·4%; footwear and related products, 28·6%; base and fabricated metals, 8·0%. Principal imports in 2001: food and beverages, 19·4%; nonelectrical and electrical machinery, 18·4%; mineral fuels, 13·8%; textiles and clothing, 10·4%; base and fabricated metals, 8·8%. Main export markets, 2001 (% of total trade): Italy, 71·6%; Greece, 13·1%; Germany, 5·6%. Main import suppliers: Italy, 36·5%; Greece, 31·5%; Turkey, 6·7%.

COMMUNICATIONS

Roads. In 2002 there were 3,220 km of main roads, 4,300 km of secondary roads and 10,480 km of other roads. There were 148,531 passenger cars in 2002, as well as 21,026 buses and coaches and 51,960 lorries and vans. There were 428 road accidents in 2000 (280 fatalities).

Rail. Total length in operation in 2000 was 400 km. Passenger-km travelled in 2003 came to 105m. and freight tonne-km to 18m. In Aug. 2003 the government announced plans to re-establish rail links with Montenegro and the European network and construct a railway to Macedonia with the financial assistance of the World Bank.

Civil Aviation. The national carrier is Albanian Airlines, a joint venture with a Kuwaiti firm. It began operations in Oct. 1995. In 2002 it flew services to Bologna, Frankfurt, İstanbul, Priština and Rome. Air civil transportation is carried out by 12 airlines, of which ten are foreign airlines and two are joint ventures. In 1999 scheduled airline traffic of Albania-based carriers flew 0·3m. km, carrying 20,000 passengers (all on international flights). The main airport is Mother Teresa International Airport at Rinas, 25 km from Tirana, which handled 356,823 passengers in 1999.

Shipping. In 2002 merchant shipping totalled 49,000 GRT. The main port is Durrës, with secondary ports being Vlorë, Sarandë and Shëngjin.

Telecommunications. In 2003 there were 222,000 telephone main lines. A state-owned mobile telephone network was set up in 1996, initially serving 8,000 subscribers. By 2003 there were 1·15m. mobile subscribers. There were 36,000 PCs in use in 2002 (8·9 for every 1,000 persons). Albania had 12,000 Internet users in 2002.

Postal Services. In 1995 there were 698 post offices. The volume of postal traffic in 2000 was 2,095,000 pieces of ordinary mail and 892,000 pieces of registered post.

SOCIAL INSTITUTIONS

Justice. A new criminal code was introduced in June 1995. The administration of justice (made up of First Instance Courts, The Courts of Appeal and the Supreme Court) is presided over by the *Council of Justice*, chaired by the President of the Republic, which appoints judges to courts. A Ministry of Justice was re-established in 1990 and a Bar Council set up. In Nov. 1993 the number of capital offences was reduced from 13 to six and the death penalty was abolished for women. In 2000 the death penalty was abolished for peacetime offences. The prison population in Nov. 2001 was 3,053 (90 per 100,000 of national population).

Religion. In 2001, 39% of the population were Muslims, mainly Sunni with some Belaktashi, 17% Roman Catholic, 10% Albanian Orthodox and the remainder other religions. The Albanian Orthodox Church is autocephalous; it is headed by an Exarch, Anastasios, Archbishop of Tirana, Durrës and All Albania, and three metropolitans. In 2001 there were 118 priests. The Roman Catholic cathedral in Shkodër has been restored and the cathedral in Tirana has been rebuilt, opening in 2002. In 2000 there were one Roman Catholic archbishop and three bishops.

Education. Primary education is free and compulsory in eight-year schools from seven to 15 years. Secondary education is also free and lasts four years. Secondary education is divided into three categories: general; technical and professional; vocational. There were, in 2003–04, 1,763 nursery schools with 79,905 pupils and 3,770 teachers; 27,248 primary school teachers with 505,141 pupils; and 142,402 pupils and 6,873 teachers at secondary schools. In 2000–01 there were five universities, one agricultural university, one technological university, one polytechnic, one academy of fine arts and one higher institute of physical education.

There were 53,255 university students registered and 1,750 academic staff in 2003–04; Tirana is the largest university, with 12,190 students in 2003–04. Adult literacy in 2001 was 85·3% (92·5% among males and 77·8% among females).

In 2000 total expenditure on education came to 3% of GNP.

Health. Medical services are free, though medicines are charged for. In 2003 there were 50 hospitals, 4,100 doctors and 11,470 nurses or midwives. In 2003 there were 9,514 hospital beds. The expenditure on health in 1999 was 12,077m. leks (7·3% of total government expenditure).

Welfare. The retirement age is 60 (men), or 55 (women); to be eligible for a state pension contributions over 35 years are required. Old-age benefits consist of a basic pension and an earnings-related increment. The basic pension is indexed according to price changes of selected commodities.

Unemployment benefit was 3,960 leks per month as of 2003.

CULTURE

World Heritage Sites. In 1992 Butrint was added to the UNESCO World Heritage List. Butrint is a settlement in the southwest of the country, near the port of Sarandë, which was inhabited from 800 BC and is now a major site of archaeological investigation.

Broadcasting. Broadcasting is regulated by the National Council for Radio-Television (NCRT), one member of which is appointed by the president, and the other six by the permanent Commission on the Media, which is composed equally of representatives of government and opposition parties. In Dec. 2000 the NCRT licensed two national television stations, 45 local television stations, 31 local radio stations and one national radio station. There are also a number of privately owned television broadcasting stations. In 2000 there were 756,000 radio receivers and 480,000 TV receivers (colour by SECAM H).

Press. In 1996 there were five national dailies (combined circulation of 116,000, at a rate of 37 per 1,000 inhabitants).

Tourism. In 2000, 32,000 foreign tourists visited Albania; tourist spending totalled US$389m. There were 102 hotels in 1999.

DIPLOMATIC REPRESENTATIVES

Of Albania in the United Kingdom (2nd Floor, 24 Buckingham Gate, London, SW1E 6LB)
Ambassador: Kastriot Robo.

Of the United Kingdom in Albania (Rruga Skenderbeg 12, Tirana)
Ambassador: Richard Jones.

Of Albania in the USA (2100 S St., NW, Washington, D.C., 20008)
Ambassador: Dr Fatos Tarifa.

Of the USA in Albania (Tirana Rruga Elbasanit 103, Tirana)
Ambassador: Marcie Ries.

Of Albania to the United Nations
Ambassador: Agim Nesho.

Of Albania to the European Union
Ambassador: Artur Kuko.

FURTHER READING

Fischer, Bernd, *Albania at War 1939–45.* Hurst, London, 1999
Hutchings, R., *Historical Dictionary of Albania.* Lanham (MD), 1997
Sjoberg, O., *Rural Change and Development in Albania.* Boulder (CO), 1992
Vickers, M., *The Albanians: a Modern History.* London, 1997
Vickers, M. and Pettifer, J., *Albania: from Anarchy to a Balkan Identity*. Farnborough, 1997
Winnifrith, T. (ed.) *Perspectives on Albania.* London, 1992
Young, A., *Albania.* [Bibliography] 2nd ed. ABC-Clio, Oxford and Santa Barbara (CA), 1997

National statistical office: Albanian Institute of Statistics, Tirana. *Director General:* Milva Ekonomi.
Website: http://www.instat.gov.al/

ALGERIA

Jumhuriya al-Jazairiya ad-Dimuqratiya ash-Shabiya (People's Democratic Republic of Algeria)

Capital: Algiers
Population projection, 2010: 35·55m.
GDP per capita, 2002: (PPP$) 5,760
HDI/world rank: 0·704/108

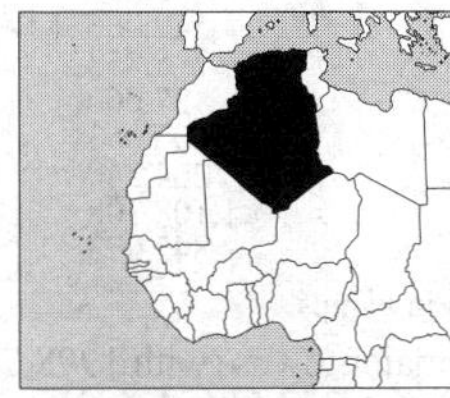

KEY HISTORICAL EVENTS

Algeria came under French control in the 1850s. French settlers developed political and economic power at the expense of the indigenous Muslim population. In Nov. 1954 the *Front de Libération Nationale* (FLN), representing the Muslim majority, declared open warfare against the French administration. There was extensive loss of life and property during the fighting which continued unabated until March 1962 when a ceasefire was agreed between the French government and the nationalists. Against the wishes of the French in Algeria, Gen. de Gaulle conceded Algerian independence on 3 July 1962.

The Political Bureau of the FLN took over the functions of government, a National Constituent Assembly was elected and the Republic was declared on 25 Sept. 1962. One of the founders of the FLN, Ahmed Ben Bella, became prime minister, and president the following year. On 15 June 1965 the government was overthrown by a junta of army officers, who established a Revolutionary Council under Col. Houari Boumédienne. After 10 years of rule, Boumédienne proposed elections for a president and a National Assembly. A new constitution was accepted in a referendum in Nov. 1976 and Boumédienne was elected president unopposed. With all parties except the FLN banned from participating, a National Assembly was elected in Feb. 1977.

On the death of the president in Dec. 1978 the Revolutionary Council again took over the government. The Islamic Salvation Front (FIS) was banned in March 1992. The head of state, Mohamed Boudiaf, was assassinated on 29 July 1992, and a campaign of terrorism by fundamentalists has continued to the present day. It is estimated that over 100,000 lives have been lost, although Algeria has emerged from the worst of the war, with most of the guerrilla activity now restricted to the countryside. Unrest among Berbers, Algeria's main ethnic community, erupted into violence in May 2001, resulting in 60 people losing their lives in the Berber region of Kabylie. In March 2002 President Bouteflika agreed to grant the Berber language official status alongside Arabic.

TERRITORY AND POPULATION

Algeria is bounded in the west by Morocco and Western Sahara, southwest by Mauritania and Mali, southeast by Niger, east by Libya and Tunisia, and north by the Mediterranean Sea. It has an area of 2,381,741 sq. km (919,595 sq. miles). Population (census 1998) 29,100,867; density, 12·2 per sq. km. 2003 estimate: 31·82m. In 2001, 57·7% of the population lived in urban areas.

The UN gives a projected population for 2010 of 35·55m.

2·5m. Algerians live in France.

83% of the population speak Arabic, 17% Berber; French is widely spoken. A law of Dec. 1996 made Arabic the sole official language, but in March 2002 Tamazight, the Berber language, was given official status and also made a national language.

The 1998 census populations of the 48 *wilayat* (provincial councils) were as follows:

Adrar	311,615	Annaba	557,818
Ain Defla	660,342	Batna	962,623
Ain Témouchent	327,331	al-Bayadh	168,789
Al-Jaza'ir (Algiers)	2,562,428	Béchar	225,546

Béjaia	856,840	Ouahran (Oran)	1,213,839
Biskra	575,858	Ouargla	445,619
Blida	784,283	al-Oued	504,401
Bordj Bou Arreridj	555,402	Oum al-Bouaghi	519,170
Bouira	629,560	Qacentina (Constantine)	810,914
Boumerdes	647,389	Relizane	642,205
Chlef	858,695	Saida	279,526
Djelfa	797,706	Sétif	1,311,413
Ghardaia	300,516	Sidi-bel-Abbès	525,632
Guelma	430,000	Skikda	786,154
Illizi	34,108	Souk Ahras	367,455
Jijel	573,208	Tamanrasset	137,175
Khenchela	327,917	at-Tarf	352,588
Laghouat	317,125	Tébessa	549,066
Mascara	676,192	Tiaret	725,853
Médéa	802,078	Tindouf	27,060[1]
Mila	674,480	Tipaza	506,053
Mostaganem	631,057	Tissemsilt	264,240
M'Sila	805,519	Tizi-Ouzou	1,108,708
Naâma	127,314	Tlemcen	842,053

[1]Excluding Saharawi refugees (170,000 in 1988) in camps.

The capital is Algiers (1998 population, 1,519,570). Other major towns (with 1998 census populations): Oran, 655,852; Constantine, 462,187; Batna, 242,514; Annaba, 215,083; Sétif, 211,859; Sidi-bel-Abbès, 180,260; Biskra, 170,956; Djelfa, 154,265; Tébassa, 153,246; Blida, 153,083; Skikda, 152,335; Béjaia, 147,076; Tiaret, 145,332; Chlef, 133,874; al-Buni, 133,471; Béchar, 131,010.

SOCIAL STATISTICS

2001 estimates: births, 618,000; deaths, 129,000; marriages, 194,273. Rates (2001 estimates): births, 20·1 per 1,000; deaths, 4·2 per 1,000. Infant mortality in 2001 was 39 per 1,000 live births. Expectation of life (2001), 70·7 years for females and 67·7 years for males. Annual population growth rate, 1992–2002, 1·8%. Fertility rate, 2001, 2·9 births per woman.

CLIMATE

Coastal areas have a warm temperate climate, with most rain in winter, which is mild, while summers are hot and dry. Inland, conditions become more arid beyond the Atlas Mountains. Algiers, Jan. 54°F (12·2°C), July 76°F (24·4°C). Annual rainfall 30" (762 mm). Biskra, Jan. 52°F (11·1°C), July 93°F (33·9°C). Annual rainfall 6" (158 mm). Oran, Jan. 54°F (12·2°C), July 76°F (24·4°C). Annual rainfall 15" (376 mm).

CONSTITUTION AND GOVERNMENT

A referendum was held on 28 Nov. 1996. The electorate was 16,434,527; turn-out was 79·6%. The electorate approved by 85·81% of votes cast a new Constitution which defines the fundamental components of the Algerian people as Islam, Arab identity and Berber identity. It was signed into law on 7 Dec. 1996. Political parties are permitted, but not if based on a separatist feature such as race, religion, sex, language or region. The terms of office of the President are limited to two, but the President's powers of nomination are widened (General-Secretary of the government, governor of the national bank, judges, chiefs of security organs and prefects). Parliament is bicameral: a 389-member *National Assembly* elected by direct universal suffrage using proportional representation, and a 144-member *Council of the Nation*, one-third nominated by the President and two-thirds indirectly elected by the 48 local authorities. The Council of the Nation debates bills passed by the National Assembly which become law if a three-quarters majority is in favour.

In a referendum on 16 Sept. 1999 voters were asked 'Do you agree with the president's approach to restore peace and civilian concord?' Turn-out was 85·1% and 98·6% of the votes cast were in favour.

National Anthem. 'Qassaman bin nazilat Il-mahiqat' ('We swear by the lightning that destroys'); words by M. Zakaria, tune by Mohamed Fawzi.

RECENT ELECTIONS

In presidential elections on 8 April 2004 Abdelaziz Bouteflika (Rassemblement National pour la Démocratie; RND) won a second term of office, gaining 85·0% of the votes cast; Ali Benflis (Front pour la Libération Nationale; FLN) received 6·4% of votes cast; Abdallah Djaballah (el-Islah), 5·0%; Said Sadi, 1·9%; Louiza Hanoune, 1·0%; and Fawzi Rebaine, 0·6%. Turn-out was 58·1%.

Parliamentary elections were held on 30 May 2002. Prime Minister Ali Benflis' FLN won 199 out of 389 seats with 34·3% of votes cast; the RND, 47 seats with 8·2%; el-Islah, 43 with 9·5%; the Movement of the Society for Peace, 38 with 7·0%; and the Workers' Party, 21 with 3·3%. Turn-out was 46·2%.

CURRENT ADMINISTRATION

President: Abdelaziz Bouteflika; b. 1937 (sworn in 27 April 1999; re-elected 8 April 2004). In March 2005 the government comprised:

Prime Minister: Ahmed Ouyahia; b. 1952 (RND; appointed 5 May 2003, having previously held office from Dec. 1995 to Dec. 1998).

Minister of State, Interior Minister: Noureddine Yazid Zerhouni. *Minister of State, Foreign Affairs Minister:* Abdelaziz Belkhadem. *Minister of Agriculture and Rural Development:* Saïd Berkat. *Commerce:* Noureddine Boukrouh. *Communication:* Boudjemaa Haichour. *Culture:* Khalida Toumi. *Energy and Mines:* Chakib Khelil. *Finance:* Abdelatif Benachenhou. *Fisheries and Marine Resources:* Smaïl Mimoune. *Health, Population and Hospital Reform:* Mourad Redjimi. *Higher Education and Scientific Research:* Rachid Harraoubia. *Housing and Urban Planning:* Mohamed Nadir Hamimid. *Industry:* El-Hachemi Djaaboub. *Information Technology and Telecommunications:* Amar Tou. *Justice and Keeper of the Seals:* Tayeb Belaiz. *Labour and Social Security:* Tayeb Louh. *Moudjahidine (War Veterans):* Mohamed Cherif Abbes. *National and Regional Development and Environment:* Chérif Rahmani. *National Education:* Boubekeur Benbouzid. *National Solidarity and Employment:* Djamel Ould Abbas. *Vocational Training:* El-Hadi Khaldi. *Public Works:* Omar Ghoul. *Relations with Parliament:* Mahmoud Khoudri. *Religious Affairs:* Bouabdellah Ghlamallah. *Small and Medium-Sized Businesses, and Handicrafts:* Mustapha Benbada. *Tourism:* Mohamed Seghir Kara. *Transport:* Mohamed Maghlaoui. *Water Resources:* Abdelmalek Sellal. *Youth and Sports:* Abdelaziz Ziari.

President's Website (Arabic and French only): http://www.elmouradia.dz

DEFENCE

Conscription is for 18 months (six months basic training and 12 months civilian tasks) at the age of 19.

Military expenditure totalled US$2,206m. in 2003 (US$69 per capita), representing 3·4% of GDP.

Army. There are six military regions. The Army had a strength of 120,000 (75,000 conscripts) in 2002. The Ministry of the Interior maintains National Security Forces of 20,000. The Republican Guard numbers 1,200 personnel and the Gendarmerie 60,000. There were in addition legitimate defence groups (self-defence militia and communal guards) numbering around 100,000.

Navy. Naval personnel in 2002 totalled 6,700. The Navy's 28 vessels included two submarines and three frigates. There are naval bases at Algiers, Annaba, Mers el Kebir and Jijel.

Air Force. The Air Force in 2002 had 10,000 personnel, 222 combat aircraft and 63 armed helicopters.

INTERNATIONAL RELATIONS

Algeria is a member of the UN, the African Union, the League of Arab States, Arab Maghreb Union, OPEC, African Development Bank, IOM, OIC and Islamic Development Bank.

ECONOMY

In 2002 agriculture accounted for 10·0% of GDP, industry 52·7% and services 37·3%.

Overview. The Algerian economy is heavily dependent on the sale of oil and gas. The government responded to the collapse of oil prices in 1986 by negotiating large loans which became unmanageable. An IMF-sponsored programme for economic reconstruction was implemented in 1994. The austerity measures taken to reduce inflation and create a free-market economy resulted in massive unemployment. 500,000 lost their jobs as a result of hundreds of companies going bankrupt. However, inflation was reduced to 5% and foreign currency reserves were replenished. Algeria's economy has grown slowly despite a high foreign investment rate in the country. The government launched a revival plan in 2001 which envisaged an expenditure of US$7bn. over three years to develop infrastructure and to support economic diversification, especially in agriculture.

Privatization policy began in earnest in 1994 as demanded by the IMF rescue package. Legislation of 1995 offered 1,200 small and 50 large businesses for sale to Algerian citizens. However, few public assets had been privatized by 2001, when new legislation was passed to simplify the process. In 2002 the Indian steel company ISPAT acquired a 70% stake in SIDER, the government-owned iron and steel producer.

Currency. The unit of currency is the *Algerian dinar* (DZD) of 100 *centimes*. Foreign exchange reserves were US$21,133m. in June 2002, with gold reserves 5·58m. troy oz. Total money supply was 1,287bn. dinars in March 2002. Inflation was 4·2% in 2001 and 1·4% in 2002. The dinar was devalued by 28·6% in April 1994.

Budget. The fiscal year starts on 1 Jan. In 2001 revenue totalled 1,505,500m. dinars and expenditure 1,334,500m. dinars.

Performance. Total GDP was US$65·9bn. in 2002. GDP growth was 4·0% in 2002 and 6·8% in 2003.

Banking and Finance. The central bank and bank of issue is the Banque d'Algérie. The *Governor* is Mohammed Laksaci. In 2002 it had total reserves of US$23·5bn. Private banking recommenced in Sept. 1995. In 2002 there were five state-owned commercial banks, four development banks, nine private banks and two foreign banks.

ENERGY AND NATURAL RESOURCES

Environment. Algeria's carbon dioxide emissions from the consumption and flaring of fossil fuels in 2002 were the equivalent of 2·6 tonnes per capita.

Electricity. Installed capacity was 6m. kW in 2000 (4·6% is hydro-electric). Production in 2000 was 24·65bn. kWh, with consumption per capita 808 kWh.

Oil and Gas. A law of Nov. 1991 permits foreign companies to acquire up to 49% of known oil and gas reserves. Oil and gas production accounted for 23·2% of GDP in 1994. Oil production in 2003 was 79·0m. tonnes; oil reserves in 2002 totalled 9·2bn. bbls. Production of natural gas in 2002 was 80·4bn. cu. metres (the fifth highest in the world); proven reserves in 2002 were 4,520bn. cu. metres.

Minerals. Output in 2001 (in 1,000 tonnes): gypsum (2000), 1,341; iron ore, 1,291; phosphate rock, 939; salt, 195; zinc, 13·5; lead (1999), 1·2. There are also deposits of mercury, silver, gold, copper, antimony, kaolin, marble, onyx, salt and coal.

Agriculture. Much of the land is unsuitable for agriculture. The northern mountains provide grazing. There were 7·67m. ha of arable land in 2001 and 0·59m. ha of permanent crops. 0·56m. ha were irrigated in 2001. In 1987 the government sold back to the private sector land which had been nationalized on the declaration of independence in 1962; a further 0·5m. ha, expropriated in 1973, were returned to some 30,000 small landowners in 1990. In 2002 the agricultural population was 13·04m. There were 93,700 tractors and 9,250 harvester-threshers in 2001.

The chief crops in 2000 were (in 1,000 tonnes): potatoes, 950; tomatoes, 800; wheat, 800; melons and watermelons, 540; dates, 430; barley, 400; onions, 380; olives, 350; oranges, 310; grapes, 180; chillies and green peppers, 155; carrots, 135.

Livestock, 2000: sheep, 18·2m.; goats, 3·4m.; cattle, 1·65m.; asses, 202,000; camels, 151,000; mules, 72,000; horses, 55,000; chickens, 110m. Livestock products, 2000 (in 1,000 tonnes): poultry meat, 200; lamb and mutton, 170; beef and veal, 117; eggs, 120; cow's milk, 1,000; sheep's milk, 220; goat's milk, 150.

Forestry. Forests covered 2·15m. ha. in 2000, or 0·9% of the total land area. The greater part of the state forests are brushwood, but there are large areas with cork-oak trees, Aleppo pine, evergreen oak and cedar. The dwarf-palm is grown on the plains, alfalfa on the tableland. Timber is cut for firewood and for industrial purposes, and bark for tanning. Timber production in 2001 was 7·40m. cu. metres.

Fisheries. There are extensive fisheries for sardines, anchovies, sprats, tuna and shellfish. The total catch in 2001 amounted to approximately 100,000 tonnes, exclusively from marine waters.

INDUSTRY

Output (in 1,000 tonnes): cement (2001), 8,710; distillate fuel oil (2000), 6,008; residual fuel oil (2000), 5,526; petrol (2000), 2,106; jet fuels (2000), 1,571; crude steel (2000), 842; pig iron (2000), 767; rolled steel (1997), 439; phosphate fertilizers (2001), 254; ammonitrates (1992), 193; concrete bars (1992), 134; steel tubes (2001), 62; bricks (2001), 1,428,000 cu. metres. Production in units: lorries (2001), 2,811 (assembled); tractors (2001), 2,105; TV sets (2001), 245,000.

Labour. In 2000 there were 5,726,000 employed persons. The main areas of activity were: public administration and defence/compulsory social security, 1,773,000; education and other community, social and personal service activities, 933,000; agriculture, hunting, fishing and forestry, 898,000; mining, quarrying and manufacturing, and electricity, gas and water supply, 721,000. By 2001 unemployment was approaching 30%.

INTERNATIONAL TRADE

Foreign debt was US$22,800m. in 2002. Foreign investors are permitted to hold 100% of the equity of companies, and to repatriate all profits.

Imports and Exports. In 2000 exports (f.o.b.) were valued at US$22,031m. and imports (c.i.f.) at US$9,152m. Main export markets in 1999 (in US$1m.): Italy, 2,942; USA, 1,755; France, 1,719; Spain, 1,329; Netherlands, 1,021. Main import suppliers (in US$1m.): France, 2,086; Italy, 907; USA, 770; Germany, 679; Spain, 508. Main imports in 1999 (in US$1m.): machinery and transport equipment, 3,035; food and live animals, 2,222; manufactured goods, 1,667; chemicals and related products, 1,073. Main exports (in US$1m.): petroleum and products, 6,940; gas, 5,227.

COMMUNICATIONS

Roads. There were, in 1999, an estimated 104,000 km of roads including 640 km of motorways. There were approximately 1,505,000 vehicles registered in 1996, of which 725,000 were passenger cars (24·8 cars per 1,000 inhabitants).

Rail. In 2000 there were 2,888 km of 1,435 mm route (283 km electrified) and 1,085 km of 1,055 mm gauge. The railways carried 7·8m. tonnes of freight and 28·3m. passengers in 2000.

Civil Aviation. The main international airport is at Algiers (Houari Boumédienne), with some international services also using Annaba, Constantine and Oran. The national carrier is the state-owned Air Algérie which in 2003 operated direct flights to Frankfurt, Geneva and London. There were direct international flights in 2003 with other airlines to Barcelona, Cairo, Casablanca, Damascus, İstanbul, Lille, Lyon, Malaga, Marseille, Milan, Montpellier, Munich, Nantes, Nice, Palma de Mallorca, Paris, Rome, Strasbourg, Toulouse, Tripoli and Tunis. In 2000 Houari Boumédienne International Airport handled 2,754,689 passengers (1,392,438 on domestic flights) and, in 1999, 14,757 tonnes of freight. In 1999 scheduled airline traffic of Algerian-based carriers flew 32·2m. km, carrying 2,937,000 passengers (1,663,000 on international flights).

Shipping. In 2001 vessels totalling 118,994,000 GRT entered ports and vessels totalling 119,074,000 GRT cleared. The state shipping line, Compagnie Nationale

Algérienne de Navigation, owned 47 vessels in 2001. The merchant shipping fleet totalled 936,000 GRT in 2002, including oil tankers 19,000 GRT.

Telecommunications. In 2002 there were 2,308,000 telephone subscribers, or 73·8 per 1,000 inhabitants, and 242,000 PCs in use (7·7 per 1,000 persons). Mobile phone subscribers numbered 400,000 in 2002. In 2002 there were approximately 500,000 Internet users. There were 7,000 fax machines in 1999.

Postal Services. There were 3,223 post offices in 1997.

SOCIAL INSTITUTIONS

Justice. The judiciary is constitutionally independent. Judges are appointed by the Supreme Council of Magistrature chaired by the President of the Republic. Criminal justice is organized as in France. The Supreme Court is at the same time Council of State and High Court of Appeal. The death penalty is in force for terrorism.

The population in penal institutions in Dec. 2001 was 34,243 (110 per 100,000 of national population).

Religion. The 1996 Constitution made Islam the state religion, established a consultative *High Islamic Council*, and forbids practices 'contrary to Islamic morality'. Over 99% of the population are Sunni Muslims. There are also around 180,000 Ibadiyah Muslims and 90,000 others. The Armed Islamic Group (GIA) vowed in 1994 to kill 'Jews, Christians and polytheists' in Algeria. Hundreds of foreign nationals, including priests and nuns, have since been killed. Signalling an increasing tolerance amongst the Muslim community, the Missionaries of Africa's house at Ghardaia Oasis was re-opened in 2000.

Education. Adult literacy in 2001 was 67·8% (77·1% among males and 58·3% among females). In 2000–01 there were 46,670 children in pre-primary education. There were 4,720,950 pupils and 169,559 teachers in primary schools in 2000–01 and 2,991,232 pupils (51% female) with 157,725 teachers in secondary schools.

In 1995–96 there were six universities, two universities of science and technology, five university centres, one agronomic institute, one telecommunications institute, one veterinary institute, one school of architecture and town planning and one *école normale supérieure*. In 1996 there were 160,000 university students and 7,947 academic staff.

In 1996 expenditure on education came to 5·1% of GNP and represented 16·4% of total government expenditure.

Health. In 1996 there were 27,650 physicians, 7,837 dentists and 3,866 pharmacists. There were 186 government hospitals in 1996 and 1,309 health centres, 510 polyclinics, 475 maternity clinics and 3,344 care centres in 1990.

Welfare. Welfare payments to 7·4m. beneficiaries on low incomes were introduced in March 1992.

CULTURE

World Heritage Sites. There are seven UNESCO sites in Algeria: Al Qal'a of Beni Hammad (inscribed in 1980), the 11th century ruined capital of the Hammadid emirs; Tassili n'Ajjer (1982), a group of over 15,000 prehistoric cave drawings; the M'zab Valley (1982), a tenth century community settlement of the Ibadites; Djémila (1982), or Cuicul, a mountainous Roman town; Tipasa (1982), an ancient Carthaginian port; Timgad (1982), a military colony founded by the Roman emperor Trajan in AD 100; the Kasbah of Algiers (1992), the medina of Algiers.

Broadcasting. The state-controlled Radiodiffusion Algérienne and Entreprise Nationale de Télévision broadcast home services in Arabic, Kabyle (Berber) and French, and an external service. There are 18 TV transmitting stations (colour by PAL). In 2000 there were 7·4m. radio receivers and in 2001 there were 3·5m. TV receivers.

Press. Algeria had 24 daily newspapers in 1998, with a combined circulation of 796,440.

Tourism. In 2000 there were 866,000 foreign tourists; spending by tourists totalled US$102m.

DIPLOMATIC REPRESENTATIVES

Of Algeria in the United Kingdom (54 Holland Park, London, W11 3RS)
Ambassador: Vacant.
Chargé d'Affaires a.i.: Omar Djamel-Eddine Bennaoum.

Of the United Kingdom in Algeria (Hilton Hotel, Pins Maritimes, El Mohammadia, Algiers 16000)
Ambassador: Brian E. Stewart.

Of Algeria in the USA (2118 Kalorama Rd, NW, Washington, D.C., 20008)
Ambassador: Idriss Jazairy.

Of the USA in Algeria (4 Chemin Cheich Bachir Ibrahimi, Algiers)
Ambassador: Richard W. Erdman.

Of Algeria to the United Nations
Ambassador: Abdallah Baali.

Of Algeria to the European Union
Ambassador: Halim Benattallah.

FURTHER READING

Ageron, C.-R., *Modern Algeria: a History from 1830 to the Present.* London, 1991
Eveno, P., *L'Algérie.* Paris, 1994
Heggoy, A. A. and Crout, R. R., *Historical Dictionary of Algeria.* Metuchen (NJ), 1995
Lawless, R. I., *Algeria.* [Bibliography] 2nd ed. ABC-Clio, Oxford and Santa Barbara (CA), 1995
Roberts, Hugh, *The Battlefield: Algeria 1998–2002, Studies in a Broken Polity.* Verso, London, 2003
Ruedy, J., *Modern Algeria: the Origins and Development of a Nation.* Indiana Univ. Press, 1992
Stone, M., *The Agony of Algeria.* Columbia University Press, 1997
Stora, B., *Histoire de l'Algérie depuis l'Indépendance.* Paris, 1994
Volpi, Frédéric, *Islam and Democracy: The Failure of Dialogue in Algeria, 1998–2001.* Pluto Press, London, 2003
Willis, M., *The Islamist Challenge in Algeria: A Political History.* New York, 1997

National statistical office: Office National des Statistiques, 8–10 rue des Moussebilines, Algiers.
Website: http://www.ons.dz

ANDORRA

Principat d'Andorra

Capital: Andorra la Vella
Population, 2000: 66,000
GDP per capita: not available

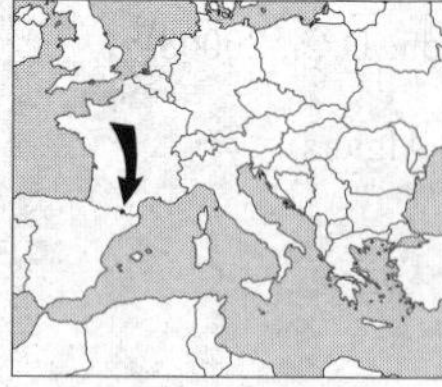

KEY HISTORICAL EVENTS
The status of Andorra was regulated by the *Paréage* of 1278 which placed Andorra under the joint suzerainty of the Comte de Foix and of the Bishop of Urgel. The rights vested in the house of Foix passed by marriage to that of Bearn and, on the accession of Henri IV, to the French crown. A democratic constitution was adopted in 1993.

TERRITORY AND POPULATION
The co-principality of Andorra is situated in the eastern Pyrenees on the French–Spanish border. The country is mountainous and has an average altitude of 1,996 metres. Area, 464 sq. km. In lieu of a census, a register of population is kept. The estimated population in 2004 was 72,320; density, 156 per sq. km.

In 1995, 95·4% of the population lived in urban areas.

The chief towns are Andorra la Vella, the capital (estimated population, 22,035 in 2004) and its suburb Escaldes-Engordany (16,402). 36·0% of the residential population are Andorran, 40·6% Spanish, 10·2% Portuguese and 6·5% French. Catalan is the official language, but Spanish and French are widely spoken.

SOCIAL STATISTICS
Births in 2001 numbered 777 (rate of 11·6 per 1,000 inhabitants) and deaths 237 (3·6 per 1,000 inhabitants). Life expectancy (2000): male, 89·8 years; female, 91·1 years. Annual population growth rate, 1992–2002, 1·8%. Fertility rate, 2001, 1·3 births per woman.

CLIMATE
Escaldes-Engordany, Jan. 35·8°F (2·1°C), July 65·8°F (18·8°C). Annual rainfall 34·9" (886 mm).

CONSTITUTION AND GOVERNMENT
The joint heads of state are the President of the French Republic and the Bishop of Urgel, the co-princes.

A new democratic constitution was approved by 74·2% of votes cast at a referendum on 14 March 1993. The electorate was 9,123; turn-out was 75·7%. The new Constitution, which came into force on 4 May 1993, makes the co-princes a single constitutional monarch and provides for a parliament, the unicameral *General Council of the Valleys*, with 28 members, two from each of the seven parishes and 14 elected by proportional representation from the single national constituency, for four years. In 1982 an *Executive Council* was appointed and legislative and executive powers were separated. The General Council elects the President of the Executive Council, who is the head of the government.

There is a *Constitutional Court* of four members who hold office for eight-year terms, renewable once.

National Anthem. 'El Gran Carlemany, mon pare' ('Great Charlemagne, my father'); words by Enric Marfany, tune by D. J. Benlloch i Vivò.

RECENT ELECTIONS
Elections to the General Council were held on 24 April 2005. The Liberal Party of Andorra won 14 seats (41·2% of the vote), the Social Democratic Party 12 (38·1%) and the Andorran Democratic Centre 2 (11·0%). Turn-out was 80·4%.

CURRENT ADMINISTRATION

In March 2005 the government comprised:

President, Executive Council: Marc Forné Molné; b. 1946 (Liberal Party of Andorra; sworn in 7 Dec. 1994 and re-elected in Feb. 1997 and March 2001). He is currently Europe's longest-serving head of government.

Minister for Foreign Affairs: Juli Minoves Triquell. *Economy:* Miquel Alvarez Marfany. *Finance:* Mireia Maestre Cortadella. *Interior and Justice:* Jordi Visent Guitart. *Territorial Planning:* Jordi Malleu Serra. *Health and Social Affairs:* Mónica Tort Codina. *Culture:* Xavier Montane Atero. *Education, Youth and Sports:* Pere Cervós Cardona. *Presidency and Tourism:* Enric Pujal Areny. *Agriculture and Environment:* Olga Adellach Coma.

Government Website (Catalan only): http://www.govern.ad

INTERNATIONAL RELATIONS

The 1993 Constitution empowers Andorra to conduct its own foreign affairs, with consultation on matters affecting France or Spain.

Andorra is a member of the UN, UNESCO, WIPO, the Council of Europe, the OSCE and the International Organization of the Francophonie.

ECONOMY

Currency. Since 1 Jan. 2002 Andorra has been using the euro. Inflation was 2·8% in 2001, rising to 3·4% in 2002.

Budget. 2001: revenue, €234,705,780; expenditure, €250,775,790.

Performance. Real GDP growth was 3·8% in 2000.

Banking and Finance. The banking sector, with its tax-haven status, contributes substantially to the economy. Leading banks include: Andbanc-Grup Agricol Reig; Banc Internacional d'Andorra SA; Banca Mora SA; Banca Privada d'Andorra SA; CaixaBank SA; and Crèdit Andorrà.

ENERGY AND NATURAL RESOURCES

Electricity. Installed capacity was 26,500 kW in 2000. Production in 1998 was 116m. kWh. 60% of Andorra's electricity comes from Spain.

Agriculture. In 2001 there were some 1,000 ha of arable land (2% of total) and 1,000 ha of permanent crops. Tobacco and potatoes are principal crops. The principal livestock activity is sheep raising.

INDUSTRY

Labour. Only 1% of the workforce is employed in agriculture, the rest in tourism, commerce, services and light industry. Manufacturing consists mainly of cigarettes, cigars and furniture.

INTERNATIONAL TRADE

Andorra is a member of the EU Customs Union for industrial goods, but is a third country for agricultural produce. There is a free economic zone.

Imports and Exports. 2000 exports, €49·5m.; imports, €1,160·0m. Main export markets (2000): Spain, 60·9%; France, 26·1%. Leading import suppliers (2000): Spain, 48·5%; France, 26·6%. The European Union accounted for 92·3% of exports in 2000 and 89·2% of imports.

COMMUNICATIONS

Roads. In 1994 there were 269 km of roads (198 km paved). Motor vehicles (2000) totalled 60,287, including 46,421 cars and 6,029 trucks and vans.

Civil Aviation. There is an airport at Seo de Urgel.

Telecommunications. In 2000 there were 34,215 telephone main lines, or 519·6 per 1,000 inhabitants. There were 25,099 mobile phone subscribers in Dec. 2000 and 24,500 Internet users in April 2001. In 1998 there were 5,000 fax machines.

SOCIAL INSTITUTIONS

Justice. Justice is administered by the High Council of Justice, comprising five members appointed for single six-year terms. The independence of judges is constitutionally guaranteed. Judicial power is exercised in civil matters in the first instance by Magistrates' Courts and a Judge's Court. Criminal justice is administered by the *Corts*, consisting of the judge of appeal, a *raonador* (ombudsman) elected by the General Council of the Valleys, a general attorney and an attorney nominated for five years alternately by each of the co-princes.

Religion. The Roman Catholic is the established church, but the 1993 Constitution guarantees religious liberty. In 2001 around 88% of the population were Catholics.

Education. Free education in French- or Spanish-language schools is compulsory: six years primary starting at six years, followed by four years secondary. A Roman Catholic school provides education in Catalan. In 1996–97 there were 18 schools altogether with 8,079 pupils.

Health. In 2000 there were two hospitals (one private, one public); in 1998 there were 166 physicians, 35 dentists, 188 nurses and 59 pharmacists.

CULTURE

World Heritage Sites. There is one UNESCO site in Andorra: Madriu-Perafita-Claror Valley (entered on the list in 2004).

Broadcasting. Servei de Telecomunicacions d'Andorra relays French and Spanish programmes. Radio Andorra is a commercial public station; Radio Valira is commercial. Number of receivers: radio (1997), 16,000; TV (2001), 36,000. Colour is by PAL.

Press. In 1996 there were three daily newspapers with a combined circulation of 4,000, at a rate of 60 per 1,000 inhabitants.

Tourism. Tourism is the main industry, averaging 11m. visitors a year and accounting for 80% of GDP.

DIPLOMATIC REPRESENTATIVES

Of Andorra in the United Kingdom (63 Westover Road, London, SW18 2RF)
Ambassador: Vacant.
Chargé d'Affaires a.i.: Maria Rosa Picart de Francis.

Of the United Kingdom in Andorra
Ambassador: Stephen J. L. Wright, CMG (resides at Madrid).

Of Andorra in the USA (2 United Nations Plaza, 25th Floor, N.Y. 10017)
Ambassador: Vacant.
Chargé d'Affaires a.i.: Jelena V. Pia-Comella.

Of USA in Andorra
Ambassador: Vacant.
Chargé d'Affaires a.i.: J. Robert Manzanares.

Of Andorra to the United Nations
Ambassador: Vacant.
Deputy Permanent Representative: Jelena V. Pia-Comella.

Of Andorra to the European Union
Ambassador: Meritxell Mateu i Pi.

FURTHER READING

Taylor, Barry, *Andorra.* [Bibliography] ABC-Clio, Oxford and Santa Barbara (CA), 1993.

National statistical office: Servie d'Estudis, Ministeri de Finances, c/Doctor Vilanova, núm. 13, Edifici Davi, Esc. c, 5è, Andorra la Vella.
Website (Catalan only): http://estudis-estadistica.finances.ad

ANGOLA

República de Angola

Capital: Luanda
Population projection, 2010: 16·84m.
GDP per capita, 2002: (PPP$) 2,130
HDI/world rank: 0·381/166

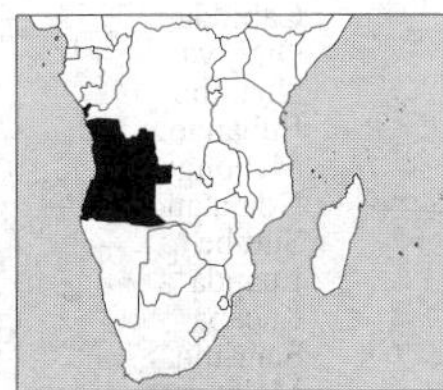

KEY HISTORICAL EVENTS

The Portuguese were dominant from the late 19th century. Angola remained a Portuguese colony until 11 June 1951, when it became an Overseas Province of Portugal.

A guerrilla war broke out in 1961 when the People's Movement for the Liberation of Angola launched an offensive to end colonial rule. After the coup d'état in Portugal in April 1974, negotiations with Portugal, the MPLA (People's Movement for the Liberation of Angola), the FNLA (National Front for the Liberation of Angola) and UNITA (National Union for the Total Liberation of Angola) led to independence on 11 Nov. 1975. The FNLA tried to seize power by force but was driven out of the capital. As independence approached, invasion from the north was combined with a South African invasion in support of UNITA. The MPLA declared independence and, subsequently, with the help of Cuban troops, defeated the FNLA in the north and drove the invading South African army out of the country. South African invasions and the occupation of large areas of Angola continued until the signing of the New York Agreement in Dec. 1988, when South Africa agreed to withdraw its forces from Angola and Namibia (and grant independence to Namibia), while Angola and Cuba agreed to the phased withdrawal of Cuban troops.

After abortive attempts to end the conflict with UNITA, a peace agreement was signed on 31 May 1991. A national army was to be formed and multi-party elections held. In Sept. 1992 the MPLA won the elections and José Eduardo dos Santos was re-elected president against UNITA leader Jonas Savimbi. But the latter rejected the election results, withdrew his generals from the unified army and went back to war, seizing an estimated 70% of the country.

On 20 Nov. 1994 a peace agreement was signed in Lusaka, allowing for UNITA to share in government.

In Jan. 1998 Jonas Savimbi, UNITA's leader, met with President dos Santos but talks soon foundered and serious fighting resumed in the north, raising fears of a major new offensive by the Angolan Armed Forces against the UNITA rebels. Meanwhile, Angolan troops fought in the Democratic Republic of the Congo alongside the forces of President Kabila in his efforts to quash a Rwandan-backed rebellion in the east of his country. They remained after the assassination of Kabila in Jan. 2001 but renewed hopes of peace resulted in their withdrawal in Jan. 2002. In Feb. 2002 Jonas Savimbi was killed in fighting with government troops. On 4 April 2002 commanders of the Angolan army and UNITA signed a ceasefire agreement. More than half a million Angolans died in the civil unrest that plagued the country for over a quarter of a century.

TERRITORY AND POPULATION

Angola is bounded in the north by the Republic of the Congo, north and northeast by the Democratic Republic of the Congo, east by Zambia, south by Namibia and west by the Atlantic Ocean. The area is 1,246,700 sq. km (481,350 sq. miles) including the province of Cabinda, an exclave of territory separated by 30 sq. km of the Democratic Republic of the Congo's territory. The population at census, 1970, was 5,646,166, of whom 14% were urban. Estimate, 2003, 13·67m.; density, 11·0 per sq. km. In 2001, 65·2% of the population were living in rural areas. Population figures are rough estimates because the civil war led to huge movements of population.

There were 0·3m. Angolan refugees in the Democratic Republic of the Congo, Zambia and the Republic of the Congo in 1995.

The UN gives a projected population for 2010 of 16·84m.

Area, population and chief towns of the provinces:

Province	*Area (in sq. km)*	*Population estimate, 1992 (in 1,000)*	*Chief town*
Bengo	31,371	196·1	Caxito
Benguela	31,788	656·6	Benguela
Bié	70,314	1,119·8	Kuito
Cabinda	7,270	152·1	Cabinda
Cunene	89,342	241·2	Ondjiva
Huambo	34,274	1,521·0	Huambo
Huíla	75,002	885·1	Lubango
Kuando-Kubango	199,049	139·6	Menongue
Kwanza Norte	24,190	385·2	Ndalatando
Kwanza Sul	55,660	694·5	Sumbe
Luanda	2,418	1,588·6	Luanda
Lunda Norte	102,783	305·9	Lucapa
Lunda Sul	45,649	169·1	Saurimo
Malanje	97,602	906·0	Malanje
Moxico	223,023	319·3	Luena
Namibe	58,137	107·3	Namibe
Uíge	58,698	802·7	Uíge
Zaire	40,130	237·5	Mbanza Congo

The most important towns (populations) are Luanda, the capital (1999, 2·55m.), Huambo (1995, 400,000), Benguela (1983, 155,000), Lobito (1983, 150,000), Lubango (1984, 105,000), Malanje (1970, 31,559) and Namibe (formerly Moçâmedes, 1981, 100,000).

The main ethnic groups are Umbundo (Ovimbundo), Kimbundo, Bakongo, Chokwe, Ganguela, Luvale and Kwanyama.

Portuguese is the official language. Bantu and other African languages are also spoken.

SOCIAL STATISTICS

Life expectancy at birth, 2001, 38·8 years for males and 41·6 years for females. 2001 births (estimates), 656,000; deaths, 246,000. Estimated birth rate in 2001 was 51·2 per 1,000 population; estimated death rate, 19·2. Annual population growth rate, 1992–2002, 2·9%. Fertility rate, 2001, 7·2 births per woman; infant mortality, 2001, 154 per 1,000 live births. Angola has one of the highest rates of child mortality in the world, at nearly 300 deaths among children under 5 per 1,000 live births in 1999.

CLIMATE

The climate is tropical, with low rainfall in the west but increasing inland. Temperatures are constant over the year and most rain falls in March and April. Luanda, Jan. 78°F (25·6°C), July 69°F (20·6°C). Annual rainfall 13" (323 mm). Lobito, Jan. 77°F (25°C), July 68°F (20°C). Annual rainfall 14" (353 mm).

CONSTITUTION AND GOVERNMENT

Under the Constitution adopted at independence, the sole legal party was the MPLA. In Dec. 1990, however, the MPLA announced that the Constitution would be revised to permit opposition parties. The supreme organ of state is the 220-member *National Assembly.* There is an executive *President* elected for renewable terms of five years, who appoints a *Council of Ministers*.

In Dec. 2002 Angola's ruling party and the UNITA party of former rebels agreed on a new constitution. The president would keep key powers, including the power to name and to remove the prime minister. The president will also appoint provincial governors, rather than letting voters elect them, but the governor must be from the party that received a majority of votes in that province. A draft constitution was submitted to the constitutional commission of the Angolan parliament for consideration in Jan. 2004.

National Anthem. 'O Pátria, nunca mais esqueceremos' ('Oh Fatherland, never shall we forget'); words by M. R. Alves Monteiro, tune by R. A. Dias Mingas.

RECENT ELECTIONS

At the presidential and parliamentary elections of 29–30 Sept. 1992 the electorate was 4,862,748. Turn-out was about 90%. Eduardo dos Santos (MPLA) was re-elected as president with 49·5% of votes cast against 40·5% for his single opponent, Jonas Savimbi (UNITA). The latter refused to accept the result. The MPLA gained 129 seats in the National Assembly with 53·7% of votes cast, and UNITA 77 with 34·1%. Ten other parties gained six seats or fewer.

On 11 April 1997 a Government of National Unity was installed, with three ministerial posts going to UNITA. Jonas Savimbi, UNITA's leader, received the specially created position of Chief of the Principal Opposition Party.

Presidential and parliamentary elections are set to take place in 2006.

CURRENT ADMINISTRATION

President: José Eduardo dos Santos; b. 1943 (MPLA; since 10 Sept. 1979; re-elected 9 Dec. 1985 and 29–30 Sept. 1992).

Prime Minister: Fernando da Piedade Dias dos Santos 'Nando'; b. 1952 (MPLA; since 6 Dec. 2002).

In March 2005 the government comprised:

Minister for Agriculture and Rural Development: Gilberto Lutucuta. *Assistance and Social Reintegration:* João Kussumua. *Commerce:* Joaquim Ekuma Muafumua. *Culture:* Boaventura Cardoso. *Education:* António Burity da Silva Neto. *Energy and Water:* José Maria Botelho de Vasconcelos. *Environment and Urban Development:* Diakunpuna Sita José. *External Relations:* João Bernardo de Miranda. *Family and Women's Affairs:* Cândida Celeste da Silva. *Finance:* José Pedro de Morais. *Fisheries:* Salomão Luheto Xirimbimbi. *Geology and Mines:* Manuel António Africano. *Health:* Sebastião Sapuile Veloso. *Hotels and Tourism:* Eduardo Jonatão Chingungi. *Industry:* Joaquim Duarte da Costa David. *Information:* Pedro Hendrik Vaal Neto. *Interior:* Osvaldo de Jesus Serra Van-Dúnem. *Justice:* Manuel da Costa Aragão. *National Defence:* Kundy Paihama. *Oil:* Desidério da Graça Veríssimo e Costa. *Planning:* Ana Dias Lourenço. *Posts and Telecommunications:* Licínio Tavares Ribeiro. *Public Administration, Employment and Social Welfare:* António Domingos Pitra da Costa Neto. *Public Works:* Francisco Higino Carneiro. *Science and Technology:* João Baptista Ngandagina. *Territorial Administration:* Virgílio Fontes Pereira. *Transport:* André Luís Brandão. *War Veterans:* Pedro José Van-Dúnem. *Youth and Sports:* José Marcos Barrica.

Government Website: http://www.angola.org

DEFENCE

Conscription is for two years. Angola has one of the worst records in terms of child soldier conscription in the world. Defence expenditure totalled US$750m. in 2003 (US$55 per capita), representing 5·7% of GDP.

Army. In 2002 the Army had 35 regiments. Total strength was estimated at 90,000. In addition the paramilitary Rapid Reaction Police numbered 10,000.

Navy. Naval personnel in 2002 totalled about 4,000 with seven operational vessels. There is a naval base at Luanda.

Air Force. The Angolan People's Air Force (FAPA) was formed in 1976 and has about 6,000 personnel. Since the elections in 1992 and the relative calm, the Air Force has been run down and serviceability of combat aircraft is low. In 2002 there were 85 combat aircraft and 40 armed helicopters.

INTERNATIONAL RELATIONS

Angola is a member of the UN, WTO, the African Union, African Development Bank, COMESA, SADC, IOM and is an ACP member state of the ACP-EU relationship.

ECONOMY

In 2002 agriculture accounted for 8·1% of GDP, industry 65·2% and services 26·7%.

Overview. Reforms are under way to introduce a market economy and restore private property. In April 2000 Angola signed a far-reaching agreement with the International Monetary Fund which stipulates economic reforms. In July 2000 the

World Bank also signed an agreement approving a series of reforms in return for help with the country's huge foreign debt.

Currency. The unit of currency is the *kwanza* (AOA), introduced in Dec. 1999, replacing the *readjusted kwanza* at a rate of 1 kwanza = 1m. readjusted kwanzas. Foreign exchange reserves were US$902m. in June 2002. Gold reserves were 46,500 troy oz in 1990. Inflation was 4,146% in 1996. It has slowed since then, and in 2003 was 98·3%. However, only Zimbabwe had a higher annual inflation rate in 2003.

Budget. Revenues in 2001 were KZr88·9bn. and expenditures KZr96·7bn.

Performance. Total GDP was US$13·2bn. in 2003. The civil war meant GDP growth in 1993 was negative, at –24·0%, but a recovery followed and in 2001 and 2002 it was 3·1% and 14·4% respectively, mainly thanks to booming diamond exports and post-war rebuilding. Angola's 14·4% growth in 2002 was among the highest in the world for the year.

Banking and Finance. The Banco Nacional de Angola is the central bank and bank of issue (*Governor*, Amadeu Mauricio). All banks were state-owned until the sector was re-opened to commercial competition in 1991. In 2002 there were three commercial banks, one development bank, one investment bank and three foreign banks.

Angola received US$1·8bn. in foreign direct investment in 2000, approximately 90% of which was in the oil sector.

ENERGY AND NATURAL RESOURCES

Environment. In 2002 Angola's carbon dioxide emissions from the consumption and flaring of fossil fuels were the equivalent of 1·2 tonnes per capita.

Electricity. Installed capacity was 0·5m. kW in 2000. Production in 2000 was 1·45bn. kWh, with consumption per capita 110 kWh.

Oil and Gas. Oil is produced mainly offshore and in the Cabinda exclave. Oil production and supporting activities contribute some 45% of Angolan GDP and provide the government with approximately US$3·5bn. annually. The oil industry is expected to invest US$3·5bn. a year in offshore Angola in the early part of the 21st century. There are plans for a new US$3·3bn. oil refinery near Lobito which is scheduled to begin operations in 2006. Only Nigeria among sub-Saharan African countries produces more oil. It is believed that there are huge oil resources yet to be discovered. Proven crude petroleum reserves in 2002 were 6bn. bbls. Total production (2003) 43·6m. tonnes. Natural gas reserves (2002) 113bn. cu. metres; production, 1998, 565m. cu. metres.

Minerals. Mineral production in Angola is dominated by diamonds and 90% of all workers in the mining sector work in the diamond industry. Production in 2002 totalled 6·0m. carats. Angola has billions of dollars worth of unexploited diamond fields. In 2000 the government regained control of the nation's richest diamond provinces from UNITA rebels. Other minerals produced (2001) include granite, 1·5m. cu. metres; marble, 100,000 cu. metres; salt, 30,000 tonnes. Iron ore, phosphate, manganese and copper deposits exist.

Agriculture. In 2001 there were 3·0m. ha of arable land and 0·3m. ha of permanent crops. 75,000 ha were irrigated in 2001. The agricultural population in 2002 was 8·50m., of whom 4·29m. were economically active. Although more than 70% of the economically active population are engaged in agriculture it only accounts for 8% of GDP. There were 10,300 tractors in 2001. Principal crops (with 2000 production, in 1,000 tonnes): cassava (3,130); maize (428); sugarcane (330); bananas (290); sweet potatoes (182); millet (102); citrus fruits (75); dry beans (68).

Livestock (2000): 4·0m. cattle, 350,000 sheep, 2·15m. goats, 800,000 pigs.

Forestry. In 2000, 69·76m. ha, or 56·0% of the total land area, was covered by forests, including mahogany and other hardwoods. Timber production in 2001 was 4·36m. cu. metres.

Fisheries. Total catch in 2001 came to 252,518 tonnes, mainly from sea fishing.

INDUSTRY

The principal manufacturing branches are foodstuffs, textiles and oil refining. Output, 2000 (in 1,000 tonnes): residual fuel oil, 595; distillate fuel oil, 558; cement (1997), 301; jet fuels, 295; flour (1998), 172; petrol, 111; beer (2003), 160m. litres; 33,000 TV sets (1992); 29,000 radio sets (1992).

Labour. In 1996 the total labour force numbered 5,144,000 (54% males).

INTERNATIONAL TRADE

In 2002 total foreign debt was US$10,134m.

Imports and Exports. Imports and exports for calendar years in US$1m.:

	1997	*1998*	*1999*	*2000*	*2001*
Imports (f.o.b.)	2,597	2,079	3,109	3,039	3,179
Exports (f.o.b.)	5,007	3,543	5,156	7,921	6,534

Main exports, 2001 (in US$1m.): crude oil, 5,690; diamonds, 689; refined oil products, 93. Chief import suppliers (1999): Portugal (18·8%); USA (14·6%); South Africa (11·9%); France (8·2%). Chief export markets (1999): USA (59·5%); China (8·2%); Taiwan (7·7%); Germany (2·4%).

COMMUNICATIONS

Roads. There were, in 2001, 51,429 km of roads (7,944 km highways; 10·4% of all roads surfaced), and in 1996 approximately 207,000 passenger cars and 25,000 commercial vehicles. Many roads remain mined as a result of the civil war; a programme of de-mining and rehabilitation is under way.

Rail. The length of railways open for traffic in 1987 was 2,952 km, comprising 2,798 km of 1,067 mm gauge and 154 km of 600 mm gauge, but much of the network was severely damaged in the civil war. Restoration and redevelopment of the network is under way, notably the Benguela Railway, linking the port city of Lobito with Huambo in Angola's rich farmlands and neighbouring Democratic Republic of the Congo and Zambia.

Civil Aviation. There is an international airport at Luanda (Fourth of February). The national carrier is Linhas Aéreas de Angola (TAAG), which operated direct flights in 2003 to Johannesburg, Kinshasa, Paris, Pointe-Noire, Rio de Janeiro, São Tomé and Windhoek. There were direct flights in 2003 with other airlines to Addis Ababa, Brussels, Libreville, Lisbon, London and Moscow. In 1999 scheduled airline traffic of Angola-based carriers flew 6·5m. km, carrying 531,000 passengers (120,000 on international flights).

Shipping. There are ports at Luanda, Lobito and Namibe, and oil terminals at Malongo, Lobito and Soyo. In 2002 the merchant fleet totalled 55,000 GRT, including oil tankers 3,000 GRT.

Telecommunications. There were 215,000 telephone subscribers in 2002, or 15·4 per 1,000 inhabitants. It is intended to privatize Angola Telecom, although no date has been set. In 2002 there were 130,000 mobile phone subscribers and 27,000 PCs were in use. In 2002 there were 41,000 Internet users.

Postal Services. In 1997 there were 80 post offices, or one for every 145,000 persons.

SOCIAL INSTITUTIONS

Justice. The Supreme Court and Court of Appeal are in Luanda. The death penalty was abolished in 1992. In 2002–03 the US government's Agency for International Development assisted in the modernization of the judicial system. Measures including the introduction of a court case numbering system were intended to reduce legal costs and attract foreign investment.

The population in penal institutions in 2002 was 4,975 (36 per 100,000 of national population).

Religion. In 2001 there were 6·44m. Roman Catholics, 1·55m. Protestants and 710,000 African Christians, and most of the remainder follow traditional animist religions. In Sept. 2003 there was one cardinal.

Education. The education system provides three levels of general education totalling eight years, followed by schools for technical training, teacher training or pre-university studies. In 2000–01 there were 1,178,485 pupils and 33,478 teachers at primary schools, 399,712 pupils and 19,798 teachers at secondary schools and (1999–2000) 7,845 students with 796 academic staff in tertiary education institutions. There is one university. Private schools have been permitted since 1991. The University of Luanda has campuses at Luanda, Huambo and Lubango. It had 8,954 students in 1991–92. The adult literacy rate was 42·0% in 1998.

In 2000–01 expenditure on education came to 3·4% of GNP.

Health. In 1997 there were 736 physicians, 10,942 nurses and 411 midwives. In 1990 there were 266 hospitals and health centres with 11,857 beds. There were 1,339 medical posts.

In the period 1990–98 only 31% of the population had access to safe drinking water. In 2000 it was estimated that 60% of the 3·9m. displaced people were suffering from malnutrition.

CULTURE

Broadcasting. In 2001 there were 710,000 TV receivers and in 1997 there were 630,000 radio receivers in Angola. The government-controlled Rádio Nacional de Angola broadcasts three programmes and an international service. There are also regional stations. Televisão Popular de Angola transmits from seven stations (colour by PAL).

Press. Angola had five daily newspapers in 1996, with a combined circulation of 128,000. The government daily is the *Jornal de Angola*. The *Diário da República* is the official gazette. There is an independent weekly, *Agora*, and there are around 100 specialized and independent publications.

Tourism. In 2000 there were 51,000 foreign tourists, bringing revenue of US$18m.

DIPLOMATIC REPRESENTATIVES

Of Angola in the United Kingdom (22 Dorset Street, London W1U 6QY)
Ambassador: António da Costa Fernandes.

Of the United Kingdom in Angola (Rua Diogo Cão 4, Luanda)
Ambassador: John Thompson, MBE.

Of Angola in the USA (2108 16th Street, NW 20009, Washington, D.C., 20036)
Ambassador: Josefina Pitra Diakite.

Of the USA in Angola (32 rua Houari Boumédienne, Miramar, Luanda)
Ambassador: Cynthia G. Efird.

Of Angola to the United Nations
Ambassador: Ismael Gaspar Martins.

Of Angola to the European Union
Ambassador: Vacant.
Chargé d'Affaires a.i.: Maria Eugénia Feijo de Almeida Ferreira dos Santos.

FURTHER READING

Anstee, M. J., *Orphan of the Cold War: the Inside Story of the Collapse of the Angolan Peace Process, 1992–93*. London, 1996
Black, Richard, *Angola*. [Bibliography] ABC-Clio, Oxford and Santa Barbara (CA), 1992
Brittain, Victoria, *Death of Dignity: Angola's Civil War*. Pluto, London, 1999
Guimarães, Fernando Andersen, *The Origins of the Angolan Civil War: Foreign Intervention and Domestic Political Conflict*. Palgrave, Basingstoke, 2001
Hodges, Tony, *Angola From Afro-Stalinism to Petro-Diamond Capitalism*. James Currey, Oxford, 2001
James, W. M., *Political History of the War in Angola*. New York, 1991
Roque, F., *Económia de Angola*. Lisbon, 1991

National statistical office: Instituto Nacional de Estatística, Luanda.

ANTIGUA AND BARBUDA

Capital: St John's
Population, 2002: 67,000
GDP per capita, 2002: (PPP$) 10,920
HDI/world rank: 0·800/55

KEY HISTORICAL EVENTS

Antigua and Barbuda make up the island nation of the Lesser Antilles in the Eastern Caribbean. Most of the population is descended from African slaves brought in during colonial times to work on sugar plantations.

As British colonies, Antigua and Barbuda formed part of the Leeward Islands Federation from 1871 until 30 June 1956 when they became a separate Crown Colony. This was part of the West Indies Federation from 3 Jan. 1958 until 31 May 1962 and became an Associated State of the UK on 27 Feb. 1967. Antigua and Barbuda gained independence on 1 Nov. 1981.

TERRITORY AND POPULATION

Antigua and Barbuda comprises three islands of the Lesser Antilles situated in the eastern Caribbean with a total land area of 442 sq. km (171 sq. miles); it consists of Antigua (280 sq. km), Barbuda, 40 km to the north (161 sq. km) and uninhabited Redonda, 40 km to the southwest (one sq. km). The population in July 2002 was 67,448 (1,400 on Barbuda); density, 153 per sq. km. Urban population (2001), 37·1%.

The chief towns are St John's, the capital on Antigua (25,000 inhabitants in 1999) and Codrington (1,400), the only settlement on Barbuda.

English is the official language; local dialects are also spoken.

SOCIAL STATISTICS

Expectation of life, 1996: males, 71·5 years, females, 75·8. Annual population growth rate, 1992–2002, 1·2%. Births, 2000, 1,528; deaths, 2000, 451. Infant mortality in 2001 was 12 per 1,000 live births; fertility rate, 2001, 1·6 births per woman.

CLIMATE

A tropical climate, but drier than most West Indies islands. The hot season is from May to Nov., when rainfall is greater. Mean annual rainfall is 40" (1,000 mm).

CONSTITUTION AND GOVERNMENT

H.M. Queen Elizabeth, as Head of State, is represented by a Governor-General appointed by her on the advice of the Prime Minister. There is a bicameral legislature, comprising a 17-member Senate appointed by the Governor-General and a 17-member House of Representatives elected by universal suffrage for a five-year term. The Governor-General appoints a Prime Minister and, on the latter's advice, other members of the Cabinet.

Barbuda is administered by a nine-member directly-elected council.

National Anthem. 'Fair Antigua and Barbuda'; words by N. H. Richards, tune by W. G. Chambers.

RECENT ELECTIONS

At the elections to the House of Representatives of 24 March 2004 the United Progressive Party (UPP) won 12 seats, the Antigua Labour Party (ALP) 4 and the Barbuda People's Movement (BPM) 1.

CURRENT ADMINISTRATION

Governor General: Sir James Beethoven Carlisle, GCMG; b. 1937 (in office since 10 June 1993).

In March 2005 the UPP government comprised:

Prime Minister and Minister of Barbuda Affairs, National Security, Foreign Affairs and International Trade: Baldwin Spencer; b. 1948 (UPP; in office since 24 March 2004).

Deputy Prime Minister and Minister of Works and the Environment: Wilmouth Daniel.

Minister of Agriculture, Food Production and Marine Affairs: Charlesworth Samuel. *Education:* Bertrand Joseph. *Finance and the Economy:* Eroll Cort. *Tourism and Civil Aviation:* Harold Lovell. *Health, Sports and Youth Affairs:* John Maginley. *Housing, Culture and Social Transformation:* Hilson Baptiste. *Justice and Legal Affairs:* Colin Derrick. *Labour, Public Administration and Empowerment:* Jacqui Quinn-Leandro. *Attorney General:* Justin Simon. *Minister without Portfolio:* Aziz Hadeed.

Government Website: http://www.antiguagov.com

DEFENCE

The Antigua and Barbuda Defence Force numbers 170. There are some 75 reserves. A coastguard service has been formed.

In 2003 defence expenditure totalled US$4m. (US$56 per capita), representing 0·6% of GDP.

Army. The strength of the Army section of the Defence Force was 125 in 2002.

Navy. There was a naval force of 45 operating three patrol craft in 2002.

INTERNATIONAL RELATIONS

Antigua and Barbuda is a member of the UN, the World Bank, ILO, IMO, IMF, UNESCO, WHO, WIPO, WTO, the Commonwealth, OAS, ACS, CARICOM, OECS and is an ACP member state of the ACP-EU relationship.

ECONOMY

In 2002 agriculture accounted for 3·7% of GDP, industry 21·7% and services 74·6%.

Currency. The unit of currency is the *Eastern Caribbean dollar* (ECD), issued by the Eastern Caribbean Central Bank. Foreign exchange reserves in May 2002 were US$84m. and total money supply was EC$334m. Inflation in 2002 was 2·2%.

Budget. The budget for 2002 envisaged recurrent revenue of EC$571·1m. and recurrent expenditure of EC$599·2m.

Performance. Real GDP growth was 1·5% in 2001 and 2·1% in 2002. Total GDP was US$0·8bn. in 2003.

Banking and Finance. The East Caribbean Central Bank based in St Kitts functions as a central bank. The *Governor* is Sir Dwight Venner. In 2002, nine commercial banks were operating (four foreign). Total national savings were EC$1,357m. in Dec. 2001.

In 1981 Antigua established an offshore banking sector which in 2002 had 21 banks registered and operating. The offshore sector is regulated by the Financial Services Regulatory Commission, a statutory body.

ENERGY AND NATURAL RESOURCES

Environment. In 2002 Antigua and Barbuda's carbon dioxide emissions from the consumption and flaring of fossil fuels were the equivalent of 7·7 tonnes per capita.

Electricity. Capacity in 2000 was 27,000 kW. Production was estimated at 99m. kWh in 2000 and consumption per capita an estimated 1,523 kWh.

Water. There is a desalination plant with a capacity of 0·6m. gallons per day, sufficient to meet the needs of the country.

Agriculture. In 2001 there were 8,000 ha of arable land and 2,000 ha of permanent crops. Cotton and fruits are the main crops. Production (2000) of fruits, 8,000 tonnes (notably melons and mangoes).

Livestock (2000): cattle, 16,000; pigs, 2,000; sheep, 12,000; goats, 12,000.

Forestry. Forests covered 9,000 ha, or 20·5% of the total land area, in 2000.

Fisheries. Total catch in 2001 came to approximately 1,583 tonnes, exclusively from sea fishing.

INDUSTRY

Manufactures include beer, cement, toilet tissue, stoves, refrigerators, blenders, fans, garments and rum (molasses imported from Guyana).

Labour. The unemployment rate in 1998 was the lowest in the Caribbean, at 4·5%. Between 1994 and 1998, 2,543 jobs were created. The average annual salary in 1998 was US$8,345 per head of population.

INTERNATIONAL TRADE

Imports and Exports. Imports in 2001 were estimated at US$321m. and exports US$39m. The main trading partners were CARICOM, the USA, the UK and Canada.

COMMUNICATIONS

Roads. In 1995 there were 384 km of main roads, 164 km of secondary roads, 320 km of rural roads and 293 km of other roads. 15,100 passenger cars and 5,700 commercial vehicles were in use in 1995. More than EC$64m. was spent to rebuild major roads and highways in the three years following damage caused by hurricanes Luis and Marilyn in 1995.

Civil Aviation. V. C. Bird International Airport is near St John's. There were flights in 2003 to Anguilla, Barbados, Dominica, Dominican Republic, Georgetown, Grenada, Kingston, London, Milan, Montego Bay, New York, Paris, Philadelphia, Puerto Rico, St Croix, St Kitts and Nevis, St Lucia, St Maarten, St Vincent, Tampa, Toronto, Trinidad and Tobago and the British and US Virgin Islands. A domestic flight links the airports on Antigua and Barbuda.

Shipping. The main port is St John's Harbour. The merchant shipping fleet of 762 vessels totalled 4,541,940 GRT in Dec. 2001. In 1997 vessels totalling 94,907,000 NRT entered ports and vessels totalling 667,126,000 NRT cleared.

Telecommunications. There were 62,300 main telephone subscribers in 2001, or 804·2 per 1,000 inhabitants. There is a mobile phone system, with 38,200 subscribers in 2002. There were 10,000 Internet users in 2002.

Postal Services. The main Post Office is located in St John's. There is another one at the airport.

SOCIAL INSTITUTIONS

Justice. Law is based on UK common law as exercised by the Eastern Caribbean Supreme Court (ECSC) on St Lucia. There are Magistrates' Courts and a Court of Summary Jurisdiction. Appeals lie to the Court of Appeal of ECSC, or ultimately to the UK Privy Council. Antigua and Barbuda was one of ten countries to sign an agreement in Feb. 2001 establishing a Caribbean Court of Justice to replace the British Privy Council as the highest civil and criminal court. In the meantime the number of signatories has risen to twelve. The court was inaugurated at Port-of-Spain, Trinidad on 16 April 2005.

The population in penal institutions in Feb. 1998 was 186 (equivalent to 278 per 100,000 of national population).

Religion. In 2001 there were 30,000 Protestants, 23,000 Anglicans and 8,000 Roman Catholics.

Education. Adult literacy was 95% in 1998. In 1999–2000 there were 13,025 pupils and 695 teachers at primary schools, and 5,276 pupils and 394 teachers at secondary schools. In 1992–93 there were 72 government primary and secondary schools. Other schools were run by religious organizations. The Antigua State College offers technical and teacher training. Antigua is a partner in the regional University of the West Indies. In 1999–2000 expenditure on education came to 3·5% of GNP.

Health. There is one general hospital, a private clinic, seven health centres and 17 associated clinics. A new medical centre at Mount St John's is set to open during 2005. In 1996 there were 75 physicians, 12 dentists, 187 nurses and 13 pharmacists.

Welfare. The state operates a Medical Benefits Scheme providing free medical attention, and a Social Security Scheme, providing age and disability pensions and sickness benefits.

CULTURE

Broadcasting. Radio and television services are provided by the government-owned Antigua and Barbuda Broadcasting Service (ABS). Other radio and/or TV stations are Observer Radio, Caribbean Radio Lighthouse (Baptist Mission), Rado ZDK (commercial), Caribbean Relay (BBC and Deutsche Welle), CTV Entertainment Systems (12 US cable channels). In 1997 there were 36,000 radio and 31,000 TV receivers.

Press. The main newspapers are The Antigua Sun and The Daily Observer. The Outlet Newspaper, the National Informer and the Worker's Voice are published weekly. The Chamber of Commerce has a monthly publication.

Tourism. Tourism is the main industry, contributing about 90% of GDP and 80% of foreign exchange earnings and related activities. In 2001 there were 193,126 staying visitors and 429,406 cruise ship arrivals. Income from tourism amounted to US$290m. in 2000.

Festivals. Of particular interest are the International Sailing Week (April–May); Annual Tennis Championship (May); Mid-Summer Carnival (July–Aug.).

Museums and Galleries. The main attractions are the Museum of Antigua and Barbuda; Coates Cottage; Aiton Place; Harmony Hall; Cedars Pottery; SOFA (Sculpture Objects Functional Art); Pigeon Point Pottery; Harbour Art Gallery; Nelson's Dockyard; Shirley Heights.

DIPLOMATIC REPRESENTATIVES

Of Antigua and Barbuda in the United Kingdom (15 Thayer St., London, W1U 3JT)
High Commissioner: Carl Roberts.

Of the United Kingdom in Antigua and Barbuda (Price Waterhouse Centre, 11 Old Parham Rd, St John's, Antigua)
High Commissioner: John White (resides at Bridgetown, Barbados).

Of Antigua and Barbuda in the USA (3216 New Mexico Av., NW, Washington, D.C., 20016)
Ambassador: Lionel Alexander Hurst.

Of the USA in Antigua and Barbuda
Ambassador: Mary E. Kramer (resides at Bridgetown).

Of Antigua and Barbuda to the United Nations
Ambassador: John W. Ashe.

Of Antigua and Barbuda to the European Union
Ambassador: Vacant.

FURTHER READING

Berleant-Schiller, Riva, *et al.*, *Antigua and Barbuda.* [Bibliography] ABC-Clio, Oxford and Santa Barbara (CA), 1995

Nicholson, Desmond, *Antigua, Barbuda and Redonda: A Historical Sketch.* St John's, 1991

ARGENTINA

República Argentina

Capital: Buenos Aires
Population projection, 2010: 41·44m.
GDP per capita, 2002: (PPP$) 10,880
HDI/world rank: 0·85/34

KEY HISTORICAL EVENTS

Prior to European colonization the two main indigenous groups—the Diaguita in the northwest and the Guarani in the south and east—developed an agricultural civilization. Europeans came to Argentina in the early 16th century. When Sebastian Cabot established the first Spanish settlement in 1526, he revealed Argentina's silver resources, possibly inspiring the name *Argentina* ('of silver'). Ten years later Pedro de Mendoza founded Buenos Aires. However, it was not until 1580 that the region's indigenous peoples, weakened by European diseases as much as by military campaigns, were finally defeated and Spanish rule established.

In 1776 Buenos Aires, an 18th-century smuggler's haunt, was made a free port at the centre of a viceroyalty comprising Argentina, Uruguay, Paraguay and Bolivia. This coincided with Buenos Aires' growing prosperity as trade with Europe increased. When Spain came under Napoleonic control the British attacked Buenos Aires—in 1806 and 1807—helping to trigger the independence movement. In 1810 the first elected government was formed in Buenos Aires, where nationalists took advantage of the weakness of the Spanish crown to implement the libertarian principles of the American and French Revolutions.

Having separated from Paraguay in 1814, Argentina gained its independence from Spain in 1816. Unable to control its outlying regions, it lost Bolivia in 1825 and Uruguay in 1828. In 1827 Argentinians joined forces with Uruguay to repel a Brazilian invasion, thereby securing independence for Uruguay and a move towards a centralized Argentinian state. However, from 1835–52 the Federalists, who favoured regional self-government, held power under Gen. Juan Manuel de Rosas. Governor of Buenos Aires from 1829, Rosas proved a formidable leader but his period in office saw Britain seize the Falkland Islands (Islas Malvinas) in 1833, while Bolivia, Paraguay and Uruguay continued to isolate the federation. In 1838, following a trade dispute with Uruguay, Argentinian political exiles gained French support in an attempt to overthrow Rosas. He remained in power until 1853 when he was ousted by Gen. Justo José de Urquiza.

The Unitarists inaugurated a new constitution and achieved a more stable government, but Urquiza's overthrow by Santiago Derquai led to another civil war. From 1865–70 Argentina was involved in the War of the Triple Alliance, joining with Uruguay and Brazil in a campaign against Paraguay. This strengthened the newly centralized Argentina and was seminal in defining the role of the military. From 1880–86 Argentina thrived under the leadership of Gen. Julio Roca. A Federalist, Roca nevertheless retained Buenos Aires as the capital. During his second term of office, Roca made peace with Chile after years of territorial dispute.

Argentina became a magnet for European immigrants, mainly Italian and Spanish, who founded the Union Civica Radical party. This became the main political force and, under the leadership of Hipólito Irigoyen, won its first presidential election in 1916.

Although Argentina remained neutral at the outbreak of the Second World War, a coup in 1943 brought to power Gen. Juan Domingo Perón, who chose to side with the USA. Perón led a regime that was autocratic but populist, winning presidential elections in 1946 and 1951 with the support of the urban working class. His success was reinforced by his second wife Eva Duarte de Perón, 'Evita', who acted as *de facto* minister of health and labour. In 1952 her death, caused by cancer, combined with Perón's increasing authoritarianism and his excommunication from the church, led to a fall in his popularity. In 1955 a coup by the armed forces sent him into exile.

In 1958 Dr Arturo Frondizi was elected president on the promise of US financial aid. He fell out of favour with the military, whose intervention continued to inform Argentinian politics. After the Peronists achieved the highest number of votes in elections in 1962, the military took control. An attempted return by Perón in 1964 was resisted by the military but it eventually allowed his re-election in 1973. With Perón's death in 1974 his third wife, María Estela Martínez de Perón, 'Isabelita', succeeded him, becoming the Americas' first woman head of state. She was deposed by a military coup two years later and the army's commander-in-chief, Gen. Jorge Videla, became president. Once in power, Videla dissolved Congress, banned trade unions, and imposed military control. Censorship and military curfews were imposed and the secret police was used extensively. His savagely repressive regime implemented what became known as the 'Dirty War'. Videla justified the 'disappearance' of 13,000–15,000 countrymen, many believed to have been tortured and executed, claiming that they threatened to undermine the government.

Videla was eventually succeeded by Gen. Leopoldo Galtieri, the army commander-in-chief. In April 1982 Galtieri, in an effort to distract attention from internal tension, invaded the Falkland Islands. The subsequent military defeat helped to precipitate Galtieri's fall in July 1982. After presidential elections were held in Oct. 1983, civilian rule was restored under Raúl Alfonsín. A failure to redress the finances of the bloated public sector, growing unemployment and four-figure inflation led to a Peronist victory in the 1989 elections, when Carlos Menem became president.

In Dec. 1990, following a failed military coup, Economy Minister Domingo Cavallo stabilized the economy, clearing the way for Menem's second term. However, by 1999, with economic recession, Menem's popularity had plummeted. He was later charged with illegal arms deals. A state of emergency was introduced in Dec. 2001 in the face of an ever-worsening economic crisis. President Fernando de la Rúa resigned on 20 Dec. 2001 after days of rioting and looting across the country. Three interim presidents held power over a period of just 11 days before Eduardo Duhalde was elected by Congress. The economy still in crisis, Duhalde held office until the election of Peronist Néstor Kirchner in May 2003.

TERRITORY AND POPULATION

The second largest country in South America, the Argentine Republic is bounded in the north by Bolivia, in the northeast by Paraguay, in the east by Brazil, Uruguay and the Atlantic Ocean, and the west by Chile. The republic consists of 23 provinces and one federal district with the following areas and estimated populations in 2001 (in 1,000):

Provinces	*Area (sq. km)*	*Population (census 2001)*	*Capital*	*Population (census 2001)*
Buenos Aires	307,571	13,827	La Plata	564
Catamarca	102,602	335	Catamarca	141
Chaco	99,633	984	Resistencia	274
Chubut	224,686	413	Rawson	22
Córdoba	165,321	3,067	Córdoba	1,268
Corrientes	88,199	931	Corrientes	315
Entre Ríos	78,781	1,158	Paraná	236
Formosa	72,066	487	Formosa	198
Jujuy	53,219	612	San Salvador de Jujuy	231
La Pampa	143,440	299	Santa Rosa	94
La Rioja	89,680	290	La Rioja	144
Mendoza	148,827	1,580	Mendoza	111
Misiones	29,801	966	Posadas	253
Neuquén	94,078	474	Neuquén	202
Río Negro	203,013	553	Viedma	47
Salta	155,488	1,079	Salta	462
San Juan	89,651	620	San Juan	113
San Luis	76,748	368	San Luis	153
Santa Cruz	243,943	197	Río Gallegos	79
Santa Fé	133,007	3,001	Santa Fé	369
Santiago del Estero	136,351	804	Santiago del Estero	231
Tierra del Fuego	21,571	101	Ushuaia	45
Tucumán	22,524	1,339	San Miguel de Tucumán	527
Federal Capital	200	2,776	Buenos Aires	2,776

Argentina also claims territory in Antarctica.

The area is 2,780,400 sq. km excluding the claimed Antarctic territory, and the population at the 2001 census was 36,260,130, giving a density of 13 per sq. km.

The UN gives a projected population for 2010 of 41·44m.

In 2001, 89·3% of the population were urban.

In April 1990 the National Congress declared that the Falklands and other British-held islands in the South Atlantic were part of the new province of Tierra del Fuego formed from the former National Territory of the same name. The 1994 Constitution reaffirms Argentine sovereignty over the Falkland Islands.

The population of the principal metropolitan areas in 2001 was: Buenos Aires, 12,046,799; Córdoba, 1,368,301; Rosario, 1,161,188; Mendoza, 848,660; Tucumán, 738,479; La Plata, 694,253.

95% speak the national language, Spanish, while 3% speak Italian, 1% Guaraní and 1% other languages. In 2002, 10,395 immigrants were granted permanent residency, down from 19,916 in 2001.

SOCIAL STATISTICS

2001 births, 683,495; deaths, 285,941. Rates, 2001 (per 1,000 population): birth, 18·2; death, 7·6. Infant mortality, 2001, 16 per 1,000 live births. Estimated life expectancy at birth, 2002, 71·5 years for males and 79·2 years for females. Annual population growth rate, 1992–2002, 1·3%; fertility rate, 2001, 2·5 births per woman.

CLIMATE

The climate is warm temperate over the pampas, where rainfall occurs in all seasons, but diminishes towards the west. In the north and west, the climate is more arid, with high summer temperatures, while in the extreme south conditions are also dry, but much cooler. Buenos Aires, Jan. 74°F (23·3°C), July 50°F (10°C). Annual rainfall 37" (950 mm). Bahía Blanca, Jan. 74°F (23·3°C), July 48°F (8·9°C). Annual rainfall 21" (523 mm). Mendoza, Jan. 75°F (23·9°C), July 47°F (8·3°C). Annual rainfall 8" (190 mm). Rosario, Jan. 76°F (24·4°C), July 51°F (10·6°C). Annual rainfall 35" (869 mm). San Juan, Jan. 78°F (25·6°C), July 50°F (10°C). Annual rainfall 4" (89 mm). San Miguel de Tucumán, Jan. 79°F (26·1°C), July 56°F (13·3°C). Annual rainfall 38" (970 mm). Ushuaia, Jan. 50°F (10°C), July 34°F (1·1°C). Annual rainfall 19" (475 mm).

CONSTITUTION AND GOVERNMENT

On 10 April 1994 elections were held for a 230-member constituent assembly to reform the 1853 constitution. The Justicialist National Movement (Peronist) gained 39% of votes cast and the Radical Union 20%. On 22 Aug. 1994 this assembly unanimously adopted a new Constitution. This reduces the presidential term of office from six to four years, but permits the President to stand for two terms. The President is no longer elected by an electoral college, but directly by universal suffrage. A presidential candidate is elected with more than 45% of votes cast, or 40% if at least 10% ahead of an opponent; otherwise there is a second round. The Constitution reduces the President's powers by instituting a *Chief of Cabinet.* The bicameral *National Congress* consists of a Senate and a Chamber of Deputies. The Senate comprises 72 members (previously consisting of three members appointed by each provincial legislature and three from the Federal District for nine years, but in the process of changing to one-third of the members being elected every two years to six-year terms). The Chamber of Deputies comprises 257 members (one-half of the members elected every two years to four-year terms) directly elected by universal suffrage (at age 18).

National Anthem. 'Oíd, mortales, el grito sagrado: Libertad' ('Hear, mortals, the sacred cry of Liberty'); words by V. López y Planes, 1813; tune by J. Blas Parera.

RECENT ELECTIONS

In the first round of presidential elections held on 27 April 2003, Carlos Menem (Peronist) won 24·4% of the vote, followed by Néstor Kirchner (Peronist) with 22·0%, Ricardo López Murphy (ind.) with 16·3%, Elisa Carrió (ind.) with 14·1% and Adolfo Rodriguez Saá (Peronist) with 14·1%. There were three other candidates. Turn-out was 77·6%. On 14 May Menem pulled out of the second round, leaving Kirchner as winner by default.

In the elections to the Chamber of Deputies on 14 Oct. 2001 the Justicialist Party won 66 of 127 seats with 37·4% of votes cast, the Alliance 35 with 23·1%, Support for an Egalitarian Republic (ARI) 8 with 7·2%, and Front for Change 4 with 4·1%. Other parties won two seats or fewer. Turn-out was 73·7%. In the elections of 2003 for the 130 seats not contested at the 2001 elections, the Justicialist Party won 67 seats, the Radical Union (formerly part of the Alliance) 25, ARI 7 and the remaining seats went to local parties.

CURRENT ADMINISTRATION

President: Néstor Carlos Kirchner; b. 1950 (Peronist; sworn in 27 May 2003).

Vice-President: Daniel Osvaldo Scioli.

In March 2005 the cabinet comprised:

Chief of the Cabinet: Alberto Fernández. *Minister of Defence:* José Pampuro. *Foreign Affairs:* Rafael Bielsa. *Education and Culture:* Daniel Filmus. *Federal Planning:* Julio de Vido. *Interior:* Dr Anibal Fernández. *Justice:* Horacio Rosatti. *Health:* Ginés González García. *Economy and Production:* Roberto Lavagna. *Labour:* Carlos Tomada. *Social Development:* Alicia Kirchner. *Secretary General of the Presidency:* Oscar Parrilli. *Secretary of State Intelligence:* Héctor Icazuriaga.

Office of the President (Spanish only): http://www.presidencia.gov.ar

DEFENCE

Conscription was abolished in 1995. In 2003 defence expenditure totalled US$2,030m. (US$53 per capita), representing 1·5% of GDP (compared to over 8% in 1981).

Army. In 2002 the Army was 41,400 strong. There are no reserves formally established or trained.

There is a paramilitary gendarmerie of 18,000 run by the Ministry of Interior.

Navy. The Argentinian Fleet (2002) included three diesel submarines, five destroyers and eight frigates. Total personnel was 16,000 including 2,000 in Naval Aviation and 2,500 marines. Main bases are at Buenos Aires, Puerto Belgrano, Mar del Plata and Ushuaia.

The Naval Aviation Service had 25 combat aircraft in 2002, including Super-Etendard strike aircraft, and 23 armed helicopters.

Air Force. The Air Force is organized into Air Operations, Air Regions, Logistics and Personnel Commands. There were (2002) 12,500 personnel and 130 combat aircraft including Mirage 5 and Mirage III jet fighters. In addition there were 29 armed helicopters.

INTERNATIONAL RELATIONS

Argentina is a member of the UN, WTO, BIS, OAS, Inter-American Development Bank, LAIA, Mercosur, IOM and the Antarctic Treaty, and is set to apply for membership of the OECD. Diplomatic relations with Britain, broken since the 1982 Falklands War, were re-opened in 1990. Praising Argentina's 'call to peace', in Nov. 1997 US President Clinton announced his intention to give the country 'major non-NATO ally' status. The alignment with US foreign policy came after years of anti-American sentiment and a policy of neutrality.

ECONOMY

Agriculture contributed 10·7% of GDP in 2002, industry 21·3% and services 57·3%.

Overview. Monetary and fiscal mismanagement and a failure to conduct state reform weakened Argentina's economy and left it vulnerable to a series of external shocks in 1997–99. The fixed exchange rate policy, which had the peso pegged at parity with the dollar, left Argentina's overvalued currency vulnerable in the international financial markets. In Dec. 2001 Argentina recorded the largest sovereign debt default in history and abandoned the Convertibility Law. The relationship with the IMF and the international community has been shaky since 2001. The IMF agreed to extend further credit to Argentina but threats to default on loans have left negotiations strained. The country has been suffering from a severe depression, with GDP shrinking 20% in four years. Poverty has increased sharply, with one Argentine out of two now living in poverty. However, post-crisis policy has helped to steer the economy towards recovery. GDP grew at 8·8% in 2003 and inflation was 3·7%. Fiscal performance has exceeded IMF expectations and monetary policy has remained resilient. Argentina is rich in natural resources. However, less than 20% of the continental area (the federal district and Buenos Aires, Santa Fé and Córdoba provinces) accounts for 92% of agricultural output, 80% of industrial production and 64% of the population.

Currency. The monetary unit is the *peso* (ARP), which replaced the austral on 1 Jan. 1992 at a rate of one peso = 10,000 australs. For nearly a decade the peso was pegged at parity with the US dollar, but it was devalued by nearly 30% in Jan. 2002 and floated in Feb. 2002. There was deflation in 2000 of 0·7% and 2001 of 1·5%, but in 2002 there was inflation of 41·0% as Argentina's economic crisis worsened. However, in 2003 there was inflation of just 3·7%, thanks to tight control of monetary policy. In 2004 inflation rose again to 6·1%. Gold reserves were 9,000 troy oz in June 2002 (4·4m. troy oz in 1995); foreign exchange reserves were US$9,621m. (US$20,780m. in June 2001). Total money supply was 15,701m. pesos in Dec. 2001.

Budget. The financial year commences on 1 Jan.

Government revenue and expenditure (in 1m. pesos):

	1998	*1999*	*2000*	*2001*
Revenue	41,188·6	39,765·2	40,346·0	37,093·9
Expenditure	45,930·4	48,056·6	48,224·7	46,013·4

Performance. The economy grew in 1998 by 3·8% but shrank by 3·4% and 0·8% in 1999 and 2000 respectively, mainly as a result of the recession in Brazil, which started in 1998, and the devaluation of the Brazilian *real* in Jan. 1999. In 2001 the economy contracted by 4·4%. As Argentina's economic crisis worsened, in 2002 the economy contracted by 10·9%. However, in 2003 there was a strong recovery, with GDP growth of 8·8%. Total GDP was US$129·7bn. in 2003. In March 2001 the economy minister, José Luis Machinea, resigned after a turbulent 15 months in which he had failed to revive a stagnant economy. As the economic situation deteriorated Argentina had a further five economy ministers in the space of just over a year. In Nov. 2001 the government tried to persuade creditors to accept a restructuring of the US$132bn. public debt, but on 23 Dec. 2001 interim President Adolfo Rodríguez Saá announced that Argentina would default on the debt payments—the biggest debt default in history. One in five Argentines now lives in extreme poverty and more than half the population lives below the official poverty line.

Banking and Finance. The total assets of the Argentine Central Bank (BCRA) in Feb. 2001 were 41·90bn. pesos. The *President* of the Central Bank is Martín Redrado. In early 2002 banks and financial markets were temporarily closed as an emergency measure in response to the economic crisis that made the country virtually bankrupt. In 2002 there were 16 government banks, 24 private commercial banks, four co-operative banks, one other national bank (Banco Hipotecario Nacional) and 17 foreign banks.

There is a main stock exchange at Buenos Aires and there are others in Córdoba, Rosario, Mendoza and La Plata.

ENERGY AND NATURAL RESOURCES

Environment. Argentina's carbon dioxide emissions from the consumption and flaring of fossil fuels in 2002 were the equivalent of 3·2 tonnes per capita.

Electricity. Installed capacity in 2002 was 25·4m. kW. Electric power production (2002) was 82,924m. kWh (5,821m. kWh nuclear); consumption per capita in 2000 was 2,437 kWh. In 2003 there were two nuclear reactors. The electricity market is almost entirely under private ownership, much of it in foreign hands.

Oil and Gas. Crude oil production (2003) was 39·0m. tonnes. Reserves were estimated at some 2·9bn. bbls. in 2002. The oil industry was privatized in 1993. Natural gas extraction in 2002 was 36·1bn. cu. metres. Reserves were about 758bn. cu. metres in 2002. The main area in production is the Neuquen basin in western Argentina, with over 40% of the total oil reserves and nearly half the gas reserves. Natural gas accounts for approximately 45% of all the energy consumed in

Argentina. In 2001 Argentina exported 13% of the natural gas produced, mainly to Chile and Uruguay.

Minerals. Minerals (with estimated production in 2002) include clays (1·6m. tonnes), salt (0·8m. tonnes), aluminium (262,000 tonnes in 2000), coal (259,000 tonnes in 2000), copper (204,027 tonnes in 2001), borates (169,000 tonnes), bentonite (88,685 tonnes), zinc (37,325 tonnes of metal), lead (12,011 tonnes of metal), silver (126 tonnes), beryllium (10 tonnes of metal in 2000), gold (32,486 kg), granite, marble and tungsten. Production from the US$1·1bn. Alumbrera copper and gold mine, the country's biggest mining project, in Catamarca province in the northwest, started in late 1997. In 1993 the mining laws were reformed and state regulation was swept away creating a more stable tax regime for investors. In Dec. 1997 Argentina and Chile signed a treaty laying the legal and tax framework for mining operations straddling the 5,000 km border, allowing mining products to be transported out through both countries.

Agriculture. In 2001 there were 33·7m. ha of arable land and 1·3m. ha of permanent crops. The agricultural population was 4·37m. in 2001, of whom 1·46m. were economically active. 1·56m. ha were irrigated in 2001.

Livestock (2001): cattle, 48,851,000; sheep, 13,561,000; goats, 3,490,000. There were 2,042,400 pigs in 2002 and 1,994,241 horses in 1998. In 2000 wool production was 38,892 tonnes; milk (in 2002), 8,110m. litres; eggs (in 2002, provisional), 380m. dozen.

Crop production (in 1,000 tonnes) in 2002–03: soybeans, 35,000; sugarcane (1998–99), 18,193; maize, 15,000; wheat, 12,300; sunflower seed, 3,800; potatoes (1997–98), 3,412. Cotton, vine, citrus fruit, olives and *yerba maté* (Paraguayan tea) are also cultivated. Wine is fast becoming a major product. Argentina is the world's leading producer of sunflower seeds, and is now the sixth largest wine producer (1·2m. tonnes in 2002) after France, Italy, Spain, USA and Australia; the value of wine exports has grown from US$19m. in 1995 to an estimated US$200m. in 2000.

Forestry. The woodland area was 34·65m. ha, or 12·7% of the total land area, in 2000. Production in 2001 included 1·44m. cu. metres of sawn wood, 4·96m. tonnes of round logs, 1·15m. tonnes of paper and cardboard and 403,000 cu. metres of chipboard. Timber production totalled 9·97m. cu. metres in 2001.

Fisheries. Fish landings in 2002 amounted to 882,815 tonnes, almost exclusively from sea fishing. Hake and squid are the most common catches.

INDUSTRY

The leading companies by market capitalization in Argentina, excluding banking and finance, in Jan. 2002 were: YPF SA (23bn. pesos), an integrated oil company; Siderca SAIC (6bn. pesos), a manufacturer of steel pipe for the energy industry; Pecom Energía SA (5bn. pesos), an energy conglomerate.

Production (in 1,000 tonnes): distillate fuel oil (2000), 10,560; cement (2001), 6,119; petrol (2000), 5,383; crude steel (2002), 4,400; pig iron (2002), 2,200; residual fuel oil (2000), 2,138; sugar (2003), 1,816; jet fuel (2000), 1,547; paper (2003), 1,394; polyethylene (2003), 547; primary aluminium (2003), 272; synthetic rubber (2000), 54. Motor vehicles produced in 2003 totalled 109,364; tyres, 9,578,000; motorcycles, 11,430.

Labour. In 2001 the economically active population totalled 15·26m., of which 10·92m. were employed; there were 1·46m. unemployed in 2000. The urban unemployment rate, which had been 12·9% in 1998, rose to a record 21·5% by May 2002 at the height of the economic crisis before falling to 15·6% in May 2003.

INTERNATIONAL TRADE

External debt was US$132,314m. in 2002.

Imports and Exports. Foreign trade (in US$1m.):

	1998	*1999*	*2000*	*2001*	*2002*	*2003*
Imports	29,531	24,103	23,889	19,158	8,470	13,119
Exports	26,434	23,309	26,341	26,543	25,709	29,566

Principal exports in 2002 (in US$1m., provisional) were fuels, mineral lubricants and related products (4,375); food industry residues (2,783); cereals (2,127); animal and vegetable oils (2,084); and vehicles (1,603).

Principal imports in 2002 (in US$1m., provisional) were nuclear reactors and machinery, and mechanical goods (1,281); organic chemical products (987); vehicles (722); and machines and electrical materials (598).

In 2002 imports (in US$1m.) were mainly from Brazil (2,517); USA (1,804); Germany (554); China, including Hong Kong (342); Japan (314); and Italy (311). Exports went mainly to Brazil (4,828); Chile (2,960); USA (2,957); Spain (1,146); China, including Hong Kong (1,176); and Netherlands (1,038).

COMMUNICATIONS

Roads. In 1999 there were 215,471 km of roads, including 734 km of motorways. The four main roads constituting Argentina's portion of the Pan-American Highway were opened in 1942. Vehicles in use in 1998 totalled 6,544,197, of which 5,047,630 were passenger cars, 1,453,335 trucks and vans, and 43,232 buses and coaches. In 2002, 3,178 people were killed in road accidents. In 2002, 101,143 new vehicles were registered.

Rail. Much of the 33,000 km state-owned network (on 1,000 mm, 1,435 mm and 1,676 mm gauges; 210 km electrified) was privatized in 1993–94. 30-year concessions were awarded to five freight operators; long-distance passenger services are run by contractors to the requirements of local authorities. Metro, light rail and suburban railway services are also operated by concessionaires.

In 2002 railways carried 17,469,000 tonnes of freight and 355,420,000 passengers.

The metro and light rail network in Buenos Aires extends to 46 km.

Civil Aviation. The main international airport is Buenos Aires Ezeiza, which handled 5,442,640 passengers on international flights out of a total of 5,537,297 passengers in 2001. The second busiest airport is Buenos Aires Aeroparque, which handled 5,051,824 passengers in 2001. It is much more important as a domestic airport, with only 581,953 passengers on international flights in 2001 but 4,469,871 on domestic flights. The national carrier, Aerolíneas Argentinas, is 15% state-owned. In 2003 it operated direct flights to Asunción, Auckland, Caracas, Florianópolis, Lima, London, Madrid, Miami, Montevideo, New York, Paris, Pôrto Alegre, Rio de Janeiro, Rome, Santa Cruz, Santiago, São Paulo and Sydney. There were direct flights in 2003 with other airlines to Barcelona, Bogotá, Cancún, Cape Town, Chicago, Cochabamba, Colonia, Dallas, Fortaleza, Frankfurt, Guayaquil, Havana, Johannesburg, Kuala Lumpur, La Paz, Los Angeles, Mexico City, Milan, the Netherlands Antilles, Panama City, Puerto Montt, Punta Cana, Punta del Este, Quito, Puerto Rico, Salvador, Varadero and Zürich.

In 2000 a total of 13·63m. passengers and 203,606 tonnes of freight were carried on domestic and international airlines. In 1998 Aerolíneas Argentinas flew 83·2m. km, carrying 4,024,600 passengers (2,060,000 on international flights).

Shipping. The merchant shipping fleet totalled 423,000 GRT in 2002, including oil tankers totalling 51,000 GRT.

Telecommunications. The telephone service Entel was privatized in 1990. The sell-off split Argentina into two monopolies, operated by Telefonica Internacional de España, and a holding controlled by France Telecom and Telecom Italia. In Nov. 2000 the industry was opened to unrestricted competition. The number of subscribers in 2002 totalled 14,509,400 (396·4 per 1,000 inhabitants). Mobile phone subscribers numbered 6,500,000 in 2002. There were 3,000,000 PCs in use in 2002 (82·0 per 1,000 persons) and 87,000 fax machines in 1998. Argentina had 4·1m. Internet users in 2002.

Postal Services. In 1997 there were 6,678 post offices. In 2002, 5·3m. telegrams were sent.

SOCIAL INSTITUTIONS

Justice. Justice is administered by federal and provincial courts. The former deal only with cases of a national character, or those in which different provinces or inhabitants of different provinces are parties. The chief federal court is the Supreme Court, with five judges whose appointment is approved by the Senate. Other federal courts are the appeal courts, at Buenos Aires, Bahía Blanca, La Plata, Córdoba, Mendoza, Tucumán and Resistencia. Each province has its own judicial system, with a Supreme Court (generally so designated) and several minor chambers. The death penalty was re-introduced in 1976 for the killing of government, military police and judicial officials, and for participation in terrorist activities. The population in penal institutions in June 1999 was 38,604 (107 per 100,000 of national population). In 2002 there were 1,340,529 crimes reported; and 23,538 guilty verdicts were passed.

The police force is centralized under the Federal Security Council.

Religion. The Roman Catholic religion is supported by the State; affiliation numbered 29·92m. in 2001. In Sept. 2003 there were four cardinals. There were 2·04m. Protestants of various denominations in 2001, 730,000 Muslims and 500,000 Jews. There were 275,000 Latter-day Saints (Mormons) in 1998.

Education. Adult literacy was 96·9% in 2001 (96·9% for both males and females). In 2001, 1,331,155 children attended pre-school institutions, 6,716,653 were in basic general education, 1,503,920 in 'multimodal' secondary schooling and 494,461 in higher non-universities.

In 2001, in the public sector, there were 33 universities; one technical university; and university institutes of aeronautics, military studies, naval and maritime studies and police studies. In the private sector, there were 42 universities, including seven Roman Catholic universities. In 2001 there were 1,196,581 students attending public universities and (1999) 171,783 at private universities. In 2000 there was a total of 117,596 academic staff in public universities.

In 2000–01 total expenditure on education came to 4·7% of GNP and 13·6% of total government spending.

Health. Free medical attention is obtainable from public hospitals. In 2001 there were 7,833 public health care institutions which had an average of 75,075 available beds. In 1992 there were 88,800 physicians.

Welfare. Until the end of 1996 trade unions had a monopoly in the handling of the compulsory social security contributions of employees, but private insurance agencies are now permitted to function alongside them.

Unique Social Security System Expenditure (in 1m. pesos):

	1999	*2000*
Retirement and pensions	17,508	17,386
Healthcare assistance and other forms of social insurance	5,249	5,440
Family allowances	1,879	1,920
Unemployment insurance, employment and training programmes	519	484
Work risks insurance	323	367
Other	2,201	2,361
Total	27,679	27,958

CULTURE

World Heritage Sites. Argentina's heritage sites as classified by UNESCO (with year entered on list) are: Los Glaciares national park (1981), the Iguazu National Park (1984), and the Ischigualasto and Talampaya Natural Parks (2000). The Cueva de las Manos (Cave of Hands, 1999), in Patagonia, contains cave art that is between 1,000 and 10,000 years old. The Península Valdés (1999) in Patagonia protects several endangered species of marine mammal. The Jesuit Block and Estancias of Córdoba (2000) are the principal buildings of the Jesuit community from the 17th and 18th century. Shared with Brazil, the Jesuit Missions of the Guaranis (1984) encompasses the ruins of five Jesuit missions. The Quebrada de Humahuaca (2003) is a valley on the Camino Inca trade route.

Broadcasting. There are state-owned, provincial, municipal and private radio stations overseen by the Secretaria de Comunicaciones, the Comité Federal de Radiodifusión, the Servicio Oficial de Radiodifusión (which also operates an external service and a station in Antarctica) and the Asociación de Teleradiodifusoras

Argentinas. There were 24·3m. radio sets in 2000 and 11·8m. TV receivers (colour by PAL N) in 2001. In 2001 there were 5·0m. cable TV subscribers.

Cinema. In 2002 there were 1,003 cinemas with an audience of approximately 27,178,000.

Press. In 1996 there were 106 daily newspapers with a combined circulation of 1·5m., a rate of 41 per 1,000 inhabitants. In 2001 a total of 13,148 book titles were published.

Tourism. In 2000, 2,949,139 tourists visited Argentina, including 567,967 from Chile, 499,831 from Paraguay, 488,007 from Uruguay and 466,016 from Brazil. Receipts in 2000 totalled US$2·90bn. In 2002 there were 7,433 hotels providing 398,653 beds.

Libraries. In 1995 there were 2,700 public libraries. They held a combined 13,496,000 volumes.

DIPLOMATIC REPRESENTATIVES

Of Argentina in the United Kingdom (65 Brook St., London, W1K 4AH)
Ambassador: Federico Mirré.

Of the United Kingdom in Argentina (Dr Luis Agote 2141/52, 1425 Buenos Aires)
Ambassador: John Hughes.

Of Argentina in the USA (1600 New Hampshire Ave., NW, Washington, D.C., 20009)
Ambassador: José Octavio Bordón.

Of the USA in Argentina (4300 Colombia, 1425 Buenos Aires)
Ambassador: Lino Gutierrez.

Of Argentina to the United Nations
Ambassador: César Mayoral.

Of Argentina to the European Union
Ambassador: D. Jorge Remes Lenicov.

FURTHER READING

Bethell, L. (ed.) *Argentina since Independence.* CUP, 1994
Biggins, Alex, *Argentina.* [Bibliography] ABC-Clio, Oxford and Santa Barbara (CA), 1991
Lewis, P., *The Crisis of Argentine Capitalism.* North Carolina Univ. Press, 1990
Manzetti, L., *Institutions, Parties and Coalitions in Argentine Politics.* Univ. of Pittsburgh Press, 1994
Romero, Luis Alberto, *A History of Argentina in the Twentieth Century;* translated from Spanish. Pennsylvania State Univ. Press, 2002
Shumway, N., *The Invention of Argentina.* California Univ. Press, 1992
Turner, Barry, (ed.) *Latin America Profiled.* Macmillan, London, 2000
Wynia, G. W., *Argentina: Illusions and Realities.* 2nd ed. Hoddesdon, 1993

National statistical office: Instituto Nacional de Estadística y Censos (INDEC). Av. Julio A. Roca 615, PB (1067) Buenos Aires. *Director:* Dr Lelio Mármora.
Website: http://www.indec.mecon.ar

ARMENIA

Hayastani Hanrapetoutiun
(Republic of Armenia)

Capital: Yerevan
Population projection, 2010: 2·99m.
GDP per capita, 2002: (PPP$) 3,120
HDI/world rank: 0·754/82

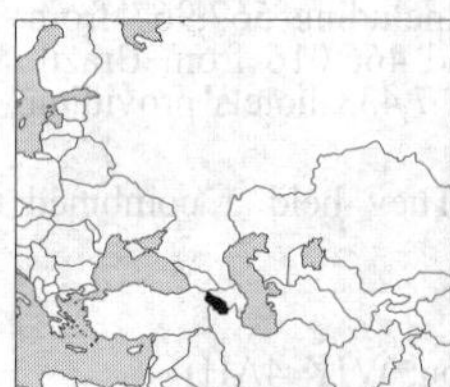

KEY HISTORICAL EVENTS

According to tradition, the kingdom was founded in the region of Lake Van by Haig, or Haik, a descendant of Noah. Historically, the region and former kingdom that was Greater Armenia lay east of the Euphrates River; Little, or Lesser, Armenia was west of the river. In 189 BC the Armenians split from the Syrians to found a native dynasty, the Artashesids. The imperialistic ambitions of King Tigranes led to war with Rome and defeated Armenia became a tributary kingdom. In the 3rd century AD it was overrun by Sassanian Persia. Armenia was the first country to adopt Christianity as its state religion, in the early 4th century. The persecution of Christians under Persian rule kindled nationalism, particularly after the partition (387) of the kingdom between Persia and Rome. However, because of its strategic location, attempts at independence were short-lived, as Armenia was the constant prey of the Persians, Byzantines and Arabs, and later of the Turkish and Russian Empires.

In the early part of the 20th century the Armenians under Turkish rule suffered brutal persecution. An estimated 1·75m. were massacred or deported to present-day Syria from their homeland in Anatolia. Armenia enjoyed a brief period of independence after the First World War but in 1920 the country was proclaimed a Soviet Socialist Republic. After the collapse of Communism, 99% of voters supported a breakaway from the Soviet Union. A declaration of independence in Sept. 1991 was followed by presidential elections after which President Ter-Petrosyan came to an agreement on economic co-operation with the other Soviet republics and joined the CIS. A new constitution adopted in July 1995 led to National Assembly elections. President Ter-Petrosyan was re-elected in Sept. 1996. OSCE observers noted 'very serious irregularities' in the conduct of the election and there were demonstrations of protest in Yerevan, leading to several deaths.

Hostilities with Azerbaijan over the enclave of Nagorno-Karabakh were brought to an end with a 1994 ceasefire. Resigning over Nagorno-Karabakh in Feb. 1998, President Ter-Petrosyan was succeeded by Robert Kocharyan, who was sworn in as president in April 1998. On 27 Oct. 1999, five men burst into the parliamentary chamber, killing the Prime Minister, Vazgen Sarkisian, and seven other officials. Aram Sarkisian, brother of the slain prime minister, was named as his successor. In April 2001 a first round of high-level talks on the settlement of the Nagorno-Karabakh conflict was held in Florida. Armenia and Azerbaijan have agreed, in principle, to continue talks.

TERRITORY AND POPULATION

Armenia covers an area of 29,743 sq. km (11,484 sq. miles). It is bounded in the north by Georgia, in the east by Azerbaijan and in the south and west by Turkey and Iran.

The population in 2001 was estimated at 3,802,400 (1,848,500 males; 1,953,900 females), of which 2,532,400 (66·6%) lived in urban areas; population density is 128 per sq. km. Armenians account for 97%, Kurds 1·6% and Russians 0·8%—in 1989, 2·6% of the population were Azeris, prior to the Nagorno-Karabakh conflict. The United Nations population estimate for 2000 was 3,112,000.

The UN gives a projected population for 2010 of 2·99m.

According to the Second Armenia-Diaspora Conference in May 2002 there are approximately 10m. Armenians worldwide.

The capital is Yerevan (1·1m. population in 2001). Other large towns are Gyumri (formerly Leninakan) (150,900 in 2001) and Vanadzor (formerly Kirovakan) (107,300 in 2001).

The official language is Armenian.

SOCIAL STATISTICS

2001 births, 32,065; deaths, 24,003; marriages, 12,302; divorces, 1,776. Rates, 2001 (per 1,000 population): births, 8·4; deaths, 6·3; marriage, 3·2; divorce, 0·5. Infant mortality, 2001, 31 per 1,000 live births. Annual population growth rate, 1992–2002, –1·3%. Life expectancy at birth, 2001, 68·7 years for men and 75·3 years for women; fertility rate, 2000, 1·1 births per woman.

CLIMATE

Summers are very dry and hot although nights can be cold. Winters are very cold, often with heavy snowfall. Yerevan, Jan. –9°C, July 28°C. Annual rainfall 318 mm.

CONSTITUTION AND GOVERNMENT

The head of state is the *President*, directly elected for five-year terms. Parliament is a 131-member *Azgayin Zhoghov* (National Assembly), with 75 deputies elected by party list and 56 chosen by direct election (vice-versa until 2002). The government is nominated by the President.

National Anthem. 'Mer Hayrenik azat, ankakh' ('Land of our fathers, free and independent'); words by M. Nalbandyan, tune by B. Kanachyan.

RECENT ELECTIONS

In presidential elections held on 19 Feb. 2003 incumbent president Robert Kocharian received 48·3% of votes cast, ahead of Stepan Demirchyan with 27·4% and Artashes Geghamyan 16·9%. Turn-out was 61·2%. The OSCE said that the election process 'fell short of international standards in several key respects'. In the run-off on 5 March 2003 between the two leading candidates Robert Kocharian won 67·5% of the vote against 32·5% for Stepan Demirchyan. Again observers claimed the elections failed to meet international standards.

Elections to the National Assembly were held on 25 May 2003. The Republican Party of Armenia (HHK) won 31 seats with 23·5% of the vote. Rule of Law Country (Orinants Erkir, OE) won 19 seats (12·3%), Ardartyun (Justice) 14 seats (13·6%), Dashnak (Armenian Revolutionary Federation) 11 seats (11·4%), National Unity 9 seats (8·8%) and the United Labour Party 6 seats (5·7%). The All Armenian Labour Party and Hanrapetutiun (Republic) both won one seat. 36 non-partisans were also elected. Turn-out was 51·5%.

CURRENT ADMINISTRATION

President: Robert Kocharian, formerly President of Nagorno-Karabakh, the Armenian-inhabited enclave in Azerbaijan; b. 1954 (in office since 4 Feb. 1998).

In March 2005 the government comprised:

Prime Minister: Andranik Markaryan; b. 1951 (HHK; appointed 12 May 2000).

Minister of Foreign Affairs: Vardan Oskanian. *Defence:* Serge Sargsian. *Justice:* Davit Harutyunian. *Education and Science:* Sergo Yeritsen. *Health:* Norair Davidyan. *Culture and Youth Affairs:* Ovik Oveyan. *Industry and Trade:* Karen Chshmaritian. *Transportation and Telecommunications:* Andranik Manukian. *Agriculture:* David Lokian. *Environment:* Vardan Ayvazian. *Finance and Economy:* Vardan Khachatrian. *Energy:* Armen Movsisyan. *Urban Development:* Aram Harutiunian. *Regional Government and Co-ordinating the Operation of Infrastructures:* Hovik Abrahamian. *Social Welfare:* Agvan Vardanian. *Cabinet Chief of Staff:* Manook Topuzian.

DEFENCE

There is conscription for 24 months. Total active forces numbered 44,160 in 2002, including 33,100 conscripts.

Defence expenditure in 2003 totalled US$700m. (US$229 per capita), representing 6·4% of GDP.

Army. Current troop levels are 38,900, plus air and defence aviation forces of 3,160 and paramilitary forces of 1,000. There are approximately 210,000 Armenians who have received some kind of military service experience within the last 15 years.

INTERNATIONAL RELATIONS

There is a dispute over the mainly Armenian-populated enclave of Nagorno-Karabakh, which lies within Azerbaijan's borders—Armenia and Azerbaijan are technically still at war.

Armenia is a member of the UN, NATO Partnership for Peace, Council of Europe, CIS, OSCE, BSE and the IOM. It is the biggest recipient of US government aid, per head of population, after Israel.

ECONOMY

In 2002 agriculture contributed 25·9% of GDP, industry 35·1% and services 39·0%.

Overview. Privatization began after independence in 1991 with the privatization of most agricultural land. In 1998 the Greek telecommunications company OTE bought a 90% stake in ArmenTel, the Armenian state company. By 1998 approximately 60% of enterprises had been privatized, rising to over 80% of medium and large enterprises and 90% of small enterprises by the end of 2000. The IMF and the World Bank have supported Armenia's privatization and economic restructuring.

Currency. In Nov. 1993 a new currency unit, the *dram* (AMD) of 100 *lumma*, was introduced to replace the rouble. Inflation, which had been 5,273% in 1994, was just 1·1% in 2002. Foreign exchange reserves were US$323m. in June 2002, gold reserves were 28,000 troy oz and total money supply was 74,904m. drams.

Budget. In 2000 total revenue was 172,132·8m. drams and total expenditure 222,886·4m. drams.

Performance. Real GDP growth was 9·6% in 2001, 12·9% in 2002 and 13·9% in 2003. Total GDP in 2003 was US$2·8bn.

Banking and Finance. The *Chairman* of the Central Bank (founded in 1993) is Tigran Sargsyan. In 2002 there were 28 commercial banks and one savings bank. There are commodity and stock exchanges in Yerevan and Gyumri.

ENERGY AND NATURAL RESOURCES

Environment. Armenia's carbon dioxide emissions from the consumption and flaring of fossil fuels in 2002 were the equivalent of 2·6 tonnes per capita.

Electricity. Output of electricity in 2000 was 5·57bn. kWh. Capacity was 3·0m. kW in 2000. Consumption per capita was 1,445 kWh in 2000. A nuclear plant closed in 1989 was re-opened in 1995 because of the blockade of the electricity supply by Azerbaijan; it was anticipated that domestic supply would be raised from four to 12 hours daily.

Minerals. There are deposits of copper, zinc, aluminium, molybdenum, marble, gold and granite.

Agriculture. The chief agricultural area is the valley of the Arax and the area round Yerevan. Here there are cotton plantations, orchards and vineyards. Almonds, olives and figs are also grown. In the mountainous areas the chief pursuit is livestock raising. In 2001 there were 495,000 ha of arable land and 65,000 ha of permanent crops. Major agricultural production (in tonnes in 2000): potatoes, 290,300; wheat, 177,800; tomatoes, 143,700; grapes, 115,800; barley, 32,900. Livestock (2000): cattle, 497,306; sheep, 539,992; pigs, 68,912; horses, 11,400; chickens, 4m.

Forestry. In 2000 forests covered 351,000 ha, or 12·4% of the total land area. Timber production in 2001 was 42,000 cu. metres.

Fisheries. Total catch in 2001 came to 866 tonnes, exclusively from inland waters.

INDUSTRY

Among the chief industries are chemicals, producing mainly synthetic rubber and fertilizers, the extraction and processing of building materials, ginning- and textile-mills, carpet weaving and food processing, including wine-making.

Labour. In 2000 the population of working age was 2·35m., of whom 1·3m. were employed: 44% in agriculture, 14% in industry. The registered unemployment rate was 9·4% of the workforce in 2002. The official average monthly salary in Jan. 2001 was 20,612 drams.

INTERNATIONAL TRADE

External debt was US$1,149m. in 2002.

Imports and Exports. Imports and exports for calendar years in US$1m.:

	1998	*1999*	*2000*	*2001*	*2002*
Imports	806·3	721·4	773·4	773·3	882·5
Exports	228·9	247·3	309·9	353·1	513·8

The main import suppliers in 2000 were Russia (14·9%), USA (11·6%), Belgium (9·5%) and Iran (9·4%). Principal export markets were Belgium (25·2%), Russia (15·0%), USA (12·7%) and Iran (9·3%). Cut diamonds and jewellery from precious metals and stones account for 45% of Armenia's exports, non-precious metals 15% and mineral products 13%. Foodstuffs account for 26% of Armenia's imports, mineral products 19%, and equipment and machinery 15%.

COMMUNICATIONS

Roads. There were 15,918 km of road network in 2000, including 7,527 km of motorways. In 1996 there were 5,760 passenger cars, buses, coaches, lorries and vans as well as 7,200 motorcycles and mopeds. There were 214 fatalities as a result of road accidents in 2000.

Rail. Total length in 2000 was 711 km of 1,000 mm gauge. Passenger-km travelled in 2000 came to 52m. and freight tonne-km to 354m.

There is a metro and a tramway in Yerevan.

Civil Aviation. There is an international airport at Yerevan (Zvartnots). The state-owned Armenian Airlines has been operational since 1995. In 2003 it operated services to Adler/Sochi, Amsterdam, Anapa, Ashgabat, Athens, Dubai, Frankfurt, Kharkiv, Krasnodar, Kyiv, Mineralnye Vody, Moscow, Nizhny Novgorod, Novosibirsk, Odesa, Paris, Samara, Simferopol, Stavropol, Tashkent, Tbilisi, Tehran, Vienna and Volgograd. There were direct flights in 2003 with other airlines to Astrakhan, Donetsk, Ekaterinburg, İstanbul, Larnaca, London, Minsk, Rostov, St Petersburg and Saratov. In 1999 scheduled airline traffic of Armenian-based carriers flew 8·2m. km, carrying 343,000 passengers (all on international flights).

Telecommunications. Telephone subscribers numbered 614,800 in 2002 (161·7 per 1,000 inhabitants) and 60,000 PCs were in use (15·8 for every 1,000 persons). There were 71,900 mobile phone subscribers in 2002. Armenia had 60,000 Internet users in 2002.

SOCIAL INSTITUTIONS

Justice. In 2000, 12,048 crimes were reported, including 127 murders or attempted murders. The population in penal institutions in Feb. 2000 was 6,789 (178 per 100,000 of national population).

Religion. Armenia adopted Christianity in AD 301, thus becoming the first Christian nation in the world. The Armenian Apostolic Church is headed by its Catholicos (Karekin II, b. 1951) whose seat is at Etchmiadzin, and who is head of all the Armenian (Gregorian) communities throughout the world. In 1995 it numbered 7m. adherents (4m. in diaspora). The Catholicos is elected by representatives of parishes. The Catholicos of the diaspora is Aram I (b. 1947) of Cilicia, with seat at Antelias. In 2001, 65% of the population belonged to the Armenian Apostolic Church.

Education. Armenia's literacy rate was 98·5% in 2001 (99·3% among males and 97·8% among females). At the end of 2000, 46,300 children (17% of those eligible) attended pre-school institutions. In 2000–01 there were 176,302 pupils in primary schools (and 13,620 teachers in 1996–97) and 292,368 pupils in secondary schools. In 2000–01 there were 25 technical colleges with 26,870 students and 19 higher educational institutions with 43,615 students. Yerevan houses the National Academy of Sciences of the Republic of Armenia (NAS RA), 43 scientific institutes, a medical institute and other technical colleges, and a state university. NAS RA is composed of more than 50 institutions and organizations with a staff of 4,500.

In 2000–01 there were seven universities (including the Yerevan State University and the American University), with 22,400 students, out of a total of 19 public higher education establishments.

Total expenditure on education in 2000–01 came to 2·9% of GNP.

Health. In 2000 there were some 12,270 doctors, 22,672 junior medical personnel and 146 hospitals with 20,795 beds.

Welfare. In 2000 there were 501,711 old age, and 58,371 other, pensioners.

CULTURE

World Heritage Sites. There are three UNESCO sites in Armenia: the Monasteries of Haghpat and Sanahin (inscribed in 1996); the Monastery of Geghard and the Upper Azat Valley (2000); the Cathedral and Churches of Echmiatsin and the Archaeological Site of Zvartnots (2000).

Broadcasting. The state-owned Armenian Radio broadcasts two national programmes and relays of Radio Moscow and Voice of America, and a foreign service, Radio Yerevan (Armenian, English, French, Spanish, Arabic, Kurdish, Russian). Television broadcasting is by the state-controlled Armenian Television (colour by SECAM H). In 2001 there were 870,000 TV receivers and in 2000 there were 700,000 radio receivers.

Press. In 2000 there were 91 daily publications.

Tourism. In 2000 there were 30,000 foreign tourists bringing in receipts of US$45m.

Libraries. There were 1,138 libraries in 2000, which lent 5·1m. items.

Theatre and Opera. 360,000 people attended 21 theatres in 2000.

Museums and Galleries. In 2000 there were 93 museums with 874,100 visitors.

DIPLOMATIC REPRESENTATIVES

Of Armenia in the United Kingdom (25A Cheniston Gdns, London, W8 6TG)
Ambassador: Vahe Gabrielyan.

Of the United Kingdom in Armenia (34 Baghramyan Avenue, Yerevan 375019)
Ambassador: Thorda Abbott-Watt.

Of Armenia in the USA (2225 R St, NW, Washington, D.C., 20008)
Ambassador: Arman Kirakossian.

Of the USA in Armenia (18 Baghramyan Avenue, Yerevan 375019)
Ambassador: John Evans.

Of Armenia to the United Nations
Ambassador: Armen Martirosian.

Of Armenia to the European Union
Ambassador: Viguen Tchitetchian.

FURTHER READING

Brook, S., *Claws of the Crab: Georgia and Armenia in Crisis.* London, 1992
Hovannisian, R. G., *The Republic of Armenia.* 4 vols. Univ. of California Press, 1996
Malkasian, M., *Gha-Ra-Bagh: the Emergence of the National Democratic Movement in Armenia.* Wayne State Univ. Press, 1996
Nersessian, V. N., *Armenia.* [Bibliography] ABC-Clio, Oxford and Santa Barbara (CA), 1993
Walker, C. J., *Armenia: The Survival of a Nation.* 2nd ed. London, 1990

National statistical office: National Statistical Service of the Republic of Armenia. *President:* Stepan L. Mnatsakanyan.
Website: http://www.armstat.am

AUSTRALIA

Commonwealth of Australia

Capital: Canberra
Population projection, 2010: 20·95m.
GDP per capita, 2002: (PPP$) 28,260
HDI/world rank: 0·946/3

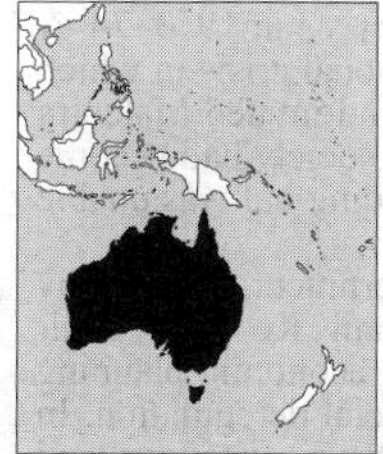

KEY HISTORICAL EVENTS

Inhabited in prehistoric times, climatic changes led to an exodus between 15,000 and 25,000 years ago. A population using stone tools was in evidence by 2,000–1,000 BC. The Aboriginal society, composed of extended family groups, numbered around 1m.

Various dates are given for the European discovery of Australia but while the Dutch, Portuguese and Spanish first charted the continent, it was the discovery of the east coast by the British Capt. James Cook in 1770 that prompted colonization. The British decided to use Australia as a penal colony; Botany Bay received the first convicts. By 1800 the colony was self-sufficient and convicts had established legal rights as crown subjects. The crossing of the Blue Mountains in 1813 was the first of many expeditions which led to the discovery of good grazing land. The colonists' diseases decimated the Aboriginal population, which fell by half to 300,000 between 1820–50.

The wool trade took off in the middle of the 19th century with the introduction of the Merino sheep. By 1850 wool accounted for 90% of all Australia's exports. With the arrival of 'free immigrants' from Britain, the population rose to 1·1m. in 1860. The economy was boosted by the discovery of copper and gold and by 1850 Victoria accounted for one third of the world's gold supply. Sydney, Melbourne, Adelaide and Perth grew during these boom decades, attaining a degree of self-rule. New South Wales, Tasmania and Victoria were granted full parliamentary control of their own affairs in 1855, with South Australia and the newly formed Queensland following in the next five years. However, the British government retained control of foreign policy and kept power of veto. In the 1890s recession the economy shrank by a third. Trade unionism grew from the 1870s and from the turn of the century until the First World War, Labor was in government in every state.

In 1901 the six colonies of New South Wales, Victoria, Queensland, South Australia, Western Australia and Tasmania were federated under the Commonwealth of Australia, becoming 'states'; Northern Territory was transferred from South Australia to the Commonwealth as a 'territory' on 1 Jan. 1911. A bicameral parliament was established and in 1907 Australia gained dominion status. By the following year there was female suffrage for the national and all state legislatives.

In 1911 a site in New South Wales was designated the Australian capital, Canberra, where the Federal Parliament opened in 1927. Australia rallied to the British cause in the First World War. Around 330,000 Australian troops served in the war—60,000 died and over 150,000 were wounded. Australia lost its markets in France, Belgium and Germany, accounting for a third of its exports. The early 1920s was a period of recovery, assisted by 200,000 immigrants from Britain. However, the economy (except for the wool industry) relied on government subsidy, leaving it exposed to the depression that followed the 1929 Crash. Under Labor public spending was cut, a 10% reduction in wages imposed and the currency devalued by 25%. Unemployment approached 30%. The recently formed United Australia Party took over the government.

The late 1930s saw deteriorating relations with Japan. When war became inevitable, Australia again rallied to the imperial cause. 100,000 Australian troops were killed or wounded. After Pearl Harbor, Darwin was attacked in 1942.

Robert Menzies led successive Liberal governments from 1949–66. Unemployment was low and the economy tripled in size in the 1950s and 1960s. In 1951 Australia entered the ANZUS group with New Zealand and the USA and three years later joined the South-East Asian Treaty Organization. Australia's new found confidence was reflected in the success of the 1956 Melbourne Olympics.

The movement for Aboriginal rights grew after the war with a strike by Aboriginal workers at Pilbara in 1946. Moderate reforms favouring the Aboriginal population were passed between 1959–67 but the assimilation policy allowed for the forced removal of large numbers of children from their families. The last of the Aboriginal reserves was taken over in the 1960s. An apology for the policy of forced removal of children was not given until the 1980s.

Gough Whitlam, who led the Labor party to power in 1972, withdrew Australian forces from Vietnam, set about modernizing the education and health programmes and funded extensive urban renewal. Government expenditure doubled over his three years in office and Australia was ill-prepared for the global oil crisis in 1973–74. A failure to win approval for the national budget led to a constitutional crisis in which the Governor-General John Kerr dismissed the prime minister and invited Malcolm Fraser to form an administration. Fraser believed that Australian society had become overly dependent on the state. He authorized cuts in public spending but was unable to counter rising unemployment and inflation.

Bob Hawke took power in 1983 at the head of a Labor government, assisted by his finance minister (and successor as prime minister), Paul Keating. Their premierships saw a shift in Labor's stance on state control and economic planning to allow for an ambitious programme of privatization and financial deregulation. In March 1986 the Australia Act abolished the remaining legislative, executive and judicial controls of the British Parliament.

A referendum to decide if Australia should become a republic was held on 6 Nov. 1999. 54·87% of votes were in favour of the monarchy. Liberal Prime Minister John Howard agreed to military involvement in UN peacekeeping in East Timor and NATO action against Serbia. Howard has pursued an interventionist foreign policy in the Pacific region and committed Australia to the US-led war in Iraq in 2003.

TERRITORY AND POPULATION

Australia, excluding external territories, covers an estimated land area of 7,692,030 sq. km, extending from Cape York (10° 41' S) in the north some 3,680 km to South East Cape, Tasmania (43° 39' S), and from Cape Byron, New South Wales (153° 39' E) in the east some 4,000 km west to Steep Point, Western Australia (113° 9' E). External territories under the administration of Australia comprise the Ashmore and Cartier Islands, Australian Antarctic Territory, Christmas Island, the Cocos (Keeling) Islands, the Coral Sea Islands, the Heard and McDonald Islands and Norfolk Island. For these *see below.*

Growth in census population has been:

1901	3,774,310	1966	11,599,498	1986	15,763,000
1911	4,455,005	1971	12,755,638	1991	16,852,258
1921	5,435,734	1976	13,915,500	1996	17,892,423
1947	7,579,358	1981	15,053,600	2001	18,972,350
1961	10,508,186				

Of the 2001 census population, 9,618,981 were females.

Population at 30 June 2004 was estimated to be 20,111,300. The UN gives a projected population for 2010 of 20·95m.

At 30 June 2002 density was 2·6 per sq. km. In 2001, 91·1% of the population lived in urban areas.

Areas and populations of the States and Territories at the 2001 census:

States and Territories	*Area (sq. km)*	*Population*	*Per sq. km*
New South Wales (NSW)	800,640	6,371,745	8·0
Victoria (Vic.)	227,420	4,644,950	20·4
Queensland (Qld.)	1,730,650	3,655,139	2·1
South Australia (SA)	983,480	1,467,261	1·5
Western Australia (WA)	2,529,880	1,851,252	0·7
Tasmania (Tas.)	68,400	456,652	6·7
Northern Territory (NT)	1,349,130	210,664	0·2
Australian Capital Territory (ACT)	2,360	311,947	132·2

Estimated population at 30 June 2004: New South Wales, 6,731,300; Victoria, 4,972,800; Queensland, 3,882,000; South Australia, 1,534,300; Western Australia, 1,982,200; Tasmania, 482,100; Northern Territory, 199,900; Australian Capital Territory, 324,000.

Resident population in capitals and other statistical districts with more than 150,000 population at 30 June 2002:

Capital	*State*	*Population*	*Capital*	*State*	*Population*
Canberra	ACT	321,400	Darwin	NT	107,400
Sydney	NSW	4,170,900	*Statistical district*		
Melbourne	Vic.	3,524,100	Newcastle	NSW	497,500
Brisbane	Qld.	1,689,100	Gold Coast[1]	Qld.	439,700
Adelaide	SA	1,114,300	Wollongong	NSW	272,100
Perth	WA	1,413,700	Sunshine Coast[2]	Qld.	191,900
Hobart	Tas.	198,000	Geelong	Vic.	161,700

[1]Includes part of Tweed Shire (in NSW). [2]Includes Caloundra, Maroochy and Noosa.

The median age of the 2001 census population was 35 years.

Australians born overseas (census 2001), 4,105,444, of whom 1,036,245 (5·5%) were from the UK. In 1998 it was estimated that 23·4% of the population was born overseas.

Aboriginals have been included in population statistics only since 1967. At the 2001 census 410,003 people identified themselves as being of indigenous origin (2·2% of the total population). A 1992 High Court ruling that the Meriam people of the Murray Islands had land rights before the European settlement reversed the previous assumption that Australia was *terra nullius* before that settlement. The Native Title Act setting up a system for deciding claims by Aborigines came into effect on 1 Jan. 1994.

Overseas arrivals and departures:

	Settler arrival numbers[1]	*Permanent departure numbers*	*Net permanent migration*
1999–2000	92,300	41,100	51,200
2000–01	107,400	46,500	60,800
2001–02	88,900	48,200	40,700
2002–03	93,900	50,500	43,500

[1]Equals the total number of people entitled to permanent residence actually arriving.

The Migration Act of Dec. 1989 sought to curb illegal entry and ensure that annual immigrant intakes were met but not exceeded. Provisions for temporary visitors to become permanent were restricted. According to the 2001 census, 74% of the population born overseas have become Australian citizens.

The national language is English.

SOCIAL STATISTICS

Life expectancy at birth, 2003, 77·8 years for males and 82·8 years for females. A World Health Organization report published in June 2000 put Australians in second place in a 'healthy life expectancy' list, with an expected 73·2 years of healthy life for babies born in 1999.

Statistics for years ended 30 June:

	Births	*Deaths*	*Marriages*	*Divorces*
1999	249,282	127,200	114,300	52,600
2000	249,600	128,100	113,400	49,900
2001	246,400	128,540	103,130	55,330
2002	251,000	133,700	105,440	54,000
2003	251,200	132,300	106,400	53,100

In 2003 the median age for marrying was 31 years for males and 29 for females. Infant mortality, 2003, was 4·8 per 1,000 live births. Population growth rate in the year ended 30 June 2004, 1·2%; fertility rate, 2003, 1·75 births per woman.

Suicide rates (per 100,000 population, 2002): 11·8 (men, 19·5; women, 5·2).

CLIMATE

Over most of the continent, four seasons may be recognized. Spring is from Sept. to Nov., summer from Dec. to Feb., autumn from March to May and winter from June to Aug., but because of its great size there are climates that range from tropical monsoon to cool temperate, with large areas of desert as well. In northern Australia there are only two seasons, the wet one lasting from Nov. to March, but rainfall amounts diminish markedly from the coast to the interior. Central and southern Queensland are subtropical, north and central New South Wales are warm temperate, as are parts of Victoria, Western Australia and Tasmania, where most rain falls in winter. Canberra, Jan. 68°F (20°C), July 42°F (5·6°C). Annual rainfall 25" (635 mm). Adelaide, Jan. 73°F (22·8°C), July 52°F (11·1°C). Annual rainfall 21" (528 mm). Brisbane, Jan. 77°F (25°C), July 58°F (14·4°C). Annual rainfall 45" (1,153 mm). Darwin, Jan. 83°F (28·3°C), July 77°F (25°C). Annual rainfall 59" (1,536 mm). Hobart, Jan. 62°F (16·7°C), July 46°F (7·8°C). Annual rainfall 23" (584 mm). Melbourne, Jan. 67°F (19·4°C), July 49°F (9·4°C). Annual rainfall 26" (659 mm). Perth, Jan. 74°F (23·3°C), July 55°F (12·8°C). Annual rainfall 35" (873 mm). Sydney, Jan. 71°F (21·7°C), July 53°F (11·7°C). Annual rainfall 47" (1,215 mm).

CONSTITUTION AND GOVERNMENT

Federal Government. Under the Constitution legislative power is vested in a Federal Parliament, consisting of the Queen, represented by a Governor-General, a Senate and a House of Representatives. Under the terms of the constitution there must be a session of parliament at least once a year.

The Senate (Upper House) comprises 76 Senators (12 for each State voting as one electorate and, as from Aug. 1974, two Senators respectively for the Australian Capital Territory and the Northern Territory). Senators representing the States are chosen for six years. The terms of Senators representing the Territories expire at the close of the day next preceding the polling day for the general elections of the House of Representatives. In general, the Senate is renewed to the extent of one-half every three years, but in case of disagreement with the House of Representatives, it, together with the House of Representatives, may be dissolved, and an entirely new Senate elected. Elections to the Senate are on the single transferable vote system; voters list candidates in order of preference. A candidate must reach a quota to be elected, otherwise the lowest-placed candidate drops out and his or her votes are transferred to other candidates.

The *House of Representatives* (Lower House) consists, as nearly as practicable, of twice as many Members as there are Senators, the numbers chosen in the several States being in proportion to population as shown by the latest statistics, but not less than five for any original State. The 150 membership is made up as follows: New South Wales, 50; Victoria, 37; Queensland, 27; South Australia, 12; Western Australia, 15; Tasmania, 5; ACT, 2; Northern Territory, 2. Elections to the House of Representatives are on the alternative vote system; voters list candidates in order of preference, and if no one candidate wins an overall majority, the lowest-placed drops out and his or her votes are transferred. The first Member for the Australian Capital Territory was given full voting rights as from the Parliament elected in Nov. 1966. The first Member for the Northern Territory was given full voting rights in 1968. The House of Representatives continues for three years from the date of its first meeting, unless sooner dissolved.

Every Senator or Member of the House of Representatives must be a subject of the Queen, be of full age, possess electoral qualifications and have resided for three years within Australia. The franchise for both Houses is the same and is based on universal (males and females aged 18 years) suffrage. Compulsory voting was introduced in 1925. If a Member of a State Parliament wishes to be a candidate in a federal election, he must first resign his State seat.

Executive power is vested in the *Governor-General*, advised by an Executive Council. The Governor-General presides over the Council, and its members hold office at his pleasure. All Ministers of State, who are members of the party or parties commanding a majority in the lower House, are members of the Executive Council under summons. A record of proceedings of meetings is kept by the Secretary to the Council. At Executive Council meetings the decisions of the Cabinet are (where necessary) given legal form, appointments made, resignations accepted, proclamations, regulations and the like made.

The policy of a ministry is, in practice, determined by the Ministers of State meeting without the Governor-General under the chairmanship of the Prime Minister. This group is known as the *Cabinet.* There are 11 Standing Committees of the Cabinet comprising varying numbers of Cabinet and non-Cabinet Ministers. In Labour governments all Ministers have been members of Cabinet; in Liberal and National Country Party governments, only the senior ministers. Cabinet meetings are private and deliberative, and records of meetings are not made public.

The Cabinet does not form part of the legal mechanisms of government; the decisions it takes have, in themselves, no legal effect. The Cabinet substantially controls, in ordinary circumstances, not only the general legislative programme of Parliament but the whole course of Parliamentary proceedings. In effect, though not in form, the Cabinet, by reason of the fact that all Ministers are members of the Executive Council, is also the dominant element in the executive government of the country.

The legislative powers of the Federal Parliament embrace trade and commerce, shipping, etc.; taxation, finance, banking, currency, bills of exchange, bankruptcy, insurance, defence, external affairs, naturalization and aliens, quarantine, immigration and emigration; the people of any race for whom it is deemed necessary to make special laws; postal, telegraph and like services; census and statistics; weights and measures; astronomical and meteorological observations; copyrights; railways; conciliation and arbitration in disputes extending beyond the limits of any one State; social services; marriage, divorce, etc.; service and execution of the civil and criminal process; recognition of the laws, Acts and records, and judicial proceedings of the States. The Senate may not originate or amend money bills. Disagreement with the House of Representatives may result in dissolution and, in the last resort, a joint sitting of the two Houses. The Federal Parliament has limited and enumerated powers, the several State parliaments retaining the residuary power of government over their respective territories. If a State law is inconsistent with a Commonwealth law, the latter prevails.

The Constitution also provides for the admission or creation of new States. Proposed laws for the alteration of the Constitution must be submitted to the electors, and they can be enacted only if approved by a majority of the States and by a majority of all the electors voting.

The Australia Acts 1986 removed residual powers of the British government to intervene in the government of Australia or the individual states.

In Feb. 1998 an Australian Constitutional Convention voted for Australia to become a republic. In a national referendum, held on 6 Nov. 1999, 54·9% voted against Australia becoming a republic.

State Government. In each of the six States (New South Wales, Victoria, Queensland, South Australia, Western Australia, Tasmania) there is a State government whose constitution, powers and laws continue, subject to changes embodied in the Australian Constitution and subsequent alterations and agreements, as they were before federation. The system of government is basically the same as that described above for the Commonwealth—i.e., the Sovereign, her representative (in this case a Governor), an upper and lower house of Parliament (except in Queensland, where the upper house was abolished in 1922), a cabinet led by the Premier and an Executive Council. Among the more important functions of the State governments are those relating to education, health, hospitals and charities, law, order and public safety, business undertakings such as railways and tramways, and public utilities such as water supply and sewerage. In the domains of education, hospitals, justice, the police, penal establishments, and railway and tramway operation, State government activity predominates. Care of the public health and recreative activities are shared with local government authorities and the Federal government; social services other than those referred to above are now primarily the concern of the Federal government; the operation of public utilities is shared with local and semi-government authorities.

Administration of Territories. Since 1911 responsibility for administration and development of the Australian Capital Territory (ACT) has been vested in Federal Ministers and Departments. The ACT became self-governing on 11 May 1989. The ACT House of Assembly has been accorded the forms of a legislature, but continues to perform an advisory function for the Minister for the Capital Territory.

On 1 July 1978 the Northern Territory of Australia became a self-governing Territory with expenditure responsibilities and revenue-raising powers broadly approximating those of a State.

National Anthem. 'Advance Australia Fair' (adopted 19 April 1984; words and tune by P. D. McCormick). The 'Royal Anthem' (i.e. 'God Save the Queen') is used in the presence of the British Royal Family.

RECENT ELECTIONS

The 41st Parliament was elected on 9 Oct. 2004.

House of Representatives. Liberal Party (LP), 74 seats and 40·5% of votes cast; Australian Labor Party (ALP), 60 seats and 37·6% of votes cast; National Party of Australia (NP), 12 (5·9%); Northern Territory Country Liberal Party, 1 (0·3%); ind. and others, 3 (2·4%).

Senate. As at March 2005 the make-up of the Senate was Liberal Party, 31; Australian Labor Party, 28; Australian Democratic Party, 7; National Party of Australia, 3; Greens, 2, Northern Territory Country Liberal Party, 1; One Nation, 1; Australian Progressive Alliance, 1; ind., 2.

CURRENT ADMINISTRATION

Governor-General: Maj.-Gen. (retd) Michael Jeffery, AC, CVO, MC; b. 1937 (took office on 11 Aug. 2003).

Following the 2004 general election a new LP–NP coalition government was formed on 26 Oct. 1994. In March 2005 the cabinet comprised:

Prime Minister: John Winston Howard; b. 1939 (LP; in office since 11 March 1996).

Deputy Prime Minister and Minister for Transport and Regional Services: John Anderson (NP). *Treasurer:* Peter Costello (LP). *Defence and Leader of the Government in the Senate:* Robert Hill (LP). *Communications, Information Technology and the Arts:* Helen Coonan (LP). *Employment and Workplace Relations, and Minister Assisting the Prime Minister for the Public Service:* Kevin Andrews (LP). *Foreign Affairs:* Alexander Downer (LP). *Environment and Heritage:* Ian Campbell (LP). *Industry, Tourism and Resources:* Ian Macfarlane (LP). *Agriculture, Fisheries and Forestry:* Warren Truss (NP). *Health and Ageing and Leader of the House of Representatives:* Tony Abbott (LP). *Education, Science and Training:* Dr Brendan Nelson (LP). *Finance and Administration:* Nicholas Minchin (LP). *Family and Community Services, and Minister Assisting the Prime Minister for the Status of Women:* Kay Patterson (LP). *Immigration and Multicultural and Indigenous Affairs:* Amanda Vanstone (LP). *Trade:* Mark Vaile (NP). *Attorney General:* Philip Ruddock (LP).

The *Speaker* is David Hawker (LP).

The *President* of the Senate is Paul Calvert (LP).

Leader of the Opposition: Kim Beazley (ALP).

Government: http://www.gov.au

DEFENCE

The Minister for Defence has responsibility under legislation for the control and administration of the Defence Force. The Chief of Defence Force Staff is vested with command of the Defence Force. He is the principal military adviser to the Minister. The Chief of Naval Staff, the Chief of the General Staff and the Chief of the Air Staff command the Navy, Army and Air Force respectively. They have delegated authority from the Chief of Defence Force Staff and the Secretary to administer matters relating to their particular Service.

2003 defence expenditure was US$11,758m., amounting to US$591 per capita and representing 2·3% of GDP.

Army. The strength of the Army was 25,150, including 2,500 women, in 2002. The effective strength of the Army Reserve was 16,200.

Women have been eligible for combat duties since 1993.

Navy. The all-volunteer Navy in 2002 was 12,750 including 990 in the Fleet Air Arm and 1,900 women. The Fleet included six diesel-powered submarines and nine frigates.

The fleet main base is at Sydney, with subsidiary bases at Cockburn Sound (Western Australia), Cairns and Darwin.

Air Force. The Royal Australian Air Force (RAAF) operated 156 combat aircraft including 35 F-111 and 71 F-18 'Hornets' in 2002. Personnel numbered 13,200, including 1,964 women. There is also an Australian Air Force Reserve, 2,000-strong.

INTERNATIONAL RELATIONS

Australia is a member of the UN, WTO, BIS, the Commonwealth, OECD, Asian Development Bank, Colombo Plan, APEC, IOM, the Pacific Islands Forum, the Pacific Community and the Antarctic Treaty.

ECONOMY

In the year ended 30 June 2003 service industries accounted for almost 80% of GDP and manufacturing 10·7%.

According to the anti-corruption organization *Transparency International*, Australia ranked 9th in the world in a 2004 survey of the countries with the least corruption in business and government. It received 8·8 out of 10 in the annual index.

Overview. The Australian economy has experienced healthy expansion for more than a decade. GDP growth averaged 3·5% between 1991 and 2004, exceeding average OECD growth by more than 1%. Significant change in the Australian economy in recent years is attributed in part to a combination of liberalization, increased competition and technological advance. Growth since 2001 has been driven by buoyant domestic demand, which has been stimulated by growth in real disposable household incomes. Strong growth has had a beneficial impact on unemployment, which has halved since the early 1990s. Notwithstanding the recent excellent economic performance, Australia's per capita GDP stands at 76% of US per capita GDP and hourly productivity levels fall short of those seen at international levels. The stock of household has risen sharply; increases in asset values have, however, ensured that only small changes in the leverage of households have been seen and monetary relaxation has helped to reduce the household debt interest burden.

The primary fiscal goal is to balance the budget on average over the course of the business cycle. There are concerns about the fiscal pressures that will be placed on the system owing to rising healthcare costs and long-term care, caused by demographic and medical technology trends. Per capita health care costs per person aged over 65 are projected to rise by more than the OECD average. In the 2003 budget the government proposed measures to increase labour force participation in a bid to boost output, reduce social security spending and increase tax receipts. A range of initiatives were introduced to contain health care expenditure and to ensure the viability of the current system.

Currency. On 14 Feb. 1966 Australia adopted a system of decimal currency. The currency unit, the Australian dollar (AUD), is divided into 100 *cents*.

Foreign exchange reserves were US$33,902m. in Dec. 2004 and gold reserves US$1,123m. Total money supply was $A166,978m. in March 2002.

The Reserve Bank of Australia forecasts an underlying inflation rate of 2·5% towards the end of 2005, rising to 2·75% by mid-2006.

Budget. In Aug. 1998 the Commonwealth government introduced a tax reform package including, from 2000, the introduction of a Goods and Services Tax (GST) at a 10% rate, with all the revenues going to the states in return for the abolition of a range of other indirect taxes; the abolition of Financial Assistance Grants to states; the abolition of wholesale sales tax (which is levied by the Commonwealth government); cuts in personal income tax; and increases in social security benefits, especially for families. In the 2004–05 Mid-Year Economic and Fiscal Outlook an underlying cash surplus of $A6·2bn. (0·7% of GDP) was anticipated in 2004–05, an increase of $A3·8bn. since the 2004–05 budget.

The Australian Government levies income taxes. State expenditure is backed by federal grants. Australian Government General Government Sector expenses and revenue outcomes (in $A1m.):

	2003–04	*2004–05*[1]
Total expenses (by function)	181,238	193,808
including		
General public services	10,848	12,404
Defence	12,937	14,349
Public order and safety	2,386	2,928
Education	13,398	14,628
Health	31,771	35,720
Social security and welfare	80,103	82,200
Housing and community amenities	1,634	1,689
Recreation and culture	2,168	2,444

	2003–04	2004–05[1]
Total expenses (by function)	181,238	193,808
including		
Fuel and energy	3,494	3,953
Agriculture, fisheries and forestry	2,038	2,402
Mining and mineral resources (other than fuels), manufacturing and construction	1,589	1,846
Transport and communications	2,816	2,873
Other economic affairs	4,286	4,955
Other purposes	11,771	11,417
Total revenue (by source)	187,559	199,443
including		
Income tax		
Individuals and other witholding	98,779	105,060
Companies	36,337	40,870
Superannuation funds	5,785	6,710
Petroleum resource rent tax	1,165	1,560
Indirect tax		
Excise duty—Petroleum products and crude oil	13,529	13,950
Other excise	7,539	7,700
Total excise duty	21,068	21,650
Customs duty	5,622	5,714
Other indirect taxes	1,002	1,140
Fringe benefit tax	3,277	3,020
Other taxes	1,420	1,898
Non-tax revenue	12,501	11,821

[1]Estimate.

Performance. GDP growth was forecast to slow from an estimated 3·5% in 2003–04 (real terms) to 3·2% in 2004–05. Severe Acute Respiratory Syndrome (SARS) and continuing international security concerns reduced GDP growth in 2003–04. The current account deficit was expected to narrow to 5% of GDP in 2004–05, reflecting an improvement in the country's terms of trade. During much of the 1990s the real GDP growth rate, along with lower inflation, made the Australian economic performance one of the best in the OECD area. In 2003 total GDP was US$518,382m. ($A777,301m.)

In March 2003 the OECD reported that 'Australia's current and recent economic outcomes place it among the top performers in the OECD. This owes much to a good combination of prudent, medium-term oriented fiscal and monetary policies, and far-reaching reforms to labour, product and financial markets in the past two decades. … Previous structural reforms are likely to continue bearing their fruits for some years.'

Banking and Finance. From 1 July 1998 a new financial regulatory framework based on three agencies was introduced by the Australian government, following recommendations by the Financial System Inquiry. The framework included changes in the role of the Reserve Bank of Australia and creation of the Australian Prudential Regulation Authority (APRA) with responsibility for the supervision of deposit-taking institutions (comprising banks, building societies and credit unions), friendly societies, life and general insurance companies and superannuation funds. It further involved replacement of the Australian Securities Commission with the Australian Securities and Investments Commission (ASIC) with responsibility for the regulation of financial services and Australia's 1·2m. companies.

The banking system comprises:

(a) The Reserve Bank of Australia is the central bank. It has two broad responsibilities—monetary policy and the maintenance of financial stability, including stability of the payments system. It also issues Australia's currency notes and provides selected banking and registry services to Commonwealth Government customers and some overseas official institutions. Within the Reserve Bank there are two Boards: the Reserve Bank Board and the Payments System Board; the *Governor* (present incumbent, Ian Macfarlane) is the Chairman of each.

At 30 June 2004 total assets of the Reserve Bank of Australia were $A75,948m., including gold and foreign exchange, $A55,173m.; and Australian dollar securities, $A19,708m. At 30 June 2004 capital and reserves were $A10,856m. and main liabilities were Australian notes on issue, $A34,022m.; and deposits, $A18,126m.

A wholly owned subsidiary of the Reserve Bank (Note Printing Australia Limited) manufactures currency notes and other security documents for Australia and for export.

(b) Four major banks: (i) The Commonwealth Bank of Australia; (ii) the Australia and New Zealand Banking Group Ltd; (iii) Westpac Banking Corporation; (iv) National Australia Bank.

(c) The Commonwealth Bank of Australia has a subsidiary—Commonwealth Development Bank. There are nine other Australian-owned banks—Adelaide Bank Ltd, AMP Bank Ltd, Bank of Queensland Ltd, Bendigo Bank Ltd, Elders Rural Bank (50% owned by Bendigo Bank Ltd), Macquarie Bank Ltd, Members Equity Pty Ltd, St George Bank Ltd and Suncorp-Metway Ltd.

(d) There are ten banks incorporated in Australia which are owned by foreign banks and 27 branches of foreign banks (these figures include five foreign banks which have both a subsidiary and a branch presence in Australia).

(e) As at 30 June 2004 there were 51 authorized banks with Australian banking assets of $A1,240·5bn., with 4,888 branches, 21,550 reported ATMs and 465,754 reported EFTPOS terminals. As at 30 June 2004 there were 14 building societies with assets of $A14·6bn. and 171 credit unions with assets of $A31·1bn.

There is an Australian Stock Exchange (ASX) in Sydney.

ENERGY AND NATURAL RESOURCES

Environment. Australia's carbon dioxide emissions from the consumption and flaring of fossil fuels were the equivalent of 21·0 tonnes per capita in 2002. An *Environmental Sustainability Index* compiled for the World Economic Forum meeting in Feb. 2002 ranked Australia 16th in the world, with 60·3%. The index measured the ability of countries to maintain favourable environmental conditions and examined various factors including pollution levels and the use or abuse of natural resources.

Electricity. Electricity supply is the responsibility of the State governments. 2002–03 total production was 201,141m. kWh (7·6% hydro-electric). In the year ended 30 June 2001 total consumption stood at 173,075m. kWh, including 50,319m. kWh by residential customers.

Oil and Gas. The main fields are Gippsland (Vic.) and Carnarvon (WA). Crude oil and condensate production was 38,705m. litres in 2000–01, an increase of 3% over the previous year. The value of oil and natural gas production in 2000–01 was estimated to total $A16·4bn. Oil reserves at the end of 2002 totalled 3·1bn. bbls. and natural gas reserves 2,550bn. cu. metres. Australia's most productive oilfield in 2000 was Laminaria in Northern Territory with peak production of around 180,000 bbls. and average production at Nov. 2000 of around 167,000 bbls. per day. Natural gas production (2002) was 34·5bn. cu. metres. Natural gas reserves (2002) totalled 2,265bn. cu. metres.

Minerals. Australia is the world's largest producer of bauxite and alumina. It is also the world's largest producer of diamonds (mostly for industrial use) and the third-largest gold producer. Black coal is Australia's major source of energy. Reserves are large (2002: 39·7bn. economically recoverable tonnes) and easily worked. The main fields are in New South Wales and Queensland. Brown coal (lignite) reserves are mined only in Victoria. In 2001–02 raw coal production was 348·0m. tonnes; lignite production, 66·7m. tonnes; and (2003–04 estimate) iron ore and concentrates, 220·7m. tonnes.

Production of other major minerals in 2003–04 (in tonnes): bauxite, 56·3m.; alumina, 16·8m.; salt (estimate), 10·7m.; manganese (estimate), 3·1m.; zinc, 1·9m.; nickel, 185,000 (content of concentrates); uranium, 9,538; silver, 2,675; gold, 264. Diamond production, 2003–04: 24·3m. carats. Australia is the world's largest producer of diamonds, ranking first for industrial-grade diamonds and second for gem-grade diamonds, after Botswana.

Agriculture. At 30 June 2002 there were an estimated 135,377 establishments mainly engaged in agriculture. Agricultural production in 2001–02 was estimated to total $A39·6bn. At 30 June 2002 the estimated total area of land under agricultural use was 447m. ha (about 58% of total land area). In 2002 there were 48·2m. ha of arable land and 24·1m. ha of crops. 2·55m. ha were irrigated in 2001–02. Important crops (2001–02): wheat (24·3m. tonnes from 11·5m. ha); barley (8·3m. tonnes from 3·7m. ha); canola (1·8m. tonnes from 1·3m. ha); oats (1·4m. tonnes from 0·78m. ha); rice (1·2m. tonnes from 0·14m. ha); sugarcane (31·4m. tonnes from 0·43m. ha). At 30 June 2002, 1·8m. tonnes of grapes were harvested from 159,000 ha of vines.

Beef cattle farming represents the largest sector, accounting for 25% of farming establishments. Livestock totals at June 2002: beef cattle and calves, 24·7m.; dairy cattle, 3·1m.; sheep and lambs, 106m.; pigs, 2·8m. Gross value of agricultural production in 2001–02, $A39·6bn., including (in $A1bn.) cattle and calves slaughtering, 7·1; sheep and lamb slaughtering, 2·1; wheat, 6·4; wool, 2·7; milk, 3·7. Livestock products (in 1,000 tonnes) at June 2002: beef, 1,996; lamb and mutton, 644; pigmeat, 396; veal, 31. 2000–01 estimates: poultry meat, 657,000 tonnes; wool, 652,000 tonnes; milk, 10,556m. litres.

Fruit and vegetable production in 2001–02 (in 1,000 tonnes): potatoes, 1,333·2; oranges, 450·6; apples, 320·5; bananas, 313·3; onions, 282·5.

Figures compiled by the Soil Association, a British organization, show that in 1999 organic crops were grown in an area covering 1·7m. ha (the largest area of any country in the world), representing 1·4% of all farmland.

Australia is the world's leading wool producer; only China has more sheep.

Forestry. The Federal government is responsible for forestry at the national level. Each State is responsible for the management of publicly owned forests. Estimated total native forest cover was 162·7m. ha at Feb. 2003 (approximately 21% of Australia's land area), made up of (in 1,000 ha): public forest, 121·6m.; privately owned, 38·9m. The major part of wood supplies derives from coniferous plantations, of which there were 988,000 ha at 30 Dec. 2002. Australia also had 638,000 ha of hardwood plantation at that date. Production of sawn timber in 2001–02 was 4,119,000 cu. metres.

Fisheries. The Australian Fishing Zone covers an area 16% larger than the Australian land mass and is the third largest fishing zone in the world, but fish production is insignificant by world standards owing to low productivity of the oceans. The major commercially exploited species are prawns, rock lobster, abalone, tuna, other fin fish, scallops, oysters and pearls. Estimated total fisheries production in 2002–03 came to 249,000 tonnes with a gross value of $A2·3bn. In the same year aquaculture production was an estimated 44,049 tonnes with a gross value of $A743·5m., which represented 32% of the total value of fisheries production.

INDUSTRY

The leading companies by market capitalization in Australia, excluding banking and finance, in May 2003 were: Telstra Corporation Ltd (US$37·8bn.), a telecommunications company; The News Corporation Ltd (US$36·2bn.); and BHP Billiton Ltd (US$20·8bn.), a resources company.

Manufacturing industry in 2002–03 contributed around 11% to Australia's GDP. In May 2004 almost 1·1m. people were employed, 11% of Australia's total employed.

Manufacturing by sector, 2000–01:

	Employment	*Labour costs in $A1m.*	*Sales of goods and services income in $A1m.*
Food, beverages and tobacco	189,600	8,173	56,626
Textiles, clothing, footwear and leather products	57,800	1,951	9,111
Wood and paper products	65,000	2,751	15,077
Printing, publishing and recorded media	91,600	4,213	15,929
Chemical, petroleum, coal and associated products	101,300	5,537	47,115
Non-metallic mineral products	37,200	1,903	9,960
Metal products	147,000	6,999	40,517
Machinery and equipment	202,200	9,621	50,645
Other manufacturing	54,200	1,772	6,963

Manufactured products in 2002–03 included: clay bricks, 1,639m.; portland cement, 7·5m. tonnes; ready-mixed concrete, 21·0m. cu. metres; tobacco and cigarettes, 19,561 tonnes; newsprint, 407m. tonnes; pig iron, 6·6m. tonnes; aviation turbine fuel, 5,149m. litres; beer, 1,727m. litres.

Labour. In 2002–03 the total workforce (persons aged 15 and over) numbered 10,074,800 (4,474,900 females). In 2002–03 there were 9,458,500 employed persons (56·0% females). In Feb. 2001 the labour force included 329,700 employers, 7,326,400 wage and salary earners and 866,900 self-employed. The majority of wage and salary earners have had their minimum wages and conditions of work prescribed in awards by the Industrial Relations Commission. In Oct. 1991 the Commission decided to allow direct employer-employee wage bargaining, provided agreements reached are endorsed by the Commission. In some States, some conditions of work (e.g., weekly hours of work, leave) are set down in State legislation. Average weekly wage, Feb. 2003, $A717·40 (men, $A862·60; women, $A564·10). Average weekly hours worked by full-time employed person, 2002–03: 42·1 hours. Four weeks annual leave is standard. In 2002–03 part-time work accounted for 28·5% of all employment in Australia and persons born overseas made up 57·7% of the total labour force.

Employees in all States are covered by workers' compensation legislation and by certain industrial award provisions relating to work injuries.

During 2002 there were 766 industrial disputes recorded which accounted for 259,000 working days lost (34% decrease on 2001). In these disputes 159,700 workers were involved.

Retail trade has overtaken the manufacturing industry as the largest employer in recent years with 15% and 12% of employed persons respectively in 2001–02. Property and business services have 11% of employed persons while health and community services employ 10%.

In Feb. 2001, 1,427,500 wage and salary earners worked in the public sector and 5,898,900 in the private sector.

The following table shows the percentage distribution of employed persons in 2001–02 according to the *Australian Standard Classification of Occupations (2nd edition)*:

	Employed persons (%)
Professionals	18·5
Intermediate clerical, sales and service workers	17·1
Tradespersons and related workers	12·8
Associate professionals	11·8
Elementary clerical, sales and service workers	9·8
Labourers and related workers	9·2
Intermediate production and transport workers	8·6
Managers and administrators	7·8
Advanced clerical and service workers	4·3

In 2002–03, 616,300 persons were unemployed, of whom 22·1% had been unemployed for more than one year. The unemployment rate in Jan. 2005 was 5·1%, the lowest since 1976.

Trade Unions. In Aug. 2002, 23·1% of all full-time employees (21·5% females) were members of a trade union. In 1999 there were 11 unions with fewer than 1,000 members and 14 unions with 50,000 or more members. Many of the larger trade unions are affiliated with central labour organizations, the oldest and by far the largest being the Australian Council of Trade Unions (ACTU) formed in 1927. In 2002, 46 unions were affiliated to ACTU, representing approximately 1·8m. workers. In July 1992 the Industrial Relations Legislation Amendment Act freed the way for employers and employees to negotiate enterprise-based awards and agreements.

INTERNATIONAL TRADE

In 1990 Australia and New Zealand completed a Closer Economic Relations agreement (initiated in 1983) which establishes free trade in goods. Net foreign debt was $A359·0bn. as at 30 June 2003 (an increase of 9·0% on the previous year). In 1998 the effect of the Asian meltdown on exports resulted increasingly in shipments of commodities and exports of manufactures and some services being redirected to other destinations, notably the USA and Europe. Merchandise exports decreased by 5% in 2002–03 against the previous year while imports rose by 11%.

Imports and Exports. Merchandise imports and exports for years ending 30 June (in $A1m.):

	Imports	*Exports*
1999–2000	110,078	97,286
2000–01	118,317	119,539
2001–02	119,681	121,176
2002–03	133,131	115,442

The Australian customs tariff provides for preferences to goods produced in and shipped from certain countries as a result of reciprocal trade agreements. These include the UK, New Zealand, Canada and Ireland.

Most valuable commodity exports, 2002–03 (in $A1m.): coal, 11,946; crude petroleum products, 5,881; non-monetary gold, 5,584; iron ore, 5,328; aluminium, 4,059; bovine meat, 3,906; aluminium ores and concentrates (including alumina), 3,587. Most valuable commodity imports, 2002–03 (in $A1m.): passenger motor vehicles, 10,283; crude petroleum oils, 7,812; aircraft, associated equipment and spacecraft, 5,481; computing equipment, 4,871; medicaments, 4,241; telecommunications equipment, 4,239.

Australia is the world's largest exporter of black coal, bauxite, lead, diamonds, mineral sands, beef and wool.

Trade by bloc or country in 2002–03 (in $A1m.):

	Exports	*Imports*
APEC	82,998	92,247
ASEAN	13,850	20,722
EU	15,841	31,400
OECD	68,323	84,752
China	8,793	13,792
Japan	21,738	16,335
South Korea	9,116	4,753
New Zealand	8,120	5,019
Singapore	4,655	4,370
Taiwan	4,314	3,401
Indonesia	2,908	4,600
Malaysia	2,147	4,262
Germany	1,579	7,953
UK	7,236	5,770
USA	10,369	22,496

COMMUNICATIONS

Roads. As at June 1999 controlled access roads (motorways excluding tolled roads) totalled 1,563 km; national highways, 18,620 km; rural arterial, 94,854 km; urban arterial, 12,398 km; rural local, 600,725 km; urban local, 84,845 km.

At 31 March 2002 registration totals were: 10,137,000 passenger vehicles, 1,820,000 light commercial vehicles, 425,000 trucks, 70,000 buses, 371,000 motorcycles.

In 2002, 1,723 persons were killed in road accidents (1,737 in the previous year).

Rail. Privatization of government railways began in Victoria in 1994 with West Coast Railway and Hoys Transport being granted seven-year franchises. A three-year extension was granted to West Coast Railway in 2001. Specialised Container Transport (SCT) won the first private rail freight franchise in 1995 followed by TNT (now Toll Holdings). Australian National Railway Commission was sold by the Commonwealth Government in Nov. 1997 and in Feb. 1999 V/Line Freight Corporation, owned by the Victorian Government, was sold to Freight Australia. Rail passenger services in Victoria were franchised in mid-1999. The Australian Railroad Group acquired Western Australia's government rail freight operation, Westrail, in Nov. 2000. In Jan. 2002 Toll Holdings and Lang acquired the rolling stock of the National Rail Corporation (NRC) and New South Wales freight carrier, FreightCorp. These two sales leave QR as the only government-owned rail freight operator in Australia.

At 30 June 2002 the total length of track was 4,017 km (broad gauge, 1,600 mm); 17,678 km (standard, 1,435 mm); 15,160 km (narrow, 1,067 mm); 4,150 km (narrow, 610 mm gauge); and 281 km (dual gauge). In 2002–203 a total of 598·6m. tonnes of freight were carried; passengers carried totalled 586m. urban (including train and tram); 9m. non-urban.

Under various Commonwealth–State standardization agreements, all the State capitals are now linked by standard gauge track. The 'AustralAsia Rail Project', which involved the construction of 1,420 km standard gauge railway between Alice Springs and Darwin, has been completed and passenger services from Adelaide through Alice Springs and on to Darwin commenced on 1 Feb. 2004.

There are also private industrial and tourist railways, and tramways in Adelaide, Melbourne and Sydney. In the latter two cities there are also metro systems.

Civil Aviation. Qantas Airways is Australia's principal international airline. In 1992 Qantas merged with Australian Airlines, and in 1993, 25% of the company was purchased by British Airways. The remainder is government-owned. Qantas relaunched Australian Airlines in Oct. 2002 to connect Asia-Pacific with Cairns and the Gold Coast. A total of 49 international airlines operated scheduled air services to and from Australia in 2001. There are 13 international airports, the main ones being Adelaide, Brisbane, Cairns, Darwin, Melbourne, Perth and Sydney. In the year ended 2002 international passenger traffic decreased by 5·9% to 16·5m.; international freight decreased by 4·6% to 634,341 tonnes; mail decreased by 5·3% to 29,206 tonnes.

Sydney (Kingsford Smith) handled the most traffic (48%) in Australia in 2002–03 (23,150,121 passengers, of which 13,524,090 on domestic flights), followed by Melbourne International (20%) and Brisbane (15%).

Internal airlines (domestic and regional) carried 31,852,000 passengers in 2000–01. Domestic airlines were deregulated in Oct. 1990.

At 6 Aug. 2001 there were 261 licensed aerodromes in Australia and its external territories. At 31 Dec. 2003 there were 12,034 registered aircraft.

Shipping. The chief ports are Brisbane, Dampier, Fremantle, Gladstone, Hay Point, Melbourne, Newcastle, Port Hedland, Port Kembla, Port Walcott, Sydney and Weipa. Dampier, Australia's busiest port, handled 92,228,000 tonnes of cargo in 2001–02. As at 30 June 2002 the trading fleet comprised 77 vessels totalling 2,028,637 DWT, 1,587,743 GRT.

Coastal cargo handled at Australian ports in 2001–02 (in gross weight tonnes): loaded, 52·4m.; unloaded, 52·8m. International trade loaded, 506·6m. tonnes; unloaded, 58·0m. tonnes. Calls to ports made by commercial ships in 2001–02 totalled 21,358 with 366 made by passenger vessels.

Telecommunications. Australian telecommunications are in the latter stages of an evolution from a state-owned monopoly. In 1989 the domestic market became a regulated monopoly with Telstra as the government-owned company providing all services and, in 1991, a duopoly (with Optus) in fixed network services. In 1993 Vodafone joined Telstra and Optus in the provision of mobile phone services. A new regulatory regime was created by the introduction of the Telecommunications Act 1997 and both markets were opened to wholesale and retail competition. There is no limit to the number of carriers that can hold licences under the new arrangements and by June 2002 a total of 83 licences had been issued. The Australian Communications Authority (ACA) and the Australian Competition and Consumer Commission (ACCC) are the primary regulators with responsibility for the industry's development.

Telephone subscribers numbered 23,169,000 in 2002 (1,178·3 per 1,000 inhabitants), and there were 11,111,000 PCs in use, or 565·1 per 1,000 persons. In Feb. 2002 there were 12·87m. mobile phone subscribers (the largest supplier being Optus, with 4·59m. subscribers) and 10·63m. Internet users.

Three telecommunications satellites are in orbit covering the entire continent.

Postal Services. Postal services are operated by Australia Post, operating under the Australian Postal Corporation Act 1989 as a government business enterprise. Revenue was $A3,733m. in 2000–01, expenditure $A3,331m. There were 3,872 corporate outlets and licensed post offices and other agencies in 2000–01, and 4,761·1m. postal items were handled.

SOCIAL INSTITUTIONS

Justice. The judicial power of the Commonwealth of Australia is vested in the High Court of Australia (the Federal Supreme Court), in the Federal courts created by the Federal Parliament (the Federal Court of Australia and the Family Court of Australia) and in the State courts invested by Parliament with Federal jurisdiction.

High Court. The High Court consists of a Chief Justice and six other Justices, appointed by the Governor-General in Council. The Constitution confers on the High Court original jurisdiction, *inter alia*, in all matters arising under treaties or affecting consuls or other foreign representatives, matters between the States of the Commonwealth, matters to which the Commonwealth is a party and matters between residents of different States. Federal Parliament may make laws conferring original jurisdiction on the High Court, *inter alia*, in matters arising under the Constitution or under any laws made by the Parliament. It has in fact conferred jurisdiction on the High Court in matters arising under the Constitution and in matters arising under certain laws made by Parliament.

The High Court may hear and determine appeals from its own Justices exercising original jurisdiction, from any other Federal Court, from a Court exercising Federal jurisdiction and from the Supreme Courts of the States. It also has jurisdiction to hear and determine appeals from the Supreme Courts of the Territories. The right of appeal from the High Court to the Privy Council in London was abolished in 1986.

Other Federal Courts. Since 1924, four other Federal courts have been created to exercise special Federal jurisdiction, i.e. the Federal Court of Australia, the Family Court of Australia, the Australian Industrial Court and the Federal Court of Bankruptcy. The Federal Court of Australia was created by the Federal Court of Australia Act 1976 and began to exercise jurisdiction on 1 Feb. 1977. It exercises such original jurisdiction as is invested in it by laws made by the Federal Parliament including jurisdiction formerly exercised by the Australian Industrial Court and the Federal Court of Bankruptcy, and in some matters previously invested in either the High Court or State and Territory Supreme Courts. The Federal Court also acts as a court of appeal from State and Territory courts in relation to Federal matters. Appeal from the Federal Court to the High Court will be by way of special leave only. The State Supreme Courts have also been invested with Federal jurisdiction in bankruptcy.

State Courts. The general Federal jurisdiction of the State courts extends, subject to certain restrictions and exceptions, to all matters in which the High Court has jurisdiction or in which jurisdiction may be conferred upon it.

Industrial Tribunals. The chief federal industrial tribunal is the Australian Conciliation and Arbitration Commission, constituted by presidential members (with the status of judges) and commissioners. The Commission's functions include settling industrial disputes, making awards, determining the standard hours of work and wage fixation. Questions of law, the judicial interpretation of awards and imposition of penalties in relation to industrial matters are dealt with by the Industrial Division of the Federal Court.

At 30 June 2003 the prison population was 23,555, an increase of almost 50% since 1993.

Each State has its own individual police service which operates almost exclusively within its State boundaries. State police investigations include murder, robbery, street-level drug dealing, kidnapping, domestic violence and motor vehicle offences. State police activities are broadly known as community policing.

The role of the Australian Federal Police (AFP) is to enforce Commonwealth criminal law and protect Commonwealth and national interests from crime in Australia and overseas. Responsibilities include combating organized crime, transnational crime, money laundering, illicit drug trafficking, e-crime, the investigation of fraud against the Australian Government and handling special references from Government. The AFP also provides a protection service to dignitaries and crucial witnesses as well as community policing services to the people of the Australian Capital Territory, Jervis Bay and Australia's External Territories.

Total Australian Federal Police personnel (excluding ACT policing) as at 30 June 2003 was 3,496, of which 2,297 were sworn employees (police members) and 1,199 unsworn employees. There are approximately 48,000 police officers in Australia.

Religion. Under the Constitution the Commonwealth cannot make any law to establish any religion, to impose any religious observance or to prohibit the free exercise of any religion. The following percentages refer to those religions with the largest number of adherents at the census of 2001. Answering the census question on religious adherence was not obligatory, however.

Christian, 68·0% of population: Catholic, 26·6%; Anglican, 20·7%; Uniting Church, 6·7%; Presbyterian and Reformed, 3·4%; Orthodox, 2·8%; Baptist, 1·6%; Lutheran, 1·3%; Pentecostal, 1·0%; Jehovah's Witnesses, 0·4%; Salvation Army, 0·4%; Churches of Christ, 0·3%; other Christian, 2·7%. Religions other than Christian 5·0%: Buddhism, 1·9%; Islam, 1·5%; Hinduism, 0·5%; Judaism, 0·4%; other religions, 0·5%; no religion, 15·5%; no statement, 11·7%.

The Anglican Synod voted for the ordination of ten women in Nov. 1992. In Sept. 2003 the Roman Catholic church had three cardinals.

Thompson, R. C., *Religion in Australia, a History.* OUP, 1995

Education. The governments of the Australian States and Territories have the major responsibility for education, including the administration and substantial funding of primary, secondary, and technical and further education. In most States, a single Education Department is responsible for these three levels but in Queensland, Western Australia and the Northern Territory, separate departments deal with school-based and technical and further education issues.

School attendance is compulsory between the ages of six and 15 years (16 years in Tasmania), at either a government school or a recognized non-government educational institution. Many children attend pre-schools for a year before entering school (usually in sessions of two–three hours, for two–five days per week). Government schools are usually co-educational and comprehensive. Non-government schools have been traditionally single-sex, particularly in secondary schools, but there is a trend towards co-education. Tuition is free at government schools, but fees are normally charged at non-government schools.

In Aug. 2004 there were 6,938 government (and 2,677 non-government) primary and secondary schools with 2,249,076 (1,082,888) full-time pupils and (Aug. 2003) 156,156 (76,910) full-time teachers.

Vocational education and training (VET) is essentially a partnership between the Commonwealth, the States and Territories and industry. The Commonwealth is involved in VET through an agreed set of national arrangements for sharing responsibility with the States and Territories. The current mechanism for giving effect to this is the Australian National Training Authority (ANTA) Agreement, which sets out the roles and responsibilities for VET: they provide two-thirds of the funding and have all of the regulatory responsibility for the sector. They are also the 'owners' of the network of public Technical and Further Education (TAFE) institutes. In 2003 publicly-funded VET programmes were offered by some 79 TAFEs and other government institutions. A further 531 community education providers and 1,339 other providers (mainly private providers) delivering VET were at least partly publicly funded. In 2003 there were over 1·7m. people enrolled in VET courses.

In 2003, 45 higher education institutions received Commonwealth Government funding. Most of these institutions operate under State and Territory legislation although several operate under Commonwealth legislation. There is also a completely privately-funded university and numerous private higher education providers in a range of specialist fields. Institutions established by appropriate legislation are autonomous and have the authority to accredit their own programmes and are primarily responsible for their own quality assurance. There were 929,952 university students in 2003. Fields of university study with the largest number of award course students in 2003 were management and commerce (27·5%); society and culture (21·8%); health (10·8%); and education (9·7%).

The higher education sector contributes a significant proportion of the research and research training undertaken in Australia. The Australian Research Council provides advice on research issues and administers the allocation of some research grants to higher education sector researchers and institutions.

The Commonwealth Government offers a number of programmes which provide financial assistance to students. The Youth Allowance is available for eligible full-time students aged 16 to 24, depending on the circumstances of study. Austudy is available to eligible full-time students aged over 25. Abstudy provides financial assistance for eligible Aboriginal and Torres Strait Islanders who undertake full-time or part-time study. AIC—the Assistance for Isolated Children scheme—provides special support to families whose children are isolated from schooling or who have physical disabilities.

Most students contribute to the cost of their higher education through the Higher Education Contribution Scheme (HECS). They can choose to make an upfront contribution (with a 25% discount) or to defer all or part of their payment until their income reaches a certain level when they must begin repaying their contribution through the taxation system. Overseas students generally pay full tuition fees. Universities are also able to offer full-fee places in postgraduate courses and to a limited number of domestic undergraduate students. In 2000 Australia hosted approximately 150,000 international students, mostly from Asia, who contributed around $A3·7bn. to the local economy in fees and expenditure on goods and services.

Total operating expenses of Australian Government on education in 2002–03 were $A41,004m. Private expenditure on education amounted to $A12,443m. The figures include government grants to the private sector which are also included in the operating expenses of Australian governments.

International education is becoming increasingly important, with 385,000 overseas students attending Australian educational institutions in 2002, compared to just 56,000 in 1988. It is now Australia's third largest service export sector. Nearly 18% of university students are foreign, the highest proportion of any country.

The adult literacy rate in 2001 was 99%.

Health. In 2002–03 there were 729 public hospitals (including 19 psychiatric hospitals) and 549 private hospitals (including acute and psychiatric hospitals); there were an average 2·6 public hospital beds per 1,000 population (down from 3·0 in 1997–98). In 2002–03 there were 164,700 registered nurses, 36,700 general medical practitioners and 10,100 physiotherapists. The Royal Flying Doctor Service serves remote areas. Estimated total government expenditure on health services (public and private sectors) in 2001–02 was $A66·6bn. ($A60·8bn in the previous year), representing 9·3% of GDP.

At 31 Dec. 2003 there were estimated to be 20,580 HIV cases, 9,380 AIDS diagnoses and 6,385 deaths following AIDS.

In 1999–2000, 21% of the adult population (aged 25 years and over) were considered obese (having a body mass index over 30), compared to 8·7% in 1990 and 7·1% in 1980.

Welfare. All Commonwealth government social security pensions, benefits and allowances are financed from the Commonwealth government's general revenue. In addition, assistance is provided for welfare services.

Age Pensions—age pensions are payable to men 65 years of age or more who have lived in Australia for a specified period and, unless permanently blind, also satisfy an income and assets test. The minimum age for women's eligibility was raised by six months to 62 years on 1 July 2001 and is being lifted in six-month increments every two years until 1 July 2013 when it will be 65 years. The qualifying age at 1 July 2004 was 62 years 6 months. In the year ending 30 June 2004, 1,876,250 age pensioners received a total of $A19,540·4m.

Disability Support Pension (DSP)—payable to persons aged 16 years or over with a physical, intellectual or psychiatric impairment of at least 20%, assessed as being unable to work for at least 30 hours a week. DSP for those of 21 years or over is paid at the same rate as Age Pensions and is subject to the same means test except for those who are permanently blind. In the year ending 30 June 2004, 696,742 disability support pensioners received a total of $A7,492·5m.

Carer Payment—payable to a person unable to support themselves due to providing constant care and attention at home for a severely disabled person aged 16 or over, or a person who is frail aged, either permanently or for an extended period. Since 1 July 1998 Carer Payment has been extended to carers of children under 16 years of age with profound disabilities. Subject to income and assets tests, the rate of Carer Payment is the same as for other pensions. In the year ending 30 June 2004, 67,260 carers received a total of $A595·8m.

Carer Allowance—supplementary payment to a person providing constant care and attention at home for an adult or child with a disability or severe medical condition. The allowance is not income or assets tested. In the year ending 30 June 2004, 297,607 carers received a total of $A965·4m.

Sickness Allowance—paid to those over school-leaving age but below Age Pension age who are unable to work or continue full-time study temporarily owing to illness or injury. Eligibility rests on the person having a job or study course to which they can return. In the year ending 30 June 2004 a total of $A85·4m. was paid to beneficiaries.

Family Tax Benefit (FTB)—replaced *Family Allowance* and *Family Tax Payment* on 1 July 2000. Family Tax Benefit Part A is paid to assist families with children under 21 years of age or dependent full-time students aged 21–24 years; Family Tax Benefit Part B provides additional assistance to families with only one income earner and children under 16 years of age or dependent full-time students aged 16–18 years. Both benefits are subject to an income and assets test. In the year ending 30 June 2004 FTB Part A and Part B payments were made to a total of 3·0m. families comprising 5·8m. children.

Parenting Payment (Single) and (Partnered)—is paid to assist those who care for children under 16, with income and assets under certain amounts, and have been an Australian resident for at least two years or a refugee or have become a lone parent while an Australian resident. Parenting Payment (Single) is paid to lone parents under pension rates and conditions; Parenting Payment (Partnered) is paid to one of the parents in the couple. [Since 1 July 2000 the basic component of Parenting Payment (Partnered) was incorporated into Family Tax Benefit with 375,233 beneficiaries transferring to Family Tax Benefit Part B.] In the year ending 30 June 2004, 449,312 Parenting Payment (Single) beneficiaries and 177,157 Parenting Payment (Partnered) beneficiaries received a total of $A5,995·1m.

Maternity Payment—was introduced in the 'More Help for Families' package in the 2004–05 budget. Recognizing the costs associated with a new baby, all families with a child born or adopted from 1 July 2004 are eligible for the payment with no income or assets test applying. This replaces the Maternity Allowance and Baby Bonus. The Maternity Immunization Allowance is not subject to an income test for children born on or after 1 Jan. 2003. In the year ended 30 June 2004 a total of $A223·3m. was paid (including Maternity Immunization Allowance).

Newstart Allowance (NSA)—payable to those who are unemployed and are over 21 years of age but less than Age Pension age. Eligibility is subject to income and assets tests and recipients must satisfy the 'activity test' whereby they are actively seeking and willing to undertake suitable paid work, including casual and part-time work. To be eligible for benefit a person must have resided in Australia for at least 12 months preceding his or her claim or intend to remain in Australia permanently; unemployment must not be as a result of industrial action by that person or by members of a union to which that person is a member. In the year ended 30 June 2004 a total of $A4,754·7m. was paid to NSA beneficiaries.

Youth Allowance—replaced five former schemes for young people, including the Youth Training Allowance. In the year ending 30 June 2004 a total of $A2,257·4m. was paid to YA beneficiaries.

Mature Age Allowance (MAA)—paid to older long-term unemployed, over 60 years of age but less than Age Pension age. MAA is non-activity tested. In the year ended June 2004 a total of $A372·5m. was paid.

Service Pensions—are paid by the Department of Veterans' Affairs. Male veterans who have reached the age of 60 years or are permanently unemployable, and who served in a theatre of war, are eligible subject to an income and assets test. The minimum age for female veterans' eligibility is being lifted from 55 to 60 years in six-month increments every two years over the period 1995–2013. The qualifying age at 1 July 2004 was 57 years. Wives of service pensioners are also eligible, provided that they do not receive a pension from the Department of Social Security. Disability pension is a compensatory payment in respect of incapacity attributable to war service. It is paid at a rate commensurate with the degree of incapacity and is free of any income test. In the year ended 30 June 2004, $A2,830·5m. of service pensions and $A2,743·6m. of disability and war widows' dependants' pensions were paid out; at 30 June 2004 there were 307,514 eligible veterans.

In addition to cash benefits, welfare services are provided, either directly or through State and local government authorities and voluntary agencies, for people with special needs.

Medicare—covers: automatic entitlement under a single public health fund to medical and optometrical benefits of 85% of the Medical Benefits Schedule fee, with a maximum patient payment for any service where the Schedule fee is charged; access without direct charge to public hospital accommodation and to inpatient and outpatient treatment by doctors appointed by the hospital; the restoration of funds for community health to approximately the same real level as 1975; a reduction in charges for private treatment in shared wards of public hospitals, and increases in the daily bed subsidy payable to private hospitals.

The Medicare programme is financed in part by a 1·5% levy on taxable incomes, with low income cut-off points, which were $A13,807 p.a. for a single person in 2001–02 and $A24,534 p.a. for a family with an extra allowance of $A2,253 for each child. A levy surcharge of 1% was introduced from 1 July 1997 for single individuals with taxable incomes in excess of $A50,000 p.a. and couples and families with combined taxable incomes in excess of $A100,000 who do not have private hospital cover through private health insurance.

Medicare benefits are available to all persons ordinarily resident in Australia. Visitors from the UK, New Zealand, Italy, Sweden, the Netherlands and Malta have immediate access to necessary medical treatment, as do all visitors staying more than six months.

CULTURE

World Heritage Sites. There are 16 sites under Australian jurisdiction that appear on the UNESCO World Heritage List. They are (with year entered on list): Great Barrier Reef (1981), Kakadu National Park (1981), Willandra Lakes Region (1981), Tasmanian Wilderness (1982), Lord Howe Island Group (1982), Uluru-Kata Tjuta National Park (1987), Central Eastern Rainforest Reserves (1987), Wet Tropics of Queensland (1988), Shark Bay (1991), Fraser Island (1992), Australian Fossil Mammal Sites (Riversleigh/Naracoorte) (1994), Heard and McDonald Islands (1997), Macquarie Island (1997), the Greater Blue Mountains Area (2000), Purnululu National Park (2003) and Royal Exhibition Building and Carlton Gardens in Melbourne (2004).

Broadcasting. Broadcasting is regulated by the Australian Broadcasting Authority (ABA), established under the Broadcasting Services Act 1992. Foreign ownership of commercial radio and TV companies is restricted to 20%. The national broadcasting service is provided by the Australian Broadcasting Corporation (ABC) (established 1932), an independent statutory corporation receiving 82% of its funding from the Federal Government and the remainder from independent sources, and the Special Broadcasting Service (established 1978). The latter provides radio and TV services in more than 100 languages. The transmission system is PAL. There are also commercial radio and TV services operated by companies under licence, subscription TV services, community radio services operated on a non-profit basis and a parliamentary radio service to state capitals, Canberra and Newcastle. The international service Radio Australia broadcasts via short-wave to Papua New Guinea and the Pacific and also via satellite to the Asia-Pacific regions in English and other languages. Digital television broadcasting commenced in the five mainland metropolitan areas on 1 Jan. 2001. As at 30 June 2001 the ABA had licensed 48 commercial TV services, 255 commercial radio services and 286 community radio services. The ABA had allocated licences for six new commercial radio and ten community radio services in 2000–01. In 2000 there were 36·7m. radio receivers.

In 2000 there were estimated to be 7·0m. TV households and 14·13m. TV sets (99% of households had at least one set). As at Sept. 2000 it was estimated there were 1·32m. pay-TV subscribers, representing 18·86% of households.

Cinema. At 30 June 2000 there were 326 cinema sites with a total of 1,514 screens, 374,000 seats and paid admissions of $A79·4m.

Press. There were 49 daily metropolitan newspapers in 2000 (two national, ten metropolitan and 37 regional). The papers with the largest circulations are the *Sunday Telegraph* (New South Wales), with an average of 724,000 per issue in 1999; the *Sunday Mail* (Queensland), with an average of 594,000 per issue; and the *Sun-Herald* (New South Wales), with an average of 591,000 per issue. At least 30 magazines have a circulation of over 85,000 copies per issue.

Tourism. In 2001–02 the total number of overseas visitors for the year stood at 4·8m. (a 2·5% increase on 1999–2000). The top source countries for visitors in

2001–02 were New Zealand (787,700); Japan (659,200); UK (627,100); USA (424,400); Singapore (295,800); and Korea (181,100). Tourism is Australia's largest single earner of foreign exchange.

Festivals. In 1999–2000 there were 152 performing arts festivals of more than two days' duration with a total income of $A103m. Attendance was estimated to be 9·9m. people.

Libraries. In the year ended 30 April 1999, almost 5·7m. people visited a national, State or local library at least once. Total government funding for libraries in 2000–01 was $A838·8m.

Theatre and Opera. Opera Australia is the largest performing arts organization in the country with almost 250 performances staged annually. In the year ended April 1999, 25·4% of the population aged 15 years and over (almost 3·8m. people) had attended at least one popular music concert; 16·5% (almost 2·5m.), at least one theatre performance; 16·3% (over 2·4m.), at least one opera or musical.

Museums and Galleries. At 30 June 2000 there were 2,049 museums, including 250 art museums and 400 historic properties, employing 37,402 people and receiving 27·5m. visitors annually. Most admissions (60%) were free of charge. Government funding represents 68% of the museums' total income of $A716m.

DIPLOMATIC REPRESENTATIVES

Of Australia in the United Kingdom (Australia House, Strand, London, WC2B 4LA)
High Commissioner: Richard Alston.

Of the United Kingdom in Australia (Commonwealth Ave., Yarralumla, Canberra)
High Commissioner: Sir Alastair Goodlad, KCMG.

Of Australia in the USA (1601 Massachusetts Ave., NW, Washington, D.C., 20036)
Ambassador: Michael J. Thawley.

Of the USA in Australia (Moonah Pl., Canberra, A.C.T. 2600)
Ambassador: John Thomas Schieffer.

Of Australia to the United Nations
Ambassador: John Dauth, LVO.

Of Australia to the European Union
Ambassador: Peter Charles Grey.

FURTHER READING

Australian Bureau of Statistics (ABS). *Year Book Australia.—Pocket Year Book Australia.—Monthly Summary of Statistics.* ABS also publish numerous specialized statistical digests.
Australian Encyclopædia. 12 vols. Sydney, 1983
Blainey, G., *A Short History of Australia.* Melbourne, 1996
The Cambridge Encyclopedia of Australia. CUP, 1994
Clark, M., *Manning Clark's History of Australia*; abridged by M. Cathcart. London, 1994
Concise Oxford Dictionary of Australian History. 2nd ed. OUP, 1995
Davison, Graeme, *et al.*, (eds.) *The Oxford Companion to Australian History.* 2nd ed. OUP, 2002
Docherty, J. D., *Historical Dictionary of Australia.* Metuchen (NJ), 1993
Foster, S. G., Marsden, S. and Russell, R. (compilers) *Federation. A guide to records.* Australian Archives, Canberra, 2000
Gilbert, A. D. and Inglis, K. S. (eds.) *Australians: a Historical Library.* 5 vols. CUP, 1988
Hirst, John, *The Sentimental Nation: The Making of the Australian Commonwealth.* OUP, 2000.—*Australia's Democracy: A Short History.* Allen and Unwin, Sydney, 2002
Irving, H. (ed.) *The Centenary Companion to Australian Federation.* CUP, 2000
Kepars, I., *Australia.* [Bibliography] 2nd ed. ABC-Clio, Oxford and Santa Barbara (CA), 1994
Knightley, Phillip, *Australia: A biography of a Nation.* Cape, London, 2000
Macintyre, S., *A Concise History of Australia.* CUP, 2000
Oxford History of Australia. vol 2: 1770–1860. OUP, 1992. vol 5: 1942–88. OUP, 1990
The Oxford Illustrated Dictionary of Australian History. OUP, 1993
Turnbull, M., *The Reluctant Republic.* London, 1994
Ward, Stuart, *Australia and the British Embrace: The Demise of the Imperial Ideal.* Melbourne Univ. Press, 2002

A more specialized title is listed under RELIGION, *above*

National library: The National Library, Canberra, ACT.
National statistical office: Australian Bureau of Statistics (ABS), Belconnen, ACT. The statistical services of the states are integrated with the Bureau.
ABS Website: http://www.abs.gov.au/

AUSTRALIAN TERRITORIES AND STATES

AUSTRALIAN CAPITAL TERRITORY

KEY HISTORICAL EVENTS

The area, now the Australian Capital Territory (ACT), was explored in 1820 by Charles Throsby who named it Limestone Plains. Settlement commenced in 1824. In 1901 the Commonwealth constitution stipulated that a land tract of at least 260 sq. km in area and not less than 160 km from Sydney be reserved as a capital district. The Canberra site was adopted by the Seat of Government Act 1908. The present site, together with an area for a port at Jervis Bay, was surrendered by New South Wales and accepted by the Commonwealth in 1909. By subsequential proclamation the Territory became vested in the Commonwealth from 1 Jan. 1911. In 1911 an international competition for the city plan was won by W. Burley Griffin of Chicago but construction was delayed by the First World War. It was not until 1927 that Canberra became the seat of government. Located on the Molonglo River surrounding an artificial lake, it was built as a compromise capital to stop squabbling between Melbourne and Sydney following the 1901 Federation of Australian States.

In 1989 self-government was proclaimed and in May the first ACT assembly was elected.

TERRITORY AND POPULATION

The total area is 2,360 sq. km, of which 60% is hilly or mountainous. Timbered mountains are located in the south and west, and plains and hill country in the north. The ACT lies within the upper Murrumbidgee River catchment, in the Murray-Darling Basin. The Murrumbidgee flows throughout the Territory from the south, and its tributary, the Molonglo, from the east. The Molonglo was dammed in 1964 to form Lake Burley Griffin. As at 30 June 2004 the estimated resident population was 324,000. Increase in the annual growth rate during 2003–04 was 0·2%. Population at the 2001 census was 311,947 (1996: 299,243).

SOCIAL STATISTICS

2003: births, 4,128; deaths, 1,414; marriages, 1,558; divorces, 1,652. Infant mortality rate (per 1,000 live births), 5·8. Expectation of life, 2003: males, 79·2 years; females, 83·8 years.

CLIMATE

ACT has a continental climate, characterized by a marked variation in temperature between seasons, with warm to hot summers and cold winters.

CONSTITUTION AND GOVERNMENT

The ACT became self-governing on 11 May 1989. It is represented by two members in the Commonwealth House of Representatives and two senators.

The parliament of the ACT, the *Legislative Assembly*, consists of 17 members elected for a three-year term. Its responsibilities are at State and Local government level. The Legislative Assembly elects a Chief Minister and a four-member cabinet.

RECENT ELECTIONS

At the elections of 16 Oct. 2004 the Labor Party won ten seats (46·9% of the vote) with the Liberal Party taking six seats (34·7%) and the Green Party one seat (9·3%).

CURRENT ADMINISTRATION

The ACT Australian Labor Party Ministry was as follows in Feb. 2005:

Chief Minister, Attorney General, Minister for Arts, Heritage, Indigenous Affairs and the Environment: Jon Stanhope.

Deputy Chief Minister, Treasurer, Minister for Economic Development, Business and Tourism, Sport, Racing and Gaming: Ted Quinlan. *Health and Planning:* Simon

Corbell. *Disability, Housing and Community Services, Urban Services, Police and Emergency Services:* John Hargreaves. *Education, Youth and Family Services, Women and Industrial Relations:* Katy Gallagher.

Speaker: Wayne Berry.

ACT Government website: http://www.act.gov.au

ECONOMY

Budget. The ACT fully participates in the federal-state model underpinning the Australian Federal System. As a city-State, the ACT Government reflects State and local (municipal) government responsibilities, which is unique within the federal system. However, the ACT is treated equitably with the States and Northern Territory regarding the distribution of federal funding.

In 2003–04 the Territory received revenues of $A2,936m. (including extraordinaries) and had expenditure of $A2,827m. (including extraordinaries) achieving a surplus of $A109m. on an accrual basis.

Banking and Finance. In March 2002 bank deposits totalled, $A6,597m.; loans, $A7,962m.; Housing Finance for Owner Occupation (all lenders), total commitments 2002–03, $A1,762m.

ENERGY AND NATURAL RESOURCES

Electricity. See NEW SOUTH WALES.

Water. ACTEW (Australian Capital Territory, Electricity & Water) provides more than 100m. litres of water each day to Canberra residents. There were 45 reservoirs in 2001–02 with a capacity of 912m. litres.

Agriculture. Sheep and/or beef cattle farming is the main agricultural activity. In 2002–03 there were 91 farming establishments with a total area of 50,000 ha.

Forestry. There is about 23,838 ha of plantation forest in the ACT (approximately 10% of the land area). Most of the area is managed for the production of softwood timber. After harvesting, 500–1,000 ha of land are planted with new pine forest each year. No native forests or woodlands have been cleared for plantation since the mid-1970s.

INDUSTRY

Manufacturing industries at June 2001 employed 4,400 persons and generated $A274m., a fall of 5% on the previous year.

Labour. In Feb. 2003 there were an estimated 171,200 employed persons and 7,600 unemployed persons. The annual average unemployment rate in the ACT has fallen since 1996–97 (7·5%) to an average of 4·2% in Feb. 2003.

In the year ending Feb. 2003, 25% of the ACT labour force was employed in public administration and defence; 14% in property and business services; 12% in retail trade. The average weekly wage in Feb. 2003 was $A1,031·80 (males $A1,122·40, females $A916·10).

Trade Unions. As at Aug. 2003 there were 37,600 people belonging to a trade union (24% of total employees).

INTERNATIONAL TRADE

Imports and Exports. In 2002–03 imports were valued at $A216·5m. ($A5·4m. in 2001–02); exports at $A4·3m. ($A10·6m. in 2001–02). Machinery and transport equipment accounted for 99% of total imports and 54% of total exports.

COMMUNICATIONS

Roads. At March 2004 there were 2,645 km of road. At 31 March 2003 there were 213,396 vehicles registered in the ACT. In the year ended Aug. 2003, 13 fatalities were caused by traffic accidents.

Civil Aviation. In 2002–03 Canberra International Airport handled an estimated 1,916,351 passengers.

Telecommunications. In 2002 there were 96,000 households with home computer access (78% of the population) and 72,000 households with home Internet access (59%).

Postal Services. See NEW SOUTH WALES.

SOCIAL INSTITUTIONS

Justice. In 2002–03 there were 47,375 criminal incidents recorded by police. During the same year there were 594 full-time sworn police officers in the ACT and 205 unsworn police staff.

Religion. At the 2001 census, 63% of the population were Christian. Of these, 45% were Roman Catholic and 29% Anglican. Non-Christian religions accounted for 5%, the largest groups being Buddhism, Islam and Hinduism.

Education. In Feb. 2004 there were 219 schools comprising 80 pre-schools, 139 primary and secondary schools (including colleges) and five special schools. Of these 176 were government schools. There was a total of 60,165 full-time students. There were four higher education institutions in 2003: the Signadou Campus of the Australian Catholic University (ACU) had 617 students enrolled; the Australian National University, 13,384 students; the University of Canberra, 11,270; and the Australian Defence Force Academy, 2,078.

Health. The ACT is serviced by two public and nine private hospitals (six of the private hospitals are day surgery only). At June 2003 there were 255 dental practitioners.

Welfare. At June 2003 there were 17,060 age pensioners (5·3% of ACT population); 6,648 persons received disability support pension (2·1%).

CULTURE

In 2000–01 total funding on culture by the ACT Government was $A30·0m., an 8% decrease on the previous year.

Tourism. In the year ended 31 Dec. 2003, 171,500 international visitors came to the ACT. Of these, the largest proportion (19%) was from the UK. At Dec. 2002 there were 266 accommodation establishments employing 4,146 persons.

FURTHER READING

Regional Statistics (Cat. no. 1362.8), Australian Capital Territory.

Australian Capital Territory in Focus (formerly *Statistical Summary*). Australian Bureau of Statistics. Annual

Sources: ACT in Focus 1307.8, Labour Force, Australia 6203.0 and *Labour Force, New South Wales and Australian Capital Territory 6201.1.*

NORTHERN TERRITORY

KEY HISTORICAL EVENTS

The Northern Territory, after forming part of New South Wales, was annexed on 6 July 1863 to South Australia. After the agreement of 7 Dec. 1907 for the transfer of the Northern Territory to the Commonwealth, it passed to the control of the Commonwealth government on 1 Jan. 1911. On 1 Feb. 1927 the Northern Territory was divided into two territories but in 1931 it was again administered as a single territory. The Legislative Council for the Northern Territory, constituted in 1947, was reconstituted in 1959. In that year, citizenship rights were granted to Aboriginal people of 'full descent'. On 1 July 1978 self-government was granted.

TERRITORY AND POPULATION

The Northern Territory's total area is 1,352,212 sq. km and includes adjacent islands. It has 5,100 km of mainland coastline and 2,100 km of coast around the islands. The greater part of the interior consists of a tableland with excellent pasturage. The southern part is generally sandy and has a small rainfall.

The population of the Territory at 30 June 2004 was an estimated 199,900. The 2001 census population was 210,664 (1996: 181,843). The capital, seat of government and principal port is Darwin, on the north coast; estimated population 68,516 at 30 June 2003. Other main centres (estimated totals) include Katherine (8,610); Alice Springs (26,229); Tennant Creek (2,983); Nhulunbuy (3,768); and Jabiru (1,164). There also are a number of large self-contained Aboriginal communities. People identifying themselves as indigenous numbered 57,600 at 30 June 2001.

SOCIAL STATISTICS

2003 totals: births, 3,790; deaths, 875; marriages, 723; divorce, 490. Infant mortality rate per 1,000 live births, 8·4. Life expectancy, 2003: 72·0 years for males, 77·3 for females. The annual rates per 1,000 population in 2003 were: births, 19·1; deaths, 4·4; marriages, 3·6; divorces, 2·5.

CLIMATE

See AUSTRALIA: Climate.

The highest temperature ever recorded in the NT was 118·9°F (48·3°C) at Finke in 1960, while the lowest recorded temperature was 18·5°F (–7·5°C) at Alice Springs in 1976.

CONSTITUTION AND GOVERNMENT

The Northern Territory (Self-Government) Act 1978 established the Northern Territory as a body politic as from 1 July 1978, with Ministers having control over and responsibility for Territory finances and the administration of the functions of government as specified by the Federal government. Regulations have been made conferring executive authority for the bulk of administrative functions.

The Northern Territory has federal representation, electing one member to the House of Representatives and two members to the Senate.

The Legislative Assembly has 25 members, directly elected for a period of four years. The *Administrator* (John Anictomatis) appoints Ministers on the advice of the Leader of the majority party.

RECENT ELECTIONS

In parliamentary elections held in Aug. 2001 the Australian Labor Party won 13 seats against 10 for the Country Liberal Party.

CURRENT ADMINISTRATION

Administrator: Ted Egan, AM.

The NT Territory Labor Party Cabinet was as follows in Feb. 2005:

Chief Minister, Minister for Territorial Development, AustralAsia Railway, Indigenous Affairs, Tourism, Arts and Museums, Young Territorians, Senior Territorians and Women's Policy: Clare Martin.

Deputy Chief Minister, Treasurer, Minister for Employment, Education and Training, and Racing, Gaming and Licensing: Sydney Stirling. *Attorney General, Minister for Justice, Health and Central Australia:* Peter Toyne. *Business and Industry, Asian Relations and Trade, Police, Fire and Emergency Services, Defence Support, Corporate and Information Services and Communications:* Paul Henderson. *Community Development, Housing, Sport and Recreation, Local Government and Regional Development:* John Ah Kit. *Transport and Infrastructure, Lands and Planning, Essential Services, Parks and Wildlife:* Chris Burns. *Mines and Energy, Primary Industry and Fisheries, and Ethnic Affairs:* Konstantine Vatskalis. *Family and Community Services, Environment and Heritage:* Marion Scrymgour.

NT Government website: http://www.nt.gov.au

ECONOMY

Budget. Revenue and expenditure in $A1m.[1]:

	2001–02	*2002–03*	*2003–04*
Revenue	2,289	2,361	2,455
Expenditure	2,307	2,362	2,450

[1]Based on Northern Territory Outcomes reports for 2001–02 and 2002–03. 2003–04 figures based on latest estimates in the Northern Territory's 2003–04 Mid-Year Report.

Using accrual uniform presentation framework standards, total revenue in 2003–04 was expected to be $A2,455m. of which $A1,997m. grants to the Northern Territory from the Commonwealth, and $A458m. Northern Territory Government own-source revenue, which includes $A256m. in state-like taxes.

Expenditure during 2003–04 included $A530m. for education; $A487m. for health; $A243m. for public order and safety; $A205m. for recreation and culture; and $A146m. for general public services.

Banking and Finance. At March 2002 there were 11 banks operating in the Territory with total deposits, $A1,549m.; loans, $A3,452m.

ENERGY AND NATURAL RESOURCES

Environment. There are 93 parks and reserves covering 43,709 sq. km. Twelve of the parks are classified as national parks, including the Kakadu and Uluru-Kata Tjuta National Park which are included on the World Heritage List.

Electricity. The Power and Water Corporation supplies power to 78 indigenous and remote communities as well as the major centres. In the year ended 30 June 2003 total electricity generated was 1,651 GWh; total consumption was 1,549m. kWh, including 1,055m. kWh by business customers.

Oil and Gas. The Timor Sea is a petroleum producing province with five fields and more than 22m. cu. ft of known gas reserves. Gas is currently supplied from the Palm Valley and Mereenie fields in the onshore Amadeus Basin to the Channel Island Power Station in Darwin via one of Australia's longest onshore gas pipelines. The value of energy mineral production in the Territory increased by 77·3% in 2000–01. The total value of oil and gas production in 2000–01 was $A2,622m., an increase of $A1,192m. over 1999–2000. This is largely a result of an increase in crude oil production which rose by 86·3% in 2000–01. The Territory produced 5,316 megalitres of crude oil and 458m. cu. metres of natural gas in 2000–01.

Minerals. Mining is the major contributor to the Territory's economy. Compared to 2001–02 the overall value of production in the mining industry decreased by 13·1% in 2002–03. Value of major mineral commodities production in 2002–03 (in $A1m.): bauxite/alumina, 594; gold, 352; manganese, 199; uranium, 154; lead/zinc concentrate, 106; diamonds, 14.

Agriculture. In the year ended June 2002 there were 406 agricultural establishments with a total area under holding of 65·2m. ha. Gross value of agricultural production in 2001–02 rose by 19% to $A321m. Beef cattle production constitutes the largest farming industry. Total value of livestock slaughter and products in 2001–02 was $A247m., an increase of 23% on the previous year. Fruit production consists mainly of mangoes, bananas and melons. The banana crop decreased significantly from 6,851 tonnes in 2001 to 3,943 tonnes in 2002 while grape production increased by 3% to 698,000 tonnes. There were eight crocodile farms in 2001 producing a total of 16,335·25 kg of meat in the period Jan.–June 2001.

Forestry. In 2001 there were 35m. ha of native forest, accounting for 26% of the Territory's total land area. Of the total native forest cover, 1% is rainforest, 23% open forest and 76% woodland. Total area of plantation forest is around 5,500 ha, consisting mainly of softwoods. Hardwood plantations of fast growing Acacia Mangium have been established on the Tiwi Islands for the production of woodchip for paper pulp. In addition, a number of operations for the production of sandalwood oil and neem products have been established near Batchelor. Teak plantations are planned for designated farmland in the Katherine/Daly development region.

Fisheries. Estimated total fisheries production in 2002–03 came to 6,001 tonnes with a gross value of $A33·0m. In the same year, aquaculture production was worth an estimated $A21·9m.

INDUSTRY

At 30 June 2000 the manufacturing industry turnover was $A1,020·2m.; 3,300 persons were employed and salaries totalled $A144·9m. In Nov. 2001, 15,102 persons were employed in the wholesale and retail trade.

Labour. The labour force totalled 102,000 in Jan. 2004, of whom 97,400 were employed. The unemployment rate was 4·5%, down from 5·7% in Jan. 2003. The average weekly wage in Nov. 2003 was $A720·10 (males $A820·20, females $A619·40).

Trade Unions. In June 1996, 26 trade unions had 19,300 members.

INTERNATIONAL TRADE

Imports and Exports. In 2003–04 the value of the Territory's exports totalled $A1,878m. Major export destinations (figures in $A1m.): China, 404; Singapore, 298; Canada, 164; Republic of Korea, 146; Hong Kong, 143. 2003–04 imports totalled $A899m. Major sources of imports for 2003–04 (figures in $A1m.): Singapore, 239; Kuwait, 107; Japan, 100; Italy, 89; USA, 57.

COMMUNICATIONS

Roads. At 30 June 2001 there were 20,627 km of roads. Registered motor vehicles at 31 Dec. 2002 numbered 126,562, including 93,002 passenger vehicles, 3,216 motorcycles and 1,420 buses. There were 48 road accident fatalities in the year ended Aug. 2003.

Rail. In 1980 Alice Springs was linked to the Trans-continental network by a standard (1,435 mm) gauge railway to Tarcoola in South Australia (830 km). A new 1,410 km standard gauge line operates between Darwin and Alice Springs. This $A1·3bn. AustralAsia Railway project links Darwin and Adelaide. The first train to complete the journey of 1,860 miles arrived in Darwin on 3 Feb. 2004.

Civil Aviation. Darwin and most regional centres in the Territory are serviced by daily flights to all State capitals and major cities. In 2003 there were direct international services connecting Darwin to Brunei, East Timor, Hong Kong, Indonesia and Singapore. In 2003 Darwin airport handled 924,000 domestic and an estimated 77,700 international passengers, and Alice Springs (2003–04), 610,000 domestic passengers.

Shipping. In 2002–03, 704 commercial vessels called at Northern Territory ports. General cargo imported in 2002–03 was 117,794 mass tonnes and general cargo exported was 216,573 mass tonnes.

Telecommunications. In 2001 there were 63,480 households with home computer access and 26,801 households with home Internet access.

Postal Services. At 30 June 1999 there were 548 Australia Post retail facilities in South Australia and Northern Territory.

SOCIAL INSTITUTIONS

Justice. Voluntary euthanasia for the terminally ill was legalized in 1995 but the law was overturned by the Federal Senate on 24 March 1997. The first person to have recourse to legalized euthanasia died on 22 Sept. 1996.

Police personnel (sworn and unsworn) at 30 June 2003, 1,178. In addition there were 49 Aboriginal community police officers. At 30 June 2002 the Territory had three prisons with a daily average of 667 prisoners held.

Education. Education is compulsory from the age of six to 15 years. There were (Aug. 2003) 32,556 full-time students enrolled in 151 government schools and 8,773 enrolled in 33 non-government schools with an additional 3,480 in pre-schools. Teaching staff totalled 2,534 in government schools and 754 in non-government schools. The proportion of Indigenous students in the Territory is high, comprising 37·8% of all primary and secondary students at Aug. 2003. Bilingual programmes operate in some Aboriginal communities where traditional Aboriginal culture prevails.

The Northern Territory University (NTU), founded in 1989 by amalgamating the existing University College of the Northern Territory and the Darwin Institute of Technology, joined with the Alice Springs' Centralian College in 2004 to form the Charles Darwin University. At 31 March 2003, 1,711 students were enrolled in higher education courses of whom 5·2% were identified as Indigenous. The Batchelor Institute of Indigenous Tertiary Education, which provides higher and vocational education and training for Aboriginal and Torres Straits Islanders, had 605 students enrolled in higher education courses in 2001. In 2002 there were 27,096 enrolments in Vocational Education and Training activities.

Health. In 2002 there were five public hospitals with a total of 569 beds and two private hospitals. Community health services are provided from urban and rural Health Centres including mobile units. Remote communities are served by resident nursing staff, aboriginal health workers and in larger communities, resident GPs. Emergency services are supported by the Aerial Medical Services throughout the Territory.

Welfare. The Aged and Disability Program administers NT and Commonwealth funds ($A32m. in 1999–2000) to provide a number of services for senior Territorians and those with a disability. At June 2002 the numbers of pensioners receiving concessions was 16,252. Concessions include allowances on electricity; water, sewerage and property rates; vehicle registrations; spectacles; urban bus travel; and interstate travel. In 2001–02 disability services expenditure was $A14,618m.

CULTURE

Broadcasting. Darwin's radio services include four ABC stations, one SBS station, two commercial stations and a community station. Darwin has two commercial, one ABC and one SBS TV service. Most other Northern Territory centres have one commercial and one national radio service, with one each of ABC, SBS and commercial television.

Tourism. In 2003–04 a total of 1·5m. people visited the Northern Territory, a decrease of 10% over the previous year. In the same year tourist expenditure was $A1·2bn. Tourism is the second largest revenue earner after the mining industry.

FURTHER READING

Profile of Australia's Northern Territory—1997/98. Protocol and Public Affairs Branch, Dept. of the Chief Minister, GPO Box 4396, Darwin

The Northern Territory: Annual Report. Dept. of Territories, Canberra, from 1911. Dept. of the Interior, Canberra, from 1966–67. Dept. of Northern Territory, from 1972

Australian Territories, Dept. of Territories, Canberra, 1960 to 1973. Dept. of Special Minister of State, Canberra, 1973–75. Department of Administrative Services, 1976

Northern Territory in Focus (formerly *Statistical Summary*). Australian Bureau of Statistics, Canberra, from 1960

Donovan, P. F., *A Land Full of Possibilities: A History of South Australia's Northern Territory 1863–1911*. 1981.—*At the Other End of Australia: The Commonwealth and the Northern Territory 1911–1978*. Univ. of Queensland Press, 1984

Heatley, A., *Almost Australians: the Politics of Northern Territory Self-Government*. Australian National Univ. Press, 1990

Powell, A., *Far Country: A Short History of the Northern Territory*. Melbourne Univ. Press, 1996

NEW SOUTH WALES

KEY HISTORICAL EVENTS

The name New South Wales was applied to the entire east coast of Australia when Capt. James Cook claimed the land for the British Crown on 23 Aug. 1770. The separate colonies of Tasmania, South Australia, Victoria and Queensland were proclaimed in the 19th century. In 1911 and 1915 the Australian Capital Territory around Canberra and Jervis Bay was ceded to the Commonwealth. New South Wales was thus gradually reduced to its present area. The first settlement was made at Port Jackson in 1788 as a penal settlement. A partially elective council was established in 1843 and responsible government in 1856.

Gold discoveries from 1851 brought an influx of immigrants, and responsible government was at first unstable, with seven ministries holding office in the five years after 1856. Bitter conflict arose from land laws enacted in 1861. Lack of transport hampered agricultural expansion.

New South Wales federated with the other Australian states to form the Commonwealth of Australia in 1901.

TERRITORY AND POPULATION

New South Wales (NSW) is situated between the 29th and 38th parallels of S. lat. and 141st and 154th meridians of E. long., and comprises 800,640 sq. km, inclusive of Lord Howe Island, 17 sq. km, but exclusive of the Australian Capital Territory (2,360 sq. km) and 70 sq. km at Jervis Bay.

The population at the 2001 census was 6,371,745 (6,038,696 at 1996 census), of which 3,226,300 were female. In 2001 there were eight people per sq. km. At 30 June 2004 the estimated resident population was 6,731,300. Although NSW comprises only 10·4% of the total area of Australia, over 33·9% of the Australian population live there. During the year ended June 2003, 36,431 permanent settlers arrived in New South Wales (35,301 June 2002).

The state is divided into 12 *Statistical Divisions*. The estimated population of these (in 1,000) at 30 June 2002 was: Sydney, 4,170·9; Hunter, 595·0; Illawarra, 405·0; Mid-North Coast, 284·5; Richmond-Tweed, 219·0; South Eastern, 195·9; Northern, 180·4; Central West, 178·6; Murrumbidgee, 153·0; North Western, 119·6; Murray, 114·1; Far West, 24·2. Population of the Statistical Subdivisions Newcastle (within Hunter) and Wollongong (within Illawarra) was 497·5 and 272·1 respectively.

Lord Howe Island, 31° 33' 4" S., 159° 4' 26" E., which is part of New South Wales, is situated about 702 km northeast of Sydney; area, 1,654 ha, of which only about 120 ha are arable; resident population, estimate (1996 census), 369. The Island, which was discovered in 1788, is of volcanic origin. Mount Gower, the highest point, reaches a height of 866 metres.

The Lord Howe Island Board manages the affairs of the Island and supervises the Kentia palm-seed industry.

SOCIAL STATISTICS

Statistics for calendar years:

	Live births	*Deaths*	*Marriages*	*Divorces*
2000	86,752	45,409	39,323	14,756
2001	84,578	44,552	36,109	16,057
2002	86,583	46,384	36,321	16,957
2003	86,344	46,111	36,872	16,285

The annual rates per 1,000 of mean estimated resident population in 2003 were: births, 12·9; deaths, 6·9; marriages, 5·5; divorces, 2·4; infant mortality, 4·6 per 1,000 live births. Expectation of life in 2003: males, 77·7 years, females, 82·9.

CLIMATE

See AUSTRALIA: Climate.

CONSTITUTION AND GOVERNMENT

Within the State there are three levels of government: the Commonwealth government, with authority derived from a written constitution; the State government with residual powers; the local government authorities with powers based upon a State Act of Parliament, operating within incorporated areas extending over almost 90% of the State.

The Constitution of New South Wales is drawn from several diverse sources; certain Imperial statutes such as the Commonwealth of Australia Constitution Act (1900); the Australian States Constitution Act (1907); an element of inherited English law; amendments to the Commonwealth of Australia Constitution Act; the (State) Constitution Act; the Australia Acts of 1986; the Constitution (Amendment) Act 1987 and certain other State Statutes; numerous legal decisions; and a large amount of English and local convention.

The Parliament of New South Wales may legislate for the peace, welfare and good government of the State in all matters not specifically reserved to the Commonwealth government. The State Legislature consists of the Sovereign, represented by the Governor, and two Houses of Parliament, the Legislative Council (upper house) and the Legislative Assembly (lower house). Australian citizens aged 18 and over, and other British subjects who were enrolled prior to 26 Jan. 1984, men and women aged 18 years and over, are entitled to the franchise. Enrolment and voting is compulsory. The optional preferential method of voting is used for both houses. The Legislative Council has 42 members elected for a term of office equivalent to two terms of the Legislative Assembly, with 21 members retiring at the same time as the Legislative Assembly elections. The whole State constitutes a single electoral district. The Legislative Assembly has 93 members elected in single-seat electoral districts for a maximum period of four years.

RECENT ELECTIONS

In elections held on 22 March 2003 the Australian Labor Party won 56 of 93 seats, the Liberal Party of Australia 18, the National Party 12 and ind. 7.

CURRENT ADMINISTRATION

In Feb. 2005 the Legislative Council consisted of the following parties: Australian Labor Party, 18; Liberal Party of Australia, 9; National Party, 4; Greens, 3; Christian Democratic Party (Fred Nile Group), 2; ind., 2; Australian Democrats, 1; Outdoor Recreation Party, 1; Shooters Party, 1; Unity, 1.

The Legislative Assembly, which was elected in 2003, consisted of the following parties in Feb. 2005: Australian Labor Party, 55 seats; Liberal Party of Australia, 20; National Party, 12; ind., 6.

Governor: Prof. Marie Bashir, AC.

The New South Wales ALP Ministry was as follows in Feb. 2005:

Premier, Minister for the Arts and for Citizenship: Robert Carr (b. 1947).

Deputy Premier, Treasurer, Minister for State Development and for Aboriginal Affairs: Dr Andrew Refshauge. *Special Minister of State, Minister for Commerce, Industrial Relations, Ageing and Disability Services:* John Della Bosca. *Infrastructure and Planning, and Natural Resources:* Craig Knowles. *Attorney General and Minister for the Environment:* Bob Debus. *Police:* Carl Scully. *Health:* Morris Iemma. *Roads, Economic Reform, Ports and Minister for the Hunter:* Michael Costa. *Transport:* John Watkins. *Education and Training:* Carmel Tebbutt. *Energy and Utilities, and Science and Medical Research:* Frank Sartor. *Community Services and Youth:* Reba Meagher. *Tourism, Sport and Recreation, and Women:* Sandra Nori. *Rural Affairs, Local Government, Emergency Services and Lands:* Tony Kelly. *Regional Development, Illawarra and Small Business:* David Campbell. *Primary Industries:* Ian Macdonald. *Juvenile Justice and Western Sydney:* Diane Beamer. *Justice and Fair Trading:* John Hatzistergos. *Gaming and Racing, and the Central Coast:* Grant McBride. *Mineral Resources:* Kerry Hickey. *Housing:* Joseph Tripodi.

Speaker of the Legislative Assembly: John Murray.

NSW Government website: http://www.nsw.gov.au

ECONOMY

Budget. Government sector revenue and expenses ($A1m.):

	2003–04	*2004–05*	*2005–06*[1]
Revenue	39,328	40,361	42,211
Expenditure	38,037	39,525	41,100

[1]Forward estimate.

In 2003–04 State government revenue from taxes amounted to $A14,932m.; grants and subsidies totalled $A16,881m.

Performance. In 2002–03 the gross state product of New South Wales represented 34·95% of Australia's total GDP.

Banking and Finance. Lending activity of financial institutions in New South Wales in 2002–03 comprised (in $A1m.): commercial, 134,274; personal, 23,102; lease financing, 2,682. In March 2002 total deposits held by banks was $A238,488m.; loans, $A245,119m.

ENERGY AND NATURAL RESOURCES

Electricity. In the year ended 30 June 2002 total consumption (including ACT total consumption) stood at 60,383m. kWh, of which 41,215m. kWh was by business customers. In 2001–02, 63,911m. kWh were produced, a decrease of 1·4% on the previous year. Coal is the main fuel source for electricity generation in the state, producing 83% of the total in the year ended 30 June 2002. Total installed capacity at 30 June 2002 was 12,147 MW.

Oil and Gas. No natural gas is produced in NSW. Almost all gas is imported from the Moomba field in South Australia plus, since 2001, a small amount from Bass Strait.

Water. Ground water represents the largest source with at least 130 communities relying on it for drinking water.

Minerals. New South Wales contains extensive mineral deposits. For the year ended 30 June 2000, turnover from 123 mining establishments in the coal and metal ore mining industries, employing 10,461 people, was $A5,660m. The value of metallic minerals produced in 2001–02 was $A1·18bn.; construction materials, $A389·5m.; industrial minerals, $A124·5m. Output of principal products, 2002–03 (in tonnes): coal, 143·1m.; zinc, 238,000; copper, 144,000; lead, 107,000; tin, 919; silver, 88; gold, 27.

Agriculture. NSW accounts for around 26% of the value of Australia's total agricultural production with a gross value of $A10·2bn. in 2001–02. In 2001–02 GDP at factor income for agriculture, forestry, hunting and fishing was $A5,808m. In that year farm income (including Australian Capital Territory) was $A2,682m., 21·3% of the Australian total agricultural income. In the year ended 30 June 2002 there were 41,651 farming establishments with a total area under holding of 63·4m. ha of which 6·64m. ha were under crops.

Principal crops in 2001–02 with production in 1,000 tonnes: wheat for grain, 8,257; barley, 1,389; sorghum, 785; canola, 716. Estimated value of crops, 2001–02, came to $A5·7bn. with wheat totalling $A2·0bn. and cotton $A0·9bn. (Data relates to farms whose estimated value of agricultural operations was $A5,000 or more at the census.)

The total area under vines in 2002 was 37,381 ha (including 3,376 ha not yet bearing fruit); winegrape production totalled 415,026 tonnes.

In the year ended June 2002 there were 2,600 ha of banana plantations, with production of 31,600 tonnes; 195,600 tonnes of oranges were produced (43% of the Australian total).

2001–02 gross value of livestock products was $A1·6bn., including wool produced, $A1·0bn.; and milk, $A434m. In 2002–03 production (in tonnes) of beef and veal, 488,000; mutton and lamb, 191,400; pig meat, 140,200.

Forestry. The area of forests managed by State Forests of NSW in 2002–03 totalled 2·9m. ha of native forest; 212,000 ha of softwood and 57,000 ha of hardwood plantation with a total yield (1999–2000) of 2·78m. cu. metres of sawlogs and veneer logs.

Fisheries. Estimated total fisheries production in 2002–03 came to 14,795 tonnes with a gross value of $A88·6m. In the same year aquaculture production was an estimated 6,186 tonnes with a gross value of $A50·6m.

INDUSTRY

A wide range of manufacturing is undertaken in the Sydney area, and there are large iron and steel works near the coalfields at Newcastle and Port Kembla. Around one-third of Australian manufacturing takes place in NSW.

Manufacturing establishments' operations, 2000–01:

Industry	*No. of persons employed*	*Wages and salaries ($A1m.)*	*Turnover ($A1m.)*	*Industry gross product ($A1m.)*
Food, beverages and tobacco	52,989	2,269·1	17,177·8	4,681·3
Textiles, clothing, footwear and leather	15,201	476·1	2,525·6	681·1
Wood and paper products	19,813	743·4	4,762·0	1,510·8
Printing, publishing and recorded media	35,299	1,633·7	6,863·0	2,688·2
Petroleum, coal, chemical and associated products	34,121	1,573·8	14,878·5	3,104·6
Non-metallic mineral products	10,991	534·5	3,021·3	1,175·5
Metal products	52,033	2,189·5	14,104·8	4,339·8
Machinery and equipment	58,744	2,559·6	13,163·1	4,115·4
Other manufacturing	16,409	525·9	2,162·9	790·7
Total manufacturing	295,600	12,505·7	78,659·1	23,067·4

Labour. In May 2003 the labour force was estimated to number 3,354,200 persons, of whom 3,152,100 were employed: 611,300 as professionals; 564,700 as intermediate clerical, sales and service workers; 390,500 as tradespersons and related workers; 275,900 as labourers and related workers; 262,900 as intermediate production and transport workers; 237,500 as managers and administrators; and 126,000 as advanced clerical and service workers. There were 202,100 unemployed (a rate of 6·0%) in May 2003. The average weekly wage in Feb. 2003 was $A950·90 (males $A1,016·50, females $A842·10).

Industrial tribunals are authorized to fix minimum rates of wages and other conditions of employment. Their awards may be enforced by law, as may be industrial agreements between employers and organizations of employees, when registered.

During 2002, 48,000 workers were directly involved in 234 industrial disputes. A total of 73,400 working days were lost.

Trade Unions. Registration of trade unions is effected under the New South Wales Trade Union Act 1881, which follows substantially the Trade Union Acts of 1871 and 1876 of England. Registration confers a quasi-corporate existence with power to hold property, to sue and be sued, etc., and the various classes of employees covered by the union are required to be prescribed by the constitution of the union. For the purpose of bringing an industry under the review of the State industrial tribunals, or participating in proceedings relating to disputes before Commonwealth tribunals, employees and employers must be registered as industrial unions, under State or Commonwealth industrial legislation respectively. Trade union membership was held by 26% of employees in Aug. 2001.

INTERNATIONAL TRADE

Imports and Exports. External commerce, exclusive of interstate trade, is included in the statement of the commerce of Australia. Overseas commerce of New South Wales in $A1m. for years ending 30 June:

	Imports	*Exports*		*Imports*	*Exports*
1998–99	42,142	17,950	2001–02	51,901	22,920
1999–2000	47,927	18,966	2002–03	55,248	20,235
2000–01	52,503	22,750	2003–04	53,774	19,025

The major commodities exported in 2003–04 (in $A1m.) were coal, 2,804; aluminium, 1,401; copper ores, 720; bovine meat, 719; medicaments, including veterinary, 691. Principal imports were computers, 4,084; passenger motor vehicles, 3,962; medicaments, including veterinary, 3,841; telecommunications equipment, 3,132.

Principal destinations of exports in 2003–04 (in $A1m.) were Japan, 4,427; USA, 1,954; New Zealand, 1,928; Republic of Korea, 1,207; China, 1,168. Major sources of supply were USA, 8,241; China, 7,424; Japan, 5,956; Germany, 2,987; UK, 2,851.

COMMUNICATIONS

Roads. At June 2003 there were 182,100 km of public roads of all sorts. The Roads and Traffic Authority of New South Wales is responsible for the administration and upkeep of major roads. In 2003 there were 20,586 km of roads under its control, comprising 3,105 km of national highways, 14,519 km of state roads and 2,962 km of regional and local roads.

The number of registered motor vehicles (excluding tractors and trailers) at 31 March 2003 was 3,944,900, including 3,163,300 passenger vehicles, 531,800 light commercial vehicles, 130,900 trucks, 18,800 buses and 100,000 motorcycles. There were 535 fatalities in road accidents in the year ended Aug. 2003.

Rail. The Rail Infrastructure Corporation (formerly known as the Rail Access Corporation) owns, operates and maintains the rail tracks and related infrastructure. It leases trackage rights to the State Rail Authority (consisting of CityRail and Countrylink), which operates passenger trains, and to the rail freight operators (state-owned FreightCorp was privatized in 2001). In 2002–03, 273·5m. passengers were carried on CityRail and 2·1m. on Countrylink. In the year ended 31 March 2001, 112m. tonnes of freight were transported. Also open for traffic are 325 km of Victorian government railways which extend over the border, 68 km of private railways (mainly in mining districts) and 53 km of Commonwealth government-owned track.

A tramway opened in Sydney in 1996. There is also a small overhead railway in the city centre.

Civil Aviation. Sydney Airport (Kingsford Smith) is the major airport in New South Wales and Australia's principal international air terminal. In 2002 it was sold to Macquarie Airports. In 2002–03 it handled a total of 23,442,248 passengers (14,158,215 on domestic flights). It is also the leading airport for freight, handling 377,460 tonnes in 2002–03. At 13 Sept. 2003 registered aircraft totalled 3,593.

Shipping. The main ports are at Sydney, Newcastle, Port Kembla and Botany Bay. In 2002–03, 655 commercial vessels called at New South Wales ports. General cargo imported in 2002–03 was 25,992,725 mass tonnes and general cargo exported was 7,919,655 mass tonnes.

Telecommunications. At 30 June 2003 there were 14·3m. mobile telephone subscribers (11·2m. in 2001). In 2002 there were 1·53m. households with home computer access (61% of all households) and 1,196,000 households home Internet access (48%).

Postal Services. At 30 June 2003 a total of 1,473 post offices, post office agencies and community mail agencies provided Australia Post services throughout NSW and the ACT.

SOCIAL INSTITUTIONS

Justice. Legal processes may be conducted in Local Courts presided over by magistrates or in higher courts (District Court or Supreme Court) presided over by judges. There is also an appellate jurisdiction. Persons charged with more serious crimes must be tried before a higher court.

Children's Courts remove children as far as possible from the atmosphere of a public court. There are also a number of tribunals exercising special jurisdiction, *e.g.* the Industrial Commission and the Compensation Court.

As at 30 June 2002 there was a daily average of 7,705 persons held in prison. There was a 23% increase in the number of prisoners between 2001–02. Police personnel (sworn and unsworn) at 30 June 2003, 18,798.

Religion. At the 2001 census of those who stated a religion, 29% were Roman Catholic and 24% Anglican. These two religions combined had over 3·3m. followers.

Education. The State government maintains a system of free primary and secondary education, and attendance at school is compulsory from six to 15 years of age. Non-government schools are subject to government inspection.

In Aug. 2002 there were 2,191 government schools with 753,700 pupils (449,482 primary and 304,218 secondary) and 50,084 teachers, and 904 non-government schools with 351,081 pupils (179,930 primary and 171,151 secondary) and 24,228 teachers. There were 289,886 students in higher education in 2002, with the largest numbers enrolled in management and commerce (27% of total enrolments) and society and culture (24%). Student enrolments in 2002: University of Sydney (founded 1850), 42,305; University of New England at Armidale (incorporated 1954), 18,202; University of New South Wales (founded 1949), 42,333; University of Newcastle (granted autonomy 1965), 23,502; University of Wollongong, 18,764; Macquarie University in Sydney (founded 1964), 27,239; University of Technology, Sydney, 29,290; University of Western Sydney, 35,361; Charles Sturt University, 39,776. Colleges of advanced education were merged with universities in 1990. Post-school technical and further education is provided at State TAFE colleges. Enrolments in 2002 totalled 526,083.

Health. In 2002–03 there were 25,281 medical practitioners, 4,153 dentists and 79,244 registered nurses. In the same year there were 218 public and 180 private hospitals.

Welfare. The number of income support payments in June 2003 included: age, 611,513; disability support, 219,820; single parent, 140,941; child care benefit, 224,820; carer payment, 26,910.

Direct State government social welfare services are limited, for the most part, to the assistance of persons not eligible for Commonwealth government pensions or benefits, and the provision of certain forms of assistance not available from the

Commonwealth government. The State also subsidizes many approved services for needy persons.

CULTURE

Broadcasting. In addition to national broadcasting, at Sept. 2001 there were 22 commercial television services (including stations whose licence covers part of NSW as well as remote satellite services) and a total of 36 AM and 48 FM commercial radio services. The first cable-pay television service commenced in Sept. 1995, and satellite-delivered services in Nov. 1995.

Tourism. In 2003–04, 1·43m. overseas visitors arrived for short-term visits, a 7·4% increase on the previous year. At 31 March 2003 there were 1,301 hotels, motels, guest houses and serviced apartments providing 62,691 rooms.

FURTHER READING

Statistical Information: The NSW Government Statistician's Office was established in 1886, and in 1957 was integrated with the Commonwealth Bureau of Census and Statistics (now called the Australian Bureau of Statistics). Its principal publications are:

New South Wales Year Book (1886/87–1900/01 under the title *Wealth and Progress of New South Wales*). Annual.—*Regional Statistics*.—*New South Wales Pocket Year Book*.—*Monthly Summary of Statistics*.—*New South Wales in Brief*.

State Library: The State Library of NSW, Macquarie St., Sydney.

QUEENSLAND

KEY HISTORICAL EVENTS

Queensland was discovered by Capt. Cook in 1770. From 1778 it was part of New South Wales and was made a separate colony, with the name of Queensland, by letters patent of 8 June 1859, when responsible government was conferred. Although by 1868 gold had been discovered, wool was the colony's principal product. The first railway line was opened in 1865. Queensland federated with the other Australian states to form the Commonwealth of Australia in 1901.

TERRITORY AND POPULATION

Queensland comprises the whole northeastern portion of the Australian continent, including the adjacent islands in the Pacific Ocean and in the Gulf of Carpentaria. Estimated area 1,730,650 sq. km.

At the 2001 census the population was 3,655,139 (1,847,409 females). At the 2001 census there were 112,772 Aboriginals and Torres Strait Islanders. Statistics on birthplaces from the 2001 census are as follows: Australia, 77·7% (81·3% in 1991); UK and Ireland, 5·1% (5·9%); New Zealand, 3·6% (2·9%); Germany, 0·6% (0·6%). The 1996 census recorded a total of 3,368,850. Estimated resident population at 30 June 2004, 3,882,000 (annual growth rate, 2·1%).

Brisbane, the capital, had at 30 June 2003 (estimate) a resident population of 1,732,978 (Statistical Division). The resident populations of the other major centres (Statistical Districts) at the 2001 Census were: Gold Coast-Tweed (including that part in New South Wales), 396,588; Sunshine Coast, 192,357; Townsville, 135,142; Cairns, 126,364; Mackay, 63,145; Rockhampton, 62,845; Bundaberg, 55,998; Gladstone, 39,003.

SOCIAL STATISTICS

Statistics (including Aboriginals) for calendar years:

	Births	*Deaths*	*Marriages*	*Divorces*
2000	47,278	22,425	22,842	10,092
2001	47,678	22,856	20,314	12,085
2002	46,908	23,584	21,264	10,920
2003	48,342	23,500	22,273	10,681

The annual rates per 1,000 population in 2003 were: births, 12·7; deaths, 6·2; marriages, 5·9; divorces, 2·8. The infant mortality rate in 2003 was 4·8 per 1,000 live births. Life expectancy, 2003: 77·6 years for males, 82·8 for females.

CLIMATE

A typical subtropical to tropical climate. High daytime temperatures during Oct. to March give a short spring and long summer. Centigrade temperatures in the hottest inland areas often exceed the high 30s before the official commencement of summer on 1 Dec. Daytime temperatures in winter are quite mild, in the low- to mid-20s. Average rainfall varies from about 150 mm in the desert in the extreme southwestern corner of the State to about 4,000 mm in parts of the sugar lands of the wet northeastern coast, the latter being the wettest part of Australia.

CONSTITUTION AND GOVERNMENT

Queensland, formerly a portion of New South Wales, was formed into a separate colony in 1859, and responsible government was conferred. The power of making laws and imposing taxes is vested in a parliament of one house—the *Legislative Assembly*—which comprises 89 members, returned from four electoral zones for three years, elected from single-member constituencies by compulsory ballot.

Queensland elects 26 members to the Commonwealth House of Representatives.

The Elections Act, 1983, provides franchise for all males and females, 18 years of age and over, qualified by six months' residence in Australia and three months in the electoral district.

RECENT ELECTIONS

Legislative Assembly elections on 7 Feb. 2004 gave the ruling Australian Labor Party (ALP) 63 seats, the National Party (NP) 15, the Liberal Party (LP) 5 and One Nation 1. Five independents were elected. The NP/LP coalition forms the opposition.

CURRENT ADMINISTRATION

Governor of Queensland: Quentin Bryce, AC (took office on 29 July 2003).

In Feb. 2005 the ALP administration was as follows:

Premier and Minister for Trade: Peter Beattie (appointed 29 June 1998).

Deputy Premier, Treasurer and Minister for Sport: Terry Mackenroth. *Education and the Arts:* Anna Bligh. *Employment, Training and Industrial Relations:* Tom Barton. *State Development and Innovation:* Tony McGrady. *Health:* Gordon Nuttall. *Public Works, Housing and Racing:* Rob Schwarten. *Police and Corrective Services:* Judy Spence. *Attorney General, Justice:* Rod Welford. *Transport and Main Roads:* Paul Lucas. *Primary Industries and Fisheries:* Henry Palaszczuk. *Natural Resources and Mines:* Stephen Robertson. *Child Safety:* Mike Reynolds. *Communities, Disability Services and Seniors:* Warren Pitt. *Tourism, Fair Trading and Wine Industry Development:* Margaret Keech. *Energy:* John Mickel. *Environment, Local Government, Planning and Women:* Desley Boyle. *Emergency Services:* Chris Cummins. *Aboriginal and Torres Strait Islander Policy:* Liddy Clarke.

QLD Government website: http://www.qld.gov.au

ECONOMY

Budget. In 2004–05 general government expenses by the state were expected to total $A23,363m.; revenue and grants received were expected to be $A24,009m.

Banking and Finance. In March 2002 deposits at all banks in Queensland totalled $A64,443m. Other lending totalled $A88,382m.

ENERGY AND NATURAL RESOURCES

Electricity. The government-owned sector of the state's electricity industry has been restructured, and since Dec. 1998 it has operated as part of the wholesale national electricity market. Part of the restructuring was the formation of a single corporation, Ergon Energy, by the amalgamation of the six former regional distribution corporations. In the year ended 30 June 2002 total consumption stood at 39,544m. kWh by 1,684,488 customers, including 27,900m. kWh by business customers. Coal is the main fuel source for electricity generation in the state, producing 45,967m. kWh in the year ended 30 June 2002; installed generation capacity stood at 10,700 MW.

Minerals. There are large reserves of coal, bauxite, gold, copper, silver, lead, zinc, nickel, phosphate rock and limestone. The state is the largest producer of black coal in Australia. Most of the coal produced comes from the Bowen Basin coalfields in central Queensland. Copper, lead, silver and zinc are mined in the northwest and the State's largest goldmines are in the north. The total value of metallic minerals in 2002–03 was $A3·54bn. In 2002–03 there were 37 coal mines in operation producing 153·6m. tonnes of saleable coal (an increase of 3·5% on the previous year); and at 30 June 2003, 10,713 persons were employed in mining.

Agriculture. Queensland is Australia's leading beef-producing state and its chief producer of fruit and vegetables. In the year ended 30 June 2002 there were 27,900 agricultural establishments farming 141·3m. ha of which 2·68m. ha were under crops. Livestock numbered (at 30 June 2002) 11,284,000 beef cattle; 6,752,000 sheep and lambs; and 643,000 pigs. Total value of wool production, 2001–02: $A189m. The gross value of agricultural commodity production in 2001–02 was $A8·1bn. (an 11% increase on the previous year) which comprised crops, $A3·9bn.; livestock disposals, $A3·7bn.; and livestock products, $A501m.

Forestry. Of a total of 54m. ha of forests and woodlands in 1999, 6% was in national parks and World Heritage areas while 7% was in State forests and timber reserves outside World Heritage sites. Queensland's plantation forests supply around 40% of Australia's wood and paper products. The forestry industry is an important part of the state's economy, employing around 17,000 people with a gross output of $A1,700m.

Fisheries. Estimated total fisheries production in 2002–03 came to 27,766 tonnes with a gross value of $A222·3m. In the same year aquaculture production was an estimated 4,366 tonnes with a gross value of $A62·9m.

INDUSTRY

In 2000–01 manufacturing industry turnover was $A40,292m. with a total of 156,500 people employed. The largest manufacturing sector was food, beverages and tobacco (2000–01 turnover: $A12,314m.).

Labour. In 2003–04 the labour force numbered 1,967,800, of whom 1,845,000 (825,600 females) were employed. In 2003–04 unemployment stood at 6·2%, the lowest total for two years. The average weekly wage in Feb. 2003 was $A820·10 (males $A856·60, females $A754·50).

Trade Unions. In Aug. 1999, 332,373 employees were members of a trade union (25·0% of total employment).

INTERNATIONAL TRADE

Imports and Exports. Total value of direct overseas imports and exports f.o.b. port of shipment for both imports and exports in 2003–04: imports, $A18,080m.; exports, $A20,093m.

Chief sources of imports in 2003–04 (in $A1m.): USA, 3,052; Japan, 2,861; China, 1,614; Papua New Guinea, 920; Germany, 861. Exports went chiefly to (in $A1m.): Japan, 5,301; Republic of Korea, 2,194; USA, 1,421; China, 1,409; India, 1,041.

Principal overseas imports were (in $A1m.): passenger vehicles, 2,446; crude petroleum, 2,074; aircraft and parts, 1,199; motor vehicles for transporting goods, 815; non-monetary gold, 575; civil engineering equipment, 538. The chief exports overseas in 2003–04 (in $A1m.) were: coal, 5,929; bovine meat, 2,375; aluminium, 891; other ores, 807; copper, 490.

COMMUNICATIONS

Roads. At 30 June 2001 there were 178,295 km of roads open to the public. Of these, 68,076 km were surfaced with sealed pavement. At 31 March 2003 motor vehicles registered totalled 2,552,061, comprising 1,999,117 passenger vehicles and motorcycles, 441,358 light commercial vehicles and 111,586 trucks, buses and prime movers. There were 286 fatalities in road accidents in the year ended Aug. 2003.

Rail. Queensland Rail is a State government-owned corporation. Total length of line, 2001–02 was 9,514 km. In 2002–03, 47·3m. passengers and 156·5m. tonnes of freight were carried.

Civil Aviation. Queensland is well served with a network of air services, with overseas and interstate connections. Subsidiary companies provide planes for taxi and charter work, and the Flying Doctor Service operates throughout western

Queensland. In 1997–98 all Federal airports were leased to private sector operators—Brisbane, Archerfield, Coolangatta, Mount Isa and Townsville Airports (the latter is operated jointly with the Department of Defence). In 2002–03 Brisbane handled 11,841,196 passengers (8,771,730 on domestic flights); Cairns, 2,900,472 passengers (1,899,991 on domestic flights). The number of aircraft registered at 30 June 1999 was 2,423.

Shipping. Queensland has 14 modern trading ports, two community ports and a number of non-trading ports. In 2002–03 general cargo imported through Queensland ports was 1,588,964 mass tonnes and general cargo exported was 4,138,321 mass tonnes. There were 1,963 commercial ship calls during 2002–03.

Telecommunications. In 2000 there were 668,000 households with home computer access (50% of all households) and 408,000 households with home Internet access (31%).

Postal Services. At 1 July 1997 there were 446 post offices and postal agencies.

SOCIAL INSTITUTIONS

Justice. Justice is administered by Higher Courts (Supreme and District), Magistrates' Courts and Children's Courts. The Supreme Court comprises the Chief Justice and 21 judges; the District Courts, 34 district court judges. Stipendiary magistrates preside over the Magistrates' and Children's Courts, except in the smaller centres, where justices of the peace officiate. A parole board may recommend prisoners for release.

Total police personnel (sworn and unsworn) at 30 June 2003 was 11,961. As at 30 June 2002 the average daily number of prisoners stood at 4,721.

Religion. Religious affiliation at the 1996 census: Roman Catholic, 25·2%; Anglican, 23·6%; Uniting Church, 9·5%; Presbyterian, 4·7%; Lutheran, 2·2%; Baptist, 1·9%; other Christian, 6·8%; non-Christian, 1·5%; no religion, 15·3%; not stated, 9·0%.

Education. Education is compulsory between the ages of six and 15 years and is provided free in government schools.

Primary and secondary education comprises 12 years of full-time formal schooling, and is provided by both the government and non-government sectors. In 2002 the State administered 1,291 schools with 284,262 primary students and 155,802 secondary students. In 2002 there were 35,071 teachers in government schools. There were 435 private schools in 2002 with 92,497 primary students and 87,026 secondary students. Educational programmes at private schools were provided by 13,803 teachers in 2002. In 2002 there were 2,061,500 subject enrolments in Vocational Education and Training activities. The seven publicly funded universities had 174,000 full-time students in 2002.

Health. At 30 June 2003 there were 175 public acute hospitals and six public psychiatric hospitals; 44 private free-standing day hospital facilities and 55 other private hospitals (including acute and psychiatric hospitals). In 2001 Queensland had the highest rate of obesity (18·5% of the State's population).

Welfare. Welfare institutions providing shelter and social care for the aged, the handicapped and children are maintained or assisted by the State. A child health service is provided throughout the State. Age, invalid, widows', disability and war service pensions, family allowances, and unemployment and sickness benefits are paid by the Federal government. The number of age and disability pensions (including wives' and carers' pensions) at 30 June 1999 was: age, 284,852; disability support, 105,276; carer, 7,770. There were 5,879 widows' and 80,318 single parent payments current at 30 June 1999, and basic family payment was being paid for 654,363 children under 16 years.

CULTURE

Broadcasting. In addition to the national networks Queensland is served by 13 public radio stations (non-profit-making), 44 commercial radio stations and three commercial TV channels.

Tourism. Overseas visitors to Queensland in the year ending June 2004 totalled 1·96m., the main source being from Asia, with Japanese tourists totalling 454,157

(23% of the total). Visitors from New Zealand accounted for 17%; UK, 14%; and USA, 7%.

FURTHER READING

Statistical Information: The Statistical Office (now Australian Bureau of Statistics, 313 Adelaide St., Brisbane) was set up in 1859. *A Queensland Official Year Book* was issued in 1901, the annual *ABC of Queensland Statistics* from 1905 to 1936 with exception of 1918 and 1922. Present publications include: *Queensland Year Book.* Annual, from 1937 (omitting 1942, 1943, 1944, 1987, 1991).—*Queensland Pocket Year Book.* Annual from 1950.—*Monthly Summary of Statistics, Queensland.* From Jan. 1961. Selected statistics available at *website:* http://www.abs.gov.au

Australian Sugar Year Book. Brisbane, from 1941
Johnston, W. R., *A Bibliography of Queensland History. Brisbane*, 1981.—*The Call of the Land: A History of Queensland to the Present Day.* Brisbane, 1982
Johnston, W. R. and Zerner, M., *Guide to the History of Queensland.* Brisbane, 1985

State library: The State Library of Queensland, Queensland Cultural Centre, PO Box 3488, South Bank, South Brisbane.

Local statistical office: Office of Economic and Statistical Research, PO Box 15037, City East, Qld 4002.

Website: http://www.oesr.qld.gov.au

SOUTH AUSTRALIA

KEY HISTORICAL EVENTS

South Australia was surveyed by Tasman in 1644 and charted by Flinders in 1802. It was made into a British province by letters of patent of Feb. 1836, and a partially elective legislative council was established in 1851. From 6 July 1863 the Northern Territory was placed under the jurisdiction of South Australia until the establishment of the Commonwealth of Australia in 1911.

TERRITORY AND POPULATION

The total area of South Australia is 983,480 sq. km. The settled part is divided into counties and hundreds. There are 49 counties proclaimed, and 536 hundreds, covering 23m. ha, of which 19m. ha are occupied. Outside this area there are extensive pastoral districts, covering 76m. ha, 49m. of which are under pastoral leases.

The estimated resident population at 30 June 2004 was estimated to be 1,534,250 (774,477 females). The 2001 census population was 1,467,261 (23,425 Aboriginal and Torres Strait Islanders). The 1996 census totalled 1,427,936.

At 30 June 2003 the Adelaide Statistical Division had an estimated 1,119,718 persons (73·3% of South Australia's total population) in 25 councils and four municipalities and other districts. Urban centres outside this area (with estimated populations at 30 June 2003) are Mount Gambier (23,571), Whyalla (21,604), Port Pirie (17,490), Port Lincoln (14,273) and Port Augusta (13,795).

SOCIAL STATISTICS

Statistics for calendar years:

	Live Births	*Deaths*	*Marriages*	*Divorces*
2000	17,859	11,843	8,227	–
2001	17,439	11,767	7,434	4,545
2002	17,481	11,578	7,373	4,409
2003	17,443	12,185	7,609	4,151

The rates per 1,000 population in 2003 were: births, 11·4; deaths, 8·0; marriages, 5·0; divorces, 2·7. The infant mortality rate in 2003 was 3·7 per 1,000 live births. Life expectancy for 2003 was 77·7 years for men and 82·7 years for women.

CONSTITUTION AND GOVERNMENT

The present Constitution dates from 24 Oct. 1856. It vests the legislative power in an elected Parliament, consisting of a Legislative Council and a House of Assembly. The former is composed of 22 members. Eleven members are elected at alternate elections for a term of at least six years and are elected on the basis of preferential proportional representation with the State as one multi-member electorate. The House of Assembly consists of 47 members elected by a preferential system of voting for the term of a Parliament (four years). Election of members of both Houses takes place by secret ballot. Voting is compulsory for those on the Electoral Roll. The qualifications of an elector are to be an Australian citizen, or a British subject who was, at some time within the period of three months commencing on 26 Oct. 1983, enrolled under the Repealed Act as an Assembly elector or enrolled on an electoral roll maintained under the Commonwealth or a Commonwealth Territory, must be at least 18 years of age and have lived in the subdivision for which the person is enrolled for at least one month. By the Constitution Act Amendment Act, 1894, the franchise was extended to women, who voted for the first time at the general election of 25 April 1896. Certain persons are ineligible for election to either House.

Electors enrolled (30 Dec. 2002) numbered 1,050,000.

The executive power is vested in a Governor appointed by the Crown and an Executive Council, consisting of the Governor and the Ministers of the Crown. The Governor has the power to dissolve the House of Assembly but not the Legislative Council, unless that Chamber has twice consecutively with an election intervening defeated the same or substantially the same Bill passed in the House of Assembly by an absolute majority.

RECENT ELECTIONS

The House of Assembly, elected on 9 Feb. 2002, consisted of the following members: Australian Labor Party (ALP), 23; Liberal Party (LIB), 20; Independent (ind.), 2; National, 1.

CURRENT ADMINISTRATION

Governor: Marjorie Jackson-Nelson, AC, CVO, MBE.

In Feb. 2005 the Labor Ministry was as follows:

Premier, Minister for Economic Development, Social Inclusion, the Arts and Volunteers: Mike Rann.

Deputy Premier, Treasurer, Minister Assisting the Premier in Economic Development, Police and Federal/State Relations: Kevin Foley. *Industry and Trade and Mineral Resources Development:* Paul Holloway. *Infrastructure, Energy, and Emergency Services:* Patrick Conlon. *Attorney-General, Justice and Multicultural Affairs:* Michael Atkinson. *Aboriginal Affairs and Reconciliation, Correctional Services and Minister Assisting the Minister for Environment and Conservation:* Terry Roberts. *Health and Minister Assisting the Premier in Social Inclusion:* Lea Stevens. *Transport, Urban Development and Planning and Science and Information Economy:* Trish White. *Environment and Conservation, Southern Suburbs and Minister Assisting the Premier in the Arts:* John Hill. *Employment, Training and Further Education, Youth and the Status of Women:* Stephanie Key. *Administrative Services, Industrial Relations, Recreation, Sport and Racing and Gambling:* Michael Wright. *Education and Children's Services and Tourism:* Jane Lomax-Smith. *Families and Communities, Housing, Ageing and Disability:* Jay Weatherill. *Agriculture, Food and Fisheries, State/Local Government Relations and Forests:* Rory McEwen (ind.). *River Murray, Regional Development, Small Business and Consumer Affairs:* Karlene Maywald (National).

Speaker: Peter Lewis (ind.).

President: Ron Roberts (ALP).

SA Government website: http://www.sa.gov.au

ECONOMY

Budget. Estimated government sector revenue and expenses ($A1m.):

	2001–02	*2002–03*	*2003–04*
Revenue	9,367	10,172	10,707
Expenditure	9,487	9,696	10,294

In 2003–04 State government revenue from taxes amounted to $A2,783m.; grants and subsidies totalled $A5,081m.

Performance. South Australia's 2002–03 gross state product represented 6·63% of Australia's total GDP.

Banking and Finance. In March 2002 total deposits held by banks was $A22,717m. and loans totalled $A29,739m.

ENERGY AND NATURAL RESOURCES

Electricity. In the year ended 30 June 2002 total consumption stood at 11,213m. kWh, including 6,813m. kWh by business customers. At June 2002 installed generation capacity stood at 3,479 MW.

Minerals. The principal metallic minerals produced are copper, iron ore, uranium oxide, gold and silver. The total value of minerals produced in 2002–03 was $A1,655·2m. including copper, $A514·6m.; natural gas, $A336·1m.; uranium oxide, $A131·3m.; opals (estimate), $A33·0m. In 2002–03 there were 4,000 persons employed in mining.

Agriculture. In the year ended 30 June 2002 there were 14,824 establishments mainly engaged in agriculture with a total area under holding of 53·5m. ha of which 4·18m. ha were under crops. The gross value of agricultural production in 2002–03 was $A4·1bn. Total value of wool production, $A403·9m. Value of chief crops in 2001–02: wheat, $A1·3bn.; barley, $A588m.; potatoes, $A135m. Production of grapes (2001–02) was 697,700 tonnes with virtually all being used for winemaking (vineyards' total area, 67,000 ha, including 6,500 ha not yet bearing). Fruit culture is extensive with citrus and orchard fruits. The most valuable vegetable crops are potatoes, onions and carrots.

Livestock, 30 June 2003: cattle, 1,401,000; sheep and lambs, 13,059,000; pigs, 381,000. Gross value of livestock slaughtered, 2002–03, $A846·7m.

Forestry. Total area of plantations at 30 June 2003 totalled 81,126 ha.

Fisheries. Estimated total fisheries production in 2002–03 came to 33,024 tonnes with a gross value of $A195·0m. In the same year aquaculture production was an estimated 12,311 tonnes with a gross value of $A278·5m.

INDUSTRY

The turnover for manufacturing industries for 2000–01 was $A23,623m.; wages and salaries totalled $A3,557m.

Industry sub-division	*Persons employed (1,000)*	*Turnover ($A1m.)*
Food, beverages and tobacco	21·1	4,881·2
Textiles, clothing, footwear and leather manufacturing	4·5	716·1
Wood and paper products manufacturing	5·9	1,374·3
Printing, publishing and recorded media	5·0	833·3
Chemical, petroleum, coal and associated products	7·2	1,614·0
Non-metallic mineral products	2·8	710·1
Metal products manufacturing	12·9	2,827·4
Machinery and equipment	33·9	7,814·0
Other manufacturing	4·6	671·2
Total	97·9	21,442·0

Labour. In Nov. 2004 the labour force stood at 767,400. There were 42,400 unemployed, a rate of 5·5%. The average weekly wage in Aug. 2004 was $A662·50 (males $A785·50, females $A526·70).

INTERNATIONAL TRADE

Imports and Exports. Overseas imports and exports in $A1m. (year ending 30 June):

	2001–02	*2002–03*	*2003–04*
Imports	5,347	5,724	5,163
Exports	9,103	8,365	7,604

Principal imports in 2003–04 were (with values in $A1m.): refined petroleum, 481; motor vehicles parts, 409; passenger motor vehicles, 384; internal combustion piston engines, 222; measuring and controlling instruments, 138. Principal exports in 2003–04 were (with values in $A1m.): alcoholic beverages, 1,411; passenger motor vehicles, 1,110; wheat, 693; copper, 398; fish 247; meat, excluding bovine, 217.

In 2003–04 the leading suppliers of imports were (with values in $A1m.): Japan, 891; USA, 652; Singapore, 547; China, 371; Canada, 311. Main export markets were USA, 1,391; UK, 784; Japan, 695; New Zealand, 557; Saudi Arabia, 444.

COMMUNICATIONS

Roads. At 30 June 1999 there were 27,117 km of sealed and 69,335 km of unsealed roads. Motor vehicles registered as at 30 June 1999: passenger vehicles, 838,485; other motor vehicles, 167,922; motorcycles, 26,129. In the year ended Aug. 2003 there were 143 road accident fatalities.

Rail. In Aug. 1997 the passenger operations of Australian National Railways were sold to Great Southern Railway and the freight operations to Australian Southern Railroad. Australian National Railways operates 4,415 km of railway in country areas. TransAdelaide operates 120 km of railway in the metropolitan area of Adelaide. In the year ended 31 March 2001, 19m. tonnes of freight were carried.

There is a tramway in Adelaide that runs from the city centre to the coast. A joint South Australia and Northern Territory project, The AustralAsia Rail Project between Alice Springs and Darwin, carried its first passenger train in Feb. 2004.

Civil Aviation. The main airport is Adelaide International Airport, which handled 4,350,836 passengers (3,841,475 on domestic flights) in 2002–03.

Shipping. There are ten state and five private deep-sea ports. In 2002–03, 1,361 commercial vessels arrived in South Australia. General cargo imported in 2002–03 was 678,338 mass tonnes and general cargo exported was 1,610,919 mass tonnes.

Telecommunications. In 1998 residential telephone penetration was 98·0% (93·6% in 1986). In 2000 there were 295,000 households with home computer access (50% of all households) and 176,000 households with home Internet access (30%).

Postal Services. At 30 June 1999 there were 548 Australia Post retail facilities in South Australia and Northern Territory.

SOCIAL INSTITUTIONS

Justice. There is a Supreme Court, which incorporates admiralty, civil, criminal, land and valuation, and testamentary jurisdiction; district criminal courts, which have jurisdiction in many indictable offences; and magistrates courts, which include the Youth Court. Circuit courts are held at several places. At 30 June 2004 the police force numbered 3,910. The average daily number of prisoners at 30 June 2003 was 1,455.

Religion. Religious affiliation at the 1996 census: Catholic, 296,048; Anglican, 228,151; Uniting Church, 180,604; Lutheran, 70,970; Orthodox, 42,053; Baptist, 26,251; Presbyterian, 23,994; other Christians, 74,868; non-Christians, 25,236; indefinite, 4,885; no religion, 310,908; not stated, 138,554.

Education. Education is compulsory for children between the ages of six and 15 years although most children are enrolled at age five or soon after. Primary and secondary education at government schools is secular and free. In Aug. 2001 there were 812 schools operating, of which 611 were government and 201 non-government schools. In that year there were 114,287 children in government and 43,500 in non-government primary schools, and 61,935 children in government and 31,800 in non-government secondary schools. In 2001 there were 167,900 enrolments in Vocational Education and Training activities. There were 30,627 students enrolled at the University of South Australia in 2002; University of Adelaide, 16,188; and Flinders University, 13,644.

Health. In 2003–04 there were 80 public hospitals and 55 private hospitals. Beds available in public and private hospitals totalled 6,553.

Welfare. The number of age and disability pensions (including wives' and carers' pensions) on 30 June 2002 was: age, 170,648; disability support, 62,977. There were 50,692 Newstart and Mature Age allowances and 35,079 single parent payments current at 30 June 2002.

CULTURE

Broadcasting. There are 131 radio stations (24 AM and 107 FM) and four commercial TV stations, one community service TV station and the national ABC service.

Tourism. In the year ended 30 June 2000 international visitors totalled 350,100 (over 50% from Europe), an increase of 12% on the previous year. At 30 June 2002 there were 236 hotels, motels, guest houses and serviced apartments with 10,955 rooms.

FURTHER READING

Statistical Information: The State office of the Australian Bureau of Statistics is at 55 Currie St., Adelaide (GPO Box 2272). Although the first printed statistical publication was the *Statistics of South Australia, 1854*, with the title altered to *Statistical Register* in 1859, there is a manuscript volume for each year back to 1838. These contain simple records of trade, demography, production, etc. and were prepared only for the information of the Colonial Office; one copy was retained in the State.

The publications of the State office include the *South Australian Year Book* (now discontinued), a monthly *South Australian Economic Indicators*, a quarterly bulletin of building activity, and approximately 40 special bulletins issued each year as particulars of various sections of statistics become available.

Gibbs, R. M., *A History of South Australia: from Colonial Days to the Present.* 3rd ed. revised, Adelaide, 1995

Prest, Wilfred, Round, Kerrie and Fort, Carol, (eds.) *The Wakefield Companion to South Australian History.* Wakefield Press, Kent Town, 2002

Whitelock, D., *Adelaide from Colony to Jubilee: a Sense of Difference.* Adelaide, 1985

State Library: The State Library of S.A., North Terrace, Adelaide.

TASMANIA

KEY HISTORICAL EVENTS

Abel Janszoon Tasman discovered Van Diemen's Land (Tasmania) on 24 Nov. 1642. The island became a British settlement in 1803 as a dependency of New South Wales. In 1825 its connection with New South Wales was terminated and in 1851 a partially elected Legislative Council was established. In 1856 a fully responsible government was inaugurated. On 1 Jan. 1901 Tasmania was federated with the other Australian states into the Commonwealth of Australia.

TERRITORY AND POPULATION

Tasmania is a group of islands separated from the mainland by Bass Strait with an area (including islands) of 68,400 sq. km, of which 63,447 sq. km form the area of the main island. The population at the 7 Aug. 2001 census was 456,652 (459,659 at 1996 census); 21,910 were born in the UK or Ireland, 11,120 in other European countries and 386,036 in Australia. The estimated resident population at 30 June 2004 was 482,100 (annual growth rate, 1·0%).

The largest cities and towns (with populations at the 2001 census) are: Hobart (191,169), Launceston (95,604), Devonport (23,030) and Burnie (18,145).

SOCIAL STATISTICS

Statistics for calendar years:

	Births	*Deaths*	*Marriages*	*Divorces*
2000	5,692	3,711	2,589	1,329
2001	6,430	3,876	2,182	1,439
2002	6,003	3,979	2,605	1,386
2003	5,752	3,965	2,599	1,336

The annual rates per 1,000 of the mean resident population in 2003 were: births, 12·1; deaths, 8·3; marriages, 5·4; divorces, 2·8. Infant mortality rate, 2003, 7·0 per 1,000 live births. Expectation of life, 2003: males, 76·6 years; females, 81·4 years.

CLIMATE

Mostly a temperate maritime climate. The prevailing westerly airstream leads to a west coast and highlands that are cool, wet and cloudy, and an east coast and lowlands that are milder, drier and sunnier.

CONSTITUTION AND GOVERNMENT

Parliament consists of the Governor, the Legislative Council and the House of Assembly. The Council has 15 members, elected by adults with six months' residence. Members sit for six years, with either two or three retiring annually. There is no power to dissolve the Council. The House of Assembly has 25 members; the maximum term for the House of Assembly is four years. Women received the right to vote in 1903. Proportional representation was adopted in 1907, the method now being the single transferable vote in five member constituencies.

A Minister must have a seat in one of the two Houses.

RECENT ELECTIONS

At the elections of July 2002 the Australian Labor Party won 14 seats in the House of Assembly, the Liberal Party 7 and the Tasmanian Greens 4.

CURRENT ADMINISTRATION

Governor: William Cox; b. 1936 (took office on 15 Dec. 2004, having been acting governor from 9 Aug. 2004–3 Dec. 2004).

The Legislative Council is predominantly independent without formal party allegiance; four members are Labor-endorsed.

In Feb. 2005 the Labor government comprised:

Premier and Treasurer: Paul Lennon (took office on 21 March 2004).

Deputy Premier and Minister for Health and Human Services, and Police and Public Safety: David Llewellyn. *Minister for Economic Development and the Arts:* Lara Giddings. *Justice, Industrial Relations, Environment and Planning, and Attorney General:* Judy Jackson. *Education and Women Tasmania:* Paula Wriedt. *Finance, Employment, Racing, Sport and Recreation:* Jim Cox. *Infrastructure, Energy and Resources:* Bryan Green. *Primary Industries and Water:* Steven Kons. *Tourism, Parks and Heritage:* Ken Bacon. *Leader of the Government in the Legislative Council:* Michael Aird.

Speaker of the House of Assembly: Michael Polley.

TAS Government website: http://www.tas.gov.au

ECONOMY

Budget. Consolidated Revenue Fund receipts and expenditure, in $A1m., for financial years ending 30 June:

	2002–03	*2003–04*
Revenue	2,551	3,212
Expenditure	2,542	2,916

In 2003–04 State government revenue from taxes amounted to $A631m.; grants and subsidies totalled $A1,997m.

Banking and Finance. In March 2002 total deposits held by banks was $A3,958m. and loans totalled $A5,540m.

ENERGY AND NATURAL RESOURCES

Electricity. Installed capacity is 2,502 MW. In the year ended 30 June 2003 total consumption stood at 9,780m. kWh, including 1,820m. kWh by residential customers.

Minerals. Output of principal metallic minerals in 2002–03 was (in 1,000 tonnes): iron ore pellets, 2,142·3; zinc, 141·9; copper, 108·1; lead, 42·2; tin, 8·5.

Agriculture. There were 4,027 agricultural establishments at 30 June 2002 occupying a total area of 1·8m. ha. Principal crops in 2000–01 (in 1,000 tonnes): potatoes, 331,018; apples, 56,105; barley, 25,992; wheat, 25,554; oats, 12,616. Gross value of recorded production from agriculture in 2000–01 was (in $A1m.): crops, 350·1; livestock products, 244·4; livestock slaughterings and other disposals, 160·4; total gross value, 755·0. Livestock, 2001–02: cattle, 661,000; sheep and lambs, 3,380,200; pigs, 18,000. Wool produced during 2001–02 was 14,268 tonnes.

Forestry. Indigenous forests, which cover a considerable part of the State, support sawmilling and woodchipping industries. Production of sawn timber in 2002–03 was 398,500 cu. metres. Newsprint and paper are produced from native hardwoods.

Fisheries. Estimated total fisheries production in 2002–03 came to 5,725 tonnes with a gross value of $A161·7m. In the same year aquaculture production was an estimated 16,659 tonnes with a gross value of $A126·5m.

INDUSTRY

The most important manufactures for export are refined metals, woodchips, newsprint and other paper manufactures, pigments, woollen goods, fruit pulp, confectionery, butter, cheese, preserved and dried vegetables, sawn timber, and processed fish products. The electrolytic-zinc works at Risdon produce zinc, sulphuric acid, superphosphate, sulphate of ammonia, cadmium and other by-products. At George Town, large-scale plants produce refined aluminium and manganese alloys. In 2000–01 employment in manufacturing establishments was 20,600; wages and salaries totalled $A776·2m.; turnover, $A5,043·6m.

Labour. In 2002–03 the labour force stood at 219,600. There were 18,900 unemployed, a rate of 8·6%. The average weekly wage in Feb. 2003 was $A826·00 (males $A863·00, females $A748·30).

Trade Unions. In 2000 Tasmania had the highest rate of trade union membership of any Australian State, at 31·3%. This compared with 34·6% in Aug. 1998 and 39·3% in Aug. 1996.

INTERNATIONAL TRADE

Imports and Exports. In 2003–04 exports totalled $A2,312m. The principal countries of destination in 2003–04 (with values in $A1m.) for overseas exports were: Japan, 589; Hong Kong, 282; USA, 275; Republic of Korea, 207; China, 160. In 2003–04 direct imports into Tasmania totalled $A699m. In that year the principal suppliers of imports were (with values in $A1m.): Indonesia, 115; Germany, 100; USA, 71. Commodities by value (in $A1m.) exported to overseas countries in 2003–04 included: zinc, 345; aluminium, 333; crustaceans, 90; bovine meat, 89. Commodities by value (in $A1m.) imported from overseas countries in 2003–04 included: ships, boats and floating structures, 172; pulp and waste paper, 68; rotating electric plant, 68.

COMMUNICATIONS

Roads. In 2001 there were approximately 24,000 km of roads open to general traffic, of which 370 km were National Highway and 3,350 km were arterial State roads. Motor vehicles registered at 31 Oct. 2001 comprised 246,367 passenger vehicles, 76,432 commercial vehicles and 8,469 motorcycles. In the year ended Aug. 2003 there were 33 road accident fatalities.

Rail. Tasmania's rail network, incorporating 867 km of railways, is primarily a freight system with no regular passenger services. There are some small tourist railways, notably the newly rebuilt 34 km Abt Wilderness Railway on the west coast.

Civil Aviation. Regular passenger and freight services connect the south, north and northwest of the State with the mainland. During 2000–01 the six main airports handled 1,825,828 passengers and 5,593·9 tonnes of freight.

Shipping. There are four major commercial ports: Burnie, Devonport, Launceston and Hobart. In 2002–03, 1,443 commercial vessels called at Tasmanian ports. General cargo imported in 2002–03 was 1,846,595 mass tonnes and general cargo exported was 2,852,972 mass tonnes. Passenger ferry services connect Tasmania with the mainland and offshore islands.

Telecommunications. In 2000 there were 84,000 households with home computer access (45% of all households) and 48,000 households with home Internet access. In 2000, 49% of all households had access to a mobile phone.

Postal Services. In April 1999 there were 34 post offices and 152 licensees.

SOCIAL INSTITUTIONS

Justice. The Supreme Court of Tasmania is a superior court of record, with both original and appellate jurisdiction, and consists of a Chief Justice and five puisne judges. There are also inferior civil courts with limited jurisdiction.

In 2000–01 there were 58,295 recorded offences, of which 51,339 were against property; 3,660 against the person; and 2,879 fraud and similar offences. Total police personnel (sworn and unsworn) at 30 June 2003 was 1,548. There are three prisons and one detention centre which received a combined total of 427 prisoners at 30 June 2002.

Religion. At the census of 2001 the following numbers of adherents of the principal religions were recorded:

Anglican Church	147,413	Other Christian	10,526
Roman Catholic	87,691	Indefinite and not stated	47,430
Uniting Church	30,376	No religion	78,672
Presbyterian	12,508	Non-Christian	2,975
Baptist	8,984		
		Total	456,652

Education. Education is controlled by the State and is free, secular and compulsory between the ages of six and 16. In 2003, 214 government schools had a total enrolment of 61,157 pupils; 67 private schools had a total enrolment of 21,219 pupils.

In 2003 there were 54,814 enrolments in Vocational Education and Training activities.

Tertiary education is offered at the University of Tasmania and the Australian Maritime College. In 2003 the University (established 1890) had 14,506 students and the Australian Maritime College 2,724 students.

Health. In 2002–03 there were 25 public hospitals with 1,136 beds and 11 private hospitals with 1,098 beds, a total of 4·7 beds per 1,000 population.

Welfare. The number of age and disability pensions (including wives' and carers' pensions) on 30 June 2001 was: age, 48,499; disability support, 21,655; carer, 2,005. There were 976 widows' and 20,217 single parent payments current at 30 June 2001, and basic family payment was being paid for 83,433 children under 16 years.

CULTURE

Broadcasting. In 2002 there were four TV broadcasters and 21 radio stations.

Press. There were three daily papers with a combined circulation of 120,710 in March 2001. The largest circulation for a Tasmanian daily is for the Saturday edition of *The Mercury*, with a circulation of 65,097.

Tourism. In 2002–03 an estimated 652,200 adult visitors arrived in Tasmania, a 25·5% increase on 2001–02.

FURTHER READING

Statistical Information: The State Government Statistical Office (200 Collins St., Hobart), established in 1877, became in 1924 the Tasmanian Office of the Australian Bureau of Statistics, but continues to serve State statistical needs as required.

Main publications: Annual Statistical Bulletins (e.g., *Demography, Agriculture, Government Finance, Manufacturing Industry* etc.).—*Tasmanian Pocket Year Book.* Annual (from 1913).—*Tasmanian Year Book.* Annual (from 1967; biennial from 1986).—Monthly *Tasmanian Statistical Indicators* (from July 1945).

E-mail address: Sales and Inquiries: client.services@abs.gov.au
Website: http://www.abs.gov.au

Kepars, I., *Tasmania.* [Bibliography] ABC-Clio, Oxford and Santa Barbara (CA), 1997

Robson, L., *A History of Tasmania. Vol. 1: Van Diemen's Land from the Earliest Times to 1855.* Melbourne, 1983.—*A History of Tasmania. Vol. 2: Colony and State from 1856 to the 1980s.* Melbourne, 1990

State library: The State Library of Tasmania, 91 Murray St., Hobart, TAS 7000.
Website: http://statelibrary.tas.gov.au

VICTORIA

KEY HISTORICAL EVENTS

The first permanent settlement was formed at Portland Bay in 1834. A government was established in 1839. Victoria, formerly a portion of New South Wales, was proclaimed a separate colony in 1851 at much the same time as gold was discovered. A new constitution giving responsible government to the colony was proclaimed on 23 Nov. 1855. This event had far-reaching effects, as the population increased from 76,162 in 1850 to 589,160 in 1864. By this time the impetus for the search for gold had waned and new arrivals made a living from pastoral and agricultural holdings and from the development of manufacturing industries. Victoria federated with the other Australian states to form the Commonwealth of Australia in 1901.

TERRITORY AND POPULATION

The State has an area of 227,420 sq. km, and, at 30 June 2004, an estimated resident population of 4,972,800 (annual growth rate, 1·2%). The 2001 census population was 4,644,950 (4,373,520 at 1996 census). Victoria has the greatest proportion of people from non-English-speaking countries of any State or Territory, with (1996 census) 2·3% from Italy, 1·4% from Greece and 1·3% from Vietnam.

Estimated population at 30 June 2002, within 11 'Statistical Divisions': Melbourne, 3,524,103; Barwon, 259,549; Goulburn, 196,545; Loddon, 169,088; Gippsland, 161,204; Central Highlands, 143,179; Western District, 100,894; Ovens-Murray, 94,264; Mallee, 91,170; East Gippsland, 81,178; Wimmera, 51,364.

SOCIAL STATISTICS

Statistics for calendar years:

	Births	*Deaths*	*Marriages*	*Divorces*
2000	59,171	32,018	26,852	12,401
2001	58,626	32,295	24,953	13,722
2002	61,478	33,772	25,058	12,987
2003	61,058	32,925	25,211	12,865

The annual rates per 1,000 of the mean resident population in 2003 were: births, 12·4; deaths, 6·7; marriages, 5·1; divorces, 2·6. Infant mortality rate, 2003, 5·1 per 1,000 live births. Expectation of life, 2003: males, 78·2 years; females, 83·1 years.

CLIMATE

See AUSTRALIA: Climate.

CONSTITUTION AND GOVERNMENT

Victoria, formerly a portion of New South Wales, was, in 1851, proclaimed a separate colony, with a partially elective Legislative Council. In 1856 responsible government was conferred, the legislative power being vested in a parliament consisting of a Legislative Council (Upper House) and a Legislative Assembly (Lower House). At present the Council consists of 44 members who are elected for two terms of the Assembly, with half of the seats up for renewal at each election. The Assembly consists of 88 members, elected for four years from the date of its first meeting unless sooner dissolved by the Governor. Members and electors of both Houses must be aged 18 years and Australian citizens or those British subjects previously enrolled as electors, according to the Constitution Act 1975. Single voting (one elector one vote) and compulsory preferential voting apply to Council and Assembly elections. Enrolment for Council and Assembly electors is compulsory. The Council may not initiate or amend money bills, but may suggest amendments in such bills other than amendments which would increase any charge. A bill shall not become law unless passed by both Houses.

In the exercise of the executive power the Governor is advised by a Cabinet of responsible Ministers. Section 50 of the Constitution Act 1975 provides that the number of Ministers shall not at any one time exceed 22, of whom not more than six may sit in the Legislative Council and not more than 17 may sit in the Legislative Assembly.

RECENT ELECTIONS

In elections to the Legislative Assembly on 30 Nov. 2002 the Labor Party (ALP) won 62 seats with 47·9% of votes cast; the Liberal Party (LP), 17 (33·9%); the National Party (NP), 7 (4·3%). Two independents were elected. The Greens took 9·7% of the vote but no seats. Turn-out was 76·3%.

In the simultaneous elections to the Legislative Council the ALP won 17 seats, the LP 3, and the NP 2. Total seats in March 2004: ALP 25, LP 15, and NP 4.

CURRENT ADMINISTRATION

Governor: John Landy, AC, MBE.

The Labor Cabinet was as follows in Feb. 2005:

Premier, Minister for Multicultural Affairs: Stephen Bracks.

Deputy Premier, Minister for the Environment, Water and Victorian Communities: John Thwaites. *Transport:* Peter Batchelor. *Local Government and Housing:* Candy Broad. *State and Regional Development, Innovation and Treasurer:* John Brumby. *Agriculture:* Bob Cameron. *Health:* Bronwyn Pike. *Education and Training:* Lynne Kosky. *Community Services and Children:* Sherryl Garbutt. *Finance, Major Projects and Workcover:* John Lenders. *Manufacturing and Export, Small Business and Financial Service:* Andre Haermeyer. *Arts and Women's Affairs:* Mary Delahunty. *Education Services, Youth Affairs and Employment:* Jacinta Allan. *Consumer Affairs, Information and Communication Technology:* Marsha Thomson. *Attorney General, Minister for Industrial Relations and Planning:* Rob Hulls. *Sport and Recreation, Commonwealth Games:* Justin Madden. *Gaming and Racing, and Tourism:* John Pandazopoulos. *Aged Care, Aboriginal Affairs:* Gavin Jennings. *Police, Emergency Services and Corrections:* Tim Holding. *Energy Industries and Resources:* Theo Theophanous.

Speaker of the Legislative Assembly: Judy Maddigan.

VIC Government website: http://www.vic.gov.au

ECONOMY

Budget. In 2004–05 general government expenses by the state were expected to total $A28,439·9m.; revenue and grants received were expected to increase by 4·5% to $A28,984·9m. ($A27,731·2m. in 2003–04).

Performance. In 2002–03 Victoria's gross state product represented 25·59% of Australia's total GDP.

Banking and Finance. The State Bank of Victoria, the largest bank in the State, provides domestic and international services for business and personal customers and is the largest supplier of housing finance in Victoria. In 1990 it ran into debt and was acquired by the Commonwealth from the Victorian government in Sept. 1990.

The 11 major trading banks in Victoria are the Commonwealth Bank of Australia, the Australia and New Zealand Banking Group, the Westpac Banking Corporation, the National Australia Bank, the Bank of Melbourne, the St George Bank, the Challenge Bank, the Metway Bank, the State Bank of New South Wales, Bendigo Bank and Citibank. Banks had a total of 1,217 branches and 1,262 agencies between them at 30 June 2000.

As at March 2002 bank deposits repayable totalled $A112,233m. and loans $A141,664m.

ENERGY AND NATURAL RESOURCES

Electricity. In the year to 30 June 2002 total production was 49,438m. kWh; total consumption stood at 39,007m. kWh, including 28,156m. kWh by business customers.

In 1993 the State government began a major restructure of the government-owned electricity industry along competitive lines. The distribution sector was privatized in 1995, and four generator companies in 1997.

About 90% of power generated is supplied by four brown-coal fired generating stations. There are two other thermal stations and three hydro-electric stations in northeast Victoria. Victoria is also entitled to approximately 30% of the output of the Snowy Mountains hydro-electric scheme and half the output of the Hume hydro-electric station, both of which are in New South Wales.

Oil and Gas. Crude oil in commercially recoverable quantities was first discovered in 1967 in two large fields offshore, in East Gippsland in Bass Strait, between 65 and 80 km from land. These fields, with 20 other fields since discovered, have been assessed as containing initial recoverable oil reserves of 4,063·4m. bbls. Estimated remaining oil reserves as at 30 June 2001 is 432·0m. bbls. Production of crude oil in the fiscal year 2002–03 was valued at about $A3·2bn. with output at 133,000 bbls. per day (15% less than the previous year).

Natural gas was discovered offshore in East Gippsland in 1965. The initial recoverable gas reserves were 272·0m. cu. metres. Estimated remaining gas reserves (30 June 2001), 117·68m. cu. metres. Production of natural gas (2000–01), 6·43m. cu. metres.

Liquefied petroleum gas is produced after extraction of the propane and butane fractions from the untreated oil and gas.

Brown Coal. Major deposits of brown coal are located in the Central Gippsland region and comprise approximately 94% of the total resources in Victoria. In 1993 the resource was estimated to be 0·2m. megatonnes, of which about 52,000 megatonnes was economically recoverable. It is young and soft with a water content of 60% to 70%. In the Latrobe Valley section of the region, the thick brown coal seams underlie an area from 10 to 30 km wide extending over approximately 70 km from Yallourn in the west to the south of Sale in the east. It can be won continuously in large quantities and at low cost by specialized mechanical plant.

The primary use of these reserves is to fuel electricity generating stations. Production of brown coal in 2000–01 was 66·0m. tonnes.

Minerals. Production, 1999–2000: basalt, 13,074,000 tonnes; sand for concrete, 4,977,000 tonnes. In 2002–03, 3,048 kg of gold were produced (around 32% of Australian gold production).

Agriculture. In the year ended 30 June 2002 there were 33,581 agricultural establishments (excluding those with an estimated value of agricultural operations less than $A5,000) with a total area of 12·8m. ha of which 2·96m. ha were under crops. Gross value of agricultural production, 2001–02, $A9·3bn. Preliminary estimates of principal crops produced in 2001–02 (in 1,000 tonnes): wheat, 2,812; barley, 1,692; canola, 355; oats, 352.

Gross value of livestock production in 2001–02 totalled $A3·1bn., including wool production $A569m.

Grape growing, particularly for winemaking, is an important crop. In 2002, 338,536 tonnes of winegrapes were produced from 38,653 ha of vineyards (including 3,618 ha not yet bearing).

Forestry. Commercial timber production is an increasingly important source of income. As at Dec. 2002 there were 360,000 ha of plantation. Of Victoria's 7·9m. ha of native forest (Dec. 2002), 6·6m. ha (83·4%) were publicly owned (3·1m. ha in conservation reserves).

Fisheries. Estimated total fisheries production in 2002–03 came to 5,576 tonnes with a gross value of $A87·2m. In the same year aquaculture production was an estimated 3,517 tonnes with a gross value of $A21·7m.

INDUSTRY

Total turnover in the manufacturing industry in 2000–01 was $A74,311·9m. At 30 June 2000 there were 292,100 persons employed in the manufacturing sector.

Labour. At Aug. 2001 there were 2,455,100 persons in the labour force (63·2% of the civilian population aged 15 years and over), of whom 2,303,100 were employed: wholesale and retail trade, 463,300; finance, insurance, property and business services, 349,800; manufacturing, 361,100; health and community services, 221,200; education, 165,700; construction, 158,100; culture, recreation, personal and other services, 143,600; transport and storage, 103,900; agriculture, forestry and fishing, 91,300; accommodation, cafes and restaurants, 91,000; government administration and defence, 80,600; communication services, 49,200; electricity, gas and water supply, 20,500; mining, 3,800. There were 152,000 unemployed persons in Aug. 2001 (6·2% of the labour force). The average weekly wage in Feb. 2003 was $A902·00 (males $A954·20, females $A807·30).

Trade Unions. There were 57 trade unions with a total membership of 680,000 at 30 June 1996.

INTERNATIONAL TRADE

Imports and Exports. The total value of the overseas imports and exports of Victoria, including bullion and specie, was as follows (in $A1m.):

	2001–02	*2002–03*	*2003–04*
Imports	37,558	42,129	40,739
Exports[1]	22,237	18,904	17,997

[1]Includes re-exports.

The chief exports in 2003–04 (in $A1m.) were: passenger motor vehicles, 1,467; aluminium, 1,081; milk and cream, 1,060; wool, 970; cheese and curd, 567. Exports in 2003–04 (in $A1m.) went mainly to New Zealand, 2,095; USA, 1,949; China, 1,889; Japan, 1,626; Saudi Arabia, 945.

The chief imports in 2003–04 (in $A1m.) were: passenger motor vehicles, 3,40; crude petroleum, 1,618; aircraft and parts, 1,571; medicaments (including veterinary), 1,012; telecommunications equipment, 945. Imports in 2003–04 (in $A1m.) came mainly from the USA, 6,530; China, 5,274; Japan, 4,963; Germany, 3,280; France, 1,926.

COMMUNICATIONS

Roads. There are over 150,000 km of roads open for general traffic, consisting of (at 31 Oct. 2000) 1,004 km of National Highways, 6,524 km of state highways and freeways, 14,710 km of main, tourist and forest roads, and (at 30 June 1999) 133,960 km of other roads and streets. The number of registered motor vehicles (other than tractors and motor cycles) at 31 March 2001 was 3,222,941. There were 321 road accident fatalities in the year ended Aug. 2003.

Rail. The railways are the property of the State and the land is owned and managed by the Victorian Rail Track Corporation (VicTrack). The railway land and infrastructure was transferred from the Public Transport Corporation (PTC) to VicTrack during privatization in 1996–99. In 1999 the non-electrified intra-State railway was leased (for a total of 45 years) to Freight Victoria (trading as Freight Australia), a private company which in May 1999 purchased the business of V/Line Freight Corporation from the State. The passenger rail businesses were franchised to the following private operators in Aug. 1999: National Express, Melbourne Transport Enterprises Pty Ltd, and Metrolink Victoria Pty Ltd.

Victoria's rail network consists of over 5,000 km of track, comprising 1,274 km of standard gauge (1,435 mm). There are 3,745 km of broad gauge (1,600 mm) of which 336 km are electrified. 849 km of standard gauge lines form part of the interstate rail network from Brisbane to Perth and are under the control of the Australian Rail Track Corporation. In the year ended 31 March 2001, 10m. tonnes of freight were carried by Freight Australia and there were a total of 139·4m. passenger boardings (11·5m. non-urban). Melbourne's tramway and light rail network extends to 241 km and is the tenth longest in the world. There were 131·4m. boardings in 2000–01.

Civil Aviation. There were 13,245,878 domestic and regional passenger movements and 3,136,420 international passenger movements in 2002–03 at Melbourne (Tullamarine) airport (Australia's second busiest airport after Sydney). Total freight handled in 2000 was 271,605 tonnes (international, 199,437; domestic, 72,168).

Shipping. The four major commercial ports are at Melbourne, Geelong, Portland and Hastings. In 2002–03, 3,687 commercial vessels called at Victorian ports. General cargo imported in 2002–03 was 9,573,802 mass tonnes and general cargo exported was 9,908,314 mass tonnes.

Telecommunications. In May 1998, 93·5% of households had a fixed telephone connected; 44·3% had mobile phones. In 2000 there were 973,000 households with home computer access (56% of all households) and 598,000 households with home Internet access (34%).

Postal Services. At June 2001 there were 1,055 retail outlets including 842 licensed post offices. Postal items handled by Australia Post in Victoria (1999–2000) totalled 1,637·2m.

SOCIAL INSTITUTIONS

Justice. There is a Supreme Court with a Chief Justice and 21 puisne judges. There are a county court, magistrates' courts, a court of licensing and a bankruptcy court.

During 1996–97 the State's prisons were replaced with new facilities developed, owned and operated by the private sector. During 1999–2000 approximately 45% of Victoria's prison population was accommodated in the three private prisons. There are ten public prisons remaining. At 30 June 2002 the daily average of prisoners held stood at 3,540. Police personnel (sworn and unsworn) at 30 June 2003, 12,924.

Religion. There is no State Church, and no State assistance has been given to religion since 1875. At the 1991 census the following were the enumerated numbers of the principal religions: Catholic, 1,237,399; Anglican, 772,632; Uniting, 342,493 (including Methodist); Orthodox, 199,063; Presbyterian, 193,300; other Christian, 255,375; Muslim, 49,617; Jewish, 33,882; Buddhist, 42,350; no religion, 612,074; not stated, 474,921.

Education. In 2002 there were 1,623 government schools with 533,417 pupils and 37,520 full-time teaching staff plus full-time equivalents of part-time teaching staff: 316,843 pupils were in primary schools and 216,574 in secondary schools. As from 1990 students attending special schools have not been identified separately and have been allocated to either primary or secondary level of education. They are integrated where possible into mainstream education. There were, in 2002, 697 non-government schools, excluding commercial colleges, with 18,830 (2000) teaching staff and 281,076 pupils; 139,821 pupils at primary schools; and 141,255 pupils at secondary schools.

All higher education institutions, excluding continuing education and technical and further education (TAFE), now fall under the Unified National System, and can no longer be split into universities and colleges of advanced education. In addition, a number of institutional amalgamations and name changes occurred in the 12 months prior to the commencement of the 1992 academic year. In 2001 there were 479,900 enrolments in Vocational Education and Training activities.

There are ten publicly funded higher education institutions including eight State universities, Marcus Oldham College and the Australian Catholic University (partly privately funded), and the Melbourne University Private, established in 1998. In 2002 there were 228,561 students in higher education.

Health. In 2002–03 there were 144 public hospitals with 11,938 beds, and 140 private hospitals with 6,628 beds. Total government outlay on health in 2002–03 was $A6,376m.

Welfare. Victoria was the first State of Australia to make a statutory provision for the payment of Age Pensions. The Act came into operation on 18 Jan. 1901, and continued until 1 July 1909, when the Australian Invalid and Old Age Pension Act came into force. The Social Services Consolidation Act, which came into operation on 1 July 1947, repealed the various legislative enactments relating to age and invalid pensions, maternity allowances, child endowment, unemployment and sickness benefits and, while following in general the Acts repealed, considerably liberalized many of their provisions.

The number of age and disability pensions (including wives' and carers' pensions) on 30 June 1999 was: age, 439,595; disability support, 136,218; carer, 10,266. There were 7,680 widows' and 84,368 single parent payments current at 30 June 1999, and basic family payment was being paid for 789,899 children under 16 years.

CULTURE

Tourism. In 1999–2000 the number of short-term overseas visitors to Australia who specified Victoria as their main destination was 685,950 (14·7% of total overseas visitors to Australia), with 466,480 nominating 'holiday' or 'visiting friends/relatives' as purpose of their visit. New Zealand represented the major source of international visitors with 19·9%; followed by the UK and Ireland (11·7%), USA (11·3%), Singapore (7·5%) and Japan (6·8%).

FURTHER READING

Australian Bureau of Statistics Victorian Office. *Victorian Year Book.—Summary of Statistics* (annual).

State library: The State Library of Victoria, 328 Swanston St., Melbourne 3000.
State statistical office: Victorian Office, 5th Floor, Commercial Union Tower, 485 LaTrobe Street, Melbourne 3000.

WESTERN AUSTRALIA

KEY HISTORICAL EVENTS

In 1791 the British navigator George Vancouver took possession of the country around King George Sound. In 1826 the government of New South Wales sent 20 convicts and a detachment of soldiers to form a settlement then called Frederickstown. The following year, Capt. James Stirling surveyed the coast from King George Sound to the Swan River, and in May 1829 Capt. Charles Fremantle took possession of the territory. In June 1829 Capt. Stirling founded the Swan River Settlement (now the Commonwealth State of Western Australia) and the towns of Perth and Fremantle. He was appointed Lieut.-Governor.

Grants of land were made to the early settlers until, in 1850, with the colony languishing, they petitioned for the colony to be made a penal settlement. Between 1850 and 1868 (in which year transportation ceased), 9,668 convicts were sent out. In 1870 partially representative government was instituted. Western Australia federated with the other Australian states to form the Commonwealth of Australia in 1901.

In the 1914–18 war Western Australia provided more volunteers for overseas military service in proportion to population than any other State. The worldwide depression of 1929 brought unemployment (30% of trade union membership), and in 1933 over two-thirds voted to leave the Federation. While there were modest improvements in the standard of living through the 1930s, it was the 1939–45 war which brought full employment. Japanese aircraft attacked the Western Australia coast in 1942. Talk of a 'Brisbane line', which would abandon the West to invasion, only served to reinforce Western Australia's sense of isolation from the rest of the nation. The post-war years saw increasing demand for wheat and wool but the 1954–55 decline in farm incomes led to diversification. Work began in the early 1950s on steel production and oil processing. Oil was discovered in 1953 but it was not until 1966 that it was commercially exploited. The discovery of deposits of iron ore in the Pilbara, bauxite in the Darling scarp, nickel in Kambalda and ilmenite from mineral sands led to the State becoming a major world supplier of mineral exports by 1965.

TERRITORY AND POPULATION

Western Australia has an area of 2,529,880 sq. km and 12,500 km of coastline.

The population at the 2001 census was 1,851,252 (1,726,095 at 1996 census). Of the total, 1,241,786 (67·8%) were born in Australia and 928,984 were females. The estimated resident population at 30 June 2004 was 1,982,200. Perth, the capital, had an estimated resident population (June 2002) of 1,413,700.

Principal local government areas outside the metropolitan area, with population at the 2001 census: Mandurah, 45,020; Albany, 29,571; Kalgoorlie-Boulder, 28,818; Bunbury, 28,682; Busselton, 22,060; Geraldton, 19,275; Roebourne, 15,974; Port Hedland, 13,099.

SOCIAL STATISTICS

Statistics for calendar years[1]:

	Births	*Deaths*	*Marriages*	*Divorces*
2000	25,093	10,668	11,000	5,276
2001	24,002	10,779	10,484	5,351
2002	23.601	11,326	10,484	5,252
2003	24,273	11,311	9,549	5,685

[1]Figures are on state of usual residence basis.

The annual rates per 1,000 of the mean resident population in 2003 were: births, 12·4; deaths, 5·8; marriages, 4·9; divorces, 2·9. Infant mortality rate, 2003, 4·1 per 1,000 live births. Expectation of life, 2003: males, 78·1 years; females, 83·0 years.

CLIMATE

Western Australia is a region of several climate zones, ranging from the tropical north to the semi-arid interior and Mediterranean-style climate of the southwest. Most of the State is a plateau between 300 and 600 metres above sea level. Except in the far southwest coast, maximum temperatures in excess of 40°C have been recorded throughout the State. The normal average number of sunshine hours per day is 8·0.

CONSTITUTION AND GOVERNMENT

The *Legislative Council* consists of 34 members elected for a term of four years. There are six electoral regions for Legislative Council elections. Four electoral regions return five members and the other two electoral regions seven members. Each member represents the entire region.

There are 57 members of the *Legislative Assembly*, each member representing one of the 57 electoral districts of the State. Members are elected for a period of up to four years. A system of proportional representation is used to elect members.

RECENT ELECTIONS

In elections to the Legislative Assembly on 26 Feb. 2005 the Labor Party (ALP) won 32 seats with 41·9% of votes cast; the Liberal Party (LP), 18 (35·6%); the National Party (NP), 5 (3·7%); ind., 2 (4·6%).

CURRENT ADMINISTRATION

Governor: Lieut.-Gen. John M. Sanderson, AC.

Lieut.-Governor and Chief Justice: David Kingsley Malcolm, AC.

In Feb. 2005 the Cabinet comprised:

Premier, Minister for Public Sector Management, Federal Affairs, Science, Citizenship and Multicultural Interests: Dr Geoff Gallop.

Deputy Premier, Treasurer, Minister for Energy: Eric Ripper. *Agriculture, Forestry and Fisheries, the Midwest, Wheatbelt and Great Southern:* Kim Chance. *Local Government and Regional Development, Heritage, the Kimberley, Pilbara and Gascoyne, Goldfields and Esperance:* Ljiljanna Ravlich. *Consumer and Employment Protection, and Indigenous Affairs:* John Kobelke. *Attorney General, Minister for Health and Electoral Affairs:* Jim McGinty. *Environment:* Dr Judy Edwards. *Police and Emergency Services, Justice and Community Safety:* Michelle Roberts. *Planning and Infrastructure:* Alannah MacTiernan. *State Development:* Clive Brown. *Education and Training:* Alan Carpenter. *Community Development, Women's Interests, Seniors and Youth, Disability Services, Culture and the Arts:* Sheila McHale. *Tourism, Small Business, Sport and Recreation, Peel and the South West:* Bob Kucera, APM. *Housing and Works, Racing and Gaming, Government Enterprises, Land Information:* Nick Griffiths.

Speaker of the Legislative Assembly: Fred Riebeling.

WA Government website: http://www.wa.gov.au

ECONOMY

Budget. Revenue and expenditure (in $A1m.) in years ending 30 June:

	2000–01	*2001–02*	*2002–03*	*2003–04*[1]
Revenue	10,597	11,035	11,771	12,049
Expenditure	10,429	10,838	11,517	11,908

[1]Projected.

A general government net operating surplus of $A142m. was projected for 2003–04. This is the fourth consecutive general government surplus since 2000–01, reinforcing the turnaround in the State's finances from the deficits recorded in the mid- to late-1990s.

Banking and Finance. In March 2002 bank deposits totalled $A32,539m., and loans $A55,412m.

ENERGY AND NATURAL RESOURCES

Electricity. Deregulation of the energy industry was passed by the Office of Energy during 1996–97. Electricity users can obtain power from Western Power or private sector operators. In the year ended 30 June 2002 Western Power customer consumption stood at 12,081m. kWh, including 8,251m. kWh by business customers.

Oil and Gas. Petroleum continued to be the State's largest resource sector with a sales increase of $A2·9bn. to $A10·6bn. in 2000–01. During the same year crude oil was the most valuable product with a 16% increase in the quantity of sales to 14bn. litres and value of sales at 52% to $A4·8bn. The State accounts for around 48% of Australia's oil and condensate production.

Western Australia has significant natural gas resources and, with a $A2·4bn. expansion of the North West Shelf liquefied natural gas (LNG) project, exports are forecast to rise by around $A1bn. Total natural gas production, 2002–03: 20,179 gigalitres.

Source: Western Australian Department of Mineral and Petroleum Resources

Minerals. Mining is a significant contributor to the Western Australia economy. The State is the world's third largest producer of iron ore and accounts for almost 88% of Australia's iron ore production.

Principal minerals produced in 2003–04 were: gold, 173 tonnes; iron ore, 193·3m. tonnes; diamonds, 24·3m. carats; crude oil (2002–03), 19,428 megalitres. Most of the State's coal production (an estimated 6·6m. tonnes in 2003–04) is used by Western Power's electricity generation.

Agriculture. In the year ended 30 June 2002 there were 12,688 establishments mainly engaged in agriculture with a total area of 109·0m. ha of which 7·53m. ha were under crops. Gross value of agricultural production in 2001–02 totalled $A5·5bn., an increase of 26% on the previous year.

Preliminary estimates of crops produced in 2001–02 (in 1,000 tonnes): wheat, 7,931; barley, 2,243; lupins for grain, 896; canola, 439; oats, 567; sugarcane, 308.

Value of livestock products in 2001–02 totalled $A656m. Total value of wool produced in 2001–02 was $A514m.

Forestry. The area of State forests and timber reserves at 30 June 2003 was 1,169,300 ha. Jarrah and Karri hardwoods supply about 0·5m. cu. metres of sawn wood and pine plantations, 1m. cu. metres of logs for panel manufacture, sawmilling and export.

Fisheries. Estimated total fisheries production in 2002–03 came to 40,446 tonnes with a gross value of $A425·8m. In the same year aquaculture production was an estimated 1,020 tonnes with a gross value of $A181·3m. Pearling is the most valuable form of aquaculture in the State with the Pearl Oyster Fishery producing an estimated $A175m. worth of pearls from wild captured and hatchery produced oysters in 2001–02.

INDUSTRY

Heavy industry is concentrated in the southwest, and is largely tied to export-orientated mineral processing, especially alumina and nickel.

The following table shows manufacturing industry statistics for 1999–2000:

Industry sub-division	*Persons employed 1,000*	*Wages and salaries $A1m.*	*Turnover $A1m.*
Food, beverages and tobacco	13·6	447·0	3,508·5
Textiles, clothing and leather products	3·2	86·2	386·6
Wood and paper products	4·3	144·0	834·9
Printing and publishing and recorded media	7·0	232·0	958·0
Petroleum, coal, chemical products	6·7	301·1	3,847·3
Non-metallic mineral products	4·6	199·4	1,250·9
Metal products	15·7	634·8	4,960·3
Machinery and equipment	12·9	468·3	2,202·1
Other manufacturing	6·3	142·6	703·0

Labour. The labour force comprised 970,900 employed and 61,300 unemployed persons in 2002–03 (an unemployment rate of 5·9%). The average weekly wage in Feb. 2003 was $A889·30 (males $A960·70, females $A752·20).

Trade Unions. In 1996 there were 54 trade unions with a total of 135,200 male members and 86,500 female members.

INTERNATIONAL TRADE

Imports and Exports. Value of foreign imports and exports (i.e. excluding interstate trade) for years ending 30 June (in $A1m.):

	2001–02	*2002–03*	*2003–04*
Imports	9,320	11,755	11,690
Exports	30,224	32,439	32,220

The chief exports in 2003–04 (in $A1m.) were: non-monetary gold, 5,554; iron ore, 5,159; crude petroleum, 3,641; natural gas, 2,174; wheat, 1,785; nickel ores, 598. Exports in 2003–04 (in $A1m.) went mainly to Japan, 6,931; China, 4,400; Republic of Korea, 3,207; India, 2,809; UK, 1,916.

The chief imports in 2003–04 (in $A1m.) were: non-monetary gold, 1,956; crude petroleum, 1,086; passenger motor vehicles, 954; refined petroleum, 572; motor vehicles for transporting goods, 420. Imports in 2003–04 (in $A1m.) came mainly from the USA, 1,340; Japan, 1,315; Indonesia, 1,246; Singapore, 870; China, 613.

COMMUNICATIONS

Roads. At 30 June 2001 there were 173,970 km of roads comprising 10,815 km of National and State highways, 6,859 km of main roads and 125,962 km of unclassified local roads. In addition, there were 29,289 km of roads in forests and national parks and 1,045 km of private roads.

New motor vehicles registered during the year ended 30 June 2001 were 77,642. In the year ended Aug. 2003 there were 152 fatalities in road accidents.

Rail. In 1999–2000, 29·5m. passenger journeys were made on urban services. In the year ended 31 March 2001, 196m. tonnes of freight were carried.

Civil Aviation. An extensive system of regular air services operates for passengers, freight and mail. In 2002–03 Perth International Airport handled 5,189,365 passengers (3,402,600 on domestic flights).

Shipping. In 2002–03, 2,781 commercial vessels called at Western Australian ports (1,569 at Fremantle). General cargo imported in 2002–03 was 2,686,346 mass tonnes and general cargo exported was 3,033,257 mass tonnes.

Telecommunications. In 2000 there were 390,000 households with home computer access (56% of all households) and 241,000 households with home Internet access.

Postal Services. In 1995 the Australia Post Corporation had 441 outlets and 722,114 delivery points in Western Australia.

SOCIAL INSTITUTIONS

Justice. Justice is administered by a Supreme Court, consisting of a Chief Justice, 16 other judges and two masters; a District Court comprising a chief judge and 20 other judges; a Magistrates Court, a Chief Stipendiary Magistrate, 37 Stipendiary Magistrates and Justices of the Peace. All courts exercise both civil and criminal jurisdiction except Justices of the Peace who deal with summary criminal matters only. Juvenile offenders are dealt with by the Children's Court. The Family Court also forms part of the justice system.

At June 2002 there was a daily average of 2,800 prisoners held. At 30 June 2003 police personnel (sworn and unsworn) stood at 6,347.

Religion. At the census of 6 Aug. 1996 the principal denominations were: Catholic, 427,848; Anglican, 410,233; Uniting, 87,549; Presbyterian and Reformed, 45,761; Baptist, 27,618; other Christian, 126,041. There were 48,294 persons practising non-Christian religions and 367,491 persons had no religion.

Education. School attendance is compulsory from the age of six until the end of the year in which the child attains 15 years. In Aug. 2002 there were 775 government primary and secondary schools (with 15,136 full-time equivalent teaching staff, excluding pre-primary teaching staff) providing free education to 250,096 primary and secondary students; in Aug. 2002 there were 308 non-government schools for 108,629 kindergarten, pre-primary, primary and secondary students (with 7,745 full-time equivalent teaching staff in Aug. 2000, excluding pre-primary teaching staff).

Higher education is available through four state universities and one private (Notre Dame). In 2001 there were 170,700 enrolments in Vocational Education and Training activities. In 2002 there was a total of 70,932 students in tertiary education at the University of Western Australia, Murdoch University, the University of Notre Dame Australia, Curtin University of Technology and the Edith Cowan University.

Health. In 2002–03 there were 93 acute public hospitals and one public psychiatric hospital, 27 acute private hospitals and 14 day hospitals.

Welfare. The Department for Community Development is responsible for the provision of welfare and community services throughout the State.

The number of age and disability pensions (including wives' and carers' pensions) on 30 June 1999 was: age, 140,033; disability support, 47,768; carer, 2,602. There were 2,473 widows' and 38,694 single parent payments current at 30 June 1999, and basic family payment was being paid for 326,692 children under 16 years.

CULTURE

Tourism. In 2002–03 there were 460,534 short-term overseas visitors. Of these, 24·3% were from the UK and Ireland, 18·5% from Singapore and 12·5% from Japan.

FURTHER READING

Statistical Information: The State Government Statistician's Office was established in 1897 and now functions as the Western Australian Office of the Australian Bureau of Statistics (Level 15, Exchange Plaza, Sherwood Court, Perth 6001). Its principal publications are: *Western Australia: Facts and Figures* (from 1989). *Monthly Summary of Statistics* (from 1958)

Broeze, F. J. A. (ed.) *Private Enterprise, Government and Society.* Univ. of Western Australia, 1993

Crowley, F. K., *Australia's Western Third: A History of Western Australia from the First Settlements to Modern Times.* (Rev. ed.) Melbourne, 1970

Stannage, C. T. (ed.) *A New History of Western Australia.* Perth, 1980

State library: Alexander Library Building, Perth.

AUSTRALIAN EXTERNAL TERRITORIES

AUSTRALIAN ANTARCTIC TERRITORY

An Imperial Order in Council of 7 Feb. 1933 placed under Australian authority all the islands and territories other than Adélie Land situated south of 60° S. lat. and lying between 160° E. long. and 45° E. long. The Order came into force with a Proclamation issued by the Governor-General on 24 Aug. 1936 after the passage of the Australian Antarctic Territory Acceptance Act 1933. The boundaries of Adélie Land were definitively fixed by a French Decree of 1 April 1938 as the islands and territories south of 60° S. lat. lying between 136° E. long. and 142° E. long. The Australian Antarctic Territory Act 1954 declared that the laws in force in the Australian Capital Territory are, so far as they are applicable and are not inconsistent with any ordinance made under the Act, in force in the Australian Antarctic Territory.

The area of the territory is estimated at 6,119,818 sq. km (2,362,875 sq. miles).

There is a research station on MacRobertson Land at lat. 67° 37' S. and long. 62° 52' E. (Mawson), one on the coast of Princess Elizabeth Land at lat. 68° 34' S. and long. 77° 58' E. (Davis), and one at lat. 66° 17' S. and long. 110° 32' E. (Casey). The Antarctic Division also operates a station on Macquarie Island.

COCOS (KEELING) ISLANDS

The Cocos (Keeling) Islands are two separate atolls comprising some 27 small coral islands with a total area of about 14·2 sq. km, and are situated in the Indian Ocean at 12° 05' S. lat. and 96° 53' E. long. They lie 2,768 km northwest of Perth. The islands are low-lying, flat and thickly covered by coconut palms, and surround a lagoon in which ships drawing up to seven metres may be anchored. There is an equable and pleasant climate, affected for much of the year by the southeast trade winds. Temperatures range over the year from 68° F (20° C) to 88° F (31·1° C) and rainfall averages 80" (2,000 mm) a year.

The main islands are: West Island (the largest, about 10 km long), home to most of the European community; Home Island, occupied by the Cocos Malay community; Direction, South and Horsburgh Islands, and North Keeling Island, 24 km to the north of the group. The population of the Territory (2001 Census) was 621, distributed between Home Island (75%) and West Island (25%). About 85% are Muslim and 15% Christian.

The islands were discovered in 1609 by Capt. William Keeling but remained uninhabited until 1826. In 1857 the islands were annexed to the Crown; the governments of Ceylon and Singapore held jurisdiction over the islands at different periods until they were placed under the authority of the Australian government as the Territory of Cocos (Keeling) Islands on 23 Nov. 1955. An *Administrator* (Evan Williams; took office in Nov. 2003), appointed by the Governor-General, is the government's representative in the Territory and is responsible to the Minister for Territories and Local Government. The Cocos (Keeling) Islands Council, established as the elected body of the Cocos Malay community in July 1979, advises the Administrator on all issues affecting the Territory.

In 1978 and 1993 the Australian government purchased the interests of the Clunies-Ross family, who had been granted the land in its entirety by Queen Victoria. A Cocos Malay co-operative was established to take over the running of the Clunies-Ross copra plantation and to engage in other business with the Commonwealth in the Territory, including construction projects.

The Islands are served by 15 km of roads and an airport on West Island, with flights operated by National Jet to Christmas Island and Perth (2003). In 1992 there was one primary school on each island, with a combined enrolment of 98 pupils and seven teachers. There were two secondary schools with 70 pupils and nine teachers and a technical school with 29 students. In 1992 there was one doctor and seven nursing personnel.

CHRISTMAS ISLAND

GENERAL DETAILS

Christmas Island is an isolated peak in the Indian Ocean, lat. 10° 25' 22" S., long. 105° 39' 59" E. It lies 360 km S. 8° E. of Java Head, and 417 km N. 79° E. from Cocos Islands, 1,310 km from Singapore and 2,623 km from Fremantle. Area: 136·7 sq. km. The climate is tropical with temperatures varying little over the year at 27° C. The wet season lasts from Nov. to April with an annual total of about 2,673 mm. The island was formally annexed by the UK on 6 June 1888, placed under the administration of the Governor of the Straits Settlements in 1889, and incorporated with the Settlement of Singapore in 1900. Sovereignty was transferred to the Australian government on 1 Oct. 1958. The population at the 2001 census was 1,508.

The legislative, judicial and administrative systems are regulated by the Christmas Island Act, 1958–73. They are the responsibility of the Commonwealth government and are operated by an Administrator. The Territory underwent major changes to its legal system when the Federal Parliament passed the Territories Law Reform Bill of 1992; Commonwealth and State laws applying in the state of Western Australia now apply in the Territory as a result, although some laws have been repealed to take into account the unique status of the Territory. The first Island Assembly was elected in Sept. 1985, and is now replaced by the elected members of the Christmas Island Shire Council.

Extraction and export of rock phosphate dust is the main industry. The government is also encouraging the private sector development of tourism.

CONSTITUTION AND GOVERNMENT

The Christmas Island Assembly has nine annually-elected members. The last elections were on 3 May 2003. All non-partisan candidates were elected unopposed.

CURRENT ADMINISTRATION

Administrator: Evan Williams (appointed Nov. 2003).

ECONOMY

Currency. The Australian dollar is legal tender.

ENERGY AND NATURAL RESOURCES

Electricity. Annual energy consumption is around 25m. kWh.

COMMUNICATIONS

Roads. The Shire of Christmas Island has responsibility for approximately 140 km of roads with the remaining 100 km of haul roads and tracks maintained by Christmas Island Phosphates and Park Australia North. In 1999 there were 1,398 registered vehicles.

Civil Aviation. In 2003 National Jet operated scheduled flights to Perth and Cocos Island.

Shipping. In 1999 there were up to seven ships a month collecting phosphate products from the island.

Postal Services. There was one post office in 1999, operated by Australia Post licensees.

SOCIAL INSTITUTIONS

Religion. About 50% of the population are Buddhists or Taoists, 16% Muslims and 30% Christians.

Education. In 1999 there were 530 students at the Christmas Island District High School; 15% were pre-primary, 60% primary and 25% secondary level pupils.

Health. There is a nine-bed hospital, the island's only one, which was completed in 1994. There are two doctors, one dentist, a director of nursing and 20 locally engaged staff. Specialists visit about every three months.

CULTURE

Broadcasting. A local radio and television station operate 24 hours per day. Local Radio VLU2 broadcasts in English, Malay and Chinese.

NORFOLK ISLAND

KEY HISTORICAL EVENTS

The island was formerly part of the colony of New South Wales and then of Van Diemen's Land (now known as Tasmania). A penal colony between 1788–1814 and 1825–55, it was separated from the state of Tasmania in 1856 and placed under the jurisdiction of the Australian State of New South Wales. Following the Norfolk Island Act 1913 (Cth), the Island was accepted as a Territory of Australia with the Australian Federal Government having jurisdiction for the Island.

TERRITORY AND POPULATION

Situated 29° 02' S. lat. 167° 57' E. long.; area 3,455 ha; permanent population (Aug. 1996), 1,470.

Descendants of the *Bounty* mutineer families constitute the 'original' settlers and are known locally as 'Islanders', while later settlers, mostly from Australia and

New Zealand, are identified as 'mainlanders'. 80% of the Island's permanent population are Australian citizens with 16% being New Zealand citizens. Descendants of the Pitcairn Islanders make up about 46% of the permanent resident population. Over the years the Islanders have preserved their own lifestyle and customs, and their language remains a mixture of West Country English, Gaelic and Tahitian.

CLIMATE

Sub-tropical. Summer temperatures (Dec.–March) average about 75°F (25°C), and 65°F (18°C) in winter (June–Sept.). Annual rainfall is approximately 50" (1,200 mm), most of which falls in winter.

CONSTITUTION AND GOVERNMENT

An Administrator, appointed by the Governor-General and responsible to the Minister for Territories and Local Government, is the senior government representative in the Territory. The seat of administration is Kingston.

The Norfolk Island Act 1979 gives Norfolk Island responsible legislative and executive government to enable it to run its own affairs. Wide powers are exercised by the Norfolk Island Legislative Assembly of nine members, elected for a period of three years, and by an Executive Council. The Norfolk Island Act also provides for consultation with the Federal Government in respect of certain types of laws proposed by Norfolk Island's Legislative Assembly.

RECENT ELECTIONS

At the last elections, on 20 Oct. 2004, only non-partisans were elected.

CURRENT ADMINISTRATION

Administrator: Grant Tambling (since 2003).

Chief Minister: Geoffrey Robert Gardner (since 2001).

ECONOMY

The office of the Administrator is financed from Commonwealth expenditure which in 1999–2000 was $A560,000; local revenue for 1999–2000 totalled $A10,300,000; expenditure, $A10,400,000.

Currency. Australian notes and coins are the legal currency.

Banking and Finance. There are two banks, Westpac and the Commonwealth Bank of Australia.

COMMUNICATIONS

Roads. There are 100 km of roads (53 km paved), some 2,800 passenger cars and 200 commercial vehicles.

Civil Aviation. In 2003 there were scheduled flights to Auckland, Brisbane, Melbourne and Sydney.

Telecommunications. In 1999 there were 1,920 telephones.

Postal Services. There is one post office located in Burnt Pine.

SOCIAL INSTITUTIONS

Justice. The Island's Supreme Court sits as required and a Court of Petty Sessions exercises both civil and criminal jurisdiction. Appeals from decisions of the Norfolk Island Supreme Court are heard by the Federal Court of Australia and by the High Court of Australia.

Religion. 40% of the population are Anglicans.

Education. A school is run by the New South Wales Department of Education covering pre-school to Year 12. It had 320 pupils at 30 June 1999.

Health. In 1999 there were two doctors, one dentist, a pharmacist and a hospital with 24 beds. Visiting specialists attend the Island on a regular basis.

CULTURE

Broadcasting. In 1999 there were 1,500 television receivers and 1,600 radio receivers.

Press. There is one weekly with a circulation of 1,200.

Tourism. In 1998–99, 35,000 visitors travelled to Norfolk Island.

HEARD AND McDONALD ISLANDS

These islands, about 2,500 miles southwest of Fremantle, were transferred from British to Australian control from 26 Dec. 1947. Heard Island is about 43 km long and 21 km wide; Shag Island is about 8 km north of Heard. The total area is 412 sq. km (159 sq. miles). The McDonald Islands are 42 km to the west of Heard. Heard is an active stratovolcano that has erupted eight times since 1910, most recently in 1993. In 1985–88 a major research programme was set up by the Australian National Antarctic Research Expeditions to investigate the wildlife as part of international studies of the Southern Ocean ecosystem. Subsequent expeditions followed from June 1990 through to 1992.

TERRITORY OF ASHMORE AND CARTIER ISLANDS

By Imperial Order in Council of 23 July 1931, Ashmore Islands (known as Middle, East and West Islands) and Cartier Island, situated in the Indian Ocean, some 320 km off the northwest coast of Australia (area, 5 sq. km), were placed under the authority of the Commonwealth. Under the Ashmore and Cartier Islands Acceptance Act, 1933, the islands were accepted by the Commonwealth as the Territory of Ashmore and Cartier Islands. It was the intention that the Territory should be administered by the State of Western Australia but owing to administrative difficulties the Territory was deemed to form part of the Northern Territory of Australia (by amendment to the Act in 1938). On 16 Aug. 1983 Ashmore Reef was declared a National Nature Reserve. The islands are uninhabited but Indonesian fishing boats fish within the Territory and land to collect water in accordance with an agreement between the governments of Australia and Indonesia. It is believed that the islands and their waters may house considerable oil reserves.

TERRITORY OF CORAL SEA ISLANDS

The Coral Sea Islands, which became a Territory of the Commonwealth of Australia under the Coral Sea Islands Act 1969, comprises scattered reefs and islands over a sea area of about 1m. sq. km. The Territory is uninhabited apart from a meteorological station on Willis Island.

FURTHER READING

Australian Department of Arts, Sport, the Environment, Tourism and Territories. *Christmas Island: Annual Report.—Cocos (Keeling) Islands: Annual Report.—Norfolk Island: Annual Report.*

AUSTRIA

Republik Österreich

Capital: Vienna
Population projection, 2010: 8·09m.
GDP per capita, 2002: (PPP$) 29,220
HDI/world rank: 0·934/14

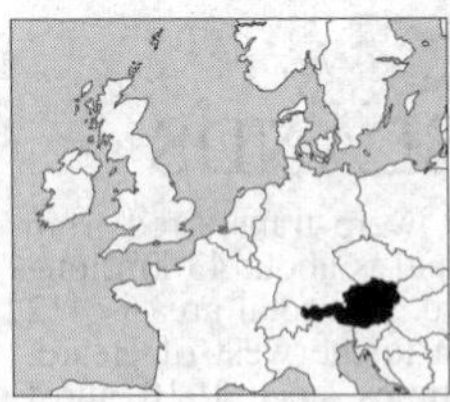

KEY HISTORICAL EVENTS

The margravate of Austria became a separate duchy in 1156. Vienna, the most important trading town on the Danube, received its town charter in 1198. In 1440 the rule of the Habsburgs was confirmed when Frederick III became Holy Roman Emperor. Austria was harried by the Ottoman Turks, under Sultan Süleyman the Magnificent. A truce was agreed after the Ottoman defeat at Vienna in 1529.

In 1740 Holy Roman Emperor Charles VI died without a male heir. By pragmatic sanction, his daughter Maria Theresa succeeded him as the first female Habsburg ruler. Her reforms doubled the size of the army and introduced public education and centralization. During the Seven Years' War (1756–63) Maria Theresa aimed to re-conquer Silesia, lost in the War of the Austrian Succession. However, the Austrians, bereft of allies, were defeated at Burkersdorf in July 1762. In 1772 Austria, Prussia and Russia carried out the first partition of Poland, with Austria gaining Galicia.

Napoléon defeated Austria in the Battle of Austerlitz in 1805, forcing Francis to surrender his title of Holy Roman Emperor. After Napoléon was exiled to Elba in 1814, the Prince von Metternich, the foreign minister, created the German confederation of 35 states and four free cities to succeed the Holy Roman Empire. An uprising in Vienna in 1848 forced the Habsburgs to flee the city. Revolution spread to Hungary but the Habsburgs refused to accept Hungary's independence and enlisted Russian aid to quell the uprising. Italian and Slavic revolts followed. In 1859, the Habsburgs were defeated in the Austro-Italian war and Italy was unified.

Austria's defeat against Prussia at the battle of Königgrätz stripped it of all powers over Germany. Emperor Francis Joseph I was forced to compromise with Hungary and negotiated the *Ausgleich* in 1867, giving Hungary its own constitution. The emperor was henceforth recognized as the Apostolic king of Hungary and emperor of Austria within the Austro-Hungarian monarchy (the Dual Monarchy).

In 1879 Austria entered the Dual Alliance with the German Reich in defence against Russian aggression. Italy joined in 1882, making a Triple Alliance. Austria tried to gain control over Serbia during the Balkan wars of 1912–13. In June 1914 the heir to the Habsburg throne, Archduke Franz Ferdinand, and his wife were assassinated in Sarajevo by a Bosnian nationalist. The refusal of Serbia to accept the blame led to an Austrian declaration of war on Serbia in July. Germany declared war on Russia and France in early August, beginning the First World War. Strikes, mutiny in the army and navy and food shortages were among the factors that defeated Austro-Hungarian forces in the spring and summer of 1918. About 1·2m. soldiers from Austria-Hungary died during the war.

In 1918 the Poles declared themselves an independent unified state; the Czechs founded an independent republic in Prague and the Southern Slavs merged with Serbia. An armistice was agreed on 3 Nov., the Hungarian government announced its separation from Austria and Austria was declared a republic. The Treaty of Saint Germain in 1919 stipulated that the German–Austrian lands were not permitted union (*Anschluss*) with Germany without the consent of the League of Nations. Austria was declared a federal state on 1 Oct. 1920.

The economic crises of the 1920s led to the rise of a nationalist movement influenced by German National Socialism (Nazism). When Engelbert Dollfuss of the conservative Christian Socialists became chancellor in 1932, he faced Nazi and Marxist opposition. After parliament was dissolved, the Social Democrats raised arms and started a civil war, won by Dollfuss with the backing of the *Heimwehr* (home defence forces). On 25 July 1934 a pro-Nazi gang murdered Dollfuss. Hitler demanded top positions for Nazi sympathizers in the Austrian cabinet. Chancellor Kurt Schuschnigg announced a plebiscite to decide upon Anschluss but on 12 March

1938 German forces marched into Austria, establishing a Nazi government led by Arthur Seyss-Inquart. On 13 April 1945 Vienna was liberated by Soviet troops. Two weeks later, Dr Karl Renner proclaimed a provisional government, recognized officially at the Potsdam conference. The forces of the Soviet Union, Britain, France and the USA occupied Austria until 1955, when full sovereignty was restored.

The first all-socialist cabinet was formed in 1970 under Chancellor Bruno Kreisky, who established economic stability and prosperity throughout the 1970s. In 1995 Austria joined the EU. In Jan. 2000 the Freedom Party, headed by the far-right leader Jörg Haider, joined the government. Although Haider, described as a 'dangerous extremist' by EU leaders, did not take a post in the government, sanctions against Austria were imposed by the European Union from Feb.–Sept. 2000. The popularity of the Freedom Party fell sharply in subsequent elections.

TERRITORY AND POPULATION

Austria is bounded in the north by Germany and the Czech Republic, east by Slovakia and Hungary, south by Slovenia and Italy, and west by Switzerland and Liechtenstein. It has an area of 83,871 sq. km (32,383 sq. miles). Population (2001 census) 8,065,166; density, 96·2 per sq. km. Previous population censuses: (1923) 6·53m., (1934) 6·76m., (1951) 6·93m., (1971) 7·49m., (1981) 7·56m., (1991) 7·80m. In 2001, 67·4% of the population lived in urban areas.

In 1991, 93·4% of residents were of Austrian nationality and 94% were German-speaking, with linguistic minorities of Slovenes (29,000), Croats (60,000), Hungarians (33,000) and Czechs (19,000). Between 1986 and 1996 the number of foreigners living in Austria more than doubled, from just over 4% to just over 9%.

The UN gives a projected population for 2010 of 8·09m.

The areas, populations and capitals of the nine federal states:

Federal States	*Area (sq. km)*	*Population at censuses (1991)*	*(2001)*	*State capitals*
Vienna (Wien)	415	1,539,848	1,562,676	Vienna
Lower Austria (Niederösterreich)	19,178	1,473,813	1,549,640	St Pölten
Burgenland	3,965	270,880	278,600	Eisenstadt
Upper Austria (Oberösterreich)	11,980	1,333,480	1,382,017	Linz
Salzburg	7,154	482,365	518,580	Salzburg
Styria (Steiermark)	16,392	1,184,720	1,185,911	Graz
Carinthia (Kärnten)	9,536	547,798	561,114	Klagenfurt
Tyrol	12,648	631,410	675,063	Innsbruck
Vorarlberg	2,601	331,472	351,565	Bregenz

The populations of the principal towns at the census of 2001 (and 1991): Vienna, 1,550,123 (1,539,848); Graz, 226,244 (237,810); Linz, 183,504 (203,044); Salzburg, 142,662 (143,978); Innsbruck, 113,392 (118,112); Klagenfurt, 90,141 (89,415); Villach, 57,497 (54,640); Wels, 56,478 (52,594); St Pölten, 49,121 (50,026).

The official language is German. For orthographical changes agreed in 1996 *see* GERMANY: Territory and Population.

SOCIAL STATISTICS

Statistics, 2001: live births, 75,458 (rate of 9·3 per 1,000 population); deaths, 74,767 (rate of 9·2 per 1,000 population); infant deaths, 365; stillborn, 471; marriages, 34,213; divorces, 20,582. In 2001 there were 1,489 suicides (rate of 18·3 per 100,000 population), of which 1,081 males and 408 females. Average annual population growth rate, 1992–2002, 0·3%. Life expectancy at birth, 2001, 81·3 years for women and 75·1 years for men. In 2001 the most popular age range for marrying was 25–29 for both males and females. Infant mortality, 2001, was 4·8 per 1,000 live births; fertility rate, 2001, 1·3 children per woman. In 2000 some 370,700 Austrians resided permanently abroad: 186,000 lived in Germany, 28,000 in Switzerland, 17,000 in South Africa, and 16,000 in both Australia and the USA. In 2002 Austria received 37,074 asylum applications, equivalent to 4·6 per 1,000 inhabitants (the highest ratio in Europe).

CLIMATE

The climate is temperate and from west to east in transition from marine to more continental. Depending to the elevation, the climate is also predominated by alpine influence. Winters are cold with snowfall. In the eastern parts summers are warm and dry.

Vienna, Jan. 0·0°C, July 20·2°C. Annual rainfall 624 mm. Graz, Jan. –1·0°C, July 19·4°C. Annual rainfall 825 mm. Innsbruck, Jan. –1·7°C, July 18·1°C. Annual rainfall 885 mm. Salzburg, Jan. –0·9°C, July 18·6°C. Annual rainfall 1,174 mm.

CONSTITUTION AND GOVERNMENT

The Constitution of 1 Oct. 1920 was restored on 27 April 1945. Austria is a democratic federal republic comprising nine states *(Länder)*, with a federal *President (Bundespräsident)* directly elected for not more than two successive six-year terms, and a bicameral National Assembly which comprises a National Council and a Federal Council.

The National Council *(Nationalrat)* comprises 183 members directly elected for a four-year term by proportional representation in a three-tier system by which seats are allocated at the level of 43 regional and nine state constituencies, and one federal constituency. Any party gaining 4% of votes cast nationally is represented in the National Council.

The Federal Council *(Bundesrat)* has 62 members appointed by the nine states for the duration of the individual State Assemblies' terms; the number of deputies for each state is proportional to that state's population. In Oct. 2004 the ÖVP held 27 of the 62 seats, the SPÖ 26, the FPÖ 5 and the Greens 4.

The head of government is a *Federal Chancellor*, who is appointed by the President (usually the head of the party winning the most seats in National Council elections). The *Vice-Chancellor*, the *Federal Ministers* and the *State Secretaries* are appointed by the President at the Chancellor's recommendation.

National Anthem. 'Land der Berge, Land am Strome' ('Land of mountains, land on the river'); words by Paula Preradovic; tune attributed to Mozart.

RECENT ELECTIONS

Elections were held on 24 Nov. 2002. The Austrian People's Party (ÖVP) won 79 seats with 42·3% of votes cast (52 with 26·9% in 1999); the Social Democratic Party (SPÖ), 69 with 36·9% (65 with 33·2%); the Freedom Party (FPÖ), 18 with 10·2% (52 with 26·9%); and the Greens, 17 with 9·0% (14 with 7·4%). Turn-out was 80·5%.

In the presidential election held on 25 April 2004 Heinz Fischer (SPÖ) won 52·4% of the vote against 47·6% for Minister for Foreign Affairs Benita Ferrero-Waldner (ÖVP). Turn-out was 70·8%.

European Parliament. Austria has 18 (21 in 1999) representatives. At the June 2004 elections turn-out was 41·8% (49·0% in 1999). The SPÖ won 7 seats with 33·5% of the votes cast (political affiliation in European Parliament: Party of European Socialists); the ÖVP, 6 with 32·7% (European People's Party–European Democrats); Liste Martin, 2 with 14·0% (non-attached); the Greens, 2 with 12·8% (Greens/ European Free Alliance); the FPÖ, 1 with 6·3% (non-attached).

CURRENT ADMINISTRATION

President: Dr Heinz Fischer; b. 1938 (SPÖ; took office on 8 July 2004).

Following the Nov. 1999 elections the ÖVP and the right-wing FPÖ agreed in Feb. 2000 to form a coalition government, with Dr Wolfgang Schüssel (ÖVP) as chancellor. In Sept. 2002 the coalition collapsed in the wake of a bitter power struggle within the FPÖ. Chancellor Schüssel called for new elections, held on 24 Nov 2002 and won by the ÖVP, which revived the coalition with the FPÖ. In March 2005 the government comprised:

Chancellor: Dr Wolfgang Schüssel; b. 1945 (ÖVP; sworn in 4 Feb. 2000).

Deputy-Chancellor and Minister for Transport, Innovation and Technology: Hubert Gorbach (FPÖ).

Minister for Foreign Affairs: Ursula Plassnik (ÖVP). *Defence:* Günther Platter (ÖVP). *Justice:* Karin Miklautsch (FPÖ). *Finance:* Karl-Heinz Grasser (ind.). *Economic Affairs and Labour:* Martin Bartenstein (ÖVP). *Interior:* Liese Prokop (ÖVP). *Agriculture, Forestry and Environment:* Josef Pröll (ÖVP). *Health Affairs and Women's Issues:* Maria Rauch-Kallat (ÖVP). *Education, Science and Culture:* Elisabeth Gehrer (ÖVP). *Social Security, Generations and Consumer Protection:* Ursula Haubner (FPÖ). *State Secretary in the Ministry for Finance:* Alfred Finz (ÖVP). *State Secretaries in the Federal Chancellery:* Franz Morak (ÖVP); Karl

Schweitzer (FPÖ). *State Secretary in the Ministry for Social Security and Generations:* Sigisbert Dolinschek (FPÖ). *State Secretaries in the Ministry for Transport, Innovation and Technology:* Helmut Kukacka (ÖVP); Eduard Mainoni (FPÖ).

Government Website: http://www.austria.gv.at

DEFENCE

The Federal President is C.-in-C. of the armed forces. Conscription is for a seven-month period, with liability for at least another 30 days' reservist refresher training spread over eight to ten years. Since 1992 the total 'on mobilization strength' of the forces has been reduced from approximately 200,000 to 110,000 troops. In 2002 approximately 1,000 personnel from so-called 'prepared units' were deployed in peace support operations in places such as Afghanistan, Bosnia, Cyprus, the Golan Heights and Syria.

Defence expenditure in 2003 totalled US$2,488m. (US$309 per capita), representing 1·0% of GDP.

Army. The army is structured in five brigades and nine provincial military commands. Two brigades are mechanized, the rest infantry brigades. The mechanized brigades are equipped with Leopard 2/A4 main battle tanks. One of three infantry brigades is earmarked for airborne operations, the second is equipped with Pandur wheeled armoured personnel carriers and the third infantry brigade is specialized in mountain operations. The artillery units are brigade-directed. M-109 armoured self-propelled guns equip the artillery battalions. In addition to these standing units, some 20 infantry battalions under the direction of the provincial military commands are available on mobilization. Active personnel, 2002, 34,600 (to be 26,100) including 17,200 conscripts. Women started to serve in the armed forces on 1 April 1998.

Air Force. The Air Force Command comprises three aviation and three air-defence regiments with about 6,500 personnel, more than 150 aircraft and a number of fixed- and mobile radar stations. Some 23 Draken interceptors equip a surveillance wing responsible for the defence of the Austrian air space and a fighter-bomber wing operates SAAB 105s. Helicopters including the S-70 Black Hawk equip six squadrons for transport/support, communication, observation, and search and rescue duties. Fixed-wing aircraft including PC-6s, PC-7s, Skyvans and in the near future C-130 Hercules are operated as trainers and for transport. The procurement of a fourth generation fighter is also planned for the near future.

INTERNATIONAL RELATIONS

Austria is a member of the UN, WTO, BIS, NATO Partnership for Peace, OECD, EU, Council of Europe, OSCE, CERN, CEI, Danube Commission, Inter-American Development Bank, Asian Development Bank, IOM and the Antarctic Treaty. Austria is a signatory to the Schengen Accord abolishing border controls between Austria, Belgium, Denmark, Finland, France, Germany, Greece, Iceland, Italy, Luxembourg, Netherlands, Norway, Portugal, Spain and Sweden.

ECONOMY

Trade and services account for about two-thirds of value added, and the industrial sector about one-third.

According to the anti-corruption organization *Transparency International*, Austria ranked equal 13th in the world in a 2004 survey of the countries with the least corruption in business and government. It received 8·4 out of 10 in the annual index.

Overview. The most important sector in the economy is the service sector, accounting for 62% of economic output. Tourism plays an important role. EU membership has led to a more liberal market and many companies have been taken over by foreign, particularly German, companies. Although the goal of a balanced budget was set for the year 2002, this was already achieved in 2001 (0·3% of GDP) and maintained in 2002 (–0·1% of GDP), despite a weaker cyclical position. There was an estimated deficit of 1·1% of GDP in 2003. The planned tax reform for 2004–05 comprised a tax relief in favour of business and private households by 1·3% of GDP (net-effect), changes to simplify the tax structure and strengthened ecological elements. A major goal of the government is to reduce Austria's tax burden further to 40% of GDP by 2010. The Austrian public pension system, absorbing around 14·5% of GDP, has been one of the most extensive in Europe. A pension reform bill passed Parliament in the spring of 2003. This will reduce the total cost of the system and therefore makes a fundamental contribution to long-term financial sustainability.

Currency. On 1 Jan. 1999 the euro (EUR) became the legal currency in Austria; irrevocable conversion rate 13·7603 schillings to one euro. The euro, which consists of 100 cents, has been in circulation since 1 Jan. 2002. There are seven euro notes in different colours and sizes denominated in 500, 200, 100, 50, 20, 10 and 5 euros, and eight coins denominated in 2 and 1 euros, then 50, 20, 10, 5, 2 and 1 cents. On the introduction of the euro there was a 'dual circulation' period before the schilling ceased to be legal tender on 28 Feb. 2002.

Inflation in Austria was 1·8% in 2002, 1·3% in 2003 and 2·1% in 2004. Foreign exchange reserves were US$12,020m. in June 2002 and gold reserves were 10·21m. troy oz. Total money supply was €9,258m. in June 2002.

Budget. The federal budget for calendar years provided revenue and expenditure as follows (in €1m.):

	2000	*2001*	*2002*	*2003*[1]
Revenue	58,247	60,403	61,803	61,459
Expenditure	55,393	58,988	59,413	57,518

[1]Provisional.

VAT is 20% (reduced rates, 12% and 6%).

Performance. Real GDP growth was 0·8% in 2001, 1·4% in 2002 and 0·7% in 2003. Total GDP was US$251·5bn. in 2003.

Banking and Finance. The Oesterreichische Nationalbank, central bank of Austria, opened on 1 Jan. 1923 but was taken over by the German Reichsbank on 17 March 1938. It was re-established on 3 July 1945. Its *Governor* is Klaus Liebscher. At 31 Dec. 2002 it had total reserves of US$13·2bn.

In the first two quarters of 2003, banking and insurance accounted for 5·8% of gross domestic product at current prices. In 2002 an average of 110,356 individuals were engaged in banking and insurance (76,475 in banking, 28,164 in insurance and 5,717 in banking and insurance), representing 3·5% of Austria's wage and salary earners.

By June 2003, 906 credit institutions and branch offices from banks located in the European Union were active in Austria. 40 credit institutions from countries outside the EU have established representative offices. The leading banks with total assets in 2002 (in €1bn) were: Bank Austria Group of Companies, 147,969; Erste Bank, 95,564; Bank für Arbeit und Wirtschaft AG–PSK, 48,842; and Raiffeisenzentralbank Österreich AG, 46,405.

There is a stock exchange in Vienna (VEX). It is one of the oldest in Europe and one of the smallest.

ENERGY AND NATURAL RESOURCES

Environment. Austria's carbon dioxide emissions from the consumption and flaring of fossil fuels were the equivalent of 8·7 tonnes per capita in 2002. An *Environmental Sustainability Index* compiled for the World Economic Forum meeting in Feb. 2002 ranked Austria seventh in the world, with 64·2%. The index measured the ability of countries to maintain favourable environmental conditions and examined various factors including pollution levels and the use or abuse of natural resources.

Austria is one of the world leaders in recycling. In 1996, 48% of all household waste was recycled.

Electricity. The Austrian electricity market was fully liberalized on 1 Oct. 2001. Installed capacity was 18·2m. kW in 2000. Production in 2000 was 69·48bn. kWh. Consumption per capita, 2000: 8,408 kWh.

Oil and Gas. The commercial production of petroleum began in the early 1930s. Production of crude oil, 2001: 1,012,132 tonnes. Crude oil reserves, 2002, were some 86m. bbls.

The Austrian gas market was fully liberalized on 1 Oct. 2002. Production of natural gas, 2001: 1,731m. cu. metres. Natural gas reserves in 2002 amounted to 24bn. cu. metres.

Minerals. The most important minerals are limestone and marble (2001 production, 23,799,657 tonnes), dolomite (2001 production, 6,171,999 tonnes), quartz and arenaceous quartz, lignite, basalt, clay and kaolin.

Agriculture. In 1998, 149,600 persons were employed in agriculture as their main occupation. In 1998 the total cultivated area amounted to 3,422,449 ha. There were 1·40m. ha of arable land in 2001 and 71,000 ha of permanent crops. There were 252,110 farms in 1999. Figures compiled by the Soil Association, a British organization, show that in 1999 Austria set aside 345,000 ha (10·1% of its agricultural land—one of the highest proportions in the world) for the growth of organic crops. Agriculture accounted for 1·4% of GDP, 4·9% of exports and 7·0% of imports in 1999.

The chief products in 2001 (area in 1,000 ha; yield in tonnes) were as follows: barley (217·5; 1,012,407); oats (31·4; 128,253); potatoes (23·1; 694,602); rye (51·2; 213,530); sugarbeets (44·7; 2,773,478); wheat (287·8; 1,508,283). Other important agricultural products include apples (410,000 tonnes in 2001) and pears (109,000 tonnes in 2001). Wine production in 2000–01 totalled 2,338,410 hectolitres.

Livestock (2001): cattle, 2,118,454; pigs, 3,440,405; sheep, 320,467; goats, 59,452; horses, 81,600 (1999); poultry, 12,571,528.

Forestry. Forested area in 2000, 3·9m. ha (47% of the land area), around three-quarters of which was coniferous. Felled timber, in 1,000 cu. metres: 1998, 14,033·5; 1999, 14,083·9; 2000, 13,276·3; 2001, 13,466·5.

Fisheries. The total catch in 2001 amounted to 362 tonnes, exclusively from inland waters.

INDUSTRY

The leading companies by market capitalization in Austria in May 2004 were: Erste Bank (US$9·3bn.), Bank Austria Creditanstalt (US$8·4bn.) and Telekom Austria (US$7·0bn.).

Production (in 1,000 tonnes): pig iron (2002), 4,600; paper and paperboard (2000), 4,386; cement (2001), 3,863; distillate fuel oil (2000), 3,724; petrol (2000), 1,819; residual fuel oil (2000), 1,002; sugar (2000), 447; sawnwood (2000), 10·39m. cu. metres; soft drinks (2001), 1,524·3m. litres; beer (2001), 852·8m. litres.

Labour. Austria has the second highest per capita income among the euro-12 countries and one of the lowest unemployment rates (4·5% in Dec. 2004). During 2000 Austria experienced its biggest fall in joblessness since the mid 1950s. Youth unemployment, at 6·0% in 2001, was also one of the lowest in the world.

In 2001 there were an average of 3,148,177 employed persons, with an average of 613,909 persons working in manufacturing; 498,307 in wholesale and retail trade, and repair of motor vehicles, motorcycles and personal and household goods; 469,707 in public administration and defence; 266,928 in real estate, renting and business activities; 247,516 in construction; and 224,178 in transport, storage and communication. In 2001 there were an average of 29,670 job vacancies.

The number of foreigners who may be employed in Austria is limited to 9% of the potential workforce. There were four strikes in 2002, with 6,305 participants (none in 2001). There were no strikes either in 1996, 1998 or 1999. Between 1993 and 2002 strikes cost Austria an average of just one day per 1,000 employees a year (the lowest in the European Union), compared to the EU average of 64 per 1,000.

Austria has one of the lowest average retirement ages but reforms passed in 1997 now make it less attractive to retire before 60. Only 15% of men and 6% of women in the 60–65 age range work, although the legal retirement ages are 60 for women and 65 for men.

Trade Unions. The 14 unions in the Austrian Trade Union Confederation (Österreichischer Gewerkschaftsbund, ÖGB) had 1,465,000 members in Dec. 1999.

INTERNATIONAL TRADE

Imports and Exports. Trade in US$1m.:

	1998	*1999*	*2000*	*2001*	*2002*
Imports f.o.b.	66,983	68,051	67,421	68,169	70,096
Exports f.o.b.	63,299	64,422	64,684	66,900	73,667

Main export markets (% of total exports) in 2001: Germany, 32·5%; Italy, 8·5%; USA, 5·3%; Switzerland, 5·2%. Main import suppliers: Germany, 40·5%; Italy, 7·2%; USA, 5·3%; France, 4·1%. Other EU-member countries accounted for 62·6% of exports and 68·4% of imports.

In 1999 principal exports were: machinery and transport equipment, 40·5%; manufactured goods, 23·6%; chemicals and related products, 7·1%. Principal imports were: machinery and transport equipment, 41·2%; manufactured goods, 17·6%; chemicals and related products, 10·0%.

Trade Fairs. Austria's largest trade fairs are the Graz International Autumn Fair (Oct.), with 1,159 exhibitors and 204,947 visitors in 1999; the Graz International Spring Fair (May), with 1,139 exhibitors and 194,607 visitors in 1999; and Aufgetischt—International Fair for the Food and Catering Trade, in Vienna (Feb.), with 925 exhibitors and 125,500 visitors in 1999. Vienna ranked as the fourth most popular convention city behind Paris, London and Brussels in 2002 according to the Union des Associations Internationales (UAI).

COMMUNICATIONS

Roads. In 2002 the road network totalled 200,000 km (Autobahn, 1,645 km; highways, 10,334 km; secondary roads, 23,657 km). On 31 Dec. 2001 motor vehicles registered numbered 5,684,244, including 4,182,027 passenger cars, 331,394 trucks, 9,902 buses and 641,434 motorcycles. There were 956 fatalities in road accidents in 2002.

Rail. The Austrian Federal Railways (ÖBB) has been restructured and was split up into ten new companies, which became operational on 1 Jan. 2005. Length of route in 2001, 5,549 km, of which 3,313 km were electrified. There are also a number of private railways with a total length of 589 km. In 2001, 183·3m. passengers and 85·8m. tonnes of freight were carried by Federal Railways. There is a metro and tramway in Vienna, and tramways in Gmunden, Graz, Innsbruck and Linz.

Civil Aviation. The national airline is Austrian Airlines, which is 51·9% state-owned. There are international airports at Vienna (Schwechat), Linz, Salzburg, Graz, Klagenfurt and Innsbruck. In 2003 services were provided by 62 other airlines. In 2001, 260,256 commercial aircraft and 15,259,661 passengers arrived and departed (11·75m. at Vienna); 115,135 tonnes of freight and 9,521 tonnes of mail were handled. In 2001 Vienna handled 11,752,175 passengers and 110,976 tonnes of freight. Austrian Airlines carried 3,608,795 passengers in 2001.

Shipping. The Danube is an important waterway. Goods traffic (in 1,000 tonnes): 10,236 in 1998; 9,987 in 1999; 10,980 in 2000; 11,634 in 2001 (including the Rhine-Main-Danube Canal). The merchant shipping fleet totalled 30,000 GRT in 2002.

Telecommunications. Österreichische Industrie Holding AG, the Austrian investment and privatization agency, holds a 47·2% stake in Telekom Austria with Telecom Italia having a 14·8% stake. There were 10,588,000 telephone subscribers in 2002 (1,297·7 per 1,000 inhabitants). Mobile phone subscribers numbered 6,415,000 in 2002 and there were 3,013,000 PCs in use (369·3 per 1,000 persons). The number of Internet users in June 2002 was approximately 3·7m.

Postal Services. The Postal Savings Bank was privatized in 2000. In 2002 there were 1,669 post offices and 120 post-agencies, the so-called 'Post-Partner'. A total of 4,541m. postal items were handled in 2000.

SOCIAL INSTITUTIONS

Justice. The Supreme Court of Justice *(Oberster Gerichtshof)* in Vienna is the highest court in civil and criminal cases. In addition, in 2002 there were four Courts of Appeal *(Oberlandesgerichte)*, 21 High Courts *(Landesgerichte)* and 166 District Courts *(Bezirksgerichte)*. There is also a Supreme Constitutional Court

(Verfassungsgerichtshof) and a Supreme Administrative Court *(Verwaltungsgerichtshof)*, both seated in Vienna. In 2001 a total of 522,710 criminal offences were reported to the police and 38,763 people were convicted of offences. The population in penal institutions in Nov. 2003 was 8,114 (100 per 100,000 of national population).

Religion. In 2001 there were 5,920,000 Roman Catholics (73·6%), 376,000 Evangelical Lutherans (4·7%), 339,000 Muslims (4·2%), 963,000 without religious allegiance (12·0%) and 439,000 others (5·5%). The Roman Catholic Church has two archbishoprics and seven bishoprics. In March 2004 there were two cardinals.

Education. In 2001–02 there were 4,923 general compulsory schools (including special education) with 75,335 teachers and 686,276 pupils. Secondary schools totalled 1,679 in 2000–01 with 523,533 pupils.

In 2001–02 there were also 123 commercial academies with 42,460 pupils and 5,527 teachers, and 76 higher schools of economic professions (secondary level) with 23,511 pupils; and 119 schools of technical and industrial training with 11,774 pupils, and 106 agricultural technical schools with 10,283 pupils. 116 professional schools had 13,095 pupils in 2001–02.

The dominant institutions of higher education are the 13 universities and six colleges of arts, which are publicly financed. In 1994 Higher Technical Study Centres (*Fachhochschul-Studiengänge*, FHS) were established, which are private, but government-dependent, institutions. In the winter term 2000–01 there were 234,937 students enrolled at the universities, 9,224 at the colleges of arts and 11,743 at 67 FHS. About 15,000 teachers (full-time equivalent) provide tertiary-level education.

In 2000–01 expenditure on education came to 5·9% of GNP and 15·1% of total government spending. The adult literacy rate in 2001 was at least 99%.

Health. In 2001 there were 35,400 doctors, 3,879 dentists, 39,332 nurses (2000) and 1,579 midwives. In 2000 there were 312 hospitals and 72,008 hospital beds. In 2002 Austria spent 7·7% of its GDP on health.

Welfare. Maternity/paternity leave is for 18 months. A new parenting allowance was introduced on 1 Jan 2002, replacing the maternity/paternity allowance. The new system is based on family benefit financed from the Family Fund instead of the insurance principle. The basic allowance is €436 per month for a maximum of three years. In June 2003 a reform of the pensions system was approved involving the reduction of pension benefits by 10%, the raising of the retirement age to 65 by increasing the workers' contribution period from 40 to 45 years and the abolition of early retirement by 2017.

CULTURE

World Heritage Sites. There are seven sites under Austrian jurisdiction. They are (with year entered on list): the historic centre of the city of Salzburg (1996); the Palace and gardens of Schönbrunn (1996); Hallstatt-Dachstein Salzkammergut cultural landscape (1997); Semmering Railway (1998); the historic centre of the city of Graz (1999); the Wachau cultural landscape (2000); and the historic centre of the city of Vienna (2001).

Austria also shares the Cultural Landscape of Fertö/Neusiedlersee site (2001) with Hungary.

Broadcasting. The 'Österreichische Rundfunk' (Austrian Broadcasting Corporation) is state-controlled. It transmits four national and nine regional radio programmes. An additional programme in English and French can be received all over the country; there is also a 24-hour foreign service (short wave). There were 2·81m. radio licenses and 2·78m. television licenses (colour by PAL) issued in 2001. There were also 1,035,703 cable TV subscribers in 2001.

Cinema. In 2001 there were 579 fixed cinemas, one drive-in cinema and 23 mobile units. Audience numbers totalled 18,832,700.

Press. There were 16 daily newspapers (seven of them in Vienna), 197 non-daily newspapers and 2,788 other periodicals in 2001. The most popular newspaper is the mass-market tabloid *Kronen-Zeitung*, which is read on a daily basis by 42% of the population. In 2001 a total of 20,192 books were published, including 7,650 new titles.

Tourism. Tourism is an important industry. In 2000–01, 17,372 hotels and boarding houses had a total of 622,746 beds available. In 2000, 17,982,000 foreigners visited Austria and tourist receipts were US$11·44bn. Tourist arrivals reached 27·3m. in 2002. Tyrol is the most popular province for visits, recording more than a third of all overnight stays in 1999. Of 115,110,685 overnight stays in tourist accommodation in 2001, 31,441,815 were by Austrians and 52,786,420 by Germans.

Festivals. The main festivals are Salzburger Festspiele, held every July–Aug. (231,432 visitors in 2002), and Bregenzer Festspiele, also held in July–Aug. (197,090 visitors in 2002). The Haydn Days in Eisenstadt, held every Sept., is also considered to be one of the leading annual festivals.

Libraries. In 1997 there were 5,642,000 library users and 26,123,000 volumes in scientific and special libraries, and 1,149,300 users and 11,252,800 volumes in public libraries.

Theatre and Opera. The attendance at federal theatres was 1,243,100 in 1999–2000.

Museums and Galleries. In 2000 there were 23,848,871 visitors to museums, exhibitions and similar attractions (10,791,674 in Vienna).

DIPLOMATIC REPRESENTATIVES

Of Austria in the United Kingdom (18 Belgrave Mews West, London, SW1X 8HU)
Ambassador: Dr Alexander Christiani.

Of the United Kingdom in Austria (Jaurèsgasse 12, 1030 Vienna)
Ambassador: John M. Macgregor, CVO.

Of Austria in the USA (3524 International Court, NW, Washington, D.C., 20008)
Ambassador: Eva Nowotny.

Of the USA in Austria (Boltzmanngasse 16, A-1091 Vienna)
Ambassador: Lyons Brown, Jr.

Of Austria to the United Nations
Ambassador: Dr Gerhard Pfanzelter.

FURTHER READING

Austrian Central Statistical Office. *Main publications: Statistisches Jahrbuch für die Republik Österreich.* New Series from 1950. Annual.—*Statistische Nachrichten.* Monthly.—*Beiträge zur österreichischen Statistik.*—*Statistik in Österreich 1918–1938.* [Bibliography] 1985.—*Veröffentlichungen des Österreichischen Statistischen Zentralamtes 1945–1985.* [Bibliography], 1990.—*Republik Österreich, 1945–1995.*

Brook-Shepherd, G., *The Austrians: a Thousand-Year Odyssey.* London, 1997
Peniston-Bird, C. M., *Vienna.* [Bibliography] ABC-Clio, Oxford and Santa Barbara (CA), 1997
Pick, Hella, *Guilty Victim: Austria from the Holocaust to Haider.* I. B. Tauris, London, 2000
Sully, M. A., *A Contemporary History of Austria.* London, 1990
Wolfram, H. (ed.) *Österreichische Geschichte.* 10 vols. Vienna, 1994

National library: Österreichische Nationalbibliothek, Josefsplatz, 1015 Vienna.
National statistical office: Austrian Central Statistical Office, POB 9000, A-1033 Vienna.
Website: http://www.statistik.at

AZERBAIJAN

Azarbaijchan Respublikasy

Capital: Baku
Population projection, 2010: 8·98m.
GDP per capita, 2002: (PPP$) 3,210
HDI/world rank: 0·746/91

KEY HISTORICAL EVENTS

In 1920 Azerbaijan was proclaimed a Soviet Socialist Republic. From 1922, with Georgia and Armenia, it formed the Transcaucasian Soviet Federal Socialist Republic. Conflict with Armenia over the enclave of Nagorno-Karabakh escalated in 1988, leading to violent expulsions of Armenians in Azerbaijan and Azeris in Armenia. In 'Black January' 1990 Soviet tanks moved in to react to rioting in Baku, and over 100 civilians were killed. War broke out between the two countries in 1992, with a ceasefire agreed in 1994. The dispute over territory remains unsettled, although negotiations in Florida in 2001 promised a peaceful solution. In 1990 it adopted a declaration of republican sovereignty and on 18 Aug. 1991 the Supreme Soviet of Azerbaijan declared independence. Under the presidency of Heydär Äliyev, elected in Oct. 1993, parliament ratified association with the CIS on 20 Sept. 1993. A treaty of friendship and co-operation was signed with Russia on 3 July 1997 and Äliyev was re-elected in Oct. 1998, although the administration of the election was criticized by international observers.

TERRITORY AND POPULATION

Azerbaijan is bounded in the west by Armenia, in the north by Georgia and the Russian Federation (Dagestan), in the east by the Caspian sea and in the south by Turkey and Iran. Its area is 86,600 sq. km (33,430 sq. miles), and it includes the Nakhichevan Autonomous Republic and the largely Armenian-inhabited Nagorno-Karabakh.

The population at the 1999 census was 7,953,000 (4,119,000 females); density, approximately 92 per sq. km. Estimate, 1 Jan. 2004, 8,265,700. At 1 Jan. 2004, 51·5% of the population lived in urban areas. There are 69 towns (one in each region), nine of which have over 50,000 people. The population breaks down into 82·7% Azerbaijanis, 5·6% Armenians, 5·6% Russians and 2·4% Lezgis (1999 census).

The UN gives a projected population for 2010 of 8·98m.

Chief cities: Baku (at 1 Jan. 2004, 1,839,800), Gandja (303,100) and Sumgait (290,700).

The official language is Azeri. On 1 Aug. 2001 Azerbaijan abolished the use of the Cyrillic alphabet and switched to using Latin script.

SOCIAL STATISTICS

In 2003: births, 113,467; deaths, 49,001; marriages, 56,091; divorces, 6,671. Rates, 2003 (per 1,000 population): births, 14·0; deaths, 6·0; infant mortality (2001, per 1,000 live births), 74. Life expectancy in 2003: 75·1 years for females and 69·5 years for males. Annual population growth rate, 1990–2003, 0·8%; fertility rate, 2003, 2·0 children per woman.

CLIMATE

The climate is almost tropical in summer and the winters slightly warmer than in regions north of the Caucasus. Cold spells do occur, however, both on the high mountains and in the enclosed valleys. There are nine climatic zones. Baku, Jan. –6°C, July 25°C. Annual rainfall 318 mm.

CONSTITUTION AND GOVERNMENT

Parliament is the 125-member *Melli-Majlis.* 100 seats are elected from single-member districts, and 25 distributed proportionally among political parties. For the majority seats there is a minimum 50% turn-out requirement. There is an 8% threshold. A constitutional referendum and parliamentary elections were held on 12

Nov. 1995. Turn-out for the referendum was 86%. The new Constitution was approved by 91·9% of votes cast. As a result of a referendum held on 24 Aug. 2002 on a number of changes to the constitution, all 125 members will be elected from single-member districts in the next parliament. The validity of the outcome of the referendum was questioned by international observers.

National Anthem. 'Azerbaijan! Azerbaijan!'; words by A. Javad, tune by U. Hajibeyov.

RECENT ELECTIONS

At elections on 15 Oct. 2003 İlham Äliyev of the New Azerbaijan Party (YAP) was elected president with 79·5% of votes cast. Isa Qämbär of the Equality Party won 12·1%, Lalä Şövket Hacıyev of National Unity won 3·3% and Ehtibar Mämmädov of the Azerbaijan National Independence Party (AMIP) won 2·7%. There were four other candidates who all received less than 1% of the vote.

At the parliamentary elections held on 5 Nov. 2000 and 7 Jan. 2001 the YAP gained 75 seats with 62·3% of votes cast; Popular Front Party gained 6 seats with 11·0%; Civil Solidarity Party, 3 seats with 6·4%; the Communist Party of Azerbaijan, 2 seats with 6·3%; Equality Party, 2 seats with 4·9%; AMIP, 2 seats with 3·9%. Five other parties took one seat each. 29 non-partisans were also elected. Turn-out was 68%.

CURRENT ADMINISTRATION

President: İlham Äliyev; b. 1961 (YAP; sworn in 31 Oct. 2003).

In March 2005 the government comprised:

Prime Minister: Artur Rasizade; b. 1935 (YAP; in office since 6 Aug. 2003, until 4 Nov. as acting prime minister).

First Deputy Prime Minister: Abbas Abbasov, Yagub Eyyubov. *Deputy Prime Ministers:* Elchin Efendiyev, Ali Hasanov, Abid Sharifov.

Minister of Foreign Affairs: Elmar Mamedyarov. *Interior:* Ramil Usubov. *Culture:* Polad Byul-Byul. *Education:* Misir Mardanov. *National Security:* Eldar Mahmudov. *Defence:* Lt.-Gen. Safar Abiyev. *Communications and Information Technologies:* Ali Abbasov. *Agriculture and Food:* Ismat Abbasov. *Justice:* Fikret Mamedov. *Health:* Ali Insanov. *Finance:* Avaz Alekperov. *Labour and Social Protection:* Ali Nagiyev. *Youth and Sport:* Abulfaz Karaev. *Economic Development:* Farhad Aliyev. *Ecology and Natural Resources:* Huseyngulu Bagirov. *Fuel and Energy Development:* Macid Karimov. *Taxation:* Fazil Mamedov. *Transport:* Ziya Mammadov.

Chairman of the National Assembly (Melli-Majlis): Murtuz Aleskerov.

Office of the President: http://www.president.az

DEFENCE

Conscription is for 17 months. Defence expenditure in 2003 totalled US$950m. (US$115 per capita), representing 3·2% of GDP.

Army. Personnel, 2002, 62,000. In addition there is a reserve force of 300,000 Azerbaijanis who have received some kind of military service experience within the last 15 years. There is also a paramilitary Ministry of the Interior militia of about 10,000 and a border guard of approximately 5,000.

Navy. The flotilla is based at Baku on the Caspian Sea and numbered about 2,200 in 2002 including six patrol craft.

Air Force. How many ex-Soviet aircraft are usable is not known but there are 48 combat aircraft and 15 armed helicopters. Personnel, 7,900 in 2002.

INTERNATIONAL RELATIONS

Azerbaijan is a member of the UN, the NATO Partnership for Peace, Council of Europe, OSCE, CIS, IMO, the World Bank, IMF, EBRD, BSEC, ECO, IOM, OIC, Islamic Development Bank and OEC. There is a dispute with Armenia over the status of the chiefly Armenian-populated Azerbaijani enclave of Nagorno-Karabakh. A ceasefire was negotiated from 1994 with 20% of Azerbaijan's land in Armenian hands and with 1m. Azeri refugees and displaced persons.

ECONOMY

In 2003 agriculture accounted for 13·1% of GDP, industry 37·8% and services 49·1%.

Currency. The *manta* (AZM) of 100 *gyapiks* replaced the rouble in Jan. 1994. Inflation was 2·8% in 2002 and 2·2% in 2003. Foreign exchange reserves were US$763m. in June 2002 and total money supply was 1,729·57bn. manats.

Budget. Government revenue and expenditure (in 1m. manats):

	2000	*2001*	*2002*	*2003*
Revenue	3,573,200	3,924,000	4,551,200	6,131,900
Expenditure	3,819,800	4,037,500	4,658,800	6,173,000

VAT accounted for 2,048,600m. manats of the 2003 budget revenue and profits tax accounted for 891,500m. manats. Of the 2003 expenditure, education accounted for 1,170,000m. manats, social security and welfare 1,070,000m. manats, law enforcement 603,400m. manats, state administration bodies 289,500m. manats and health 276,600m. manats.

Performance. Total GDP was US$7·1bn. in 2003. Azerbaijan has one of the fastest growing economies in the world. Real GDP growth was 11·1% in 2000, 9·9% in 2001, 10·6% in 2002 and 11·2% in 2003. This was largely thanks to foreign investment into the country and the oil boom.

Banking and Finance. The central bank and bank of issue is the National Bank (*Chairman*, Dr Elman Rustamov). In 2003 there were two state-owned banks (International Bank of Azerbaijan and the United Joint Stock Bank). In 2003 there were 46 privately-owned commercial banks of varying size.

ENERGY AND NATURAL RESOURCES

Environment. Azerbaijan's carbon dioxide emissions from the consumption and flaring of fossil fuels were the equivalent of 4·2 tonnes per capita in 2002.

Electricity. Output was 21·1bn. kWh in 2003; consumption per capita in 2000 was 2,404 kWh. Capacity in 2000 was 5·2m. kW.

Oil and Gas. The most important industry is crude oil extraction. Baku is at the centre of oil exploration in the Caspian. Partnerships with Turkish, western European and US companies have been forged.

In 2003 oil reserves totalled 7·0bn. bbls. A century ago Azerbaijan produced half of the world's oil, but production today is less than 1% of the total. An average of 15·0m. tonnes of oil are produced annually. Oil production in 2003 was 113m. bbls. In July 1999 BP Amoco announced a major natural gas discovery in the Shakh Deniz offshore field, with reserves of at least 700bn. cu. metres and perhaps as much as 1,000bn. cu. metres. There were proven reserves of 850bn. cu. metres in 2002. Natural gas production in 2003 amounted to 5·1bn. cu. metres.

Accords for the construction of an oil pipeline from Baku, the Azerbaijani capital, on the Caspian Sea through Georgia to Ceyhan in southern Turkey, and a gas pipeline from Turkmenistan through Azerbaijan and Georgia, to Erzurum in northeastern Turkey, were signed in Nov. 1999. Work on the oil pipeline, which is expected to become operational before the end of 2005, began in Sept. 2002.

Minerals. The republic is rich in natural resources: iron, bauxite, manganese, aluminium, copper ores, lead, zinc, precious metals, sulphur pyrites, nepheline syenites, limestone and salt. Cobalt ore reserves have been discovered in Dashkasan, and Azerbaijan has the largest iodine-bromine ore reserves of the former Soviet Union (the Neftchala region has an iodine-bromine mill).

Agriculture. In 2003 the total area devoted to agriculture was 4·8m. ha, of which 1·8m. ha was under crop and 223,774 ha were orchards and vineyards. In 2003 there were 1·80m. ha of arable land and 0·23m. ha of permanent crops. 1·42m. ha were irrigated in 2003. In 2003, 40% of the economically active population was engaged in agriculture. Principal crops include grain, cotton, rice, grapes, citrus fruit, vegetables, tobacco and silk.

Output of main agricultural products (in 1,000 tonnes) in 2003: wheat, 1,547; potatoes, 769; tomatoes, 421; melons and watermelons, 357; barley, 334; apples, 154.

Livestock (2003): cattle, 2·24m.; sheep, 6·68m.; goats, 604,000; chickens, 18m. Livestock products (2003, in 1,000 tonnes): beef and veal, 67; lamb and mutton, 39; cow's milk, 1,147; eggs, 38.

Forestry. In 2003 forests covered 1,037,000 ha, or 12·0% of the total land area. Timber production in 2001 was 14,000 cu. metres.

Fisheries. About ten tonnes of caviar from the Caspian sturgeon are produced annually. Total fish catch in 2003 came to approximately 23,300 tonnes, exclusively from inland waters.

INDUSTRY

There are oil extraction and refining, oil-related machinery, iron and steel, aluminium, copper, chemical, cement, building materials, timber, synthetic rubber, salt, textiles, food and fishing industries. Production (2003) in 1,000 tonnes: residual fuel oil, 2,470; distillate fuel oil, 1,641; cement, 1,012; petrol, 720; bread and bakery products, 686; jet fuel, 631. Output of other products: footwear (2003), 455,900 pairs; 17,000 drilling and boring machines (1997).

Labour. In 2003 the economically active workforce numbered 3,747,000. The main areas of activity were: agriculture, hunting and forestry, 1,497,000; wholesale and retail trade/repair of motor vehicles, motorcycles and personal and household goods, 618,300; education, 330,000; public administration and defence/compulsory social security, 265,000. The unemployment rate in 2003 was 10·9%. The average monthly salary in 2003 was 368,974 manats.

INTERNATIONAL TRADE

Total external debt was US$1,598m. in 2003.

Imports and Exports. In 2003 imports (f.o.b.) were valued at US$2,626·4m. and exports (f.o.b.) at US$2,591·7m.

Petroleum and related products accounted for approximately 85% of exports in 2003. Cotton, chemicals, tobacco, beverages, air conditioners, wool and refrigerators are also important exports. Principal imports are machinery, power, cereals, steel tubes, sugar and sweets.

The main export markets in 2003 were Italy (51·7%), France (8·1%), Israel (5·3%), Russia (5·3%), Georgia (4·3%), Turkey (4·1%). Leading import suppliers were Russia (21·3%), UK (10·9%), Turkey (7·4%), Turkmenistan (7·2%), Germany (6·5%).

COMMUNICATIONS

Roads. There were 25,021 km of roads (6,897 km highways and main roads) in 2003. Passenger cars in use in 2003 totalled 370,439 (45 per 1,000 inhabitants). In addition, there were 77,019 trucks and vans and 18,781 buses and coaches. There were 837 fatalities as a result of road accidents in 2003.

Rail. Total length in 2003 was 2,112 km of 1,520 mm gauge (1,270 km electrified). Passenger-km travelled in 2003 came to 654m. and freight tonne-km to 7·70bn.

There is a metro and tramway in Baku and a tramway in Sumgait.

Civil Aviation. There is an international airport at Baku. Azerbaijan Airlines had international flights in 2003 to Aktau, Aleppo, Ankara, Dubai, İstanbul, Kabul, Kyiv, London, Paris, Tbilisi, Tehran, Tel Aviv, Trabzon and Urumqi. There were direct flights in 2003 with other airlines to Almaty, Ashgabat, Bishkek, Donetsk, Ekaterinburg, Frankfurt, Kazan, Mineralnye Vody, Minsk, Moscow, Nizhnevartovsk, Novosibirsk, Omsk, St Petersburg, Samara, Surgut, Tashkent, Tyumen and Volgograd. In 1999 Azerbaijan Airlines flew 10·4m. km, carrying 571,700 passengers (187,500 on international flights).

Shipping. In 2002 merchant shipping totalled 633,000 GRT (including oil tankers 175,000 GRT). In 2000 vessels totalling 5,118,000 NRT entered ports and vessels totalling 703,000 NRT cleared.

Telecommunications. Telephone subscribers numbered 1,793,800 in 2002 (220·3 per 1,000 inhabitants) including 870,000 mobile phone subscribers. In 2003 there were 2,170 fax machines. Internet users numbered 300,000 in 2002.

Postal Services. There were 1,673 post offices in 1997.

SOCIAL INSTITUTIONS

Justice. The number of reported crimes in 2003 was 15,206, including 285 murders or attempted murders (449 in 1997). There were 187 crimes per 1,000 inhabitants and 94% of crimes were solved (80% in 1997).

The population in penal institutions in Jan. 2003 was 17,795 (217 per 100,000 of national population).

The death penalty was abolished in 1998.

Religion. In 2003 the population was 92% Muslim (mostly Shia), the balance being mainly Russian Orthodox, Armenian Apostolic and Judaism.

Education. In 2003–04 there were 603,894 pupils and 40,876 teachers at 4,533 primary schools, and 1,070,636 pupils at secondary schools. There were 110,891 children enrolled at pre-school institutions. In 2003 there were 175,229 students at 42 institutes of higher education and 60 specialized secondary schools. There were 33 institutes of higher education in Baku, with 95,068 students in 2003–04 (including correspondence students). The Azerbaijan Academy of Sciences, founded in 1945, has 31 research institutes. Adult literacy was estimated to be 99% in 2003.

In 2003 total expenditure on education came to 3·3% of GNP and represented 18·8% of total government expenditure.

Health. In 2003 there were 734 hospitals with 68,000 beds. In 2003 there were 29,687 physicians, 2,275 dentists, 59,531 nurses, 1,842 pharmacists and 9,803 midwives.

Welfare. In Jan. 2004 there were 751,000 age pensioners and 576,000 other pensioners.

CULTURE

World Heritage Sites. There is one UNESCO site in Azerbaijan: the Walled City of Baku with the Shirvanshah's Palace and Maiden Tower (2000). The site was damaged by an earthquake in 2000.

Broadcasting. The government-controlled Azerbaijan Radio broadcasts two national and one regional programme, a relay of Radio Moscow and a foreign service, Radio Baku (Azeri, Arabic, Iranian and Turkish). There are a number of private TV and radio stations. In 2001 there were 2·5m. TV receivers and in 2000 there were 177,000 radio receivers.

Cinema. In 2000 there were 607 cinemas.

Press. In 1997 Azerbaijan published 270 different newspapers and 45 magazines. In 1995, 422 newspapers were registered with the Ministry of Justice, but only about 50 were actually appearing. There is one daily, published by parliament, with a circulation of 5,000, and two independent thrice-weeklies with a combined circulation of 30,000.

Tourism. In 2003 there were 1,066,000 foreign tourists; spending by tourists totalled US$63m. in 2000.

Libraries. There are 4,124 public libraries (2003).

Theatre and Opera. Azerbaijan had 27 professional theatres in 2003.

Museums and Galleries. There were 159 museums including a National Museum of History in 2003.

DIPLOMATIC REPRESENTATIVES

Of Azerbaijan in the United Kingdom (4 Kensington Court, London, W8 5DL)
Ambassador: Rafael Ibrahimov.

Of the United Kingdom in Azerbaijan (45 Khagani St, AZ1000 Baku)
Ambassador: Dr Laurie Bristow.

Of Azerbaijan in the USA (2741 34th St, Washington, D.C., NW, 20008)
Ambassador: Hafiz Mir Jalal Pashayev.

Of the USA in Azerbaijan (83 Azadliq Prospect, Baku 37007)
Ambassador: Reno L. Harnish, III.

Of Azerbaijan to the United Nations
Ambassador: Yashar Aliyev.

Of Azerbaijan to the European Union
Ambassador: Arif Mamedov.

FURTHER READING

Swietochowski, T., *Russia and a Divided Azerbaijan.* Columbia University Press, 1995
Van Der Leeuw, C., *Azerbaijan.* Saint Martin's Press, New York, 1999

NAKHICHEVAN

This territory, on the borders of Turkey and Iran, forms part of Azerbaijan although separated from it by the territory of Armenia. Its population in 1989 was 95·9% Azerbaijani. It was annexed by Russia in 1828. In June 1923 it was constituted as an Autonomous Region within Azerbaijan. On 9 Feb. 1924 it was elevated to the status of Autonomous Republic. The 1996 Azerbaijani Constitution defines it as an Autonomous State within Azerbaijan.

Area, 5,500 sq. km (2,120 sq. miles); population (Jan. 1994), 315,000. Capital, Nakhichevan (66,800).

70% of the people are engaged in agriculture, of which the main branches are cotton and tobacco growing. Fruit and grapes are also produced.

In 1989–90 there were 219 primary and secondary schools with 60,200 pupils, and 2,200 students in higher educational institutions.

In Jan. 1990 there were 381 doctors and 2,445 junior medical personnel.

NAGORNO-KARABAKH

Established on 7 July 1923 as an Autonomous Region within Azerbaijan, in 1989 the area was placed under a 'special form of administration' subordinate to the USSR government. In Sept. 1991 the regional Soviet and the Shaumyan district Soviet jointly declared a Nagorno-Karabakh republic, which declared itself independent with a 99·9% popular vote (only the Armenian community took part in this vote as the Azeri population had already been expelled from Nagorno-Karabakh) in Dec. 1991. The autonomous status of the region was meanwhile abolished by the Azerbaijan Supreme Soviet in Nov. 1991, and the capital renamed Khankendi. A presidential decree of Jan. 1992 placed the region under direct rule. Azeri-Armenian fighting for possession of the region culminated in its occupation by Armenia in 1993 (and the occupation of seven other Azerbaijani regions outside it), despite attempts at international mediation. Since May 1994 there has been a ceasefire. Negotiations on settlements are conducted within the OSCE Minsk Group.

Area, 4,400 sq. km (1,700 sq. miles); population (Jan. 1990), 192,400. Capital, Khankendi (33,000). Populated by Armenians (76·9% at the 1989 census) and Azerbaijanis (21·5%).

In presidential elections held on 11 Aug. 1997 the hard-line independence candidate Arkady Gukasyan received more than 89% of votes cast, and was sworn in on 8 Sept. He was re-elected on 11 Aug. 2002 with 88·4% of votes cast. Legislative elections were held on 18 June 2000. The Democratic Artsakh Party, which supports President Gukasyan, won 13 seats; the Armenian Revolutionary Federation 9; the Armenakan Party 1; and independents 10. The *Prime Minister* is Anushavan Danielyan.

Main industries are silk, wine, dairying and building materials. Crop area is 67,200 ha; cotton, grapes and winter wheat are grown. There are 33 collective and 38 state farms.

In 1989–90, 34,200 pupils were studying in primary and secondary schools, 2,400 in colleges and 2,100 in higher educational institutions.

BAHAMAS

Commonwealth of The Bahamas

Capital: Nassau
Population projection, 2010: 336,000
GDP per capita, 2000: (PPP$) 17,012
HDI/world rank: 0·815/51

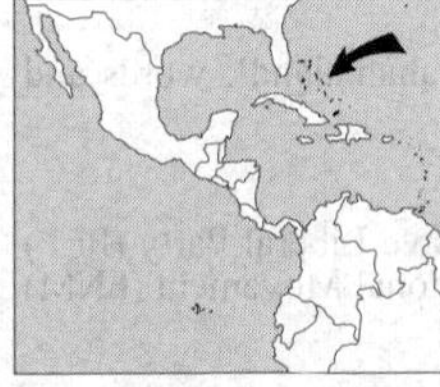

KEY HISTORICAL EVENTS

First inhabited in the 9th century by the Lucayans, a branch of the Arawaks, the Bahamas received their name 'Baja Mar' (low sea) from Christopher Columbus who landed on San Salvador in 1492. Colonized by English puritans from Bermuda during the 17th century, the Bahamas were later plagued by notorious pirates such as Blackbeard, until they were driven out by Governor Woodes Rogers in 1718. The Bahamas played an important part in the American Civil War: blockaded by the Union navy in 1861, the islanders traded Confederate cotton with Britain and supplied military equipment to the Confederacy. During Prohibition the Bahamas prospered as a rum-smuggling base but experienced a severe economic downturn when the Prohibition law was repealed in 1933. An important Atlantic base during WWII, the tourist industry benefited greatly from Cuba's closure to western visitors in the 1950s. Internal self-government with cabinet responsibility was introduced on 7 Jan. 1964 and full independence achieved on 10 July 1973.

TERRITORY AND POPULATION

The Commonwealth of The Bahamas consists of over 700 islands and inhabited cays off the southeast coast of Florida extending for about 260,000 sq. miles. Only 22 islands are inhabited. Land area, 5,382 sq. miles (13,939 sq. km).

The areas and populations of the 19 divisions used for the most recent census in 2000 were as follows:

	Area (in sq. km)	*Population*		*Area (in sq. km)*	*Population*
New Providence	207	210,832	Spanish Wells	26	1,527
Grand Bahama	1,373	46,994	San Salvador	163	970
Abaco	1,681	13,170	Inagua	1,551	969
Eleuthera	484	7,999	Berry Islands	31	709
Andros	5,954	7,686	Acklins	497	428
Exuma and Cays	290	3,571	Crooked Island	241	350
Long Island	596	2,992	Mayaguana	285	259
Biminis	23	1,717	Rum Cay	78	80
Cat Island	388	1,647	Ragged Island	36	72
Harbour Island	8	1,639			

Total census population for 2000 was 303,611 (155,833 females).

The UN gives a projected population for 2010 of 336,000.

In 2001, 88·8% of the population were urban. The capital is Nassau on New Providence Island (212,432 in 2000); the other large town is Freeport (45,000 in 1999) on Grand Bahama.

English is the official language. Creole is spoken among Haitian immigrants.

SOCIAL STATISTICS

1999: births, 6,367; deaths, 1,567. Rates, 1999 (per 1,000 population): birth, 21·4; death, 5·3; marriage (1996), 9·3; infant mortality (per 1,000 live births), 2001, 13. Expectation of life was 63·8 years for males and 70·6 years for females in 2001. Annual population growth rate, 1992–2002, 1·5%; fertility rate, 2001, 2·3 children per woman.

CLIMATE

Winters are mild and summers pleasantly warm. Most rain falls in May, June, Sept. and Oct., and thunderstorms are frequent in summer. Rainfall amounts vary over the islands from 30" (750 mm) to 60" (1,500 mm). Nassau, Jan. 71°F (21·7°C), July 81°F (27·2°C). Annual rainfall 47" (1,179 mm).

CONSTITUTION AND GOVERNMENT

The Commonwealth of The Bahamas is a free and democratic sovereign state. Executive power rests with Her Majesty the Queen, who appoints a Governor-General to represent her, advised by a Cabinet whom he appoints. There is a bicameral legislature. The *Senate* comprises 16 members all appointed by the Governor-General for five-year terms, nine on the advice of the Prime Minister, four on the advice of the Leader of the Opposition, and three after consultation with both of them. The *House of Assembly* consists of 40 members elected from single-member constituencies for a maximum term of five years.

National Anthem. 'Lift up your head to the rising sun, Bahamaland'; words and tune by T. Gibson.

RECENT ELECTIONS

In parliamentary elections held on 2 May 2002 the Progressive Liberal Party (PLP) won 50·8% of votes cast and 29 out of 40 seats, the Free National Movement (FNM) 41·1% (7) and ind. 5·2% (4). Turn-out was 82·4%.

CURRENT ADMINISTRATION

Governor-General: Dame Ivy Dumont; b. 1930 (appointed 13 Nov. 2001).

In March 2005 the cabinet was composed as follows:

Prime Minister and Minister of Finance: Perry Christie; b. 1943 (PLP; sworn in 3 May 2002).

Deputy Prime Minister and Minister of National Security: Cynthia Pratt. *Agriculture, Fisheries and Local Government:* Alfred Grey. *Transportation and Aviation:* Glenys Hanna-Martin. *Foreign Affairs and Public Service:* Fred Mitchell. *Education:* Alfred Sears. *Financial Services and Investments:* Allyson Maynard-Gibson. *Health and Environment:* Marcus Bethel. *Housing and National Insurance:* Shane Gibson. *Labour and Immigration:* Vincent Peet. *Social Services and Community Development:* Melanie Griffin. *Trade and Industry:* Leslie Miller. *Youth, Sports and Culture:* Neville Wisdom. *Tourism:* Obie Wilchcombe. *Justice:* Vacant.

Office of the Prime Minister: http://www.opm.gov.bs

DEFENCE

The Royal Bahamian Defence Force is a primarily maritime force tasked with naval patrols and protection duties in the extensive waters of the archipelago. Personnel in 2002 numbered 860 (including 70 women), and the base is at Coral Harbour on New Providence Island.

In 2003 defence expenditure totalled US$29m. (US$91 per capita), representing 0·6% of GDP.

Navy. The Navy operates ten vessels including seven patrol craft, plus four aircraft.

INTERNATIONAL RELATIONS

The Commonwealth of The Bahamas is a member of the UN, OAS, Inter-American Development Bank, the Commonwealth, ACS, CARICOM, FAO, IBRD, ICAO, ILO, IMF, Intelsat, ITU, UNESCO, UNIDO, WHO, WIPO, IOM and is an ACP member state of the ACP-EU relationship.

ECONOMY

Services contributed an estimated 92% of GDP in 1997.

Overview. The government is committed to free enterprise. The National Investment Policy, designed to attract investment, focuses on the tourism and financial services sectors.

Currency. The unit of currency is the *Bahamian dollar* (BSD) of 100 *cents*. American currency is generally accepted. Inflation was 2·0% in 2002. Foreign exchange reserves were US$461m. in June 2002 and total money supply was B$812m.

Budget. Government revenue and expenditure (in B$1m.):

	1997	*1998*	*1999*	*2000*	*2001*
Revenue	729·0	761·3	869·1	937·2	920·3
Expenditure	829·3	807·2	884·4	916·2	964·4

The main sources of revenue are import duties, stamp duty from land sales, work permits and residence fees, and accommodation tax. There is no direct taxation.

Performance. The Bahamas experienced a recession during the period 1988–94; this was mainly due to the recession in the USA leading to a fall in the number of American tourists. The economy has been growing since, and there are continuing efforts to diversify. Freeport's tax-free status was extended by 25 years in 1995, and import duties were reduced in the 1996–97 budget.

Real GDP growth was 4·9% in 2000 but the general downturn in the world economy resulted in negative growth of 2·0% in 2001. There was a slight recovery in 2002, with growth of 0·7%. Total GDP in 2003 was US$5·3bn.

Banking and Finance. The Central Bank of The Bahamas was established in 1974. Its *Governor* is Julian Francis. The Bahamas is an important centre for offshore banking. Financial business produces about 20% of GDP. In 2001, 356 banks and trust companies were licensed, about half being branches of foreign companies. Leading Bahamian-based banks include The Bank of Bahamas Ltd., The Commonwealth Bank Ltd. and Private Investment Bank Ltd. There is also a Development Bank.

The Bahamas was one of 15 countries and territories named in a report in June 2000 as failing to co-operate in the fight against international money laundering. The Financial Action Task Force on Money Laundering was set up by the G7 group of major industrialized nations.

A stock exchange, the Bahamas International Securities Exchange (BISX) based in Nassau, was inaugurated in May 2000.

Weights and Measures. The Bahamas follows the USA in using linear, dry and liquid measure.

ENERGY AND NATURAL RESOURCES

Environment. The carbon dioxide emissions of the Bahamas from the consumption and flaring of fossil fuels were the equivalent of 10·9 tonnes per capita in 2002.

Electricity. In 2000 installed capacity was 0·4m. kW, all thermal. Output in 2000 was approximately 1·66bn. kWh; consumption per capita in 2000 was an estimated 5,479 kWh.

Oil and Gas. The Bahamas does not have reserves of either oil or gas, but oil is refined in the Bahamas. The Bahamas Oil Refining Company (BORCO), in Grand Bahama, operates as a terminal which trans-ships, stores and blends oil.

Minerals. Aragonite is extracted from the seabed.

Agriculture. In 2001 there were some 8,000 ha of arable land and 4,000 ha of permanent crops. Production (in 1,000 tonnes), 2000: sugarcane, 45; fruit, 22 (notably grapefruit, lemons and limes); vegetables, 21.

Livestock (2000): cattle, 1,000; sheep, 6,000; goats, 15,000; pigs, 6,000; chickens, 5m.

Forestry. In 2000 forests covered 842,000 ha or 84·1% of the total land area. Timber production in 2001 was 17,000 cu. metres.

Fisheries. The estimated total catch in 2001 amounted to 9,290 tonnes, mainly lobsters, and exclusively from sea fishing. Total value in 1995 of fish landings was B$59·7m.

INDUSTRY

Tourism and offshore banking are the main industries. Two industrial sites, one in New Providence and the other in Grand Bahama, have been developed as part of an industrialization programme. The main products are pharmaceutical chemicals, salt and rum.

Labour. A total of 144,355 persons were in employment in April 1998 (excluding armed forces). The main areas of activity were: construction, 21·1%; wholesale and retail trade, restaurants and hotels, 21·1%; community, social and personal services, 18·9%; financing, insurance, real estate and business services, 18·4%. Unemployment was 6·9% in 2001.

Trade Unions. In 1996 there were 43 unions, the largest being The Bahamas Hotel, Catering and Allied Workers' Union (5,000 members).

INTERNATIONAL TRADE

Public-sector foreign debt was US$372,862 in Dec. 1997. There is a freeport zone of Grand Bahama. Although a member of CARICOM, the Bahamas is not a signatory to its trade protocol.

Imports and Exports. Imports and exports for calendar years in US$1m.:

	1997	*1998*	*1999*	*2000*	*2001*
Imports f.o.b.	1,410·7	1,737·1	1,808·1	2,176·4	1,764·7
Exports f.o.b.	295·0	362·9	379·9	805·3	614·1

The principal exports are oil products and trans-shipments, chemicals, fish, rum and salt. In 1997 the main export markets were USA (77%) and France (12%); the USA was the source of 91% of imports.

COMMUNICATIONS

Roads. There were about 2,693 km of roads in 1999 (57·4% paved). In 1996 there were around 46,000 passenger cars and 12,000 lorries and vans.

Civil Aviation. There are international airports at Nassau and Freeport (Grand Bahama Island). The national carrier is the state-owned Bahamasair, which in 2003 flew to Fort Lauderdale, Miami, Orlando and the Turks and Caicos Islands, as well as providing services between different parts of the Bahamas. There were direct flights in 2003 with other airlines to Atlanta, Baltimore, Boston, Charlotte, Cincinnati, Cleveland, Daytona Beach, Detroit, Hartford, Havana, Houston, Key West, Kingston, London, Manchester, Melbourne, Milwaukee, Montreal, New York, Philadelphia, Pittsburgh, Raleigh, Richmond, Rochester, Salt Lake City, San Diego, Tampa, Trinidad, Toronto, Washington, D.C. and West Palm Beach. In 1999 scheduled airline traffic of Bahamas-based carriers flew 6·8m. km, carrying 1,719,000 passengers (944,000 on international flights).

Shipping. The Bahamas' shipping registry consisted of a fleet of 35·8m. GRT in 2002, a figure exceeded only by the fleets of Panama and Liberia. There were 1,295 vessels in 2000, including 259 tankers.

Telecommunications. New Providence and most of the other major islands have automatic telephone systems in operation, interconnected by a radio network, while local distribution within the islands is by overhead and underground cables. In 2002 there were 248,300 telephone subscribers, or 795·9 per 1,000 inhabitants. International operator-assisted and direct dialling telephone services are available to all major countries. There were 121,800 mobile phone subscribers in 2002 and 500 fax machines in 1995. There were 60,000 Internet users in 2002.

Postal Services. In 1998 there were 138 post offices.

SOCIAL INSTITUTIONS

Justice. English Common Law is the basis of the Bahamian judicial system, although there is a large volume of Bahamian Statute Law. The highest tribunal in the country is the Court of Appeal. New Providence has 15 Magistrates' Courts and Grand Bahama has three.

The strength of the police force (1995) was 2,223 officers.

There were 64 murders in 1999 (a rate of 21·5 per 100,000 population). The death penalty is in force, the most recent execution being carried out in Jan. 2000. The population in penal institutions in Oct. 2002 was 1,280 (410 per 100,000 of national population).

Religion. In 2001, 44% of the population were Protestant, 16% Roman Catholic, 10% Anglican and the remainder other religions.

Education. Education is compulsory between five and 16 years of age. The adult literacy rate in 2001 was 95·5% (94·6% among males and 96·3% among females). In 2003 there were 206 schools (45 independent). In 1999–2000 there were 33,145 pupils with 2,400 teachers in primary schools and 44,137 pupils with 1,710 teachers in secondary education. Courses lead to The Bahamas General Certificate of

Secondary Education (BGCSE). Independent schools provide education at primary, secondary and high school levels.

The four institutions offering higher education are: the government-sponsored College of The Bahamas, established in 1974; the University of the West Indies (regional), affiliated with the Bahamas since 1960; The Bahamas Hotel Training College, sponsored by the Ministry of Education and the hotel industry; and The Bahamas Technical and Vocational Institute, established to provide basic skills. Several schools of continuing education offer secretarial and academic courses.

Health. In 1996 there was a government general hospital (436 beds) and a psychiatric/geriatric care centre (502 beds) in Nassau, and a hospital in Freeport (82 beds). The Family Islands, comprising 20 health districts, had 13 health centres and 107 main clinics in 1996. There were two private hospitals (86 beds) in New Providence in 1993. In 1996 there were 419 physicians, 72 dentists and 648 nurses.

Welfare. Social Services are provided by the Department of Social Services, a government agency which grants assistance to restore, reinforce and enhance the capacity of the individual to perform life tasks, and to provide for the protection of children in the Bahamas. The Department's divisions comprise: community support services, child welfare, family services, senior citizens, Family Island and research planning, training and community relations.

CULTURE

Broadcasting. The Broadcasting Corporation of the Bahamas is a government-owned company which operates five radio broadcasting stations and a TV service with one channel, ZNS TV 13. In 1998, five independent radio stations were operating. There were 75,200 television receivers in 2000 and 215,000 radio receivers in 1997. TV colour is by NTSC. There is cable TV on Grand Bahama, New Providence and the majority of the Family Islands.

Press. There were three national dailies and one weekly in 1998.

Tourism. Tourism is the most important industry, accounting for about 70% of GDP. In 1998 there were 1,590,000 stop-over and 1,730,000 cruise-ship visitors. Tourist expenditure was US$1,814m. in 2000.

DIPLOMATIC REPRESENTATIVES

Of the Bahamas in the United Kingdom (10 Chesterfield St, London, W1J 5JL)
High Commissioner: Basil G. O'Brien, CMG.

Of the United Kingdom in the Bahamas (3rd Floor, Ansbacher House, East St, Nassau)
High Commissioner: Roderick Gemmell, OBE.

Of the Bahamas in the USA (2220 Massachusetts Ave., NW, Washington, D.C., 20008)
Ambassador: Joshua Sears.

Of the USA in the Bahamas (Mosmar Bldg, Queen St, Nassau)
Ambassador: Vacant.
Chargé d'Affaires a.i.: Robert M. Witajewski.

Of the Bahamas to the United Nations
Ambassador: Paulette Bethel.

Of the Bahamas to the European Union
Ambassador: Basil G. O'Brien, CMG.

FURTHER READING

Cash, P., *et al.*, *Making of Bahamian History.* London, 1991
Craton, M. and Saunders, G., *Islanders in the Stream: a History of the Bahamian People.* 2 vols. Univ. of Georgia Press, 1998

National statistical office: Department of Statistics, PO Box N-3904, Nassau
Website: http://www.bahamas.gov.bs/statistics

BAHRAIN

Al-Mamlaka Al-Bahrayn
(Kingdom of Bahrain)

Capital: Manama
Population projection, 2010: 828,000
GDP per capita, 2002: (PPP$) 17,170
HDI/world rank: 0·843/40

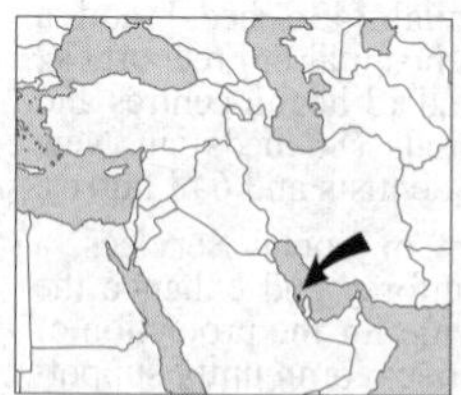

KEY HISTORICAL EVENTS

Bahrain was controlled by the Portuguese from 1521 until 1602. The Khalifa family gained control in 1783 and has ruled since that date. British assistance was sought to retain independence and from 1861 until 1971 Bahrain was in all but name a British protectorate. Bahrain declared its independence in 1971. Shaikh Isa bin Salman Al-Khalifa became the Amir. A constitution was ratified in June 1973 providing for a National Assembly of 30 members, popularly elected for a four-year term, together with all members of the cabinet (appointed by the Amir). However, in 1975 the National Assembly was dissolved and the Amir began ruling by decree. In 1987 the main island was joined to the Saudi mainland by a causeway. In Feb. 2002 Bahrain became a kingdom, with the Amir proclaiming himself king.

TERRITORY AND POPULATION

The Kingdom of Bahrain forms an archipelago of 36 low-lying islands in the Persian Gulf, between the Qatar peninsula and the mainland of Saudi Arabia. The total area is 720 sq. km.

The island of Bahrain (578 sq. km) is connected by a 2·4 km causeway to the second largest island, Muharraq to the northeast, and by a causeway with the island of Sitra to the east. A causeway links Bahrain with Saudi Arabia. From Sitra, oil pipelines and a causeway carrying a road extend out to sea for 4·8 km to a deep-water anchorage.

Total census population in 2001 was 650,604. Population (2003 est.) 689,418 (males, 396,278; females, 293,140), of which 427,955 were Bahraini and 261,463 non-Bahraini. The population density was 957 per sq. km in 2003. In 2001, 92·5% of the population were urban.

The UN gives a projected population for 2010 of 828,000.

There are 12 regions: Central, Eastern, Hamad Town, Hidd Town, Isa Town, Jidhafs, Manama, Muharraq, Northern, Rifa'a, Sitra, Western. Manama, the capital and commercial centre, had a 2001 census population of 153,395. Other towns (2001 census population) are Muharraq (91,939), Rifa'a (79,985), Jidhafs (52,450), Sitra (43,910) and Isa Town (36,883).

Arabic is the official language. English is widely used in business.

SOCIAL STATISTICS

Statistics 2002: births, 13,576 (Bahraini, 10,539); deaths, 2,035 (Bahraini, 1,672). Rates (per 1,000 population) in 2002: birth, 20·2; death, 3·0. Infant mortality (per 1,000 live births), 13 (2001). Life expectancy at birth, 2001, was 72·1 years for men and 75·7 years for women. Annual population growth rate, 1992–2002, 3·0%; fertility rate, 2001, 2·4 children per woman. In 2002 there were 4,909 marriages and 838 divorces.

The Shia make up 65% of the national population, half of whom are under 15.

CLIMATE

The climate is pleasantly warm between Dec. and March but from June to Sept. the conditions are very hot and humid. The period June to Nov. is virtually rainless. Bahrain, Jan. 66°F (19°C), July 97°F (36°C). Annual rainfall 5·2" (130 mm).

CONSTITUTION AND GOVERNMENT

The ruling family is the Al-Khalifa who have been in power since 1783.

The constitution changing Bahrain from an Emirate to a Kingdom dates from 14 Feb. 2002. The new constitutional hereditary monarchy has a bicameral legislature, inaugurated on 14 Dec. 2002. National elections for a legislative body took place on 24 and 31 Oct. 2002 (the first since the National Assembly was adjourned 27 years earlier). One chamber (*House of Deputies*) is a directly elected assembly while the second (upper) chamber, a *Shura* consultative council of experts, is appointed by the government. Both chambers have 40 members. All Bahraini citizens over the age of 21—men and women—are able to vote for the elected assembly. In the Oct. 2002 national elections women stood for office for the first time.

National Anthem. 'Bahrain ona, baladolaman' ('Our Bahrain, secure as a country'); words by M. S. Ayyash, tune anonymous.

RECENT ELECTIONS

On 24 and 31 Oct. 2002 the first national elections since Dec. 1973 were held. Despite a call from opposition parties for the election to be boycotted, turn-out was over 50%. 21 out of 40 seats were won by secular candidates, with the remaining seats going to Sunni and Shia representatives. There were eight women among a total of 177 candidates running for the legislature, although males won all of the seats.

CURRENT ADMINISTRATION

The present king (formerly Amir), HH Shaikh Hamad bin Isa Al-Khalifa, KCMG (b. 1950), succeeded on 6 March 1999 and became king on 14 Feb. 2002.

In March 2005 the cabinet was composed as follows:

Prime Minister: Shaikh Khalifa bin Salman Al-Khalifa; b. 1936. He is currently the longest-serving prime minister of any sovereign country, having been Bahrain's prime minister since it became independent in Aug. 1971.

Deputy Prime Minister and Minister of Islamic Affairs: Shaikh Abdullah bin Khalid Al-Khalifa. *Deputy Prime Minister and Minister of Foreign Affairs:* Shaikh Mohammed bin Mubarak Al-Khalifa.

Minister of Defence: Shaikh Khalifa bin Ahmed Al-Khalifa. *Electricity and Water:* Shaikh Abdulla bin Salman Al-Khalifa. *Finance:* Sheikh Ahmad ibn Muhammad Al-Khalifa. *Health:* Nada Abbas Haffadh. *Works and Housing:* Fahmi bin Ali Al-Jowdar. *Industry and Commerce:* Dr Hassan bin Abdullah Fakhro. *Information:* Dr Mohammed Abd Al-Ghaffar. *Interior:* Gen. Rashed bin Abdullah bin Ahmed Al-Khalifa. *Justice:* Dr Mohammed Ali bin Al-Shaikh Mansoor Al-Sitri. *Labour:* Dr Majeed bin Mohsin Al-Alawi. *Social Affairs:* Dr Fatima Ahmed Al-Beloushi. *Municipalities and Agriculture:* Ali Saleh Al-Saleh. *Oil:* Shaikh Isa bin Ali Hamad Al-Khalifa. *Prime Minister's Court:* Shaikh Khalid bin Abdulla Al-Khalifa. *Transportation:* Shaikh Ali bin Khalifa bin Salman Al-Khalifa. *Education:* Majid Ali Al-Nuaymi.

Government Website: http://www.bahrain.gov.bh

DEFENCE

The Crown Prince is C.-in-C. of the armed forces. An agreement with the USA in Oct. 1991 gave port facilities to the US Navy and provided for mutual manoeuvres.

Military expenditure totalled US$314m. in 2002 (US$435 per capita), representing 4·0% of GDP.

Army. The Army consists of one armoured brigade, one infantry brigade, one artillery brigade, one special forces battalion and one air defence battalion. Personnel, 2002, 8,500. In addition there is a National Guard of approximately 900 and a paramilitary police force of 9,000.

Navy. The Naval force based at Mina Sulman numbered 1,000 in 2002.

Air Force. Personnel (2002), 1,200. Equipment includes 30 combat aircraft and 40 armed helicopters.

INTERNATIONAL RELATIONS

Bahrain is a member of the UN, WTO, the League of Arab States, the Gulf Co-operation Council, OAPEC (Organization of Arab Petroleum Exporting Countries), OIC and Islamic Development Bank.

In March 2001 the International Court of Justice ruled on a long-standing dispute between Bahrain and Qatar over the boundary between the two countries and ownership of certain islands. Both countries accepted the decision.

ECONOMY

In 2002 industry accounted for 42·8% of GDP and services 56·6%.

Currency. The unit of currency is the *Bahraini dinar* (BHD), divided into 1,000 *fils*. In June 2002 foreign exchange reserves were US$1,675m., total money supply was BD602m. and gold reserves were 150,000 troy oz. In 2002 there was deflation, of 1·0%. The previous four years had also seen deflation.

In 2001 the six Gulf Arab states—Bahrain, along with Kuwait, Oman, Qatar, Saudi Arabia and the United Arab Emirates—signed an agreement to establish a single currency by 2010.

Budget. Government revenue and expenditure (in BD1m.):

	1996	*1997*	*1998*	*1999*	*2000*	*2001*
Revenue	615·2	633·2	516·6	653·5	1,065·9	969·3
Expenditure	581·3	620·0	644·6	699·3	777·0	826·6

Performance. Total GDP in 2001 was US$7·9bn. Real GDP growth was 4·8% in 2001 and 4·1% in 2002.

Banking and Finance. The Bahrain Monetary Agency (*Governor*, Rasheed Mohammed Al Maraj) has central banking powers. In 2001 Bahrain had 51 offshore banking units. Offshore banking units may not engage in local business; their assets totalled US$62,503m. in March 1996. In 2001 there were six locally incorporated commercial banks, ten foreign commercial banks and two specialized financial institutions. There were also several investment banks.

There is a stock exchange in Manama linked with those of Kuwait and Oman.

ENERGY AND NATURAL RESOURCES

Environment. Bahrain's carbon dioxide emissions from the consumption and flaring of fossil fuels in 2002 were the equivalent of 33·1 tonnes per capita, among the highest in the world.

Electricity. In 2000 installed capacity was 1·4m. kW; about 6·30bn. kWh were produced in 2000. Electricity consumption per capita was an estimated 9,113 kWh in 2000.

Oil and Gas. In 1931 oil was discovered. Operations were at first conducted by the Bahrain Petroleum Co. (BAPCO) under concession. In 1975 the government assumed a 60% interest in the oilfield and related crude oil facilities of BAPCO. Oil reserves in 2002 were 125m. bbls. Production (2000) was 1·9m. tonnes. Refinery distillation output amounted to 12·7m. tonnes in 2000.

There were known natural gas reserves of 91bn. cu. metres in 2002. Production in 2002 was 9·2bn. cu. metres. Gas reserves are government-owned.

Water. Water is obtained from artesian wells and desalination plants and there is a piped supply to Manama, Muharraq, Isa Town, Rifa'a and most villages.

Minerals. Aluminium is Bahrain's oldest major industry after oil and gas; production in 2001 was 522,000 tonnes.

Agriculture. In 2001 there were 2,000 ha of arable land and 4,000 ha of permanent crops. There are about 900 farms and smallholdings (average 2·5 ha) operated by about 2,500 farmers who produce a wide variety of fruits (22,000 tonnes in 2000) including dates (17,000 tonnes). In 2000 an estimated 12,000 tonnes of vegetables were produced. The major crop is alfalfa for animal fodder.

Livestock (2000): cattle, 11,000; camels, 1,000; sheep, 18,000; goats, 16,000.

In 2000 an estimated 5,000 tonnes of lamb and mutton, 5,000 tonnes of poultry meat, 3,000 tonnes of eggs and 14,000 tonnes of fresh milk were produced. Agriculture contributed 1% of GDP in 1997.

Fisheries. The total catch in 2001 was 11,230 tonnes, exclusively from sea fishing.

INDUSTRY

Industry is being developed with foreign participation: aluminium smelting (and ancillary industries), shipbuilding and repair, petrochemicals, electronics assembly and light industry.

Traditional crafts include boatbuilding, weaving and pottery.

Labour. The workforce (estimate 2003) was 328,865 of which 136,215 were Bahraini. There were 16,965 unemployed persons in 2001.

Trade Unions. Trade unions have been permitted since 2002; all unions belong to the General Federation of Workers Trade Unions in Bahrain (GFWTUB).

INTERNATIONAL TRADE

Totally foreign-owned companies have been permitted to register since 1991.

Bahrain, along with Kuwait, Oman, Qatar, Saudi Arabia and the United Arab Emirates began the implementation of a customs union in Jan. 2003.

Imports and Exports. In 2002 imports (f.o.b.) totalled US$4,672·9m. and exports (f.o.b.) US$5,785·6m. In 1999 mineral fuels and related materials made up 62% of exports and 35% of imports. In 1999 the main export markets were Saudi Arabia, USA and India; the main import sources were Australia, Saudi Arabia, USA and UK.

COMMUNICATIONS

Roads. A 25-km causeway links Bahrain with Saudi Arabia. In 2002 there were 3,459 km of roads (76·7% paved), including 428 km of main roads and 474 km of secondary roads. Bahrain has one of the densest road networks in the world. In 2002 there were 249,121 vehicles in use, including 206,544 passenger cars (307·3 per 1,000 inhabitants). In 2000 there were 1,656 road accidents resulting in 53 deaths.

Civil Aviation. Bahrain has a 25% share (with Oman, Qatar and UAE) in Gulf Air. In 2000 Bahrain International Airport handled 3·38m. passengers (all on international flights) and 146,800 tonnes of freight. In 1999 scheduled airline traffic of Bahrain-based carriers flew 20·8m. km, carrying 1,307,000 passengers (all on international flights).

Shipping. In 2002 the merchant fleet totalled 288,000 GRT, including oil tankers 81,000 GRT. The port of Mina Sulman is a free transit and industrial area; about 800 vessels are handled annually.

Telecommunications. The government has a 37% stake in Bahrain Telecommunications (BATELCO). The telecommunications industry was fully liberalized on 1 July 2004. In 2002 there were 564,400 telephone subscribers (846·4 per 1,000 inhabitants) and 107,000 PCs were in use (160·4 for every 1,000 persons). There were 389,000 mobile phone subscribers in 2002 and 6,900 fax machines in 1999. Bahrain had 165,000 Internet users in 2002.

Postal Services. There were 13 post offices in 1998.

SOCIAL INSTITUTIONS

Justice. The new constitution which came into force in Feb. 2002 includes the creation of an independent judiciary. The State Security Law and the State Security Court were both abolished in the lead-up to the change to a constitutional monarchy.

The population in penal institutions in Dec. 1997 was 911 (155 per 100,000 of national population).

Religion. Islam is the state religion. In 2001, 87% of the population were Muslim (65% Shia and 22% Sunni). There are also Christian, Jewish, Bahai, Hindu and Parsee minorities.

Education. Adult literacy was 87·9% in 2001 (male, 91·1%; female, 83·2%). Government schools provide free education from primary to technical college level. Schooling is in three stages: primary (six years), intermediate (three years) and secondary (three years). Secondary education may be general or specialized. In 2000–01 there were 62,917 primary school pupils, 28,972 intermediate school pupils and 23,366 secondary school pupils; there were a total of 192 schools and 7,128 teachers in 2000–01. There was also one religious institute with 460 male students and 44 teachers.

In the private sector there were 33 schools with 23,600 pupils and 1,579 teachers in 1993–94. There were two universities (1994–95) with 7,019 students in attendance; as well as 3,711 persons attending adult education centres.

In 2000–01 total expenditure on education came to 3·1% of GNP and 11·4% of total government spending.

Health. There is a free medical service for all residents. In 2003 there were 1,295 physicians, 186 dentists, 3,156 nurses and 158 pharmacists. In 2003 there were ten general hospitals (four government; six private) and 21 health centres. In 1996 there were five maternity hospitals.

Welfare. In 1976 a pensions, sickness benefits and unemployment, maternity and family allowances scheme was established. Employers contribute 7% of salaries and Bahraini employees 11%. In 1994, 36,612 persons received state benefit payments totalling BD3,715,158. A total of BD5,975,700 was paid out to pensioners, and BD306,600 to recipients of social insurance.

CULTURE

Broadcasting. Radio Bahrain is government-controlled, Bahrain Television part-commercial. In 1997 there were 338,000 radio receivers and in 2001 there were 280,000 TV receivers (colour by PAL).

In 1998 there were six television channels—two in English and four in Arabic—as well as a satellite channel.

Cinema. There were six cinemas in 2002; the total attendance was 1,207,520.

Press. There were five daily newspapers in 2003. In 1996 the daily newspapers had a combined circulation of 67,000, at a rate of 117 per 1,000 inhabitants.

Tourism. In 2000 there were 2,420,000 foreign tourists, spending US$469m. In 1994 there were 44 hotels with 5,175 beds.

Libraries. In 2003 there were ten public libraries; a total of 190,756 books were borrowed in that year.

DIPLOMATIC REPRESENTATIVES

Of Bahrain in the United Kingdom (30 Belgrave Square, London SW1X 8QB)
Ambassador: Shaikh Khalid bin Ahmed Al-Khalifa.

Of the United Kingdom in Bahrain (21 Government Ave., Manama 306, PO Box 114, Bahrain)
Ambassador: Robin Lamb.

Of Bahrain in the USA (3502 International Dr., NW, Washington, D.C., 20008)
Ambassador: Khalifa Ali Al-Khalifa.

Of the USA in Bahrain (Building No. 979, Road No. 3119, Block 331, Zinj District, Manama)
Ambassador: William T. Monroe.

Of Bahrain to the United Nations
Ambassador: Tawfeeq Ahmed Khalil Almansoor.

Of Bahrain to the European Union
Ambassador: Haya bint Rashid Al-Khalifa.

FURTHER READING

Bahrain Monetary Authority. *Quarterly Statistical Bulletin.*
Central Statistics Organization. *Statistical Abstract.* Annual

Al-Khalifa, A. and Rice, M. (eds.) *Bahrain through the Ages.* London, 1993
Al-Khalifa, H. bin I., *First Light: Modern Bahrain and its Heritage.* London, 1995

National statistical office: Central Statistics Organization, Council of Ministers, Manama.

BANGLADESH

Gana Prajatantri Bangladesh (People's Republic of Bangladesh)

Capital: Dhaka
Population projection, 2010: 167·17m.
GDP per capita, 2002: (PPP$) 1,700
HDI/world rank: 0·509/138

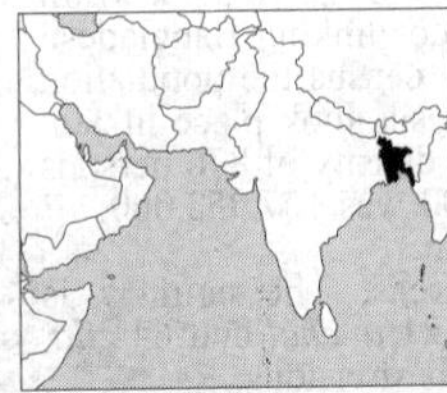

KEY HISTORICAL EVENTS

India's Maurya Empire established Buddhism in Bengal (*Bangla*) in the 3rd century BC. The Buddhist Pala Dynasty ruled Bengal and Bihar independently from 750 AD, exporting Buddhism to Tibet. Hinduism regained dominance under the Sena Dynasty in the 11th century until the Muslim invasions in 1203–04. Rule from Delhi was broken in the 14th century by local Bengali kings. The Afghan adventurer Sher Shah conquered Bengal in 1539 and defeated the Mughal Emperor Humayun, creating an extensive administrative empire in North India. However, Mughal power was re-established by Akbar in 1576.

The Portuguese arrived in the 15th century, drawn to the rich Bengali cotton trade. They were followed by the Dutch and the British, whose East India Company was centred at Calcutta. The Nawab of Bengal was defeated by Robert Clive's army at the Battle of Plassey in 1757. British rule was maintained through the mainly Hindu *zamindar* land-owners and the Company was replaced by the Crown in 1858.

The partition of Bengal in 1905 was an attempt to undermine the nationalist influence of the *bhadralok*, the Hindu middle-classes, by forming a Muslim-dominated eastern province. Religious violence increased and political interests were represented by newly formed parties, including the All-India Muslim League. The partition was reversed in 1912. Tensions between the Muslim and Hindu communities escalated in the 1930s. The League suffered electoral defeat in 1936 but calls for a Muslim state were strengthened by the Pakistan Resolution of 1940. An agreement between Hindu and Muslim leaders to create an independent, secular Bengal was resisted by Mahatma Gandhi. Further violence, such as the Great Calcutta Killing in 1946, put pressure on the administration and India was hastily partitioned—East Bengal was united with the north-western Muslim provinces as Pakistan. East Pakistan (as East Bengal became under the 1956 constitution) received 0·7m. Muslims, mainly from Bihar and West Bengal, while over 2·5m. Hindus left for India.

Relations with West Pakistan were strained from the outset. Bengali demands for recognition of their language and resentment of preferential investment in their western partner led to the formation of the Awami League in 1949 to represent Bengali interests. Led by Sheikh Mujibur Rahman (Mujib), the Awami League triumphed as part of the 'United Front' in elections in 1954 but its government was dismissed by Governor-General Ghulam Mohammad after two months. A military government was installed from 1958–62 and in 1966 Mujib was arrested. Civilian government was again suspended in 1969 and in elections in 1970–71 the Awami League won all East Pakistani seats. While talks to form a government foundered, President Yahya Khan sent troops to the East and suspended the assembly, provoking a civil disobedience campaign. On 25 March 1971 the army began a crackdown. Members of the Awami League were arrested or fled to Calcutta, where they declared a provisional Bengali government. 10m. Bengalis fled to India to escape the bloody repression. India, with Soviet support, invaded on 3 Dec. 1971, forcing the surrender of the Pakistani army on 16 Dec. Mujib was released to become prime minister of independent Bangladesh.

Bangladesh suffered famine in 1974 and disorder led to Mujib assuming the presidency with dictatorial powers. Assassinated in Aug. 1975, a coup brought to power Maj.-Gen. Zia ur-Rahman, who turned against the former ally, India. Zia was assassinated in 1981. Hussain Mohammad Ershad became martial law administrator in 1982 and president in 1983. Ershad's National Party triumphed in parliamentary elections in May 1986 but presidential elections in Oct. were boycotted by opposition parties. A campaign of demonstrations and national strikes forced Ershad's resignation in 1990. Zia's widow, Khaleda, became prime minister after her Bangladesh Nationalist Party (BJD) won nearly half the seats. The Awami League's victory in 1996 brought Mujib's daughter, Sheikh Hasina Wajed, to the premiership but Khaleda Zia returned to power in 2001.

TERRITORY AND POPULATION

Bangladesh is bounded in the west and north by India, east by India and Myanmar and south by the Bay of Bengal. The area is 56,977 sq. miles (147,570 sq. km). In 1992 India granted a 999-year lease of the Tin Bigha corridor linking Bangladesh with its enclaves of Angarpota and Dahagram. At the 1991 census the population was 111,455,000 (54,141,000 females). The most recent census took place in Jan. 2001; population, 129,247,233 (65,841,419 males), giving a density of 876 persons per sq. km. The United Nations population estimate for 2000 was 137,952,000.

The UN gives a projected population for 2010 of 167·17m.

In 2001, 76·4% of the population lived in rural areas. The country is administratively divided into six divisions, subdivided into 21 *anchal* and 64 *zila*. Area (in sq. km) and population (in 1,000) in 2001 of the six divisions:

	Area	*Population*
Barisal division	13,297	8,514
Chittagong division	33,771	25,187
Dhaka division	31,119	40,592
Khulna division	22,274	15,185
Rajshahi division	34,513	31,478
Sylhet division	12,596	8,291

The populations of the chief cities (2001 census) were as follows:

Dhaka[1]	5,644,235	Tongi	295,883	Jessore	187,098
Chittagong[2]	2,199,590	Rangpur	264,158	Comilla	176,713
Khulna[3]	811,490	Narayanganj	241,694	Dinajpur	165,131
Rajshahi[4]	402,646	Mymensingh	236,989	Nawabganj	160,838
Sylhet	299,431	Barisal	212,253	Bogra	157,570

[1]Metropolitan area, 10,403,597. [2]Metropolitan area, 3,361,244.
[3]Metropolitan area, 1,287,987. [4]Metropolitan area, 678,728.

The official language is Bengali. English is also in use for official, legal and commercial purposes.

SOCIAL STATISTICS

1998 births, 2,629,000; deaths, 634,000. In 1998 the birth rate was 19·9 per 1,000 population; death rate, 4·8; marriage rate, 1997, 10·0; infant mortality, 2001, 51 per 1,000 live births. Life expectancy at birth, 2001, 60·9 years for females and 60·1 years for males. Annual population growth rate, 1992–2002, 2·3%. The fertility rate dropped from 4·5 births per woman in 1991 to 3·6 births per woman in 2001. Bangladesh has made some of the best progress in recent years in reducing child mortality. The number of deaths per 1,000 live births among children under five was reduced from nearly 150 in 1990 to 77 in 2001.

CLIMATE

A tropical monsoon climate with heat, extreme humidity and heavy rainfall in the monsoon season, from June to Oct. The short winter season (Nov.–Feb.) is mild and dry. Rainfall varies between 50" (1,250 mm) in the west to 100" (2,500 mm) in the southeast and up to 200" (5,000 mm) in the northeast. Dhaka, Jan. 66°F (19°C), July 84°F (28·9°C). Annual rainfall 81" (2,025 mm). Chittagong, Jan. 66°F (19°C), July 81°F (27·2°C). Annual rainfall 108" (2,831 mm). In mid-1998 the Ganges and other rivers flowing into Bangladesh burst their banks causing a deluge that covered two-thirds of the country. More than 22m. were made homeless and 700 died in the floods.

CONSTITUTION AND GOVERNMENT

Bangladesh is a unitary republic. The Constitution came into force on 16 Dec. 1972 and provides for a parliamentary democracy. The head of state is the *President*, elected by parliament every five years, who appoints a *Vice-President*. A referendum of Sept. 1991 was in favour of abandoning the executive presidential system and opted for a parliamentary system. Turn-out was low. An amendment to the constitution in 1996 allowed for a caretaker government, which the president may instal to supervise elections should the parliament be dissolved. There is a *Council of Ministers* to assist and advise the President. The President appoints the government ministers.

Following a constitutional amendment made in May 2004 parliament has one chamber of 345 members, 300 directly elected every five years by citizens over 18 and 45 reserved for women, elected by the 300 MPs based on proportional representation in parliament. Prior to the amendment the parliament had just contained 300 directly elected members.

National Anthem. 'Amar Sonar Bangla, ami tomay bhalobashi' ('My golden Bengal, I love you'); words and tune by Rabindranath Tagore.

RECENT ELECTIONS

Iajuddin Ahmed was declared president-elect on 5 Sept. 2002 after the opposition Bangladesh Awami League failed to put forward a rival candidate.

In parliamentary elections of 1 Oct. 2001 the Bangladesh Jatiyatabadi Dal (BJD) and its coalition partners gained 47% of votes cast. The BJD itself gained 191 seats, with allies the Jamaat-e-Islami Bangladesh (JIB) gaining 18, the Jatiya Dal-Naziur (JD-N) 4 and the Islami Oikya Jote (IOJ) 2. The Bangladesh Awami League (BAL) gained 62 seats (40%), the Jatiya Dal-Ershad (JD-E) 14 (7·5%) with remaining seats going to other parties. Turn-out was 74·9%.

CURRENT ADMINISTRATION

President: Iajuddin Ahmed; b. 1931 (since 6 Sept. 2002).

In March 2005 the government comprised:

Prime Minister and Minister of Defence, Chittagong Hill Tracts Affairs, Cabinet Affairs, Energy and Mineral Resources, Primary and Mass Education, and Establishment: Khaleda Zia; b. 1945 (BJD; sworn in 10 Oct. 2001).

Minister of Agriculture: M. K. Anwar. *Commerce:* Altaf Hossain Chowdhury. *Communications:* Nazmul Huda. *Education:* Osman Faruq. *Environment and Forestry:* Tariqul Islam. *Finance and Planning:* Saifur Rahman. *Fisheries and Livestock:* Abdullah Al-Noman. *Food and Disaster Management:* Chowdhury Kamal Ibne Yusuf. *Foreign Affairs:* Morshed Khan. *Health and Family Welfare:* Dr Khandaker Mosharraf Hossain. *Housing and Public Works:* Mirza Abbas. *Industries:* Matiur Rahman Nizami. *Information:* Shamsul Islam. *Law, Justice and Parliamentary Affairs:* Moudud Ahmed. *Local Government, Rural Development and Co-operatives:* Abdul Mannan Bhuiyan. *Post and Telecommunications:* Aminul Haque. *Science and Information and Communication Technology:* Dr Abdul Moyeen Khan. *Shipping:* Akbar Hossain. *Social Welfare:* Ali Ahsan Mohammed Mujahid. *Textiles and Jute:* Shahjahan Siraj. *Water Resources:* Hafizuddin Ahmad Bir Bakram. *Women and Children's Affairs:* Khurshid Jahan Haque. *Minister without Portfolio:* Abdul Matin Chowdhury.

Government Website: http://www.bangladesh.gov.bd

DEFENCE

The supreme command of defence services is vested in the President. Defence expenditure in 2003 totalled US$645m. (US$5 per capita), representing 1·2% of GDP.

Army. Strength (2002) 120,000. There is also an armed police reserve, 5,000 strong, 20,000 security guards (Ansars) and the Bangladesh Rifles (border guard) numbering 38,000. There is a further potential reserve Ansar force of 180,000.

Navy. Naval bases are at Chittagong, Dhaka, Kaptai, Khulna and Mongla. The fleet comprises five frigates, ten missile craft, four torpedo craft and 19 patrol craft. Personnel, 2002, 10,500.

Air Force. There are four fighter squadrons and three helicopter squadrons. Personnel strength (2002) 6,500. There were 83 combat aircraft in 2002.

INTERNATIONAL RELATIONS

Bangladesh is a member of the UN, WTO, the Commonwealth, Asian Development Bank, Colombo Plan, IOM, Organization of the Islamic Conference, SAARC, Islamic Development Bank and the Non-Aligned Movement.

ECONOMY

In 2002 agriculture accounted for 22·7% of GDP, industry 26·4% and services 50·9%.

Overview. Bangladesh is ranked 36th in world poverty rankings with 36·9% of the population below the international US$1 a day poverty line. The agricultural sector accounts for nearly two-thirds of employment with rice as the single most important product. The government has followed prudent macro policies and has undertaken IMF structural reforms, which have strengthened economic performance. Despite these recent improvements Bangladesh has suffered lower foreign direct investment than other fast growing countries in East Asia owing to an unreliable power supply, high real interest rates, corruption and weaknesses in law and order. Bangladesh's efforts to decrease poverty and increase stability have been hindered by a weak banking system, limited public resources and natural disasters.

Currency. The unit of currency is the *taka* (BDT) of 100 *poisha*, which was floated in 1976. Foreign exchange reserves in June 2002 were US$1,543m. and gold reserves 112,000 troy oz. Inflation was 3·8% in 2002. Total money supply was Tk.231,658m. in May 2002.

Budget. The fiscal year ends on 30 June. Budget, 2002–03: revenue, Tk.326bn.; expenditure, Tk.448bn.

Performance. Real GDP growth was 4·8% in 2001 and 4·9% in 2002. Total GDP was US$51·9bn. in 2003. Corporate earnings grew by 9% in 1997. Trade liberalization measures were introduced 1994–96.

Banking and Finance. Bangladesh Bank is the central bank (*Governor*, Dr Fakhruddin Ahmed). There are four nationalized commercial banks, 16 private commercial banks, nine foreign commercial banks and ten development finance organizations. In 1999 the Bangladesh Bank had Tk.9,118m. deposits. In 1999 Sonali Bank was the largest of the nationalized commercial banks with deposits of Tk.170,961m.

There are stock exchanges in Dhaka and Chittagong.

Weights and Measures. The metric system was introduced from July 1982, but some imperial and traditional measures are still in use. One *tola* = 11·66 g; one *maund* = 37·32 kg = 40 *seers*; one *seer* = 0·93 kg.

ENERGY AND NATURAL RESOURCES

Environment. Bangladesh's carbon dioxide emissions from the consumption and flaring of fossil fuels in 2002 were the equivalent of 0·2 tonnes per capita.

Electricity. Installed capacity, 2000, 3·5m. kW. Electricity generated, 2000, about 15·55bn. kWh; consumption per capita in 2000 was an estimated 113 kWh.

Oil and Gas. In 2002 Bangladesh had proven natural gas reserves of 300,000m. cu. metres in about 20 mainly onshore fields. Some international companies believe the actual figure to be very much higher. Total natural gas production in 2002 amounted to 11·2bn. cu. metres.

Water. A Ganges water-sharing accord was signed with India in 1997, ending a 25-year dispute which had hindered and dominated relations between the two countries.

By 2000 it was estimated that 85m. people out of the total population of 128m. had been accidentally poisoned over the previous 30 years through arsenic-contaminated drinking water. A World Health Organization report has described it as 'the largest mass poisoning of a population in history'.

Minerals. The principal minerals are lignite, limestone, china clay and glass sand. There are reserves of good-quality coal of 300m. tonnes. Production, 2001–02: limestone, 32,000 tonnes; kaolin, 8,100 tonnes.

Agriculture. In 1995 the agricultural population was 106·18m., of whom 39·18m. were economically active. There were 8·09m. ha of arable land in 2001 and 0·4m.

ha of permanent crops. 4·42m. ha were irrigated in 2001. Bangladesh is a major producer of jute: production, 2000, 1·53m. tonnes. Rice is the most important food crop; production in 2000 (in 1m. metric tonnes), 35·82. Other major crops (1m. tonnes): sugarcane, 6·95; wheat, 1·90; potatoes, 1·70; bananas, 0·56.

Livestock in 2000: cattle, 23,652,000; goats, 33,800,000; sheep, 1,121,000; buffalo, 828,000; chickens, 139,000,000. Livestock products in 2000 (tonnes): beef and veal, 170,000; goat meat, 127,000; poultry meat, 112,000; goat milk, 1,296,000; cow milk, 755,000; buffalo milk, 22,000; sheep milk, 22,000; eggs, 132,000. Bangladesh is the second largest producer of goat milk, after India.

Forestry. In 2000 the area under forests was 1·33m. ha, or 10·2% of the total land area. Timber production in 2001 was 28·42m. cu. metres.

Fisheries. Bangladesh is a major producer of fish and fish products. There are 500,000 sea- and 800,000 inland-fishermen, with 1,249 mechanized boats, including 52 trawlers, and 3,317 motor boats. The total catch in 2001 amounted to approximately 1,000,000 tonnes, of which 670,000 tonnes came from inland waters. Only China and India have larger annual catches of freshwater fish.

INDUSTRY

Manufacturing contributes around 11% of GDP. The principal industries are jute and cotton textiles, tea, paper, newsprint, cement, chemical fertilizers and light engineering. Production, in 1,000 tonnes: cement (2000–01), 2,340; nitrogenous fertilizer (2001), 1,875; jute goods (2001–02), 536; sugar (2002), 229. Output of other products: cotton woven fabrics (2000–01), 63m. sq. metres; cigarettes (2000–01), 20·1bn. units; television sets (2001), 133,000 units; bicycles (2000–01), 13,000 units.

Labour. In 2000 the economically active workforce totalled 51,764,000 over the age of 15 years (32,369,000 males). The main areas of activity (in 1,000) were as follows: agriculture, hunting, forestry and fishing, 32,171; wholesale and retail trade, restaurants and hotels, 6,275; manufacturing, 3,783; community, social and personal services, 2,969; transport, storage and communication, 2,509; construction, 1,099. On average, wage rates (US$0·23 an hour, 1997) are among the lowest of developing countries. In 1999–2000, 3·3% of the workforce aged 15 or over were unemployed.

INTERNATIONAL TRADE

Foreign companies are permitted wholly to own local subsidiaries. Tax concessions are available to foreign firms in the export zones of Dhaka and Chittagong. Foreign debt was US$17,037m. in 2002.

Imports and Exports. The main exports are jute and jute goods, tea, hides and skins, newsprint, fish and garments, and the main imports are machinery, transport equipment, manufactured goods, minerals, fuels and lubricants.

Imports and exports for calendar years in US$1m.:

	1998	*1999*	*2000*	*2001*	*2002*
Imports f.o.b.	6,715·7	7,535·5	8,052·9	8,133·4	7,714·0
Exports f.o.b.	5,141·4	5,458·3	6,399·2	6,084·7	6,078·4

In 1998, 39% of exports went to the USA, 9% to France, 9% to Germany and 7% to the UK. 15% of imports in 1998 came from India, 10% from China, 7% from Japan and 6% from Singapore.

Since the early 1980s the garment industry has developed from virtually nothing to earn some 70% of the country's hard currency. Garment exports in 1997 earned US$3·5bn.

COMMUNICATIONS

Roads. In 1999 the total road network covered 207,486 km, including 19,775 km of national roads and 17,297 km of secondary roads. Some 10,000 km of roads were destroyed in the floods of 1998. In 1998 there were 30,361 buses and coaches, 42,425 trucks and lorries, 2,235 taxis (1995), 46,561 motorized rickshaws (1995) and 57,068 passenger cars. In 1995 there were also 411,000 rickshaws and 727,000 bullock carts. There were 5,820 road accidents in 1998, resulting in 3,375 fatalities.

Rail. In 1999 there were 2,706 km of railways, comprising 884 km of 1,676 mm gauge and 1,822 km of metre gauge. Passenger-km travelled in 1999 came to 3·68bn. and freight tonne-km to 896m.

Civil Aviation. There are international airports at Dhaka (Zia) and Chittagong, and eight domestic airports. Biman Bangladesh Airlines is state-owned. In addition to domestic routes, in 2003 it operated international services to Abu Dhabi, Bahrain, Bangkok, Bombay, Brussels, Calcutta, Dammam, Delhi, Doha, Dubai, Frankfurt, Hong Kong, Jeddah, Karachi, Kathmandu, Kuala Lumpur, Kuwait, London, Muscat, New York, Paris, Rangoon (Yangon), Riyadh, Rome, Singapore and Tokyo. There were direct flights in 2003 with other airlines to Madinah, Paro, Tashkent and Tehran. In 2000 Dhaka's Zia International Airport handled 2,585,317 passengers (2,101,201 on international flights) and 113,333 tonnes of freight. In 1999 Biman Bangladesh Airlines flew 21·0m. km, carrying 1,215,400 passengers (891,600 on international flights).

Shipping. There are sea ports at Chittagong and Mongla, and inland ports at Dhaka, Chandpur, Barisal, Khulna and five other towns. There are 8,000 km of navigable inland waterways. The Bangladesh Shipping Corporation owned 18 ships in 1994. Total tonnage registered, 2002, 432,000 GRT (including oil tankers 63,000 GRT). In 1993–94 the two sea ports handled 8·20m. tonnes of imports and 1·66m. tonnes of exports. In 1999–2000 vessels totalling 6,509,000 NRT entered ports and vessels totalling 2,949,000 NRT cleared. The Bangladesh Inland Water Transport Corporation had 288 vessels in 1994. 70·29m. passengers were carried in 1992–93.

Telecommunications. Telephone subscribers numbered 1,757,000 in 2002 (13·2 per 1,000 inhabitants), of which 1,075,000 were mobile phone subscribers. International communications are by the Indian Ocean Intelsat IV satellite. There were 450,000 PCs in use in 2002 (3·4 for every 1,000 persons) and 40,000 fax machines in 1995. Bangladesh had 204,000 Internet users in 2002.

Postal Services. There were 9,093 post offices in 1997.

SOCIAL INSTITUTIONS

Justice. The Supreme Court comprises an Appellate and a High Court Division, the latter having control over all subordinate courts. Judges are appointed by the President and retire at 65. There are benches at Comilla, Rangpur, Jessore, Barisal, Chittagong and Sylhet, and courts at District level.

The population in penal institutions in 2002 was 64,866 (45 per 100,000 of national population).

The death penalty is still in force. In 2004 there were 12 executions.

Religion. Islam is the state religion. In 2001 the population was 87% Muslim and 12% Hindu.

Education. In 2000–01 there were 17·7m. pupils and 309,341 teachers at primary schools; 10·3m. pupils and 269,237 teachers in secondary schools; 878,537 students and 47,137 academic staff in tertiary education. In 1993–94 there were 80 professional colleges with 43,503 students and 2,752 teachers.

In 1995–96 there were five universities, an Islamic university, an open university and universities of agriculture, engineering and technology, and science and technology; there were five teacher training colleges, five medical, three law and two fine arts colleges, an institute of ophthalmology and a rehabilitation institute. In 1997 there were 67,282 university students and 4,015 academic staff. Adult literacy was 40·6% in 2001 (49·9% among males and 30·8% among females).

In 2000–01 total expenditure on education came to 2·5% of GNP and 15·7% of total government spending.

Health. In 1997 there were 976 hospitals, with the equivalent of four beds per 10,000 persons. There were 27,546 physicians, 938 dentists, 15,408 nurses and 13,211 midwives in 1997.

CULTURE

World Heritage Sites. There are three UNESCO sites in Bangladesh: the Historic Mosque City of Bagerhat (inscribed on the list in 1985); the Ruins of the Buddhist Vihara at Paharpur (1985); the Sundarbans (1997), 140,000 ha of mangrove forest.

Broadcasting. The government-controlled Bangladesh Betam and part-commercial Bangladesh Television transmit a home service and an external service radio programmes, and a TV programme (colour by PAL). In 2000 there were 6·4m. radio receivers and in 2001 there were 2·2m. TV receivers.

Press. In 1996 there were 37 daily newspapers with a combined circulation of 1·1m., at a rate of 9·3 per 1,000 inhabitants. In 1994, 1,258 book titles were published (122 in English).

Tourism. In 2000 there were 200,000 foreign tourists. Receipts totalled US$59m.

Libraries. Dhaka is home to The United States Information Centre, The British Council, and The Central Public Library (which also has branches outside the capital).

Theatre and Opera. The principal theatres are the Dhaka Theatre and the Nagorik Theatre.

Museums and Galleries. The main museums are: The National Museum; Muktijuddha Judughar (War of Liberation Museum); and The Bangabandhu Memorial Museum.

DIPLOMATIC REPRESENTATIVES

Of Bangladesh in the United Kingdom (28 Queen's Gate, London, SW7 5JA)
High Commissioner: Mofazzal Karim.
(There are also Assistant High Commissioners in Birmingham and Manchester)

Of the United Kingdom in Bangladesh (United Nations Rd, Baridhara, Dhaka 12)
High Commissioner: Anwar Choudhury.

Of Bangladesh in the USA (3510 International Drive, NW, Washington, D.C., 20008)
Ambassador: Syed Hasan Ahmed.

Of the USA in Bangladesh (Madani Ave., Baridhara, Dhaka 1212)
Ambassador: Harry K. Thomas, Jr.

Of Bangladesh to the United Nations
Ambassador: Iftekhar Ahmed Chowdhury.

Of Bangladesh to the European Union
Ambassador: Syed Maudud Ali.

FURTHER READING

Bangladesh Bureau of Statistics. *Statistical Yearbook of Bangladesh.—Statistical Pocket Book of Bangladesh.*

Ahmed, A. F. S., *Bangladesh: Tradition and Transformation.* Dhaka, 1987
Hajnoczy, R., *Fire of Bengal.* Bangladesh Univ. Press, 1993
Muhith, A. M. A., *Issues of Governance in Bangladesh.* Mowla Brothers, Dhaka, 2000
Rashid, H. U., *Foreign Relations of Bangladesh.* Rishi Publications, Varanasi, 2001
Tajuddin, M., *Foreign Policy of Bangladesh: Liberation War to Sheikh Hasina.* National Book Organisation, New Delhi, 2001
Ziring, L., *Bangladesh from Mujib to Ershad: an Interpretive Study.* OUP, 1993

National statistical office: Bangladesh Bureau of Statistics, Ministry of Planning, Dhaka
Website: http://www.bbsgov.org/

BARBADOS

Capital: Bridgetown
Population projection, 2010: 276,000
GDP per capita, 2002: (PPP$) 15,290
HDI/world rank: 0·888/29

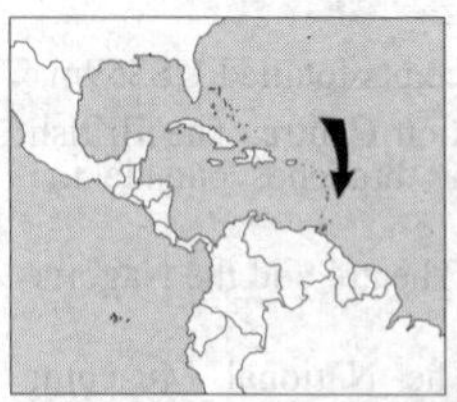

KEY HISTORICAL EVENTS

Barbados was settled by the British during the 1620s and developed as a sugar plantation economy, initially on the basis of slavery until its abolition in the 1840s. In 1951 universal suffrage was introduced, followed in 1954 by cabinet government. Full internal self-government was attained in Oct. 1961. On 30 Nov. 1966 Barbados became an independent sovereign state within the Commonwealth.

TERRITORY AND POPULATION

Barbados lies to the east of the Windward Islands. Area 166 sq. miles (430 sq. km). In 2000 the census population was 268,792. 2003 estimate: 272,229; density 528·7 per sq. km.

The UN gives a projected population for 2010 of 276,000.

In 2001, 50·5% of the population were urban. Bridgetown is the principal city: population (including suburbs), 133,000 in 1999. Other main towns are Oistins, Holetown and Speightstown.

The official language is English.

SOCIAL STATISTICS

In 2003: births, 3,748; deaths, 2,274; birth rate, 13·0 per 1,000 population; death rate, 8·4; infant mortality, 9·9 per 1,000 live births. Expectation of life, 2001, males 74·3 years and females 79·3. Population growth rate, 2003, 0·3%; fertility rate, 2001, 1·5 children per woman.

CLIMATE

An equable climate in winter, but the wet season, from June to Nov., is more humid. Rainfall varies from 50" (1,250 mm) on the coast to 75" (1,875 mm) in the higher interior. Bridgetown, Jan. 76°F (24·4°C), July 80°F (26·7°C). Annual rainfall 51" (1,275 mm).

CONSTITUTION AND GOVERNMENT

The head of state is the British sovereign, represented by an appointed Governor-General. The bicameral Parliament consists of a Senate and a House of Assembly. The *Senate* comprises 21 members appointed by the Governor-General, 12 being appointed on the advice of the Prime Minister, two on the advice of the Leader of the Opposition and seven at the Governor-General's discretion. The *House of Assembly* comprises 30 members elected every five years. In 1963 the voting age was reduced to 18.

The *Privy Council* is appointed by the Governor-General after consultation with the Prime Minister. It consists of 12 members and the Governor-General as chairman. It advises the Governor-General in the exercise of the royal prerogative of mercy and in the exercise of his disciplinary powers over members of the public and police services.

National Anthem. 'In plenty and in time of need'; words by Irvine Burgie, tune by V. R. Edwards.

RECENT ELECTIONS

In the general election of 21 May 2003 the Barbados Labour Party (BLP) gained 23 seats (55·8% of the total vote) and the Democratic Labour Party (DLP) 7 seats (44·1%).

CURRENT ADMINISTRATION

Governor-General: Sir Clifford Husbands, GCMG, KA; b. 1926.

In March 2005 the government comprised:

Prime Minister, Minister of Finance and Economic Affairs, and Civil Service: Owen S. Arthur; b. 1950 (BLP; appointed 7 Sept. 1994).

Deputy Prime Minister, Attorney General, Minister of Home Affairs: Mia Amor Mottley. *Minister of Agriculture and Rural Development:* Erskine Griffith. *Commerce, Consumer Affairs and Business Development:* Lynette Eastmond. *Education, Youth Affairs and Sports:* Reginald Farley. *Energy and Public Utilities:* Anthony Wood. *Foreign Affairs and Foreign Trade:* Billie A. Miller. *Health:* Dr Jerome Walcott. *Housing, Lands and the Environment:* Elizabeth Thompson. *Industry and International Business:* Dale Marshall. *Labour and Social Security:* Rawle C. Eastmond. *Public Works:* Gline Arley Clarke. *Social Transformation:* Hamilton Lashley. *Tourism and International Transport:* Noel Anderson Lynch.

Government of Barbados Information Network: http://www.barbados.gov.bb

DEFENCE

The Barbados Defence Force has a strength of about 610. In 2003 defence expenditure totalled US$13m. (US$48 per capita), representing 0·5% of GDP.

Army. Army strength was 500 with reserves numbering 430 in 2002.

Navy. A small maritime unit numbering 110 (2002) operates five patrol vessels. The unit is based at St Ann's Fort Garrison, Bridgetown.

INTERNATIONAL RELATIONS

Barbados is a member of the UN, WTO, OAS, Inter-American Development Bank, ACS, CARICOM, the Commonwealth and is an ACP member state of the ACP-EU relationship.

ECONOMY

In 2003 agriculture accounted for 4% of GDP, industry 16% and services 80%.

Currency. The unit of currency is the *Barbados dollar* (BDS$) of 100 *cents*, which is pegged to the US dollar at BDS$2=US$1. Inflation was 1·6% in 2003. Total money in circulation was BDS$2,242m. in March 2003. Foreign exchange reserves were USS$506m. in March 2003.

Budget. The financial year runs from April. Capital expenditure for 2003–04 was BDS$253·7m.; current expenditure for the same period was BDS$2,048·3m. The budget for 2003–04 put total revenue at an estimated BDS$1,850·5m. and recurrent expenditure at BDS$2,080·5m.

VAT at 15% was introduced in Jan. 1997.

Performance. Total GDP in 2003 was US$2·7bn. Barbados has been experiencing a recession, with the economy shrinking by 2·7% in 2001 and 1·8% in 2002. There were signs of a slight recovery in 2003.

Banking and Finance. The central bank and bank of issue is the Central Bank of Barbados (*Governor,* Dr Marion Williams), which had total assets of BDS$1,248·5m. in Dec. 2003. The provisional figures for the total assets of commercial banks in Dec. 2003 were BDS$6,812·6m. and savings banks' deposits BDS$5,493·8m.

In 2003 there were 4,635 international business companies, 413 exempt insurance companies and 51 offshore banks. In addition, there were three commercial banks, one regional development bank, one National Bank (scheduled for privatization), three foreign banks and seven trust companies.

There is a stock exchange which participates in the regional Caribbean exchange.

Weights and Measures. Both Imperial and metric systems are in use.

ENERGY AND NATURAL RESOURCES

Environment. Carbon dioxide emissions from the consumption and flaring of fossil fuels in Barbados in 2002 were the equivalent of 6·0 tonnes per capita.

Electricity. Production in 2003, 900·5m. kWh. Capacity in 2000 was 0·2m kW. Consumption per capita was an estimated 2,961 kWh in 2003.

Oil and Gas. Crude oil production in 2003 was 370,909 bbls. and reserves in 2002 were 2·5m. bbls.

Output of gas (2003) 22·4m. cu. metres, and reserves (2003) 130m. cu. metres. Production of Liquid Petroleum Gas (LPG) was 3,691 bbls. in 2003.

Agriculture. The agricultural sector accounted for 4·4% of GDP in 2003, down from 24% in 1967. Of the total labour force in 2003, 4·6% were employed in agriculture. Of the total area of Barbados (42,995 ha), about 16,000 ha are arable land, which is intensively cultivated. In 2003, 7,515 ha were under sugarcane cultivation. Production, 2003 (in tonnes): sugarcane, 48,500; sweet potatoes, 2,610; cucumbers, 2,018; okra, 1,446; tomatoes, 1,234; yams, 1,234; carrots, 1,012; cabbages, 640.

Meat and dairy products, 2003 (in tonnes): poultry, 11,458; cow milk, 7,017; pork, 1,756; eggs, 1,620; beef, 346.

Livestock (2000): cattle, 23,000; sheep, 41,000; pigs, 33,000; chickens, 4m.

Forestry. Timber production in 2001 was 5,000 cu. metres.

Fisheries. In 2003 there were 954 fishing vessels employed during the flying-fish season. The catch in 2003 was 2,400 tonnes, exclusively from sea fishing.

INDUSTRY

Industry has traditionally been centred on sugar, but there is also light manufacturing and component assembly for export. In 2003, 36,300 tonnes of raw sugar were produced.

Labour. In 2003 the workforce was 145,500, of whom 129,500 were employed. Unemployment stood at 11·0%, down from 24·5% in 1993.

Trade Unions. About one-third of employees are unionized. The Barbados Workers' Union was founded in 1938 and has the majority of members. There are also a National Union of Public Workers and two teachers' unions.

INTERNATIONAL TRADE

External debt was BDS$2,224m. in 2004 (provisional).

Imports and Exports. In 2004 exports (excluding petroleum products) were valued at BDS$498m., and imports at BDS$2,752m.

The main import suppliers in 2004 were the USA (37·0%), followed by Trinidad and Tobago (18·9%), UK (6·0%) and Canada (3·9%). Principal export markets in 2004 were the USA (15·4%), followed by Trinidad and Tobago (11·0%), UK (10·5%) and Jamaica (5·2%).

The main exports are electrical components, sugar, rum, cement, chemicals and petroleum (re-export) products. Main imports are foodstuffs, cars, chemicals, mineral fuels, and machinery and equipment.

COMMUNICATIONS

Roads. There were 1,793 km of roads in 2000. In 2004 there were 86,240 cars; 10,748 lorries, vans and pickups; 5,896 buses, coaches and taxis; 1,156 other commercial vehicles. There were 29 deaths as a result of road accidents in 2000.

Civil Aviation. The Grantley Adams International Airport is 16 km from Bridgetown. In 2001 it handled 1,763,500 passengers (all on international flights) and 14,094 tonnes of freight.

Shipping. There is a deep-water harbour at Bridgetown. 665,595 tonnes of cargo were handled in 1994. Shipping registered in 2002 totalled 328,000 GRT, including oil tankers 8,000 GRT. The number of merchant vessels entering in 2001 was 2,087 of 18·6m. net tonnes.

Telecommunications. In Dec. 2001 there were 127,632 telephone main lines (474·8 per 1,000 inhabitants), 39,789 of which were business lines. There were 28,000 PCs in use in 2002 (104·1 per 1,000 inhabitants). Barbados had 53,100 mobile phone subscribers in 2001 and 30,000 Internet users in 2002. In 1995 there were 1,800 fax machines.

Postal Services. There is a general post office in Bridgetown and 16 branches on the island.

SOCIAL INSTITUTIONS

Justice. Justice is administered by the Supreme Court and Justices' Appeal Court, and by magistrates' courts. All have both civil and criminal jurisdiction. There is a Chief Justice, three judges of appeal, five puisne judges of the Supreme Court and nine magistrates. The death penalty is authorized. Final appeal lies to the Privy Council in London. Barbados was one of ten countries to sign an agreement in Feb. 2001 establishing a Caribbean Court of Justice to replace the British Privy Council as the highest civil and criminal court. In the meantime the number of signatories has risen to twelve. The court was inaugurated at Port-of-Spain, Trinidad on 16 April 2005.

The population in penal institutions in Nov. 2003 was 992 (367 per 100,000 of national population).

Police. The strength of the police service in 1996 was 1,221.

Religion. In 2001, 63% of the population were Protestants, 5% Roman Catholics and the remainder other religions.

Education. The adult literacy rate was 99·7% in 2001 (males, 99·7%; females, 99·7%). In 2002–03 there were 25,265 primary and 20,375 secondary school pupils in government schools and 3,730 primary and 1,139 secondary pupils in private schools. There were 23 public and eight private secondary schools in 2003. Education is free in all government-owned and government-maintained institutions from primary to university level.

In 2000–01 total expenditure on education came to 7·3% of GNP and 18·5% of total government spending.

In 2002–03 the University of the West Indies in Barbados (founded 1963) had 4,363 students, the Community College had 3,697, the Samuel Jackman Prescod Polytechnic had 2,972 and Erdiston Teachers' College had 223 students.

Health. In 2001 there was one general hospital, one psychiatric hospital, five district hospitals, eight health centres and two private hospitals with 35 beds. There were 2,049 hospital beds and 420 doctors in the same year.

Welfare. The National Insurance and Social Security Scheme provides contributory sickness, age, maternity, disability and survivors benefits. Sugar workers have their own scheme.

CULTURE

Broadcasting. The Caribbean Broadcasting Corporation is a government-owned commercial TV and radio service. There are two other commercial services. In 2001 there were 202,000 radios (749 per 1,000 persons) and 88,000 television sets (326 per 1,000 persons). Colour is by NTSC.

Cinema. In 2001 there were two cinemas and one drive-in cinema for 600 cars.

Press. In 2003 there were two daily newspapers, the *Barbados Advocate* (est. 1895) and the *Daily Nation* (est. 1973), and a weekly business publication, the *Broad Street Journal*. The *Daily Nation* has an average daily circulation of 25,000; the *Barbados Advocate*, 15,000.

Tourism. There were 531,211 foreign tourists in 2003, plus 559,119 cruise ship arrivals, bringing revenue of BDS$1,493·8m. and contributing 11·8% of the country's GDP.

Festivals. The National Cultural Foundation organizes three annual national festivals: the nine-day Congaline Carnival which begins in the last week of April; Crop Over, a three-week festival held from mid-July until Aug.; the National Independence Festival of Creative Arts (NIFCA) which runs throughout Nov.

Libraries. The National Library Service operates seven branch libraries around the island and the Adult and Children's libraries in Bridgetown.

Museums and Galleries. There are four museums: the Barbados Museum at Bridgetown, which is housed in the former British military prison; Sunbury Plantation House; Hutson Sugar Museum; Tyrol Cot Heritage Village.

DIPLOMATIC REPRESENTATIVES

Of Barbados in the United Kingdom (1 Great Russell St., London, WC1B 3ND)
High Commissioner: L. Edwin Pollard.

Of the United Kingdom in Barbados (Lower Collymore Rock, Bridgetown)
High Commissioner: John White.

Of Barbados in the USA (2144 Wyoming Ave., NW, Washington, D.C. 20008)
Ambassador: Michael I. King.

Of the USA in Barbados (PO Box 302, Bridgetown)
Ambassador: Mary E. Kramer.

Of Barbados to the United Nations
Ambassador: Christopher Hackett.

Of Barbados to the European Union
Ambassador: Errol L. Humphrey.

FURTHER READING

Beckles, H., *A History of Barbados: from Amerindian Settlement to Nation-State.* Cambridge Univ. Press, 1990

Hoyos, F. A., *Tom Adams: a Biography.* London, 1988.—*Barbados: A History from the Amerindians to Independence.* 2nd ed. London, 1992

National statistical office: Barbados Statistical Service, Fairchild Street, Bridgetown.

BELARUS

Respublika Belarus

Capital: Minsk
Population projection, 2010: 9·61m.
GDP per capita, 2002: (PPP$) 5,520
HDI/world rank: 0·790/62

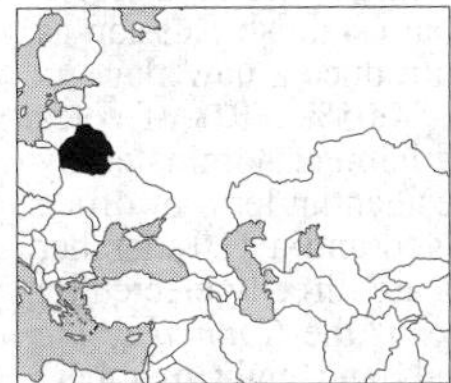

KEY HISTORICAL EVENTS

Belarus was fully integrated with Russia until the Gorbachev reforms of the mid-1980s encouraged demands for greater freedom. On 25 Aug. 1991 Belarus declared its independence and in Dec. it became a founder member of the CIS. The Communists retained power in Belarus despite formidable opposition and it was not until a new constitution was adopted in March 1994 that the economic reformers began to influence events. Alyaksandr Lukashenka was elected president in July 1994. By 1996, only 11% of state enterprises had been privatized and the government remains pro-Russian, striving for eventual unification with Russia within the Russia–Belarus Union. A referendum held over 9–24 Nov. 1996 extended the President's term of office from three to five years and increased his powers to rule by decree. The last parliamentary elections were criticized by the OSCE for a lack of transparency.

TERRITORY AND POPULATION

Belarus is situated along the western Dvina and Dnieper. It is bounded in the west by Poland, north by Latvia and Lithuania, east by Russia and south by Ukraine. The area is 207,600 sq. km (80,155 sq. miles). The capital is Minsk. Other important towns are Homel, Vitebsk, Mahilyou, Bobruisk, Hrodno and Brest. On 2 Nov. 1939 western Belorussia was incorporated with an area of over 108,000 sq. km and a population of 4·8m. Census population, 1999, 10,045,237. Estimated population, 2004, 9,849,100; density, 47·4 per sq. km.

The UN gives a projected population for 2010 of 9·61m.

In 2001, 69·6% of the population lived in urban areas. Major ethnic groups: 78% Belorussians, 13% Russians, 4% Poles, 3% Ukrainians, 1% Jews, 1% others.

Belarus comprises six provinces. Areas and estimated populations:

Province	*Area sq. km*	*Population 2004*	*Capital*	*Population 2004*
Brest	32,300	1,462,900	Brest	298,300
Homel	40,400	1,505,400	Homel	481,100
Hrodno	25,000	1,146,100	Hrodno	314,800
Mahilyou	29,000	1,169,200	Mahilyou	365,100
Minsk	40,800	3,244,400	Minsk	1,741,300
Vitebsk	40,100	1,321,100	Vitebsk	342,300

Belorussian is the national language. Russian is also spoken.

SOCIAL STATISTICS

2001 births, 91,677 (rate of 9·2 per 1,000 population); deaths, 139,904 (rate of 14·0 per 1,000 population); marriages, 68,697; divorces, 40,850. In 1999 abortions totalled 1,451 per 1,000 live births—one of the highest rates in the world. In 2001 there were 4·1 divorces per 1,000 population, also one of the highest rates in the world. Annual population growth rate, 1992–2002, –0·4%. Life expectancy at birth, 2001, was 64·3 years for men and 75·0 years for women. Infant mortality, 2001, 9·1 per 1,000 live births; fertility rate, 2001, 1·3 children per woman.

CLIMATE

Moderately continental and humid with temperatures averaging 20°F (–6°C) in Jan. and 64°F (18°C) in July. Annual precipitation is 22–28" (550–700 mm).

CONSTITUTION AND GOVERNMENT

A new Constitution was adopted on 15 March 1994. It provides for a *President* who must be a citizen of at least 35 years of age, have resided for ten years in Belarus and whose candidacy must be supported by the signatures of 70 deputies or 100,000 electors. At a referendum held on 20 Oct. 2004, 86·2% of votes cast were in favour of the abolition of the two-term limit on the presidency. The vote was widely regarded as fraudulent.

There is an 11-member *Constitutional Court*. The chief justice and five other judges are appointed by the President.

Four referendums held on 14 May 1995 gave the President powers to dissolve parliament; work for closer economic integration with Russia; establish Russian as an official language of equal status with Belorussian; and introduce a new flag.

At a further referendum of 9–24 Nov. 1996 turn-out was 84·05%. 79% of votes cast were in favour of the creation of an upper house of parliament nominated by provincial governors and 70% in favour of extending the presidential term of office by two years to five years. The Supreme Soviet was dissolved and a 110-member lower *House of Representatives* established, whose members are directly elected by universal adult suffrage every four years. The upper chamber is the *Council of the Republic* (64 seats; 56 members elected by regional councils and eight members appointed by the president, all for four-year terms). In practice, since 1996 the Belorussian parliament has only had a ceremonial function.

National Anthem. 'Magutny Bozha' ('Mighty God'); words by Natalla Arsiennieva, tune by Mikola Revienski.

RECENT ELECTIONS

Parliamentary elections were held on 17 Oct. 2004. A total of 107 out of 110 deputies were elected, all supporters of the government, with 12 of them representing political parties. The remaining three seats were to be decided in a second round which has yet to take place. The results of the first round have been widely disputed.

Presidential elections were held on 9 Sept. 2001. Alyaksandr Lukashenka was re-elected with 75·6% of votes cast against 15·4% for Uladzimir Hancharyk and 2·5% for Syarhey Haydukevich. The election took place amid accusations of vote rigging. No independent observers were allowed to watch the count. However, experts estimated that the opposition actually gained between 30% and 40% of the votes. Turn-out was 83·9%.

CURRENT ADMINISTRATION

President: Alyaksandr Lukashenka; b. 1955 (sworn in 20 July 1994 and re-elected in 2001).

Prime Minister: Sergei Sidorsky; b. 1954 (took office on 19 Dec. 2003).

In March 2005 the government comprised:

First Deputy Prime Minister: Vladimir Semashko. *Deputy Prime Ministers:* Andrei Kobyakov; Vladimir Drahzin; Anatoly Tyutyunov; Ivan Bambiza.

Minister for Architecture and Construction: Gennady Kurochkin. *Internal Affairs:* Vladimir Naumov. *Housing and Communal Services:* Vladimir Belokhvostov. *Health:* Ludmila Postoyalko. *Foreign Affairs:* Sergei Martynov. *Information:* Vladimir Rusakevich. *Culture:* Leonid Gulyako. *Defence:* Leonid Maltsev. *Education:* Alexander Radkov. *Tax Collection:* Anna Deiko. *Emergencies (acting):* Enver Bariyev. *Natural Resources and Environmental Protection:* Leonty Khoruzhik. *Industry:* Anatoly Rusetsky. *Communication:* Vladimir Goncharenko. *Agriculture and Food:* Leonid Rusak. *Sports and Tourism:* Yuri Sivakov. *Statistics and Analysis:* Vladimir Zinovsky. *Trade:* Aleksandr Kulichkov. *Transport and Communications:* Mikhail Borovoy. *Labour and Social Protection:* Antonina Morova. *Economy:* Nikolai Zaychenko. *Finance:* Nikolai Korbut. *Energy:* Eduard Tovpenets. *Justice:* Viktor Golovanov.

Government Website (Russian only): http://www.government.by

DEFENCE

Conscription is for 9–12 months. A treaty with Russia of April 1993 co-ordinates their military activities. All nuclear weapons had been transferred to Russia by Dec. 1996. Total active armed forces in 2002 numbered 79,800, including 30,000 conscripts and 4,000 women.

Defence expenditure in 2003 totalled US$2,400m. (US$243 per capita), representing 4·0% of GDP.

Army. There is a motor rifle division, three independent mobile brigades, one artillery division and one artillery regiment. In 2002 army personnel numbered 29,300. In addition there were 289,500 reserves.

Air Force. In 2002 the Air Force operated 212 combat aircraft, including MiG-23s, MiG-29s, Su-24s, Su-25s and Su-27s, and 58 attack helicopters. Personnel, 2002, 22,000 including 10,200 in Air Defence.

INTERNATIONAL RELATIONS

A treaty of friendship with Russia was signed on 21 Feb. 1995. A further treaty signed by the respective presidents on 2 April 1997 provided for even closer integration.

Belarus is a member of the UN, CIS, IMF, the World Bank, European Bank, OSCE, CEI and the NATO Partnership for Peace.

ECONOMY

In 2002 agriculture contributed 11·8% of GDP, industry 37·0% and services 51·2%. In 1999 an estimated 20% of economic output was being produced by the private sector.

Currency. The rouble was retained under an agreement of Sept. 1993 and a treaty with Russia on monetary union of April 1994. Foreign currencies ceased to be legal tender in Oct. 1994. In Nov. 2000 President Lukashenka and President Putin of Russia agreed the introduction of a single currency. The Russian rouble was introduced on a non-cash basis on 1 July 2003 with a single currency unit scheduled for introduction in Jan. 2008. The inflation rate in 1994 was 2,434%. It has since been declining and in 2002 was 42·6%. Foreign exchange reserves in June 2002 were US$392m. and total money supply was 1,047·53bn. roubles.

Budget. Government revenue and expenditure (in 1bn. roubles):

	1996	*1997*	*1998*	*1999*	*2000*	*2001*
Revenue	58·99	117·87	206·59	876·23	2,646·11	4,938·20
Expenditure	62·51	121·79	213·23	933·88	2,639·80	5,080·21

In 2000 tax revenue totalled 2,447·22bn. roubles (including domestic taxes on goods and services, 1,016·56bn. roubles) and non-tax revenue 172·47bn. roubles. Main items of expenditure were: social security and welfare, 1,018·17bn. roubles; agriculture, forestry, fisheries and hunting, 219·53bn. roubles; general public services, 121·25bn. roubles; defence, 113·06bn. roubles.

Performance. Real GDP growth was 4·7% in both 2001 and 2002. Total GDP in 2003 was US$17·5bn. It was predicted in 2000 that GDP would increase by between 24% and 33% by 2005.

Banking and Finance. The central bank is the National Bank (*Chairman*, Petr P. Prokopovich). In 2003 there were 28 commercial banks. There is a stock exchange in Minsk.

ENERGY AND NATURAL RESOURCES

Environment. Carbon dioxide emissions from the consumption and flaring of fossil fuels in Belarus were the equivalent of 6·0 tonnes per capita in 2002.

Electricity. Installed capacity was 7·8m. kW in 2000. Production was 26·10bn. kWh in 2000. Consumption per capita in 2000 was 3,330 kWh.

Oil and Gas. In 2000 output of crude petroleum totalled 1·9m. tonnes; reserves in 2002 were 198m. bbls. Natural gas production in 2000 was 261m. cu. metres; in 2002 reserves were 2·8bn. cu. metres.

Minerals. Particular attention has been paid to the development of the peat industry with a view to making Belarus as far as possible self-supporting in fuel. There are over 6,500 peat deposits. There are rich deposits of rock salt and of iron ore.

Agriculture. Belarus is hilly, with a general slope towards the south. It contains large tracts of marshland, particularly to the southwest.

Agriculturally, it may be divided into three main sections—Northern: growing flax, fodder, grasses and breeding cattle for meat and dairy produce; Central: potato growing and pig breeding; Southern: good natural pasture land, hemp cultivation and cattle breeding for meat and dairy produce. In 2002 agriculture employed 12·1% of the workforce.

Output of main agricultural products (in 1m. tonnes) in 2000: potatoes, 8·50; barley, 1·70; rye, 1·45; sugarbeet, 1·50; wheat, 0·95; cabbage, 0·52; oats, 0·52; milk, 4·32; eggs, 0·19. In 2000 there were 4·33m. cattle; 3·57m. pigs; 221,000 horses; and 30m. chickens.

Since 1991 individuals may own land and pass it to their heirs, but not sell it. In 2001 there were 6·13m. ha of arable land and 124,000 ha of permanent crops. There were 2,700 farms in 1993. The private and commercial sectors accounted for 38% of the value of agricultural output in 1993 (particularly potatoes and vegetables). It was predicted in 2000 that agricultural output would increase by between 20% and 30% by 2005.

Forestry. Forests occupied 9·40m. ha, or 45·3% of the land area, in 2000. There are valuable reserves of oak, elm, maple and white beech. Timber production in 2001 was 6·27m. cu. metres.

Fisheries. Fish landings in 2001 amounted to 943 tonnes, exclusively from inland waters.

INDUSTRY

There are food-processing, chemical, textile, artificial silk, flax-spinning, motor vehicle, leather, machine-tool and agricultural machinery industries. Output in 1,000 tonnes: residual fuel oil (2000), 4,629; distillate fuel oil (2000), 3,847; fertilizers (1995), 3,350; petrol (2000), 1,964; cement (2000), 1,847; wheat flour (1995), 1,417; crude steel (1997), 1,220. Output of other products: 10,356m. cigarettes (2000); 812,000 refrigerators (2000); 532,000 TV sets (2000); 26,500 tractors (1995); 13,002 lorries (1997); beer (2003), 200m. litres; footwear (1995), 13m. pairs; woven cotton (1997), 48m. sq. metres; linen fabrics (1995), 41·5m. sq. metres. Machine-building equipment and chemical products are also important. Most industry is still state-controlled.

Labour. In 2001 the labour force totalled 4,519,000. In 2001, out of 4,417,000 economically active people, 1,300,000 were in industry; 660,000 in agriculture; 500,000 in education; 420,000 in trade and public catering, material and technical supply and sale. In 2002 there were 130,500 unemployed persons, or 3·0% of the workforce.

Trade Unions. Trade unions are grouped in the Federation of Trade Unions of Belarus.

INTERNATIONAL TRADE

Foreign debt was US$908m. in 2002.

Imports and Exports. In 2002 imports were valued at US$9,092m. and exports at US$8,021m. The main import suppliers in 2002 were Russia (65·1%), Germany (7·6%), Ukraine (3·2%), Italy (2·4%) and Poland (2·4%). Principal export markets were Russia (49·6%), Latvia (6·5%), United Kingdom (6·2%), Germany (4·3%) and the Netherlands (3·5%). Main import commodities are petroleum, natural gas, rolled metal and coal. Export commodities include machinery and transport equipment, diesel fuel, synthetic fibres and consumer goods.

COMMUNICATIONS

Roads. In 2002 there were 79,990 km of motor roads (86·7% paved), including 15,371 km of national roads. There were 1,548,472 passenger cars in use in 2002 (156 per 1,000 inhabitants). In 2000 public transport totalled 9,235m. passenger-km and freight 8,982m. tonne-km. There were 1,594 fatalities as a result of road accidents in 2000.

Rail. In 2000 there were 5,512 km of 1,520 mm gauge railways (874 km electrified). Passenger-km travelled in 2000 came to 17·7bn. and freight tonne-km to 31·4bn. There is a metro in Minsk.

Civil Aviation. The main airport is Minsk International 2, which handled 400,000 passengers (all international) and 2,600 tonnes of freight in 2000. The national carrier is Belavia. In 2003 Belavia flew on domestic routes and operated international services to Adler/Sochi, Baku, Berlin, Frankfurt, Hurghada, İstanbul, Kaliningrad, Kyiv, Larnaca, London, Moscow, Paris, Prague, Rome, Shannon, Stockholm, Tashkent, Tbilisi, Tel Aviv, Vienna, Warsaw and Yerevan. In 1999 scheduled airline traffic of Belarus-based carriers flew 8·0m. km, carrying 212,000 passengers (all on international flights).

Shipping. In 2002 inland waterways carried 2m. passenger-km and 59m. tonne-km of freight.

Telecommunications. In 2002 there were 3,432,400 telephone subscribers (346·3 per 1,000 inhabitants). There are plans to privatize Beltelecom, the state monopoly, in 2007. There were 462,600 mobile phone subscribers in 2002 and 24,000 fax machines in 1999. Belarus had 808,700 Internet users in 2002.

Postal Services. In 1998 there were 3,852 post offices.

SOCIAL INSTITUTIONS

Justice. The death penalty is retained following the constitutional referendum of Nov. 1996 and was used in 2000.

135,540 crimes were reported in 2000. In Dec. 2001 there were 55,156 prisoners, giving Belarus one of the highest rates of imprisonment in the world, with 554 prisoners per 100,000 population.

Religion. The Orthodox is the largest church. There is a Roman Catholic archdiocese of Minsk and Mahilyou, and five dioceses embracing 455 parishes. In 2001, 32% of the population were Belorussian Orthodox and 18% Roman Catholics. In Sept. 2003 there was one cardinal.

Education. Adult literacy rate in 2001 was 99·7% (male, 99·8%; female, 99·6%). There were 254,595 children and 52,459 teachers at pre-school institutions in 2000–01, 551,486 pupils and 32,166 teachers at primary schools, 980,603 pupils and 105,312 teachers in secondary schools, and 437,995 students and 40,470 academic staff at institutions of tertiary education.

In 2001 there were 58 state higher educational establishments including: four universities; specialized universities of agriculture, culture, economics, information technology and radio-electronics, linguistics, teacher training and transport; academies of agriculture, arts, music, physical culture and sport, and a polytechnical academy; four medical, three polytechnical and three teacher training institutes, and institutes of agriculture, co-operation, light industry technology, machine-building and veterinary science. In 2001–02 there were 301,800 people enrolled at state higher education establishments.

In 1999–2000 total expenditure on education came to 6·0% of GNP.

Health. In 2002 there were 44,800 doctors (45·3 per 10,000 population); and, in 1999, 4,522 dentists, 47,343 nurses and 5,826 midwives. In 1995 there were nine hospitals with 74 beds per 10,000 persons.

Welfare. To qualify for an old-age pension men must be age 60 with 25 years of insurance coverage and women must be 55 with 20 years of insurance coverage. Minimum old-age pension is 25% of the average per capita subsistence budget. The maximum pension is 75% of wage base. The minimum unemployment benefit is the minimum wage and the maximum benefit is twice the minimum wage. The minimum wage in 2001 was 3,600 roubles a month. Benefits are adjusted periodically according to changes in the minimum wage.

CULTURE

World Heritage Sites. The Mir Castle Complex, begun in the 15th century, was entered on the UNESCO World Heritage List in 2000. Belarus also shares the UNESCO Belovezhskaya Pushcha/Bialowieza Forest site (inscribed in 1979 and 1992) with Poland.

Broadcasting. The government-controlled Belarus Radio broadcasts two national programmes and various regional programmes, a foreign service (Belorussian, German) and a shared relay with Radio Moscow. Belarus Television broadcasts on one channel (colour by SECAM H). In 2001 there were 3·5m. TV receivers and in 2000 there were 3·0m. radio receivers.

Press. There were 20 dailies in 1998, with a total average circulation of 1,559,000, a ratio of 152 per 1,000 inhabitants. In 1998 a total of 6,073 book titles were published.

Tourism. In 2001 there were 61,000 foreign tourists.

DIPLOMATIC REPRESENTATIVES

Of Belarus in the United Kingdom (6 Kensington Court, London, W8 5DL)
Ambassador: Dr Alyaksei Mazhukhou.

Of the United Kingdom in Belarus (37 Karl Marx St., Minsk 220030)
Ambassador: Brian M. Bennett.

Of Belarus in the USA (1619 New Hampshire Avenue, NW, Washington, D.C., 20009)
Ambassador: Mikhail Khvostov.

Of the USA in Belarus (46 Starovilenskaya, Minsk 220002)
Ambassador: George Krol.

Of Belarus to the United Nations
Ambassador: Andrei Dapkiunas.

Of Belarus to the European Union
Ambassador: Vacant.
Deputy Head of Mission: Aleksandr Baichorov.

FURTHER READING

Marples, D. R., *Belarus: from Soviet Rule to Nuclear Catastrophe*. London, 1996
Zaprudnik, J., *Belarus at the Crossroads in History*. Boulder (CO), 1993

National statistical office: Ministry of Statistics and Analysis of the Republic of Belarus, Minsk.
Website: http://www.belstat.gov.by

BELGIUM

Royaume de Belgique
Koninkrijk België
(Kingdom of Belgium)

Capital: Brussels
Population projection, 2010: 10·43m.
GDP per capita, 2002: (PPP$) 27,570
HDI/world rank: 0·942/6

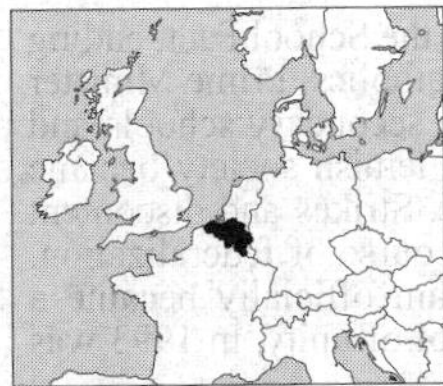

KEY HISTORICAL EVENTS

Burgundian rule in the Low Countries began in 1369 with the marriage of Philip the Bold, duke of Burgundy to Margaret of Flanders. The 1477 marriage of Mary of Burgundy to Maximilian of Habsburg, later Holy Roman Emperor, brought three centuries of Habsburg rule. Brugge (Bruges) was overtaken by Antwerp in the 1490s as the principal trading and financial centre of northwest Europe. Philip the Handsome married the Spanish heiress, Juana the Mad, in 1496. The imposition of a new ecclesiastical hierarchy unified opposition to Spanish rule. Philip II of Spain sent the duke of Alba to stamp out Protestantism. Although Alba managed to reassert Philip's authority in the south, his armies were unable to regain the provinces north of the Rhine. However, a measure of unity was achieved at the Pacification of Ghent after the 'Spanish Fury' of 1576—Spanish troops massacred 7,000 in Antwerp. The Union of Arras (1579) accepted the sovereignty of the Spanish king, supported Catholicism and ended the revolt of the southern provinces. In reaction the northern provinces drew up the Union of Utrecht, thus creating the Dutch Republic.

By the Treaty of Utrecht in 1713, the Spanish Netherlands came under the Austrian Habsburgs. The reign of Archduchess Maria Theresa saw great economic gains in the Netherlands and the beginning of industrial capitalism. Joseph II abolished local privileges and attacked the power of the Catholic Church, provoking his 'Belgian' subjects into revolt in 1789. Although Léopold II reasserted Austrian authority, Republican France invaded Belgium in 1795. Military conscription and religious persecution led to peasant uprisings in 1798.

After Napoléon's defeat in 1814 the Congress of Vienna reunified the Belgians and the Dutch in the Kingdom of the Netherlands under William of Orange. Despite cultural and linguistic affinities, the relationship was uneasy. Belgium's French-speaking elite was alienated by the declaration of Dutch as the official language. The two economies were in contrast, the Dutch being primarily mercantile while the Belgian was geared towards industry. The Belgians revolted in 1830. Repelled by the French, King William accepted the loss of Belgium in 1838 and Limburg and Luxembourg were partitioned. Prince Léopold of Saxe-Coburg was installed as king of the Belgians.

The Schools War dominated the political agenda and saw a conservative counter-offensive with the establishment of a network of independent Catholic schools. A conservative Catholic victory in 1884 brought to the premiership Auguste Beernaert, who gave the Flemish language the same rights as French. In the Belgian Congo, acquired as a personal possession by King Léopold II in 1885, abuse and exploitation became legendary. After international condemnation, the 'Congo Free State' was formally annexed by Belgium in 1908, thus curbing Léopold's excesses. Belgian neutrality was violated by Germany in 1914 after Albert I's refusal to allow German free passage. Albert remained with his army on the Yser River throughout the First World War, supported by Allied troops. Belgium was awarded the provinces of Eupen and Malmédy and jurisdiction over Ruanda-Urundi from the defeated Germany. Constitutional changes after the war included the formal linguistic separation of Flanders and Wallonia (excluding Brussels).

Germany invaded Belgium on 10 May 1940. Capitulation after just 18 days made King Léopold III unpopular, despite his refusal to flee to London with the government. An underground army was active for much of the Second World War. Insurgents managed to protect the port of Antwerp, crucial for Allied support, during the liberation of Belgium in Sept. 1944.

In 1951 Léopold was persuaded to abdicate in favour of his son, Baudouin. Belgium embarked on a policy of European unity under the leadership of Prime Minister Paul-Henri Spaak. Economic union with Luxembourg was re-established and extended to include the Netherlands, forming the Benelux Economic Union. In 1949 Belgium joined the North Atlantic Treaty Organization (NATO) and in 1951 the European Coal and Steel Community (ECSC). Encouraged by the success of the ECSC, the European Economic Community (EEC) was created in Rome on 25 March 1957. The growing strength of the independence movement in the Belgian Congo led to a hurried withdrawal in 1960. Rwanda and Burundi became independent in 1962.

A milestone in domestic politics was reached in 1958 with the School Pact, ending a century of conflict between secularists and conservative Catholics. Prime Minister Gaston Eyskens negotiated a guarantee of funding for state secondary schools and private religious schools. Relations between Walloon and Flemish society became more difficult as a result of the decline of Walloon industry. Strikes and discontent with the distribution of state subsidies set Belgium on the course of federalization. After the division of Brabant along linguistic lines Belgium officially became a federal state in 1993. The death of King Baudouin, a symbol of unity, in 1993 was met with widespread grief.

TERRITORY AND POPULATION

Belgium is bounded in the north by the Netherlands, northwest by the North Sea, west and south by France, and east by Germany and Luxembourg. Its area is 30,528 sq. km. The Belgian exclave of Baarle-Hertog in the Netherlands has an area of seven sq. km and a population (1996) of 2,702. Population (2001 census), 10,296,350. Population (at 1 Jan. 2004), 10,396,421 (5,309,245 females); density, 340·6 per sq. km. There were 850,077 resident foreign nationals as at 1 Jan. 2003. In 2001, 97·4% of the population lived in urban areas.

The UN gives a projected population for 2010 of 10·43m.

Dutch (Flemish) is spoken by the Flemish section of the population in the north, French by the Walloon south. The linguistic frontier passes south of the capital, Brussels, which is bilingual. Some German is spoken in the east. Each language has official status in its own community. (Bracketed names below signify French/Dutch and where relevant English alternatives.)

Area, population and chief towns of the ten provinces on 1 Jan. 2004:

Province	*Area (sq. km)*	*Population*	*Chief Town*
Flemish Region			
Antwerp	2,867	1,668,812	Antwerpen (Anvers/Antwerp)
East Flanders	2,982	1,373,720	Gent (Gand/Ghent)
West Flanders	3,144	1,135,802	Brugge (Bruges)
Flemish Brabant	2,106	1,031,904	Leuven (Louvain)
Limbourg	2,422	805,786	Hasselt
Walloon Region			
Hainaut (Henegouwen)	3,786	1,283,200	Mons (Bergen)
Liège (Luik)	3,862	1,029,605	Liège (Luik)
Namur (Namen)	3,666	452,856	Namur (Namen)
Walloon Brabant	1,091	360,717	Wavre (Waver)
Luxembourg	4,440	254,120	Arlon (Aarlen)

Population of the regions on 1 Jan. 2004: Brussels Capital Region, 999,899; Flemish Region, 6,016,024; Walloon Region, 3,380,498 (including the German-speaking Region, 71,571 in 2003).

The most populous towns, with population on 1 Jan. 2004:

Brussel (Bruxelles/Brussels)[1]	999,899	Mechelen (Malines)	76,981
Antwerpen (Anvers/Antwerp)	455,148	Aalst (Alost)	76,852
Gent (Gand/Ghent)	229,344	La Louvière	76,784
Charleroi	200,608	Kortrijk (Courtrai)	73,984
Liège (Luik)	185,488	Hasselt	69,127
Brugge (Bruges)	117,025	St Niklaas (St Nicolas)	68,820
Namur (Namen)	106,213	Oostende (Ostende/Ostend)	68,273
Mons (Bergen)	91,185	Tournai (Doornik)	67,341
Leuven (Louvain)	89,777	Genk	63,550

Seraing	60,579	Verviers	52,804
Roeselare (Roulers)	55,273	Mouscron (Moeskroen)	52,290

[1]19 communes.

SOCIAL STATISTICS

Statistics for calendar years:

	Births	*Deaths*	*Marriages*	*Divorces*	*Immigration*[1]	*Emigration*[1]
1999	113,469	104,904	44,171	26,423	521,684	509,432
2000	114,883	104,903	45,123	27,002	511,180	486,051
2001	114,172	103,447	42,110	29,314	524,626	489,263
2002	111,225	105,642	40,434	30,628	542,191	500,885
2003	112,149	107,039	41,805	31,373	552,608	512,592

[1]Including internal.

In 2002 Belgium received 18,805 asylum applications, equivalent to 1·8 per 1,000 inhabitants. Annual population growth rate, 1992–2002, 0·3%. Life expectancy at birth, 2002, was 75·6 years for men and 81·7 years for women. 2003 birth rate (per 1,000 population): 10·8; death rate: 10·3. Infant mortality, 2001, 5 per 1,000 live births; fertility rate, 2001, 1·5 children per woman.

A UNICEF report published in 2000 showed that 4·4% of children in Belgium live in poverty (in households with income below 50% of the national median).

CLIMATE

Cool temperate climate influenced by the sea, giving mild winters and cool summers. Brussels, Jan. 36°F (2·2°C), July 64°F (17·8°C). Annual rainfall 33" (825 mm). Ostend, Jan. 38°F (3·3°C), July 62°F (16·7°C). Annual rainfall 31" (775 mm).

CONSTITUTION AND GOVERNMENT

According to the constitution of 1831, Belgium is a constitutional, representative and hereditary monarchy. The legislative power is vested in the King, the federal parliament and the community and regional councils. The King convokes parliament after an election or the resignation of a government, and has the power to dissolve it in accordance with Article 46 of the Constitution.

The reigning King is **Albert II,** born 6 June 1934, who succeeded his brother, Baudouin, on 9 Aug. 1993. Married on 2 July 1959 to Paola Ruffo di Calabria, daughter of Don Fuleo and Donna Luisa Gazelli de Rossena. *Offspring:* Prince Philippe, Duke of Brabant, b. 15 April 1960; Princess Astrid, b. 5 June 1962; Prince Laurent, b. 19 Oct. 1963. Prince Philippe married Mathilde d'Udekem d'Acoz, 4 Dec. 1999. *Offspring:* Princess Elizabeth, b. 25 Oct. 2001; Prince Gabriel, b. 20 Aug. 2003. Princess Astrid married Archduke Lorenz of Austria, 22 Sept. 1984. *Offspring:* Prince Amedeo, b. 21 Feb. 1986; Princess Maria Laura, b. 26 Aug. 1988; Prince Joachim, b. 9 Dec. 1991; Princess Luisa Maria, b. 11 Oct. 1995; Princess Laetitia Maria, b. 23 April 2003. Prince Laurent married Claire Coombs, 12 April 2003. *Offspring:* Princess Louise, b. 6 Feb. 2004.

The Dowager Queen. Queen Fabiola de Mora y Aragón, daughter of the Conde de Mora y Aragón and Marqués de Casa Riera; married to King Baudouin on 15 Dec. 1960. *Sister of the King.* Josephine Charlotte, Princess of Belgium, b. 11 Oct. 1927; married to Prince Jean of Luxembourg, 9 April 1953. *Half-brother and half-sisters of the King.* Prince Alexandre, b. 18 July 1942; Princess Marie Christine, b. 6 Feb. 1951; Princess Maria-Esmeralda, b. 30 Sept. 1956.

A constitutional amendment of June 1991 permits women to accede to the throne.

The King receives a basic annual tax-free sum from the civil list of €6,048,000 for the duration of his reign; Queen Fabiola receives €1,115,000; Prince Philippe, €768,400; Princess Astrid and Prince Laurent, €272,000 each. These figures are adapted annually in accordance with the general price index.

Constitutional reforms begun in Dec. 1970 culminated in May 1993 in the transformation of Belgium from a unitary into a 'federal state, composed of communities and regions'. The communities are three in number and based on language: Flemish, French and German. The regions also number three, and are based territorially: Flemish, Walloon and the Capital Brussels.

Since 1995 the federal parliament has consisted of a 150-member *Chamber of Representatives*, directly elected by obligatory universal suffrage from 20 constituencies on a proportional representation system for four-year terms; and a *Senate* of 71 members (excluding senators by right, i.e. certain members of the

Royal Family). 25 senators are elected by a Flemish, and 15 by a French, electoral college; 21 are designated by community councils (ten Flemish, ten French and one German). These senators co-opt a further ten senators (six Flemish and four French).

The federal parliament's powers relate to constitutional reform, federal finance, foreign affairs, defence, justice, internal security, social security and some areas of public health. The Senate is essentially a revising chamber, though it may initiate certain legislation, and is equally competent with the Chamber of Representatives in matters concerning constitutional reform and the assent to international treaties.

The number of ministers in the federal government is limited to 15. The Council of Ministers, apart from the Prime Minister, must comprise an equal number of Dutch- and French-speakers. Members of parliament, if appointed ministers, are replaced in parliament by the runner-up on the electoral list for the minister's period of office. Community and regional councillors may not be members of the Chamber of Representatives or Senate.

National Anthem. 'La Brabançonne'; words by C. Rogier, tune by F. van Campenhout. The Flemish version is 'O Vaderland, o edel land der Belgen' ('Oh Fatherland, noble land of the Belgians').

RECENT ELECTIONS

Elections to the 150-member Chamber of Representatives were held on 18 May 2003. The Flemish Liberal and Democratic Party (VLD) won 25 seats with 15·4% of votes cast; The Socialist Party (PS) won 25 seats (13·0%); the Reformist Movement (MR) won 24 seats (11·4%); SPA (Socialist Party Different)-Spirit coalition won 23 seats (14·9% of the vote); the Christian Democratic and Flemish Party (CD&V) won 21 seats (13·3%); the Vlaams Blok (Flemish Block, VB) won 18 seats (11·6%); the Humanist Democratic Centre (CDH) won 8 seats (5·5%); Ecolo won 4 seats (3·1%); the New Flemish Alliance (N-VA) won 1 seat (3·1%); and the National Front (FN) won 1 seat (2·0%). Agalev (2·5%) and Vivant (1·2%) won no seats. Prime Minister Guy Verhofstadt's VLD won two more seats than in the 1999 elections.

Voting for the 40 electable seats in the Senate took place on the same day. SPA-Spirit and VLD both won 7 seats; CD&V and PS won 6; MR and VB, 5; CDH, 2; and Ecolo and FN 1. There are also 31 indirectly elected senators.

European Parliament. Belgium has 24 (25 in 1999) representatives. At the June 2004 elections turn-out was 90·8% (95·0% in 1999). The CD&V/N-VA won 4 seats with 17·4% of the vote (political affiliation in European Parliament: European People's Party–European Democrats); the PS, 4 with 13·5% (Party of European Socialists); the VB, 3 with 14·3% (non-attached); the VLD-Vivant, 3 with 13·6% (Alliance of Liberals and Democrats for Europe); SPA-Spirit, 3 with 11·0% (Party of European Socialists); the MR, 3 with 10·4% (Alliance of Liberals and Democrats for Europe); the CDH, 1 with 5·7% (European People's Party–European Democrats); Groen!, 1 with 4·9% (Greens/European Free Alliance); Ecolo, 1 with 3·7% (Greens/European Free Alliance); the Christian-Social Party, 1 with 0·2% (European People's Party–European Democrats).

CURRENT ADMINISTRATION

In March 2005 the coalition government comprised:

Prime Minister: Guy Verhofstadt; b. 1953 (VLD; in office since 12 July 1999 and re-elected on 18 May 2003).

Deputy Prime Ministers: Laurette Onkelinx (PS; also *Minister of Justice*); Didier Reynders (MR; also *Minister of Finance*); Johan Vande Lanotte (SPA; also *Minister of Budget and Private Enterprise*); Patrick Dewael (VLD: also *Minister of Interior*).

Minister for the Civil Service, Social Integration, Urban Policy and Equal Opportunities: Christian Dupont (PS). *Defence:* André Flahaut (PS). *Development Co-operation:* Armand De Decker (MR). *Economy, Energy, Foreign Trade and Science:* Marc Verwilghen (VLD). *Employment:* Freya Van den Bossche (SPA). *Environment and Pensions:* Bruno Tobback (SPA). *Foreign Affairs:* Karel De Gucht (VLD). *Middle Classes and Agriculture:* Sabine Laruelle (MR). *Social Affairs and Public Health:* Rudy Demotte (PS). *Transport:* Renaat Landuyt (SPA).

Government Website: http://www.belgium.fgov.be

DEFENCE

Conscription was abolished in 1995 and the Armed Forces were restructured, with the aim of progressively reducing the size and making more use of civilian personnel. The Interforces Territorial Command is responsible for assignments to assure the safety of the National Territory and for logistic support in those fields which are mutual for the different forces.

In 2003 defence expenditure totalled US$3,923m. (US$379 per capita), representing 1·3% of GDP.

Army. The Army has a joint service territorial command and an operations command HQ. There is a mechanized infantry division, a combat support division, a parachute commando brigade and a light aviation group. Total strength (2002) 26,400 including 1,500 women. In addition there are 71,500 army reserves.

Navy. The naval forces, based at Ostend and Zeebrugge, include three frigates. Naval personnel (2002) totalled 2,400.

The naval air arm comprises three general utility helicopters.

Air Force. The Belgian Royal Air Force has a strength of (2002) 8,600 personnel. There are three fighter-ground attack squadrons, one fighter-ground attack reconnaissance squadron, two fighter squadrons, two transport squadrons, three training squadrons and one search and rescue squadron. Equipment includes 90 combat aircraft, including F-16s, plus 45 in store.

INTERNATIONAL RELATIONS

Belgium is a member of the UN, WTO, NATO, BIS, OECD, EU, Council of Europe, WEU, OSCE, CERN, Inter-American Development Bank, Asian Development Bank, IOM, Antarctic Treaty and the International Organization of the Francophonie. Belgium is a signatory to the Schengen Accord abolishing border controls between Austria, Belgium, Denmark, Finland, France, Germany, Greece, Iceland, Italy, Luxembourg, the Netherlands, Norway, Portugal, Spain and Sweden.

ECONOMY

Services contributed 71·8% of GDP in 2002, with industry accounting for 26·9% and agriculture 1·3%.

According to the anti-corruption organization *Transparency International*, Belgium ranked equal 17th in the world in a 2004 survey of the countries with the least corruption in business and government. It received 7·5 out of 10 in the annual index.

Overview. A slowdown since 2000 is attributed to the deterioration of the international business climate, which has led to lower business profitability and a diminished demand for Belgian exports. Belgium's economy is one of the most open in the world and is closely interlinked with that of Germany, France and the Netherlands. In 2001 the share of external trade in goods and services in GDP was 88%. However, Belgium has lost export market share at approximately 1% per year over recent years. This loss can be explained by the dominance in Belgium's export profile of intermediate products such as chemicals and steel, which have lower structural growth than other products. The shift from the Belgian franc to the euro in 2002 was conducted with comparative ease. Inflexibilities in the labour market, including low labour mobility and wage inflexibility, have contributed to relatively high unemployment rates. Whilst the unemployment rate in 2002 was relatively low at 7·3%, more than 60% of the unemployed have been so for over two years and over 80% for at least one year. The sectoral composition of the economy has changed since 1985; the share of GDP accounted for by the industry sector has fallen from 32% in 1985 to 27% whilst that of the service sector has increased from 65% in 1985 to 72% of GDP. Agriculture's share, at just over 1%, has halved since 1985.

Currency. On 1 Jan. 1999 the euro (EUR) became the legal currency in Belgium; irrevocable conversion rate BEF40·3399 to EUR1. The euro, which consists of 100 cents, has been in circulation since 1 Jan. 2002. There are seven euro notes in different colours and sizes denominated in 500, 200, 100, 50, 20, 10 and 5 euros, and eight coins denominated in 2 and 1 euros, then 50, 20, 10, 5, 2 and 1 cents. On the introduction of the euro there was a 'dual circulation' period before the Belgian franc ceased to be legal tender on 28 Feb. 2002. Euro banknotes in circulation on 1 Jan. 2002 had a total value of €24·0bn.

In June 2002 gold reserves were 8·29m. troy oz (20·54m. troy oz in 1995) and foreign exchange reserves US$8,517m. Total money supply was €10,626m. in June 2002. Inflation was 1·6% in 2002 and 1·7% in 2003.

Budget. Federal government receipts and expenditure in €1m.:

	1999	*2000*	*2001*	*2002*
Revenue	67,754	72,628	74,500	73,592
Expenditure	71,468	73,753	76,750	74,306

Tax revenue in 2002 was €67,513m.; non-tax revenue, €6,079m. VAT is 21% (reduced rates, 12% and 10%).

Performance. Real GDP growth was 0·7% in 2001, 0·9% in 2002, 1·3% in 2003 and (provisional) 2·7% in 2004. Total GDP in 2003 was US$302·2bn.

With regard to the downturn of 2001 and 2002 the Feb. 2003 *OECD Economic Survey* reported that 'Economic activity slowed sharply from the beginning of 2000, with growth reaching a trough in the fourth quarter of 2001 before recovering somewhat in 2002. The slowdown in the Belgian economy was largely in step with that in the euro-zone economy although, as usual, the Belgian cycle slightly leads the euro-zone cycle … and has larger amplitude …. The main cause of the slowdown was the deterioration in the international business climate, which resulted in less demand for Belgian exports and reduced business profitability.'

Banking and Finance. The National Bank of Belgium was established in 1850. The *Governor*—in 2004, Guy Quaden—is appointed for a five-year period. Its shares are listed on Euronext (Brussels); half of them are nominative held by the state.

The law of 22 Feb. 1998 has adapted the status of the National Bank of Belgium in view of the realization of the Economic and Monetary Union.

The National Bank of Belgium is within the ESCB-framework in charge of the issue of banknotes, the execution of exchange rate policy and monetary policy. Furthermore, it is the Bank of banks and the cashier of the federal state.

The law of 4 Dec. 1990 on financial transactions and financial markets defines the legal framework for collective investment institutions, the sole object of which is the collective investment of capital raised from the public. It transposes into Belgian legislation the European Directive of 20 Dec. 1985 on the co-ordination of laws, regulations and administrative provisions relating to undertakings for collective investment in transferable securities.

The law of 6 April 1995 relating to secondary markets, status and supervision of investment firms, intermediaries and investment consultants, provides the credit institutions with direct access to securities' stock exchanges. Stock exchange legislation was also subject to an important reform. The law fundamentally modifies the competitive environment and strengthens exercise conditions for securities' dealers.

On 31 Dec. 2003, 109 credit institutions with a balance sheet totalling €891bn. were established in Belgium: 61 governed by Belgian law and 48 by foreign law. 399 collective investment institutions (132 Belgian and 267 foreign) were marketed in Belgium and supervised by the Banking, Finance and Insurance Commission; and 82 investment firms were operating in Belgium with the approval of the Banking, Finance and Insurance Commission.

There is a stock exchange (a component of Euronext) in Brussels. Euronext was created in Sept. 2000 through the merger of the Amsterdam, Brussels and Paris bourses.

ENERGY AND NATURAL RESOURCES

Environment. Belgium's carbon dioxide emissions from the consumption and flaring of fossil fuels were the equivalent of 14·2 tonnes per capita in 2002.

Electricity. The production of electricity amounted to 83·9bn. kWh in 2000; consumption per capita (2000) was 8,608 kWh. 57% of production in 2000 was nuclear-produced. Belgium had seven nuclear reactors in 2003. Installed capacity (2000) was 15·7m. kW.

Minerals. Belgium's mineral resources are very limited; the most abundantly occurring mineral is calcite.

Agriculture. There were, in 2001, 1,390,191 ha under cultivation, of which 845,779 ha were arable land. There were 55,000 farms in 2003. The agricultural sector employs 2·7% of the workforce.

Chief crops	*Area in ha* 2000	2001	*Produce in tonnes* 1998	1999	2000
Wheat	204,022	173,270	1,733,046	1,490,247	1,633,854
Barley	48,570	51,504	374,500	387,564	333,381
Oats	5,341	—	28,468	42,552	28,887
Rye	1,098	—	7,130	3,971	4,781
Potatoes	65,845	62,157	2,455,777	3,059,162	2,921,871
Beet (sugar)	90,858	95,553	5,364,649	7,112,021	6,151,978
Beet (fodder)	6,713	5,970	676,396	738,315	670,224
Tobacco	388	380	1,308	1,314	1,166

In 2003 there were 32,093 horses, 2,778,077 cattle, 146,030 sheep, 26,237 goats and 6,538,609 pigs.

Forestry. In 2000 forest covered 671,890 ha (22·2% of the total land area). Timber production in 2001 was 4·19m. cu. metres.

Fisheries. In 2002 the fishing fleet had a total tonnage of 24,276 GRT. Total catch, 2001, 30,209 tonnes, almost entirely from marine waters.

INDUSTRY

The leading companies by market capitalization in Belgium, excluding banking and finance, in May 2004 were: Electrabel (US$18·0bn.), Belgium's leading energy producer; Interbrew SA (US$13·2bn.); and Belgacom (US$11·7bn.), a telecommunications company.

Output in 1,000 tonnes: distillate fuel oil (2000), 12,501; crude steel (2002), 11,300; cement (2000), 8,000; residual fuel oil (2000), 7,990; petrol (2000), 5,311; beer (2003), 1,565·0m. litres; mineral water (1998), 809·7m. litres; cigarettes (2001), 14·7bn. units. Output of sugar factories and refineries (1998), 995,053 tonnes.

Labour. Retirement age is flexible for men and 60–65 years for women. In 2002 (Labour Force Survey), 69,278 persons worked in the primary sector (agriculture, fishing and mining), 1,034,693 in the secondary sector (industry and construction) and 2,965,861 in the tertiary sector (services). The unemployment rate was 8·0% in Dec. 2004. In French-speaking Wallonia the rate is more than double that in Flemish-speaking Flanders. In 2002 the participation rate of the active population in the labour market was one of the lowest in the EU, at 59·9%.

Trade Unions. The main trade union organizations are the Confederation of Christian Trade Unions (CSC/ACV), the Belgian Socialist Confederation of Labour (FGTB/ABVV) and the Federation of Liberal Trade Unions of Belgium (CGSLB/ACLVB).

INTERNATIONAL TRADE

In 1922 the customs frontier between Belgium and Luxembourg was abolished; their foreign trade figures are amalgamated.

Imports and Exports. Imports and exports for three calendar years (in €1m.):

	Imports	*Exports*
1999	154,635	168,091
2000	192,195	203,953
2001	197,402	209,933

Leading imports and exports (in €1m.):

	Imports 2000	2001	*Exports* 2000	2001
Machinery and appliances	36,778	35,859	33,850	32,530
Chemicals and pharmaceutical products	25,154	30,336	30,492	33,968
Transport equipment	24,072	25,564	27,718	32,070
Mineral products	18,757	18,682	10,892	10,261
Precious stones and precious metals	14,657	13,455	15,555	14,419
Base metals	14,216	13,434	17,039	16,255
Plastics and rubber	11,204	11,327	16,647	16,597

	Imports 2000	*Imports* 2001	*Exports* 2000	*Exports* 2001
Textile and textile articles	9,265	9,385	11,230	11,511
Food industry	6,903	7,510	10,892	10,261
Paper and applications	5,694	5,467	5,705	5,471

Trade by selected countries (in €1m.):

	Imports from 2000	*Imports from* 2001	*Exports to* 2000	*Exports to* 2001
China	1,340	1,675	4,011	4,307
France	35,846	36,491	24,354	26,424
Germany	34,531	38,157	32,553	31,900
India	3,467	3,009	1,732	1,679
Ireland	1,619	1,679	4,301	6,602
Israel	3,805	3,066	2,373	2,153
Italy	11,285	12,098	7,515	8,289
Japan	2,420	2,196	5,949	5,630
Luxembourg	4,144	4,095	1,080	1,141
Netherlands	25,753	25,444	33,584	33,417
Spain	7,339	8,051	3,488	3,784
Sweden	3,194	2,891	4,395	4,500
Switzerland	3,081	3,025	1,678	1,733
UK	20,230	21,160	16,500	15,196
USA	11,919	11,749	14,392	13,701

In 2000 other EU-member countries accounted for 74·0% of exports and 68·1% of imports.

Trade Fairs. Brussels ranks as the second most popular convention city in the world behind Paris according to the Union des Associations Internationales (UAI), hosting 2·1% of all international meetings held in 2002.

COMMUNICATIONS

Roads. Length of roads, 2002: motorways, 1,729 km; other state roads, 12,610 km; provincial roads, 1,349 km; local roads, about 133,340 km. Belgium has one of the densest road networks in the world. The number of motor vehicles registered on 1 Aug. 2003 was 5,816,339, including 4,820,868 passenger cars, 15,060 buses, 556,397 trucks, 47,102 non-agricultural tractors, 319,480 motorcycles and 57,432 special vehicles. Road accidents caused 1,486 fatalities in 2001.

Rail. The main Belgian lines were a State enterprise from their inception in 1834. In 1926 the *Société Nationale des Chemins de Fer Belges (SNCB)* was formed to take over the railways. The State is sole holder of the ordinary shares of SNCB, which carry the majority vote at General Meetings. The length of railway operated in 2000 was 3,471 km (electrified, 2,705 km). Revenue in 1998 was BEF81,715m.; expenditure, BEF75,441m. In 2003, 55·73m. tonnes of freight were carried; and, in 2000, 153·3m. passengers.

The regional transport undertakings *Société Régionale Wallonne de Transport* and *Vlaamse Vervoermaatschappij* operate electrified light railways around Charleroi (19 km) and from De Panne to Knokke (68 km). There is also a metro and tramway in Brussels (165 km), and tramways in Antwerp (180 km) and Ghent (29 km).

Civil Aviation. The former national airline SABENA (*Société anonyme belge d'exploitation de la navigation aérienne*) was set up in 1923. In 1997 its fleet comprised 33 aircraft. In 1999 SABENA flew 179·1m. km, carrying 9,965,200 passengers. However, in Nov. 2001 it filed for bankruptcy after failing to secure financial assistance from its part-owner Swissair, which itself was on the verge of collapse. Its successor, Delta Air Transport (DAT), a former SABENA subsidiary, was given a new identity in Feb. 2002 as SN Brussels Airlines. Some 60 other airlines also operate services, including Ryanair and Virgin Express, which flies more people out of Brussels National Airport than any other airline. The busiest airport is Brussels National Airport (Zaventem), which handled 15,194,097 passengers in 2003 and 676,400 tonnes of freight in 2000. Charleroi is the second busiest airport in terms of passenger numbers and Liège the third busiest.

Shipping. On 1 Jan. 1999 the merchant fleet was composed of 19 vessels of 345,058 tonnes. There were eight shipping companies in 1997. In 2001 vessels totalling 436,927,000 NRT entered ports and vessels totalling 422,703,000 NRT cleared. In

2002, 131,619,000 tonnes of cargo were handled at the port of Antwerp, with total container throughput 4,777,000 TEUs (twenty-foot equivalent units). Antwerp is Europe's second busiest port in terms of cargo handled after Rotterdam.

The length of navigable inland waterways was 1,493·3 km in 1995. 104m. tonnes of freight were carried on inland waterways in 1998.

Telecommunications. In 2002 telephone subscribers numbered 13,267,900 (1,282·4 per 1,000 inhabitants) and there were 2·5m. PCs in use (241·6 for every 1,000 persons). Belgium had 8,135,500 mobile phone subscribers in 2002. In Aug. 2002 there were 3·76m. Internet users. There were 190,000 fax machines in 1996.

Postal Services. In 1996 there were 1,637 post offices. In 1998 a total of 3,713m. pieces of mail were processed.

SOCIAL INSTITUTIONS

Justice. Judges are appointed for life. There is a court of cassation, five courts of appeal and assize courts for political and criminal cases. There are 27 judicial districts, each with a court of first instance. In each of the 222 cantons is a justice and judge of the peace. There are also various special tribunals. There is trial by jury in assize courts. The death penalty, which had been in abeyance for 45 years, was formally abolished in 1991.

The Gendarmerie ceased to be part of the army in Jan. 1992.

The population in penal institutions in 2004 was 9,249 (89 per 100,000 of national population).

In Aug. 2003 a new act reformed war crimes legislation introduced in 1993 which allowed for charges to be brought against foreign nationals accused of abuses committed outside Belgian jurisdiction. The amendment requires that either accuser or defendant be a citizen of or resident in Belgium.

Religion. There is full religious liberty, and part of the income of the ministers of all denominations is paid by the State. In 2001 there were 8·31m. Roman Catholics. Numbers of clergy, 1996: Roman Catholic, 3,899; Protestant, 84; Anglican, 9; Jews, 26; Greek Orthodox, 39. There are eight Roman Catholic dioceses subdivided into 260 deaneries. In Sept. 2003 there were three cardinals. The Protestant (Evangelical) Church is under a synod. There is also a Central Jewish Consistory, a Central Committee of the Anglican Church and a Free Protestant Church.

Education. Following the constitutional reform of 1988, education is the responsibility of the Flemish and Walloon communities. There were (2000–01) 400,805 pupils and 27,118 teachers in pre-primary schools; 771,889 pupils and 63,626 teachers in primary schools; 1,125,256 pupils and 115,262 teachers (1996–97) in secondary schools; and 359,265 students and 23,041 academic staff in tertiary education. There were 17 universities and 134 non-university colleges and institutes in 1996–97. There are five royal academies of fine arts and five royal conservatoires at Brussels, Liège, Ghent, Antwerp and Mons.

Total expenditure on education in 1999–2000 amounted to 5·8% of GNP and represented 11·6% of total government expenditure.

The adult literacy rate in 2001 was at least 99%.

Health. On 1 Jan. 1998 there were 39,240 physicians, 7,360 dentists and 14,597 pharmacists. Hospital beds numbered 75,360 in 1995. Total health spending accounted for 9·1% of GDP in 2002. In Jan. 2000 the Belgian government agreed to decriminalize the use of cannabis. Euthanasia became legal on 24 Sept. 2002. The Belgian Chamber of Representatives had given its approval on 16 May 2002 to a measure adopted by the Senate on 26 Oct. 2001. Belgium was the second country to legalize euthanasia, after the Netherlands.

Welfare. Expenditure in 2000: social security (wage earners) €39,114·47m., (self employed) €3,315·46m.; pensions €5,712·17m.

CULTURE

World Heritage Sites. Belgium has eight sites which have been included on the UNESCO world heritage list. They are: the Flemish Beguinages (1998); the four lifts on the Canal du Centre and their environs (1998); La Grand Place in Brussels (1998); the belfries of Flanders and Wallonia (1998); the historic centre of Bruges (2000);

the major town houses of the architect Victor Horta in Brussels (2000); the Neolithic flint mines at Spiennes (2000); and Notre Dame cathedral in Tournai (2000).

Broadcasting. Broadcasting is organized according to the language communities. VRT, RTBF and BRF fulfil the public service of broadcasting in Dutch, French and German respectively. TV colour is by PAL.

VRT (*Vlaamse Radio- en Televisieomroep*) is organized by decree as a public-sector public-limited company. It has seven radio and three TV services: Radio 1, Radio 2, Klara, Studio Brussel, Radio Donna, DAB klassiek and RVi; TV1, Canvas and Ketnet. In July 2000 VRT started a new branch, e-VRT, which is responsible for the organization and development of a truly multimedia e-service platform and e-service network in Flanders.

RTBF has five radio and three TV services: La Première, FW, Musique 3, Bruxelles Capitale, Radio 21; RTBF International, La Une, La Deux.

BRF transmits a radio programme from three stations.

There are also four commercial networks: VTM (Dutch, cable only), VT4 (under British licence; Dutch, cable only), RTL-TVI (French, one station), Canal Plus (pay TV; French, three channels; Dutch, two channels).

Number of receivers: radios, 8·1m. (2000); TVs, 5·6m. (2001).

Press. In 1996 there were 30 daily newspapers with a combined circulation of 1,625,000, at a rate of 161 per 1,000 inhabitants.

Tourism. *Internal Tourism.* In 2003, 29,019,000 tourist nights were spent in 3,490 establishments in accommodation for 619,841 persons. In 2001 the number of overnight stays accounted for by leisure, holiday and recreation was 22,033,903, with 2,932,483 for congresses and conferences, and 3,408,532 for other business purposes. Total number of tourists reached 10,641,144 (7,520,461 leisure, 1,465,996 conference, 1,654,687 for other business purposes).

National Tourism. In 1998, 10,972,140 Belgians went on holiday. They spent 6,799,990 nights abroad and 4,172,150 in Belgium. 6,883,752 Belgians went on holiday for four nights or more spending 5,262,232 nights abroad and 1,626,884 in Belgium. Belgian tourists tend to organize holidays themselves. They prefer to travel by car to France for long holidays and stay in hotels. In 1996 they spent on average BEF19,651 per holiday of four nights and more.

DIPLOMATIC REPRESENTATIVES

Of Belgium in the United Kingdom (103 Eaton Sq., London, SW1W 9AB)
Ambassador: Baron Thierry de Gruben.

Of the United Kingdom in Belgium (Rue d'Arlon 85, 1040 Brussels)
Ambassador: Richard Kinchen, MVO.

Of Belgium in the USA (3330 Garfield St., NW, Washington, D.C., 20008)
Ambassador: Franciskus Van Daele.

Of the USA in Belgium (Blvd. du Régent 27, 1000 Brussels)
Ambassador: Tom C. Korologos.

Of Belgium to the United Nations
Ambassador: Johan Verbeke.

FURTHER READING

The Institut National de Statistique. *Statistiques du commerce extérieur* (monthly). *Bulletin de Statistique* (bi-monthly). *Annuaire Statistique de la Belgique* (from 1870).—*Annuaire statistique de poche* (from 1965).
Service Fédéral d'Information. *Guide de l'Administration Fédérale.* Occasional

Deprez, K., and Vos, L., *Nationalism in Belgium—Shifting Identities, 1780–1995*. London 1998
Fitzmaurice, J., *The Politics of Belgium: a Unique Federalism*. Farnborough, 1996
Hermans, T. J., *et al.*, (eds.) *The Flemish Movement: a Documentary History.* London, 1992

National statistical office: Institut National de Statistique, Rue de Louvain 44, 1000 Brussels.
Service Fédérale d'Information: POB 3000, 1040 Brussels 4.
Website: http://statbel.fgov.be

BELIZE

Capital: Belmopan
Population projection, 2010: 291,000
GDP per capita, 2002: (PPP$) 6,080
HDI/world rank: 0·737/99

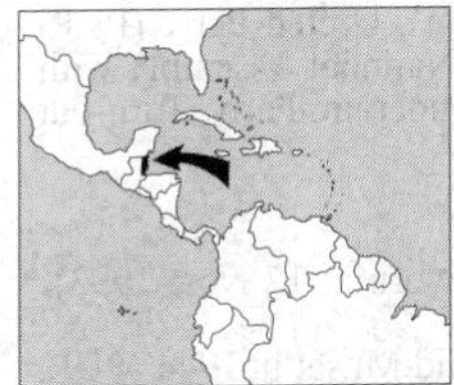

KEY HISTORICAL EVENTS

From the 17th century, British settlers, later joined by British soldiers and sailors disbanded after the capture of Jamaica from Spain in 1655, governed themselves under a form of democracy by public meeting. A constitution was granted in 1765 and, with some modification, continued until 1840 when an executive council was created. In 1862 what was then known as British Honduras was declared a British colony with a legislative assembly and a Lieut.-Governor under the Governor of Jamaica. The administrative connection with Jamaica was severed in 1884. Universal suffrage was introduced in 1964 and thereafter the majority of the legislature were elected rather than appointed. In June 1974 British Honduras became Belize. Independence was achieved on 21 Sept. 1981 and a new constitution introduced.

TERRITORY AND POPULATION

Belize is bounded in the north by Mexico, west and south by Guatemala and east by the Caribbean. Fringing the coast there are three atolls and some 400 islets (cays) in the world's second longest barrier reef (140 miles), which was declared a world heritage site in 1996. Area, 22,964 sq. km.

There are six districts as follows, with area, population and chief city:

District	*Area (in sq. km)*	*Population 2000*	*Chief City*	*Population 2000*
Belize	4,204	68,197	Belize City	49,050
Cayo	5,338	52,564	San Ignacio	13,260
Corozal	1,860	32,708	Corozal	7,888
Orange Walk	4,737	38,890	Orange Walk	13,483
Stann Creek	2,176	24,548	Dangriga	8,814
Toledo	4,649	23,297	Punta Gorda	4,329

Population (2000 census), 240,204 (121,278 males); density, 10·5 per sq. km.

The UN gives a projected population for 2010 of 291,000.

In 2001, 51·9% of the population were rural. In 1995 some 45,000 Belizeans were working abroad.

The capital is Belmopan (1996 population, 6,490).

English is the official language. Spanish is widely spoken. In 1996 the main ethnic groups were Mestizo (Spanish-Maya), 44%; Creole (African descent), 30%; Mayans, 11%; and Garifuna (Caribs), 7%.

SOCIAL STATISTICS

2001 births (est.), 7,100; deaths (est.), 1,300. In 2001 (est.) the birth rate per 1,000 was 29·0 and the death rate 5·3; infant mortality in 2001 was 34 per 1,000 live births; there were 1,517 marriages in 1999. Life expectancy in 2001 was 70·2 years for males and 73·4 for females. Annual population growth rate, 1992–2002, 2·5%; fertility rate, 2001, 3·0 children per woman.

CLIMATE

A tropical climate with high rainfall and small annual range of temperature. The driest months are Feb. and March. Belize City, Jan. 74°F (23·3°C), July 81°F (27·2°C). Annual rainfall 76" (1,890 mm).

CONSTITUTION AND GOVERNMENT

The head of state is the British sovereign, represented by an appointed Governor-General. The Constitution, which came into force on 21 Sept. 1981, provided for a National Assembly, with a five-year term, comprising a 29-member *House of Representatives* elected by universal suffrage, and a *Senate* consisting of eight members, five appointed by the Governor-General on the advice of the Prime

Minister, two on the advice of the Leader of the Opposition and one on the advice of the Belize Advisory Council.

National Anthem. 'O, Land of the Free'; words by S. A. Haynes, tune by S. W. Young.

RECENT ELECTIONS

In parliamentary elections held on 5 March 2003 the People's United Party (PUP) of Prime Minister Said Musa won 22 of the 29 seats in the National Assembly with 53·2% of votes cast against 7 and 45·6% for the United Democratic Party. Turn-out was 78·9%.

CURRENT ADMINISTRATION

Governor-General: Sir Colville Young, GCMG; b. 1932 (sworn in 17 Nov. 1993).

In March 2005 the cabinet comprised as follows:

Prime Minister and Minister for Finance and Defence: Said Musa; b. 1944 (PUP; sworn in 28 Aug. 1998 and re-elected for a second term in March 2003).

Deputy Prime Minister and Minister of Natural Resources and the Environment: John Briceño. *Home Affairs and Investment:* Ralph Fonseca. *Housing:* Servulo Baeza. *Foreign Affairs, Foreign Trade, National Emergency Management, Tourism and Information:* Godfrey Smith. *National Development:* Assad Shoman. *Public Sevice, Works and Transport:* José Coye. *Health, Energy and Communications:* Vildo Marin. *Local Government, Labour and Rural Development:* Marcial Mes. *Agriculture and Fisheries:* Michael Espat. *Human Development:* Sylvia Flores. *Attorney General, Education, Culture, Youth and Sports:* Francis Fonseca.

Government Website: http://www.belize.gov.bz

DEFENCE

The Belize Defence Force numbers 1,050 (2002) with a reserve militia of 700. There is an Air Wing and a Maritime Wing.

In 2003 defence expenditure totalled US$19m. (US$73 per capita), representing 2·4% of GDP.

INTERNATIONAL RELATIONS

Belize is a member of the UN, WTO, the Commonwealth, OAS, Inter-American Development Bank, ACS, CARICOM, IOM and is an ACP member state of the ACP-EU relationship.

ECONOMY

In 2002 agriculture accounted for 15·1% of GDP, industry 19·7% and services 65·2%.

Currency. The unit of currency is the *Belize dollar* (BZD) of 100 *cents.* Since 1976 $B2 has been fixed at US$1. Total money supply was $B352m. in June 2002 and foreign exchange reserves were US$91m. There was inflation of 1·2% in 2002.

Budget. Revenues in 2001 were $B450·9m. and expenditures $B581·1m. Tax revenues accounted for 71·5% of total revenues; current expenditure accounted for 57·4% of total expenditures.

Performance. Real GDP growth was 5·3% in 2001 and 3·5% in 2002. Total GDP in 2002 was US$0·8bn.

Banking and Finance. A Central Bank was established in 1981 (*Governor*, Jorge Meliton Auil) and in 2001 had deposits of $B148m. There were (2001) one development bank and six other banks.

ENERGY AND NATURAL RESOURCES

Environment. Carbon dioxide emissions from the consumption and flaring of fossil fuels in Belize were the equivalent of 3·6 tonnes per capita in 2002.

Electricity. Installed capacity in 2000 was 43,000 kW. Production was 137m. kWh in 2000 and consumption per capita in 2000 was 648 kWh. Supply, 110 and 220 volts; 60 Hz. A rural electrification unit was set up in 1991.

Agriculture. In 2001 there were 65,000 ha of arable land and 39,000 ha of permanent crops. Production, 2000 (in 1,000 tonnes): sugarcane, 1,181; oranges, 190; bananas, 75. Livestock (1996): cattle, 59,000; pigs, 24,000; horses, 5,000; mules, 4,000; chickens, 1m.

Forestry. In 2000, 1,348,000 ha (59·1% of the total land area) were under forests. Timber production in 2001 was 188,000 cu. metres.

Fisheries. There were (1995) 13 registered fishing co-operatives. The total catch in 2001 amounted to 14,370 tonnes, exclusively from sea fishing.

INDUSTRY

Manufacturing is mainly confined to processing agricultural products and timber. There is also a clothing industry. Sugar production was 118,500 tonnes in 2002; molasses, 46,500 in 1995.

Labour. In 1999 the economically active labour force totalled 150,395; the unemployment rate in 1999 was 12·8%.

Trade Unions. There were 14 accredited unions in 1997.

INTERNATIONAL TRADE

External debt was US$835m. in 2002.

Imports and Exports. Imports (f.o.b.) in 2002 totalled US$500·3m. (US$488·7m. in 2001); exports (f.o.b.) in 2002 amounted to US$310·4m. (US$275·0m. in 2001). Main exports in 1999 were: sugar (23%), shellfish (18%), orange juice (18%), clothes (11%) and bananas (9%); main imports were machinery and transport equipment (27%), manufactured goods (16%), food and live animals (15%) and petroleum and related products (14%). Main export markets in 1999: USA (48%), UK (25%), Denmark (7%) and Mexico (4%). Main import suppliers were USA (52%), Mexico (12%), Cuba (10%) and UK (4%).

COMMUNICATIONS

Roads. In 1998 there were 543 km of main roads and 2,329 km of other roads. In 1998 there were 9,930 passenger cars in use and 11,340 trucks and vans. There were 49 deaths as a result of road accidents in 1998.

Civil Aviation. There is an international airport (Philip S. W. Goldson) in Belize City. The national carrier is Maya Island Air, which in 2003 operated domestic services and international flights to Flores (Guatemala). There were direct flights in 2003 with other airlines to Boston, Charlotte, Dallas, Houston, Indianapolis, Las Vegas, McAllen, Miami, Montego Bay, New York, Raleigh, San Pedreo Sula, San Salvador and Washington, D.C. In 2000 Philip S. W. Goldson International handled 492,385 passengers (363,811 on international flights).

Shipping. The main port is Belize City, with a modern deep-water port able to handle containerized shipping. There are also ports at Commerce Bight and Big Creek. In 2002 the merchant marine totalled 1,473,000 GRT, including oil tankers 236,000 GRT. Nine cargo shipping lines serve Belize, and there are coastal passenger services to the offshore islands and Guatemala.

Telecommunications. Telephone subscribers numbered 83,800 in 2002, or 331·2 per 1,000 inhabitants. In 2002 there were 51,700 mobile telephone subscribers and 35,000 PCs in use (138·3 per 1,000 inhabitants). In 1995 there were 1,000 paging users, 300 voice mail users and 500 fax machines. In 2002 Belize had 30,000 Internet users.

Postal Services. In 1997 there were 134 post offices.

SOCIAL INSTITUTIONS

Justice. Each of the six judicial districts has summary jurisdiction courts (criminal) and district courts (civil), both of which are presided over by magistrates. There is a Supreme Court, a Court of Appeal and a Family Court. There is a Director of Public Prosecutions, a Chief Justice and two Puisne Judges. Belize was one of ten countries to sign an agreement in Feb. 2001 establishing a Caribbean Court of

Justice to replace the British Privy Council as the highest civil and criminal court. In the meantime the number of signatories has risen to twelve. The court was inaugurated at Port-of-Spain, Trinidad on 16 April 2005.

In 1995 the police force was 450 strong. The population in penal institutions in June 1999 was 1,097 (459 per 100,000 of national population).

Religion. In 2001, 58% of the population was Roman Catholic and 34% Protestant.

Education. The adult literacy rate was 93·4% in 2001 (93·6% among males and 93·3% among females). Education is in English. State education is managed jointly by the government and the Roman Catholic and Anglican Churches. It is compulsory for children between six and 14 years and primary education is free. In 2000–01 there were 45,246 pupils at primary schools and 24,331 at secondary schools. There are two government-maintained special schools for disabled children. There is a teachers' training college. The University College of Belize opened in 1986. The University of the West Indies maintains an extramural department in Belize City.

In 2000–01 total expenditure on education came to 6·8% of GNP and 20·9% of total government spending.

Health. In 1998 there were seven hospitals with 23 beds per 10,000 persons. There were 155 physicians, 26 dentists, 404 nurses, 30 pharmacists and 230 midwives in 1998. Medical services in rural areas are provided by health care centres and mobile clinics.

CULTURE

World Heritage Sites. The Belize Barrier Reef Reserve System was inscribed on the UNESCO World Heritage List in 1996.

Broadcasting. The Broadcasting Corporation of Belize operates a national broadcasting service. 60% of programmes are in English, the remainder in Spanish and the Amerindian languages. There is also a commercial radio station. There are two commercial TV channels (colour by NTSC). In 1997 there were some 133,000 radio sets and in 2001 there were 45,000 TV sets in use.

Press. There were four weekly newspapers and several monthly magazines in 1995.

Tourism. In 2001 there were 185,700 tourist visitors, of which 106,300 were US citizens and 48,100 arrived on cruise ships. Tourism receipts totalled US$120·5m. in 2001, representing 17·7% of GDP.

DIPLOMATIC REPRESENTATIVES

Of Belize in the United Kingdom (3rd Floor, 45 Crawford Place, London, W1H 4LP)
High Commissioner: Alexis Rosado.

Of the United Kingdom in Belize (PO Box 91, Belmopan, Belize)
High Commissioner: Alan Jones.

Of Belize in the USA (2535 Massachusetts Av., NW, Washington, D.C., 20008)
Ambassador: Lisa M. Shoman.

Of the USA in Belize (Gabourel Lane, Belize City)
Ambassador: Russell F. Freeman.

Of Belize to the United Nations
Ambassador: Stuart M. Leslie.

Of Belize to the European Union
Ambassador: Yvonne Hyde.

FURTHER READING

Leslie, Robert, (ed.) *A History of Belize: Nation in the Making.* 2nd ed. Cubola Productions, Benque Viejo, 1995

Shoman, Assad, *Thirteen Chapters of a History of Belize.* Angelus Press, Belize City, 1994

Sutherland, Anne, *The Making of Belize: Globalization in the Margins.* Bergin & Garvey, London, 1998

Wright, Peggy and Coutts, Brian E., *Belize.* [Bibliography] 2nd ed. ABC-Clio, Oxford and Santa Barbara (CA), 1993

National statistical office: Central Statistical Office, Belmopan.
Website: http://www.cso.gov.bz

BENIN

République du Bénin

Capital: Porto-Novo
Population projection 2010: 8·07m.
GDP per capita, 2002: (PPP$) 1,070
HDI/world rank: 0·421/161

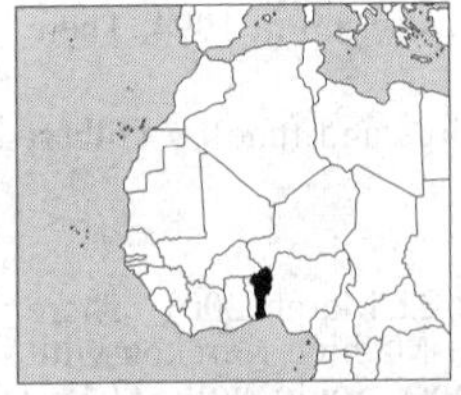

KEY HISTORICAL EVENTS

The People's Republic of Benin is the former Republic of Dahomey. Dahomey was a powerful, well-organized state from the 17th century, trading extensively in slaves through the port of Whydah with the Portuguese, British and French. On the coast an educated African elite grew up in the 19th century.

After the defeat of Dahomey, and the abolition of the monarchy, the French occupied territory inland up to the River Niger and created the colony of Dahomey as part of French West Africa. The African elite protested at French rule as African nationalism grew after the Second World War.

After Dahomey became independent on 1 Aug. 1960 civilian government was interrupted by long periods of military rule. In Oct. 1972 Gen. Mathieu Kérékou seized power and installed a new left-wing regime committed to socialist policies. A constitution was adopted in 1977, based on a single Marxist-Leninist party, the *Parti de la Révolution Populaire du Bénin* (PRPB). Benin is beset with economic problems, factional fighting and frequent plots to overthrow the regime.

TERRITORY AND POPULATION

Benin is bounded in the east by Nigeria, north by Niger and Burkina Faso, west by Togo and south by the Gulf of Guinea. The area is 112,622 sq. km, and the population (census 2002) 6,769,914; density, 60·1 per sq. km.

The UN gives a projected population for 2010 of 8·07m.

In 2001, 57·0% of the population were rural.

The areas and populations of the 12 departments are as follows:

Province	*Sq. km*	*Census 2002*	*Province*	*Sq. km*	*Census 2002*
Alibori	25,683	521,093	Donga	10,691	350,062
Atacora	20,459	549,417	Littoral	79	665,100
Atlantique	3,233	801,683	Mono	1,396	360,037
Borgou	25,310	724,171	Ouémé	2,835	730,772
Collines	13,561	535,923	Plateau	1,865	407,116
Couffo	2,404	524,586	Zou	5,106	599,954

Major towns, with 2002 census population: Cotonou, 665,100; Porto-Novo, 223,552; Parakou, 149,819; Bohicon, 65,974; Abomey, 59,672.

In 1992 the main ethnic groups numbered (in 1,000): Fon, 1,930; Yoruba, 590; Adja, 540; Aizo, 420; Bariba, 420; Somba, 320; Fulani, 270. The official language is French. Over half the people speak Fon.

SOCIAL STATISTICS

2001 (estimates) births, 264,000; deaths, 83,000. Rates, 2001 estimates (per 1,000 population): births, 41·3; deaths, 13·0. Infant mortality, 2001 (per 1,000 live births), 94. Expectation of life in 2001 was 48·6 years for males and 53·2 for females. Annual population growth rate, 1992–2002, 2·8%. Fertility rate, 2001, 5·8 children per woman.

CLIMATE

In coastal parts there is an equatorial climate, with a long rainy season from March to July and a short rainy season in Oct. and Nov. The dry season increases in length from the coast, with inland areas having rain only between May and Sept. Porto-Novo, Jan. 82°F (27·8°C), July 78°F (25·6°C). Annual rainfall 52" (1,300 mm). Cotonou, Jan. 81°F (27·2°C), July 77°F (25°C). Annual rainfall 53" (1,325 mm).

CONSTITUTION AND GOVERNMENT

The Benin Party of Popular Revolution (PRPB) held a monopoly of power from 1977 to 1989.

In Feb. 1990 a 'National Conference of the Active Forces of the Nation' proclaimed its sovereignty and appointed Nicéphore Soglo Prime Minister of a provisional government. At a referendum in Dec. 1990, 93·2% of votes cast were in favour of the new constitution, which has introduced a presidential regime. The *President* is directly elected for renewable five-year terms. Parliament is the unicameral *National Assembly* of 83 members elected by proportional representation for four-year terms.

A 30-member advisory *Social and Economic Council* was set up in 1994. There is a *Constitutional Court.*

National Anthem. 'L'Aube Nouvelle' ('New Dawn'); words and tune by Gilbert Dagnon.

RECENT ELECTIONS

Presidential elections were held in two rounds on 4 and 22 March 2001. There were four candidates for the first round, won by President Mathieu Kérékou with 45·4% of votes cast, ahead of former president Nicéphore Soglo with 27·1%. Following the withdrawal of both Nicéphore Soglo and the third-placed candidate, both of whom claimed that the election had been flawed, President Kérékou was re-elected with 84·06% of votes cast in the run-off against the fourth-placed candidate, Bruno Amoussou. Turn-out in the first round was 87·7% and in the second round 53·4%.

Parliamentary elections were held on 30 March 2003. The Presidential Movement won 52 of 83 seats (of which the Union for the Benin of the Future 31, the African Movement for Development and Progress 9, the Key Force 5 and smaller parties 7), the Rebirth of Benin 15, the Party of Democratic Renewal 11, the Star Alliance 3, and the New Alliance 2.

CURRENT ADMINISTRATION

President: Mathieu Kérékou; b. 1933 (Action Front for Renewal and Development; sworn in 4 April 1996 and re-elected 22 March 2001, having previously been president from 26 Oct. 1972 to 4 April 1991).

In March 2005 the government comprised:

Minister of Foreign Affairs and African Integration: Rogatien Biaou. *Justice, Legislation and Human Rights:* Dorothée Sossa. *Communications, Promotion of New Technologies:* Frédéric Dohou. *Technical and Vocational Education:* Alain François Adihou. *Higher Education and Scientific Research:* Kiémoko Bagnan. *Primary and Secondary Education:* Rafiatou Karimou. *Labour, Civil Service and Administrative Reform:* Aboubakar Arouna. *Mines, Energy and Water Resources:* Kamarou Fassassi. *Environment, Housing and Urban Affairs*: Jules Assogba. *Finance and Economy:* Cosme Sehlin. *Public Health:* Dorothée Akoko Gazard. *Family Affairs, Social Welfare and Solidarity:* Lea Hounkpe. *Interior, Security and Decentralization:* Gen. Seydou Mama Sika. *Commerce, Industry, Promotion of Employment:* Massiyatou Latoundji. *Public Works and Transport:* Jeanne Marie Omichessan. *Agriculture, Husbandry and Fisheries:* Fatiou Akplogan. *Youth, Sports and Leisure:* Jean-Baptiste Edayé. *Culture, Handicrafts and Tourism:* Antoine Dayori. *Relations with Institutions, Civil Society and Beninese Abroad:* Valentin Aditi Houde. *Minister of State for National Defence:* Pierre Osho. *Minister of State for Development and Planning:* Zul Kiff Salami.

Government Website: http://www.gouv.bj

DEFENCE

There is selective conscription for 18 months. Defence expenditure totalled US$60m. in 2003 (US$9 per capita), representing 1·6% of GDP.

Army. The Army strength (2002) was 4,300, with an additional 2,500-strong paramilitary gendarmerie.

Navy. Personnel in 2002 numbered 100; the force is based at Cotonou.

Air Force. The Air Force has suffered a shortage of funds and operates no combat aircraft. Personnel, 2002, 150.

INTERNATIONAL RELATIONS

Benin is a member of the UN, WTO, the African Union African Development Bank, ECOWAS, IOM, OIC, Islamic Development Bank, International Organization of the Francophonie and is an ACP member state of the ACP-EU relationship.

ECONOMY

Agriculture accounted for 36·0% of GDP in 2002, industry 14·3% and services 49·7%.

Currency. The unit of currency is the *franc CFA* (XOF) with a parity of 655·957 francs CFA to one euro. Total money supply was 351,786m. francs CFA in May 2002 and foreign exchange reserves were US$563m. Gold reserves in June 2000 were 11,000 troy oz. Inflation was 2·4% in 2002.

Budget. The fiscal year is the calendar year. In 2001 revenue was 281bn. francs CFA and expenditure 353bn. francs CFA.

Performance. Real GDP growth was 5·0% in 2001 and 6·0% in 2002. Total GDP was US$3·5bn. in 2003.

Banking and Finance. The bank of issue and the central bank is the regional Central Bank of West African States (BCEAO). The *Governor* is Charles Konan Banny. In Dec. 2001 it had total assets of 5,517,700m. francs CFA. There are five private commercial banks, one savings bank (total deposits 15,758m. francs CFA in 1997) and three credit institutions. The Caisse Autonome d'Amortissement du Bénin manages state funds.

ENERGY AND NATURAL RESOURCES

Environment. Benin's carbon dioxide emissions from the consumption and flaring of fossil fuels in 2002 were the equivalent of 0·3 tonnes per capita.

Electricity. Installed capacity in 2000 was 55,000 kW. In 2000 production was 56m. kWh; Benin also imported 375m. kWh. A solar energy programme was initiated in 1993. Consumption per capita in 2000 was 70 kWh.

Oil and Gas. The Semé oilfield, located 15 km offshore, was discovered in 1968. Production commenced in 1982 and was 44,000 tonnes in 1999. Crude petroleum reserves in 2002 were 8m. bbls.

Agriculture. Benin's economy is underdeveloped, and is dependent on subsistence agriculture. In 1998, 3·23m. persons depended on agriculture, of whom 1·47m. were economically active. Small independent farms produce about 90% of output. In 2001, 2·0m. ha were arable and 0·27m. ha permanent crops; 12,000 ha were irrigated in 2001. There were 185 tractors in 2001. The chief agricultural products, 2000 (in 1,000 tonnes) were: cassava, 2,026; yams, 1,773; maize, 663; seed cotton, 435; cottonseed, 240; sorghum, 136; groundnuts, 81.

Livestock, 2000: cattle, 1,438,000; sheep, 645,000; goats, 1,183,000; pigs, 470,000; poultry, 23m.

Forestry. In 2000 there were 2·65m. ha of forest (24·0% of the total land area), mainly in the north. Timber production in 2001 was 6·27m. cu. metres.

Fisheries. Total catch, 2001, 38,415 tonnes, of which freshwater fish approximately 78% and marine fish 22%.

INDUSTRY

Only about 2% of the workforce is employed in industry. The main activities include palm-oil processing, brewing and the manufacture of cement, sugar and textiles. Also important are cigarettes, food, construction materials and petroleum. Production (in 1,000 tonnes): cement (2000), 759; palm oil (2000), 15; wheat flour (1999), 9; beer (2002), 57m. litres.

Labour. The labour force numbered 2,490,000 in 1996 (52% males). Approximately half of the economically active population is engaged in agriculture, fishing and forestry.

Trade Unions. In 1973 all trade unions were amalgamated to form a single body, the *Union Nationale des Syndicats des Travailleurs du Bénin*. In 1990 some unions declared their independence from this Union, which itself broke its links with the PRPB. In 1992 there were three trade union federations.

INTERNATIONAL TRADE

Commercial and transport activities, which make up 36% of GDP, are extremely vulnerable to developments in neighbouring Nigeria, with which there is a significant amount of illegal trade. Foreign debt was US$1,843m. in 2002.

Imports and Exports. Imports (f.o.b.) in 2001, US$553·0m.; exports (f.o.b.), US$373·5m.

Principal export markets, 1999: Brazil, 19·8%; India, 15·5%; Indonesia, 10·0%; Thailand, 5·3%; Bangladesh, 4·7%. Principal import suppliers: France, 22·0%; Côte d'Ivoire, 10·5%; Togo, 5·6%; China, 5·1%; USA, 5·1%.

Main imports in 1998 were: manufactured goods (19%); refined oil (19%); food and live animals (18%); machinery and transport equipment (17%). The main exports were: cotton (47%); uranium ores (30%); cigarettes (6%).

COMMUNICATIONS

Roads. There were 6,787 km of roads in 1999 (including 10 km of motorways), of which 20% were surfaced. Passenger cars in use in 1996 totalled 37,772, and there were also 7,554 buses and coaches plus approximately 250,000 motorcycles and mopeds. In 1996, 412 people died in road accidents.

Rail. There are 458 km of metre-gauge railway. In 2000, 0·7m. passengers were carried and 0·3m. tonnes of freight.

Civil Aviation. The international airport is at Cotonou (Cadjehoun), which in 2000 handled 250,000 passengers (all on international flights) and 4,100 tonnes of freight. In 1999 scheduled airline traffic of Benin-based carriers flew 3·0m. km, carrying 84,000 passengers (all on international flights). In 2003 Trans African Airlines flew to Abidjan, Bamako, Brazzaville, Dakar, Lomé and Pointe-Noire; Trans Air Benin operated services to Abidjan, Brazzaville and Lomé and Aero Benin flew to Bamako, Brazzaville, Johannesburg, Libreville and Ouagadougou.

Shipping. There is a port at Cotonou. In 2002 the merchant fleet totalled 1,000 GRT. In 2000 vessels entering totalled 1,184,000 NRT.

Telecommunications. In 2002 there were 281,400 telephone subscribers (28·6 per 1,000 persons), of which 218,800 were mobile phone subscribers. There were 12,000 PCs in use in 2002 and 1,100 fax machines in 1996. Benin had 50,000 Internet users in 2002.

Postal Services. In 1998 there were 178 post offices.

SOCIAL INSTITUTIONS

Justice. The Supreme Court is at Cotonou. There are Magistrates Courts and a *tribunal de conciliation* in each district. The legal system is based on French civil law and customary law.

The population in penal institutions in Sept. 2000 was 4,961 (81 per 100,000 of national population).

Religion. Some 51% of the population follow traditional animist beliefs. In 2001 there were 1·37m. Roman Catholics and 1·32m. Muslims. In Sept. 2003 there was one cardinal.

Education. Adult literacy rate was 38·6% in 2001 (53·5% among males and 24·6% among females). In 2000–01 there were 1,054,936 pupils in primary schools with 19,710 teachers and (1999–2000) 229,228 pupils in secondary schools with 9,803 teachers. The University of Benin (Cotonou) had 9,000 students and 240 academic staff in 1994–95.

In 2000–01 total expenditure on education came to 3·2% of GNP.

Health. In 1995 there were 312 physicians, 16 dentists, 1,116 nurses, 85 pharmacists and 432 midwives. Hospital bed provision was just two for every 10,000 persons in 1993.

CULTURE

World Heritage Sites. The Royal Palaces of Abomey joined the World Heritage List in 1985. They preserve the remains of the palaces of 12 kings who ruled between 1625 and 1900.

Broadcasting. The media are overseen by the nine-member Haute Autorité de l'Audiovisuel et de la Communication. The government-controlled Office de Radiodiffusion et Télévision du Bénin broadcasts a radio programme from Cotonou and a regional programme from Parakou, and a TV service (colour by SECAM V) from Cotonou. In 1997 there were 620,000 radio receivers and in 2001 there were 76,000 TV receivers.

Press. In 1999 there were 13 daily newspapers with a circulation of 32,500, at a rate of 5·3 per 1,000 inhabitants.

Tourism. In 2002 there were 72,000 foreign tourists. Receipts totalled US$60m.

DIPLOMATIC REPRESENTATIVES

Of Benin in the United Kingdom
Ambassador: Edgar-Yves Monnou (resides at Paris).
Honorary Consul: Lawrence Landau (Dolphin House, 16 The Broadway, Stanmore, Middlesex HA7 4DW).

Of the United Kingdom in Benin
Ambassador: Richard Gozney, CMG (resides at Abuja, Nigeria).

Of Benin in the USA (2124 Kalorama Road, NW, Washington, D.C., 20008)
Ambassador: Segbe Cyrille Oguin.

Of the USA in Benin (Rue Caporal Bernard Anani, Cotonou)
Ambassador: Wayne E. Neill.

Of Benin to the United Nations
Ambassador: Joël Wassi Adechi.

Of Benin to the European Union
Ambassador: Euloge Hinvi.

FURTHER READING

Bay, E., *Wives of the Leopard: Gender, Politics, and Culture in the Kingdom of Dahomey.* University Press of Virginia, 1998

Eades, Jerry S. and Allen, Christopher, *Benin.* [Bibliography] ABC-Clio, Oxford and Santa Barbara (CA), 1996

National statistical office: Institut National de la Statistique et de l'Analyse Economique, 01 BP 323, Cotonou.
Website (French only): http://www.insae.bj

BHUTAN

Druk-yul

(Kingdom of Bhutan)

Capital: Thimphu
Population projection, 2010: 2·71m
GDP per capita, 2001: (PPP$) 1,833
HDI/world rank: 0·536/134

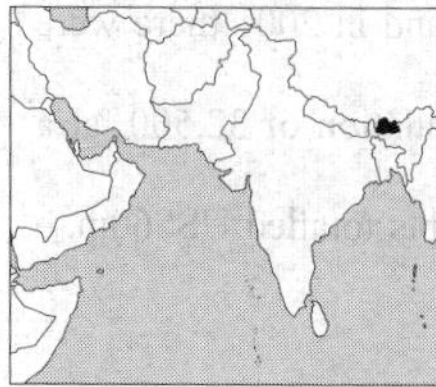

KEY HISTORICAL EVENTS

A sovereign kingdom in the Himalayas, Bhutan was governed by a spiritual ruler and a temporal ruler—the Dharma and Deb Raja—from the 17th century. The interior was organized into districts controlled by governors and fort commanders. These officials formed the electoral council appointing the Deb Raja. During the 19th century civil wars were fought between district governors for the office of the Deb Raja. The election became a formality and the governors of Tongsa and Paro were the most frequently chosen because they were the strongest. In 1863 a British attempt to bring stability to Bhutan led to war on the frontier with India.

In 1907 the office of Dharma Raja came to an end. The governor of Tongsa, Ugyen Wangchuk, was then chosen Maharajah of Bhutan, the throne becoming hereditary in his family (the title is now King of Bhutan). He concluded a treaty with the British in 1910 allowing internal autonomy but British control of foreign policy. The treaty was renewed with the Government of India in 1949. In the early 1990s, tens of thousands of 'illegal immigrants', mostly Nepali-speaking Hindus, were forcibly expelled. More than ten years on, there are still nearly 90,000 people claiming to be Bhutanese refugees in camps set up by the UNHCR in eastern Nepal.

TERRITORY AND POPULATION

Bhutan is situated in the eastern Himalayas, bounded in the north by Tibet and on all other sides by India. In 1949 India retroceded 83 sq. km of Dewangiri, annexed in 1865. Area about 18,000 sq. miles (46,500 sq. km); population estimate, 2002, 2·19m., giving a density of 47 per sq. km.

The UN gives a projected population for 2010 of 2·71m.

In 2001, 92·6% of the population lived in rural areas. Only Rwanda has a larger proportion of its population living in rural areas. A Nepalese minority makes up 30–35% of the population, mainly in the south. The capital is Thimphu (1999, 28,000 population).

The official language is Dzongkha.

SOCIAL STATISTICS

1995 (estimates) births, 74,000 (rate of 41·4 per 1,000 population); deaths, 25,000 (rate of 14·4 per 1,000 population). Life expectancy at birth, 2001, was 61·3 years for men and 63·8 years for women. Infant mortality, 2001, 74 per 1,000 live births. Annual population growth rate, 1992–2002, 2·8%; fertility rate, 2001, 5·2 children per woman.

CLIMATE

The climate is largely controlled by altitude. The mountainous north is cold, with perpetual snow on the summits, but the centre has a more moderate climate, though winters are cold, with rainfall under 40" (1,000 mm). In the south, the climate is humid sub-tropical and rainfall approaches 200" (5,000 mm).

CONSTITUTION AND GOVERNMENT

There is no formal constitution. The monarchy acts in consultation with a National Assembly (*Tshogdu*), which was reinstituted in 1953. But King Wangchuck is leaning towards democracy. In July 1998 the National Assembly was given the right to dismiss him. This has 150 members and meets at least once a year. 105 members are elected from village constituencies, 10 are nominated by the Buddhist clergy and 35 are appointed by the King from among the bureaucracy and the government to represent him. All serve for a three-year term. All Bhutanese over 30 years may be candidates.

The reigning King is **Jigme Singye Wangchuck** (b. 1955), who succeeded his father Jigme Dorji Wangchuck (died 21 July 1972).

In 1907 the Trongsa Penlop (the governor of the province of Trongsa in central Bhutan), Sir Ugyen Wangchuk, GCIE, KCSI, was elected as the first hereditary Maharaja of Bhutan. The Bhutanese title is *Druk Gyalpo*, and his successor is now addressed as King of Bhutan. Educated in Britain, King Wangchuk is opposed to certain western influences such as television and jeans. The stated goal is to increase Gross National Happiness.

12 monastic representatives are elected by the central and regional ecclesiastical bodies, while the remaining members are nominated by the King, and include members of the Council of Ministers (the Cabinet) and the Royal Advisory Council.

National Anthem. 'Druk tsendhen koipi gyelknap na' ('In the Thunder Dragon Kingdom'); words by Dasho Shinkar Lam, tune by A. Tongmi.

CURRENT ADMINISTRATION

In March 2005 the government comprised:

Prime Minister and Minister for Trade and Industry: Lyonpo Yeshey Zimba; b. 1952 (in office since 20 Aug. 2004, previously in office July 2000–Aug. 2001).

Chairman of the Royal Advisory Council: Rinzin Gyaltshen. *Chief Justice:* Sonam Tobgye. *Minister of Agriculture:* Sangay Ngedup. *Education:* Thinley Gyamtso. *Finance:* Wangdi Norbu. *Foreign Affairs:* Khandu Wangchuck. *Health:* Jigmi Singay. *Home and Cultural Affairs:* Jigme Thinley. *Information and Communication:* Leki Dorji. *Labour and Human Resources:* Ugyen Tshering. *Works and Human Settlements:* Kinzang Dorji.

Government Website: http://www.bhutan.gov.bt/

DEFENCE

In 2003 defence spending totalled US$22m. (US$25 per capita), representing 3·3% of GDP.

Army. In 1996 there was an army of 6,000 men. Three to five weeks militia training was introduced in 1989 for senior students and government officials, and three months training for some 10,000 volunteers from the general population in 1990 and 1991. Since 1992 only refresher training has been implemented.

INTERNATIONAL RELATIONS

Bhutan is a member of the UN, Asian Development Bank, Colombo Plan and SAARC.

ECONOMY

Agriculture accounted for 33·7% of GDP in 2002, with industry accounting for 39·4% and services 26·9%.

Overview. The 8th development plan (1997–2002) allowed for expenditure of Nu35,169m. Hydro-electric power and industries were stressed. The 9th development plan (2003–07) focuses on decentralization, and aims to bring electricity to 15,000 rural households as part of a plan to make Bhutan fully electrified by 2020, supported by the Asian Development Bank.

Currency. The unit of currency is the *ngultrum* (BTN) of 100 *chetrum*, at parity with the Indian rupee. Indian currency is also legal tender. Foreign exchange reserves were US$273m. in May 2002. Total money supply in May 2002 was Nu4,922m. In 2002 inflation was 5·0%.

Budget. Current provincial revenue and expenditure in Nu1m. for fiscal years ending 30 June:

	1997–98	*1998–99*	*1999–2000*	*2000–01*	*2001–02*[1]
Revenue	3,133·0	3,656·9	4,585·4	4,975·7	5,140·6
Expenditure	4,588·4	7,284·0	8,334·2	10,716·5	9,813·7

[1]Provisional.

Performance. Real GDP growth was 6·6% in 2001 and 7·7% in 2002. Total GDP in 2003 was US$0·6bn.

Banking and Finance. The Royal Monetary Authority (founded 1982; *Managing Director,* Sonam Wangchuk) acts as the central bank. Deposits (Dec. 1995) Nu2,816·3m. Foreign exchange reserves in 1997: US$120m. The Bank of Bhutan, a commercial bank, was established in 1968. The headquarters are at Phuentsholing with 26 branches throughout the country. It is 80%-owned by the government of Bhutan and 20%-owned by the Indian government. There is another commercial bank (the Bhutan National Bank), a development bank (the Bhutan Development Finance Corporation) and a stock exchange in Thimphu.

ENERGY AND NATURAL RESOURCES

Environment. Bhutan's carbon dioxide emissions from the consumption and flaring of fossil fuels in 2002 were the equivalent of 0·1 tonnes per capita.

Electricity. Installed capacity in 2000 was 362,000 kW (of which 350,000 kW hydro-electric). Production (2000) was approximately 1·8bn. kWh. In 1995, 38 towns and 297 villages had electricity. Consumption per capita in 2000 was an estimated 201 kWh. Bhutan exports electricity to India.

Minerals. Large deposits of limestone, marble, dolomite, slate, graphite, lead, copper, coal, talc, gypsum, beryl, mica, pyrites and tufa have been found. Most mining activity (principally limestone, coal, slate and dolomite) is on a small-scale. Output, 1998 estimates: limestone, 272,000 tonnes; dolomite, 255,000 tonnes; coal (2000 estimate), 50,000 tonnes.

Agriculture. The area under cultivation in 1996 was 0·36m. ha. In 2001 there were 145,000 ha of arable land and 20,000 ha of permanent crops. The chief products (2000 production in 1,000 tonnes) are maize (70), oranges (58), rice (50), potatoes (34), wheat (20) and sugarcane (13).

Livestock (2000): cattle, 435,000; pigs, 75,000; sheep, 59,000; goats, 42,000; horses, 30,000.

Forestry. In 2000, 3·02m. ha (64·2% of the land area) were forested. Timber production in 2001 was 4·42m. cu. metres.

Fisheries. The total catch in 2001 amounted to an estimated 300 tonnes, exclusively from inland waters.

INDUSTRY

Industries in Bhutan include cement, wood products, processed fruits, alcoholic beverages and calcium carbide. 2001 production: cement, 160,000 tonnes; veneer sheets, 16,000 cu. metres; particle board, 12,000 cu. metres; plywood, 4,000 cu. metres. In 2001 there were 12,878 licensed industrial establishments, of which 8,536 were construction, 3,773 service and 569 manufacturing industries. The latter included 317 forest-based companies, 116 agriculture-based and 46 mineral-based.

Labour. In 1996 the labour force totalled 888,000 (60% males).

INTERNATIONAL TRADE

External debt in 2002 amounted to US$377m. and cumulative debt service payments in 1999 totalled US$7m.

Financial support is received from India, the UN and other international aid organizations.

Imports and Exports. Trade with India dominates but oranges and apples, timber, cardamom and liquor are also exported to the Middle East, Singapore and Europe. Exports in 1999 amounted to US$116·0m. and imports to US$182·1m. In 1997–98 India accounted for 70·5% of imports and 94·5% of exports.

COMMUNICATIONS

Roads. In 2000 there were about 3,691 km of roads, of which 1,591 km were highways and main roads. In 2002 there were 10,071 cars; 770 buses and coaches; 2,747 trucks and vans plus 8,371 motorcycles and mopeds. A number of sets of traffic lights were installed during the late 1990s but all have subsequently been removed as they were considered to be eyesores. There had previously been just one set.

Civil Aviation. In 2003 Druk-Air flew from Paro to Bangkok, Delhi, Dhaka, Kathmandu, Calcutta and Rangoon (Yangon). In 1999 scheduled airline traffic of

Bhutan-based carriers flew 1·0m. km, carrying 31,000 passengers (all on international flights).

Telecommunications. In 2002 there were 19,600 telephone subscribers (28·4 per 1,000 inhabitants). There were 1,500 fax machines in 1998 and 10,000 PCs (14·5 for every 1,000 persons) were in use in 2002. The country's first Internet cafe was opened in March 2000 in the capital Thimphu. There were 10,000 Internet users in 2002.

Postal Services. In 1997 there were 106 post offices. Prior to the opening of the country to tourism in 1974 the main source of foreign exchange was the sale of commemorative postage stamps.

SOCIAL INSTITUTIONS

Justice. The High Court consists of eight judges appointed by the King. There is a Magistrate's Court in each district, under a *Thrimpon*, from which appeal is to the High Court at Thimphu. The death penalty, not used for 40 years, was abolished in 2004.

Religion. The state religion of Bhutan is the Drukpa Kagyupa, a branch of Mahayana Buddhism. There are also Hindu and Muslim minorities.

Education. In 2004 there were 24,533 pupils and 707 teachers in community primary schools, 26,508 pupils and 752 teachers in primary schools and 79,729 pupils with 2,630 teachers in secondary schools. In 1996 there were 1,795 pupils and 203 teachers in technical, vocational and tertiary-level schools. There were 1,248 students and 61 teachers in seven private schools. Adult literacy was 42% in 1998.

In 2000–01 total expenditure on education came to 5·1% of GNP and 12·9% of total government spending.

Health. In 1997 there were 28 hospitals with 16 beds per 10,000 inhabitants, and 101 physicians. There were (1996) 32 dispensaries, 97 basic health units, 10 indigenous dispensaries, 454 outreach clinics, 19 malaria centres and 3 training institutes. In 1994 beds totalled 970; there were 578 paramedics in 1994. Free health facilities are available to 90% of the population.

CULTURE

Broadcasting. In 1994 there were 52 radio stations for internal administrative communications, and 13 hydro-met stations. Bhutan Broadcasting Service (autonomous since 1992) broadcasts a daily programme in English, Sharchopkha, Dzongkha and Nepali. The first television station was launched in 1999. Satellite and cable television are illegal. In 2001 there were 18,000 TV receivers and in 1997 there were 37,000 radio receivers.

Cinema. There are two cinemas in Thimphu and four others.

Press. There is one weekly newspaper, published in English, Dzongkha and Nepali. Total circulation (1996) about 12,000.

Tourism. Bhutan was not formally opened to foreign tourists until 1974, but tourism is now the largest source of foreign exchange. In 2000, 8,000 tourists visited Bhutan; revenue totalled US$9m.

DIPLOMATIC REPRESENTATIVES

Of Bhutan to the United Nations
Ambassador: Daw Penjo.

Of Bhutan to the European Union
Ambassador: Bap Kesang.

FURTHER READING

Crossette, B., *So Close to Heaven: The Vanishing Buddhist Kingdoms of the Himalayas.* New York, 1995
Das, B. N., *Mission to Bhutan: a Nation in Transition.* New Delhi, 1995
Hutt, M., *Bhutan: Perspectives on Conflict and Dissent.* London, 1994
Savada, A. M. (ed.) *Nepal and Bhutan: Country Studies.* Washington, D.C., 1993
Sinha, A. C., *Bhutan: Ethnic Identity and National Dilemma.* New Delhi, 1998

National statistical office: Central Statistical Organization, Thimphu.

BOLIVIA

República de Bolivia

Capital: Sucre
Seat of government: La Paz
Population projection, 2010: 9·99m
GDP per capita, 2002: (PPP$) 2,460
HDI/world rank: 0·681/114

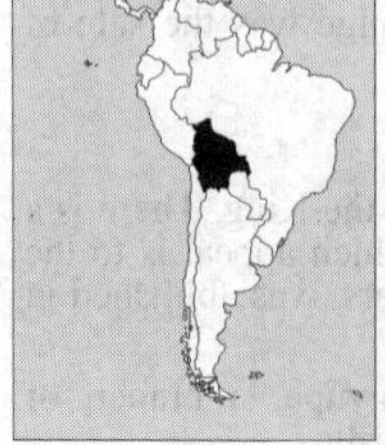

KEY HISTORICAL EVENTS

Bolivia was part of the Inca Empire until conquered by the Spanish in the 16th century. Independence was won and the Republic of Bolivia was proclaimed on 6 Aug. 1825. During the first 154 years of its independence, Bolivia had 189 governments, many of them installed by coups. In the 1960s the Argentinian revolutionary and former minister of the Cuban government, Ernesto 'Che' Guevara, was killed in Bolivia while fighting with a left-wing guerrilla group. In 1971 Bolivian instability reached a peak with the brief establishment of a revolutionary Popular Assembly during the regime of Gen. Torres. Later repression under Gen. Hugo Banzer took a heavy toll on the left-wing parties. Banzer was followed by a succession of military-led governments until civilian rule was restored in Oct. 1982 when Dr Siles Zuazo became president. He introduced a period of economic reform embracing free markets and open trade, since when 'Bolivia has been a model of democratic stability'. (*The Economist*, 24 June 2000).

TERRITORY AND POPULATION

Bolivia is a landlocked state bounded in the north and east by Brazil, south by Paraguay and Argentina, and west by Chile and Peru, with an area of some 424,165 sq. miles (1,098,581 sq. km). A coastal strip of land on the Pacific passed to Chile after a war in 1884. In 1953 Chile declared Arica a free port and Bolivia has certain privileges there.

Population (2001 census): 8,274,325 (62·9% urban); density, 7·5 per sq. km.

The UN gives a projected population for 2010 of 9·99m.

Area and population of the departments (capitals in brackets) at the 1992 and 2001 censuses:

Departments	*Area (sq. km)*	*Census 1992*	*Census 2001*
Beni (Trinidad)	213,564	276,174	362,521
Chuquisaca (Sucre)	51,524	453,756	531,522
Cochabamba (Cochabamba)	55,631	1,110,205	1,455,711
La Paz (La Paz)	133,985	1,900,786	2,350,466
Oruro (Oruro)	53,588	340,114	391,870
Pando (Cobija)	63,827	38,072	52,525
Potosí (Potosí)	118,218	645,889	709,013
Santa Cruz (Santa Cruz)	370,621	1,364,389	2,029,471
Tarija (Tarija)	37,623	291,407	391,226
Total	1,098,581	6,420,792	8,274,325

Population (2001, in 1,000) of the principal towns: Santa Cruz, 1,116; La Paz, 790; El Alto, 647; Cochabamba, 517; Oruro, 201; Sucre, 194; Tarija, 136; Potosí, 133.

Spanish is the official and commercial language. The Amerindian languages Aymará and Quechua are spoken exclusively by 22% and 5·2% of the population respectively; Tupi Guaraní is also spoken. Indigenous peoples account for 71% of the population.

SOCIAL STATISTICS

In 2000 births totalled an estimated 265,000 (birth rate of 32·4 per 1,000 population); deaths totalled an estimated 72,000 (rate, 8·8 per 1,000); infant mortality (2001), 60 per 1,000 live births, the highest in South America. Expectation of life (2001) was 61·3 years for men and 65·4 years for women. Annual population growth rate, 1992–2002, 2·2%. Fertility rate, 2001, 4·1 children per woman, also the highest in South America.

CLIMATE

The varied geography produces different climates. The low-lying areas in the Amazon Basin are warm and damp throughout the year, with heavy rainfall from Nov. to March; the Altiplano is generally dry between May and Nov. with sunshine but cold nights in June and July, while the months from Dec. to March are the wettest. La Paz, Jan. 55·9°F (13·3°C), July 50·5°F (10·3°C). Annual rainfall 20·8" (529 mm). Sucre, Jan. 58·5°F (14·7°C), July 52·7°F (11·5°C). Annual rainfall 20·1" (510 mm).

CONSTITUTION AND GOVERNMENT

Bolivia's first constitution was adopted on 19 Nov. 1826. The *President* is elected by universal suffrage for a five-year term. If 50% of the vote is not obtained, the result is determined by a secret ballot in Congress amongst the leading two candidates. The President appoints the members of his Cabinet. There is a bicameral legislature; the *Senate* comprises 27 members, three from each department, and the *Chamber of Deputies* 130 members, all serving terms of five years. The *Vice-President* is also the *President* of the National Congress. A constitutional amendment of 1996 introduced direct elections for 65 deputies; the remainder are nominated by party leaders. Voting is compulsory.

National Anthem. 'Bolivianos, el hado propicio' ('Bolivians, the propitious fate'); words by I. de Sanjinés, tune by B. Vincenti.

RECENT ELECTIONS

Presidential elections were held on 30 June 2002. Former president Gonzalo Sánchez de Lozada (the Nationalist Revolutionary Movement) won 22·5% of votes cast against 20·9% for Evo Morales (Movement Towards Socialism), 20·91% for Manfred Reyes Villa (New Republican Force) and 16·3% for former president Jaime Paz Zamora (Movement of the Revolutionary Left). Turn-out was 63·4%. In the run-off held on 4 Aug. 2002 Gonzalo Sánchez de Lozada was elected president by parliament with 84 votes against 43 for Evo Morales.

In elections to the Chamber of Deputies, also held on 30 June 2002, the Nationalist Revolutionary Movement/Movement Free Bolivia won 36 seats with 26·9% of the vote, Movement Towards Socialism 27 with 11·9%, Movement of Revolutionary Left 26 with 19·8%, New Republican Force 25 with 26·5%, Indegenious Pachakuti Movement 6 with 2·2%, Citizens' Solidarity Union 5 with 5·3%, Nationalist Democratic Alliance 4 with 3·1%, Socialist Party 1 with 0·7%.

CURRENT ADMINISTRATION

President: Carlos Diego Mesa Gilbert; b. 1953 (Nationalist Revolutionary Movement; in office since resignation of Gonzalo Sánchez de Lozada on 17 Oct. 2003).

Vice-President: Vacant.

In March 2005 the cabinet was composed as follows:

Minister of Foreign Relations and Worship: Juan Ignacio Siles del Valle. *Presidency:* José Galindo Néder. *Government:* Saúl Lara. *National Defence:* Gonzalo Arredondo Millán. *Sustainable Development:* Erwin Aguilera. *Finance:* Luis Carlos Jemio. *Economic Development:* Wálter Kreidler. *Agriculture:* Víctor Gabriel Barrios. *Services and Public Works:* René Gómez. *Education:* María Soledad Quiroga. *Health and Sports:* Rosario Quiroga. *Labour:* Audalia Zurita. *Mining and Minerals:* Jorge Espinoza. *Hydrocarbons:* Guillermo Torrez Orias. *Without Portfolio Responsible for Popular Participation:* Gloria Ardaya. *Without Portfolio Responsible for Indigenous Affairs:* Pedro Ticona.

Government Website (Spanish only): http://www.bolivia.gov.bo

DEFENCE

There is selective conscription for 12 months at the age of 18 years. There has been optional pre-military training for high school pupils since 1998.

In 2003 defence expenditure totalled US$131m. (US$15 per capita), representing 1·7% of GDP.

Army. There are six military regions. Strength (2002): 25,000 (18,000 conscripts), including a Presidential Guard infantry regiment under direct headquarters command.

Navy. A small force exists for river and lake patrol duties. Personnel in 2002 totalled 3,500, including 1,700 marines. There were six Naval Districts in 2002, covering Lake Titicaca and the rivers, each with one flotilla.

Air Force. The Air Force, established in 1923, has 37 combat aircraft and 16 armed helicopters. Personnel strength (2002) about 3,000 (2,000 conscripts).

INTERNATIONAL RELATIONS

Bolivia is a member of the UN, WTO, OAS, Inter-American Development Bank, LAIA, the Andean Group, IOM and the Amazon Pact, and is an associate member of Mercosur.

ECONOMY

In 2002 agriculture accounted for 14·6% of GDP, industry 33·3% and services 52·1%.

Overview. The New Economic Policy includes a 'capitalization' programme (partial privatization and 50% distribution of shares to pension funds for adult citizens). State enterprises in oil and gas, telecommunications, electricity, railways, airlines and tin were capitalized between 1995–98. Water privatization in Cochabamba in 2000 was revoked after riots over tariffs.

Currency. The unit of currency is the *boliviano* (BOB) of 100 *centavos*, which replaced the *peso* on 1 Jan. 1987 at a rate of one boliviano = 1m. pesos. Inflation was 0·9% in 2002. In June 2002 foreign exchange reserves were US$557m., total money supply was 4,163m. bolivianos and gold reserves totalled 911,000 troy oz.

Budget. Government revenue and expenditure (in 1m. bolivianos):

	1996	*1997*	*1998*	*1999*	*2000*	*2001*
Revenue	6,564·7	7,092·3	8,300·8	8,638·3	9,278·7	9,168·1
Expenditure	8,627·4	9,193·7	10,339·8	11,166·9	12,314·4	14,089·9

Performance. Real GDP growth was 1·5% in 2001 and 2·8% in 2002. Total GDP was US$8·0bn. in 2003.

Banking and Finance. The Central Bank (*President*, Juan Antonio Morales Anaya) is the bank of issue. In 2000 there were eight commercial banks and five foreign banks.

There are stock exchanges in La Paz and Santa Cruz.

ENERGY AND NATURAL RESOURCES

Environment. In 2002 Bolivia's carbon dioxide emissions from the consumption and flaring of fossil fuels were the equivalent of 1·0 tonnes per capita.

Electricity. Installed capacity was 1·3m. kW in 2000. Production from all sources (2000), 3·95bn. kWh; consumption per capita was 475 kWh in 2000.

Oil and Gas. There are petroleum and natural gas deposits in the Santa Cruz–Camiri areas. Production of oil in 2000 was 11,424,058 bbls. Reserves in 2002 were 441m. bbls. Work has begun on a US$1·9bn. pipeline from eastern Bolivia to São Paulo in Brazil. Natural gas output was 5·4bn. cu. metres in 2002 with proven reserves of 680bn. cu. metres in 2002.

Minerals. Mining accounts for 5·76% of GDP (1996 estimate). Tin-mining had been the mainstay of the economy until the collapse of the international tin market in 1985. Estimated production, 2001 (in tonnes): zinc, 141,226; tin (2000), 12,039; lead (2000), 9,090; antimony (2000), 2,072; wolfram (2000), 671; silver, 408; gold, 12,395 kg.

Agriculture. The agricultural population was 3·17m. in 2002, of whom 1·56m. were economically active. There were 2·90m. ha of arable land in 2001 and 0·20m. ha of permanent crops. Output in 1,000 tonnes in 2000 was: sugarcane, 3,602; soybeans, 1,232; potatoes, 927; bananas, 695; maize, 653; cassava, 515; rice, 310; plantains, 187. In 1992, 77,000 tonnes of coca (the source of cocaine) were grown.

Since 1987 Bolivia has received international (mainly US) aid to reduce the amount of coca grown, with compensation for farmers who co-operate.

Livestock, 2000: cattle, 6,725,000; sheep, 8,752,000; pigs, 2,793,000; goats, 1,500,000; asses and mules, 712,000; horses, 322,000; chickens, 74m.

Forestry. Forests covered 53·07m. ha (48·9% of the land area) in 2000. Tropical forests with woods ranging from the 'iron tree' to the light balsa are exploited. Timber production in 2001 was 2·72m. cu. metres.

Fisheries. In 2001 the total catch was 5,940 tonnes, exclusively from inland waters.

INDUSTRY

In 1998 it was estimated that the industrial sector employed a total of 51,214 persons. The principal manufactures are mining, petroleum, smelting, foodstuffs, tobacco and textiles.

Labour. Out of 3,884,251 people (54·8% male) in employment in 2001, 44·1% were in agriculture, ranching and hunting, 14·0% in retail and repair, 9·2% in industrial manufacturing, 4·9% in construction and 4·6% in transport, storage and communications. The unemployment rate in 2000 was 11·5%. In 2002 the minimum wage was 420 bolivianos a month.

Trade Unions. Unions are grouped in the Confederación de Obreros Bolivianos.

INTERNATIONAL TRADE

An agreement of Jan. 1992 with Peru gives Bolivia duty-free transit for imports and exports through a corridor leading to the Peruvian Pacific port of Ilo from the Bolivian frontier town of Desaguadero, in return for Peruvian access to the Atlantic via Bolivia's roads and railways. The mining code of 1991 gives tax incentives to foreign investors. Foreign debt was US$4,867m. in 2002.

Imports and Exports. In 2002 imports (f.o.b.) amounted to US$1,532·1m. (US$1,477·4m. in 2001); exports (f.o.b.) US$1,298·7m. (US$1,284·8m. in 2001). Main exports (2001 provisional, in US$1m.): soybeans and products, 272·9; natural gas, 237·4; zinc, 120·7; gold, 89·9; food products, 58·1; tin, 51·1; silver ore, 48·9; other fuels, 47·4; wood and products, 41·1. Main import commodities are road vehicles and parts, machinery for specific industries, cereals and cereal preparations, general industrial machinery, chemicals, petroleum, food, and iron and steel.

Main export markets, 2001 (provisional, in US$1m.): Brazil, 286·7; Colombia, 186·0; Switzerland, 175·4; USA, 156·8; Venezuela, 96·1; UK, 72·3. Main import suppliers, 2001 (provisional, in US$1m.): Argentina, 289·1; USA, 281·7; Brazil, 277·3; Chile, 142·6; Peru, 107·1; China, 69·7.

Imports and exports pass chiefly through the ports of Arica and Antofagasta in Chile, Mollendo-Matarani in Peru, through La Quiaca on the Bolivian-Argentine border and through river-ports on the rivers flowing into the Amazon.

COMMUNICATIONS

Roads. The total length of the road system was about 60,282 km in 2002, of which 12,431 km were national roads. Total vehicles in use in 2002 was 85,119, including 26,229 passenger cars and 30,539 trucks and vans.

Rail. In 1994 the state railway ENFE network totalled 3,697 km of metre gauge, comprising unconnected Eastern (1,423 km) and Andina (2,274 km) systems. Passenger-km travelled in 2000 came to 259m. and freight tonne-km to 856m.

Civil Aviation. The two international airports are La Paz (El Alto) and Santa Cruz (Viru Viru). The national airlines are the state-owned Aerosur (domestic services only) and Lloyd Aéreo Boliviano (97·5% state-owned), which in 2003 ran scheduled services to Buenos Aires, Bogotá, Cancún, Córdoba, Cuzco, Havana, Lima, Manaus, Mexico City, Miami, Panama City, Rio de Janeiro, Salta, Santiago, São Paulo and Trinidad, as well as internal services. There were direct flights in 2003 with other airlines to Arica, Caracas, Iquique and Montevideo. In 1999 Lloyd Aéreo Boliviano flew 18·8m. km, carrying 1,525,900 passengers (658,800 on international flights).

Shipping. Lake Titicaca and about 19,000 km of rivers are open to navigation. In 2002 the merchant marine totalled 358,000 GRT, including oil tankers 242,000 GRT.

Telecommunications. In 2002 there were 1,436,600 telephone subscribers (172·2 per 1,000 persons), including 872,700 mobile phone subscribers (104·6 per 1,000 persons). There were 190,000 PCs in use (22·8 per 1,000 persons). There were five Internet Service Providers in 1999; Internet users numbered 270,000 in 2002.

Postal Services. In 1998 there were 171 post offices, or one for every 46,500 persons.

SOCIAL INSTITUTIONS

Justice. Justice is administered by the Supreme Court, superior department courts (of five or seven judges) and courts of local justice. The Supreme Court, with headquarters at Sucre, is divided into two sections, civil and criminal, of five justices each, with the Chief Justice presiding over both. Members of the Supreme Court are chosen on a two-thirds vote of Congress. The death penalty was abolished for ordinary crimes in 1997.

The population in penal institutions in June 1999 was 8,315 (102 per 100,000 of national population).

Religion. The Roman Catholic church was disestablished in 1961. It is under a cardinal (in Sucre), an archbishop (in La Paz), six bishops and vicars apostolic. It had 7·54m. adherents in 2001. In 2001, 89% of the population were Roman Catholics and 9% Protestants. In Sept. 2003 there was one cardinal.

Education. Adult literacy was 86·0% in 2001 (male, 92·3%; female, 79·9%). Primary instruction is free and obligatory between the ages of six and 14 years. In 1999 there were 13,365 schooling facilities. In 2000–01 there were 1,492,023 pupils and 61,546 teachers in primary schools, 874,669 pupils and 39,192 teachers in secondary schools, and 278,763 students and 12,809 academic staff in tertiary education. The national rate of school attendance (6–19-year-olds) reached 74·3% in 1998.

In 1994–95 there were seven universities, two technical universities, one Roman Catholic university, one musical conservatory, and colleges in the following fields: business, six; teacher training, four; industry, one; nursing, one; technical teacher training, one; fine arts, one; rural education, one; physical education, one. In 1997 state universities had 162,538 students and 7,490 teaching staff. In 1998 there were 35 private universities with 32,253 students and 3,538 teaching staff.

In 2000–01 total expenditure on education came to 5·7% of GNP and 23·1% of total government expenditure.

Health. In 1998 there were 2,561 doctors and 5,077 nurses; and 230 hospitals with 9,185 hospital beds (one per 897 persons).

Welfare. The pensions and social security systems in Bolivia were reformed in 1996. Instead of a defined-benefit publicly managed pension system, a defined-contribution system based on privately managed individual capitalization accounts was introduced. There are now two funds: the Collective Capitalization Fund, made up of 50% of the shares of capitalized companies formerly owned by the state, and the Individual Capitalization Fund, made up of contributions of those associated to the new system with a monthly income of above US$50. A solidarity bonus, BONOSOL—worth approximately US$250 a year—is paid to all Bolivians over the age of 65.

CULTURE

World Heritage Sites. There are six UNESCO World Heritage sites in Bolivia: the City of Potosí (inscribed on the list in 1987), the largest industrial mining complex of the 16th century; the Jesuit Missions of the Chiquitos (1990), six settlements for converted Indians built between 1696 and 1760; the Historic City of Sucre (1991), containing 16th century colonial architecture; El Fuerte de Samaipata (1998), a pre-Hispanic sculptured rock and political and religious centre; Noel Kempff Mercado National Park (2000), a 1,523,000 ha park in the Amazon Basin; and Tiwanaku: Spiritual and Political Centre of the Tiwanaku Culture (2000), monumental remains from AD 500 to 900.

Broadcasting. The broadcasting authority is the Dirección General de Telecomunicaciones. In 1999 there were 321 radio stations. Broadcasts are in Spanish, Aymará and Quechua. There were 5·51m. radios in 2000. There were 48 television stations in 1997 and 990,000 televisions (colour by NTSC) in 2000.

Cinema. In 1999 there were 27 cinemas, with a total attendance for the year of 1·4m.

Press. There were 18 daily newspapers in 1996 with a combined circulation of 420,000, at a rate of 55 per 1,000 inhabitants.

Tourism. In 2000 there were 306,000 foreign tourists, bringing revenue totalling US$160m.

DIPLOMATIC REPRESENTATIVES

Of Bolivia in the United Kingdom (106 Eaton Sq., London, SW1W 9AD)
Ambassador: Gonzalo Montenegro.

Of the United Kingdom in Bolivia (Avenida Arce 2732, La Paz)
Ambassador: William Sinton, OBE.

Of Bolivia in the USA (3014 Massachusetts Ave, NW, Washington, D.C., 20008)
Ambassador: Jaime Aparicio Otero.

Of the USA in Bolivia (Avenida Arce 2780, La Paz)
Ambassador: David N. Greenlee.

Of Bolivia to the United Nations
Ambassador: Ernesto Araníbar Quiroga.

Of Bolivia to the European Union
Ambassador: Fernando Laredo Aguayo.

FURTHER READING

Fifer, J. V., *Bolivia.* [Bibliography] ABC-Clio, Oxford and Santa Barbara (CA), 2000
Klein, H., *Bolivia: The Evolution of a Multi-Ethnic Society.* OUP, 1982

National statistical office: Instituto Nacional de Estadistica, Av. José Carrasco 1391, CP 6129, La Paz.
Website (Spanish only): http://www.ine.gov.bo/

BOSNIA-HERZEGOVINA

Republika Bosna i Hercegovina

Capital: Sarajevo
Population projection, 2010: 4·27m.
GDP per capita, 2001: (PPP$) 5,970
HDI/world rank: 0·781/66

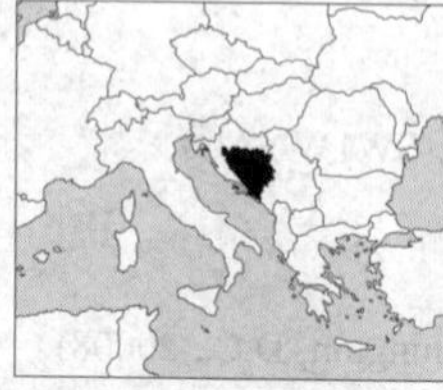

KEY HISTORICAL EVENTS

Settled by Slavs in the 7th century, Bosnia was conquered by the Turks in 1463 when much of the population was gradually converted to Islam. At the Congress of Berlin (1878) the territory was assigned to Austro-Hungarian administration under nominal Turkish suzerainty. Austria-Hungary's outright annexation in 1908 generated international tensions which contributed to the outbreak of the First World War. After 1918 Bosnia Hercegovina became part of a new kingdom of Serbs, Croats and Slovenes under the Serbian monarchy. Its name was changed to Yugoslavia in 1929. (See SERBIA AND MONTENEGRO for developments up to and beyond the Second World War.)

On 15 Oct. 1991 the National Assembly adopted a 'Memorandum on Sovereignty', the Serbian deputies abstaining. This envisaged Bosnian autonomy within a Yugoslav federation. Though boycotted by Serbs, a referendum in March 1992 supported independence. In March 1992 an agreement was reached by Muslims, Serbs and Croats to set up three autonomous ethnic communities under a central Bosnian authority.

Bosnia-Herzegovina declared itself independent on 5 April 1992. Fighting broke out between the Serb, Croat and Muslim communities, with particularly heavy casualties and destruction in Sarajevo, leading to extensive Muslim territorial losses and an exodus of refugees. UN-sponsored ceasefires were repeatedly violated.

On 13 Aug. 1992 the UN Security Council voted to authorize the use of force if necessary to ensure the delivery of humanitarian aid to besieged civilians. Internationally sponsored peace talks were held in Geneva in 1993, but Serb-Muslim-Croat fighting continued.

In Dec. 1994 Bosnian Serbs and Muslims signed a countrywide interim ceasefire. Bosnian Croats also signed in Jan. 1995. However, Croatian Serbs and the Muslim secessionist forces under Fikret Abdić did not sign the agreement, and fighting continued. On 16 June 1995 Bosnian government forces launched an attack to break the Bosnian Serb siege of Sarajevo. On 11 July Bosnian Serb forces began to occupy UN security zones despite retaliatory NATO air strikes, and on 28 Aug. shelled Sarajevo.

To stop the shelling of UN safe areas, more than 60 NATO aircraft attacked Bosnian Serb military installations on 30–31 Aug. On 26 Sept. in Washington the foreign ministers of Bosnia, Croatia and Yugoslavia (the latter negotiating for the Bosnian Serbs) agreed a draft Bosnian constitution under which a central government would handle foreign affairs and commerce and a Serb Zone, and a Muslim-Croat Federation would run their internal affairs. A ceasefire came into force on 12 Oct. 1995.

In Dayton (Ohio) on 21 Nov. 1995 the prime ministers of Bosnia, Croatia and Yugoslavia initialled a US-brokered agreement to end hostilities. The Bosnian state was divided into a Croat-Muslim Federation containing 51% of Bosnian territory and a Serb Republic containing 49%. A central government authority representing all ethnic groups with responsibility for foreign and monetary policy and citizenship issues was established, and free elections held. On 20 Dec. 1995 a NATO contingent (IFOR) took over from UN peacekeeping forces to enforce the Paris peace agreements and set up a 4-km separation zone between the Serb and Muslim-Croat territories. After a year IFOR was replaced by SFOR, a 'Stabilization Force'.

On 2 Dec. 2004 a 7,000-strong European Union force 'EUFOR' took over from SFOR.

'Bosnia is not now a failed state, but it is a center for the trafficking of women and narcotics, a hide-out for war criminals and a steady drain on Western aid and defense budgets. It's not likely to collapse soon, but neither will foreign troops and administrators likely be able to safely pull out for many years to come'. (*International Herald Tribune*, 13 Nov. 2002).

TERRITORY AND POPULATION

The republic is bounded in the north and west by Croatia and in the east and southeast by Serbia and Montenegro. It has a coastline of only 20 km with no harbours. Its area is 51,129 sq. km. The capital is Sarajevo (estimated population, 2003: 380,000).

Population at the 1991 census: 4,377,033, of which the predominating ethnic groups were Muslims (1,905,829), Serbs (1,369,258) and Croats (755,892). Population of the principal cities in 1991: Sarajevo, 415,631 (est. 1999, 522,000); Banja Luka, 142,644; Zenica, 96,238. By 1996, following the civil war, 1,319,250 Bosnians had taken refuge abroad, including 0·45m. in Serbia and Montenegro, 0·32m. in Germany, 0·17m. in Croatia and 0·12m. in Sweden. Population estimate, 2002: 4·07m.

The UN gives a projected population for 2010 of 4·27m.

In 1999 Bosnia-Herzegovina had the fastest-growing population in Europe, with a rise of 4·6% on the 1998 figure. In 2001, 56·6% of the population lived in rural areas.

The official language is Serbo-Croat.

SOCIAL STATISTICS

2002 births, 35,587; deaths, 30,155. Rates per 1,000, 2002: birth, 9·3; death, 7·9. Annual population growth rate, 1992–2002, 0·4%. Life expectancy at birth, 2001, was 71·1 years for men and 76·5 years for women. Infant mortality, 2001, 15 per 1,000 live births; fertility rate, 2001, 1·3 children per woman.

CLIMATE

The climate is generally continental with steady rainfall throughout the year, although in areas nearer the coast it is more Mediterranean.

CONSTITUTION AND GOVERNMENT

On 18 March 1994, in Washington, Bosnian Muslims and Croats reached an agreement for the creation of a federation of cantons with a central government responsible for foreign affairs, defence and commerce. It was envisaged that there would be a president elected by a two-house legislature alternating annually between the nationalities.

On 31 May 1994 the National Assembly approved the creation of the Muslim Croat federation. Alija Izetbegović remained the unitary states' President. An interim government with Hasan Muratović as Prime Minister was formed on 30 Jan. 1996.

The Dayton Agreement including the new constitution was signed and came into force on 14 Dec. 1995. The government structure was established in 1996 as follows:

Heading the state is a three-member *Presidency* (one Croat, one Muslim, one Serb) with a rotating president. The Presidency is elected by direct universal suffrage, and is responsible for foreign affairs and the nomination of the prime minister. There is a two-chamber parliament: the *House of Representatives* (which meets in Sarajevo) comprises 42 directly elected deputies, two-thirds Croat and Muslim and one-third Serb; and the *House of Peoples* (which meets in Lukavica) comprises five Croat, five Muslim and five Serb delegates.

Below the national level the country is divided into two self-governing entities along ethnic lines.

The Bosniak-Croat **Federation of Bosnia and Herzegovina** (Federacija Bosna i Hercegovina) is headed by a President and Vice-President, alternately Croat and Muslim, a 98-member Chamber of Representatives and a 74-member Chamber of

Peoples. The **Serb Republic** (Republika Srpska) is also headed by an elected President and Vice-President, and there is a National Assembly of 83 members, elected by proportional representation.

Central government is conducted by a *Council of Ministers*, which comprises Muslim and Serb Co-Prime Ministers and a Croat Deputy Prime Minister. The Co-Prime Ministers alternate in office every week.

National Anthem. 'Intermezzo'; tune by Dusan Sestić; no words.

RECENT ELECTIONS

Elections were held on 5 Oct. 2002 for the Presidium and the federal parliament. Seats for the three-member rotating presidency went to Serb, Croat and Muslim nationalist parties. The elected members were as follows: Sulejman Tihić (Muslim; Party of Democratic Action—SDA); Dragan Čović (Croat; Croatian Democratic Community—HDZ); and Mirko Šarović (Serb; Social Democratic Party—SDS). In the parliamentary elections, the Party for Democratic Action won ten seats with 32·5% of the vote, against five seats for both the Croat Democratic Union and the Serb Democratic Party.

CURRENT ADMINISTRATION

Presidency Chairman: Borislav Paravac (Serb; SDS; took rotating presidency on 28 Oct. 2004). *Presidency Members:* Ivo Miro Jović (Croat, HDZ); Sulejman Tihić (Muslim; SDA).

In March 2005 the cabinet comprised:

Prime Minister: Adnan Terzić (Muslim; SDA); b. 1960 (sworn in 23 Dec. 2002).

Minister of Civil Affairs: Safet Halilović. *Defence:* Nikola Radovanović. *Finance and Treasury:* Ljerka Marić. *Foreign Affairs:* Mladen Ivanić. *Foreign Trade and Economic Relations:* Dragan Doko. *Human Rights and Refugees:* Mirsad Kebo. *Justice:* Slobodan Kovać. *Security:* Bariša Čolak. *Transportation and Communications:* Branko Dokić.

UN High Representative: Lord Ashdown (UK); b. 1941 (sworn in 27 May 2002).

Office of the High Representative: http://www.ohr.int

DEFENCE

Defence expenditure in 2003 totalled US$152m. (US$37 per capita), representing 2·2% of GDP.

An EU-led peacekeeping contingent 'EUFOR' took over military operations from the NATO-led 'SFOR' on 2 Dec. 2004. Its mission is to focus on the apprehension of indicted war criminals and counter-terrorism, and provide advice on defence reform.

Army. The forces of the Federation of Bosnia and Herzegovina (composed of the Army of Bosnia and Herzegovina and the Croatian Defence Council) numbered 13,200 in 2002, with the personnel of the Serb Republic's armed forces totalling 6,600. In 2002 the forces of the Federation of Bosnia and Herzegovina had 203 main battle tanks and those of the Serb Republic had 137 main battle tanks. There are no armed forces at the state level except for border guards and the Brcko-district police. Under the supervision of the Defence Reform Commission, military change has been rapid. In early 2004 a state-level civilian-led command and control structure was set up, including a Defence Ministry, incorporating the forces of both the Federation of Bosnia and Herzegovina and the Serb Republic.

INTERNATIONAL RELATIONS

Bosnia-Herzegovina is a member of the UN, BIS, OSCE and the Central European Initiative.

The Serb Republic and Yugoslavia (now Serbia and Montenegro) signed an agreement on 28 Feb. 1997 establishing 'special parallel relations' between them. The agreement envisages co-operation in cultural, commercial, security and foreign policy matters, allows visa-free transit of borders and includes a non-aggression pact. A customs agreement followed on 31 March.

ECONOMY

In 2002 agriculture accounted for 14·9% of GDP, industry 32·1% and services 52·9%.

Currency. A new currency, the *konvertibilna marka* (BAM) consisting of 100 *pfennig*, was introduced in June 1998. Initially trading at a strict 1-to-1 against the Deutsche Mark, it is now pegged to the euro at a rate of 1·95583 convertible marks to the euro. Inflation was 0·1% in 2003 (0·3% in 2002). Total money supply was 3,117m. convertible marks in June 2002.

Budget. Revenue in 2001 was 1,653m. convertible marks; expenditure was 1,888m. convertible marks.

Performance. Bosnia-Herzegovina had one of the fastest growing economies in the world during the second half of the 1990s. Real GDP growth was 60·8% in 1996 and 30·4% in 1997, although it has slowed since then and was 4·5% in 2001 and 3·8% in 2002. Total GDP was US$6·9bn. in 2003.

Banking and Finance. There is a Central Bank (*Governor:* Kemal Kozarić). In 2001 there were 69 commercial banks (50 in the Federation and 19 in the Serb Republic). There are stock exchanges in Banja Luka and Sarajevo.

ENERGY AND NATURAL RESOURCES

Environment. Bosnia-Herzegovina's carbon dioxide emissions from the consumption and flaring of fossil fuels in 2002 were the equivalent of 4·7 tonnes per capita.

Electricity. Installed capacity was 2·7m. kW in 2000. Production in 2000 was 10·43bn. kWh. In 2000 consumption per capita was 2,355 kWh.

Minerals. Output: lignite (2000), 5·3m. tonnes; hard coal (2000), 3·5m. tonnes; aluminium (2001), 175,000 tonnes; iron ore (2001), 100,000 tonnes; bauxite (2001), 75,000 tonnes.

Agriculture. In 2001 there were 690,000 ha of arable land and 150,000 ha of permanent crops. 2000 yields (in 1,000 tonnes): maize, 900; potatoes, 365; wheat, 275; cabbages, 120; plums, 90; barley, 64. Livestock in 2000: cattle, 462,000; sheep, 672,000; pigs, 150,000; poultry, 3m.

Forestry. In 2000 forests covered 2·27m. ha, or 44·6% of the total land area. Timber production in 2001 was 3·82m. cu. metres.

Fisheries. Estimated total fish catch in 2001: 2,500 tonnes (exclusively freshwater).

INDUSTRY

Output (in 1,000 tonnes): cement (2000), 300; crude steel (2001), 80. Other products (1990): cars, 38,000 units; tractors, 34,000 units; lorries, 16,000 units; televisions, 21,000 sets.

Labour. The labour force totalled 1,719,000 in 1996 (62% males). Unemployment in 2004 was nearly 40%.

INTERNATIONAL TRADE

External debt was US$2,515m. in 2002.

Imports and Exports. In 2002 exports (f.o.b.) totalled US$1,115·0m. and imports (f.o.b.) US$4,518·7m.

In 2000 main export markets were Italy, 31·5%; Germany, 13·8%; Slovenia, 7·6%. Principal import sources in 2000 were Slovenia, 16·1%; Germany, 13·6%; Italy, 13·0%. In 2000 the EU accounted for 65·4% of Bosnia-Herzegovina's exports and 43·8% of imports.

COMMUNICATIONS

Roads. In 1999 there were an estimated 21,846 km of roads (1996, 3,722 km of highways or main roads). There were 96,182 passenger cars in use in 1996 (23 per

1,000 inhabitants) and 9,783 vans and trucks. There were 199 road accident fatalities in 1996.

Rail. There were 1,021 km of railways in 1991 (795 km electrified); they carried 554m. passenger-km and 1,946m. tonne-km of freight. It is estimated that up to 80% of the rail network was destroyed in the civil war, and it was not until July 2001 that the first international services were resumed. There are three state-owned rail companies—the Bosnia and Herzegovina railway company (ZBH), the Herzeg-Bosnia Railway company (ZHB), and the Serb Republic Railway and Transport Company (ZTP).

Civil Aviation. There are international airports at Sarajevo (Butmir) and Banja Luka. In 2003 there were direct flights to Amsterdam, Belgrade, Budapest, Copenhagen, Düsseldorf, Gothenburg, İstanbul, Ljubljana, London, Munich, Oslo, Rome, Stockholm, Vienna, Zagreb and Zürich. In 2000 Sarajevo handled 355,000 passengers (all international) and 1,200 tonnes of freight.

Telecommunications. Telephone subscribers totalled 1,651,600 in 2002, equivalent to 432·9 per 1,000 inhabitants. There were 748,800 mobile phone subscribers in 2002 (196·3 per 1,000 inhabitants) and 100,000 Internet users (26·2 per 1,000 inhabitants). There had been just 7,000 mobile phone subscribers in 1997. Three state-owned companies run the telephone networks in different parts of the country, the largest of which is the Sarajevo-based PTT Bih.

Postal Services. In 1998 there were 210 post offices. A total of 9·8m. pieces of mail were processed in 1998.

SOCIAL INSTITUTIONS

Justice. The population in penal institutions in April 2003 was 2,283.

Police. The European Union Police Mission (EUPM) in Bosnia and Herzegovina, the EU's first civilian crisis management operation, took over from the UN's International Police Task Force on 1 Jan. 2003. It aims to help the authorities develop their police forces to the highest European and international standards.

Religion. In 2001 there were estimated to be 1,690,000 Sunni Muslims, 1,180,000 Serbian Orthodox, 710,000 Roman Catholics and 350,000 followers of other religions. In Sept. 2003 the Roman Catholic church had one cardinal.

Education. In 1990–91 there were 543,500 pupils in 2,205 primary schools (23,400 teachers), 173,100 in 238 secondary schools (9,000 teachers) and 37,500 in 44 tertiary schools (2,800 teachers). In 1995 there were four universities.

Health. In 1998 there were 4,813 physicians (one for every 699 persons), 640 dentists, 15,241 nurses and 370 pharmacists. In 1996 there were 48 hospital beds per 10,000 inhabitants.

Welfare. There were 380,000 pensions in 1990 (including 140,000 old age).

CULTURE

Broadcasting. In 2000 there were 900,000 radio receivers and 411,000 TV receivers.

Press. There were two daily newspapers in 1995 with a combined circulation of 520,000, at a rate of 146 per 1,000 inhabitants.

Tourism. In 2000 there were 110,000 foreign tourists, bringing revenue of US$17m.

DIPLOMATIC REPRESENTATIVES

Of Bosnia-Herzegovina in the United Kingdom (5–7 Lexham Gardens, London, W8 5JJ)
Ambassador: Jadranka Negodić.

Of the United Kingdom in Bosnia-Herzegovina (8 Tina Ujevića, Sarajevo)
Ambassador: Ian Cliff, OBE.

Of Bosnia-Herzegovina in the USA (2109 E Street, NW, Washington, D.C., 20037)
Ambassador: Igor Davidović.

Of the USA in Bosnia-Herzegovina (Alipasina 43, 71000, Sarajevo)
Ambassador: Douglas L. McElhaney.

Of Bosnia-Herzegovina to the United Nations
Ambassador: Mirza Kušljugić.

Of Bosnia-Herzegovina to the European Union
Ambassador: Zdenko Martinović.

FURTHER READING

Bert, W., *The Reluctant Superpower: United States Policy in Bosnia, 1991–1995*. New York, 1997
Burg, Steven L. and Shoup, Paul S., *The War in Bosnia-Herzegovina.* New York, 1999
Cigar, N., *Genocide in Bosnia: the Policy of Ethnic Cleansing.* Texas Univ. Press, 1995
Fine, J. V. A. and Donia, R. J., *Bosnia-Hercegovina: a Tradition Betrayed.* Farnborough, 1994
Friedman, F., *The Bosnian Muslims: Denial of a Nation*. Boulder (CO), 1996
Garde, P., *Journal de Voyage en Bosnie-Herzégovine*. Paris, 1995
Holbrooke, R., *To End a War*. Random House, London, 1998
Malcolm, N., *Bosnia: a Short History*. 2nd ed. London, 1996
O'Ballance, E., *Civil War in Bosnia, 1992–94.* London, 1995
Rieff, D., *Slaughterhouse: Bosnia and the Failure of the West*. New York, 1997
Sells, M. A., *The Bridge Betrayed: Religion and Genocide in Bosnia*. California Univ. Press, 1996

National statistical office: Bosnia-Herzegovina Statistics Agency, Trg Bosne i Hercegovine Br. 1, 71000 Sarajevo. *Director:* Derviš Đurđević.

BOTSWANA

Republic of Botswana

Capital: Gaborone
Population projection, 2010: 1·77m.
GDP per capita, 2002: (PPP$) 8,170
HDI/world rank: 0·589/128

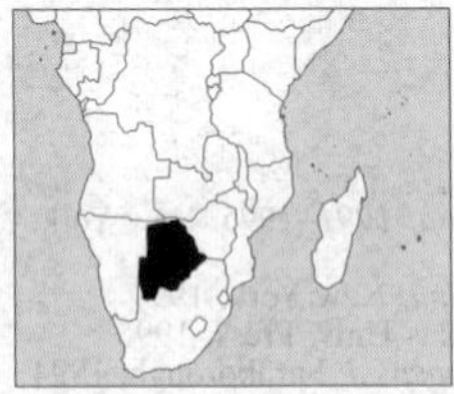

KEY HISTORICAL EVENTS

The Tswana or Batswana people are the principal inhabitants of the country formerly known as Bechuanaland. The territory was declared a British protectorate in 1895. Britain ruled through her High Commissioner in South Africa until the post was abolished in 1964. Frequent suggestions for the addition of Bechuanaland and the other two High Commission Territories to South Africa were rejected, the Africans being strongly against the idea. Economically, however, the country was very closely tied to that of South Africa and has remained so. In Dec. 1960 Bechuanaland received its first constitution. Further constitutional change brought full self-government in 1965 and full independence on 30 Sept. 1966. For years Botswana had great difficulties with the neighbouring settler regime in Rhodesia, until that country became Zimbabwe in 1980. Relations with South Africa were also strained until the ending of apartheid. Today the country enjoys stability and a fast-growing economy.

TERRITORY AND POPULATION

Botswana is bounded in the west and north by Namibia, northeast by Zambia and Zimbabwe, and east and south by South Africa. The area is 581,730 sq. km. Population (2001 census), 1,680,863; density, 2·9 per sq. km. In 2001, 49·4% of the population was urban.

The UN gives a projected population for 2010 of 1·77m.

In 2001, 50·6% of the population were rural. Between 1990 and 1995 there was a 10% rise in the urban population every year, the largest percentage increase anywhere in the world in the same period.

The country is divided into ten districts (Central, Chobe, Ghanzi, Kgalagadi, Kgatleng, Kweneng, Ngamiland, Ngwaketse, North East and South East).

The main towns (with population, 2001) are Gaborone (186,007), Francistown (83,023), Molepolole (54,561), Selebi-Phikwe (49,849), Maun (43,776), Serowe (42,444), Kanye (40,628), Mahalapye (39,719), Mochudi (36,962), Mogoditshane (32,843) and Lobatse (29,689).

The official languages are Setswana and English. Setswana is spoken by over 90% of the population and English by approximately 40%. More than ten other languages, including Herero, Hottentot, Kalanga, Mbukushu, San, and Sekgalagadi are spoken in various tribal areas.

SOCIAL STATISTICS

2001 (estimates) births, 49,000; deaths, 21,000. Rates, 2001 estimates (per 1,000 population): births, 28·9; deaths, 12·4. Infant mortality, 2001 (per 1,000 live births), 56. Expectation of life in 2001 was 43·3 years for males and 46·0 for females. Life expectancy has declined dramatically over the last ten years as a result of the impact of AIDS. In 2001, 35·3% of all adults were infected with HIV, with well over half of those aged between 25 and 29 being HIV positive. Annual population growth rate, 1992–2002, 2·1%. Fertility rate, 2001, 3·3 children per woman.

CLIMATE

In winter, days are warm and nights cold, with occasional frosts. Summer heat is tempered by prevailing northeast winds. Rainfall comes mainly in summer, from Oct. to April, while the rest of the year is almost completely dry with very high sunshine amounts. Gaborone, Jan. 79°F (26·1°C), July 55°F (12·8°C). Annual rainfall varies from 650 mm in the north to 250 mm in the southeast. The country is prone to droughts.

CONSTITUTION AND GOVERNMENT

The Constitution adopted on 30 Sept. 1966 provides for a republican form of government headed by the President with three main organs: the Legislature, the Executive and the Judiciary. The executive rests with the President who is responsible to the National Assembly. The President is elected for five-year terms by the National Assembly.

The *National Assembly* consists of 63 members, of which 57 are elected by universal suffrage, four are specially elected members and two, the President and the Speaker, are *ex officio*.

Elections are held every five years. Voting is on the first-past-the-post system.

There is also a *House of Chiefs* to advise the government. It consists of the Chiefs of the eight tribes who were autonomous during the days of the British protectorate, plus four members elected by and from among the sub-chiefs in four districts; these 12 members elect a further three politically independent members.

National Anthem. 'Fatshe leno la rona' ('Blessed be this noble land'); words and tune by K. T. Motsete.

RECENT ELECTIONS

In National Assembly elections held on 30 Oct. 2004 the Botswana Democratic Party (BDP) gained 44 seats with 51·7% of the vote, the Botswana National Front 12 with 26·1% and the Botswana Congress Party 1 with 16·6%. Turn-out was 77·1%.

CURRENT ADMINISTRATION

President: Festus Mogae; b. 1939 (BDP; sworn in on 1 April 1998).

Vice-President: Lieut.-Gen. Seretse Ian Khama.

In March 2005 the cabinet was as follows:

Minister of Finance and Development Planning: Baledzi Gaolathe. *Foreign Affairs:* Lieut.-Gen. Mompati Merafhe. *Communications, Science and Technology:* Pelonomi Venson. *Health:* Prof. Sheila Tlou. *Works and Transport:* Lesego Motsumi. *Environment, Wildlife and Tourism:* Capt. Kitso Mokaila. *Mineral Resources, Energy and Water Affairs:* Charles Tibone. *Education:* Jacob Nkate. *Labour and Home Affairs:* Major-Gen. Moeng Pheto. *Agriculture:* Johnny Swartz. *Lands and Housing:* Ramadeluka Seretse. *Local Government:* Dr Margaret Nasha. *Trade and Industry:* Neo Moroka. *Presidential Affairs and Public Administration:* Phandu Skelemani.

Government Website: http://www.gov.bw

DEFENCE

In 2003 defence expenditure totalled US$304m. (US$177 per capita), representing 3·8% of GDP.

Army. The Army personnel (2002) numbered 8,500. There is also a 1,000-strong paramilitary force.

Air Force. The Air Wing operated 30 combat aircraft in 2002 and numbered 500.

INTERNATIONAL RELATIONS

Botswana is a member of the UN, WTO, the Commonwealth, the African Union, African Development Bank, SADC and is an ACP member state of the ACP-EU relationship.

ECONOMY

Services accounted for 51·9% of GDP in 2002, industry 45·6% and agriculture 2·5%.

Overview. The theme of the Ninth National Development Plan (2003–09) is 'Towards Realisation of Vision 2016: Sustainable and Diversified Development through Competitiveness in Global Markets'. Real GDP growth is projected to average 5·5% annually over the six-year duration of the Plan.

Currency. The unit of currency is the *pula* (BWP) of 100 *thebe*. Inflation was 6·7% in July 2004. Foreign exchange reserves were US$5,163m. in Aug. 2004. Total money supply was P2,409m. in May 2002.

Budget. The fiscal year begins in April. Government finance for recent years (in P1m.):

	2001–02	*2002–03*	*2003–04*
Revenue	7,907·5	8,829·1	9,746·7
Expenditure	8,143·3	9,469·9	10,082·2

2003–04 revenue (in P1m.) comprised: mineral taxes, 4,930·0; customs pool, 1,394·1; other revenue, 3,422·6. Expenditure included: recurrent, 7,327·6; development, 2,462·6.

Performance. Real GDP is estimated to have grown by 6·7% in 2002–03. In 2003 total GDP at constant prices was US$3·7bn. (P18·03bn.).

Banking and Finance. There were five commercial banks in 2004. Total assets were P24,718·2m. at July 2004. The Bank of Botswana (*Governor*, Linah Mohohlo), established in 1976, is the central bank. The National Development Bank, founded in 1964, has six regional offices, and agricultural, industrial and commercial development divisions. The Botswana Co-operative Bank is banker to co-operatives and to thrift and loan societies. The government-owned Post Office Savings Bank (Botswana Post) operates throughout the country.

There is a stock exchange in Gaborone.

ENERGY AND NATURAL RESOURCES

Environment. Botswana's carbon dioxide emissions from the consumption and flaring of fossil fuels in 2002 were the equivalent of 2·2 tonnes per capita.

Electricity. Installed capacity was 132,000 kW in 2003. Production in 2000 was approximately 1·1bn. kWh. The coal-fired power station at Morupule supplies cities and major towns.

Water. Surface water resources are about 18,000m. cu. metres a year.

Minerals. Botswana is the world's biggest diamond producer in terms of value; in 2003 the total value was estimated to be US$2·5bn. Debswana, a partnership between the government and De Beers, runs three mines producing around 30m. carats a year, with plans to double the capacity of the largest mine from 6m. to 12m. carats a year. Coal reserves are estimated at 17bn. tonnes. There is also copper, salt and soda ash. Mineral production, 2003: diamonds, 30m. carats (the second largest quantity after Australia); coal, 823,000 tonnes; salt, 30,000 tonnes; copper, 8,000 tonnes; gold, 9 kg.

Agriculture. 70% of the total land area is desert. 80% of the population is rural, 71% of all land is 'tribal', protected and allocated to prevent over-grazing, maintain small farmers and foster commercial ranching. Agriculture provides a livelihood for over 70% of the population, but accounts for only 2·4% of GDP (2003). In 2003, 360,000 ha were arable and 3,000 ha permanent crops. There were 7,000 tractors in 2004 and 102 harvester-threshers. Cattle-rearing is the chief industry after diamond-mining, and the country is more a pastoral than an agricultural one, crops depending entirely upon the rainfall. In 2001, 300,000 persons were economically active in agriculture. In 2002 there were: cattle, 3·1m.; goats, 1·1m.; asses, 330,000; sheep, 273,000; chickens, 866,000. In 1995, 80% of cattle were owned by traditional farmers, about half owning fewer than 20 head. A serious outbreak of cattle lung disease in 1995–96 led to the slaughter of around 300,000 animals.

Production (2002, in tonnes): maize, 16,447; sorghum, 15,807; sunflower seeds, 2,250; pulses, 1,907; other crops (including vegetables), 7,694.

17% of the land is set aside for wildlife conservation and 20% for wildlife management areas, with four national parks and game reserves.

Forestry. Forests covered 139,000 sq. km, or 25·2% of the total land area, in 2003. There are forest nurseries and plantations. Concessions have been granted to harvest 7,500 cu. metres in Kasane and Chobe Forestry Reserves, and up to 2,500 cu. metres in the Masame area. In 2001, 745,000 cu. metres of roundwood were cut.

Fisheries. In 2003 the total catch was 121 tonnes, exclusively from inland waters.

INDUSTRY

The most important sector is the diamond industry. Meat is processed, and beer, soft drinks, textiles and foodstuffs manufactured. Rural technology is being developed and traditional crafts encouraged. In June 2003 there were 16,773 enterprises operating in Botswana, of which a third were in the wholesale and retail trade.

Labour. In 2001, 266,607 persons were in formal employment. At the 2001 census there were 270,679 paid employees (including informal employment) and 28,764 self-employed. A further 76,101 persons worked on a non-cash basis, for example as family helpers. 60,757 were seeking work. In March 1994 there were 12,342 Botswana nationals employed in the mines of South Africa. In 1991 there were 57,001 building workers, 34,322 in trade and 29,325 in domestic service. Botswana's biggest individual employer is the Debswana Diamond Company, with a workforce (1997) of nearly 6,000. In 2003 the unemployment rate was 23·8%.

INTERNATIONAL TRADE

Botswana is a member of the Southern African Customs Union (SACU) with Lesotho, Namibia, South Africa and Swaziland. There are no foreign exchange restrictions. External debt in 2003 totalled US$422m. (P2,058m.).

Imports and Exports. In 2003 imports (f.o.b.) totalled US$2,107·5m. More than three-quarters of all imports are from the SACU countries, the main commodities being machinery and electrical equipment, foodstuffs, vehicles and transport equipment, textiles and petroleum products.

In 2003 exports (f.o.b.) totalled US$2,975·5m., including diamonds, vehicles, copper, nickel and beef.

Principal import sources in 1998 were Southern African Customs Union (SACU), 74·9%; South Korea, 4·8%; Zimbabwe, 3·9%; UK, 3·4%. Main export markets were UK, 55·5%; SACU 17·2%; Zimbabwe 2·9%; USA, 1·0%.

COMMUNICATIONS

Roads. In 2004 the total road network was estimated to be 21,133 km (8,916 km national roads). In Nov. 2004 there were 220,663 motor vehicles registered. As of 15 Nov. 2004 there were 455 deaths in road accidents during 2004.

Rail. The main line from Mafeking in South Africa to Bulawayo in Zimbabwe traverses Botswana. With three branches the total length was 888 km in 2000. Passenger-km travelled in 2000 came to 89m. and freight tonne-km to 1,282m.

Civil Aviation. There are international airports at Gaborone (Sir Seretse Khama) and at Maun and six domestic airports. The national carrier is the state-owned Air Botswana. In 2003 direct flights were operated to Harare and Johannesburg. In 1998 Air Botswana flew 2·6m. km, carrying 123,700 passengers (92,500 on international flights). In Oct. 1999 an Air Botswana pilot who had been suspended two months earlier crashed an empty passenger plane into the airline's two serviceable aeroplanes at Gaborone Airport, killing himself and destroying the airline's complete fleet in the process. In 2000 Gaborone handled 224,794 passengers (170,186 on international flights).

Telecommunications. Botswana had 778,000 telephone subscribers in 2002 (400 per 1,000 inhabitants), including 765,000 mobile phone subscribers. Botswana has the second highest mobile phone penetration rate in Africa, after South Africa. There were 112,000 PCs in use in 2003 and 5,200 fax machines. In 2001 Internet users numbered 80,000.

Postal Services. There were 113 post offices and 70 postal agencies in Nov. 2004. The Botswana Post offers many services including Western Union Money Transfers.

SOCIAL INSTITUTIONS

Justice. Law is based on the Roman-Dutch law of the former Cape Colony, but judges and magistrates are also qualified in English common law. The Court of Appeal has jurisdiction in respect of criminal and civil appeals emanating from the High Court, and in all criminal and civil cases and proceedings. Magistrates' courts and traditional courts are in each administrative district. As well as a national police force there are local customary law enforcement officers. The death penalty is still in force. In 2003 there were four executions. The population in penal institutions in Nov. 2003 was 5,890 (327 per 100,000 of national population).

Religion. Freedom of worship is guaranteed under the Constitution. About 43% of the population is Christian. Non-Christian religions include Bahais, Muslims and Hindus.

Education. Adult literacy rate in 2001 was 78·1% (male, 75·3%; female, 80·6%). Basic free education, introduced in 1986, consists of seven years of primary and three years of junior secondary schooling. In 2001 enrolment in 780 primary schools was 326,481 with 13,128 teachers, and 151,847 pupils at secondary level with 9,261 teachers. In 2001 there were 1,404 students in teacher training colleges. There is one university (12,286 students in 2001–02).

In 2003–04 expenditure on education came to US$797·4m.

Health. In 2004 there were 16 primary hospitals, one mental hospital, three referral hospitals, 15 health centres, 257 clinics and 366 health posts. There were also 761 stops for mobile health teams. In 2004 there were 89 doctors and 2,129 nurses in government health facilities. There are other private health facilities with more personnel.

CULTURE

World Heritage Sites. Tsodilo was created a UNESCO World Heritage Site in 2001. It is the site of over 4,500 prehistoric rock paintings in the Kalahari Desert.

Broadcasting. The government-controlled Radio Botswana broadcasts daily on two channels in both English and Setswana. There is also the government-run Botswana Television (BTV) which covers almost the whole country and a commercial television company that transmits on a 50 km-radius from Gaborone (colour by PAL). There were 254,000 radio sets in 2000 and 74,000 TV sets in 2001. Most broadcasts are in English.

Press. The government owned *Daily News* is distributed free. There are also six weekly independent newspapers. *The Gazette, The Botswana Guardian, The Voice, Mokgosi, Sunday Standard* and *The Mid-Week Sun* are middle-of-the-road politically. For a more distinctive political slant there is a daily independent paper *Mmegi* (The Reporter). The press in Botswana is free from censorship.

Tourism. There were 1·1m. foreign visitors in 2003 with tourism receipts totalling US$356m.

DIPLOMATIC REPRESENTATIVES

Of Botswana in the United Kingdom (6 Stratford Pl., London, W1C 1AY)
High Commissioner: Roy Warren Blackbeard.

Of the United Kingdom in Botswana (Private Bag 0023, Gaborone)
High Commissioner: David Merry, CBE.

Of Botswana in the USA (1531–1533 New Hampshire Ave., NW, Washington, D.C., 20037)
Ambassador: Lapologang Caesar Lekoa.

Of the USA in Botswana (PO Box 90, Gaborone)
Ambassador: Joseph Huggins.

Of Botswana to the United Nations
Ambassador: Alfred M. Dube.

Of Botswana to the European Union
Ambassador: Sasara George.

FURTHER READING

Central Statistics Office. *Statistical Bulletin* (Quarterly).
Ministry of Information and Broadcasting. *Botswana Handbook.—Kutlwano* (Monthly).
Molomo, M. G. and Mokopakgosi, B. (eds.) *Multi-Party Democracy in Botswana.* Harare, 1991
Perrings, C., *Sustainable Development and Poverty Alleviation in Sub-Saharan Africa: the Case of Botswana.* London, 1995
Wiseman, John, *Botswana.* [Bibliography] ABC-Clio, Oxford and Santa Barbara (CA), 1992

National statistical office: Central Statistics Office, Private Bag 0024, Gaborone.
Website: http://www.cso.gov.bw

BRAZIL

República Federativa do Brasil

Capital: Brasília (Federal District)
Population projection, 2010: 192·88m.
GDP per capita, 2002: (PPP$) 7,770
HDI/world rank: 0·775/72

KEY HISTORICAL EVENTS

Before the Portuguese discovery and occupation of Brazil there was a large indigenous population. The first Portuguese contact with Brazil was Pedro Alvares Cabral who left Lisbon in 1500 to sail along the Cape of Good Hope route discovered by Vasco da Gama in 1497–98. Setting a more westerly course he was carried farther westward, landing in a place he named *Terra do Brasil*. Early Portuguese economic activity revolved around the exploitation of the huge timber (Brazilwood) resources. This was superseded by sugarcane and, to a lesser extent, tobacco, industries requiring large-scale labour. Millions of Africans were enslaved and shipped to the region.

Portuguese settlers conquering the Brazilian interior in the late 17th century discovered gold at Minas Gerais. Rio de Janeiro benefited greatly from mining wealth and in 1763 became the colonial capital in place of Salvador. As Brazilian government became increasingly centralized nationalism burgeoned, most famously in the failed rebellion against the Portuguese led by Joaquim José da Silva Xavier (Tiradentes) in 1789. In 1807 an invasion of Portugal by the French forces of Napoléon Bonaparte forced the royal family to take refuge in Rio, declaring it the temporary capital of the Portuguese Empire. While in Brazil King João VI initiated reforms which ended Portugal's commercial monopoly and in 1815 granted Brazil equal status with Portugal in the United Kingdom of Portugal, Brazil and the Algarves. On his return to Portugal João's son, Pedro, became Brazil's regent.

Pedro's regency ran into trouble when the Cortes in Lisbon repealed many of João's reforms for the former colony and sought to reduce it to colonial status. Pedro called for Brazilian independence and on 1 Dec. 1822 he was crowned Constitutional Emperor and Perpetual Defender of Brazil. The United States recognized Brazil's independence in May 1824 followed by Portugal itself in 1825. Pedro was forced to abdicate in 1831 following a disastrous war with Argentina. His son, Pedro II, freed himself of political influences after a long minority. He ruled for nearly 50 years and despite a series of uprisings, Brazil remained relatively stable.

Pedro was instrumental in the overthrow of Juan Manuel de Rosas in Argentina in the 1850s and became involved in Uruguay's civil war in the 1860s. In the 1870s the three nations united to repel the advances of the Paraguayan forces of Francisco Solano López. Pedro outlawed the slave trade in 1854. Emancipation was achieved in 1888 when three quarters of a million slaves were freed without compensation to their owners. In 1889 Gen. Manuel Deodoro da Fonseca led a military revolt, forcing Pedro's abdication. In 1891 Brazil became a Federal Republic with Fonseca as its first president. Forced to resign when he attempted to bypass congress, he was succeeded by Floriano Peixoto. He, in turn, was replaced by Brazil's first civilian president, Prudente de Morais, the first of a succession of leaders who enjoyed relative peace as Brazil grew rich on coffee exports.

By the 1920s there was growing resentment at the wealth of the coffee barons and in 1922 a failed military coup initiated eight years of civil strife. Amid economic crisis in 1930 Getulio Vargas was swept to power by a military junta that dismissed the elected government. The constitution of 1934 provided for universal suffrage and three years later a new constitution, drafted in the aftermath of a failed coup, gave Vargas greatly extended power. In Oct. 1945 the military forced Vargas to step down but he returned to power in 1950. Brazil's economic problems spiralled and in 1954 Vargas was implicated in the attempted murder of a journalist. When the High Command demanded his resignation, Vargas committed suicide.

Juscelino Kubitschek, popularly known as JK, was elected president in 1956. He instigated massive public expenditure including road and hydroelectric schemes and the creation of a new capital, Brasília. It was hoped these programmes would be the catalyst for the development of Brazil's huge interior but instead brought uncontrollable inflation. There followed 20 years of military rule. The generals benefited from the Brazilian economic miracle in the late 1960s and '70s, when the economy was growing by more than 10% per year. However, uncoordinated growth led to rampant bureaucracy, corruption and inflation. In 1980 a militant working-class movement sprang up under the leadership of Luiz Inácio Lula da Silva (Lula), opening the way to a slow return to democratic government. The transition from military to civilian rule was marked by economic chaos, with finance ministers changing frequently and foreign debt reaching CR$115,000m. In the presidential run-off of Dec. 1989 Fernando Collor de Mello narrowly defeated Lula.

By 1992 Collor's government had failed to reach many of its targets and was embroiled in scandals and corruption. After Itamar Franco, Collor's vice-president, took office, inflation leapt towards 3,000% but his fourth finance minister, Fernando Henrique Cardoso, achieved successful economic reforms. In 1994 Cardoso was elected president. He oversaw a radical privatization programme, the lowering of trade barriers and the introduction of a new currency, the *real*. He won a second term in 1998 but he was forced to devalue the real, which lost 35% of its value against the dollar in two months. In Cardoso's second term public debt reached US$260bn. and the government was forced to reduce spending on health and welfare while increasing taxes. In the 2002 presidential elections Cardoso's successor, José Serra, was defeated by Lula. As the country's first elected socialist president, he pledged to combat Brazil's widespread poverty while co-operating with the business sector and international community.

TERRITORY AND POPULATION

Brazil is bounded in the east by the Atlantic and on its northern, western and southern borders by all the South American countries except Chile and Ecuador. The total area (including inland water) is 8,514,877 sq. km. Population as at censuses of 1996 and 2000:

Federal Unit and Capital	*Area (sq. km)*	*Census 1996*	*Census 2000*
North	3,853,327		
Rondônia (Porto Velho)	237,576	1,229,306	1,379,787
Acre (Rio Branco)	152,581	483,593	557,526
Amazonas (Manaus)	1,570,746	2,389,279	2,812,557
Roraima (Boa Vista)	224,299	247,131	324,397
Pará (Belém)	1,247,690	5,510,849	6,192,307
Amapá (Macapá)	142,815	379,459	477,032
Tocantins (Palmas)	277,621	1,048,642	1,157,098
North-East	1,554,257[1]		
Maranhão (São Luís)	331,983	5,222,183	5,651,475
Piauí (Teresina)	251,529	2,673,085	2,843,278
Ceará (Fortaleza)	148,826	6,809,290	7,430,661
Rio Grande do Norte (Natal)	52,797	2,558,660	2,776,782
Paraíba (João Pessoa)	56,440	3,305,616	3,443,825
Pernambuco (Recife)	98,312	7,399,071	7,918,344
Alagoas (Maceió)	27,768	2,633,251	2,822,621
Sergipe (Aracajú)	21,910	1,624,020	1,784,475
Bahia (Salvador)	564,693	12,541,675	13,070,250
South-East	924,511		
Minas Gerais (Belo Horizonte)	586,528	16,672,613	17,891,494
Espírito Santo (Vitória)	46,078	2,802,707	3,097,232
Rio de Janeiro (Rio de Janeiro)	43,696	13,406,308	14,391,282
São Paulo (São Paulo)	248,209	34,119,110	37,032,403
South	576,410		
Paraná (Curitiba)	199,315	9,003,804	9,563,458
Santa Catarina (Florianópolis)	95,346	4,875,244	5,356,360
Rio Grande do Sul (Porto Alegre)	281,749	9,634,688	10,187,798

Federal Unit and Capital	Area (sq. km)	Census 1996	Census 2000
Central West	1,606,372		
Mato Grosso (Cuiabá)	903,358	2,235,832	2,504,353
Mato Grosso do Sul (Campo Grande)	357,125	1,927,834	2,078,001
Goiás (Goiânia)	340,087	4,514,967	5,003,228
Distrito Federal (Brasília)	5,802	1,821,946	2,051,146
Total	8,514,877	157,070,163	169,799,170

[1]Including disputed areas between states of Piauí and Ceará.

Population density, 19·9 per sq. km. The 2000 census showed 83,576,015 males and 86,233,155 females. The urban population comprised 81·7% of the population in 2001.

The UN gives a projected population for 2010 of 192·88m.

The official language is Portuguese.

Population of principal cities (2000 census):

São Paulo	10,434,252	São Luis	870,028	Contagem	538,017
Rio de Janeiro	5,857,904	Maceió	797,759	Ribeirão Preto	504,923
Salvador	2,443,107	Duque de Caxias	775,456	Uberlândia	501,214
Belo Horizonte	2,238,526	Teresina	715,360	Sorocaba	493,468
Fortaleza	2,141,402	Natal	712,317	Cuiabá	483,346
Brasília	2,051,146	São Bernardo do Campo	703,177	Feira de Santana	480,949
Curitiba	1,587,315	Campo Grande	663,216	Aracajú	461,949
Recife	1,422,905	Osasco	652,593	Niterói	459,451
Manaus	1,405,835	Santo André	649,331	Juiz de Fora	456,796
Porto Alegre	1,360,590	João Pessoa	597,934	São João de Meriti	449,476
Belém	1,280,614	Joboatão dos Guararapes	581,556	Londrina	447,065
Goiânia	1,093,007	São José dos Campos	539,313	Joinville	429,604
Guarulhos	1,072,717			Santos	417,983
Campinas	969,396			Campos dos Goytacazes	406,279
Nova Iguaçu	920,599				
São Gonçalo	891,119				

The principal metropolitan areas (census, 2000) were São Paulo (17,834,664), Rio de Janeiro (10,872,768), Belo Horizonte (4,811,760), Porto Alegre (3,655,834), Recife (3,335,704), Salvador (3,018,285), Fortaleza (2,975,703), Curitiba (2,725,629) and Belém (1,794,981).

Approximately 54% of the population of Brazil is white, 40% mixed white and black, and 5% black. There are some 260,000 native Indians.

SOCIAL STATISTICS

2002: births, 2,581,055 (rate of 19·7 per 1,000 population); deaths, 958,475 (6·7 per 1,000 population). Life expectancy in 2001 was 63·7 for males and 72·3 for females. Annual population growth rate, 1992–2002, 1·4%; infant mortality, 2002, 28 per 1,000 live births; fertility rate, 2002, 2·2 children per woman.

CLIMATE

Because of its latitude, the climate is predominantly tropical, but factors such as altitude, prevailing winds and distance from the sea cause certain variations, though temperatures are not notably extreme. In tropical parts, winters are dry and summers wet, while in Amazonia conditions are constantly warm and humid. The northeast *sertão* is hot and arid, with frequent droughts. In the south and east, spring and autumn are sunny and warm, summers are hot, but winters can be cold when polar air-masses impinge. Brasília, Jan. 72°F (22·3°C), July 68°F (19·8°C). Annual rainfall 60" (1,512 mm). Belém, Jan. 78°F (25·8°C), July 80°F (26·4°C). Annual rainfall 105" (2,664 mm). Manaus, Jan. 79°F (26·1°C), July 80°F (26·7°C). Annual rainfall 92" (2,329 mm). Recife, Jan. 80°F (26·6°C), July 77°F (24·8°C). Annual rainfall 75" (1,907 mm). Rio de Janeiro, Jan. 83°F (28·5°C), July 67°F (19·6°C). Annual rainfall 67" (1,758 mm). São Paulo, Jan. 75°F (24°C), July 57°F (13·7°C). Annual rainfall 62" (1,584 mm). Salvador, Jan. 80°F (26·5°C), July 74°F (23·5°C). Annual rainfall 105" (2,669 mm). Porto Alegre, Jan. 75°F (23·9°C), July 62°F (16·7°C). Annual rainfall 59" (1,502 mm).

CONSTITUTION AND GOVERNMENT

The present Constitution came into force on 5 Oct. 1988, the eighth since independence. The *President* and *Vice-President* are elected for a four-year term. To be elected candidates must secure 50% plus one vote of all the valid votes, otherwise a second round of voting is held to elect the President between the two most voted candidates. Voting is compulsory for men and women between the ages of 18 and 70 apart from illiterates (for whom it is optional); it is also optional for persons from 16 to 18 years old and persons over 70. A referendum on constitutional change was held on 21 April 1993. Turn-out was 80%. 66·1% of votes cast were in favour of retaining a republican form of government, and 10·2% for re-establishing a monarchy. 56·4% favoured an executive presidency, 24·7% parliamentary supremacy.

A constitutional amendment of June 1997 authorizes the re-election of the President for one extra term of four years.

Congress consists of an 81-member *Senate* (three Senators per federal unit) and a 513-member *Chamber of Deputies*. The Senate is two-thirds directly elected (50% of these elected for eight years in rotation) and one-third indirectly elected. The Chamber of Deputies is elected by universal franchise for four years. There is a *Council of the Republic* which is convened only in national emergencies.

Baaklini, A. I., *The Brazilian Legislature and Political System*. London, 1992

Martinez-Lara, J., *Building Democracy in Brazil: the Politics of Constitutional Change*. London, 1996

National Anthem. 'Ouviram do Ipiranga. . .' ('They hear the river Ipiranga'); words by J. O. Duque Estrada, tune by F. M. da Silva.

RECENT ELECTIONS

In the first round of presidential elections held on 6 Oct. 2002, Luiz Inácio Lula da Silva (Workers' Party) won 46·4% of votes cast, twice as many votes as his nearest opponent, José Serra (Brazilian Social Democracy Party), who won 23·2%. The two other candidates, Anthony Garotinho and Ciro Gomes, won 17·9% and 12% respectively. In the run-off held on 27 Oct. 2002 Luiz Inácio Lula da Silva won 61·3% against 38·7% for José Serra, the biggest ever winning margin in a Brazilian presidential election.

Parliamentary elections were also held on 6 Oct. 2002 for both the Chamber of Deputies and the Senate.

In the elections to the 513-seat Chamber of Deputies, the Workers' Party (PT) won 91 seats; the Liberal Front Party (PFL), 84; the Brazilian Democratic Movement Party (PMDB), 74; the Brazilian Social Democracy Party (PSDB), 71; the Brazilian Progressive Party (PPB), 49; the Liberal Party (PL), 26; the Brazilian Labour Party (PTB), 26; the Brazilian Socialist Party (PSB), 22; the Democratic Labour Party (PDT), 21; the Socialist People's Party (PPS), 15; the Communist Party of Brazil (PCdoB), 12; others, 22. Following the election a ten-party coalition government was formed, but in Dec. 2004 the Brazilian Democratic Movement Party left it.

Following the Senate elections the Brazilian Democratic Movement Party had 19 seats; the Liberal Front Party, 19; the Worker's Party, 14; the Brazilian Social Democracy Party, 11; the Democratic Labour Party, 5; the Brazilian Socialist Party, 4; the Liberal Party, 3; the Brazilian Labour Party, 3; the Socialist People's Party, 1; the Democratic Socialist Party, 1; and the Brazilian Progressive Party, 1.

CURRENT ADMINISTRATION

President: Luiz Inácio Lula da Silva 'Lula'; b. 1945 (Workers' Party; sworn in on 1 Jan. 2003).

Vice-President and Minister of Defence: José Alencar.

In March 2005 the coalition government was composed as follows:

Minister of Agrarian Development: Miguel Rossetto. *Agriculture:* João Roberto Rodrigues. *Chief of Staff:* José Dirceu. *Communications:* Eunício Oliveira. *Culture:* Gilberto Gil. *Development, Industry and Foreign Trade:* Luiz Fernando Furlan. *Education:* Tarso Genro. *Environment:* Marina Silva. *Finance:* Antônio Palocci. *Foreign Relations:* Celso Amorim. *Health:* Humberto Costa. *Justice:* Márcio Tomaz Bastos. *Labour:* Ricardo Berzoíni. *Mines and Energy:* Dilma Rousseff.

National Integration: Ciro Gomes. *Planning and Administration:* Vacant. *Science and Technology:* Eduardo Campos. *Sport:* Agnelo Queiroz. *Tourism:* Walfrido Mares Guia. *Transport:* Anderson Adauto. *Urban Affairs:* Olívio Dutra. *Social Development and Hunger Alleviation:* Patrus Ananias. *Social Welfare:* Amir Lando.

Government Website (Portuguese only): http://www.brasil.gov.br

DEFENCE

Conscription is for 12 months, extendable by six months.

In 2003 defence expenditure totalled US$9,274m. (US$53 per capita), representing 1·8% of GDP.

Army. There are seven military commands and 12 military regions. Strength, 2002, 189,000 (40,000 conscripts). There is an additional potential first-line 1,115,000 of whom 400,000 are subject to immediate recall. There is a second-line reserve of 225,000 and a paramilitary Public Police Force of some 385,600.

Navy. The principal ship of the Navy and Brazil's only aircraft carrier is the 32,700-tonne *São Paulo* (formerly the French *Foch*), commissioned in 1963 and purchased in 2000. There are also four diesel submarines and 14 frigates including four bought from the UK in 1995 and 1996. Fleet Air Arm personnel only fly helicopters.

Naval bases are at Rio de Janeiro, Recife, Belém, Florianópolis and Salvador, with river bases at Ladario and Manaus.

Active personnel, 2002, totalled 48,600 (3,200 conscripts), including 13,900 Marines and 1,150 in Naval Aviation.

Air Force. The Air Force has an air defence command, tactical command, maritime command, transport command and training command. Personnel strength (2002) 50,000 (5,000 conscripts). There were 264 combat aircraft in 2002, including Mirage F-103s and F-5Es, and 29 armed helicopters.

INTERNATIONAL RELATIONS

Brazil is a member of the UN, WTO, BIS, OAS, Inter-American Development Bank, LAIA, Mercosur, IOM and the Antarctic Treaty.

ECONOMY

Agriculture accounted for 5·8% of GDP in 2003, industry 19·1% and services 75·1%.

Overview. Economic growth slowed after 2000. In 2002 the economy experienced a sharp decline in external capital flows, a depreciation of the *real*, a sharp rise in the trade balance, high inflation and a drop in rollover rates on domestic debt. Brazil's financial variables improved in 2003 owing to the authorities' strong commitment to sound macroeconomic policies and an improvement in the external economy. The economy is well endowed in natural and human resources and has a substantial industrial base. Brazil has an important role in promoting regional integration, and also plays an important part in multilateral negotiations, such as trade liberalization and action against climate change. In the 1990s Brazil undertook market reforms and moved towards an outward orientated development strategy after several decades of inward orientated development policies. In comparison to other countries in the region, import penetration is still low signalling that the economy is still relatively closed to trade. Since 1999 there has been a free-floating exchange rate. High inflation was broken in 1995 and since 1999 monetary policy has been led by a 4% inflation target.

Currency. The unit of currency is the *real* (equal to 100 *centavos*), which was introduced on 1 July 1994 to replace the former *cruzeiro real* at a rate of 1 real (R$1) = 2,750 cruzeiros reais (CR$2,750). The *real* was devalued in Sept. 1994, March 1995, June 1995 and Jan. 1999. Inflation fell from nearly 2,076% in 1994 to 3·2% in 1998. There was inflation of 9·3% in 2003. In June 2002 foreign exchange reserves were US$41,838m.; gold reserves totalled 0·46m. troy oz (4·57m. troy oz in 1995). Total money supply in May 2002 was R$74,988m.

Budget. 2000 (in R$1m.): revenue was 235,062 (158,781 in 1999) and expenditure 247,253 (163,709 in 1999). Internal federal debt, July 1996, was R$176,478m. Internal states and municipalities (main securities outstanding), R$49,672m.

Performance. Real GDP growth was 1·9% in 2002 and 0·5% in 2003. In March 1999 an IMF agreement introduced a tight monetary policy with an emphasis on reducing the ratio of debt to GDP. Total GDP in 2003 was US$492·3bn.

Banking and Finance. On 31 Dec. 1964 the Banco Central do Brasil (*President*, Henrique Meirelles) was founded as the national bank of issue and at Dec. 2002 had total reserves of US$37·84bn.

The Bank of Brazil (founded in 1853 and reorganized in 1906) is a state-owned commercial bank; it had 2,927 branches in 2000 throughout the country. The largest private banks are Banco Bradesco, Banco Itaú and Unibanco. On 31 Dec. 1996 deposits were R$33,604m. In 2000 there were 190 banking establishments with 14,892 branches (26 commercial banks with 3,352 branches and 164 multiple banks with 11,540 branches), plus 19 investment banks with 45 branches.

In Nov. 1998 the IMF announced a US$41·5bn. financing package to help shore up the Brazilian economy. In Aug. 2001 it gave approval for a new US$15bn. stand-by credit, and in Aug. 2002 granted an additional US$30bn. loan to try to prevent a financial meltdown that was threatening to devastate the region.

Brazil received US$22·5bn. worth of foreign direct investment in 2001, down from a record US$33·5bn. in 2000. Spain was the leading investor in 2000, providing 21·3% of foreign capital, ahead of the USA.

There is a stock exchange in São Paulo.

ENERGY AND NATURAL RESOURCES

Environment. Brazil's carbon dioxide emissions from the consumption and flaring of fossil fuels in 2002 were the equivalent of 2·0 tonnes per capita.

Brazil has the world's biggest river system and about a quarter of the world's primary rainforest. Current environmental issues are deforestation in the Amazon Basin, air and water pollution in Rio de Janeiro and São Paulo (the world's fourth largest city), and land degradation and water pollution caused by improper mining activities. Contaminated drinking water causes 70% of child deaths.

Electricity. Hydro-electric power accounts for nearly 90% of Brazil's total electricity output. Although Brazil was only the tenth largest electricity producer overall in the world in 2000, it was the second largest producer of hydro-electric power. Installed electric capacity (2000) was 73·1m. kW, of which 60·8m. kW hydro-electric. In July 2001 the government announced that supply would be increased by 20,000 MW by the end of 2003 to help solve the country's worst energy crisis in modern times. There were two nuclear power plants in 2003, supplying some 1·5% of total output. Production (2000) 348,000 GWh. Consumption per capita in 2000 was 2,345 kWh.

Oil and Gas. There are 13 oil refineries, of which 11 are state-owned. Crude oil production (2003), 76·8m. tonnes. Crude oil reserves were estimated at 8·3bn. bbls. in 2002. Brazil began to open its markets in 1999 by inviting foreign companies to drill for oil, and in 2000 the monopoly of the state-owned Petrobrás on importing oil products was removed.

Gas production (2002), 9·1bn. cu. metres with reserves of 230bn. cu. metres. One of the most significant developments has been the construction of the 3,150-km Bolivia–Brazil gas pipeline, one of Latin America's biggest infrastructure projects, costing around US$2bn. (£1·2bn.). The pipeline runs from the Bolivian interior across the Brazilian border at Puerto Suárez-Corumbá to the far southern port city of Porto Alegre. Gas from Bolivia began to be pumped to São Paulo in 1999.

Minerals. The chief minerals are bauxite, gold, iron ore, manganese, nickel, phosphates, platinum, tin and uranium. Output figures, 1999 (in 1,000 tonnes): phosphate rock, 27,000; bauxite (2000), 13,224; salt (2002), 7,000; hard coal (2000), 6,712; asbestos (crude ore), 3,950; manganese ore, 1,674; aluminium (2001), 1,131; magnesite, 869; graphite, 650; chrome (crude ore), 420; zinc (2001), 111; barytes, 49; nickel ore (2002), 45; copper (2000), 32; zirconium, 29; tin (tin content), 13; lead (lead content in concentrate), 10. Deposits of coal exist in Rio Grande do Sul, Santa Catarina and Paraná. Total reserves were estimated at 11,950m. tonnes in 2000.

Iron is found chiefly in Minas Gerais, notably the Cauê Peak at Itabira. The government is opening up iron-ore deposits in Carajás, in the northern state of Pará, with estimated reserves of 35,000m. tonnes, representing a 66% concentration of high-grade iron ore. Total output of iron ore, 2001, mainly from the Vale do Rio Doce mine at Itabira, was 208·7m. tonnes. Brazil is the second largest producer of iron ore after China.

Gold is chiefly from Pará, Mato Grosso and Minas Gerais; total production (2001), 53·2 tonnes. Silver output (2001), 46 tonnes. Diamond output in 2002 was 700,000 carats, mainly from Minas Gerais and Mato Grosso.

Agriculture. In 2002 the agricultural population was 31·22m. There were 4·86m. farms in 1995. There were 58·87m. ha of arable land in 2001 and 7·6m. ha of permanent crops. 2·91m. ha were irrigated in 2001.

Production (in tonnes):

	2002	*2003*		*2002*	*2003*
Apples	875,388	841,821	Onions	1,222,124	1,229,848
Bananas	6,422,855	6,800,981	Oranges	18,530,625	16,917,558
Beans	3,064,288	3,302,038	Pineapples (1,000 fruits)	1,433,234	1,440,013
Cassava	23,065,577	22,961,082	Potatoes	3,126,411	3,089,016
Coconut (1,000 fruits)	1,928,236	1,985,661	Rice	10,457,093	10,334,603
Coffee	2,649,609	1,987,079	Soya	42,124,898	51,919,440
Cotton	2,166,014	2,199,268	Sugarcane	364,391,016	396,012,158
Grapes	1,148,648	1,067,422	Tomatoes	3,251,046	3,708,602
Maize	35,932,962	48,327,323	Wheat	3,105,658	6,153,500

Brazil is the world's leading producer of sugarcane, oranges and coffee (and the second largest consumer of coffee after the USA). Harvested coffee area, 2003, 2,408,023 ha, principally in the states of Minas Gerais, Espírito Santo, São Paulo and Paraná. Harvested cocoa area, 2003, 605,930 ha. Bahia furnished 84% of the output in 1998. Two crops a year are grown. Brazil accounts for more than a quarter of annual coffee production worldwide. Harvested castor-bean area, 2003, 134,485 ha. Tobacco is grown chiefly in Rio Grande do Sul and Santa Catarina.

Rubber is produced chiefly in the states of São Paulo, Mato Grosso, Bahia, Espírito Santo and Minas Gerais. Output, 2003, 156,318 tonnes.

Livestock, 2003: cattle, 195·6m.; pigs, 32·3m.; sheep, 14·6m.; goats, 9·6m.; horses, 5·8m.; mules, 1·3m.; asses, 1·2m.; chickens and other poultry, 921·3m. Livestock products, 2002 (in 1,000 tonnes): beef and veal, 7,136; pork, bacon and ham, 2,100; poultry meat, 7,229; cow's milk, 22,635; hen's eggs, 1,550; wool (2003), 11; honey (2003), 30.

Forestry. With forest lands covering 543,905,000 ha in 2000, only Russia had a larger area of forests. In 2000, 64·3% of the total land area of Brazil was under forests. The annual loss of 2,309,000 ha of forests between 1990 and 2000 was the biggest in any country in the world over the same period. Nevertheless, an independent study commissioned by NASA has found that the rate of deforestation was on the decline and stated that the government had been extremely active since 1990 in reducing the rate of illegal deforestation. In 1996 the government ruled that Amazonian landowners could log only 20% of their holdings, instead of 50%, as had previously been permitted. Timber production in 2001 totalled 236·42m. cu. metres, a figure exceeded only in the USA, India and China. In 1997 the government's environmental agency, Ibama, levied fines of nearly US$11m. on illicit loggers. In 2001 Ibama seized 25,600 cu. metres (US$40m. worth) of illegally-cut mahogany.

Fisheries. In 2001 the fishing industry had a catch of approximately 770,000 tonnes (74% sea fishing and 26% inland).

INDUSTRY

The leading companies by market capitalization in Brazil, excluding banking and finance, in May 2004 were: Petróleo Brasileiro SA (Petrobras), US$27·2bn.; Companhia Vale do Rio Doce, the world's largest iron ore producer (US$18·7bn.); and Companhia de Bebidas das Americas (AmBev), a beverage company (US$10·0bn.).

The main industries are textiles, shoes, chemicals, cement, lumber, iron ore, tin, steel, aircraft, motor vehicles and parts, and other machinery and equipment. The National Iron and Steel Co. at Volta Redonda, State of Rio de Janeiro, furnishes a substantial part of Brazil's steel. Production (in 1,000 tonnes), 2001: cement, 38,735; crude steel (2002), 29,600; pig iron (2002), 29,600; cast iron (2000), 27,854; distillate fuel oil (2000), 25,811; sugar (2002), 23,567; rolled steel (2000), 18,201; residual fuel oil (2000), 17,894; petrol (2000), 13,701; paper (2000), 7,100. Output of other products in 2001: 5·46m. TV sets; 3·37m. refrigerators; 34·4m. rubber tyres for motor vehicles; 1·72m. motor vehicles (2002); beer, 6,790·5m. litres; soft drinks, 6,226·1m. litres.

Labour. In 2003 a total of 79,251,000 persons were in employment (46,401,000 males), including: 16,409,000 engaged in agriculture, hunting, forestry and fishing; 14,047,000 in wholesale and retail trade; 11,387,000 in manufacturing; 5,158,000 in construction. A constitutional amendment of Oct. 1996 prohibits the employment of children under 14 years. However, in 2000 more than 14% of children between 10 and 14 were working. At May 2004 there was a minimum monthly wage of R$260. In 2000, 7·1% of the workforce was unemployed (7·5% in 1999).

Trade Unions. The main union is the United Workers' Centre (CUT).

INTERNATIONAL TRADE

In 1990 Brazil repealed most of its protectionist legislation. Import tariffs on some 13,000 items were reduced in 1995. In 1991 the government permitted an annual US$100m. of foreign debt to be converted into funds for environmental protection. Total foreign debt in 2002 was US$227,932m. (the highest of any developing country).

Imports and Exports. Imports and exports for calendar years (in US$1m.):

	1999	*2000*	*2001*	*2002*
Imports	49,272	55,783	55,572	47,219
Exports	48,011	55,086	58,223	60,362

Principal imports in 1999 were: machinery and transport equipment, 42·9%; chemicals, 18·4%; manufactured goods, 10·0%; petroleum and related products, 9·0%; and food and live animals, 6·9%.

Principal exports in 1999 were: machinery and transport equipment, 23·7%; food and live animals, 21·6%, including coffee (5·1%), oilcake (3·1%), orange juice (2·6%) and sugar (2·4%); iron ore, 5·7%; footwear, 2·7%; and aluminium, 2·5%. Brazil is the world's leading sugar exporter.

Main export markets, 2000: USA, 23·9%; Argentina, 11·3%; Netherlands, 5·1%; Germany, 4·6%; Japan, 4·5%; Italy, 3·9%. Main import suppliers: USA, 23·1%; Argentina, 12·3%; Germany, 7·9%; Japan, 5·3%; Italy, 3·9%; France, 3·4%.

COMMUNICATIONS

Roads. In 2000 there were 1,724,929 km of roads, of which 94,871 km were paved. In 2000 there were 33,707,640 vehicles registered. Some 56% of freight is carried by truck. In 1998 there were 120,442 road accidents resulting in 5,305 deaths.

Rail. The Brazilian railways have largely been privatized: all six branches of the large RFFSA network are now under private management. In 2000 RFFSA (Rede Ferroviária Federal S.A.) had a route-length of 21,316 km and FERROBAN (Ferrovias Bandeirantes S.A.) a route-length of 4,235 km. Total route-length nationwide was 29,283 km in 2000. Two-thirds is narrow (1·0 metre) gauge, the rest either broad (1·60) or a mix of the two. Passenger-km travelled in 2000 came to 5·85bn. and freight tonne-km to 154·87bn.

There are several important independent freight railways, including the Vitoria à Minas (898 km in 1993), the Ferroeste (238 km), the Carajas (1,076 km in 1991) and the Amapa (194 km). There are metros in São Paulo (44 km), Rio de Janeiro (23 km), Belo Horizonte (14 km), Porto Alegre (28 km), Brasília (38·5 km) and Recife (25 km).

Civil Aviation. There are major international airports at Rio de Janeiro-Galeão (Antonio Carlos Jobim International) and São Paulo (Guarulhos) and some international flights from Brasília, Porto Alegre, Recife and Salvador. The three main airlines are Viação Aérea Rio Grande do Sul (Varig), with 33% of the market, TAM and Viação Aérea São Paulo (Vasp). In 1999 Varig carried 10,064,000 passengers, TAM carried 4,775,000 passengers and VASP 4,190,000 passengers.

Brazil's busiest airport is Guarulhos (São Paulo), which handled 13,163,000 passengers in 2000 (up from 6·45m. in 1992) and 348,200 tonnes of freight, followed by Congonhas (São Paulo) with 7,757,514 passengers (in 1998), and Rio de Janeiro with 5,416,000 passengers and 117,900 tonnes of freight in 2000.

Shipping. Inland waterways, mostly rivers, are open to navigation over some 43,000 km. Tubarão and Itaqui are the leading ports. In 2002 Santos, the leading container port, handled 1·22m. TEUs (twenty-foot equivalent units). During 1997, 28,973 vessels entered and cleared the Brazilian ports; vessels totalling 88,562,000 NRT entered ports in 2001 and vessels totalling 258,962,000 NRT cleared. In 2000 the merchant fleet comprised 505 vessels (77 oil tankers). In 2002 total tonnage registered was 3·45m. GRT, including oil tankers 1·40m. GRT.

Telecommunications. The state-owned telephone system was privatized in 1998. There were 73,691,000 telephone subscribers in 2002 (423·8 per 1,000 inhabitants). Mobile phone services were opened to the private sector in 1996. By 2002 there were 34,881,000 mobile phone subscribers. There were 13·98m. Internet users in Sept. 2002, up from 3·1m. in July 1999. In 2002 PCs numbered 13·0m. (74·8 per 1,000 persons) and in 1997 there were 500,000 fax machines.

Postal Services. In 2000 there were 25,957 post offices. A total of 5,223m. pieces of mail were handled in 1998.

SOCIAL INSTITUTIONS

Justice. There is a Supreme Federal Court of Justice at Brasília composed of 11 judges, and a Supreme Court of Justice; all judges are appointed by the President with the approval of the Senate. There are also Regional Federal Courts, Labour Courts, Electoral Courts and Military Courts. Each state organizes its own courts and judicial system in accordance with the federal Constitution.

In Dec. 1999 President Cardoso created the country's first intelligence agency (the Brazilian Intelligence Agency) under civilian rule. It replaced informal networks which were a legacy of the military dictatorship, and will help authorities crack down on organized drug gangs.

The prison population was 285,000 in June 2003 (160 per 100,000 of national population). Brazil's annual murder rate, in excess of 25 per 100,000 population, is on the increase and is more than four times that of the USA.

Religion. In 2000 there were 124,977,000 Roman Catholics (including syncretic Afro-Catholic cults having spiritualist beliefs and rituals) and 26,167,000 Evangelical Protestants, with 2,684,000 followers of other religions. Roman Catholic estimates in 1991 suggest that 90% were baptized Roman Catholic but only 35% were regular attenders. In 1991 there were 338 bishops and some 14,000 priests. In Sept. 2003 there were eight cardinals. There are numerous sects, some evangelical, some African-derived (e.g. *Candomble*).

Education. Elementary education is compulsory from seven to 14. Adult literacy in 2001 was 87·3 % (male, 87·4%; female, 87·2%). There were 50,646 literacy classes in 1993 with 1,584,147 students and 75,413 teachers. In 2003 there were 94,741 pre-primary schools, with 5,155,676 pupils and 270,576 teachers; 169,075 primary schools, with 34,438,749 pupils and 1,603,851 teachers; 21,980 secondary schools, with 9,072,942 pupils and 488,376 teachers; and 1,637 higher education institutions, with 3,479,913 students and 227,844 teachers. In 2003, 97·2% of children between the ages of seven and 14 were enrolled at schools. However, only a third of Brazilian teenagers attend school. In Jan. 2001 President Cardoso announced a National Education Plan that involves teaching 10m. young people and adults to read and write within five years and eradicating illiteracy within a decade.

There were 1,859 universities in Brazil in 2003, of which 207 were public and 1,652 were private. Of the 207 public universities, 83 were federal, 65 were state and 59 were municipal institutions.

In 2000–01 total expenditure on education came to 4·0% of GNP and 10·4% of total government expenditure.

Health. In 1999 there were 48,815 hospitals and clinics (26,209 private), of which 7,806 were for in-patients (5,193 private). There were a total of 484,945 hospital beds in 1999 (341,871 private). In 1997 there were 205,828 doctors, 137,600 dentists, 67,760 nurses and 51,847 pharmacists.

Brazil has been one of the most successful countries in the developing world in the campaign against AIDS. It is reported to have reduced AIDS-related deaths by 40% between 1996 and 2000.

Welfare. Old-age pensions begin at 65 years (men) or 60 years (women) for employees and the urban self-employed, and ages 60 (men) or 55 (women) for the rural self-employed. To qualify there must be at least 35 years contributions for men or 30 years contributions for women. The maximum monthly pension was R$1,869·34 in June 2003.

Unemployment benefits vary depending on insurance but, as a general rule, cover 50% of average earnings in the last three months of employment, up to three times the minimum wage. The minimum benefit is 100% of the minimum monthly wage (R$260 in May 2004).

Family allowances are granted to low-income families with one or more children under the age of 14 or with disabled children attending school. In 2003, R$13·48 a month was provided for each child.

CULTURE

World Heritage Sites. The sites under Brazilian jurisdiction entered on the UNESCO world heritage list (with year entered) are: the Historic Town of Ouro Preto (1980), the centre of the gold rush founded at the end of the 17th century; the Historic Centre of Olinda (1982), founded by the Portuguese in the 16th century; the Jesuit Missions of the Guaranis (1984), the ruins of five Jesuit missions; the centre of Salvador de Bahia, Brazil's first capital (1549–1763); and the Sanctuary of Bom Jesus do Congonhas, an ornate church dating to the late 18th century (both 1985); the Iguaçu National Park (1986); Brasília (1987), Brazil's purpose built capital city; Serra da Capivara National Park (1991) including cave paintings over 25,000 years old; the Historic Centre of São Luis (1997), which has examples of late 17th-century architecture; the Historic Centre of Diamantina, a colonial village inhabited by diamond prospectors in the 18th century; the Discovery Coast Atlantic Forest Reserves; and Atlantic Forest Southeast Reserves, covering 470,000 ha over 25 protected areas (all 1999); the Pantanal Conservation Area; and Jaú National Park, covering over 2,250,000 ha of Amazon basin (both 2000); the Cerrado Protected Areas, comprising Chapada dos Veadeiros and Emas National Parks; Brazilian Atlantic Islands, comprising Fernando de Noronha and Atol das Rocas Reserves; and the Historic Centre of Goiás, established by colonizing powers in the 18th and 19th centuries (all 2001).

Broadcasting. In 1995 there were 2,033 radio and 119 television stations (colour by PAL M). In 2000 there were 74m. radio receivers and in 2001 there were 60m. television receivers.

Press. In 1998 there were 372 daily newspapers with a combined circulation of 7,163,000, at a rate of 43 per 1,000 inhabitants.

Tourism. In 2000, 5,313,000 tourists visited Brazil. Argentina is the country of origin of the largest number of visitors, ahead of the USA, Uruguay and Paraguay. Receipts in 2000 totalled US$4·23bn.

Festivals. New Year's Eve in Rio de Janeiro is always marked with special celebrations, with a major fireworks display over the bay at Copacabana Beach. Immediately afterwards, preparations start for Carnival, which in 2006 will be held from 25–28 Feb.

Libraries. In 1993 Brazil had a National Library with 5·28m. volumes, and in 1994 a total of 2,739 public libraries.

DIPLOMATIC REPRESENTATIVES

Of Brazil in the United Kingdom (32 Green St., London, W1K 7AT)
Ambassador: José Maurício Bustani.

Of the United Kingdom in Brazil (Setor De Embaixadas Sul, Quadro 801, Conjunto K, CP70.408-900, Brasília, DF *or* Av. das Nações, CP07-0586, 70.359, Brasília, DF)
Ambassador: Peter Collecott, CMG.

Of Brazil in the USA (3006 Massachusetts Ave., NW, Washington, D.C. 20008)
Ambassador: Roberto Abdenur.

Of the USA in Brazil (Av. das Nações, Lote 03, Quadra 801, CEP: 70403-900, Brasília, D.F.)
Ambassador: John Danilovich.

Of Brazil to the United Nations
Ambassador: Ronaldo Mota Sardenberg.

Of Brazil to the European Union
Ambassador: José Alfredo Graca Lima.

FURTHER READING

Instituto Brasileiro de Geografia e Estatística. *Anuário Estatistico do Brasil.—Censo Demográfico de 1991.—Indicadores IBGE.* Monthly
Boletim do Banco Central do Brasil. Banco Central do Brasil. Brasília. Monthly

Baer, W., *The Brazilian Economy: Growth and Development.* 4th ed. New York, 1995
Dickenson, John, *Brazil.* [Bibliography] 2nd ed. ABC-Clio, Oxford and Santa Barbara (CA), 1997
Eakin, Marshall C., *Brazil: The Once and Future Country.* New York, 1997
Fausto, Boris, *A Concise History of Brazil.* CUP, 1999
Font, M. A., *Coffee, Contention and Change in the Making of Modern Brazil.* Oxford, 1990
Guirmaraes, R. P., *Politics and Environment in Brazil: Ecopolitics of Development in the Third World.* New York, 1991
Stepan, A. (ed.) *Democratizing Brazil: Problems of Transition and Consolidation.* OUP, 1993
Turner, Barry, (ed.) *Latin America Profiled.* Macmillan, London, 2000
Welch, J. H., *Capital Markets in the Development Process: the Case of Brazil.* London, 1992

For other more specialized titles see under CONSTITUTION AND GOVERNMENT *above.*

National library: Biblioteca Nacional, Avenida Rio Branco 21939, Rio de Janeiro, RJ.
National statistical office: Instituto Brasileiro de Geografia e Estatística (IBGE), Rua General Canabarro 666, 20.271-201 Maracanã, Rio de Janeiro, RJ.
Website: http://www.ibge.gov.br

BRUNEI

Negara Brunei Darussalam—
State of Brunei Darussalam

Capital: Bandar Seri Begawan
Population projection, 2010: 415,000
GDP per capita, 1998: (PPP$) 16,779
HDI/world rank: 0·867/33

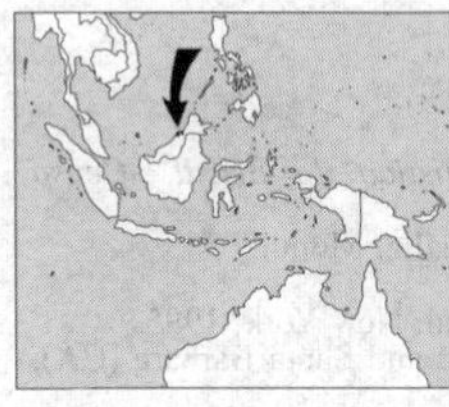

KEY HISTORICAL EVENTS

Brunei became an independent Sultanate in the 15th century, controlling most of Borneo, its neighbouring islands and the Suhi Archipelago. By the end of the 16th century, however, the power of Brunei was on the wane. By the middle of the 19th century the State had been reduced to its present limits. Brunei became a British protectorate in 1888. The discovery of major oilfields in the western end of the State in the 1920s brought economic stability to Brunei and created a new style of life for the population. Brunei was occupied by the Japanese in 1941 and liberated by the Australians in 1945. Self-government was introduced in 1959 but Britain retained responsibility for foreign affairs. In 1965 constitutional changes were made which led to direct elections for a new Legislative Council. Full independence and sovereignty were gained in Jan. 1984.

TERRITORY AND POPULATION

Brunei, on the coast of Borneo, is bounded in the northwest by the South China Sea and on all other sides by Sarawak (Malaysia), which splits it into two parts, the smaller portion forming the Temburong district. Area, 2,226 sq. miles (5,765 sq. km). Population (2001 census) 332,844 (168,925 males), giving a density of 57·8 per sq. km.

The UN gives a projected population for 2010 of 415,000.

In 2001, 72·7% of the population lived in urban areas. The four districts are Brunei/Muara (1995: 195,000), Belait (60,000), Tutong (32,500), Temburong (8,500). The capital is Bandar Seri Begawan (estimate 1999: 85,000); other large towns are Kuala Belait (1991: 21,163) and Seria (1991: 21,082). Ethnic groups include Malays 64% and Chinese 20%.

The official language is Malay but English is in use.

SOCIAL STATISTICS

2000 births, 7,481; deaths, 965. Rates, 2000: birth per 1,000 population, 22·1; death, 2·9. There were 2,184 marriages in 2000. Life expectancy in 2001: males, 74·0 years; females, 78·7. Annual population growth rate, 1992–2002, 2·6%. Infant mortality, 2001, 6 per 1,000 live births; fertility rate, 2001, 2·6 children per woman.

CLIMATE

The climate is tropical marine, hot and moist, but nights are cool. Humidity is high and rainfall heavy, varying from 100" (2,500 mm) on the coast to 200" (5,000 mm) inland. There is no dry season. Bandar Seri Begawan, Jan. 80°F (26·7°C), July 82°F (27·8°C). Annual rainfall 131" (3,275 mm).

CONSTITUTION AND GOVERNMENT

The Sultan and Yang Di Pertuan of Brunei Darussalam is HM Paduka Seri Baginda Sultan Haji Hassanal Bolkiah Mu'izzadin Waddaulah. He succeeded on 5 Oct. 1967 at his father's abdication and was crowned on 1 Aug. 1968. On 10 Aug. 1998 his son, Oxford-graduate Prince Al-Muhtadee Billah, was inaugurated as Crown Prince and heir apparent.

On 29 Sept. 1959 the Sultan promulgated a Constitution, but parts of it have been in abeyance since Dec. 1962. In Sept. 2004 the Constitution was amended and parliament reconvened for the first time since 1984. The amendment allows for the first elections since 1962. A third of the members of the new 45-member parliament will be directly elected. The Sultan is both the head of state and head of government.

A Council of Cabinet Ministers, appointed and presided over by the Sultan, exercises executive powers. There is also a unicameral Legislative Council (*Majlis Masyuarat Megeri*) whose members are at present also appointed by the Sultan, which has a consultative role.

National Anthem. 'Ya Allah, lanjutkan lah usia' ('O God, long live His Majesty'); words by P. Rahim, tune by I. Sagap.

CURRENT ADMINISTRATION

In March 2005 the Council of Ministers was composed as follows:

Prime Minister, Minister of Defence and of Finance: The Sultan.

Minister of Foreign Affairs: Prince Haji Mohammad Bolkiah. *Home Affairs:* Pehin Dato Haji Isa bin Ibrahim. *Education:* Pehin Dato Haji Abdul Aziz bin Umar. *Health:* Abu Bakar bin Apong. *Industry and Primary Resources:* Pehin Dato Haji Abdul Rahman bin Mohammad Taib. *Religious Affairs:* Pehin Dato Dr Haji Mohammad Zain bin Serudin. *Development:* Ahmed bin Jumaat. *Culture, Youth and Sports:* Pehin Dato Haji Hussain bin Mohammad Yusof. *Communications:* Dato Haji Zakaria bin Sulaiman.

Government Website: http://www.brunei.gov.bn

DEFENCE

In 2003 military expenditure totalled US$259m. (US$726 per capita), representing 5·1% of GDP.

Army. The armed forces are known as the Task Force and contain the naval and air elements. Only Malays are eligible for service. Strength (2002) 4,900, including 250 women.

There is a 2,000-strong paramilitary Gurkha reserve unit.

Navy. The Royal Brunei Armed Forces Flotilla includes three fast missile-armed attack craft. Personnel in 2002 numbered 1,000 (80 women). The Flotilla is based at Muara.

Air Wing. The Air Wing of the Royal Brunei Armed Forces was formed in 1965. Personnel (2002), 1,100 (75 women). There are no combat aircraft.

INTERNATIONAL RELATIONS

Brunei is a member of the UN, WTO, the Commonwealth, APEC, Mekong Group, ASEAN, OIC and Islamic Development Bank.

ECONOMY

In 1998 agriculture accounted for 2·8% of GDP, industry 44·5% and services 52·7%. The fall in oil prices in 1997–98 led to the setting up of an Economic Council to advise the Sultan on reforms. An investigation was mounted into the affairs of the Amedeo Corporation, Brunei's largest private company run by Prince Jefri, the Sultan's brother.

Currency. The unit of currency is the *Brunei dollar* (BND) of 100 cents, which is at parity with the Singapore dollar (also legal tender). In 2002 there was deflation, of 2·0%.

Budget. Revenues in 1998 were B$2·8bn. Expenditure in 1998 was B$4·3bn.

Performance. Real GDP growth in the wake of the general downturn in the world economy was just 0·8% in 2001 but there was then growth of 3·0% in 2002. Total GDP in 1998 was US$4·9bn.

Banking and Finance. The Brunei Currency Board is the note-issuing monetary authority. In 2002 there were three commercial banks, six foreign banks and one off-shore bank. Total bank assets in 1993 were B$6,567·7m.

The International Brunei Exchange Ltd. (IBX) established an international securities exchange in May 2002.

ENERGY AND NATURAL RESOURCES

Environment. Brunei's carbon dioxide emissions from the consumption and flaring of fossil fuels were the equivalent of 14·8 tonnes per capita in 2002.

Electricity. Installed capacity was 0·5m. kW in 2000. Production in 2000 was approximately 2·43bn. kWh and consumption per capita in 2000 an estimated 7,201 kWh.

Oil and Gas. The Seria oilfield, discovered in 1929, has passed its peak production. The high level of crude oil production is maintained through the increase of offshore oilfields production. Production was 10·5m. tonnes in 2003. The crude oil is exported directly, and only a small amount is refined at Seria for domestic uses. There were proven oil reserves of 1·4bn. bbls. in 2002.

Natural gas is produced (11·5bn. cu. metres in 2002) at one of the largest liquefied natural gas plants in the world and is exported to Japan. There were proven reserves of 390bn. cu. metres in 2002.

Agriculture. In 2001 there were 3,000 ha of arable land and 4,000 ha of permanent crops. The main crops produced in 2000 were (estimates, in 1,000 tonnes): vegetables, 9; fruit, 6 (notably bananas and pineapples); cassava, 2.

Livestock in 2000: cattle, 2,000; buffaloes, 6,000; pigs, 6,000; goats, 4,000; chickens, 6m.

Forestry. Forests covered 442,000 ha, or 83·9% of the total land area, in 2000. Most of the interior is under forest, containing large potential supplies of serviceable timber. Timber production in 2001 was 229,000 cu. metres.

Fisheries. The 2001 catch totalled 1,492 tonnes, almost exclusively from marine waters.

INDUSTRY

Brunei depends primarily on its oil industry. Other minor products are rubber, pepper, sawn timber, gravel and animal hides.

Labour. The labour force totalled 131,000 in 1996 (66% males).

INTERNATIONAL TRADE

Imports and Exports. In 2001 imports totalled B$2,076m.; exports, B$6,522m. In 1998 liquefied natural gas accounted for 52·6% of exports and crude oil 33·7%. In 2001 Singapore supplied 23% of imports, Malaysia 22% and the USA 9%. Japan took 46% of all exports, South Korea 12% and Thailand 12%.

COMMUNICATIONS

Roads. There were an estimated 1,150 km of roads in 1999. The main road connects Bandar Seri Begawan with Kuala Belait and Seria. In 2000 there were 115,476 private cars and 13,740 vans and trucks. There were 45 fatalities in road accidents in 1999.

Civil Aviation. Brunei International Airport (Bandar Seri Begawan) handled 949,000 passengers (all international) in 1999. The national carrier is the state-owned Royal Brunei Airlines (RBA). In 2003 RBA operated services to Abu Dhabi, Bangkok, Brisbane, Calcutta, Darwin, Denpasar Bali, Dubai, Frankfurt, Hong Kong, Jakarta, Jeddah, Kota Kinabalu, Kuala Lumpur, Kuching, London, Manila, Perth, Shanghai, Singapore, Surabaya and Taipei. In 1997 RBA flew 35·3m. km, carrying 876,800 passengers (all on international flights).

Shipping. Regular shipping services operate from Singapore, Hong Kong, Sarawak and Sabah to Bandar Seri Begawan, and there is a daily passenger ferry between Bandar Seri Begawan and Labuan. In 2002 merchant shipping totalled 483,000 GRT. In 2002 vessels totalling 1,735,000 NRT entered ports and vessels totalling 1,732,000 NRT cleared.

Telecommunications. There is a telephone network linking the main centres. In 2001 there were 225,400 telephone subscribers (or 659·2 per 1,000 inhabitants), including 137,000 mobile phone subscribers. In 2002 there were 27,000 PCs (76·7 for every 1,000 persons). There were 35,000 Internet users in 2001 and 2,000 fax machines in 1995.

Postal Services. There were 18 post offices in 1998.

SOCIAL INSTITUTIONS

Justice. The Supreme Court comprises a High Court and a Court of Appeal and the Magistrates' Courts. The High Court receives appeals from subordinate courts in the districts and is itself a court of first instance for criminal and civil cases. The Judicial Committee of the Privy Council in London is the final court of appeal. Shariah Courts deal with Islamic law. 25,310 crimes were reported in 1993.

The Royal Brunei Police numbers 1,750 officers and men (1997). In addition, there are 500 additional police officers mostly employed on static guard duties. The population in penal institutions in 2002 was 454 (133 per 100,000 of national population).

Religion. The official religion is Islam. In 2001, 67% of the population were Muslim (mostly Malays). There are Buddhist and Christian minorities.

Education. The government provides free education to all citizens from pre-school up to the highest level at local and overseas universities and institutions. In 2000–01 there were 9,837 children in pre-primary education; 44,981 pupils and 3,753 teachers in primary education; 35,945 pupils in secondary education; 3,984 students and 483 academic staff in tertiary education. The University of Brunei Darussalam was founded in 1985; in 1996 there were also six technical and vocational colleges (one teacher training college) and an institute of advanced education.

Adult literacy rate, 2001, 91·6% (male, 94·6%; female, 88·1%). Total expenditure on education came to 3·0% of GNP (1998–99) and 9·1% of total government spending (2000–01).

Health. Medical and health services are free to citizens and those in government service and their dependants. Citizens are sent overseas, at government expense, for medical care not available in Brunei. Flying medical services are provided to remote areas. In 1995 there were ten hospitals; and in 1996 there were 259 physicians, 26 dentists and 1,229 nurses.

CULTURE

Broadcasting. Radio Television Brunei operates on medium- and shortwaves in Malay, English, Chinese and Nepali. Number of receivers: radio (2000), 363,000; television (2001), 215,000 (colour by PAL).

Press. In 1996 there was one local newspaper with a circulation of 21,000.

Tourism. In 2000 there were 984,000 foreign tourists. In 1998 receipts totalled US$37m.

DIPLOMATIC REPRESENTATIVES

Of Brunei in the United Kingdom (19/20 Belgrave Sq., London, SW1X 8PG)
High Commissioner: Penigran Haji Yunus.

Of the United Kingdom in Brunei (PO Box 2197, Bandar Seri Begawan 8674)
High Commissioner: Andrew Caie.

Of Brunei in the USA (3520 International Court, NW, Washington, D.C., 20008)
Ambassador: Pengiran Anak Dato Haji Puteh.

Of the USA in Brunei (3rd Floor, Teck Guan Plaza, Jalan Sultan, Bandar Seri Begawan 2085)
Ambassador: Gene Christy.

Of Brunei to the United Nations
Ambassador: Shofry bin Abdul Ghafor.

Of Brunei to the European Union
Ambassador: Vacant.
Chargé d'Affaires a.i.: Amalina Murad.

FURTHER READING

Ministry of Finance Statistics Department. *Brunei Darussalam Statistical Yearbook.*

Cleary, M. and Wong, S. Y., *Oil, Economic Development and Diversification in Brunei.* London, 1994

Horton, A. V. M., *A Critical Guide to Source Material Relating to Brunei with Special Reference to the British Residential Era, 1906–1959.* Bordesley, 1995

Saunders, G., *History of Brunei.* OUP, 1996

National statistical office: Ministry of Finance Statistics Department.

BULGARIA

Republika Bulgaria

Capital: Sofia
Population projection, 2010: 7·46m.
GDP per capita, 2002: (PPP$) 7,130
HDI/world rank: 0·796/56

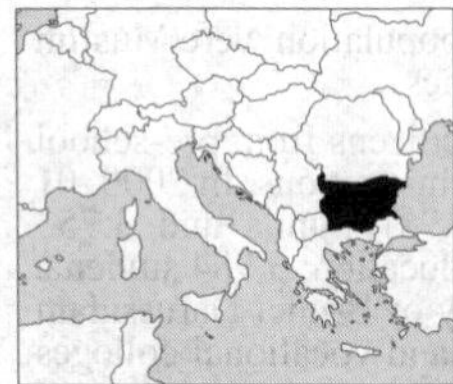

KEY HISTORICAL EVENTS

The Bulgarians take their name from an invading Asiatic horde (Bulgars) and their language from the Slav population, with whom they merged after 680. The Bulgarians carved out empires against a background of conflict with Byzantium and Serbia but after the Serb-Bulgarian defeat at Kosovo in 1389 Bulgaria finally succumbed to Ottoman encroachment. The Ottoman empire's decline, however, engendered rebellion which met with brutal repression, provoking great power intervention. By the Treaty of Berlin (1878), Macedonia and Thrace reverted to Turkey, Eastern Rumelia became semi-autonomous and Bulgaria proper became a principality under Turkish suzerainty.

After Austria annexed Bosnia in 1908, Bulgaria declared itself independent. To block Austrian expansion into the Balkans, Russia encouraged Greece, Serbia, Montenegro and Bulgaria to attack Turkey (First Balkan War, 1912), but in the dispute which followed over the territorial spoils Bulgaria failed to secure her claims against her formal allies by force (Second Balkan War, 1913). Territorial aspirations led Bulgaria to join the First World War on the German side.

Economic decline caused by the war produced social unrest. Ferdinand was forced to abdicate in favour of his son, Boris III, in Oct. 1918. Bedevilled by Macedonian terrorism and the effects of the world economic depression, parliamentary government was ended by a military coup in May 1934. In 1935 Boris established a royal dictatorship under which political parties were banned. Boris died in 1943 and was succeeded by a regency.

Increasingly drawn into the German economic orbit, Bulgaria joined the Nazis against Britain in March 1941. In Sept. 1944 the Soviet Union declared war and sent its troops across the frontiers. The Communist-dominated Fatherland Front formed a government and a referendum in 1946 abolished the monarchy. Demonstrations in Sofia in Nov. 1989, occasioned by the Helsinki Agreement ecological conference, broadened into demands for political reform. In Dec. the National Assembly approved 21 measures of constitutional reform, including the abolition of the Communist Party's sole right to govern. But attempts at economic reform led to strikes and unrest. In 1996 Petar Stoyanov was elected as an anti-Communist pro-reform President. In the election the following April the anti-Communist Union of Democratic Forces (UDF) coalition, led by Ivan Kostov and Alexander Bozhkov, swept back to power.

Bulgaria was one of seven countries to join NATO in 2004. It has an EU membership target date of 2007.

TERRITORY AND POPULATION

The area of Bulgaria is 110,994 sq. km (42,855 sq. miles). It is bounded in the north by Romania, east by the Black Sea, south by Turkey and Greece, and west by Serbia and Montenegro and the Republic of Macedonia. The country is divided into nine regions.

Area and population in 2001 (census):

Region	*Area (sq. km)*	*Population*	*Region*	*Area (sq. km)*	*Population*
Bourgas	14,724	802,932	Rousse	10,843	702,292
Haskovo	13,824	816,874	Sofia (city)	1,311	1,173,811
Lovech	15,150	924,505	Sofia (region)	19,021	930,958
Montana	10,607	559,449	Varna	11,929	887,222
Plovdiv	13,585	1,175,628	*Total*	*110,994*	*7,973,671*

The capital, Sofia, has regional status.

The population of Bulgaria at the census of 1992 was 8,472,724 (females, 4,515,936); population density 76·3 per sq. km. Bulgaria's population has been declining since the mid-1980s. It has been falling at such a rate that by 2001 it was the same as it had been in the early 1960s. In 2001, 67·5% of the population were urban.

The UN gives a projected population for 2010 of 7·46m.

Population of principal towns (2001 census): Sofia, 1,096,389; Plovdiv, 340,638; Varna, 314,539; Bourgas, 193,316; Rousse, 162,128; Stara Zagora, 143,989; Pleven, 122,149; Sliven, 100,695; Dobrich, 100,379.

Ethnic groups at the 2001 census: Bulgarians, 6,655,210; Turks, 746,664; Roma (Gypsies), 370,908.

Bulgarian is the official language.

SOCIAL STATISTICS

2002: live births, 66,499; deaths, 112,617; marriages, 29,218; divorces, 10,203. Rates per 1,000 population, 2002: birth, 8·5; death, 14·3; marriage, 3·7; divorce, 1·3; infant mortality, 14 per 1,000 live births (2001). Legal abortions totalled 50,824 in 2002. In 2001 the most popular age range for marrying was 25–29 for males and 20–24 for females. Expectation of life in 2001 was 67·4 years among males and 74·6 years among females. Annual population growth rate, 1992–2002, –0·8%; fertility rate, 2001, 1·1 children per woman (one of the lowest rates in the world).

CLIMATE

The southern parts have a Mediterranean climate, with winters mild and moist and summers hot and dry, but further north the conditions become more Continental, with a larger range of temperature and greater amounts of rainfall in summer and early autumn. Sofia, Jan. 28°F (–2·2°C), July 69°F (20·6°C). Annual rainfall 25·4" (635 mm).

CONSTITUTION AND GOVERNMENT

A new constitution was adopted at Turnovo in July 1991. The *President* is directly elected for not more than two five-year terms. Candidates for the presidency must be at least 40 years old and have lived for the last five years in Bulgaria. American-style primary elections were introduced in 1996; voting is open to all the electorate.

The 240-member *National Assembly* is directly elected by proportional representation. The President nominates a candidate from the largest parliamentary party as Prime Minister.

National Anthem. 'Gorda stara planina' ('Proud and ancient mountains'); words and tune by T. Radoslavov.

RECENT ELECTIONS

Presidential elections were held in two rounds on 11 and 18 Nov. 2001. Georgi Parvanov won the first round against five opponents with 36·4% of votes cast; turn-out was 39·2%. He also won the run-off round against the incumbent president Petar Stoyanov, with 54·1% of votes cast; turn-out was 54·4%.

At the elections of 17 June 2001 the National Movement Simeon II, the party of former King Simeon II, won 120 of the 240 seats with 42·7% of the vote; incumbent prime minister Ivan Kostov's United Democratic Forces coalition (consisting of the Union of Democratic Forces, the Bulgarian Agrarian People's Union-PU, the Democratic Party, the Bulgarian Social Democratic Party and the National Democratic Party) won 51 seats with 18·2%; the Coalition for Bulgaria (headed by the Bulgarian Socialist Party) won 48 seats with 17·1%; and the Movement for Rights and Freedoms (consisting of the Movement for Rights and Freedoms, the Liberal Union and Euroroma) won 21 seats with 7·5%. Turn-out was 66·7%.

Parliamentary elections were scheduled to take place on 25 June 2005.

CURRENT ADMINISTRATION

President: Georgi Parvanov; b. 1957 (Bulgarian Socialist Party; in office since 22 Jan. 2002).

Vice-President: Angel Marin.

In March 2005 the National Movement Simeon II-Movement for Rights and Freedoms-Coalition for Bulgaria coalition government comprised:

Chairman of the Council of Ministers: Simeon Borisov Sakskoburggotski (former King Simeon II); b. 1937 (National Movement Simeon II; sworn in 24 July 2001).

Deputy Prime Ministers: Nikolay Vassilev (also *Minister of Transport and Communications*), Plamen Panayotov.

Minister of Agriculture and Forestry: Nihat Kabil. *Civil Service:* Dimitar Kalchev. *Culture and Tourism:* Nina Chilova. *Defence:* Nikolay Svinarov. *Economy:* Milko Kovachev. *Education and Science:* Igor Damyanov. *Energy and Energy Resources:* Miroslav Sevlievski. *Environment and Water:* Dolores Arsenova. *European Affairs:* Meglena Kuneva. *Finance:* Milen Velchev. *Foreign Affairs:* Solomon Passy. *Health:* Slavcho Bogoev. *Interior:* Georgi Petkanov. *Justice:* Anton Stankov. *Labour and Social Policy:* Christina Christova. *Regional Development and Public Works:* Valentin Cerovski. *Youth and Sport:* Vassil Ivanov. *Minister without Portfolio:* Filiz Husmenova.

Government Website: http://www.government.bg

DEFENCE

Conscription is nine months (six months for university graduates).

Defence expenditure in 2003 totalled US$471m. (US$60 per capita), representing 2·4% of GDP. In 1985 the total had been US$1,424m.

Army. There are three military districts based around Sofia, Plovdiv and Sliven. In 2002 the Army had a strength of 31,050 including conscripts. In addition there are reserves of 303,000, 12,000 border guards and 18,000 railway and construction troops.

Navy. The Navy, all ex-Soviet or Soviet-built, includes one old diesel submarine and one small frigate. The Naval Aviation Wing operates nine armed helicopters. The naval headquarters are at Varna (Northern Command) and Bourgas (Southern Command), and there are further bases at Atiya, Vidin, Balchik and Sozopol. Personnel in 2002 totalled 4,370 (2,000 conscripts).

Air Force. The Air Force had (2002) 17,780 personnel. There are 232 combat aircraft, including MiG-21s, MiG-23s and Su-25s, and 43 attack helicopters.

INTERNATIONAL RELATIONS

Bulgaria is a member of the UN, WTO, BIS, NATO, Council of Europe, OSCE, CEI, BSEC, Danube Commission, IOM, Antarctic Treaty and the International Organization of the Francophonie, and is an Associate Member of the EU and an Associate Partner of the WEU. At the European Union's Helsinki Summit in Dec. 1999 Bulgaria, along with five other countries, was invited to begin full negotiations for membership in Feb. 2000. Entry into the EU is likely to be in 2007 at the earliest. It became a member of NATO on 29 March 2004.

ECONOMY

Agriculture accounted for 10·7% of GDP in 2002, industry 25·6% and services 63·7%.

Overview. Bulgaria is classified by the World Bank as a lower-middle income country. Its key sectors are agriculture, tourism, light industry and services. After economic and political crises in 1996–97 the country embarked on a reform programme aimed at ensuring long-term macroeconomic stability. Since the implementation of these reforms inflation has remained low, the country has experienced growth of 4·5% per year and foreign direct investment has been raised to 7% of GDP. In 2003 Bulgaria further tightened fiscal policy, saving half the revenue over-performance and reducing the deficit to 0·4% of GDP. Macroeconomic policies and structural reforms are aimed at entering the European Union. The EU has offered a favourable assessment of the Bulgarian economy and in 2003 it was declared to be a fully functioning market economy. Bulgaria has recently reached two important landmarks in its development path: it joined NATO in March 2004, and in June 2004 it successfully completed EU negotiations. Bulgaria is considered by the European Commission to be on track for EU accession in 2007, provided that the reform momentum is maintained.

Currency. The unit of currency is the *lev* (BGN) of 100 *stotinki*. In May 1996 the lev was devalued by 68%. A new *lev* was introduced on 5 July 1999, at 1 new *lev* = 1,000 old *leva*. Runaway inflation (123·0% in 1996 rising to 1,061% in 1997) forced the closure of 14 banks in 1996. However, by 2003 the rate was down to 2·3%. In June 1997 the new government introduced a currency board financial system which stabilized the lev and renewed economic growth. Under it, the lev is pegged to the euro at one euro = 1·95583 new leva. Foreign exchange reserves were estimated to be US$3,835m. in June 2002; gold reserves were 513,000 troy oz. Total money supply was 4,603m. leva in April 2002.

Budget. The fiscal year is the calendar year.

Government revenue and expenditure (in 1m. new leva):

	1997	*1998*	*1999*	*2000*	*2001*
Revenue	5,558·0	7,380·4	8,005·7	9,124·5	9,874·3
Expenditure	5,733·2	7,227·6	8,122·7	9,444·8	10,212·6

VAT was first introduced in 1995. In 1996 it was increased from 18% to 22%, but then lowered from 1 Jan. 1999 to 20%.

Performance. Total GDP in 2003 was US$19·9bn. Real GDP growth was 4·9% in 2002 and 4·3% in 2003. In 1997–98 the country pulled itself back from economic and financial disaster. Its success in stabilizing the economy, in the wake of the collapse of the banking system and the lurch into hyperinflation in early 1997, has exceeded expectations.

Banking and Finance. The National Bank (*Governor*, Ivan Iskrov) is the central bank and bank of issue. There is also a Currency Board, established in 1997. The DSK Bank became the last state bank to be privatized in 2003. There were 34 commercial banks in 2003. Foreign direct investment totalled US$1,419m. in 2003 (26% from privatization revenues).

There is a stock exchange in Sofia.

ENERGY AND NATURAL RESOURCES

Environment. Bulgaria's carbon dioxide emissions from the consumption and flaring of fossil fuels were the equivalent of 5·8 tonnes per capita in 2002.

Electricity. Bulgaria has little oil, gas or high-grade coal, and energy policy is based on the exploitation of its low-grade coal and hydro-electric resources. But the country is a major distribution centre for energy in the Black Sea region, a fact underlined by the 1997 deal with Russia which guarantees gas supplies to Bulgaria, while clearing the way for the construction of a transit gas pipeline between Russia and western Turkey. In 2003 there were four nuclear reactors in use, at the country's sole nuclear power plant in Kozloduy (dating from the 1970s). In Dec. 2002 it was announced that the two oldest of six reactors would close in 2003, with a further two to follow by 2006. The closure of the oldest reactor was a condition for the country's EU membership, proposed for 2007. To compensate, the government plans to complete a nuclear plant in Belene, started in the 1980s but suspended in 1990 because of lack of funds and environmental protests. Installed electrical capacity was 11·0m. kW in 2000. Output, 2000, 40·92bn. kWh (48% thermal, 44% nuclear and 8% hydro-electric). Consumption per capita: 4,567 kWh (2000).

Oil and Gas. Oil is extracted in the Balchik district on the Black Sea, in an area 100 km north of Varna, and at Dolni Dubnik near Pleven. There are refineries at Bourgas (annual capacity 5m. tonnes) and Dolni Dubnik (7m. tonnes). Crude oil production (2000) was 42,000 tonnes; natural gas (2000), 15m. cu. metres.

Minerals. Production in 2000: lignite, 26·31m. tonnes; iron ore (1999), 466,000 tonnes; coal, 118,000 tonnes. There are also deposits of gold, silver and copper.

Agriculture. In 2002 the total area of land in agricultural use was 5,796,208 ha (52·2% of the overall territory of the country); there were 3,080,829 ha under crops (including 2,217,560 ha for cereals), 2,502,723 ha of permanent grassland (including meadows and orchards), and 212,656 ha of perennial plantations. By 1999, 60% of Bulgarian households worked a plot of land, often on a part-time basis. In 2000 around 25% of the labour force was employed in agriculture. There were 25,000 tractors in use in 2001 and 5,500 harvester-threshers.

Legislation of 1991 and 1992 provided for the redistribution of collectivized land to its former owners up to 30 ha. In 2002 there were 37,836 registered agricultural producers, including 33,633 individual farmers.

Production in 2000 (in 1,000 tonnes): wheat, 2,800; maize, 937; barley, 684; potatoes, 566; grapes, 450; tomatoes, 446; sunflower seeds, 438; melons and watermelons, 384; chillies and green peppers, 207; cucumbers and gherkins, 170; cabbages, 140. Bulgaria is a leading producer of attar of roses (rose oil). Bulgaria produced 139,000 tonnes of wine in 2000. Other products (in 1,000 tonnes) in 2000: meat, 445; cow milk, 1,200; goat milk, 200; sheep milk, 106; eggs, 90.

Livestock (2000, in 1,000): cattle, 682; sheep, 2,549; pigs, 1,512; goats, 1,046; poultry, 14,000.

Forestry. In 2000 forests covered 3·69m. ha, or 33·4% of the total land area; natural forest covered 2·72m. ha and forest plantations 0·97m. ha. Timber production in 2001 totalled 3·99m. cu. metres.

Fisheries. In 2001 total catch was 6,530 tonnes, mainly from sea fishing. As recently as 1988 the catch amounted to 106,000 tonnes.

INDUSTRY

In 1996 there were 342,261 registered economic units. Units by ownership: state, 9,682; municipal, 9,820; joint-stock companies, 3,588; co-operatives, 5,410; social organizations, 6,306; associations, 2,483; foreign ventures, 9,005; resident, 307,448. Industrial gross output rose by 0·7% in real terms in 2001 and 2·6% in 2002.

Output in 1,000 tonnes: cement (2001), 2,088; crude steel (2000), 2,023; distillate fuel oil (2000), 1,934; nitrogenous fertilizers (1997), 1,846; rolled steel (2000), 1,455; residual fuel oil (2000), 1,127; pig iron (2002), 1,100; petrol (2000), 1,017; sulphuric acid (2001), 620; paper (2002), 171. Production of other products: cotton (1997), 98m. sq. metres; woven wool (1997), 17m. sq. metres; 26·7bn. cigarettes (2001); 145,000 refrigerators (2001).

Labour. There is a 42½-hour five-day working week. The average wage in 2000 was 225 new leva per month. In 2001 the labour force numbered 3,412,600. A total of 2,940,300 persons were in employment in 2001 (excluding the armed forces), with the leading areas of activity as follows: agriculture, fishing, forestry and hunting, 774,100; manufacturing, 591,800; wholesale and retail trade/repair of motor vehicles, motorcycles and personal and household goods, 355,200; transport, storage and communications, 214,200; and health and social work, 138,300. Unemployment was 11·7% in Sept. 2004, the lowest rate in five years.

Trade Unions. The former official Central Council of Trade Unions reconstituted itself in 1990 as the Confederation of Independent Trade Unions; in 2003 it had 390,000 members. An independent white-collar trade union movement, Podkrepa, was formed in 1989; there were an estimated 109,000 members in 2003.

INTERNATIONAL TRADE

Legislation in force as of Feb. 1992 abolished restrictions imposed in 1990 on the repatriation of profits and allows foreign nationals to own and set up companies in Bulgaria. Western share participation in joint ventures may exceed 50%. Total foreign debt was US$10,462m. in 2002.

Imports and Exports. Imports and exports (f.o.b.) for calendar years in US$1m.:

	1998	*1999*	*2000*	*2001*	*2002*
Imports	4,574·2	5,087·4	6,000·1	6,693·3	7,286·6
Exports	4,193·5	4,006·4	4,824·6	5,113·0	5,692·1

Leading export commodities are non-precious metals and articles, textile materials and articles, mineral products and chemical industry produce. Leading import commodities are mineral products, machinery and apparatus, electrical equipment and parts, textile materials and articles, and transportation facilities.

Main export markets in 2001: Italy, 15·0%; Germany, 9·6%; Greece, 8·8%; Turkey, 8·1%; Belgium, 5·6%; France, 5·6%. Leading import suppliers: Russia, 19·9%; Germany, 15·3%; Italy, 9·6%; Turkey, 3·8%; Ukraine, 3·2%; USA, 2·6%. Trade with the EU has been steadily growing, with exports to the EU increasing from 39% of all exports in 1996 to 56% in 2000, and imports from the EU rising from 35% of the total in 1996 to 51% in 2000.

COMMUNICATIONS

Roads. In 2002 Bulgaria had 37,077 km of roads, including 328 km of motorways and 2,991 km of main roads. In 2002 there were 2,254,222 passenger cars (287·0 per 1,000 inhabitants), 262,641 trucks and vans, 44,255 buses and coaches, and 220,296 motorcycles and mopeds. In 2000 public transport totalled 8·60bn. passenger-km. There were 6,886 road accidents in 2000 with 1,012 fatalities.

Rail. In 2000 there were 4,320 km of 1,435 mm gauge railway (2,744 km electrified). Passenger-km travelled in 2000 came to 3·47bn. and freight tonne-km to 5·54bn.

There is a tramway and a metro in Sofia.

Civil Aviation. There is an international airport at Sofia (Vrazhdebna), which handled 1,128,000 passengers (1,049,000 on international flights) and 9,400 tonnes of freight in 2000. The bankrupt former state-owned Balkan Bulgarian Airlines was replaced by Balkan Air Tour in 2002 as the new national flag carrier. In 2003 Balkan Air Tour operated direct services to Berlin, Brussels, Budapest, Copenhagen, Frankfurt, Lisbon, London, Madrid, Moscow, Paris, Prague, Rome, Stockholm, Tel Aviv, Vienna, Warsaw and Zürich. The independent Hemus Air operated services in 2003 to Athens, Beirut, Bucharest, Damascus, Dubai, Larnaca, Tirana and Tripoli. In 1999 Balkan Bulgarian Airlines flew 18·5m. km, carrying 695,400 passengers (627,400 on international flights).

Shipping. In 2002 the merchant fleet totalled 889,000 GRT, including oil tankers 114,000 GRT. Bourgas is a fishing and oil-port. Varna is the other important port. There is a rail ferry between Varna and Ilitchovsk (Ukraine). In 2002, 15·5m. tonnes of cargo were carried on international and coastal sea traffic; 60,000 passengers and 1·6m tonnes of freight were carried on inland waterways.

Telecommunications. The Bulgarian Telecommunications Company was privatized in Jan. 2004. Only about 15% of local exchanges had been digitalized by early 1999. There were 4,463,900 telephone subscribers in 2001 (550·6 per 1,000 inhabitants) and 405,000 PCs in use in 2002 (51·9 per 1,000 persons). Bulgaria had 630,000 Internet users in 2002. There were 2,597,500 mobile phone subscribers in 2002 and 1,500 fax machines in 1997.

Postal Services. In 1998 there were 3,303 post offices.

SOCIAL INSTITUTIONS

Justice. A law of Nov. 1982 provides for the election (and recall) of all judges by the National Assembly. There are a Supreme Court, 28 provincial courts (including Sofia) and regional courts. Jurors are elected at the local government elections. The Prosecutor General and judges are elected by the Supreme Judicial Council established in 1992.

The population in penal institutions in Sept. 2003 was 10,500 (134 per 100,000 of national population). The maximum term of imprisonment is 20 years. The death penalty was abolished for all crimes in 1998.

Religion. 'The traditional church of the Bulgarian people' (as it is officially described) is that of the Eastern Orthodox Church. It was disestablished under the 1947 Constitution. In 1953 the Bulgarian Patriarchate was revived. The Patriarch is Maksim (enthroned 1971). The seat of the Patriarch is at Sofia. There are 11 dioceses (each under a Metropolitan), ten bishops, 2,600 parishes, 1,500 priests, 120 monasteries (with about 400 monks and nuns), 3,700 churches and chapels, one seminary and one theological college.

In 2002 there were some 80,000 Roman Catholics with 51 priests and 54 parishes in three bishoprics. At the 2001 census, 6,638,870 Christians were recorded and 966,978 Muslims (Pomaks). There is a Chief Mufti elected by regional muftis.

Education. Adult literacy rate in 2001 was 98·5% (male, 99·0%; female, 98·0%). Education is free, and compulsory for children between the ages of 7 and 16.

In 2003–04 there were 6,648 educational establishments: 3,278 kindergartens, 2,823 general and special schools, 496 vocational schools and 51 higher education institutions. There were 122,986 teaching staff (22,532 in higher education) and 1,451,284 pupils and students (228,468 in higher education); 114 schools (with 8,721 pupils) and 14 higher institutions (with 32,802 students) were private. There are eight state universities, four private universities and several specialized higher education institutions, some of which have university status. The Academy of Sciences was founded in 1869.

In 2001–02 total expenditure on education came to 3·6% of GNP.

Health. All medical services are free. Private medical services were authorized in Jan. 1991. In 1998 there were 288 hospitals with 104 beds per 10,000 inhabitants.

There were 28,823 physicians, 5,324 dentists, 47,434 nurses, 1,230 pharmacists and 5,923 midwives in 1998. In 2000 health spending represented 4·3% of GDP.

Welfare. In 2002 the official retirement age was 61 years 6 months (men) and 56 years 6 months (women). However, the age level is to be increased gradually until 2009 when the retirement ages will be 63 (men) and 60 (women). The minimum old-age pension is 115% of the social pension (44 leva a month).

The family allowance is 8·54 leva a month for each child below age 16 (or age 18 if the child attends secondary school).

Unemployment benefits are calculated as 60% of average earnings for the previous nine months.

CULTURE

World Heritage Sites. There are nine Bulgarian sites that appear on the UNESCO World Heritage List. They are (with year entered on list): Boyana Church (1979); Madara Rider (1979), an 8th century sculpture carved into a rockface; Rock-hewn Churches of Ivanovo (1979); Thracian Tomb of Kazanlak (1979); Ancient City of Nessebar (1983); Srebarna Nature Reserve (1983); Pirin National Park (1983); Rila Monastery (1983); Thracian tomb of Sveshtari (1985).

Broadcasting. Broadcasting is under the aegis of the state-controlled Bulgarian National Radio and Bulgarian Television. There are four national and six regional radio programmes. There are two TV programmes; Bulgaria also receives transmissions from the French satellite channel TV5. There are two independent TV channels—Nova TV (New Television) and 7 Dni (7 Days). Colour programmes are by the SECAM V system. Radio receivers in 1997, 4·5m.; televisions in 2000, 3·7m.

Press. In 2000 there were 43 daily newspapers with a combined daily circulation of 1·40m., giving a rate of 173 per 1,000 persons. A total of 4,971 book titles were published in 1999, including 1,803 in literature, 1,029 in social sciences and 715 in applied sciences.

Tourism. There were 3,531,567 foreign tourists in 2003. Most arrived from Serbia and Montenegro, Macedonia, Greece and Germany. In 2003, 903,133 Bulgarians made visits abroad as tourists. Earnings from tourism were US$963m. in 2000.

DIPLOMATIC REPRESENTATIVES

Of Bulgaria in the United Kingdom (186–188 Queen's Gate, London, SW7 5HL)
Ambassador: Valentin Dobrev.

Of the United Kingdom in Bulgaria (9 Moskovska St., Sofia 1000)
Ambassador: Jeremy Hill.

Of Bulgaria in the USA (1621 22nd St., NW, Washington, D.C., 20008)
Ambassador: Elena Borislavova Poptodorova.

Of the USA in Bulgaria (16 Kozyak St., 1407 Sofia)
Ambassador: James Pardew.

Of Bulgaria to the United Nations
Ambassador: Stefan Tafrov.

Of Bulgaria to the European Union
Ambassador: Stanislav Daskalov.

FURTHER READING

Central Statistical Office. *Statisticheski Godishnik.—Statisticheski Spravochnik* (annual).—*Statistical Reference Book of Republic of Bulgaria* (annual).

Crampton, Richard J., *A Concise History of Bulgaria*. CUP, 1997

Melone, A., *Creating Parliamentary Government: The Transition to Democracy in Bulgaria*. Ohio State Univ. Press, 1998

National statistical office: Natsionalen Statisticheski Institut, Sofia. *President:* Alexander Hadjiiski.
Website: http://www.nsi.bg/

BURKINA FASO

République Démocratique du Burkina Faso

Capital: Ouagadougou
Population projection, 2010: 16·02m.
GDP per capita, 2002: (PPP$) 1,100
HDI/world rank: 0·302/175

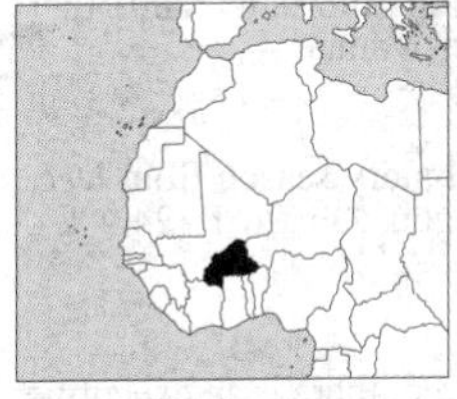

KEY HISTORICAL EVENTS

Formerly known as Upper Volta, the country's name was changed in 1984 to Burkina Faso, meaning 'the land of honest men'. The area it covers was settled by farming communities until their invasion by the Mossi people in the 11th century, who successfully resisted Islamic crusades and attacks by neighbouring empires for seven centuries until conquered by the French between 1895 and 1903.

France made Upper Volta a separate colony in 1919, only to abolish it as such in 1932, dividing its territory between the Ivory Coast (now Côte d'Ivoire), French Sudan (now Mali) and Niger. In 1947 the territory of Upper Volta was reconstituted. Upper Volta remained a desperately poor country often hit by drought, particularly in 1972–74 and again in 1982–84. The military has held power for most of the period after independence. In Aug. 1983 a coup brought to power Capt. Thomas Sankara, a leading radical, who headed a left-wing regime. Sankara was overthrown and killed in a coup on 15 Oct. 1987, the fifth since 1960, led by his friend Capt. Blaise Compaoré.

TERRITORY AND POPULATION

Burkina Faso is bounded in the north and west by Mali, east by Niger and south by Benin, Togo, Ghana and Côte d'Ivoire. Area: 267,950 sq. km; 1996 census population, 10,312,609 (83·1% rural in 2001), giving a density of 38·4 per sq. km. 2002 estimate: 12,662,000.

The UN gives a projected population for 2010 of 16·02m.

The largest cities in 1996 were Ouagadougou, the capital (709,736), Bobo-Dioulasso (309,711), Koudougou (72,490), Ouahigouya (52,193), Banfora (49,724), Pouytenga (35,720) and Kaya (33,958).

Areas and populations of the 45 provinces:

Province	*Sq. km*	*Population 1998*	*Province*	*Sq. km*	*Population 1998*
Balé	4,595	149,925	Mouhoun	6,668	239,063
Bam	4,084	216,098	Nahouri	3,754	131,557
Banwa	5,882	204,386	Namentenga	6,464	275,226
Bazéga	3,963	214,367	Nayala	3,919	143,454
Bougouriba	2,812	73,538	Noumbiel	2,736	51,424
Boulgou	6,692	411,418	Oubritenga	2,778	204,935
Boulkiemdé	4,269	423,779	Oudalan	9,797	110,185
Comoé	15,277	243,082	Passoré	3,867	281,317
Ganzourgou	4,178	289,464	Poni	7,365	201,371
Gnagna	8,468	357,097	Sanguié	5,178	236,740
Gourma	11,117	298,801	Sanmatenga	9,281	497,188
Houet	11,568	354,417	Séno	6,863	214,436
Ioba	3,289	163,874	Sissili	7,136	147,842
Kadiogo	2,805	189,813	Soum	12,222	263,028
Kénédougou	8,137	196,236	Sourou	5,765	195,724
Komondjari	5,048	54,487	Tapoa	14,594	250,798
Kompienga	7,029	44,190	Tuy	5,639	165,072
Kossi	7,324	233,129	Yagha	6,468	127,156
Koulpélogo	2,497	192,861	Yatenga	6,990	421,975
Kouritenga	2,622	256,957	Ziro	5,139	11,680
Kourwéogo	1,588	118,239	Zondoma	1,758	134,590
Léraba	3,129	94,377	Zoundwéogo	3,604	190,686
Loroum	3,592	113,153			

The principal ethnic groups are the Mossi (49%), Fulani (8%), Mandé (7%), Bobo (7%), Gourmantché (7%), Gourounsi (7%), Bissa (4%), Lobi-Dagari (4%) and Sénoufo (2%).

French is the official language.

SOCIAL STATISTICS

Births, 1996, 499,000; deaths, 212,000. Birth rate (1996) per 1,000 population, 47·0; death, 20·0. Annual population growth rate, 1992–2002, 2·9%. Expectation of life at birth, 2001, 46·4 years for females and 45·0 for males. Infant mortality, 2001 (per 1,000 live births), 104. Fertility rate, 2001, 6·8 children per woman.

CLIMATE

A tropical climate with a wet season from May to Nov. and a dry season from Dec. to April. Rainfall decreases from south to north. Ouagadougou, Jan. 76°F (24·4°C), July 83°F (28·3°C). Annual rainfall 36" (894 mm).

CONSTITUTION AND GOVERNMENT

At a referendum in June 1991 a new constitution was approved; there is an executive presidency. Parliament consists of the 111-member *National Assembly*, elected by universal suffrage. The *Chamber of Representatives*, a consultative body representing social, religious, professional and political organizations, was abolished in 2002. There is also an *Economic and Social Council*. In April 2000 parliament passed a law reducing presidential terms from seven to five years, with a maximum of two terms. The new law will not affect President Blaise Compaoré's current seven-year term, which expires in Nov. 2005.

National Anthem. 'Contre la férule humiliante' ('Against the shameful fetters'); words by T. Sankara, tune anonymous.

RECENT ELECTIONS

At the presidential elections of 15 Nov. 1998 Blaise Compaoré was re-elected by 87·5% of votes cast against two other candidates.

Parliamentary elections were held on 5 May 2002. The Congress for Democracy and Progress (CDP) won 57 out of 111 seats, the Alliance for Democracy and the Federation-African Democratic Rally (ADF-RDA) 17, and the Party for Democracy and Progress (PDP) 10. Turn-out was 64·1%.

Presidential elections are scheduled to take place in Nov. 2005.

CURRENT ADMINISTRATION

President: Capt. Blaise Compaoré; b. 1951 (CDP; in office since 1987, most recently re-elected on 15 Nov. 1998).

In March 2005 the government comprised:

Prime Minister: Paramanga Ernest Yonli; b. 1956 (CDP; sworn in 7 Nov. 2000).

Minister of State and Minister for Foreign Affairs and Regional Co-operation: Youssouf Ouédraogo. *Minister of Agriculture, Water and Water Resources:* Salif Diallo. *Animal Resources:* Alphonse Bonou. *Civil Service and State Reform:* Lassané Sawadogo. *Arts, Tourism and Culture:* Mahamoudou Ouédraogo. *Defence:* Yéro Boli. *Economy and Development:* Seydou Bouda. *Employment, Labour and Youth:* Alain Lodovic Tou. *Energy and Mines:* Abdoulaye Abdoulkader Cissé. *Environment:* Laurent Sédogo. *Finance and Budget:* Jean-Baptiste Compaoré. *Health:* Bédouma Alain Yoda. *Trade, Industry and Crafts:* Bénoît Ouattara. *Justice and Keeper of the Seals:* Boureima Badini. *Human Rights Promotion:* Monique Ilboudo. *Basic Education and Mass Literacy:* Mathieu Ouédraogo. *Infrastructure, Housing and Transport:* Hippolyte Lingani. *Information:* Joseph Kahoun. *Post and Telecommunications:* Justin Tiéba Thiombiano. *Relations with Parliament:* Adama Fofana. *Security:* Djibrill Yipéné Bassolé. *Secondary and Higher Education and Scientific Research:* Laya Sawadogo. *Social Affairs and National Solidarity:* Mariam Lamizana. *Territorial Administration and Decentralization:* Moumouni Fabré. *Sports and Leisure:* Tioundoum Sessouma. *Promotion of Women:* Marie Gisèle Guigma.

Office of the Prime Minister: http://www.primature.gov.bf

DEFENCE

There are six military regions. All forces form part of the Army. Defence expenditure totalled US$55m. in 2003 (US$5 per capita), representing 1·3% of GDP.

Army. Strength (2002), 5,800 with a paramilitary Gendarmerie of 4,200. In addition there is a People's Militia of 45,000.

Air Force. Personnel total (2002), 200 with five combat aircraft.

INTERNATIONAL RELATIONS

Burkina Faso is a member of the UN, WTO, the African Union, African Development Bank, ECOWAS, IOM, OIC, Islamic Development Bank, International Organization of the Francophonie and is an ACP member state of the ACP-EU relationship.

ECONOMY

In 2002 agriculture accounted for 31·0% of GDP, industry 18·0% and services 50·9%.

Currency. The unit of currency is the *franc CFA* (XOF) with a parity of 655·957 francs CFA to one euro. Foreign exchange reserves were US$260m. in May 2002 and total money supply was 256,913m. francs CFA. Gold reserves were 11,000 troy oz in June 2000. There was deflation in 2000, of 0·3%, but then inflation in 2001 and 2002, of 4·9% and 2·3% respectively.

Budget. Total revenues in 2001 were 376·3bn. francs CFA and expenditures 457·5bn. francs CFA.

Performance. Real GDP growth was 4·6% in both 2001 and 2002. Total GDP was US$4·2bn. in 2003.

Banking and Finance. The bank of issue which functions as the central bank is the regional Central Bank of West African States (BCEAO; *Governor*, Charles Konan Banny). There are seven other banks and three credit institutions. There is a stock exchange in Ouagadougou.

ENERGY AND NATURAL RESOURCES

Environment. Burkina Faso's carbon dioxide emissions from the consumption and flaring of fossil fuels in 2002 were the equivalent of 0·1 tonnes per capita.

Electricity. Production of electricity (2000) was about 284m. kWh. There are five thermal power stations with a total capacity in 2000 of 48,000 kW. Hydro-electric capacity in 2000 was 30,000 kW, giving a total installed capacity of 78,000 kW in 2000. Consumption per capita was an estimated 25 kWh in 2000.

Minerals. There are deposits of manganese, zinc, limestone, phosphate and diamonds. Gold production was 886 kg in 1999.

Agriculture. In 2001 there were 3·95m. ha of arable land and 52,000 ha of permanent crops. 25,000 ha were irrigated in 2001. There were 1,995 tractors in 2001. The agricultural population in 2002 totalled 10·45m., of whom 5·47m. were economically active. Production (2000, in 1,000 tonnes): sorghum, 1,100; millet, 900; sugarcane, 400; maize, 350; seed cotton, 300; groundnuts, 205; cottonseed, 175; cotton lint, 125; rice, 88.

Livestock (2000): cattle, 4·70m.; sheep, 6·59m.; goats, 8·40m.; pigs, 610,000; asses, 491,000; chickens, 22m. Livestock products, 2000 (in 1,000 tonnes): beef and veal, 52; goat meat, 22; poultry meat, 26; cow's milk, 163; eggs, 18.

Forestry. In 2000 forests covered 7,089,000 ha, or 25·9% of the total land area. Timber production in 2001 was 11·84m. cu. metres.

Fisheries. In 2001 total catch was approximately 8,500 tonnes, exclusively from inland waters. There is some fish farming.

INDUSTRY

In 2002 manufacturing contributed 14·5% of GDP, primarily food-processing and textiles. Industry is underdeveloped and employs only 1% of the workforce. The country's manufactures are mainly restricted to basic consumer goods and processed foods. Output of major products, in 1,000 tonnes: vegetable oil (2000), 31; sugar (1999), 30; soap (1999), 13; flour (2002), 10; beer (2003), 55·0m. litres; printed fabric (2000), 275,000 sq. metres.

Labour. In 1996 the labour force was 5,419,000 (53% males). Over 90% of the economically active population are engaged in agriculture, fishing and forestry.

Trade Unions. There were six federations in 1999: Confédération Générale de Travailleurs de Burkina (CGTB), Union syndicale des travailleurs du Burkina (USTB), Union générale des travailleurs du Burkina (UGTB), Confédération syndicale Burkinabe (CSB), Confédération nationale des travailleurs Burkinabe (CNTB) and Organisation nationale des syndicats libres (ONSL).

INTERNATIONAL TRADE

Foreign debt was US$1,580m. in 2002.

Imports and Exports. In 2001 imports totalled US$504·2m. and exports US$228·0m. Principal import suppliers, 2000: Côte d'Ivoire, 22·7%; France, 22·4%; Japan, 5·6%; China, 4·1%; USA, 3·7%. Principal export markets: France, 21·6%; Côte d'Ivoire, 11·5%; Belgium-Luxembourg, 8·4%; Italy, 7·7%; Singapore, 5·6%. Cotton is the main export, accounting for about half of the country's export income.

COMMUNICATIONS

Roads. The road system comprised an estimated 12,100 km in 1996, of which 5,720 km were national, 3,030 km regional and 3,290 km other roads. Only 1,900 km are asphalted. There were an estimated 56,430 vehicles in use in 1996, including 38,220 passenger cars (3·6 per 1,000 inhabitants).

Rail. The railway from Abidjan in Côte d'Ivoire to Kaya (622 km of metre gauge within Burkina Faso) is operated by the mixed public-private company Sitarail, a concessionaire to both governments. The railways carried 0·6m. passengers and 0·2m. tonnes of freight in 1993.

Civil Aviation. The international airports are Ouagadougou (which handled 188,000 passengers in 2000) and Bobo-Dioulasso. The national carrier is Air Burkina (66% state-owned), which in 2003 flew to Abidjan, Bamako, Cotonou, Dakar, Lomé and Niamey in addition to operating on domestic routes. In 1999 scheduled airline traffic of Burkina Faso-based carriers flew 3·9m. km, carrying 147,000 passengers (132,000 on international flights).

Telecommunications. There were 154,200 telephone subscribers in 2002, equivalent to 12·9 per 1,000 inhabitants, of which mobile phone subscribers numbered 89,900. In 2002, 19,000 PCs were in use (1·6 per 1,000 persons). There were 25,000 Internet users in 2002.

Postal Services. There were 85 post offices in 1998.

SOCIAL INSTITUTIONS

Justice. Civilian courts replaced revolutionary tribunals in 1993. A law passed in April 2000 split the supreme court into four separate entities—a constitutional court, an appeal court, a council of state and a government audit office.

Religion. In 2001 there were 5·96m. Muslims and 2·04m. Christians (mainly Roman Catholic). Many of the remaining population follow traditional animist religions.

Education. In 2001 adult literacy was 24·8% (male, 34·9%; female, 14·9%), the second lowest in the world after Niger. The 1994–96 development programme established an adult literacy campaign, and centres for the education of 10–15-year-old non-school-attenders. In 2000–01 there were 19,007 teachers and 901,321 pupils in primary schools. During the period 1990–95 only 24% of females of primary school age were enrolled in school. In 2000–01 there were 199,278 pupils and 6,432 teachers in secondary schools, and in 2001–02 there were 15,535 students in higher education. There is a university at Ouagadougou, with over 8,000 students.

Health. In 1993 there were 78 hospitals with five beds per 10,000 inhabitants.

CULTURE

Broadcasting. Radio and television services (colour by NTSC) are provided by the state-controlled Radiodiffusion-Télévision Burkina. Radio Bobo is a regional service and there is a commercial radio station. In 2000 there were 428,000 radio receivers and in 2001 there were 150,000 television receivers.

Press. There were four dailies (one government-owned) with a combined circulation of 14,000 in 1996. There were nine non-dailies and periodicals in 1995.

Tourism. In 2001 there were 128,000 foreign tourists. Receipts totalled US$34m.

DIPLOMATIC REPRESENTATIVES

Of Burkina Faso in the United Kingdom
Ambassador: Kadré Désiré Ouedraogo (resides at Brussels).
Honorary Consul: Stuart Singer (5 Cinnamon Row, Plantation Wharf, London SW11 3TW).

Of the United Kingdom in Burkina Faso
Ambassador: David Coates (resides at Abidjan, Côte d'Ivoire).

Of Burkina Faso in the USA (2340 Massachusetts Ave., NW, Washington, D.C., 20008)
Ambassador: Tertius Zongo.

Of the USA in Burkina Faso (602 avenue Raoul Follereau, 01 BP 35, Ouagadougou 01)
Ambassador: J. Anthony Holmes.

Of Burkina Faso to the United Nations
Ambassador: Michel Kafando.

Of Burkina Faso to the European Union
Ambassador: Kadré Désiré Ouedraogo.

FURTHER READING

Decalo, Samuel, *Burkina Faso.* [Bibliography] ABC-Clio, Oxford and Santa Barbara (CA), 1994

Nnaji, B. O., *Blaise Compaoré: Architect of the Burkina Faso Revolution.* Lagos, 1991

National statistical office: Institut National de la Statistique et de la Démographie (INSD), 555 Boulevard de l'Indépendance, 01 BP 374, Ouagadougou.
Website (French only): http://www.insd.bf

BURUNDI

Republika y'Uburundi

Capital: Bujumbura
Population projection, 2010: 8·63m.
GDP per capita, 2002: (PPP$) 630
HDI/world rank: 0·339/173

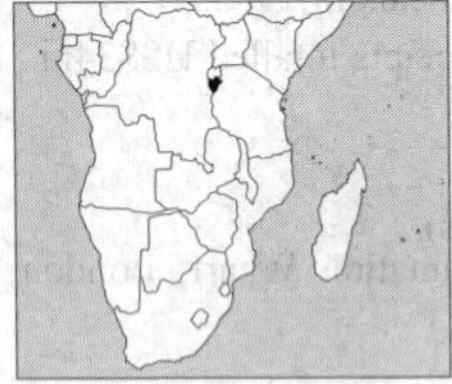

KEY HISTORICAL EVENTS

From 1890 Burundi was part of German East Africa and from 1919 part of Ruanda-Urundi administered by Belgium as a League of Nations mandate. Internal self-government was granted on 1 Jan. 1962, followed by independence on 1 July 1962. In April 1972 fighting broke out between rebels from both Burundi and neighbouring countries and the ruling Tutsi, apparently with the intention of destroying the Tutsi hegemony. Up to 120,000 died. On 1 Nov. 1976 President Micombero was deposed by the Army, as was President Bagaza on 3 Sept. 1987. Pierre Buyoya assumed the presidency on 1 Oct. 1987.

On 1 June 1993 President Buyoya was defeated in elections by Melchior Ndadaye, who thus became the country's first elected president and the first Hutu president, but on 21 Oct. President Ndadaye and six ministers were killed in an attempted military coup. A wave of Tutsi-Hutu massacres broke out, costing thousands of lives. On 6 April 1994 the new president, Cyprien Ntaryamira, was also killed, possibly assassinated, together with the President of Rwanda.

On 25 July 1996 the army seized power, installing Maj. Pierre Buyoya, a Tutsi, as president for the second time. In June 1998 Maj. Buyoya drew up a settlement for a power-sharing transitional government and the replacement of the prime minister by two vice-presidents, one Hutu and one Tutsi. Extremists on both sides denounced the agreement. An attempted coup in April 2001 failed. In July 2001 it was agreed that a three-year transitional government should be installed with Pierre Buyoya as president and Domitien Ndayizeye, a Hutu, as vice-president for the first 18 months, after which the roles would be reversed. A further attempted coup shortly after the announcement of the agreement also failed, although fighting continued. A ceasefire accord was eventually signed in Dec. 2002 by the government and the Forces for the Defence of Democracy (FDD), the country's principal rebel movement. In Oct. 2003 the FDD and the government sealed a peace deal to end the civil war and put into practice the ceasefire agreed in 2002. More than 200,000 people have been killed in civil conflict since 1993.

TERRITORY AND POPULATION

Burundi is bounded in the north by Rwanda, east and south by Tanzania and west by the Democratic Republic of the Congo, and has an area (including inland water) of 27,834 sq. km (10,759 sq. miles). The population at the 1990 census was 5,292,793; estimate (2002) 6,688,000, giving a population density of 240 per sq. km. Only 9·3% of the population was urban in 2001 (90·7% rural).

The UN gives a projected population for 2010 of 8·63m.

There are 17 regions, all named after their chief towns. Area and population:

Region	*Area (in sq. km.)*	*Population (1999)*
Bubanza	1,089	289,060
Bujumbura Mairie	87	319,098
Bujumbura Rural	1,089	436,896
Bururi	2,465	437,931
Cankuzo	1,965	172,477
Cibitoke	1,636	385,438
Gitega	1,979	628,872
Karusi	1,457	384,187
Kayanza	1,233	458,815
Kirundo	1,703	502,171
Makamba	1,960	357,492
Muramvya	696	252,833
Muyinga	1,836	485,347

Region	Area (in sq. km.)	Population (1999)
Mwaro	840	229,013
Ngozi	1,474	601,382
Rutana	1,959	244,939
Ruyigi	2,339	304,567

The capital, Bujumbura, had an estimated population of 321,000 in 1999. The second largest town, Gitega, had a population in 1990 of 102,000.

There are three ethnic groups—Hutu (Bantu, forming over 83% of the total); Tutsi (Nilotic, less than 15%); Twa (pygmoids, less than 1%). The local language is Kirundi. French is also an official language. Kiswahili is spoken in the commercial centres.

SOCIAL STATISTICS

1998 estimates: births, 291,000; deaths, 116,000. Rates, 1998 estimates (per 1,000 population): birth, 47·2; death, 18·8. Life expectancy at birth, 2001, was 39·9 years for men and 41·0 years for women. Infant mortality, 2001, 114 per 1,000 live births. Annual population growth rate, 1992–2002, 1·3%; fertility rate, 2001, 6·8 children per woman.

CLIMATE

An equatorial climate, modified by altitude. The eastern plateau is generally cool, the easternmost savanna several degrees hotter. The wet seasons are from March to May and Sept. to Dec. Bujumbura, Jan. 73°F (22·8°C), July 73°F (22·8°C). Annual rainfall 33" (825 mm).

CONSTITUTION AND GOVERNMENT

The Constitution of 1981 provided for a one-party state. In Jan. 1991 the government of President Buyoya, leader of the sole party, the Party of Unity and National Progress (Uprona), proposed a new constitution which was approved by a referendum in March 1992 (with 89% of votes cast in favour), legalizing parties not based on ethnic group, region or religion and providing for presidential elections by direct universal suffrage. On 28 Feb. 2005 citizens voted overwhelmingly to adopt a new constitution laying the foundations for the end of a 12-year civil war.

Burundi has a bicameral legislature, consisting of the *Transitional National Assembly* of 185 members under the transitional government inaugurated on 1 Nov. 2001, with members elected by popular vote to serve five-year terms, and the *Senate* of 53 members.

In July 2001 agreement was reached on President Pierre Buyoya's presidency for the first 18 months of a three-year transition period of multi-ethnic broad-based government. In accordance with the terms of the Arusha peace accord, initially he was being assisted by Hutu Vice-President Domitien Ndayizeye, after which the roles were to be reversed for the second 18 months. The transitional government was established on 1 Nov. 2001. On 30 April 2003 Domitien Ndayizeye became president but Alphonse Marie Kadege, like Pierre Buyoya a Tutsi from the Party of Unity and National Progress, became the vice-president. In Oct. 2004 the transitional government was extended for a further six months, with elections scheduled for 22 April 2005. In April 2005 the transitional period was extended for a further four months and a new deadline of 19 Aug. 2005 set for elections. The success of the referendum in Feb. 2005 held under 1993 electoral laws was seen as proof that presidential elections need not be postponed further.

National Anthem. 'Uburundi Bwacu' ('Dear Burundi'); words by a committee, tune by M. Barengayabo.

RECENT ELECTIONS

At the presidential elections of 1 June 1993 the electorate was 2·36m.; turn-out was 97·18%. Melchior Ndadaye was elected against former President Buyoya and one other opponent with 64·79% of votes cast, and was sworn in on 10 July 1993.

Following Ndadaye's assassination Cyprien Ntaryamira was elected President by the National Assembly on 13 Jan. 1994 to serve out President Ndadaye's five-year term of office. After Ntaryamira's death and possible assassination, Sylvestre Ntibantunganya (b. 1956; Frodebu) was elected *President* by the National Assembly on 5 Sept. 1994 against five opponents.

At the parliamentary elections of 29 June 1993, 740 candidates stood representing 6 parties. The Front for Democracy in Burundi (Frodebu) gained 65 seats with 71·4% of votes cast, and Uprona, 16 with 21·4%. A number of Frodebu MPs elected in June 1993 have been killed in the meantime. 40 additional members were elected on 16 July 1998.

CURRENT ADMINISTRATION

On 30 April 2003 Domitien Ndayizeye (b. 1953; Frodebu) was installed as *President* in accordance with the agreement reached in July 2001 on a three-year transition period of multi-ethnic broad-based government. The *Vice-President* is Frédéric Ngenzebuhoro (Uprona).

In March 2005 the transitional government also comprised:

Minister of Foreign Affairs and Co-operation: Thérence Sinunguruza. *Interior:* Vacant. *Justice and Keeper of the Seals:* Didace Kiganahe. *National Defence:* Maj.-Gen. Vincent Niyungeko. *Planning, Development and Reconstruction:* Séraphine Wakana. *Communal Development:* Cyrille Hicintuka. *Reintegration and Resettlement of Displaced and Repatriated Persons:* Françoise Ngendahayo. *Peace Mobilization and National Reconciliation:* Antoine Butoyi. *Land Management, Environment and Tourism:* Albert Mbonerane. *Agriculture and Livestock:* Pierre Ndikumagenge. *Handicrafts, Professional Training and Adult Literacy:* Godefroid Hakizimana. *Employment and Social Security:* Dismas Nditabiriye. *Public Security:* Donatien Sindakira. *Civil Service:* Gaspard Kobako. *Finance:* Athanase Gahungu. *Commerce and Industry:* Thomas Minani. *National Education:* Salvator Nthabose. *Social Action and Promotion of Women:* Marie Goretti Nduwimana. *Youth, Sports and Culture:* Barnabé Muteragiranwa. *Health:* Jean Kamana. *Communication and Government Spokesperson:* Onésime Nduwimana. *Public Works and Equipment:* Salvator Ntahomenyereye. *Transport and Telecommunications:* Séverin Ndikumugongo. *Energy and Mining:* André Nkundikije. *Institutional Reforms, Human Rights and Parliamentary Relations:* Déogratias Rungwamihigo. *Minister of State in Charge of Good Governance:* Pierre Nkurunziza.

Government Website (French only): http://www.burundi-gov.org

DEFENCE

Armed forces personnel, including the Gendarmerie, totalled 45,500 in 2002.

Defence expenditure totalled US$42m. in 2003 (US$6 per capita), representing 7·2% of GDP.

Army. The Army had a strength (2002) of 40,000 including an air wing.

Air Force. There were 200 air wing personnel in 2002 with four combat aircraft and one combat helicopter.

INTERNATIONAL RELATIONS

Burundi is a member of the UN, WTO, the African Union, African Development Bank, COMESA, International Organization of the Francophonie, and is an ACP member state of the ACP-EU relationship.

ECONOMY

Agriculture accounted for 49·3% of GDP in 2002, industry 19·4% and services 31·3%.

Currency. The unit of currency is the *Burundi franc* (BIF) of 100 *centimes.* There was deflation in 2002 of 1·3%. In June 2002 gold reserves were 1,000 troy oz and foreign exchange reserves US$26m. Total money supply was 481,193m. Burundi francs in April 2002.

Budget. Government revenue and expenditure (in 1m. Burundi francs):

	1995	*1996*	*1997*	*1998*	*1999*
Revenue	48,397	46,401	46,253	66,333	72,047
Expenditure	76,403	75,405	80,800	98,061	105,181

Performance. In 2002 real GDP growth was 4·5%, following growth of 2·2% in 2001. Total GDP in 2003 was US$0·7bn.

Banking and Finance. The Bank of the Republic of Burundi is the central bank and bank of issue. Its *Governor* is Salvator Toyi. In 1999 it had deposits of 11·23bn.

Burundi francs. There are seven commercial banks, a development bank and a co-operative bank.

ENERGY AND NATURAL RESOURCES

Environment. Burundi's carbon dioxide emissions from the consumption and flaring of fossil fuels in 2002 were the equivalent of 0·1 tonnes per capita.

Electricity. Installed capacity was 44,000 kW in 2000. Production was about 128m. kWh in 2000. Consumption per capita in 2000 was 75 kWh.

Minerals. Gold is mined on a small scale. Deposits of nickel (280m. tonnes) and vanadium remain to be exploited. There are proven reserves of phosphates of 17·6m. tonnes.

Agriculture. The main economic activity is agriculture, which contributed 49% of GDP in 2002. In 2001, 0·90m. ha were arable and 0·36m. ha permanent crops. 74,000 ha were irrigated in 2001. There were 170 tractors in 2001. Beans, cassava, maize, sweet potatoes, groundnuts, peas, sorghum and bananas are grown according to the climate and the region.

The main cash crop is coffee, of which about 95% is arabica. It accounts for 90% of exports, and taxes and levies on coffee constitute a major source of revenue. A coffee board (OCIBU) manages the grading and export of the crop. Production (2000) 19,000 tonnes. The main agricultural crops (2000 production, in 1,000 tonnes) are bananas (1,514), sweet potatoes (687), cassava (657), dry beans (187), sugarcane (174), maize (118), taro (81), sorghum (61), rice (52), peas (30) and potatoes (24).

Livestock (2000): 550,000 goats, 390,000 cattle, 120,000 sheep, 50,000 pigs and 4m. chickens.

Forestry. Forests covered 94,000 ha, or 3·7% of the total land area, in 2000. Timber production in 2001 was 8·29m. cu. metres, the majority of it for fuel.

Fisheries. There is a small commercial fishing industry on Lake Tanganyika. In 2001 the total catch was 8,964 tonnes, exclusively from inland waters.

INDUSTRY

The industrial sector is underdeveloped, although a few firms manufacture consumer products, and some process cotton and coffee. In 2001 production of sugar totalled 26,000 tonnes. Other major products are beer (87·5m. litres in 2003), cigarettes (286m. units in 2000) and blankets (141,854 units in 2000).

Labour. In 1996 the labour force was 3,337,000 (51% males).

INTERNATIONAL TRADE

With Rwanda and the Democratic Republic of the Congo, Burundi forms part of the Economic Community of the Great Lakes. Foreign debt was US$1,204m. in 2002.

Imports and Exports. Imports and exports for calendar years in US$1m.:

	1998	*1999*	*2000*	*2001*	*2002*
Imports f.o.b.	123·5	97·3	107·9	108·3	104·0
Exports f.o.b.	64·0	55·0	49·1	39·2	31·0

Main exports are coffee, manufactures and tea. Main export markets, 1999: Belgium, 31%; Switzerland, 18%; UK, 14%. Main import suppliers, 1999: Belgium, 15%; Saudi Arabia, 13%; Italy, 12%.

COMMUNICATIONS

Roads. In 1999 there were 14,480 km of roads of which 7·1% were paved. An estimated 37,240 vehicles were in use in 1996, including 19,200 passenger cars (2·8 per 1,000 inhabitants).

Civil Aviation. There were direct flights to Addis Ababa, Douala, Entebbe/Kampala, Kigali and Nairobi in 2003. In 1998 scheduled airline traffic of Burundi-based carriers flew 800,000 km, carrying 12,000 passengers (all on international flights). Bujumbura International airport handled 52,257 passengers and 3,898 tonnes of freight in 2000.

Shipping. There are lake services from Bujumbura to Kigoma (Tanzania) and Kalémie (Democratic Republic of the Congo). The main route for exports and imports is via Kigoma, and thence by rail to Dar es Salaam.

Telecommunications. In 2002 there were 74,100 telephone subscribers (10·6 per 1,000 inhabitants), including 52,000 mobile phone subscribers. 5,000 PCs were in use in 2002 (0·7 per 1,000 persons). In 1996 there were 4,000 fax machines. The number of Internet users in 2002 was 8,400.

Postal Services. In 1998 there were 28 post offices, equivalent to one for every 225,000 persons (the lowest ratio of any country).

SOCIAL INSTITUTIONS

Justice. There is a Supreme Court, an appeal court and a court of first instance at Bujumbura, and provincial courts in each provincial capital.

The population in penal institutions in 2002 was 8,647 (129 per 100,000 of national population). The death penalty is in force.

Religion. In 2001 there were 4·05m. Roman Catholics with an archbishop and three bishops. About 3% of the population are Pentecostal, 1% Anglican and 1% Muslim, while the balance follow traditional tribal beliefs.

Education. Adult literacy rate was 49·2% in 2001 (56·9% among males and 42·0% among females). In 2000–01 there were 750,589 pupils in primary schools with 14,955 teachers and 113,427 pupils in secondary schools. In 2000–01 there were 6,289 students in higher education institutes with 507 teachers. In 1995–96 there were 3,750 students and 170 academic staff at the university.

In 2000–01 total expenditure on education came to 3·5% of GNP.

Health. In 1993 there were 354 doctors and 1,270 nurses. In 1996 there was less than one hospital bed per 10,000 inhabitants.

CULTURE

Broadcasting. Broadcasting is provided by the state-controlled *Radiodiffusion et Télévision du Burundi*. In 2000 there were 1·26m. radio receivers and in 2001 there were 200,000 TV (colour by SECAM V) receivers.

Press. There was (1996) one daily newspaper *(Le Renouveau)* with a circulation of 20,000.

Tourism. There were 30,000 foreign tourists in 2000. Receipts totalled US$1m.

DIPLOMATIC REPRESENTATIVES

Of Burundi in the United Kingdom (26 Armitage Road, London, NW11 8RD)
Ambassador: Ferdinand Nyabenda (resides at Brussels).

Of the United Kingdom in Burundi
Ambassador: Sue Hogwood, MBE (resides at Kigali, Rwanda).

Of Burundi in the USA (2233 Wisconsin Ave., NW 212, Washington, D.C., 20007)
Ambassador: Antoine Ntamobwa.

Of the USA in Burundi (PO Box 1720, Ave. des Etats-Unis, Bujumbura)
Ambassador: James Yellin.

Of Burundi to the United Nations
Ambassador: Marc Nteturuye.

Of Burundi to the European Union
Ambassador: Ferdinand Nyabenda.

FURTHER READING

Daniels, Morna, *Burundi.* [Bibliography] ABC-Clio, Oxford and Santa Barbara (CA), 1992
Lemarchand, R., *Burundi: Ethnic Conflict and Genocide.* CUP, 1996

National statistical office: Service des Etudes et Statistiques, Ministère du Plan, Bujumbura.

CAMBODIA

Preah Reach Ana Pak Kampuchea
(Kingdom of Cambodia)

Capital: Phnom Penh
Population projection, 2010: 16·61m.
GDP per capita, 2002: (PPP$) 2,060
HDI/world rank: 0·568/130

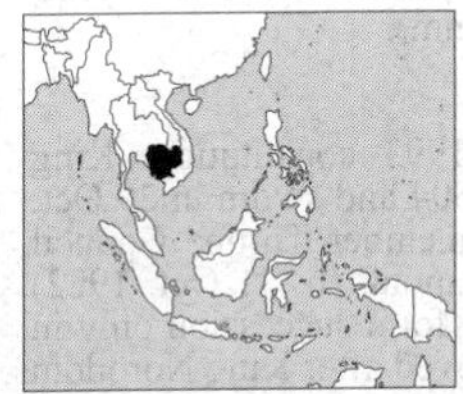

KEY HISTORICAL EVENTS

Cambodia was made a French protectorate in 1863. A nationalist movement began in the 1930s, and anti-French feeling strengthened in 1940–41 when the French submitted to Japanese demands for bases in Cambodia. Anti-French guerrillas, active from 1945, gave the impetus to a communist-led revolution. A fragile peace was established before Cambodia gained independence in 1953 but in 1967 the Khmer Rouge took up arms to support peasants against a rice tax. Their aim was to establish a communist rice-growing dynasty, a combination of Maoism and ancient xenophobic nationalism. From 1970 hostilities extended throughout most of the country involving US and North Vietnamese forces. During 1973 direct US and North Vietnamese participation came to an end, leaving a civil war which continued with large-scale fighting between the Khmer Republic, supported by US arms, and the United National Cambodian Front including 'Khmer Rouge' communists, supported by North Vietnam and China. After unsuccessful attempts to capture Phnom Penh in 1973 and 1974, the Khmer Rouge defeated the American backed leader Lon Nol in April 1975, when the remnants of the republican forces surrendered the city.

From 1975 the Khmer Rouge instituted a harsh and highly centralized regime. All cities and towns were forcibly evacuated and the citizens set to work in the fields. In 1978, in response to repeated border attacks, Vietnam invaded Cambodia. On 7 Jan. 1979 Phnom Penh was captured by the Vietnamese, and the Prime Minister, Pol Pot, fled. Over 2m. Cambodian lives were lost from 1975 to 1979. On 23 Oct. 1991 the warring factions and 19 countries signed an agreement in Paris instituting a ceasefire in Cambodia to be monitored by UN troops. Following the election of a constituent assembly in May 1993, a new constitution was promulgated on 23 Sept. 1993 restoring parliamentary monarchy. The Khmer Rouge continued hostilities, refusing to take part in the 1993 elections. By 1996 the Khmer Rouge had split into two warring factions. The leader of one, Ieng Sary, who had been sentenced to death in his absence for genocide, was pardoned by the King in Sept. 1996. In early Nov. 1996 Ieng Sary and some 4,000 of his forces threw in their lot with government forces.

In July 1997 Hun Sen, the second prime minister, engineered a coup which led to the exiling of first prime minister, Prince Norodom Ranariddh. However, on 30 March 1998 he returned with a Japanese-brokered plan to ensure 'fair and free' elections. These took place on 26 July 1998 against a background of violence and general intimidation. Hun Sen's Cambodian People's Party declared victory.

King Norodom Sihanouk abdicated in Oct. 2004 for health reasons and was succeeded by one of his sons, Norodom Sihamoni.

TERRITORY AND POPULATION

Cambodia is bounded in the north by Laos and Thailand, west by Thailand, east by Vietnam and south by the Gulf of Thailand. It has an area of about 181,035 sq. km (69,898 sq. miles).

Population, 11,437,656 (1998 census), of whom 5,926,248 were females. In 1994, 88·6% of the population were Khmer, 5·5% Vietnamese and 3·1% Chinese. In 2001, 82·6% of the population lived in rural areas. 2002 population estimate: 13,818,000.

The UN gives a projected population for 2010 of 16·61m.

The capital, Phnom Penh, had an estimated population of 938,000 in 1999. Other cities are Kompong Cham and Battambang. Ethnic composition, 1994: Khmer, 89%; Vietnamese, 5%; Chinese, 3%; Cham, 2%; Lao-Thai, 1%.

Khmer is the official language.

SOCIAL STATISTICS

1996 estimated births, 429,000; deaths, 156,000. Rates, 1996 estimates (per 1,000 population): births, 43·5; deaths, 15·8. Infant mortality, 2001 (per 1,000 live births), 97. Expectation of life in 2001 was 55·2 years for males and 59·4 for females. Annual population growth rate, 1992–2002, 2·8%. Fertility rate, 2001, 4·9 children per woman.

CLIMATE

A tropical climate, with high temperatures all the year. Phnom Penh, Jan. 78°F (25·6°C), July 84°F (28·9°C). Annual rainfall 52" (1,308 mm).

CONSTITUTION AND GOVERNMENT

A parliamentary monarchy was re-established by the 1993 constitution. King Norodom Sihamoni (b. 14 May 1953; appointed 14 Oct. 2004 and sworn in 29 Oct. 2004) was chosen in the first ever meeting of the nine-member Throne Council following the abdication of his father King Norodom Sihanouk (b. 31 Oct. 1922) on health grounds. As the Cambodian constitution allowed for a succession only in the event of the monarch's death, a new law had to be approved after King Norodom Sihanouk announced his abdication.

Cambodia has a bicameral legislature. There is a 122-member *National Assembly*, which on 14 June 1993 elected Prince Sihanouk head of state. On 21 Sept. it adopted a constitution (promulgated on 23 Sept.) by 113 votes to five with two abstentions making him monarch of a parliamentary democracy. Its members are elected by popular vote to serve five-year terms. There is also a 61-member *Senate*, established in 1999.

National Anthem. 'Nokoreach' ('Royal state'); words by Chuon Nat, tune adapted from a Cambodian folk song.

RECENT ELECTIONS

Parliamentary elections were held on 27 July 2003. Under the UN-brokered constitution, a party had to win two-thirds of seats in the 122-member Parliament in order to form a government. With an 81% turn-out, the Cambodian People's Party (KPK) won 68 seats with 47·5% of the vote, the royalist FUNCINPEC party of Prince Norodom Ranariddh won 24 seats with 20·5% and the party of the government critic Sam Rainsy won 31 seats with 22·1%.

CURRENT ADMINISTRATION

In June 2004, nearly a year after elections, the KPK and FUNCINPEC agreed to form a coalition government, including the Sam Rainsy Party.

In March 2005 the government comprised:

Prime Minister: Hun Sen; b. 1951 (KPK; sworn in on 30 Nov. 1998 and reappointed 14 July 2004).

Deputy Prime Ministers: Sar Kheng (also *Co-Minister for Internal Affairs*), Prince Norodom Sirivudh (also *Co-Minister for Internal Affairs*), Sok An (also *Minister in Charge of the Office of the Council of Ministers*), Lu Lay Sreng (also *Minister of Rural Development*), Gen. Tea Banh (also *Co-Minister for Defence*), Hor Nam Hong (also *Minister of Foreign Affairs and International Co-operation*), Nhiek Bun Chhay (also *Co-Minister for Defence*).

Minister of State for Economy and Finance: Keat Chhon. *Commerce:* Cham Prasidh. *Land Management, Urban Affairs and Construction:* Im Chhun Lim. *Parliamentary Affairs and Inspection:* Mem Som An. *Planning:* Chhay Than. *Environment:* Dr Mok Mareth. *Religious Affairs:* Khun Haing. *Education, Youth and Sports:* Kol Pheng. *Without Portfolio:* You Hockry, Hong Sun Huot, Khy Taing Lim, Veng Sereyvuth, Nhim Vanda, Tav Senghuor, Serey Kosal.

Minister of Agriculture, Forestry and Fisheries: Chan Sarun. *Industry, Mines and Energy:* Suy Sem. *Social Affairs, War Veterans and Youth Rehabilitation:* Ith Sam Heng. *Water Resources:* Lim Kean Hor. *Information:* Khieu Kanharith. *Justice:* Ang Vong Vathana. *Post and Telecommunications:* So Khun. *Health:* Nuth Sokhom. *Public Works and Transport:* Sun Chanthol. *Culture:* Prince Sisowath Panara Sirivudh. *Tourism:* Lay Prohas. *Women's Affairs:* Ing Kantha Phavi. *Labour and Vocational Training:* Nhep Bun Chin.

Government Website: http://www.camnet.com.kh/ocm

DEFENCE

The King is C.-in-C. of the armed forces. Defence expenditure in 2003 totalled US$68m. (US$5 per capita), representing 1·7% of GDP.

Army. Strength (2002) 75,000. There are also provincial forces numbering some 45,000 and paramilitary local forces organized at village level.

Navy. Naval personnel in 2002 totalled about 3,000 including a naval infantry of 1,500.

Air Force. Aviation operations were resumed in 1988 under the aegis of the Army. Personnel (2002), 2,000. There are 24 combat aircraft but serviceability is in doubt.

INTERNATIONAL RELATIONS

Cambodia is a member of the UN, WTO, Asian Development Bank, ASEAN, Mekong Group, IOM and the International Organization of the Francophonie.

ECONOMY

Agriculture accounted for 35·6% of GDP in 2002, industry 28·0% and services 36·4%.

Currency. The unit of currency is the *riel* (KHR) of 100 *sen*. Foreign exchange reserves were US$718m. in June 2002. Total money supply in May 2002 was 713,831m. riels. Inflation in 2002 was 3·3%.

Budget. In 2001 revenues were 1,520bn. riels and expenditures 2,329bn. riels.

Performance. Real GDP growth was 6·3% in 2001 and 5·5% in 2002. Total GDP in 2003 was US$4·3bn.

Banking and Finance. The National Bank of Cambodia (*Governor,* Chea Chanto) is the bank of issue. In 2001 there were operating: one state-owned bank; three specialized banks; 12 locally-incorporated private banks; and five foreign banks. In 2001, 11 banks were closed for failing to comply with new banking legislation.

ENERGY AND NATURAL RESOURCES

Electricity. Installed capacity was 35,000 kW in 2000. Production (2000) was around 229m. kWh. Consumption per capita in 2000 was an estimated 17 kWh. A long-term plan for hydro-electricity has been issued by the government.

Water. In 1995, 65% of the urban and 26% of the rural population had access to safe water.

Minerals. There are phosphates and high-grade iron-ore deposits. Some small-scale gold panning and gem (mainly zircon) mining is carried out.

Agriculture. The majority of the population is engaged in agriculture, fishing or forestry. Before the spread of war, the high productivity provided for a low but well-fed standard of living for the peasant farmers, the majority of whom owned the land they worked before agriculture was collectivized. A relatively small proportion of the food production entered the cash economy. The war and unwise pricing policies led to a disastrous reduction in production, so much so that the country became a net importer of rice. Private ownership of land was restored by the 1989 Constitution. In 2001 there were 3·70m. ha of arable land and 107,000 ha of permanent crops.

A crop of 3·76m. tonnes of rice was produced in 2000. Production of other crops, 2000 (in 1,000 tonnes): bananas, 147; sugarcane, 140; maize, 95; cassava, 68; oranges, 63; coconuts, 56.

Livestock (2000): cattle, 3·0m.; pigs, 2·60m.; buffaloes, 710,000; poultry, 13m.

Forestry. Some 9·34m. ha, or 52·9% of the land area, were covered by forests in 2000. Nearly half of the forested area in 1995 was reserved by the government to be awarded to concessionaires. Such areas are not at present worked to any extent. The remainder is available for exploitation by the local residents, and as a result some areas are over-exploited and conservation is not practised. Timber exports have been banned since Dec. 1996. In 1990 the area under forests was 10·65m. ha. There are substantial reserves of pitch pine. Rubber plantations are a valuable asset with production at around 40,000 tonnes per year. There are plans to expand the area under rubber cultivation from 50,000 ha to 800,000 ha. Timber production in 2001 was 10·04m. cu. metres. In 1997 forestry represented 43% of foreign trade.

Fisheries. 2001 catch was approximately 397,200 tonnes (360,000 tonnes from inland waters).

INDUSTRY

Some development of industry had taken place before the spread of open warfare in 1970, but little was in operation by the 1990s except for rubber processing, seafood processing, jute sack making and cigarette manufacture. Garment manufacture, rice milling, wood and wood products, rubber, cement and textiles production are the main industries. In the private sector small family concerns produce a wide range of goods. Light industry is generally better developed than heavy industry.

Labour. In 1996 the labour force was 5,322,000. Females constituted 52% of the labour force in 1999—the highest proportion of women in the workforce anywhere in the world. More than 60% of the economically active population are engaged in agriculture, fishing and forestry.

INTERNATIONAL TRADE

Foreign investment has been encouraged since 1989. Legislation of 1994 exempts profits from taxation for eight years, removes duties from various raw and semi-finished materials and offers tax incentives to investors in tourism, energy, the infrastructure and labour-intensive industries. External debt was US$2,907m. in 2002.

Imports and Exports. Imports and exports for calendar years in US$1m.:

	1998	*1999*	*2000*	*2001*	*2002*
Imports f.o.b.	1,165·8	1,591·0	1,939·3	2,094·0	2,313·5
Exports f.o.b.	800·5	1,129·3	1,401·1	1,571·2	1,750·1

The main exports are timber, rubber, soybeans and sesame. Main imports include cigarettes, construction materials, petroleum products, machinery and motor vehicles. Principal export destinations, 1998: USA (37%), Singapore (17%), Thailand (10%) and Germany (9%). Major import sources, 1998: Thailand (16%), Hong Kong (12%), Singapore (9%) and Mainland China (9%).

COMMUNICATIONS

Roads. There were about 12,323 km of roads in 2000, of which 16·2% were paved. 312,303 passenger cars were in use in 2000, 18,918 buses and coaches, and 49,036 trucks and vans. There were 196 fatalities in road accidents in 1999.

Rail. Main lines link Phnom Penh with Sisophon near the Thai border and the port of Kompong Som (total 601 km, metre gauge). After a long period of disruption owing to political unrest, limited services were restored on both lines in 1992. Passenger-km travelled in 2000 came to 15m. and freight tonne-km to 91m.

Civil Aviation. Pochentong airport is 8 km from Phnom Penh and handled 861,000 passengers (641,000 on international flights) in 2000. There are regular domestic services, and in 2003 Mekong Airlines flew to Hong Kong, Kuala Lumpur and Singapore, President Airlines flew to Hong Kong and Taipei, and Royal Phnom Penh Airways and Siem Riep Airways International operated services to Bangkok.

Shipping. There is an ocean port at Kompong Som; the port of Phnom Penh can be reached by the Mekong (through Vietnam) by ships of between 3,000 and 4,000 tonnes. In 2002 merchant shipping totalled 2,426,000 GRT, including oil tankers 141,000 GRT.

Telecommunications. There are telephone exchanges in all the main towns. In 2002 Cambodia had 415,400 telephone subscribers (30·1 per 1,000 persons), of which mobile phone subscribers numbered 380,000. In 2002, 91·5% of all telephone subscribers were mobile phone subscribers—among the highest ratios of mobile to fixed-line subscribers in the world. There were 27,000 PCs in use in 2002 (2·0 for every 1,000 persons) and 3,000 fax machines in 1997. In 2002 there were 30,000 Internet users.

Postal Services. In 1998 there were 56 post offices, or one for every 204,000 persons.

SOCIAL INSTITUTIONS

Justice. The population in penal institutions in 2002 was 6,128. In March 2003 the government announced plans to establish a special court in partnership with the UN to try leaders of the former Khmer Rouge regime.

Religion. The Constitution of 1989 reinstated Buddhism as the state religion; it had 10·8m. adherents in 2001. About 2,800 monasteries were active in 1994. There are small Roman Catholic and Muslim minorities.

Education. In 2001–02 there were 2,705,453 pupils and 54,519 teachers in 5,741 primary schools, and in general secondary education 24,884 teachers for 465,039 pupils. In 1994–95 there were 16,350 students in vocational establishments. There is a university (with 8,400 students and 350 academic staff in 1995–96) and a fine arts university. Adult literacy in 2001 was 68·7% (male, 80·5%; female, 58·2%).

In 2000–01 total expenditure on education came to 1·9% of GNP and 10·1% of total government spending.

Health. In 1998 there were 3,464 physicians, 210 dentists, 8,608 nurses and 3,359 midwives.

CULTURE

World Heritage Sites. Angkor was inscribed on the UNESCO World Heritage List in 1992. The Archeological Park contains the Temple of Angkor Wat and the Bayon Temple at Angkor Thom.

Broadcasting. Broadcasting is provided by the state-owned Voice of the People of Cambodia and Cambodian Television (colour by PAL). In 2000 there were 1·48m. radio sets and in 2001 there were 102,000 TV sets.

Press. There are 21 newspapers, two of which are in English.

Tourism. In 2000 there were 466,000 foreign visitors, up from 25,000 in 1991. Tourist numbers in the 1990s increased at a faster rate in Cambodia than in any other country. Receipts in 2000 totalled US$228m.

DIPLOMATIC REPRESENTATIVES

Of Cambodia in the United Kingdom (Wellington Building, 28–32 Wellington Rd, London, NW8 9SP)
Ambassador: Hor Nambora.

Of the United Kingdom in Cambodia (29 Street 75, Phnom Penh)
Ambassador: Stephen Bridges.

Of Cambodia in the USA (4530 16th Street, NW, Washington, D.C., 20011)
Ambassador: Ronald Eng.

Of the USA in Cambodia (16–18, St. 228, Phnom Penh)
Ambassador: Charles A. Ray.

Of Cambodia to the United Nations
Ambassador: Chem Widhya.

Of Cambodia to the European Union
Ambassador: Vacant.
Roving Ambassador (Francophonie): Yao Chant Rith.

FURTHER READING

Chandler, D. P., *A History of Cambodia*. 2nd ed. Boulder (CO), 1996
Jarvis, Helen, *Cambodia.* [Bibliography] ABC-Clio, Oxford and Santa Barbara (CA), 1997
Martin, M. A, *Cambodia: A Shattered Society.* California Univ. Press, 1994
Peschoux, C., *Le Cambodge dans la Tourmente: le Troisième Conflit Indochinois, 1978–1991.* Paris, 1992.—*Les 'Nouveaux' Khmers Rouges.* Paris, 1992
Short, Philip, *Pol Pot: The History of a Nightmare.* John Murray, London, 2004

National statistical office: National Institute of Statistics, Ministry of Planning, 386 Monivong Boulevard, Phnom Penh.
Website: http://www.nis.gov.kh/

CAMEROON

République du Cameroun—
Republic of Cameroon

Capital: Yaoundé
Population projection, 2010: 17·78m.
GDP per capita, 2002: (PPP$) 2,000
HDI/world rank: 0·501/141

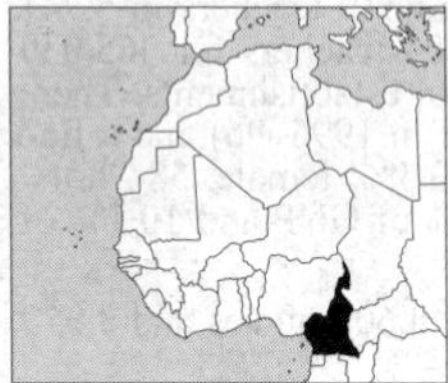

KEY HISTORICAL EVENTS

The name Cameroon derives from *camarães* (prawns), introduced by Portuguese navigators. Called Kamerun in German and Cameroun in French, the estuary was later called the Cameroons River by British navigators. The Duala people living there were traders, selling slaves and later palm oil to Europeans. On 12 July 1884 they signed a treaty establishing German rule over Kamerun. Originally covering the Duala's territory on the Wouri, this German colony later expanded to cover a large area inland, home to a number of African peoples. In the First World War Allied forces occupied the territory which was partitioned between France and Britain. British Cameroons consisted of British Southern Cameroons and British Northern Cameroons, adjoining Nigeria. France's mandated territory of Cameroun occupied most of the former German colony. The Dualas continued to take the lead in anti-colonial protest.

In 1946 the French and British territories became Trust Territories of the UN. In French Cameroun the *Union des Populations du Cameroun* (UPC), founded in 1948, became the major nationalist party, calling for independence and 'reunification' with British Cameroons. In Dec. 1956, when elections were held prior to self-government, the UPC began a guerrilla war against the French and the new Cameroonian government. On 1 Jan. 1960 French Cameroun gained independence. The UPC guerrillas were largely defeated by 1963. On 11 Feb. 1961 British Southern Cameroons voted in a referendum to join ex-French Cameroun, while British Northern Cameroons chose to join Nigeria. The country's name was changed to the Republic of Cameroon in 1984.

TERRITORY AND POPULATION

Cameroon is bounded in the west by the Gulf of Guinea, northwest by Nigeria, east by Chad and the Central African Republic, and south by the Republic of the Congo, Gabon and Equatorial Guinea. The total area (including inland water) is 475,440 sq. km. On 29 March 1994 Cameroon asked the International Court of Justice to confirm its sovereignty over the oil-rich Bakassi Peninsula, occupied by Nigerian troops. The dispute continued for eight years, with Equatorial Guinea also subsequently becoming involved. In Oct. 2002 the International Court of Justice rejected Nigeria's claims and awarded the peninsula to Cameroon. All parties agreed to accept the Court's judgment. Population (1987 census) 10,494,000. Estimate (July 2003) 15,746,200; density, 33·0 per sq. km.

The UN gives a projected population for 2010 of 17·78m.

In 2001, 50·4% of the population were rural.

The areas, estimated populations and chief towns of the ten provinces are:

Province	*Sq. km*	*Estimate 2001*	*Chief town*	*Estimate 2001*
Adamaoua	63,691	723,600	Ngaoundéré	189,800
Centre	68,926	2,501,200	Yaoundé	1,248,200
Est	109,011	755,100	Bertoua	173,000
Extrême-Nord	34,246	2,721,500	Maroua	271,700
Littoral	20,239	2,202,300	Douala	1,494,700
Nord (Bénoué)	65,576	1,227,000	Garoua	356,900
Nord-Ouest	17,810	1,840,500	Bamenda	316,100
Ouest	13,872	1,982,100	Bafoussam	242,000
Sud	47,110	534,900	Ebolowa	79,500
Sud-Ouest	24,471	1,242,700	Buéa	47,300

The population is composed of Sudanic-speaking people in the north (Fulani, Sao and others) and Bantu-speaking groups, mainly Bamileke, Beti, Bulu, Tikar, Bassa and Duala, in the rest of the country. The official languages are French and English.

SOCIAL STATISTICS

1995 births, 526,000 (rate of 39·9 per 1,000 population); deaths, 164,000 (rate of 12·4 per 1,000 population). Annual population growth rate, 1992–2002, 2·4%. Infant mortality, 2001, 96 per 1,000 live births. Life expectancy in 2001: males, 46·6 years; females, 49·4. Fertility rate, 2001, 4·8 children per woman.

CLIMATE

An equatorial climate, with high temperatures and plentiful rain, especially from March to June and Sept. to Nov. Further inland, rain occurs at all seasons. Yaoundé, Jan. 76°F (24·4°C), July 73°F (22·8°C). Annual rainfall 62" (1,555 mm). Douala, Jan. 79°F (26·1°C), July 75°F (23·9°C). Annual rainfall 160" (4,026 mm).

CONSTITUTION AND GOVERNMENT

The 1972 Constitution, subsequently amended, provides for a *President* as head of state and government. The President is directly elected for a five-year term, and there is a *Council of Ministers* whose members must not be members of parliament.

The *National Assembly*, elected by universal adult suffrage for five years, consists of 180 representatives. After 1966 the sole legal party was the Cameroon People's Democratic Movement (RDPC), but in Dec. 1990 the National Assembly legalized opposition parties.

National Anthem. 'O Cameroon, Thou Cradle of our Fathers'/'O Cameroun, Berceau de nos Ancêtres'; words by R. Afame, tune by R. Afame, S. Bamba and M. Nko'o.

RECENT ELECTIONS

Presidential elections were held on 11 Oct. 2004. Incumbent Paul Biya was re-elected with 70·9% of the votes ahead of John Fru Ndi with17·4%, Adamou Ndam Njoya with 4·5% and Garga Haman Adji with 3·7%. The opposition denounced the election as fraudulent. Turn-out was 82·8%.

The most recent National Assembly elections were held on 30 June 2002. The conservative Rassemblement Démocratique du Peuple Camerounais (RDPC) won 133 seats, the Social-Democratic Front (SDF) 21, the Union Démocratique du Cameroun (UDC) 5, the Union des Populations du Cameroun (UPC) 3, and others won 18 seats.

CURRENT ADMINISTRATION

President: Paul Biya; b. 1933 (RDPC; assumed office 6 Nov. 1982, elected 14 Jan. 1984, re-elected 24 April 1988, also 10 Oct. 1992, 12 Oct. 1997 and once again re-elected 11 Oct. 2004).

In March 2005 the cabinet comprised:

Prime Minister: Ephraïm Inoni; b. 1947 (RDPC; in office since 8 Dec. 2004).

Deputy Prime Minister for Justice, Guardian of the Seals: Amadou Ali.

Minister of State for Culture: Ferdinand Léopold Oyono. *Planning, Programming and Regional Development:* Augustin Frederick Kodock. *Posts and Telecommunications:* Bello Bouba Maigari. *Territorial Administration and Decentralization (Interior):* Marafa Hamidou Yaya. *Town Planning and Housing:* Lekene Donfack. *Secretary General at the Presidency:* Jean Marie Atangana Mebara.

Minister for Agriculture: Clobaire Tchatat. *Basic Education:* Adama Haman. *Commerce:* Luc Magoire Mbarga Atangana. *Communication:* Pierre Moukoko Mbonjo. *Economy and Finance:* Polycarpe Abah Abah. *Employment and Professional Training:* Zacharie Perevet. *Energy and Water Resources:* Alphonse Siyam Siwé. *Environment and Nature Protection:* Pierre Hélé. *External Relations:*

Laurent Esso. *Forests and Wildlife:* Egbe Achu Hilman. *Health:* Urbain Olanguena Awono. *Higher Education:* Jacques Fame Ndongo. *Industry, Mines and Technological Development:* Charles Salé. *Labour and Social Insurance:* Robert Nkili. *Lands and Land Titles:* Louis Marie Abogo Nkono. *Livestock, Fisheries and Animal Industries:* Aboubakari Sarki. *Promotion of Women and Family Affairs:* Suzanne Bombak. *Public Service and Administrative Reforms:* Benjamin Amama Amama. *Public Works:* Martin Okouda. *Scientific Research and Innovation:* Madeleine Tchuenté. *Secondary Education:* Louis Bapes Bapes. *Small and Medium-Sized Enterprises, Social Economy and Handicrafts:* Bernard Messengue Avom. *Social Affairs:* Cathérine Bakang Mbock. *Sports and Physical Education:* Philippe Mbarga Mboa. *Tourism:* Baba Hamadou. *Transport:* Dakole Daissala. *Youth:* Adoum Garoua. *Minister Delegate at the Presidency in Charge of Defence:* Remy Ze Meka.

Office of the President: http://www.camnet.cm/celcom/homepr.htm

DEFENCE

The President of the Republic is C.-in-C. of the armed forces. Defence expenditure totalled US$172m. in 2003 (US$11 per capita), representing 1·4% of GDP.

Army. Total strength (2002) is 12,500 and includes a Presidential Guard; there is a Gendarmerie 9,000 strong.

Navy. Personnel in 2002 numbered 1,300. There are bases at Douala (HQ), Limbe and Kribi.

Air Force. Aircraft availability is low because of funding problems. Personnel (2002), 300. There are 15 combat aircraft.

INTERNATIONAL RELATIONS

Cameroon is a member of the UN, WTO, the Commonwealth, the African Union, African Development Bank, OIC, Islamic Development Bank, International Organization of the Francophonie, the Lake Chad Basin Commission and is an ACP member state of the ACP-EU relationship.

ECONOMY

In 2002 agriculture accounted for 44·2% of GDP, industry 19·1% and services 36·7%.

Overview. Agriculture is the economy's key sector, employing two-thirds of the working population. Cameroon's primary export is oil, contributing nearly half of GDP in 2002. Export crops have suffered from low world prices, ageing plantations and disruption in the coffee and cocoa sector. Since the devaluation of the currency in 1994, annual inflation has decreased from 32·5% to 4·5% in 2003. Cameroon's external debt was significantly reduced by the devaluation, though remained high at 80% of GDP in 2001. Privatization commenced fairly late, in 1995. In the first two waves of reform, privatization has been undertaken and completed in the major export, infrastructure, banking and insurance sectors. Despite structural reforms to the economy, Cameroon's major weaknesses, corruption and poor resource management, remain severe. Cameroon signed a new agreement with the IMF in 2000 giving it access to US$139m. Cameroon's exchange rate is pegged to the euro.

Currency. The unit of currency is the *franc CFA* (XAF) with a parity of 655·957 francs CFA to one euro. In April 2002 foreign exchange reserves were US$508m. (negligible in 1997) and total money supply was 644,230m. francs CFA. Gold reserves were 30,000 troy oz in June 2002. Inflation in 2003 was 4·5%.

Budget. The financial year used to end on 30 June but since 2003 has been the calendar year. In 2000–01 revenues totalled 1,326bn. francs CFA and expenditures 1,175bn. francs CFA.

VAT, introduced in 1999, is 17%.

Performance. Real GDP growth was 5·3% in 2001 and 6·5% in 2002. Total GDP in 2003 was US$12·4bn.

Banking and Finance. The *Banque des Etats de l'Afrique Centrale* (*Governor*, Jean-Félix Mamalepot) is the sole bank of issue. There are in addition nine commercial banks, three development banks and five other financial institutions.

The Douala Stock Exchange was opened in April 2003.

ENERGY AND NATURAL RESOURCES

Environment. Cameroon's carbon dioxide emissions from the consumption and flaring of fossil fuels in 2002 were the equivalent of 0·4 tonnes per capita.

Electricity. Installed capacity in 2000 was 0·9m. kW. Total production in 2000 was 3·44bn. kWh (97% hydro-electric), with consumption per capita (2000) 231 kWh.

Oil and Gas. Oil production (2003), mainly from Kole oilfield, was 3·5m. tonnes. In 2002 there were proven reserves of 400m. bbls. In June 2000 the World Bank approved funding for a 1,000-km US$4bn. pipeline to run from 300 new oil wells in Chad through Cameroon to the Atlantic Ocean. Oil started pumping in July 2003. Revenues are projected to reach US$20m. per annum.

Minerals. Tin ore and limestone are extracted. There are deposits of aluminium, bauxite, uranium, nickel, gold, cassiterite and kyanite. Aluminium production in 2001 was 81,000 tonnes.

Agriculture. In 2001 there were 5·96m. ha of arable land and 1·20m. ha of permanent crops. 33,000 ha were irrigated in 2001. There were 500 tractors in 2001. Main agricultural crops (with 2000 production in 1,000 tonnes): cassava, 2,067; plantains, 1,403; sugarcane, 1,350; bananas, 850; maize, 850; sorghum, 500; yams, 260; seed cotton, 220; sweet potatoes, 180; dry beans, 170; groundnuts, 160; palm oil, 140; cocoa beans, 120; pumpkins and squash, 120.

Livestock (2000): 5·9m. cattle; 3·88m. sheep; 3·85m. goats; 1·43m. pigs; 30m. chickens.

Livestock products (in 1,000 tonnes), 2000: beef and veal, 90; pork, bacon and ham, 18; lamb and mutton, 17; goat meat, 15; poultry meat, 24; cow's milk, 125; goat's milk, 42; eggs, 14.

Forestry. Forests covered 23·86m. ha in 2000 (51·3% of the total land area), ranging from tropical rain forests in the south (producing hardwoods such as mahogany, ebony and sapele) to semi-deciduous forests in the centre and wooded savannah in the north. Timber production in 2001 was 10·99m. cu. metres.

Fisheries. In 2001 the total catch was 111,031 tonnes (58,531 tonnes from sea fishing).

INDUSTRY

Manufacturing is largely small-scale, with only some 30 firms employing more than 10 workers. Output in 1,000 tonnes: cement (2001), 980; distillate fuel oil (2000), 459; residual fuel oil (2000), 397; petrol (2000), 323; kerosene (2000), 250; sugar (2002), 104. In 2001, 374m. litres of beer and 2·8bn. cigarettes were produced. There are also factories producing shoes, soap, oil and food products.

Labour. In 1996 the workforce numbered 5,500,000 (62% males), of whom over 50% were occupied in agriculture.

Trade Unions. The principal trade union federation is the *Organisation des syndicats des travailleurs camerounais* (OSTC), established on 7 Dec. 1985 to replace the former body, the UNTC.

INTERNATIONAL TRADE

Foreign debt was US$8,502m. in 2002.

Imports and Exports. In 1999 total imports amounted to US$1,315·8m. and exports to US$1,587·7m.

Principal exports (in US$1m.), 1999: crude oil, 552·1; sawn wood, 191·1; cocoa, 162·5; coffee, 121·0; aluminium, 94·5.

Main export markets, 1999: Italy, 22%; France, 18%; Spain, 13%. Main import suppliers: France, 28%; Nigeria, 12%; Germany, 6%.

COMMUNICATIONS

Roads. There were about 34,300 km of classified roads in 1999, of which 4,300 km were paved. In 1996 there were 98,000 passenger cars and 64,350 commercial vehicles.

Rail. Cameroon Railways (*Regifercam*), 1,016 km in 2000, link Douala with Nkongsamba and Ngaoundéré, with branches from M'Banga to Kumba and Makak to M'Balmayo. In 2000 railways carried 1·4m. passengers and 1·8m. tonnes of freight.

Civil Aviation. There are 45 airports including three international airports at Douala, Garoua and Yaoundé (Nsimalen). In 2000 Douala handled 419,000 passengers (339,000 on international flights). In 2003 Cameroon Airlines (Camair), the national carrier, operated on domestic routes and provided international services to Abidjan, Bamako, Bangui, Brazzaville, Bujumbura, Cotonou, Dakar, Johannesburg, Kigali, Kinshasa, Lagos, Libreville, Malabo, N'Djaména, Paris and Pointe-Noire.

In 1999 scheduled airline traffic of Cameroon-based carriers flew 6·0m. km, carrying 293,000 passengers (204,000 on international flights).

Shipping. In 2002 the merchant marine totalled 17,000 GRT. In 2001 vessels totalling 1,243,000 NRT entered ports.

The main port is Douala; other ports are Bota, Campo, Garoua (only navigable in the rainy season), Kribi and Limbo-Tiko.

Telecommunications. In 2002 there were 785,500 telephone subscribers, or 49·7 per 1,000 inhabitants. There were 675,700 mobile phone subscribers in 2002 and 72,000 PCs were in use (4·6 per 1,000 persons). Cameroon had 60,000 Internet users in 2002.

Postal Services. There were 377 post offices in 1997.

SOCIAL INSTITUTIONS

Justice. The Supreme Court sits at Yaoundé, as does the High Court of Justice (consisting of nine titular judges and six surrogates all appointed by the National Assembly). There are magistrates' courts situated in the provinces.

The population in penal institutions in 2002 was 20,000 (129 per 100,000 of national population).

Religion. In 2001 there were 4·18m. Roman Catholics, 3·35m. Muslims and 3·27m. Protestants. Some of the population follow traditional animist religions. In Sept. 2003 there was one cardinal.

Education. In 2000–01 there were 5,310 teachers for 125,674 children in pre-primary schools and (1999–2000) 32,246 teachers for 2,237,083 pupils in primary schools. In 2000–01 there were 554,830 secondary level pupils in general programmes.

In 2000–01, 68,495 students were in tertiary education. In 1991 there were 33 teacher training colleges and five new institutions of higher education. Total staff: 1,086. In 1994–95 there were six universities and one Roman Catholic university, four specialized *Ecoles Nationales*, an *Ecole Supérieure* for posts and telecommunications, six specialized institutes, a national school of administration and magistracy and a faculty of Protestant theology. In 1995–96 there were 15,220 university students and 830 academic staff. The adult literacy rate in 2001 was 72·4% (79·9% among males and 65·1% among females).

In 2000–01 total expenditure on education came to 3·4% of GNP and 12·5% of total government spending.

Health. In 1988 there were 629 hospitals with 27 beds per 10,000 inhabitants. In 1996 there were 1,031 physicians, 56 dentists, 5,112 nurses and 70 midwives.

CULTURE

World Heritage Sites. The Dja Faunal Reserve was inscribed on the UNESCO World Heritage List in 1987. Surrounded by the Dja River, it is one of Africa's largest rainforests.

Broadcasting. The state-controlled Cameroon Radio Television provides home, national, provincial and urban radio programmes and a TV service. Colour is by PAL. In 2000 there were 2·4m. radio receivers and in 2001 there were 1·1m. TV receivers.

Press. There was (1997) one national government-owned daily newspaper with a circulation of 66,000 and about 100 other periodicals, including 20 weeklies.

Tourism. In 2000 there were 277,000 foreign tourists, bringing revenue of US$39m.

DIPLOMATIC REPRESENTATIVES

Of Cameroon in the United Kingdom (84 Holland Park, London, W11 3SB)
High Commissioner: Dr Samuel Libock Mbei.

Of the United Kingdom in Cameroon (Ave. Winston Churchill, BP 547, Yaoundé)
High Commissioner: Richard Wildash, LVO.

Of Cameroon in the USA (2349 Massachusetts Ave., NW, Washington, D.C., 20008)
Ambassador: Jérôme Mendouga.

Of the USA in Cameroon (Rue Nachtigal, BP 817, Yaoundé)
Ambassador: Niels Marquardt.

Of Cameroon to the United Nations
Ambassador: Martin Belinga-Eboutou.

Of Cameroon to the European Union
Ambassador: Isabelle Bassong.

FURTHER READING

National statistical office: Direction de la Statistique et de la Comptabilité Nationale, Ministère du Plan et de l'Aménagement du Territoire, Yaoundé.

Ardener, E., *Kingdom on Mount Cameroon: Studies in the History of the Cameroon Coast 1500–1970.* Berghahn Books, Oxford, 1996

DeLancey, M. W., *Cameroon: Dependence and Independence.* London, 1989

CANADA

Capital: Ottawa
Population projection, 2010: 33·07m.
GDP per capita, 2002: (PPP$) 29,480
HDI/world rank: 0·943/4

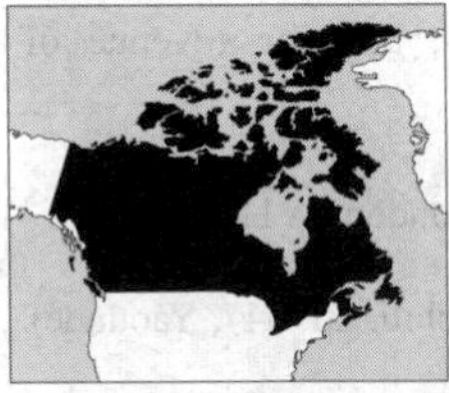

KEY HISTORICAL EVENTS

The first human habitation in Canada dates from the last stages of the Pleistocene Ice Age up to 30,000 years ago. Mongoloid hunter-gatherers from Asia were the forefathers of Canada's First Nations, numerous self-governing tribes consisting of 12 major language groups.

In 1497 John Cabot was commissioned by King Henry VII of England to chart the coasts around Labrador and Newfoundland. The Frenchman, Jacques Cartier, discovered the Gulf of St Lawrence in 1534 and claimed it for the French crown. Fisheries were set up by the English and French, who traded iron and other goods with natives in exchange for valuable furs, mostly beaver. The French sent Samuel de Champlain in 1604 to establish a fur trade and organize a settlement in an area called Acadia (now New Brunswick, Nova Scotia and Prince Edward Island). The French traded with the Algonquin and Huron and supported them during fierce raids by the Iroquois, who became the fur trading allies of the Dutch and then the English.

In opposition to French expansion, England sent explorers such as Martin Frobisher, William Baffin and Henry Hudson to claim new territory. Colonies sprang up along the English coast and the Hudson Bay Company was formed in 1670 to gain a fur-trading monopoly over the area. In 1713 the Treaty of Utrecht gave England complete control of the Hudson Bay territory, Acadia and Newfoundland. France, however, retained Cape Breton Island, the St Lawrence Islands and fishing rights in Newfoundland. Led by General Wolfe, Britain's victory over France at the Battle of the Plains of Abraham in 1759 gained Quebec, and in 1760 Montreal too was taken. The Treaty of Paris ceded all French Canadian territory to the British. The Quebec Act of 1774 allowed French Canadians religious and linguistic freedom and recognized French civil law.

After the American war against Britain in Canada in 1812, large numbers of English, Scottish and Irish settlers swelled the English speaking population. Following a report by Lord Durham, Upper Canada (mostly English-speaking) and Lower Canada (mostly French) were united under one central government in 1841. Nova Scotia, New Brunswick and the Canadas (now Ontario and Quebec) were united in 1867 as the Dominion of Canada. The Constitution Act confirmed the language and legal rights of the French. The 1890s were a period of growth and stability. Mineral resources were found in British Columbia and Ontario as well as gold which precipitated the Klondike gold rush of 1897. The Yukon territory was established in 1898 to ensure Canadian jurisdiction over the exploitation of gold. The provinces of Saskatchewan and Alberta were created in 1905.

When the First World War broke out in 1914 thousands of Canadians volunteered to fight. Around 60,000 men died in the battles of Ypres, Vimy Ridge and Passendaele, and another 173,000 were wounded. Canada participated as an independent state at the Paris Peace Conference and joined the League of Nations. To meet the objections of French Canadians who had bitterly opposed conscription, Prime Minister Robert Laird Borden formed a joint government of Liberals and Conservatives comprising English-speaking Unionists and the French-speaking Liberals.

Women's suffrage was granted in 1918. In 1931 the Statute of Westminster granted Canada complete independence. In the same year Norway formally recognized the Canadian title to the Sverdrup group of Arctic islands. Canada thus holds sovereignty in the whole Arctic sector north of the Canadian mainland.

Canada's contribution in the Second World War was even more extensive although casualties were lower. A post-war plan introduced unemployment insurance, family allowances, veterans' benefits, subsidized housing, health plans and improved pensions. Canada became a founder member of the United Nations. In 1949

Newfoundland (including Labrador) became a Canadian province thus completing the Confederation.

For 20 years after 1950 Canada enjoyed growth, prosperity and a 'baby boom'. The face of industrial Canada changed with the discovery of radium, petroleum and natural gas. During Lester Pearson's five years as prime minister Canada gained a national flag, a social security system and medical care for all its citizens.

Having chosen Pierre Trudeau to succeed Pearson, the Liberals won the 1968 election. At the same time there was a revival of French nationalism, especially in Quebec, with the formation of the Parti Québécois (PQ) led by René Levasque. Keen to preserve national unity, Trudeau passed the Official Languages Act in 1969 which affirmed the equality of French and English in all governmental activities. However, in 1970 he had to send troops into Quebec following the murder of the Labour minister, Pierre Laporte, by the separatist Front de Libération du Québec. In 1976 a pledge on separatism won the PQ the provincial election and French became the official language of Quebec. A referendum to make the province an independent country was rejected by Quebec voters in 1980.

The Conservative leader Brian Mulroney negotiated a free trade agreement with the United States that came into force in 1989. This was followed in 1994 by North American Free Trade Agreement (NAFTA) with the USA and Mexico. A recession in the early nineties forced Mulroney to resign in 1993. He was replaced by Kim Campbell, Canada's first female prime minister. In the Oct. election of that year, Campbell and the Conservatives suffered a major defeat retaining only two of their 154 seats. Led by Jean Chrétien, the Liberals won 177 seats and the Reform Party 52 seats. The PQ became the major opposition party with 54 seats.

Another referendum on Quebec's independence from Canada failed narrowly in 1995. In 1998 the Supreme Court ruled that Quebec was prohibited from declaring itself independent without first negotiating an agreement with the federal government and other provinces. Chrétien was returned for a third term in Nov. 2000 with an increased majority.

TERRITORY AND POPULATION

Canada is bounded in the northwest by the Beaufort Sea, north by the Arctic Ocean, northeast by Baffin Bay, east by the Davis Strait, Labrador Sea and Atlantic Ocean, south by the USA and west by the Pacific Ocean and USA (Alaska). The area is 9,984,670 sq. km, of which 891,163 sq. km are fresh water. 2001 census population, 30,007,094 (15,693,393 females), giving a density of 3·0 per sq. km. In 2001, 79·7% of the population were urban. Population estimate, 1 July 2003, 31,629,700.

The UN gives a projected population for 2010 of 33·07m.

Population at previous censuses:

1851	2,436,297	1911	7,206,643	1971	21,568,311
1861	3,229,633	1921	8,787,949	1976[1]	22,992,604
1871	3,689,257	1931	10,376,786	1981	24,343,181
1881	4,324,810	1941	11,506,655	1986[1]	25,309,331
1891	4,833,239	1951	14,009,429	1991	27,296,859[2]
1901	5,371,315	1961	18,238,247	1996[1]	28,848,761[2]

[1]It became a statutory requirement to conduct a census every five years in 1971.
[2]Excludes data from incompletely enumerated Indian reserves and Indian settlements.

Of the total population in 2001, 80·9% were Canadian-born. Alberta had the biggest population increase between 1996 and 2001 with 10·3%, whilst Newfoundland had the biggest population reduction with –7·0%, more than double the 2·9% rate of decline recorded between 1991 and 1996.

The population (2001) born outside Canada in the provinces was in the following ratio (%): Alberta, 14·9; British Columbia, 26·1; Manitoba, 12·1; New Brunswick, 3·1; Newfoundland, 1·6; Northwest Territories, 6·4; Nova Scotia, 4·6; Nunavut, 1·7; Ontario, 26·8; Prince Edward Island, 3·1; Quebec, 9·9; Saskatchewan, 5·0; Yukon, 10·6.

Figures for the 2001 census population according to ethnic origin (leading categories), were[1]:

Canadian	11,682,680	Scottish	4,157,210
English	5,978,875	Irish	3,822,660
French	4,668,410	German	2,742,765

Italian	1,270,370	Dutch	923,310
Chinese	1,094,700	Polish	817,085
Ukrainian	1,071,060	East Indian	713,330
North American Indian	1,000,890		

[1]Census respondents who reported multiple ethnic origins are counted for each origin they reported.

The aboriginal population (those persons identifying with at least one aboriginal group, and including North American Indian, Métis or Inuit) numbered 976,305 in 2001. In 2001, 59·1% of the population gave their mother tongue as English and 22·9% as French (English and French are both official languages); Chinese was reported as the third most common language, accounting for 2·9% of the total population. In 2001, 1·8m. residents were immigrants who arrived between 1991 and 2001, accounting for 6·2% of the total population; 58% came from Asia (including the Middle East), 20% from Europe, 11% from the Caribbean, Central and South America, 8% from Africa, and 3% from the USA.

Populations of Census Metropolitan Areas (CMA) and Cities (proper), 2001 census:

	CMA	*City proper*		*CMA*	*City proper*
Toronto	4,682,897	2,481,494	Halifax	359,183	119,292
Montreal	3,426,350	1,039,534	Victoria	311,902	74,125
Vancouver	1,986,965	545,671	Windsor	307,877	208,402
Ottawa-Hull	1,063,664	—	Oshawa	296,298	139,051
Ottawa	—	774,072	Saskatoon	225,927	196,811
Hull	—	66,246	Regina	192,800	178,225
Calgary	951,395	878,866	St John's	172,918	99,182
Edmonton	937,845	616,014	Sudbury	155,601	85,354
Quebec	682,757	169,076	Chicoutimi-Jonquière	154,938	—
Winnipeg	671,274	619,544	Chicoutimi	—	60,008
Hamilton	662,401	490,268	Jonquière	—	54,842
London	432,451	336,539	Sherbrooke	153,811	75,916
Kitchener	414,284	190,399	Abbotsford	147,370	115,463
St Catharines-Niagara	377,009	—	Kingston	146,838	114,195
St Catharines	—	129,170	Trois Rivières	137,507	46,295
Niagara Falls	—	78,815	Saint John	122,678	69,661

SOCIAL STATISTICS

Statistics for period from July–June:

	Live births	*Deaths*
1999–2000	336,912	217,229
2000–01	327,107	219,114
2001–02	332,806	222,833
2002–03	331,522	227,630

Average annual population growth rate, 1992–2002, 1·0%. Birth rate, 2002–03 (per 1,000 population), 10·5; death rate, 7·2. Marriages, 2002, numbered 146,738; divorces, 70,155. In 1997 the most popular age range for marrying was 25–29 for both males and females, followed by 30–34 for males and 20–24 for females. Suicides, 1999, 4,074 (13·8 per 100,000 population). Life expectancy at birth, 2001, was 76·5 years for men and 81·8 years for women. Infant mortality, 2001, 5 per 1,000 live births; fertility rate, 2001, 1·6 children per woman.

CLIMATE

The climate ranges from polar conditions in the north to cool temperate in the south, but with considerable differences between east coast, west coast and the interior, affecting temperatures, rainfall amounts and seasonal distribution. Winters are very severe over much of the country, but summers can be very hot inland. *See* individual provinces for climatic details.

CONSTITUTION AND GOVERNMENT

In Nov. 1981 the Canadian government agreed on the provisions of an amended constitution, to the end that it should replace the British North America Act and that its future amendment should be the prerogative of Canada. These proposals were adopted by the Parliament of Canada and were enacted by the UK Parliament as the Canada Act of 1982. This was the final act of the UK Parliament in Canadian constitutional development. The Act gave to Canada the power to amend the Constitution according to procedures determined by the Constitutional Act 1982. The latter added to the Canadian Constitution a charter of Rights and Freedoms, and provisions which recognize the nation's multi-cultural heritage, affirm the existing rights of native peoples, confirm the principle of equalization of benefits among the provinces, and strengthen provincial ownership of natural resources.

Under the Constitution legislative power is vested in Parliament, consisting of the Queen, represented by a Governor-General, a Senate and a House of Commons. The members of the *Senate* are appointed until age 75 by summons of the Governor-General under the Great Seal of Canada. Members appointed before 2 June 1965 may remain in office for life. The Senate consists of 105 senators: 24 from Ontario, 24 from Quebec, 10 from Nova Scotia, 10 from New Brunswick, 6 from Manitoba, 6 from British Columbia, 6 from Alberta, 6 from Saskatchewan, 6 from Newfoundland, 4 from Prince Edward Island, 1 from the Yukon Territory, 1 from the Northwest Territories, and 1 from Nunavut. Each senator must be at least 30 years of age and reside in the province for which he or she is appointed. The *House of Commons*, currently of 301 members, is elected by universal secret suffrage, by a first-past-the-post system, for five-year terms. Representation is based on the population of all the provinces taken as a whole with readjustments made after each census. As a result of the 2001 census, there will be 308 members of the House of Commons after the next election. State of the parties in the Senate (Jan. 2005): Liberals, 58; Conservatives, 23; Progressive Conservatives, 3; independents, 5; vacant, 16.

The First Nations have representation in the *Assembly of First Nations* (National Chief: Phil Fontaine, elected July 2003).

The office and appointment of the Governor-General are regulated by letters patent of 1947. In 1977 the Queen approved the transfer to the Governor-General of functions discharged by the Sovereign. The Governor-General is assisted by a *Privy Council* composed of Cabinet Ministers.

Canadian Parliamentary Guide. Annual. Ottawa

Bejermi, J., *Canadian Parliamentary Handbook.* Ottawa, 1993

Cairns, A. C., *Charter versus Federalism: the Dilemmas of Constitutional Reform.* Montreal, 1992

Canada: The State of the Federation. Queen's Univ., annual

Forsey, E. A., *How Canadians Govern Themselves.* Ottawa, 1991

Fox, P. W. and White, G., *Politics Canada.* 7th ed. Toronto, 1991

Hogg, P. W., *Constitutional Law of Canada.* 3rd ed. Toronto, 1992

Kaplan, W. (ed.) *Belonging: the Meaning and Future of Canadian Citizenship.* McGill-Queen's Univ. Press, 1993

Kernaghan, K., *Public Administration in Canada: a Text.* Scarborough, 1991

Mahler, G., *Contemporary Canadian Politics, 1970–1994: an Annotated Bibliography.* 2 vols. Westport (CT), 1995

Osbaldston, G. F., *Organizing to Govern.* Toronto, 1992

Reesor, B., *The Canadian Constitution in Historical Perspective.* Scarborough, 1992

Tardi, G., *The Legal Framework of Government: a Canadian Guide.* Aurora, 1992

National Anthem. 'O Canada, our home and native land'/'O Canada, terre de nos aïeux'; words by A. Routhier, tune by C. Lavallée.

RECENT ELECTIONS

At the elections of 28 June 2004 the Liberal Party (Lib.) gained 135 seats (172 in 2000) with 36·7% (40·8% in 2000) of votes cast; the Conservative Party 99 (in 2000 the Conservative Alliance won 66 and the Progressive Conservatives 12) with 29·6% (25·5% and 12·2% in 2000); the Bloc Québécois (BQ) 54 with 12·4% (38 in 2000 with 10·7%); the New Democratic Party 19 with 15·7% (13 in 2000 with 8·5%). The Green Party polled 4·3% and took no seats. One independent was elected. Turnout was a record low of 60·5% (62·9% in 2000).

CURRENT ADMINISTRATION

Governor-General: Adrienne Clarkson (b. 1939; term of office originally Oct. 1999–Oct. 2004 and now extended until Sept. 2005).

In March 2005 the Liberal cabinet comprised:

Prime Minister: Paul Martin; b. 1938 (took office on 12 Dec. 2003).

Deputy Prime Minister and Minister of Public Safety and Emergency Preparedness: Anne McLellan. *Leader of the Government in the Senate:* Jacob

Austin. *Leader of the Government in the House of Commons:* Tony Valeri. *Minister of the Environment:* Stéphane Dion. *Finance:* Ralph Goodale. *Industry:* David Emerson. *Health:* Ujjal Dosanjh. *International Trade:* James Scott Peterson. *Indian Affairs and Northern Development and Federal Interlocutor for Métis and Non-Status Indians:* Andy Scott. *Labour and Housing:* Joseph Fontana. *Western Economic Diversification:* Stephen Owen. *Veterans Affairs:* Albina Guarnieri. *Public Works and Government Services:* Scott Brison. *Foreign Affairs:* Pierre Pettigrew. *National Revenue:* John McCallum. *Agriculture and Agri-Food:* Andrew Mitchell. *Fisheries and Oceans:* Geoff Regan. *Transport:* Jean Lapierre. *National Defence:* William Graham. *Justice and Attorney General:* Irwin Cotler. *Citizenship and Immigration:* Giuseppe 'Joseph' Volpe. *Canadian Heritage:* Liza Frulla. *Natural Resources:* John Efford. *Social Development:* Ken Dryden. *Atlantic Canada Opportunities Agency:* Joseph McGuire. *International Co-operation:* Aileen Carroll. *President of the Queen's Privy Council for Canada and Minister of Intergovernmental Affairs, Human Resources and Skills Development:* Lucienne Robillard. *President of the Treasury Board:* Reg Alcock.

The *Leader of the Opposition* is Stephen Harper.

Office of the Prime Minister: http://www.pm.gc.ca

DEFENCE

The armed forces are unified and organized in functional commands: Land Forces (army), Air Command (air forces) and Maritime Command (naval and naval air forces). In 2002 the armed forces numbered 52,300 (6,100 women); reserves, 35,400.

Military expenditure totalled US$10,118m. in 2003 (US$320 per capita), representing just 1·2% of GDP, the lowest share of GDP since before the Second World War. However, in Feb. 2005 Finance Minister Ralph Goodale announced the biggest increase in defence spending in the past 20 years.

Army. The Land Forces numbered 19,300 in 2002 including 1,600 women. Reserves include a Militia of 14,000 and 3,500 Canadian Rangers.

Navy. The naval combatant force, which forms part of the Maritime Command of the unified armed forces, is headquartered at Halifax (Nova Scotia), and includes two diesel submarines (commissioned but not yet operational), four destroyers and 12 helicopter-carrying frigates. Naval personnel in 2002 numbered about 9,000, with 4,000 reserves. The main bases are Halifax, where about two-thirds of the fleet is based, and Esquimalt (British Columbia).

Air Force. The air forces numbered 13,500 in 2002 (1,700 women) with 140 combat aircraft.

INTERNATIONAL RELATIONS

Canada is a member of the UN, WTO, NATO, the Commonwealth, OAS, OECD, OSCE, APEC, BIS, Inter-American Development Bank, Asian Development Bank, IOM, Antarctic Treaty and the International Organization of the Francophonie.

ECONOMY

Services accounted for 71% of GDP in 2001, industry 27% and agriculture 2%.

According to the anti-corruption organization *Transparency International*, Canada ranked 12th in the world in a 2004 survey of the countries with the least corruption in business and government. It received 8·5 out of 10 in the annual index.

Overview. Canada has experienced strong economic growth since the mid 1990s, considered by the OECD to be a consequence of increased hourly productivity growth rates. There was a slowdown in 2003, with average annual per capita growth of approximately 2·5%. The USA accounts for a quarter of Canada's exports. Canada is still substantially behind the USA in terms of income per capita. The income gap between the two countries started to narrow in the late 1990s. This is partly a result of reforms, which have increased flexibility, improved fiscal consolidation and established a credible monetary framework. The improved macroeconomic framework has helped to lower sustainable real interest rates and has increased the effectiveness of counter-cyclical monetary policy. Although the current framework has been considered successful, the Bank of Canada and the government are committed to evaluating the current inflation target range by the end of 2006. Structural unemployment remains high; in 2003 it was one percentage point above the G7 average, in part owing to generous social assistance and unemployment insurance schemes. Canada is better prepared than most OECD countries to cope with an ageing population. However, problems remain with healthcare spending—further growth in healthcare costs could make the fiscal position unsustainable.

Currency. The unit of currency is the *Canadian dollar* (CAD) of 100 *cents.* In June 2002 gold reserves were 0·86m. troy oz and foreign exchange reserves totalled US$32,831m. Total money supply was $258,252m. CDN in June 2002. Inflation was 2·6% in 2001, 2·2% in 2002 and 2·8% in 2003.

Budget. Consolidated federal, provincial, territorial and local government revenue and expenditure for fiscal years ending 31 March (in $1m. CDN):

	1999–2000	*2000–01*	*2001–02*	*2002–03*
Revenue	414,170	445,311	435,520	440,746
Expenditure	401,520	422,656	435,885	440,006

In 2002–03 revenue included (in $1m. CDN): income taxes, 179,631; consumption taxes, 96,845; property and related taxes, 43,291; sales of goods and services, 35,071; contributions to social security plans, 30,027. Expenditure included: social services, 117,109; health, 81,720; education, 65,002; debt charges, 51,642.

On 1 Jan. 1991 a 7% Goods and Services Tax (GST) was introduced, superseding a 13·5% Manufacturers' Sales Tax.

Performance. Total GDP was US$834,390m. in 2003. Real GDP growth was 1·8% in 2001, 3·4% in 2002 and 2·0% in 2003.

Banking and Finance. The Bank of Canada (established 1935) is the central bank and bank of issue. The *Governor* (David Dodge) is appointed by the Bank's directors for seven-year terms. The Minister of Finance owns the capital stock of the Bank on behalf of Canada. Banks in Canada are chartered under the terms of the Bank Act, which imposes strict conditions on capital reserves, returns to the federal government, types of lending operations, ownership and other matters. As of July 2002 there were 14 domestic banks, 33 foreign bank subsidiaries and 20 foreign bank branches operating in Canada through over 8,000 branches and managing over $1·7trn. CDN in assets. Chartered banks accounted collectively for over 70% of the total assets of the Canadian financial services sector, with the six largest domestic banks (Canadian Imperial Bank of Commerce, Bank of Nova Scotia, Bank of Montreal, National Bank of Canada, TD Canada Trust and Royal Bank of Canada) accounting for over 90% of the total assets held by the banking industry. In 2002 Canada had the highest number of automated bank machines per capita in the world (with nearly 18,000 ABMs) and the highest penetration levels of electronic banking channels (such as debit cards, Internet banking and telephone banking). In 2000 chartered banks employed over 235,000 people in Canada and had a payroll of approximately $16·1bn. CDN. The First Nations Bank was founded in Dec. 1996 to provide finance to Inuit and Indian entrepreneurs.

The activities of banks are monitored by the federal Office of the Superintendent of Financial Institutions (OSFI), which reports to the Minister of Finance. Canada's federal financial institutions legislation is reviewed at least every five years. Significant legislative changes were made in 1992, updating the regulatory framework and removing barriers separating the activities of various types of financial institutions. In 1999 legislation was passed allowing foreign banks to establish operations in Canada without having to set up Canadian-incorporated subsidiaries. In 2001 Bill C-8, establishing the Financial Consumer Agency of Canada (the FCAC), was implemented. It aimed to foster competition in the financial sector and provide a holding company option allowing additional organizational flexibility to banks and insurance companies. The FCAC is responsible for enforcing consumer-related provisions of laws governing federal financial institutions.

There are stock exchanges at Calgary (Alberta Stock Exchange), Montreal, Toronto, Vancouver and Winnipeg.

ENERGY AND NATURAL RESOURCES

Environment. Canada's carbon dioxide emissions from the consumption and flaring of fossil fuels in 2002 were the equivalent of 18·9 tonnes per capita. An

Environmental Sustainability Index compiled for the World Economic Forum meeting in Feb. 2002 ranked Canada fourth in the world, with 70·6%. The index measured the ability of countries to maintain favourable environmental conditions and examined various factors including pollution levels and the use or abuse of natural resources.

Electricity. Generating capacity, 2000, 118·0m. kW. Production, 2000, 590·13bn. kWh (358·41bn. kWh hydro-electric, 158·68bn. kWh thermal and 72·80bn. kWh nuclear); consumption per capita was 18,030 kWh in 2000. In 2003 there were 17 nuclear reactors in use.

Oil and Gas. Oil reserves in 2002 were 6·9bn. bbls.; gas (2002), 1,700,000m. cu. metres. Production of crude petroleum, 2002, 135·6m. tonnes; natural gas (2002), 183·5bn. cu. metres. Canada is the third largest producer of natural gas, after Russia and the USA. Canada's first off-shore field, 250 km off Nova Scotia, began producing in June 1992.

Water. Annual average water usage in Canada is 1,600 cu. metres per person—less than in the USA but nearly twice the average for an industrialized nation.

Minerals. Mineral production in 1,000 tonnes: sand and gravel (2001), 238,795; lignite (2000), 35,359; coal (2000), 33,804; iron ore (2001), 27,900; salt (2002), 13,000; gypsum and anhydrite (2000), 9,232; aluminium (2001), 2,583; lime (2001), 2,235; peat (2001), 1,280; zinc (2001), 1,012; copper (2001), 633; asbestos (2001), 262; nickel (2002), 178 (content of concentrate); lead (2001), 154; uranium (2002), 11·6 (the highest of any country in the world); cobalt (2001), 5·3; silver (2001), 1·27; gold (2001), 159 tonnes; diamonds (2002), 5·0m. carats.

Agriculture. Grain growing, dairy farming, fruit farming, ranching and fur farming are all practised. In 2000, 2·4% of the economically active population was engaged in agriculture.

According to 2001 census the total land area was 9,012,112 sq. km, of which 675,039 sq. km were on farms. There were 264,925 farms in 2001; average size, 273·6 ha. Average farm receipts in 2001 totalled $155,104 CDN. Total farm cash receipts (2003), $34,122,273,000 CDN. There were 732,521 tractors in 2001 and 115,803 harvester-threshers.

The following table shows the value of receipts for selected agricultural commodities in 2003 (in $1m. CDN):

Crops	*13,055*	*Livestock and products*	*16,213*
Barley	387	Beef	5,194
Canola	1,755	Dairy	4,496
Corn for grain	784	Hogs	3,390
Soybeans	715	Poultry	1,785
Wheat	2,441		
Other crops	6,966		

Output (in 1,000 tonnes) and harvested area (in 1,000 ha) of crops:

	Output		*Harvested Area*	
	1999	*2000*	*1999*	*2000*
Wheat	26,900	26,804	10,367	10,963
Barley	13,196	13,468	4,069	4,551
Rapeseeds	8,798	7,119	5,564	4,816
Maize	9,161	6,827	1,141	1,088
Potatoes	4,268	4,569	157	158
Oats	3,641	3,389	1,398	1,299
Peas	2,252	2,864	835	1,220
Soybeans	2,781	2,703	1,004	1,061
Lentils	724	914	497	688
Sugarbeets	744	821	17	15
Linseeds	1,022	693	777	591
Tomatoes	683	670	9	8
Chick-peas	197	387	139	283
Carrots	294	279	9	8
Beans	294	261	150	158
Rye	387	260	169	115
Onions	181	189	5	5
Cabbages	180	167	9	8
Sunflower seeds	122	119	79	69

Canada is the world's leading barley and rapeseed producer and the second largest producer of oats.

Livestock. In parts of Saskatchewan and Alberta, stockraising is still carried on as a primary industry, but the livestock industry of the country at large is mainly a subsidiary of mixed farming. The following table shows the numbers of livestock (in 1,000) by provinces in 2001:

Provinces	*Milch cows*	*Total cattle and calves*	*Sheep and lambs*	*Pigs*
Newfoundland and Labrador	4·7	9·5	7·9	2·7
Prince Edward Island	14·6	84·8	3·6	126·1
Nova Scotia	23·9	108·4	24·9	124·9
New Brunswick	19·0	91·2	9·6	137·0
Quebec	407·2	1,362·8	254·1	4,267·4
Ontario	363·5	2,140·7	337·6	3,457·3
Manitoba	42·4	1,424·4	84·8	2,540·2
Saskatchewan	30·1	2,899·5	149·4	1,109·8
Alberta	84·0	6,615·2	307·3	2,027·5
British Columbia	71·4	814·9	83·3	165·8
Total	1,061·0	15,551·4	1,262·4	13,958·8

Other livestock totals (2000): horses, 385,000; chickens, 158m.; turkeys, 5m.

Livestock products. Slaughterings in 2000: pigs, 19·96m.; cattle, 3·77m.; sheep, 0·53m. Production, 2000 (in 1,000 tonnes): pork, bacon and ham, 1,675; beef and veal, 1,260; poultry meat, 1,065; horsemeat, 18; lamb and mutton, 11; cow's milk, 8,090; hens' eggs, 357; cheese, 351; honey, 32; hides, 94.

Fruit production in 2002, in 1,000 tonnes: apples, 382; grapes, 67; blueberries, 65; cranberries, 52; peaches and nectarines, 29; strawberries, 25; pears, 15; raspberries, 15.

Forestry. Forests make up nearly half of Canada's landmass and 10% of the world's forest cover. Forestry is of great economic importance, and forestry products (pulp, newsprint, building timber) constitute Canada's most valuable exports. In 2002 Canada had 417·6m. ha of forest land, about 56% (234·5m. ha) of which was classed as commercial forest. 2·8m. ha were burned by forest fires in 2002.

In 2001, 176·69m. cu. metres of roundwood was produced.

Fur Trade. In 2001, 1,019,400 wildlife pelts (valued at $23,496,600 CDN) and 1,147,100 ranch-raised pelts (valued at $49,971,300 CDN) were produced.

Fisheries. In 2002 landings of commercial fisheries totalled 1,101,376 tonnes; primary fisheries production was valued at $2·8bn. CDN (of which commercial marine $2·1bn. CDN). In 2001 the total catch was 1,063,915 tonnes (more than 96% from sea fishing); Atlantic landings totalled 879,636 tonnes and Pacific landings 184,279 tonnes. Value of sea fisheries landed in 2001 totalled $2,098m. CDN.

INDUSTRY

The leading companies by market capitalization in Canada, excluding banking and finance, in May 2004 were: The Thomson Corporation (US$21·4bn.), a media and photography company; BCE Inc. (US$18·5bn.), a telecommunications company; and EnCana (US$18·3bn.), an oil and gas company.

Value of manufacturing shipments for all industries in 2003 was $545,765·2m. CDN. Principal manufactures in 1,000 tonnes: petrol (2000), 30,981; distillate fuel oil (2000), 28,198; paper and paperboard (2001), 19,828; crude steel (2002), 16,000; cement (producers' shipments, 2001), 12,986; mechanical wood pulp (2001), 11,409; pig iron (2002), 8,700; newsprint (2001), 8,376; residual fuel oil (2000), 6,564; jet fuel (2000), 4,114; sulphuric acid (2001), 3,846; kerosene (2000), 1,487; synthetic rubber (1998), 191; sugar (2002), 64. Output of other products: 2·6m. motor vehicles (2003); 44·4bn. cigarettes (2001); sawn timber (2001), 47·70m. cu. metres; chipboard (2001), 10·73m. cu. metres; plywood (2001), 2·33m. cu. metres.

Labour. In 2001 there were (in 1,000), 15,076·8 (6,967·1 females) in employment, with principal areas of activity as follows: wholesale and retail trade/repair of motor vehicles, motorcycles and personal and household goods, 2,649·6; manufacturing, 2,274·5; real estate, renting and business activities, 1,776·7; health and social work,

1,542·1; transport, storage and communications, 1,162·4; hotels and restaurants, 976·0; education, 966·2; construction, 839·6; public administration and defence/compulsory social security, 764·0. In Jan. 2005 the unemployment rate stood at 7·0%.

In 2001, 2,231,145 working days were lost in industrial disputes.

Trade Unions. Union membership in Jan. 2002 was 4,178,000, of whom 72·8% belonged to the Canadian Labour Congress. Individual unions with the largest memberships in Jan. 2002 were the Canadian Union of Public Employees (521,600), National Union of Public and General Employees (325,000), National Automobile, Aerospace, Transportation and General Workers Union of Canada (238,000) and United Food and Commercial Workers International Union (220,800).

A trade union to which the majority of employees in a unit suitable for collective bargaining belong generally has certain rights and duties. An employer is required to negotiate with that union to determine wage rates and other working conditions of employees. The employer, trade union and employees affected are bound by the resulting agreement. Generally, work stoppages do not take place until an established conciliation or mediation procedure has been carried out, and are prohibited while an agreement is in effect.

INTERNATIONAL TRADE

A North American Free Trade Agreement (NAFTA) between Canada, Mexico and the USA was signed on 7 Oct. 1992 and came into force on 1 Jan. 1994.

Imports and Exports. Trade in US$1m.:

	1998	*1999*	*2000*	*2001*	*2002*
Imports f.o.b.	204,617	220,203	243,889	226,495	227,240
Exports f.o.b.	220,539	248,494	289,468	272,359	264,078

Canada is heavily dependent on foreign trade. In 2002 exports of goods and services were equivalent to 41% of GDP and imports equivalent to 37%; merchandise exports to the USA accounted for over 33·5% of GDP. Main export markets, 2002 (in $1m. CDN): USA, 346,990·6; Japan, 10,291·6; United Kingdom, 6,239·4; other EU countries, 16,496·4; other OECD countries, 12,341·9; other countries, 21,945·3. Main import suppliers, 2002 (in $1m. CDN): USA, 254,929·0; Japan, 11,732·2; United Kingdom, 10,312·4; other EU countries, 25,863·3; other OECD countries, 19,670·3; other countries, 33,952·1.

Main categories of exports, 2002 (in $1m. CDN): machinery and equipment, 97,303·8 (aircraft and other transport equipment, 22,784·1; industrial and agricultural machinery, 20,281·0); automotive products, 97,030·3 (passenger cars and chassis, 49,815·4; motor vehicle parts, 29,357·8); industrial goods and materials, 70,232·5 (chemicals, plastics and fertilizers, 24,302·7; metals and alloys, 22,214·3); energy products, 49,542·0 (crude petroleum, 18,795·3; natural gas, 18,359·4); forestry products, 37,197·9 (lumber and sawmill products, 17,761·1; newsprint and other paper and paperboard products, 12,986·4). Imports, 2002 (in $1m. CDN): machinery and equipment, 105,866·7 (industrial and agricultural machinery, 27,553·0; office machines and equipment, 15,699·6); automotive products, 81,449·6 (motor vehicle parts, 43,454·6); industrial goods and materials, 68,873·1 (chemicals and plastics, 25,724·1; metals and metal ores, 16,475·1).

COMMUNICATIONS

Roads. In 2002 there were 1,408,800 km of roads, including 85,800 km of highways, national or main roads, 114,600 km of secondary or regional roads and 16,900 km of motorways.

The National Highway System, spanning almost 25,000 km, includes the Trans-Canada Highway and other major east–west and north–south highways. While representing only 3% of total road infrastructure, the system carries about 30% of all vehicle travel in Canada.

Registered road motor vehicles totalled 18,868,756 in 2003; they comprised 17,755,082 passenger cars and light vehicles, 660,437 trucks and truck tractors (weighing at least 4,500 kg), 79,875 buses and 373,362 motorcycles and mopeds.

In 2001 freight transport totalled 87,522m. tonne-km.

There were 2,778 fatalities (a rate of 8·9% deaths per 100,000 population) in road accidents in 2001.

Rail. Canada has two great trans-continental systems: the Canadian National Railway system (CN), a body privatized in 1995 which operated 31,764 km of routes in 2000, and the Canadian Pacific Railway (CP), operating 22,590 km. A government-funded organization, VIA Rail, operates passenger services in all regions of Canada; 3·8m. passengers were carried in 2003. There are several provincial and private railways operating 17,528 km (2000).

There are metros in Montreal, Toronto and Vancouver, and tram/light rail systems in Calgary, Edmonton and Toronto.

Civil Aviation. Civil aviation is under the jurisdiction of the federal government. The technical and administrative aspects are supervised by Transport Canada, while the economic functions are assigned to the National Transportation Agency.

The busiest Canadian airport is Toronto (Lester B. Pearson International), which in 2000 handled 28,930,000 passengers (16,612,000 on international flights), ahead of Vancouver International, with 16,007,000 passengers (8,306,000 on domestic flights) and Montreal (Dorval International), with 8,493,000 passengers (5,751,000 on domestic flights). Toronto is also the busiest airport for freight, handling 392,000 tonnes in 2000.

Air Canada (privatized in July 1989) took over its main competitor, Canadian Airlines, in April 2000. In 1999 Air Canada flew 356·6m. km and carried 16,520,600 passengers, and Canadian Airlines International flew 211·9m. km and carried 7,496,900 passengers (3,667,300 on international flights).

Shipping. In 2000 the merchant marine comprised 861 vessels over 100 GRT including 25 oil tankers. Total tonnage, 2002, 2·80m. GRT, including oil tankers 0·40m. GRT. In 2001 vessels totalling 92,790,000 NRT entered ports and vessels totalling 121,712,000 NRT cleared.

Canada's leading port in terms of cargo handled is Vancouver. Other major ports are Saint John, Fraser River, Montreal and Quebec.

The major canals are those of the St Lawrence Seaway. Main commodities moved along the seaway are grain, iron ore, coal, other bulk and steel. The St Lawrence Seaway Management Corporation was established in 1998 as a non-profit making corporation to operate the Canadian assets of the seaway for the federal government under a long-term agreement with Transport Canada.

In 2003 total traffic on the Montreal-Lake Ontario (MLO) section of the seaway was 28,900,440 tonnes; on the Welland Canal section it was 31,870,466 tonnes. There were 3,886 vessel transits in 2003, generating $62,257,197 CDN in toll revenue.

Telecommunications. In 2002 there were 31,811,100 telephone subscribers (1,012·6 per 1,000 persons). Canada had 16·84m. Internet users in March 2002. There were 15·3m. PCs in use in 2002 (487·0 for every 1,000 persons) and 11,849,000 mobile phone subscribers (377·2 for every 1,000 persons). There were 1·1m. fax machines in 1997.

Postal Services. The Canada Post Corporation processed 10·7bn. pieces of mail in 2003. Revenue from operations reached $6·3bn. CDN, an increase of $190m. CDN over 2002. Consolidated net income for 2003 was $253m. CDN, an increase of $182m. CDN over 2002. The Corporation had 23,765 retail points of access at the end of 2003.

SOCIAL INSTITUTIONS

Justice. The courts in Canada are organized in a four-tier structure. The Supreme Court of Canada, based in Ottawa, is the highest court, having general appellate jurisdiction in civil and criminal cases throughout the country. It is comprised of a Chief Justice and eight puisne judges appointed by the Governor-in-Council, with a minimum of three judges coming from Quebec. The second tier consists of the Federal Court of Appeal and the various provincial courts of appeal. The third tier consists of the Federal Court (which replaced the Exchequer Court in 1971), the Tax Court of Canada and the provincial and territorial superior courts (which include both a court of general trial jurisdiction and a provincial court of appeal). The majority of cases are heard by the provincial courts, the fourth tier in the hierarchy. They are generally divided within each province into various divisions defined by the subject matter of their respective jurisdictions (for example a Traffic Division, a Small Claims Division, a Family Division and a Criminal Division).

There were 2,353,926 Criminal Code Offences (excluding traffic) reported in 2000. There were 963 violent crimes per 100,000 population in 2003. In 2003 there were 548 homicides in Canada, giving a rate of 1·7 homicides per 100,000 population (the lowest rate since 1967). The population in penal institutions in 2001 was 31,624 (102 per 100,000 of national population). The death penalty was abolished for all crimes in 1998.

Police. Total police personnel in Canada in June 2000 numbered 56,020. There were 7,658 female police officers, up from 3,573 in June 1990. Policing costs in 1999 totalled $6·4bn. CDN.

Royal Canadian Mounted Police (RCMP). The RCMP is a civil force maintained by the federal government. Established in 1873 as the North-West Mounted Police, it became the Royal North-West Mounted Police in 1904. Its sphere of operations was expanded in 1918 to include all of Canada west of Thunder Bay. In 1920 the force absorbed the Dominion Police, its headquarters was transferred from Regina to Ottawa, and its title was changed to Royal Canadian Mounted Police. The force is responsible to the Solicitor-General of Canada and is controlled by a Commissioner who is empowered to appoint peace officers in all the provinces and territories of Canada.

The responsibilities of the RCMP are national in scope. The administration of justice within the provinces, including the enforcement of the Criminal Code of Canada, is the responsibility of provincial governments, but all the provinces except Ontario and Quebec have entered into contracts with the RCMP to enforce criminal and provincial laws under the direction of the respective Attorneys-General. In addition, in these eight provinces the RCMP is under agreement to provide police services to municipalities. The RCMP is also responsible for all police work in the Yukon, Northwest Territories and Nunavut, enforcing federal law and territorial ordinances. The 14 Divisions, alphabetically designated, make up the strength of the RCMP across Canada; they comprise 52 sub-divisions which include 800 detachments. Headquarters Division, as well as the Office of the Commissioner, is located in Ottawa.

Assisting the criminal investigation work of the RCMP is the Directorate of Identification Services. Its services, together with those of divisional and sub-divisional units, and of six Forensic Laboratories, are available to police forces throughout Canada. The Canadian Police Information Centre (CPIC) at RCMP Headquarters, a national computer network, is staffed and operated by the RCMP. Law Enforcement agencies throughout Canada have access to information on stolen vehicles, licences and wanted persons.

In Feb. 2001 the Force had a total strength of 20,000 including regular members, special constables, civilian members and public service employees. It maintained 8,677 motor vehicles, 92 police service dogs and 156 horses.

The Force has 14 divisions actively engaged in law enforcement, one Headquarters Division and one training division. Marine services are divisional responsibilities and the Force currently has 402 boats at various points across Canada. The Air Directorate has stations throughout the country and maintains a fleet of 21 fixed-wing aircraft and eight helicopters.

Religion. Membership of religious denominations (according to census analysis):

	1991	*2001*	*% change 1991–2001*
Anglican Church of Canada	2,188,110	2,035,500	–7·0
Canadian Baptist Ministries	663,360	729,470	10·0
Christian Orthodox	387,395	479,620	23·8
Lutheran Church	636,205	606,590	–4·7
Pentecostal Assemblies of Canada	436,435	369,475	–15·3
Presbyterian Church	636,295	409,830	–35·6
Roman Catholic Church	12,203,625	12,793,125	4·8
United Church of Canada	3,093,120	2,839,125	–8·2

Membership of other denominations in 2001 (census figures): Jehovah's Witnesses, 154,745; Jews, 329,995; Latter-day Saints (Mormons), 104,750; Mennonites, 191,465; Muslims, 579,640; Salvation Army, 87,785. In Sept. 2003 the Roman Catholic church had five cardinals.

Education. Under the Constitution the provincial legislatures have powers over education. These are subject to certain qualifications respecting the rights of denominational and minority language schools. School board revenues derive from local taxation on real property, and government grants from general provincial revenue.

In 1999–2000 there were 15,595 elementary and secondary public and private schools with 5,397,068 pupils and 301,757 teachers; there were also 199 community colleges with 408,781 students.

Enrolment for Indian and Inuit children in elementary/secondary schools for 1999–2000: federal schools, 1,708; band-operated schools, 71,823; provincial/private schools, 45,839; giving a total of 119,370 students funded by the Department of Indian and Northern Affairs (DIAND). However, this total represents only a portion of Indian and Inuit students attending elementary/secondary schools.

There were 75 universities in 1999–2000 with 590,663 students and 33,801 teachers. According to 2001 census data, between 1991 and 2001 the proportion of adults aged 25 or over with university credentials grew from 15% to 20%; another 16% had a college diploma in 2001 (up from 12% in 1991) and 12% had a trade certificate. In all, the number of Canadians aged 25 and over with university, college or trade credentials grew by 2·7m. (a 39% increase) between 1991 and 2001.

The adult literacy rate in 2001 was at least 99%.

In 2000–01 public education expenditure represented 5·5% of GDP.

Health. Constitutional responsibility for healthcare services rests with the provinces and territories. Accordingly, Canada's national health insurance system consists of an interlocking set of provincial and territorial hospital and medical insurance plans conforming to certain national standards rather than a single national programme. The Canada Health Act (which took effect from April 1984 and consolidated the original federal health insurance legislation) sets out the national standards that provinces and territories are required to meet in order to qualify for full federal health contributions, including: provision of a comprehensive range of hospital and medical benefits; universal population coverage; access to necessary services on uniform terms and conditions; portability of benefits; and public administration of provincial and territorial insurance plans. Starting in the fiscal year 1996–97 the federal government's contribution to provincial health and social programmes was consolidated into a single block transfer—the Canada Health and Social Transfer (CHST). Funding is transferred to provinces as a combination of cash contributions and tax transfers, the latter being the federal government's largest transfer. In 2002–03 the provinces and territories received a total of $35·7bn. CDN in CHST, of which $16·6bn. CDN was in tax transfers. Over and above these health transfers, the federal government also provides financial support for such provincial and territorial extended healthcare service programmes as nursing-home care, certain home care services, ambulatory healthcare services and adult residential care services.

The approach taken by Canada is one of state-sponsored health insurance. The advent of insurance programmes produced little change in the ownership of hospitals, almost all of which are owned by non-government non-profit corporations, or in the rights and privileges of private medical practice. Patients are free to choose their own general practitioner. Except for a small percentage of the population whose care is provided for under other legislation (such as serving members of the Canadian Armed Forces and inmates of federal penitentiaries), all residents are eligible, regardless of whether they are in the workforce. Benefits are available without upper limit so long as they are medically necessary, provided any registration obligations are met.

In addition to the benefits qualifying for federal contributions, provinces and territories provide additional benefits at their own discretion. Most fund their portion of health costs out of general provincial and territorial revenues. Most have charges for long-term chronic hospital care geared, approximately, to the room and board portion of the OAS–GIS payment mentioned under Welfare *below*. Health spending accounted for 9·6% of GDP in 2002.

In 2001 there were 58,546 physicians, giving a rate of 187 per 100,000 population; there were 57 dentists per 100,000 population. In 2002 the regulated nursing workforce numbered 296,200.

Welfare. The social security system provides financial benefits and social services to individuals and their families through programmes administered by federal, provincial and municipal governments and voluntary organizations. Federally, Human Resources and Skills Development is responsible for research into the areas of social issues, provision of grants and contributions for various social services and the administration of income security programmes, including the Old Age Security (OAS) programme, the Guaranteed Income Supplement, the Spouse's Allowance and the Canada Pension Plan (CPP).

The Old Age Security pension is payable to persons 65 years of age and over who satisfy the residence requirements stipulated in the Old Age Security Act. The amount payable, whether full or partial, is also governed by stipulated conditions, as is the payment of an OAS pension to a recipient who absents himself from Canada. OAS pensioners with little or no income apart from OAS may, upon application, receive a full or partial supplement known as the Guaranteed Income Supplement (GIS). Entitlement is normally based on the pensioner's income in the preceding year, calculated in accordance with the Income Tax Act. The spouse of an OAS pensioner, aged 60 to 64, meeting the same residence requirements as those stipulated for OAS, may be eligible for a full or partial Spouse's Allowance (SPA). SPA is payable, on application, depending on the annual combined income of the couple (not including the pensioner spouse's basic OAS pension or GIS). In 1979 the SPA programme was expanded to include a spouse, who is eligible for SPA in the month the pensioner spouse dies, until the age of 65 or until remarriage (Extended Spouse's Allowance). Since Sept. 1985 SPA has also been available to low income widow(er)s aged 60–64 regardless of the age of their spouse at death.

As of 1 July 2004 the basic OAS pension was $466·63 CDN monthly; the maximum Guaranteed Income Supplement was $554·59 CDN monthly for a single pensioner or a married pensioner whose spouse was not receiving a pension or a Spouse's Allowance, and $361·24 CDN monthly for each spouse of a married couple where both were pensioners.

The Canada Pension Plan is designed to provide workers with a basic level of income protection in the event of retirement, disability or death. Benefits may be payable to a contributor, a surviving spouse or an eligible child. Actuarially adjusted retirement benefits may begin as early as age 60 or as late as age 70. Benefits are determined by the contributor's earnings and contributions made to the Plan. Contribution is compulsory for most employed and self-employed Canadians aged 18 to 65. The CPP does not operate in Quebec, which has exercised its constitutional prerogative to establish a similar plan. In 2004 the maximum retirement pension payable under CPP was $814·17 CDN; the maximum disability pension was $992·80 CDN; and the maximum surviving spouse's pension was $488·50 CDN (for survivors 65 years of age and over) or 60% of the retirement pension which the deceased contributor would have received at age 65. The survivor pension payable to a surviving spouse under 65 (maximum of $454·42 CDN in 2004) is composed of two parts: a flat-rate component and an earnings-related portion.

As projections indicated that the CPP was lacking sufficient assets to meet long-term obligations, contribution rates were increased from 6% in 1997 to 9·9% of maximum pensionable earnings by 2003. The Canada Pension Plan Investment Board, an independent investment organization separate from the CPP, was established to invest excess CPP funds in a diversified portfolio of securities, beginning operations in April 1998. In 2004 the range of yearly pensionable earnings was from $3,500 CDN to $40,500 CDN. In June 1999 over 5m. Canadians received Canada or Quebec Pension Plan benefits. Social security agreements co-ordinate the operation of the Old Age Security and the CPP with the comparable social security programmes of certain other countries.

Canada Child Tax Benefit (CCTB) is a tax-free monthly payment made to eligible families to help them with the cost of raising children under 18. Included with the CCTB is the National Child Benefit Supplement (NCBS), a monthly benefit for low-income families with children.

CULTURE

World Heritage Sites. Sites under Canadian jurisdiction which appear on UNESCO's world heritage list are (with year entered on list): L'Anse aux Meadows National Historic Site (1978), the remains of an 11th-century Viking settlement in Newfoundland; Nahanni National Park (1978); Dinosaur Provincial Park (1979), in

Alberta, a major area for fossil discoveries; SGaang Gwaii (Anthony Island) (1981), illustrating the Haida people's art and way of life; Head-Smashed-In Buffalo Jump (1981), in southwest Alberta, incorporating an aboriginal camp—the name relates to the aboriginal custom of killing buffalo by chasing them over a precipice; Wood Buffalo National Park (1983); Canadian Rocky Mountain Parks (1984), incorporating the neighbouring parks of Banff, Jasper, Kootenay and Yoho, as well as the Mount Robson, Mount Assiniboine and Hamber provincial parks, and the Burgess Shale fossil site; Historic District of Quebec (1985), retaining aspects of its French colonial past; Gros Morne National Park (1987), in Newfoundland; Old Town Lunenburg (1995), a well-preserved British colonial settlement; Miguasha Park (1999), among the world's most important fossil sites. Two UNESCO World Heritage Sites fall under joint Canadian and US jurisdiction: Kluane/Wrangell-St Elias/Glacier Bay/ Tatshenshini-Alsek (1979), parks in the Yukon Territory, British Columbia and Alaska; Waterton Glacier International Peace Park (1995), in Alberta and Montana.

Broadcasting. The Canadian Radio-Television and Telecommunications Commission is an independent authority established by parliament in 1968 to regulate the broadcasting and telecommunications systems. The Canadian Broadcasting Corporation operates two national TV networks, one in English and one in French, and there are three private TV networks (colour by NTSC). In 2002 there were 785 cable TV licences (the number having decreased following the CRTC's decision not to regulate cable systems that serve small and rural communities and have fewer than 2,000 subscribers) and there were 7,623,000 subscribers to cable television. There were 21·5m. TV receivers in 2001 and 32·2m. radio receivers in 2000.

There were 1,959 originating radio stations operating in 2003, of which 432 were AM and 1,527 FM.

Press. In 2003 there were 101 daily papers with a total average circulation of 4·93m.; *The Toronto Star* had the largest circulation at 460,000, then *The Globe and Mail* with 315,000. There were 1,071 non-daily papers in 2003, with a circulation of 21,235,000. In 2000–01 a total of 15,744 book titles were published.

Tourism. In 2000 there were 20,423,000 foreign tourists, around 90% of whom were from the USA. The next biggest tourist markets are the UK, Japan, France and Germany. Revenue from visitors was US$10,768m.

Festivals. The Quebec Winter Festival is held each Feb. The Montreal Jazz Festival is in June while the Calgary Stampede (the world's largest rodeo, incorporating a series of concerts and a carnival) is in July. Also in July are the Ottawa International Jazz Festival, the Québec Festival d'Été/Summer Festival (featuring music and art performances) and the Montréal Juste Pour Rire/Just for Laughs comedy festival. The Toronto international film festival takes place in Sept. and the Vancouver international film festival is the following month. Canada Day, held each July, is marked nationwide with firework displays, parades and parties.

Libraries. In 2002 the National Library and the National Archives of Canada amalgamated to create the Library and Archives of Canada. In 1999 the National Library held 6,955,000 volumes and public libraries had a total of 75,033,000 volumes.

Museums and Galleries. In 1999 there were 2,600 heritage institutions (including museums, historic sites, archives, exhibition centres, planetariums and observatories, aquariums and zoos, and botanical gardens); attendance totalled 118·3m. visits (including 26·5m. visits to museums) and operating revenues were $1·5bn. CDN.

DIPLOMATIC REPRESENTATIVES

Of Canada in the United Kingdom (Macdonald House, 1 Grosvenor Sq., London, W1K 4AB)
High Commissioner: Mel Cappe.

Of the United Kingdom in Canada (80 Elgin St., Ottawa, K1P 5K7)
High Commissioner: David Reddaway, CMG, MBE.

Of Canada in the USA (501 Pennsylvania Ave., NW, Washington, D.C., 20001)
Ambassador: Frank McKenna.

Of the USA in Canada (490 Sussex Drive, Ottawa, K1N 1G8)
Ambassador: Argeo Paul Cellucci.

Of Canada to the United Nations
Ambassador: Allan Rock.

Of Canada to the European Union
Ambassador: Jeremy K. B. Kinsman.

FURTHER READING

Canadian Annual Review. From 1960
Canadian Encyclopedia. 2nd ed. 4 vols. Edmonton, 1988

Brown, R. C., *An Illustrated History of Canada.* Toronto, 1991
Cook, C., *Canada after the Referendum of 1992.* McGill-Queens Univ. Press, 1994
Dawson, R. M. and Dawson, W. F., *Democratic Government in Canada.* 5th ed. Toronto Univ. Press, 1989
Ingles, E., *Canada.* [Bibliography] ABC-Clio, Oxford and Santa Barbara (CA), 1990
Jackson, R. J., *Politics in Canada: Culture, Institutions, Behaviour and Public Policy.* 2nd ed. Scarborough (Ont.), 1990
Longille, P., *Changing the Guard: Canada's Defence in a World in Transition.* Toronto Univ. Press, 1991
Silver, A. I. (ed.) *Introduction to Canadian History.* London, 1994

Other more specialized titles are listed under CONSTITUTION AND GOVERNMENT *above.*

National library: The National Library of Canada, Ottawa, Ontario. *Librarian:* Roch Carrier.
National statistical office: Statistics Canada, Ottawa, K1A 0T6.
Website: http://www.statcan.ca/

CANADIAN PROVINCES

GENERAL DETAILS

The ten provinces each have a separate parliament and administration, with a Lieut.-Governor, appointed by the Governor-General in Council at the head of the executive. They have full powers to regulate their own local affairs and dispose of their revenues, provided only that they do not interfere with the action and policy of the central administration. Among the subjects assigned exclusively to the provincial legislatures are: the amendment of the provincial constitution, except as regards the office of the Lieut.-Governor; property and civil rights; direct taxation for revenue purposes; borrowing; management and sale of Crown lands; provincial hospitals, reformatories, etc.; shop, saloon, tavern, auctioneer and other licences for local or provincial purposes; local works and undertakings, except lines of ships, railways, canals, telegraphs, etc., extending beyond the province or connecting with other provinces, and excepting also such works as the Canadian Parliament declares are for the general good; marriages, administration of justice within the province; education. On 18 July 1994 the federal and provincial governments signed an agreement easing inter-provincial barriers on government procurement, labour mobility, transport licences and product standards. Federal legislation of Dec. 1995 grants provinces a right of constitutional veto.

For the administration of the three territories *see* Northwest Territories, Nunavut, Yukon Territory *below.*

Areas of the ten provinces and three territories (Northwest Territories, Nunavut and Yukon) (in sq. km) and population at recent censuses:

Province	*Land area*	*Total land and fresh water area*	*Population, 1991*[1, 2]	*Population, 1996*	*Population, 2001*[1]
Newfoundland (Nfld.)	373,872	405,212	568,474	551,792	512,930
Prince Edward Island (PEI)	5,660	5,660	129,765	134,557	135,294
Nova Scotia (NS)	53,338	55,284	899,942	909,282	908,007
New Brunswick (NB)	71,450	72,908	723,900	738,133	729,498
Quebec (Que.)	1,365,128	1,542,056	6,895,963	7,138,795	7,237,479
Ontario (Ont.)	917,741	1,076,395	10,084,885	10,753,573	11,410,046
Manitoba (Man.)	553,556	647,797	1,091,942	1,113,898	1,119,583
Saskatchewan (Sask.)	591,670	651,036	988,928	990,237	978,933
Alberta (Alta.)	642,317	661,848	2,545,553	2,696,826	2,974,807

Province	Land area	Total land and fresh water area	Population, 1991[1, 2]	Population, 1996	Population, 2001[1]
British Columbia (BC)	925,186	944,735	3,282,061	3,724,500	3,907,738
Nunavut (Nvt.)	1,936,113	2,093,190			26,745[3]
Northwest Territories (NWT)	1,183,085	1,346,106	57,649	64,402	37,360[4]
Yukon Territory (YT)	474,391	482,443	27,797	30,766	28,674

[1]Excludes data from incompletely enumerated Indian reserves and Indian settlements.
[2]Comparison of the 1991 census data with data from earlier censuses is affected by a change in the definition of the 1991 census population. Persons in Canada on student authorizations, Minister's permits, and as refugee claimants were enumerated in the 1991 census but not in previous censuses. These persons are referred to as non-permanent residents.
[3]Nunavut only came into existence in 1999.
[4]The population of the Northwest Territories declined so steeply between 1996 and 2001 because of the formation of Nunavut, previously part of the Northwest Territories, in 1999.

Local Government. Under the terms of the British North America Act the provinces are given full powers over local government. All local government institutions are, therefore, supervised by the provinces, and are incorporated and function under provincial acts.

The acts under which municipalities operate vary from province to province. A municipal corporation is usually administered by an elected council headed by a mayor or reeve, whose powers to administer affairs and to raise funds by taxation and other methods are set forth in provincial laws, as is the scope of its obligations to, and on behalf of, the citizens. Similarly, the types of municipal corporations, their official designations and the requirements for their incorporation vary between provinces. The following table sets out the classifications as at the 2001 census:

	Federal electoral districts	Economic regions	Census divisions
Nfld.	7	4	10
PEI	4	1	3[1]
NS	11	5	18[1]
NB	10	5	15[1]
Que.	75	17	99[2]
Ont.	106	11	49[3]
Man.	14	8	23
Sask.	14	6	18
Alta.	28	8	19
BC	36	8	28[4]
Nvt.	1	1	3[5]
NWT	1	1	2[5]
YT	1	1	1[6]

[1]Counties.
[2]3 census divisions, 3 communautés urbaines, 93 municipalités régionales de comté.
[3]21 counties, 10 districts, 7 census divisions, 1 district municipality, 7 regional municipalities, 3 united counties. [4]1 region, 27 regional districts. [5]Regions. [6]Territory.

Justice. The administration of justice within the provinces, including the enforcement of the Criminal Code of Canada, is the responsibility of provincial governments, but all the provinces except Ontario and Quebec have entered into contracts with the Royal Canadian Mounted Police (RCMP) to enforce criminal and provincial law. In addition, in these eight provinces the RCMP is under agreement to provide police services to municipalities.

ALBERTA

KEY HISTORICAL EVENTS

The southern half of Alberta was administered from 1670 as part of Rupert's land by the Hudson's Bay Company. Trading posts were set up after 1783 when the North West Company took a share in the fur trade. In 1869 Rupert's land was transferred from the Hudson's Bay Company (which had absorbed its rival in 1821) to the new Dominion and in the following year this land was combined with the former Crown land of the North Western Territories to form the Northwest Territories. In 1882 'Alberta' first appeared as a provisional 'district', consisting of the southern half of the present province. In 1905 the Athabasca district to the north was added when provincial status was granted to Alberta.

TERRITORY AND POPULATION

The area of the province is 661,848 sq. km, 642,317 sq. km being land area and 16,531 sq. km water area. The population at the 2001 census was 2,974,807. Alberta has the fastest growing population of any Canadian province, with a 10·3% increase since the 1996 census. The urban population (2001), centres of 1,000 or over, was 80·9% and the rural 19·1%. Population (15 May 2001) of the 14 cities, as well as the two specialized municipalities: Calgary, 878,866; Edmonton, 616,104; Red Deer, 67,707; Lethbridge, 67,374; St Albert, 53,081; Medicine Hat, 51,249; Grande Prairie, 36,983; Airdrie, 20,382; Leduc, 15,032; Spruce Grove, 15,983; Camrose, 14,854; Fort Saskatchewan, 13,121; Lloydminster (Alberta portion), 13,148; Wetaskiwin, 11,154; Specialized Municipality of Wood Buffalo (Fort McMurray), 41,466; Specialized Municipality of Strathcona County (Sherwood Park), 71,986.

SOCIAL STATISTICS

Births in 2001 numbered 37,006 (a rate of 11·5 per 1,000 population) and deaths 18,068 (rate of 5·9 per 1,000 population). There were 17,981 marriages in 2002 and 8,291 divorces.

CLIMATE

Alberta has a continental climate of warm summers and cold winters—extremes of temperature. For the capital city, Edmonton, the hottest month is usually July (mean 17·5°C), while the coldest are Dec. and Jan. (–12°C). Rainfall amounts are greatest between May and Sept. In a year, the average precipitation is 461 mm (19·6") with about 129·6 cm of snowfall.

CONSTITUTION AND GOVERNMENT

The constitution of Alberta is contained in the British North America Act of 1867, and amending Acts; also in the Alberta Act of 1905, passed by the Parliament of the Dominion of Canada, which created the province out of the then Northwest Territories. The province is represented by five members in the Senate and 26 in the House of Commons of Canada.

The executive is vested nominally in the Lieut.-Governor, who is appointed by the federal government, but actually in the Executive Council or the Cabinet of the legislature. Legislative power is vested in the Assembly in the name of the Queen.

Members of the 83-member Legislative Assembly are elected by the universal vote of adults, 18 years of age and older.

RECENT ELECTIONS

In elections on 22 Nov. 2004 Premier Ralph Klein's Conservative Party won 47% of the vote (taking 61 of 83 seats), the Liberal Party 29% (17), the New Democrats 10% (4) and the Alberta Alliance 9% (1).

CURRENT ADMINISTRATION

Lieut.-Governor: Normie Kwong (sworn in 20 Jan. 2005).

As of Feb. 2005 the members of the Executive Council were as follows:

Premier, President of Executive Council: Ralph Klein (b. 1942; Progressive Conservative).

Deputy Premier and Minister of Finance: Shirley McClellan. *Advanced Education:* Dave Hancock. *Justice and Attorney General:* Ron Stevens. *Heath and Wellness:* Iris Evans. *International and Intergovernmental Relations:* Ed Stelmach. *Education:* Gene Zwozdesky. *Energy:* Greg Melchin. *Community Development:* Gary Mar. *Infrastructure and Transportation:* Lyle Oberg. *Human Resources and Employment:* Mike Cardinal. *Environment:* Guy Boutilier. *Children's Services:* Heather Forsyth. *Innovation and Science:* Victor Doerksen. *Sustainable Resource Development:* David Coutts. *Aboriginal Affairs and Northern Development:* Pearl Calahasen. *Government Services:* Ty Lund. *Economic Development:* Clint Dunford. *Gaming:* Gordon Graydon. *Municipal Affairs:* Rob Renner. *Restructuring and Government Efficiency:* Luke Ouellette. *Solicitor General:* Harvey Cenaiko. *Seniors and Community Support:* Yvonne Fritz. *Agriculture, Food and Rural Development:* Doug Horner.

Office of the Premier: http://www.gov.ab.ca/premier

ECONOMY

GDP per person in 2003 was $54,075 CDN.

Budget. The budgetary revenue and expenditure (in $1m. CDN) for years ending 31 March were as follows:

	1997–98	*1998–99*	*1999–2000*	*2000–01*	*2001–02*
Revenue	17,815	16,882	20,168	25,597	22,027
Expenditure	15,156	15,788	17,377	19,024	20,919

Performance. Real GDP growth was 5·4% in 2000.

Banking and Finance. Personal income *per capita* (2001), $30,993 CDN.

ENERGY AND NATURAL RESOURCES

Environment. There are five national parks in Alberta totalling 63,045 sq. km, the largest area of any province in Canada. There are also 518 parks and protected areas in Alberta covering 2,752,969 ha.

Oil and Gas. Oil sands underlie some 60,000 sq. km of Alberta, the four major deposits being: the Athabasca, Cold Lake, Peace River and Buffalo Head Hills deposits. Some 7% (3,250 sq. km) of the Athabasca deposit can be exploited through open-pit mining. The rest of the Athabasca, and all the deposits in the other areas, are deeper reserves which must be developed through *in situ* techniques. These reserves reach depths of 760 metres. In 2001, 86,679,000 cu. metres of crude oil were produced with gross sales value of $18,234·8m. CDN. Alberta produced 69% of Canada's crude petroleum output in 2001. 18,608,000 cu. metres of synthetic crude oil were produced in 2000.

Natural gas is found in abundance in numerous localities. In 2001, 133,283,000 cu. metres valued at $26,303·7m. CDN were produced in Alberta.

Minerals. Coal production in 2001 was 30,911,020 tonnes with 6,893,677 tonnes of coal being exported.

Value of total mineral production was $49,832·5m. CDN in 2001.

Agriculture. There were 53,652 farms in Alberta in 2001 with a total area of 21,067,486 ha. About 9,728,181 ha are land in crop (2001 census). The majority of farms are made up of cattle, followed by grains and oilseed, and wheat. For particulars of livestock *see* CANADA: Agriculture.

Farm cash receipts in 2001 totalled $8,322·0m. CDN of which crops contributed $2,299·4m. CDN, livestock and products $5,186·7m. CDN, and direct payments $835·9m. CDN.

Forestry. Forest land in 1999 covered some 38,210,000 ha. In 1999, 42,210 ha of forest was harvested.

Fisheries. The largest catch in commercial fishing is whitefish. Perch, tullibee, walley, pike and lake trout are also caught in smaller quantities. Commercial fish production in 2000–01 was 2,023 tonnes, value $3·27m. CDN.

INDUSTRY

The leading manufacturing industries are food and beverages, petroleum refining, metal fabricating, wood industries, primary metal, chemical and chemical products and non-metallic mineral products.

Manufacturing shipments had a total value of $42,552·0m. CDN in 2001. Greatest among these shipments were (in $1m. CDN): food, 9,143; refined petroleum and coal products, 7,449; chemicals and chemical products, 7,010; machinery, 3,363; fabricated metal products, 2,716; wood products, 2,200; computer and electronic products, 2,004; paper and allied products, 1,503; non-metal mineral products, 1,202; and primary metal, 1,008.

Total retail sales in 2001 were $34,602m. CDN, as compared to 2000 with $31,712m. CDN in sales. Main sales in 2001 were (in $1m. CDN): automobiles, 9,309·4; food, 7,316·0; general merchandise, 3,859·4; fuel 2,638·5; and automotive parts, accessories and services, 2,068·0.

Labour. In 2001 the labour force was 1,710,700 (771,600 females), of whom approximately 1,632,100 (736,900) were employed. In 2001 a total of 44,100 new jobs were created. Alberta's unemployment rate dropped to 4·6% in 2001, compared to the national average of 7·2%.

INTERNATIONAL TRADE

Imports and Exports. Alberta's domestic commodity exports were valued at $56·9bn. CDN in 2001. The largest export markets were the USA, Japan, China, Mexico and

South Korea, which together accounted for approximately 94% of Alberta's international exports. Mining and energy accounted for 71% of exports in 2001.

COMMUNICATIONS

Roads. In 2002 there were 16,012 km of primary highways, 14,717 km secondary highways and 137,298 km of local municipal roads.

On 31 March 2002 there were 2,296,748 motor vehicles registered, including 1,067,625 passenger vehicles.

Rail. In 2002 the length of main railway lines was 7,067 km. There are light rail networks in Edmonton (12·3 km) and Calgary (32·7 km).

Civil Aviation. Calgary International is a major international airport. It handled 8,090,000 passengers (5,751,000 on domestic flights) in 2000.

Telecommunications. The primary telephone system is owned and operated by the Telus Corporation. Telus Corporation had 1,998,366 telephone subscriber lines (including residential and business lines) in service in 2002.

SOCIAL INSTITUTIONS

Justice. The Supreme Judicial authority of the province is the Court of Appeal. Judges of the Court of Appeal and Court of Queen's Bench are appointed by the Federal government and hold office until retirement at the age of 75. There are courts of lesser jurisdiction in both civil and criminal matters. The Court of Queen's Bench has full jurisdiction over civil proceedings. A Provincial Court which has jurisdiction in civil matters up to $2,000 CDN is presided over by provincially appointed judges. Youth Courts have power to try boys and girls 12–17 years old inclusive for offences against the Young Offenders Act.

The jurisdiction of all criminal courts in Alberta is enacted in the provisions of the Criminal Code. The system of procedure in civil and criminal cases conforms as nearly as possible to the English system. In 2001, 276,860 Criminal Code offences were reported, including 70 homicides.

Education. Schools of all grades are included under the term of public school (including those in the separate school system, which are publicly supported). The same board of trustees controls the schools from kindergarten to university entrance. In 2001–02 there were approximately 547,830 pupils enrolled in grades 1–12, including private schools and special education programmes. The University of Alberta (in Edmonton), founded in 1907, had, in 2001–02, 32,248 students; the University of Calgary had 26,654 students; Athabasca University had 24,136 students; the University of Lethbridge had 6,217 students. Alberta has 30 post-secondary institutions including four universities and two technical colleges.

CULTURE

Tourism. Alberta attracted more than 5,067,000 visitors from outside the province in 2000. It is known for its mountains, museums, parks and festivals. Total tourism receipts in 2000 were $4·9bn. CDN.

FURTHER READING

Savage, H., Kroetsch, R., Wiebe, R., *Alberta.* NeWest Press, 1993

Economic Development Edmonton, *Edmonton Info: Edmonton's Official Fact Book 1999.* Edmonton, 1999

Statistical office: Alberta Finance, Statistics, Room 259, Terrace Bldg, 9515–107 St., Edmonton, AB T5K 2C3.

Websites: http://www.alberta-canada.com; http://www.discoveralberta.com

BRITISH COLUMBIA

KEY HISTORICAL EVENTS

British Columbia, formerly known as New Caledonia, was first administered by the Hudson's Bay Company. In 1849 Vancouver Island was given crown colony status and in 1853 the Queen Charlotte Islands became a dependency. The discovery of gold on the Fraser river and the following influx of population resulted in the creation in 1858 of the mainland crown colony of British Columbia, to which the Strikine Territory (established 1862) was later added. In 1866 the two colonies were united.

TERRITORY AND POPULATION

British Columbia has an area of 944,735 sq. km of which land area is 926,492 sq. km. The capital is Victoria. The province is bordered westerly by the Pacific Ocean and Alaska Panhandle, northerly by the Yukon and Northwest Territories, easterly by the Province of Alberta and southerly by the USA along the 49th parallel. A chain of islands, the largest of which are Vancouver Island and the Queen Charlotte Islands, affords protection to the mainland coast.

The population at the 2001 census was 3,907,738; 2002 estimate, 4·1m.

The principal metropolitan areas and cities and their population census for 2001 are as follows: Metropolitan Vancouver, 1,986,965; Metropolitan Victoria, 325,754; Abbotsford (amalgamated with Matsqui), 115,463; Kelowna, 96,298; Kamloops, 77,281; Nanaimo, 73,000; Prince George, 72,406; Chilliwack, 62,927; Vernon, 33,494; Mission, 31,272; Penticton, 30,985; Campbell River, 29,465; North Cowichan, 26,148; Cranbrook, 18,476; Port Alberni, 17,743.

SOCIAL STATISTICS

Births in 2002–03 numbered 40,134 (a rate of 9·7 per 1,000 population) and deaths 28,757 (rate of 7·0 per 1,000 population). There were 21,247 marriages and 10,125 divorces in 2002.

CLIMATE

The climate is cool temperate, but mountain influences affect temperatures and rainfall considerably. Driest months occur in summer. Vancouver, Jan. 36°F (2·2°C), July 64°F (17·8°C). Annual rainfall 58" (1,458 mm).

CONSTITUTION AND GOVERNMENT

The British North America Act of 1867 provided for eventual admission into Canadian Confederation, and on 20 July 1871 British Columbia became the sixth province of the Dominion.

British Columbia has a unicameral legislature of 79 elected members. Government policy is determined by the Executive Council responsible to the Legislature. The Lieut.-Governor is appointed by the Governor-General of Canada, usually for a term of five years, and is the head of the executive government of the province.

The Legislative Assembly is elected for a maximum term of five years. There are 79 electoral districts. Every Canadian citizen 18 years and over, having resided a minimum of six months in the province, duly registered, is entitled to vote. The province is represented in the Federal Parliament by 36 members in the House of Commons and six Senators.

RECENT ELECTIONS

At the Legislative Assembly elections of 16 May 2001 the Liberal Party won 58% of the vote and 77 of the 79 available seats. The other two seats went to the New Democratic Party.

CURRENT ADMINISTRATION

Lieut.-Governor: Iona Campagnolo, PC, OM, OBC (sworn in 25 Sept. 2001).

The Liberal Executive Council comprised in Feb. 2005:

Premier, President of the Executive Council: Gordon Campbell.

Minister of Children and Family Development: Stan Hagen. *Education:* Tom Christensen. *Attorney General and Minister Responsible for Treaty Negotiations:* Geoff Plant. *Solicitor General and Minister of Public Safety:* Rich Coleman. *Intergovernmental Relations:* Sindi Hawkins. *Finance:* Colin Hansen. *Early Childhood Development:* Linda Reid. *Community, Aboriginal Affairs and Women's Services:* Murray Coell. *Women's and Seniors' Services:* Wendy McMahon. *Advanced Education:* Ida Chong. *Skills Development and Labour:* Graham Bruce. *Agriculture, Food and Fisheries:* John van Dongen. *Energy and Mines:* Richard Neufeld. *Water, Land and Air Protection:* Bill Barisoff. *Forests:* Mike de Jong. *Health Services:* Shirley Bond. *Immigration and Multicultural Services:* Patrick

Wong. *Mental Health and Addiction Services:* Brenda Locke. *Mining:* Pat Bell. *Forestry Operations:* Roger Harris. *Transportation:* Kevin Falcon. *Provincial Revenue:* Rick Thorpe. *Human Resources:* Susan Brice. *Sustainable Resource Management:* George Abbott. *Management Services:* Joyce Murray. *Small Business and Economic Development:* John Les. *Resort Development:* Patty Sahota.

Office of the Premier: http://www.gov.bc.ca/prem

ECONOMY

GDP per person in 2003 was $35,041 CDN.

Budget. Total revenue in 2003–04 was $28,175m. CDN (own source revenue, $24,248m. CDN; general purpose transfers, $3,151m. CDN; special purpose transfers, $776m. CDN). Total expenditures in 2003–04 amounted to $30,896m. CDN (including: health, $11,181m. CDN; education, $6,797m. CDN; social services, $4,445m. CDN; debt charges, $2,538m. CDN; resource conservation and industrial development, $1,761m. CDN; transport and communication, $1,727m. CDN; protection of persons and property, $1,143m. CDN).

Banking and Finance. At Oct. 1997 Canadian chartered banks maintained 925 branches and had total assets of $146·3bn. CDN in British Columbia. In 1997 credit unions at 96 locations had total assets of $20·4bn. CDN. Several foreign banks have Canadian head offices in Vancouver and several others have branches.

ENERGY AND NATURAL RESOURCES

Electricity. Generation in 2003 totalled 63,051 GWh (56,689 GWh from hydro-electric sources), of which 14,717 GWh were delivered outside the province. Available within the province were 60,176 GWh (with imports of 11,842 GWh).

Oil and Gas. In 2001 natural gas production, from the northeastern part of the province, was valued at $5·18bn. CDN.

Water. Canada accounts for a quarter of the world's fresh water supply, a third of which is located in British Columbia. An extensive hydro-electric generation system has been developed in the province.

Minerals. Coal, copper, gold, zinc, silver and molybdenum are the most important minerals produced but natural gas amounts to approximately half of the value of mineral and fuel extraction. The value of mineral and petroleum products production in 2002 was estimated at $7·23bn. CDN. Coal production (from the northeastern and southeastern regions) was valued at $1·0bn. CDN. Copper was the most valuable metal with production totalling $599m. CDN in 2002; gold production amounted to $336m. CDN.

Agriculture. Only 3% of the total land area is arable or potentially arable. Farm holdings (20,290 in 2001) cover 2·6m. ha. with an average size of 127 ha. Farm cash receipts in 2003 were estimated at $2·2bn. CDN, led by floriculture and nursery products valued at $439m. CDN, dairy products valued at $393m. CDN and vegetables valued at $329m. CDN. For particulars of livestock *see* CANADA: Agriculture.

Forestry. Around 49·9m. ha are considered productive forest land of which 48·0m. ha are provincial crown lands managed by the Ministry of Forests. Approximately 96% of the forested land is coniferous. The total timber harvest in 2002 was 69·8m. cu. metres. Output of forest-based products, 2002: lumber, 33·56m. cu. metres; plywood, 1·68m. cu. metres; pulp, 4·49m. tonnes; newsprint, paper and paperboard, 2·90m. tonnes.

Fisheries. In 2003 the total landed value of the catch was $630m. CDN; wholesale value $1bn. CDN. Salmon (wild and farmed) generated 44% of the wholesale value of seafood products, followed by shellfish, groundfish and herring. The seafood sector supported 11,200 jobs in 2001.

INDUSTRY

The value of shipments from all manufacturing industries reached $37·2bn. CDN in 2003 and accounted for around 10% of the province's GDP.

Labour. In 2003 the labour force averaged 2,202,000 persons with 2,023,000 employed (47% female) and 179,000 unemployed (8·1%). Of the employed workforce 1·60m. were in service industries and 422,000 in goods production. There were 321,000 employed in trade, 212,000 in healthcare and social assistance, 206,000 in manufacturing, 165,000 in accommodation and food industries, 127,000 in finance and related business, 122,000 in construction, 114,000 in transportation and warehousing, 92,000 in public administration, 34,000 in agriculture, 29,000 in forestry, 13,000 in mining and 5,000 in fishing and trapping.

Trade Unions. In 2003, 34% of the province's paid workers were unionized. The largest unions are: Canadian Union of Public Employees (63,999 members in early 2003); B.C. Government and Service Employees' Union and affiliates (approximately 60,000); and B.C. Teachers' Federation (43,876 in 1997).

INTERNATIONAL TRADE

Imports and Exports. Exports in 2003 totalled $28,550m. CDN in value, while imports amounted to $31,258m. CDN. The USA is the largest market for products exported through British Columbia customs ports ($18,928m. CDN in 2003), followed by Japan ($3,621m. CDN) and People's Republic of China, including Hong Kong ($1,278m. CDN).

The leading exports in 2001 were: wood products, $10,327m. CDN; paper and allied products, $5,421m. CDN; food, $4,149m. CDN; fabricated metal products, $1,577m. CDN; machinery, $1,467m. CDN.

COMMUNICATIONS

Roads. In 2001 there were 42,440 km of provincial highway, of which 23,710 km were paved. In 2003, 1,829,000 passenger cars and 589,000 commercial vehicles were registered.

Rail. The province is served by two transcontinental railways, the Canadian Pacific Railway and the Canadian National Railway. Passenger service is provided by VIA Rail, a Crown Corporation, and the publicly owned British Columbia Railway. In 1995 the American company Amtrak began operating a service between Seattle and Vancouver after a 14-year hiatus. British Columbia is also served by the freight trains of the B.C. Hydro and Power Authority, the Northern Alberta Railways Company and the Burlington Northern and Southern Railways Inc. The combined route-mileage of mainline track operated by the CPR, CNR and BCR totals 6,800 km. The system also includes CPR and CNR wagon ferry connections to Vancouver Island, between Prince Rupert and Alaska, and interchanges with American railways at southern border points. A metro line was opened in Vancouver in 1986 (29 km). A commuter rail service linking Vancouver and the Fraser Valley was established in 1995 (69 km).

Civil Aviation. International airports are located at Vancouver and Victoria. Total passenger arrivals and departures on scheduled services made by 33 foreign and domestic airlines were 14·3m. in 2003 at Vancouver and 1·1m. in 1997 at Victoria. Daily interprovincial and intraprovincial flights serve all main population centres. Small public and private airstrips are located throughout the province.

Shipping. The major ports are Vancouver (the largest dry cargo port on the North American Pacific coast), Prince Rupert and ports on the Fraser River. Other deep-sea ports include Nanaimo, Port Alberni, Campbell River, Powell River, Kitimat, Stewart and Squamish. Total cargo shipped through the port of Vancouver during 2003 was 66·7m. tonnes. 953,000 cruise passengers visited Vancouver in 2003.

British Columbia Ferries—one of the largest ferry systems in the world—connect Vancouver Island with the mainland and also provide service to other coastal points; in 2003, 21·3m. passengers and 8·3m. vehicles were carried. Service by other ferry systems is also provided between Vancouver Island and the USA. The Alaska State Ferries connect Prince Rupert with centres in Alaska.

Telecommunications. The British Columbia Telephone Company had (1997) approximately 2·5m. customers. In 2000 there were 800,000 cellular phone subscribers in the province.

SOCIAL INSTITUTIONS

Justice. The judicial system is composed of the Court of Appeal, the Supreme Court, County Courts and various Provincial Courts, including Magistrates' Courts and

Small Claims Courts. The federal courts include the Supreme Court of Canada and the Federal Court of Canada.

In 2002, 478,635 Criminal Code offences were reported, including 126 homicides.

Education. Education, free up to Grade XII level, is financed jointly from municipal and provincial government revenues. Attendance is compulsory from the age of five to 16. There were approximately 656,150 pupils enrolled in 1,707 public schools from kindergarten to Grade 12 in Sept. 2003.

The universities had a full-time enrolment of approximately 85,497 for 2002–03. Non-vocational enrolment at leading institutions (2002–03): the University of British Columbia, 39,224; Simon Fraser University, 21,684; University of Victoria, 17,975; University of Northern British Columbia, 3,630; Royal Roads University, 2,984. The regional colleges in 1996 were: Camosun College, Victoria; Capilano College, North Vancouver; Cariboo College, Kamloops; College of New Caledonia, Prince George; Douglas College, New Westminister; East Kootenay Community College, Cranbrook; Fraser Valley College, Chilliwack/Abbotsford; Kwantlen College, Surrey; Malaspina College, Nanaimo; North Island College, Comox; Northern Lights College, Dawson Creek/Fort St John; Northwest Community College, Terrace/Prince Rupert; Okanagan College, Kelowna with branches at Salmon Arm and Vernon; Selkirk College, Castlegar; Vancouver Community College, Vancouver; Langara College, Vancouver.

There are also the British Columbia Institute of Technology, Burnaby; Emily Carr College of Art and Design, Vancouver; Open Learning Institute, Richmond. A televised distance education and special programmes through KNOW, the Knowledge Network of the West, is provided.

Health. The government operates a hospital insurance scheme giving universal coverage after a qualifying period of three months' residence in the province. The province has come under a national medicare scheme which is partially subsidized by the provincial government and partially by the federal government. In March 2003 there were approximately 8,400 acute care and rehabilitation hospital beds. The provincial government spent an estimated $11·8bn. CDN on health programmes during 2004–05. 39% of the government's total expenditure was for health care.

CULTURE

Broadcasting. In 2001 there were ten television broadcasting stations in operation, with 84% of households subscribing to cable television. In July 1997 there were 130 radio stations originating in British Columbia.

Tourism. British Columbia's greatest attractions are Vancouver, and the provincial parks and ecological reserves that make up the Protected Areas System. The entire Tatshenshini-Alsek region, almost 1m. ha in northwestern B.C., has been protected as a Class A provincial park and nominated as a World Heritage Site. In 2002 there were 13,302 campsites and 3,000 km of hiking trails. In 2003, 21·87m. tourists spent $8·95n. CDN in the province.

FURTHER READING

Barman, J., *The West beyond the West: a History of British Columbia.* Toronto Univ. Press, 1991

Statistical office: BC STATS, Ministry of Finance and Corporate Relations, P.O. Box 9410, Stn. Prov. Govt., Victoria V8W 9V1.

MANITOBA

KEY HISTORICAL EVENTS

Manitoba was known as the Red River Settlement before it entered the dominion in 1870. During the 18th century its only inhabitants were fur-trappers, but a more settled colonization began in the 19th century. The area was administered by the Hudson's Bay Company until 1869 when it was purchased by the new dominion. In 1870 it was given provincial status. It was enlarged in 1881 and again in 1912 by the addition of part of the Northwest Territories.

TERRITORY AND POPULATION

The area of the province is 250,114 sq. miles (647,797 sq. km), of which 213,728 sq. miles are land and 36,386 sq. miles water. From north to south it is 1,225 km, and at the widest point it is 793 km.

Population estimate, 1 July 2003, was 1,162,776. The 2001 census showed the following figures for areas of population of over 10,000 people: Winnipeg, the province's capital and largest city, 671,274; City of Brandon, 39,716; City of Thompson, 13,256; City of Portage la Prairie, 12,978; Rural Municipality of Springfield, 12,602; Rural Municipality of Hanover, 10,789; Rural Municipality of St Andrews, 10,695.

SOCIAL STATISTICS

Births in 2002 numbered 14,332 (a rate of 12·4 per 1,000 population) and deaths 9,881 (rate of 8·6 per 1,000 population).

CLIMATE

The climate is cold continental, with very severe winters but pleasantly warm summers. Rainfall amounts are greatest in the months May to Sept. Winnipeg, Jan. –3°F (–19·3°C), July 67°F (19·6°C). Annual rainfall 21" (539 mm).

CONSTITUTION AND GOVERNMENT

The provincial government is administered by a *Lieut.-Governor* assisted by an *Executive Council* (Cabinet), which is appointed from and responsible to a *Legislative Assembly* of 57 members elected for five years. Women were enfranchised in 1916. The Electoral Division Act, 1955, created 57 single-member constituencies and abolished the transferable vote. There are 26 rural electoral divisions and 31 urban electoral divisions. The province is represented by six members in the Senate and 14 in the House of Commons of Canada.

RECENT ELECTIONS

In elections to the Legislative Assembly held on 3 June 2003 the New Democratic Party won 35 out of 57 seats (49·2% of the vote), the Progressive Conservative Party 20 seats (36·9%) and the Liberal Party 2 seats (12·8%).

CURRENT ADMINISTRATION

Lieut.-Governor: John Harvard, PC, OM; b. 1938 (took office on 30 June 2004).

The members of the New Democratic Party Ministry in Feb. 2005 were:

Premier, President of the Executive Council, Minister of Federal-Provincial Relations: Gary A. Doer; b. 1948.

Deputy Premier, Minister of Agriculture, Food and Rural Initiatives: Rosann Wowchuk. *Water Stewardship:* Steve Ashton. *Energy, Science and Technology:* David Walter Chomiak. *Aboriginal and Northern Affairs:* Oscar Lathlin. *Justice and Attorney General, Keeper of the Great Seal:* Gord Mackintosh. *Culture, Heritage and Tourism:* Eric Robinson. *Advanced Education and Training:* Diane McGifford. *Health:* Tim Sale. *Transportation and Government Services:* Ron Lemieux. *Finance:* Gregory F. Selinger. *Intergovernmental Affairs and Trade:* Scott Smith. *Conservation:* Stan Struthers. *Labour and Immigration:* Nancy Allan. *Industry, Economic Development and Mines:* Jim Rondeau. *Education, Citizenship and Youth:* Peter Bjornson. *Family Services and Housing:* Christine Melnick. *Healthy Living:* Theresa Oswald.

Manitoba Government Website: http://www.gov.mb.ca

ECONOMY

Nominal GDP in Manitoba grew 3·5% in 2002 to $35·9bn. CDN.

Budget. Provincial revenue and expenditure (current account, excluding capital expenditures, debt/pension repayment and transfers from/to the Fiscal Stabilization Fund) for fiscal years ending 31 March (in $1m. CDN):

	2000–01	*2001–02*	*2002–03*[1]	*2003–04*[2]
Revenue	6,752	6,747	6,990	7,314
Expenditure	6,615	6,738	6,967	7,256

[1]Forecast. [2]Budgeted figure.

Performance. Manitoba's economy grew 3·1% in real terms in 2002, up from 1·5% growth in 2001.

ENERGY AND NATURAL RESOURCES

Electricity. The province's electrical utility, Manitoba Hydro, has a total net generating capacity of 5,466,000 kW. In the year ending 31 March 2003 the provincial Crown corporation produced 29,178m. kWh of electricity. In 2002–03 scheduled power purchases from elsewhere in Canada and the USA totalled 3,043m. kWh. Manitoba provided 18,953m. kWh to its domestic customers. Energy sold outside Manitoba was 9,735m. kWh. This represented a decline in extraprovincial sales for the first time in six years. Revenue declined to $463m. CDN, $125m. CDN less than revenues reported in 2001–02. Of total extraprovincial revenue, $379m. CDN or 82% was derived from the US market while $84m. CDN or 18% was from sales to other Canadian provinces.

Oil and Gas. The value of oil production in 2002 was $152·6m. CDN, up 10·5% from 2001.

Minerals. Principal minerals mined are nickel, zinc, copper, gold and small quantities of silver. The value of mineral production declined 4% in 2002 to $982m. CDN. At $398m. CDN, nickel is Manitoba's most important mineral product, accounting for 40·5% of the province's total value of mineral production. Zinc accounted for 11% of the value of mineral production in 2002. Copper, which accounts for 9% of Manitoba's mineral production, saw moderate declines in both price and volume of production in 2002.

Agriculture. Rich farmland is the main primary resource, although the area in farms is only about 14% of the total land area. In 2002 total farm cash receipts increased by 2·9% to $3·76bn. CDN. Crop receipts surged 24·4% to $1·85bn. CDN while livestock receipts fell 5·2% to $1·7bn. CDN. Crop receipts accounted for 52% of total market receipts while livestock accounted for 48%. The growth of a number of non-traditional crops, such a dry beans and potatoes, underscores the continuing diversification of Manitoba's agricultural base. Manitoba's share of Canada's dry bean production has increased from 7% in 1993 to 57% in 2002. For particulars of livestock *see* CANADA: Agriculture.

Fisheries. From about 57,000 sq. km of rivers and lakes, the value of fisheries production to fishers was about $32·2m. CDN in 2001–02 representing about 14,800 tonnes of fish. Whitefish, sauger, pickerel and pike are the principal varieties of fish caught.

INDUSTRY

Manitoba's diverse manufacturing sector is the province's largest industry, accounting for approximately 12·5% of total GDP. The value of manufacturing shipments grew 0·6% in 2002 to $11·5bn. CDN.

Labour. Manitoba's total employment rose by 9,100 in 2002 (3,500 full-time and 5,600 part-time jobs), a 1·6% increase, bringing employment to a record-high level of 567,000. Manitoba had the lowest unemployment rate among the Canadian provinces at 5·2%. It also had the lowest youth unemployment rate in the country at 10·2%.

INTERNATIONAL TRADE

Products grown and manufactured in Manitoba find ready markets in other parts of Canada, in the USA, particularly the upper Midwest region, and in other countries.

Imports and Exports. In 2002 Manitoba merchandise exports to the US rose 1% to $7·6bn. CDN. Manitoba is the only province in Canada to record higher exports to the USA in 2001 and 2002. Merchandise exports to the USA comprise 82% of Manitoba's total foreign merchandise exports. In 2002 merchandise exports to Japan (Manitoba's second-most important foreign market) increased 3·2% while exports declined to Mexico, Hong Kong, Belgium and China. Manufacturing industries' exports, which account for about two-thirds of Manitoba's total foreign exports, increased by 1%. Gains were posted by four of the five largest manufacturing industry categories. Leading growth export industries include machinery, printing and wood products.

COMMUNICATIONS

Roads. Highways and provincial roads total 18,500 km, with 2,800 bridges and other structures. In 2003 there were 498,880 passenger vehicles (including taxis),

118,823 trucks, 51,122 farm trucks, 27,978 off-road vehicles and 9,138 motorcycles registered in the province.

Rail. The province has about 5,650 km of commercial track, not including industrial track, yards and sidings. Most of the track belongs to the country's two national railways. Canadian Pacific owns about 1,950 km and Canadian National about 2,400 km. The Hudson Bay Railway, operated by Denver-based Omnitrax, has about 1,300 km of track. Fort Worth-based Burlington Northern's railcars are moved in Manitoba on CN and CP tracks and trains.

Civil Aviation. In 2003 there were 61 domestic commercial aviation operators flying from bases in Manitoba. Three were designated private. Fifty-four air taxi companies were licensed to carry fewer than ten passengers; and six commuter operations were licensed to carry up to 19 passengers. Twelve national airlines were licensed to carry more than 19 passengers. Five foreign airlines were landing in the province (cargo and passenger). In addition, 36 aerial services were licensed (largely for agricultural chemical spraying).

Telecommunications. In 2002 Manitoba Telecom Services provided over 700,000 access services on its wireline network, more than 230,000 cellular subscribers and more than 115,000 Internet access customers.

SOCIAL INSTITUTIONS

Justice. In 2002, 129,935 Criminal Code offences (excluding traffic offences) were reported in Manitoba (a ratio of 11,290 per 100,000 people), including 36 homicides (a ratio of three per 100,000 people).

Education. Education is controlled through locally elected school divisions. There were 179,287 students enrolled in the province's public schools in the 2003–04 school year. Student teacher ratios (including all instructors but excluding school-based administrators) averaged one teacher for every 18·1 students.

Manitoba has four universities with a total full- and part-time undergraduate and graduate enrolment for the 2003–04 academic year of 39,500. They are the University of Manitoba, founded in 1877; the University of Winnipeg; Brandon University; and the Collège universitaire de Saint Boniface.

Community colleges in Brandon, The Pas and Winnipeg offer two-year diploma courses in a number of fields, as well as specialized training in many trades. They also give a large number and variety of shorter courses, both at their campuses and in many communities throughout the province. Provincial government expenditure on education and training for the 2003–04 fiscal year is budgeted at $1·59bn. CDN.

CULTURE

Tourism. Between 2000 and 2002 Manitoba's tourism sector grew 28% and now brings in $1·3bn. CDN a year. Tourism and related industries have created 60,000 jobs in the province, employing one in ten people. For the period ending 30 Nov. 2002 the total number of overseas tourists entering Manitoba for one or more nights increased by 1·4%. Manitoba was the only Canadian jurisdiction to record positive growth of overseas tourists in the period in question.

FURTHER READING

General Information: Inquiries may be addressed to Manitoba Government Inquiry. *e-mail:* mgi@gov.mb.ca

NEW BRUNSWICK

KEY HISTORICAL EVENTS

Visited by Jacques Cartier in 1534, New Brunswick was first explored by Samuel de Champlain in 1604. With Nova Scotia, it originally formed one French colony called Acadia. It was ceded by the French in the Treaty of Utrecht in 1713 and became a permanent British possession in 1759. It was first settled by British colonists in 1764 but was separated from Nova Scotia, and became a province in June 1784 as a result of the great influx of United Empire Loyalists. Responsible government came into being in 1848 and consisted of an executive council, a legislative council (later abolished) and a House of Assembly. In 1867 New Brunswick entered the Confederation.

TERRITORY AND POPULATION

The area of the province is 28,150 sq. miles (72,908 sq. km), of which 27,587 sq. miles (71,450 sq. km) is land area. The Census counted 729,498 people in New Brunswick on 15 May 2001. At this time, the most frequently reported ethnic origin, whether reported alone or in combination with other origins, was Canadian (58%). French was the second most frequently reported ancestry (27%), followed by English (23%), Irish (19%) and Scottish (18%). A total of 16,990 persons in New Brunswick identified themselves as Aboriginal (that is, as a North American Indian, Métis or Inuit) in 2001. The six urban centres of the province and their respective populations based on 2001 census figures are: Saint John, 122,678; Moncton, 117,727; Fredericton (capital), 81,346; Bathurst, 23,935; Edmundston, 22,173; Campbellton (part only), 13,310. The official languages are English and French.

SOCIAL STATISTICS

Births in 2002 numbered 7,102 (a rate of 9·8 per 1,000 population) and deaths 6,203 (rate of 8·8 per 1,000 population). There were 3,818 marriages and 1,461 divorces in 2002.

CLIMATE

A cool temperate climate, with rain in all seasons but temperatures modified by the influence of the Gulf Stream. Annual average total precipitation in Fredericton: 1,131 mm. Warmest month, July (average high) 25·6°C.

CONSTITUTION AND GOVERNMENT

The government is vested in a Lieut.-Governor, appointed by the Queen's representative in New Brunswick, and a Legislative Assembly of 55 members, each of whom is individually elected to represent the voters in one constituency or riding. The political party with the largest number of elected representatives, after a Provincial election, forms the government.

The province has ten appointed members in the Canadian Senate and elects ten members in the House of Commons.

RECENT ELECTIONS

Elections to the provincial assembly were held on 9 June 2003. The Progressive Conservative Party (PC) won 28 seats (with 45·5% of the vote), the Liberal Party (LIB) 26 seats (44·3%) and the New Democratic Party (NDP) one seat (9·7%). The governing PCs lost 19 seats, including four ministers.

CURRENT ADMINISTRATION

Lieut.-Governor: Herménégilde Chiasson; b. 1946 (took office on 26 Aug. 2003).

The members of the PC cabinet were as follows in Feb. 2005:

Premier, President of Executive Council Office, and Minister for Regional Development Corporation: Bernard Lord; b. 1965.

Deputy Premier, Minister of Supply and Services: Dale Graham. *Justice, Attorney General:* Bradley Green, QC. *Business New Brunswick:* Peter Mesheau. *Intergovernmental and International Relations:* Percy Mockler. *Finance:* Jeannot Volpé. *Agriculture, Fisheries and Aquaculture:* David Alward. *Health and Wellness:* Elvy Robichaud. *Training and Employment Development:* Margaret-Ann Blaney. *Environment and Local Government:* Brenda Fowlie. *Transportation:* Paul Robichaud. *Public Safety:* Wayne Steeves. *Natural Resources:* Keith Ashfield. *Energy:* Bruce Fitch. *Office of Human Resources:* Rose-May Poirier. *Family and Community Services:* Tony J. Huntjens. *Education:* Madeleine Dubé. *Tourism and Parks:* L. Joan MacAlpine.

Government of New Brunswick Website: http://www.gnb.ca

ECONOMY

GDP per capita in 2001 was $27,217 CDN. Personal income was $18,115m. CDN; personal income per capita was $24,153 CDN.

Budget. The ordinary budget (in $1m. CDN) is shown as follows (financial years ended 31 March):

	1998	*1999*	*2000*	*2001*	*2002*
Gross revenue	4,474·1	4,486·4	4,366·6	4,707·2	4,707·2
Gross expenditure	4,439·2	4,650·7	4,297·6	4,488·0	4,725·2

Funded debt and capital loans outstanding (exclusive of Treasury Bills) as of 31 March 1998 was $6,685·1m. CDN.

ENERGY AND NATURAL RESOURCES

Electricity. Hydro-electric, thermal and nuclear generating stations of NB Power had an installed capacity of 3,769 MW at 31 March 2002, consisting of 15 generating stations. The sale of out-of-province power accounted for 17·8% of revenue in 2002–03. Total revenue amounted to $1,273m. CDN.

Oil and Gas. In 2002 Enbridge Gas New Brunswick continued developing the natural gas distribution system in the province, which is now available in Fredericton, Moncton, St John, St George and Oromocto.

Minerals. The total value of minerals produced in 2002 reached $652·3m. CDN. The top four contributors to mineral production are zinc, lead, copper and peat, accounting for 72·9% of total value in 2002. In 2000 New Brunswick ranked first in Canada for the production of zinc, bismuth and lead, third for silver and sixth for copper.

Agriculture. The total area under crops is estimated at 135,008 ha. Farms numbered 3,034 and averaged 149 ha (census 2001). Potatoes account for 33% of total farm cash receipts and dairyproducts 11%. New Brunswick is self-sufficient in fluid milk and supplies a processing industry. For particulars of livestock, *see* CANADA: Agriculture. Farm cash receipts in 2002 were $421·2m. CDN.

Forestry. New Brunswick contains some 6m. ha of productive forest lands. The value of manufacturing shipments for the wood-related industries in 2002 was just over $3·8bn. CDN. The paper and allied industry group is the largest component of the industry, contributing 55·2% of forestry output. In 2002 nearly 15,750 people were employed in all aspects of the forest industry.

Fisheries. Commercial fishing is one of the most important primary industries of the province, employing 7,123 in 1999. Landings in 2002 (122,225 tonnes) amounted to $194m. CDN. In 2001 molluscs and crustaceans ranked first with a value of $153m. CDN, 87·6% of the total landed value. Exports in 2001, totalling $644·8m. CDN, went mainly to the USA and Japan.

INDUSTRY

Important industries include food and beverages, paper and allied industries, and timber products.

Labour. New Brunswick's labour force increased by 2·4% in 2002 to 385,700 while employment increased to 345,000. Goods producing industries employed 79,700 and the service-producing industries employed 253,700. Nearly 20% of the industrial labour force work in Saint John. In 2002 unemployment was 10·4%.

INTERNATIONAL TRADE

Imports and Exports. New Brunswick's location, with deepwater harbours open throughout the year and container facilities at Saint John, makes it ideal for exporting. The main exports include lumber, woodpulp, newsprint, refined petroleum products and electricity. In 2002 the major trading partners of the province were the USA with 89·2% of total exports, followed by Japan with 2·4% and the UK with 1·4% of total exports. Exports reached $8,160·8m. CDN while imports totalled $5,720m. CDN in 2002.

COMMUNICATIONS

Roads. There are 21,423 km of roads in the Provincial Highway system, of which 8,333 km consists of arterial, collector and local roads that provide access to most areas. The main highway system, including approximately 964 km of the Trans-Canada Highway, links the province with the principal roads in Quebec, Nova Scotia and Prince Edward Island, as well as the Interstate Highway System in the eastern seaboard states of the USA. At 31 March 2002 total road motor vehicle registrations numbered 549,061 of which 370,990 were passenger automobiles, 147,149 were truck and truck tractors, 13,406 motorcycles and mopeds, and 4,387 other vehicles.

Rail. New Brunswick is served by the Canadian National Railways, Springfield Terminal Railway, New Brunswick Southern Railway, New Brunswick East Coast Railway, Le Chemin de fer de la Matapédia et du Golfe and VIA Rail. The Salem-Hillsborough rail is popular with tourists.

Civil Aviation. There are three major airports at Fredericton, Moncton and Saint John. There are also a number of small regional airports.

Shipping. New Brunswick has five major ports. The Port of Saint John handles approximately 20m. tonnes of cargo each year including forest products, steel, potash and petroleum. The Port of Belledune is a deep-water port and open all year round. Other ports are Dalhousie, Bayside/St Andrews and Miramichi.

Telecommunications. In 1996 the New Brunswick Telephone Co. Ltd had 542,887 access lines in service.

SOCIAL INSTITUTIONS

Justice. In 2002, 56,856 Criminal Code offences were reported, including nine homicides.

Education. Public education is free and non-sectarian.

There were, in Sept. 2002, 120,600 students (including kindergarten) and 7,469 full-time equivalent/professional educational staff in the province's 342 schools.

There are four universities. The University of New Brunswick at Fredericton (founded 13 Dec. 1785 by the Loyalists, elevated to university status in 1823, and reorganized as the University of New Brunswick in 1859) had 9,007 full-time students at the Fredericton campus and 3,017 full-time students at the Saint John campus (2002–03); the Université de Moncton at Moncton, 5,089 full-time students; St Thomas University at Fredericton, 2,897 full-time students; Mount Allison University at Sackville had 2,199 full-time students.

CULTURE

Broadcasting. The province is served by 57 radio stations and a number of television stations, the majority of which broadcast exclusively in English; the remainder broadcast in French (some radio stations are bilingual).

Press. In 2002 New Brunswick had five daily newspapers (one in French), and 23 weekly newspapers, five in French and two bilingual.

Tourism. New Brunswick has a number of historic buildings as well as libraries, museums and other cultural sites. Tourism is one of the leading contributors to the economy. In 2002 tourism revenues reached $1·2bn. CDN.

FURTHER READING

Industrial Information: Dept. of Business New Brunswick, Fredericton. *Economic Information:* Dept. of Finance, New Brunswick Statistics Agency, Fredericton. *General Information:* Communications New Brunswick, Fredericton.

NEWFOUNDLAND AND LABRADOR

KEY HISTORICAL EVENTS

Archaeological finds at L'Anse-au-Meadow in northern Newfoundland show that the Vikings established a colony here in about AD 1000. This site is the only known Viking colony in North America. Newfoundland was discovered by John Cabot on 24 June 1497, and was soon frequented in the summer months by the Portuguese, Spanish and French for its fisheries. It was formally occupied in Aug. 1583 by Sir Humphrey Gilbert on behalf of the English Crown but various attempts to colonize the island remained unsuccessful. Although British sovereignty was recognized in 1713 by the Treaty of Utrecht, disputes over fishing rights with the French were not finally settled till 1904. By the Anglo-French Convention of 1904, France renounced her exclusive fishing rights along part of the coast, granted under the Treaty of Utrecht, but retained sovereignty of the offshore islands of St Pierre and Miquelon. Self-governing from 1855, the colony remained outside of the Canadian confederation in 1867 and continued to govern itself until 1934, when a commission of government appointed by the British Crown assumed responsibility for governing the colony and Labrador. This body controlled the country until union with Canada in 1949.

TERRITORY AND POPULATION

Area, 405,212 sq. km (156,452 sq. miles), of which freshwater, 31,340 sq. km (12,100 sq. miles). In March 1927 the Privy Council decided the boundary between Canada and Newfoundland in Labrador. This area, now part of the Province of Newfoundland and Labrador, is 294,330 sq. km (113,641 sq. miles) of land area.

Newfoundland island's coastline is punctuated with numerous bays, fjords and inlets, providing many good deep water harbours. Approximately one-third of the area is covered by water. Grand Lake, the largest body of water, has an area of about 530 sq. km. Good agricultural land is generally found in the valleys of the Terra Nova River, the Gander River, the Exploits River and the Humber River, which are also heavily timbered. The Strait of Belle Isle separates the island from Labrador to the north. Bordering on the Canadian province of Quebec, Labrador is a vast, pristine wilderness and extremely sparsely populated (approximately 10 sq. km per person). Labrador's Lake Melville is 2,934 sq. km and its highest peak, Mount Caubvick, is 5,577 ft.

The population at the 2001 census was 512,930. The population is declining at a faster rate than any other Canadian province, with a drop of 7·0% between the censuses of 1996 and 2001.

The capital of the province is the City of St. John's (2001 census population, 99,182). The other cities are Mt Pearl (24,964 in 2001) and Corner Brook (20,103); important towns are Conception Bay South (19,772), Grand Falls-Windsor (13,340), Gander (9,651), Paradise (9,598), Happy Valley-Goose Bay (7,969), Labrador City (7,744), Stephenville (7,101), Marystown (5,908), Portugal Cove-St Philip's (5,866), Bay Roberts (5,237), Clarenville (5,104) and Channel-Port aux Basques (4,637).

SOCIAL STATISTICS

Births in 2002 numbered 4,618 (a rate of 8·9 per 1,000 population) and deaths 4,252 (rate of 8·2 per 1,000 population). There were 2,959 marriages in 2002 and 842 divorces.

CLIMATE

The cool temperate climate is marked by heavy precipitation, distributed evenly over the year, a cool summer and frequent fogs in spring. St. John's, Jan. –4°C, July 15·8°C. Annual rainfall 1,240 mm.

CONSTITUTION AND GOVERNMENT

Until 1832 Newfoundland was ruled by a British Governor. In that year a Legislature was brought into existence, but the Governor and his Executive Council were not responsible to it. Under the constitution of 1855, the government was administered by the Governor appointed by the Crown with an Executive Council responsible to the House of Assembly.

Parliamentary government was suspended in 1933 on financial grounds and Government by Commission was inaugurated on 16 Feb. 1934. Confederation with Canada was approved by a referendum in July 1948. In the Canadian Senate on 18 Feb. 1949 Royal Assent was given to the terms of union of Newfoundland and Labrador with Canada, and on 23 March 1949, in the House of Lords, London, Royal Assent was given to an amendment to the British North America Act, made necessary by the inclusion of Newfoundland and Labrador as the tenth Province of Canada.

The province is represented by six members in the Senate and by seven members in the House of Commons of Canada.

RECENT ELECTIONS

Elections were held on 21 Oct. 2003. The Progressive Conservative Party (PC) won 34 of the 48 seats in the House of Assembly (with 58·7% of the vote), defeating the ruling Liberal Party (Lib.) of Premier Roger Grimes, which won 12 seats (33·2%). The New Democratic Party (NDP) won 2 seats (6·9%).

CURRENT ADMINISTRATION

Lieut.-Governor: Edward M. Roberts; b. 1940 (assumed office 1 Nov. 2002).

In Feb. 2005 the Progressive Conservative Cabinet was composed as follows:

Premier and Minister for Intergovernmental Affairs and Business: Danny Williams; b. 1950 (sworn in on 6 Nov. 2003).

Minister of Education: Tom Hedderson. *Environment and Conservation:* Tom Osborne. *Finance and President of the Treasury Board:* Loyola Sullivan. *Fisheries and Aquaculture, and Responsible for Labrador Affairs:* Trevor Taylor. *Government Services:* Dianne Whalen. *Health and Community Services:* John Ottenheimer. *Human Resources, Labour and Employment and Responsible for Housing and the Status of Women:* Joan Burke. *Innovation, Trade and Rural Development:* Kathy Dunderdale. *Justice and Attorney General:* Tom Marshall. *Natural Resources and Government House Leader:* Ed Byrne. *Municipal and Provincial Affairs:* Jack Byrne. *Tourism, Culture and Recreation:* Paul Shelley. *Transportation, Works and Responsible for Aboriginal Affairs:* Tom Rideout.

Speaker of the House of Assembly: Harvey Hodder.

Office of the Premier: http://www.premier.gov.nl.ca/premier

ECONOMY

GDP growth for 2003 was expected to be 4·3%. Inflation was estimated to be 2·2% in 2003.

Budget. Government budget in $1,000 CDN in fiscal years ending 31 March:

	2001–02	*2002–03*	*2003–04*[1]
Gross Revenue	3,800,799	3,896,047	3,916,285
Gross Expenditure	3,684,975	3,831,485	4,017,878

[1]Estimate.

ENERGY AND NATURAL RESOURCES

Electricity. Newfoundland and Labrador is served by two physically independent electrical systems with a total of 7,401 MW of operational electrical generating capacity. In 2002 total provincial electricity generation equalled 43·9bn. kWh, of which about 94% was from hydro-electric sources. Electricity service for a total of 254,000 retail customers is provided by two utilities and regulated by the Board of Commissioners of Public Utilities.

Oil and Gas. Since 1965, 140 wells have been drilled on the Continental Margin of the Province. Only the Hibernia discovery had commercial capability with production starting in the early 1990s. In 2002 oil production from Hibernia reached 65·9m. bbls. 2003 production was expected to increase to around 78m. bbls. The Terra Nova development produced oil in Jan. 2002 and is permitted to produce almost 59m. bbls. annually.

Minerals. The mineral resources are vast but only partially documented. Large deposits of iron ore, with an ore reserve of over 5,000m. tonnes at Labrador City, Wabush City and in the Knob Lake area, are supplying approximately half of Canada's production. Other large deposits of iron ore are known to exist in the Julienne Lake area. The Central Mineral Belt, which extends from the Smallwood Reservoir to the Atlantic coast near Makkovik, holds uranium, copper, beryllium and molybdenite potential.

The percentage share of mineral shipment value in 2002 stood at 91% for iron ore. Other major mineral products were gold, silver, pyrophyllite, limestone and gypsum. The value of mineral shipments in 2002 totalled $792m. CDN.

Agriculture. The value of farm production in 2002 was $82·7m. CDN, an increase of 1·7% on 2001. Dairy products accounted for 34% of total receipts, hens and chickens 20%, eggs 13% and floriculture and nursery 13%. For particulars of livestock *see* CANADA: Agriculture.

Forestry. The forestry economy in the province is mainly dependent on the operation of three newsprint mills—Corner Brook Pulp and Paper and Abitibi-

Consolidated (which operates two mills). In 2002 the estimated value of newsprint exported totalled $541m. CDN, a decrease of 20% over 2001. Lumber mills and saw-log operations produced 144m. flat bd ft in 2001–02.

Fisheries. Closure of the northern cod and other groundfish fisheries has switched attention to secondary seafood production and aquaculture. The total catch in 2002 increased by 2·5% to 267,500 tonnes valued at $515m. CDN. Crab, shrimp and cod together accounted for 59·4% of total landings and 80% of landed value. 16,200 people were employed in the fishing industry in 2002.

INDUSTRY

The total value of manufacturing shipments in 2002 was $2·24bn. CDN, an increase of 1·7% on 2001. This consisted largely of fish products, refined petroleum and newsprint.

Labour. In 2002 those in employment numbered 213,900 with 12,400 workers employed in manufacturing. The unemployment rate was 16·9% in 2002 (16·1% in 2001).

Trade Unions. In 2002 union membership was 39% of the employed workforce. The Newfoundland and Labrador Federation of Labour (NLFL) has 50,000 members; the Newfoundland and Labrador Association of Public and Private Employees (NAPE) has 19,000.

COMMUNICATIONS

Roads. In 2001 there were 8,938 km of roads, of which 6,990 were paved. In 2002 there were 261,842 motor vehicles registered.

Rail. In 1997 the Quebec North Shore and Labrador Railway operated both freight and passenger services on its 588 km main line from Sept-Iles, Quebec, to Shefferville, Quebec and its 58 km spur line from Ross Bay Junction to Labrador City, Newfoundland. In 1996 freight totalled 20·8m. tonnes (iron ore, 20·0m. tonnes).

Civil Aviation. The province is linked to the rest of Canada by regular air services provided by Air Canada and a number of smaller air carriers.

Shipping. At Jan. 2004 there were 1,822 ships on register in Newfoundland. Marine Atlantic, a federal crown corporation, provides a freight and passenger service all year round from Channel-Port aux Basques to North Sydney, Nova Scotia; and seasonal ferries connect Argentia with North Sydney, and Lewisporte with Goose Bay, Labrador.

Telecommunications. Telephone access lines numbered 262,856 in 1993 (193,987 private). There were 3,384 public pay phones.

Postal Services. There were 459 full service post office outlets in March 1996.

SOCIAL INSTITUTIONS

Justice. In 2002, 33,939 Criminal Code offences were reported, including two homicides.

Education. In 2002–03 total enrolment for elementary and secondary education was 84,268; full time teachers numbered 6,065; total number of schools was 317. The Memorial University, offering courses in arts, science, engineering, education, nursing and medicine, had 14,000 full-time students in 1999–2000.

CULTURE

Tourism. In 2002, 439,444 non-resident tourists (427,706 in 2001) spent approximately $302·5m. CDN in the province.

FURTHER READING

Statistical office: Newfoundland Labrador Statistics Agency, POB 8700, St. John's, NL A1B 4J6.
Website: http://www.nfstats.gov.nf.ca/

NOVA SCOTIA

KEY HISTORICAL EVENTS

Nova Scotia was visited by John and Sebastian Cabot in 1497–98. In 1605 a number of French colonists settled at Port Royal. The old name of the colony, Acadia, was changed in 1621 to Nova Scotia. The French were granted possession of the colony by the Treaty of St-Germain-en-Laye (1632). In 1654 Oliver Cromwell sent a force to occupy the settlement. Charles II, by the Treaty of Breda (1667), restored Nova Scotia to the French. It was finally ceded to the British by the Treaty of Utrecht in 1713. In the Treaty of Paris (1763) France resigned all claims and in 1820 Cape Breton Island united with Nova Scotia. Representative government was granted as early as 1758 and a fully responsible legislative assembly was established in 1848. In 1867 the province entered the dominion of Canada.

TERRITORY AND POPULATION

The area of the province is 21,345 sq. miles (55,284 sq. km), of which 20,594 sq. miles are land area and 751 sq. miles water area. The population at the 2001 census was 908,007.

Population of the major urban areas (2001 census): Halifax Regional Municipality, 359,110; Cape Breton Regional Municipality, 105,965. Principal towns (2001 estimates): Truro, 12,264; New Glasgow, 10,060; Amherst, 9,718; Bridgewater, 7,778; Yarmouth, 7,565; Kentville, 5,536.

SOCIAL STATISTICS

Births in 2002–03 numbered 8,710 (a rate of 9·3 per 1,000 population) and deaths 8,243 (rate of 8·8 per 1,000 population). There were 4,899 marriages in 2002 and 1,990 divorces.

CLIMATE

A cool temperate climate, with rainfall occurring evenly over the year. The Gulf Stream moderates the temperatures in winter so that ports remain ice-free. Halifax, Jan. 23·7°F (–4·6°C), July 63·5°F (17·5°C). Annual rainfall 54" (1,371 mm).

CONSTITUTION AND GOVERNMENT

Under the British North America Act of 1867 the legislature of Nova Scotia may exclusively make laws in relation to local matters, including direct taxation within the province, education and the administration of justice. The legislature of Nova Scotia consists of a Lieut.-Governor, appointed and paid by the federal government, and holding office for five years, and a House of Assembly of 52 members, chosen by popular vote at least every five years. The province is represented in the Canadian Senate by ten members, and in the House of Commons by 11.

RECENT ELECTIONS

At the provincial elections of 5 Aug. 2003 the Progressive Conservatives won 25 seats (36·3% of the vote), the New Democratic Party 15 seats (31·0%) and the Liberals 12 (31·4%). Turn-out was 63%.

CURRENT ADMINISTRATION

Lieut.-Governor: Myra Freeman, ONS.

The members of the Progressive Conservative Ministry in Feb. 2005 were:

Premier, President of the Executive Council and Minister of Intergovernmental Affairs: John F. Hamm.

Deputy Premier, Deputy President of the Executive Council, Minister of Transportation and Public Works: Ronald Russell. *Minister of Economic Development:* Ernest Fage. *Justice and Attorney General, Aboriginal Affairs, Chair of Treasury and Policy Board:* Michael G. Baker QC. *Education:* Jamie Muir. *Finance:* Peter G. Christie. *Tourism, Immigration, Culture and Heritage, and Health Promotion:* Rodney MacDonald. *Health, Chair of the Senior Citizens' Secretariat:* Angus MacIsaac. *Community Services:* David Morse. *Energy:* Cecil Clarke. *Service Nova Scotia and Municipal Relations:* Barry Barnet. *Environment and Labour:* Kerry Morash. *Natural Resources:* Richard Hurlburt. *Agriculture and Fisheries, and Acadian Affairs:* Chris d'Entremont. *Human Resources:* Carolyn Bolivar-Getson.

Speaker of the House of Assembly: Murray Scott.

Government of Nova Scotia Website: http://www.gov.ns.ca

ECONOMY

Budget. Summary of operations and net funding requirements for the consolidated entity (in $1m. CDN) for fiscal years ending 31 March:

	2001[1]	*2002*[2]	*2003*[3]
Revenues	5,240·1	5,423·4	5,628·6
Net Programme Expenditures/Expenses	4,472·1	4,570·1	4,756·5
Net Debt Servicing Costs	940·2	883·1	892·8
Pension Valuation Adjustment	(66·8)	(23·0)	(13·6)
Total Net Expenditures/Expenses	5,354·6	5,430·2	5,635·7
Consolidation Adjustment	(279·7)	(1·2)	–
Net Income from Government Business Enterprises	308·9	22·5	10·0
Unusual Item	30·9	–	–
Surplus (Deficit)	(54·2)	14·5	2·8

[1]Actual. [2]Forecast. [3]Estimate.

Performance. GDP (market prices) was $27,102m. CDN in 2002, an increase of just over 3·9% on 2001. GDP per person in 2002 was $29,017 CDN.

Banking and Finance. Revenue is derived from provincial sources, payments from the federal government under the equalization agreements and the Canada Health and Social Transfer (CHST).

In the fourth quarter of 2002 deposits with chartered banks totalled $7,893m. CDN.

ENERGY AND NATURAL RESOURCES

Electricity. In 2002 production was 12,117,399 kWh, of which 96% came from thermal sources and the rest from hydro-electric, wind and tidal sources.

Oil and Gas. Significant finds of offshore natural gas are currently under development. Gas is flowing to markets in Canada and the USA (the pipeline was completed in 1999). Total marketable gas receipts for 2002 was 5·2bn. cu. metres.

Minerals. Principal minerals in 2002 were: gypsum, 7·4m. tonnes, valued at $86·9m. CDN; stone, 8·2m. tonnes, valued at $55·6m. CDN. Total value of mineral production in 2002 was $1·3bn. CDN.

Agriculture. In 2001 there were 3,923 farms in the province with 119,221 ha of land under crops. Dairying, poultry and egg production, livestock and fruit growing are the most important branches. Farm cash receipts for 2002 were $408·2m. CDN. Cash receipts from sale of dairy products were $93·4m. CDN, with total milk and cream sales of 172·9m. litres. The production of poultry meat in 2002 was 36,413 tonnes, of which 32,713 tonnes were chicken and 3,700 tonnes were turkey. Egg production in 2002 was 17·6m. dozen. For particulars of livestock *see* CANADA: Agriculture.

The main fruit crops in 2002 were apples, 37,758 tonnes; blueberries, 18,053 tonnes; strawberries, 2,109 tonnes.

Forestry. The estimated forest area of Nova Scotia is 15,830 sq. miles (40,990 sq. km), of which about 28% is owned by the province. Softwood species represented 85·4% of the 6,066,392 cu. metres of the forest round products produced in 2002. Employment in the forest sector was 3,900 persons in 2002.

Fisheries. The fisheries of the province in 2002 had a landed value of $731m. CDN of sea fish; including lobster fishery, $334m. CDN; and scallop fishery, $120m. CDN. Aquaculture production in 2001 was 8,067 tonnes with a value of $29·7m. CDN; finfish accounted for 81% of total value while shellfish made up the remainder.

INDUSTRY

The number of manufacturing establishments was 1,097 in 2001; the number of employees was 38,621; wages and salaries, $1,324m. CDN. The value of shipments in 2001 was $8,706m. CDN, and the leading industries were food, paper production, and plastic and rubber products.

Labour. In 2002 the labour force was 474,200 (225,700 females), of whom 428,400 (206,800) were employed. The provincial unemployment rate stood at 9·7% while the participation rate was 62·8%.

Trade Unions. Total union membership in 2002 was 103,100 or 28·1% of employees. The largest union membership was in the service sector, followed by public administration and defence.

INTERNATIONAL TRADE

Imports and Exports. Total of imports and exports to and from Nova Scotia (in $1m. CDN):

	1999	*2000*	*2001*	*2002*
Imports	4,523	5,429	5,594	5,138
Exports	4,082	5,219	5,807	5,352

The main exports in 2002 included fish and fish products, natural gas and paper. Major trading partners were the USA with 81·6% of total exports, followed by Japan and the United Kingdom.

COMMUNICATIONS

Roads. In 2002 there were 26,000 km of highways, of which 13,600 km were paved. The Trans Canada and 100 series highways are limited access, all-weather, rapid transit routes. The province's first toll road opened in Dec. 1997. In the fiscal year 2001–02 total road vehicle registrations numbered 546,260 and over 600,000 persons had road motor vehicle operators licences.

Rail. The province has a 805 km network of mainline track operated predominantly by Canadian National Railways. The Cape Breton and Central Nova Scotia Railway operates between Truro and Cape Breton Island. The Windsor and Hantsport Railway operates in the Annapolis Valley region. VIA Rail operates the Ocean for six days a week, a transcontinental service between Halifax and Montreal.

Civil Aviation. There is direct air service to all major Canadian points, and international scheduled services in 2003 to Bermuda, Boston, Frankfurt, Kansas City, London, New York and Omaha. Halifax International Airport is the largest airport, and there are also major airports at Yarmouth and Sydney.

Shipping. Ferry services connect Nova Scotia to the provinces of Newfoundland, Prince Edward Island and New Brunswick as well as to the USA. The deep-water, ice-free Port of Halifax handles about 14m. tonnes of cargo annually.

Telecommunications. In 1996 there were 565,874 access lines (372,794 residential and 193,080 business). There were 59·8 access lines per 100 population and 98·3% of households had telephones. Household Internet use was 57·4% in 2001.

Postal Services. The postal service is provided by the Federal Crown Corporation Canada Post.

SOCIAL INSTITUTIONS

Justice. The Supreme Court (Trial Division and Appeal Division) is the superior court of Nova Scotia and has original and appellate jurisdiction in all civil and criminal matters unless they have been specifically assigned to another court by Statute. An appeal from the Supreme Court, Appeal Division, is to the Supreme Court of Canada.

For the year ending 31 March 2002 there were 1,507 admissions to provincial sentenced custody. In 2002, 71,890 Criminal Code offences were reported, including nine homicides.

Religion. The population is predominantly Christian. In 2001, 36·6% were Roman Catholic, 15·9% were United Church, 13·4% Anglicans, 10·6% Baptist and 2·5% Presbyterian.

Education. Public education in Nova Scotia is free, compulsory and undenominational through elementary and high school. Attendance is compulsory to the age of 16. There were 460 elementary-secondary public schools, with 9,304 full-time teachers and 153,450 pupils, in 2001–02. The province has eleven degree-granting institutions. The Nova Scotia Agricultural College is located at Truro. The Technical University of Nova Scotia, which grants degrees in engineering and architecture, amalgamated with Dalhousie University and is now known as DalTech.

Health. A provincial retail sales tax of 8% provides funds for free hospital in-patient care up to ward level and free medically required services of physicians. The Queen Elizabeth II Hospital in Halifax is the overall referral hospital for the province and, in many instances, for the Atlantic region. The Izaak Walton Killam Hospital provides similar regional specialization for children.

Welfare. General and specialized welfare services in the province are under the jurisdiction of the Department of Community Services. The provincial government funds all of the costs.

CULTURE

Broadcasting. Nova Scotia has 22 radio stations and nine television stations. In 1996 there were 85 operating cable television systems with 243,683 subscribers.

Press. Nova Scotia has approximately 50 newspapers, including eight dailies. Daily newspapers with the largest circulations are *The Chronicle Herald and Mail-Star* of Halifax, *The Daily News* of Dartmouth and *The Cape Breton Post* of Sydney.

Tourism. Tourism revenues were $1·3bn. CDN in 2002. Total number of visitors in 2002 was 2,180,400.

FURTHER READING

Nova Scotia Statistical Review. N. S. Department of Finance, Halifax, 2003
Nova Scotia Facts at a Glance. N. S. Department of Finance, Halifax, 2003

Statistical office: Statistics Division, Department of Finance, POB 187, Halifax, Nova Scotia B3J 2N3.
Website: http://www.gov.ns.ca/finance/statisti/

ONTARIO

KEY HISTORICAL EVENTS

The French explorer Samuel de Champlain explored the Ottawa River from 1613. The area was governed by the French, first under a joint stock company and then as a royal province, from 1627 and was ceded to Great Britain in 1763. A constitutional act of 1791 created there the province of Upper Canada, largely to accommodate loyalists of English descent who had immigrated after the United States war of independence. Upper Canada entered the Confederation as Ontario in 1867.

TERRITORY AND POPULATION

The area is 415,596 sq. miles (1,076,395 sq. km), of which some 354,340 sq. miles (917,741 sq. km) are land area and some 61,256 sq. miles (158,654 sq. km) are lakes and fresh water rivers. The province extends 1,050 miles (1,690 km) from east to west and 1,075 miles (1,730 km) from north to south. It is bounded in the north by the Hudson and James Bays, in the east by Quebec, in the west by Manitoba, and in the south by the USA, the Great Lakes and the St Lawrence Seaway.

The census population in 2001 was 11,410,046. Population of the principal cities (2001 census):

Toronto[1]	2,481,494	Markham	208,615	Richmond Hill	132,030
Ottawa	774,072	Windsor	208,402	St Catharines	129,170
Mississauga	612,925	Kitchener	190,399	East York[1]	115,185
North York[1]	608,288	Thunder Bay	190,016	Cambridge	110,372
Scarborough[1]	593,297	Vaughan	182,022	Gloucester	110,264
Hamilton	490,286	Burlington	150,836	Guelph	106,170
Etobicoke[1]	338,117	York[1]	150,255	Barrie	103,710
London	336,539	Oakville	144,738	Brantford	86,417
Brampton	325,428	Oshawa	139,051	Sudbury	85,354

[1]The new City of Toronto was created on 1 Jan. 1998 through the amalgamation of seven municipalities: Metropolitan Toronto and six local area municipalities of Toronto, North York, Scarborough, Etobicoke, East York and York.

There are over 1m. French-speaking people and 0·25m. native Indians. An agreement with the Ontario government of Aug. 1991 recognized Indians' right to self-government.

SOCIAL STATISTICS

Births in 2003–04 numbered 128,455 (a rate of 10·4 per 1,000 population) and deaths 87,296 (a rate of 7·1 per 1,000 population). In 2002 there were 61,615 marriages and 26,170 divorces; in 2002 life expectancy was 77·7 years for males and 82·2 years for females.

CLIMATE

A temperate continental climate, but conditions can be quite severe in winter, though proximity to the Great Lakes has a moderating influence on temperatures. Ottawa, average temperature, Jan. –10·8°C, July 20·8°C. Annual rainfall (including snow) 911 mm. Toronto, average temperature, Jan. –4·5°C, July 22·1°C. Annual rainfall (including snow) 818 mm.

CONSTITUTION AND GOVERNMENT

The provincial government is administered by a *Lieut.-Governor*, a cabinet and a single-chamber 103-member *Legislative Assembly* elected by a general franchise for a period of no longer than five years. The minimum voting age is 18 years.

RECENT ELECTIONS

At the elections on 2 Oct. 2003 to the Legislative Assembly, the Liberal Party won 72 of a possible 103 seats (with 46·4% of the vote), defeating the governing Progressive Conservative Party of Premier Ernie Eves, which took 24 seats (34·6%). The New Democratic Party (NDP) took 7 seats (14·7%).

CURRENT ADMINISTRATION

Lieut.-Governor: James K. Bartleman, O.Ont; b. 1939 (in office since March 2002).

In Feb. 2005 the Executive Council comprised:

Premier, President of the Council and Minister of Intergovernmental Affairs: Dalton McGuinty; b. 1955 (sworn in 23 Oct. 2003).

Minister of Community Safety and Correctional Services: Monte Kwinter. *Finance:* Greg Sorbara. *Economic Development and Trade:* Joe Cordiano. *Children and Youth Services and Citizenship and Immigration:* Dr Marie Bountrogianni. *Municipal Affairs, Housing and Seniors:* John Gerretsen. *Community and Social Services and Women's Issues:* Sandra Pupatello. *Attorney General, Minister for Native Affairs and for Democratic Renewal:* Michael Bryant. *Agriculture and Food:* Steve Peters. *Labour:* Chris Bentley. *Culture and Francophone Affairs:* Madeleine Meilleur. *Consumer and Business Services:* Jim Watson. *Tourism and Recreation:* Jim Bradley. *Natural Resources:* David Ramsay. *Northern Development and Mines:* Rick Bartolucci. *Energy, Chair of Cabinet and Government House Leader:* Dwight Duncan. *Education:* Gerard Kennedy. *Public Infrastructure Renewal and Deputy Government House Leader:* David Caplan. *Environment:* Leona Dombrowsky. *Health and Long-Term Care:* George Smitherman. *Training, Colleges and Universities:* Mary Anne Chambers. *Transportation:* Harinder Takhar. *Chair of the Management Board of Cabinet:* Gerry Phillips.

Office of the Premier: http://www.premier.gov.on.ca

ECONOMY

GDP per person in 2002 was $37,049 CDN.

Budget. Provincial revenue and expenditure (in $1m. CDN) for years ending 31 March:

	1998–99	*1999–2000*	*2000–01*	*2001–02*	*2002–03*[1]
Gross revenue	55,786	62,931	63,824	63,886	66,391
Gross expenditure	57,788	61,909	61,940	63,442	65,907

[1]Estimate.

Gross revenue and expenditure figures reflect accrual and consolidation accounting as recommended by the Public Sector Accounting and Auditing Board of the Canadian Institute of Chartered Accountants. Transactions on behalf of Ontario Hydro are excluded.

Performance. In 2003 real GDP grew at a rate of 1·6% (3·7% in 2002).

ENERGY AND NATURAL RESOURCES

Electricity. Ontario Power Generation recorded for the calendar year 2003 an installed generating capacity of 24,300 MW. Primary energy made available (2003), 109bn. kWh. In 2001 there were 68 hydro-electric, six fossil fuel and five nuclear stations operating. The industry has since been deregulated and Ontario Power Generation now has the province's 80 generating stations. In 1999 Ontario Hydro served 108 direct industrial customers, almost 1m. retail customers (homes, farms and small businesses) and 90 municipal utilities, who in turn serve over 3m. customers.

Oil and Gas. Ontario is Canada's leading petroleum refining region. The province's five refineries have an annual capacity of 170m. bbls. (27m. cu. metres).

Minerals. The total value of mineral production in 2002 was $5·7bn. CDN. In 2003 the most valuable commodities (production in $1m. CDN) were: gold, 1,253; nickel, 1,192; cement, 614; stone, 506; sand and gravel, 410; copper, 393. Total direct employment in the mining industry was 14,000 (9,000, metals) in 2002.

Agriculture. In 2001, 59,728 census farms operated on 5,466,256 ha, with total farm receipts of $8·49bn. CDN. Net farm income in 2003 totalled $138m. CDN. For particulars of livestock *see* CANADA: Agriculture.

Forestry. The forested area totals 69·1m. ha, approximately 65% of Ontario's total area. Composition of Ontario forests: conifer, 56%; mixed, 26%; deciduous, 18%. The total growing stock (62% conifer, 38% hardwood) equals 5·3bn. cu. metres with an annual harvest level of 23m. cu. metres.

INDUSTRY

Ontario is Canada's most industrialized province, with GDP in 2003 of $494,501m. CDN, or 40·6% of the Canadian total. Manufacturing accounts for 21·1% of Ontario's GDP.

Leading manufacturing industries include: motor vehicles and parts; office and industrial electrical equipment; food processing; chemicals; and steel.

In 1998 Ontario was responsible for about 54% ($171,870m. CDN) of Canada's merchandise exports; motor vehicles and parts accounted for about 45%.

Labour. In 2003 the labour force was 6,694,000, of whom 6,229,000 were employed. The major employers (2001 in thousands) were: manufacturing, 984; trade, 951 (wholesale, 279; retail, 672); health care and social assistance, 532; professional, scientific and technical services, 429; accommodation and food services, 380. The unemployment rate in 2003 was 7·0%. In 1999 total labour income was $185,099m. CDN.

INTERNATIONAL TRADE

Imports and Exports. Ontario's exports were $189·1bn. CDN in 2003, down from $206·5bn. CDN in 2002. Imports were $209·9bn. CDN in 2003, down from $224·7bn. CDN.

COMMUNICATIONS

Roads. Almost 40% of the population of North America is within one day's drive of Ontario. There were, in 1998, 159,456 km of roads (municipal, 143,000). Motor licences (on the road) numbered (1999) 8,961,741, of which 5,521,803 were passenger cars, 1,189,414 commercial vehicles, 27,938 buses, 1,616,152 trailers, 103,469 motorcycles and 361,292 snow vehicles.

Rail. In 1999 there were 14 provincial short lines plus the provincially-owned Ontario Northland Railway and 12 federal railways. The Canadian National and Canadian Pacific Railways operate in Ontario. Total track length, approximately 12,500 km. There is a metro and tramway network in Toronto.

Civil Aviation. Toronto's Lester B. Pearson International Airport is Canada's busiest, serving approximately 29m. passengers annually.

Shipping. The Great Lakes/St Lawrence Seaway, a 3,747 km system of locks, canal and natural water connecting Ontario to the Atlantic Ocean, has 95,000 sq. miles of navigable waters and serves the water-borne cargo needs of four Canadian provinces and 17 American States.

Telecommunications. The telephone service in 1998 was provided by 30 independent systems and Bell Canada.

SOCIAL INSTITUTIONS

Justice. In 2003 there were 6,097 criminal code offences per 100,000 population, compared to a national average of 8,132 per 100,000 population.

Education. There is a provincial system of publicly financed elementary and secondary schools as well as private schools. In 1998–99 publicly financed elementary and secondary schools had a total enrolment of 2,128,642 pupils and 117,098 teachers. In 2001–02, of the $64,270m. CDN total expenditure, 18·5% was on education.

There are 18 universities (Brock, Carleton, Dominicain, Guelph, Lakehead, Laurentian, McMaster, Nipissing, Ottawa, Queen's, Ryerson, Toronto, Trent, Waterloo, Western Ontario, Wilfred Laurier, Windsor and York), the Royal Military College of Canada and the University of Ontario Institute of Technology as well as one institute of equivalent status (Ontario College of Art and Design) with full-time enrolment for 2000–01 of 242,411. All receive operating grants from the Ontario government. There are also 25 publicly financed Colleges of Applied Arts and Technology (CAAT), with a full-time enrolment of 136,170 in 1998–99.

Operating expense (including capital expense) by the Ontario government on education for 1997–98 was $9,470m. CDN.

Health. Ontario Health Insurance Plan healthcare services are available to eligible Ontario residents at no cost. The Ontario Health Insurance Plan (OHIP) is funded, in part, by an Employer Health Tax.

FURTHER READING

Statistical Information: Annual publications of the Ontario Ministry of Finance include: *Ontario Statistics; Ontario Budget; Public Accounts; Financial Report.*

PRINCE EDWARD ISLAND

KEY HISTORICAL EVENTS

The first recorded European visit was by Jacques Cartier in 1534, who named it Isle St-Jean. In 1719 it was settled by the French, but was taken from them by the English in 1758, annexed to Nova Scotia in 1763, and constituted a separate colony in 1769. Named Prince Edward Island in honour of Prince Edward, Duke of Kent, in 1799, it joined the Canadian Confederation on 1 July 1873.

TERRITORY AND POPULATION

The province lies in the Gulf of St Lawrence, and is separated from the mainland of New Brunswick and Nova Scotia by Northumberland Strait. The area of the island is 2,185 sq. miles (5,660 sq. km). The population in 2003 (provisional) was 137,781. Population of the principal cities (2001): Charlottetown (capital), 32,245; Summerside, 14,654.

SOCIAL STATISTICS

Births in 2002–03 numbered 1,384 (a rate of 10·1 per 1,000 population) and deaths 1,213 (rate of 8·8 per 1,000 population). There were 901 marriages and 258 divorces in 2002.

CLIMATE

The cool temperate climate is affected in winter by the freezing of the St Lawrence, which reduces winter temperatures. Charlottetown, Jan. –3°C to –11°C, July 14°C to 23°C. Annual rainfall 853·5 mm.

CONSTITUTION AND GOVERNMENT

The provincial government is administered by a Lieut.-Governor-in-Council (Cabinet) and a Legislative Assembly of 27 members who are elected for up to five years.

RECENT ELECTIONS

At provincial elections on 29 Sept. 2003 the Progressive Conservatives won 23 of the available 27 seats (with 54·29% of the vote) and the Liberals took four seats (42·66%). The New Democratic Party won no seats (3·06%).

CURRENT ADMINISTRATION

Lieut.-Governor: J. Léonce Bernard, OPEI; b. 1943 (sworn in 28 May 2001).

The PC Executive Council was composed as follows in Feb. 2005:

Premier, President of the Executive Council and Minister Responsible for Intergovernmental Affairs: Patrick G. Binns; b. 1948.

Provincial Treasurer: Mitchell Murphy. *Minister for Development and Technology:* Michael Currie. *Agriculture, Fisheries and Aquaculture:* Kevin MacAdam. *Education and Attorney General:* Mildred Dover. *Health and Social Services:* Chester Gillan. *Environment, Energy and Forestry:* James Ballem. *Transportation and Public Works:* Gail Shea. *Community and Cultural Affairs:* Elmer MacFadyen. *Tourism:* Philip Brown.

Office of the Premier: http://www.gov.pe.ca/premier

ECONOMY

Budget. Total revenue in 2002–03 was $1,045m. CDN (own source revenue, $662m. CDN; general purpose transfers, $334m. CDN; special purpose transfers, $49m.). Total expenditures in 2002–03 amounted to $1,074m. CDN (including: health, $310m. CDN; education, $229m. CDN; debt charges, $111m. CDN; social services, $103m. CDN).

ENERGY AND NATURAL RESOURCES

Electricity. Prince Edward Island's electricity supply in 2003 was 1,138,554 MWh, an increase of 5·7% over the preceding year. All but 4% was accessed from other provinces, via an underwater cable which spans the Northumberland Strait. Wind generated power accounted for 11% of the total capacity within the province in 2003.

Oil and Gas. In 1999 Prince Edward Island had more than 400,000 ha under permit for oil and natural gas exploration.

Agriculture. Total area of farmland occupies approximately half of the total land area of 566,177 ha. Farm cash receipts in 2003 were $353m. CDN, with cash receipts from potatoes accounting for about 50% of the total. Cash receipts from dairy products, hogs and cattle followed in importance. For particulars of livestock, *see* CANADA: Agriculture.

Forestry. Total forested area is 280,000 ha. Of this 87% is owned by 12,000 woodlot owners. Most of the harvest takes place on private woodlots. The forest cover is 23% softwood, 29% hardwood and 48% mixed wood. In 2003 the volume of wood harvested reached 677,031 cu. metres, an increase of 5·2% on the previous year. The total value of wood industry shipments was $50·6m. CDN in 2003.

Fisheries. The total catch of 147m. lb in 2003 had a landed value of $169·6m. CDN. Lobsters accounted for $108·3m. CDN, around two-thirds of the total value; other shellfish, $47·1m. CDN; pelagic and estuarial, $10·7m. CDN; groundfish, $0·6m. CDN; seaplants, $2·7m. CDN.

INDUSTRY

Value of manufacturing shipments for all industries in 2003 was $1,356·1m. CDN. In 2003 (provisional) provincial GDP in constant prices for manufacturing was $394·9m. CDN; construction, $160·7m. CDN. In 2003 the total value of retail trade was $1,318·0m. CDN.

Labour. The average weekly wage (industrial aggregate) rose from $540·77 CDN in 2002 to $547·04 CDN in 2003. The labour force averaged 78,500 in 2004, with employment averaging 69,600. The unemployment rate was 11·1% in 2003.

COMMUNICATIONS

Roads. In 1999 there were 3,500 km of paved highway and 1,900 km of unpaved road as well as 1,200 bridge structures. The Confederation Bridge, a 12·9 km two-lane bridge that joins Borden-Carleton with Cape Jourimain in New Brunswick, was opened in June 1997. A bus service operates twice daily to the mainland.

Civil Aviation. In 2003 Air Canada provided daily services from Charlottetown to Halifax and Toronto. Canadian Airlines International operated daily services to Boston and Halifax, and there were also services to Moncton, Montreal and St John.

Shipping. Car ferries link the Island to New Brunswick year-round, with ice-breaking ferries during the winter months. Ferry services are operated to Nova Scotia from late April to mid-Dec. A service to the Magdalen Islands (Quebec) operates from 1 April to 31 Jan. The main ports are Summerside and Charlottetown, with additional capacity provided at Souris and Georgetown.

Telecommunications. In 1999 there were 88,577 telephone lines in service.

SOCIAL INSTITUTIONS

Justice. In 2003, there were 8,619 Criminal Code offences per 100,000 population, including one homicide.

Education. In 2003–04 there were 10,731 elementary students and 12,352 secondary students in both private and public schools. There is one undergraduate university (3,294 full-time and 599 part-time students), a veterinary college (237 students), and a Master of Science programme (33 students), all in Charlottetown. Holland College provides training for employment in business, applied arts and technology, with approximately 2,500 full-time students in post-secondary and vocational career programmes. The college offers extensive academic and career preparation programmes for adults.

Estimated government expenditure on education, 2000–01, $183·4m. CDN.

CULTURE

Tourism. The value of the tourist industry was estimated at $350m. CDN in 2003, with 1·1m. visitors in that year.

FURTHER READING

Baldwin, D. O., *Abegweit: Land of the Red Soil.* Charlottetown, 1985

QUEBEC—QUÉBEC

KEY HISTORICAL EVENTS

Quebec was known as New France from 1534 to 1763; as the province of Quebec from 1763 to 1790; as Lower Canada from 1791 to 1846; as Canada East from 1846 to 1867, and when, by the union of the four original provinces, the Confederation of the Dominion of Canada was formed, it again became known as the province of Quebec (Québec).

The Quebec Act, passed by the British Parliament in 1774, guaranteed to the people of the newly conquered French territory in North America security in their religion and language, their customs and tenures, under their own civil laws. In a referendum on 20 May 1980, 59·5% voted against 'separatism'. At a further referendum on 30 Oct. 1995, 50·6% of votes cast were against Quebec becoming 'sovereign in a new economic and political partnership' with Canada. The electorate was 5m.; turn-out was 93%. On 20 Aug. 1998 Canada's supreme court ruled that Quebec was prohibited by both the constitution and international law from seceding unilaterally from the rest of the country, but that a clear majority in a referendum would impose a duty on the Canadian government to negotiate. Both sides claimed victory.

TERRITORY AND POPULATION

The area of Quebec (as amended by the Labrador Boundary Award) is 1,542,056 sq. km (595,388 sq. miles), of which 1,365,128 sq. km is land area (including the Territory of Ungava, annexed in 1912 under the Quebec Boundaries Extension Act). The population at the 2001 census was 7,237,479.

Principal cities (2001 census populations): Montreal, 1,039,534; Laval, 343,005; Quebec (capital), 169,076; Longueuil, 128,016; Gatineau, 103,207; Montreal North,

82,408 (1999 estimate); Saint-Laurent, 77,391; Sherbrooke, 75,916; Saint-Hubert, 75,912; LaSalle, 73,983; Beauport, 72,813; Sainte-Foy, 72,547; Charlesbourg, 70,310; Saint-Léonard, 69,604; Hull, 66,246; Brossard, 65,026; Verdun, 60,564; Chicoutimi, 60,008; Jonquière, 54,842.

SOCIAL STATISTICS

Births in 2002–03 numbered 71,964 (a rate of 9·6 per 1,000 population) and deaths 54,585 (rate of 7·3 per 1,000 population). There were 21,987 marriages and 16,499 divorces in 2002.

CLIMATE

Cool temperate in the south, but conditions are more extreme towards the north. Winters are severe and snowfall considerable, but summer temperatures are quite warm. Quebec, Jan. –12·5°C, July 19·1°C. Annual rainfall 1,123 mm. Montreal, Jan. –10·7°C, July 20·2°C. Annual rainfall 936 mm.

CONSTITUTION AND GOVERNMENT

There is a Legislative Assembly consisting of 125 members, elected in 125 electoral districts for four years.

RECENT ELECTIONS

At the elections of 14 April 2003 the Liberal Party won 76 seats with 45·9% of votes cast, the Parti Québécois won 45 seats with 33·2% and the Action Démocratique won four seats with 18·3%.

CURRENT ADMINISTRATION

Lieut.-Governor: Lise Thibault (took office on 30 Jan. 1997).

Members of the Quebec Liberal Party Cabinet in Feb. 2005:

Premier and President of Executive Council: Jean Charest; b. 1958.

Deputy Premier and Minister of Public Security: Jacques Dupuis. *Government Administration and Chair of the Conseil du trésor:* Monique Jérôme-Forget. *Finance:* Michel Audet. *International Relations:* Monique Gagnon-Tremblay. *Health and Social Services:* Philippe Couillard. *Education, Recreation and Sports:* Jean-Marc Fournier. *Justice:* Yvon Marcoux. *Economic Development, Innovation and Export Trade:* Claude Béchard. *Agriculture, Fisheries and Food:* Yvon Vallières. *Sustainable Development and Parks:* Thomas Mulcair. *Natural Resources and Wildlife:* Pierre Corbeil. *Transport:* Michel Després. *Municipal Affairs and Regions:* Nathalie Normandeau. *Culture and Communications:* Line Beauchamp. *Government Services:* Pierre Reid. *Revenue:* Lawrence Bergman. *Employment and Social Solidarity:* Michelle Courchesne. *Tourism:* Françoise Gauthier. *Families, Seniors and the Status of Women:* Carole Théberge. *Labour:* Laurent Lessard. *Immigration and Cultural Communities:* Lise Thériault.

In addition to the above, the Cabinet also includes 'Ministers for' (full ministers who assist senior ministers).

Government of Quebec Website: http://www.gouv.qc.ca

ECONOMY

GDP per person in 2003 was $33,856 CDN.

Budget. Revenue and expenditure (in $1,000 CDN) for fiscal years ending 31 March:

	1999–2000	*2000–01*	*2001–02*	*2002–03*[1]
Revenue	47,410,000	51,049,000	50,309,000	52,706,000
Expenditure	47,403,000	49,672,000	51,237,000	52,706,000

[1]Preliminary.

The total net debt at 31 March 2000 was $88,886m. CDN.

ENERGY AND NATURAL RESOURCES

Electricity. Water power is one of the most important natural resources of Quebec. Its turbine installation represents about 40% of the aggregate of Canada. At the end of 1997 the installed generating capacity was 34,972 MW. Production, 1997, was 166,255 MWh.

Water. There are 4,500 rivers and 500,000 lakes in Quebec, which possesses 3% of the world's freshwater resources.

Minerals. For 1999 the value of mineral production (metal only) was $2,224m. CDN. Chief minerals: iron ore (confidential); gold, $495·5m. CDN; copper, $314·0m. CDN; zinc, $294·7m. CDN. Non-metallic minerals produced include: asbestos ($160·8m. CDN), titanium-dioxide (confidential), industrial lime, dolomite and brucite, quartz and pyrite. Among the building materials produced were: sand and gravel, $834·0m. CDN; cement, $246·6m. CDN; stone, $218·4m. CDN; lime (confidential).

Agriculture. In 1995 the agricultural area was 3,445,000 ha. The yield of the principal crops was (1998 in 1,000 tonnes):

Crops	*Yield*	*Crops*	*Yield*
Tame hay	4,300	Barley	425
Corn for grain	2,690	Soya	390
Fodder corn	1,520	Oats for grain	197
Potatoes	475	Mixed grains	111

About 38,000 farms were operating in 1995. Cash receipts, 1998, $4,882m. CDN (dairy products, 30·8%; crops, 24·6%; livestock, 21·9%; poultry and eggs, 10·7%). In 1996, 33,906 census farms reported total gross farm receipts of $2,500 CDN or more. For particulars of livestock *see* CANADA: Agriculture.

Forestry. Forests cover an area of 757,900 sq. km. 518,164 sq. km are classified as productive forests, of which 448,929 sq. km are provincial forest land and 66,198 sq. km are privately owned. Quebec leads the Canadian provinces in pulp and paper production, having nearly half of the Canadian estimated total.

In 1999 production of lumber was: softwood and hardwood, 17,897,000 cu. metres; pulp and paper, 10,092,000 tonnes.

Fisheries. The principal fish are cod, herring, red fish, lobster and salmon. Total catch of sea fish, 1999, 55,257 tonnes, valued at $134m. CDN.

INDUSTRY

In 1999 there were 10,176 industrial establishments in the province; employees, 500,906; salaries and wages, $17,769m. CDN; cost of materials, $63,702m. CDN; value of shipments, $113,079m. CDN. Among the leading industries are petroleum refining, pulp and paper mills, smelting and refining, dairy products, slaughtering and meat processing, motor vehicle manufacturing, women's clothing, sawmills and planing mills, iron and steel mills, commercial printing.

Labour. In 1999 there were 3,357,400 persons (1,507,500 female) in employment.

INTERNATIONAL TRADE

Imports and Exports. In 1999 the value of Canadian exports through Quebec custom ports was $45,404m. CDN; value of imports, $43,656m. CDN.

COMMUNICATIONS

Roads. In 1998 there were 29,140 km of roads and 4,496,376 registered motor vehicles.

Rail. There were (1998) 6,621 km of railway. There is a metro system in Montreal (64 km).

Civil Aviation. There are two international airports, Dorval (Montreal) and Mirabel (Laurentides).

Telecommunications. In 1997, 3,028,318 households (98·9%) had telephones.

SOCIAL INSTITUTIONS

Justice. In 1998, 467,530 Criminal Code offences were reported. In 2002 there were 118 homicides.

Education. Education is compulsory for children aged 6–16. Pre-school education and elementary and secondary training are free in some 2,527 public schools. In July 1998 the number of school boards was reduced to 72. These were organized along linguistic lines, 60 French, nine English and three special school boards that served native students in the Cote-Nord and Nord-du-Quebec regions. Just under 10% of the student population attends private schools: in 1999–2000, 272 establishments were authorized to provide pre-school, elementary and secondary education. After six years of elementary and five years of secondary school education, students enter Cegeps, a post-secondary educational institution. In 1999–2000 college, pre-university and technical training for young and adult students was provided by 48 Cegeps, 11 government schools and 77 private establishments.

In 1999–2000 in pre-kindergartens there were 15,174 pupils; in kindergartens, 89,223; in primary schools, 573,102; in secondary schools, 674,964; in colleges (post-secondary, non-university), 219,144; and in classes for children with special needs, 135,838. In 1998–99 the school boards had a total of 92,746 teachers (57,456 full-time and 32,290 part-time).

Expenditure of the Departments of Education for 1999–2000, $9,521·1m. CDN net. This included $1,511·2m. CDN for universities, $5,450·1m. CDN for public primary and secondary schools, $272·1m. CDN for private primary and secondary schools and $1,255·6m. CDN for colleges.

In 1999–2000 the province had nine universities: six French-language universities: Laval (Quebec, founded 1852), Montreal University (opened 1876 as a branch of Laval, independent 1920), Sherbrooke University (founded 1954), University of Quebec (founded 1968) and two others; and three English-language universities, McGill (Montreal, founded 1821), Bishop (Lennoxville, founded 1845) and the Concordia University (Montreal, granted a charter 1975). In 1999 there were 137,183 full-time university students and 94,691 part-time.

Health. Quebec's socio-health network consisted of 478 public and private establishments in 2001, of which 348 were public.

CULTURE

Broadcasting. In 1998 there were 50 television and 171 radio stations.

Press. In 2000 there were 11 French- and three English-language daily newspapers.

FURTHER READING

Dickinson, J. A. and Young, B., *A Short History of Quebec.* 2nd ed. Harlow, 1994
Gagnon, A.- G., *Québec.* [Bibliography] ABC-Clio, Oxford and Santa Barbara (CA), 1998
Young, R. A., *The Secession of Quebec and the Future of Canada.* McGill-Queen's Univ. Press, 1995

Statistical office: Bureau de la Statistique du Québec, 117 rue Saint-André, Québec G1K 3Y3

SASKATCHEWAN

KEY HISTORICAL EVENTS

Saskatchewan derives its name from its major river system, which the Cree Indians called 'Kis-is-ska-tche-wan', meaning 'swift flowing'. It officially became a province when it joined the Confederation on 1 Sept. 1905.

In 1670 King Charles II granted to Prince Rupert and his friends a charter covering exclusive trading rights in 'all the land drained by streams finding their outlet in the Hudson Bay'. This included what is now Saskatchewan. The trading company was first known as The Governor and Company of Adventurers of England; later as the Hudson's Bay Company. In 1869 the Northwest Territories was formed, and this included Saskatchewan. In 1882 the District of Saskatchewan was formed. By 1885 the North-West Mounted Police had been inaugurated, with headquarters in Regina (now the capital), and the Canadian Pacific Railway's transcontinental line had been completed, bringing a stream of immigrants to southern Saskatchewan. The Hudson's Bay Company surrendered its claim to territory in return for cash and land around the existing trading posts.

TERRITORY AND POPULATION

Saskatchewan is bounded in the west by Alberta, in the east by Manitoba, in the north by the Northwest Territories and in the south by the USA. The area of the province is 251,365 sq. miles (651,036 sq. km), of which 228,444 sq. miles is land area and 22,921 sq. miles is water. The population at the 2001 census was 978,933; it was estimated at 994,843 in July 2003. Population of cities, 2001 census: Saskatoon, 196,811; Regina (capital), 178,225; Prince Albert, 34,291; Moose Jaw, 32,131; Yorkton, 15,105; Swift Current, 14,821; North Battleford, 13,692; Estevan, 10,242; Weyburn, 9,534; Lloydminster, 7,840; Melfort, 5,559; Humboldt, 5,161.

SOCIAL STATISTICS

Births in 2001–02 numbered 11,733 (a rate of 11·6 per 1,000 population) and deaths 8,818 (rate of 8·7 per 1,000 population). There were 5,067 marriages and 1,959 divorces in 2002.

CLIMATE

A cold continental climate, with severe winters and warm summers. Rainfall amounts are greatest from May to Aug. Regina, Jan. 0°F (–17·8°C), July 65°F (18·3°C). Annual rainfall 15" (373 mm).

CONSTITUTION AND GOVERNMENT

The provincial government is vested in a Lieut.-Governor, an Executive Council and a Legislative Assembly, elected for five years. Women were given the franchise in 1916.

RECENT ELECTIONS

In elections on 5 Nov. 2003 the New Democrats (NDP) won 30 of 58 seats (44·62% of the vote); the Saskatchewan Party (SP), 28 (39·35%). The Liberal Party received 14·17% of the vote but did not win any seats.

CURRENT ADMINISTRATION

Lieut.-Governor: Dr Lynda M. Haverstock, SOM (took office 21 Feb. 2000).

The New Democratic Party ministry comprised as follows in Feb. 2005:

Premier, President of the Executive Council: Lorne Calvert.

Deputy Premier and Minister of Rural Revitalization: Clay Serby. *Health and Seniors:* John Nilson. *Learning and Information Technology:* Andrew Thomson. *Culture, Youth and Recreation, Provincial Secretary:* Joan Beatty. *Highways, Transportation and First Nations and Métis Relations:* Maynard Sonntag. *Northern Affairs:* Buckley Belanger. *Finance:* Harry Van Mulligen. *Community Resources, Employment, Disability Issues and Gaming:* Joanne Crofford. *Corrections and Public Safety:* Peter Prebble. *Environment:* David Forbes. *Government Relations:* Len Taylor. *Industry and Resources:* Eric Cline. *Labour and Status of Women:* Debra Higgins. *Justice and Attorney General:* Frank Quennell. *Crown Management Board, Public Service Commission and Immigration:* Pat Atkinson. *Agriculture and Food:* Mark Wartman.

Office of the Premier: http://www.gov.sk.ca/govinfo/premier

ECONOMY

GDP per capita in 2002 was $34,298 CDN.

Budget. Budget and net assets (years ending 31 March) in $1,000 CDN:

	1999–2000	*2000–01*	*2001–02*	*2002–03*
Budgetary revenue	6,629,490	6,382,400	6,041,700	6,094,300
Budgetary expenditure	6,785,466	5,967,986	6,302,624	6,319,255

ENERGY AND NATURAL RESOURCES

Agriculture used to dominate the history and economics of Saskatchewan, but the 'prairie province' is now a rapidly developing mining and manufacturing area. It is a major supplier of oil, has the world's largest deposits of potash and the net value of its non-agricultural production accounted for (2002 estimate) 93·8% of the provincial economy.

Electricity. The Saskatchewan Power Corporation generated 16,755m. kWh in 2002.

Minerals. In 2002 mineral sales were valued at $8,266m. CDN, including (in $1m. CDN): petroleum, 4,705·7; potash, 1,717·2; natural gas, 913·7; coal and others,

885·5; sodium sulphate, 23·0; salt, 21·4. Other major minerals included copper, zinc, potassium sulphate, ammonium sulphate, bentonite, coal, uranium, gold and base metals.

Agriculture. Saskatchewan normally produces about two-thirds of Canada's wheat. Wheat production in 2002 (in 1,000 tonnes) was 7,484 (9,851 in 2001) from 15·1m. acres; barley, 2,526 from 5·2m. acres; canola, 1,656 from 4·4m. acres; oats, 1,049 from 2·6m. acres; flax, 445 from 1·2m. acres; rye, 28 from 85,000 acres. Livestock (1 July 2003): cattle and calves, 3·3m.; swine, 1·3m.; sheep and lambs, 145,000. Poultry in 2002: chickens, 21·5m.; turkeys, 758,000. Cash income from the sale of farm products in 2002 was $6,356m. CDN. At the June 2001 census there were 50,598 farms in the province, each being a holding of one acre or more with sales of $250 CDN or more during the previous year.

The South Saskatchewan River irrigation project, the main feature of which is the Gardiner Dam, was completed in 1967. It will ultimately provide for an area of 0·2m. to 0·5m. acres of irrigated cultivation in Central Saskatchewan. As of 2002, 243,077 acres were intensively irrigated. Total irrigated land in the province, 337,284 acres.

Forestry. Half of Saskatchewan's area is forested, but only 115,000 sq. km are of commercial value at present. Forest products valued at $356m. CDN were produced in 2001–02.

Fur Production. In 2000–01 wild fur production was estimated at $1,910,908 CDN. Ranch-raised fur production amounted to $31,226 CDN in 2000 and $11,426 CDN in 2001.

Fisheries. The lakeside value of the 2002–03 commercial fish catch of 3·5m. kg was $4·6m. CDN.

INDUSTRY

In 2001 there were 1,004 manufacturing establishments, employing 20,376 persons. In 2002 manufacturing contributed $2,054·2m. CDN and construction $1,238·9m. CDN to total GDP at basic prices of $28,114·2m. CDN.

Labour. In 2002 the labour force was 511,100 (232,000 females), of whom 482,000 (220,500) were employed.

COMMUNICATIONS

Roads. In 2002 there were 26,249 km of provincial highways and 198,348 km of municipal roads (including prairie trails). Motor vehicles registered totalled 721,999 (2002). Bus services are provided by two major lines.

Rail. In 2002 there were approximately 9,908 km of railway track.

Civil Aviation. There were two major airports and 148 airports and landing strips in 2002.

Telecommunications. There were 613,695 telephone network access services to the Saskatchewan Telecommunications system in 2002.

Postal Services. In 2002 there were 475 post offices (excluding sub-post offices).

SOCIAL INSTITUTIONS

Justice. In 2002, 135,262 Criminal Code offences were reported, including 27 homicides.

Education. The Saskatchewan education system in 2002–03 consisted of 99 school divisions and three comprehensive school boards, of which one is Protestant and 19 are Roman Catholic Separate School Divisions, serving 116,271 elementary pupils, 59,715 high-school students and 1,589 students enrolled in special classes. In addition, the Saskatchewan Institute of Applied Science and Technology (SIAST) had approximately 12,000 full-time and 29,000 part-time and extension course registration students in 2002–03. There are also eight regional colleges with an enrolment of approximately 30,126 students in 2001–02.

The University of Saskatchewan was established at Saskatoon in 1907. In 2001–02 it had 15,368 full-time students, 4,101 part-time students and 961 full-time academic staff. The University of Regina, established in 1974, had 8,975 full-time and 3,205 part-time students and 388 full-time academic staff in 2001–02.

CULTURE

Broadcasting. In 2002 there were 50 TV and re-broadcasting stations, and 28 AM and FM radio stations.

Tourism. An estimated 1·6m. out-of-province tourists spent $480m. CDN in 2002.

FURTHER READING

Archer, J. H., *Saskatchewan: A History*. Saskatoon, 1980
Arora, V., *The Saskatchewan Bibliography*. Regina, 1980

Statistical office: Bureau of Statistics, 5th Floor, 2350 Albert St., Regina, SK, S4P 4A6.

THE NORTHWEST TERRITORIES

KEY HISTORICAL EVENTS

The Territory was developed by the Hudson's Bay Company and the North West Company (of Montreal) from the 17th century. The Canadian government bought out the Hudson's Bay Company in 1869 and the Territory was annexed to Canada in 1870. The Arctic Islands lying north of the Canadian mainland were annexed to Canada in 1880.

A plebiscite held in March 1992 approved the division of the Northwest Territories into two separate territories. (For the new territory of Nunavut see CONSTITUTION AND GOVERNMENT, *below*, and NUNAVUT on page 405).

TERRITORY AND POPULATION

The Northwest Territories comprises all that portion of Canada lying north of the 60th parallel of N. lat. except those portions within Nunavut, the Yukon Territory and the provinces of Quebec and Newfoundland. The total area of the Territories was 3,426,320 sq. km, but since the formation of Nunavut is now 1,346,106 km. Of its five former administrative regions—Fort Smith, Inuvik, Kitikmeot, Keewatin and Baffin—only Fort Smith and Inuvik remain in the Northwest Territories. The population at the 1991 census was 57,649, 37% of whom were Inuit (Eskimo), 16% Dene (Indian) and 7% Metis. The formation of Nunavut in 1999 out of the Northwest Territories resulted in a large decline in the population. The population at the 2001 census was 37,360. The capital is Yellowknife, population (2001); 16,541. Other main centres (with population in 2001): Hay River (3,510), Inuvik (2,894), Fort Smith (2,185), Rae-Edzo (1,552). Iqaluit and Rankin Inlet, formerly in the Northwest Territories, are now in Nunavut. In Aug. 2003 an agreement was reached for the Tlicho First Nation to assume control over 39,000 sq. km of land in the Northwest Territories (including Canada's two diamond mines), creating the largest single block of First Nation-owned land in Canada.

SOCIAL STATISTICS

Births in 2002–03 numbered 606 (a rate of 14·5 per 1,000 population) and deaths 175 (rate of 4·2 per 1,000 population). There were 144 marriages and 68 divorces in 2002.

CLIMATE

Conditions range from cold continental to polar, with long hard winters and short cool summers. Precipitation is low. Yellowknife, Jan. mean high –24·7°C, low –33°C; July mean high 20·7°C, low 11·8°C. Annual rainfall 26·7 cm.

CONSTITUTION AND GOVERNMENT

The Northwest Territories is governed by a Premier, with a cabinet (the Executive Council) of eight members including the Speaker, and a Legislative Assembly, who choose the premier and ministers by consensus. There are no political parties. The Assembly is composed of 19 members elected for a four-year term of office. A Commissioner of the Northwest Territories is the federal government's senior representative in the Territorial government. The seat of government was transferred from Ottawa to Yellowknife when it was named Territorial Capital on 18 Jan. 1967. On 10 Nov. 1997 the governments of Canada and the Northwest Territories signed an agreement so that the territorial government could assume full responsibility to manage its elections.

The Territorial government has assumed most of the responsibility for the administration of the Northwest Territories but political control of Crown lands. In a Territory-wide plebiscite in April 1982, a majority of residents voted in favour of dividing the Northwest Territories into two jurisdictions, east and west. Constitutions for an eastern and western government have been under discussion since 1992. A referendum was held in Nov. 1992 among the Inuit on the formation of a third territory, **Nunavut** ('Our Land'), in the eastern Arctic. Nunavut became Canada's third territory on 1 April 1999.

RECENT ELECTIONS

On 24 Nov. 2003, 19 non-partisan members (MLAs) were returned to the 15th Legislative Assembly. There were 58 candidates, five of whom were unopposed.

CURRENT ADMINISTRATION

Commissioner: Tony Whitford, b. 1941 (took office in April 2005).

Members of the Executive Council of Ministers in Feb. 2005:

Premier, Chairman of the Executive Council, Minister for Aboriginal Affairs: Joseph Handley; b. 1943.

Deputy Premier and Minister of Finance, Public Works and Services: Floyd Roland. *Government House Leader and Minister of Education, Culture and Employment and Justice:* Charles Dent. *Resources, Wildlife and Economic Development:* Brendan Bell. *Transportation, and Municipal and Community Affairs:* Michael McLeod. *Health and Social Services:* J. Michael Miltenberger.

Speaker: Paul Delorey.

Government of the Northwest Territories Website: http://www.gov.nt.ca

ECONOMY

GDP per person in 2003 was $85,983 CDN, the highest of any Canadian province or territory.

Budget. Total revenue in 2002–03 was $976m. CDN (own source revenue, $449m. CDN; general purpose transfers, $411m. CDN; special purpose transfers, $116m. CDN). Total expenditures in 2002–03 amounted to $1,021m. CDN (including: health, $203m. CDN; education, $187m. CDN; social services, $104m. CDN).

ENERGY AND NATURAL RESOURCES

Oil and Gas. Oil production was 1,535,000 cu. metres in 2000, down from 1,640,000 cu. metres in 1999. Natural gas production in 2000 was 541m. cu. metres, up from 110m. cu. metres in 1999.

Minerals. Mineral production in 2000: gold, 4,372 kg (valued at $58,148,000 CDN); silver, 1 tonne ($248,000 CDN); diamonds, 2,558 carats ($638,161,000 CDN); sand and gravel, 539,000 tonnes ($4,805,000 CDN); stone, 184,000 tonnes ($2,848,000 CDN). Total mineral production in 2000 was valued at $1·14bn. CDN.

Forestry. Forest land area in the Northwest Territories consists of 61·4m. ha, about 18% of the total land area. The principal trees are white and black spruce, jack-pine, tamarack, balsam poplar, aspen and birch. In 1996, 202,000 cu. metres of timber were produced.

Trapping and Game. Wildlife harvesting is the largest economic activity undertaken by aboriginal residents in the Northwest Territories. The value of the subsistence food harvest is estimated at $28m. CDN annually in terms of imports replaced. Fur-trapping (the most valuable pelts being white fox, wolverine, beaver, mink, lynx, and red fox) was once a major industry, but has been hit by anti-fur campaigns. In 1999–2000, 37,124 pelts worth $842,049 CDN were sold.

Fisheries. Fish marketed through the Freshwater Fish Marketing Corporation in 1996–97 totalled 1,742,700 kg at a value of $1,725,000 CDN, principally whitefish, northern pike and trout.

INDUSTRY

Co-operatives. There are 37 active co-operatives, including two housing co-operatives and two central organizations to service local co-operatives, in the Northwest Territories. They are active in handicrafts, furs, fisheries, retail stores, hotels, cable TV, post offices, petroleum delivery and print shops. Total revenue in 2000 was about $97m. CDN.

COMMUNICATIONS

Roads. The Mackenzie Route connects Grimshaw, Alberta, with Hay River, Pine Point, Fort Smith, Fort Providence, Rae-Edzo and Yellowknife. The Mackenzie Highway extension to Fort Simpson and a road between Pine Point and Fort Resolution have both been opened.

Highway service to Inuvik in the Mackenzie Delta was opened in spring 1980, extending north from Dawson, Yukon as the Dempster Highway. The Liard Highway connecting the communities of the Liard River valley to British Columbia opened in 1984.

In 2000 there were 27,703 vehicle registrations, including 21,630 passenger cars and 1,881 trucks and 2,841 trailers.

Rail. There is one small railway system in the north which runs from Hay River, on the south shore of Great Slave Lake, 435 miles south to Grimshaw, Alberta, where it connects with the Canadian National Railways, but it is not in use.

Civil Aviation. In 2000 there were 132,775 take-offs and landings in the Northwest Territories.

Shipping. A direct inland-water transportation route for about 1,700 miles is provided by the Mackenzie River and its tributaries, the Athabasca and Slave rivers. Subsidiary routes on Lake Athabasca, Great Slave Lake and Great Bear Lake total more than 800 miles. Communities in the eastern Arctic are resupplied by ship each summer via the Atlantic and Arctic Oceans or Hudson Bay.

Telecommunications. Telephone service is provided to nearly all communities in the Northwest Territories. Those few communities without service have high frequency or very high frequency radios for emergency use.

Postal Services. There is a postal service in all communities.

SOCIAL INSTITUTIONS

Education. The Education System in the Northwest Territories is comprised of eight regional bodies (boards) that have responsibilities for the K-12 education programme. Three of these jurisdictions are located in Yellowknife; a public school authority, a catholic school authority and a Commission scolaire francophone that oversees a school operating in Yellowknife, and one in Hay River.

For the 2000–01 school year there were 49 public plus two (small) private schools operating in the NWT. Within this system there were 667 teachers, including Aboriginal Language Specialists, for 9,855 students. 98% of students have access to high school programmes in their home communities. There is a full range of courses available in the school system, including academic, French immersion, Aboriginal language, cultural programmes, technical and occupational programmes.

A range of post secondary programmes are available through the Northwest Territories' Aurora College. The majority of these programmes are offered at the three main campus locations: Inuvik, Yellowknife and Fort Smith.

Health. In 2004 there were eight separate regional boards. Expenditure on health totalled $159·4m. CDN in 1999–2000.

Welfare. Welfare services are provided by professional social workers. Facilities included (1993) for children: seven group homes and two residential treatment centres.

CULTURE

Broadcasting. In 2000 CBC operated radio stations at Yellowknife and Inuvik. There is an English language CBC-owned television station at Yellowknife. There are also two other television broadcasting stations based in Yellowknife.

FURTHER READING

Annual Report of the Government of the Northwest Territories
Government Activities in the North, 1983–84. Indian and Northern Affairs, Canada
NWT Data Book 90/91. Yellowknife, 1991

Zaslow, M., *The Opening of the Canadian North 1870–1914.* Toronto, 1971

NUNAVUT

KEY HISTORICAL EVENTS

Inuit communities started entering and moving around what is now the Canadian Arctic between 4500 BC and AD 1000. By the 19th century these communities were under the jurisdiction of the Northwest Territories. In 1963 the Canadian government first introduced legislation to divide the territory, a proposal that failed at the order paper stage. In 1973 the Comprehensive Land Claims Policy was established which sought to define the rights and benefits of the Aboriginal population in a land claim settlement agreement. The Northwest Territories Legislative Assembly voted in favour of dividing the territory in 1980, and in a public referendum of 1982, 56% of votes cast were also for the division. In 1992 the proposed boundary was ratified in a public vote and the Inuit population approved their land claim settlement. A year later, the Nunavut Act (creating the territory) and the Nunavut Land Claim Agreement Act were passed by parliament. Iqaluit was selected as the capital in 1995.

On 15 Feb. 1999 Nunavut held elections for its Legislative Assembly and on 1 April 1999 the territory was officially designated and the government inaugurated.

TERRITORY AND POPULATION

The total area of the region is 2,093,190 sq. km or about 21% of Canada's total mass, making Nunavut Canada's largest territory. It contains seven of Canada's 12 largest islands and two thirds of the country's coastline. The territory is divided into three regions: Qikiqtaaluk (Baffin), Kivalliq (Keewatin) and Kitikmeot. The total population at the 1996 census was 24,720 (12,910 males, 11,810 females) or 97 persons per 10,000 sq. km; at the 2001 census the population was 26,745. 85% of the population are Inuit. The population is divided up into 28 communities of which the largest is in the capital Iqaluit, numbering 4,500.

The native Inuit language is Inuktitut.

SOCIAL STATISTICS

Births in 2002–03 numbered 727 (a rate of 25·0 per 1,000 population) and deaths 130 (rate of 4·5 per 1,000 population). Nunavut's birth rate is the highest in Canada and is more than twice the national average of 10·5 per 1,000 births. 56% of the population are under 25 years of age. Life expectancy, 1996: males, 67 years; females, 72.

CLIMATE

Conditions range from cold continental to polar, with long hard winters and short cool summers. In Iqaluit there can be as little as four hours sunshine per day in winter and up to 21 hours per day at the summer solstice. Iqaluit, Jan. mean high –22°C; July mean high, 15°C.

CONSTITUTION AND GOVERNMENT

Government is by a Legislative Assembly of 19 elected members, who then choose a leader and ministers by consensus. There are no political parties. The government is being established in evolutionary stages, a process which began in 1993 and is scheduled for completion in 2009. It is intended that government be highly decentralized, consisting of ten departments spread over 11 different communities.

Inuktitut will be the working language of government but government agencies will also offer services in English and French. Although the Inuits will be the dominant force in public government, non-Inuit citizens have the same voting rights.

RECENT ELECTIONS

Legislative Assembly elections were held on 16 Feb. 2004. There were 82 non-partisan candidates; 17 men and 2 women were elected.

CURRENT ADMINISTRATION

Commissioner: Ann Meekitjuk Hanson (took office in April 2005).

In Feb. 2005 the cabinet was as follows:

Premier and Minister of Executive and Intergovernmental Affairs and of Justice: Paul Okalik; b. 1964 (took office on 1 April 1999 and re-elected in 2004).

Deputy Premier, Minister of Health and Social Services and Responsible for the Status of Women: Levinia Brown. *Finance and Government House Leader:* Leona Aglukkaq. *Environment:* Olayuk Akesuk. *Community and Government Services:* Peter Kilabuk. *Education, Energy and Responsible for Homelessness and Immigration:* Ed Picco. *Economic Development and Transportation:* David Simailak. *Culture, Language, Elders and Youth and Human Resources:* Louis Tapardjuk.

Government of Nunavut Website: http://www.gov.nu.ca

ECONOMY

While the cost of living in Nunavut is around 160–200% that of southern Canadians, the average household income is $31,471 CDN compared to $45,251 CDN for Canada as a whole. With unemployment running high, transport costs expensive and education limited, self-sufficiency is unlikely to be achieved soon.

Currency. The Canadian dollar is the standard currency.

Budget. Total revenue in 2002–03 was $959m. CDN (own source revenue, $115m. CDN; general purpose transfers, $649m. CDN; special purpose transfers, $195m.). Total expenditures in 2002–03 amounted to $1,035m. CDN (including: education, $199m. CDN; health, $168m. CDN; housing, $134m. CDN).

Banking and Finance. Few banks have branches in the province. Iqaluit has two automated cash machines and stores are increasingly installing debit card facilities.

ENERGY AND NATURAL RESOURCES

Minerals. There are two lead and zinc mines operating in the High Arctic region. There are also known deposits of copper, gold, silver and diamonds.

Hunting and Trapping. Most communities still rely on traditional foodstuffs such as caribou and seal. The Canadian government now provides meat inspections so that caribou and musk ox meat can be sold across the country.

Fisheries. Fishing is still very important in Inuit life. The principal catches are shrimp, scallop and arctic char.

INDUSTRY

The main industries are mining, tourism, fishing, hunting and trapping and arts and crafts production.

Labour. Unemployment was running at 20·7% in 1999.

COMMUNICATIONS

Roads. There is one 21-km government-maintained road between Arctic Bay and Nanisivik. There are a few paved roads in Iqaluit and Rankin Inlet, but most are unpaved. Some communities have local roads and tracks but Kivalliq has no direct land connections with southern Canada.

Civil Aviation. There are air connections between communities and a daily air connection between Iqaluit and Montreal/Ottawa.

Shipping. There is an annual summer sea-lift by ship and barge for transport of construction materials, dry goods, non-perishable food, trucks and cars.

Telecommunications. There are telephone services in all communities except for Bathurst Inlet and Umingmaktok. Because of the wide distances between communities, there is a very high rate of Internet use in Nunavut. However, line speeds are slow and there is a problem with satellite bounce.

Postal Services. There is no door-to-door delivery service, so correspondence has to be retrieved from post offices.

SOCIAL INSTITUTIONS

Justice. A territorial court has been put in place. Policing is by the Royal Canadian Mounted Police (RCMP).

Education. Approximately one third of Nunavut's population aged over 15 have less than Grade 9 schooling. Training and development is seen as central to securing a firm economic foundation for the province. The Canadian government has pledged $40m. CDN for recruiting and training Inuit employees into Nunavut public service.

Courses in computer science, business management and public administration may be undertaken at Arctic College. In 1997–98 there were 39 schools with 7,770 students.

Health. There is one hospital in Iqaluit. 26 health centres provide nursing care for communities. For more specialized treatment, patients of Qikiqtaaluk may be flown to Montreal, patients in Kivalliq to Churchill or Winnipeg and patients in Kitikmeot to Yellowknife's Stanton Regional Hospital.

CULTURE

Broadcasting. The Canadian Broadcasting Corporation (CBC) North transmits television to Iqaluit and other communities. The Inuit Broadcasting Corporation (IBC) transmits in Inuktitut and Television Northern Canada (TVNC) is devoted to programming by and for northerners and native citizens. There are 5½ hours of Inuktitut television programming per week. Cable satellite television is also widely available. CBC is the only local radio station accessible in all Nunavut communities.

Tourism. Auyuittuq National Park is one of the principal tourist attractions, along with the opportunity of seeing Inuit life first-hand. Under the terms of the land claim settlement, three more national parks are planned. It is also hoped that the publicity surrounding the new territory will encourage visitors.

FURTHER READING

The Nunavut Handbook, Raincoast Books, Vancouver, 1999

YUKON TERRITORY

KEY HISTORICAL EVENTS

The territory owes its fame to the discovery of gold in the Klondike at the end of the 19th century. Formerly part of the Northwest Territories, the Yukon was joined to the Dominion as a separate territory on 13 June 1898.

Yukon First Nations People lived a semi-nomadic subsistence lifestyle in the region long before it was established as a territory. The earliest evidence of human activity was found in caves containing stone tools and animal bones estimated to be 20,000 years old. The Athapaskan cultural linguistic tradition to which most Yukon First Nations belong is more than 1,000 years old. The territory's name comes from the native 'Yu-kun-ah' for the great river that drains most of this area.

The Yukon was created as a district of the North West Territories in 1895. The Klondike Gold Rush in the late 1890s saw the invasion of thousands of stampeders pouring into the gold fields of the Canadian northwest. Population at the peak of the rush reached 40,000. This event spurred the federal government to set up basic administrative structures in the Yukon. The territory was given the status of a separate geographical and political entity with an appointed legislative council in 1898. In 1953 the capital was moved south from Dawson City to Whitehorse, where most of the economic activity was centred. The federal government granted the Yukon responsible government in 1979.

TERRITORY AND POPULATION

The territory consists of one city, three towns, four villages, two hamlets, 13 unincorporated communities and eight rural communities. It is situated in the northwestern region of Canada and comprises 482,443 sq. km of which 8,052 sq. km is fresh water.

The population at the 2001 census was 28,674.

Principal centres in 2001 were Whitehorse, the capital, 19,058; Dawson City, 1,251; Watson Lake, 912; Haines Junction, 531; Faro, 313.

The Yukon represents 4·8% of Canada's total land area.

SOCIAL STATISTICS

Births in 2002–03 numbered 333 (a rate of 10·9 per 1,000 population) and deaths 145 (rate of 4·7 per 1,000 population). There were 143 marriages and 90 divorces in 2002.

CLIMATE

Temperatures in the Yukon are usually more extreme than those experienced in the southern provinces of Canada. A cold climate in winter with moderate temperatures in summer provide a considerable annual range of temperature and moderate rainfall.

Whitehorse, Jan. –18·7°C (–2·0°F), July 14°C (57·2°F). Annual precipitation 268·8 mm. Dawson City, Jan. –30·7°C (–23·3°F), July 15·6°C (60·1°F). Annual precipitation 182·7 mm.

CONSTITUTION AND GOVERNMENT

The Yukon was constituted a separate territory on 13 June 1898. The Yukon Legislative Assembly consists of 17 elected members and functions in much the same way as a provincial legislature. The seat of government is at Whitehorse. It consists of an executive council with parliamentary powers similar to those of a provincial cabinet. The Yukon government consists of 12 departments, as well as a Women's Directorate and four Crown corporations.

RECENT ELECTIONS

At elections held on 4 Nov. 2002 the Yukon Party took 12 of the available 18 seats; the New Democratic Party 5; and the Liberals 1.

CURRENT ADMINISTRATION

Commissioner: Jack Cable; b. 1934 (took office on 1 Oct. 2000).

In Feb. 2005 the Yukon Party Ministry comprised:

Premier, Minister Responsible for Executive Council Office, including Devolution, Land Claims and Youth Directorate, and Minister of Finance: Dennis Fentie.

Minister of Health, Social Services and Environment: Peter Jenkins. *Education and Justice:* John Edzerza. *Tourism and Culture:* Elaine Taylor. *Energy, Mines and Resources:* Archie Lang. *Highways and Public Works, and Community Services:* Glenn Hart. *Economic Development:* Jim Kenyon.

Government of Yukon Website: http://www.gov.yk.ca

ECONOMY

The key sectors of the economy are government, tourism, finance, insurance and real estate.

Budget. Total revenue in 2003–04 was $660m. CDN (own source revenue, $126m. CDN; general purpose transfers, $468m. CDN; special purpose transfers, $65m. CDN). Total expenditures in 2003–04 amounted to $679m. CDN (including: education, $118m. CDN; health, $96m. CDN; social services, $92m. CDN).

Performance. GDP at market prices in 2000 was $1,124m. CDN. Mining, oil and gas production was estimated at $72·8m. CDN in 1998 and revenue from agriculture, forestry, hunting and fishing was estimated at $4m. CDN. In the manufacturing sector, shipments were valued at $2·3m. CDN in 2000. GDP per person in 2000 was $36,258 CDN.

ENERGY AND NATURAL RESOURCES

Environment. The Yukon is recognized as a critical habitat for many species of rare and endangered flowers, big game animals, birds of prey and migratory birds. There are 278 species of birds and 38 species of fish. The vegetation is classified as sub-arctic and alpine.

Three national parks (total area 36,572 sq. km), five territorial parks (7,861 sq. km), two ecological reserves (181 sq. km), eight wildlife management areas (10,651 sq. km) and one wildlife sanctuary (6,450 sq. km) have been established to protect fragile and significant areas for the future.

Electricity. The Yukon currently depends on imported refined petroleum products for about 16% of the energy it uses. At the same time, 94·6% (2000 figure) of the territory's electrical supply comes from four utility-owned hydro-electrical facilities.

Hydro-generated power is supplemented with diesel power plants which are located in most communities. Current capacity is 130·2 MW combined hydrodiesel-generated power. Total generation for 2000 was 268 GWh.

Oil and Gas. In 1997 the Yukon Oil and Gas Act was passed, replacing the federal legislation. This Act provides for the transfer of responsibility for oil and gas resources to Yukon jurisdiction. Five unexplored oil and gas basins with rich potential exist. Current net production is about 1·7m. cu. metres of natural gas per day.

Minerals. Gold and silver are the chief minerals. There are also deposits of lead, zinc, copper, tungsten and iron ore. Gold deposits, both hard rock and placer, are being mined.

Estimates for 2000 mineral production: gold, $51·6m. CDN; and silver, $0·3m. CDN. Total: $51·9m. CDN.

Agriculture. Many areas have suitable soils and climate for the production of forages, cereal grains and vegetables, domestic livestock and game farming. The greenhouse industry is the Yukon's largest horticulture sector.

In 1996 there were 160 farms operating full- and part-time. The total area of farms was 9,890 ha of which 2,248 ha are in field crop.

Farm receipts in 1996 were estimated at $3·5m. CDN. Total farm capital, 1996, was $45m. CDN.

Forestry. The forests, covering 275,000 sq. km of the territory, are part of the great Boreal forest region of Canada, which covers 57% of the Yukon. Forestry products include posts and beams for the construction industry, roof trusses, niche products and timber.

Production from forestry was 145·0m. cu. metres in 1999–2000. Fuel wood represents approximately $4m. CDN to $5m. CDN in direct employment and petroleum substitution in the Yukon annually.

Fur Trade. The fur-trapping industry is considered vital to rural and remote residents and especially First Nations people wishing to maintain a traditional lifestyle. Preliminary fur production in 2000 (mostly marten, muskrat, beaver, lynx and wolverine) was valued at $296,896 CDN.

Fisheries. Commercial fishing concentrates on chinook salmon, chum salmon, lake trout and whitefish.

INDUSTRY

The key sectors of the economy are tourism and government.

Labour. The 2000 labour force was 15,242, of whom 13,475 were employed.

INTERNATIONAL TRADE

Imports and Exports. In 2000 exports made up 35·2% of Yukon goods and services produced. In 2000 exports were valued at $396m. CDN.

COMMUNICATIONS

Roads. The Alaska Highway and branch highway systems connect Yukon's main communities with Alaska, the Northwest Territories, southern Canada and the United States. The 735-km Dempster Highway north of Dawson City connects with Inuvik, on the Arctic coast. In 2000 there were 4,712·5 km of roads maintained by the Yukon Territorial government: 3,178·1 km, Alaska Highway; 1,534·4 km is secondary. Vehicles registered in 2000 totalled 23,915 (excluding buses, motorcycles and trailers), including 21,149 passenger vehicles.

Rail. The 176-km White Pass and Yukon Railway connected Whitehorse with year-round ocean shipping at Skagway, Alaska, but was closed in 1982. A modified passenger service was restarted in 1988 to take cruise ship tourists from Skagway to Carcross, Yukon, over the White Pass summit.

Civil Aviation. Whitehorse has an international airport with direct daily flights from Vancouver, Alaska and the Northwest Territories. In the summer there are regular scheduled flights from Europe. There are ten airports throughout the territory, with many smaller airstrips and aerodromes in remote areas. Commercial airlines offering charter services are located throughout the territory.

Shipping. The majority of goods are shipped into the territory by truck over the Alaska and Stewart-Cassiar Highways. Some goods are shipped through the ports of Skagway and Haines, Alaska, and then trucked to Whitehorse for distribution throughout the territory.

Telecommunications. All telephone and telecommunications, including Internet access in most communities, are provided by Northwestel, a subsidiary of Bell Canada Enterprises.

SOCIAL INSTITUTIONS

Education. The Yukon Department of Education operates (with the assistance of elected school boards) the territory's 28 schools, both public and private, from kindergarten to grade 12. In 2001 there were 5,579 pupils. There are also one French First Language school and one Roman Catholic school. The total enrolment figure for 1999–2000 was 5,332. The Whitehorse campus is the administrative and programme centre for 13 other campuses located throughout the territory. In 1999–2000 a total of 664 full-time and 4,668 part-time students enrolled in programmes and courses.

Health. In 2000 there were two hospitals with 61 staffed beds, four nursing stations, nine health treatment centres, 55 resident doctors and 15 dentists. The territorial government operates a medical travel programme to send patients to nearby provinces for specialized treatment not available in the territory.

CULTURE

Broadcasting. There are three radio stations in Whitehorse and 15 low-power relay radio transmitters operated by CBC, and six operated by the Yukon government. CHON-FM, operated by Northern Native Broadcasting, is broadcast to virtually all Yukon communities by satellite. There are also 27 basic and 36 extended pay-cable TV channels in Whitehorse, and private cable operations in some communities. Live CBC national television and TVNC is provided by satellite and relayed to all communities.

Press. In 2000 there were one daily and one semi-weekly newspaper in Whitehorse, and a semi-weekly (summer only) and a monthly newspaper in Dawson City. In total, the territory publishes ten newspapers which range in publication from daily to annual.

Tourism. In 1999 there were about 280,500 visitors, generating revenues of $160m. CDN. Primary tourist activities are related to highway travel, wilderness adventure and historical and cultural interests.

Tourism is the largest private sector employer. In 1999, 66% of employed Yukon people were working for businesses that reported some level of tourism revenue. 20% of businesses generate more than 33% of gross revenues from tourism.

FURTHER READING

Annual Report of the Government of the Yukon.
Yukon Executive Council, *Annual Statistical Review.*

Berton, P., *Klondike.* (Rev. ed.) Toronto, 1987
Coates, K. and Morrison, W., *Land of the Midnight Sun: A History of the Yukon.* Edmonton, 1988

There is a Yukon Archive at Yukon College, Whitehorse.

CAPE VERDE

República de Cabo Verde

Capital: Praia
Population projection, 2010: 529,000
GDP per capita, 2002: (PPP$) 5,000
HDI/world rank: 0·717/105

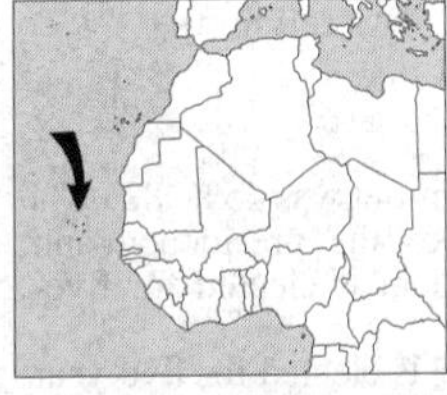

KEY HISTORICAL EVENTS

During centuries of Portuguese rule the islands were gradually peopled with Portuguese, slaves from Africa, and people of mixed African-European descent who became the majority. While retaining some African culture, the Cape Verdians spoke Portuguese or the Portuguese-derived Crioulo (Creole) language and became Catholics. In 1956 nationalists from Cape Verde and Portuguese Guinea formed the *Partido Africano da Independência da Guiné e Cabo Verde* (PAIGC). In the 1960s the PAIGC waged a successful guerrilla war. On 5 July 1975 Cape Verde became independent, ruled by the PAIGC, which was already the ruling party in the former Portuguese colony of Guinea-Bissau. But resentment at Cape Verdians' privileged position in Guinea-Bissau led to the end of the ties between the two countries' ruling parties. Although the PAIGC retained its name in Guinea-Bissau, in Jan. 1981 it was renamed the *Partido Africano da Independência do Cabo Verde* (PAICV) in Cape Verde. The Constitution of 1981 made the PAICV the sole legal party but in Sept. 1990 the National Assembly abolished its monopoly and free elections were permitted.

TERRITORY AND POPULATION

Cape Verde is situated in the Atlantic Ocean 620 km off west Africa and consists of ten islands (Boa Vista, Brava, Fogo, Maio, Sal, Santa Luzia, Santo Antão, São Nicolau, São Tiago and São Vicente) and five islets. The islands are divided into two groups, named Barlavento (windward) and Sotavento (leeward). The total area is 4,033 sq. km (1,557 sq. miles). The 2000 census population was 434,625, giving a density of 107·8 per sq. km. In 2001, 63·3% of the population lived in urban areas.

The UN gives a projected population for 2010 of 529,000.

About 600,000 Cape Verdeans live abroad.

Areas and populations of the islands:

Island	*Area (sq. km)*	*Population Census 1990*	*Population Census 2000*
Santo Antão	779	43,845	47,170
São Vicente[1]	227	51,277	67,163
São Nicolau	388	13,665	13,661
Sal	216	7,715	14,816
Boa Vista	620	3,452	4,209
Barlavento	*2,230*	*119,954*	*147,019*
Maio	269	4,969	6,754
São Tiago	991	175,691	236,627
Fogo	476	33,902	37,421
Brava	67	6,975	6,804
Sotavento	*1,803*	*221,537*	*287,606*

[1]Including Santa Luzia island, which is uninhabited.

The main towns are Praia, the capital, on São Tiago (76,000, 1999 estimate) and Mindelo on São Vicente (47,109, 1990 census). Ethnic groups: Mixed, 71%; Black, 28%; White, 1%. The official language is Portuguese; a creole (Crioulo) is in ordinary use.

SOCIAL STATISTICS

1998 births, 15,460; 1996 deaths, 2,786. 1998 birth rate, 37·1 per 1,000 population; 1996 death rate, 7·0. Annual population growth rate, 1992–2002, 2·2%. Annual emigration varies between 2,000 and 10,000. Life expectancy at birth, 2001, was

66·6 years for men and 72·4 years for women. Infant mortality, 2001, 29 per 1,000 live births; fertility rate, 2001, 3·3 children per woman.

CLIMATE

The climate is arid, with a cool dry season from Dec. to June and warm dry conditions for the rest of the year. Rainfall is sparse, rarely exceeding 5" (127 mm) in the northern islands or 12" (304 mm) in the southern ones. There are periodic severe droughts. Praia, Jan. 72°F (22·2°C), July 77°F (25°C). Annual rainfall 10" (250 mm).

CONSTITUTION AND GOVERNMENT

The Constitution was adopted in Sept. 1992.

A constitutional referendum was held on 28 Dec. 1994; turn-out was 45%. 82·06% of votes cast favoured a reform extending the powers of the presidency and strengthening the autonomy of local authorities. The President is elected for five-year terms by universal suffrage.

The 72-member *National Assembly* (*Assembleia Nacional*) is elected for five-year terms.

National Anthem. 'Sol, suor, o verde e mar' ('Sun, sweat, the green and the sea'); words and tune by A. Lopes Cabral.

RECENT ELECTIONS

Elections for the *National Assembly* of 72 members were held on 14 Jan. 2001. Turn-out was 57·8%. Three parties stood. The PAICV won 40 seats with 49·9% of votes cast, the Movement for Democracy (MPD) won 30 seats with 40·8% and the Democratic Alliance for Change won 2 with 6·2%.

In the presidential elections which took place on 11 Feb. 2001 Pedro Pires won 46·5% of the vote and Carlos Veiga 45·9%, with 2 other candidates winning less than 4% each, qualifying the two former prime ministers for a run-off. Turn-out was 50%. After the 25 Feb. 2001 run-off, Pires was confirmed as the victor with 75,828 votes (49·43%) against Veiga's 75,811 (49·42%), a difference of just 17 votes. Turn-out was 59%.

CURRENT ADMINISTRATION

President: Pedro Pires; b. 1934 (PAICV; sworn in 22 March 2001).

In March 2005 the government comprised:

Prime Minister: José Maria Neves; b. 1959 (PAICV; sworn in 1 Feb. 2001).

Senior Minister for Health: Dr Basílio Mosso Ramos. *Senior Minister for Infrastructure and Transport:* Manuel Inocêncio Sousa. *Minister for Foreign Affairs, Co-operation and Communities:* Dr Víctor Borges. *Internal Administration:* Dr Júlio Lopes Correira. *Defence and Parliamentary Affairs:* Dr Armindo Cipriano Maurício. *Education and Human Resources:* Dr Filomena Martins. *Environment, Agriculture and Fisheries:* Dr Maria Brito Neves. *Justice:* Cristina Fontes Lima. *Economy, Growth and Competitiveness:* João Pereira Silva. *Finance and Planning:* Dr João Serra. *Labour and Solidarity:* Dr Sidónio Monteiro. *State Reform and Public Administration:* Dr Ilídio da Cruz.

Government Website (Portuguese only): http://www.governo.cv

DEFENCE

There is selective conscription. Defence expenditure totalled US$5m. in 2003 (US$11 per capita), representing 1·5% of GDP.

Army. The Army is composed of two battalions and had a strength of 1,000 in 2002.

Navy. There is a coast guard of 100 (2002).

Air Force. The Air Force had under 100 personnel and no combat aircraft in 2002.

INTERNATIONAL RELATIONS

Cape Verde is a member of the UN, the African Union, African Development Bank, ECOWAS, IOM, the International Organization of the Francophonie and is an ACP member state of the ACP-EU relationship.

ECONOMY

Agriculture accounted for 10·7% of GDP in 2002, industry 16·4% and services 72·8%.

Currency. The unit of currency is the *Cape Verde escudo* (CVE) of 100 *centavos*. Foreign exchange reserves were US$63m. in June 2002 and total money supply was 20,893m. escudos. There was inflation in 2002 of 1·8% (3·8% in 2001).

Budget. In 2001 revenue totalled 14,900m. escudos and expenditure 21,200m. escudos.

Performance. Real GDP growth was 3·8% in 2001 and 4·6% in 2002. Total GDP in 2003 was US$0·8bn.

Banking and Finance. The Banco de Cabo Verde is the central bank (*Governor*, Amaro Alexandre da Luz) and bank of issue, and was also previously a commercial bank. Its latter functions have been taken over by the Banco Comercial do Atlântico, mainly financed by public funds. The Caixa Econômica de Cabo Verde (CECV) has been upgraded into a commercial and development bank. Two foreign banks have also been established there. In addition, the Fundo de Solidariedade Nacional acts as the country's leading savings institution while the Fundo de Desenvoluimento Nacional administers public investment resources and the Instituto Caboverdiano channels international aid.

ENERGY AND NATURAL RESOURCES

Environment. Cape Verde's carbon dioxide emissions from the consumption and flaring of fossil fuels in 2002 were the equivalent of 0·4 tonnes per capita.

Electricity. Installed capacity was 7,000 kW in 2000. Production was around 43m. kWh in 2000. Consumption per capita in 2000 was an estimated 101 kWh.

Minerals. Salt is obtained on the islands of Sal, Boa Vista and Maio. Volcanic rock (pozzolana) is mined for export. There are also deposits of kaolin, clay, gypsum and basalt.

Agriculture. Some 10–15% of the land area is suitable for farming. In 2001, 39,000 ha were arable and 2,000 ha permanent crops, mainly confined to inland valleys. 3,000 ha were irrigated in 2001. The chief crops (production, 2000, in 1,000 tonnes) are: sugarcane, 13; maize, 11; bananas, 6; cabbages, 6; coconuts, 6; mangoes, 5; sweet potatoes, 4; tomatoes, 4.

Livestock (2000): 640,000 pigs, 110,000 goats, 22,000 cattle, 14,000 asses.

Forestry. In 2000 the woodland area was 85,000 ha, or 21·1% of the total land area.

Fisheries. In 2001 the total catch was 9,653 tonnes (mainly tuna), exclusively from marine waters. About 200 tonnes of lobsters are caught annually.

INDUSTRY

The main industries are the manufacture of paint, beer, soft drinks, rum, flour, cigarettes, canned tuna and shoes.

Labour. In 1996 the workforce was 157,000 (62% males).

INTERNATIONAL TRADE

Foreign debt was US$414m. in 2002.

Imports and Exports. Imports and exports (f.o.b.) for calendar years in US$1m.:

	1998	*1999*	*2000*	*2001*	*2002*
Imports	218·8	239·0	225·7	231·5	278·0
Exports	32·7	26·0	38·3	37·2	41·8

Main exports in 1997: road vehicles (43%), refined petroleum (29%), footwear (7%) and fish and shellfish (4%). Leading export markets, 2000: Portugal, 80·1%; USA, 11·4%; Spain, 3·5%. Main import suppliers, 2000: Portugal, 52·4%; Netherlands, 13·0%; France, 4·4%. Approximately 90% of food is imported.

COMMUNICATIONS

Roads. In 1999 there were estimated 1,100 km of roads (78% paved); and in 1996 there were 3,280 private cars and 820 commercial vehicles.

Civil Aviation. Amilcar Cabral International Airport, at Espargos on Sal, is a major refuelling point on flights to Africa and Latin America. A new airport, Francisco Mendes Airport, has been built at Praia, and was opened in 2003. Transportes Aéreos de Cabo Verde (TACV), the national carrier, provided services to most of the other islands in 2003, and internationally to Abidjan, Amsterdam, Bamako, Bissau, Conakry, Dakar, Fortaleza, Las Palmas, Lisbon, Madrid, Milan, Munich, Paris and Zürich. In 2000 Amilcar Cabral International Airport handled 489,000 passengers (254,000 on international flights) and 3,500 tonnes of freight. In 1999 scheduled airline traffic of Cape Verde-based carriers flew 5·5m. km, carrying 252,000 passengers (114,000 on international flights).

Shipping. The main ports are Mindelo and Praia. In 2002 the merchant marine totalled 16,000 GRT. There is a state-owned ferry service between the islands.

Telecommunications. There were 113,100 telephone subscribers in 2002 (257·7 per 1,000 persons), including 42,900 mobile phone subscribers, and 35,000 PCs were in use. In 1996 there were approximately 1,000 fax machines. The number of Internet users in 2002 was 16,000.

Postal Services. In 1998 there were 54 post offices.

SOCIAL INSTITUTIONS

Justice. There is a network of People's Tribunals, with a Supreme Court in Praia. The Supreme Court is composed of a minimum of five Judges, of whom one is appointed by the President, one elected by the National Assembly and the other by the Supreme Council of Magistrates.

The population in penal institutions in Dec. 1999 was 755 (178 per 100,000 of national population).

Religion. In 2001, 83% of the population were Roman Catholic and 8% were followers of other religions.

Education. Adult literacy in 2001 was 74·9% (male, 84·9%; female, 67·0%). Primary schooling is followed by lower (13–15 years) and upper (16–18 years) secondary education options. In 2000–01 there were 3,214 primary school teachers for 90,640 pupils; and 1,372 teachers (1997–98) for 45,545 pupils at secondary schools. In 1990 there were 531 students and 52 teachers at a technical school, 211 students and 53 teachers in three teacher-training colleges and about 500 students at foreign universities.

In 1998–99 total expenditure on education came to 4·4% of GNP.

Health. In 1996 there were two central and three regional hospitals, 15 health centres, 22 dispensaries and 60 community health clinics. There were 66 physicians, 213 nurses and six pharmacists in 1996.

CULTURE

Broadcasting. There are two national radio stations and a national TV service. Portuguese and French international radio and TV services also broadcast to Cape Verde. There were 73,000 radio receivers in 1997 and 44,000 television receivers in 2001.

Press. In 1996 there were three national newspapers—a state-owned bi-weekly, and a weekly and a fortnightly, owned by political parties. Total circulation approximates 12,000, but publication is suspended from time to time owing to shortage of paper.

Tourism. Tourism is in the initial stages of development. In 2002 there were 126,000 foreign tourists; spending by tourists totalled US$66m. Some 50% of tourists originate from Portugal, 15% from Germany and 7% from France.

DIPLOMATIC REPRESENTATIVES

Of Cape Verde in the United Kingdom
Ambassador: Vacant (resides at Brussels).
2nd Secretary: Clara Manuela da Luz Delgado.

Of the United Kingdom in Cape Verde
Ambassador: Peter Newall (resides at Dakar, Senegal).

Of Cape Verde in the USA (3415 Massachusetts Ave., NW, Washington, D.C., 20007)
Ambassador: José Brito.

Of the USA in Cape Verde (Rua Abilio Macedo 81, Praia)
Ambassador: Donald C. Johnson.

Of Cape Verde to the United Nations
Ambassador: Fátima Veiga.

Of Cape Verde to the European Union
Ambassador: Fernando Jorge Wahnon Ferreira.

FURTHER READING

Lobban, R., *Cape Verde: Crioulo Colony to Independent Nation.* Westview Press, Boulder (CO), 1998

Meintel, D., *Race, Culture, and Portuguese Colonialism in Cabo Verde.* Syracuse Univ. Press, 1984

Shaw, Caroline E., *Cape Verde Islands.* [Bibliography] ABC-Clio, Oxford and Santa Barbara (CA), 1991

National statistical office: Instituto Nacional de Estatística, Praia.
Website (Portuguese only): http://www.ine.cv/

CENTRAL AFRICAN REPUBLIC

Capital: Bangui
Population projection, 2010: 4·27m.
GDP per capita, 2002: (PPP$) 1,170
HDI/world rank: 0·361/169

République Centrafricaine

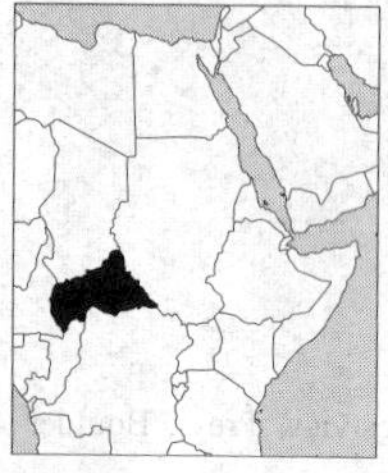

KEY HISTORICAL EVENTS

Central African Republic became independent on 13 Aug. 1960, after having been one of the four territories of French Equatorial Africa. A Constitution of 1976 provided for the country to be a parliamentary democracy to be known as the Central African Empire. President Bokassa became Emperor Bokassa I. He was overthrown in 1979. In 1981 General André Kolingba took power, initiating a gradual return to constitutional rule.

On 5 June 1996, following an army mutiny, President Patassé accepted an agreement brokered by France which led to the formation of a government of national unity. But mutineers demanded the replacement of President Patassé. France chaired a mediation committee of various neighbouring French-speaking states, and an agreement to end the mutiny was signed in 1997 and a peacekeeping force from neighbouring states, MISAB, was set up. Conflicts between the mutineers and MISAB continued until a ceasefire was concluded on 2 July 1997. There was an attempted coup on 28 May 2001, allegedly led by Gen. André Kolingba, who had been the country's military ruler from 1981 to 1993. However, it failed following several days of fighting in and around the capital, Bangui. Fighting erupted once more in Oct. 2002 after another coup attempt. In March 2003 a further coup saw Gen. François Bozizé, a former army chief, seize power.

TERRITORY AND POPULATION

The republic is bounded in the north by Chad, east by Sudan, south by the Democratic Republic of the Congo and the Republic of the Congo, and west by Cameroon. The area (including inland water) covers 622,984 sq. km (240,534 sq. miles). The population at the 1988 census was 2,463,616; 2003 census (provisional), 3,151,072, giving a density of 5 per sq. km. In 2001, 58·3% of the population were rural.

The UN gives a projected population for 2010 of 4·27m.

The areas, populations and capitals of the prefectures are as follows:

Prefecture	*Sq. km*	*2003 census (provisional)*	*Capital*
Bamingui-Bangoran	58,200	38,437	Ndele
Bangui[1]	67	531,763	Bangui
Basse-Kotto	17,604	203,887	Mobaye
Haute-Kotto	86,650	69,514	Bria
Haut-M'bomou	55,530	38,184	Obo
Kemo	17,204	98,881	Sibut
Lobaye	19,235	214,137	M'baiki
Mambere Kadéi	30,203	289,688	Berbérati
M'bomou	61,150	132,740	Bangassou
Nana Grebizi	19,996	87,341	Kaga-Bandoro
Nana-Mambere	26,600	184,594	Bouar
Ombella-M'poko	31,835	304,025	Bimbo
Ouaka	49,900	224,076	Bambari
Ouham	50,250	280,772	Bossangoa
Ouham-Pendé	32,100	325,567	Bozoum
Sangha M'baéré	19,412	89,871	Nola
Vakaga	46,500	37,595	Birao

[1]Autonomous commune.

The capital, Bangui, had a census population (provisional) in 2003 of 531,763. Other main towns, with 2003 census populations (provisional), are Bimbo (114,086), Bebérati (59,414), Carnot (37,339), Bambari (33,273) and Bouar (29,753).

There are a number of ethnic groups, the largest being Gbaya (23·7%), Banda (23·4%) and Mandja (14·7%) at the 1988 census.

Sango (spoken by 89% of the population in 1988) and French are the official languages.

SOCIAL STATISTICS

1996 births, 131,000; deaths, 58,000. Rates, 1996 estimates (per 1,000 population): births, 40·0; deaths, 17·6. Infant mortality, 2001 (per 1,000 live births), 115. Expectation of life in 2001 was 39·1 years for males and 41·8 for females. Annual population growth rate, 1992–2002, 2·1%. Fertility rate, 2001, 5·0 children per woman.

CLIMATE

A tropical climate with little variation in temperature. The wet months are May, June, Oct. and Nov. Bangui, Jan. 31·9°C, July 20·7°C. Annual rainfall 1,289·3 mm. Ndele, Jan. 36·3°C, July 30·5°C. Annual rainfall 203·6 mm.

CONSTITUTION AND GOVERNMENT

Under the Constitution adopted by a referendum on 21 Nov. 1986, the sole legal political party was the *Rassemblement Démocratique Centrafricain*. In Aug. 1992 the Constitution was revised to permit multi-party democracy. Further constitutional reforms followed a referendum in Dec. 1994, including the establishment of a *Constitutional Court*. The President is elected by popular vote for not more than two terms of six years, and appoints and leads a Council of Ministers. There is a 109-member *National Assembly*. Following the coup of March 2003 Gen. François Bozizé suspended the constitution and dissolved parliament. However, at a referendum in Dec. 2004, 90·4% of voters approved the adoption of a new constitution; voter participation was 77·4%. The new constitution resembles the previous one but permits the president to serve not more than two terms of five years. It also provides for the appointment of the prime minister from the political party with a parliamentary majority.

National Anthem. 'La Renaissance' ('Rebirth'); words by B. Boganda, tune by H. Pepper.

RECENT ELECTIONS

At the presidential elections held on 13 March 2005 there were 11 presidential candidates. Incumbent president Gen. François Bozizé received 42·9% of the vote, ahead of former prime minister Martin Ziguélé (Liberation Movement of the Central African People) with 23·5% and former president André Kolingba (Central African Democratic Rally) 16·4%. In the second round on 8 May 2005 Gen. François Bozizé won 64·7% of the vote against Martin Ziguélé who won 35·3%. Turn-out was 64·6%.

In National Assembly elections on 13 March and 8 May 2005 the National Convergence coalition gained 42 seats (including the National Unity Party with 3 seats and the Movement for Democracy and Development with 2), the Liberation Movement of the Central African People 11, the Central African Democratic Rally 8, Social Democratic Party 4, Patriotic Front for Progress 2, Alliance for Democracy and Progress 2, the Londo Association 1 and ind. 34.

CURRENT ADMINISTRATION

Former army chief Gen. François Bozizé seized power on 15 March 2003 in a coup and the following day declared himself president, saying that he had dissolved the National Assembly and government. A transitional government was formed comprising representatives of civil society and all political parties. Gen. Bozizé has said that a transition period will last between one and three years, after which elections would be held to decide on a new government. Bozizé reshuffled the transitional government in Dec. 2003 and again in Sept. 2004. In March. 2005 it comprised the following:

President and Minister of Defence: Gen. François Bozizé; b. 1946 (since 16 March 2003).

Vice-President and Minister for Communication: Vacant.

Prime Minister and Minister of Finance, Budget and the Economy: Célestin Gaombalet; b. 1941 (took office on 15 Dec. 2003).

Minister of State responsible for National Education, Literacy, Higher Education and Research: Karim Meckassoua.

Minister of Communications, National Reconciliation and Culture: Joseph Kiticki-Kouamba. *Planning, Economy, Finance, Budget and International Co-operation:* Daniel Nditifei-Boysembe. *Foreign Affairs, Regional Integration and the Francophonie:* Charles Hervé Wénézoui. *Justice, Keeper of the Seals:* Vacant. *Interior:* Michel Salle. *Energy and Mines:* Sylvain Ndoutingaï. *Agriculture and Livestock:* Parfait-Anicet Mbay. *Public Health and Population:* Nestor Mamadou Nali. *Equipment and Transport:* Sonny Mpokomandji. *Family, Social Affairs and National Solidarity:* Solange Pagonendji Ndackala. *Commerce, Industry and the Promotion of the Private Sector:* Didier Wangue. *Water, Forests, Hunting and Fishing:* Denis Kossi-Bella. *Civil Service, Labour and Social Security:* Jacques Bothy. *Restoration of Public Buildings, Town Planning and Housing:* Abraham Ngoto Bouloum. *Posts and Telecommunications:* Idris Salao. *Tourism and Craft Industry Development:* Bruno Dacko. *Youth, Sports, Arts and Culture:* Lieut.-Col. Guy Kolingba. *Minister Responsible for the General Secretariat of Government and Relations with Parliament:* Me Zarambaud Assingambi.

DEFENCE

Selective national service for a two-year period is in force.

Defence expenditure totalled US$29m. in 2003 (US$8 per capita), representing 2·3% of GDP.

Army. The Army consisted (2002) of about 1,400 personnel. There is a territorial defence regiment, a combined arms regiment and a support/HQ regiment. In addition there are some 1,000 personnel in the paramilitary Gendarmerie.

Navy. The Army includes a small naval wing operating a handful of patrol craft.

Air Force. Personnel strength (2002) about 150. There are no combat aircraft.

INTERNATIONAL RELATIONS

The Central African Republic is a member of the UN, WTO, the African Union, African Development Bank, Lake Chad Commission, the International Organization of the Francophonie and is an ACP member state of the ACP-EU relationship.

ECONOMY

Agriculture accounted for 56·5% of GDP in 2002, industry 22·3% and services 21·2%.

Currency. The unit of currency is the *franc CFA* (XAF) with a parity of 655·957 francs CFA to one euro. Total money supply in April 2002 was 103,991m. francs CFA and foreign exchange reserves were US$123m. Gold reserves were 11,000 troy oz in June 2002. In 2002 there was inflation of 2·3%.

Budget. In 2001 expenditure totalled 97,200m. francs CFA and revenue 63,200m. francs CFA.

Performance. Total GDP in 2003 was US$1·2bn. Real GDP growth was 0·8% in 2002 (1·0% in 2001).

Banking and Finance. The *Banque des Etats de l'Afrique Centrale* (*BEAC*) acts as the central bank and bank of issue. The *Governor* is Jean-Félix Mamalepot. There are three commercial banks, a development bank and an investment bank.

ENERGY AND NATURAL RESOURCES

Environment. The Central African Republic's carbon dioxide emissions from the consumption and flaring of fossil fuels in 2002 were the equivalent of 0·1 tonnes per capita.

Electricity. Installed capacity was 36,890 kW in 2000. Production in 2000 totalled 127·7m. kWh (approximately 98% hydro-electric). Consumption per capita in 2000 was 31 kWh.

Minerals. In 2001, 360,000 carats of gem diamonds and 120,000 carats of industrial diamonds were mined; and, in 2000, 12·3 kg of gold. In 2000, 633,000 kg of sheet aluminium were produced. There are also oil, uranium and other mineral deposits which are for the most part unexploited.

Agriculture. In 1998 the agricultural population numbered 2·59m. persons, of whom 1·24m. were economically active. In 2001, 1·93m. ha were arable and 90,000 ha permanent crops. The main crops (production 2000, in 1,000 tonnes) are cassava, 500; yams, 360; bananas, 115; groundnuts, 105; maize, 101; taro, 100; plantains, 82; seed cotton, 35.

Livestock, 2000: cattle, 2·95m.; goats, 2·60m.; sheep, 210,000; pigs, 650,000; chickens, 4m.

Forestry. There were 22·91m. ha of forest in 2000, or 36·8% of the total land area. The extensive hardwood forests, particularly in the southwest, provide mahogany, obeche and limba. Timber production in 2001 was 3·06m. cu. metres.

Fisheries. The catch in 2001 was approximately 15,000 tonnes, exclusively from inland waters.

INDUSTRY

The small industrial sector includes factories producing wood products, cotton fabrics, footwear, beer and radios. Output: sugar (2001), 13,000 tonnes; oils and fats (2000), 7,000 tonnes; beer (2003), 12·2m. litres; cotton fabrics (1992), 5·32m. metres; sawnwood (2001), 150,000 cu. metres.

Labour. In 1996 the labour force was 1,623,000 (53% males).

INTERNATIONAL TRADE

External debt was US$1,066m. in 2002.

Imports and Exports. Exports in 2000 totalled US$181m. (US$178m. in 1999); imports in 2000 totalled US$247m. (US$253m. in 1999).

Main export markets, 2000: Belgium-Luxembourg, 64·7%; Spain, 6·3%; France, 3·2%; Taiwan, 3·2%. Main import suppliers, 1999: France, 33·8%; Cameroon, 12·2%; Belgium-Luxembourg, 7·4%; UK, 4·1%. Main exports are diamonds, coffee, timber and cotton. Main imports include food, textiles, petroleum products, machinery, electrical equipment and motor vehicles.

COMMUNICATIONS

Roads. There were 24,307 km of roads in 1998, including 5,398 km of highways or main roads. In 1997 there were 966 passenger cars and 662 commercial vehicles. There were 77 road accident deaths in 2000.

Civil Aviation. There is an international airport at M'Poko, near Bangui, which handled 56,000 passengers (52,000 on international flights) in 2000. In 2003 there were direct services operating to Douala, Khartoum, Nyala, Paris and Yaoundé. In 1999 scheduled airline traffic of Central African Republic-based carriers flew 3·0m. km, carrying 84,000 passengers (all on international flights).

Shipping. Timber and barges are taken to Brazzaville (Republic of the Congo).

Telecommunications. There were 21,600 telephone subscribers in 2002 (equivalent to 5·5 per 1,000 persons), including 12,600 mobile phone subscribers, and 8,000 PCs were in use (2·0 per 1,000 persons). In 1997 there were 300 fax machines. The number of Internet users in 2002 was 5,000.

Postal Services. In 1998 there were 35 post offices.

SOCIAL INSTITUTIONS

Justice. The Criminal Court and Supreme Court are situated in Bangui. There are 16 high courts throughout the country. The population in penal institutions in 2001 was 4,168 (110 per 100,000 of national population).

Religion. In 2001 there were 660,000 Roman Catholics, 560,000 Muslims and 520,000 Protestants. Traditional animist beliefs are still widespread.

Education. Adult literacy rate was 48·2% in 2001 (60·8% among males and 36·6% among females).

In 2000–01 there were an estimated 457,000 pupils at the *fondamental 1* (lower primary) level being taught in 2,147 schools by 4,555 teachers; and 47,267 pupils at 143 *fondamental 2* and secondary schools with 913 teachers. The University of Bangui, founded in 1969, had 3,590 students and 140 academic staff in 1995–96. In 2000–01 there were 5,523 students in higher education.

In 1998–99 total expenditure on education came to 1·9% of GNP.

Health. In 1990 there were 255 hospitals and health centres with 4,120 beds (4,126 beds in 2000). In 2000 there were 114 doctors, 179 midwives and 217 state qualified nurses. The government's healthcare budget for 2000 was 5·4m. francs CFA and foreign aid amounted to 5·3m. francs CFA.

In the period 1990–98 only 38% of the population had access to safe drinking water.

CULTURE

World Heritage Sites. The Manovo-Gounda St Floris National Park was inscribed on the UNESCO World Heritage List in 1988. Poaching and violence closed the park to tourism in 1997.

Broadcasting. Broadcasting is provided by the state-controlled Radiodiffusion-Télévision Centrafricaine. There were 280,000 radio receivers in 2000 and 22,000 TV sets in 2001 (colour by SECAM V).

Press. In 1996 there were three daily newspapers with a circulation of 6,000, giving a rate of 1·8 per 1,000 inhabitants.

Tourism. In 1998 there were 20,000 foreign tourists, bringing revenue of US$6m.

DIPLOMATIC REPRESENTATIVES

Of Central African Republic in the United Kingdom
Ambassador: Vacant.
First Counsellor: Germain Gresenguet (resides at Paris).

Of the United Kingdom in Central African Republic
Ambassador: Richard Wildash, LVO (resides at Yaoundé, Cameroon).

Of Central African Republic in the USA (1618 22nd St., NW, Washington, D.C., 20008)
Ambassador: Emmanuel Touaboy.

Of the USA in Central African Republic (Ave. David Dacko, Bangui)
Ambassador: Vacant.
Chargé d'Affaires a.i.: James Panos.

Of Central African Republic to the United Nations
Ambassador: Fernand Poukré-Kono.

Of Central African Republic to the European Union
Ambassador: Armand-Guy Zounguere-Sokambi.

FURTHER READING

Kalck, P., *Historical Dictionary of the Central African Republic.* Scarecrow Press, Metuchen, (NJ), 1992.—*Central African Republic.* [Bibliography] ABC-Clio, Oxford and Santa Barbara (CA), 1993

Titley, B., *Dark Age: The Political Odyssey of Emperor Bokassa*. McGill-University Press, Montreal, 1997

National statistical office: Division des Statistiques, des Etudes Economiques et Sociales, BP 696, Bangui.
Website (French only): http://www.stat-centrafrique.com

CHAD

République du Tchad

Capital: N'Djaména
Population projection, 2010: 10·54m.
GDP per capita, 2002: (PPP$) 1,020
HDI/world rank: 0·379/167

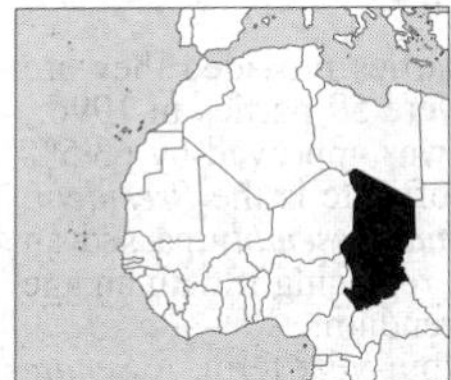

KEY HISTORICAL EVENTS

France proclaimed a protectorate over Chad in 1900 and in July 1908 the territory was incorporated into French Equatorial Africa. It became a separate colony in 1920, and in 1946 one of the four constituent territories of French Equatorial Africa. It achieved full independence on 11 Aug. 1960. Conflicts between the government and secessionist groups, particularly in the Muslim north and centre, began in 1965 and developed into civil war. In 1982 forces led by Hissène Habré gained control of the country. In June 1983 Libyan-backed forces re-occupied some territory but a ceasefire took effect in Sept. 1987. Rebel forces of the Popular Salvation Movement led by Idriss Déby entered Chad from Sudan in Nov. 1990. On 4 Dec. 1990 Déby declared himself President. In Feb. 2000 Hissène Habré was charged with torture and barbarity and put under house arrest in Senegal, where he had lived since being toppled in 1990.

TERRITORY AND POPULATION

Chad is bounded in the west by Cameroon, Nigeria and Niger, north by Libya, east by Sudan and south by the Central African Republic. In Feb. 1994 the International Court of Justice ruled that the Aozou Strip along the Libyan border, occupied by Libya since 1973, was part of Chad. Area, 1,284,000 sq. km. At the 1993 census the population was 6,279,931 (5,929,192 settled, of whom 1,327,570 were urban and 359,069 nomadic). 2002 population estimate, 8,363,000; density, 7 per sq. km.

The UN gives a projected population for 2010 of 10·54m.

In 2001, 75·8% of the population were rural. The capital is N'Djaména with 998,000 inhabitants (1999 estimate), other large towns being (1993 census figures) Moundou (282,103), Sarh (193,753), Bongor (196,713), Abéché (187,936) and Doba (185,461).

The areas, populations and chief towns of the 14 prefectures were:

Prefecture	*Area sq. km*	*Population (1993 census)*	*Capital*
Batha	88,800	288,458	Ati
Biltine	46,850	184,807	Biltine
Borkou-Ennedi-Tibesti	600,350	73,185	Faya (Largeau)
Chari-Baguirmi	82,910	1,251,906	N'Djaména
Guéra	58,950	306,253	Mongo
Kanem	114,520	279,927	Mao
Lac	22,320	252,932	Bol
Logone Occidental	8,695	455,489	Moundou
Logone Oriental	28,035	441,064	Doba
Mayo-Kebbi	30,105	825,158	Bongor
Moyen-Chari	45,180	738,595	Sarh
Ouaddaï	76,240	543,900	Abéché
Salamat	63,000	184,403	Amtiman
Tandjilé	18,045	453,854	Laï

The official languages are French and Arabic, but more than 100 different languages and dialects are spoken. The largest ethnic group is the Sara of southern Chad (27·7% of the total population), followed by the Sudanic Arabs (11·5%).

SOCIAL STATISTICS

2001 estimates: births, 398,000; deaths, 138,000. Rates, 2001 estimates (per 1,000 population): births, 49·1; deaths, 17·0. Annual rate of growth, 1992–2002, 3·1%. Expectation of life in 2001 was 43·5 years among males and 45·7 among females. Infant mortality, 2001 (per 1,000 live births), 117. Fertility rate, 2001, 6·7 children per woman.

CLIMATE

A tropical climate, with adequate rainfall in the south, though Nov. to April are virtually rainless months. Further north, desert conditions prevail. N'Djaména, Jan. 75°F (23·9°C), July 82°F (27·8°C). Annual rainfall 30" (744 mm).

CONSTITUTION AND GOVERNMENT

After overthrowing the regime of Hissène Habré, Idriss Déby proclaimed himself *President* and was sworn in on 4 March 1991.

A law of Oct. 1991 permits the formation of political parties provided they are not based on regionalism, tribalism or intolerance. There were 59 parties in 1996.

At a referendum on 31 March 1996 a new Constitution was approved by 63·5% of votes cast. It defines Chad as a unitary state. The head of state is the *President*, elected by universal suffrage. On 26 May 2004 the *National Assembly* passed an amendment scrapping the two-term limit on the presidency, replacing it with an age limit of 70. To become law, it must be approved by a referendum.

The *National Assembly* has 155 members, elected for a four-year term. A *Senate* was stipulated in the 1996 constitution, but has yet to be created.

National Anthem. 'Peuple tchadien, debout et à l'ouvrage' ('People of Chad, arise and to the task'); words by L. Gidrol, tune by P. Villard.

RECENT ELECTIONS

Presidential elections were held on 20 May 2001. Turn-out was 80·9%. Incumbent Idriss Déby won re-election, with 67·4% of the vote, against 13·9% for Ngarlejy Yorongar, 6·5% for Saleh Kabzabo and 5·1% for Wadal Abdelkader Kamougue.

In parliamentary elections held on 21 April 2002 the Patriotic Salvation Movement (MPS) of President Idriss Déby won 102 seats, the Rally for Democracy and Progress (RDP) 12, the Federation Action for the Republic 11, the National Rally for Development and Progress 5, the National Union for Democracy and Renewal 5 and the Union for Renewal and Democracy 3. Turn-out was 52·8%.

CURRENT ADMINISTRATION

President: Lt.-Gen. Idriss Déby; b. 1954 (MPS; in office since 1990 and re-elected 3 July 1996 and 20 May 2001).

In March 2005 the government comprised:

Prime Minister: Pascal Yoadimnadji; b. 1950 (appointed on 3 Feb. 2005).

Minister of State, Minister of Foreign Affairs and African Co-operation: Nagoum Yamassoum. *Minister of Agriculture:* Laokein Medar. *Civil Service, Labour and Employment:* Mahamat Nour Mallaye. *Commerce, Industry and Handicrafts:* Routouang Yoma Golom. *Communications and Government Spokesman:* Natoingar Bailodji Barthelemy. *Culture, Youth and Sports:* Baradine Haroun. *Economy and Finance:* Ngeyam Djaibe. *Environment and Water Resources:* Adoum Diar. *Higher Education, Scientific Research and Vocational Training:* Prof. Avocksouma Djona. *Justice, Keeper of the Seals:* Kalzeubé Pahimi. *Livestock:* Mahamat Abdoulaye. *Mines and Energy:* Nasser Mahamat Hassan. *National Defence, Veterans and War Victims:* Emmanuel Nadingar. *National Education:* Mahamat Maouloud Izzadine. *Oil Resources:* Youssouf Abassallah. *Planning, Development and Co-operation:* Mahamat Ali Hassan. *Post and Telecommunications:* Dr Brahim Seid. *Public Health:* Aziza Baroud. *Public Security and Immigration:* Abderahman Moussa. *Public Works and Transport:* Adoum Younousmi. *Regional Planning, Urban Planning and Housing:* Sandjima Dounia. *Social Action and Family Affairs:* Fatime Kimto. *Territorial Administration:* Mahamat Zène Bada. *Tourism Development:* Oumar Kadjallami Boukar. *Secretary General of the Government, Minister in Charge of Relations with Parliament:* Abakar Mallah.

President of the National Assembly: Nassour Guelendksia (MPS).

President's Website (French only): http://www.tit.td/presidence.html

DEFENCE

There are seven military regions. Total armed forces personnel numbered 30,350 in 2002, including republican guards. Defence expenditure totalled US$34m. in 2003 (US$4 per capita), representing 1·3% of GDP.

Army. In 2002 the strength was 25,000. In addition there was a paramilitary Gendarmerie of 4,500 and a Republican Guard of 5,000.

Air Force. Personnel (2002) about 350 including two combat aircraft and two combat helicopters.

INTERNATIONAL RELATIONS

Chad is a member of the UN, WTO, the African Union, African Development Bank, Lake Chad Basin Commission, OIC, Islamic Development Bank, the International Organization of the Francophonie and is an ACP member state of the ACP-EU relationship.

ECONOMY

Agriculture accounted for 38·7% of GDP in 2002, industry 15·4% and services 45·8%.

Overview. Over 30 years of civil war have left Chad dependent on external aid, chiefly from the IMF, the World Bank and the EU. Economic development suffers from political turmoil, droughts and primitive infrastructure. However, thanks to the development of the Chad-Cameroon oil pipeline and the Doba oilfield, the economy is set to improve dramatically. The agricultural sector employs around 90% of the population and accounts for 35% of GDP. Cotton has traditionally been the core export, but has suffered bad harvests. The country is among the world's leading exporters of gum arabic. Chad is a member of CAEMU (the Central African Economic and Monetary Union). As the currency is pegged to the euro and managed by La Banque Centrale des Etats de l'Afrique Centrale, the government has no influence over monetary policy.

Currency. The unit of currency is the *franc CFA* (XAF) with a parity of 655·957 francs CFA to one euro. Inflation in 2002 was 5·2%, down from 12·4% in 2001. Foreign exchange reserves were US$154m. in April 2002 and total money supply was 161,104m. francs CFA. Gold reserves were 11,000 troy oz in June 2002.

Budget. Revenues in 2000 were 128·2bn. francs CFA and expenditures 203·2bn. francs CFA.

Performance. Real GDP growth was 8·5% in 2001 and 9·7% in 2002, thanks mainly to the acceleration of the construction of an oil pipeline from Chad to Cameroon. The pipeline will allow Chad to export its oil riches to the world market. Chad became the world's newest oil producer in 2003, and as a result in 2004 was expected to be the world's fastest growing economy. In 2003 total GDP was US$2·6bn.

Banking and Finance. The *Banque des Etats de l'Afrique Centrale* (*Governor*, Jean-Félix Mamalepot) is the bank of issue. Other leading banks include: Banque Agricole du Soudan au Tchad; Banque Commerciale du Chari; Banque Internationale de l'Afrique au Tchad; Commercial Bank Tchad; Financial Bank Tchad; and Société Générale Tchadienne de Banque.

ENERGY AND NATURAL RESOURCES

Electricity. Installed capacity was 29,000 kW in 2000. Production in 2000 amounted to an estimated 92m. kWh. Consumption per capita was an estimated 12 kWh—the lowest in the world—in 2000.

Oil and Gas. The oilfield in Kanem préfecture has been linked by pipeline to a new refinery at N'Djaména but production has remained minimal. There is a larger oilfield in the Doba Basin. In June 2000 the World Bank approved funding for a 1,070-km US$4bn. pipeline to run from 300 new oil wells in Chad through Cameroon to the Atlantic Ocean. Oil started pumping in July 2003 making Chad the world's newest oil producer. Crude oil production in 2003 was 2·1m. tonnes. Revenues are expected to reach US$80m. per annum.

Minerals. Salt (about 4,000 tonnes per annum) is mined around Lake Chad, and there are deposits of uranium, gold, iron ore and bauxite. There are small-scale workings for gold and iron.

Agriculture. Some 80% of the workforce is involved in subsistence agriculture and fisheries. In 2001, 3·60m. ha were arable and 30,000 ha permanent crops. There were 175 tractors in 2001. Cotton growing (in the south) and animal husbandry (in the central zone) are the most important branches. Production, 2000 (in 1,000 tonnes): sorghum, 567; groundnuts, 372; millet, 321; sugarcane, 315; cassava, 255; seed cotton, 235; yams, 230; rice, 131; cottonseed, 125; cotton lint, 90; maize, 87.

Livestock, 2000: cattle, 5,595,000; goats, 5,050,000; sheep, 2,500,000; camels, 715,000; chickens, 5m.

Forestry. In 2000 the area under forests was 12·69m. ha, or 10·1% of the total land area. Timber production in 2001 was 6·76m. cu. metres.

Fisheries. Total catches, from Lake Chad and the Chari and Logone rivers, were approximately 84,000 tonnes in 2001.

INDUSTRY

Output: cotton fibre (1998), 86,260 tonnes; sugar (2002), 32,000 tonnes; soap (1996), 2,958 tonnes; edible oil (1996), 12·55m. litres; beer (2003), 21·6m. litres; cigarettes (2000), 30m. packets; bicycles (1996), 3,444 units.

Labour. In 1996 the labour force was 3,145,000 (56% males). In 1994 approximately 70% of the economically active population were engaged in agriculture, fishing and forestry.

INTERNATIONAL TRADE

External debt was US$1,281m. in 2002.

Imports and Exports. Exports in 2000 totalled US$233m. (US$242m. in 1999); imports in 2000 totalled US$450m. (US$474m. in 1999).

Main export markets in 1997 were Portugal, 29·9%; Germany, 14·2%; Thailand, 7·5%; Costa Rica, 6·0%; Hong Kong, 4·8%; Taiwan, 4·8%. Main import suppliers were France, 41·3%; Nigeria, 10·1%; Cameroon, 7·2%; India, 5·8%; Belgium-Luxembourg, 5·1%; Italy, 4·3%. Cotton exports in 1994, 28,857m. francs CFA; cattle, 15,401 francs CFA. Apart from cotton and cattle, other important exports are textiles and fish. The principal imports are machinery and transportation equipment, industrial goods, petroleum products and foodstuffs.

COMMUNICATIONS

Roads. In 1999 there were estimated to be 33,400 km of roads, of which only 0·8% were surfaced. Approximately 10,560 passenger cars were in use in 1996, plus 14,550 trucks and vans, and 3,640 motorcycles and mopeds.

Civil Aviation. There is an international airport at N'Djaména, from which there were direct flights in 2003 to Addis Ababa, Bamako, Bangui, Douala, Garoua, Kano, Paris, Tripoli and Yaoundé. In 1999 scheduled airline traffic of Chad-based carriers flew 2·9m. km, carrying 84,000 passengers (all on international flights). In 2000 N'Djaména handled 17,000 passengers and 2,300 tonnes of freight.

Telecommunications. In 2002 telephone subscribers numbered 46,000 (5·8 per 1,000 persons) and there were 13,000 PCs in use (1·7 per 1,000 persons). There were 200 fax machines in 1999. There were 34,200 mobile phone subscribers in 2002. Internet users numbered 15,000 in 2002.

Postal Services. In 1998 there were 36 post offices, or one for every 201,900 persons.

SOCIAL INSTITUTIONS

Justice. There are criminal courts and magistrates courts in N'Djaména, Moundou, Sarh and Abéché, with a Court of Appeal situated in N'Djaména.

The population in penal institutions in 2002 was 3,883 (46 per 100,000 of national population).

The death penalty is still in force. In 2003 there were nine executions (the first since 1991).

Religion. The northern and central parts of the country are predominantly Muslim. In 2001 there were estimated to be 4,690,000 Muslims, 1,770,000 Roman Catholics and 1,250,000 Protestants. Traditional beliefs are still widespread.

Education. In 1999–2000 there were 913,547 pupils in primary schools with 13,313 teachers and 137,269 pupils in secondary schools with 4,260 teachers. In 1999–2000 there were 5,901 students with 409 academic staff at institutes of tertiary education. Adult literacy rate was 44·2% in 2001 (male, 53·0%; female, 35·8%).

In 1999–2000 total expenditure on education came to 2·0% of GNP.

Health. In 1994 there were 3,962 hospital beds, 217 doctors, 878 nurses, 130 midwives and 10 pharmacists.

Chad has made significant progress in the reduction of undernourishment in the past 15 years. Between the period 1990–92 and 2000–02 the proportion of undernourished people declined from 58% of the population to 34%.

CULTURE

Broadcasting. The state-controlled Radiodiffusion Nationale Tchadienne broadcasts a national and three regional services in French, Arabic and Sara. There were 1·99m. radio sets in 2000. Television is being developed (colour by SECAM V) by the state-controlled Télé-Tchad, and there were 13,500 TV receivers in 2001.

Press. In 1998 there were two daily newspapers with a circulation of 1,560, giving a rate of one per 4,760 inhabitants.

Tourism. There were 44,000 foreign tourists in 2000; spending by tourists in 1998 totalled US$10m.

DIPLOMATIC REPRESENTATIVES

Of Chad in the United Kingdom
Ambassador: Abderahim Yacoub Ndiaye (resides at Brussels).

Of the United Kingdom in Chad
Ambassador: Richard Wildash, LVO (resides at Yaoundé, Cameroon).

Of Chad in the USA (2002 R. St., NW, Washington, D.C., 20009)
Ambassador: Hassaballah Ahmat Soubiane.

Of the USA in Chad (Ave. Felix Eboue, N'Djaména)
Ambassador: Mark M. Wall.

Of Chad to the United Nations
Ambassador: Mahamat Ali Adoum.

Of Chad to the European Union
Ambassador: Abderahim Yacoub N'diaye.

FURTHER READING

Joffe, Emille and Day-Viaud, Valerie (eds.) *Chad.* [Bibliography] ABC-Clio, Oxford and Santa Barbara (CA), 1995

National statistical office: Direction de la Statistique des Etudes Economiques et Démographiques, Ministère du Plan et de la Cooperation, N'Djaména.

CHILE

República de Chile

Capital: Santiago (Administrative), Valparaíso (Legislative)
Population projection, 2010: 17·11m.
GDP per capita, 2002: (PPP$) 9,820
HDI/world rank: 0·839/43

KEY HISTORICAL EVENTS

The earliest settlements in Chile date from around 10,500 BC. Prior to the arrival of Europeans, the indigenous peoples included the Atacameno, living in small settlements in the northern deserts, the Araucanians, farmers in the more temperate valleys of central Chile, and the Chono—Alacaluf and Yahgan nomads from the mountainous southern areas.

Ferdinand Magellan was the first European to glimpse what is now Chile in 1520. Twenty years later a Spanish expeditionary force, headed by Pedro de Valdivia, established the settlement of Santiago. In the next ten years the Spanish built fortified towns at Concepción, La Serena, Valdivia and Villarrica. But with violent opposition from the native population, the colony remained a frontier, dependent on the Viceroyalty of Peru. Gold was discovered but the wealth it generated was minimal compared with the riches of Mexico and Peru.

Attempts by successive governors to make peace with the natives ended in failure and sporadic fighting continued throughout the 17th and 18th centuries. After Habsburg rule over Spain ended in 1700, the French Bourbon monarchy gave the *audiencia* of Chile (based in Santiago) greater independence from the Viceroyalty of Peru. One of the most charismatic governors of the Bourbon era was the Irish-born Ambrosio O'Higgins, who outlawed forced labour and strengthened economic links with Argentina. By the end of the 18th century Chile was engaging in direct trade with Europe. Freer trade brought with it knowledge of politics abroad, particularly the spread of liberalism in Europe and American independence. Napoléon's invasion of Spain in 1807 led to greater autonomy. In 1810 the Santiago aristocracy announced their intention to govern the colony. Chile's first government was led by José Miguel Carrera Verdugo and Bernardo O'Higgins (son of the former governor), who favoured independence. 1814 saw the start of the Spanish Reconquest. O'Higgins and other Chilean rebels escaped to Argentina, where they won the support of the revolutionary government in Buenos Aires. Their joint forces freed Chile in 1817, defeating the Spaniards at the Battle of Chacabuco.

From 1817–23 Bernardo O'Higgins ruled Chile, proclaiming independence on 12 Feb. 1818. His authoritarian style and attempted land reforms together with a succession of poor harvests forced him to abdicate in 1823. Political stability and economic revival in the 1830s was underpinned by discoveries of silver and copper in northern Chile and coal around Concepción. In the period after 1860, known as the 'Liberal Republic', Britain became the main trading partner and British entrepreneurs invested in the construction of railways and the modernization of the ports.

A border war with Bolivia and Peru (1879–83) was followed by a civil war, forcing a change from presidential republic to parliamentary democracy. The Democratic Party was formed in 1887 to represent artisans and urban workers, while the Radical Party was backed by the middle class. A Socialist Party was established in 1901. By the start of the 20th century Chilean society was polarized, with parts of Santiago and Valparaíso mirroring prosperous and elegant European cities, while the masses remained largely poverty stricken and illiterate.

The outbreak of the First World War brought disaster to the Chilean economy, as Britain and Germany were leading trading partners. In the 1920s the constitution was amended, establishing a presidential republic, separating church and state, and enshrining labour and welfare legislation. The military dictatorship of Carlos Ibáñez de Campo led to improvements in education but failed to address the economic power of the oligarchs. A democratic-leftist coalition, the Popular Front, took power following the elections of 1938. Chile remained neutral in the Second World War until 1942, when President Juan Antonio Ríos declared war on Germany, Italy and Japan. The post-war years were characterized by slow economic growth and spiralling inflation. Salvador Allende Gossens, elected president in 1970, adopted a socialist programme. In Sept. 1973, with covert American support, the armed forces staged a coup and Allende died during an assault on the presidential palace. Gen. Augusto Pinochet Ugarte was installed as president. The military closed Congress, censored the media, purged the universities and banned Marxist parties and union activities. Over 3,000 of Allende's supporters lost their lives, over 30,000 were forced into exile and more than 130,000 were arrested over a three-year period. The return to market capitalism led to steady economic improvement from 1976 but falling copper prices and mounting foreign debt caused spiralling inflation and growing unemployment in the early 1980s. In 1981 a new constitution was approved, guaranteeing an eight-year extension to Pinochet's rule but also allowing a transition to civilian government. The first free elections since the 1973 coup took place in Dec. 1989 after which Patricio Aylwin Azócar headed a coalition of left and centrist parties. The 1990s saw a rapid strengthening of the economy, underpinned by foreign investment.

Pinochet remained head of the military until 1998, after which he claimed his constitutional right to become a senator for life (and hence immune from prosecution). While visiting Britain for medical treatment in 1998, Pinochet was arrested and held on human rights charges instigated by Spain. In early 2000 he returned to Chile after the British government ruled he was too ill to be extradited to Spain to face charges. On his election in Jan. 2000, Ricardo Lagos Escobar, leader of the Coalition of Parties for Democracy (CPD), pledged to reform the labour code, increase the minimum wage and introduce unemployment insurance. In March 2003 Lagos' government faced allegations of financial corruption. Pinochet was stripped of his immunity by a Chilean court in May 2004.

TERRITORY AND POPULATION

Chile is bounded in the north by Peru, east by Bolivia and Argentina, and south and west by the Pacific Ocean. The area is 756,096 sq. km (291,928 sq. miles) excluding the claimed Antarctic territory. Many islands to the west and south belong to Chile: the Islas Juan Fernández (147 sq. km with 488 inhabitants in 1992) lie about 600 km west of Valparaíso, and the volcanic Isla de Pascua (Easter Island or Rapa Nui, 164 sq. km with 2,764 inhabitants in 1992), lies about 3,000 km west-northwest of Valparaíso. Small uninhabited dependencies include Sala y Goméz (400 km east of Easter Is.), San Félix and San Ambrosio (1,000 km northwest of Valparaíso, and 20 km apart) and Islas Diego Ramírez (100 km southwest of Cape Horn).

In 1940 Chile declared, and in each subsequent year has reaffirmed, its ownership of the sector of the Antarctic lying between 53° and 90° W. long., and asserted that the British claim to the sector between the meridians 20° and 80° W. long. overlapped the Chilean by 27°. Seven Chilean bases exist in Antarctica. A law of 1955 put the governor of Magallanes in charge of the 'Chilean Antarctic Territory' which has an area of 1,250,000 sq. km and a population (1992) of 1,945.

The population at the census of April 2002 was 15,116,435 (7,668,740 females); density, 20 per sq. km. 86·2% of the population lived in urban areas in 2002.

The UN gives a projected population for 2010 of 17·11m.

Area, population and capitals of the 13 regions:

Region	*Sq. km*	*Population (2002 census)*	*Capital*	*Population (2002 census)*
Aisén del Gral. Carlos Ibáñez del Campo	108,494	91,492	Coihaique	50,041
De Antofagasta	126,049	493,984	Antofagasta	296,905
De La Araucanía	31,842	869,535	Temuco	245,347
De Atacama	75,176	254,336	Copiapó	129,091
Del Bíobío	37,063	1,861,562	Concepción	216,061
De Coquimbo	40,580	603,210	La Serena	160,148
Del Libertador Gral B. O'Higgins	16,387	780,627	Rancagua	214,344
De Los Lagos	67,013	1,073,135	Puerto Montt	175,938
De Magallanes y de la Antártica Chilena	132,297	150,826	Punta Arenas	119,496
Del Maule	30,296	908,097	Talca	201,797
Metropolitana de Santiago	15,403	6,061,185	Santiago	4,668,473

Region	Sq. km	Population (2002 census)	Capital	Population (2002 census)
De Tarapacá	59,099	428,594	Iquique	216,419
De Valparaíso	16,396	1,5389,435	Valparaíso	275,982

Other large towns (June 2002 populations) are: Puente Alto (458,906), Viña del Mar (350,221), Talcahuano (288,666), San Bernardo (262,623), Arica (189,743), Chillán (176,863), Coquimbo (141,796), Osorno (135,204) and Calama (135,526).

69·7% of the population is mixed or mestizo, 20% are of European descent and 10·3% declared themselves to be indigenous Amerindians of the Araucanian, Fuegian and Chango groups. Language and culture remain of European origin, with 998,385 Araucanian-speaking (mainly Mapuche) Indians the only sizeable minority.

The official language is Spanish.

SOCIAL STATISTICS

2000 births, 248,893; deaths, 78,814; marriages, 66,607. Rates, 2000 (per 1,000 population): birth, 17·2; death, 5·2. Divorce was only made legal in 2004; abortion remains illegal. Annual population growth rate, 1992–2002, 1·4%. Infant mortality, 2000 (per 1,000 live births), 8·9. In 2000 the most popular age range for marrying was 25–29 for males and 20–24 for females. Expectation of life at birth (2001): males 72·8 years, females 78·8 years. Chile has the highest life expectancy in South America. Fertility rate, 2000, 2·1 children per woman.

CLIMATE

With its enormous range of latitude and the influence of the Andean Cordillera, the climate of Chile is very complex, ranging from extreme aridity in the north, through a Mediterranean climate in Central Chile, where winters are wet and summers dry, to a cool temperate zone in the south, with rain at all seasons. In the extreme south, conditions are very wet and stormy. Santiago, Jan. 67°F (19·5°C), July 46°F (8°C). Annual rainfall 15" (375 mm). Antofagasta, Jan. 69°F (20·6°C), July 57°F (14°C). Annual rainfall 0·5" (12·7 mm). Valparaíso, Jan. 64°F (17·8°C), July 53°F (11·7°C). Annual rainfall 20" (505 mm).

CONSTITUTION AND GOVERNMENT

A new Constitution was approved by 67·5% of the voters on 11 Sept. 1980 and came into force on 11 March 1981. It provided for a return to democracy after a minimum period of eight years. Gen. Pinochet would remain in office during this period after which the government would nominate a single candidate for President. At a plebiscite on 5 Oct. 1988 President Pinochet was rejected as a presidential candidate by 54·6% of votes cast.

The *President* is directly elected for a non-renewable six-year term. Parliament consists of a 120-member *Chamber of Deputies* and a *Senate* of 49 members (38 by popular vote, nine appointed or 'institutional' members and two former presidents). In Oct. 2004 Senate voted to make the Senate fully elected, by abolishing the non-elected senators with effect from March 2006 and similarly eliminating life seats for former presidents.

Santiago is the administrative capital of Chile, but since 11 March 1990 Valparaíso has been the legislative capital.

National Anthem. 'Dulce patria, recibe los votos' ('Sweet Fatherland, receive the vows'); words by E. Lillo, tune by Ramón Carnicer.

RECENT ELECTIONS

In the presidential run-off held on 16 Jan. 2000 leftist Ricardo Lagos (Party for Democracy/PPD) polled 51·3%, defeating the conservative Joaquín Lavin (Independent Democratic Union/UDI). Four other candidates had participated in the first round of voting on 12 Dec. 1999.

In elections to the Chamber of Deputies on 16 Dec. 2001 the Independent Democratic Union (UDI) won 35 seats, the Christian Democratic Party (PDC) 24, National Renewal (RN) 22, Party for Democracy (PPD) 21, the Socialist Party (PS) 11, the Social Democratic Radical Party (PRSD) 6, ind. 1. Member parties of the Coalition of Parties for Democracy/CPD (PDC, PPD, PS and PRSD) won 62 of the 120 seats (with 47·9% of votes cast) against 57 seats (44·3%) for the Alliance for

Chile/APC (UDI, RN). After partial elections to the Senate on the same day the composition in the Senate was: PDC, 12; UDI, 11; RN, 7; PS, 5; PPD, 3; appointed members, 10.

Parliamentary and presidential elections are scheduled to take place on 14 Dec. 2005.

CURRENT ADMINISTRATION

In March 2005 the CPD government comprised:

President: Ricardo Lagos; b. 1938 (PPD; sworn in 11 March 2000).

Minister of Agriculture: Jaime Campos Quiroga. *Defence:* Jaime Ravinet. *Economy and Energy:* Jorge Rodríguez Grossi. *Education:* Sergio Bitar Chacra. *Finance:* Nicolás Eyzaguire Guzmán. *Foreign Affairs:* Ignacio Walker Prieto. *Health:* Pedro García Aspillaga. *Housing, Urbanism and Public Lands:* Sonia Tschorne. *Interior:* José Miguel Insulza Salinas. *Justice:* Luis Bates Hidalgo. *Mining:* Alfonso Dulanto Rencoret. *Labour and Social Security:* Ricardo Solari Saaverdra. *Planning and Co-operation:* Yasna Provoste. *Public Works, Transportation and Telecommunications:* Jaime Estévez. *National Women's Service:* Cecilia Pérez Díaz. *General Secretary of the Government:* Francisco Vidal Salinas. *General Secretary of the Presidency:* Eduardo Dockendorff Vallejos.

Government Website (Spanish only): http://www.gobiernodechile.cl

DEFENCE

Military service is currently for one year in the Army and 22 months in the Navy and Air Force, but conscription is set to be phased out in 2006.

In 2003 defence expenditure totalled US$2,537m. (US$161 per capita), representing 3·9% of GDP. In 1985 defence spending had accounted for 10·0% of GDP.

Army. A modernization plan of 1995 provided for the transformation of the seven Army divisions into three garrisons—North, Centre-South and Austral—independent and adapted to the terrains in which they operate. Strength (2002): 45,000 (20,700 conscripts) with 50,000 reserves. There is a 36,800-strong paramilitary force of Carabineros.

Navy. The principal ships of the Navy are three ex-British destroyers, three diesel submarines and three frigates. There is a Naval Air Service numbering 600 personnel with 13 combat aircraft.

Naval personnel in 2002 totalled 23,000 (1,000 conscripts) including 3,800 marines and 1,300 Coast Guard. There are HQs at Valaparaíso, Talcahuano, Puerto Montt, Punta Arenas, Puerto Williams and Iquique.

Air Force. Strength (2002) was 12,500 personnel (700 conscripts). There are 76 combat aircraft made up largely of Mirage jets.

INTERNATIONAL RELATIONS

Chile is a member of the UN, WTO, OAS, Inter-American Development Bank, LAIA, APEC, IOM and the Antarctic Treaty, and has a free trade agreement with Mercosur.

ECONOMY

Agriculture accounted for 8·8% of GDP in 2002, industry 34·3% and services 56·9%.

According to the anti-corruption organization *Transparency International*, Chile ranked 20th in the world in a 2004 survey of the countries with the least corruption in business and government. It received 7·4 out of 10 in the annual index, making it Latin America's least corrupt nation.

Overview. In 2002 Chile was the sixth largest economy in Latin America and one of the region's most open economies, with a volume of trade to GDP ratio greater than 50%. Since the mid-1980s Chile has experienced the largest GDP per capita growth in Latin America. During the 1990s Chile had the highest share of foreign direct investment to GDP. Between 1984–97 the economy experienced consistently high growth. Chile experienced negative growth of –0·8% in 1999 but the economy grew an average of 3·3% annually between 2000 and 2003. Chile's macroeconomic framework has undergone significant structural changes. Inflation targeting policy commenced in the early 1990s. Inflation declined gradually in the last decade, from 30% in 1990 to 3% in 1999. A floating exchange rate was adopted in 1999 and in 2000 the government defined a medium term fiscal policy rule in which it gave up future discretion over the underlying fiscal stance. Chile suffers from one of the most unequal income distributions among emerging market economies. The government has been urged by the World Bank to prioritize social goals, including improving access to health care and education and reducing poverty.

Currency. The unit of currency is the *Chilean peso* (CLP) of 100 *centavos*. The peso was revalued 3·5% against the US dollar in Nov. 1994. In Sept. 1999 the managed exchange-rate system was abandoned and the peso allowed to float. Inflation was 1·1% in 2003. In June 2002 gold reserves were 12,000 troy oz (1·22m. troy oz in Jan. 2000); foreign exchange reserves were US$14,612m. Total money supply in June 2002 was 3,722·29bn. pesos.

Budget. The fiscal year is the calendar year.

Central government revenue and expenditure (in 1bn. pesos):

	1997	*1998*	*1999*	*2000*	*2001*
Revenue	7,525·4	7,907·0	7,910·1	9,114·5	9,795·6
Expenditure	6,902·2	7,775·2	8,412·4	9,058·1	9,908·2

VAT is 16–18%.

Performance. Real GDP growth averaged 7·7% between 1991 and 1997, leading to Chile being labelled the 'tiger of South America'. In 1998 GDP growth was 3·2%. In 1999 the economy contracted by 0·8%, but there was then growth of 4·5% in 2000, 3·4% in 2001, 2·2% in 2002 and 3·3% in 2003. Total GDP in 2003 was US$72·4bn.

Banking and Finance. Banking is regulated by legislation of 1995. The Superintendencia de Bancos e Instituciones Financieras, affiliated to the finance ministry, is the banking supervisory authority. There is a Central Bank and a State Bank. The Central Bank was made independent of government control in March 1990. The *President* is Vittorio Corbo. There were 13 domestic and 23 foreign banks in 2001. In Dec. 2001 deposits in domestic banks totalled 17,440,672m. pesos; in foreign banks, 6,062,888m. pesos, and in other finance companies, 184,226m. pesos.

There are stock exchanges in Santiago and Valparaíso.

ENERGY AND NATURAL RESOURCES

Environment. Chile's carbon dioxide emissions from the consumption and flaring of fossil fuels in 2002 were the equivalent of 3·5 tonnes per capita.

Electricity. Installed capacity was 10·4m. kW in 2000. Production of electricity was 41·3bn. kWh in 2000, of which just over 46% was hydro-electric. Consumption per capita in 2000 was 2,406 kWh.

Oil and Gas. Production of crude oil, 2000, was 270,000 tonnes. Gas production, 2000, was 106 petajoules. Chile imports much of the natural gas it consumes from neighbouring Argentina.

Minerals. The wealth of the country consists chiefly in its minerals. Chile is the world's largest copper producer; copper is the most important source of foreign exchange and government revenues. Production, 2000, 4,617,885 tonnes. Coal is low-grade and difficult to mine, made possible by state subsidies. Production, 2000, 503,350 tonnes.

Output of other minerals, 2000 (in tonnes): iron, 8,728,927; limestone, 5,395,215; salt, 5,082,911; iron pellets, 4,502,456; manganese, 41,716; lignite (1997), 36,000; molybdenum, 33,639; zinc (2001), 32,762; silver (2001), 1,348. Gold (42,673 kg in 2001), lithium, nitrate, iodine and sodium sulphate are also produced.

Agriculture. In 2001, 1·98m. ha were arable land and 0·32m. ha permanent crops. 1·9m. ha were irrigated in 2001. Some 54,000 tractors were in use in 2001 and 8,900 harvester-threshers.

Principal crops were as follows:

Crop	Area harvested, 1,000 ha 2000	Production, 1,000 tonnes 2000	Crop	Area harvested, 1,000 ha 2000	Production, 1,000 tonnes 2000
Sugarbeets	46	2,882	Oats	89	344
Wheat	407	1,746	Onions	6	282
Tomatoes	22	1,267	Rice	28	143
Potatoes	63	1,210	Pumpkins	5	100
Maize	82	778	Carrots	4	97

Fruit production, 2000 (in 1,000 tonnes): apples, 1,135; grapes, 935; peaches and nectarines, 250; pears, 230; plums, 205; lemons and limes, 120; oranges, 92. Wine production in 2001 totalled 5,658,000 hectolitres.

Livestock, 2000: cattle, 3,900,000; sheep, 3,800,000; pigs, 1,900,000; goats, 760,000; horses, 400,000; poultry, 42m. Livestock products, 2000 (in 1,000 tonnes): pork, bacon and ham, 265; beef and veal, 226; poultry meat, 378; milk, 1,990; eggs, 95.

Since 1985 agricultural trade has been consistently in surplus. Wine exports rose from US$52m. in 1990 to US$593m. in 2001.

Forestry. In 2000, 15·54m. ha, or 20·7% of the total land area, was under forests. There were 13·4m. ha of natural forest and woodland (larch, araucaria, lenga, coihue, oak are important species) and 2·1m. ha of planted forest. Timber production in 2001 was 25·7m. cu. metres.

Fisheries. Chile has 4,200 km of coastline and exclusive fishing rights to 1·6m. sq. km. There are 220 species of edible fish. The catch in 2001 was 4,150,966 tonnes and came entirely from sea fishing. Exports of fishery commodities in 2000 were valued at US$1·78bn., against imports of US$47·96m. Fish farms produced 99,300 tonnes of salmon in 2001.

INDUSTRY

The leading companies by market capitalization in Chile, excluding banking and finance, in Jan. 2002 were: Compañía de Petróleos de Chile SA (COPEC), 3trn. pesos; Compañía de Telecomunicaciones de Chile SA (Telefónica CTC Chile), 2trn. pesos; and Endesa Chile (Empresa Nacional de Electricida SA), 2trn. pesos.

Output of major products in 2001 (in 1,000 tonnes): distillate fuel oil (2000), 3,716; cement, 2,833; sulphuric acid, 2,736; petrol (2000), 2,170; residual fuel oil (2000), 1,592; cellulose, 1,373; sugar (2002), 576; fishmeal, 503; iron or steel plates, 403; newsprint, 225; paper and cardboard, 113. Output of other products: soft drinks, 2,212·1m. litres; beer, 337·4m. litres; 20,136 motor vehicles; 3·25m. motor tyres.

Labour. In 2001 there were 5,326,370 people in employment (1,738,120 women). In Dec. 2001, 1,497,620 persons were employed in social or personal services, 1,011,360 in trade, 756,830 in manufacturing, 704,390 in agriculture, forestry and fisheries, 413,380 in building and 427,080 in transport and communications. In 2004 there was a monthly minimum wage of 120,000 pesos. In Jan. 2001, 9·1% of the workforce was unemployed, up from 6·1% in 1997 although down from a peak of 11·4% in Aug. 1999.

Trade Unions. Trade unions were established in the mid-1880s.

INTERNATIONAL TRADE

In Sept. 1991 Chile and Mexico signed the free trade Treaty of Santiago envisaging annual tariff reductions of 10% from Jan. 1992. On 1 Oct. 1996 Chile joined the Mercosur free trade zone, but continues to act unilaterally in trade with third countries.

Foreign debt was US$41,945m. in 2002.

Imports and Exports. Trade in US$1m.:

	1998	*1999*	*2000*	*2001*	*2002*
Exports f.o.b.	16,323	17,162	19,210	18,466	18,340
Imports f.o.b.	18,363	14,735	17,091	16,411	15,827

In 2001 the principal exports were (in US$1m.): manufactures, 8,304·9; minerals, 7,510·2 (of which copper, 6,673·4, equivalent to 37·8% of all exports); agricultural products, 1,710·8. Major export markets (in US$1m.), 2001: USA, 3,451·4; Japan, 2,140·2; UK, 1,231·4; China, 1,069·6; Brazil, 834·6; Mexico, 828·1; Italy, 800·8. Major import suppliers (in US$1m.), 2001: Argentina, 3,063·8; USA, 2,888·7; Brazil, 1,498·6; China, 1,052·9; Germany, 699·2.

COMMUNICATIONS

Roads. In 2001 there were 79,605 km of roads, but only 20·2% were hard-surfaced. There were 2,132 km of motorways and 16,056 km of main roads. In 2001 there were 1,172,572 private cars, 747,311 trucks and vans, 160,586 buses and coaches and 41,271 motorcycles and mopeds. In 2000 there were 40,926 road accidents resulting in 1,698 deaths.

Rail. The total length of state railway (EFE) lines was (2001) 4,024 km, including 1,051 km electrified, of broad- and metre-gauge. EFE is now mainly a passenger carrier, and carried 16·1m. passengers in 2001. Freight operations are in the hands of the semi-private companies Ferronor, which carried 5·9m. tonnes in 2001, and Pacifico, which carried 5·5m. tonnes in 2001. The Antofagasta (Chili) and Bolivia Railway (973 km, metre-gauge) links the port of Antofagasta with Bolivia and Argentina, and carried 3·5m. tonnes in 2001. Passenger-km travelled in 2001 came to 1,105m. and freight tonne-km to 925m.

There are metro systems in Santiago (40·4 km) and Viña del Mar.

Civil Aviation. There are 389 airports, with an international airport at Santiago (Comodoro Arturo Merino Benítez). The largest airline is Línea Aérea Nacional Chile (Lan-Chile), which in 2001 flew 70·3m. km and carried 5,046,600 passengers, followed by Línea Aérea de Colore (Ladeco), which in 1998 flew 15·1m. km and carried 1,148,100 passengers. In 2000 Santiago handled 5,778,000 passengers (3,187,000 on international flights) and 292,800 tonnes of freight.

Shipping. The mercantile marine in 2001 totalled 647,820 GRT, including oil tankers 160,179 GRT. The five major ports, Valparaíso, San Antonio, Antofagasta, Arica and Iquique, are state-owned; there are 11 smaller private ports. Valparaíso, the largest port, handled 4,469,302 tonnes of freight in 2001.

Telecommunications. In 2001 there were 3,505,000 telephone main lines, equivalent to 227·6 for every 1,000 persons, and in 2002 there were 1,796,000 PCs in use (119·3 for every 1,000 persons). There were 3,575,000 Internet users in 2002. Mobile phone subscribers numbered 6,445,700 in 2002 and there were 40,000 fax machines in 1997.

Postal Services. In 2002 there were 752 post offices.

SOCIAL INSTITUTIONS

Justice. There are a High Court of Justice in the capital, 17 courts of appeal distributed over the republic, courts of first instance in the departmental capitals and second-class judges in the sub-delegations.

The population in penal institutions in Dec. 2002 was 36,214 (232 per 100,000 of national population).

The death penalty for ordinary crimes was abolished in 2001.

Religion. In 2001 Chile had an estimated 11·81m. Roman Catholics. In Jan. 2002 there were five archbishops, 25 bishops and two vicars apostolic. In Sept. 2003 there were three cardinals. 13·2% of the population defined themselves as evangelical in Jan. 2002. There were 478,000 Latter-day Saints in 1998 and 130,000 Jews in 1991.

Education. In 2001 there were 287,196 children at pre-primary schools; 146,918 teachers (imparting primary and/or secondary education) for 2·36m. primary school pupils; and 850,713 pupils at secondary level. Adult literacy rate in 2001 was 95·9% (male, 96·1%; female, 95·7%).

In 2001 there were 479,487 students in higher education. There were 60 universities with 339,200 students, 51 professional institutes with 86,392 students and 111 technical education centres with 53,895 students.

In 1998–99 total expenditure on education came to 3·8% of GNP and represented 16·1% of total government expenditure.

Health. There were 846 hospitals and 19,000 doctors in 2002, and 1,012 dentists in the national health service and 3,677 university nurses in 2000.

Welfare. In 1981 Chile abolished its state-sponsored pension plan and became the first country to establish private mandatory retirement savings. The system is managed by competitive private companies called AFPs (Pension Fund Administrators). Employees are required to save 13% of their pay. In May 2002 it had 6,477,244 members and assets of 24,016,805m. pesos. In 1995 about 25% of adults had private health insurance.

CULTURE

World Heritage Sites. Chile's three UNESCO protected sites are the Rapa Nui National Park, the Churches of Chiloé and the Historic Quarter of the Seaport of Valparaíso. Entered on the list in 1995, the Rapa Nui National Park encompasses much of the coastline of Easter Island and protects the shrines and statues (*Moai*) carved between the 10th–16th centuries. On the island of Chiloé off the Araucanian coastline, wooden churches were built by Jesuit missionaries at the turn of the 17th century. The churches were entered on the list in 2000. The Valparaíso site was inscribed on the list in 2003 as a model of urban and architectural development in 19th-century Latin America.

Broadcasting. In 2002 there were 1,341 radio broadcasting stations (including repeaters), 1,173 FM and 168 AM. In Sept. 1999 there were five television channels operating in UHF frequencies on the national territory. 18 other channels were operating on VHF through 400 frequencies. Both data included four university channels (three VHF and one UHF frequency). In Dec. 2002 the Televisión Nacional de Chile covered the whole of the country through 170 transmitters. In 2000 there were 5·2m. radio sets and in 2001 there were 4·4m. TV sets.

Press. In 2002 there were 76 national daily newspapers; in 1996 Chile's newspapers had a combined circulation of 1·4m.

Tourism. There were 1,723,107 foreign visitors in 2001. Tourist receipts were US$788m. in 2001.

DIPLOMATIC REPRESENTATIVES

Of Chile in the United Kingdom (12 Devonshire St., London, W1G 7DS)
Ambassador: Mariano Fernández.

Of the United Kingdom in Chile (Av. El Bosque Norte 0125, Piso 2, Las Condes, Santiago)
Ambassador: Richard Wilkinson, CVO.

Of Chile in the USA (1732 Massachusetts Ave., NW, Washington, D.C., 20036)
Ambassador: Andrés Bianchi Larre.

Of the USA in Chile (Av. Andrés Bello 2800, Las Condes, Santiago)
Ambassador: Craig A. Kelly.

Of Chile to the United Nations
Ambassador: Heraldo Muñoz.

Of Chile to the European Union
Ambassador: Alberto Van Klaveren Stork.

FURTHER READING

Banco Central de Chile. *Boletín Mensual.*
Bethell, L. (ed.) *Chile since Independence.* CUP, 1993
Collier, S. and Sater, W. F., *A History of Chile, 1808–1994*. CUP, 1996
Hickman, J., *News From the End of the Earth: A Portrait of Chile.* Hurst, London, 1998
Hojman, D. E., *Chile: the Political Economy of Development and Democracy in the 1990s.* London, 1993.—(ed.) *Change in the Chilean Countryside: from Pinochet to Aylwin and Beyond.* London, 1993
Oppenheim, L. H., *Politics in Chile: Democracy, Authoritarianism and the Search for Development.* Boulder (CO), 1993

National statistical office: Instituto Nacional de Estadísticas (INE), Santiago.
Website (Spanish only): http://www.ine.cl/

CHINA

Zhonghua Renmin Gonghe Guo
(People's Republic of China)

Capital: Beijing (Peking)
Population projection, 2010: 1,364·88m.
GDP per capita, 2002: (PPP$) 4,580
HDI/world rank: 0·745/94

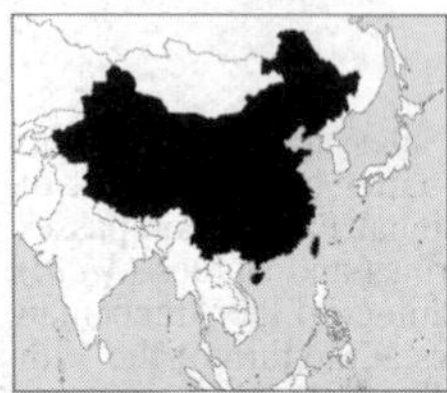

KEY HISTORICAL EVENTS

An embryonic Chinese state emerged in the fertile Huang He (Yellow River) basin before 4000 BC. Chinese culture reached the Chang Jiang (Yangtze) basin by 2500 BC and within 500 years the far south was also within the Chinese orbit. About 1500 BC writing developed using recognizable Chinese characters. Around 1000 BC under the Zhou dynasty, a centralized administration developed. In about 500 BC a court official, Kongfuzi (Confucius), outlined his vision of society. Confucianism, which introduced a system of civil service recruitment through examination, remained the principal Chinese belief system until the mid-20th century.

In 221 BC the ruler of the Warring State of Qin became the first emperor of China. He built an empire extending from the South China Sea to the edge of Central Asia, where work was begun on the Great Wall of China. The Qin dynasty standardized laws, money and administration throughout the empire but it was short-lived. By 206 BC the state had divided into three.

Reunification came gradually under the Han dynasty (202 BC–AD 200), then the Jin (265–316) and Sui (589–612) dynasties, interspersed by a period of inter-state war and anarchy. Reunification was achieved by the Tang dynasty, whose rule brought new prosperity to China from 618–917. Eventually the Tang empire too collapsed as separatism grew.

In 1126 nomads from Manchuria invaded the north, defeating the Song dynasty (960–1127) north of the Chang Jiang. The northern invaders were overthrown by the Mongols, led by Genghis Khan (c. 1162–1227), who went on to claim the rest of China. In 1280 their ruler Kublai Khan (1251–94), who had founded the Yuan dynasty in 1271, swept into southern China. The Mongol Yuan dynasty adopted Chinese ways but was overthrown by a nationalist uprising in 1368 which established the Ming dynasty.

The Ming empire collapsed in a peasants' revolt in 1644. Within months the peasants' leader was swept aside by the invasion of the Manchus, whose Qing dynasty ruled China until 1911.

Preoccupied with threats from the north, China neglected its southern coastal frontier where European traders were attempting to open up the country. The Portuguese, who landed on the Chinese coast in 1516, were followed by the Dutch in 1622 and the English in 1637. In the two Opium Wars (1838–42; 1856–58), Britain forced China to allow the import of opium from India into China, while Britain, France, Germany and other European states gained concessions in 'treaty ports' that virtually came under foreign rule. In 1860 British and French forces invaded Beijing and burnt the imperial palace. Defeat in the Sino-Japanese War (1894–95) resulted in the loss of Taiwan and Korea.

The xenophobic Boxer Rebellion, led by members of a secret society called the Fists of Righteous Harmony, broke out in 1900. The Guangxu emperor (1875–1908) attempted modernization in the Hundred Days Reform, but was taken captive by the conservative dowager empress who harnessed the Boxer Rebellion to her own ends. The rebellion was put down by European troops in 1901. China was then divided into zones of influence between the major European states and Japan.

The turning point came in 1911 when a revolution led by the Kuomintang (Guomintang or Nationalist movement) of Sun Yet-sen (Sun Zhong Shan; 1866–1925) overthrew the emperor. In 1916 Sun founded a republic in southern China on Soviet lines. After Sun's death the nationalist movement was taken over by his ally Chiang Kai-shek (Jiang Jie Shi; 1887–1976). In April 1927 he tried to suppress the Chinese Communist Party in a bloody campaign in which thousands of Communists were slaughtered. The remains of the party fled to the far western province of Jiangxi, beyond the reach of the Nationalists. In 1928 Chiang's army entered Beijing. With the greater part of the country reunited under Chiang's rule, he formed a government in Nanjing, which became the capital of China.

In 1934 the Communists were forced to retreat from Jiangxi province. Led by Mao Zedong (Mao Tse-tung; 1893–1976) they trekked for more than a year on the 5,600-mile Long March. Harried during their journey, they were besieged by the Nationalists when they eventually took refuge in Shaanxi province.

Against this backdrop of civil unrest, the Japanese invaded Manchuria in 1931, and by 1937 had seized Beijing and most of coastal China. At the end of the World War II, the Soviet sponsored Communist Party marched into Manchuria beginning a civil war. On 1 Oct. 1949 Mao declared the People's Republic of China in Beijing. Chiang fled with the remains of his Nationalist forces to the island of Taiwan, where he established a rival Chinese administration. It was not until 1978 that the USA recognized the People's Republic of China.

In 1950 China invaded Tibet. China posted 'volunteers' to fight alongside Communist North Korea during the Korean War (1950–53). There were clashes on the Soviet border in the 1950s and the Indian border in the 1960s. A Soviet-style five-year plan was put into action in 1953, but the two Communist powers fell out over their different interpretations of Marxist orthodoxy. Chinese research into atomic weapons culminated in the testing of the first Chinese atomic bomb in 1964.

Mao introduced the collectivization of farms in 1955. In 1956 he encouraged intellectual debate letting a 'hundred flowers bloom'. However, the new freedoms led to the questioning of the role of the party. Strict controls were reimposed and free-thinkers were sent to work in the countryside to be 're-educated'. In May 1958 Mao launched another ill-fated policy, the Great Leap Forward. To promote rapid industrialization and socialism, the collectives were reorganized into larger units. Neither the resources nor trained labour were available for this huge task. As relations with the Soviet Union cooled, a rapprochement with the United States was achieved in the early 1970s.

By the mid-1960s, Mao became the centre of a personality cult. Mao's 'Thoughts' were published in the 'Little Red Book'. In 1964 Mao set the Cultural Revolution in motion. Anyone who lacked enthusiasm for Mao Zedong Thought was denounced. After Mao's death in 1976, the Gang of Four, led by Mao's widow Chang Ch'ing, attempted to seize power. After these hard-liners were denounced and arrested, China came under the control of Deng Xiaoping, who emphasized economic reform. The country was opened to Western investment. Special Economic Zones and 'open cities' were designated and private enterprise gradually returned.

Greatly improved standards of living and a thriving economy increased expectations for civil liberties. The demand for political change climaxed in demonstrations by workers and students in April 1989, following the funeral of Communist Party leader Hu Yaobang. In Beijing the demonstrators were evicted from Tiananmen Square by the military who opened fire, killing more than 1,500. Hard-liners took control of the government, and martial law was imposed from May 1989 to Jan. 1990. Since then a more liberal regime has focused on economic development. Hong Kong was returned to China from British rule in 1997 and Macao from Portuguese rule in 1999. The late 1990s saw a cautious extension of civil liberties.

For the background to the handover of Hong Kong in 1997, see page 450.

TERRITORY AND POPULATION

China is bounded in the north by Russia and Mongolia; east by North Korea, the Yellow Sea and the East China Sea, with Hong Kong and Macao as enclaves on the southeast coast; south by Vietnam, Laos, Myanmar, India, Bhutan and Nepal; west by India, Pakistan, Afghanistan, Tajikistan, Kyrgyzstan and Kazakhstan. The total area (including Taiwan, Hong Kong and Macao) is estimated at 9,572,900 sq. km (3,696,100 sq. miles). A law of Feb. 1992 claimed the Spratly, Paracel and Diaoyutasi Islands. An agreement of 7 Sept. 1993 at prime ministerial level settled Sino-Indian border disputes which had first emerged in the war of 1962.

China's fifth national census was held on 1 Nov. 2000. According to preliminary results, the total population of the 31 provinces, autonomous regions and municipalities on the mainland was 1,265,830,000 (612,280,000 females, representing 48·37%); density, 132 per sq. km. The population rose by 132,150,000 (or 11·66%) since the census in 1990. There were 455,940,000 urban residents, accounting for 36·1% of the population. The proportion of the population living in urban areas has more than doubled since 1975. An estimated 300m. people have migrated from the countryside to cities since the economy was opened up in the late 1970s, and a further 300m. are expected to move to towns and cities by 2020.

The UN gives a projected population for 2010 of 1,364·88m.

China is set to lose its status as the world's most populous country to India by 2040, and according to UN projections its population will begin to decline between 2035 and 2040.

1979 regulations restricting married couples to a single child, a policy enforced by compulsory abortions and economic sanctions, have been widely ignored, and it was admitted in 1988 that the population target of 1,200m. by 2000 would have to be revised to 1,270m. Since 1988 peasant couples have been permitted a second child after four years if the first born is a girl, a measure to combat infanticide. In 1999 China started to implement a more widespread gradual relaxation of the one-child policy.

An estimated 34m. persons of Chinese origin lived abroad in 2000.

A number of widely divergent varieties of Chinese are spoken. The official 'Modern Standard Chinese' is based on the dialect of North China. Mandarin in one form or another is spoken by 885m. people in China, or around 70% of the population of mainland China. The Wu language and its dialects has some 77m. native speakers and Cantonese 66m. The ideographic writing system of 'characters' is uniform throughout the country, and has undergone systematic simplification. In 1958 a phonetic alphabet (*Pinyin*) was devised to transcribe the characters, and in 1979 this was officially adopted for use in all texts in the Roman alphabet. The previous transcription scheme (Wade) is still used in Taiwan and Hong Kong.

Mainland China is administratively divided into 22 provinces, five autonomous regions (originally entirely or largely inhabited by ethnic minorities, though in some regions now outnumbered by Han immigrants) and four government-controlled municipalities. These are in turn divided into 332 prefectures, 658 cities (of which 265 are at prefecture level and 393 at county level), 2,053 counties and 808 urban districts.

Government-controlled municipalities	*Area (in 1,000 sq. km)*	*Population (2000 census, in 1,000)*	*Density per sq. km (in 2000)*	*Capital*
Beijing	16·8	13,820	823	—
Chongqing	82·0	30,090	367	—
Shanghai	6·2	16,740	2,700	—
Tianjin	11·3	10,010	886	—
Provinces				
Anhui	139·9	59,860	428	Hefei
Fujian	123·1	34,710	282	Fuzhou
Gansu[1]	366·5	25,620	70	Lanzhou
Guangdong[1]	197·1	86,420	438	Guangzhou
Guizhou[1]	174·0	35,250	203	Guiyang
Hainan[1]	34·3	7,870	229	Haikou
Hebei[1]	202·7	67,440	333	Shijiazhuang
Heilongjiang[1]	463·6	36,890	80	Haerbin
Henan	167·0	92,560	554	Zhengzhou
Hubei[1]	187·5	60,280	321	Wuhan
Hunan[1]	210·5	64,400	306	Changsha
Jiangsu	102·6	74,380	723	Nanjing
Jiangxi	164·8	41,400	251	Nanchang
Jilin[1]	187·0	27,280	146	Changchun
Liaoning[1]	151·0	42,380	281	Shenyang
Qinghai[1]	721·0	5,180	7	Xining
Shaanxi	195·8	36,050	184	Xian
Shandong	153·3	90,790	592	Jinan
Shanxi	157·1	32,970	210	Taiyuan
Sichuan[1]	487·0	83,290	171	Chengdu
Yunnan[1]	436·2	42,880	98	Kunming
Zhejiang[1]	101·8	46,770	459	Hangzhou

Autonomous regions	*Area (in 1,000 sq. km)*	*Population (2000 census, in 1,000)*	*Density per sq. km (in 2000)*	*Capital*
Guangxi Zhuang	220·4	44,890	204	Nanning
Inner Mongolia	1,177·5	23,760	20	Hohhot
Ningxia Hui	66·4	5,620	85	Yinchuan
Tibet[2]	1,221·6	2,620	2	Lhasa
Xinjiang Uighur	1,646·9	19,250	12	Urumqi

[1]Also designated minority nationality autonomous area. [2]See also Tibet below.

Population of largest cities in 2000: Shanghai, 14·35m.; Beijing (Peking), 11·51m.; Chongqing, 9·69m.; Guangzhou (Canton), 8·52m.; Wuhan, 8·31m.; Tianjin, 7·50m.; Shenzhen, 7·01m.; Dongguan, 6·45m.; Shenyang, 5·30m.; Xian, 4·48m.; Chengdu, 4·33m.; Nanjing, 3·62m.; Haerbin, 3·48m.; Dalian, 3·25m.; Changchun, 3·23m.; Kunming, 3·04m.; Jinan, 3·00m.; Guiyang, 2·99m.; Zibo, 2·82m.; Qingdao, 2·72m.; Zhengzhou, 2·59m.; Taiyuan, 2·56m.; Chaoyang, 2·47m.; Hangzhou, 2·45m.; Zhongshan, 2·36m.; Nanhai, 2·13m.; Changsha, 2·12m.; Fuzhou, 2·12m.; Lanzhou, 2·09m.; Xiamen, 2·05m.; Zaozhuang, 2·00m.; Shijiazhuang, 1·97m.; Jilin, 1·95m.; Linyi, 1·94m.; Wenzhou, 1·92m.; Puning, 1·86m.; Nanchang, 1·84m.; Nanchong, 1·77m.; Nanning, 1·77m.; Urumqi (Wulumuqi), 1·75m.; Fuyang, 1·72m.; Yantai, 1·72m.; Tangshan, 1·71m.; Shunde, 1·69m.; Xuzhou, 1·68m.; Baotou, 1·67m.; Hefei, 1·66m.; Tianmen, 1·61m.; Liuan, 1·60m.; Suizhou, 1·60m.; Suzhou, 1·60m.; Nanyang, 1·58m.; Ningbo, 1·57m.; Anshan, 1·56m.; Tengzhou, 1·55m.; Pizhou, 1·54m.; Qiqihaer, 1·54m.; Taian, 1·54m.; Datong, 1·53m.

China has 56 ethnic groups. According to the 2000 census 1,159,400,000 people (91·6%) were of Han nationality and 106,430,000 (8·4%) were from national minorities (including Zhuang, Manchu, Hui, Miao, Uighur, Yi, Tujia, Mongolian and Tibetan). Compared with the 1990 census, the Han population increased by almost 116,920,000 (11·2%), while the ethnic minorities increased by 15,230,000 (16·7%). Non-Han populations predominate in the autonomous regions, most notably in Tibet where national minorities accounted for 97·2% of the population in 1994.

Li Chengrui, *The Population of China.* Beijing, 1992

Tibet

After the 1959 revolt was suppressed, the Preparatory Committee for the Autonomous Region of Tibet (set up in 1955) took over the functions of local government, led by its Vice-Chairman, the Panchen Lama, in the absence of its Chairman, the Dalai Lama, who had fled to India in 1959. In Dec. 1964 both the Dalai and Panchen Lamas were removed from their posts and on 9 Sept. 1965 Tibet became an Autonomous Region. 301 delegates were elected to the first People's Congress, of whom 226 were Tibetans. The senior spiritual leader, the Dalai Lama, is in exile. He was awarded the Nobel Peace Prize in 1989. Following the death of the 10th Panchen Lama (Tibet's second most important spiritual leader) in Jan. 1989, the Dalai Lama announced Gendu Choekyi Nyima (b. 1989) as the 11th Panchen Lama in May 1995. Beijing rejected the choice and appointed Gyaltsen Norbu (b. 1989) in his place. Gendu Choekyi Nyima has been missing since 1995.

The borders were opened for trade with neighbouring countries in 1980. In July 1988 Tibetan was reinstated as a 'major official language', competence in which is required of all administrative officials. Monasteries and shrines have been renovated and reopened. There were some 15,000 monks and nuns in 1987. In 1984 a Buddhist seminary in Lhasa opened with 200 students. A further softening of Beijing's attitude towards Tibet was shown during President Bill Clinton's visit to China in June 1998. Jiang Zemin, China's president, said he was prepared to meet the Dalai Lama provided he acknowledged Chinese sovereignty over Tibet and Taiwan. In Sept. 2002 direct contact between the exiled government and China was re-established after a nine-year gap.

At the 2000 census Tibet had a population of 2·62m., of which 2·42m. were Tibetans and the remainder from other ethnic groups. The average population density was 2·02 persons per sq. km, although the majority of residents live in the southern and eastern parts of the region. Birth rate (per 1,000), 2000, 17·6; death rate, 6·6. Population of the Lhasa (capital) region in 2000 was 403,700. Expectation of life was 67 years in 2000.

In 2000, 1·24m. people were in employment: 909,800 worked in agriculture, forestry, animal husbandry and fisheries; 73,300 in wholesale and retail services; 57,300 in government and party institutions and social organizations; 35,600 in construction; 33,100 in transport and communications; 32,400 in education, culture and media; 28,700 in manufacturing; and 12,400 in health and social welfare. Output in 2000 included 120,000 cu. metres of timber, 493,200 tonnes of cement, 196,628 tonnes of chromium ore, 441,900 garments and 591 tonnes of traditional Chinese medicines. Electricity output in 2000 was 66m. kWh.

In 2000 the total sown area was 230,850 ha (dry fields, 229,760 ha; paddy fields, 1,080 ha). Output (in 1,000 tonnes), 2000: total major crops, 962; including qingke barley, 597; wheat, 307; rice, 5. Livestock numbered 22·6m. in 2000: including 5·3m. cattle; 10·4m. sheep; 5·9m. goats; and 0·2m. pigs.

In 2000 there were 22,503 km of roads (21,842 km in 1990). There are airports at Lhasa and Bangda providing external links. 148,877 tourists visited Tibet in 2000. In 2000 plans were announced to build a railway of some 900 km to link Lhasa with the town of Golmud, which already has a link with the city of Xining. It would be the highest railway in the world. The Chinese government approved the plan on 8 Feb. 2001 with the aim of completing the link by 2008.

By 2000 Tibet had about 4,250 primary schools (including those run by villages); 106 secondary schools (90 middle schools, 16 vocational and polytechnic schools); and 4 higher education institutes (Tibet University, Tibet Ethnic College, Tibet Institute of Agriculture and Animal Husbandry, and Tibetan Medical College). There were more than 300,000 pupils and students.

In 2000 there were 11,027 medical personnel (including 5,262 doctors) and 1,237 medical institutions, with a total of 6,348 beds.

Barnett, R. and Akiner, S. (eds.) *Resistance and Reform in Tibet.* Farnborough, 1994

Margolis, Eric, *War at the Top of the World: The Struggle for Afghanistan, Kashmir and Tibet.* Routledge, New York, 2001

Pinfold, John, *Tibet* [Bibliography]. Oxford and Santa Barbara (CA), 1991

Schwartz, R. D., *Circle of Protest: Political Ritual in the Tibetan Uprising.* Farnborough, 1994

Smith, W. W., *A History of Tibet: Nationalism and Self-Determination*. Oxford, 1996

SOCIAL STATISTICS

Births, 2001, 17,020,000; deaths, 8,180,000. 2001 birth rate (per 1,000 population), 13·38; death rate, 6·43. The birth rate has declined each year since 1987. There were 8,420,044 marriages and 1,212,863 divorces in 2000. In April 2001 parliament passed revisions to the marriage law prohibiting bigamy and cohabitation outside marriage. The Ministry of Health estimated in 2001 that the suicide rate in China was about 22 per 100,000 population. China is the only major country in which the suicide rate is higher among females—over half the world's women suicides occur in China. In 1996 the most popular age for marrying was 25–29 for both men and women. Life expectancy at birth, 2001, was 68·6 years for men and 72·9 years for women. Infant mortality, 2001, 31 per 1,000 live births. Fertility rate, 2001, 1·8 births per woman. Annual population growth rate, 1992–2002, 0·9%. The number of people living on less than US$1 a day at purchasing power parity declined from 470m. in 1990 to 261m. in 2000.

CLIMATE

Most of China has a temperate climate but, with such a large country, extending far inland and embracing a wide range of latitude as well as containing large areas at high altitude, many parts experience extremes of climate, especially in winter. Most rain falls during the summer, from May to Sept., though amounts decrease inland. Monthly average temperatures and annual rainfall (2000): Beijing (Peking), Jan. 20·5°F (–6·4°C), July 85·3°F (29·6°C). Annual rainfall 14·6" (371·1 mm). Chongqing, Jan. 45·8°F (7·7°C), July 83·3°F (28·5°C). Annual rainfall 39·8" (1,010 mm). Shanghai, Jan. 41·2°F (5·1°C), July 84·5°F (29·1°C). Annual rainfall 52·4" (1,332 mm). Tianjin, Jan. 20·3°F (–6·5°C), July 83·8°F (28·8°C). Annual rainfall 18·0" (459 mm).

CONSTITUTION AND GOVERNMENT

On 21 Sept. 1949 the *Chinese People's Political Consultative Conference* met in Beijing, convened by the Chinese Communist Party. The Conference adopted a

'Common Programme' of 60 articles and the 'Organic Law of the Central People's Government' (31 articles). Both became the basis of the Constitution adopted on 20 Sept. 1954 by the 1st National People's Congress, the supreme legislative body. The Consultative Conference continued to exist after 1954 as an advisory body. Three further constitutions have been promulgated under Communist rule—in 1975, 1978 and 1982 (currently in force). The latter was partially amended in 1988, 1993 and 1999, endorsing the principles of a socialist market economy and of private ownership.

The unicameral *National People's Congress* is the highest organ of state power. Usually meeting for one session a year, it can amend the constitution and nominally elects and has power to remove from office the highest officers of state. There are 2,989 members of the Congress, who are elected to serve five-year terms by municipal, regional and provincial people's congresses. The Congress elects a *Standing Committee* (which supervises the *State Council*) and the *President* and *Vice-President* for a five-year term. When not in session, Congress business is carried on by the *Standing Committee*.

The *State Council* is the supreme executive organ and comprises the Prime Minister, Deputy Prime Ministers and State Councillors.

The *Central Military Commission* is the highest state military organ.

National Anthem. 'March of the Volunteers'; words by Tien Han, tune by Nieh Erh.

RECENT ELECTIONS

Elections of delegates to the 10th *National People's Congress* were held between Dec. 2002 and Feb. 2003 by municipal, regional and provincial people's congresses. At its annual session in March 2003 the Congress elected Hu Jintao as *President* and Zeng Qinghong as *Vice-President*.

CURRENT ADMINISTRATION

President and Chairman of Central Military Commission: Hu Jintao; b. 1942 (Chinese Communist Party; elected 15 March 2003).

Deputy President: Zeng Qinghong.

In March 2005 the government comprised:

Prime Minister: Wen Jiabao; b. 1942 (Chinese Communist Party; appointed 16 March 2003).

Deputy Prime Ministers: Huang Ju, Wu Yi (also *Minister of Health*), Zeng Peiyan, Hui Liangyu.

Minister of Agriculture: Du Qinglin. *Civil Administration:* Li Xueju. *Commerce:* Bo Xilai. *Construction:* Wang Guangtao. *Culture:* Sun Jiazheng. *Education:* Zhou Ji. *Finance:* Jin Renqing. *Foreign Affairs:* Li Zhaoxing. *Information Industry:* Wang Xudong. *Justice:* Zhang Fusen. *Labour and Social Security:* Zheng Silin. *National Land Resources:* Tian Fengshan. *National Defence:* Cao Gangchuan. *National Security:* Xu Yongyue. *Personnel:* Zhang Bolin. *Public Security:* Zhou Yongkang. *Railways:* Liu Zhijun. *Science and Technology:* Xu Guanhua. *Supervision:* Li Zhilun. *Transportation:* Zhang Chunxian. *Water Resources:* Wang Shucheng.

Ministers heading State Commissions: *Family Planning*, Zhang Weiqing. *Nationalities Affairs*, Li Dezhu. *Development and Reform*, Ma Kai. *Science, Technology and Industry for National Defence*, Zhang Yunchuan.

De facto power is in the hands of the Communist Party of China, which had 66m. members in 2002. There are eight other parties, all members of the Chinese People's Political Consultative Conference.

The members of the Standing Committee of the Politburo in March 2005 were Hu Jintao (*General Secretary*), Wen Jiabao, Luo Gan, Wu Bangguo, Zeng Qinghong, Huang Ju, Jia Qinglin, Li Changchun, Wu Guanzheng.

Government Website (Chinese only): http://www.govonline.cn

DEFENCE

The Chinese president is chairman of the State and Party's Military Commissions. China is divided into seven military regions. The military commander also commands the air, naval and civilian militia forces assigned to each region.

Conscription is compulsory but for organizational reasons selective: only some 10% of potential recruits are called up. Service is for two years. A military academy to train senior officers in modern warfare was established in 1985.

Defence expenditure in 2003 totalled US$55,948m. (US$43 per capita) and represented 3·9% of GDP. Only the USA and Russia spent more on defence in 2003. In the period 1999–2003 China's spending on major conventional weapons was the highest in the world at US$11·8bn., although in 2003 India overtook China as the leading recipient.

Nuclear Weapons. Having carried out its first test in 1964, there have been 45 tests in all at Lop Nur, in Xinjiang (the last in 1996). The nuclear arsenal consisted of approximately 402 warheads in Jan. 2004 according to the Stockholm International Peace Research Institute. China has been helping Pakistan with its nuclear efforts. Despite China's official position, *Deadly Arsenals*, published by the Carnegie Endowment for International Peace, alleges that the Chinese government is secretly pursuing chemical and biological weapons programmes.

Army. The Army (PLA: 'People's Liberation Army') is divided into main and local forces. Main forces, administered by the seven military regions in which they are stationed, but commanded by the Ministry of Defence, are available for operation anywhere and are better equipped. Local forces concentrate on the defence of their own regions. There are 21 Integrated Group Armies comprising 44 infantry divisions, nine armoured divisions, 12 armoured brigades, one mechanized infantry, 22 motorized infantry brigades, six artillery divisions, 15 artillery brigades, one anti-tank brigade, eight surface-to-air missile brigades, 13 anti-aircraft artillery brigades and three army aviation regiments. Total strength in 2002 was 1·60m. including some 800,000 conscripts. Reserve forces are undergoing major reorganization on a provincial basis but are estimated to number some 500–600,000.

In Sept. 2003 it was announced that the strength of the PLA was to be reduced by 200,000 as part of a move to modernize the military.

There is a paramilitary People's Armed Police force estimated at 1·5m. under PLA command.

Navy. The naval arm of the PLA comprises one nuclear-powered ballistic missile armed submarine, five nuclear-propelled fleet submarines, one diesel-powered cruise missile submarine and some 61 patrol submarines. Surface combatant forces include 21 missile-armed destroyers, 42 frigates and some 93 missile craft.

There is a land-based naval air force of about 472 combat aircraft, primarily for defensive and anti-submarine service. The force includes H-5 torpedo bombers, Q-5 fighter/ground attack aircraft J-6 (MiG-19) and J-7 (MiG-21) fighters.

The naval arm is split into a North Sea Fleet, an East Sea Fleet and a South Sea Fleet.

In 2002 naval personnel were estimated at 250,000, including 26,000 in the naval air force and 40,000 conscripts.

Air Force. There are five air corps and 32 air divisions. Up to four squadrons make up an air regiment and three air regiments form an air division. The Air Force has an estimated 1,900 combat aircraft.

Equipment includes J-7 (MiG-21) interceptors and fighter-bombers, H-5 (Il-28) jet bombers, H-6 Chinese-built copies of Tu-16 strategic bombers, Q-5 fighter-bombers (evolved from the MiG-19) and Su-27 fighters supplied by Russia. About 100 of a locally-developed fighter designated J-8 (known in the West as 'Finback') are in service.

Total strength (2002) was 420,000 (160,000 conscripts), including 220,000 in air defence organization. The Air Force headquarters are in Beijing.

INTERNATIONAL RELATIONS

The People's Republic of China is a member of UN (and its Security Council), WTO, BIS, the Asian Development Bank, APEC, Mekong Group and the Antarctic Treaty. China joined the WTO in Dec. 2001.

China is heavily dependent on foreign aid. In 2000 it received US$1·7bn., more than any other country.

ECONOMY

In 2002 agriculture accounted for 15·4% of GDP, industry 51·1% and services 33·5%.

It has been estimated that corruption cost China US$150bn. in the 1990s, or between 13% and 16% of the country's GDP.

Overview. China ranks among the world's top ten economies is currently one of the fastest-growing. In purchasing power parity terms, China is the second largest economy in the world. The economy has grown by an average of 9% per year over the last 25 years.

During the last decade economic growth has been predominantly fuelled by a rapid expansion of industry and investment. A tenth five-year plan covers 2001–05; there is also a 15-year strategic plan, the 'Long-Term Target for 2010'. The five-year plan has as its guiding principles the spread of market forces, economic restructuring, making technological progress the driving force for economic growth, improving living standards, and co-ordinating economic and social development. Market development is being encouraged by building the institutional, legal, social, human and physical infrastructure needed to invigorate private investment and rapid growth. Private enterprise, which did not exist until the late 1970s, now accounts for over 30% of national output. A further policy goal is to increase integration with the world economy—in 2001 China gained accession to the World Trade Organization. Since 1993 the Chinese authorities have embarked upon the goal of achieving full exchange rate convertibility and capital account liberalization. Progress has been slow and deliberate in a bid to overcome weaknesses in the domestic financial sector and to reduce the risk of over-exposure to capital flows before sufficient institutional development has occurred.

Until 1978 industry was dominated by state-owned enterprises. Since then, much of the increase in manufacturing has been produced by collective enterprises, e.g., by private entrepreneurs working with foreign investors. However, the state sector contains the most capital-intensive industries. Government revenue is strong thanks to high industrial profits and improvements in tax administrations. This has enabled the government to increase social security spending and to cope with public investment, interest costs and civil service wage bills. China faces several economic and social challenges in the future including the reformation of bulky state-owned industries, the overhaul of the financial sector and raising the incomes of China's rural poor.

Currency. The currency is called Renminbi (*i.e.,* People's Currency). The unit of currency is the *yuan* (CNY) which is divided into ten *jiao*, the *jiao* being divided into ten *fen*. The yuan was floated to reflect market forces on 1 Jan. 1994 while remaining state-controlled. Since then the People's Bank of China has maintained the yuan at about 8·28 to the US dollar, allowing it to fluctuate but only by a fraction of 1% in closely supervised trading. The yuan became convertible for current transactions from 1 Dec. 1996. Total money supply in June 2002 was 6,565·77bn. yuan and gold reserves were 16·08m. troy oz. Foreign exchange reserves were US$609·9bn. in Dec. 2004 (US$73·6bn. in 1995). Only Japan, with US$844·5bn., had more. Inflation, which had been 24·1% in 1994, was 0·7% in 2001. There was then deflation in 2002, of 0·8%, and inflation in 2003, of 1·2%.

Budget. Total revenue and expenditure (in 1bn. yuan):

	1997	*1998*	*1999*	*2000*	*2001*	*2002*
Revenue	865·1	987·6	1,144·4	1,339·5	1,637·1	1,891·4
Expenditure	923·3	1,079·8	1,318·8	1,588·7	1,884·4	2,201·2

Total revenue in the central budget for 2001 was 917·1bn. yuan, comprising 857·8bn. yuan in revenue collected by central government and 59·3bn. yuan transferred to central government from local authorities. Total expenditure in the central budget amounted to 1,176·9bn. yuan, of which 575·4bn. yuan of expenditure for the central government and 601·5bn. yuan in the form of subsidies for local authorities. Local government revenue in 2001 came to 1,380·8bn. yuan (779·3bn. yuan in revenue collected by local authorities and 601·5bn. yuan in central government subsidies) and expenditure amounted to 1,368·3bn. yuan (1,309·0bn. yuan of expenditure in local budgets and 59·3bn. yuan transferred to central government). The 247·3bn. yuan deficit in 2001 increased to 309·8bn. in 2002.

Performance. GDP totalled US$1,409·8bn. in 2003. It is forecast that by 2050 China will have overtaken the USA to become the world's largest economy. GDP growth was officially put at 7·1% in 1999 (the slowest rate for a decade), but then 8·0% in 2000. In 2001 there was 7·3% growth, rising to 8·0% in 2002, 9·3% in 2003 and 9·5% in 2004. In spite of high growth in recent years, China's GDP per capita at purchasing power parity was $4,020 in 2001 compared to the high human development average of $23,135.

Banking and Finance. The People's Bank of China is the central bank and bank of issue (*Governor:* Zhou Xiaochuan). There are three state policy banks—the State Development Bank, Export and Import Bank of China and Agricultural Development Bank of China—and four national specialized banks (the Bank of China, Industrial and Commercial Bank of China, Agricultural Bank of China and China Construction Bank). The Bank of China is responsible for foreign banking operations. In April 2003 the China Banking Regulatory Commission was launched, taking over the role of regulating and supervising the country's banks and other deposit-taking financial institutions from the central bank. Legislation of 1995 permitted the establishment of commercial banks; credit co-operatives may be transformed into banks, mainly to provide credit to small businesses. In 2001 there were over 44,000 rural credit co-operatives and 3,200 urban credit co-operatives. In mid-2002 deposits in rural co-operatives amounted to 1,870bn. yuan and loans reached 1,360bn. yuan. Insurance is handled by the People's Insurance Company.

Savings deposits in various forms in all banking institutions totalled 14,363bn. yuan at the end of 2001. Loans amounted to 11,230bn. yuan.

There are stock exchanges in the Shenzhen Special Economic Zone and in Shanghai. A securities trading system linking six cities (Securities Automated Quotations System) was inaugurated in 1990 for trading in government bonds.

In 2003 China received a record US$53·5bn. worth of foreign direct investment, the second highest total behind Luxembourg. Annual FDI is now ten times that of the early 1990s.

Weights and Measures. The metric system is in general use alongside traditional units of measurement.

ENERGY AND NATURAL RESOURCES

Environment. China's carbon dioxide emissions from the consumption and flaring of fossil fuels in 2002 accounted for 13·5% of the world total (the second highest after the USA) and were equivalent to 2·6 tonnes per capita. An *Environmental Sustainability Index* compiled for the World Economic Forum meeting in Feb. 2002 ranked China 129th in the world out of 142 countries analysed, with 38·5%. The index measured the ability of countries to maintain favourable environmental conditions and examined various factors including pollution levels and the use or abuse of natural resources.

Electricity. Installed generating capacity in 2002 was 353m. kW, compared with 254m. kW in 1997. In 2002 electricity output was 1,654,000 GWh, an 11·7% increase over 2001. Consumption per capita was 1,057 kWh in 2000. Rapidly increasing demand has meant that more than half of China's provinces have had to ration power. Sources of energy in 2001 as percentage of total energy production: coal, 67·7%; crude oil, 20·6%; hydro-electric power, 8·3%; natural gas, 3·4%. In 2003 there were eight nuclear reactors in use with a further three under construction. Generating electricity is not centralized; local units range between 30 and 60 MW of output. In Dec. 2002 China formally broke up its state power monopoly, creating instead five generating and two transmission firms. The Three Gorges dam project on the Yangtze river, launched in 1993 and scheduled for completion in 2009, is intended to produce abundant hydro-electricity (as well as helping flood control); the first three 700,000-kW generators in service at the project's hydro-power station began commercial operation in July 2003. When the project is completed in 2009, its 26 generators will have a combined capacity of 18·2 GW.

Oil and Gas. On-shore oil reserves are found mainly in the northeast (particularly the Daqing and Liaohe fields) and northwest. There are off-shore fields in the continental shelves of east China. Crude oil production was 169m. tonnes in 2002. Proven reserves in 2002 were 18·3bn. bbls.

The largest natural gas reserves are located in the western and north-central regions. Production was 32·6bn. cu. metres in 2002, with proven reserves of 1,510bn. cu. metres.

Minerals. At the end of 2001 there were 156 varieties of proven mineral deposits in China, making it the third richest in the world in total reserves. Recoverable deposits of coal totalled 1,003·3bn. tonnes, mainly distributed in north China (particularly Shanxi province and the Inner Mongolia Autonomous Region). Coal production was 1,380m. tonnes in 2002, an 18·9% increase on 2001.

Iron ore reserves were 45·7bn. tonnes in 2001. Deposits are abundant in the anthracite field of Shanxi, in Hebei and in Shandong, and are found in conjunction with coal and worked in the northeast. Production in 2001 was 217m. tonnes, making China the world's leading iron ore producer.

Tin ore is plentiful in Yunnan, where the tin-mining industry has long existed. Tin production was 62,000 tonnes in 2002.

China is a major producer of wolfram (tungsten ore). Mining of wolfram is carried on in Hunan, Guangdong and Yunnan.

Salt production was 35·0m. tonnes in 2002; gold production was 162 tonnes in 2000. Output of other minerals (in 1,000 tonnes) in 2001: bauxite, 9,500; aluminium (2002), 4,300; zinc, 1,700; lead (1997), 650; copper, 588; diamonds, 1,185,000 carats. Other minerals produced: nickel, barite, bismuth, graphite, gypsum, mercury, molybdenum, silver. Reserves (in tonnes) of salt, 402,400m.; phosphate ore, 15,766m.; sylvite, 458m.

Agriculture. Agriculture accounted for approximately 15·4% of GDP in 2002, compared to over 50% in 1949 at the time of the birth of the People's Republic of China and over 30% in 1980. In 2000 areas harvested for major crops were (in 1m. ha): rice, 30·50; wheat, 26·65; maize, 22·54; soybeans, 9·03; rapeseed, 7·80; sweet potatoes, 6·21. Intensive agriculture and horticulture have been practised for millennia. Present-day policy aims to avert the traditional threats from floods and droughts by soil conservancy, afforestation, irrigation and drainage projects, and to increase the 'high stable yields' areas by introducing fertilizers, pesticides and improved crops. In spite of this, 18·1m. ha of land were flooded in 1996 and 20·1m. ha were covered by drought. In Aug. 1998 more than 21m. ha, notably in the Yangtze valley, were under water as China experienced some of its worst flooding in recent times. The 2002 flood season claimed over 1,500 lives.

'Township and village enterprises' in agriculture comprise enterprises previously run by the communes of the Maoist era, co-operatives run by rural labourers and individual firms of a certain size. Such enterprises employed 130·8m. people in 2001. There were 2,026 state farms in 2000 with 3·92m. employees. In 2001 there were 244·32m. rural households. The rural workforce in 2001 was 490·85m., of whom 324·5m. were employed in agriculture, fishing or land management. Net per capita annual peasant income, 2001: 2,366 yuan. Around 44% of the total workforce is engaged in agriculture, down from 68% in 1980. According to the 2000 census, rural residents accounted for 63·9% of the population.

In 2001 there were 143,625,000 ha of arable land and 11,650,000 ha of permanent cropland; 54·8m. ha were irrigated. There were 1,112,617 tractors in 2001 and 200,000 harvester-threshers.

Agricultural production of main crops (in 1m. tonnes), 2000: rice, 190·17; sweet potatoes, 121·02; maize, 105·23; wheat, 99·37; sugarcane, 70·20; potatoes, 62·04; watermelons, 38·38; cabbages, 20·21; tomatoes, 19·31; cucumbers and gherkins, 17·18; soybeans, 15·40; groundnuts, 15·07; seed cotton, 13·05; onions, 12·18; aubergines, 11·91; rapeseeds, 11·35; cottonseed, 8·70; pears, 8·62; chillies and green peppers, 8·14; sugarbeets, 7·70; tangerines and mandarins, 7·61; garlic, 6·47. Tea production in 2000 was just 721,000 tonnes. China is the world's leading producer of a number of agricultural crops, including rice, sweet potatoes, wheat, potatoes, watermelons, groundnuts and honey. The gross value of agricultural output in 2001 was 2,617,960m. yuan. Agricultural production during the period 1990–97 grew on average by 4·4% every year. Only Vietnam among Asian countries achieved higher annual agricultural growth over the same period.

Livestock, 2000: pigs, 437,551,000; goats, 148,401,000; sheep, 131,095,000; cattle, 104,582,000; buffaloes, 22,599,000; horses, 8,916,000; chickens, 3·62bn.; ducks, 612m. China has more sheep, goats, pigs, horses and chickens than any other country. China also has more than two-thirds of the world's ducks. Meat production in 2000 was 64·44m. tonnes; milk, 7·84m. tonnes; eggs, 19·24m. tonnes; honey, 256,000 tonnes. China is the world's leading producer of meat and eggs.

Powell, S. G., *Agricultural Reform in China: from Communes to Commodity Economy, 1978–1990.* Manchester Univ. Press, 1992

Forestry. In 2000 the area under forests was 163·48m. ha, or 17·5% of the total land area. The average annual increase in forest cover of 1,806,000 ha between 1990 and 2000 was the highest of any country in the world. Total roundwood production in 2001 was 284·91m. cu. metres, making China the world's third largest timber producer (8·6% of the world total in 2001). It is the world's leading importer of roundwood, accounting for 15·1% of world timber imports in 2001.

Fisheries. Total catch, 2001: 16,529,389 tonnes, of which 14,379,457 tonnes were from marine waters. China's annual catch is the largest in the world, and currently accounts for approximately 18% of the world total. In 1989 the annual catch had been just 5·3m. tonnes.

INDUSTRY

The leading companies by market capitalization in China in Feb. 2004 were: PetroChina (US$90·7bn.), an oil and gas company; China Mobile (US$65·4bn.), a mobile telecommunications company; and Sinopec (US$51·9bn.), also an oil and gas company.

Industry accounted for 51·1% of GDP in 2002, up from 21% in 1949 when the People's Republic of China came into existence. Cottage industries persist into the 21st century. Modern industrial development began with the manufacture of cotton textiles and the establishment of silk filatures, steel plants, flour mills and match factories. In 1999 there were 7,929,900 industrial enterprises. 61,300 were state-owned, 1,659,800 were collectives and 6,126,800 were individually owned. A law of 1988 ended direct state control of firms and provided for the possibility of bankruptcy.

Output of major products, 2002 (in tonnes): cement, 725m. (more than a third of the world total); rolled steel, 192·9m.; crude steel, 181·5m.; pig iron, 170·7m.; distillate fuel oil (2000), 70·8m.; petrol (2000), 41·3m.; chemical fertilizers, 37·9m.; paper and paperboard (2001), 37·9m.; sulphuric acid, 30·5m.; residual fuel oil (2000), 20·5m.; sugar, 9·26m.; cotton yarn, 8·50m. Also produced in 2002: cloth, 3,220m. metres; woollen fabrics (1996), 459·5m. metres; beer (2003), 25,404·8m. litres; 184m. watches (2001); 119·6m. mobile telephones; 81·8m. clocks (1997); 56·50m. radios (1996); 51·55m. TV sets; 59·62m. cameras (2001); 31·55m. air conditioners; 29m. bicycles (2000); 15·99m. refrigerators; 14·64m. micro-computers; 13·42m. washing machines (2001); 10·41m. motorcycles and scooters (2001); 3·25m. motor vehicles; 2,207 ships. China is the world's leading steel producer.

The gross value of industrial output in 1999 was 12,611,100m. yuan.

Labour. The employed population at the 1990 census was 647·2m. (291·1m. female). By the end of 2002 it had risen to 737·4m. (7·15m. more than in 2001), of whom 489·6m. worked in rural areas (1·25m. fewer than in 2001) and 247·8m. in urban areas (8·4m. more than in 2001). In June 2003 China's registered jobless was 4·2%, with 7·95m. registered unemployed in the country's cities. Between 1995 and 2002, 15m. jobs were lost owing to the closure of state-owned factories. In 2000 there were 333·55m. people working in agriculture, hunting, forestry and fisheries; 80·43m. in manufacturing; 46·86m. in wholesale and retail trade, restaurants and hotels; 35·52m. in construction; and 20·29m. in transport, storage and communication.

By 2001 China had more than 2m. private companies employing 22m. people. It was not until the late 1970s that the private sector even came into existence in China.

The average non-agricultural annual wage in 2001 was 10,870 yuan: 6,867 yuan, urban collectives; 11,178 yuan, state-owned enterprises; 12,140 yuan, other enterprises. There is a 6-day 48-hour working week. Minimum working age was fixed at 16 in 1991. There were 120,000 labour disputes in 1999, up from 8,000 in 1989.

Trade Unions. The All-China Federation of Trade Unions, founded in 1925, is headed by Wang Zhaoguo. In 2003 there were 103m. members. It consists of 31 federations of trade unions. Its National Congress convenes every five years.

INTERNATIONAL TRADE

Foreign debt was US$168,255m. in 2002.

There are five Special Economic Zones at Shenzhen, Xiamen, Zhuhai, Shantou and Hainan in which concessions are made to foreign businessmen. The Pudong New Area in Shanghai is also designated a special development area. Since 1979 joint ventures with foreign firms have been permitted. A law of April 1991 reduced taxation on joint ventures to 33%. There is no maximum limit on the foreign share of the holdings; the minimum limit is 25%.

In May 2000 the US granted normal trade relations to China, a progression after a number of years when China was accorded 'most favoured nation' status. China subsequently joined the World Trade Organization on 11 Dec. 2001.

Pearson, M. M., *Joint Ventures in the People's Republic of China: the Control of Foreign Direct Investment under Socialism.* Princeton Univ. Press, 1991

Imports and Exports. Trade in US$1m.:

	1997	*1998*	*1999*	*2000*	*2001*	*2002*
Imports f.o.b.	136,448	136,915	158,734	214,657	232,058	281,484
Exports f.o.b.	182,670	183,529	194,716	249,131	266,075	325,651

Major exports in 1999 (in US$1bn.): electrical machinery and equipment, 32·9; textiles and clothing, 27·3; power generation equipment, 19·1; footwear and parts thereof, 8·7; toys and games, 7·7; iron and steel, 6·4. Imports: electrical machinery and equipment, 35·2; power generation equipment, 27·8; plastics and articles thereof, 11·6; mineral fuels and oil, 8·9; iron and steel, 8·8; inorganic and organic chemicals, 6·5. Chinese exports have doubled in just over five years, largely thanks to foreign investment. China is now the world's largest importer of steel, having overtaken the USA in 2002.

Main export markets in 2000: USA, 33·2%; Hong Kong, 26·7%; Japan, 17·9%; Germany, 5·0%. Main import suppliers, 2000; Hong Kong, 21·8%; Japan, 18·6%; South Korea, 10·3%; USA, 9·6%. Customs duties with Taiwan were abolished in 1980. Trade with the European Union is fast expanding, having doubled since 1999.

COMMUNICATIONS

Roads. The total road length in 2002 was 1,765,000 km, including 25,000 km of expressways. 10,563m. tonnes of freight and 14,027m. persons were transported by road in 2001. The number of civil motor vehicles reached 18·02m., including 9·93m. buses and cars and 7·65m. trucks in 2001. There were 412,860 traffic accidents in 1999, with 83,529 fatalities.

Rail. In 2001 there were 70,100 km of railway including 22,600 km multiple-tracked and 17,000 km electrified. Gauge is standard except for some 600 mm track in Yunnan. Passenger-km travelled in 2001 came to 476·7bn. and freight tonne-km to 1,457·5bn. There are metro systems in Beijing, Guangzhou and Shanghai.

Civil Aviation. There are major international airports at Beijing, Shanghai (Hongqiao and Pu Dong airports) and Guangzhou (Baiyun). At the end of 2001 there were 139 airports for regular flights. The national and major airlines are state-owned, except Shanghai Airlines (75% municipality-owned, 25% private) and Shenzhen Airlines (private). The leading Chinese airlines operating scheduled services in 1999 were China Southern Airlines (13,266,700 passengers), China Eastern Airlines (8,253,100), Air China (6,521,200), China Southwest Airlines (4,507,600), China Northern Airlines (4,034,000), China Yunnan Airlines (3,018,500), China Northwest Airlines (2,882,500) and Xinjiang Airlines (1,361,400). Other Chinese airlines include Changan Airlines, China National Aviation, Fujian Airlines, Hainan Airlines, Shandong Airlines, Shanghai Airlines, Shanxi Airlines, Shenzhen Airlines, Sichuan Airlines and Xiamen Airlines.

In 1999 the busiest airport was Beijing, with 21,691,000 passengers (16,073,000 on domestic flights), followed by Guangzhou (Baiyun), with 12,791,000 passengers (11,527,000 on domestic flights) and Shanghai (Hongqiao), with 12,139,000 passengers (7,481,000 on domestic flights). By the end of 2001 China had a total of 1,143 scheduled flight routes, of which 1,009 were domestic air routes, reaching 130 cities, and 134 were international air routes, reaching 62 cities in 33 countries.

Shipping. In 2000 the merchant fleet consisted of 3,322 vessels (561 oil tankers), totalling 16·50m. GRT (oil tankers, 2·25m. GRT).

In 2001, 1,426m. tonnes of freight were handled in major coastal ports, including: Shanghai, 220·9m tonnes; Ningbo, 128·5m.; Guangzhou (Canton), 128·2m.; Tianjin, 113·7m.; Qinhuangdao, 113·0m.; Qingdao, 104·0m.; Dalian, 100·5m. Cargo traffic at Tianjin grew at an average annual rate of 17·3% between 1998 and 2002, the highest rate of growth of any port in the world over the same period. In 1993, 125·08m. tonnes of freight were carried. Shanghai handled 6·33m. 20-ft equivalent units (TEUs) in 2001, making it the world's fifth busiest container port in terms of number of containers handled. Construction began in 2002 on the 14·31bn. yuan Yangshan deep-water port that should make Shanghai the world's third busiest port. On completion in 2020 it is estimated that it will have a capacity of 13m. TEUs.

In Jan. 2001 the first legal direct shipping links between the Chinese mainland and Taiwanese islands in more than 50 years were inaugurated.

Inland waterways totalled 121,500 km in 2001. 1,326·7m. tonnes of freight and 186·45m. passengers were carried. In June 2003 the Three Gorges Reservoir on the Chang Jiang River, the largest water control project in the world, reached sufficient depth to support the resumption of passenger and cargo shipping.

Telecommunications. In 2003 there were 263·0m. main telephone lines (209·2 per 1,000 persons) and 269·0m. mobile phone subscribers (214·0 per 1,000 persons), making China the biggest market for both fixed-line users and mobile phones in the world. The two main mobile operators are China Mobile and China Unicom. The main landline operators are China Telecom and China Netcom. There were 59·1m. Internet users in 2002. At the beginning of 1998 there had only been around 500,000 users. By 2007 Chinese is expected to have overtaken English as the most-used language on the Internet. In 2002, 35·5m. PCs were in use (27·6 per 1,000 inhabitants). There were 2m. fax machines in 1997.

Postal Services. There were 112,204 post offices in 1998. The use of *Pinyin* transcription of place names has been requested for mail to addresses in China (*e.g.*, 'Beijing' *not* 'Peking').

SOCIAL INSTITUTIONS

Justice. Six new codes of law (including criminal and electoral) came into force in 1980, to regularize the legal unorthodoxy of previous years. There is no provision for *habeas corpus*. The death penalty has been extended from treason and murder to include rape, embezzlement, smuggling, fraud, theft, drug-dealing, bribery and robbery with violence. There were 3,400 reported executions in 2004 (although there are believed to have been more). Nearly 90% of the recorded annual executions take place in China. 'People's courts' are divided into some 30 higher, 200 intermediate and 2,000 basic-level courts, and headed by the Supreme People's Court. The latter, the highest state judicial organ, tries cases, hears appeals and supervises the people's courts. It is responsible to the National People's Congress and its Standing Committee. People's courts are composed of a president, vice-presidents, judges and 'people's assessors' who are the equivalent of jurors. 'People's conciliation committees' are charged with settling minor disputes. There are also special military courts. Procuratorial powers and functions are exercised by the Supreme People's Procuracy and local procuracies.

The population in penal institutions in 2002 was 1,512,000 (117 per 100,000 of national population).

Religion. Non-religious persons account for 52% of the population. The government accords legality to five religions only: Buddhism, Islam, Protestantism, Roman Catholicism and Taoism. Confucianism, Buddhism and Taoism have long been practised. Confucianism has no ecclesiastical organization and appears rather as a philosophy of ethics and government. Taoism—of Chinese origin—copied Buddhist ceremonial soon after the arrival of Buddhism two millennia ago. Buddhism in return adopted many Taoist beliefs and practices. A more tolerant attitude towards religion had emerged by 1979, and the government's Bureau of Religious Affairs was reactivated.

Ceremonies of reverence to ancestors have been observed by the whole population regardless of philosophical or religious beliefs.

A new quasi-religious movement, Falun Gong, was founded in 1992, but has since been banned by the authorities. The movement claims it has some 100m. adherents, although the Chinese government has maintained the real number is closer to 2m.

Muslims are found in every province of China, being most numerous in the Ningxia-Hui Autonomous Region, Yunnan, Shaanxi, Gansu, Hebei, Honan, Shandong, Sichuan, Xinjiang and Shanxi. They totalled 18,360,000 in 2001.

Roman Catholicism has had a footing in China for more than three centuries. In 2002 there were an estimated 4m. Catholic believers, 4,000 clergy and 4,600 churches and meeting places. Catholics are members of the Patriotic Catholic Association, which declared its independence from Rome in 1958. Protestants are members of the All-China Conference of Protestant Churches. In 2002 they numbered 10m. There were an estimated 76,540,000 Christians in total in 2001.

In 2001 there were also estimated to be 256,260,000 Chinese folk-religionists, 152,990,000 atheists, 108,110,000 Buddhists and 1,280,000 advocates of traditional beliefs.

Legislation of 1994 prohibits foreign nationals from setting up religious organizations.

Education. An educational reform of 1985 planned to phase in compulsory nine-year education consisting of six years of primary schooling and three years of secondary schooling, to replace a previous five-year system.

In mainland China the 2000 population census revealed the following levels of educational attainment: 45·71m. people had finished university education; 141·09m. had received senior secondary education; 429·89m. had received junior secondary education; and 451·91m. had had primary education. 85·07m. people over 15 years of age or 6·72% of the population were illiterate, although this compared favourably with a 15·88% rate of illiteracy recorded in the 1990 census. In 2000 there were 175,836 kindergartens with 22·44m. children and 856,000 teachers; 553,662 primary schools with 130·13m. pupils and 5·86m. teachers; 89,763 secondary schools (of which: 14,564 senior secondary; 62,704 junior secondary; 3,646 specialized; and 8,849 vocational) with 83·61m. pupils and 4·48m. teachers. There were also 378,000 children at 1,539 special education schools. Institutes of higher education, including universities, numbered 1,225 in 2001, with 7·19m. students (a substantial increase from 5·56m. in 2000) and 532,000 teachers. A national system of student loans was established in 1999. Every year 25,000 Chinese go abroad to study, making it the largest exporter of students in the world.

There are more than 1,300 non-governmental private higher education institutions (including 12 private universities) with 1·5m. students, or 39% of the total college and university students nationwide.

There is an Academy of Sciences with provincial branches. An Academy of Social Sciences was established in 1977.

In 1999 total expenditure on education came to 334,904m. yuan; government appropriation was 228,717m. yuan.

Health. Medical treatment is free only for certain groups of employees, but where costs are incurred they are partly borne by the patient's employing organization.

At the end of 2001 there were 330,000 health institutions throughout China, with a total of 3·19m. beds. The 4·49m. health workers included 2·09m. doctors and 1·28m. senior and junior nurses. There were also 6,025 anti-epidemic and disease prevention stations with 220,000 health workers, and 2,539 maternal and child healthcare institutions with 80,000 health workers. Rural townships had 50,000 commune hospitals with 740,000 beds and 1·03m. health workers. 89·7% of villages across China had medical stations, employing 1·28m. rural doctors and health workers.

Approximately 1m. Chinese were HIV-infected in 2002. Some suggestions indicate that there may be as many as 10m. HIV-positive people by 2010.

In the first half of 2003 China was struck by an epidemic of a pneumonia-type virus identified as SARS (severe acute respiratory syndrome). The virus was first detected in southern China and was subsequently reported in over 30 other countries. According to the Ministry of Health, by the time the outbreak had been contained a total of 5,327 cases had been reported on the Chinese mainland; 4,959 patients were cured and discharged from hospital, and 349 died.

In 1996 some 62% of males smoked, but fewer than 4% of females. The rate among males has been gradually rising over the past 15 years whilst that among females has gradually gone down.

In 2001 approximately 142m. people, then representing 11% of the population, were undernourished. In 1979, 22% of the population had been undernourished.

Welfare. In 2000 there were 42,103 social welfare institutions with 843,000 inmates. Numbers (in 1,000) of beneficiaries of relief funds: persons in poor rural households,

16,676; in poor urban households, 1,556; persons in rural households entitled to 'the five guarantees' (food, clothing, medical care, housing, education for children or funeral expenses), 2,706; retired, laid-off or disabled workers, 497. The major relief funds (in 1,000 yuan) in 2000 were: families of deceased or disabled servicemen, 10,766,050; poor households, 1,648,260; orphaned, disabled, old and young persons, 1,957,370; urban and rural welfare homes (1999), 2,866,620.

CULTURE

Beijing will host the Olympic Games in 2008, from 8 to 24 Aug. Shanghai will be hosting Expo 2010.

World Heritage Sites. There are 30 sites in the People's Republic of China that appear on the UNESCO World Heritage List. They are (with year entered on list): the Great Wall of China (1987), Zhoukoudian, the Peking Man site (1987), Beijing imperial palaces (1987), mausoleum of first Qing dynasty emperor, Beijing (1987), Taishan mountain (1987), Mogao Caves (1987), Huangshan mountain (1990), Huanglong Scenic Reserve (1992), Jiuzhaigou National Reserve (1992), Wulingyuan Scenic Reserve (1992), Chengde summer palace and temples (1994), Potala palace, Lhasa (1994), Wudang mountain (1994), Qufu temple, cemetery and mansion of Confucius (1994), the Leshan Buddha (1996), Mount Emei Scenic Reserve (1996), Lijiang old town (1997), Ping Yao old town (1997), Suzhou classical gardens (1997), Summer Palace, Beijing (1998), Temple of Heaven, Beijing (1998), Mount Wuyi (1999), Dazu rock carvings (1999), Mount Qincheng and Dujiangyan irrigation system (2000), Xidi and Hongcun ancient villages, Anhui (2000), Longmen grottoes (2000), Ming and Qing dynasty tombs (2000), the Yungang Grottoes (2001), the Three Parallel Rivers of Yunnan Protected Areas (2003) and the Capital Cities and Tombs of the Ancient Koguryo Kingdom (2004).

Broadcasting. In 2000 there were 370m. television receivers in China (the greatest number in any country in the world). In 1980 there had been just 9m., representing an increase of 361m. between 1980 and 2000, or more TV sets than were in use in the USA (the country with the second highest number of sets) in 2000. At the end of 2001 there were 358 TV stations, offering programmes to 94·1% of the total population. China Central Television, the largest national station, features 11 channels with a daily air time of more than 200 hours. Cable TV subscribers numbered 88·03m. by the end of 2001 (compared to 50m. in 1997). There were 311 radio broadcasting stations and 770 medium- and short-wave transmitting and relaying stations throughout China at the end of 2001, reaching 92·9% of the population. The Central People's Broadcasting Station, the official radio broadcasting station, has seven channels (including services to Taiwan) and broadcasts for over 100 hours a day. In 2000 there were 428m. radio receivers (only the USA has more).

Cinema. There were 4,639 cinemas in 1995. A total of 88 feature films and 66 scientific, documentary and cartoon films were produced in 2001.

Press. China has two news agencies: Xinhua (New China) News Agency (the nation's official agency) and China News Service. In 2002 there were 2,137 newspapers and about 8,700 magazines; 21,600m. copies of newspapers and 2,900m. copies of magazines were published in 2001. In 1980 there were fewer than 400 newspapers. The Communist Party newspaper is *Renmin Ribao* (People's Daily), which had a daily circulation of 2·1m. in 1999. The most widely read newspaper is *Sichuan Ribao* (Sichuan Daily), with a daily circulation of 8·0m. in 1999. In July 2003 the State Administration of Press and Publication abolished compulsory subscription to state newspapers and magazines and funding for subscription-dependent publications, which amount to 40% of the press. By Nov. 2003, 673 newspapers had ceased publication.

There are over 560 publishing houses, producing 6,300m. volumes of books in 2001.

Tourism. 31,229,000 tourists visited in 2000. The World Tourism Organization predicts that China will overtake France as the world's most visited destination by 2020 and become the world's fourth most important source of tourists to other countries. More than 16·5m. Chinese travelled abroad in 2002, nearly double the 1998 figure. Income from tourists in 2000 was US$16,231m.

Festivals. The lunar New Year, also known as the 'Spring Festival', is a time of great excitement for the Chinese people. The festivities get under way 22 days prior to the New Year date and continue for 15 days afterwards. Dates of the lunar New Year: Year of the Rooster, 9 Feb. 2005; Year of the Dog, 29 Jan. 2006. Lantern Festival, or Yuanxiao Jie, is an important, traditional Chinese festival, which is on the 15th of the first month of the Chinese New Year. Guanyin's Birthday is on the 19th day of the second month of the Chinese lunar calendar. Guanyin is the Chinese goddess of mercy. Tomb Sweeping Day, as the name implies, is a day for visiting and cleaning the ancestral tomb and usually falls on 5 April. Dragon Boat Festival is called Duan Wu Jie in Chinese. The festival is celebrated on the 5th of the 5th month of the Chinese lunar calendar. The Moon Festival is on the 15th of the 8th lunar month. It is sometimes called Mid-Autumn Festival. The Moon Festival is an occasion for family reunion.

Libraries. At the end of 2001 there were 2,689 public libraries. The National Library of China, with 22m. items, is the largest library in Asia. Shanghai library is China's biggest provincial-level library.

Museums and Galleries. There were 1,394 museums in 2001, of which 118 were in Beijing.

DIPLOMATIC REPRESENTATIVES

Of China in the United Kingdom (49–51 Portland Pl., London, W1B 1JL)
Ambassador: Zha Peixin.

Of the United Kingdom in China (11 Guang Hua Lu, Jian Guo Men Wai, Beijing 100600)
Ambassador: Sir Christopher Hum, KCMG.

Of China in the USA (2300 Connecticut Ave., NW, Washington, D.C. 20008)
Ambassador: Yang Jiechi.

Of the USA in China (Xiu Shui Bei Jie 3, 100600 Beijing)
Ambassador: Clark T. Randt, Jr.

Of China to the United Nations
Ambassador: Wang Guangya.

Of China to the European Union
Ambassador: Guan Chengyuan.

FURTHER READING

State Statistical Bureau. *China Statistical Yearbook*
China Directory [in Pinyin and Chinese]. Tokyo, annual
Adshead, S. A. M., *China in World History.* Macmillan, London, 1999
Baum, R., *Burying Mao: Chinese Politics in the Age of Deng Xiaoping.* Princeton Univ. Press, 1994
Becker, Jasper, *The Chinese.* John Murray, London, 2000
Brown, Raj, *Overseas Chinese Merchants.* Macmillan, London, 1999
The Cambridge Encyclopaedia of China. 2nd ed. CUP, 1991
The Cambridge History of China. 14 vols. CUP, 1978 ff.
Chang, David Wen-Wei and Chuang, Richard Y., *The Politics of Hong Kong's Reversion to China.* Macmillan, London, 1999
Cook, Sarah, Yao, Shujie and Zhuang, Juzhong, (eds.) *The Chinese Economy Under Transition.* Macmillan, London, 1999
De Crespigny, R., *China This Century.* 2nd ed. OUP, 1993
Dixin, Xu and Chengming, Wu, (eds.) *Chinese Capitalism, 1522–1840.* Macmillan, London, 1999
Dreyer, J. T., *China's Political System: Modernization and Tradition.* 2nd ed. London, 1996
Evans, R., *Deng Xiaoping and the Making of Modern China.* London, 1993
Fairbank, J. K., *The Great Chinese Revolution 1800–1985.* London, 1987.—*China: a New History.* Harvard Univ. Press, 1992
Glassman, R. M., *China in Transition: Communism, Capitalism and Democracy.* New York, 1991
Goldman, M., *Sowing the Seeds of Democracy in China: Political Reform in the Deng Xiaoping Era.* Harvard Univ. Press, 1994
Hayford, C. W., *China.* [Bibliography] ABC-Clio, Oxford and Santa Barbara (CA), 1997
Ho, Samuel P. S. and Kueh, Y. Y. (eds.) *Sustainable Economic Development in South China.* Macmillan, London, 1999

Huang, R., *China: a Macro History.* 2nd ed. Armonk (NY), 1997
Hunter, A. and Sexton, J., *Contemporary China.* Macmillan, London, 1999
Kruger, Rayne, *All Under Heaven: A Complete History of China.* John Wiley, Chichester, 2004
Lieberthal, K. G., *From Revolution through Reform.* New York, 1995.—and Lampton, D. M. (eds.) *Bureaucracy, Politics and Decision-Making in Post-Mao China.* California Univ. Press, 1992
Lu, Aiguo, *China and the Global Economy Since 1840.* Macmillan, London, 1999
Ma, Jun, *Chinese Economy in the 1990s.* Macmillan, London, 1999
MacFarquhar, R. (ed.) *The Politics of China: the Eras of Mao and Deng.* 2nd ed. CUP, 1997.—*The Origins of the Cultural Revolution.* 3 vols. Columbia Univ. Press, 1998
Mackerras, C. and Yorke, A., *The Cambridge Handbook of Contemporary China.* CUP, 1991
Mok, Ka-Ho, *Social and Political Development in Post-Reform China.* Macmillan, London, 1999
Nolan, Peter, *China and the Global Economy.* Palgrave, Basingstoke, 2001
Phillips, R. T., *China Since 1911.* London, 1996
Roberts, J. A. G., *A History of China.* Palgrave, Basingstoke, 2001
Saich, Tony, *Governance and Politics of China.* 2nd ed. Palgrave Macmillan, Basingstoke, 2004
Schram, S. (ed.) *Mao's Road to Power: Revolutionary Writings 1912–1949.* 4 vols. Harvard, 1998
Shen, Xiobai, *The Chinese Road to High Technology.* Macmillan, London, 1999
Sheng Hua, *et al., China: from Revolution to Reform.* London, 1992
Shirk, S. L., *The Political Logic of Economic Reform in China.* Univ. of California Press, 1993
Short, Philip, *Mao: A Life.* Henry Holt, New York and Hodder and Stoughton, London, 2000
Spence, Jonathan, D., *The Chan's Great Continent: China in Western Minds.* W. W. Norton, New York, 1998.—*Mao Zedong.* Viking, New York and Weidenfeld & Nicolson, London, 2000
Suyin, H., *Eldest Son, Zhou Enlai and The Making of Modern China.* Kodansha Globe, 1995
Turner, Barry, (ed.) *China Profiled.* Macmillan, London, 1999
Womack, B. (ed.) *Contemporary Chinese Politics in Historical Perspective.* CUP, 1992
Yan, Yanni, *International Joint Ventures in China.* Macmillan, London, 1999
Yeung, Henry Wai-Cheung and Olds, Kristopher, (eds.) *The Globalisation of Chinese Business Firms.* Macmillan, London, 1999
Zhang, Xiao-Guang, *China's Trade Patterns and International Comparative Advantage.* Macmillan, London, 1999

Other more specialized titles are listed under TERRITORY AND POPULATION; TIBET; AGRICULTURE; INTERNATIONAL TRADE.

National statistical office: National Bureau of Statistics, 75 Yuetan Nanjie, Beijing 100826.
Website: http://www.stats.gov.cn/

HONG KONG

Xianggang

KEY HISTORICAL EVENTS

Hong Kong island and the southern tip of the Kowloon peninsula were ceded in perpetuity to the British Crown in 1841 and 1860 respectively. The area lying immediately to the north of Kowloon known as the New Territories was leased to Britain for 99 years in 1898. Talks began in Sept. 1982 between Britain and China over the future of Hong Kong after the lease expiry in 1997. On 19 Dec. 1984 the two countries signed a Joint Declaration by which Hong Kong became, with effect from 1 July 1997, a Special Administrative Region of the People's Republic of China enjoying a high degree of autonomy, and vested with executive, legislative and independent judicial power, including that of final adjudication. The existing social and economic systems were to remain unchanged for another 50 years. This 'one country, two systems' principle, embodied in the Basic Law, became the constitution for the Hong Kong Special Administrative Region of the People's Republic of China.

TERRITORY AND POPULATION

Hong Kong ('Xianggang' in Mandarin *Pinyin*) island is situated off the southern coast of the Chinese mainland 32 km east of the mouth of the Pearl River. The area of the island is 79·99 sq. km. It is separated from the mainland by a fine natural harbour. On the opposite side is the peninsula of Kowloon (46·27 sq. km). Total area of the Territory is 1,091 sq. km, a large part of it being steep and unproductive hillside. Country parks and special areas cover over 40% of the land area. Since 1945 the government has reclaimed over 5,400 ha from the sea, principally from the seafronts of Hong Kong and Kowloon, facing the harbour. The 'New Territories' are on the mainland, north of Kowloon.

Based on the results of the 2001 population census Hong Kong's resident population in March 2001 was 6,708,389 and the population density 6,237 per sq. km. 59·7% of the population was born in Hong Kong, 33·7% in other parts of China and 6·6% in the rest of the world.

In 2001, 100% of the population lived in urban areas. Some 10,600 persons emigrated in 2001. The British Nationality Scheme enables persons to acquire citizenship without leaving Hong Kong. There were 53,655 legal entrants (one-way permit holders) from the mainland of China in 2001.

The UN gives a projected population for 2010 of 7·54m.

The official languages are Chinese and English.

SOCIAL STATISTICS

Annual population growth rate, 2001, 0·9%. Vital statistics, 2001: known births, 48,200; known deaths, 33,400; registered marriages, 32,800. Rates (per 1,000): birth, 7·2; death, 5·0; marriage, 4·8; infant mortality, 2001, 2·6 per 1,000 live births (one of the lowest rates in the world). Expectation of life at birth, 2001: males, 78·4 years; females, 84·6. The median age for marrying in 2001 was 31·3 years for males and 28·1 for females. Total fertility rate, 2001, 0·9 child per woman.

CLIMATE

The climate is sub-tropical, tending towards temperate for nearly half the year, the winter being cool and dry and the summer hot and humid, May to Sept. being the wettest months. Normal temperatures are Jan. 60°F (15·8°C), July 84°F (28·8°C). Annual rainfall 87" (2,214·3 mm).

THE BRITISH ADMINISTRATION

Hong Kong used to be administered by the Hong Kong government. The Governor was the head of government and presided over the *Executive Council*, which advised the Governor on all important matters. The last British Governor was Chris Patten. In Oct. 1996 the Executive Council consisted of three *ex officio* members and ten appointed members, of whom one was an official member. The chief functions of the *Legislative Council* were to enact laws, control public expenditure and put questions to the administration on matters of public interest. The Legislative Council elected in Sept. 1995 was, for the first time, constituted solely by election. It comprised 60 members, of whom 20 were elected from geographical constituencies, 30 from functional constituencies encompassing all eligible persons in a workforce of 2·9m., and ten from an election committee formed by members of 18 district boards. A president was elected from and by the members.

At the elections on 17 Sept. 1995 turn-out for the geographical seats was 35·79%, and for the functional seats (21 of which were contested), 40·42%. The Democratic Party and its allies gained 29 seats, the Liberal Party 10 and the pro-Beijing Democratic Alliance 6. The remaining seats went to independents.

CONSTITUTION AND GOVERNMENT

In Dec. 1995 the Standing Committee of China's National People's Congress set up a Preparatory Committee of 150 members (including 94 from Hong Kong) to oversee the retrocession of Hong Kong to China on 1 July 1997. In Nov. 1996 the Preparatory Committee nominated a 400-member Selection Committee to select the Chief Executive of Hong Kong and a provisional legislature to replace the Legislative Council. The Selection Committee was composed of Hong Kong residents, with 60 seats reserved for delegates to the National People's Congress and appointees of the People's Political Consultative Conference. On 11 Dec. 1996 Tung Chee Hwa was elected Chief Executive by 80% of the Selection Committee's votes.

On 21 Dec. 1996 the Selection Committee selected a provisional legislature which began its activities in Jan. 1997 while the Legislative Council was still functioning. In Jan. 1997 the provisional legislature started its work by enacting legislation which would be applicable to the Hong Kong Special Administrative Region and compatible with the Basic Law.

Constitutionally Hong Kong is a Special Administrative Region of the People's Republic of China. The Basic Law enables Hong Kong to retain a high degree of autonomy. It provides that the legislative, judicial and administrative systems which were previously in operation are to remain in place. The Special Administrative Region Government is also empowered to decide on Hong Kong's monetary and economic policies independent of China.

In July 1997 the first-past-the-post system of returning members from geographical constituencies to the Legislative Council was replaced by proportional representation. There were 20 directly elected seats out of 60 for the first elections to the Legislative Council following Hong Kong's return to Chinese sovereignty, increasing in accordance with the Basic Law to 24 for the 2000 election with 36 indirectly elected. In the Sept. 2004 Legislative Council election 30 of the 60 seats were directly elected.

In July 2002 a new accountability or 'ministerial' system was introduced, under which the Chief Executive nominates for appointment 14 policy secretaries, who report directly to the Chief Executive. The Chief Executive is aided by the Executive Council, consisting of the three senior Secretaries of Department (the Chief Secretary, the Financial Secretary and the Secretary for Justice) and eleven other secretaries plus five non-officials.

RECENT ELECTIONS

In the Legislative Council election held on 12 Sept. 2004 turn-out was 55·6%, up from 43·6% at the 2000 vote. 30 of the 60 seats were directly elected, the other 30 being returned by committees and professional associations. Pro-Beijing parties won 34 of the 60 seats (34 in 2000) including 12 of the 30 that were directly elected; pro-democracy parties won 25 (22 in 2000), including 18 of the 30 that were directly elected. An independent won the remaining seat (independents won four seats in 2000).

CURRENT ADMINISTRATION

In March 2005 the government of the Hong Kong Special Administrative Region comprised:

Chief Executive (acting) and Chief Secretary for Administration: Donald Tsang, OBE, JP; b. 1944 (since 12 March 2005).

Financial Secretary: Henry Tang, JP. *Secretary for Justice:* Elsie Leung Oi-sie, JP. *Commerce, Industry and Technology:* John Tsang Chun-wah, JP. *Housing, Planning and Lands:* Michael Suen. *Education and Manpower:* Arthur Li. *Health, Welfare and Food:* York Chow. *Civil Service:* Joseph Wong. *Home Affairs:* Dr Patrick Ho. *Security:* Ambrose Lee. *Economic Development and Labour:* Stephen Ip Shu-kwan. *Environment, Transport and Works:* Dr Sarah Liao. *Financial Services and the Treasury:* Frederick Ma Si-hang. *Constitutional Affairs:* Stephen Lam, JP.

Government Website: http://www.info.gov.hk

ECONOMY

Industry accounted for 12·4% of GDP in 2002 and services 87·5%.

According to the anti-corruption organization *Transparency International*, Hong Kong ranked 16th in the world in a 2004 survey of the countries and regions with the least corruption in business and government. It received 8·0 out of 10 in the annual index.

Income tax is a flat 15% and only 25% of the population pay any tax at all. 6% of the population pays 80% of the total income tax bill. Hong Kong represents 20% of China's total worth.

Overview. The economy witnessed a prolonged economic downturn between 1997 and 2003. In this period the economy experienced three recessions and suffered three major shocks. Between 1997–98 it was hit by the Asian financial crisis, between 2001–02 the economy suffered from the US-led global economic downturn and in 2003 outbreaks of SARS dampened economic growth. The financial system has remained resilient in the face of external shocks. Hong Kong's banking system and financial markets are the third largest in the Asia-Pacific region and Hong Kong is the region's most open economy. Property prices have fallen since the bursting of the property price bubble and between 1999–2003 the economy experienced asset price deflation, weak import prices and consumer price deflation, a reflection of weak demand. The unemployment rate reached record levels in mid-2002. The fiscal balance was in surplus between 1985–97 but gradually deteriorated after 1998, leading to consolidated deficits of 5% of GDP in 2001.

Currency. The unit of currency is the *Hong Kong dollar* (HKD) of 100 *cents*. Banknotes are issued by the Hongkong and Shanghai Banking Corporation and the Standard Chartered Bank, and, from May 1994, the Bank of China. Total money supply was HK$216,760m. in May 2002. In June 2002 gold reserves were 67,000 troy oz and in Feb. 1998 foreign exchange reserves US$112,335m. (US$55,398m. in 1995). Hong Kong has been experiencing deflation every year since 1999. There was deflation of 3·0% in 2002 and 2·6% in 2003.

Budget. The total government revenue and expenditure for financial years ending 31 March were as follows (in HK$1m.):

	1998	*1999*	*2000*	*2001*	*2002*
Revenue[1]	281,226	216,115	232,995	225,060	175,559
Expenditure[2]	194,241	218,811	214,533	224,791	238,585

[1]Including the change in the net worth of investments up to 31 Oct. 1998.
[2]Excluding Capital Investment Fund.

Public expenditure in 2002 (based on revised estimates 2001–02) was divided as follows (HK$1bn.): education, 52·6; support, 35·7; health, 34·0; housing, 33·2; social welfare, 30·7; security, 28·1; infrastructure, 24·7; economic, 14·1; environment and food, 11·3; community and external affairs, 8·5.

The final reserve balance as at 31 March 2002 was HK$372·5bn.

Performance. Total GDP was US$158,596m. in 2003. Following real GDP growth of 5·1% in 1997, the economy contracted in 1998 by 5·0%, representing Hong Kong's most severe recession since the 1970s. There was then growth of 3·4% in 1999 and 10·2% in 2000, including 14·1% in the first quarter of 2000. GDP growth was only 0·6% in 2001, but then 2·3% in 2002.

Banking and Finance. The Hong Kong Monetary Authority acts as a central bank. The *Chief Executive* is Joseph Yam. As at Dec. 2003 there were 133 banks licensed under the Banking Ordinance, of which 26 were locally incorporated, 46 restricted licence banks, 45 deposit-taking companies and 94 representative offices of foreign banks. Licensed bank deposits were HK$2,601,971m. in June 1997; restricted licence bank deposits were HK$62,033m. There are three banks of issue: Bank of China (Hong Kong); The Hong Kong and Shanghai Banking Corporation; and Standard Chartered Bank.

In March 2000 the stock exchange, the futures exchange and the clearing settlement merged into Hong Kong Exchanges and Clearing (HKEx). The summer of 1997 saw record highs on the Hang Seng index (16,365 in July 1997 compared with 10,681 in July 1996). In July 1997 the average daily turnover was HK$19,500m.

Weights and Measures. The metric system is standard but British Imperial and traditional Chinese measurements are still in use.

ENERGY AND NATURAL RESOURCES

Environment. Hong Kong's carbon dioxide emissions from the consumption and flaring of fossil fuels in 2002 were the equivalent of 8·8 tonnes per capita.

Electricity. Installed capacity was 11·6m. kW in 2000. Production in 2000 was 31·33bn. kWh. Consumption in 2000 was 40·35bn. kWh.

Water. There are 17 impounding reservoirs with a total capacity of 586m. cu. metres. Raw water is also purchased from the Guangdong Province of China (729m. cu. metres in 2001). Consumption in 2001 was 940m. cu. metres.

Agriculture. The local agricultural industry is directed towards the production of high quality fresh food through intensive land use and modern farming techniques. Out of the territory's total land area of 1,097 sq. km, only 27 sq. km is currently farmed. In 1999 local production accounted for 11·7% of fresh vegetables, 18·2% of live poultry and 22·2% of live pigs consumed. Pig production increased by about 17% compared with the previous year. Crop production continued to fall as vegetable prices fell and land was redeveloped for other uses. The common crops cultivated are leafy vegetables, high value cut flowers and ornamental plants. In 1999, 48,000 tonnes of vegetables were produced. Poultry production was 12,650 tonnes. There were 415,400 pigs in 1999.

Forestry. Timber production in 1995 was 200,000 cu. metres.

Fisheries. In 1999 the capture and mariculture fisheries supplied about 36% of seafood consumed in Hong Kong and pond fish farm produced about 10% of the freshwater fish consumed. The capture fishing industry employs some 5,170 fishing vessels and some 12,900 local fishermen. In 2001 the industry produced an estimated 173,972 tonnes of fisheries produce. Some 75,000 tonnes were supplied for local consumption and the remainder landed or exported outside Hong Kong. On the other hand, there are 26 fish culture zones occupying a total sea area of 209 ha with some 1,450 licensed operators. The estimated production in 1999 was 1,250 tonnes, or 7% of local consumption of live marine fish. The inland fish ponds, covering a total of 1,094 ha, produced 4,500 of freshwater fish in 1999. The first phase of the artificial reefs programme was successfully completed in 1999 with more than 110 species of fish recorded on the reefs.

INDUSTRY

The leading companies by market capitalization in Hong Kong, excluding banking and finance, in May 2004 were: Hutchison Whampoa (US$28·4bn.), a diversified industrial conglomerate; Sun Hung Kai Properties (US$20·5bn.), a real estate company; and Cheung Kong Holdings (US$17·4bn.), also a real estate company.

An economic policy based on free enterprise and free trade, a skilled workforce, an efficient commercial infrastructure, the modern and efficient sea-port (including container shipping terminals) and airport facilities, a geographical position relative to markets in North America and traditional trading links with the UK all contribute to Hong Kong's success as a modern industrial territory. Links with China have been growing increasingly strong in recent years and will remain so.

In Sept. 2001 there were 19,801 manufacturing establishments employing 209,329 persons. Other establishment statistics by product type (and persons engaged) were: printing, publishing and allied industries, 4,778 (42,963); textiles and clothing, 3,696 (58,821); plastics, 973 (5,938); electronics, 748 (20,939); watches and clocks, 347 (2,945); shipbuilding, 325 (3,173); electrical appliances, 49 (390).

Labour. In 2001 the size of the labour force (synonymous with the economically active population) was 3,427,100 (1,461,900 females). The persons engaged in Sept. 2001 included 1,027,000 people in wholesale, retail and import/export trades, restaurants and hotels, 437,000 in finance, insurance, real estate and business services, 209,000 in manufacturing, 177,000 in the civil service and 77,000 in construction sites (manual workers only).

The seasonally-adjusted unemployment rate for July–Sept. 2002 was 7·4%, compared to the equivalent rate for July–Sept. 1997 of 2·1%.

EXTERNAL ECONOMIC RELATIONS

Imports and Exports. Industry is mainly export-oriented. In 2001 the total value of imports (c.i.f.) was HK$1,586·2bn. and total exports (f.o.b.) HK$1,481·0bn. In 2001, 36·9% of total exports went to the mainland of China, 22·3% to the USA, 5·9% to Japan, 3·7% to the United Kingdom and 3·5% to Germany. The main suppliers of imports were the mainland of China (43·5%), Japan (11·3%), Taiwan (6·9%), USA (6·7%) and Singapore (4·6%).

In 2001 domestic exports included (in HK$1m.): clothing and accessories, 72,240; electrical machinery and parts, 20,322; textiles and fabrics, 8,193; parts and accessories suitable for use solely with office machines and automatic data processing machines, 4,705. The chief import items were consumer goods (537,967), raw materials and semi-manufactures (511,367), capital goods (428,147) and foodstuffs (60,353).

Visible trade normally carries an adverse balance which is offset by a favourable balance of invisible trade, in particular transactions in connection with air transportation, shipping, tourism and banking services.

Hong Kong has a free exchange market. Foreign merchants may remit profits or repatriate capital. Import and export controls are kept to the minimum, consistent with strategic requirements.

COMMUNICATIONS

Roads. In 1998 there were 1,865 km of roads, more than 900 km of which were in the New Territories. There are eight major road tunnels, including two under Victoria Harbour. In 1999 there were 390,000 passenger cars, 116,000 trucks and vans, 19,000 buses and coaches, and 33,000 motorcycles and mopeds. There were 14,714 road accidents in 1999, 217 fatal. A total of 14·8m. tonnes of cargo were transported by road in 1996.

Rail. The railway network covers around 143 km. The electrified Kowloon-Canton Railway runs for 34 km from the terminus at Hung Hom in Kowloon to the border point at Lo Wu. It carried 255m. passengers in 1998. In 1996, 939,000 tonnes of cargo were transported by rail. A light rail system (32 km and 57 stops) is operated by the Kowloon-Canton Railway Corporation in Tuen Mun, Yuen Long and Tin Shui Wai; it carried 105m. passengers in 1998.

The electric tramway on the northern shore of Hong Kong Island commenced operating in 1904 and has a total track length of 16 km. The Peak Tram, a funicular railway connecting the Peak district with the lower levels in Victoria, has a track length of 1,365 metres and a capacity of 120 passengers per trip.

A metro, the Mass Transit Railway system, comprises 74 km with 43 stations and carried 2·3m. passengers per weekday in 1998.

The Airport Express Line (35 km) opened in 1998 and carried a total of 3·9m. passengers in that year.

In 1996 a total of 3·9m. passenger journeys were made on public transport (including local railways, buses, etc.).

Civil Aviation. The new Chek Lap Kok airport, built on reclaimed land off Lantau Island to the west of Hong Kong, opened on 6 July 1998, replacing Hong Kong International Airport (Kai Tak), which was situated on the north shore of Kowloon Bay. More than 70 airlines now operate scheduled services to and from Hong Kong. Cathay Pacific Airways, one of the three Hong Kong-based airlines, operates more than 530 passenger and cargo services weekly to Europe (including 18 passenger and 10 cargo services per week to the UK), the Far and Middle East, South Africa, Australasia and North America. Cathay Pacific flew 197·6m. km in 1999 and carried 12,321,256 passengers in 2002. Hong Kong Dragon Airlines provides scheduled services to 19 cities in Mainland China and nine other destinations in Asia plus 14 cargo services per week to seven destinations (including six weekly services to the UK). AHK Air Hong Kong Ltd., an all-cargo operator, provides seven weekly scheduled services to and from Hong Kong with Incheon, Tokyo and Osaka as destinations. In 2002 (provisional figures), 206,640 aircraft arrived and departed and 33m. passengers and 2·48m. tonnes of freight were carried on aircraft. Hong Kong International Airport handled more international freight in 2001 than any other airport.

Hong Kong–Taipei and vice-versa is the most flown airline route in the world, with 5·43m. passengers flying between the two cities in 2001.

Shipping. The port of Hong Kong handled 17·8m. 20-ft equivalent units in 2001, making it the world's busiest container port. The Kwai Chung Container Port has 18 berths with 5,754 metres of quay backed by 217 ha of cargo handling area. Merchant shipping in 2002 totalled 16,164,000 GRT, including oil tankers 2,450,000 GRT. In 2001, 37,350 ocean-going vessels, 116,190 river cargo vessels and 61,200 river passenger vessels called at Hong Kong. In 2001, 178m. tonnes of freight were handled. In 2002 vessels totalling 372,415,000 NRT entered ports and vessels totalling 372,574,000 NRT cleared.

Telecommunications. In Dec. 2001 there were 4,940,525 telephones (731 per 1,000 population), of which 1,764,623 were for business use and 2,161,151 were residential lines. There were also 411,099 fax lines.

The local fixed telecommunications network services (FTNS) market in Hong Kong was liberalized in 1995. Apart from the incumbent FTNS operator at that time, three new local FTNS operators were licensed. In July 1999 the Government invited the industry to apply for licences to operate local wireless fixed networks. On 18 Jan. 2000 the Government announced that five licences for the local fixed wireless FTNS services would be provided. This would further increase the choice of consumers in the local fixed market.

In Dec. 2000 there were six mobile phone operators providing 11 networks in Hong Kong. There were only 687,600 mobile phone subscribers in 1995, since when the sector has expanded substantially. In 2002 there were 6,395,700 mobile phone subscribers (94% of Hong Kong's population). In addition there were 29 radio paging operators in Nov. 2000 serving 333,990 users. The Internet market has also seen considerable growth. In April 2002 there were 4·35m. Internet users, up from 1·85m. in June 2000.

The external telecommunications services market has been fully liberalized since 1 Jan. 1999, and the external telecommunications facilities market was also liberalized starting from 1 Jan. 2000.

In 2002 there were 2·86m. PCs in use (422·9 per 1,000 persons).

Postal Services. In Dec. 2002 there were 131 post offices. In 2001 Hongkong Post handled 1,360m. letters and 923,000 parcels.

SOCIAL INSTITUTIONS

Justice. The Hong Kong Act of 1985 provided for Hong Kong ordinances to replace English laws in specified fields.

The courts of justice comprise the Court of Final Appeal (inaugurated 1 July 1997) which hears appeals on civil and criminal matters from the High Court; the High Court (consisting of the Court of Appeal and the Court of First Instance); the Lands Tribunal which determines on statutory claims for compensation over land and certain landlord and tenant matters; the District Court (which includes the Family Court); the Magistracies (including the Juvenile Court); the Coroner's Court; the Labour Tribunal, which provides a quick and inexpensive method of settling disputes between employers and employees; the Small Claims Tribunal deals with monetary claims involving amounts not exceeding HK$50,000; and the Obscene Articles Tribunal.

While the High Court has unlimited jurisdiction in both civil and criminal matters, the District Court has limited jurisdiction. The maximum term of imprisonment it may impose is seven years. Magistracies exercise criminal jurisdiction over a wide range of offences, and the powers of punishment are generally restricted to a maximum of two years' imprisonment or a fine of HK$100,000.

After being in abeyance for 25 years, the death penalty was abolished in 1992.

71,962 crimes were reported in 1998, of which 14,682 were violent crimes. 40,422 people were arrested in 1998, of whom 9,207 were for violent crimes. The prison population was 12,900 in Sept. 2003 (184 per 100,000 of national population).

Religion. In 2001 there were 4,970,000 Buddhists and Taoists, 290,000 Protestants and 280,000 Roman Catholics. The remainder of the population are followers of other religions.

Education. Adult literacy was 93·5% in 2001 (96·9% among males and 89·6% among females). Universal basic education is available to all children aged from six to 15 years. In around three-quarters of the ordinary secondary day schools teaching has been in Cantonese since 1998–99, with about a quarter of ordinary secondary day schools still using English. In 1998 there were 175,073 pupils in 744 kindergartens (all private), 476,802 full-time students in 832 ordinary primary day schools (some 10·7% in private schools) and 455,872 in 37 government, 352 aided and 82 private ordinary secondary day schools.

There were 15,204 full-time and 32,543 part-time students enrolled in the seven Technical Institutes in the academic year 1998–99, and 5,220 full-time and 9,454 part-time students enrolled in the two Technical Colleges. The Hong Kong Technical Institutes and the Hong Kong Technical Colleges were renamed the Hong Kong Institute of Vocational Education in 1999.

The University of Hong Kong (founded 1911) had 10,687 full-time and 2,985 part-time students in the academic year of 1998–99, the Chinese University of Hong Kong (founded 1963), 10,271 full-time and 2,224 part-time students, the Hong Kong University of Science and Technology (founded 1991), 6,446 full-time and 710 part-time students, the Hong Kong Polytechnic University (founded 1972 as the Hong Kong Polytechnic), 11,646 full-time and 6,778 part-time students, the City University of Hong Kong (founded 1984 as the City Polytechnic of Hong Kong), 11,123 full-time and 5,241 part-time students, the Hong Kong Baptist University (founded 1956 as the Hong Kong Baptist College), 4,185 full-time and 517 part-time students, the Lingnan University (founded 1967 as the Lingnan College), 2,133 full-time and three part-time students, and the Hong Kong Institute of Education (founded 1997), 3,037 full-time and 5,954 part-time students.

Estimated total government expenditure on education in 1999–2000 was HK$55·2bn. In 2000–01 total expenditure on education came to 4·0% of GNP and 22·9% of total government spending.

Health. The Department of Health (DH) is the Government's health adviser and regulatory authority. The Hospital Authority (HA) is an independent body responsible for the management of all public hospitals. In 2002 there were 9,021 doctors on the local list, equivalent to 1·5 doctors per 1,000 population. In 2001 there were 1,900 dentists, 42,000 nurses and 136 midwives. In 2002 the total number of hospital beds was 35,100, including 29,432 beds in 41 public hospitals under the HA and 2,928 beds in 12 private hospitals. The bed-population ratio was 5·2 beds per thousand population.

The Chinese Medicine Ordinance was passed by the Legislative Council in July 1999 to establish a statutory framework to control the practice, use, manufacture and trading of Chinese medicine.

Recurrent spending on health amounts to US$4·15bn. (HK$324bn.), an increase of 4% in real terms over the latest estimated spending for 2001–02.

Welfare. Social welfare programmes include social security, family services, child care, services for the elderly, medical social services, youth and community work, probation, and corrections and rehabilitation. 181 non-governmental organizations are subsidized by public funds.

The government gives non-contributory cash assistance to needy families, unemployed able-bodied adults, the severely disabled and the elderly. Caseload as at 31 Dec. 2002 totalled 266,571. Victims of natural disasters, crimes of violence and traffic accidents are financially assisted. Estimated total government expenditure on social welfare for 2002–03 was HK$32·1bn.

CULTURE

Broadcasting. Broadcasting is regulated by the Broadcasting Authority, a statutory body comprising three government officers and nine non-official members.

There is a public broadcasting station, Radio Television Hong Kong (colour by PAL), which broadcasts seven channels (three Chinese, one English, one bilingual and one Putonhua service, and one for the relay of the BBC World Service), six of which provide a 24-hour service. Hong Kong Commercial Broadcasting Co. Ltd and Metro Broadcast Co. Ltd transmit commercial sound programmes on six channels. Television Broadcasts Ltd and Asia Television Ltd transmit domestic free television programme services in English and Chinese on four channels. Hong Kong Cable Television Ltd offers over 30 TV channels on a subscription basis. The PCCW VOD Ltd launched the world's first commercial scale video-on-demand programme service in March 1998. Four new domestic pay television service licences have been granted respectively to Hong Kong Network TV Ltd, Galaxy Satellite Broadcasting Ltd, Yes Television (Hong Kong) Ltd and Pacific Digital Media (HK) Corp. Ltd. These new services are expected to bring in over 100 television channels. There are four non-domestic television programme services in Hong Kong. Hutchvision Hong Kong broadcasts by satellite to the entire Asian region on 30 TV channels. Galaxy Satellite Broadcasting Ltd offers by satellite two channels covering Asia, Australia, Middle East, South Africa and part of Europe. The third and fourth non-domestic television programme service licensees are APT Satellite Glory Ltd and Starbucks (HK) Ltd.

In 2001 there were 3·39m. TV receivers and in 2000 there were 4·56m. radio receivers.

Press. In 1999 there were 45 newspapers including 22 Chinese-language dailies, three English dailies, six other Chinese and eight other English papers, one bilingual paper and five other language papers. The newspapers with the highest circulation figures are all Chinese-language papers—*The Sun*, *Apple Daily* and *Oriental Daily*. In 1999 there were 722 periodicals of which 452 were Chinese, 152 English, 106 bilingual and 12 in other languages. Circulation of dailies in 1996 was 5m. At 800 newspapers per 1,000 inhabitants, Hong Kong has one of the highest rates of circulation in the world. A number of news agency bulletins are registered as newspapers.

Tourism. There were 16,566,000 visitor arrivals in 2002. Tourism receipts totalled HK$64,282·1m. in 2001.

FURTHER READING

Statistical Information: The Census and Statistics Department is responsible for the preparation and collation of government statistics. These statistics are published mainly in the *Hong Kong Monthly Digest of Statistics.* The Department also publishes monthly trade statistics, economic indicators and an annual review of overseas trade, etc. *Website:* http://www.info.gov.hk/censtatd/

Hong Kong [various years] Hong Kong Government Press
Brown, J. M. (ed.) *Hong Kong's Transitions, 1842–1997.* London, 1997
Buckley, R., *Hong Kong: the Road to 1997.* CUP, 1997
Cameron, N., *An Illustrated History of Hong Kong.* OUP, 1991
Cottrell, R., *The End of Hong Kong: the Secret Diplomacy of Imperial Retreat.* London, 1993
Courtauld, C. and Holdsworth, M., *The Hong Kong Story.* OUP, 1997
Flowerdew, J., *The Final Years of British Hong Kong: the Discourse of Colonial Withdrawal.* Hong Kong, 1997
Keay, J., *Last Post: the End of Empire in the Far East.* London, 1997
Lo, C. P., *Hong Kong.* London, 1992
Lo, S.-H., *The Politics of Democratization in Hong Kong.* London, 1997
Morris, J., *Hong Kong: Epilogue to an Empire.* 2nd ed. [of *Hong Kong: Xianggang*]. London, 1993
Roberti, M., *The Fall of Hong Kong: China's Triumph and Britain's Betrayal.* 2nd ed. Chichester, 1997
Roberts, E. V., *et al.*, *Historical Dictionary of Hong Kong and Macau.* Metuchen (NJ), 1993
Scott, Ian, *Hong Kong.* [Bibliography] ABC-Clio, Oxford and Santa Barbara (CA), 1990
Shipp, S., *Hong Kong, China: a Political History of the British Crown Colony's Transfer to Chinese Rule.* Jefferson (NC), 1995
Tsang, S. Y., *Hong Kong: an Appointment with China.* London, 1997
Wang, G. and Wong, S. L. (eds.) *Hong Kong's Transition: a Decade after the Deal.* OUP, 1996
Welsh, F., *A History of Hong Kong.* 3rd ed. London, 1997
Yahuda, M., *Hong Kong: China's Challenge.* London, 1996

MACAO

KEY HISTORICAL EVENTS

Macao was visited by Portuguese traders from 1513 and became a Portuguese colony in 1557. Initially sovereignty remained vested in China, with the Portuguese paying an annual rent. In 1848–49 the Portuguese declared Macao a free port and established jurisdiction over the territory. On 6 Jan. 1987 Portugal agreed to return Macao to China on 20 Dec. 1999 under a plan in which it would become a special administrative zone of China, with considerable autonomy.

TERRITORY AND POPULATION

The Macao Special Administrative Region, which lies at the mouth of the Pearl River, comprises a peninsula (8·7 sq. km) connected by a narrow isthmus to the People's Republic of China, on which is built the city of Santa Nome de Deus de Macao, and the islands of Taipa (6·3 sq. km), linked to Macao by a 2-km bridge, and Colôane (7·6 sq. km) linked to Taipa by a 2-km causeway. The total area of Macao is 27·3 sq. km. Land is being reclaimed from the sea. The population (2001 census) was 435,235 (266,370 females). Population on 31 Dec. 2003, 448,495 (232,879 females); density, 16,428 people per sq. km. The population increased by 1·5% in 2003. An estimated 98·8% of the population lived in urban areas in 1995. The official languages are Chinese and Portuguese, with the majority speaking the Cantonese dialect.

The UN gives a projected population for 2010 of 491,000.

In Dec. 2003, 32,167 foreigners were legally registered for residency in Macao. There were 2,451 legal immigrants from mainland China.

SOCIAL STATISTICS

2003: births, 3,212 (7·2 per 1,000 population); deaths, 1,474 (3·3); marriages, 1,309 (2·9); divorces, 440 (1·0). Infant mortality, 2001, 4·3 per 1,000 live births. Life expectancy at birth (1998–2001), 78·9 years.

CLIMATE

Sub-tropical tending towards temperate, with an average temperature of 23·0°C. The number of rainy days is around a third of the year. Average annual rainfall varies from 47–87" (1,200–2,200 mm). It is very humid from May to Sept.

CONSTITUTION AND GOVERNMENT

Macao's constitution is the 'Basic Law', promulgated by China's National People's Congress on 31 March 1993 and in effect since 20 Dec. 1999. It is a Special Administrative Region (SAR) of the People's Republic of China, and is directly under the Central People's Government while enjoying a high degree of autonomy.

RECENT ELECTIONS

At the elections held on 23 Sept. 2001 pro-Beijing candidates and pro-business candidates each won four seats, with the pro-democracy New Democratic Macau Association winning two. Turn-out was 52%.

Edmund Ho was re-elected chief executive for a second term on 29 Aug. 2004, receiving 296 out of 300 votes in the Election Committee.

CURRENT ADMINISTRATION

Chief Executive: Hau-wah (Edmund) Ho; b. 1955 (appointed 20 Dec. 1999 and re-elected 29 Aug. 2004).

Government Website: http://www.macau.gov.mo

ECONOMY

Gaming is of major importance to the economy of Macao, accounting for around one third of total GDP (2002) and providing billions of dollars in taxes. In 2003, 7·5% of the workforce was directly employed by the casinos.

Currency. The unit of currency is the *pataca* (MOP) of 100 *avos* which is tied to the Hong Kong dollar at parity. Inflation was –2·6% in 2002 and –1·6% in 2003. Foreign exchange reserves were US$4,343m. in 2003. Total money supply was 8,790m. patacas in 2003.

Budget. Final budget figures for 2003 were: revenue, 15,578·0m. patacas; expenditure, 15,578·0m. patacas. Actual figures were: revenue, 18,370·6m. patacas; expenditure, 15,713·0m. patacas.

Performance. Real GDP growth was an estimated 10·0% in 2002 and 15·6% in 2003. Total GDP in 2003 was US$7·9bn.

Banking and Finance. There are two note-issuing banks in Macao—the Macao branch of the Bank of China and the Macao branch of the Banco Nacional Ultramarino. The Monetary Authority of Macao functions as a central bank (*Director,* Teng Ling Seng). Commercial business is handled (2003) by 23 banks, 10 of which are local and 13 foreign. Total deposits, 2003 (including non-resident deposits), 124,977·4m. patacas. There are no foreign-exchange controls within Macao.

ENERGY AND NATURAL RESOURCES

Environment. Macao's carbon dioxide emissions from the consumption and flaring of fossil fuels in 2002 were the equivalent of 3·8 tonnes per capita.

Electricity. Installed capacity was 0·49m. kW in 2003; production, 1·72bn. kWh; net import, 179·8m. kWh.

Oil and Gas. 311,324,000 litres of fuel oil were imported in 2003.

Fisheries. The catch in 2001 was approximately 1,500 tonnes.

INDUSTRY

Although the economy is based on gaming and tourism there is a light industrial base of textiles and garments. In 2002 the number of manufacturing establishments was 1,162 (textiles and clothing, 500; metal products, 138; foods, 119; publishing and printing, 117).

Labour. In 2003 a total of 202,588 people were in employment, including 37,077 (18·3%) in manufacturing; 32,824 (16·2%), wholesale and retail trade, repair of motor vehicles, motorcycles and personal and household goods; 23,469 (11·6%), community, social and other personal services; 22,114 (10·9%), hotels, restaurants and similar activities; 17,812 (8·8%), public administration, defence and compulsory social security; 16,283 (8·0%), construction. Employment in 2003 was 60·9% of the labour force (62·3% in 2002); unemployment rate stood at 6·0% (6·3% in 2002).

INTERNATIONAL TRADE

Imports and Exports. In 2003 imports were valued at 22,097m. patacas, of which the main products were consumer goods, raw materials and semi-manufactured goods, capital goods, fuels and lubricants. Main markets for imports (in 1m. patacas): mainland China, 9,489·9; Hong Kong, 2,794·4; European Union, 2,643·3.

2003 exports were valued at 20,700m. patacas, of which the main products were textiles and garments, machinery and apparatus, footwear, cement and toys. Main markets for exports (in 1m. patacas): 10,320·2, USA; 4,724·6, European Union.

COMMUNICATIONS

Roads. In 2003 there were 345·2 km of roads. In 2003 there were 58,667 passenger cars in use (131 cars per 1,000 inhabitants), 1,317 buses and coaches (excluding school buses), 3,863 trucks and vans, and 66,399 motorcycles and mopeds. In 2003 there were 17 fatalities in 11,764 traffic accidents.

Civil Aviation. An international airport opened in Dec. 1995. In 2003 Macau International Airport handled 2,904,118 passengers and 141,223 tonnes of freight (including transit cargo). In 2003 Air Macau flew to Bangkok, Beijing, Chengdu, Guilin, Haikou, Kaohsiung, Kota Kinabalu, Kuala Lumpur, Kunming, Manila, Nanjing, Ningbo, Shanghai, Singapore, Taipei and Xiamen. It flew a total of 11·5m. km in 1998 and carried 1,270,600 passengers in 1999.

Shipping. Regular services connect Macao with Hong Kong, 65 km to the northeast. In 2002 merchant shipping totalled 4,000 GRT. In 2003 cargo vessel departures by flag totalled 2,451,106 NRT.

Telecommunications. In 2003 there were 538,652 telephone subscribers (1,201 per 1,000 inhabitants), 364,031 mobile phone subscribers and 59,401 Internet subscribers. There were 7,300 fax machines in 1997 and 92,000 PCs in use (210·2 for every 1,000 persons) in 2002.

Postal Services. 21,076,438 letters and parcels were posted in 2003.

SOCIAL INSTITUTIONS

Justice. There is a judicial district court, a criminal court and an administrative court with 24 magistrates in all.

In 2003 there were 9,920 crimes, of which 5,445 were against property. There were 928 persons in prison in 2003.

Religion. Non-religious persons account for 62% of the population. About 17% are Buddhists and 7% Roman Catholics.

Education. There are three types of schools: public, church-run and private. In 2002–03 there were 142 schools and colleges with 110,266 students and 5,324 teachers. Numbers of schools and colleges by category (number of students at the end of the 2002–03 academic year): pre-primary, 62 (12,737); primary, 83 (41,535); secondary, 56 (41,551); technical/professional secondary, 4 (2,448); higher, 12 (11,995). In 2002–03 there were 132 adult education institutions with a total of 86,578 students enrolled.

In 2003 total expenditure on education came to 2·9% of GNP and 15·2% of total government spending.

Health. In 2003 there were 986 doctors, 91 dentists and 1,010 nurses. In 2003 there were 444 inhabitants per doctor and 447 per hospital bed.

CULTURE

Broadcasting. One government and one private commercial radio station are in operation on medium-waves broadcasting in Portuguese and Chinese. Number of receivers (2000), 215,300. Macao receives television broadcasts from Hong Kong and in 1984 a public bilingual TV station began operating. There were, in 2001, 126,600 receivers (colour by PAL).

Press. In 2003 there were 11 daily newspapers (three in Portuguese and eight in Chinese) and six weekly newspapers (one in Portuguese and five in Chinese), plus four Chinese periodicals.

Tourism. Tourism is one of the mainstays of the economy. In 2003 there were 11·9m. visitors. 5·7m. were from mainland China, 4·6m. from Hong Kong and 1·0m. from Taiwan. Receipts in 2003 totalled US$4,836m.

FURTHER READING

Direcção de Serviços de Estatística e Censos. *Anuário Estatístico/Yearbook of Statistics Macau in Figures*. Macao, Annual.
Porter, J., *Macau, the Imaginary City: Culture and Society, 1557 to the Present*. Oxford, 1996
Roberts, E. V., *Historical Dictionary of Hong Kong and Macau*. Metuchen (NJ), 1993

Statistics and Census Service Website: http://www.dsec.gov.mo

TAIWAN[1]

'Republic of China'

KEY HISTORICAL EVENTS

Taiwan, christened Ilha Formosa (beautiful island) by the Portuguese, was ceded to Japan by China by the Treaty of Shimonoseki in 1895. After the Second World War the island was surrendered to Gen. Chiang Kai-shek who made it the headquarters for his crumbling Nationalist Government. Until 1970 the USA supported Taiwan's claims to represent all of China. Only in 1971 did the government of the People's Republic of China manage to replace that of Chiang Kai-shek at the UN. In Jan. 1979 the UN established formal diplomatic relations with the People's Republic of China, breaking off all formal ties with Taiwan. Taiwan itself has continued to reject all attempts at reunification, and although there have been frequent threats from mainland China to precipitate direct action (including military manoeuvres off the Taiwanese coast) the prospect of confrontation with the USA supports the status quo.

In July 1999 President Lee Teng-hui repudiated Taiwan's 50-year-old One China policy—the pretence of a common goal of unification—arguing that Taiwan and China should maintain equal 'state to state' relations. This was a rejection of Beijing's view that Taiwan is no more than a renegade Chinese province which must be reunited with the mainland, by force if necessary. In the Presidential election of 18 March 2000 Chen Shui-bian, leader of the Democratic Progressive Party, was elected, together with Annette Lu Hsiu-bien as his Vice-President. Both support independence although Chen Shui-bian has made friendly gestures towards China and has distanced himself from colleagues who want an immediate declaration of independence.

TERRITORY AND POPULATION

Taiwan lies between the East and South China Seas about 100 miles from the coast of Fujian. The territories currently under the control of the Republic of China include Taiwan, Penghu (the Pescadores), Kinmen (Quemoy), and the Matsu Islands, as well as the archipelagos in the South China Sea. Off the Pacific coast of Taiwan are Green Island and Orchid Island. To the northeast of Taiwan are the Tiaoyutai Islets. The total area of Taiwan Island, the Penghu Archipelago and the Kinmen area (including the fortified offshore islands of Quemoy and Matsu) is 13,973 sq. miles (36,188 sq. km). Population (2001), 22,405,568. The ethnic composition is 84% native Taiwanese (including 15% of Hakka), 14% of Mainland Chinese, and 2% aborigine of Malayo-Polynesian origin. There are also 420,892 aboriginals of Malay origin. Population density: 619 per sq. km.

Taiwan's administrative units comprise (with 2001 populations): two special municipalities: Taipei, the capital (2·69m.) and Kaohsiung (1·48m.); five cities

[1]See note on transcription of names in CHINA: Territory and Population.

outside the county structure: Chiayi (265,109), Hsinchu (361,958), Keelung (390,966), Taichung (983,694), Tainan (740,846); 16 counties (*hsien*): Changhwa (1,313,994), Chiayi (563,365), Hsinchu (446,300), Hualien (353,139), Ilan (465,799), Kaohsiung (1,236,958), Miaoli (560,640), Nantou (541,818), Penghu (92,268), Pingtung (909,364), Taichung (1,502,274), Tainan (1,109,397), Taipei (3,610,252), Taitung (244,612), Taoyuan (1,792,962), Yunlin (743,562).

SOCIAL STATISTICS

In 2001 the birth rate was 11·65 per 1,000 population; death rate, 5·71 per 1,000; rate of growth, 0·56% per annum. Life expectancy: males, 72·87 years; females, 78·79 years. Infant mortality, 6·62 per 1,000 live births.

CLIMATE

The climate is subtropical in the north and tropical in the south. The typhoon season extends from July to Sept. The average monthly temperatures of Jan. and July in Taipei are 59·5°F (15·3°C) and 83·3°F (28·5°C) respectively, and average annual rainfall is 84·99" (2,158·8 mm). Kaohsiung's average monthly temperatures of Jan. and July are 65·66°F (18·9°C) and 83·3°F (28·5°C) respectively, and average annual rainfall is 69·65" (1,769·2 mm).

CONSTITUTION AND GOVERNMENT

The ROC Constitution is based on the Principles of Nationalism, Democracy and Social Wellbeing formulated by Dr Sun Yat-sen, the founding father of the Republic of China. The ROC government is divided into three main levels: central, provincial/municipal and county/city each of which has well-defined powers.

The central government consists of the Office of the President, the National Assembly, which is specially elected only for constitutional amendment, and five governing branches called '*yuan*', namely the Executive Yuan, the Legislative Yuan, the Judicial Yuan, the Examination Yuan and the Control Yuan. The additional Article 4 of the Constitution stipulates that, beginning with the fourth Legislative Yuan (1999), the Legislative Yuan shall have 225 members.

From 5 May to 23 July 1997 the *Additional Articles of the Constitution of the Republic of China* underwent yet another amendment. As a result a resolution on the impeachment of the President or Vice President is no longer to be instituted by the Control Yuan but rather by the Legislative Yuan. The Legislative Yuan has the power to pass a no-confidence vote against the premier of the Executive Yuan, while the president of the Republic has the power to dissolve the Legislative Yuan. The premier of the Executive Yuan is now directly appointed by the president of the Republic. Hence the consent of the Legislative Yuan is no longer needed.

In Dec. 2003 a law came into effect allowing for referendums to be held.

National Anthem. 'San Min Chu I'; words by Dr Sun Yat-sen, tune by Cheng Mao-yun.

RECENT ELECTIONS

Presidential elections took place on 20 March 2004. Incumbent Chen Shui-bian (Democratic Progressive Party) won 50·1% of the vote against 49·9% for Lien Chan (Nationalist Party/Kuomintang). Turn-out was 80·3%. Chen Shui-bian was sworn in for a second term on 20 May 2004 but Lien Chan made an appeal to the High Court to overturn the result. The High Court judged against Lien Chan, who in Feb. 2005 declared an intention to challenge the ruling.

Elections to the Legislative Yuan were held on 11 Dec. 2004. The Democratic Progressive Party won 89 seats with 35·7% of votes cast; the Nationalist Party, 79 seats (32·8%); the People First Party, 34 seats (13·9%); the Taiwan Solidarity Union, 12 seats (7·8%); the Non-Partisan Solidarity Union, 6 seats (3·9%); the New Party, 1 seat (0·1%); ind., 4 seats (3·9%).

Elections for an *ad hoc* National Assembly charged with amending the constitution were held on 14 May 2005. The Democratic Progressive Party took 127 of 300 seats (with 42·5% of the vote), the Nationalist Party 117 (38·9%), the Taiwan Solidarity Union 21 (7·1%), the People First Party 18 (6·1%) and the Jhang Ya Jhong Union 5 (1·7%). Turn-out was 23·4%.

CURRENT ADMINISTRATION

President: Chen Shui-bian; b. 1951 (Democratic Progressive Party; sworn in 20 May 2000 and re-elected in March 2004).

Vice President: Annette Lu Hsiu-lien.

Prime Minister and *President of the Executive Yuan:* Frank Hsieh; b. 1946 (Democratic Progressive Party; sworn in 1 Feb. 2005). There are eight ministries under the Executive Yuan: Interior; Foreign Affairs; National Defence; Finance; Education; Justice; Economic Affairs; Transport and Communications.

Vice-President of the Executive Yuan and Minister for the Consumer Protection Commission: Vacant. *President, Control Yuan:* Fredrick Chien. *President, Examination Yuan:* Yao Chia-wen. *President, Judicial Yuan:* Yueh-sheng Weng. *President, Legislative Yuan:* Wang Jin-ping. *Secretary General, Executive Yuan:* Arthur Iap. *Minister of Foreign Affairs:* Chen Tang-shan. *Defence:* Lee Jye. *Interior:* Su Jia-chyuan. *Finance:* Lin Chuan. *Education:* Tu Cheng-shen. *Economic Affairs:* Ho Mei-yueh. *Justice:* Shih Mao-lin. *Transport and Communications:* Lin Ling-san. *Health:* Chen Chien-jen. *Ministers without Portfolio:* Hu Sheng-cheng; Lin Yi-fu; Chen Chi-mai; Lin Sheng-feng; Lin Ferng-ching; Fu Li-yeh; Kuo Yao-chi (also *Chair of the Public Construction Commission*).

In addition to the Mongolian and Tibetan Affairs Commission and the Overseas Chinese Affairs Commission, a number of commissions and subordinate organizations have been formed with the resolution of the Executive Yuan Council and the Legislature to meet new demands and handle new affairs. Examples include the Environmental Protection Administration, which was set up in 1987 as public awareness of pollution control rose; the Mainland Affairs Council, which was established in 1990 to handle the thawing of relations between Taiwan and the Chinese mainland; and the Fair Trade Commission, which was established in 1992 to promote a fair trade system. Since 1995 even more commissions have been set up to provide a wider scope of services: the Public Construction Commission was set up in July 1995, the Council of Aboriginal Affairs in Dec. 1996, and the National Council on Physical Fitness and Sports in July 1997.

These commissions and councils are headed by:

Agricultural Council: Lee Ching-lung. *Atomic Energy Council:* Ouyang Min-shen. *Central Election Commission:* Masa Chang. *Council for Hakka Affairs:* Luo Wen-jia. *Coast Guard Administration:* Shi Hwei-yow. *Cultural Affairs:* Chen Chi-nan. *Economic Planning and Development Council:* Hu Sheng-cheng. *Environmental Protection Administration:* Chang Juu-en. *Fair Trade Commission:* Hwang Tzong-leh. *Indigenous Peoples' Council:* Chen Chien-nien. *Labour Affairs Council:* Chen Chu. *Mainland Affairs Council:* Wu Jau-shieh. *Mongolian and Tibetan Affairs Commission:* Hsu Chih-hsiung. *National Council on Physical Fitness and Sports:* Chen Chuan-show. *National Palace Museum:* Shih Shou-chien. *National Science Council:* Wu Maw-kuen. *National Youth Commission:* Cheng Li-chiun. *Overseas Chinese Affairs Commission:* Chang Fu-mei. *Research, Development and Evaluation Commission:* Yeh Jiunn-rong. *Veterans Affairs Commission:* Kao Hua-chu.

Government Website: http://www.gio.gov.tw

DEFENCE

Conscription is for two years.

Defence expenditure in 2003 totalled US$6,632m. (US$293 per capita), representing 2·4% of GDP.

Army. The Army was estimated to number about 190,000 in 2000, including military police. Army reserves numbered 2·7m. In addition the Ministry of Justice, Ministry of Interior and the Ministry of Defence each command paramilitary forces totalling 25,000 personnel in all. The Army consists of Army Corps, Defence Commands, Airborne Cavalry Brigades, Armoured Brigades, Motorized Rifle Brigades, Infantry Brigades, Special Warfare Brigades and Missile Command.

Navy. Active personnel in the Navy in 2000 totalled 50,000. There are 425,000 naval reservists. The operational and land-based forces consist of four submarines, 16 destroyers and 21 frigates. There is a naval air wing operating 31 combat aircraft and 21 armed helicopters.

Air Force. Units in the operational system are equipped with aircraft that include locally developed IDF, F-16, Mirage 2000-5 and F-5E fighter-interceptors. There were 50,000 Air Force personnel in 2000 and 334,000 reservists.

INTERNATIONAL RELATIONS

By a treaty of 2 Dec. 1954 the USA pledged to defend Taiwan, but this treaty lapsed one year after the USA established diplomatic relations with the People's Republic of China on 1 Jan. 1979. In April 1979 the Taiwan Relations Act was passed by the US Congress to maintain commercial, cultural and other relations between USA and Taiwan through the American Institute in Taiwan and its Taiwan counterpart, the Co-ordination Council for North American Affairs in the USA, which were accorded quasi-diplomatic status in 1980. The People's Republic took over the China seat in the UN from Taiwan on 25 Oct. 1971. In May 1991 Taiwan ended its formal state of war with the People's Republic. Taiwan became a member of the World Trade Organization on 1 Jan. 2002.

In Nov. 2000 Taiwan had formal diplomatic ties with 29 countries and maintained substantive relations with over 100 countries and territories around the globe.

ECONOMY

Overview. Taiwan has made a successful transition from an agricultural economy to one based on sophisticated high-tech electronics. The agricultural, industrial and service sectors account for approximately 2%, 20% and 68% of GDP respectively. Taiwan has experienced average economic growth of 8% during the last three decades; economic growth has been driven primarily by high value added manufacturing and exports, mainly in electronics and computers. Government intervention in investment and foreign trade has decreased since the early 1990s. In 1989 the government began a programme to privatize government-owned enterprises, including banks, telecommunication firms and industrial firms. The Asian financial crisis had a relatively little effect on Taiwan. The economy has, however, suffered recent setbacks, partly owing to policy co-ordination problems and bad debts in the banking system. The economy went into a recession in 2001, when the economy experienced the first year of negative growth ever recorded and unemployment reached record levels. Strong export performance has stimulated a recovery.

Currency. The unit of currency is the *New Taiwan dollar* (TWD) of 100 *cents*. Gold reserves were 13·55m. oz in Oct. 2000. There was deflation in both 1999 and 2000, of 1·4% and 1·6% respectively. Foreign exchange reserves were US$241·7bn. in Dec. 2004.

Budget. As a result of the constitutional amendment to abolish the provincial government from the fiscal year 2000 the central government budget has been enlarged to include the former provincial government. The central government's general budget for the fiscal year 2002 (beginning on 1 Jan.) was NT$1,518,724m. Expenditure planned: 18·1% on education, science and culture; 17·6% on economic development; 17·5% on social security; 15% on defence.

Performance. Taiwan sustained rapid economic growth at an annual rate of 9·2% from 1960 up to 1990. The rate slipped to 6·4% in the 1990s and 5·9% in 2000; Taiwan suffered from the Asian financial crisis, though less than its neighbours. Consumer prices showed increasing stability, rising at an average annual rate of 6·3% from 1960 to 1989, 2·9% in the 1990s and 1·3% in 2000. In 2001 global economic sluggishness and the events of 11 Sept. in the USA severely affected Taiwan's economy, which contracted by 2·2%. Per capita GNP stood at US$12,876, while consumer prices remained almost unchanged. Subsequent economic recovery led to growth of 3·9% in 2002, 3·3% in 2003 and 5·7% in 2004.

Banking and Finance. The Central Bank of China (reactivated in 1961) regulates the money supply, manages foreign exchange and issues currency. The *Governor* is Perng Fai-nan. The Bank of Taiwan is the largest commercial bank and the fiscal agent of the government. There are seven domestic banks, 38 commercial banks and 36 foreign banks. Government banks are scheduled for privatization by 2006 and it is proposed that the government will sell its commercial bank holdings by 2010.

There are two stock exchanges in Taipei.

ENERGY AND NATURAL RESOURCES

Environment. Taiwan's carbon dioxide emissions from the consumption and flaring of fossil fuels in 2002 were the equivalent of 10·2 tonnes per capita.

Electricity. Output of electricity in 2001 was 188·5m. MWh; total installed capacity was 35,568 MW, of which 77·1% is held by the Taiwan Power Company. There were six units in three nuclear power stations in 2003. Consumption per capita stood at 4,257 litres of oil equivalent in 2001.

Oil and Gas. Crude oil production in 2001 was 40·6m. litres; natural gas, 849m. cu. metres.

Minerals. Coal production ceased by 2001 because of competitive imports and increasing local production costs.

Agriculture. In 2001 the cultivated area was 848,743 ha, of which 438,974 ha were paddy fields. Rice production totalled 1,396,274 tonnes. Livestock production was valued at more than NT$101,205m., accounting for 28·67% of Taiwan's total agricultural production value.

Forestry. Forest area, 2001: 2,101,719 ha. Forest reserves: trees, 357,492,423 cu. metres; bamboo, 1,109m. poles. Timber production, 26,401 cu. metres.

Fisheries. In 2001 Taiwan's fishing fleet totalled 27,018 vessels (12,942 were powered craft); the catch was approximately 1·32m. tonnes. NT$89,813m. worth of fish was produced. Of this, 52% came from far-sea fishing, 26% from inland aquaculture, 14% from offshore fishing and 5% from coastal fishing. More than 40% of the catch was exported, with the biggest items being big eye tuna and albacore (long-finned tuna).

INDUSTRY

The largest companies in Taiwan by market capitalization in May 2004 were Taiwan Semicon. Mnfg (US$34·1bn.), Chunghwa Telecom (US$15·6bn.) and Cathay Financial Holdings (US$14·3bn.).

Output (in tonnes) in 1999: cement, 18·2m.; steel bars, 1·4m.; pulp, 0·3m.; sugar, 0·3m.; cotton fabrics, 1,061m. sq. metres; portable computers, 9·95m. units; desktop computers, 3·01m. units. Taiwan is the third largest information technology producer after the USA and Japan. The IT sector has replaced traditional industries as the engine for growth.

Labour. In Sept. 2002 the total labour force was 9·97m., of whom 9·44m. were employed. Of the employed population, 55·09% worked in the service sector (including 22·70% in trade and 16·11% in accommodation and eating and drinking establishments); 37·28% in industry (including 27·05% in manufacturing and 7·64% in construction); and 7·63% in agriculture, forestry and fisheries. The unemployment rate was 5·32%.

INTERNATIONAL TRADE

Restrictions on the repatriation of investment earnings by foreign nationals were removed in 1994.

Imports and Exports. Total trade, in US$1m.:

	1996	*1997*	*1998*	*1999*	*2000*	*2001*
Imports	102,370	114,425	104,665	110,690	140,011	107,237
Exports	115,942	122,081	110,582	121,591	148,321	122,866

In 2001 the main export markets were the USA (22·5%), Hong Kong (21·9%), Japan (10·4%) and Germany (3·6%). The main import suppliers were Japan (24·1%), the USA (17·0%), South Korea (6·3%) and Germany (4·0%).

Principal exports, in US$1bn.: machinery and electrical equipment, 66·85; textiles, 12·63; basic metals and articles, 11·33; plastic and rubber products, 7·99; vehicles and transport equipment, 4·44; toys, games and sports equipment, 1·79; footwear, headwear and umbrellas, 0·79. By 2001 high-tech products were responsible for more than 54% of exports.

Principal imports, in US$1bn.: machinery and electrical equipment, 47·55; minerals, 12·76; chemicals, 10·23; basic metals and articles, 7·78; precision instruments, clocks and watches, and musical instruments, 6·21; vehicles and transport equipment, 4·24; textile products, 2·36.

COMMUNICATIONS

Roads. In 2002 there were 37,299 km of roads. 17·9m. motor vehicles were registered including 5·0m. passenger cars, 25,000 buses, 700,000 trucks and 12·0m. motorcycles. 1,091m. passengers and 301m. tonnes of freight were transported (including urban buses) in 2001. There were 64,264 road accidents, resulting in 3,344 fatalities.

Rail. In 2001 freight traffic amounted to 16·9m. tonnes and passenger traffic to 165m. Total route length was 2,363 km. A metro system opened in Taipei in 1996.

Civil Aviation. There are currently two international airports: Chiang Kai-shek International at Taoyuan near Taipei, and Kaohsiung International in the south. In addition there are 14 domestic airports: Taipei, Hualien, Taitung, Taichung, Tainan, Chiayi, Pingtung, Makung, Chimei, Orchid Island, Green Island, Wangan, Kinmen and Matsu (Peikan). A second passenger terminal at Chiang Kai-shek International Airport opened in July 2000 as part of a US$800m. expansion project, which included aircraft bays, airport connection roads, a rapid transit link with Taipei, car parks and the expansion of air freight facilities, begun in 1989. The planned facilities are designed to allow the airport to handle an additional 14m. passengers annually by the year 2010.

In June 2002, 38 airlines including code-share airlines provided flights to destinations in Taiwan, of which 32 foreign and six Taiwanese carriers—China Airlines (CAL), EVA Airways, Far Eastern Air Transport Corp., Mandarin Airlines (MDA; CAL's subsidiary), Trans Asia Airways (TNA) and UNI Airways—operated international services. In 2001, 44·1m. passengers and 1·3m. tonnes of freight were flown.

Taipei–Hong Kong and vice-versa was the most flown airline route in the world in 2001, with 5·43m. passengers flying between the two cities.

Shipping. Maritime transportation is vital to the trade-oriented economy of Taiwan. At the end of 2001 Taiwan's shipping fleet totalled 249 national-flagged ships (over 100 GRT), amounting to 4·7m. GRT and 7·4m. DWT. There are six international ports: Kaohsiung, Keelung, Hualien, Taichung, Anping and Suao. The first two are container centres, Kaohsiung handling 7·54m. 20-ft equivalent units in 2001, making it the world's fourth busiest container port in terms of number of containers handled. Suao port is an auxiliary port to Keelung. In Jan. 2001 the first legal direct shipping links between Taiwanese islands and the Chinese mainland in more than 50 years were inaugurated.

Telecommunications. In 2002 there were 37,004,800 telephone subscribers (1,647·8 per 1,000 inhabitants) and PCs numbered 8·89m. (395·7 per 1,000 inhabitants). Taiwan's biggest telecommunications firm, the state-owned Chunghwa Telecom, lost its fixed-line monopoly in Aug. 2001. In 2002 there were 23,905,400 mobile phone subscribers, equivalent to 1,061·5 per 1,000 persons—the highest rate anywhere in the world. There were approximately 8·59m. Internet users in 2002. In 1997 there were 2,496,090 radio pager subscribers.

SOCIAL INSTITUTIONS

Justice. The Judicial Yuan is the supreme judicial organ of state. Comprising 15 grand justices, since 2003 these have been nominated and, with the consent of the Legislative Yuan, appointed by the President of the Republic. The grand justices hold meetings to interpret the Constitution and unify the interpretation of laws and orders. There are three levels of judiciary: district courts and their branches deal with civil and criminal cases in the first instance; high courts and their branches deal with appeals against judgments of district courts; the Supreme Court reviews judgments by the lower courts. There is also the Supreme Administrative Court, high administrative courts and a Commission on the Disciplinary Sanctions of Public Functionaries. Criminal cases relating to rebellion, treason and offences against friendly relations with foreign states are handled by high courts as the courts of first instance.

The death penalty is still in force. There were seven confirmed executions in 2003. The population in penal institutions on 30 Sept. 2002 was approximately 39,000 (135 per 100,000 of national population).

Religion. According to the registered statistics of Municipality, County and City Government there were 827,135 Taoists in 2001 (and 7,714 temples), 382,437 Protestants (and 2,387 churches), 216,495 Buddhists (and 1,966 temples) and 182,814 Catholics (and 728 churches). In Sept. 2003 there was one cardinal.

Education. Since 1968 there has been compulsory education for six to 15 year olds with free tuition. The illiteracy rate dropped to 4·21% in 2001 and is still falling. In 2001 there were 2,611 elementary schools with 103,501 teachers and 1,925,491 pupils; 1,181 secondary schools with 98,609 teachers and 1,684,499 students; 154 schools of higher education, including 57 universities, 78 colleges and 19 junior colleges, with 44,769 teachers and 1,189,225 students. Almost one-quarter of the total population attend an educational institution.

Health. In 2001 there was one physician serving every 733 persons, one doctor of Chinese medicine per 5,631 persons and one dentist per 2,505 persons. Some 114,179 beds were provided by the 92 public and 501 private hospitals, averaging nearly 57 beds per 10,000 persons. In addition to the 492 public and 17,136 private clinics, there were 369 health stations and 503 health rooms serving residents in the sparsely populated areas. Acute infectious diseases were no longer the number one killer. Malignant neoplasms, cerebrovascular diseases, heart diseases and accidents and adverse effects were the first four leading causes of death.

Welfare. A universal health insurance scheme came into force in March 1995 as an extension to 13 social insurance plans which cover only 59% of Taiwan's population. Premium shares among the government, employer and insured are varied according to the insured statuses. By the end of 2001 about 21·65m. people or 96% of the population were covered by the National Health Insurance programme.

CULTURE

Broadcasting. At Oct. 2002 there were 174 radio stations, one public and four commercial TV services and 65 cable systems. June 1997 saw the inauguration of a fourth over-the-air television station—The Kaohsiung-based Formosa Television—which is affiliated with the Democratic Progressive Party and telecasts on VHF low-band. A Public Television Law was promulgated on 18 June 1997. In 2001 there were 9·9m. TV receivers (colour by NTSC).

Press. There were 267 domestic news agencies, 454 newspapers and 7,236 periodicals in 2001.

Tourism. In 2002, 2,617,137 tourists visited Taiwan and 7,189,334 Taiwanese made visits abroad.

FURTHER READING

Statistical Yearbook of the Republic of China. Taipei, annual. *The Republic of China Yearbook.* Taipei, annual. *Taiwan Statistical Data Book.* Taipei, annual. *Annual Review of Government Administration, Republic of China.* Taipei, annual.

Arrigo, L. G., *et al.*, *The Other Taiwan: 1945 to the Present Day.* New York, 1994
Cooper, J. F., *Historical Dictionary of Taiwan.* Metuchen (NJ), 1993
Hughes, C., *Taiwan and Chinese Nationalism: National Identity and Status in International Society.* London, 1997
Lee, W.-C., *Taiwan.* [Bibliography] ABC-Clio, Oxford and Santa Barbara (CA), 1990
Long, S., *Taiwan: China's Last Frontier.* London, 1991
Moody, P. R., *Political Change in Taiwan: a Study of Ruling Party Adaptability.* New York, 1992
Smith, H., *Industry Policy in Taiwan and Korea in the 1980s*. Edward Elgar, Cheltenham, 2000
Tsang, S. (ed.) *In the Shadow of China: Political Developments in Taiwan since 1949.* Farnborough, 1994

National library: National Central Library, Taipei (established 1986).
National Statistics Website: http://www.stat.gov.tw

COLOMBIA

República de Colombia

Capital: Bogotá
Population projection, 2010: 48·96m.
GDP per capita, 2002: (PPP$) 6,370
HDI/world rank: 0·773/73

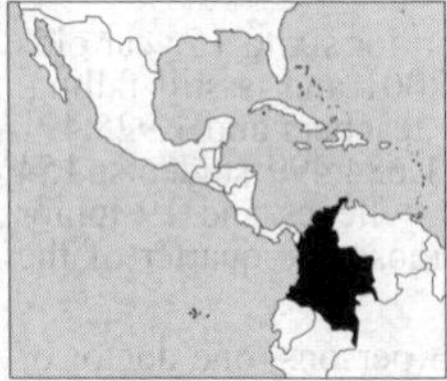

KEY HISTORICAL EVENTS

In 1564 the Spanish Crown appointed a President of New Granada, which included the territories of Colombia, Panama and Venezuela. In 1718 a viceroyalty of New Granada was created. This viceroyalty gained its independence from Spain in 1819, and together with the present territories of Panama, Venezuela and Ecuador was officially constituted as the state of 'Greater Colombia'. This new state lasted only until 1830 when it split up into Venezuela, Ecuador and the republic of New Granada, later renamed *Estados Unidos de Colombia*. The constitution of 5 Aug. 1886, forming the Republic of Colombia, abolished the sovereignty of the states, converting them into departments with governors appointed by the President of the Republic. The department of Panama, however, became an independent country in 1903. Conservatives and Liberals fought a civil war from 1948 to 1957 (*La Violencia)* during which some 300,000 people were killed. Subsequently, powerful drugs lords have made violence endemic. Two Marxist guerrilla forces are active, the Colombian Revolutionary Armed Forces (FARC), and the smaller National Liberation Army (ELN). They are opposed by a well-armed paramilitary organization which emerged after the setting up of rural self-defence groups. Killings and other abuses by paramilitary squads, guerrillas and the military in 1996 made it the most infamous year in the nation's history for human rights violations. On average, ten Colombians were killed every day for political or ideological reasons, while one person disappeared every two days.

There were hopes of a fresh start in 1998 when Andrés Pastrana was elected president. Offers to talk peace were taken up by the rebels and by their paramilitary enemies. But political differences are wide, with FARC demanding sweeping agrarian reform and a redistribution of wealth. FARC controls around 40% of the country including areas which produce the bulk of illegal drugs. Approximately 80% of the cocaine and 60% of the heroin sold in the USA originates in Colombia. In Feb. 2002, following the kidnapping of a prominent senator, President Pastrana broke off three years of peace talks. In May 2002 Álvaro Uribe Vélez became president, but within days of his inauguration, amidst mounting violence, he called a state of emergency.

TERRITORY AND POPULATION

Colombia is bounded in the north by the Caribbean Sea, northwest by Panama, west by the Pacific Ocean, southwest by Ecuador and Peru, northeast by Venezuela and southeast by Brazil. The estimated area is 1,141,748 sq. km (440,829 sq. miles). Population census (1993), 33,109,840; density, 29·0 per sq. km. Population estimate, 2002: 43·51m.

The UN gives a projected population for 2010 of 48·96m.

In 2001, 75·5% lived in urban areas. Bogotá, the capital (estimate 1999): 6,276,000.

The following table gives population estimates for departments and their capitals for 1999:

Departments	*Area (sq. km)*	*Population*	*Capital*	*Population*
Amazonas	109,665	69,000	Leticia	30,000[1]
Antioquia	63,612	5,300,000	Medellín	1,958,000
Arauca	23,818	232,000	Arauca	69,000[1]
Atlántico	3,388	2,081,000	Barranquilla	1,226,000
Bogotá[2]	1,587	6,276,000	—	—
Bolívar	25,978	1,951,000	Cartagena	877,000
Boyacá	23,189	1,355,000	Tunja	118,000[1]
Caldas	7,888	1,094,000	Manizales	362,000

Departments	Area (sq. km)	Population	Capital	Population
Caquetá	88,965	410,000	Florencia	115,000[1]
Casanare	44,640	278,000	Yopal	69,000[1]
Cauca	29,308	1,234,000	Popayán	218,000[1]
César	22,905	944,000	Valledupar	297,000[1]
Chocó	46,530	406,000	Quibdó	123,000[1]
Córdoba	25,020	1,308,000	Montería	321,000
Cundinamarca	22,623	2,099,000	Bogotá[1]	—
Guainía	72,238	36,000	Puerto Inírida	20,000[1]
Guaviare	42,327	114,000	San José del Guaviare	54,000[1]
Huila	19,890	911,000	Neiva	322,000
La Guajira	20,848	475,000	Riohacha	115,000[1]
Magdalena	23,188	1,260,000	Santa Marta	343,000[1]
Meta	85,635	686,000	Villavicencio	314,000
Nariño	33,268	1,603,000	Pasto	379,000
Norte de Santander	21,658	1,316,000	Cúcuta	624,000
Putumayo	24,885	324,000	Mocoa	30,000[1]
Quindío	1,845	552,000	Armenia	284,000[1]
Risaralda	4,140	928,000	Pereira	457,000
San Andrés y Providencia	44	71,000	San Andrés	61,000[1]
Santander	30,537	1,939,000	Bucaramanga	521,000
Sucre	10,917	779,000	Sincelejo	214,000[1]
Tolima	23,562	1,293,000	Ibagué	420,000[1]
Valle del Cauca	22,140	4,104,000	Cali	2,111,000
Vaupés	65,268	29,000	Mitú	14,000[1]
Vichada	100,242	80,000	Puerto Carreño	12,000[1]

[1]1997. [2]Capital District.

Ethnic divisions (1996): mestizo 58%, white 20%, mulatto 14%, black 4%, mixed black-Indian 3%, Indian 1%.

The official language is Spanish.

SOCIAL STATISTICS

2000 estimates: births, 734,000; deaths, 184,000. Rates, 2000 estimates (per 1,000 population): births 17·4; deaths, 4·4. Annual population growth rate, 1992–2002, 1·8%. Life expectancy at birth, 2001, was 68·6 years for men and 75·0 years for women. Infant mortality, 2001, 19 per 1,000 live births; fertility rate, 2001, 2·7 children per woman.

CLIMATE

The climate includes equatorial and tropical conditions, according to situation and altitude. In tropical areas, the wettest months are March to May and Oct. to Nov. Bogotá, Jan. 58°F (14·4°C), July 57°F (13·9°C). Annual rainfall 42" (1,052 mm). Barranquilla, Jan. 80°F (26·7°C), July 82°F (27·8°C). Annual rainfall 32" (799 mm). Cali, Jan. 75°F (23·9°C), July 75°F (23·9°C). Annual rainfall 37" (915 mm). Medellín, Jan. 71°F (21·7°C), July 72°F (22·2°C). Annual rainfall 64" (1,606 mm).

CONSTITUTION AND GOVERNMENT

Simultaneously with the presidential elections of May 1990, a referendum was held in which 7m. votes were cast for the establishment of a special assembly to draft a new constitution. Elections were held on 9 Dec. 1990 for this 74-member 'Constitutional Assembly' which operated from Feb. to July 1991. The electorate was 14·2m.; turn-out was 3·7m. The Liberals gained 24 seats, M19 (a former guerrilla organization), 19. The Assembly produced a new constitution which came into force on 5 July 1991. It stresses the state's obligation to protect human rights, and establishes constitutional rights to healthcare, social security and leisure. Indians are allotted two Senate seats. Congress may dismiss ministers, and representatives may be recalled by their electors.

The *President* is elected by direct vote for a single term of four years and may only serve one term. A vice-presidency was instituted in July 1991.

The legislative power rests with a *Congress* of two houses, the *Senate*, of 102 members, and the *House of Representatives*, of 166 members, both elected for four years by proportional representation. Congress meets annually at Bogotá on 20 July.

National Anthem. 'O! Gloria inmarcesible' ('Oh unfading Glory!'); words by R. Núñez, tune by O. Síndici.

RECENT ELECTIONS

Presidential elections were held on 26 May 2002, in which Álvaro Uribe Vélez (independent) won with 53·1% of votes cast, against 31·8% for his nearest rival, Horacio Serpa Uribe (Liberal Party). Turn-out was 46·8%.

Congressional elections were held on 10 March 2002. Unlike the 1998 elections, which were marred by vote-buying, fraud, kidnapping and violence, the balloting process was largely peaceful. This was in spite of warnings of violence from FARC and their apparent involvement in the kidnapping of a presidential candidate and the assassination of an opposition-member senator in the weeks prior to the ballot. In the elections to the Senate candidates from the two largest parties, the Colombian Conservative Party and the Liberal Party, were routed by independents. The Liberal Party won 28 seats, down from 56, the Colombian Conservative Party won 13, down from 17, with independent candidates accounting for the remainder. In elections to the House of Representatives the Liberal Party won 54 seats, the Colombian Conservative Party 21, the Coalition Party 17, the Radical Change Party 7 and the Liberal Opening Party 5, with the remaining seats going to smaller parties.

CURRENT ADMINISTRATION

President: Álvaro Uribe Vélez; b. 1952 (ind.; sworn in 7 Aug. 2002).

Vice President: Francisco Santos Calderón.

In March 2005 the government comprised:

Minister of Interior and Justice: Sabas Pretelt de la Vega. *Finance:* Alberto Carrasquilla Barrera. *Defence:* Jorge Alberto Uribe Echavarría. *Agriculture and Rural Development:* Andrés Felipe Arias Leyva. *Social Welfare:* Diego Palacio Betancourt. *Mines and Energy:* Luis Ernesto Mejía Castro. *National Education:* Cecilia María Vélez White. *Communications:* Martha Pinto de De Hart. *Trade, Industry and Tourism:* Jorge Humberto Botero. *Foreign Relations:* Carolina Barco Isakson. *Environment, Housing and Territorial Development:* Sandra Suárez Pérez. *Transport:* Andrés Uriel Gallego Henao. *Culture:* María Consuelo Araújo Castro.

Office of the President (Spanish only): http://www.presidencia.gov.co

DEFENCE

Selective conscription at 18 years is for two years' service. In 2003 defence expenditure totalled US$3,234m. (US$73 per capita), representing 4·2% of GDP. In 1985 expenditure had been US$823m.

Army. Personnel (2002) 136,000 (conscripts, 63,800); reserves number 54,700. The national police numbered (2002) 104,600.

Navy. The Navy has two diesel powered submarines, two midget submarines and four small frigates. Naval personnel in 2002 totalled 15,000. There are also two brigades of marines numbering 10,000. An air arm operates light reconnaissance aircraft.

The Navy's main ocean base is Cartagena with Pacific bases at Buenaventura and Málaga. There are in addition numerous river bases.

Air Force. The Air Force has been independent of the Army and Navy since 1943, when its reorganization began with US assistance. It has 58 combat aircraft and 23 combat helicopters. There are two fighter-bomber squadrons (one with Mirage 5s and one with Kfirs). Total strength (2002), 7,000 personnel (3,900 conscripts).

INTERNATIONAL RELATIONS

Colombia is a member of the UN, WTO, OAS, Inter-American Development Bank, the Andean Group, ALADI/LAIA, ACS, IOM and the Antarctic Treaty.

It was announced in Aug. 2000 that Colombia would receive US$1·3bn. in anti drug-trafficking aid (mostly of a military nature) from the USA as part of 'Plan Colombia', a five-year long series of projects intended to serve as a foundation for stability and peace of which the focal point is the fight against drugs. By Aug. 2003 the USA had given aid amounting to US$2·4bn.

ECONOMY

In 2002 agriculture accounted for 13·9% of GDP, industry 30·2% and services 55·9%.

Overview. Latin America's fifth largest economy suffers from civil war, vast illegal drugs production and an unsustainable fiscal deficit. The country produces 80% of the world's cocaine and it is estimated that trade in illegal drugs accounts for 3–8% of GDP. Core agricultural exports are coffee and bananas. Manufacturing has suffered high interest rates and a strong currency in recent years. Mining, one of Colombia's major export industries, accounts for just 5% of GDP. Oil production has increased thanks to newly discovered reserves. In 2002 the USA granted US$104m. for increased military spending, which the government aims to increase by a third (US$1bn.) each year until 2007.

Currency. The unit of currency is the *Colombian peso* (COP) of 100 *centavos.* Inflation was 6·3% in 2002, the lowest rate in more than 30 years. In June 2002 gold reserves were 327,000 troy oz and foreign exchange reserves were US$10,188m. Total money supply was 17,289bn. pesos in June 2002.

Budget. Government revenue and expenditure (in 1bn. pesos):

	1995	*1996*	*1997*	*1998*	*1999*
Revenue	9,524	12,048	15,283	16,592	18,760
Expenditure	11,290	15,363	19,584	23,492	28,536

Performance. In 1999 Colombia experienced its worst recession since the 1930s, with GDP shrinking by 4·2%. There was a recovery in 2000, with growth at 2·9%. In 2001 there was growth of 1·4% and in 2002 growth of 1·5%. Total GDP in 2003 was US$77·6bn.

Banking and Finance. In 1923 the Bank of the Republic (*Governor*, José Dario Uribe Escobar) was inaugurated as a semi-official central bank, with the exclusive privilege of issuing banknotes. Its note issues must be covered by a reserve in gold of foreign exchange of 25% of their value. Interest rates of 40% plus are imposed.

There are 24 commercial banks, of which 18 are private or mixed, and six official. There is also an Agricultural, Industrial and Mining Credit Institute, a Central Mortgage Bank and a Social Savings Bank. Demand deposits totalled 11,256bn. pesos in Dec. 2002. The Superintendencia Bancaria acts as a supervising body.

There are stock exchanges in Bogotá, Medellín and Cali.

Weights and Measures. The metric system is standard but traditional Spanish weights and measures are still used, *e.g., botella* (750 grammes), *galón* (5 *botellas*), *vara* (70 cm) and *fanegada* (1,000 square varas).

ENERGY AND NATURAL RESOURCES

Environment. In 2002 Colombia's carbon dioxide emissions from the consumption and flaring of fossil fuels were the equivalent of 1·4 tonnes per capita.

Electricity. Installed capacity of electric power (2000) was 12·7m. kW. In 2000 production was 43·94bn. kWh and consumption per capita 1,039 kWh.

Oil and Gas. Crude oil production (2003) 27·9m. tonnes. Natural gas production in 2002 totalled 6·2bn. cu. metres. In 2002 there were proven oil reserves of 1·9bn. bbls. and proven gas reserves of 130bn. cu. metres.

Minerals. Production (2001): gold, 21,813 kg; silver, 7,242 kg; platinum (1998), 14,016 troy oz. Other important minerals include: copper, lead, mercury, manganese, nickel and emeralds (of which Colombia accounts for about half of world production).

Coal production (2000): 38·36m. tonnes; iron ore (2000): 660,000 tonnes; salt production (1998): 159,621 tonnes.

Agriculture. There is a wide range of climate and, consequently, crops. In 2001 there were 2·52m. ha of arable land and 1·73m. ha of permanent crops.

Production, 2000 (in 1,000 tonnes): sugarcane, 37,000; potatoes, 2,705; plantains, 2,689; rice, 2,100; cassava, 1,956; bananas, 1,570; maize, 1,010; coffee, 630. Colombia is the third largest coffee producer in the world after Brazil and Vietnam. Coca was cultivated in 2000 on approximately 135,000 ha, up from 40,000 ha in

1992. Coca leaf production in 2000 totalled 88,000 tonnes, making Colombia the world's largest producer of coca leaves, the raw material for cocaine.

Livestock (2000): 26,000,000 cattle; 2,800,000 pigs; 2,200,000 sheep; 2,450,000 horses; 100m. chickens. Meat production, 2000: beef and veal, 754,000 tonnes; poultry meat, 520,000 tonnes; pork, bacon and ham, 152,000 tonnes.

Forestry. In 2000 the area under forests was 49·6m. ha, or 47·8% of the total land area. Timber production in 2001 was 12·5m. cu. metres.

Fisheries. Total catch (2001) was approximately 125,000 tonnes, of which about 80% was from marine waters.

INDUSTRY

Production (in tonnes): cement (2001), 6,776,000; petrol (2000), 4,900,000; distillate fuel oil (2000), 3,038,000; residual fuel oil (2000), 2,922,000; sugar (2002), 2,522,637; steel ingots (1998), 264,466; soft drinks (2001), 1,832·5m. litres; beer (2001), 1,421·3m. litres; passenger cars (1998), 49,807 units; industrial vehicles (1998), 14,162 units.

Labour. The economically active workforce in 2001 was 18·65m., of which 16·62m. were employed. The main areas of activity in 2001 were: wholesale and retail trade, restaurants and hotels (employing 4·19m. persons); community, social and personal services (3·74m.); and agriculture, hunting, forestry and fishing (3·49m.). The unemployment rate in 2002 was 15·7%.

INTERNATIONAL TRADE

Foreign companies are liable for basic income tax of 30% and surtax of 7·5%. Since 1993 tax on profit remittance has started at 12%, reducing (except for oil companies) to 7% after three years. Foreign debt was US$33,853m. in 2002.

The Group of Three (G-3) free trade pact with Mexico and Venezuela came into effect on 1 Jan. 1995.

Imports and Exports. In US$1m.:

	1999	*2000*	*2001*	*2002*
Exports f.o.b.	12,037	13,620	12,772	12,303
Imports f.o.b.	10,262	11,090	12,269	12,077

Main export markets, 2000: USA (50·0%), Venezuela (9·9%), Ecuador (3·5%), Germany (3·2%). Major import suppliers, 2000: USA (33·7%), Venezuela (8·2%), Japan (4·6%), Brazil (4·4%). Main exports in 1999 were (in US$1m.): crude oil (3,334·4), chemicals and related products (1,163·7), coal (835·2), bananas (559·5), cut flowers (550·4) and clothing (426·6).

COMMUNICATIONS

Roads. Total length of roads was 112,988 km in 1999 (including 16,575 km of main roads), of which 14·4% were paved. Of the 3,700-km Simón Bolívar highway, which runs from Caracas in Venezuela to Guayaquil in Ecuador, the Colombian portion is complete. Motor vehicles in 1999 numbered 2,122,495, of which 1,803,201 were passenger cars, 184,495 vans and trucks, and 134,799 buses and coaches.

Rail. The National Railways (2,532 km of route, 914 mm gauge) went into liquidation in 1990 prior to takeover of services and obligations by three new public companies in 1992. Freight tonne-km came to 373m. in 1999. Total rail track, 3,304 km. A metro system operates in Medellín.

Civil Aviation. There are international airports at Barranquilla, Bogotá (Eldorado), Cali, Cartagena, Medellín and San Andrés. The national carriers are Avianca and ACES. In 1998 Avianca flew 48·5m. km and carried 3,924,100 passengers; ACES flew 20·1m. km and carried 2,078,500 passengers in 1997. The busiest airport is Bogotá, which in 2000 handled 7,154,312 passengers (5,234,807 on domestic flights) and 372,957 tonnes of freight.

Shipping. Vessels entering Colombian ports in 1995 unloaded 13,806,000 tonnes of imports and loaded 26,284,000 tonnes of exports. In 2000 vessels totalling 52,442,000 NRT entered ports and vessels totalling 50,787,000 NRT cleared. The merchant marine totalled 68,000 GRT in 2002, including oil tankers 6,000 GRT.

The Magdalena River is subject to drought, and navigation is always impeded during the dry season, but it is an important artery of passenger and goods traffic. The river is navigable for 1,400 km; steamers ascend to La Dorada, 953 km from Barranquilla.

Telecommunications. In 2002 there were 12,363,000 telephone subscribers (285·6 for every 1,000 inhabitants) and 2,133,000 PCs in use (49·3 for every 1,000 persons). The number of Internet users was 2·0m. in 2002. Mobile phone subscribers numbered 4,596,000 in 2002 and there were 242,000 fax machines in 1999.

Postal Services. In 1998 there were 1,354 post offices.

SOCIAL INSTITUTIONS

Justice. The July 1991 constitution introduced the offices of public prosecutor and public defence. There is no extradition of Colombians for trial in other countries. The Supreme Court, at Bogotá, of 20 members, is divided into three chambers—civil cassation (six), criminal cassation (eight), labour cassation (six). Each of the 61 judicial districts has a superior court with various sub-dependent tribunals of lower juridical grade.

In 2003 there were 23,013 murders (a rate of around 52 per 100,000 persons), down 20% on the 2002 total. Colombia's murder rate is among the highest in the world. In 2003 the reported number of kidnappings numbered 2,200, the highest in the world, albeit down 26% on the 2002 total.

The police force numbered 73,176 in 1989. Colombia abolished the death penalty in 1997. The population in penal institutions in May 2001 was 54,034 (126 per 100,000 of national population).

Religion. The religion is Roman Catholic (39·59m. adherents in 2001), with the Cardinal Archbishop of Bogotá as Primate of Colombia and nine other archbishoprics. There are also 44 bishops, 8 apostolic vicars, 5 apostolic prefects and 2 prelates. In 1990 there were 1,546 parishes and 4,020 priests. In Sept. 2003 there were three cardinals. Other forms of religion are permitted so long as their exercise is 'not contrary to Christian morals or the law'. In 2001 there were 3·48m. followers of other religions.

Education. Primary education is free but not compulsory. Schools are both state and privately controlled. In 2000–01 there were 53,357 teachers for 1,070,482 children in pre-primary schools; 197,374 teachers for 5,221,018 pupils in primary schools; and 3,568,889 pupils with 185,588 teachers in secondary schools. In 1995 there were 235 higher education establishments with 562,716 students.

In 1995–96 in the public sector there were 20 universities, one open university, three technological universities, and universities of education, educational technology and industry. There were also two colleges of public administration, one school of police studies, one institute of fine art, one polytechnic and one conservatory. In the private sector there were 25 universities, four Roman Catholic universities, one college of education and one school of administration. There were eight public, and 44 private, other institutions of higher education. In 1994–95 there were 208,394 university students.

Adult literacy in 2001 was 91·9% (91·9% among both males and females).

In 2000–01 total expenditure on education came to 5·2% of GNP and represented 17·4% of total government expenditure.

Health. In 1997 there were 1,165 hospitals with 47,236 beds. Medical personnel was as follows: doctors, 40,355; dentists, 22,121; nurses, 13,558; auxiliaries, 38,723.

Welfare. The retirement age is 60 (men), or 55 (women); to be eligible for a state pension 1,000 weeks of contributions are required. The minimum social insurance pension is equal to the minimum wage. If a private pension is less than the minimum pension set by law, the government makes up the difference.

Unemployment benefit is a month's wage for every year of employment.

CULTURE

World Heritage Sites. Colombia's heritage sites as classified by UNESCO (with year entered on list) are: the Port, Fortresses and Group of Monuments, Cartagena

(1984)—on the Caribbean coast, Cartagena was one of the first cities to be founded in South America; Los Katios National Park (1994); the Historic Centre of Santa Cruz de Mompox (1995), or Mompós, was a focal point for colonization and a vital trade post between the Caribbean coast and the interior; the National Archaeological Park of Tierradentro (1995) contains statues and elaborately decorated underground tombs dating from the 6th–10th centuries; the San Agustín Archaeological Park (1995) protects religious monuments and sculptures from the 1st–8th centuries.

Broadcasting. There are five radio companies overseen by the Dirección General de Radiocomunicaciones. Instituto Nacional de Radio y Televisión transmits on three networks (colour by NTSC) and rents air time to 26 commercial companies. In 2000 there were 21·6m. radio sets and in 2001 there were 12·3m. TV sets. There are 33 television broadcast stations.

Press. There were 37 daily newspapers in 1996, with daily circulation totalling 1·8m.

Tourism. In 2000 there were 530,000 foreign tourists, bringing revenue of US$1,028m.

DIPLOMATIC REPRESENTATIVES

Of Colombia in the United Kingdom (Flat 3a, 3 Hans Cres., London, SW1X 0LN)
Ambassador: Dr Alfonso Lopez-Cabellero.

Of the United Kingdom in Colombia (Edificio Ing. Barings, Carrera 9 No 76–49, Piso 9, Bogotá)
Ambassador: Tom Duggin.

Of Colombia in the USA (2118 Leroy Pl., NW, Washington, D.C., 20008)
Ambassador: Luis Alberto Moreno.

Of the USA in Colombia (Carrera 45 # 22D-45, Bogotá)
Ambassador: William B. Wood.

Of Colombia to the United Nations
Ambassador: María Angela Holguín-Cuellar.

Of Colombia to the European Union
Ambassador: Nicolas Echavarría Mesa.

FURTHER READING

Departamento Administrativo Nacional de Estadística. *Boletin de Estadistica.* Monthly.

Davis, Robert H., *Historical Dictionary of Colombia.* 2nd ed. Metuchen (NJ), 1994.—*Colombia.* [Bibliography] ABC-Clio, Oxford and Santa Barbara (CA), 1990

Dudley, Steven, *Walking Ghosts: Murder and Guerrilla Politics in Colombia.* Routledge, London, 2004

Thorp, R., *Economic Management and Economic Development in Peru and Colombia.* London, 1991

National statistical office: Departamento Administrativo Nacional de Estadística (DANE), AA 80043, Zona Postal 611, Bogotá.
Website (Spanish only): http://www.dane.gov.co/

COMOROS

Union des Iles Comores

Capital: Moroni
Population projection, 2010: 927,000
GDP per capita, 2002: (PPP$) 1,690
HDI/world rank: 0·530/136

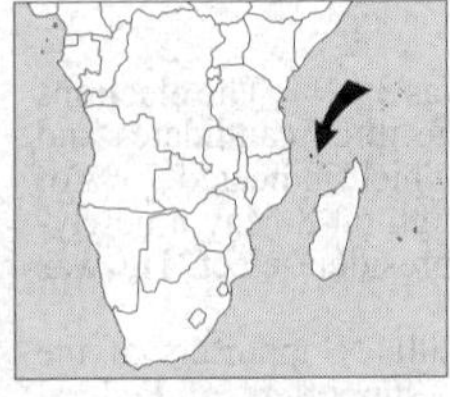

KEY HISTORICAL EVENTS

The three islands forming the present state became French protectorates at the end of the 19th century and were proclaimed colonies in 1912. With neighbouring Mayotte they were administratively attached to Madagascar from 1914 until 1947 when the four islands became a French Overseas Territory, achieving internal self-government in Dec. 1961. In referendums held on each island on 22 Dec. 1974, the three western islands voted overwhelmingly for independence, while Mayotte voted to remain French. There have been more than 20 coups or attempted takeovers since independence, with recent years being marked by political disruption. In 1997 the islands of Anjouan and Mohéli attempted to secede from the federation.

In April 1999 an agreement was brokered on a federal structure for the three main islands—Grand Comore, Anjouan and Mohéli—to be known as the Union of Comoros Islands. However, the delegates from Anjouan did not sign the agreement. Violence broke out in the capital, Moroni, against Anjouans living there. A military coup followed on 30 April 1999, led by Col. Azaly Assoumani. He subsequently dissolved the government and the constitution, declaring a transitional government.

TERRITORY AND POPULATION

The Comoros consist of three islands in the Indian Ocean between the African mainland and Madagascar with a total area of 1,862 sq. km (719 sq. miles). The population at the 1991 census was 446,817; provisional census population, 2003, 590,151; density, 317 per sq. km.

The UN gives a projected population for 2010 of 927,000.

In 2001, 66·2% of the population were rural.

	Area (sq. km)	*Population (2003 census, provisional)*	*Chief town*
Njazídja (Grande Comore)	1,148	295,655	Moroni
Nzwani (Anjouan)	424	259,099	Mutsamudu
Mwali (Mohéli)	290	35,378	Fomboni

Estimated population of the chief towns (2002): Moroni, 40,275; Mutsamudu, 21,558; Domoni, 13,254; Fomboni, 13,053.

The indigenous population are a mixture of Malagasy, African, Malay and Arab peoples; the vast majority speak Comorian, an Arabized dialect of Swahili, but a small proportion speak Makua (a Bantu language) or one of the official languages, French and Arabic.

SOCIAL STATISTICS

1996 births, 26,100; deaths, 5,900. Birth rate per 1,000 population, 1996, 45·8; death, 10·3. Annual population growth rate, 1992–2002, 3·0%. Infant mortality, 59 per 1,000 live births (2001). Expectation of life in 2001 was 58·8 years among men and 61·6 among females. Fertility rate, 2001, 5·1 children per woman.

CLIMATE

There is a tropical climate, affected by Indian monsoon winds from the north, which gives a wet season from Nov. to April. Moroni, Jan. 81°F (27·2°C), July 75°F (23·9°C). Annual rainfall, 113" (2,825 mm).

CONSTITUTION AND GOVERNMENT

At a referendum on 23 Dec. 2001, 77% of voters approved a new constitution that keeps the three islands as one country while granting each one greater autonomy.

The *President of the Union* is Head of State.

There used to be a *Federal Assembly* comprised of 42 democratically elected officials and a 15-member *Senate* chosen by an electoral college, but these were dissolved after the 1999 coup. A new 33-member *Federal Parliament* was established following the elections of April 2004.

National Anthem. 'Udzima wa ya Masiwa' ('The union of the islands'); words by S. H. Abderamane, tune by K. Abdallah and S. H. Abderamane.

RECENT ELECTIONS

Presidential elections were held on 14 April 2002. Turn-out was 39·1%. The elections were marred by violence and were boycotted by two of the three candidates and by most of the voters of Anjouan. On 22 April the results, which indicated 75% of votes cast for Col. Azaly Assoumani, were cancelled, although on 8 May a newly-appointed electoral commission confirmed Assoumani as president-elect. He was subsequently sworn in as president on 26 May.

Parliamentary elections were held on 18 and 25 April 2004. Supporters of the three regional presidents won 12 of the 18 elected seats; supporters of Federal President Azaly Assoumani won six. Holding a majority, the regional presidents each appointed five legislators.

CURRENT ADMINISTRATION

President of the Union: Col. Azaly Assoumani; b. 1959 (sworn in 26 May 2002, having previously seized power in a coup on 30 April 1999 and having been president until 21 Jan. 2002).

President of Anjouan: Mohamed Bacar. *President of Grande Comore:* Mze Soule El Bak. *President of Mohéli:* Mohamed Fazul.

In March 2005 the government comprised:

Vice President of the Union Responsible for Administrative Services in Anjouan and Minister of Solidarity, Health, Population, Social Protection and State Reform: Caabi El Yachroutu. *Vice President of the Union Responsible for Administrative Services in Mohéli and Minister of Justice, Islamic Affairs, Human Rights and Parliamentary Relations:* Ben Massoundi Rachidi.

Minister of State for Foreign Affairs and Co-operation: Souef Mohamed Elamine. *Finance and Budget:* Ahamadi Abdoulbastoi. *Defence, Homeland Security, Strategic Infrastructures, Communication and Government Spokesperson:* M'Saidie Houmed. *Economy, Foreign Trade and Industrial Development:* Maoulana Charif. *Rural Development, Fisheries, Handicrafts and Environment:* Mohamed Abdoulhamid. *Planning and Land Management:* Said Hamza. *National and Higher Education and Research:* Yahaya Mohamed Iliassa.

Secretary of State for Co-operation: Moustradroine Abdou. *Homeland Security and Communication:* Abdou Madi Mari.

Office of the President: http://www.presidence-uniondescomores.com

DEFENCE

Army. The Army was reorganized after a failed coup in Sept. 1995.

Navy. One landing craft with ramps was purchased in 1981. Two small patrol boats were supplied by Japan in 1982. Personnel in 1996 numbered about 200.

INTERNATIONAL RELATIONS

Comoros is a member of the UN, the League of Arab States, African Development Bank, COMESA, OIC, Islamic Development Bank and the International Organization of the Francophonie, and an ACP member state of the ACP-EU relationship.

ECONOMY

Agriculture accounted for 40·9% of GDP in 2002, industry 11·9% and services 47·2%.

Currency. The unit of currency is the *Comorian franc* (KMF) of 100 *centimes.* It is pegged to the euro at 491·96775 *Comorian francs* to the euro. Foreign exchange reserves were US$76m. in June 2002 and total money supply was 24,586m. Comorian francs. There was inflation of 3·3% in 2002.

Budget. Revenues were 15·6bn. Comorian francs and expenditures 17·7bn. Comorian francs in 2000.

Performance. Real GDP growth was 1·9% in 2001 and 2·5% in 2002. In 2003 total GDP was US$0·3bn.

Banking and Finance. The Central Bank is the bank of issue. Chief commercial banks include the Banque Internationale des Comores, the Banque de Développement des Comores and the Banque pour l'Industrie et le Commerce-Comores.

ENERGY AND NATURAL RESOURCES

Environment. Carbon dioxide emissions from the consumption and flaring of fossil fuels were the equivalent of 0·1 tonnes per capita in 2002.

Electricity. In 2000 installed capacity was 6,000 kW. Production was around 19m. kWh in 2000; consumption per capita was an estimated 27 kWh in 2000.

Agriculture. 80% of the economically active population depends upon agriculture, which (including fishing, hunting and forestry) contributed 41% to GDP in 2002. There were 80,000 ha of arable land in 2001 and 52,000 ha of permanent crops. The chief product was formerly sugarcane, but now vanilla, copra, maize and other food crops, cloves and essential oils (citronella, ylang-ylang, lemon grass) are the most important products. Production (2000 in 1,000 tonnes): coconuts, 75; bananas, 59; cassava, 53; rice, 17; copra, 9; taro, 9; sweet potatoes, 6.

Livestock (2000): goats, 140,000; cattle, 52,000; sheep, 20,000; asses, 5,000.

Forestry. In 2000 the area under forest was 8,000 ha, or 4·3% of the total land area. The forested area has been severely reduced because of the shortage of cultivable land and ylang-ylang production. In 2001, 9,000 cu. metres of timber were cut.

Fisheries. Fishing is on an individual basis, without modern equipment. The catch totalled to be 12,180 tonnes in 2001.

INDUSTRY

Branches include perfume distillation, textiles, furniture, jewellery, soft drinks and the processing of vanilla and copra.

Labour. The workforce in 1996 was 286,000 (58% males).

INTERNATIONAL TRADE

Total foreign debt was US$270m. in 2002.

Imports and Exports. In 2000 imports amounted to US$43·7m. and exports to US$11·9m.

Main export markets, 2000: France, 38·6%; USA, 19·9%; Germany, 6·6%. Main import suppliers, 2000: France, 36·6%; Pakistan, 13·7%; Kenya, 10·8%. The main exports are vanilla (US$6·2m. in 1995), cloves, ylang-ylang, essences, cocoa, copra and coffee. Principal imports are rice (US$14·1m. in 1995), petroleum products (US$7·7m. in 1995), cement, meat, vehicles, and iron and steel.

COMMUNICATIONS

Roads. In 1999 there were 880 km of roads, of which 76·5% were paved.

Civil Aviation. There is an international airport at Moroni (International Prince Said Ibrahim). In 2000 it handled 103,000 passengers (79,000 on international flights).

Shipping. In 2002 the merchant marine totalled 407,000 GRT.

Telecommunications. There were 10,300 telephone main lines in 2002 (13·5 per 1,000 persons) and 4,000 PCs in use (5·5 per 1,000 persons). In 1995 there were 200 fax machines. Internet users numbered 3,200 in 2002.

Postal Services. In 1998 there were 37 post offices.

SOCIAL INSTITUTIONS

Justice. French and Muslim law is in a new consolidated code. The Supreme Court comprises seven members, two each appointed by the President and the Federal Assembly, and one by each island's Legislative Council. The death penalty is authorized for murder. The last execution was in 1996.

Religion. Islam is the official religion: 98% of the population are Muslims; there is a small Christian minority. Following the coup of April 1999 the federal government discouraged the practice of religions other than Islam, with Christians especially facing restrictions on worship.

Education. After two pre-primary years at Koran school, which 50% of children attend, there are six years of primary schooling for seven- to 13-year-olds followed by a four-year secondary stage attended by 25% of children. Some 5% of 17- to 20-year-olds conclude schooling at *lycées*. There were 97,706 pupils with 2,723 teachers in primary schools in 2000–01 and 24,324 pupils at secondary schools in 1999–2000. There were 714 students in tertiary education in 1999–2000.

The adult literacy rate in 2001 was 56·0% (63·3% among males and 48·8% among females).

In 1998–99 total expenditure on education came to 3·8% of GNP.

Health. In 1997 there were 64 physicians, 180 nurses and 74 midwives. In 1995 there were 29 hospital beds per 10,000 inhabitants.

CULTURE

Broadcasting. The state-controlled Radio Comoros broadcasts in French and Comorian. In 1997 there were 90,000 radio and 1,000 television receivers.

Press. There was one weekly newspaper in 1997.

Tourism. In 2000 there were 24,000 foreign tourists (around a third from France), bringing revenue of US$15m.

DIPLOMATIC REPRESENTATIVES

Of the United Kingdom in the Comoros
Ambassador: Brian Donaldson (resides at Antananarivo, Madagascar).

Of the Comoros in the USA (Temporary: c/o the Permanent Mission of the Union of the Comoran Islands to the United Nations, 430 E 50th Street, N.Y. 10022)
Ambassador: Vacant.

Of the USA in the Comoros
Ambassador: John Price (resides at Port Louis, Mauritius).

Of the Comoros to the United Nations
Ambassador: Vacant.
Chargé d'Affaires a.i.: Mahmoud M. Aboud.

Of the Comoros to the European Union
Ambassador (Designate): Sultan Chouzour.

FURTHER READING

Ottenheimer, M. and Ottenheimer, H. J., *Historical Dictionary of the Comoro Islands.* Metuchen (NJ), 1994

CONGO, DEMOCRATIC REPUBLIC OF THE (FORMERLY ZAÏRE)

République Démocratique du Congo

Capital: Kinshasa
Population projection, 2010: 64·71m.
GDP per capita, 2002: (PPP$) 650
HDI/world rank: 0·365/168

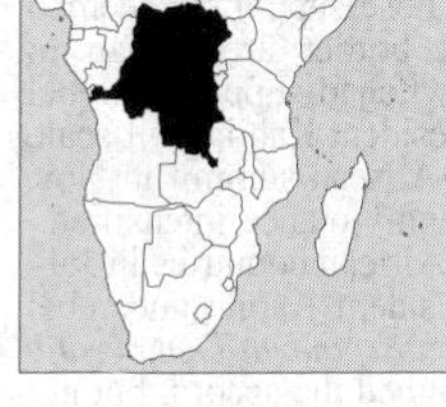

KEY HISTORICAL EVENTS

Bantu tribes migrated to the Congo basin from the north-west in the first millennium AD, forming several kingdoms and many smaller forest communities. Kongo emerged as a kingdom on the Atlantic coast in the 14th century. King Nzinga Mbemba entered into diplomatic relations with Portugal after 1492. Christian missionaries, who baptized the king Affonso, caused divisions in Kongo society; the Portuguese were expelled in 1526, only to be welcomed back after attacks by the Jagas in the late 16th century.

The Luba kingdom was centred on the marshy Upemba depression in the south-east. Expansion began in the late 18th century under Ilungu Sungu. A tribute system extended Luba power and established trading relations with East Africa. In central Congo the Kuba kingdom was established in the 17th century as a federation of Bantu groups. Agriculture became the mainstay of the Kuba economy, strengthened by the introduction of American crops by Europeans. Trade made the Kuba elite, especially the Bushoong group, wealthy and encouraged the development of art and decorated cloth. Kuba thrived until the incursions of the Nsapo in the late 19th century.

King Léopold II of the Belgians claimed the Congo Basin as a personal possession in 1885. Exploitation of the native population provoked international condemnation. The Belgian government responded by annexing the Congo in 1908. Political representation was denied the Congolese until 1957, when the colonial administration introduced the *statut des villes* in response to the revolutionary demands of the *Alliance des BaKongo* (Abako). Political violence increased, instigated by the *Mouvement National Congolais* (MNC), led by Patrice Lumumba. Local elections were held in Dec. 1959 and in Jan. 1960 the Belgian government announced a rapid independence programme. After general elections in May, the Republic of the Congo became independent on 1 June 1960, with Lumumba as prime minister and Joseph Kasavubu, the Abako leader, as president.

The country descended into anarchy, with the mineral-rich Katanga region declaring independence. Lumumba was ousted and in 1961 was assassinated. Only in 2002 did Belgium admit to participating in his murder. Lieut.-Gen. Joseph-Désiré Mobutu (later Sésé Séko) seized power in 1965. At first he was seen as a strongman who could hold together a huge, unstable country comprising hundreds of tribes and language groups. He changed the country's name to Zaïre in 1971. In the 1970s he was feted by the USA, which used Zaïre as a springboard for operations into neighbouring Angola where western-backed Unita rebels were locked in civil war with a Cuban and Soviet backed government. Because Mobutu was useful in the fight against Communism the brutality and repressiveness of his regime was ignored.

After armed insurrection by Tutsi rebels in the province of Kivu, the government alleged pro-Tutsi intervention by the armies of Burundi and Rwanda and on 25 Oct. 1996 declared a state of emergency. By Dec. the secessionist forces of Laurent-Désiré Kabila, the *Alliance des Forces Démocratiques pour la Libération du Congo-Zaïre* (AFDL), had begun to drive the regular Zaïrean army out of Kivu and an attempt was made to establish a rebel administration, called 'Democratic Congo'. In the face of continuing rebel military successes and the disaffection of the army, the Government accepted a UN resolution demanding the immediate cessation of hostilities. The Security Council asked the rebels to make a public declaration of their acceptance. However, they continued in their victorious advance westwards, capturing Kisangani on 15 March 1997, then Kasai and Shaba, giving Kabila control of eastern Zaïre, and crucially the country's mineral wealth. After a futile attempt to deploy Serbian mercenaries, Mobutu succumbed to pressure—particularly from the USA and South Africa—agreeing to meet Kabila, an occasion that had all the trappings of a symbolic surrender. Mobutu fled on the night of 15–16 May 1997. He died of cancer four months later. Described as one of the most destructive tyrants of the African independence era, it is said that his personal fortune, if ever recovered, could wipe out his country's national debt.

On coming to power Kabila changed the name of the country to the Democratic Republic of the Congo. Hopes for democratic and economic renewal were soon disappointed. The Kabila regime relied too closely on its military backup, mainly Rwandans and eastern Congolese from the Tutsi minority. Those supporters seemed more interested in eliminating tribal enemies in eastern border areas than in establishing democracy. As a result, Rwanda and Uganda switched support to rebel forces. When Zimbabwe and Angola sent in troops to help President Kabila, full-scale civil war threatened. A ceasefire was negotiated at a Franco-African summit in Nov. 1998 but the military build-up continued into the new year and violence intensified.

A ceasefire was signed by leaders from more than a dozen African countries in July 1999 to bring the civil war between the government of President Kabila and rebel forces to an end. Rival factions of the *Rassemblement Congolais pour la Démocratie* (RCD), the main rebel group opposed to the president, also signed the accord, but not until Sept. The threat remained of an early return to outright civil war.

'On the third anniversary of Kabila's assumption of power, a dispatch from the Panafrican News Agency reviewed the Democratic Republic of the Congo's condition:– Basic infrastructure is in total decay. Major sections of trunk "A" roads ... are not usable. Proposals for the rehabilitation of other facilities, such as hospitals, industries, manufacturing, and other structures, have also been stalled. On the social front, dirt and environmental decay have spewed all sorts of diseases. Smallpox, diarrhoea, sleeping sickness, among others, have come back in force while AIDS, malaria and poliomyelitis continue to devastate a population already weakened by under-nourishment... More than 60 per cent of the country's working population is not at work...' (*The New Yorker*, 25 Sept. 2000).

On 16 Jan. 2001 President Kabila was assassinated, allegedly by one of his own bodyguards. Kabila was succeeded by his son Joseph.

Prospects for peace improved dramatically in Feb. 2001 when the UN Security Council approved a plan for the disengagement of the warring factions that would allow the eventual deployment of 3,000 UN-supported peacekeepers. In early 2002 talks between the government and rebels on how to end the conflict ended without a satisfactory agreement embracing all factions. However, talks were resumed and in July 2002 the presidents of the Democratic Republic of the Congo and neighbouring Rwanda signed a peace deal that was expected to be the first stage towards ending the war which has claimed more than 3m. lives. In Oct. 2002 Rwanda completed the withdrawal of its forces. The Democratic Republic of the Congo and Uganda also signed a peace agreement.

The conflict, described as Africa's first continental war, had drawn in Zimbabwe, Angola and Namibia (and, for a time, Sudan and Chad) on the side of the government, which controls the west of the country, while Rwanda and Uganda backed other rival factions. The RCD, which controls areas in the east, was backed by Rwanda, while Uganda supported the *Mouvement de Libération du Congo* (MLC), based in the north and northeast of the country. Burundi also had troops in the country, allied to the Rwandans, although they stayed close to the border with Burundi. In addition to the huge death toll, large numbers of people were displaced and sought asylum in Tanzania and Zambia. In Dec. 2002 the government and leading rebel forces reached an agreement on power-sharing. Joseph Kabila was to remain as president, with a transitional power-sharing government, until elections scheduled for Nov. 2005.

TERRITORY AND POPULATION

The Democratic Republic of the Congo is bounded in the north by the Central African Republic, northeast by Sudan, east by Uganda, Rwanda, Burundi and Lake

Tanganyika, south by Zambia, southwest by Angola and northwest by the Republic of the Congo. There is a 37-km stretch of coastline which gives access to the Atlantic Ocean, with the Angolan exclave of Cabinda to the immediate north, and Angola itself to the south. Area, 2,344,798 sq. km (905,327 sq. miles). At the 1988 census the population was 34·7m. Estimate (2002) 48,874,000 (70% rural, 1999); density, 21 per sq. km.

The UN gives a projected population for 2010 of 64·71m.

More than 200,000 refugees who escaped the fighting between Hutus and Tutsis in Rwanda and Burundi in 1994 are still in the Democratic Republic of the Congo (out of 1m. who came originally), and there are also 100,000 Angolan and 100,000 Sudanese refugees in the country.

Area and populations (1998 estimate) of the provinces (plus Kinshasa City), with their chief towns (1994 population estimates):

Region	*Area (sq. km)*	*Population (in 1,000)*	*Chief town*	*Population*
Bandundu	295,658	5,201	Bandundu	. . .
Bas-Congo	53,920	2,835	Matadi	172,730
Equateur	403,292	4,820	Mbandaka	169,841
Kasai Occidental	154,742	3,337	Kananga	393,030
Kasai Oriental	170,302	3,830	Mbuji-Mayi	806,475
Katanga	496,877	4,125	Lubumbashi	851,381
Maniema	132,250	1,247	Kindu	. . .
Nord-Kivu	59,483	3,564	Goma	109,094
Orientale	503,239	5,566	Kisangani	417,517
Sud-Kivu	65,070	2,838	Bukavu	201,569
Kinshasa City[1]	9,965	4,787	Kinshasa	4,885,000[2]

[1]Neutral city. [2]1999 figure.

Other large cities (with estimated 1994 population): Kolwezi (417,810), Likasi (299,118), Kikwit (182,142), Tshikapa (180,860).

The population is Bantu, with minorities of Sudanese (in the north), Nilotes (northeast), Pygmies and Hamites (in the east). French is the official language, but of more than 200 languages spoken, four are recognized as national languages: Kiswahili, Tshiluba, Kikongo and Lingala. Lingala has become the *lingua franca* after French.

SOCIAL STATISTICS

1997 births, 2,263,000; deaths, 788,000. Rates (1997 estimates, per 1,000 population); birth, 47·7; death, 16·6. Annual population growth rate, 1992–2002, 2·4%. Infant mortality in 2001 was 129 per 1,000 live births. Expectation of life in 2001 was 39·6 years for men and 41·7 for females. Fertility rate, 2001, 6·7 children per woman.

CLIMATE

The climate is varied, the central region having an equatorial climate, with year-long high temperatures and rain at all seasons. Elsewhere, depending on position north or south of the Equator, there are well-marked wet and dry seasons. The mountains of the east and south have a temperate mountain climate, with the highest summits having considerable snowfall. Kinshasa, Jan. 79°F (26·1°C), July 73°F (22·8°C). Annual rainfall 45" (1,125 mm). Kananga, Jan. 76°F (24·4°C), July 74°F (23·3°C). Annual rainfall 62" (1,584 mm). Kisangani, Jan. 78°F (25·6°C), July 75°F (23·9°C). Annual rainfall 68" (1,704 mm). Lubumbashi, Jan. 72°F (22·2°C), July 61°F (16·1°C). Annual rainfall 50" (1,237 mm).

CONSTITUTION AND GOVERNMENT

The 1978 constitution stipulated a one-party system. In 1991 Marshal Mobutu Sésé Séko convened a national conference for the transition to multi-party democracy. This led to a new constitution, approved in 1994.

Gen. Laurent-Désiré Kabila seized power on 17 May 1997 but the civil war continued. He assumed the powers of both chief of state and head of government. A new constitution came into force in 1998. A ceasefire, brokered by President Frederick Chiluba of Zambia, was signed by Sept. 1999 by all major groups involved in the civil war. All parties agreed to administer the areas under their control at the time. Kabila was assassinated in Jan. 2001 and was succeeded by his son, Joseph. The ban on political parties was lifted in May 2001. In Dec. 2002 the commitments laid down in the Lusaka peace agreement of 1999 were settled by the main groups. In April 2003 a new constitution was adopted, providing for the installation of a provisional government agreed by rival factions, to rule for two years. A power-sharing transitional government was announced on 30 June 2003.

The 240-member *Constituent and Legislative Assembly* was appointed in Aug. 2000 by former President Laurent Désiré Kabila. In Aug. 2003 a new bicameral parliament of 500 members and 120 senators met in Kinshasa. The representatives were chosen from the groups that comprise the new transitional government.

National Anthem. 'Debout Congolais' ('Stand up, Congolese'); words and tune by J. Lutumba and S. Boka.

RECENT ELECTIONS

The Democratic Republic of the Congo's first elections since independence in 1960 are set to take place in Nov. 2005.

CURRENT ADMINISTRATION

President: Joseph Kabila; b. 1971 (in office since 17 Jan. 2001).

On 30 June 2003 a new transitional government was announced, composed of members of the former government (f.g.), the political opposition (p.o.), the *Rassemblement Congolais pour la Démocratie* (RCD-Goma), the *Rassemblement Congolais pour la Démocratie-Nationale* (RCD-N), the *Rassemblement Congolais pour la Démocratie-Mouvement de Libération* (RCD-ML), the *Mouvement de Libération du Congo* (MLC) and the *Mayi-Mayi*. Several members of civil society (c.s.) were also appointed. In March 2005 the government comprised:

Vice-Presidents: Jean-Pierre Bemba (MLC), Abdoulaye Yerodia Ndombasi (f.g.), Arthur Z'ahidi Ngoma (p.o.) and Azarias Ruberwa (RCD-Goma).

Minister for the Interior, Decentralization and Security: Théophile Mbemba Fundu (f.g.). *Foreign Affairs and International Co-operation:* Raymond Ramazani Baya (MLC). *Regional Co-operation:* Mbusa Nyamwisi (RCD-ML). *Defence, Demobilization and War Veterans:* Adolphe Onusumba (RCD-Goma). *Family and Women's Affairs:* Faida Mwangila (RCD-Goma). *Justice:* Honorius Kisimba Ngoy (p.o.). *Human Rights:* Marie-Madeleine Kalala (c.s.). *Press and Information:* Henri Mova Sakanyi (f.g.). *Planning:* Alexis Thambwe Mwamba (MLC). *Budget:* François Mwamba Tshishimbi (RCD-Goma). *Finance:* Pierre André Futa (f.g.). *Economy:* Floribert Bokanga (RCD-Goma). *Industry and Small and Medium Enterprises:* Jean Mbuyu Lunyongola (f.g.). *Mines:* Ingele Ifoto (p.o.). *Energy:* Pierre Muzumba Mwana Ombe (f.g.). *External Trade:* Chantal Ngalula Mulumba (RCD-N). *State Properties:* Célestin Mvunabandi (RCD-Goma). *Civil Service:* Athenase Matenda Kyelu (c.s.). *Agriculture:* Paul Musafiri (MLC). *Rural Development:* Pardonne Kaliba Munanga (Mayi-Mayi). *Posts and Telecommunications:* Gertrude Kitembo (RCD-Goma). *Scientific Research:* Gérard Kamanda Wa Kamanda (p.o.). *Public Works and Infrastructure:* José Makila (MLC). *Transport and Communications:* Eva Makasa (p.o.). *Environment:* Anselme Enerunga (Mayi-Mayi). *Tourism:* José Engbanda (MLC). *Land Affairs:* Venant Tshipasa (p.o.). *Health:* Emile Bongeli Yekolo (f.g.). *University and Higher Education:* Jean-Pierre Lola Kisanga (RCD-Goma). *Primary, Secondary and Professional Education:* Constant Ndom Nda Ombel (MLC). *Labour and Social Welfare:* Balamage Nkolo (RCD-Goma). *Social Affairs:* Laurent-Charles Otete (p.o.). *Youth and Sports:* Roger Nimy (MLC). *Humanitarian Affairs and Solidarity:* Catherine Nzuzi Wa Mbombo (p.o.). *Culture and Arts:* Christophe Muzungu (f.g.). *Urban Affairs:* John Tibasima (RCD-ML).

DEFENCE

Following the overthrow of the Mobutu regime in May 1997, the former Zaïrean armed forces were in disarray. In June 2003 command of ground forces and naval forces were handed over to the RCD-Goma and MLC factions respectively as part of the power-sharing transitional government. Supreme command of the armed forces will remain in the hands of the former government faction.

A UN mission, MONUC, has been in the Democratic Republic of the Congo since 1999. It currently numbers 11,500 (growing to 16,000) and ranks among the largest peacekeeping forces in the world.

Defence expenditure totalled US$946m. in 2002 (US$18 per capita), representing 21·7% of GDP.

Army. The total strength of the Army was estimated at 79,000 (2002). There is an additional paramilitary National Police Force of unknown size. There are thought to be ten infantry brigades, one presidential guard brigade, one mechanized infantry brigade and one commando brigade.

Navy. Naval strength is estimated at 900. The main coastal base is at Matadi.

INTERNATIONAL RELATIONS

The Democratic Republic of the Congo is a member of the UN, WTO, the African Union, African Development Bank, COMESA, IOM, International Organization of the Francophonie and is an ACP member state of the ACP-EU relationship.

ECONOMY

Agriculture accounted for 57·1% of GDP in 2002 (one of the highest percentages of any country), industry 12·1% and services 30·8%.

Following the end of the civil war in 2002, several donor countries and institutions agreed to a development aid package worth US$2·5bn.

Currency. The unit of currency is the *Congo franc* which replaced the former *zaïre* in July 1998. The value of the new currency fell by two-thirds in the six months following its launch. Foreign exchange reserves were US$83m. in Dec. 1996. Gold reserves were 54,000 troy oz in 1997. Inflation, which reached 23,760% in 1994, had declined to 27·7% by 2002. In May 2001 the franc was floated in an effort to overcome the economic chaos caused by three years of state control and inter-regional war.

Budget. In 2001 total revenue was 66,644m. Congo francs and total expenditure was 139,200m. Congo francs. International economic aid has been made dependent on a coherent plan to revive the economy and progress on democracy and human rights.

Performance. GDP growth was –4·3% in 1999, –6·2% in 2000 and –2·1% in 2001. However, following the end of the five-year long war the economy grew by 3·0% in 2002. In Feb. 1998 GDP was reported to be 65% lower than it was in 1960, when the country gained independence. Total GDP in 2003 was US$5·6bn.

Banking and Finance. The central bank, the Banque Centrale du Congo (*Governor*, Jean-Claude Masangu), achieved independence in May 2002. There are 14 commercial banks. The largest is the Banque Commerciale Congolaise, in which the Société Générale of Belgium has a 25% stake through its subsidiary, Belgolaise. Other banks include Citibank and Stanbic. A 40% state-owned investment bank, Société Financière de Développement (Sofide), lends mainly to agriculture and manufacturing.

ENERGY AND NATURAL RESOURCES

Electricity. Production (2000), 5·5bn. kWh. A dam at Inga, on the River Congo near Matadi, has a potential capacity in excess of 42,000 MW. Installed capacity was 3·2m. kW in 2000. Consumption per capita was 87 kWh in 2000.

Oil and Gas. Offshore oil production began in Nov. 1975; crude production (1999) was 1·1m. tonnes. Reserves in 2002 were 187m. bbls. There is an oil refinery at Kinlao-Muanda.

Minerals. Production, 2001 (in 1,000 tonnes): coal (2000), 96; copper, 23; cobalt, 5; gold, 50 kg; diamonds (2002), 18·2m. carats. Only Australia, Botswana and Russia produce more diamonds. The country holds an estimated 80% of the world's coltan (columbite-tantalite) reserves. Coal, tin and silver are also found. The most important mining area is in the province of Katanga.

Agriculture. There were, in 2001, 6·70m. ha of arable land and 1·18m. ha of permanent crops. 11,000 ha were irrigated in 2001. There were 2,430 tractors in 2001. The main agricultural crops (2000 production in 1,000 tonnes) are: cassava, 15,959; plantains, 1,800; sugarcane, 1,669; maize, 1,184; rice, 383; groundnuts, 382; sweet potatoes, 370; bananas, 312; yams, 255; papayas, 213; mangoes, 206; pineapples, 196; oranges, 185; palm oil, 157; dry beans, 122; palm kernels, 63; taro, 62.

Livestock (2000): goats, 4,131,000; pigs, 1,049,000; sheep, 925,000; cattle, 882,000; poultry, 22m.

Forestry. Forests covered 135·21m. ha in 2000, or 59·6% of the land area. Timber production in 2001 was 69·73m. cu. metres.

Fisheries. The catch for 2001 was approximately 208,448 tonnes, almost entirely from inland waters.

INDUSTRY

The main manufactures are foodstuffs, beverages, tobacco, textiles, rubber, leather, wood products, cement and building materials, metallurgy and metal extraction, metal items, transport vehicles, electrical equipment and bicycles. Main products in 1,000 tonnes : cement (1999), 100; steel (2001), 80; sugar (2002), 65; soap (1995), 47; tyres (1995), 50,000 units; printed fabrics (1995), 15·73m. sq. metres; shoes (1995), 1·6m. pairs; beer (2003), 149·6m. litres.

Labour. In 1996 the workforce was 19·62m. (56% males). Agriculture employs around 65% of the total economically active population.

INTERNATIONAL TRADE

With Burundi and Rwanda, the Democratic Republic of the Congo forms part of the Economic Community of the Great Lakes. External debt was US$8,726m. in 2002.

Imports and Exports. Exports in 2001 were US$868·2m. (US$823·5m. in 2000); imports were US$703·9m. (US$697·1m. in 2000). Main commodities for export are diamonds, copper, coffee, cobalt and crude oil; and for import: consumer goods, foodstuffs, mining and other machinery, transport equipment and fuels. Principal export markets in 1999 were Belgium-Luxembourg, 63·8%; USA, 19·0%; Finland, 4·1%; Italy, 3·0%. Principal import suppliers were South Africa, 22·0%; Belgium, 15·8%; Nigeria, 10·0%; Zambia, 5·3%.

COMMUNICATIONS

Roads. In 1996 there were approximately 33,130 km of motorways and main roads, 40,500 km of secondary roads and 83,400 km of other roads. There were an estimated 787,000 passenger cars in use in 1996 (16·9 per 1,000 inhabitants) plus 538,000 trucks and vans.

Rail. There was 5,138 km of track on three gauges in 1995, of which 858 km was electrified. However, the length of track in use was severely reduced by the civil strife in late 1996 and the early part of 1997. In 2000, 1·3m. passengers were carried and 1·5m. tonnes of freight.

Civil Aviation. There is an international airport at Kinshasa (Ndjili). Other major airports are at Lubumbashi (Luano), Bukavu, Goma and Kisangani. The national carrier is Congo Airlines. In 1996 Kinshasa handled 344,000 passengers (192,000 on domestic flights) and 96,300 tonnes of freight.

Shipping. The River Congo and its tributaries are navigable to 300-tonne vessels for about 14,500 km. Regular traffic has been established between Kinshasa and Kisangani as well as Ilebo, on the Lualaba (*i.e.*, the river above Kisangani), on some tributaries and on the lakes. The Democratic Republic of the Congo has only 37 km of sea coast. In 2002 merchant shipping totalled 13,000 GRT. Matadi, Kinshasa and Kalemie are the main seaports.

Telecommunications. Telephone subscribers numbered 570,000 in 2002, or 10·8 per 1,000 inhabitants, including 560,000 mobile phone subscribers. With 98·2% of all telephone subscribers being mobile users, no other country has such a high ratio of mobile subscribers to landline subscribers. In 1995 there were 5,000 fax machines. In 2002 there were 50,000 Internet users.

Postal Services. In 1998 there were 497 post offices.

SOCIAL INSTITUTIONS

Justice. There is a Supreme Court at Kinshasa, 11 courts of appeal, 36 courts of first instance and 24 'peace tribunals'. The death penalty is in force.

Religion. In 2001 there were 21·99m. Roman Catholics, 16·95m. Protestants, 7·17m. Kimbanguistes (African Christians) and 0·75m. Muslims. Animist beliefs persist. In Sept. 2003 there was one cardinal.

Education. In 1994–95 there were 14,885 primary schools with 121,054 teachers for 5·4m. pupils, and 1·5m. pupils in secondary schools. In 1994–95 there were 93,266 students at university level. In higher education there were three universities (Kinshasa, Kisangani and Lubumbashi) in 1994–95, 14 teacher training colleges and 18 technical institutes in the public sector; and 13 university institutes, four teacher training colleges and 49 technical institutes in the private sector. Adult literacy rate was 62·7% in 2001 (male, 74·2%; female, 51·8%).

Health. In 1996 there were 3,224 physicians, 514 dentists and 20,652 nurses.

The Democratic Republic of the Congo has been one of the least successful countries in the battle against undernourishment in the past 15 years. The proportion of the population classified as undernourished increased from 32% in 1990–92 to 71% by 2000–02.

CULTURE

World Heritage Sites. Sites under Democratic Republic of the Congo jurisdiction which appear on UNESCO's world heritage list are (with year entered on list): Virunga National Park (1979); Kahuzi-Biega National Park (1980); Garamba National Park (1980); Salonga National Park (1984); and Okapi Wildlife Reserve (1996).

Broadcasting. Broadcasting is provided by government-controlled radio and television stations (colour by SECAM V). There is also an educational radio station. There were 18·7m. radio sets in 2000 and 6·5m. TV receivers in 1997.

Press. In 1996 there were nine daily newspapers with a combined circulation of 124,000.

Tourism. In 2000 there were 103,000 foreign tourists; spending by tourists in 1998 totalled US$2m.

DIPLOMATIC REPRESENTATIVES

Of the Democratic Republic of the Congo in the United Kingdom (281 Gray's Inn Rd, London, WC1X 8QF)
Ambassador: Henri N'Swana.

Of the United Kingdom in the Democratic Republic of the Congo (83 Ave. du Roi Baudouin, Kinshasa)
Ambassador: Jim Atkinson.

Of the Democratic Republic of the Congo in the USA (1800 New Hampshire Ave., NW, Washington, D.C., 20009)
Ambassador: Faida Mitifu.

Of the USA in the Democratic Republic of the Congo (498 Lukusa Ave., Gombe/Kinshasa)
Ambassador: Roger A. Meece.

Of the Democratic Republic of the Congo to the United Nations
Ambassador: Ileka Atoki.

Of the Democratic Republic of the Congo to the European Union
Ambassador: Jean-Pierre Mavungu-di-Ngoma.

FURTHER READING

Hochschild, Adam, *King Leopold's Ghost: A Study of Greed, Terror and Heroism in Colonial Africa.* Macmillan, London, 1999

Leslie, W. J., *Zaïre: Continuity and Political Change in an Oppressive State.* Boulder (CO), 1993

Williams, D. B., *et al., Zaïre.* [Bibliography] 2nd ed. ABC-Clio, Oxford and Santa Barbara (CA), 1995

Wrong, Michaela, *In the Footsteps of Mr Kurtz: Living on the Brink of Disaster in the Congo.* Fourth Estate, London, 2000

CONGO, REPUBLIC OF THE

République du Congo

Capital: Brazzaville
Population projection, 2010: 4·53m.
GDP per capita, 2002: (PPP$) 980
HDI/world rank: 0·494/144

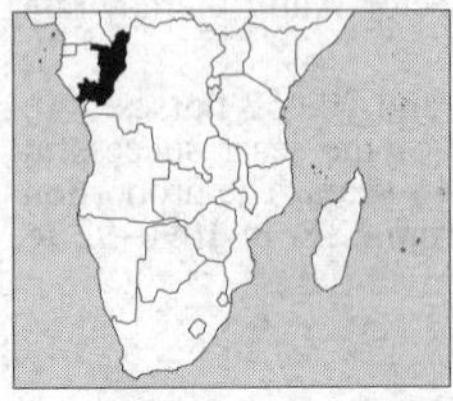

KEY HISTORICAL EVENTS

First occupied by France in 1882, the Congo became a territory of French Equatorial Africa from 1910–58, and then a member state of the French Community. Between 1940 and 1944, thanks to Equatorial Africa's allegiance to General de Gaulle, he named Brazzaville the capital of the Empire and Liberated France. Independence was granted in 1960. A Marxist-Leninist state was introduced in 1970. Free elections were restored in 1992 but violence erupted when in June 1997 President Lissouba tried to disarm opposition militia ahead of a fresh election. There followed four months of civil war with fighting concentrated on Brazzaville which became a ghost town. In Oct. Gen. Sassou-Nguesso proclaimed victory, having relied upon military support from Angola. President Lissouba went into hiding in Burkina Faso. A peace agreement signed in Nov. 1999 between President Sassou-Nguesso and the Cocoye and Ninja militias brought a period of relative stability.

TERRITORY AND POPULATION

The Republic of the Congo is bounded by Cameroon and the Central African Republic in the north, the Democratic Republic of the Congo to the east and south, Angola and the Atlantic Ocean to the southwest and Gabon to the west, and covers 341,821 sq. km. At the census of 1996 the population was 2,591,271. Estimated population in 2002, 3,634,000; density, 10·6 per sq. km.

The UN gives a projected population for 2010 of 4·53m.

In 2001, 66·0% of the population were urban. Census population of major cities in 1996: Brazzaville, the capital, 856,410; Pointe-Noire, 455,131; Loubomo (Dolisie), 79,852; N'Kayi, 46,727; Ouesso, 17,784; Mossendjo, 16,458.

Area, census population and county towns of the regions in 1996 were:

Region	*Sq. km*	*Population*	*County town*
Bouenza	12,258	236,566	Madingou
Capital District	100	856,410	Brazzaville
Cuvette }	74,850	{ 112,946	Owando
Cuvette Ouest }		{ 49,422	Ewo
Kouilou	13,650	532,179	Pointe-Noire
Lékoumou	20,950	75,734	Sibiti
Likouala	66,044	66,252	Impfondo
Niari	25,918	199,988	Loubomo (Dolisie)
Plateaux	38,400	139,371	Djambala
Pool	33,955	265,180	Kinkala
Sangha	55,795	57,223	Ouesso

Main ethnic groups are: Kongo (48%), Sangha (20%), Teke (17%) and M'Bochi (12%).

French is the official language. Kongo languages are widely spoken. Monokutuba and Lingala serve as lingua francas.

SOCIAL STATISTICS

1997 births, 100,000; deaths, 45,000. Rates, 1997 estimates (per 1,000 population): births, 38·8; deaths, 17·3. Infant mortality, 2001 (per 1,000 live births), 81. Expectation of life in 2001 was 46·7 years for males and 50·3 for females. Annual population growth rate, 1992–2002, 3·2%. Fertility rate, 2001, 6·3 children per woman.

CLIMATE

An equatorial climate, with moderate rainfall and a small range of temperature. There is a long dry season from May to Oct. in the southwest plateaux, but the

Congo Basin in the northeast is more humid, with rainfall approaching 100" (2,500 mm). Brazzaville, Jan. 78°F (25·6°C), July 73°F (22·8°C). Annual rainfall 59" (1,473 mm).

CONSTITUTION AND GOVERNMENT

A new constitution was approved in a referendum held in Jan. 2002. Under the new constitution the president's term of office is increased from five to seven years. The constitution provides for a new two-chamber assembly consisting of a house of representatives and a senate. The president may also appoint and dismiss ministers. 84·3% of voters were in favour of the draft constitution and 11·3% against. Turn-out was 78%, despite calls from opposition parties for a boycott. The new constitution came into force in Aug. 2002.

There is a 137-seat *National Assembly*, with members elected for a five-year term in single-seat constituencies, and a 66-seat *Senate*, with members elected for a six-year term (one third of members every two years).

National Anthem. 'La Congolaise'; words and tune by Jean Royer and others.

RECENT ELECTIONS

Presidential elections were held on 10 March 2002. Incumbent Denis Sassou-Nguesso won with 89·4% of votes cast, against 2·7% for Joseph Kignoumbi Kia Mboungou. The turn-out was 74·7%. The election represented the first time that Sassou-Nguesso was elected to the presidency, having seized power in 1979 and again in 1997.

Parliamentary elections were held on 26 May and 22 June 2002. President Denis Sassou-Nguesso's Congolese Labour Party won 52 out of 137 seats; his allies, 31; the Union for Democracy and Republic, 6; the Pan-African Union for Social Development, 4. Non-partisans and other political formations won the remaining seats.

CURRENT ADMINISTRATION

President: Denis Sassou-Nguesso; b. 1943 (Congolese Labour Party; sworn in 25 Oct. 1997 for a second time and re-elected in March 2002, having previously held office 1979–92).

In March 2005 the government comprised:

Prime Minister: Isidore Mvouba; b. 1954 (Congolese Labour Party; since 7 Jan. 2005).

State Minister of Planning, Economic Integration and Territorial Development: Pierre Moussa. *Foreign Affairs and Francophonie Affairs:* Rodolphe Adada. *Civil Service and State Reform:* Jean-Martin Mbemba. *Hydrocarbons:* Jean-Baptiste Tati Loutard.

Minister of Agriculture, Livestock and Fisheries: Jeanne Dambedzet. *Commerce, Consumer Affairs and Supplies:* Adélaïde Moundélé-Ngollo. *Communications, in Charge of Relations with Parliament and Government Spokesperson:* Alain Akoualat. *Construction, Urbanism and Housing:* Claude Alphonse Nsilou. *Culture, Arts and Tourism:* Jean Claude Gakosso. *Economy, Finance and Budget:* Pacifique Issoïbéka. *Energy and Water Resources:* Bruno Jean-Richard Itoua. *Equipment and Public Works:* Florent Ntsiba. *Forestry and the Environment:* Henri Djombo. *Health and Population:* Dr Alphonse Gando. *Higher Education:* Henri Ossebi. *Industrial Development and Promotion of the Private Sector:* Emile Mabondzot. *Justice, Guardian of the Seals and Human Rights:* Gabriel Entcha-Ebia. *Labour, Employment and Social Security:* Gilbert Ondongo. *Land Reform:* Lamyr Nguelé. *Maritime Economy and Merchant Marine:* Louis-Marie Nombo Mavoungou. *Mines, Mining Industry and Geology:* Pierre Oba. *Posts and Telecommunications, in Charge of Technological Development:* Philippe Mvouvo. *Primary and Secondary Education and Literacy:* Rosalie Kama. *Promotion of Women and the Involvement of Women in Development:* Jeanne Françoise Lekomba. *Scientific Research and Technical Innovation:* Pierre Ernest Abandzounou. *Security and Public Order:* Paul Mbot. *Small and Medium-Sized Businesses, and Handicrafts:* Martin Parfait Aimé Coussoud-Mavoungou. *Social Affairs, Solidarity, Humanitarian Action, Disabled War Veterans and Family Affairs:* Emilienne Raoul. *Sports and Youth Affairs:* Marcel Mbani. *Technical and Vocational Training:* Pierre Michel Nguimbi. *Territorial Administration and Decentralization:* François Ibovi.

Transport and Civil Aviation: André Okombi Salissa. *Presidency, in Charge of Co-operation and Development:* Justin Ballay Megot. *Presidency, in Charge of Defence:* Brig. Gen. Jacques Yvon Ndolou.

DEFENCE

In 2003 military expenditure totalled US$112m. (US$30 per capita), representing 3·1% of GDP.

Army. Total personnel (2002) 8,000. There is a Gendarmerie of 2,000.

Navy. Personnel in 2002 totalled about 800. The Navy is based at Pointe Noire.

Air Force. The Air Force had (2002) about 1,200 personnel and 12 combat aircraft, most of which are in store.

INTERNATIONAL RELATIONS

The Republic of the Congo is a member of the UN, WTO, the African Union, African Development Bank, IOM, International Organization of the Francophonie and is an ACP member state of the ACP-EU relationship.

ECONOMY

Agriculture produced 6·3% of GDP in 2002, industry 63·3% and services 30·4%.

Currency. The unit of currency is the *franc CFA* (XAF) with a parity of 655·957 francs CFA to one euro. Total money supply in April 2002 was 238,885m. francs CFA and foreign exchange reserves were US$51m. Gold reserves were 11,000 troy oz in June 2002. In 2002 there was inflation of 3·3%.

Budget. Total revenue in 2000 was 604·52bn. francs CFA (637·40bn. francs CFA forecast for 2001) and total expenditure was 584·80bn. francs CFA (524·90bn. francs CFA forecast for 2001).

Performance. Total GDP in 2003 was US$3·5bn. Real GDP growth was 3·6% in 2001 and 3·5% in 2002.

Banking and Finance. The *Banque des Etats de l'Afrique Centrale* (*Governor,* Jean-Félix Mamalepot) is the bank of issue. There are four commercial banks and a development bank, in all of which the government has majority stakes. There is also a co-operative banking organization (Mutuelle Congolaise de l'Epargne et de Crédit).

ENERGY AND NATURAL RESOURCES

Environment. Carbon dioxide emissions from the consumption and flaring of fossil fuels in 2002 were the equivalent of 0·9 tonnes per capita.

Electricity. Installed capacity was 0·1m. kW in 2000. Total production in 2000 was 300m. kWh and consumption per capita 162 kWh.

Oil and Gas. Oil was discovered in the mid-1960s when Elf Aquitaine was given exclusive rights to production. Elf still has the lion's share but Agip Congo is also involved in oil exploitation. In 2000 production was 13·2m. tonnes. Proven reserves in 2002 were 1·5bn. bbls., including major off-shore deposits. Oil provides about 90% of government revenue and exports. There is a refinery at Pointe-Noire, the second largest city. Gas reserves were estimated at 119bn. cu. metres in 2002.

Minerals. A government mine produces several metals; gold and diamonds are extracted by individuals. There are reserves of potash (4·5m. tonnes), iron ore (1,000m. tonnes), and also clay, bituminous sand, phosphates, zinc and lead.

Agriculture. In 2001 there were 175,000 ha of arable land and 45,000 ha of permanent crops. There were some 700 tractors and 85 thresher-harvesters in use in 2001. Production (2000, in thousand tonnes): cassava, 790; sugarcane, 450; plantains, 78; bananas, 52; avocados, 25; groundnuts, 22; sweet potatoes, 22; palm oil, 17; yams, 14.

Livestock (2000): cattle, 77,000; pigs, 46,000; sheep, 116,000; goats, 285,000; poultry, 2m.

Forestry. In 2000 equatorial forests covered 22·06m. ha (64·6% of the total land area). In 2001, 2·42m. cu. metres of timber were produced, mainly okoumé from the south and sapele from the north. Timber companies are required to replant, and to process at least 60% of their production locally. Before the development of the oil industry, forestry was the mainstay of the economy.

Fisheries. The catch for 2001 was an estimated 42,000, of which approximately half was from inland waters and half from marine waters.

INDUSTRY

There is a growing manufacturing sector, located mainly in the four major towns, producing processed foods, textiles, cement, metal goods and chemicals. Industry produced 65·2% of GDP in 2001, including 4·1% from manufacturing. Production (2000): residual fuel oil, 206,000 tonnes; distillate fuel oil, 62,000 tonnes; petrol, 40,000 tonnes; kerosene, 21,000 tonnes; cigarettes (1994), 655m. cartons; beer (2003), 66·0m. litres; veneer sheets (2001), 12,000 cu. metres; cotton textiles (1993), 1·8m. metres; footwear (1992), 300,000 pairs.

Labour. In 1996 the labour force was 1,105,000 (57% males). More than 50% of the economically active population were engaged in agriculture.

Trade Unions. In 1964 the existing unions merged into one national body, the Confédération Syndicale Congolaise. The 40,000-strong *Confédération Syndicale des Travailleurs Congolais* split off from the latter in 1993.

INTERNATIONAL TRADE

Foreign debt was US$5,152m. in 2002.

Imports and Exports. Imports and exports for calendar years in US$1m.:

	1998	*1999*	*2000*	*2001*	*2002*
Imports f.o.b.	558	523	455	681	691
Exports f.o.b.	1,368	1,560	2,492	2,055	2,289

Apart from crude oil, other significant commodities for export are lumber, plywood, sugar, cocoa, coffee and diamonds. Principal imported commodities are intermediate manufactures, capital equipment, construction materials, foodstuffs and petroleum products. Main export markets in 1999 were Taiwan, 31·5%; USA, 22·8%; South Korea, 15·3%; Germany, 6·7%; France, 2·6%. Main import suppliers were France, 23·2%; Italy, 7·8%; USA, 7·8%; Hong Kong, 4·9%; Belgium, 3·8%.

COMMUNICATIONS

Roads. In 1999 there was an estimated 12,800 km of roads, of which 9·7% were surfaced. Vehicles in use in 1996 numbered 53,000, including approximately 37,240 passenger cars (14 per 1,000 inhabitants). There were 124 deaths in road accidents in 1994.

Rail. A railway (510 km, 1,067 mm gauge) connects Brazzaville with Pointe-Noire via Loubomo and Bilinga, and a branch links Mont-Belo with Mbinda on the Gabon border. Total length is 900 km. In 2000 railways carried 84m. passenger-km and 85m. tonne-km of freight.

Civil Aviation. The principal airports are at Brazzaville (Maya Maya) and Pointe-Noire. In 2003 Trans Air Congo operated services to Abidjan, Cotonou and Lomé, as well as domestic services. Trans African Airlines flew to Abidjan, Bamako, Cotonou, Dakar and Lomé. In 2000 Brazzaville handled 412,000 passengers (335,000 on domestic flights) and 57,400 tonnes of freight.

Shipping. The only seaport is Pointe-Noire. The merchant marine totalled 3,000 GRT in 2002. There are some 5,000 km of navigable rivers, and river transport is an important service for timber and other freight as well as passengers. There are hydrofoil connections from Brazzaville to Kinshasa.

Telecommunications. There were 243,800 telephone subscribers in 2002 (74·1 per 1,000 persons) and 13,000 PCs were in use (4·0 per 1,000 persons). In 2002 there were 221,800 mobile phone subscribers. There were 5,000 Internet users in 2002. In 1995 there were 100 fax machines.

Postal Services. There were 114 post offices in 1995.

SOCIAL INSTITUTIONS

Justice. The Supreme Court, Court of Appeal and a criminal court are situated in Brazzaville, with a network of *tribunaux de grande instance* and *tribunaux d'instance* in the regions.

Religion. In 2001 there were 1·43m. Roman Catholics, 0·49m. Protestants and 0·36m. Kimbanguistes (African Christians). Traditional animist beliefs are still widespread.

Education. In 2000–01 there were 9,880 teachers for 500,921 pupils at primary schools; 7,668 secondary school teachers for 197,184 pupils; and 13,403 students at university level. Adult literacy rate in 2001 was 81·8% (male, 88·2%; female, 75·9%).

In 1999–2000 total expenditure on education came to 5·5% of GNP and 12·6% of total government spending.

Health. In 1990 there were 33 hospital beds per 10,000 inhabitants. In 1995 there were 632 physicians, 4,663 dentists and 160 midwives.

CULTURE

Broadcasting. Broadcasting is under the aegis of the government-controlled Radiodiffusion-Télévision Congolaise, which transmits a national and a regional radio programme and a programme in French. There were 424,000 radio and 114,000 TV receivers in 2000.

Press. In 1996 there were six daily newspapers with a combined circulation of 20,000.

Tourism. There were 26,000 foreign tourists in 2000, bringing revenue of US$11m.

DIPLOMATIC REPRESENTATIVES

Of the Republic of the Congo in the United Kingdom
Ambassador: Henri Marie Joseph Lopes (resides at Paris).
Honorary Consul: Louis Muzzu (4 Wendle Court, 131–137 Wandsworth Road, London SW8 2LH).

Of the United Kingdom in the Republic of the Congo
Ambassador: Jim Atkinson (resides at Kinshasa).

Of the Republic of the Congo in the USA (4891 Colorado Ave., NW, Washington, D.C., 20011)
Ambassador: Serge Mombouli.

Of the USA in the Republic of the Congo (Rue Léon Jacob, Brazzaville)
Ambassador: Robin Renee Sanders.

Of the Republic of the Congo to the United Nations
Ambassador: Basile Ikouebe.

Of the Republic of the Congo to the European Union
Ambassador: Jacques Obia.

FURTHER READING

Fegley, Randall, *Congo.* [Bibliography] ABC-Clio, Oxford and Santa Barbara (CA), 1993
Thompson, V. and Adloff, R., *Historical Dictionary of the People's Republic of the Congo.* 2nd ed. Metuchen (NJ), 1984

National statistical office: Centre National de la Statistique et des Etudes Economiques, BP 2031, Brazzaville.
Website (French only): http://www.cnsee.org

COSTA RICA

República de Costa Rica

Capital: San José
Population projection, 2010: 4·70m.
GDP per capita, 2002: (PPP$) 8,840
HDI/world rank: 0·834/45

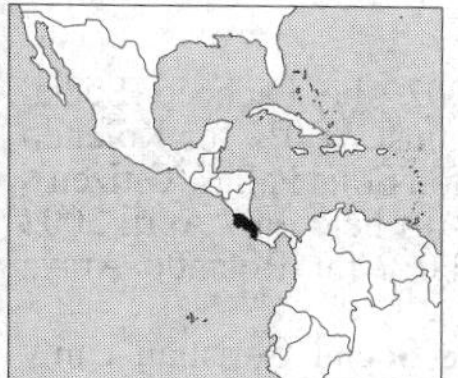

KEY HISTORICAL EVENTS

Discovered by Columbus in 1502 on his last voyage, Costa Rica (Rich Coast) was part of the Spanish viceroyalty of New Spain from 1540 to 1821, then of the Central American Federation until 1838 when it achieved full independence. Coffee was introduced in 1808 and became a mainstay of the economy, helping to create a peasant land-owning class. In 1948 accusations of election fraud led to a six-week civil war, at the conclusion of which José Figueres Ferrer won power at the head of a revolutionary junta. A new constitution abolished the army. In 1986 Oscar Arias Sánchez was elected president. He promised to prevent Nicaraguan anti-Sandinista (*contra*) forces using Costa Rica as a base. In 1987 he received the Nobel Peace Prize as recognition of his Central American peace plan, agreed to by the other Central American states. Costa Rica was beset with economic problems in the early 1990s when several politicians, including President Calderón, were accused of profiting from drug trafficking.

TERRITORY AND POPULATION

Costa Rica is bounded in the north by Nicaragua, east by the Caribbean, southeast by Panama, and south and west by the Pacific. The area is estimated at 51,100 sq. km (19,730 sq. miles). The population at the census of July 2000 was 3,810,179; density, 71·4 per sq. km. In 2001, 59·5% of the population were urban.

The UN gives a projected population for 2010 of 4·70m.

There are seven provinces (with 2000 population): Alajuela (716,286); Cartago (432,395); Guanacaste (264,238); Heredia (354,732); Limón (339,295); Puntarenas (357,483); San José (1,345,750). The largest cities, with estimated 2000 populations, are San José (346,600); Limón (62,000); and Alajuela (53,900).

The population is mainly of Spanish (85%) and mixed (8%) descent. About 3% are Afro-Caribbean (including some 70,000 speakers of an English Creole along the Caribbean coast). There is a residual Amerindian population of about 10,000.

Spanish is the official language.

SOCIAL STATISTICS

Statistics for calendar years:

	Marriages	*Births*	*Deaths*
1998	24,831	76,982	14,708
1999	25,613	78,526	15,052
2000	24,436	78,178	14,944
2001	23,730	76,401	15,609

2001 rates per 1,000 population: births, 19·2; deaths, 3·9. Annual population growth rate, 1992–2002, 2·4%. Life expectancy at birth, 2001, was 75·6 years for men and 80·3 years for women. Infant mortality, 2000, 10·2 per 1,000 live births; fertility rate, 2000, 2·4 children per woman.

CLIMATE

The climate is tropical, with a small range of temperature and abundant rain. The dry season is from Dec. to April. San José, Jan. 66°F (18·9°C), July 69°F (20·6°C). Annual rainfall 72" (1,793 mm).

CONSTITUTION AND GOVERNMENT

The Constitution was promulgated in Nov. 1949. The legislative power is vested in a single-chamber *Legislative Assembly* of 57 deputies elected for four years. The *President* and two *Vice-Presidents* are elected for four years; the candidate receiving the largest vote, provided it is over 40% of the total, is declared elected, but a second ballot is required if no candidate gets 40% of the total. Elections are normally held on the first Sunday in Feb.

The President may appoint and remove members of the cabinet.

National Anthem. 'Noble patria, tu hermosa bandera' ('Noble fatherland, thy beautiful banner'); words by J. M. Zeledón Brenes, tune by M. M. Gutiérrez.

RECENT ELECTIONS

In the first round of presidential elections held on 3 Feb. 2002 Abel Pacheco (Social Christian Unity Party/PUSC) won 38·6% of votes cast against 31·0% for Rolando Araya Monge (National Liberation Party) and 26·2% for Ottón Solís Fallas (Citizen's Action Party). Turn-out was 68·9%. In the presidential run-off held on 7 April 2002 Abel Pacheco won with 58·0% of votes cast against 42·0% for Rolando Araya Monge.

At the parliamentary elections held on 3 Feb. 2002 the Social Christian Unity Party (PUSC) won 19 seats with 29·8% of the vote, the National Liberation Party 17 (27·1%), the Citizen's Action Party 14 (21·9%), Libertarian Movement 6 (9·3%) and Costa Rican Renewal Party 1 (3·6%). Turn-out was 66·6%.

CURRENT ADMINISTRATION

President: Dr Abel Pacheco de la Espriella; b. 1933 (PUSC; sworn in 8 May 2002).

In March 2005 the government comprised:

First Vice President and Minister of Planning and of the Presidency: Lineth Saborío Chaverri. *Second Vice President:* Luis Fishman. *Minister of Agriculture and Livestock:* Rodolfo Coto Pacheco. *Culture, Youth and Sports:* Guido Sáenz González. *Economy and Industry:* Gilberto Barrantes. *Education:* Dr Manuel Bolaños Salas. *Environment and Energy:* Carlos Manuel Rodríguez. *Finance:* Federico Carrillo. *Foreign Relations and Religion:* Roberto Tovar Faja. *Foreign Trade:* Manuel González. *Health:* María del Rocio Sáenz. *Housing:* Helio Fallas Venegas. *Justice:* Patricia Vega. *Labour and Social Security:* Fernando Trejos. *Planning:* Danilo Chaverri Soto. *Public Security, Government and Police:* Rogelio Vicente Ramos Martínez. *Public Works and Transportation:* Randall Quirós Bustamante. *Science and Technology:* Fernando Gutiérrez Ortíz. *Tourism:* Rodrigo Castro Fonseca. *Women's Affairs:* Georgina Vargas. *Minister without Portfolio:* Rosalia Gil.

Government Website (Spanish only): http://www.casapres.go.cr

DEFENCE

In 2003 defence expenditure totalled US$101m. (US$25 per capita), representing 0·6% of GDP.

Army. The Army was abolished in 1948, and replaced by a Civil Guard numbering 4,400 in 2002. In addition there is a Border Security Police of 2,000 and a Rural Guard, also 2,000-strong.

Navy. The paramilitary Maritime Surveillance Unit numbered (2002) 300.

Air Wing. The Civil Guard operates a small air wing equipped with 11 light planes and helicopters.

INTERNATIONAL RELATIONS

Costa Rica is a member of the UN, WTO, OAS, Inter-American Development Bank, CACM, ACS and IOM.

ECONOMY

Agriculture accounted for 8·4% of GDP in 2002, industry 29·1% and services 62·4%.

Currency. The unit of currency is the *Costa Rican colón* (CRC) of 100 *céntimos.* The official rate is used for all imports on an essential list and by the government and autonomous institutions, and a free rate is used for all other transactions. In June 2002 total money supply was 641,189m. colones, foreign exchange reserves were US$1,426m. and gold reserves were 2,000 troy oz. Inflation was 9·1% in 2002.

Budget. In 2001 total revenue was 1,202·00bn. colones (1,025·89bn. colones in 2000) and total expenditure 1,269·56bn. colones (1,095·16bn. colones in 2000).

Performance. Costa Rica, said to be the most stable country in Central America, experienced GDP growth of 8·4% in 1998 and 8·2% in 1999, although then only 1·8% in 2000, 1·1% in 2001 and 2·8% in 2002. Total GDP in 2003 was US$17·5bn.

Banking and Finance. The bank of issue is the Central Bank (founded 1950) which supervises the national monetary system, foreign exchange dealings and banking operations. The bank has a board of seven directors appointed by the government, including *ex officio* the Minister of Finance and the Planning Office Director. The *Governor* is Francisco de Paula Gutiérrez Gutiérrez.

There are three state-owned banks (Banco de Costa Rica, Banco Nacional de Costa Rica and Banco Popular y de Desarrollo Comunal), 17 private banks and one credit co-operative.

There is a stock exchange in San José.

Weights and Measures. The metric system is obligatory but Imperial Spanish measurements are still used.

ENERGY AND NATURAL RESOURCES

Environment. Costa Rica's carbon dioxide emissions from the consumption and flaring of fossil fuels in 2002 were the equivalent of 1·3 tonnes per capita. An *Environmental Sustainability Index* compiled for the World Economic Forum meeting in Feb. 2002 ranked Costa Rica ninth in the world, with 63·2%. The index measured the ability of countries to maintain favourable environmental conditions and examined various factors including pollution levels and the use or abuse of natural resources.

Electricity. Installed capacity was 1·7m. kW in 2000. Production was 7·23bn. kWh in 2000; consumption per capita in 2000 was 1,889 kWh.

Minerals. In 2001 gold output was 100 kg and salt production was 37,000 tonnes.

Agriculture. Agriculture is a key sector, with 243,000 people (including hunting, forestry and fisheries) being economically active in 2002. There were 0·23m. ha of arable land in 2001 and 0·3m. ha of permanent crops. The principal agricultural products are coffee, bananas and sugar. Cattle are also of great importance. Production figures for 2000 (in 1,000 tonnes): sugarcane, 4,000; bananas, 2,700; rice, 264; melons, 177; coffee, 164; palm oil, 134; oranges, 126; plantains, 90; watermelons, 77; potatoes, 74; pineapples, 43; papayas, 36.

Livestock (2000): cattle, 1·71m.; pigs, 390,000; horses, 115,000; chickens, 17m.

Forestry. In 2000 forests covered 1·97m. ha, or 38·5% of the land area. Timber production in 2001 was 5·16m. cu. metres.

Fisheries. Total catch in 2001 amounted to 34,733 tonnes, mostly from sea fishing.

INDUSTRY

The main manufactured goods are foodstuffs, palm oil, textiles, fertilizers, pharmaceuticals, furniture, cement, tyres, canning, clothing, plastic goods, plywood and electrical equipment.

Labour. In July 2001 there were 1,552,920 people in employment. In July 2001 there were 100,397 unemployed persons, or 6·1% of the workforce. The main area of employment is transport, storage and communications (303,000 people in 2002), followed by agriculture, hunting, forestry and fisheries (243,000 in 2002).

Trade Unions. There are two main trade unions, *Rerum Novarum* (anti-Communist) and *Confederación General de Trabajadores Costarricenses* (Communist).

INTERNATIONAL TRADE

A free trade agreement was signed with Mexico in March 1994. Some 2,300 products were freed from tariffs, with others to follow over ten years. External debt was US$4,834m. in 2002.

Imports and Exports. The value of imports and exports in US$1m. was:

	1999	*2000*	*2001*	*2002*
Imports c.i.f.	5,996	6,025	5,745	6,523
Exports f.o.b.	6,577	5,813	4,923	5,259

Chief exports: manufactured goods and other products, coffee, bananas, sugar, cocoa. Major export markets, 2000: USA, 33·9%; Nicaragua, 6·9%; Guatemala, 6·8%; Germany, 5·3%. Main import suppliers: USA, 33·5%; Mexico, 8·4%; Venezuela, 7·2%; Japan, 4·5%.

COMMUNICATIONS

Roads. In 2002 there were 35,303 km of roads, including 7,270 km of main roads. On the Costa Rica section of the Inter-American Highway it is possible to motor to Panama during the dry season. The Pan-American Highway into Nicaragua is metalled for most of the way and there is now a good highway open almost to Puntarenas. Motor vehicles, 2002, numbered 651,030 (367,832 passenger cars). There were 336 fatalities as a result of road accidents in 2000.

Rail. The nationalized railway system *(Incofer)* was closed in 1994.

Civil Aviation. There is an international airport at San José (Juan Santamaria). The national carrier is Líneas Aéreas Costarriquenses (LACSA), which in 1999 flew 23·9m. km and carried 922,600 passengers. In 2000 San José handled 2,159,215 passengers (1,994,829 on international flights) and 77,137 tonnes of freight.

Shipping. The chief ports are Limón on the Atlantic and Caldera on the Pacific. The merchant marine totalled 4,000 GRT in 2002. In 2002 vessels totalling 2,101,000 NRT entered ports and vessels totalling 2,101,000 NRT cleared.

Telecommunications. There were 1,497,700 telephone subscribers in 2002 (361·5 per 1,000 inhabitants) and 817,000 PCs in use (197·2 for every 1,000 persons). The government has 202 telegraph offices and 88 official telephone stations. In 2002 mobile phone subscribers numbered 459,800 and in 1997 there were 8,500 fax machines. Costa Rica had 800,000 Internet users in 2002.

Postal Services. In 1998 there were 134 post offices.

SOCIAL INSTITUTIONS

Justice. Justice is administered by the Supreme Court and five appeal courts divided into five chambers—the Court of Cassation, the Higher and Lower Criminal Courts, and the Higher and Lower Civil Courts. There are also subordinate courts in the separate provinces and local justices throughout the republic. Capital punishment may not be inflicted.

The population in penal institutions in June 1999 was 8,526 (229 per 100,000 of national population).

Religion. Roman Catholicism is the state religion; it had 3·38m. adherents in 2001. There is entire religious liberty under the constitution. The Archbishop of Costa Rica has six bishops at Alajuela, Ciudad Quesada, Limón, Puntarenas, San Isidro el General and Tilarán. There were 360,000 Protestants in 2001. The remainder of the population are followers of other religions.

Education. The adult literacy rate in 2001 was 95·7% (95·6% among males and 95·8% among females). Primary instruction is compulsory and free from six to 15 years; secondary education (since 1949) is also free. Primary schools are provided and maintained by local school councils, while the national government pays the teachers, besides making subventions in aid of local funds. In 2002 there were 3,904 public and private primary schools with 31,266 teachers and administrative staff and 537,191 enrolled pupils, and 580 public and private secondary schools with 20,549 teachers and 284,841 pupils. In 1999 there was 1 university and 1 technological institute in the public sector, and 8 universities, 1 Adventist university and 1 university of science and technology in the private sector. There were also four other institutions of higher education. In 1999 there were 59,947 university students.

In 2000–01 total expenditure on education came to 4·8% of GNP, representing 20·0% of total government expenditure.

Health. In 2000 there were 3,333 doctors, 346 dentists, 1,214 nurses, 272 pharmacists and (1999) 29 hospitals. In 1997 there were 14 beds per 10,000 inhabitants.

CULTURE

World Heritage Sites. Costa Rica's two UNESCO protected sites are: Cocos Island National Park (1997); and the Area de Conservación Guanacaste (1999), an important dry forest habitat. Costa Rica also shares a UNESCO site with Panama: the Talamanca Range-La Amistad Reserves (1983), an important cross-breeding site for North and South American flora and fauna.

Broadcasting. There were 980,000 radio sets in 1997 and 930,000 television receivers in 2000 (colour by NTSC).

Press. There were six daily newspapers in 1996 with a combined circulation of 320,000, at a rate of 88 per 1,000 inhabitants.

Tourism. In 2000 there were 1,106,000 foreign tourists, bringing revenue of US$1,102m.

Theatre and Opera. There are eight national theatres.

Museums and Galleries. Costa Rica has three museums.

DIPLOMATIC REPRESENTATIVES

Of Costa Rica in the United Kingdom (Flat 1, 14 Lancaster Gate, London, W2 3LH)
Ambassador: Vacant.
Chargé d'Affaires a.i.: Sylvia Ugalde.

Of the United Kingdom in Costa Rica (Edificio Centro Colón, 11th Floor, Apartado 815, San José 1007)
Ambassador: Georgina Butler.

Of Costa Rica in the USA (2114 S Street, NW, Washington, D.C., 20008)
Ambassador: Tomás Dueñas.

Of the USA in Costa Rica (Pavas, Frente Centro Comercial, San José)
Ambassador: Vacant.
Chargé d'Affaires a.i.: Douglas M. Barnes.

Of Costa Rica to the United Nations
Ambassador: Bruno Stagno.

Of Costa Rica to the European Union
Ambassador: María Salvadora Ortíz Ortíz.

FURTHER READING

Biesanz, R., *et al.*, *The Costa Ricans.* Hemel Hempstead, 1982
Bird, L., *Costa Rica: Unarmed Democracy.* London, 1984
Creedman, T. S., *Historical Dictionary of Costa Rica.* 2nd ed. Metuchen (N.J.), 1991
Stansifer, Charles L., *Costa Rica.* [Bibliography] ABC-Clio, Oxford and Santa Barbara (CA), 1991

National statistical office: Instituto Nacional de Estadística y Censos, San José.
Website (Spanish only): http://www.inec.go.cr/

CÔTE D'IVOIRE

République de la Côte d'Ivoire
(Republic of the Ivory Coast)

Capital: Yamoussoukro
Seat of government: Abidjan
Population projection, 2010: 18·53m.
GDP per capita, 2002: (PPP$) 1,520
HDI/world rank: 0·399/163

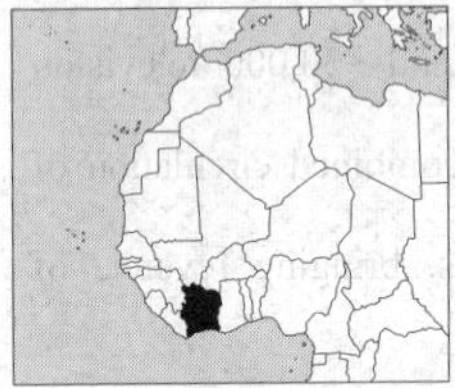

KEY HISTORICAL EVENTS

France obtained rights on the coast in 1842 but did not occupy the territory until 1882. In the early 1870s a French offer to exchange Côte d'Ivoire with the British for the Gambia, which bisected the French colony of Senegal, was refused. Rumours of gold later rekindled French interest and in 1889 Côte d'Ivoire was declared a French protectorate. Governors appointed from France administered the colony using a system of centralized rule that allowed little room for local participation. In 1946 Côte d'Ivoire's first political party, the Democratic Party of Côte d'Ivoire, was created under the leadership of Félix Houphouët-Boigny who eventually adopted a policy of co-operation with the French authorities. By the mid-1950s the country had become the wealthiest in French West Africa and in 1958 Côte d'Ivoire became an autonomous republic within the French Community. Côte d'Ivoire achieved full independence on 7 Aug. 1960, with Félix Houphouët-Boigny as its first president.

On 23 Dec. 1999 President Henri Konan Bédié was ousted in a military coup led by Gen. Robert Guéï, the country's military chief from 1990 to 1995. On 6 Oct. 2000 a state of emergency was declared ahead of a Supreme Court announcement on the candidates allowed to stand for the presidential election on 22 Oct. 2000. After Robert Guéï declared himself the winner in the election, a violent uprising in which over 2,000 people were killed resulted in Gen. Guéï fleeing to Benin. The veteran opposition candidate Laurent Gbagbo was then declared the rightful winner. In Sept. 2002 there was a failed coup attempt by mutinous soldiers that claimed more than 20 lives, including those of both Gen. Guéï and the interior minister. Since then, Côte d'Ivoire has descended further into civil war.

TERRITORY AND POPULATION

Côte d'Ivoire is bounded in the west by Liberia and Guinea, north by Mali and Burkina Faso, east by Ghana, and south by the Gulf of Guinea. It has an area (including inland water) of 322,460 sq. km. The population at the 1998 census was 15,366,672; density, 47·7 per sq. km. The population was 56·0% rural in 2001. Population estimate (2002): 16·36m.

The UN gives a projected population for 2010 of 18·53m.

Since 2000 the country has been divided into 19 regions comprising 58 departments.

Areas, populations (1998 census) and capitals of the regions are:

Region	*Area (in sq. km)*	*Population*	*Capital*
Agnéby	9,080	525,211	Agboville
Bafing	8,720	139,251	Touba
Bas-Sassandra	25,800	1,395,251	San-Pédro
Denguélé	20,600	222,446	Odienné
Dix-Huit Montagnes	16,600	936,510	Man
Fromager	6,900	542,992	Gagnoa
Haut-Sassandra	15,200	1,071,977	Daloa
Lacs	8,920	476,235	Yamoussoukro
Lagunes	14,200	3,733,413	Abidjan
Marahoué	8,500	554,807	Bouaflé
Moyen-Cavally	14,150	508,733	Guiglo
Moyen-Comoé	6,900	394,761	Abengourou
N'zi-Comoé	19,560	633,927	Dimbokro
Savanes	40,323	929,673	Korhogo
Sud-Bandama	10,650	682,021	Divo

Region	*Area (in sq. km)*	*Population*	*Capital*
Sud-Comoé	6,250	459,487	Aboisso
Vallée du Bandama	28,530	1,080,509	Bouaké
Worodougou	21,900	378,463	Séguéla
Zanzan	38,000	701,005	Bondoukou

In 2000 the population of Abidjan stood at 3,790,000. Other major towns (with 1998 census population): Bouaké, 461,618; Yamoussoukro, 299,243; Daloa, 173,107; Korhogo, 142,093.

There are about 60 ethnic groups, the principal ones being the Baoulé (23%), the Bété (18%) and the Sénoufo (15%). A referendum held in July 2000 on the adoption of a new constitution set eligibility conditions for presidential candidates (the candidate and both his parents had to be Ivorian). This excluded a northern Muslim leader and in effect made foreigners out of millions of Ivorians. The north of the country is predominantly Muslim and the south predominantly Christian and animist.

Approximately 30% of the population are immigrants, in particular from Burkina Faso, Mali, Guinea and Senegal.

French is the official language.

SOCIAL STATISTICS

1996 births, 627,000; deaths, 232,000. Rates, 1996 estimates (per 1,000 population): births, 42·5; deaths, 15·7. Infant mortality (per 1,000 live births), 102 (1999). Expectation of life in 2001 was 41·2 years for males and 42·1 for females. Annual population growth rate, 1992–2002, 2·1%. Infant mortality, 2001, 102 per 1,000 live births; fertility rate, 2001, 4·8 births per woman. 29% of the population are migrants.

CLIMATE

A tropical climate, affected by distance from the sea. In coastal areas, there are wet seasons from May to July and in Oct. and Nov., but in central areas the periods are March to May and July to Nov. In the north, there is one wet season from June to Oct. Abidjan, Jan. 81°F (27·2°C), July 75°F (23·9°C). Annual rainfall 84" (2,100 mm). Bouaké, Jan. 81°F (27·2°C), July 77°F (25°C). Annual rainfall 48" (1,200 mm).

CONSTITUTION AND GOVERNMENT

The 1960 Constitution was amended in 1971, 1975, 1980, 1985, 1986, 1990, 1998 and 2000. The sole legal party was the Democratic Party of Côte d'Ivoire, but opposition parties were legalized in 1990. There is a 225-member *National Assembly* elected by universal suffrage for a five-year term. The *President* is also directly elected for a five-year term (renewable). He appoints and leads a Council of Ministers.

In Nov. 1990 the National Assembly voted that its Speaker should become President in the event of the latter's incapacity, and created the post of Prime Minister to be appointed by the President. Following the death of President Houphouët-Boigny on 7 Dec. 1993, the speaker, Henri Konan Bédié, proclaimed himself head of state till the end of the presidential term in Sept. 1995.

Following the coup of Dec. 1999 a referendum was held on 23 July 2000 on the adoption of a new constitution, which set eligibility conditions for presidential candidates (the candidate and both his parents must be Ivorian), reduced the voting age from 21 to 18, and abolished the death penalty. It also offered an amnesty to soldiers who staged the coup and the junta, but committed the junta to hand over power to an elected civilian head of state and parliament within six months of the proclamation of the text. Approximately 87% of votes cast were in favour of the new constitution. This was subsequently adopted on 4 Aug. 2000.

National Anthem. 'L'Abidjanaise'; words by M. Ekra and others, tune by P. M Pango.

RECENT ELECTIONS

Presidential elections were held on 22 Oct. 2000, but were boycotted by the former ruling Parti Démocratique de Côte d'Ivoire/PDCI and the Rassemblement des Républicains/RDR. Laurent Gbagbo (Front Populaire Ivorienne/FPI) obtained 59·4% of votes cast against 32·7% for Robert Guéï, who had seized power in a coup in Dec. 1999. Initially Robert Guéï claimed victory but following a violent uprising accepted defeat (the first time in Africa that a popular rising had succeeded in toppling a military regime). There were three other candidates.

The National Assembly elections were held on 10 Dec. 2000 and 14 Jan. 2001. The Ivorian People's Front (FPI) won 96 seats; the Democratic Party (PDCI) won 94 seats; Rally of the Republicans, 5. There were also two vacant seats.

CURRENT ADMINISTRATION

President: Laurent Gbagbo; b. 1945 (FPI; assumed office 26 Oct. 2000).

In March 2003 a power-sharing unity government was formed with the hope of bringing to an end six months of civil war. In March 2005 the transitional government comprised:

Prime Minister: Seydou Diarra; b. 1933 (ind.; sworn in on 10 Feb. 2003 for a second time, having previously been prime minister for five months in 2000).

Minister of State for Agriculture: Amadou Gon Coulibaly (RDR). *Communications:* Guillaume Soro (MPCI). *Economic Infrastructure:* Patrick Achi (PDCI). *Economy and Finance:* Paul Bohoun Bouabré (FPI). *Environment:* Angèle Gnonsoa (Parti Ivorien des Travailleurs). *Foreign Affairs:* Mamadou Bamba (PDCI). *Health and Population:* Toiqueuse Mabri (Union pour la Démocratie et la Paix en Côte d'Ivoire). *Justice:* Henriette Diabaté (RDR). *Mines and Energy:* Léon Monnet (FPI). *Regional Integration and African Union:* Théodore Mel Eg (Union Démocratique Citoyenne). *Territorial Administration:* Issa Diakité (Mouvement Patriotique de Côte d'Ivoire). *Transport:* Anaki Kobenan (Mouvement des Forces de l'Avenir).

Minister of Administrative Reform: Eric Kahé (Union pour la Démocratie et la Paix en Côte d'Ivoire). *Animal Production and Fishery Resources:* Kobenan Kouassi Adjoumani (PDCI). *Commerce:* Amadou Soumahoro (RDR). *Culture and Francophonie:* Melan Messou (PDCI). *Defence:* René Amani (ind.). *Fight Against AIDS:* Christine Adjobi (FPI). *Handicrafts:* Moussa Dosso (Mouvement Patriotique de Côte d'Ivoire). *Higher Education:* Zémogo Fofana (RDR). *Housing and Town Planning:* Raymond N'Doli (FPI). *Human Rights:* Victorine Wodié (Parti Ivorien des Travailleurs). *Industry and Promotion of the Private Sector:* Jeannot Ahoussou Kouadio (PDCI). *Internal Security:* Martin Bléou (ind.). *Labour and Civil Service:* Hubert Oulaye (FPI). *National Education:* Amani N'Guessan Michel (FPI). *National Reconciliation:* Sébastien Danon Djédjé (FPI). *New Information Technologies and Telecommunications:* Hamed Bakayoko (RDR). *Planning and Development:* Brito Nama Boniface (PDCI). *Relations with the Institutions of the Republic:* Alfonse Douaty (FPI). *Religion:* Désiré Gnonkonté Gnessoa (PDCI). *Scientific Research:* Mamadou Koné (Mouvement Patriotique de Côte d'Ivoire). *Small and Medium Enterprises:* Roger Banchi (Mouvement Populaire Ivoirien du Grand Ouest). *Solidarity, Health and Social Security:* Clotilde Ohouochi (FPI). *Sports and Leisure:* Michel Gueu (Mouvement Patriotique de Côte d'Ivoire). *Technical Education and Professional Training:* Youssouf Soumahoro (PDCI). *Tourism:* Marcel Tanoh (RDR). *War Victims, Displaced and Exiled Persons:* Messamba Koné (Mouvement Patriotique de Côte d'Ivoire). *Water and Forests:* Assoa Adou (FPI). *Women, Family and Children:* Jeanne Peuhmond (RDR). *Youth and Civil Protection:* Tuo Fozié (Mouvement Patriotique de Côte d'Ivoire).

Government Website: http://www.primature.gov.ci

DEFENCE

There is selective conscription for six months. Defence expenditure totalled US$172m. in 2003 (US$10 per capita), representing 1·2% of GDP.

Army. Total strength (2002), 6,500. In addition there is a Presidential Guard of 1,350, a Gendarmerie of 7,600 and a Militia of 1,500.

Navy. Personnel in 2002 totalled 900 with the force based at Locodjo (Abidjan).

Air Force. There are five Alpha Jet light strike combat aircraft, although only one or two are operational. Personnel (2002) 700.

INTERNATIONAL RELATIONS

Côte d'Ivoire is a member of the UN, WTO, the African Union, African Development Bank, UEMOA, ECOWAS, IOM, OIC, Islamic Development Bank,

International Organization of the Francophonie and is an ACP member state of the ACP-EU relationship.

ECONOMY

Agriculture accounted for 26·2% of GDP in 2002, industry 20·4% and services 53·4%.

Overview. Austerity measures were introduced in May 1990. A privatization programme, concentrating on the agro-industrial sectors, was introduced in 1992. 54 companies from an initial list of 60 had been privatized by mid-1999, when 20 additional companies were listed.

Currency. The unit of currency is the *franc CFA* (XOF) with a parity of 655·957 francs CFA to one euro. Foreign exchange reserves were US$1,273m. in May 2002 and total money supply was 1,338·30bn. francs CFA. In 2000 gold reserves were 45,000 troy oz. Inflation was 3·1% in 2002.

Budget. Government revenue and expenditure (in 1bn. francs CFA):

	1998	*1999*	*2000*	*2001*
Revenue	1,392·2	1,283·3	1,238·1	1,335·9
Expenditure	1,557·3	1,521·5	1,351·2	1,297·3

VAT is 25%.

Performance. Real GDP growth was 0·3% in 2001 but there was then a recession with the economy contracting by 1·8% in 2002. Total GDP in 2003 was US$13·7bn.

Banking and Finance. The regional *Banque Centrale des Etats de l'Afrique de l'Ouest* is the central bank and bank of issue. The *Governor* is Charles Konan Banny. In 2002 there were 13 commercial banks and six credit institutions. The African Development Bank is based in Abidjan.

ENERGY AND NATURAL RESOURCES

Environment. Carbon dioxide emissions from the consumption and flaring of fossil fuels in 2002 were the equivalent of 0·3 tonnes per capita.

Electricity. The electricity industry was privatized in 1990. Installed capacity was 1·2m. kW in 2000. Production in 2000 amounted to 3·62 bn. kWh, with consumption per capita 221 kWh.

Oil and Gas. Petroleum has been produced (offshore) since Oct. 1977. Production (1999), 1·5m. tonnes. Oil reserves, 2002, 100m. bbls. Natural gas reserves, 2002, 30bn. cu. metres; production (2000), 1,550m. cu. metres.

Minerals. Côte d'Ivoire has large deposits of iron ores, bauxite, tantalite, diamonds, gold, nickel and manganese, most of which are untapped. Gold production has steadily increased with 3·2 tonnes being produced in 2000. In 2001 diamond production totalled 320,000 carats.

Agriculture. In 2002 the agricultural population was 9·09m., of whom 3·13m. were economically active. In 1998 agriculture accounted for 66% of exports. There were 3·10m. ha of arable land in 2001 and 4·40m. ha of permanent crops. 73,000 ha were irrigated in 2001. There were 3,800 tractors in 2001 and 70 harvester-threshers. Côte d'Ivoire is the world's largest producer and exporter of cocoa beans, with an output of 1·30m. tonnes in 2000 (more than 41% of the world total). It is also a leading coffee producer, with 365,000 tonnes in 2000. The cocoa and coffee industries have for years relied on foreign workers, but tens of thousands have left the country since the 1999 coup resulting in labour shortages. Other main crops, with 2000 production figures in 1,000 tonnes, are: yams (2,923), cassava (1,673), plantains (1,405), rice (1,162), sugarcane (1,155), maize (571), taro (365), seed cotton (270), palm oil (242), bananas (241), pineapples (226), coconuts (193), groundnuts (144), cottonseed (140), cotton lint (130), tomatoes (130) and natural rubber (119). Côte d'Ivoire is the biggest producer of rubber in Africa.

Livestock, 2000: 1·35m. cattle, 1·39m. sheep, 1·09m. goats, 280,000 pigs and 30m. chickens.

Forestry. In 2000 the rainforest covered 7·12m. ha, or 22·4% of the total land area. Products include teak, mahogany and ebony. In 2001, 12·08m. cu. metres of roundwood were produced.

Fisheries. The catch in 2001 amounted to 73,556 tonnes, of which 63,026 tonnes were from marine waters.

INDUSTRY

Industrialization has developed rapidly since independence, particularly food processing, textiles and sawmills. Output in 2000 (in 1,000 tonnes): distillate fuel oil, 1,103; cement (2001), 650; petrol, 554; kerosene, 536; residual fuel oil, 443; sugar, 189; sawnwood (2001), 630,000 cu. metres; veneer sheets (2001), 296,000 cu. metres.

Labour. In 1996 the workforce was 5·7m. (67% males).

Trade Unions. The main trade union is the *Union Générale des Travailleurs de Côte d'Ivoire*, with over 100,000 members.

INTERNATIONAL TRADE

External debt was US$11,816m. in 2002.

Imports and Exports. Imports and exports for calendar years in US$1m.:

	1998	*1999*	*2000*	*2001*	*2002*
Imports f.o.b.	2,886·5	2,766·0	2,401·8	2,417·7	2,432·0
Exports f.o.b.	4,606·5	4,661·4	3,888·0	3,945·9	5,166·5

Principal exports, 2001: cocoa beans and products, 33·2%; crude petroleum and petroleum products, 13·7%; wood and wood products, 7·1%. Principal imports, 2001: crude and refined petroleum, 28·8%; food products, 22·5%; machinery and transport equipment, 20·4%. Main export markets, 1999: France, 14·4%; Netherlands, 13·4%; USA, 8·5%; Brazil, 7·7%; Mali, 4·7%. Main import suppliers, 1999: France, 25·9%; Italy, 5·6%; USA, 5·2%; Germany, 4·3%; Japan, 4·3%.

Trade Fairs. A major international farming and livestock trade show, SARA, takes place every other year in Nov. and attracts exhibitors from around the world.

COMMUNICATIONS

Roads. In 1999 roads totalled about 50,400 km, of which 4,900 km were paved. There were about 456,000 motor vehicles in 1996 (293,000 cars, or 18·1 per 1,000 inhabitants, and 163,000 trucks and vans).

Rail. From Abidjan a metre-gauge railway runs to Léraba on the border with Burkina Faso (639 km), and thence through Burkina Faso to Ouagadougou and Kaya. Operation of the railway in both countries is franchised to the mixed public-private company Sitarail.

Civil Aviation. There is an international airport at Abidjan (Felix Houphouet Boigny Airport), which in 2000 handled 946,000 passengers (all on international flights) and 20,900 tonnes of freight. The national carrier is the state-owned Air Ivoire, which in 1997 flew 1·3m. km and carried 72,100 passengers. It provides domestic services and in 2003 operated international flights to Accra, Bamako, Conakry, Cotonou, Dakar, Douala, Libreville, Lomé, Niamey and Ouagadougou. There were direct flights in 2003 with other airlines to Addis Ababa, Banjul, Beirut, Bobo Dioulasso, Brazzaville, Brussels, Cairo, Casablanca, Freetown, Johannesburg, Lagos, Monrovia, Nairobi, Nouakchott, Paris, Pointe-Noire and Tripoli.

Shipping. The main ports are Abidjan and San-Pédro. Abidjan handled 15m. tonnes of cargo for the first time in 1998 and is the busiest port in West Africa. Some US$200m. have been earmarked for continued expansion of the port. In 2002 the merchant marine totalled 9,000 GRT, including oil tankers 1,000 GRT.

Telecommunications. In 2002 there were 1,363,200 telephone subscribers, or 82·7 per 1,000 inhabitants, and there were 154,000 PCs in use (9·3 per 1,000 persons). Since liberalization in 1995 the telecommunications sector has quickly progressed to become the West African leader and second only to that in South Africa in the continent as a whole. Mobile phone subscribers numbered 1,027,100 in 2002. In 2002 there were 90,000 Internet users.

Postal Services. In 1998 there were 373 post offices.

SOCIAL INSTITUTIONS

Justice. There are 28 courts of first instance and three assize courts in Abidjan, Bouaké and Daloa, two courts of appeal in Abidjan and Bouaké, and a supreme court in Abidjan. Côte d'Ivoire abolished the death penalty in 2000.

Religion. In 2001 there were 6·3m. Muslims (mainly in the north) and 4·3m. Christians (chiefly Roman Catholics in the south). Although Christians are in the majority among Ivorians, when Côte d'Ivoire's large immigrant population is taken into account Muslims are in the majority. Traditional animist beliefs are also practised. In Sept. 2003 the Roman Catholic church had one cardinal.

Education. The adult literacy rate in 2001 was 49·7% (60·3% among males and 38·4% among females). There were, in 2000–01, 2,046,861 pupils with 44,424 teachers in primary schools and 663,636 pupils with 23,184 teachers at secondary schools. In 2000–01 there were 115,413 students at higher education institutions. In 1995–96 there was one university with 21,000 students and 730 academic staff, and three university centres. There were six other institutions of higher education.

In 2000–01 expenditure on education came to 4·9% of GNP and 21·5% of total government spending.

Health. In 1993 there were five hospital beds per 10,000 inhabitants. In 1996 there were 1,318 physicians, 4,568 nurses and 2,196 midwives.

CULTURE

World Heritage Sites. UNESCO world heritage sites in Côte d'Ivoire are: Taï National Park (inscribed on the list in 1982); and the Comoé National Park (1983).

Broadcasting. The government-controlled Radiodiffusion Télévision Ivoirienne is responsible for broadcasting. There were 1m. television sets (colour by SECAM V) in 2001 and 2·2m. radio receivers in 2000.

Press. In 1996 there were 12 daily newspapers with a combined circulation of 231,000, at a rate of 17 per 1,000 inhabitants.

Tourism. There were 301,000 foreign tourists in 1998; spending by tourists in 2000 totalled US$57m.

DIPLOMATIC REPRESENTATIVES

Of Côte d'Ivoire in the United Kingdom (2 Upper Belgrave St., London, SW1X 8BJ)
Ambassador: Yousoufou Bamba.

Of the United Kingdom in Côte d'Ivoire (3rd Floor, Immeuble 'Bank of Africa', angle Av. Terrasson de Fougères et Rue Gourgas Plateau, Abidjan)
Ambassador: David Coates.

Of Côte d'Ivoire in the USA (2424 Massachusetts Ave., NW, Washington, D.C., 20008)
Ambassador: Daouda Diabate.

Of the USA in Côte d'Ivoire (5 Rue Jesse Owens, Abidjan)
Ambassador: Aubrey Hooks.

Of Côte d'Ivoire to the United Nations
Ambassador: Djessan Philippe Djangone-Bi.

Of Côte d'Ivoire to the European Union
Ambassador: Marie Gosset.

FURTHER READING

Direction de la Statistique. *Bulletin Mensuel de Statistique.*

Daniels, Morna, *Côte d'Ivoire.* [Bibliography] ABC-Clio, Oxford and Santa Barbara (CA), 1996

National statistical office: Institut National de la Statistique, BP V 55, Abidjan 01.
Website (French only): http://www.ins.ci

CROATIA

Republika Hrvatska

Capital: Zagreb
Population projection, 2010: 4·35m.
GDP per capita, 2002: (PPP$) 10,240
HDI/world rank: 0·830/48

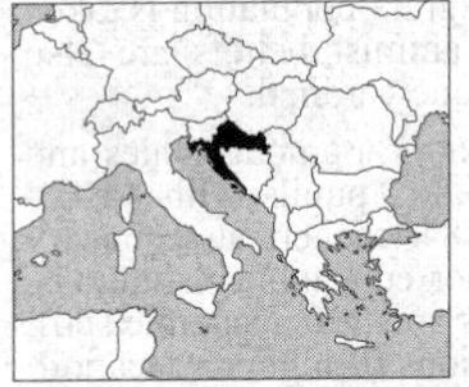

KEY HISTORICAL EVENTS

Croatia was united with Hungary in 1091 and remained under Hungarian administration until the end of the First World War. On 1 Dec. 1918 Croatia became a part of the new Kingdom of Serbs, Croats and Slovenes, which was renamed Yugoslavia in 1929. During the Second World War an independent fascist (Ustaša) state was set up under the aegis of the German occupiers. During the Communist period Croatia became one of the six 'Socialist Republics' constituting the Yugoslav federation led by Marshal Tito. With the collapse of Communism, an independence movement gained momentum.

In a referendum on 19 May 1991, 94·17% of votes cast were in favour of Croatia becoming an independent sovereign state with the option of joining a future Yugoslav confederation as opposed to remaining in the existing Yugoslav federation. The Krajina and other predominantly Serbian areas of Croatia wanted union with Serbia and seized power. Croatian forces and Serb insurgents backed by federal forces became embroiled in a conflict throughout 1991 until the arrival of a UN peacekeeping mission at the beginning of 1992 and the establishment of four UN peacekeeping zones ('pink zones'). In early May 1995 Croatian forces re-took Western Slavonia from the Serbs and opened the Zagreb-Belgrade highway. In a 60-hour operation mounted on 4 Aug. 1995 the former self-declared Serb Republic of Krajina was occupied, provoking an exodus of 180,000 Serb refugees. Croats who had left the area in 1991 began to return. On 12 Nov. 1995 the Croatian government and Bosnian Serbs reached an agreement to place Eastern Slavonia, the last Croatian territory still under Bosnian Serb control, under UN administration.

TERRITORY AND POPULATION

Croatia is bounded in the north by Slovenia and Hungary and in the east by Serbia and Montenegro and Bosnia-Herzegovina. It includes the areas of Dalmatia, Istria and Slavonia which no longer have administrative status. Its area is 56,542 sq. km. Population at the 2001 census was 4,437,460 (4,784,265 in 1991), of whom the predominating ethnic groups were Croats (90%) and Serbs (5%); population density, 78·5 per sq. km. The significant population decrease, popularly called 'the white plague', is seen as a serious social problem.

The UN gives a projected population for 2010 of 4·35m.

In 2001, 58·1% of the population lived in urban areas.

The area and population (2001 census) of the 20 counties and one city:

County	*Area (in sq. km)*	*Population*	*Capital*
Bjelovarska-Bilogorska	2,638	133,084	Bjelovar
Brodsko-Posavska	2,027	176,765	Slavonski Brod
Dubrovačko-Neretvanska	1,782	122,870	Dubrovnik
Istarska	2,813	206,344	Pazin
Karlovačka	3,622	141,787	Karlovac
Koprivničko-Križevačka	1,734	124,467	Koprivnica
Krapinsko-Zagorska	1,230	142,432	Krapina
Ličko-Senjska	5,350	53,677	Gospić
Međimurska	730	118,426	Čakovec
Osječko-Baranjska	4,149	330,506	Osijek
Požeško-Slavonska	1,821	85,831	Požega
Primorsko-Goranska	3,590	305,505	Rijeka
Šibensko-Kninska	2,994	112,891	Šibenik
Sisačko-Moslavačka	4,448	185,387	Sisak

County	Area (in sq. km)	Population	Capital
Splitsko-Dalmatinska	4,524	463,676	Split
Varaždinska	1,260	184,769	Varaždin
Virovitičko-Podravska	2,021	93,389	Virovitica
Vukovarsko-Srijemska	2,448	204,768	Vukovar
Zadarska	3,643	162,045	Zadar
Zagrebačka	3,078	309,696	Zagreb
Zagreb (city)	640	779,145	Zagreb

Zagreb, the capital, had a 2001 population of 691,724. Other major towns (with 2001 census population): Split (188,694), Rijeka (143,800) and Osijek (90,411).

At the beginning of 1991 there were some 0·6m. resident Serbs. A law of Dec. 1991 guaranteed the autonomy of Serbs in areas where they are in a majority after the establishment of a permanent peace.

The official language is Croatian.

SOCIAL STATISTICS

2002: births, 40,094; deaths, 50,569; marriages, 22,806; divorces, 4,496. Suicides (2000), 926. 2002 rates: birth, 9·0 per 1,000 population; death, 11·4; marriage, 5·1; divorce (1998), 0·9. Suicide rate, 2000, 21·1 per 100,000 population. Infant mortality, 2001, seven per 1,000 live births. Annual population growth rate, 1992–2002, –0·6%. In 2001 the most popular age range for marrying was 25–29 for males and 20–24 for females. Life expectancy at birth, 2001, was 70·0 years for males and 77·9 years for females. Fertility rate, 2001, 1·7 children per woman.

CLIMATE

Inland Croatia has a central European type of climate, with cold winters and hot summers, but the Adriatic coastal region experiences a Mediterranean climate with mild, moist winters and hot, brilliantly sunny summers with less than average rainfall. Average annual temperature and rainfall: Dubrovnik, 16·6°C and 1,051 mm. Zadar, 15·6°C and 963 mm. Rijeka, 14·3°C and 1,809 mm. Zagreb, 12·4°C and 1,000 mm. Osijek, 11·3°C and 683 mm.

CONSTITUTION AND GOVERNMENT

A new constitution was adopted on 21 Dec. 1990. The *President* is elected for renewable five-year terms. There is a unicameral Parliament (*Hrvatski Sabor*), consisting of 152 deputies. It has 140 members elected from multi-seat constituencies for a four-year term, five seats are reserved for national minorities and six members representing Croatians abroad are chosen by proportional representation. The upper house, the *Chamber of Counties*, was abolished in 2001.

National Anthem. 'Lijepa nasva domovino' ('Beautiful our homeland'); words by A. Mihanović, tune by J. Runjanin.

RECENT ELECTIONS

Presidential elections were held on 2 Jan. 2005. Incumbent Stipe Mesić (Croatian People's Party) received 48·9% of the vote, Jadranka Kosor (Croatian Democratic Union) 20·3% and Boris Mikšić (ind.) 17·8%. There were ten other candidates. Turn-out was 50·6%. As a result a second round was required. In the run-off on 16 Jan. 2005 Stipe Mesić received 65·9% of votes cast, against 34·1% for Jadranka Kosor.

Elections to the Sabor were held on 23 Nov. 2003. The Croatian Democratic Union (HDZ) won 66 of 152 seats (33·9% of the vote); an alliance of the Social Democratic Party of Croatia, the Istrian Democratic Assembly, Libra and the Liberal Party won 43 seats with 22·6% (of which the Social Democratic Party of Croatia 34 seats); an alliance of the Croatian People's Party and the Littoral and Highland Region Alliance won 11 with 8·0%; the Croatian Peasant Party won 10 with 7·2%; the Croatian Party of Rights won 8 seats with 6·4%. Other parties won three seats or fewer; non-partisans took four seats. Turn-out was 61·7%.

CURRENT ADMINISTRATION

President: Stipe Mesić; b. 1934 (Croatian People's Party; sworn in 18 Feb. 2000 and re-elected on 2 Jan. 2005).

Following the election of 23 Nov. 2003 a coalition government was formed between the Croatian Democratic Union and the alliance of the Croatian Social Liberal Party and Democratic Centre.

In March 2005 the government comprised:

Prime Minister: Ivo Sanader; b. 1953 (Croatian Democratic Union; sworn in 23 Dec. 2003).

Deputy Prime Ministers: Jadranka Kosor (also *Minister of the Family, Veterans' Affairs and Intergenerational Solidarity*); Damir Polančec.

Minister of Foreign Affairs and European Integration: Kolinda Grabar-Kitarović. *Finance:* Ivan Šuker. *Defence:* Berislav Rončević. *Interior:* Marijan Mlinarić. *Economy, Labour and Entrepreneurship:* Branko Vukelić. *Sea, Tourism, Transport and Development:* Božidar Kalmeta. *Agriculture, Forestry and Water Management:* Petar Čobanković. *Environmental Protection, Physical Planning and Construction:* Marina Matulović Dropulić. *Health and Social Welfare:* Neven Ljubičić. *Culture:* Božo Biškupić. *Justice:* Vesna Škare Ožbolt. *Science, Education and Sports:* Dragan Primorac.

Government Website: http://www.vlada.hr/

DEFENCE

Conscription is for six months. Defence expenditure in 2003 totalled US$596m. (US$134 per capita), representing 2·1% of GDP.

Army. The country is divided into six operations zones. Personnel, 2002, 45,000 (around 20,000 conscripts). Paramilitary forces include an armed police of 10,000. There are 40,000 reserves in 27 Home Defence regiments and 100,000 regular Army reservists.

Navy. In 2002 the fleet included one submarine for special operations and one missile-armed corvette. Total personnel in 2002 numbered about 3,000 including two companies of marines.

Air Force. Personnel, 2002, 3,000 (including Air Defence and 1,320 conscripts). There are 24 combat aircraft including 20 MiG-21s, and 22 armed helicopters.

INTERNATIONAL RELATIONS

Croatia is a member of the UN, WTO, BIS, NATO Partnership for Peace, the Council of Europe, OSCE, the Central European Initiative, the Danube Commission, the Inter-American Development Bank and the IOM. Croatia applied for European Union membership in 2003 and was accepted as an official candidate country in 2004.

ECONOMY

Agriculture contributed 8·9% of GDP in 2002, industry 29·3% and services 61·8%.

Overview. Croatia has experienced average growth rates of 4·5% per annum and consistently low inflation since the mid-1990s. The country witnessed strong industrial production and retail sales in 2003 although private sector activity started to slow down in 2004. Structural reforms including privatization have been successfully undertaken in the last decade. Bankruptcy, company and labour laws have been modernized in a bid to harmonize with EU standards. According to the OECD, deeper reforms are needed in the legal system and in the labour market, and greater privatization is needed outside the telecommunications and banking sectors in order to boost corporate governance and competitiveness. The external position has been gradually worsening despite good performances in other areas. External debt increased to 75% of GDP in 2003; according to the IMF this is more than twice the average of that in emerging markets and higher than that in the other Central and Eastern European countries. Domestic investment has grown faster than savings since the mid-1990s, creating persistent current account deficits, leaving the debt profile increasingly vulnerable to external shocks, particularly in the event of currency depreciation. In 2003 fiscal discipline waned as the fiscal deficit increased to 6·3% of GDP, overshooting its target of 4·5%. In 2004 the newly elected government resumed efforts to maintain fiscal consolidation, to improve transparency in the fiscal accounts, to rein in quasi-fiscal operations and to strengthen public expenditure and debt management.

Currency. On 30 May 1994 the *kuna* (HRK; a name used in 1941–45) of 100 *lipa* replaced the Croatian dinar at one kuna = 1,000 dinars. Foreign exchange reserves were US$5,506m. in June 2002. Gold reserves have been negligible since Sept. 2001. Inflation was 1·8% in 2003 (2·2% in 2002). Total money supply was 26,715m. kuna in May 2002.

Budget. Government revenue and expenditure (1m. kuna):

	1996	*1997*	*1998*	*1999*	*2000*	*2001*
Revenue	47,696	52,945	63,173	61,358	63,817	65,843
Expenditure	48,407	54,362	63,079	68,889	73,269	73,796

Expenditure by function (2001, in 1m. kuna): social security and welfare, 31,610; health, 11,815; education, 5,896. VAT at 22% was introduced in 1997.

Performance. Real GDP growth was 3·8% in 2001 and 5·2% in 2002. Total GDP was US$28·3bn. in 2003.

Banking and Finance. The National Bank of Croatia (*Governor*, Zeljko Rohatinski) is the bank of issue. In 2001 there were 43 registered banks. The largest banks are Zagrebačka Banka, with assets in 2000 of US$2·8bn., and Privredna Banka Zagreb. There are stock exchanges in Zagreb and Varaždin.

Total foreign direct investments from 1993 to Sept. 2001 amounted to US$5,927·5m., principally from Austria (US$1,739m.), Germany (US$1,199m.) and the USA (US$1,189m).

ENERGY AND NATURAL RESOURCES

Environment. Croatia's carbon dioxide emissions from the consumption and flaring of fossil fuels in 2002 were the equivalent of 4·4 tonnes per capita. An *Environmental Sustainability Index* compiled for the World Economic Forum meeting in Feb. 2002 ranked Croatia 12th in the world, with 62·5%. The index measured the ability of countries to maintain favourable environmental conditions and examined various factors including pollution levels and the use or abuse of natural resources.

Electricity. Installed capacity in 2000 was 3·8m. kW. Output was 10·70bn. kWh in 2000, with consumption per capita 3,356 kWh in 2000.

Oil and Gas. In 2000, 1·1m. tonnes of crude oil were produced. Natural gas output in 2000 totalled 1·7bn. cu. metres and reserves were 34bn. cu. metres in 2002.

Minerals. Production (in 1,000 tonnes): salt (2001), 33.

Agriculture. Agriculture and fishing generate approximately 9% of GDP. At the 1993 census 409,647 persons subsisted on agriculture. Agricultural land totals 3·15m. ha (63·4% is cultivated). There were 1·46m. ha of arable land in 2001 and 127,000 ha of permanent crops. Production (in 1,000 tonnes, 2000): wheat, 1,080; maize, 800; sugarbeets, 770; potatoes, 500; grapes, 394; wine, 209; barley, 125.

Livestock, 2000: cattle, 427,000; sheep, 528,000; pigs, 1,233,000; chickens, 11m. Animal products, 2000: milk, 641,000 tonnes; meat, 125,000 tonnes; eggs, 49,000 tonnes; cheese, 19,000 tonnes.

Forestry. Forests covered 1·96m. ha in 2002, of which 80% are state owned. In 2001, 3·47m. cu. metres of roundwood were produced.

Fisheries. In 2002 there were 15 fish-processing factories. Total catch in 2001 was 18,090 tonnes, almost exclusively from sea fishing.

INDUSTRY

The largest company in Croatia in Jan. 2003 was Pliva (market capitalization of 9,360·3m. kuna), a pharmaceuticals company.

In 2001 industrial production growth totalled 6% in comparison with 2000. Production, 2000: cement, 3·25m. tonnes; cotton fabrics and blankets (1998), 16·75m. sq. metres; wool fabrics and blankets (1998), 6·55m. sq. metres; beer (2001), 379·9m. litres.

Labour. In 2001 the number of employees was 1,469,500 and unemployment was 24·7%. Among 15 to 30-year-olds unemployment is around 40%. The main areas of activity in 2001 were manufacturing (employing 305,600 persons), agriculture, hunting and forestry (224,500), wholesale and retail trade/repair of motor vehicles, motorcycles and personal and household goods (211,300) and public administration and defence/compulsory social security (105,500).

INTERNATIONAL TRADE

Croatia has accepted responsibility for 29·5% of the US$4,400m. commercial bank debt of the former Yugoslavia. Total foreign debt was US$15,347m. in 2002.

Imports and Exports. Exports in 2002 were valued at US$4,994·6m. Imports for 2002 came to US$10,273·9m.

Main exports in 1999 were: machinery and transport equipment, 29·1%; manufactured goods, 14·9%; clothing, 12·3%; chemicals, 11·1%; food and live animals, 6·8%; refined petroleum products, 6·2%. Principal imports in 1999 were: machinery and transport equipment, 34·7%; manufactured goods, 16·8%; chemicals, 11·7%; petroleum products, 8·7%; foodstuffs, 7·2%. In 2001 the main export markets were (in US$1m.): Italy (1,104); Germany (689); Bosnia-Herzegovina (560); Slovenia (426); Austria (268). Main import suppliers (in US$1m.): Germany (1,547); Italy (1,524); Slovenia (712); Russia (654); Austria (630).

COMMUNICATIONS

Roads. There were 28,344 km of roads in 2002 (including 455 km of motorways). In 1999, 84·6% of roads were paved. In 2000 there were 1,124,825 passenger cars, 4,660 buses and coaches, and 116,768 vans and trucks. 84m. passengers and 5·69m. tonnes of freight were carried by public transport in 1998. There were 655 deaths in road accidents in 2000.

Rail. There were 2,727 km of 1,435 mm gauge rail in 2000 (983 km electrified). In 2000 railways carried 17·6m. passengers and 10·1m. tonnes of freight.

Civil Aviation. There are international airports at Zagreb (Pleso), Split and Dubrovnik. The national carrier is Croatia Airlines. In 1999 scheduled airline traffic of Croatian-based carriers flew 9·6m. km, carrying 838,000 passengers (503,000 on international flights). In 2000 Zagreb handled 1,139,000 passengers (784,000 on international flights) and 5,300 tonnes of freight, Split handled 514,000 passengers (353,000 on international flights) and Dubrovnik 387,000 passengers (276,000 on international flights).

Shipping. The main port is Rijeka, which handled 8·9m. tonnes of freight in 2000 (2·6m. dry cargo). There were 168 ocean-going vessels in 1995, totalling 3·29m. DWT. 132 of the vessels (94·09% of tonnage) were registered under foreign flags. In 2002 total GRT was 835,000, including oil tankers 8,000 GRT. Provisional figures for 1998 show that 12·75m. passengers and 15·71m. tonnes of cargo were transported. In 2002 vessels totalling 24,436,000 NRT entered ports and vessels totalling 20,577,000 NRT cleared.

Telecommunications. The repair and expansion of the telecommunications industry has been made a high priority in the development process of the country. In 1999 Deutsche Telekom acquired a 35% stake in Croatian Telecom from the Croatian government. The telephone density (the number of lines per 1,000 population) rose from 17·2% in 1990 to 35% in 1998.

In 2002 there were 4,157,000 telephone subscribers, equivalent to 858·2 per 1,000 persons, and 760,000 PCs (156·9 per 1,000 persons). Mobile phone subscribers numbered 2,340,000 in 2002, and in 1997 there were 50,200 fax machines. The number of Internet users in 2002 was 789,000.

Postal Services. In 1998 there were 1,168 post offices.

SOCIAL INSTITUTIONS

Justice. The population in penal institutions in Dec. 2001 was 2,584 (59 per 100,000 of national population).

Religion. In 2001 there were 3,890,000 Roman Catholics, 250,000 Serbian Orthodox and 100,000 Sunni Muslims. The remainder of the population were followers of other religions. In Sept. 2003 there was one cardinal.

Education. In 2003–04 there were 1,067 pre-school institutions with 89,212 children and 7,020 childcare workers; 2,138 primary schools with 393,421 pupils and 28,335 teachers; 665 secondary schools with 195,340 pupils and 20,073 teachers. In 2002–03 there were 102 institutes of higher education with 121,722 students and 6,748 (1998–99) academic staff. In 2002 there were four universities (Zagreb, Osijek, Rijeka and Split). Adult literacy rate in 2001 was 98·4% (male, 99·4%; female, 97·4%).

In 1999–2000 total expenditure on education came to 4·3% of GNP; in 1998–99 expenditure on education accounted for 10·4% of total government expenditure.

Health. In 1997 there were 70 hospitals with 63 beds per 10,000 inhabitants. In 1998 there were 9,766 physicians, 2,802 dentists, 20,216 nurses, 1,940 pharmacists and 1,407 midwives.

Welfare. The official retirement age is 62 years (men) and 57 years (women). However, this is set to rise gradually until 2008 when it will be 65 (men) and 60 (women). The old-age pension is dependent on wages earned in relation to the average wage of all employed persons. The minimum old-age pension is defined for every year of the qualifying period as 0·825% of the average gross salary of all employees in 1998. This amount (39·86 kuna from Jan. 2002) is adjusted for inflation. The minimum unemployment benefit was 725 kuna a month in 2002 and the maximum benefit was 900 kuna a month.

CULTURE

World Heritage Sites. Croatia has six UNESCO protected sites: the Old City of Dubrovnik (entered on the List in 1979), known as the 'Pearl of the Adriatic' and medieval Ragusa, an important maritime republic; the Historic Complex of Split with the Palace of Diocletian (1979), including Roman Emperor Diocletian's mausoleum, now the cathedral; Plitvice Lakes National Park (1979), a series of lakes and waterfalls and a habitat for bears and wolves; the Episcopal Complex of the Euphrasian Basilica in the Historical Centre of Poreč (1997); the Historic City of Trogir (1997), a Venetian city based on a Hellenistic plan; and the Cathedral of St James in Šibenik (2000), built in the Gothic and Renaissance styles between 1431–1535.

Broadcasting. Broadcasting is controlled by the state Croatian Radio-Television (colour by PAL). In 1998 there were 108 radio and ten television stations. In 2000 there were 1·12m. radio receivers and 1·31m. television receivers.

Cinema. There were 141 cinemas with a total attendance of 2·3m in 1999. Three feature films were made in 1998.

Press. In 1996 there were ten daily newspapers with a combined circulation of 515,000, at a rate of 115 per 1,000 inhabitants. An amendment of March 1996 to the criminal code makes it an offence for the press to defame the government. In 1999 a total of 2,309 book titles were published.

Tourism. In 2000 there were a total of 6·62m. tourists (5·34m. foreign tourists, including 920,000 Germans and 886,000 Italians) staying 38·41m. tourist nights. In 2002 there were 160,000 hotel beds and 306,000 beds in private accommodation. The tourist industry is now recovering following the 1991–95 war, although the events in neighbouring Yugoslavia in 1999 resulted in the number of tourists for the year declining to 4·75m. In 2000 tourism accounted for more than 15% of GDP. The industry directly employs about 10% of the population.

Festivals. Croatia has a number of cultural and traditional festivals, including the Zagreb Summer Festival (July–Aug.); the International Folk Dance Festival in

Zagreb (July); Dubrovnik Summer Festival (July–Aug.); Split Summer (July–Aug.); Alka Festival (traditional medieval tilting), Sinj (Aug.).

Libraries. In 1995 there were 232 public libraries, one National library and 134 Higher Education libraries. They held a combined 12,683,000 volumes for 1,233,600 registered users.

DIPLOMATIC REPRESENTATIVES

Of Croatia in the United Kingdom (21 Conway St., London, W1T 6BN)
Ambassador: Josip Paro.

Of the United Kingdom in Croatia (Ivana Lucica 4, 10000 Zagreb)
Ambassador: Nicholas R. Jarrold.

Of Croatia in the USA (2343 Massachusetts Ave., NW, Washington, D.C., 20008)
Ambassador: Neven Jurica.

Of the USA in Croatia (Thomasa Jeffersona 2, 10010 Zagreb)
Ambassador: Ralph Frank.

Of Croatia to the United Nations
Ambassador: Vacant.
Chargé d'Affaires a.i.: Ivan Nimac.

Of Croatia to the European Union
Ambassador: Mirjana Mladineo.

FURTHER READING

Central Bureau of Statistics. *Statistical Yearbook, Monthly Statistical Report, Statistical Information, Statistical Reports.*

Carmichael, Cathie, *Croatia.* [Bibliography] ABC-Clio, Oxford and Santa Barbara (CA), 1999
Jovanovic, Nikolina, *Croatia: A History.* Translated from Croatian. Hurst, London, 2000
Stallaerts, R. and Laurens, J., *Historical Dictionary of the Republic of Croatia.* Metuchen (NJ), 1995
Tanner, M. C., *A Nation Forged in War.* Yale, 1997

National statistical office: Central Bureau of Statistics, 3 Ilica, 10000 Zagreb. *Director:* Marijan Gredelj.
Website: http://www.dzs.hr/

CUBA

República de Cuba

Capital: Havana
Population projection, 2010: 11·46m.
GDP per capita, 2000: (PPP$) 5,259
HDI/world rank: 0·809/52

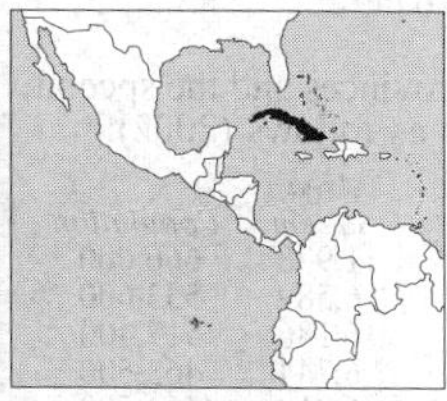

KEY HISTORICAL EVENTS

Cuba's first inhabitants were the Taíno, Ciboney and Guanahatabey tribes. Christopher Columbus arrived in Cuba in 1492 and a permanent settlement was established by Diego Velázquez in 1511. Oppression and European diseases virtually exterminated the indigenous population within 50 years and African slaves were imported as replacements. In 1607 Havana was declared the capital.

Resistance to Spanish rule grew after the removal of Cuban delegates from the Spanish Cortes in 1837. Repeated offers by the USA to buy Cuba were rejected. Slavery was suppressed from the 1850s though not abolished until 1886. The first rebellion, the Ten-Year War, broke out in 1868 and was led by Gen. Máximo Gómez. An assembly was granted in 1869. However, José Martí y Pérez created the Cuban Revolutionary Party from New York and launched an invasion of Cuba in 1895 with Gómez and Antonio Maceo. The USA intervened in 1898, winning control of Cuba from Spain at the Treaty of Paris. Municipal elections in 1900 rejected annexationist policies and Cuba achieved independence in 1902. The Platt Amendment allowed for US intervention to preserve independence and stability and awarded the USA control of Guantánamo Bay. At the request of President Estrada Palma, US forces were installed on the island between 1906 and 1909. In 1912 and 1917 there were further instances of American intervention to protect national interests.

Gerardo Machado's dictatorial presidency began in 1925 and was ended by a coup in 1933. The Revolt of the Sergeants brought Fulgencio Batista y Zaldívar to power. The Platt Amendment was revoked and in 1940 a socially progressive constitution was inaugurated. Batista was returned at disputed elections in 1940 but was voted out of office four years later. He ran for re-election in 1952 but, with little chance of victory, led a bloodless coup before elections could be held, suspending the constitution and instigating a repressive and corrupt regime.

Fidel Castro, imprisoned in 1953 after a failed revolt, arrived from Mexico with 80 men in 1956. Castro and Che Guevara led a guerrilla war from the Sierra Maestra mountains and, despite US financial support, Batista fled after revolutionaries seized Havana in Jan. 1959. The USA recognized the new regime but relations soon deteriorated. Castro, as prime minister, launched a nationalization programme, seizing American assets and outlawing foreign land ownership. In Oct. 1960 the USA's trade embargo began and diplomatic relations were broken in Jan. 1961. Close relations between Cuba and the USSR provoked covert US support for the doomed Bay of Pigs invasion in April 1961, in which an offensive by a group of exiled Cubans was defeated by Castro's troops. Castro declared Cuba to be a socialist state. In 1962 the USA and USSR neared nuclear conflict during the Cuban Missile Crisis, with the US Navy imposing a blockade on Cuba from 22 Oct. until 22 Nov. to force the USSR to withdraw Soviet missile bases. In return, the USA guaranteed not to invade Cuba. Between 1965 and 1973, 250,000 Cubans left for America on Freedom Flights agreed between the two nations. In 1976 a new constitution consolidated Castro's power as head of state, government and the Armed Forces.

Cuba continued to receive financial aid and technical advice from the USSR until the early 1990s when subsidies were suspended. This led to a 40% drop in GDP between 1989 and 1993. The USA has maintained an economic embargo against the island and relations between Cuba and the USA have remained embittered, although contact between the two countries has been growing in recent years. From Jan. 2002 suspected al-Qaeda and Taliban prisoners were brought from Afghanistan to the military prison at the American naval base at Guantánamo Bay.

TERRITORY AND POPULATION

The island of Cuba forms the largest and most westerly of the Greater Antilles group and lies 135 miles south of the tip of Florida, USA. The area is 110,861 sq. km, and comprises the island of Cuba (104,748 sq. km); the Isle of Youth (Isla de la Juventud, formerly the Isle of Pines; 2,398 sq. km); and some 1,600 small isles ('cays'; 3,715 sq. km). Population, census (2002), 11,177,743, giving a density of 100·8 per sq. km. In 2001, 75·5% of the population were urban.

The UN gives a projected population for 2010 of 11·46m.

The area, population and density of population of the 14 provinces and the special Municipality of the Isle of Youth (Isla de la Juventud) were as follows (2002):

	Area sq. km	*Population*		*Area sq. km*	*Population*
Ciudad de La Habana	727	2,175,900	Matanzas	11,978	666,000
Santiago de Cuba	6,170	1,043,200	Las Tunas	6,589	533,600
Holguín	9,301	1,037,700	Guantánamo	6,186	517,400
Villa Clara	8,662	836,200	Sancti Spíritus	6,744	463,500
Granma	8,372	837,200	Ciego de Avila	6,910	414,500
Camagüey	15,990	792,800	Cienfuegos	4,178	399,000
Pinar del Río	10,925	740,200			
La Habana	5,731	713,100	Isla de la Juventud	2,398	80,700

The capital city, Havana, had a population in 2000 of 2,186,632. Other major cities (2000 populations in 1,000): Santiago de Cuba (443), Camagüey (308), Holguín (262), Santa Clara (211), Guantánamo (209), Pinar del Río (148), Bayamo (144), Cienfuegos (139), Las Tunas (139) and Matanzas (125).

The official language is Spanish.

SOCIAL STATISTICS

2001 births, 138,718; deaths, 79,395; marriages, 54,345; divorces, 37,260; suicides (1996), 2,015. Rates, 2001: birth, 12·4 per 1,000 population; death, 7·1; marriage, 4·8; divorce, 3·3; suicide (1996), 18·3. Infant mortality rate, 2001, 6·2 per 1,000 live births. Annual population growth rate, 1992–2002, 0·4%. Life expectancy in 2001 was 74·6 years for males and 78·5 for females. The fertility rate in 2001 was 1·6 births per woman.

CLIMATE

Situated in the sub-tropical zone, Cuba has a generally rainy climate, affected by the Gulf Stream and the N.E. Trades, although winters are comparatively dry after the heaviest rains in Sept. and Oct. Hurricanes are liable to occur between June and Nov. Havana, Jan. 72°F (22·2°C), July 82°F (27·8°C). Annual rainfall 48" (1,224 mm).

CONSTITUTION AND GOVERNMENT

A Communist Constitution came into force on 24 Feb. 1976. It was amended in July 1992 to permit direct parliamentary elections and in June 2002 to make the country's socialist system 'irrevocable'.

Legislative power is vested in the *National Assembly of People's Power*, which meets twice a year and consists of 609 deputies elected for a five-year term by universal suffrage. Lists of candidates are drawn up by mass organizations (trade unions, etc.). The National Assembly elects a 31-member *Council of State* as its permanent organ. The Council of State's President, who is head of state and of government, nominates and leads a Council of Ministers approved by the National Assembly.

National Anthem. 'Al combate corred bayameses' ('Run, Bayamans, to the combat'); words and tune by P. Figueredo.

RECENT ELECTIONS

Elections to the National Assembly were held on 19 Jan. 2003. All 609 candidates were from the National Assembly of People's Power and received the requisite 50% of votes for election. No other parties are allowed.

CURRENT ADMINISTRATION

President: Dr Fidel Castro Ruz (b. 1927) became *President* of the Council of State on 3 Dec. 1976; re-elected for five years on 24 Feb. 1998 and again on 6 March

2003. He is also First Secretary of the Cuban Communist Party, President of the Council of Ministers and C.-in-C. of the National Defence Council.

In March 2005 the government comprised:

First Vice-President of the Council of State and of the Council of Ministers, Minister of the Revolutionary Armed Forces: Gen. Raúl Castro Ruz (Fidel Castro's younger brother and his designated successor).

Vice-Presidents of the Council of Ministers: Osmany Cienfuegos Gorriarán, José Ramón Fernández Alvarez, José Luis Rodríguez García (also *Minister of Economy and Planning*), Pedro Miret Prieto, Otto Rivero Torres. *Secretary of the Council of Ministers:* Carlos Lage Dávila.

Minister of Agriculture: Alfredo Jordán Morales. *Auditing and Control:* Lina Olinda Pedraza Rodríguez. *Basic Industries:* Yadira García Vera. *Construction:* Fidel Figueroa de la Paz. *Culture:* Abel Prieto Jiménez. *Domestic Trade:* Barbara Castillo Cuesta. *Education:* Luis Gómez Gutiérrez. *Finance and Prices:* Georgina Barreiro Fajardo. *Fishing Industry:* Alfredo López Valdés. *Food Industry:* Alejandro Roca Iglesias. *Foreign Investment and Economic Co-operation:* Marta Lomas Morales. *Foreign Relations:* Felipe Pérez Roque. *Foreign Trade:* Raúl de la Nuez Ramírez. *Higher Education:* Fernando Vecino Alegret. *Information Science and Communications:* Roberto Ignacio González Planas. *Interior:* Gen. Abelardo Colomé Ibarra. *Iron, Steel and Engineering Industries:* Fernando Acosta Santana. *Justice:* Roberto Díaz Sotolongo. *Labour and Social Security:* Alfredo Morales Cartaya. *Light Industry:* Jesús Pérez Othón. *Public Health:* José Ramón Balaguer Cabrera. *Science, Technology and Environment:* Vacant. *Sugar Industry:* Div. Gen. Ulises Rosales del Toro. *Tourism:* Manual Marrero Cruz. *Transport:* Carlos Manuel Pazo Torrado. *Ministers without Portfolio:* Wilfredo López Rodríguez; Ricardo Cabrisas Ruiz.

The Congress of the Cuban Communist Party (PCC) elects a Central Committee of 225 members, which in turn appoints a Political Bureau comprising 26 members.

Government Website: http://www.cubagob.cu

DEFENCE

The National Defence Council is headed by the president of the republic. Conscription is for two years.

In 2003 defence expenditure totalled US$1,200m. (US$106 per capita), representing 4·0% of GDP.

Army. The strength was estimated at 35,000 (including conscripts and Ready Reservists) in 2002. Border Guard and State Security forces total 26,500. The Territorial Militia is estimated at 1m. (reservists), all armed. In addition there is a Youth Labour Army of 70,000 and a Civil Defence Force of 50,000.

Navy. Personnel in 1999 totalled about 5,000 conscripts including about 550 marines. The Navy has five patrol and coastal combatants, six mine warfare vessels and one support vessel. Main bases are at Cabañas and Holguín. The USA still occupies the Guantánamo naval base.

Air Force. In 2002 the Air Force had a strength of some 8,000 and about 130 combat aircraft of which only around 25 are thought to be operational. They include MiG-29, MiG-23 and MiG-21 jet fighters.

INTERNATIONAL RELATIONS

Cuba is a member of the UN, WTO, OAS, LAIA, ACS, Antarctic Treaty and SELA (Latin American Economic System).

ECONOMY

Agriculture accounted for an estimated 6·4% of GDP in 1998, industry 36·9% and services 56·7%.

Overview. With the end to subsidies from the former Soviet Union, the economy has had to cope with a fall in tourism, low export prices and hurricane damage. The US trade embargo on Cuba, imposed in 1963, blocks the island's access to funds from the International Monetary Fund and the World Bank. Agriculture accounts for 6% of GDP and employs 24% of the active workforce. The chief export crops are sugar and coffee. The industrial sector accounts for 37% of GDP. Output from the cigar industry increased in the late 1990s. The country's black market is bigger than its legal economy and basic economic activities (e.g. the sale of milk and bread) take place in the informal sector. There are no joint ventures with foreigners or foreign ownership of property. The currency is not convertible. The government employs 75% of the labour force, who receive housing and food subsidies but low wages. After the economic crisis of the early 1990s, growth has picked up through the legalization of the use of the US dollar and the promotion of dollar-based tourism with a parallel dollar economy.

Currency. The unit of currency is the *Cuban peso* (CUP) of 100 *centavos*, which is not convertible, although an official exchange rate is announced daily reflecting any changes in the strength of the US dollar. The US dollar ceased to be legal tender in 2004. 9,710m. pesos were in circulation in 1998. Inflation was negative in 1999, at –0·5%.

Budget. The 2002 revenue totalled 16,051bn. pesos and expenditure 17,051bn. pesos. Hard-currency earners and the self-employed became liable to a 10–50% income tax in Nov. 1995.

Performance. A combination of poor commodity export prices and a poor sugar harvest slowed down Cuba's economic growth in 1998 to 1·2%, below the government's original target of 2·5–3·5%. In 1999, however, growth was an impressive 6·2%, and 2000 saw growth of 5·6%. GDP in 1997 was estimated to be only 80% of that in 1984.

Banking and Finance. The Central Bank of Cuba (*Governor*, Francisco Soberón Valdés) replaced the National Bank of Cuba as the central bank in June 1997. On 14 Oct. 1960 all banks were nationalized. Changes to the banking structure beginning in 1996 divested the National Bank of its commercial functions, and created new commercial and investment institutions. The Grupa Nueva Banca has majority holdings in each institution of the new structure. There were eight commercial banks in March 2002 and 18 local non-banking financial institutions. In addition, there were 13 representative offices of foreign banks and four representative offices of non-banking financial institutions. All insurance business was nationalized in Jan. 1964. A National Savings Bank was established in 1983.

Weights and Measures. The metric system is legally compulsory, but the American and old Spanish systems are much used. The sugar industry uses the Spanish long ton (1·03 tonnes) and short ton (0·92 tonne). Cuba sugar sack = 329·59 lb or 149·49 kg. Land is measured in *caballerias* (of 13·4 ha or 33 acres).

ENERGY AND NATURAL RESOURCES

Environment. Cuba's carbon dioxide emissions from the consumption and flaring of fossil fuels were the equivalent of 3·0 tonnes per capita in 2002.

Electricity. Installed capacity was 4·3m. kW in 2000. Production was 15·7bn. kWh in 2002; consumption per capita in 2000 was 1,343 kWh.

Oil and Gas. Crude oil production (2000), 2·7m. tonnes. There were known natural gas reserves of 14bn. cu. metres in 2002. Natural gas production (2000), 589m. cu. metres.

Minerals. Iron ore abounds, with deposits estimated at 3,500m. tonnes. In 2000 output of salt was 177,000 tonnes; refractory chrome, 56,300 tonnes; copper concentrate, 1,346 tonnes. Other minerals are nickel (2001, 72,619 tonnes), cobalt, silica and barytes. Nickel is Cuba's second largest foreign exchange earner, after tourism. Gold and silver are also worked.

Agriculture. In 1959 all land over 30 *caballerias* was nationalized and eventually turned into state farms. In 2001 there were 3·63m. ha of arable land and 0·84m. ha of permanent crops. 870,000 ha were irrigated in 2001. Under legislation of 1993, state farms were re-organized as 'units of basic co-operative production'. Unit workers select their own managers, and are paid an advance on earnings. 294,700 persons were employed in these units in 1995. In 1963 private holdings were reduced to a maximum of five *caballerías*. In 1994 farmers were permitted to trade on free market principles after state delivery quotas had been met.

The most important product is sugar and its by-products, but in 1998 the harvest suffered a series of weather disasters reducing production to 3·2m. tonnes (3·4m. tonnes in 1995–96), the smallest crop for 50 years. By 2000 production had risen again to 3·6m. tonnes. Production of other important crops in 2000 was (in 1,000 tonnes): oranges, 441; rice, 369; potatoes, 344; plantains, 329; grapefruit and pomelos, 233; cassava, 210; sweet potatoes, 195; maize, 185; bananas, 133; tomatoes, 129.

In 2000 livestock included 4·7m. cattle; 2·8m. pigs; 450,000 horses; 310,000 sheep; 140,000 goats; 15m. chickens.

Forestry. Cuba had 2·35m. ha of forests in 2000, representing 21·4% of the land area. These forests contain valuable cabinet woods, such as mahogany and cedar, besides dye-woods, fibres, gums, resins and oils. Cedar is used locally for cigar boxes, and mahogany is exported. In 2001, 1·70m. cu. metres of roundwood were produced.

Fisheries. Fishing is the third most important export industry, after sugar and nickel. The total catch was approximately 56,000 tonnes in 2001, of which 51,400 tonnes were from marine waters.

INDUSTRY

The gross value of the manufacturing industry in 1998 was 4,290·7m. pesos. All industrial enterprises had been state-controlled, but in 1995 the economy was officially stated to comprise state property, commercial property based on activity by state enterprises, joint co-operative and private property. Production (in 1,000 tonnes): sugar (2002), 3,522; cement (2000), 1,633; residual fuel oil (2000), 780; petrol (2000), 492; distillate fuel oil (2000), 405; sulphuric acid (1989), 381; steel (1998), 278; complete fertilizers (1998), 157; tobacco (1998), 40. Also in 1998: 160m. cigars; textiles, 54m. sq. metres. The sugar industry, the backbone of the country's economy for much of its history, is being restructured. Up to half of Cuba's sugar mills are facing closure.

Labour. In 1998 the labour force was 6,621,522, with 3,753,600 in employment. Self-employment was legalized in 1993. Under legislation of Sept. 1994 employees made redundant must be assigned to other jobs or to strategic social or economic tasks; failing this, they are paid 60% of former salary.

Trade Unions. The Workers' Central Union of Cuba groups 23 unions.

INTERNATIONAL TRADE

Foreign debt to non-communist countries was US$12·3bn. in 2000. Since July 1992 foreign investment has been permitted in selected state enterprises, and Cuban companies have been able to import and export without seeking government permission. Foreign ownership is recognized in joint ventures. A free-trade zone opened at Havana in 1993. In 1994 the productive, real estate and service sectors were opened to foreign investment. Legislation of 1995 opened all sectors of the economy to foreign investment except defence, education and health services. 100% foreign-owned investments and investments in property are now permitted.

The Helms-Burton Law of March 1996 gives US nationals the right to sue foreign companies investing in Cuban estate expropriated by the Cuban government.

Imports and Exports. In 2001 exports totalled US$1,661m. and imports US$4,788m. The principal exports are sugar, minerals, tobacco, fish and coffee. Sugar accounts for more than half of Cuba's export revenues, but revenues have been gradually declining and are now only a tenth of the 1990 total.

In 1999 the chief export markets (as % of total) were: Russia, 23·3; Canada, 14·5; Netherlands, 12·9; Spain, 8·0; China, 3·6. The chief import sources (as % of total) were: Spain, 19·5; France, 8·2; Canada, 8·1; China, 7·7; Italy, 7·0.

COMMUNICATIONS

Roads. In 1999 there were estimated to be 60,858 km of roads (including 638 km of motorways), of which 29,820 km were paved. Vehicles in use in 1997 included 172,500 passenger cars (15·6 per 1,000 inhabitants) and 156,600 trucks and vans. There were 1,309 fatalities as a result of road accidents in 1997.

Rail. There were (2000) 4,807 km of public railway (1,435 mm gauge), of which 147 km was electrified. Passenger-km travelled in 2000 came to 1,853m. and freight tonne-km to 804m. In addition, the large sugar estates have 7,162 km of lines in total on 1,435 mm, 914 mm and 760 mm gauges.

Civil Aviation. There is an international airport at Havana (Jose Martí). The state airline Cubana operates all services internally, and in 2003 had international flights from Havana to Bogotá, Buenos Aires, Cancún, Caracas, Curaçao, Fort de France, Guatemala City, Guayaquil, Kingston, Las Palmas, London, Madrid, Mexico City, Montego Bay, Montreal, Moscow, Panama City, Paris, Pointe-à-Pitre, Quito, Rome, San José (Costa Rica), Santiago, Santo Domingo, São Paulo and Toronto. Cubana flew 26·2m. km in 1999 and carried 1,259,000 passengers (683,000 on international flights). In 2000 Havana Jose Martí International handled 2,425,000 passengers (2,001,200 on international flights) and 20,526 tonnes of freight.

Shipping. There are 11 ports, the largest being Havana, Cienfuegos and Mariel. The merchant marine in 2002 totalled 103,000 GRT, including oil tankers 5,000 GRT.

Telecommunications. There were 583,000 telephone subscribers in 2001 (51·9 for every 1,000 persons) and 359,000 PCs in use in 2002 (31·8 for every 1,000 persons). Mobile phone subscribers numbered 17,900 in 2002 and there were 400 fax machines in 1995. There were 12,000 Internet users in 2001.

Postal Services. In 1998 there were 1,855 post offices, or one for every 5,990 persons.

SOCIAL INSTITUTIONS

Justice. There is a Supreme Court in Havana and seven regional courts of appeal. The provinces are divided into judicial districts, with courts for civil and criminal actions, and municipal courts for minor offences. The civil code guarantees aliens the same property and personal rights as those enjoyed by nationals.

The 1959 Agrarian Reform Law and the Urban Reform Law passed on 14 Oct. 1960 have placed certain restrictions on both. Revolutionary Summary Tribunals have wide powers.

The death penalty is still in force. In 2003 there were three executions.

The population in penal institutions in 1997 was approximately 33,000 (297 per 100,000 of national population).

Religion. Religious liberty was constitutionally guaranteed in July 1992. 40% of the population were estimated to be Roman Catholics in 2001. In 1994 Cardinal Jaime Ortega (b. 1936) was nominated Primate by the Pope. In Sept. 2003 there was one cardinal. In 2002 there were 180 Roman Catholic priests, approximately half of them foreign nationals. There is a seminary in Havana which had 61 students in 1996. There is a bishop of the American Episcopal Church in Havana; there are congregations of Methodists in Havana and in the provinces as well as Baptists and other denominations. Cults of African origin (mainly Santería) still persist.

Education. Education is compulsory (between the ages of six and 14), free and universal. In 1996–97 there were 154,520 pre-primary pupils with 6,970 teachers; in 2002–03 there were 9,397 elementary schools with 93,000 teachers for 873,700 pupils; and 2,032 secondary schools with 85,600 teachers for 992,000 pupils. There were 192,000 students in higher education in 2002–03.

There are four universities, and ten teacher training, two agricultural, four medical and ten other higher educational institutions.

The adult literacy rate was 96·8% in 2001 (96·9% among males and 96·7% among females).

In 2000–01 total expenditure on education came to 8·7% of GNP and 15·1% of total government spending.

Health. In 2002 there were 67,079 physicians, 9,955 dentists and (1996) 76,013 nurses. There were 266 hospitals in 2002; in 1993 there were 65 beds per 10,000 population.

Free medical services are provided by the state polyclinics, though a few doctors still have private practices.

Welfare. The official retirement age is 60 (men) or 55 (women). However, the qualifying age falls to 55 (men) or 50 (women) if the last 12 years of employment or 75% of employment was in dangerous or arduous work. The minimum pension in 2003 was 59 pesos a month, or 79 pesos a month, or 80% of wages, depending on average earnings and the number of years of employment. The maximum pension is 90% of average earnings.

Cuba has a sickness and maternity support programme.

CULTURE

World Heritage Sites. There are seven sites in Cuba that appear on the UNESCO World Heritage List. They are (with the year entered on list): Old Havana and its fortifications (1982), Trinidad and the Valley de los Ingenios (19th century sugar mills; 1988), San Pedro de la Roca Castle in Santiago de Cuba (1997), Desembarco del Granma National Park (marine terraces; 1999), Vinales Valley (1999), the 19th-century coffee plantations at Sierra Maestra (2000) and Alejandro de Humboldt National Park (2001).

Broadcasting. There are five national radio networks, provincial and local stations and an external service, Radio Habana (Spanish, Arabic, Creole, English, Esperanto, French, Guaraní, Portuguese and Quechua). There are two TV channels (colour by NTSC). There were 5·32m. radio receivers in 2000 and 2·82m. TV sets in 2001.

Press. There were (2000) two daily newspapers with a combined circulation of 600,000.

Tourism. Tourism is Cuba's largest foreign exchange earner, and for some years was growing by nearly 20% per year. Ironically, with Cuba's sympathy for rebel causes, the country was one of the most seriously affected by the huge drop in visitors following the attacks on New York and Washington of 11 Sept. 2001. There were 1,656,000 foreign tourists in 2002 (1,741,000 in 2000 and 1,735,900 in 2001). Total receipts from tourism in 2000 amounted to US$1,756m.

DIPLOMATIC REPRESENTATIVES

Of Cuba in the United Kingdom (167 High Holborn, London, WC1 6PA)
Ambassador: José Fernandez de Cossío.

Of the United Kingdom in Cuba (Calle 34, No. 702/4, entre 7 ma Avenida y 17 Miramar, Havana)
Ambassador: Paul Hare, LVO.

Of Cuba to the United Nations
Ambassador: Orlando Requeijo Gual.

Of Cuba to the European Union
Ambassador: Rodrigo Malmierca Diaz.

The USA broke off diplomatic relations with Cuba on 3 Jan. 1961 but Cuba has an Interests Section in the Swiss Embassy in Washington, D.C., and the USA has an Interests Section in the Swiss Embassy in Havana.

FURTHER READING

Bethell, L. (ed.) *Cuba: a Short History.* CUP, 1993
Bunck, J. M., *Fidel Castro and the Quest for a Revolutionary Culture in Cuba.* Pennsylvania State Univ. Press, 1994
Cabrera Infantye, G., *Mea Cuba*; translated into English from Spanish. London, 1994
Cardoso, E. and Helwege, A., *Cuba after Communism.* Boston (Mass.), 1992
Eckstein, S. E., *Back from the Future: Cuba under Castro.* Princeton Univ. Press, 1994
Fursenko, A. and Naftali, T., *'One Hell of a Gamble': Khrushchev, Castro and Kennedy, 1958–1964.* New York, 1997
Gott, Richard, *Cuba: A New History.* Yale Univ. Press, 2004
Levine, Robert, *Secret Missions to Cuba: Fidel Castro, Bernardo Benes, and Cuban Miami.* Palgrave Macmillan, Basingstoke, 2002
May, E. R. and Zelikow, P. D., *The Kennedy Tapes: Inside the White House during the Cuban Missile Crisis.* Belknap Press/Harvard Univ. Press, 1997
Mesa-Lago, C. (ed.) *Cuba: After the Cold War.* Pittsburgh Univ. Press, 1993
Stubbs, J., *et al.*, *Cuba.* [Bibliography] ABC-Clio, Oxford and Santa Barbara (CA), 1996
Sweig, Julia, *Inside the Cuban Revolution.* Harvard Univ. Press, 2002
Thomas, Hugh, *Cuba, or the Pursuit of Freedom.* Eyre & Spottiswoode, London, 1971; Picador, London, 2001

CYPRUS

Kypriaki Dimokratia—
Kibris Çumhuriyeti
(Republic of Cyprus)

Capital: Nicosia
Population projection, 2010: 838,000
GDP per capita, 2001: (PPP$) 21,190
HDI/world rank: 0·883/30

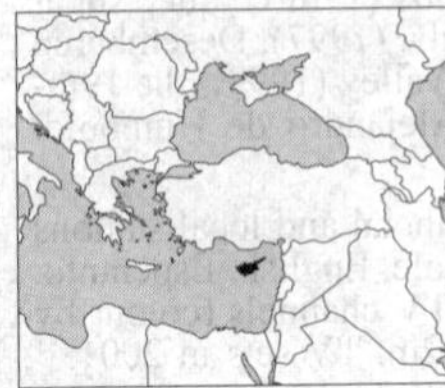

KEY HISTORICAL EVENTS

In 1193 the island became a Frankish kingdom, in 1489 a Venetian dependency, and in 1751 was conquered by the Turks. In 1914 the island was annexed by Great Britain and on 1 May 1925 it was given the status of a Crown Colony. In the 1930s the Greek Cypriots began to agitate for *enosis* (union with Greece). In 1955 they started a guerrilla movement (EOKA) against the British, with Archbishop Makarios, the head of the Greek Orthodox Church in Cyprus, as leader. In 1959 the Greek and Turkish Cypriots agreed on a constitution for an independent Cyprus and Makarios was elected President. On 16 June 1960 Cyprus became an independent state. In Dec. 1963 the Turkish Cypriots withdrew from the government. Fighting between Turkish and Greek Cypriots led to a UN peacekeeping force being sent in. Turkey invaded the island on 20 July 1974, eventually occupying the northern part. 0·2m. Greek Cypriots fled to live as refugees in the south. In 1975 a Turkish Cypriot Federated State was proclaimed. Rauf Denktaş was appointed President. In 1983 the Turkish state unilaterally proclaimed itself the 'Turkish Republic of Northern Cyprus' (TRNC). In 1991 the UN rejected Rauf Denktaş' demands for the recognition of sovereignty for the TRNC, including a right to secession. In 1998 a proposal by Rauf Denktaş that the Greek and Turkish communities should join in a federation that recognizes 'the equal and sovereign status of Cyprus' Greek and Turkish parts' was rejected by the Greek and Cypriot governments. Greece is threatening to block progress on Turkey's application for EU membership until the Cyprus question is resolved. In 2002 Cyprus was nominated as one of ten countries eligible for EU membership in 2004; the TRNC would be included only if UN-brokered talks to reunify the country succeeded. In Nov. 2002 the UN presented a peace plan to the Greek Cypriot and Turkish Cypriot leaders for a 'common' state with two 'component' states, along the lines of Switzerland and its cantons. In March 2003 UN-brokered talks to pave the way for the reunification of Cyprus collapsed. However, as a goodwill measure the 'Turkish Republic of Northern Cyprus' opened the Green Line separating the island's two sections in April 2003. In a referendum held in both the Greek-speaking and the Turkish-speaking areas of Cyprus on 24 April 2004, Greek Cypriots rejected a UN plan to reunite the island while Turkish Cypriots voted in favour. As a result, in the short term, EU benefits and laws will apply only to the Greek Cypriot community. Cyprus became a member of the European Union on 1 May 2004.

TERRITORY AND POPULATION

The island lies in the Mediterranean, about 60 km off the south coast of Turkey and 90 km off the coast of Syria. Area, 3,572 sq. miles (9,251 sq. km). The Turkish-occupied area is 3,335 sq. km. Population by ethnic group:

Ethnic group	*1960 census*	*1973 census*	*1992*	*2000*
Greek Cypriot	452,291	498,511	599,200	647,100
Turkish Cypriot	104,942	116,000	94,500	87,800
Others	16,333	17,267	20,000	24,200
Total	573,566	631,778	713,700	759,100

Estimated population, 2000, 759,100; density, 82 per sq. km.

The UN gives a projected population for 2010 of 838,000.

70·2% of the population lived in urban areas in 2001. Principal towns with populations (2000 estimate): Nicosia (the capital), 199,100; Limassol, 159,800; Larnaca, 70,500; Paphos, 40,900.

As a result of the Turkish occupation of the northern part of Cyprus, 0·2m. Greek Cypriots were displaced and forced to find refuge in the south. The urban centres of Famagusta, Kyrenia and Morphou were completely evacuated. *See below* for details on the 'Turkish Republic of Northern Cyprus'. (The 'TRNC' was unilaterally declared as a 'state' in 1983 in the area of the Republic of Cyprus, which has been under Turkish occupation since 1974, when Turkish forces invaded the island. The establishment of the 'TRNC' was declared illegal by UN Security Resolutions 541/83 and 550/84. The 'TRNC' is not recognized by any country in the world except Turkey). Nicosia is a divided city, with the UN-patrolled Green Line passing through it.

Greek and Turkish are official languages. English is widely spoken.

SOCIAL STATISTICS

2000 births, 9,557; deaths, 6,059; marriages, 9,775; divorces, 1,337. Rates, 2000 (per 1,000 population): birth, 12·6; death, 8·0; marriage, 12·6; divorce, 1·8. Life expectancy at birth, 2001, was 75·8 years for males and 80·4 years for females. Annual population growth rate, 1992–2002, 1·2%; infant mortality, 2000, 5·6 per 1,000 live births; fertility rate, 2000, 1·8 children per woman. In 2000 the average age of first marriage was 28·9 years for men and 26·1 years for women.

CLIMATE

The climate is Mediterranean, with very hot, dry summers and variable winters. Maximum temperatures may reach 112°F (44·5°C) in July and Aug., but minimum figures may fall to 22°F (–5·5°C) in the mountains in winter, when snow is experienced. Rainfall is generally between 10" and 27" (250 and 675 mm) and occurs mainly in the winter months, but it may reach 48" (1,200 mm) in the Troodos mountains. Nicosia, Jan. 50°F (10·0°C), July 83°F (28·3°C). Annual rainfall 19·6" (500 mm).

CONSTITUTION AND GOVERNMENT

Under the 1960 Constitution executive power is vested in a *President* elected for a five-year term by universal suffrage, and exercised through a Council of Ministers appointed by him or her. The *House of Representatives* exercises legislative power. It is elected by universal suffrage for five-year terms, and consists of 80 members, of whom 56 are elected by the Greek Cypriot and 24 by the Turkish Cypriot community. Voting is compulsory, and is by preferential vote in a proportional representation system with reallocation of votes at national level. As from Dec. 1963 the Turkish Cypriot members have ceased to attend.

National Anthem. 'Segnoriso apo tin kopsi' ('Always shall I know you'); words by D. Solomos, tune by N. Mantzaros.

RECENT ELECTIONS

Parliamentary elections were held on 27 May 2001. The Communist Progressive Party of the Working People (AKEL) won 34·7% of the vote and 20 seats, the Democratic Rally (DISI) won 34·0% and 19 seats, the Democratic Party (DIKO) 14·8% and 9 seats and the Social Democrats Movement (KISOS) 6·5% and 4 seats. Four other parties won a single seat each. The electorate was 467,182 and turn-out 91·8%. For the first time in a parliamentary election those aged 18 to 21 were able to vote.

Presidential elections held on 16 Feb. 2003 were won by Tassos Papadopoulos, with 51·5% of the vote, against 38·8% for incumbent Glafcos Clerides and 6·6% for Alekos Markidis. Turn-out was 95·9%.

European Parliament. Cyprus has six representatives. At the June 2004 elections turn-out was 71·4%. The DISI won 2 seats with 28·2% of votes cast (political affiliation in European Parliament: European People's Party–European Democrats); AKEL, 2 with 27·9% (European Unitary Left/Nordic Green Left); DIKO, 1 with 17·1% (Alliance of Liberals and Democrats for Europe); Gia tin Evropi (For Europe), 1 with 10·8% (European People's Party–European Democrats).

CURRENT ADMINISTRATION

President: Tassos Papadopoulos; b. 1934 (Democratic Party; sworn in on 28 Feb. 2003).

In March 2005 the Council of Ministers consisted of:

Minister of Foreign Affairs: George Iacovou. *Interior:* Andreas Christou. *Defence:* Kyriacos Mavronicolas. *Agriculture, Natural Resources and Environment:* Efthimios Efthimiou. *Commerce, Industry and Tourism:* George Lillikas. *Health:* Andreas Gavrielides. *Communications and Works:* Charis Thrasou. *Finance:* Iacovos Keravnos. *Education and Culture:* Pefkios Georgiades. *Labour and Social Insurance:* Christos Taliadoros. *Justice and Public Order:* Doros Thedorou. *Government Spokesman:* Kypros Chrysostomides. *Undersecretary to the President:* Christodoulos Pashiardis.

Government Website: http://www.cyprus.gov.cy

DEFENCE

Conscription is for 26 months. Defence expenditure in 2003 totalled US$294m. (US$382 per capita), representing 2·3% of GDP. At the end of 1998 the President cancelled a US$450m. contract with Russia for the deployment of S-300 anti-aircraft missiles on the island and negotiated to place them on Crete instead.

National Guard. Total strength (2002) 10,000 (8,700 conscripts). There is also a paramilitary force of 500 armed police.

There are two British bases (Army and Royal Air Force) and some 3,190 personnel. Greek (1,250) and UN peacekeeping (1,206; UNFICYP) forces are also stationed on the island.

There are approximately 35,000 Turkish troops stationed in the occupied area of Cyprus. The Turkish Cypriot army amounts to 5,000 troops, with 26,000 reservists and a paramilitary armed police of approximately 150.

Navy. The Maritime Wing of the National Guard operates two vessels. In the Turkish-occupied area of Cyprus the Coast Guard operates six patrol craft.

Air Force. The Air Wing of the National Guard operates a handful of aircraft and helicopters.

INTERNATIONAL RELATIONS

Cyprus is a member of the UN, WTO, the Commonwealth, EU, Council of Europe, OSCE and IOM. It became a member of the EU on 1 May 2004.

ECONOMY

Overview. Core exports are agricultural products (vegetables and citrus fruits), transport equipment and textiles. Tourism accounts for 20% of the economy. With one of southern Europe's highest rates of Internet penetration, the country is promoting investment in information technology and financial and medical services. The financial sector accounts for 20% of GDP. There is a wide economic divide between the Turkish north and the Greek south of Cyprus. The south, with a per capita income of 83% of the EU average, has potential for strong economic growth. Per capita income in the north is 20% of that in the south. Using the Turkish lira as currency, the north lacks an independent monetary policy, suffers from high inflation and relies on Turkey for fiscal transfers and trade. The informal economy accounts for 30–40% of GDP.

Since the start of the EU accession negotiations, a tight fiscal policy has reduced the budget deficit by 50%. The Cypriot pound has been pegged to the euro since Jan. 1999. The Greek Cypriot government is planning to spend around €200m. to improve the infrastructure in the north, subject to reunification. As an EU member, the island would be granted €278m. to balance the gap between the north and the south.

Currency. The *Cyprus pound* (CYP) is divided into 100 *cents*. Inflation was 2·0% in 2001, rising to 2·8% in 2002. In June 2002 gold reserves were 465,000 troy oz and foreign exchange reserves were US$2,539m. In Dec. 2001 total money supply was £C1,081m.

Budget. Revenue in 2000 (1999) was £C1·87bn. (£C1·59bn.) and expenditure £C2·02bn. (£C1·79bn.). Main sources of revenue in 2000 (in £C1m.) were: direct taxes, 558·1; indirect taxes, 653·5; social security contributions, 244·0.

Main divisions of expenditure in 2000 (in £C1m.): wages and salaries, 526·3; social security payments, 304·0; education, 233·7; goods and services, 160·9; health, 127·6; pensions and gratuities, 112·0; commodity subsidies, 79·5.

Development expenditure for 2000 (in £C1m.) included 42·3 for roads, 16·9 for water development, 12·7 for rural development and 11·9 for agriculture, forests and fisheries.

The outstanding domestic debt at 31 Dec. 2000 was £C2,457·7m. and the foreign debt was £C825·6m.

VAT is 15%.

Performance. Real GDP growth was 4·1% in 2001 but only 1·8% in 2002. Total GDP in 2003 was US$11·4bn. GDP per capita in 2000 was 83% of the European Union average, the highest percentage of any of the EU candidate countries.

Banking and Finance. The Central Bank of Cyprus, established in 1963, is the bank of issue. It regulates money supply, credit and foreign exchange and supervises the banking system. The *Governor* is Christodoulos Christodoulou.

In 1997 there were nine commercial banks (three foreign) and three specialized banks (co-operative, development and mortgage). The leading banks are Bank of Cyprus, Cyprus Popular Bank and Hellenic Bank.

At 31 Dec. 1997 total deposits in banks were £C6,483m. Cyprus has a fast-growing offshore sector—in 2000 there were more than 40,000 offshore companies registered on the island.

There is a stock exchange in Nicosia.

ENERGY AND NATURAL RESOURCES

Environment. Carbon dioxide emissions from the consumption and flaring of fossil fuels in Cyprus were the equivalent of 10·4 tonnes per capita in 2002.

Electricity. Installed capacity was 1·0m. kW in 2000. Production in 2002 was 3·75bn. kWh and consumption 3,401m. kWh.

Water. In 1997, £C16·6m. was spent on water dams, water supplies, hydrological research and geophysical surveys. Existing dams had (1997) a capacity of 299m. cu. metres.

Minerals. The principal minerals extracted in 2000 were (in tonnes): gypsum, 138,000; bentonite, 125,000; umber and other ochres, 12,000; copper, 5,000.

Agriculture. 28% of the government-controlled area is cultivated. There were 72,000 ha of arable land in 2001 and 41,000 ha of permanent crops. 40,000 ha were irrigated in 2001. About 8·7% (2000) of the economically active population were engaged in agriculture.

Chief agricultural products in 2000 (1,000 tonnes): milk, 193·8; citrus fruit, 127·2; potatoes, 117·0; grapes, 108·0; meat, 100·6; cereals (wheat and barley), 47·6; fresh fruit, 37·3; olives, 21·0; carrots, 1·9; other vegetables, 134·0; eggs, 14·0m. dozen.

Livestock in 2000: cattle, 54,200; sheep, 246,000; goats, 378,600; pigs, 408,400; poultry, 3,660,000.

Forestry. Total forest area in 2000 was 172,000 ha (18·6% of the land area). In 2001, 18,000 cu. metres of timber were produced.

Fisheries. The total catch in 2001 amounted to 75,803 tonnes.

INDUSTRY

The most important industries in 2000 were: food, beverages and tobacco, textiles, wearing apparel and leather, chemicals and chemical petroleum, rubber and plastic products, metal products, machinery and equipment, wood and wood products including furniture. Manufacturing industry in 2000 contributed about 11·0% of the GDP.

Labour. Out of 303,206 people in employment in the period March–June 2001, 53,839 were in wholesale and retail trade/repair of motor vehicles, motorcycles and personal and household goods; 37,720 in manufacturing; and 29,439 in construction. The unemployment rate was 3·1% in Sept. 2003.

Trade Unions. About 80% of the workforce is organized and the majority of workers belong either to the Pancyprian Federation of Labour or the Cyprus Workers Confederation.

INTERNATIONAL TRADE

Imports and Exports. Trade figures for calendar years were (in £C1,000):

	1997	*1998*	*1999*	*2000*
Imports[1]	1,899,339	1,904,738	1,970,905	2,401,826
Exports	640,015	551,134	542,919	591,864

[1]Excludes military goods.

Chief imports, 2000 (in £C1m.):

Machinery, electrical equipment, sound and television recorders	408·6
Prepared foodstuffs, beverages and tobacco	331·2
Mineral products	313·9
Vehicles, aircraft, vessels and equipment	270·7
Products of chemical or allied industries	174·7
Textiles and textile articles	172·3
Base metal and articles of base metal	122·4
Plastics and rubber and articles thereof	84·2
Pulp, waste paper and paperboard and articles thereof	80·1
Vegetable products	76·4
Articles of stone, plaster, cement, etc., ceramic and glass products	50·6
Optical, photographic, medical, musical and other instruments, clocks and watches	48·5
Live animals and animal products	35·5
Footwear, headgear, umbrellas, prepared leathers, etc.	33·1
Wood and articles, charcoal, cork, etc.	31·1
Pearls, precious stones and metals, semi-precious stones and articles	29·1

Chief domestic exports, 2000 (in £C1,000):

Medicinal and pharmaceutical products	30,859
Clothing	22,456
Cigarettes	16,192
Citrus fruit	12,795
Potatoes	12,328
Cement	10,911
Cheese	8,717
Fruit, preserved and juices	6,741
Wine	6,232
Footwear	6,126

Main export markets, 2001: UK, 16·6%; Greece, 9·2%; Russia, 9·0%; Syria, 7·5%; Lebanon, 5·8%. Main import suppliers, 2001: UK, 10·7%; USA, 10·5%; Italy, 8·9%; Greece, 8·7%; Germany, 7·1%.

COMMUNICATIONS

Roads. In 2003 the total length of roads in the government-controlled area was 11,593 km. The asphalted roads maintained by the Ministry of Communications and Works (Public Works Department) by the end of 2000 totalled 2,359 km. Construction of new asphalted roads in 2000 totalled 240 km. In 2001 there were an estimated 280,069 passenger cars, 3,003 buses and coaches, 116,795 trucks and vans and 41,985 motorcycles and mopeds. There were 94 deaths as a result of road accidents in 2002.

The area controlled by the government of the Republic and that controlled by the 'TRNC' are now served by separate transport systems, and there are no services linking the two areas.

Civil Aviation. Nicosia airport has been closed since the Turkish invasion in 1974. It is situated in the UN controlled buffer zone. There are international airports at Larnaca (the main airport) and Paphos. In 2000, 6,125,211 passengers and 33,477 tonnes of commercial freight went through these airports. Both are set to be expanded with a view to increasing annual capacity by 3m. In 2000 Larnaca handled 4,745,249 passengers (all on international flights) and 32,077 tonnes of freight. In 2000 Paphos handled 1,379,962 passengers (all on international flights) and 1,396 tonnes of freight. The national carrier is Cyprus Airways, which is 69·62% state-owned. Cyprus Airways flew 21·1m. km in 2000, carrying 1,452,608 passengers (all on international flights).

Shipping. The two main ports are Limassol and Larnaca. In 2000, 5,289 ships of 20,570,975 net registered tons entered Cyprus ports carrying 6,901,088 tonnes of cargo from, to and via Cyprus. In 2002 the merchant marine totalled 23·0m. GRT, including oil tankers 3·6m. GRT. The fleet consisted of 1,735 vessels (185 tankers). In 2002 vessels totalling 20,154,000 NRT entered ports. The port in Famagusta has been closed to international traffic since the Turkish invasion in 1974.

Telecommunications. Telephone subscribers numbered 845,400 in 2002 (1,207·7 for every 1,000 inhabitants) and there were 193,000 PCs in use (275·7 per 1,000 persons). There were 417,900 mobile phone subscribers in 2002. Cyprus had 210,000 Internet users in 2002. In 1995 there were 7,000 fax machines. The Cyprus Telecommunications Authority provides telephone and data transmission services nationally, and to 253 countries automatically. The liberalization of the telecommunications market began in Aug. 2003 when the Electricity Authority of Cyprus was awarded a licence to provide landline telephone services.

Postal Services. In 2000 there were 51 post offices and 992 postal agencies.

SOCIAL INSTITUTIONS

Justice. There is a Supreme Court, Assize Courts and District Courts. The Supreme Court is composed of 13 judges, one of whom is the President of the Court. The Assize Courts have unlimited criminal jurisdiction, and may order the payment of compensation up to £C3,000. The District Courts exercise civil and criminal jurisdiction, the extent of which varies with the composition of the Bench.

A Supreme Council of Judicature, consisting of the President and Judges of the Supreme Court, is entrusted with the appointment, promotion, transfers, termination of appointment and disciplinary control over all judicial officers, other than the Judges of the Supreme Court. The Attorney-General (Alecos Markides) is head of the independent Law Office and legal advisor to the President and his Ministers.

The population in penal institutions in Sept. 2002 was 345 (49 per 100,000 of national population).

The death penalty was abolished for all crimes in 2002.

Religion. The Greek Cypriots are Greek Orthodox Christians, and the Turkish Cypriots are Muslims (mostly Sunnis of the Hanafi sect). There are also small groups of the Armenian Apostolic Church, Roman Catholics (Maronites and Latin Rite) and Protestants (mainly Anglicans). *See also* CYPRUS: Territory and Population.

Education. *Greek-Cypriot Education.* Elementary education is compulsory and is provided free in six grades to children between 5 years 8 months and 11 years 8 months. There are also schools for the deaf and blind, and eight schools for handicapped children. In 1999–2000 the Ministry of Education and Culture ran 223 kindergartens for children in the age group 2½–5; there were also 115 communal and 89 private kindergartens. There were 366 primary schools with 63,715 pupils and 3,711 teachers in 1999–2000.

Secondary education is also free and attendance for the first cycle is compulsory. The secondary school is six years—three years at the gymnasium followed by three years at the *lykeion* (lyceum) or three years at one of the technical schools which provide technical and vocational education for industry. In 1999–2000 there were 130 secondary schools with 5,313 teachers and 69,043 pupils.

Post-secondary education is provided at seven public institutions: the University of Cyprus, which admitted its first students in Sept. 1992 and had 2,589 students by 1999–2000; the Higher Technical Institute, which provides courses lasting three to four years for technicians in civil, electrical, mechanical and marine engineering; a two-year Forestry College (administered by the Ministry of Agriculture, Natural Resources and Environment); the Higher Hotel Institute (Ministry of Labour and Social Insurance); the Mediterranean Institute of Management (Ministry of Labour and Social Insurance); the School of Nursing (Ministry of Health) which runs courses lasting two to three years; the Cyprus Police Academy which provides a three-year training programme.

There are also various public and private institutions which provide courses at various levels. These include the Apprenticeship Training Scheme and Evening

Technical Classes, and other vocational and technical courses organized by the Industrial Training Authority.

In 2001 the adult literacy rate was 97·2% (98·8% among males, 95·7% among females). The percentage of the population aged 20 years and over that has attended school was 95·9% in 1997. In 2000–01 total expenditure on education came to 5·7% of GNP.

Health. In 2000 there were 1,800 doctors, 619 dentists, 2,931 nurses and 584 pharmacists. There were 115 hospitals and clinics (excluding psychiatric hospitals) in 2000.

Welfare. The administration of social security services is in the hands of the Ministry of Labour and Social Insurance, with the Ministry of Health providing medical services through public clinics and hospitals on a means test. The exception is for medical treatment for employment accidents, which is given free to all insured employees and financed by the Social Insurance Scheme.

CULTURE

World Heritage Sites. There are three sites under Cypriot jurisdiction in the World Heritage List: Paphos (entered on the list in 1980); the churches of the Troodos region (1985, 2001); and Choirokoitia (1998). Paphos was a site of worship of the goddess Aphrodite. The Troodos region has one of the largest groups of Byzantine churches and monasteries. The Neolithic settlement of Choirokhoitia dates from the 7th to the 4th millennium BC.

Broadcasting. Cyprus Broadcasting Corporation has three radio channels and broadcasts mainly in Greek, but also in Turkish, English and Armenian. The Corporation also broadcasts on two TV channels (colour by SECAM H). A law of June 1990 permits the operation of commercial radio and TV stations. In 1994 there were two independent radio stations broadcasting nationwide and numerous radio stations broadcasting locally. There were also two private TV stations operating and one private Pay-TV. There are also two foreign broadcasting stations. In 1997 there were 310,000 radio sets and in 2001 there were 266,000 TV sets.

Cinema. In the government-controlled area there were 24 cinemas and 28 screens in 1999. In 1999 gross box office receipts came to £C2·6m.

Press. In 2000 there were eight daily newspapers with a circulation of 87,000; and 38 other newspapers with a circulation of 200,000.

Tourism. There were 2,696,732 tourist arrivals in 2001, an increase of 0·4% on 2000. Visitors from the UK account for some 50% of all tourist arrivals. Tourist spending in 2001 totalled £C1,277m.

Libraries. In 1995 there were 117 public libraries, one National library and one non-specialized library, holding a combined 454,000 volumes for 30,051 registered users.

Museums and Galleries. In 1999 there were 29 museums which received 764,319 visitors.

DIPLOMATIC REPRESENTATIVES

Of Cyprus in the United Kingdom (93 Park St., London, W1K 7ET)
High Commissioner: Petros Eftychiou.

Of the United Kingdom in Cyprus (Alexander Pallis St., Nicosia)
High Commissioner: Lyn Parker.

Of Cyprus in the USA (2211 R Street, NW, Washington, D.C., 20008)
Ambassador: Euripides L. Evriviades.

Of the USA in Cyprus (Metochiou and Ploutarchou Streets, Engomi, Nicosia)
Ambassador: Michael Klosson.

Of Cyprus to the United Nations
Ambassador: Andreas Mavroyiannis.

Of Cyprus to the European Union
Ambassador: Theophilos Theophilou.

FURTHER READING

Calotychos, V., *Cyprus and Its People: Nation, Identity and Experience in an Unimaginable Community 1955–1997.* Westview, Oxford, 1999

Christodolou, D., *Inside the Cyprus Miracle: the Labours of an Embattled Mini-Economy.* Univ. of Minnesota Press, 1992

Kitromilides, P. M. and Evriviades, M. L., *Cyprus.* [Bibliography] 2nd ed. ABC-Clio, Oxford and Santa Barbara (CA), 1995

Salem N. (ed.) *Cyprus: a Regional Conflict and its Resolution.* London, 1992

Statistical Information: Statistical Service of the Republic of Cyprus, Michalakis Karaolis Street, 1444 Nicosia.
Website: http://www.mof.gov.cy/mof/cystat/statistics.nsf

'TURKISH REPUBLIC OF NORTHERN CYPRUS (TRNC)'

KEY HISTORICAL EVENTS

See CYPRUS: Key Historical Events.

TERRITORY AND POPULATION

The Turkish Republic of Northern Cyprus occupies 3,355 sq. km (about 33% of the island of Cyprus) and its census population in 1996 was 200,587. The population was estimated to be 219,000 in 2004. Distribution of population by districts (1996): Nicosia, 89,818; Famagusta, 72,054; Kyrenia, 38,715.

CONSTITUTION AND GOVERNMENT

The Turkish Republic of Northern Cyprus was proclaimed on 15 Nov. 1983. The 50 members of the Legislative Assembly are elected under a proportional representation system.

RECENT ELECTIONS

Presidential elections were held on 17 April 2005. Prime Minister Mehmet Ali Talat (Republican Turkish Party-United Forces) won 55·6% against Derviş Eroğlu (National Unity Party), who claimed 22·7%. Turn-out was 69·6%.

In parliamentary elections on 20 Feb. 2005 the Republican Turkish Party-United Forces (CTP-BG) won 24 seats and 44·5% of the vote, ahead of the National Union Party with 19 and 31·7%, the Democrat Party with 6 and 13·5% and the Peace and Democracy Movement with 1 and 5·8%. Turn-out was 80·8%.

CURRENT ADMINISTRATION

President: Mehmet Ali Talat; b. 1952 (sworn in 24 April 2005).

Following the parliamentary election of Feb. 2005 the CTP-BG and the DP renewed their coalition. After the presidential election of April 2005 Mehmet Ali Talat resigned his premiership to take up the presidency and approved a new CTP-BG/DP cabinet consisting of:

Prime Minister: Ferdi Sabit Soyer; b. 1952 (CTP; took office on 26 April 2005).

Deputy Prime Minister and Foreign Minister: Serdar Denktaş (DP).

Minister for Public Works and Transport: Salih Usar (CTP). *Finance:* Ahmet Uzun (CTP). *Youth and Sports:* Özkan Yorgancıoğlu (CTP). *Health and Social Aid:* Eşref Vaiz (CTP). *Interior:* Özkan Murat (CTP). *Agriculture and Forestry:* Hüseyin Öztoprak (DP). *Education and Culture:* Canan Öztoprak (CTP). *Labour and Social Security:* Sonay Adem (CTP). *Economy:* Derviş Kemal Deniz (DP).

President of Legislative Assembly: Fatma Ekenoğlu.

Government Website: http://www.trncgov.com

DEFENCE

In 2004, 35,000 members of Turkey's armed forces were stationed in the TRNC with 441 main battle tanks. TRNC forces comprise seven infantry battalions with a total personnel strength of 5,000. Conscription is for two years.

INTERNATIONAL RELATIONS

In April 2004 the European Union pledged to release almost US$310m. as a reward for approval of a UN plan to reunify the island, although it will not be coming into force as it was rejected by the Greek Cypriot south.

ECONOMY

Currency. The Turkish lira is used.

Budget. Revenue in 2003 (in US$1m.) was 696·1 (of which local revenues 404·3 and foreign aid and loans 291·8); expenditure, 691·4.

Banking and Finance. 46 banks, including 21 offshore banks, were operating in 2004. Control is exercised by the Central Bank of the TRNC.

ENERGY AND NATURAL RESOURCES

Agriculture. Agriculture accounted for 10·6% of GDP in 2003 (provisional figure).

INTERNATIONAL TRADE

Exports earned US$49·3m. in 2003. Imports cost US$415·2m. Customs tariffs with Turkey were reduced in July 1990. There is a free port at Famagusta.

COMMUNICATIONS

Civil Aviation. There is an international airport at Ercan. In 2004 there were flights to Adana, Ankara, Antalya, Dalaman, İstanbul and İzmir with Turkish Airlines and Cyprus Turkish Airlines.

SOCIAL INSTITUTIONS

Education. In 2003 there were 15,482 pupils and 1,156 teachers in primary schools; 15,910 pupils and 1,504 teachers in secondary and general high schools; 1,985 students and 435 teachers in technical and vocational schools; and 29,054 students in higher education. There are four private colleges and five universities.

Health. In 2002 there were 338 doctors, 115 dentists, 167 pharmacists and 1,121 beds in state hospitals and private clinics.

CULTURE

Broadcasting. There are five local radio stations: Radio Bayrak (BRTK) broadcasts in several languages including Greek, Arabic and English. There are five local television channels. Colour is by PAL. In 1994 there were 108,800 TV and radio sets.

Press. In 2004 there were ten daily and three weekly newspapers.

Tourism. There were 469,867 tourists in 2003, of which 340,083 were from Turkey and 129,784 from other countries. Tourist earnings totalled US$388·3m. in 1995.

FURTHER READING

North Cyprus Almanack, London, 1987
Dodd, C. H. (ed.) *The Political, Social and Economic Development of Northern Cyprus.* Huntingdon, 1993
Hanworth, R., *The Heritage of Northern Cyprus.* Nicosia, 1993
Ioannides, C. P., *In Turkey's Image: the Transformation of Occupied Cyprus into a Turkish Province.* New Rochelle (NY), 1991

CZECH REPUBLIC

Česká Republika

Capital: Prague
Population projection, 2010: 10·16m.
GDP per capita, 2002: (PPP$) 15,780
HDI/world rank: 0·868/32

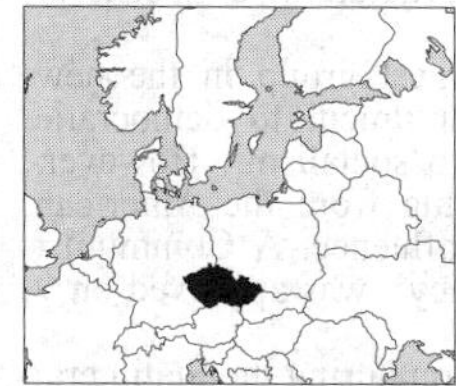

KEY HISTORICAL EVENTS

What is now the Czech Republic was originally inhabited by Celts around the 4th century BC. The Celtic Boii tribe gave the country its Latin name—Boiohaemum (Bohemia)—but was driven out by Germanic tribes. Slav tribes were well established by the 6th century. The Great Moravian Empire, comprising Bohemia, Moravia and Slovakia, reached its height under Moravian ruler Svatopluk, but was engulfed and destroyed by the Magyars around 903–07.

In 1041 Bohemia became a fief of the Holy Roman Empire. A period of prosperity followed, aided by the immigration of German miners and merchants. Bohemia expanded in the 13th century under the last Přemysl kings. John of Luxembourg succeeded in 1310. John's son Charles (1346–78) became Holy Roman Emperor as Charles IV (Charles I of Bohemia) in 1355. He declared Prague the capital of the German Empire. Charles fostered commercial and cultural development in Bohemia's Golden Age, founding Prague University in 1348.

Dissatisfaction with the Catholic church in the 14th and 15th centuries climaxed with the Hussite Revolution, the clerical reform movement associated with Jan Hus. Hus was condemned as a heretic and burnt at the stake in Constance in 1415. Anti-Hussite rulings by Wenceslas IV led to the first 'Defenestration of Prague' in 1419, when Catholic councillors were thrown from the Town Hall windows. In the ensuing Hussite wars Sigismund, the Hungarian Holy Roman Emperor, failed to recover the Bohemian crown. Five crusades were launched against the Hussites in the years 1420–31, all of which were defeated.

In 1526 the Habsburgs re-introduced Roman Catholicism. Religious divisions during the Counter-Reformation led to the second Defenestration of Prague. Two Catholic governors and their secretary were thrown from a window of Prague Castle, the catalyst for the Thirty Years' War (1618–48). Habsburg forces wiped out a third of the Bohemian population. The throne of Bohemia was made hereditary in the Habsburg Dynasty and the most important offices transferred to Vienna. In the Enlightenment era of the late 18th century, Empress Maria Theresa granted freedom of worship and movement to the peasantry. Bohemia and Moravia each became independent parts of the Habsburg Monarchy.

The revival of the Czech nation, which began as a cultural movement promoting the Czech language, soon progressed into a struggle for political emancipation. The First World War brought complete estrangement between the Czechs and the Bohemian Germans. Tomáš Garrigue Masaryk, the Czech nationalist leader, went into exile in London, where he campaigned for a post-war independent Czechoslovak state. In 1918 he secured the support of US president Woodrow Wilson for Czech and Slovak unity and on 18 Oct. 1918 a provisional government was recognized by the Allies. A republic was proclaimed with Masaryk as president and Edvard Beneš as foreign minister.

In Nov. 1935 Masaryk was succeeded by Beneš. Adolf Hitler stirred up nationalist agitation among the Sudeten Germans in Czechoslovakia, which had relied on its 1925 pact with France for defence against Germany. However, at the Munich Conference of 29 Sept. 1938 France sided with Britain and Italy in signing an agreement stipulating that all districts with a German population of more than 50% should be ceded to Germany. This legitimized the annexing of the Czech Sudetenland to Germany. Beneš resigned and on 15 March 1939 Hitler's troops invaded Prague. Slovakia declared itself independent under the fascist leadership of Jozef Tiso, though it was allied to the Germans, and the Czech lands became the German Protectorate of Bohemia-Moravia.

Resistance was brutally crushed and on 17 Nov. 1939 German occupiers closed down all Czech universities. In 1940 the Gestapo transformed the town of Terezín

(Theresienstadt) near Prague into a concentration camp, evacuating the pre-war population to accommodate 140,000 Jews from all parts of the Reich. 85,000 were then transported to death camps in the East. Liberation by the Soviet Army and US forces was completed in 1945 following an insurrection on 5 May. Territories taken by Germans, Poles and Hungarians were restored to Czechoslovakia. Subcarparthian Ruthenia (now in Ukraine) was transferred to the USSR. German or Hungarian Czechs had their citizenship taken away unless they were naturalized Czechs or Slovaks. A total of 2·7m. Germans were expelled.

In the 1946 elections the Communists became the largest group in the new Constituent National Assembly. Its leaders pledged commitment to democratic traditions while pursuing a 'specific Czechoslovak road to socialism'. However, Czechoslovakia was pressurized by Stalin into withdrawing from the American Marshall plan, seen by Moscow as a threat to its own influence. A Communist constitution, declaring Czechoslovakia a 'people's democracy', was approved on 9 May 1948.

Between 200,000 and 280,000 suffered death or persecution during the Stalin era. The Soviet five-year economic plans emphasized engineering, arms production and heavy industry and all farms were collectivized. The founding of COMECON on 1 Jan. 1949 and the signing of the Warsaw Pact in 1955 limited Czechoslovakia's trading partners to the Eastern bloc. A new constitution, introduced in 1960, reinforced the power of the Communist Party and changed the country's name to the Socialist Republic of Czechoslovakia (ČSSR).

The failure of the third five-year plan allowed the introduction of a mixed economy and cultural liberalization—the Prague Spring of 1968. Alexander Dubček pursued 'socialism with a human face'. New political bodies were formed, breaking the monopoly of the Communist Party, press censorship was abolished and restraints on freedom of expression relaxed. The reforms caused unrest in Moscow. Warsaw Pact troops invaded on 20–21 Aug. Dubček and other party leaders were then abducted to Moscow and forced to sign an agreement to keep Soviet troops stationed in Czechoslovakia. The only surviving reform was the introduction of the federal system on 1 Jan. 1969. Separate Czech and Slovak states came into force within a Czechoslovak federation. On 17 April Dubček was forced from office and replaced with the hard-liner, Gustáv Husák.

The fall of the Berlin Wall on 9 Nov. 1989 galvanized the pro-democracy movement, forcing the resignation of the entire CPCz leadership on 24 Nov. Civic Forum (OF) in the Czech Republic and the Public Against Violence (VPN) in Slovakia were formed to co-ordinate the 'Velvet Revolution', and an interim 'Government of National Understanding' with a minority of Communists took over. Václav Havel was unanimously elected president of Czechoslovakia by the Federal Assembly on 29 Dec. 1989.

The first free elections since the Second World War were held in June 1990, with a turn-out of 96·4%. The Communists were roundly defeated, and Civic Forum won 52% of the votes. After the 1992 elections the Czech right-wing Civic Democratic party (ODS) formed a coalition led by Václav Klaus. In Slovakia, Vladimír Mečiar's Democratic Slovakia party and other post-communists were successful in the elections. A continuing Slovak desire for independence from Prague led to a 'velvet divorce' on 1 Jan. 1993. Klaus' Czech Republic embarked on a series of radical reforms, impressing Western investors with his Thatcherite rhetoric. A programme of mass privatization was implemented and the early to mid-nineties were a time of economic boom. However, many of the tough policies were not fully implemented and an increasing number of financial scandals associated with the Klaus administration forced him to resign on 18 Nov. 1997. The Czech Republic became a member of NATO in 1999 and of the European Union on 1 May 2004.

TERRITORY AND POPULATION

The Czech Republic is bounded in the west by Germany, north by Poland, east by Slovakia and south by Austria. Minor exchanges of territory to straighten their mutual border were agreed between the Czech Republic and Slovakia on 4 Jan. 1996, but the Czech parliament refused to ratify them on 24 April 1996. Its area is 78,866 sq. km (30,450 sq. miles). At the 2001 census the population was 10,230,060 (51·3% female); density, 129·7 per sq. km. In 2001, 74·6% of the population lived in urban areas.

The UN gives a projected population for 2010 of 10·16m.

There are 14 administrative regions *(Kraj)*, one of which is the capital, Prague (Praha).

Region	*Chief city*	*Area in sq. km*	*Population 2001 census*
Jihočeský	České Budějovice	10,056	625,267
Jihomoravský	Brno	7,067	1,127,718
Karlovarský	Karlovy Vary	3,315	304,343
Královéhradecký	Hradec Králové	4,757	550,724
Liberecký	Liberec	3,163	428,184
Moravskoslezský	Ostrava	5,555	1,269,467
Olomoucký	Olomouc	5,139	639,369
Pardubický	Pardubice	4,519	508,281
Plzeňský	Plzeň (Pilsen)	7,560	550,688
Praha (Prague)	—	496	1,169,106
Středočeský	Praha (Prague)	11,014	1,122,473
Ústecký	Ústí nad Labem	5,335	820,219
Vysočina	Jihlava	6,925	519,211
Zlínský	Zlín	3,965	595,010

The estimated population of the principal towns in 2002 (in 1,000):

Prague (Praha)	1,162	Liberec	98	Havířov	85
Brno	371	České Budějovice	96	Zlín	80
Ostrava	314	Hradec Králové	96	Kladno	70
Plzeň	164	Ústí nad Labem	95	Most	68
Olomouc	102	Pardubice	90	Karviná	64

At the 2001 census 90·4% of the population was Czech, 3·7% Moravian and 1·9% Slovak. There were also (in 1,000): Poles, 52; Germans, 39; Roma (Gypsies), 12; Silesians, 11.

The official language is Czech.

SOCIAL STATISTICS

2002 births, 92,786; deaths, 108,243; marriages, 52,732; divorces, 31,758. Rates (per 1,000 population), 1999: birth, 9·1; death, 10·6; marriage, 5·2; divorce, 3·1. Life expectancy at birth, 2001, 72·1 years for males and 78·5 years for females. In 2002 the most popular age for marrying was 26 for males and 25 for females. Annual population growth rate, 1990–99, 0·0%. Infant mortality, 2002, 4·1 per 1,000 live births; fertility rate, 2002, 1·2 children per woman.

CLIMATE

A humid continental climate, with warm summers and cold winters. Precipitation is generally greater in summer, with thunderstorms. Autumn, with dry clear weather, and spring, which is damp, are each of short duration. Prague, Jan. 29·5°F (–1·5°C), July 67°F (19·4°C). Annual rainfall 19·3" (483 mm). Brno, Jan. 31°F (–0·6°C), July 67°F (19·4°C). Annual rainfall 21" (525 mm).

CONSTITUTION AND GOVERNMENT

The Constitution of 1 Jan. 1993 provides for a parliament comprising a 200-member *Chamber of Deputies*, elected for four-year terms by proportional representation, and an 81-member *Senate* elected for six-year terms in single-member districts, 27 senators being elected every two years. The main function of the Senate is to scrutinize proposed legislation. Senators must be at least 40 years of age, and are elected on a first-past-the-post basis, with a run-off in constituencies where no candidate wins more than half the votes cast. For the House of Representatives there is a 5% threshold; votes for parties failing to surmount this are redistributed on the basis of results in each of the eight electoral districts.

There is a *Constitutional Court* at Brno, whose 15 members are nominated by the President and approved by the Senate for ten-year terms.

The *President* of the Republic is elected for a five-year term by both chambers of parliament. He or she must be at least 40 years of age. The President names the Prime Minister at the suggestion of the Speaker.

National Anthem. 'Kde domov můj?' ('Where is my homeland?'); words by J. K. Tyl, tune by F. J. Škroup.

RECENT ELECTIONS

Former prime minister Václav Klaus (Civic Democratic Party/ODS) was elected president on 28 Feb. 2003 by parliament. He won the lower house 115–81 over Jan Sokol (Czech Social Democratic Party), but Sokol won the Senate 47–32. A second round was also inconclusive. In the third round, in which votes from both chambers were counted together, Klaus won a majority with 142 votes against 124 for Sokol. Previous attempts to elect a president on 15 Jan. and 24 Jan. 2003 had both failed.

Elections to the National Assembly were held on 14 and 15 June 2002; turn-out was 58·0%. The Czech Social Democratic Party (ČSSD) gained 70 seats with 30·2% of votes cast; the Civic Democratic Party (ODS) gained 58 with 24·5%; the Communist Party of Bohemia and Moravia (KSČM), 41 with 18·5%; and Koalice, the coalition of the Christian and Democratic Union (KDU), the Czechoslovak People's Party (ČSL), the Freedom Union (US) and the Democratic Union (DU), 31 with 14·3%. Following the elections a coalition government was formed between ČSSD and Koalice.

Elections for a third of the seats in the Senate were held on 5, 6, 12 and 13 Nov. 2004. As a result ODS had 34 seats in the Senate; ind. 19; Koalice (the coalition of four), 15; ČSSD, 6; and a number of parties held either one or two seats.

European Parliament. The Czech Republic has 24 representatives. At the June 2004 elections turn-out was 27·9%. The ODS won 9 seats with 30·0% of votes cast (political affiliation in European Parliament: European People's Party–European Democrats); KSČM, 6 with 20·3% (European Unitary Left/Nordic Green Left); SN–ED (Association of Independents–European Democrats Alliance), 3 with 11·0% (European People's Party–European Democrats); KDU–ČSL, 2 with 9·6% (European People's Party–European Democrats); ČSSD, 2 with 8·8% (Party of European Socialists); Klub Nezavisli (Independent), 2 with 8·2% (one non-attached; one Independence and Democracy Group).

CURRENT ADMINISTRATION

President: Václav Klaus; b. 1941 (ODS; sworn in on 7 March 2003).

In April 2005 the ČSSD-Koalice government comprised:

Prime Minister: Jiří Paroubek; b. 1952 (ČSSD; appointed on 25 April 2005).

First Deputy Prime Minister and Minister of Finance: Bohuslav Sobotka. *Deputy Prime Minister and Minister of Labour and Social Affairs:* Zdeněk Škromach. *Deputy Prime Minister and Minister of Justice:* Pavel Němec. *Deputy Prime Minister and Minister of Transport:* Milan Šimonovský. *Deputy Prime Minister:* Martin Jahn.

Minister of Agriculture: Petr Zgarba. *Culture:* Pavel Dostál. *Defence:* Karel Kühnl. *Education, Youth and Sports:* Petra Buzková. *Environment:* Libor Ambrozek. *Foreign Affairs:* Cyril Svoboda. *Health:* Milada Emerová. *Industry and Trade:* Milan Urban. *Informatics:* Dana Bérová. *Interior:* František Bublan. *Regional Development:* Radko Martínek. *Minister without Portfolio for Legislation:* Pavel Zářecký.

Government Website: http://www.vlada.cz

DEFENCE

Conscription ended in Dec. 2004 when the armed forces became all-volunteer. Defence expenditure in 2003 totalled US$1,871m. (US$183 per capita), representing 2·2% of GDP.

Army. Strength (2002) 36,370 (15,500 conscripts). There are also paramilitary Border Guards (4,000-strong) and Internal Security Forces (1,600).

Air Force. The Air Force has a strength of some 11,300 and is organized into two main structures—Tactical Air Force and Air Defence. There are 44 combat aircraft (L-159s and MiG-21s) and 34 attack helicopters in all.

INTERNATIONAL RELATIONS

In 1974 the Federal Republic of Germany and Czechoslovakia annulled the Munich agreement of 1938. On 14 Feb. 1997 the Czech parliament ratified a declaration of German–Czech reconciliation, with particular reference to the Sudeten German problems.

The Czech Republic is a member of the UN, WTO, BIS, NATO, OECD, EU, Council of Europe, OSCE, CEFTA, CERN, CEI, IOM, and the Antarctic Treaty, and is an associate partner of the WEU. The Czech Republic became a member of the EU on 1 May 2004. A referendum held on 13–14 June 2003 approved accession, with 77·3% of votes cast for membership and 22·7% against. In 2000 a visa requirement for Russians entering the country was introduced as one of the conditions for EU membership.

ECONOMY

Agriculture accounted for 3·7% of GDP in 2002, industry 39·6% and services 56·7%. In 2002 an estimated 82·2% of economic output was produced by the private sector.

Overview. Macroeconomic policies have supported economic recovery while progress with structural reform promises long-term growth. Growth has been supported by strong private consumption (reflecting rapid growth of wages and lending to households), rising goods exports and a sizeable fiscal surplus. Fiscal policy is in need of adjustment owing to a widening fiscal deficit, a high tax burden and an ageing population. At the beginning of the economic transition, the private sector accounted for 4% of GDP. By 2001 it had increased to 80% of GDP, owing to bank privatization and selling of the major utilities. This has led to a structural change in the Czech economy and increased the number of service companies and small businesses. However, some large firms are still under the control of state-owned banks, and the state retains minority shares in most heavy industrial enterprises. Privatization increased the country's attraction for foreign investors, although it increased unemployment in the process. The Czech Republic has been successful in attracting foreign direct investment. Much of the FDI goes towards generating exports; the EU is the largest export market, consuming approximately 70% of exports.

Currency. The unit of currency is the *koruna* (CEK) or crown of 100 *haler*, introduced on 8 Feb. 1993 at parity with the former Czechoslovakian koruna. Gold reserves were 443,000 troy oz in June 2002; foreign currency reserves were US$21,136m. Inflation, which reached 10·7% in 1998, was brought down to 1·8% in 2002 and was just 0·1% in 2003. It then went up to 2·8% in 2004. The koruna became convertible on 1 Oct. 1995. In May 1997 the koruna was devalued 10% and allowed to float. Total money supply was Kč. 692,300m. in Dec. 2002.

Budget. Revenue and expenditure in Kč. 1m.:

	1996	*1997*	*1998*	*1999*	*2000*	*2001*
Revenue	536,135	560,146	594,027	624,630	649,363	729,506
Expenditure	556,269	591,839	637,413	670,717	729,756	831,759

Expenditure by category, 2001 (in Kč. 1m.): social security and welfare, 293,611; health, 143,647; education, 77,669; public order and safety, 39,789.

VAT, introduced on 1 Jan. 1993, is 22% (reduced rate, 5%).

Performance. In 2003 real GDP growth was 2·9% (2·0% in 2002 and 3·1% in 2001). Total GDP was US$85·4bn. in 2003.

Banking and Finance. The central bank and bank of issue is the Czech National Bank (*Governor*, Zdeněk Tůma), which also acts as banking supervisor and regulator. Decentralization of the banking system began in 1991, and private banks began to operate. The Czech banking sector accounted for 78·3% of total financial sector assets at the end of 2002, representing Kč. 2,504bn. or 110% of GDP in 2002. The only legal form of domestically operating banks are joint stock companies (27 at 30 June 2003) and branches of foreign banks (nine at 30 June 2003). The Commercial Bank and Investment Bank are privatized nationwide networks with a significant government holding. Specialized banks include the Czech Savings Bank and the Czech Commercial Bank (for foreign trade payments). Private banks tend to be on a regional basis, many of them agricultural banks. In Nov. 1997 the cabinet agreed to sell off large stakes in three of the largest state-held banks to individual foreign investors through tenders, in preparation for European Union entry. In June 2000 the country's fourth largest bank, Československá obchodní banka (CSOB), acquired the operations of the third largest bank, Investiční a Poštovní banka (IPB). The newly-formed institution became the country's largest bank, with assets of US$16·6bn. in Dec. 1999. Other major banks are Komerční banka (assets of US$10·8bn. in Dec. 1999) and Česká Spořitelna (assets of US$9·6bn.). Foreign shareholders controlled 94·5% of the total assets of the banking sector at June 2003, most of them from EU countries. Other capital market participants are subject to the supervision of the Czech Securities Commission. Savings deposits were Kč. 1,467,270m. in 2002.

Foreign direct investment, which was only US$1·29bn. in 1997, rose to US$39·4bn. in 2002.

A stock exchange was founded in Prague in 1992.

ENERGY AND NATURAL RESOURCES

Environment. The Czech Republic's carbon dioxide emissions from the consumption and flaring of fossil fuels in 2002 were the equivalent of 10·1 tonnes per capita.

Electricity. Installed capacity was 16·3m. kW in 2002. Production in 2002 was 76·35bn. kWh. 72% of electricity was produced by thermal power stations (mainly using brown coal), 25% was nuclear and the rest was from hydro-electric generation and autoproduction. In 2003 there were six nuclear reactors in operation. Consumption per capita in 2002 was 4,836 kWh.

Oil and Gas. Natural gas reserves in 2002 totalled 2·1bn. cu. metres. Production in 2000 was 207m. cu. metres. In 2002 crude petroleum reserves were 15m. bbls.; production was 175,000 tonnes in 2000.

Minerals. There are hard coal and lignite reserves (chief fields: Most, Chomutov, Kladno, Ostrava and Sokolov). Lignite production in 2000 was 50·3m. tonnes; coal production was 14·9m. tonnes.

Agriculture. In 2002 there were 4,273,000 ha of agricultural land. In 2002 there were 3·07m. ha of arable land and 0·97m. ha of permanent crops. Approximately 24,000 ha were irrigated in 2001. 31·1% of agricultural land was state-owned, 61% co-operative, 4·4% private and 2·2% public. Agriculture employs just 4·9% of the workforce—the smallest proportion of any of the ex-Communist countries in eastern Europe.

A law of May 1991 returned land seized by the Communist regime to its original owners, to a maximum of 150 ha of arable to a single owner.

Main agricultural production figures, 2002 (1,000 tonnes): wheat, 3,867; sugarbeets, 3,833; barley, 1,793; potatoes, 901; rapeseed, 710; apples, 339; maize, 304; rye, 119.

Livestock, 2003: cattle, 1·47m.; pigs, 3·36m.; sheep, 103,000; poultry, 27m. In 2002 production of meat was 787,000 tonnes; cheese, 146,000 tonnes; milk, 2,728m. litres; 1,829m. eggs.

Forestry. In 2002 forests covered 2,643,000 ha (34% of the total land area). Timber production in 2002 was 14·54m. cu. metres.

Fisheries. Ponds created for fish-farming number 21,800 and cover about 41,000 ha, the largest of them being two lakes in southern Bohemia. Fish landings in 2002 amounted to 24,193 tonnes, entirely from inland waters.

INDUSTRY

The leading companies by market capitalization in the Czech Republic, excluding banking and finance, in Jan. 2002 were: Český Telecom a.s. (Kč. 111bn.); ČEZ (České Energetické Závody a.s.), Kč. 45bn.; and Philip Morris CR a.s. (Kč. 23bn.), a tobacco company.

In 2002 there were 1,607,151 small private businesses (of which 21,331 were incorporated), 220,461 companies and partnerships (of which 15,260 were joint-stock companies), 12,085 co-operatives and 995 state enterprises. Output, 2002, included: crude steel, 6·5m. tonnes; pig iron, 4·8m. tonnes; cement (2001), 3·6m. tonnes; 1,141,000 TV sets (2000); 428,000 motor cars (2000); beer, 1,798·7m. litres; soft drinks (2001), 1,601·7m. litres.

Labour. In 2002 the economically active population numbered 5,139,000. The major areas of activity were 1·32m. persons employed in mining and manufacturing; 619,800 in trade; 425,200 in construction; 367,600 in transport, storage and communications; and 325,700 in public administration and defence. In Dec. 2004 the unemployment rate was 8·3%. Workers in the Czech Republic put in among the longest hours of any country in the world. In 2002 the average worker put in 1,980 hours. The average monthly wage was Kč. 18,133 in 2002. Pay increases are regulated in firms where wages grow faster than production. Fines are levied if wages rise by more than 15% over four years. In 1996, 11,500 employees were involved in industrial disputes resulting in a loss of 16,400 working days.

INTERNATIONAL TRADE

A memorandum envisaging a customs union and close economic co-operation was signed with Slovakia in Oct. 1992. An agreement of Dec. 1992 with Hungary, Poland and Slovakia abolished tariffs on raw materials and goods, where exports do not compete directly with locally produced items, and envisaged tariff reductions on agricultural and industrial goods in 1995–97.

Foreign debt was US$26,281m. in 2002. There were 10,599 joint ventures in June 1993.

Imports and Exports. Trading with EU and EFTA countries has increased significantly while trading with all post-communist states has decreased.

Trade, 2002, in US$1m. (2001 in brackets): imports f.o.b., 40,720 (36,482); exports f.o.b., 38,480 (33,404). Main export markets, 2000: Germany, 41·8%; Slovakia, 8·5%; Austria, 6·6%; Poland, 5·5%; France, 3·8%. Main import suppliers, 2000: Germany, 34·2%; Slovakia, 6·1%; Austria, 5·7%; Russia, 5·7%; France, 5·6%. In 1999 the EU accounted for 69·2% of Czech exports and 64·0% of imports.

Main exports in 1999 were: machinery and transport equipment, 43·1% (15·1% was road vehicles and 9·7% was electrical machinery); manufactured goods, 26·5%; chemicals, 6·6%. Main imports in 1999 were: machinery and transport equipment, 40·3% (10·1% was electrical machinery and 7·7% was road vehicles); manufactured goods, 21·0%; chemicals, 11·2%; foodstuffs, 4·6%; petroleum products, 4·2%.

COMMUNICATIONS

Roads. In 2002 there were 518 km of motorways, 6,102 km of highways and main roads, 14,668 km of secondary roads and 34,134 km of other roads, forming a total network of 55,422 km. Passenger cars in use in 2002 numbered 3,647,067 (356 per 1,000 inhabitants), and there were also 323,434 commercial vehicles and 21,340 buses and coaches. Motorcycles numbered 760,219. In 2000 passenger transport totalled 73,392m. passenger-km (63,840m. passenger-km private transport) and freight 39,036m. tonne-km. There were 1,431 deaths as a result of road accidents in 2002.

Rail. In 2002 Czech State Railways had a route length of 9,600 km (1,435 mm gauge), of which 2,926 km were electrified. Passenger-km travelled in 2002 came to 6·60bn. and freight tonne-km to 15·81bn. There is a metro (50 km) and tram/light rail system (496 km) in Prague, and tram/light rail networks in Brno, Liberec, Most, Olomouc, Ostrava, Plzeň and Teplice-Trecianské.

Civil Aviation. There are international airports at Prague (Ruzyné), Ostrava (Mosnov) and Brno (Turany). The national carrier is Czech Airlines, which is 68·1% state-owned. In 2002 it flew 68·0m. km and carried 4,243,000 passengers (all on international flights). In 2000 Prague handled 5,527,524 passengers (5,476,067 on international flights) and 30,284 tonnes of freight, Ostrava handled 107,387 passengers and Brno 106,009 passengers.

Shipping. 1·7m. tonnes of freight were carried by inland waterways in 2002. Merchant shipping totalled 16,000 GRT in 1997.

Telecommunications. In 2002 there were 12,285,600 telephone subscribers, or 1,211·1 for every 1,000 inhabitants, and 1·8m. PCs (177·4 per 1,000 persons). Český Telecom and České Radiokomunikace, the two main telecommunications companies, are partly privatized. The government privatized Český Telecom in April 2005 by agreeing to sell a 51·1% stake to the Spanish telecommunications firm Telefónica. Mobile phone subscribers numbered 8·61m. in 2002 (848·8 per 1,000 population) and there were 102,000 fax machines in 1999. There were 2·60m. Internet users in 2002.

Postal Services. In 2002 there were 3,407 post offices.

SOCIAL INSTITUTIONS

Justice. The post-Communist judicial system was established in July 1991. This provides for a unified system of civil, criminal, commercial and administrative courts. Commercial courts arbitrate in disputes arising from business activities. Administrative courts examine the legality of the decisions of state institutions when appealed by citizens. In addition, there are military courts which operate under the jurisdiction of the Ministry of Defence. There is a Supreme Court, and a hierarchy of courts under the Ministry of Justice at republic, region and district level. District courts are courts of first instance. Cases are usually decided by senates comprising a judge and two associate judges, though occasionally by a single judge. (Associate judges are citizens in good standing over the age of 25 who are elected for four-year terms). Regional courts are courts of first instance in more serious cases and also courts of appeal for district courts. Cases are usually decided by a senate of two judges and three associate judges, although occasionally by a single judge. There is also a Supreme Administrative Court. The Supreme Court interprets law as a guide to other courts and functions also as a court of appeal. Decisions are made by senates of three judges. Judges are appointed for life by the National Council.

There is no death penalty. In 2002, 372,341 crimes were reported, of which 40·7% were solved. The population in penal institutions in Oct. 2003 was 17,360.

Religion. In 2003 there were 25 registered churches and religious societies. In 2001 church membership was estimated to be: Roman Catholic, 2,740,800; Evangelical Church of the Czech Brethren, 117,200; Hussites, 99,100; Eastern Orthodox, 23,000; Silesian Evangelicals, 14,000. 6,040,000 persons were classified as atheist or non-religious, and there were 331,000 adherents of other religions.

Miloslav Vlk (b. 1932) was installed as Archbishop of Prague and Primate of Czechoslovakia in 1991. The national Czech church, created in 1918, took the name 'Hussite' in 1972. In 1991 it had a patriarch, five bishops and 300 pastors (40% women). In 1991 there were also around a dozen other Protestant churches, the largest being the Evangelical which unites Calvinists and Lutherans, and numbered about 200,000. In Sept. 2003 the Roman Catholic church had two cardinals.

Education. Elementary education up to age 15 is compulsory. 52% of children continue their education in vocational schools and 48% move on to secondary schools.

In 2003–04 there were nine universities, four technical universities, one university for economics, one for agriculture, one for agriculture and forestry, one for veterinary sciences, one for pharmaceutical sciences, one for chemical technology, four academies for performing arts, music and dramatic arts, fine arts and arts, architecture and industrial design, and a higher school of teacher training. Together, these 24 higher education institutions had 219,514 students in 2002–03 and 13,641 teaching staff.

In 2002 total expenditure on education came to Kč. 106,569m., or 4·68% of GNP.

The adult literacy rate in 2002 was at least 99%.

Health. In 2002 there were 201 hospitals with a provision of 65 beds per 10,000 inhabitants. There were 42,447 physicians, 6,697 dentists, 91,213 nurses, 4,785 pharmacists and 4,602 midwives in 1999. In 2001 the Czech Republic spent 7·3% of its GDP on health.

Welfare. Since 1 Jan. 1996 the retirement age has been gradually increasing by two months per year for men and by four months per year for women. The target retirement age, from 1 Jan. 2007, is 62 years (men) and 57 to 61 (women), according to the number of children raised.

The old-age pension is calculated as a flat-rate basic amount of Kč. 1,310 plus an earnings-related percentage calculated on personal assessment and the number of years of insurance. In 2002 the minimum monthly pension was Kč. 2,080.

To qualify for unemployment benefit the applicant must have been in employment for at least 12 months in the previous three years. The maximum unemployment benefit in 2002 was Kč. 10,250 per month.

CULTURE

World Heritage Sites. Sites under Czech jurisdiction which appear on UNESCO's world heritage list are (with year entered on list): Historic Centre of Prague (1992);

Historic Centre of Český Krumlov (1992); Historic Centre of Telč (1992); Pilgrimage Church of St John of Nipomuk at Zelena Hora in Zdar nad Sazavou (1994); Kutná Hora—the Historical Town Centre with the Church of Saint Barbara and the Cathedral of our Lady at Sedlec (1995); Lednice-Valtice Cultural Landscape (1996); Holašovice Historical Village Reservation (1998); Gardens and Castle at Kroměříž (1998); Litomyšl Castle (1999); Holy Trinity Column in Olomouc (2000); Tugendhat Villa in Brno (2001); and the Jewish Quarter and St Procopius' Basilica in Třebíč (2003).

Broadcasting. Broadcasting is the responsibility of the independent Board for Radio and Television. Czech Television (CTV, colour by SECAM H) and Czech Radio are public corporations. The former Czechoslovakian broadcasting stations in the Czech Republic have become a second service. There is also a nationwide private TV company and two radio companies as well as local private stations. There were 5·5m. TV receivers in 2001 and 8·27m. radio receivers in 1997.

Cinema. In 2002 there were 665 cinemas; attendance for the year was 10·7m.

Press. There were 93 daily newspapers in 2002 with a total readership of 2,620,000 (256 per 1,000 inhabitants). There were also 3,636 non-dailies with total readership of 4,200,000 (410 per 1,000 inhabitants).

Tourism. There were 16,031,000 foreign tourists in 1999; foreign currency income from tourism was US$3,035m. Tourism accounted for 6·5% of GDP in 1996.

Libraries. In 2002 there were 6,043 libraries, one National library and 1,096 national libraries. They held a combined 51,178,000 volumes for 1,600,000 registered users.

Museums and Galleries. In 2002 there were 331 museums hosting a combined 8,726,000 visitors.

DIPLOMATIC REPRESENTATIVES

Of the Czech Republic in the United Kingdom (26 Kensington Palace Gdns, London, W8 4QY)
Ambassador: Štefan Füle.

Of the United Kingdom in the Czech Republic (Thunovská 14, 118 00 Prague 1)
Ambassador: Anne Fyfe Pringle.

Of the Czech Republic in the USA (3900 Spring of Freedom St., NW, Washington, D.C., 20008)
Ambassador: Martin Palous.

Of the USA in the Czech Republic (Tržiste 15, 118 01 Prague 1)
Ambassador: William J. Cabaniss, Jr.

Of the Czech Republic to the United Nations
Ambassador: Hynek Kmoniček.

Of the Czech Republic to the European Union
Ambassador: Pavel Telička.

FURTHER READING

Czech Statistical Office. *Statistical Yearbook of the Czech Republic.*
Havel, V., *Disturbing the Peace.* London, 1990.—*Living in Truth: Twenty-Two Essays.* London, 1990.—*Summer Meditations.* London, 1992
Kalvoda, J., *The Genesis of Czechoslovakia.* New York, 1986
Krejcí, Jaroslav and Machonin, Pavel, *Czechoslovakia 1918–1992: A Laboratory for Social Change.* Macmillan, London, 1996
Leff, C. S., *National Conflict in Czechoslovakia: The Making and Remaking of a State, 1918–1987.* Princeton, 1988
Lunt, Susie, *Prague.* [Bibliography] ABC-Clio, Oxford and Santa Barbara (CA), 1997
Simmons, M., *The Reluctant President: a Political Life of Vaclav Havel.* London, 1992
Turner, Barry, (ed.) *Central Europe Profiled.* Macmillan, London, 2000

National statistical office: Czech Statistical Office, Na Padesátém 81, 100 82 Prague 10.
Website: http://www.czso.cz

DENMARK

Kongeriget Danmark (Kingdom of Denmark)

Capital: Copenhagen
Population projection, 2010: 5·46m.
GDP per capita, 2002: (PPP$) 30,940
HDI/world rank: 0·932/17

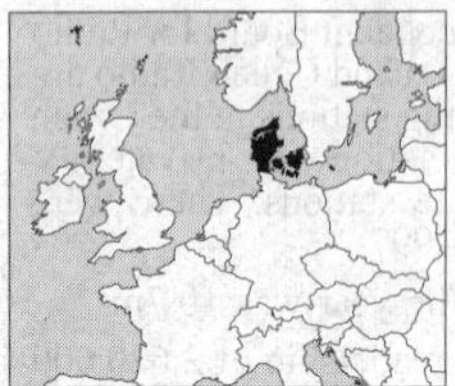

KEY HISTORICAL EVENTS

Evidence of habitation exists from the Bølling period (12500–12000 BC). By 7700 BC reindeer hunters were settled on the Jutland Peninsula and around 3900 BC agriculture developed. Metal tools and weapons were imported in the Dagger Period (*c.* 2000 BC) but established trading stations on the coast did not appear until around AD 300. The first towns developed in the Germanic Iron Age (AD 400–750).

Danish Vikings first attacked England's northeast coast in 793. They then expanded raiding expeditions to the Flemish and French coastal trading stations, where they began to settle. Denmark was converted to Christianity in 860. In about 900 Harold Bluetooth became the first king of Denmark and Skåne (southern Sweden). His grandson, Canute the Great, fought successfully to incorporate England into his North Sea Empire and from 1018–35, Denmark, England and Norway were one kingdom. By 1200 Skåne, Halland and Blekinge in the South of Sweden were part of the Danish kingdom.

In the 13th century agriculture was boosted by the expansion of fishing. Economic growth strengthened German influence. Under the Hanseatic League, German entrepreneurs were granted trade concessions for herring, salt and grain and also played a leading role in the country's political affairs. Valdemar IV Atterdag was crowned king in 1340. He challenged the privileges of the Hanseatic League, and was brought into conflict with Sweden. In 1361 Valdemar took Gotland in one of Nordic history's bloodiest battles. The Hanseatic merchants bought protection with a large donation to the Danish exchequer and then attacked Danish positions along the Sound to give Germany control over the approaches to the Baltic. When the king died in 1375, his daughter Margaret (married to King Håkon of Norway) claimed the throne on behalf of her five-year-old son Olav. After Håkon's death she became regent of Norway and succeeded in defeating Sweden, thus clearing the way to a Nordic union. In 1397, after her son's death, her nephew Erik of Pomerania became king of Denmark, Norway and Sweden. In 1412 Erik was opposed by the Swedish nobles who resented being taxed to finance Danish wars in northern Germany. When Erik abdicated, Christian I was elected king of Denmark and Norway in 1448.

By the 16th century Scandinavia was divided into two states, Denmark-Norway (including Iceland and Greenland) and Sweden-Finland. Christian IV (1577–1648) is regarded as one of Denmark's greatest rulers. Around this time overseas colonies were established, such as Tranquebar (India), Danish Gold Coast (Ghana) and the Danish West Indies (the US Virgin Islands). However, in 1626 Denmark was defeated in the Thirty Years' War. Denmark lost Gotland and the Norwegian territories of Jämtland and Härjedalen to Sweden. In 1660 Sweden gained Skåne, Halland and Blekinge. In the Great Northern War, Denmark allied itself with Russia, the Netherlands and France.

In the Napoleonic Wars, Denmark allied itself to France. The price Denmark had to pay was signing away its rights to Norway, which it did by the treaty of Kiel in 1814. Danish possessions were now reduced to Iceland, Greenland, the Faroes and Schleswig-Holstein. Holstein was lost to Germany in 1863 and Schleswig a year later. The surrender of so much rich agricultural land, with nearly a million inhabitants, brought Denmark to the edge of bankruptcy. Bishop Grundtvig (founder of the folk high-schools), who reconciled patriotism with a reduced status for Denmark in European affairs, had a great social influence. In 1901 the Left Reform Party came to power to introduce free trade, democratization of the education system and changes in the revenue system to make income rather than land the criterion for taxation. The First World War gave neutral Denmark an improved export market, but there was a shortage of raw materials. In 1929 a social democrat government, led by Thorvald Stauning, combined rural and urban interests in one of the most ambitious programmes of social reforms ever mounted.

In 1939, when the Second World War broke out, Denmark again declared neutrality. On 9 April 1940 German troops entered and occupied the country. The Germans permitted Danish self-government until resistance brought on a state of emergency. After the liberation a liberal government was elected with Knud Kristensen as prime minister. Kristensen's campaign for the return of southern Schleswig from Germany brought down his government in 1947. Denmark joined NATO in 1949.

With its share of the Marshall Plan, Denmark entered on a new industrial revolution. By the mid-1950s manufacturing equalled that of agriculture. In 1953 the Social Democrats returned to power where they remained until the mid-1960s. By then the rate of inflation was higher than in any comparable country. Jens Otto Krag took Denmark into the European Union, making Copenhagen the bridge between the Nordic capitals and Brussels. In 1981 the voting age was reduced from 20 to 18. Poul Schlüter became the first Conservative prime minister since 1901 when he formed a Conservative-led minority government in 1982. After several general elections and government reshuffles, a scandal over Tamil refugees forced him to resign in 1993.

Under a Social Democratic-led coalition, the economy improved. Following the 2001 election, a right-wing government came to power. The new prime minister, Anders Fogh Rasmussen, is a strong supporter of the EU who favours joining EMU (European Monetary Union), though this was rejected in a referendum in 2000.

TERRITORY AND POPULATION

Denmark is bounded in the west by the North Sea, northwest and north by the Skagerrak and Kattegat straits (separating it from Norway and Sweden), and south by Germany. A 16-km long fixed link with Sweden was opened in July 2000 when the Øresund motorway and railway bridge between Copenhagen and Malmö was completed.

Administrative divisions		*Area (sq. km) 2004*	*Population 1 Jan. 2004*	*Population per sq. km 2004*
København (Copenhagen)	(city)	88	501,664	5,684·6
Frederiksberg	(borough)	9	91,721	10,458·5
Københavns	(county)	528	618,407	1,170·6
Frederiksborg	(county)	1,347	373,688	277·3
Roskilde	(county)	891	237,089	266·0
Vestsjælland	(county)	2,984	302,479	101·4
Storstrøm	(county)	3,398	261,884	77·1
Bornholm	(county)	589	43,774	74·4
Fyn	(county)	3,486	475,082	136.3
Sønderjylland	(county)	3,939	252,936	64·2
Ribe	(county)	3,132	224,595	71·7
Vejle	(county)	2,997	355,691	118·7
Ringkøbing	(county)	4,854	274,830	56·6
Aarhus	(county)	4,561	653,472	143·3
Viborg	(county)	4,123	234,659	56·9
Nordjylland	(county)	6,173	492,669	80·3
Total		43,098	5,397,640	125·2

Statistics Denmark gives a projected population for 2010 of 5·46m.

In 2004 an estimated 85·4% of the population lived in urban areas. In 2004, 92·8% of the inhabitants were born in Denmark, including the Faroe Islands and Greenland.

On 1 Jan. 2004 the population of the capital, Copenhagen (comprising Copenhagen, Frederiksberg and Gentofte municipalities), was 662,089; Aarhus, 228,547; Odense, 145,554; Aalborg, 121,549; Esbjerg, 72,550; Randers, 55,739; Kolding, 54,941; Vejle, 49,917; Horsens, 49,652; Roskilde, 44,205.

The official language is Danish.

SOCIAL STATISTICS

Statistics for calendar years:

	Live births	Marriages	Divorces	Deaths	Emigration	Immigration
1999	66,220	35,439	13,537	59,179	41,340	50,236
2000	67,084	38,388	14,381	57,998	43,417	52,915
2001	65,458	36,567	14,597	58,338	43,980	55,984
2002	64,149	37,210	15,304	58,610	43,481	52,778
2003	64,682	35,041	15,763	57,574	43,466	49,754

2003 rates per 1,000 population: birth, 12·0; death, 10·7. Single-parent births: 1999, 44·9%; 2000, 44·6%; 2001, 44·6%; 2002, 44·6%; 2003, 44·9%. Denmark is the only west European country in which the percentage of births out of wedlock has declined in the past ten years. Annual population growth rate, 1992–2002, 0·3%. Suicide rate, 2000 (per 100,000 population) was 13·7 (men, 20·2; women, 7·3). Life expectancy at birth, 2002–03, was 74·9 years for males and 79·5 years for females. In 2003 the most popular age range for marrying was 30–34 for males and 25–29 for females. Infant mortality, 2003, 4·4 per 1,000 live births. Fertility rate, 2003, 1·8 births per woman. In 2003 Denmark received 4,593 asylum applications, equivalent to 0·9 per 1,000 inhabitants. In July 2002 a controversial new immigration law was introduced in an attempt to deter potential asylum seekers.

CLIMATE

The climate is much modified by marine influences and the effect of the Gulf Stream, to give winters that may be both cold or mild and often cloudy. Summers may be warm and sunny or chilly and rainy. Generally the east is drier than the west. Long periods of calm weather are exceptional and windy conditions are common. Copenhagen, Jan. 33°F (0·5°C), July 63°F (17°C). Annual rainfall 650 mm. Esbjerg, Jan. 33°F (0·5°C), July 61°F (16°C). Annual rainfall 800 mm. In general 10% of precipitation is snow.

CONSTITUTION AND GOVERNMENT

The present constitution is founded upon the Basic Law of 5 June 1953. The legislative power lies with the Queen and the *Folketing* (parliament) jointly. The executive power is vested in the monarch, who exercises authority through the ministers.

The reigning Queen is **Margrethe II,** b. 16 April 1940; married 10 June 1967 to Prince Henrik, b. Count de Monpezat. She succeeded to the throne on the death of her father, King Frederik IX, on 14 Jan. 1972. *Offspring:* Crown Prince Frederik, b. 26 May 1968, married 14 May 2004 Mary Elizabeth Donaldson, b. 5 Feb. 1972; Prince Joachim, b. 7 June 1969; married 18 Nov. 1995 Alexandra Manley, b. 30 June 1964 (*Offspring:* Prince Nikolai William Alexander Frederik, b. 28 Aug. 1999; Prince Felix Henrik Valdemar Christian, b. 22 July 2002).

Sisters of the Queen. Princess Benedikte, b. 29 April 1944; married 3 Feb. 1968 to Prince Richard of Sayn-Wittgenstein-Berleburg; Princess Anne-Marie, b. 30 Aug. 1946; married 18 Sept. 1964 to King Constantine of Greece.

The crown was elective from the earliest times but became hereditary by right in 1660. The direct male line of the house of Oldenburg became extinct with King Frederik VII on 15 Nov. 1863. In view of the death of the king, without direct heirs, the Great Powers signed a treaty at London on 8 May 1852, by the terms of which the succession to the crown was made over to Prince Christian of Schleswig-Holstein-Sonderburg-Glücksburg, and to the direct male descendants of his union with the Princess Louise of Hesse-Cassel. This became law on 31 July 1853. Linked to the constitution of 5 June 1953, a new law of succession, dated 27 March 1953, has come into force, which restricts the right of succession to the descendants of King Christian X and Queen Alexandrine, and admits the sovereign's daughters to the line of succession, ranking after the sovereign's sons.

The Queen receives a tax-free annual sum of 59·7m. kroner from the state (2004).

The judicial power is with the courts. The monarch must be a member of the Evangelical-Lutheran Church, the official Church of the State, and may not assume major international obligations without the consent of the Folketing. The Folketing consists of one chamber. All men and women of Danish nationality of more than 18 years of age and permanently resident in Denmark possess the franchise, and are eligible for election to the Folketing, which is at present composed of 179 members; 135 members are elected by the method of proportional representation in 17 constituencies. In order to attain an equal representation of the different parties, 40 additional seats are divided among such parties which have not obtained sufficient returns at the constituency elections. Two members are elected for the Faroe Islands and two for Greenland. The term of the legislature is four years, but a general election may be called at any time. The Folketing convenes every year on the first Tuesday in Oct. Besides its legislative functions, every six years it appoints judges who, together with the ordinary members of the Supreme Court, form the *Rigsret*, a tribunal which can alone try parliamentary impeachments.

National Anthem. 'Kong Kristian stod ved højen mast' ('King Christian stood by the lofty mast'); words by J. Ewald, tune by J. E. Hartmann.

RECENT ELECTIONS

Parliamentary elections were held on 8 Feb. 2005; turn-out was 84·5%. The Liberal Party (V) won 52 seats, with 29·1% of votes cast (56 seats with 31·3% in 2001); the Social Democratic Party (SD) 47 with 25·9% (52 with 29·1%); the Danish People's Party (DF) 24 with 13·2% (22 with 12·0%); the Conservative Party (KF) 18 with 10·3% (16 with 9·1%); the Radical Liberal Party (RV) 17 with 9·2% (9 with 5·2%); the Socialist People's Party (SF) 11 with 6·0% (12 with 6·4%); the Unity List—the Red Greens (E) 6 with 3·4% (4 with 2·4%). Four remaining seats go to representative parties from the Faroe Islands and Greenland.

European Parliament. Denmark has 14 (16 in 1999) representatives. At the June 2004 elections turn-out was 47·9% (49·9% in 1999). The SD won 5 seats with 32·7% of votes cast (political affiliation in European Parliament: Party of European Socialists); V, 3 with 19·4% (Alliance of Liberals and Democrats for Europe); KF, 1 with 11·3% (European People's Party–European Democrats); the June Movement, 1 with 9·1% (Independence and Democracy Group); the SF, 1 with 8·0% (Greens/European Free Alliance); DF, 1 with 6·8% (Union for a Europe of Nations); RV, 1 with 6·4% (Alliance of Liberals and Democrats for Europe); the People's Anti-EU Movement, 1 with 5·2% (European Unitary Left/Nordic Green Left).

CURRENT ADMINISTRATION

Following the 2001 election a coalition government of the Liberal Party (V) and Conservatives (KF) was formed. The coalition was re-elected in Feb. 2005. The government relies on the support of the far-right, anti-immigrant Danish People's Party, although it is not represented in the cabinet. In March 2005 the government comprised:

Prime Minister: Anders Fogh Rasmussen; b. 1953 (V; sworn in 27 Nov. 2001).

Minister of Culture: Brian Mikkelsen (KF). *Defence:* Søren Gade (V). *Economic and Business Affairs:* Bendt Bendtsen (KF). *Education and Ecclesiastical Affairs:* Bertel Haarder (V). *Employment:* Claus Hjort Frederiksen (V). *Environment and Nordic Co-operation:* Connie Hedegaard (KF). *Family and Consumer Affairs:* Lars Barfoed (KF). *Finance:* Thor Pedersen (V). *Food, Agriculture and Fisheries:* Hans Christian Schmidt (V). *Foreign Affairs:* Dr Per Stig Møller (KF). *Interior and Health:* Lars Løkke Rasmussen (V). *Justice:* Lene Espersen (KF). *Refugees, Immigration and Integration:* Rikke Hvilshøj (V). *Development Co-operation:* Ulla Tørnæs (V). *Science, Technology and Innovation:* Helge Sander (V). *Social Affairs and Gender Equality:* Eva Kjer Hansen (V). *Taxation:* Kristian Jensen (V). *Transport and Energy:* Flemming Hansen (KF).

Office of the Prime Minister: http://www.statsministeriet.dk

DEFENCE

Pursuant to the new Defence Agreement covering 2005–09 the Danish defence system will be completely restructured. A new security mechanism is being built from scratch to make it relevant in today's security environment. The entire transformation process centres on increasing Denmark's deployable capabilities. The composition of armed forces personnel has changed to 60:40 in favour of operational elements. Change has been accomplished by establishing so-called functional services in a number of areas formerly run by each individual service, and by reducing the staff- and support structure.

Denmark will be able simultaneously to deploy 2,000 soldiers on international missions and offer considerable High Readiness forces to NATO or coalition partners. The Armed Forces as a whole have been professionalized. Formal conscription still exists, but no specific combat training takes place. New conscripts train for four months in basic Homeland Defence, for example fire fighting, relief work during *force majeure* and basic weapons handling. The 20% of conscripts expected to sign up for additional time undergo military training focussing on participation in international operations for eight months and then deploy on an international assignment for six months.

The overall organization of the Danish Armed Forces includes the Ministry of Defence (MoD), the Danish Defence Command, the Army, the Navy, the Air Force and several joint service institutions and authorities; to this should be added the Home Guard, which is an integral part of Danish military defence. The Chief of Defence (CHOD), answering to the Minister of Defence, is in full command of the Army, the Navy and the Air Force.

Denmark has a compulsory military service with mobilization based on The Constitution of 1849. This states that it is the duty of every fit man to contribute to the national defence. In 2004 defence expenditure totalled US$2,750m. (US$519 per capita), representing 1·2% of GDP.

Army. The Danish Army is comprised of field army formations and local defence forces. The peacetime strength of the Danish Army is approximately 13,200. The Army's military wartime establishment would be about 46,000. The Danish Army is organized in two brigades, the first made up of professional soldiers and the second functioning as a training structure for conscripts.

Navy. The peacetime strength of the Royal Danish Navy is approximately 4,100. The naval wartime establishment would be about 7,300. The two main naval bases are located at Frederikshavn and Korsør.

Air Force. The peacetime strength of the Royal Danish Air Force is approximately 4,100. The wartime establishment would be about 11,600. The Royal Danish Air Force consists of Tactical Air Command Denmark and the Danish Air Materiel Command.

Home Guard (Hjemmeværnet). The overall Home Guard organization comprises the Home Guard Command, the Army Home Guard, the Naval Home Guard, the Air Force Home Guard and supporting institutions. The personnel are recruited on a voluntary basis. The personnel establishment of the Home Guard is approximately 57,000 soldiers.

INTERNATIONAL RELATIONS

In a referendum in June 1992 the electorate voted against ratifying the Maastricht Treaty for closer political union within the EU. Turn-out was 82%. 50·7% of votes were against ratification, 49·3% in favour. However, a second referendum on 18 May 1993 reversed this result, with 56·8% of votes cast in favour of ratification and 43·2% against. Turn-out was 86·2%. In a referendum held on 28 Sept. 2000 Danish voters rejected their country's entry into the common European currency, 53·2% opposing membership of the euro against 46·8% voting in favour. Turn-out was 87·6%.

Denmark gave US$1·7bn. in international aid in 2003, which at 0·84% of GNI made it the second most generous country as a percentage of its gross national income, after Norway.

Denmark is a member of the UN, WTO, BIS, NATO, OECD, the EU, Council of Europe, OSCE, CERN, Nordic Council, Council of the Baltic Sea States, Inter-American Development Bank, Asian Development Bank, IOM and the Antarctic Treaty. On 19 Dec. 1996 Denmark acceded to the Schengen Accord of June 1990 which abolishes border controls between Denmark, Austria, Belgium, Finland, France, Germany, Greece, Iceland, Italy, Luxembourg, the Netherlands, Norway, Portugal, Spain and Sweden.

ECONOMY

In 2002 agriculture accounted for 2·6% of GDP, industry 26·5% and services 70·9%.

According to the Berlin-based organization *Transparency International*, in 2004 Denmark ranked equal third in having the least corruption in business and government of any country in the world. It received 9·5 out of 10 in a corruption perceptions index.

Overview. Consumer prices and wage rates have risen slightly faster than the EU average. The size of the public sector is falling but the state sector is one of the most efficient and transparent in the world and there is little public pressure for reducing the role of the state. The EU Commission, the IMF and the OECD all urge Denmark to lower its tax level to stimulate labour supply. Generous student grants, early retirement benefits and disability compensation have resulted in 25% of the working age population living on some form of social welfare assistance. Monetary policy for the euro area has been appropriate for the Danish economy.

Currency. The monetary unit is the *Danish krone* (DKK) of 100 *øre*. Inflation was 2·4% in 2002, 2·1% in 2003 and 1·2% in 2004. Foreign exchange reserves were 236,300m. kroner in 2003 and gold reserves 2·14m. troy oz. In June 2000 the money supply was 387,135m. kroner.

While not participating directly in EMU, the Danish krone is pegged to the new currency in ERM-2, the successor to the exchange rate mechanism.

Budget. The following shows the actual revenue and expenditure in central government accounts for the calendar years 2002 and 2003, the approved budget figures for 2004 and the budget for 2005 (in 1,000 kroner):

	2002	*2003*	*2004*	*2005*
Revenue[1]	438,721,400	436,932,600	454,819,900	476,544,600
Expenditure[1]	409,903,800	420,626,700	440,347,700	451,486,600

[1]Receipts and expenditures of special government funds and expenditures on public works are included.

The 2005 budget envisaged revenue of 142,312·7m. kroner from income and property taxes and 228,720·0m. kroner from consumer taxes. The central government debt on 31 Dec. 2003 amounted to 535,838m. kroner.

VAT is 25%.

Performance. In 1999 a growth rate of 2·6% was recorded, followed by 2·8% in 2000, 1·6% in 2001, 1·0% in 2002 and 0·5% in 2003. Total GDP in 2003 was US$212·4bn.

The *OECD Economic Survey* of July 2003 reported: 'The Danish economy has continued to perform well despite the weak international economic climate. The macroeconomic policy framework provides a sound underpinning for a policy stance that aims to guide the country safely through short-term developments by steadfastly focusing on medium-term priorities rather than allowing itself to be blown off course. This steady-as-she goes approach enables policymakers to concentrate most of their efforts on addressing the longer-term challenges it faces.'

Banking and Finance. On 31 Dec. 2001 the accounts of the National Bank (*Chairman of the Board of Governors*, Bodil Nyboe Andersen) balanced at 295,286m. kroner. The assets included official net foreign reserves of 148,427m. kroner. The liabilities included notes and coins totalling 47,299m. kroner. On 31 Dec. 2000 there were 97 commercial banks and savings banks, with deposits of 757,625m. kroner.

The two largest commercial banks are Den Danske Bank and Unibank, which merged with MeritaNordbanken in 2000 and now forms part of the Stockholm-based Nordea group. The supervisory boards of all banks must include public representation.

There is a stock exchange in Copenhagen.

ENERGY AND NATURAL RESOURCES

Environment. Denmark's carbon dioxide emissions from the consumption and flaring of fossil fuels in 2002 were the equivalent of 10·3 tonnes per capita.

Electricity. Installed capacity was 12·9m. kW in 2003. Production (2003), 43,757m. kWh. Consumption per capita in 2003 was 6,378 kWh. In 2003 some 5,560 wind turbines produced 13% of output.

Oil and Gas. Oil production was (2003) 18·3m. tonnes with 1,700m. bbls. of proven reserves. Production of natural gas was (2003) 7·1bn. cu. metres with 136bn. cu. metres of proven reserves.

Wind. Denmark is one of the world's largest wind-power producers, with an installed capacity of 2,886 MW at the end of 2002. Denmark generates 13% of its electricity from wind, the highest proportion of any country.

Agriculture. Agriculture accounted for 11·0% of exports and 2·6% of imports in 2001. Land ownership is widely distributed. In May 2003 there were 48,613 holdings with at least 5 ha of agricultural area (or at least a production equivalent to that from 5 ha of barley). There were 9,829 small holdings (with less than 10 ha), 21,605 medium-sized holdings (10–50 ha) and 17,181 holdings with more than 50 ha. Approximately 5·0% of all agricultural land is used for organic farming. There were 28,232 agricultural workers in 2003. In 2003 Denmark had 2·29m. ha of arable land and 8,000 ha of permanent crops.

In 2003 the cultivated area was (in 1,000 ha): grain, 1,487; green fodder and grass, 622; set aside, 207; root crops, 94; other crops, 217; pulses, 31; total cultivated area, 2,658.

	Area (1,000 ha)				Production (in 1,000 tonnes)			
Chief crops	*2000*	*2001*	*2002*	*2003*[1]	*2000*	*2001*	*2002*	*2003*[1]
Wheat	628	634	577	664	4,693	4,664	4,059	4,701
Barley	741	744	825	710	3,980	3,966	4,121	3,776
Potatoes	39	38	38	36	1,645	1,543	1,504	1,412
Rye	51	65	46	33	263	332	230	169
Oats	45	60	55	50	233	292	276	260
Other root crops	77	70	68	58	4,498	4,048	4,102	3,404

[1]Provisional figures.

Livestock, 2002 (in 1,000): pigs, 12,732; cattle, 2,000; sheep, 131; horses, 38; poultry, 20,580.

Production (in 1,000 tonnes) in 2002: pork and bacon, 1,892; beef, 169; milk, 4,445; cheese, 318; eggs, 81; butter, 47.

In 2001 tractors numbered 123,000 and harvester-threshers 23,300.

Forestry. The area under forests in 2000 was 486,000 ha, or 11·3% of the total land area. Timber production in 2003 was 1·81m. cu. metres.

Fisheries. The total value of the fish caught was (in 1m. kroner): 1950, 156; 1955, 252; 1960, 376; 1965, 650; 1970, 854; 1975, 1,442; 1980, 2,888; 1985, 3,542; 1990, 3,485; 1995, 3,020; 2000, 3,141; 2003, 2,748.

In 2001 the total catch was 1,510,439 tonnes, almost exclusively from sea fishing. Denmark is the leading fishing nation in the EU.

INDUSTRY

The leading companies by market capitalization in Denmark, excluding banking and finance, in May 2004 were: Novo Nordisk A/S (US$16·3bn.), a healthcare company; A.P. Møller-Mærsk (US$28·1bn.), a shipping company; and TDC A/S (US$7·3bn.), formerly Tele Danmark.

The following table is of gross value added by kind of activity (in 1m. kroner; 1995 constant prices):

	2001	*2002*[1]	*2003*[1]
Total	1,017,068	1,026,029	1,031,246
Agriculture, fishing and quarrying	50,709	49,822	51,301
Manufacturing	168,651	168,472	168,614
Electricity, gas and water supply	22,551	21,147	20,330
Construction	51,335	51,666	50,285
Trade, hotels and restaurants	163,810	166,055	167,569
Transport, storage and communications	94,756	97,430	99,960
Financial intermediation, business activities	250,356	253,699	254,808
Public and personal services	256,357	260,939	262,407
Financial intermediation services indirectly measured	–41,457	–43,201	–44,028

[1]Provisional or estimated figures.

In the following table 'number of jobs' refers to 18,530 local activity units including single-proprietor units (Nov. 2002):

Branch of industry	*Number of employees*
Food, beverages and tobacco	84,425
Textiles, wearing apparel, leather	12,022
Wood and wood products	14,898
Paper products	55,170
Refined petroleum products	646

Branch of industry	*Number of employees*
Chemicals and man-made fibres	29,806
Rubber and plastic products	22,296
Non-metallic mineral products	17,560
Basic metals	53,669
Machinery and equipment	67,004
Electrical and optical equipment	53,118
Transport equipment	15,158
Furniture, other manufactures	30,379
Total manufacturing	456,511

Labour. In 2003 the labour force was 2,860,636. 35·2% of the working population in 2002 were in public and personal services; 18·0% in wholesale and retail trade, hotels and restaurants; 16·7% in manufacturing; 13·7% in financial intermediation, commerce etc.; 6·4% in transport, storage and telecommunications; 6·1% in construction; 3·7% in agriculture, fisheries and quarrying; and 0·5% in electricity, gas and water supply. In 2003, 439,120 persons were employed in manufacturing. Retirement age is 67. In Dec. 2004 the unemployment rate was 5·1%. In 2003 Denmark lost 22 working days to strikes per 1,000 employees.

INTERNATIONAL TRADE

Imports and Exports. In 2003 imports totalled 369,700·9m. kroner and exports 429,272·2m. kroner.

Imports and exports (in 1m. kroner) for calendar years:

	2002[1]		2003[1]	
Leading commodities	*Imports*	*Exports*	*Imports*	*Exports*
Live animals, meat and meat preparations	4,146	29,335	4,575	27,270
Dairy products and eggs	2,927	11,051	2,840	10,797
Fish, crustaceans, etc. and preparations	9,599	16,250	9,197	15,365
Cereals and cereal preparations	3,287	5,185	3,275	5,164
Fodder for animals	5,387	4,435	5,344	4,205
Wood and cork	4,492	980	4,699	771
Textile fibres, yarns, fabrics, etc.	8,523	8,501	8,060	8,210
Mineral fuels, lubricants, etc.	15,127	28,346	16,063	28,857
Chemicals and plastics	18,190	13,944	17,601	14,313
Medicine and pharmaceutical products	10,564	30,374	11,296	32,190
Metals, manufacture of metals	28,298	19,598	28,079	19,614
Machinery, electrical, equipment, etc.	102,951	110,380	94,723	101,124
Transport equipment	41,632	19,320	36,201	17,117
Furniture, etc.	5,653	15,754	6,068	15,773
Clothing and clothing accessories	17,985	14,931	17,780	15,048

[1]Excluding trade not distributed.

Distribution of foreign trade (in 1m. kroner) according to countries of origin and destination for 2003:

Countries	*Imports*[1]	*Exports*[1]
Austria	4,643·5	4,440·9
Belgium	12,814·5	7,879·7
Canada	1,220·8	3,612·8
China	13,622·5	5,010·4
Finland	8,568·2	13,713·0
France and Monaco	17,926·7	21,706·6
Germany	85,582·6	79,685·1
Greece	900·8	3,388·5
Greenland	2,117·4	2,405·0
Hong Kong	1,589·3	3,984·5
Ireland	4,466·1	6,485·4
Italy	15,340·5	14,397·1
Japan	3,154·6	13,322·4
Netherlands	25,616·2	19,960·8
Norway	16,688·9	24,538·3
Poland	6,721·2	6,777·0
Russia	3,966·3	5,703·5
Singapore	3,119·9	1,853·4
South Korea	4,228·6	2,389·0
Spain	6,478·5	13,466·4

Countries	*Imports*[1]	*Exports*[1]
Sweden	47,708·5	54,381·0
Switzerland	4,184·0	4,882·7
Turkey	3,368·4	2,006·2
United Kingdom	25,947·0	36,454·0
United States of America	11,988·6	26,178·0

[1]Excluding trade not distributed.

In 2003 other European Union member countries accounted for 64·8% of exports and 70·1% of imports.

COMMUNICATIONS

Roads. Denmark proper had (1 Jan. 2004) 1,027 km of motorways, 649 km of other state roads, 9,682 km of other provincial roads and 60,717 km of commercial roads. Motor vehicles registered at 1 Jan. 2004 comprised 1,894,649 passenger cars, 34,896 trucks, 365,112 vans, 17,217 taxi cabs (including 11,296 for private hire), 14,132 buses and 87,779 motorcycles. There were 8,844 road accidents in 2003, resulting in 432 fatalities.

Rail. In 2003 there were 2,273 km of State railways of 1,435 mm gauge (641 km electrified), which carried 154m. passengers and 7·71m. tonnes of freight. There were also 495 km of private railways. A metro system was opened in Copenhagen in 2002.

Civil Aviation. The main international airport is at Copenhagen (Kastrup), and there are also international flights from Aalborg, Aarhus, Billund and Esbjerg. The Scandinavian Airlines System (SAS) resulted from the 1950 merger of the three former Scandinavian airlines. SAS Denmark A/S is the Danish partner (SAS Norge ASA and SAS Sverige AB being the other two). Denmark and Norway each hold two-sevenths of the capital of SAS and Sweden three-sevenths.

On 1 Jan. 2001 Denmark had 1,089 aircraft with a capacity of 23,110 seats. In 2001 there were 305,636 take-offs and landings to and from abroad, and 335,392 to and from Danish airports, including local flights. Copenhagen (Kastrup) handled 9,124,447 departing passengers in 2001, Billund 849,761, Aalborg 348,390 and Aarhus 327,399.

Shipping. On 1 Jan. 2004 the merchant fleet consisted of 660 vessels (above 20 GRT) totalling 7·3m. GRT. In 2003, 45m. tonnes of cargo were unloaded and 35m. tonnes were loaded in Danish ports; traffic by passenger ships and ferries is not included.

Telecommunications. In 2003 there were 8,380,100 telephone subscribers (1,552 per 1,000 persons), including 4,767,300 mobile phone subscribers. In June 2002 there were 3·37m. Internet users (62·73% of the population). There were 3·1m. PCs in use in 2002 (576·8 per 1,000 persons).

Postal Services. In 2001 there were 1,083 post offices.

SOCIAL INSTITUTIONS

Justice. The lowest courts of justice are organized in 82 tribunals *(byretter)*, where minor cases are dealt with by a single judge. The tribunal at Copenhagen has one president and 49 other judges; and Aarhus one president and 15 other judges; the other tribunals have one to 11 judges. Cases of greater consequence are dealt with by the two High Courts *(Landsretterne)*; these courts are also courts of appeal for minor cases. The Eastern High Court in Copenhagen has one president and 65 other judges; and the Western in Viborg one president and 38 other judges. From these an appeal lies to the Supreme Court in Copenhagen, composed of a president and 18 other judges. Judges under 65 years of age can be removed only by judicial sentence.

In 2003 there were 15,735 convictions for males and 1,722 for females for violations of the criminal code, fines not included. In 2003 the daily average population in penal institutions was 3,641 (67·6 per 100,000 of national population).

Religion. There is complete religious liberty. The state church is the Evangelical-Lutheran to which 84·3% of the population belonged in 2002. It is divided into ten dioceses, each with a Bishop. The Bishop together with the Chief Administrative Officer of the county make up the diocesan-governing body, responsible for all matters of ecclesiastical local finance and general administration. Bishops are appointed by the Crown after an election by the clergy and parish council members.

Each diocese is divided into a number of deaneries (111 in the whole country), each with its Dean and Deanery Committee, who have certain financial powers.

Education. Education has been compulsory since 1814. The first stage of the Danish education system is the basic school (education at first level). This starts with an optional pre-school year (education preceding the first level) and continues up to and including the optional 10th year in the *folkeskole* (municipal primary and lower secondary school). In 2003, 704,668 pupils attended education at first level and second level, first stage. Of this group, 69,165 began their education at pre-school, while 156,953 attended grades 8 to 10.

Of all students leaving basic school in 1997–98, 76·1% had commenced further education after a period of three months. Almost half the students had elected to attend general upper-secondary education (general programmes of education at secondary level, second stage), while 27% opted for a vocational education at secondary level, second stage.

Education that qualifies students for tertiary level education is called general upper-secondary education and comprises general upper-secondary education (general programmes of education at second level, second stage), such as *gymnasium* (upper-secondary school), higher preparatory examination, and adult upper-secondary level courses as well as general/vocational upper secondary education at the vocational education institutions. In 2003, 103,674 students attended general upper-secondary education.

Higher education is divided into three levels: short-cycle higher education involves two years of training, sometimes practical, after completion of upper-secondary education (31,350 students in 2003); medium-cycle higher education involves two–four years of mainly theoretical training (71,580 students in 2003); long-cycle higher education requires more than four years of education, mainly theoretical, divided between a bachelors' degree and a candidate programme (51,196 students in bachelors' programmes in 2003 and 57,030 in the candidate programme). Universities, 1997–98: the University of Copenhagen (founded 1479), 29,389 students; the University of Aarhus (founded in 1928), 17,901 students; the University of Odense (founded in 1964), 9,127 students; the University of Aalborg (founded in 1974), 8,927 students; Roskilde University Centre (founded in 1972), 5,719 students. The Technical University of Denmark had 6,372 students in 1997–98. Eight engineering colleges had 6,126 students.

Other types of post-secondary education (2002): the Royal Veterinary and Agricultural University had 3,240 students; the Danish School of Pharmacy, 1,189 students; 7 colleges of economics, business administration and modern languages, 17,354 students; 2 schools of architecture, 2,326 students; 7 academies of music, 1,399 students; 2 schools of library and information science, 958 students; the Educational University of Denmark, 2,737 students; 4 schools of social work, 2,213 students; the Danish School of Journalism, 963 students; 9 colleges of physiotherapy, 3,794 students; 2 schools of Midwifery Education, 294 students; 2 colleges of home economics, 873 students; the School of Visual Arts, 186 students; 23 schools of nursing, 9,772 students; 3 military academies, 586 students.

In 2002 total expenditure on education came to 15% of total government spending.

The adult literacy rate in 2003 was at least 99%.

Health. In 2001 there were 15,598 doctors (292 per 100,000 persons), 4,619 dentists, 51,669 nurses, 39,197 auxiliary nurses and 1,308 midwives. There were 68 hospitals in 2002 (provision of 1 bed per 210 population in 1996). In 2002 Denmark spent 8·8% of its GDP on health. In 2004 an estimated 31% of men and 32% of women smoked. The rate among women is one of the highest in the world.

Welfare. The main body of Danish social welfare legislation is consolidated in seven acts concerning: (1) public health security, (2) sick-day benefits, (3) social pensions (for early retirement and old age), (4) employment injuries insurance, (5) employment services, unemployment insurance and activation measures, (6) social assistance including assistance to handicapped, rehabilitation, child and juvenile guidance, daycare institutions, care of the aged and sick, and (7) family allowances.

Public health security, covering the entire population, provides free medical care, substantial subsidies for certain essential medicines together with some dental care, and a funeral allowance. Hospitals are primarily municipal and treatment is normally free. All employed workers are granted daily sickness allowances; others can have limited daily sickness allowances. Daily cash benefits are granted in the case of temporary incapacity because of illness, injury or childbirth to all persons in paid employment. The benefit is paid up to the rate of 100% of the average weekly earnings. There is, however, a maximum rate of 3,016 kroner a week.

Social pensions cover the entire population. Entitlement to the old-age pension at the full rate is subject to the condition that the beneficiary has been ordinarily resident in Denmark for 40 years. For a shorter period of residence, the benefits are reduced proportionally. The basic amount of the old-age pension in Jan. 2004 was 163,968 kroner a year to married couples and 111,924 to single persons. Various supplementary allowances, depending on age and income, may be payable with the basic amount. The retirement age is 65, or 67 for those born before 1 July 1939. Depending on health and income, persons aged 60–64 (60–66 for those born before 1 July 1939) may apply for an early retirement pension. Persons over 65 (or 67) years of age are entitled to the basic amount. The pensions to a married couple are calculated and paid to the husband and the wife separately. Early retirement pension to a disabled person is payable at ages 18–64 (or 66) years, at a rate of 166,740 kroner to a single person. Early retirement pensions may be subject to income regulation. The same applies to the old-age pension.

Employment injuries insurance provides for disability or survivors' pensions and compensations. The scheme covers practically all employees.

Employment services are provided by regional public employment agencies. Insurance against unemployment provides daily allowances and covers about 85% of the unemployed. The unemployment insurance system is based on state subsidized insurance funds linked to the trade unions. The unemployment insurance funds had a membership of 2,147,015 in Nov. 2004.

The *Social Assistance Act* comprises three acts (the act on active social policy, the act on social service and the act on integration of foreigners). From these acts individual benefits are applied, in contrast to the other fields of social legislation which apply to fixed benefits. Total social expenditure, including hospital and health services, statutory pensions, etc. amounted in the financial year 2003 to 420,123·7m. kroner.

CULTURE

World Heritage Sites. Denmark has four sites on the UNESCO World Heritage List: the burial mounds, runic stones and church at Jelling (inscribed on the list in 1994); Roskilde Cathedral (1995); Kronborg Castle (2000); and Ilulissat Icefjord (2004), the sea mouth of Sermeq Kujalleq in Greenland.

Broadcasting. *Danmarks Radio* is the government broadcasting station and is financed by household licence fees. Television is broadcast by *Danmarks Radio* and *TV2* with colour programmes by PAL system. Number of licences (2003): TV, 2·15m., including 2·14m. colour sets. Denmark had 1·28m. cable TV subscribers in 2003. There were 7·2m. radio receivers in 2000 and 4·6m. television receivers in 2001.

Cinema. In 2003 there were 379 auditoria. Total attendance in 2003 was 12·3m.; in 2003 net box office receipts came to 582m. kroner. 33 full-length films were made in 2003.

Press. In 2003 there were 32 daily newspapers with a combined circulation of 1·38m. The newspaper with the largest average circulation in the period Jan.–June 2003 was *Jyllands-Posten* (172,000 on weekdays and 231,000 on Sundays), followed by *Berlingske Tidende* (142,000 on weekdays and 165,000 on Sundays) and *Politiken* (137,000 on weekdays and 173,000 on Sundays).

Tourism. In 2003, 3,352,000 foreign tourists visited Denmark. In 2001 tourists spent some 39,078m. kroner. Foreigners spent 5,925,000 nights in hotels and 3,557,000 nights at camping sites in 2003.

Libraries. In 2002 there were 764 public libraries, one National library and 43 Higher Education libraries. They held a combined 100,385,000 volumes.

DIPLOMATIC REPRESENTATIVES

Of Denmark in the United Kingdom (55 Sloane St., London, SW1X 9SR)
Ambassador: Tom Risdahl Jensen.

Of the United Kingdom in Denmark (Kastelsvej 36–40, DK-2100, Copenhagen Ø)
Ambassador: Sir Nicholas Browne, KBE, CMG.

Of Denmark in the USA (3200 Whitehaven St., NW, Washington, D.C., 20008)
Ambassador: Ulrik Andreas Federspiel.

Of the USA in Denmark (Dag Hammarskjölds Allé 24, DK-2100, Copenhagen Ø)
Ambassador: Vacant.
Chargé d'Affaires a.i.: Sally M. Light.

Of Denmark to the United Nations
Ambassador: Ellen Margrethe Løj.

FURTHER READING

Statistical Information: Danmarks Statistik (Sejrøgade 11, DK-2100 Copenhagen Ø. *Website:* http://www.dst.dk/) was founded in 1849 and reorganized in 1966 as an independent institution; it is administratively placed under the Minister of Economic Affairs. Its main publications are: *Statistisk Årbog* (Statistical Yearbook). From 1896: *Statistiske Efterretninger* (Statistical News). *Konjunkturstatistik* (Main indicators); *Statistisk Tiårsoversigt* (Statistical Ten-Year Review).

Dania polyglotta. Annual Bibliography of Books . . . in Foreign Languages Printed in Denmark. State Library, Copenhagen. Annual
Kongelig Dansk Hof og Statskalender. Copenhagen. Annual
Jespersen, Knud J. V., *History of Denmark.* Palgrave Macmillan, Basingstoke, 2004
Petersson, O., *The Government and Politics of the Nordic Countries.* Stockholm, 1994
Turner, Barry, (ed.) *Scandinavia Profiled.* Macmillan, London, 2000

National library: Det kongelige Bibliotek, P.O.B. 2149, DK-1016 Copenhagen K. *Director:* Erland Kolding Nielsen.
National statistical office: Statistics Denmark, Copenhagen. *Director General:* Jan Plovsing.
Website: http://www.dst.dk/

THE FAROE ISLANDS

Føroyar/Færøerne

KEY HISTORICAL EVENTS

A Norwegian province till the peace treaty of 14 Jan. 1814, the islands have been represented by two members in the Danish parliament since 1851. In 1852 they were granted an elected parliament which in 1948 secured a degree of home-rule. The islands are not part of the EU. Recently, negotiations for independence were given a push by the prospect of exploiting offshore oil and gas.

TERRITORY AND POPULATION

The archipelago is situated due north of Scotland, 300 km from the Shetland Islands, 675 km from Norway and 450 km from Iceland, with a total land area of 1,399 sq. km (540 sq. miles). There are 17 inhabited islands (the main ones being Streymoy, Eysturoy, Vágoy, Suðuroy, Sandoy and Borðoy) and numerous islets, all mountainous and of volcanic origin. Population in Dec. 2002 was 47,700; density, 34·1 per sq. km. In 1995 an estimated 67·9% of the population lived in rural areas. The capital is Tórshavn (16,000 residents in 1999) on Streymoy.

The official languages are Faroese and Danish.

SOCIAL STATISTICS

Birth rate per 1,000 inhabitants (2002), 15·0; death rate, 8·3. Life expectancy at birth for total population (1996 est.), 77·83.

CONSTITUTION AND GOVERNMENT

The parliament comprises 32 members elected by proportional representation by universal suffrage at age 18. Parliament elects a government of at least three members which administers home rule. Denmark is represented in parliament by the chief administrator. A referendum was to be held on 26 May 2001 on the government's plan to move towards full sovereignty, but it was called off after the Danish prime minister at the time Poul Nyrup Rasmussen stated that subsidies would cease after four years if the islanders voted for independence.

RECENT ELECTIONS

Parliamentary elections were held on 20 Jan. 2004: the Party for People's Government (TF) won 8 seats with 21·7% of the vote; the Union Party (SF) won 7 seats (23·7%); the Equality Party/Social Democrats (JF) won 7 seats (21·8%); the People's Party (FF) won 7 seats (20·6%); the Centre Party (MF) won 2 seats (5·2%); and the Self-Government Party (SSF) won 1 seat (4·6%).

CURRENT ADMINISTRATION

High Commissioner: Birgit Kleis (b. 1956; appointed 2001).

Prime Minister: Jóannes Eidesgaard; b. 1951 (JF; took office on 3 Feb. 2004).

ECONOMY

Currency. Since 1940 the currency has been the Faroese *króna* (kr.) which remains freely interchangeable with the Danish krone.

Budget. In 2002 revenues totalled 3,726m. kr and expenditures 3,586m. kr.

Banking and Finance. The largest bank is the state-owned Føroya Banki. There are four other banks.

ENERGY AND NATURAL RESOURCES

Environment. Carbon dioxide emissions from the consumption and flaring of fossil fuels in 2002 were the equivalent of 14·7 tonnes per capita.

Electricity. Installed capacity was 93,000 kW in 2000. Total production in 2000 was estimated at 188m. kWh, of which approximately 44% was hydro-electric. There are five hydro-electric stations at Vestmanna on Streymoy and one at Eiði on Eysturoy. Consumption per capita was an estimated 4,087 kWh in 2000.

Agriculture. Only 2% of the surface is cultivated; it is chiefly used for sheep and cattle grazing. Potatoes are grown for home consumption. Livestock (2002): sheep, 68,000; cattle, 2,000.

Fisheries. Deep-sea fishing now forms the most important sector (90%) of the economy, primarily in the 200-mile exclusive zone, but also off Greenland, Iceland, Svalbard and Newfoundland and in the Barents Sea. Total catch (2001) 524,837 tonnes, primarily cod, coalfish, redfish, mackerel, blue whiting, capelin, prawns and herring.

INTERNATIONAL TRADE

Imports and Exports. Exports f.o.b. amounted to US$477·9m. in 1999; US$315·0m. was fish, US$26·4m. was seafood and US$17·9m. was ships and boats. Imports c.i.f. were US$477·5m. in 1999; US$174·5m. was machinery and transport equipment (34% of which was trawlers), US$89·4m. was foodstuffs and US$57·1m. was manufactured goods. Denmark supplied 28% of imports, Norway 26% and Germany 7%; Denmark took 32% of exports, UK 21% and France 9%.

COMMUNICATIONS

Roads. In 1995 there were 458 km of highways, 11,528 passenger cars and 2,901 commercial vehicles.

Civil Aviation. The airport is on Vágoy, from which there are regular services to Aberdeen, Billund, Copenhagen and Reykjavík.

Shipping. The chief port is Tórshavn, with smaller ports at Klaksvik, Vestmanna, Skálafjørður, Tvøroyri, Vágur and Fuglafjørður. In 2002 merchant shipping totalled 200,000 GRT, including oil tankers 80,000 GRT.

Telecommunications. In 2002 there were 23,000 telephone main lines in use. There were 30,700 mobile phone subscribers in 2002 and 25,000 Internet users.

SOCIAL INSTITUTIONS

Religion. About 80% are Evangelical Lutherans and 20% are Plymouth Brethren, or belong to small communities of Roman Catholics, Pentecostal, Adventists, Jehovah's Witnesses and Bahai.

Education. In 2000–01 there were 5,570 primary and 2,507 secondary school pupils (total of 670 teachers).

Health. In 1995 there were 85 physicians, 40 dentists, 412 nurses, ten pharmacists and 19 midwives. In 1994 there were three hospitals with 297 beds.

CULTURE

Broadcasting. Radio and TV broadcasting (colour by PAL) are provided by Utvarp Føroya and Sjónvarp Føroya respectively. In 2000 there were 102,000 radio and 46,800 TV receivers.

Press. In 1996 there was one daily newspaper with a circulation of 6,000.

FURTHER READING

Árbók fyri Føroyar. Annual.
Rutherford, G. K. (ed.) *The Physical Environment of the Færoe Islands.* The Hague, 1982
Wylie, J., *The Faroe Islands: Interpretations of History.* Lexington, 1987

National statistical office: Hagstova Føroya, Statistics Faroe Islands.
Website (Faeroese only): http://www.hagstova.fo

GREENLAND

Grønland/Kalaallit Nunaat

KEY HISTORICAL EVENTS

A Danish possession since 1380, Greenland became an integral part of the Danish kingdom on 5 June 1953. Following a referendum in Jan. 1979, home rule was introduced from 1 May 1979.

TERRITORY AND POPULATION

Area, 2,166,086 sq. km (840,000 sq. miles), made up of 1,755,437 sq. km of ice cap and 410,449 sq. km of ice-free land. The population, 1 Jan. 2000, numbered 56,124; density, 0·03 sq. km. In 2000, 45,714 persons were urban (81%); 49,369 were born in Greenland and 6,755 were born outside Greenland. 2000 population of West Greenland, 51,069; East Greenland, 3,462; North Greenland (Thule/Qaanaaq), 864; and 729 not belonging to any specific municipality. The capital is Nuuk (Godthåb), with a population in 1999 of 13,445.

The predominant language is Greenlandic. Danish is widely used in matters relating to teaching, administration and business.

SOCIAL STATISTICS

Registered live births (2001), 936; deaths (1999), 482. Number of abortions (2001): 809. Birth rate per 1,000 population (1999), 16·9; death rate per 1,000 population (1999), 8·6. In 1999 suicide was the cause of death in 11% of all deaths. Annual growth rate (2000), 0·1%.

CONSTITUTION AND GOVERNMENT

There is a 31-member Home Rule Parliament, which is elected for four-year terms and meets two to three times a year. The seven-member cabinet is elected by parliament. Ministers need not be members of parliament. In accordance with the Home Rule Act, the Greenland Home Rule government is constituted by an elected parliament, *Landstinget* (The Greenland Parliament), and an administration headed by a local government, *Landsstyret* (The Cabinet).

Greenland elects two representatives to the Danish parliament (*Folketing*). Denmark is represented by an appointed High Commissioner.

RECENT ELECTIONS

At parliamentary elections held on 3 Dec. 2002 Siumut (Social Democratic) won 10 of 31 seats and 28% of votes cast, Inuit Ataqatigiit (leftist) 8 and 25%, Atássut (Liberal) 7 and 20%, and the Democrats 5 and 16%. Turn-out was 75%.

CURRENT ADMINISTRATION

The coalition government of Siumut and Inuit Ataqatigiit was formed in Sept. 2003.

Prime Minister: Hans Enoksen; b. 1956 (Siumut; in office since 14 Dec. 2002).

High Commissioner: Peter Lauritzen (appointed 2002).

Greenland Homerule Website: http://www.nanoq.gl

ECONOMY

Currency. The Danish krone is the legal currency.

Budget. The budget (*finanslovsforslag*) for the following year must be approved by the Home Rule Parliament (*Landstinget*) no later than 31 Oct.

The following table shows the actual revenue and expenditure as shown in Home Rule government accounts for the calendar years 1997–99 and the approved budget figures for 2000 and 2001. Figures are in 1,000 kroner.

	1997	*1998*	*1999*	*2000*	*2001*
Revenue	4,178	4,304	4,511	4,646	4,687
Expenditure	4,089	4,366	4,393	4,342	4,652

Performance. Following a period of recession between 1990–93, the economy has been growing since 1994, although at a rate well below the OECD average in recent years. In 2001 GDP at market prices was 9,088m. kroner and gross national disposable income was 12,281m. kroner. In 1998 the real GNP growth rate was 7·8%.

Banking and Finance. There are two private banks, Grønlandsbanken and Sparbank Vest.

ENERGY AND NATURAL RESOURCES

Environment. Greenland's carbon dioxide emissions from the consumption and flaring of fossil fuels in 2002 were the equivalent of 10·2 tonnes per capita.

Electricity. Installed capacity was 0·1m. kW in 2000. Production in 2000 was about 263m. kWh.

Oil and Gas. Imports of fuel and fuel oil (1999), 171,523 tonnes worth 256m. kroner.

Agriculture. Livestock, 1999: sheep, 21,007; reindeer, 2,106. There are approximately 57 sheep-breeding farms in southwest Greenland.

Fisheries. Fishing and product-processing are the principal industry. The total catch in 2001 was 158,485 tonnes. In 1999 prawns accounted for almost 64% of the country's economic output. Greenland halibut and other fish made up around 26%. In 1999, 190 large whales were caught and 3,981 smaller cetacean mammals, such as porpoise (subject to the International Whaling Commission's regulations); and in 1998, 167,506 seals.

INDUSTRY

Six shipyards repair and maintain ships and produce industrial tanks, containers and steel constructions for building.

Labour. At 1 Jan. 2000 the potential labour force was 36,434.

INTERNATIONAL TRADE

Imports and Exports. In 2001 imports totalled 2,466m. kroner and exports 2,251m. kroner. Principal import commodities were food, beverages and tobacco products (17·3%); mineral fuels (16·6%); goods for construction industry (9·2%); machinery (7·0%). Main export commodities were fish and fish products (87·2%), notably shrimp and crab.

Principal import sources, 2000: Denmark, 72·8%; Norway, 8·9%; Japan, 2·6%; Germany, 2·4%. Main export markets, 2000: Denmark, 86·0%; Japan, 6·6%; USA, 4·7%; Thailand, 1·4%.

COMMUNICATIONS

Roads. There are no roads between towns. Registered vehicles (1999): passenger cars, 2,226; lorries and trucks, 1,332; total (including others), 4,026.

Civil Aviation. Number of passengers to/from Greenland (1999): 100,094. Domestic flights—number of passengers (1999): aeroplanes, 169,732; helicopters, 62,155. Air Greenland operates domestic services and international flights to Denmark. There are international airports at Kangerlussuaq (Søndre Strømfjord), Narsarsuaq and Kulusuk and 18 local airports/heliports with scheduled services. There are cargo services to Denmark, Iceland and Canada.

Shipping. There are no overseas passenger services. In 1998, 100,969 passengers were carried on coastal services. There are cargo services to Denmark, Iceland and St John's (Canada).

Telecommunications. In 2002 there were 45,300 telephone subscribers (798·5 per 1,000 inhabitants). There were 13,600 mobile phone subscribers in Dec. 1999. In Dec. 2000 Internet users numbered 17,800.

SOCIAL INSTITUTIONS

Justice. The High Court in Nuuk comprises one professional judge and two lay magistrates, while there are 18 district courts under lay assessors.

The population in penal institutions in 2000 was 74 (131 per 100,000 of national population).

Religion. About 80% of the population are Evangelical Lutherans. In 1998 there were 17 parishes with 81 churches and chapels, and 22 ministers.

Education. Education is compulsory from six to 15 years. A further three years of schooling are optional. Primary schools (2001–02) had 11,368 pupils and 1,191 teachers; secondary schools, 682 pupils.

Health. The medical service is free to all citizens. There is a central hospital in Nuuk and 15 smaller district hospitals. In 1998 there were 83 doctors.

Non-natural death occurred in approximately one-fifth of all deaths in 1999. Suicide is the most dominant non-natural cause of death. There were 63 reported cases of tuberculosis in 1999 and 633 cases of venereal disease. Reported cases of syphilis had decreased from 37 in 1991 to 1 in 1999. In 1998, 17 cases of HIV were reported while a total of eight new HIV-positive cases were reported in 1999.

Welfare. Pensions are granted to persons who are 63 or above. The right to maternity leave has been extended to two weeks before the expected birth and up to 20 weeks after birth against a total of 21 weeks in earlier regulations. The father's right to one week's paternity leave in connection with the birth has been extended to three weeks as from 1 Jan. 2000. Wage earners who are members of SIK (The National Workers' Union) receive financial assistance (unemployment benefit) according to fixed rates, in case of unemployment or illness.

CULTURE

Broadcasting. The government Kalaallit Nunaata Radioa provides broadcasting services, and there are also local services. In 1997 there were estimated to be 27,000 radio and 22,000 TV sets (colour by NTSC). Several towns have local television stations.

Press. There are two national newspapers.

Tourism. In 1999 visitors stayed 205,573 nights in hotels (including 105,227 Greenlandic visitors) at 31 hotels.

FURTHER READING

Greenland 19xx and *Greenland 20xx: Statistical Yearbook* has been published annually since 1989 by Statistics Greenland in Greenlandic/Danish. *Greenland 2001–2002* in English
Gad, F., *A History of Greenland.* 2 vols. London, 1970–73
Miller, K. E., *Greenland.* [Bibliography] ABC-Clio, Oxford and Santa Barbara (CA), 1991
Greenland National Library, P.O. Box 1011, DK-3900 Nuuk

National statistical office: Statistics Greenland, PO Box 1025, DK-3900 Nuuk.
Website: http://www.statgreen.gl

DJIBOUTI

Jumhouriyya Djibouti
(Republic of Djibouti)

Capital: Djibouti
Population projection, 2010: 773,000
GDP per capita, 2002: (PPP$) 1,990
HDI/world rank: 0·454/154

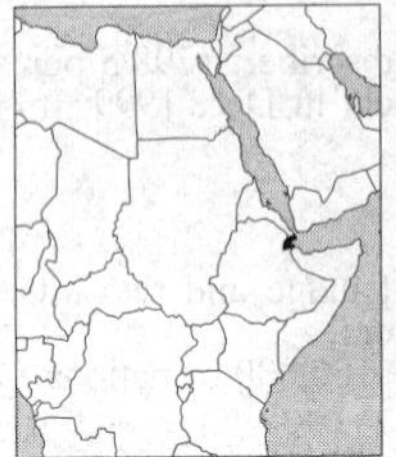

KEY HISTORICAL EVENTS

At a referendum held on 19 March 1967, 60% of the electorate voted for continued association with France rather than independence. France affirmed that the Territory of the Afars and the Issas was destined for independence but no date was fixed. Independence as the Republic of Djibouti was achieved on 27 June 1977. Afar rebels in the north, belonging to the Front for the Restoration of Unity and Democracy (FRUD), signed a 'Peace and National Reconciliation Agreement' with the government on 26 Dec. 1994, envisaging the formation of a national coalition government, the redrafting of the electoral roll and the integration of FRUD militants into the armed forces and civil service.

TERRITORY AND POPULATION

Djibouti is in effect a city-state surrounded by a semi-desert hinterland. It is bounded in the northwest by Eritrea, northeast by the Gulf of Aden, southeast by Somalia and southwest by Ethiopia. The area is 23,200 sq. km (8,958 sq. miles). The population was estimated in 2002 at 688,000 (84·2% urban in 2001), of whom about half were Somali (Issa, Gadaboursi and Issaq), 35% Afar, and some Europeans (mainly French) and Arabs. 2002 density, 30 per sq. km.

The UN gives a projected population for 2010 of 773,000.

There are five administrative districts (areas in sq. km): Ali-Sabieh (2,400); Dikhil (7,200); Djibouti (600); Obock (5,700); Tadjoura (7,300). The capital is Djibouti (1999 population, 523,000).

French and Arabic are official languages; Somali and Afar are also spoken.

SOCIAL STATISTICS

1995 births, 23,500; deaths, 9,500. Birth rate in 1995, 38·8 per 1,000 population; death rate, 15·6. Annual population growth rate, 1992–2002, 2·3%. Infant mortality, 2001, 100 per 1,000 live births. Expectation of life, 2001: 44·9 years for men, 47·3 for women. Fertility rate, 2001, 5·9 children per woman.

CLIMATE

Conditions are hot throughout the year, with very little rain. Djibouti, Jan. 78°F (25·6°C), July 96°F (35·6°C). Annual rainfall 5" (130 mm).

CONSTITUTION AND GOVERNMENT

After a referendum at which turn-out was 70%, a new constitution was approved on 4 Sept. 1992 by 96·63% of votes cast, which permits the existence of up to four political parties. Parties are required to maintain an ethnic balance in their membership. The *President* is directly elected for a renewable six-year term. Parliament is a 65-member *Chamber of Deputies* elected for five-year terms.

National Anthem. 'Hinjinne u sara kaca' ('Arise with strength'); words by A. Elmi, tune by A. Robleh.

RECENT ELECTIONS

In the presidential election on 8 April 2005 Ismail Omar Guelleh was re-elected with 100% of the votes cast. There were no other candidates. Turn-out was 78·9%.

At the parliamentary elections of 10 Jan. 2003—the first free multi-party general elections since independence—the Union for a Presidential Majority, a coalition of RPP (People's Rally for Progress) and FRUD (Front for the Restoration of Unity and Democracy), won all 65 seats with 62·2% of votes cast, against 36·9% for the Union for a Democratic Alternative. Turn-out was 48%.

CURRENT ADMINISTRATION

President: Ismail Omar Guelleh; b. 1947 (RPP; sworn in 8 May 1999).

In March 2005 the Council of Ministers comprised:

Prime Minister: Dilleita Mohamed Dilleita; b. 1958 (RPP; sworn in 7 March 2001).

Minister of Agriculture, Fisheries and Livestock: Dini Abdallah Bililis. *Commerce and Industry:* Saleban Omar Oudine. *Communications, Culture, Post and Telecommunications, Government Spokesperson:* Rifki Abdoulkader Bamakhrama. *Defence:* Ougoureh Kifleh Ahmed. *Economy, Finance and Privatization:* Yacin Elmi Bouh. *Education:* Abdi Ibrahim Absieh. *Employment and National Solidarity:* Mohamed Barkat Abdillahi. *Energy and Natural Resources:* Mohamed Ali Mohamed. *Foreign Affairs, International Co-operation and Parliamentary Relations:* Ali Abdi Farah. *Health:* Dr Banoita Tourab Saleh. *Housing, Town Planning, Environment and Territorial Administration:* Abdallah Adillahi Miguil. *Interior and Decentralization:* Abdoulkader Doualeh Waïs. *Justice, Penal and Muslim Affairs, and Human Rights:* Ismail Ibrahim Houmed. *Presidential Affairs:* Osman Ahmed Moussa. *Transport:* Elmi Obsieh Waïs. *Youth, Sports, Leisure and Tourism:* Otban Goïta Moussa.

Government Website (French only): http://www.presidence.dj

DEFENCE

France maintains a naval base and forces numbering 2,900 under an agreement renewed in Feb. 1991. Defence expenditure totalled US$24m. in 2003 (US$34 per capita), representing 3·9% of GDP.

Army. There are three Army commands: North, Central and South. The strength of the Army in 2002 was 8,000. There is also a paramilitary Gendarmerie of some 1,400, and an Interior Ministry National Security Force of 2,500.

Navy. A coastal patrol is maintained. Personnel (2002), 200.

Air Force. There is a small air force with no combat aircraft. Personnel (2002), 250.

INTERNATIONAL RELATIONS

Djibouti is a member of the UN, WTO, the African Union, African Development Bank, COMESA, OIC, Islamic Development Bank, the League of Arab States, the Intergovernmental Authority on Development, the International Organization of the Francophonie and is an ACP member state of the ACP-EU relationship.

ECONOMY

Agriculture accounted for 3·6% of GDP in 1997, industry 20·5% and services 75·8%.

Currency. The currency is the *Djibouti franc* (DJF), notionally of 100 *centimes*. Foreign exchange reserves were US$72m. in June 2002 and total money supply was 31,286m. Djibouti francs. Inflation was 0·6% in 2002.

Budget. Revenues in 2000 were 23·7bn. Djibouti francs and expenditures 38·2bn. Djibouti francs.

Performance. Real GDP growth was 1·9% in 2001 and 2·6% in 2002. Total GDP in 2003 was US$0·6bn.

Banking and Finance. The Banque Nationale de Djibouti is the bank of issue (*Governor*, Djama Mahamoud Haid). There are three commercial banks and a development bank.

ENERGY AND NATURAL RESOURCES

Environment. Djibouti's carbon dioxide emissions from the consumption and flaring of fossil fuels in 2002 were the equivalent of 2·8 tonnes per capita.

Electricity. Installed capacity in 2000 was 88,000 kW. Production in 2000 was around 192m. kWh; consumption per capita was an estimated 304 kWh in 2000.

Agriculture. Approximately 1·3m. ha were permanent pasture in 1994. There were 1,000 ha of arable land in 2001. Production is dependent on irrigation which in 2000 covered 1,000 ha. Vegetable production (2000) 24,000 tonnes. The most common crops are tomatoes and dates. Livestock (2000): cattle, 269,000; sheep, 465,000; goats, 513,000; camels, 67,000. Livestock products, 2000: meat, 9,000 tonnes; milk, 8,000 tonnes.

Forestry. In 2000 the area under forests was 6,000 ha, or 0·3% of the total land area.

Fisheries. In 2001 the catch was approximately 350 tonnes, entirely from sea fishing.

INDUSTRY

Labour. In 1991 the estimated labour force totalled 282,000, with 75% employed in agriculture, 14% in services and 11% in industry. A 40-hour working week is standard. Unemployment in 1994 was estimated at 30%.

INTERNATIONAL TRADE

Foreign debt totalled US$335m. in 2002.

Imports and Exports. The main economic activity is the operation of the port; in 1990 only 36% of imports were destined for Djibouti. Exports are largely re-exports. In 1998 imports totalled US$238·8m. and exports US$59·1m. The chief imports are cotton goods, sugar, cement, flour, fuel oil and vehicles; the chief exports are hides, cattle and coffee (transit from Ethiopia).

Main export markets, 1998 (% of total trade): Somalia, 53·0%; Yemen, 22·5%; Ethiopia, 5·0%. Main import suppliers, 1998: France, 12·5%; Ethiopia, 12·0%; Italy, 9·2%.

COMMUNICATIONS

Roads. In 1999 there were estimated to be 2,890 km of roads, of which 12·6% were hard-surfaced. An estimated 9,200 passenger cars were in use in 1996 (17·2 per 1,000 inhabitants), plus 2,040 vans and trucks.

Rail. For the line from Djibouti to Addis Ababa, of which 97 km lie within Djibouti, *see* ETHIOPIA: Communications. Traffic carried is mainly in transit to and from Ethiopia.

Civil Aviation. There is an international airport at Djibouti (Ambouli), 5 km south of Djibouti. Djibouti-based carriers are Daallo Airlines and Djibouti Airlines. They operated flights in 2003 to Addis Ababa, Asmara, Borama, Bossaso, Burao, Dire Dawa, Dubai, Galcaio, Hargeisa, Jeddah, London, Mogadishu, Paris and Ta'iz.

Shipping. Djibouti is a free port and container terminal. 950 ships berthed in 1989 (including 177 warships), totalling 3·87m. NRT. 3,211 passengers embarked or disembarked, and 0·87m. tonnes of cargo were handled (1·48m. tonnes in 1992). In 2002 the merchant marine totalled 3,000 GRT.

Telecommunications. There were 25,100 telephone subscribers in 2002 (38·3 for every 1,000 inhabitants) and 10,000 PCs in use. Mobile phone subscribers numbered 15,000 in 2002. In 1999 there were 100 fax machines. Djibouti had 4,500 Internet users in 2002.

Postal Services. There were 12 post offices in 1998.

SOCIAL INSTITUTIONS

Justice. There is a Court of First Instance and a Court of Appeal in the capital. The judicial system is based on Islamic law. The death penalty was abolished for all crimes in 1994.

The population in penal institutions in Dec. 1999 was 384 (61 per 100,000 of national population).

Religion. In 2001, 96% of the population were Muslim; there were small Roman Catholic, Protestant and Orthodox minorities.

Education. Adult literacy in 2001 was 65·5% (76·1% of men; 55·5% of women). In 2000–01 there were 42,692 pupils and 1,199 teachers in primary schools, and

18,808 pupils and 791 teachers in secondary schools. In 2000–01 there were 496 students at tertiary education institutions.

In 1998–99 total expenditure on education came to 3·4% of GNP.

Health. In 1993 there were 2 hospitals, 6 medical centres and 21 dispensaries. There were 60 physicians, 7 dentists, 315 nurses and 8 pharmacists in 1996.

CULTURE

Broadcasting. The state-run *Radiodiffusion-Télévision de Djibouti* broadcasts in French, Somali, Afar and Arabic. There is a television transmitter in Djibouti, broadcasting for 35 hours a week. Number of receivers: radio (1997), 52,000; TV (2001), 50,000 (colour by SECAM V).

Tourism. There were 21,000 foreign tourists in 1998, spending US$4m.

DIPLOMATIC REPRESENTATIVES

Of Djibouti in the United Kingdom
Ambassador: Vacant (resides at Paris).
Chargé d'Affaires a.i.: Mourad Houssien Monti.

Of the United Kingdom in Djibouti
Ambassador: Robert Dewar (resides at Addis Ababa, Ethiopia).

Of the USA in Djibouti (Plateau du Serpent Blvd., Djibouti)
Ambassador: Marguerita Ragsdale.

Of Djibouti to the United Nations and in the USA (1156 15th Street, NW, Suite 515, Washington, D.C., 20005)
Ambassador: Roble Olhaye.

Of Djibouti to the European Union
Ambassador: Mohamed Moussa Chehem.

FURTHER READING

Direction Nationale de la Statistique. *Annuaire Statistique de Djibouti*
Schraeder, Peter J., *Djibouti.* [Bibliography] ABC-Clio, Oxford and Santa Barbara (CA), 1991

National statistical office: Direction Nationale de la Statistique, Ministère du Commerce, des Transports et du Tourisme, BP 1846, Djibouti.

DOMINICA

Commonwealth of Dominica

Capital: Roseau
Population 2001: 72,000
GDP per capita, 2002: (PPP$) 5,640
HDI/world rank: 0·743/95

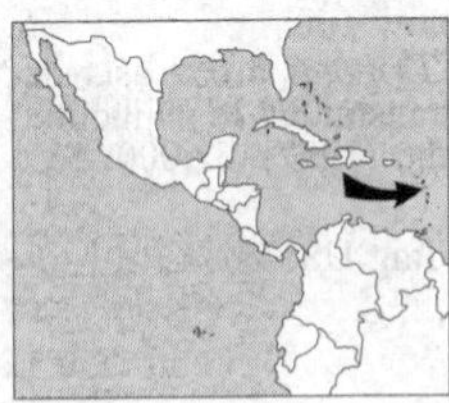

KEY HISTORICAL EVENTS

Dominica was discovered by Columbus on Sunday (hence the island's name), 3 Nov. 1493. But it was French settlers who began to create plantations on the island. Recognizing the island's strategic position, control was contested between the British and French until it was awarded to the British in 1783. In March 1967 Dominica became an Associated State of the UK, with internal self-government, and an independent republic as the Commonwealth of Dominica on 3 Nov. 1978.

TERRITORY AND POPULATION

Dominica is an island in the Windward group of the West Indies situated between Martinique and Guadeloupe. It has an area of 750 sq. km (290 sq. miles) and a provisional population at the 2001 census of 71,242. The population density in 2001 was 95·0 per sq. km.

In 2001, 71·3% of the population were urban. The chief town, Roseau, had 24,000 inhabitants in 1999.

The population is mainly of African and mixed origins, with small white and Asian minorities. There is a Carib settlement of about 500, almost entirely of mixed blood.

The official language is English, although 95% of the population speak a French Creole.

SOCIAL STATISTICS

Births, 2000, 1,199 (rate of 16·8 per 1,000 population); deaths, 503 (rate of 7·0); marriages (1999), 339 (rate of 4·7); divorces (1999), 61 (rate of 0·9). Life expectancy, 1996, 77·4 years; male 74·5, female 80·4. Annual population growth rate, 1992–2002, 0·0%. Infant mortality rate, 2001, 14 per 1,000 live births. Fertility rate, 2001, 1·8 births per woman.

CLIMATE

A tropical climate, with pleasant conditions between Dec. and March, but there is a rainy season from June to Oct., when hurricanes may occur. Rainfall is heavy, with coastal areas having 70" (1,750 mm) but the mountains may have up to 225" (6,250 mm). Roseau, Jan. 76°F (24·2°C), July 81°F (27·2°C). Annual rainfall 78" (1,956 mm).

CONSTITUTION AND GOVERNMENT

The head of state is the *President*, nominated by the Prime Minister and the Leader of the Opposition, and elected for a five-year term (renewable once) by the House of Assembly. The *House of Assembly* has 30 members, of whom 21 members are elected and nine nominated by the President.

National Anthem. 'Isle of beauty, isle of splendour'; words by W. Pond, tune by L. M. Christian.

RECENT ELECTIONS

Elections were held on 5 May 2005. The Dominica Labour Party (DLP) won 12 of the 21 available seats (10 in 2000), the United Workers Party (UWP) won 8 seats (9 in 2000) and independent candidates won 1 seat (0 in 1995). The Dominica Freedom Party (DFP), previously part of the coalition government, did not win any seats. The DLP formed the government without the need for a coalition partner.

CURRENT ADMINISTRATION

President: Dr Nicholas Liverpool; b. 1934 (took office on 2 Oct. 2003).

Prime Minister, Minister of Finance and Planning, and Caribbean Affairs: Roosevelt Skerrit; b. 1972 (DLP; sworn in 8 Jan. 2004). He is currently the youngest head of government in the world.

In May 2005 the cabinet comprised:

Minister of Foreign Affairs, Trade, Labour and Public Services: Charles Savarin. *Housing, Lands, Communications, Energy and Ports:* Reginald Austrie. *Tourism, Industry and Public Sector Affairs:* Yvor Nassief. *Health and Social Security:* John Fabien. *Community Development, Gender Affairs, Culture and Information:* Matthew Walter. *Agriculture, Fisheries and the Environment:* Colin McIntyre. *Education, Human Resource Development, Sports and Youth Affairs:* Vince Henderson. *Public Works and Utilities:* Ambrose George. *Immigration, Legal Affairs and Attorney General:* Ian Douglas.

INTERNATIONAL RELATIONS

Dominica is a member of the UN, WTO, the Commonwealth, OAS, ACS, CARICOM, OECS, the International Organization of the Francophonie and is an ACP member state of the ACP-EU relationship.

ECONOMY

Agriculture accounted for 18·6% of GDP in 2002, industry 21·0% and services 60·4%.

Currency. The *East Caribbean dollar* and the US dollar are legal tender. Foreign exchange reserves were US$34m. in May 2002 and total money supply was EC$113m. Inflation was negative in 2001, at –0·3%.

Budget. Revenues for the fiscal year 2000–01 were EC$194·9m. and expenditures EC$270·8m.

Performance. Real GDP growth was 0·7% in 2000 but Dominica then went into recession, with the economy contracting by 4·6% in 2001 and 3·6% in 2002. In 2003 total GDP was US$0·3bn.

Banking and Finance. The East Caribbean Central Bank based in St Kitts and Nevis functions as a central bank. The *Governor* is Sir Dwight Venner. In 2001 there were five commercial banks (four foreign, one domestic), a development bank and a credit union. Dominica is affiliated to the Eastern Caribbean Securities Exchange in Basseterre, St Kitts and Nevis.

ENERGY AND NATURAL RESOURCES

Environment. Carbon dioxide emissions from the consumption and flaring of fossil fuels in 2002 were the equivalent of 1·4 tonnes per capita.

Electricity. Installed capacity was 13,000 kW in 2000. Production in 2000 was 77m. kWh. Consumption per capita in 2000 was 1,069 kWh. There is a hydro-electric power station.

Agriculture. Agriculture employs 26% of the labour force. In 2001 there were 5,000 ha of arable land and 15,000 ha of permanent crops. Production (2000, in 1,000 tonnes): bananas, 31; grapefruit and pomelos, 21; coconuts, 12; taro, 11; oranges, 8; plantains, 8; yams, 8. Livestock (2000): cattle, 13,000; goats, 10,000; sheep, 8,000; pigs, 5,000.

Forestry. In 2000 forests covered 46,000 ha, or 61·3% of the total land area.

Fisheries. In 2001 fish landings were estimated at 1,150 tonnes, exclusively from sea fishing.

INDUSTRY

Manufactures include soap (10,500 tonnes in 2001), coconut oil, copra, cement blocks, furniture and footwear.

Labour. Around 25% of the economically active population are engaged in agriculture, fishing and forestry. In 2003 the minimum wage was US$0·75 an hour. The unemployment rate in 2003 was 15·7%.

INTERNATIONAL TRADE

Total foreign debt was US$207m. in 2002.

Imports and Exports. In 2001 imports (c.i.f.) totalled US$115·3m. and exports (f.o.b.) US$44·4m. Main exports in 1999: soap (US$17·0m.), bananas (US$16·7m.), fruit, perfumes and sand. Main export markets were (2000): UK, 24·8%; Jamaica, 23·7%; France, 8·5%; Antigua and Barbuda, 7·4%; USA, 7·4%. Main imports (1999): machine and transport equipment (US$34·4m.), food (US$23·8m.), manufactured goods (US$23·8m.), chemicals (US$16·7m.) and refined petroleum products (US$7·4m.). Main import suppliers, 2000: USA, 37·5%; Trinidad and Tobago, 16·3%; UK, 7·7%; Japan, 6·3%; Canada, 4·2%.

COMMUNICATIONS

Roads. In 1999 there were an estimated 780 km of roads, of which 393 km were paved. Approximately 7,000 passenger cars and 2,800 commercial vehicles were in use in 1994.

Civil Aviation. There are international airports at Melville Hall and Cane Field. In 2003 there were direct flights to Anguilla, Antigua, Barbados, British Virgin Islands, Grenada, Guadeloupe, Martinique, Puerto Rico, St Kitts, St Lucia, St Maarten, St Vincent, Trinidad and the US Virgin Islands.

Shipping. There are deep-water harbours at Roseau and Woodbridge Bay. Roseau has a cruise ship berth. In 2002 merchant shipping totalled 4,000 GRT. In 1998 vessels totalling 2,218,000 NRT entered ports.

Telecommunications. There were 34,800 telephone subscribers in 2002, equivalent to 445·7 per 1,000 inhabitants, and 7,000 PCs were in use (89·7 for every 1,000 persons). In 2002 there were 9,400 mobile phone subscribers and in 1995 approximately 300 fax machines were in use. Dominica had 12,500 Internet users in 2002.

Postal Services. In 1994 there were 64 post offices, or one for every 1,090 persons.

SOCIAL INSTITUTIONS

Justice. There is a supreme court and 12 magistrates courts. Law is based on UK common law as exercised by the Eastern Caribbean Supreme Court on St Lucia. Final appeal lies to the UK Privy Council. Dominica was one of twelve countries to sign an agreement establishing a Caribbean Court of Justice to replace the British Privy Council as the highest civil and criminal court. The court was inaugurated at Port-of-Spain, Trinidad on 16 April 2005.

The police force has a residual responsibility for defence. The population in penal institutions in June 1999 was 298 (equivalent to 420 per 100,000 of national population).

Religion. 70% of the population was Roman Catholic in 2001.

Education. In 1998 adult literacy was 94%. Education is free and compulsory between the ages of five and 15 years. In 2000–01 there were 552 teachers and 11,430 pupils in primary schools, and 374 teachers and 7,456 pupils in general secondary level education. In 1992–93 there were 484 students and 34 teaching staff at higher education institutions. In 1999–2000 total expenditure on education came to 5·6% of GNP.

Health. In 1994 there were 53 hospitals and health centres with 25 beds per 10,000 inhabitants. There were 38 physicians, 10 dentists and 361 nurses in 1998. Large numbers of professional nurses take up employment abroad, especially in the USA, causing a shortage of healthcare workers in Dominica.

CULTURE

World Heritage Sites. Dominica has one site on the UNESCO World Heritage List: Morne Trois Pitons National Park (1997), a tropical forest centred on the Morne Trois Pitons volcano.

Broadcasting. Radio and television broadcasting is provided by the part government-controlled, part-commercial Dominica Broadcasting Corporation.

There are also two religious radio networks, two commercial TV channels (colour by NTSC) and a commercial cable service. There were 46,000 radios in 1997 and 15,700 TV sets in 2000.

Cinema. There is one cinema with a seating capacity of 1,000.

Press. In 1994 there were three newspapers, including one government and one independent weekly.

Tourism. There were 69,000 foreign tourists in 2000; in 1998 there were 239,000 cruise ship arrivals. Tourism receipts in 2000 totalled US$47m.

DIPLOMATIC REPRESENTATIVES

Of Dominica in the United Kingdom (1 Collingham Gdns, South Kensington, London, SW5 0HW)
Acting High Commissioner: Agnes Adonis.

Of the United Kingdom in Dominica
High Commissioner: John White (resides at Bridgetown, Barbados).

Of Dominica in the USA (3216 New Mexico Ave., NW, Washington, D.C., 20016)
Ambassador: Vacant.

Of the USA in Dominica
Ambassador: Mary E. Kramer (resides at Bridgetown).

Of Dominica to the United Nations
Ambassador: Crispin Gregoire.

Of Dominica to the European Union
Ambassador: George Bullen.

FURTHER READING

Baker, P. L., *Centring the Periphery: Chaos, Order and the Ethnohistory of Dominica.* McGill-Queen's Univ. Press, 1994
Honychurch, L., *The Dominica Story: a History of the Island.* 2nd ed. London, 1995
Myers, R. A., *Dominica.* [Bibliography] ABC-Clio, Oxford and Santa Barbara (CA), 1987

National statistical office: Central Statistical Office, Kennedy Avenue, Roseau.

DOMINICAN REPUBLIC

República Dominicana

Capital: Santo Domingo
Population projection, 2010: 9·60m.
GDP per capita, 2002: (PPP$) 6,640
HDI/world rank: 0·738/98

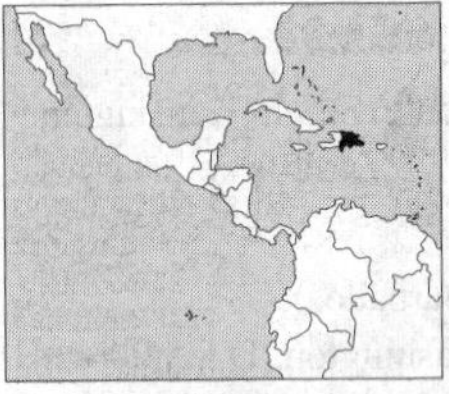

KEY HISTORICAL EVENTS

Columbus discovered the island of Santo Domingo, which he called La Isla Española, and which for a time was also known as Hispaniola. The city of Santo Domingo, founded by his brother, Bartholomew, in 1496, is the oldest city in the Americas. The western third of the island—now the Republic of Haiti—was later occupied and colonized by the French, to whom the Spanish colony of Santo Domingo was also ceded in 1795. In 1808 the Dominican population routed the French at the battle of Palo Hincado. Eventually, with the aid of a British naval squadron, the French were forced to return the colony to Spanish rule, from which it declared its independence in 1821. It was invaded and held by the Haitians from 1822 to 1844, when the Dominican Republic was founded and a constitution adopted.

Thereafter the rule was dictatorship interspersed with brief democratic interludes. Between 1916 and 1924 the country was under US military occupation. From 1930 until his assassination in 1961, Rafael Trujillo was one of Latin America's legendary dictators. The conservative pro-American Joaquin Balaguer was president from 1966 to 1978. In 1986 Balaguer returned to power at the head of the Socialist Christian Reform Party, leading the way to economic reforms. But there was violent opposition to spending cuts and general austerity. The 1996 elections brought in a reforming government pledged to act against corruption.

TERRITORY AND POPULATION

The Dominican Republic occupies the eastern portion (about two-thirds) of the island of Hispaniola, the western division forming the Republic of Haiti. The area is 48,137 sq. km (18,586 sq. miles). The area and 2002 census populations of the provinces and National District (Santo Domingo area) were:

	Area (in sq. km)	*Population*		*Area (in sq. km)*	*Population*
La Altagracia	2,474	182,020	Peravia	998	232,233
Azua	2,532	208,857	Puerto Plata	1,857	312,706
Bahoruco	1,282	91,480	La Romana	654	219,812
Barahona	1,739	179,239	Salcedo	440	96,356
Dajabón	1,021	62,046	Samaná	854	91,875
Distrito Nacional			Sánchez Ramírez	1,196	151,179
(Santo Domingo area)	1,401	2,731,294	San Cristóbal	1,266	532,880
Duarte	1,605	283,805	San José de Ocoa[1]	650	—
Elías Piña	1,426	63,879	San Juan	3,569	241,105
Espaillat	839	225,091	San Pedro de Macorís	1,255	301,744
Hato Mayor	1,329	87,631	Santiago	2,839	908,250
Independencia	2,006	50,833	Santiago Rodríguez	1,111	59,629
María Trinidad Sánchez	1,272	135,727	Santo Domingo[2]	1,296	—
Monseñor Nouel	992	167,618	El Seíbo	1,787	89,261
Monte Cristi	1,924	111,014	Valverde	823	158,293
Monte Plata	2,632	180,376	La Vega	2,287	385,101
Pedernales	2,075	21,207			

[1]Created in 2002; formerly part of Peravia. [2]Created in 2001; formerly part of Distrito Nacional.

Census population (2002), 8,562,541 (4,297,326 females). In 2001 the population was 66·0% urban.

The UN gives a projected population for 2010 of 9·60m.

Population of the main towns (1993, in 1,000): Santo Domingo, the capital, 3,523 (1999); Santiago de los Caballeros, 1,289 (1995); La Romana, 140; San Pedro de Macorís, 125; San Francisco de Macorís, 108.

The population is mainly composed of a mixed race of European (Spanish) and African blood. The official language is Spanish; about 0·15m. persons speak a Haitian-French Creole.

SOCIAL STATISTICS

1996 births, 190,000; deaths, 46,000. Rates, 1996: birth, 23·5 (per 1,000 population); death, 5·7. Annual population growth rate, 1992–2002, 1·7%. Life expectancy, 2001, 64·4 years for males and 69·3 for females. Infant mortality, 2001, 41 per 1,000 live births. Fertility rate, 2001, 2·8 children per woman.

CLIMATE

A tropical maritime climate with most rain falling in the summer months. The rainy season extends from May to Nov. and amounts are greatest in the north and east. Hurricanes may occur from June to Nov. Santo Domingo, Jan. 75°F (23·9°C), July 81°F (27·2°C). Annual rainfall 56" (1,400 mm).

CONSTITUTION AND GOVERNMENT

The constitution dates from 28 Nov. 1966. The *President* is elected for four years, by direct vote, and has executive power. A constitutional amendment of Aug. 1994 prohibits the president from serving consecutive terms. In 1994 the constitution was amended to allow for a second round of voting in a presidential election, when no candidate secures an absolute majority in the first ballot. There is a bicameral legislature, the *Congress*, comprising a 30-member Senate (one member for each province and one for the National District of Santo Domingo) and a 149-member *Chamber of Deputies*, both elected for four-year terms. Citizens are entitled to vote at the age of 18, or less when married.

National Anthem. 'Quisqueyanos valientes, alcemos' ('Valiant Quisqueyans, Let us raise our voices'); words by E. Prud'homme, tune by J. Reyes.

RECENT ELECTIONS

Presidential elections were held on 16 May 2004. Leonel Antonio Fernández Reyna of the Dominican Liberation Party/PLD won 57·1% of the votes, incumbent Rafael Hipólito Mejía Domínguez of the Dominican Revolutionary Party/PRD 33·6% and Eduardo Estrella of the Social Christian Reformist Party/PRSC 8·8%. Turn-out was 72·8%.

Parliamentary elections were held on 16 May 2002. In the election to the Chamber of the Deputies the PRD won 73 seats, the PLD 41 and the PRSC 36. In the Senate elections on the same day, the PRD won 29 seats, the PLD 1 and the PRSC 1.

CURRENT ADMINISTRATION

President: Leonel Antonio Fernández; b. 1953 (PLD; sworn in 16 Aug. 2004, having previously been president from 1996–2000).

Vice-President: Rafael Alburquerque.

In March 2005 the government comprised:

Secretary of State for Agriculture: Amílcar Romero. *Armed Forces:* Rear Adm. Sigfrido Pared Pérez. *Culture:* José Rafael Lantigua. *Education:* Alejandrina Germán. *Environment and Natural Resources:* Maximiliamo Puig. *Finance:* Vicente Bengoa. *Foreign Relations:* Carlos Morales Troncoso. *Higher Education, Science and Technology:* Ligia Amada de Melo. *Industry and Commerce:* Francisco Javier García. *Interior and Police:* Franklin Almeyda. *Labour:* José Ramón Fadul. *Presidency:* Danilo Medina. *Public Health and Social Welfare:* Sabino Báez. *Public Works and Communications:* Manuel de Jesús Pérez. *Sport:* Felipe Jay Payano. *Tourism:* Félix Jiménez. *Women:* Gladis Gutiérrez. *Youth:* Manuel Crespo.

Office of the President: http://www.presidencia.gov.do

DEFENCE

In 2003 defence expenditure totalled US$162m. (US$19 per capita), representing 1·0% of GDP.

Army. There are three defence zones. The Army has a strength (2002) of about 15,000 and includes a special forces unit and a Presidential Guard. There is a paramilitary National Police 15,000-strong.

Navy. The Navy is equipped with former US vessels. Personnel in 2002 totalled 4,000, based at Santo Domingo and Las Calderas.

Air Force. The Air Force, with HQ at San Isidoro, has 16 combat aircraft. Personnel strength (2002), 5,500.

INTERNATIONAL RELATIONS

The Dominican Republic is a member of the UN, WTO, OAS, Inter-American Development Bank, ACS, IOM and is an ACP member state of the ACP-EU relationship.

ECONOMY

In 2002 agriculture accounted for 11·8% of GDP, industry 32·9% and services 55·2%.

Currency. The unit of currency is the *peso* (DOP) of 100 *centavos*. Gold reserves were 18,000 troy oz in June 2002 and foreign exchange reserves US$876m. Total money supply was RD$37,826m. in March 2002. Inflation was 5·2% in 2002.

Budget. Central government budgetary revenue in 2000 was RD$54,318·3m. (RD$45,535·5m. in 1999) and expenditure RD$51,507·4m. (RD$47,234·2m. in 1999). Tax revenue in 2000 was RD$47,853·0m.; non-tax revenue, RD$3,310·5m.; capital revenue, RD$27·1m.

Performance. Real GDP growth was 3·2% in 2001, rising to 4·1% in 2002. Total GDP in 2003 was US$15·9bn.

Banking and Finance. In 1947 the Central Bank was established (*Governor*, Héctor Valdez Albizu). Its total assets were RD$34,958·7m. in 1993. In 2002 there were 12 commercial banks, two foreign banks and nine development banks.

The Santo Domingo Securities Exchange is a member of the Association of Central American Stock Exchanges (Bolcen).

The Dominican Republic was one of 15 countries and territories named in a report in June 2000 as failing to co-operate in the fight against international money laundering. The Financial Action Task Force on Money Laundering was set up by the G7 group of major industrialized nations.

Weights and Measures. The metric system is in force but US units are in common use. Rural land is measured with the *tarea* (624 sq. metres).

ENERGY AND NATURAL RESOURCES

Environment. Carbon dioxide emissions from the consumption and flaring of fossil fuels in 2002 were the equivalent of 2·1 tonnes per capita.

Electricity. Installed capacity was 3·6m. kW in 2000. Production was 9·70bn. kWh in 2000; consumption per capita was 1,139 kWh.

Minerals. Bauxite output in 1988 was 167,800 tonnes, but had declined to nil by 1992. Output: nickel (2002), 38,859 tonnes; gold (1999), 651 kg. Gold production had been declining over the previous few years and has since been suspended.

Agriculture. Agriculture and processing are the chief sources of income, sugar cultivation being the principal industry. In 2001 there were 1·1m. ha of arable land and 500,000 ha of permanent cropland. 275,000 ha were irrigated in 2001.

Production, 2000 (in 1,000 tonnes): sugarcane, 4,785; rice, 527; bananas, 422; plantains, 343; tomatoes, 286; mangoes, 180; coconuts, 173; oranges, 131.

Livestock in 2000: 1·90m. cattle; 539,000 pigs; 330,000 horses; 170,000 goats; 46m. chickens. Livestock products, 2000 (in 1,000 tonnes): poultry meat, 254; beef and veal, 69; pork, bacon and ham, 61; eggs, 61; milk, 398.

Forestry. Forests and woodlands covered 1·38m. ha in 2000, representing 28·4% of the total land area. In 2001, 562,000 cu. metres of timber were cut.

Fisheries. The total catch in 2001 was 13,217 tonnes, mainly from sea fishing.

INDUSTRY

Production, 2000 (in 1,000 tonnes): cement (2001), 2,758; residual fuel oil, 599; sugar (2002), 516; kerosene, 394; distillate fuel oil, 385; petrol, 345; rum (1995–96), 395·6m. litres; beer (2003), 337·0m. litres; cigarettes (1999), 4·0bn. units.

Labour. In 2001 the labour force was 3,710,000. In 1997 the unemployment rate was 15·9%.

INTERNATIONAL TRADE

Foreign debt was US$6,256m. in 2002.

Imports and Exports. Imports f.o.b. in 2002 totalled US$8,882·5m. (US$8,779·3m. in 2001); exports in 2002 totalled US$5,183·4m. (US$5,276·3m. in 2001). Main exports, 1995: ferronickel, 31·6%; raw sugar, 13·3%; coffee, 10·6%; cocoa, 7·1%; gold, 5·4%. Main imports (in US$1m.): oil and products, 21·7%; agricultural products, 17·2%.

Main export markets, 1997: USA, 54%; Belgium, 12%; Puerto Rico, 7%. Main import suppliers: USA, 56%; Venezuela, 23%; Mexico, 9%.

COMMUNICATIONS

Roads. In 1999 the road network covered an estimated 12,600 km, of which 6,224 km were paved. In 1996 there were 224,000 passenger cars (29·8 per 1,000 inhabitants), 137,000 trucks and vans, and 14,550 buses and coaches. In 1998 there were 1,494 road accidents resulting in 1,683 deaths.

Rail. In 1995 the total length was 757 km, comprising 375 km of the Central Romana Railroad, 142 km of the Dominican Republic Government Railway between Guayubin and the port of Pepillo, and 240 km operated by the sugar industry.

Civil Aviation. There are international airports at Santo Domingo (Las Americas), Puerto Plata and Punta Cana. Air Santo Domingo operates scheduled domestic services and international services to Puerto Rico. In 2000 Santo Domingo was the busiest airport, handling 4,652,000 passengers, followed by Puerto Plata (estimated at 2,023,000 passengers) and Punta Cana (1,745,000).

Shipping. The main ports are Santo Domingo, Puerto Plata, La Romana and Haina. In 2002 the merchant marine totalled 9,000 GRT. In 2001 vessels totalling 13,892,000 NRT entered and vessels totalling 2,507,000 NRT cleared.

Telecommunications. In 2002 there were 2,609,600 telephone subscribers (299·7 for every 1,000 inhabitants). Mobile phone subscribers numbered 1,700,600 in 2002 and there were 2,500 fax machines in 1995. The number of Internet users in 2002 was 300,000.

Postal Services. In 1998 there were 239 post offices.

SOCIAL INSTITUTIONS

Justice. The judicial power resides in the Supreme Court of Justice, the courts of appeal, the courts of first instance, the communal courts and other tribunals created by special laws, such as the land courts. The Supreme Court, consisting of a president and eight judges chosen by the Senate, and the procurator-general, appointed by the executive, supervises the lower courts. Each province forms a judicial district, as does the National District, and each has its own procurator fiscal and court of first instance; these districts are subdivided, in all, into 97 municipalities, each with one or more local justices. The death penalty was abolished in 1924.

The population in penal institutions in June 2003 was 16,789 (193 per 100,000 of national population).

Religion. The religion of the state is Roman Catholic; there were 7·11m. adherents in 2001. Protestants numbered 560,000 in 2001. In Sept. 2003 there was one cardinal.

Education. Primary instruction is free and compulsory for children between seven and 14 years of age; there are also secondary, normal, vocational and special schools, all of which are either wholly maintained by the State or state-aided. In 2001–02 there were 1,399,844 primary school pupils and 756,240 pupils at secondary level. There are four universities, three Roman Catholic universities, one Adventist university, three technological universities and one Roman Catholic university college, and five other higher education institutions. Adult literacy was 84·0% in 2001 (84·0% among both males and females).

In 1999–2000 total expenditure on education came to 2·6% of GNP and 15·7% of total government spending.

Health. In 1997 there were 17,315 physicians, 1,879 dentists, 8,600 nurses and 372 pharmacists. There were 723 government hospitals in 1992.

CULTURE

World Heritage Sites. The Dominican Republic has one site on the UNESCO World Heritage List: the Colonial City of Santo Domingo (1990)—founded in 1492, it is the site of the first cathedral and university in the Americas.

Broadcasting. There were (1994) more than 170 broadcasting stations in Santo Domingo and other towns; this includes the two government stations. There were seven television stations (colour by NTSC). In 2000 there were 1·51m. radio and 810,000 television receivers.

Press. In 2000 there were nine dailies with a combined circulation of 230,000.

Tourism. There were 2,977,000 foreign tourists in 2000 (394,000 cruise ship arrivals in 1998). Tourism receipts in 2000 totalled US$2,918m. For some 15 years the Dominican Republic has been experiencing annual growth of 10% or more in both tourist arrivals and hotel capacity. In Dec. 1998 there were 41,600 hotel rooms (11,400 in 1987).

DIPLOMATIC REPRESENTATIVES

Of the Dominican Republic in the United Kingdom (139 Inverness Terrace, London, W2 6JF)
Ambassador: Vacant.
Chargé d'Affaires a.i.: Francisco Comprés.

Of the United Kingdom in the Dominican Republic (Edificio Corominas Pepin, Ave. 27 de Febrero 233, Santo Domingo)
Ambassador: Andy Ashcroft.

Of the Dominican Republic in the USA (1715 22nd St., NW, Washington, D.C., 20008)
Ambassador: Flavio Dario Espinal.

Of the USA in the Dominican Republic (Calle Cesar Nicolas Penson, Santo Domingo)
Ambassador: Hans H. Hertell.

Of the Dominican Republic to the United Nations
Ambassador: Marino de Jesús Villanueva Callot.

Of the Dominican Republic to the European Union
Ambassador: Clara Quiñones de Longo.

FURTHER READING

Black, J. K., *The Dominican Republic: Politics and Development in an Unsovereign State.* London, 1986

Schoenhals, K., *Dominican Republic.* [Bibliography] ABC-Clio, Oxford and Santa Barbara (CA), 1990

National statistical office: Oficina Nacional de Estadística, Av. México esq. Leopoldo Navarro, Edificio Oficinas Gubernamentales 'Juan Pablo Duarte' Pisos 8 y 9 Gazcue, Santo Domingo.
Website (Spanish only): http://www.one.gov.do/

EAST TIMOR

República Democrática de Timor-Leste (Democratic Republic of East Timor)

Capital: Dili
Population projection, 2010: 976,000
GDP per capita: not available
GNI per capita: $520
HDI/world rank: 0·436/158

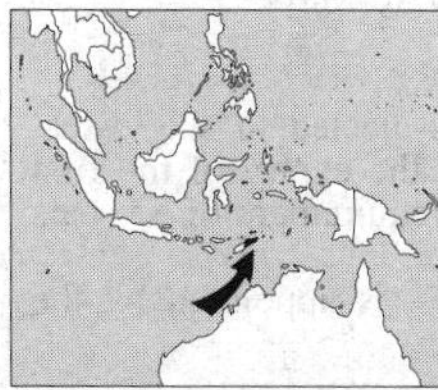

KEY HISTORICAL EVENTS

Portugal abandoned its former colony, with its largely Roman Catholic population, in 1975, when it was occupied by Indonesia and claimed as the province of Timor Timur. The UN did not recognize Indonesian sovereignty over the territory. An independence movement, the Revolutionary Front for an Independent East Timor (FRETILIN), maintained a guerrilla resistance to the Indonesian government which resulted in large-scale casualties and alleged atrocities. On 24 July 1998 Indonesia announced a withdrawal of troops from East Timor and an amnesty for some political prisoners, although no indication was given of how many of the estimated 12,000 troops and police would pull out. On 5 Aug. Indonesia and Portugal reached agreement on the outlines of an autonomy plan which would give the Timorese the right to self-government except in foreign affairs and defence.

In a referendum on the future of East Timor held on 30 Aug. 1999 the electorate was some 450,000 and turn-out was nearly 99%. 78·5% of voters opted for independence, but pro-Indonesian militia gangs wreaked havoc both before and after the referendum. The militias accused the UN of rigging the poll. There was widespread violence in and around Dili, the provincial capital, with heavy loss of life, and thousands of people were forced to take to the hills after intimidation. East Timor's first democratic election took place on 30 Aug. 2001 in a ballot run by the UN, with FRETILIN winning 57% of the vote and 55 of the 88 seats in the new constituent assembly. East Timor became an independent country on 20 May 2002 but unrest continues.

TERRITORY AND POPULATION

East Timor has a total land area of 17,222 sq. km (6,649 sq. miles), consisting of the mainland (14,609 sq. km), the enclave of Oscússu-Ambeno in West Timor (2,461 sq. km), and the islands of Ataúro to the north (144 sq. km) and Jaco to the east (8 sq. km). The mainland area incorporates the eastern half of the island of Timor. Oscússu-Ambeno lies westwards, separated from the main portion of East Timor by a distance of some 100 km. The island is bound to the south by the Timor Sea and lies approximately 500 km from the Australian coast.

The UN population estimate for East Timor in 2001 was 738,000; density, 43 per sq. km. The largest city is Dili, East Timor's capital. In 1999 its population was an estimated 180,000.

The UN gives a projected population for 2010 of 976,000.

The ethnic East Timorese form the majority of the population. Non-East Timorese, comprising Portuguese and West Timorese as well as persons from Sumatra, Java, Sulawesi and other parts of Indonesia, are estimated to constitute approximately 20% of the total population.

During Indonesian occupation the official language was Bahasa Indonesia. East Timor's new constitution designates Portuguese and Tetum (the region's *lingua franca*) as the official languages, and English and Bahasa Indonesia as working languages.

SOCIAL STATISTICS

Based on UN figures for the period 1995–2000: birth rate, 32 per 1,000; death rate, 15 per 1,000; fertility rate, 4·3 births per woman; annual population growth rate, 1·7%; life expectancy at birth, 48 years.

From having the world's highest rate of infant mortality in the early 1980s, East Timor's infant mortality rate has dropped to around 60 per 1,000 live births in 1999, although the figure varies widely between urban and rural areas.

CLIMATE

In the north there is an average annual temperature of over 24°C (75°F), weak precipitation—below 1,500 mm (59") annually—and a dry period lasting five months. The mountainous zone, between the northern and southern parts of the island, has high precipitation—above 1,500 mm (59")—and a dry period of four months. The southern zone has precipitation reaching 2,000 mm (79") and is permanently humid. The monsoon season extends from Nov. to May.

CONSTITUTION AND GOVERNMENT

There is a 88-seat *National Parliament*, with 13 members elected in single-seat constituencies and 75 by proportional representation. After the expiry of the first term the number of seats will be reduced, with a minimum requirement of 52 seats and a maximum of 65.

The *President*, who is elected for a period of five years, is appointed by the *National Parliament*.

National Anthem. 'Eh! Foho Ramelau, Foho Ramelau !' ('Hey, Mount Ramelau, Mount Ramelau!'); words by F. Borja da Costa, tune by A. Araujo.

RECENT ELECTIONS

Presidential elections were held on 14 April 2002. Former separatist guerrilla leader Xanana Gusmão (FRETILIN) won a landslide victory with 82·6% of votes cast against 17·3% for Xavier do Amaral, his single rival. Turn-out was 86%. Amaral, who served as president of East Timor for nine days in 1975, in the short period between Portuguese withdrawal and Indonesian occupation, declared that his intention to run for the presidency was solely to provide the electorate with a choice of candidates.

Elections to the 75-member national assembly took place on 30 Aug. 2001, the anniversary of the referendum for independence two years earlier. The Frente Revolucionária do Timor Leste Independente (FRETILIN; Revolutionary Front for an Independent East Timor) won 57·37% of the vote and took 43 seats with 208,531 votes. The Partido Democrático (PD; Democratic Party) won 8·72% of votes cast and 7 seats; the Partido Social Democrata (PSD; Social Democratic Party) won 8·18% and 6 seats; the Associação Social-Democrata Timorense (ASDT) 7·84% and 6 seats; the União Democrática Timorense (UDT) 2·36% and 2 seats; the Partido do Povo de Timor (PPT) 2·01% and 2 seats. Other parties won less than 2% of the vote. In elections to the district assembly, held on the same day, FRETILIN secured 12 of the 13 seats, giving them a total of 55 seats in the 88-seat constituent assembly. Turn-out for the elections was 91·3%. 23 of the seats went to women.

CURRENT ADMINISTRATION

President: Xanana Gusmão; b. 1946 (ind.; sworn in 20 May 2002).

In March 2005 the government was comprised as follows:

Prime Minister and Minister for Development and the Environment: Marí Bim Amude Alkatiri (FRETILIN).

Deputy Prime Minister: Ana Maria Pessoa Pereira da Silva Pinto.

Minister for Foreign Affairs and Co-operation: José Ramos Horta. *Justice:* Domingos Maria Sarmento. *Finance:* Madalena Brites Boavida. *Internal Administration:* Rogerio Tiago Lobato. *Health:* Rui Maria de Araujo. *Education, Culture and Youth:* Armindo Maia. *Agriculture and Fisheries:* Estanislau Aleixo da Silva. *Transportation, Communications and General Employment:* Ovidio Amaral.

Government Website: http://www.gov.east-timor.org

DEFENCE

Training began in 2001 with the aim of deploying 1,500 full-time personnel and 1,5000 by reservists by 2004. A 650-strong East Timor Defence Force became operational in 2002.

INTERNATIONAL RELATIONS

East Timor is a member of the UN, the IMF and the Asian Development Bank.

ECONOMY

Currency. The official currency is the US dollar. The Australian dollar and the Indonesian rupiah, both previously used, no longer serve as legal tender.

Performance. Total GDP in 2003 was US$0·3bn.

ENERGY AND NATURAL RESOURCES

Electricity. In 1996 only a quarter of households in East Timor had electricity.

Oil and Gas. Although current production is small, the Timor Gap, an area of offshore territory between East Timor and Australia, is one of the richest oil fields in the world outside the Middle East. Potential revenue from the area is estimated at US$11bn. The area is split into three zones with a central 'zone of occupation' (occupying 61,000 sq. km). Royalties on oil discovered within the central zone were split equally between Indonesia and Australia following the Timor Gap Treaty which came into force on 9 Feb. 1991. Questions over East Timor's rights to oil revenue from the area have arisen following the 1999 independence referendum.

Minerals. Gold, iron sands, copper and chromium are present.

Agriculture. Although the presence of sandalwood was one of the principal reasons behind Portuguese colonization, its production has declined in recent years. In 2001 there were 70,000 ha of arable land and 10,000 ha of permanent crops. Coffee is grown extensively.

Fisheries. The total fish catch in 2001 was 356 tonnes.

INDUSTRY

Labour. In 2000 the unemployment rate exceeded 80% of the labour force.

INTERNATIONAL TRADE

Imports and Exports. All basic goods such as rice, sugar and flour are imported. Coffee and cattle are important exports.

COMMUNICATIONS

Civil Aviation. There is an international airport at Dili.

SOCIAL INSTITUTIONS

Religion. Over 90% of East Timor's population are Roman Catholic, with Protestants, Muslims, Hindus and Buddhists accounting for the remainder.

DIPLOMATIC REPRESENTATIVES

Of the United Kingdom in East Timor (Pantai Kelapa, PO Box 194, The Post Office, Dili)
Ambassador: Tina Redshaw.

Of East Timor in the USA (3415 Massachusetts Ave., NW, Washington, D.C., 20007)
Ambassador: José Luis Guterres.

Of the USA in East Timor (Avenido do Portugal, Farol, Dili)
Ambassador: Grover Joseph Rees, III.

Of East Timor to the United Nations
Ambassador: José Luis Guterres.

Of East Timor to the European Union
Ambassador: José Antonio Amorim Dias.

FURTHER READING

Carey, P. and Bentley, G. C. (eds.) *East Timor at the Crossroads: the Forging of a Nation.* London, 1995

Kohen, Arnold S., *From the Place of the Dead: Bishop Belo and the Struggle for East Timor.* Lion, Oxford, 2000

Rowland, Ian, *Timor.* [Bibliography] ABC-Clio, Oxford and Santa Barbara (CA), 1992

ECUADOR

República del Ecuador

Capital: Quito
Population projection, 2010: 14·27m.
GDP per capita, 2002: (PPP$) 3,580
HDI/world rank: 0·735/100

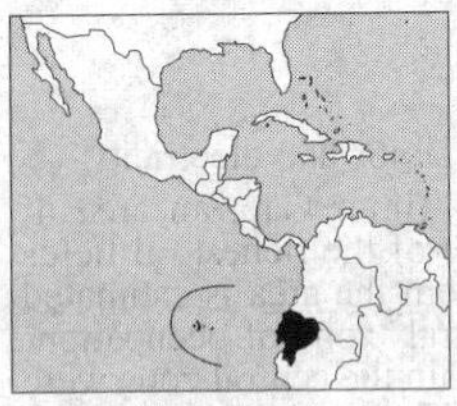

KEY HISTORICAL EVENTS

In 1532 the Spaniards founded a colony in Ecuador, then called Quito. In 1821 a revolt led to the defeat of the Spaniards at Pichincha and thus independence from Spain. On 13 March 1830, Quito became the Republic of Ecuador. Political instability was endemic. From the mid-1930s, President José Maria Velasco Ibarra gave more continuity to the presidential regimes, although he was deposed by military coups from four of his five presidencies.

From 1963 to 1966 and from 1976 to 1979 military juntas ruled the country. The second of these juntas produced a new constitution which came into force on 10 Aug. 1979. Since then presidencies have been more stable but civil unrest continued in the wake of economic reforms and attempts to combat political corruption.

In Jan. 2000 President Mahaud declared a state of emergency as protesters demanded his resignation over his handling of the country's economic crisis. There was a coup on 21 Jan., but after five hours in control the military junta handed power to the former vice-president, Gustavo Noboa.

TERRITORY AND POPULATION

Ecuador is bounded in the north by Colombia, in the east and south by Peru and in the west by the Pacific ocean. The frontier with Peru has long been a source of dispute. It was delimited in the Treaty of Rio, 29 Jan. 1942, when, after being invaded by Peru, Ecuador lost over half her Amazonian territories. Ecuador unilaterally denounced this treaty in Sept. 1961. Fighting between Peru and Ecuador began again in Jan. 1981 over this border issue but a ceasefire was agreed in early Feb. Following a confrontation of soldiers in Aug. 1991 the foreign ministers of both countries signed a pact creating a security zone, and took their cases to the UN in Oct. 1991. On 26 Jan. 1995 further armed clashes broke out with Peruvian forces in the undemarcated mutual border area ('Cordillera del Cóndor'). On 2 Feb. talks were held under the auspices of the guarantor nations of the 1942 Protocol of Rio de Janeiro (Argentina, Brazil, Chile and the USA), but fighting continued. A ceasefire was agreed on 17 Feb., which was broken, and again on 28 Feb. On 25 July 1995 an agreement between Ecuador and Peru established a demilitarized zone along their joint frontier. The frontier was re-opened on 4 Sept. 1995. Since 23 Feb. 1996 Ecuador and Peru have signed three further agreements to regulate the dispute. The dispute was settled in Oct. 1998. Confirming the Peruvian claim that the border lies along the high peaks of the Cóndor, Ecuador gained navigation rights on the Amazon within Peru.

No definite figure of the area of the country can yet be given. One estimate of the area of Ecuador is 272,045 sq. km, excluding the litigation zone between Peru and Ecuador, which is 190,807 sq. km, but including the **Galápagos** Archipelago (8,010 sq. km), situated in the Pacific ocean about 960 km west of Ecuador, and comprising 13 islands and 19 islets. These were discovered in 1535 by Fray Tomás de Berlanga and had a population of 10,207 in 1996. They constitute a national park, and had about 80,000 visitors in 1995.

The population is an amalgam of European, Amerindian and African origins. Some 40% of the population is Amerindian: Quechua, Swiwiar, Achuar and Zaparo. In May 1992 they were granted title to the 1m. ha of land they occupy in Pastaza.

The official language is Spanish. Quechua and other languages are also spoken.

Census population in 2001, 12,156,608; density, 45 per sq. km. In 2001, 63·4% lived in urban areas.

The UN gives a projected population for 2010 of 14·27m.

The population was distributed by provinces as follows in 2001 (census figures):

Province	*Sq. km*	*Population*	*Capital*	*Population*
Azuay	8,124·7	599,546	Cuenca	277,374
Bolívar	3,939·9	169,370	Guaranda	20,742
Cañar	3,122·1	194,529	Azogues	27,866
Carchi	3,605·1	206,981	Tulcán	47,359
Chimborazo	6,569·3	403,632	Riobamba	124,807
Cotopaxi	6,071·9	349,540	Latacunga	51,689
El Oro	5,850·1	525,763	Machala	204,578
Esmeraldas	15,239·1	385,223	Esmeraldas	95,124
Guayas	20,502·5	3,309,034	Guayaquil	1,985,379
Imbabura	4,559·3	344,044	Ibarra	108,535
Loja	11,026·5	404,835	Loja	118,532
Los Ríos	7,175·0	650,178	Babahoyo	76,869
Manabi	18,878·8	1,186,025	Portoviejo	171,847
Morona-Santiago	25,690·0	115,412	Macas	13,602
Napo	11,430·9	79,139	Tena	16,669
Orellana	22,500·0	86,493	Francisco de Orellana	18,298
Pastaza	29,773·7	61,779	Puyo	24,432
Pichincha	12,914·7	2,388,817	Quito	1,399,378
Sucumbíos	18,327·5	128,995	Nueva Loja	34,106
Tungurahua	3,334·8	441,034	Ambato	154,095
Zamora-Chinchipe	23,110·8	76,601	Zamora	10,355
Galápagos	8,010·0	18,640	Puerto Baquerizo Moreno	4,908
Non-delimited zones	2,288·8	72,588		

SOCIAL STATISTICS

2001 estimates: births, 328,000; deaths, 68,000. Rates, 2001 estimates (per 1,000 population): birth, 26·0; death, 5·4. Life expectancy at birth, 2001, was 68·0 years for males and 73·2 years for females. Annual population growth rate, 1992–2002, 1·8%. Infant mortality, 2001, 24 per 1,000 live births; fertility rate, 2001, 2·9 children per woman. In 1998 the most popular age for marrying was 20–24 for both men and women.

CLIMATE

The climate varies from equatorial, through warm temperate to mountain conditions, according to altitude, which affects temperatures and rainfall. In coastal areas, the dry season is from May to Dec., but only from June to Sept. in mountainous parts, where temperatures may be 20°F colder than on the coast. Quito, Jan. 59°F (15°C), July 58°F (14·4°C). Annual rainfall 44" (1,115 mm). Guayaquil, Jan. 79°F (26·1°C), July 75°F (23·9°C). Annual rainfall 39" (986 mm).

CONSTITUTION AND GOVERNMENT

A new constitution came into force on 10 Aug. 1998. It provides for an executive president and a vice-president to be directly elected by universal suffrage. The president appoints and leads a *Council of Ministers*, and determines the number and functions of the ministries that comprise the executive branch. The new constitution strengthened the executive branch by eliminating mid-term congressional elections and by restricting congress' power to challenge and remove cabinet ministers.

Legislative power is vested in a *National Congress* of 100 members, popularly elected by province. Voting is obligatory for all literate citizens of 18–65 years.

National Anthem. 'Salve, Oh Patria, mil veces, Oh Patria' ('Hail, Oh Fatherland, a thousand times, Oh Fatherland'); words by J. L. Mera, tune by A. Neumane.

RECENT ELECTIONS

Dissatisfaction with President Fabián Alarcón led to presidential elections in 1998. Jamil Mahuad, candidate of the centre-right Popular Democracy party (DP), won in the second round of the presidential election on 12 July 1998, with 51·3% of the votes, against 48·7% for Alvaro Noboa, a populist businessman. In the first round on 31 May he had defeated five other candidates to win 35·3% of the vote. After a coup in Jan. 2000 Noboa (who was elected vice-president) replaced Jamil Mahuad as president. In the first round of presidential elections held on 20 Oct. 2002 Col.

Lucio Gutiérrez (the instigator of the coup) won 20·3% of the vote, against 17·4% for Alvaro Noboa. In the run-off held on 24 Nov. 2002 Gutiérrez won 54·3% against 45·7% for Noboa.

In *National Congress* elections on 20 Oct. 2002 the Social Christian Party (PSC) won 25 seats, the Party of the Democratic Left (ID) 16, the Ecuadorian Roldosist Party (PRE) 15, the National Action Institutional Renewal Party (PRIAN) 10, the 21 January Patriotic Society (PSP) 9, the Pluri–National Pachakutik Movement–New Country (MUPP–NP) 6, the Popular Democratic Movement (MPD) 5, the People's Democracy–Christian Democrat Union (DP–UDC) 4 and the Socialist Party of Ecuador–Wide Front (PS–FA) 3. Independent candidates won the remaining 7 seats.

CURRENT ADMINISTRATION

President: Dr Alfredo Palacio; b. 1939 (sworn in 20 April 2005).

Vice-President: Alejandro Serrano.

In May 2005 the cabinet comprised:

Minister of Agriculture and Livestock: Pablo Rizzo. *Defence:* Gen. Aníbal Solón. *Economy and Finance:* Rafael Correa. *Education and Culture:* Consuelo Yánez. *Energy and Mines:* Vacant. *Environment:* Anita Albán. *Foreign Relations:* Antonio Parra. *Foreign Trade, Industrialization, Fishing and Competitiveness:* Dr Oswaldo Molestina. *Government and Police:* Mauricio Gándara. *Labour and Human Resources:* Vacant. *Public Health:* Wellington Sandoval. *Public Works and Communications:* Derliz Palacios. *Social Welfare:* Alberto Rigail. *Tourism:* María Isabel Salvador. *Urban Development and Housing:* Armando Bravo.

Office of the President (Spanish only): http://www.presidencia.gov.ec

DEFENCE

Military service is selective, with a one-year period of conscription. The country is divided into four military zones, with headquarters at Quito, Guayaquil, Cuenca and Pastaza.

In 2003 defence expenditure totalled US$640m. (US$49 per capita), representing 2·4% of GDP.

Army. Strength (2002) 50,000, with about 100,000 reservists.

Navy. Navy combatant forces include two diesel submarines and two ex-UK frigates. The Maritime Air Force has eight aircraft but no combat aircraft. Naval personnel in 2002 totalled 5,500 including some 1,700 marines.

Air Force. The Air Force had a 2002 strength of about 4,000 personnel and 79 combat aircraft, and includes Jaguars, Mirage F-1s and Kfirs.

INTERNATIONAL RELATIONS

Ecuador is a member of the UN, WTO, OAS, Inter-American Development Bank the Andean Group, LAIA, IOM and the Antarctic Treaty.

ECONOMY

Agriculture accounted for 9·0% of GDP in 2002, industry 28·3% and services 62·6%.

Overview. A reform programme was announced in 1992, including the privatization of 20 state-owned enterprises. A new economic plan was promulgated in Nov. 1996, envisaging privatization of the oil and electricity sectors, but in 1998 privatization was put on hold as the sale of 35% of state telecommunications companies was suspended in April 1998 owing to a lack of serious bidders. Congress approved the Economic Transformation Law on 1 March 2000 to introduce flexibility into the labour market and encourage further private investment in the oil, electrical and telecommunications sectors.

Currency. The monetary unit is the US dollar. Inflation was 12·6% in 2002, down from 37·7% in 2001. In March 2000 the government passed a law to phase out the former national currency, the *sucre*, to be replaced by the US dollar, and in April bank cash machines began dispensing dollars instead of sucres. On 11 Sept. 2000 the dollar became the only legal currency. Foreign exchange reserves were US$880m. in June 2002 and gold reserves 845,000 troy oz.

Budget. Revenues in 2002 were US$4,526m. and expenditures US$4,694m.

In 2000 VAT was increased from 10% to 12% and corporate tax from 15% to 25%.

Performance. Ecuador experienced a recession in 1999, with the economy shrinking by 6·3%, partly owing to years of mismanagement and partly to El Niño. There was a recovery in 2000, however, with the growth rate reaching 2·8%. In 2001 growth was 5·1%, the highest in Latin America, followed in 2002 by growth of 3·4%. Total GDP in 2003 was US$26·9bn.

Banking and Finance. The Central Bank of Ecuador (*President of the Directorate*, Mauricio Pareja), the bank of issue, with a capital and reserves of US$1,557m. at 31 Dec. 1995, is modelled after the Federal Reserve Banks of the USA; through branches opened in 16 towns, it now deals in mortgage bonds. There are five other state banks, 16 commercial banks, four foreign banks and a *Multibanco*. All commercial banks must be affiliated to the Central Bank. Legislation of May 1994 liberalized the financial sector. The national monetary board is based in Quito.

There are stock exchanges in Quito and Guayaquil.

Weights and Measures. The metric system is standard but some US measures are used.

ENERGY AND NATURAL RESOURCES

Environment. Ecuador's carbon dioxide emissions from the consumption and flaring of fossil fuels were the equivalent of 1·7 tonnes per capita in 2002.

Electricity. Installed capacity was 3·49m. kW in 2000. Production was 10·61bn. kWh in 2000; consumption per capita was 839 kWh.

Oil and Gas. Production of crude oil in 2000 was 20·9m. tonnes. Estimated reserves, 2002, 4,600m. bbls. In 1999 natural gas production was 772m. cu. metres. Estimated reserves (2002), 109bn. cu. metres.

Minerals. Main products are silver, gold, copper and zinc. The country also has some iron, uranium, lead, coal, cobalt, manganese and titanium.

Agriculture. There were 1·62m. ha of arable land in 2001 and 1·37m. ha of permanent crops. In 2002, 24·5% of the economically active population worked in agriculture.

50,000 ha of rich virgin land in the Santo Domingo de los Colorados area has been set aside for settlement by medium and large landowners. A law of 1994 restricts the redistribution of land to small farmers to land which has lain fallow for more than three years.

The staple export products are bananas and coffee. Main crops, in 1,000 tonnes, in 2000: bananas, 6,816; sugarcane, 6,200; rice, 1,520; potatoes, 788; maize, 747; plantains, 476; palm oil, 268; cassava, 184; soybeans, 170; oranges, 157; coffee, 133. Ecuador's annual banana crop is exceeded only by that of India.

Livestock, 2000: cattle, 5·11m.; sheep, 2·13m.; pigs, 2·87m.; horses, 521,000; goats, 284,000; asses, 269,000; chickens, 130m.

Forestry. Excepting the agricultural zones and a few arid spots on the Pacific coast, Ecuador is a vast forest. 10·56m. ha, or 38·1% of the land area, was forested in 2000, but much of the forest is not commercially accessible. In 2001, 10·92m. cu. metres of roundwood were produced.

Fisheries. In 1993 primary sea export products were valued at US$498·9m. Fish landings in 2001 were 586,570 tonnes (almost entirely from sea fishing).

INDUSTRY

Industry produced 29·4% of GDP in 2001, including 11·7% from manufacturing. Manufacturing showed an annual increase of 2·9% in 2001. Main products include (2000, in 1,000 tonnes): residual fuel oil, 3,914; cement (1999), 2,262; distillate fuel oil, 1,751; petrol, 1,302.

Labour. Out of 3,673,200 people in urban employment in 2001, 1,026,700 were in wholesale and retail trade/repair of motor vehicles, motorcycles and personal and household goods; 610,600 in manufacturing; 244,600 in transport, storage and communications; and 239,800 in agriculture, hunting and forestry. In June 2001, 10·4% of the workforce was unemployed, down from 14·1% in June 2000.

Trade Unions. The main trade union federation is the United Workers' Front.

INTERNATIONAL TRADE

Most restrictions on foreign investment were removed in 1992 and the repatriation of profits was permitted. Foreign debt was US$16,452m. in 2002.

Imports and Exports. Imports and exports for calendar years, in US$1m.:

	1998	*1999*	*2000*	*2001*	*2002*
Imports f.o.b.	5,458	3,028	3,743	5,325	6,196
Exports f.o.b.	4,326	4,615	5,137	4,862	5,192

Ecuador is the world's leading exporter of bananas (US$954·4m. in 1999), with approximately a third of world banana exports. Other major exports (1999, in US$1m.): crude oil, 1,312·3; shrimps, 608·5; fish, 256·1; cut flowers, 180·4; cocoa, 102·7. Main export markets, 1999 (in US$1m.): USA, 1,708·2 (38·4%); Colombia, 227·2; Panama, 219·5; South Korea, 213·5; Italy, 208·1. Main import suppliers: USA, 918·5 (30·4%); Colombia, 363·4; Venezuela, 193·2; Japan, 142·0; Germany, 126·0. Main imports were (in US$1m.): machinery and transport equipment, 869·8; chemicals, 663·8; manufactured goods, 498·4; petroleum and petroleum products, 143·1; cereals, 134·8.

COMMUNICATIONS

Roads. In 2002 there were 43,197 km of roads. In 2001 there were 529,359 passenger cars (43·5 per 1,000 inhabitants) and 54,698 lorries and vans. There were 1,177 fatalities in road accidents in 1999.

In 1998 storms and floods on the coast, caused by El Niño, resulted in 2,000 km of roads being damaged or destroyed.

Rail. The railway network, once 971 km long, now has a total length of just 204 km. In 2002 passenger-km travelled came to 33m.

Civil Aviation. There are international airports at Quito (Mariscal Sucre) and Guayaquil (Simon Bolivar). The main Ecuadorian carriers are Tame Linea Aerea del Ecuador and Icaro. In 2000 Quito handled 1,953,859 passengers (1,036,578 on domestic flights) and 111,867 tonnes of freight, and Guayaquil handled 1,285,583 passengers (686,964 on domestic flights) and 38,471 tonnes of freight.

Shipping. Ecuador has three major seaports, of which Guayaquil is the most important, and six minor ones. In 2002 the merchant navy totalled 313,000 GRT of ocean-going vessels, including oil tankers 219,000 GRT. In 2001 vessels totalling 3,064,000 NRT entered ports and vessels totalling 18,761,000 NRT cleared.

Telecommunications. In 2002 there were 2,987,000 telephone subscribers, equivalent to 230·8 for every 1,000 persons, and 403,000 PCs were in use (31·1 for every 1,000 persons). Mobile phone subscribers numbered 1,560,900 in 2002 and there were 30,000 fax machines in 1995. Ecuador had 537,900 Internet users in 2002.

Postal Services. In 1998 there were 315 post offices.

SOCIAL INSTITUTIONS

Justice. The Supreme Court in Quito, consisting of a President and 30 Justices, comprises ten chambers each of three Justices. It is also a Court of Appeal. There is a Superior Court in each province, comprising chambers (as appointed by the Supreme Court) of three magistrates each. The Superior Courts are at the apex of a hierarchy of various tribunals. There is no death penalty.

The population in penal institutions in June 2002 was 7,716 (59 per 100,000 of national population).

Religion. The state recognizes no religion and grants freedom of worship to all. In 2001 there were 11·91m. Roman Catholics. There were also small numbers of Protestants and followers of other faiths. In Sept. 2003 there was one cardinal.

Education. In 2000–01 there were 199,588 pre-primary pupils with 13,755 teachers. Primary education is free and compulsory. Private schools, both primary and secondary, are under some state supervision. In 2000–01 there were 1·96m. pupils and 84,758 teachers in primary schools; and 936,406 pupils with 79,231 teachers in secondary schools. In the public sector in 1995–96 there were: 9 universities, 3

Roman Catholic, 12 technical, 1 agricultural and 2 polytechnical universities, 2 institutes of technology and 1 military polytechnic; and in the private sector: 2 universities, 1 Roman Catholic and 1 technological university. Adult literacy was 91·8% in 2001 (male, 93·4%; female, 90·3%).

In 2000–01 total expenditure on education came to 1·7% of GNP and 8·0% of total government spending.

Health. In 1995 there were 474 hospitals with 16 beds per 10,000 inhabitants. There were 15,212 physicians, 1,788 dentists, 5,212 nurses and 802 midwives in 1995.

Welfare. Those who qualify for a pension must be aged 55 and have 360 months of contributions if born before 30 Nov. 1946, or be aged 65 with 180 months of contributions. A scheme to change the age of retirement to 60 with 360 months of contributions is to be phased in gradually by Feb. 2006. In 2003 the minimum monthly pension was US$25, and the maximum pension was US$125.

Social insurance providing lump-sum benefits for unemployment is gradually being phased out in favour of a system linking payments to income and length of employment.

CULTURE

World Heritage Sites. Ecuador has four sites on the UNESCO World Heritage List: the Galápagos Islands (inscribed on the list in 1978 and 2001); the City of Quito (1978); Sangay National Park (1983); and the Historic Centre of Santa Ana de los Ríos de Cuenca (1999).

Broadcasting. There were 5·2m. radio sets in 2000 and 2·9m. TV receivers in 2001 (colour by NTSC).

Press. There were 36 daily newspapers in 2000, with a circulation of 1,220,000.

Tourism. Foreign tourists numbered 615,000 in 2000, with spending of US$402m.

DIPLOMATIC REPRESENTATIVES

Of Ecuador in the United Kingdom (Flat 3b, 3 Hans Cres., London, SW1X 0LS)
Ambassador: Eduardo Cabezas.

Of the United Kingdom in Ecuador (Citiplaza Bldg., Naciones Unidas Ave., & Republica de El Salvador, 14th Floor, Quito)
Ambassador: Richard Lewington.

Of Ecuador in the USA (2535 15th St., NW, Washington, D.C., 20009)
Ambassador: Raúl Gangotena Rivadeneira.

Of the USA in Ecuador (Avenida 12 de Octubre y Avenida Patria, Quito)
Ambassador: Kristie A. Kenney.

Of Ecuador to the United Nations
Ambassador: Luis Gallegos Chiriboga.

Of Ecuador to the European Union
Ambassador: Méntor Villagomez Merino.

FURTHER READING

Hidrobo, J. A., *Power and Industrialization in Ecuador.* Boulder (CO), 1993
Pineo, R. F., *Social and Economic Reform in Ecuador.* Univ. Press of Florida, 1996
Roos, W. and van Renterghem, O., *Ecuador in Focus: A Guide to the People, Politics and Culture.* Interlink Publishing Group, Northampton (MA), 1997
Selverston-Scher, M., *Ethnopolitics in Ecuador: Indigenous Rights and the Strengthening of Democracy.* Lynne Rienner Publishers, 2001

National statistical office: Instituto Nacional de Estadistica y Censos (INEC), Juan Larrea 534 y Riofrío, Quito.
Website (Spanish only): http://www.inec.gov.ec/

EGYPT

Jumhuriyat Misr al-Arabiya
(Arab Republic of Egypt)

Capital: Cairo
Population projection, 2010: 82·59m.
GDP per capita, 2002: (PPP$) 3,810
HDI/world rank: 0·653/120

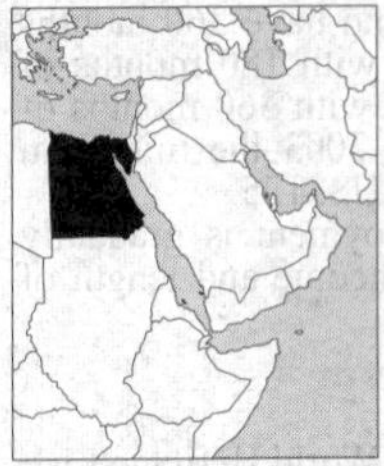

KEY HISTORICAL EVENTS

There is evidence of Neolithic habitation along the Nile and there was agricultural activity by 6000 BC. Around 3100 BC Menes united Upper and Lower Egypt and so began the rule of 31 successive pharaonic dynasties. This period was marked by three phases. The Old Kingdom, which lasted from c. 2575–2150 BC, was governed centrally from Memphis and saw the construction of the Giza pyramids. The Middle Kingdom (c. 2050–1650 BC) saw Egypt reach its zenith culturally and intellectually. The era finished with the incursions of the Hyksos, a nomadic Asiatic tribe. The New Kingdom came into being with the expulsion of the Hyksos around 1550 BC and lasted until 1050 BC. It saw Egypt achieve its greatest territorial dominance, with Syria, Palestine and northern Iraq all under Egyptian jurisdiction.

The last Pharaoh was ousted by Persian invading forces under Cambyses in 525 BC. The Persians remained in power until overrun by Alexander the Great around 330 BC. He founded the port city of Alexandria, including its great lighthouse, and made it the commercial and cultural centre of the Greek world. On his death in 305 BC, Ptolemy of Macedonia seized power, establishing a dynasty which lasted until 30 BC and the suicide of Cleopatra. Egypt then became a province of the Roman empire until Islamic forces took control in AD 642.

Under the successive rule of Turkish, Arabic and Mameluke leaders, Egypt gained an increasingly Arabic Islamic culture. In 1517 it was absorbed into the Ottoman empire. Napoleonic forces seized the country between 1798 and 1801, but were forced to flee by a combined Anglo-Ottoman force. Muhammad Ali (1805–40) succeeded in establishing a hereditary dynasty of Khedives but with the opening of the Suez Canal in 1869 and Britain's purchase of the Khedives' shares, Egypt's strategic importance paved the way for foreign intervention and domination. Egypt came under the control of Britain after 1882 until limited independence in 1922.

In the Second World War (1939–45) Egypt supported the Allies. Following a revolution in July 1952 led by Gen. Neguib, King Farouk abdicated in favour of his son but in 1953 the monarchy was abolished. Neguib became president but encountered opposition from the military when he attempted to move towards a parliamentary republic. Col. Gamal Abdel Nasser became head of state on 14 June 1954 (president from 1956), and remained in office until he died on 28 Sept. 1970. In 1956 Egypt nationalized the Suez Canal, a move which led Britain, France and Israel to mount military attacks against Egypt until forced by the UN and the USA to withdraw.

The 1960s and 1970s saw constant conflict with Israel until President Muhammad Anwar Sadat, who succeeded Nasser, made a dramatic peace treaty with Israel in March 1979. Sadat was assassinated on 6 Oct. 1981, and was succeeded by the vice-president, Lieut.-Gen. Muhammad Hosni Mubarak.

TERRITORY AND POPULATION

Egypt is bounded in the east by Israel and Palestine, the Gulf of Aqaba and the Red Sea, south by Sudan, west by Libya and north by the Mediterranean. The total area (including inland waters) is 1,001,450 sq. km, but the cultivated and settled area, that is the Nile Valley, Delta and oases, covers only 35,189 sq. km. A number of new desert cities are being developed to entice people away from the overcrowded Nile valley. Population density in this latter, 1992, 1,557·9 per sq. km. In 2001, 57·3% of the population were rural. In 2001 the population was 69,079,000.

The UN gives a projected population for 2010 of 82·59m.

1·9m. Egyptians were living abroad in 2002.

Area, population and capitals of the governorates (1986 and 1996 censuses):

Governorate	*Area (in sq. km)*	*Population (1986 census)*	*Population (1996 census)*	*Capital*
Alexandria	2,679	2,917,327	3,328,196	Alexandria
Aswan	679	801,408	973,671	Aswan
Asyut	1,553	2,223,034	2,802,185	Asyut
Behera	10,130	3,257,168	3,981,209	Damanhur
Beni Suef	1,322	1,442,981	1,860,180	Beni Suef
Cairo	214	6,052,836	6,789,497	Cairo
Dakahlia	3,471	3,500,470	4,223,665	Mansura
Damietta	589	741,264	914,614	Damietta
Fayum	1,827	1,544,047	1,989,881	Fayum
Gharbia	1,942	2,870,960	3,404,827	Tanta
Giza	85,153	3,700,054	4,779,865	Giza
Ismailia	1,442	544,427	715,009	Ismailia
Kafr El Shaikh	3,437	1,800,129	2,222,920	Kafr El Shaikh
Kalyubia	1,001	2,514,244	3,302,860	Benha
Luxor	55	—	360,503	Luxor
Matruh	212,112	160,567	211,866	Matruh
Menia	2,262	2,648,043	3,308,875	Menia
Menufia	1,532	2,227,087	2,758,499	Shibin Al Kom
New Valley	376,505	113,838	141,737	Al Kharija
Port Said	72	399,793	469,553	Port Said
Qena	1,796	2,252,315	2,441,420	Qena
Red Sea	203,685	90,491	155,695	El Gurdakah
Sharkia	4,180	3,420,119	4,287,848	Zagazig
North Sinai	27,574	171,505	252,750	Al Arish
South Sinai	33,140	28,988	54,495	At Tur
Suez	17,840	326,820	417,610	Suez
Suhag	1,547	2,455,134	3,125,000	Suhag

Principal cities, with estimated 1998 populations (in 1,000): Cairo, 7,109; Alexandria, 3,485; Giza, 2,326; Shubra Al Khayma, 912; Port Said, 492; Suez, 437.

Smaller cities, with 1996 populations (in 1,000): Mahalla Al Kubra, 395; Hulwan, 372; Tanta, 371; Mansura, 369; Luxor (Uqsur), 361; Asyut, 343; Zagazig, 267; Fayum, 261; Ismailia, 254; Kafr Ad Dawwar, 232; Aswan, 219; Damanhur, 212; Menia, 201; Beni Suef, 172; Qena, 171; Suhag, 170; Shibin Al Kom, 160; Benha, 146; Kafr Ash Shaikh, 125.

The official language is Arabic, although French and English are widely spoken.

SOCIAL STATISTICS

Births, 1999, 1,693,025 (27·0 per 1,000 population); deaths, 401,433 (6·4). Marriages, 1999, 525,000 (rate per 1,000 population, 8·4); divorces, 1999, 73,000 (1·2). Annual population growth rate, 1992–2002, 1·9%. In 1991 the average family size was 4·3 and 40% of the population was under 40 years. Life expectancy at birth, 2001, was 66·3 years for males and 70·4 years for females. Fertility rate, 2001, 3·0 births per woman; infant mortality, 2001, 35 per 1,000 live births. Egypt has made some of the best progress in recent years in reducing child mortality. The number of deaths per 1,000 live births among children under five was reduced from more than 100 in 1990 to only just over 50 in 1999.

In the Human Development Index, or HDI (measuring progress in countries in longevity, knowledge and standard of living), Egypt's index achieved the second largest improvement during the last quarter of the 20th century, rising from 0·430 in 1975 to 0·635 in 1999. Only Indonesia recorded a greater increase.

CLIMATE

The climate is mainly dry, but there are winter rains along the Mediterranean coast. Elsewhere, rainfall is very low and erratic in its distribution. Winter temperatures are comfortable everywhere, but summer temperatures are very high, especially in the south. Cairo, Jan. 56°F (13·3°C), July 83°F (28·3°C). Annual rainfall 1·2" (28 mm). Alexandria, Jan. 58°F (14·4°C), July 79°F (26·1°C). Annual rainfall 7" (178 mm). Aswan, Jan. 62°F (16·7°C), July 92°F (33·3°C). Annual rainfall (trace). Giza, Jan. 55°F (12·8°C), July 78°F (25·6°C). Annual rainfall 16" (389 mm). Ismailia, Jan. 56°F (13·3°C), July 84°F (28·9°C). Annual rainfall 1·5" (37 mm). Luxor, Jan. 59°F (15°C), July 86°F (30°C). Annual rainfall (trace). Port Said, Jan. 58°F (14·4°C), July 78°F (27·2°C). Annual rainfall 3" (76 mm).

CONSTITUTION AND GOVERNMENT

The Constitution was approved by referendum on 11 Sept. 1970. It defines Egypt as 'an Arab Republic with a democratic, socialist system' and the Egyptian people as 'part of the Arab nation'. The *President* is nominated by the People's Assembly and confirmed by plebiscite for a six-year term. In March 2005 parliament approved a proposal by President Mubarak to amend the constitution to allow for multi-candidate presidential elections. The President may appoint one or more *Vice-Presidents*.

The *People's Assembly* consists of 454 members, 444 directly elected and ten appointed by the president. An upper house, the *Shura Council*, was established in 1980, but it has a consultative role only. It has 264 members, 176 elected by popular vote and 88 appointed by the president. There is a *Constitutional Court*.

The President appoints the Prime Minister and a Council of Ministers. It is traditional for two ministers to be Coptic Christians.

National Anthem. 'Biladi' ('My homeland'); words and tune by S. Darwish.

RECENT ELECTIONS

Elections for the People's Assembly were held in three rounds on 18 and 29 Oct. and 13 Nov. 2000. Turn-out was low. The National Democratic Party (NDP) gained 388 seats (including 35 'independents'); non-partisans, 37; Wafd, 7; Al-Tagamu, 6; Nasserites, 3; Liberal Party, 1.

On 26 Sept. 1999 a referendum was held to confirm the People's Assembly's nomination of Hosni Mubarak for a fourth term as president. Turn-out was 79% with Mubarak gaining 93·97% support.

CURRENT ADMINISTRATION

President: Hosni Mubarak; b. 1928 (NDP; first sworn in 14 Oct. 1981 and most recently re-elected in Sept. 1999).

In March 2005 the cabinet comprised:

Prime Minister: Ahmad Mahmoud Nazif; b. 1952 (NDP; sworn in 14 July 2004).

Minister of Agriculture and Land Reclamation: Ahmed Abd-El Moneim El Leithy. *Civil Aviation:* Ahmed Mohammed Shafique. *Transport:* Esam Abd El-Aziz Ahmed Sharaf. *Electricity and Energy:* Hassan Ahmed Younis. *Defence and Military Production:* Field Marshal Mohamed Hussein Tantawi. *Information:* Anas el-Fiqqi. *Foreign Affairs:* Ahmed Ali Ahmed Abou Elgheit. *International Co-operation:* Fayza Abu el-Naga. *Justice:* Mahmoud Abo Elleil Rashed. *Culture:* Farouk Abdel Aziz Hosni. *Finance:* Yousef Boutrous Ghali. *Religious Affairs (Awqaf):* Mahmoud Hamdi Zakzouk. *Industry and Technology Development:* Ali al-Saidi. *Health and Population:* Dr Mohammad Awad Tag El-Din. *Foreign Trade and Industry:* Rasheed Mohamed Rasheed Hussein. *Education:* Ahmed Gamal El-Din Abd El-Fattah Mousa. *Higher Education:* Amr Salama. *Petroleum:* Amin Sameh Fahmy. *Interior:* Habib Ibrahim Al-Adly. *Tourism:* Ahmed Alaa El-Din Amin El-Maghrabi. *Irrigation and Water Resources:* Mahmoud Abd Al-Halim Abu-Zeid. *Housing, Utilities and Urban Communities:* Dr Mohammad Ibrahim Soliman. *Communications and Information Technology:* Tarek Mohamed Kamel Mahmoud. *Social Affairs and Insurance:* Almina al-Guindi. *Investment:* Mahmoud Safwat Mohyee El-Din. *Manpower and Immigration:* Ahmed El-Amawy. *Planning:* Osman Mohammed Osman. *Supply and Internal Trade:* Hassan Ali Khedr. *Youth:* Mamdouh Ahmed El Beltagy.

Office of the President: http://www.presidency.gov.eg

DEFENCE

Conscription is selective, and for one–three years (followed by refresher training over a period of up to nine years). Military expenditure totalled US$2,732m. in 2003 (US$40 per capita), representing 4·0% of GDP. According to *Deadly Arsenals*, published by the Carnegie Endowment for International Peace, Egypt has a chemical and biological weapons programme.

Army. Strength (2002) 320,000 (250,000 conscripts). In addition there were 250,000 reservists, a Central Security Force of 150,000, a National Guard of 60,000 and 20,000 Border Guards.

Navy. Major surface combatants include one destroyer and ten frigates. A small shore-based naval aviation branch operates 24 helicopters. There are naval bases at

Al Ghardaqah, Alexandria, Hurghada, Mersa Matruh, Port Said, Port Tewfik, Safaqa and Suez. Naval personnel in 2002 totalled 19,000.

Air Force. Until 1979 the Air Force was equipped largely with aircraft of USSR design, but subsequent re-equipment involves aircraft bought in the West, as well as some supplied by China. Strength (2002) is about 29,000 personnel (10,000 conscripts), 128 attack helicopters and 608 combat aircraft including F-16s, MiG-21s, *Alpha Jets* and *Mirages*.

INTERNATIONAL RELATIONS

Egypt is a member of the UN, WTO, the League of Arab States, OAPEC (Organization of Arab Petroleum Exporting Countries), the African Union, African Development Bank, COMESA, IOM, OIC, Islamic Development Bank and the International Organization of the Francophonie.

ECONOMY

In 2002 agriculture accounted for 16·5% of GDP, industry 34·8% and services 48·7%.

Overview. With slowing growth since 2000, conditions have worsened with the fall in tourism revenues since 11 Sept. 2001. The service sector dominates the economy, with tourism and the Suez Canal as important revenue earners. Egypt is chiefly a cash economy with basic banking services. There is a large informal market. Each year Egypt receives US$2bn. in military and civilian assistance from the USA. In Feb. 2002 foreign donors agreed US$10·3bn. in aid over three years. Excessive bureaucracy is a concern. Following reforms since the early 1990s, by 2000 around 50% of state-owned enterprises were fully privatized. By the end of 2000 a total of 172 state-owned enterprises had been sold, generating US$3·9bn. However, privatization has stalled. Foreign investment has financed a development project in the Sinai Peninsula and Upper Egypt that aims to increase the inhabited area of the country from 6% to 20% in 20 years.

Currency. The monetary unit is the *Egyptian pound* (EGP) of 100 *piastres*. Inflation was 2·5% in 2002. Faced with slowing economic activity, the country devalued the Egyptian pound four times in 2001. In Jan. 2003 the Egyptian pound was allowed to float against the dollar after years of a government-controlled foreign exchange regime. In May 2002 foreign exchange reserves were US$12,587m. and gold reserves 2·43m. troy oz. Total money supply in May 2002 was £E70,345m.

Budget. The financial year runs from 1 July. Revenues in 2000–01 were £E97,938m. and expenditures £E111,669m. Main sources of revenue were income and profits taxes, 28·4%; sales taxes, 18·4%; customs duties, 13·3%; oil revenue, 4·7%. Current expenditure accounted for 76·7% of total expenditures and capital expenditure 23·3%.

Performance. Real GDP growth was 3·2% in 2002 and 3·1% in 2003. Total GDP in 2003 was US$82·4bn.

Banking and Finance. The Central Bank of Egypt (founded 1960) is the central bank and bank of issue. The *Governor* is Farouk el-Okdah.

In 1999, four major public-sector commercial banks accounted for some 70% of all banking assets: the National Bank of Egypt (the largest bank, with assets of nearly £E74bn.), the Banque Misr, the Bank of Alexandria and the Banque du Caïre. There were 62 banks in total in 2002. Foreign banks have only been allowed to operate since 1996.

Foreign direct investment inflows, which were US$1,235m. in 2000, fell to just US$237m. in 2003.

There are stock exchanges in Cairo and Alexandria.

Weights and Measures. The metric system is official with the exception of the *feddan* (= 0·42 ha) to measure land. However, other traditional measures are still in use: *Kadah* = 1·91 litres; *Rob* = 4 kadahs; *Keila* = 8 kadahs; *Ardeb* = 96 kadahs; *Dirhem* = 3·12 grammes; *Rotl* = 144 dirhems (0·449 kg); *Oke* = 400 dirhems; *Qantar* = 100 rotls or 36 okes.

ENERGY AND NATURAL RESOURCES

Environment. Egypt's carbon dioxide emissions from the consumption and flaring of fossil fuels in 2002 were the equivalent of 2·0 tonnes per capita.

Electricity. Installed capacity was 17·7m. kW in 2000. Electricity generated in 2000 was 76·28bn. kWh. Consumption per capita was an estimated 1,192 kWh in 2000. Electricity sector investments reached approximately £E25bn. in 1996–97. The use of solar energy is expanding.

Oil and Gas. Oil was discovered in 1909. Oil policy is controlled by the state-owned Egyptian General Petroleum Corporation, whole or part-owner of the production and refining companies. Oil reserves in 2002 were 3·7bn. bbls. Production of crude oil has been declining from a record 42·8m. tonnes in 1996 to 34·8m. tonnes in 2000.

As a result of a series of new discoveries in 1999 and 2000 gas reserves have been steadily increasing. Annual revenue from future natural gas exports could exceed US$1·5bn. 2002 total production amounted to 22·7bn. cu. metres. There were proven natural gas reserves of 1,533bn. cu. metres in 2002.

Water. The Aswan High Dam, completed in 1970, allows for a perennial irrigation system.

The Mubarak Pumping Station, the world's largest, has been operational since Jan. 2003. Located behind the Aswan High Dam at Lake Nasser, since its inauguration it has been pumping 14·5m. cu. metres of water per day into a 67 km canal to irrigate approximately 540,000 feddans of desert land in Toshka.

Minerals. Production (2002 estimates, in tonnes): salt, 2·40m.; iron ore, 2·30m.; phosphate, 1·50m.; kaolin, 0·30m.; aluminium, 0·19m.; quartz (1995–96), 90,393; asbestos, 2,000.

Agriculture. There were 2·86m. ha of arable land in 2001 and 0·48m. ha of permanent crops. In 1996, of the total cultivated area 18·4% was reclaimed desert. Irrigation is vital to agriculture and is being developed by government programmes; it now reaches most cultivated areas and in 2001 covered 3·34m. ha. The Nile provides 85% of the water used in irrigation, some 55,000m. cu. metres annually. There were 89,527 tractors in 2001 and 2,370 harvester-threshers.

In 1994 there were 5,214 agricultural co-operatives. 0·71m. feddan of land had been distributed by 1991 to 0·35m. families under an agrarian reform programme. In 2001, 5·07m. persons were engaged in agriculture. Cotton, sugarcane and rice are subject to government price controls and procurement quotas.

Output (in 1,000 tonnes), 2000: sugarcane, 15,668; wheat, 6,564; maize, 6,395; tomatoes, 6,354; rice, 5,597; sugarbeets, 2,560; melons and watermelons, 2,225; potatoes, 1,784; oranges, 1,550; grapes, 1,008; dry onions, 1,000; sorghum, 950; dates, 890; pumpkins and squash, 650; seed cotton 644; bananas, 620; aubergines, 562; cabbages, 500; tangerines and mandarins, 450; apples, 410; peaches and nectarines, 400; cottonseed, 389; chillies and green peppers, 369; broad beans, 354; garlic, 301. Egypt is Africa's largest producer of a number of crops, including wheat, rice, tomatoes, potatoes and oranges.

Livestock, 2000: cattle, 3·18m.; sheep, 4·45m.; buffaloes, 3·20m.; goats, 3·30m.; asses, 3·05m.; camels, 120,000; chickens, 88m. Livestock products in 2000 (in 1,000 tonnes): buffalo milk, 2,079; cow milk, 1,645; meat, 1,391; eggs, 170. 464,000 tonnes of cheese were produced in 2000, making Egypt the largest cheese producer in Africa.

Forestry. In 2001, 16·60m. cu. metres of roundwood were produced.

Fisheries. The catch in 2001 was 428,651 tonnes, of which 295,422 tonnes were freshwater fish.

INDUSTRY

According to the Financial Times Survey (FT 500), the largest companies by market capitalization in Egypt on 4 Jan. 2001 were MobiNil (US$1,860·4m.), the Egyptian mobile phone provider; and Orascom Telecom (US$1,375·3m.).

Almost all large-scale enterprises are in the public sector, and these account for about two-thirds of total output. The private sector, dominated by food processing and textiles, consists of about 150,000 small and medium businesses, most employing fewer than 50 workers. Industrial production in 2001 showed a growth rate of 0·7% compared to 2000, although manufacturing grew by 4·5%.

Production, in 1,000 tonnes: cement (2001), 26,811; residual fuel oil (2000), 11,171; distillate fuel oil (2000), 5,759; petrol (2000), 5,100; fertilizers (1997–98),

4,634; crude steel (2002), 4,300; sugar (2001–02), 1,555; tobacco (1997–98), 595; paper and paperboard (2001), 460; cotton yarn (1997–98), 275. Motor vehicles (2002), 46,479 units; washing machines (1999), 252,000 units; cigarettes (2000), 53·0bn. units.

Labour. In 2002–03 the labour force was 19·9m. In 1999, 27·6% of the economically active workforce were engaged in wholesale and retail trade, restaurants and hotels; 14·9% in transport, storage and communication; 13·2% in mining and quarrying; and 9·9% in agriculture, hunting, forestry and fishing. Unemployment was 9·9% in 2003. The high birth rate of the 1980s has meant that there are now some 800,000 new entrants into the job market annually.

INTERNATIONAL TRADE

Foreign debt totalled US$30,750m. in 2002.

Imports and Exports. In 2002 exports (f.o.b.) were valued at US$7,118m.; imports (f.o.b.) were valued at US$12,879m. Services accounted for 64·1% of exports in 1998—mainly from travel and tourism—the highest percentage of any country.

Export of principal commodities in 1999: petroleum and petroleum products, 36·0%; cotton yarn and fabrics, 10·1%; clothing, 7·9%; foodstuffs, 7·9%; chemicals, 7·5%; cotton, 6·8%; aluminium, 3·3%. Imports: machinery and transport equipment, 26·2%; foodstuffs, 18·3%; manufactured goods, 18·0%; chemical products, 11·5%; mineral fuels, 6·1%. Egypt exports less than 20% of its manufactured goods. Much higher exports are deemed necessary to accelerate growth and job creation.

Main export markets, 2001: Italy, 15·0%; USA, 14·4%; UK, 9·3%; France, 4·7%; Germany, 4·1%. Main import suppliers in 2001: USA, 18·6%; Italy, 6·6%; Germany, 6·5%; France, 4·9%; China, 4·4%. Trade between Egypt and the European Union represented 35% of Egypt's foreign trade in 1999.

COMMUNICATIONS

Roads. In 1999 there were about 26,000 km of highways and main roads, 25,000 km of secondary roads and 13,000 km of other roads. The road link between Sinai and the mainland across the Suez Canal was opened in 1996. Vehicles (in 1,000), 1996: passenger cars, 1,354 (22 per 1,000 inhabitants); trucks and vans, 397; motorcycles, 418; buses, 38.

Rail. In 2000 there were 5,062 km of state railways (1,435 mm gauge), of which 62 km were electrified. Passenger-km travelled in 2000 came to 73·6bn. and freight tonne-km to 4·0bn.

There are tramway networks in Cairo and Alexandria, and a metro (62·5 km) opened in Cairo in 1987.

Civil Aviation. There are international airports at Cairo, Luxor, Alexandria and a new one which opened at Marsa Alam in 2001. The national carrier is Egyptair, which flew 67·7m. km in 1999 and carried 4,620,100 passengers (3,064,000 on international flights). In 2000 Cairo handled 8,633,307 passengers (6,384,961 on international flights) and 170,329 tonnes of freight. Luxor was the second busiest in 2000, with 2,313,000 passengers.

Shipping. In 2002 the merchant marine totalled 1,275,000 GRT, including oil tankers 223,000 GRT. In 2000 vessels totalling 69,801,000 NRT entered ports and vessels totalling 54,142,000 NRT cleared. Dockyards for containerized shipping were constructed in Alexandria, Dekheila, Damietta and Port Said in 1995–96, with two more planned for Adabeya and the Suez Canal. Egypt's largest port is Damietta, which handles 14m. tonnes of cargo annually.

Suez Canal. The Suez Canal was opened for navigation on 17 Nov. 1869 and nationalized in June 1956. By the convention of Constantinople of 29 Oct. 1888, the canal is open to vessels of all nations and is free from blockade, except in time of war. It is 173 km long (excluding 11 km of approach channels to the harbours), connecting the Mediterranean with the Red Sea. It is being deepened from 16 to 17 metres and widened from 365 to 415 metres to permit the passage of vessels of 180,000 DWT.

In 2002, 13,411 vessels (net tonnage, 445m.) went through the canal. In 2002, 369m. tonnes of cargo were transported and in 1994 a total of 15,800 passengers were carried. Toll revenue in 2002 was US$1,964m. Tolls for tankers were reduced by 20% after Jan. 1996.

Telecommunications. In 2002 there were 11,924,700 telephone subscribers (181·7 per 1,000 persons) and 1·12m. PCs were in use (17·1 per 1,000 persons). The government hopes to privatize Telecom Egypt by the end of 2005. In 2002 mobile phone subscribers numbered 4,494,700 and there were 1,900,000 Internet users. There were 34,000 fax machines in 1999.

Postal Services. There were 7,488 post offices in 1998, or one for every 8,810 persons.

SOCIAL INSTITUTIONS

Justice. The court system comprises: a Court of Cassation with a bench of five judges which constitutes the highest court of appeal in both criminal and civil cases; five Courts of Appeal with three judges; Assize Courts with three judges which deal with all cases of serious crime; Central Tribunals with three judges which deal with ordinary civil and commercial cases; Summary Tribunals presided over by a single judge which hear minor civil disputes and criminal offences. Contempt for religion and what is judged to be a false interpretation of the Koran may result in prison sentences.

The population in penal institutions in 1998 was approximately 80,000 (121 per 100,000 of national population). The death penalty is in force. There were six confirmed executions in 2004.

Religion. Islam is constitutionally the state religion. In 2001 there were 58·1m. Sunni Muslims. Some 9% of the population are Coptic Christians, the remainder being Roman Catholics, Protestants or Greek Orthodox, with a small number of Jews. A Patriarch heads the Coptic Church, and there are 25 metropolitans and bishops in Egypt; four metropolitans for Ethiopia, Jerusalem, Khartoum and Omdurman, and 12 bishops in Ethiopia. The Copts use the Diocletian (or Martyrs') calendar, which begins in AD 284. In Sept. 2003 the Roman Catholic church had one cardinal.

Education. The adult literacy rate in 2001 was 56·1% (67·2% among males and 44·8% among females). Free compulsory education is provided in primary schools (eight years). Secondary and technical education is also free. Approximately 98% of girls and 90% of boys are enrolled in the primary school system. In 2001–02 there were 4,312 pre-primary schools with 413,725 pupils and (2000–01) 17,327 teachers. In 2001–02 there were 7,141,303 primary school pupils at 15,653 schools, and (2000–01) 352,911 teachers; and, in 2001–02, 7,993 preparatory schools with 4,393,211 pupils and 1,783 general secondary schools with 1,162,879 pupils and (2000–01) 490,648 teachers. In 2001–02 there were 990,222 students in commercial secondary schools, 933,875 in industrial secondary schools and 225,311 in agricultural secondary schools.

Al Azhar institutes educate students who intend enrolling at Al Azhar University, one of the world's oldest universities and Sunni Islam's foremost seat of learning. In 2000 in the Al Azhar system there were 2,996 institutes with 605,960 pupils.

In 2002–03 there were 12 state universities, the Al Azhar university and five private universities including a French and a German university. There were 2·0m. students enrolled in university and higher education.

Education expenditure in 1998 was between 6% and 7% of GDP.

Health. In 1998 there were 7,411 hospitals with 19 beds per 10,000 inhabitants. There were 129,000 physicians, 15,211 dentists and 141,770 nurses in 1998. In 2002–03 health expenditure represented 2·2% of GDP.

Welfare. In 2002–03 there were 18·6m. welfare beneficiaries including 7·4m. recipients of pensions.

CULTURE

World Heritage Sites. There are six sites under Egyptian jurisdiction that appear on the UNESCO World Heritage List. The first five were entered on the list in 1979. They are: Memphis and its Necropolis (the Pyramid Fields from Giza to Dahshur);

Ancient Thebes with its Necropolis; Nubian Monuments from Abu Simbel to Philae; Islamic Cairo; and Abu Mena. Memphis was considered one of the Seven Wonders of the World. Ancient Thebes was the capital of Egypt during the period of the middle (c. 2000 BC) and new (c. 1600 BC) kingdoms. The Nubian monuments include the temples of Ramses II in Abu Simbel and the Sanctuary of Isis in Philae. Islamic Cairo, founded in the 10th century, became the centre of the Islamic world. Abu Mena was an early Christian holy city.

The Saint Catherine Area was added to the list in 2002. It included Saint Catherine's Monastery, an outstanding example of an Orthodox Christian monastic settlement, dating from the 6th century AD. The area is centred on Mount Sinai (Jebel Musa or Mount Horeb).

Broadcasting. The Ministry of Information operates domestic television and radio stations through the Egyptian Radio and Television Union. Two private satellite stations have been broadcasting since 2001, Dream TV and al-Mihwar. The state holds a monopoly on radio broadcasting. Number of radio receivers in 2000, 21·9m.; TV receivers (2001), 14·9m. Colour is by SECAM V.

Press. In 1999 there were 16 dailies with a total average circulation of 2·08m. To set up a newspaper requires permission from the prime minister. In 1998 a total of 1,410 book titles were published.

Tourism. There were a record 6·04m. foreign tourists in 2003, spending a record US$4·4bn. Tourism is the leading source of foreign revenue and employs nearly 150,000 people. Expenditure by Egyptian tourists abroad in 1995 was US$1·28bn., up from US$52m. in 1986. No other country increased its overseas tourist expenditure at such a rate over the same ten-year period.

Libraries. In 1998 there were 307 public libraries and 55 National libraries. They held a combined 3,740,000 volumes.

DIPLOMATIC REPRESENTATIVES

Of Egypt in the United Kingdom (26 South Street, London, W1K 1DW)
Ambassador: Gehad Refaat Madi.

Of the United Kingdom in Egypt (Ahmed Ragheb St., Garden City, Cairo)
Ambassador: Sir Derek Plumbly, KCMG.

Of Egypt in the USA (3521 International Court, NW, Washington, D.C., 20008)
Ambassador: Nabil Fahmy.

Of the USA in Egypt (8 Kamal el-Din Salah St., Garden City, Cairo)
Ambassador: C. David Welch.

Of Egypt to the United Nations
Ambassador: Maged Abdelfattah Abdelaziz.

Of Egypt to the European Union
Ambassador: Soliman Awaad.

FURTHER READING

CAPMAS, *Statistical Year Book, Arab Republic of Egypt*
Abdel-Khalek, G., *Stabilization and Adjustment in Egypt*. Edward Elgar, Cheltenham, 2001
Daly, M. W. (ed.) *The Cambridge History of Egypt*. 2 vols. CUP, 2000
Hopwood, D., *Egypt: Politics and Society 1945–1990*. 3rd ed. London, 1992
Ibrahim, Fouad N. and Ibrahim, Barbara, *Egypt: An Economic Geography*. I. B. Tauris, London, 2001
King, J. W., *Historical Dictionary of Egypt*. 2nd ed. Revised by A. Goldschmidt. Metuchen (NJ), 1995
Malek, J. (ed.) *Egypt*. Univ. of Oklahoma Press, 1993
Raymond, André, *Cairo*. Harvard Univ. Press, 2001
Rodenbeck, M., *Cairo—the City Victorious*. Picador, London, 1998
Rubin, Barry, *Islamic Fundamentalism in Egyptian Politics*. Palgrave Macmillan, Basingstoke, 2002
Vatikiotis, P. J., *History of Modern Egypt: from Muhammad Ali to Mubarak*. London, 1991

National statistical office: Central Agency for Public Mobilization and Statistics (CAPMAS), Nasr City, Cairo.
Website: http://www.capmas.gov.eg

EL SALVADOR

República de El Salvador

Capital: San Salvador
Population projection, 2010: 7·15m.
GDP per capita, 2002: (PPP$) 4,890
HDI/world rank: 0·720/103

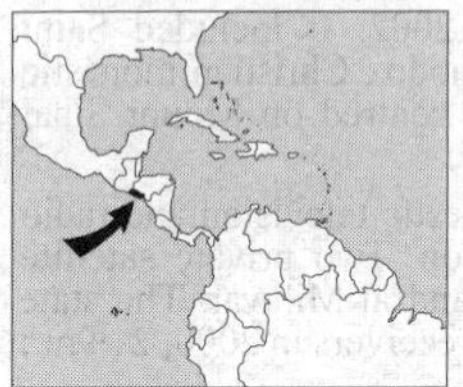

KEY HISTORICAL EVENTS

Conquered by Spain in 1526, El Salvador remained under Spanish rule until 1821. Thereafter, El Salvador was a member of the Central American Federation comprising the states of El Salvador, Guatemala, Honduras, Nicaragua and Costa Rica until this federation was dissolved in 1839. In 1841 El Salvador declared itself an independent republic.

The country's history has been marked by political violence. The repressive dictatorship of President Maximiliano Hernandez Martínez lasted from 1931 to 1944 when he was deposed as were his successors in 1948 and 1960. The military junta that followed gave way to more secure presidential succession although left-wing guerrilla groups were fighting government troops in the late 1970s. As the guerrillas grew stronger and gained control over a part of the country, the USA sent economic aid and assisted in the training of Salvadorean troops. A new constitution was enacted in Dec. 1983 but the presidential election was boycotted by the main left-wing organization, the Favabundo Marti National Liberation Front (FMLN). Talks between the government and the FMLN in April 1991 led to constitutional reforms in May, envisaging the establishment of civilian control over the armed forces and a reduction in their size. On 16 Jan. 1992 the government and the FMLN signed a peace agreement.

TERRITORY AND POPULATION

El Salvador is bounded in the northwest by Guatemala, northeast and east by Honduras and south by the Pacific Ocean. The area (including 247 sq. km of inland lakes) is 21,041 sq. km. Population (1992 census), 5,047,925 (female 52%); 2002 estimate, 6·38m., giving a population density of 303 per sq. km.

The UN gives a projected population for 2010 of 7·15m.

In 2001, 61·3% of the population were urban. In 2004, 2m. Salvadoreans were living abroad, mainly in the USA.

The republic is divided into 14 departments. Areas (in sq. km) and 2000 estimated populations:

Department	*Area*	*Population*	*Chief town*	*Population*
Ahuachapán	1,240	319,800	Ahuachapán	33,800
Cabañas	1,104	152,800	Sensuntepeque	16,800
Chalatenango	2,017	196,600	Chalatenango	15,900
Cuscatlán	756	203,000	Cojutepeque	44,500
La Libertad	1,653	682,100	Nueva San Salvador	136,900
La Paz	1,224	292,900	Zacatecoluca	33,700
La Unión	2,074	289,000	La Unión	23,100
Morazán	1,447	173,500	San Francisco	13,500
San Miguel	2,077	480,300	San Miguel	159,700
San Salvador	886	1,985,300	San Salvador	479,600[1]
San Vicente	1,184	161,100	San Vicente	32,800
Santa Ana	2,023	550,200	Santa Ana	164,500
Sonsonate	1,226	450,100	Sonsonate	58,300
Usulatán	2,130	338,300	Usulután	44,000

[1]Greater San Salvador conurbation (1992), 1,522,126.

The official language is Spanish.

SOCIAL STATISTICS

2001 births, 138,354; deaths, 29,559. Rates (2001, per 1,000 population): births, 21·6; deaths, 4·6. Life expectancy at birth in 2001 was 67·3 years for males and 73·3 years for females. Annual population growth rate, 1992–2002, 1·9%. Infant mortality, 2001, 33 per 1,000 live births; fertility rate, 2001, 3·0 births per woman.

CLIMATE

Despite its proximity to the equator, the climate is warm rather than hot, and nights are cool inland. Light rains occur in the dry season from Nov. to April, while the rest of the year has heavy rains, especially on the coastal plain. San Salvador, Jan. 71°F (21·7°C), July 75°F (23·9°C). Annual rainfall 71" (1,775 mm). San Miguel, Jan. 77°F (25°C), July 83°F (28·3°C). Annual rainfall 68" (1,700 mm).

CONSTITUTION AND GOVERNMENT

A new Constitution was enacted in Dec. 1983. Executive power is vested in a *President* and *Vice-President* elected for a non-renewable term of five years. There is a *Legislative Assembly* of 84 members elected by universal suffrage and proportional representation: 64 locally and 20 nationally, for a term of three years.

National Anthem. 'Saludemos la patria orgullosos' ('We proudly salute the Fatherland'); words by J. J. Cañas, tune by J. Aberle.

RECENT ELECTIONS

Presidential elections were held on 21 March 2004. Antonio Saca (Nationalist Republican Alliance; ARENA) received 57·7% of votes cast, ahead of Schafik Hándal (National Liberation Front) with 35·7%, Héctor Silva Argüello (United Democratic Centre–Christian Democratic Party) with 3·9% and José Rafael Machuca Zelaya (National Conciliation Party) with 2·7%.

In parliamentary elections on 16 March 2003 the FMLN (National Liberation Front) gained 31 of a possible 84 seats in the Legislative Assembly, ARENA 27, the National Conciliation Party 16, the United Democratic Centre 5 and the Christian Democratic Party 5. Turn-out was 40%.

CURRENT ADMINISTRATION

President: Antonio Saca; b. 1965 (ARENA; sworn in 1 June 2004).

In March 2005 the cabinet comprised:

Vice-President: Ana Vilma de Escobar.

Minister of Agriculture and Livestock: Mario Salaverría. *Economy:* Yolanda de Gavidia. *Defence:* Gen. Otto Romero. *Environment:* Hugo Barrera. *Finance:* Guillermo López Suárez. *Foreign Affairs:* Francisco Laínez. *Health:* José Guillermo Maza. *Governance:* René Figueroa. *Labour:* José Espinal. *Education:* Darlyn Meza. *Public Works:* David Gutiérrez. *Tourism:* Luis Cardenal.

Office of the President (Spanish only): http://www.casapres.gob.sv

DEFENCE

There is selective conscription for one year. In 2003 defence expenditure totalled US$106m. (US$16 per capita), representing 0·7% of GDP.

Army. Strength (2002): 15,000 (4,000 conscripts). The National Civilian Police numbers 12,000 and is scheduled to be increased to 16,000.

Navy. A small coastguard force based largely at Acajutla, with 700 (2002) personnel. There was also (2002) one company of Naval Infantry numbering 90.

Air Force. Strength (2002): 1,100 personnel (200 conscripts). There are 23 combat aircraft and 21 armed helicopters.

INTERNATIONAL RELATIONS

El Salvador is a member of the UN, WTO, OAS, Inter-American Development Bank, CACM, ACS and IOM.

ECONOMY

Agriculture accounted for 8·7% of GDP in 2002, industry 30·3% and services 61·0%.

Currency. The *dollar* (USD) replaced the *colón* as the legal currency of El Salvador in 2003. Inflation was 1·9% in 2002. Foreign exchange reserves were US$1,669m. and gold reserves 469,000 troy oz in June 2002. Total money supply was ₡9,608m. in Dec. 2000.

Budget. Central government budgetary revenue totalled US$1,481·3m. in 2001; expenditure, US$1,968·6m.

Performance. Real GDP growth was 1·8% in 2001 and 2·3% in 2002. Total GDP in 2003 was US$14·4bn.

Banking and Finance. The bank of issue is the Central Reserve Bank (*President*, Luz María Serpas de Portillo), formed in 1934 and nationalized in 1961. There are 15 commercial banks (two foreign). Individual private holdings may not exceed 5% of the total equity.

There is a stock exchange in San Salvador, founded in 1992.

Weights and Measures. The metric system is standard with US gallons.

ENERGY AND NATURAL RESOURCES

Environment. El Salvador's carbon dioxide emissions from the consumption and flaring of fossil fuels were the equivalent of 0·9 tonnes per capita in 2002.

Electricity. Installed capacity in 2000 was 601,000 kW, of which 395,000 kW hydro-electric. Production in 2000 was 3·55bn. kWh; consumption per capita was 676 kWh in 2000.

Minerals. El Salvador has few mineral resources. In 2002 an estimated 3·2m. tonnes of limestone were produced. Annual marine salt production averages 30,000 tonnes.

Agriculture. 27% of the land surface is given over to arable farming. There were 660,000 ha of arable land in 2001 and 250,000 ha of permanent crops. In 1995, 32·4% of the working population was engaged in agriculture. Large landholdings have been progressively expropriated and redistributed in accordance with legislation initiated in 1980. By 1994 some 12,000 individuals had received plots of 4–5 ha.

Since the mid-19th century El Salvador's economy has been dominated by coffee. Cotton is the second main commercial crop. Production, in 1,000 tonnes (2000): sugarcane, 5,145; maize, 588; sorghum, 157; coffee, 138; coconuts, 86; dry beans, 71; bananas, 70; rice, 48.

Livestock (2000): 1,212,000 cattle, 300,000 pigs, 96,000 horses, 8m. chickens. Livestock products (2000, in 1,000 tonnes): beef and veal, 34; pork, bacon and ham, 8; poultry, 48; milk, 401; eggs, 53.

Forestry. Forest area was 121,000 ha (5·8% of the land area) in 2000. In the national forests, dye woods are found, and valuable hardwoods including mahogany, cedar and walnut. Balsam trees abound: El Salvador is the world's principal source of this medicinal gum. In 2001, 5·20m. cu. metres of roundwood were cut.

Fisheries. The catch in 2001 was 17,747 tonnes (90% from marine waters).

INDUSTRY

Production, in 1,000 tonnes: cement (2001), 1,174; residual fuel oil (2000), 537; sugar (2002), 476; distillate fuel oil (2000), 163; petrol (2000), 140; paper and paperboard (2001), 56. Traditional industries include food processing and textiles.

Labour. Out of 2,412,800 people in employment in 2002, 688,500 were in wholesale and retail trade/repair of motor vehicles, motorcycles and personal and household goods/hotels and restaurants; 458,400 in agriculture, forestry and hunting; 434,100 in manufacturing; and 155,400 in health and social work, and other community, social and personal service activities. There were 160,200 unemployed persons, or 6·2% of the workforce, in 2002.

INTERNATIONAL TRADE

In May 1992 El Salvador, Guatemala and Honduras agreed to create a free trade zone for almost all goods and capital. External debt was US$5,828m. in 2002.

Imports and Exports. Imports and exports in calendar years (in US$1m.):

	1998	*1999*	*2000*	*2001*	*2002*
Imports f.o.b.	3,765·2	3,890·4	4,702·8	4,796·0	4,922·3
Exports f.o.b.	2,459·5	2,534·3	2,963·2	2,890·8	3,016·8

Principal import suppliers, 1999: USA, 37·5%; Guatemala, 11·8%; Mexico, 8·4%; Japan, 4·1%. Principal export markets, 1999: Guatemala, 23·4%; USA, 21·3%; Honduras, 14·7%; Germany, 9·0%. Main import commodities are chemicals and chemical products, transport equipment, and food and beverages; main export commodities are coffee, paper and paper products, and clothing.

COMMUNICATIONS

Roads. In 1999 there were an estimated 10,029 km of roads, including 327 km of motorways. Vehicles in use in 1997: passenger cars, 177,500; trucks and vans, 151,800. There were 656 fatalities in road accidents in 1997.

Rail. The railways are run by the National Railways of El Salvador. Route length (operational) in 2002: 283 km. There is a link to the Guatemalan system. Passenger-km travelled in 1999 came to 8m. and freight tonne-km to 19m.

Civil Aviation. The international airport is El Salvador International in San Salvador. The national carrier is Taca International Airlines, which flew 27·6m. km in 1999, carrying 1,624,100 passengers. It flies to various destinations in the USA, Mexico and all Central American countries. In 2000 El Salvador International handled 1,256,347 passengers on international flights and 32,397 tonnes of international freight.

Shipping. The main ports are Acajutla and Cutuco. Merchant shipping totalled 6,000 GRT in 2002. In 1999 vessels totalling 3,374,000 NRT entered ports and vessels totalling 566,000 NRT cleared.

Telecommunications. The telephone system has been privatized and is owned by two international telephone companies. In 2002 there were 1,556,500 telephone subscribers (241·0 per 1,000 inhabitants) and 163,000 PCs in use (25·2 for every 1,000 persons). There were 888,800 mobile phone subscribers in 2002. Internet users numbered 30,000 in 2002.

Postal Services. In 1998 there were 289 post offices.

SOCIAL INSTITUTIONS

Justice. Justice is administered by the Supreme Court (six members appointed for three-year terms by the Legislative Assembly and six by bar associations), courts of first and second instance, and minor tribunals.

Following the disbanding of security forces in Jan. 1992 a new National Civilian Police Force was created which numbered 12,000 by 2002.

El Salvador has among the highest annual murder rates in the world, at 55 per 100,000 peeople.

The population in penal institutions in July 2002 was 10,278 (158 per 100,000 of national population).

Religion. In 2001 there were 4,880,000 Roman Catholics. Under the 1962 Constitution, churches are exempted from the property tax; the Catholic Church is recognized as a legal person, and other churches are entitled to secure similar recognition. There is an archbishop in San Salvador and bishops at Santa Ana, San Miguel, San Vicente, Santiago de María, Usulután, Sonsonate and Zacatecoluca. There were about 1,070,000 Protestants in 2001 and 290,000 followers of other religions.

Education. The adult literacy rate in 2001 was 79·2% (81·9% among males and 76·6% among females). Education, run by the state, is free and compulsory. In 2000–01 there were 203,133 pupils in nursery schools, 940,457 in primary schools and 429,579 in secondary schools. In 1995–96 in the public sector there were three universities; in the private sector there were 21 universities and 14 specialized universities (1 American, 3 Evangelical, 1 Roman Catholic, 1 Open and 1 each for business, integrated education, polytechnic, science and development, teaching, science and technology, technical studies and technology). In 2000–01 there were 118,491 students and 7,285 academic staff in tertiary education.

In 1999–2000 total expenditure on education came to 2·4% of GNP and 13·4% of total government spending.

Health. In 1993 there were 78 hospitals with 17 beds per 10,000 inhabitants. There were 6,177 physicians, 5,604 dentists and 12,851 nurses in 1997.

Welfare. The Social Security Institute now administers the sickness, old age and death insurance, covering industrial workers and employees earning up to ₡700 a month. Employees in other private institutions with higher salaries are included but are excluded from the medical and hospital benefits.

CULTURE

World Heritage Sites. El Salvador has one site on the UNESCO World Heritage List: the Joya de Cerén Archaeological Site (1993), a pre-Hispanic farming community preserved under volcanic ash.

Broadcasting. Broadcasting is under the control of the Administración Nacional de Telecomunicaciones. There are six commercial television channels, a government-owned channel and two educational channels sponsored by the Ministry of Education. In 2000 there were 2·97m. radio receivers and in 2001 there were 1·49m. television sets (colour by NTSC).

Press. In 1998 there were four daily newspapers with a combined circulation of 171,000, at a rate of 28 per 1,000 inhabitants.

Tourism. There were 795,000 foreign tourists in 2000, spending US$254m.

DIPLOMATIC REPRESENTATIVES

Of El Salvador in the United Kingdom (Mayfair House, 39 Great Portland St., London, W1W 7JZ)
Ambassador: Eduardo Ernesto Vilanova-Molina.

Of the United Kingdom in El Salvador (embassy in San Salvador closed in July 2003)
Ambassador: Richard Lavers (resides at Guatemala City).

Of El Salvador in the USA (2308 California St., NW, Washington, D.C., 20008)
Ambassador: Rene A. León Rodríguez.

Of the USA in El Salvador (Urbanización Santa Elena, Antiguo Cuscatlán, San Salvador)
Ambassador: Hugh Douglas Barclay.

Of El Salvador to the United Nations
Ambassador: Carmen María Gallardo Hernández.

Of El Salvador to the European Union
Ambassador: Héctor Gonzalez Urrutia.

FURTHER READING

Kufeld, A., *El Salvador.* NY, 1991
Montgomery, T. S., *Revolution in El Salvador: Origins and Evolution.* Boulder (CO), 1982

National statistical office: Dirección General de Estadística y Censos, Calle Arce, San Salvador.

EQUATORIAL GUINEA

República de Guinea Ecuatorial

Capital: Malabo
Population projection, 2010: 590,000
GDP per capita, 2000: (PPP$) 15,073
HDI/world rank: 0·703/109

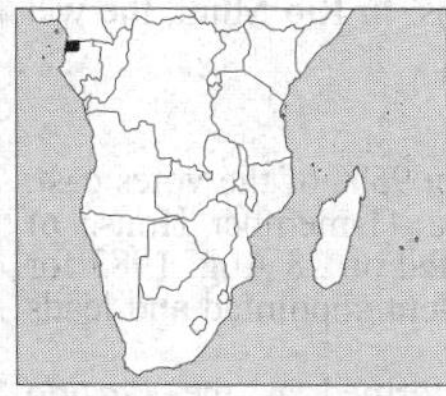

KEY HISTORICAL EVENTS

Equatorial Guinea consists of the island of Bioko, for centuries called Fernando Po; other smaller islands and the mainland territory of Rio Muni. Fernando Po was named after the Portuguese navigator Fernão do Po. The island was then ruled for three centuries by Portugal until 1778 when it was ceded to Spain. For some decades after taking possession of Fernando Po, Spain did not effectively occupy it and allowed Britain to establish a naval base at Clarence (later Santa Isabel), which was important for the suppression of slave trading over a wide area. Spain asserted its rule from the 1840s. On Fernando Po the Spanish grew cocoa on European-owned plantations using imported African labour. This traffic led to an international scandal in 1930 when Liberians were found to be held in virtual slavery. Later many Nigerians were employed, often in poor conditions.

African nationalist movements began in the 1950s. Internal self-government was granted in 1963. In 1969 Spain suspended the constitution but then, under pressure to grant independence, agreed on condition of its approval by a referendum, which was given on 11 Aug. 1969. The two parts of Equatorial Guinea were united under Macías Nguema who established single-party rule. Up to a third of the population was killed or else left the country. Macías was declared President-for-Life in July 1972 but was overthrown by a military coup on 3 Aug. 1979.

A constitution approved by a referendum on 3 Aug. 1982 restored some institutions but a Supreme Military Council remained the sole political body until constitutional rule was resumed on 12 Oct. 1982.

TERRITORY AND POPULATION

The mainland part of Equatorial Guinea is bounded in the north by Cameroon, east and south by Gabon, and west by the Gulf of Guinea, in which lie the islands of Bioko (formerly Macías Nguema, formerly Fernando Póo) and Annobón (called Pagalu from 1973 to 1979). The total area is 28,051 sq. km (10,831 sq. miles) and the population at the 1994 census was 406,151. Estimate (July 2003), 510,500; density, 18 per sq. km. Another 110,000 are estimated to remain in exile abroad.

The UN gives a projected population for 2010 of 590,000.

In 2001, 50·8% of the population were rural.

The seven provinces are grouped into two regions—Continental (C), chief town Bata; and Insular (I), chief town Malabo—with areas and populations as follows:

	Sq. km	*Census 1994 (estimate)*	*Chief town*
Annobón (I)	17	2,800	San Antonio de Palea
Bioko Norte (I)	776	75,100	Malabo
Bioko Sur (I)	1,241	12,600	Luba
Centro Sur (C)	9,931	60,300	Evinayong
Kié-Ntem (C)	3,943	92,800	Ebebiyin
Litoral (C)	6,665[1]	100,000	Bata
Wele-Nzas (C)	5,478	62,500	Mongomo

[1]Including the adjacent islets of Corisco, Elobey Grande and Elobey Chico (17 sq. km).

In 2003 the capital, Malabo, had an estimated population of 92,900.

The main ethnic group on the mainland is the Fang, which comprises 85% of the total population; there are several minority groups along the coast and adjacent islets. On Bioko the indigenous inhabitants (Bubis) constitute 60% of the population there, the balance being mainly Fang and coast people. On Annobón the indigenous inhabitants are the descendants of Portuguese slaves and still speak a Portuguese patois. The official language is Spanish.

SOCIAL STATISTICS

1997 births, 17,400; deaths, 6,100. Birth rate (per 1,000 population, 1997 estimate): 39·3; death, 13·7. Life expectancy (2001): male, 47·6 years; female, 50·4. Annual population growth rate, 1992–2002, 2·6%. Infant mortality, 2001, 101 per 1,000 live births; fertility rate, 2001, 5·9 births per woman.

CLIMATE

The climate is equatorial, with alternate wet and dry seasons. In Rio Muni, the wet season lasts from Dec. to Feb.

CONSTITUTION AND GOVERNMENT

A Constitution was approved in a plebiscite in Aug. 1982 by 95% of the votes cast. It provided for an 11-member Council of State, and for a 41-member House of Representatives of the People, the latter being directly elected on 28 Aug. 1983 for a five-year term and re-elected on 10 July 1988. The President appointed and leads a Council of Ministers.

On 12 Oct. 1987 a single new political party was formed as the *Partido Democrático de Guinea Ecuatorial.*

A referendum on 17 Nov. 1991 approved the institution of multi-party democracy, and a law to this effect was passed in Jan. 1992. The electorate is restricted to citizens who have resided in Equatorial Guinea for at least ten years. A parliament created as a result, the *Cámara de Representantes del Pueblo* (*House of People's Representatives*), has 80 seats, with members elected for a five year term by proportional representation in multi-member constituencies.

National Anthem. 'Caminemos pisando las sendas' ('Let us journey treading the pathways'); words by A. N. Miyongo, tune anonymous.

RECENT ELECTIONS

At the *National Assembly* elections on 25 April 2004, boycotted by most opposition parties, the ruling Democratic Party of Equatorial Guinea (PDGE) won 68 of the 100 seats with 47·5% of the vote, its allies (the so-called 'democratic opposition') won 30 with 40·5% and the Convergence for Social Democracy won 2 with 6·0%.

Presidential elections were held on 15 Dec. 2002. President Nguema Mbasogo was re-elected with 97·1% of votes cast, against 2·2% for Celestino Bonifacio Bacalé. Opposition parties withdrew their candidates during polling, citing irregularities.

CURRENT ADMINISTRATION

President of the Supreme Military Council: Brig.-Gen. Teodoro Obiang Nguema Mbasogo; b. 1943 (PDGE; in office since 1979, most recently re-elected in 2002).

In March 2005 the government comprised:

Prime Minister: Miguel Abia Biteo Borico; b. 1961 (PDGE; sworn in 14 June 2004).

First Deputy Prime Minister and Minister of Internal Affairs: Marcelino Oyono Ntutumu. *Second Deputy Prime Minister, in Charge of Social Affairs and Human Rights:* Ricardo Mangue Obama Nfubea.

Minister of Foreign Affairs and International Co-operation: Micha Ondo Bilé. *Justice and Religion:* Angel Masié Mibuy. *Economy, Commerce and Promotion:* Jaime Ela Ndong. *Interior and Local Corporations:* Clemente Engonga Nguema Onguene. *National Defence:* Gen. Antomio Mba Nguema. *National Security:* Col. Manuel Nguema Mba. *Planning, Economic Development and Public Investment:* Carmelo Modu Acusé Bindang. *Mines, Industry and Energy:* Atanasio Ela Ntugu Nsa. *Finance and Budget:* Marcelino Owono Edu. *Women's Development:* Jesusa Obono Engono. *Health and Social Welfare:* Justino Obama Nvé. *Fisheries and Environment:* Fortunato Ofa Mbo. *Labour and Social Security:* Enrique Mercader Costa. *Transport, Technology, Posts and Communications:* Demetrio Elo Ndong Nsefumu. *Education, Science and Sports:* Cristobal Meñana Ela. *Agriculture and Forestry:* Teodoro Nguema Obiang Mangue. *Information, Tourism, Culture and*

Government Spokesperson: Alfonso Nsue Mokuy. *Infrastructure and Urban Planning:* Aniceto Ebiaka Muete. *Minister of State at the Presidency:* Alejandro Evuna Owono Asangono. *Secretary General of the Government in Charge of Administrative Co-ordination and Relations with Parliament:* Antonio Martin Ndong Ntutumu.

DEFENCE

In 2003 defence expenditure totalled US$6m. (US$12 per capita), representing 0·2% of GDP.

Army. The Army consists of three infantry battalions with (2002) 1,100 personnel. There is also a paramilitary Guardia Civil.

Navy. A small force, numbering 120 in 2002 and based at Malabo and Bata, operates four inshore patrol craft.

Air Force. There are no combat aircraft or armed helicopters. Personnel (2002), 100.

INTERNATIONAL RELATIONS

Equatorial Guinea is a member of the UN, the African Union, African Development Bank and the International Organization of the Francophonie, and is an ACP member state of the ACP-EU relationship.

ECONOMY

Agriculture accounted for 8·9% of GDP in 2002, industry 86·0% (the highest percentage of any country) and services 5·0%.

Currency. On 2 Jan. 1985 the country joined the Franc Zone and the *ekpwele* was replaced by the *franc CFA* (XAF) which now has a parity value of 655·957 francs CFA to one euro. Foreign exchange reserves were US$77m. in April 2002 and total money supply was 68,514m. francs CFA. Inflation in 2002 was 12·0%.

Budget. In 1998 revenue was 76,974m. francs CFA and expenditure 80,728m. francs CFA. Oil revenue accounts for more than two-thirds of revenues; current expenditure accounted for 63·6% of total expenditures in 1998.

Performance. Equatorial Guinea is one of the world's fastest growing economies thanks to the rapid expansion of its oil sector. The economy grew by a record 82·0% in 1997. The growth rate was 37·5% in 2001, 19·0% in 2002 and 14·7% in 2003. In 1997, 1998, 1999 and 2001 Equatorial Guinea's real GDP growth was the highest in the world. In 2003 total GDP was US$2·9bn.

Banking and Finance. The *Banque des Etats de l'Afrique Centrale* (*Governor*, Jean-Félix Mamalepot) became the bank of issue in Jan. 1985. There are two commercial banks (Caisse Commune d'Epargne et d'Investissement Guinea Ecuatorial; Société Générale des Banques GE) and two development banks.

ENERGY AND NATURAL RESOURCES

Environment. Carbon dioxide emissions from the consumption and flaring of fossil fuels in 2002 were the equivalent of 8·3 tonnes per capita.

Electricity. There are two hydro-electric plants. Installed capacity was 18,000 kW in 2000. Production was around 23m. kWh in 2000; consumption per capita in 2000 was an estimated 50 kWh.

Oil and Gas. Oil production started in 1992, and in 2003 totalled 12·3m. tonnes, up from 5·6m. tonnes in 2000. In 2002 Equatorial Guinea's oil production increased at a faster rate than that of any other country. Mobil is the biggest operator in the country but other US-based oil companies are investing heavily. Since oil in commercial quantities was discovered in 1995 Equatorial Guinea has attracted more than US$3bn. in foreign direct investment.

Natural gas reserves were 100bn. cu. metres in 2002.

Minerals. There is some small-scale alluvial gold production.

Agriculture. There were 130,000 ha of arable land in 2001 and 100,000 ha of permanent crops. Subsistence farming predominates, and in 2002 approximately

69% of the economically active population were engaged in agriculture. Production (in 1,000 tonnes, in 2000): cassava, 45; sweet potatoes, 36; bananas, 20; coconuts, 6; cocoa beans, 4; coffee, 4. Plantations in the hinterland have been abandoned by their Spanish former owners and, except for cocoa and coffee, commercial agriculture is under serious difficulties. Livestock (2000): cattle, 5,000; goats, 8,000; pigs, 5,000; sheep, 36,000.

Forestry. In 2000 forests covered 1·75m. ha, or 62·5% of the total land area. Timber production in 2001 totalled 811,000 cu. metres.

Fisheries. The total catch in 2001 was estimated to be 3,500 tonnes (71% from sea fishing). Tuna and shellfish are caught.

INDUSTRY

The once-flourishing light industry collapsed under the Macías regime. Oil production is now the major activity. Production of veneer sheets, 2001, 15,000 cu. metres. Food processing is also being developed.

Labour. In 1996 the labour force was 171,000 (65% males). The wage-earning non-agricultural workforce is small. The average monthly wage was 14,000 francs CFA in 1992.

INTERNATIONAL TRADE

Foreign debt was US$260m. in 2002.

Imports and Exports. In 2001 imports totalled 593·4bn. francs CFA and exports 1,346·7bn. francs CFA.

Main export markets, 1998: USA, 62·0%; Spain, 17·3%; China, 8·9%; France, 3·4%; Japan, 3·4%. Main import suppliers, 1998: USA, 35·4%; France, 15·0%; Cameroon, 9·9%; Spain, 9·9%; UK, 6·2%. Principal export commodities are petroleum, cocoa and timber; principal import commodities are machinery and transport equipment, and petroleum and petroleum products.

COMMUNICATIONS

Roads. In 1999 the road network covered 2,880 km. Most roads are in a state of disrepair. Vehicles in use numbered 2,040 (1,520 passenger cars, or 3·3 per 1,000 inhabitants, and 540 vans and trucks) in 1996.

Civil Aviation. There is an international airport at Malabo. There were international flights in 2003 to Cotonou, Douala, Libreville, Madrid, Yaoundé and Zürich. In 1998 Malabo handled 54,000 passengers.

Shipping. Bata is the main port, handling mainly timber. The other ports are Luba, formerly San Carlos (bananas, cocoa), in Bioko, and Malabo, Evinayong and Mbini on the mainland. Ocean-going shipping totalled 29,000 GRT in 2002.

Telecommunications. Telephone services are rudimentary. In 2002 there were 35,800 telephone subscribers (73·4 for every 1,000 persons) and the number of PCs in use was 4,000 (7·2 per 1,000 persons). There were 32,000 mobile phone subscribers in 2002. In 1995 there were around 100 fax machines. In 2002 Internet users numbered 1,800.

Postal Services. There were 23 post offices in 1994.

SOCIAL INSTITUTIONS

Justice. The Constitution guarantees an independent judiciary. The Supreme Tribunal, the highest court of appeal, is located at Malabo. There are Courts of First Instance and Courts of Appeal at Malabo and Bata.

Religion. Christianity was proscribed under President Macias but reinstated in 1979. In 2001 there were 390,000 Roman Catholics with the remainder of the population followers of other religions.

Education. In 2000–01 there were 596 teachers for 16,654 children in pre-primary schools; 1,754 teachers for 72,791 pupils in primary schools; and (1999–2000) 20,679 secondary pupils with 836 teachers. In 1993 there were 2 teacher training colleges, 2 post-secondary vocational schools and 1 agricultural institute. Adult literacy was 84·2% in 2001 (male, 92·8%; female, 76·0%). The rate for males is second only to Zimbabwe among African countries. In 2000–01 total expenditure on education came to 1·9% of GNP.

Health. In 1988 there were 29 hospital beds per 10,000 inhabitants. There were 105 physicians, 4 dentists, 169 nurses and 9 midwives in 1996.

CULTURE

Broadcasting. Two radio programmes are broadcast by the state-controlled Radio Nacional de Guinea Ecuatorial and Televisión Nacional. There is also a commercial radio network, and a cultural programme produced with Spanish collaboration. In 1997 there were 180,000 radio and 4,000 TV receivers (colour by SECAM).

Press. In 1996 there was one daily newspaper with a circulation of 2,000, at a rate of 4·9 per 1,000 inhabitants.

Tourism. Foreign tourists brought in revenue of US$2m. in 1998.

DIPLOMATIC REPRESENTATIVES

Of Equatorial Guinea in the United Kingdom
Ambassador: Eduardo Ndong Elo Nzang (resides at Paris).

Of the United Kingdom in Equatorial Guinea
Ambassador: Richard Wildash, LVO (resides at Yaoundé, Cameroon).

Of Equatorial Guinea in the USA (2020 16th St., NW, Washington, D.C., 20009)
Ambassador: Teodoro Biyogo Nsue Okomo.

Of Equatorial Guinea to the United Nations
Ambassador: Lino Sima Ekua Avomo.

Of Equatorial Guinea to the European Union
Ambassador: Victorino Nka Obiang Maye.

The USA does not have an embassy in Equatorial Guinea; US relations with Equatorial Guinea are handled through the US Embassy in Yaoundé, Cameroon.

FURTHER READING

Fegley, Randall, *Equatorial Guinea, an African Tragedy.* New York, 1989
Liniger-Goumaz, M., *Guinea Ecuatorial: Bibliografía General.* Geneva, 1974–91
Molino, A. M. del, *La Ciudad de Clarence.* Madrid, 1994

National statistical office: Dirección General de Estadísticas y Cuentas Nacionales.
Website (Spanish only): http://www.dgecnstat-ge.org

ERITREA

Capital: Asmara
Population projection, 2010: 5·26m.
GDP per capita, 2002: (PPP$) 890
HDI/world rank: 0·439/156

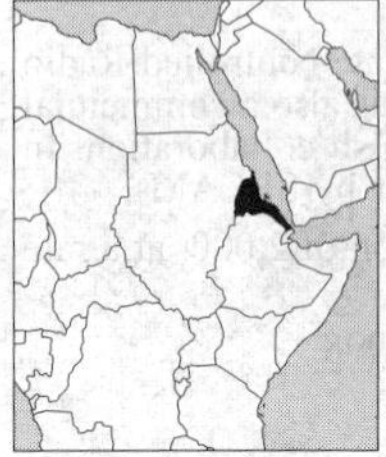

KEY HISTORICAL EVENTS

Italy was the colonial ruler from 1890 until 1941 when Eritrea fell to British forces and a British protectorate was set up. This ended in 1952 when the UN sanctioned federation with Ethiopia. In 1962 Ethiopia became a unitary state and Eritrea was incorporated as a province. Eritreans began an armed struggle for independence under the leadership of the Eritrean People's Liberation Front (EPLF) which culminated successfully in the capture of Asmara on 24 May 1991. Thereafter the EPLF maintained a *de facto* independent administration recognized by the Ethiopian government. Sovereignty was proclaimed on 24 May 1993. In 1999 fighting broke out along the border with Ethiopia. After the failure of international mediation, the 13-month long-truce between Eritrea and Ethiopia ended in May 2000. Ethiopia launched a major offensive in the ongoing war over territorial disputes and claimed victory. In June both sides agreed to an Organization of African Unity peace deal to end the two-year border war.

TERRITORY AND POPULATION

Eritrea is bounded in the northeast by the Red Sea, southeast by Djibouti, south by Ethiopia and west by Sudan. Some 300 islands form the Dahlak Archipelago, most of them uninhabited. For the dispute with Yemen over the islands of Greater and Lesser Hanish *see* YEMEN: Territory and Population. Its area is 121,100 sq. km (46,800 sq. miles). Population, 2003 estimate, 4,362,300 (80·9% rural in 2001); density, 36·0 per sq. km.

The UN gives a projected population for 2010 of 5·26m.

In 1995, 1m. Eritreans lived abroad, 0·5m. as refugees in Sudan. A UN Programme for Refugee Reintegration and Rehabilitation of Resettlement Areas in Eritrea (PROFERI) is in operation.

There are six regions: Anseba, Debub, Debubawi Keyih Bahri, Gash Barka, Maekel and Semenawi Keyih Bahri. The capital is Asmara (2002 estimated population, 500,600). Other large towns (with 2002 populations) are Keren (74,800) and Adi Ugri (25,700). An agreement of July 1993 gives Ethiopia rights to use the ports of Assab and Massawa.

48% of the population speak Tigrinya and 31% Tigré, and there are seven other indigenous languages. Arabic is spoken on the coast and along the Sudanese border, and English is used in secondary schools. Arabic and Tigrinya are the official languages.

SOCIAL STATISTICS

Births, 1995, 131,000; deaths, 48,000. Rates, 1995 (per 1,000 population): birth, 41·4; death, 15·2. Annual population growth rate, 1992–2002, 2·4%. Life expectancy at birth, 2001, was 50·9 years for males and 54·1 years for females. Infant mortality, 2001, 72 per 1,000 live births; fertility rate, 2001, 5·4 births per woman.

CLIMATE

Massawa, Jan. 78°F (25·6°C), July 94°F (34·4°C). Annual rainfall 8" (193 mm).

CONSTITUTION AND GOVERNMENT

A referendum to approve independence was held on 23–25 April 1993. The electorate was 1,173,506. 99·8% of votes cast were in favour.

The transitional government consists of the *President* and a 150-member *National Assembly.* It elects the President, who in turn appoints the *State Council* made up of 14 ministers and the governors of the ten provinces. The President chairs both the State Council and the National Assembly.

National Anthem. 'Ertra, Ertra, Ertra' ('Eritrea, Eritrea, Eritrea'); words by S. Beraki, tune by I. Meharezghi and A. Tesfatsion.

RECENT ELECTIONS

In the presidential and legislative elections in May 1997, President Afewerki was re-elected to office. National assembly elections, postponed in 1998, were set to take place before the end of 2003 but have been put back indefinitely. In the meantime several dissident politicians have been jailed.

CURRENT ADMINISTRATION

President: Issaias Afewerki; b. 1945 (PFDJ; elected 22 May 1993 and re-elected in May 1997).

In March 2005 the ministers in the State Council were:

Minister of Agriculture: Arefaine Berhe. *Construction:* Abraha Asfaha. *Defence:* Sebhat Ephrem. *Education:* Osman Saleh. *Energy and Mining:* Tesfai Ghebreselassie. *Finance:* Berhane Abrehe. *Fisheries and Maritime Resources:* Ahmed Haj Ali. *Foreign Affairs:* Ali Said Abdella. *Health:* Saleh Meki. *Information:* Naizghi Kiflu. *Justice:* Fozia Hashim. *Labour and Human Welfare:* Askalu Menkerios. *Land, Water and Environment:* Woldemichael Ghebremariam. *Tourism:* Amna Nur Husayn. *National Development:* Wolday Futur. *Trade and Industry:* Giorgis Teklemikael. *Transport and Communications:* Woldemikael Abraha.

DEFENCE

Conscription for 18 months was introduced in 1994 for all Eritreans between the ages of 18 and 40, with some exceptions. It has since been reduced to 16 months. The total strength of all forces was estimated at 172,200 in 2002.

Defence expenditure totalled US$73m. in 2003 (US$17 per capita and 9·2% of GDP).

Army. The army had a strength of around 170,000 in 2002. There were an additional 120,000 reservists available.

Navy. Most of the former Ethiopian Navy is now in Eritrean hands. The main bases and training establishments are at Massawa, Assab and Dahlak. Personnel numbered 1,400 in 2002.

Air Force. Personnel numbers were estimated at 800 in 2002. There were over 17 combat aircraft including MiG-23s, MiG-21s and MiG-29s.

INTERNATIONAL RELATIONS

A border dispute between Eritrea and Ethiopia broke out in May 1998. Eritrean troops took over the border town of Badame after a skirmish between Ethiopian police units and armed men from Eritrea. Ethiopia maintained that Badame and Sheraro, a nearby town, had always been part of Ethiopia and called Eritrea's action an invasion. An agreement ending hostilities was signed in June 2000, followed by a peace accord in Dec. A buffer zone has been created to separate the armies.

Eritrea is a member of the UN, the African Union, African Development Bank, COMESA, the Intergovernmental Authority on Development and is an ACP member state of the ACP-EU relationship.

ECONOMY

In 2002 agriculture accounted for 12·9% of GDP, industry 25·0% and services 62·1%.

Eritrea's resources are meagre, the population small and poorly-educated; communications are difficult and there is a shortage of energy.

Currency. A new currency, the *nakfa*, has replaced the Ethiopian currency, the *birr*. However, its introduction led to tensions with Ethiopia, adversely affecting cross-border trade. Inflation was 16·9% in 2002.

Budget. Revenues in 2001 were 3,362m. nafka and expenditures 4,545m. nafka.

Performance. Total GDP in 2003 was US$0·7bn. The economy expanded by 10·2% in 2001 following the end of the conflict with neighbouring Ethiopia but then by only 1·8% in 2002.

Banking and Finance. The central bank is the National Bank of Eritrea (*Governor*, Tequie Beyene). All banks and financial institutions are state-run. There is a Commercial Bank of Eritrea with 15 branches, an Eritrean Investment and Development Bank with 13 branches, a Housing and Commercial Bank of Eritrea with seven branches and an Insurance Corporation.

ENERGY AND NATURAL RESOURCES

Environment. Carbon dioxide emissions from the consumption and flaring of fossil fuels were the equivalent of 0·2 tonnes per capita in 2002.

Electricity. Installed capacity was 0·2m. kW in 2000. Electricity is provided to only some 10% of the population. Total production was around 216m. kWh in 2000.

Minerals. There are deposits of gold, silver, copper, zinc, sulphur, nickel, chrome and potash. Basalt, limestone, marble, sand and silicates are extracted. Oil exploration is taking place in the Red Sea. Salt production totals 200,000 tonnes annually.

Agriculture. Agriculture engaged approximately 77% of the economically active population in 2002. Several systems of land ownership (state, colonial, traditional) co-exist. In 1994 the PFDJ proclaimed the sole right of the state to own land. There were 500,000 ha of arable land in 2001 and 3,000 ha of permanent crops. 21,000 ha were irrigated in 2001. There were 463 tractors in 2001 and 125 harvester-threshers. Main agricultural products, 2000 (in 1,000 tonnes): sorghum, 100; potatoes, 35; barley, 25; millet, 25; maize, 12; wheat, 10. Livestock, 2000: cattle, 1·80m.; sheep, 1·54m.; goats, 1·50m.; camels, 73,000; chickens, 1m.

Forestry. In 2000 forests covered 1·59m. ha, or 13·5% of the total land area. Timber production in 2001 was 2·29m. cu. metres.

Fisheries. The total catch in 2001 was 8,820 tonnes, exclusively from marine waters, but a joint French–Eritrean project to assess fish stocks in the Red Sea suggests a sustainable yield of up to 70,000 tonnes a year.

INDUSTRY

Light industry was well developed in the colonial period but capability has declined. Processed food, textiles, leatherwear, building materials, glassware and oil products are produced. Industrial production accounted for 22·5% of GDP in 2001, with the manufacturing sector providing 10·8%.

Labour. In 1996 the labour force was 1,649,000 (53% males).

INTERNATIONAL TRADE

Eritrea is dependent on foreign aid for most of its capital expenditure. Total external debt in 2002 was US$528m.

Imports and Exports. In 2000 exports were valued at US$36·8m. and imports at US$471·4m.

The main exports are drinks, leather and products, textiles and oil products. The leading imports are machinery and transport equipment, basic manufactures, and food and live animals.

Principal import suppliers in 1998 were Italy, 17·4%; United Arab Emirates, 16·2%; Germany, 5·7%; UK, 4·5%; USA, 4·2%. Principal export markets, 1998:

Sudan, 27·2%; Ethiopia, 26·5%; Japan, 13·2%; United Arab Emirates, 7·3%; Italy, 5·3%.

COMMUNICATIONS

Roads. There were some 4,010 km of roads in 1999, around 875 km of which were paved. A tarmac road links the capital Asmara with one of the main ports, Massawa. In 1996 passenger cars in use numbered 5,940 (1·5 per 1,000 inhabitants). About 500 buses operate regular services.

Rail. In 2000 the reconstruction of the 117 km Massawa–Asmara line reached Embatkala, thus opening up an 80 km stretch from Massawa on the coast. In 2003 the line was re-built right through to Asmara.

Civil Aviation. There is an international airport at Asmara (Yohannes IV Airport). In 2003 there were scheduled flights to Cairo, Djibouti, Dubai, Frankfurt, Jeddah, Milan, Nairobi and Sana'a. In 2000 Asmara handled 103,000 passengers (88,000 on international flights) and 7,300 tonnes of freight.

Shipping. Massawa is the main port; Assab used to be the main port for imports to Ethiopia. Both were free ports for Ethiopia until the onset of hostilities. Merchant shipping totalled 21,000 GRT in 2002.

Telecommunications. International telephone links were restored in 1992. There were 35,900 telephone subscribers in 2002 (9·0 for every 1,000 inhabitants) and 10,000 PCs were in use (2·5 per 1,000 inhabitants). In 1995 there were 800 fax machines. In 2002 Eritrea had 9,000 Internet users.

Postal Services. In 1996 there were 37 post offices, equivalent to one for every 91,900 persons.

SOCIAL INSTITUTIONS

Justice. The legal system derives from a decree of May 1993.

Religion. Half the population are Sunni Muslims (along the coast and in the north), and half Coptic Christians (in the south).

Education. Adult literacy was about 56·7% in 2001 (68·2% among males and 34·6% among females). In 2000–01 there were 298,691 pupils and 6,668 teachers in primary schools, and 142,124 pupils at secondary schools with 2,710 teachers. There is one university, with 3,200 students and 250 academic staff in 1994–95. In 1998–99 total expenditure on education came to 4·1% of GNP.

Health. In 1993 there were 10 small regional hospitals, 32 health centres and 65 medical posts. In 1996 there were 108 physicians, 4 dentists, 574 nurses and 79 midwives.

Eritrea has one of the highest rates of undernourishment of any country. The proportion of the population classified as undernourished was 73% in the period 2000–02, up from 68% in 1995–97.

CULTURE

Broadcasting. There is daily radio and TV broadcasting. In 2001 there were 150,000 TV receivers and in 2000 there were 1,650,000 radio receivers.

Press. There is a government daily in Arabic and Tigrinya. In Sept. 2001 the government closed down the country's eight independent newspapers. A number of journalists have been jailed.

Tourism. There were 113,000 foreign tourists in 2001. Receipts in 2000 totalled US$36m.

DIPLOMATIC REPRESENTATIVES

Of Eritrea in the United Kingdom (96 White Lion Street, London, N1 9PF)
Ambassador: Negassi Sengal Ghebrezghi.

Of the United Kingdom in Eritrea (66–68 Mariam Ghimbi Street, PO Box 5584, Asmara)
Ambassador: Mike Murray.

Of Eritrea in the USA (1708 New Hampshire Avenue, NW, Washington, D.C., 20009)
Ambassador: Girma Asmerom.

Of the USA in Eritrea (Franklin D. Roosevelt St., PO Box 211, Asmara)
Ambassador: Scott H. DeLisi.

Of Eritrea to the United Nations
Ambassador: Ahmed Tahir Baduri.

Of Eritrea to the European Union
Ambassador: Aldebrhan Weldegiorgis.

FURTHER READING

Connel, D., *Against All Odds: a Chronicle of the Eritrean Revolution.* Red Sea Press, Trenton (NJ), 1993
Fegley, Randall, *Eritrea.* [Bibliography] ABC-Clio, Oxford and Santa Barbara (CA), 1995
Henze, Paul, *Eritrea's War: Confrontation, International Response, Outcome, Prospects.* Shama, Addis Ababa, 2001
Lewis, R., *Eritrea: Africa's Newest Country.* Christian Aid, London, 1993
Negash, Tekeste and Tronvoll, Kjetil, *Brothers at War: Making Sense of the Eritrean–Ethiopian War.* Ohio Univ. Press and James Currey, Oxford, 2001
Wrong, Michaela, *I Didn't Do It For You: How the World Betrayed a Small African Nation.* Fourth Estate, London, 2005

ESTONIA

Eesti Vabariik
(Republic of Estonia)

Capital: Tallinn
Population projection, 2010: 1·23m.
GDP per capita, 2002: (PPP$) 12,260
HDI/world rank: 0·853/36

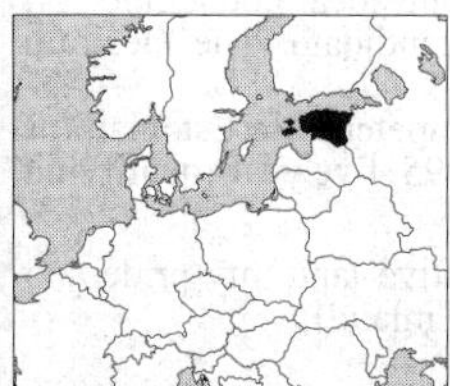

KEY HISTORICAL EVENTS

Estonia was part of the Holy Roman Empire until it became a Swedish possession in the 17th century. On Sweden's defeat by Peter the Great, Estonia passed to the Russian Empire in 1721. The workers' and soldiers' Soviets, which came to prominence in 1917, were overthrown with the assistance of British naval forces in May 1919 and a democratic republic proclaimed. In March 1934 this regime was, in turn, overthrown by a fascist coup. The secret protocol of the Soviet-German agreement of 23 Aug. 1939 assigned Estonia to the Soviet sphere of interest. An ultimatum (16 June 1940) led to the formation of the Estonian Soviet Socialist Republic. At a referendum in March 1991, 77·8% of votes cast were in favour of independence. A fully independent status was conceded by the USSR State Council on 6 Sept. 1991. Estonia was admitted to the Council of Europe in 1993, and became a member of NATO in March 2004 and the European Union in May 2004.

TERRITORY AND POPULATION

Estonia is bounded in the west and north by the Baltic Sea, east by Russia and south by Latvia. There are 1,521 offshore islands, of which the largest are Saaremaa and Hiiumaa, but only 12 are permanently inhabited. Area, 45,227 sq. km (17,462 sq. miles); population, 1,370,052 (2000 census), giving a density of 30·3 per sq. km. Estimate, Jan. 2003: 1,356,000.

The UN gives a projected population for 2010 of 1·23m.

As of 1 Jan. 2001, 66·6% of the population lived in urban areas. Of the whole population, Estonians accounted for 67·9%, Russians 25·6%, Ukrainians 2·1%, Belorussians 1·3% and Finns 0·9%. The capital is Tallinn (population, 397,200 or 29·3%). Other large towns are Tartu (101,200), Narva (67,800), Kohtla-Järve (46,800) and Pärnu (44,800). There are 15 counties, 47 towns and 202 rural municipalities.

The official language is Estonian.

SOCIAL STATISTICS

2003 registered births, 13,198; deaths, 18,231. Rates (per 1,000 population): birth, 9·7; death, 13·4. There were 10,834 induced abortions in 2002. Expectation of life in 2002 was 65·2 years for males and 77·0 for females. The annual population growth rate in the period 1992–2002 was –1·4%, giving Estonia one of the fastest declining populations of any country. Infant mortality in 2002 was 5·7 per 1,000 births. In 2002 total fertility rate was 1·37 births per woman.

CLIMATE

Because of its maritime location Estonia has a moderate climate, with cool summers and mild winters. Average daily temperatures in 2000: Jan. –2·5°C; July 16·3°C. Rainfall is heavy, 500–700 mm per year, and evaporation low.

CONSTITUTION AND GOVERNMENT

A draft constitution drawn up by a constitutional assembly was approved by 91·1% of votes cast at a referendum on 28 June 1992. Turn-out was 66·6%. The constitution came into effect on 3 July 1992. It defines Estonia as a 'democratic state guided by the rule of law, where universally recognized norms of international law are an inseparable part of the legal system.' It provides for a 101-member national assembly (*Riigikogu*) elected for four-year terms. There are 12 electoral districts with eight to 12 mandates each. Candidates may be elected: a) by gaining more than 'quota', i.e.

the number of votes cast in a district divided by the number of its mandates; b) by standing for a party which attracts for all of its candidates more than the quota, in order of listing; c) by being listed nationally for parties which clear a 5% threshold and eligible for the seats remaining according to position on the lists. The head of state is the *President*, elected by the Riigikogu for five-year terms. Presidential candidates must gain the nominations of at least 20% of parliamentary deputies. If no candidate wins a two-thirds majority in any of three rounds, the Speaker convenes an electoral college, composed of parliamentary deputies and local councillors. At this stage any 21 electors may nominate an additional candidate. The electoral college elects the President by a simple majority.

Citizenship requirements are two years residence and competence in Estonian for existing residents. For residents immigrating after 1 April 1995, five years qualifying residence is required.

National Anthem. 'Mu isamaa, mu õnn ja rõõm' ('My native land, my pride and joy'); words by J. V. Jannsen, tune by F. Pacius (same as Finland).

RECENT ELECTIONS

Parliamentary elections were held on 2 March 2003; turn-out was 58·2%. The Estonian Centre Party (Kesk) won 28 of the 101 seats (with 25·4% of the total votes); Union for the Republic—Res Publica (ResP), 28 seats (24·6%); Estonian Reform Party (Reform), 19 seats (17·7%); Estonian People's Union (Rahvaliit), 13 (13·3%); Pro Patria Union (Isamaa), 7 seats (7·3%); People's Party Moderates (Mõõdukad), 6 seats (7·0%). Two other parties failed to win seats.

A special government assembly elected the president after two rounds of votes on 21 Sept. 2001. There were four candidates. In the run-off for the presidency Arnold Rüütel won with 186 votes against 155 for Toomas Savi.

European Parliament. Estonia has six representatives. At the June 2004 elections turn-out was 26·9%. The Social Democratic Party (was Mõõdukad) won 3 seats with 36·8% of votes cast (political affiliation in European Parliament: Party of European Socialists); Kesk, 1 with 17·5% (Alliance of Liberals and Democrats for Europe); Reform, 1 with 12·2% (Alliance of Liberals and Democrats for Europe); Isamaa, 1 with 10·5% (European People's Party–European Democrats).

CURRENT ADMINISTRATION

President: Arnold Rüütel; b. 1928 (sworn in 8 Oct. 2001).

In April 2005 the Reform-Kesk-Rahvaliit coalition government comprised:

Prime Minister: Andrus Ansip; b. 1956 (Reform; in office since 13 April 2005).

Minister of Agriculture: Ester Tuiksoo (Rahvaliit). *Culture:* Raivo Palmaru (Kesk). *Defence:* Jaak Jõerüüt (Reform). *Economic Affairs and Communications:* Edgar Savisaar (Kesk). *Education and Research:* Mailis Reps (Kesk). *Environment:* Villu Reiljan (Rahvaliit). *Finance:* Aivar Sõerd (Rahvaliit). *Foreign Affairs:* Urmas Paet (Reform). *Internal Affairs:* Kalle Laanet (Kesk). *Justice:* Rein Lang (Reform). *Population and Ethnic Affairs:* Paul-Eerik Rummo (Reform). *Regional Affairs:* Jaan Õunapuu (Rahvaliit). *Social Affairs:* Jaak Aab (Kesk).

Government Website: http://www.riik.ee

DEFENCE

The President is the head of national defence. Conscription is eight to 11 months for men and voluntary for women. Conscientious objectors may opt for 16 months civilian service instead.

Defence expenditure in 2003 totalled US$203m. (US$150 per capita), representing 2·0% of GDP.

The Estonian Defence Forces (EDF) regular component is divided into the Army, the Air Force and the Navy.

Army. The army consists of nine army-training battalions (six for infantry, one for air defence, one for artillery and one for peace operations). Annually around 3,000 conscripts are trained for reserve. The total number of personnel in the Army in 2000 was 4,535 (1,420 officers and NCOs and contract soldiers; 2,290 conscripts and 825 civilians).

Navy. The Navy consists of the Naval Staff (Naval HQ), the Naval Base, and the Mine Countermeasures (MCM) Squadron. The total number of personnel in the Navy in 2000 was 385 (110 officers and NCOs and contract soldiers, 220 conscripts and 55 civilians). Estonia, Latvia and Lithuania have established a joint naval unit 'BALTRON' (Baltic Naval Squadron), with bases at Tallinn in Estonia, Liepāja, Riga and Ventspils in Latvia, and Klaipėda in Lithuania.

Air Force. The Air Force consists of an Air Force Staff, Air Force Base, and Air Surveillance Battalion. The total number of personnel in the Air Force is 200 (120 officers and NCOs and contract soldiers, 50 conscripts and 30 civilians).

INTERNATIONAL RELATIONS

Estonia is a member of the UN, WTO, BIS, NATO, EU, the Council of Europe, OSCE, Council of the Baltic Sea States, IOM and is an associate partner of the WEU. Estonia became a member of NATO on 29 March 2004 and of the EU on 1 May 2004. Estonia held a referendum on EU membership on 14 Sept. 2003, in which 66·9% of votes cast were in favour of accession, with 33·1% against.

ECONOMY

Agriculture contributed 4% of GDP in 2003, industry 21% and services 75%.

Overview. According to the IMF 'the Estonian experience has demonstrated clearly that a free and open trade regime is key to strong economic performance'. Since independence, Estonia has been among the fastest growing of the EU accession countries, with per capita GDP almost doubling between 1993–2003 to reach about 45% of the EU average in purchasing power parity terms. Exports include machinery, electrical equipment, wood and textile products. Tourism is important. Finland and Sweden are core business partners in investment and tourism. The transition to a market economy was helped by proximity to Nordic countries. The cornerstone of economic reform was the introduction of the new currency, tight budgetary policies, privatization and trade liberalization. In 1999 many tariff and non-tariff barriers were abolished in line with WTO rules. Privatization of large and medium-sized enterprises has been successful with the private sector contributing 80% of GDP in 2002. Telecommunications and banking industries have been opened up.

Currency. The unit of currency is the *kroon* (EKR) of 100 *sents*. The kroon is pegged to the euro at a rate of 15·6466 *krooni* to one euro. Foreign exchange reserves were US$914m. in June 2002 and gold reserves 8,000 troy oz. Inflation was 1·3% in 2003, down from 3·6% in 2002. Total money supply in June 2002 was 25,936m. krooni. In June 2004 the kroon was included in the Exchange Rate Mechanism II (ERM II); the fixed exchange rate with the euro remains unchanged. There are no restrictions on the free movement of capital between Estonia and foreign countries.

Budget. Government budgetary revenue and expenditure in 1m. krooni for calendar years:

	2000	*2001*	*2002*	*2003*[1]
Revenue	26,773·0	31,285·6	36,125·2	41,382·1
Expenditure	27,373·3	30,295·7	34,103·6	37,001·9

[1]Provisional.

Tax revenue provided 32,372·9m. krooni in 2002, non-tax revenue totalled 3,215·7m. krooni and grants 536·6m. krooni. The standard rate of income tax is 26%; VAT is 18% (reduced rate, 5%).

Performance. The real GDP growth rate was 5·1% in 2003—among the highest rates in the region—following growth of 6·4% in 2001 and 7·2% in 2002. Growth was supported by the increasing import demand of the European Union. Total GDP in 2003 was US$8·5bn.

Banking and Finance. A central bank, the Bank of Estonia, was re-established in 1990 (*Governor*, Vahur Kraft). The Estonian Investment Bank was established in 1992 to provide financing for privatized and private companies. Since 1 Jan. 1996 banks have been required to have an equity of at least 50m. krooni. As of Dec. 2004 there were six Estonian authorized commercial banks, three foreign banks' branches and five foreign banks' representative offices. As a result of a wave of mergers the two largest groups, Hansabank and the Union Bank of Estonia, control 80% of the market. Total assets and liabilities of commercial banks at Nov. 2004 were 128,211m. krooni. The Estonian Banking Association was founded in 1992.

A stock exchange opened in Tallinn in 1996.

ENERGY AND NATURAL RESOURCES

Environment. Estonia's carbon dioxide emissions from the consumption and flaring of fossil fuels in 2002 were the equivalent of 9·1 tonnes per capita.

Electricity. Estonia is a net electricity exporter. In 2001 installed capacity was 3·2m. kW in 2001, with production of 7·9bn. kWh. Consumption per capita was 5,540 kWh in 2000. In 1999, 92% of electricity was produced by burning oil shale. Wind power is being utilized on a small scale on Saaremaa and Hiiumaa.

Oil and Gas. Recoverable oil shale deposits were estimated at 1,500m. tonnes in 2000. A factory for the production of gas from shale and a 208 km-pipeline from Kohtla-Järve supplies shale gas to Tallinn, and exports to St Petersburg. Natural gas is imported from Russia.

Minerals. Oil shale is the most valuable mineral resource. Production volume has decreased (from 21m. tonnes in 1990 to 12m. tonnes in 2001) because of falls in exports and domestic electricity consumption, and an increase in the use of natural gas. Peatlands occupy about 22% of Estonia's territory; there are extensive deposits, of which an estimated 1·5bn. tonnes were classed as recoverable reserves in 2001. Phosphorites and super-phosphates are found and refined, and lignite (11·73m. tonnes in 2000), limestone, dolomite, clay, sand and gravel are mined.

Agriculture. In the course of the 1990s the proportion of agriculture in the gross national product decreased from 15% to 4%. Farming employed 6·1% of the population in 2003. At 1 Jan. 2001 there were 60,895 private farms and 709 state agricultural enterprises and co-operatives. In 2000 there were 1·43m. ha of agricultural land of which 1·12m. ha were arable and 0·30m. ha were natural grassland. There were 19,000 ha of permanent crops in 2001. Total agricultural output in 2003 was valued at 7,044m. krooni, including: animal production 3,388m. krooni; crop production, 2,616m. krooni; agricultural services and other non-agricultural production, 1,040m. krooni.

Output of main agricultural products (in 1,000 tonnes) in 2003: barley, 254; potatoes, 244; wheat, 145; oats, 63; rye, 23.

In 2003 there were 253,900 cattle, 29,900 sheep, 340,800 pigs and 2,096,000 chickens.

Livestock products (in 1,000 tonnes), 2003: meat, 105; milk, 611; eggs, 15.

Forestry. In 2000, 2·06m. ha were covered by forests, which provide material for sawmills, furniture, and the match and pulp industries, as well as wood fuel. Private, municipal and state ownership of forests is allowed. In 2001 the annual timber cut was 10·20m. cu. metres, of which approximately 55% was from private forests.

Fisheries. In 2000 the Estonian fishing fleet numbered 170 vessels over 12 metres; 6,690 people were employed in active fishing. The total catch in 2001 totalled in 2001 was 126,902 tonnes.

INDUSTRY

The leading companies by market capitalization in Estonia, excluding banking and finance, in Jan. 2002 were: Eesti Telekom (12bn. krooni); Norma (830m. krooni), a car seatbelt producer; and Merko Ehitus (719m. krooni), a construction company.

Important industries are engineering, metalworking, food products, wood products, furniture and textiles. In 2001 manufacturing accounted for 16·5% of GDP.

Labour. The workforce in 2003 totalled 660,500, of whom 594,300 were employed. The monthly average gross wage in 2003 was 6,723 krooni. The unemployment rate in 2003 was 10·0%, compared with 13·7% in 2000.

Retirement age was 63 years for both men and women in 1998.

Trade Unions. The main trade union organization in Estonia is the Estonian Association of Trade Unions, which represents the interests of industrial, service, trade, public and agricultural employees.

INTERNATIONAL TRADE

Direct investment position in Estonia by countries as of 31 Dec. 2003: Sweden, 42·8%; Finland, 27·0%; USA, 5·5%; Netherlands, 3·0%; Denmark, 2·6%; Germany, 2·5%; Norway, 2·5%. Estonia's direct investment position abroad by countries as of 31 Dec. 2004: Lithuania, 45·4%; Latvia, 28·4%; Cyprus, 14·0%; Italy, 4·4%; Ukraine, 2·5%. Direct foreign investment in Estonia as at 31 Dec. 2003 totalled 80,792·3m. krooni. Estonia's direct investment abroad as at 31 Dec. 2003 totalled 12,668m. krooni.

External debt was US$3,703m. in 2002.

Imports and Exports. Exports in 2003 (and 2002) were valued at US$5,299·3m. (US$4,829·7m.); imports, US$7,602·5m. (US$6,734·9m.).

Main export markets, 2003: Finland, 25·9%; Sweden, 15·3%; Germany, 9·9%; Latvia, 7·0%; UK, 4·2%. Main import suppliers in 2003: Finland, 15·9%; Germany, 11·3%; Sweden, 8·8%; Russia, 8·6%; China, 4·5%.

Around 80% of Estonian trade is with EU member countries, and 41% with Finland and Sweden alone.

COMMUNICATIONS

Roads. As of 1 Jan. 2004 there were 16,452 km of national roads (29·4% of the total Estonian road and street network of 55,592 km), of which 52·3% were paved. In 2003 there were 433,982 registered passenger cars in use, plus 83,400 trucks and vans, 5,400 buses and coaches, and 8,100 motorcycles and mopeds. There were 1,928 road accidents and 164 fatalities in 2003.

Rail. Length of railways in 2002 was 968 km (1,520 mm gauge), of which 132 km was electrified. In 2003, 5·06m. passengers and 65·6m. tonnes of freight were carried.

Civil Aviation. In 2002 there were 38 airports in Estonia. There is an international airport at Tallinn (Ulemiste), which handled 554,898 passengers (550,255 on international flights) and 2,417 tonnes of freight in 2000. Estonian aviation companies handled 336,200 passengers and 5,500 tonnes of goods in 1999. The national carrier is Estonian Air, 34% state-owned. In 2003 Estonian Air operated services to Copenhagen, Frankfurt, Hamburg, Kyiv, London, Moscow, Paris, Riga, Stockholm and Vilnius. In 1999 it flew 6·0m. km, carrying 291,300 passengers (all on international flights). In Jan. 2000 there were 124 aircraft in Estonia.

Shipping. There are six major shipping companies, all of which are privatized. There are ice-free, deep-water ports at Tallinn and Muuga (state-owned). Tallinn handled 85% of the total turnover of goods in Estonia in 2000. The port of Tallinn makes most of its money by shipping out Russian oil and importing goods destined for Russia. In 2002 the merchant shipping fleet comprised 33 vessels of 1,000 GRT or over.

Telecommunications. Estonia had 1,356,000 telephone subscribers in 2002 (1,000·7 per 1,000 persons) and 285,000 PCs (210·3 per 1,000 persons). There were 881,000 mobile phone subscribers in 2002 and 13,000 fax machines in 1999. In Feb. 2000 the Estonian parliament voted to guarantee Internet access to its citizens. The number of Internet users in 2002 was 444,000.

Postal Services. As of 1 Jan. 2004, the state-owned Eesti Post had 12 main post offices, 395 other post offices and 154 postal agencies, employing 4,237.

SOCIAL INSTITUTIONS

Justice. A post-Soviet criminal code was introduced in 1992. There is a three-tier court system with the State Court at its apex, and there are both city and district courts. The latter act as courts of appeal. The State Court is the final court of appeal, and also functions as a constitutional court. There are also administrative courts for petty offences. Judges are appointed for life. City and district judges are appointed by the President; State Court judges are elected by Parliament.

In 2003, 53,595 crimes were recorded; there were 38 murders and attempted murders (down from 200 in 1999). There are nine prisons; in May 2003, 4,874 persons were in custody (361 per 100,000 of national population—one of the highest rates in Europe).

The death penalty was abolished for all crimes in 1998.

Religion. There is freedom of religion in Estonia and no state church, although most of the population is Lutheran. The Estonian Orthodox Church owed allegiance to Constantinople until it was forcibly brought under Moscow's control in 1940; a synod of the free Estonian Orthodox Church was established in Stockholm. Returning from exile, it registered itself in 1993 as the Estonian Apostolic Orthodox Church. By an agreement in 1996 between the Moscow and Constantinople Orthodox Patriarchates, there are now two Orthodox jurisdictions in Estonia. In 2000 there were 152,000 Lutherans and 144,000 Orthodox. Other Christian denominations, including Methodist, Baptist and Roman Catholic, are also represented.

Education. Adult literacy rate in 2001 was at least 99%. There are nine years of comprehensive school starting at age six, followed by three years secondary school. In 2002–03 there were 636 general education schools: 65 nursery/primary, 52 primary, 279 basic and 240 secondary/upper secondary. Of these, 525 were Estonian-language, 89 Russian-language and 22 mixed-language. There were 45 schools for children with special needs. The total number of pupils at basic school level in general education in 2002–03 was 165,486 (115,204 at urban schools and 50,282 at rural schools). At the start of the 2003–04 academic year there were 65,659 higher education students studying at six public universities, six private universities, seven state higher schools and 17 private higher schools; 11 vocational educational institutions also provide higher education.

In 2001 central government expenditure on education came to 2,136·9m. krooni. In 1999–2000 total education expenditure came to 7·6% of GNP.

Health. Estonia had 51 hospitals (14 private) in 2002, down from 78 hospitals (28 private) in 1999. There were 8,248 hospital beds in 2002. In 2003 there were 4,293 doctors (1,245 in private medicine).

Welfare. In 2003 there were 0·37m. pensioners. The average monthly pension was 1,816 krooni in 2003. An official poverty line was introduced in 1993 (then 280 krooni per month). Persons receiving less are entitled to state benefit. Unemployment benefit was 400 krooni a month in 2003.

CULTURE

World Heritage Sites. Estonia has one site on the UNESCO World Heritage List: the Historic Centre (Old Town) of Tallinn (1997).

Broadcasting. There were over 30 radio stations in Estonia in 2000. Public service radio, Estonian Radio, operates four channels, three in Estonian and one in languages of national minorities, mainly Russian. In 2000 there were four TV channels with nationwide networks (colour by PAL): Estonian State Television and three commercial channels. The Broadcasting Council is the regulatory body for public service broadcasting and has nine members nominated by Riigikogu (the Estonian Parliament). There were 900,000 TV receivers in 2001 and 1·50m. radio receivers in 2000.

Cinema. In 1997 there were 200 cinemas. Attendances in cinemas totalled 875,000 in 1999. Three full-length films were made in 1999.

Press. In 2000 there were 109 officially registered newspapers, including 82 in Estonian; and 956 periodicals, including 778 in Estonian. *The Baltic Times* is an English-language weekly.

Tourism. There were 1·1m. foreign visitors in 2000 who spent US$505m., 18% of Estonia's GDP.

Festivals. Festivals include: International Folklore Festival, BALTICA, which is staged every three years; Festival of Baroque Music; Jazz festival, JAZZKAAR; Pärnu International Documentary and Anthropology Film Festival and the Viljandi Folk Music Festival. Estonia's Song Festival, which was first held in 1869, is held every five years and is next scheduled to take place in 2009.

Baltoscandal, an international theatre festival which takes place every two years, celebrated its 8th staging in June 2004.

Libraries. The Eesti Rahvusraamatukogu (National Library of Estonia), which opened in 1993, hosts exhibitions of local and international art. Other libraries include the Tallinn Tartu University Library (1802); Technical University Library (1919); and the Estonian Academic Library (1946). In 1997 there were 743 public libraries, two National libraries and 33 Higher Education libraries. They held a combined 18,116,000 volumes for 1,073,000 registered users.

Theatre and Opera. Most performances are in the Estonian language with the exception of the Russian Drama Theatre, and the Estonia Opera and Ballet Theatre which sometimes performs operas in their original language. There were nine state theatres and one municipal in 2000.

DIPLOMATIC REPRESENTATIVES

Of Estonia in the United Kingdom (16 Hyde Park Gate, London, SW7 5DG)
Ambassador: Kaja Tael.

Of the United Kingdom in Estonia (Wismari 6, 10136 Tallinn)
Ambassador: Nigel Haywood.

Of Estonia in the USA (2131 Massachusetts Ave., NW, Washington, D.C., 20008)
Ambassador: Juri Luik.

Of the USA in Estonia (Kentmanni 20, 15099 Tallinn)
Ambassador: Aldona Zofia Wos.

Of Estonia to the United Nations
Ambassador: Tiina Intelmann.

Of Estonia to the European Union
Ambassador: Väino Reinart.

FURTHER READING

Statistical Office of Estonia. *Statistical Yearbook.*
Ministry of the Economy. *Estonian Economy.* Annual
Hood, N., *et al.*, (eds.) *Transition in the Baltic States*. London, 1997
Lieven, A., *The Baltic Revolution: Estonia, Latvia, Lithuania and the Path to Independence.* 2nd ed. Yale Univ. Press, 1994
Misiunas, R.-J. and Taagepera, R., *The Baltic States: Years of Dependence 1940–1991.* 2nd ed., Farnborough, 1993
Smith, I. A. and Grunts, M. V., *The Baltic States.* [Bibliography] ABC-Clio, Oxford and Santa Barbara (CA), 1993
Taagepera, R., *Estonia: Return to Independence.* Boulder (CO), 1993

National statistical office: Statistical Office of Estonia, Tallinn.
Website: http://www.stat.ee/

ETHIOPIA

Federal Democratic Republic of Ethiopia

Capital: Addis Ababa
Population projection, 2010: 83·53m.
GDP per capita, 2002: (PPP$) 780
HDI/world rank: 0·359/170

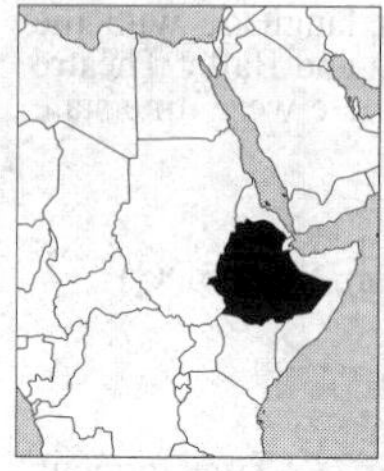

KEY HISTORICAL EVENTS

The ancient empire of Ethiopia has its legendary origin in the meeting of King Solomon and the Queen of Sheba. The empire developed at Askum in the north in the centuries before and after the birth of Christ as a result of Semitic immigration from South Arabia. Ethiopia's subsequent history is one of sporadic expansion southwards and eastwards, checked from the 16th to early 19th centuries by devastating wars with Muslims and Gallas. Modern Ethiopia dates from the reign of the Emperor Theodore (1855–68). Menelik II (1889–1913) defeated the Italians in 1896 and thereby safeguarded the empire's independence in the scramble for Africa.

In 1923 the heir to the throne, Ras Tafari (crowned Emperor Haile Selassie five years later), succeeded in getting Ethiopia admitted as an independent country to the League of Nations. However, the League was ineffective in preventing a second Italian invasion in 1936. The emperor fled the country, only returning when the Allied forces defeated the Italians in 1941.

In 1950 the former Italian colony of Eritrea, from 1941 under British military administration, was handed over to Ethiopia. Thereafter, a secessionist movement fought a guerrilla war for independence under the Eritrean Peoples' Liberation Front (EPLF). A military government, known as the Dirgue, assumed power on 12 Sept. 1974 under the leadership of Lieut. Col. Mengistu Haile Miriam. It deposed the emperor, abolished the monarchy and mounted an agricultural collectivization programme. In 1977 Somalia invaded Ethiopia and took control of the Ogaden region. After a counter offensive with Soviet and Cuban support the area was recaptured. Following ever-increasing territorial gains by the insurgent Ethiopian People's Revolutionary Democratic Front (EPRDF) and the EPLF, Mengistu fled the country. In July 1991 a conference of 24 political groups, called to appoint a transitional government, agreed a democratic charter. Eritrea seceded, and became independent, on 24 May 1993. In 1999 fighting broke out along Ethiopia's border with Eritrea. After the failure of international mediation, the 13-month long-truce between Ethiopia and Eritrea ended in May 2000. Ethiopia launched a major offensive in the ongoing war over territorial disputes and claimed victory. In June both sides agreed to an Organization of African Unity peace deal to end the two-year border war. Economic progress, including market-led reforms, raised hopes of higher living standards until three successive years of drought left food resources seriously depleted. Widespread malnutrition was alleviated by international aid.

TERRITORY AND POPULATION

Ethiopia is bounded in the northeast by Eritrea, east by Djibouti and Somalia, south by Kenya and west by Sudan. It has a total area of 1,127,127 sq. km. The secession of Eritrea in 1993 left Ethiopia without a coastline. An Eritrean–Ethiopian agreement of July 1993 gives Ethiopia rights to use the Eritrean ports of Assab and Massawa.

The first census was carried out in 1984: population, 42,019,418 (without Eritrea, 39,570,266). 1994 census population: 49,218,178. Estimate (2002), 69·03m. (84·1% rural in 2001); density, 61 per sq. km.

The UN gives a projected population for 2010 of 83·53m.

Ethiopia has eleven administrative divisions—eight states (Afar, Amhara, Benshangul/Gumaz, Gambella, Oromia, the Peoples of the South, Somalia and Tigre) and three cities (Addis Ababa, Dire Dawa and Harar).

The population of the capital, Addis Ababa, was 2,534,000 in 1999. Other large towns (1994 populations): Dire Dawa, 164,851; Nazret, 127,842; Harar, 122,932; Mekele, 119,779; Jimma, 119,717.

There are six major ethnic groups (in % of total population in 1996): Oromo, 31%; Amhara, 30%; Tigrinya, 7%; Gurage, 5%; Somali, 4%; Sidamo, 3%. There are also some 60 minor ethnic groups and 286 languages are spoken. The *de facto* official language is Amharic (which uses its own alphabet), though Oromo-speakers form the largest group.

SOCIAL STATISTICS

Births, 1999, 2,186,000; deaths, 1,062,000. Rates per 1,000 population, 1999: births, 34·2; deaths, 16·6. Expectation of life at birth in 2001 was 44·6 years for males and 46·7 years for females. Annual population growth rate, 1992–2002, 2·8%; infant mortality, 2001, 116 per 1,000 live births; fertility rate, 2001, 6·8 births per woman.

CLIMATE

The wide range of latitude produces many climatic variations between the high, temperate plateaus and the hot, humid lowlands. The main rainy season lasts from June to Aug., with light rains from Feb. to April, but the country is very vulnerable to drought. Addis Ababa, Jan. 59°F (15°C), July 59°F (15°C). Annual rainfall 50" (1,237 mm). Harar, Jan. 65°F (18·3°C), July 64°F (17·8°C). Annual rainfall 35" (897 mm). Massawa, Jan. 78°F (25·6°C), July 94°F (34·4°C). Annual rainfall 8" (193 mm).

CONSTITUTION AND GOVERNMENT

A 548-member constituent assembly was elected on 5 June 1994; turn-out was 55%. The EPRDF gained 484 seats. On 8 Dec. 1994 it unanimously adopted a new federal Constitution which provided for the creation of a federation of nine regions based (except the capital and the southern region) on a predominant ethnic group. These regions have the right of secession after a referendum. The *President*, a largely ceremonial post, is elected by parliament, the 548-member *Council of People's Representatives*. There is also an upper house, the 108-member *Federal Council*.

National Anthem. 'Yazegennat keber ba-Ityop yachchen santo' ('In our Ethiopia our civic pride is strong'); words anonymous, tune by S. Lulu.

RECENT ELECTIONS

Elections to the Council of People's Representatives took place on 14 May 2000. The Oromo People's Democratic Organization (OPDO) took 183 seats; Amhara National Democratic Movement (ANDM) 146; Southern Ethiopia People's Democratic Front (SEPDO) 112; Tigre People's Liberation Front (TPLF) 40; Afar National Democratic Party (ANDP) 8; Benshangul Gumuz Peoples' Democratic United Party (BGBDUP) 6; 11 other parties won four seats or fewer. Non-partisans took 13 seats. The four main parties belong to the Ethiopian People's Revolutionary Democratic Front.

CURRENT ADMINISTRATION

President: Girma Wolde-Giyorgis; b. 1925 (elected 8 Oct. 2001).

In March 2005 the government comprised:

Prime Minister: Meles Zenawi; b. 1955 (TPLF; appointed 22 Aug. 1995).

Deputy Prime Ministers: Kassu Ilala (also *Minister of Infrastructure*); Adisu Legesse (also *Minister of Agriculture and Rural Development*).

Minister of Defence: Abadula Gemeda. *Capacity Building:* Tefera Walwa. *Education:* Genet Zewdie. *Federal Affairs:* Abay Tsehay. *Finance and Economic Development:* Sufyan Ahmad. *Foreign Affairs:* Seyoum Mesfin. *Health:* Kebede Tadesse. *Information:* Bereket Simon. *Cabinet Affairs:* Adelo Berhanu. *Justice:* Harika Haroye. *Labour and Social Affairs:* Hassan Abdella. *Mines and Energy:* Mohammed Dirir. *Revenue:* Getachew Belay. *Trade and Industry:* Girma Birru. *Water Resources:* Shiferaw Jarso. *Youth, Sports and Culture:* Teshome Toga.

Ethiopian Parliament: http://www.ethiopar.net

DEFENCE

In 2003 defence expenditure totalled US$326m. (US$5 per capita), representing 4·9% of GDP.

Army. Following the overthrow of President Mengistu's government Ethiopian armed forces were constituted from former members of the Tigray People's Liberation Front. The strength of the armed forces is estimated at 252,500 (2002).

Air Force. Owing to its role in the war with Eritrea aircraft operability has improved. There were 55 combat aircraft in 2002, including MiG-21s and MiG-23s, and 30 armed helicopters. Personnel were estimated at 2,500 in 2002.

INTERNATIONAL RELATIONS

A border dispute between Ethiopia and Eritrea broke out in May 1998. Eritrean troops took over the border town of Badame after a skirmish between Ethiopian police units and armed men from Eritrea. Ethiopia maintained that Badame and Sheraro, a nearby town, had always been part of Ethiopia and called Eritrea's action an invasion. An agreement ending hostilities was signed in June 2000, followed by a peace accord in Dec. A buffer zone has been created to separate the armies.

Ethiopia is a member of the UN, the African Union, African Development Bank, COMESA, the Intergovernmental Authority on Development and is an ACP member state of the ACP-EU relationship.

ECONOMY

Agriculture accounted for 42·3% of GDP in 2002, industry 11·1% and services 46·5%.

Overview. An Economic Reform Programme, instituted in 1992, aimed at stabilizing the economy and deregulating economic activities to prepare for a free-market economy. An Economic Rehabilitation and Reconstruction Programme (ERRP), launched in 1991–92, eased foreign exchange regulations and a privatization programme began in 1995. Economic growth has been hampered by drought, leading to widespread food shortages.

Currency. The *birr* (ETB), of 100 *cents*, is the unit of currency. The birr was devalued in Oct. 1992. In May 2002 total money supply was 12,976m. birr, foreign exchange reserves were US$638m. and gold reserves 205,000 troy oz. There was deflation in 2001, of 7·1%, and again in 2002, of 7·2%.

Budget. The fiscal year ends on 6 July. Revenue, 1999–2000, 11,222m. birrs; expenditure, 17,184m. birrs.

Performance. Real GDP growth was 1·2% in 2002 (7·7% in 2001). Total GDP was US$6·6bn. in 2003.

Banking and Finance. The central bank and bank of issue is the National Bank of Ethiopia (founded 1964; *Governor*, Teklewold Atnafu). The country's largest bank is the state-owned Commercial Bank of Ethiopia. The complete monopoly held by the bank ended with deregulation in 1994, but it still commands about 90% of the market share. There are eight other banks. On 1 Jan. 1975 the government nationalized all banks, mortgage and insurance companies.

Weights and Measures. The metric system is official. Traditional units include the *feresula* (= approximately 17 kg), and the *gasha* (based on family land-ownership), which is officially 40 ha but can be up to 120 ha.

ENERGY AND NATURAL RESOURCES

Environment. Carbon dioxide emissions from the consumption and flaring of fossil fuels were the equivalent of 0·1 tonnes per capita in 2002.

Electricity. Installed capacity in 2000 was 0·5m. kW. Production in 2000 was 1·70bn. kWh. Hydro-electricity accounts for 97% of generation. Consumption per capita was 28 kWh in 2000. Supply: 220 volts; 50 Hz.

Oil and Gas. The Calub gas field in the southeast of Ethiopia had reserves estimated at 25bn. cu. metres in 2002.

Minerals. Gold and salt are produced. Lege Dembi, an open-pit gold mine in the south of the country, has proven reserves of over 62 tonnes and produces more than five tonnes a year.

Agriculture. Small-scale farmers make up about 85% of Ethiopia's population. There were 10·7m. ha of arable land in 2001 and 750,000 ha of permanent crops. 190,000 ha were irrigated in 2001. There were 3,000 tractors in 2001 and 100 harvester-threshers. By 1993, 96% of agricultural land was worked by smallholdings averaging 0·5–1·5 ha. Land remains the property of the state, but individuals are granted rights of usage which can be passed to their children, and produce may be sold on the open market instead of compulsorily to the state at low fixed prices.

Coffee is by far the most important source of rural income. Main agricultural products (2000, in 1,000 tonnes): maize, 2,600; sugarcane, 2,300; wheat, 1,220; sorghum, 1,190; barley, 750; potatoes, 340; millet, 320; broad beans, 280; yams, 250; coffee, 230. Teff (*Eragrastis abyssinica*) and durra are also major products.

Livestock, 2000: cattle, 35·0m.; sheep, 21·0m.; goats, 16·8m.; asses, 5·20m.; horses, 2·75m.; camels, 1·06m.; chickens, 56m.

Forestry. In 2000 forests covered 4·59m. ha, representing 4·2% of the land area. Ethiopia is Africa's leading roundwood producer, with removals totalling 91·28m. cu. metres in 2001.

Fisheries. The catch in 2001 was 15,390 tonnes, entirely from inland waters.

INDUSTRY

Most public industrial enterprises are controlled by the state. Industrial activity is centred around Addis Ababa. Processed food, cement, textiles and drinks are the main commodities produced. Industrial production accounted for 11·1% of GDP in 2001, including 7·0% from manufacturing.

Labour. The labour force in 1996 was 25,392,000 (59% males); it was estimated by the UN that 30% were unemployed. Coffee provided a livelihood to a quarter of the population.

INTERNATIONAL TRADE

Foreign debt was US$6,522m. in 2002.

Imports and Exports. Imports and exports for calendar years in US$1m.:

	1998	*1999*	*2000*	*2001*	*2002*
Imports f.o.b.	1,359·8	1,387·2	1,131·4	1,625·8	1,455·0
Exports f.o.b.	560·3	467·4	486·0	455·6	480·2

Principal exports (2000): coffee (53·0%); leather (8·5%). Other important exports include sugar, pulses and cattle. Principal imports: machinery and apparatus (19·8%); refined petroleum (19·6%); road vehicles (12·0%); chemicals and chemical products (11·3%).

Coffee accounts for about half of the country's export earnings. In 1997, 103,000 tonnes of coffee were exported, earning around US$360m. (£220m.) compared to just US$160m. (£100m.) in 1993.

Main export markets, 2000: Germany, 19·6%; Japan, 11·7%; Djibouti, 10·7%; Saudi Arabia, 8·1%. Major import suppliers: Yemen, 19·1%; Italy, 8·9%; Japan, 8·2%; China, 7·7%.

COMMUNICATIONS

Roads. There were 33,297 km of roads in 2002, only 12% of which were paved. Passenger cars in use in 2002 numbered 67,614 (one per 1,000 inhabitants) and there were also 34,102 trucks and vans, and 18,067 buses and coaches. In 1999 there were 1,274 deaths in road accidents.

In 1998 a US$500m. deal was signed with the World Bank for road and power development projects.

Rail. The Ethiopian-Djibouti Railway has a length of 782 km (metre-gauge), but much of the route is in need of renovation. Passenger-km travelled in 1998–99 came to 151m. and freight tonne-km to 90m.

Civil Aviation. There are international airports at Addis Ababa (Bole) and Dire Dawa. The national carrier is the state-owned Ethiopian Airlines. In 2003 it served 43 international and 25 domestic destinations. In 1999 scheduled airline traffic of Ethiopian-based carriers flew 28·5m. km, carrying 861,000 passengers (617,000 on international flights). In 2000 Addis Ababa (Bole) handled 1,040,623 passengers and 27,237 tonnes of freight.

Shipping. Merchant shipping totalled 82,000 GRT in 2002, including oil tankers 2,000 GRT.

Telecommunications. All the main centres are connected with Addis Ababa by telephone or radio telegraph. In 2002 there were 404,200 telephone subscribers (6·0 per 1,000 persons), including 50,400 mobile phone subscribers. There were 100,000 PCs in use in 2002 (1·5 per 1,000 persons) and 3,100 fax machines in 1999. In 2002 Ethiopia had 50,000 Internet users.

Postal Services. In 1998 there were 534 post offices, or one for every 112,000 persons.

SOCIAL INSTITUTIONS

Justice. The legal system is based on the Justinian Code. A new penal code came into force in 1958 and Special Penal Law in 1974. Codes of criminal procedure, civil, commercial and maritime codes have since been promulgated. Provincial and district courts have been established, and High Court judges visit the provincial courts on circuit. The Supreme Court at Addis Ababa is presided over by the Chief Justice.

Religion. About 59% of the population are Christian, mainly belonging to the Ethiopian Orthodox Church, and 32% Sunni Muslims. Amhara, Tigreans and some Oromos are Christian. Somalis, Afars and some Oromos are Muslims. About 5% of the population follow traditional animist beliefs.

Education. The adult literacy rate in 2001 was 40·3% (48·1% among males and 32·4% among females). Primary education commences at seven years and continues with optional secondary education at 13 years. Up to the age of 12, education is in the local language of the federal region. In 2000–01 there were 6,650,841 pupils at primary schools with 121,077 teachers, and 1,495,445 pupils with 25,984 (1995–96) teachers at secondary schools. During the period 1990–95 only 19% of females of primary school age were enrolled in school. In 1994–95 there was one university with 19,200 students and 900 academic staff, and one agricultural university with 1,551 students and 324 academic staff. There were two institutes of health sciences and water technology; and two colleges—one of teacher training and one of town planning.

In 2000–01 expenditure on education came to 4·8% of GNP and 13·8% of total government spending.

Health. Population per hospital bed, 1994–95, 293,787; population per health centre, 22,242. In the period 1990–98 only 25% of the population had access to safe drinking water.

CULTURE

World Heritage Sites. There are seven sites in Ethiopia that appear on the UNESCO World Heritage List. They are (with the year entered on list): the Rock-hewn Churches at Laibela (1978), 11 monolithic 13th century churches; Simien National Park (1978); Fasil Ghebbi, Gondar Region (1979), a 16th century fortress city; Aksum (1980), the capital of the ancient Kingdom of Aksum, containing tombs and castles dating from the first millennium AD; the Lower Valley of the Awash (1980), an important palaeontological site; the Lower Valley of the Omo (1980), where *Homo gracilis* was discovered; and Tiya (1980), a group of archeological sites south of Addis Ababa.

Broadcasting. The government-run Voice of Ethiopia broadcasts a national programme and an external service in English. The government-controlled Ethiopian Television (colour by PAL) transmits about 28 hours a week. Private radio stations have been permitted since 2004. In 2000 there were 11·8m. radio receivers and in 2001 there were 370,000 TV receivers.

Press. In 1998 there were two daily newspapers with a combined circulation of 23,000 and 78 non-dailies and periodicals.

Tourism. In 2000 there were 125,000 foreign visitors. Revenue from tourists in 2000 totalled US$24m.

Calendar. The Julian calendar remains in use; the year has 13 months (12 months with 30 days and one month with five or six, depending on the leap-year). It begins on 11 Sept. (Gregorian) and is seven or eight years behind the Gregorian calendar.

DIPLOMATIC REPRESENTATIVES

Of Ethiopia in the United Kingdom (17 Prince's Gate, London, SW7 1PZ)
Ambassador: Fisseha Adugna.

Of the United Kingdom in Ethiopia (Fikre Mariam Abatechan St., Addis Ababa)
Ambassador: Robert Dewar.

Of Ethiopia in the USA (3506 International Drive, NW, Washington, D.C., 20008)
Ambassador: Ayele Kassahun.

Of the USA in Ethiopia (Entoto St., Addis Ababa)
Ambassador: Aurelia B. Brazeal.

Of Ethiopia to the United Nations
Ambassador: Vacant.
Chargé d'Affaires a.i.: Zenna Teruneh.

Of Ethiopia to the European Union
Ambassador: Ato Berhane Gebre-Christos.

FURTHER READING

Alemneh Dejene. *Environment, Famine and Politics in Ethiopia: a View from the Village.* Boulder (Colo.), 1991
Araia, G., *Ethiopia: the Political Economy of Transition.* Univ. Press of America, 1995
Crummey, Donald, *Land and Society in the Christian Kingdom of Ethiopia: From the Thirteenth to the Twentieth Century.* Univ. of Illinois Press and James Currey, Oxford, 2000
Henze, Paul B., *Layers of Time: A History of Ethiopia.* Hurst, London, 2000
Marcus, H. G., *A History of Ethiopia.* California Univ. Press, 1994
Mekonnen, T. (ed.) *The Ethiopian Economy: Structure, Problems and Policy Issues.* Addis Ababa, 1992
Munro-Hay, Stuart and Pankhurst, Richard, *Ethiopia.* [Bibliography] ABC-Clio, Oxford and Santa Barbara (CA), 1995
Negash, Tekeste and Tronvoll, Kjetil, *Brothers at War: Making Sense of the Eritrean–Ethiopian War.* Ohio Univ. Press and James Currey, Oxford, 2001
Pankhurst, Richard, *The Ethiopians.* Oxford, 1999
Tiruneh, A., *The Ethiopian Revolution: a Transformation from an Aristocratic to a Totalitarian Autocracy.* CUP, 1993

National statistical office: Central Statistical Office, Addis Ababa.

FIJI ISLANDS

Capital: Suva
Population projection, 2010: 890,000
GDP per capita, 2002: (PPP$) 5,440
HDI/world rank: 0·758/81

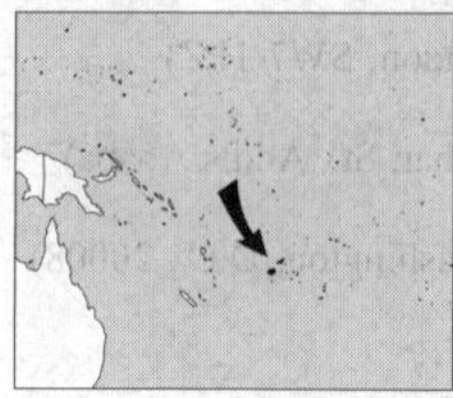

KEY HISTORICAL EVENTS

The Fiji Islands were first recorded in detail by Capt. Bligh after the mutiny of the Bounty (1789). In the 19th century the demand for sandalwood attracted merchant ships. Deserters and shipwrecked men stayed. Tribal wars were bloody and general until Fiji was ceded to Britain on 10 Oct. 1874. Fiji gained independence on 10 Oct. 1970. It remained an independent state within the Commonwealth with a Governor-General appointed by the Queen until 1987. In the general election of 12 April 1987 a left-wing coalition came to power with the support of the Indian population who outnumbered the indigenous Fijians by 50% to 44%. However, it was overthrown in a military coup. A month later, Fiji declared itself a Republic and Fiji's Commonwealth membership lapsed.

In 1990 a new coalition restored civilian rule but made it impossible for Fijian Indians to hold power. A rapprochement with Indian leaders led to an agreement to restore multi-racial government in 1998. Fiji rejoined the Commonwealth in 1997. On 27 July 1998 a new constitution changed the country's name from Fiji to Fiji Islands.

A coup was staged in May 2000 under the leadership of George Speight, a failed businessman. His main aim was to exclude Indians from the government. An interim government, excluding Speight supporters, was appointed on 3 July 2000 to rule for 18 months. On 26 July George Speight and 400 of his supporters were arrested. On 18 Feb. 2002 Speight was sentenced to death although this was subsequently commuted to life imprisonment.

TERRITORY AND POPULATION

The Fiji Islands comprise 332 islands and islets (about one-third are inhabited) lying between 15° and 22° S. lat. and 174° E. and 177° W. long. The largest is Viti Levu, area 10,429 sq. km (4,027 sq. miles); next is Vanua Levu, area 5,556 sq. km (2,145 sq. miles). The island of Rotuma (47 sq. km, 18 sq. miles), about 12° 30' S. lat., 178° E. long., was added to the colony in 1881. Total area, 7,055 sq. miles (18,272 sq. km). Total population (1996 census), 775,077 (females, 381,146); ethnic groups: Fijian, 393,575; Indian, 338,818; part-European/European, 14,788; Chinese, 4,939; other Pacific islanders, 10,463; Rotuman, 9,727; other, 2,767. Population density (1996), 42·4 per sq. km. 2002 population estimate: 830,000. In 2001, 50·2% of the population lived in urban areas.

The UN gives a projected population for 2010 of 890,000.

Population estimate of the capital, Suva, in 1999 was 196,000. Other large towns, with 1996 populations, are Lautoka (42,917), Nadi (30,791) and Labasa (24,187).

English is the official language; Fijian and Hindustani are also spoken.

SOCIAL STATISTICS

Births, 1999, 16,916; deaths, 3,603; marriages (1998), 8,058. 1999 birth rate per 1,000 population, 21·0; death rate per 1,000 population, 4·5. Annual population growth rate, 1992–2002, 1·2%. Life expectancy at birth in 2001 was 67·7 years for males and 71·1 years for females. Infant mortality, 2001, 18 per 1,000 live births; fertility rate, 2001, 3·0 births per woman.

CLIMATE

A tropical climate, but oceanic influences prevent undue extremes of heat or humidity. The S. E. Trades blow from May to Nov., during which time nights are cool and rainfall amounts least. Suva, Jan. 80°F (26·7°C), July 73°F (22·8°C). Annual rainfall 117" (2,974 mm).

CONSTITUTION AND GOVERNMENT

The executive authority of the State is vested in the *President*, who is appointed by the Bose Levu Vakaturaga (Great Council of Chiefs). The *Prime Minister* is appointed by the President. The Prime Minister must establish a multi-party cabinet. The President's term of office is five years.

A new Constitution unanimously passed by Parliament and assented to by H.E. the President came into force on 27 July 1998. The country's name was changed from Fiji to Fiji Islands and the people were to be known as Fiji Islanders instead of Fijians. The new Constitution also does away with an indigenous Prime Minister and has a 71-seat *House of Representatives* (Lower House), with 46 elected on a communal role and 25 from an open electoral roll. Of the 46, 23 will be elected from a roll of voters registered as Fijians, 19 from a roll of voters registered as Indians, one from a roll of voters registered as Rotumans and three from a roll of voters registered who are none of these. The Upper House or *Senate* has 34 members, 24 appointed by the Great Council of Chiefs, nine appointed by the president, and one appointed by the Council of Rotuma.

Parliament was reopened in Oct. 2001, having been suspended following a coup in May 2000. In July 2003 the supreme court declared that, according to the constitution, the government must include members of the opposition. Laisenia Qarase, who replaced Mahendra Chaudhry as prime minister after the 2000 coup, had excluded MPs from the Indian-dominated Labour party following general elections in 2001. In Nov. 2004 the Labour party leadership declined the offered cabinet positions, preferring instead to form an official opposition.

National Anthem. 'God Bless Fiji'; words by M. Prescott, tune anonymous.

RECENT ELECTIONS

Mahendra Chaudhry, the Labour Party leader, became the country's first Indian prime minister in 1999, but was ousted in the coup of May 2000 after just over a year in office. In parliamentary elections held between 25 Aug.–2 Sept. 2001 Soqosoqo Duavata ni Leweniavanua (Fiji United Party) won 32 out of 71 seats ahead of the Fiji Labour Party with 27. Other parties won six seats or fewer.

CURRENT ADMINISTRATION

President: Ratu Josefa Iloilo; b. 1920 (appointed as interim president on 18 July 2000; re-appointed as president for a five-year term on 15 March 2001).

Vice President: Ratu Joni Madraiwiwi.

In March 2005 the government comprised:

Prime Minister, Minister for National Reconciliation and Unity, Fijian Affairs, Culture and Heritage: Laisenia Qarase (sworn in 10 Sept. 2001, having previously been interim prime minister from 4 July 2000 to 14 March 2001 and from 16 March 2001 until officially taking office). He named a cabinet that did not include any members of the Indian-dominated Labour party in defiance of the constitution, which states that any party with eight or more seats is entitled to ministerial positions.

Minister of Agriculture, Sugar and Land Resettlement: Ilaitia Tuisese. *Commerce, Business Development and Investment:* Tomasi Vuetilovoni. *Education:* Ro Teimumu Kepa. *Finance and National Planning:* Ratu Jone Kubuabola. *Fisheries and Forests:* Konisi Yabaki. *Foreign Affairs and External Trade:* Kaliopate Tavola. *Health:* Solomone Naivalu. *Home Affairs, Immigration and National Disaster Management:* Josefa Vosanibola. *Information, Communications and Media Relations:* Dr Ahmed Ali. *Justice and Attorney General:* Qoriniasi Bale. *Labour, Industrial Relations and Productivity:* Kenneth Zinck. *Lands and Mineral Resources:* Ratu Naiqama Lalabalavu. *Local Government, Housing, Squatter Settlement and Environment:* Pio Wong. *Multi-Ethnic Affairs:* Vacant. *Public Enterprises and Public Sector Reform:* Jonetani Galuinadi. *Regional Development:* Ted Young. *Tourism:* Pita Nacuva. *Transport and Civil Aviation:* Simione Kaitani. *Women, Social Welfare and Poverty Alleviation:* Asenaca Caucau. *Works and Energy:* Savenaca Draunidalo. *Youth, Employment Opportunities and Sports:* Isireli Leweniqila.

Fiji Islands Government Online: http://www.fiji.gov.fj

DEFENCE

In 2003 defence expenditure totalled US$33m. (US$40 per capita), representing 1·5% of GDP.

Army. Personnel in 2002 numbered 3,200 including 300 recalled reserves. More than 600 of these are actively involved in UN and peacekeeping operations. There is an additional reserve force of 6,000.

Navy. A small naval division of the armed forces numbered 300 in 2002.

INTERNATIONAL RELATIONS

The Fiji Islands is a member of the UN, WTO, the Commonwealth, the Asian Development Bank, the Colombo Plan, the Pacific Community, the Pacific Islands Forum and is an ACP member state of the ACP-EU relationship.

ECONOMY

Agriculture accounted for 16·2% of GDP in 2002, industry 27·0% and services 56·8%.

Currency. The unit of currency is the *Fiji dollar* (FJD) of 100 *cents.* In June 2002 total money supply was $F661m., foreign exchange reserves were US$332m. and gold reserves 1,000 troy oz. Inflation in 2002 was 1·9%. The Fiji dollar was devalued by 20% in Jan. 1998.

Budget. Revenues in 2002 totalled $F949·4m. and expenditures $F1,345·3m.

VAT of 10% was introduced in 1992.

Performance. There was a recession in 2000, with the economy shrinking by 3·2%, but 2001 saw a recovery, with growth of 4·3%. In 2002 there was real GDP growth of 4·4%. Total GDP in 2003 was US$2·3bn.

Banking and Finance. The central bank and bank of issue is the Reserve Bank of Fiji (*Governor*, Savenaca Narube). Total assets were $F493·07m. in June 1996. The National Bank is a government-owned commercial bank. The Fiji Development Bank has assets totalling $F356·01m. There are six foreign banks in the country, one commercial bank, one development bank and two merchant banks. Total assets of commercial banks were $F1,797·92m. in June 1996.

The South Pacific Stock Exchange is based in Suva.

ENERGY AND NATURAL RESOURCES

Environment. Carbon dioxide emissions from the consumption and flaring of fossil fuels in 2002 were the equivalent of 1·1 tonnes per capita.

Electricity. The Fiji Electricity Authority is responsible for the generation, transmission and distribution of electricity in the country. It operates six separate supply systems. The largest energy project is one of hydro-electricity generating 95% of the main island's electric needs. Two rural hydro schemes have been completed, one generating 100 kW and the other 800 kW. In 1994 there were seven thermal and one hydro-electric power stations.

Installed capacity in 2000 was 0·2m. kW. Production in 2000 was 545m. kWh with consumption per capita an estimated 670 kWh.

Minerals. The main gold-mine accounts for almost one tenth of the country's exports and employs about 1,700 people. Gold is one of the Fiji Islands' main exports. Gold production, 2001, was 3,858 kg.

Agriculture. With a total land area of 1·8m. ha, only 16% is suitable for farming. In 2001 there were 200,000 ha of arable land and 85,000 ha of permanent crops. Arable land: 24% sugarcane, 23% coconut and 53% other crops. Production figures for 2000 (in 1,000 tonnes): sugarcane, 2,250; coconut, 215; cassava, 30; taro, 27; rice, 18; copra, 14; sweet potatoes, 8. Ginger is becoming increasingly important.

Livestock (2000): cattle, 350,000; horses, 44,000; goats, 235,000; pigs, 115,000; chickens, 4m. Products, 2000 (in 1,000 tonnes): beef and veal, 10; pork, bacon and ham, 4; poultry meat, 8; eggs, 4. Total production of milk was 58,000 tonnes in 2000.

Forestry. Forests covered 815,000 ha—44·6% of the land area—in 2000. Forestry contributed around 1·2% of GDP in 1998. It is the fifth most important export commodity, valued at $F34m. in 1996. Hardwood plantations covered over 48,000 ha in 1996. In 2000 Fiji Pine Ltd had nearly 42,000 ha of softwood plantations. Roundwood production in 2001 was 510,000 cu. metres.

Fisheries. The catch in 2001 was 42,972 tonnes, of which 37,051 tonnes came from sea fishing. In 1997 fisheries accounted for 2% of GDP. Mainstay of export fisheries are the skipjack and albacore tuna for canning. There was an increase in export of fresh and chilled tuna from 53 tonnes in 1989 to over 3,000 tonnes in 1995.

INDUSTRY

The Tax Free Factory scheme was instituted in 1987 as an encouragement to industry. In 1991 it was replaced by the Trade Free Zones (TFZ), of which there were 131 in 2001. However, the scheme is being gradually phased out. The main industries are tourism, garments (a major beneficiary of the TFZ scheme) and sugar, which in 2001 accounted for 19·2%, 12·3% and 8·5% of GDP respectively. In 1987 garments accounted for less than 1% of GDP.

Output (in tonnes): sugar (2002), 334,200; cement (2003), 100,000; flour (2003), 63,559; animal feed (2003), 41,095; coconut oil (2003), 7,523; soap, washing powder and detergents (2003), 3,192; beer (2003), 15·0m. litres; soft drinks (2003), 79·4m. litres; cigarettes (2001), 389m. (units). Garment production was valued at $F129·1m. in 2003.

Labour. Approximately 301,500 persons were in paid employment in 1996. In 2002 there were 23,000 people out of work and seeking employment—the number of unemployed people doubled between 1996 and 2002.

INTERNATIONAL TRADE

The Tax Free Factory/Tax Free Zone Scheme was introduced in 1987 to stimulate investment and encourage export-oriented businesses.

Foreign debt was US$210m. in 2002.

Imports and Exports. Imports totalled $F1·8m. in 2001; exports $F1·2m.

Chief exports are sugar, gold, prepared and preserved fish, timber, ginger and molasses. Main export markets, 2001: Australia, 25·6%; USA, 22·5%; UK, 15·1%. Principal import suppliers, 2001: Australia, 39·8%; New Zealand, 18·7%; Singapore, 5·5%.

COMMUNICATIONS

Roads. Total road length in 1999 was an estimated 3,440 km, of which almost half were surfaced. There were a total of 30,000 passenger cars and 29,000 lorries and vans in 1996. In 1997, 73 fatalities were caused by road accidents.

Rail. Fiji Sugar Cane Corporation runs 600 mm gauge railways at four of its mills on Viti Levu and Vanua Levu, totalling 595 km.

Civil Aviation. There are international airports at Nadi and Suva. The national carrier is Air Pacific (78% government-owned). In 2003 it provided services to Australia, Japan, New Zealand, USA and a number of Pacific island nations. Air Fiji only operates on domestic routes. In 2000 Nadi handled 816,000 passengers (700,000 on international flights).

Shipping. The three ports of entry are Suva, Lautoka and Levuka. Ocean-going shipping totalled 27,000 GRT in 2000, including oil tankers 1,000 GRT. Inter-island shipping fleet is a mix of private and government vessels. A total of 620 foreign vessels called into the Suva port in 1995, 318 and 109 respectively in Lautoka and Levuka. Altogether 7,189 ships including local ships, yachts and foreign vessels called into the three major ports.

Telecommunications. There were 187,400 telephone subscribers in 2002 (224·7 for every 1,000 population). In 1998, 40% of subscribers were business customers and 60% residential. There were over 500 cardphones located around the country in 1998 and approximately 80 in rural areas. In 2002 there were 89,900 mobile phone subscribers and 40,000 PCs in use (48·0 per 1,000 persons). There were 2,800 fax machines in use in 1999 and Internet users numbered 50,000 in 2002.

Postal Services. There were 318 post offices in 1998, or one for every 2,520 persons. A total of 40m. pieces of mail were processed in 1998.

SOCIAL INSTITUTIONS

Justice. An independent Judiciary is guaranteed under the constitution. A High Court has unlimited original jurisdiction to hear and determine any civil or criminal proceedings under any law. The High Court also has jurisdiction to hear and determine constitutional and electoral questions including the membership of the House of Representatives. The Chief Justice of the Fiji Islands is appointed by the President after consultation with the Prime Minister.

The Fiji Islands' Court of Appeal, of which the Chief Justice is *ex officio* President, is formed by three specially appointed Justices of Appeal, appointed by the President after consultation with the Judicial and Legal Services Commission. Generally, any person convicted of an offence has a right of appeal from the High Court of Appeal. The final appellant court is the Supreme Court. Most matters coming before the Superior Courts originate in Magistrates' Courts.

The population in penal institutions in 2002 was 897 (108 per 100,000 of national population).

Police. In 1997 the Royal Fiji Police Force had a total strength of 1,915.

Religion. In 2001 the population consisted of 53% Christians, 38% Hindus, 8% Muslims and 1% others.

Education. Adult literacy rate was 93·2% in 2001 (95·2% among males and 91·2% among females). Total enrolment in 2003: primary schools, 142,781 (with 5,107 teachers); secondary schools, 68,178 (with 3,935 teachers). Enrolment in 1996: teacher training, 903 (with 92 teachers); vocational/technical education, 1,876. The number of registered schools totalled 1,261. Of these there were 391 pre-schools, 16 special schools, 698 primary schools, 151 secondary schools and 5 post secondary schools.

The University of the South Pacific, which is located in Suva, serves 12 countries in the South Pacific region. The Fiji Islands also has a college of agriculture, school of medicine and nursing, an institute of technology, a primary school teacher training college and an advanced college of education.

In 2000–01 total expenditure on education came to 5·1% of GNP and 17·0% of total government spending.

Health. In 1997 there were 25 hospitals with 1,805 beds; 409 doctors, 36 dentists and 1,742 nurses.

Through its national health service system, the government continues to provide the bulk of health services both in the curative and public health programmes. In 1998, 41% of adults in the Fiji Islands aged 15 and over smoked—the second highest percentage of any country, after Russia.

CULTURE

Broadcasting. There are two major radio stations, Island Network Corporation Ltd and Communications Fiji Ltd. Each has its own unique programmes to suit the culture, age and taste of the nation's radio audience. Fiji Television Company is a commercial network that has one free to air and two pay channels (colour by NTSC). In 2001 there were 95,100 TV receivers and in 1997 there were 500,000 radio receivers.

Press. There are two daily newspapers, *Fiji Times and Herald* and *The Daily Post*. Vernacular newspapers are also published by these two, including *Nai Lalakai*, *Nai Volasiga* and *Shanti Dut*. Other locally produced periodicals are the *Review*, *Island's Business*, *Fiji First*, *Pacific Islands Monthly* and *Marama Vou*.

Tourism. Visitor arrivals in 2000 totalled 294,000, earning US$171m.

DIPLOMATIC REPRESENTATIVES

Of the Fiji Islands in the United Kingdom (34 Hyde Park Gate, London, SW7 5DN)
High Commissioner: Emitai Lausiki Boladuadua.

Of the United Kingdom in the Fiji Islands (Victoria House, 47 Gladstone Rd, Suva)
High Commissioner: Charles Mochan.

Of the Fiji Islands in the USA (2233 Wisconsin Ave., NW, Washington, D.C., 20007)
Ambassador: Vacant.
Chargé d'Affaires a.i.: Paula Navunisaravi.

Of the USA in the Fiji Islands (31 Loftus St., Suva)
Ambassador: David Lyon.

Of the Fiji Islands to the United Nations
Ambassador: Isikia Savua.

Of the Fiji Islands to the European Union
Ambassador: Isikeli Uluinairai Mataitoga.

FURTHER READING

Bureau of Statistics. *Annual Report; Current Economic Statistics*. Quarterly

Reserve Bank of Fiji. *Quarterly Review*

Gorman, G. E. and Mills, J. J., *Fiji.* [Bibliography] ABC-Clio, Oxford and Santa Barbara (CA), 1994

Lal, B. J., *Broken Waves: a History of the Fiji Islands in the Twentieth Century.* Univ. of Hawaii Press, 1992

Sutherland, W., *Beyond the Politics of Race: an Alternative History of Fiji to 1992.* Australian National Univ. Press, 1992

National statistical office: Bureau of Statistics, POB 2221, Government Buildings, Suva.

FINLAND

Suomen Tasavalta—
Republiken Finland

Capital: Helsinki
Population projection, 2010: 5·31m.
GDP per capita, 2002: (PPP$) 26,190
HDI/world rank: 0·935/13

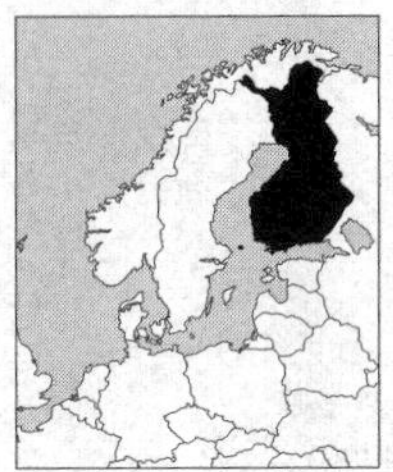

KEY HISTORICAL EVENTS

During the Viking era Finland's location on the trade route between Russia and Sweden brought prosperity and conflict, with attacks frequently made on Finnish trading posts by the Swedes and the Danes. In the 12th century economic and religious rivalry between Sweden and Russia was centred on Finland. By 1323 Russia was forced to recognize a boundary marking off Swedish control including all of western and southern Finland. Finland remained a duchy of Sweden until 1581 when it was made a grand duchy.

In the 18th century Russian forces conquered the southeast territory. The rest of the country was ceded to Russia by the treaty of Hamina in 1809 when Finland became an autonomous grand duchy retaining its laws and institutions under a grand duke, the tsar of Russia. Throughout the 19th century Finland remained in Russia's shadow. With the appointment of General Bobrikov as governor-general in 1898, the army was put under Russian command, the Russian language was made compulsory and decision-making reverted to the tsar's appointees.

Resistance first took the form of non-cooperation but as the Russian revolutionary movement gathered pace, their allies in Finland became bolder. In June 1904 Bobrikov was assassinated and in 1916 the Marxists won an absolute majority in parliamentary elections. Following the Russian Revolution Finland declared its independence in Dec. 1917. This was recognized by the Russian Bolsheviks on 31 Dec. A major breach between the left and right parties in Finland resulted in the Whites (the government forces) taking the western, Russian-controlled province of Ostrobothnia in Jan. 1918 while the Reds (the left-wing forces, supported by the Bolsheviks) seized power in the south. Civil war ensued which the government forces won, led by General Gustaf Mannerheim and aided by German troops. In the summer of 1919 Finland became a republic with K. J. Ståhlberg elected as its first president.

In the 1930s fascism entered domestic politics with the emergence of the Lapua Movement. After an unsuccessful coup attempt in 1932 the movement was banned. As Europe was anticipating German aggression, the Finns were taking up arms to resist Moscow's territorial demands. Outnumbered and outmatched, their hopes were pinned on foreign involvement. When this failed to materialize, there was no option but to give the Russians all they wanted, including the Karelian Isthmus. The 1940 treaty, which ended the Winter War, required the resettlement of 12% of the Finnish population. Fearing worse to come from the Soviet Union, Helsinki opened up contacts with the Germans, allowing transit for military traffic in return for food and armaments.

There followed the German invasion of Russia, a campaign that Mannerheim, in justifying the active participation of his army, described as a 'holy war' to restore Finnish borders. Having achieved this objective, the Finns wanted out, a desire which became all the more determined as the German advance ground to a halt at Stalingrad. But there was no basis for a settlement and the Finns could only wait for the inevitable Russian counter-attack. When it came, retreating Germans took revenge by devastating everything in their path.

Having fought first against Russia then against Germany, the country emerged from the Second World War defeated, demoralized and in political disarray. As president, Mannerheim appointed a government that gave roughly equal representation to the social democrats, communists and the farmers' party. When Mannerheim, who had turned 78 and was ailing fast, was persuaded to stand down in mid-term, Prime Minister Juho Paasikivi was the obvious successor. The peace treaty with Russia was signed in Feb. 1947. Finland lost 12% of her border territory to the Soviet Union, including the country's second largest city of Viipuri and the port and province of Petsamo on the Arctic coast. With a large part of the province of Karelia taken over by the Russians, the frontier was moved back from a distance of only 31 km from Leningrad to a new line 180 km from the former Russian capital. 400,000 people had to be resettled and limitations were imposed on the Finnish armed forces. For a time it seemed as if nothing less than an administration directly answerable to Moscow would satisfy the Russians but Paasikivi succeeded in shifting the emphasis away from Russian ambitions for making Finland an ally towards the more attractive prospect of the two countries' entering into a joint security arrangement, allowing Finland to stand aside from big power politics. Though most of the nation's productive capacity had survived the war intact and the export demand for wood products was strong, the Russian demands caused a severe shortage of skilled labour and consumer goods. Wages and prices climbed steeply, fuelling inflation.

Prime Minister Urho Kekkonen worked hard to establish good personal relations with the Russians. But in 1952 he put up a plan for 'a neutral alliance between the Scandinavian countries', which 'would remove even the theoretical threat of an attack … via Finland's territory'. In reality, a Scandinavian alliance, neutral or otherwise, was impracticable since Denmark and Norway had only recently joined NATO. Moscow congratulated Finland on pursuing the course of 'strict neutrality', indicating that Russia was prepared to recognize Finland as neutral.

In 1955 Finland negotiated the departure of the last Soviet troops on Finnish territory and joined the United Nations—but stayed out of the Warsaw Pact. In 1956 Kekkonen succeeded Paasikivi as president. A succession of weak governments consolidated presidential power and confirmed Kekkonen as the only leader capable of handling the Russians. When he suggested forming relations with the European Community, Russia demanded military bases on Finnish soil. He warned Moscow that if military consultations went ahead there would be a war scare in Scandinavia, possibly leading to counter-measures by the West. When the Soviet Union backed down Kekkonen was elected for a second six-year term by an overwhelming majority.

In 1981 Mauno Koivisto replaced the ailing Kekkonen. At first, he adopted the foreign policy of his predecessor but with the collapse of the Soviet Union at the end of the 1980s he was able to move Finland towards closer ties with Western Europe. Koivisto played a major role in dismantling the 1948 Treaty and in the early 1990s fostered close relations with the EU, leading to membership in 1995.

TERRITORY AND POPULATION

Finland, a country of lakes and forests, is bounded in the northwest and north by Norway, east by Russia, south by the Baltic Sea and west by the Gulf of Bothnia and Sweden. The most recent ten-yearly census took place on 31 Dec. 2000. The area and the population of Finland on 31 Dec. 2003 (Swedish names in brackets):

Provinces (in italics) and Regions	*Area (sq. km)*[1]	*Population*	*Population per sq. km*
Etelä-Suomi (Södra Finland)	*30,173*	*2,116,914*	*70·2*
Uusimaa (Nyland)	6,366	1,338,180	210·2
Itä-Uusimaa (Östra Nyland)	2,747	91,689	33·4
Kanta-Häme (Egentliga Tavastland)	5,204	166,648	32·0
Päijät-Häme (Päijänne-Tavastland)	5,133	198,434	38·7
Kymenlaakso (Kymmenedalen)	5,106	185,662	36·4
Etelä-Karjala (Södra Karelen)	5,618	133,301	24·3
Itä-Suomi (Östra Finland)	*48,727*	*582,781*	*12·0*
Etelä-Savo (Södra Savolax)	14,137	162,296	11·5
Pohjois-Savo (Norra Savolax)	16,808	251,356	15·0
Pohjois-Karjala (Norra Karelen)	17,782	169,129	9·5
Länsi-Suomi (Västra Finland)	*74,185*	*1,848,269*	*24·9*
Varsinais-Suomi (Egentliga Finland)	10,624	452,444	42·6
Satakunta	8,289	234,777	28·3
Pirkanmaa (Birkaland)	12,272	457,317	37·3

Provinces (in italics) and Regions	*Area (sq. km)*[1]	*Population*	*Population per sq. km*
Keski-Suomi (Mellersta Finland)	16,582	266,082	16·0
Etelä-Pohjanmaa (Södra Österbotten)	13,458	193,954	14·4
Pohjanmaa (Österbotten)	7,675	173,111	22·6
Keski-Pohjanmaa (Mellersta Österbotten)	5,286	70,584	13·4
Lappi (Lappland)	*93,004*	*186,917*	*2·0*
Oulu (Uleåborg)	*56,857*	*458,504*	*8·1*
Pohjois-Pohjanmaa (Norra Österbotten)	35,290	371,931	10·5
Kainuu (Kajanaland)	21,567	86,573	4·0
Ahvenanmaa (Åland)	*1,527*	*26,347*	*17·3*
Total	304,473	5,219,732	17·1

[1]Excluding inland water area which totals 33,672 sq. km.

The semi-autonomous province of the **Åland Islands** (Ahvenanmaa) occupies a special position as a demilitarized area and is 93% Swedish-speaking. **Åland** elects a 30-member parliament (*Lagting*), which in turn elects the provincial government (*Landskapsstyrelse*). It has a population of 26,000. The capital is Mariehamn (Maarianhamina).

The growth of Finland's population, which was 421,500 in 1750, has been:

End of year	*Urban*[1]	*Semi-urban*[2]	*Rural*	*Total*	*Percentage urban*
1800	46,600	. . .	786,100	832,700	5·6
1900	333,300	. . .	2,322,600	2,655,900	12·5
1950	1,302,400	. . .	2,727,400	4,029,800	32·3
1970	2,340,300	. . .	2,258,000	4,598,300	50·9
1980	2,865,100	. . .	1,922,700	4,787,800	59·8
1990	2,846,220	803,224	1,349,034	4,998,500	56·9
2000	3,167,668	898,860	1,114,587	5,181,115	61·1
2001	3,190,897	899,120	1,104,884	5,194,901	61·4
2002	3,225,913	882,617	1,097,765	5,206,295	62·0
2003	3,242,443	884,308	1,092,981	5,219,732	62·1

The classification urban/rural has been revised as follows: [1]Urban—at least 90% of the population lives in urban settlements, or in which the population of the largest settlement is at least 15,000. [2]Semi-urban—at least 60% but less than 90% live in urban settlements, or the population of the largest settlement is more than 4,000 but less than 15,000.

The population on 31 Dec. 2003 by language spoken: Finnish, 4,803,343; Swedish, 289,868; other languages, 124,817; Lappish, 1,704.

The projected population for 2010 is 5·31m.

The principal towns with resident population, 31 Dec. 2003, are (Swedish names in brackets):

Helsinki (Helsingfors)—capital	559,330	Rauma (Raumo)	36,869
Espoo (Esbo)	224,231	Lohja (Lojo)	36,004
Tampere (Tammerfors)	200,966	Kokkola (Karleby)	35,756
Vantaa (Vanda)	184,039	Kajaani	35,713
Turku (Åbo)	175,059	Rovaniemi	35,081
Oulu (Uleåborg)	125,928	Tuusula	33,952
Lahti	98,253	Seinäjoki	31,696
Kuopio	88,250	Kouvola	31,339
Jyväskylä	82,409	Kerava (Kervo)	31,170
Pori (Björneborg)	76,189	Imatra	29,969
Lappeenranta (Villmanstrand)	58,897	Nokia	28,090
Vaasa (Vasa)	56,953	Savonlinna (Nyslott)	27,536
Kotka	54,618	Riihimäki	26,654
Joensuu	52,659	Salo	24,794
Hämeenlinna (Tavastehus)	46,909	Raisio (Reso)	23,430
Mikkeli (St Michel)	46,511	Kemi	23,056
Porvoo (Borgå)	46,217	Varkaus	22,761
Hyvinkää (Hyvinge)	43,169	Iisalmi	22,647
Järvenpää	37,114	Tornio (Torneå)	22,198

In 2003, 62·0% of the population lived in urban areas. Nearly one-fifth of the total population lives in the Helsinki metropolitan region.

Finnish and Swedish are the official languages. Sami is spoken in Lapland.

SOCIAL STATISTICS

Statistics in calendar years:

	Living births	*Of which outside marriage*	*Still-born*	*Marriages*	*Deaths (exclusive of still-born)*	*Emigration*
1996	60,723	21,484	231	24,464	49,167	10,587
1997	59,329	21,659	221	23,444	49,108	9,854
1998	57,108	21,244	211	24,023	49,262	10,817
1999	57,574	22,273	177	24,271	49,345	11,966
2000	56,742	22,247	231	26,150	49,339	14,311
2001	56,189	22,222	185	24,830	48,550	13,153
2002	55,555	22,156	176	26,969	49,418	12,891
2003	56,630	22,649	178	25,815	48,996	12,083

In 2003 the rate per 1,000 population was: births, 11; deaths, 9; marriages, 5; infant deaths (per 1,000 live births), 3·1. Annual population growth rate, 1994–2003, 0·3%. In 2003 the suicide rate per 100,000 population was 32·0 among men and 9·8 among women, giving Finland one of the highest suicide rates in Europe. Life expectancy at birth, 2003, 75·1 years for males and 81·8 years for females. In 2003 the most popular age range for marrying was 25–29 for both males and females. Fertility rate, 2003, 1·7 births per woman. In 2003 Finland received 3,221 asylum applications, equivalent to 0·6 per 1,000 inhabitants.

A UNICEF report published in 2000 showed that 4·3% of children in Finland live in poverty (in households with income below 50% of the national median), the third lowest percentage of any country behind Sweden and Norway.

CLIMATE

A quarter of Finland lies north of the Arctic Circle. The climate is severe in winter, which lasts about six months, but mean temperatures in the south and southwest are less harsh, 21°F (–6°C). In the north, mean temperatures may fall to 8·5°F (–13°C). Snow covers the ground for three months in the south and for over six months in the far north. Summers are short but quite warm, with occasional very hot days. Precipitation is light throughout the country, with one third falling as snow, the remainder mainly as rain in summer and autumn. Helsinki (Helsingfors), Jan. 30·2°F (–1·0°C), July 68·4°F (20·2°C). Annual rainfall 27·9" (708·7 mm).

CONSTITUTION AND GOVERNMENT

Finland is a republic governed by the constitution of 1 March 2000 (which replaced the previous constitution dating from 1919). Although the president used to choose who formed the government, under the new constitution it is the responsibility of parliament to select the prime minister. The government is in charge of domestic and EU affairs with the president responsible for foreign policy ‘in co-operation with the government’.

Parliament consists of one chamber (*Eduskunta*) of 200 members chosen by direct and proportional election by all citizens of 18 or over. The country is divided into 15 electoral districts, with a representation proportional to their population. Every citizen over the age of 18 is eligible for parliament, which is elected for four years, but can be dissolved sooner by the president.

The *president* is elected for six years by direct popular vote. In the event of no candidate winning an absolute majority, a second round is held between the two most successful candidates.

National Anthem. ‘Maamme’/‘Vårt land’ (‘Our land’); words by J. L. Runeberg, tune by F. Pacius (same as Estonia).

RECENT ELECTIONS

Presidential elections were held on 16 Jan. 2000 with a second round on 6 Feb. In the first round SDP candidate Tarja Halonen came first with 40·0%, followed by Esko Aho (KESK) with 34·4%. There were five other candidates. In the run-off Halonen won with 51·6% against 48·4% for Aho. Turn-out was around 80%.

At the elections for the 200-member parliament on 16 March 2003, turn-out was 69·6%. The Centre Party (KESK) won 55 seats with 24·7% of votes cast (48 seats in 1999), the ruling Social Democratic Party (SDP) 53 with 24·5% (51 seats in 1999), the National Rally Party (KOK) 40 with 18·5%, the Left Wing League 19 with 9·9% (19), the Greens 14 with 8·0%, the Christian Democrats 7 with 5·3% and the Swedish People's Party (SFP) 8 with 4·6%. Turn-out was 69·6%. Following the March 2003 election 37·5% of the seats in parliament were held by women.

European Parliament. Finland has 14 (16 in 1999) representatives. At the June 2004 elections turn-out was 41·1% (30·1% in 1999). The KOK won 4 seats with 23·7% of votes cast (political affiliation in European Parliament: European People's Party–European Democrats); Centre Party, 4 with 23·3% (Alliance of Liberals and Democrats for Europe); the SDP, 3 with 21·1% (Party of European Socialists); Green League, 1 with 10·4% (Greens/European Free Alliance); Left Wing League, 1 with 9·1% (European Unitary Left/Nordic Green Left); the SFP, 1 with 5·7% (Alliance of Liberals and Democrats for Europe).

CURRENT ADMINISTRATION

President: Tarja Halonen; b. 1943 (Social Democrat; sworn in 1 March 2000).

The Council of State (Cabinet) is composed of a coalition of the Centre Party (KESK), the Social Democratic Party (SDP) and the Swedish People's Party (SFP). Prime Minister Anneli Jäätteenmäki, who took office on 17 April 2003, resigned on 18 June and was deputized by Antti Kalliomäki. Defence Minister Matti Vanhanen was elected prime minister by parliament on 24 June. The 18-member cabinet, consisting of ten men and eight women, comprised in March 2005:

Prime Minister: Matti Vanhanen; b. 1955 (KESK; sworn in 24 June 2003).

Deputy Prime Minister and Minister of Finance: Antti Kalliomäki (SDP). *Foreign Affairs:* Erkki Tuomioja (SDP). *Justice:* Johannes Koskinen (SDP). *Education:* Tuula Haatainen (SDP). *Culture:* Tanja Karpela (KESK). *Interior:* Kari Rajamäki (SDP). *Trade and Industry:* Mauri Pekkarinen (KESK). *Transport and Communications:* Leena Luhtanen (SDP). *Social Affairs and Health:* Sinikka Mönkäre (SDP). *Health and Social Services:* Liisa Hyssälä (KESK). *Labour:* Tarja Filatov (SDP). *Defence:* Seppo Kääriäinen (KESK). *Environment:* Jan-Erik Enestam (SFP). *Regional and Municipal Affairs:* Hannes Manninen (KESK). *Foreign Trade and Development:* Paula Lehtomäki (KESK). *Agriculture and Forestry:* Juha Korkeaoja (KESK). *Minister at the Ministry of Finance:* Ulla-Maj Wideroos (SFP).

The *Speaker* is Paavo Lipponen.

Government Website: http://www.valtioneuvosto.fi

DEFENCE

Conscript service is 6–12 months. Total strength of trained and equipped reserves is about 485,000 (to be 350,000).

Defence expenditure totalled about US$2·2m. in 2004 (1·4% of GDP).

Army. The Army consists of 1 armoured training brigade, 3 readiness brigades, 3 infantry training brigades, 3 jaeger regiments, 1 artillery brigade, 3 brigade artillery regiments, 2 air defence regiments, 1 engineer regiment (including ABC school), 3 brigade engineer battalions, 1 signals regiment, 4 brigade signals battalions and a reserve officer school. Total strength of 27,300 (21,600 conscripts).

Frontier Guard. This comes under the purview of the Ministry of the Interior, but is militarily organized to participate in the defence of the country. It is in charge of border surveillance and border controls. It is also responsible for conducting maritime search and rescue operations. If necessary in the interests of defence capability, the frontier troops or parts thereof may be attached to the Defence Forces. Personnel, 2004, 3,200 (professional) with a potential mobilizational force of 22,000 (to be 8,500).

Navy. The organization of the Navy was changed on 1 July 1998. The Coastal Defence, comprising the coast artillery and naval infantry, was merged into the navy.

About 50% of the combatant units are kept manned, with the others on short-notice reserve and re-activated on a regular basis. Naval bases exist at Upinniemi (near Helsinki), Turku and Kotka. Naval Infantry mobile troops are trained at Tammisaari. Total personnel strength (2004) was 6,800, of whom 4,500 were conscripts.

Air Force. Personnel (2004), 4,500 (1,500 conscripts). Equipment included 63 F-18 Hornets.

INTERNATIONAL RELATIONS

Finland is a member of the UN, WTO, BIS, NATO Partnership for Peace, OECD, EU, Council of Europe, OSCE, CERN, Nordic Council, Council of the Baltic Sea States, Inter-American Development Bank, Asian Development Bank, IOM and the Antarctic Treaty. Finland has acceded to the Schengen Accord, which abolishes border controls between Finland, Austria, Belgium, Denmark, France, Germany, Greece, Iceland, Italy, Luxembourg, the Netherlands, Norway, Portugal, Spain and Sweden.

ECONOMY

Agriculture accounted for 4% of GDP in 2003, industry 31% and services 65%.

According to the Berlin-based organization *Transparency International*, Finland has the least corruption in business and government of any country in the world. It received 9·7 out of 10 in the corruption perceptions index published in 2004.

Overview. Sound macroeconomic policies and economic openness have led the recovery from the recession of the early 1990s. A surplus in central government finances has been achieved by cutting taxes to boost the economy and by a tight control of expenditure. Fiscal policy in 2002 promoted growth in domestic demand. Income tax paid by households, pensioners' social security contribution and employers' national pension contributions have been reduced. In the last decade there has been a structural shift from a resource-based to a knowledge-based economy. The basic metals and forestry industry have given way to ICT (Information and Communications Technology). Finland ranks as one of the world's leading ICT producers.

Currency. On 1 Jan. 1999 the euro (EUR) became the legal currency in Finland; irrevocable conversion rate 5·94573 marks to one euro. The euro, which consists of 100 cents, has been in circulation since 1 Jan. 2002. There are seven euro notes in different colours and sizes denominated in 500, 200, 100, 50, 20, 10 and 5 euros, and eight coins denominated in 2 and 1 euros, then 50, 20, 10, 5, 2 and 1 cents. On the introduction of the euro there was a 'dual circulation' period before the mark ceased to be legal tender on 28 Feb. 2002. Euro banknotes in circulation on 1 Jan. 2002 had a total value of €8·0bn.

Inflation in 2002 was 1·6%, declining to 0·9% in 2003. Foreign exchange reserves were US$7,904m. in June 2002 and gold reserves 1·58m. troy oz. Total money supply was €5,189m. in June 2002.

Budget. Revenue and expenditure for the calendar years 2000–04 in €1m:

	2000	*2001*	*2002*	*2003*	*2004*[1]
Revenue	37,756	35,426	36,353	36,413	37,065
Expenditure	38,472	36,072	35,511	36,897	37,065

[1]Proposed figure.

Of the total revenue in 2003, 34% derived from income and property tax, 28% from value added tax, 13% from excise duties, 6% from other taxes and similar revenue and 19% from miscellaneous sources. Of the total expenditure, 2003, 23% went to health and social security, 16% to education and culture, 7% to agriculture and forestry, 5% to defence, 5% to transport and 44% to other expenditure.

VAT is 22% (reduced rates, 17% and 8%).

At the end of Dec. 2003 the central government debt totalled €63,320m. Domestic debt amounted to €62,079m.; foreign debt, €1,241m.

Performance. Real GDP growth was 1·1% in 2001, rising to 2·2% in 2002, 2·4% in 2003 and (provisional) 3·7% in 2004. Total GDP was US$160·8bn. in 2003.

In March 2003 the OECD reported that 'Finland was more severely affected than most other euro area countries by the global downturn in 2001, but has also recovered more quickly in 2002. ... One factor underlying the more severe downturn was the global slump in demand for ICT (information and communication technology) goods and the importance of this sector in the Finnish economy, although more traditional exports particularly those of the forestry industry also experienced a sharp contraction.'

Finland was placed first in the world in the Growth Competitiveness Index and second behind the USA in the Business Competitiveness Index in the World Economic Forum's *Global Competitiveness Report 2004–05*.

Banking and Finance. The central bank is the Bank of Finland (founded in 1811), operating under the guarantee and supervision of parliament. The Bank is a member of the European System of Central Banks. As a member of the euro area, the Bank issues euro banknotes and coins in Finland by permission of the European Central Bank. The *Governor* is Erkki Liikanen.

At the end of 2003 the deposits in banking institutions totalled €66,424m. and the loans granted by them €81,842m.

The most important groups of banking institutions in 2003 were:

	Number of institutions	*Number of branches*	*Deposits (€1m.)*	*Loans (€1m.)*
Commercial banks	11	493	36,747	49,303
Savings banks	40	232	5,737	5,504
Co-operative banks	284	509	21,392	21,570
Foreign banks	8	29	1,975	5,465

The three largest banks are Nordea Bank Finland (formed in 1997 as MeritaNordbanken when Nordbanken of Sweden merged with Merita of Finland), Sampo Bank (formerly Leonia) and OKO Bank. In March 2000 MeritaNordbanken acquired Denmark's Unidanmark, thereby becoming the Nordic region's biggest bank in terms of assets. It has also become Europe's leading Internet bank, by July 2000 having 1·4m. Internet banking clients. By early 2001 approximately 40% of the Finnish population were using e-banking, the highest percentage in any country.

There is a stock exchange in Helsinki, which is one of the best performers among small industrialized nations. In 1999 share prices rose by 125%.

In 2003 Finland received US$2·8bn. worth of foreign direct investment.

ENERGY AND NATURAL RESOURCES

Environment. Finland's carbon dioxide emissions in 2002 were the equivalent of 12·0 tonnes per capita. An *Environmental Sustainability Index* compiled for the World Economic Forum meeting in Feb. 2002 ranked Finland first in the world, with 73·9%. The index measured the ability of countries to maintain favourable environmental conditions and examined various factors including pollution levels and the use or abuse of natural resources.

Electricity. Installed capacity was 17·7m. kW at the beginning of 2004. Production was 71,617m. kWh. in 2002 (15% hydro-electric) and 71,229m. kWh in 2001 (18% hydro-electric). Consumption per capita in 2002 was an estimated 16,047 kWh. In 2003 there were four nuclear reactors, which contributed 30% of production in 2002. In May 2002 parliament approved the construction of a fifth reactor. Supply: 220 volts; 50 Hz.

Water. Finland has abundant surface water and groundwater resources relative to its population and level of consumption. The total groundwater yield is estimated to be 10–30m. cu. metres a day, of which some 6m. is suitable for water supplies. Approximately 15% of this latter figure is made use of at the present time. A total of 2–4% of Finland's exploitable water resources are utilized each year.

Minerals. Notable of the mines are Pyhäsalmi (zinc–copper), Orivesi (gold ore), Hitura (nickel) and Keminmaa (chromium). In 2002 the metal content (in tonnes) of the output of zinc ore was 34,100; of copper ore, 11,200; of nickel ore, 2,500; of chromium, 248,000.

Agriculture. The cultivated area covers only 7% of the land, and of the economically active population 5% were employed in agriculture and forestry in 2003. In 2003 there were 2·21m. ha of arable land. The arable area was divided in 2003 into 73,714 farms (including 636 farms with under one hectare of arable land). The distribution of this area by the size of the farms was: less than 5 ha cultivated, 6,031 farms; 5–20 ha, 27,486 farms; 20–50 ha, 27,904 farms; 50–100 ha, 10,063 farms; over 100 ha, 2,230 farms.

Agriculture accounted for 0·9% of exports and 1·9% of imports in 2001.

The principal crops (area in 1,000 ha, yield in 1,000 tonnes) were in 2003:

Crop	*Area*	*Yield*	*Crop*	*Area*	*Yield*
Barley	530·7	1,697·4	Hay	101·2	344·6
Oats	425·5	1,294·5	Wheat	191·6	679·0
Potatoes	28·7	617·4	Rye	30·7	72·8

The total area under cultivation in 2003 was 2,212,100 ha. Approximately 7·2% of all agricultural land is used for organic farming. Production of dairy butter in 2003 was 58,402 tonnes; and of cheese, 97,486 tonnes.

Livestock (2003): horses, 60,200 (including trotting and riding horses, and ponies); cattle, 1,000,200; pigs, 1,374,900; poultry, 3,947,100; reindeer, 197,000.

Forestry. Forests covered 23·1m. ha in 2002, or 75·8% of the total land area. The productive forest land covers 20·3m. ha. Timber production in 2003 was 55·0m. cu. metres. Finland is one of the largest producers of roundwood in Europe. Finland's per capita consumption of roundwood is the highest in the world, at 12·32m. cu. metres per person in 2001.

Fisheries. The catch in 2002 was 103,640 tonnes, of which 98,423 tonnes came from sea fishing. In 2003 there were 223 food fish production farms in operation, of which 69 were freshwater farms. Their total production amounted to 12,558 tonnes. In addition there were 104 fry-farms and 294 natural food rearers, most of these in freshwater.

INDUSTRY

The leading companies by market capitalization in Finland, excluding banking and finance, in May 2004 were: Nokia Oyj (US$67·0bn.), the world's leading mobile phone producer; Stora Enso (US$10·7bn.), a forest-products company; and Fortum (US$9·8bn.), an energy company.

Forests are still Finland's most crucial raw material resource, although the metal and engineering industry has long been Finland's leading branch of manufacturing, both in terms of value added and as an employer. In 2002 there were 29,224 establishments in industry (of which 26,766 were manufacturing concerns) with 439,089 personnel (of whom 418,736 were in manufacturing). Gross value of industrial production in 2002 was €102,207m., of which manufacturing accounted for €96,179m.

Labour. In 2003 the labour force was 2,365,000 (52% males). In 2003, 68·3% of the economically active population worked in services, 19·9% in manufacturing and 15·3% in trade and restaurants. In 2004 unemployment was 8·9%, up from 3·2% in 1990, but down from 16·6% in 1994.

Trade Unions. There are three labour organizations: the Confederation of Unions for Academic Professionals—Akateemisten Toimihenkilöiden Keskusjarjesto (AKAVA); the Finnish Confederation of Salaried Employees—Toimihenkilo-keskusjarjesto (STTK); and the Central Organization of Finnish Trade Unions (SAK). According to an incomes policy agreement reached by the central labour market organizations in Nov. 2004, which is in force until Sept. 2007, wages and salaries were to be raised by 1·9% in March 2005 and by 1·4% in June 2006. The government has undertaken to cut taxes on wages and salaries to support moderate pay increases.

INTERNATIONAL TRADE

At the start of the 1990s a collapse in trade with Russia led to the worst recession in the country's recent history. Today, exports to Russia are less than 8% of the total.

Imports and Exports. In 1960 wood and paper industry dominated exports with their 69% contribution, but today the metal and engineering industry is the largest export sector.

Imports and exports for calendar years, in €1m.:

	2000	*2001*	*2002*	*2003*
Imports	36,837	35,891	35,611	36,775
Exports	49,484	47,800	47,245	46,378

Industry	*Exports 2003*
Metal, Engineering, Electronics	55%
Forest Industry	26%
Chemical Industry	6%
Other	13%

Use of Goods	*Imports 2003*
Raw materials, production necessities	38%
Investment goods	22%
Durable consumer goods	12%
Energy	12%
Other	16%

Region	*Exports 2003*	*Imports 2003*
European Union	53%	55%
Other Europe	20%	23%
Developing Countries	14%	12%
EFTA	4%	4%
Other Countries	9%	6%

Trade with principal partners in 2003 was as follows (in €1m.):

	Imports	*Exports*		*Imports*	*Exports*
Australia	283	333	Italy	1,376	1,845
Austria	398	462	Japan	1,507	985
Belgium	872	1,296	Netherlands	1,466	2,169
Brazil	214	212	Norway	1,012	1,118
Canada	123	510	Poland	353	863
China	1,582	1,283	Portugal	166	272
Czech Republic	251	214	Russia	4,367	3,477
Denmark	1,541	1,030	South Korea	329	316
Estonia	1,032	1,138	Spain	604	1,297
France	1,777	1,732	Sweden	4,064	4,590
Germany	5,513	5,491	Switzerland	430	449
Greece	104	392	Taiwan	264	295
Hong Kong	101	408	Turkey	217	374
Hungary	377	357	UK	1,936	3,740
Ireland	386	234	USA	1,711	3,760

COMMUNICATIONS

Roads. In Jan. 2004 there were 78,197 km of public roads, of which 50,539 km were paved. At the end of 2003 there were 2,274,577 registered cars, 77,015 lorries, 250,107 vans and pick-ups, 10,358 buses and coaches and 14,942 special automobiles. Road accidents caused 379 fatalities in 2003.

Rail. In 2003 the total length of the line operated was 5,851 km (2,400 km electrified), all of it owned by the State. The gauge is 1,524 mm. In 2003, 55·9m. passengers and 43·5m. tonnes of freight were carried. There is a metro (21·2 km) and tram/light rail network (83·5 km) in Helsinki.

Civil Aviation. The main international airport is at Helsinki (Vantaa), and there are also international airports at Turku, Tampere, Rovaniemi and Oulu. The national carrier is Finnair. Scheduled traffic of Finnish airlines covered 98m. km in 2003. The number of passengers was 7·6m. and the number of passenger-km 14,008,000; the air transport of freight and mail amounted to 278·8m. tonne-km. Helsinki-Vantaa handled 9,710,920 passengers in 2003 (7,026,302 on international flights) and 88,116 tonnes of freight and mail. Oulu is the second busiest airport, handling 669,882 passengers in 2003, and Rovaniemi the third busiest, with 364,898 in 2003.

Shipping. The total registered mercantile marine in 2003 was 626 vessels of 1,484,711 GRT. In 2003 the total number of vessels arriving in Finland from abroad was 30,037 and the goods discharged amounted to 51·8m. tonnes. The goods loaded for export from Finnish ports amounted to 39·9m. tonnes.

The lakes, rivers and canals are navigable for about 6,300 km. Timber floating has some importance, and there are about 9,149 km of floatable inland waterways. In 2000 bundle floating was about 0·9m. tonnes.

Telecommunications. In 2003 there were 2,568,000 telephone main lines in use and 4,747,000 mobile telephone subscribers. In spring 2004 around 94% of Finnish households owned at least one mobile phone. The rate among 18- and 19-year-olds is almost 100%. In mid-1999 approximately 19% of Finnish households only had a mobile phone and did not have a fixed-line phone at all. The Finnish company Nokia is the world's biggest manufacturer of mobile phones, having a 36% share of the world mobile phone market. It is by far the biggest company in Finland, accounting for 4·5% of the country's GDP in 2000 and more than half the value of its stock exchange. The biggest operator is Sonera (formerly Telecom Finland). Approximately 50% of all voice and data traffic streams through the company's networks, and approximately 60% of all mobile users are Sonera customers. In 2003 Sonera and the Swedish telecommunications operator Telia merged. Finland has the lowest rates in Europe for both fixed and mobile phone calls.

There were 2·3m. PCs in use in 2002 (441·7 per 1,000 persons) and 198,000 fax machines in 1997. Finland had 2·73m. Internet users in May 2004. According to the World Economic Forum's *Global Information Technology Report 2002–2003* Finland is the country best placed to reap the economic and social benefits of the Internet.

Postal Services. In 2003 there were 293 primary post offices and 1,053 agents providing postal services in Finland. Finland Post Group is now exposed to competition in its business operations, with the exception of addressed letter mail for which it holds a licence for nationwide delivery.

SOCIAL INSTITUTIONS

Justice. The lowest court of justice is the District Court. In most civil cases a District Court has a quorum of three legally qualified members. In criminal cases as well as in some cases related to family law the District Court has a quorum with a chair and three lay judges. In the preliminary preparation of a civil case and in a criminal case concerning a minor offence, a District Court is composed of the chair only. From the District Court an appeal lies to the courts of appeal in Turku, Vaasa, Kuopio, Helsinki, Kouvola and Rovaniemi. The Supreme Court sits in Helsinki. Appeals from the decisions of administrative authorities are in the final instance decided by the Supreme Administrative Court, also in Helsinki. Judges can be removed only by judicial sentence. Two functionaries, the Chancellor of Justice and the Ombudsman or Solicitor-General, exercise control over the administration of justice. The former acts also as counsel and public prosecutor for the government; the latter is appointed by Parliament.

At the end of 2003 the daily average number of prisoners was 3,578 of which 205 were women. The number of convictions in 2003 was 283,768, of which 218,883 were for minor offences with a maximum penalty of fines, and 26,678 with penalty of imprisonment. 11,604 of the prison sentences were unconditional.

Religion. Liberty of conscience is guaranteed to members of all religions. National churches are the Lutheran National Church and the Greek Orthodox Church of Finland. The Lutheran Church is divided into eight bishoprics (Turku being the archiepiscopal see), 80 provostships and 567 parishes. The Greek Orthodox Church is divided into three bishoprics (Kuopio being the archiepiscopal see) and 27 parishes, in addition to which there are a monastery and a convent.

Percentage of the total population at the end of 2003: Lutherans, 84·2; Greek Orthodox, 1·1; others, 0·6; not members of any religion, 13·5.

Education. Number of institutions, teachers and students (2003).

Primary and Secondary Education:

	Number of institutions	*Teachers*[1]	*Students*
First-level Education (Lower sections of the comprehensive schools, grades I–VI)	4,248	51,263	400,368[2]
Second-level Education General education (Upper sections of the comprehensive schools, grades VII–IX, and upper secondary general schools)			318,862
Vocational and Professional Education	281[3]	13,548[3, 4]	174,659

[1]Data for teachers refers to 2002.
[2]Including pre-primary education (12,434 pupils) in comprehensive schools.
[3]Numbers of institutions for vocational and professional education refer to secondary and tertiary education.
[4]Number of teachers for vocational and professional education refer to secondary and tertiary education.

Tertiary Education. Vocational and professional education at tertiary education level was provided for 154 students in 2003. In 2003 polytechnic education was provided at 31 polytechnics with 129,875 students and 5,844 teachers (2002). In 2003, 24·6% of the population aged 15 years or over had been through tertiary education.

University Education. Universities with the number of teachers and students in 2003:

	Founded[1]	Teachers	Students Total	Students Women
Universities				
Helsinki	1640	1,648	37,486	23,886
Turku (Swedish)	1918	362	6,725	4,116
Turku (Finnish)	1922	793	15,226	9,715
Tampere	1925	608	14,800	9,761
Jyväskylä	1934	702	13,668	8,728
Oulu	1958	848	15,127	7,333
Vaasa	1968	164	4,850	2,652
Joensuu	1969	403	7,561	4,844
Kuopio	1972	336	5,938	3,917
Lapland	1979	192	4,099	2,835
Universities of Technology				
Helsinki	1849	514	14,599	3,094
Tampere	1965	332	11,889	2,408
Lappeenranta	1969	213	5,549	1,482
Schools of Economics and Business Administration				
Helsinki (Swedish)	1909	100	2,375	1,020
Helsinki (Finnish)	1911	152	4,206	1,836
Turku (Finnish)	1950	100	2,122	1,068
Universities of Art				
Academy of Fine Arts	1848	25	220	119
University of Art and Design	1871	147	1,507	925
Sibelius Academy	1882	239	1,481	815
Theatre Academy	1943	55	418	232
Total		7,933	169,846	90,786

[1]Year when the institution was founded regardless of status at the time.

Adult Education. Adult education provided by educational institutions in 2003.

Type of institution	*Participants*[1]
General education institutions[2]	1,914,000
Vocational and professional education institutions	558,000
Permanent polytechnics	90,500
Universities[3]	141,100
Summer universities	75,400
	2,779,000

[1]Participants are persons who have attended adult education courses run by educational institutions in the course of the calendar year. The same person may have attended a number of different courses and has been recorded as a participant in each one of them.
[2]Including study centres.
[3]Adult education at continuing education centres of universities.

In 2002 total expenditure on education came to 6·4% of GNP and 12·8% of total government spending.

The adult literacy rate in 2003 was almost 100%.

Health. In 2003 there were 16,433 physicians, 4,607 dentists and 37,656 hospital beds. The average Finnish adult smokes 3·5 cigarettes a day and drinks 9·4 litres of alcohol a year.

In 2002 Finland spent 7·3% of its GDP on health.

Welfare. The Social Insurance Institution administers general systems of old-age pensions (to all persons over 65 years of age and disabled younger persons) and of health insurance. An additional system of compulsory old-age pensions paid for by the employers is in force and works through the Central Pension Security Institute. Systems for other public aid are administered by the communes and supervised by the National Social Board and the Ministry of Social Affairs and Health.

The total cost of social security amounted to €36,908m. in 2002. Out of this €16,593m. (45%) was spent on old age and disability, €8,879m. (24%) on health, €5,557m. (15%) on family allowances and child welfare, €3,509m. (10%) on unemployment and €2,372m. (6%) on general welfare purposes and administration. Out of the total expenditure, 39·2% was financed by employers, 23·7% by the State, 19·6% by local authorities, 11·0% by the insured and 6·5% by property income.

CULTURE

World Heritage Sites. Finland has five sites on the UNESCO world heritage list: Old Rauma harbour (1991); the sea fortress of Suomenlinna (1991); the old church of Petäjävesi (1994); Verla groundwood and board mill (1996); and the Bronze Age burial site of Sammallahdenmäki (1999).

Broadcasting. There are four national television channels: *TV1*, *TV2*, *MTV3* and *Channel Four*. The Finnish Broadcasting Company, YLE, is the biggest national radio and television service provider. YLE operates two analogue and five digital national television channels. The second biggest television broadcaster, the privately owned Commercial *MTV3*, has one nationwide channel and one cable channel. The private TV channel, *Channel Four Finland*, started in 1997. In addition, the coverage of the Swedish-language channel *SVT Europa* with programmes from the Swedish channels 1 and 2 extends over southern Finland. There are some 38 local TV stations that mainly relay foreign and domestic programmes over cable and radio waves, in addition to locally produced material. On 31 Dec. 2003 the number of television licences was 2,016,753. The government decided upon the digitalization of the distribution of television and radio broadcasting in the mid 1990s. In 2004 the transmission area covered 94% of Finnish households. Examples of the commercial digital channels are the sports channel (*Urheilukanava*), *SubTV* and the shopping channel *TV5*. There were 3·52m. TV receivers in 2001.

The only radio broadcaster with full nationwide coverage is YLE. It transmits three analogue national channels in Finnish and two in Swedish, as well as various regional channels, including one in Sami in Lapland. In addition YLE has three digital radio channels. At the end of 2003 there were 67 local radio stations. Two of them, the news and music stations Nova and Classic, cover almost 60% of the population. There were 8·4m. radio receivers in 2000.

Cinema. In 2003 there were 338 cinema halls. In 2003 total attendance was 7·7m. and gross box office receipts came to €56·4m. 177 films premiered of which fourteen were Finnish.

Press. Finland has 53 newspapers that are published four to seven times a week, nine of which are in Swedish, and 150 with one to three issues per week. The total circulation of all newspapers is 3·2m. There are 5,042 registered periodicals with a total circulation of over 17m. In terms of total circulation of dailies relative to population, Finland ranks second in Europe after Norway. Most newspapers are bought on subscription rather than from newsstands. Only two newspapers depend entirely on newsstand sales. The five bestselling newspapers in 2003 were: *Helsingin Sanomat* (average daily circulation, 439,618 copies), *Ilta-Sanomat* (198,829), *Aamulehti* (136,331), *Iltalehti* (121,267) and *Turun Sanomat* (111,517). The bestselling newspaper in the Swedish language is *Hufvudstadsbladet*, 50,094.

In 2003 a total of 12,309 book titles were published.

Tourism. There were 21,047,444 foreign tourists in 2003; the income from tourism was €1,656m. and the expenses were €2,150m.

Spas, leisure centres and amusement parks are popular tourism destinations for the Finns, while international tourists favour churches and other religious attractions as well as spas and leisure centres. Major international tourist attractions include Uspensky Cathedral, Helsinki Cathedral and Suomenlinna (all in Helsinki). Helsinki's churches and Santa Park in Rovaniemi are particularly popular among foreigners, who account for the majority of their visitors.

Festivals. Major festivals are the Helsinki Festival Week, the Maritime Festival in Kotka, the Lakeside Blues Festival in Järvenpää, Pori Jazz Festival, Kaustinen Folk Music Festival, Tampere Theatre Festival and Seinäjoki's Tango Festival.

Libraries. The Helsinki University Library doubles as a National Library. The collections of the university libraries and major research libraries comprise in total

53·9m. volumes (of which the university libraries have 21·8m.). In total, they issued 19·4m. loans (university libraries 14·0m.) in 2003.

The revised Public Library Act, which came into force on 1 Jan. 1999, requires each municipality to provide basic library services free of charge. The public library network is comprehensive with 968 libraries altogether. These are complemented by 191 mobile units with over 15,807 service stops. The Helsinki City Library doubles as a Central Library in this sector. Additionally the country is divided into 19 regions with a Regional Central Library providing supplementary services. In 2003 there were over 2·4m. registered borrowers, who represent 47% of the population. The number of loans issued totalled 108·4m.

Theatre and Opera. A new Opera House and a new 14,000-seat Arena Show Hall opened in 1999 in Helsinki. The city hosts both the National Theatre and the National Opera. All major cities have theatres and showhalls. In the summer season open air theatres are very popular. In 2003 there were 13,239 performances in total with over 2·5m. tickets sold.

Museums and Galleries. The National Museum as well as the National Gallery (the Atheneum) are located in Helsinki. The new Museum of Modern Art (Kiasma) was opened in Helsinki in 1998 and a new Ethnographic Museum and a media centre, also in Helsinki, opened in 1999. Major cities all host their own art galleries and local museums. The Alvar Aalto Museum is located in Jyväskylä in central Finland. In 2003 there were 163 museums with full-time personnel. The number of exhibitions was 1,275 and there were 4·5m. visitors.

DIPLOMATIC REPRESENTATIVES

Of Finland in the United Kingdom (38 Chesham Pl., London, SW1X 8HW)
Ambassador: Jaako Laajava.

Of the United Kingdom in Finland (Itäinen Puistotie 17, 00140 Helsinki)
Ambassador: Matthew Kirk.

Of Finland in the USA (3301 Massachusetts Ave., NW, Washington, D.C., 20008)
Ambassador: Jukka Valtasaari.

Of the USA in Finland (Itäinen Puistotie 14B, Helsinki 00140)
Ambassador: Earle I. Mack.

Of Finland to the United Nations
Ambassador: Kirsti Lintonen.

FURTHER READING

Statistics Finland. *Statistical Yearbook of Finland* (from 1879).—*Bulletin of Statistics* (quarterly, from 1971).
Constitution Act and Parliament Act of Finland. Helsinki, 1984
Suomen valtiokalenteri—Finlands statskalender (State Calendar of Finland). Helsinki. Annual
Facts About Finland. Helsinki. Annual (Union Bank of Finland)
Finland in Figures. Helsinki, Annual
Jakobson, M., *Myth and Reality.* Helsinki, 1987
Kirby, D. G., *Finland in the Twentieth Century.* 2nd ed. London, 1984
Klinge, M., *A Brief History of Finland.* Helsinki, 1987
Petersson, O., *The Government and Politics of the Nordic Countries.* Stockholm, 1994
Screen, J. E. O., *Finland.* [Bibliography] 2nd ed. ABC-Clio, Oxford and Santa Barbara (CA), 1997
Singleton, F., *The Economy of Finland in the Twentieth Century.* Univ. of Bradford Press, 1987.—*A Short History of Finland.* 2nd edition. CUP, 1998
Tillotson, H. M., *Finland at Peace and War, 1918–1993.* London, 1993
Turner, Barry, (ed.) *Scandinavia Profiled.* Macmillan, London, 2000

National statistical office: Statistics Finland, FIN-00022.
Website: http://www.stat.fi/

FRANCE

République Française

Capital: Paris
Population projection, 2010: 61·89m.
GDP per capita, 2002: (PPP$) 26,920
HDI/world rank: 0·932/16

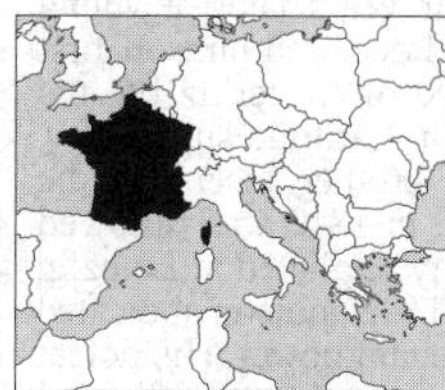

KEY HISTORICAL EVENTS

The Dordogne has evidence of Mousterian industry from 40,000 BC and of Cro-Magnon man of the Upper Paleolithic period. With the end of the Ice Age, agricultural settlement became established around 7000 BC. By the beginning of the 8th century BC, Celtic tribes from Central Europe were in the Rhône valley of Gaul while the Greeks were building cities such as Massalia (Marseilles) along the southern coast.

The Romans crossed the Alps into southern France (Provence) in 121 BC; Julius Caesar conquered the rest of Gaul in 52 BC. Roman rule was threatened by Germanic ('barbarian') incursions from the north and east. Many of these tribes were assimilated as *foederati* (treaty nations) into the Gallo-Roman Empire but they assumed authority in their domains as Roman government receded in the 4th and 5th centuries. After the repulse of Attila and his Huns in 451, the Salian Franks emerged as the strongest of the Germanic tribes under their leader Merovius. The Merovingians remained in power for two centuries but their rule, weakened by internecine warfare, gave way to the Carolingian dynasty in 751. Having extended his empire over Germany and Italy, Charlemagne was crowned emperor of the West by the pope in 800.

After Charlemagne's death in 814 the Carolingians failed to maintain the integrity of their empire; in 987 Hugh Capet, duke of the Franks, ousted the legitimate claimant to the throne and appointed himself king. When Charles IV died in 1328 the Capetian dynasty gave way to the House of Valois. The refusal of King Edward III of England to accept Philippe de Valois' claim to the French throne led to the Hundred Years War (1337–1453). The Treaty of Brétigny (1360) ceded Aquitaine to England but fighting continued. In 1415 Henry V of England was victorious at Agincourt. By marrying the daughter of Charles IV he gained the right of succession to the French throne. The war continued between his son Henry VI and the dauphin Charles (VI) who enlisted the help of Joan of Arc. After leading a series of successful campaigns against the English, she was captured, tried as a heretic by a court of Burgundian ecclesiastics and burnt at the stake in Rouen in 1431. Nevertheless, the English were driven from all their French possessions except Calais by 1453.

The reign of Louis XI (1461–83) saw the beginnings of a modern state with provincial governments responsible to the king. However, François I (1515–47) is considered to be France's first Renaissance monarch and an important patron of the arts. Between 1562–98 the protestant Huguenots and the Spanish-supported Catholic League fought the Wars of Religion. The civil war reached its peak with the 1572 St Bartholomew's Day Massacre, in which 20,000 Huguenots were killed, before ending with Henry of Navarre's conversion to Catholicism. He did not abandon his Huguenot roots, however, and the 1598 Edict of Nantes guaranteed Protestants political and religious rights.

After Henry's assassination in 1610, the young Louis XIII took the throne. Between 1624–42 Cardinal Richelieu, Louis' chief minister, set about establishing absolute royal power, a policy continued by his successor, Cardinal Mazarin. On Mazarin's death, Louis XIV (1643–1715) was able to govern alone. The king formally revoked the Edict of Nantes and once again imposed Catholicism on France. His successor, Louis XV, married Maria, the daughter of the deposed king of Poland, drawing France into the War of the Polish Succession. Further costly military disasters followed including the Seven Years' War, in which France lost her colonies in India, North America and the West Indies.

When Louis XVI succeeded in 1774, he supported the American colonies in their struggle for independence from England, a policy that disseminated revolutionary and democratic ideals in France. The French Revolution erupted in 1789. Riots broke out all over France, culminating in the storming of the Bastille in Paris on 14 July. A new legislative assembly was formed and although the moderate Girondins held power at the start, the more extreme followers of Danton, Robespierre and Marat—the Jacobins—seized power and in 1792 declared a republic.

On 21 Jan. 1793 Louis XVI was guillotined in the Place de la Révolution. A reign of terror led by Robespierre followed in which thousands died. In 1795 the 'Directory of Five' was appointed to run the country. Four years later, a young general, Napoléon Bonaparte, overthrew the government and declared himself first consul. In 1805 he defeated Austria and Russia at the Battle of Austerlitz but the British naval victory at Trafalgar the same year gave Britain maritime supremacy. Napoléon's best troops were bogged down supporting his brother Joseph in the Peninsula War in Spain and his success at Borodino, Russia, in 1812 was followed by the army's forced retreat from Moscow. The Prussian army retaliated at Leipzig, entered France and forced the surrender of Paris in March 1814. Napoléon abdicated in 1814 and retired to Elba but later that year attempted to regain power. His defeat in 1815 at Waterloo ended his 'Hundred Days' reign. He was exiled to the island of St Helena where he died in 1821.

The monarchy was restored under the Bourbon family. A revolution in 1830 brought Louis Philippe, son of the duke of Orleans, to the throne as a constitutional monarch. This 'July Monarchy' was overthrown in 1848 and superseded by the Second Republic, with Louis Napoléon (nephew of Napoléon I) elected president. In 1852 he took the title of Emperor Napoléon III. Defeat in the Franco-Prussian War (1870–71) led to Napoléon being deposed and the proclamation of the Third Republic. But German troops advanced on Paris and after a four-month siege Paris capitulated in Jan. 1871. Alsace and Lorraine were annexed by Germany.

Although Paris was saved from occupation during the First World War, ten departments were overrun and four long years of trench warfare followed. The tide began to turn against Germany in 1916 with the Battle of the Somme, the French stand at Verdun and the arrival of the Americans in 1917. An Armistice was signed on 11 Nov. 1918. By the end of the war France had lost a total of 1·3m. men. The 'Maginot Line', a supposedly impregnable barrier running along the German frontier, was constructed to defend France from German aggression but was sidestepped by the advancing German forces in 1939. The French government capitulated and a pro-German government presided over by Marshal Pétain was established at Vichy. A truce was signed with Germany agreeing to German occupation in the northern third of the country and collaborationist control in the south. General Charles de Gaulle established the Forces Françaises Libres (Free French Forces) and declared the Comité National Français to be the true French government-in-exile with its headquarters first in London and then in Algiers. In Aug. 1944 de Gaulle returned to a liberated Paris to head a provisional government.

In Oct. 1946 the Fourth Republic was established. Despite frequent changes of government and defeat in Indo-China, France returned to economic prosperity. In 1957 a European common market was established of which France, West Germany, Italy and the Benelux countries were founder members.

Between 1954–62 France was embroiled in civil war with Algeria. In 1958 de Gaulle returned first as prime minister and then, by popular vote, as the first president of the newly declared Fifth Republic. In 1962 Algeria gained independence. Strikes and student riots in Paris in 1968 precipitated overdue reforms. The National Assembly was dissolved and, although the Gaullists were returned to power, de Gaulle's referendum proposing further decentralization was defeated and in 1969 he resigned. In 1981 the Socialist leader François Mitterrand was elected president. He implemented widespread social reforms but a recession in 1983 forced him to take unpopular deflationary measures.

When the ailing Mitterrand's term of office expired in 1995, the right-wing Jacques Chirac was elected president but after the Socialists won an Assembly majority in 1997, the Socialist leader Lionel Jospin became prime minister. The right and leftwing *cohabitation* lasted five years until Jospin was defeated in first round presidential elections. Chirac's second electoral success was consolidated by the moderate right taking an Assembly majority in the 2002 elections.

TERRITORY AND POPULATION

France is bounded in the north by the English Channel *(La Manche)*, northeast by Belgium and Luxembourg, east by Germany, Switzerland and Italy, south by the Mediterranean (with Monaco as a coastal enclave), southwest by Spain and Andorra, and west by the Atlantic Ocean. The total area is 543,965 sq. km. Paris is the most populous agglomeration in Europe, with a population of over 9·7m. More than 14% of the population of Paris are foreign and 19% are foreign born.

Population (1999 census), 58,518,748; density, 108 persons per sq. km. Population estimate, 2002: 59,492,000.

The UN gives a projected population for 2010 of 61·89m.

In 2001, 75·5% of the population lived in urban areas.

The growth of the population has been as follows:

Census	*Population*	*Census*	*Population*	*Census*	*Population*
1801	27,349,003	1946	40,506,639	1975	52,655,802
1861	37,386,313	1954	42,777,174	1982	54,334,871
1901	38,961,945	1962	46,519,997	1990	56,615,155
1921	39,209,518	1968	49,778,540	1999	58,518,748
1931	41,834,923				

According to the 1999 census, there were 3·26m. people of foreign extraction in France (5·6% of the population). The largest groups of foreigners with residence permits in 1999 were: Portuguese (573,000), Algerians (545,000) and Moroccans (445,000). France's Muslim population, at 5m., is the highest in Europe.

Controls on illegal immigration were tightened in July 1991. Automatic right to citizenship for those born on French soil was restored in 1997 by the new left-wing coalition government. New immigration legislation, which came into force in 1998, brought in harsher penalties for organized traffic in illegal immigrants and extended asylum laws to include people whose lives are at risk from non-state as well as state groups. It also extended nationality at the age of 18 to those born in France of non-French parents, provided they have lived a minimum of five years in France since the age of 11.

The areas, populations and chief towns of the 22 metropolitan regions at the 1999 census were as follows:

Regions	*Area (sq. km)*	*Population*	*Chief town*
Alsace	8,280	1,734,145	Strasbourg
Aquitaine	41,309	2,908,359	Bordeaux
Auvergne	26,013	1,308,878	Clermont-Ferrand
Basse-Normandie	17,589	1,422,193	Caen
Bourgogne (Burgundy)	31,582	1,610,067	Dijon
Bretagne (Brittany)	27,209	2,906,197	Rennes
Centre	39,151	2,440,329	Orléans
Champagne-Ardenne	25,606	1,342,363	Reims
Corse (Corsica)	8,680	260,196	Ajaccio
Franche-Comté	16,202	1,117,059	Besançon
Haute-Normandie	12,318	1,780,192	Rouen
Île-de-France	12,011	10,925,011	Paris
Languedoc-Roussillon	27,376	2,295,648	Montpellier
Limousin	16,942	710,939	Limoges
Lorraine	23,542	2,310,376	Nancy
Midi-Pyrénées	45,348	2,551,687	Toulouse
Nord-Pas-de-Calais	12,414	3,996,588	Lille
Pays de la Loire	32,082	3,222,061	Nantes
Picardie	19,399	1,857,834	Amiens
Poitou-Charentes	25,809	1,640,068	Poitiers
Provence-Alpes-Côte d'Azur	31,400	4,506,151	Marseilles
Rhône-Alpes	43,698	5,645,407	Lyons

The 22 regions are divided into 96 metropolitan *départements*, which, in 2001, consisted of 36,565 communes.

Populations of the principal conurbations (in descending order of size) and towns at the 1999 census:

	Conurbation	*Town*		*Conurbation*	*Town*
Paris	9,644,507[1]	2,147,857	Lille	1,000,900[2]	191,164
Marseilles–Aix-en-Provence	1,349,772[3]	807,071	Nice	888,784	345,892
			Toulouse	761,090	398,423
Lyons	1,348,832[4]	453,187	Bordeaux	753,931	218,948

	Conurbation	*Town*		*Conurbation*	*Town*
Nantes	544,932	277,728	Caen	199,490	117,157
Toulon	519,640	166,442	Le Mans	194,825	150,605
Douai–Lens	518,727	. . .[5]	Dunkerque	191,173	72,333
Strasbourg	427,245	267,051	Pau	181,413	80,610
Grenoble	419,334	156,203	Bayonne	178,965	41,778
Rouen	389,862	108,758	Limoges	173,299	137,502
Valenciennes	357,395	42,343	Perpignan	162,678	107,241
Nancy	331,363	105,830	Amiens	160,815	139,210
Metz	322,526	127,498	Nîmes	148,889	137,740
Tours	297,631	137,046	Saint-Nazaire	136,886	68,616
Saint-Étienne	291,960	183,522	Annecy	136,815	52,100
Montpellier	287,981	229,025	Besançon	134,376	122,308
Rennes	272,263	212,494	Thionville	130,480	42,205
Orléans	263,292	116,559	Troyes	128,945	62,612
Béthune	259,198	28,522	Poitiers	119,371	87,012
Clermont-Ferrand	258,541	141,004	Valence	117,448	66,568
Avignon	253,580	88,312	Lorient	116,174	61,844
Le Havre	248,547	193,259	La Rochelle	116,157	80,055
Dijon	236,953	153,815	Chambéry	113,457	57,592
Mulhouse	234,445	112,002	Montbéliard	113,059	28,766
Angers	226,843	156,327	Genève–Annemasse	106,673	. . .[6]
Reims	215,581	191,325	Calais	104,852	78,170
Brest	210,055	156,217	Angoulême	103,746	46,324

[1]Including Boulogne-Billancourt (107,042), Argenteuil (95,416), Montreuil (91,146), Versailles (88,476), Saint-Denis (86,871), Nanterre (86,219), Créteil (82,630), Aulnay-sous-Bois (80,315), Vitry-sur-Seine (79,322).
[2]Including Roubaix (98,039), Tourcoing (94,204).
[3]Including Aix-en-Provence (137,067).
[4]Including Villeurbanne (127,299), Vénissieux (56,487).
[5]Including Douai (44,742), Lens (36,823).
[6]Including Annemasse (27,659).

France has 6 national parks, 35 regional national parks and 132 nature reserves.

Languages. The official language is French. Breton and Basque are spoken in their regions. The *Toubon* legislation of 1994 seeks to restrict the use of foreign words in official communications, broadcasting and advertisements (a previous such decree dated from 1975). The Constitutional Court has since ruled that imposing such restrictions on private citizens would infringe their freedom of expression.

SOCIAL STATISTICS

Statistics for calendar years:

	Births	*Deaths*	*Marriages*	*Divorces*
1998	738,080	534,005	271,361	116,349
1999	744,791	537,661	286,191	116,813
2000	774,782	530,864	297,922	114,005
2001	770,945	531,485	288,255	112,631
2002	761,630	534,183	279,087	115,860
2003	760,300[1]	549,600[1]	273,100[1]	125,200[1]

[1]Provisional.

Live birth rate (2002) was 12·8 per 1,000 population; death rate, 9·0; marriage rate, 4·7; divorce rate, 2·0. 44·3% of births in 2002 were outside marriage. In 1999 the most popular age range for marrying was 25–29 for both males and females. Abortions were legalized in 1975; there were an estimated 164,000 in 1997. Life expectancy at birth, 2001, 74·9 years for males and 82·6 years for females. Annual population growth rate, 1992–2002, 0·4%. From 1990–95 the suicide rate per 100,000 population was 20·1 (men, 29·6; women, 11·1). Infant mortality, 2001, 4 per 1,000 live births; fertility rate, 2001, 1·8 births per woman. In 2002 France received 50,798 asylum applications, equivalent to 0·9 per 1,000 inhabitants.

CLIMATE

The northwest has a moderate maritime climate, with small temperature range and abundant rainfall; inland, rainfall becomes more seasonal, with a summer maximum, and the annual range of temperature increases. Southern France has a Mediterranean climate, with mild moist winters and hot dry summers. Eastern France has a continental climate and a rainfall maximum in summer, with thunderstorms prevalent. Paris, Jan. 37°F (3°C), July 64°F (18°C). Annual rainfall 22·9" (573 mm). Bordeaux, Jan. 41°F (5°C), July 68°F (20°C). Annual rainfall 31·4" (786 mm). Lyons, Jan. 37°F (3°C), July 68°F (20°C). Annual rainfall 31·8" (794 mm).

CONSTITUTION AND GOVERNMENT

The Constitution of the Fifth Republic, superseding that of 1946, came into force on 4 Oct. 1958. It consists of a preamble, dealing with the Rights of Man, and 92 articles.

France is a republic, indivisible, secular, democratic and social; all citizens are equal before the law (Art. 2). National sovereignty resides with the people, who exercise it through their representatives and by referendums (Art. 3). Constitutional reforms of July 1995 widened the range of issues on which referendums may be called. Political parties carry out their activities freely, but must respect the principles of national sovereignty and democracy (Art. 4).

A constitutional amendment of 4 Aug. 1995 deleted all references to the 'community' (*communauté*) between France and her overseas possessions, representing an important step towards the constitutional dismantling of the former French colonial empire.

The head of state is the President, who sees that the Constitution is respected; ensures the regular functioning of the public authorities, as well as the continuity of the state; is the protector of national independence and territorial integrity (Art. 5). As a result of a referendum held on 24 Sept. 2000 the President is elected for five years by direct universal suffrage (Art. 6). Previously the term of office had been seven years. The President appoints (and dismisses) a Prime Minister and, on the latter's advice, appoints and dismisses the other members of the government (*Council of Ministers*) (Art. 8); presides over the Council of Ministers (Art. 9); may dissolve the National Assembly, after consultation with the Prime Minister and the Presidents of the two Houses (Art. 12); appoints to the civil and military offices of the state (Art. 13). In times of crisis, the President may take such emergency powers as the circumstances demand; the National Assembly cannot be dissolved during such a period (Art. 16).

Parliament consists of the National Assembly and the Senate. The National Assembly is elected by direct suffrage by the second ballot system (by which candidates winning 50% or more of the vote in their constituencies are elected, candidates winning less than 12·5% are eliminated and other candidates go on to a second round of voting); the Senate is elected by indirect suffrage (Art. 24). Since 1996 the National Assembly has convened for an annual nine-month session. It comprises 577 deputies, elected by a two-ballot system for a five-year term from single-member constituencies (555 in Metropolitan France, 22 in the overseas departments and dependencies), and may be dissolved by the President.

The *Senate* comprises 321 senators elected for nine-year terms (one-third every three years) by an electoral college in each Department or overseas dependency, made up of all members of the Departmental Council or its equivalent in overseas dependencies, together with all members of Municipal Councils within that area. The *Speaker* of the Senate deputizes for the President of the Republic in the event of the latter's incapacity. Senate elections were last held on 26 Sept. 2004.

The *Constitutional Council* is composed of nine members whose term of office is nine years (non-renewable), one-third every three years; three are appointed by the President of the Republic, three by the President of the National Assembly, three by the President of the Senate; in addition, former Presidents of the Republic are, by right, life members of the Constitutional Council (Art. 56). It oversees the fairness of the elections of the President (Art. 58) and Parliament (Art. 59), and of referendums (Art. 60), and acts as a guardian of the Constitution (Art. 61). Its *President* is Pierre Mazeaud (appointed 27 Feb. 2004).

The *Economic and Social Council* advises on Government and Private Members' Bills (Art. 69). It comprises representatives of employers', workers' and farmers' organizations in each Department and Overseas Territory.

Ameller, M., *L'Assemblée Nationale.* Paris, 1994

Duhamel, O. and Mény, Y., *Dictionnaire Constitutionnel.* Paris, 1992

Elgie, R. (ed.) *Electing the French President: the 1995 Presidential Election.* Macmillan, London, 1996

National Anthem. 'La Marseillaise'; words and tune by C. Rouget de Lisle.

RECENT ELECTIONS

At the first round of presidential elections on 21 April 2002 Jacques Chirac gained the largest number of votes (19·87% of those cast) against 15 opponents. His nearest rivals were the National Front leader Jean-Marie Le Pen, who came second with 16·86% of votes cast, and incumbent prime minister Lionel Jospin, with 16·17%. The result caused a series of anti-Le Pen protest rallies across France. Socialist leaders urged their supporters to vote for Chirac in the second round run-off between Chirac and Le Pen in order that the extreme right-wing leader might be kept from gaining power. In the second round of voting, held on 5 May 2002, Jacques Chirac won a second consecutive presidential term in a landslide victory, with 82·21% of votes cast against 17·79% for Le Pen. Turn-out was 79·7%.

Elections to the National Assembly were held on 9 and 16 June 2002. The Union for the Presidential Majority (UMP)—formed by the Rassemblement pour la République (Rally for the Republic) and the Démocratie Libérale (Liberal Democracy)—the allies of President Jacques Chirac, gained an overwhelming parliamentary majority with 357 seats, winning 33·7% of votes cast; the Socialist Party (PS), 140 seats with 24·1%; the Union for French Democracy (UDF), 29 seats with 4·8%; the Communist Party (PCF), 21 seats with 4·8%; the Greens, 3 seats with 4·5%. Despite winning 11·3% of votes cast, the National Front (FN) failed to gain a single seat. The result brought to an end five years of 'cohabitation', with a right-wing president and a socialist prime minister.

In March 2002 only 55 out of 564 deputies were women. The proportion of women deputies, at 9·8%, is the lowest of any EU-member country.

Following the election held on 26 Sept. 2004, the Senate was composed of (by group, including affiliates): UMP, 155; the Socialist Group, 97; the Centrist Group, 33; Républicain, Communiste et Citoyen (RCC), 23; Democratic and Social European Rally, 15; Unattached, 8. In Oct. 1998 Christian Poncelet (RPR) was elected *Speaker* for a three-year term. He was re-elected for a further term in Oct. 2001 and again in Oct. 2004.

European Parliament. France has 78 (87 in 1999) representatives. At the June 2004 elections turn-out was 43·1% (47·0% in 1999). The PS won 31 seats with 28·9% of votes cast (political affiliation in European Parliament: Party of European Socialists); Union pour un Mouvement Populaire, 17 with 16·6% (European People's Party–European Democrats); UDF, 11 with 12·0% (Alliance of Liberals and Democrats for Europe); the FN, 7 with 9·8% (non-attached); the Greens, 6 with 7·4% (Greens/European Free Alliance); Mouvement pour la France, 3 with 6·7% (Independence and Democracy Group); PCF, 2 with 5·3% (European Unitary Left/Nordic Green Left); Union de la Gauche, 1 with 1·4% (European Unitary Left/Nordic Green Left).

CURRENT ADMINISTRATION

President: Jacques Chirac; b. 1932 (RPR; sworn in 17 May 1995 and re-elected 5 May 2002).

After the presidential election of May 2002 the Socialist Prime Minister Lionel Jospin resigned and an interim centre-right government was installed. Following the parliamentary elections of June 2002 all of the cabinet members were confirmed in their posts. Prime Minister Raffarin and his government resigned on 30 March 2004 after poor results in regional elections. Raffarin was immediately reappointed and a cabinet reshuffle carried out. In March 2005 the cabinet comprised:

Prime Minister: Jean-Pierre Raffarin; b. 1948 (Liberal Democracy; sworn in 6 May 2002).

Minister of the Economy, Finance and Industry: Thierry Breton. *National Education, Higher Education and Research:* François Fillon. *Interior, Domestic Security and Local Freedoms:* Dominique de Villepin. *Employment, Labour and Social Cohesion:* Jean-Louis Borloo. *Justice and Keeper of the Seals:* Dominique Perben. *Defence and Veterans' Affairs:* Michèle Alliot-Marie. *Foreign Affairs, Co-operation and Francophony:* Michel Barnier. *Solidarity, Health and the Family:* Philippe Douste-Blazy. *Capital Works, Transportation, Land Management, Tourism and Maritime Affairs:* Gilles de Robien. *Civil Service and Administrative Reform:* Renaud Dutreil. *Agriculture, Food, Fisheries and Rural Affairs:* Dominique Bussereau. *Environment and Sustainable Development:* Serge Lepeltier. *Culture and*

Communication: Renaud Donnedieu de Vabres. *Overseas Departments and Territories:* Brigitte Girardin. *Youth, Sport and Community:* Jean-François Lamour. *Parity and Professional Equality:* Nicole Ameline. *Small and Medium-Sized Enterprises, Trade, Small-Scale Industry, the Professions and Consumer Affairs:* Christian Jacob.

President of the National Assembly: Jean-Louis Debré.

Office of the Prime Minister: http://www.premier-ministre.gouv.fr/

DEFENCE

The President of the Republic is the supreme head of defence policy and exercises command over the Armed Forces. He is the only person empowered to give the order to use nuclear weapons. He is assisted by the Council of Ministers, which studies defence problems, and by the Defence Council and the Restricted Defence Committee, which formulate directives.

Legislation of 1996 inaugurated a wide-ranging reform of the defence system over 1997–2002, with regard to the professionalization of the armed forces (brought about by the ending of military conscription and consequent switch to an all-volunteer defence force), the modification and modernization of equipment and the restructuring of the defence industry. In 2003 defence expenditure totalled US$45,695m. (equivalent to US$765 per capita). Defence spending as a proportion of GDP has fallen from 3·9% in 1985 to 2·6% in 2003.

French forces are not formally under the NATO command structure, although France signed the NATO strategic document on eastern Europe in Nov. 1991. The Minister of Defence attends informal NATO meetings which have an agenda of French interest, but not the formal twice-yearly meetings. Since Dec. 1995 France has taken a seat on the NATO Military Committee. In early 2004 there were 33,441 French military personnel stationed outside France, in a number of countries including Afghanistan, Bosnia-Herzegovina, Côte d'Ivoire, the Democratic Republic of the Congo and Macedonia.

Conscription was for ten months, but France officially ended its military draft on 27 June 2001 with a reprieve granted to all conscripts (barring those serving in civil positions) on 30 Nov. 2001.

Nuclear Weapons. Having carried out its first test in 1960, there have been 210 tests in all. The last French test was in 1996 (this compares with the last UK test in 1991 and the last US test in 1993). The nuclear arsenal consisted of approximately 348 warheads in Jan. 2004 according to the Stockholm International Peace Research Institute.

Arms Trade. France was the world's fourth largest exporter after the USA, the UK and Russia in 2002, with sales worth US$1,800m., or 7·1% of the world total.

Army. The Army comprises the Logistic Force (CFLT), based in Montlhéry with two logistic brigades, and the Land Force Command (CFAT), based in Lille. Apart from the Franco-German brigade, there are 12 brigades, each made up of between four and seven battalions, including one airmobile brigade.

Personnel numbered (2002) 168,126 (5,544 volunteers and 11,240 women) including 16,500 marines and a Foreign Legion of 8,000. There were 242,500 reserves in 2002. The 1997–2002 Programming Act provided for the following force at the end of the transitional period: 16,000 officers, 50,000 NCOs, 66,500 army enlistees, 5,500 volunteers, 34,000 civilians and 30,000 reservists. Equipment levels in 2001 included 809 main battle tanks and 410 helicopters.

Gendarmerie. The paramilitary police force exists to ensure public security and maintain law and order, as well as participate in the operational defence of French territory as part of the armed forces. It consisted in 2002 of 98,135 personnel including 15,203 volunteers, 5,705 women and 2,020 civilians. It comprises a territorial force of 69,000 personnel throughout the country, a mobile force of 17,025 personnel and specialized formations including the Republican Guard, the Air Force and Naval Gendarmeries, and an anti-terrorist unit.

Navy. The missions of the Navy are to provide the prime element of the French independent nuclear deterrent through its force of strategic submarines; to assure the security of the French offshore zones; to contribute to NATO's missions; and to provide on-station and deployment forces overseas in support of French territorial interests and UN commitments. French territorial seas and economic zones are organized into two maritime districts (with headquarters in Brest and Toulon).

The strategic deterrent force comprises four nuclear-powered strategic-missile submarines, including two of four new-generation ships of a new, much larger, class, *Le Triomphant* and *Le Téméraire*, which entered service in 1997 and 1999.

Until it was withdrawn from service in 2000, the *Foch*, of 33,000 tonnes, was the principal surface ship. The 40,000-tonne nuclear-powered replacement *Charles de Gaulle*, which was launched at Brest in 1994, commissioned in Oct. 2000. There is one cruiser, the *Jeanne d'Arc*, completed in 1964 and used in peacetime as a training vessel. Other surface combatants include four destroyers and 26 frigates.

The naval air arm, *Aviation Navale*, numbers some 6,800 personnel. Operational aircraft include Super-Etendard nuclear-capable strike aircraft, Etendard reconnaissance aircraft and maritime Rafale combat aircraft. A small Marine force of 1,700 *Fusiliers Marins* provides assault groups.

Personnel in 2002 numbered 54,433, including 1,613 volunteers, 3,328 women and 10,157 civilians. There were 97,000 reserves in 2002.

Air Force. Created in 1934, the Air Force was reorganized in June 1994. The Conventional Forces in Europe (CFE) Agreement imposes a ceiling of 800 combat aircraft. In 2002 there were 355 combat aircraft, 100 transport aircraft and 290 aircraft for training purposes.

Personnel (2002) 69,667 (1,942 volunteers; 8,210 women; 6,003 civilians). Air Force reserves in 2002 numbered 79,500.

INTERNATIONAL RELATIONS

France is a member of the UN, WTO, BIS, the Council of Europe, WEU, EU, OSCE, OECD, CERN, Inter-American Development Bank, Asian Development Bank, the Pacific Community, IOM, Antarctic Treaty and the International Organization of the Francophonie. France is a signatory to the Schengen Accord, which abolishes border controls between France, Austria, Belgium, Denmark, Finland, Germany, Greece, Iceland, Italy, Luxembourg, the Netherlands, Norway, Portugal, Spain and Sweden.

At a referendum in Sept. 1992 to approve the ratification of the Maastricht treaty on European union of 7 Feb. 1992, 12,967,498 votes (50·81%) were cast for and 12,550,651 (49·18%) against.

France is the focus of the *Communauté Francophone* (French-speaking Community) which formally links France with many of its former colonies in Africa. A wide range of agreements, both with members of the Community and with other French-speaking countries, extend to economic and technical matters, and in particular to the disbursement of overseas aid.

ECONOMY

Agriculture accounted for 2·7% of GDP in 2002, industry 24·9% and services 72·4%.

Overview. France ranks among the world's top five economies. The agricultural sector is larger than that of other OECD countries, with agriculture contributing approximately 3% of GDP and employing 5% of the workforce. France enjoys high per capita income and business sector productivity but has a high tax burden and one of the largest fiscal deficits in the euro area. Since monetary policy is now set for the euro area as a whole the government has only the budget as an instrument to influence domestic demand. According to the IMF, strengthening the fiscal framework is essential. In 2004, owing to structural relaxation of fiscal policy, the budget deficit exceeded the 3% target set by the European Stability and Growth Pact. Tax cuts and additional government spending have not as yet been offset by savings elsewhere in the budget. The IMF maintains that rigid labour markets have had a severe adverse impact on the budget. To alleviate these problems the government has limited the adoption of the 35-hour workweek and has also phased out some public employment programmes. Public expenditure has been put under pressure, with health care running above budget. The health system is more expensive than in most OECD countries and nearly 10% of GDP is spent on health. Fiscal policy also faces the challenge posed by the ageing population, which is expected to result in the ratio of people retired to those employed doubling by 2030.

Currency. On 1 Jan. 1999 the euro (EUR) became the legal currency in France; irrevocable conversion rate 6·55957 francs to one euro. The euro, which consists of 100 cents, has been in circulation since 1 Jan. 2002. There are seven euro notes in different colours and sizes denominated in 500, 200, 100, 50, 20, 10 and 5 euros, and eight coins denominated in 2 and 1 euros, then 50, 20, 10, 5, 2 and 1 cents. On the introduction of the euro there was a 'dual circulation' period before the franc ceased to be legal tender on 17 Feb. 2002. Euro banknotes in circulation on 1 Jan. 2002 had a total value of €84·2bn.

Foreign exchange reserves were US$23,338m. in June 2002 and gold reserves 97·25m. troy oz (81·89m. troy oz in 1997). Inflation was 1·9% in 2002 and 2·1% in 2003. Total money supply was €62,266m. in June 2002.

Franc Zone. 13 former French colonies (Benin, Burkina Faso, Cameroon, Central African Republic, Chad, Comoros, the Republic of the Congo, Côte d'Ivoire, Gabon, Mali, Niger, Senegal and Togo), the former Spanish colony of Equatorial Guinea and the former Portuguese colony of Guinea-Bissau are members of a Franc Zone, the CFA (*Communauté Financière Africaine*). Comoros uses the Comorian franc. The *franc CFA* is pegged to the euro at a rate of 655·957 francs CFA to one euro. The franc CFP *(Comptoirs Français du Pacifique)* is the common currency of French Polynesia, New Caledonia and Wallis and Futuna. It is pegged to the euro at 119·3317422 francs CFP to the euro.

Budget. Receipts and expenditure in €1m.:

	2001	*2002*	*2003*
Revenue	662,110	674,870	688,770
Expenditure	683,500	723,130	749,390

Principal sources of revenue in 2003: social security contributions, €258·90bn.; taxes on goods and services, €165·61bn.; taxes on income, profits and capital gains, €159·99bn. Main items of expenditure by economic type in 2003: social benefits, €367·54bn.; compensation of employees, €167·86bn.; grants, €70·26bn.

The standard rate of VAT is 19·6% (reduced rates, 5·5% and 2·1%). In 2003 the top rate of income tax was 49·58% and corporate tax was 33·3%.

In both 2002 and 2003 the budget deficit exceeded 3%, the target set by the European Stability and Growth Pact, reaching 3·2% in 2002 and 4·1% in 2003.

Ministère de l'Economie, des Finances et du Plan. *Le Budget de l'Etat: de la Préparation à l'Exécution.* Paris, 1995

Performance. Real GDP growth was 2·1% in 2001, 1·1% in 2002 and 0·6% in 2003, rising to 2·3% (provisional) in 2004. Total GDP in 2003 was US$1,748bn.

The July 2003 *OECD Economic Survey* warns: 'Over the medium-term in the absence of substantial reforms, the ageing of the population risks to threaten economic and fiscal equilibrium.'

Banking and Finance. The central bank and bank of issue is the *Banque de France* (*Governor*, Christian Noyer, appointed 2003), founded in 1800, and nationalized on 2 Dec. 1945. The Governor is appointed for a six-year term (renewable once) and heads the nine-member Council of Monetary Policy.

The National Credit Council, formed in 1945 to regulate banking activity and consulted in all political decisions on monetary policy, comprises 51 members nominated by the government; its president is the Minister for the Economy; its Vice-President is the Governor of the Banque de France.

In 1996 there were 1,445 banks and other credit institutions, including 400 shareholder-owned banks and 342 mutual or savings banks. Four principal deposit banks were nationalized in 1945, the remainder in 1982; the latter were privatized in 1987. The banking and insurance sectors underwent a flurry of mergers, privatizations, foreign investment, corporate restructuring and consolidation in 1997, in both the national and international fields. The largest banks in 2003 by assets were: Crédit Agricole (US$989,863m.), BNP Paribas (US$986,128m.) and Société Générale (US$679,250m.). In 2004 the largest banks by market value were BNP Paribas (US$53,143m.), Société Générale (US$37,405m.) and Crédit Agricole (US$37,069m.).

The state savings organization *Caisse Nationale d'Epargne* is administered by the post office on a giro system. There are also commercial savings banks (*caisses d'epargne et de prévoyance*). Deposited funds are centralized by a non-banking body, the *Caisse de Dépôts et Consignations*, which finances a large number of local authorities and state-aided housing projects, and carries an important portfolio of transferable securities.

France attracted a record US$50·47bn. worth of foreign direct investment in 2001, although in 2003 this fell slightly to US$46·98m.

There is a stock exchange (Bourse) in Paris; it is a component of Euronext, which was created in Sept. 2000 through the merger of the Paris, Brussels and Amsterdam bourses.

ENERGY AND NATURAL RESOURCES

Environment. France's carbon dioxide emissions from the consumption and flaring of fossil fuels in 2002 were the equivalent of 6·8 tonnes per capita. An *Environmental Sustainability Index* compiled for the World Economic Forum meeting in Feb. 2002 ranked France 33rd in the world, with 55·5%. The index measured the ability of countries to maintain favourable environmental conditions and examined various factors including pollution levels and the use or abuse of natural resources.

Electricity. The state-owned monopoly Electricité de France is responsible for power generation and supply under the Ministry of Industry. Installed capacity was 116·6m. kW in 2000. Electricity production in 2000: 546·71bn. kWh, of which 75·9% was nuclear. Hydro-electric power contributes about 13·1% of total electricity output. Consumption per capita in 2000 was 8,099 kWh. In 2002 France was the European Union's biggest exporter of electricity with 93·7bn. kWh. Electricité de France is Europe's leading electricity producer, generating 486bn. kWh in 2002.

France, not rich in natural energy resources, is at the centre of Europe's nuclear energy industry. In 2003 there were 59 nuclear reactors in operation—more than in any other country in the world apart from the USA—with a generating capacity of 63,473 MW. Only Lithuania has a higher percentage of its electricity generated through nuclear power.

Oil and Gas. In 2000, 1·4m. tonnes of crude oil were produced. The greater part came from the Parentis oilfield in the Landes. Reserves in 2002 totalled 148m. bbls. The importation and distribution of natural gas is the responsibility of the government monopoly Gaz de France. Production of natural gas (2000) was 1·6bn. cu. metres. Gas reserves were 14bn. cu. metres in 2002.

Minerals. France is a significant producer of nickel, uranium, iron ore, bauxite, potash, pig iron, aluminium and coal. Société Le Nickel extracts in New Caledonia and is the world's third largest nickel producer.

Coal production in 2002 was 2·1m. tonnes. Coal reserves in Dec. 2001 were 36m. tonnes, but France's last coal mine closed in April 2004. Production of other principal minerals and metals, in 1,000 tonnes: salt (2002), 7,100; aluminium (2001), 462; potash salts (2001), 257; gold (2000), 2,632 kg.

Agriculture. France has the highest agricultural production in Europe. In 2000 the agricultural sector employed about 885,000 people, down from 1,869,000 in 1980. Agriculture accounts for 14·5% of exports and 11·4% of imports.

In 2000 there were 664,000 holdings (average size 42 ha), down from over 1m. in 1988. Co-operatives account for between 30–50% of output. There were 1,264,000 tractors and 91,000 harvester-threshers in 2001. Although the total number of tractors has been declining steadily in recent years, increasingly more powerful ones are being used. In 1997, 368,000 tractors in use were of 80 hp or higher, compared to 96,000 in 1979.

Of the total area of France (54·9m. ha), the utilized agricultural area comprised 29·63m. ha in 2001. 18·45m. ha were arable, 10·05m. ha were under pasture, and 1·14m. ha were under permanent crops including vines (0·90m. ha).

Area under cultivation and yield for principal crops:

	Area (1,000 ha)			*Production (1,000 tonnes)*		
	1998	*1999*	*2000*	*1998*	*1999*	*2000*
Wheat	5,235	5,114	5,266	39,809	37,002	37,529
Sugarbeets	456	442	414	31,156	32,919	31,454
Maize	1,797	1,759	1,834	15,191	15,656	16,469
Barley	1,631	1,534	1,573	10,591	9,539	9,927

	Area (1,000 ha)			Production (1,000 tonnes)		
	1998	1999	2000	1998	1999	2000
Potatoes	164	171	169	6,053	6,645	6,652
Rapeseeds	1,145	1,369	1,225	3,734	4,469	3,572
Peas	640	510	465	3,775	3,179	2,507
Sunflower seeds	782	799	720	1,713	1,868	1,824

Production of principal fruit crops (in 1,000 tonnes) as follows:

	1998	1999	2000
Apples	2,210	2,643	2,537
Peaches	202	280	272
Melons	324	322	314
Pears	260	300	271
Plums	205	185	214

Total fruit and vegetable production in 2000 was 19,075,000 tonnes. Other important vegetables include tomatoes (898,000 tonnes in 2000), carrots (450,000 tonnes), cauliflowers (412,000 tonnes) and onions (361,000 tonnes). France is the world's leading producer of sugarbeets. Total area under cultivation and yield of grapes from the vine (2000): 745,000 ha; 7·63m. tonnes. Wine production (2002): 5,200,000 tonnes. France is the largest wine producer in the world, having overtaken Italy in 1999. Consumption in France has declined dramatically in recent times, from nearly 120 litres per person in 1966 to 57 litres per person in 2001.

Figures compiled by the Soil Association, a British organization, show that in 1999 France set aside 220,000 ha (1% of its agricultural land) for the growth of organic crops, compared to the EU average of 2·2%.

Livestock (2000, in 1,000): cattle, 20,527; pigs, 14,635; sheep, 10,004; goats, 1,191; horses, 349; chickens, 233,000; turkeys, 42,000; ducks, 24,000. Livestock products (2000, in 1,000 tonnes): pork, bacon and ham, 2,315; beef and veal, 1,590; lamb and mutton, 130; poultry, 2,022; horse, 10; eggs, 1,050. Milk production, 2000 (in 1,000 tonnes): cow, 24,890; sheep, 247; goat, 483. Cheese production, 1,668,000 tonnes. France is the second largest cheese producer in the world after the USA.

Source: SCEES/Agreste

Forestry. Forestry is France's richest natural resource and employs 550,000 people. In 2000 forest covered 15·05m. ha (27·4% of the land area). In 1990 the area under forests had been 14·23m. ha, or 25·9% of the land area. 65% of forest is privately owned. 51,000 ha of land in France is reforested annually. Timber production in 2001 was 38·81m. cu. metres.

Fisheries. In 2002 there were 8,088 fishing vessels totalling 229,762 GRT, and (in 1996) 16,556 fishermen. Catch in 2001 was 606,194 tonnes, of which 604,064 tonnes were from marine waters.

INDUSTRY

The leading companies by market capitalization in France, excluding banking and finance, in May 2004 were: Total Fina Elf SA (US$122·9bn.), an integrated oil company; Aventis (US$63·7bn.), a pharmaceuticals and biotechnology company; and France Telecom (US$59·3bn.).

The industrial sector employs about 19% of the workforce. In 2000 capacity utilization in industry was approaching 88%. Chief industries: steel, chemicals, textiles, aircraft, machinery, electronic equipment, tourism, wine and perfume.

Industrial production (in 1,000 tonnes): distillate fuel oil (2000), 34,596; cement (2001), 20,652; crude steel (2002), 20,300; petrol (2000), 17,231; pig iron (2002), 13,500; residual fuel oil (2000), 11,090; jet fuel (2000), 6,030; sulphuric acid (2001), 2,051; caustic soda (1999), 777. France is one of the biggest producers of mineral water, with 6,283m. litres in 2001; soft drinks production in 2000, 2,276m. litres; beer production in 2001, 1,572m. litres; cigarette production in 2001, 41·8bn. units.

Engineering production (in 1,000 units): passenger cars (2002), 3,009; car tyres (2001), 63,790; television sets (2002), 5,375; radio sets (2002), 3,357.

Labour. Out of an economically active population of 23,529,000 in March 2000, 44·7% were women. By sector, 71·5% worked in services (58·1% in 1980), 24·4% in industry and construction (33·1% in 1980) and 4·1% in agriculture (8·8% in 1980). Some 5m. people work in the public sector at national and local level. It was estimated in 1997 that 51% of households have no-one working in the private sector.

A new definition of 'unemployed' was adopted in Aug. 1995, omitting persons who had worked at least 78 hours in the previous month. The unemployment rate has risen over the past few years, from 8·5% in 2001 to 9·6% in 2004.

Conciliation boards (*Conseils de Prud'hommes*) mediate in labour disputes. They are elected for five-year terms by two colleges of employers and employees. Between 1989 and 1998 strikes cost France an average of 45 days per 1,000 employees a year, compared to the EU average of 85 per 1,000. In July 2003 the minimum wage (SMIC) was raised to €7·19 an hour (€1,090·48 a month for a 35-hour week); it affected about 2·1m. wage-earners in July 2003. The net average annual wage was 130,790 francs (€19,938) in 1999. Retirement age is 60, although the average actual age for retirement is 57. A five-week annual holiday is statutory.

In March 2005 the National Assembly voted by 350 to 135 to amend the working hours law restricting the legal working week to 35 hours, introduced by the former Socialist government between 1998–2000. Under the new proposals employees can, in agreement with their employer, work up to 48 hours per week. There is no change in the legal working week: any increased hours are on a voluntary basis. The proposal also allows for the increase of overtime hours from 180 to 220 per year, payable at 125% of the normal hourly rate (110% for businesses employing fewer than 20 people until 2008).

Trade Unions. The main trade union confederations are as follows: the Communist-led CGT (Confédération Générale du Travail), founded 1895; the CGT-FO (Confédération Générale du Travail–Force Ouvrière) which broke away from the CGT in 1948; the CFTC (Confédération Française des Travailleurs Chrétiens), founded in 1919 and divided in 1964, with a breakaway group retaining the old name and the main body continuing under the new name of CFDT (Confédération Française Démocratique du Travail); and the CGC-CFE (Confédération Générale des Cadres-Confédération Française de l'Encadrement) formed in 1946, which represents managerial and supervisory staff. The main haulage confederation is the FNTR; the leading employers' association is the CNPF, often referred to as the *Patronat*. Unions are not required to publish membership figures, but in 2002 the two largest federations, the CFDT and CGT, had an estimated 0·89m. and 0·65m. members respectively.

Although France has the lowest rate of trade union membership in Europe (9% in 2000, compared to 29% in the UK, 30% in Germany and over 90% in Sweden), its trade unionists have considerable clout: they run France's welfare system; staff the country's dispute-settling industrial tribunals (*conseils de prud'hommes*); and fix national agreements on wages and working conditions. A union call to strike is invariably answered by more than a union's membership.

INTERNATIONAL TRADE

Imports and Exports. In 2003 imports (c.i.f.) totalled US$363·60bn. (US$309·03bn. in 2002); exports (f.o.b.), US$358·81bn. (US$307·48bn. in 2002). Principal imports include: oil, machinery and equipment, chemicals, iron and steel, and foodstuffs. Major exports: metals, chemicals, industrial equipment, consumer goods and agricultural products.

In 2003 chemicals, manufactured goods classified chiefly by material and miscellaneous manufactured articles accounted for 42·3% of France's imports and 39·4% of exports; machinery and transport equipment 36·9% of imports and 42·9% of exports; food, live animals, beverages and tobacco 8·4% of imports and 13·1% of exports; mineral fuels, lubricants and related materials 9·6% of imports and 2·6% of exports; and crude materials, inedible, animal and vegetable oil and fats 2·8% of imports and 2·0% of exports.

In 2002 the chief import sources (as % of total imports) were as follows: Germany, 17·3%; Italy, 9·1%; USA, 7·9%; UK, 7·4%; Spain, 7·2%. The chief export markets (as % of total) were: Germany, 14·5%; UK, 10·4%; Spain, 9·8%; Italy, 9·1%; USA, 8·0%. Imports from fellow European Union members accounted for 60·0% of all imports, and exports to other European Union members constituted 62·3% of the total.

Trade Fairs. Paris ranks as the most popular convention city in the world according to the Union des Associations Internationales (UAI), hosting 2·5% of all international meetings held in 2002.

COMMUNICATIONS

Roads. In 2002 there were 893,100 km of road, including 12,000 km of motorway. France has the longest road network in the EU. Around 90% of all freight is transported by road. In 2002 there were 29,160,000 passenger cars, 5,903,000 lorries and vans, 81,000 buses, and 2,321,000 motorcycles and scooters (1998). The average distance travelled by a passenger car in 2002 was 14,000 km. Road passenger traffic in 1998 totalled 753·1bn. passenger-km. In 2002 there were 7,655 road deaths (12·9 per 100,000 population), down from 8,160 in 2001.

Rail. In 1938 all the independent railway companies were merged with the existing state railway system in a Société Nationale des Chemins de Fer Français (SNCF), which became a public industrial and commercial establishment in 1983. Legislation came into effect in 1997 which vested ownership of the railway infrastructure (track and signalling) in a newly established public corporation, the French Rail Network (RFF). The RFF is funded by payments for usage from the SNCF, government and local subventions and authority capital made available by the state derived from the proceeds of privatization. The SNCF remains responsible for maintenance and management of the rail network. The legislation also envisages the establishment of regional railway services which receive funds previously given to the SNCF as well as a state subvention. These regional bodies negotiate with SNCF for the provision of suitable services for their area. SNCF is the most heavily indebted and subsidized company in France.

In 2001 the RFF-managed network totalled 31,385 km of track (14,464 km electrified). High-speed TGV lines link Paris to the south and west of France, and Paris and Lille to the Channel Tunnel (Eurostar). The high-speed TGV line appeared in 1983; it had 2,110 km of track in 2001, and another 4,000 km planned by 2015. Services from London through the Channel Tunnel began operating in 1994. Rail passenger traffic in 2001 totalled 71·6bn. passenger km and freight tonne-km came to 50·4bn.

The Paris transport network consisted in 2000 of 211·3 km of metro (297 stations), 115 km of regional express railways and 20 km of tramway. There are metros in Lille (45·0 km), Lyons (29·4 km), Toulouse (10·0 km), Marseilles (19·5 km) and Rennes (9·4 km), and tram/light railway networks in Grenoble (20·6 km), Lille (23·0 km), Lyons (18·7 km), Marseilles (3·1 km), Montpellier (15·2 km), Nantes (38·5 km), Orléans (17·9 km), Rouen (15·4 km), St Étienne (9·3 km) and Strasbourg (28·0 km).

Civil Aviation. The main international airports are at Paris (Charles de Gaulle), Paris (Orly), Bordeaux (Mérignac), Lyons (Satolas), Marseilles-Provence, Nice-Côte d'Azur, Strasbourg (Entzheim), Toulouse (Blagnac), Clermont-Ferrand (Aulunat) and Nantes (Atlantique). The following had international flights to only a few destinations in 2003: Brest, Caen, Carcassonne, Le Havre, Le Touquet, Lille, Pau, Rennes, Rouen and Saint-Étienne. The national airline, Air France, was 54·4% state-owned but merged in Oct. 2003 with the Dutch carrier KLM to form Air France-KLM. In the process the share owned by the French state fell to 44·0%. In Dec. 2004 the government announced that it would sell off a further 18·4% of its stake. In 1999 Air France flew 636·8m. km, carrying 37,027,900 passengers (19,141,000 on international flights). In 2001 Charles de Gaulle airport handled 47,930,187 passengers (42,859,153 on international flights) and 1,069,677 tonnes of freight. Only Heathrow handled more international passengers in 2001. Orly was the second busiest airport, handling 23,010,946 passengers (17,336,729 on domestic flights) and 80,491 tonnes of freight. Nice was the third busiest for passengers, with 8,992,373 (4,607,370 on international flights).

In April 2003 Air France announced that Concorde, the world's first supersonic jet which began commercial service in 1976, would be permanently grounded from Oct. 2003.

Shipping. In 2000 the merchant fleet comprised 808 vessels (of 100 gross tons or more) totalling 4·82m. GRT, including 68 tankers of 2·70m. GRT. In 2001 vessels totalling 2,225m. NRT entered ports. In 1993 from a total of 215 vessels (all sizes; GRT: 3,928,000), 212m. tonnes of cargo were unloaded, including 130m. tonnes of crude and refined petroleum products, 93m. tonnes were loaded; total passenger traffic was 29·2m. Chief ports: Marseilles, Le Havre, Dunkerque, Saint-Nazaire and Calais.

France has extensive inland waterways. Canals are administered by the public authority France Navigable Waterways (FVN). In 1993 there were 8,500 km of navigable rivers, waterways and canals (of which 1,647 km were accessible to vessels over 3,000 tons), with a total traffic of 59·8m. tonnes.

Telecommunications. France Télécom became a limited company on 1 Jan. 1997. In 2002 there were 72,579,700 telephone subscribers, or 1,217·0 for every 1,000 inhabitants, and there were 20·7m. PCs in use (equivalent to 347·1 per 1,000 persons). Mobile phone subscribers numbered 38,585,300 in 2002. The largest operators are Orange France, with a 48% share of the market, and SFR, with a 34% share. In 1997 there were 2·8m. fax machines in use. France had 16·97m. Internet users in May 2002—just over 28% of the population.

Postal Services. There were 17,038 post offices in 1998. A total of 26,115m. pieces of mail were processed in 1998, or 436 items per person. La Poste is a public enterprise under autonomous management responsible for mail delivery and financial services.

SOCIAL INSTITUTIONS

Justice. The system of justice is divided into two jurisdictions: the judicial and the administrative. Within the judicial jurisdiction are common law courts including 473 lower courts (*tribunaux d'instance*, 11 in overseas departments), 181 higher courts (*tribunaux de grande instance*, 5 *tribunaux de première instance* in the overseas territories) and 454 police courts (*tribunaux de police*, 11 in overseas departments).

The *tribunaux d'instance* are presided over by a single judge. The *tribunaux de grande instance* usually have a collegiate composition, but may be presided over by a single judge in some civil cases. The *tribunaux de police*, presided over by a judge on duty in the *tribunal d'instance*, deal with petty offences (*contraventions*); correctional chambers (*chambres correctionelles*, of which there is at least one in each *tribunal de grande instance*) deal with graver offences (*délits*), including cases involving imprisonment up to five years. Correctional chambers normally consist of three judges of a *tribunal de grande instance* (a single judge in some cases). Sometimes in cases of *délit*, and in all cases of more serious *crimes*, a preliminary inquiry is made in secrecy by one of 569 examining magistrates (*juges d'instruction*), who either dismisses the case or sends it for trial before a public prosecutor.

Within the judicial jurisdiction are various specialized courts, including 191 commercial courts (*tribunaux de commerce*), composed of tradesmen and manufacturers elected for two years initially, and then for four years; 271 conciliation boards (*conseils de prud'hommes*), composed of an equal number of employers and employees elected for five years to deal with labour disputes; 437 courts for settling rural landholding disputes (*tribunaux paritaires des baux ruraux*, 11 in overseas departments); and 116 social security courts (*tribunaux des affaires de sécurité sociale*).

When the decisions of any of these courts are susceptible of appeal, the case goes to one of the 35 courts of appeal (*cours d'appel*), composed each of a president and a variable number of members. There are 104 courts of assize (*cours d'assises*), each composed of a president who is a member of the court of appeal, and two other magistrates, and assisted by a lay jury of nine members. These try crimes involving imprisonment of over five years. The decisions of the courts of appeal and the courts of assize are final. However, the Court of Cassation (*cour de cassation*) has discretion to verify if the law has been correctly interpreted and if the rules of procedure have been followed exactly. The Court of Cassation may annul any judgment, following which the cases must be retried by a court of appeal or a court of assizes.

The administrative jurisdiction exists to resolve conflicts arising between citizens and central and local government authorities. It consists of 36 administrative courts (*tribunaux administratifs*, of which eight are in overseas departments and territories) and 15 administrative courts of appeal (*cours administratives d'appel*, of which eight are in overseas departments and territories). The Council of State is the final court of appeal in administrative cases, though it may also act as a court of first instance.

Cases of doubt as to whether the judicial or administrative jurisdiction is competent in any case are resolved by a *Tribunal de conflits* composed in equal measure of members of the Court of Cassation and the Council of State. In 1997 the government restricted its ability to intervene in individual cases of justice.

Penal code. A revised penal code came into force on 1 March 1994, replacing the *Code Napoléon* of 1810. Penal institutions consist of: (1) *maisons d'arrêt*, where persons awaiting trial as well as those condemned to short periods of imprisonment are kept; (2) punishment institutions – (a) central prisons (*maisons centrales*) for those sentenced to long imprisonment, (b) detention centres for offenders showing promise of rehabilitation, and (c) penitentiary centres, establishments combining (a) and (b); (3) hospitals for the sick. Special attention is being paid to classified treatment and the rehabilitation and vocational re-education of prisoners including work in open-air and semi-free establishments. Juvenile delinquents go before special judges in 139 (11 in overseas departments and territories) juvenile courts (*tribunaux pour enfants*); they are sent to public or private institutions of supervision and re-education.

The first Ombudsman (*Médiateur*) was appointed for a six-year period in Jan. 1973. The present incumbent is Jean-Paul Delevoye (appointed April 2004).

Capital punishment was abolished in Aug. 1981. In metropolitan France the detention rate in July 2001 was 84·3 prisoners per 100,000 population, up from 50 per 100,000 in 1975. The average period of detention in 2001 was 10·2 months. The principal offences committed were: theft, 27·2%; rape and other sexual assaults, 21·0%; drug-related offences, 16·8%. The population of the 186 penal establishments (three for women) in July 2001 was 49,718 including 1,746 women.

Weston, M., *English Reader's Guide to the French Legal System.* Oxford, 1991

Religion. A law of 1905 separated church and state. In 2000 there were 100 Roman Catholic dioceses in metropolitan France and (1996) 112 bishops. In Sept. 2003 there were seven cardinals. In 2001 there were 38·69m. Roman Catholics (over 65% of the population), 4·18m. Muslims, 0·72m. Protestants and 0·59m. Jews. France has both the highest number of Muslims and of Jews of any EU member country. An estimated 9·23m. people were non-religious in 2001 and there were 2·38m. atheists.

Education. The primary, secondary and higher state schools constitute the 'Université de France'. Its Supreme Council of 84 members has deliberative, administrative and judiciary functions, and as a consultative committee advises respecting the working of the school system; the inspectors-general are in direct communication with the Minister. For local education administration France is divided into 25 academic areas, each of which has an Academic Council whose members include a certain number elected by the professors or teachers. The Academic Council deals with all grades of education. Each is under a Rector, and each is provided with academy inspectors, one for each department.

Compulsory education is provided for children of 6–16. The educational stages are as follows:

1. Non-compulsory pre-school instruction for children aged 2–5, to be given in infant schools or infant classes attached to primary schools.

2. Compulsory elementary instruction for children aged 6–11, to be given in primary schools and certain classes of the *lycées*. It consists of three courses: preparatory (one year), elementary (two years) and intermediary (two years). Children with special needs are cared for in special institutions or special classes of primary schools.

3. Lower secondary education (*Enseignement du premier cycle du Second Degré*) for pupils aged 11–15, consists of four years of study in the *lycées* (grammar schools), *Collèges d'Enseignement Technique* or *Collèges d'Enseignement Général*.

4. Upper secondary education (*Enseignement du second cycle du Second Degré*) for pupils aged 15–18: (1) *Long, général* or *professionel* provided by the *lycées* and leading to the *baccalauréat* or to the *baccalauréat de technicien* after three years; and (2) *Court*, professional courses of three, two and one year are taught in the *lycées d'enseignement professionel*, or the specialized sections of the *lycées*, CES or CEG.

The following table shows the number of schools in 2002–03 and the numbers of teachers and pupils in 2000–01:

	Number of Schools	Teachers	Pupils
Nursery	18,460	132,447	2,443,116
Primary	39,329	204,727	3,837,902
Secondary	11,389	506,304	5,876,047

Higher education is provided by the state free of charge in the universities and in special schools, and by private individuals in the free faculties and schools. Legislation of 1968 redefined the activities and workings of universities. Bringing several disciplines together, 780 units for teaching and research (*UER—Unités d'Enseignement et de Recherche*) were formed which decided their own teaching activities, research programmes and procedures for checking the level of knowledge gained. They and the other parts of each university must respect the rules designed to maintain the national standard of qualifications. The UERs form the basic units of the 69 state universities and three national polytechnic institutes (with university status), which are grouped into 25 *Académies*. There are also five Catholic universities in Paris, Angers, Lille, Lyons and Toulouse; and private universities. There were 2,031,743 students in higher education in 2000–01.

Outside the university system, higher education (academic, professional and technical) is provided by over 400 schools and institutes, including the 177 *Grandes Écoles*, which are highly selective public or private institutions offering mainly technological or commercial curricula. These have an annual output of about 20,000 graduates, and in 1994–95 there were also 71,271 students in preparatory classes leading to the *Grandes Écoles;* in 1993–94, 232,844 students were registered in the Sections de Techniciens Supérieurs, 71,273 in the Écoles d'Ingénieurs.

Adult literacy rate in 2001 was at least 99%.

In 2000–01 total expenditure on education came to 5·7% of GNP and represented 11·4% of total government expenditure.

Health. Ordinances of 1996 created a new regional regime of hospital administration and introduced a system of patients' records to prevent abuses of public health benefits. In 2002 there were 4,671 hospitals with a provision of 115 beds per 10,000 persons. There were 177,585 physicians, 39,736 dentists, 291,287 nurses, 58,609 pharmacists and 12,718 midwives in 1997.

In 2002 France spent 9·7% of its GDP on health, public spending amounting to 76·0% of the total. A survey published by the World Health Organization in June 2000 to measure health systems in all of the sovereign countries and find which country has the best overall health care ranked France in first place.

The average French adult smokes 4·0 cigarettes a day, compared to a European Union average of 4·5, and drinks 14·1 litres of alcohol a year, compared to a European Union average of 11·1 litres. France has the highest alcohol consumption per person of any EU member country. It has the lowest rate of cardiovascular disease in the EU, but the highest rate of cancer among men.

Welfare. An order of 4 Oct. 1945 laid down the framework of a comprehensive plan of Social Security and created a single organization which superseded the various laws relating to social insurance, workmen's compensation, health insurance, family allowances, etc. All previous matters relating to Social Security are dealt with in the Social Security Code, 1956; this has been revised several times. The Chamber of Deputies and Senate, meeting as Congress on 19 Feb. 1996, adopted an important revision of the Constitution giving parliament powers to review annually the funding of social security (previously managed by the trade unions and employers' associations), and to fix targets for expenditure in the light of anticipated receipts.

In 2002 the welfare system accounted for €381bn., representing 35% of GDP. In 1997, 6m. people were dependent on the welfare system. The Social Security budget had a deficit of some 13bn. francs in 1998.

Contributions. The general social security contribution (CSG) introduced in 1991 was raised by 4% to 7·5% in 1997 by the Jospin administration in an attempt to dramatically reduce the deficit on social security spending, effectively almost doubling the CSG. All wage-earning workers or those of equivalent status are insured regardless of the amount or the nature of the salary or earnings. The funds for the general scheme are raised mainly from professional contributions, these being fixed within the limits of a ceiling and calculated as a percentage of the salaries. The calculation of contributions payable for family allowances, old age and industrial injuries relates only to this amount; on the other hand, the amount payable for sickness, maternity expenses, disability and death is calculated partly within the limit of the 'ceiling' and partly on the whole salary. These contributions are the responsibility of both employer and employee, except in the case of family allowances or industrial injuries, where they are the sole responsibility of the employer.

Self-employed Workers. From 17 Jan. 1948 allowances and old-age pensions were paid to self-employed workers by independent insurance funds set up within their own profession, trade or business. Schemes of compulsory insurance for sickness were instituted in 1961 for farmers, and in 1966, with modifications in 1970, for other non-wage-earning workers.

Social Insurance. The orders laid down in Aug. 1967 ensure that the whole population can benefit from the Social Security Scheme; at present all elderly persons who have been engaged in the professions, as well as the surviving spouse, are entitled to claim an old-age benefit.

Sickness Insurance refunds the costs of treatment required by the insured and the needs of dependants.

Maternity Insurance covers the costs of medical treatment relating to the pregnancy, confinement and lying-in period; the beneficiaries being the insured person or the spouse.

Insurance for Invalids is divided into three categories: (1) those who are capable of working; (2) those who cannot work; (3) those who, in addition, are in need of the help of another person. According to the category, the pension rate varies from 30 to 50% of the average salary for the last ten years, with additional allowance for home help for the third category.

Old-Age Pensions for workers were introduced in 1910 and are now fixed by the Social Security Code of 28 Jan. 1972. Since 1983 people who have paid insurance for at least 37½ years (150 quarters) receive at 60 a pension equal to 60% of basic salary. People who have paid insurance for less than 37½ years but no less than 15 years can expect a pension equal to as many 1/150ths of the full pension as their quarterly payments justify. In the event of death of the insured person, the husband or wife of the deceased person receives half the pension received by the latter. Compulsory supplementary schemes ensure benefits equal to 70% of previous earnings. In 2003 the duration an employee had to work in order to qualify for a pension was raised from 37½ years to 40 years, to take effect by 2008.

Family Allowances. A controversial programme of means-testing for Family Allowance was introduced in 1997 by the new administration. The Family Allowance benefit system comprises: (a) Family allowances proper, equivalent to 25·5% of the basic monthly salary for two dependent children, 46% for the third child, 41% for the fourth child, and 39% for the fifth and each subsequent child; a supplement equivalent to 9% of the basic monthly salary for the second and each subsequent dependent child more than ten years old, and 16% for each dependent child over 15 years. (b) Family supplement for persons with at least three children or one child aged less than three years. (c) Ante-natal grants. (d) Maternity grant is equal to 260% of basic salary. Increase for multiple births or adoptions, 198%; increase for birth or adoption of third or subsequent child, 457%. (e) Allowance for specialized education of handicapped children. (f) Allowance for orphans. (g) Single parent allowance. (h) Allowance for opening of school term. (i) Allowance for accommodation, under certain circumstances. (j) Minimum family income for those with at least three children. Allowances (b), (g), (h) and (j) only apply to those whose annual income falls below a specified level.

Workmen's Compensation. The law passed by the National Assembly on 30 Oct. 1946 forms part of the Social Security Code and is administered by the Social

Security Organization. Employers are invited to take preventive measures. The application of these measures is supervised by consulting engineers (assessors) of the local funds dealing with sickness insurance, who may compel employers who do not respect these measures to make additional contributions; they may, in like manner, grant rebates to employers who have in operation suitable preventive measures. The injured person receives free treatment, the insurance fund reimburses the practitioners, hospitals and suppliers chosen freely by the injured. In cases of temporary disablement, the daily payments are equal to half the total daily wage received by the injured. In case of permanent disablement, the injured person receives a pension, the amount of which varies according to the degree of disablement and the salary received during the past 12 months.

Unemployment Benefits vary according to circumstances (full or partial unemployment) which are means-tested.

Ambler, J. S. (ed.) *The French Welfare State: Surviving Social and Ideological Change.* New York Univ. Press, 1992

CULTURE

World Heritage Sites. There are 27 sites under French jurisdiction that appear of the UNESCO world heritage list. They are (with year entered on list): Mont-Saint-Michel and its Bay, the Versailles Palace and Park, the church and hill at Vézelay (Burgundy), the Decorated Grottoes of the Vézère Valley (Dordogne) and Chartres Cathedral (all 1979); Fontainebleau Palace and Park, Amiens Cathedral, Orange's Roman theatre and Arch de Triomphe, the Roman and Romanesque monuments of Arles and Fontenay's Cistercian Abbey (all 1981); the Royal Saltworks of Arc-et-Senans, Franche-Comté (1982); Nancy's Place Stanislas, Place de la Carrière and Place d'Alliance, the Church of Saint-Savin, Poitou-Charentes, and Cape Girolata, Cape Porto, Scandola Nature Reserve and the Piana Calanches in Corsica (all 1983); the Pont du Gard Roman aqueduct, Languedoc (1985); Strasbourg-Grande île (1988); the Banks of the Seine and Reims's Notre Dame Cathedral, Abbey of Saint-Remi and Tau Palace (both 1991); Bourges Cathedral (1992); Avignon's historic centre (1995); the Canal du Midi, Languedoc (1996); the Historic Fortified City of Carcassonne (1997); Lyons' historic sites and the route of Santiago de Compostela (both 1998); Saint-Emilion Jurisdiction (1999); the Loire Valley between Sully-sur-Loire and Chalonnes (2000); and Provins, the Town of Medieval Fairs (2001).

France also shares the Pyrénées–Mount Perdu site (1997) with Spain.

Broadcasting. The broadcasting authority (an independent regulatory commission) is the *Conseil Supérieur de l'Audiovisuel (CSA).* Public radio is provided by *Radio France*, *Réseau France outre-mer* (*RFO*) and *Radio France Internationale* (*RFI*). *Radio France* broadcasts nationwide on *France Info, France Inter, France Musiques, France Culture, France Bleu*; locally via 40 radio stations plus *FIP* and *Le Mouv'*, both of which serve a number of cities; and Europe-wide on *Hector*, *France Culture Europe* and *Elisa*. In Oct. 1998 there were 3,229 private local radio stations. *Réseau France outre-mer* has two networks, *RFO 1* and *RFO 2*, which broadcast in the French Overseas Departments and Territories. An external service, *Radio France Internationale*, was founded in 1931 (as 'Poste Coloniale'), and broadcasts in 18 languages.

There are three public national TV channels that together form the *France Télévision* group—*France 2*, *France 3* and *France 5*. Until the mid-1990s, French state controlled television was protected from competition by legislation but under pressure from the private sector and cable companies, the two public channels were re-named and *France Télévision* was created in 1992 to manage them. The third channel, *La Cinquième*, started up in 1994, mainly as an education service and was renamed *France 5* in 2002. The four main terrestrial private channels broadcasting nationwide are: TF1, a former state channel privatized in 1987; M6, established in 1987; Arte, a joint Franco-German cultural channel; and Canal+, a subscription channel. Colour is by SECAM H. French TV broadcasts (terrestrial and satellite) must contain at least 60% EU-generated programmes and 50% of these must be French.

France has been broadcasting via satellite since 1984 with a combined service relaying programmes from Belgian and Swiss as well as French satellites. More satellites have been added including TDF1and TDF2 broadcasting for Arte, Canal+ and Radio France. Télécom A and Télécom B transmit for the principal TV stations and from 1995, Astra, Eutelsat and Télécom satellites have been broadcasting to the majority of households able to receive television. Digital Television arrived in 1996 and three new satellites, Canal Satellite, Télévision par Satellite and AB Sat, were launched. There were 853 TV channels altogether in 2002. In 2002 there were 8·8m. satellite and cable TV subscribers.

In addition to specialized French national channels, foreign channels are also transmitted to approximately 1·5m. French households via cable.

There were about 55·9m. radio receivers in use in 2000 and 37·5m. TV sets in 2001.

Cinema. There were 4,762 cinemas in 1998. Attendances totalled 185·8m. in 2001 (130·2m. in 1995); gross box office receipts came to €1,013·9m. in 2001. A record 204 full-length films were made in 2001. In 1996 French films took 37% of the national market, but in 1998 this dropped to 27%. Around 360 new screens were to be opened between 1998 and 2000.

Press. There were 74 daily papers (11 nationals, 63 provincials) in 2002. The leading dailies are: *Ouest France* (average circulation, 762,000); *Le Parisien* (average circulation, 458,000); *L'Équipe* (average circulation, 384,000); *Le Monde; Le Figaro; Sud Ouest; Voix du Nord; Le Dauphiné Libéré*. The *Journal de Dimanche* is the only national Sunday paper. In 2002 total daily press circulation was 12·7m. copies. In 1999 a total of 49,808 book titles were published.

Tourism. There were 75,500,000 foreign tourists in 2000; tourism receipts in 2000 were US$29·9bn. France is the most popular tourist destination in the world, and receipts from tourism in 2000 were exceeded only in the USA and Spain. The most visited tourist attractions in 2002 were Disneyland Paris (13·1m.), the Eiffel Tower (6·2m.) and the Louvre (5·8m.). Around 11m. foreigners a year visit Paris. Countries of origin of visitors to France in 2002: UK, 19·4%; Germany, 18·6%; Netherlands, 16·4%; Belgium and Luxembourg, 11·0%; Italy, 10·2%; Switzerland, 4·0%; Spain, 3·9%; USA, 3·9%. There were 583,578 classified hotel rooms in 18,563 hotels in 2000. 39,000 new jobs were created in 2000 through tourism.

Festivals. *Religious Festivals.* Assumption of the Blessed Virgin Mary (15 Aug.) and All Saints Day (1 Nov.) are both Public Holidays.

Cultural Festivals. The Grande Parade de Montmartre, Paris (1 Jan.); the Carnival of Nice (Feb.–March); the Fête de la Victoire (8 May), celebrates victory in World War Two; the May Feasts take place in Nice regularly throughout May; the prestigious Cannes Film Festival, which has been running since 1946, lasts two weeks in mid-May; the Avignon Festival is a celebration of theatre that attracts average attendances of 140,000 each year and runs for most of July; Bastille Day (14 July) sees celebrations, parties and fireworks across the country. The Festival International d'Art Lyrique, focusing on classical music, opera and ballet, takes place in Aix-en-Provence every July. There are also annual festivals of opera at Orange (July–Aug.) and baroque music at Ambronay (Sept.–Oct.).

Libraries. In 1997 there were 2,577 public libraries, two National libraries and 186 Higher Education libraries; they held a combined 125,772,000 volumes. There were 295,229,000 visits to the libraries in 1997.

Museums and Galleries. In 2001, 12m. people visited France's 33 national museums: the Musée du Louvre received 5·16m. visitors; the Château de Versailles, 2·59m.; the Musée d'Orsay, 1·67m.

DIPLOMATIC REPRESENTATIVES

Of France in the United Kingdom (58 Knightsbridge, London, SW1X 7JT)
Ambassador: Gérard Errera.

Of the United Kingdom in France (35 rue du Faubourg St Honoré, 75383 Paris Cedex 08)
Ambassador: Sir John Eaton Holmes, KBE, CVO, CMG.

Of France in the USA (4101 Reservoir Rd, NW, Washington, D.C., 20007)
Ambassador: Jean-David Levitte.

Of the USA in France (2 Ave. Gabriel, Paris)
Ambassador: Howard H. Leach.

Of France to the United Nations
Ambassador: Jean-Marc de la Sablière.

FURTHER READING

Institut National de la Statistique et des Études Économiques: *Annuaire statistique de la France* (from 1878); *Bulletin mensuel de statistique* (monthly); *Documentation économique* (bi-monthly); *Economie et Statistique* (monthly); *Tableaux de l'Économie Française* (biennially, from 1956); *Tendances de la Conjoncture* (monthly).

Agulhon, Maurice, *De Gaulle: Histoire, Symbole, Mythe.* Plon, Paris, 2000
Agulhon, Maurice and Nevill, Antonia, *The French Republic, 1879–1992.* Blackwell, Oxford, 1993
Ardagh, John, *France in the New Century: Portrait of a Changing Society.* Viking, London, 1999
Ardant, P., *Les Institutions de la Ve République.* Paris, 1992
Balladur, E., *Deux Ans à Matignon.* Paris, 1995
Bell, David, *Presidential Power in Fifth Republic France.* Berg, Oxford, 2000.—*Parties and Democracy in France: Parties under Presidentialism.* Ashgate, Aldershot, 2000
Chafer, Tony and Sackur, Amanda, (eds.) *French Colonial Empire and the Popular Front.* Macmillan, London, 1999
Chazal, C., *Balladur.* [in French] Paris, 1993
Cole, Alistair, Le Galès, Patrick and Levy, Jonah, (eds.) *Developments in French Politics 3.* Palgrave Macmillan, Basingstoke, 2005
Cubertafond, A., *Le Pouvoir, la Politique et l'État en France.* Paris, 1993
L'État de la France. Paris, annual
Friend, Julius W., *The Long Presidency: France in the Mitterrand Years, 1981–95.* Westview, Oxford, 1999
Gildea, R., *France since 1945.* OUP, 1996
Guyard, Marius-François, (ed.) *Charles de Gaulle: Mémoires.* Gallimard, Paris, 2000
Hollifield, J. F. and Ross, G., *Searching for the New France.* Routledge, London, 1991
Hudson, G. L., *Corsica.* [World Bibliographic Series, vol. 202] Oxford, 1997
Jack, A., *The French Exception.* Profile Books, London, 1999
Jones, C., *The Cambridge Illustrated History of France.* CUP, 1994
Knapp, Andrew, *Parties and the Party System in France: A Disconnected Democracy?* Palgrave Macmillan, Basingstoke, 2004
Lacoutre, Jean, *Mitterrand: Une histoire de Français.* 2 vols. Seuil, Paris, 1999
Lewis-Beck, Michael S., *The French Voter: Before and After the 2002 Elections.* Palgrave Macmillan, Basingstoke, 2004
MacLean, Mairi, *The Mitterrand Years: Legacy and Evaluation.* Macmillan, London, 1999
McMillan, J. F., *Twentieth-Century France: Politics and Society in France, 1898–1991.* 2nd ed. [of *Dreyfus to De Gaulle*]. Arnold, London, 1992
Menon, Anand, *France, NATO and the Limits of Independence, 1918–97.* Macmillan, London, 1999
Milner, Susan and Parsons, Nick, (eds.) *Reinventing France: State and Society in the 21st Century.* Palgrave Macmillan, Basingstoke, 2004
Noin, D. and White, P., *Paris.* John Wiley, Chichester, 1998
Peyrefitte, Alain, *C'était de Gaulle.* Fayard, Paris, 2000
Popkin, J. D., *A History of Modern France.* New York, 1994
Price, Roger, *A Concise History of France.* CUP, 1993
Raymond, Gino G. (ed.) *Structures of Power in Modern France.* Macmillan, London, 1999
Stevens, Anne, *Government and Politics of France.* Palgrave Macmillan, Basingstoke, 2003
Tiersky, Ronald, *Mitterrand in Light and Shadow.* Macmillan, London, 1999.—*François Mitterrand: The Last French President.* St Martin's Press, New York, 2000
Tippett-Spiritou, Sandy, *French Catholicism.* Macmillan, London, 1999
Turner, Barry, (ed.) *France Profiled.* Macmillan, London, 1999
Zeldin, T., *The French.* Harvill Press, London, 1997

(Also see specialized titles listed under relevant sections, above.)

National statistical office: Institut National de la Statistique et des Études Économiques (INSEE), 75582 Paris Cedex 12.
Website: http://www.insee.fr/

DEPARTMENTS AND TERRITORIES OVERSEAS

Départements (DOM) et Territoires (TOM) d'Outre-Mer

GENERAL DETAILS

These fall into six categories: *Overseas Departments* (French Guiana, Guadeloupe, Martinique, Réunion); *Departmental Collectivities* (Mayotte); *Territorial Collectivities* (New Caledonia, St Pierre and Miquelon); *Overseas Countries* (French Polynesia); *Overseas Territories* (Southern and Antarctic Territories, Wallis and Futuna); and *Dependencies* (Bassas da India, Clipperton Island, Europa Island, Glorieuses Islands, Juan de Nova Island, Tromelin Island).

FURTHER READING

Aldrich, R. and Connell, J., *France's Overseas Frontier: Départements et Territoires d'Outre-Mer.* CUP, 1992

OVERSEAS DEPARTMENTS

Départements d'Outre-Mer

FRENCH GUIANA

Guyane Française

KEY HISTORICAL EVENTS

A French settlement on the island of Cayenne was established in 1604 and the territory between the Maroni and Oyapock rivers finally became a French possession in 1817. Convict settlements were established from 1852, that on Devil's Island being the most notorious; all were closed by 1945. On 19 March 1946 the status of French Guiana was changed to that of an Overseas Department.

TERRITORY AND POPULATION

French Guiana is situated on the northeast coast of Latin America, and is bounded in the northeast by the Atlantic Ocean, west by Suriname, and south and east by Brazil. It includes the offshore Devil's Island, Royal Island and St Joseph, and has an area of 85,534 sq. km. Population at the 1999 census: 157,213. The UN gives a projected population for 2010 of 208,000. In 1995, 76·4% lived in urban areas. The chief towns are (with 1999 census populations): the capital, Cayenne (50,594 inhabitants), Saint-Laurent-du-Maroni (19,210) and Kourou (19,107). About 58% of inhabitants are of African descent.

The official language is French.

SOCIAL STATISTICS

2002 births, 5,276; deaths, 665. 49% of the population are migrants. Annual growth rate, 1995–99, 4·3%.

CLIMATE

Equatorial type climate with most of the country having a main rainy season between April and July and a fairly dry period between Aug. and Dec. Both temperatures and humidity are high the whole year round. Cayenne, Jan. 26°C, July 29°C. Annual rainfall 3,202 mm.

CONSTITUTION AND GOVERNMENT

French Guiana is administered by a General Council of 19 members directly elected for five-year terms, and by a Regional Council of 31 members. It is represented in the National Assembly by two deputies; in the Senate by one senator. The French government is represented by a Prefect. There are two *arrondissements* (Cayenne and Saint Laurent-du-Maroni) sub-divided into 22 communes and 19 cantons.

CURRENT ADMINISTRATION

Prefect: Ange Mancini.

President of the General Council: Pierre Désert (Entente Démocratique).

President of the Regional Council: Antoine Karam (Parti Socialiste de Guyanais).

ECONOMY

Currency. Since 1 Jan. 2002 the euro has been the official currency as in metropolitan France.

Performance. In 2000 GDP was €1,729m.; GDP per capita was €10,550. Real GDP growth was –10·5% in 2000.

Banking and Finance. The Caisse Centrale de Coopération Economique is the bank of issue. In 2001 commercial banks included the Banque Nationale de Paris-Guyane, Crédit Populaire Guyanais and Banque Française Commerciale.

ENERGY AND NATURAL RESOURCES

Electricity. Installed capacity was 0·1m. kW in 2000. Production in 2000 was about 455m. kWh.

Minerals. Placer gold mining is the most important industry in French Guiana. In 2001, 3,971 kg of gold were produced.

Agriculture. There were 12,000 ha of arable land in 2001 and 4,000 ha of permanent crops. Principal crops (2002 estimates, in 1,000 tonnes): rice, 20; cassava, 10; cabbages, 6; sugarcane, 5.

Livestock (2002): 9,000 cattle; 10,000 pigs; 3,000 sheep; 220,000 poultry (1993).

Forestry. The country has immense forests which are rich in many kinds of timber. In 1995 forests covered 79,900 sq. km, or 90·6% of the total land area. Roundwood production (2001) 139,000 cu. metres. The trees also yield oils, essences and gum products.

Fisheries. The catch in 2001 was an estimated 5,194 tonnes. Shrimps account for nearly 55% of the total catch.

INDUSTRY

Important products include rum, rosewood essence and beer. The island has sawmills and one sugar factory.

Labour. The economically active population (1993) was 46,300. In July 2003 the minimum wage (SMIC) was raised to €7·19 an hour (€1,090·48 a month for a 35-hour week). 8,324 persons were registered unemployed in 1994.

INTERNATIONAL TRADE

Imports and Exports. Imports (2000), €1,910m.; exports (2000), €1,274m. Main import suppliers are France, the USA and Trinidad and Tobago. Leading export markets are France, Switzerland and the USA.

COMMUNICATIONS

Roads. There were (1996) 356 km of national and 366 km of departmental roads. In 1993 there were 29,100 passenger cars and 10,600 commercial vehicles.

Civil Aviation. In 2000 Rochambeau International Airport (Cayenne) handled 435,421 passengers and 6,053 tonnes of freight. The base of the European Space Agency (ESA) is located near Kourou and has been operational since 1979.

Shipping. 359 vessels arrived and departed in 1993; 249,160 tonnes of petroleum products and 230,179 tonnes of other products were discharged, and 69,185 tonnes of freight loaded. Chief ports: Cayenne, St-Laurent-du-Maroni and Kourou. There are also inland waterways navigable by small craft.

Telecommunications. In 1999 there were 49,200 telephone main lines (282·6 per 1,000 population). There were 138,200 mobile phone subscribers in 2002 and 70,000 PCs in use (291·6 for every 1,000 persons). In Dec. 1999 there were 2,000 Internet users.

SOCIAL INSTITUTIONS

Justice. At Cayenne there is a *tribunal d'instance* and a *tribunal de grande instance*, from which appeal is to the regional *cour d'appel* in Martinique.

The population in penal institutions in April 2003 was 5,900 (324 per 100,000 population).

Religion. In 2001 approximately 55% of the population was Roman Catholic.

Education. Primary education is free and compulsory. In 2001–02 there were 33,813 pupils at pre-elementary and primary schools, and 21,439 at secondary level. In 1993, 644 students from French Guiana attended the Henri Visioz Institute, which forms part of the University of Antilles-Guyana (8,290 students in 1993).

Health. In 1996 there were 25 hospitals with a provision of 143 beds per 10,000 inhabitants. There were (1994) 213 doctors, 38 dentists, 47 pharmacists, 40 midwives and 495 nursing personnel.

CULTURE

Broadcasting. *Radiodiffusion Française d'Outre-Mer-Guyane* broadcasts for 133 hours each week on medium- and short-waves, and FM in French. Television is broadcast for 60 hours each week on two channels. In 1997 there were 104,000 radio receivers and in 1998 there were 37,000 TV receivers; colour is by SECAM.

Press. There was (1996) one daily newspaper with a circulation of 1,000, and a second paper published four times a week has a circulation of 5,500.

Tourism. Total number of tourists (2002), 65,000; receipts totalled US$45m.

FURTHER READING

Crane, Janet, *French Guiana.* [Bibliography] ABC-Clio, Oxford and Santa Barbara (CA), 1998

GUADELOUPE

KEY HISTORICAL EVENTS

The islands were discovered by Columbus in 1493. The Carib inhabitants resisted Spanish attempts to colonize. A French colony was established on 28 June 1635, and apart from short periods of occupancy by British forces, Guadeloupe has since remained a French possession. On 19 March 1946 Guadeloupe became an Overseas Department.

TERRITORY AND POPULATION

Guadeloupe consists of a group of islands in the Lesser Antilles with a total area of 1,705 sq. km. The two main islands, Basse-Terre (to the west) and Grande-Terre (to the east), are joined by a bridge over a narrow channel. Adjacent to these are the islands of Marie-Galante (to the southeast), La Désirade (to the east), and the Îles des Saintes (to the south); the islands of St Martin and St Barthélemy lie 250 km to the northwest.

Island	*Area (sq. km)*	*1999 populations*	*Chief town*
St Martin[1]	53[2]	29,078	Marigot
St Barthélemy	21	6,852	Gustavia
Basse-Terre	848	172,693	Basse-Terre
Grande-Terre	590	196,767	Pointe-à-Pitre
Îles des Saintes	13	2,998	Terre-de-Bas
La Désirade	22	1,620	Grande Anse
Marie-Galante	158	12,488	Grand-Bourg

[1]Northern part only; the southern third is Dutch.
[2]Includes uninhabited Tintamarre.

Population at the last census (1999), 422,496. The UN gives a projected population for 2010 of 460,000. An estimated 99·4% of the population were urban in 1995. Population of principal towns (1999): Les Abymes, 63,054; Saint-Martin, 29,078; Pointe-à-Pitre, 20,948; Basse-Terre, 12,410. Basse-Terre is the seat of government, while larger Pointe-à-Pitre is the department's main economic centre and port; Les Abymes is a 'suburb' of Pointe-à-Pitre.

French is the official language, but Creole is spoken by the vast majority, except on St Martin.

SOCIAL STATISTICS

2000: live births, 7,659; deaths, 2,602; marriages (1998), 3,510. 1998 estimates (per 1,000 population): birth rate, 15·5; death rate, 6·0. Annual growth rate, 1995–99, 1·5%. Life expectancy at birth, 1990–95, 71·1 years for males and 78·0 years for females.

CLIMATE

Warm and humid. Pointe-à-Pitre, Jan. 74°F (23·4°C), July 80°F (26·7°C). Annual rainfall 71" (1,814 mm).

CONSTITUTION AND GOVERNMENT

Guadeloupe is administered by a General Council of 42 members directly elected for six-year terms (assisted by an Economic and Social Committee of 40 members) and by a Regional Council of 41 members. It is represented in the National Assembly by four deputies; in the Senate by two senators; and on the Economic and Social Council by one councillor. There are four *arrondissements,* sub-divided into 42 cantons and 34 communes, each administered by an elected municipal council. The French government is represented by an appointed Prefect.

CURRENT ADMINISTRATION

Prefect: Paul Girot de Langlade.

President of the General Council: Jacques Gillot.

President of the Regional Council: Victorin Lurel.

ECONOMY

Currency. Since 1 Jan. 2002 the euro has been the official currency as in metropolitan France.

Performance. In 2000 GDP was €5,593m.; GDP per capita was €13,071. Real GDP growth was 4·9% in 2000.

Banking and Finance. The Caisse Française de Développement is the official bank of the department. The main commercial banks in 1995 (with number of branches) were: Banque des Antilles Françaises (six), Banque Régionale d'Escompte et de Depôts (five), Banque Nationale de Paris (eight), Crédit Agricole (18), Banque Française Commerciale (eight), Société Générale de Banque aux Antilles (five), Crédit Lyonnais (six), Crédit Martiniquais (three), Banque Inschauspé et Cie (one).

ENERGY AND NATURAL RESOURCES

Electricity. Total production (2000): 1·22bn. kWh. Installed capacity was 0·4m. kW in 2000.

Agriculture. Chief products (2002 estimates, in 1,000 tonnes): sugarcane, 798; bananas, 115; yams, 10; plantains, 9; pineapples, 7. Other fruits and vegetables are also grown for both export and domestic consumption.

Livestock (2002): cattle, 85,000; goats, 28,000; pigs, 19,000.

Forestry. In 1995 forests covered 89,000 ha, or 47·3% of the total land area (down from 51·5% in 1990). Timber production in 2001 was 15,000 cu. metres.

Fisheries. Total catch in 2001 amounted to an estimated 10,100 tonnes, exclusively from sea fishing.

INDUSTRY

The main industries are sugar refining, food processing and rum distilling, carried out by small and medium-sized businesses. Other important industries are cement production and tourism.

Labour. The economically active population in 1997 was approximately 125,900. In July 2003 the minimum wage (SMIC) was raised to €7·19 an hour (€1,090·48 a month for a 35-hour week). 46,360 persons were registered unemployed in 1994.

INTERNATIONAL TRADE

Imports and Exports. Total imports (2000): €2,010m.; total exports (2000): €538m. Main export commodities are bananas, sugar and rum. Main import sources in 1998 were France, 63·4%; Germany, 4·4%; Italy, 3·5%; Martinique, 3·4%. Main export markets were France, 68·5%; Martinique, 9·4%; Italy, 4·8%; Belgium-Luxembourg, 3·3%.

COMMUNICATIONS

Roads. In 1996 there were 3,200 km of roads. In 1993 there were 101,600 passenger cars and 37,500 commercial vehicles. There were 83 road-related fatalities in 1996.

Civil Aviation. Air France and six other airlines call at Guadeloupe airport. In 2000 there were 35,245 arrivals and departures of aircraft, and 1,974,350 passengers, at Le Raizet (Pointe-à-Pitre) airport. There are also airports at Marie-Galante, La Désirade, St Barthélemy and St Martin. Most domestic services are operated by Air Caraibes.

Shipping. In 1996 Port Autonome was visited by 2,014 cargo vessels carrying 2·9m. tonnes of freight and by 1,328 passenger ships.

Telecommunications. Guadeloupe had 204,900 main telephone lines in 2000 and 323,500 mobile phone subscribers in 2002. There were 111,000 PCs in use in 2001 and 3,400 fax machines in 1995. Internet users numbered 4,000 in Dec. 1999.

SOCIAL INSTITUTIONS

Justice. There are four *tribunaux d'instance* and two *tribunaux de grande instance* at Basse-Terre and Pointe-à-Pitre; there is also a court of appeal and a court of assizes.

The population in penal institutions in April 2003 was 695 (159 per 100,000 population).

Religion. The majority of the population are Roman Catholic.

Education. Education is free and compulsory from six to 16 years. In 2001–02 there were 63,310 pupils at pre-elementary and primary schools, and 52,770 at secondary level. In 1993 there were 4,308 students from Guadeloupe at the University of Antilles-Guyana (out of total number of 8,290).

Health. In 1995 there were 13 public hospitals and 16 private clinics. In 1996 there were 690 physicians, 129 dentists, 1,640 nurses, 220 pharmacists and 140 midwives.

CULTURE

Broadcasting. *Radiodiffusion Française d'Outre-Mer* broadcasts for 17 hours a day in French. There is a local region radio station, and several private stations. There are two television channels (one regional; one satellite) broadcasting for six hours a day (colour by SECAM V). There were (1997) 113,000 radio and (1999) 118,000 TV receivers.

Press. There was (1996) one daily newspaper with a circulation of 30,000.

Tourism. Tourism is the chief economic activity. In 1998 there were 693,000 tourists plus 334,000 cruise ship arrivals. Tourism receipts in 2000 totalled US$418m.

MARTINIQUE

KEY HISTORICAL EVENTS

Discovered by Columbus in 1502, Martinique became a French colony in 1635 and apart from brief periods of British occupation the island has since remained under French control. On 19 March 1946 its status was altered to that of an Overseas Department.

TERRITORY AND POPULATION

The island, situated in the Lesser Antilles between Dominica and St Lucia, occupies an area of 1,128 sq. km. Population at last census (1999), 381,427; density, 338 per sq. km. The UN gives a projected population for 2010 of 404,000. An estimated 93·3% of the population were urban in 1995. Population of principal towns (1999 census): the capital and main port Fort-de-France, 94,049; Le Lamentin, 35,460; Schoelcher, 20,845; Sainte-Marie, 20,098; Rivière-Pilote, 13,057; La Trinité, 12,890.

French is the official language but the majority of people speak Creole.

SOCIAL STATISTICS

2000: live births, 5,950; deaths, 2,756. 1998 estimates per 1,000 population: birth rate, 15·3; death rate, 6·6. Annual growth rate, 1995–99, 0·2%. Life expectancy at birth, 1990–95, 73·0 years for males and 79·5 years for females.

CLIMATE

The dry season is from Dec. to May, and the humid season from June to Nov. Fort-de-France, Jan. 74°F (23·5°C), July 78°F (25·6°C). Annual rainfall 72" (1,840 mm).

CONSTITUTION AND GOVERNMENT

The island is administered by a General Council of 45 members directly elected for six-year terms and by a Regional Council of 42 members. The French government is represented by an appointed Prefect. There are four *arrondissements*, sub-divided into 45 cantons and 34 communes, each administered by an elected municipal council. Martinique is represented in the National Assembly by four deputies, in the Senate by two senators and on the Economic and Social Council by one councillor.

CURRENT ADMINISTRATION

Prefect: Yves Dassonville; b. 1948 (took office on 8 Feb. 2004).

President of the General Council: Claude Lise.

President of the Regional Council: Alfred Marie-Jeanne.

ECONOMY

Main sectors of activity: tradeable services, distribution, industry, building and public works, transport and telecommunications, agriculture and tourism.

Currency. Since 1 Jan. 2002 the euro has been the official currency as in metropolitan France.

Performance. In 2000 GDP was €5,496m.; GDP per capita was €14,283. Real GDP growth was 0·7% in 2000.

Banking and Finance. The Agence Française de Développement is the government's vehicle for the promotion of economic development in the region. There were five commercial banks, four co-operative banks, one savings bank, five investment companies and two specialized financial institutions in 1999.

ENERGY AND NATURAL RESOURCES

Electricity. A network of 4,262 km of cables covers 98% of Martinique and supplies more than 142,000 customers. Electricity is produced by two fuel-powered electricity stations. Total production (2000): 1·09bn. kWh. Installed capacity (2000): 0·4m. kW.

Agriculture. In 1997 there were 3,035 ha under sugarcane, 11,200 ha under bananas and 600 ha under pineapples. Production (2002 estimates, in 1,000 tonnes): bananas, 310; sugarcane, 207; plantains, 16; pineapples, 10.

Livestock (2002): 25,000 cattle; 34,000 sheep; 35,000 pigs; 17,000 goats; 295,000 poultry (1997).

Forestry. In 1995 there were 38,000 ha of forest, or 35·8% of the total land area (down from 37·7% in 1990). Timber production in 2001 was 12,000 cu. metres.

Fisheries. The catch in 2001 was 6,200 tonnes, exclusively from sea fishing.

INDUSTRY

Some food processing and chemical engineering is carried out by small and medium-size businesses. There were 14,839 businesses in 2000. There is an important cement industry; 11 rum distilleries and an oil refinery, with an annual treatment capacity of 0·75m. tonnes. Martinique has five industrial zones.

Labour. In 1998, 6·6% of the working population were in agriculture; 15·1% in industry; 23·8% in retail; 34·1% in services; 16·9% in distribution. In July 2003 the minimum wage (SMIC) was raised to €7·19 an hour (€1,090·48 a month for a 35-hour week). The economically active population in 1999 was 166,800. In 1999, 48,667 persons were unemployed.

INTERNATIONAL TRADE

Imports and Exports. Martinique has a structural trade deficit owing to the nature of goods traded. It imports high-value-added goods (foodstuffs, capital goods, consumer goods and motor vehicles) and exports agricultural produce (bananas) and refined oil.

In 2000 imports were valued at €1,958m.; exports at €585m. Main trading partners: France, EU, French Guiana and Guadeloupe. Trade with France accounted for 63% of imports and 61% of exports in 1995.

COMMUNICATIONS

Roads. Martinique has 2,176 km of roads. In 1993 there were 108,300 passenger cars and 32,200 commercial vehicles.

Civil Aviation. There is an international airport at Fort-de-France (Lamentin). In 2000 it handled 1,645,468 passengers and 15,755 tonnes of freight.

Shipping. The island is visited regularly by French, American and other lines. The main sea links to and from Martinique are ensured by CGM Sud. It links Martinique to Europe and some African and American companies. Since 1995 new scheduled links have been introduced between Martinique, French Guiana, Haiti and Panama. These new links facilitate exchanges between Martinique, Latin America and the Caribbean, especially Cuba. In 1993, 2,856 vessels called at Martinique and discharged 80,605 passengers and 1,612,000 tonnes of freight, and embarked 82,119 passengers and 789,000 tonnes of freight.

Telecommunications. In 2001 there were 458,100 telephone subscribers, or 1,145·3 per 1,000 inhabitants, and 54,000 PCs in use (equivalent to 133·3 for every 1,000 persons). There were 319,900 mobile phone subscribers in 2002 and 20,000 fax machines in 1995. The main operator is France Télécom. In Dec. 1999 there were 5,000 Internet users.

SOCIAL INSTITUTIONS

Justice. Justice is administered by two lower courts (*tribunaux d'instance*), a higher court (*tribunal de grande instance*), a regional court of appeal, a commercial court and an administrative court.

The population in penal institutions in April 2003 was 643 (164 per 100,000 population).

Religion. In 2001, 87% of the population was Roman Catholic.

Education. Education is compulsory between the ages of six and 16 years. In 2002–03 there were 51,926 pupils in nursery and primary schools, and 47,770 pupils in secondary schools. There were 29 institutes of higher education in 1994. In 1993, 3,670 students from Martinique were registered at the University of Antilles-French Guyana (out of a total of 8,290).

Health. In 1995 there were eight hospitals, three private clinics and seven nursing homes. Total number of beds, 2,100. There were 680 physicians, 130 dentists, 1,700 nurses, 230 pharmacists and 150 midwives in 1996.

CULTURE

Broadcasting. *Radio Diffusion Française d'Outre-Mer* broadcasts on FM wave, and operates two channels (one satellite). There are also two commercial TV stations. In 1997 there were 82,000 radio receivers and in 1999 there were 66,000 TV receivers (colour by SECAM V).

Press. In 1996 there was one daily newspaper with a circulation of 30,000.

Tourism. In 1999 there were 564,303 tourists plus 339,086 cruise ship arrivals. Tourism receipts totalled US$302m. in 2000. In 1999 there were 122 hotels, with 6,051 rooms.

FURTHER READING

Crane, Janet, *Martinique.* [Bibliography] ABC-Clio, Oxford and Santa Barbara (CA), 1995

RÉUNION

KEY HISTORICAL EVENTS

Réunion (formerly Île Bourbon) became a French possession in 1638 and remained so until 19 March 1946, when its status was altered to that of an Overseas Department.

TERRITORY AND POPULATION

The island of Réunion lies in the Indian Ocean, about 880 km east of Madagascar and 210 km southwest of Mauritius. It has an area of 2,507 sq. km. Population on 1 Jan. 2001: 728,400, giving a density of 291 per sq. km. An estimated 67·7% of the population were rural in 1995. The capital is Saint-Denis (population, 1999: 132,338); other large towns are Saint-Pierre (69,358), Saint-Paul (88,254) and le Tampon (60,701).

The UN gives a projected population for 2010 of 821,000.

French is the official language, but Creole is also spoken.

SOCIAL STATISTICS

2001: births, 14,541; deaths, 3,740; marriages, 3,344; divorces, 934. Birth rate per 1,000 population (2001), 19·8; death rate, 5·1. Annual growth rate, 1995–99, 1·3%. Life expectancy at birth, 2000, 70·6 years for males and 78·7 years for females. Infant mortality, 1998, 8·0 per 1,000 live births; fertility rate, 1998, 2·8 births per woman.

CLIMATE

There is a sub-tropical maritime climate, free from extremes of weather, although the island lies in the cyclone belt of the Indian Ocean. Conditions are generally humid and there is no well-defined dry season. Saint-Denis, Jan. 80°F (26·7°C), July 70°F (21·1°C). Annual rainfall 56" (1,400 mm).

CONSTITUTION AND GOVERNMENT

Réunion is administered by a General Council of 47 members directly elected for six-year terms, and by a Regional Council of 45 members. Réunion is represented in the National Assembly in Paris by five deputies; in the Senate by three senators; and in the Economic and Social Council by one councillor. There are 4 *arrondissements* sub-divided into 47 cantons and 24 communes, each administered by an elected municipal council. The French government is represented by an appointed Commissioner.

CURRENT ADMINISTRATION

Prefect: Dominique Vian.

President of the General Council: Nassimah Dindar-Mangrolia.

President of the Regional Council: Paul Vergès.

ECONOMY

Currency. Since 1 Jan. 2002 the euro has been the official currency as in metropolitan France. Owing to its geographical location, Réunion was by two hours the first territory to introduce the euro.

Performance. GDP was €7,615m. in 1998; real GDP growth was 4·1% in 1998. GDP per capita (1998) was €10,907.

Banking and Finance. The Institut d'Émission des Départements d'Outre-mer has the right to issue bank-notes. Banks operating in Réunion are the Banque de la Réunion (Crédit Lyonnais), the Banque Nationale de Paris Intercontinentale, the Crédit Agricole de la Réunion, the Banque Française Commerciale (BFC) CCP, Trésorerie Générale and the Banque de la Réunion pour l'Économie et le Développement (BRED).

ENERGY AND NATURAL RESOURCES

Electricity. Production (2001), 1,871m. kWh. Consumption per capita (2000), 2,208 kWh. Installed capacity (2000): 0·4m. kW.

Agriculture. There were 34,000 ha of arable land in 2001 and 3,000 ha of permanent crops. Main agricultural products: sugarcane, 1,835,000 (2001); maize, 17,000 (2001 estimate); pineapples, 10,000 (2001 estimate); cabbages, 8,000 (2001 estimate); cauliflowers, 8,000 (2001 estimate).

Livestock (2002): 78,000 pigs, 30,000 cattle, 37,000 goats, 12,000 poultry (1997). Meat production (1999, in tonnes): pork, 11,810; beef and veal, 1,660; poultry, 13,550. Milk production (1999), 19,726 hectolitres.

Forestry. There were 100,916 ha of forest in 1998, or 40·3% of the total land area. Timber production in 2001 was 36,000 cu. metres.

Fisheries. In 2001 the catch was 5,406 tonnes, almost entirely from marine waters. Deep-sea fishing (1999) is mainly for blue marlin, sail-fish, blue-fin tuna and sea bream.

INDUSTRY

The major industries are electricity and sugar. Food processing, chemical engineering, printing and the production of perfume, textiles, leathers, tobacco, wood and construction materials are carried out by small and medium-sized businesses. At the beginning of 1994 there were 9,465 craft businesses employing about 20,000 persons. Production of sugar was 215,600 tonnes in 1999; rum, 74,154 hectolitres (pure alcohol) in 1999.

Labour. The workforce was 284,300 in 2000. In July 2003 the minimum wage (SMIC) was raised to €7·19 an hour (€1,090·48 a month for a 35-hour week). In 2000, 130,400 persons were registered unemployed, a rate of 42·1%. Among the under 25s the unemployment rate is nearly 60%

INTERNATIONAL TRADE

Imports and Exports. Trade in 1m. French francs:

	1996	*1997*	*1998*	*1999*	*2000*	*2001*
Imports	14,214	14,262	15,310	15,828	17,908	18,728
Exports	1,071	1,250	1,215	1,267	1,489	1,502

The chief export is sugar, accounting for 53·7% of total exports (1999). In 1999, 62·2% of trade was with France.

COMMUNICATIONS

Roads. There were, in 2001, 2,914 km of roads and 258,400 registered vehicles. In 1999 the County Council was operating bus services to all towns.

Civil Aviation. In 2000, 736,499 passengers and 17,206 tonnes of freight arrived at, and 730,980 passengers and 8,934 tonnes of freight departed from, Roland Garros Saint-Denis airport.

Shipping. 753 vessels visited the island in 2000, unloading 2,783,700 tonnes of freight and loading 482,300 tonnes at Port-Réunion.

Telecommunications. There were 269,500 telephone main lines in 1999, or 388·6 per 1,000 inhabitants, and 32,000 PCs in use (46·3 per 1,000 persons). There were 489,800 mobile phone subscribers in 2002. In 1995 there were 1,900 fax machines. Internet users numbered 10,000 in July 2000.

Postal Services. In 1996 there were 824 post offices.

SOCIAL INSTITUTIONS

Justice. There are three lower courts (*tribunaux d'instance*), two higher courts (*tribunaux de grande instance*), one appeal, one administrative court and one conciliation board.

The population in penal institutions in April 2003 was 1,071 (143 per 100,000 population).

Religion. In 2001, 82% of the population was Roman Catholic.

Education. In 2002–03 there were 121,926 pupils in primary schools and 100,020 in secondary schools. In 1999–2000 secondary education was provided in 27 *lycées*, 73 colleges and 13 technical *lycées*. The *Université Française de l'Océan Indien* (founded 1971) had 13,371 students in 1999–2000.

Health. In 2000 there were 17 hospitals with 2,734 beds, 1,595 doctors, 364 dentists, 342 pharmacists, 221 midwives and 2,906 nursing personnel.

CULTURE

Broadcasting. *Radiodiffusion Française d'Outre-Mer* broadcasts in French on medium- and short-waves for more than 18 hours a day. There are two national television channels (*RFD1* and *Tempo*) and three independent channels (*Antenne Réunion, Canal Réunion/Canal* + and *Parabole Réunion*). Colour transmission is by SECAM V. In 1998 there were 130,000 TV receivers and in 1997 there were 173,000 radio receivers.

Press. There were (2000) three daily newspapers (*Quotidien, Journal de l'Île, Témoignages*), two weekly (*Visu, Télé Magazine*), three monthly (*Memento, Via, l'Eco Austral*) and two fortnightly magazines (*Leader* and *Attitude*), with a combined circulation of 57,000.

Tourism. Tourism is a major resource industry. There were 430,000 visitors in 2000 (81·6% French). Receipts (2000) totalled €276m. In Jan. 2001 accommodation included 60 hotels, 126 country lodges (*gîtes ruraux*), 269 bed and breakfast houses, 22 stopover lodges (*gîtes d'étape*) and 22 mountain huts.

FURTHER READING

Institut National de la Statistique et des Etudes Économiques: *Tableau Économique de la Réunion.* Paris (annual)

Bertile, W., *Atlas Thématique et Régional.* Réunion, 1990

DEPARTMENTAL COLLECTIVITIES

Collectivités Départementales

MAYOTTE

KEY HISTORICAL EVENTS

Mayotte was a French colony from 1843 until 1914 when it was attached, with the other Comoro islands, to the government-general of Madagascar. The Comoro group was granted administrative autonomy within the French Republic and became an Overseas Territory. When the other three islands voted to become independent (as the Comoro state) in 1974, Mayotte voted against and remained a French dependency. In Dec. 1976, following a further referendum, it became a Territorial Collectivity.

On 11 July 2001 Mayotte became a Departmental Collectivity—a constitutional innovation—as a result of a referendum. This was denounced by the Comorian authorities, who claim Mayotte as part of the Union of the Comoro Islands.

TERRITORY AND POPULATION

Mayotte, east of the Comoro Islands, had a total population at the 2002 census of 160,265 (population density of 426 persons per sq. km). The estimated population for 2003 is 183,400. The whole territory covers 376 sq. km (144 sq. miles). It consists of a main island (362 sq. km) with (2003 estimate) 158,500 inhabitants, containing the chief town, Mamoudzou (45,485 inhabitants in 2002); and the smaller island of Pamanzi (11 sq. km) lying 2 km to the east (24,900 estimated for 2003) containing the old capital of Dzaoudzi (12,066 in 2002).

The spoken language is Shimaoré (akin to Comorian, an Arabized dialect of Swahili), but French remains the official, commercial and administrative language.

CLIMATE

The dry and sunniest season is from May to Oct. The hot but rainy season is from Nov. to April. Average temperatures are 27°C from Dec. to March and 24°C from May to Sept.

CONSTITUTION AND GOVERNMENT

The island is administered by a General Council of 19 members, directly elected for a six-year term. The French government is represented by an appointed Prefect. In accordance with the legislation of 11 July 2001 executive powers were transferred from the prefect to the president of the General Council in March 2004. Mayotte is represented by one deputy in the National Assembly and by one member in the Senate. There are 17 communes, including two on Pamanzi.

RECENT ELECTIONS

At the General Council elections on 21 and 28 March 2004 the Union pour un Mouvement Populaire (UMP) won nine seats (with 22·8% of the vote), the Mouvement Départmentaliste Mahorais (MDM) won six (23·3%) and the Mouvement Républicain et Citoyen (MRC) won two (8·9%). The Mouvement Populaire Mahorais (MPM) and Diverse Gauche (DVG) won one seat each. The Parti Socialiste (PS) took 10·2% of the vote but no seats.

CURRENT ADMINISTRATION

Prefect: Jean-Paul Kihl.

President of the General Council: Saïd Omar Oili (ind.).

ECONOMY

Currency. Since 1 Jan. 2002 the euro has been the official currency as in metropolitan France.

Banking and Finance. The Institut d'Emission d'Outre-mer and the Banque Française Commerciale both have branches in Dzaoudzi and Mamoudzou.

ENERGY AND NATURAL RESOURCES

Agriculture. The area under cultivation in 1998 was 14,400 ha. Mayotte is the world's second largest producer of ylang-ylang essence. Important cash crops include cinnamon, ylang-ylang, vanilla and coconut. The main food crops (1997) were bananas (30,200 tonnes) and cassava (10,000 tonnes). Livestock (1997): cattle, 17,000; goats, 25,000; sheep, 2,000.

Forestry. There are some 19,750 ha of forest, of which 1,150 is primary, 15,000 secondary and 3,600 badlands (uncultivable or eroded).

Fisheries. A lobster and shrimp industry has been created. Fish landings in 2001 totalled 5,500 tonnes.

INDUSTRY

Labour. In 1994, 18·5% of the active population was engaged in public building and works. Unemployment rate, 1997, 41%.

INTERNATIONAL TRADE

Imports and Exports. In 1999 imports totalled US$96·2m. and exports US$1·9m. Main export commodities are ylang-ylang, vanilla, cinnamon and coconut. Main imports sources in 1997: France, 66%; South Africa, 14%. Main export destinations, 1997: France, 80%; Comoros, 15%.

COMMUNICATIONS

Roads. In 2002 there were 224 km of main roads, all of which are paved, and 1,528 motor vehicles.

Civil Aviation. There is an airport at Pamandzi, with scheduled services in 2002 provided to the Comoros, Kenya, Madagascar, Mozambique, Réunion, Seychelles and South Africa.

Shipping. There are services provided by Tratringa and Ville de Sima to Anjouan (Comoros) and Moroni (Comoros).

Telecommunications. In 2001 there were 10,000 telephone main lines, or 69·8 per 1,000 inhabitants. There were 21,700 mobile phone subscribers in 2002.

SOCIAL INSTITUTIONS

Justice. There is a *tribunal de première instance* and a *tribunal supérieur d'appel*.

Religion. The population is 97% Sunni Muslim, with a small Christian (mainly Roman Catholic) minority.

Education. In 1994 there were 25,805 pupils in nursery and primary schools, and 6,190 pupils at seven *collèges* and one *lycée* at secondary level. There were also 1,922 pupils enrolled in pre-professional classes and professional *lycées*. There is a teacher training college.

Health. There were two hospitals with 100 beds in 1994. In 1985 there were nine doctors, one dentist, one pharmacist, two midwives and 51 nursing personnel.

CULTURE

Broadcasting. Broadcasting is conducted by *Radio-Télévision Française d'Outre-Mer* (RFO-Mayotte) with one hour a day in Shimaoré. *Télé Mayotte RFO* on Petite Terre transmits from 6 a.m. to around midnight every day. There are two private radio stations. In 2000 there were an estimated 40,000 radio and 5,000 TV receivers; colour is by SECAM. Since 1999, two satellite TV programmes have been available.

Press. There are two newspapers: *Kwezi*, published twice a week, and *Mayotte Hebdo*, published once a week.

Tourism. In 2001 there were 23,000 visitors. In 1999, 44% came from Réunion, 42% from mainland France and 14% from other countries. The average length of stay was 11 to 14 days.

TERRITORIAL COLLECTIVITIES

Collectivités Territoriales

NEW CALEDONIA

Nouvelle-Calédonie

KEY HISTORICAL EVENTS

From the 11th century Melanesians settled in the islands that now form New Caledonia and dependencies. James Cook was the first European to arrive on Grande Terre on 4 Sept. 1774. The first European settlers (English Protestants and French

Catholics) came in 1840. In 1853 New Caledonia was annexed by France and was used as a penal colony, taking in 21,000 convicts by 1897. Nickel was discovered in 1863, the mining of which provoked revolt among the Kanak tribes. During the Second World War, New Caledonia was used as a military base by the USA. Having fought for France during the war, the Kanaks were awarded citizenship in 1946. Together with most of its former dependencies, New Caledonia was made an Overseas Territory in 1958. It became a Territorial Collectivity under the Nouméa Accord of May 1998, which agreed on a gradual handover of responsibilities and the creation of New Caledonian citizenship. A referendum on independence will be held between 2013 and 2018.

TERRITORY AND POPULATION

The territory comprises Grande Terre (New Caledonia mainland) and various outlying islands, all situated in the southwest Pacific (Melanesia) with a total land area of 18,575 sq. km (7,172 sq. miles). New Caledonia has the second biggest coral reef in the world. The population (1996 census) was 196,836, including 67,151 Europeans (majority French), 86,788 Melanesians (Kanaks), 7,825 Vietnamese and Indonesians, 5,171 Polynesians, 17,763 Wallisians and Futunians, 1,318 others. Density, 10 per sq. km. In 1996 an estimated 60·4% of the population lived in urban areas. The estimated population at 1 Jan. 2001 was 212,709. The UN gives a projected population for 2010 of 258,000. The capital, Nouméa, had 76,293 inhabitants in 1996.

There are four main islands (or groups of):

Grande Terre An area of 16,372 sq. km (about 400 km long, 50 km wide) with a population (1996 census) of 170,365. A central mountain range separates a humid east coast and a drier temperate west coast. The east coast is predominantly Melanesian; the Nouméa region predominantly European; and the rest of the west coast is of mixed population.

Loyalty Islands 100 km (60 miles) east of New Caledonia, consisting of four large islands: Maré, Lifou, Uvéa and Tiga. It has a total area of 1,981 sq. km and a population (1996) of 20,877.

Isle of Pines A tourist and fishing centre 50 km (30 miles) to the southeast of Nouméa, with an area of 152 sq. km and a population (1996) of 1,671.

Bélep Archipelago About 50 km northwest of New Caledonia, with an area of 70 sq. km and a population (1996) of 923.

The remaining islands are very small and have no permanent inhabitants.

At the 1996 census there were 341 tribes (which have legal status under a high chief) living in 160 reserves, covering a surface area of 392,550 ha (21% of total land), and representing about 28·7% of the population. 80,443 Melanesians belong to a tribe.

New Caledonia has a remarkable diversity of Melanesian languages (29 vernacular), divided into four main groups (Northern, Central, Southern and Loyalty Islands). There were 53,556 speakers (1996). In 2000 six Melanesian languages were taught in schools.

SOCIAL STATISTICS

2000: live births, 4,564; deaths, 1,075; marriages, 995; divorces, 159. Annual growth rate, 1·65%. Life expectancy at birth, 1990–95, 69·7 years for males and 74·7 years for females. Infant mortality, 1990–95, 22 per 1,000 live births; fertility rate, 2·7 births per woman.

CLIMATE

2000: Nouméa, Jan. 25·8°C, July 20·4°C (average temperature, 23·8°C; max. 33·5°C, min. 14·3°C). Annual rainfall 1,294 mm.

CONSTITUTION AND GOVERNMENT

Subsequent to the referendum law of 9 Nov. 1988, the organic and ordinary laws of 19 March 1999 define New Caledonia's new statute. Until then an 'Overseas Territory', New Caledonia became a Territorial Collectivity with specific status endowed with wide autonomy. New Caledonia's institutions comprise the congress, government, economic and social council (CES), the customary senate and customary councils. The congress is made up of 54 members called 'Councillors of New Caledonia', from the provincial assemblies. The 11-member government is elected by congress on a proportional ballot from party lists. The president is elected by majority vote of all members. Each member is allocated to lead and control a given sector in the administration. The government's mandate ends when the mandate of the Congress that elected it comes to an end. New Caledonia is represented by two deputies and one senator in the French parliament.

RECENT ELECTIONS

On 8 Nov. 1998 there was a referendum for the agreement of the Nouméa accords. Nearly 72% of those who voted approved. Turn-out was 74·2%. Voting was restricted to those people resident in New Caledonia before 1998.

In elections to the Territorial Congress on 9 May 2004, the conservative Rassemblement-UMP and Our Future Together (Avénir Ensemble; AE) won 16 seats each, the National Liberation Front of the Socialist Kanaks (FLNKS) 8, the Caledonian Union 7 and the National Front 4. Turn-out was 76%.

CURRENT ADMINISTRATION

High Commissioner: Daniel Constantin; b. 1940 (took office on 31 July 2002).

Congress elected Marie-Noëlle Thémereau as president of the government on 10 June 2004 but the resignation of three ministers brought down the government. The congressional vote on 24 June was split between Thémereau and her predecessor, Pierre Frogier. Thémereau won the vote on 29 June.

President: Marie-Noëlle Thémereau; b. 1949 (AE; took office on 10 June 2004).

Vice-President: Déwé Gorodey (Palika/FLNKS).

President of the Congress: Harold Martin (AE).

ECONOMY

Currency. The unit of currency is the franc CFP (XPF), with a parity of 119·3317422 francs CPF to the euro. 211,396m. francs CFP were in circulation in Dec. 2000.

Budget. The budget for 2000 balanced at 74,904m. francs CFP.

Performance. Total GDP was US$2·7bn in 2001.

Banking and Finance. In 2000 the banks were: Banque Calédonienne d'Investissement (BCI), the Bank of Hawaii-Nouvelle-Calédonie (BoH-NC), the Banque Nationale de Paris/Nouvelle-Calédonie (BNP/NC), the Société Générale Calédonienne de Banque (SGCB) and the Caisse d'Epargne.

ENERGY AND NATURAL RESOURCES

Environment. Carbon dioxide emissions from the consumption and flaring of fossil fuels in 2002 were the equivalent of 8·6 tonnes per capita.

Electricity. Production (2000): 1,645m. kWh. Installed capacity was 0·4m. kW in 2000.

Minerals. A wide range of minerals has been found in New Caledonia including: nickel, copper and lead, gold, chrome, gypsum and platinum metals. The nickel deposits are of special value, being without arsenic, and constitute between 20–40% of the world's known nickel resources located on the mainland.

Production of nickel ore (2000): 128,289 tonnes, of which garnieritic ore (108,302 tonnes) and lateritic ore (19,987).

Agriculture. According to the 1996 census, 4,663 persons worked in the agricultural sector. In 2001 there were an estimated 7,000 ha of arable land and 6,000 ha of permanent crops. In 1999 livestock numbered: pigs, 38,000; goats, 16,000; deer, 13,000; horses, 11,000; poultry, 877,000; cattle (2000), 122,000. The chief products are beef, pork, poultry, coffee, copra, maize, fruit and vegetables. Production (2002 estimates, in 1,000 tonnes): coconuts, 16; yams, 11; cassava, 3; sweet potatoes, 3.

Forestry. There were 698,000 ha of forest in 1995, or 38·2% of the total land area (down from 38·3% in 1990). Timber production (2001), 5,000 cu. metres.

Fisheries. Total catch in 2001 was approximately 3,337 tonnes. In 1998 there were 291 fishing boats (1,950 GRT). Aquaculture (consisting mainly of saltwater prawns) provides New Caledonia's second highest source of export income after nickel.

INDUSTRY

Up until the end of the 1970s the New Caledonia economy was almost totally dependent on the nickel industry. Subsequently transformation or processing industries gained in importance to reach levels similar to those in metallurgic industries.

Labour. The employed population (1996) was 64,377. In July 2001 the guaranteed monthly minimum wage was 100,000 francs CFP. In 2002 the unemployment rate stood at 10·5%.

INTERNATIONAL TRADE

Imports and Exports. In 2000 the balance of trade showed a deficit of 41,312m. francs CFP. Imports and exports in 1m. francs CFP:

	1997	*1998*	*1999*	*2000*
Imports	97,700	99,531	112,887	119,766
Exports	55,912	40,621	52,387	78,454

In 2000, 38·8% of imports came from France, 16·8% from Australia and 14·9% from other countries of European Union. In 2000, 20·6% of exports went to France and 26·6% to Japan. In 1999 ferro-nickel accounted for 54·8% of exports, nickel ore 18·8% and nickel matte 13·9%. Machinery and apparatus accounted for 20·0% of imports, food 16·2% and transportation equipment 15·6%.

COMMUNICATIONS

Roads. In 2000 there were 5,432 km of roads and 83,554 vehicles. In 1999 road accidents inured 983 and killed 58 persons.

Civil Aviation. New Caledonia is connected by air routes with Australia, Japan, Vanuatu, Wallis and Futuna, Fiji Islands and French Polynesia. Regular domestic air services are provided by Air Calédonie from Magenta aerodrome in Nouméa. In 2000 there were 288,322 passengers recorded at Magenta Aerodrome. Internal services with Air Calédonie link Nouméa to a number of domestic airfields.

In 2000, 359,381 passengers and 5,243 tonnes of freight were carried via La Tontouta International Airport, near Nouméa.

Shipping. In 1999, 510 vessels entered New Caledonia, unloading 1,254,662 tonnes of freight, loading 4,007,049 tonnes (including 3·8m. tonnes of nickel ore).

Telecommunications. In 2002 there were 132,000 telephone subscribers (589·3 per 1,000 inhabitants). There were 80,000 mobile phone subscribers in 2002 and 2,200 fax machines in 1995. New Caledonia has had Internet access since 1995. In 2002 there were 30,000 Internet users.

Postal Services. In 2000 there were 36 post offices.

SOCIAL INSTITUTIONS

Justice. There are courts at Nouméa, Koné and Wé (on Lifou Island), a court of appeal, a labour court and a joint commerce tribunal. There were 4,054 cases judged in the magistrates courts in 1999; 280 went before the court of appeal, 26 were sentenced in the court of assizes.

The population in penal institutions in April 2003 was 315 (139 per 100,000 population).

Religion. There were about 130,000 Roman Catholics in 2001.

Education. In 1999 there were 36,667 pupils and 1,628 teachers in 284 primary schools; 27,877 pupils and 2,212 teachers in 85 secondary schools; and 1,866 students at university with 89 teaching staff. By decree of 1999 the New Caledonia campus of the French University of the Pacific (UFP), established in 1987, was separated from the campus, to become University of New Caledonia (UNC).

Health. In 1999 there were 418 doctors, 106 dentists, 91 pharmacists and 1,209 paramedical personnel. There were 26 socio-medical districts, with four hospitals, three private clinics for a total of 838 beds.

Welfare. There are two main forms of social security cover: Free Medical Aid provides total sickness cover for non-waged persons and low-income earners; the Family Benefit, Workplace Injury and Contingency Fund for Workers in New Caledonia (CAFAT). There are also numerous mutual benefit societies. In 1999 Free Medical Aid had 56,894 beneficiaries; CAFAT had approximately 150,000 beneficiaries.

CULTURE

Broadcasting. Television broadcasting was, for a long time, limited to one or two state-owned stations (today Télé Nouvelle-Calédonie and Tempo). A private channel (Canal+) began broadcasting in 1994, and in late 1999 a digital selection of 13 pay-channels (Canal'Sat) was launched. By the end of 2001 Canal Calédonie had 17,000 Canal'Sat subscribers and 18,000 Canal+ subscribers.

There were 111,000 TV sets in 2001 and 107,000 radio receivers in 1997.

Press. In 2001 there was one daily newspaper, *Les Nouvelles Calédoniennes*.

Tourism. In 2000 New Caledonia welcomed 109,587 tourists (Japan, 23·8%; Australia, 16·4%; France, 16·4%; New Zealand, 8·7%). Spending by tourists totalled US$110m. in 2000. In 1999 there were 82 hotels providing 2,398 beds.

FURTHER READING

Institut de la Statistique et des Etudes Économiques: *Tableaux de l'Économie Calédonienne/ New Caledonia: Facts & Figures (TEC 2003)* (every three years)*; Informations Statistiques Rapides de Nouvelle-Calédonie* (monthly).

Imprimerie Administrative, Nouméa: *Journal Officiel de la Nouvelle Calédonie.*

Local statistical office: Institut Territorial de la Statistique et des Études Économiques, BP 823, 98845 Nouméa.

ST PIERRE AND MIQUELON

Îles Saint-Pierre et Miquelon

KEY HISTORICAL EVENTS

The only remaining fragment of the once-extensive French possessions in North America, the archipelago was settled from France in the 17th century. It was a French colony from 1816 until 1976, an overseas department until 1985, and is now a Territorial Collectivity.

TERRITORY AND POPULATION

The archipelago consists of two islands off the south coast of Newfoundland, with a total area of 242 sq. km, comprising the Saint-Pierre group (26 sq. km) and the Miquelon-Langlade group (216 sq. km). The population (1999 census) was 6,316 of whom 3,169 were female. This total population figure represents a decrease of 76 from the 1990 census. Approximately 88% of the population lives on Saint-Pierre. The chief town is St Pierre.

The official language is French.

SOCIAL STATISTICS

2000: births, 51; deaths, 35; marriages, 24; divorces, 7.

CONSTITUTION AND GOVERNMENT

The Territorial Collectivity is administered by a General Council of 19 members directly elected for a six-year term. It is represented in the National Assembly in Paris by one deputy, in the Senate by one senator and in the Economic and Social Council by one councillor. The French government is represented by a Prefect.

RECENT ELECTIONS

At the General Council elections on 19 and 26 March 2000, 11 seats went to Défense des Intérêts de l'Archipel, 3 to Volonté Insulaire, 2 to Expérience et Innovation, 2 to Cap sur l'Avenir and 1 to Miquelon 2000.

CURRENT ADMINISTRATION

Prefect: Albert Dupuy.

President of the General Council: Marc Plantegenest.

ECONOMY

Currency. Since 1 Jan. 2002 the euro has been the official currency as in metropolitan France.

Budget. The budget for 2000 balanced at 270m. French francs.

Banking and Finance. Banks include the Banque des Îles Saint-Pierre et Miquelon, the Crédit Saint-Pierrais and the Caisse d'Épargne.

A Development Agency was created in 1996 to help with investment projects.

ENERGY AND NATURAL RESOURCES

Environment. Carbon dioxide emissions from the consumption and flaring of fossil fuels in 2002 were the equivalent of 10·9 tonnes per capita.

Electricity. Production (2000): 39m. kWh. Installed capacity (2000): 27,000 kW.

Agriculture. The islands, being mostly barren rock, are unsuited for agriculture, but some vegetables are grown and livestock is kept for local consumption.

Fisheries. In June 1992 an international tribunal awarded France a 24-mile fishery and economic zone around the islands and a 10·5-mile-wide corridor extending for 200 miles to the high seas. The 2000 catch amounted to 1,261 tonnes, chiefly snow crab, cod, lumpfish, shark and scallops. A Franco-Canadian agreement regulating fishing in the area was signed in Dec. 1994. The total annual catch has declined dramatically in the past 15 years.

INDUSTRY

In 1994 there were 351 businesses (including 144 services, 69 public works, 45 food trade, 8 manufacturing and 2 agriculture). The main industry, fish processing, resumed in 1994 after a temporary cessation due to lack of supplies in 1992. Diversification activities are in progress (aquaculture, sea products processing, scallops plant).

Labour. The economically active population in 2000 was 3,261. In July 2003 the minimum wage (SMIC) was raised to €7·19 an hour (€1,090·48 a month for a 35-hour week). In 1996, 11% of the labour force was registered as unemployed.

INTERNATIONAL TRADE

Imports and Exports. Trade in 1m. French francs (2000): imports, 371 (51% from Canada); exports, 50.

COMMUNICATIONS

Roads. In 2000 there were 117 km of roads, of which 80 km were surfaced. There were 2,508 passenger cars and 1,254 commercial vehicles in use.

Civil Aviation. Air Saint–Pierre connects St Pierre with Halifax, Montreal, Sydney (Nova Scotia) and St John's (Newfoundland). In addition, a new airport capable of receiving medium-haul aeroplanes was opened in 1999.

Shipping. St Pierre has regular services to Fortune and Halifax in Canada. In 1999, 893 vessels called at St Pierre; 17,067 tonnes of freight were unloaded and 3,020 tonnes were loaded.

Telecommunications. There were 4,900 telephones in 2000.

SOCIAL INSTITUTIONS

Justice. There is a court of first instance and a higher court of appeal at St Pierre.

Religion. The population is chiefly Roman Catholic.

Education. Primary instruction is free. In 2000 there were three nursery and five primary schools with 799 pupils; three secondary schools with 564 pupils; and two technical schools with 199 pupils.

Health. In 2000 there was one hospital with 45 beds, one convalescent home with 20 beds, one retirement home with 40 beds; 15 doctors and one dentist.

CULTURE

Broadcasting. *Radio Télévision Française d'Outre Mer* (RFO) broadcasts in French on medium waves and on two television channels (one satellite). In 2000 there were 35 cable television channels from Canada and USA. In 2000 there were also approximately 4,900 radio and 4,500 television sets in use.

Tourism. In 2000 there were 10,090 visitors.

OVERSEAS COUNTRIES

Pays d'Outre-Mer

FRENCH POLYNESIA

Territoire de la Polynésie Française

KEY HISTORICAL EVENTS

French protectorates since 1843, these islands were annexed to France 1880–82 to form 'French Settlements in Oceania', which opted in Nov. 1958 for the status of an overseas territory within the French Community.

TERRITORY AND POPULATION

The total land area of these five archipelagoes, comprising 130 volcanic islands and coral atolls (76 inhabited) scattered over a wide area in the eastern Pacific, is 4,167 sq. km. The population (2002 census) was 245,516; density, 59 per sq. km. At Dec.1998 French forces stationed in Polynesia numbered 2,119 (based mostly on Tahiti and the Hao atoll) and employed 1,162 Polynesian citizens. In 1995 an estimated 56·4% of the population lived in urban areas.

The UN gives a projected population for 2010 of 270,000.

The official languages are French and Tahitian.

The islands are administratively divided into five *circonscriptions* as follows:

Windward Islands (Îles du Vent) (184,224 inhabitants, 2002) comprise Tahiti with an area of 1,042 sq. km and 150,707 inhabitants in 1996; Mooréa with an area of 132 sq. km and 11,682 inhabitants in 1996; Maiao (Tubuai Manu) with an area of 9 sq. km; and the smaller Mehetia and Tetiaroa. The capital is Papeete, Tahiti (79,024 inhabitants in 1996, including suburbs).

Leeward Islands (Îles sous le Vent) comprise the five volcanic islands of Raiatéa, Tahaa, Huahine, Bora-Bora and Maupiti, together with four small atolls (Tupai, Mopelia, Scilly, Bellinghausen), the group having a total land area of 404 sq. km and 30,221 inhabitants in 2002. The chief town is Uturoa on Raiatéa. The Windward and Leeward Islands together are called the Society Archipelago (Archipel de la Société). Tahitian, a Polynesian language, is spoken throughout the archipelago and used as a *lingua franca* in the rest of the territory.

Marquesas Islands 12 islands lying north of the Tuamotu Archipelago, with a total area of 1,049 sq. km and 8,712 inhabitants in 2002. There are six inhabited islands: Nuku Hiva, Ua Pou, Ua Uka, Hiva Oa, Tahuata, Fatu Hiva; and six smaller (uninhabited) ones; the chief centre is Taiohae on Nuku Hiva.

Austral or Tubuai Islands lying south of the Society Archipelago, comprise a 1,300 km chain of volcanic islands and reefs. There are five inhabited islands (Rimatara,

Rurutu, Tubuai, Raivavae and, 500 km to the south, Rapa), with a combined area of 148 sq. km (6,386 inhabitants in 2002); the chief centre is Mataura on Tubuai.

Tuamotu Archipelago consists of two parallel ranges of 76 atolls (53 inhabited) lying north and east of the Society Archipelago, and has a total area of 690 sq. km, with 15,973 inhabitants in 2002. The most populous atolls are Rangiroa (1,913 inhabitants in 1996), Hao (1,356 in 1996) and Manihi (769 in 1996).

The Mururoa and Fangataufa atolls in the southeast of the group were ceded to France in 1964 by the Territorial Assembly, and were used by France for nuclear tests from 1966–96. The Pacific Testing Centre (CEP) was dismantled in 1998. A small military presence remains to ensure permanent radiological control.

SOCIAL STATISTICS

2000: births, 4,900; deaths, 1,013 (estimate). Annual population growth rate, 2·2%. Life expectancy at birth, 1990–95, 68·3 years for males and 73·8 years for females. Infant mortality, 1990–95, 11 per 1,000 live births; fertility rate, 3·1 births per woman.

CLIMATE

Papeete. Jan. 81°F (27·1°C), July 75°F (24°C). Annual rainfall 83" (2,106 mm).

CONSTITUTION AND GOVERNMENT

Under the 1984 Constitution, the Territory is administered by a Council of Ministers, whose President is elected by the Territorial Assembly from among its own members; the President appoints a Vice-President and 14 other ministers. French Polynesia is represented in the French Assembly by two deputies and in the Senate by one senator. The French government is represented by a High Commissioner. The Territorial Assembly comprises 41 members elected every five years from five constituencies by universal suffrage, using the same proportional representation system as in metropolitan French regional elections. To be elected a party must gain at least 5% of votes cast.

In Dec. 2003 French Polynesia's status was changed from that of an Overseas Territory to an Overseas Country within the French Republic. The statute gives the government in Papeete more powers and allows it to change some laws.

RECENT ELECTIONS

Elections were held on 23 May 2004. The People's Front-Rally for the Republic (TH-RPR), the party of President Gaston Flosse, won 28 seats and the Union for Democracy (UPD) won 27 seats. New Star (Fetia Api) and the Nicole Bouteau List took one seat each. Following by-elections on 13 Feb. 2005 after elections in one of the districts had been declared invalid the TH-RPR and the UPD each held 27 seats and the Alliance for a New Democracy (alliance of New Star and the Nicole Bouteau List) 3 seats. In the presidential vote held on 13 March 2005 in the Assembly Oscar Temaru (UPD) defeated Gaston Tong Sang (TH-RPR) by 29 votes to 26.

CURRENT ADMINISTRATION

High Commissioner: Michel Mathieu; b. 1944 (took office on 17 Nov. 2001).

President: Oscar Temaru; b. 1944 (UPD; took office for a second time on 3 March 2005).

ECONOMY

In decline since 1993, the economy has shown signs of recovery since 1997.

Currency. The unit of currency is the franc CFP (XPF). Up to 31 Dec. 1998, its parity was to the French franc: 1 franc CFP = 0·055 French francs; from 1 Jan. 1999 parity was linked to the euro: 119·3317422 francs CPF = one euro.

Budget. Revenues totalled 108·0bn. francs CPF in 2001 and expenditures 140·7bn. francs CPF.

Performance. Total GDP in 2001 was US$3·4bn.

Banking and Finance. There are four commercial banks: Banque de Tahiti, Banque de Polynésie, Société de Crédit et de Développement de l'Océanie and the Banque Westpac.

ENERGY AND NATURAL RESOURCES

French Polynesia is heavily dependent on external sources for its energy. By 1999 it was estimated that production of solar energy was in the region of 2,700 hours a year.

Environment. Carbon dioxide emissions from the consumption and flaring of fossil fuels in 2002 were the equivalent of 2·7 tonnes per capita.

Electricity. Production (2000) was 407m. kWh, of which approximately 29% was hydro-electric. Consumption per capita in 2000 was 1,747 kWh.

Oil and Gas. In 1997 over 236,000 tonnes of combustible products were imported (with a value of 346m. French francs), mainly from Australia and Hawaii; 8,600 tonnes of gas was imported.

Agriculture. Agriculture used to be the primary economic sector but now accounts for only a modest 8% (1997) of GDP. Important products are copra (coconut trees cover the coastal plains of the mountainous islands and the greater part of the low-lying islands) and the nono fruit, which has medicinal value. Production in 1,000 tonnes (2002 estimates): coconuts, 88; copra, 10; cassava, 6; sugarcane, 3. Tropical fruits, such as bananas, pineapples and oranges, are grown for local consumption.

Livestock (2002): cattle 11,000; pigs 34,000; goats 16,000; poultry (1995) 297,700.

Forestry. In 1999 there was between 4,000 and 5,000 ha of forest, around half of it exploitable. The industry remains embryonic.

Fisheries. Polynesia has an exclusive zone of 5·2m. sq. km, one of the largest in the world. The industry employs some 2,000 people, including 700 traditional fishermen. Catch (2001): 15,404 tonnes, almost exclusively from sea fishing.

INDUSTRY

Some 2,218 industrial enterprises employ 5,800 people. Principal industries include food and drink products, cosmetics, clothing and jewellery, furniture-making, metalwork and shipbuilding.

INTERNATIONAL TRADE

Imports and Exports. Polynesia imports a great deal and exports very little. Total imports (2001), 135·6bn. francs CFP; total exports, 18·7bn. francs CFP.

The chief exports are coconut oil, fish, nono juice, mother of pearl and cultured pearls. Pearl production in particular has increased in recent years. Representing 27% of the world market, Polynesia is the world's second largest producer of pearls after Australia. It is the second largest industry in Polynesia after tourism, and employs some 4,000 islanders.

Major trading partners: France, Japan (66% of pearl exports), Hong Kong, the USA and the EU, with France accounting for over 38% of total imports and around 25% of exports in 1997, and the EU as a whole 52% of imports.

COMMUNICATIONS

Roads. There were estimated to be 2,590 km of roads in 1999, 67% bitumenized.

Civil Aviation. The main airport is at Papeete (Tahiti-Faa'a). Air France and nine other international airlines (including Air New Zealand, Quantas and Lan Chile) connect Tahiti International Airport with Paris, Auckland, Honolulu, Los Angeles, Osaka, Santiago, Tokyo and many Pacific islands. In 2000 Papeete handled 1,553,132 passengers (849,540 on domestic flights) and 11,429 tonnes of freight.

Shipping. Ten shipping companies connect France, San Francisco, New Zealand, Japan, Australia, southeast Asia and most Pacific locations with Papeete. In 1997, 727,000 tonnes of cargo were unloaded and 28,000 tonnes loaded at Papeete's main port. Around 1·4m. people pass through the port each year.

Telecommunications. Number of telephone subscribers in 2002 was 142,500 (593·7 per 1,000 inhabitants); mobile phone subscribers (2002), 90,000. In 1997 there were 2,900 fax machines. In 2002 there were 35,000 Internet users.

Postal Services. In 1999 there were 56 post offices.

SOCIAL INSTITUTIONS

Justice. There is a *tribunal de première instance* and a *cour d'appel* at Papeete. The population in penal institutions in April 2003 was 291 (120 per 100,000 population).

Religion. In 2001 there were approximately 119,000 protestants (about 49% of the population) and 94,000 Roman Catholics (39%).

Education. In 1998–99 there were 77,300 pupils and 5,200 teachers in 316 schools (46,800 in 255 primary schools; 30,500 in secondary school). The French University of the Pacific (UFP) has a campus on Tahiti. The South Pacific University Institute for Teacher Training (part of UFP) has three colleges: in French Polynesia, Wallis and Futuna, and in Nouméa (New Caledonia), where it is headquartered. In 1997–98, 2,200 students followed university courses.

Health. In 1999 there were 1 territorial hospital centre, 4 general hospitals, 1 specialist hospital and 2 private clinics, with a total of 855 beds. Medical personnel numbered 1,590 persons, including 384 doctors (175 per 100,000 inhabitants), 94 dentists and 51 pharmacists. Health spending accounted for 10·2% of GDP in 1997.

Welfare. In 1997, 202,760 people benefited from social welfare.

CULTURE

Broadcasting. There are three TV broadcasters (one public, two independent): *Radio Télévision Française d'Outre-mer* (RFO) which broadcasts on two channels in French, Tahitian and English; *Canal + Polynésie*; and *Telefenua* which broadcasts across 16 channels. There are also 11 private radio stations. Number of receivers: radio (1999), 40,350; TV (2001), 54,400 (colour by SECAM H).

Press. In 1999 there were two daily newspapers.

Tourism. Tourism is the main industry. There were 252,000 tourist arrivals in 2000. Total revenue (1999) US$394m.

FURTHER READING

Local statistical office: Institut Statistique de Polynésie Française, Papeete.
Website (French only): http://www.ispf.pfl

OVERSEAS TERRITORIES

Territoires d'Outre-Mer

SOUTHERN AND ANTARCTIC TERRITORIES

Terres Australes et Antarctiques Françaises (TAAF)

The Territory of the TAAF was created on 6 Aug. 1955. It comprises the Kerguelen and Crozet archipelagoes, the islands of Saint-Paul and Amsterdam (formerly Nouvelle Amsterdam), all in the southern Indian Ocean, and Terre Adélie. Since 2 April 1997 the administration has had its seat in Saint-Pierre, Réunion; before that it was in Paris. The Administrator is assisted by a seven-member consultative council which meets twice yearly in Paris; its members are nominated by the government for five years. The 15-member Polar Environment Committee, which in 1993 replaced the former Consultative Committee on the Environment (est. 1982), meets at least once a year to discuss all problems relating to the preservation of the environment.

The French Institute for Polar Research and Technology was set up to organize scientific research and expeditions in Jan. 1992. The staff of the permanent scientific stations of the TAAF (120 in 1998) is renewed every 6 or 12 months and forms the only population.

Administrateur Supérieur. Michel Champon.

Kerguelen Islands Situated 48–50° S. lat., 68–70° E. long.; consists of one large and 85 smaller islands, and over 200 islets and rocks, with a total area of 7,215 sq. km (2,786 sq. miles) of which Grande Terre occupies 6,675 sq. km (2,577 sq. miles). It was discovered in 1772 by Yves de Kerguelen, but was effectively occupied by France only in 1949. Port-aux-Français has several scientific research stations (56 members). Reindeer, trout and sheep have been acclimatized.

Crozet Islands Situated 46° S. lat., 50–52° E. long.; consists of five larger and 15 tiny islands, with a total area of 505 sq. km (195 sq. miles). The western group includes Apostles, Pigs and Penguins islands; the eastern group, Possession and Eastern islands. The archipelago was discovered in 1772 by Marion Dufresne, whose first mate, Crozet, annexed it for Louis XV. A meteorological and scientific station (17 members) at Base Alfred-Faure on Possession Island was built in 1964.

Amsterdam and **Saint-Paul Islands** Situated 38–39° S. lat., 77° E. long. Amsterdam, with an area of 54 sq. km (21 sq. miles) was discovered in 1522 by Magellan's companions; Saint-Paul, lying about 100 km to the south, with an area of 7 sq. km (2·7 sq. miles), was probably discovered in 1559 by Portuguese sailors. Both were first visited in 1633 by the Dutch explorer, Van Diemen, and were annexed by France in 1843. They are both extinct volcanoes. The only inhabitants are at Base Martin de Vivies (est. 1949 on Amsterdam Island), including several scientific research stations, a hospital, communication and other facilities (20 members). Crayfish are caught commercially on Amsterdam.

Terre Adélie Comprises that section of the Antarctic continent between 136° and 142° E. long., south of 60° S. lat. The ice-covered plateau has an area of about 432,000 sq. km (166,800 sq. miles), and was discovered in 1840 by Dumont d'Urville. A research station (27 members) is situated at Base Dumont d'Urville, which is maintained by the French Institute for Polar Research and Technology.

WALLIS AND FUTUNA

Wallis et Futuna

KEY HISTORICAL EVENTS

French dependencies since 1842, the inhabitants of these islands voted on 22 Dec. 1959 by 4,307 votes out of 4,576 in favour of exchanging their status to that of an overseas territory, which took effect from 29 July 1961.

TERRITORY AND POPULATION

The territory comprises two groups of islands in the central Pacific (total area 274 sq. km, provisional census population 14,944 in 2003). The Îles de Hoorn lie 255 km northeast of the Fiji Islands and consist of two main islands: Futuna (64 sq. km, 4,873 inhabitants) and uninhabited Alofi (51 sq. km). The Wallis Archipelago lies another 160 km further northeast, and has an area of 159 sq. km (10,071 inhabitants). It comprises the main island of Uvéa (60 sq. km) and neighbouring uninhabited islands, with a surrounding coral reef. The capital is Mata-Utu (2003 provisional census population of 1,191) on Uvéa. Wallisian and Futunian are distinct Polynesian languages.

SOCIAL STATISTICS

Estimates per 1,000 population, 1998: birth rate, 23·0; death rate, 4·8.

CONSTITUTION AND GOVERNMENT

A Prefect represents the French government and carries out the duties of head of the territory, assisted by a 20-member Territorial Assembly directly elected for a five-year term, and a six-member Territorial Council, comprising the three traditional chiefs and three nominees of the Prefect agreed by the Territorial

Assembly. The territory is represented by one deputy in the French National Assembly, by one senator in the Senate, and by one member on the Economic and Social Council. There are three districts: Singave and Alo (both on Futuna), and Wallis; in each, tribal kings exercise customary powers assisted by ministers and district and village chiefs.

RECENT ELECTIONS

Territorial Assembly elections were held on 10 March 2002. Rassemblement pour la République–La Voix des Peuples Wallisens et Futuniens won 13 of the 20 seats, with 7 going to Parti Socialiste–Union Populaire pour Wallis et Futuna.

CURRENT ADMINISTRATION

Senior Administrator: Xavier de Furst.

President of the Territorial Assembly: Apeleto Likuvalu.

ECONOMY

Currency. The unit of currency is the franc CFP (XPF), with a parity of 119·3317422 francs CPF to the euro.

Budget. The budget for 1997 balanced at 120,100m. French francs.

Banking and Finance. There is a branch of Banque Indosuez at Mata-Utu.

ENERGY AND NATURAL RESOURCES

Electricity. There is a thermal power station at Mata-Utu.

Agriculture. The chief products are bananas, coconuts, copra, cassava, yams and taro.

Livestock (2002): 25,000 pigs; 7,000 goats.

Fisheries. The catch in 2001 was estimated at 300 tonnes.

COMMUNICATIONS

Roads. There are about 100 km of roads on Uvéa.

Civil Aviation. There is an airport on Wallis, at Hihifo, and another near Alo on Futuna. Eight flights a week link Wallis and Futuna. Air Calédonie International operates two flights a week to Nouméa (three in the summer) and two flights a week to Nadi.

Shipping. A regular cargo service links Mata-Utu (Wallis) and Singave (Futuna) with Nouméa (New Caledonia). In 2002 merchant shipping totalled 158,000 GRT.

Telecommunications. There were 1,400 main telephone lines in 1997.

Postal Services. There were six post offices in 1986.

SOCIAL INSTITUTIONS

Justice. There is a court of first instance, from which appeals can be made to the court of appeal in New Caledonia.

Religion. The majority of the population is Roman Catholic.

Education. In 1993 there were 3,624 pupils in primary schools and 1,777 in secondary schools. The South Pacific University Institute for Teacher Training, founded in 1992 (part of the French University of the Pacific, UFP) has three colleges: in Wallis and Futuna, French Polynesia and Nouméa (New Caledonia), where it is headquartered.

Health. In 1991 there was one hospital with 60 beds, and four dispensaries.

CULTURE

Broadcasting. Since Aug. 2000 Réseau Française d'Outre-Mer (RFO) Wallis et Futuna radio has broadcast 24 hours a day. Télé Wallis et Futuna is the only television station.

DEPENDENCIES

Dépendances

BASSAS DA INDIA

Île Bassas da India

KEY HISTORICAL EVENTS

The island was annexed by France in 1897. Its present status, an entity administered by France but not part of any other French territory, was established in 1960. The island is claimed by Madagascar.

TERRITORY AND POPULATION

Bassas da India is an uninhabited Indian Ocean atoll surrounded by reefs. It lies 380 km west of Madagascar and 460 km from the African mainland, and covers an area of 0·2 sq. km. The entire surface of the atoll is made of volcanic rock. Most of the island is submerged under water at high tide.

CONSTITUTION AND GOVERNMENT

The island is administered from St Denis, in Réunion, although it is not legally part of that territory.

CLIPPERTON ISLAND

Île Clipperton

KEY HISTORICAL EVENTS

In the 18th century the island was the hideout of a pirate, John Clipperton, for whom it was named. In 1855 it was claimed by France, and in 1897 by Mexico. It was awarded to France by international arbitration in 1935.

TERRITORY AND POPULATION

Clipperton Island is a Pacific atoll, 3 km long, some 1,120 km south-west of the coast of Mexico. It covers an area of 7 sq. km and is uninhabited.

CONSTITUTION AND GOVERNMENT

The island is administered from Papeete, in French Polynesia, although it is not legally part of that territory.

ECONOMY

The island is occasionally visited by tuna fishermen.

EUROPA ISLAND

Île Europa

KEY HISTORICAL EVENTS

The island was annexed by France in 1897. Its present status, an entity administered by France but not part of any other French territory, was established in 1960. The island is claimed by Madagascar.

TERRITORY AND POPULATION

The island, which lies 350 km west of Madagascar, is low and flat. It covers an area of 28 sq. km. There is no permanent population, although there is a small French military garrison and a meteorological station.

CONSTITUTION AND GOVERNMENT

The island is administered from St Denis, in Réunion, although it is not legally part of that territory.

GLORIEUSES ISLANDS

Îles Glorieuses

KEY HISTORICAL EVENTS

The islands were claimed by France in 1892. Their present status, an entity administered by France but not part of any other French territory, was established in 1960. The islands are claimed by Madagascar.

TERRITORY AND POPULATION

The Glorieuses Islands (also known as Glorioso) are two lush tropical islands, Ile du Lys and Grande Glorieuse, plus a number of rocky outcrops, Les Rochers. The group lies between Madagascar and Mayotte and have an area of 5 sq. km. There is no permanent population although there is a French military garrison, a meteorological station and a radio station on Grande Glorieuse.

CONSTITUTION AND GOVERNMENT

The islands are administered from St Denis, in Réunion, although they are not legally part of that territory.

JUAN DE NOVA ISLAND

Île Juan de Nova

KEY HISTORICAL EVENTS

The island was discovered by a 15th century Spanish navigator for whom it was named. In 1897 it was claimed by France. Its present status, an entity administered by France but not part of any other French territory, was established in 1960. The island is claimed by Madagascar.

TERRITORY AND POPULATION

Situated in the Mozambique Channel between Madagascar and Mozambique, the island has an area of 4·4 sq. km. There is no permanent population although there is a small French military garrison that runs a meteorological station. There is also a small civilian workforce to mine the island's guano.

CONSTITUTION AND GOVERNMENT

The island is administered from St Denis, in Réunion, although it is not legally part of that territory.

ECONOMY

About 12,000 tonnes of guano are mined annually and are taken to the jetty on what is probably the world's shortest railway system.

TROMELIN ISLAND

Île Tromelin

KEY HISTORICAL EVENTS

The island was explored by French navigators in 1776. In 1814 it was claimed by France and annexed to Réunion. Its present status, an entity administered by France but not part of any other French territory, was established in 1960. The island is claimed by Madagascar.

TERRITORY AND POPULATION

Tromelin, which is 535 km north-west of Réunion, covers an area of 1 sq. km. There is no permanent population although there is a meteorological station.

CONSTITUTION AND GOVERNMENT

The island is administered from St Denis, in Réunion, although it is not legally part of that territory.

GABON

République Gabonaise

Capital: Libreville
Population projection, 2010: 1·51m.
GDP per capita, 2002: (PPP$) 6,590
HDI/world rank: 0·648/122

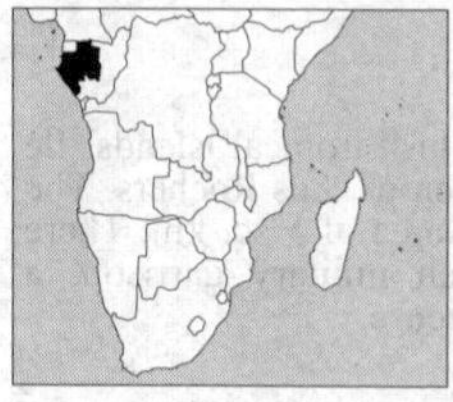

KEY HISTORICAL EVENTS

Between the 16th and 18th centuries, the Fang and other peoples in the region of present-day Gabon were part of a federation of chiefdoms. The country's capital, Libreville, grew from a settlement of slaves who were rescued from captivity by the French in 1849. Colonized by France around this period, the territory was annexed to French Congo in 1888. There was resistance by the indigenous people between 1905 and 1911 to the depredations of colonial rule, but the country became a separate colony in 1910 as one of the four territories of French Equatorial Africa. Gabon became an autonomous republic within the French Community on 28 Nov. 1958 and achieved independence on 17 Aug. 1960.

TERRITORY AND POPULATION

Gabon is bounded in the west by the Atlantic Ocean, north by Equatorial Guinea and Cameroon and east and south by the Republic of the Congo. The area covers 267,667 sq. km. Its population at the 1993 census was 1,014,976; density, 3·8 per sq. km. In 2001, 82·1% of the population were urban. 2002 estimate, 1,305,000; density, 4·9 per sq. km.

The UN gives a projected population for 2010 of 1·51m.

The capital is Libreville (523,000 inhabitants, 1999 estimate), other large towns (1993 census) being Port-Gentil (79,225), Franceville (31,183), Oyem (22,404) and Moanda (21,882).

Provincial areas, populations (in 1,000) and capitals:

Province	*Area in sq. km*	*Population 1993 census*	*Capital*
Estuaire	20,740	463,187	Libreville
Haut-Ogooué	36,547	104,301	Franceville (Masuku)
Moyen-Ogooué	18,535	42,316	Lambaréné
Ngounié	37,750	77,781	Mouila
Nyanga	21,285	39,430	Tchibanga
Ogooué-Ivindo	46,075	48,862	Makokou
Ogooué-Lolo	25,380	43,915	Koulamoutou
Ogooué-Maritime	22,890	97,913	Port-Gentil
Woleu-Ntem	38,465	97,271	Oyem

The largest ethnic groups are the Fangs (25%) in the north and the Bapounou (24%) in the south. There are some 40 smaller groups. French is the official language.

SOCIAL STATISTICS

2003 estimates: births, 41,000; deaths, 16,000. Estimated rates, 2003 (per 1,000 population): births, 31; deaths, 12. Annual population growth rate, 1992–2002, 2·6%. Expectation of life at birth, 2002, 55·7 years for males and 57·6 years for females. Infant mortality, 2001, 60 per 1,000 live births; fertility rate, 2001, 5·4 births per woman.

CLIMATE

The climate is equatorial, with high temperatures and considerable rainfall. Mid-May to mid-Sept. is the long dry season, followed by a short rainy season, then a dry season again from mid-Dec. to mid-Feb., and finally a long rainy season once more. Libreville, Jan. 80°F (26·7°C), July 75°F (23·9°C). Annual rainfall 99" (2,510 mm).

CONSTITUTION AND GOVERNMENT

On 21 March 1997 the government presented to the Parliament legislation aimed at reforming the constitution in a number of key areas: notably, the bill mandated the creation of a Vice-President of the Republic, the extension of the presidential term of office from five to seven years, and the transformation of the Senate into an Upper Chamber of Parliament. Gabon has a bicameral legislature, consisting of a 120-member *National Assembly* (with members elected by direct, popular vote to serve five-year terms) and a 91-member *Senate* (elected for six-year terms in single-seat constituencies by local and departmental councillors). At a referendum on electoral reform on 23 July 1995, 96·48% of votes cast were in favour; turn-out was 63·45%. The 1991 Constitution provides for an Executive *President* directly elected for a five-year term (renewable once only). In July 2003 Gabon's parliament approved an amendment to the constitution that allows the president to seek re-election indefinitely. The head of government is the *Prime Minister*, who appoints a Council of Ministers.

National Anthem. 'La concorde' ('The Concord'); words and tune by G. Damas Aleka.

RECENT ELECTIONS

Presidential elections were held on 6 Dec. 1998. President Bongo was re-elected against eight opponents with 66·6% of votes cast.

Elections for the National Assembly were held in two rounds on 9 and 23 Dec. 2001. The Gabonese Democratic Party (PDG) won 85 seats, the National Woodcutters' Rally 6, the Gabonese Party of Progress 3, the Social Democratic Party 2 and the People's Unity Party 1. Non-partisans took 11 seats.

CURRENT ADMINISTRATION

President: El Hadj Omar Bongo Ondimba; b. 1935 (PDG; succeeded 2 Dec. 1967, re-elected in 1973, 1979, 1986, 1993 and 1998).

Vice President: Didjob Divungi Di Ndinge.

In March 2005 the Council of Ministers comprised:

Prime Minister: Jean-François Ntoutoume-Emane; b. 1939 (sworn in 23 Jan. 1999).

Deputy Prime Ministers: Emmanuel Ondo-Metogho (also *Minister of Town and Country Planning*); Antoine de Padoue Mboumbou Miyakou (also *Minister of the City*); Paul Mba Abessole (also *Minister of Transport and Civil Aviation*).

Minister of State for Economy, Finance, Budget and Privatization: Paul Toungui. *Foreign Affairs, Co-operation and Francophony Affairs:* Jean Ping. *Housing, Town Planning and Land Registry:* Jacques Adiahénot. *Missions and Reform:* Pierre Claver Maganga Moussavou. *Planning and Development Programmes:* Casimir Oyé Mba. *Public Health:* Paulette Missambo. *Small and Medium-Sized Enterprises and Industries:* Jean-Rémy Pendy-Bouyiki.

Minister of Agriculture, Livestock and Rural Development: Faustin Boukoubi. *Civil Service, Administrative Reform and State Modernization:* Egide Boundono-Simangoye. *Commerce and Industrial Development:* Paul Biyoghé-Mba. *Communication and Information Technology:* Mehdi Teale. *Culture and Arts:* Pierre Amoughe Mba. *Defence:* Ali Bongo Ondimba. *Family, Child Welfare and Women's Affairs:* Angélique Ngoma. *Forest Economy, Water and Fisheries:* Emile Doumba. *Higher Education and Scientific Research:* Vincent Moulengui Boukossou. *Interior and Decentralization:* Clotaire Christian Ivala. *Justice and Keeper of the Seals:* Honorine Dossou Naki. *Labour and Employment:* Jean Boniface Assélé. *Merchant Marine:* Alice Lamou. *Mines, Energy, Oil and Hydraulic Resources:* Richard Onouviet. *National Education:* François Engongah Owono. *National Solidarity and Social Affairs:* André Mba Obame. *Posts and Telecommunications:* Daniel Ona Ondo. *Public Security:* Pascal Désiré Missongo. *Public Works, Equipment and Construction:* Gen. Idriss Ngari. *Relations with Parliament and Government Spokesperson:* René Ndemezo Obiang. *State Control and Inspections:* Martin Mabala. *Tourism and Handicrafts:* Jean Massima. *Vocational Training and Social Rehabilitation:* Barnabé Ndaki. *Youth and Sports:* Alfred Mabicka.

DEFENCE

In 2003 military expenditure totalled US$15m. (US$12 per capita), representing 0·2% of GDP.

Army. The Army totalled (2002) 3,200. A referendum of 23 July 1995 favoured the transformation of the Presidential Guard into a republican guard. There is also a paramilitary Gendarmerie of 2,000. France maintains a 750-strong marine infantry battalion.

Navy. There is a small naval flotilla, 500 strong in 2002.

Air Force. Personnel (2002) 1,000. There are ten combat aircraft including nine Mirage 5s and five armed helicopters.

INTERNATIONAL RELATIONS

Gabon is a member of the UN, WTO, IMF, World Bank, African Development Bank, the African Union, Islamic Development Bank, Economic and Monetary Community of Central Africa (CEMAC), Economic Community of the Central African States (CEEAC), Islamic Conference, International Organization of the Francophonie, Movement of Non-Aligned Countries and is an ACP member state of the ACP-EU relationship.

ECONOMY

Agriculture accounted for 7·6% of GDP in 2002, industry 46·4% and services 46·0%.

Overview. Five-year development plans, of which there were five after 1966, have been replaced by three-year rolling investment plans.

Currency. The unit of currency is the *franc CFA* (XAF) with a parity of 655·957 francs CFA to one euro. Foreign exchange reserves were US$38m. in April 2002 and total money supply was 343,048m. francs CFA. Gold reserves were 13,000 troy oz in June 2002. Inflation was 0·2% in 2002.

Budget. In 2000 revenue totalled 1,207·6bn. francs CFA and expenditure 786bn. francs CFA. Oil revenues account for nearly two-thirds of all revenues.

Performance. Gabon experienced a recession in 1999 and 2000, with the economy shrinking by 10·6% and 1·9% respectively. A slight recovery followed in 2001, with growth of 2·0%. Total GDP in 2003 was US$5·6bn.

Banking and Finance. The *Banque des États de l'Afrique Centrale* (*Governor*, Jean-Félix Mamalepot) is the bank of issue. There are five commercial banks. The largest are Banque Internationale pour le Commerce et l'Industrie du Gabon, BGFIBANK and Union Gabonaise de Banque, which between them had 80% of the market share in 2003.

ENERGY AND NATURAL RESOURCES

Environment. Gabon's carbon dioxide emissions from the consumption and flaring of fossil fuels in 2002 were the equivalent of 3·7 tonnes per capita.

Electricity. Installed capacity was 0·4m. kW in 2000. The semi-public *Société d'énergie et d'eau du Gabon* produced 1·35bn. kWh in 2000 (approximately 52% hydro-electric and 48% thermal). Consumption per capita was 1,123 kWh in 2000.

Oil and Gas. Proven oil reserves (2002), 2·5bn. bbls. Production, 2003, 12·0m. tonnes. There were proven natural gas reserves of 99bn. cu. metres in 2002. Natural gas production (2000) was 1·1bn. cu. metres.

Minerals. There are an estimated 200m. tonnes of manganese ore and 850m. tonnes of iron ore deposits. Gold, zinc and phosphates also occur. Output, 2001: manganese ore, 1·57m. tonnes.

Agriculture. There were 325,000 ha of arable land in 2001 and 170,000 ha of permanent crops. 15,000 ha were irrigated in 2001. The major crops (estimated production, 2000, in 1,000 tonnes) are: plantains, 280; cassava, 225; sugarcane, 176; yams, 150; taro, 59; maize, 31; groundnuts, 17; bananas, 12. Other important products include palm oil, sweet potatoes and soybeans.

Livestock (2000): 36,000 cattle, 198,000 sheep, 91,000 goats, 213,000 pigs.

Forestry. Equatorial forests covered 21·83m. ha in 2000, or 84·7% of the total land area. Timber production in 2001 was 3·10m. cu. metres.

In 2002 President Bongo announced that a tenth of the country would be transformed into 13 national parks covering nearly 30,000 sq. km. Gabon is likely to need US$85m. over a seven-year period to build the national parks.

Fisheries. The catch in 2001 was 40,457 tonnes, of which 30,607 tonnes were from marine waters. Industrial fleets account for about 25% of the catch.

INDUSTRY

Most manufacturing is based on the processing of food (particularly sugar), timber and mineral resources, cement and chemical production and oil refining. Production figures (2000) in 1,000 tonnes: residual fuel oil, 283; cement (2001), 240; distillate fuel oil, 185; kerosene, 23; beer (2001), 86·7m. litres; soft drinks (2001), 57·8m. litres.

Labour. The workforce in 1996 numbered 519,000 (56% males). Around 60% of the economically active population are engaged in agriculture. In 1993 the legal minimum monthly wage was 1,200 francs CFA. There is a 40-hour working week.

INTERNATIONAL TRADE

Foreign debt was US$3,533m. in 2002. The government retains the right to participate in foreign investment in oil and mineral extraction.

Imports and Exports. In 2001 imports totalled 629bn. francs CFA and exports 1,942bn. francs CFA. Machinery and mechanical equipment accounted for 26·4% of imports in 1997, food and agricultural products 23·1%, consumer products 15·5% and transport equipment 11·5%. Crude petroleum and petroleum products constituted 77·1% of exports in 1997, and wood 14·5%. Main export markets, 1997: USA, 68·2%; France, 8·1%; Japan, 3·2%. Main import suppliers: France, 39·1%; Belgium, 9·7%; USA, 8·1%.

COMMUNICATIONS

Roads. In 2000 there were an estimated 8,464 km of roads (9·9% asphalted); and in 1996 some 24,750 passenger cars plus 16,490 trucks and vans. There were 293 deaths in road accidents in 2000.

Rail. The 657-km standard gauge Transgabonais railway runs from the port of Owendo to Franceville. Total length of railways, 2000, 649 km. In 2000, 237,000 passengers and 3·1m. tonnes of freight were transported.

Civil Aviation. There are international airports at Libreville (Léon M'Ba Airport), Port-Gentil and Franceville (Masuku); scheduled internal services link these to a number of domestic airfields. The national carrier is Air Gabon (80% state-owned). Libreville, the main airport, handled 754,000 passengers and 14,900 tonnes of freight in 2000. In 1999 scheduled airline traffic of Gabonese-based carriers flew 8·0m. km, carrying 423,000 passengers (226,000 on international flights).

Shipping. In 2002 the merchant marine totalled 13,000 GRT, including oil tankers 1,000 GRT. Owendo (near Libreville), Mayumba and Port-Gentil are the main ports. In 2000, 18m. tonnes of cargo were handled at the ports. Rivers are an important means of inland transport.

Telecommunications. In 2003 Gabon had 338,400 telephone subscribers (300,000 mobile and 38,400 landline) and 30,000 PCs were in use. There were 28·7 main telephone lines per 1,000 inhabitants and 224·4 mobile phone subscribers per 1,000 inhabitants. There were 500 fax machines in 1997. In 2002 there were 25,000 Internet users.

Postal Services. There were 54 post offices in 2000.

SOCIAL INSTITUTIONS

Justice. There are *tribunaux de grande instance* at Libreville, Port-Gentil, Lambaréné, Mouila, Oyem, Franceville (Masuku) and Koulamoutou, from which cases move progressively to a central Criminal Court, Court of Appeal and Supreme Court, all three located in Libreville. Civil police number about 900.

Religion. In 2001 there were 0·69m. Roman Catholics, 0·22m. Protestants and 0·17m. followers of African Christian sects. The majority of the remaining population follow animist beliefs. There are about 12,000 Muslims.

Education. The adult literacy rate in 2000 was 71·0%. Education is compulsory between 6–16 years. In 2000–01 there were 265,714 pupils and 5,399 teachers in primary schools, and 101,681 pupils with 2,727 (1996–97) teachers at secondary schools; in 1996–97 there were 6,703 students in 11 technical and professional schools and 76 students in 2 teacher-training establishments.

In 1996–97 there was one university at Libreville (the Omar Bongo University) and one university of science and technology at Franceville (Masuku), with a total of 6,800 students and 506 academic staff. In 2004 a university of health sciences (previously part of the Omar Bongo University) was created in Libreville.

In 2000–01 total expenditure on education came to 4·6% of GNP.

Health. In 1995 there were 292 doctors, 8 dentists and 23 pharmacists; and in 1989, 240 midwives and 759 nurses. In 1999 there were 25 hospitals, 63 medical centres and 413 dispensaries.

CULTURE

Broadcasting. Broadcasting is the responsibility of the state-controlled Radiodiffusion Télévision Gabonaise (RTG), which transmits two national radio programmes and provincial services. RTG has two TV channels (one national). In 2000 there were eight private radio stations and two private TV channels. In 2000 there were 630,000 radio sets and in 2001 there were 400,000 TV sets (colour by SECAM).

Press. In 2000 there was one government-controlled daily newspaper (*L'Union*).

Tourism. There were 155,000 foreign tourists in 2000, spending US$7m.

DIPLOMATIC REPRESENTATIVES

Of Gabon in the United Kingdom (27 Elvaston Place, London, SW7 5NL)
Ambassador: Alain Mansah-Zoguelet.

Of the United Kingdom in Gabon
Ambassador: Richard Wildash, LVO (resides at Yaoundé, Cameroon).

Of Gabon in the USA (2034 20th St., NW, Suite 200, Washington, D.C., 20009)
Ambassador: Jules M. Ogouebandja.

Of the USA in Gabon (Blvd de la Mer, Libreville)
Ambassador: Barrie R. Walkley.

Of Gabon to the United Nations
Ambassador: Denis Dangue Réwaka.

Of Gabon to the European Union
Ambassador: René Makongo.

FURTHER READING

Barnes, J. F. G., *Gabon: Beyond the Colonial Legacy*. Boulder (Colo.), 1992
Gardinier, David E. (ed.) *Historical Dictionary of Gabon*. 2nd ed. Metuchen (NJ), 1994.—*Gabon*. [Bibliography] ABC-Clio, Oxford and Santa Barbara (CA), 1992
Saint Paul, M. A., *Gabon: the Development of a Nation*. London, 1989

National statistical office: Direction Générale de la Statistique et des Études Économiques, Ministère de la Planification et de la Programmation du Développement, Libreville.

THE GAMBIA

Republic of The Gambia

Capital: Banjul
Population projection, 2010: 1·68m.
GDP per capita, 2002: (PPP$) 1,690
HDI/world rank: 0·452/155

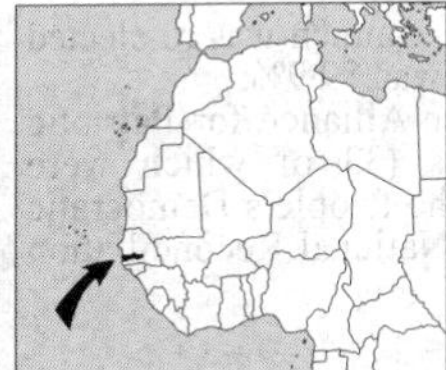

KEY HISTORICAL EVENTS

The Gambia was discovered by the early Portuguese navigators, but they did not settle. During the 17th century companies of merchants obtained trading charters and established a settlement on the river, which, from 1807, was controlled from Sierra Leone. The Gambia became an independent member of the Commonwealth on 18 Feb. 1965 and a republic within the Commonwealth on 24 April 1970.

TERRITORY AND POPULATION

The Gambia takes its name from the River Gambia, and consists of a strip of territory never wider than 10 km on both banks. It is bounded in the west by the Atlantic Ocean and on all other sides by Senegal. The area is 10,689 sq. km, including 2,077 sq. km of inland water. Population (census provisional, 2003), 1,364,507; density, 128 per sq. km. In 2001, 68·8% of the population were rural.

The UN gives a projected population for 2010 of 1·68m.

The largest ethnic group is the Mandingo, followed by the Wolofs, Fulas, Jolas and Sarahuley. The country is administratively divided into the capital, Banjul (2003 census provisional, 357,238) plus five other administrative divisions.

The five rural divisions, with their areas, populations and chief towns are (listed west to east, or upriver):

Division	*Area in sq. km*	*Population 2003 census*	*Chief town*
Western	1,764	392,987	Brikama
North Bank	2,256	172,806	Kerewan/Farafenni
Lower River	1,618	72,546	Mansa Konko
Central River	2,894	185,897	Jangjangbureh
Upper River	2,069	183,033	Basse

The official language is English.

SOCIAL STATISTICS

1995 births, 46,000; deaths, 20,000. 1995 birth rate per 1,000 population, 41·6; death rate, 18·3. Annual population growth rate, 1992–2002, 3·3%. Expectation of life, 2001, was 52·2 years for males and 55·2 for females. Fertility rate, 2001, 4·9 births per woman; infant mortality, 2001, 91 per 1,000 live births. The Gambia has made some of the best progress in recent years in reducing child mortality. The number of deaths per 1,000 live births among children under five was reduced from around 130 in 1990 to approximately 80 in 1999.

CLIMATE

The climate is characterized by two very different seasons. The dry season lasts from Nov. to May, when precipitation is very light and humidity moderate. Days are warm but nights quite cool. The SW monsoon is likely to set in with spectacular storms and produces considerable rainfall from July to Oct., with increased humidity. Banjul, Jan. 73°F (22·8°C), July 80°F (26·7°C). Annual rainfall 52" (1,295 mm).

CONSTITUTION AND GOVERNMENT

The 1970 constitution provided for an executive *President* elected directly for renewable five-year terms. The President appoints a *Vice-President* who is the government's chief minister. The single-chamber *National Assembly* has 53 members (48 elected by universal adult suffrage for a five-year term and 5 appointed by the President).

A referendum of 8 Aug. 1996 approved a new constitution by 70·4% of votes cast. Under this, the ban on political parties imposed in July 1994 was lifted.

Members of the ruling Military Council resigned from their military positions before joining the Alliance for Patriotic Reorientation and Construction (APRC).

National Anthem. 'For The Gambia, our homeland'; words by V. J. Howe, tune traditional.

RECENT ELECTIONS

Presidential elections were held on 18 Oct. 2001. President Jammeh was re-elected against four opponents with 53·0% of votes cast. Turn-out was 89·9%.

Parliamentary elections were held on 17 Jan. 2002. The Alliance for Patriotic Reorientation and Construction (APRC) won 45 seats (33 of which were unopposed because of boycotting by opposition parties), the People's Democratic Organization for Independence and Socialism 2, and the National Reconciliation Party 1.

CURRENT ADMINISTRATION

President: Rtd Col. Yahya Jammeh; b. 1965 (APRC; seized power 22 July 1994; elected 26 Sept. 1996 and re-elected in 2001).

In March 2005 the government comprised:

Vice-President and Secretary of State for Women's Affairs: Isatou Njie Saidy.

Secretary of State for Agriculture: Vacant. *Works, Construction and Infrastructure:* Bala Garba-Jahumpa. *Local Government and Lands:* Ismaila Sambou. *Finance and Economic Affairs:* Margaret Keita. *Foreign Affairs:* Mousa Gibril Bala-Gaye. *Interior and Religious Affairs:* Samba Bah. *Trade, Industry and Employment:* Sidi Moro Sanneh. *Forestry and Environment:* Edward Singhatey. *Education:* Fatou Faye. *Fisheries and Water Resources:* Bai Mass Taal. *Health and Social Affairs:* Tamsir Mbowe. *Justice and Attorney General:* Raymond Sock. *Tourism and Culture:* Susan Waffa-Ogoo. *Youth and Sports:* Samba Faal. *Communications, Information and Technology:* Amadou Scattred Janneh.

Office of the President: http://www.statehouse.gm/

DEFENCE

The Gambian National Army, 800 strong, has two infantry battalions and one engineer squadron.

The marine unit of the Army consisted in 2002 of 70 personnel operating three inshore patrol craft, based at Banjul.

Defence expenditure totalled US$2m. in 2003 (US$1 per capita), representing 0·6% of GDP.

INTERNATIONAL RELATIONS

The Gambia is a member of the UN, WTO, the Commonwealth, the African Union, African Development Bank, ECOWAS, IOM, OIC, Islamic Development Bank and is an ACP member state of the ACP-EU relationship.

ECONOMY

Agriculture accounted for 25·8% of GDP in 2002, industry 14·2% and services 60·0%.

Currency. The unit of currency is the *dalasi* (GMD), of 100 *butut.* Inflation was 8·6% in 2002. Foreign exchange reserves were US$94m. in May 2002. Total money supply in May 2002 was 1,343m. dalasis.

Budget. In 1999 revenues were 944·5m. dalasis and expenditures 1,118·2m. dalasis.

Performance. Real GDP growth was 5·8% in 2001 but there then followed a recession, with the economy shrinking by 3·1% in 2002. Total GDP was US$0·4bn. in 2003.

Banking and Finance. The Central Bank of The Gambia (founded 1971; *Governor*, Momodou Clerke Bajo) is the bank of issue. There are six other banks: Standard Chartered, Trust Bank, Arab Gambian Islamic Bank, Continent Bank, First International and the International Bank for Commerce and Industry.

ENERGY AND NATURAL RESOURCES

Environment. Carbon dioxide emissions from the consumption and flaring of fossil fuels in 2002 were the equivalent of 0·2 tonnes per capita.

Electricity. Installed capacity was 29,000 kW in 2000. Production was 132m. kWh in 2000; consumption per capita in 2000 was 95 kWh.

Oil and Gas. President Jammeh announced in Feb. 2004 that large quantities of oil had been discovered in waters off the Gambia's coast.

Minerals. Heavy minerals, including ilmenite, zircon and rutile, have been discovered in Sanyang, Batokunku and Kartong areas.

Agriculture. About 68% of the population depend upon agriculture. There were 0·25m. ha of arable land in 2001 and 5,000 ha of permanent crops. Almost all commercial activity centres upon the marketing of groundnuts, which is the only export crop of financial significance; in 2000 an estimated 126,000 tonnes were produced. Cotton is also exported on a limited scale. Rice is of increasing importance for local consumption. Major products (2000 estimates, in 1,000 tonnes), are: groundnuts, 126; millet, 76; rice, 29; maize, 21; sorghum, 18; cassava, 6; palm oil, 3; palm kernels, 2.

Livestock (2000): 370,000 cattle, 270,000 goats, 195,000 sheep and 1m. poultry.

Forestry. In 2000 forests covered 481,000 ha, or 48·1% of the land area. Timber production in 2001 was 724,000 cu. metres.

Fisheries. The total catch in 2001 was estimated at 34,527 tonnes, of which 32,027 tonnes were from marine waters.

INDUSTRY

Labour. The labour force in 1996 totalled 579,000 (55% males). Around 78% of the economically active population are engaged in agriculture.

INTERNATIONAL TRADE

Foreign debt was US$573m. in 2002.

Imports and Exports. Imports and exports in US$1m.:

	1995	*1996*	*1997*	*1998*	*1999*
Imports c.i.f.	214·6	219·2	256·0	257·2	193·7
Exports f.o.b.	18·7	12·8	8·6	25·6	8·2

In 1998, US$13·2m. of groundnuts were exported, US$2·5m. of fish and seafood and US$2·5m. of vegetables and fruit. Chief imports in 1998 were: machinery and transport equipment, US$52·9m.; rice, US$40·7m.; and manufactured goods, US$37·1m.

Main import suppliers in 1999 were (in US$1m.): Germany, 26·8; UK, 20·6; France, 13·0; China, 12·4. Leading export destinations in 1999 were (in US$1m.): Belgium, 2·1; UK, 1·4; Germany, 0·9; Spain, 0·7.

COMMUNICATIONS

Roads. There were some 2,700 km of roads in 1999, of which 956 km were paved. Number of vehicles (1996): 8,640 passenger cars; 9,000 trucks and vans.

Civil Aviation. There is an international airport at Banjul (Yundum). The national carrier is Gambia International Airlines. Banjul handled 301,756 passengers in 2000 (all on international flights) and 2,236 tonnes of freight.

Shipping. The chief port is Banjul. Ocean-going vessels can travel up the Gambia River as far as Kuntaur. The merchant marine totalled 2,000 GRT in 2002.

Telecommunications. The Gambia had 138,300 telephone subscribers in 2002, or 100·8 per 1,000 population, and there were 19,000 PCs in use (13·8 per 1,000 persons). Mobile phone subscribers numbered 100,000 in 2002 and there were 1,100 fax machines in 1997. In 2002 there were 25,000 Internet users.

Postal Services. There are several post offices and agencies; postal facilities are also afforded to all towns.

SOCIAL INSTITUTIONS

Justice. Justice is administered by a Supreme Court consisting of a chief justice and puisne judges. The High Court has unlimited original jurisdiction in civil and criminal matters. The Supreme Court is the highest court of appeal and succeeds the judicial committee of the Privy Council in London. There are Magistrates Courts in each of the divisions plus one in Banjul and two in nearby Kombo St Mary's Division—eight in all. There are resident magistrates in provincial areas. There are also Muslim courts, district tribunals dealing with cases concerned with customary law, and two juvenile courts.

The death penalty was abolished in 1993 but restored by decree in 1995.

Religion. More than 90% of the population is Muslim. Banjul is the seat of an Anglican and a Roman Catholic bishop. There is a Methodist mission. A few sections of the population retain their original animist beliefs.

Education. The adult literacy rate in 2001 was 37·8% (45·0% among males and 30·9% among females). In 2000–01 there were 156,839 pupils with 4,186 teachers at primary schools and 56,179 pupils with 2,207 teachers at secondary schools. In 1993–94 there were 1,591 students at 155 institutions of higher education, which comprise The Gambia College, a technical training institute, a management development institute, a multi-media training institute, a hotel training school, and centres for self-development and skills training, and continuing education.

In 2000–01 total expenditure on education came to 2·7% of GNP and 14·2% of total government spending.

Health. In 1994 there were 2 hospitals, 1 clinic, 10 health centres and some 60 dispensaries. There were 43 physicians, 155 nurses, 6 pharmacists and 102 midwives in 1997.

CULTURE

World Heritage Sites. The Gambia has one site on the UNESCO World Heritage List: James Island and Related Sites (inscribed on the list in 2003), containing important evidence of early Afro-European encounters and the slave trade.

Broadcasting. Gambia Radio and Television Services (GRTS) broadcasts radio and television programmes in English and some other local languages. There are four private commercial radio stations and three community radio stations. TV operations started in 1995 and programmes are transmitted countrywide and beyond (colour by PAL). In 2000 there were 520,000 radio receivers and in 2001 there were 20,000 television receivers.

Press. There is a government-owned daily; an independent newspaper appears five times a week, there are two weeklies, several news-sheets and a monthly.

Tourism. Tourism is The Gambia's biggest foreign exchange earner. In 1999 there were 96,000 foreign tourists; spending by tourists in 1998 totalled US$49m.

DIPLOMATIC REPRESENTATIVES

Of The Gambia in the United Kingdom (57 Kensington Ct., London, W8 5DG)
High Commissioner: Gibril Seman Joof.

Of the United Kingdom in The Gambia (48 Atlantic Rd, Fajara, Banjul)
High Commissioner: Eric Jenkinson.

Of The Gambia in USA (1155 15th St, Suite 1000, NW, Washington, D.C., 20005)
Ambassador: Dodou Bammy Jagne.

Of the USA in The Gambia (Fajara (East), Kairaba Ave., Banjul)
Ambassador: Joseph D. Stafford, III.

Of The Gambia to the United Nations
Ambassador: Crispin Grey-Johnson.

Of The Gambia to the European Union
Ambassador: Yusupha Alieu Kah.

FURTHER READING

Hughes, A. and Perfect, D., *Political History of The Gambia, 1816–1992.* Farnborough, 1993

GEORGIA

Sakartvelos Respublika
(Republic of Georgia)

Capital: Tbilisi
Population projection, 2010: 4·84m.
GDP per capita, 2002: (PPP$) 2,260
HDI/world rank: 0·739/97

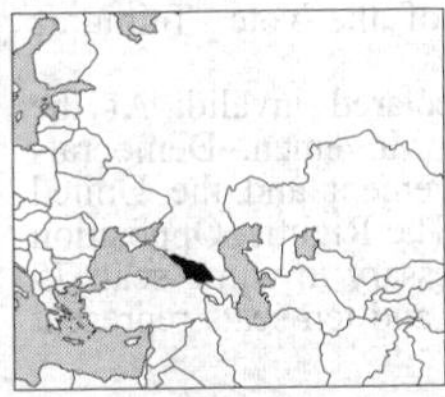

KEY HISTORICAL EVENTS

The independent Georgian Social Democratic Republic was declared on 26 May 1918 and was recognized by the Russian Soviet Federal Socialist Republic on 7 May 1920. In 1936 the Georgian Soviet Socialist Republic became one of the constituent republics of the USSR. Following nationalist successes at elections in Oct. 1990, the Supreme Soviet resolved on a transition to full independence and on 9 April 1991 unanimously declared the republic an independent state. President Zviad Gamsakhurdia was deposed by armed insurrection on 6 Jan. 1992 and a military council took control. After elections in which he gained 95% of votes cast, Eduard Shevardnadze became *de facto* head of state in Oct. 1992. On 22 Oct. 1993 Georgia joined the CIS. Supporters of the deposed president Gamsakhurdia were in intermittent conflict with the government, mainly in Mingrelia, but suffered heavy defeats once Russian support became available via the CIS. Ethnic conflict has been rife in the two autonomous republics of South Ossetia and Abhkazia. Civil war broke out with South Ossetia in 1990 and Abhkazia in 1992 and 1998. Georgia has since moved closer to the West but economic reforms have been slow in coming and industry and agriculture are both in need of investment. In Nov. 2003 Eduard Shevardnadze resigned after opposition forces stormed parliament in protest against alleged fixing of elections three weeks earlier.

TERRITORY AND POPULATION

Georgia is bounded in the west by the Black Sea and south by Turkey, Armenia and Azerbaijan. Area, 69,700 sq. km (26,900 sq. miles). Its census population in 2002 was 4,371,535 (excluding Abkhazia and South Ossetia); density (excluding Abkhazia and South Ossetia), 76 per sq. km.

The UN gives a projected population for 2010 of 4·84m. (including Abkhazia).

In 2001, 56·5% of the population lived in urban areas. The capital is Tbilisi (2002 population estimate, 1·08m.). Other important towns are Kutaisi (186,000; 2002), Batumi (122,000; 2002), Sukhumi (121,000; 1991), Rustavi (116,500; 2002), Gori (49,500; 2002) and Poti (47,000; 2002).

Georgians accounted for 83·8% of the 2002 census population; others included 6·5% Azerbaijanis, 5·7% Armenians and 1·5% Russians. Georgia includes the Autonomous Republics of Abkhazia and Adjaria and the former Autonomous Region of South Ossetia.

Georgian is the official language. Armenian, Russian and Azeri are also spoken.

SOCIAL STATISTICS

2001 estimates: births, 40,400; deaths, 39,300. Rates, 2001 estimates: birth, 7·8 per 1,000 population; death, 7·5 per 1,000. Annual population growth rate, 1992–2002, –0·5%. Life expectancy, 2001, 69·2 years for males and 77·4 years for females. Infant mortality, 2001, 24 per 1,000 live births; fertility rate, 2001, 1·4 births per woman.

CLIMATE

The Georgian climate is extremely varied. The relatively small territory covers different climatic zones, ranging from humid sub-tropical zones to permanent snow and glaciers. In Tbilisi summer is hot: 25–35°C. Nov. sees the beginning of the Georgian winter and the temperature in Tbilisi can drop to –8°C; however, average temperature ranges from 2–6°C.

CONSTITUTION AND GOVERNMENT

A new Constitution of 24 Aug. 1995 defines Georgia as a presidential republic with federal elements. The head of state is the *President*, elected by universal suffrage for not more than two five-year terms. The 235-member *Supreme Council* is elected by a system combining 85 single-member districts with proportional representation based on party lists. There is a 5% threshold.

National Anthem. 'Dideba zetsit kurtheuls' ('Praise be to the Heavenly Bestower of Blessings'); words anonymous, tune by K. Potskhverashvili.

RECENT ELECTIONS

At the presidential election held on 4 Jan. 2004 Mikhail Saakashvili of the United National Movement was elected president with 96·3% of the vote. Teimuraz Shashiashvili took 1·9%. Turn-out was 88·0%.

The parliamentary elections of 2 Nov. 2003 were declared invalid. At the parliamentary elections of 28 March 2004 the National Movement–Democrats (formed through the merger of the United National Movement and the United Democrats) won 67·0% of the vote (135 of the 235 seats). The Rightist Opposition won 7·6% (15 seats). No other party achieved the 7% necessary to win a seat. 75 seats were taken in single-seat constituencies in Nov. 2003 and ten seats represent Abkhazians.

CURRENT ADMINISTRATION

President: Mikhail Saakashvili; b. 1967 (National Movement–Democrats; sworn in on 25 Jan. 2004).

In March 2005 the government comprised:

Prime Minister: Zurab Noghaideli; b. 1964 (National Movement–Democrats; sworn in on 17 Feb. 2005).

Deputy Prime Minister and Minister of Justice: Konstantin Kemularia.

Minister of Agriculture and Food: Mikhail Svimonishvili. *Culture and Sports:* Giorgi Gabashvili. *Defence:* Irakli Okruashvili. *Education:* Kakha Lomaia. *Environment:* Giorgi Papuashvili. *Finance and Revenue:* Valery Chechelashvili. *Foreign Affairs:* Salome Zurabishvili. *Energy:* Nika Gilauri. *Health and Social Welfare:* Lado Chipashvili. *Interior:* Vano Merabishvili. *Refugees:* Eter Astemirova. *Economic Development:* Alex Alexishvili.

The *Speaker* is Nino Burjanadze.

Georgian Parliament: http://www.parliament.ge

DEFENCE

The total strength of the Armed Forces consists of 17,500 personnel. In 2002 some 4,000 Russian troops and 12,130 peacekeeping forces were stationed in Georgia. The UN has some 107 observers from 23 countries.

Defence expenditure in 2003 totalled US$350m. (US$68 per capita), representing 2·7% of GDP.

Army. The Army totals 8,620. In addition there are 250,000 reservists and a paramilitary border guard estimated at 5,400.

Navy. Former Soviet facilities at Poti have been taken over. The headquarters are at Tbilisi. Personnel, 2002, 1,830.

Air Force. Personnel, 2002, 1,250. Equipment includes Su-17 and Su-25 fighter-bombers.

INTERNATIONAL RELATIONS

Georgia is a member of the UN, WTO, CIS, NATO Partnership for Peace, Council of Europe, OSCE, WTO, BSEC and IOM.

ECONOMY

Agriculture accounted for 20·6% of GDP in 2002, industry 24·3% and services 55·0%.

Overview. Georgia is a small lower-income transition economy. After independence in 1991, civil war and the loss of markets in the former Soviet Union led to economic collapse. Georgia suffered the worst declines experienced by any of the transition economies, with exports declining by 90% and output falling by 70%. Georgia's economy suffered political tensions, declining standards of living and low tax revenues that undermined the funding of basic state functions. The 1996–99 programme of reforms, supported by the IMF, focused on building national institutions, privatization, energy sector rehabilitation, land reform and fiscal consolidation. Georgia made progress towards macroeconomic stabilization in the late 1990s although this progress was thwarted by internal fragmentation, drought and the 1998 financial crisis in Russia. The second round of IMF supported programmes, from 2001–04, brought the recovery of growth and of price stability. The IMF notes that several areas of weakness still remain, notably a lack of fiscal consolidation, strong interest groups and corruption hampering reforms, the under-development of financial markets and the slow progress of privatization.

Currency. The unit of currency is the *lari* (GEL) of 100 *tetri*, which replaced coupons at 1 lari = 1m. coupons on 25 Sept. 1995. Inflation was 5·6% in 2002, having been 163% in 1995 and 15,606% in 1994. Gold reserves are negligible. Total money supply was 394m. laris in June 2002.

Budget. Revenues in 2002 totalled 928·6m. laris and expenditures 920·5m. laris. Tax revenue accounted for 83·1% of total revenues; current expenditure accounted for 99·7% of total expenditures.

Performance. Real GDP growth was 4·7% in 2001, 5·5% in 2002 and 11·1% in 2003. In both 1996 and 1997 growth had exceeded 10%, but prior to that the economy had suffered a sharp downturn, contracting by 45% in 1992, 29% in 1993 and 10% in 1994. Of all the former Soviet republics Georgia's economy, along with that of Moldova, has suffered the most since 1989 when political and economic reforms took place across central and eastern Europe. In 2002 the level of GDP was estimated to be only 38% of that in 1989. Total GDP was US$3·9bn. in 2003.

Between 1990 and 1996 the average annual real growth in GNP per capita was –19·3% (the lowest of any country in the world).

Banking and Finance. The *Governor* of the Central Bank is Irakli Managadze. In 1996 there were 65 commercial banks. One foreign bank had a representative office.

ENERGY AND NATURAL RESOURCES

Environment. Carbon dioxide emissions from the consumption and flaring of fossil fuels in Georgia were the equivalent of 1·7 tonnes per capita in 2002.

Electricity. The many fast-flowing rivers provide an important hydro-electric resource. Installed capacity was 4·6m. kW in 2000. Production in 2000 was 7·40bn. kWh; consumption per capita in 2000 was 1,452 kWh.

Oil and Gas. Output (2000) of crude petroleum, 110,000 tonnes. A 920 km long oil pipeline is under construction from an offshore Azerbaijani oil field in the Caspian Sea across Azerbaijan and Georgia to a new oil terminal at Supsa, near Poti, on the Black Sea Coast. The US$600m. pipeline started pumping oil in early 1999 and will have an ultimate capacity of some 15m. tonnes of oil a year. The pipeline allowed Georgia to create 25,000 new jobs. However, Georgia is still heavily dependent on Russia for natural gas. Accords for the construction of a second oil pipeline through Georgia and a gas pipeline were signed in Nov. 1999, to take oil from Azerbaijan to Turkey via Georgia and gas from Turkmenistan to Turkey via Azerbaijan and Georgia. Work on the oil pipeline, which is expected to become operational before the end of 2005, began in Sept. 2002. Natural gas production was 61m. cu. metres in 2000.

Minerals. Manganese deposits are calculated at 250m. tonnes. Other important minerals are coal, barytes, clays, gold, diatomite shale, agate, marble, alabaster, iron and other ores, building stone, arsenic, molybdenum, tungsten and mercury. Output of coal in 2000 was estimated to be 7,000 tonnes.

Agriculture. Agriculture plays an important part in Georgia's economy, contributing 20·6% of GDP in 2002. In 2001 there were 795,000 ha of arable land and 268,000 ha permanent crops. 469,000 ha were irrigated in 2001.

Output of main agricultural products (in 1,000 tonnes) in 2000: potatoes, 480; tomatoes, 325; maize, 225; grapes, 200; cabbages, 125; wine, 116; apples, 115; wheat, 84; watermelons (including melons, pumpkins and squash), 70.

Livestock, 2000: cattle, 1,122,000; sheep, 560,000; pigs, 411,000; chickens, 8m. Livestock products, 2000 (in 1,000 tonnes): meat, 105; milk, 721; eggs, 24.

Forestry. There were 2·99m. ha of forest in 2000, or 43·7% of the total land area.

Fisheries. The catch in 2001 was 1,830 tonnes, down from 147,688 tonnes in 1989.

INDUSTRY

Industry accounted for 24·3% of GDP in 2002. There is a metallurgical plant and a motor works. There are factories for processing tea, creameries and breweries. There are also textile and silk industries.

Production (in 1,000 tonnes): cement (2001), 335; nitrogenous fertilizer (2000), 99; flour (2002), 78; steel (2000), 49; footwear (2001), 45,000 pairs; beer (2002), 27·0m. litres; spirits (2002), 2·1m. litres; cigarettes (2001), 1,615m. units.

Labour. The economically active workforce numbered 1,877,600 in 2001 (966,600 males), including: 989,600 in agriculture, hunting and forestry; 181,500 in wholesale and retail trade/repair of motor vehicles, motorcycles and personal and household goods; 138,700 in education; 105,600 in public administration and defence/compulsory social security; and 102,400 in manufacturing. The unemployment rate was 11·0% in 2001. Approximately 500,000 Georgians, or a tenth of the population, work in Russia, but in Dec. 2000 Russia began requiring Georgians to have a visa to visit the country.

INTERNATIONAL TRADE

Total foreign debt was US$1,838m. in 2002. The debt was mainly as a result of the importing of natural gas from Turkmenistan.

Imports and Exports. In 2002 Georgian exports (f.o.b.) amounted to US$583·4m. and imports (f.o.b.) US$1,041·6m. Major commodities imported are fuel, grain and other foods, machinery and parts, and transport equipment. Major commodities for export are iron and steel products, food and beverages, machinery, textiles and chemicals. Main export markets, 2000: Turkey, 22·7%; Russia, 21·1%; Germany, 10·4%; Azerbaijan, 6·4%. Main import suppliers, 2000: Turkey, 16·0%; Russia, 14·1%; USA, 10·1%; Azerbaijan, 8·5%.

COMMUNICATIONS

Roads. There were 20,229 km of roads in 2002 (93·5% hard-surfaced). Passenger cars in use in 2002 numbered 251,961 (56·3 per 1,000 inhabitants), and there were also 45,470 trucks and vans and 24,134 buses and coaches. In 2002 there were 515 road deaths.

Rail. Total length is 1,562 km of 1,520 mm gauge (1,544 km electrified). In 2000 railways carried 2·3m. tonnes of freight and 11·5m. passengers. There is a metro system in Tbilisi.

Civil Aviation. The main airport is at Tbilisi (Novo-Alexeyevka). The main Georgian carrier is Airzena Georgian Airlines. In 2003 it had flights to Amsterdam, Frankfurt, Kyiv, Paris, Prague, Tel Aviv and Vienna. In 2000 Tbilisi airport handled 271,820 passengers (270,011 on international flights) and 7,529 tonnes of freight.

Shipping. In 2002 sea-going shipping totalled 569,000 GRT, of which oil tankers accounted for 41,000 GRT.

Telecommunications. There were 1,152,100 telephone subscribers in 2002, or 233·5 per 1,000 persons, and PCs numbered 156,000. Mobile phone subscribers numbered 503,600 in 2002 and there were 500 fax machines in 1995. In 2002 there were 73,500 Internet users.

Postal Services. There were 1,190 post offices in 1997.

SOCIAL INSTITUTIONS

Justice. The population in penal institutions in Sept. 2002 was 7,343 (198 per 100,000 of national population). The death penalty was abolished in 1997.

Religion. The Georgian Orthodox Church has its own organization under Catholicos (patriarch) Ilya II who is resident in Tbilisi. In 2001 there were 1·8m. Georgian

Orthodox, 550,000 Sunni Muslims, 280,000 Armenian Apostolic (Orthodox) and 130,000 Russian Orthodox.

Education. In 2000–01 there were 1,195 pre-primary schools with 6,958 teachers for 72,790 pupils; and 3,409 primary schools with 17,732 teachers for 276,389 pupils. In 1999–2000 there were 467,249 pupils at secondary level with 62,517 teachers; and 140,627 students at institutions of higher education. There is one university and one technical university, with (1996) a total of 34,590 students and 6,464 academic staff. Adult literacy rate in 2001 was over 99%.

Health. Georgia had 57,100 hospital beds in 1994. In 1998 there were 22,236 physicians, 1,800 dentists, 24,174 nurses, 469 pharmacists and 1,586 midwives.

Welfare. In 1994 there were 804,000 age and 355,000 other pensioners.

CULTURE

World Heritage Sites. Georgia has three sites on the UNESCO World Heritage List: City-Museum Reserve of Mtskheta (inscribed on the list in 1994), churches of the former Georgian capital; Bagrati Cathedral and Gelati Monastery (1994); and Upper Svaneti (1996), a mountainous area of medieval villages.

Broadcasting. The government-controlled Georgian Radio broadcasts two national and three regional programmes, and a foreign service, Radio Georgia (English, Russian). There are local independent TV stations in ten towns. The main independent TV station is *Rustavi-2*. Colour is by SECAM V. In 2000 there were 2·79m. radio receivers and in 2001 there were 1·76m. TV receivers.

Press. In 2000 there were 35 dailies with a combined daily circulation of 25,705.

Tourism. Investment in tourism has increased substantially in recent years, and large numbers of hotels have been built. In 2000 there were 387,000 foreign tourists bringing in receipts of US$413m.

DIPLOMATIC REPRESENTATIVES

Of Georgia in the United Kingdom (4 Russell Gardens, London, W14 8EZ)
Ambassador: Amiran Kavadze.

Of the United Kingdom in Georgia (Sheraton Metechi Palace Hotel, 380003 Tbilisi)
Ambassador: Donald MacLaren of MacLaren.

Of Georgia in the USA (1615 New Hampshire Ave., NW, Suite 300, Washington, D.C., 20009)
Ambassador: Levan Mikeladze.

Of the USA in Georgia (25 Antoneli Street, 380026 Tbilisi)
Ambassador: Richard M. Miles.

Of Georgia to the United Nations
Ambassador: Revaz Adamia.

Of Georgia to the European Union
Ambassador: Konstantin Zaldastanishvili.

FURTHER READING

Brook, S., *Claws of the Crab: Georgia and Armenia in Crisis.* London, 1992
Gachechiladze, R., *The New Georgia: Space, Society, Politics*. London, 1995
Nasmyth, P., *Georgia: a Rebel in the Caucasus.* London, 1992
Suny, R. G., *The Making of the Georgian Nation.* 2nd ed. Indiana Univ. Press, 1994

State Department for Statistics Website: http://www.statistics.ge

ABKHAZIA

Area, 8,600 sq. km (3,320 sq. miles); population (Jan. 1990), 537,500. Capital Sukhumi (1990 population, 121,700). This area, the ancient Colchis, saw the establishment of a West Georgian kingdom in the 4th century and a Russian protectorate in 1810. In March 1921 a congress of local Soviets proclaimed it a Soviet Republic, and its status as an Autonomous Republic, within Georgia, was confirmed on 17 April 1930 and again by the Georgian Constitution of 1995.

Ethnic groups (1989 census) Georgians, 45·7%; Abkhazians, 17·8%; Armenians, 14·6%; and Russians, 14·3%.

In July 1992 the Abkhazian parliament declared sovereignty under the presidency of Vladislav Ardzinba and the restoration of its 1925 constitution. Fighting broke out as Georgian forces moved into Abkhazia. On 3 Sept. and on 19 Nov. ceasefires were agreed, but fighting continued into 1993 and by Sept. Georgian forces were driven out. On 15 May 1994 Georgian and Abkhazian delegates under Russian auspices signed an agreement on a ceasefire and deployment of 2,500 Russian troops as a peacekeeping force. On 26 Nov. 1994 parliament adopted a new Constitution proclaiming Abkhazian sovereignty. CIS economic sanctions were imposed in Jan. 1996. Parliamentary elections were held on 23 Nov. 1996. Neither the constitution nor the elections were recognized by the Georgian government or the international community. Fighting flared up between rival militia forces again in May 1998 after Abkhazian forces ejected thousands of ethnic Mingrelian and Georgian refugees who had returned to the southern Abkhazian region of Gali. After the fighting in 1998, the worst in five years, both sides declared a ceasefire. Up to 20,000 Georgians lost their homes. Abkhazia has expressed a desire to join the Russian Federation, but Russia is wary of the request.

Abkhazia, and notably Sukhumi, the capital, have seen living standards plunge dramatically. There are no Internet links, no mobile phones and no hotels. There is very little work and practically no money.

President: Sergei Bagapsh (elected on 3 Oct. 2004). Georgian officials declared the election illegal. The Supreme Court eventually decided to hold new elections within two months, although parliament voted on 26 Nov. 2004 to recognize Sergei Bagapsh as the winner of the election. In the new elections held on 12 Jan. 2005 Sergei Bagapsh was elected with 90·1% of the votes, against 4·5% for Yakub Lakoba.

Prime Minister: Akeksandr Ankvab (appointed on 14 Feb. 2005).

The republic has coal, electric power, building materials and light industries. Main crops are tobacco, tea, grapes, oranges, tangerines and lemons. Crop area: 43,900 ha.

Livestock, 1 Jan. 1987: 147,300 cattle, 127,900 pigs, 28,800 sheep and goats.

In 1990–91 there were 16,700 children attending pre-school institutions. There is a university at Sukhumi with 3,000 students and 270 academic staff in 1995–96. In 1990 there were 2,100 students at colleges and 7,700 students at other institutions of higher education.

In Jan. 1990 there were 2,500 doctors and 6,600 junior medical personnel.

ADJARIA

Area, 2,900 sq. km (1,160 sq. miles); provisional census population (2002): 376,016. Capital, Batumi (2002 provisional census population, 121,806, mostly Sunni Muslim). Adjaria fell under Turkish rule in the 17th century, and was annexed to Russia (rejoining Georgia) after the Berlin Treaty of 1878. On 16 July 1921 the territory was constituted as an Autonomous Republic within the Georgian SSR, a status confirmed by the Georgian Constitution of 1995. In Jan. 2004 Adjarian leader Aslan Abashidze refused to acknowledge the central government of Mikhail Saakashvili and declared a state of emergency. Fearing a Georgian invasion, Abashidze destroyed road and rail links to the rest of Georgia but was forced to step down on 6 May after popular demonstrations in Batumi. Saakashvili imposed direct rule over Adjaria. Elections were held on 20 June 2004. Saakashvili's Victorious Adjaria group took 72·1% of the vote and 28 of the 30 seats in the *Supreme Council*, Adjaria's parliament. Two seats went to the Republican Party (13·5% of the vote).

Ethnic groups (1989 census): Georgians, 82·8%; Russians, 7·7%; Armenians 4%.

Chairman of the Supreme Council: Mikheil Makharadze.

Prime Minister: Levan Varshalomidze.

Elections were held in Sept. 1996. A coalition of the Citizens' Union of Georgia and the All-Georgian Union of Revival gained a majority of seats.

Adjaria specializes in sub-tropical agricultural products. These include tea, citruses, bamboo, eucalyptus, tobacco, etc. Livestock (Jan. 1990): 112,300 cattle, 6,200 pigs, 7,000 sheep and goats.

There is a port and a shipyard at Batumi, oil-refining, food-processing and canning factories, clothing, building materials, pharmaceutical factories, etc.

In 1990–91, 77,239 pupils were engaged in study at all levels.

In Jan. 1990 there were 1,700 doctors and 4,400 junior medical personnel.

SOUTH OSSETIA

Area, 3,900 sq. km (1,505 sq. miles); population (Jan. 1990), 99,800 (ethnic groups at the 1989 census; Ossetians 66% and Georgians 29%). Capital, Tskhinvali (34,000). This area was populated by Ossetians from across the Caucasus (North Ossetia), driven out by the Mongols in the 13th century. The region was set up within the Georgian SSR on 20 April 1922. Formerly an Autonomous Region, its administrative autonomy was abolished by the Georgian Supreme Soviet on 11 Dec. 1990, and it has been named the Tskhinvali Region.

Fighting broke out in 1990 between insurgents wishing to unite with North Ossetia (in the Russian Federation) and Georgian forces. By a Russo-Georgian agreement of July 1992 Russian peacekeeping forces moved into a seven-km buffer zone between South Ossetia and Georgia pending negotiations. An OSCE peacekeeping force has been deployed since 1992.

At elections not recognized by the Georgian government on 10 Nov. 1996, Lyudvig Chibirov was elected president. Though maintaining a commitment to independence, President Chibirov came to a political agreement with the Georgian government in 1996 that neither force nor sanctions should be applied. In July 2003 his successor, President Eduard Kokoyty, asked Vladmir Putin to let South Ossetia become a member of the Russian Federation. Georgian President Mikhail Saakashvili, who took office in Jan. 2004, has made clear his wish to revive the authority of the Georgian government in the regions.

Presidential elections in Dec. 2001 were won by Eduard Kokoyty.

Main industries are mining, timber, electrical engineering and building materials.

In 1989–90 there were 21,200 pupils in elementary and secondary schools. There were 6,525 children in pre-school institutions.

In Jan. 1987 there were 511 doctors and 1,400 hospital beds.

GERMANY

Bundesrepublik Deutschland
(Federal Republic of Germany)

Capital: Berlin
Seat of Government: Berlin/Bonn
Population projection, 2010: 82·58m.
GDP per capita, 2002: (PPP$) 27,100
HDI/world rank: 0·925/19

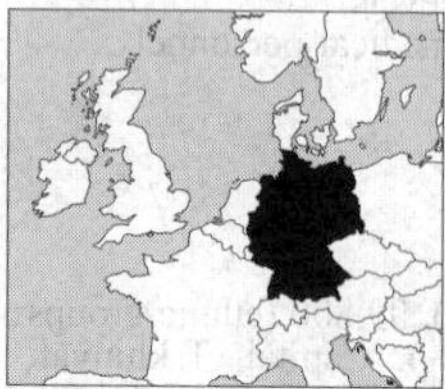

KEY HISTORICAL EVENTS

From the 8th century BC the Celts predominated in most of the area of modern Germany but by about 500 BC Germanic tribes had settled in the Celtic lands. The Roman Empire established its boundaries along the Rhine and the Danube rivers but attempts to move further east were abandoned after Varius was defeated in AD 9 by Germanic forces under Arminius. Christianity was introduced under Emperor Constantine and the first bishopric north of the Alps was established in Trier in AD 314.

At the start of the 5th century, the Huns overran the area and forced the Saxons north. However the Franks, the founders of a civilized German state, gradually asserted themselves over all the other Germanic people. Charlemagne succeeded to the Frankish throne in 768, founding what was later known as the First Reich (Empire). The Franks continued to expand until their influence stretched from Rome to the North Sea and from the Pyrenees to the River Elbe. The pope crowned Charlemagne emperor on Christmas Day 800, creating what was later known as the Holy Roman Empire, but the empire was too unwieldy to survive Charlemagne's death in 814. The Treaty of Verdun in 843 divided the realm into a Germanic Central Europe and a Latin (French) Western Europe. The Saxon Otto the Great, the first to associate German kingship with the office of the Holy Roman Emperor, crushed the increasing power of the hereditary duchies in the 10th century.

After an intense feud with the Guelfs (of Bavaria; later denoting anti-imperial loyalties), the Hohenstaufens (of Swabia) gained supremacy. Frederick Barbarossa, descended from both dynasties, led several expeditions to subjugate Italy and died on the Third Crusade. The Golden Bull of 1356 established the method for electing an emperor by setting up an electoral college composed of seven princes, representing the church and nobility. The title of Holy Roman Emperor nearly always went to an outsider and increasingly to members of the Austrian Habsburg dynasty. In 1273 Count Rudolph IV was the first Habsburg to be crowned king of the Germans.

Founded as a defence and trading league at Lübeck, the Hanseatic League combated piracy and established Germanic economic and political domination of the Baltic and North Sea. In the 14th century the bubonic plague wiped out a quarter of the German population. In the early part of the 15th century, the unpopularity of the church was linked to corruption coupled with a growing trade in the sale of indulgences. In 1517 Martin Luther, an Augustinian monk, nailed 95 Theses (arguments against indulgences) to the door of Wittenberg Castle Church. Marking the beginning of the Reformation, Luther challenged the power of the pope, the privileged position of the priests and the doctrine of transubstantiation.

The Habsburg Charles I of Spain was elected emperor in 1519. Luther was excommunicated in 1520 but was given haven in Wartburg Castle where he translated the Bible into German, the first vernacular translation. His doctrine of 'justification by faith alone', with its apparent invitation to resist the authority of the church, led the way to many of the small independent German states joining the Protestant cause. The Peace of Augsburg gave rulers of each state the right to decide on their own religious practices.

After Luther died in 1546 the Catholics launched a counter reformation setting in train dynastic and religious conflicts. The Thirty Years' War devastated Germany and reduced the population by as much as a third. The Peace of Westphalia (1648) deprived the emperor of much of his authority. While the Habsburgs struggled to hold on to the title of Holy Roman Emperor, Brandenburg-Prussia under the Hohenzollern family grew into a powerful independent state with its capital in

Berlin. Under Frederick the Great, Prussia annexed Silesia, provoking the Habsburgs into the Seven Years' War. The Prussian forces were seriously overextended but Frederick annexed most of Poland, helped by the collapse of the alliance between Austria and Russia in 1772.

When Napoléon Bonaparte defeated Austria in 1802 he redrew the map of Germany. All but a few of the free German cities and all the ecclesiastical territories were stripped of their independence. Bavaria, Württemberg and Saxony were raised to the status of kingdoms. In 1806 the Holy Roman Empire was officially abolished. Prussia played a vital role in the defeat of Napoléon at Waterloo in 1815; the Congress of Vienna, which determined the structure of post-Napoleonic Europe, established Prussian dominance in German affairs. A German Confederation was created and each state was represented in the Frankfurt-based Diet. Failed harvests in the late 1840s led to armed rebellions. The Diet was disbanded and the Prussian army seized power. Realizing the importance of industrial might, Prussia became the driving force for creating a single internal German market.

In 1862 Wilhelm I appointed as chancellor Otto von Bismarck, who introduced widespread reforms including universal male suffrage. Bismarck persuaded Austria to back him in a war against Denmark, resulting in the recapture of Schleswig and Holstein. In a subsequent row with Austria over the spoils, Austria was crushed and forced out of German affairs. The previously neutral Hanover and Hesse-Kassel joined the other small German states under Prussia to form a North German Confederation. Bismarck rallied all the German states in 1870 to provoke a war with France. The outcome of the Franco-Prussian War of 1870–71 was the defeat of France and the creation of a united Germany (including the long disputed provinces of Alsace and Lorraine). Wilhelm I of Prussia was named *Kaiser* (emperor) of the 'Second Reich'.

Kaiser Wilhelm II's ambition for military supremacy divided Europe into two hostile camps. Germany was allied once more with Austria and Italy. France and Russia, united in common mistrust of the German speaking nations, drew Britain closer to them. In June 1914 a Bosnian Serb nationalist assassinated the Austrian Archduke Franz Ferdinand at Sarajevo. Austria threatened Serbia with war, causing Russia to mobilize in defence of her Slavic neighbours. Assuming the advantage of striking first, Germany attacked France, beginning the First World War. Belgium's neutrality (guaranteed by Britain) was violated when the German armies marched through on their way to France, obliging Britain to declare war on Germany on 4 Aug. 1914.

In 1917 the United States entered the war. Although the Bolshevik revolution in Russia that same year gained Germany a reprieve, allowing the transfer of vast numbers of troops from the eastern to western fronts, the respite was short-lived. Troops returning from Russia agitated against the war. At the same time, the German lines were weakened by over-extension. On 8 Aug. 1918 the German defences were finally broken. The Kaiser abdicated on 9 Nov. and a republic was proclaimed. An armistice ended the war on 11 Nov. 1918.

A new constitution was drawn up at Weimar in 1919. Under the Treaty of Versailles the rich industrial regions of Saarland and Alsace-Lorraine were ceded to France and Upper Silesia was given to a resurrected Poland. A corridor to the east cut off East Prussia from the rest of the country and all Germany's overseas colonies were confiscated. The Rhineland was declared a demilitarized zone and the size of the armed forces was severely limited. The German economy was burdened with a heavy reparations bill, which contributed to a collapse of the currency.

With the help of US loans, the currency was re-established by Oct. 1924 and reparation payments were scaled down. However, the National Socialist German Workers' Party (Nazis), led by Adolf Hitler, attracted political extremists and misfits whose views mixed the extremes of right and left wing opinion. After Hitler led a failed *Putsch* in Bavaria in 1923 he was convicted of high treason. He used his nine months in prison to write his political manifesto, *Mein Kampf*. In 1929 the Wall Street crash set in motion worldwide financial chaos, which proved fertile ground for Hitler's ideas. Helped by a campaign of terror by his storm troopers, Hitler was sworn in as chancellor on 30 Jan. 1933. He declared himself president of the Third Reich in 1934.

Hitler's policies embraced a theory of Aryan racial supremacy that led to the slaughter of millions of Jews, gypsies and other non-Aryan 'undesirables'. His ambition to dominate Europe started with the annexation (*Anschluss*) of Austria and German-speaking Czechoslovakia in 1938. Britain and France, persuaded that Hitler had no further territorial demands, accepted the Munich peace agreement. But Hitler went on to take Bohemia-Moravia and invade Poland, having signed a non-aggression pact with Russia. Realizing that the Munich agreement was a sham, Britain and France declared war on Germany.

The fall of Poland was quickly followed by the occupation of the Low Countries and France in 1940. Hitler bombarded Britain from the air and turned to the east, subduing the Balkans and invading the Soviet Union in June 1941. In Dec. Hitler's Japanese allies attacked the United States naval base at Pearl Harbor provoking America to declare war on the Axis powers. By the end of 1942 Germany was hopelessly overextended and in retreat from Russia. Defeat in North Africa came in May 1943. The Allies invaded France in June 1944, liberating Paris in Aug. while Russian troops advanced from the east. On 30 April 1945, as Soviet forces marched into Berlin, Hitler committed suicide. Germany surrendered unconditionally on 7 May 1945, bringing the Third Reich to an end.

Allied forces occupied Germany—the UK, the USA and France held the west and the USSR the east. Berlin was divided into four sectors. By 1948 it had become clear that there would be no agreement between the occupying powers on Germany's future. Accordingly, the western allies united their zones into one unit in March 1948. In protest, the USSR withdrew from the Allied Control Council, blockaded Berlin until May 1949 and consolidated control of eastern Germany, establishing the German Democratic Republic (GDR). A People's Council, appointed in 1948, drew up a constitution, which came into force in Oct. 1949, providing for a communist state of five Länder with a centrally planned economy. Berlin was closed as a migration route to the west by the construction of a concrete wall in 1961. In 1953 there were popular revolts against food shortages and collectivization.

In Sept. 1949 the Western occupation forces transferred power to the Federal Republic of Germany and sovereignty was granted in 1955. The first chancellor, Konrad Adenauer (1949–63), was committed to the reunification of Germany and refused to acknowledge the GDR. It was not until 1972 that the two German states signed an agreement of mutual recognition and intent to co-operate. Post-war West Germany experienced rapid population and economic growth, joining in creating the European Coal and Steel Community in 1951 and the European Economic Community in 1957. In Jan. 1957 the Saarland was returned to full German control and in 1973 the Federal Republic entered the UN. In the autumn of 1989 movements for political liberalization in the GDR and re-unification with Federal Germany gathered strength. Erich Honecker and other long-serving Communist leaders were dismissed in Oct.–Nov. The Berlin Wall was opened on 9 Nov.

Following reforms in the GDR in Nov. 1989, President Gorbachev withdrew Soviet objections to German re-unification. On 18 May 1990 Federal Germany and the GDR signed a treaty extending Federal Germany's currency, together with its economic, monetary and social legislation, to the GDR. On 12 Sept. the Treaty on the Final Settlement with Respect to Germany was signed by the Federal Republic of Germany, the GDR and the four wartime allies: France, the USSR, the UK and the USA. The Federal Assembly (*Bundestag*) moved from Bonn to the renovated *Reichstag* in Berlin in 1999.

TERRITORY AND POPULATION

Germany is bounded in the north by Denmark and the North and Baltic Seas, east by Poland, east and southeast by the Czech Republic, southeast and south by Austria, south by Switzerland and west by France, Luxembourg, Belgium and the Netherlands. Area: 357,034 sq. km. Population estimate, 31 Dec. 2002: 82,536,700 (42,191,800 females). Of the total population, 65,527,200 lived in the former Federal Republic of Germany (excluding West Berlin), 13,617,000 in the five new states of the former German Democratic Republic (excluding East Berlin) and 3,392,400 in Berlin; density, 231 per sq. km. In 2001, 87·7% of the population lived in urban areas. There were 38·94m. households in May 2003; 14·42m. were single-person and 12·24m. had a female principal breadwinner. Germany has an ageing population. The proportion of the population over 60 has been steadily rising, and that of the under 20s steadily declining. By the mid-1990s the number of over 60s had surpassed the number of under 20s and now stands at 25% of the total population.

The UN gives a projected population for 2010 of 82·58m.

On 14 Nov. 1990 Germany and Poland signed a treaty confirming Poland's existing western frontier and renouncing German claims to territory lost as a result of the Second World War.

The capital is Berlin; the Federal German government moved from Bonn to Berlin in 1999.

The Federation comprises 16 *Bundesländer* (states). Area and population:

Bundesländer	*Area in sq. km*	*Population (in 1,000) 1987 census*	*2003 estimate*	*Density per sq. km (2003)*
Baden-Württemberg (BW)	35,752	9,286	10,707[1]	299[1]
Bavaria (BY)	70,549	10,903	12,423	176
Berlin (BE)[2]	892	. .	3,388	3,800
Brandenburg (BB)[3]	29,477	. . .	2,575	87
Bremen (HB)	404	660	663	1,641
Hamburg (HH)	755	1,593	1,734	2,296
Hessen (HE)	21,115	5,508	6,089	288
Lower Saxony (NI)	47,618	7,162	8,002[1]	168[1]
Mecklenburg-West Pomerania (MV)[3]	23,174	. . .	1,732	75
North Rhine-Westphalia (NW)	34,082	16,712	18,080	530
Rhineland-Palatinate (RP)	19,853	3,631	4,059	204
Saarland (SL)	2,568	1,056	1,061	413
Saxony (SN)[3]	18,414	. . .	4,321	235
Saxony-Anhalt (ST)[3]	20,447	. . .	2,523	123
Schleswig-Holstein (SH)	15,763	2,554	2,823	179
Thuringia (TH)[3]	16,172	. . .	2,373	147

[1]June 2004. [2]1987 census population of West Berlin: 2,013,000. [3]Reconstituted in 1990 in the Federal Republic.

On 31 Dec. 2003 there were 7,334,800 resident foreigners, including 1,877,700 Turks, 601,300 Italians, 568,200 Serbs and Montenegrins and 354,600 Greeks. More than 1·6m. of these were born in Germany. Germany's Muslim population, at 3·2m., is the second highest in Europe after that of France. In 2003 Germany received 50,563 asylum applications, compared to 438,200 in 1992. The main countries of origin in 2003 were Turkey, Serbia and Montenegro, Iraq, Russia and China. Tighter controls on entry from abroad were applied as from 1993. 140,731 persons were naturalized in 2003, of whom 56,244 were from Turkey. In 2002 there were 623,300 emigrants and 842,500 immigrants. New citizenship laws were introduced on 1 Jan. 2000, whereby a child of non-Germans will have German citizenship automatically if the birth is in Germany, if at the time of the birth one parent has made Germany his or her customary legal place of abode for at least eight years, and if this parent has had an unlimited residence permit for at least three years. Previously at least one parent had to hold German citizenship for the child to become a German national.

Populations of the 83 towns of over 100,000 inhabitants in Dec. 2002 (in 1,000):

Town (and Bundesland)	*Population (in 1,000)*	*Ranking by population*
Aachen (NW)	247·7	28
Augsburg (BY)	259·2	26
Bergisch Gladbach (NW)	105·9	76
Berlin (BE)	3,392·4	1
Bielefeld (NW)	324·8	18
Bochum (NW)	388·9	16
Bonn (NW)	308·9	19
Bottrop (NW)	120·8	61
Braunschweig (NI)	245·4	29
Bremen (HB)	543·0	10
Bremerhaven (HB)	119·1	65
Chemnitz (SN)	252·6	27
Cologne (NW)	968·6	4
Cottbus (BB)	103·8	77
Darmstadt (HE)	139·0	54
Dortmund (NW)	590·8	6
Dresden (SN)	480·2	15
Duisburg (NW)	508·7	12
Düsseldorf (NW)	571·9	9
Erfurt (TH)	200·0	38
Erlangen (BY)	102·2	80
Essen (NW)	585·5	8
Frankfurt am Main (HE)	643·7	5
Freiburg im Breisgau (BW)	210·2	36
Fürth (BY)	111·8	70
Gelsenkirchen (NW)	274·9	22
Gera (TH)	108·1	73
Göttingen (NI)	123·7	59
Hagen (NW)	201·1	37
Halle (ST)	239·4	30
Hamburg (HH)	1,728·8	2
Hamm (NW)	184·6	42
Hanover (NI)	517·3	11
Heidelberg (BW)	142·6	52
Heilbronn (BW)	120·7	62
Herne (NW)	173·6	44
Hildesheim (NI)	103·4	78
Ingolstadt (BY)	118·4	67
Jena (TH)	100·5	82

Town (and Bundesland)	*Population (in 1,000)*	*Ranking by population*	*Town (and Bundesland)*	*Population (in 1,000)*	*Ranking by population*
Karlsruhe (BW)	281·3	21	Oldenburg (NI)	157·4	50
Kassel (HE)	194·1	40	Osnabrück (NI)	164·6	47
Kiel (SH)	233·3	32	Paderborn (NW)	141·5	53
Koblenz (RP)	107·9	75	Pforzheim (BW)	118·8	66
Krefeld (NW)	239·2	31	Potsdam (BB)	131·4	56
Leipzig (SN)	494·8	13	Recklinghausen (NW)	123·9	58
Leverkusen (NW)	160·3	49	Regensburg (BY)	128·0	57
Lübeck (SH)	213·3	35	Remscheid (NW)	118·3	68
Ludwigshafen am Rhein (RP)	162·4	48	Reutlingen (BW)	112·1	69
			Rostock (MV)	198·3	39
Magdeburg (ST)	228·2	33	Saarbrücken (SL)	182·5	43
Mainz (RP)	186·1	41	Salzgitter (NI)	110·8	71
Mannheim (BW)	308·8	20	Siegen (NW)	108·3	72
Moers (NW)	108·0	74	Solingen (NW)	164·7	46
Mönchengladbach (NW)	263·1	25	Stuttgart (BW)	588·5	7
Mülheim a. d. Ruhr (NW)	172·2	45	Trier (RP)	100·2	83
			Ulm (BW)	119·2	63=
Munich (BY)	1,234·7	3	Wiesbaden (HE)	271·6	23
Münster (NW)	268·9	24	Witten (NW)	102·4	79
Neuss (NW)	151·6	51	Wolfsburg (NI)	122·3	60
Nuremberg (BY)	493·4	14	Wuppertal (NW)	363·5	17
Oberhausen (NW)	220·9	34	Würzburg (BY)	131·6	55
Offenbach am Main (HE)	119·2	63=	Zwickau (SN)	100·9	81

The official language is German. Minor orthographical amendments were agreed in 1995. An agreement between German-speaking countries in Vienna on 1 July 1996 provided for minor orthographical changes and established a Commission for German Orthography in Mannheim. There have been considerable objections within Germany, particularly in the North, and many *Bundesländer* are to decide their own language programmes for schools. Generally, both old and new spellings are acceptable.

SOCIAL STATISTICS

Calendar years:

	Marriages	*Live births*	*Of these to single parents*	*Deaths*	*Divorces*
1998	417,420	785,034	157,117	852,382	192,416
1999	430,674	770,744	170,634	846,330	190,590
2000	418,550	766,999	179,574	838,797	194,630
2001	389,591	734,475	183,816	828,541	197,498
2002	391,963	719,250	187,961	841,686	204,214
2003	—	707,000[1]	—	854,000[1]	—

[1]Provisional.

Of the 391,963 marriages in 2002, 36,594 involved a foreign male and 46,909 involved a foreign female. The average age of bridegrooms in 2002 was 35·4 years, and of brides 32·3. The average first-time marrying age for men was 31·8 and for women 28·8.

Rates (per 1,000 population), 2002: birth, 8·7; death, 10·2; marriage, 4·8; infant mortality, 4·2 per 1,000 births; stillborn rate, 3·7 per 1,000 births. Life expectancy, 2001: men, 74·9 years; women, 81·0. Suicide rates, 2002, per 100,000 population, 13·5 (men, 20·1; women, 7·2). Annual population growth rate, 1992–2002, 0·2%; fertility rate, 2001, 1·3 births per woman.

Legislation of 1995 categorizes abortions as illegal, but stipulates that prosecutions will not be brought if they are performed in the first three months of pregnancy after consultation with a doctor. The annual abortion rate, at under ten per 1,000 women aged 15–44, is among the lowest in the world.

Since 1 Aug. 2001 same-sex couples have been permitted to exchange vows at registry offices. The law also gives them the same rights as heterosexual couples in inheritance and insurance law.

A UNICEF report published in 2000 showed that 10·7% of children in Germany live in poverty (in households with income below 50% of the national median). The report also showed that the poverty rate of children in lone-parent families was 51·2%, compared to 6·2% in two-parent families.

CLIMATE

Oceanic influences are only found in the northwest where winters are quite mild but stormy. Elsewhere a continental climate is general. To the east and south, winter temperatures are lower, with bright frosty weather and considerable snowfall. Summer temperatures are fairly uniform throughout. Berlin, Jan. 31°F (–0·5°C), July 66°F (19°C). Annual rainfall 22·5" (563 mm). Cologne, Jan. 36°F (2·2°C), July 66°F (18·9°C). Annual rainfall 27" (676 mm). Dresden, Jan. 30°F (–0·1°C), July 65°F (18·5°C). Annual rainfall 27·2" (680 mm). Frankfurt, Jan. 33°F (0·6°C), July 66°F (18·9°C). Annual rainfall 24" (601 mm). Hamburg, Jan. 31°F (–0·6°C), July 63°F (17·2°C). Annual rainfall 29" (726 mm). Hanover, Jan. 33°F (0·6°C), July 64°F (17·8°C). Annual rainfall 24" (604 mm). Munich, Jan. 28°F (–2·2°C), July 63°F (17·2°C). Annual rainfall 34" (855 mm). Stuttgart, Jan. 33°F (0·6°C), July 66°F (18·9°C). Annual rainfall 27" (677 mm).

CONSTITUTION AND GOVERNMENT

The Basic Law (*Grundgesetz*) was approved by the parliaments of the participating *Bundesländer* and came into force on 23 May 1949. It is to remain in force until 'a constitution adopted by a free decision of the German people comes into being'. The Federal Republic is a democratic and social constitutional state on a parliamentary basis. The federation is constituted by the 16 *Bundesländer* (states). The Basic Law decrees that the general rules of international law form part of the federal law. The constitutions of the *Bundesländer* must conform to the principles of a republican, democratic and social state based on the rule of law. Executive power is vested in the *Bundesländer,* unless the Basic Law prescribes or permits otherwise. Federal law takes precedence over state law.

Legislative power is vested in the *Bundestag* (Federal Assembly) and the *Bundesrat* (Federal Council). The Bundestag is currently composed of 603 members and is elected in universal, free, equal and secret elections for a term of four years. A party must gain 5% of total votes cast in order to gain representation in the Bundestag, although if a party has three candidates elected directly, they may take their seats even if the party obtains less than 5% of the national vote. The electoral system combines relative-majority and proportional voting; each voter has two votes, the first for the direct constituency representative, the second for the competing party lists in the *Bundesländer*. All directly elected constituency representatives enter parliament, but if a party receives more 'indirect' than 'direct' votes, the first name in order on the party list not to have a seat becomes a member—the number of seats is increased by the difference ('overhang votes'). Thus the number of seats in the Bundestag varies, but is 598 regular members (for the 2002 election, down from 656 for the previous elections since reunification) plus the 'overhang votes'. The Bundesrat consists of 69 members appointed by the governments of the *Bundesländer* in proportions determined by the number of inhabitants. Each *Bundesland* has at least three votes.

The Head of State is the Federal *President,* who is elected for a five-year term by a *Federal Convention* specially convened for this purpose. This Convention consists of all the members of the Bundestag and an equal number of members elected by the *Bundesländer* parliaments in accordance with party strengths, but who need not themselves be members of the parliaments. No president may serve more than two terms. Executive power is vested in the Federal government, which consists of the Federal *Chancellor*, elected by the Bundestag on the proposal of the Federal President, and the Federal Ministers, who are appointed and dismissed by the Federal President upon the proposal of the Federal Chancellor.

The Federal Republic has exclusive legislation on: (1) foreign affairs; (2) federal citizenship; (3) freedom of movement, passports, immigration and emigration, and extradition; (4) currency, money and coinage, weights and measures, and regulation of time and calendar; (5) customs, commercial and navigation agreements, traffic in goods and payments with foreign countries, including customs and frontier protection; (6) federal railways and air traffic; (7) post and telecommunications; (8) the legal status of persons in the employment of the Federation and of public law corporations under direct supervision of the Federal government; (9) trade marks, copyright and publishing rights; (10) co-operation of the Federal Republic and the *Bundesländer* in the criminal police and in matters concerning the protection of the constitution, the establishment of a Federal Office of Criminal Police, as well as the combating of international crime; (11) federal statistics.

In the field of finance the Federal Republic has exclusive legislation on customs and financial monopolies and concurrent legislation on: (1) excise taxes and taxes on transactions, in particular, taxes on real-estate acquisition, incremented value and on fire protection; (2) taxes on income, property, inheritance and donations; (3) real estate, industrial and trade taxes, with the exception of the determining of the tax rates.

Federal laws are passed by the Bundestag and after their adoption submitted to the Bundesrat, which has a limited veto. The Basic Law may be amended only upon the approval of two-thirds of the members of the Bundestag and two-thirds of the votes of the Bundesrat.

Die Bundesrepublik Deutschland: Staatshandbuch. Cologne, annual

National Anthem. 'Einigkeit und Recht und Freiheit' ('Unity and right and freedom'); words by H. Hoffmann, tune by J. Haydn.

RECENT ELECTIONS

On 23 May 2004 Horst Köhler was elected Federal President by the Federal Convention, defeating Gesine Schwan, the government's candidate, in the first round.

Bundestag elections were held on 22 Sept. 2002. The Social Democratic Party (SPD) of Chancellor Gerhard Schröder won 251 seats with 38·5% of votes cast (298 seats with 40·9% in 1998); the Christian Democratic Union/Christian Social Union (CDU/CSU; the CSU is a Bavarian party where the CDU does not stand) won 248 with 38·5% (245 with 35·2%); the Greens/Alliance 90, 55 with 8·6% (47 with 6·6%); the Free Democratic Party (FDP), 47 with 7·4% (44 with 6·2%); and the Party for Democratic Socialism (PDS; former Communists), 2 with 4·3% (35 with 5·2%). Turn-out was 79·1%. With the SPD renewing its alliance with the Greens, the new government had a nine-seat majority in the Bundestag.

European Parliament. Germany has 99 representatives. At the June 2004 elections turn-out was 43·0% (45·2% in 1999). The CDU won 40 seats with 36·5% of votes cast (political affiliation in European Parliament: European People's Party–European Democrats); the SPD, 23 with 21·5% (Party of European Socialists); the Greens, 13 with 11·9% (Greens/European Free Alliance); the CSU, 9 with 9·0% (European People's Party–European Democrats); the FDP, 7 with 6·1% (Alliance of Liberals and Democrats for Europe); PDS, 7 with 6·1% (European Unitary Left/Nordic Green Left).

CURRENT ADMINISTRATION

Federal President: Horst Köhler; b. 1943 (CDU; sworn in 1 July 2004).

In Oct. 1998 an SPD–Green party coalition was formed, the first time that the Green party had entered national government in Germany. Following elections in Sept. 2002 a new SPD–Green cabinet was formed. In March 2005 the cabinet was composed as follows:

Chancellor: Gerhard Schröder; b. 1944 (SPD; sworn in on 27 Oct. 1998 and re-elected in Sept. 2002).

Vice-Chancellor and Foreign Minister: Joschka Fischer (Greens/Alliance 90). *Interior:* Otto Schily (SPD). *Justice:* Brigitte Zypries (SPD). *Finance:* Hans Eichel (SPD). *Economy and Labour:* Wolfgang Clement (SPD). *Consumer Protection, Food and Agriculture:* Renate Künast (Greens/Alliance 90). *Defence:* Peter Struck (SPD). *Family Affairs, Senior Citizens, Women and Youth:* Renate Schmidt (SPD). *Health and Social Security:* Ulla Schmidt (SPD). *Transport, Housing and Construction:* Manfred Stolpe (SPD). *Environment, Nature Conservation and Nuclear Safety:* Jürgen Trittin (Greens/Alliance 90). *Education and Research:* Edelgard Bulmahn (SPD). *Economic Co-operation and Development:* Heidemarie Wieczorek-Zeul (SPD).

The leader of the opposition Christian Democratic Union (CDU) is Angela Merkel, an East German liberal, who was elected to succeed Wolfgang Schäuble in March 2000 in the wake of the financial scandal which had previously brought down Helmut Kohl. However, Edmund Stoiber of the Christian Social Union (the CDU's sister party in Bavaria) was chosen instead of Angela Merkel as the conservative challenger to Gerhard Schröder for the federal election of Sept. 2002.

President of the Bundestag: Wolfgang Thierse (SPD; elected Oct. 1998).
Government Website: http://www.bundesregierung.de

DEFENCE

Conscription was reduced from ten months to nine months from Jan. 2002. In July 1994 the Constitutional Court ruled that German armed forces might be sent on peacekeeping missions abroad. Germany has increased the number of professionals available for military missions abroad and sent troops to Afghanistan as part of the international alliance against terrorism in the aftermath of 11 Sept. 2001. The first time that German armed forces were deployed in this way since the Second World War, the move provoked controversy in Germany. Since Jan. 2001 women have been allowed to serve in all branches of the military on the same basis as men.

In 2003 defence expenditure totalled US$35,145m. (US$426 per capita), representing 1·5% of GDP.

Army. The Army is organized in the Army Forces Command. The equipment of the former East German army is in store. Total strength was (2003) 191,350 (conscripts 73,450). There are Army reserves of 297,300.

The Territorial Army is organized into five Military Districts, under three Territorial Commands. Its main task is to defend rear areas and remains under national control even in wartime.

Navy. The Fleet Commander operates from a modern Maritime Headquarters at Glücksburg, close to the Danish border.

The fleet includes 14 diesel coastal submarines, two destroyers and 12 frigates. The main naval bases are at Wilhelmshaven, Olpenitz, Kiel, Eckernförde and Warnemünde.

The Naval Air Arm, 3,720 strong, is organized into three wings and includes 65 combat aircraft (Tornados and Atlantics) and 22 armed helicopters.

Personnel in 2003 numbered 25,650, including 4,950 conscripts.

Air Force. Since 1970 the *Luftwaffe* has comprised the following commands: German Air Force Tactical Command, German Air Force Support Command (including two German Air Force Regional Support Commands—North and South) and General Air Force Office. Personnel in 2003 was 67,500 (16,100 conscripts). There were 376 combat aircraft, including *Tornados*, F-4Fs, T-37Bs and T-38As.

INTERNATIONAL RELATIONS

A treaty of friendship with Poland signed on 17 June 1991 recognized the Oder-Neisse border and guaranteed minorities' rights in both countries.

Germany is a member of the UN, WTO, NATO, BIS, OECD, EU, Council of Europe, WEU, OSCE, CERN, Council of the Baltic Sea States, Danube Commission, Inter-American Development Bank, Asian Development Bank, IOM and the Antarctic Treaty. Germany is a signatory to the Schengen Accord which abolishes border controls between Germany, Austria, Belgium, Denmark, Finland, France, Greece, Iceland, Italy, Luxembourg, the Netherlands, Norway, Portugal, Spain and Sweden.

ECONOMY

Services accounted for 69·2% of GDP in 2002, industry (manufacturing and construction) 29·6% and agriculture 1·2%.

According to the anti-corruption organization *Transparency International*, Germany ranked 15th in the world in a 2004 survey of the countries with the least corruption in business and government. It received 8·2 out of 10 in the annual index.

Overview. Germany is the third largest economy in the world, after the USA and Japan. GDP growth has steadily declined from 4·5% per annum in the 1960s to an average of 0·6% in the past four years. GDP growth currently ranks, together with Italy, as the worst performer in the euro zone. Low growth is attributed to weaknesses in the labour market which have been amplified by reunification and the high cost of restructuring the economy of the former GDR. Labour utilization has diminished owing to high and inflexible labour costs, generous unemployment benefits and early retirement policies. Household income and consumption have become stagnant, as a result of structural difficulties, with private consumption growth significantly lower than the euro average since 2001.

In 2004 the budget deficit was 3·7%, greater than the 3% target set by the European Stability and Growth Pact. The ratio of public debt to GDP, at 65%, is also greater than that of the 60% specified in the pact, leaving little scope for expansionary fiscal policy. According to the IMF 'ambitious reforms to improve the flexibility of the labour market and a substantial reduction of entitlements and subsidies, […] will be key to correcting the fiscal imbalance permanently.' Tax reform has been instigated since 2000 to revive the economy. The basic income tax rate fell from 25·9% in 1998 to 17% in 2003–04. From 2001 the corporation tax rate dropped from 30% and 40% (a split rate system) to a unified 25%. Further tax cuts equivalent to 0·7% and 0·2% of GDP in 2004 and 2005 respectively are hoped to further improve the fiscal stance. In June 2003 Chancellor Schröder won support from his party for Agenda 2010, a series of social and economic reforms. The agenda comprises pension, labour market and health care reforms, which aim to reduce key structural weaknesses. Unemployment benefits and social security have been amalgamated for long-term claimants (known as the Hartz IV reforms). The IMF suggests, however, that reforms beyond Agenda 2010 need to be developed and implemented to support higher potential growth and fiscal consolidation in the long run.

Currency. On 1 Jan. 1999 the euro (EUR) became the legal currency in Germany; irrevocable conversion rate 1·95583 DM (deutschemark) to one euro. The euro, which consists of 100 cents, has been in circulation since 1 Jan. 2002. There are seven euro notes in different colours and sizes denominated in 500, 200, 100, 50, 20, 10 and 5 euros, and eight coins denominated in 2 and 1 euros, then 50, 20, 10, 5, 2 and 1 cents. It was still possible to make cash transactions in German marks until 28 Feb. 2002, although formally the mark had ceased to be legal tender on 31 Dec. 2001. Euro banknotes in circulation on 1 Jan. 2002 had a total value of €254·2bn.

Foreign exchange reserves were US$42,260m. in June 2002 and gold reserves were 110·79m. troy oz (95·18m. troy oz in 1997). Only the USA, with 262·00m. troy oz, had more in June 2002. Total money supply was €93,977m. in June 2002. Inflation was 1·6% in 2004, up from 1·1% in 2003.

Budget. In 2002, 2003 and 2004 the budget deficit exceeded 3%, the target set by the European Stability and Growth Pact. In 2004 it reached 3·7%.

In July 2000 Chancellor Schröder pushed through the largest tax-cutting package in Germany's history. From 2001 corporation tax was cut from 40%/30% to 25%. The top rate of income tax was gradually to be reduced from 51% to 42% in 2005. In March 2003 Schröder announced 'Agenda 2010', a major economic reform package. It includes cuts in unemployment benefits, enhanced legislation to ease job protection rules and trimmed state pensions. The health system, among the world's most expensive, is also a core target. The boldest reform package in German post-war history, 'Agenda 2010' has encountered criticism from trade unionists and left-wingers within the SPD. In July 2003 the German government announced that it would bring forward the tax cuts scheduled for 2005 and combine them with those planned for 2004, bringing the total tax cut for 2004 to €15·5bn.

Since 1 Jan. 1979 tax revenues have been distributed as follows: *Federal government.* Income tax, 42·5%; capital yield and corporation tax, 50%; turnover tax, 67·5%; trade tax, 15%; capital gains, insurance and accounts taxes, 100%; excise duties (other than on beer), 100%. *Bundesländer.* Income tax, 42·5%; capital yield and corporation tax, 50%; turnover tax, 32·5%; trade tax, 15%; other taxes, 100%. *Local authorities.* Income tax, 15%; trade tax, 70%; local taxes, 100%.

VAT is 16% (reduced rate, 7%).

Budget for 2004 (in €1m.):

	All public authorities	*Federal portion*
	Current	
Revenue		
Taxes	439,721	197,677
Economic activities	18,111	4,193
Interest	4,059	1,028
Current allocations and subsidies	136,936	4,307
Other receipts	34,796	8,577
minus equalising payments	120,504	. .
	513,119	215,782

	All public authorities	*Federal portion*
	Capital	
Revenue		
Sale of assets	15,602	7,783
Allocations for investment	21,933	2
Repayment of loans	9,015	4,163
Public sector borrowing	326	. . .
minus equalising payments	17,348	. . .
	29,528	11,948
Excess revenue	702	. . .
Total revenues	543,349	227,730
	Current	
Expenditure		
Staff	173,208	27,325
Materials	68,630	17,536
Interest	67,284	37,655
Allocations and subsidies	353,556	152,786
minus equalising payments	120,504	. . .
	542,174	235,302
	Capital	
Expenditure		
Construction	25,728	5,517
Acquisition of property	8,021	1,613
Allocations and subsidies	41,023	13,636
Loans	10,325	3,685
Acquisition of shares	2,354	565
Repayments in the public sector	701	. . .
minus equalising payments	17,348	. . .
	70,804	25,016
Excess expenditure	–4,505	–3,019
Total expenditures	608,473	257,299

Performance. In 2002 growth real GDP growth was just 0·1%, the lowest since 1993, and in 2003 the economy contracted by 0·1%, although Germany came out of recession in the second half of the year. In 2004 the economy grew by 1·7%, the best performance since 2000. Total GDP in 2003 was US$2,400·7bn., the third highest behind the USA and Japan. Germany was ranked third in the Business Competitiveness Index in the World Economic Forum's *Global Competitiveness Report 2004–05*.

According to the Jan. 2003 *OECD Economic Survey* 'In the wake of the unification boom Germany has been for a number of years an economy characterized by weak domestic demand and lower growth than in many other OECD countries. Low employment growth and a high share of structural unemployment are highlighting the need for comprehensive labour market reform. These developments have been shaped by long drawn-out adjustment to the exceptional unification shock as well as increased vulnerability to adverse external shocks. Growth has been very low since 2001, and the projected recovery relies strongly on the expansion of world trade.'

Banking and Finance. The Deutsche Bundesbank (German Federal Bank) is the central bank and bank of issue. Its duty is to protect the stability of the currency. It is independent of the government but obliged to support the government's general policy. Its Governor is appointed by the government for eight years. The *President* is Axel Weber. Its assets were US$874,706m. in June 2001. Ranked by total assets it is the third largest bank in the world. Its market capitalization in June 2001 was US$45·7bn. The largest private banks are the Deutsche Bank, HypoVereinsbank, Dresdner Bank and Commerzbank. The former GDR central bank Staatsbank has become a public commercial bank. In April 2001 Dresdner Bank accepted a takeover offer from Allianz, the country's largest insurance company.

In 2003 there were 2,466 credit institutes, including 357 banks, 489 savings banks, 25 mortgage lenders and 1,394 credit societies. They are represented in the wholesale market by the 13 public sector *Bundesländer* banks. Total assets, 2003, €6,470,882m. Savings deposits were €600,378m. in 2003. By Oct. 2000 approximately 6% of the German population were using e-banking.

A single stock exchange, the Deutsche Börse, was created in 1992, based on the former Frankfurt stock exchange in a union with the smaller exchanges in Berlin,

Bremen, Düsseldorf, Hamburg, Hanover, Munich and Stuttgart. Frankfurt processes 90% of equities trading in the country.

Germany attracted US$12·87bn. worth of foreign direct investment in 2003, compared to a record US$198·28bn. in 2000.

Gull, L. *et al., The Deutsche Bank, 1870–1995*. London, 1996

ENERGY AND NATURAL RESOURCES

Environment. Germany's carbon dioxide emissions from the consumption and flaring of fossil fuels were the equivalent of 10·2 tonnes per capita in 2002. An *Environmental Sustainability Index* compiled for the World Economic Forum meeting in Feb. 2002 ranked Germany 50th in the world, with 52·5%. The index measured the ability of countries to maintain favourable environmental conditions and examined various factors including pollution levels and the use or abuse of natural resources.

Germany is one of the world leaders in recycling. In 1996, 48% of all household waste was recycled. In 1998 recycling included 81% of glass, 81% of steel and 86% of aluminium cans.

Electricity. Installed capacity in 2001 was 117·19m. kW. In 2003 there were 18 nuclear reactors in operation, but in Dec. 2001 the German parliament decided to decommission the country's nuclear reactors over the next two decades. Production of electricity was 569·33bn. kWh in 2001, of which about 19% was nuclear. There is a moratorium on further nuclear plant construction. Consumption per capita was 7,113 kWh in 2000. In April 1998 the electricity market was liberalized, leading to huge cuts in bills for both industrial and residential customers. In June 2000 Veba and Viag merged to form E.ON, which became the world's largest private energy service provider.

By 2010 it is hoped that renewable energy sources, which currently account for 6% of electric power, will constitute 10% of the total.

Oil and Gas. The chief oilfields are in Emsland (Lower Saxony). In 2003, 3·8m. tonnes of crude oil were produced. Natural gas production was 17·4bn. cu. metres in 2002. Natural gas reserves were 320bn. cu. metres and crude petroleum reserves 364m. bbls. in 2002.

Wind. Germany is the world's leading producer of wind-power. By the end of 2003 there were 15,387 wind turbines with a total rated power of 14,609 MW (37% of the world total).

Minerals. The main production areas are: North Rhine-Westphalia (for coal, iron and metal smelting-works), Central Germany (for lignite) and Lower Saxony (Salzgitter for iron ore; the Harz for metal ore).

Production (in 1,000 tonnes), 2003: lignite, 180,523; coal, 28,869; salt, 15,700. In 2000 recoverable coal reserves were estimated at 67bn. tonnes. Germany is the world's largest lignite producer and the third largest salt producer after the USA and China.

Agriculture. In 2001 there were 11·81m. ha of arable land and 207,000 ha of permanent crops. Sown areas in 2003 (in 1,000 ha) included: wheat, 2,967·4; barley, 2,081·7; fodder, 1,541·4; rape, 1,267·6; rye, 531·1; maize, 468·9; sugarbeets, 445·5; potatoes, 284·4; oats, 260·9. Crop production, 2003 (and 1994) (in 1,000 tonnes): fodder, 47,017·5 (52,187·9); sugarbeets (2002), 26,464·8 (24,211·3); wheat, 19,287·9 (16,480·5); barley, 10,636·5 (10,902·5); potatoes, 9,812·8 (9,668·6); rapeseed, 3,637·7 (2,895·5); maize, 3,455·7 (2,446·0); rye, 2,278·7 (3,450·6); oats, 1,196·0 (1,663·0). Germany is the world's largest producer of hops (30,000 tonnes in 2000) and the second largest producer of both barley and rye.

In 2001 Germany set aside 3·7% of its agricultural land for the growth of organic crops. Organic food sales for Germany in 2000 were valued at US$2·4bn. (the second highest in the world behind the USA).

In 2003 there were 420,697 farms, of which 70,642 were between two and five ha and 28,463 over 100 ha. In 2003 there were 388,600 farmers assisted by 434,100 household members and 480,600 hired labourers (289,200 of them seasonal).

In 2003 wine production was 811·0m. litres.

Livestock, 2003 (in 1,000): beef cattle, 13,643·7; milch cows, 4,372·0; sheep, 2,697·0; pigs, 26,334·3; horses, 524·8; poultry, 109,793·5. Livestock products, 2003 (in 1,000 tonnes): milk, 28,533; meat, 5,415; cheese, 1,816; eggs (2002), 870.

Forestry. Forest area in 2001 was 8,984,000 ha, of which about half was owned by the State. Timber production was 42·38m. cu metres in 2002. In recent years depredation has occurred through pollution with acid rain.

Fisheries. The total catch in 2001 was 211,282 tonnes (188,464 tonnes from marine waters). In 2000 the fishing fleet consisted of 44 ocean-going vessels and 2,247 coastal cutters.

INDUSTRY

The leading companies by market capitalization in Germany, excluding banking and finance, in May 2004 were: Deutsche Telekom (US$70·5bn.); Siemens AG, an electronic and electric equipment producer (US$63·2bn.); and SAP, a software and computer services company (US$50·9bn.).

In 2002 a total of 723,333 firms were registered, 564,697 of which were classified as sole traders.

Output of major industrial products, 2003 (in 1,000 tonnes): distillate fuel oil (2000), 46,449; crude steel, 44,800; cement, 32,243; pig iron, 29,400; unleaded petrol, 24,660; rolled steel (2001), 23,757; household plastics, 13,531; residual fuel oil (2000), 13,116; paper, 10,550; flour, 4,572; jet fuels (2000), 4,311; sulphuric acid (2002), 1,732; nitrogenous fertilizers, 1,292; synthetic fibre, 388; passenger cars, 5,605,000 units; household dishwashing machines, 3,971,000 units; refrigerators, 2,773,000 units; glass bottles, 10,403m. units; radio sets (2001), 4,746,000; TV sets, 763,000; beer, 9,893m. litres; soft drinks (excluding milk-based beverages), 25,984m. litres.

Labour. Retirement age is normally 65 years. At May 2003 the workforce was 40·79m. (18·17m. females), of whom 36·17m. (16·18m. females) were working and 4·62m. (1·99m. females) were unemployed. In May 2003 there were 29·80m. employees, 3·74m. self-employed, 2·24m. civil servants and 385,000 helping other family members. 3·70m. foreign workers were employed in 2003. Of the 2003 workforce the year average for the number of employees in each industry was as follows: 10,562,000 in the public and private service sector, 7,460,000 in the mining, processing and manufacturing industries, 5,570,000 in the retail, hotel and catering industries, 2,934,000 in the civil service, 2,917,000 in real estate and corporate services, 2,400,000 in the construction industry, 1,834,000 in transport and communications, 1,305,000 in banking and insurance, 857,000 in agriculture, forestry and fisheries and 277,000 in energy and water services. In 2003 there were 354,726 job vacancies. By 2000 there was a shortfall of 75,000 people in the information technology industry. In Aug. 2000 Germany launched a 'Green Card' project, aimed at attracting 20,000 telecommunication and information technology specialists from non-European Union countries in a bid to make up for the shortfall in qualified personnel. The card will authorize the holder to unrestricted employment in Germany for five years. By Aug. 2001 more than 8,000 recruits had found work. The standardized unemployment rate was 9·8% in 2004, up from 8·7% in 2002 and 9·6% in 2003; the rate in the former GDR is more than double that in the states of the former Federal Republic of Germany. In Jan. 2005 the number of people out of work reached 5m., the highest total since the 1930s. In June 2001, 47% of those unemployed were women and 34·3% were long-term unemployed. The number of people in employment in May 2003 was 36,172,000.

Trade Unions. Germany's largest trade union is *Vereinigte Dienstleistungsgewerkschaft*, or *ver.di*, created in March 2001 as a result of the merger of five smaller unions. Representing 3m. workers in the service industry, it is the largest trade union outside of China.

The majority of trade unions belong to the *Deutscher Gewerkschaftsbund* (DGB, German Trade Union Federation), which had 7,363,367 (2,350,267 women) members in Dec. 2003. It functions as an umbrella organization for its eight member unions. DGB unions are organized in industrial branches such that only one union operates within each enterprise. The official GDR trade union organization (FDGB) was merged in the Deutscher Gewerkschaftsbund. Trade union membership declined significantly during the 1990s, from 11·8m. in 1991 to 8·3m. in 1999. Strikes are not legal unless called by a union with the backing of 75% of members. Certain public service employees are contractually not permitted to strike. 163,281 days were lost through strikes in 2003, up substantially from 2001 (26,833 days lost). Between 1989 and 1998 strikes cost Germany an average of 11 days per 1,000 employees a year, compared to the EU average of 85 per 1,000.

INTERNATIONAL TRADE

In 2002 Germany had its highest ever annual trade surplus, at €132·8bn. for the year compared to €95·5bn. a year earlier. The annual trade surplus in 2003 was €129·6bn.

Imports and Exports. Trade in €1m.:

	2000	*2001*	*2002*	*2003*
Imports	538,311	542,774	518,532	531,970
Exports	597,440	638,268	651,320	661,613

Most important trading partners in 2003 (trade figures in €1m.). Imports: France, 48,832; Netherlands, 44,404; USA, 39,046; Italy, 33,670; UK, 31,961; Belgium, 25,770; Austria, 21,025; Japan, 19,139; Switzerland, 19,035. Exports: France, 70,006; USA, 61,669; UK, 55,307; Italy, 48,785; Netherlands, 40,997; Austria, 35,187; Belgium, 33,366; Spain, 32,504; Switzerland, 25,902.

Distribution of imports and exports by commodities in 2003 (in €1m.): finished goods, 374,524 and 567,782; semi-finished goods, 31,433 and 24,293; foodstuffs, 35,625 and 24,465; raw materials, 42,249 and 7,525; drinks and tobacco, 5,637 and 4,803; live animals, 458 and 550.

Germany is the second largest trading nation in the world after the USA, but in 2003 took over from the USA as the world's leading exporter.

Trade Fairs. Germany has a number of major annual trade fairs, among the most important of which are Internationale Grüne Woche Berlin (International Green Week Berlin—Exhibition for the Food Industry, Agriculture and Horticulture), held in Berlin in Jan.; Ambiente (for high quality consumer goods and new products), held in Frankfurt in Feb.; ITB Berlin (International Tourism Exchange), held in Berlin in March; CeBit (World Business Fair for Office Automation, Information Technology and Telecommunications), held in Hanover in March; Hannover Messe (the World's Leading Fair for Industry, Automation and Innovation), held in Hanover, in April; Internationale Funkausstellung Berlin (Your World of Consumer Electronics), held in Berlin in late Aug./early Sept.; and Frankfurter Buchmesse (Frankfurt Book Fair) held in Frankfurt in Oct. Hanover's trade fair site is the largest in Europe and Frankfurt's the second largest.

COMMUNICATIONS

Roads. In 2003 the total length of the road network was 231,581 km, including 12,037 km of motorway *(Autobahn)*, 41,246 km of federal highways and 86,868 km of secondary roads. The motorway network is the largest in Europe. On 1 Jan. 2004 there were 54,082,200 motor vehicles, including: passenger cars, 45,022,900 (approximately one car for every two persons); trucks, 2,586,300; buses, 86,500; motorcycles, 3,745,000. In 2000, 7,943m. passengers were transported by long-distance road traffic. The estimated average distance travelled by a passenger car in the year 1998 was 12,700 km. In 2003, 311,900 motorists were arrested at the scene of an accident (resulting in injury) for driving offences, of which 14,658 were alcohol related and 58,207 for exceeding speed limits. Road casualties in 2003 (and 2002) totalled 468,783 (483,255), with 462,170 injured (476,413) and 6,613 killed (6,842). In 2002 there were 8·3 fatalities per 100,000 population.

Rail. Legislation of 1993 provides for the eventual privatization of the railways, but in 2004 DB Regio, part of Deutsche Bahn, still had almost 90% of the market. On 1 Jan. 1994 West German Bundesbahn and the former GDR Reichsbahn were amalgamated as the Deutsche Bahn, a joint-stock company in which track, long-distance passenger traffic, regional passenger traffic, goods traffic and railway stations/services are run as five separate administrative entities. These were intended after 3–5 years to become themselves companies, at first under a holding company, and ultimately independent. Initially the government will hold all the shares. Length of railway in 2002 was 44,324 km (1,435 mm gauge) of which 19,751 km were electrified. There were 5,256 stations in 2002. 2,028m. passengers were carried in 2003 and 296·9m. tonnes of freight.

There are metros in Berlin (136 km), Hamburg (95 km), Frankfurt am Main (51 km), Munich (63 km) and Nuremberg (23 km), and tram/light rail networks in 56 cities.

Civil Aviation. Lufthansa, the largest carrier, was set up in 1953 and was originally 75% state-owned. The government sold its final shares in 1997. Other airlines include Condor, Deutsche-British Airways, Hapag Lloyd, Eurowings, LTU International Airways, Air Berlin and Germanwings. Lufthansa flew 629·9m. km in 1999, carrying 41,892,700 passengers (27,276,400 on international flights). In 2002 civil aviation had 651 aircraft over 20 tonnes (602 jets).

In 2003 there were 73·07m. passenger arrivals and 72·28m. departures. Main international airports: Bremen, Cologne-Bonn, Düsseldorf, Frankfurt am Main, Hamburg (Fuhlsbüttel), Hanover, Leipzig, Munich, Nuremberg, Stuttgart and three at Berlin (Tegel, Tempelhof and Schönefeld). Airports at Dortmund, Dresden, Frankfurt (Hahn), Lübeck, Paderborn, Rostock and Saarbrücken are used for only a few scheduled international flights in addition to domestic flights.

In 2003 Frankfurt am Main handled 48,025,000 passengers (37,087,000 on international flights in 1999) and 1,519,602 tonnes of freight. It is the busiest airport in Europe in terms of freight handled. Munich was the second busiest German airport in terms of passenger traffic in 2003 (23·95m.) but third for freight. Cologne-Bonn was the second busiest in 2003 for freight, with 517,577 tonnes, but only sixth for passenger traffic.

Shipping. At 31 Dec. 2003 the mercantile marine comprised 982 ocean-going vessels of 6,110,000 GRT. Sea-going ships in 2003 carried 254·83m. tonnes of cargo. Navigable rivers and canals have a total length of 7,472 km. The inland-waterways fleet on 31 Dec. 2003 included 966 motor freight vessels totalling 1·14m. tonnes and 332 tankers of 509,098 tonnes. 219·99m. tonnes of freight were transported in 2003. In 2002 vessels totalling 958,945,000 NRT entered ports and vessels totalling 958,503,000 NRT cleared. The busiest port, Hamburg, handled 98·6m. tonnes of cargo in 2003, ranking it third in Europe behind Rotterdam and Antwerp. Hamburg is Europe's second busiest container port after Rotterdam.

Telecommunications. Telecommunications were deregulated in 1989. On 1 Jan. 1995, three state-owned joint-stock companies were set up: Deutsche Telekom, Postdienst and Postbank. The partial privatization of Deutsche Telekom began in Nov. 1996.

In 2002 there were 113,763,000 telephone subscribers, equivalent to 1,378·3 per 1,000 population. In 2001, 96·4% of all households had a private telephone. There were 35·6m. PCs in use in 2002 (431·3 per 1,000 persons). In 2002 Germany had 60,043,000 mobile phone subscribers, the highest number in any European country. T-Mobile and D2 Vodafone are the largest networks, each having around 40% of the market share. Germany is the country with the second highest number of Internet users in Europe after the UK, with approximately 32·1m. in Aug. 2002 (nearly 39% of the population). In 2002, 16·4% of households had fax transmitters.

Postal Services. In 2002 there were 12,683 post offices and 5,030 affiliated agents. A total of 17,998m. pieces of mail were processed in 2002.

SOCIAL INSTITUTIONS

Justice. Justice is administered by the federal courts and by the courts of the *Bundesländer*. In criminal procedures, civil cases and procedures of non-contentious jurisdiction the courts on the state level are the local courts *(Amtsgerichte)*, the regional courts *(Landgerichte)* and the courts of appeal *(Oberlandesgerichte)*. Constitutional federal disputes are dealt with by the Federal Constitutional Court *(Bundesverfassungsgericht)* elected by the Bundestag and Bundesrat. The *Bundesländer* also have constitutional courts. In labour law disputes the courts of the first and second instance are the labour courts and the *Bundesland* labour courts, and in the third instance the Federal Labour Court *(Bundesarbeitsgericht)*. Disputes about public law in matters of social security, unemployment insurance, maintenance of war victims and similar cases are dealt with in the first and second instances by the social courts and the *Bundesland* social courts and in the third instance by the Federal Social Court *(Bundessozialgericht)*. In most tax matters the finance courts of the *Bundesländer* are competent, and in the second instance the Federal Finance Court *(Bundesfinanzhof)*. Other controversies of public law in non-constitutional matters are decided in the first and second instance by the administrative and the higher administrative courts *(Oberverwaltungsgerichte)* of the *Bundesländer*, and in the third instance by the Federal Administrative Court *(Bundesverwaltungsgericht)*.

For the inquiry into maritime accidents the admiralty courts *(Seeämter)* are competent on the state level and in the second instance the Federal Admiralty Court *(Bundesoberseeamt)* in Hamburg.

The death sentence was abolished in the Federal Republic of Germany in 1949 and in the German Democratic Republic in 1987.

The population in penal institutions in 2003 was 62,288. 1,774 prisoners were serving life sentences.

Religion. In 2002 there were 26,211,000 Protestants in 16,356 parishes, 26,466,000 Roman Catholics in 13,099 parishes; and in 2003, 102,472 Jews with 32 rabbis and 72 synagogues.

There are seven Roman Catholic archbishoprics (Bamberg, Berlin, Cologne, Freiburg, Hamburg, Munich and Freising, Paderborn) and 27 bishoprics. Chairman of the German Bishops' Conference is Cardinal Karl Lehmann, Bishop of Mainz. A concordat between Germany and the Holy See dates from 10 Sept. 1933. In April 2005 Cardinal Joseph Ratzinger, former archbishop of Munich and Freising, was elected Pope as Benedict XVI. In March 2005 there were eight cardinals.

The Evangelical (Protestant) Church (EKD) consists of 24 member-churches including seven Lutheran Churches, eight United-Lutheran-Reformed, two Reformed Churches and one Confederation of United member Churches: 'Church of the Union'. Its organs are the Synod, the Church Conference and the Council under the chairmanship of Dr Wolfgang Huber. There are also some 12 Evangelical Free Churches.

Education. Education is compulsory for children aged 6 to 15. After the first four (or six) years at primary school *(Grundschulen)* children attend post-primary *(Hauptschulen)*, secondary modern *(Realschulen)*, grammar *(Gymnasien)*, or comprehensive schools *(Integrierte Gesamtschulen)*. Secondary modern school lasts six years and grammar school nine. Entry to higher education is by the final Grammar School Certificate (*Abitur*—Higher School Certificate). There are also schools for physically disabled children and those with other special needs *(Sonderschulen)*.

In 2002–03 there were 3,225 kindergartens with 54,787 pupils and 3,985 teachers; 17,057 primary schools with 3,144,307 pupils and 188,463 teachers; 3,487 special schools with 429,275 pupils and 69,619 teachers; 10,553 secondary modern schools with 2,745,570 pupils and 173,897 teachers; 3,154 grammar schools with 2,296,724 pupils and 155,142 teachers; 953 comprehensive schools with 619,366 pupils and 47,965 teachers.

In 2002–03 there were 676,131 working teachers, of whom 450,550 were female.

The adult literacy rate in 2001 was at least 99%.

In 2002 total expenditure on education came to €88·39bn. In 2000–01 total expenditure on education came to 4·6% of GNP and represented 9·9% of total government expenditure.

Vocational education is provided in part-time, full-time and advanced vocational schools (*Berufs-, Berufsaufbau-, Berufsfach-* and *Fachschulen,* including *Fachschulen für Technik* and *Schulen des Gesundheitswesens)*. Occupation-related, part-time vocational training of six to 12 hours per week is compulsory for all (including unemployed) up to the age of 18 years or until the completion of the practical vocational training. Full-time vocational schools comprise courses of at least one year. They prepare for commercial and domestic occupations as well as specialized occupations in the field of handicrafts. Advanced full-time vocational schools are attended by pupils over 18. Courses vary from six months to three or more years.

In 2002–03 there were 9,850 full- and part-time vocational schools with 2,699,669 students and 116,800 teachers.

Higher Education. In the winter term of the 2003–04 academic year there were 366 institutes of higher education *(Hochschulen)* with 2,016,231 students, including 100 universities (1,408,871 students), six teacher training colleges (20,214), 16 theological seminaries (2,532), 52 schools of art (31,564), 163 technical colleges (514,315) and 29 management schools (38,735). Only 317,463 students (15·7%) were in their first year.

Health. In 2003 there were 304,117 doctors (368 doctors for every 100,000 people), 64,484 dentists (2002) and 53,691 pharmacists. In 2001 there were 2,240 hospitals with 552,680 beds (67 for every 10,000 people). In 2002 Germany spent 10·9% of its GDP on health, public spending amounting to 78·5% of the total. In 2002 total expenditure on health came to €134·96bn.

Welfare. *Social Health Insurance* (introduced in 1883). Wage-earners and apprentices, salaried employees with an income below a certain limit and social insurance pensioners are compulsorily insured within the state system. Voluntary insurance is also possible.

Benefits: medical treatment, medicines, hospital and nursing care, maternity benefits, death benefits for the insured and their families, sickness payments and out-patients' allowances. Economy measures of Dec. 1992 introduced prescription charges related to recipients' income.

As part of a series of measures to tackle a funding shortfall in the health service, a patient charge of €10 was introduced from Jan. 2004, payable for the first visit only per quarter to a doctor.

50·75m. persons were insured in 2003 (28·95m. compulsorily). Number of cases of incapacity for work (2002) totalled 36·16m., and the number of working days lost were 269·73m. (men) and 224·76m. (women). Total disbursements in 2002 were €134,328m.

Accident Insurance (introduced in 1884). Those insured are all persons in employment or service, apprentices and the majority of the self-employed and the unpaid family workers.

Benefits in the case of industrial injuries and occupational diseases: medical treatment and nursing care, sickness payments, pensions and other payments in cash and in kind, surviving dependants' pensions.

Number of insured in 2002, 57·63m.; number of current pensions, 1,121,741; total disbursements, €9,969m.

Workers' and Employees' Old-Age Insurance Scheme (introduced in 1889). All wage-earners and salaried employees, the members of certain liberal professions and—subject to certain conditions—self-employed craftsmen are compulsorily insured. The insured may voluntarily continue to insure when no longer liable to do so or increase the insurance.

Benefits: measures designed to maintain, improve and restore the earning capacity; pensions paid to persons incapable of work, old age and surviving dependants' pensions.

Number of insured in May 2000, 43·13m. (20·28m. women); number of current pensions (in July 2003), 23·74m.; pensions to widows and widowers, 5·40m. Total disbursements in 2002, €247,456m.

There are also special retirement and unemployment pension schemes for miners and farmers, assistance for war victims and compensation payments to members of German minorities in East European countries expelled after the Second World War and persons who suffered damage because of the war or in connection with the currency reform.

Family Allowances. €28·88bn. were dispensed to 9·12m. recipients (1·04m. foreigners) in 2003 on behalf of 15·16m. children. Paid child care leave is available for three years to mothers or fathers.

Unemployment Allowances. In 2003, 2·02m. persons (0·84m. women) were receiving unemployment benefit and 1·22m. (0·80m. women) earnings-related benefit. Total expenditure on these and similar benefits (e.g. short-working supplement, job creation schemes) was €56·85bn. in 2003. Unemployment assistance was abolished in Jan. 2005 and replaced with a new so-called 'Unemployment benefit II'. The new benefit is no longer tied to the former income of the recipient but is around the same flat-rate level as the social assistance benefit. The time an unemployed person can receive an earnings-related benefit will be reduced to a standard 12 months.

Public Welfare (introduced in 1962). In 2002, €24·65bn. were distributed to 2·77m. recipients (1·55m. women).

Public Youth Welfare. For supervision of foster children, official guardianship, assistance with adoptions and affiliations, social assistance in juvenile courts, educational assistance and correctional education under a court order. A total of €17·11bn. was spent on recipients in 2001.

Pension Reform. A major reform of the German pension system became law on 11 May 2001. The changes entail a cut in the value of the average state pension from 70% to approximately 67% of average final earnings by 2030. There will be incentives in the form of tax concessions and direct payments to encourage individuals to build up supplementary provision by contributing up to 4% of their earnings into private-sector personal pensions. In the long term these could supply up to 40% of overall pension income, with 60% coming from the state as opposed to 85% prior to the changes.

CULTURE

World Heritage Sites. Germany has 30 sites on the UNESCO World Heritage List (date of inscription on the list in brackets): Aachen Cathedral (1978), begun in the 8th century under Charlemagne; Speyer Cathedral (1981), founded in 1030 and constructed in the Romanesque style; Würzburg Residence, with the Court Gardens and Residence Square (1981), an 18th century Baroque palace; Pilgrimage Church of Wies (1983), an 18th century Baroque-Rococo church; Castles of Augustusburg and Falkenlust at Brühl (1984), early examples of 18th century Rococo architecture; St Mary's Cathedral and St Michael's Church at Hildesheim (1985), Romanesque constructions from the 11th century; Roman Monuments in Trier (1986), a Roman colony from the 1st century, and the Cathedral of St Peter and Church of Our Lady; Hanseatic City of Lübeck (1987), founded in the 12th century; Palaces and Parks of Potsdam and Berlin (1990), an eclectic mix of 150 buildings covering 500 hectares built between 1730 and 1916; Abbey and Altenmünster of Lorsch (1992), an example of Carolignian architecture; Mines of Rammelsberg and Historic Town of Goslar (1991), with a well-preserved historic centre; Town of Bamberg (1993), the country's biggest intact historical city core; Maulbronn Monastery Complex (1993), a former Cistercian abbey over 850 years old; Collegiate Church, Castle, and Old Town of Quedlinburg (1994), capital of the East Franconian German Empire; Völklingen Ironworks (1994), a preserved 19th/20th centuries ironworks; Messel Pit Fossil site (1995), containing important fossils from 57m.–36m. BC; Cologne Cathedral (1996), a Gothic masterpiece begun in 1248; Bauhaus and its sites in Weimar and Dessau (1996), buildings of the influential early-20th century architectural movement; Luther Memorials in Eisleben and Wittenberg (1996), including his birthplace, baptism church, and religious sites; Classical Weimar (1998), a cultural epicentre during the 18th and early 19th centuries; Museumsinsel (Museum Island), Berlin (1999), including Altes Museum, Bodemuseum, Neues Museum and Pergamonmuseum; Wartburg Castle (1999), dating from the feudal period and rebuilt in the 19th century—Luther translated the New Testament here; Garden Kingdom of Dessau-Wörlitz (2000), an 18th century landscaped garden in the Enlightenment style; Monastic Island of Reichenau (2000), on Lake Constance, incorporating medieval churches and the remains of an 8th century Benedictine monastery; Zollverein Coal Mine Industrial Complex in Essen (2001), a 20th century mining complex with modernist buildings; Upper Middle Rhine Valley (2002), a 65 km-stretch of one of Europe's most important historical transport conduits; Historic Centres of Stralsund and Wismar (2002), Hanseatic towns; Dresden Elbe Valley (2004); Town Hall and Roland on the Marketplace of Bremen (2004).

In addition, Germany and Poland are jointly responsible for Muskauer Park/Park Muzakowski (2004), a landscaped park astride the Neisse river.

Broadcasting. There are two public service broadcasting companies—ARD (*Arbeitsgemeinschaft der öffentlich-rechtlichen Rundfunkanstalten der Bundesrepublik Deutschland*) and ZDF (*Zweites Deutsches Fernsehen*)—plus many private and regional stations, notably RTL and SAT1. ARD is the co-ordinating body for television and radio. It represents public-right broadcasters and organizes co-operation between them. Deutsche Welle Fernsehen (DW-tv) is the foreign service broadcaster. Most German households now subscribe to cable television. In 2003 there were 36·45m. TV licences. There were 21·8m. cable TV subscribers in 2001.

Public service radio is provided by ARD and ZDF via DeutschlandRadio. Private radio stations also broadcast in the regions. Deutsche Welle (DW-radio) broadcasts overseas. In 2003 there were 41·63m. radio licences.

Cinema. In 2003 there were 4,705 cinemas with a total seating capacity of 889,702. In 2003, 80 feature films were made. A total of 149m. visits to the cinema were made in 2003; gross box office receipts came to €850·0m. in 2003. In 2001 German films took 18% of the national market, up from 10% in 1998.

Press. The daily press is mainly regional. The dailies with the highest circulation are (average figures for Jan.–March 2001): the tabloid *Bild* (Hamburg, 4·40m. copies per day); *Westdeutsche Allgemeine Zeitung* (Essen, 0·56m.); *Süddeutsche Zeitung* (Munich, 0·44m.); and *Frankfurter Allgemeine Zeitung* (0·41m.). Other important opinion leaders are the weeklies *Die Zeit*, *Die Woche* and *Rheinischer Merkur*. *Bild* has the highest circulation of any paper in Europe. In 2000, 355 newspapers and 408 newsstand magazines were published with respective circulations of 24m. and 127m. The seven main Sunday papers sold 4·5m. copies. The total circulation of daily newspapers in Germany is the highest in Europe. 78% of the population over the age of 14 regularly read a daily newspaper. There are also 230 online newspapers. Among magazines the most widely read are *stern* (7·51m. copies per issue according to figures published in July 2001), *Focus* and *Der Spiegel*. In 2003 a total of 61,538 book titles were published.

Tourism. In 2003 there were 53,771 places of accommodation with 2,515,139 beds (including 13,098 hotels with 939,227 beds). 17,299,236 foreign visitors and 88,995,509 tourists resident in Germany spent a total of 315,127,500 nights in holiday accommodation. Berlin is the most visited city with 4,952,798 visitors in 2003, and Bavaria the most visited *Bundesland* with 21,890,555 (4,091,640 visited Munich). More foreign visitors were from the Netherlands (2,167,071) than any other country, with USA second (1,672,263) followed by 1,588,945 visitors from UK. In 2003 tourism brought in €20,318m.

Festivals. The Munich Opera Festival takes place annually in June–July, and the Wagner Festspiele (the Wagner Festival) in Bayreuth is held from late July to the end of Aug. The Oberammergau Passion Play, which takes place every ten years, was last held in 2000. Karneval (Fasching in some areas), in Jan./Feb./March, is a major event in the annual calendar in cities such as Cologne, Munich, Düsseldorf and Mainz. The Berlin Love Parade, which takes place in mid-July, is Europe's second largest street party. Oktoberfest, Munich's famous beer festival which first began in 1810, takes place each year in late Sept. and early Oct. and regularly attracts 7m. visitors.

Libraries. In 2002 there were 10,326 public libraries, seven national libraries and 246 Higher Education libraries; they and other libraries held a combined 338,757,000 volumes. There were 11,453,000 active users in 2002, with 369,671,000 loans.

Theatre and Opera. In 2001–02 there were 151 theatre companies, performing on 721 stages. Audiences totalled 19·29m.

Museums and Galleries. In 2002 there were 4,892 museums which attracted 101,219,000 visitors.

DIPLOMATIC REPRESENTATIVES

Of Germany in the United Kingdom (23 Belgrave Sq., 1 Chesham Place, London, SW1X 8PZ)
Ambassador: Thomas Matussek.

Of the United Kingdom in Germany (Wilhelmstrasse 70, 10117 Berlin)
Ambassador: Sir Peter J. Torry, KCMG.

Of Germany in the USA (4645 Reservoir Rd, NW, Washington, D.C., 20007)
Ambassador: Wolfgang Ischinger.

Of the USA in Germany (Neustädtische Kirchstr. 4, 10117 Berlin)
Ambassador: Daniel Coats.

Of Germany to the United Nations
Ambassador: Gunter Pleuger.

FURTHER READING

Statistisches Bundesamt. *Statistisches Jahrbuch für die Bundesrepublik Deutschland; Wirtschaft und Statistik* (monthly, from 1949); *Das Arbeitsgebiet der Bundesstatistik* (latest issue 1997; Abridged English version: *Survey of German Federal Statistics*).

Ardagh, J., *Germany and the Germans*. 3rd ed. London, 1996
Balfour, M., *Germany: the Tides of Power.* Routledge, London, 1992
Bark, D. L. and Gress, D. R., *A History of West Germany, 1945–1991.* 2nd ed. 2 vols. Oxford, 1993
Betz, H. G., *Postmodern Politics in Germany.* London, 1991
Blackbourn, D., *Fontana History of Germany, 1780–1918: The Long Nineteenth Century.* Fontana, London, 1997
Blackbourn, D. and Eley, G., *The Peculiarities of German History*. Oxford University Press, 1985
Carr, W., *A History of Germany, 1815–1990.* 4th ed. Edward Arnold, London, 1995
Childs, D., *Germany in the 20th Century.* London, 1991.—*The Stasi: The East German Intelligence and Security Service.* Macmillan, London, 1999
Dennis, M., *The German Democratic Republic: Politics, Economics and Society.* Pinter, London, 1987
Edinger, L. J., *West German Politics*. Columbia Univ. Press, New York, 1986
Fulbrook, Mary, *A Concise History of Germany.* CUP, 1991.—*The Divided Nation: A History of Germany, 1918–1990.* CUP, 1992.—*German National Identity After the Holocaust.* Polity, Oxford, 1999.—*Interpretation of the Two Germanies, 1945–1997*. Macmillan, London, 1999
Glees, A., *Reinventing Germany: German Political Development since 1945*. Berg, Oxford, 1996
Heneghan, Tom, *Unchained Eagle: Germany After the Wall.* Reuters, London, 2000
Huelshoff, M. G., *et al.*, (eds.) *From Bundesrepublik to Deutschland: German Politics after Reunification.* Michigan Univ. Press, 1993
Kielinger, T., *Crossroads and Roundabouts, Junctions in German-British Relations*. Bonn, 1997
Langewiesche, Dieter, *Liberalism in Germany.* Macmillan, London, 1999
Loth, W., *Stalin's Unwanted Child—The Soviet Union, the German Question and the Founding of the GDR*. St Martin's Press, New York, 1998
Maier, C. S., *Dissolution: The Crisis of Communism and the End of East Germany*. Princeton Univ. Press, N.J., 1997
Marsh, D., *The New Germany: At the Crossroads.* London, 1990
Merkl, Peter H. (ed.) *The Federal Republic of Germany at Fifty: The End of a Century of Turmoil.* Macmillan, London, 1999
Müller, Jan-Werner, *Another Country: German Intellectuals, Unification and National Identity.* Yale, New Haven (CT) and London, 2000
Neville, P., *Appeasing Hitler: The Diplomacy of Sir Neville Henderson*. Macmillan, London, 1999
Nicholls, A. J., *The Bonn Republic: West German Democracy, 1945–1990*. Addison-Wesley, Harlow, 1998
Olsen, Jonathan, *Nature and Nationalism: Right-wing Ecology and the Politics of Identity in Contemporary Germany.* Macmillan, London, 2000
Orlow, D., *A History of Modern Germany, 1871 to the Present.* 4th ed. Prentice Hall, New York, 1994
Padgett, Stephen, Paterson, William E. and Smith, Gordon, (eds.) *Developments in German Politics 3.* Palgrave Macmillan, Basingstoke, 2003
Parkes, K. S., *Understanding Contemporary Germany*. Routledge, London, 1996
Pulzer, P., *German Politics, 1945–1995*. OUP, 1995
Sa'adah, Anne, *Germany's Second Chance: Trust, Justice and Democratization.* Harvard Univ. Press, 1999
Schmidt, H., *Handeln für Deutschland.* Berlin, 1993
Schwartz, H-P., translator, Willmot, L., *Konrad Adenauer Vol 1: From the German Empire to the Federal Republic, 1876–1952*. Berghahn Books, Oxford and New York, 1995
Schwartz, H-P., translator, Willmot, L., *Konrad Adenauer Vol 2: The Statesman: 1952–1967*. Berghahn Books, Oxford and New York, 1997
Schweitzer, C.-C., Karsten, D., Spencer, R., Cole, R. T., Kommers, D. P. and Nicholls, A. J. (eds.) *Politics and Government in Germany, 1944–1994: Basic Documents*. 2nd ed. Berghahn Books, Oxford, 1995
Sereny, Gitta, *The German Trauma: Experiences and Reflections, 1938–99.* Penguin Press, London, 2000
Sinn, G. and Sinn, H.-W., *Jumpstart: the Economic Reunification of Germany.* MIT Press, Boston (MA), 1993
Smyser, W. R., *The Economy of United Germany: Colossus at the Crossroads.* New York, 1992.—*From Yalta to Berlin: The Cold War Struggle over Germany.* St Martin's, New York and Macmillan, London, 1999
Speirs, Ronald and Breuilly, John, (eds.) *Germany's Two Unifications: Anticipations, Experiences, Responses.* Palgrave Macmillan, Basingstoke, 2005
Stürmer, M., *Die Grenzen der Macht.* Berlin, 1992
Taylor, R., *Berlin and its Culture*. Yale Univ. Press, 1997
Thompson, W. C., *et al.*, *Historical Dictionary of Germany*. Scarecrow Press, Metuchen (NJ), 1995

Turner, Barry, (ed.) *Germany Profiled.* Macmillan, London, 1999
Turner, H. A., *Germany from Partition to Reunification.* 2nd ed. [of *Two Germanies since 1945*]. Yale Univ. Press, 1993
Tusa, A., *The Last Division – A History of Berlin, 1945–1989.* Perseus Books, Reading, Mass., 1997
Wallace, I., *East Germany: the German Democratic Republic.* [Bibliography] ABC-Clio, Oxford and Santa Barbara (CA), 1987
Watson, A., *The Germans: Who Are They Now?* 2nd ed. London, 1994
Wende, Peter, *History of Germany.* Palgrave Macmillan, Basingstoke, 2004
Williams, C., *Adenauer: The Father of the New Germany.* Little, Brown, London, 2000

Other more specialized titles are listed under CONSTITUTION AND GOVERNMENT *and* BANKING AND FINANCE, *above.*

National statistical office: Statistisches Bundesamt, D-65189 Wiesbaden, Gustav Stresemann Ring 11. *President:* Johann Hahlen. *Website:* http://www.destatis.de
National libraries: Deutsche Bibliothek, Zeppelinallee 4–8; Frankfurt am Main. *Director:* Elisabeth Niggemann; (Berliner) Staatsbibliothek Preussischer Kulturbesitz, Potsdamer Str. 33, Postfach 1407, D-10785 Berlin. *Director:* Barbara Schneider-Kempf.

THE BUNDESLÄNDER

BADEN-WÜRTTEMBERG

KEY HISTORICAL EVENTS

The *Bundesland* is a combination of former states. Baden (the western part of the present *Bundesland*) became a united margravate in 1771, after being divided as Baden-Baden and Baden-Durlach since 1535; Baden-Baden was predominantly Catholic, and Baden-Durlach predominantly Protestant. The margrave became an ally of Napoleon, ceding land west of the Rhine and receiving northern and southern territory as compensation. In 1805 Baden became a grand duchy and in 1806 a member state of the Confederation of the Rhine, extending from the Main to Lake Constance. In 1815 it was a founder-state of the German Confederation. A constitution was granted by the grand duke in 1818, but later rulers were less liberal and there was revolution in 1848, put down with Prussian help. The grand Duchy was abolished and replaced by a *Bundesland* in 1919.

In 1949 Baden was combined with Württemberg to form three states; the three joined as one in 1952.

Württemberg, having been a duchy since 1495, became a kingdom in 1805 and joined the Confederations as did Baden. A constitution was granted in 1819 and the state remained liberal. In 1866 the king allied himself with Austria against Prussia, but in 1870 joined Prussia in war against France. The liberal monarchy came to an end with the abdication of William II in 1918, and Württemberg became a state of the German Republic. In 1945 the state was divided between Allied occupation authorities but the divisions ended in 1952.

TERRITORY AND POPULATION

Baden-Württemberg comprises 35,752 sq. km, with a population (at 30 June 2004) of 10,706,805 (5,450,845 females, 5,255,960 males).

The *Bundesland* is divided into four administrative regions, nine urban and 35 rural districts, and numbers 1,111 communes. The capital is Stuttgart.

SOCIAL STATISTICS

Statistics for calendar years:

	Live births	*Marriages*	*Divorces*	*Deaths*
2000	106,182	55,422	22,050	95,354
2001	101,366	51,382	22,774	94,096
2002	99,604	51,946	23,794	95,110
2003	97,596	50,693	25,091	97,229

CONSTITUTION AND GOVERNMENT

The *Bundesland* Baden-Württemberg is a merger of Baden, Württemberg-Baden and Württemberg-Hohenzollern. The merger was approved by a plebiscite held on

9 Dec. 1951, when 70% of the population voted in its favour. It has six votes in the Bundesrat.

RECENT ELECTIONS

At the elections to the 128-member Diet of 25 March 2001, turn-out was 62·6%. The Christian Democrats won 63 seats with 44·8% of the vote, the Social Democrats 45 with 33·3%, the Free Democrats 10 with 8·1% and the Greens 10 with 7·7%. The Republicans only received 4·4% of the vote, and therefore won no seats.

CURRENT ADMINISTRATION

Günther Oettinger (CDU) is *Prime Minister.*

Government Website: http://www.baden-wuerttemberg.de

ECONOMY

Performance. GDP in 2003 was €291,204m., which amounted to 14·7% of Germany's total GDP. Manufacturing industries (*Verarbeitendes Gewerbe*) provide around 28·2% of GDP (33·1% in 1991). Real GDP growth in 2003 was –0·2%. Services enterprises account for nearly 61·6% of GDP, compared to 51·8% as recently as 1991.

Banking and Finance. There is a stock exchange in Stuttgart. Turnover of shares and bonds in 2003 was €49·9bn.

ENERGY AND NATURAL RESOURCES

Electricity. Hydro-electric power is a significant source of electricity in the *Bundesland.*

Agriculture. Area and yield of the most important crops:

	Area (in 1,000 ha)			*Yield (in 1,000 tonnes)*		
	2001	*2002*	*2003*	*2001*	*2002*	*2003*
Wheat	218·4	222·6	206·4	1,623·9	1,511·7	1,219·3
Sugarbeet	20·9	22·3	20·6	1,266·0	1,484·4	988·7
Barley	201·5	195·1	201·7	1,121·2	1,058·9	1,021·6
Potatoes	6·8	7·9	6·8	240·2	269·4	183·5
Oats	42·8	41·5	44·0	235·9	204·5	216·9
Rye	10·3	8·9	6·7	57·3	48·0	30·2

Livestock in May 2004 (in thousands): cattle, 1,079·6 (including 385·4 milch cows); pigs, 2,178·9; sheep, 306·0; poultry, 5,061·8 (May 2003).

Forestry. Total area covered by forests is 13,584 sq. km or 38% of the total area.

INDUSTRY

Baden-Württemberg is one of Germany's most industrialized states. In 2003, 8,753 establishments (with 20 or more employees) employed 1,230,227 persons; of these, 271,360 were employed in machine construction (excluding office machines, data processing equipment and facilities); 240,210 in car manufacture; 198,622 in electrical engineering; 20,267 in the textile industry.

Labour. Economically active persons totalled 4,984,000 at the 1%-EU-sample survey of May 2003: 4·42m. were employees and 567,000 were self-employed (including family workers); 1,948,200 were engaged in power supply, mining, manufacturing and building; 979,200 in commerce and transport; 105,000 in agriculture and forestry; 1,951,500 in other industries and services. There were 336,895 unemployed in 2003, a rate of 6·9%.

INTERNATIONAL TRADE

Imports and Exports. Total imports (2003): €83,997m. Total exports: €106,840m., of which €55,729m. went to the EU. Machinery exports totalled €23,616m. and automotive exports €27,224m.

COMMUNICATIONS

Roads. On 1 Jan. 2004 there were 27,416 km of 'classified' roads, comprising 1,028 km of Autobahn, 4,408 km of federal roads, 9,908 km of first-class and 12,072 km of second-class highways. Motor vehicles, at 1 Jan. 2004, numbered 7,384,358, including 6,083,702 passenger cars, 9,635 buses, 299,639 lorries, 337,845 tractors and 555,351 motorcycles.

Civil Aviation. The largest airport in Baden-Württemberg is at Stuttgart, which in 2003 handled 7,418,000 passengers and 17,448 tonnes of freight. There are two further regional airports, 14 helicopter landing fields and numerous smaller airstrips.

Shipping. The harbour in Mannheim is the largest in Baden-Württemberg. In 2003 it handled 7·0m. tonnes of freight, compared to 6·2m. tonnes in Karlsruhe.

SOCIAL INSTITUTIONS

Justice. There are a constitutional court *(Staatsgerichtshof)*, two courts of appeal, 17 regional courts, 108 local courts, a *Bundesland* labour court, nine labour courts, a *Bundesland* social court, eight social courts, a finance court, a higher administrative court *(Verwaltungsgerichtshof)* and four administrative courts.

Religion. On 1 Jan. 2000, 38·7% of the population were Protestants and 43·2% were Roman Catholics.

Education. In 2003–04 there were 2,722 primary schools *(Grund- und Hauptschulen)* with 35,644 teachers and 665,601 pupils; 585 special schools with 10,706 teachers and 55,199 pupils; 462 intermediate schools with 12,762 teachers and 247,412 pupils; 423 high schools with 19,873 teachers and 313,302 pupils; 46 *Freie Waldorf* schools with 1,505 teachers and 21,529 pupils. Other general schools had 560 teachers and 10,248 pupils in total; there were also 762 vocational schools with 402,716 pupils. There were 38 *Fachhochschulen* (colleges of engineering and others) with 70,841 students in winter term 2003–04.

In the winter term 2003–04 there were nine universities (Freiburg, 20,663 students; Heidelberg, 23,492; Konstanz, 8,891; Tübingen, 20,801; Karlsruhe, 16,077; Stuttgart, 19,217; Hohenheim, 5,070; Mannheim, 12,135; Ulm, 6,767); six teacher-training colleges with 20,214 students; five colleges of music with 2,702 students; and three colleges of fine arts with 1,404 students.

Health. In 2003 the 320 hospitals in Baden-Württemberg had 63,366 beds and treated 1,954,286 patients. The average occupancy rate was 75·8%.

Welfare. In 2002 there were 223,000 persons receiving benefits of all kinds. 2002 expenditure on social welfare was €2,116m.

CULTURE

Tourism. In 2003, 13,096,338 visitors spent a total of 37,069,432 nights in Baden-Württemberg. Only Bavaria of the German *Bundesländer* recorded more overnight stays.

FURTHER READING

Statistical Information: Statistisches Landesamt Baden-Württemberg (P.O.B. 10 60 33, 70049 Stuttgart) (*President:* Dr Gisela Meister-Scheufelen), publishes: *Statistisches Monatsheft* (monthly); *Statistisch-prognostischer Bericht* (latest issue 2004); *Statistisches Taschenbuch* (latest issue 2004).

State libraries: Württembergische Landesbibliothek, Konrad-Adenauer-Str. 8, 70173 Stuttgart. Badische Landesbibliothek Karlsruhe, Erbprinzenstr. 15, 76133 Karlsruhe.

BAVARIA

Bayern

KEY HISTORICAL EVENTS

Bavaria was ruled by the Wittelsbach family from 1180. The duchy remained Catholic after the Reformation, which made it a natural ally of Austria and the Habsburg Emperors.

The present boundaries were reached during the Napoleonic wars, and Bavaria became a kingdom in 1806. Despite the granting of a constitution and parliament, radical feeling forced the abdication of King Ludwig I in 1848. Maximilian II was followed by Ludwig II who allied himself with Austria against Prussia in 1866, but was reconciled with Prussia and entered the German Empire in 1871. In 1918 the King Ludwig III abdicated. The first years of republican government were filled with unrest, attempts at the overthrow of the state by both communist and right-wing groups culminating in an unsuccessful coup by Adolf Hitler in 1923.

The state of Bavaria included the Palatinate from 1214 until 1945, when it was taken from Bavaria and added to the Rhineland. The present *Bundesland* of Bavaria was formed in 1946. Munich became capital of Bavaria in the reign of Albert IV (1467–1508) and remains capital of the *Bundesland*.

TERRITORY AND POPULATION

Bavaria has an area of 70,549 sq. km. The capital is Munich. There are seven administrative regions, 25 urban districts, 71 rural districts, 222 unadopted areas and 2,056 communes, 991 of which are members of 314 administrative associations (as of 31 Dec. 2003). The population (31 Dec. 2003) numbered 12,423,386 (6,079,009 males, 6,344,377 females).

SOCIAL STATISTICS

Statistics for calendar years:

	Live births	*Marriages*	*Divorces*	*Deaths*
2000	120,765	63,038	27,250	118,846
2001	115,964	60,226	28,347	117,930
2002	113,818	60,686	29,503	119,755
2003	111,536	59,009	29,992	121,778

CONSTITUTION AND GOVERNMENT

The Constituent Assembly, elected on 30 June 1946, passed a constitution on the lines of the democratic constitution of 1919, but with greater emphasis on state rights; this was agreed upon by the Christian Social Union (CSU) and the Social Democrats (SPD). Bavaria has six seats in the Bundesrat. The CSU replaces the Christian Democratic Party in Bavaria.

RECENT ELECTIONS

At the Diet elections on 21 Sept. 2003 the CSU won 124 seats with 60·7% of votes cast, the SPD 41 with 19·6% and the Greens 15 with 7·7%. The Free Democratic Party took 2·6% but won no seats. Turn-out was 57·1%.

CURRENT ADMINISTRATION

The *Prime Minister* is Dr Edmund Stoiber (CSU).

Government Website: http://www.bayern.de

ECONOMY

Performance. Real GDP growth in 2003 was 0·2%, compared to the national growth rate of –0·1%. Real GDP growth in 2004 was 2·3%, which was the highest in Germany (along with Saxony), compared to the national growth rate of 1·7%.

ENERGY AND NATURAL RESOURCES

Agriculture. Area and yield of the most important products:

	Area (in 1,000 ha)			*Yield (in 1,000 tonnes)*		
	2001	*2002*	*2003*	*2001*	*2002*	*2003*
Sugarbeet	71·6	74·1	71·7	4,460·9	5,272·8	3,979·5
Wheat	465·8	468·1	435·9	3,269·4	3,103·0	2,559·7
Barley	458·2	451·2	466·7	2,579·7	2,382·6	2,174·2
Potatoes	50·0	51·6	51·0	1,811·1	2,094·6	1,576·4
Oats	51·9	51·4	57·4	249·5	217·0	262·6
Rye	49·5	42·4	31·1	249·2	212·1	120·8

Livestock, 2003: 3,780,900 cattle (including 1,334,100 milch cows); 82,200 horses (2001); 478,400 sheep; 3,780,100 pigs; 9,599,700 poultry (2001).

INDUSTRY

In 2003, 7,934 establishments (with 20 or more employees) employed 1,180,751 persons; of these, 195,182 were employed in the manufacture of machinery and equipment, 180,087 in the manufacture of motor vehicles and 34,745 in the manufacture of textiles and textile products.

Labour. The economically active persons totalled 5,827,000 at the 1% sample survey of the microcensus of 2004. Of the total, 5,046,000 were employees, 693,000 were self-employed, 88,000 were unpaid family workers; 1,985,000 worked in power supply, mining, manufacturing and building; 1,273,000 in commerce, hotels and restaurants, and transport; 175,000 in agriculture and forestry; 2,394,000 in other services.

COMMUNICATIONS

Roads. There were, on 1 Jan. 2004, 41,769 km of 'classified' roads, comprising 2,299 km of Autobahn, 6,780 km of federal roads, 13,943 km of first-class and 18,748 km of second-class highways. Number of motor vehicles on 1 Jan. 2004 was 9,053,383, including 7,195,111 passenger cars, 379,419 lorries, 14,709 buses and 736,537 motorcycles.

Civil Aviation. Munich airport handled 23,954,387 passengers (15,547,073 on international flights) and 141,100 tonnes of freight in 2003. Nuremberg handled 3,212,799 (2,039,317 on international flights) and 10,537 tonnes of freight in 2003.

SOCIAL INSTITUTIONS

Justice. There are a constitutional court *(Verfassungsgerichtshof)*, a supreme *Bundesland* court *(Oberstes Landesgericht)*, three courts of appeal, 22 regional courts, 72 local courts, two *Bundesland* labour courts, 11 labour courts, a *Bundesland* social court, seven social courts, two finance courts, a higher administrative court *(Verwaltungsgerichtshof)* and six administrative courts. The supreme *Bundesland* court *(Oberstes Landesgericht)* is scheduled to be abolished by 30 June 2006. Since 1 Jan. 2005 new cases have been transferred to the courts of appeal.

Religion. At the census of 25 May 1987 there were 67·2% Roman Catholics and 23·9% Protestants.

Education. In 2003–04 there were 2,870 primary schools with 48,614 teachers and 820,363 pupils; 373 special schools with 8,175 teachers and 62,356 pupils; 343 intermediate schools with 12,064 teachers and 212,010 pupils; 405 high schools with 22,794 teachers and 341,296 pupils; 231 part-time vocational schools with 8,208 teachers and 292,617 pupils, including 49 special part-time vocational schools with 1,061 teachers and 14,973 pupils; 760 full-time vocational schools with 5,252 teachers and 70,568 pupils including 343 schools for public health occupations with 1,715 teachers and 20,277 pupils; 357 advanced full-time vocational schools with 2,055 teachers and 26,765 pupils; 130 vocational high schools *(Berufsoberschulen, Fachoberschulen)* with 2,389 teachers and 39,302 pupils.

In 2003–04 there were 12 universities with 171,997 students (Augsburg, 14,181; Bamberg, 8,153; Bayreuth, 8,726; Eichstätt, 4,447; Erlangen-Nürnberg, 23,161; München, 46,203; Passau, 8,002; Regensburg, 17,215; Würzburg, 18,183; the Technical University of München, 19,887; München, University of the Federal Armed Forces *(Universität der Bundeswehr)*, 2,903; the college of politics, München, 936; plus the college of philosophy, München, 447, and two philosophical-theological colleges with 209 students in total (Benediktbeuern, 92; Neuendettelsau, 117). There were also five colleges of music, two colleges of fine arts and one college of television and film, with 3,468 students in total; 20 vocational colleges *(Fachhochschulen)* with 68,702 students including one for the civil service *(Bayerische Beamtenfachhochschule)* with 3,607 students.

Welfare. In Dec. 2003 there were 226,475 persons receiving benefits of all kinds.

CULTURE

Tourism. In June 2003 there were 14,019 places of accommodation (with nine beds or more) providing beds for 559,243 people. In 2003 they received 21,890,555 guests of whom 4,240,774 were foreigners. They stayed an average of 3·2 nights each, totalling 69,325,984 nights (8,873,677 nights stayed by foreign visitors).

Festivals. Oktoberfest, Munich's famous beer festival, takes place each year from the penultimate Saturday in Sept. through to the first Sunday in Oct. (extended to

3 Oct. if the last Sunday of the festival falls on 1 or 2 Oct.). There were 5·9m. visitors at the 171st Oktoberfest in 2004.

FURTHER READING

Statistical Information: Bayerisches Landesamt für Statistik und Datenverarbeitung, Neuhauser Str. 8, 80331 Munich. *President:* Dr Peter Bauer. It publishes: *Statistisches Jahrbuch für Bayern.* 1894 ff.—*Bayern in Zahlen.* Monthly (from Jan. 1947).—*Zeitschrift des Bayerischen Statistischen Landesamts.* July 1869–1943; 1948 ff.—*Beiträge zur Statistik Bayerns.* 1850 ff.—*Statistische Berichte.* 1951 ff.—*Kreisdaten.* 1972–2001 (from 2003 incorporated in *Statistisches Jahrbuch für Bayern*).—*Gemeindedaten.* 1973 ff.

State Library: Bayerische Staatsbibliothek, Munich. *Director General:* Dr Hermann Leskien.

BERLIN

KEY HISTORICAL EVENTS

After the end of World War II, Berlin was divided into four occupied sectors, each with a military governor from one of the victorious Allied Powers (the USA, the Soviet Union, Britain and France). In March 1948 the USSR withdrew from the Allied Control Council and in June blockaded West Berlin until May 1949. In response, the allies flew food and other supplies into the city in what became known as the Berlin Airlift. On 30 Nov. 1948 a separate municipal government was set up in the Soviet sector which led to the political division of the city. In contravention of the special Allied status agreed for the city, East Berlin became 'Capital of the GDR' in 1949 and thus increasingly integrated into the GDR as a whole. In West Berlin, the formal authority of the western allies lasted until 1990.

On 17 June 1953 the protest by workers in East Berlin against political oppression and economic hardship was suppressed by Soviet military forces. To stop refugees, the east German government erected the Berlin Wall to seal off West Berlin's borders on 13 Aug. 1961.

The Berlin Wall was breached on 9 Nov. 1989 as the regime in the GDR bowed to the internal pressure which had been building for months. East and West Berlin were amalgamated on the re-unification of Germany in Oct. 1990. In April 1994 the *Bundesland* governments of Berlin and Brandenburg agreed to merge the two *Bundesländer* in 1999 or 2002, subject to the approval of their respective parliaments, and of their electorates in referendums held in May 1996. In Berlin 53·4% of votes were cast in favour, but in Brandenburg 62·8% were against. A further referendum on the proposed merger is likely to take place in the next few years.

With the move of the national government, the parliament (Bundestag), and the federal organ of the *Bundesländer* (Bundesrat) in 1999, Berlin is once again a capital city.

TERRITORY AND POPULATION

The area is 891·75 sq. km. Population, 31 Dec. 2003, 3,388,477 (1,737,274 females), including 447,325 foreign nationals; density, 3,799·8 per sq. km.

SOCIAL STATISTICS

Statistics for calendar years:

	Live births	*Marriages*	*Divorces*	*Deaths*
1999	29,856	14,635	10,001	34,996
2000	29,695	14,119	9,631	33,335
2001	28,624	12,903	8,731	32,826
2002	28,801	12,800	9,322	33,492
2003	28,723	12,390	10,102	33,146

CONSTITUTION AND GOVERNMENT

According to the constitutions of Sept. 1950 and Oct. 1995, Berlin is simultaneously a *Bundesland* of the Federal Republic and a city. It is governed by a House of Representatives (of at least 130 members); executive power is vested in a Senate, consisting of the Governing Mayor, two Mayors and not more than eight senators. Since 1992 adherence to the constitution has been watched over by a Constitutional Court.

After a proposed merger was rejected by Brandenburg in the 1996 referendum, a Joint Berlin-Brandenburg Co-operation Council was set up.

Berlin has four seats in the Bundesrat.

RECENT ELECTIONS

In Dec. 1999 a CDU–SPD coalition government was formed, but the 'grand coalition' that had held power for more than ten years collapsed on 7 June 2001. The Social Democrats announced their withdrawal after the authorities had accumulated huge debts. At the elections of 21 Oct. 2001 turn-out was 68·1%. The Social Democratic Party (SPD) won 44 seats with 29·7% of votes cast; the Christian Democratic Union (CDU) 35, with 23·8%; the Party of Democratic Socialism (former Communists) 33, with 22·6%; the Free Democratic Party 15, with 9·9%; and the Greens 14, with 9·1%. Initially the SPD had coalition talks with the Free Democratic Party and the Greens, but these broke down. Thus the SPD formed a coalition with the Party of Democratic Socialism, the successor to the former German Democratic Republic's Communist Party, who thereby had their first share of power in Berlin since the fall of the Wall.

CURRENT ADMINISTRATION

The *Governing Mayor* is Klaus Wowereit (SPD).

Government Website: http://www.berlin.de

ECONOMY

Berlin's real GDP growth was –1·3% in 2003.

INDUSTRY

In 2003 there were 919 industrial concerns employing 106,832 people. The main industries in terms of percentage of the labour force employed were: electronics, 27·8%; paper, printing and publishing, 13·7%; food and tobacco, 12·5%; chemicals, 11·1%; machine-building, 10·9%; vehicle production, 8·6%; metallurgy, 7·9%.

Labour. In 2003 the workforce was 1,514,000. There were 306,462 persons registered unemployed in 2003 and 5,324 on short time. An average of 8,279 jobs were available at any one time in 2003. The unemployment rate in 2003 was 18·1%.

COMMUNICATIONS

Roads. On 1 Jan. 2004 there were 5,328·7 km of roads (251·4 km of 'classified' roads, made up of 68·6 km of Autobahn and 182·8 km of federal roads). In Jan. 2004, 1,427,966 motor vehicles were registered, including 1,226,299 passenger cars, 82,513 lorries, 2,508 buses and 92,611 motorcycles. There were 127,986 road accidents in 2003 of which 15,029 involved badly damaged vehicles or injured persons, of whom there were 16,770.

Civil Aviation. 187,023 flights were made from Berlin's three airports—Tegel, Tempelhof and Schönefeld—in 2003, carrying a total of 13,124,186 passengers.

SOCIAL INSTITUTIONS

Justice. There are a court of appeal *(Kammergericht)*, a regional court, nine local courts, a *Bundesland* Labour court, a labour court, a *Bundesland* social court, a social court, a higher administrative court, an administrative court and a finance court.

Religion. In Dec. 2003 membership and number of places of worship for major religions was as follows:

Religion	*Members*	*Places of Worship*
Protestant	773,971	461[1]
Roman Catholic	307,619	171
Jewish	12,211	8
Muslim	208,829	106[1]

[1]2001.

Education. In the autumn of 2003 there were 348,148 pupils attending schools. There were 450 primary schools with 149,149 pupils, 60 schools for practical education with 14,948 pupils, 99 special schools with 13,738 pupils, 84 secondary modern schools with 30,056 pupils, 121 grammar schools with 86,742 pupils and 64 comprehensive schools with 49,919 pupils. In 2002–03 there were two universities and one technical university, four arts colleges and 11 technical colleges. There were an estimated 143,540 students in higher education.

Health. In 2003 there were 69 hospitals with 20,991 beds, 6,737 doctors, 3,108 dentists and 872 pharmacies.

CULTURE

Tourism. In 2003 Berlin had 560 places of accommodation providing 68,779 beds for 4,952,798 visitors.

FURTHER READING

Statistical Information: The Statistisches Landesamt Berlin was founded in 1862 (Alt-Friedrichsfelde 60, 10315 Berlin (Lichtenberg)). *Director:* Prof. Dr Ulrike Rockmann. It publishes: *Statistisches Jahrbuch* (from 1867): *Berliner Statistik* (monthly, from 1947).—*100 Jahre Berliner Statistik* (1962). *Website (German only):* http://www.statistik-berlin.de

Read, A., and Fisher, D., *Berlin, Biography of a City*. London, 1994
Taylor, R., *Berlin and its Culture*. London, 1997
Wallace, Ian, *Berlin.* [Bibliography] ABC-Clio, Oxford and Santa Barbara (CA), 1993

State Library: Zentral- und Landesbibliothek, Blücherplatz 1, D-10961 Berlin. *Director:* Dr Claudia Lux.

BRANDENBURG

KEY HISTORICAL EVENTS

For the proposed merger with Berlin *see* BERLIN: Key Historical Events.

Brandenburg surrounds the new capital city of Germany, Berlin, but the people of the state voted against the recommendations of the Berlin House of Representatives and the Brandenburg State Parliament that the two states should merge around the year 2000. The state capital, Potsdam, is the ancient city of the Emperor Frederic II 'The Great' who transformed the garrison town of his father Frederic I 'The Soldier' into an elegant city.

TERRITORY AND POPULATION

The area is 29,477 sq. km. Population on 31 Dec. 2003 was 2,574,521 (1,301,523 females). There are four urban districts, 14 rural districts and 438 communes (31 Dec. 2003). The capital is Potsdam.

SOCIAL STATISTICS

Statistics for calendar years:

	Live births	*Marriages*	*Divorces*	*Deaths*
2000	18,444	9,804	6,010	26,068
2001	17,692	9,774	6,043	25,889
2002	17,704	9,650	5,829	26,494
2003	17,970	9,974	6,107	26,862

CONSTITUTION AND GOVERNMENT

The *Bundesland* was reconstituted on former GDR territory on 14 Oct. 1990. Brandenburg has four seats in the Bundesrat and 16 in the Bundestag.

After a proposed merger was rejected by Brandenburg in the 1996 referendum, a Joint Berlin-Brandenburg Co-operation Council was set up.

At a referendum on 14 June 1992, 93·5% of votes cast were in favour of a new constitution guaranteeing direct democracy and the right to work and housing.

RECENT ELECTIONS

At the Diet elections on 19 Sept. 2004 the Social Democrats (SPD) won 33 seats with 31·9% of the vote; the Party of Democratic Socialism (PDS, former Communists) 29, with 28·0%; the Christian Democrats (CDU) 20, with 19·4%; the extreme right-wing German People's Union (DVU) 6, with 6·1%. Turn-out was 56·6%.

CURRENT ADMINISTRATION

The *Prime Minister* is Matthias Platzeck (SPD).

Government Website: http://www.brandenburg.de

ECONOMY

Performance. GDP in 2003 was €45,010m. (nominal).

ENERGY AND NATURAL RESOURCES

Electricity. Power stations in Brandenburg produced 36,861m. kWh in 2003. A minimal amount was produced from hydro-electric power.

Agriculture. Area and yield of the most important crops:

	Area (in 1,000 ha)			*Yield (in 1,000 tonnes)*		
	2001	*2002*	*2003*	*2001*	*2002*	*2003*
Wheat	131·5	139·2	145·4	858·8	828·8	574·3
Rye	253·2	231·0	170·9	1,350·8	945·6	504·2
Sugarbeet	11·3	12·1	11·2	561·0	597·2	465·3
Potatoes	12·3	11·5	11·4	380·2	345·5	303·8
Barley	84·9	78·2	82·9	547·8	375·2	245·4
Rape	99·6	111·3	112·3	330·0	296·0	223·6
Oats	15·8	16·2	20·2	63·8	55·7	42·2

Livestock on 3 May 2003: cattle, 614,337 (including 181,472 milch cows); pigs, 769,084; sheep, 140,287; horses, 17,633; poultry (2001), 7,452,804.

INDUSTRY

In 2003, 1,129 establishments (20 or more employees) in the mining and manufacturing industries employed 86,858 persons, the main areas being: vehicle construction (12,318); the food industry (10,619); manufacturing of metal products (9,062); machine construction (7,124); glassworks, ceramics, processing stones and earthenware (5,653); chemical industries (4,828); and mining and quarrying (4,759). There were 771 companies (with 20 or more employees) in the building industry, employing 32,644 persons.

Labour. In April 2003 at the 1%-sample of the microcensus, 1,117,100 persons were economically active, of which 557,600 white-collar and 379,000 manual workers, 108,300 self-employed and family assistants, and 72,000 civil servants. At 31 Dec. 2003 there were 244,332 unemployed persons (19·8%).

INTERNATIONAL TRADE

Imports and Exports. Total imports (2003): €5,507m. Total exports: €5,077m.

COMMUNICATIONS

Roads. On 1 Jan. 2004 there were 1,670,470 registered vehicles including 1,407,645 passenger cars.

SOCIAL INSTITUTIONS

Education. In 2003–04 there were 1,005 schools providing general education (including special schools) with 277,526 pupils and 64 vocational schools with 76,154 pupils.

In the winter term 2003–04 there were three universities and ten colleges with 39,614 students.

CULTURE

Tourism. In 2003 there were 1,492 places of accommodation (with nine or more beds), including 483 hotels, providing a total of 77,878 beds (31 July 2003). 2,956,091 visitors spent a total of 8,452,025 nights in Brandenburg in 2003.

FURTHER READING

Statistical office: Landesbetrieb für Datenverarbeitung und Statistik Land Brandenburg, Dortustrasse 46, D-14467 Potsdam. It publishes *Statistisches Jahrbuch Land Brandenburg* (since 1991). *Website (German only):* http://www.lds-bb.de/sixcms/list.php/lds

BREMEN

Freie Hansestadt Bremen

KEY HISTORICAL EVENTS

The state is dominated by the Free City of Bremen and its port, Bremerhaven. In 1815, when it joined the German Confederation, Bremen was an autonomous city and Hanse port with important Baltic trade. In 1827 the expansion of trade inspired the founding of Bremerhaven on land ceded by Hanover at the confluence of the Geest and Weser rivers. Further expansion followed the founding of the Norddeutscher Lloyd Shipping Company in 1857. Merchant shipping, associated trade and fishing were dominant until 1940 but there was diversification in the post-war years. In 1939 Bremerhaven was absorbed by the Hanoverian town of Wesermünde. The combined port was returned to the jurisdiction of Bremen in 1947.

TERRITORY AND POPULATION

The area of the *Bundesland*, consisting of the two urban districts and ports of Bremen and Bremerhaven, is 404 sq. km. Population, 31 Dec. 2003, 663,129 (320,815 males, 342,314 females).

SOCIAL STATISTICS

Statistics for calendar years:

	Live births	*Marriages*	*Divorces*	*Deaths*
2000	6,070	3,275	1,814	7,638
2001	5,831	3,153	1,805	7,473
2002	5,484	3,130	1,742	7,668
2003	5,577	3,094	1,797	7,658

CONSTITUTION AND GOVERNMENT

Political power is vested in the 100-member House of Burgesses *(Bürgerschaft)* which appoints the executive, called the Senate. Bremen has three seats in the Bundesrat.

RECENT ELECTIONS

At the elections of 25 May 2003 the Social Democratic Party won 40 seats with 42·3% of votes cast; the Christian Democratic Union 29 with 29·9%; the Greens 12 with 12·8%; the Free Democratic Party 1 with 4·2%; and the German People's Union 1 with 2·3%. The *Partei Rechtsstaatlicher Offensive* took 4·3% of the vote but secured no seats. Turn-out was 61·4%.

CURRENT ADMINISTRATION

The Burgomaster is Dr Henning Scherf (Social Democrat).

Government Website: http://www.bremen.de

ENERGY AND NATURAL RESOURCES

Agriculture. Agricultural area comprised (2001) 11,741 ha. Livestock (2 May 1999): 12,612 cattle (including 3,502 milch cows); 1,792 pigs; 301 sheep; 1,099 horses; 10,866 poultry.

INDUSTRY

In 2002, 355 establishments (20 or more employees) employed 64,005 persons; of these, 24,891 were employed in the production of cars and car parts and other vehicles; 5,388 were employed in machine construction; 3,524 in electrical engineering; 1,996 in shipbuilding (except naval engineering); 1,278 in coffee and tea processing.

Labour. The economically active persons totalled 276,000 at the microcensus of April 2001. Of the total, 248,000 were employees, 26,000 self-employed; 83,000 in commerce, trade and communications, 68,000 in production industries, 122,000 in other industries and services.

COMMUNICATIONS

Roads. On 1 Jan. 2003 there were 98 km of 'classified' roads, of which 59 km were Autobahn and 39 km federal roads. Registered motor vehicles on 1 Jan. 2003 numbered 339,583, including 292,885 passenger cars, 18,433 lorries, 520 buses, 2,918 tractors and 19,648 motorcycles.

Civil Aviation. Bremen airport handled 1,639,834 passengers (1,004,261 on international flights) in 2003.

Shipping. Vessels entered in 2002, 8,911 of 136,878,644 GRT; cleared, 8,811 of 135,989,781 GRT. Sea traffic, 1999, incoming 21,066,000 tonnes; outgoing, 14,970,000 tonnes.

SOCIAL INSTITUTIONS

Justice. There are a constitutional court *(Staatsgerichtshof)*, a court of appeal, a regional court, three local courts, a *Bundesland* labour court, two labour courts, a *Bundesland* social court, a finance court, a higher administrative court and an administrative court.

Religion. At the census of 25 May 1987, 61% of the population were Protestants and 10% Roman Catholics.

Education. In 2003 there were 386 new system schools with 5,000 teachers and 70,437 pupils; 22 part-time vocational schools with 17,058 pupils; 24 full-time vocational schools with 2,603 pupils; four advanced vocational schools (including institutions for the training of technicians) with 667 pupils; ten schools for public health occupations with 780 pupils. In 1999 there were 27 special schools with 668 teachers and 2,709 pupils.

In the winter term 2002–03, 20,064 students were enrolled at the University of Bremen and 357 at the International University of Bremen. In addition to the universities there were four other colleges in 2002–03 with 10,164 students.

CULTURE

Tourism. Bremen had 89 places of accommodation providing 9,192 beds for 713,964 visitors in 2003.

FURTHER READING

Statistical Information: Statistisches Landesamt Bremen (An der Weide 14–16, P. B. 101309, D-28195 Bremen), founded in 1850. *Director:* Reg. Dir. Jürgen Dinse. Its current publications include: *Statistisches Jahrbuch Bremen* (from 1992).—*Statistische Mitteilungen* (from 1948).—*Statistische Monatsberichte* (from 1954).—*Statistische Berichte* (from 1956).—*Statistisches Handbuch Bremen (1950–60,* 1961; *1960–64,* 1967; *1965–69,* 1971; *1970–74,* 1975; *1975–80*, 1982; *1981–85,* 1987).—*Bremen im statistischen Zeitvergleich 1950–1976.* 1977.—*Bremen in Zahlen,* 2004.

State and University Library: Bibliotheksstr., D-28359 Bremen. *Director:* Annette Rath-Beckmann.

HAMBURG

Freie und Hansestadt Hamburg

KEY HISTORICAL EVENTS

Hamburg was a free Hanse town owing nominal allegiance to the Holy Roman Emperor until 1806. In 1815 it became part of the German Confederation, sharing a seat in the Federal Diet with Lübeck, Bremen and Frankfurt. During the Empire it retained its autonomy. By 1938 it had become the third largest port in the world and its territory was extended by the cession of land (three urban and 27 rural districts) from Prussia. After World War II, Hamburg became a *Bundesland* of the Federal Republic with its 1938 boundaries.

TERRITORY AND POPULATION

Total area, 755·3 sq. km (2003), including the islands Neuwerk and Scharhörn (7·6 sq. km). Population (31 Dec. 2003), 1,734,100 (842,600 males, 891,500 females). The *Bundesland* forms a single urban district (*Stadtstaat)* with seven administrative subdivisions.

SOCIAL STATISTICS

Statistics for calendar years:

	Live births	*Marriages*	*Divorces*	*Deaths*
2000	16,159	7,865	4,645	18,210
2001	15,786	7,020	4,328	17,869
2002	15,707	6,999	4,560	18,424
2003	15,916	6,959	4,989	18,072

CONSTITUTION AND GOVERNMENT

The constitution of 6 June 1952 vests the supreme power in the House of Burgesses *(Bürgerschaft)* of 121 members. The executive is in the hands of the Senate, whose members are elected by the Bürgerschaft. Hamburg has three seats in the Bundesrat.

RECENT ELECTIONS

The elections of 29 Feb. 2004 had the following results: Christian Democrats, 63 seats with 47·2% of votes cast; Social Democrats, 41 with 30·5%; the Greens, 17 with 12·3%; Pro DM/Schill, no seats (3·1%); Free Democrats, no seats (2·8%). 11 other parties stood. Turn-out was 68·7%.

CURRENT ADMINISTRATION

The First Burgomaster is Ole von Beust (Christian Democrat).

Government Website: http://www.hamburg.de

ENERGY AND NATURAL RESOURCES

Agriculture. The agricultural area comprised 13,736 ha in 2003.

Livestock (2003): cattle, 7,129 (including 1,087 milch cows); pigs, 1,441; horses, 3,268; sheep, 2,848; poultry, 7,507.

INDUSTRY

In June 2003, 532 establishments (with 20 or more employees) employed 97,369 persons; of these, 24,408 were employed in manufacturing transport equipment (including motor vehicles, aircraft and ships), 14,744 in manufacturing machinery, 11,531 in manufacturing electrical and optical equipment, 6,692 in manufacturing chemical products and 6,091 in mineral oil industry.

Labour. The economically active persons totalled 785,000 at the 1%-sample survey of the microcensus of May 2003. Of the total, 678,000 were employees and 107,000 were self-employed or unpaid family workers; 221,000 were engaged in commerce and transport, 154,000 in power supply, mining, manufacturing and building, 8,000 in agriculture and forestry, 402,000 in other industries and services.

COMMUNICATIONS

Roads. In 2004 there were 3,956 km of roads, including 82 km of Autobahn, 150 km of federal roads. Number of motor vehicles (1 Jan. 2004), 960,406, of which 836,001 were passenger cars, 54,399 lorries, 1,621 buses, 47,334 motorcycles and 21,051 other motor vehicles.

Civil Aviation. Hamburg airport handled 9,365,984 passengers (5,041,074 on international flights) and 23,609 tonnes of freight in 2003.

Shipping. Hamburg is the largest sea port in Germany.

Vessels		*2001*	*2002*	*2003*
Entered:	Number	12,333	11,606	11,503
	Tonnage (gross)	115,383,156	120,683,288	129,782,091
Cleared:	Number	12,344	11,650	11,514
	Tonnage (gross)	115,135,138	120,970,345	128,961,988

SOCIAL INSTITUTIONS

Justice. There is a constitutional court *(Verfassungsgericht)*, a court of appeal *(Oberlandesgericht)*, a regional court *(Landgericht)*, eight local courts *(Amtsgerichte)*, a *Bundesland* labour court, a labour court, a *Bundesland* social court, a social court, a finance court, a higher administrative court and an administrative court.

Religion. In 2003, 32·7% of the population went to the Evangelical Church and Free Churches, whilst 10·3% were Roman Catholic.

Education. In 2003 there were 419 schools of general education (not including *Internationale Schule*) with 181,550 pupils; 45 special schools with 7,525 pupils; 43 part-time vocational schools with 33,778 pupils; 40 schools with 4,939 pupils in manual instruction classes; 47 full-time vocational schools with 11,615 pupils; nine economic secondary schools with 2,250 pupils; two technical *Gymnasien* with 445 pupils; 21 advanced vocational schools with 3,359 pupils; 30 schools for public health occupations with 2,412 pupils; and 18 technical superior schools with 2,036 pupils.

In the winter term 2003–04 there was one university with 39,250 students; one technical university with 5,689 students; one college of music and one college of fine arts with 1,493 students in total; one university of the *Bundeswehr* with 1,888 students; one university of economics and political sciences with 2,753 students; four professional colleges with a total of 18,986 students.

Health. In 2002 there were 35 hospitals with 12,503 beds, 9,200 doctors and 1,750 dentists.

CULTURE

Broadcasting. In 2003 there was one public broadcasting service as well as seven private broadcasters.

Tourism. At Dec. 2003 there were 274 places of accommodation with 30,802 beds. Of the 2,956,012 visitors in 2003, 19·0% were foreigners.

FURTHER READING

Statistical Information: Statistisches Amt für Hamburg und Schleswig-Holstein (Standort Hamburg, Steckelhörn 12, D-20457 Hamburg). *Directors:* Wolfgang Bick, Dr Hans-Peter Kirschner. Publications: *Hamburg in Zahlen, Statistische Berichte, Statistisches Jahrbuch, Hamburger Statistische Porträts, Statistik Magazin.*

Hamburger Sparkasse, *Hamburg: von Altona bis Zollspieker.* Hamburg, 2002
Hamburgische Gesellschaft für Wirtschaftsförderung mbH, *Hamburg.* Oldenburg, 1993
Klessmann, E., *Geschichte der Stadt Hamburg.* 7th ed. Hamburg, 1994
Kopitzsch, F. and Brietzke, D., *Hamburgische Biografie, Personenlexikon.* Vol. 1. Hamburg, 2001
Kopitzsch, F. and Tilgner, D., *Hamburg Lexikon.* Hamburg, 1998
Möller, I., *Hamburg.* 2nd ed. Stuttgart, 1999
Schubert, D. and Harms, H., *Wohnen am Hafen.* Hamburg, 1993
Schütt, E. C., *Die Chronik Hamburgs.* Hamburg, 1991

State Library: Staats- und Universitätsbibliothek, Carl von Ossietzky, Von-Melle-Park 3, D-20146 Hamburg. *Director:* Prof. Dr Peter Rau.

HESSEN

KEY HISTORICAL EVENTS

The *Bundesland* consists of the former states of Hesse-Darmstadt and Hesse-Kassel, and Nassau. Hesse-Darmstadt was ruled by the Landgrave Louis X from 1790. He became grand duke in 1806 with absolute power, having dismissed the parliament in 1803. However, he granted a constitution and bicameral parliament in 1820. Hesse-Darmstadt lost land to Prussia in the Seven Weeks' War of 1866, but retained its independence, both then and as a state of the German Empire after 1871. In 1918 the grand duke abdicated and the territory became a state of the German Republic. In 1945 areas west of the Rhine were incorporated into the new *Bundesland* of Rhineland-Palatinate, areas east of the Rhine became part of the *Bundesland* of Greater Hesse.

Hesse-Kassel was ruled by the Landgrave William IX from 1785 until he became Elector in 1805. In 1807 the Electorate was absorbed into the Kingdom of Westphalia (a Napoleonic creation), becoming independent again in 1815 as a state of the German Confederation. In 1831 a constitution and parliament were granted but the Electors remained strongly conservative.

In 1866 the Diet approved alliance with Prussia against Austria; the Elector nevertheless supported Austria. He was defeated by the Prussians and exiled and

Hesse-Kassel was annexed to Prussia. In 1867 it was combined with Frankfurt and some areas taken from Nassau and Hesse-Darmstadt to form a Prussian province (Hesse-Nassau). In 1801 Nassau west of the Rhine passed to France; Napoléon also took the northern state in 1806. The remnant of the southern states allied in 1803 and three years later they became a duchy. In 1866 the duke supported Austria against Prussia and the duchy was annexed by Prussia as a result. In 1944 the Prussian province of Hesse-Nassau was split in two: Nassau and Electoral Hesse, also called Kurhessen. The following year these were combined with Hesse-Darmstadt as the *Bundesland* of Greater Hesse which became known as Hessen.

TERRITORY AND POPULATION

Area, 21,115 sq. km. The capital is Wiesbaden. There are three administrative regions with five urban and 21 rural districts and 426 communes. Population, 31 Dec. 2003, was 6,089,428 (2,981,511 males, 3,107,917 females).

SOCIAL STATISTICS

Statistics for calendar years:

	Live births	*Marriages*	*Divorces*	*Deaths*
2000	58,817	32,516	14,905	60,345
2001	56,228	29,832	15,078	59,370
2002	55,324	30,472	15,785	60,367
2003	54,400	29,613	16,288	61,508

CONSTITUTION AND GOVERNMENT

The constitution was put into force by popular referendum on 1 Dec. 1946. Hessen has five seats in the Bundesrat.

RECENT ELECTIONS

At the Diet elections on 2 Feb. 2003 the Christian Democratic Union (CDU) won 56 of 110 seats, with 48·8% of votes cast (up from 43·4% in 1999), the Social Democratic Party (SPD) 33 with 29·1% (down from 39·4% in 1999), the Greens 12 with 10·1% and the Free Democratic Party (FDP) 9 with 7·9%.

CURRENT ADMINISTRATION

The cabinet is headed by *Prime Minister* Roland Koch (Christian Democrats; CDU).

Government Website: http://www.hessen.de

ECONOMY

Performance. In 2003 the gross domestic product at market prices (GDP) was unchanged at 1995 constant prices in comparison with the previous year. The total amount was €185·0 bn. in 2003. The GDP per person engaged in labour productivity was €62,140 in 2003 (€61,276 in 2002).

ENERGY AND NATURAL RESOURCES

Electricity. Electricity production in 2003 was 22,337m. kWh (gross) and 19,785m. kWh (net). Total electricity consumption in 2002 was 33,893m. kWh.

Oil and Gas. Gas consumption in 2003 was 68,063m. kWh. All gas was imported from other parts of Germany.

Agriculture. Area and yield of the most important crops:

	Area (in 1,000 ha)			*Yield (in 1,000 tonnes)*		
	2001	*2002*	*2003*	*2001*	*2002*	*2003*
Wheat	146·4	148·9	147·5	1,180·2	1,054·9	1,030·5
Sugarbeet	18·4	18·8	18·6	1,001·6	1,108·9	995·8
Barley	109·6	105·0	104·2	670·2	594·9	541·3
Potatoes	4·7	4·7	5·1	172·6	153·0	172·2
Rape	51·3	53·5	56·3	178·2	173·6	161·4
Oats	17·5	16·9	19·1	83·3	72·7	103·7
Rye	20·1	17·5	13·8	121·7	103·6	74·3

Livestock, May 2003: cattle, 504,770 (including 161,561 milch cows); pigs, 819,310; sheep, 183,666; horses, 35,817; poultry, 1·55m.

INDUSTRY

In Sept. 2004, 3,153 establishments (with 20 or more employees) employed 428,406 persons; of these, 62,401 were employed in the chemical industry; 57,792 in machine construction; 54,636 in car building; 36,778 in production of metal products.

Labour. The economically active persons totalled 2,743,100 at the 1% sample survey of the microcensus of May 2003. Of the total, 2,407,200 were employees, 304,300 self-employed, 31,600 unpaid family workers; 783,500 were engaged in power supply, mining, manufacturing and building, 663,000 in commerce, transport, hotels and restaurants, 43,800 in agriculture and forestry and 1,252,900 in other services.

COMMUNICATIONS

Roads. On 1 Jan. 2004 there were 16,724 km of 'classified' roads, comprising 957 km of Autobahn, 3,476 km of federal highways, 7,241 km of first-class highways and 5,051 km of second-class highways. Motor vehicles licensed on 1 Jan. 2004 totalled 4,223,592, including 3,548,806 passenger cars, 6,245 buses, 183,529 lorries, 136,953 tractors and 296,269 motorcycles.

Civil Aviation. Frankfurt/Main airport is one of the most important freight airports in the world. In 2003, 458,865 aeroplanes took off and landed, carrying 48,359,320 passengers, 1,548,014 tonnes of air freight and 126,726 tonnes of air mail.

Shipping. Frankfurt/Main harbour and Hanau harbour are the two most important harbours. In 2003, 9·8m. tonnes of goods were imported into the *Bundesland* and 2·2m. tonnes were exported.

SOCIAL INSTITUTIONS

Justice. There are a constitutional court *(Staatsgerichtshof)*, a court of appeal, nine regional courts, 58 local courts, a *Bundesland* labour court, 12 labour courts, a *Bundesland* social court, seven social courts, a finance court, a higher administrative court *(Verwaltungsgerichtshof)* and five administrative courts.

Religion. In 2002 the churches in Hessen reported 2,592,000 Protestants and 1,588,000 Roman Catholics.

Education. In 2002 there were 1,256 primary schools with 285,010 pupils (including *Förderstufen*); 162 intermediate schools with 53,133 pupils; 20,052 teachers in primary and intermediate schools; 232 special schools with 4,488 teachers and 25,927 pupils; 167 high schools with 9,672 teachers and 140,071 pupils; 213 *Gesamtschulen* (comprehensive schools) with 12,534 teachers and 194,371 pupils; 118 part-time vocational schools with 130,415 pupils; 263 full-time vocational schools with 49,452 pupils; 108 advanced vocational schools with 11,271 pupils; 8,639 teachers in the vocational schools.

In the winter term 2003–04 there were four universities (Frankfurt/Main, 42,420 students; Giessen, 22,121; Kassel, 18,582; Marburg/Lahn, 19,332); one technical university in Darmstadt (20,588); two private *Wissenschaftliche Hochschulen* (1,100); 16 *Fachhochschulen* (51,794); two Roman Catholic theological colleges and one Protestant theological college with a total of 307; one college of music and two colleges of fine arts with 1,512 students in total.

CULTURE

Press. In 2003 there were 82 newspapers published in Hessen with a combined circulation of 2·0m.

Tourism. In 2002, 9·4m. visitors stayed 23·8m. nights in Hessen.

FURTHER READING

Statistical Information: The Hessisches Statistisches Landesamt (Rheinstr. 35–37, D-65175 Wiesbaden). *President:* Eckart Hohmann. Main publications: *Statistisches Jahrbuch für das Land Hessen* (biannual).—*Staat und Wirtschaft in Hessen* (monthly).—*Statistische Berichte.—Hessische Gemeindestatistik* (annual, 1980 ff.). *Website (German only):* http://www.statistik-hessen.de

State Library: Hessische Landesbibliothek, Rheinstr. 55–57, D-65185 Wiesbaden. *Director:* Dr Marianne Dörr.

LOWER SAXONY

Niedersachsen

KEY HISTORICAL EVENTS

The *Bundesland* consists of the former states of Hanover, Oldenburg, Schaumburg-Lippe and Brunswick. It does not include the cities of Bremen or Bremerhaven. Oldenburg, Danish from 1667, passed to the bishopric of Lübeck in 1773; the Holy Roman Emperor made it a duchy in 1777. As a small state of the Confederation after 1815 it supported Prussia, becoming a member of the Prussian Zollverein (1853) and North German Confederation (1867). The grand duke abdicated in 1918 and was replaced by an elected government.

Schaumburg-Lippe was a small sovereign principality. As such it became a member of the Confederation of the Rhine in 1807 and of the German Confederation in 1815. Surrounded by Prussian territory, it also joined the Prussian-led North German Confederation in 1867. Part of the Empire until 1918, it then became a state of the new republic.

Brunswick, a small duchy, was taken into the Kingdom of Westphalia by Napoléon in 1806 but restored to independence in 1814. In 1830 the duke, Charles II, was forced into exile and replaced in 1831 by his more liberal brother, William. The succession passed to a Hanoverian claimant in 1913 but the duchy ended with the Empire in 1918.

As a state of the republican Germany, Brunswick was greatly reduced under the Third Reich. Its boundaries were restored by the British occupation forces in 1945.

Hanover was an autonomous Electorate of the Holy Roman Empire whose rulers were also kings of Great Britain from 1714 to 1837. From 1762 they ruled almost entirely from England. After Napoleonic invasions Hanover was restored in 1815. A constitution of 1819 made no radical change and had to be followed by more liberal versions in 1833 and 1848. Prussia annexed Hanover in 1866; it remained a Prussian province until 1946. On 1 Nov. 1946 all four states were combined by the British military administration to form the *Bundesland* of Lower Saxony.

TERRITORY AND POPULATION

Lower Saxony has an area of 47,618 sq. km, and is divided into eight urban districts, 38 rural districts and 1,023 communes; capital, Hanover.

Population, on 30 June 2004, was 8,001,671 (3,920,356 males; 4,081,315 females).

SOCIAL STATISTICS

Statistics for calendar years:

	Live births	*Marriages*	*Divorces*	*Deaths*
2000	79,436	45,233	18,367	82,901
2001	75,239	41,781	19,485	82,517
2002	73,193	42,391	21,044	83,512
2003	70,563	40,827	21,921	85,336

CONSTITUTION AND GOVERNMENT

The *Bundesland* Niedersachsen was formed on 1 Nov. 1946 by merging the former Prussian province of Hanover with Brunswick, Oldenburg and Schaumburg-Lippe. Lower Saxony has seven seats in the Bundesrat.

RECENT ELECTIONS

At the Diet elections on 2 Feb. 2003 the Christian Democratic Union won 91 of 183 seats, receiving 48·3% of votes cast (up from 35·9% in 1998), the Social Democratic Party 63 with 33·4% (down from 47·9% in 1998), the Free Democrats 15 with 8·1% and the Greens 14 with 7·6%.

CURRENT ADMINISTRATION

The *Prime Minister* is Christian Wulff (CDU).

Government Website (German only): http://www.niedersachsen.de

ECONOMY

Banking and Finance. 214 credit institutions were operating in 2003. Deposits totalled €50,111m.

ENERGY AND NATURAL RESOURCES

Electricity. Electricity production in 2003 was 58,875m. kWh. Consumption in 2003 was 53,141m. kWh.

Agriculture. Area and yield of the most important crops:

	Area (in 1,000 ha)			*Yield (in 1,000 tonnes)*		
	2001	*2002*	*2003*	*2001*	*2002*	*2003*
Sugarbeet	115	117	114	6,289	6,369	6,627
Potatoes	122	123	126	5,529	4,948	4,588
Wheat	390	412	405	3,463	2,925	2,972
Barley	306	295	297	2,016	1,548	1,631
Rye	156	132	104	1,114	761	582
Oats	23	24	26	113	96	129

Livestock, 3 May 2004: cattle, 2,584,700 (including 740,800 milch cows); pigs, 7,574,900; sheep, 278,200. 3 May 2003: horses, 89,300; poultry, 59,550,900.

Fisheries. In 1999 the yield of sea and coastal fishing was 32,117 tonnes valued at 66·5m. DM.

INDUSTRY

In Sept. 2003, 4,044 establishments employed 541,131 persons; of these 54,788 were employed in electrical engineering; 50,775 in machine construction.

Labour. The economically active persons totalled 3,325,000 in April 2004. Of the total, 2,917,000 were employees, 356,600 self-employed, 51,700 unpaid family workers; 992,300 were engaged in power supply, mining, manufacturing and building, 785,300 in commerce and transport, 118,100 in agriculture and forestry and 1,429,600 in other industries and services.

COMMUNICATIONS

Roads. At 1 Jan. 2004 there were 28,195 km of 'classified' roads, comprising 1,354 km of Autobahn, 4,853 km of federal roads, 8,318 km of first-class and 13,669 km of second-class highways. Number of motor vehicles, 1 Jan. 2004, was 5,378,884 including 4,440,092 passenger cars, 244,407 lorries, 8,454 buses, 234,288 tractors and 376,148 motorcycles.

Rail. In 2003, 28·5m. tonnes of freight came into the *Bundesland* by rail and 21·6m. tonnes left by rail.

Civil Aviation. 77,089 planes landed at Hanover airport in 2003, which saw 2,443,499 passenger arrivals and 2,461,174 departures. 3,153 tonnes of freight left by air and 2,167 tonnes came in.

SOCIAL INSTITUTIONS

Justice. There are a constitutional court *(Staatsgerichtshof)*, three courts of appeal, 11 regional courts, 79 local courts, a *Bundesland* labour court, 15 labour courts, a *Bundesland* social court, eight social courts, a finance court, a higher administrative court and seven administrative courts.

Religion. On 25 May 1987 (census) there were 66·1% Protestants and 19·6% Roman Catholics.

Education. In 2003–04 there were 1,873 primary schools with 347,627 pupils; 950 post-primary schools with 240,717 pupils; 291 special schools with 40,024 pupils; 417 secondary modern schools with 121,426 pupils; 236 grammar schools with 164,808 pupils; 34 co-operative comprehensive schools with 36,606 pupils; and 33 integrated comprehensive schools with 27,052 pupils.

In the winter term 2003–04 there were seven universities (Göttingen, 23,011 students; Hanover, 24,152; Hildesheim, 3,674; Lüneburg, 6,748; Oldenburg, 11,220; Osnabrück, 10,678; Vechta, 2,223); two technical universities (Braunschweig, 13,501; Clausthal, 2,717); the medical college of Hanover (3,208); the veterinary college in Hanover (1,893).

Health. At Dec. 2003 there were 25,824 doctors and 209 hospitals with 5·9 beds per 1,000 population.

CULTURE

Broadcasting. Norddeutscher Rundfunk is the public broadcasting service for Lower Saxony.

Tourism. In 2003, 9,536,805 guests spent 32,339,890 nights in Lower Saxony.

FURTHER READING

Statistical Information: The Niedersächsisches Landesamt für Statistik, Postfach 910764, D-30427 Hanover. *Head of Division:* President Karl-Ludwig Strelen. Main publications are: *Statistische Monatshefte Niedersachsen* (from 1947).—*Statistische Berichte Niedersachsen.—Statistisches Taschenbuch Niedersachsen 2004* (biennial).

State Libraries: Niedersächsische Staats- und Universitätsbibliothek, Platz der Göttinger Sieben 1, D-37073 Göttingen. *Director:* Prof. Dr Elmar Mittler; Niedersächsische Landesbibliothek, Waterloostr. 8, D-30169 Hanover. *Director:* Dr Georg Ruppelt.

MECKLENBURG-WEST POMERANIA

Mecklenburg-Vorpommern

KEY HISTORICAL EVENTS

Pomerania was at one time under Swedish control while Mecklenburg was an independent part of the German Empire. The two states were not united until after the Second World War, and after a short period when it was subdivided into three districts under the GDR, it became a state of the Federal Republic of Germany in 1990. The people of the region speak a dialect known as Plattdeutsch (Low German). The four main cities of this state are Hanseatic towns from the period when the area dominated trade with Scandinavia. Rostock on the North Sea coast became the home of the GDR's biggest shipyards.

TERRITORY AND POPULATION

The area is 23,174 sq. km. It is divided into six urban districts, 12 rural districts and 964 communes. Population on 31 Dec. 2003 was 1,732,226 (873,977 females). It is the most sparsely populated of the German *Bundesländer*, with a population density of 75 per sq. km in 2003. The capital is Schwerin.

SOCIAL STATISTICS

Statistics for calendar years:

	Live births	*Marriages*	*Divorces*	*Deaths*
2000	13,319	8,083	3,951	17,460
2001	12,968	7,869	4,021	17,179
2002	12,504	7,901	3,505	17,333
2003	12,782	7,872	3,677	17,715

CONSTITUTION AND GOVERNMENT

The *Bundesland* was reconstituted on former GDR territory in 1990. It has three seats in the Bundesrat.

RECENT ELECTIONS

At the Diet elections of 22 Sept. 2002 the Social Democrats (SPD) won 33 seats with 40·6% of the vote; the Christian Democrats (CDU), 25, with 31·3%; and the Party of Democratic Socialism (PDS, former Communists), 13, with 16·4%.

CURRENT ADMINISTRATION

The *Prime Minister* is Dr Harald Ringstorff (SPD).

Government Website: http://www.mecklenburg-vorpommern.de

ENERGY AND NATURAL RESOURCES

Agriculture. Area and yield of the most important crops:

	Area (in 1,000 ha)			*Yield (in 1,000 tonnes)*		
	2001	*2002*	*2003*	*2001*	*2002*	*2003*
Wheat	297·2	324·2	338·6	2,333·5	2,309·0	2,153·4
Sugarbeet	27·9	27·8	27·0	1,334·0	1,357·4	1,381·0

	Area (in 1,000 ha)			*Yield (in 1,000 tonnes)*		
	2001	*2002*	*2003*	*2001*	*2002*	*2003*
Barley	148·8	115·9	140·9	1,151·3	712·8	764·0
Rape	207·9	237·1	227·3	858·8	755·9	756·9
Potatoes	15·9	15·4	16·3	580·9	555·1	543·6
Rye	111·0	87·1	54·3	737·1	467·4	263·0
Oats	12·0	12·0	13·2	58·9	50·9	56·5

Livestock in 2003: cattle, 565,079 (including 182,210 milch cows); pigs, 688,122; sheep, 109,241; horses, 12,480; poultry, 8,235,352.

Fisheries. Sea catch, 2003: 19,528 tonnes (751 tonnes frozen, 18,777 tonnes fresh). Freshwater catch, 2003: 598 tonnes (mainly carp, trout and eels). Fish farming, 2003: 478 tonnes.

INDUSTRY

In 2003 there were 693 enterprises (with 20 or more employees) employing 48,665 persons.

Labour. 725,400 persons (334,000 females) were employed at the 1%-sample survey of the microcensus of May 2003, including 360,100 white-collar workers, 259,600 manual workers and 66,500 self-employed and family assistants. 39,200 persons were employed as officials. Employment by sector (on average for the year 2003): public and private services, 252,700; trade, guest business, transport and communications, 188,400; financing, leasing and services for enterprises, 89,900; manufacturing, 72,600; construction, 68,100; agriculture, forestry and fisheries, 33,100; mining, energy and water resources, 6,500; total, 712,000.

COMMUNICATIONS

Roads. In 2003 there were 9,878 km of 'classified' roads, comprising 443 km of Autobahn, 2,076 km of federal roads, 3,239 km of first-class and 4,120 km of second-class highways. Number of motor vehicles at 1 Jan. 2004 was 1,054,043, including 891,044 passenger cars, 72,796 lorries, 1,944 buses and 49,840 motorcycles.

Shipping. There is a lake district of some 554 lakes greater than 0·1 sq. km. The ports of Rostock, Stralsund and Wismar are important for ship-building and repairs. In 2003 the cargo fleet consisted of 101 vessels (including one tanker) of 1,434,000 GT. Sea traffic, 2003, incoming 12,781,495 tonnes; outgoing 10,723,335 tonnes.

SOCIAL INSTITUTIONS

Justice. There is a court of appeal (*Oberlandesgericht*), four regional courts (*Landgerichte*), 21 local courts (*Amtsgerichte*), four labour courts, four social courts, a finance court and two administrative courts.

Religion. In 2003 the Evangelical Lutheran Church of Mecklenburg had 216,600 adherents, 235 pastors and 309 parishes. Roman Catholics numbered 57,800, with 56 priests and 64 parishes. The Pomeranian Evangelical Church had 116,000 adherents, 134 pastors and 268 parishes in 2003.

Education. In 2003 there were 257 primary schools, 26 comprehensives, 96 secondary schools and 92 special needs schools. There are universities at Rostock and Greifswald with (in 2003–04) 22,435 students and 4,958 academic staff, and five institutions of equivalent status with 9,936 students and 1,113 academic staff.

CULTURE

Tourism. In July 2003 there were 2,628 places of accommodation (with nine or more beds) providing a total of 164,282 beds. 5,145,948 guests stayed an average of 4·3 nights each in 2003.

FURTHER READING

Statistical Office: Statistisches Landesamt Mecklenburg-Vorpommern, Postfach 120135, D-19018 Schwerin.

Main publications are: *Statistische Hefte* (formerly *Statistische Monatshefte*) *Mecklenburg-Vorpommern* (since 1991); *Gemeindedaten Mecklenburg-Vorpommern* (since 1999; electronic); *Statistische Berichte* (since 1991; various); *Statistisches Jahrbuch Mecklenburg-Vorpommern* (since 1991); *Statistische Sonderhefte* (since 1992; various). *Website (German only):* http://www.statistik-mv.de

NORTH RHINE-WESTPHALIA

Nordrhein-Westfalen

KEY HISTORICAL EVENTS

Historical Westphalia consisted of many small political units, most of them absorbed by Prussia and Hanover before 1800. In 1807 Napoléon created a Kingdom of Westphalia for his brother Joseph. This included Hesse-Kassel, but was formed mainly from the Prussian and Hanoverian lands between the rivers Elbe and Weser.

In 1815 the kingdom ended with Napoléon's defeat. Most of the area was given to Prussia, with the small principalities of Lippe and Waldeck surviving as independent states. Both joined the North German Confederation in 1867. Lippe remained autonomous after the end of the Empire in 1918; Waldeck was absorbed into Prussia in 1929.

In 1946 the occupying forces combined Lippe with most of the Prussian province of Westphalia to form the *Bundesland* of North Rhine-Westphalia. On 1 March 1947 the allied Control Council formally abolished Prussia.

TERRITORY AND POPULATION

The *Bundesland* comprises 34,082 sq. km. It is divided into five administrative regions, 23 urban districts, 31 rural districts and 396 communes. Capital: Düsseldorf. Population, 31 Dec. 2003, 18,079,686.

SOCIAL STATISTICS

Statistics for calendar years:

	Live births	*Marriages*	*Divorces*	*Deaths*
1999	176,578	99,645	45,105	188,851
2000	175,144	97,508	45,201	187,736
2001	167,752	89,529	46,913	184,824
2002	163,434	89,803	47,208	188,333
2003	159,883	87,768	50,962	190,794

CONSTITUTION AND GOVERNMENT

Since Oct. 1990 North Rhine-Westphalia has had six seats in the Bundesrat.

RECENT ELECTIONS

The Diet elected on 14 May 2000 consisted of 102 Social Democrats (42·8% of votes cast), 88 Christian Democrats (37·0%), 24 Free Democrats (9·8%) and 17 Greens (7·1%). Turn-out was 56·7%.

CURRENT ADMINISTRATION

North Rhine-Westphalia is governed by Social Democrats (SPD) and the Greens.

Prime Minister: Peer Steinbrück (SPD).

Government Website (German only): http://www.nrw.de

ECONOMY

North Rhine-Westphalia has the highest GDP of any German *Bundesland*—€464·0bn. in 2002 out of a total of €2,063·0bn. Foreign direct investment is also higher than in any other *Bundesland*.

Budget. The predicted total revenue for 2003 was €47,892·1m. and the predicted total expenditure was also €47,892·1m.

ENERGY AND NATURAL RESOURCES

Agriculture. Area and yield of the most important crops:

	Area (in 1,000 ha)			*Yield (in 1,000 tonnes)*		
	2000	*2001*	*2002*	*2000*	*2001*	*2002*
Sugarbeet	70·5	71·1	71·3	4,377·3	3,939·1	4,045·6
Wheat	262·4	257·1	259·1	2,095·5	2,356·4	2,132·6
Potatoes	32·9	30·1	29·9	1,584·9	1,282·9	1,298·4
Barley	190·6	193·1	189·2	1,203·3	1,420·1	1,273·5
Rye	26·2	25·3	22·9	160·9	184·1	156·6
Oats	23·5	22·2	22·0	115·0	122·4	103·1

Livestock, 3 May 2002: cattle, 1,432,217 (including 387,461 milch cows); pigs, 6,092,905; sheep, 205,215; poultry, 10,772,733 (2001).

INDUSTRY

In Sept. 2002, 10,394 establishments (with 20 or more employees) employed 1,355,697 persons: 299,316 were employed in metal production and manufacture of metal goods; 226,335 in machine construction; 147,075 in manufacture of office machines, computers, electrical and precision engineering and optics; 127,215 in the chemical industry; 100,648 in motor vehicle manufacture; 99,991 in production of food and tobacco. 66% of the workforce is now employed in the services industry. Of the total population, 7·5% were engaged in industry.

Labour. The economically active persons totalled 7,620,000 at the 1%-sample survey of the microcensus of April 2002. Of the total, 6,847,000 were employees, 698,000 self-employed and 75,000 unpaid family workers; 2,457,000 were engaged in power supply, mining, manufacturing, water supply and building, 1,752,000 in commerce, hotel trade and transport, 116,000 in agriculture, forestry and fishing, and 3,295,000 in other industries and services.

COMMUNICATIONS

Roads. There were (1 Jan. 2003) 29,679 km of 'classified' roads, comprising 2,173 km of Autobahn, 5,083 km of federal roads, 12,619 km of first-class and 9,804 km of second-class highways. Number of motor vehicles (1 Jan. 2003): 11,255,936, including 9,579,221 passenger cars, 505,265 lorries, 17,826 buses and 799,194 motorcycles.

Civil Aviation. In 2002, 88,988 aircraft landed at Düsseldorf, bringing 7,288,751 incoming passengers; and 60,609 aircraft landed at Cologne-Bonn, bringing 2,650,664 incoming passengers.

SOCIAL INSTITUTIONS

Justice. There are a constitutional court *(Verfassungsgerichtshof)*, three courts of appeal, 19 regional courts, 130 local courts, three *Bundesland* labour courts, 30 labour courts, one *Bundesland* social court, eight social courts, three finance courts, a higher administrative court and seven administrative courts.

Religion. On 25 May 1987 (census) there were 35·2% Protestants and 49·4% Roman Catholics.

Education. In 2002 there were 4,202 primary schools with 61,556 teachers and 1,074,051 pupils; 707 special schools with 16,743 teachers and 102,068 pupils; 550 intermediate schools with 18,825 teachers and 343,085 pupils; 264 *Gesamtschulen* (comprehensive schools) with 17,903 teachers and 239,048 pupils; 627 high schools with 33,241 teachers and 541,286 pupils; there were 301 part-time vocational schools with 371,853 pupils; 193 vocational preparatory year schools with 19,053 pupils; 297 full-time vocational schools with 110,376 pupils; 188 full-time vocational schools leading up to vocational colleges with 18,919 pupils; 263 advanced full-time vocational schools with 42,782 pupils; 549 schools for public health occupations with 15,963 teachers and 42,180 pupils.

In the winter term 2002–03 there were 13 universities (Bielefeld, 19,369 students; Bochum, 34,143; Bonn, 37,293; Cologne (Köln), 58,812; Dortmund, 24,278; Düsseldorf, 24,835; Essen, 20,662; Münster, 42,511; Paderborn, 13,453; Siegen, 11,143; Witten, 1,099; Wuppertal, 14,205; the Technical University of Aachen, 29,376); four Roman Catholic and two Protestant theological colleges with a total of 617 students. There were also four colleges of music, three colleges of fine arts with 5,204 students in total; 24 *Fachhochschulen* (vocational colleges) with 104,593 students.

Health. In 2001 there were 462 hospitals in North Rhine-Westphalia with 134,883 beds, which had an average occupancy rate of 79·3%.

CULTURE

Tourism. At Dec. 2002 there were 5,438 places of accommodation (nine beds or more) providing 277,834 beds altogether. In 2002, 14,373,206 visitors (2,533,008 foreigners) spent 36,335,584 nights in North Rhine-Westphalia.

FURTHER READING

Statistical Information: The Landesamt für Datenverarbeitung und Statistik Nordrhein-Westfalen (Mauerstr. 51, D-40476 Düsseldorf) was founded in 1946, by amalgamating the provincial statistical offices of Rhineland and Westphalia. *President:* Jochen Kehlenbach. The Landesamt publishes (from 1949): *Statistisches Jahrbuch Nordrhein-Westfalen.* More than 550 other publications yearly. *Website (German only):* http://www.lds.nrw.de

Bundesland Library: Universitätsbibliothek, Universitätsstr. 1, D-40225 Düsseldorf. *Director:* Dr Irmgard Siebert.

RHINELAND-PALATINATE

Rheinland-Pfalz

KEY HISTORICAL EVENTS

The *Bundesland* was formed from the Rhenisch Palatinate and the Rhine valley areas of Prussia, Hesse-Darmstadt, Hesse-Kassel and Bavaria.

From 1214 the Palatinate was ruled by the Bavarian house of Wittelsbach, with its capital as Heidelberg. In 1797 the land west of the Rhine was taken into France, and Napoléon divided the eastern land between Baden and Hesse. In 1815 the territory taken by France was restored to Germany and allotted to Bavaria. The area and its neighbours formed the strategically important Bavarian Circle of the Rhine. The rule of the Wittelsbachs ended in 1918 but the Palatinate remained part of Bavaria until the American occupying forces detached it in 1946. The new *Bundesland*, incorporating the Palatinate and other territory, received its constitution in April 1947.

TERRITORY AND POPULATION

Rhineland-Palatinate has an area of 19,853 sq. km. It comprises 12 urban districts, 24 rural districts and 2,305 other communes. The capital is Mainz. Population (at 31 Dec. 2003), 4,058,682 (2,069,555 females).

SOCIAL STATISTICS

Statistics for calendar years:

	Live births	*Marriages*	*Divorces*	*Deaths*
2000	37,826	22,129	10,416	42,088
2001	35,781	20,608	10,301	42,222
2002	34,741	20,800	11,187	42,669
2003	34,083	20,123	11,567	43,933

CONSTITUTION AND GOVERNMENT

The constitution of the *Bundesland* Rheinland-Pfalz was approved by the Consultative Assembly on 25 April 1947 and by referendum on 18 May 1947, when 579,002 voted for and 514,338 against its acceptance. It has four seats in the Bundesrat.

RECENT ELECTIONS

At the elections of 25 March 2001 the Social Democratic Party won 49 seats of the 101 in the state parliament with 44·7% of votes cast; the Christian Democrats 38 with 35·3% (their worst result ever in Rheinland-Pfalz); the Free Democrats 8 with 7·8%; and the Greens 6 with 5·2%; turn-out was 62·1%.

CURRENT ADMINISTRATION

The coalition cabinet is headed by Kurt Beck (b. 1949; Social Democrat).

Government Website: http://www.rlp.de

ENERGY AND NATURAL RESOURCES

Agriculture. Area and yield of the most important products:

	Area (1,000 ha)			*Yield (1,000 tonnes)*		
	2001	*2002*	*2003*	*2001*	*2002*	*2003*
Sugarbeet	19·8	21·8	21·7	1,094·2	1,449·5	1,006·4
Barley	121·2	104·1	112·0	582·9	511·7	538·5
Wheat	84·2	95·0	87·1	603·9	650·5	522·6

	Area (1,000 ha)			Yield (1,000 tonnes)		
	2001	2002	2003	2001	2002	2003
Potatoes	8·7	9·6	8·8	267·9	310·9	252·4
Oats	11·9	10·4	11·2	45·9	39·7	47·4
Rye	11·3	12·3	8·5	66·6	73·9	41·3
Wine	62·7	61·8	61·4	5,959·4[1]	6,635·4[1]	5,585·0[1]

[1]1,000 hectolitres.

Livestock (2003, in 1,000): cattle, 410·5 (including milch cows, 126·6); sheep, 130·2; pigs, 340·8; horses, 23·4; poultry, 1,676·7.

Forestry. Total area covered by forests in Dec. 2003 was 8,111·7 sq. km or 40·8% of the total area.

INDUSTRY

In 2003, 2,258 establishments (with 20 or more employees) employed 289,169 persons; of these 59,743 were employed in the chemical industry; 35,519 in machine construction; 20,583 in processing stoneware and earthenware; 16,916 in electrical equipment manufacture; 4,021 in leather goods and footwear.

Labour. The economically active persons totalled 1,799,500 in 2003. Of the total, 1,591,600 were employees, 182,700 were self-employed, 25,200 were unpaid family workers; 559,500 were engaged in power supply, mining, manufacturing and building, 413,000 in commerce, transport, hotels and restaurants, 46,900 in agriculture and forestry, 779,700 in other industries and services.

COMMUNICATIONS

Roads. In 2004 there were 18,441 km of 'classified' roads, comprising 862 km of Autobahn, 2,992 km of federal roads, 7,181 km of first-class and 7,406 km of second-class highways. Number of motor vehicles, 1 Jan. 2004, was 2,895,764, including 2,376,656 passenger cars, 125,112 lorries, 5,620 buses, 136,475 tractors and 216,524 motorcycles.

SOCIAL INSTITUTIONS

Justice. There are a constitutional court *(Verfassungsgerichtshof)*, two courts of appeal, eight regional courts, 46 local courts, a *Bundesland* labour court, five labour courts, a *Bundesland* social court, four social courts, a finance court, a higher administrative court and four administrative courts.

Religion. On 25 May 1987 (census) there were 37·7% Protestants and 54·5% Roman Catholics.

Education. In 2003 there were 997 primary schools with 8,937 teachers and 172,632 pupils; 606 secondary schools with 17,738 teachers and 301,493 pupils; 141 special schools with 2,566 teachers and 17,668 pupils; 109 vocational and advanced vocational schools with 5,228 teachers and 125,750 pupils.

In higher education, in the winter term 2004–05 (provisional figures) there were the University of Mainz (34,257 students), the University of Kaiserslautern (8,591 students), the University of Trier (12,913 students), the University of Koblenz-Landau (10,314 students), the *Deutsche Hochschule für Verwaltungswissenschaften* in Speyer (499 students), the *Wissenschaftliche Hochschule für Unternehmensführung* (Otto Beisheim Graduate School) in Vallendar (447 students), the Roman Catholic Theological College in Trier (295 students) and the Roman Catholic Theological College in Vallendar (100 students). There were also nine *Fachhochschulen* with 29,583 students and three *Verwaltungsfachhochschulen* with 1,960 students.

CULTURE

Tourism. In 2002, 3,707 places of accommodation provided 155,513 beds for 6,147,406 visitors.

FURTHER READING

Statistical Information: Statistisches Landesamt Rheinland-Pfalz (Mainzer Str., 14–16, D-56130 Bad Ems). *President:* Jörg Berres. Its publications include: *Statistisches Taschenbuch Rheinland-Pfalz* (from 1948); *Statistische Monatshefte Rheinland-Pfalz* (from 1958); *Statistik von Rheinland-Pfalz* (from 1946) 390 vols. to date; *Rheinland-Pfalz im Spiegel der Statistik* (from 1968); *Rheinland-Pfalz—seine kreisfreien Städte und Landkreise* (1992); *Rheinland-Pfalz heute* (from 1973).

SAARLAND

KEY HISTORICAL EVENTS

Long disputed between Germany and France, the area was occupied by France in 1792. Most of it was allotted to Prussia at the close of the Napoleonic wars in 1815. In 1870 Prussia defeated France and when, in 1871, the German Empire was founded under Prussian leadership, it was able to incorporate Lorraine. This part of France was the Saar territory's western neighbour so the Saar was no longer a vulnerable boundary state. It began to develop industrially, exploiting Lorraine coal and iron.

In 1919 the League of Nations took control of the Saar until a plebiscite of 1935 favoured return to Germany. In 1945 there was a French occupation, and in 1947 the Saar was made an international area, but in economic union with France. In 1954 France and Germany agreed that the Saar should be a separate and autonomous state, under an independent commissioner. This was rejected by referendum and France agreed to return Saarland to Germany; it became a *Bundesland* of the Federal Republic on 1 Jan. 1957.

TERRITORY AND POPULATION

Saarland has an area of 2,568 sq. km. Population, 31 Dec. 2003, 1,061,376 (515,641 males, 545,735 females). It comprises six rural districts and 52 communes. The capital is Saarbrücken.

SOCIAL STATISTICS

Statistics for calendar years:

	Live births	*Marriages*	*Divorces*	*Deaths*
2000	8,783	5,856	3,066	12,311
2001	8,196	5,417	3,100	12,316
2002	7,879	5,289	2,981	12,371
2003	7,598	5,141	2,867	12,852

CONSTITUTION AND GOVERNMENT

Saarland has three seats in the Bundesrat.

RECENT ELECTIONS

At the elections to the Saar Diet of 5 Sept. 2004 the Christian Democrats (CDU) won 27 seats with 47·5% of votes cast and the Social Democrats (SDP) 18 with 30·8%. The Greens and the Free Democrats each won 3 seats. Turn-out was 55·5%.

CURRENT ADMINISTRATION

Saarland is governed by Christian Democrats in Parliament. The *Prime Minister* is Peter Müller (Christian Democrat).

Government Website: http://www.saarland.de

ENERGY AND NATURAL RESOURCES

Electricity. In 2003 electricity production was 12,554m. kWh. End-user consumption totalled 7,235m. kWh in 2001.

Oil and Gas. 7,575m. kWh of gas was used in 2003.

Agriculture. The cultivated area (2001) occupied 114,618 ha or 44·6% of the total area.

Area and yield of the most important crops:

	Area (in 1,000 ha)			*Yield (in 1,000 tonnes)*		
	2002	*2003*	*2004*	*2002*	*2003*	*2004*
Wheat	9·3	8·2	8·7	61·7	44·1	61·1
Barley	6·6	7·0	7·2	34·2	31·7	36·3
Rye	4·3	3·3	3·9	24·9	14·5	25·4
Oats	2·9	3·5	3·3	11·8	13·9	15·4
Potatoes	0·2	0·2	0·2	5·7	4·4	5·8

Livestock, May 2002: cattle, 60,904 (including 14,215 milch cows); pigs, 18,621; sheep, 15,498; May 2001: horses, 5,142; poultry, 207,017.

Forestry. The forest area comprises nearly 33·4% of the total (256,929 ha).

INDUSTRY

In June 2003, 502 establishments (with 20 or more employees) employed 99,381 persons; of these 25,306 were engaged in manufacturing of motor vehicles, parts and accessories, 12,168 in machine construction, 10,803 in iron and steel production, 7,774 in coalmining, 3,503 in steel construction and 2,482 in electrical engineering. In 2003 the coalmines produced 5·6m. tonnes of coal. Two blast furnaces and eight steel furnaces produced 3·9m. tonnes of pig-iron and 5·0m. tonnes of crude steel.

Labour. The economically active persons totalled 426,300 at the 1%-sample survey of the microcensus of May 2003. Of the total, 383,000 were employees and 40,200 self-employed; 127,600 were engaged in power supply, mining, manufacturing and building, 104,200 in commerce and transport, 6,700 in agriculture and forestry, and 187,900 in other industries and services.

COMMUNICATIONS

Roads. At 1 Jan. 2004 there were 2,037 km of classified roads, comprising 240 km of Autobahn, 329 km of federal roads, 848 km of first-class and 620 km of second-class highways. Number of motor vehicles, 31 Dec. 2003, 749,303, including 634,792 passenger cars, 33,304 lorries, 1,341 buses, 15,158 tractors and 56,788 motorcycles.

Shipping. During 2003, 964 ships docked in Saarland ports, bringing 1·7m. tonnes of freight. In the same period 509 ships left the ports, carrying 853,985 tonnes of freight.

SOCIAL INSTITUTIONS

Justice. There are a constitutional court *(Verfassungsgerichtshof)*, a regional court of appeal, a regional court, ten local courts, a *Bundesland* labour court, three labour courts, a *Bundesland* social court, a social court, a finance court, a higher administrative court and an administrative court.

Religion. In 2002, 66·5% of the population were Roman Catholics and 19·7% were Protestants.

Education. In 2004–05 there were 269 primary schools with 39,614 pupils; 41 special schools with 4,094 pupils; 55 *Realschulen*, *Erweiterte Realschulen* and *Sekundarschulen* with 29,132 pupils; 35 high schools with 30,345 pupils; 15 comprehensive high schools with 11,014 pupils; four *Freie Waldorfschulen* with 1,314 pupils; four business and technical grammar schools with 645 pupils; two evening intermediate schools with 349 pupils; one evening high school and one Saarland College with 287 pupils; 37 part-time vocational schools with 20,470 pupils; year of commercial basic training: 59 institutions with 3,331 pupils; 16 advanced full-time vocational schools and schools for technicians with 2,236 pupils; 46 full-time vocational schools with 3,859 pupils; 33 *Fachoberschulen* (full-time vocational schools leading up to vocational colleges) with 6,945 pupils; 39 schools for public health occupations with 2,556 pupils. The number of pupils attending the vocational schools amounts to 40,042.

In the winter term 2004–05 there was the University of the Saarland with 14,988 students; one academy of fine art with 285 students; one academy of music and theatre with 334 students; one vocational college (economics and technics) with 3,304 students; one vocational college for social affairs with 287 students; and one vocational college for public administration with 392 students.

Health. In 2002 the 28 hospitals in the Saarland contained 7,497 beds and treated 266,245 patients. The average occupancy rate was 83·6%. There were also 21 out-patient and rehabilitation centres which treated 37,786 patients in 2002. On average they were using 81·8% of their capacity.

CULTURE

Tourism. In 2003, 15,120 beds were available in 291 places of accommodation (of nine or more beds). 662,809 guests spent 2,066,346 nights in the Saarland, staying an average of 3·1 days each.

FURTHER READING

Statistical Information: Statistisches Landesamt Saarland (Virchowstrasse 7, D-66119 Saarbrücken). *Chief:* Michael Sossong. The most important publications are: *Statistisches Jahrbuch Saarland,* from 1999.—*Saarland in Zahlen* (special issues).—*Einzelschriften zur Statistik des Saarlandes,* from 1950.—*Statistik-Journal* (monthly), from 1996. *Website (German only):* http://www.statistik.saarland.de

Born, M., *Geographische Inselkunde des Saarlandes.* Saarbrücken, 1980
Herrmann, H.-W., *et al., Das Saarland: Politische, wirtschaftliche und kulturelle Entwicklung.* Saarbrücken, 1989
Matthias, K., *Wirtschaftsgeographie des Saarlandes.* Saarbrücken, 1980.—*Wirtschaftsraum Saarland* (published in collaboration with the Industrie- und Handelskammer des Saarlandes). Oldenburg, 1990
Staerk, D., *Das Saarlandbuch.* Saarbrücken, 1981

SAXONY

Freistaat Sachsen

KEY HISTORICAL EVENTS

The former kingdom of Saxony was a member state of the German Empire from 1871 until 1918, when it became the state of Saxony and joined the Weimar Republic. After the Second World War it was one of the five states in the German Democratic Republic until German reunification in 1990. It has been home to much of Germany's cultural history. In the 18th century, the capital of Saxony, Dresden, became the cultural capital of northern Europe earning the title 'Florence of the North', and the other great eastern German city, Leipzig, was a lively commercial city with strong artistic trends. The three cities of Dresden, Chemnitz and Leipzig formed the industrial heartland of Germany which, after World War II, was the manufacturing centre of the GDR.

TERRITORY AND POPULATION

The area is 18,414 sq. km. It is divided into three administrative regions, seven urban districts, 22 rural districts and 522 communes. Population on 31 Dec. 2003 was 4,321,437 (2,218,669 females, 2,102,768 males); density, 235 per sq. km. The capital is Dresden.

SOCIAL STATISTICS

Statistics for calendar years:

	Live births	*Marriages*	*Divorces*	*Deaths*
2000	33,139	16,482	8,775	50,428
2001	31,943	15,421	8,430	49,244
2002	31,518	15,188	8,515	50,096
2003	32,079	14,778	8,946	50,669

CONSTITUTION AND GOVERNMENT

The *Bundesland* was reconstituted as the Free State of Saxony on former GDR territory in 1990. It has four seats in the Bundesrat.

RECENT ELECTIONS

At the Diet elections of 19 Sept. 2004 the Christian Democratic Union won 55 seats, with 41·1% of the vote; the Party of Democratic Socialism (former Communists), 31, with 23·6%; the Social Democratic Party, 13, with 9·8%; the extreme right-wing National Democratic Party, 12, with 9·2%; the Free Democrats, 7, with 5·9%; and the Greens, 6, with 5·1%. Turn-out was 59·6%.

CURRENT ADMINISTRATION

The *Prime Minister* is Georg Milbradt (b. 1945; Christian Democrat).

Government Website: http://www.sachsen.de

ENERGY AND NATURAL RESOURCES

Agriculture. Area and yield of the most important crops:

	Area (in 1,000 ha)			*Yield (in 1,000 tonnes)*		
	2002	*2003*	*2004*	*2002*	*2003*	*2004*
Maize	69·5	77·7	79·3	2,528·1	2,106·6	2,605·3
Fodder	183·7	180·9	185·2	1,504·2	987·3	1,545·7
Wheat	172·9	167·4	174·7	1,070·8	823·4	1,414·1
Barley	138·8	141·1	134·9	715·7	602·3	911·9
Potatoes	8·3	8·0	8·1	284·2	221·0	322·4
Rye	41·9	31·9	39·6	204·0	119·3	266·1

Livestock in May 2004 (in 1,000): cattle, 505 (including milch cows, 202); pigs, 616; sheep, 142.

INDUSTRY

In Sept. 2004, 2,953 establishments (with 20 or more employees) employed 230,641 persons.

Labour. The unemployment rate was 19·7% in Dec. 2004.

COMMUNICATIONS

Roads. On 1 Jan. 2004 there were 455·5 km of autobahn and 2,472·8 km of main roads. On 1 Jan. 2004 there were 2,656,821 registered motor vehicles, including 2,281,719 motor cars, 226,547 lorries and tractors, 4,406 buses and 121,567 motorcycles.

Civil Aviation. Leipzig airport handled 2,194,000 passengers (1,399,000 on international flights) in 2000.

SOCIAL INSTITUTIONS

Religion. In 2003, 21·6% of the population belonged to the Evangelical Church and 3·6% were Roman Catholic.

Education. In 2004–05 there were 859 primary schools (*Grundschulen*) with 104,159 pupils and 9,689 teachers; 469 secondary schools (*Mittelschulen*) with 134,425 pupils and 11,873 teachers; 154 grammar schools (*Gymnasien*) with 101,898 pupils and 8,444 teachers; and 168 high schools (*Förderschulen*) with 21,628 pupils and 3,468 teachers. There were 834 professional training schools with 169,366 students and 7,184 teachers and three *Freie Waldorfschulen* (private) with 1,174 pupils and 102 teachers. In 2003–04 there were seven universities with 74,039 students, ten polytechnics with 25,139 students, seven art schools with 2,700 students and two management colleges with 1,125 students.

Health. In 2003 there were 87 hospitals with 29,156 beds. There were 14,066 doctors and 3,814 dentists.

CULTURE

Tourism. In 2003 there were 111,535 beds in places of accommodation (totalling 2,144 in 2003). There were 5,125,603 visitors during the year.

FURTHER READING

Statistical office: Statistisches Landesamt des Freistaates Sachsen, Postfach 105, D-01911 Kamenz. It publishes *Statistisches Jahrbuch des Freistaates Sachsen* (since 1990).

SAXONY-ANHALT

Sachsen-Anhalt

KEY HISTORICAL EVENTS

Saxony-Anhalt has a short history as a state in its own right. Made up of a patchwork of older regions ruled by other states, Saxony-Anhalt existed between 1947 and 1952 and then, after reunification in 1990, it was re-established. Geographically, it lies at the very heart of Germany and despite the brevity of its federal status, the region has some of the oldest heartlands of German culture.

TERRITORY AND POPULATION

The area is 20,447 sq. km. It is divided into three administrative regions, three urban districts, 21 rural districts and 1,197 communes. Population in 2003 was 2,522,941. The capital is Magdeburg.

SOCIAL STATISTICS

Statistics for calendar years:

	Live births	*Marriages*	*Divorces*	*Deaths*
2000	18,723	10,310	5,823	30,175
2001	18,073	9,359	5,829	29,621
2002	17,617	9,274	5,838	30,159
2003	16,889	9,314	5,863	29,632

CONSTITUTION AND GOVERNMENT

The *Bundesland* was reconstituted on former GDR territory in 1990. It has four seats in the Bundesrat.

RECENT ELECTIONS

At the Diet election on 21 April 2002 the CDU received 38·2% of votes cast giving them 48 of 115 seats, the PDS (former Communists) 21·8% (25 seats), the SPD 21·3% (25 seats), the Free Democratic Party 13·1% (17) and the Green Party 2·1%. Turn-out was 56·5%.

CURRENT ADMINISTRATION

The *Prime Minister* is Wolfgang Böhmer (CDU).

Government Website (German only): http://www.sachsen-anhalt.de

ENERGY AND NATURAL RESOURCES

Agriculture. Area and yield of the most important crops:

	Aea (in 1,000 ha)			*Yield (in 1,000 tonnes)*		
	2001	*2002*	*2003*	*2001*	*2002*	*2003*
Cereals	608·1	587·2	559·5	4,362·8	3,577·2	3,312·3
Sugarbeet	50·2	51·8	50·3	2,546·6	2,618·8	2,246·4
Potatoes	14·0	13·8	14·1	584·3	556·1	465·1
Maize	12·8	13·6	23·7	112·4	120·1	122·8

Livestock in 2003 (in 1,000): cattle, 364·6 (including milch cows, 142·9); pigs, 820·0; sheep, 123·7.

INDUSTRY

In 2003, 1,360 establishments (with 20 or more employees) employed 109,433 persons; of these, 48,790 were employed in basic industry, 32,261 in capital goods industry and 20,336 in the food industry. Major sectors are extraction of metal, metal working, metal articles, the nutrition industry, mechanical engineering and the chemical industry.

Labour. The economically active persons totalled 1,050,900 in April 2003. Of the total, 964,100 were employees, 80,300 self-employed, 6,500 unpaid family workers; 314,400 were engaged in power supply, mining, manufacturing and building, 248,400 in commerce and transport, 37,900 in agriculture and forestry, 450,200 in other industries and services.

COMMUNICATIONS

Roads. In 2003 there were 360 km of motorways, 2,359 km of main and 3,778 km of local roads. At 1 Jan. 2004 there were 1,531,416 registered motor vehicles, including 1,312,060 passenger cars, 98,365 lorries, 2,612 buses and 70,351 motorcycles.

SOCIAL INSTITUTIONS

Religion. There are Saxon and Anhalt branches of the Evangelical Church. There were some 0·2m. Roman Catholics in 1990.

Education. In 2003–04 there were 1,206 schools with 249,595 pupils. There were ten universities and institutes of equivalent status with 48,715 students.

CULTURE

Tourism. 1,023 places of accommodation provided 50,440 beds in Dec. 2003. There were 2,142,285 visitors during the year.

FURTHER READING

Statistical office: Statistisches Landesamt Sachsen-Anhalt, Postfach 20 11 56, D-06012 Halle (Saale). It publishes *Statistisches Jahrbuch des Landes Sachsen-Anhalt* (since 1991).

SCHLESWIG-HOLSTEIN

KEY HISTORICAL EVENTS

The *Bundesland* is formed from two states formerly contested between Germany and Denmark.

Schleswig was a Danish dependency ruled since 1474 by the King of Denmark as Duke of Schleswig. He also ruled Holstein, its southern neighbour, as Duke of Holstein, but he did so recognizing that it was a fief of the Holy Roman Empire. As such, Holstein joined the German Confederation which replaced the Empire in 1815.

Disputes between Denmark and the powerful German states were accompanied by rising national feeling in the duchies, where the population was part-Danish and part-German. There was war in 1848–50 and in 1864, when Denmark surrendered its claims to Prussia and Austria. Following her defeat of Austria in 1866 Prussia annexed both duchies.

North Schleswig (predominantly Danish) was awarded to Denmark in 1920. Prussian Holstein and south Schleswig became the present *Bundesland* in 1946.

TERRITORY AND POPULATION

The area of Schleswig-Holstein is 15,763 sq. km. It is divided into four urban and 11 rural districts and 1,127 communes. The capital is Kiel. The population (estimate, 31 Dec. 2003) numbered 2,823,171 (1,379,707 males, 1,443,464 females).

SOCIAL STATISTICS

Statistics for calendar years:

	Live births	*Marriages*	*Divorces*	*Deaths*
2000	26,920	17,849	7,641	29,821
2001	25,681	16,773	7,604	29,667
2002	24,914	17,037	8,194	29,902
2003	24,216	16,985	8,293	30,543

CONSTITUTION AND GOVERNMENT

The *Bundesland* has four seats in the Bundesrat.

RECENT ELECTIONS

At the elections of 20 Feb. 2005 the Christian Democrats won 30 of the 69 available seats with 40·2% of votes cast, the Social Democrats 29 with 38·7%, the Free Democrats 4 with 6·6%, the Greens 4 with 6·2% and the (Danish) South Schleswig Voters Association 2 with 6·6%. Turn-out was 66·6%.

CURRENT ADMINISTRATION

The *Prime Minister* is Peter Harry Carstensen (b. 1947; CDU).

Government Website (German only): http://www.schleswig-holstein.de

ENERGY AND NATURAL RESOURCES

Agriculture. Area and yield of the most important crops:

	Area (in 1,000 ha)			*Yield (in 1,000 tonnes)*		
	2001	*2002*	*2003*	*2001*	*2002*	*2003*
Wheat	195	219	217	1,911	1,776	1,866
Sugarbeet	13	14	13	715	744	686

	Area (in 1,000 ha)			Yield (in 1,000 tonnes)		
	2001	2002	2003	2001	2002	2003
Barley	76	50	69	618	323	514
Potatoes	6	6	6	218	187	200
Rye	34	24	16	245	154	108
Oats	9	10	9	51	52	54

Livestock, Nov. 2003: 1,228,174 cattle (including 375,129 milch cows); 1,397,664 pigs. May 2003: 363,075 sheep; 53,050 horses; 2,515,593 poultry.

Fisheries. In 2003 the yield of small-scale deep-sea and inshore fisheries was 62,844 tonnes valued at €63·4m.

INDUSTRY

In 2003 (average), 1,414 mining, quarrying and manufacturing establishments (with 20 or more employees) employed 131,742 persons; of these, 21,468 were employed in machine construction; 19,701 in food and related industries; 10,108 in electrical engineering; 5,699 in shipbuilding (except naval engineering).

Labour. The economically active persons totalled 1,244,000 in 2003. Of the total, 1,090,000 were employees, 141,000 were self-employed, 13,000 unpaid family workers; 335,000 were engaged in commerce and transport, 287,000 in power supply, mining, manufacturing and building, 43,000 in agriculture and forestry, and 580,000 in other industries and services.

COMMUNICATIONS

Roads. There were (1 Jan. 2002) 9,888 km of 'classified' roads, comprising 485 km of Autobahn, 1,673 km of federal roads, 3,631 km of first-class and 4,098 km of second-class highways. In 2004 the number of motor vehicles was 1,886,816, including 1,552,152 passenger cars, 94,580 lorries, 2,979 buses, 71,460 tractors and 132,183 motorcycles.

Shipping. The Kiel Canal (*Nord-Ostsee-Kanal*) is 98·7 km long; in 2002, 38,562 vessels of 49m. NRT passed through it.

SOCIAL INSTITUTIONS

Justice. There are a court of appeal, four regional courts, 27 local courts, a *Bundesland* labour court, five labour courts, a *Bundesland* social court, four social courts, a finance court, an upper administrative court and an administrative court.

Religion. At the census of 25 May 1987, 73% of the population were Protestants and 6% Roman Catholics.

Education. In 2003–04 there were 650 primary schools with 7,273 teachers and 121,138 pupils; 284 elementary schools with 3,179 teachers and 46,059 pupils; 171 intermediate schools with 4,230 teachers and 65,452 pupils; 107 grammar schools (*Gymnasien*) with 5,544 teachers and 73,608 pupils; 26 comprehensive schools with 1,397 teachers and 17,226 pupils; 171 other schools (including special schools) with 2,370 teachers and 16,856 pupils; 383 vocational schools with 4,364 teachers and 89,557 pupils.

In the winter term of the academic year 2003–04 there were 26,426 students at the three universities (Kiel, Flensburg and Lübeck) and 18,938 students at 11 further education colleges.

CULTURE

Tourism. 4,768 places of accommodation provided 177,233 beds in 2003 for 4,512,002 visitors.

FURTHER READING

Statistical Information: Statistisches Amt für Hamburg und Schleswig-Holstein (Fröbel Str. 15–17, D-24113 Kiel). *Directors:* Dr Hans-Peter Kirschner, Wolfgang Bick. Publications: *Statistisches Taschenbuch Schleswig-Holstein,* since 1954.—*Statistisches Jahrbuch Schleswig-Holstein,* since 1951.—*Statistische Monatshefte Schleswig-Holstein,* since 1949.—*Statistische Berichte,* since 1947.—*Beitrage zur historischen Statistik Schleswig-Holstein,* from 1967.—*Lange Reihen,* from 1977. *Website (German only):* http://www.statistik-sh.de

Baxter, R. R., *The Law of International Waterways.* Harvard Univ. Press, 1964
Brandt, O., *Grundriss der Geschichte Schleswig-Holsteins.* 5th ed. Kiel, 1957
Handbuch für Schleswig-Holstein. 28th ed. Kiel, 1996

State Library: Schleswig-Holsteinische Landesbibliothek, Kiel, Schloss. *Director:* Prof. Dr Dieter Lohmeier.

THURINGIA

Thüringen

KEY HISTORICAL EVENTS

Thuringia with its capital Erfurt is criss-crossed by the rivers Saale, Werra and Weisse Elster and dominated in the south by the mountains of the Thuringian Forest. Martin Luther spent his exile in Eisenach where he translated the New Testament into German while he lived in protective custody in the castle. Weimar became the centre of German intellectual life in the 18th century. In 1919 Weimar was the seat of a briefly liberal Republic. Only ten miles from Weimar lies Buchenwald, the site of a war-time Nazi concentration camp, which is now a national monument to the victims of fascism.

TERRITORY AND POPULATION

The area is 16,172 sq. km. Population on 31 Dec. 2003 was 2,373,157 (1,206,894 females); density, 147 per sq. km. It is divided into six urban districts, 17 rural districts and 1,006 communes. The capital is Erfurt.

SOCIAL STATISTICS

Statistics for calendar years:

	Live births	*Marriages*	*Divorces*	*Deaths*
2000	17,577	9,067	4,878	26,081
2001	17,351	8,575	4,748	25,499
2002	17,007	8,597	5,301	26,000
2003	16,911	8,372	5,558	26,220

CONSTITUTION AND GOVERNMENT

The *Bundesland* was reconstituted on former GDR territory in 1990. It has four seats in the Bundesrat.

RECENT ELECTIONS

At the Diet elections of 13 June 2004 the Christian Democrats (CDU) won 45 seats, with 43·0% of the vote; the Party of Democratic Socialism (PDS) 28, with 26·1%; and the Social Democrats (SPD) 15, with 14·5%. Turn-out was 53·8%.

CURRENT ADMINISTRATION

The *Prime Minister* is Dieter Althaus (CDU).

Government Website: http://www.thueringen.de

ENERGY AND NATURAL RESOURCES

Agriculture. Area and yield of the most important crops:

	Area (in 1,000 ha)			*Yield (in 1,000 tonnes)*		
	2001	*2002*	*2003*	*2001*	*2002*	*2003*
Wheat	215·3	217·2	208·0	1,624·3	1,335·6	1,277·7
Barley	126·1	118·9	124·4	814·0	644·6	637·7
Sugarbeet	10·8	11·2	10·8	562·7	609·7	537·0
Potatoes	2·8	2·7	2·6	110·0	105·1	75·3
Rye	16·4	13·7	9·1	118·7	88·3	51·9
Oats	6·7	6·9	8·6	37·7	33·3	40·6

Livestock, 3 May 2003: 366,882 cattle (including 126,962 milch cows); 710,521 pigs; 234,963 sheep; 8,645 horses; 4,679,089 poultry.

INDUSTRY

In 2003, 1,912 establishments (with 20 or more employees) employed 143,913 persons; of these, 66,129 were employed by producers of materials and supplies, 40,150 by producers of investment goods, 9,369 by producers of durables and 28,265 by producers of non-durables.

Labour. The economically active persons totalled 1,029,500 in May 2003, including 493,500 professional workers, 390,500 manual workers and 92,000 self-employed. 358,600 were engaged in production industries, 223,400 in commerce, transport and communications, 30,200 persons in agriculture and forestry, and 417,300 in other sectors. There were 205,642 persons registered unemployed in Dec. 2003 (102,413 females) and 4,768 on short time; the unemployment rate was 17·7%.

COMMUNICATIONS

Roads. At 1 Jan. 2004 there were 383 km of motorways, 1,950 km of federal roads, 5,492 km of first- and second-class highways and 2,431 km of district highways. Number of motor vehicles, Jan. 2004, 1,507,873, including 1,275,159 private cars, 99,818 lorries, 2,789 buses, 39,761 tractors and 76,341 motorcycles.

SOCIAL INSTITUTIONS

Religion. In 2002, 199,611 persons were Roman Catholic and 643,174 persons were Protestant. In 2003, 550 were Jewish.

Education. In 2003–04 there were 486 primary schools with 54,563 pupils, 294 core curriculum schools with 80,318 pupils, 110 grammar schools with 67,826 pupils and 99 special schools with 15,971 pupils; there were 86,150 pupils in technical and professional education, and 4,956 in professional training for the disabled.

In the winter term 2003–04 there were 11 universities and colleges with 49,193 students enrolled.

Health. In 2003 there were 49 hospitals with 16,917 beds. There were 7,721 doctors (one doctor per 307 population).

Welfare. 2003 expenditure on social welfare was €498m.

CULTURE

Tourism. In July 2003, 1,417 places of accommodation (with nine or more beds) received 2,793,300 visitors who stayed 8,174,800 nights.

FURTHER READING

Statistical information: Thüringer Landesamt für Statistik (Postfach 900163, D-99104 Erfurt; Europaplatz 3, D-99091 Erfurt). *President:* Günter Krombholz. Publications: *Statistisches Jahrbuch Thüringen,* since 1993. *Kreiszahlen für Thüringen*, since 1995. *Gemeindezahlen für Thüringen*, since 1998. *Thüringen-Atlas*, since 1999. *Statistische Monatshefte Thüringen*, since 1994. *Statistische Berichte,* since 1991. *Faltblätter*, since 1991. *Website (German only):* http://www.tls.thueringen.de

State library: Thüringer Universitäts- und Landesbibliothek, Jena.

GHANA

Republic of Ghana

Capital: Accra
Population projection, 2010: 24·12m.
GDP per capita, 2002: (PPP$) 2,130
HDI/world rank: 0·568/131

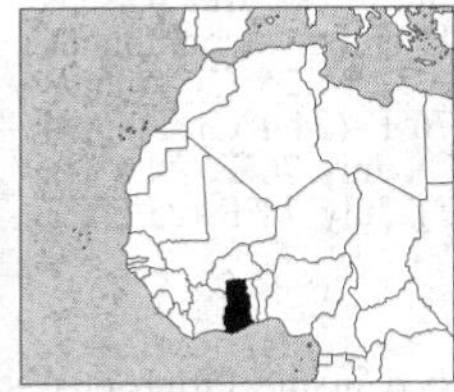

KEY HISTORICAL EVENTS

By the 17th century, strong chiefdoms and warrior states, notably the Ashanti, dominated the territory. The Ashanti state was strengthened by its collaboration with the slave trade but by 1874 it had been conquered by Britain and made a colony. The hinterland became a protectorate in 1901. British rule was challenged after the Second World War by Kwame Nkrumah and the Convention People's Party (CPP), formed in 1949. The state of Ghana came into existence on 6 March 1957 when the former Colony of the Gold Coast with the Trusteeship Territory of Togoland attained Dominion status. The country was declared a Republic within the Commonwealth on 1 July 1960 with Dr Kwame Nkrumah as the first President.

In 1966 the Nkrumah regime was overthrown by the military who ruled until 1969 when they handed over to a civilian regime under a new constitution. On 13 Jan. 1972 the armed forces regained power. In 1979 the Supreme Military Council (SMC) was toppled in a coup led by Flight-Lieut. J. J. Rawlings. The new government permitted elections already scheduled and these resulted in a victory for Dr Hilla Limann and his People's National Party. However, on 31 Dec. 1981 another coup led by Flight-Lieut. Rawlings dismissed the government and Parliament, suspended the constitution and established a Provisional National Defence Council to exercise all government powers. A new pluralist democratic constitution was approved by referendum in April 1992. The Fourth Republic was proclaimed on 7 Jan. 1993.

TERRITORY AND POPULATION

Ghana is bounded west by Côte d'Ivoire, north by Burkina Faso, east by Togo and south by the Gulf of Guinea. The area is 238,533 sq. km; the 2000 census population was 18,845,265, giving a density of 79·0 persons per sq. km. The United Nations population estimate for 2000 was 19,593,000.

The UN gives a projected population for 2010 of 24·12m.

In 2001, 63·6% of the population was rural. 1m. Ghanaians lived abroad in 1995.

Ghana is divided into ten regions:

Regions	*Area (sq. km)*	*Population, census 2000*	*Capital*
Ashanti	24,389	3,600,358	Kumasi
Brong-Ahafo	39,557	1,798,058	Sunyani
Central	9,826	1,593,888	Cape Coast
Eastern	19,323	2,101,650	Koforidua
Greater Accra	3,245	2,903,753	Accra
Northern	70,384	1,805,428	Tamale
Upper East	8,842	919,549	Bolgatanga
Upper West	18,476	575,579	Wa
Volta	20,570	1,630,254	Ho
Western	23,921	1,916,748	Sekondi-Takoradi

In 1999 the capital, Accra, had a population of 1,904,000. Other major cities with 1988 estimated populations: Kumasi, 385,192; Tamale, 151,069; Tema, 109,975; Sekondi-Takoradi, 103,653.

About 44% of the population are Akan. Other tribal groups include Moshi-Dagomba (16%), Ewe (13%) and Ga (8%). About 75 languages are spoken; the official language is English.

SOCIAL STATISTICS

1995 births, 676,000; deaths, 191,000. Birth rate (per 1,000 population), 1995: 39·3; death rate, 11·0. 2001 life expectancy, 56·2 years for men and 59·3 for women. Infant mortality, 57 per 1,000 live births (2001). Annual population growth rate, 1992–2002, 2·4%; fertility rate, 2001, 4·3 births per woman.

CLIMATE

The climate ranges from the equatorial type on the coast to savannah in the north and is typified by the existence of well-marked dry and wet seasons. Temperatures are relatively high throughout the year. The amount, duration and seasonal distribution of rain is very marked, from the south, with over 80" (2,000 mm), to the north, with under 50" (1,250 mm). In the extreme north, the wet season is from March to Aug., but further south it lasts until Oct. Near Kumasi, two wet seasons occur, in May and June and again in Oct., and this is repeated, with greater amounts, along the coast of Ghana. Accra, Jan. 80°F (26·7°C), July 77°F (25°C). Annual rainfall 29" (724 mm). Kumasi, Jan. 77°F (25°C), July 76°F (24·4°C). Annual rainfall 58" (1,402 mm). Sekondi-Takoradi, Jan. 77°F (25°C), July 76°F (24·4°C). Annual rainfall 47" (1,181 mm). Tamale, Jan. 82°F (27·8°C), July 78°F (25·6°C). Annual rainfall 41" (1,026 mm).

CONSTITUTION AND GOVERNMENT

After the coup of 31 Dec. 1981, supreme power was vested in the Provisional National Defence Council (PNDC), chaired by Flight-Lieut. Jerry John Rawlings.

A new constitution was approved by 92·6% of votes cast at a referendum on 28 April 1992. The electorate was 8,255,690; turn-out was 43·8%. The constitution sets up a presidential system on the US model, with a multi-party parliament and an independent judiciary. The *President* is elected by universal suffrage for a four-year term renewable once.

The unicameral *Parliament* has 230 members, elected for a four-year term in single-seat constituencies.

National Anthem. 'God bless our Homeland, Ghana'; words by the government, tune by P. Gbeho.

RECENT ELECTIONS

Presidential elections were held on 7 Dec. 2004. Incumbent John Agyekum Kufuor of the New Patriotic Party (NPP) won 52·5% of the vote and John Atta Mills of the National Democratic Congress (NDC) 44·6%. There were two other candidates. In parliamentary elections, the NPP won 128 of 230 seats, the NDC 94, the People's National Convention 4, the Convention People's Party 3 and ind. 1.

CURRENT ADMINISTRATION

President: John Agyekum Kufuor; b. 1938 (NPP; sworn in 7 Jan. 2001 and re-elected in Dec. 2004).

Vice-President: Aliu Mahama.

In March 2005 the government comprised the following:

Senior Minister and Leader of Government Economic Team: Joseph Henry Mensah. *Minister of Defence:* Dr Kwame Addo-Kufuor. *Local Government and Rural Development:* Charles Bintim. *Foreign Affairs:* Nana Akufo Addo. *Interior:* Papa Owusu Ankomah. *Information:* Dan Botwe. *Justice and Attorney General:* Ayikoi Otoo. *Parliamentary Affairs:* F. K. Owusu-Ajapong. *Food and Agriculture:* Ernest Debrah. *Finance and Economic Planning:* Kwadwo Baah Wiredu. *Regional Co-operation and NEPAD:* Kofi Konadu Apraku. *Trade and Industry:* Alan Kyeremanteng. *Private Sector Development:* Kwamina Bartels. *Fisheries:* Gladys Asmah. *Tourism and Modernization of the Capital City:* Jake Obetsebi-Lamptey. *Works and Housing:* Hackman Owusu Agyeman. *Road Transport:* Richard Anane. *Ports, Harbours and Railways:* Christopher Ameyaw-Akumfi. *Communications:* Albert Kan-Dapaah. *Energy:* Prof. Mike Oquaye. *Lands, Forestry and Mines:* Prof. Dominic Kwaku Fobih. *Education and Sports:* Yaw Osafo-Maafo. *Health:* Major Courage Quashigah. *Women and Children's Affairs:* Hajia Alima Mahama. *Manpower, Youth and Employment:* Joseph Adda. *Environment and Science:* Christine Churcher.

Government Website: http://www.ghana.gov.gh

DEFENCE

Defence expenditure totalled US$23m. in 2003 (US$1 per capita), representing 0·3% of GDP.

Army. Total strength (2002), 5,000.

Navy. The Navy, based at Sekondi and Tema, numbered 1,000 in 2002 including support personnel.

Air Force. There are air bases at Takoradi and Tamale. Personnel strength (2002), 1,000. There were 19 combat aircraft.

INTERNATIONAL RELATIONS

Ghana is a member of the UN, WTO, the Commonwealth, the African Union, African Development Bank, ECOWAS and is an ACP member state of the ACP-EU relationship.

ECONOMY

Agriculture accounted for 36·0% of GDP in 2002, industry 24·3% and services 39·7%.

Overview. Ghana is committed to the reform programmes of the IMF and World Bank and is one of Africa's biggest borrowers. In 1996 aid amounted to 11% of GDP, or four times the value of Ghana's exports. A privatization programme was inaugurated in 1988. By April 2000, 132 state-owned enterprises had been sold off to become 232 privately-owned companies. A further 168 were set to be privatized. Privatization deals raised US$804m. between 1990 and 1996, including the Ashanti Goldfields sell-off worth more than US$400m. On 27 April 2004 Ashanti Goldfields completed its merger with South Africa's AngloGold to form the world's largest gold mining company in terms of reserves, under the new name of AngloGold Ashanti. Only South Africa among sub-Saharan African nations has raised more from privatization. Building, tourism, technology and financial services account for more than 46% of national income.

Currency. The monetary unit is the *cedi* (GHC) of 100 *pesewas* (P). In 1995 inflation was running at nearly 60% but by 2002 was down to 14·8%. Foreign exchange reserves were US$238m. in April 2002 and gold reserves 281,000 troy oz in May 2002. Total money supply in Sept. 2001 was ₵3,867·83bn.

Budget. In 2000 revenues totalled ₵5,385bn. and expenditures ₵7,525bn.

Performance. Average GDP growth in the ten years to 1998 was 4·5%—almost twice the African average. Real GDP growth was 4·2% in 2001 and 4·5% in 2002. Total GDP was US$7·7bn. in 2003.

Banking and Finance. The Bank of Ghana (*Governor,* Dr Paul Acquah) was established in 1957 as the central bank and bank of issue. At Dec. 1995 its total assets were ₵3,272,946·6m. There were in 1998 nine commercial banks, four merchant banks and 130 rural banks. There are two discount houses. Banks are required to have a capital base of at least 6% of net assets. At Dec. 1995 assets of commercial banks totalled ₵1,900,327·1m.

Foreign investment is actively encouraged with the Ghana Free Zone Scheme offering particular incentives such as full exemption of duties and levies on all imports for production and exports from the zones, full exemption on tax on profits for ten years, and no more than 8% after ten years. It is a condition of the scheme that at least 70% of goods made within the zones must be exported. Within 18 months of the scheme being set up in 1995, 50 projects had been registered.

There is a stock exchange in Accra.

ENERGY AND NATURAL RESOURCES

Ghana is facing an energy crisis, with power cuts of up to 12 hours a day because drought has caused the level of Lake Volta to drop to below the danger level.

Environment. Ghana's carbon dioxide emissions from the consumption and flaring of fossil fuels in 2002 were the equivalent of 0·3 tonnes per capita.

Electricity. Installed capacity was 1·2m. kW in 2000. Production (2000) 7·55bn. kWh, mainly from two hydro-electric stations operated by the Volta River Authority, Akosombo (six units) and Kpong (four units). Consumption per capita was 417 kWh in 2000. A drought in 1998 caused power cuts, with over 99% of electricity being hydro-electric. It is planned that electricity production will become less dependent on hydro-electric stations and more so on gas, with the construction of a 600 km pipeline forming part of the proposed West African Gas Pipeline Project.

Oil and Gas. Ghana is pursuing the development of its own gas fields and plans to harness gas at the North and South Tano fields located off the western coast. Natural gas reserves, 2002, totalled 23bn. cu. metres. Oil reserves in 2002 were 17m. bbls.

Minerals. Gold is one of the mainstays of the economy; Ghana ranks second only to South Africa among African gold producers. Production in 2001 was 68,700 kg. In 2002 diamond production was 963,000 carats; manganese, 1·14m. tonnes; bauxite, 684,000 tonnes; aluminium, 117,000 tonnes.

Agriculture. The rural poor earn little and many small farmers have reverted to subsistence farming. The agricultural population in 2002 was 12·97m., of whom 5·74m. were economically active. There were 3·70m. ha of arable land in 2001 and 2·20m. ha of permanent crops. 11,000 ha were irrigated in 2001. There were 3,600 tractors in 2001. In southern and central Ghana main food crops are maize, rice, cassava, plantains, groundnuts, yam and taro, and in northern Ghana groundnuts, rice, maize, sorghum, millet and yams. Agriculture presently operates at only 20% of its potential and is an area that is to be a major focus of investment.

Production of main food crops, 2000 (in 1,000 tonnes): cassava, 7,845; yams, 3,249; plantains, 2,046; taro, 1,707; maize, 1,014; cocoa beans, 398; coconuts, 305; sorghum, 302; chillies and green peppers, 270; oranges, 270. Cocoa is the main cash crop. The government estimates that more than 40% of the population relies either directly or indirectly on cocoa as a source of income. It contributes approximately 13% of GDP. Ghana is the second largest cocoa bean producer in the world after Côte d'Ivoire, and the second largest producer of both yams and taro, after Nigeria.

Livestock, 2000: cattle, 1·28m.; sheep, 2·56m.; pigs, 350,000; goats, 2·80m.; chickens, 18m.

Forestry. There were 6·34m. ha of forest in 2000, or 27·8% of the total land area. Reserves account for some 30% of the total forest lands. Timber production in 2001 was 21·98m. cu. metres.

Fisheries. In 2001 total catch was 445,287 tonnes, of which 370,787 tonnes came from sea fishing.

INDUSTRY

Ghana's industries include mining, lumbering, light manufacturing and food processing.

Labour. In 1996 the labour force was 8,393,000. Females constituted 51% of the workforce in 1999. Only Cambodia had a higher percentage of females in its workforce.

In 1994 there were 37,000 persons registered as unemployed.

INTERNATIONAL TRADE

Foreign debt was US$7,338m. in 2002.

Imports and Exports. In 2002 exports (f.o.b.) totalled US$2,015·2m.; imports (f.o.b.) were valued at US$2,705·1m. Principal exports, 1999: cocoa, 35%; manufactured goods (including wood products, aluminium, iron and steel), 18%; timber, 8%; and gold, 8%. Principal imported commodities: machinery and transport equipment, 38%; petroleum, 16%; manufactured goods, 13%; foodstuffs, 11%. Main export markets, 1999: UK, 23%; Netherlands, 14%; Italy, 6%; Burkina Faso, 5%; USA, 5%. Main import suppliers: UK, 10%; USA, 9%; Nigeria, 8%; Belgium, 7%; Germany, 7%; Netherlands, 7%.

COMMUNICATIONS

Roads. In 2001 there were 46,179 km of roads, including 21 km of motorways. About 18·4% of all roads are hard-surfaced. A Road Sector Strategy and Programme to develop the road network ran from 1995 to 2000. There were 90,000 passenger cars in use in 1996, equivalent to 4·7 per 1,000 inhabitants.

Rail. Total length of railways in 2000 was 953 km of 1,067 mm gauge. In 2000 railways carried 1·0m. tonnes of freight and 2·2m. passengers.

Civil Aviation. There is an international airport at Accra (Kotoka). The national carrier is the state-owned Ghana Airways. In 1999 scheduled airline traffic of Ghana-based carriers flew 9·1m. km, carrying 304,000 passengers (all on international flights). Accra handled 602,000 passengers (592,000 on international flights) in 2000.

Shipping. The chief ports are Tema and Takoradi. In 2002, 6·8m. tonnes of cargo were handled at Tema and 3·4m. tonnes at Takoradi. There is inland water transport on Lake Volta. In 2002 the merchant marine totalled 126,000 GRT, including oil tankers 8,000 GRT. The Volta, Ankobra and Tano rivers provide 168 km of navigable waterways for launches and lighters.

Telecommunications. Ghana Telecom was privatized in 1996. In 2002 Ghana had 723,800 telephone subscribers, or 33·4 for every 1,000 inhabitants, and there were 82,000 PCs in use (3·8 per 1,000 persons). Mobile phone subscribers numbered 449,400 in 2002. There were 170,000 Internet users in 2002. In 1999 there were 5,000 fax machines.

Postal Services. In 1998 there were 1,010 post offices.

SOCIAL INSTITUTIONS

Justice. The Courts are constituted as follows:

Supreme Court. The Supreme Court consists of the Chief Justice who is also the President, and not less than four other Justices of the Supreme Court. The Supreme Court is the final court of appeal in Ghana. The final interpretation of the constitution is entrusted to the Supreme Court.

Court of Appeal. The Court of Appeal consists of the Chief Justice with not less than five other Justices of the Appeal court and such other Justices of Superior Courts as the Chief Justice may nominate. The Court of Appeal is duly constituted by three Justices. The Court of Appeal is bound by its own previous decisions and all courts inferior to the Court of Appeal are bound to follow the decisions of the Court of Appeal on questions of law. Divisions of the Appeal Court may be created, subject to the discretion of the Chief Justice.

High Court of Justice. The Court has jurisdiction in civil and criminal matters as well as those relating to industrial and labour disputes including administrative complaints. The High Court of Justice has supervisory jurisdiction over all inferior Courts and any adjudicating authority and in exercise of its supervisory jurisdiction has power to issue such directions, orders or writs including writs or orders in the nature of habeas corpus, certiorari, mandamus, prohibition and quo qarrantto. The High Court of Justice has no jurisdiction in cases of treason. The High Court consists of the Chief Justice and not less than 12 other judges and such other Justices of the Superior Court as the Chief Justice may appoint.

Under the Provisional National Defence Council which ruled from 1981 to 2001 public tribunals were established in addition to the traditional courts of justice.

The population in penal institutions in 2002 was 11,624 (58 per 100,000 of national population).

Religion. An estimated 30% of the population are Muslim and 24% Christian, with 38% adherents to indigenous beliefs and 8% other religions. In Sept. 2003 the Roman Catholic church had one cardinal.

Education. Schooling is free and compulsory, and consists of six years of primary, three years of junior secondary and three years of senior secondary education. In 1990, 75% of eligible children attended primary, and 39% secondary, school. In 2000–01 there were 2·48m. pupils in primary schools with 75,087 teachers; and 1·03m. pupils with 55,549 teachers in secondary schools. University education is free. There are two universities, one university each for development studies, and science and technology. In 1994–95 there were 11,225 university students and 779 academic staff. There were also six polytechnics, seven colleges and 38 teacher training colleges. Adult literacy in 2001 was 72·7% (81·1% among men and 64·5% among women). In 1970 adult literacy was just 31%.

In 1999–2000 total expenditure on education came to 4·2% of GNP.

Health. Provision of doctors, 1994: one per 22,970 population. Provision of hospital beds, 1994: one per 638 population. At the end of 1995 there were 15,890 cases of AIDS, mainly women.

Ghana has been one of the most successful countries in reducing undernourishment in the past 15 years. Between 1990–02 and 2000–02 the proportion of undernourished people declined from 37% of the population to just 13%. The proportion of the population with access to safe water increased from 35% in 1980 to 65% in 1996.

CULTURE

World Heritage Sites. Ghana has two sites on the UNESCO World Heritage List: Forts and Castles, Volta, Greater Accra, Central and Western Regions (inscribed on the list in 1979), Portuguese trading posts built between 1482 and 1786 along the coast; Asante Traditional Buildings (1980), the remains of the Asante civilization that peaked in the 18th century.

Broadcasting. The Ghana Broadcasting Corporation is an autonomous statutory body. In April 2000 there were three free television stations, three satellite/cable services and 49 commercial radio stations. There were 1·1m. TV receivers (colour by PAL) in 2001 and 13·9m. radio receivers in 2000.

Press. There were (1996) four daily newspapers with a combined circulation of 250,000.

Tourism. There were 399,000 foreign tourists in 2000, spending US$386m.

DIPLOMATIC REPRESENTATIVES

Of Ghana in the United Kingdom (13 Belgrave Sq., London, SW1X 8PN)
High Commissioner: Isaac Osei.

Of the United Kingdom in Ghana (Osu Link, off Gamel Abdul Nasser Ave., Accra)
High Commissioner: Gordon Wetherell.

Of Ghana in the USA (3512 International Dr., NW, Washington, D.C., 20008)
Ambassador: Fritz Kwabena Poku.

Of the USA in Ghana (Ring Rd. East, Accra)
Ambassador: Mary C. Yates.

Of Ghana to the United Nations
Ambassador: Nana Effah-Apentang.

Of Ghana to the European Union
Ambassador: Kobina Wudu.

FURTHER READING

Carmichael, J., *Profile of Ghana.* London, 1992.—*African Eldorado: Ghana from Gold Coast to Independence.* London, 1993

Herbst, J., *The Politics of Reform in Ghana, 1982–1991.* California Univ. Press, 1993

Myers, Robert A., *Ghana.* [Bibliography] ABC-Clio, Oxford and Santa Barbara (CA), 1991

Petchenkine, Y., *Ghana in Search of Stability, 1957–1992.* New York, 1992

Rathbone, R., *Nkrumah and the Chiefs: The Politics of Chieftaincy in Ghana.* Currey, Oxford, 2000

Ray, D. I., *Ghana: Politics, Economics and Society.* London, 1986

Rimmer, D., *Staying Poor: Ghana's Political Economy, 1950–1990.* Oxford, 1993

Rothchild., D. (ed.) *Ghana: the Political Economy of Recovery.* Boulder (Colo.), 1991

National statistical office: Statistical Service, Accra.

GREECE

Elliniki Dimokratia
(Hellenic Republic)

Capital: Athens
Population projection, 2010: 10·99m.
GDP per capita, 2002: (PPP$) 18,720
HDI/world rank: 0·902/24

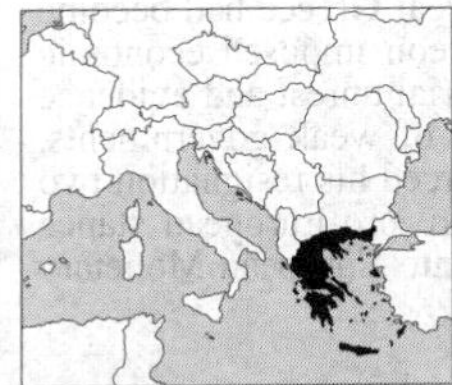

KEY HISTORICAL EVENTS

The land which is now Greece was first inhabited between 2000–1700 BC by tribes from the North. This period was followed by the Mycenaean Civilization which was overthrown by the Dorians at the end of the 12th century BC. Its dominant citadels were at Tiryns and Mycenae. What little is known about this period is from stories such as those by Homer written in the 9th or 8th century BC.

The following period, known as the Greek Dark Ages, ended by the 6th century BC when the *polis*, or city state, was formed. Built mainly on coastal plains, the two principal cities were Sparta and Athens. Based on ideas of democracy and meritocracy, and rich in theatre, art and philosophy, the *polis* was the pinnacle of the Greek Classical Age. It was the era of Euripydes, Theusidades and Socrates. With strong trade links, Greece also had territories in Southern Italy, Sicily, Southern France and Asia Minor.

Two Persian invasions in the 5th century were checked at Marathon (490 BC) and Thermopylae (480 BC) where Spartans held off a great force of Persian soldiers. In 431 BC rivalry between the dominant city states erupted into the Peloponnesian War. Eventually in 404 BC Sparta emerged victorious against Athens, but in the next century Sparta itself fell to Thebes (371 BC).

Led by Philip II of Macedon, the Macedonians defeated the city states in 338 BC. The *poleis* were forced to unify under his rule. With Plato and Aristotle active at this time, the latter serving as a tutor to Philip's son Alexander, this was a period of rich cultural heritage. When Philip was assassinated in 336 BC, Alexander succeeded him at the age of 20. He spent the next thirteen years on a relentless campaign to expand the Macedonian territories. The Greek Empire stretched to the edge of India and encompassed most of the known civilized world.

Following Alexander's death in 323 BC, the empire gradually disintegrated. By the end of the 2nd century AD, the Romans had defeated the Macedonians and Greece was incorporated into the Roman Empire. It remained in Roman hands until it became part of the Byzantine Empire in the 4th century AD. Byzantium was populated with Greek-speaking Christians with its power base in Constantinople.

Over the next six centuries Greece was invaded by Franks, Normans and Arabs but remained part of the Byzantine Empire. Following the Empire's decline in the 11th century, Greece was incorporated into the Ottoman Empire in 1460. Apart from a period under Venetian control between 1686–1715, Greece was part of Turkey until the Greek War of Independence.

Greece broke away from the Ottoman Empire in the 1820s and was declared a kingdom under the protection of Great Britain, France and Russia. Many Greeks were left outside the new state but Greece's area increased by 70%, the population growing from 2·8m. to 4·8m., after the Treaty of Bucharest (1913) recognized Greek sovereignty over Crete.

King Constantine opted for neutrality in the First World War, while Prime Minister Venezelos favoured the Entente powers. This National Schism led to British and French intervention which deposed Constantine on 11 June 1917. When his son Alexander died on 25 Oct. 1920, he returned and reigned until 1922. He was forced to abdicate by a coup after defeat by Turkey and the loss of Smyrna. The Treaty of Lausanne (1923) recognized Smyrna as Turkish with Eastern Thrace and the islands of Imvros and Tenedos, all of which had been ceded to Greece by the 1920 Treaty of Sevres. An exchange of Christian and Muslim populations followed. Resistance to Italian demands brought Greece into the Second World War when Germany had to come to the aid of the hard-pressed Italians. Athens was occupied on 27 April 1941. The occupation lasted until 15 Oct. 1944.

A communist led insurrection in 1946–47 was put down with the help of British and, later, US troops. Peace came after 1949.

The late 1950s saw the emergence of the Left, capitalizing on the movement for union with Cyprus and unease over NATO membership (1952). A military coup in 1967 led to the authoritarian rule of the 'Colonels' headed by George Papadopoulos. A republic was declared on 29 July 1973. The dictatorship collapsed in 1974 giving way to a civilian government of national unity. The monarchy was abolished by a referendum on 8 Dec. 1974. The 1981 election brought Andreas Papandreou to power and the head of a socialist government. Earlier that year Greece had become the tenth member of the EU. Re-elected in 1985, Papandreou imposed economic austerity to combat inflation and soaring budgets but industrial unrest and evidence of widespread corruption led to his fall and a succession of weak governments. Papandreou returned to power in Oct. 1993 but ill-health forced his resignation two years later. His successor Constantinos Simitis took a more pro-European stance instituting economic reforms to prepare the way for entry into European Monetary Union (EMU).

TERRITORY AND POPULATION

Greece is bounded in the north by Albania, the Former Yugoslav Republic of Macedonia (FYROM) and Bulgaria, east by Turkey and the Aegean Sea, south by the Mediterranean and west by the Ionian Sea. The total area is 131,957 sq. km (50,949 sq. miles), of which the islands account for 25,042 sq. km (9,669 sq. miles).

The population was 10,964,020 (5,537,574 females) according to the census of March 2001; density, 83·1 per sq. km.

The UN gives a projected population for 2010 of 10·99m.

In 2001, 60·4% of the population lived in urban areas. There were 166,031 resident foreign nationals in 1991. A further 5m. Greeks are estimated to live abroad.

In 1987 the territory of Greece was administratively reorganized into 13 *regions* comprising in all 51 *departments*. Areas and populations according to the 2001 census:

Region/Department	*Area in sq. km*	*Population*	*Chief town*
Aegean Islands	*9,113*	*508,807*	
Chios	904	53,408	Chios
Cyclades	2,572	112,615	Hermoupolis
Dodecanese	2,705	190,071	Rhodes
Lesbos	2,154	109,118	Mytilene
Samos	778	43,595	Samos
Attica[1]	*3,808*	*3,761,810*	*Athens*
Central Greece and Euboea	*21,100*	*829,758*	
Aetolia and Acarnania	5,447	224,429	Messolonghi
Boeotia	3,211	131,085	Levadeia
Euboea	3,908	215,136	Chalcis
Evrytania	2,045	32,053	Karpenissi
Phocis	2,121	48,284	Amphissa
Phthiotis	4,368	178,771	Lamia
Crete	*8,336*	*601,131*	
Canea	2,376	150,387	Canea
Heraklion	2,641	292,489	Heraklion
Lassithi	1,823	76,319	Aghios Nikolaos
Rethymnon	1,496	81,936	Rethymnon
Epirus	*9,203*	*353,820*	
Arta	1,612	78,134	Arta
Ioannina	4,990	170,239	Ioannina
Preveza	1,086	59,356	Preveza
Thesprotia	1,515	46,091	Hegoumenitsa
Ionian Islands	*2,307*	*212,984*	
Cephalonia	935	39,488	Argostoli
Corfu	641	111,975	Corfu
Leucas	325	22,506	Leucas
Zante	406	39,015	Zante
Macedonia	*34,174*	*2,424,765*	
Cavalla	2,109	145,054	Cavalla
Chalcidice	2,945	104,894	Polygyros
Drama	3,468	103,975	Drama
Florina	1,863	54,768	Florina

Region/Department	Area in sq. km	Population	Chief town
Grevena	2,338	37,947	Grevena
Imathia	1,712	143,618	Veroia
Kastoria	1,685	53,483	Kastoria
Kilkis	2,614	89,056	Kilkis
Kozani	3,562	155,324	Kozani
Mount Athos[2]	336	2,262	Karyai
Pella	2,506	145,797	Edessa
Pieria	1,506	129,846	Katerini
Serres	3,970	200,916	Serres
Thessaloniki (Salonika)	3,560	1,057,825	Thessaloniki
Peloponnese	*21,440*	*1,155,019*	
Achaia	3,209	322,789	Patras
Arcadia	4,419	102,035	Tripolis
Argolis	2,214	105,770	Nauplion
Corinth	2,290	154,624	Corinthos
Elia	2,681	193,288	Pyrgos
Laconia	3,636	99,637	Sparti
Messenia	2,991	176,876	Calamata
Thessaly	*13,930*	*753,888*	
Karditsa	2,576	129,541	Karditsa
Larissa	5,351	279,305	Larissa
Magnesia	2,636	206,995	Volos
Trikala	3,367	138,047	Trikala
Thrace	*8,578*	*362,038*	
Evros	4,242	149,354	Alexandroupolis
Rhodope	2,543	110,828	Comotini
Xanthi	1,793	101,856	Xanthi

[1]Attica is both region and department. [2]Autonomous region.

The largest cities (2001 census populations) are Athens (the capital), 745,514 (total agglomeration of Greater Athens, 3,187,734); Thessaloniki (agglomeration), 800,764; Patras (agglomeration), 185,668; Piraeus (municipality), 175,697; Heraklion (agglomeration), 144,642; Peristerion (municipality), 137,918; Larissa, 124,786; Volos (agglomeration), 116,031 in 1991; Kallithea (municipality), 109,609. Greater Athens, composed of the capital city, the port of Piraeus and a number of suburbs, contains about one third of the Greek population. It also contains about 50% of the country's industry and is the principal commercial, financial and diplomatic centre. Efforts have, however, been made to decentralize the economy. The second city, Thessaloniki, with its major port, has grown rapidly in population and industrial development.

The Monastic Republic of **Mount Athos** (or Agion Oros, i.e. 'Holy Mountain'), the easternmost of the three prongs of the peninsula of Chalcidice, is a self-governing community composed of 20 monasteries. The peninsula is administered by a Council of four members and an Assembly of 20 members, one deputy from each monastery. The Constitution of 1927 gives legal sanction to the Charter of Mount Athos, drawn up by representatives of the 20 monasteries on 20 May 1924, and its status is confirmed by the 1952 and 1975 Constitutions. Women are not permitted to enter. Population, 2001, 2,262.

The modern Greek language had two contesting literary standard forms, the archaizing *Katharevousa* ('purist'), and a version based on the spoken vernacular, 'Demotic'. In 1976 Standard Modern Greek was adopted as the official language, with Demotic as its core.

SOCIAL STATISTICS

2001: 102,282 live births; 102,559 deaths; 58,491 marriages; 11,500 divorces; 588 still births; 4,351 births to unmarried mothers. 2001 rates: birth (per 1,000 population), 9·4; death, 9·4; marriage, 5·3; divorce, 1·0. Annual population growth rate, 1992–2002, 0·7%. Over 1990–98 the suicide rate per 100,000 population was 3·8 (men, 6·1; women, 1·6). Expectation of life at birth, 2001, 75·6 years for males and 80·8 years for females. In 1998 the most popular age range for marrying was 25–29 for both males and females. Infant mortality, 2001, five per 1,000 live births; fertility rate, 2001, 1·3 births per woman. In 2002 Greece received 5,664 asylum applications, equivalent to 0·5 per 1,000 inhabitants.

CLIMATE

Coastal regions and the islands have typical Mediterranean conditions, with mild, rainy winters and hot, dry, sunny summers. Rainfall comes almost entirely in the winter months, though amounts vary widely according to position and relief. Continental conditions affect the northern mountainous areas, with severe winters, deep snow cover and heavy precipitation, but summers are hot. Athens, Jan. 48°F (8·6°C), July 82·5°F (28·2°C). Annual rainfall 16·6" (414·3 mm).

CONSTITUTION AND GOVERNMENT

Greece is a presidential parliamentary democracy. A new Constitution was introduced in June 1975. The 300-member *Chamber of Deputies* is elected for four-year terms by proportional representation. There is a 3% threshold. Extra seats are awarded to the party which leads in an election. The Chamber of Deputies elects the head of state, the *President*, for a five-year term.

National Anthem. 'Imnos eis tin Eleftherian' ('Hymn to Freedom'); words by Dionysios Solomos, tune by N. Mantzaros.

RECENT ELECTIONS

Karolos Papoulias was elected president by the 300-member parliament on 8 Feb. 2005, receiving 279 votes. No other candidates stood.

Parliamentary elections were held on 7 March 2004. Turn-out was 76·5%. Seats gained (and % of vote): New Democracy (ND), 165 (45·4%); Pasok (Panhellenic Socialist Movement), 117 (40·6%); Communist Party, 12 (5·9%); Coalition of the Left and Progress (SIN), 6 (3·3%).

European Parliament. Greece has 24 (25 in 1999) representatives. At the June 2004 elections turn-out was 62·8% (70·1% in 1999). ND won 11 seats with 43·1% of votes cast (political affiliation in European Parliament: European People's Party–European Democrats); Pasok, 8 with 34·0% (Party of European Socialists); Communist Party, 3 with 9·5% (European Unitary Left/Nordic Green Left); the SIN, 1 with 4·2% (European Unitary Left/Nordic Green Left); the Populist Orthodox Rally (LAOS), 1 with 4·1% (Independence and Democracy Group).

CURRENT ADMINISTRATION

President: Karolos Papoulias; b. 1929 (sworn in 12 March 2005).

In March 2005 the New Democracy Government comprised:

Prime Minister and Minister of Culture: Dr Konstantinos 'Kostas' Karamanlis; b. 1956 (sworn in 10 March 2004).

Minister of Economy and Finance: Georgios Alogoskoufis. *Foreign Affairs:* Petros Moliviatis. *Defence:* Spilios Spiliotopoulos. *Interior, Public Administration and Decentralization:* Prokopis Pavlopoulos. *Development:* Dimitris Sioufas. *Environment, Land Planning and Public Works:* Giorgos Souflias. *Education and Religion:* Marietta Giannakou. *Employment and Social Protection:* Panos Panagiotopoulos. *Health and Social Solidarity:* Nikitas Kaklamanis. *Agricultural Development and Food:* Savvas Tsitouridis. *Justice:* Anastasios Papaligouras. *Transport and Communications:* Michalis Liapis. *Public Order:* Georgios Voulgarakis. *Mercantile Marine:* Manolis Kefalogiannis. *Macedonia and Thrace:* Nikos Tsiartsionis. *Tourism:* Dimitris Avramopoulos. *Aegean and Island Policy:* Aristotelis Pavlidis. *Minister of State and Government Spokesman:* Thodoris Rousopoulos.

Office of the Prime Minister: http://www.primeminister.gr

DEFENCE

Prior to 2001 conscription was generally: (Army) 18 months, (Navy) 21 months, (Air Force) 20 months. However, following a gradual shortening of military service, by 2003 conscription was 12 months in the Army, 14 in the Air Force and 15 in the Navy.

In 2003 defence expenditure totalled US$7,169m. (US$671 per capita), representing 4·1% of GDP (the highest percentage in the EU). In the period 1999–2003 Greece's spending on major conventional weapons, at US$4·4bn., was the third highest behind China and India.

Army. The Field Army is organized in three military regions, with one Army, two command, five corps and five divisional headquarters. Total Army strength (2002) 114,000 (81,000 conscripts, 2,700 women). There is also a Territorial Defence Force/National Guard of 35,000 whose role is internal security.

Navy. The current strength of the Hellenic Navy includes eight diesel submarines, two destroyers and 12 frigates. Main bases are at Salamis, Patras and Soudha Bay (Crete). Personnel in 2002 totalled 19,000 (9,800 conscripts, 1,300 women).

Air Force. The Hellenic Air Force (HAF) had a strength (2002) of 33,000 (7,521 conscripts, 1,520 women). There were 418 combat aircraft including A-7s, F-4s, F-5s, F-16s, Mirage F-1s and Mirage 2000s. The HAF is organized into Tactical and Air Training Commands.

INTERNATIONAL RELATIONS

Greece is a member of the UN, WTO, BIS, NATO, OECD, EU, WEU, Council of Europe, OSCE, CERN, BSEC, IOM, the Antarctic Treaty and the International Organization of the Francophonie. Greece is a signatory to the Schengen Accord which abolishes border controls between Greece, Austria, Belgium, Denmark, Finland, France, Germany, Iceland, Italy, Luxembourg, the Netherlands, Norway, Portugal, Spain and Sweden. On 19 April 2005 Greece became the sixth European Union member to ratify the new EU constitution. The parliament approved the treaty by 268 votes to 17, with 15 abstentions.

ECONOMY

Agriculture accounted for 7·3% of GDP in 2002 (the highest percentage in the EU), industry 22·4% and services 70·3%.

Overview. GDP is among the lowest in the EU. Prior to the accession of the ten new members in May 2004 the agricultural sector was the largest in the EU. The industrial base is small compared to other EU countries. Industry contributes between 22–24% of GDP and manufacturing 12–13%. Until the early 1990s, the state was responsible for up to 70% of all industrial assets but in 1998 the government began a programme of privatization to meet with its criteria for joining the EMU. Greece became a member of the eurozone in Jan. 2000. The Maastricht convergence criteria required tight fiscal policy and left little margin for social spending. Growth since 2001 has outpaced that of the euro area; real output is estimated to have grown by 4% per year, boosted by high levels of investment driven by low interest rates and by the fact that Greece was awarded the 2004 Olympic Games. The present tax system is complex and inequitable and rigidities in the labour market must be tackled if unemployment is to be pushed much below 10%, according to the OECD.

Currency. In June 2000 EU leaders approved a recommendation for Greece to join the European single currency, the euro, and on 1 Jan. 2001 the euro (EUR) became the legal currency; irrevocable conversion rate 340·750 drachmas to 1 euro. The euro, which consists of 100 cents, has been in circulation since 1 Jan. 2002. There are seven euro notes in different colours and sizes denominated in 500, 200, 100, 50, 20, 10 and 5 euros, and eight coins denominated in 2 and 1 euros, then 50, 20, 10, 5, 2 and 1 cents. On the introduction of the euro there was a 'dual circulation' period before the drachma ceased to be legal tender on 28 Feb. 2002. Euro banknotes in circulation on 1 Jan. 2002 had a total value of €13·4bn.

Inflation was 3·5% in 2003 (3·6% in 2002). Foreign exchange reserves were US$6,509m. and gold reserves 3·86m. troy oz in June 2002. Total money supply in June 2002 was €7,683m.

Budget. Ordinary budget revenue in 2002 (in €1m.): 38,920 (tax revenue, 35,284); expenditure: 36,637.

In 2003 the budget deficit exceeded 3%, the target set by the European Stability and Growth Pact, reaching 3·2%.

VAT is 18% (reduced rates, 8% and 4%).

Performance. Real GDP growth was 3·6% in 2002 and 4·5% in 2003. Greece has had economic growth above the EU average every year since 1996. Total GDP in 2003 was US$173·0bn.

Banking and Finance. The central bank and bank of issue is the Bank of Greece. Its *Governor* is Nicholas Garganas. There were 39 commercial banks in 2002 (17 Greek and 22 foreign). Total assets of all banks were 41,819bn. drachmas in 1999. The six leading banks in 2000 accounted for nearly 80% of assets of all Greek banks. Ranked by size of assets the largest banks were National Bank of Greece, Alpha Bank, Agricultural Bank, Commercial Bank of Greece, EFG Eurobank and Piraeus Bank. Foreign direct investment is extremely low, at just US$47m. in 2003.

There is a stock exchange in Athens.

ENERGY AND NATURAL RESOURCES

Environment. Carbon dioxide emissions from the consumption and flaring of fossil fuels in Greece were the equivalent of 9·5 tonnes per capita in 2002.

Electricity. Installed capacity in 2000 was 11·1m. kW. 72% of power is supplied by lignite-fired power stations. A national grid supplies the mainland, and islands near its coast. Power is produced in remoter islands by local generators. Total production in 2000 was 48·48bn. kWh; consumption per capita in 2000 was 4,925 kWh. Electricity supply is: domestic, 220v, 50 cycles AC; industrial, 280v, AC 3 phase.

Oil and Gas. Output of crude petroleum, 2000, 256,000 tonnes; proven reserves, 2002, 9m. bbls. The oil sector plays a critical role in the Greek economy, accounting for more than 70% of total energy demand. Supply is mostly imported but oil prospecting is intensifying. Natural gas was introduced in Greece in 1997 through a pipeline from Russia, and an additional source of supply is liquefied natural gas from Algeria. Demand for natural gas is in its infancy; however, in 2000 production ran to 51m. cu. metres. The public monopoly in natural gas, DEPA, has developed only a few sales contracts to some large industrial groups, outside a large contract with DEH.

Minerals. Greece produces a variety of ores and minerals, including (with production, in tonnes): asbestos ore (4·0m. in 1998), bauxite (1,931,497 in 2001), magnesite (483,296 in 2001), aluminium (168,000 in 2000), caustic magnesia (115,000 in 2002), nickel ore (22,670 in 2002), iron-pyrites (18,737 in 1995), zinc (16,900 in 2000), chromite (2,273 in 1999), silver (62 in 2001), marble (white and coloured) and various other earths. There is little coal, and the lignite is of indifferent quality (63·89m. tonnes, 2000). Salt production (2000) 244,709 tonnes.

Agriculture. In 2001 there were 2·72m. ha of arable land and 1·13m. ha of permanent crops.

The Greek economy was traditionally based on agriculture, with small-scale farming predominating, except in a few areas in the north. There were 817,100 farms in 2000. However, there has been a steady shift towards industry and although agriculture still employs nearly 17% of the population, it accounted for only 7% of GDP in 2002. Nevertheless, prior to the accession of the ten new member countries in May 2004 Greece had a higher percentage of its population working in agriculture than any other European Union member country. Agriculture accounts for 33·1% of exports and 17·9% of imports.

Production (2000, in 1,000 tonnes):

Sugarbeets	2,906	Oranges	950
Olives	2,000	Peaches and nectarines	900
Tomatoes	1,960	Potatoes	890
Maize	1,850	Cottonseed	650
Wheat	1,770	Watermelons	650
Seed cotton	1,250	Olive oil	443
Grapes	1,200	Wine	430

Livestock (2000, in 1,000): 590 cattle, 9,041 sheep, 5,293 goats, 906 pigs, 78 asses, 37 mules, 33 horses, 28,000 poultry. Livestock products, 2000 (in 1,000 tonnes): milk, 1,990; meat, 499; cheese, 240.

Forestry. Area covered by forests in 2000 was 3·60m. ha, or 27·9% of the total land area. Timber production in 2001 was 2·17m. cu. metres.

Fisheries. Total catch in 2001 was 94,388 tonnes, mainly from sea fishing. In 1998, 17,093 fishermen were active. 10,000 kg of sponges were produced in 1998.

INDUSTRY

The leading companies by market capitalization in Greece, excluding banking and finance, in May 2004 were: Hellenic Telecommunications Organization SA (OTE) (US$6·6bn.); OPAP, a lottery and sports betting company (US$6·1bn.); and Coca-Cola HBC SA (CCHBC), formerly the Hellenic Bottling Company (US$5·9bn.).

The main products are canned vegetables and fruit, fruit juice, beer, wine, alcoholic beverages, cigarettes, textiles, yarn, leather, shoes, synthetic timber, paper, plastics, rubber products, chemical acids, pigments, pharmaceutical products, cosmetics, soap, disinfectants, fertilizers, glassware, porcelain sanitary items, wire and power coils and household instruments.

Production in 1,000 tonnes: cement, 15,563 (2001); residual fuel oil, 7,510 (2000); distillate fuel oil, 5,647 (2000); petrol, 3,758 (2000); jet fuels, 2,087 (2000); crude steel, 1,835 (2002); fertilizers, 1,030 (1998); iron (concrete-reinforcing bars), 835 (1998); alumina, 709 (2001); sulphuric acid, 515 (2001); packing materials, 302 (1998); soap, washing powder, detergents, 241 (1998); textile yarns, 149 (1998); soft drinks, 675·4m. litres (2001); beer, 450·2m. litres (2001); wine, 147·0m. litres (2001); cigarettes, 33·3bn. units (2001); glass, 230,351 sq. metres (1998).

Although manufacturing accounts for more than 21% of GDP, Greece's performance is hampered by the proliferation of small, traditional, low-tech firms, often run as family businesses. Food, drink and tobacco processing are the most important sectors, but there are also some steel mills and several shipyards. Shipping is of prime importance to the economy. In addition, there are major programmes under way in the fields of power, irrigation and land reclamation.

Labour. Of the total workforce of 4,406,700 in the period April–June 2003, 4,014,500 persons were employed. 682,500 were engaged in wholesale and retail trade; 638,200 in agriculture, animal breeding, hunting and forestry; 514,000 in manufacturing; and 317,800 in construction. Automatic index-linking of wages was abolished at the end of 1990. Since 1989 a statutory minimum of wage-bills must be spent on training (0·45%). Retirement age is 65 years for men and 60 for women, although most men retire before the age of 60. Unemployment was 10·5% in June 2004; youth unemployment in 2002 was nearly 26%.

Trade Unions. The status of trade unions is regulated by the Associations Act 1914. Trade union liberties are guaranteed under the Constitution, and a law of June 1982 altered the unions' right to strike.

The national body of trade unions is the Greek General Confederation of Labour.

INTERNATIONAL TRADE

Following the normalization of their relations, Greece lifted its trade embargo (imposed in Feb. 1994) on Macedonia on 13 Oct. 1995. There are quarrels with Turkey over Cyprus, oil rights under the Aegean and ownership of uninhabited islands close to the Turkish coast.

Imports and Exports. In 2002 exports (f.o.b.) were valued at US$9,868m. and imports (f.o.b.) at US$31,320m. In 2000 principal exports were: food, 14·6% (notably fruit and nuts); clothing and apparel, 12·8%; refined petroleum, 12·5%; machinery and apparatus, 9·8%; aluminium, 4·2%. Principal imports in 2000 were: machinery and apparatus, 18·6%; chemicals and chemical products, 11·5%; crude petroleum, 10·1%; road vehicles, 9·5%; food products, 9·1%.

In 2001 Germany was the leading export market (12·3% of the total), followed by Italy (9·2%), UK (6·4%) and USA (5·3%). Italy was the principal supplier of imports (13·5% of the total), ahead of Germany (13·4%), France (7·1%) and the Netherlands (5·7%). Fellow EU member countries accounted for 46·7% of exports in 2001 and 54·8% of all imports.

COMMUNICATIONS

Roads. There were, in 1999, an estimated 117,000 km of roads, including 470 km of motorways, 9,100 km of national roads and 31,300 km of secondary roads. Number of motor vehicles in 2000: 3,195,065 passenger cars, 1,057,422 trucks and vans, 781,361 motorcycles and 27,037 buses. There are approximately 312 passenger cars per 1,000 population. There were 1,654 road deaths in 2002. With 15·7 deaths per 100,000 population in 2002, Greece has among the highest death rates in road accidents of any industrialized country. Road projects include improved links to Turkey and Bulgaria.

Rail. In 1997 the state network, Hellenic Railways (OSE), totalled 2,503 km including 1,565 km of 1,435 mm gauge, 887 km of 1,000 mm gauge, and 51 km of 750 mm gauge. Railways carried 3·2m. tonnes of freight and 14·9m. passengers in 2000. The Greek Railways Organization is investing US$23bn. in the link from Athens to the northern Bulgarian border. A 52-km long metro opened in Athens in Jan. 2000.

Civil Aviation. There are international airports at Athens (Spata 'Eleftherios Venizelos') and Thessaloniki-Makedonia. The airport at Spata opened in March 2001 and is Europe's newest airport. The old airport at Hellenikon has now closed down. The national carrier is Olympic Airways, serving some 30 towns and islands. Several failed attempts to privatize the company by selling a 51% stake led to its restructuring and the establishment of a new company, Olympic Airlines. Apart from the international airports, there are a further 25 provincial airports all connected by regular services operated by Olympic Airways. 6·27m. passengers were carried in 1999, of whom 3·64m. were on domestic and 2·63m. on international flights. Olympic Airways operates routes from Athens to all important cities of the country, Europe, the Middle East and USA. In 1999 Athens airport (Hellenikon) handled 10,335,000 passengers (6,164,000 on international flights).

Shipping. In 2002 the merchant navy totalled 28,783,000 GRT, of which oil tankers 14,562,000 GRT. Greek-owned ships under foreign flags numbered 127 of 2,785,865 GRT in 1997. In 2001 vessels totalling 45,973,000 NRT entered ports and vessels totalling 23,970,000 NRT cleared.

There is a canal (opened 9 Nov. 1893) across the Isthmus of Corinth (about 7 km). The principal seaports are Piraeus, Thessaloniki, Patras, Volos, Igoumenitsa and Heraklion. Greece has 123 seaports with cargo and passenger handling facilities. Container terminals at the port of Piraeus are to be expanded to 1m. TEUs (twenty-foot equivalent units).

Telecommunications. In 2001 Greece had 13,569,700 telephone subscribers (equivalent to 1,280·6 per 1,000 inhabitants) and 900,000 PCs were in use (or 81·7 per 1,000 persons). Mobile phone subscribers numbered 9,314,300 in 2002 and there were 1,704,900 Internet users. In 1999 there were 40,000 fax machines.

Postal Services. In 1998 there were 1,125 post offices, or one for every 8,590 persons. A total of 465,274,000 letters and 3,186,000 parcels were dispatched worldwide in 1996. Total receipts were valued at 78,550m. drachmas and expenses at 92,515m. drachmas.

SOCIAL INSTITUTIONS

Justice. Judges are appointed for life by the President after consultation with the judicial council. Judges enjoy personal and functional independence. There are three divisions of the courts—administrative, civil and criminal—and they must not give decisions which are contrary to the Constitution. Final jurisdiction lies with a Special Supreme Tribunal.

The Ombudsman (*Synigoros*), Giorgos Kaminis, was appointed for a five-year term in April 2003. In the period 1998–2002 a total of 41,865 complaints were submitted, relating to: State–Citizen Relations (36·10%), Social Welfare (28·97%), Quality of Life (22·00%) and Human Rights (12·93%).

The population in penal institutions in Dec. 2002 was 8,500 (80 per 100,000 of national population). The death penalty was abolished for ordinary crimes in 1993.

Religion. The Christian Eastern (Greek) Orthodox Church is the established religion to which 91% of the population belong. It is under an archbishop and 67 metropolitans, one archbishop and seven metropolitans in Crete, and four metropolitans in the Dodecanese. The head of the Greek Orthodox Church is Archbishop Christodoulos Paraskevaides of Athens and All Greece (b. 1939). Roman Catholics have three archbishops (in Naxos and Corfu and, not recognized by the State, in Athens) and one bishop (for Syra and Santorin). The Exarchs of the Greek Catholics and the Armenians are not recognized by the State. There are 360,000 Muslims.

Complete religious freedom is recognized by the Constitution of 1974, but proselytizing from, and interference with, the Greek Orthodox Church is forbidden.

Education. Public education is provided in nursery, primary and secondary schools, starting at 5½–6½ years of age and free at all levels. Adult literacy rate, 2001, 97·3% (male 98·5%; female 96·1%).

In 2001–02 there were 5,694 nursery schools with 10,211 teachers and 144,055 pupils; 6,074 primary schools with 49,842 teachers and 647,041 pupils; 3,244 high schools (lycea) with 54,123 teachers and 589,669 pupils; 677 secondary technical, vocational and ecclesiastic schools with 13,980 teachers and 161,222 students. In third level education there were 68 technical, vocational and ecclesiastic schools with 10,652 teachers and 112,605 students; and 18 universities with 10,708 academic staff and 163,256 students. In 1998–99 there was also one teacher training school with 159 teachers and 895 students.

In 2000–01 total expenditure on education came to 3·7% of GNP and in 1999–2000 represented 7·0% of total government expenditure.

Health. Doctor and hospital treatment within the Greek national health system is free, but patients have to pay 25% of prescription charges. Those living in remote areas can reclaim a proportion of private medical expenses. In 2000 there were 337 hospitals and sanatoria with a total of 52,495 beds in 1998. There were 174 health centres in 1998. There were 43,030 doctors and 11,638 dentists (1997). In 2002 Greece spent 9·5% of its GDP on health. Greeks smoke on average 3,020 cigarettes a year.

Welfare. The majority of employees are covered by the Social Insurance Institute, financed by employer and employee contributions. Benefits include pensions, medical expenses and long-term disability payments. Social insurance expenditure in 2000 totalled 8,215bn. drachmas.

CULTURE

Patras will be the European Capital of Culture for 2006. The title attracts large European Union grants.

World Heritage sites. Greece has 16 sites on the UNESCO World Heritage List, they are: the Temple of Apollo Epicurius at Bassae (1986); the archaeological site of Delphi (1987); The Acropolis, Athens (1987); Mount Athos (1988); Meteora (1988); the Paleochristian and Byzantine monuments of Thessaloniki (1988); the Archaeological Site of Epidaurus (1988); the Medieval City of Rhodes (1988); the archaeological site of Olympia (1989); Mystras (1989); Delos (1990); the monasteries of Daphni, Hossios Luckas and Nea Moni of Chios (1990); the Pythagoreion and Heraion of Samos (1992); the archaeological site of Vergina (1996); the archaeological sites of Mycenae and Tiryns (1999); and the historical sites on the Island of Patmos (1999).

Broadcasting. *Elliniki Radiophonia Tileorasis* (ERT), the Hellenic National Radio and Television Institute, is the government broadcasting station. There are four national and regional programmes, and an external service, Voice of Greece (16 languages). ERT broadcasts two TV programmes (colour by SECAM H). Number of receivers: radio (2000), 5·2m.; television (2001), 5·5m.

Press. There were 207 daily newspapers published in 1998. In 1998 a total of 5,914 book titles were published.

Tourism. Tourism is Greece's biggest industry with an estimated revenue for 2000 of US$9·22bn., contributing approximately 7% of GDP. Tourists in 2000 numbered 13·6m. There were 607,614 hotel beds in 2000 (285,956 in 1981). A total of 61,303,000 nights were spent in hotels in 2000 (provisional), 46,636,000 by foreigners and 14,667,000 by nationals.

Festivals. There are many festivals throughout the year, notably: The feast of St. Basil (1 Jan.); Gynaecocracy (8 Jan., female dominion); Carnival Season (mid-Feb. to mid-March); Independence Day (25 March); Feast of St George (23 April); Anastenaria (21–23 May, firewalking); Navy Week (end of June/beginning of July); Athens Lycabettus Theatre artistic performances (June–Aug.); Athens Festival (June–Sept.); Epidaurus Festival (July–Sept.); Philipi and Thasos Festival

(July–Sept.); Dodoni Festival (July–Sept.); Athens Wine Festival and Ithaca Music Festival (end of July); Olympus Festival (Aug.); Epirotika Festival (Aug.); Kos Hippokrateia Festival (Aug.); Thessaloniki Film Festival and Festival of Popular Song (Sept.–Oct.); National Anniversary Procession (28 Oct.).

Libraries. In 1997 there were 829 public libraries, two National libraries and 64 Higher Education libraries; they held a combined 18,159,000 volumes. There were 7,521,000 visits to the libraries in 1997.

Theatre and Opera. There are two National Theatres and one Opera House.

Museums and Galleries. Amongst Greece's most important museums are the Acropolis Museum, the Museum of the City of Athens, the National Archaeological Museum and the National Historical Museum. In 1999 there were 89 museums and 182 galleries visited by 1,814,823 guests.

DIPLOMATIC REPRESENTATIVES

Of Greece in the United Kingdom (1A Holland Park, London, W11 3TP)
Ambassador: Anastase Scopelitis.

Of the United Kingdom in Greece (1 Ploutarchou St., 106 75 Athens)
Ambassador: Sir David C. A. Madden, KCMG.

Of Greece in the USA (2221 Massachusetts Ave., NW, Washington, D.C., 20008)
Ambassador: George Savvaides.

Of the USA in Greece (91 Vasilissis Sophias Blvd., 101 60 Athens)
Ambassador: Charles P. Ries.

Of Greece to the United Nations
Ambassador: Adamantios Th. Vassilakis.

FURTHER READING

Clogg, Richard, *A Concise History of Greece.* 2nd ed. CUP, 2002
Jougnatos, G. A., *Development of the Greek Economy, 1950–91: an Historical, Empirical and Econometric Analysis.* London, 1992
Legg, K. R. and Roberts, J. M., *Modern Greece: A Civilization on the Periphery.* Oxford, 1997
Pettifer, J., *The Greeks: the Land and the People since the War.* London, 1994
Sarafis, M. and Eve, M. (eds.) *Background to Contemporary Greece.* London, 1990
Tsakalotos, E., *Alternative Economic Strategies: the Case of Greece.* Aldershot, 1991
Veremis, T., *The Military in Greek Politics: From Independence to Democracy.* C. Hurst, London, 1997
Woodhouse, C. M., *Modern Greece: a Short History.* rev. ed. London, 1991

National statistical office: National Statistical Service; 14–16 Lycourgou St., Athens.
Website: http://www.statistics.gr/

GRENADA

Capital: St George's
Population, 2001: 101,000
GDP per capita, 2002: (PPP$) 7,280
HDI/world rank: 0·745/93

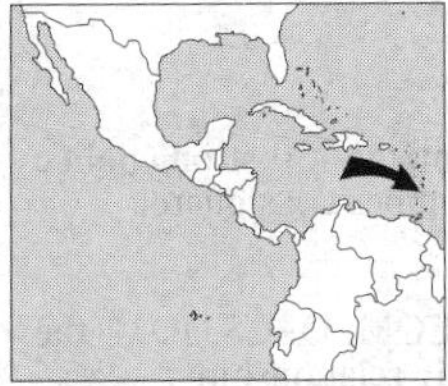

KEY HISTORICAL EVENTS

Grenada became an independent nation within the Commonwealth on 7 Feb. 1974. The 1973 Constitution was suspended in 1979 following a revolution. On 19 Oct. 1983 the army took control after a power struggle led to the killing of the prime minister. At the request of a group of Caribbean countries, Grenada was invaded by US-led forces on 25–28 Oct. On 1 Nov. a State of Emergency was imposed which ended with the restoration of the 1973 Constitution.

TERRITORY AND POPULATION

Grenada is the most southerly island of the Windward Islands with an area of 133 sq. miles (344 sq. km); the state also includes the Southern Grenadine Islands to the north, chiefly Carriacou (58·3 sq. km) and Petit Martinique. The total population at the 2001 census was 102,632; density, 298 per sq. km.

In 2001, 61·6% of the population were rural. The Borough of St George's, the capital, had 35,559 inhabitants in 2001. 85% of the population is of African descent, 11% of mixed origins, 3% Indian and 1% white.

The official language is English. A French-African patois is also spoken.

SOCIAL STATISTICS

Births, 2001, 1,899; deaths, 727. Rates per 1,000 population, 2001: birth, 18·8; death, 7·2. Life expectancy, 2000: 68 years for males, 73 years for females. Infant mortality, 2001, 20 per 1,000 live births. Annual population growth rate, 1995–2001, 0·4%; fertility rate, 2001, 3·5 births per woman.

CLIMATE

The tropical climate is very agreeable in the dry season, from Jan. to May, when days are warm and nights quite cool, but in the wet season there is very little difference between day and night temperatures. On the coast, annual rainfall is about 60" (1,500 mm) but it is as high as 150–200" (3,750–5,000 mm) in the mountains. Average temperature, 27°C.

CONSTITUTION AND GOVERNMENT

The head of state is the British sovereign, represented by an appointed Governor-General. There is a bicameral legislature, consisting of a 13-member *Senate,* appointed by the Governor-General, and a 15-member *House of Representatives,* elected by universal suffrage.

National Anthem. 'Hail Grenada, land of ours'; words by I. M. Baptiste, tune by L. A. Masanto.

RECENT ELECTIONS

At the elections of 27 Nov. 2003 for the House of Representatives the New National Party (NNP) won 8 seats, with 49·9% of the votes cast, against 7 and 45·1% for the National Democratic Congress.

CURRENT ADMINISTRATION

Governor-General: Sir Daniel Williams.

In March 2005 the government comprised:

Prime Minister, Minister of Information, National Security, Business and Private Sector Development, Youth Development and Information Communication Technology: Dr Keith Mitchell; b. 1946 (NNP; in office since 22 June 1995).

Minister of Health, Social Security and the Environment: Ann David Antoine. *Foreign Affairs and International Trade, Carriacou and Petit Martinique Affairs, and Legal Affairs:* Elvin Nimrod. *Finance and Planning:* Anthony Boatswain. *Agriculture, Lands, Forestry, Fisheries, Public Utilities, Energy and the Marketing and National Importing Board:* Gregory Bowen. *Education and Labour:* Claris Charles. *Tourism, Civil Aviation, Culture and the Performing Arts:* Brenda Hood. *Social Development:* Yolande Bain Joseph. *Sports, Community Development and Co-operatives:* Roland Bhola. *Communications, Works and Transport:* Clarice Modeste-Curwen. *Attorney General:* Raymond Anthony.

DEFENCE

Royal Grenada Police Force. Modelled on the British system, the 730-strong police force includes an 80-member paramilitary unit and a 30-member coastguard.

INTERNATIONAL RELATIONS

Grenada is a member of the UN, WTO, OAS, ACS, CARICOM, OECS, IOM, the Commonwealth and is an ACP member state of the ACP-EU relationship.

ECONOMY

Agriculture accounted for 7·5% of GDP in 2002, industry 22·6% and services 69·8%.

Currency. The unit of currency is the *Eastern Caribbean dollar* (EC$). Foreign exchange reserves were US$69m. in May 2002. Total money supply in May 2002 was EC$228m. Inflation was 3·0% in 2002.

Budget. In 2001 current revenue was EC$326·4m. and current expenditure EC$257·0m. Capital expenditure was EC$125·0m. Income tax has been abolished. VAT is 25% (reduced rate, 5%).

Performance. Grenada has been experiencing a recession, with the economy shrinking by 3·3% in 2001 and by 0·5% in 2002, although in 2003 there were signs of a slight recovery. Total GDP in 2003 was US$0·4bn.

Banking and Finance. Grenada is a member of the Eastern Caribbean Central Bank. The *Governor* is Sir Dwight Venner. In 2002 there were three commercial banks and four foreign banks. The Grenada Agricultural Bank was established in 1965 to encourage agricultural development; in 1975 it became the Grenada Agricultural and Industrial Development Corporation. In 1995 bank deposits were EC$666·8m. (US$249·7m.). Total foreign currency deposits in 1995 amounted to US$11·8m.

Grenada is affiliated to the Eastern Caribbean Securities Exchange in Basseterre, St Kitts and Nevis.

ENERGY AND NATURAL RESOURCES

Environment. Grenada's carbon dioxide emissions from the consumption and flaring of fossil fuels in 2002 were the equivalent of 2·3 tonnes per capita.

Electricity. Installed capacity in 2000 was 27,000 kW. Production in 2000 was 118m. kWh, with consumption per capita 1,168 kWh.

Agriculture. There were 2,000 ha of arable land in 2001 and 10,000 ha of permanent crops. Principal crop production (2000, in 1,000 tonnes): coconuts, 7; sugarcane, 7; bananas, 5; avocados, 2; grapefruit and pomelos, 2; mangoes, 2. Nutmeg, corn, pigeon peas, citrus, root-crops and vegetables are also grown, in addition to small scattered cultivations of cotton, cloves, cinnamon, pimento, coffee and fruit trees. Grenada is the second largest producer of nutmeg in the world, after Indonesia.

Livestock (2000): cattle, 4,000; sheep, 13,000; goats, 7,000; pigs, 5,000.

Forestry. In 2000 the area under forests was 5,000 ha, or 14·7% of the total land area.

Fisheries. The catch in 2001 was 2,247 tonnes, entirely from marine waters.

INDUSTRY

Main products are wheat flour, soft drinks, beer, animal feed, rum and cigarettes.

Labour. In 1993 the labour force was estimated at 27,820. Unemployment was 11% in Dec. 2000.

INTERNATIONAL TRADE

Total external debt amounted to US$339m. in 2002.

Imports and Exports. In 2002 exports totalled US$59·7m. The principal exports were: electronic components, 36·1%; nutmeg, 19·7%; fish, 6·8%. In 2002 imports totalled US$233·2m. Major import commodities were: machinery and transport equipment, 27·4%; food, 16·6%; chemicals and chemical products, 11·1%.

In 1999 the main export destinations were the Netherlands (19·8%), the USA (18·7%), Germany (11·0%), St Lucia (6·9%), France (5·5%) and Barbados (5·2%). Main import suppliers were the USA (41·8%), Trinidad and Tobago (21·4%), the UK (8·0%), Japan (5·4%), Canada (3·5%) and Barbados (2·8%).

COMMUNICATIONS

Roads. In 1999 there were about 1,040 km of roads, of which 638 km were hard-surfaced.

Civil Aviation. The main airport is Point Salines International. Union Island and Carriacou have smaller airports. There were direct flights from Point Salines in 2003 to Anguilla, Antigua, Barbados, the British Virgin Islands, Dominica, Frankfurt, London, Montego Bay, New York, Philadelphia, Puerto Rico, St Kitts, St Lucia, St Maarten, St Vincent, Tobago and Trinidad. In 1998 Point Salines handled 330,000 passengers (317,000 on international flights) and 1,700 tonnes of freight.

Shipping. The main port is at St George's; there are eight minor ports. Total number of containers handled in 1991 was 5,161; cargo landed, 187,039 tonnes; cargo loaded, 24,786 tonnes. Sea-going shipping totalled 1,000 GRT in 2002.

Telecommunications. Telephone subscribers numbered 41,100 in 2002 (387·7 per 1,000 persons) and there were 14,000 PCs in use (132·1 for every 1,000 persons). There were 7,600 mobile phone subscribers in 2002 and 300 fax machines in 1999. In 2002 Grenada had 15,000 Internet users.

Postal Services. In 1994 there were 58 post offices.

SOCIAL INSTITUTIONS

Justice. The Grenada Supreme Court, situated in St George's, comprises a High Court of Justice, a Court of Magisterial Appeal (which hears appeals from the lower Magistrates' Courts exercising summary jurisdiction) and an Itinerant Court of Appeal (to hear appeals from the High Court). Grenada was one of ten countries to sign an agreement in Feb. 2001 establishing a Caribbean Court of Justice to replace the British Privy Council as the highest civil and criminal court. In the meantime the number of signatories has risen to twelve. The court was inaugurated at Port-of-Spain, Trinidad on 16 April 2005. For police *see* DEFENCE, *above*.

The population in penal institutions in June 2002 was 297 (equivalent to 333 per 100,000 of national population).

Religion. At the 2001 census 53% of the population were Roman Catholic, 14% Anglican and the remainder other religions.

Education. Adult literacy was 96% in 1998. In 2000–01 there were 15,974 pupils in primary schools (765 teachers) and 8,312 pupils (439 teachers) in secondary schools. In 2000–01 the teacher-pupil ratio was 1:21 in primary schools and 1:19 in secondary schools. The Grenada National College was established in 1988. There is also a branch of the University of the West Indies. 12·3% of the 2001 budget was allocated to education.

Health. In 1996 there were three general hospitals with a provision of 35 beds per 10,000 inhabitants. There were 96 physicians, 14 dentists, 232 nurses and 47 pharmacists in 1996. 16·2% of the 2001 budget was allocated to health.

CULTURE

Broadcasting. The government-owned Grenada Broadcasting Corporation operates Radio Grenada and Grenada Television. There are also four independent radio stations. Grenada Television transmits on three channels (colour by NTSC). A private cable TV company provides services on 25 channels, and there is a religious TV service. In 1997 there were 57,000 radio and 33,000 TV sets.

Press. In 1993 there were 5 weekly, 1 monthly and 2 bi-monthly newspapers.

Tourism. In 2001 there were 123,351 overnight visitors and 147,300 cruise ship arrivals. Tourism receipts totalled US$67m. in 2000. Tourism contributed 7·5% of GDP in 2000.

DIPLOMATIC REPRESENTATIVES

Of Grenada in the United Kingdom (5 Chandos Street, London, W1G 9DG)
High Commissioner: Joslyn R. Whiteman.

Of the United Kingdom in Grenada
High Commissioner: John White (resides at Bridgetown, Barbados).

Of Grenada in the USA (1701 New Hampshire Ave., NW, Washington, D.C., 20009)
Ambassador: Denis Antoine.

Of the USA in Grenada
Ambassador: Mary E. Kramer (resides at Bridgetown).

Of Grenada to the United Nations
Ambassador: Ruth Elizabeth Rouse.

Of Grenada to the European Union
Ambassador: Joan Marie Coutain.

FURTHER READING

Ferguson, J., *Grenada: Revolution in Reverse.* London, 1991
Heine, J. (ed.) *A Revolution Aborted: the Lessons of Grenada.* Pittsburgh Univ. Press, 1990

GUATEMALA

República de Guatemala

Capital: Guatemala City
Population projection, 2010: 14·58m.
GDP per capita, 2002: (PPP$) 4,080
HDI/world rank: 0·649/121

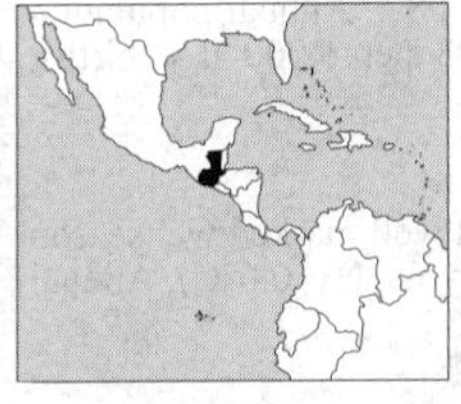

KEY HISTORICAL EVENTS

From 1524 Guatemala was part of a Spanish captaincy-general, comprising the whole of Central America. It became independent in 1821 and formed part of the Confederation of Central America from 1823 to 1839. The overthrow of the right-wing dictator Jorge Ubico in 1944 opened a decade of left-wing activity which alarmed the USA. In 1954 the leftist regime of Jacob Arbenz Guzmán was overthrown by a CIA-supported coup. A series of right-wing governments failed to produce stability while the toll on human life and the violation of human rights was such as to cause thousands of refugees to flee to Mexico. Elections to a National Constituent Assembly were held on 1 July 1984, and a new constitution was promulgated in May 1985. Amidst violence and assassinations, the presidential election was won by Marco Vinicio Cerezo Arévalo. On 14 Jan. 1986 Cerezo's civilian government was installed—the first for 16 years and only the second since 1954. Violence continued, however, and there were frequent reports of torture and killings by right-wing 'death squads'. The presidential and legislative elections of Nov. 1995 saw the return of open politics for the first time in over 40 years. Meanwhile the Guatemalan Revolutionary Unit (URNG) declared a ceasefire. On 6 May and 19 Sept. 1996 the government agreed reforms to military, internal security, judicial and agrarian institutions. A ceasefire was concluded in Oslo on 4 Dec. 1996 and a final peace treaty was signed on 29 Dec. 1996. In Nov. 1999 the country's first presidential elections took place since the end of the 36-year-long civil war, which had claimed over 200,000 lives.

TERRITORY AND POPULATION

Guatemala is bounded on the north and west by Mexico, south by the Pacific ocean and east by El Salvador, Honduras and Belize, and the area is 108,889 sq. km (42,042 sq. miles). In March 1936 Guatemala, El Salvador and Honduras agreed to accept the peak of Mount Montecristo as the common boundary point.

The population was 11,237,196 at the census of Nov. 2002; density, 103 per sq. km.

The UN gives a projected population for 2010 of 14·58m.

In 2001, 60·0% of the population were rural. In 1996, 44% were Amerindian, of 21 different groups descended from the Maya; 56% Mestizo (mixed Amerindian and Spanish). 60% speak Spanish, with the remainder speaking one or a combination of the 23 Indian dialects.

Guatemala is administratively divided into 22 departments, each with a governor appointed by the president. Population, 2002:

Departments	*Area (sq. km)*	*Population*	*Departments*	*Area (sq. km)*	*Population*
Alta Verapaz	8,686	776,246	Petén	35,854	366,735
Baja Verapaz	3,124	215,915	Quezaltenango	1,951	624,716
Chimaltenango	1,979	446,133	Quiché	8,378	655,510
Chiquimula	2,376	302,485	Retalhuleu	1,858	241,411
El Progreso	1,922	139,490	Sacatepéquez	465	248,019
Escuintla	4,384	538,746	San Marcos	3,791	794,951
Guatemala City	2,126	2,541,581	Santa Rosa	2,955	301,370
Huehuetenango	7,403	846,544	Sololá	1,061	307,661
Izabal	9,038	314,306	Suchitepéquez	2,510	403,945
Jalapa	2,063	242,926	Totonicapán	1,061	339,254
Jutiapa	3,219	389,085	Zacapa	2,690	200,167

In 1999 Guatemala City, the capital, had a population of 3,119,000. Populations of other major towns, 1995 estimates (in 1,000): Quezaltenango, 104; Escuintla, 70; Mazatenango, 43; Retalhuleu, 40; Puerto Barrios, 39.

SOCIAL STATISTICS

Births, 2002, 297,885; deaths, 46,224. 2002 rates per 1,000 population: birth, 26·5; death, 4·1. Life expectancy, 2001: male 62·5 years, female 68·4. Annual population growth rate, 1992–2002, 2·7%. Infant mortality, 2001, 43 per 1,000 live births; fertility rate, 2001, 4·6 births per woman.

CLIMATE

A tropical climate, with little variation in temperature and a well marked wet season from May to Oct. Guatemala City, Jan. 63°F (17·2°C), July 69°F (20·6°C). Annual rainfall 53" (1,316 mm).

CONSTITUTION AND GOVERNMENT

A new Constitution, drawn up by the Constituent Assembly elected on 1 July 1984, was promulgated in June 1985 and came into force on 14 Jan. 1986. In 1993, 43 amendments were adopted, reducing *inter alia* the President's term of office from five to four years. The President and Vice-President are elected by direct election (with a second round of voting if no candidate secures 50% of the first-round votes) for a non-renewable four-year term. The unicameral *Congreso de la República* comprises 140 members, elected partly from constituencies and partly by proportional representation to serve four-year terms.

National Anthem. '¡Guatemala! Feliz' ('Happy Guatemala'); words by J. J. Palma, tune by R. Alvárez.

RECENT ELECTIONS

In a run-off for the presidency on 28 Dec. 2003 Óscar Berger Perdomo of the Gran Alianza Nacional (GANA, Grand National Alliance) won with 54·1% of the vote against Álvaro Colom Caballeros of the Unidad Nacional de la Esperanza (UNE, National Union of Hope). A further seven candidates had participated in the first round of voting on 9 Nov. 2003. Combined turn-out was 45·8%.

Congressional elections were held on 9 Nov. 2003: the Gran Alianza Nacional (composed of the Patriotic Party, the Reformist Movement and the National Solidarity Party) won 49 seats with 24·3% of the vote; the Frente Republicano Guatemalteco (FRG, Guatemalan Republican Front) won 42 seats (19·7%); the UNE won 33 seats (26·4%); the Partido de Avanzade Nacional (PAN, National Advancement Party) won 16 seats (10·9%). Seven other parties failed to win seats. Turn-out was 54·5%.

CURRENT ADMINISTRATION

President: Óscar Berger Perdomo; b. 1946 (GANA; sworn in 14 Jan. 2004).

Vice-President: Dr Eduardo Stein Barillas; b. 1945 (took office on 14 Jan. 2004).

In March 2005 the government comprised:

Minister of Agriculture, Livestock and Food: Alvaro Aguilar. *Communications, Transportation and Public Works:* Eduardo Castillo. *Defence:* Gen. César Méndez Pinelo. *Education:* María del Carmen Aceña. *Energy and Mining:* Roberto González. *Culture:* Manuel Salazar. *Public Finance:* María Antonieta de Bonilla. *Foreign Affairs:* Jorge Briz Abularach. *Health:* Marco Tulio Sosa. *Government:* Carlos Vielman. *Labour:* Jorge Gallardo. *Economy:* Marcio Cuevas. *Environment and Natural Resources:* Mario Dary.

Government Website (Spanish only): http://www.guatemala.gob.gt

DEFENCE

There is selective conscription for 30 months. In 2003 defence expenditure totalled US$102m. (US$8 per capita), representing 0·4% of GDP.

Army. The Army numbered (2002) 29,200 (23,000 conscripts) and is organized in 15 military zones. It includes a special forces unit. The Presidential Guard was disbanded in 2003. There is a paramilitary national police of 7,000, treasury police of 2,500 and a trained reserve of 35,000.

Navy. A naval element of the combined armed forces was (2002) 1,500 strong of whom 650 are marines for maintenance of riverine security. Main bases are Santo Tomás de Castilla (on the Atlantic Coast) and Puerto Quetzal (Pacific).

Air Force. There is a small Air Force with 10 combat aircraft and 12 armed helicopters (although fewer than half are operational). Strength was (2002) 700.

INTERNATIONAL RELATIONS

Guatemala is a member of the UN, WTO, OAS, Inter-American Development Bank, CACM, ACS and IOM.

ECONOMY

In 2002 agriculture accounted for 22·5% of GDP, industry 19·3% and services 58·2%.

Overview. Guatemala has the third highest per capita income in Central America. However, owing to a highly unequal income distribution with approximately 50% of the overall population living in poverty, Guatemala's social indicators rank among the lowest in the region. The signing of the UN-sponsored peace accords in 1996, which ended 36 years of civil war, was followed by an ambitious programme aimed at addressing social problems, improving social capital, raising productivity and mobilizing domestic resources. The progress of the programme was, however, slower than forecast. The Guatemalan authorities have presented revised programmes incorporating the agenda of the 1996 peace accords. In early 2002 a medium-term poverty reduction strategy (PRS) was introduced to enhance economic growth and improve social conditions. The strategy set specific goals to be reached by 2005 such as reducing extreme poverty by 3%, raising economic growth to more than 4% per year and improving the quality of education, health and rural development. Despite significant accomplishments since 1996, overall compliance with the peace commitments has been uneven. According to the World Bank, to achieve growth targets Guatemala needs to strengthen its institutions by improving property rights, dismantling excessive regulation and reducing crime rates.

Currency. The unit of currency is the *quetzal* (CTQ) of 100 *centavos*, established on 7 May 1925. In June 2002 foreign exchange reserves were US$2,222m., total money supply was Q.20,561m. and gold reserves were 222,000 troy oz. Inflation was 6·3% in 2002.

Budget. Government revenue and expenditure (in Q.1m.):

	1997	*1998*	*1999*	*2000*	*2001*
Revenue	9,627·7	11,856·2	13,967·1	15,205·8	17,656·2
Expenditure	10,418·7	13,486·0	16,373·7	18,220·8	21,035·1

VAT is 10%.

Performance. Real GDP growth was 2·3% in 2001 and 2·2% in 2002. Total GDP in 2003 was US$24·7bn.

Banking and Finance. The Banco de Guatemala is the central bank and bank of issue (*President*, Lizardo Sosa López). Constitutional amendments of 1993 placed limits on its financing of government spending. In 2002 there were 27 national banks (four state-owned and 23 private). The international banks and the foreign banks are authorized to operate as commercial banks.

There are two stock exchanges.

Weights and Measures. The metric system is official but the imperial is still used locally.

ENERGY AND NATURAL RESOURCES

Environment. Carbon dioxide emissions from the consumption and flaring of fossil fuels in 2002 were the equivalent of 0·8 tonnes per capita.

Electricity. Installed capacity in 2000 was 1·3m. kW. Production, 2000, 6·05bn. kWh. Consumption per capita in 2000 was 469 kWh.

Oil and Gas. There were proven natural gas reserves in 2002 of 2·8m. cu. metres. Production (1998), 11m. cu. metres. In 2002 crude petroleum reserves were 526m. bbls.; in 2000 output was 1·0m. tonnes.

Minerals. There are deposits of gold, silver and nickel.

Agriculture. There were 1·36m. ha of arable land in 2001 and 0·55m. ha of permanent crops. 130,000 ha were irrigated in 2001. Production, 2000 (in 1,000 tonnes): sugarcane, 17,150; maize, 1,109; bananas, 733; coffee, 295; tomatoes, 150; lemons and limes, 117; melons, 115. Rubber development schemes are under way, assisted by US funds. Guatemala is one of the largest sources of essential oils (citronella and lemongrass). Arable land: 12%; permanent crops: 4%; meadows and pastures: 12%; forest and woodland: 40%; other: 32%.

Livestock (2000): cattle, 2·30m.; pigs, 825,000; sheep, 551,000; horses, 120,000; goats, 110,000; chickens, 24m.

Forestry. In 2000 the area under forests was 2·85m ha, or 26·3% of the total land area. Mahogany and cedar are grown, and chick, a chewing gum base, is produced. Timber production in 2001 was 15·34m. cu. metres.

Fisheries. In 2001 the total catch was approximately 10,100 tonnes (7,300 tonnes from inland waters).

INDUSTRY

Manufacturing contributed 12·9% of GDP in 2001. The principal industries are food and beverages, tobacco, chemicals, hides and skins, textiles, garments and non-metallic minerals. Cement production in 2000 was 2,039,000 tonnes; raw sugar production was 1,661,000 tonnes in 2001. New industries include electrical goods, plastic sheet and metal furniture.

Labour. In 1995 the workforce totalled 3,316,723 including: agriculture, 1,513,600; commerce, 572,011; services, 439,719; manufacturing, 439,121; building, 214,102; transport and communications, 77,476; finance, 40,474.

There is a working week of a maximum of 44 hours.

Trade Unions. There are three federations for private sector workers.

INTERNATIONAL TRADE

In May 1992 Guatemala, El Salvador and Honduras agreed to create a free trade zone and standardize import duties. External debt was US$4,676m. in 2002.

Imports and Exports. Values in US$1m. were:

	1998	*1999*	*2000*	*2001*	*2002*
Imports f.o.b.	4,255·7	4,225·7	4,742·0	5,142·0	5,578·4
Exports f.o.b.	2,846·9	2,780·6	3,085·1	2,859·8	2,628·4

In 1999 the principal exports were: coffee, 22·9%; chemicals, 13·1%; manufactured goods, 11·3%; sugar, 7·9%; bananas, 5·9%. Main imports were: machinery and transport equipment, 35·4%; manufactured goods, 16·6%; chemicals, 16·3%; foodstuffs, 10·2%; petroleum and related products, 8·9%.

Main export markets, 1999: USA, 34·3%; El Salvador, 14·5%; Honduras, 8·5%; Costa Rica, 4·9%; Nicaragua, 4·2%; Germany, 4·0%; Mexico, 4·0%. Main import suppliers: USA, 41·6%; Mexico, 11·0%; El Salvador, 5·6%; Venezuela, 4·5%; Japan, 4·0%; Panama, 3·2%; Costa Rica, 3·1%.

COMMUNICATIONS

Roads. In 1999 there were 14,118 km of roads, of which 74 km were motorways. 34·5% of all roads were paved in 1999. There is a highway from coast to coast via Guatemala City. There are two highways from the Mexican to the Salvadorean frontier: the Pacific Highway serving the fertile coastal plain and the Pan-American Highway running through the highlands and Guatemala City. Passenger cars numbered 578,733 in 2000, and there were 42,219 trucks and vans and 11,017 buses and coaches.

Rail. The state-owned Ferrocarriles de Guatemala operated 903 km of railway in 2000, linking east and west coast seaports to Guatemala City, with branch lines to the north and south borders. Passenger-km travelled in 1994 came to 991m. and freight tonne-km in 2000 to 2·2bn.

Civil Aviation. There are international airports at Guatemala City (La Aurora) and Flores. In 2000 La Aurora handled 1,258,919 passengers and 58,118 tonnes of freight. In 1999 scheduled airline traffic of Guatemalan-based carriers flew 5·3m. km, carrying 506,000 passengers (472,000 on international flights).

Shipping. The chief ports on the Atlantic coast are Puerto Barrios and Santo Tomás de Castilla: on the Pacific coast, Puerto Quetzal and Champerico. Merchant shipping totalled 9,000 GRT in 2002. In 1997 vessels totalling 4,505,000 NRT entered ports and vessels totalling 3,815,000 NRT cleared.

Telecommunications. The government own and operate the telecommunications services. In 2002 there were 2,423,100 telephone subscribers, or 202·0 for every 1,000 persons, and 173,000 PCs were in use (14·4 for every 1,000 persons). There were 1,577,100 mobile phone subscribers in 2002 and 10,000 fax machines in use in 1999. Guatemala had 400,000 Internet users in 2002.

Postal Services. There were 540 post offices in 1994.

SOCIAL INSTITUTIONS

Justice. Justice is administered in a Constitution Court, a Supreme Court, six appeal courts and 28 courts of first instance. Supreme Court and appeal court judges are elected by Congress. Judges of first instance are appointed by the Supreme Court.

The death penalty is authorized for murder and kidnapping. Two executions were carried out in 2000.

A new National Civil Police force under the authority of the Minister of the Interior was created in 1996. It was 19,000-strong in 2002.

The population in penal institutions in Sept. 1999 was 8,460 (71 per 100,000 of national population).

Religion. Roman Catholicism is the prevailing faith (8·9m. adherents in 2001) and there is a Roman Catholic archbishopric. In Sept. 2003 there was one cardinal. The remainder of the population are followers of other religions (mainly Evangelical Protestants).

Education. In 2000–01 there were 1,909,389 pupils at primary schools and 503,884 pupils at secondary level. The adult literacy rate in 2001 was 69·2% (male, 76·6%; female, 61·8%). In 1994–95 there were five universities with 70,233 students and 4,450 academic staff.

In 2000–01 total public expenditure on education came to 1·7% of GNP and 11·4% of total government spending.

Health. Guatemala had 9,812 physicians and 1,367 dentists in 1997. There were 49 hospitals, 257 country health centres and 1,288 community health clinics in 2000.

Welfare. A comprehensive system of social security was outlined in a law of 30 Oct. 1946.

CULTURE

World Heritage Sites. Guatemala has three sites on the UNESCO World Heritage List: Tikal National Park (inscribed on the list in 1979); Antigua Guatemala (1979); and the Archaeological Park and Ruins of Quiriguá (1981).

Broadcasting. There are five government, six educational and 84 commercial radio broadcasting services. There are four commercial TV stations and one government station. There is also reception by US television satellite. There were 1·7m. TV receivers (colour by NTSC) in 2001 and 902,000 radio sets in 2000.

Press. In 2002 there were 11 daily newspapers.

Tourism. Tourism is an important source of foreign exchange (US$518m. in 2000). There were 826,000 foreign tourists in 2000.

DIPLOMATIC REPRESENTATIVES

Of Guatemala in the United Kingdom (13 Fawcett St., London, SW10 9HN)
Ambassador: Vacant.
Chargé d'Affaires a.i.: Danilo Rodríguez-Marcucci.

Of the United Kingdom in Guatemala (Avenida La Reforma 16-00, Zona 10, Edificio Torre Internacional, Nivel 11, Guatemala City)
Ambassador: Richard Lavers.

Of Guatemala in the USA (2220 R. St., NW, Washington, D.C., 20008)
Ambassador: Guillermo Castillo.

Of the USA in Guatemala (7–01 Avenida de la Reforma, Zone 10, Guatemala City)
Ambassador: John R. Hamilton.

Of Guatemala to the United Nations
Ambassador: Jorge Skinner-Klée Arenales.

Of Guatemala to the European Union
Ambassador: Edmond Mulet-Lesieur.

FURTHER READING

Jonas, Susanne, *Of Centaurs and Doves: Guatemala's Peace Process.* Westview Press, Boulder (CO), 2001

Woodward, R. L., *Guatemala.* [Bibliography] 2nd ed. ABC-Clio, Oxford and Santa Barbara (CA), 1992

National library: Biblioteca Nacional, 5a Avenida y 8a Calle, Zona 1, Guatemala City.
National Institute of Statistics Website (Spanish only): http://www.segeplan.gob.gt/ine

GUINEA

République de Guinée

Capital: Conakry
Population projection, 2010: 9·99m.
GDP per capita, 2002: (PPP$) 2,100
HDI/world rank: 0·425/160

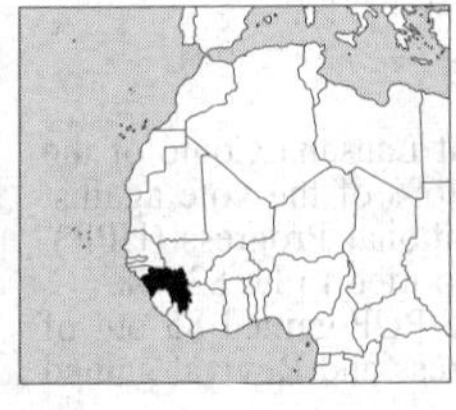

KEY HISTORICAL EVENTS

In 1888 Guinea became a French protectorate, in 1893 a colony, and in 1904 a constituent territory of French West Africa. Forced labour and other colonial depredations ensued, although a form of representation was introduced in 1946. The independent Republic of Guinea was proclaimed on 2 Oct. 1958, after the territory of French Guinea had decided to leave the French community. Guinea became a single-party state. In 1980 the armed forces staged a coup and dissolved the National Assembly. Following popular disturbances a multi-party system was introduced in April 1992.

In 2000 fierce fighting broke out between Guinean government troops and rebels, believed to be a mix of Guinean dissidents and mercenaries from Liberia and Sierra Leone. More than 250,000 refugees were caught up in what the United Nations High Commissioner for Refugees described as the world's worst refugee crisis.

TERRITORY AND POPULATION

Guinea is bounded in the northwest by Guinea-Bissau and Senegal, northeast by Mali, southeast by Côte d'Ivoire, south by Liberia and Sierra Leone, and west by the Atlantic Ocean.

The area is 245,857 sq. km (94,926 sq. miles). In 1996 the census population was 7,164,823 (density 29·1 per sq. km). 2002 estimate: 8,385,000.

The UN gives a projected population for 2010 of 9·99m.

The capital is Conakry. In 2001, 72·1% of the population were rural.

Guinea is divided into seven provinces and a special zone (national capital). These are in turn divided into 33 administrative regions. The major divisions (with their areas in sq. km) are: Boké, 34,231; Conakry (special zone—national capital), 308; Faranah, 38,272; Kankan, 71,085; Kindia, 26,749; Labé, 21,150; Mamou, 13,560; Nzérékoré, 40,502.

The main towns are Conakry (population estimate, 1999, 1,764,000), Kindia, Nzérékoré, Kankan and Labé.

The ethnic composition is Fulani (40·3%, predominant in Moyenne-Guinée), Malinké (or Mandingo, 25·8%, prominent in Haute-Guinée), Susu (11%, prominent in Guinée-Maritime), Kissi (6·5%) and Kpelle (4·8%) in Guinée-Forestière, and Dialonka, Loma and others (11·6%).

The official language is French.

SOCIAL STATISTICS

Births, 1997, 311,000; deaths, 135,000. Rates, 1997: birth, 42·0 per 1,000 population; death, 18·2; infant mortality, 109 per 1,000 live births (2001). Life expectancy, 2001, 48·1 years for males and 48·9 for females. Annual population growth rate, 1992–2002, 2·4%; fertility rate, 2001, 6·0 births per woman.

CLIMATE

A tropical climate, with high rainfall near the coast and constant heat, but conditions are a little cooler on the plateau. The wet season on the coast lasts from May to Nov., but only to Oct. inland. Conakry, Jan. 80°F (26·7°C), July 77°F (25°C). Annual rainfall 172" (4,293 mm).

CONSTITUTION AND GOVERNMENT

There is a 114-member *National Assembly*, 38 of whose members are elected on a first-past-the-post system, and the remainder from national lists by proportional representation.

On 11 Nov. 2001 a referendum was held in which 98·4% of votes cast were in favour of President Conté remaining in office for a third term, requiring an amendment to the constitution (previously allowing a maximum two presidential terms). The referendum, which also increased the presidential mandate from five to seven years, was boycotted by opposition parties.

National Anthem. 'Peuple d'Afrique, le passé historique' ('People of Africa, the historic past'); words anonymous, tune by K. Fodeba.

RECENT ELECTIONS

Presidential elections were held on 21 Dec. 2003. President Lansana Conté of the Party of Unity and Progress (PUP) was re-elected with 95·6% of the vote against 4·4% won by Mamadou Bhoye Barry of the Union for National Progress (UPR). Opposition parties boycotted the elections. Turn-out was reported to be 82·8%.

Parliamentary elections took place on 30 June 2002. The PUP gained 85 out of 114 seats with 61·6% of votes cast and the Union for Progress and Revival gained 20 seats with 26·6%. The turn-out was 72·5%.

CURRENT ADMINISTRATION

President: Gen. Lansana Conté; b. 1934 (PUP; seized power 3 April 1984, most recently re-elected 21 Dec. 2003).

Prime Minister: Cellou Dalein Diallo (since 9 Dec. 2004).

In March 2005 the cabinet comprised:

Minister of Agriculture and Animal Husbandry: Jean Paul Sarr. *Commerce, Industry and Small- and Medium-Scale Enterprise:* Dr Djéné Saran Camara. *Posts and Telecommunications:* Jean-Claude Sultan. *Co-operation:* Elhadj Thierno Habib Diallo. *Economy and Finance:* Mady Kaba Camara. *Employment and Public Administration:* Alpha Ibrahima Kéira. *Mining and Geology:* Ahmed Tidiane Souaré. *Environment:* Abdel Kader Sangaré. *Fishing and Aquaculture:* Vacant. *Foreign Affairs:* Fatoumata Kaba. *Information:* Hadja Aïssatou Bella Diallo. *Justice and Keeper of the Seals:* Sylla Mamadou Syma. *Higher Education and Scientific Research:* Sékou Décasy Camara. *Planning:* Eugène Camara. *Public Works:* Bana Sidibé. *Pre-University and Civic Education:* Galéma Guilavogui. *Public Health:* Dr Amara Cissé. *Security:* Ousmane Camara. *Social Affairs and Promotion of Women and Children:* Mariama Aribot. *Technical Teaching and Professional Training:* Ibrahima Soumah. *Territorial Administration and Decentralization:* Kiridi Bangoura. *Tourism, Hotels and Handicrafts:* Hadja Koumba Diakité. *Transport:* Aliou Condé. *Urban Planning and Housing:* Ouo-Ouo Blaise Foromou. *Water Power and Energy:* Dioubaté Hadj Fatoumata Binta. *Youth, Sports and Culture:* Fodé Soumah. *Secretary General of the Government:* Elhadj Oury Baïlo Diallo.

Government Website (French only): http://www.guinee.gov.gn

DEFENCE

Conscription is for two years. Defence expenditure totalled US$71m. in 2003 (US$9 per capita), representing 1·9% of GDP.

Army. The Army of 8,500 (2002) includes 7,500 conscripts. There are also three paramilitary forces: People's Militia (7,000), Gendarmerie (1,000) and Republican Guard (1,600).

Navy. A small force of 400 (2002) operates from bases at Conakry and Kakanda.

Air Force. Personnel (2002) 800. There were eight combat aircraft including MiG-17s and MiG-21s.

INTERNATIONAL RELATIONS

Guinea is a member of the UN, WTO, the African Union, African Development Bank, ECOWAS, IOM, OIC, Islamic Development Bank, International Organization of the Francophonie and is an ACP member state of the ACP-EU relationship.

ECONOMY

Agriculture produced 24·2% of GDP in 2002, industry 36·6% and services 39·1%.

Currency. The monetary unit is the *Guinean franc* (GNF). Inflation in 2002 was 3·0%. In June 2002 foreign exchange reserves were US$192m. and total money supply was 600,100m. Guinean francs.

Budget. Revenue for 2002 was 909,700m. Guinean francs and expenditure 1,281,800m. Guinean francs.

Of total government revenue in 2002, tax revenue accounted for 76·2%, grants 16·0% and non-tax revenue 7·8%. Current expenditure accounted for 61·5% of total expenditure and capital expenditure 38·5%. VAT was applied to non-essential goods in July 1996.

Performance. Real GDP growth in 2002 was 4·2% (3·8% in 2001). Total GDP in 2003 was US$3·6bn.

Banking and Finance. In 1986 the Central Bank (*Governor*, Mohamed Alkhaly Daffé) and commercial banking were restructured, and commercial banks returned to the private sector. There were seven commercial banks in 2002. There is an Islamic bank.

ENERGY AND NATURAL RESOURCES

Environment. Guinea's carbon dioxide emissions from the consumption and flaring of fossil fuels in 2002 were the equivalent of 0·2 tonnes per capita.

Electricity. In 2000 installed capacity was 0·2m. kW. Production was approximately 569m. kWh in 2000; consumption per capita was an estimated 70 kWh.

Minerals. Mining produced 16% of GDP in 1999. Guinea possesses over 25% of the world's bauxite reserves and is the second largest producer after Australia. Output: bauxite (2001), 15,700,000 tonnes; alumina (2002), 701,936 tonnes; diamonds (2001), 370,000 carats; gold (2000), 13,104 kg. There are also deposits of granite, iron ore, chrome, copper, lead, manganese, molybdenum, nickel, platinum, uranium and zinc.

Agriculture. Subsistence agriculture supports about 70% of the population. There were 890,000 ha of arable land in 2001 and 635,000 ha of permanent crops. 95,000 ha were irrigated in 2001. The chief crops (production, 2000, in 1,000 tonnes) are: cassava, 870; rice, 750; plantains, 429; sugarcane, 220; groundnuts, 182; bananas, 150; sweet potatoes, 135; maize, 90; yams, 88; mangoes, 83; pineapples, 72; palm kernels, 52; palm oil, 50; seed cotton, 50; taro, 29; coffee, 21; cotton lint, 21.

Livestock (2000): cattle, 2·37m.; goats, 864,000; sheep, 687,000; pigs, 54,000; chickens, 9m.

Forestry. The area under forests in 2000 was 6·93m. ha, or 28·2% of the total land area. In 2001, 12·14m. cu. metres of roundwood were cut.

Fisheries. In 2001 the total catch was approximately 90,000 tonnes, almost entirely from sea fishing.

INDUSTRY

Manufacturing accounted for 4·4% of GDP in 2001. Cement, corrugated and sheet iron, beer, soft drinks and cigarettes are produced.

Labour. In 1996 the labour force was 3,565,000 (53% males). The agricultural sector employs 80% of the workforce.

INTERNATIONAL TRADE

Foreign debt was US$3,401m. in 2002. Imports require authorization and there are restrictions on the export of capital.

Imports and Exports. Imports and exports for calendar years in US$1m.:

	1998	*1999*	*2000*	*2001*	*2002*
Imports f.o.b.	572·0	581·7	587·1	561·9	668·4
Exports f.o.b.	693·0	635·7	666·3	731·0	886·0

Main imports by value, 2000: refined petroleum, 25%; food, 18%; machinery and apparatus, 10%; road vehicles, 9%. Principal import suppliers, 2000: Côte d'Ivoire,

21%; France, 20%; Belgium, 8%; USA, 8%; Japan, 6%. Main exports by value, 1998: bauxite, 46%; gold, 18%; alumina, 14%; diamonds, 7%. Principal export markets, 2000: France, 33%; USA, 13%; Spain, 10%; Ireland, 9%; Germany, 6%.

COMMUNICATIONS

Roads. In 1999 there were about 4,300 km of main and national roads, 7,960 km of secondary roads and 18,200 km of other roads. 16·5% of all roads were paved in 1999. In 1996 there were 14,100 passenger cars, or two per 1,000 inhabitants, and 21,000 trucks and vans.

Rail. A railway connects Conakry with Kankan (662 km) and is to be extended to Bougouni in Mali. A line 134 km long linking bauxite deposits at Sangaredi with Port Kamsar was opened in 1973 (carried 12·5m. tonnes in 1993), a third line links Conakry and Fria (144 km; carried 1m. tonnes in 1993) and a fourth, the Kindia Bauxite Railway (102 km) linking Débéle with Conakry, carried 3m. tonnes in 1994.

Civil Aviation. There is an international airport at Conakry (Gbessia). In 2003 there were scheduled flights to Abidjan, Accra, Bamako, Banjul, Bissau, Brussels, Casablanca, Dakar, Freetown, Lagos and Paris. In 2000 Conakry handled 243,000 passengers (227,000 on international flights) and 4,600 tonnes of freight. In 1999 scheduled airline traffic of Guinean-based carriers flew 800,000 km, carrying 59,000 passengers (all on international flights).

Shipping. There are ports at Conakry and for bauxite exports at Kamsar (opened 1973). Merchant shipping totalled 12,000 GRT in 2002.

Telecommunications. The Société des Télécommunications de Guinée is 40% state-owned. In 2002 there were 116,800 telephone subscribers, equivalent to 15·2 per 1,000 population, and 42,000 PCs in use (5·5 per 1,000 persons). There were 90,800 mobile phone subscribers in 2002 and 3,200 fax machines in use in 1999. In 2002 Guinea had 35,000 Internet users.

Postal Services. In 1998 there were 96 post offices, or one for every 47,400 persons.

SOCIAL INSTITUTIONS

Justice. There are *tribunaux du premier degré* at Conakry and Kankan, and a *juge de paix* at Nzérékoré. The High Court, Court of Appeal and Superior Tribunal of Cassation are at Conakry. The death penalty is in force, and was used in 2001 for the first time in 17 years.

The population in penal institutions in 2002 was 3,070 (37 per 100,000 of national population).

Religion. 79% of the population are Muslim, 9% Christian. Traditional animist beliefs are still found.

Education. In 1998 adult literacy was 36·0%. In 2000–01 there were 853,623 pupils with 19,244 teachers in primary schools; and 232,567 pupils with 5,099 teachers (1997–98) in general education in secondary schools. In 1995 there were 28,311 pupils (6,143 girls) and 1,407 teachers in 61 *lycées* and 8,569 pupils (3,013) and 1,268 teachers in 55 institutions of professional education. In 1996 there were two universities with 5,735 students and 525 academic staff.

Besides French, there are eight official languages taught in schools: Fulani, Malinké, Susu, Kissi, Kpelle, Loma, Basari and Koniagi.

In 2000–01 total expenditure on education came to 2·0% of GNP and 25·6% of total government spending.

Health. In 1991 there were 38 hospitals, with the equivalent of five beds per 10,000 population. In 1988 there were 3,382 beds; there were also 930 doctors (1995), 22 dentists (1988), 197 pharmacists (1991), 372 midwives (1995) and 3,983 trained nursing personnel (1995).

CULTURE

World Heritage Sites. Guinea shares one site with Côte d'Ivoire on the UNESCO World Heritage List: Mount Nimba Strict Nature Reserve (inscribed on the list in

1981). The dense forested slopes are home to viviparous toads and chimpanzees among other fauna.

Broadcasting. Broadcasting is the responsibility of the state-controlled Radiodiffusion Télévision Guinéenne. There were 357,000 TV receivers (colour by SECAM H) in 2001 and 422,000 radio receivers in 2000.

Press. There is one daily newspaper (circulation 20,000).

Tourism. There were 33,000 foreign tourists in 2000 bringing in revenue of US$12m.

DIPLOMATIC REPRESENTATIVES

Of Guinea in the United Kingdom
Ambassador: Ibrahima Haïara Chérif (resides at Paris).
Consul General: Lansana Keita (7 Waterloo Place, London, SW1Y 4BN).

Of the United Kingdom in Guinea (4th Floor, ETI-Bull Building, Boulevard du Commerce, Commune de Kaloum, Conakry)
Ambassador: Helen Horn, MBE.

Of Guinea in the USA (2112 Leroy Pl., NW, Washington, D.C., 20008)
Ambassador: Alpha Oumar Rafiou Barry.

Of the USA in Guinea (Rue KA 038, Conakry)
Ambassador: Jackson McDonald.

Of Guinea to the United Nations
Ambassador: Alpha Ibrahima Sow.

Of Guinea to the European Union
Ambassador: Kazaliou Balde.

FURTHER READING

Bulletin Statistique et Economique de la Guinée. Monthly. Conakry

Binns, Margaret, *Guinea.* [Bibliography] ABC-Clio, Oxford and Santa Barbara (CA), 1996

National statistical office: Direction Nationale de la Statistique, BP 221, Conakry.
Website (French only): http://www.stat-guinee.org

GUINEA-BISSAU

Republica da Guiné-Bissau

Capital: Bissau
Population projection, 2010: 1·83m.
GDP per capita, 2002: (PPP$) 710
HDI/world rank: 0·350/172

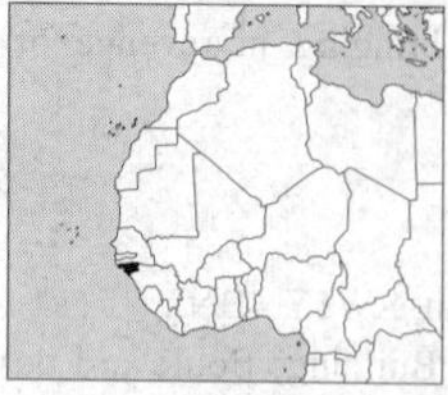

KEY HISTORICAL EVENTS

Portugal was the major power in the area throughout the colonial period. In 1974, after the Portuguese revolution, Portugal abandoned the struggle to keep Guinea-Bissau and independence was formally recognized on 10 Sept. 1974. In 1975 Cape Verde also became independent but the two countries remained separate sovereign states. On 14 Nov. 1980 a coup d'état was in part inspired by resentment in Guinea-Bissau over the privileges enjoyed by Cape Verdians. Guineans obtained a more prominent role under the new government. On 16 May 1984 a new constitution was approved based on Marxist principles but after 1986 there was a return to private enterprise in an attempt to solve critical economic problems and to lift the country out of poverty. A year-long civil war broke out in 1998 between army rebels and the country's long-time ruler. Neighbouring Senegal and Guinea sent troops in to aid the government. On 7 May 1999 President João Bernardo Vieira was ousted in a military coup led by former chief of staff Gen. Ansumane Mané, whom the president had dismissed in 1998. Following the coup Mané briefly headed a military junta before National Assembly speaker Malam Bacai Sanhá took power as acting president. After presidential elections in Nov. 1999 and Jan. 2000 Kumba Ialá gained the presidency in a landslide victory. Marking a change towards a democratic future in Guinea-Bissau's politics, Ialá rejected a demand made by the outgoing junta for special consultative status following the elections. Kumba Ialá was overthrown in a coup in Sept. 2003 led by army chief of staff Gen. Veríssimo Correia Seabra.

TERRITORY AND POPULATION

Guinea-Bissau is bounded by Senegal in the north, the Atlantic Ocean in the west and by Guinea in the east and south. It includes the adjacent archipelago of Bijagós. Area, 36,125 sq. km (13,948 sq. miles). Population (1991 census), 983,367. Population estimate, 2002: 1,454,600 (736,000 females); density, 40·2 per sq. km. The capital, Bissau, had an estimated 274,000 inhabitants in 1999. In 2001, 67·7% of the population were rural.

The UN gives a projected population for 2010 of 1·83m.

The area, population, and chief town of the capital and the eight regions:

Region	*Area in sq. km*	*Population (1991 census)*	*Chief town*
Bissau City	78	197,610	—
Bafatá	5,981	143,377	Bafatá
Biombo	838	60,420	Quinhámel
Bolama	2,624	26,691	Bolama
Cacheu	5,175	146,980	Cacheu
Gabú	9,150	134,971	Gabú
Oio	5,403	156,084	Farim
Quinara	3,138	44,793	Fulacunda
Tombali	3,736	72,441	Catió

The main ethnic groups were (1998) the Balante (30%), Fulani (20%), Manjaco (14%), Mandingo (13%) and Papeis (7%). Portuguese remains the official language, but Crioulo is spoken throughout the country.

SOCIAL STATISTICS

Births, 1997, 46,000; deaths, 19,000. 1997 birth rate, 39·2 per 1,000 population; death rate, 15·9. Annual population growth rate, 1992–2002, 3·0%. Life expectancy in 2001 was 46·7 years for women and 43·5 for men. Infant mortality, 2001, 130 per 1,000 live births; fertility rate, 2001, 6·0 births per woman.

CLIMATE

The tropical climate has a wet season from June to Nov., when rains are abundant, but the hot, dry Harmattan wind blows from Dec. to May. Bissau, Jan. 76°F (24·4°C), July 80°F (26·7°C). Annual rainfall 78" (1,950 mm).

CONSTITUTION AND GOVERNMENT

A new Constitution was promulgated on 16 May 1984. The Revolutionary Council, established following the 1980 coup, was replaced by a 15-member Council of State, while in April 1984 a new National People's Assembly was elected comprising 150 representatives elected by and from the directly-elected regional councils for five-year terms. The sole political movement was the *Partido Africano da Independência da Guiné e Cabo Verde* (PAIGC), but in Dec. 1990 a policy of 'integral multi-partyism' was announced, and in May 1991 the National Assembly voted unanimously to abolish the law making the PAIGC the sole party. The *President* is Head of State and Government and is elected for a five-year term. The *National Assembly* has 100 members. After the coup of Sept. 2003, a transitional government was appointed by the National Transition Council (CNT) which governed until elections in March 2004. The CNT, which was to function as the parliament until the elections, comprised 25 military officers and 31 representatives of 23 political parties and eight groups from civil society.

National Anthem. 'Sol, suor, o verde e mar' ('Sun, sweat, the green and the sea'); words and tune by A. Lopes Cabral. (Same as Cape Verde.)

RECENT ELECTIONS

Presidential elections were held in two rounds on 28 Nov. 1999 and 16 Jan. 2000. After the first round Kumba Ialá (Party for Social Renewal) and Malam Bacai Sanhá (African Party for the Independence of Guinea and Cape Verde) out-polled four opponents and went into a run-off. At the second round turn-out was 69%. Ialá won with 72% of the vote.

At the parliamentary elections on 28 March 2004 turn-out was 76·3%. The African Party for the Independence of Guinea and Cape Verde (PAIGC) won 33·9% of the vote (45 of 100 seats), the Party for Social Renewal (PRS) 26·5% (35 seats) and the United Social Democratic Party (PUSD) 17·6% (17 seats). The Electoral Union (UE) took two seats and the United Popular Alliance (APU) one seat.

CURRENT ADMINISTRATION

Interim President: Henrique Rosa; b. 1946 (took office on 28 Sept. 2003).

In April 2005 the government comprised:

Prime Minister: Carlos Gomes Júnior (PAIGC); b. 1949 (since 10 May 2004).

Minister for the Presidency of the Council of Ministers, for Social Communication and Relations with Parliament: Daniel Gomes. *Foreign Affairs, International Co-operation and Communities:* Soares Sambú. *Defence:* Martinho Dafa Cabi. *Internal Administration:* Dr Aladji Joaquim Mumini Embalo. *Administrative Reform, Civil Service and Labour:* Pedro Augusto Godinho Gomes. *Economy:* Issuf Sanhá. *Finance:* João Aladji Fadiá. *Social Solidarity, Family and the Fight against Poverty:* Dr Eugénia Araujo Saldanha. *Education:* Marciano Silva Barbeiro. *Agriculture and Rural Development:* João de Carvalho. *Public Works, Construction and Urbanization:* Domingos Simões Pereira. *Transport and Communications:* Raimundo Pereira. *Fishing:* Dr Helena Nosoline Embaló. *Energy and Natural Resources:* Rui Araújo. *Industry, Handicrafts and Commerce:* Adiatu Djalo Nandigna. *Justice:* Filomeno Lobo de Pina. *Health:* Dr Odete Semedo. *War Veterans:* Isabel Buscardini.

President of the Assembly: Francisco Benante (PAIGC).

DEFENCE

There is selective conscription. Defence expenditure totalled US$9m. in 2003 (US$6 per capita), representing 4·0% of GDP.

Army. Army personnel in 2002 numbered 6,800. There is a paramilitary Gendarmerie 2,000 strong.

Navy. The naval flotilla, based at Bissau, numbered 350 in 2002.

Air Force. Formation of a small Air Force began in 1978. Personnel (2002) 100 with three combat aircraft (MiG-17s).

INTERNATIONAL RELATIONS

Guinea-Bissau is a member of the UN, WTO, the African Union, African Development Bank, ECOWAS, IOM, OIC, Islamic Development Bank, International Organization of the Francophonie and is an ACP member state of the ACP-EU relationship.

ECONOMY

In 2002 agriculture accounted for 62·4% of GDP (one of the highest percentages of any country), industry 13·1% and services 24·5%.

Currency. On 2 May 1997 Guinea-Bissau joined the French Franc Zone, and the *peso* was replaced by the franc CFA at 65 pesos = one franc CFA. The *franc CFA* (XOF) has a parity rate of 655·957 francs CFA to one euro. Foreign exchange reserves were US$84m. in May 2002. Inflation was 3·3% in 2002. Total money supply in May 2002 was 77,011m. francs CFA.

Budget. Revenue in 2001 was 47,530m. francs CFA; expenditure totalled 63,162m. francs CFA.

Performance. GDP growth was 0·2% in 2001, but there then followed a recession with the economy contracting by 7·2% in 2002. Total GDP in 2003 was US$0·2bn.

Banking and Finance. The bank of issue and the central bank is the regional Central Bank of West African States (BCEAO). The *Governor* is Charles Konan Banny. There are four other banks (Banco da Africa Occidental; Banco Internacional de Guiné-Bissau; Caixa de Crédito de Guiné; Caixa Económica Postal).

The stock exchange of the Economic and Monetary Union of West Africa is in Abidjan.

ENERGY AND NATURAL RESOURCES

Environment. Carbon dioxide emissions from the consumption and flaring of fossil fuels in 2002 were the equivalent of 0·3 tonnes per capita.

Electricity. Installed capacity in 2000 was 21,000 kW. Production was about 58m. kWh in 2000; consumption per capita was an estimated 48 kWh.

Minerals. Mineral resources are not exploited. There are estimated to be 200m. tonnes of bauxite and 112m. tonnes of phosphate.

Agriculture. Agriculture employs 80% of the labour force. There were 300,000 ha of arable land in 2001 and 248,000 ha of permanent crops. Chief crops (production, 2000, in 1,000 tonnes) are: rice, 138; coconuts, 46; cashew nuts, 42; plantains, 38; millet, 35; sorghum, 26; groundnuts, 19; cassava, 17; maize, 10; copra, 9; palm kernels, 9; sugarcane, 6.

Livestock (2000): cattle, 530,000; pigs, 345,000; goats, 325,000; sheep, 285,000; chickens, 1m.

Forestry. The area covered by forests in 2000 was 2·19m. ha, or 60·5% of the total land area. In 2001, 592,000 cu. metres of roundwood were cut.

Fisheries. Total catch in 2001 came to approximately 5,000 tonnes, of which 96% was from sea fishing. Revenue from fishing licences may be worth as much as 45% of government revenue.

INDUSTRY

Manufacturing accounted for 10·1% of GDP in 2001. Output of main products: vegetable oils (3·4m. litres in 2000), sawnwood (16,000 tonnes in 2001), soap (2,500 tonnes in 2000) and animal hides and skins (1,400 tonnes in 2001).

Labour. The labour force in 1996 was 514,000 (60% males).

INTERNATIONAL TRADE

Foreign debt totalled US$699m. in 2002.

Imports and Exports. Trade in US$1m.:

	1997	*1998*	*1999*	*2000*	*2001*
Imports f.o.b.	62·5	51·1	65·6	85·6	79·8
Exports f.o.b.	48·9	25·9	51·2	62·1	47·2

Main exports in 2001 were: cashew nuts, 95·6%; cotton, 2·3%; logs, 1·5%. Imports: foodstuffs, 18·7%; transport equipment, 13·2%; equipment and machinery, 7·7%. Guinea-Bissau supplies more than 10% of the world market of cashew nuts. Principal imports are foodstuffs, transport equipment, machinery, fuel and lubricants.

Main export markets, 2001: India, 85·6%; Portugal, 3·8%; Senegal, 2·5%; France, 1·7%. Main import suppliers, 2001: Portugal, 30·9%; Senegal, 28·3%; China, 11·3%; Netherlands, 6·8%.

COMMUNICATIONS

Roads. In 1999 there were about 4,400 km of roads, of which 2,400 km were national roads; and in 1996, 7,120 passenger cars (5·7 per 1,000 inhabitants) and 5,640 trucks.

Civil Aviation. The national carrier is Transportes Aéreos de Guiné-Bissau. There is an international airport serving Bissau (Osvaldo Vieira). In 2003 there were scheduled flights to Banjul, Conakry, Dakar, Lisbon, Nouakchott, Praia and Sal.

Shipping. The main port is Bissau; minor ports are Bolama, Cacheu and Catió. In 2002 the merchant marine totalled 6,000 GRT.

Telecommunications. Telephone subscribers numbered 11,200 in 2002 (8·9 per 1,000 persons) and there were 500 fax machines in 1998. In 2002 there were 5,000 Internet users.

Postal Services. In 1996 there were 18 post offices.

SOCIAL INSTITUTIONS

Justice. The death penalty was abolished for all crimes in 1993.

Religion. In 2001 about 38% of the population were Muslim and about 12% Christian (mainly Roman Catholic). The remainder held traditional animist beliefs.

Education. Adult literacy was 39·6% in 2001 (male, 55·2%; female, 24·7%). Some 60% of children of primary school age attend school. In 1999–2000 there were 150,041 pupils at primary schools (3,405 teachers), 25,736 at secondary schools (1,226 teachers) and 463 students in tertiary education. In 1999–2000 total expenditure on education came to 2·3% of GNP and 4·8% of total government spending.

Health. In 1993 there were 10 private, two national and four regional hospitals with a total of 1,300 beds. There were 125 dispensaries. In 1996 there were 194 physicians, 11 dentists, 1,277 nurses and 148 midwives.

CULTURE

Broadcasting. In 2000 there were 56,000 radio receivers. A television service started in 1989 (colour by SECAM V). In 2001 there were 44,000 TV receivers.

Press. In 1996 there were three newspapers, including one privately owned.

DIPLOMATIC REPRESENTATIVES

Of Guinea-Bissau in the United Kingdom
Chargé d'Affaires a.i.: Fali Embalo (resides at Paris).
Honorary Consul: Mabel Figueirdo da Fonseca Smith (PO Box 393, Tunbridge Wells, Kent, TN4 9YZ).

Of the United Kingdom in Guinea-Bissau
Ambassador: Peter Newall (resides at Dakar, Senegal).

Of Guinea-Bissau in the USA (PO Box 33813, Washington, D.C., 20033)
Ambassador: Vacant.
Chargé d'Affaires a.i.: Henrique Adriano Da Silva.

Of the USA in Guinea-Bissau
Ambassador: Richard Roth (resides at Dakar, Senegal).

Of Guinea-Bissau to the United Nations
Ambassador: Alfredo Lopes Cabral.

Of Guinea-Bissau to the European Union
Ambassador: Vacant.
Chargé d'Affaires a.i.: Serafim Ianga.

FURTHER READING

Forrest, J. A., *Guinea-Bissau: Power, Conflict and Renewal in a West African Nation.* Boulder (CO), 1992

Galli, Rosemary, *Guinea-Bissau.* [Bibliography] ABC-Clio, Oxford and Santa Barbara (CA), 1990

National statistical office: Instituto Nacional de Estadística e Censos (INEC), CP 06 Bissau.
Website (Portuguese only): http://www.stat-guinebissau.com

GUYANA

Co-operative Republic of Guyana

Capital: Georgetown
Population projection, 2010: 769,000
GDP per capita, 2002: (PPP$) 4,260
HDI/world rank: 0·719/104

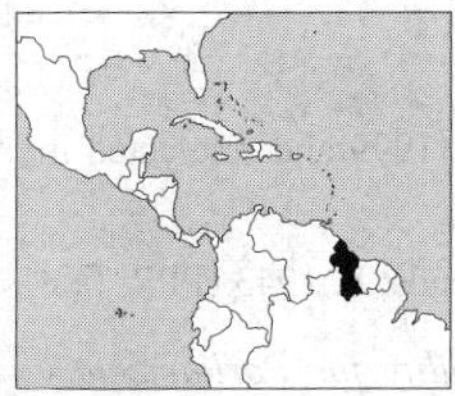

KEY HISTORICAL EVENTS

First settled by the Dutch West Indian Company about 1620, the territory was captured by Britain to whom it was ceded in 1814 and named British Guiana. To work the sugar plantations African slaves were transported to Guyana in the 18th century and East Indian and Chinese indentured labourers in the 19th century. From 1950 the anti-colonial struggle was spearheaded by the People's Progressive Party (PPP) led by Cheddi Jagan and Forbes Burnham. By the time internal autonomy was granted in 1961 Burnham had split with Jagan to form the more moderate People's National Congress (PNC). Guyana became an independent member of the Commonwealth in 1966 with Burnham as the first prime minister, later president. By the 1980s, desperate economic straits had forced Guyana to seek outside help which came on condition of restoring free elections. Dr Jagan returned to power in 1992. Following his death in March 1997 his wife, Janet Jagan, was sworn in as President.

TERRITORY AND POPULATION

Guyana is situated on the northeast coast of Latin America on the Atlantic Ocean, with Suriname on the east, Venezuela on the west and Brazil on the south and west. Area, 83,044 sq. miles (215,083 sq. km). In 1991 the census population was 723,800; density 3·4 per sq. km. Estimated population (2002), 763,000.

The UN gives a projected population for 2010 of 769,000.

Guyana has the highest proportion of rural population in South America, with only 36·7% living in urban areas in 2001. Ethnic groups by origin: 49% Indian, 36% African, 7% mixed race, 7% Amerindian and 1% others. The capital is Georgetown (1999 population, 275,000); other towns are Linden, New Amsterdam, Rose Hall and Corriverton.

Venezuela demanded the return of the Essequibo region in 1963. It was finally agreed in March 1983 that the UN Secretary-General should mediate. There was also an unresolved claim (1984) by Suriname for the return of an area between the New River and the Corentyne River.

The official language is English.

SOCIAL STATISTICS

Births, 1997, 29,000; deaths, 7,000. 1997 birth rate per 1,000 population, 34·7; death rate, 8·6. Life expectancy at birth in 2001; male 60·1 years and female 66·5 years. Annual population growth rate, 1992–2002, 0·4%. Infant mortality, 2001, 54 per 1,000 live births; fertility rate, 2001, 2·4 births per woman.

CLIMATE

A tropical climate, with rainy seasons from April to July and Nov. to Jan. Humidity is high all the year but temperatures are moderated by sea-breezes. Rainfall increases from 90" (2,280 mm) on the coast to 140" (3,560 mm) in the forest zone. Georgetown, Jan. 79°F (26·1°C), July 81°F (27·2°C). Annual rainfall 87" (2,175 mm).

CONSTITUTION AND GOVERNMENT

A new Constitution was promulgated in Oct. 1980. There is an *Executive Presidency*, and a 68-member *National Assembly*, with 65 members elected by popular vote, one elected Speaker of the National Assembly and two non-voting members appointed by the president. Elections for five-year terms are held under the single-list system of proportional representation, with the whole of the country forming one electoral area and each voter casting a vote for a party list of candidates.

National Anthem. 'Dear land of Guyana'; words by A. L. Luker, tune by R. Potter.

RECENT ELECTIONS

Bharrat Jagdeo and the People's Progressive Party (PPP) won the presidential and parliamentary elections of 19 March 2001. In the presidential election incumbent Bharrat Jagdeo received 209,031 votes (53·1% of the vote), with former president Desmond Hoyte of the People's National Congress (PNC) receiving 164,074 (41·7%). The PPP won 35 seats with 52·6% of votes in the parliamentary election, compared to 27 and 41·5% for the PNC.

CURRENT ADMINISTRATION

President: Bharrat Jagdeo; b. 1964 (PPP; sworn in 11 Aug. 1999 and re-elected in March 2001).

In March 2005 the government comprised:

Prime Minister and Minister of Public Works: Samuel Hinds; b. 1943 (PPP; first sworn in 9 Oct. 1992 and now in office for the third time).

Minister in the Office of the President with Responsibility for Parliamentary Affairs: Reepu Daman Persaud. *Attorney General and Minister of Legal Affairs:* Doodnauth Singh. *Cabinet Secretary:* Roger Luncheon. *Minister of Finance:* Sasenarine Kowlessar. *Foreign Affairs:* Samuel Rudolph Insanally. *Foreign Trade:* Clement Rohee. *Health:* Leslie Ramsammy. *Education:* Henry Jeffrey. *Home Affairs:* Ronald Gajraj. *Trade, Industry and Tourism:* Manzoor Nadir. *Amerindian Affairs:* Carolyn Rodrigues. *Housing and Water:* Shaik Baksh. *Culture, Youth and Sports:* Gail Teixeira. *Information:* Vacant. *Local Government:* Harripersaud Nokta. *Human Services, Social Security and Labour:* Dale Bisnauth. *Public Service:* Jennifer Westford. *Agriculture:* Satyadeow Sawh. *Fisheries, Crops and Livestock:* Satyadeow Sawah. *Transport and Hydraulics:* Carl Anthony Xavier.

Government Information Agency Website: http://www.gina.gov.gy

DEFENCE

In 2003 defence expenditure totalled US$5m. (US$7 per capita), representing 0·7% of GDP. The army, navy and air force are combined in a 1,600-strong Guyana Defence Force.

Army. The Guyana Army had (2002) a strength of 1,400 including 500 reserves. There is a paramilitary Guyana People's Militia 1,500 strong.

Navy. The Maritime Corps is an integral part of the Guyana Defence Force. In 2002 it had 100 personnel and one patrol and coastal combatant plus two boats. It is based at Georgetown and New Amsterdam.

Air Force. The Air Command has no combat aircraft. It is equipped with light aircraft and helicopters. Personnel (2002) 100.

INTERNATIONAL RELATIONS

In June 2000 a maritime dispute arose between Guyana and Suriname over offshore oil exploration.

Guyana is a member of the UN, WTO, the Commonwealth, OAS, Inter-American Development Bank, ACS, CARICOM, OIC and is an ACP member state of the ACP-EU relationship.

ECONOMY

Agriculture accounted for 30·8% of GDP in 2002, industry 28·6% and services 40·6%.

Overview. State control was reduced during the 1990s, with some privatization.

Currency. The unit of currency is the *Guyana dollar* (GYD) of 100 *cents*. Inflation was 5·3% in 2002. Foreign exchange reserves were US$280m. in June 2002 and total money supply was G$26·31bn.

Budget. Revenues in 1999 totalled G$36,544m. (tax revenue, 91·6%) and expenditures G$41,983m. (current expenditure, 71·2%).

Performance. GDP growth in 2000 was negative, at –1·3%, but was followed by a recovery, with growth in 2001 of 2·3% and in 2002 of 1·1%. Total GDP was US$0·7bn. in 2003.

Banking and Finance. The bank of issue is the Bank of Guyana (*Acting Governor*, Lawrence Williams), established 1965. There are five commercial banks and three foreign-owned. At March 1996 the total assets of commercial banks were G$62,587·9m. Savings deposits were G$26,564·2m.

ENERGY AND NATURAL RESOURCES

Environment. Guyana's carbon dioxide emissions from the consumption and flaring of fossil fuels were the equivalent of 2·2 tonnes per capita in 2002.

Electricity. Capacity in 2000 was 0·3m. kW. In 2000 production was 894m. kWh and consumption per capita 1,158 kWh.

Minerals. Placer gold mining commenced in 1884, and was followed by diamond mining in 1887. In 2001 output of bauxite was 1,985,000 tonnes, and of gold 14,183 kg. Other minerals include copper, tungsten, iron, nickel, quartz and molybdenum.

Agriculture. In 2001 Guyana had 480,000 ha of arable land and 30,000 ha of permanent crops. 150,000 ha were irrigated in 2001. Agricultural production, 2000 (in 1,000 tonnes): sugarcane, 3,000; rice, 600; coconuts, 56; cassava, 26; plantains, 14; bananas, 12; pineapples, 7.

Livestock (2000): cattle, 220,000; sheep, 130,000; goats, 79,000; pigs, 20,000; chickens, 13m. Livestock products, 2000 (in 1,000 tonnes): meat, 17; milk, 13; eggs, 7.

Forestry. In 2000 the area under forests totalled 16·88m. ha (78·5% of the land area). 25% of the country's energy needs are met by wood fuel. Timber production in 2001 was 1·19m. cu. metres.

Fisheries. Fish landings in 2001 came to 53,405 tonnes, of which 99% was from sea fishing.

INDUSTRY

The main industries are agro-processing (sugar, rice, timber and coconut) and mining (gold and diamonds). There is a light manufacturing sector, and textiles and pharmaceuticals are produced by state and private companies. Production: sugar (2002), 331,068 tonnes; rum (2002), 14·6m. litres; beer (2001), 8·1m. litres; soft drinks (2002), 4,251,000 cases; textiles (1995), 322m. metres; footwear (1995), 54,132 pairs; margarine (1995), 1,262,420 kg; edible oil (1995), 2,388,120 litres; refrigerators (1995), 2,763 units; paint (1995), 923,847 litres.

Labour. In 1996 the labour force was 353,000 (67% males).

INTERNATIONAL TRADE

Guyana's external debt in 2002 was US$1,459m.

Imports and Exports. In 2002 exports were valued at US$494·9m. and imports at US$563·1m. Principal commodities exported, 2002: gold, 27·5%; sugar, 24·1%; shrimps, 10·6%. Rice, timber and bauxite are also exported. Main commodities imported, 2002: consumer goods, 28·0%; fuels and lubricants, 22·3%; capital goods, 20·1%. Main export markets in 1999: Canada, 22%; USA, 22%; UK, 18%; Netherlands Antilles, 11%. Major import suppliers, 1999: USA, 29%; Trinidad and Tobago, 18%; Netherlands Antilles, 16%; UK, 7%.

COMMUNICATIONS

Roads. In 1999 there were an estimated 7,970 km of roads, of which 590 km were paved. Passenger cars numbered 24,000 in 1993 and commercial vehicles 9,000.

Rail. There is a government-owned railway in the North West District, while the Guyana Mining Enterprise operates a standard gauge railway of 133 km from Linden on the Demerara River to Ituni and Coomacka.

Civil Aviation. There is an international airport at Georgetown (Timehri). In 2003 there were direct flights to Anguilla, Antigua, Barbados, Dominica, Miami, New York, Paramaribo, Port of Spain, St Kitts and the British Virgin Islands. In 1999 scheduled airline traffic of Guyana-based carriers flew 1·7m. km, carrying 70,000 passengers.

Shipping. The major port is Georgetown; there are two other ports. In 2002 merchant shipping totalled 15,000 GRT. There are 217 nautical miles of river navigation. There are ferry services across the mouths of the Demerara, Berbice and Essequibo rivers.

Telecommunications. The inland public telegraph and radio communication services are operated by the Guyana Telephone and Telegraph Company Ltd. In 2002 there were 167,700 telephone subscribers, equivalent to 190·8 per 1,000 population, and 24,000 PCs in 2000 (or 27·3 for every 1,000 persons). Mobile phone subscribers numbered 87,300 in 2002. There were 125,000 Internet users in 2002.

Postal Services. In 1997 there were 85 post offices.

SOCIAL INSTITUTIONS

Justice. The law, both civil and criminal, is based on the common and statute law of England, save that the principles of the Roman–Dutch law have been retained for the registration, conveyance and mortgaging of land.

The Supreme Court of Judicature consists of a Court of Appeal, a High Court and a number of courts of summary jurisdiction. Guyana was one of ten countries to sign an agreement in Feb. 2001 establishing a Caribbean Court of Justice to replace the British Privy Council as the highest civil and criminal court. In the meantime the number of signatories has risen to twelve. The court was inaugurated at Port-of-Spain, Trinidad on 16 April 2005.

In 1996 there were 4,563 reported serious crimes, including 88 homicides. The population in penal institutions in July 2001 was 1,507 (175 per 100,000 of national population).

Religion. In 2001, 40% of the population were Protestant and Roman Catholic, 35% Hindu and 9% Muslim.

Education. In 1999–2000 there were 407 pre-primary schools with 2,218 teachers for 36,955 pupils; 428 primary schools with 3,951 teachers for 105,800 pupils; and 408 secondary schools with 3,371 teachers for 62,495 pupils. In 1999–2000 there were 7,496 students at university level.

Adult literacy in 2001 was 98·6% (male, 99·0%; female, 98·2%). The literacy rates are the highest in South America.

In 1999–2000 total expenditure on education came to 4·5% of GNP and 8·6% of total government spending.

Health. In 1994 there were 30 hospitals (five private), 162 health centres and 14 health posts. In 1997 there were 38·8 hospital beds per 10,000 population. There were 214 physicians, 35 dentists, 504 nurses, 40 pharmacists and 165 midwives in 1996.

CULTURE

Broadcasting. The Guyana Broadcasting Corporation has two radio programmes. There were 85,000 TV receivers (colour by PAL) in 2001 and 420,000 radio receivers in 1997. The Guyana Television Broadcasting Company (GTV) is state-owned and there are 12 private stations relaying US satellite services.

Cinema. In 1997 there were 18 cinemas.

Press. In 2000 there were two daily newspapers with a combined circulation of 56,750.

Tourism. There were 104,000 foreign visitors in 2002; receipts totalled US$49m.

Festivals. There are a number of Christian, Hindu and Muslim festivals throughout the year.

Libraries. There is a National Library in Georgetown.

Museums and Galleries. The Guyana National Museum contains a broad selection of animal life and Guyanese heritage. Castellani House, the National Gallery, is home to the finest art collection in Guyana.

DIPLOMATIC REPRESENTATIVES

Of Guyana in the United Kingdom (3 Palace Ct., London, W2 4LP)
High Commissioner: Laleshwar K. N. Singh.

Of the United Kingdom in Guyana (44 Main St., Georgetown)
High Commissioner: Stephen Hiscock.

Of Guyana in the USA (2490 Tracy Pl., NW, Washington, D.C., 20008)
Ambassador: Bayney R. Karran.

Of the USA in Guyana (99–100 Young and Duke Streets, Kingston, Georgetown)
Ambassador: Roland W. Bullen.

Of Guyana to the United Nations
Ambassador: Samuel Rudolph Insanally.

Of Guyana to the European Union
Ambassador: Kenneth F. S. King.

FURTHER READING

Braveboy-Wagner, J. A., *The Venezuela-Guyana Border Dispute: Britain's Colonial Legacy in Latin America.* London, 1984

Daly, V. T., *A Short History of the Guyanese People.* 3rd. ed. London, 1992

Williams, B. F., *Stains on My Name, War in My Veins: Guyana and the Politics of Cultural Struggle.* Duke Univ. Press, 1992

National statistical office: Bureau of Statistics, Avenue of the Republic and Brickdam, Georgetown.

HAITI

République d'Haïti

Capital: Port-au-Prince
Population projection, 2010: 9·13m.
GDP per capita, 2002: (PPP$) 1,610
HDI/world rank: 0·463/153

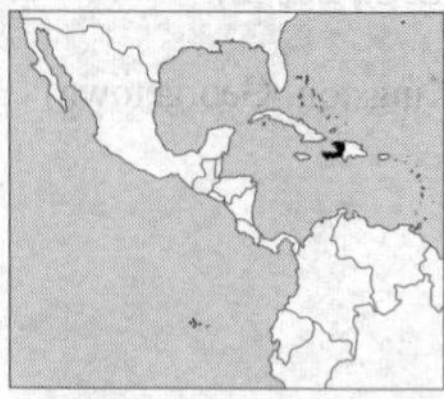

KEY HISTORICAL EVENTS

In the 16th century, Spain imported large numbers of African slaves whose descendants now populate the country. The colony subsequently fell under French rule. In 1791 a slave uprising led to the 13-year-long Haitian Revolution. In 1801 Toussaint Louverture, one of the leaders of the revolution, succeeded in eradicating slavery. He proclaimed himself governor-general for life over the whole island. He was captured and sent to France, but Jean-Jacques Dessalines, one of his generals, led the final battle that defeated Napoléon's forces. The newly-named Haiti declared its independence on 1 Jan. 1804, becoming the first independent black republic in the world. Ruled by a succession of self-appointed monarchs, Haiti became a republic in the mid-19th century. From 1915 to 1934 Haiti was under United States occupation.

A corrupt regime was dominated by François Duvalier from 1957 to 1964 when he was succeeded by his son, Jean-Claude Duvalier. He fled the country on 7 Feb. 1986. After a period of military rule, Father Jean-Bertrand Aristide was elected president in Dec. 1990.

On 30 Sept. 1991 President Aristide was deposed by a military junta and went into exile. Under international pressure, parliament again recognized Aristide as president in June 1993. However, despite a UN led naval blockade, the junta showed no sign of stepping down. 20,000 US troops moved into Haiti on 19 Sept. in an uncontested occupation. President Aristide returned to office on 15 Oct. 1994 and on 1 April 1995 a UN peacekeeping force (MANUH) took over from the US military mission. Aristide was succeeded by René Préval who was generally assumed to be a stand-in for his predecessor. Jean-Bertrand Aristide subsequently won the presidential elections held in Nov. 2000. In Dec. 2001 there was an unsuccessful coup led by former police and army officers. After armed rebels took control of the north of the country President Aristide stood down in Feb. 2004 and fled into exile.

TERRITORY AND POPULATION

Haiti is bounded in the east by the Dominican Republic, to the north by the Atlantic and elsewhere by the Caribbean Sea. The area is 27,700 sq. km (10,695 sq. miles). The Île de la Gonave, some 40 miles long, lies in the gulf of the same name. Among other islands is La Tortue, off the north peninsula. Provisional census population (2003), 7,929,048. Population density, 286 per sq. km. In 2001, 63·7% of the population were rural.

The UN gives a projected population for 2010 of 9·13m.

Areas, provisional census populations (2003) and chief towns of the nine departments:

Department	*Area (in sq. km)*	*Population*	*Chief town*
Artibonite	4,984	1,070,397	Gonaïves
Centre	3,675	566,043	Hinche
Grande Anse	3,310	603,894	Jérémie
Nord	2,106	773,546	Cap Haïtien
Nord-Est	1,805	300,493	Fort-Liberté
Nord-Ouest	2,176	445,080	Port-de-Paix
Ouest	4,827	3,093,699	Port-au-Prince
Sud	2,794	627,311	Les Cayes
Sud-Est	2,023	449,585	Jacmel

The capital is Port-au-Prince (1999 estimated population, 990,558; urban agglomeration, 1,977,036); other towns are Cap Haïtien (113,555 in 1999), Gonaïves (63,690 in 1997), Saint-Marc (49,128 in 1997) and Les Cayes (48,838 in 1997). Most of the population is of African or mixed origin.

The official languages are French and Créole. Créole is spoken by all Haitians; French by only a small minority.

SOCIAL STATISTICS

1995 births, 247,000; deaths, 92,000. Birth rate (per 1,000 population), 1995, 34·7; death rate, 12·9. Annual population growth rate, 1992–2002, 1·4%. Expectation of life at birth, 2001, 48·5 years for males and 49·8 years for females. Infant mortality, 2001, 79 per 1,000 live births; fertility rate, 2001, 4·1 births per woman.

In the Human Development Index, or HDI (measuring progress in countries in longevity, knowledge and standard of living), Haiti is the lowest-ranked country outside of Africa.

CLIMATE

A tropical climate, but the central mountains can cause semi-arid conditions in their lee. There are rainy seasons from April to June and Aug. to Nov. Hurricanes and severe thunderstorms can occur. The annual temperature range is small. Port-au-Prince, Jan. 77°F (25°C), July 84°F (28·9°C). Annual rainfall 53" (1,321 mm).

CONSTITUTION AND GOVERNMENT

The 1987 Constitution, ratified by a referendum, provides for a bicameral legislature (an 83-member *Chamber of Deputies* and a 27-member *Senate*), and an executive *President*, directly elected for a five-year term. The President can stand for a second term but only after a five-year interval.

National Anthem. 'La Dessalinienne'; words by J. Lhérisson, tune by N. Geffrard.

RECENT ELECTIONS

Presidential elections were held on 26 Nov. 2000. There were seven candidates. Jean-Bertrand Aristide was elected with 91·8% of votes cast. However, most opposition parties refused to recognize the result, with doubts being cast over the accuracy of the counting process.

Much delayed parliamentary elections were held on 21 May and 30 July 2000. In the vote for the Chamber of Deputies, Fanmi Lavalas (Water Fall Family/FL) won 72 of the available 82 seats, Mouvement Chrétien National (Christian National Movement/Mochrena) 3, Parti Louvri Baryé (Open the Gate Party/PLB), 2, Espace (Space/E) 2, Eskanp-Korega (EK) 1, Organisation de Peuple en Lutte (Organization of Struggling People/OPL) 1 and 1 seat went to a non-partisan. In elections for the Senate held on 21 May, 30 July and 26 Nov. 2000, FL took 26 of the 27 seats and PLB one seat.

CURRENT ADMINISTRATION

Provisional President: Boniface Alexandre; b. 1940 (Chief Justice; sworn in 29 Feb. 2004 after the deposition of President Jean-Bertrand Aristide).

In March 2005 the interim government comprised:

Prime Minister: Gérard Latortue; b. 1934 (sworn in 12 March 2004).

Minister of Foreign Affairs: Hérard Abraham. *Justice and Public Security:* Bernard Gousse. *Education, Youth, Sport and Culture:* Pierre Buteau. *Economy and Finance:* Henry Bazin. *Planning and International Co-operation:* Roland Pierre. *Commerce, Industry and Tourism:* Jacques Fritz Kénol. *Environment:* Yves André Wainwright. *Agriculture, Natural Resources and Rural Development:* Philippe Mathieu. *Public Health and Population:* Dr Josette Bijoux. *Public Works, Transport and Communications:* Fritz Adrien. *Social Affairs:* Pierre Claude Calixte. *Interior and National Security:* Georges Moïse. *Haitians Living Abroad:* Alix Baptiste. *Women's Affairs and Rights:* Adeline Magloire Chancy. *Minister without Portfolio, Responsible for Liaison with the Presidency:* Robert Ulysse.

DEFENCE

After the restoration of civilian rule in 1994 the armed forces and police were disbanded and an Interim Public Security Force formed, although this was later also dissolved. In 1995 a new police force—Police Nationale d'Haiti (PNH)—was recruited from former military personnel and others not implicated in human rights violations. The PNH currently has about 5,300 members. A UN peacekeeping force, MINUSTAH, consists of over 8,000 military personnel and civilian police.

In 2003 defence expenditure totalled US$22m. (US$3 per capita), representing 0·8% of GDP.

Army. The Army was disbanded in 1995.

Navy. A small Coast Guard, based at Port-au-Prince, is being developed. It had 30 personnel in 2002.

Air Force. The Air Force was disbanded in 1995.

INTERNATIONAL RELATIONS

In July 2004 international donors pledged more than US$1bn. in aid to help rebuild Haiti in addition to more than US$400m. previously committed. More than US$2bn. in aid had been given to Haiti over the previous ten years.

Haiti is a member of the UN, WTO, OAS, Inter-American Development Bank, ACS, CARICOM, IOM, International Organization of the Francophonie and is an ACP member state of the ACP-EU relationship.

ECONOMY

Agriculture accounted for 27·1% of GDP in 2002, industry 16·3% and services 56·5%.

Currency. The unit of currency is the *gourde* (HTG) of 100 *centimes.* Total money supply in June 2002 was 10,763m. gourdes. Inflation in 2002 was 8·7%. In April 2002 foreign exchange reserves were US$185m.

Budget. In 2001 revenues were 6,509m. gourdes (of which general sales tax 31·3% and customs duties 27·2%) and expenditures 8,728m. gourdes (current expenditure 81·9%).

Performance. There was a recession in both 2001 and 2002, with the economy contracting by 1·1% and 0·9% respectively. Total GDP in 2003 was US$2·7bn.

Banking and Finance. The Banque Nationale de la République d'Haïti is the central bank and bank of issue (*Governor*, Raymond Magloire). In 1999 there were 12 commercial banks (three foreign-owned) and a development bank.

Weights and Measures. The metric system and British imperial and US measures are in use.

ENERGY AND NATURAL RESOURCES

Environment. Carbon dioxide emissions from the consumption and flaring of fossil fuels in 2002 were the equivalent of 0·2 tonnes per capita. An *Environmental Sustainability Index* compiled for the World Economic Forum meeting in Feb. 2002 ranked Haiti 137th in the world out of the 142 countries analysed, with 34·8%. The index measured the ability of countries to maintain favourable environmental conditions and examined various factors including pollution levels and the use or abuse of natural resources.

Electricity. Most of the country is only provided with around four hours of electricity a day, supplied by the state-owned Electricité d'Haiti. Installed capacity was 0·3m. kW in 2000. Production in 2000 was 635m. kWh, with consumption per capita 80 kWh.

Minerals. Until the supply was exhausted in the 1970s, a small quantity of bauxite was mined.

Agriculture. There were 780,000 ha of arable land in 2001 and 320,000 ha of permanent crops. 65% of the workforce, mainly smallholders, make a living by agriculture carried on in seven large plains, from 0·2m. to 25,000 acres, and in 15 smaller plains down to 2,000 acres. Irrigation is used in some areas and in 2001 covered 75,000 ha. The main crops are (2000 production, in 1,000 tonnes): sugarcane, 800; cassava, 338; bananas, 323; plantains, 290; mangoes, 250; maize, 203; yams, 200; sweet potatoes, 180; rice, 130; sorghum, 98. Livestock (2000): cattle, 1·43m.; goats, 1·94m.; pigs, 1·0m.; horses, 500,000; chickens, 6m.

Forestry. The area under forests in 2000 was 88,000 ha, or 3·2% of the total land area. In 2001, 2·21m. cu. metres of roundwood were cut.

Fisheries. The total catch in 2001 was estimated to be 5,000 tonnes, of which 90% was from marine waters.

INDUSTRY

Manufacturing is largely based on the assembly of imported components: toys, sports equipment, clothing, electronic and electrical equipment. Textiles, steel, soap, chemicals, paint and shoes are also produced. Many jobs were lost to other Central American and Caribbean countries during the 1991–94 trade embargo, after President Aristide was deposed.

Labour. In 1996 the labour force was 3,209,000 (57% males). The unemployment rate in July 1998 was around 60%.

Trade Unions. Whilst at least six unions exist, their influence is very limited.

INTERNATIONAL TRADE

Foreign debt was US$1,248m. in 2002.

Imports and Exports. In 2001 exports totalled US$293·3m. and imports US$1,061·5m. The leading imports are petroleum products, foodstuffs, textiles, machinery, animal and vegetable oils, chemicals, pharmaceuticals, raw materials for transformation industries and vehicles. The USA is by far the leading trading partner. Main import suppliers in 1999 were USA, 60%; Dominican Republic, 4%; France, 3%; Japan, 3%. The USA accounted for 90% of exports in 1999.

COMMUNICATIONS

Roads. Total length of roads was estimated at 4,160 km in 1999, of which 1,010 km were surfaced. There were 32,000 passenger cars in 1996 (4·4 per 1,000 inhabitants), plus 21,000 trucks and vans.

Civil Aviation. There is an international airport at Port-au-Prince. Cap Haïtien also has scheduled flights to the Turks and Caicos Islands. In 2003 there were international flights to Aruba, Boston, Cayenne, Curaçao, Fort de France, Kingston, Miami, Montego Bay, Montreal, New York, Panama City, Paramaribo, Pointe-à-Pitre, Raleigh/Durham, St Maarten, Santiago (Cuba), Santiago (Dominican Republic), Santo Domingo and Washington, D.C. In 2000 Port-au-Prince handled 924,000 passengers (781,000 on international flights) and 15,300 tonnes of freight.

Shipping. Port-au-Prince and Cap Haïtien are the principal ports, and there are 12 minor ports. In 2002 the merchant marine totalled 1,000 GRT. In 1997 vessels totalling 1,304,000 NRT entered ports.

Telecommunications. The state telecommunications agency is Teleco. Telephone subscribers in 2002 numbered 270,000 (32·5 for every 1,000 inhabitants), including 140,000 mobile phone subscribers. In 2002 there were approximately 80,000 Internet users.

Postal Services. There were 85 post offices in 1998. The postal service is fairly reliable in the capital and major towns. Many businesses, however, prefer to use express courier services (DHL and Federal Express).

SOCIAL INSTITUTIONS

Justice. The Court of Cassation is the highest court in the judicial system. There are four Courts of Appeal and four Civil Courts. Judges are appointed by the President. The legal system is basically French.

The population in penal institutions in June 1999 was 4,152 (53 per 100,000 of national population).

Religion. Since the Concordat of 1860 Roman Catholicism has been given special recognition, under an archbishop with nine bishops. The Episcopal Church has one bishop. 60% of the population are nominally Roman Catholic, while other Christian churches number perhaps 20%. Probably two-thirds of the population to some extent adhere to Voodoo, recognized as an official religion in 2003.

Education. The adult literacy rate in 2001 was 50·8% (52·9% among males and 48·9% among females). Education is divided into nine years 'education fondamentale', followed by four years to 'Baccalaureate' and university/higher education. The school system is based on the French system and instruction is in

French and Créole. About 20% of education is provided by state schools; the remaining 80% by private schools, including Church and Mission schools.

In 1994–95 there were 360 primary schools (221 state, 139 religious), 21 public *lycées*, 123 private secondary schools, 18 vocational training centres and 42 domestic science centres.

There is a state university, several private universities and an Institute of Administration and Management.

In 2000–01 total expenditure on education came to 1·1% of GNP and 10·9% of total government spending.

Health. In 1996 there were 773 physicians and 2,630 nurses. There were 49 hospitals with a provision of ten beds per 10,000 population in 1994. In the period 1990–98 only 37% of the population had access to safe drinking water.

CULTURE

World Heritage Sites. Haiti has one site on the UNESCO World Heritage List: National History Park—Citadel, Sans-Souci, Ramiers (inscribed on the list in 1982), 19th century monuments to independence.

Broadcasting. Under the aegis of the Conseil National des Télécommunications, radio and TV programmes (colour by SECAM V) are broadcast by Radio Nationale and Télévision Nationale. There is a privately-owned cable TV company, and several privately-owned radio stations. There were 395,000 radio and 36,000 TV sets in 2000.

Press. There were two daily newspapers in 1998. In 1995 the press had a combined circulation of 45,000, at a rate of six per 1,000 inhabitants.

Tourism. In 2000 there were 140,000 foreign tourists, spending US$54m. Cruise ship arrivals in 1998 numbered 246,000. There are only about 1,000 hotel rooms in the whole country.

Libraries. There is a public library, Bibliothèque Nationale, in Port-au-Prince. A private library open to scholars, Bibliothèque des Frères de l'Instruction Chrétienne, is nearby.

Museums and Galleries. The main museums are MUPANAH and the Musée de l'Art Haïtien, both in Port-au-Prince. There are at least 20 private art shops in Port-au-Prince and major towns.

DIPLOMATIC REPRESENTATIVES

Of Haiti in the United Kingdom. The Embassy closed on 30 March 1987.

Of the United Kingdom in Haiti
Ambassador: Andy Ashcroft (resides at Santo Domingo, Dominican Republic).

Of Haiti in the USA (2311 Massachusetts Ave., NW, Washington, D.C., 20008)
Ambassador: Vacant.
Chargé d'Affaires a.i.: Harry Frantz Leo.

Of the USA in Haiti (Harry Truman Blvd., Port-au-Prince)
Ambassador: James B. Foley.

Of Haiti to the United Nations
Ambassador: Vacant.

Of Haiti to the European Union
Ambassador: Yolette Azor-Charles.

FURTHER READING

Chambers, F., *Haiti.* [Bibliography] 2nd ed. ABC-Clio, Oxford and Santa Barbara (CA), 1994
Heinl, Robert & Nancy, revised by Michael Heinl, *Written in Blood.* Univ. Press of America, 1996
Nicholls, D., *From Dessalines to Duvalier: Race, Colour and National Independence in Haiti.* 2nd ed. CUP, 1992.
Thomson, I., *Bonjour Blanc: a Journey through Haiti.* London, 1992
Weinstein, B. and Segal, A., *Haiti: the Failure of Politics.* New York, 1992

National library: Bibliothèque Nationale, Rue du Centre, Port-au-Prince.

HONDURAS

República de Honduras

Capital: Tegucigalpa
Population projection, 2010: 8·03m.
GDP per capita, 2002: (PPP$) 2,600
HDI/world rank: 0·672/115

KEY HISTORICAL EVENTS

Discovered by Columbus in 1502, Honduras was ruled by Spain until independence in 1821. Political instability was endemic throughout the 19th and most of the 20th century. The end of military rule seemed to come in 1981 when a general election gave victory to the more liberal and non-military party, PLH (Partido Liberal de Honduras). Power, however, remained with the armed forces. Internal unrest continued into the 1990s with politicians and military leaders at loggerheads, particularly over attempts to investigate violations of human rights. In Oct. 1998 Honduras was devastated by Hurricane Mitch, the worst natural disaster to hit the area in modern times.

TERRITORY AND POPULATION

Honduras is bounded in the north by the Caribbean, east and southeast by Nicaragua, west by Guatemala, southwest by El Salvador and south by the Pacific Ocean. The area is 112,492 sq. km (43,433 sq. miles). In 2001 the census population was 6,535,344 (3,304,386 females), giving a density of 58 per sq. km. In 2001, 53·6% of the population were urban.

The UN gives a projected population for 2010 of 8·03m.

The chief cities and towns are (2001 census populations): Tegucigalpa, the capital (819,867), San Pedro Sula (483,384), La Ceiba (126,721), Choloma (126,042), El Progreso (94,797), Choluteca (76,135), Comayagua (60,078), Danlí (47,310), Catacamas (35,995), Juticalpa (33,698).

Areas and 2001 populations of the 18 departments:

Department	*Area (in sq. km)*	*Population*	*Department*	*Area (in sq. km)*	*Population*
Atlántida	4,372	344,099	Intibucá	3,123	179,862
Choluteca	3,923	390,085	Islas de la Bahía	236	38,073
Colón	4,360	246,708	La Paz	2,525	156,560
Comayagua	8,249	352,881	Lempira	4,228	250,067
Copán	5,124	288,766	Ocotepeque	1,630	108,029
Cortés	3,242	1,202,510	Olancho	23,905	419,561
El Paraíso	7,489	350,054	Santa Bárbara	5,024	342,054
Francisco Morazán	8,619	1,180,676	Valle	1,665	151,841
Gracias a Dios	16,997	67,384	Yoro	7,781	465,414

The official language is Spanish. The Spanish-speaking population is of mixed Spanish and Amerindian descent (90%), with 7% Amerindians.

SOCIAL STATISTICS

Births, 1997 estimates, 187,000; deaths, 32,000. 1997 birth rate, 32·6 per 1,000 population; death rate, 5·6. 2001 life expectancy, 66·4 years for men and 71·3 for women. Annual population growth rate, 1992–2002, 2·8%. Infant mortality, 2001, 31 per 1,000 live births; fertility rate, 2001, 3·9 births per woman.

CLIMATE

The climate is tropical, with a small annual range of temperature but with high rainfall. Upland areas have two wet seasons, from May to July and in Sept. and Oct. The Caribbean Coast has most rain in Dec. and Jan. and temperatures are generally higher than inland. Tegucigalpa, Jan. 66°F (19°C), July 74°F (23·3°C). Annual rainfall 64" (1,621 mm).

CONSTITUTION AND GOVERNMENT

The present Constitution came into force in 1982. The *President* is elected for a four-year term. Members of the *National Congress* (total 128 seats) and municipal mayors are elected simultaneously on a proportional basis, according to combined votes cast for the Presidential candidate of their party.

National Anthem. 'Tu bandera' ('Thy Banner'); words by A. C. Coello, tune by C. Hartling.

RECENT ELECTIONS

Presidential and parliamentary elections took place on 25 Nov. 2001. In the presidential elections Ricardo Maduro won with 52·9% of votes cast, against 43·4% for his chief rival, Rafael Piñeda Ponce. In the elections to the National Congress, the Partido Nacional (PN) of Ricardo Maduro won 61 seats with 46·6% of the vote, while the Partido Liberal (PL) won 55 seats with 39·3%. The remaining seats went to the Partido de Unificación Democrática (PUD), 5 seats; the Partido de Inovación y Unidad-Social Democracia (PINU), 4; and the Partido Demócrata Cristiano de Honduras (PDCH), 3.

Congressional and presidential elections are scheduled to take place on 27 Nov. 2005.

CURRENT ADMINISTRATION

President: Ricardo Maduro; b. 1946 (PN; sworn in 27 Jan. 2002).

First Vice-President: Vicente Williams. *Second Vice-President:* Armida de López Contreras. *Third Vice-President:* Alberto Díaz Lobo.

In March 2005 the government consisted of:

Minister of Agriculture and Livestock: Mariano Jiménez. *Culture, Arts and Sports:* Vacant. *Defence:* Federico Brevé Travieso. *Education:* Roberto Martínez Lozano. *Finance:* William Chong Wong. *Foreign Relations:* Leonidas Rosa Bautista. *Industry and Commerce:* Norman García. *Interior and Justice:* Jorge Ramón Hernández Alcerro. *Labour and Social Security:* German Leitzelar Vidaurreta. *Natural Resources and Environment:* Patricia Panting. *Presidency:* Luis Consenza Jiménez. *Public Employees' Retirement and Pensions (INJUPEMP):* David Mendoza Lupiac. *Public Health:* Elías Lizardo Zelaya. *Public Works, Transportation and Housing:* Jorge Carranza Díaz. *Security:* Óscar Álvarez. *Tourism:* Thiery Pierrefeu Midence. *Ministers without Portfolio:* Carlos Vargas; Johnny Roberto Kafaty; Camilo Atala; Eduardo Kafaty; Ramón Medina Luna.

Honduran Parliament (Spanish only): http://www.congreso.gob.hn

DEFENCE

Conscription was abolished in 1995. In 2003 defence expenditure totalled US$53m. (US$8 per capita), representing 0·8% of GDP.

Army. The Army numbered (2002) 5,500. There is also a paramilitary Public Security Force of 6,000.

Navy. Personnel (2002), 1,000 including 400 marines. Bases are at Puerto Cortés, Puerto Castilla and Amapala.

Air Force. There were 49 combat aircraft in 2002 including F-5E/F Tiger II fighters. Total strength was (2002) about 1,800 personnel.

INTERNATIONAL RELATIONS

Honduras is a member of the UN, WTO, OAS, Inter-American Development Bank, CACM, ACS and IOM.

ECONOMY

Agriculture accounted for 13·4% of GDP in 2002, industry 30·6% and services 56·0%.

Currency. The unit of currency is the *lempira* (HNL) of 100 *centavos*. Foreign exchange reserves were US$1,526m. and gold reserves 21,000 troy oz in June 2002. Inflation was 7·7% in 2002. Total money supply in May 2002 was 11,610m. lempiras.

Budget. In 1999 revenues were 14,621m. lempiras and expenditures 18,198m. lempiras.

Performance. Real GDP growth was 3·3% in 2001 and 2·0% in 2002. Total GDP in 2003 was US$6·9bn.

Banking and Finance. The central bank of issue is the Banco Central de Honduras (*President,* Maria Elena Mondragón de Villar). It had total reserves at Dec. 2002 of US$1,531m. There is an agricultural development bank, Banadesa, for small grain producers, a state land bank and a network of rural credit agencies managed by peasant organizations. The Central American Bank for Economic Integration (BCIE) has its head office in Tegucigalpa. In 1999 there were 40 private banks, including four foreign.

There are stock exchanges in Tegucigalpa and San Pedro Sula.

Weights and Measures. The metric system is official but some local measures are used, such as the *manzana* (= 0·7 ha) and the *vara* (= 88 mm).

ENERGY AND NATURAL RESOURCES

Environment. Carbon dioxide emissions from the consumption and flaring of fossil fuels in 2002 were the equivalent of 0·8 tonnes per capita.

Electricity. Installed capacity was 0·9m. kW in 2000 (0·4m. kW hydro-electric). Production in 2000 was 3·68bn. kWh (77% hydro-electric); consumption per capita (2000) was 617 kWh.

Minerals. Output in 2002: zinc, 46,339 tonnes; lead (1998), 10,400 tonnes; silver, 52,877 kg. Small quantities of gold are mined, and there are also deposits of tin, iron, copper, coal, antimony and pitchblende.

Agriculture. There were 1·07m. ha of arable land in 2001 and 0·36m. ha of permanent crops. Legislation of 1975 provided for the compulsory redistribution of land, but in 1992 the grounds for this were much reduced, and a 5-ha minimum area for land titles abolished. Members of the 2,800 co-operatives set up in 1975 received individual shareholdings which can be broken up into personal units. Since 1992 women may have tenure in their own right. The state monopoly of the foreign grain trade was abolished in 1992. In 1996 the Agricultural Incentive Program was created (Ley de Incentivo Agrícola, LIA) which involves the redistribution of land for agricultural development.

Crop production in 2000 (in 1,000 tonnes): sugarcane, 3,896; maize, 534; bananas, 453; plantains, 250; coffee, 196; palm oil, 150; melons, 102; dry beans, 85; oranges, 80; pineapples, 71; sorghum, 65.

Livestock (2000): cattle, 1·95m.; pigs, 800,000; horses, 179,000; mules, 70,000; chickens, 18m.

Forestry. In 2000 forests covered 5·38m. ha, or 48·1% of the total land area. In 2001, 9·55m. cu. metres of roundwood were cut.

Fisheries. Shrimps and lobsters are important catches. The total catch in 2001 was 7,451 tonnes, almost entirely from sea fishing.

INDUSTRY

Industry is small-scale and local. 2001 output (in 1,000 tonnes): cement, 1,100; raw sugar, 316; wheat flour (1996), 100; fabrics (1995), 11,641 metres; beer (2003), 96·1m. litres; rum (1995), 2·37m. litres.

Labour. The workforce was 2,438,000 in Sept. 2001. Of 2,334,600 persons in employment in Sept. 2001, 766,800 were in agriculture, hunting, forestry and fishing, 559,200 in wholesale and retail trade and restaurants and hotels, 380,300 in community, social and personal services and 356,000 in manufacturing. Unemployment rate, Sept. 2001: 4·2%.

Trade Unions. About 346,000 workers were unionized in 1994.

INTERNATIONAL TRADE

In May 1992 Honduras, El Salvador and Guatemala agreed to create a free trade zone. Import duties are to be standardized. Foreign debt was US$5,395m. in 2002.

Imports and Exports. Imports (f.o.b.) in 2002 were valued at US$2,804·4m. and exports (f.o.b.) at US$1,930·4m.

Main exports are bananas, coffee, shrimps and lobsters, fruit, lead and zinc, timber, and refrigerated meats. Main imports are machinery and electrical equipment, industrial chemicals, and mineral products and lubricants. Principal export markets, 1999: USA, 57·3%; El Salvador, 10·1%; Guatemala, 7·7%; Germany, 4·6%; Japan, 3·5%; Spain, 1·8%. Principal import suppliers, 1999: USA, 48·8%; Guatemala, 7·7%; El Salvador, 6·1%; Mexico, 5·2%; Panama, 4·3%; Japan, 4·0%.

COMMUNICATIONS

Roads. Honduras is connected with Guatemala, El Salvador and Nicaragua by the Pan-American Highway. Out of a total of 13,603 km of roads in 1999, 20·4% were paved. In 1999 there were 326,541 passenger cars, 18,419 buses and coaches, 40,903 trucks and vans, and 90,890 motorcycles and mopeds.

Rail. The small government-run railway was built to serve the banana industry and is confined to the northern coastal region and does not reach Tegucigalpa. In 1995 there were 595 km of track in three gauges, which in 1994 carried 1m. passengers and 1·2m. tonnes of freight.

Civil Aviation. There are four international airports: San Pedro Sula (Ramon Villeda) and Tegucigalpa (Toncontín) are the main ones, plus Roatún and La Ceiba, with over 80 smaller airstrips in various parts of the country. In addition to domestic flights and services to other parts of central America and the Caribbean, there were flights in 2003 to Barcelona, Dallas/Fort Worth, Houston, Las Vegas, Los Angeles, Madrid, Miami, New Orleans, New York, Oklahoma City, Orange County, Phoenix and San Jose. In 2000 San Pedro Sula handled 636,000 passengers (507,000 on international flights) and 20,500 tonnes of freight, and Tegucigalpa handled 499,000 passengers (281,000 on international flights) and 8,400 tonnes of freight.

Shipping. The largest port is Puerto Cortés on the Atlantic coast. There are also ports at Henecán (on the Pacific) and Puerto Castilla and Tela (northern coast). In 2002 the merchant marine totalled 933,000 GRT, including oil tankers 214,000 GRT. Honduras is a flag of convenience registry.

Telecommunications. In 2002 there were 649,000 telephone subscribers, or 96·7 for every 1,000 persons, and 91,000 PCs were in use (13·6 for every 1,000 persons). There were 326,500 mobile phone subscribers in 2002. Honduras had 168,600 Internet users in 2002.

Postal Services. There were 435 post offices in 1995.

SOCIAL INSTITUTIONS

Justice. Judicial power is vested in the Supreme Court, with nine judges elected by the National Congress for four years; it appoints the judges of the courts of appeal, and justices of the peace.

There were 2,155 homicides in 2000. Honduras has among the highest murder rates in the world.

The population in penal institutions in June 2002 was 11,502 (172 per 100,000 of national population).

Religion. Roman Catholicism is the prevailing religion (5,740,000 followers in 2001), but the constitution guarantees freedom to all creeds, and the State does not contribute to the support of any. In 2001 there were 690,000 Evangelical Protestants with the remainder of the population followers of other faiths. In Sept. 2003 there was one cardinal.

Education. Adult literacy in 2001 was 75·6% (male, 75·4%; female, 75·7%). Education is free, compulsory (from 7 to 12 years) and secular. There is a high drop-out rate after the first years in primary education. In 2000–01 there were 120,141 children in pre-primary schools (6,167 teachers); 1,094,792 children in primary schools (32,144 teachers); 310,053 pupils in general education in secondary schools (12,480 teachers in 1995); and 90,620 students in tertiary education (5,549 academic staff). In 1995 there were eight universities or specialized colleges.

In 1998–99 expenditure on education came to 4·2% of GNP.

Health. In 1997 there were 4,896 physicians, 989 dentists and 6,152 nurses. In 1994 there were 29 public hospitals and 32 private, with 4,737 beds, and 849 health centres.

CULTURE

World Heritage Sites. Honduras has two sites on the UNESCO World Heritage List: Maya Site of Copán (inscribed on the list in 1980), a centre of the Mayan civilization abandoned in the early 10th century; and Río Plátano Biosphere Reserve (1982), one of the few remains of the Central American rain forest.

Broadcasting. There were six commercial TV channels in 1993 (colour by NTSC) and various radio stations (mostly local). There were 640,000 TV sets in 2001 and 2·62m. radio receivers in 2000.

Press. Honduras had eight national daily papers in 1998, with a combined circulation of 240,000.

Tourism. In 2000 there were 408,000 foreign tourists, spending US$240m.

DIPLOMATIC REPRESENTATIVES

Of Honduras in the United Kingdom (115 Gloucester Pl., London, W1U 6JT)
Ambassador: Hernán Antonio Bermúdez-Aguilar.

Of the United Kingdom in Honduras. The embassy closed on 28 Nov. 2003.
Ambassador: Richard Lavers (resides at Guatemala City).

Of Honduras in the USA (3007 Tilden St., NW, Washington, D.C., 20008)
Ambassador: Mario Miguel Canahuati.

Of the USA in Honduras (Av. La Paz, Tegucigalpa)
Ambassador: Larry L. Palmer.

Of Honduras to the United Nations
Ambassador: Manuel Acosta Bonilla.

Of Honduras to the European Union
Ambassador: Teodolinda Banegas de Makris.

FURTHER READING

Banco Central de Honduras. *Honduras en Cifras 1990–92.* Tegucigalpa, 1993

Howard-Reguindin, Pamela F., *Honduras.* [Bibliography] ABC-Clio, Oxford and Santa Barbara (CA), 1992

Meyer, H. K. and Meyer, J. H., *Historical Dictionary of Honduras.* 2nd ed. Metuchen (NJ), 1994

National statistical office: Instituto Nacional de Estadísticas, Tegucigalpa.
Website: http://www.ine-hn.org

HUNGARY

Magyar Köztársaság
(Hungarian Republic)

Capital: Budapest
Population projection, 2010: 9·55m.
GDP per capita, 2002: (PPP$) 13,400
HDI/world rank: 0·848/38

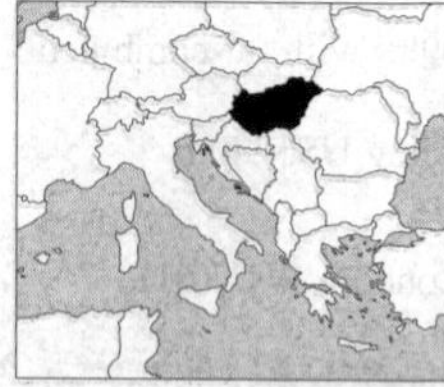

KEY HISTORICAL EVENTS

Records date back to 9 BC, when the Romans subdued the Celts to establish the Western region as Pannonia, centred on Aquincum. From the 5th century Romans and Celts retreated before the Huns who were followed by the Avars in the 7th century and the Magyars in the 9th. It was then that the name *On ogur* ('ten arrows') was given to the Magyar federation that was to become Hungary. The founding of Hungary is put at 896 after which Árpád, leader of one of the Magyar tribes, forged a dynasty that ruled Hungary until 1301. The death of Andrew III, the last Árpád, led to a seven-year interregnum, after which, with two exceptions, Hungary was ruled by foreign kings.

Lájos (Louis) the Great (1342–82), the son of Charles Robert of Anjou, pursued successful expansionist policies, achieving a golden age of prosperity. Having succeeded to the Hungarian throne in 1387, Sigismund of Luxembourg became Holy Roman Emperor in 1410. He and his successors were constantly under threat from the Ottoman Turks. In 1456 János Hunyadi, a military governor, broke the siege of Belgrade to keep the Turks at bay for another 70 years. In 1457 the Diet appointed Hunyadi's son Matthias Corvinus as king. Ambitious to become Holy Roman Emperor, Matthias sent a crusade against the Hussite King of Bohemia in 1468, gained control of Moravia and Silesia and conquered part of Austria to make Vienna his capital.

Matthias was an enlightened if despotic king. He built up one of Europe's finest libraries—destroyed a century later by the Ottomans. His successors could do little to hold off the Turks, to whom Belgrade was lost in 1521. The Hungarians lost ignominiously to the Turks under Suleiman II at the battle of Mohács on 29 Aug. 1526. Hungary was partitioned, the largest section going to the Turks, royal Hungary to the Habsburgs and Transylvania, though theoretically autonomous, becoming a vassal state of the Ottomans. The Ottoman siege of Vienna in 1683 was repulsed by the Habsburgs, marking a turning point for the Turks who, by 1699, had ceded most of their Hungarian territory. The Habsburgs became hereditary rulers pursuing a policy of divide and rule, guaranteeing political freedom for the three 'nations'—the ethnic Magyar, Saxon and Székelys groups.

In March 1848 the Hungarian Diet renounced Viennese rule. However, national minorities such as the Croats, the Romanians, Serbs and Slovaks demanded the same rights. In the War of Independence, fighting broke out between the Hungarians and the Austrians, the Hungarians being led by Lajos Kossuth (1802–94).

When Emperor Franz Joseph I took the throne in 1848, the Hungarians refused to recognize him, provoking an Austrian invasion, assisted by Russia. The aftermath of the war brought mass executions and direct rule from Vienna. Kossuth escaped into exile. Austria recognized the need for a compromise with Hungary. The *Ausgleich* created a dual monarchy to preside over the Austro-Hungarian Empire. Hungary gained internal autonomy with foreign affairs and defence as joint responsibilities.

On 28 June 1914 a Bosnian Serb assassinated the Habsburg Archduke Franz Ferdinand in Sarajevo. Austria-Hungary declared war on Serbia a month later, precipitating the First World War. Hungary became a republic in Nov. 1918. By the Treaty of Versailles, new countries including Czechoslovakia and Yugoslavia were created, reducing Hungary's territory by two-thirds and the population by a half. Transylvania was handed over to Romania.

In 1919 the Hungarian Kingdom was restored under Count Miklós Horthy, who ruled as regent in the absence of a monarch and appointed a chiefly aristocratic government. An alliance with Nazi Germany drew Hungary into fighting against the Soviet army in 1941. In March 1944 the Germans occupied Hungary and Horthy was forced to abdicate. Around 400,000 Jews are estimated to have been murdered. With civilian and military losses, almost a million Hungarians died in the war.

Under Soviet occupation, post-war Communist rule was established in 1948–49. Mátyás Rákosi and his Hungarian Workers Party headed the People's Republic under a dictatorship which went unchallenged until Stalin's death in 1953 when Rákosi was ousted by reformers led by Imre Nagy. Nagy began what he called 'the new stage in building socialism', which entailed industrial and economic reforms and the restoration of human rights.

Nagy was forced out of office in April 1955. On 23 Oct. 1956 student demonstrations demanded democracy and Nagy's reinstatement as prime minister. Local revolutionary committees were set up and a general strike was called. Under Soviet influence, János Kádár formed a counter-government with Soviet military backing; the Soviet Army marched into Budapest on 4 Nov., swiftly crushing all resistance. Nagy and several of his associates were hanged on 16 June 1958. Many opponents of the regime were deported to labour camps in the Soviet Union and over 200,000 people fled the country.

János Kádár was party leader from 1956–89. The New Economic Mechanism (NEM) of 1968 relaxed price controls, acknowledged the profit motive, improved manufacturing quality and shifted the emphasis from heavy to light industry. The old guard of the Hungarian Socialist Workers' Party was gradually phased out. A committee investigated the events of 1956, concluding that it had been a popular uprising and not a counter-revolution. The reburial of Imre Nagy on 16 June 1989 in Heroes' Square, Budapest was attended by a quarter of a million people. The first free elections to the National Assembly took place on 25 March 1990. Hungary became a member of NATO in 1999 and of the European Union on 1 May 2004.

TERRITORY AND POPULATION

Hungary is bounded in the north by Slovakia, northeast by Ukraine, east by Romania, south by Croatia and Serbia and Montenegro, southwest by Slovenia and west by Austria. The peace treaty of 10 Feb. 1947 restored the frontiers as of 1 Jan. 1938. The area of Hungary is 93,030 sq. km (35,919 sq. miles).

At the census of 1 Jan. 1990 the population was 10,374,823 (5,389,919 females); 1 Feb. 2001 census population, 10,197,119.

The UN gives a projected population for 2010 of 9·55m.

Hungary's population has been falling at such a steady rate since 1980 that its 2000 population was the same as that in the mid 1960s.

64·8% of the population was urban in 2001; population density, 2001, 109·6 per sq. km. Ethnic minorities, 1995: Roma (Gypsies), 4%; Germans, 2·6%; Serbs, 2%; Slovaks, 0·8%; Romanians, 0·7%. A law of 1993 permits ethnic minorities to set up self-governing councils. There is a worldwide Hungarian diaspora of nearly 2·5m. (1·5m. in the USA; 200,000 in Israel; 140,000 in Canada; 140,000 in Germany), and Hungarian minorities (totalling 3·2m. in 1992) in Romania (1·7m.), Slovakia (0·6m.), Serbia and Montenegro (0·35m., mainly in Vojvodina) and Ukraine (0·16m.).

Hungary is divided into 19 counties (*megyék*) and the capital, Budapest, which has county status.

Area (in sq. km) and population (in 1,000) of counties and county towns:

Counties	*Area*	*2002 population*	*Chief town*	*2000 population*
Bács-Kiskun	8,445	546	Kecskemét	105
Baranya	4,430	406	Pécs	158
Békés	5,631	399	Békéscsaba	65
Borsod-Abaúj-Zemplén	7,247	749	Miskolc	182
Csongrád	4,263	428	Szeged	164
Fejér	4,359	429	Székesfehérvár	106
Győr-Moson-Sopron	4,089	435	Győr	127
Hajdú-Bihar	6,211	552	Debrecen	210
Heves	3,637	327	Eger	58
Jász-Nagykún-Szolnok	5,582	419	Szolnok	78
Komárom-Esztergom	2,265	317	Tatabánya	72
Nógrád	2,544	221	Salgótarján	45

Counties	*Area*	*2002 population*	*Chief town*	*2000 population*
Pest	6,393	1,089	Budapest	1,852[1]
Somogy	6,036	337	Kaposvár	67
Szabolcs-Szatmár-Bereg	5,937	588	Nyíregyháza	113
Tolna	3,703	250	Szekszárd	36
Vas	3,336	269	Szombathely	83
Veszprém	4,613	375	Veszprém	66
Zala	3,784	299	Zalaegerszeg	63
Budapest	525	1,740	(has county status)	

[1]1999 figure.

The official language is Hungarian. 96·6% of the population have Hungarian as their mother tongue. Ethnic minorities have the right to education in their own language.

SOCIAL STATISTICS

2001: births, 97,047; deaths, 132,183; marriages, 43,583; divorces, 24,379. In 2000 the number of births rose for the first time in a decade. There were 2,979 suicides in 2001. Rates (per 1,000 population), 2001: birth, 9·5; death, 13·0; marriage, 4·3; divorce, 2·4. Annual population growth rate, 1992–2002, –0·4%. In 1999 the suicide rate per 100,000 population was 33·1, with the rate among men nearly three times as high as that among women. In 2001 the most popular age range for marrying was 25–29 for males and 20–24 for females. Expectation of life at birth, 2001, 67·3 years for males and 75·7 years for females (the lowest of any OECD member country). Infant mortality, 2001, 8 per 1,000 live births. Fertility rate, 2001, 1·3 births per woman.

CLIMATE

A humid continental climate, with warm summers and cold winters. Precipitation is generally greater in summer, with thunderstorms. Dry, clear weather is likely in autumn, but spring is damp and both seasons are of short duration. Budapest, Jan. 32°F (0°C), July 71°F (21·5°C). Annual rainfall 25" (625 mm). Pécs, Jan. 30°F (–0·7°C), July 71°F (21·5°C). Annual rainfall 26·4" (661 mm).

CONSTITUTION AND GOVERNMENT

On 18 Oct. 1989 the National Assembly approved by an 88% majority a constitution which abolished the People's Republic, and established Hungary as an independent, democratic, law-based state.

The head of state is the *President*, who is elected for five-year terms by the National Assembly.

The single-chamber *National Assembly* has 386 members, made up of 176 individual constituency winners, 152 allotted by proportional representation from county party lists and 58 from a national list. It is elected for four-year terms. A *Constitutional Court* was established in Jan. 1990 to review laws under consideration.

National Anthem. 'Isten áldd meg a magyart' ('God bless the Hungarians'); words by Ferenc Kölcsey, tune by Ferenc Erkel.

RECENT ELECTIONS

Ferenc Mádl was elected President by the National Assembly on 6 June 2000 by 243 votes to 96. In two previous rounds he had failed to achieve the required two-thirds majority.

In the Hungarian parliamentary elections on 7 and 21 April 2002 the centre-right coalition of Fidesz-Hungarian Civic Party (Fidesz-MPP) and the Hungarian Democratic Forum (MDF) won 188 seats with 41·1% of the votes, against 178 seats and 42·1% for the Hungarian Socialist Party (MSzP). The remaining 20 seats in the 386-seat National Assembly went to the Alliance of Free Democrats (SzDSz) who received 5·5% of votes cast. Parties which failed to win seats included the Hungarian Justice and Life Party (4·4%), the Centre Party (3·9%), the Worker's Party (2·8%) and the Independent Party of Smallholders, Agrarian Workers and Citizens (0·8%). Turn-out was 70·5%. Following the elections, a coalition was formed between the Hungarian Socialist Party and the Alliance of Free Democrats, giving them a total of 198 seats. Fidesz-MPP leader Viktor Orbán conceded defeat and a government was subsequently formed with Péter Medgyessy as prime minister.

European Parliament. Hungary has 24 representatives. At the June 2004 elections turn-out was 38·5%. Fidesz-MPP won 12 seats with 47·4% of votes cast (political affiliation in European Parliament: European People's Party–European Democrats); the MSzP, 9 with 34·3% (Party of European Socialists); the SzDSz, 2 with 7·7% (Alliance of Liberals and Democrats for Europe); the MDF, 1 with 5·3% (European People's Party–European Democrats).

CURRENT ADMINISTRATION

President: Ferenc Mádl; b. 1931 (sworn in 4 Aug. 2000).

In April 2005 the MSzP-SzDSz coalition government consisted of:

Prime Minister: Ferenc Gyurcsány; b. 1961 (MSzP; acting from 27 Aug. to 28 Sept. 2004 and sworn in on 29 Sept. 2004).

Head of Prime Minister's Office: Péter Kiss. *Minister of Agriculture and Regional Development:* Imre Németh. *Defence:* Ferenc Juhász. *Economic Affairs and Transport:* János Kóka. *Education:* Bálint Magyar. *Employment and Labour:* Gábor Csizmár. *Environment and Water Management:* Miklós Persányi. *Finance:* János Veres. *Foreign Affairs:* Ferenc Somogyi. *Health, Social and Family Affairs:* Jenő Rácz. *Information Technology and Telecommunications:* Kálmán Kovács. *Interior:* Mónika Lamperth. *Justice:* József Petrétei. *Cultural Heritage:* András Bozóki. *Youth, Family Affairs and Equal Opportunities:* Kinga Göncz. *Minister without Portfolio in Charge of Regional Development and Housing:* István Kolber. *Minister without Portfolio in Charge of EU Affairs:* Etele Baráth.

Office of the Prime Minister: http://www.meh.hu

DEFENCE

The President of the Republic is C.-in-C. of the armed forces.

Men between the ages of 18 and 23 are liable for six months' conscription, or two years of civilian service.

Defence expenditure in 2003 totalled US$1,589m. Per capita spending in 2003 was US$157. The 2003 expenditure represented 1·9% of GDP, compared to 6·8% in 1985.

Army. The strength of the Army was (2002) 23,600 (including 16,500 conscripts). There is an additional force of 12,000 border guards. Army reserves number 74,950.

Navy. The Danube Flotilla, the maritime wing of the Army, consisted of some 290 personnel in 1999. It is based at Budapest.

Air Force. The Air Force had a strength (2002) of 7,700 (including conscripts). There were 37 combat aircraft in 2002, including MiG-21s, MiG-23s, MiG-29s and Su-22s, plus 55 in store, and 49 attack helicopters.

INTERNATIONAL RELATIONS

Hungary is a member of the UN, WTO, BIS, NATO, OECD, EU, Council of Europe, OSCE, CEFTA, CERN, CEI, Danube Commission, IOM, Antarctic Treaty, and is an Associate Partner of the WEU. Hungary held a referendum on EU membership on 12 April 2003, in which 83·8% of votes cast were in favour of accession, with 16·2% against, although turn-out was only 45·6%. It became a member of the EU on 1 May 2004. On 20 Dec. 2004 Hungary became the second European Union member to ratify the new EU constitution. The parliament approved the treaty by 304 votes to nine. In 2000 Hungary introduced a visa requirement for Russians entering the country as one of the conditions for EU membership.

Hungary has had a long-standing dispute with Slovakia over the Gabčíkovo-Nagymaros Project, involving the building of dam structures in both countries for the production of electric power, flood control and improvement of navigation on the Danube as agreed in a treaty signed in 1977 between Hungary and Czechoslovakia. In late 1998 Slovakia and Hungary signed a protocol easing tensions between the two nations and settling differences over the dam.

ECONOMY

Agriculture accounted for 4·3% of GDP in 2002, industry 31·2% and services 64·5%. In 2003 the private sector was responsible for an estimated 80% of economic output.

Overview. In 2000 Hungary boasted the strongest economic performance in the East European region, with export-led GDP growth of 5·2% that year. Growth then declined annually in 2001–03, but was projected to rise again by about 4% in 2004 owing to higher private investment, a recovery of exports and stronger industrial output. The economy is largely service based, following the decline in industrial contribution to GDP in the years after communism. In Oct. 2001 the National Bank moved the exchange rate from a crawling-peg regime to a managed float regime to speed up growth and as a first step towards European monetary union. A privatization law was adopted in 1995; the privatization process should be complete by 2006, with only 37 companies remaining in state ownership. FDI has redirected trade from east to west and modernized production.

Currency. A decree of 26 July 1946 instituted a new monetary unit, the *forint* (HUF) of 100 *fillér*. The forint was made fully convertible in Jan. 1991 and moves in a 15% band against the euro either side of a central rate of €1=276·1 forints. Inflation had been 28·2% in 1995, was down to 5·3% in 2002 and in 2003 was 4·7%, the lowest rate in more than 20 years. Foreign exchange reserves were US$9,695m. in June 2002 and gold reserves 101,000 troy oz. Total money supply in April 2002 was 2,662·29bn. forints.

Budget. Central government revenues totalled 6,338·1bn. forints in 2002 (5,707·5bn. forints in 2001); expenditures totalled 7,161·8bn. forints in 2002 (5,968·6bn. forints in 2001). Principal sources of revenue in 2002: social security contributions, 2,159·1bn. forints; taxes on goods and services, 2,032·0bn. forints; taxes on income, profits and capital gains, 1,355·4bn. forints. Main items of expenditure by economic type in 2002: social benefits, 2,598·5bn. forints; grants, 1,028·2bn. forints; compensation of employees, 996·8bn. forints.

VAT is 25·0% (reduced rate, 12%).

Performance. Real GDP growth was 4·2% in 1999, rising in 2000 to an impressive 5·2%. The economy then grew by only 3·8% in 2001, but this was still more than double the EU average. Real growth slipped to 3·5% in 2002 and 2·9% in 2003. Total GDP was US$82·8bn. in 2003.

Banking and Finance. In 1987 a two-tier system was established. The National Bank (*Director,* Zsigmond Járai) remained the central state financial institution. It is responsible for the operation of monetary policy and the foreign exchange system. In 2001 there were 42 commercial banks, five specialized financial institutions and a central corporation of banking companies. In 1998 there were 241 savings co-operatives. The largest bank is OTP Bank Rt. (the National Savings and Commercial Bank of Hungary), with assets in 2002 of 2,393bn. forints. Other leading banks are K+H (Hungarian Commercial and Credit Bank) and MKB (Hungarian Foreign Trade Bank). A law of June 1991 sets capital and reserve requirements, and provides for foreign investment in Hungarian banks. Permission is needed for investments of more than 10%. Privatization of the banking system is well under way.

At the end of 2002 foreign direct investments totalled US$35·9bn.

The Hungarian International Trade Bank opened in London in 1973. In 1980 the Central European International Bank was set up in Budapest with seven western banks holding 66% of the shares.

A stock exchange was opened in Budapest in Jan. 1989.

ENERGY AND NATURAL RESOURCES

Environment. Hungary's carbon dioxide emissions from the consumption and flaring of fossil fuels in 2002 were the equivalent of 5·7 tonnes per capita. An *Environmental Sustainability Index* compiled for the World Economic Forum meeting in Feb. 2002 ranked Hungary 11th in the world, with 62·7%. The index measured the ability of countries to maintain favourable environmental conditions and examined various factors including pollution levels and the use or abuse of natural resources.

Electricity. Installed capacity in 2000 was 8·3m. kW, about a quarter of which is nuclear. There is an 880 MW nuclear power station at Paks with four reactors. It produced an estimated 36% of total output in 2002. In 2003 Hungary produced 34·1bn. kWh of electricity and 8·9bn. kWh were imported. Total consumption in

2003 (including domestic consumption, power station consumption, network losses and exports) was 43bn. kWh. Consumption per capita in 2000 was 3,834 kWh.

Oil and Gas. Oil and natural gas are found in the Szeged basin and Zala county. Oil production in 2000 was 1·1m. tonnes. Gas production in 2000 was 3·0bn. cu. metres, with proven reserves of 65bn. cu. metres in 2002.

Minerals. Production in 1,000 tonnes: lignite (2000), 14,033; bauxite (2001), 1,000; hard coal (2000), 744.

Agriculture. Agricultural land was collectivized in 1950. It was announced in 1990 that land would be restored to its pre-collectivization owners if they wished to cultivate it. A law of April 1994 restricts the area of land that may be bought by individuals to 300 ha, and prohibits the sale of arable land and land in conservation zones to companies and foreign nationals. Today, although 90% of all cultivated land is in private hands, most farms are little more than smallholdings. In 2003 the agricultural area was 5·87m. ha (equivalent to 63% of the total land area); arable land constituted 4·52m. ha.

Agricultural production has dropped drastically since 1989. Production figures (2003, in 1,000 tonnes): maize, 4,532 (6,747 in 1989); wheat, 2,941 (6,509 in 1989); sugarbeets, 1,812 (5,277 in 1989); sunflower seeds, 992; barley, 810; potatoes, 582; grapes, 581; apples, 508.

Livestock has also drastically decreased since 1989 from 7·7m. pigs to 5·1m. by 2003, from 1·6m. cattle to 770,000, and from 2·1m. sheep to 1·1m. Thus the pig stock, cattle stock and sheep stock have all declined to levels not seen in fifty years.

The north shore of Lake Balaton and the Tokaj area are important wine-producing districts. Wine production in 2002 was 380,000 tonnes.

Forestry. The forest area in 2003 was 1·77m. ha, or 19·1% of the land area. Timber production in 2001 was 5·81m. cu. metres.

Fisheries. There are fisheries in the rivers Danube and Tisza and Lake Balaton. In 2003 there were 33,100 ha of commercial fishponds. In 2001 total catch was 6,638 tonnes, exclusively from inland fishing.

INDUSTRY

The leading companies by market capitalization in Hungary, excluding banking and finance, in Jan. 2002 were: Magyar Távközlési Rt. (MATÁV), the telecommunications company (1trn. forints); MOL Magyar Olaj-és Gázipari Rt (Hungarian Oil and Gas Plc), 489bn. forints; and Richter Gedeon Rt. (335bn. forints), a pharmaceuticals company.

Manufacturing output grew by an average of 8·5% annually between 1992 and 2002.

Important items include food and beverages, chemicals and chemical products, motor vehicles, refined petroleum products, base metals and computers. Production (in 1,000 tonnes): cement (2001), 3,500; distillate fuel oil (2000), 2,466; crude steel (2000), 1,969; rolled steel (2001), 1,900; residual fuel oil (2000), 1,442; petrol (2000), 1,249; plastics (2002), 1,136; fertilizers (2000), 781; alumina (2001), 300; sulphuric acid (2001), 80; radio sets (2001), 3,459,000 units; refrigerators (2001), 1,058,000 units; beer (2003), 750·0m. litres.

Labour. In 2001 out of an economically active population of 4,093,000 there were 3,860,000 employed persons, of which 3,296,000 were employees. Among the employed persons, 59·6% worked in services, 34·2% in industry and construction, and 6·2% in agriculture. Average gross monthly wages in 2001: 103,558 forints. Minimum monthly wage, 2004, 53,000 forints. In Dec. 2004 Hungary had an unemployment rate of 6·2%. Retirement age: men, 60; women, 55.

Trade Unions. The former official Communist organization (National Council of Trade Unions), renamed the National Confederation of Hungarian Trade Unions (MSZOSZ), groups 70 organizations and claimed 240,000 members in 2003. A law of 1991 abolished its obligatory levy on pay packets. Other major workers' organizations are (with 2003 membership): the Association of Autonomous Trade Unions (ASZSZ, 150,000); Co-operation Forum of Trade Unions (SZEF, 270,000); Confederation of Unions of Professionals (ESZT, 85,000); Democratic League of Independent Trade Unions (Liga, 100,000); National Federation of Workers' Councils (MOSZ, 56,000).

INTERNATIONAL TRADE

Hungary is a member of CEFTA, along with the Czech Republic, Poland, Slovakia and Slovenia. Foreign debt was US$34,958m. in 2002. An import surcharge imposed in March 1995 was abolished in July 1997.

Imports and Exports. In 2002 the value of exports was US$34,792m. and that of imports US$36,911m. (up from US$31,080m. and US$33,318m. respectively in 2001). Hungary's foreign trade has been expanding at a very fast rate, with the value of both its exports and its imports doubling between 1996 and 2002. Machinery and transport equipment accounted for 57·5% of exports and 51·5% of imports in 2001, and manufactured goods 31·0% of exports and 35·3% of imports. 75% of exports go to European Union member countries, the highest share of any of the central and eastern European countries that joined the EU in May 2004. The share of CIS countries is only around 2%. In 2001, 34·9% of exports went to Germany and 26·4% of imports came from Germany. Italy was the second biggest supplier of imports in 2001 (8·3% of the total) and Austria the second biggest market for exports (8·7%). In 2001, 1·5% of exports went to Russia, down from 13·1% in 1992. An import surcharge which was imposed in March 1995 was abolished in July 1997.

COMMUNICATIONS

Roads. In 2002 there were 159,568 km of roads, including 533 km of motorways and 30,460 km of main roads. Passenger cars numbered (2002) 2,629,500; trucks, vans and special-purpose vehicles, 369,300; buses, 17,900; and motorcycles, 10,200. In 2003 there were 19,976 road accidents with 1,135 fatalities.

Rail. In 2003 the rail network was 7,685 km in length; 49·9m. tonnes of freight and 159·8m. passengers were carried. There is a metro in Budapest (30·1 km), and tram/light rail networks in Budapest (161·2 km), Debrecen, Miskolc and Szeged.

Civil Aviation. Budapest airport (Ferihegy) handled 4,482,000 passengers in 2002 (all on international flights) and 42,380 tonnes of freight. The national carrier is Malév, which is 99·95% owned by the state. It carried 2,354,080 passengers in 2003.

Shipping. There are 1,622 km of navigable waterways. In 2002, along the Hungarian section of the Danube River, 4,801 vessels entered the country on their way to a Hungarian destination, 4,916 vessels left Hungary for other countries and 3,331 vessels were in transit. In 2003, 2·06m. tonnes of cargo and 1·42m. passengers were carried. Merchant shipping totalled 4,000 GRT in 2002. The Hungarian Shipping Company (MAHART) has agencies at Amsterdam, Alexandria, Algiers, Beirut, Rijeka and Trieste. It has 23 ships and runs scheduled services between Budapest and Esztergom.

Telecommunications. There were 10,288,400 main telephone subscribers in 2002, equivalent to 1,007·5 per 1,000 population, and 1,100,000 PCs in use (108·4 per 1,000 persons). Matav, the privatized former national telephone company, still has more than 80% of the fixed line market. Hungary had 6,862,800 mobile phone subscribers in 2002 (68% of the population). Internet users numbered 1·6m. in 2002. In 1999 there were 180,000 fax machines.

Postal Services. In 2001 there were 2,581 post offices.

SOCIAL INSTITUTIONS

Justice. The administration of justice is the responsibility of the Procurator-General, elected by Parliament for six years. There are 111 local courts, 20 labour law courts, 20 county courts, six district courts and a Supreme Court. Criminal proceedings are dealt with by the regional courts through three-member councils and by the county courts and the Supreme Court in five-member councils. A new Civil Code was adopted in 1978 and a new Criminal Code in 1979.

Regional courts act as courts of first instance; county courts as either courts of first instance or of appeal. The Supreme Court acts normally as an appeal court, but may act as a court of first instance in cases submitted to it by the Public Prosecutor. All courts, when acting as courts of first instance, consist of one professional judge and two lay assessors, and, as courts of appeal, of three professional judges. Local government Executive Committees may try petty offences.

Regional and county judges and assessors are elected by the appropriate local councils; members of the Supreme Court by Parliament.

The Office of Ombudsman was instituted in 1993. He or she is elected by parliament for a six-year term, renewable once.

There are also military courts of the first instance. Military cases of the second instance go before the Supreme Court.

The death penalty was abolished in Oct. 1990.

The population in penal institutions in Nov. 2003 was 16,700 (165 per 100,000 of national population). There were 87,476 convictions of adults and 6,726 of juvenile offenders in 2003; 34% of convictions resulted in custodial sentences (most of them suspended). 18,000 crimes against the person were detected in 2003, including 227 homicides.

Religion. Church-state affairs are regulated by a law of Feb. 1990 which guarantees freedom of conscience and religion and separates church and state by prohibiting state interference in church affairs. Religious matters are the concern of the Department for Church Relations, under the auspices of the Prime Minister's Office.

According to the 2001 census, 51·9% of the population was Roman Catholic (5·3m. people), 15·9% Calvinist (1·6m.), 3·0% Lutheran (0·3m.) and 2·6% Greek Catholic (0·27m.). Adherents to smaller Christian faiths, including Baptists, other Protestant groups, Adventists and a range of Orthodox denominations, numbered around 98,000. About 0·1% of the population was Jewish in 2001.

The Primate of Hungary is Péter Erdő, Archbishop of Esztergom-Budapest, installed in Jan. 2003. There are 11 dioceses, all with bishops or archbishops. There is one Uniate bishopric. In Sept. 2003 the Roman Catholic church had two cardinals.

Education. Adult literacy rate in 2001 was 99·3% (male, 99·5%; female, 99·2%). Education is free and compulsory from six to 14. Primary schooling ends at 14; thereafter education may be continued at secondary, secondary technical or secondary vocational schools, which offer diplomas entitling students to apply for higher education, or at vocational training schools which offer tradesmen's diplomas. Students at the latter may also take the secondary school diploma examinations after two years of evening or correspondence study. Optional religious education was introduced in schools in 1990.

In 2003–04 there were: 4,610 kindergartens with 31,383 teachers and 327,500 pupils; 3,748 primary schools with 89,784 teachers and 913,600 pupils; and 1,622 secondary schools (including vocational schools) with 38,479 teachers and 531,400 pupils (of which 438,100 were full-time). 409,075 students were enrolled in tertiary education at 68 institutions in 2003–04: of these, 366,947 were at university and college level (204,910 full-time and 162,037 part-time). In 1990 only 11% of 18- to 23-year-olds were enrolled in higher education. By 2000 the proportion had risen to 35% and the target for 2010 is 50%.

There were, in 1999–2000, 201 schools for special needs with 45,245 pupils and 7,244 teachers. Schools for ethnic minorities, 1997–98: kindergartens, 386, with 20,440 pupils and 993 teachers; primary schools, 390, with 53,021 pupils and 1,357 teachers; secondary schools, 27, with 2,310 pupils and 179 teachers.

In 2000–01 total expenditure on education came to 5·2% of GNP and 14·1% of total government spending.

Health. In 1999 there were 36,386 doctors and 84,247 hospital beds; in 1998 there were 5,671 dentists, 4,789 pharmacists, 2,227 midwives and 51,965 nurses. While there is an excess supply of doctors, there are too few nurses and wages for both groups are exceptionally low. In 1998 there were 167 hospitals with 83 beds per 10,000 inhabitants. Spending on health accounted for 6·8% of GDP in 2001.

Welfare. In 1998 the Hungarian parliament decided to place the financial funds of health and pension insurance under government supervision. The self-governing bodies which had previously been responsible for this were dissolved. Medical treatment is free. Patients bear 15% of the cost of medicines. Sickness benefit is 75% of wages, old age pensions (at 60 for men, 55 for women) 60–70%. In 2003, 1·9trn. forints was spent on pensions and pension-like benefits for 3·05m. recipients (old age 53%, disability or reduced working ability 34%, and widows and other pensions 13%); the average monthly amount of benefit per capita was 50,428 forints. Family and child benefits totalled about 2·5% of GDP in 2001. On a monthly basis as of Jan. 2004, 1·3m. families were receiving family allowance on behalf of 2·1m. children, child care allowance was being paid for 164,000 children and 82,000 were receiving child care fee.

CULTURE

World Heritage Sites. Sites under Hungarian jurisdiction which appear on UNESCO's world heritage list are (with year entered on list): the Cultural Landscape of Fertö/Neusiedlersee (2001), an area on the border with Austria that has acted as a meeting place for different cultures for 8,000 years; Budapest, and specifically the Banks of the Danube and the Buda Castle Quarter (1987); Hollókő (1987), a preserved settlement developed during the 17th and 18th centuries; Millenary Benedictine Monastery of Pannonhalma and its Natural Environment (1996), first settled by Benedictine monks in 996; Hortobágy National Park (1999), a large area of plains and wetlands in eastern Hungary; Pécs (Sopianae) Early Christian Cemetery (2000), a series of decorated tombs dating from the 4th century; Tokaj Wine Region Historic Cultural Landscape (2002).

Hungary also shares a UNESCO site with Slovakia: the Caves of Aggtelek and Slovak Karst (1995 and 2000), a complex of 712 temperate-zone karstic caves.

Broadcasting. The government network *Magyar Rádio* broadcasts four programmes on medium wave and FM and also regional programmes, including transmissions in German, Romanian and Serbo-Croat. There are four other networks, three of them commercial. There are five national television channels, three of which are state-owned. *Magyar Televizió* operates two TV channels (colour by PAL). *Duna Televizió* broadcasts to Hungarians abroad. The two national private TV channels are *tv2* and *RTL-KLUB*. There are approximately 220 other commercial television stations and 30 private radio stations. There were 7·05m. radios in use and 4·45m. TV sets in 2000.

Cinema. There were 628 cinemas in 1998; attendances in 1999 totalled 13·40m. In 1997, 12 full-length feature films were made.

Press. In 2000 there were 40 daily newspapers with a combined circulation of 1,625,000, at a rate of 162 per 1,000 inhabitants. The most widely read newspaper is the free tabloid *Metro*. In 2000 there were 167 non-dailies. A total of 8,837 book titles were published in 2001 in 32·62m. copies.

Tourism. In 2000 there were 15·57m. foreign tourists. 11·1m. Hungarians travelled abroad in 2001. Revenue from foreign tourists in 2000 was US$3·42bn. 8% of GDP is produced by tourism.

Festivals. The Budapest Spring Festival, comprising music, theatre, dance etc., takes place in March. The Balaton Festival is in May and the Szeged Open-Air Theatre Festival is in July–Aug.

Libraries. In 2001 there were 3,429 public libraries and three National libraries. They held a combined 45,630,000 volumes for 1,416,000 registered users.

Theatre and Galleries. There were 776 museums and galleries in 1997. 466,000 people visited museums in 2003.

DIPLOMATIC REPRESENTATIVES

Of Hungary in the United Kingdom (35 Eaton Pl., London, SW1X 8BY)
Ambassador: Béla Szombati.

Of the United Kingdom in Hungary (Harmincad Utca 6, Budapest 1051)
Ambassador: John Nichols.

Of Hungary in the USA (3910 Shoemaker St., NW, Washington, D.C., 20008)
Ambassador: András Simonyi.

Of the USA in Hungary (Szabadság Tér 12, Budapest V)
Ambassador: George Herbert Walker.

Of Hungary to the United Nations
Ambassador: László Molnár.

Of Hungary to the European Union
Ambassador: Péter Balázs.

FURTHER READING

Central Statistical Office. *Statisztikai Évkönyv.* Annual since 1871.—*Magyar Statisztikai Zsebkönyv.* Annual.—*Statistical Yearbook.*—*Statistical Handbook of Hungary.*—*Monthly Bulletin of Statistics.*
Bozóki, A., *et al.*, (eds.) *Post-Communist Transition: Emerging Pluralism in Hungary.* London, 1992
Burawoy, M. and Lukács, J., *The Radiant Past: Ideology and Reality in Hungary's Road to Capitalism.* Chicago Univ. Press, 1992
Cox, T. and Furlong, A. (eds.) *Hungary: the Politics of Transition.* London, 1995
Geró, A., *Modern Hungarian Society in the Making: the Unfinished Experience*; translated from Hungarian. Budapest, 1995
Kontler, László, *A History of Hungary.* Palgrave Macmillan, Basingstoke, 2002
Mitchell, K. D. (ed.) *Political Pluralism in Hungary and Poland: Perspectives on the Reforms.* New York, 1992
Molnár, Miklós, *A Concise History of Hungary*. CUP, 2001
Sárközi, Mátyás, *Budapest.* [Bibliography] ABC-Clio, Oxford and Santa Barbara (CA), 1997
Szekely, I. P., *Hungary: an Economy in Transition.* CUP, 1993
Turner, Barry, (ed.) *Central Europe Profiled.* Macmillan, London, 2000

National library: Széchenyi Library, Budapest.
National statistical office: Központi Statisztikai Hivatal/Central Statistical Office, Keleti Károly u. 5/7, H-1024 Budapest. *Director:* Dr Péter Pukli.
Website: http://www.ksh.hu/

ICELAND

Lyðveldið Ísland
(Republic of Iceland)

Capital: Reykjavík
Population projection, 2010: 303,000
GDP per capita, 2002: (PPP$) 29,750
HDI/world rank: 0·941/7

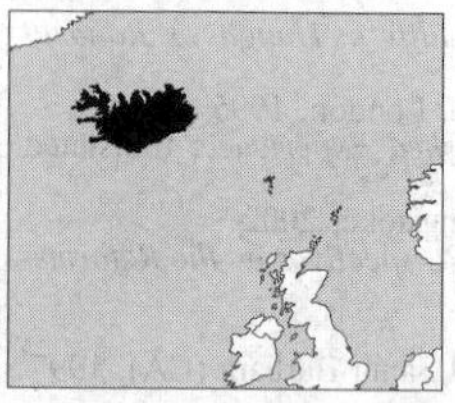

KEY HISTORICAL EVENTS

Scandinavia's North Atlantic outpost was first settled by Irish monks in the early 9th century but migrants from Scandinavia and Norse settlements in the British Isles drove them out in 874. A ruling class of chieftains, known as the *godar,* established thefirst ever democratic national assembly, the *Alþingi* (Althing), in 930. Primarily an adjudicating body, it also served as a legislature and a fair. In 1000 it adopted Christianity by majority decision as Iceland's official religion. Bishoprics were established at Skálholt in 1056 and at Hólar in 1106. In the mid-13th century the *godar* were persuaded to swear allegiance to the king of Norway, bringing Iceland under Norwegian rule but leaving it with relative autonomy. When Norway was joined with Denmark in 1380, Iceland retained the Althing and its own code of law.

In the 14th century the expansion of fishing to satisfy European demand stimulated agriculture and other basic industries. Iceland's economic progress was checked when birchwood, the only indigenous wood, became severely depleted. Coupled with over-grazing, this led to soil erosion and put an end to crop growth. In the 15th century Iceland fell victim to the Black Death, losing around half of the population on two occasions. In the first half of the 16th century Denmark imposed Lutheranism, resistance to which ended after the execution of the bishop of Hólar in 1550. In 1602 a royal decree gave all foreign trading rights in Iceland exclusively to Danish merchants. This restriction, which lasted until 1787, virtually ended Iceland's contacts with England and Germany. Climatic and volcanic conditions in the 1780s brought famine that killed one-fifth of the population.

In the 1830s a Danish consultative assembly was formed in which Iceland was given two seats. Denmark's transition to a system of representative democratic government after 1848 did not extend to Iceland. The Althing decided that 1874, the year that marked a thousand years of settlement, should be chosen as the year for a new constitution. This provided the Althing with legislative if not executive control. During this period the strains of population growth forced mass emigration to North America. In 1904 Iceland achieved home rule. In 1918 Iceland became a separate state under the Danish crown, with only foreign affairs remaining under Danish jurisdiction.

In 1944, when Denmark was occupied by Nazi Germany, Iceland declared independence. Iceland was occupied peacefully by Britain in 1940 but US troops took over a year later. They improved roads and docks and built an airport. Iceland joined NATO and in 1951 a defence agreement with the United States allowed for an increase in the number of troops 'to defend Iceland and ... to ensure the security of the seas around the country'. Greater integration with Europe came with joining the European Free Trade Association in 1970.

Fish was central to the economy, accounting for 90% of exports. In 1950 one mile was added to the three-mile offshore zone that Iceland had administered since 1901. When, in 1958, the limit was extended to 12 miles, Britain sent naval vessels to protect its trawlers from harassment. This was the first Cod War, a cat-and-mouse game between the British navy and coastguard patrols which continued until 1961. In 1971, however, a left-wing government extended the offshore zone to 50 miles. Despite a clear contravention of treaty commitment, Iceland gained sympathy when the European Community announced an extension of its jurisdiction over the continental shelf to a limit of 200 miles. Iceland followed suit and after 1976 British and other fishing vessels were banned from Icelandic waters.

TERRITORY AND POPULATION

Iceland is an island in the North Atlantic, close to the Arctic Circle. Area, 102,819 sq. km (39,698 sq. miles).

There are eight regions:

Region	*Inhabited land (sq. km)*	*Mountain pasture (sq. km)*	*Waste-land (sq. km)*	*Total area (sq. km)*	*Popula-tion (31 Dec. 2003)*
Capital area } Southwest Peninsula }	1,266	716	–	1,982	181,917 / 16,953
West	5,011	3,415	275	8,701	14,438
Western Peninsula	4,130	3,698	1,652	9,470	7,837
Northland West	4,867	5,278	2,948	13,093	9,145
Northland East	9,890	6,727	5,751	22,368	26,835
East } South }	16,921	17,929	12,555	21,991 / 25,214	11,887 / 21,558
Iceland	42,085	37,553	23,181	102,819	290,570

Of the population of 290,570 in 2003, 21,109 were domiciled in rural districts and 269,461 (92·7%) in towns and villages (of over 200 inhabitants). Population density (2003), 2·8 per sq. km.

The UN gives a projected population for 2010 of 303,000.

The population is almost entirely Icelandic. In 2003 foreigners numbered 10,180 (1,856 Polish, 870 Danish, 609 Filipino, 551 German, 529 Serb and Montenegrin, 521 US, 474 Thai, 370 British, 326 Swedish, 323 Norwegian).

The capital, Reykjavík, had on 31 Dec. 2003 a population of 112,490; other towns were: Akranes, 5,588; Akureyri, 16,086; Bolungarvík, 944; Dalvík, 1,461; Eskifjörður, 972; Garðabær, 8,878; Grindavík, 2,434; Hafnarfjörður, 21,207; Húsavík, 2,368; Ísafjörður, 2,596; Keflavík, 7,963; Kópavogur, 25,352; Neskaupstaður, 1,400; Njarðvík, 2,825; Ólafsfjörður, 994; Sauðárkrókur, 2,620; Selfoss, 5,068; Seltjarnarnes, 4,577; Seyðisfjörður, 730; Siglufjörður, 1,434; Vestmannaeyjar, 4,344.

The official language is Icelandic.

SOCIAL STATISTICS

Statistics for calendar years:

	Live births	*Still-born*	*Marriages*	*Divorces*	*Deaths*	*Infant deaths*	*Net immigration*
2000	4,329	14	1,777 (12 same sex)	545	1,823	13	1,714
2001	4,091	11	1,484 (13 same sex)	551	1,725	11	968
2002	4,090	7	1,652 (9 same sex)	529	1,821	9	–275
2003	4,143	4	1,473 (12 same sex)	531	1,827	10	–133

2003 rates per 1,000 population: births, 14·3; deaths, 6·3. 64% of births are to unmarried mothers, the highest percentage in Europe. Population growth rate, 2003, 0·7%. In 2003 the most popular age range for marrying was 30–34 for both males and females. Life expectancy, 2003: males, 78·7 years; females, 82·5. Infant mortality, 2003, 2·4 per 1,000 live births (one of the lowest rates in the world); fertility rate, 2003, 1·99 births per woman.

CLIMATE

The climate is cool temperate oceanic and rather changeable, but mild for its latitude because of the Gulf Stream and prevailing S.W. winds. Precipitation is high in upland areas, mainly in the form of snow. Reykjavík, Jan. 33·8°F (1·0°C), July 51·6°F (10·9°C). Annual rainfall 31·4" (792 mm).

CONSTITUTION AND GOVERNMENT

The President is elected by direct, popular vote for a period of four years.

The *Alþingi* (parliament) is elected in accordance with the electoral law of 1999, which provides for an *Alþingi* of 63 members. The country is divided into a minimum of six and a maximum of seven constituencies. There are currently six constituencies: Northwest (10 seats); Northeast (10 seats); South (10); Southwest (11); Reykjavík north (11); and Reykjavík south (11).

National Anthem. 'Ó Guð vors lands' ('Oh God of Our Country'); words by M. Jochumsson, tune by S. Sveinbjörnsson.

RECENT ELECTIONS

President Ólafur Ragnar Grímsson was reappointed for a second term on 1 Aug. 2000, no opposing candidates having come forward. On 26 June 2004 he stood for popular election and gained 85·6% of the vote. Baldur Ágústsson won 12·5% and Ástþór Magnússon won 1·9%. Turn-out was 63·0%.

In the parliamentary election held on 10 May 2003, the conservative Independence Party (SSF) won 22 of the 63 seats with 33·7% of the votes cast, the Alliance (SF)—consisting of the People's Alliance, the People's Party and the Alliance of the Women's List—20 with 31·0%, the Progressive Party (FSF) 12 with 17·7%, the Left-Green Alliance (VG) 5 with 8·8% and the Liberal Party (FF) 4 with 7·4%. Turn-out was 87·5%.

CURRENT ADMINISTRATION

President: Ólafur Ragnar Grímsson; b. 1943 (People's Alliance; sworn in 1 Aug. 1996, reappointed 1 Aug. 2000 and re-elected on 26 June 2004).

In March 2005 the government, formed by the Independence Party (SSF/IP) and the Progressive Party (FSF/PP), comprised:

Prime Minister: Halldór Ásgrímsson; b. 1947 (PP; sworn in 15 Sept. 2004).

Minister of Foreign Affairs: Davíð Oddsson (IP). *Finance:* Geir H. Haarde (IP). *Social Affairs:* Árni Magnússon (PP). *Fisheries:* Árni Mathiesen (IP). *Justice and Ecclesiastical Affairs:* Björn Bjarnason (IP). *Agriculture:* Guðni Ágústsson (PP). *Environment:* Sigríður Anna Þórðardóttir (IP). *Health and Social Security:* Jón Kristjánsson (PP). *Education, Science and Culture:* Þorgerður Katrín Gunnarsdóttir (IP). *Industry, Commerce and Nordic Co-operation:* Valgerður Sverrisdóttir (PP). *Communications:* Sturla Böðvarsson (IP).

Government Offices of Iceland Website: http://www.stjr.is

DEFENCE

Iceland possesses no armed forces. Under the North Atlantic Treaty, US forces are stationed in Iceland as the Iceland Defence Force.

Navy. There is a paramilitary coastguard of 120.

INTERNATIONAL RELATIONS

Iceland is a member of the UN, WTO, BIS, NATO, OECD, EFTA, OSCE, the Council of Europe, the Nordic Council and Council of the Baltic Sea States, and is an Associate Member of the WEU. Iceland has acceded to the Schengen Accord, which abolishes border controls between Iceland, Austria, Belgium, Denmark, Finland, France, Germany, Greece, Italy, Luxembourg, the Netherlands, Norway, Portugal, Spain and Sweden.

ECONOMY

Agriculture and fishing contributed 11·1% of GDP in 2003, industry 21·4%, and services 67·5%.

According to the anti-corruption organization *Transparency International*, Iceland ranked equal third in the world in a 2004 survey of the countries with the least corruption in business and government. It received 9·5 out of 10 in the annual index.

Overview. The economy has experienced strong growth since the mid-1990s as a result of the liberalization of financial markets, inflation reduction programmes, privatization and fiscal consolidation. As a result, per capita income increased from one-tenth above OECD average income in 1995 to one-fifth above in 2003. Some weaknesses in the economy persist. The agricultural, housing and energy sectors suffer from government-induced distortions, exports are exposed to destabilizing external shocks and household debt is high.

Currency. The unit of currency is the *króna* (ISK) of 100 *aurar* (singular: *eyrir*). Foreign exchange markets were deregulated on 1 Jan. 1992. The krona was devalued 7·5% in June 1993. Inflation was 6·7% in 2001, 4·8% in 2002 and 2·1% in 2003; the average annual rate during the period 1992–2001 was 3·2%. Foreign exchange

The Political World

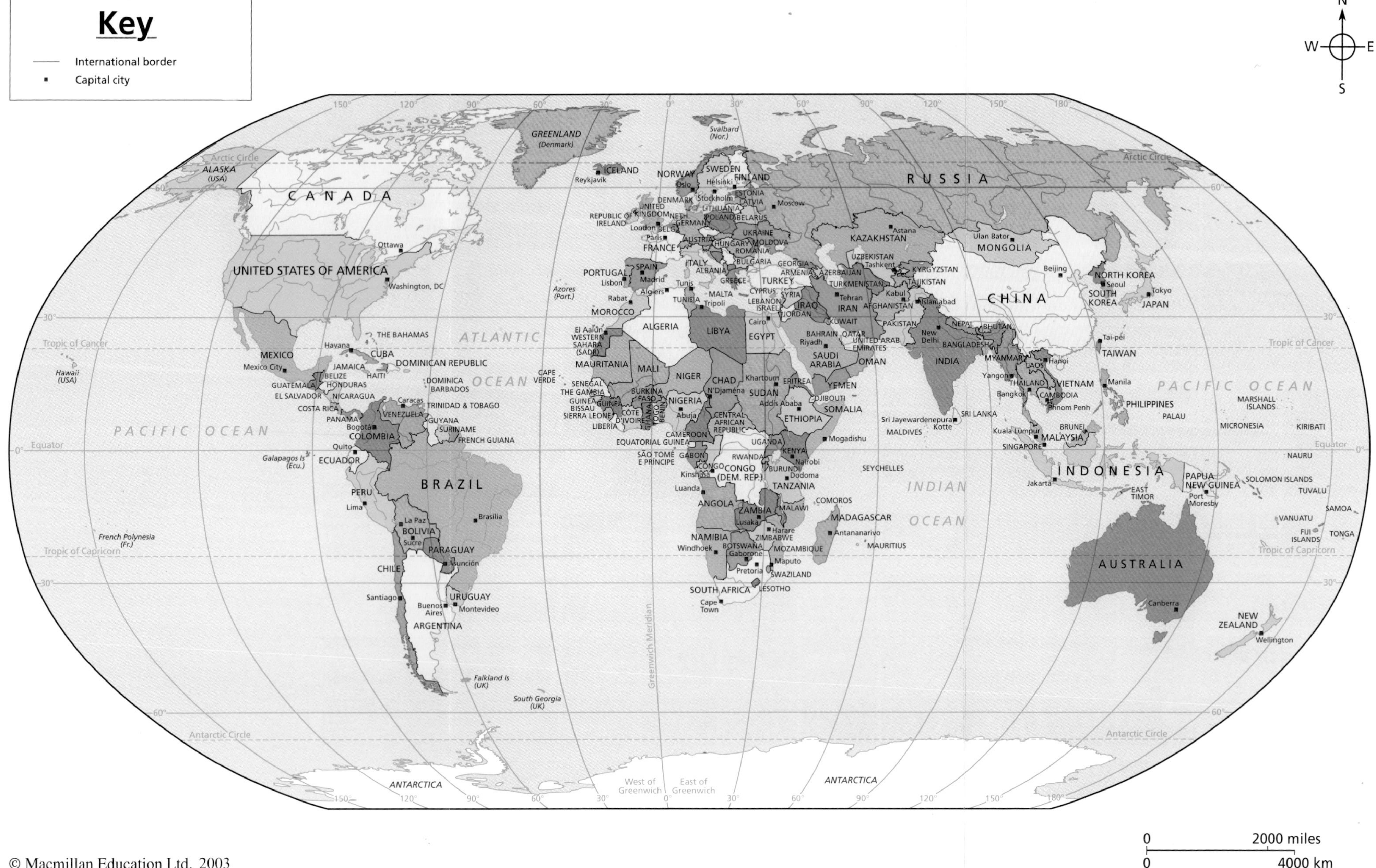

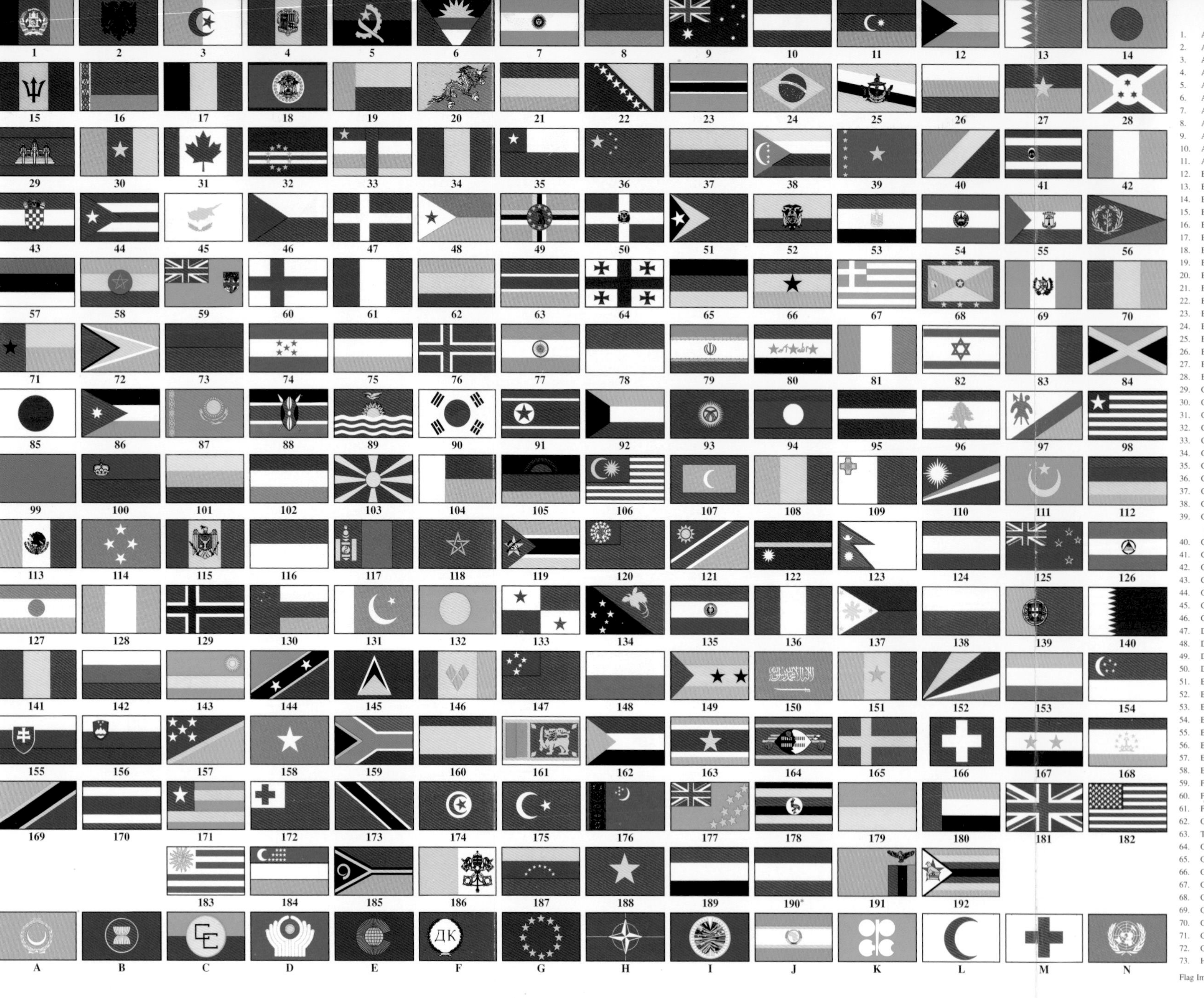

KEY

1. Afghanistan
2. Albania
3. Algeria
4. Andorra
5. Angola
6. Antigua and Barbuda
7. Argentina
8. Armenia
9. Australia
10. Austria
11. Azerbaijan
12. Bahamas
13. Bahrain
14. Bangladesh
15. Barbados
16. Belarus
17. Belgium
18. Belize
19. Benin
20. Bhutan
21. Bolivia
22. Bosnia-Hercegovina
23. Botswana
24. Brazil
25. Brunei
26. Bulgaria
27. Burkina Faso
28. Burundi
29. Cambodia
30. Cameroon
31. Canada
32. Cape Verde
33. Central African Republic
34. Chad
35. Chile
36. China, People's Republic of
37. Colombia
38. Comoros
39. Congo, Democratic Republic of (former Zaïre)
40. Congo, Republic of
41. Costa Rica
42. Côte d'Ivoire
43. Croatia
44. Cuba
45. Cyprus
46. Czech Republic
47. Denmark
48. Djibouti
49. Dominica
50. Dominican Republic
51. East Timor
52. Ecuador
53. Egypt
54. El Salvador
55. Equatorial Guinea
56. Eritrea
57. Estonia
58. Ethiopia
59. Fiji Islands
60. Finland
61. France
62. Gabon
63. The Gambia
64. Georgia
65. Germany
66. Ghana
67. Greece
68. Grenada
69. Guatemala
70. Guinea
71. Guinea-Bissau
72. Guyana
73. Haiti
74. Honduras
75. Hungary
76. Iceland
77. India
78. Indonesia
79. Iran
80. Iraq
81. Ireland
82. Israel
83. Italy
84. Jamaica
85. Japan
86. Jordan
87. Kazakhstan
88. Kenya
89. Kiribati
90. Korea (South)
91. Korea (North)
92. Kuwait
92. Kyrgyzstan
94. Laos
95. Latvia
96. Lebanon
97. Lesotho
98. Liberia
99. Libya
100. Liechtenstein
101. Lithuania
102. Luxembourg
103. Macedonia
104. Madagascar
105. Malawi
106. Malaysia
107. Maldives
108. Mali
109. Malta
110. Marshall Islands
111. Mauritania
112. Mauritius
113. Mexico
114. Micronesia
115. Moldova
116. Monaco
117. Mongolia
118. Morocco
119. Mozambique
120. Myanmar
121. Namibia
122. Nauru
123. Nepal
124. Netherlands
125. New Zealand
126. Nicaragua
127. Niger
128. Nigeria
129. Norway
130. Oman
131. Pakistan
132. Palau
133. Panama
134. Papua New Guinea
135. Paraguay
136. Peru
137. Philippines
138. Poland
139. Portugal
140. Qatar
141. Romania
142. Russia
143. Rwanda
144. St Kitts and Nevis
145. St Lucia
146. St Vincent and the Grenadines
147. Samoa
148. San Marino
149. São Tomé and Príncipe
150. Saudi Arabia
151. Senegal
152. Seychelles
153. Sierra Leone
154. Singapore
155. Slovakia
156. Slovenia
157. Solomon Islands
158. Somalia
159. South Africa
160. Spain
161. Sri Lanka
162. Sudan
163. Suriname
164. Swaziland
165. Sweden
166. Switzerland
167. Syria
168. Tajikistan
169. Tanzania
170. Thailand
171. Togo
172. Tonga
173. Trinidad and Tobago
174. Tunisia
175. Turkey
176. Turkmenistan
177. Tuvalu
178. Uganda
179. Ukraine
180. United Arab Emirates
181. United Kingdom
182. United States of America
183. Uruguay
184. Uzbekistan
185. Vanuatu
186. Vatican City
187. Venezuela
188. Vietnam
189. Yemen
190. Yugoslavia*
191. Zambia
192. Zimbabwe

*Now Serbia and Montenegro. New flag to be confirmed.

FLAGS OF INTERNATIONAL ORGANIZATIONS

A. Arab League
B. Association of South East Asian Nations (ASEAN)
C. Caricom
D. Commonwealth of Independent States (CIS)
E. Commonwealth
F. Danube Commission
G. Europe
H. North Atlantic Treaty Organization (NATO)
I. Organization of American States (OAS)
J. Organization of African Unity (OAU)
K. Organization of Oil Exporting Countries (OPEC)
L. Red Crescent
M. Red Cross
N. United Nations Organization (UNO)

reserves were US$366m. and gold reserves 62,000 troy oz in June 2002. Note and coin circulation at 31 Dec. 2003 was 8,391m. kr.

Budget. Total central government revenue and expenditure for calendar years (in 1m. kr.):

	1998	*1999*	*2000*	*2001*	*2002*	*2003*
Revenue	170,500	198,900	212,600	227,100	237,000	251,500
Expenditure	164,300	183,300	195,600	222,600	241,700	266,100

Central government debt was 277,000m. kr. on 31 Dec. 2003, of which the foreign debt amounted to 112,005m. kr. VAT is 24·5% (reduced rate, 14%).

Performance. GDP in 2003 totalled US$10·5bn. Real GDP growth was 2·2% in 2001, but there was then a recession in 2002 with the economy shrinking by 0·5%, followed by a recovery in 2003 with growth of 4·3%.

Banking and Finance. The Central Bank of Iceland (founded 1961; *Chairman of the Board of Governors*, Birgir Ísleifur Gunnarsson) is responsible for note issue and carries out the central banking functions. There were 27 savings banks in 2002. The government had by 2003 sold to the public its shares in two banks. On 31 Dec. 2003 the accounts of the Central Bank balanced at 87,307m. kr. Commercial bank deposits were 369,605m. kr., and deposits in the 29 savings banks 87,307m. kr.

There is a stock exchange in Reykjavík.

ENERGY AND NATURAL RESOURCES

Iceland is aiming to become the world's first 'hydrogen economy'; its buses started to convert to fuel cell-powered vehicles in late 2003. Ultimately it aims to run all its transport and even its fishing fleet on hydrogen produced in Iceland.

Environment. Iceland's carbon dioxide emissions from the consumption and flaring of fossil fuels in 2002 were the equivalent of 10·8 tonnes per capita. An *Environmental Sustainability Index* compiled for the World Economic Forum meeting in Feb. 2002 ranked Iceland eighth in the world, with 63·9%. The index measured the ability of countries to maintain favourable environmental conditions and examined various factors including pollution levels and the use or abuse of natural resources.

Electricity. The installed capacity of public electrical power plants at the end of 2003 totalled 1·5m. kW; installed capacity of hydro-electric plants was 1,150,700 kW. Total electricity production in public-owned plants in 2003 amounted to 8,495m. kWh; in privately owned plants, 5m. kWh. Virtually all of Iceland's electricity is produced from hydro power and geothermal energy. Consumption per capita was estimated in 2003 to be 29,367 kWh (one of the highest in the world).

Agriculture. Of the total area, about six-sevenths is unproductive, but only about 1·3% is under cultivation, which is largely confined to hay and potatoes. Arable land totalled 15,500 ha in 2003. In 2003 the total hay crop was 2,287,936 cu. metres; the crop of potatoes, 7,090 tonnes; of tomatoes, 1,074 tonnes; and of cucumbers, 896 tonnes. Livestock (end of 2003): sheep, 463,006; horses, 71,412; cattle, 66,035 (milch cows, 24,904); pigs, 3,852; poultry, 48,953. Livestock products (2003, in tonnes): lamb, 8,792; milk, 108,384; cheese, 4,190; butter and dairy margarines, 1,447.

Forestry. In 2000 forests covered 31,000 ha, or approximately 0·3% of the total land area.

Fisheries. Fishing is of vital importance to the economy. Fishing vessels at the end of 2003 numbered 1,872,with a gross tonnage of 183,725. Total catch in 2000: 1,980,163; 2001: 1,986,584; 2002: 2,133,327; 2003: 1,979,545. Virtually all the fish caught is from marine waters. Iceland has received international praise for its management system which aims to avoid the over-fishing that has decimated stocks in other parts of the world. In 2003 fisheries accounted for 9·7% of GDP, down from 16·8% in 1996. The per capita consumption of fish and fishery products is the second highest in the world, after that of the Maldives.

Fishery limits were extended from 12 to 50 nautical miles in 1972 and to 200 nautical miles in 1975.

INDUSTRY

Production, 2002, in 1,000 tonnes: aluminium, 285·3; ferro-silicon, 120·6; diatomite, 26·4; and 82·6 of cement was sold.

Labour. In 2003 the economically active population was 162,400, of which 3·4% were unemployed. In the period 1993–2002 Iceland averaged 554 working days lost to strikes per 1,000 employees—the highest number in any western European country. In 2003 agriculture and fishing employed 6·9% of the economically active population, industry 21·7% (including manufacturing except fish processing 10·4%) and services 71·4% (including health services and social work 15·8% and wholesale, retail trade and repairs 13·1%).

Trade Unions. In 2002 trade union membership was 85·4% of the workforce.

INTERNATIONAL TRADE

The economy is heavily trade-dependent.

Imports and Exports. Total value of imports (c.i.f.) and exports (f.o.b.) in 1m. kr.:

	1999	*2000*	*2001*	*2002*	*2003*
Imports	182,322	203,222	220,874	207,608	216,525
Exports	144,928	149,273	196,582	204,303	182,580

Main imports, 2003 (in 1m. kr.): road vehicles, 20,959; petroleum and products, 15,605; electrical machinery and appliances, 14,197. Main exports, 2003 (in 1m. kr.): fish, crustaceans, molluscs and preparations thereof, 97,950; non-ferrous metals, 34,280; fodder for animals (excluding unmilled cereals), 11,938; iron and steel, 6,071.

Value of trade with principal countries for three years (in 1,000 kr.):

	2001		*2002*		*2003*	
	Imports (c.i.f.)	*Exports* (f.o.b.)	*Imports* (c.i.f.)	*Exports* (f.o.b.)	*Imports* (c.i.f.)	*Exports* (f.o.b.)
Belgium	4,120,900	2,798,900	3,683,600	3,209,700	4,828,200	3,215,800
China	6,352,400	905,200	6,112,300	1,310,100	7,719,200	1,327,300
Denmark	19,077,600	8,282,100	17,654,200	9,417,400	17,389,000	9,315,300
Finland	3,724,200	1,326,500	3,478,300	1,867,100	3,188,900	1,336,000
France	6,982,600	7,687,900	6,436,300	7,500,700	6,919,100	7,381,500
Germany	26,908,800	29,292,200	22,165,400	37,747,900	25,578,800	31,829,300
Italy	6,802,900	2,517,100	6,206,700	2,762,900	10,100,700	2,464,700
Japan	7,297,600	6,838,600	6,514,200	6,766,400	8,266,600	5,914,800
Netherlands	14,554,400	21,442,100	12,504,900	22,059,400	13,355,200	20,459,900
Norway	17,234,600	10,384,300	16,600,600	9,332,600	15,009,000	8,157,400
Portugal	1,223,400	10,816,300	1,011,500	8,865,000	1,022,500	6,916,400
Russia	3,551,200	715,700	7,898,200	1,704,600	6,054,000	1,034,000
Spain	4,341,800	10,538,600	3,852,800	10,693,900	3,936,300	11,546,500
Sweden	12,757,400	2,084,700	12,294,300	2,174,300	13,995,000	2,348,900
Switzerland	3,039,300	6,400,000	2,225,500	3,056,400	2,610,300	3,555,900
UK	16,609,600	35,839,100	15,459,600	35,739,000	16,096,600	31,990,100
USA	24,505,600	20,329,900	23,024,800	21,988,800	16,122,900	16,927,300

COMMUNICATIONS

Roads. On 31 Dec. 2003 the length of the public roads (including roads in towns) was 13,004 km. Of these 8,208 km were main and secondary roads and 4,796 km were provincial roads. Total length of surfaced roads was 4,331 km. A ring road of 1,400 km runs just inland from much of the coast; about 80% of it is smooth-surfaced. Motor vehicles registered at the end of 2003 numbered 183,813, of which 168,578 were passenger cars and 21,235 lorries; there were also 2,747 motorcycles. There were 20 fatal road accidents in 2003 with 23 persons killed.

Civil Aviation. Icelandair is the national carrier. In 2003 it served 13 destinations in western Europe and six in north America as well as operating domestic services. In 1999 it carried 1·3m. passengers. The main international airport is at Keflavík (Leifsstöd), with Reykjavík for flights to the Faroe Islands, Greenland and domestic services. Keflavík handled 1,368,496 passengers in 2003 (of which 211,904 transit passengers) and 40,554 tonnes of freight.

Shipping. Total registered vessels, 1,129 (228,231 gross tonnage) in 2003; of these, 943 were sea-going fishing vessels.

Telecommunications. In 2003 the number of telephone main lines was 192,552; mobile phone subscribers, 279,670 (more than 95% of the population—among the highest penetration rates in the world). In 2002 there were 130,000 PCs (451·4 per 1,000 persons); and, in 1995, 80,000 fax machines. There were 195,000 Internet users in 2003, 67·5% of the total population (the highest percentage in the world).

Postal Services. At the end of 2003 the number of post offices was 100.

SOCIAL INSTITUTIONS

Justice. In 1992 jurisdiction in civil and criminal cases was transferred from the provincial magistrates to eight new district courts, separating the judiciary from the prosecution. From the district courts there is an appeal to the Supreme Court in Reykjavík, which has eight judges. The population in penal institutions in Sept. 2002 was 107 (37 per 100,000 of national population).

Religion. The national church, the Evangelical Lutheran, is endowed by the state. There is complete religious liberty. The affairs of the national church are under the superintendence of a bishop. In 2004, 250,661 (86·3%) of the population were members of it (93·2% in 1980). 13,155 persons (4·5%) belonged to Lutheran free churches. 22,331 persons (7·7%) belonged to other religious organizations and 7,144 persons (2·5%) did not belong to any religious community.

Education. Primary education is compulsory and free from 6–15 years of age. Optional secondary education from 16 to 19 is also free. In 2003 there were 44,809 pupils in primary schools, 21,901 in secondary schools (18,885 on day courses) and 15,466 tertiary-level students (12,800 on day courses). Some 14% of tertiary-level students study abroad.

There are eight universities and specialized colleges at the tertiary level in Iceland. The largest is the University of Iceland in Reykjavík (founded 1911). There is also a university in Akureyri (founded 1987). Total enrolment of these two institutions was 6,100 students in 1997–98. In Reykjavík there are a teachers' university, a technical college, business colleges and an agricultural university.

In 2003 public sector spending on education was 6·5% of GNP.

The adult literacy rate in 2001 was at least 99%.

Health. In 2002 there were 23 hospitals with 2,228 beds, equivalent to 78 per 10,000 population. There were 1,047 doctors in 2003, 2,342 nurses and 273 pharmacists in 2002 and 283 dentists in 2000. In 2003 there were 3·6 doctors per 1,000 inhabitants. Iceland has one of the lowest alcohol consumption rates in Europe, at 6·52 litres of alcohol per adult per year (2003). In 2002 Iceland spent 9·9% of its GDP on health.

Welfare. The main body of social welfare legislation is consolidated in six acts:

(i) The social security legislation (a) health insurance, including sickness benefits; *(b)* social security pensions, mainly consisting of old age pension, disablement pension and widows' pension, and also children's pension; *(c)* employment injuries insurance.

(ii) The unemployment insurance legislation, where daily allowances are paid to those who have met certain conditions.

(iii) The subsistence legislation. This is controlled by municipal government.

(iv) The tax legislation. Prior to 1988 children's support was included in the tax legislation. Since 1988 family allowances are paid directly to all children age 0–15 years. The amount is increased with the second child in the family, and children under the age of seven get additional benefits. Single parents receive additional allowances.

(v) The rehabilitation legislation.

(vi) Child and juvenile guidance.

Health insurance covers the entire population. Citizenship is not demanded and there is a six-month waiting period. Most hospitals are both municipally and state run, a few solely state run and all offer free medical help. Medical treatment out of hospitals is partly paid by the patient; the same applies to medicines, except medicines of lifelong necessary use, which are paid in full by the health insurance. Dental care is partly paid by the state for children under 17 years old and also for old age and disabled pensioners. Sickness benefits are paid to those who lose income because of periodical illness.

The pension system is composed of the public social security system and some 90 private pension funds. The social security system pays basic old age and disablement pensions of a fixed amount regardless of past or present income, as well as supplementary pensions to individuals with low present income. The pensions are index-linked, i.e. are changed in line with changes in wage and salary rates in the labour market. In the public social security system, entitlement to old age and disablement pensions at the full rates is subject to the condition that the beneficiary has been resident in Iceland for 40 years at the age period of 16–67. For shorter periods of residence, the benefits are reduced proportionally. Entitled to old age pension are all those who are 67 years old, and have been residents in Iceland for three years of the age period of 16–67. Old age and disablement pension are of equally high amount; in the year 2004 the total sum was 254,988 kr. for an individual. Married pensioners receive double the basic pension. Pensioners with little or no other income are entitled to an income supplement; in 2004 the maximum annual income supplement was 520,688 kr.

The employment injuries insurance covers medical care, daily allowances, disablement pension and survivors' pension and is applicable to practically all employees.

CULTURE

World Heritage Sites. There is one UNESCO site in Iceland: Þingvellir National Park (2004), located on an active volcanic site.

Broadcasting. The state-owned public service, The Icelandic State Broadcasting Service, broadcasts two national and three regional radio programmes and one national TV channel. In addition, 27 privately owned radio stations and 10 private TV stations were in operation in 2003. At 31 Dec. 2003, 93,501 colour TV sets were licensed (497 black and white).

Cinema. There were 23 cinemas with 46 screens in 2003 of which the capital had seven cinemas and 27 screens. Total admissions numbered 1,445,783 in 2003, with the Reykjavík area accounting for 1,277,546. In 2002 gross box office receipts came to 1,149·9m. kr. Four full-length Icelandic films were released in 2002; the most successful was Baltasar Kormákur's *The Sea*.

Press. In 2002 there were three daily newspapers and 22 non-daily newspapers (13 paid-for and nine free).

Iceland publishes more books per person than any other country in the world. In 2002, 1,192 volumes of books and 775 volumes of booklets were published.

Tourism. There were 308,768 visitors in 2003; revenue totalled 37,285m. kr. Overnight stays in hotels and guest houses in 2003 numbered 1,260,501 (of which foreign travellers, 970,256; and Icelanders, 290,245). Tourism accounts for more than 13% of foreign currency earnings. Between 1990 and 2000 the number of visitors increased on average by 7% every year.

Festivals. The Reykjavík Arts Festival, an annual programme of international artists and performers, is held every May–June.

Libraries. The National and University Library of Iceland is in Reykjavík and contains 901,000 volumes. The seven University libraries contain 205,074 volumes, the 43 special libraries 360,854 volumes. There are 57 public libraries with 2,235,658 volumes.

Theatre and Opera. In 2003 there were six professional theatres operated on a yearly basis (of which five were in the capital region) and 18 professional theatre groups (all in the capital region). In 2003 there were 188,869 admissions to performances of the professional theatres, 67,044 admissions to the National Theatre and 78,106 admissions to the City Theatre and Idno Theatre. Total audience of the Icelandic Opera was 11,907.

There is one symphonic orchestra operated on a regular basis, the Icelandic Symphony Orchestra. In 2002 the orchestra performed 76 times within the country and abroad, with audiences totalling 40,090.

Museums and Galleries. In 2002 there were 107 museums, botanical gardens, aquariums and zoos in operation, with a total of 1,108,259 visitors. The National Museum re-opened in Sept. 2004 after extensive renovation, so received no visitors in 2002. The National Gallery received 28,459 visitors and 97,878 attended the Reykjavík Municipal Art Museum.

DIPLOMATIC REPRESENTATIVES

Of Iceland in the United Kingdom (2A Hans Street, London, SW1X 0JE)
Ambassador: Sverrir Hakur Gunnlaugsson.

Of the United Kingdom in Iceland (Laufásvegur 31, 101 Reykjavík)
Ambassador: Alp Mehmet, MVO.

Of Iceland in the USA (1156 15th Street NW, Suite 1200, Washington, D.C., 20005)
Ambassador: Helgi Ágústsson.

Of the USA in Iceland (Laufásvegur 21, 101 Reykjavík)
Ambassador: James I. Gadsen.

Of Iceland to the United Nations
Ambassador: Hjálmar W. Hannesson.

Of Iceland to the European Union
Ambassador: Kjartan Jóhansson.

FURTHER READING

Statistics Iceland, *Landshagir* (Statistical Yearbook of Iceland).—*Hagtíðindi* (Statistical Series)
Central Bank of Iceland. *Monetary Bulletin.—The Economy of Iceland.* (Latest issue 2004)
Byock, Jesse, *Viking Age Iceland.* Penguin, London, 2001
Hastrup, K., *A Place Apart: An Anthropological Study of the Icelandic World*. Clarendon Press, Oxford, 1998
Karlsson, G., *The History of Iceland*. Univ. of Minnesota Press, 2000
Lacy, T., *Ring of Seasons: Iceland—Its culture and history*. University of Michigan Press, 1998
McBride F. R., *Iceland.* [Bibliography] 2nd ed. ABC-Clio, Oxford and Santa Barbara (CA), 1996
Smiley, Jane, (ed.) *The Sagas of Icelanders: A Selection.* Penguin, London, 2002
Turner, Barry, (ed.) *Scandinavia Profiled.* Macmillan, London, 2000

National statistical office: Statistics Iceland, Bogartúni 21a, IS-150 Reykjavík.
Website: http://www.hagstofa.is
National library: Landsbókasafn Islands.—Háskólabókasafn, Reykjavík, *Librarian:* Sigrún Klara Hannesdóttir.

INDIA

Bharat
(Republic of India)

Capital: New Delhi
Population projection, 2010: 1,173·81m.
GDP per capita, 2002: (PPP$) 2,670
HDI/world rank: 0·595/127

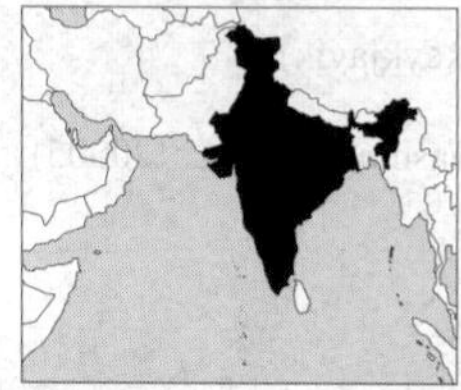

Map. Based upon Survey of India Map with the permission of the Surveyor General of India. The responsibility for the correctness of internal details rests with the pubisher. The territorial waters of India extend into the sea to a distance of 12 nautical miles measured from the appropriate base line. The external boundaries and coastlines of India agree with the Record/Master Copy certified by the Survey of India.

KEY HISTORICAL EVENTS

Approximately 7,000 years ago the valley of the Indus was one of the cradles of civilization. From the Indus Valley, Dravidian peoples spread agriculture and fixed settlements gradually across India, arriving in the far south by about 4,000 years ago. The Indus Valley Harappan civilization, a Bronze Age culture, flourished from around 2300 to 1500 BC and had links with western Asian civilizations in Iran. Writing, fine jewellery and textile production, town planning, metalworking and pottery were the hallmarks of an advanced urban society.

At the same time, another Bronze Age civilization existed in the Ganges Valley. This civilization, whose links were with south-eastern Asia, was based on a rice-growing rural economy. Around 1500 BC a pastoral people, the Aryans, invaded the Indus Valley from Iran and Central Asia. Their arrival completed the destruction of the Harappan civilization and shifted the balance of power in the subcontinent to the Ganges Valley.

The Aryans took over northern and central India, merging their culture with that of the Dravidians. The caste system, still a feature of Indian society, dates back to the Dravidians, but the languages of northern and central India, and the polytheistic religion that is now followed by the majority of the inhabitants of the subcontinent, are both Aryan in origin. From these two cultures, a Hindu civilization emerged.

By 800 BC a series of Hindu kingdoms had developed in the Ganges Valley. This region gave birth to one of the world's great religions: Buddhism. Prince Gautama, the Buddha (*c.* 563–483 BC), renounced a life of wealth to seek enlightenment. His creed of non-violence was spread throughout India and, later, south-eastern Asia.

Chandragupta Maurya (reigned 321–297 BC) conquered most of northern India before his ascetic death from self-imposed starvation. His grandson, Ashoka, ruled an empire that stretched from the Deccan to Afghanistan from *c.* 272–*c.* 231, but he is mainly remembered for his enthusiasm for Buddhist pacifism. Attacked by enemies who did not share this creed, the Mauryan empire collapsed soon after Ashoka's death.

Although no Hindu state managed to unite India, the Hindu religion and culture proved powerful influences throughout the region. By about 500 BC Sri Lanka was within the Hindu sphere of influence. Over the next 800 years Hindu kingdoms were established in Burma, Cambodia, Sumatra, Thailand and Java. From the 4th century BC, Indian merchants spread Buddhism through south-eastern Asia.

While Indian religion and culture spread south and east, an invasion from the west threatened to change the subcontinent. In AD 713 a Muslim army conquered Sind. For the next 300 years, Islamic rulers were largely confined to what is now Pakistan, but in 1000 a raid by the ruler of Ghazni (now in Afghanistan) overran the Punjab. During the 11th and 12th centuries the Hindu states of the Ganges Valley were toppled by Muslim invaders.

In the north, the Delhi Sultanate was replaced by the Mughal Empire. Founded by Babur (reigned 1526–30), it was extended by Akbar the Great (reigned 1556–1605) who conquered Baluchistan, Gujarat, Bengal, Orissa, Rajasthan, Afghanistan and Bihar. In his campaign against Gujarat, Akbar marched his army 800 km (500 miles) in only 11 days. His grandson, Shah Jahan (reigned 1628–58), was a pleasure-seeking ruler, who is remembered for constructing the Taj Mahal as a memorial to his favourite wife.

The decline of the Mughal Empire began under Shah Jahan's son, Aurangzeb I (reigned 1658–1707). Aurangzeb persecuted Hindus with a vengeance. Inter-community violence and wars against Hindu states weakened the empire. Throughout the 18th century, disputed successions and fears of assassination diverted the Mughal emperors. By the close of the 18th century the last emperor was nominal ruler of the environs of Delhi.

By the 16th century, European traders were established along India's coasts. In 1510 the Portuguese took Goa, which remained the centre of the fragmented possessions of Portuguese India until 1962. The creation of the (English) East India Company in 1600 heralded the beginning of what was to become the British Indian Empire. The main threat to British rule in India was France. Although the East India Company controlled parts of Bengal and the Ganges Valley, France was supreme in the Deccan where French forces, and Indian rulers allied to France, held sway over an area twice the size of France itself.

In the 1750s Britain and France fought out their European wars overseas. The defeat of French forces, and France's Indian allies, at the battle of Plassey (1757), by British forces led by Robert Clive (1725–74), confirmed British rule in Bengal and Bihar and ejected France from the Deccan. Henceforth, France was restricted to five small coastal possessions.

Founded by Sivaji (1627–80), the Maratha state was the major power in central and southern India in the 17th and 18th centuries. The Hindu Sivaji came into conflict with the fanatical Muslim Mughal emperor Aurangzeb, who imprisoned Sivaji. After his famous escape from captivity, concealed in a fruit basket, Sivaji made himself emperor of his Maratha state in 1674. This pious monarch ruled competently, establishing an efficient administration, but by the time of his grandson, Shahu (reigned 1707–27), the power of the Maratha emperors had been eclipsed by that of their hereditary chief minister, the Peshwa. In 1727 the Peshwa Baji Rao I (reigned 1720–40) effectively replaced the emperor and established his own dynasty. Baji Rao made the Maratha state the strongest in India. His descendant, Baji Rao II (reigned 1795–1817), raised a weakened state against the British and was crushed. He had been the last important Indian monarch outside British influence.

During the first half of the 19th century, wars against Sind (1843) and the Sikhs in Punjab (1849) extended the borders of British India. By the middle of the 19th century about 60% of the subcontinent was controlled by the East India Company. The remaining 40% was divided between about 620 Indian states, which were, in theory, still sovereign and ruled by their own maharajas, sultans, nawabs and other monarchs, each advised by a British resident. The Indian states ranged from large entities the size of European countries (states such as Hyderabad, Baroda, Mysore and Indore) to tiny states no bigger than an English parish.

Landless peasants and dispossessed princes united in their opposition to British rule. In 1857 a mutiny by soldiers of the East India Company quickly spread into full-scale rebellion. Throughout India those who resented the speed and nature of the changes brought about by British rule made one final attempt to eject the occupiers. The Indian Mutiny took 14 months to put down.

After the Mutiny the British government replaced the East India Company as the ruler of the Indian colonial empire (1858), and the modernization of India began apace. Emphasis was placed on building up an Indian infrastructure, particularly roads and railways. The participation of Indians within the civil administration, the construction of a vast national railway system and the imposition of the English language, through the many new schools, colleges and universities, did much to forge an Indian identity. But industry in India was not modernized, in part through fear of competition. In 1877 the Indian Empire was proclaimed and Queen Victoria became Empress of India (Kaiser-i-Hind).

The divisions fostered by religion proved stronger than any new sense of a national Indian identity. The (Hindu-dominated) Indian National Congress, the forerunner of the Congress Party, first met in 1885, and in 1906 the rival Muslim League was founded. Demands for Home Rule grew in the early years of the 20th century, and nationalist feeling was fuelled when British troops fired without warning on a peaceful nationalist protest meeting—the Amritsar Massacre (1919).

Realizing that change was inevitable, the British government reformed the administration through two Acts of Parliament in 1919 and 1935. These created an Indian federation, effectively removing many of the differences between the Crown territories and the Indian states. These acts granted a new Indian government limited autonomy. The pace of reform was, however, too slow for Indian popular opinion.

In 1920 the Congress party began a campaign of non-violence and non-cooperation with the British colonial authorities, led by the charismatic figure of Mahatma Gandhi (1869–1948). By the start of World War II (1939–45), relations between the Hindu and Muslim communities in India had broken down, and the Muslims were demanding a separate independent Islamic state, later Pakistan.

In 1945 Britain had neither the will nor the resources to maintain the Indian Empire. In 1947 India was divided into India, a predominantly Hindu state led by Jawaharlal (Pandit) Nehru (1889–1964) of the Congress Party, and Pakistan, a Muslim state led by Mohammad Ali Jinnah (1876–1948) of the Muslim League. Partition brought enormous upheaval. More than 70m. Hindus and Muslims became refugees as they trekked across the new boundaries. Many thousands were killed in intercommunal violence. The border remained disputed in many places. Tension increased when Gandhi was assassinated by a Hindu fundamentalist (1948). In 1950 India became a republic.

Tension between India and Pakistan erupted into war in 1947–49 when the two countries fought over Kashmir. The region was divided along a ceasefire line, although neither side recognized this as an international border. India and Pakistan went to war again over Kashmir in 1965, and in 1971 when Bangladesh (formerly East Pakistan) gained its independence as a result of Indian military intervention. Indian forces saw action in 1961 when Indian troops invaded and annexed Portuguese India and in 1962 in a border war with China.

In 1966 Nehru's daughter Indira Gandhi (1917–84) became premier. Under Mrs Gandhi, India continued to assert itself as a regional power and the rival of Pakistan. Although non-aligned, India developed close relations with the Soviet Union. In spite of being the world's largest democracy, India was wracked by local separatism and communal unrest. From 1975 to 1977 Mrs Gandhi imposed a much-criticized state of emergency. Her actions split the Congress Party, allowing Morarji Desai (1896–1995) of the Janata Party to form India's first non-Congress administration. However, his alliance of parties soon shattered and a wing of Congress, led by Mrs Gandhi, was returned to power in 1980.

Violence in Sikh areas, fanned by demands by militant Sikhs for an independent homeland (called Khalistan), increased tensions. In 1984 Mrs Gandhi ordered that the Golden Temple in Amritsar be stormed after it had been turned into a storehouse for weapons by Sikh extremists. Soon afterwards, Mrs Gandhi was assassinated by her Sikh bodyguards.

Mrs Gandhi was succeeded as premier by her son, Ranjiv (1944–91), during whose period of office India became involved in Sri Lanka, supporting the central government against the separatist Tamil Tigers movement. Ranjiv Gandhi was assassinated by a Tamil Tiger suicide bomber during the 1991 election campaign. By 1989 personality clashes had shattered the unity of the once all-powerful Congress Party. Since then coalitions have held office. The right-wing Hindu nationalist Bharatiya Janata Party (BJP) has been part of most these. Support for the BJP increased following violence between Hindus and Muslims over a campaign, which began in 1990, to build a Hindu temple on the site of a mosque in the holy city of Ayodhya.

After the fall of the Soviet Union (1991), India gradually abandoned state ownership and some elements of protectionism. Privatization has been accompanied by an economic revolution that has seen the development of high tech industries. At the same time, India has become a nuclear power, exploding its first nuclear device in 1974. Along with Pakistan, India has yet to sign the Comprehensive Nuclear-Test-Ban Treaty.

There have been 35,000 deaths since the outbreak of the Kashmir insurgency in 1988. Negotiations with Pakistan over the future of the disputed territory of Kashmir began in July 1999. In May 2001 India ended its six-month long ceasefire. It then invited Pakistan's government to enter talks, which ended with hopes of avoiding further violence. In Dec. 2001, in an attack on the Indian parliament by suicide bombers, 13 people died. Although no group claimed responsibility, Kashmiri separatists were blamed. However, Pakistani President Pervez Musharraf's subsequent crackdown on militants helped to bring the two countries back from the brink of war. Tension between India and Pakistan increased following an attack on an Indian army base in Indian-occupied Kashmir on 14 May 2002. The attack, which killed 31 people, was linked to Islamic terrorists infiltrating the Kashmir valley from Pakistan. It drew widespread criticism of President Musharraf for failing to combat terrorism in the disputed region. In Feb. 2002, 58 Hindu pilgrims returning from Ayodhya were killed when their train was set on fire following a confrontation with a Muslim crowd at Godhra in Gujarat. The incident led to three months of intermittent communal rioting, during which at least 800 Muslims died in attacks by Hindus. Relations between India and Pakistan cooled following terrorist bombings in Bombay (Mumbai). Since then, however, the situation has improved, leading *The Economist* to write in its 17 Jan. 2004 issue: "Mr Vajpayee has pulled off a reconciliation with President Pervez Musharraf of Pakistan, setting the two countries on the most promising, if uncertain, path to peace for years."

TERRITORY AND POPULATION

India is bounded in the northwest by Pakistan, north by China (Tibet), Nepal and Bhutan, east by Myanmar, and southeast, south and southwest by the Indian Ocean. The far eastern states and territories are almost separated from the rest by Bangladesh. The area (excluding the Pakistan and China-occupied parts of Jammu and Kashmir) is 3,166,414 sq. km. A Sino-Indian agreement of 7 Sept. 1993 settled frontier disputes dating from the war of 1962. Population (excluding occupied Jammu and Kashmir), 2001 census population: 1,027,015,247 (495,738,169 females), giving a density of 324 persons per sq. km. There are also 20m. Indians and ethnic Indians living abroad, notably in Malaysia, the USA, Saudi Arabia, the UK and South Africa. 72·2% of the population was rural in 2001 (Goa being the most urban state, at 49·8%; and Himachal Pradesh the most rural, at 90·2%). More than 45% of Indians are under 20.

The UN gives a projected population for 2010 of 1,173·81m.

By 2050 India is expected to have a population of 1·53bn. and is projected to have overtaken China as the world's most populous country.

Area and population of states and union territories:

States	*Area in sq. km*	*Population 2001 census*	*Density per sq. km (2001)*
Andhra Pradesh (And P)	275,069	75,727,541	275
Arunachal Pradesh (Arun P)	83,743	1,091,117	13
Assam (Ass)	78,438	26,638,407	340
Bihar (Bih)	94,163	82,878,796	880
Chhattisgarh (Chh)	135,191	20,795,956	154
Goa	3,702	1,343,998	363
Gujarat (Guj)	196,022	50,596,992	258
Haryana (Har)	44,212	21,082,989	477
Himachal Pradesh (Him P)	55,673	6,077,248	109
Jammu and Kashmir (J and K)[1]	101,387	10,069,917	99
Jharkhand (Jha)	79,714	26,909,428	338
Karnataka (Kar)	191,791	52,733,958	275
Kerala (Ker)	38,863	31,838,619	819
Madhya Pradesh (MP)	308,245	60,385,118	196
Maharashtra (Mah)	307,713	96,752,247	314
Manipur (Man)	22,327	2,388,634	107
Meghalaya (Meg)	22,429	2,306,069	103
Mizoram (Miz)	21,081	891,058	42
Nagaland (Nag)	16,579	1,988,636	120
Orissa (Or)	155,707	36,706,920	236
Punjab (Pun)	50,362	24,289,296	482
Rajasthan (Raj)	342,239	56,473,122	165
Sikkim (Sik)	7,096	540,493	76
Tamil Nadu (TN)	130,058	62,110,839	478
Tripura (Tri)	10,486	3,191,168	304
Uttar Pradesh (UP)	240,928	166,052,859	689
Uttaranchal (Uan)	53,483	8,479,562	159
West Bengal (WB)	88,752	80,221,171	904

	Area in sq. km	Population 2001 census	Density per sq. km (2001)
Union Territories			
Andaman and Nicobar Islands (ANI)	8,249	356,265	43
Chandigarh (Chan)	114	900,914	7,903
Dadra and Nagar Haveli (DNH)	491	220,451	449
Daman and Diu (D and D)	112	158,059	1,411
Delhi (Del)	1,483	13,782,976	9,294
Lakshadweep (Lak)	32	60,595	1,894
Pondicherry (Pon)	480	973,829	2,029

[1]Excludes the area occupied by Pakistan and China.

Urban agglomerations with populations over 2m., together with their core cities at the 2001 census:

	State/ Union Territory	Urban agglomeration	Core city
Bombay (Mumbai)	Maharashtra	16,368,084	11,914,348
Calcutta (Kolkata)	West Bengal	13,216,546	4,580,544
Delhi	Delhi	12,791,458	9,817,439
Madras (Chennai)	Tamil Nadu	6,424,624	4,216,268
Bangalore	Karnataka	5,686,844	4,292,223
Hyderabad	Andhra Pradesh	5,533,640	3,449,878
Ahmedabad	Gujarat	4,519,278	3,515,361
Pune (Poona)	Maharashtra	3,755,525	2,540,069
Surat	Gujarat	2,811,466	2,433,787
Kanpur	Uttar Pradesh	2,690,486	2,532,138
Jaipur	Rajasthan	2,324,319	2,324,319
Lucknow	Uttar Pradesh	2,266,933	2,207,340
Nagpur	Maharashtra	2,122,965	2,051,320

Smaller urban agglomerations and cities with populations over 250,000 (with 2001 census populations, in 1,000):

Agra (UP)	1,321	Dhanbad (Jha)	1,064	Ludhiana (Pun)	1,395
Ahmadnagar (Mah)	347	Dhule (Mah)	341	Madurai (TN)	1,195
Ajmer (Raj)	490	Durgapur (WB)	493	Malegaon (Mah)	409
Akola (Mah)	400	Erode (TN)	391	Mangalore (Kar)	539
Alappuzha (Ker)	283	Faridabad Complex (Har)	1,055	Mathura (UP)	319
Aligarh (UP)	668	Firozabad (UP)	432	Meerut (UP)	1,074
Allahabad (UP)	1,050	Gaya (Bih)	394	Moradabad (UP)	641
Alwar (Raj)	266	Ghaziabad (UP)	969	Muzaffarnagar (UP)	331
Amravati (Mah)	549	Gorakhpur (UP)	625	Muzaffarpur (Bih)	305
Amritsar (Pun)	1,011	Gulbarga (Kar)	436	Mysore (Kar)	786
Asansol (WB)	1,090	Guntur (And P)	515	Nanded (Mah)	431
Aurangabad (Mah)	892	Guwahati (Ass)	815	Nashik (Mah)	1,152
Barddhaman (WB)	286	Gwalior (MP)	866	Nellore (And P)	405
Bareilly (UP)	730	Hisar (Har)	263	Nizamabad (And P)	287
Belgaum (Mah)	506	Hubli-Dharwad (Kar)	786	Panipat (Har)	354
Bellary (Kar)	317	Ichalkaranji (Mah)	286	Parbhani (Mah)	259
Bhagalpur (Bih)	350	Indore (MP)	1,639	Patiala (Pun)	323
Bhavnagar (Guj)	518	Jabalpur (MP)	1,117	Patna (Bih)	1,707
Bhilai (Chh)	924	Jalandhar (Pun)	709	Pondicherry (Pon)	506
Bhilwara (Raj)	280	Jalgaon (Mah)	369	Raipur (Chh)	699
Bhiwandi (Mah)	621	Jammu (J and K)	608	Rajahmundry (And P)	408
Bhopal (MP)	1,455	Jamnagar (Guj)	558	Rajkot (Raj)	1,002
Bhubaneswar (Or)	657	Jamshedpur (Jha)	1,102	Rampur (UP)	282
Bijapur (Kar)	253	Jhansi (UP)	463	Ranchi (Jha)	863
Bikaner (Raj)	529	Jodhpur (Raj)	856	Rohtak (Har)	295
Bilaspur (Chh)	330	Junagadh (Guj)	252	Rourkela (OR)	484
Bokaro Steel City (Jha)	498	Kakinada (And P)	369	Sagar (MP)	309
Brahmapur (OR)	290	Kharagpur (WB)	296	Saharanpur (UP)	453
Chandigarh (Chan)	809	Kochi (Ker)	1,355	Salem (TN)	749
Chandrapur (Mah)	298	Kolhapur (Mah)	498	Sangli-Miraj (Mah)	448
Coimbatore (TN)	1,446	Kollam (Ker)	380	Shahjahanpur (UP)	323
Cuddapah (And P)	261	Korba (Chh)	316	Shiliguri (WB)	470
Cuttack (Or)	588	Kota (Raj)	705	Shillong (Meg)	268
Darbhanga (Bih)	267	Kozhikode (Ker)	880	Shimoga (Kar)	274
Davangere (Kar)	364	Kurnool (And P)	321	Sholapur (Mah)	873
Dehra Dun (Uan)	528	Latur (Mah)	300	Srinagar (J and K)	971
				Thalassery (Ker)	498

Thiruvananthapuram (Ker)	889	Tiruppur (TN)	543	Vijayawada (And P)	1,011
Thrissur (Ker)	330	Udaipur (Raj)	389	Visakhapatnam (And P)	1,329
Tiruchirapalli (TN)	847	Ujjain (MP)	431	Warangal (And P)	577
Tirunelveli (TN)	432	Vadodara (Guj)	1,492	Yamunanagar (Har)	307
Tirupati (And P)	302	Varanasi (UP)	1,212		
		Vellore (TN)	388		

SOCIAL STATISTICS

Many births and deaths go unregistered. The Registrar General's data suggests a birth rate for 2003 of 23·3 per 1,000 population and a death rate of 8·5, which would indicate in a year approximately 24,860,000 births and 9,070,000 deaths. The growth rate is, however, slowing, and by 2003 had dropped below 1·5%, having been over 2% in 1991. Expectation of life at birth, 2003, 62·9 years for males and 64·4 years for females.

Marriages and divorces are not registered. The minimum age for a civil marriage is 18 for women and 21 for men; for a sacramental marriage, 14 for females and 18 for males. Population growth rate, 1991–2001, 21·35% (the lowest since 1961–71). Infant mortality, 2002, 60 per 1,000 live births; fertility rate, 2002, 2·9 births per woman. Child deaths (under the age of five) were more than halved between 1980 and 2001, from 172 per 1,000 in 1980 to only 72 per 1,000 in 2001.

CLIMATE

India has a variety of climatic sub-divisions. In general, there are four seasons. The cool one lasts from Dec. to March, the hot season is in April and May, the rainy season is June to Sept., followed by a further dry season until Nov. Rainfall, however, varies considerably, from 4" (100 mm) in the N.W. desert to over 400" (10,000 mm) in parts of Assam.

Range of temperature and rainfall: New Delhi, Jan. 57°F (13·9°C), July 88°F (31·1°C). Annual rainfall 26" (640 mm). Bombay, Jan. 75°F (23·9°C), July 81°F (27·2°C). Annual rainfall 72" (1,809 mm). Calcutta, Jan. 67°F (19·4°C), July 84°F (28·9°C). Annual rainfall 64" (1,600 mm). Cherrapunji, Jan. 53°F (11·7°C), July 68°F (20°C). Annual rainfall 432" (10,798 mm). Darjeeling, Jan. 41°F (5°C), July 62°F (16·7°C). Annual rainfall 121" (3,035 mm). Hyderabad, Jan. 72°F (22·2°C), July 80°F (26·7°C). Annual rainfall 30" (752 mm). Kochi, Jan. 80°F (26·7°C), July 79°F (26·1°C). Annual rainfall 117" (2,929 mm). Madras, Jan. 76°F (24·4°C), July 87°F (30·6°C). Annual rainfall 51" (1,270 mm). Patna, Jan. 63°F (17·2°C), July 90°F (32·2°C). Annual rainfall 46" (1,150 mm).

On 26 Dec. 2004 an undersea earthquake centred off the Indonesian island of Sumatra caused a huge tsunami that flooded coastal areas in southern India resulting in 16,000 deaths. In total there were 290,000 deaths in twelve countries.

CONSTITUTION AND GOVERNMENT

The Constitution was passed by the Constituent Assembly on 26 Nov. 1949 and came into force on 26 Jan. 1950. It has since been amended 86 times.

India is a republic and comprises a Union of 28 States and seven Union Territories. Each State is administered by a Governor appointed by the President for a term of five years while each Union Territory is administered by the President through a Lieut.-Governor or an administrator appointed by him. The head of the Union (head of state) is the *President* in whom all executive power is vested, to be exercised on the advice of ministers responsible to Parliament. The President, who must be an Indian citizen at least 35 years old and eligible for election to the House of the People, is elected by an electoral college of all the elected members of Parliament and of the state legislative assemblies, holds office for five years and is eligible for re-election. There is also a *Vice-President* who is *ex officio* chairman of the Council of States.

There is a *Council of Ministers* to aid and advise the President; this comprises Ministers who are members of the Cabinet and Ministers of State and deputy ministers who are not. A Minister who for any period of six consecutive months is not a member of either House of Parliament ceases to be a Minister at the expiration of that period. The *Prime Minister* is appointed by the President; other Ministers are appointed by the President on the Prime Minister's advice. The salary of each Minister is Rs 12,000 per month.

Parliament consists of the President, the *Council of States* (*Rajya Sabha*) and the *House of the People* (*Lok Sabha*). The Council of States, or the Upper House, consists of not more than 250 members; in Oct. 2003 there were 233 elected members and 12 members nominated by the President. The election to this house is indirect; the representatives of each State are elected by the elected members of the Legislative Assembly of that State. The Council of States is a permanent body not liable to dissolution, but one-third of the members retire every second year. The House of the People, or the Lower House, consists of 545 members, 543 directly elected on the basis of adult suffrage from territorial constituencies in the States, and the Union territories; in Feb. 2004 there were 536 elected members, two nominated members and seven vacancies. The House of the People unless sooner dissolved continues for a period of five years from the date appointed for its first meeting; in emergency, Parliament can extend the term by one year.

State Legislatures. For every State there is a legislature which consists of the Governor, and (a) two Houses, a Legislative Assembly and a Legislative Council, in the States of Bihar, Jammu and Kashmir, Karnataka, Madhya Pradesh (where it is provided for but not in operation), Maharashtra and Uttar Pradesh, and (b) one House, a Legislative Assembly, in the other States. Every Legislative Assembly, unless sooner dissolved, continues for five years from the date appointed for its first meeting. In emergency the term can be extended by one year. Every State Legislative Council is a permanent body and is not subject to dissolution, but one-third of the members retire every second year. Parliament can, however, abolish an existing Legislative Council or create a new one, if the proposal is supported by a resolution of the Legislative Assembly concerned.

Legislation. The various subjects of legislation are enumerated in three lists in the seventh schedule to the constitution. List I, the Union List, consists of 97 subjects (including defence, foreign affairs, communications, currency and coinage, banking and customs) with respect to which the Union Parliament has exclusive power to make laws. The State legislature has exclusive power to make laws with respect to the 66 subjects in list II, the State List; these include police and public order, agriculture and irrigation, education, public health and local government. The powers to make laws with respect to the 47 subjects (including economic and social planning, legal questions and labour and price control) in list III, the Concurrent List, are held by both Union and State governments, though the former prevails. But Parliament may legislate with respect to any subject in the State List in circumstances when the subject assumes national importance or during emergencies.

Fundamental Rights. Two chapters of the constitution deal with fundamental rights and 'Directive Principles of State Policy'. 'Untouchability' is abolished, and its practice in any form is punishable. The fundamental rights can be enforced through the ordinary courts of law and through the Supreme Court of the Union. The directive principles cannot be enforced through the courts of law; they are nevertheless fundamental in the governance of the country.

Citizenship. Under the Constitution, every person who was on the 26 Jan. 1950 domiciled in India and (a) was born in India or (b) either of whose parents was born in India or (c) who has been ordinarily resident in the territory of India for not less than five years immediately preceding that date became a citizen of India. Special provision is made for migrants from Pakistan and for Indians resident abroad. The right to vote is granted to every person who is a citizen of India and who is not less than 18 years of age on a fixed date and is not otherwise disqualified.

Parliament. Parliament and the state legislatures are organized according to the following schedule (figures show distribution of seats in Oct. 2003 for the Lok Sabha, the Rajya Sabha and the State Legislatures):

	Parliament		*State Legislatures*	
States:	*House of the People (Lok Sabha)*	*Council of States (Rajya Sabha)*	*Legislative Assemblies (Vidhan Sabhas)*	*Legislative Councils (Vidhan Parishads)*
Andhra Pradesh	42	18	294	–
Arunachal Pradesh	2	1	60	–
Assam	14	7	126	–
Bihar	40	16	243	96
Chhattisgarh	11	5	90	–
Goa	2	1	40	–

	Parliament		State Legislatures	
	House of the People (Lok Sabha)	Council of States (Rajya Sabha)	Legislative Assemblies (Vidhan Sabhas)	Legislative Councils (Vidhan Parishads)
States:				
Gujarat	26	11	182	–
Haryana	10	5	90	–
Himachal Pradesh	4	3	68	–
Jammu and Kashmir	6	4	87[1]	36[2]
Jharkhand	14	6	81	–
Karnataka	28	12	224	75
Kerala	20	9	140	–
Madhya Pradesh	29	11	230	–
Maharashtra	48	19	288	78
Manipur	2	1	60	–
Meghalaya	2	1	60	–
Mizoram	1	1	40	–
Nagaland	1	1	60	–
Orissa	21	10	147	–
Punjab	13	7	117	–
Rajasthan	25	10	200	–
Sikkim	1	1	32	–
Tamil Nadu	39	18	234	–
Tripura	2	1	60	–
Uttar Pradesh	80	31	403	108
Uttaranchal	5	3	30	–
West Bengal	42	16	295[3]	–
Union Territories:				
Andaman and Nicobar Islands	1	–	–	–
Chandigarh	1	–	–	–
Dadra and Nagar Haveli	1	–	–	–
Delhi	7	3	70	–
Daman and Diu	1	–	–	–
Lakshadweep	1	–	–	–
Pondicherry	1	1	30	–
Nominated by the President under Article 80 (1) (a) of the Constitution	–	12	–	–
Total	545[4]	245	4,081	393[4]

[1]Excludes 24 seats for Pakistan-occupied areas of the State which are in abeyance.
[2]Excludes seats for the Pakistan-occupied areas.
[3]Includes one nominated minority community representative.
[4]Includes two nominated members to represent Anglo-Indians.

Language. The Constitution provides that the official language of the Union shall be Hindi in the Devanagari script. Hindi is spoken by over 30% of the population. It was originally provided that English should continue to be used for all official purposes until 1965. But the Official Languages Act 1963 provides that, after the expiry of this period of 15 years from the coming into force of the Constitution, English might continue to be used, in addition to Hindi, for all official purposes of the Union for which it was being used immediately before that day, and for the transaction of business in Parliament. According to the Official Languages (Use for official purposes of the Union) Rules 1976, an employee may record in Hindi or in English without being required to furnish a translation thereof in the other language and no employee possessing a working knowledge of Hindi may ask for an English translation of any document in Hindi except in the case of legal or technical documents.

The 58th amendment to the Constitution (26 Nov. 1987) authorized the preparation of a Constitution text in Hindi.

The following 18 languages are included in the Eighth Schedule to the Constitution (with 2003 estimate of speakers): Assamese (16·6m.), Bengali (88·6m.), Gujarati (51·7m.), Hindi (429·1m.), Kannada (41·7m.), Kashmiri (1·1m.), Konkani (2·2m.), Malayalam (38·6m.), Manipuri (1·6m.), Marathi (79·5m.), Nepali (2·7m.), Oriya (35·7m.), Punjabi (29·8m.), Sanskrit (fewer than 1m.), Sindhi (2·7m.), Tamil (67·4m.), Telugu (84·0m.), Urdu (55·3m.).

Thakur, R., *The Government and Politics of India*. London, 1995

National Anthem. 'Jana-gana-mana' ('Thou art the ruler of the minds of all people'); words and tune by Rabindranath Tagore.

RECENT ELECTIONS

Presidential elections were held on 18 July 2002. A. P. J. Abdul Kalam was elected against one opponent with 89·6% of votes cast.

Parliamentary elections were held in four phases between 20 April and 10 May 2004. Turn-out was 57·9%. The Indian National Congress and its allies gained 217 seats and received 34·6% of votes cast (112 seats in 1999), with the Indian National Congress (INC) winning 145 seats; the National Democratic Alliance gained 185 seats and received 35·3% of the vote (182 seats in 1999), with the Bharatiya Janata Party (BJP) winning 138 seats; the Left Front (LF) won 59 seats; Samajwadi Party (SP) 36; Bahujan Samaj Party (BSP) 19; Janata Dal (Secular) (JD(S)) 4; ind. 4; Rashtriya Lok Dal (RLD) 3. A total of ten other parties won either one or two seats and two members were nominated by the president.

Singh, V. B., *Elections in India: Data Handbook on Lok Sabha Elections, 1986–91.* Delhi, 1994

CURRENT ADMINISTRATION

President: A. P. J. Abdul Kalam; b. 1931 (sworn in 25 July 2002).

Vice-President: Bhairon Singh Shekhawat.

After the 2004 elections, despite emotional appeals from her supporters, Congress President Sonia Gandhi declined the premiership on 18 May. Manmohan Singh became India's first Sikh prime minister on 22 May.

In March 2005 the INC-led 12-party coalition government was composed as follows:

Prime Minister: Manmohan Singh; b. 1932 (INC; sworn in 22 May 2004).

Minister of Defence: Pranab Mukherjee (INC). *Human Resource Development:* Arjun Singh (INC). *Agriculture, Food and Civil Supplies, Consumer Affairs and Public Distribution:* Sharad Pawar (Nationalist Congress Party). *Railways:* Lalu Prasad Yadav (RJD). *Home Affairs:* Shivraj Patil (INC). *Chemicals and Fertilizers and Steel:* Ram Vilas Paswan (Lok Jan Shakti Party). *Coal:* Shibu Soren (Jharkhand Mukti Morcha). *Parliamentary Affairs and Urban Development:* Ghulam Nabi Azad (INC). *Information and Broadcasting and Culture:* S. Jaipal Reddy (INC). *Labour and Employment:* Chandra Shekhar Rao (Telangana Rashtra Samithi). *Finance:* P. Chidambaram (INC). *Mines:* Sish Ram Ola (INC). *Small-Scale, Agro and Rural Industries:* Mahavir Prasad (INC). *Tribal Affairs and Development of the North East:* P. R. Kyndiah (INC). *Shipping, Road Transport and Highways:* T. R. Baalu (Dravida Progressive Federation; DMK). *Textiles:* Shankersinh Vaghela (INC). *External Affairs:* K. Natwar Singh (INC). *Commerce and Industry:* Kamal Nath (INC). *Law and Justice:* H. R. Bhardwaj (INC). *Power:* P. M. Sayeed (INC). *Rural Development:* Raghubansh Prasad Singh (RJD). *Water Resources:* Priya Ranjan Dasmunsi (INC). *Petroleum and Natural Gas and Panchayati Raj:* Mani Shankar Aiyar (INC). *Youth and Sports:* Sunil Dutt (INC). *Social Justice and Empowerment:* Meira Kumar (INC). *Environment and Forests:* A. Raja (Dravida Progressive Federation; DMK). *Communication and Information Technology:* Dayanidhi Maran (Dravida Progressive Federation; DMK). *Health and Family Welfare:* Anbumani Ramdoss (Pattali Makkal Katchi).

Office of the Prime Minister: http://www.pmindia.nic.in

DEFENCE

The Supreme Command of the Armed Forces is vested in the President. As well as armed forces of 1,250,000 personnel in 2003, there are nearly 200,000 active paramilitary forces including members of the Border Security Force based mainly in the troubled Jammu and Kashmir region. Military service is voluntary but, under the amended constitution, it is regarded as a fundamental duty of every citizen to perform National Service when called upon. Defence expenditure in 2003 was US$15,508m. (US$15 per capita and 2·6% of GDP). In the period 1999–2003 India's spending on major conventional weapons was second only to that of China, at US$7·8bn.—in 2000, 2001 and 2002 China's expenditure was higher, although in 2003 that of India (at US$3·6bn.) was the highest in the world. In Sept. 2003 India announced that it would be buying 66 Hawk trainer fighter jets, with delivery expected by 2009. In Oct. 2003 agreement was reached for India to purchase Israel's sophisticated US$1bn. Phalcon early-warning radar system.

Nuclear Weapons. India's first nuclear test was in 1974. Its most recent tests were a series of five carried out in May 1998. According to the Stockholm International Peace Research Institute, India's nuclear arsenal was estimated to consist of between 30 and 40 nuclear warheads in Jan. 2004. India, known to have a nuclear weapons programme, has not signed the Comprehensive Nuclear-Test-Ban-Treaty, which is intended to bring about a ban on any nuclear explosions. According to *Deadly Arsenals*, published by the Carnegie Endowment for International Peace, India has chemical weapons and has a biological weapons research programme.

Army. The Army is organized into five commands each divided into areas, which in turn are subdivided into sub-areas.

The strength of the Army in 2003 was 1·1m. There are 30 divisions of infantry, two armoured divisions and two mechanical divisions: in all there are 355 infantry battalions, 290 artillery regiments and 55 tank battalions. Officers are trained at the Indian Military Academy, Dehra Dun (Uttaranchal). An Aviation Corps of 14 squadrons operates helicopters locally-built under licence. Army reserves number 300,000 with a further 500,000 personnel available as a second-line reserve force. There is a volunteer Territorial Army of 40,000. There are numerous paramilitary groups including the Ministry of Defence *Rashtriya Rifles* (numbering 40,000), the Indo-Tibetan Border Police (32,400), the State Armed Police (400,000), the Civil Defence (453,000), the Central Industrial Security Force (95,000) and the Ministry of Home Affairs Assam Rifles (52,500).

Navy. The Navy has three commands; Eastern (at Visakhapatnam), Western (at Bombay) and Southern (at Kochi), the latter a training and support command. The fleet is divided into two elements, Eastern and Western; and well-trained, all-volunteer personnel operate a mix of Soviet and western vessels. In May 2003 India held joint naval exercises with Russia in the Arabian Sea for the first time since the collapse of the Soviet Union.

The principal ship is the light aircraft carrier, *Viraat*, formerly HMS *Hermes*, of 29,000 tonnes, completed in 1959 and transferred to the Indian Navy in 1987 after seeing service in the Falklands War. In 2003 India began construction of another aircraft carrier and began negotiations to purchase a third from the Russian navy. The fleet includes 12 Soviet-built diesel submarines and four new German-designed boats. There are also 23 destroyers and frigates. The Naval Air force, 5,000 strong, operates 35 combat aircraft (including 20 Sea Harriers) and 75 armed helicopters. Main bases are at Bombay (main dockyard), Goa, Visakhapatnam and Calcutta on the sub-continent, Port Blair in the Andaman Islands and Lakshadweep on the Laccadive Islands.

Naval personnel in 2002 numbered 53,000 including 5,000 Naval Air Arm and 1,200 marines.

Air Force. Units of the IAF are organized into five operational commands—Western at Delhi, Central at Allahabad, Eastern at Shillong, Southern at Thiruvananthapuram and South-Western at Gandhinagar. The air force has 110,000 personnel.

Equipment includes nearly 800 combat aircraft, in 43 squadrons of aircraft, and 32 armed helicopters. Major combat types include Su-30s, MiG-21s, MiG-23s, MiG-27s, MiG-29s, *Jaguars* and Mirage 2000s. Air Force reserves numbered 140,000 in 2003.

INTERNATIONAL RELATIONS

India is a member of the UN, WTO, BIS, the Commonwealth, Asian Development Bank, Colombo Plan, SAARC and the Antarctic Treaty.

ECONOMY

Agriculture accounted for 22·7% of GDP in 2002, industry 26·6% and services 50·7%.

In the late 1990s there were ever-increasing signs of a divide between the south and west, where a modern economy is booming in cities such as Bangalore, Hyderabad and Madras, and the poorer and politically volatile areas in the north and east.

Overview. In recent years India's economic growth rate has risen, poverty has declined from 36% of the population in 1993–94 to 26% in the early 2000s and social indicators have improved. Economic reforms initiated in 1991 have helped India to become one of the world's fastest-growing economies. Foreign investment rose from almost nothing in the 1990s to US$2bn. per year. The economy has expanded by an average of 6% per annum since the early 1990s. Financial market confidence in India is strong, with returns of 83% in 2003, the highest among emerging markets. Manufacturing is the most regulated sector and the weakest performer while services, the least regulated sector, is the strongest performer. The economy remains fairly closed and is placed amongst the most restrictive countries by the IMF. A large, educated English-speaking labour force has helped economic development and the country is an exporter of IT and software workers. India has developed a diversified industrial base and a relatively large and sophisticated financial sector. Its IT sector has experienced rapid growth, with revenues estimated at US$8bn. in 2000. Software exports accounted for 14% of total merchandise exports in 2001.

Currency. A decimal system of coinage was introduced in 1957. The Indian *rupee* (INR) is divided into 100 *paise*. The paper currency consists of Reserve Bank notes and Government of India currency notes.

Foreign exchange reserves were US$54,703m. in June 2002 and gold reserves 11·50m. troy oz. Inflation was 4·3% in 2002 and 3·8% in 2003.

The official exchange rate was abolished on 1 March 1993; the rupee now has a single market exchange rate and is convertible. The pound sterling is the currency of intervention. Total money supply in May 2002 was Rs 4,191·12bn.

Budget. Revenue and expenditure of the central government for years ending 31 March, in Rs 1m.:

	2001–02	*2002–03*	*2003–04*
Revenue	2,573,600	2,958,000	3,222,300
Expenditure	3,559,200	4,041,100	4,446,100

Breakdown of revenue and expenditure of the central government for 1999–2000, in Rs 1m.:

Revenue		*Expenditure*	
Current Revenue	2,326,900	Economic Affairs and Services	492,600
Tax	*1,717,500*	Defence	467,900
including:		General Public Services including Public Order	195,900
Domestic taxes on goods and services	653,500	Housing and Community Amenities	156,200
Tax on incomes, profits and capital gains	575,600	Other	1,700,500
Non-tax	*609,400*	including Interest Payments	868,800
Capital Revenue	22,800		

VAT was introduced on 1 April 2005, at 12·5% (reduced rate, 4%).

Performance. India has one of the fastest-growing economies in Asia. Real GDP growth for 1998 was 5·8%, indicating that India managed to avoid the worst of the Asian crisis. In 1999 a growth rate of 6·7% was recorded, followed by 5·4% in 2000, 4·9% in 2001, 5·0% in 2002 and 7·2% in 2003. Critics claim that growth needs to be at least 8% in order to tackle the country's poverty. Recent years have seen a growing disparity between the performance of India's richest states, mainly in the south and the west, and the poorest states, generally in the east and the north.

Total GDP in 2003 was US$599·0bn.

Banking and Finance. The Reserve Bank, the central bank for India, was established in 1934 and started functioning on 1 April 1935 as a shareholder's bank; it became a nationalized institution on 1 Jan. 1949. It has the sole right of issuing currency notes. The *Governor* is Yaga Venugopal Reddy. The Bank acts as adviser to the government on financial problems and is the banker for central and state governments, commercial banks and some other financial institutions. It manages the rupee public debt of central and state governments and is the custodian of the country's exchange reserve.

The commercial banking system consisted of 298 scheduled banks (*i.e.*, banks which are included in the 2nd schedule to the Reserve Bank Act) in Dec. 1999. 223 of these were in the public sector, of which 196 were Regional Rural Banks. The other 27 (which comprise the State Bank of India and its seven associate banks and 19 nationalized banks) were regular commercial banks and account for more than 75% of deposits and about 75% of bank credit of all scheduled commercial banks. Total deposits in commercial banks, March 2002, stood at Rs 11,234,160m. The business of non-scheduled banks forms less than 0·1% of commercial bank business. The State Bank of India acts as the agent of the Reserve Bank for transacting government business as well as undertaking commercial functions. In 2002 India received US$3·4bn. worth of foreign direct investment.

There are stock exchanges in Ahmedabad, Bombay, Calcutta, Delhi, Madras and 18 other centres.

Weights and Measures. The metric system is official but Imperial measurements are still used in commerce. Frequent use is made in figures of the terms *lakh* (=100,000) and *crore* (= 10m).

ENERGY AND NATURAL RESOURCES

Environment. India's carbon dioxide emissions from the consumption and flaring of fossil fuels were equivalent to 0·98 tonnes per capita in 2002, well below the global average and the lowest figure for any major industrial country. A 2003 report issued by the US Department of Energy stated that India was the world's fifth largest emitter of carbon dioxide but that in 2000 emissions decreased by 0·6% to 292m. tonnes of carbon. An *Environmental Sustainability Index* compiled for the World Economic Forum meeting in Feb. 2002 ranked India 116th in the world out of 142 countries analysed, with 41·6%. The index measured the ability of countries to maintain favourable environmental conditions and examined various factors including pollution levels and the use or abuse of natural resources.

Electricity. Installed capacity in 2000 was 93m. kW. In 2002 nearly 520,000 villages out of 600,000 had electricity. Production of electricity in 2001 was 533·3bn. kWh, of which approximately 81·7% came from thermal stations, 3·4% from nuclear stations and 14·5% from hydro-electric stations. In 2003 there were 14 nuclear reactors in use. An additional eight reactors were either under construction or approved to start construction. Electricity consumption per capita in 2001 was 473 kWh.

Oil and Gas. The Oil and Natural Gas Corporation Ltd and Oil India Ltd are the only producers of crude oil. Production 2001–02, 32·0m. tonnes. The main fields are in Assam and Gujarat and offshore in the Gulf of Cambay (the Bombay High field). India imports 70% of its annual oil requirement. There were proven reserves of 5·4bn. bbls. in 2002. Oil refinery capacity, 2002, was 2·3m. bbls. daily. Natural gas production, 2002, 28·4bn. cu. metres with 760bn. cu. metres of proven reserves in 2002.

Water. By 2000, 76·34m. ha of irrigation potential had been created of which 57·24m. ha was utilized. Irrigation projects have formed an important part of all the Five-Year Plans. The possibilities of diverting rivers into canals being nearly exhausted, the emphasis is now on damming the monsoon surplus flow and diverting that. Ultimate potential of irrigation is assessed at 110m. ha by 2025, total cultivated land being 185m. ha.

A Ganges water-sharing accord was signed with Bangladesh in 1997, ending a 25-year dispute which had hindered and dominated relations between the two countries.

Minerals. The coal industry was nationalized in 1973. Production, 2000, 316m. tonnes; recoverable reserves were estimated at 77bn. tonnes (1997). Production of other minerals (in 1,000 tonnes): iron ore (2001), 79,200; lignite (2000), 22,406; salt (2002), 14,800; bauxite (2001), 8,585; copper ore (1996–97), 3,900; chromite (2002), 1,900; manganese ore (1996–97), 1,836; aluminium (2001), 624; silver (2001), 49,500 kg; gold (2001), 3,700 kg. Other important minerals are lead, zinc, limestone, apatite and phosphorite, dolomite, magnesite and uranium. Value of mineral production, 1996–97, Rs 330,204·3m. of which mineral fuels produced Rs 275,053m., metallic minerals Rs 24,295m. and non-metallic Rs 11,392·4m.

Agriculture. About 70% of the people are dependent on the land for their living. The farming year runs from July to June through three crop seasons: kharif (monsoon); rabi (winter) and summer. In 2001 there were 161,750,000 ha of arable land and 8,150,000 ha of permanent cropland. 54,800,000 ha were irrigated in 2001. There were 1,525,000 tractors and 4,200 harvester-threshers in 2001. The average size of holding for the whole of India in 1991 was 1·57 ha. Of the total 71m. rural households possessing operational holdings, 34% hold on the average less than 0·2 ha of land each.

Agricultural production, 2000 (in 1,000 tonnes): sugarcane, 315,000; rice, 134,150; wheat, 74,251; potatoes, 23,500; mangoes, 15,642; bananas, 13,900; maize, 11,500; coconuts, 11,100; sorghum, 9,500; millet, 9,000; seed cotton, 6,172; rapeseed, 6,120; aubergines, 6,100; groundnuts, 6,100; cassava, 5,800; tomatoes, 5,500; onions, 5,467; soybeans, 5,400; chick-peas, 5,350; cauliflowers, 5,250; dry beans, 4,340; cabbages, 4,250; cottonseed, 4,115; pumpkins and squash, 3,400. Jute is grown in West Bengal (70% of total yield), Bihar and Assam: total yield, 1,740,000 tonnes. The coffee industry is growing: the main cash varieties are Arabica and Robusta (main growing areas Karnataka, Kerala and Tamil Nadu). India is the world's leading producer of a number of agricultural crops, including mangoes, millet, bananas and chick-peas.

The tea industry is important, with production concentrated in Assam, West Bengal, Tamil Nadu and Kerala. India is the world's largest tea producer. The 2000 crop was 749,000 tonnes; exports in 1997, 203,000 tonnes, valued at US$432m.

Livestock (2000): cattle, 218·8m.; goats, 123·0m.; buffaloes, 93·8m.; sheep, 57·9m.; pigs, 16·5m.; asses, 1·0m.; camels, 1·0m.; horses, 990,000; chickens, 402m. There are more cattle and buffaloes in India than in any other country.

Fertilizer consumption in 1996–97 was 14·31m. tonnes.

Opium. By international agreement the poppy is cultivated under licence, and all raw opium is sold to the central government. Opium, other than for wholly medical use, is available only to registered addicts.

Forestry. The lands under the control of the state forest departments are classified as 'reserved forests' (forests intended to be permanently maintained for the supply of timber, etc., or for the protection of water supply, etc.), 'protected forests' and 'unclassed' forest land. In 2000 the total forest area was 64·11m. ha (21·6% of the land area). Main types are teak and sal. About 16% of the area is inaccessible, of which about 45% is potentially productive. In 2001, 296·23m. cu. metres of roundwood were produced, making India the second largest producer after the USA (8·9% of the world total in 2001). Most states have encouraged planting small areas around villages.

Fisheries. Total catch (2001) was 3,762,600 tonnes, of which Kerala, Tamil Nadu and Maharashtra produced about half. Of the total catch, 2,787,890 tonnes were marine fish. There were 46,918 mechanized boats in 1994–95. There were also 31,726 motorized traditional crafts and 159,481 traditional crafts in 1994–95. There were 11,440 fishermen's co-operatives with 1,250,379 members in 1995–96; total sales, Rs 1,495m. (1994–95).

INDUSTRY

The leading companies by market capitalization in India, excluding banking and finance, in May 2004 were: the Oil & Natural Gas Corporation Ltd (ONGC), US$19·7bn.; Reliance Industries, a chemical production company (US$13·2bn.); and Indian Oil (US$8·6bn.).

The information technology industry has become increasingly important, leading Prime Minister Atal Vajpayee to state in 1999 that 'I believe that IT is India's tomorrow'. In 1994–95 the software industry had been valued at just Rs 63,450m., but by 1998–99 it was worth Rs 247,815m., with a forecast for 1999–2000 of a further rapid expansion, making it worth Rs 361,000m. (US$8,390m.).

There is expansion in petrochemicals, based on the oil and associated gas of the Bombay High field, and gas from Krishna-Godavari Basin, Rajasthan, Tripura, Assam and Bassein field. Small industries numbering 2·72m. (initial outlay on capital equipment of less than Rs 30m.) are important; they employ about 15·26m. and produced (1995–96) goods worth Rs 3,164,210m.

Industrial production, 2000 unless otherwise indicated (in 1,000 tonnes): cement, 99,227; distillate fuel oil, 39,447; crude steel (2002), 28,800; pig iron (2002), 24,300; sugar (2002), 19,525; residual fuel oil, 11,245; nitrogenous fertilizers, 11,025; kerosene, 8,321; petrol, 7,849; sulphuric acid, 5,540; paper and paperboard (2001), 3,973; phosphate fertilizer, 3,745; jute goods (1995–96), 1,114; man-made fibre and yarn (1995–96), 468; 3,756,000 motorcycles, mopeds and scooters; 2,854,719 diesel engines (2001); 1,648,000 electric motors (2001); 859,927 cars and lorries (2002); 60·58bn. cigarettes (2001).

Labour. At the 2001 census there were 402·5m. workers, of whom 127·6m. were cultivators; 107·4m. agricultural labourers; and 16·4m. worked in household industry, manufacturing, processing, servicing and repairs. Workdays lost by industrial disputes, 1999, 26·79m., through strikes and lockouts.

The unemployment rate was 5·2% of the workforce in 1997.

Companies. The total number of companies limited by shares at work as on 31 March 2002 was 589,246; estimated paid-up capital was Rs 3,870,239m. Of these, 76,279 were public limited companies with an estimated paid-up capital of Rs 2,587,149m., and 512,967 private limited companies (Rs 1,283,090m.).

During 2001–02 there were 21,059 new limited companies registered in the Indian Union under the Companies Act 1956 with a total authorized capital of Rs 53,156m.; 14 were government companies (Rs 5,781m.). There were 479 companies with unlimited liability and 3,007 companies with liability limited by guarantee and association not for profit also registered in 2001–02. During 2001–02, 760 non-government companies with an aggregate paid-up capital of Rs 144·7m. went into liquidation or were struck off the register.

On 31 March 2002 there were 1,261 government companies at work with a total paid-up capital of Rs 1,099,155m.; 658 were public limited companies and 603 were private limited companies. There were 587,985 non-government companies at work on 31 March 2002. Of these 75,621 were public limited companies and 512,364 were private limited companies.

On 31 March 2002, 1,285 companies incorporated elsewhere were reported to have a place of business in India; 241 were of UK and 286 of US origin.

Co-operative Movement. In 1995–96 there were 411,000 co-operative societies with a total membership of 197·8m. These included Primary Co-operative Marketing Societies, State Co-operative Marketing Federations and the National Agricultural Co-operative Marketing Federation of India. There were also State Co-operative Commodity Marketing Federations, and 29 general purpose and 16 Special Commodities Marketing Federations.

There were, in 1995–96, 28 State Co-operative Banks, 362 District Central Co-operative Banks, 90,783 Primary Agricultural Credit Societies, 20 State Land Development Banks, and 2,970 Primary Land Development Banks which provide long-term credits.

Trade Unions. The Indian National Trade Union Congress (INTUC) had 3,987 affiliated unions with a total membership of 6,726,569 in March 2000.

INTERNATIONAL TRADE

Foreign investment is encouraged by a tax holiday on income up to 6% of capital employed for five years. There are special depreciation allowances, and customs and excise concessions, for export industries. Proposals for investment ventures involving up to 51% foreign equity require only the Reserve Bank's approval under new liberalized policy. In Feb. 1991 India resumed trans-frontier trade with China, which had ceased in 1962.

Foreign debt was US$104,429m. in 2002.

Imports and Exports. The external trade of India (excluding land-borne trade with Tibet and Bhutan) was as follows (in Rs 100,000):

	Imports	*Exports and Re-exports*
1999–2000	21,552,844	15,956,139
2000–01	23,087,276	20,357,101
2001–02	24,519,972	20,901,797

The distribution of commerce by countries was as follows in the year ended 31 March 2002 (in Rs 100,000):

Countries	*Exports to*	*Imports from*	*Countries*	*Exports to*	*Imports from*
Afghanistan	11,623	8,357	Brazil	104,450	146,974
Argentina	30,818	207,937	Canada	278,910	252,497
Australia	199,363	622,903	China	454,004	971,192
Austria	36,405	37,113	Czech Republic	19,594	18,423
Bahrain	36,052	63,912	Denmark	72,424	57,523
Bangladesh	477,958	28,194	Egypt	220,686	47,664
Belgium	663,213	1,317,727	France	450,689	402,640

Countries	Exports to	Imports from	Countries	Exports to	Imports from
Germany	852,901	967,238	Poland	51,653	14,972
Hong Kong	1,128,560	347,609	Qatar	23,371	43,730
Hungary	22,270	11,406	Romania	5,429	23,094
Indonesia	254,535	494,476	Russia	380,669	255,393
Iran	120,676	135,360	Saudi Arabia	394,142	221,284
Israel	204,131	204,001	Senegal	10,985	63,715
Italy	575,415	336,125	Singapore	463,713	621,945
Japan	720,355	1,023,680	South Africa	168,326	687,191
Jordan	38,582	100,038	Spain	322,972	80,494
North Korea	76,339	1,523	Sri Lanka	300,885	32,134
South Korea	224,807	544,341	Sweden	73,575	191,821
Kuwait	98,364	35,143	Switzerland	195,109	1,369,115
Malaysia	368,989	540,605	Taiwan	171,742	266,729
Mexico	113,243	29,681	Tanzania	43,295	36,290
Morocco	26,494	127,045	Thailand	301,954	201,779
Myanmar	29,041	178,572	Tunisia	22,115	49,675
Nepal	102,280	169,756	Turkey	104,471	33,078
Netherlands	412,001	222,467	UAE	1,188,381	436,423
New Zealand	29,669	39,189	UK	1,030,561	1,222,440
Nigeria	268,574	41,548	Ukraine	38,353	79,588
Norway	25,895	22,881	USA	4,060,175	1,502,112
Pakistan	68,679	30,883	Vietnam	104,051	9,019
Philippines	118,175	45,233	Yemen	70,460	22,802

The value (in Rs 100,000) of the leading articles of merchandise was as follows in the year ended 31 March 2002:

Exports	*Value*
Carpet products (excluding silk)	178,759
Cashew nuts	164,713
Coffee	109,492
Cotton yarn, fabrics and made-up articles	1,465,492
Drugs, pharmaceuticals and fine chemicals	983,292
Dyes, intermediates and coal tar chemicals	262,199
Electronic goods	558,599
Engineering goods	2,740,621
Gems and jewellery	3,484,506
Handicrafts (excluding handmade carpets)	261,806
Inorganic and organic agro-chemicals	392,827
Iron ore	203,355
Leather garments	180,635
Leather goods	194,182
Man-made yarn, fabrics and made-up articles	507,892
Marine products	589,686
Meat preparations	119,304
Oil meals	226,293
Petroleum, crude oil and related products	994,815
Plastics and linoleum	470,889
Processed minerals	167,550
Ready-made garments, including clothing accessories of all textile materials	2,387,762
Residual chemicals and allied products	182,562
Rice	317,414
Rubber manufactured products (except footwear)	178,074
Spices	149,697
Tea	171,922

Imports	*Value*
Artificial resins, plastic materials etc.	321,480
Chemical materials and products	211,964
Coal, coke and briquettes, etc.	545,274
Computer software in physical form	103,272
Electronic goods	1,803,719
Fertilizers, manufactured	216,879
Gold	1,988,920
Inorganic chemicals	568,157
Iron and steel	375,877
Machinery other than electric and electronic	1,416,846
Manufactures of metals	194,124
Medicinal and pharmaceutical products	202,658

Imports	*Value*
Metalliferous ores and metal scrap	545,462
Newsprint	117,055
Non-ferrous metal	308,686
Organic chemicals	767,028
Pearls, precious and semi-precious stones	2,204,599
Petroleum, crude oil and related products	6,676,986
Professional instruments other than electronic	496,507
Project goods	271,355
Pulp and waste paper	140,525
Pulses	316,016
Silver	196,460
Textile yarn, fabrics and made-up articles	140,745
Transport equipment	548,187
Vegetable oils (edible)	646,497
Wood and wood products	258,387

Technology industries have become increasingly important in recent years, with software exports having grown more than 50% annually each year during the 1990s. In 1998–99 software exports were worth Rs 109,400m. (US$2,650m.), with 61% going to the USA and Canada, and 23% to Europe. Exports grew by 67·5% in 1998–99 compared to 1997–98.

In 2001–02 the main export markets (percentage of total trade) were: USA, 19·4%; United Arab Emirates, 5·7%; Hong Kong, 5·4%; UK, 4·9%; Japan, 3·4%. Main import suppliers in 2001–02 were: USA, 6·1%; Switzerland, 5·6%; Belgium, 5·4%; UK, 5·0%; Japan, 4·2%.

COMMUNICATIONS

Roads. In 1999 there were 2·53m. km of roads, of which 1·45m. km were surfaced. Roads are divided into six main administrative classes, namely: national highways, state highways, other public works department (PWD) roads, *Panchayati Raj* roads, urban roads and project roads. The national highways (49,585 km in 1999) connect capitals of states, major ports and foreign highways. The national highway system is linked with the UN Economic and Social Commission for Asia and the Pacific international highway system. The state highways are the main trunk roads of the states, while the other PWD roads and *Panchayati Raj* roads connect subsidiary areas of production and markets with distribution centres, and form the main link between headquarters and neighbouring districts. A US$12bn. ten-year highway plan is currently under way that aims to have India's main cities, ports and regions linked by more than 13,000 km of highways by 2009.

There were (2000) 6,042,000 passenger cars, 35,490,000 motorcycles and scooters, 559,000 buses and coaches, and 2,681,000 trucks and vans. In 1998 there were 298,052 road accidents resulting in 62,721 deaths.

Rail. The Indian railway system is government-owned (under the control of the Railway Board). Following reconstruction there are 16 zones, seven of which were created in 2002:

Zone	*Headquarters*	*Year of Creation*
Central	Bombay	1951
Southern	Madras	1951
Western	Bombay	1951
Eastern	Calcutta	1952
Northern	Delhi	1952
North Eastern	Gorakhpur	1952
South Eastern	Calcutta	1955
North East Frontier	Guwahati	1958
South Central	Secunderabad	1966
East Central	Hajipur	2002
East Coast	Bhubaneswar	2002
North Central	Allahabad	2002
North Western	Jaipur	2002
South East Central	Bilaspur	2002
South Western	Hubli	2002
West Central	Jabalpur	2002

The total length of the Indian railway network is 63,000 km (14,600 electrified), with the Northern zone having the longest network, at 11,040 km.

The Konkan Railway (760 km of 1,676 mm gauge) linking Roha and Mangalore opened in 1996. It is operated as a separate entity.

Principal gauges are 1,676 mm (40,620 km) and 1 metre (18,501 km), with networks also of 762 mm and 610 mm gauge (3,794 km).

Passenger-km travelled in 2001–02 came to 493·5bn. and freight tonne-km to 333·2bn. Revenue (1995–96) from passengers, Rs 61,244·9m.; from goods, Rs 152,904m.

There are metros in Calcutta (16·4 km), Delhi (23·0 km) and Madras (15·5 km).

Civil Aviation. The main international airports are at Bombay, Calcutta, Delhi (Indira Gandhi), Madras and Thiruvananthapuram, with some international flights from Ahmedabad, Amritsar, Bangalore, Calicut, Goa and Hyderabad. Air transport was nationalized in 1953 with the formation of two Air Corporations: Air India for long-distance international air services, and Indian Airlines for air services within India and to adjacent countries. Domestic air transport has been opened to private companies, the largest of which is Jet Airways. In 1999 Indian Airlines carried 5,912,100 passengers, Jet Airways 4,647,400 and Air India 3,132,600 passengers.

In 2003 Air India operated routes to Africa (Dar es Salaam and Nairobi); to Mauritius; to Europe (Frankfurt, London, Moscow, Paris, Vienna and Zürich); to western Asia (Abu Dhabi, Al Ain, Bahrain, Damman, Doha, Dubai, Jeddah, Kuwait, Muscat and Riyadh); to east Asia (Bangkok, Hong Kong, Jakarta, Kuala Lumpur, Osaka, Seoul, Singapore and Tokyo); and to North America (Chicago and New York). Indian Airlines operated international flights in 2003 to Almaty, Bahrain, Bangkok, Bishkek, Colombo, Dhaka, Doha, Dubai, Fujairah, Kathmandu, Kuala Lumpur, Kuwait, Malé, Muscat, Rangoon (Yangon), Ras-al-Khaimah, Sharjah and Singapore. Flights from Delhi to Lahore were restored in Jan. 2004. India's first budget airline, Air Deccan, began operations in 2003.

In 2000 Bombay was the busiest airport, handling 11,538,006 passengers (6,934,116 on domestic flights) and 287,800 tonnes of freight, followed by Delhi, with 8,395,736 passengers (4,900,597 on domestic flights) and 235,425 tonnes of freight.

Shipping. In 2000 the merchant fleet comprised 987 vessels (of 100 gross tons or more) totalling 6·66m. GRT, including 122 oil tankers of 3·00m. GRT. Cargo traffic of major ports, 2001–02, was as follows:

Port	*Total (1m. tonnes)*	*Unloaded (1m. tonnes)*	*Loaded (1m. tonnes)*	*Transshipment (1m. tonnes)*
Bombay	26·71	16·14	9·21	1·38
Cochin	12·21	10·15	2·07	0·00
Haldia	25·12	18·50	6·62	0·01
Jawaharlal Nehru	24·09	12·18	11·01	0·91
Kandla	37·85	28·52	7·77	1·57
Madras	36·46	23·22	13·14	0·10
Mormugao	22·93	4·60	18·31	0·02
New Mangalore	17·51	8·77	8·75	0·00
Paradip	21·13	6·66	14·48	0·00
Tuticorin	13·23	9·91	3·32	0·00
Visakhapatnam	44·37	17·87	16·91	9·57

There are about 3,700 km of major rivers navigable by motorized craft, of which 2,000 km are used. Canals, 4,300 km, of which 900 km are navigable by motorized craft.

Telecommunications. The telephone system is in the hands of the Telecommunications Department, except in Delhi and Bombay, which are served by a public corporation. Telephone subscribers numbered 53,903,000 in 2002, equivalent to 51·7 for every 1,000 persons; 3·68m. people were still on the waiting list for a line in 1999. There were 12·69m. mobile phone subscribers and 7·50m. PCs in use in 2002, and 150,000 fax machines in 1997. India had 16,580,000 Internet users in 2002.

Postal Services. In 1998 there were 153,021 post offices. India has more post offices than any other country. In 1998 a total of 16,394m. pieces of mail were processed, or 16 items per person.

SOCIAL INSTITUTIONS

Justice. All courts form a single hierarchy, with the Supreme Court at the head, which constitutes the highest court of appeal. Immediately below it are the High

Courts and subordinate courts in each state. Every court in this chain administers the whole law of the country, whether made by Parliament or by the state legislatures.

The states of Andhra Pradesh, Assam (in common with Nagaland, Meghalaya, Manipur, Mizoram, Tripura and Arunachal Pradesh), Bihar, Gujarat, Himachal Pradesh, Jammu and Kashmir, Karnataka, Kerala, Madhya Pradesh, Maharashtra (in common with Goa and the Union Territories of Daman and Diu, and Dadra and Nagar Haveli), Orissa, Punjab (in common with the state of Haryana and the Union Territory of Chandigarh), Rajasthan, Tamil Nadu (in common with the Union Territory of Pondicherry), Uttar Pradesh, West Bengal and Sikkim each have a High Court. There is a separate High Court for Delhi. For the Andaman and Nicobar Islands the Calcutta High Court, for Pondicherry the High Court of Madras and for Lakshadweep the High Court of Kerala are the highest judicial authorities. The Allahabad High Court has a Bench at Lucknow, the Bombay High Court has Benches at Nagpur, Aurangabad and Panaji, the Gauhati High Court has Benches at Kohima, Aizwal, Imphal and Agartala, the Madhya Pradesh High Court has Benches at Gwalior and Indore, the Patna High Court has a Bench at Ranchi and the Rajasthan High Court has a Bench at Jaipur. Judges and Division Courts of the Guwahati High Court also sit in Meghalaya. Similarly, judges and Division Courts of the Calcutta High Court also sit in the Andaman and Nicobar Islands. High Courts have also been established in the new states of Chhattisgarh, Jharkhand and Uttaranchal. Below the High Court each state is divided into a number of districts under the jurisdiction of district judges who preside over civil courts and courts of sessions. There are a number of judicial authorities subordinate to the district civil courts. On the criminal side magistrates of various classes act under the overall supervision of the High Court.

In Oct. 1991 the Supreme Court upheld capital punishment by hanging. In 2004 there were two executions, the first ones since 1995.

The population in penal institutions in June 2002 was 304,893 (29 per 100,000 of national population).

Police. The states control their own police forces. The Home Affairs Minister of the central government co-ordinates the work of the states. The Indian Police Service provides senior officers for the state police forces. The Central Bureau of Investigation functions under the control of the Cabinet Secretariat.

The cities of Pune, Ahmedabad, Nagpur, Bangalore, Calcutta, Madras, Bombay, Delhi and Hyderabad have separate police commissionerates.

Religion. India is a secular state; any worship is permitted, but the state itself has no religion. The principal religions in 2001 were: Hindus, 759m.; Sunni Muslims, 92m.; Shia Muslims, 31m.; Sikhs, 22m.; Protestants, 15m.; Roman Catholics, 14m.; Buddhists, 7m.; Jains, 4m. In Sept. 2003 the Roman Catholic church had five cardinals.

Education. Adult literacy was 58·0% in 2001 (69·0% among males and 46·4% among females). Of the states and territories, Kerala and Mizoram have the highest rates.

Educational Organization. Education is the concurrent responsibility of state and Union governments. In the Union Territories it is the responsibility of the central government. The Union government is also directly responsible for the central universities and all institutions declared by parliament to be of national importance; the promotion of Hindi as the federal language and co-ordinating and maintaining standards in higher education, research, science and technology. Professional education rests with the Ministry or Department concerned. There is a Central Advisory Board of Education to advise the Union and the State governments on any educational question which may be referred to it.

School Education. The school system has four stages: primary, middle, secondary and senior secondary.

Primary education is imparted either at independent primary (or junior basic) schools or primary classes attached to middle or secondary schools. The period of instruction varies from four to five years and the medium of instruction is in most cases the mother tongue of the child or the regional language. Free primary education is available for all children. Legislation for compulsory education has been passed by some state governments and Union Territories but it is not practicable to enforce compulsion when the reasons for non-attendance are socio-economic.

There are residential schools for country children. The period for the middle stage varies from two to three years.

Higher Education. Higher education is given in arts, science or professional colleges, universities and all-India educational or research institutions. In 1995–96 there were 166 universities, four institutes established under state legislature act, 11 institutions of national importance and 37 institutions deemed as universities. Of the universities, 13 are central: Aligarh Muslim University; Banaras Hindu University; Delhi University; Hyderabad University; Jamia Millia Islamia, New Delhi; Jawaharlal Nehru University; North Eastern Hill University; Visva Bharati; Pondicherry University; Baba Sahib B. R. Ambedkar University; Assam University; Tezpur University; and Nagaland University. The rest are state universities. Total enrolment at universities, 1995–96, 6,425,624, of which 5,667,400 were undergraduates. Women students numbered 2,191,138.

Technical Education. The number of institutions awarding degrees in engineering and technology in 1996–97 was 418, and those awarding diplomas, 1,029; the former admitted 328,399 students, the latter 357,891 including 58,454 female students.

Adult Education. The Directorate of Adult Education, established in 1971, is the national resource centre.

There is also a National Literacy Mission.

Educational statistics for 2001–02:

Type of recognized institution	*No. of institutions*	*No. of students on rolls*	*No. of teachers*
Primary/junior basic schools	664,041	113,900,000	1,928,000
Middle/senior basic schools	219,626	44,800,000	1,468,000
High/higher secondary schools[1]	133,492	30,500,000	1,777,000
Colleges for professional education	2,409	237,509[2]	—
Colleges for general education	8,737	6,425,624[2]	239,488[2]

[1]Including Junior Colleges. [2]1996–97.

Expenditure. Total budgeted central expenditure on revenue account of education and other departments 1997–98 was estimated at Rs 46,383m. Total public expenditure on education, sport, arts and youth welfare during the Eighth (1992–97) Plan, Rs 212,170·2m.; Seventh Plan spending on adult education, Rs 3,007m. in the central and Rs 6,098m. in the state sectors. In 1999–2000 total expenditure on education came to 4·1% of GNP and 12·7% of total government spending.

Health. Medical services are primarily the responsibility of the states. The Union government has sponsored major schemes for disease prevention and control which are implemented nationally.

Total central expenditure on health and family welfare in 1997–98 was Rs 14,166·2m. on revenue account. In 1991 there were 15,067 hospitals, and in 1992, 410,875 doctors. In 1993 there were an estimated 1,364 people per hospital bed.

In 2001 approximately 221m. people, representing 21% of the population, were undernourished. In 1979, 38% of the population had been undernourished.

Approximately 3·7m. Indians are HIV-infected, a number only exceeded in South Africa (and equivalent to nearly 9% of all the people believed to be infected worldwide). Some suggestions indicate that there may be as many as 15m. HIV-positive people by 2010.

CULTURE

World Heritage Sites. There are 26 sites under Indian jurisdiction that appear on the UNESCO World Heritage List. They are (with year entered on list): Ajanta Caves (1983), Ellora Caves (1983), Agra Fort (1983), Taj Mahal (1983), Sun Temple, Konarak (1984), Monuments at Mahabalipuram (1985), Kaziranga National Park (1985), Manas Wildlife Sanctuary (1985), Keoladeo National Park (1985), Churches and Convents of Goa (1986), Monuments at Khajuraho (1986), Monuments at Hampi (1986), Fatehpur Sikri (1986), Monuments at Pattadakal (1987), Elephanta Caves (1987), Brihadisvara Temple, Thanjavur (1987), Sundarbans National Park (1987), Nanda Devi National Park (1988), Buddhist Monuments at Sanchi (1989), Humayan's Tomb, Delhi (1993), Qutb Minar and its Monuments, Delhi (1993), Darjeeling Himalayan Railway (1999), Mahabodhi Temple Complex at Bodh Gaya (2002), the Rock Shelters of Bhimbetka (2003), Champaner-Pavagadh

Archaeological Park (2004) and the Chhatrapati Shivaji Terminus—formerly Victoria Terminus (2004) in Bombay.

Broadcasting. The national television (Doordarshan) and radio (All India Radio, or Akashwani) networks are state-owned. Satellite broadcasting is dominated by AajTak, Star and Zee TV. In March 1997 there were 187 radio stations and 297 transmitters, 19 channels and 41 programme production centres. Television reached 85·8% of the population, through a network of 834 transmitters (colour by PAL). There were estimated to be 123m. radio sets and 79m. TV sets in 2000. There were 18m. cable TV subscribers in 1997—approximately 29% of households that had TV licences. By 2001 the number of TV sets had increased to 85m. and cable subscribers to 40m.

Cinema. In 1997 there were 21,801 cinemas with a total attendance of 3·58bn. In 1990, 948 full length films were produced.

Press. There were 41,000 registered newspapers in March 1996, with a total circulation of 72·3m. In 1994 there were 369 dailies in 18 languages with a total circulation of 20m. Hindi papers have the highest number and circulation, followed by English, then Urdu, Bengali and Marathi. The newspaper with the highest circulation is *Kerala Kaumudi* (daily average of 1·7m. copies in 1999). In 1998 a total of 14,085 book titles were published.

It was estimated in 1999 that 29% of the electorate of 620m. for the general election had no access to any sort of news media.

Tourism. In 2000 there were 2,641,000 foreign tourists, spending US$3·30bn. Of 2,359,000 foreign tourists in 1998, over 360,000 were from the UK, 229,000 from the USA and 107,000 from Sri Lanka.

Calendar. The Indian National Calendar, adopted in 1957, is dated from the Saka era (Indian dynasty beginning AD 78). It uses the same year-length as the Gregorian calendar (also used for administrative and informal purposes) but begins on 22 March. Local and religious variations are also used.

DIPLOMATIC REPRESENTATIVES

Of India in the United Kingdom (India House, Aldwych, London, WC2B 4NA)
High Commissioner: Kamalesh Sharma.

Of the United Kingdom in India (Chanakyapuri, New Delhi 110021)
High Commissioner: Sir Michael Arthur, KCMG.

Of India in the USA (2107 Massachusetts Ave., NW, Washington, D.C., 20008)
Ambassador: Ronen Sen.

Of the USA in India (Shanti Path, Chanakyapuri, New Delhi 110021)
Ambassador: David C. Mulford.

Of India to the United Nations
Ambassador: Nirupam Sen.

Of India to the European Union
Ambassador: Pradeep Kumar Singh.

FURTHER READING

Bhambhri, C. P., *The Political Process in India, 1947–91*. Delhi, 1991
Bose, S. and Jalal, A. (eds.) *Nationalism, Democracy and Development: State and Politics in India*. OUP, 1997
Brown, J., *Modern India: The Origins of an Asian Democracy*. 2nd ed. OUP, 1994
Derbyshire, I., *India*. [Bibliography] 2nd ed. ABC-Clio, Oxford and Santa Barbara (CA), 1995
Gupta, D. C., *Indian Government and Politics*. 3rd ed. London, 1992
Jaffrelot, C. (ed.) *L'Inde Contemporain de 1950 à nos Jours*. Paris, 1996
James, L., *Raj: The Making and Unmaking of British India*. Little, Brown, London, 1997
Joshi, V. and Little, I. M. D., *India's Economic Reforms, 1991–2000*. Oxford, 1996
Keay, John, *India: A History*. HarperCollins, London, 2000
Khilnani, S., *The Idea of India*. London, 1997
King, R., *Nehru and the Language Politics of India*. OUP, 1997
Metcalf, Barbara D. and Metcalf, Thomas R., *A Concise History of India*. CUP, 2001
Mohan, C. Raja, *Crossing the Rubicon: The Shaping of India's New Foreign Policy*. Penguin India, New Delhi, 2003
New Cambridge History of India. 2nd ed. 5 vols. CUP, 1994–96
Robb, Peter, *A History of India*. Palgrave Macmillan, Basingstoke, 2002
Vohra, R., *The Making of India: A Historical Survey*. Armonk (NY), 1997

National statistical office: Ministry of Statistics and Programme Implementation.
Website: http://mospi.nic.in
Census India Website: http://www.censusindia.net
Other more specialized titles are listed under CONSTITUTION AND GOVERNMENT *and* RECENT ELECTIONS, *above*.

STATES AND TERRITORIES

The Republic of India is composed of the following 28 States and seven centrally administered Union Territories:

States	*Capital*	*States*	*Capital*
Andhra Pradesh	Hyderabad	Maharashtra	Bombay
Arunachal Pradesh	Itanagar	Manipur	Imphal
Assam	Dispur	Meghalaya	Shillong
Bihar	Patna	Mizoram	Aizawl
Chhattisgarh	Raipur	Nagaland	Kohima
Goa	Panaji	Orissa	Bhubaneswar
Gujarat	Gandhinagar	Punjab	Chandigarh
Haryana	Chandigarh	Rajasthan	Jaipur
Himachal Pradesh	Shimla	Sikkim	Gangtok
Jammu and Kashmir	Srinagar	Tamil Nadu	Madras
Jharkhand	Ranchi	Tripura	Agartala
Karnataka	Bangalore	Uttar Pradesh	Lucknow
Kerala	Thiruvananthapuram	Uttaranchal	Dehra Dun
Madhya Pradesh	Bhopal	West Bengal	Calcutta

Union Territories. Andaman and Nicobar Islands; Chandigarh; Dadra and Nagar Haveli; Daman and Diu; Delhi; Lakshadweep; Pondicherry.

ANDHRA PRADESH

KEY HISTORICAL EVENTS

Constituted a separate state on 1 Oct. 1953, Andhra Pradesh was the undisputed Telugu-speaking area of Madras. To this region was added, on 1 Nov. 1956, the Telangana area of the former Hyderabad State, comprising the districts of Hyderabad, Medak, Nizamabad, Karimnagar, Warangal, Khammam, Nalgonda and Mahbubnagar, parts of the Adilabad district, some taluks of the Raichur, Gulbarga and Bidar districts and some revenue circles of the Nanded district. On 1 April 1960, 221·4 sq. miles in the Chingleput and Salem districts of Madras were transferred to Andhra Pradesh in exchange for 410 sq. miles from Chittoor district. The district of Prakasam was formed on 2 Feb. 1970. Hyderabad was split into two districts on 15 Aug. 1978 (Ranga Reddy and Hyderabad). A new district, Vizianagaram, was formed in 1979.

TERRITORY AND POPULATION

Andhra Pradesh is in south India and is bounded in the south by Tamil Nadu, west by Karnataka, north and northwest by Maharashtra, northeast by Chhattisgarh and Orissa and east by the Bay of Bengal. The state has an area of 275,069 sq. km and a population (2001 census) of 75,727,541; density, 275 per sq. km. The principal language is Telugu. Cities with over 250,000 population (2001 census), *see* INDIA: Territory and Population. Other large cities (2001): Anantapur, 243,359; Ramagundam, 236,623; Karimnagar, 215,782; Eluru, 215,343; Khamman, 196,763; Vizianagaram, 195,462; Machilipatnam, 183,370; Chirala, 166,877; Proddutur, 164,932; Adoni, 161,125; Nandyal, 156,216; Chittoor, 152,966; Ongole, 152,945; Tenali, 149,839; Bheemavaram, 141,975; Mahbubnagar, 139,483; Adilabad, 128,196; Hindupur, 125,056; Mancherial, 118,047; Guntakal, 117,403; Srikakulam, 117,066; Gudivada, 112,245; Nalgonda, 111,745; Madanapalle, 107,262; Kottagudem, 105,265; Dharmavaram, 103,400; Tadepalligudem, 102,303.

SOCIAL STATISTICS

Growth rate 1991–2001, 13·86%.

CONSTITUTION AND GOVERNMENT

Andhra Pradesh has a unicameral legislature; the Legislative Council was abolished in June 1985. There are 294 seats in the Legislative Assembly. For administrative purposes there are 23 districts in the state. The capital is Hyderabad.

RECENT ELECTIONS

At the State Assembly elections held on 20 and 26 April 2004 the Congress Alliance won 226 seats—of which 185 (38·2% of the vote) for the INC, 26 (6·6%) for Telangana Rashtra Samithi, 9 (2·0%) for the CPI-M and 6 (1·5%) for the CPI. The Telugu Desam Party won 47 seats (37·1%) and the BJP 2 (2·6%). Four other parties received a total of 8 seats and 11 independents were elected.

CURRENT ADMINISTRATION

Governor: Sushil Kumar Shinde; b. 1941 (took office on 4 Nov. 2004).

Chief Minister: Y. S. Rajasekhara Reddy; b. 1949 (took office on 14 May 2004).

ECONOMY

Budget. Budget estimate, 2002–03: receipts on revenue account, Rs 256,747·9m.; expenditure, Rs 281,205·0m. Annual plan, 2002–03: Rs 112,995·0m.

ENERGY AND NATURAL RESOURCES

Electricity. There are 13 hydro-electric plants, 11 thermal stations and two gas-based units. Installed capacity, 2000, 7,341 MW, power generated (1999) 6,480m. kWh. By Nov. 1996 all 27,358 villages were electrified and 1·74m. electric pump sets energized.

Oil and Gas. Crude oil is refined at Visakhapatnam in Andhra Pradesh. Oil/gas structures are found in Krishna-Godavari basin which encompasses an area of 20,000 sq. km on land and 21,000 sq. km up to 200 metres isobath off-shore. In 2001, 1,604m. cu. metres of natural gas were produced. Reserves of the land basin are estimated at 760 metric tonnes of oil and oil equivalent of gas.

Water. In 2000, more than 120 irrigation projects had created irrigation potential of 6m. ha. The Telugu Ganga joint project with Tamil Nadu, now in execution, will irrigate about 233,000 ha, besides supplying drinking water to Madras city (Tamil Nadu).

Minerals. The state is an important producer of asbestos and barytes. The Cuppadah basin is a major source of uranium and other minerals. Other important minerals are copper ore, coal, iron and limestone, steatite, mica and manganese.

Agriculture. There were (1999) about 10·7m. ha of cropped land, of which 6·8m. ha were under foodgrains. Irrigated area, 2000, 6m. ha. Production in 1999 (in tonnes): bananas, 13·73m.; pulses, 10·94m.; foodgrains, 10·37m. (rice, 8·51m.); oil seeds, 1·3m.; sugarcane, 0·2m.

Livestock (1993): cattle, 10·95m.; buffaloes, 9·13m.; sheep, 7·77m.; goats, 4·32m. There are also an estimated 100m. chickens.

Forestry. In 1999 it was estimated that forests occupy 15·7% of the total area of the state, or 43,290 sq. km; main forest products are teak, eucalyptus, cashew, casuarina, softwoods and bamboo.

Fisheries. Production 2001–02, 578,000 tonnes of marine and freshwater fish and crustaceans. This represents 10% of India's catch. The state has a coastline of 974 km.

INDUSTRY

The main industries are textile manufacture, sugar-milling, machine tools, pharmaceuticals (Andhra Pradesh commands 40% of India's pharmaceuticals industry), electronic equipment, heavy electrical machinery, aircraft parts and paper-making. There is an oil refinery at Visakhapatnam, where India's major shipbuilding yards are situated. A major steel plant at Visakhapatnam and a railway repair shop at Tirupati are functioning. At 31 March 1997 there were 1,536 large and medium industries employing 644,480 persons, and 124,209 small-scale industries employing 1m. There are cottage industries and sericulture. District Industries Centres have been set up to promote small-scale industry. Tourism is growing; the main centres are Hyderabad, Nagarjunasagar, Warangal, Arakuvalley, Horsley Hills and Tirupati.

COMMUNICATIONS

Roads. In 2002 there were 198,000 km of roads in the state including national roads. Number of vehicles as of 31 March 1997 was 2,783,220, including 2,287,029 motorcycles and scooters, 177,516 cars and jeeps and 187,863 goods vehicles.

Rail. There are 5,073 route-km of railway.

Civil Aviation. There are airports at Hyderabad, Tirupati, Vijayawada and Visakhapatnam, with regular scheduled services to Bombay, Delhi, Calcutta, Bangalore, Madras and Bhubaneswar. International flights are operated from Hyderabad to Bangkok, Dubai, Jeddah, Kuala Lumpur, Kuwait, Muscat, Sharjah and Singapore.

Shipping. The chief port is Visakhapatnam, which handles 44·6m. tonnes of cargo annually. There are minor ports at Kakinada, Machilipatnam, Bheemunipatnam, Narsapur, Krishnapatnam, Nizampatnam, Vadarevu and Kalingapatnam.

SOCIAL INSTITUTIONS

Justice. The high court of Judicature at Hyderabad has a Chief Justice and and a sanctioned strength of 39 judges.

Religion. At the 2001 census Hindus accounted for 89·14% of the population, Muslims 8·91%, Christians 1·83%, Jains 0·04%, Sikhs 0·03%, Buddhists 0·03%.

Education. In 2001, 61·11% of the population were literate (70·85% of men and 51·17% of women). There were, in 1999, 51,836 primary schools (6,237,700 students); 8,713 upper primary (2,440,000); 8,819 high schools (3,732,000). Education is free for children up to 14.

In 1995–96 there were 1,818 junior colleges (676,455 students). In 1996–97 there were 805 degree colleges (427,652 students); 46 oriented colleges and 18 universities: Osmania University, Hyderabad; Andhra University, Waltair; Sri Venkateswara University, Tirupati; Kakatiya University, Warangal; Nagarjuna University, Guntur; Sri Jawaharlal Nehru Technological University, Hyderabad; Hyderabad University, Hyderabad; N. G. Ranga Agricultural University, Hyderabad; Sri Krishnadevaraya University, Anantapur; Smt. Padmavathi Mahila Vishwavidyalayam (University for Women), Tirupati; Dr B. R. Ambedkar Open University, Hyderabad; Patti Sriramulu Telugu University, Hyderabad; N. T. R. University of Health Science, Vijayawada; Moulana Azad National Urdu University, Hyderabad; Dravidian University, Chittoor; Rashtriya Sanskrit Vidyapeeth, Tirupati; Sri Satya Sai Institute of Higher Learning, Prashanti Nilayam; National Academy of Legal Studies and Research University, Hyderabad.

Health. There were (1996) 1,947 allopathic hospitals and dispensaries, 550 Ayurvedic hospitals and dispensaries, 193 Unani and 283 homoeopathy hospitals and dispensaries. There were also 181 nature cure hospitals and (in 1999) 1,360 primary health centres. Number of beds in hospitals was 32,116.

ARUNACHAL PRADESH

KEY HISTORICAL EVENTS

Before independence the North East Frontier Agency of Assam was administered for the viceroy by a political agent working through tribal groups. After independence it became the North East Frontier Tract, administered for the central government by the Governor of Assam. In 1972 the area became the Union Territory of Arunachal Pradesh; statehood was achieved in Dec. 1986.

TERRITORY AND POPULATION

The state is in the extreme northeast of India and is bounded in the north by China, east by Myanmar, west by Bhutan and south by Assam and Nagaland. It has 13 districts and comprises the former frontier divisions of Kameng, Tirap, Subansiri, Siang and Lohit; it has an area of 83,743 sq. km and a population (2001 census) of 1,091,117; density, 13 per sq. km.

The state is mainly tribal; there are 106 tribes using about 50 tribal dialects.

SOCIAL STATISTICS

Growth rate 1991–2001, 26·21%.

CONSTITUTION AND GOVERNMENT

There is a Legislative Assembly of 60 members. The capital is Itanagar (population, 2001, 34,970).

RECENT ELECTIONS

At the State Assembly elections held on 7 Oct. 2004 the India National Congress Party won 34 seats; the Bharatiya Janata Party, 9; the Nationalist Congress Party, 2; the Arunachal Congress, 2; ind., 13.

CURRENT ADMINISTRATION

Governor: Shailendra Kumar Singh; b. 1932 (since 16 Dec. 2004).

Chief Minister: Gegong Apang (since 3 Aug. 2003; previously in office from 1980–99).

ECONOMY

Budget. Total estimated receipts, 2000–01, Rs 11,843m.; total estimated expenditure, Rs 11,451m. Plan outlay, 2000–01, Rs 6,400m.

ENERGY AND NATURAL RESOURCES

Electricity. Total installed capacity (1999), 45·43 MW. Power generated (1999): 66·28m. units. 2,188 out of 3,257 villages have electricity.

Oil and Gas. Production, 2001, 31,000 tonnes of crude oil and 23m. cu. metres of gas. Crude oil reserves are estimated at nearly 30m. tonnes.

Minerals. Coal reserves are estimated at 90·23m. tonnes; dolomite, 154·13m. tonnes; limestone, 409·35m. tonnes.

Agriculture. Production of foodgrains, 1999, 204,000 tonnes.

Forestry. Area under forest, 51,540 sq. km; revenue from forestry (1995–96) Rs 402m.

INDUSTRY

In 1996 there were 18 medium and 3,306 small industries, 80 craft or weaving centres and 225 sericulture centres. Most of the medium industries are forest-based. Industries include coal, textiles, jute, iron and steel, chemicals, tea and leather.

COMMUNICATIONS

Roads. Total length of roads in the state, 12,280 km of which 9,855 km are surfaced. There were 14,821 vehicles in 1995–96. The state had 393 km of national highway in 2000. Four towns are linked by air services.

SOCIAL INSTITUTIONS

Religion. At the 2001 census Hindus accounted for 37·04% of the population, Buddhists 12·88%, Christians 10·29%, Muslims 1·38%, Sikhs 0·14%, Jains 0·01%, others 36·22%.

Education. In 2001, 54·74% of the population were literate (64·07% of men and 44·24% of women). There were (1996–97) 1,256 primary schools with 147,676 students, 301 middle schools with 42,197 students, 157 high and higher secondary schools with 24,951 students, six colleges and two technical schools. Arunachal University, established in 1985, had four colleges and 3,240 students in 1994–95.

Health. There are (1996) 13 hospitals, ten community health centres, 42 primary health centres and 260 sub-centres. There are two TB hospitals and 11 leprosy and other hospitals. Total number of beds, 2,539.

FURTHER READING

Bose, M. L., *History of Arunachal Pradesh.* Concept Publications, New Delhi, 1997

ASSAM

KEY HISTORICAL EVENTS

Assam first became a British Protectorate at the close of the first Burmese War in 1826. In 1832 Cachar was annexed; in 1835 the Jaintia Hills were included in the East India Company's dominions, and in 1839 Assam was annexed to Bengal. In 1874 Assam was detached from Bengal and made a separate chief commissionership. On the partition of Bengal in 1905, it was united to the Eastern Districts of Bengal under a Lieut.-Governor. From 1912 the chief commissionership of Assam was revived, and in 1921 a governorship was created. On the partition of India almost the whole of the predominantly Muslim district of Sylhet was merged with East Bengal (Pakistan). Dewangiri in North Kamrup was ceded to Bhutan in 1951. The Naga Hill district, administered by the Union government since 1957, became part of Nagaland in 1962. The autonomous state of Meghalaya within Assam, comprising the districts of Garo Hills and Khasi and Jaintia Hills, came into existence on 2 April 1970, and achieved full independent statehood in Jan. 1972, when it was also decided to form a Union Territory, Mizoram (now a state), from the Mizo Hills district.

TERRITORY AND POPULATION

Assam is in northeast India, almost separated from central India by Bangladesh. It is bounded in the west by West Bengal, north by Bhutan and Arunachal Pradesh, east by Nagaland, Manipur and Myanmar, south by Meghalaya, Bangladesh, Mizoram and Tripura. The area of the state is now 78,438 sq. km. Population (2001 census) 26,638,407; density, 340 per sq. km. Principal towns with population (2001 census): Guwahati, 814,575; Silchar, 184,285; Dibrugarh, 137,879; Jorhat, 135,091; Nagaon, 123,054; Tinsukia, 108,102; Tezpur, 83,028; Bongaigaon, 76,397; Dhubri, 63,965. The principal language is Assamese.

The central government is surveying the line of a proposed boundary fence to prevent illegal entry from Bangladesh.

SOCIAL STATISTICS

Growth rate 1991–2001, 18·85%.

CONSTITUTION AND GOVERNMENT

Assam has a unicameral legislature of 126 members. The capital is Dispur. The state has 23 districts.

RECENT ELECTIONS

In the elections of 10 May 2001 the Indian National Congress (INC) took 70 seats, Asom Gana Parishad 20 and Bharatiya Janata Party (BJP) 8.

CURRENT ADMINISTRATION

Governor: Lt Gen. (Retd) Ajai Singh (took office on 5 June 2003).

Chief Minister: Tarun Gogoi; b. 1936 (took office on 18 May 2001).

ECONOMY

Budget. The budget estimates for 2001 showed receipts of Rs 91,576m. and expenditure of Rs 100,124m.

ENERGY AND NATURAL RESOURCES

Electricity. In 2000 there was an installed capacity of 574 MW. In 1998, 77% of villages had electricity. New power stations are under construction at Lakwa, and Karbi-Langpi hydro-electricity project.

Oil and Gas. Assam contains important oilfields and produces about 16% of India's crude oil. Production (1999): crude oil, 5·00m. tonnes; gas (1999), 1,333m. cu. metres.

Minerals. Coal production (1999), 921,000 tonnes. The state also has limestone, refractory clay, dolomite and corundum.

Agriculture. Assam produces 50% of India's tea—in 2003 there were 1,196 registered tea estates in the state. Production in 1998 was 425·4m. kg. 82% of the cultivable area is used. Over 72% of the cultivated area is under food crops, of which the most important is rice. Total foodgrains, 1997, 3·53m. tonnes. Main cash crops: tea, jute, cotton, oilseeds, sugarcane, fruit and potatoes. Wheat production, 100,000 tonnes in 2000; rice, 3·9m. tonnes; pulses, 64,688 tonnes. Cattle are important.

Forestry. In 2000 there were 17,420 sq. km of reserved forests under the administration of the Forest Department and 6,000 sq. km of unclassed forests, altogether about 39% of the total area of the state. Revenue from forests, in 1999, Rs9,590m.

INDUSTRY

Sericulture and hand-loom weaving, both silk and cotton, are important home industries together with the manufacture of brass, cane and bamboo articles. The main heavy industry is petro-chemicals; there are four oil refineries in the region. Other industries include manufacturing paper, nylon, electronic goods, cement, fertilizers, sugar, jute and plywood products, rice and oil milling.

There were 23,218 small-scale industries in 2000. In 1999, 1·1m. persons were employed in state-run enterprises.

COMMUNICATIONS

Roads. In 1998 there were 33,064 km of road maintained by the Public Works Department. There were 2,034 km of national highway in 1999. There were 373,962 motor vehicles in the state in 1998–99.

Rail. The route-km of railways in 1999 was 3,722 km, of which 2,392 km was broad gauge.

Civil Aviation. Daily scheduled flights connect the principal towns with the rest of India. There are airports at Guwahati, Tezpur, Jorhat, North Lakhimpur, Silchar and Dibrugarh.

Shipping. Water transport is important in Lower Assam; the main waterway is the Brahmaputra River. Cargo carried in 1998 was 50,334 tonnes.

SOCIAL INSTITUTIONS

Justice. The seat of the High Court is Guwahati. It has a Chief Justice and Justice and a sanctioned strength of 19 judges.

Religion. At the 1991 census Hindus numbered 15,047,293; Muslims, 6,373,204; Christians, 744,367; Buddhists, 64,008; Sikhs, 21,910; Jains, 20,645.

Education. In 2001, 64·28% of the population were literate (71·93% of men and 56·03% of women). In 1999–2000 there were 31,888 primary/junior basic schools with 3,293,835 students; 8,019 middle/senior basic schools with 1,406,818 students; 4,514 high/higher secondary schools with 1,465,518 students. There were 247 colleges for general education, six medical colleges, three engineering and one agricultural, 24 teacher-training colleges, and a fisheries college at Raha. There were five universities: Assam Agricultural University, Jorhat; Dibrugarh University, Dibrugarh with 86 colleges and 55,982 students (1992–93); Gauhati University, Guwahati with 128 colleges and 80,363 students (1992–93); and two central universities, at Silchar and Tezpur.

Health. In 2000 there were 164 hospitals (12,900 beds), 618 primary health centres and 323 dispensaries.

BIHAR

KEY HISTORICAL EVENTS

Bihar was part of Bengal under British rule until 1912 when it was separated together with Orissa. The two were joined until 1936 when Bihar became a separate province. As a state of the Indian Union it was enlarged in 1956 by the addition of land from West Bengal.

The state contains the ethnic areas of North Bihar, Santhal Pargana and Chota Nagpur. In 1956 certain areas of Purnea and Manbhum districts were transferred to West Bengal. In 2000 the state of Jharkhand was carved from the mineral-rich southern region of Bihar, substantially reducing the state's revenue-earning power.

TERRITORY AND POPULATION

Bihar is in north India and is bounded north by Nepal, east by West Bengal, south by the new state of Jharkhand, southwest and west by Uttar Pradesh. After the formation of Jharkhand the area of Bihar is 94,163 sq. km (previously 173,877 sq. km). Population (2001 census), 82,878,796, with a density of 880 per sq. km. Population of principal towns, *see* INDIA: Territory and Population. Other large towns (2001): Biharsharif, 231,972; Arrah, 203,395; Munger, 187,311; Chapra, 178,835; Katihar, 175,169; Purnea, 171,235; Sasaram, 131,042; Dinapur Nizamat, 130,339; Saharsa, 124,015; Hajipur, 119,276; Dehri, 119,007; Bettiah, 116,692; Siwan, 108,172; Motihari, 101,506.

The state is divided into 37 districts. The capital is Patna.

The official language is Hindi (spoken by 80·9% at the 2001 census), the second, Urdu (9·9%), and the third, Bengali (2·9%).

SOCIAL STATISTICS

Growth rate 1991–2001, 28·43%.

CONSTITUTION AND GOVERNMENT

Bihar has a bicameral legislature. The Legislative Assembly consists of 243 elected members, and the Council 96. In March 2005 the state was put under president's rule after the elections had resulted in a hung assembly.

RECENT ELECTIONS

In elections held on 3, 15 and 23 Feb. 2005 the Rashtriya Janata Dal retained power winning 74 of 243 seats; Janata Dal (United), 55; Bharatiya Janata Party, 38; Lok Janshakti Party, 30; Indian National Congress, 10; Communist Party of India (Marxist-Leninist) (Liberation), 7; Samajwadi Party, 4; Communist Party of India, 3; Nationalist Congress Party, 3; Bahujan Samaj Party, 2; ind., 17.

CURRENT ADMINISTRATION

Governor: Buta Singh; b. 1934 (took office on 5 Nov. 2004).

ECONOMY

Budget. The budget estimates for 2001–02 showed total receipts of Rs 68,020m. and expenditure of Rs 66,806m. The creation of Jharkhand in 2000 removed two-thirds of Bihar's revenue.

ENERGY AND NATURAL RESOURCES

Electricity. Installed capacity (2000–01) 3,170 MW. Power generated in Bihar and Jharkhand (1994–95), 2,700m. kWh. There were (2001) 26,115 villages with electricity. Bihar has a higher percentage of villages without electricity than most Indian states. Hydro-electric projects in hand will add about 149·2 MW capacity.

Minerals. Before the creation of the new state of Jharkhand, Bihar was very rich in minerals. The truncated state has only deposits of bauxite, mica, glass sand and salt.

Agriculture. (Including Jharkhand). The irrigated area was 4·13m. ha in 1993–94. Cultivable land, 11·6m. ha, of a total area of 17·4m. ha. Total cropped area, 1991–92, 9·79m. ha. Production (1995–96): rice, 6·91m. tonnes; wheat, 4·18m.; total foodgrains, 13·07m. Other food crops are maize, rabi and pulses. Main cash crops are jute, sugarcane, oilseeds, tobacco and potatoes.

Forests in 1995 covered 26,561 sq. km. There are 12 protected forests.

INDUSTRY

(Including Jharkhand). Iron, steel and aluminium are produced and there is an oil refinery. Other important industries are heavy engineering, machine tools, fertilizers, electrical engineering, manufacturing drugs and fruit processing. There were 500 large and medium industries and 163,000 small and handicraft units in 1996–97.

COMMUNICATIONS

Roads. (Including Jharkhand). In March 1997 the state had 87,836 km of roads, including 2,118 km of national highway and 4,192 km of state highway, and 15,526 km of district roads. Passenger transport has been nationalized. There were 1,329,709 motor vehicles registered in March 1996.

Rail. (Including Jharkhand). The North Eastern, South Eastern and Eastern railways traverse the state; route-km, 1995–96, 5,283 km.

Civil Aviation. There are airports at Patna and Gaya with regular scheduled services to Calcutta and Delhi.

Shipping. (Including Jharkhand). The length of waterways open for navigation is 1,300 km.

SOCIAL INSTITUTIONS

Justice. There is a High Court (constituted in 1916) at Patna with a Chief Justice, 31 puisne judges and four additional judges.

Police. The police force is under a Director General of Police; in 1990 there were 1,097 police stations.

Religion. At the 2001 census Hindus numbered 82·4% of the population.

Education. At the census of 2001, 47·53% of the population were literate (60·32% of males and 33·57% of females). There were, 1996–97, 4,149 high and higher secondary schools with 1,080,321 pupils, 13,834 middle schools with 2·42m. pupils and 53,652 primary schools with 9,626,855 pupils. Education is free for children aged 6–11.

There are 12 universities: Patna University (founded 1917) with 14,699 students (1994–95); Babasaheb Bhimrao Ambedkar Bihar University, Muzaffarpur (1952) with 95 colleges, and 84,873 students (1989–90); Tilka Manjhi Bhagalpur University (1960) with 140,718 students (1990–91); Kameshwara Singh Darbhanga Sanskrit University (1961); Magadh University, Gaya (1962) with 186 colleges and 122,019 students (1994–95); Lalit Narayan Mithila University (1972), Darbhanga; Rajendra Agricultural University, Samastipur (1970); Nalanda Open University, Nalanda; BN Mandal University, Madhepura; Indira Gandhi University of Medical Sciences, Sheikhpura; Jai Prakash University, Chapra; and Veer Kunwar Singh University, Arrah. Including Jharkhand, there were 742 degree colleges, 11 engineering colleges, 31 medical colleges and 15 teacher training colleges in 1996–97. Ranchi University, Bisra Agricultural College and Sidhu Kanhu University, all formerly in Bihar, are now part of Jharkhand.

Health. (Including Jharkhand). In 1986 there were 1,289 hospitals and dispensaries with 28,997 beds in 1992.

CULTURE

Tourism. The main tourist centres are Bodh Gaya, Patna, Nalanda, Sasaram, Rajgir and Vaishali.

CHHATTISGARH

KEY HISTORICAL EVENTS

The state was carved from sixteen mainly tribal districts of Madhya Pradesh and became the twenty-sixth state of India on 1 Nov. 2000. Chhattisgarh has been under the administrative control of many different rulers during its history, which can be traced back to the 4th century. Originally known as South Kosala, archaeological excavations made in recent times indicate that the region was a hive of artistic and cultural experimentation in ancient times. During the Sarabhapuriyas, Nalas, Pandavamsis and Kalchuris dynasties between the 6th and 8th centuries vast numbers of brick temples were built in the area. The British took control of the area from the Mahrattas in the early 19th century. Despite possessing its own cultural identity Chhattisgarh was constantly swallowed up by other regions and in 1956, as a direct result of the Indian Union of 1949, it was made part of the new region of Madhya Pradesh. For several years locals in Chhattisgarh voiced the grievance that their region was effectively a 'colony' of Madhya Pradesh, maintaining that the revenue generated by their region, which was termed the 'rice bowl of Madhya Pradesh' and was also rich in minerals, was insufficiently re-invested in the area itself. In 2000 the National Democratic Alliance successfully negotiated the passage of a bill through both houses of the Indian parliament which carved out three new Indian states, Chhattisgarh among them.

TERRITORY AND POPULATION

Chhattisgarh is in central eastern India and is bounded by the new state of Jharkhand to the east, Orissa to the southeast, Andhra Pradesh to the south and Maharashtra and Madhya Pradesh to the west. Chhattisgarh has an area of 135,191 sq. km. Population (2001 census) 20,795,956; density, 154 per sq. km. The principal languages are Hindi and Chhattisgarhi.

Cities with over 250,000 population, *see* INDIA: Territory and Population. Other large cities (2001): Rajnandgaon, 143,727; Raigarh, 115,740; Jagdalpur, 103,216.

SOCIAL STATISTICS

Growth rate 1991–2001, 18·06%.

CONSTITUTION AND GOVERNMENT

Chhattisgarh is the twenty-sixth state of India. In creating Chhattisgarh it was decided that the 90 members of the Madhya Pradesh Legislative Assembly from Chhattisgarhi districts would become the members of the new state's legislative assembly. For administrative purposes the region is divided into 16 districts. The council of ministers consists of 15 cabinet ministers and eight ministers of state.

The capital and seat of government is at Raipur.

RECENT ELECTIONS

At elections in Dec. 2003 the Bharatiya Janata Party won 50 seats and the Congress (I) Party took 36. Other parties won three seats.

CURRENT ADMINISTRATION

Governor: Lieut.-Gen. (retd) Krishna Mohan Seth; b. 1939 (since 2 June 2003).

Chief Minister: Dr Raman Singh; b. 1952 (took office 8 Dec. 2003).

ENERGY AND NATURAL RESOURCES

Electricity. Of the 19,720 villages in Chhattisgarh, 18,070 have electricity.

Water. 1·21m. ha of land is under irrigation. 44,750 residential areas have sufficient drinking water supplies while 7,315 residential areas only have partial supplies and 2,751 areas have insufficient supplies. In total there were 102,063 hand pumps in the state and 701 water fulfilment plans in place in 1999.

Minerals. The state has extensive mineral resources including (1999 estimates): over 27,000m. tonnes of tin ore, 2,000m. tonnes of iron ore, 525m. tonnes of dolomite (accounting for 24% of India's entire share) and 73m. tonnes of bauxite. There are also significant deposits of limestone, copper ore, rock phosphate, corundum, tin, coal and manganese ore. Deobogh in the Raipur district contains deposits of diamonds.

Agriculture. Agriculture is the occupation for 1·7m. of the population (around 80%). 5·8m. ha of land is agricultural and the area provides food grain for over 600 rice mills. The great plains of Chhattisgarh produce 10,000 varieties of rice. Other crops include maize, millet, groundnuts, soybeans and sunflower. More than 25% of the land in Chhattisgarh is double cropped.

COMMUNICATIONS

Roads. Total length of roads (1999) was 33,182 km. State highways connect Raipur to neighbouring states and to Jagdalpur and Kondagaon in the south of Chhattisgarh and Durg and Rajnandgaon in the west.

Rail. Raipur is at the centre of the state's railway network, linking Chhattisgarh to the states of Orissa and Madhya Pradesh.

SOCIAL INSTITUTIONS

Education. In 2001, 65·18% of the population were literate (77·86% of men and 52·40% of women). There are three universities in Chhattisgarh. Ravishankar University (founded 1964), at Raipur, had 89 affiliated colleges (1992–93); Indira Gandhi Krishi Vishwavidyalaya, Raipur, a music and fine arts institution (founded in 1956); and Guru Ghasidas University, Bilaspur which had 58 colleges and 34,717 students (1992–93).

GOA

KEY HISTORICAL EVENTS

The coastal area was captured by the Portuguese in 1510 and the inland area was added in the 18th century. In Dec. 1961 Portuguese rule was ended and Goa incorporated into the Indian Union as a Territory together with Daman and Diu. Goa was granted statehood as a separate unit on 30 May 1987. Daman and Diu remained Union Territories.

TERRITORY AND POPULATION

Goa, bounded on the north by Maharashtra and on the east and south by Karnataka, has a coastline of 105 km. The area is 3,702 sq. km. Population (2001 census) 1,343,998; density, 363 per sq. km. Marmagao is the largest town; population (urban agglomeration, 2001) 104,689. The capital is Panaji; population (urban agglomeration, 2001) 98,915. The state has two districts. There are 183 village Panchayats. The languages spoken are Konkani (official language; 51·5%), Marathi 33·4%, Kannada 4·6%, Hindi and English.

SOCIAL STATISTICS

Growth rate 1991–2001, 14·89%.

CONSTITUTION AND GOVERNMENT

The Indian Parliament passed legislation in March 1962 by which Goa became a Union Territory with retrospective effect from 20 Dec. 1961. On 30 May 1987 Goa attained statehood. There is a Legislative Assembly of 40 members. In March 2005 the state was put under president's rule following a controversy over a vote of confidence in the Legislative Assembly.

RECENT ELECTIONS

Of the 40 seats available at the elections for the State Assembly on 30 May 2002, the Bharatiya Janata Party won 17; Indian National Congress 16; United Goans Democratic Party, 3; Maharashtrawadi Gomantak Party, 2; Nationalist Congress Party, 1; ind., 1.

CURRENT ADMINISTRATION

Governor: S. C. Jamir; b. 1931 (took office on 17 July 2004).

ECONOMY

Budget. The total budget for 2001–02 was Rs 21,377m. Receipts Rs 22,125m.

ENERGY AND NATURAL RESOURCES

Electricity. In 1996 installed capacity was 0·16m. MW, but Goa receives most of its power supply from the states of Maharashtra and Karnataka. In 2001, 360 villages and 44 towns had electricity.

Minerals. Resources include bauxite, ferro-manganese ore and iron ore, all of which are exported. Iron ore production (1992–93) 12,435,334 tonnes. There are also reserves of limestone and clay.

Agriculture. Agriculture is the main occupation, important crops being rice, pulses, ragi, mango, cashew and coconuts. Area under rice (2001) 57,207 ha; production, 128,100 tonnes. Area under pulses 13,250 ha, sugarcane 1,250 ha, cashew nuts 53,767 ha. Total production of foodgrains, 2001, 138,000 tonnes.

Government poultry and dairy farming schemes produced 94m. eggs and 29,000m. litres of milk in 1992–93. Poultry (2001), 780,000; cattle (2001), 88,000.

Forestry. Forests covered 1,250 sq. km in 1995.

Fisheries. Fish is the state's staple food. In 1995–96 the catch of seafish was 84,210 tonnes. There is a coastline of about 104 km and about 2,850 (1994–95) active fishing vessels.

INDUSTRY

In 2001 there were 891 factories registered with a workforce of 39,938. There were 6,127 small-scale industries registered employing 43,312 persons. Production included: nylon fishing nets, ready made clothing, electronic goods, pesticides, pharmaceuticals, tyres, footwear, fertilizers, automotive components and shipbuilding.

COMMUNICATIONS

Roads. There were 7,419 km of roads in 1993–94 (National Highway, 224 km). Motor vehicles numbered 211,756 in March 1996.

Rail. In 1995–96 there were 79 km of route. In 2003 plans were announced for a monorail system.

Civil Aviation. An airport at Dabolim is connected with Agatti, Bangalore, Bombay, Delhi, Kochi, Kozhikode, Pune and Madras. It also receives international charter flights and scheduled flights from Kuwait and Sharjah.

Shipping. There are seaports at Panaji, Marmagao and Margao.

SOCIAL INSTITUTIONS

Justice. There is a bench of the Bombay High Court at Panaji.

Religion. At the 2001 census 65% of the population were Hindus, 30% Christians and 5% Muslims.

Education. In 2001, 82·32% of the population were literate (88·88% of men and 75·51% of women). In 2001 there were 1,268 primary schools (97,457 students), 440 middle schools (72,726 students) and 445 high and higher secondary schools (85,217 students). In 1996–97 there were also two engineering colleges, four medical colleges, two teacher-training colleges, 21 other colleges and six polytechnic institutes. Goa University, Taleigao (1985) had 33 colleges and 16,977 students in 1994–95.

Health. In 2001 there were 120 hospitals (4,865 beds), 201 rural medical dispensaries, health and sub-health centres and 268 family planning units.

FURTHER READING

Hutt, A., *Goa: A Traveller's Historical and Architectural Guide*. Buckhurst Hill, 1988

GUJARAT

KEY HISTORICAL EVENTS

The Gujarati-speaking areas of India were part of the Moghul empire, coming under Mahratta domination in the late 18th century. In 1818 areas of present Gujurat around the Gulf of Cambay were annexed by the British East India Company. The remainder consisted of a group of small principalities, notably Baroda, Rajkot, Bhavnagar and Nawanagar. British areas became part of the Bombay Presidency.

At independence all the area now forming Gujarat became part of Bombay State except for Rajkot and Bhavnagar which formed the state of Saurashtra until incorporated in Bombay in 1956. In 1960 Bombay State was divided and the Gujarati-speaking areas became Gujarat.

In early 2002 at least 800 people, mostly Muslims, were killed in Gujarat in ethnic violence involving Hindus and the Muslim minority.

TERRITORY AND POPULATION

Gujarat is in western India and is bounded in the north by Pakistan and Rajasthan, east by Madhya Pradesh, southeast by Maharashtra, south and west by the Indian ocean and Arabian sea. The area of the state is 196,022 sq. km and the population (2001 census) 50,596,992; density, 258 per sq. km. The chief cities, *see* INDIA: Territory and Population. Other important towns (2001 census) are: Navsari (232,420), Surendranagar (219,828), Anand (218,064), Porbandar (197,414), Nadiad (196,679), Gandhinagar (195,891), Morbi (178,148), Bharuch (176,531), Veraval (157,869), Gandhidham (151,475), Valsad (145,650), Mehesana (141,367), Bhuj (136,327), Godhra (131,144), Palanpur (122,279), Patan (113,568), Anklesvar (112,648), Dahod (112,087), Kalol (112,025), Jetpur (104,301), Botad (100,059). Gujarati and Hindi in the Devanagari script are the official languages.

SOCIAL STATISTICS
Growth rate 1991–2001, 22·48%.

CLIMATE
Summers are intensely hot: 33–45°C. Winters: 7–13°C. Monsoon season: 22–36°C. Annual rainfall varies from 35 cm to 189 cm.

CONSTITUTION AND GOVERNMENT
Gujarat has a unicameral legislature, the *Legislative Assembly*, which has 182 elected members.

The capital is Gandhinagar. There are 25 districts.

RECENT ELECTIONS
In elections held in Dec. 2002 the Bharatiya Janata Party retained power with an increased majority, winning 126 seats against 51 for Congress, with ind. and others winning four seats.

CURRENT ADMINISTRATION
Governor: Nawal Kishore Sharma; b. 1925 (took office on 24 July 2004).

Chief Minister: Shri Narendrabhai Modi; b. 1950 (took office on 7 Oct. 2001).

ECONOMY
Budget. The budget estimates for 2004–05 showed revenue receipts of Rs 208,136·7m. and revenue expenditure of Rs 237,863·3m.

Banking and Finance. At March 2004 there were 3,668 branches of commercial banks in the State with combined deposits of Rs 846,810m. Total credit advanced was Rs 366,820m.

ENERGY AND NATURAL RESOURCES
Electricity. In March 2004 total installed capacity was 8,713 MW and 17,940 villages had electricity.

Oil and Gas. There are large crude oil and gas reserves. Production, 2002–03: crude oil, 6·0m. tonnes; gas, 3,324m. cu. metres.

Water. Water resources are limited. In 2003 irrigation potential was 6·49m. ha.

Minerals. Chief minerals produced in 2002–03 (in tonnes) included limestone (18m.), lignite (5·7m.), bauxite (1·7m.), quartz and silica (865,305), crude china clay (129,084), dolomite (128,519), calcareous and sea sand (4,000 in 1999–2000) and agate stone (68). Value of production (2002–03) Rs 51,221m. Reserves of coal lie under the Kalol and Mehsana oil and gas fields. The deposit, mixed with crude petroleum, is estimated at 100,000m. tonnes.

Agriculture. 3·5m. ha of the cropped area was irrigated in June 2003.

Production of principal crops, 2002–03: foodgrains, 3·6m. tonnes (wheat, 0·86m. tonnes); rice, 0·6m. tonnes from 481,000 ha; pulses, 327,000 tonnes; cotton, 1·69m. bales of 170 kg. Tobacco and groundnuts are important cash crops.

Livestock (1997): buffaloes, 6·29m.; other cattle, 6·75m.; sheep and goats, 6·54m.; horses and ponies, 14,381.

Forestry. Forests covered 18,940 sq. km in March 2003 (9·66% of total area). The State has four National Parks and 21 sanctuaries.

Fisheries. There were (1997) 158,000 people engaged in fisheries. In 2002–03 there were 30,098 fishing vessels and the catch was 777,905 tonnes.

INDUSTRY

Gujarat ranks among India's most industrialized states. In 2003 there were 286,185 small-scale units and (2001) 18,880 factories including 3,293 chemical and chemical products factories, 2,275 textile factories, 1,736 non-metallic mineral products factories, 1,700 machinery and equipment factories and 876 rubber and plastic products factories. There were 251 industrial estates in 2002–03. Principal industries are textiles, general and electrical engineering, oil-refining, fertilizers, petrochemicals, machine tools, automobiles, heavy chemicals, pharmaceuticals, dyes, sugar, soda ash, cement, man-made fibres, salt, sulphuric acid, paper and paperboard.

In 2002 state production of soda-ash was 1·88m. tonnes, salt production was 13·08m. tonnes and cement production 10·78m. tonnes.

COMMUNICATIONS

Roads. At March 2002 there were 74,018 km of roads. Gujarat State Road Transport Corporation operated 18,507 routes. Number of vehicles at the end of March 2004, 7,087,490.

Rail. In 2002–03 the state had 5,186 route-km of railway line.

Civil Aviation. Sardar Vallabhbhai Patel International Airport at Ahmedabad is the main airport. There are some international flights and regular internal services between Ahmedabad and Bombay, Delhi and Jaipur, and within Gujarat between Ahmedabad and Bhavnagar, Bhuj, Rajkot and Vadodara (Baroda). There are five other airports: Jamnagar (which also has some international flights), Kandla, Keshod, Porbandar and Surat.

Shipping. The largest port is Kandla. There are 40 other ports. Cargo handled at the ports in 2003–04 totalled 130·9m. tonnes (41·5m. tonnes at Kandla).

Telecommunications. There were 2,775,500 telephone connections and 2,073,035 mobile phone connections in the state at the end of March 2004.

Postal Services. There were 9,023 post offices and 1,258 telegraph offices at the end of March 2004.

SOCIAL INSTITUTIONS

Justice. The High Court of Judicature at Ahmedabad has a Chief Justice and 30 puisne judges.

Religion. At the 2001 census Hindus numbered 89% of the population; Muslims, 9%; Jains, 1%; Christians, 0·6%.

Education. In 2001, 69·97% of the population were literate (80·50% of males and 58·60% of females). Primary and secondary education up to Standard XII are free. Education above Standard XII is free for girls. In 2002–03 there were 41,339 primary schools with 8·47m. students and 7,308 secondary schools with 2·48m. students.

There are 11 universities in the state. Gujarat University, Ahmedabad, founded in 1950, is teaching and affiliating; it has 154 affiliated colleges and 143,692 students (all student figures for 1998–99). The Maharaja Sayajirao University of Vadodara (1949) is residential and teaching; it has 12 colleges and 26,511 students. The Sardar Patel University, Vallabh-Vidyanagar (1955), has 20 constituent and affiliated colleges and 17,913 students. Saurashtra University at Rajkot (1968) has 113 affiliated colleges and 72,234 students. South Gujarat University at Surat (1967) has 58 colleges and 59,600 students. Bhavnagar University (1978) is residential and teaching with 15 affiliated colleges and 11,195 students. North Gujarat University was established at Patan in 1986 and has 73 colleges and 54,720 students. Gujarat Vidyapith at Ahmedabad is deemed a university under the University Grants Commission Act. There are also Gujarat Agricultural University, Banaskantha, Gujarat Ayurved University, Jamnagar and Dr Babasaheb Ambedkar Open University, Ahmedabad.

There are 31 engineering and technical colleges, 36 polytechnics, 50 medical colleges and nine agricultural colleges. There are also 339 arts, science and commerce colleges, 42 teacher-training colleges and 31 law colleges. There were 0·4m. students enrolled in 1998–99 in all colleges.

Health. At March 2004 there were 271 community health centres, 1,067 primary health centres and 7,274 sub-centres. There were 25 general hospitals, 23 cottage hospitals (2000) and 22 Taluka-level hospitals. In 2003–04, 41·3m. patients were treated.

CULTURE

Press. At June 2004 there were 2,445 newspapers and periodicals of which 2,255 were published in Gujarati, 85 in English and 75 in Hindi.

Tourism. There are many sights of religious pilgrimage as well as archaeological sights, attractive beaches, the Lion Sanctuary of Gir Forest and the Wild Ass Sanctuary in Kachchh. Mahatma Gandhi's birthplace at Porbandar is also a popular tourist attraction.

FURTHER READING

Desai, I. F., *Untouchability in Rural Gujarat.* Bombay, 1977
Sharma, R. N., *Gujurat Holocaust (Communalism in the Land of Gandhi).* Delhi, 2002

HARYANA

KEY HISTORICAL EVENTS

The state of Haryana, created on 1 Nov. 1966 under the Punjab Reorganization Act, 1966, was formed from the Hindi-speaking parts of the state of Punjab (India). It comprises the districts of Ambala, Bhiwani, Faridabad, Fatehabad, Gurgaon, Hisar, Jhajjar, Jind, Kaithal, Karnal, Kurukshetra, Mahendragarh, Panchkula, Panipat, Rewari, Rohtak, Sirsa, Sonipat and Yamunanagar.

TERRITORY AND POPULATION

Haryana is in north India and is bounded north by Himachal Pradesh, east by Uttar Pradesh, south and west by Rajasthan and northwest by Punjab. Delhi forms an enclave on its eastern boundary. The state has an area of 44,212 sq. km and a population (2001 census) of 21,082,989; density, 477 per sq. km. Principal cities, *see* INDIA: Territory and Population. Other large towns (2001) are: Gurgaon (229,243), Sonipat (225,151), Karnal (222,017), Bhiwani (169,424), Ambala (168,003), Sirsa (160,129), Panchkula Urban Estate (140,992), Jind (136,089), Bahadurgarh (131,924), Thanesar (122,704), Kaithal (117,226). The principal language is Hindi.

SOCIAL STATISTICS

Growth rate 1991–2001, 28·06%.

CONSTITUTION AND GOVERNMENT

The state has a unicameral legislature with 90 members. The capital (shared with Punjab) is Chandigarh. Its transfer to Punjab, intended for 1986, has been postponed. There are 19 districts.

RECENT ELECTIONS

In the elections of 3 Feb. 2005 the Indian National Congress won 67 seats, the Indian National Lok Dal 9, the Bharatiya Janata Party 2, the Bahujan Samaj Party 1, the Nationalist Congress Party 1 and ind. 10.

CURRENT ADMINISTRATION

Governor: A. R. Kidwai; b. 1920 (took office on 7 July 2004).

Chief Minister: Bhupinder Singh Hooda; b. 1947 (took office on 5 March 2005).

ECONOMY

Budget. Budget estimates for 2002–03 show revenue income of Rs 104,091·4m. and revenue expenditure of Rs 114,057·9m.

ENERGY AND NATURAL RESOURCES

Electricity. Approximately 1,000 MW are supplied to Haryana, mainly from the Bhakra Nangal system. In 1999 installed capacity was 8,301 MW and all the villages had electric power.

Minerals. Minerals include placer gold, barytes, tin and rare earths. Value of production, 1987–88, Rs 40m.

Agriculture. Haryana has sandy soil and erratic rainfall, but the state shares the benefit of the Sutlej-Beas scheme. Agriculture employs over 82% of the working population; in 1981 there were about 0·9m. holdings (average 3·7 ha), and the gross irrigated area was 2·05m. ha in 1993–94. Area under foodgrains, 1995–96, 4·02m. ha. Foodgrain production, 1999–2000, 10·36m. tonnes (rice 2·59m. tonnes in 2000, wheat 7·35m. tonnes in 1995–96); pulses, 416,400 tonnes in 1995–96; cotton, 1·5m. bales of 170 kg in 1995–96; sugar (gur) and oilseeds are important. Haryana produces a surplus of wheat and rice.

Forestry. Forests covered 603 sq. km in 1995.

INDUSTRY

Haryana has a large market for consumer goods in neighbouring Delhi. In 1996–97 there were 916 large and medium scale industries and 138,759 small units providing employment to about 1m. persons, and 56,012 rural industrial units. The main industries are cotton textiles, agricultural machinery and tractors, woollen textiles, scientific instruments, glass, cement, paper and sugar milling, cars, tyres and tubes, motorcycles, bicycles, steel tubes, engineering goods, electrical and electronic goods. An oil refinery at Panipat was commissioned in 1999 and includes a diesel hydro desulphurization plant.

COMMUNICATIONS

Roads. There were (2002) 29,524 km of metalled roads—including 656 km of national highways, 3,135 km of state highways and 1,587 km of district highways—linking all villages. Road transport is nationalized. There were 954,563 motor vehicles in 1995–96. Haryana roadways carried 1·75m. passengers daily in 2002 with a fleet of 3,411 buses.

Rail. The state is crossed by lines from Delhi to Agra, Ajmer, Ferozepur and Chandigarh. Route km, 1995–96, 1,452 km. The main stations are at Ambala and Kurukshetra.

Civil Aviation. There is no airport within the state but Delhi is on its eastern boundary.

SOCIAL INSTITUTIONS

Justice. Haryana shares the High Court of Punjab and Haryana at Chandigarh.

Religion. At the 2001 census Hindus numbered 89% of the population; Sikhs, 5·8%; Muslims, 4·6%.

Education. In 2001, 68·59% of the population were literate (79·25% of men and 56·31% of women). In 1996–97 there were 5,651 primary schools with 1,981,993 students, 3,233 high and higher secondary schools with 511,377 students, 1,631 middle schools with 832,886 students and 129 colleges of arts, science and commerce, nine engineering and technical colleges and ten medical colleges. There are four universities: Haryana Agricultural University, Hisar; Kurukshetra University, Kurukshetra with 70 colleges and 80,000 students (1999); Maharshi Dayanand University, Rohtak; and Guru Jambeshwar University, Hisar.

Health. In 2003 there were 49 hospitals, 64 community health centres, 402 primary health centres and 2,299 health sub-centres. A further 12 primary health centres were under construction.

HIMACHAL PRADESH

KEY HISTORICAL EVENTS

Thirty small hill states were merged to form the Territory of Himachal Pradesh in 1948; the state of Bilaspur was added in 1954 and parts of the Punjab in 1966. The whole territory became a state in Jan. 1971. The state is a Himalayan area of hill-tribes, rivers and forests. Its main component areas are Chamba, a former princely state, dominated in turn by Moghuls and Sikhs before coming under British influence in 1848; Bilaspur, an independent Punjab state until it was invaded by Gurkhas in 1814 (the British East India Company forces drove out the Gurkhas in 1815); Simla district around the town built by the Company near Bilaspur on land reclaimed from Gurkha troops (the summer capital of India from 1865 until 1948); Mandi, a princely state until 1948; Kangra and Kullu districts, originally Rajput areas which had become part of the British-ruled Punjab. They were incorporated into Himachal Pradesh in 1966 when the Punjab was reorganized.

TERRITORY AND POPULATION

Himachal Pradesh is in north India and is bounded north by Kashmir, east by Tibet, southeast by Uttaranchal, south by Haryana, southwest and west by Punjab. The area of the state is 55,673 sq. km and the population (2001 census) 6,077,248; density, 109 per sq. km. Principal languages are Hindi and Pahari. The capital is Shimla, population (2001 census) of the urban agglomeration, 144,578.

SOCIAL STATISTICS

Growth rate 1991–2001, 17·53%.

CONSTITUTION AND GOVERNMENT

Full statehood was attained, as the 18th State of the Union, on 25 Jan. 1971. On 1 Sept. 1972 districts were reorganized and three new districts created, Solan, Hamirpur and Una, making a total of 12.

There is a unicameral *Legislative Assembly*.

RECENT ELECTIONS

Elections were held in Feb. 2003 in 65 of the 68 constituencies. Congress won 40 seats; Bharatiya Janata Party (BJP), 16; ind. 6; other parties, 3.

CURRENT ADMINISTRATION

Governor: Vishnu Sadashiv Kokje; b. 1939 (took office on 8 May 2003).

Chief Minister: Virbhadra Singh; b. 1934 (since 6 March 2003, for a third time).

ECONOMY

Budget. Budget estimates for 2000–01 showed receipts of Rs 39,854m. and expenditure of Rs 48,860m.

ENERGY AND NATURAL RESOURCES

Electricity. All 16,881 villages have electricity. Installed capacity (1995–96), 288·7 MW. The state has huge hydropower potential—there is an estimated potential of 20,376 MW (14·5% of India's potential). In 2003 there was installed capacity of 3,942 MW, with a further 7,060 MW under execution. There were 13,436 substations and 70,323 km of power lines in 2003. The Nathpa Jhakri project is India's largest hydroelectric power plant. The plant, which incorporates a 28 km power tunnel, came online in Oct. 2003. Electricity generated (1999), 1,485m. kWh.

Water. An artificial confluence of the Sutlej and Beas rivers has been made, directing their united flow into Govind Sagar Lake.

Minerals. The state has rock salt, slate, gypsum, limestone, barytes, dolomite, pyrites, copper, gold and sulphur. However, Himachal Pradesh supplies only 0·2% of the national mineral output.

Agriculture. Farming employs 71% of the people. Irrigated area is 17% of the area sown. There are about 2,000 tea planters cultivating 2,063 ha. Main crops are seed potatoes, off season vegetables, wheat, maize, rice and fruits such as apples, peaches, apricots, hops, kiwi fruit, strawberries and flowers; 436,000 tonnes of fruits were produced in 1999.

Production (2001): foodgrains 1,599,000 tonnes (of which maize 768,000 tonnes, wheat 637,000 tonnes, rice 137,000 tonnes), plus vegetables 627,000 tonnes, ginger 2,900 tonnes.

Livestock (1992 census): buffaloes, 701,000; other cattle, 2,152,000; goats and sheep, 2·19m.

Forestry. Himachal Pradesh forests cover 66·2% of the state and supply the largest quantities of coniferous timber in northern India. The forests also ensure the safety of the catchment areas of the Yamuna, Sutlej, Beas, Ravi and Chenab rivers. Commercial felling of green trees has been totally halted and forest working nationalized. Area under forests, 37,033 sq. km.

INDUSTRY

The main sources of employment are the forests and their related industries; there are factories making turpentine and rosin. The state also makes fertilizers, cement, electronic items, TV sets, watches, computer parts, electronic toys and video cassettes. Sericulture is a major industry. There is a foundry and a brewery. Other industries include salt production and handicrafts, including weaving. The state has 173 large and medium units, 27,000 small scale units (providing employment for 140,000 people), seven industrial estates and 21 industrial areas. 300 mineral based industries have also been established.

COMMUNICATIONS

Roads. The national highway from Chandigarh runs through Shimla; other main highways from Shimla serve Kullu, Manali, Kangra, Chamba and Pathankot. The rest are minor roads. Pathankot is also on national highways from Punjab to Kashmir. Length of roads (1999), 25,773 km; number of vehicles (1995–96), 119,037; number of transport buses (1995–96), 1,692.

Rail. There is a line from Chandigarh to Shimla, and the Jammu-Delhi line runs through Pathankot. A Nangal-Talwara rail link has been approved by the central government. There are two narrow gauge lines, from Shimla to Kalka (96 km) and Jogindernagar to Pathankot (103 km), and a broad gauge line from Una to Nangal (16 km). Route-km in 2003, 256 km.

Civil Aviation. The state has airports at Bhuntar near Kullu, at Jubbarhatti near Shimla and at Gaggal in Kangra district. There are also 12 state-run helipads across the state.

SOCIAL INSTITUTIONS

Justice. The state has its own High Court at Shimla with eight judges.

Religion. At the 2001 census Hindus accounted for 96% of the population; Muslims, 1·7%; Buddhists, 1·2%.

Education. In 2001, 77·13% of the population were literate (86·02% of men and 68·08% of women). There were (1996–97) 7,732 primary schools with 728,870 students, 1,037 middle schools with 371,622 students, 1,228 high and higher secondary schools with 271,596 students, 62 (including 18 private) arts, science and commerce colleges, one engineering college, two medical colleges, one teacher training college and three universities. The universities are Himachal Pradesh University, Shimla (1970) with 48 affiliated colleges and 32,773 students (1992–93), Himachal Pradesh Agricultural University, Palampur (1978) and Dr Y. S. Parmar University of Horticulture and Forestry, Solan (1985).

Health. There were (Dec. 1996) 80 hospitals (9,525 beds), 286 primary and community health centres and 1,831 sub-health centres, and 838 allopathic and Ayurvedic dispensaries.

FURTHER READING

Verma, Vishwashwar, *The Emergence of Himachal Pradesh: A Survey of Constitutional Development.* Indus Publishing Company, New Delhi, 1995

JAMMU AND KASHMIR

KEY HISTORICAL EVENTS

The state of Jammu and Kashmir was brought into being in 1846 at the close of the First Sikh War. By the Treaty of Amritsar, Gulab Singh, *de facto* ruler of Jammu and Ladakh, added Kashmir to his existing territories, in consideration of his agreeing to pay the indemnity imposed by the British on the defeated Sikh empire.

Of the state's three component parts, Ladakh and Kashmir were ancient polities, Ladakh having been an independent kingdom since the tenth century AD until its conquest by Gulab Singh's armies in 1834–42. Kashmir lost its independence to the Mughal empire in 1586, and was conquered in turn by the Afghans (1756) and the Sikhs (1819). Jammu was a collection of small principalities, until these were consolidated by Gulab Singh and his brothers in the early nineteenth century.

British supremacy was recognized until the Indian Independence Act, 1947, when all states decided on accession to India or Pakistan. Kashmir asked for standstill agreements with both. Pakistan agreed, but India wanted further discussion with the government of Jammu and Kashmir State. Meantime the state was subject to armed attack from Pakistan and the Maharajah acceded to India on 26 Oct. 1947 by signing the Instrument of Accession. India approached the UN in Jan. 1948, and the conflict ended by ceasefire in Jan. 1949, the major part of the state remaining with India, but a significant amount of territory in the north and west going to Pakistan. Hostilities between the two countries broke out in 1965 and again in 1971, but notwithstanding bilateral agreements—the Tashkent Declaration (Jan. 1966) and the Simla Agreement (July 1972)—the issue remains unresolved. With Muslims a majority of its population, both India and Pakistan regard the state as a touchstone of their divergent political raisons d'être—Pakistan as a Muslim nation, and India a secular one—and hence their position as non-negotiable. Intermittent violence between nationalistic factions has led to further negotiations between India and Pakistan with both sides pledging a peaceful solution. In Dec. 2002 the new provincial government promised to open talks with separatist groups.

TERRITORY AND POPULATION

The state is in the extreme north and is bounded north by China, east by Tibet, south by Himachal Pradesh and Punjab and west by Pakistan. The area is 222,236 sq. km, of which about 84,100 sq. km is occupied by Pakistan and 36,749 sq. km by China; the population of the territory on the Indian side of the line in the 2001 census, was 10,069,917. Srinagar (population, 2001, 971,357) is the summer and Jammu (607,642) the winter capital. The official language is Urdu; other commonly spoken languages are Kashmiri, Hindi, Dogri, Gujri, Pahari, Ladakhi and Punjabi.

SOCIAL STATISTICS

Growth rate 1991–2001, 29·04%.

CONSTITUTION AND GOVERNMENT

The Maharajah's son, Yuvraj Karan Singh, took over as Regent in 1950 and, on the ending of hereditary rule (17 Oct. 1952), was sworn in as Sadar-i-Riyasat. On his father's death (26 April 1961) Yuvraj Karan Singh was recognized as Maharajah by the Indian government. The permanent Constitution of the state came into force in part on 17 Nov. 1956 and fully on 26 Jan. 1957. There is a bicameral legislature; the Legislative Council has 36 members and the Legislative Assembly has 87. Since the 1967 elections the six representatives of Jammu and Kashmir in the central House of the People are directly elected; there are four representatives in the Council of States. After a period of President's rule, a National Conference–Indira Congress coalition government was formed in March 1987. The government was dismissed and the state was brought under President's rule on 18 July 1990.

The state has 14 districts.

RECENT ELECTIONS

Elections to the State Assembly were held in four rounds between 16 Sept. and 8 Oct. 2002. The ruling pro-India National Conference won 28 of the 87 seats (57 in 1996); the Indian Congress Party won 20 (7 in 1996); the People's Democratic Party, 16; and the Bharatiya Janata Party, 1 (8 in 1996). Despite ongoing violence and voter intimidation throughout the elections, turn-out was estimated at 46%. Following the elections, a coalition government was formed by the Indian Congress Party, the People's Democratic Party and other smaller parties.

CURRENT ADMINISTRATION

Governor: Lt.-Gen. (Retd) Sriniwas Kumar Sinha; b. 1926 (since 4 June 2003).

Chief Minister: Mufti Mohammad Sayeed; b. 1936 (took office on 2 Nov. 2002).

ECONOMY

Budget. Budget estimates for 2000–01 show total receipts of Rs 57,158m. and total expenditure of Rs 77,483m.

ENERGY AND NATURAL RESOURCES

Electricity. The state has exploitable hydropower potential of about 15,000 MW. The gas turbine station at Srinagar is an important contributor. Installed capacity (2002) 1,781 MW; 95% of the villages had electricity in 2000.

Minerals. Minerals include coal, bauxite and gypsum.

Agriculture. About 80% of the population are supported by agriculture. Rice, wheat and maize are the major cereals. The total area under foodgrains (1998–99) was estimated at 908,000 ha. Total foodgrains produced, 1998–99, 1·45m. tonnes (rice, 0·55m. tonnes; wheat, 0·43m. tonnes); pulses, 17,000 tonnes. Fruit is important: production, 1994–95, 0·9m. tonnes; exports, 0·76m. tonnes.

Irrigated area, 1993–94, 442,000 ha.

Livestock (1982): cattle, 2,325,200; buffaloes, 5,631,000; goats, 1,003,900; sheep, 1,908,700; horses, 973,000; and poultry, 2,406,760.

Forestry. Forests cover about 20,443 sq. km (1995), forming an important source of revenue, besides providing employment to a large section of the population.

INDUSTRY

There are two central public sector industries and 30 medium-scale. There are 35,576 small units (1994–95) employing over 125,000. There are industries based on horticulture; traditional handicrafts are silk spinning, wood-carving, papier mâché and carpet-weaving. 750 tonnes of silk cocoons were produced in 1994–95.

The handicraft sector employed 0·26m. persons and had a production turnover of Rs 2,500m. in 1995–96.

COMMUNICATIONS

Roads. Kashmir is linked with the rest of India by the motorable Jammu–Pathankot road. The Jawahar Tunnel, through the Banihal mountain, connects Srinagar and Jammu, and maintains road communication with the Kashmir Valley during the winter months. In 2000 there were 13,093 km of roads.

There were 195,125 motor vehicles in 1995–96.

Rail. Kashmir is linked with the Indian railway system by the line between Jammu and Pathankot; route-km of railways in the state, 2002, 77 km.

Civil Aviation. Major airports are at Srinagar and Jammu. There is a third airport at Leh. There are services connecting Jammu with Amritsar, Chandigarh, Delhi and Srinagar; and services connecting Srinagar with Ahmedabad, Amritsar, Bombay, Chandigarh, Delhi, Jammu and Leh.

Telecommunications. There were 202 telephone exchanges and 54,644 telephones in 1994–95.

Postal Services. There were 1,583 post offices in 1994.

SOCIAL INSTITUTIONS

Justice. The High Court, at Srinagar and Jammu, has a Chief Justice and four puisne judges.

Religion. The majority of the population, except in Jammu, are Muslims (making it the only Indian state to have a Muslim majority). In 2003, 65% of the population of the state was estimated to be Muslim and 30% Hindu.

Education. The proportion of literate people was 54·46% in 2001 (65·75% of men and 41·82% of women). Education is free. There were (1996–97) 1,351 high and higher secondary schools with 227,699 students, 3,104 middle schools with 405,598 students and 10,483 primary schools with 893,005 students. Jammu University (1969) has five constituent and 13 affiliated colleges, with 15,278 students (1992–93); Kashmir University (1948) has 18 colleges (17,000 students, 1992–93); there are two other universities: Sher-E-Kashmir University of Agricultural Sciences and Technology and Hemwati Nandan Bahuguna Garhwal University at Srinagar. There are four medical colleges, two engineering and technology colleges, four polytechnics, eight oriental colleges and an Ayurvedic college, 34 arts, science and commerce colleges and four teacher training colleges.

Health. In 1993–94 there were 43 hospitals with 9,256 beds, 264 primary health centres and 1,740 sub-centres, and 35 community health centres. There is a National Institute of Medical Sciences.

FURTHER READING

Lamb, A., *Kashmir: a Disputed Legacy, 1846–1990.* Hertingfordbury, 1991.
Wirsing, R. G., *India, Pakistan and the Kashmir Dispute: on Regional Conflict and its Resolution.* London, 1995

JHARKHAND

KEY HISTORICAL EVENTS

The state was carved from Bihar and became the twenty-eighth state of India on 15 Nov. 2000. Located in the plateau regions of eastern India, Jharkhand (literally meaning land of forests) is mentioned in ancient Indian texts as an area inaccessible to the rest of India owing to its unforgiving terrain and the warring nature of the tribes living in its forests. The Mughals attacked the region in 1385 and again in 1616, arresting the King of Jharkhand and imprisoning him while they collected money from local chieftains. During the 17th century Jharkhand was a part of the Mughal empire and spread over areas of present-day Madhya Pradesh and Bihar. The East India Company was granted revenue-collecting power of the area in 1765 and the permanent settlement of 1796 increased the company's grip on the area. In 1858 sovereignty was transferred to the English crown. From 1793 until 1915 there were periodic tribal rebellions throughout Jharkhand against the British. In 1912 Jharkhand was constituted as part of the province of Bihar and Orissa after the former was separated from West Bengal. The Jharkhand Party submitted a request for Jharkhand to become a separate state to the State Reorganisation Committee in 1955. In 2000 a separate Jharkhand state was formed after legislation initiated by the National Democratic Alliance. The new state comprised a large area of southern Bihar but not any parts of West Bengal or Orissa as had been originally proposed.

TERRITORY AND POPULATION

Jharkhand is in central eastern India and is bounded by Bihar to the north, West Bengal to the east, Orissa to the south and the new state of Chhattisgarh to the west. Jharkhand has an area of 79,714 sq. km. Population (2001 census) 26,909,428; density: 338 per sq. km. Cities with over 250,000 population, *see* INDIA: Territory and Population. Other large cities (2001): Phusro (174,367), Hazaribag (135,446), Adityapur (119,221), Deogar (112,501), Ramgarh (110,497), Chirkunda (106,200), Giridih (105,212).

SOCIAL STATISTICS

Growth rate 1991–2001, 23·19%.

CONSTITUTION AND GOVERNMENT

Jharkhand is the twenty-eighth state of India. After the region was carved from Bihar it was decided that the 81 Members of the Legislative Assembly (MLAs) from Jharkhandi districts would become the members of the new state's legislative assembly. For administrative purposes the region is divided into 18 districts.

The capital and seat of government is at Ranchi.

RECENT ELECTIONS

In elections held on 3, 15 and 23 Feb. 2005 the Bharatiya Janata Party won 30 of 81 seats; Jharkhand Mukti Morcha, 17; Indian National Congress, 9; Rashtriya Janata Dal, 7; Janata Dal (United), 6; ind. and other parties, 12.

CURRENT ADMINISTRATION

Governor: Syed Sibtey Razi; b. 1939 (took office on 10 Dec. 2004).

Chief Minister: Arjun Munda; b. 1968 (took office on 12 March 2005).

ECONOMY

Budget. Budget estimates for Jharkhand in 2002 showed it had receipts of Rs 37,070m. and expenditure of Rs 36,560m. The formation of Jharkhand in 2000 substantially weakened the economy of Bihar, which lost 55% of its revenue but only 45% of its population. Jharkhand's annual plan of outlay for 2001–02 was Rs 19,000m.

ENERGY AND NATURAL RESOURCES

Minerals. Jharkhand is very rich in minerals, with about 40% of national production, including 90% of the country's cooking coal deposits, 40% of its copper, 37% of known coal reserves and 2% of iron ore. Other important minerals: bauxite, quartz, building stones and ceramics, graphite, limestone, kyanite, manganese, lead and silver. The state has 183 coal mines with an annual production of 59·9m. tonnes. Annually the state mines 8·6m. tonnes of iron ore, 1·0m. tonnes of bauxite, 18,700 tonnes manganese, 1·2m. tonnes of copper ores and 50,000 tonnes of fire clays.

INDUSTRY

There is a major engineering corporation in Jharkhand as well as India's largest steel plant at Bokaro. Other important industries are aluminium and copper plants, forging, explosives, refractories and glass production. Jharkhand contains large thermal plants at Patratu, Tenughat, Chandrapura and Bokaro.

COMMUNICATIONS

Roads. National highways connect Ranchi to the neighbouring states of Bihar in the north, West Bengal to the east and Orissa to the south. State highways connect to the new state of Chhattisgarh in the west. Jharkhand has a total length of about 6,450 km of state highways, 1,660 km of national highways and 400 km of district highways.

Rail. Ranchi and the steel city of Bokaro are at the hub of the state's railway network linking Jharkhand to its neighbouring states as well as to Calcutta.

SOCIAL INSTITUTIONS

Education. In 2001, 54·13% of the population were literate (87·94% of men and 39·38% of women). There are five universities: Ranchi University (founded 1960), with 106 colleges and 55,731 students (1994–95); Bisra Agricultural University at Ranchi (1980); Sidhu Kanhu University at Dumka; Binova Bhave University at Hazaribag; B. I. T. Mesra University at Ranchi (formerly Birla Institute of Technology). There are two law colleges, two agricultural colleges, five engineering colleges and ten medical colleges.

Health. There were 83 hospitals in 2003.

CULTURE

Tourism. The main tourist centre is Ranchi.

KARNATAKA

KEY HISTORICAL EVENTS

The state of Karnataka, constituted as Mysore under the States Reorganization Act, 1956, brought together the Kannada-speaking people distributed in five states, and consisted of the territories of the old states of Mysore and Coorg, the Bijapur, Kanara and Dharwar districts and the Belgaum district (except one taluk) in former Bombay, the major portions of the Gulbarga, Raichur and Bidar districts in former Hyderabad, the South Kanara district (apart from the Kasaragod taluk) and the Kollegal taluk of the Coimbatore district in Madras. The state was renamed Karnataka in 1973.

TERRITORY AND POPULATION

The state is in south India and is bounded north by Maharashtra, east by Andhra Pradesh, south by Tamil Nadu and Kerala, west by the Indian ocean and northeast by Goa. The area of the state is 191,791 sq. km, and its population (2001 census),

52,733,958; density, 275 per sq. km. Principal cities, *see* INDIA: Territory and Population. The capital is Bangalore. Other large towns (2001) are: Tumkur (248,592), Raichur (205,634), Bidar (172,298), Hospet (163,284), Bhadravati (160,392), Robertson Pet (156,961), Hassan (133,317), Mandya (131,211), Udupi (127,060), Chitradurga (125,060), Kolar (113,299), Gangawati (101,397), Chikmagalur (101,022).

Kannada is the language of administration and is spoken by about 66% of the people. Other languages include Urdu (9%), Telugu (8·2%), Marathi (4·5%), Tamil (3·6%), Tulu and Konkani.

SOCIAL STATISTICS

Growth rate 1991–2001, 17·25%.

CONSTITUTION AND GOVERNMENT

Karnataka has a bicameral legislature. The Legislative Council has 75 members. The Legislative Assembly consists of 224 elected members.

The state has 27 districts grouped in four divisions: Bangalore, Belgaum, Gulbarga and Mysore.

RECENT ELECTIONS

At the state elections on 20 and 26 April 2004 the BJP won 79 seats (with 28·3% of the vote); the INC, 65 (35·3%); the Janata Dal (Secular), 58 (20·8%); Janata Dal (United), 5 (2·1%). 13 independents were elected. Turn-out was 64·8%.

CURRENT ADMINISTRATION

Governor: Triloki Nath Chaturvedi; b. 1928 (took office on 21 Aug. 2002).

Chief Minister: Dharam Singh; b. 1936 (since 28 May 2004).

ECONOMY

Budget. Budget estimates, 2000–01: revenue receipts, Rs 200,252m.; revenue expenditure, Rs 200,615m.

ENERGY AND NATURAL RESOURCES

Electricity. In 1999 the state's installed capacity was 6,652·1 MW. Electricity generated, 1994–95, 16,830m. kWh. 26,483 villages had electricity in March 1996.

Minerals. Karnataka is an important source of gold and silver. The state produces 84% of India's gold. The estimated reserves of high grade iron ore are 8,798m. tonnes. These reserves are found mainly in the Chitradurga belt. The National Mineral Development Corporation of India has indicated total reserves of nearly 332m. tonnes of magnesite and iron ore (with an iron content ranging from 25 to 40) which have been found in Kudremukh Ganga-Mula region in Chikmagalur District. Value of production (1992–93) Rs 2,590m. The estimated reserves of manganese are over 320m. tonnes.

Limestone is found in many regions; deposits (1992–93) are about 5,892m. tonnes. Karnataka is the largest producer of chromite. It is one of only two states in India producing magnesite. The other minerals of industrial importance are corundum and garnet. Karnataka produces 63% of India's moulding sand annually and 57% of the country's quartzite, and is the only producer of felsite.

Agriculture. Agriculture forms the main occupation of more than three-quarters of the population. Physically, Karnataka divides into four regions—the coastal region, the southern and northern plains, comprising roughly the districts of Bangalore, Tumkur, Chitradurga, Kolar, Bellary, Mandya and Mysore, and the hill country, comprising the districts of Chikmagalur, Hassan and Shimoga. Rainfall is heavy in the hill country, and there is dense forest. The greater part of the plains are cultivated. Coorg district is essentially agricultural.

The main food crops are rice paddy and jowar, and ragi which is also about 30% of the national crop. Total foodgrains production (1998–99), 8·80m. tonnes (including rice 3·33m. tonnes); pulses 0·48m. tonnes. Sugar, groundnut, castor-seed, safflower, mulberry silk and cotton are important cash crops. The state grows about 70% of the national coffee crop.

Production, 1998–99: sugarcane, 28·33m. tonnes; cotton (1998–99), 985,000 tonnes.

Livestock (1992–93): buffaloes, 4·07m.; other cattle, 10·18m.; sheep, 4·73m.; goats, 3·89m.

Forestry. Total forest in the state (2000) is 38,284 sq. km, producing sandalwood, bamboo and other timbers.

Fisheries. The catch in 1998 totalled 140,000 tonnes. Catches are declining rapidly owing to overfishing and pollution.

INDUSTRY

There were 7,765 factories, 125 industrial estates and 5,176 industrial sheds employing 818,000 in March 1994. In 1994–95, 163,524 small industries employed 1,076,312 persons. The Vishveshwaraiah Iron and Steel Works is situated at Bhadravati, while at Bangalore are national undertakings for the manufacture of aircraft, machine tools, telephones, light engineering and electronics goods. The Kudremukh iron ore project is of national importance. An oil refinery is in operation at Mangalore. Other industries include textiles, vehicle manufacture, cement, chemicals, sugar, paper, porcelain and soap. In addition, much of the world's sandalwood is processed, the oil being one of the most valuable productions of the state. Sericulture is a more important cottage industry giving employment, directly or indirectly, to about 2·7m. persons; production of raw silk, 2000, 9,000 tonnes, over two-thirds of national production.

COMMUNICATIONS

Roads. In 1999 the state had 137,520 km of roads, including 2,000 km of national highway and 73,000 km of state highway. There were (31 March 1996) 2,249,890 motor vehicles.

Rail. In 1999 there were 3,192 km of railway (including 149 km of narrow gauge) in the state.

Civil Aviation. There are airports at Bangalore, Hubli, Mysore, Mangalore, Bellary and Belgaum, with regular scheduled services to Bombay, Calcutta, Delhi and Madras. Bangalore is being upgraded to an international airport—the present airport already receives international flights from a number of destinations. A new Bangalore international airport is under construction at Devanahalli, 34 km from the city.

Shipping. Mangalore is a deep-water port for the export of mineral ores. Karwar is being developed as an intermediate port.

SOCIAL INSTITUTIONS

Justice. The seat of the High Court is at Bangalore. It has a Chief Justice and 42 puisne judges.

Religion. At the 2001 census Hindus were 85·6% of the population; Muslims, 11·6%; Christians, 1·5%.

Education. In 2001, 67·04% of the population were literate (76·29% of men and 57·50% of women). In 1996–97 the state had 22,870 primary schools with 6,507,805 students, 18,485 middle schools with 2,158,487 students, 7,644 high and higher secondary schools with 1,270,794 students, 172 polytechnic and 125 medical colleges, 49 engineering and technology colleges, 761 arts, science and commerce colleges and 12 universities. Education is free up to pre-university level.

Universities: Mysore (1916); Karnataka (1949) at Dharwar; University of Agricultural Sciences (1964) at Hebbal, Bangalore; Bangalore; Gulbarga; Kannada; Mangalore; University of Agricultural Sciences, Dharwad; Kuvempu University, Shimoga; Karnataka State Open University, Mysore; Rajiv Gandhi University of Health Sciences, Bangalore; Visveswaraiah Technological University, Nehrunagar; and National Law School of India.

Mysore has six university and 125 affiliated colleges; Karnataka, five and 240; Bangalore, 204 affiliated; Hebbal, eight constituent colleges.

The Indian Institute of Science, Bangalore and the Manipal Academy of Higher Education have the status of a university.

Health. There were in 2003, 293 hospitals, 622 primary health units and dispensaries, 1,297 primary health centres and 7,793 health subcentres. Total number of beds in 2003, about 50,000.

KERALA

KEY HISTORICAL EVENTS

The state of Kerala was created in 1956, bringing together the Malayalam-speaking areas. It includes most of the former state of Travancore-Cochin and small areas from the state of Madras. Cochin, a safe harbour, was an early site of European trading in India. In 1795 the British took it from the Dutch and British influence remained dominant. Travancore was a Hindu state which became a British protectorate in 1795, having been an ally of the British East India Company for some years. Cochin and Travancore were combined as one state in 1947, reorganized and renamed Kerala in 1956.

TERRITORY AND POPULATION

Kerala is in south India and is bounded north by Karnataka, east and southeast by Tamil Nadu, southwest and west by the Indian ocean. The state has an area of 38,863 sq. km. The 2001 census showed a population of 31,838,619; density, 819 per sq. km. Chief cities, *see* INDIA: Territory and Population. Other principal towns (2001): Palakkad (197,281), Kottayam (172,867), Malappuram (170,364), Cherthala (141,512), Guruvayur (138,676), Kanhangad (129,364), Vadakara (123,965).

Languages spoken in the state are Malayalam, Tamil and Kannada.

SOCIAL STATISTICS

The growth rate during the period 1991–2001, at 9·42%, was the lowest of any Indian state.

CONSTITUTION AND GOVERNMENT

The state has a unicameral legislature of 140 elected (and one nominated) members including the Speaker.

The state has 14 districts. The capital is Thiruvananthapuram.

RECENT ELECTIONS

At the elections of 10 May 2001 the Indian National Congress party won 62 seats, the Communist Party of India (Marxist) (CPM) 23 and the Muslim League Kerala State Committee 16.

CURRENT ADMINISTRATION

Governor: Raghunandan Lal Bhatia; b. 1921 (took office on 23 June 2004).

Chief Minister: Oommen Chandy; b. 1943 (took office on 31 Aug. 2004).

ECONOMY

Budget. Budget estimates for 2000–01 showed revenue receipts of Rs 135,665m.; expenditure Rs 135,761m.

ENERGY AND NATURAL RESOURCES

Electricity. Installed capacity (1999–2000), 1,775·5 MW. The Idukki hydro-electric plant produced 3,064m. kWh and the Sabarigiri scheme 1,674m. kWh. All villages have electricity. The state had a power deficit until the inauguration of the Kayamkulam thermal power plant in 1999.

Minerals. The beach sands of Kerala contain monazite, ilmenite, rutile, zircon, sillimanite, etc. There are extensive white clay deposits; other minerals of commercial importance include titanium, copper, magnesite, china clay, limestone, quartz sand and lignite. Iron ore has been found at Kozhikode (Calicut).

Agriculture. Area under irrigation in 1995–96 was 644,000 ha; six irrigation projects were under execution in 1996–97. The chief agricultural products are rice, tapioca, coconut, arecanut, cashew nut, oilseeds, pepper, sugarcane, rubber, tea, coffee and cardamom. About 98% of Indian black pepper and about 95% of Indian rubber is produced in Kerala. Production of principal crops, 2000: total rice, 770,686 tonnes (from 349,774 ha); tapioca, 2,563,512 tonnes; coconuts, 5,167m. nuts; rubber, 572,820 tonnes; pepper, 56,431 tonnes; coffee, 60,470 tonnes; tea, 71,295 tonnes; cashew nuts, 46,366 tonnes; ginger, 38,607 tonnes; sugarcane, 47,767 tonnes.

Livestock (1987): buffaloes, 329,000; other cattle, 3·4m.; goats, 1·6m. In 1995–96 milk production was 2·24m. tonnes; egg production, 1,991m.

Forestry. Forest occupied 10,815 sq. km in 2000, including teak, sandalwood, ebony and blackwood and varieties of softwood. Net forest revenue, 1995–96, Rs 1,607·7m.

Fisheries. Fishing is a flourishing industry; the total catch in 1995–96 was 582,000 tonnes (of which marine, 532,000 tonnes). Fish exports, 78,896 tonnes in 1995–96.

INDUSTRY

There are numerous cashew and coir factories. Important industries are rubber, tea, coffee, tiles, automotive tyres, watches, electronics, oil, textiles, ceramics, fertilizers and chemicals, pharmaceuticals, zinc-smelting, sugar, cement, rayon, glass, matches, pencils, monazite, ilmenite, titanium oxide, rare earths, aluminium, electrical goods, paper, shark-liver oil, etc. The state has a refinery and a shipyard at Kochi (Cochin).

The number of factories registered under the Factories Act 1948 in 2000 was 18,340, with daily average employment of 0·41m. There were 20,006 small-scale units in 2000; 0·78m. persons were employed in small-scale units on 31 March 1996.

COMMUNICATIONS

Roads. In 2000 there were 21,730 km of roads in the state (national and state highways, 4,113 km; district roads, 4,992 km). There were 1·91m. motor vehicles in 2000.

Rail. There is a coastal line from Mangalore in Karnataka which connects with Tamil Nadu. In 1995–96 there were 1,053 route-km of track.

Civil Aviation. There are airports at Kozhikode, Kochi and Thiruvananthapuram with regular scheduled internal services to Delhi, Bombay and Madras. In addition Kochi has international flights to a number of destinations in the Gulf states plus Colombo and Singapore, and Kozhikode and Thiruvananthapuram also have flights to the Gulf.

Shipping. Port Kochi, administered by the central government, is one of India's major ports; in 1983 it became the out-port for the Inland Container Depot at Coimbatore in Tamil Nadu. There are 12 other ports and harbours.

SOCIAL INSTITUTIONS

Justice. The High Court at Ernakulam has a Chief Justice and 29 puisne judges.

Religion. At the 2001 census there were Hindus accounted for 57·5% of the population, Muslims 23·5% and Christians 18·5%.

Education. Kerala is the most literate Indian state, with 25·63m. literate people at the 2001 census (90·92%; 94·20% of men and 87·86% of women). Education is free up to the age of 14.

In 2000 there were 6,726 primary schools with 2·79m. students, 2,968 upper primary schools with 1·84m. students and 3,511 high and higher secondary schools with 1·07m. students. There were 169 junior colleges in 1996–97 with 210,074 pupils.

Kerala University (established 1937) at Thiruvananthapuram is affiliating and teaching; in 1995–96 it had 52 affiliated colleges with 113,569 students. The University of Kochi is federal, and for post-graduate studies only. The University of Calicut (established 1968) is teaching and affiliating and has 95 affiliated colleges with 122,343 students (1995–96). Kerala Agricultural University (established 1971) has seven constituent colleges. Mahatma Gandhi University at Kottayam was established in 1983 and has 64 affiliated colleges with 112,992 students (1995–96). There are two other universities, Sree Sankaracharya University at Ernakulam and

Kannur (formerly Malabar) University. There were also (2000) seven medical colleges, 20 pharmacy colleges, three dental colleges, four homeopathy colleges, 32 engineering colleges, 59 technology colleges, three nursing colleges, 19 teacher training colleges and 191 arts and science colleges.

Health. In 2000 there were 1,425 hospitals and health centres, including 113 Ayurvedic hospitals and 30 homeopathic hospitals. There were 41,462 hospital beds plus 2,604 beds in Ayurvedic hospitals and 970 beds in homeopathic clinics and hospitals.

FURTHER READING

Jeffrey, R., *Politics, Women and Well-Being: How Kerala Became a Model.* London, 1992

MADHYA PRADESH

KEY HISTORICAL EVENTS

The state was formed in 1956 to bring together the Hindi-speaking districts of the area including the 17 Hindi districts of the old Madhya Pradesh, most of the former state of Madhya Bharat, the former states of Bhopal and Vindhya Pradesh and a former Rajput enclave, Sironj. This was an area which the Mahrattas took from the Moghuls between 1712 and 1760. The British overcame Mahratta power in 1818 and established their own Central Provinces. Nagpur became the Province's capital and was also the capital of Madhya Pradesh until in 1956 boundary changes transferred it to Maharashtra. The present capital, Bhopal, was the centre of a Muslim princely state from 1723. An ally of the British against the Mahrattas, Bhopal (with neighbouring small states) became a British-protected agency in 1818. After independence Bhopal acceded to the Indian Union in 1949. The states of Madhya Bharat and Vindhya Pradesh were then formed as neighbours, and in 1956 were combined with Bhopal and Sironj and renamed Madhya Pradesh. In 2000 sixteen mainly tribal districts were carved from Madhya Pradesh to form the new state of Chhattisgarh.

TERRITORY AND POPULATION

The state is in central India and is bounded north by Uttar Pradesh, east by the new state of Chhattisgarh, south by Maharashtra, and west by Gujarat and Rajasthan. Owing to the creation of Chhattisgarh, Madhya Pradesh is no longer the largest Indian state in size. Its revised area is 308,245 sq. km (previously 443,446 sq. km), making it the second largest state in the country (after Rajasthan). Population (2001 census), 60,385,118 (31,456,873 males); density, 196 per sq. km.

Cities with over 250,000 population, *see* INDIA: Territory and Population. Other large cities (2001): Ratlam, 233,480; Dewas, 230,658; Satna, 229,323; Burhanpur, 194,360; Murwara, 186,738; Singrauli, 185,580; Rewa, 183,232; Khandwa, 171,976; Bhind, 153,768; Chhindwara, 153,635; Morena, 150,890; Shivpuri, 146,859; Guna, 137,132; Damoh, 127,939; Vidisha, 125,457; Mandsaur, 117,532; Nimach, 112,691; Itarsi, 109,288; Chhatarpur, 109,021; Khargone, 103,980.

Hindi, Marathi, Urdu and Gujarati are spoken. In April 1990 Hindi, which predominates in the state, became the sole official language.

CONSTITUTION AND GOVERNMENT

Madhya Pradesh is one of the nine states for which the Constitution provides a bicameral legislature, but the Vidhan Parishad or Upper House (to consist of 90 members) has yet to be formed. The Vidhan Sabha or Lower House has 230 elected members.

For administrative purposes the state has been split into nine revenue divisions with a Commissioner at the head of each; the headquarters of these are located at Bhopal, Gwalior, Hoshangabad, Indore, Jabalpur, Morena, Rewa, Sagar and Ujjain. There are 22,029 *gram* (village) panchayats, 313 *janpad* (intermediate) panchayats and 45 *zila* (district) panchayats, following the creation of 16 new districts in administrative reforms of 1999 and the creation of Chhattisgarh in 2000.

The seat of government is at Bhopal.

RECENT ELECTIONS
Following the election in Dec. 2003, the Bharatiya Janata Party (BJP) won power with 173 seats (117 in 1998). The Congress (I) Party declined from 170 seats in 1998 to 38. Other parties won 19 seats.

CURRENT ADMINISTRATION
Governor: Balram Jakhar; b. 1923 (took office on 30 June 2004).

Chief Minister: Babulal Gaur; b. 1930 (took office on 23 Aug. 2004).

ECONOMY
Budget. Budget estimates for 2001–02 showed revenue receipts of Rs 125,184m. and expenditure of Rs 162,770m. Annual plan, 2002–03, Rs 48,209m.

ENERGY AND NATURAL RESOURCES
Electricity. Madhya Pradesh is rich in low-grade coal suitable for power generation, and also has immense potential for hydro-electric energy. Total installed capacity, 2000–01, 2,941 MW. Power generated, 14,009m. kWh in 2000–01. There are eight hydro-electric power stations of 747·5 MW installed capacity. 50,306 out of 51,806 villages had electricity by 2000–01.

Water. Major irrigation projects include the Chambal Valley scheme (started in 1952 with Rajasthan), the Tawa project in Hoshangabad district, the Barna and Hasdeo schemes, the Mahanadi canal system and schemes in the Narmada valley at Bargi and Narmadasagar. Area under irrigation, 1999–2000, 4·28m. ha.

Minerals. Much of the state's extensive mineral deposits were in the area that has now become the new state of Chhattisgarh. In 2000–01 (1996 figures in brackets) there were 25·04m. tonnes (8,001m.) of limestone, 0·25m. tonnes (126·8m.) of bauxite, 4·04m. tonnes (26,853m.) of coal, and 0·92m. tonnes (2,186·2m.) of iron ore. In 2001–02 the output of diamonds was 73,981 carats and manganese ore 0·43m. tonnes. In 2001–02 revenue from minerals was Rs 5·39m. (Rs 8,500m. in 1997–98) and coal output was 4·4m. tonnes (43·0m. in 1999–2000).

Agriculture. The creation of the new state of Chhattisgarh, previously known as the 'rice bowl' of Madhya Pradesh, in 2000 had serious implications for the state. Agriculture is the mainstay of the state's economy and 76·8% of the people are rural. 43·7% of the land area is cultivable, of which 16·6% is irrigated. Production of principal crops, 2001–02 (in tonnes): foodgrains, 8·93m.; pulses, 3·96m.; cotton, 0·23m. bales of 170 kg.

Livestock (1997; Madhya Pradesh and Chhattisgarh combined): buffaloes, 6·64m.; other cattle, 34·88m.; sheep, 6·56m.; goats, 6·47m.

Forestry. The forested area totals 95,200 sq. km, or about 30·9% of the state. The forests are chiefly of sal, saja and teak species. They are the chief source in India of best-quality teak; they also provide firewood for about 60% of domestic fuel needs, and form valuable watershed protection. Forest revenue, 2001–02, Rs 32·5m.

INDUSTRY
The major industries are steel, aluminium, paper, cement, motor vehicles, ordnance, textiles and heavy electrical equipment. Other industries include electronics, telecommunications, sugar, fertilizers, straw board, vegetable oil, refractories, potteries, textile machinery, steel casting and re-rolling, industrial gases, synthetic fibres, drugs, biscuit manufacturing, engineering, optical fibres, plastics, tools, rayon and art silk. The number of heavy and medium industries in the state is 805; the number of small-scale establishments in production is 497,000.

There are 23 'growth centres' in operation, and five under development. The Government of India has proposed setting up a Special Economic Zone at Indore.

COMMUNICATIONS
Roads. Total length of roads is 68,100 km. The length of national highways is 4,720 km and state highway 6,500 km. In March 2002 there were 3,173,000 motor vehicles.

Rail. The main rail route linking northern and southern India passes through Madhya Pradesh. Bhopal, Bina, Gwalior, Indore, Itarsi, Jabalpur, Katni, Khandwa, Ratlam and Ujjain are important junctions for the central, south, eastern and western networks. Route length (1998–99), 5,764·8 km.

Civil Aviation. There are domestic airports at Bhopal, Gwalior, Indore and Khajuraho with regular scheduled services to Bombay, Delhi, Agra, Varanasi and Raipur.

SOCIAL INSTITUTIONS

Justice. The High Court of Judicature at Jabalpur has a Chief Justice and 29 puisne judges. Its benches are located at Gwalior and Indore. A National Institute of Law and a National Judicial Academy have been set up at Bhopal.

Religion. At the 2001 census Hindus numbered 92%; Muslims, 5%.

Education. In 2001, 64·11% of the population were literate (76·80% of men and 50·28% of women). Education is free for children aged up to 14.

In 1998 there were 81,000 primary schools (63,712 in 2001) with 10·33m. students, 20,000 middle schools with 3·46m. students and 7,000 high and higher secondary schools (8,471 in 2001) with 2·03m. students.

Universities: Dr Harisingh Gour University (established 1946), at Sagar, had 97 affiliated colleges and 74,386 students in 1992–93; Rani Durgavati University at Jabalpur (1957) had 46 affiliated colleges and 45,315 students; Vikram University (1957), at Ujjain, had 83 affiliated colleges and 39,723 students; Devi Ahilya University at Indore (1964) had 32 affiliated colleges and 28,196 students; Jiwaji University (1963), at Gwalior, had 60 affiliated colleges and (1991–92) 58,825 students; Awadhesh Pratap Singh University, Rewa had 81 colleges and 24,960 students; Barkatullah Vishwavidyalaya, Bhopal had 44 colleges and 18,817 students; Makhanlal Chaturvedi Rashtriya Patrakarita Vishwavidhyalaya Bhopal; Mahatma Gandhi Chitrakoot Gramodoya Vishwavidhayalaya, Chitrakoot; Rajiv Gandhi Technology University, Bhopal; Indira Kala Sangeet Vishwavidyalaya, Khairagarh; Jawaharlal Nehru Krishi University, Jabalpur; Bhoj Open University, Bhopal; the Maharshi Mahesh Yogi Vedic Vishwavidyalaya, Jabalpur. In 1999 there were 413 government colleges (15 of which were lost to Chhattisgarh in 2000), 252 private colleges (14 of which were lost to Chhattisgarh in 2000), 30 engineering colleges (all to be affiliated to the Rajiv Ghandi Technology University), seven medical colleges, 44 polytechnics, five institutions of architecture and 30 management institutes.

Health. In 2001–02 there were 45 district hospitals, 57 urban civil hospitals, 1,194 primary health centres, 8,835 sub-health centres, 229 community health centres, seven TB hospitals and two TB sanatoriums.

MAHARASHTRA

KEY HISTORICAL EVENTS

The Bombay Presidency of the East India Company began with a trading factory, made over to the Company in 1668. The Presidency expanded, overcoming the surrounding Mahratta chiefs until Mahratta power was finally conquered in 1818. After independence Bombay State succeeded the Presidency; its area was altered in 1956 by adding Kutch and Saurashtra and the Marathi-speaking areas of Hyderabad and Madhya Pradesh, and taking away Kannada-speaking areas (which were added to Mysore). In 1960 the Bombay Reorganization Act divided Bombay State between Gujarati and Marathi areas, the latter becoming Maharashtra. The state of Maharashtra consists of the following districts of the former Bombay State: Ahmadnagar, Akola, Amravati, Aurangabad, Bhandara, Bhir, Buldana, Chanda, Dhulia (West Khandesh), Greater Bombay, Jalgaon (East Khandesh), Kolaba, Kolhapur, Nagpur, Nanded, Nashik, Osmanabad, Parbhani, Pune, Ratnagiri, Sangli, Satara, Sholapur, Thane, Wardha, Yeotmal; certain portions of Thane and Dhulia districts have become part of Gujarat.

TERRITORY AND POPULATION

Maharashtra is in central India and is bounded north by Madhya Pradesh, east by Chhattisgarh, south by Andhra Pradesh, Karnataka and Goa, west by the Indian ocean and northwest by Daman and Gujarat. The state has an area of 307,713 sq. km. The population in 2001 (census) was 96,752,247; density, 314 per sq. km. In 2001 the area of Greater Bombay was 603 sq. km and its population 16·4m. For other principal cities, *see* INDIA: Territory and Population. Other large towns (2001): Jalna (235,529), Bhusawal (187,524), Vasai (174,382), Yavatmal (141,970), Bid (138,091), Kamthi (137,056), Gondia (120,878), Virar (118,945), Wardha (110,070), Satara (108,043), Achalpur (107,304), Barsi (104,786), Panvel (104,031).

The official language is Marathi.

SOCIAL STATISTICS

Growth rate 1991–2001, 22·57%.

CONSTITUTION AND GOVERNMENT

Maharashtra has a bicameral legislature. The Legislative Council has 78 members. The Legislative Assembly has 288 elected members and one member nominated by the Governor to represent the Anglo-Indian community.

The Council of Ministers consists of the Chief Minister, 16 other Ministers and 19 Ministers of State.

The capital is Bombay (Mumbai). The state has 35 districts.

RECENT ELECTIONS

At the elections held on 13 Oct. 2004 the Nationalist Congress Party won 71 of the 288 seats, the Indian National Congress 69, Shiv Sena 62, the Bharatiya Janata Party 54, the Communist Party of India (Marxist) 3, other parties 10 and ind. 19. Turnout was 63·4%.

CURRENT ADMINISTRATION

Governor: S. M. Krishna; b. 1932 (took office on 6 Dec. 2004).

Chief Minister: Vilasrao Deshmukh; b. 1945 (since 1 Nov. 2004; first in office 1999–2003).

ECONOMY

Budget. Budget estimates, 2000–01: revenue receipts, Rs 374,303m.; revenue expenditure, Rs 366,869m.

ENERGY AND NATURAL RESOURCES

Electricity. Installed capacity, 1998, 8,231 MW. All villages have electricity. Output, 2001, 53,013m. kWh.

Oil and Gas. Bombay High (offshore) produced 14·25m. tonnes of crude oil and 17,200,000 cu. metres of natural gas in 2001. Oil production has declined by one-third since the early 1990s. A recovery plan for the ageing field began in 2001. This involves drilling 145 new wells and laying about 245 km of sub-sea pipeline. The plan is scheduled to be completed in 2006.

Minerals. The state has coal, silica sand, dolomite, kyanite, chromite, limestone, iron ore, manganese and bauxite. Value of mineral production, 2001, Rs 21,340m. of which 94% is contributed by coal. Coal production in 2000–01 was 28·8m. tonnes. Manganese is the second most valuable mineral.

Agriculture. 3·3m. ha of the cropped area of 21·4m. ha are irrigated. In normal seasons the main food crops are rice, wheat, jowar, bajra and pulses. Main cash crops: cotton, sugarcane, groundnuts. Production, 2000–01 (in tonnes): foodgrains, 11·9m. (rice, 2·4m., wheat, 1·11m.); pulses, 1·7m.; cotton, 476,000; sugarcane, 36·5m.; groundnuts, 0·6m.

Livestock (1992 census, in 1,000): buffaloes, 5,447; other cattle, 17,441; sheep and goats, 13,015; poultry, 32,189.

Forestry. Forests occupied 64,300 sq. km in 1995–96. Value of forest products in 1996–97, Rs 2,820m.

Fisheries. In 2000–01 the marine fish catch was estimated at 403,000 tonnes and the inland fish catch at 123,000 tonnes; in 1995–96, 18,038 boats, including 8,552 mechanized, were used for marine fishing.

INDUSTRY

Industry is concentrated mainly in Bombay, Nashik, Pune and Thane. The main groups are chemicals and products, textiles, electrical and non-electrical machinery, petroleum and products, aircraft, rubber and plastic products, transport equipment, automobiles, paper, electronic items, engineering goods, pharmaceuticals and food products. The state industrial development corporation invested Rs 77,020m. in 21,452 industrial units in 1994–95. In June 1995 there were 26,642 working factories employing 1·2m. people. In Dec. 1996 there were 203,882 small scale industries employing 1·63m. people.

COMMUNICATIONS

Roads. In 2001 there were 260,000 km of roads, of which nearly 200,000 km were surfaced. There were 7,194,000 motor vehicles on 1 Jan. 2001, of which about 25% were in Greater Bombay. Passenger and freight transport has been nationalized.

Rail. The total length of railway in 2001 was 5,459 km; 66% was broad gauge, 14% metre gauge and 20% narrow gauge. The main junctions and termini are Bombay, Dadar, Manmad, Akola, Nagpur, Pune and Sholapur.

Civil Aviation. The main airport is Bombay, which has national and international flights. Nagpur airport is on the route from Bombay to Calcutta and there are also airports at Pune and Aurangabad.

Shipping. Maharashtra has a coastline of 720 km. Bombay is the major port, and there are 48 minor ports.

SOCIAL INSTITUTIONS

Justice. The High Court has a Chief Justice and 60 judges. The seat of the High Court is Bombay, but it has benches at Nagpur, Aurangabad and Panaji (Goa).

Religion. At the 2001 census 81% of the population were Hindus, 9·7% Muslims and 6·3% Buddhists.

Education. The number of literate people, according to the 2001 census, was 64·57m. (77·27%; 86·27% of men and 67·51% of women). In 2001 there were 10,225 high and 3,981 higher secondary schools with (1995) 2,795,567 pupils; 15,070 middle schools with (1995) 4,753,257 pupils; and 66,369 primary schools with (1995) 11,685,598 pupils. There are 111 engineering and technology colleges, 156 medical colleges (including dental and Ayurvedic colleges), 244 teacher training colleges, 152 polytechnics and 820 arts, science and commerce colleges.

Bombay University, founded in 1857, is mainly an affiliating university. It has 276 colleges with a total (1993–94) of 234,469 students. Nagpur University (1923) is both teaching and affiliating. It has 258 colleges with 95,664 students. Pune University, founded in 1948, is teaching and affiliating; it has 167 colleges and 151,990 students. The SNDT Women's University had 33 colleges with a total of 33,343 students. Dr B. R. Ambedkar Marathwada University, Aurangabad was founded in 1958 as a teaching and affiliating body to control colleges in the Marathwada or Marathi-speaking area, previously under Osmania University; it has 190 colleges and 195,806 students. Shivaji University, Kolhapur, was established in 1963 to control affiliated colleges previously under Pune University. It has 205 colleges and 115,553 students. Amravati University has 130 colleges and 74,484 students. Other universities are: Marathwada Krishi Vidyapeeth, Parbhani; Y. Chavan Maharashtra Open University, Nashik; North Maharashtra University, Jalgaon, with 101 colleges and 66,092 students; Mahatma Phule Krishi University, Rahuri; Dr Punjabrao Deshmukh Krishi University, Akola; Konkan Krishi University, Dapoli; Dr Babasaheb Ambedkar Technological University, Lonere; Swami Ramanand Teerth Marathwad University, Nanded; Tilak Maharashtra Vidyapeeth, Pune; Bharati Vidyapeeth, Pune; Gokhale Institute of Politics and Economics, Pune; Deccan College, Pune; Indian Institute of Technology, Bombay; Indira Gandhi Institute of Developmental Research, Bombay; International Institute for Population Sciences, Bombay; Tata Institute of Social Sciences, Bombay. The Central Institute of Fisheries Education in Bombay also has university-equivalent status.

Health. In 1995 there were 736 hospitals (124,701 beds), 1,418 dispensaries and 1,695 primary health centres, 161 primary health units and 2,154 TB hospitals and clinics.

MANIPUR

KEY HISTORICAL EVENTS

Formerly a state under the political control of the government of India, Manipur entered into interim arrangements with the Indian Union on 15 Aug. 1947 and the political agency was abolished. The administration was taken over by the government of India on 15 Oct. 1949 under a merger agreement, and it was centrally administered by the government of India through a Chief Commissioner. In 1950–51 an Advisory form of government was introduced. In 1957 this was replaced by a Territorial Council of 30 elected and two nominated members. Later, in 1963, a Legislative Assembly of 30 elected and three nominated members was established under the government of Union Territories Act 1963. Because of the unstable party position in the Assembly, it had to be dissolved on 16 Oct. 1969 and president's rule introduced. The status of the administrator was raised from Chief Commissioner to Lieut.-Governor with effect from 19 Dec. 1969. On 21 Jan. 1972 Manipur became a state and the status of the administrator was changed from Lieut.-Governor to Governor. In June 2001 Manipur was placed under central rule, but ceased to be so after the 2002 elections.

TERRITORY AND POPULATION

The state is in northeast India and is bounded north by Nagaland, east by Myanmar, south by Myanmar and Mizoram, and west by Assam. Manipur has an area of 22,327 sq. km and a population (2001 census) of 2,388,634; density, 107 per sq. km. The valley, which is about 1,813 sq. km, is 800 metres above sea-level. The largest city is Imphal with a population of 245,967 (2001 census). The hills rise in places to 3,000 metres, but are mostly about 1,500–1,800 metres. The average annual rainfall is 165 cm. The hill areas are inhabited by various hill tribes who constitute about one-third of the total population of the state. There are about 30 tribes and sub-tribes falling into two main groups of Nagas and Kukis. Manipuri and English are the official languages. A large number of dialects are spoken.

SOCIAL STATISTICS

Growth rate 1991–2001, 30·02%.

CONSTITUTION AND GOVERNMENT

Manipur has a Legislative Assembly of 60 members, of which 19 are from reserved tribal constituencies. There are nine districts. The capital is Imphal.

RECENT ELECTIONS

Elections were held in Feb. 2002. The Indian National Congress party (INC) won 19 seats; the Federal Party of Manipur (FPM), 13; the Manipur State Congress Party (MSCP), 6; the Bharatiya Janata Party (BJP), 4; Samata Party, 3; others, 15. Following the elections a Secular Progressive Front (SPF) was installed in government, comprising the INC, the MSCP, the Nationalist Congress Party and the Communist Party of India.

CURRENT ADMINISTRATION

Governor: Shivinder Singh Sidhu; b. 1929 (took office on 6 Aug. 2004).

Chief Minister: Okram Ibobi Singh; b. 1948 (took office on 7 March 2002).

ECONOMY

Budget. Budget estimates for 2000–01 show revenue of Rs 12,220·2m. and expenditure of Rs 12,453·3m.

ENERGY AND NATURAL RESOURCES

Electricity. Installed capacity (2002) is 45 MW from diesel and hydro-electric generators. This has been augmented since 1981 by the North Eastern Regional Grid and by the Lotak and Irang Hep schemes. In March 1996 there were 2,015 villages with electricity.

Water. The main power, irrigation and flood-control schemes are the Loktak Lift Irrigation scheme (irrigation potential, 40,000 ha); the Singda scheme (potential 4,000 ha, and improved water supply for Imphal); the Thoubal scheme (potential 34,000 ha); and four other large projects. By 1994–95, 59,100 ha had been irrigated.

Minerals. Chromite is the only significant mineral resource—it is extracted from a single mine.

Agriculture. Rice is the principal crop; with wheat, maize and pulses. Total foodgrains, 1998, 365,000 tonnes (rice, 352,000 tonnes).

Agricultural workforce, 453,040. Only 0·21m. ha are cultivable, of which 158,000 ha are under paddy. Fruit and vegetables are important in the valley, including pineapples, oranges, bananas, mangoes, pears, peaches and plums. Soil erosion, produced by shifting cultivation, is being halted by terracing. Fruit production in 1993–94, 0·11m. tonnes.

Forestry. Forests occupied about 17,418 sq. km in 1998. The main products are teak, jurjan, pine; there are also large areas of bamboo and cane, especially in the Jiri and Barak river drainage areas, yielding about 0·3m. tonnes annually. Total revenue from forests, 1990–91, Rs 9·95m.

Fisheries. Landings in 1995–96, 12,500 tonnes.

INDUSTRY

Handloom weaving is a cottage industry. Manipur is one of the least industrialized states of India. Location, limited infrastructure and insufficient power hold back industrial development. Larger-scale industries include the manufacture of bicycles and TV sets, sugar, cement, starch, vegetable oil and glucose. Sericulture produces about 45 tonnes of raw silk annually. Estimated non-agricultural workforce, 229,000.

COMMUNICATIONS

Roads. Length of road (1995), 7,003 km; number of vehicles (1996–97) 65,223. A national highway from Kaziranga (Assam) runs through Imphal to the border with Myanmar. The total length of national highway in 2000 was 954 km.

Rail. A railway link was opened in 1990, linking Karong with the Assamese railway system.

Civil Aviation. There is an airport at Imphal with regular scheduled services to Delhi and Calcutta.

SOCIAL INSTITUTIONS

Religion. At the 2001 census Hindus numbered nearly 58% of the population; Christians, 34%; Muslims, 7%.

Education. In 2001, 68·87% of the population were literate (77·87% of men and 59·70% of women). In 1996–97 there were 2,548 primary schools with 230,230 students, 555 middle schools with 106,200 students, 553 high and higher secondary schools with 66,160 students, 50 colleges, one medical college, two teacher training colleges, three polytechnics, Manipur University with 62 colleges and 52,352 students (1997–98) and an agricultural university (Central Agricultural University, Imphal).

Health. In 1996–97 there were 93 hospitals and public health centres, 52 dispensaries, 16 community health centres, 420 sub-centres and 58 other facilities.

MEGHALAYA

KEY HISTORICAL EVENTS

The state was created under the Assam Reorganization (Meghalaya) Act 1969 and inaugurated on 2 April 1970. Its status was that of a state within the State of Assam until 21 Jan. 1972 when it became a fully-fledged state of the Union. It consists of the former Garo Hills district and United Khasi and Jaintia Hills district of Assam.

TERRITORY AND POPULATION

Meghalaya is bounded in the north and east by Assam, south and west by Bangladesh. The area is 22,429 sq. km and the population (2001 census) 2,306,069; density, 103 per sq. km. The people are mainly of the Khasi, Jaintia and Garo tribes. The main languages of the state are Khasi, Jaintia, Garo and English.

SOCIAL STATISTICS

Growth rate 1991–2001, 29·94%.

CONSTITUTION AND GOVERNMENT

Meghalaya has a unicameral legislature. The Legislative Assembly has 60 seats.

There are seven districts. The capital is Shillong (population, 2001 census, 267,881 in the urban agglomeration).

RECENT ELECTIONS

In elections held in Feb. 2003 the Indian National Congress won 22 seats; Nationalist Congress Party, 14; United Democratic Party, 9; ind., 5; other parties, 10.

CURRENT ADMINISTRATION

Governor: Mundakkal Matthew Jacob; b. 1928 (took office on 19 June 1995).

Chief Minister: D. D. Lapang; b. 1934 (since 4 March 2003; also 1992–93).

ECONOMY

Budget. Budget estimates for 2001–02 showed revenue receipts of Rs 13,211·3m. and expenditure of Rs 13,548·3m.

ENERGY AND NATURAL RESOURCES

Electricity. Total installed capacity (2000–01) was 185·2 MW. 2,580 villages out of 4,902 had electricity in March 2001.

Minerals. The Khasi Hills, Jaintia Hills and Garo Hills districts produce coal, sillimanite (95% of India's total output), limestone, fire clay, dolomite, feldspar, quartz and glass sand. The state also has deposits of coal (estimated reserves 600m. tonnes), limestone (3,000m.), fire clay (6m.) and sandstone which are so far virtually untapped. Coal production in 2000–01 was 5,149,000 tonnes; limestone production in 2000–01 was 585,000 tonnes.

Agriculture. About 71% of the people depend on agriculture. Principal crops are rice, maize, potatoes, cotton, oranges, ginger, tezpata, areca nuts, jute, mesta, bananas and pineapples. Production 2000–01 (in tonnes) of principal crops: rice, 179,000; potatoes, 144,000; ginger, 45,000; jute, 36,000; citrus fruits, 32,000; maize, 24,000; cotton, 8,000; rape and mustard, 5,000. Poultry and pigs are the principal livestock.

Forestry. Forests covered 9,496 sq. km in 2002. Forest products are one of the state's chief resources.

INDUSTRY

Apart from agriculture the main source of employment is the extraction and processing of minerals; there are also important timber processing mills and cement factories. Other industries include electronics, tantalum capacitors, beverages and watches. The state has five industrial estates, two industrial areas and one growth centre. In 1995–96 there were 58 registered factories and 2,533 small-scale industries. In 2000, 17,800 workers were involved in manufacturing and processing.

There were also, in 2001–02, 1,812 sericultural villages, six sericultural farms, eight silk units and nine weaving centres. In 2000 there were more than 5,400 *khadi* and village industrial units.

COMMUNICATIONS

Roads. Three national highways run through the state for a distance of 520 km. In 2000–01 there were 7,598 km of surfaced and unsurfaced roads, of which 3,523 km were surfaced. Total number of motor vehicles in 2000–01 was 67,076, including 13,464 trucks, 12,853 private cars and 2,463 buses.

Rail. The state has only 1 km of railways, but this does not connect the state with the national network. The nearest station is 103 km outside the state. There is a plan to extend the national network to Byrnihat, 20 km inside Meghalaya.

Civil Aviation. Umroi airport (35 km from Shillong) connects the state with main air services. There are regular flights to Calcutta. Umroi is to be upgraded to receive larger aircraft. However, the main airport serving the state is Borjhar, at Guwahati, 21 km across the state border but only 124 km from Shillong. Guwahati has air links with several major north Indian cities.

SOCIAL INSTITUTIONS

Justice. The Guwahati High Court is common to Assam, Meghalaya, Nagaland, Manipur, Mizoram, Tripura and Arunachal Pradesh—there are 19 judges. There is a bench of the Guwahati High Court at Shillong.

Religion. At the 2001 census Christians numbered 64·8% of the population; Hindus, over 14·5%; Khasi, 6·2%.

Education. In 2001, 63·31% of the population were literate (66·14% of men and 60·41% of women). In 2000–01 the state had 4,685 primary and middle schools with 445,443 students, and 1,613 senior middle, secondary and higher secondary schools with 181,068 students. There were 35 colleges and other institutions of higher education including ten teacher training schools, one college and one polytechnic, with a total enrolment of 31,975 students. The North Eastern Hill University started functioning at Shillong in 1973; in 1993–94 it had 41 colleges and 54,803 students.

Health. In 2000–01 there were ten government hospitals, 88 primary health centres and 12 additional health centres, 38 government dispensaries and 413 sub-centres. Total beds (hospitals and health centres), 2,377. There were 389 doctors, 384 staff nurses and 915 paramedics.

MIZORAM

KEY HISTORICAL EVENTS

On 21 Jan. 1972 the former Mizo Hills District of Assam was created a Union Territory. A long dispute between the Mizo National Front (originally Separatist) and the central government was resolved in 1986. Mizoram became a state by the Constitution (53rd Amendment) and the State of Mizoram Acts, July 1986.

TERRITORY AND POPULATION

Mizoram is one of the easternmost Indian states, lying between Bangladesh and Myanmar, and having on its northern boundaries Tripura, Assam and Manipur. There are eight districts. The area is 21,081 sq. km and the population (2001 census) 891,058; density, 42 per sq. km. The main languages spoken are Mizo and English.

SOCIAL STATISTICS

Growth rate 1991–2001, 29·18%.

CONSTITUTION AND GOVERNMENT

Mizoram has a unicameral Legislative Assembly with 40 seats. The capital is Aizawl (population, 2001, 229,714 in the urban agglomeration).

RECENT ELECTIONS
In the elections of Nov. 2003 distribution of seats was: Mizo National Front, 20; Mizoram People's Conference, 5; Indian National Congress, 11; others and ind., 4.

CURRENT ADMINISTRATION
Governor: Amolak Rattan Kohli; b. 1942 (took office on 18 May 2001).

Chief Minister: Pu Zoramthanga; b. 1944 (took office on 3 Dec. 1998).

ECONOMY
Budget. Budget estimates for 2000–01 show revenue receipts of Rs 9,227m. and expenditure of Rs 9,848m.

ENERGY AND NATURAL RESOURCES
Electricity. There are 19 power stations and an installed capacity (2002) of 87·75 MW. 631 out of 764 villages had electricity in 2002.

Agriculture. About 60% of the people are engaged in agriculture, either on terraced holdings or in shifting cultivation. Total production of foodgrains, 1998–99, 127,000 tonnes (rice, 111,000 tonnes; oilseeds, 12,000).

Forestry. Total forest area, 2000, 18,576 sq. km.

INDUSTRY
Handloom weaving and other cottage industries are important. The state had (1992) 2,300 small scale industrial units, including furniture industries, steel fabrication, TV manufacturing, truck and bus body building.

COMMUNICATIONS
Roads. Aizawl is connected by road with Silchar in Assam. Total length of roads in 2000, about 6,840 km of which 885 km are national highways, 225 km are state highways, 3,471 km are classed as major highways and 935 km as village roads. 341 of Mizoram's 764 villages are served by all-weather roads, although 85 villages do not have any roads. There were 29,353 motor vehicles in 2000 of which 767 were buses, 12,847 private cars, and 357 tractors and trailers.

Rail. There is a metre-gauge rail link at Bairabi, 130 km from Aizawl.

Civil Aviation. Lengpui Airport, Aizawl is connected by air with Silchar in Assam and with Calcutta three days a week.

SOCIAL INSTITUTIONS
Religion. At the 2001 census Christians numbered over 85·5% of the population; Buddhists, 8%; Hindus, 5%.

Education. In 2001, 88·49% of the population were literate (90·69% of men and 86·13% of women). In 1998–99 there were 1,318 primary schools with over 130,000 students, 733 middle schools with 45,000 students, and 345 high and higher secondary schools with 23,000 students; there were 29 colleges, one teacher training college, three teacher training schools, one polytechnic and 29 junior colleges. Mizoram does not have any universities.

Health. In 2000–01 there were ten hospitals, 60 health centres and over 300 health sub-centres. Total beds, over 1,450. The state pays particular attention to immunization programmes.

NAGALAND

KEY HISTORICAL EVENTS
The state was created in 1961, effective 1963. It consisted of the Naga Hills district of Assam and the Tuensang Frontier Agency. The agency was a British-supervised tribal area on the borders of Myanmar. Its supervision passed to the government of India at independence, and in 1957 Tuensang and the Naga Hills became a Centrally Administered Area, governed by the central government through the Governor of Assam.

A number of Naga leaders fought for independence until a settlement was reached with the Indian government at the Shillong Peace Agreement of 1975. However, calls for a greater Naga state, potentially incorporating parts of neighbouring Manipur, Arunachal Pradesh and Assam, continued to be voiced, notably through the National Socialist Council of Nagaland (NSCN), which had been active since 1954. The national government and NSCN met in Delhi in early Jan. 2003 to hold their first joint talks in 37 years, after which the NSCN declared 'the war is over'.

TERRITORY AND POPULATION

The state is in the northeast of India and is bounded in the north by Arunachal Pradesh, west by Assam, east by Myanmar and south by Manipur. Nagaland has an area of 16,579 sq. km and a population (2001 census) of 1,988,636; density, 120 per sq. km. The major towns are the capital, Kohima (2001 population, 78,584) and Dimapur (107,382). Other towns include Wokha, Mon, Zunheboto, Mokokchung and Tuensang. The chief tribes in numerical order are: Angami, Ao, Sumi, Konyak, Chakhesang, Lotha, Phom, Khiamngan, Chang, Yimchunger, Zeliang-Kuki, Rengma, Sangtam and Pochury. The main languages of the state are English, Hindi and Nagamese.

SOCIAL STATISTICS

Growth rate 1991–2001, 64·41% (the highest rate of any Indian state).

CONSTITUTION AND GOVERNMENT

An Interim Body (Legislative Assembly) of 42 members elected by the Naga people and an Executive Council (Council of Ministers) of five members were formed in 1961, and continued until the State Assembly was elected in Jan. 1964. The Assembly has 60 members. The Governor has extraordinary powers, which include special responsibility for law and order.

The state has eight districts (Dimapur, Kohima, Mon, Zunheboto, Wokha, Phek, Mokokchung and Tuensang). The capital is Kohima.

RECENT ELECTIONS

At the elections to the State Assembly in Feb. 2003 the Indian National Congress party won 20 seats (53 in 1998); Nagaland People's Front, 19; BJP, 6; Nagaland Democratic Movement, 5; ind., 4; other parties, 4. Results for two seats were not available.

CURRENT ADMINISTRATION

Governor: Shyamal Datta; b. 1941 (took office on 28 Jan. 2002).

Chief Minister: Neiphi-u Rio; b. 1950 (took office on 6 March 2003).

ECONOMY

Budget. Budget estimates for 2000–01 showed total receipts of Rs 15,283m. and expenditure of Rs 14,998m.

ENERGY AND NATURAL RESOURCES

Electricity. Installed capacity (1997) 4·26 MW—five projects under construction or nearing completion will add 27 MW of installed capacity; all towns and villages have electricity.

Oil and Gas. Oil has been located in three districts. Reserves are estimated at 600m. tonnes.

Minerals. In addition to oil, other minerals include: coal, limestone, marble, chromite, magnesite, nickel, cobalt, chromium, iron ore, copper ore, clay, glass sand and slate.

Agriculture. 90% of the people derive their livelihood from agriculture. The Angamis, in Kohima district, practise a fixed agriculture in the shape of terraced slopes, and wet paddy cultivation in the lowlands. In the other two districts a traditional form of shifting cultivation (*jhumming*) still predominates, but some farmers have begun tea and coffee plantations and horticulture. About 61,000 ha were under terrace cultivation and 74,040 ha under *jhumming* in 1994–95.

Production of rice (1999) was 187,000 tonnes, total foodgrains 227,300 tonnes and pulses 13,000 tonnes.

Forestry. Forests, including open forests, covered 14,221 sq. km in 1999, of which forest area excluding open forest was 8,630 sq. km.

INDUSTRY

There is a forest products factory at Tijit; a paper-mill (100 tonnes daily capacity) at Tuli, a distillery unit and a sugar-mill (1,000 tonnes daily capacity) at Dimapur, and a cement factory (50 tonnes daily capacity) at Wazeho. Bricks and TV sets are also made, and there are 1,850 small units. There is a ceramics plant and sericulture is also important.

COMMUNICATIONS

Roads. There is a national highway from Kaziranga (Assam) to Kohima and on to Manipur. There are state highways connecting Kohima with the district headquarters. Total length of roads in 1999, over 15,500 km, of which 365 km are national highway and 1,094 km state highway. There were 95,020 motor vehicles registered in 1994–95.

Rail. Dimapur has a rail-head. Railway route-km in 2000, 60 km.

Civil Aviation. Dimapur has a daily air service to Calcutta. The state government plans to upgrade the airport to receive international flights.

SOCIAL INSTITUTIONS

Justice. A permanent bench of the Guwahati High Court has been established in Kohima. There are 19 judges.

Religion. At the 2001 census Christians formed 87% of the population; Hindus 10% and Muslims under 2%.

Education. In 2001, 67·11% of the population were literate (71·77% of men and 61·92% of women). In 1996–97 there were 1,414 primary schools with 271,932 students, 416 middle schools with 63,437 students, 244 high and higher secondary schools with 24,547 students, 36 colleges, two teacher training colleges and two polytechnics. The North Eastern Hill University opened at Kohima in 1978. Nagaland University was established in 1994.

Health. In 1995–96 there were 32 hospitals (1,051 beds), 27 primary and five community health centres, 65 dispensaries, 243 sub-centres, five TB centres and 30 leprosy centres.

FURTHER READING

Aram, M., *Peace in Nagaland*. New Delhi, 1974

ORISSA

KEY HISTORICAL EVENTS

Orissa was divided between Mahratta and Bengal rulers when conquered by the British East India Company, the Bengal area in 1757 and the Mahratta in 1803. The area which now forms the state then consisted of directly controlled British districts and a large number of small princely states with tributary rulers. The British districts were administered as part of Bengal until 1912 when, together with Bihar, they were separated from Bengal to form a single province. Bihar and Orissa were separated from each other in 1936. In 1948 a new state government took control of the whole state, including the former princely states (except Saraikella and Kharswan which were transferred to Bihar, and Mayurbhanj which was not incorporated until 1949).

In Oct. 1999 Orissa was hit by a devastating cyclone which resulted in more than 10,000 deaths.

TERRITORY AND POPULATION

Orissa is in eastern India and is bounded north by Jharkhand, northeast by West Bengal, east by the Bay of Bengal, south by Andhra Pradesh and west by

Chhattisgarh. The area of the state is 155,707 sq. km, and its population (2001 census), 36,706,920; density 236 per sq. km. Cities with over 250,000 population at 2001 census, *see* INDIA: Territory and Population. Other large cities (2001): Sambalpur, 226,966; Puri, 157,610; Baleshwar, 156,274; Baripada, 100,593. The principal and official language is Oriya.

SOCIAL STATISTICS

Growth rate 1991–2001, 15·94%.

CONSTITUTION AND GOVERNMENT

The Legislative Assembly has 147 members.

The state consists of 30 districts.

The capital is Bhubaneswar (18 miles south of Cuttack).

RECENT ELECTIONS

At the state elections of 20 and 26 April 2004 the Biju Janata Dal won 61 seats (with 27·4% of the vote); the INC, 28 (34·8%); the BJP, 32 (17·1%); the Jharkhand Mukti Morcha, 4 (1·8%); and the Orissa Gana Parishad, 2 (1·3%). Eight independents were elected and two other parties received one seat each.

CURRENT ADMINISTRATION

Governor: Rameshwar Thakur; b. 1927 (took office on 17 Nov. 2004).

Chief Minister: Naveen Patnaik; b. 1946 (took office on 5 March 2000).

ECONOMY

Budget. Budget estimates, 2000–01, showed total receipts of Rs 124,216m. and total expenditure of Rs 121,046m.

ENERGY AND NATURAL RESOURCES

Electricity. The Hirakud Dam Project on the river Mahanadi irrigates 628,000 acres and has an installed capacity of 307·5 MW. There are other projects under construction; hydro-electric power is now serving a large part of the state. Other hydro-power projects are Balimela (360 MW), Upper Kolab (320 MW) and Rengali (250 MW). Total installed capacity (2002) 1,693 MW. In March 1996, 32,068 villages had electricity.

Minerals. Orissa is India's leading producer of chromite (97% of national output), bauxite (71%), iron ore (33% of national reserves), dolomite (50%), manganese ore (32%), graphite (80%), iron ore (16%), fire-clay (34%), limestone (20%) and quartz-quartzite (18%). Kaliapani is the centre of chromite mining and processing. Daitari is the major centre for iron production. Production in 1995–96 (1,000 tonnes): coal, 32,660; iron ore, 9,330; bauxite, 2,420; limestone, 2,380; chromite, 1,650; dolomite, 1,350; manganese ore, 630. Value of production in 1995–96 was Rs 16,340m.

Agriculture. The cultivation of rice is the principal occupation of about 80% of the workforce, and only a very small amount of other cereals is grown. Production of foodgrains (1998–99) totalled 6·35m. tonnes from 4·7m. ha (rice 6·2m. tonnes, wheat 60,000 tonnes); pulses, 0·28m. tonnes; oilseeds, 0·21m. tonnes; sugarcane, 1,114,000 tonnes. Turmeric is cultivated in the uplands of the districts of Ganjam, Phulbani and Koraput, and is exported.

Livestock (1993): buffaloes, 1·04m.; other cattle, 9·2m.; sheep, 1·87m.; goats, 5·4m.; 15·91m. poultry including ducks (1995).

Forestry. Forests occupied 58,135 sq. km in 1999 (37·3% of the state). The most important species are sal, teak, kendu, sandal, sisu, bija, kusum, kongada and bamboo.

Fisheries. There were, in 1999, over 600 fishery co-operative societies. Fish production in 2002 was 1·3m. tonnes of marine fish (including crustaceans) and 140,000 tonnes of freshwater fish. About 170,000 people depend upon sea fishing for a living. Hundreds of fishing boats are engaged in illegal shrimp fishing. The state has four fishing harbours.

INDUSTRY

289 large and medium industries are in operation (1995–96), mostly based on minerals: steel, pig iron, ferrochrome, ferromanganese, ferrosilicon, aluminium, cement, automotive tyres and synthetic fibres.

Other industries of importance are sugar, glass, paper, fertilizers, caustic soda, salt, industrial explosives, heavy machine tools, a coach-repair factory, a re-rolling mill, textile mills and electronics. There is an oil refinery. In the past decade there has been much investment and expansion in biotechnology, electronics, leather and marine-based industries. Also, there were 49,611 small-scale industries in 1995–96 employing 349,800 persons, and 1,342,561 artisan units providing employment to 2·33m. persons. Handloom weaving and the manufacture of baskets, wooden articles, hats and nets, silver filigree work and hand-woven fabrics are specially well known.

COMMUNICATIONS

Roads. On 31 March 1996 length of roads was: state highway, 4,360 km; national highway, 1,625 km; other roads, 212,490 km. There were 658,401 motor vehicles in 1995–96. A 144-km expressway, part national highway, connects the Daitari mining area with Paradip Port.

Rail. The route-km of railway in 2001 was 2,261 km, of which 143 km was narrow gauge.

Civil Aviation. There is an airport at Bhubaneswar with regular scheduled services to New Delhi, Calcutta, Visakhapatnam and Hyderabad.

Shipping. Paradip was declared a 'major' port in 1966; it handled 23·9m. tonnes of traffic in 2002–03. There are minor ports at Bahabalpur and Gopalpur.

SOCIAL INSTITUTIONS

Justice. The High Court of Judicature at Cuttack has a Chief Justice and 16 puisne judges.

Religion. At the 2001 census Hindus numbered 94·7% of the population, Christians 2·1% and Muslims 1·8%.

Education. The percentage of literate people in the population in 2001 was 63·61% (males, 75·95%; females, 50·97%).

In 1996–97 there were 42,104 primary schools with 3·95m. students, 12,096 middle schools with 1·3m. students and 6,198 high and higher secondary schools with 945,000 students. There are ten engineering and technology colleges, 20 medical colleges, 13 teacher training colleges, 15 engineering schools/polytechnics, 497 arts, science and commerce colleges and 440 junior colleges.

Utkal University was established in 1943 at Cuttack and moved to Bhubaneswar in 1962; it is both teaching and affiliating. It has 368 affiliated colleges and 14,000 students (1993–94). Berhampur University has 33 affiliated colleges with 33,755 students, and Orissa University of Agriculture and Technology has eight constituent colleges with 641 students. Sambalpur University has 97 affiliated colleges and 43,982 students. Sri Jagannath Sanskrit Viswavidyalaya at Puri was established in 1981 for oriental studies.

Health. There were (1999–2000) 180 hospitals, 150 dispensaries, 1,351 primary health centres and units, and 5,929 health subcentres, with a total of 13,786 beds. There were also 462 homeopathic and 519 Ayurvedic dispensaries.

CULTURE

Tourism. Tourist traffic is concentrated mainly on the 'Golden Triangle' of Konark, Puri, and Bhubaneswar and its temples. Tourists also visit Gopalpur, the Similipal National Park, Nandankanan and Chilka Lake, Bhiar-Kanika and Ushakothi Wildlife Sanctuary.

PUNJAB (INDIA)

KEY HISTORICAL EVENTS

The Punjab was constituted an autonomous province of India in 1937. In 1947 the province was partitioned between India and Pakistan into East and West Punjab respectively. The name of East Punjab was changed to Punjab (India) under the Constitution of India. On 1 Nov. 1956 the erstwhile states of Punjab and Patiala and East Punjab States Union (PEPSU) were integrated to form the state of Punjab. On 1 Nov. 1966, under the Punjab Reorganization Act, 1966, the state was reconstituted as a Punjabi-speaking state comprising the districts of Gurdaspur (excluding Dalhousie), Amritsar, Kapurthala, Jullundur, Ferozepur, Bhatinda, Patiala and Ludhiana; parts of Sangrur, Hoshiarpur and Ambala districts; and part of Kharar tehsil. The remaining area comprising 47,000 sq. km and an estimated (1967) population of 8·5m. was shared between the new state of Haryana and the Union Territory of Himachal Pradesh. The existing capital of Chandigarh was made joint capital of Punjab and Haryana; its transfer to Punjab alone (scheduled for 1986) has been delayed while the two states seek agreement as to which Hindi-speaking districts shall be transferred to Haryana in exchange.

TERRITORY AND POPULATION

The Punjab is in north India and is bounded at its northernmost point by Kashmir, northeast by Himachal Pradesh, southeast by Haryana, south by Rajasthan, west and northwest by Pakistan. The area of the state is 50,362 sq. km, with a population (2001 census) of 24,289,296; density, 482 per sq. km. Cities with over 250,000 population at 2001 census, *see* INDIA: Territory and Population. Other principal towns (2001): Bathinda (217,389); Pathankot (168,275); Hoshiarpur (148,243); Batala (147,753); Moga (124,624); Abohar (124,303); S.A.S. Nagar (123,284); Maler Kotla (106,802); Khanna (103,059); Phagwara (102,111). The official language is Punjabi.

SOCIAL STATISTICS

Growth rate 1991–2001, 19·76%.

CONSTITUTION AND GOVERNMENT

Punjab (India) has a unicameral legislature, the Legislative Assembly, of 117 members. Presidential rule was imposed in May 1987 after outbreaks of communal violence. In March 1988 the Assembly was officially dissolved.

There are 17 districts. The capital is Chandigarh.

RECENT ELECTIONS

Legislative Assembly elections were held on 13 Feb. 2002. The Congress Party (INC) won 62 seats, the Shiromani Akali Dal (SAD) 41, the Bharatiya Janata Party (BJP) 3, ind. 9 and the Communist Party of India (CPI) 2.

CURRENT ADMINISTRATION

Governor: Gen. S. F. Rodrigues; b. 1933 (took office on 16 Nov. 2004).

Chief Minister: Capt. Amarinder Singh; b. 1942 (took office on 27 Feb. 2002).

ECONOMY

Budget. Budget estimates, 2000–01, showed revenue receipts of Rs 159,597m. and revenue expenditure of Rs 159,725m.

ENERGY AND NATURAL RESOURCES

Electricity. Installed capacity, 2001–02, was 4,743 MW; all villages had electricity. There are nine major hydro electric plants—Shanan, UBDC, Anandpur Sahib, RSDHEP, Mukerian, Nadampur, Daudhar, Rohti and Thuhi. The per capita consumption of electricity in Punjab is higher than in any other Indian state, at 821 units (kWh) per annum in 2000–01.

Agriculture. About 75% of the population depends on agriculture, which is technically advanced. The irrigated area rose from 2·21m. ha in 1950–51 to 4·2m.

ha in 1996–97. 95·1% of cropland in Punjab is irrigated. In 2001 wheat production was 15·5m. tonnes; rice, 9·1m.; potatoes, 10·0m; kinnow, 0·2m; plus large amounts of chillies, mangoes, grapes, pears, peaches and lemons. Total foodgrains, 24·90m. tonnes; oilseeds, 61,000 tonnes; sugarcane, 1·3m. tonnes. Cotton, 1·91m. bales of 170 kg, representing 12·4% of India's cotton. Punjab contributes 22·6% of India's wheat. Agriculture in Punjab is more advanced and mechanized than in most other parts of India. Emphasis has recently been on diversification with new crops including hyola seeds, soybeans, sunflower, spring maize and floriculture, and the use of bio-fertilizers.

Livestock (1977 census): buffaloes, 4,110,000; other cattle, 3·31m.; sheep and goats, 1,219,600; horses and ponies, 75,900; poultry, 5·5m.

Forestry. In 1999 there were 1,387 sq. km of forest land.

INDUSTRY

In March 2001 the number of registered industrial units was 202,356, employing about 1,184,550 people. In 2001 there were 620 large and medium industries and 201,736 small industrial units, investment Rs 43,310m. The chief manufactures are metals, textiles (especially hosiery and fabrics), yarn, sports goods, hand tools, sugar, bicycles, electronic goods, machine tools, hand tools, automobiles and vehicle parts, surgical goods, vegetable oils, tractors, chemicals and pharmaceuticals, fertilizers, food processing, electronics, railway coaches, paper and newsprint, cement, engineering goods and telecommunications items. There is an oil refinery.

COMMUNICATIONS

Roads. The total length of roads in 2001 was 50,389 km, including 1,729 km national highways—seven national highways pass through the state. All villages in the state are connected to metalled roads. State transport services cover 1·9m. effective km daily with a fleet of 3,426 buses carrying a daily average of over 1·2m. passengers. Coverage by private operators is estimated at 40%. There were 1,915,059 vehicles in 1995–96.

Rail. The Punjab possesses an extensive system of railway communications, served by the Northern Railway. Route-km (1995–96), 2,121 km.

Civil Aviation. There is an airport at Amritsar, and Chandigarh airport is on the northeastern boundary; both have regular scheduled services to Delhi, Jammu, Srinagar and Leh. There are also Vayudoot services to Ludhiana. Amritsar is now an international airport with charter flights from Europe and from several Middle East destinations.

SOCIAL INSTITUTIONS

Justice. The Punjab and Haryana High Court exercises jurisdiction over the states of Punjab and Haryana and the territory of Chandigarh. It is located in Chandigarh. In 2003 it consisted of a Chief Justice and 40 puisne judges.

Religion. At the 2001 census Sikhs numbered 63% of the population; Hindus, 34·5%; Muslims, over 1·5%.

Education. Compulsory education was introduced in April 1961; at the same time free education was introduced up to 8th class for boys and 9th class for girls as well as fee concessions. The aim is education for all children of 6–11. In 2001, 69·95% of the population were literate (75·63% of men and 63·55% of women).

In 1996–97 there were 12,590 primary schools with 2,081,965 students, 2,545 middle schools with 968,762 students, 2,159 high schools with 490,888 students and 1,134 higher secondary schools with 259,718 students.

Punjab University was established in 1882 at Lahore as an examining, teaching and affiliating body. It divided in 1947 with the Indian part moving to Shimla, and in 1956 moved again to Chandigarh (in 1993–94 it had 94 colleges and 77,868 students). In 1962 Punjabi University was established at Patiala (it had 66 colleges with 40,712 students) and Punjab Agricultural University at Ludhiana. Guru Nanak Dev University was established at Amritsar in 1969 to mark the 500th anniversary celebrations for Guru Nanak Dev, first Guru of the Sikhs (it had 85 colleges and 80,330 students, 1992–93). The Thapar Institute of Engineering and Technology, at

Patiala, has university status and there is also the Baba Farid University of Health Science, at Faridkot. Altogether there are 293 affiliated colleges.

Health. There were (2000) 207 hospitals, 12 hospitals/health centres, 55 community health centres, 38 community primary health centres, 446 primary health centres, and 1,470 dispensaries and clinics. There were six Ayurvedic hospitals and 507 Ayurvedic dispensaries, plus one homeopathic hospital and 105 homeopathic dispensaries. There were over 25,000 hospital beds in 2000.

FURTHER READING

Singh, Khushwant, *A History of the Sikhs.* 2 vols. OUP, 1999
Singh Tatla, Darshan and Talbot, Ian, *Punjab.* [Bibliography] ABC-Clio, Oxford and Santa Barbara (CA), 1995

RAJASTHAN

KEY HISTORICAL EVENTS

The state is in the largely desert area formerly known as Rajputana. The Rajput princes were tributary to the Moghul emperors when they were conquered by the Mahrattas' leader, Mahadaji Sindhia, in the 1780s. In 1818 Rajputana became a British protectorate and was recognized during British rule as a group of princely states including Jaipur, Jodhpur and Udaipur. After independence the Rajput princes surrendered their powers and in 1950 were replaced by a single state government. In 1956 the state boundaries were altered; small areas of the former Bombay and Madhya Bharat states were added, together with the neighbouring state of Ajmer. Ajmer had been a Moghul power base; it was taken by the Mahrattas in 1770 and annexed by the British in 1818. In 1878 it became Ajmer-Merwara, a British province, and survived as a separate state until 1956.

TERRITORY AND POPULATION

Rajasthan is in northwest India and is bounded north by Punjab, northeast by Haryana and Uttar Pradesh, east by Madhya Pradesh, south by Gujarat and west by Pakistan. Since the area of Madhya Pradesh was reduced by the creation of Chhattisgarh in 2000, Rajasthan has become the largest Indian state in size, with an area of 342,239 sq. km. Population (2001 census), 56,473,122; density 165 per sq. km. For chief cities, *see* INDIA: Territory and Population. Other major towns (2001): Ganganagar (222,833), Bharatpur (205,104), Pali (187,571), Sikar (185,506), Tonk (135,663), Hunumangarh (129,654), Beawar (125,923), Kishangarh (116,156), Gangapur (105,336), Churu (101,853), Jhunjhunun (100,476). The main languages spoken are Rajasthani and Hindi.

SOCIAL STATISTICS

Growth rate 1991–2001, 28·33%.

CONSTITUTION AND GOVERNMENT

There is a unicameral legislature, the Legislative Assembly, having 200 members. The capital is Jaipur. There are 32 districts.

RECENT ELECTIONS

After the election in Dec. 2003 the Bharatiya Janata Party came to power. BJP, 120 seats; Congress (I), 56; others, 24.

CURRENT ADMINISTRATION

Governor: Pratibha Patil; b. 1934 (took office on 8 Nov. 2004).

Chief Minister: Vasundhara Raje; b. 1953 (took office on 8 Dec. 2003).

ECONOMY

Budget. Estimates for 2000–01 show total revenue receipts of Rs 172,340m., and expenditure of Rs 172,403m.

ENERGY AND NATURAL RESOURCES

Electricity. Installed capacity in March 2001, 4,000 MW; 30,620 villages (March 1996) and 514,758 wells had electric power.

Minerals. There are 64 different minerals mined in the state. It is the sole producer of garnet and jasper in India, and by far the leading producer of zinc, calcite, gypsum and asbestos. Others include silver, tungsten, granite, marble, kaolin (44% of India's production), dolomite, lignite, lead (80% of India's production), fluorite (59% of India's production), emeralds, soapstone, feldspar (70% of India's production), copper, barytes (53% of India's production), limestone and salt. Total revenue from minerals in 2002, Rs 3,000m. Four blocs are being explored for mineral oils and gas.

Agriculture. The state has suffered drought and encroaching desert for several years. The cultivable area is (1999) about 25·6m. ha, of which 4·65m. ha is irrigated. Production of principal crops (in tonnes), 1999: pulses, 2·64m.; total foodgrains, 11·40m. (wheat, 6·7m.; rice, 190,000); cotton, 868,000 tonnes.

The total irrigable area of the state is 13·6m. ha, which is 53% of the cultivable area. The Indira Gandhi Nahar Canal—India's largest irrigation project—is the main canal system, of which 189 km of main canal, 204 km of feeder and more than 3,400 km of distributors have been built. There were 37,560 villages with full or partial drinking water facilities in Jan. 2004, out of 37,889 villages.

Livestock (1992): buffaloes, 7·75m.; other cattle, 11·6m.; sheep, 12·17m.; goats, 15·06m.; horses and ponies, 28,000; camels, 731,000.

Forestry. Forests covered 13,353 sq. km in 1999, of which 9,632 sq. km was protected.

INDUSTRY

In 2001 there were 221,369 small industrial units with an investment of Rs 31,160·6m. and employment of 857,000. Of these units 45,705 were agro-based, 26,842 forest-based, 27,397 metal-working and 24,861 textiles. There were 212 industrial estates in 2001. 10,244 medium-size and large factories were recorded in 2001. Total capital investment (1993–94) Rs 13,160m. Chief manufactures are textiles, dyeing, printing cloth, cement, glass, sugar, sodium, oxygen and acetylene units, pesticides, insecticides, dyes, caustic soda, calcium, carbide, synthetic fibres, fertilizers, shaving equipment, automobiles and automobile components, tyres, watches, nylon tyre cords and refined copper. The state is a major textile centre and is the leading producer of polyester and viscose yarns in India and the second largest producer of suiting material; out of 862 spinning mills in India, 69 are in Rajasthan.

COMMUNICATIONS

Roads. In 2001 there were 150,870 km of roads in Rajasthan including 61,520 km of good and surfaced roads. The state government gives a road length of 85,008 km in 1999 for surfaced roads—there were 4,453 km of national highways and 8,898 km of state highways. A total of 12 national highways crossed the state. Motor vehicles numbered 3·6m. in 2003.

Rail. Jodhpur, Marwar, Udaipur, Ajmer, Jaipur, Kota, Bikaner and Sawai Madhopur are important junctions of the northwestern network. Route km (2003) 5,924. The major cities of the state are integrated with the national broad-gauge network.

Civil Aviation. There are airports at Jaipur (Sanganer Airport), Jodhpur, Kota and Udaipur with regular scheduled services by Indian Airlines to Delhi, Bombay and Ahmedabad. Sanganer has been upgraded and now receives charter international flights as well as scheduled flights from Dubai and other gulf destinations.

SOCIAL INSTITUTIONS

Justice. The seat of the High Court is at Jodhpur. There is a Chief Justice and 32 puisne judges. There is also a bench of High Court judges at Jaipur.

Religion. At the 2001 census Hindus numbered 89% of the population; Muslims, 8%; Sikhs, nearly 1·5%.

Education. The proportion of literate people to the total population was 61·03% at the 2001 census; 76·46% of men and 44·34% of women.

In 2001 there were 35,015 primary schools with 7,540,000 students, 16,336 middle schools with 2,327,000 students, 4,124 high schools and 1,923 higher secondary schools with 1,560,000 students between them. Elementary education is free but not compulsory.

In 2001 there were 280 colleges. Rajasthan University, established at Jaipur in 1947, is teaching and affiliating; in 1993–94 it had 135 colleges and 160,000 students. There are 11 other universities: Rajasthan Agricultural University, Bikaner; Mohanlal Sukhadia University, Udaipur; Maharishi Dayanand Saraswati University, Ajmer; Jai Narayan Vyas University, Jodhpur; Kota Open University, Kota; National Law University, Jodhpur; Rajasthan Sanskrit University, Jaipur; Birla Institute of Science and Technology, Pilani; Jain Vishwa Bharti, Ladnu; Rajasthan Vidyapeeth, Udaipur; Vanasthali Vidyapeeth, Vanasthali. There are also 280 colleges: 111 government colleges (including teacher-training colleges and 27 polytechnics), 75 government colleges and research institutes, 92 non-aided colleges and two other institutes.

Health. In 1999 there were 266 hospitals, 262 community health centres, 1,646 primary health centres and 9,640 sub-centres. There were 34,066 beds in hospitals in 1995–96.

FURTHER READING

Sharma, S. K. and Sharma, Usha (eds.) *History and Geography of Rajasthan.* New Delhi, 2000

SIKKIM

KEY HISTORICAL EVENTS

A small Himalayan kingdom between Nepal and Bhutan, Sikkim was independent in the 1830s although in continual conflict with larger neighbours. In 1839 the British took the Darjeeling district. British political influence increased during the 19th century, as Sikkim was the smallest buffer between India and Tibet. However, Sikkim remained an independent kingdom ruled by the 14th-century Namgyal dynasty. In 1950 a treaty was signed with the government of India, declaring Sikkim an Indian Protectorate. Indian influence increased from then on. Internal political unrest came to a head in 1973, and led to the granting of constitutional reforms in 1974. Agitation continued until Sikkim became a 'state associated with the Indian Union' later that year. In 1975 the king was deposed and Sikkim became an Indian state, a change approved by referendum.

TERRITORY AND POPULATION

Sikkim is in the Eastern Himalayas and is bounded north by Tibet, east by Tibet and Bhutan, south by West Bengal and west Nepal. Area, 7,096 sq. km. It is inhabited chiefly by the Lepchas, a tribe indigenous to Sikkim, the Bhutias, who originally came from Tibet, and the Nepalis, who entered from Nepal in large numbers in the late 19th and early 20th century. Population (2001 census), 540,493; density, 76 per sq km. The capital is Gangtok (population of 29,162 at the 2001 census).

English is the principal language. Lepcha, Bhutia, Nepali and Limboo also have official status.

SOCIAL STATISTICS

Growth rate 1991–2001, 32·98%.

CONSTITUTION AND GOVERNMENT

The Assembly has 32 members.

The official language of the government is English. Lepcha, Bhutia, Nepali and Limboo have also been declared official languages.

Sikkim is divided into four districts for administration purposes, Gangtok, Mangan, Namchi and Gyalshing being the headquarters for the Eastern, Northern, Southern and Western districts respectively.

RECENT ELECTIONS

At the State Assembly election of 10 May 2004 the Sikkim Democratic Front won 31 seats (71·1% of the vote) and the INC took one seat (26·1%).

CURRENT ADMINISTRATION

Governor: V. Rama Rao; b. 1926 (took office on 25 Oct. 2002).

Chief Minister: Pawan Kumar Chamling; b. 1950 (took office on 12 Dec. 1994).

ECONOMY

Budget. Budget estimates for 2000–01 showed receipts of Rs 114,360m. and expenditure of Rs 116,300m.

ENERGY AND NATURAL RESOURCES

Electricity. Installed capacity (1999) 35·9 MW. There are four hydro-electric power stations. All villages had electricity in 1991.

Minerals. Copper, zinc and lead are mined.

Agriculture. There are 70,000 ha of cultivable land. The economy is mainly agricultural; main food crops are cardamom, ginger, rice, maize, millet, wheat and barley; cash crops are mandarin oranges, apples, potatoes and buckwheat. Foodgrain production, 1999, 98,000 tonnes (maize, 56,000; rice, 21,000 tonnes; wheat, 14,000 tonnes); potatoes, 28,000 tonnes; pulses, 6,000 tonnes. Tea is grown. Medicinal herbs are exported. Sericulture produces 179 kg of silk per annum.

Forestry. Forests occupied about 3,127 sq. km in 1995 and the potential for a timber and wood-pulp industry is being explored.

INDUSTRY

Small-scale industries include cigarettes, distilling, tanning, fruit preservation, carpets and watchmaking. Local crafts include carpet weaving, making handmade paper, wood carving and silverwork. The State Trading Corporation of Sikkim stimulates trade in indigenous products.

COMMUNICATIONS

Roads. There are 2,376 km of roads, all on mountainous terrain. Of these 40 km are national highways and 678 km state highways. 1,445 km are surfaced and 931 km unsurfaced. There are 18 major bridges. Public transport and road haulage is nationalized. There were 8,997 motor vehicles in 1995–96.

Rail. The nearest railhead is at Shiliguri (115 km from Gangtok).

Civil Aviation. The nearest airport is at Bagdogra (128 km from Gangtok), linked to Gangtok by helicopter service.

Telecommunications. There are 1,445 telephones (1987) and 37 wireless stations.

SOCIAL INSTITUTIONS

Religion. At the 2001 census Hindus accounted for 68% of the population, Buddhists 27% and Christians just over 3%.

Education. In 2001, 69·68% of the population were literate (76·73% of men and 61·46% of women). Sikkim had (1999) 739 pre-primary schools with 23,538 students, 335 primary schools with 84,986 students, 122 junior high schools with 23,949 students, 72 high schools with 3,331 students and 27 higher secondary schools with 1,484 students. Education is free up to class XII; text books are free up to class V. There are 500 adult education centres. There is also a training institute for primary teachers, two degree colleges and a teacher training college.

Health. There are five state hospitals, 24 primary health centres and 147 sub-primary health centres, with a total of 920 beds. Some 9,700 patients were treated in 1998.

CULTURE

Broadcasting. A radio broadcasting station, Akashvani Gangtok, was built in 1982, and a permanent station in 1983. Gangtok also has a low-power TV transmitter.

TAMIL NADU

KEY HISTORICAL EVENTS

The first trading establishment made by the British in the Madras State was at Peddapali (now Nizampatnam) in 1611 and then at Masulipatnam. In 1639 the

English were permitted to make a settlement at the place which is now Madras, and Fort St George was founded. By 1801 the whole of the country from the Northern Circars to Cape Comorin (with the exception of certain French and Danish settlements) had been brought under British rule.

Under the provisions of the States Reorganization Act, 1956, the Malabar district (excluding the islands of Laccadive and Minicoy) and the Kasaragod district taluk of South Kanara were transferred to the new state of Kerala; the South Kanara district (excluding Kasaragod taluk and the Amindivi Islands) and the Kollegal taluk of the Coimbatore district were transferred to the new state of Mysore; and the Laccadive, Amindivi and Minicoy Islands were constituted a separate Territory. Four taluks of the Trivandrum district and the Shencottah taluk of Quilon district were transferred from Travancore-Cochin to the new Madras State. On 1 April 1960, 1,049 sq. km from the Chittoor district of Andhra Pradesh were transferred to Madras in exchange for 844 sq. km from the Chingleput and Salem districts. In Aug. 1968 the state was renamed Tamil Nadu.

TERRITORY AND POPULATION

Tamil Nadu is in south India and is bounded north by Karnataka and Andhra Pradesh, east and south by the Indian Ocean and west by Kerala. Area, 130,058 sq. km. Population (2001 census), 62,110,839; density 478 per sq. km. Tamil is the principal language and has been adopted as the state language with effect from 14 Jan. 1958. For the principal towns, *see* INDIA: Territory and Population. Other large towns (2001 census): Tuticorin (242,860), Thanjavur (215,725), Nagercoil (208,149), Dindigul (196,619), Kanchipuram (188,349), Kumbakonam (160,827), Cuddalore (158,569), Karur (153,123), Neyveli (138,387), Tiruvannamalai (130,301), Pollachi (127,993), Arcot (126,975), Karaikkudi (125,185), Rajapalaiyam (121,982), Sivakasi (121,312), Pudukkottai (108,947), Bhavani (104,285), Vaniyambadi (103,841), Coonoor (101,234), Gudiyatham (100,021). The capital is Madras (Chennai).

SOCIAL STATISTICS

Growth rate 1991–2001, 15·39%.

CONSTITUTION AND GOVERNMENT

There is a unicameral legislature; the Legislative Assembly has 234 members. There are 30 districts.

RECENT ELECTIONS

In elections held on 10 May 2001 the All India Anna Dravida Munnetra Kazagam gained 132 seats, Dravida Munnetra Kazagam 31, the Tamil Maanila Congress (Moopanar) 23 and the Pattali Makkal Katchi 20.

CURRENT ADMINISTRATION

Governor: Surjit Singh Barnala; b. 1925 (since 3 Nov. 2004; in office for the second time).

Chief Minister: Jayaram Jayalalitha; b. 1948 (since 2 March 2002; in office for the third time).

ECONOMY

Budget. Budget estimates for 1997–98, revenue receipts, Rs 126,410·5m., revenue expenditure, Rs 143,776·2m. Annual plan, 1997–98, Rs 40,000m.

ENERGY AND NATURAL RESOURCES

Electricity. Installed capacity in 1995–96 was 5,067 MW, of which 1,948 MW was hydro-electricity and 2,970 MW thermal. All villages were supplied with electricity. The Kalpakkam nuclear power plant became operational in 1983; capacity, 330 MW.

Minerals. The state has magnesite, salt, coal, lignite, chromite, bauxite, limestone, manganese, mica, quartz, gypsum and feldspar.

Agriculture. The land is a fertile plain watered by rivers flowing east from the Western Ghats, particularly the Cauvery and the Tambaraparani. Temperature ranges between 6°C and 40°C, rainfall between 442 mm and 934 mm. Of the total land area (13m. ha), 7,158,464 ha were cropped and 298,659 ha of waste were cultivable in 1996. The staple food crops grown are paddy, maize, jawar, bajra, pulses and millets. Important commercial crops are sugarcane, oilseeds, cashew nuts, cotton, tobacco, coffee, tea, rubber and pepper. Production, 1995–96 (in tonnes): total foodgrains, 9·16m. (rice, 7·56m.); pulses, 359,700.

Livestock (1993): buffaloes, 3,116,647; other cattle, 9,318,666; sheep, 5,865,989; goats, 5,938,475; poultry, 21,454,890.

Forestry. Forest area, 1993–94, 2·14m. ha, of which 1,948,627 ha were reserved forest. Forests cover about 17·21% of land area. Main products are teak, soft wood, wattle, sandalwood, pulp wood, cashew and cinchona bark.

Fisheries. In 1995–96, 448,000 tonnes of fish were produced; marine, 340,000 tonnes.

INDUSTRY

The number of working factories was 18,480 in 1994, employing 1m. workers. In 1993–94 there were 178,114 small industries employing over 1·6m. persons. The biggest central sector project is Salem steel plant. Cotton textiles is one of the major industries. There were 449 cotton textile mills in 1991–92 and many spinning mills supplying yarn to the decentralized handloom industry. Other important industries are cement, sugar, manufacture of textile machinery, power-driven pumps, bicycles, electrical machinery, tractors, cars, rubber tyres and tubes, bricks and tiles, and silk.

Main exports: cotton goods, tea, coffee, spices, engineering goods, car ancillaries, leather and granite.

Trade Unions. In 1994 there were 5,981 registered trade unions. Work-days lost by strikes and lockouts in 1994, 1,668,484.

COMMUNICATIONS

Roads. On 31 March 1992 the state had 172,936 km of national and state highways, major and other district roads. In 1995–96 there were 2,771,845 registered motor vehicles.

Rail. On 31 March 1996 there were 4,005 route-km. Madras and Madurai are the main centres.

Civil Aviation. There are airports at Madras, Tiruchirapalli and Madurai, with regular scheduled services to Bombay, Calcutta and Delhi. Madras is an international airport and the main centre of airline routes in south India. In 2000 Madras handled 3,887,993 passengers (2,153,532 on domestic flights) and 104,972 tonnes of freight.

Shipping. Madras and Tuticorin are the chief ports. Important minor ports are Cuddalore and Nagapattinam. Madras handled 26·5m. tonnes of cargo in 1993–94, Tuticorin, 6·7m. The Inland Container Depot at Coimbatore has a capacity of 50,000 tonnes of export traffic; it is linked to Cochin (Kerala).

SOCIAL INSTITUTIONS

Justice. There is a High Court at Madras with a Chief Justice and 26 judges.

Police. Strength of police force, 1 Jan. 1995, 76,447.

Religion. At the 1991 census Hindus numbered 49,532,052 (88·67%); Christians, 3,179,410 (5·69%); Muslims, 3,052,717 (5·47%).

Education. At the 2001 census 73·47% of the population were literate (82·33% of men and 64·55% of women).

Education is free up to pre-university level. In 1996–97 there were 30,619 primary schools with 6·8m. students, 5,503 middle schools with 3·51m. students, 3,574 high schools with 1,465,631 students and 2,734 higher secondary schools with 0·69m. students. There are also 78 medical colleges, 74 engineering and technology colleges, 22 teacher training colleges and 280 general education colleges.

There are 13 universities. Madras University (founded in 1857) is affiliating and teaching (it had 119 colleges and 125,082 students in 1993–94); Annamalai

University, Annamalainagar (founded 1929) is residential; Madurai Kamaraj University (founded 1966) is an affiliating and teaching university; ten others include one agricultural university, Mother Theresa Women's University, and Tamil University, Thanjavur. There are four institutions which are deemed to be universities.

Health. There were (1993–94) 427 hospitals, 484 dispensaries (of which 56 were Indian medicine and homoeopathy), 1,683 primary health centres and 8,681 health sub-centres; total number of beds, 48,128.

CULTURE

Tourism. In 1992, 203,985 foreign tourists visited the state.

FURTHER READING

Statistical Information: The Department of Statistics (Fort St George, Madras) was established in 1948 and reorganized in 1953. Main publications: *Annual Statistical Abstract; Decennial Statistical Atlas; Season and Crop Report; Quinquennial Wages Census; Quarterly Abstract of Statistics.*

TRIPURA

KEY HISTORICAL EVENTS

Tripura is a Hindu state of great antiquity having been ruled by the Maharajahs for 1,300 years before its accession to the Indian Union on 15 Oct. 1949. With the reorganization of states on 1 Sept. 1956 Tripura became a Union Territory, and was so declared on 1 Nov. 1957. The Territory was made a State on 21 Jan. 1972.

TERRITORY AND POPULATION

Tripura is bounded by Bangladesh, except in the northeast where it joins Assam and Mizoram. The major portion of the state is hilly and mainly jungle. It has an area of 10,486 sq. km and a population of 3,191,168 (2001 census); density, 304 per sq. km.

The official languages are Bengali and Kokbarak. Manipuri is also spoken.

SOCIAL STATISTICS

Growth rate 1991–2001, 15·74%.

CONSTITUTION AND GOVERNMENT

The territory has four districts, namely Dhalai, North Tripura, South Tripura and West Tripura. The capital is Agartala (population, 2001, 189,327).

RECENT ELECTIONS

The Communist Party of India (Marxist) won the Legislative Assembly elections in Feb. 2003 with 38 seats; Congress won 13; Indigenous National Party of Tripura (INPT), 6; others, 3.

CURRENT ADMINISTRATION

Governor: Dinesh Nandan Sahaya; b. 1936 (took office on 2 June 2003).

Chief Minister: Manik Sarkar; b. 1949 (took office on 11 March 1998).

ECONOMY

Budget. Budget estimates, 1994–95, showed expenditure of Rs 3,605m. Annual plan outlay for 1997–98 was Rs 4,370m.

ENERGY AND NATURAL RESOURCES

Electricity. Installed capacity (1995–96), 69·36 MW; there were (March 1996) 3,640 villages with electricity out of a total of 4,856.

Agriculture. About 24% of the land area is cultivable. The tribes practise shifting cultivation, but this is being replaced by modern methods. The main crops are rice, wheat, jute, mesta, potatoes, oilseeds and sugarcane. Foodgrain production (1995–96), 477,100 tonnes. There are 55 registered tea gardens producing 5,432,000 kg per year, and employing 14,170 in 1994–95.

Forestry. Forests covered 5,538 sq. km in 1995, about 53% of the land area. They have been much depleted by clearance for shifting cultivation and, recently, for refugee settlements of Bangladeshis. About 8% of the forest area still consists of dense natural forest; losses elsewhere are being replaced by plantation. Commercial rubber plantation has also been encouraged. In 1994–95, 30,328 ha were under new rubber plantations.

INDUSTRY

Tea is the main industry. There is also a jute mill producing about 15 tonnes per day and employing about 2,000. Main small industries: aluminium utensils, rubber, saw-milling, soap, piping, fruit canning, handloom weaving and sericulture. There were 1,174 registered factories which employed 31,912 persons, and 700 notified factories with 3,000 workers in 1995–96. 330,980 persons were employed in handloom, handicrafts and sericulture industries in 1995–96.

COMMUNICATIONS

Roads. Total length of roads (1995–96) 5,760 km, of which 2,258 km were surfaced. On 31 March 1996 vehicles registered totalled 34,683, of which 4,701 were trucks.

Rail. There is a railway between Kumarghat and Kalkalighat (Assam). Route-km in 1995–96, 45 km.

Civil Aviation. There is one airport and three airstrips. The airport (Agartala) has regular scheduled services to Calcutta.

SOCIAL INSTITUTIONS

Religion. At the 1991 census Hindus numbered 2,384,934; Muslims, 196,495; Buddhists, 128,260; Christians, 46,472; Sikhs, 740; Jains, 301.

Education. In 2001, 73·66% of the population were literate (81·47% of men and 65·41% of women). In 1996–97 there were 2,045 primary schools (434,143 pupils); 411 middle schools (126,129); 558 high and higher secondary schools (82,273). There were 14 colleges of general education, one engineering college, one teacher training college and one polytechnic. Tripura University, established in 1987, has 20 affiliated colleges with 20,000 students.

Health. There were (1995–96) 27 hospitals, with 2,171 beds, 548 dispensaries, 818 doctors and 729 nurses. There were 53 primary health centres and 67 family planning centres.

UTTAR PRADESH

KEY HISTORICAL EVENTS

In 1833 the then Bengal Presidency was divided into two parts, one of which became the Presidency of Agra. In 1836 the Agra area was styled the North-West Province and placed under a Lieut.-Governor. In 1877 the two provinces of Agra and Oudh were placed under one administrator, styled Lieut.-Governor of the North-West Province and Chief Commissioner of Oudh. In 1902 the name was changed to 'United Provinces of Agra and Oudh', under a Lieut.-Governor, and the Lieut.-Governorship was altered to a Governorship in 1921. In 1935 the name was shortened to 'United Provinces'. On independence, the states of Rampur, Banaras and Tehri-Garwhal were merged with United Provinces. In 1950 the name of the United Provinces was changed to Uttar Pradesh. In 2000 the new state of Uttaranchal was carved from the northern, mainly mountainous, region of Uttar Pradesh.

TERRITORY AND POPULATION

Uttar Pradesh is in north India and is bounded north by the new state of Uttaranchal and Nepal, east by Bihar and Jharkhand, south by Madhya Pradesh and Chhattisgarh and west by Rajasthan, Haryana and Delhi. After the formation of Uttaranchal the area of Uttar Pradesh is 240,928 sq. km (previously 294,411 sq. km). Population (2001 census), 166,052,859; density, 689 per sq. km. Despite the decline in the population caused by the creation of Uttaranchal, Uttar Pradesh still has the highest population of any of the Indian states. If Uttar Pradesh were a separate country it would have the sixth highest population (after China, India, USA, Indonesia and Brazil). Cities with more than 250,000 population, *see* INDIA: Territory and Population. Other important towns (2001 census): Farrukhabad (242,558), Hapur (211,987), Etawah (211,460), Maunath Bhanjan (210,071), Faizabad (208,164), Mirzapur (205,264), Sambhal (182,930), Bulandshahr (176,256), Rae Bareli (169,285), Bahraich (168,376), Amroha (164,890), Jaunpur (159,996), Sitapur (151,827), Fatehpur (151,757), Budaun (148,138), Unnao (144,917), Modinagar (139,642), Orai (139,444), Banda (139,387), Hathras (126,352), Pilibhit (124,082), Gonda (122,164), Lakhimpur (120,566), Mughal Sarai (116,246), Hardoi (112,474), Lalitpur (111,810), Etah (107,098), Basti (106,985), Azamgarh (104,943), Deoria (104,222), Chandausi (103,757), Ghazipur (103,283), Ballia (102,226), Mainpuri (102,007), Sultanpur (100,085). The sole official language has been Hindi since April 1990.

SOCIAL STATISTICS

Growth rate 1991–2001, 25·80%.

CONSTITUTION AND GOVERNMENT

Uttar Pradesh has had an autonomous system of government since 1937. There is a bicameral legislature. The Legislative Council has 108 members; the Legislative Assembly has 403.

There are 14 administrative divisions, each under a Commissioner, and 70 districts.

The capital is Lucknow.

RECENT ELECTIONS

Elections were held in Feb. 2002. The Samajwadi Party (SP) won 145 seats; the Bharatiya Janata Party (BJP), 107; the Bahujan Samaj Party (BSP), 98; the Indian National Congress (INC), 25; ind. and others, 26.

CURRENT ADMINISTRATION

Governor: Thanjavelu Rajeshwar; b. 1926 (took office on 8 July 2004).

Chief Minister: Mulayam Singh Yadav; b. 1939 (took office on 29 Aug. 2003).

ECONOMY

Budget. Budget estimates for 1996–97 showed revenue receipts of Rs 155,963·2m.; expenditure, Rs 194,039·9m. Annual plan outlay, 1997–98, Rs 70,800m.

ENERGY AND NATURAL RESOURCES

Electricity. The state had, 1995–96, an installed capacity of 6,049 MW. There were 85,657 villages with electricity in March 1996, out of a total of 112,804.

Minerals. The state has magnesite, china-clay, coal, granite, sandstone, copper-lead-zinc, dolomite, limestone, soapstone, bauxite, diaspore, ochre, phosphorite, pyrophyllite, silica sand and steatite reserves among others. In 1995–96 about 13m. tonnes of minerals were produced.

Agriculture. Agriculture occupies 78% of the workforce. 10·13m. ha are irrigated. The state is India's largest producer of foodgrains; production (1995–96), 38·94m. tonnes (rice 10·4m. tonnes, wheat 22·2m. tonnes); pulses, 2·25m. tonnes. The state is one of India's main producers of sugar; production of sugarcane (1995–96), 119·9m. tonnes. There were (1995–96) 1,965 veterinary centres for cattle.

Forestry. In 1995 forests covered about 51,663 sq. km. However, much of this area is now in the new state of Uttaranchal.

INDUSTRY

Sugar production is important; other industries include oil refining, aluminium smelting, edible oils, textiles, distilleries, brewing, leather working, agricultural engineering, paper, automobile tyres, fertilizers, cement, jute, glass, heavy electricals, chemicals, automobiles and synthetic fibres. Large public-sector enterprises have been set up in electrical engineering, pharmaceuticals, locomotive building, general engineering, electronics and aeronautics. Village and small-scale industries are important; there were 0·64m. small units in 1995–96 providing employment to 1·19m. people. The state had 1,661 large and medium industries with an investment of Rs 223,002m. and employing 0·57m. persons in 1995–96.

COMMUNICATIONS

Roads. There were, 31 March 1995, 185,575 km of roads. In 1995–96 there were 2,977,275 motor vehicles of which 2,057,408 were two-wheelers.

Rail. Lucknow is the main junction of the northern network; other important junctions are Agra, Kanpur, Allahabad, Mughal Sarai and Varanasi. Route-km in 1995–96, 8,934 km.

Civil Aviation. There are airports at Lucknow, Kanpur, Varanasi, Allahabad, Agra, Gorakhpur and five other places.

SOCIAL INSTITUTIONS

Justice. The High Court of Judicature at Allahabad (with a bench at Lucknow) has a Chief Justice and 63 puisne judges including additional judges. There are 63 sessions divisions in the state.

Religion. At the 1991 census Hindus numbered 113,712,829; Muslims, 24,109,684; Sikhs, 675,775; Christians, 383,477; Buddhists, 221,443; Jains, 176,259.

Education. At the 2001 census 77·77m. people were literate (57·36%; 70·23% of men and 42·98% of women). In 1996–97 there were 91,093 primary schools with 16·26m. students, 19,917 middle schools with 5·63m. students, 2,628 high schools with 2,329,904 students and 4,375 higher secondary schools with 1,167,552 students.

Universities: Allahabad University (founded 1887); Agra University (1927); the Banaras Hindu University, Varanasi (1916); Lucknow University (1921); Aligarh Muslim University (1920) with four colleges and 13,437 students in 1993–94; Roorkee University (1949), formerly Thomason College of Civil Engineering (established in 1847); Gorakhpur University (1957) with 33 colleges and 96,504 students; Sampurnanand Sanskrit Vishwavidyalaya, Varanasi (1958); Kanpur University (1966); Ch. Charan Singh University (1966), with 82 colleges and 96,004 students in 1993–94; H. N. Bahuguna Garhwal University, Srinagar (1973); C. S. Azad University of Agriculture and Technology, Kanpur (1975); Narendra Deva University of Agriculture and Technology, Faizabad (1975); Dr Ram Manohar Lohia Awadh, Faizabad (1975; 32 colleges and 64,142 students); Rohilkhand University, Bareilly (1975; 32 colleges and 86,996 students); Bundelkhand University, Jhansi (1975); Purvanchal University, Jaunpur (1987).

There are also five institutions with university status: Gurukul Kangri Vishwavidyalaya, Hardwar; Indian Veterinary Research Institute; Central Institute of Higher Tibetan Studies; Sanjay Gandhi Post-Graduate Institute of Medical Sciences; and Dayal Bagh Educational Institute. There are 35 medical colleges, 18 engineering colleges, 62 teacher training colleges and 550 arts, science and commerce colleges.

Health. In 1994–95 there were 5,011 allopathic, 2,690 Ayurvedic and Unani and 1,149 homoeopathic hospitals and dispensaries. There were also 3,766 primary health centres and 20,153 sub-centres, and TB hospitals and clinics.

FURTHER READING

Hasan, Z., *Quest for Power: Oppositional Movements and Post-Congress Politics in Uttar Pradesh.* OUP, 1998

Lieten, G. K. and Srivastava, R., *Unequal Partners: Power Relations, Devolution and Development in Uttar Pradesh.* Sage Publications, New Delhi, 1999

Misra, S., *A Narrative of Communal Politics, Uttar Pradesh, 1937–39.* Sage Publications, New Delhi, 2001

UTTARANCHAL

KEY HISTORICAL EVENTS

The state was carved from Uttar Pradesh and became the twenty-seventh state of India on 9 Nov. 2000. It is located in the hilly and mountainous region of the northern border of the Indian subcontinent. The regions of Kumaon and Garhwal contained in the new state were referred to as Uttarakhand in ancient Hindu scriptures. The Chinese suppression of revolt in Tibet in 1959 saw a rapid influx of Tibetan exiles to the region and the Indo-Chinese conflict of 1962 persuaded the Indian government to initiate a modernization programme throughout the Indian Himalayas that resulted in the development of roads and communication networks in the previously backward region. From the 1970s the hill people began to agitate for their districts to be separated from Uttar Pradesh, which had been established in 1950. On 1 Aug. 2000 the Uttar Pradesh Reorganisation bill was passed, allowing for a separate state, called Uttaranchal, to incorporate 12 hill districts and, controversially, the lowland area of Udham Singh Nagar.

TERRITORY AND POPULATION

Uttaranchal is located in northern India and is bounded in the northeast by China and in the east by Nepal. The state of Uttar Pradesh is to the southwest, Haryana to the west and Himachal Pradesh to the northwest. Uttaranchal has an area of 53,483 sq. km. Population (2001 census), 8,479,562; density, 159 per sq. km. The principal languages are the Hindi dialects of Garhwali and Kumaoni. Cities with over 250,000 population, *see* INDIA: Territory and Population. Other large cities (2001 census): Hardwar (220,433), Haldwani (159,020), Roorkee (114,811).

SOCIAL STATISTICS

Growth rate 1991–2001, 19·20%.

CONSTITUTION AND GOVERNMENT

Uttaranchal is the twenty-seventh state of India. After the region was carved from Uttar Pradesh it was decided that the 22 Members of the Legislative Assembly (MLAs) from Uttaranchali districts would become the members of the new state's Legislative Assembly. Subsequently this was increased to 30 when the provisional assembly was established, and ultimately it is scheduled to have 70 members. For administrative purposes the region is divided into 13 districts.

The interim capital and seat of government is at Dehra Dun.

RECENT ELECTIONS

On the formation of the new state the Bharatiya Janata Party (BJP) was the single largest party with 17 seats, enabling them to form a majority administration in the 23-seat assembly with Nityanand Swamy becoming the state's first chief minister.

State assembly elections were held in Feb. 2002. The Indian National Congress party (INC) won 36 seats; the Bharatiya Janata Party (BJP), 19; the Bahujan Samaj Party (BSP), 7; the Uttarakhand Kranti Dal (UKKD), 4; the Nationalist Congress Party (NCP), 1; ind. and others, 3.

CURRENT ADMINISTRATION

Governor: Sudarshan Agarwal; b. 1931 (took office on 8 Jan. 2003).

Chief Minister: Narain Dutt Tiwari; b. 1925 (took office on 2 March 2002).

ENERGY AND NATURAL RESOURCES

Electricity. The state has a potential hydroelectric capacity of 40,000 MW. Government figures claim that more than 75% of the state's 17,000 villages have electricity.

Water. Uttaranchal suffers from an acute shortage of water for drinking and irrigation. Only 10% of the water potential is currently utilized.

Minerals. There are deposits of limestone, gypsum, iron ore, graphite and copper.

Agriculture. Agriculture is the occupation for approximately 50% of the population. Subsistence farming is the norm, as only 9% of the land in the state is cultivable.

Forestry. Approximately 65%–70% of the state's area is covered in forest.

INDUSTRY

Tourism is by far the most important industry. The state can offer ski resorts, adventure tourism, mountaineering, hiking and several areas of religious interest.

Other industries include: horticulture, floriculture, fruit-processing and medicine production. In the Terai region there are around 350 industrial units and 130 in the Doon Valley.

COMMUNICATIONS

Roads. There are 23 km of roads for every 100 sq. km of land in the state. State highways link Uttaranchal to the neighbouring states of Himachal Pradesh, Haryana and Uttar Pradesh. The state remains very inaccessible in parts.

Rail. Four main railway lines in the south of the state link several districts to Uttar Pradesh and Himachal Pradesh. Railways along the foothills connect Dehra Dun, Hardwar, Rishikesh, Roorkee, Kotdwaar, Ram Nagar, Kathgodam and Tanakpur. The rest of the state is not connected to the rail network.

Civil Aviation. There are airports at Dehra Dun and Udham Singh Nagar.

SOCIAL INSTITUTIONS

Education. In 2001, 77·28% of the population were literate (84·01% of men and 60·26% of women).

WEST BENGAL

KEY HISTORICAL EVENTS

Bengal was under the overlordship of the Moghul emperor and ruled by a Moghul governor (*nawab*) who declared himself independent in 1740. The British East India Company based at Calcutta was in conflict with the *nawab* from 1756 until 1757 when British forces defeated him at Plassey and installed their own *nawab* in 1760. The French were also in Bengal; the British captured their trading settlement at Chandernagore in 1757 and in 1794, restoring it to France in 1815.

The area of British Bengal included modern Orissa and Bihar, Bangladesh and (until 1833) Uttar Pradesh. Calcutta was the capital of British India from 1772 until 1912.

The first division into East and West took place in 1905–11 and was not popular. However, at Partition in 1947 the East (Muslim) chose to join what was then East Pakistan (now Bangladesh), leaving West Bengal as an Indian frontier state and promoting a steady flow of non-Muslim Bengali immigrants from the East. In 1950 West Bengal received the former princely state of Cooch Behar and, in 1954, Chandernagore. Small areas were transferred from Bihar in 1956.

TERRITORY AND POPULATION

West Bengal is in northeast India and is bounded north by Sikkim and Bhutan, east by Assam and Bangladesh, south by the Bay of Bengal, southwest by Orissa, west by Jharkhand and Bihar and northwest by Nepal. The total area of West Bengal is 88,752 sq. km. Its population (2001 census) was 80,221,171; density, 904 per sq. km. The capital is Calcutta (Kolkata). Population of chief cities, *see* INDIA: Territory and Population. Other major towns (2001): Habra, 239,170; Ingraj Bazar (English Bazar), 224,392; Raiganj, 175,064; Haldia, 170,695; Baharampur, 170,343; Medinipur, 153,349; Krishnanagar, 148,645; Ranaghat, 145,172; Balurghat, 143,095; Santipur, 138,195; Bankura, 128,811; Navadvip, 125,346; Khardaha, 116,252; Birnagar, 115,104; Alipur Duar, 114,069; Puruliya, 113,766; Basirhat, 113,120; Darjiling (Darjeeling), 109,163; Coch Behar, 102,922; Bangaon, 102,115; Chakdaha, 101,278; Jalpaiguri, 100,212.

The principal language is Bengali.

SOCIAL STATISTICS

Growth rate 1991–2001, 17·84%.

CONSTITUTION AND GOVERNMENT

The state of West Bengal came into existence as a result of the Indian Independence Act, 1947. The territory of Cooch-Behar State was merged with West Bengal on 1 Jan. 1950, and the former French possession of Chandernagore became part of the state on 2 Oct. 1954. Under the States Reorganization Act, 1956, certain portions of Bihar State (an area of 3,157 sq. miles with a population of 1,446,385) were transferred to West Bengal.

The Legislative Assembly has 295 seats (294 elected and one nominated).

For administrative purposes there are three divisions (Jalpaiguri, Burdwan and Presidency), under which there are 18 districts, including Calcutta. The Calcutta Metropolitan Development Authority has been set up to co-ordinate development in the metropolitan area (1,350 sq. km). For the purposes of local self-government there are 16 *zilla parishads* (district boards) excluding Darjeeling, 328 *panchayat samities* (regional boards), one *siliguri mahakuma parishad* and 3,247 *gram* (village) *panchayats*. There are 113 municipalities, six Corporations and 11 Notified Areas. The Calcutta Municipal Corporation is headed by a mayor in council.

RECENT ELECTIONS

In elections held on 10 May 2001, 143 seats went to the Communist Party of India (Marxist), 60 went to the All India Trinamool Congress, 26 to the Indian National Congress, 25 to the All India Forward Bloc and 17 to the Revolutionary Socialist Party. In winning the election the Communists retained power for a sixth consecutive term.

CURRENT ADMINISTRATION

Governor: Gopalkrishna Gandhi; b. 1945 (took office on 14 Dec. 2004).

Chief Minister: Buddhadeb Bhattacharjee; b. 1944 (since 6 Nov. 2000).

ECONOMY

Budget. Budget estimates for 1998–99, revenue receipts Rs 115,827m. and expenditure Rs 132,740·9m. Plan outlay for 1998–99 was Rs 48,061·2m.

ENERGY AND NATURAL RESOURCES

Electricity. Installed capacity, 1997–98, 6,293 MW; 29,341 villages had electricity in Nov. 1998.

Water. The largest irrigation and power scheme under construction is the Teesta Barrage (irrigation potential, 533,520 ha). Other major irrigation schemes are the Mayurakshi Reservoir, Kangsabati Reservoir, Mahananda Barrage and Aqueduct and Damodar Valley. In 1997–98 there were 11,030 tubewells, 7,170 open dugwells and 3,353 riverlift irrigation schemes.

Minerals. Value of production, 1998, Rs 13,244m. The state has coal (the Raniganj field is one of the three biggest in India) including coking coal. Coal production (1998) 16·54m. tonnes.

Agriculture. About 5·90m. ha were under rice-paddy in 1997–98. Total foodgrain production, 1997–98 (provisional), 14·35m. tonnes (rice 13·24m. tonnes, wheat 810,000 tonnes); pulses, 125,700 tonnes; oilseeds, 386,600 tonnes; jute, 7·5m. bales of 180 kg; tea (1995), 170·3m. kg. The state produces 76·3% of the national output of jute and *mesta* (1997–98).

Livestock (1998 census): 17,832,000 cattle; 998,000 buffaloes; 1,462,000 sheep; 15,648,000 goats; and 46,219,000 poultry.

Forestry. The recorded forest area (1997–98) was 13,451 sq. km.

Fisheries. Landings, 1997–98, 950,000 tonnes, of which inland 786,000 tonnes. During 1997–98 Rs 318·6m. was invested in fishery schemes. The state is the largest inland fish producer in the country.

INDUSTRY

The total number of registered factories, 1997 (provisional), was 11,213 (excluding defence factories); average daily employment, 1997, 905,088. The coalmining industry, 1996, had 105 units with average daily employment of 95,864.

There is a large automobile factory at Uttarpara, and an aluminium rolling-mill at Belur. There is a steel plant at Burnpur (Asansol) and a spun pipe factory at Kulti. Durgapur has a large steel plant and other industries under the state sector—a thermal power plant, coke oven plant, fertilizer factory, alloy steel plant and ophthalmic glass plant. There is a locomotive factory at Chittaranjan and a cable factory at Rupnarayanpur. A refinery and fertilizer factory are operating at Haldia. Other industries include chemicals, engineering goods, electronics, textiles, automobile tyres, paper, cigarettes, distillery, aluminium foil, tea, pharmaceuticals, carbon black, graphite, iron foundry, silk and explosives.

Small industries are important; 490,158 units were registered at 31 March 1998, employing 3m. persons. The silk industry is also important; 667,000 persons were employed in the handloom industry in the organized sector in 1997–98.

COMMUNICATIONS

Roads. In 1996 the total length of roads was 74,459 km. On 31 March 1996 the state had 1,198,733 motor vehicles.

Rail. The route-km of railways within the state (1997–98) is 3,784·96 km. The main centres are Asansol, New Jalpaiguri and Kharagpur. There is a metro in Calcutta (16·4 km).

Civil Aviation. The main airport is Calcutta which has national and international flights. In 2000 it handled 2,622,484 passengers (2,048,766 on domestic flights) and 53,755 tonnes of freight. The second airport is at Bagdogra in the extreme north, which has regular scheduled services to Calcutta and Delhi.

Shipping. Calcutta is the chief port: a barrage has been built at Farakka to control the flow of the Ganges and to provide a rail and road link between North and South Bengal. A second port has been developed at Haldia, between the present port and the sea, which is intended mainly for bulk cargoes. West Bengal possesses 779 km of navigable canals.

SOCIAL INSTITUTIONS

Justice. The High Court of Judicature at Calcutta has a Chief Justice and 45 puisne judges. The Andaman and Nicobar Islands come under its jurisdiction.

Police. In March 1995 the police force numbered about 56,550, under a director-general and an inspector-general. Calcutta has a separate force under a commissioner directly responsible to the government; its strength was about 22,000 in March 1995.

Religion. At the 1991 census Hindus numbered 50,866,624; Muslims, 16,075,836; Christians, 383,477; Buddhists, 203,578; Sikhs, 55,392; Jains, 34,355.

Education. In 2001, 69·22% of the total population were literate (men, 77·58%; women, 60·22%). In 1998–99 (provisional) there were 52,123 primary schools, 2,648 junior high schools and 8,077 high and higher secondary schools with 1,881,226 students. Education is free up to higher secondary stage. There are ten universities.

The University of Calcutta (founded 1857) is affiliating and teaching; in 1993–94 it had 212 colleges and 150,000 students. Visva Bharati, Santiniketan, was established in 1951 and is residential and teaching; it had 5,226 students in 1993–94. The University of Jadavpur, Calcutta (1955), had 7,087 students in 1992–93. Burdwan University was established in 1960; in 1992–93 there were 91,379 students. Kalyani University was established in 1960 (2,520 students in 1993–94). The University of North Bengal (1962) had 34,000 students in 1993–94. Rabindra Bharati University had 8,309 students in 1992–93. Bidhan Chandra Krishi Viswavidyalaya (1974) had 389 students in 1992–93. There is also Vidyasagar University, Medinipur. Bengal Engineering College has university status. There are 12 engineering and technology colleges, 19 medical colleges, 24 teacher training colleges, 41 polytechnics and 308 arts, science and commerce colleges.

Health. As at 31 March 1998 (provisional) there were 405 hospitals, 2,651 clinics, 1,266 health centres and 8,126 sub-centres with a total of 69,371 beds, and 571 dispensaries.

FURTHER READING

Chatterjee, P., *The Present History of West Bengal: Essays in Political Criticism.* OUP, 1997

UNION TERRITORIES

ANDAMAN AND NICOBAR ISLANDS

The Andaman and Nicobar Islands are administered by the President of the Republic of India acting through a Lieut.-Governor. There is a 30-member Pradesh Council, five members of which are selected by the Administrator as advisory counsellors. The seat of administration is at Port Blair, which is connected with Calcutta (1,255 km away) and Madras (1,190 km) by steamer service which calls about every ten days; there are air services from Calcutta and Madras. Roads in the islands, 733 km black-topped and 48 km others. There are two districts.

The population (2001 census) was 356,265. The area is 8,249 sq. km and the density 43 per sq. km. There are 457 villages and one town. Growth rate 1991–2001, 26·94%. Port Blair (2001), 100,186.

The climate is tropical, with little variation in temperature. Heavy rain (125" annually) is mainly brought by the southwest monsoon. Humidity is high. The islands were severely affected by the tsunami of 26 Dec. 2004.

Budget figures for 2002–03 show total revenue receipts of Rs 885m., and total expenditure on revenue account of Rs 3,850m.

There is installed capacity of 38,805 KW. 479 villages are electrified.

In 2001, 26,524 ha were under cultivation, of which 10,885 ha were under rice. 48,167 tonnes of rice were grown. There were 70,923 goats, 60,180 cattle and 42,836 pigs in 2001.

In 2002, 25,561 tonnes of fish were landed. There were 1,966 registered fishing boats in 2002 and 2,721 fishermen.

There are 7,171 sq. km of forests, of which 4,242 sq. km are protected. In 2002, 4,712 cu. metres of sawn timber were extracted.

There are 1,502 km of paved roads and 45 km of other roads.

In 2003 there were 48 factories and 1,479 small-scale industrial units, employing 5,032 people.

In 2001 there were 207 primary schools with 43,000 students, 56 middle schools with 23,000 students, 45 high schools with 11,000 students and 48 higher secondary schools with 4,000 students. There is a teachers' training college, two polytechnics and two colleges. Literacy (2001 census), 81·18% (86·07% of men and 75·29% of women).

In 2003 there were three hospitals, 28 health centres and 107 primary health sub-centres.

Lieut.-Governor. Ram Kapse; b. 1933 (sworn in 5 Jan. 2004).

The **Andaman Islands** lie in the Bay of Bengal, 193 km from Cape Negrais in Myanmar, 1,255 from Calcutta and 1,190 from Madras. Five large islands grouped together are called the Great Andamans, and to the south is the island of Little Andaman. There are some 239 islets and a total of 572 islands, islets and rocks, the two principal groups being the Ritchie Archipelago and the Labyrinth Islands. The Great Andaman group is about 467 km long and, at the widest, 51 km broad.

The original inhabitants live in the forests by hunting and fishing. The total population of the Andaman Islands (including about 430 aboriginals) was 240,089 in 1991. Main aboriginal tribes: Andamanese, Onges, Jarawas and Sentinelese.

The Great Andaman group, densely wooded (forests covered 7,615 sq. km in 1995), contains hardwood and softwood and supplies the match and plywood industries. Annually the Forest Department export about 25,000 tonnes of timber to the mainland. Coconut, coffee and rubber are cultivated. The islands are slowly being made self-sufficient in paddy and rice, and now grow approximately half their annual requirements. Livestock (1982): 27,400 cattle, 9,720 buffaloes, 17,600 goats and 21,220 pigs. Fishing is important. There is a sawmill at Port Blair and a coconut-oil mill. Little Andaman has a palm-oil mill.

The islands possess a number of harbours and safe anchorages, notably Port Blair in the south, Port Cornwallis in the north and Elphinstone and Mayabandar in the middle.

The **Nicobar Islands** are situated to the south of the Andamans, 121 km from Little Andaman. The Danes were in possession 1756–1869, and then the British until 1947. There are 19 islands, seven uninhabited; total area, 1,841 sq. km. The islands are usually divided into three sub-groups (southern, central and northern), the chief islands in each being respectively Great Nicobar, Camotra with Nancowrie and Car Nicobar. There is a harbour between the islands of Camotra and Nancowrie, Nancowrie Harbour.

The population numbered, in 1991, 39,208, including about 22,200 of Nicobarese and Shompen tribes. The coconut and areca nut are the main items of trade, and coconuts are a major item in the people's diet.

CHANDIGARH

On 1 Nov. 1966 the city of Chandigarh and the area surrounding it was constituted a Union Territory. Population (2001), 900,914; density, 7,903 per sq. km; growth rate 1991–2001, 40·33%. Area, 114 sq. km. It serves as the joint capital of both Punjab (India) and the state of Haryana, and is the seat of a High Court. The city, which had a population of 808,796 inhabitants at the 2001 census, will ultimately be the capital of just the Punjab; joint status is to last while a new capital is built for Haryana.

Budget for 2000–01 showed revenue of Rs 4,730m. and expenditure of Rs 6,327m.

There is some cultivated land and some forest (27·5% of the territory).

In 2001 there were 280 factories, of which 15 were large and medium scale factories and about 2,100 small scale industries, employing 24,000 people.

In 1996–97 there were 44 primary schools (60,012 students), 33 middle schools (34,095 students), 50 high schools (18,510 students) and 47 higher secondary schools (16,710 students). There were also two engineering and technology colleges, 12 arts, science and commerce colleges, two polytechnic institutes and a university (Panjab University). Other institutes have university status: Chandigarh College of Architecture; the Chandigarh Government College of Art; Chandigarh Institute of Postgraduate Medicinal Education and Research; Punjab Engineering College.

In 2001, 81·76% of the population were literate (85·65% of men and 78·65% of women).

In 2000 there were 43 dispensaries, 16 general hospitals and 72 private hospitals with a total of 2,530 beds.

Administrator. Gen. S. F. Rodrigues; b. 1933 (took office as Governor of Punjab on 16 Nov. 2004).

DADRA AND NAGAR HAVELI

GENERAL DETAILS

Formerly Portuguese, the territories of Dadra and Nagar Haveli were occupied in July 1954 by nationalists, and a pro-India administration was formed; this body made a request for incorporation into the Union on 1 June 1961. By the 10th amendment to the constitution the territories became a centrally administered Union Territory with effect from 11 Aug. 1961, forming an enclave at the southernmost point of the border between Gujarat and Maharashtra, approximately 30 km from the west coast. Area 491 sq. km; population (census 2001), 220,451; density 449 per sq. km; growth rate 1991–2001, 59·20%. There is an Administrator appointed by the government of India. The day-to-day business is done by various departments, co-ordinated by the Secretaries, Assistant Secretary, Collector and Resident Deputy Collector. The capital is Silvassa, which had a population of 21,890 at the 2001 census. 78·82% of the population is tribal and organized in 140 villages. Languages used are dialects classified under Bhilodi (91·1%), Bhilli, Gujarati, Marathi and Hindi.

CURRENT ADMINISTRATION

Administrator: O. P. Kelkar (since 19 July 1999).

ECONOMY

Budget. The budget for 2001–02 shows revenue receipts of Rs 1,178·3m. and revenue expenditure of Rs 507 was Rs 1,212·2m.; budget estimate was Rs 552·8m. under Plan Sector and Rs 3,688·4m. under Non-Plan Sector.

ENERGY AND NATURAL RESOURCES

Electricity. Electricity is supplied from Central Grid, and all villages have been electrified. A major sub-station at Kharadpada village has been completed.

Water. As a result of a joint project with the governments of Gujarat, Goa and Daman and Diu there is a reservoir at Damanganga with irrigation potential of 5,900 ha. Drinking water is made available through wells and piped water supply schemes.

Minerals. There are few natural mineral resources although there is some ordinary sand and quarry stone.

Agriculture. Farming is the chief occupation, and 22,352 ha were under net crop in 2001–02. Much of the land is terraced and there is a 100% subsidy for soil conservation. The major food crops are rice and ragi; wheat, small millets and pulses are also grown. There is a coverage of lift irrigation over 6,736 ha. There are nine veterinary aid centres, a veterinary hospital, an agricultural research centre and breeding centres to improve strains of cattle and poultry. During 2001–02 the administration distributed 152 tonnes of high-yielding paddy and wheat seed and 1,574 tonnes of manures and fertilizers.

Forestry. 20,359 ha or 40·8% of the total area is forest, mainly of teak, sadad and khair. In 1985 a moratorium was imposed on commercial felling to preserve the environmental function of the forests and ensure local supplies of firewood, timber and fodder. The tribals have been given exclusive right to collect minor forest produce from the reserved forest area for domestic use. 92 sq. km of reserved forest was declared a wildlife sanctuary in 2000.

Fisheries. There is some inland fishing in water reservoir project areas and individual ponds. During 2001–02 the total catch was 55 tonnes.

INDUSTRY

There is no heavy industry, and the Territory is a ‘No Polluting Industry District’. Industrial estates for small and medium scales have been set up at Pipariya, Masat and Khadoli. In March 2002 there were 1,317 small scale and 383 medium scale units employing 37,297 people.

Labour. The Labour Enforcement Office ensures the application of the Monitoring of Minimum Wages Act (1948), the Industrial Disputes Act (1947), the Contract Labour (Regulation and Abolition) Act (1970) and the Workmen’s Compensation Act (1923). During 2001–02, 81 cases under the Industrial Disputes Act were settled. Under the Contract Labour (Regulation and Abolition) Act (1970), 53 certificates of registration and 56 licences were issued to the industrial establishment. 19 cases under the Workman’s Compensation Act (1923) were settled.

Trade Unions. There is one trade union registered under the Trade Union Act.

COMMUNICATIONS

Roads. In 2002 there were 580 km of road of which 545·45 km were surfaced. Out of 72 villages, 68 are connected by all-weather road. There were 27,300 motor vehicles in 2001–02. The National Highway no. 8 passes through Vapi, 18 km from Silvassa.

Rail. Although there are no railways in the territory the line from Bombay to Ahmedabad runs through Vapi, 18 km from Silvassa.

Civil Aviation. The nearest airport is at Bombay, 180 km from Silvassa.

Telecommunications. There are six telephone exchanges, one telex exchange and one wireless station. The Telephone Department has provided over 6,000 telephone connections.

Postal Services. There is currently one post and telegraph office with three sub-post offices and 41 branch post offices covering 66 villages.

SOCIAL INSTITUTIONS

Justice. The territory is under the jurisdiction of the Bombay (Maharashtra) High Court. There is a District and Sessions Court and one Junior Division Civil Court at Silvassa.

Religion. Numbers of religious followers (2001 census): Hindu, 95% of the population; Muslims, 2·5%; Christians, 1·5%.

Education. Literacy was 60·03% of the population at the 2001 census (73·32% of men and 42·99% of women). In 2001–02 there were 195 primary and middle schools (35,637 students) and 17 high and higher secondary schools (8,887 students).

Health. The territory had (2001–02) a civil hospital, 6 primary health centres, 36 sub-centres, three dispensaries and a mobile dispensary. A Community Health Centre has been established at Khanvel, 20 km from Silvassa. The Pulse Polio Immunisation programme was organized in 1999 and 54,128 polio doses were provided to children below five years of age. There has been a sharp fall in the incidence of malaria, especially cerebral malaria, owing to the sustained efforts of the administration. Hepatitis B vaccination of all inmates in the social welfare hostels was completed with the co-operation of voluntary organizations. A blood testing centre has been established for HIV testing.

Welfare. The Social Welfare Department implements the welfare schemes for poor Scheduled castes, Scheduled tribes, women and physically disabled persons, etc.

CULTURE

Broadcasting. There is a low power Government of India TV transmission centre.

Press. One daily newspaper and two fortnightly news magazines are published.

Tourism. The territory is a rural area between the industrial centres of Bombay and Surat-Vapi. The Tourism Department is developing areas of natural beauty to promote eco-friendly tourism. Several gardens and the Madhuban Dam are among the tourist sites. A lion safari park has been set up at Vasona over 20 ha. About 380,000 visitors came to Dadra and Nagar Haveli during 2000. The government completed a tourist accommodation complex at Silvassa in 1999.

DAMAN AND DIU

GENERAL DETAILS

Daman (Damão) on the Gujarat coast, 100 miles (160 km) north of Bombay, was seized by the Portuguese in 1531 and ceded to them (1539) by the Shar of Gujarat. The island of Diu, captured in 1534, lies off the southeast coast of Kathiawar (Gujarat); there is a small coastal area. Former Portuguese forts on either side of the entrance to the Gulf of Cambay, in Dec. 1961 the territories were occupied by India and incorporated into the Indian Union; they were administered as one unit together with Goa, to which they were attached until 30 May 1987, when Goa was separated from them and became a state.

TERRITORY AND POPULATION

The territory has an area of 112 sq. km and a population of 158,059 at the 2001 census. Density, 1,411 sq. km. Daman has an area of 72 sq. km, population (2001) 113,949; Diu, 40 sq. km, population 44,110. Daman is the capital of the territory. The main language spoken is Gujarati.

The chief towns are (with 2001 populations) Daman (35,743) and Diu (21,576).

Daman and Diu have been governed as parts of a Union Territory since Dec. 1961, becoming the whole of that Territory on 30 May 1987. There are two districts.

The main activities are tourism, fishing and tapping the toddy palm (preparing palm tree sap for consumption). In Daman there is rice-growing, some wheat and dairying. Diu has fine tourist beaches, grows coconuts and pearl millet, and processes salt.

SOCIAL STATISTICS
Growth rate 1991–2001, 55·59%.

CURRENT ADMINISTRATION
Administrator: O. P. Kelkar (since 19 July 1999).

ECONOMY
Fishing is the main economic activity. Tourism is developing.

Budget. The budget for 2000–01 shows revenue receipts of Rs 713·0m. and revenue expenditure of Rs 553·5m.

SOCIAL INSTITUTIONS
Education. In 2001, 81·09% of the population were literate (88·40% of men and 70·37% of women). In 1996–97 there were 53 primary schools with 14,531 students, 20 middle schools with 6,834 students, 20 high schools with 3,220 students and 3 higher secondary schools with 1,202 students. There is a degree college and a polytechnic.

DELHI

GENERAL DETAILS
Delhi became a Union Territory on 1 Nov. 1956 and was designated the National Capital Territory in 1995.

TERRITORY AND POPULATION
The territory forms an enclave near the eastern frontier of Haryana and the western frontier of Uttar Pradesh in north India. Delhi has an area of 1,483 sq. km. Its population (2001 census) is 13,782,976 (density per sq. km, 9,294). Growth rate 1991–2001, 46·31%. In the rural area of Delhi there are 231 villages and 27 census towns. They are distributed in five community development blocks.

CONSTITUTION AND GOVERNMENT
The Lieut.-Governor is the Administrator. Under the New Delhi Municipal Act 1994 New Delhi Municipal Council is nominated by central government and replaces the former New Delhi Municipal Committee.

RECENT ELECTIONS
Elections for the 70-member Legislative Assembly were held in Dec. 2003; the Congress Party formed the government. The Indian National Congress won 47 seats (52 in 1998); Bharatiya Janata Party, 15 (20 in 1998); others, 3.

CURRENT ADMINISTRATION
Lieut.-Governor: B. L. Joshi (took office 9 June 2004).

Chief Minister: Sheila Dikshit (took office on 3 Dec. 1998).

ECONOMY
Budget. Estimates for 2003–04 show revenue receipts of Rs 98,000m. and expenditure of Rs 98,000m.

ENERGY AND NATURAL RESOURCES
Minerals. The Union Territory has deposits of kaolin (chine clay), quartzite and fire clay.

Agriculture. The contribution to the economy is not significant. In 1995–96 about 53,900 ha were cropped (of which 36,000 ha were irrigated). Animal husbandry is increasing and mixed farms are common. Chief crops are wheat, bajra, paddy, sugarcane, gram, jowar and vegetables. Buffaloes are kept as a source of milk; pigs and goats are kept for meat.

INDUSTRY

The modern city is the largest commercial centre in northern India and an important industrial centre. Since 1947 a large number of industrial units have been established; these include factories for the manufacture of razor blades, sports goods, electronic goods, bicycles and parts, plastic and PVC goods including footwear, textiles, chemicals, fertilizers, medicines, hosiery, leather goods, soft drinks and hand tools. The largest single industry is the manufacture of garments. There are also metal forging, casting, galvanizing, electro-plating and printing enterprises. The number of industrial units functioning was about 126,000 in 1996–97; average number of workers employed was 1·14m. Production was worth Rs 63,100m. and investment was about Rs 25,240m. in 1996–97.

Some traditional handicrafts, for which Delhi was formerly famous, still flourish; among them are ivory carving, miniature painting, gold and silver jewellery and papier mâché work. The handwoven textiles of Delhi are particularly fine; this craft is being successfully revived.

Delhi is a major market for manufactures, imports and agricultural goods; there are specialist fruit and vegetable, food grain, fodder, cloth, bicycle, hosiery, dry fruit and general markets.

COMMUNICATIONS

Roads. Five national highways pass through the city. There were (2000–01) 3,456,579 registered motor vehicles. There were 41,483 buses in 2000–01.

Rail. Delhi is an important rail junction with three main stations: New Delhi, Delhi Junction and Hazrat Nizamuddin. There is an electric ring railway for commuters (route-km in 1995–96, 214). The first of three lines of the Delhi metro system opened in 2002: when complete it will consist of 34·5 km subway, 35·5 km elevated and 111 km surface running.

Civil Aviation. Indira Gandhi International Airport operates international flights; Palam airport operates internal flights.

SOCIAL INSTITUTIONS

Religion. At the 1991 census Hindus numbered 7,882,164; Muslims, 889,641; Sikhs, 455,657; Jains, 94,672; Christians, 83,152; Buddhists, 13,906; others, 1,452.

Education. The proportion of literate people to the total population was 81·82% at the 2001 census (87·37% of males and 75·00% of females). In 1996–97 there were 2,184 primary schools with 1,146,691 students, 559 middle schools with 535,511 students, 324 high schools with 676,209 students and 994 higher secondary schools with 460,334 students. There are nine engineering and technology colleges, nine medical colleges and 25 polytechnics.

The University of Delhi was founded in 1922; it had 66 affiliated colleges and 189,332 students in 1994–95. There are also Jawaharlal Nehru University, Indira Gandhi National Open University, the Jamia Millia Islamia University, the Guru Gobind Singh Indraprastha University, Jamia Hamdard University and Shri Lal Bahadur Shastri Rashtriya Sanskrit Vidyapeeth University; the Indian Institute of Technology at Hauz Khas; the Indian Agricultural Research Institute at Pusa; the All India Institute of Medical Science at Ansari Nagar and the Indian Institute of Public Administration are the other important institutions.

Health. In 2001 there were 11 government hospitals plus 71 private hospitals, 167 government dispensaries plus 489 other dispensaries, 73 mobile health clinics and 64 school health clinics.

CULTURE

Press. Delhi publishes major daily newspapers, including the *Times of India*, *Hindustan Times*, *The Hindu*, *Indian Express*, *National Herald*, *Patriot*, *Economic Times*, *The Pioneer*, *The Observer of Business and Politics*, *Financial Express*, *Statesman*, *Asian Age* and *Business Standard* (all in English); *Nav Bharat Times*, *Rashtriya Sahara*, *Jansatta* and *Hindustan* (in Hindi); and three Urdu dailies.

LAKSHADWEEP

The territory consists of an archipelago of 36 islands (ten inhabited), about 300 km off the west coast of Kerala. It was constituted a Union Territory in 1956 as the Laccadive, Minicoy and Amindivi Islands, and renamed in Nov. 1973. The total area of the islands is 32 sq. km. The northern portion is called the Amindivis. The remaining islands are called the Laccadives (except Minicoy Island). The inhabited islands are: Androth (the largest), Amini, Agatti, Bitra, Chetlat, Kadmat, Kalpeni, Kavaratti, Kiltan and Minicoy. Androth is 4·8 sq. km, and is nearest to Kerala. An Advisory Committee associated with the Union Home Minister and an Advisory Council to the Administrator assist in the administration of the islands; these are constituted annually. Population (2001 census), 60,595, nearly all Muslims. Density, 1,894 per sq. km; growth rate 1991–2001, 17·19%. The language is Malayalam, but the language in Minicoy is Mahl. Budget for 2000–01 showed revenue of Rs 90·3m. and expenditure of Rs 1,370m. Installed electric capacity (1998) 8,120 kW. A solar power plant is under construction at Kadmat and wind generated plants at Kavaratti and Agatti. Guaranteeing supplies of potable water is problematic in most islands. Rain water harvesting schemes have been introduced as well as desalination plants. There are several small factories processing fibre from coconut husks: in 2002 these employed 316 workers. There are two handicraft training centres. The islands have great tourist potential. The major industry is fishing—in 1999 there were 375 registered fishing boats. The principal catches are tuna and shark. Tuna is canned at a factory at Minicoy. There is an experimental pearl culture scheme at the uninhabited island of Bangarem. In 2001, 87·52% of the population were literate (93·15% of men and 81·56% of women). There were, in 1996–97, nine high schools (2,043 students) and nine nursery schools (1,197 students), 19 junior basic schools (9,015 students), four senior basic schools (4,797 students) and two junior colleges. There are two hospitals and seven primary health centres plus 14 health sub-centres. The staple products are copra and fish; coconut is the only major crop. Headquarters of administration, Kavaratti, population 10,113 (2001 census), on Kavaratti Island. An airport, with Vayudoot services, opened on Agatti Island in April 1988. The islands are also served by ship from the mainland and have helicopter inter-island services. There are two catamaran-type high-speed inter-island ferries and four barges. The islands have 253 km of roads, of which 124 km have paved surfaces.

Administrator. K. S. Mehra (took office on 19 June 2001).

PONDICHERRY

GENERAL DETAILS

Formerly the chief French settlement in India, Pondicherry was founded by the French in 1673, taken by the Dutch in 1693 and restored to the French in 1699. The English took it in 1761, restored it in 1765, re-took it in 1778, restored it a second time in 1785, re-took it a third time in 1793 and finally restored it to the French in 1816. Administration was transferred to India on 1 Nov. 1954. A Treaty of Cession (together with Karaikal, Mahé and Yanam) was signed on 28 May 1956; instruments of ratification were signed on 16 Aug. 1962 from which date (by the 14th amendment to the Indian Constitution) Pondicherry, comprising the four territories, became a Union Territory.

TERRITORY AND POPULATION

The territory is composed of enclaves on the Coromandel Coast of Tamil Nadu and Andhra Pradesh, with Mahé forming two enclaves on the coast of Kerala. The total area of Pondicherry is 480 sq. km, divided into 11 enclaves that are grouped into four Districts. On Tamil Nadu coast: Pondicherry (290 sq. km; population, 2001 census, 735,004), Karaikal (161; 170,640). On Kerala coast: Mahé (9; 36,823). On Andhra Pradesh coast (although the enclave lies back from the shore but at no point does its territory touch the coast): Yanam (20; 31,362). Total population (2001 census), 973,829; density, 2,029 per sq. km. Pondicherry Municipality had (2001) 220,748 inhabitants and the urban agglomeration had 505,715 inhabitants. The principal languages spoken are Tamil, Telugu, Malayalam, French and English.

SOCIAL STATISTICS

Growth rate 1991–2001, 20·56%. In 1990 family schemes had reduced the birth rate to 19·9 per 1,000 and the infant mortality rate to 34·79 per 1,000 live births.

CONSTITUTION AND GOVERNMENT

By the government of Union Territories Act 1963 Pondicherry is governed by a Lieut.-Governor, appointed by the President, and a Council of Ministers responsible to a Legislative Assembly.

RECENT ELECTIONS

In the elections of 10 May 2001 the Indian National Congress–Tamil Maanila Congress (Moopanar) gained 13 seats, Dravida Munnetra Kazhagam plus allies 12, All India Anna Dravida Munnetra Kazhagam plus allies 3, and others 2.

CURRENT ADMINISTRATION

Lieut.-Governor: M. M. Lakhera; b. 1937 (sworn in 7 July 2004).

Chief Minister: N. Rangaswamy; b. 1950 (took office on 27 Oct. 2001).

ECONOMY

Budget. Budget estimates for 2000–01 showed expenditure of Rs 8,534·7m. Total expenditure Rs 8,304·2m.

ENERGY AND NATURAL RESOURCES

Electricity. Power is bought from neighbouring states. All 11 towns and 263 villages have electricity. Consumption, 1999–2000, 1,535 units per head. Total consumption, 1,239·7m. units.

Agriculture. Nearly 45% of the population is engaged in agriculture and allied pursuits; 90% of the cultivated area is irrigated. The main food crop is rice. Foodgrain production, 61,900 tonnes in 1999. Rice production, 57,900 tonnes from 43,600 ha in 1999; principal cash crops are sugarcane (240,200 tonnes) and groundnuts; minor food crops include cotton, ragi, bajra and pulses.

Fisheries. In 1999 the marine catch was 38,620 tonnes. There was also a prawn catch of 4,532 tonnes.

INDUSTRY

There were, 1999, 40 large and 112 medium-scale enterprises manufacturing items such as textiles, sugar, cotton yarn, spirits and beer, potassium chlorate, rice bran oil, vehicle parts, soap, amino acids, paper, plastics, steel ingots, washing machines, glass and tin containers and bio polymers. These factories employed 40,000 people. There were also 6,199 small industrial units (1999) engaged in varied manufacturing.

COMMUNICATIONS

Roads. There were (1992–93) 3,282 km of roads of which 1,248 km were surfaced. Motor vehicles (March 1996) 119,290.

Rail. Pondicherry is connected to Villupuram Junction. Route-km in 2001, 11 km.

Civil Aviation. The nearest main airport is Madras.

SOCIAL INSTITUTIONS

Education. In 2001, 81·49% of the population were literate (88·89% of men and 74·13% of women). There were, in 1996–97, 178 pre-primary schools (15,107 pupils), 350 primary schools (103,201), 120 middle schools (64,617), 89 high schools (28,731) and 52 higher secondary schools (11,168). There were (1996–97) seven general education colleges, two medical colleges, a law college, an engineering college, an agricultural college and a dental college, and four polytechnics. Pondicherry University had, in 1994–95, 19 colleges and 9,910 students.

Health. In 1999 there were 8 hospitals, 41 health centres and 75 sub-centres, and 12 dispensaries. There were 1,759 hospital beds and 312 beds at health centres.

INDONESIA

Republik Indonesia

Capital: Jakarta
Population projection, 2010: 238·37m.
GDP per capita, 2002: (PPP$) 3,230
HDI/world rank: 0·692/111

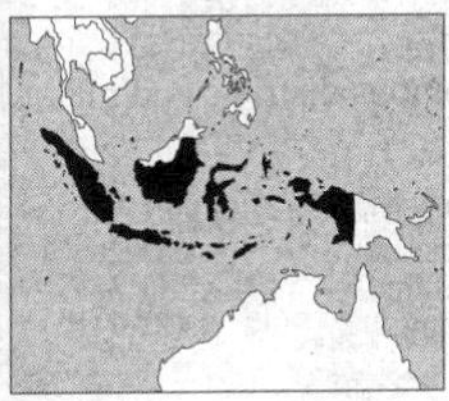

KEY HISTORICAL EVENTS

In the 16th century Portuguese traders settled in some of the islands which now comprise Indonesia but were ejected by the British who in turn were ousted by the Dutch in 1595. From 1602 the Netherlands East India Company controlled the area until the dissolution of the Company in 1798. The Netherlands government then ruled the colony from 1816 until 1941 when it was occupied by the Japanese until 1945. On 17 Aug. 1945 nationalist leaders proclaimed an independent republic. On 27 Dec. 1949 the Netherlands conceded unconditional sovereignty.

In 1960 President Sukarno assumed power and dissolved political parties. In their place he set up the National Front and a supreme state body called the Provisional People's Consultative Assembly. On 11–12 March 1966 the military commanders under the leadership of Lieut.-Gen. Suharto took over executive power while leaving President Sukarno as the head of state. The Communist party, which had twice attempted to overthrow the government, was outlawed. On 22 Feb. 1967 Sukarno handed over all his powers to Gen. Suharto. Re-elected president at five-year intervals, on the final occasion on 10 March 1998, Suharto presided over a booming economy but one which was characterized by corruption and croneyism. The weaknesses became apparent when, in 1997, a failure of economic confidence spread from Japan across Asia. By May 1998 Indonesia had regressed to the verge of civil war. As food prices doubled, then trebled, riots broke out in Jakarta destroying homes and shops. The risk of society fragmenting along ethnic and religious lines was emphasized by the particular sufferings of the Chinese community. President Suharto was forced to stand down on 21 May 1998 and was succeeded by his Vice-President, Bacharuddin Jusuf Habibie, who promised political and economic reforms. Continuing protest centred on the Suharto family which until recently exercised control over large parts of the Indonesian economy. Several of the country's discontented regions are wanting to break free.

In Aug. 1999 East Timor, the former Portuguese colony which Indonesia invaded in 1975, voted for independence, a move that was eventually approved by the Indonesian parliament after violent clashes between independence supporters and pro-Indonesian militia groups. It gained independence from Indonesia on 20 May 2002.

In Nov. 1999 up to 1m. people took to the streets in the province of Aceh, in the far west of the country, seeking a referendum on independence. One of the founder provinces of the Republic of Indonesia, there were fears that Aceh's possible secession would threaten the break-up of the country. More than 5,000 people were killed there during the 1990s, and rebellions in a number of other Indonesian provinces were suppressed with heavy loss of life. In Dec. 2002 the government and the separatist Free Aceh Movement signed a peace deal to end the violence. In exchange for disarmament, Aceh was granted autonomy and self-government from 2004.

In Oct. 2002 around 200 people, mainly foreign nationals, died in a car bomb explosion outside a nightclub in Bali. A second bomb exploded near a US consulate. The Indonesian and Australian governments blamed al-Qaeda.

On 26 Dec. 2004 Indonesia, along with a number of other south Asian countries, was hit by a devastating tsunami following an undersea earthquake. The death toll in Indonesia alone was put at 237,000, almost exclusively in the province of Aceh.

TERRITORY AND POPULATION

Indonesia, with a land area of 730,020 sq. miles (1,890,754 sq. km), consists of 17,507 islands (6,000 of which are inhabited) extending about 3,200 miles east to west through three time-zones (East, Central and West Indonesian Standard time) and 1,250 miles north to south. The largest islands are Sumatra, Java, Kalimantan (Indonesian Borneo), Sulawesi (Celebes) and Papua, formerly West Papua (the western part of New Guinea). Most of the smaller islands except Madura and Bali are grouped together. The two largest groups of islands are Maluku (the Moluccas) and Nusa Tenggara (the Lesser Sundas). On the island of Timor, Indonesia is bounded in the east by East Timor.

Population at the 2000 census was 206,264,595 (58·0% rural in 2001); density, 102 per sq. km. Indonesia has the fourth largest population in the world, after China, India and the USA.

The UN gives a projected population for 2010 of 238·37m.

Area, population and chief towns of the provinces, autonomous districts and major islands:

	Area (in sq. km)	*Population (2000 census)*	*Chief town*	*Population (1990 census)*
Bali	5,633	3,151,162	Denpasar	261,263[1]
Nusa Tenggara Barat	20,153	4,009,261	Mataram	141,387[1]
Nusa Tenggara Timur	47,351	3,952,279	Kupang	403,110[1]
Bali and Nusa Tenggara	73,137	11,112,702		
Banten	8,651	8,098,780	Serang	...[2]
DKI Jakarta[3]	664	8,389,443	Jakarta	8,259,266
Jawa Barat	34,597	35,729,537	Bandung	2,026,893
Jawa Tengah	32,549	31,228,940	Semarang	1,005,316
Jawa Timur	47,922	34,783,640	Surabaya	2,421,016
Yogyakarta[3]	3,186	3,122,268	Yogyakarta	412,392
Java	127,569	121,352,608		
Kalimantan Barat	146,807	4,034,198	Pontianak	387,112
Kalimantan Selatan	43,546	2,985,240	Banjarmasin	443,738
Kalimantan Tengah	153,564	1,857,000	Palangkaraya	60,447[1]
Kalimantan Timur	230,277	2,455,120	Samarinda	335,016
Kalimantan	574,194	11,331,558		
Irian Jaya Barat[4]	...	...	Manokwari	...[2]
Maluku	46,975	1,205,539	Amboina	206,260
Maluku Utara	30,895	785,059	Ternate	...[2]
Papua[4]	365,466	2,220,934	Jayapura	149,618[1]
Maluku and Papua	443,336	4,211,532		
Gorontalo	12,215	835,044	Gorontalo	...[2]
Sulawesi Barat[5]	...	...	...	...[2]
Sulawesi Selatan[5]	62,365	8,059,627	Makassar	913,196
Sulawesi Tengah	63,678	2,218,435	Palu	298,584[1]
Sulawesi Tenggara	38,140	1,821,284	Kendari	41,021[1]
Sulawesi Utara	15,273	2,012,098	Menado	275,374
Sulawesi	191,671	14,946,488		
Aceh[3, 6]	51,937	3,930,905	Banda Aceh	143,409
Bangka-Belitung	16,171	900,197	Pangkalpinang	...[2]
Bengkulu	19,789	1,567,432	Bengkulu	146,439
Jambi	53,437	2,413,846	Jambi[7]	301,359
Kepulauan Riau[8]	...	...	Tanjung Pinang	...[2]
Lampung	35,384	6,741,439	Bandar Lampung	457,900[9]
Riau[8]	94,560	4,957,627	Pakanbaru	341,328
Sumatera Barat	42,899	4,248,931	Padang	477,344
Sumatera Selatan	93,083	6,899,675	Palembang	1,084,483
Sumatera Utara	73,587	11,649,655	Medan	1,685,972
Sumatra	480,847	43,309,707		

[1]1980 census. [2]Province created since 1990. [3]Autonomous District. [4]Irian Jaya Barat, formerly part of Papua, was created in 2003. [5]Sulawesi Barat, formerly part of Sulawesi Selatan, was created in 2004. [6]The population of Aceh was reduced by about 237,000 as a result of the tsunami that struck Indonesia on 26 Dec. 2004. [7]Formerly Telanaipura. [8]Kepulauan Riau, formerly part of Riau, was created in 2002. [9]Estimate.

The capital, Jakarta, had a population of 8·35m. in 2000. Other major cities (2000 estimates in 1m.): Surabaya, 2·60; Bandung, 2·14; Medan, 1·90; Bekasi, 1·66; Palembang, 1·45; Semarang, 1·35.

The principal ethnic groups are the Acehnese, Bataks and Minangkabaus in Sumatra, the Javanese and Sundanese in Java, the Madurese in Madura, the Balinese in Bali, the Sasaks in Lombok, the Menadonese, Minahasans, Torajas and Buginese in Sulawesi, the Dayaks in Kalimantan, the Irianese in Papua and the Ambonese in the Moluccas. There were some 6m. Chinese resident in 1991.

Bahasa Indonesia is the official language; Dutch is spoken as a colonial inheritance.

SOCIAL STATISTICS

Estimated births, 2001, 4,620,000; deaths, 1,533,000. 2001 birth rate, 22·0 per 1,000 population; death rate, 7·3. Life expectancy in 2001 was 64·3 years for men and 68·2 for women. Annual population growth rate, 1992–2002, 1·4%. Infant mortality, 2001, 33 per 1,000 live births; fertility rate, 2001, 2·4 births per woman.

In the Human Development Index, or HDI (measuring progress in countries in longevity, knowledge and standard of living), Indonesia's index improved the most of any country during the last quarter of the 20th century, rising from 0·456 in 1975 to 0·677 in 1999.

CLIMATE

Conditions vary greatly over this spread of islands, but generally the climate is tropical monsoon, with a dry season from June to Sept. and a wet one from Oct. to April. Temperatures are high all the year and rainfall varies according to situation on lee or windward shores. Jakarta, Jan. 78°F (25·6°C), July 78°F (25·6°C). Annual rainfall 71" (1,775 mm). Padang, Jan. 79°F (26·1°C), July 79°F (26·1°C). Annual rainfall 177" (4,427 mm). Surabaya, Jan. 79°F (26·1°C), July 78°F (25·6°C). Annual rainfall 51" (1,285 mm).

On 26 Dec. 2004 an undersea earthquake centred off Sumatra caused a huge tsunami that flooded large areas along the coast of north-western Indonesia resulting in 237,000 deaths. In total there were 290,000 deaths in twelve countries.

CONSTITUTION AND GOVERNMENT

The constitution originally dates from Aug. 1945 and was in force until 1949; it was restored on 5 July 1959.

The political system is based on *pancasila*, in which deliberations lead to a consensus. There is a 550-member *Dewan Perwakilan Rakyat* (House of People's Representatives), with members elected for a five-year term by proportional representation in multi-member constituencies. The constitution was changed on 10 Aug. 2002 to allow for direct elections for the president and the vice-president.

There is no limit to the number of presidential terms. Although predominantly a Muslim country, the constitution protects the religious beliefs of non-Muslims.

National Anthem. 'Indonesia, tanah jang mulia' ('Indonesia, our native land'); words and tune by W. R. Supratman.

RECENT ELECTIONS

Elections to the House of People's Representatives were held on 5 April 2004. The Party of the Functional Groups (Golkar) won 128 seats with 21·6% of the vote; the Indonesian Democratic Party of Struggle (PDIP) won 109 seats with 18·5%; United Development Party (PPP) 58 with 8·2%; Democrat Party (PD) 57 with 7·5%; National Awakening Party (PKB) 52 with 10·6%; National Mandate Party (PAN) 52 with 6·4%; Prosperous Justice Party (PKS) 45 with 7·3%; Reform Star Party (PBR) 13 with 2·4%; Crescent Star Party (PBB) 11 with 2·6%; National Democracy Unity Party (PDK) 5 with 1·2%. The Concern for the Nation Functional Party (PKPB) and the Pioneers' Party (PP) won two seats each. The Indonesian National Party-Marhaenisme, Freedom Bull National Party (PNBK), Justice and Unity Party of Indonesia (PKPI) and the Indonesian Democratic Vanguard Party (PPDI) won one seat each. Turn-out was 84·5%.

Indonesia's first direct presidential election took place in 2004. In the first round held on 5 July 2004 Susilo Bambang Yudhoyono (PD) won 33·6% of the vote, incumbent Megawati Sukarnoputri (PDIP) 26·2%, Wiranto (Golkar) 22·2%, Amien Rais (PAN) 14·9% and Hamzah Haz (PPP) 3·1%. The run-off held on 20 Sept. 2004 was won by Susilo Bambang Yudhoyono, with 60·9% of votes cast, against 39·1% for Megawati Sukarnoputri.

CURRENT ADMINISTRATION

President: Susilo Bambang Yudhoyono; b. 1949 (PD; sworn in 20 Oct. 2004).
Vice-President: Jusuf Kalla.

In March 2005 the cabinet was composed as follows:

Co-ordinating Ministers: (Political, Legal and Security Affairs) Widodo Adi Sucipto; *(Economic Affairs)* Aburizal Bakrie; *(People's Welfare)* Alwi Shihab.

Minister of Foreign Affairs: Hassan Wirajuda. *Justice and Human Rights:* Hamid Awaluddin. *Defence:* Juwono Sudarsono. *Religious Affairs:* Muhammad Maftuh Basyuni. *Education:* Bambang Soedibyo. *Health:* Fadilah Supari. *Finance:* Yusuf Anwar. *Trade:* Mari E. Pangestu. *Manpower and Transmigration:* Fahmi Idris. *Agriculture:* Anton Apriyantono. *Forestry:* M. S. Kaban. *Industry:* Adung Nitimiharja. *Transportation:* Hatta Radjasa. *Maritime Affairs and Fisheries:* Freddy Numberi. *Social Services:* Bachtiar Chamsyah. *Energy and Mineral Resources:* Purnomo Yusgiantoro. *Home Affairs:* Mohamed Maaruf. *Public Works:* Joko Kirmanto. *Culture and Tourism:* Jero Wacik.

Government Website: http://www.indonesia.go.id

DEFENCE

There is selective conscription for two years. Defence expenditure in 2003 totalled US$6,443m. (US$30 per capita), representing 3·0% of GDP.

Army. Army strength in 2002 was estimated at 230,000 with a strategic reserve (KOSTRAD) of 30,000 and further potential mobilizable reserves of 400,000.

There is a paramilitary police some 194,000 strong; and a part-time local auxiliary forces, KAMRA (People's Security), which numbers around 40,000.

Navy. The Navy in 2002 numbered about 40,000, including 12,000 in the Commando Corps and 1,000 in the Naval Air Arm. Combatant strength includes two diesel submarines and 17 frigates. The Naval Air Arm operates 17 armed helicopters.

The Navy's principal command is split between the Western Fleet, at Teluk Ratai (Jakarta), and the Eastern Fleet, at Surabaya.

Air Force. Personnel (2002) approximately 27,000. There were 90 combat aircraft, including A-4s, F-16s, F-5s and British Aerospace *Hawks.*

INTERNATIONAL RELATIONS

Indonesia is in dispute with Malaysia over sovereignty of two islands in the Celebes Sea. Both countries have agreed to accept the Judgment of the International Court of Justice.

Indonesia is a member of the UN, WTO, OPEC, Asian Development Bank, Colombo Plan, APEC, ASEAN, Mekong Group, OIC and Islamic Development Bank.

ECONOMY

Agriculture accounted for 17·1% of GDP in 2002, industry 44·2% and services 38·7%.

Overview. Indonesia has made strong progress in achieving macroeconomic stability. In 2003 the government decided not to renew an IMF-supported programme. In the early 2000s growth averaged 3·5–4%. Investment in 2003 was approximately 20% of GDP, 10 percentage points below levels before the 1997 Asian financial crisis. Investment has shifted towards property. The role played by exports in stimulating growth has been less than in other Asian countries. Exports to China grew by 60% in 2003. Lower inflation, below 6% in 2003, has enabled Bank Indonesia to lower interest rates and public debt, standing at 67% of GDP in 2003. Progress has been made in restructuring and strengthening the banking sector although weaknesses remain. Half the banking sector is state-owned and the restructuring of non-performing loans is not always conducted on the basis of commercial viability. A government White Paper, published in 2003, includes measures to achieve a healthy fiscal position, lower inflation and adequate international reserves.

Currency. The monetary unit is the *rupiah* (IDR) notionally of 100 *sen.* Annual inflation was running at 58·0% in 1998 but had fallen to 3·8% by 2000 before rising to 11·5% in 2001 and further to 11·9% in 2002. Foreign exchange reserves were US$28,127m. and gold reserves 3·10m. troy oz in June 2002. Total money supply in Dec. 2001 was 170,509·0bn. rupiahs.

Budget. The fiscal year used to start 1 April but since 2001 has been the calendar year. Revenue in 2001 was 307,927bn. rupiahs and expenditure was 359,038bn. rupiahs. Tax accounted for 63·9% of revenue. Main items of expenditure: social security and welfare, 8·6%; general public services, 4·6%; education, 3·7%; and defence, 3·0%.

Performance. Economic growth was 4·5% in 1997 but declined dramatically in 1998 to –13·1%. There was a slight recovery in 1999, with growth of 0·8%, followed by growth of 4·9% in 2000, 3·4% in 2001 and 3·7% in 2002. The Asian economic crisis of 1997 affected Indonesia more than any other country. In 2003 total GDP was US$208·3bn.

Banking and Finance. The Bank Indonesia, successor to De Javasche Bank established by the Dutch in 1828, was made the central bank of Indonesia on 1 July 1953. Its *Governor* is Burhanuddin Abdullah. It had an original capital of 25m. rupiahs, a reserve fund of 18m. rupiahs and a special reserve of 84m. rupiahs. In Jan. 2000 independent auditors declared that the bank was technically bankrupt. In response the IMF stated that future loans would probably depend on recapitalization and an internal reorganization.

In 2003 there were 138 commercial banks, 26 regional government banks, 76 private national banks and 31 foreign banks and joint banks. The leading banks are Bank Madiri (with assets of US$27·9bn. in Dec. 2002), Bank BNI and Bank Central Asia. All state banks are authorized to deal in foreign exchange.

The government owns one Savings Bank, Bank Tabungan Negara, and 1,000 Post Office Savings Banks. There are also over 3,500 rural and village savings banks and credit co-operatives. At least 16 banks closed in the wake of the 1997 financial crisis.

There is a stock exchange in Jakarta.

ENERGY AND NATURAL RESOURCES

Environment. Indonesia's carbon dioxide emissions from the consumption and flaring of fossil fuels in 2002 were the equivalent of 1·4 tonnes per capita.

Electricity. Installed capacity in 2000 was 25·4m. kW and production 99·51bn. kWh (13·72bn. kWh hydro-electric). Consumption per capita was 473 kWh in 2000. 68,045 villages were supplied with electricity in 1999.

Oil and Gas. The importance of oil in the economy is declining. The 2003 output of crude oil was 57·5m. tonnes. Proven reserves in 2002 totalled 5·0bn. bbls. Natural gas production, 2002, was 70·6bn. cu. metres with 2,620bn. cu. metres of proven reserves. In Jan. 2001 a 640-km gas pipeline linking Indonesia's West Natuna field with Singapore came on stream. It is expected to provide Singapore with US$8bn. worth of natural gas over a 20-year period.

Minerals. The high cost of extraction means that little of the large mineral resources outside Java is exploited; however, there is copper mining in Papua, nickel mining and processing on Sulawesi, and aluminium smelting in northern Sumatra. Open-cast coal mining has been conducted since the 1890s, but since the 1970s coal production has been developed as an alternative to oil. Reserves are estimated at 28,000m. tonnes. Coal production (2000), 76·8m. tonnes. Other minerals: copper concentrate (1998), 2·9m. tonnes; bauxite (2001), 1,237,000 tonnes; salt (1998 estimate), 650,000 tonnes; iron ore (2000), 489,000 tonnes; nickel (2002), 122,000 tonnes (content of nickel ores and concentrates); tin (1998), 50,833 tonnes; silver (2001), 348 tonnes; gold (2001), 166 tonnes.

Agriculture. There were 20·50m. ha of arable land in 2001 and 13·1m. ha of permanent crops. 4·82m. ha were irrigated in 2001. Production (2000, in 1,000 tonnes): rice, 51,000; sugarcane, 21,400; cassava, 16,347; coconuts, 16,235; maize, 9,169; bananas, 3,377; cabbages, 1,750; sweet potatoes, 1,627; palm kernels, 1,600; natural rubber, 1,488; copra, 1,380; soybeans, 1,198; groundnuts, 1,000; potatoes, 924; dry beans, 900; mangoes, 827; onions, 805; oranges, 645; cucumbers and gherkins, 580. Annual nutmeg production is 6,000 tonnes, more than two-thirds of the world total. Indonesia is the world's largest producer of coconuts.

Livestock (2000): goats, 14·12m.; cattle, 12·10m.; pigs, 9·35m.; sheep, 7·50m.; buffaloes, 2·86m.; horses, 579,000; chickens, 800m.; ducks, 26m.

Forestry. In 2000 the area under forests was 104·99m. ha, or 58·0% of the total land area. The annual loss of 1,312,000 ha between 1990 and 2000 was exceeded during the same period only in Brazil. In 2001, 119·21m. cu. metres of roundwood were cut, most of it fuelwood and charcoal.

Fisheries. In 2001 total catch was 4,203,830 tonnes, of which 3,897,270 tonnes were sea fish. In 1997 there were 191,270 motorized and 371,007 other fishing vessels.

INDUSTRY

The largest company in Indonesia by market capitalization in May 2004 was Telekomunikasi Indonesia (US$8·0bn.).

There are shipyards at Jakarta Raya, Surabaya, Semarang and Amboina. There are textile factories, large paper factories, match factories, automobile and bicycle assembly works, large construction works, tyre factories, glass factories, a caustic soda and other chemical factories. Production (2000, in 1,000 tonnes): cement, 22,789; distillate fuel oil, 14,401; residual fuel oil, 11,421; petrol, 7,997; kerosene, 7,494; fertilizers (2002), 7,038; paper and paperboard (2001), 6,995; palm oil, 6,900; sugar (1998), 1,493; plywood (2001), 7·3m. cu. metres; 4,937,000 radio sets (1999); 804,000 TV sets (1998); 342,500 cars and lorries (2002); 254·3bn. cigarettes (1999). Indonesia is the third largest producer of plywood after the USA and China.

Labour. In 2001 the labour force was 98,812,000. 43·8% of employed persons worked in agriculture, forestry, hunting and fisheries, 19·2% in trade, restaurants and hotels, 13·3% in manufacturing and 12·1% in community, social and personal services. National daily average wage, 1996, 4,073 rupiahs. Unemployment in 2001 was 8·1%.

Trade Unions. Workers have a constitutional right to organize and under a law passed in Feb. 2003 have a right to be paid during lawful strikes. Between 1994 and 1996 there were more than 2,000 strikes involving 1m. workers. In Feb. 2003 the Indonesian Trade Union Congress (KSPI), supported by the International Confederation of Free Trade Unions, was inaugurated. It represents 3·1m. members and encompasses 12 industrial federations.

INTERNATIONAL TRADE

Since 1992 foreigners have been permitted to hold 100% of the equity of new companies in Indonesia with more than US$50m. part capital, or situated in remote provinces. Foreign debt was US$132,208m. in 2002.

Pressure on Indonesia's currency and stock market led to an appeal to the IMF and World Bank for long-term support funds in Oct. 1997. A bail-out package worth US$38,000m. was eventually agreed on condition that Indonesia tightened financial controls and instituted reforms, including the establishment of an independent privatization board, liberalizing foreign investment, cutting import tariffs and phasing out export levies.

Imports and Exports. Imports and exports in US$1m.:

	1998	*1999*	*2000*	*2001*	*2002*
Imports f.o.b.	31,942	30,598	40,366	34,669	35,652
Exports f.o.b.	50,371	51,242	65,406	57,364	58,773

Principal export items: gas and oil, forestry products, manufactured goods, rubber, coffee, fishery products, coal, copper, tin, pepper, palm products and tea. Main export markets, 2001: Japan, 20·0%; USA, 15·0%; Singapore, 10·8%. Principal import items: machinery and transport equipment, basic manufactures and chemicals. Main import suppliers, 2001: Japan, 18·8%; Singapore, 10·2%; South Korea, 9·8%.

COMMUNICATIONS

Roads. In 1999 there were about 342,700 km of roads (27,357 km of highways or main roads in 1997), of which 158,700 km were surfaced. Motor vehicles, 1998: passenger cars, 2,772,500; buses and coaches, 628,000; trucks and vans, 1,592,600; motorcycles, 12,651,800. There were 272 fatalities in road accidents in 1996.

Rail. In 1997 the national railways totalled 6,458 km of 1,067 mm gauge, comprising 4,967 km on Java (of which 125 km electrified) and 1,491 km on

Sumatra. Passenger-km travelled in 2001 came to 18·27bn. and freight tonne-km in 1998 to 4·96bn.

Civil Aviation. Garuda Indonesia is the state-owned national flag carrier. Merpati Nusantara Airlines is their domestic subsidiary. There are international airports at Jakarta (Sukarno-Hatta), Denpasar (on Bali), Medan (Sumatra), Pekanbaru (Sumatra), Ujung Pandang (Sulawesi), Manado (Sulawesi), Solo (Java) and Surabaya Juanda (Java). Jakarta is the busiest airport, in 2000 handling 9,950,000 passengers (5,387,000 on domestic flights) and 292,300 tonnes of freight. Denpasar handled 3,970,000 and Surabaya Juanda 2,444,000 passengers in 2000. In 1999 scheduled airline traffic of Indonesia-based carriers flew 121·8m. km, carrying 8,047,000 passengers (1,927,000 on international flights).

Shipping. There are 16 ports for ocean-going ships, the largest of which is Tanjung Priok, which serves the Jakarta area and has a container terminal. In 2002 cargo traffic at Tanjung Priok totalled 39·3m. tonnes. The national shipping company Pelajaran Nasional Indonesia (PELNI) maintains inter-island communications. Jakarta Lloyd maintains regular services between Jakarta, Amsterdam, Hamburg and London. In 1995 the merchant marine comprised 535 ocean-going ships totalling 4·13m. DWT. 95 vessels (36·22% of total tonnage) were registered under foreign flags. In 2002 total tonnage registered came to 3·72m. GRT, including oil tankers 827,000 GRT. In 2002 vessels totalling 361,246,000 net registered tons entered ports and vessels totalling 86,554,000 NRT cleared.

Telecommunications. In 2002 there were 19,450,000 telephone subscribers (91·7 per 1,000 population) and 2,519,000 PCs in use (11·9 for every 1,000 persons). There were 11,700,000 mobile phone subscribers in 2002 and 185,000 fax machines in use in 1999. Indonesia had 8·0m. Internet users in 2002, up from 400,000 in 2000.

Postal Services. In 1998 there were 20,139 post offices.

SOCIAL INSTITUTIONS

Justice. There are courts of first instance, high courts of appeal in every provincial capital and a Supreme Court of Justice for the whole of Indonesia in Jakarta.

In civil law the population is divided into three main groups: Indonesians, Europeans and foreign Orientals, to whom different law systems are applicable. When, however, people from different groups are involved, a system of so-called 'inter-gentile' law is applied.

The present criminal law, which has been in force since 1918, is codified and is based on European penal law. This law is equally applicable to all groups of the population. The death penalty is still in use. In 2004 there were three executions, the first ones in three years.

The population in penal institutions in 2001 was 62,886 (29 per 100,000 of national population).

Religion. Religious liberty is granted to all denominations. In 2001 there were 185·1m. Muslims (making Indonesia the world's biggest Muslim country), 12·8m. Protestants and 7·6m. Roman Catholics. There were also significant numbers of Hindus and Buddhists. In Sept. 2003 there was one cardinal.

Education. Adult literacy in 2001 was 87·3% (92·1% among males and 82·6% among females). In 2000–01 there were 28,690,131 pupils and 1,289,720 teachers at primary schools, and 14,828,085 pupils and 1,040,081 teachers at secondary schools. Number of students in higher education (2000–01), 3,017,887. In 1994–95 in the state sector there were 31 universities and one open university, and 13 institutes of higher education, including ten teacher training colleges. In the private sector there were 66 universities and 25 specialized universities. There were 19 institutes of higher education in the private sector, including 12 teacher training colleges.

In 2000–01 total expenditure on education came to 1·6% of GNP and 9·6% of total government spending.

Health. In 1997 there were 31,887 doctors and dentists, 155,911 nurses and midwives and 5,440 pharmacies. There were 1,090 hospitals in 1997, with a provision of six beds per 10,000 population.

Welfare. The official retirement age is 55. There are currently no unemployment benefits or family allowance programmes.

CULTURE

World Heritage Sites. There are seven UNESCO sites in Indonesia (the first four inscribed in 1991): Borobudur Temple Compounds, Ujung Kulon National Park, Komodo National Park, Prambanan Temple Compounds, Sangiran Early Man Site (1996), Lorentz National Park (1999) and the Tropical Rainforest Heritage of Sumatra (2004).

Broadcasting. Radio Republik Indonesia, under the Department of Information, operates 49 stations. There were 32m. television receivers (colour by PAL) in 2001 and 33m. radio sets in 2000.

Press. In 1998 there were 172 daily newspapers (total average circulation of 4,713,000 at a rate of 23 per 1,000 inhabitants).

Tourism. In 2001 there were 5,154,000 foreign tourists, spending US$5·40bn. 1,477,000 were from Singapore, 611,000 from Japan, 485,000 from Malaysia and 398,000 from Australia. In Feb. 2004 the government introduced a US$25 fee for a 30-day visa and a US$10 fee for a 3-day visa.

Festivals. Independence from the Dutch is celebrated on 17 Aug. with musical and theatrical performances, carnivals and sporting events. The military parades on Armed Forces Day (5 Oct.) and women are celebrated on Kartini Day (21 April) in memory of Raden Ajeng Kartini, a symbol of female emancipation. In Bali the Hindu new year is marked by a day of silence, *Nyepi*, followed by a day of feasting. Muslim, Hindu, Buddhist and Christian festivals are marked throughout the country.

DIPLOMATIC REPRESENTATIVES

Of Indonesia in the United Kingdom (38 Grosvenor Sq., London, W1X 9AD)
Ambassador: Vacant.
Chargé d'Affaires a.i.: Eddy Pratomo.

Of the United Kingdom in Indonesia (Jalan M.H. Thamrin 75, Jakarta 10310)
Ambassador: Charles Humfrey, CMG.

Of Indonesia in the USA (2020 Massachusetts Ave., NW, Washington, D.C., 20036)
Ambassador: Soemadi Djoko M. Brotodiningrat.

Of the USA in Indonesia (Medan Merdeka Selatan 5, Jakarta)
Ambassador: B. Lynn Pascoe.

Of Indonesia to the United Nations
Ambassador: Rezlan Ishar Jenie.

Of Indonesia to the European Union
Ambassador: Abdurachman Mattalitti.

FURTHER READING

Central Bureau of Statistics. *Statistical Yearbook of Indonesia.—Monthly Statistical Bulletin: Economic Indicator.*

Elson, R. E., *Suharto; a Political Biography.* CUP, 2001

Forrester, Geoff, (ed.) *Post-Soeharto Indonesia: Renewal or Chaos?* St Martin's Press, New York, 1999

Forrester, Geoff and May, R. J. (eds.) *The Fall of Soeharto.* Hurst, London, 1999

Friend, Theodore, *Indonesian Destinies.* Belknap Press, Harvard Univ. Press, 2003

Kingsbury, Damien, *The Politics of Indonesia.* 2nd ed. OUP, 2002

Krausse, G. H. and Krausse, S. C. E., *Indonesia.* [Bibliography] ABC-Clio, Oxford and Santa Barbara (CA), 1994

Ricklefs, M. C., *A History of Modern Indonesia since c. 1200.* 3rd ed. Palgrave, Basingstoke, 2001

Schwarz, Adam, *A Nation in Waiting: Indonesia's Search for Stability.* Revised ed. Westview Press, Boulder (CO), 1999

Schwarz, Adam and Paris, Jonathan, (eds.) *The Politics of Post-Suharto Indonesia.* New York, 1999

Vatikiotis, M. R. J., *Indonesian Politics under Suharto: Order, Development and Pressure for Change.* 2nd ed. London, 1994

National statistical office: Central Bureau of Statistics, POB 1003, Jakarta, 10010.
Website: http://www.bps.go.id

IRAN

Jomhuri-e-Eslami-e-Iran
(Islamic Republic of Iran)

Capital: Tehran
Population projection, 2010: 75·54m.
GDP per capita, 2002: (PPP$) 6,690
HDI/world rank: 0·732/101

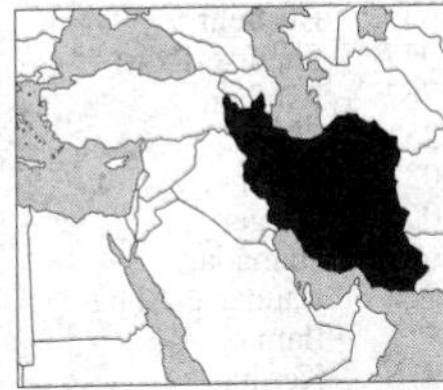

KEY HISTORICAL EVENTS

Persia was ruled by the Shahs as an absolute monarchy from the 16th century until 1906, when the first constitution was granted and a national assembly established. After a coup in 1921, Reza Khan began his rise to power. He was declared Shah on 12 Dec. 1925 and as closer relations with Europe were developed in the mid-1930s so the name Iran began to be used in the west instead of Persia. When in the Second World War Iran supported Germany, the Allies occupied the country and forced Reza Shah to abdicate in favour of his son. The British controlled oil industry was nationalized in March 1951 in line with the policy of the National Front Party whose leader, Dr Muhammad Mussadeq, became prime minister in April 1951. He was opposed by the Shah who fled the country until Aug. 1953 when the monarchists staged a coup which led to Mussadeq being deposed. The Shah's policy, which included the redistribution of land to small farmers and the enfranchisement of women, was opposed by the Shia religious scholars who considered it to be contrary to Islamic teaching. Despite economic growth, unrest was caused by the Shah's repressive measures and his extensive use of the Savak, the secret police. The opposition led by Ayatollah Ruhollah Khomeini, the Shia Muslim spiritual leader who had been exiled in 1965, was particularly successful. Following intense civil unrest in Tehran, the Shah left Iran with his family on 17 Jan. 1979 (and died in Egypt on 27 July 1980). The Ayatollah Khomeini returned from exile on 1 Feb. 1979, the Shah's government resigned and parliament dissolved itself on 11 Feb. Following a referendum in March, an Islamic Republic was proclaimed. The constitution gave supreme authority to a religious leader (*wali faqih*), a position held by Ayatollah Khomeini for the rest of his life. In Sept. 1980 border fighting with Iraq escalated into full-scale war. A UN-arranged ceasefire took place on 20 Aug. 1988, and in Aug. 1990, following Iraq's invasion of Kuwait, Iraq offered peace terms and began the withdrawal of troops from Iranian soil. Approximately 30,000 political opponents of the regime are believed to have been executed shortly after the end of the war.

In 1997 the election of Mohammad Khatami as president signalled a shift away from Islamic extremism. A clampdown on Islamic vigilantes who wage a violent campaign against western 'decadence' is the latest sign of a cautiously liberal integration of the constitution. But the conservative faction led by the spiritual leader Ayatollah Ali Khamenei retains huge power including the final say on defence and foreign policy.

In July 1999 riot police fought pitched battles with pro-democracy students in Tehran in the worst unrest since the revolution in 1979. Since then there have been further cautious moves towards a more liberal society, though the Islamic leaders remain bitterly divided on the degree of overlap between politics and religion.

TERRITORY AND POPULATION

Iran is bounded in the north by Armenia, Azerbaijan, the Caspian Sea and Turkmenistan, east by Afghanistan and Pakistan, south by the Gulf of Oman and the Persian Gulf, and west by Iraq and Turkey. It has an area (including inland water) of 1,648,195 sq. km (636,368 sq. miles), but a vast portion is desert. Population (1996 census): 60,055,488 (2001, 64·7% urban). Population density: 36 per sq. km. The United Nations population estimate for 2000 was 66,443,000.

The UN gives a projected population for 2010 of 75·54m.

In 2001 Iran had 1·9m. refugees, mostly from Afghanistan. Only Pakistan has more refugees.

The areas, populations and capitals of the 28 provinces *(ostan)* were:

Province	*Area (sq. km)*	*Census 1996*	*Estimate 2002*	*Capital*
Ardabil	17,881	1,168,011	1,204,410	Ardabil
Azarbayejan, East	47,830	3,325,540	3,378,242	Tabriz
Azarbayejan, West	39,487	2,496,320	2,774,804	Orumiyeh
Bushehr	23,191	743,675	796,639	Bushehr
Chahar Mahal and Bakhtyari	16,201	761,168	794,077	Shahr-e-Kord
Esfahan	107,027	3,923,255	4,316,767	Esfahan
Fars	122,416	3,817,036	4,135,251	Shiraz
Gilan	14,106	2,241,896	2,310,033	Rasht
Golestan	20,891	1,426,288	1,555,058	Gorgan
Hamadan	19,547	1,677,957	1,718,627	Hamadan
Hormozgan	71,193	1,062,155	1,235,816	Bandar-e-Abbas
Ilam	20,151	487,886	550,971	Ilam
Kerman	181,814	2,004,328	2,215,376	Kerman
Kermanshah	24,641	1,778,596	1,962,176	Kermanshah
Khorasan	302,766	6,047,661	6,094,888	Mashhad
Khuzestan	63,238	3,746,772	4,506,816	Ahvaz
Kohgiluyeh and Boyer Ahmad	15,563	544,356	627,517	Yasuj
Kordestan	29,151	1,346,383	1,492,007	Sanandaj
Lorestan	28,392	1,584,434	1,671,706	Khorramabad
Markazi	29,406	1,228,812	1,300,778	Arak
Mazandaran	23,064	2,602,008	2,742,885	Sari
Qazvin	15,502	968,257	1,066,317	Qazvin
Qom	11,237	853,044	971,280	Qom
Semnan	96,816	501,447	563,959	Semnan
Sistan and Baluchestan	178,431	1,722,579	2,086,170	Zahedan
Tehran	18,637	10,343,965	11,689,301	Tehran
Yazd	73,467	750,769	841,370	Yazd
Zanjan	21,841	900,890	936,985	Zanjan

At the 1996 census the populations of the principal cities were:

	Population		*Population*
Tehran	6,758,845[1]	Arak	380,755
Mashhad	1,887,405	Ardabil	340,386
Esfahan	1,266,072	Yazd	326,776
Tabriz	1,191,043	Qazvin	291,117
Shiraz	1,053,025	Zanjan	286,295
Karaj	940,968	Sanandaj	277,808
Ahvaz	804,980	Bandar-e-Abbas	273,578
Qom	777,677	Khorramabad	272,815
Kermanshah	692,986	Eslamshahr	265,450
Orumiyeh	435,200	Borujerd	217,804
Zahedan	419,518	Abadan	206,073
Rasht	417,748	Dezful	202,639
Hamadan	401,281	Khorramshahr	105,636
Kerman	384,991		

[1]1999 population, 6,934,750.

The national language is Farsi or Persian, spoken by 45% of the population in 1986. 28% spoke related languages, including Kurdish (9%) and Luri in the west, Gilaki and Mazandarami in the north, and Baluchi in the southeast; 22% speak Turkic languages, primarily in the northwest. Iranians, who are Persians, not Arabs, are less emotionally connected to the plight of the Arab Palestinians than people in other parts of the Middle East. The majority of Iranians are not instinctively anti-American.

SOCIAL STATISTICS

1999 births, 1,177,557; deaths, 374,838. Birth rate (1999, per 1,000 population), 18·8; death rate, 6·0. Iran has one of the youngest populations in the world, with about 55% of the current population being under the age of 25. Abortion is illegal, but a family planning scheme was inaugurated in 1988. Expectation of life at birth,

2001, 71·3 years for females and 68·5 years for males. Infant mortality, 2001, 35 per 1,000 live births. Annual population growth rate, 1992–2002, 1·4%; fertility rate, 2001, 2·9 births per woman. Iran has had one of the largest reductions in its fertility rate of any country in the world over the past 25 years, having had a rate of 6·4 births per woman in 1975. The suicide rate is 25 for every 100,000 people—more than twice the world average.

CLIMATE

Mainly a desert climate, but with more temperate conditions on the shores of the Caspian Sea. Seasonal range of temperature is considerable, as is rain (ranging from 2" in the southeast to 78" in the Caspian region). Winter is normally the rainy season for the whole country. Abadan, Jan. 54°F (12·2°C), July 97°F (36·1°C). Annual rainfall 8" (204 mm). Tehran, Jan. 36°F (2·2°C), July 85°F (29·4°C). Annual rainfall 10" (246 mm).

CONSTITUTION AND GOVERNMENT

The Constitution of the Islamic Republic was approved by a national referendum in Dec. 1979. It gives supreme authority to the *Spiritual Leader* (*wali faqih*), which position was held by Ayatollah Khomeini until his death on 3 June 1989. Ayatollah Seyed Ali Khamenei was elected to succeed him on 4 June 1989. Following the death of the previous incumbent, Ayatollah Ali Khamenei was proclaimed the *Source of Knowledge (Marja e Taghlid)* at the head of all Shia Muslims in Dec. 1994.

The 86-member *Assembly of Experts* was established in 1982. It is popularly elected every eight years. Its mandate is to interpret the constitution and select the Spiritual Leader. Candidates for election are examined by the *Council of Guardians*.

The *Islamic Consultative Assembly* has 290 members, elected for a four-year term in single-seat constituencies. All candidates have to be approved by the 12-member *Council of Guardians*.

The *President* of the Republic is popularly elected for not more than two four-year terms and is head of the executive; he appoints Ministers subject to approval by the *Islamic Consultative Assembly (Majlis)*.

Legislative power is held by the Islamic Consultative Assembly, directly elected on a non-party basis for a four-year term by all citizens aged 17 or over. A new law passed in Oct. 1999 raised the voting age from 16 to 17, thus depriving an estimated 1·5m. young people from voting. Two-thirds of the electorate is under 30. Voting is secret but ballot papers are not printed; electors must write the name of their preferred candidate themselves. Five seats are reserved for religious minorities. All legislation is subject to approval by the *Council of Guardians* who ensure it is in accordance with the Islamic code and with the Constitution. The Spiritual Leader appoints six members, as does the judiciary.

National Anthem. 'Sar zad az ofogh mehr-e khavaran' ('Rose from the horizon the affectionate sun of the East'); words by a group of poets, tune by Dr Riahi.

RECENT ELECTIONS

Presidential elections held on 8 June 2001 produced a second landslide victory for incumbent Mohammad Khatami. He promised to continue fighting for democratic reforms which were blocked during his preceding tenure by the hardline clerical establishment. There were ten candidates. Mohammad Khatami was elected with 78·3% of votes cast (up from 69% at the 1997 election), against 15·9% for Ahmad Tavakoli and 2·7% for defence minister Ali Shamkhani. Turn-out was 67%.

Elections to the Islamic Consultative Assembly were held on 20 Feb. 2004. Conservatives won 156 seats, allies of President Mohammad Khatami 40 and ind. 30. In the second round of elections held on 7 May 2004 conservatives won 40 of 57 seats, reformists 8 and ind. 9.

Elections to the Assembly of Experts were held on 23 Oct. 1998; turn-out was 46%. Conservative candidates won 54 seats, 13 went to moderates and the remaining 21 went to conservative-allied independents.

Presidential elections were scheduled to take place on 17 June 2005.

CURRENT ADMINISTRATION

In March 2005 the cabinet was composed as follows:

President: Ali Mohammad Khatami-Ardakani; b. 1943 (sworn in 3 Aug. 1997 and re-elected in 2001).

First Vice President: Mohammad Reza Aref-Yazdi.

Vice President for Atomic Energy: Gholamreza Aghazedeh-Khoi. *Vice President for Cultural Heritage:* Hossein Marashi. *Vice President for Environmental Protection:* Dr Masoomeh Ebtekar. *Vice President for Legal and Parliamentary Affairs:* Majid Ansari. *Vice President for Martyrs and War Veterans' Affairs:* Hossein Dehghan. *Vice President for Physical Training:* Mohsen Mehr-Alizadeh. *Vice President for Planning and Management:* Mohammad Satari-Far. *Government Spokesperson:* Dr Abdullah Ramezanzadeh. *Minister of Foreign Affairs:* Dr Kamal Kharrazi. *Oil:* Bijan Namdar-Zanganeh. *Interior:* Abdol Vahed Musavi-Lari. *Economic Affairs and Finance:* Safdar Hosseini. *Agriculture Jihad:* Muhammad Hojjati. *Commerce:* Mohammad Shariatmadar. *Energy:* Habibollah Bitaraf. *Roads and Transport:* Seyyed Mohammad Rahmati. *Industry and Mines:* Eshaq Jahangiri. *Housing and Urban Development:* Dr Ali Abdolalizadeh. *Labour and Social Affairs:* Naser Khaleghi. *Health, Treatment and Medical Education:* Masud Pezekhsian. *Education and Training:* Morteza Haji-Qaem. *Science, Research and Technology:* Dr Jafar Tofiqi Dari. *Justice:* Mohammad Esmael Shoushtari. *Defence and Armed Forces Logistics:* V. Adm. Ali Shamkhani. *Islamic Culture and Guidance:* Ahmad Masjed-Jamei. *Co-operatives:* Ali Sufi. *Intelligence and Security:* Mohammad Ali Yunesi. *Information and Communications Technology:* Dr Seyed Ahmad Motamedi. *Welfare and Social Security:* Mohammad Hossein Sharifzadegan.

Speaker of the Islamic Consultative Assembly (*Majlis*)*:* Gholam Ali Hadad-Adel.

Presidency Website: http://www.president.ir

DEFENCE

Two years' military service is compulsory. Military expenditure totalled US$3,051m. in 2003 (equivalent to US$46 per capita), representing 2·4% of GDP, compared to 7·7% in 1985.

Nuclear Weapons. Although Iran is a member of the Non-Proliferation Treaty (NPT), it may be developing weapons using its nuclear power programme. In July 2003 United Nations inspectors announced that they had found enriched uranium in environmental samples, increasing US suspicion that Iran is not using nuclear energy just to generate electricity. Iran has successfully tested Shahab-3 medium-range ballistic missiles with a known range of 1,300 km, and in Aug. 2004 tested a new version that analysts believe may have a range of 2,000 km. According to *Deadly Arsenals*, published by the Carnegie Endowment for International Peace, Iran has a chemical and biological weapons programme.

Army. Strength (2002), 325,000 (about 220,000 conscripts). Reserves are estimated to be around 350,000, made up of ex-service volunteers.

Revolutionary Guard (*Pasdaran Inqilab*). Numbering some 125,000, the Guard is divided between ground forces (100,000), naval forces (some 20,000) and marines (5,000). It controls the Basij, a volunteer 'popular mobilization army' of about 300,000, which can number 1m. strong in wartime.

Navy. The fleet includes six submarines (including three ex-Soviet *Kilo* class) and three ex-UK frigates. Personnel numbered 18,000 in 2002 including 2,000 in Naval Aviation and 2,600 marines.

The Naval Aviation wing operated five combat aircraft and 19 armed helicopters. The main naval bases are at Bandar-e-Abbas, Bushehr and Chah Bahar.

Air Force. In 2002 there were 306 combat aircraft including US F-14 Tomcat, F-5E Tiger II and F-4D/E Phantom II fighter-bombers, and a number of MiG-29 interceptors and Su-24 strike aircraft. The serviceability of the aircraft varies with only 60–80% operational.

Strength (2002) estimated at 52,000 personnel (about 15,000 air defence).

INTERNATIONAL RELATIONS

Iran's foreign policy has been much less doctrinaire since the election to the presidency in May 1997 of Mohammad Khatami. In April 2001 Iran and Saudi Arabia signed a security pact to fight drug trafficking and terrorism, 13 years after the two countries had broken off relations.

Iran is a member of the UN, OPEC, ECO, Colombo Plan, IOM, OIC and Islamic Development Bank.

ECONOMY

Agriculture accounted for 11·7% of GDP in 2002, industry 40·6% and services 47·7%.

Overview. The Fourth Five-Year Development Plan is running from 2005–10. At the beginning of 1991 about 70% of industry was state-owned, much of it nationalized after the 1979 revolution, but the government is now committed to partial privatization. Strategic heavy industry will remain in the public sector.

Currency. The unit of currency is the *rial* (IRR) of which 10 = 1 *toman*. In March 2005 the Iranian rial was fixed at a rate of IRR 9,090 to the US dollar. Gold reserves were 5·42m. troy oz in March 1996. Inflation in 2002 was 15·8%. Total money supply in Feb 2002 was 130,015bn. rials.

Budget. Revenues in 2001–02 totalled 180,975bn. rials and expenditures 168,992bn. rials. Petroleum and natural gas revenues accounted for 57·0% of all revenues and taxes 23·0%. Current expenditure accounted for 66·6% of all expenditures.

Performance. Real GDP growth was 5·9% in 2001 and 6·7% in 2002. Total GDP in 2003 was US$136·8bn.

Banking and Finance. The Central Bank is the note issuing authority and government bank. Its *Governor* is Ebrahim Sheibani. All other banks and insurance companies were nationalized in 1979, and re-organized into new state banking corporations, of which there were five in 1994. In April 2000 the government announced that it would permit the establishment of private banks for the first time since the revolution in 1979, ending the state monopoly on banking. The first private bank since the revolution came into existence in Aug. 2001 with the creation of Bank-e-Eqtesadi Novin (Modern Economic Bank). In 2002 there were 11 commercial banks, two development banks, one housing bank and around 30 foreign banks.

A stock exchange re-opened in Tehran in 1992.

ENERGY AND NATURAL RESOURCES

Environment. Iran's carbon dioxide emissions from the consumption and flaring of fossil fuels were the equivalent of 5·3 tonnes per capita in 2002.

Electricity. Total installed capacity in 2000 was 30·6m. kW; production (2000), 116·33bn. kWh (112·65bn. kWh thermal and 3·68bn. kWh hydro-electric). Consumption per capita in 2000 was about 1,827 kWh. Iran's first nuclear reactor is being built by Russia at Bushehr and is scheduled to be commissioned before the end of 2006.

Oil and Gas. Iran has 11·4% of proven global oil reserves. Oil is its chief source of revenue. The main oilfields are in the Zagros Mountains where oil was first discovered in 1908. Oil companies were nationalized in 1979 and operations of crude oil and natural gas exploitation are now run by the National Iranian Oil Company. Refining operations of crude oil are run by the National Company for Refining and Distribution of Oil Products. Iran produced 166·9m. tonnes of oil in 2002 (4·7% of the world total oil output); in 2003 it had reserves amounting to 130·7bn. bbls. (only Saudi Arabia had more). In 1999 the most important discovery in more than 30 years was made, with the Azadegan oilfield in the southwest of the country being found to have reserves of approximately 26bn. bbls. In 2001 revenue from oil exports amounted to US$14bn. (US$19bn. in 2000). Iran depends on oil for some 86% of its exports, but domestic consumption has been increasing to such an extent that it is now as high as exports.

Iran has nearly 15% of proven global gas reserves. A deal reached in Nov. 1997 between Gazprom, the Russian gas company, and Total, the French energy group, involved the investment of US$2,000m. into the development of a gas field.

In Dec. 1997 the first natural gas pipeline linking Iran with the Caspian Sea via Turkmenistan was opened. The 200-km line links gas fields in western Turkmenistan to industrial markets in northern Iran. Natural gas production (2002): 64·5bn. cu. metres. Natural gas reserves in 2002 were 23,000bn. cu. metres, the second largest behind Russia.

Minerals. Production (in 1,000 tonnes): gypsum (1999–2000), 10,834; iron ore (1999–2000), 10,776; decorative stone (1999), 7,700; crude steel (2002), 7,300; salt (1999), 1,600; coal (2000), 1,394; chromite (1999), 255; zinc and lead (1999), 182; bauxite (2000), 140; copper (2001), 140; aluminium (1999), 137; manganese (1999), 104. It was announced in Feb. 2003 that uranium deposits had been discovered in central Iran. In Nov. 2003 the International Atomic Energy Agency announced that Iran had admitted to enriching uranium at an electric plant outside Tehran.

Agriculture. Agriculture accounted for approximately 12·7% of GDP in 2000. There were 14·27m. ha of arable land in 2001 and 2·28m. ha of permanent crops. 7·5m. ha were irrigated in 2001.

Crop production (2000, in 1,000 tonnes): wheat, 8,088; sugarbeet, 4,332; potatoes, 3,658; tomatoes, 3,191; grapes, 2,505; sugarcane, 2,367; rice (paddy), 1,971; barley, 1,686; watermelons, 1,650; onions, 1,344; cucumbers and gherkins, 1,343; maize, 1,036; dates, 870; pistachios, 304. Iran's annual production of dates and pistachios is the highest in the world.

Livestock (2000): 55·0m. sheep; 26·0m. goats; 8·1m. cattle; 500,000 buffaloes; 1·6m. asses; 386m. chickens.

Forestry. Approximately 4·5% of Iran is forested (7·30m. ha), much of it in the Caspian region. Timber production in 2001 was 1·32m. cu. metres.

Fisheries. In 2001 total catch was 336,450 tonnes (262,805 tonnes from sea fishing).

INDUSTRY

Major industries: petrochemical, automotive, food, beverages and tobacco, textiles, clothing and leather, wood and fibre, paper and cardboard, chemical products, non-metal mining products, basic materials, machinery and equipment, copper, steel and aluminium. The textile industry uses local cotton and silk; carpet manufacture is an important industry. The country's steel industry is the largest in the Middle East; crude steel production in 2002 totalled 7·3m. tonnes.

Production includes: cement (2000), 23·3m. tonnes; cottonseed oil (1998), 994,000 tonnes; sugar (1998), 863,200 tonnes; stockings (2000), 18·5m. pairs; building bricks (2000), 10,077m. units.

Labour. The economically active population numbered 20m. in 2002, of which 17·6m. were employed. Approximately 12·2% of the workforce are unemployed and 800,000 Iranians enter the workforce every year.

INTERNATIONAL TRADE

There had been a limit on foreign investment, but legislation of 1995 permits foreign nationals to hold more than 50% of the equity of joint ventures with the consent of the Foreign Investment Board. Foreign debt was US$9,154m. in 2002.

Imports and Exports. Imports and exports for calendar years in US$1m.:

	1996	*1997*	*1998*	*1999*	*2000*
Imports f.o.b.	14,989	14,123	14,286	13,433	15,207
Exports f.o.b.	22,391	18,381	13,118	21,030	28,345

Main imports: machinery and motor vehicles, iron and steel, chemicals, pharmaceuticals, food. Main exports: oil, carpets, pistachios, leather and caviar. Petroleum and crude oil exports (1996): 2,620,000 bbls. a day. Crude oil exports account for 85% of hard currency earnings. Carpet exports are the second largest hard currency earner. Main export markets in 1998–99: UK, 16·8%; Japan, 15·7%; Italy, 8·6%; United Arab Emirates, 6·7%; Greece, 5·0%; South Korea, 5·0%. Main import suppliers, 1998–99: Germany, 11·6%; Italy, 8·3%; Japan, 7·0%; Belgium, 6·3%; United Arab Emirates, 5·3%; Argentina, 4·4%.

COMMUNICATIONS

Roads. In 1998 the total length of roads was 167,157 km, of which 890 km were freeways, 24,940 km main roads, 38,043 km (asphalted) by-roads, 15,370 km (gravelled) by-roads, 30,195 km asphalted rural roads and 57,719 km other rural roads. In 1996 there were 1,793,000 passenger cars; 692,000 vans and lorries; 2,565,585 motorcycles and mopeds. In 1999 there were 16,858 road accidents resulting in 2,313 deaths.

Rail. The State Railways totalled 6,688 km in 2000, of which 148 km were electrified. In 2000 the railways carried 11·7m. passengers and 25·2m. tonnes of freight. An isolated 1,676 mm gauge line (94 km) in the southeast provides a link with Pakistan Railways. A rail link to Turkmenistan was opened in May 1996. A metro system was opened in Tehran in 1999.

Civil Aviation. There are international airports at Tehran (Mehrabad), Shiraz and Bandar-e-Abbas. Tehran is the busiest airport, in 2000 handling 8,474,000 passengers (6,473,000 on domestic flights). The Imam Khomeini International Airport, construction of which began in 1977 before being halted in 1979, was inaugurated in Feb. 2004. The first flight arrived at the airport in May 2004 but it was then shut down by Iran's Revolutionary Guard, citing breaches of security by the foreign operators. The state-owned Iran Air carried 5·8m. passengers and 38,343 tonnes of freight in 1998–99.

Shipping. In 2002 the merchant fleet totalled 4·13m. GRT, including oil tankers totalling 2·14m. GRT. In 1998–99, 4,447 ships loaded and unloaded 31·0m. and 41·1m. tonnes of goods respectively (including oil products). In 2001 vessels totalling 67,267,000 NRT entered ports.

Telecommunications. In 2002 there were 14,387,100 telephone main lines, equivalent to 220·1 per 1,000 population, and 4·9m. PCs in use (75·0 for every 1,000 persons). In 2002 mobile phone subscribers numbered 2,187,000 and in 1999 there were 30,000 fax machines in use. Iran had 3,168,000 Internet users in 2002.

Postal Services. In 1998 there were 13,699 post offices. 274m. pieces of mail were processed during the year, or 4·2 items per person.

SOCIAL INSTITUTIONS

Justice. A legal system based on Islamic law (*Sharia*) was introduced by the 1979 constitution. A new criminal code on similar principles was introduced in Nov. 1995. The President of the Supreme Court and the public Prosecutor-General are appointed by the Spiritual Leader. The Supreme Court has 16 branches and 109 offences carry the death penalty. To these were added economic crimes in 1990. The population in penal institutions in April 2002 was 163,526 (226 per 100,000 of national population). There were 159 confirmed executions in 2004.

Police. Women rejoined the police force in 2003 for the first time since the 1979 revolution.

Religion. The official religion is the Shia branch of Islam. Adherents numbered approximately 85% of the population in 2001; 5% were Sunni Muslims. However, less than 2% of the population now attend Friday prayers.

Education. Adult literacy in 2001 was 77·1% (83·8% among males and 70·2% among females). Most primary and secondary schools are state schools. Elementary education in state schools and university education is free; small fees are charged for state-run secondary schools. In 2001–02 there were 7,513,015 pupils and 309,260 teachers at 68,836 primary schools, 9,416,272 pupils and 344,042 teachers at secondary schools, and 1,566,509 pupils and 79,235 academic staff at institutions of higher education. Female students now outnumber male students at the state universities.

In 1994–95 there were 30 universities, 30 medical universities, 12 specialized universities (one agriculture, one art, one oil engineering, four teacher training, five technology) and two open (distance-learning) universities. There were 733,527 students and 46,747 academic staff in tertiary education in 2000–01.

In 2000–01 total expenditure on education came to 4·4% of GNP and represented 20·4% of total government expenditure.

Health. There were 717 hospitals in 2001, with 109,152 beds. In 2001 medical personnel totalled 295,325 of which 152,396 were paramedics. There were 25,988 nurses and 8,105 midwives.

Welfare. The official retirement ages are 60 years (men) or 55 (women). However, these ages drop to 50 years (men) or 45 (women) if the individual has spent between 20 and 25 years of work in an unhealthy or physically demanding environment. The minimum old-age pension is 50% of earnings but not less than 696,460 rials a month (the minimum wage of an unskilled labourer), plus food coupons. The maximum pension is 100% of earnings up to 1,970,000 rials a month.

The minimum unemployment benefit is 55% of average earnings. The maximum can not exceed 80% of average earnings.

CULTURE

World Heritage Sites. There are six sites in Iran (all inscribed in 1979 except for Takht-e Soleyman, in 2003, and Bam and Pasargadae in 2004): Tchogha Zanbil, the ruins of the holy city of the kingdom of Elam founded around 1250 BC; Persepolis, the palace complex founded by Darius I in 518 BC and capital of the Achaemenid empire (the first Persian empire); Meidan Imam, the square built in Esfahan by Abbas I in the early 17th century, which is bordered on all sides by monumental buildings linked by a series of arcades; Takht-e Soleyman, a Sasanian royal residence with important Zoroastrian religious architecture and decoration; Bam and its Cultural Landscape, a fortified medieval town where 26,000 people lost their lives in the earthquake of Dec. 2003; and Pasargadae, the first dynastic capital of the great multicultural Achaemenid Empire in Western Asia.

Broadcasting. Broadcasting is controlled by the government agency, Islamic Republic of Iran Broadcasting (IRIB). Both television and radio operate under a single organization, the National Iranian Radio and Television Organization (NIRT), established by an Act of Parliament in 1967, which in 1990 employed some 11,620 people. There are two national radio stations (Radio One and Radio Two) and 27 regional radio stations, including a Koran service and an external service (Voice of the Islamic Republic of Iran, which broadcasts in 20 languages). There are no commercial radio stations; radio broadcasting is a state monopoly. There were (1997) 138 radio transmitters in operation. There are four television networks (colour by SECAM H). There were 17·9m. radio receivers in 2000 and 11·1m. television receivers in 2001.

Cinema. There were 312 cinemas with an attendance in 2001 of 33m.

Press. In 2000 there were 117 daily and 259 weekly newspapers. Approximately 80% of the Iranian press is printed in Farsi; much of the remaining 20% is in English or Arabic. As the power struggle continues between the conservative religious establishment and the Khatami government more than 70 reform-minded newspapers have been closed down since 1999.

In 1999 a total of 14,783 book titles were published.

Tourism. There were 1,402,160 foreign tourists in 2001, spending US$441m.

Calendar. The Iranian year is a solar year starting on varying dates between 19 and 22 March. The current solar year is 1384 (20 March 2005 to 19 March 2006). The Islamic *hegira* (622 AD, when Mohammed left Makkah for Madinah) year 1426 corresponds to 10 Feb. 2005–30 Jan. 2006, and is the current lunar year.

Libraries. In 2001 there were 1,502 libraries affiliated to the Ministry of Culture and Islamic Guidance.

DIPLOMATIC REPRESENTATIVES

Of Iran in the United Kingdom (16 Prince's Gate, London, SW7 1PT)
Ambassador: Seyed Mohammad Hossein Adeli.

Of the United Kingdom in Iran (143 Ferdowsi Ave., Tehran 11344)
Ambassador: Richard Dalton, CMG.

The USA does not have diplomatic relations with Iran, but Iran has an Interests Section in the Pakistani Embassy in Washington, D.C., and the USA has an Interests Section in the Swiss Embassy in Tehran.

Of Iran to the United Nations
Ambassador: M. Jarad Zarif.

Of Iran to the European Union
Ambassador: Abolghasem Delfi.

FURTHER READING

Abdelkhah, Fariba, *Being Modern in Iran.* Columbia Univ. Press, 1999
Abrahamian, E., *Khomeinism: Essays on the Islamic Republic.* Univ. of California Press, 1993
Amuzegar, J., *Iran's Economy Under the Islamic Republic.* London, 1992
Ansari, Ali M., *Modern Iran Since 1921: The Pahlavis and After.* Pearson Longman, Harlow, 2003
Daneshvar, P., *Revolution in Iran.* London, 1996
Ehtesami, A., *After Khomeini: the Iranian Second Republic.* London, 1994
Foran, J., *Fragile Resistance: Social Transformation in Iran from 1500 to the Revolution.* Boulder (Colo.), 1993
Fuller, G. E., *Centre of the Universe: Geopolitics of Iran.* Boulder (Colo.), 1992
Hunter, S. T., *Iran after Khomeini.* New York, 1992
Kamrava, M., *Political History of Modern Iran: from Tribalism to Theocracy.* London, 1993
Kinzer, Stephen, *All the Shah's Men: an American Coup and the Roots of Middle East Terror.* John Wiley, Indianapolis, 2003
Lahsaelzadeh, A., *Contemporary Rural Iran.* London, 1993
Martin, Vanessa, *Creating an Islamic State: Khomeini and the Making of a New Iran.* I. B. Tauris, London and New York, 2000
Mir-Hosseini, Ziba, *Islam and Gender: The Religious Debate in Contemporary Iran.* Princeton Univ. Press, 1999
Modaddel, M., *Class, Politics and Ideology in the Iranian Revolution.* Columbia Univ. Press, 1992
Moin, Baqer, *Khomeini: Life of the Ayatollah.* I. B. Tauris, London, 1999
Omid, H., *Islam and the Post-Revolutionary State in Iran.* London, 1994
Rahnema, A. and Behdad, S. (eds.) *Iran After the Revolution: the Crisis of an Islamic State.* London, 1995

National statistical office: Statistical Centre of Iran, Dr Fatemi Avenue, Tehran 1414663111, Iran.
Website: http://www.sci.org.ir/

IRAQ

Jumhouriya al 'Iraqia
(Republic of Iraq)

Capital: Baghdad
Population projection, 2010: 30·29m.
GDP per capita, 1998: (PPP$) 3,197

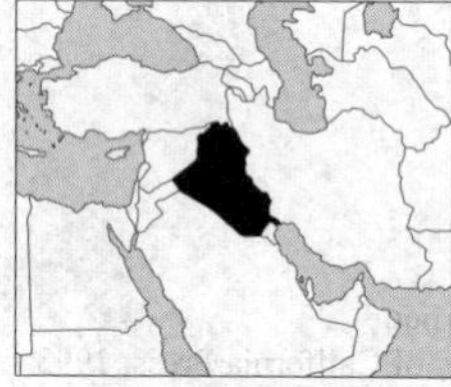

KEY HISTORICAL EVENTS

Iraq, formerly Mesopotamia, was part of the Ottoman Empire from 1534 until it was captured by British forces in 1916. Under a League of Nations mandate, administered by Britain, Amir Faisal Ibn Hussain was crowned king in 1921. On 3 Oct. 1932 Britain's mandate expired and Iraq became an independent country. The ruling Hashemite dynasty was overthrown by a military coup on 14 July 1958. King Faisal II and Nuri al Said, the prime minister, were killed. A republic was established, controlled by a military-led Council of Sovereignty under Gen. Qassim. In 1963 Qassim was overthrown and Gen. Abdul Salam Aref became president, with a partial return to a civilian government, but on 17 July 1968 a successful coup was mounted by the Ba'ath Party. Gen. Ahmed Al Bakr became president, prime minister and chairman of a newly established nine-member Revolutionary Command Council. In July 1979 Saddam Hussein, the vice-president and a Sunni Muslim, became president in a peaceful transfer of power.

In Sept. 1980 Iraq invaded Iran in a dispute over territorial rights in the Shatt-al-Arab waterway, developing into a full-scale war. A UN-arranged ceasefire took place on 20 Aug. 1988 and UN-sponsored peace talks continued in 1989. On 15 Aug. 1990 Iraq offered peace terms and began the withdrawal of troops from Iranian soil.

Early on 2 Aug. 1990 Iraqi forces invaded and rapidly overran Kuwait, meeting little resistance. The UN Security Council voted to impose economic sanctions on Iraq until it withdrew from Kuwait and the USA sent a large military force to Saudi Arabia. Further Security Council resolutions included authorization for the use of military force if Iraq did not withdraw by 15 Jan. 1991. On the night of 16–17 Jan. coalition forces began an air attack on strategic targets in Iraq. A land offensive followed on 24 Feb. The Iraqi army was routed. Kuwait City was liberated on 27 Feb. and on 28 Feb. Iraq agreed to the conditions of a provisional ceasefire, including withdrawal from Kuwait. Subsequent Kurdish and Shia rebellions were brutally suppressed.

In June 1991 UNSCOM, the United Nations Special Commission, conducted its first chemical weapons inspection in Iraq in accordance with UN Resolution 687. In Sept. a UN Security Council resolution permitted Iraq to sell oil worth US$1,600m. to pay for food and medical supplies. In Oct. the Security Council voted unanimously to prohibit all Iraqi nuclear activities. Imports of materials used in the manufacture of nuclear, biological or chemical weapons were banned, and UN weapons inspectors received wide powers to examine and retain data throughout Iraq.

In Aug. 1992 the USA, UK and France began to enforce an air exclusion zone over southern Iraq in response to the government's persecution of Shia Muslims. Following Iraqi violations of this zone and incursions over the Kuwaiti border, US, British and French forces made air and missile attacks on Iraqi military targets in Jan. 1993. On 10 Nov. 1994 Iraq recognized the independence and boundaries of Kuwait. In the first half of 1995 UN weapons inspectors secured information on an extensive biological weapons programme. At the beginning of Sept. 1996 Iraqi troops occupied the town of Arbol in a Kurdish safe haven in support of the Kurdish Democratic Party faction which was at odds with another Kurdish faction, the Patriotic Union of Kurdistan. On 3 Sept. 1996 US forces fired missiles at targets in southern Iraq and extended the no-fly area northwards to the southern suburbs of Baghdad.

Relations with the USA deteriorated further in 1997 when Iraq refused co-operation with UN weapons inspectors. On 29 Oct. the Iraqi Revolutionary Command Council announced that it had 'postponed' a decision to stop working with UNSCOM but it demanded that there should be no American nationals among the UN inspectors. The UN team suspended its operations in Iraq and the Security Council warned Saddam Hussein of 'serious consequences' if he carried out his threat to expel the Americans.

While the USA and the UK threatened retaliatory action, the larger Arab countries with Russia, China and France urged compromise. However, a renewal of hostilities looked probable until late Feb. 1998 when Kofi Annan, the UN Secretary General, forged an agreement in Baghdad allowing for 'immediate, unconditional and unrestricted access' to all suspected weapons sites. Then, in Aug. 1998, Saddam Hussein engineered another stand-off with the UN arms inspectors, demanding a declaration that Iraq had rid itself of all weapons of mass destruction. This the UN chief inspector refused to do. In Nov. all UN personnel left Iraq as the USA threatened air strikes unless Iraq complied with UN resolutions. Russia and France urged further diplomatic efforts, but on 16 Dec. the USA and Britain launched air and missile attacks aimed at destroying Saddam Hussein's arsenal of nuclear, chemical and biological weapons.

In Feb. 2000 the UN Security Council nominated Sweden's Hans Blix to head the new arms inspectorate to Iraq but he was refused entry into the country. In Feb. 2001 the USA and Britain launched a further series of air attacks on military targets in and around Baghdad. A new UN Security Council resolution was passed in May 2002. Constituting the biggest change since the introduction of an Oil-for-Food scheme in 1996 administered by the UN to alleviate suffering, the new resolution limited import restrictions to a number of specific sensitive goods. The UN and Iraq held a series of talks in early 2002 on the possible resumption of weapons inspections, but without reaching any agreement. In Sept. 2002, as the threat of a US attack on Iraq increased, provisional agreement was given to the return of weapons inspectors but shortly afterwards conditions were imposed which made it unlikely that inspections would resume. In Nov. 2002 the UN Security Council adopted Resolution 1441, holding Iraq in 'material breach' of disarmament obligations. Weapons inspectors under the leadership of Hans Blix returned to Iraq four years after their last inspections, but US and British suspicion that the Iraq regime was failing to comply led to increasing tension, resulting in the USA, the UK and Spain reserving the right to disarm Iraq without the need for a further Security Council resolution. Other Security Council members, notably China, France, Germany and Russia, opposed the proposed action.

On 20 March 2003 US forces, supported by the UK, began a war aimed at 'liberating Iraq'. UK troops entered Iraq's second city, Al-Basrah, on 6 April. On 9 April 2003 American forces took control of central Baghdad, effectively bringing an end to Saddam Hussein's rule. Widespread looting and disorder followed the fall of the capital. The bloodless capture of Tikrit, Saddam Hussein's hometown, on 14 April marked the end of formal Iraqi resistance. Jay Garner, a retired US general, arrived in Baghdad on 21 April to head the Office of Reconstruction and Humanitarian Assistance for Iraq and to oversee the transition to an interim Iraqi administration. Garner was replaced as civil administrator on 12 May by Paul Bremer. An interim government was planned until democratic elections could be held. On 22 May the UN Security Council voted to lift economic sanctions against Iraq and to support the US and UK occupation 'until an internationally recognized, representative government is established by the people of Iraq'. Only Syria opposed the resolution by boycotting the session. A 25-man Iraqi-led governing council met in Baghdad for the first time in July 2003.

Resistance to the occupying forces increased from late summer. Bomb attacks in Aug. targeted the UN's Baghdad office, killing the UN special representative. Ayatollah Mohammed Baqr al-Hakim was assassinated with 100 others in Najaf. Saddam Hussein was captured by American forces at Al-Dawr, near Tikrit, on 13 Dec. 2003. In Feb. 2004 over 100 Kurds were killed in attacks in Irbil and the Shia community suffered 270 deaths in Baghdad and Karbala. In May 2004 accusations surfaced of abuse of Iraqi prisoners by American and British soldiers.

On 30 Jan. 2005 Iraqis elected a Transitional National Assembly in their first democratic elections, won by the Shia-dominated United Iraqi Alliance. Jalal Talabani became the country's new president on 6 April 2005.

TERRITORY AND POPULATION

Iraq is bounded in the north by Turkey, east by Iran, southeast by the Persian Gulf, south by Kuwait and Saudi Arabia, and west by Jordan and Syria. In April 1992 the UN Boundary Commission redefined Iraq's border with Kuwait, moving it slightly northwards in line with an agreement of 1932. Area, 434,128 sq. km. Population, 1997 census, 22,046,244; density, 50·8 per sq. km. 2002 population estimate: 24,556,000. In 1998, 75·9% of the population lived in urban areas.

The UN gives a projected population for 2010 of 30·29m.

The areas, populations and capitals of the governorates:

Governorate	*Area in sq. km*	*Population 1997 census*	*Capital*
Al-Anbar	138,501	1,023,776	Ar-Ramadi
Babil (Babylon)	6,468	1,181,751	Al-Hillah
Baghdad	734	5,423,964	Baghdad
Al-Basrah	19,070	1,556,445	Al-Basrah
Dahuk	6,553	402,970	Dahuk
Dhi Qar	12,900	1,184,796	An-Nasiriyah
Diyala	19,076	1,135,223	Ba'qubah
Irbil	14,471	1,095,992	Irbil
Karbala	5,034	594,235	Karbala
Maysan	16,072	637,126	Al-Amarah
Al-Muthanna	51,740	436,825	As-Samawah
An-Najaf	28,824	775,042	An-Najaf
Ninawa (Nineveh)	37,323	2,042,852	Mosul
Al-Qadisiyah	8,153	751,331	Ad-Diwaniyah
Salah ad-Din	24,751	904,432	Samarra
As-Sulaymaniyah	17,023	1,362,739	As-Sulaymaniyah
Ta'mim	10,282	753,171	Kirkuk
Wasit	17,153	783,614	Al-Kut

The most populous cities are Baghdad (the capital), population of 4,689,000 in 1999; Irbil, 1,743,000 in 1995; Mosul, 879,000 in 1995. Other large cities included Kirkuk, Al-Basrah, As-Sulaymaniyah and An-Najaf.

The population is approximately 80% Arab, 17% Kurdish (mainly in the north of the country) and 3% Turkmen, Assyrian, Chaldean or other. Shia Arabs (predominantly in the south of the country) constitute approximately 60% of the total population and Sunni Arabs (principally in the centre) 20%.

The national language is Arabic. Other languages spoken are Kurdish (official in Kurdish regions), Assyrian and Armenian.

SOCIAL STATISTICS

2000 estimates: births, 792,000; deaths, 177,000; marriages, 171,000. Birth and death rates, 2000 (per 1,000 population): births, 34·1; deaths, 7·6. Life expectancy in 2000: 61·7 years for males and 64·7 for females. Annual population growth rate, 1992–2002, 2·9%. Infant mortality, 1999: 108 per 1,000 live births, up from 90 per 1,000 live births as far back as 1970, the largest increase anywhere in the world over the same period. Fertility rate, 2002: 4·9 births per woman. Maternal mortality rate per 10,000 live births, 1999: 29·4.

CLIMATE

The climate is mainly arid, with small and unreliable rainfall and a large annual range of temperature. Summers are very hot and winters cold. Al-Basrah, Jan. 55°F (12·8°C), July 92°F (33·3°C). Annual rainfall 7" (175 mm). Baghdad, Jan. 50°F (10°C), July 95°F (35°C). Annual rainfall 6" (140 mm). Mosul, Jan. 44°F (6·7°C), July 90°F (32·2°C). Annual rainfall 15" (384 mm).

CONSTITUTION AND GOVERNMENT

Until the fall of Saddam Hussein, the highest state authority was the Revolutionary Command Council (RCC) but some legislative power was given to the 220-member *National Assembly*. The only legal political grouping was the National Progressive

Front (founded 1973) comprising the Arab Socialist Renaissance (Ba'ath) Party and various Kurdish groups, but a law of Aug. 1991 legalized political parties provided they were not based on religion, racism or ethnicity.

In July 2003 a 25-man Iraqi-led governing council met in Baghdad for the first time since the US-led war in an important staging post towards full self-government. The temporary Coalition Provisional Authority was dissolved on 28 June 2004. Power was handed over to the interim Iraqi government which assumed full sovereign powers for governing Iraq. It became a transitional government after elections in Jan. 2005. The transitional National Assembly aims to draft a new constitution by 15 Aug. 2005 which is scheduled to be voted on in a nationwide referendum by 15 Oct. Elections for a permanent government are to be held by 15 Dec. with elected officials set to take office by 31 Dec. 2005.

National Anthem. 'Watanum Mede, al alufqi janalia' ('A homeland which extended its wings over the horizon'); words by S. Jabar Al Kamali, tune by W. G. Gholmieh.

RECENT ELECTIONS

On 15 Oct. 2002 a referendum was held to determine whether President Saddam Hussein should remain in office for a further seven years. The electorate was 11·4m. It was announced that turn-out was 100% and that 100% of votes cast were in favour. In a previous referendum in 1995, 99·96% of votes were declared in favour.

On 30 Jan. 2005 Iraqis elected a 275-member Transitional National Assembly in their first-ever democratic elections. The Shia-dominated United Iraqi Alliance won 140 seats with 48·2% of the vote, the Democratic Patriotic Alliance of Kurdistan 75 with 25·7%, Prime Minister Iyad Allawi's Iraqi List 40 with 13·8% and President Ghazi al-Yawer's Iraqiyun (Iraqis) List 5 with 1·8%. Eight other groups won three seats or fewer. Turn-out was 59·9%.

CURRENT ADMINISTRATION

On 6 April 2005 Iraq's parliament chose Jalal Talabani, a Kurd, as the country's new interim president, with Sheikh Ghazi al-Yawer, a Sunni Arab, and Adil Abdel-Mahdi, a Shia, as the vice presidents.

President: Jalal Talabani; b. 1933 (sworn in 7 April 2005).

Vice Presidents: Sheikh Ghazi al-Yawer; Adil Abdel-Mahdi.

Following the elections of 30 Jan. 2005 a new government was partially formed in April 2005 and completed in May 2005. The cabinet consisted of:

Prime Minister: Ibrahim al-Jaafari; b. 1947 (sworn in 3 May 2005).

Deputy Prime Ministers: Ahmed Chalabi; Ruz Nuri Shawis; Abed Mutlak al-Jiburi.

Minister of Defence: Saadoun al-Duleimi. *Foreign Affairs:* Hoshyar Zebari. *Interior:* Baqir Solagh. *Justice:* Abdel Hussein Shandal. *Finance:* Ali Abdel Amir Allawi. *Health:* Abdel Muttalib Mohammed Ali. *Communication:* Juwan Fouad Masum. *Environment, and Human Rights (acting):* Nermin Othman. *Housing:* Jasim Mohammed Jaafar. *Public Works:* Nesreen Mustafa Berwari. *Science and Technology:* Basimah Yusuf Butrus. *Planning:* Barham Salih. *Trade:* Abdel Basit Karim Mawloud. *Sport and Youth:* Talib Aziz Zayni. *Transportation:* Salam al-Malaki. *Displacement and Migration:* Suhaylah Abd-Jaafar. *Irrigation:* Abdul Latif Rasheed. *Labour:* Idris Hadi. *Education:* Abdel Falah Hassan. *Higher Education:* Sami al-Muzaffar. *Agriculture:* Ali al-Bahadili. *Culture:* Nuri Farhan al-Rawi. *Industry:* Osama al-Nujaifi. *Oil:* Ibrahim Bahr al-Uloum. *Electricity:* Mihsin Shlash.

DEFENCE

Following the downfall of Saddam Hussein, recruitment began in July 2003 for a new army run by the US military. Saddam Hussein's forces numbered 400,000 at their peak.

Army. A professional New Iraqi Army is being created to replace Saddam's army with a professional force. In April 2004 army personnel numbered 2,400.

In July 2004 the Civil Defense Corps (23,100 personnel in April 2004) was disbanded and converted into a National Guard. It has an end-strength objective of 61,900.

Navy. A 400-strong Coastal Defense Force has been established. It began operations in Oct. 2004.

Air Force. An Army Air Corps has been established and, at Feb. 2005, had a total of 14 fully trained Iraqi pilots. There were a total of 162 personnel in Aug. 2004.

INTERNATIONAL RELATIONS

Iraq is a member of the UN, the League of Arab States, OPEC, OIC and Islamic Development Bank.

ECONOMY

The oil sector accounted for 76·1% of GDP in 2001; agriculture accounted for 7·8%, manufacturing 1·6% and services 13·8%.

Overview. In Sept. 2003 the USA put the cost of rebuilding Iraq at a minimum of US$50bn. and possibly as much as US$75bn., although the planning minister of Iraq's US-backed government, Mahdi al-Hafiz, subsequently put the figure at US$100bn. Iraq's Governing Council announced in Sept. 2003 that the economy is to be privatized, apart from the oil industry, and opened up to foreign investment. World Bank estimates indicate that Iraq's GDP declined by about 4% in 2002 and a further 30% in 2003, although it was projected to increase by around 52% in 2004.

Currency. From 15 Oct. 2003 a new national currency, the new *Iraqi dinar* (NID), was introduced to replace the existing currencies in circulation in the south and north of the country.

Budget. On 13 Oct. 2003 the Iraqi minister of finance announced the post-Saddam Iraqi national budget for 2004, projecting total revenues of about 19·26trn. new Iraqi dinars (US$13bn.) and total expenditures of 20·15trn. new Iraqi dinars (US$13·5bn.). The deficit is funded through refunds from cancelled Oil-for-Food contracts. The UN terminated the Oil-for-Food programme in Nov. 2003, with surplus funds being transferred to the Development Fund for Iraq (administered by the Coalition Provisional Authority). An international conference was held in Madrid, Spain in Oct. 2003 to help raise additional funds for reconstruction and development.

Banking and Finance. All banks were nationalized in 1964. Following the Gulf War in 1991 the formation of private banks was approved, although they were prohibited from conducting international transactions. A new post-Saddam banking law in Oct. 2003 authorized private banks to process international payments, remittances and foreign currency letters of credit. There are 17 private banks. Six foreign banks will also be licensed to operate in the Iraqi market. The Trade Bank of Iraq has been established as an export credit agency to facilitate trade financing. The independent Central Bank of Iraq is the sole bank of issue; its *Governor* is Sinan Mohammed Rida Al-Shabibi. All domestic interest rates were liberalized on 1 March 2004.

ENERGY AND NATURAL RESOURCES

Environment. Iraq's carbon dioxide emissions from the consumption and flaring of fossil fuels were the equivalent of 3·2 tonnes per capita in 2002. An *Environmental Sustainability Index* compiled for the World Economic Forum meeting in Feb. 2002 ranked Iraq 139th in the world out of 142 countries analysed, with 33·2%. The index measured the ability of countries to maintain favourable environmental conditions and examined various factors including pollution levels and the use or abuse of natural resources.

Electricity. Before the war in March–April 2003 installed capacity was 4,400 MW. Despite post-war looting and sabotage, production had recovered and by Oct. 2003 the generating capacity was back to pre-war levels. The Ministry of Electricity planned to increase capacity to 6,000 MW during the summer of 2004, rising to 9,000 MW before the end of 2005.

Oil and Gas. Proven oil reserves at the end of 2003 totalled 115·0bn. bbls. Only Saudi Arabia and Iran have more reserves. Crude oil production in 2002 totalled 99·7m. tonnes. Since 1991 sanctions against Iraq have held back oil sales of some

US$100,000m. The restoration of significant oil production and the resumption of exports have been priorities since the war in March–April 2003. According to the US Defense Department, production in Dec. 2003 reached 2·3m. bbls. a day and exports 1·5m. bbls. a day.

At the end of 2002 Iraq had natural gas reserves of 3,100bn. cu. metres.

Minerals. The principal minerals extracted are phosphate rock (100,000 tonnes in 2002) and sulphur (98,000 tonnes in 2002).

Agriculture. There were 5·75m. ha of arable land in 2001 and 0·34m. ha of permanent crops. 3·53m. ha were irrigated in 2001. Production (2001 estimates, in 1,000 tonnes): melons and watermelons, 575; wheat, 550; tomatoes, 500; barley, 465; dates, 400; oranges, 270; grapes, 265; cucumbers and gherkins, 215; potatoes, 150; rice, 130.

Livestock (2000): cattle, 1·35m.; sheep, 6·78m.; goats, 1·60m.; asses, 380,000; chickens, 23m.

Forestry. In 2000 forests covered 799,000 ha, representing 1·8% of the land area. Timber production in 2001 was 111,000 cu. metres.

Fisheries. Catches in 2001 totalled approximately 20,800 tonnes, of which about 60% from marine waters.

INDUSTRY

Iraq is still relatively under-developed industrially. Production figures (2000, in 1,000 tonnes): residual fuel oil, 7,710; distillate fuel oil, 6,800; petrol, 3,011; cement (2001), 2,000; kerosene, 1,005; jet fuel, 557.

Labour. In 1996 the labour force was 5,573,000 (75% males). Unemployment had risen to 70% by Oct. 2003. In Sept. 2003 the US civil administrator signed an order implementing a new 11-tier salary scale for all public employees, replacing a temporary scale in effect since the collapse of the Saddam regime.

INTERNATIONAL TRADE

Imports and Exports. Imports and exports (in US$1m.):

	2000	*2001*	*2002*
Imports (c.i.f.)	3,330	5,190	9,817
Exports (f.o.b.)	14,289	11,041	9,990

Crude oil is the main export commodity. Manufactures and food are the main import commodities. Post-war crude oil exports are estimated to have risen from 0·2m. bbls. a day in June 2003 to 1·5m. bbls. a day in Dec. 2003. Imports and exports have both increased significantly since the Saddam era.

COMMUNICATIONS

Roads. In 1999 there were an estimated 45,550 km of roads, of which 84·3% were paved. Vehicles in use in 1996 included 773,000 passenger cars and 272,500 lorries and vans. In 1996 there were 1,338 road accidents resulting in 1,573 deaths. Post-war road reconstruction from 2003 is expected to require considerable funding, owing to heavy military use and lack of maintenance. There is a missing 150-km section of the Al-Basrah–Baghdad–Jordan expressway (the country's main artery) that is in need of completion.

Rail. In 2000 railways comprised 2,603 km of 1,435 mm gauge route. Passenger-km travelled in 2000 came to 0·38bn. and freight tonne-km to 0·87bn. In 2003, five main lines were in operation, serving 107 stations.

Civil Aviation. In 2000 there were international flights for the first time since the 1991 Gulf War, with air links being established between Iraq and Egypt, Jordan and Syria. In 2003 the two international airports at Baghdad and Al-Basrah were undergoing post-war reconstruction. Major domestic airports are at Mosul, Kirkuk and Irbil.

Shipping. The merchant fleet in 2002 had a total tonnage of 188,000 GRT, including oil tankers 59,000 GRT. A 565-km canal was opened in 1992 between Baghdad and the Persian Gulf for shipping, irrigation, the drainage of saline water and the reclamation of marsh land. Iraq has six seaports, although its single deep-water port is at Umm Qasr.

Telecommunications. In 2002 there were 675,000 main telephone lines (28 per 1,000 population). There were 20,000 mobile phone subscribers in 2002. Internet users in 2002 numbered 25,000. Satellite connections are the primary international telecommunications link. The Coalition Provisional Authority awarded three regional mobile telecommunications licences in Oct. 2003.

SOCIAL INSTITUTIONS

Justice. Up until the war in March–April 2003, for civil matters: the court of cassation in Baghdad; six courts of appeal at Al-Basrah, Baghdad (2), Babil (Babylon), Mosul and Kirkuk; 18 courts of first instance with unlimited powers and 150 courts of first instance with limited powers, all being courts of single judges. In addition, six peace courts had peace court jurisdiction only. 'Revolutionary courts' dealt with cases affecting state security.

For religious matters: the Sharia courts at all places where there were civil courts, constituted in some places of specially appointed Qadhis (religious judges) and in other places of the judges of the civil courts. For criminal matters: the court of cassation; six sessions courts (two being presided over by the judge of the local court of first instance and four being identical with the courts of appeal). Magistrates' courts at all places where there were civil courts, constituted of civil judges exercising magisterial powers of the first and second class. There were also a number of third-class magistrates' courts, powers for this purpose being granted to municipal councils and a number of administrative officials.

The death penalty was introduced for serious theft in 1992; amputation of a hand for theft in 1994. It is believed that during the Saddam era there were hundreds of executions annually. The death penalty was suspended in April 2003 after the fall of Saddam, but reinstated in Aug. 2004.

In the immediate aftermath of the war, the justice system was idle but by July 2003 an estimated 100 courts were functioning. All Baghdad criminal court functions were consolidated into two operational courthouses. In Dec. 2003 the Governing Council established the Iraqi Special Tribunal to try senior members of the Saddam regime for war crimes, crimes against humanity and genocide.

Police. A new post-war national police force is being established. In Sept. 2004 the end-strength objective was 135,000; in Oct. 2004 the police forces numbered 43,900. The personnel includes both former officers who are being retrained and new recruits.

Religion. The constitution proclaims Islam the state religion, but also stipulates freedom of religious belief and expression. In 2001 the population was 97% Muslim; there were also 750,000 Christians. *See also* TERRITORY AND POPULATION.

Education. Primary and secondary education is free; primary education became compulsory in 1976. Primary school age is 6–12. Secondary education is for six years, of which the first three are termed intermediate. The medium of instruction is Arabic; Kurdish is used in primary schools in northern districts.

According to UNESCO, in 2000–01 there were: 68,400 kindergarten pupils; 4·03m. primary school children with 190,650 teachers; and 1·36m. secondary school pupils with 81,500 teachers. Adult literacy rate was 56% in 2000 (male, 68%; female, 43%). Most schools were closed in March–April 2003 when UNICEF estimates that 200 were destroyed and a further 2,750 looted. By Oct. 2003 all 22 universities and 43 technical institutes and colleges were open, as were nearly all primary and secondary schools. Expenditure on education in 2003 was an estimated US$384·5m.

Health. According to the World Health Organization, in 2002 there were (per 10,000 population): 5·1 physicians, 1·0 dentist, 0·7 pharmacists, 12·7 hospital beds, and 20 nurses and midwifery personnel (2001 figure). There are approximately 240 hospitals and 1,200 primary health care clinics operating in post-war Iraq, with around 100,000 health professionals and staff affiliated to the Ministry of Health, 80% of whom are women.

CULTURE

World Heritage Sites. Iraq has two UNESCO World Heritage Sites: Hatra (inscribed on the list in 1985), a large fortified city of the Parthian (Persian) Empire; and Ashur (Qal'at Sherqat) (2003), the first capital and the religious centre of the Assyrians from the 14th to the 9th centuries BC.

Broadcasting. In 2000 there were 5·03m. radio and 1·88m. TV receivers (colour by SECAM H). The ban on satellite dishes, enforced while Saddam Hussein was in power, has now been lifted.

Press. In 1996 there were four main daily newspapers (one of which is in English) with a combined circulation of 407,000.

Tourism. In 2000 there were 78,000 foreign tourists; spending by tourists in 1998 totalled US$13m.

DIPLOMATIC REPRESENTATIVES

On 6 Feb. 1991 Iraq broke off diplomatic relations with the United Kingdom and the USA. Jordan looks after Iraqi interest in the UK.

Of the United Kingdom in Iraq (International Zone, Baghdad)
Ambassador: Edward Chaplin, CMG, OBE.

Of Iraq to the United Nations
Ambassador: Samir Shakir Mahmood Sumaidaie.

Of Iraq to the European Union
Ambassador: Vacant.

FURTHER READING

Aburish, S. K., *Saddam Hussein: The Politics of Revenge*. Bloomsbury, London, 2000
Anderson, Liam and Stansfield, Gareth, *The Future of Iraq: Dictatorship, Democracy or Division?* Palgrave Macmillan, Basingstoke, 2004
Blix, Hans, *Disarming Iraq: The Search for Weapons of Mass Destruction*. Bloomsbury, London, 2004
Butler, R., *Saddam Defiant: The Threat of Weapons of Mass Destruction and the Crisis of Global Security*. Weidenfeld & Nicolson, London, 2000
Mackey, Sandra, *The Reckoning: Iraq and the Legacy of Saddam Hussein*. W. W. Norton, New York, 2002
Sluglett, Marion Farouk and Sluglett, Peter, *Iraq Since 1958: From Revolution to Dictatorship*. 3rd ed. I. B. Tauris, London, 2001
Tripp, Charles, *A History of Iraq*. 2nd ed. CUP, 2002

IRELAND

Éire

Capital: Dublin
Population projection, 2010: 4·22m.
GDP per capita, 2002: (PPP$) 36,360
HDI/world rank: 0·936/10

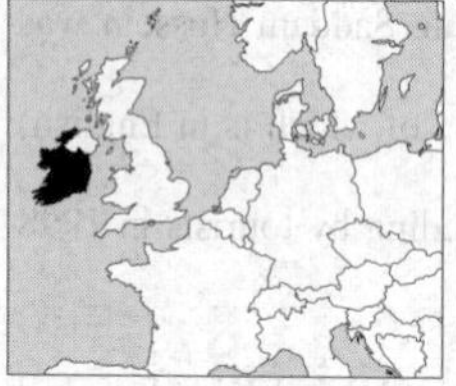

KEY HISTORICAL EVENTS

Around 7500 BC Mesolithic hunter-gatherers travelled across the land bridge that connected southwest Scotland with northern Ireland. From the sixth century BC, the island was invaded by Celtic tribes, including the Gaels, who established pastoral communities within massive stone forts. The Gaels also created settlements in Scotland (Dál Riata) and west Wales. Christian missionaries reached Ireland in the third century AD. St Patrick, born in Britain, lived and preached in Ireland from *c.* 432 until his death *c.* 465. Christianity found a haven in Ireland in contrast to much of northern Europe, ravaged by fragmentary forces following the collapse of the Roman Empire. Later, Irish missionaries took Celtic Christianity to Britain and continental Europe. By the fifth century AD there were five leading Gaelic kingdoms: Ulster, Leinster, Munster, Connacht and Meath. Vikings first appeared on the Irish coast in the late seventh century. A full-scale Viking invasion in 795 heralded more than two hundred years of Scandinavian influence. Dublin became a key outpost in the Viking diaspora.

In the 13th century Anglo-Norman adventurers began to establish themselves in Ireland. Dublin Castle was built in 1204 and the first parliament sat there in 1264. Edward Bruce, the brother of Robert Bruce, king of Scotland, landed in Ulster in 1315 to take control of most of Ireland north of Dublin, but his troops left a trail of destruction and soon lost support for his Celtic kingdom. Bruce was defeated and killed at Dundalk in 1317. The descendants of the Anglo-Norman settlers identified with the native Irish, whose language, habits, and laws they adopted. Richard II made two unsuccessful expeditions to Ireland, in 1394 and 1399, to reassert royal authority. In the 15th century the authority of the English crown became limited to the Pale, a coastal district around Dublin.

King Edward IV, of the House of York, came to the English throne in 1461 and appointed Gerald (Gearóid Mór) FitzGerald, earl of Kildare, as viceroy of Ireland. He was replaced in 1494 by Sir Edward Poynings, whose Poynings Laws removed the legal rights of the Irish parliament to legislate independently. With this one interlude, the FitzGeralds (Geraldines) ruled Ireland for over half a century. Henry VIII introduced the Reformation to Ireland in 1537 and began to dissolve the monasteries. Elizabeth I removed the Irish chiefdoms from their positions of power. An uprising in Munster in the early 1570s was quickly suppressed and only Ulster provided resistance to Tudor domination. Open rebellion ended in 1607 with the 'Flight of the Earls'. The English crown seized the earls' lands and in 1609 Ulster-Scottish and English settlers were invited to colonize. Swathes of land were cleared of farms and woodland, and 23 walled towns were created, including Belfast. The Irish in Ulster rebelled against the planters in 1641 and Owen Roe O'Neill led the Confederate forces. A provisional government was established at Kilkenny and by the end of 1642 O'Neill controlled the whole island apart from Dublin and parts of Ulster.

After the execution of Charles I in 1649, the Protector, Oliver Cromwell, was determined to rout royalists and avenge the 1641 massacre of the Ulster planters. With his New Model Army, Cromwell stormed Drogheda and murdered its garrison of 2,000 men. Wexford followed and by 1652 all of Ireland was in Cromwellian hands. Hundreds of thousands of acres of land were confiscated and given to new Protestant settlers. The English monarchy was restored in 1660 and Protestant power was reasserted when William of Orange claimed the English crown. The deposed James II led a French force into Ireland. In the spring of 1689 only the walled towns of Derry/Londonderry and Enniskillen remained in Protestant hands. Londonderry held out for 15 weeks until William's forces defeated James at the Battle of the Boyne. The Catholic defeat was followed by more confiscation of land and the introduction of the Penal Laws, which prevented Catholics from buying freehold land, holding public office or bearing arms.

The principles of the French Revolution found their most powerful expression in Ireland in the Society of United Irishmen, which, led by the Protestant lawyer Theobald Wolfe Tone, mounted a rebellion in 1798. Without the expected French assistance, the rebellion was crushed. The British prime minister, William Pitt, was convinced that the 'Irish problem' could be solved by union with Britain and Catholic emancipation. The first goal was achieved in 1801 but Protestant opposition prevented the enactment of the latter until 1829, accomplished largely through the efforts of Daniel O'Connell. The Irish representatives in the British Parliament, led by O'Connell, also fought for repeal of the Act of Union and land reform. Between 1845–49 a blight wiped out the potato crop, the staple food of the Irish population. Of a population of 8·5m. almost 1m. died of starvation and well over 1m. emigrated, mostly to the United States. Irish Catholics in the United States formed the Fenian movement, dedicated to achieving full Irish independence.

Charles Parnell, a Home Rule League MP, came to the fore of the nationalist movement in 1877. After the Home Rule Party brought down the Conservative government by voting with the Liberals, William Gladstone attempted to introduce a Home Rule Bill. This was defeated in 1886 and 1893. In 1905 the Irish political leader and journalist Arthur Griffith founded Sinn Féin to achieve independence. A Home Rule Bill was finally passed in 1914 but the act was suspended for the duration of the First World War. The Irish Republican Brotherhood (IRB) plotted a rebellion while Britain was at war, soliciting German support. On Easter Monday 1916 the IRB seized the General Post Office in Dublin and Patrick Pearse read out the proclamation of the Republic of Ireland. The Easter Rising was over in under a week and 16 of the rebel leaders were executed. Sinn Féin, linked in the Irish public's mind with the rising, scored a dramatic victory in the parliamentary elections of 1918. Its members refused to take their seats in Westminster, declared the *Dáil Éireann* ('Diet of Ireland') and proclaimed the Irish republic. The British outlawed Sinn Féin and the Dáil, which went underground and associated military groups including the Irish Republican Army (IRA) engaged in guerrilla warfare against British troops known as the Black and Tans.

A new Home Rule Bill was passed in 1920, establishing two parliaments, one in Belfast and the other in Dublin. The Unionists of the six counties accepted this scheme, and a Northern Parliament was elected in May 1921. Sinn Féin rejected the plan, but in autumn 1921 British Prime Minister Lloyd George negotiated a treaty granting Catholic Ireland dominion status within the British Empire. Michael Collins managed to gain approval in the Dáil by a slim majority but the Republicans, led by Eamonn de Valera, rejected the treaty. A brutal civil war, in which Collins was assassinated, ended with the creation of the Irish Free State in Jan. 1922. In 1932 de Valera, leader of the Fianna Fáil party, became prime minister (taoiseach). Five years later he brought in a new constitution establishing the sovereign nation of Éire and abolishing the oath of allegiance to the British crown.

Éire was neutral in the Second World War. In 1948 Prime Minister John Costello demanded total independence and reunification with the six counties of Northern Ireland. Full independence as the Republic of Ireland came the following year and in 1955 Ireland was admitted to the United Nations, but nothing came of the claim to the six Ulster counties. Trouble in the North flared up in the late 1960s over Catholic demands for civil rights and equality in the allocation of housing. On 1 Jan. 1973 the Republic of Ireland joined the European Economic Community. The 1990s were marked by an economic upturn, buoyed by EU subsidies and foreign investment. In the north, a ceasefire between the IRA and Protestant militias in 1994 formed the basis for the signing of the Good Friday Agreement in April 1998. On 2 Dec. 1999 the Irish constitution was amended to remove the articles laying claim to Northern Ireland. Prime Minister Bertie Ahern, who came to power in 1997, took Ireland into the single European currency in Jan. 2001.

For details of recent peace negotiations see Northern Ireland *on page 1718.*

TERRITORY AND POPULATION

The Republic of Ireland lies in the Atlantic Ocean, separated from Great Britain by the Irish Sea to the east, and bounded in the northeast by Northern Ireland (UK). In

2002, 59·6% of the population lived in urban areas. The population at the 2002 census was 3,917,203 (1,971,039 females), giving a density of 55·7 persons per sq. km. The total population in April 2003 was estimated at 3·98m., the highest figure since 1871 when the census recorded a population of 4·05m.

The UN gives a projected population for 2010 of 4·22m.

The capital is Dublin (Baile Átha Cliath). Town populations, 2002: Greater Dublin, 1,004,614; Cork, 186,239; Limerick, 83,147; Galway, 66,163; Waterford, 46,736.

Counties and Cities[1]	Area in ha[2]	Population, 2002 Males	Females	Totals
Province of Leinster				
Carlow	89,655	23,403	22,611	46,014
Dublin City	11,758	237,813	257,968	495,781
Dun Laoghaire-Rathdown	12,638	91,337	100,455	191,792
Fingal	45,467	97,409	99,004	196,413
Kildare	169,540	82,735	81,209	163,944
Kilkenny	207,289	40,540	39,799	80,339
Laoighis	171,990	30,131	28,643	58,744
Longford	109,116	15,794	15,274	31,068
Louth	82,613	50,489	51,332	101,821
Meath	234,207	67,733	66,272	134,005
Offaly	200,117	32,185	31,478	63,663
South Dublin	22,364	117,516	121,319	238,835
Westmeath	183,965	35,960	35,898	71,858
Wexford	236,685	58,170	58,426	116,596
Wicklow	202,662	56,800	57,876	114,676
Total of Leinster	1,980,066	1,038,015	1,067,564	2,105,579
Province of Munster				
Clare	345,004	52,063	51,214	103,277
Cork City	3,953	59,263	63,799	123,062
Cork	746,042	163,054	161,713	324,767
Kerry	480,689	66,572	65,955	132,527
Limerick City	2,087	26,128	27,895	54,023
Limerick	273,504	61,503	59,778	121,281
Tipperary, N. R.	204,627	30,864	30,146	61,010
Tipperary, S. R.	225,845	39,999	39,122	79,121
Waterford City	4,103	21,782	22,812	44,594
Waterford	181,556	28,890	28,062	56,952
Total of Munster	2,467,410	550,118	550,496	1,100,614
Province of Connacht				
Galway City	5,057	31,015	34,817	65,832
Galway	609,820	73,352	69,893	143,245
Leitrim	159,003	13,324	12,475	25,799
Mayo	558,605	59,149	58,297	117,446
Roscommon	254,819	27,583	26,1918	53,774
Sligo	183,752	28,771	29,429	58,200
Total of Connacht	1,771,056	233,194	231,102	464,296
Province of Ulster (part of)				
Cavan	193,177	29,015	27,531	56,546
Donegal	486,091	69,016	68,559	137,575
Monaghan	129,508	26,806	25,787	52,593
Total of Ulster (part of)	808,776	124,837	121,877	246,714
Total	7,027,308	1,946,164	1,971,039	3,917,203

[1]Cities were previously known as County Boroughs.
[2]Area details provided by Ordnance Survey.

The official languages are Irish (the national language) and English; according to the National Survey of Languages of 1994, Irish is spoken as a mother tongue only by 2% of the population, in certain western areas (Gaeltacht), and is no longer a compulsory subject at school.

SOCIAL STATISTICS

Statistics for six calendar years:

	Births	Marriages	Deaths		Births	Marriages	Deaths
1997	52,775	15,631	31,581	2000	54,789	18,526	32,608
1998	53,969	16,783	31,563	2001	57,354	19,246	30,212
1999	53,924	18,526	32,608	2002[1]	60,521	20,047	29,348

[1]Provisional figures—based on year of registration.

2002 rates (provisional): birth, 15·5; death, 7·5; marriage, 5·1. Annual population growth rate, 1993–2003, 1·1%. Expectation of life at birth, 2001, 74·1 years for males and 79·4 years for females.

In 2002 the suicide rate per 100,000 population (provisional) was 11·5 (men, 19·1; women, 4·1). Infant mortality in 2002, 5·1 per 1,000 live births; fertility rate (2002), 2·0 births per woman.

At a referendum on 24 Nov. 1995 on the legalization of civil divorce the electorate was 1,628,580; 818,852 votes were in favour, 809,728 against. In 2002 Ireland received 11,634 asylum applications, equivalent to 3·1 per 1,000 inhabitants.

The estimated number of immigrants in the year to April 2003 was 50,500 while emigrants numbered 20,700 in the same period. Immigration is estimated to have peaked at 66,900 in the twelve months to April 2002. 40% of emigrants went to countries other than the EU and the USA, while 45% of all immigrants originated from outside the EU and USA.

A UNICEF report published in 2000 showed that 16·8% of children in Ireland live in poverty (in households with income below 50% of the national median), compared to 2·6% in Sweden. The report also showed that the poverty rate of children in lone-parent families was 46·4%, compared to 14·2% in two-parent families.

CLIMATE

Influenced by the Gulf Stream, there is an equable climate with mild southwest winds, making temperatures almost uniform over the whole country. The coldest months are Jan. and Feb. (39–45°F, 4–7°C) and the warmest July and Aug. (57–61°F, 14–16°C). May and June are the sunniest months, averaging 5·5 to 6·5 hours each day, but over 7 hours in the extreme southeast. Rainfall is lowest along the eastern coastal strip. The central parts vary between 30–44" (750–1,125 mm), and up to 60" (1,500 mm) may be experienced in low-lying areas in the west. Dublin, Jan. 40°F (4°C), July 59°F (15°C). Annual rainfall 30" (750 mm). Cork, Jan. 42°F (5°C), July 61°F (16°C). Annual rainfall 41" (1,025 mm).

CONSTITUTION AND GOVERNMENT

Ireland is a sovereign independent, democratic republic. Its parliament exercises jurisdiction in 26 of the 32 counties of the island of Ireland. The first Constitution of the Irish Free State came into operation on 6 Dec. 1922. Certain provisions which were regarded as contrary to the national sentiments were gradually removed by successive amendments, with the result that at the end of 1936 the text differed considerably from the original document. On 14 June 1937 a new Constitution was approved by Parliament and enacted by a plebiscite on 1 July 1937. This Constitution came into operation on 29 Dec. 1937. Under it the name Ireland (Éire) was restored. It states that the whole island of Ireland is the national territory, but that, pending its reintegration, laws enacted by Parliament have the same area and extent of application as those of the former Irish Free State.

The head of state is the *President*, whose role is largely ceremonial, but who has the power to refer proposed legislation which might infringe the Constitution to the Supreme Court.

The *Oireachtas* or National Parliament consists of the President, a House of Representatives (*Dáil Éireann*) and a Senate (*Seanad Éireann*). The *Dáil*, consisting of 166 members, is elected by adult suffrage on the Single Transferable Vote system in constituencies of three, four or five members. Of the 60 members of the Senate, 11 are nominated by the *Taoiseach* (Prime Minister), six are elected by the universities and the remaining 43 are elected from five panels of candidates established on a vocational basis, representing the following public services and interests: (1) national language and culture, literature, art, education and such professional interests as may be defined by law for the purpose of this panel; (2)

agricultural and allied interests, and fisheries; (3) labour, whether organized or unorganized; (4) industry and commerce, including banking, finance, accountancy, engineering and architecture; (5) public administration and social services, including voluntary social activities. The electing body comprises members of the *Dáil*, Senate, county boroughs and county councils.

A maximum period of 90 days is afforded to the Senate for the consideration or amendment of Bills sent to that House by the *Dáil*, but the Senate has no power to veto legislative proposals.

No amendment of the Constitution can be effected except with the approval of the people given at a referendum.

National Anthem. 'Amhrán na bhFiann' ('The Soldier's Song'); words by P. Kearney, tune by P. Heeney.

RECENT ELECTIONS

A general election was held on 17 May 2002: Fianna Fáil (FF) gained 81 seats with 41·5% of votes cast (in 1997, 77 seats); Fine Gael (FG), 31 with 22·5% (54); Labour Party (L), 21 with 10·8% (17); Progressive Democrats (PD), 8; Green Party (G), 6; Sinn Féin, 5; Socialist Party, 1; ind., 13.

Following elections to the Senate on 16 and 17 July 2002, FF held 30 of the 60 seats, FG had 15, L had 5, PD had 4 and non-partisans and others held 6 seats.

Presidential elections would have taken place on 22 Oct. 2004, but incumbent Mary McAleese (FF) was reappointed unopposed as no other candidates secured the necessary backing for an election to take place.

European Parliament. Ireland has 13 (15 in 1999) representatives. At the June 2004 elections turn-out was 59·7%. Fine Gael won 5 seats with 27·8% of votes cast (political affiliation in European Parliament: European People's Party–European Democrats); Fianna Fáil, 4 with 29·5% (Union for a Europe of Nations); Sinn Féin, 1 with 11·1% (European Unitary Left/Nordic Green Left); Labour Party, 1 with 10·6% (Party of European Socialists). Two independents were elected (one Alliance of Liberals and Democrats for Europe; one Independence and Democracy Group).

CURRENT ADMINISTRATION

President: Mary McAleese (b. 1951; FF), elected out of five candidates on 30 Oct. 1997 and inaugurated 11 Nov. 1997, and appointed for a second term on 1 Oct. 2004.

Following the 2002 election the coalition government that had held office since 1997 between Fianna Fáil (FF) and the Progressive Democrats (PD) was renewed. In March 2005 it was composed as follows:

Taoiseach (Prime Minister): Bertie Ahern; b. 1951 (FF; sworn in 26 June 1997 and re-elected in 2002).

Tánaiste (Deputy Prime Minister), Minister for Health and Children: Mary Harney (b. 1953; PD). *Defence:* Willie O'Dea (b. 1952; FF). *Agriculture and Food:* Mary Coughlan (b. 1965; FF). *Finance:* Brian Cowen (b. 1960; FF). *Foreign Affairs:* Dermot Ahern (b. 1955; FF). *Education and Science:* Mary Hanafin (b. 1959; FF). *Communications, Marine and Natural Resources:* Noel Dempsey (b. 1953; FF). *Community, Rural and Gaeltacht Affairs:* Eamon Ó Cuív (b. 1952; FF). *Enterprise, Trade and Employment:* Micheál Martin (b. 1960; FF). *Transport:* Martin Cullen (b. 1954; FF). *Justice, Equality and Law Reform:* Michael McDowell (b. 1949; PD). *Environment and Local Government:* Dick Roche (b. 1947; FF). *Arts, Sport and Tourism:* John O'Donoghue (b. 1956; FF). *Social and Family Affairs:* Séamus Brennan (b. 1948; FF).

There are 17 Ministers of State.

Attorney General: Rory Brady.

Speaker of Dail Éireann: Rory O'Hanlon.

Government Website: http://www.irlgov.ie

DEFENCE

Supreme command of the Defence Forces is vested in the President. Exercise of the supreme command is regulated by law (Defence Act 1954). Military Command is exercised by the government through the Minister for Defence who is the overall commander of the Defence Forces.

The Defence Forces comprise the Permanent Defence Force (the regular Army, the Air Corps and the Naval Service) and the Reserve Defence Force (comprising a First Line Reserve of members who have served in the Permanent Defence Force, a second-line Territorial Army Reserve and a second-line Naval Reserve).

A review of the Reserve Forces is almost complete. The total strength of the Permanent Defence Force in Dec. 2002 was 10,559 (including 472 women). The total strength of the Reserve was 13,743. The Defence Forces had some 483 personnel involved with 19 different peace-support missions throughout the world in Dec. 2002.

Defence expenditure in 2003 totalled €702m. (US$803m.), equivalent to €178 (US$204) per capita, representing 0·5% of GDP.

Army. The Army strength in Dec. 2002 was 8,620 personnel with 13,249 reservists. There is a Training Centre at the Curragh, Co. Kildare and a Logistics Base, with elements located at the Curragh and Dublin for force level logistical support.

Navy. The Naval Service is based at Haulbowline in Co. Cork. The strength in Dec. 2002 was 1,034 with 422 reserves. It operates eight patrol craft.

Air Corps. The Air Corps has its headquarters at Casement Aerodrome, Baldonnel, Co. Dublin. The Air Corps is a stand-alone Corps which does not form an intrinsic part of the new Army Brigade structure. The Air Corps strength in Dec. 2002 was 905 personnel with 72 reservists. It operates 17 fixed-wing aircraft and 13 helicopters.

INTERNATIONAL RELATIONS

Ireland is a member of the UN, WTO, BIS, OECD, EU, the Council of Europe, the OSCE and IOM.

ECONOMY

Agriculture accounted for 3·3% of GDP in 2002, industry 41·2% and services 55·5%.

According to the anti-corruption organization *Transparency International*, Ireland ranked equal 17th in the world in a 2004 survey of the countries with the least corruption in business and government. It received 7·5 out of 10 in the annual index.

Overview. The extraordinary growth experienced in Ireland in the late 1990s has given way to a more sustainable pace of expansion since 2001. Growth decreased to 2% in 2003. The slowdown follows the burst of the ICT bubble and also reflects a deterioration in Irish cost competitiveness. In particular, competitiveness has been eroded by large wage gains, low productivity in the sheltered sector and the expansionary effects of low interest rates since joining EMU. The unemployment rate reached a historical low of 3·7% in the first half of 2001, rising to 4·6% in 2003. Inflation has been persistently high since 2001 and the inflation rate is the highest in the euro area as a result of rapid price increases in the service sector.

Currency. On 1 Jan. 1999 the euro (EUR) became the legal currency in Ireland; irrevocable conversion rate 0·787564 Irish pounds to 1 euro. The euro, which consists of 100 cents, has been in circulation since 1 Jan. 2002. There are seven euro notes in different colours and sizes denominated in 500, 200, 100, 50, 20, 10 and 5 euros, and eight coins denominated in 2 and 1 euros, then 50, 20, 10, 5, 2 and 1 cents. On the introduction of the euro there was a 'dual circulation' period before the Irish pound ceased to be legal tender on 9 Feb. 2002. Euro banknotes in circulation on 1 Jan. 2002 had a total value of €6·8bn.

Inflation was 4·6% in 2002 and 3·5% in 2003. The Central Bank has the sole right of issuing legal tender notes; token coinage is issued by the Minister for Finance through the Bank. Gold reserves were 176,000 troy oz in June 2002 and foreign exchange reserves US$4,648m. Total money supply was €3,616m. in June 2002.

Budget. Current revenue and expenditure (in €1m.):

Current Revenue	*2002*	*2003*
Customs duties	134	137
Excise duties	4,441	4,572
Capital taxes	778	1,657
Stamp duties	1,167	1,688
Income tax	9,063	9,162

Current Revenue	*2002*	*2003*
Corporation tax	4,803	5,161
Value-added tax	8,885	9,721
Levies	23	5
Non-tax revenue	2,231	1,054
Total	31,525	33,157
Current expenditure		
Debt service	1,669	2,027
Industry and labour	1,228	1,212
Agriculture	1,317	1,227
Fisheries, Forestry, Tourism	253	283
Health	7,788	8,729
Education	4,808	5,449
Social Welfare	9,529	10,515
Other (voted)	5,302	5,611
Other (non-voted)	1,143	1,276
Gross current	33,037	36,330
Less: Receipts, e.g. social security	6,880	7,539
Net total (including non-voted central fund)	26,157	28,791

VAT as at 1 Jan. 2004 was 21% (reduced rate 13·5%).

Total public capital programme expenditure amounted to €5,290m. (net voted capital expenditure) in 2003, with provision for €5,481m. in 2004. The general government debt at the end of 2003 is estimated at €36·3bn., 33·1% of GDP, and is forecast to remain around 33% of GDP in the medium term.

Performance. During the late 1990s Ireland had the fastest-growing economy in the European Union, with real GDP growth in 2000 of 9·9% following growth averaging 9·7% over the previous five years. Real GDP growth has slowed since then, but at 3·7% in 2003 is still one of the best performing economies in the EU. From a GDP per head of only 69% of the EU average in 1987, it was estimated to have risen to 136% of the EU average by 2003. GNP in Ireland is much lower than GDP owing to profit repatriations by multi-nationals and foreign debt servicing. Ireland's GNP per head is about 99% of the EU average. Total GDP in 2003 was US$148·6bn.

Banking and Finance. The Central Bank (founded in 1943) replaced the Currency Commission as the note-issuing authority. In 2003 the Central Bank was renamed the Central Bank and Financial Services Authority of Ireland (CBFSAI). The CBFSAI has two component entities: the Central Bank and the Irish Financial Services Regulatory Authority. It has the power of receiving deposits from banks and public authorities, of rediscounting Exchequer bills and bills of exchange, of making advances to banks against such bills or against government securities, of fixing and publishing rates of interest for rediscounting bills, or buying and selling certain government securities and securities of any international bank or financial institution formed wholly or mainly by governments. The CBFSAI also collects and publishes information relating to monetary and credit matters. The Central Bank Acts, 1971, 1989 and 1997, together with the Building Societies Act, 1989, the Investment Intermediaries Act, 1995 and the Stock Exchange Act, 1995, gave further powers to the CBFSAI in the regulation and supervision of financial institutions and payment systems.

The Board of Directors of the Central Bank consists of a Governor, appointed for a seven-year term by the President on the advice of the government, and twelve directors, all appointed by the Minister for Finance. The *Governor* is John Hurley. In 2003 the Bank's net profit was €60·04m.; €321·73m. was paid to the Exchequer.

In 2004 the Irish Financial Services Regulatory Authority was responsible for the regulation of 80 credit institutions (including branches). There are three State banks—ICC Bank, ACC Bank and the Trustee Savings Bank.

At 30 April 2004 total assets of within-the-State offices of all credit institutions amounted to €629·5bn.

The Dublin stock exchange has been affiliated to the London exchange since 1973.

ENERGY AND NATURAL RESOURCES

Environment. Ireland's carbon dioxide emissions from the consumption and flaring of fossil fuels in 2002 were the equivalent of 11·5 tonnes per capita.

Electricity. The total generating capacity in 2004 was 5,592 MW, as averaged on a daily basis. This included wind generation, small renewable and small Combined Heat and Power (CHP). In 2003 there were approximately 1,804,680 customers connected to the network consuming 22,286 GWh.

Oil and Gas. Over 0·6m. sq. km of the Irish continental shelf has been designated an exploration area for oil and gas; at the furthest point the limit of jurisdiction is 520 nautical miles from the coast. It has been established that there is potential for discoveries both offshore and onshore. In the offshore there is a vast Continental Shelf in which a number of major basins and troughs have been identified. Much of the shelf remains unexplored but from 1971 to date 121 offshore exploration wells and 45 appraisal/development wells (166 wells in total) have been drilled, and since 1965 a total of 381 offshore surveys have been carried out.

Natural gas reserves in 2002 totalled 20bn. cu. metres. Production in 2000 was 1·2bn. cu. metres and consumption 4·2bn. cu. metres. 80% of natural gas supplies for the Irish Market are imported through the two sub-sea interconnectors connecting Ireland with Scotland and the remaining 20% is supplied from the Kinsale Head gas field, 50 km off the south coast of Ireland.

Natural gas transmission and distribution is currently carried out by Bord Gáis Éireann (Irish Gas Board). The liberalization of the Irish gas market is underway; in July 2004 all non-domestic natural gas customers became eligible to choose their own natural gas supplier. Full market opening is anticipated to take place during 2005, when all remaining end users will be eligible to choose any licensed natural gas supplier.

Peat. The country has very little indigenous coal, but possesses large reserves of peat, the development of which is handled largely by Bord na Móna (Peat Board). To date, the Board has acquired and developed 85,000 ha of bog and has 27 locations around the country. In the year ending 31 March 2001 the Board sold 2·8m. tonnes of milled peat for use in five milled peat electricity generating stations. 301,000 tonnes of briquettes were produced for sale to the domestic heating market. Bord na Móna also sold 136m. cu. metres of horticultural peat, mainly for export. It is estimated that some 1m. tonnes of privately-produced peat was consumed in the same period.

Minerals. Lead and zinc concentrates are important. In 1997 mineable resources stood at over 6m. tonnes of zinc and over 1m. tonnes of lead. Metal content of concentrates production, 2001: zinc, 287,000 tonnes; lead, 50,100 tonnes. Gypsum, limestone and aggregates are important, and there is some production of silver (contained in lead) and dolomite. About 50 companies are involved in exploration, which is centred on base metals, but with interest also in gold, gem minerals, industrial minerals and coal. There is a thriving sand, gravel and aggregate extraction industry, employing some 7,500 people.

Agriculture. The CSO's Quarterly National Household Survey showed in the quarter of March–May 2003 that there were 113,200 people whose primary source of income was from agriculture. A total of 240,100 people worked on farms on a regular basis, working the equivalent of 158,100 full-time jobs. There were 136,500 farm holdings in Ireland, almost all of which were family farms. Average farm size was 32·0 ha. 43% of farms were under 20 ha. 13% of farmers were under 35 and 41% were over 55. In 2001 there were 1·05m. ha of arable land in Ireland and 2,000 ha of permanent crops.

Agriculture, fisheries and forestry represented 3·5% of GDP in 2002 (provisional). 90% of the agricultural area was devoted to grass in 2002. In 2003 beef and milk production accounted for 57% of goods output at producer prices.

Figures at June 2002: barley accounted (in ha) for 176,000; wheat, 102,700; oats, 18,800; other cereals, 1,800; potatoes, 15,400. Production figures (in 1,000 tonnes): sugarbeets, 1,313; barley, 963; wheat, 867; potatoes, 519; oats, 134.

Goods output at producer prices including changes in stock for 2003 was estimated at €4·7bn.; operating surplus (aggregate income) was €2·5bn. Direct income payments, financed or co-financed by the EU, amounted to €1·6bn. It is estimated that net subsidies (subsidies on products plus subsidies on production less taxes on products and taxes on production) represented 63% of aggregate income. Livestock (June 2003 provisional): cattle, 6,924,100; sheep, 6,964,400. (June 2002) pigs, 1,769,500; poultry, 12,708,600.

Forestry. Total forest area by the end of 2000 was 649,812 ha (9% of total land area). Timber production in 2001 was 2·45m. cu. metres.

Fisheries. In 1999 approximately 17,600 people were engaged full- or part-time in the sea fishing industry; in 2002 the fishing fleet consisted of 1,448 vessels. The quantities and values of fish landed during 1999 were: wetfish, 253,245·8 tonnes, value IR£105,870,387·16; shellfish, 53,801·0 tonnes, value IR£59,822,930·48. Total quantity (2001): 356,309 tonnes; total value (1999), IR£165,693,317·64. The main types of fish caught in 1999 were horse mackerel (59,609·0 tonnes), mackerel (58,201·2 tonnes), herring (45,334·2 tonnes) and blue whiting (35,880·0 tonnes). More than 98% of fish caught is from sea fishing.

INDUSTRY

The leading companies by market capitalization in Ireland in May 2004 were: Allied Irish Banks (US$12·3bn.); Bank of Ireland (US$11·9bn.); and CRH plc (US$11·2bn.), a building materials company.

Enterprise Ireland. Enterprise Ireland was established in 1998 to provide an integrated development package specifically for indigenous firms. Its mission is 'to help client companies develop a sustainable competitive advantage leading to profitable sales, exports and employment'. Enterprise Ireland brings together the key marketing, technology, enterprise development, business training and science and innovation initiatives through which the Government supports the growth of Irish manufacturing and internationally traded sectors.

County Enterprise Boards. The 35 City and County Enterprise Boards (CEB's), which were established in Oct. 1993, are locally controlled enterprise development companies established in each county and local urban authority area in Ireland. The function of the Boards is to develop indigenous enterprise potential and to stimulate economic activity at a local level. This is primarily achieved through the provision of financial support for the development of micro enterprise (ten employees or fewer).

IDA Ireland. The IDA was established by the Irish government in 1969 but its remit was altered in 1993 when responsibility for development of indigenous industry was moved to Enterprise Ireland. The objective of IDA Ireland is to stimulate and support regional and economic development in Ireland by attracting and expanding foreign investment in key business sectors.

Today, Ireland is recognized as a base for a wide range of activities, from software development, business and information technology to international services and pharmaceuticals. Over 1,300 foreign-owned enterprises have established businesses in Ireland.

Shannon Development. Shannon Development, which was established in 1959, is the regional economic development company responsible for industrial, tourism and rural development in the Shannon region. Its regional mandate covers Counties Clare, Limerick, North Tipperary, South Offaly and North Kerry.

Forfás. Forfás is the policy advisory and co-ordination board for industrial development and science and technology. It is the statutory agency through which powers are delegated to Enterprise Ireland for the promotion of indigenous enterprise and to IDA Ireland for the promotion of inward investment.

The main functions of Forfás are to advise the Minister on matters relating to industrial policy, to advise on the development and co-ordination of policy for Enterprise Ireland, and IDA Ireland, and encourage the development of industry, technology, marketing and human resources.

The Chairman of Forfás is Eoin O'Driscoll and its Chief Executive is Martin Cronin.

The census of industrial production for 2001 gives the following details of the values (in €1m.) of gross and net output for the principal manufacturing industries.

	Gross output	*Net output*
Mining and quarrying	1,054·4	551·2
Manufacture of food products, beverages and tobacco	17,001·0	8,347·7
Manufacture of textiles and textile products	736·4	352·9
Manufacture of leather and leather products	63·3	18·7
Manufacture of wood and wood products	796·9	310·0
Manufacture of pulp, paper and paper products; publishing and printing	10,020·6	8,502·6
Manufacture of chemicals, chemical products and man-made fibres	26,392·0	20,868·1
Manufacture of rubber and plastic products	1,143·1	561·3
Manufacture of other non-metallic mineral products	1,453·8	774·1
Manufacture of basic metals and fabricated metal products	1,909·7	882·6
Manufacture of machinery and equipment n.e.c.	1,754·7	789·9
Manufacture of electrical and optical equipment	32,004·1	13,726·8
Manufacture of transport equipment	1,080·4	476·6
Manufacturing n.e.c.	1,553·7	644·6
Electricity, gas and water supply	2,928·5	1,492·6
Total (all industries)	99,892·6	58,299·8

In 2000 gross output was €94,951·1m. and net output €55,160·7m.

Labour. The total labour force for 2003 was estimated to be 1,859,700, of which 81,400 were out of work. With the birth rate having peaked around 1980 there is currently a marked increase in the numbers entering the workforce. The unemployment rate in 2004 was 4·5% (among the lowest in the EU), down from nearly 16% in 1993. Of those at work in 2003, 1,172,600 were employed in the services sector, 492,600 in the industrial sector and 113,200 in the agricultural sector. Employment rose by approximately 51% between 1991 and 2001—more than twice as much as in any other industrialized country. The retirement age is 65 years.

Trade Unions. The number of trade unions in Dec. 2002 was 46; total membership, 532,076. The six largest unions accounted for 68% of total membership. A series of three-year social pacts, which, in addition to covering a range of economic and social policy measures, include provision for pay increases, have been negotiated between the government, trade unions and employees' organizations since 1987. The fifth such agreement concluded in Feb. 2000, the Programme for Prosperity and Fairness (PPF), provided pay increases of 15% of basic pay in the public and private sectors of the economy over the period of the agreement, 2000–02. Owing to escalating inflation a further compensatory 1% lump sum payment was negotiated, for payment in March 2001. The third phase increase (4%) in the public service was not to be paid earlier than Oct. 2002 and was dependent on the establishment of performance indicators by April 2001 and the achievement of sectoral targets by April 2002.

The PPF agreement expired for some workers in the private sector in Dec. 2002; depending on start dates, for others the agreement continued into 2003. The PPF pay element expired in Oct. 2003 for the public service. Talks to negotiate a successor to the PPF collapsed in Dec. 2002.

INTERNATIONAL TRADE

Imports and Exports. In 2002 exports accounted for 94% of GDP (both merchandise and service). This showed a slight decrease on the 2001 level which was just over 96% of GDP. Value of imports and exports of merchandise for calendar years (in €1m.):

	1999	*2000*	*2001*	*2002*
Imports	44,327	55,909	57,384	53,303
Exports	66,956	83,889	92,690	93,724

The values of the chief imports and total exports are shown in the following table (in €1m.):

	Imports		*Exports*	
	2001	*2002*	*2001*	*2002*
Animal and vegetable oils and waxes	123	115	24	28
Beverages and tobacco	679	757	985	1,001
Chemicals	6,341	6,998	32,281	39,313

	Imports		*Exports*	
	2001	*2002*	*2001*	*2002*
Live animals and food	3,116	3,135	5,801	5,679
Machinery and transport equipment	30,224	27,892	37,607	32,759
Manufactured articles	6,300	6,068	8,969	8,068
Manufactured goods	4,391	4,290	1,955	1,839
Mineral fuels and lubricants	2,219	1,740	297	361
Raw materials	799	788	953	855

Ireland is one of the most trade-dependent countries in the world. Exports constitute an increasing share of the economy's output of goods and services. In 2002 the total value of merchandise exports amounted to just over €93·7bn. (the highest ever level), which generated a trade surplus of €38·4bn. In 2002 merchandise exports to the EU countries accounted for 63·7% of total exports while merchandise imports from the EU accounted for 59·4% of total imports. Information technology has become increasingly important, and by 1999 Ireland had become the largest exporter of software products in the world.

Import and export totals for Ireland's top ten export markets in 2002 (€1m.):

	Imports		*Exports*	
	2001	*2002*	*2001*	*2002*
Belgium	864	791	4,431	3,519
France	2,752	2,252	5,532	4,668
Germany	3,521	3,533	11,671	6,744
Italy	1,185	1,092	3,309	3,593
Japan	1,991	2,012	3,261	2,642
Netherlands	1,860	1,822	4,237	3,410
Spain	646	676	2,283	2,231
Switzerland	530	557	2,706	3,121
United Kingdom	20,481	19,860	22,630	22,431
United States of America	8,700	8,504	15,694	16,385

COMMUNICATIONS

Roads. At 31 Dec. 2003 there were 95,811 km of public roads, consisting of 2,746 km of National Primary Roads (including 176 km of motorway), 2,685 km of National Secondary Roads, 11,607 km of Regional Roads and 78,773 km of Local Roads.

Number of licensed motor vehicles at 31 Dec. 2002: private cars, 1,447,908; public-service vehicles, 25,342; goods vehicles, 233,069; agricultural vehicles, 66,665; motorcycles, 33,147; other vehicles, 43,915. In 2002 a total of 376 people were killed in 346 fatal accidents.

Rail. The total length of railway open for traffic at 31 Dec. 1993 was 1,919 km (478 km electrified), all 1,600 mm gauge. A massive investment in public transport infrastructure is taking place in Ireland. Over the period 2000–06 €235m. is being invested in Dublin suburban rail alone.

Railway statistics for years ending 31 Dec.	*2001*	*2002*
Passengers (journeys)	34,206,000	35,370,000
Km run by passenger train	12,356,000	12,602,000
Freight (tonne-km)	515,754,000	426,307,000
Km run by freight trains	4,133,000	2,895,000
Receipts (IR£)	197,088,000	198,780,000
Expenditure (IR£)	378,843,000	396,127,000

A light railway system was launched in Dublin in 2004.

Civil Aviation. Aer Lingus and Ryanair are the two major airlines operating in Ireland.

Aer Lingus was founded in 1936 as a State-owned enterprise. Its principal business is the provision of passenger and cargo services to the UK, Europe and the USA. Ryanair began operations in 1985 and now operates to a range of destinations in the UK and Europe.

In addition to Aer Lingus and Ryanair, there are 16 other independent air transport operators. The main operators in this group are Aer Arann Express and Cityjet.

The principal airports (Dublin, Shannon and Cork) are operated by the state-owned Aer Rianta cpt. In 2002 Dublin handled 15·08m. passengers and 116,700 tonnes of freight. Shannon handled 2·35m. passengers and 48,100 tonnes of freight.

Cork was the third busiest, with 1·87m. passengers and 12,900 tonnes of freight. In 2003 Ireland's three state airports catered for almost 16m. passengers in Dublin, 2·4m. in Shannon and 2·2m. in Cork to give over 20m. passengers, up almost 6% on 2002.

There are six privately owned regional airports. The government part funds the scheduled services from Dublin to five of these airports and to the City of Derry airport in Northern Ireland to ensure efficient and speedy access to the more isolated regions of the state for both business and tourist travellers. The principal focus of growth during 2003 was the European market with the Dublin–London air route amongst the busiest in Europe.

Shipping. The merchant fleet totalled 269,693 GRT in 2002. Total cargo traffic passing through the country's ports amounted to 44,919,000 tonnes in 2002. Dublin handled 22·2m. tonnes of cargo in 2002 and Cork 9·4m. tonnes.

Inland Waterways. The principal inland waterways open to navigation are the Shannon Navigation (270 km), which includes the Shannon-Erne Waterway (Ballinamore/Ballyconnell Canal), and the Grand Canal and Barrow Navigation (249 km). The Waterways Service of the Department of Arts, Culture and the Gaeltacht is responsible for the waterways system as a public amenity. Merchandise traffic has now ceased and navigation is confined to pleasure craft operated either privately or commercially. The Royal Canal (146 km) from Dublin to Mullingar (53 km) was reopened for navigation in 1995.

Telecommunications. The Minister for Public Enterprise, a member of the government, has overall policy responsibility for the development of the sector. Among the key elements of the government's policy is the objective of creating a fully open and competitive telecommunications market that will stimulate investment in advanced information infrastructure and services in Ireland and develop Ireland as a global leader in the growth of Internet-based industries and electronic commerce.

The Director of Telecommunications Regulation, established by legislation as an independent officer with a separate office and staff in June 1997, is responsible for licensing of operators, allocation of numbers and radio frequency spectrum, supervision of network interconnection arrangements and other regulatory functions.

Ireland's telecommunications sector has been fully liberalized with effect from 1 Dec. 1998 when the last remaining elements of Telecom Éireann's (now called Eircom) exclusive privilege were removed. All elements of the market are now open to competition from other licensed operators. The three licensed mobile telephone operators are Vodafone, O2 and Meteor.

The Government has also sold the state's entire remaining stake of 50·1% in Eircom by way of an initial public offering of shares in the company. The sale took place in July 1999 and was the 2nd largest European privatization in that year.

eircom plc—Operational Information. The dominant operator in the telecommunications sector is eircom plc (previously Telecom Éireann). Telecom Éireann was a statutory body set up under the Postal and Telecommunications Services Act, 1983. In 1996, 20% of the State's holding was sold to KPN/Telia, a Dutch–Swedish consortium, who had an option of a further 15%, which was taken up in July 1999. In 1998 the government concluded an Employee Share Ownership Scheme under which 14·9% of the company was to be made available to employees and also held an Initial Public Offer (IPO) of shares in the company in July 1999. In Oct. 1999 the newly-privatized Telecom Éireann became eircom plc.

The level of network digitalization is 100%. In 2002 there were 4,944,000 telephone subscribers, equivalent to 1,257·7 per 1,000 inhabitants. Mobile phone customers numbered 3·0m. in 2002 and there were 1,654,000 PCs in use (420·8 per 1,000 persons). In 2004 Irish mobile phone subscribers sent 3·74bn. text messages in total (89 messages per subscriber per month). There were 1·31m. Internet users in Sept. 2002 and 132,500 were connected to broadband in Dec. 2004.

Postal Services. Postal services are provided by An Post, a statutory body established under the Postal and Telecommunications Services Act, 1983. In 1998 there were 1,912 post offices. A total of 748m. pieces of mail were handled during 1998, equivalent to 70 per person. An Post also offers a range of services to the business community through a dedicated unit, Special Delivery Services, and subsidiaries PostGEM, PrintPost and Precision Marketing Information. A range of services are provided through the Post Office network including Savings and Investments, passport applications, bill payments, National Lottery products and the payment of Social Welfare benefits on an agency basis for the State.

SOCIAL INSTITUTIONS

Justice. The Constitution provides that justice shall be administered in public in Courts established by law by Judges appointed by the President on the advice of the government. The jurisdiction and organization of the Courts are dealt with in the Courts (Establishment and Constitution) Act, 1961, the Courts (Supplemental Provisions) Acts, 1961–91, and the Courts and Court Officers Acts, 1995–2002. These Courts consist of Courts of First Instance and a Court of Final Appeal, called the Supreme Court. The Courts of First Instance are the High Court with full original jurisdiction and the Circuit and the District Courts with local and limited jurisdictions. A judge may not be removed from office except for stated misbehaviour or incapacity and then only on resolutions passed by both Houses of the Oireachtas. Judges are appointed by the President on the advice of Government. Judges of the Supreme Court and High Court are appointed from among practising Barristers or Solicitors of not less than 12 years standing or by the elevation of an existing member of the judiciary. Judges of the Circuit Court are appointed from among practising Barristers or Solicitors of not less than ten years standing or a County Registrar who has practised as a Barrister or Solicitor for not less than ten years before being appointed to that post or by the elevation of a District Court Judge. Judges of the District Court are appointed from among practising Barristers or Solicitors of not less than ten years standing.

The Supreme Court, which consists of the Chief Justice (who is *ex officio* an additional judge of the High Court) and seven ordinary judges, may sit in two Divisions and has appellate jurisdiction from all decisions of the High Court. The President may, after consultation with the Council of State, refer a Bill, which has been passed by both Houses of the Oireachtas (other than a money bill and certain other bills), to the Supreme Court for a decision on the question as to whether such Bill or any provision thereof is repugnant to the Constitution.

The High Court, which consists of a President (who is *ex officio* an additional Judge of the Supreme Court) and 31 ordinary judges (or 32 when a High Court Judge is appointed as a Commissioner of the Law Reform Commission, as is currently the case), has full original jurisdiction in and power to determine all matters and questions, whether of law or fact, civil or criminal. In all cases in which questions arise concerning the validity of any law having regard to the provisions of the Constitution, the High Court alone exercises original jurisdiction. The High Court on Circuit acts as an appeal court from the Circuit Court.

The Court of Criminal Appeal consists of the Chief Justice or an ordinary Judge of the Supreme Court, together with either two ordinary judges of the High Court or the President and one ordinary judge of the High Court. It deals with appeals by persons convicted on indictment where the appellant obtains a certificate from the trial judge that the case is a fit one for appeal, or, in case such certificate is refused, where the court itself, on appeal from such refusal, grants leave to appeal. The decision of the Court of Criminal Appeal is final, unless that court, the Attorney-General or the Director of Public Prosecutions certifies that the decision involves a point of law of exceptional public importance, in which case an appeal is taken to the Supreme Court.

The Offences against the State Act, 1939 provides in Part V for the establishment of Special Criminal Courts. A Special Criminal Court sits without a jury. The rules of evidence that apply in proceedings before a Special Criminal Court are the same as those applicable in trials in the Central Criminal Court. A Special Criminal Court is authorized by the 1939 Act to make rules governing its own practice and procedure. An appeal against conviction or sentence by a Special Criminal Court may be taken to the Court of Criminal Appeal. On 30 May 1972 Orders were made establishing a Special Criminal Court and declaring that offences of a particular class or kind (as set out) were to be scheduled offences for the purposes of Part V of the Act, the effect of which was to give the Special Criminal Court jurisdiction to try persons charged with those offences.

The High Court exercising criminal jurisdiction is known as the Central Criminal Court. It consists of a judge or judges of the High Court, nominated by the President of the High Court. The Court tries criminal cases which are outside the jurisdiction of the Circuit Court.

The Circuit Court consists of a President (who is *ex officio* an additional judge of the High Court) and 33 ordinary judges. The country is divided into eight circuits. The jurisdiction of the court in civil proceedings is subject to a financial ceiling, save by consent of the parties, in which event the jurisdiction is unlimited. In criminal matters it has jurisdiction in all cases except murder, treason, piracy, rape, serious and aggravated sexual assault and allied offences. The Circuit Court acts as an appeal court from the District Court. The Circuit Court also has jurisdiction in the Family Law area such as divorce.

The District Court, which consists of a President and 54 ordinary judges, has summary jurisdiction in a large number of criminal cases where the offence is not of a serious nature. In civil matters the Court has jurisdiction in contract and tort (except slander, libel, seduction, slander of title and false imprisonment) where the claim does not exceed €6,348·69; in proceedings founded on hire-purchase and credit-sale agreements, the jurisdiction is also €6,348·69. The District Court also has jurisdiction in Family Law matters such as maintenance, custody, access and the issuing of barring orders. The District Court also has jurisdiction in a large number of licensing (intoxicating liquor) matters.

All criminal cases, except those of a minor nature, and those tried in the Special Criminal Court, are tried by a judge and a jury of 12. Generally, a verdict need not be unanimous in a case where there are not fewer than 11 jurors if ten of them agree on the verdict.

The Courts Service Act, 1998, provided for the transfer of responsibility for the day to day management of the Courts from the Minister for Justice, Equality and Law Reform to a new body known as the Courts Service. The Board of the Courts Service consists of 17 members including members of the judiciary, the legal profession, staff and trade union representatives, a representative of court users, a person with commercial/financial experience and a Chief Executive Officer. The Courts Service was formally established on 9 Nov. 1999. While the Minister retains political responsibility to the Oireachtas, the courts are now administered independently by the Board and CEO.

At 31 Dec. 2003 the police force, the Garda Síochána, had a total staff of 12,210. There were 103,360 headline offences recorded in 2003, of which 37,184 were detected, and non-headline offences resulted in proceedings against 292,279 persons; there were 45 murders in 2003 (1·24 per 100,000 population). The National Juvenile Office received 19,915 referrals relating to 17,043 individual children during 2003. The population in penal institutions in Sept. 2003 was 3,366 (85 per 100,000 of national population).

Religion. According to the census of population taken in 2002 the principal religious professions were as follows:

	Leinster	*Munster*	*Connacht*	*Ulster (part of)*	*Total*
Roman Catholics	1,828,097	995,728	424,019	214,762	3,462,606
Church of Ireland (including Protestants)	67,877	26,183	9,773	11,778	115,611
Other Christian religion n.e.c.	13,892	5,036	1,672	803	21,403
Presbyterians	8,447	2,056	1,086	8,984	20,582
Muslims (Islamic)	13,233	3,683	1,731	500	19,147
Methodists	5,778	2,574	812	869	10,033
Orthodox	7,570	1,884	657	326	10,437
Other stated religions	24,803	10,003	3,599	1,621	40,026
Not stated or no religion	135,882	53,458	20,947	7,071	217,358

Seán Brady (b. 1939) is the Roman Catholic Cardinal of Armagh and Primate of All Ireland. In Sept. 2003 there were two cardinals.

In May 1990 the General Synod of the Church of Ireland voted to ordain women.

Education. In 2001 total expenditure on education came to 5·1% of GNP and 13·0% of total government spending. The adult literacy rate in 2001 was at least 99%.

Elementary. Elementary education is free and was given in about 3,283 national schools (including 128 special schools) in 2002–03. The total number of pupils on rolls in 2002–03 was 443,720, including pupils in special schools and classes; the number of teachers of all classes was about 24,700 in 2002–03, including remedial teachers and teachers of special classes. The total expenditure for first level education during the financial year ended 31 Dec. 2003 was €2,119·7m. The total salaries for teachers for 1998, including superannuation etc., was €1,684·2m.

Special. Special provision is made for children with disabilities in special schools which are recognized on the same basis as primary schools, in special classes attached to ordinary schools and in certain voluntary centres where educational services appropriate to the needs of the children are provided. Integration of children with disabilities in ordinary schools and classes is encouraged wherever possible, if necessary with special additional support. There are also part-time teaching facilities in hospitals, child guidance clinics, rehabilitation workshops, special 'Saturday-morning' centres and home teaching schemes. Special schools (2002–03) numbered 128 with approximately 6,807 pupils. There were also some 9,384 pupils enrolled in about 1,001 special classes within ordinary schools. There is a National Education Officer for travelling children.

Secondary. Voluntary secondary schools are under private ownership and are conducted in most cases by religious orders. These schools receive grants from the State and are open to inspection by the Department of Education. The number of recognized secondary schools during the school year 2002–03 was 410, and the number of pupils in attendance was 189,093. There were 12,447 teachers in 2002–03.

Vocational Education Committee schools provide courses of general and technical education. Pupils are prepared for State examinations and for entrance to universities and institutes of further education. The number of vocational schools during the school year 2002–03 was 247, the number of full-time students in attendance was 98,233 and the number of teachers 5,933. These schools are controlled by the local Vocational Education Committees; they are financed mainly by State grants and also by contributions from local rating authorities and Vocational Education Committee receipts. These schools also provide adult education facilities for their own areas.

Comprehensive and Community Schools. Comprehensive schools which are financed by the State combine academic and technical subjects in one broad curriculum so that pupils may be offered educational options suited to their needs, abilities and interests. Pupils are prepared for State examinations and for entrance to universities and institutes of further education. The number of comprehensive and community schools during the school year 2002–03 was 89 and the number of students in attendance was 51,905. These schools also provide adult education facilities for their own areas and make facilities available to voluntary organizations and to the adult community generally.

The total current expenditure from public funds for second level and further education for 2003 was €2,304·8m.

Education Third-Level. Traditionally, the third-level education system in Ireland has comprised the university sector, the technical and technological colleges and the colleges of education, all of which are substantially funded by the State and are autonomous. In the mid- and late 1990s a number of independent private colleges came into existence, offering a range of mainly business-related courses conferring professional qualifications and, in some instances, recognized diplomas and certificates. Numbers in third-level education have expanded dramatically since the mid-1960s, from 21,000 full-time students in 1965 to over 129,000 in 2002–03.

University education is provided by the National University of Ireland, founded in Dublin in 1908, by the University of Dublin (Trinity College), founded in 1592, and by the Dublin City University and the University of Limerick established in 1989. The National University comprises four constituent universities—NUI Dublin, NUI Cork, NUI Galway and NUI Maynooth.

St Patrick's College, Maynooth, Co. Kildare is a national seminary for Catholic priests and a pontifical university with the power to confer degrees up to doctoral level in philosophy, theology and canon law.

Besides the University medical schools, the Royal College of Surgeons in Ireland (a long-established independent medical school) provides medical qualifications which are internationally recognized. Courses to degree level are available at the National College of Art and Design, Dublin.

There are five Colleges of Education for training primary school teachers. For degree awarding purposes, three of these colleges are associated with Trinity College, one with Dublin City University and one with the University of Limerick. There are also two Home Economics Colleges for teacher training, one associated with Trinity College and the other with the National University of Ireland, Galway.

Institutes of Technology in 14 centres (Athlone, Blanchardstown, Carlow, Cork, Dundalk, Dun Laoghaire, Galway, Letterkenny, Limerick, Sligo, Tallaght, Tipperary, Tralee and Waterford) provide vocational and technical education and training for trade and industry from craft to professional level through certificate, diploma and some degree courses. These colleges (with the exception of Blandchardstown, Dun Laoghaire and Tipperary) were established on a statutory basis on 1 Jan. 1993. Prior to this they operated under the aegis of the Vocational Education Committees (VECs) for their areas. Dun Laoghaire College of Art and Design was designated under the RTC Act 1992, from 1 April 1997. The Dublin Institute of Technology (DIT) was also established on a statutory basis on 1 Jan. 1993. Prior to this it operated under the aegis of City of Dublin VEC. The DIT provides certificate, degree and diploma level courses in engineering, architecture, business studies, catering, music, etc. The Hotel and Catering College in Killybegs continues to operate under the aegis of Co. Donegal VEC.

Total full-time enrolments in the Institutes of Technology/Other Technological Colleges in the 2002–03 academic year were approximately 51,507. The Higher Education and Training Awards Council (HETAC) was established by the Government on 11 June 2001, under the Qualifications (Education and Training) Act 1999. HETAC is the qualifications awarding body for third-level educational and training institutes outside the university sector. It is the successor to the National Council for Educational Awards (NCEA).

The total full-time enrolment at third-level in institutions aided by the Department of Education and Science in 2002–03 was 129,283. Whereas in the late 1970s only one in five school leavers went on to university, now at least six out of ten are doing so.

The total current expenditure from public funds on third-level education during the financial year ended 31 Dec. 2003 was approximately €1,388·3m.

Agricultural. Teagasc, the Agriculture and Food Development Authority, is the State agency responsible for providing advisory, training, research and development services for the agriculture and food industries. Full-time instruction in agriculture is provided for all sections of the farming community. Training for young entrants, adult farmers, rural dwellers and the food industry is provided from eight colleges, local training centres and research centres.

Health. Health boards are responsible for administering health services in Ireland. There are currently ten health boards established: three area health boards located in the eastern region under the guidance of the Eastern Regional Health Authority (ERHA) and seven regional health boards covering the rest of the country. Each health board is responsible for the provision of health and social services in its area. The boards provide many of the services directly and they arrange for the provision of other services by health professionals, private health service providers, voluntary hospitals and voluntary/community organizations.

A health service reform programme is currently being implemented which will result in the most significant structural changes in the Irish health services in recent decades. The existing health boards will be replaced by a single Health Service Executive (HSE) with four regional administrative areas. A Health Information and Quality Authority (HIQA) will also be established.

Everybody ordinarily resident in Ireland has either full or limited eligibility for the public health services.

A person who satisfies the criteria of a means test receives a medical card, which confers Category 1 or full eligibility on them and their dependants. This entitles the holder to the full range of public health and hospital services, free of charge, i.e. family doctor, drugs and medicines, hospital and specialist services as well as dental, aural and optical services. Maternity care and infant welfare services are also provided.

The remainder of the population has Category 2 or limited eligibility. Category 2 patients receive public consultant and public hospital services subject to certain charges. Persons in Category 2 are liable for a hospital in-patient charge of €55 per night up to a maximum of €550 in any 12 consecutive months (with effect from 1 Jan. 2005). There is no charge for out-patient services. However, persons in Category 2 are liable for a charge of €55 if they attend the Accident and Emergency Department of a hospital without a letter from a General Practitioner.

The Long Term Illness Scheme entitles persons to free drugs and medicines, which are prescribed in respect of 15 specific illnesses. The needs of individuals with significant or ongoing medical expenses are met by a range of other schemes, which provide assistance towards the cost of prescribed drugs and medicines. The *Drug Payment Scheme* was introduced on 1 July 1999 and replaced the Drug Cost Subsidisation Scheme (DCSS) and the Drug Refund Scheme (DRS). Under this scheme no individual or family will have to pay more than €78 in any calendar month for approved prescribed drugs, medicines and appliances for use by the person or his/her family in that month.

Services for People with Disabilities: The Department of Health and Children provides, through the health boards and the Eastern Regional Health Authority, a wide range of services for people with disabilities. These include day care, home support (including personal assistance services), therapy services, training, employment, sheltered work and residential respite care. The following allowances and grants for eligible people with disabilities come under the aegis of the Department of Health and Children and are administered by the health boards and the Eastern Regional Health Authority:

Blind Welfare Allowance—provides supplementary financial support to unemployed blind persons who are not maintained in an institution and who are in receipt of a Department of Social, Community and Family Affairs payment, such as Disability Allowance, Blind Pension or Old Age Pension.

Rehabilitative Training Bonus—payable to persons who are attending approved rehabilitative training programmes. The payment of €31·80 replaced the Disabled Persons Rehabilitation Allowance (DPRA) from 1 Aug. 2001.

Domiciliary Care Allowance (DCA)—provides home care for severely disabled or mentally handicapped children up to the age of 16. The maximum rate of DCA in Jan. 2005 was €225·20 per month.

Infectious Diseases Maintenance Allowance (IDMA)—payable to a person who is unable to make reasonable and proper provision for their own maintenance or the maintenance of their dependants because they are undergoing treatment for one of the infectious diseases specified in the IDMA regulations. The personal adult rate in Jan. 2005 was €134·80 per week.

Mobility Allowance—provides financial assistance to severely disabled persons who are unable to walk or use public transport in order to finance the occasional taxi journey. At Jan. 2005 the monthly higher rate, payable only to those who do not benefit from the 'Disabled Drivers and Disabled Passengers Scheme', was €156. The lower rate was €78.

Motorized Transport Grant—provides financial assistance to disabled persons who require a car to obtain or retain employment or who have transport needs because they live in very isolated areas. The maximum grant in Jan. 2005 was €4,690.

Respite Care Grant (RCG)—an annual payment of €835 to help carers obtain respite care (at June 2004).

Spending Allowance for Persons in Long-Stay Institutions—provides basic spending money for people with disabilities and other eligible people in long stay institutions (e.g. residential accommodation) who have no other source of income to help them meet the cost of basic necessities. The maximum rate in Jan. 2005 was €24·40 per week.

Health Contributions—A health contribution of 2% of income is payable by those with Category 2 eligibility. Employers meet the levy in respect of those employees who have a medical card.

In 2003 there were 59 publicly funded acute hospitals in operation with an 85% occupancy rate. The average number of in-patient beds available for use over the year was 12,300. There were 96,499 wholetime equivalent numbers employed in health board/regional authority and voluntary/joint board hospitals and homes for the mentally handicapped at 31 Dec. 2003. Of these 6,792 were medical/dental staff, 12,690 were health and social care professionals and 33,766 were nursing staff. In 2002 Ireland spent 7·3% of its GDP on health.

Welfare. The Department of Social and Family Affairs is responsible for the day-to-day administration and delivery of social welfare schemes and services through a network of local, regional and decentralized offices. The Department's local delivery of services is structured on a regional basis. There are a total of ten regions, with offices in Waterford, Cork, Limerick, Galway, Longford, Sligo, Dundalk and three in the Dublin area.

Social Welfare Schemes. The social welfare supports can be divided into three categories:

—*Social Insurance (Contributory)* payments made on the basis of a Pay Related Social Insurance (PRSI) record. Such payments are funded by employers, employees and the self-employed. Any deficit in the fund is met by Exchequer subvention.

—*Social Assistance (Non Contributory)* payments made on the basis of satisfying a means test. These payments are financed entirely by the Exchequer.

—*Universal payments* such as Child Benefit or Free Travel which do not depend on PRSI or a means test.

The Social Welfare Appeals Office (SWAO) is an independent office responsible for determining appeals against decisions on social welfare entitlements.

There are, in addition, five statutory agencies under the aegis of the Department:

—*the Combat Poverty Agency* which has responsibilities in the areas of advice to the Minister, research, action programmes and public information in relation to poverty. It also initiates and evaluates pilot schemes aimed at overcoming poverty and examines the nature, causes and extent of poverty in the state.

—*the Pensions Board* which has the function of promoting the security of occupational pensions, their development and the general issue of pensions coverage.

—*Comhairle* which has the function of ensuring that all citizens have easy access to the highest quality of information, advice and advocacy on social services.

—*Family Support Agency* which aims to support families, promote the continuity of stability in family life, prevent marital breakdown and foster a supportive community environment for families at a local level. It does so by providing a family mediation service, by developing marriage and relationship counselling, undertaking research and by advising the Minister on its functions and family issues.

—*Office of the Pensions Ombudsman* which investigates and decides complaints and disputes involving occupational pension schemes and Personal Retirement Savings Accounts (PRSAs). The Ombudsman is independent of the Minister and the Department in the performance of his functions.

In 2003 social welfare expenditure accounted for 9·6% of GNP.

CULTURE

Cork is the European Capital of Culture for 2005. The title attracts large European Union grants.

World Heritage Sites. There are two sites under Irish jurisdiction which appear on the UNESCO world heritage list. They are (with year put on list): Archaeological Ensemble of the Bend of the Boyne (1993), the three principal sites of the Brúna Bóinne Complex, a major centre of prehistoric megalithic art; Skellig Michael (1996), a monastic complex on a craggy island from the 7th century.

Broadcasting. Public service broadcasting is provided by Radio Telefís Éireann (RTÉ), a statutory body established under the Broadcasting Authority Acts 1960–2001. RTÉ is financed principally by TV licence and advertising. In 1996 a total of 972,069 TV licences were issued. Legislation enacted in 1988 provided for the establishment of the Independent Radio and Television Commission to arrange provision of independent commercial radio stations and an independent TV service. There were (1996) 21 local commercial radio stations, ten community radio stations, two special interest Irish language radio stations, one independent national radio station and four hospital radio stations. There were 2·66m. radio receivers in 2000 and 1·52m. TV receivers (colour by PAL) in 2001. An Irish-language TV channel, TG4, broadcasts for 19 hours a day. At the end of Sept. 2004, 857,000 persons subscribed to pay TV via cable/MMDS and satellite, 55% of which subscribed to digital TV.

Cinema. As at April 2004 there were 321 cinema screens. 66 new films were made in 2001.

Press. In 2004 there were six weekday newspapers and six Sunday newspapers (all in English) with a combined circulation of 1,492,099 for Jan. to June 2004.

Tourism. Total number of overseas tourists in 2002 was 6,065,000 compared to 5,990,000 in 2001 (a 1·3% increase). In 2002 earnings from all visits to Ireland, including cross-border visits, amounted to €3,985m. In 2002, 59% of visits were from Great Britain. In 2002 Irish residents made 4,634,000 visits abroad (a 9·9% increase on 2001).

Festivals. Ireland's national holiday, St. Patrick's Day (17 March), is celebrated annually.

Libraries. In 1997 there were 351 public libraries, two National libraries and 30 Higher Education libraries; they held a combined 17,128,000 volumes. There were 848,000 registered public library users in 1996.

DIPLOMATIC REPRESENTATIVES

Of Ireland in the United Kingdom (17 Grosvenor Pl., London, SW1X 7HR)
Ambassador: Dáithí O'Ceallaigh.

Of the United Kingdom in Ireland (29 Merrion Rd, Ballsbridge, Dublin, 4)
Ambassador: Stewart Eldon CMG, OBE.

Of Ireland in the USA (2234 Massachusetts Ave., NW, Washington, D.C., 20008)
Ambassador: Noel Fahey.

Of the USA in Ireland (42 Elgin Rd, Ballsbridge, Dublin)
Ambassador: James C. Kenny.

Of Ireland to the United Nations
Ambassador: Richard Ryan.

FURTHER READING

Central Statistics Office. *National Income and Expenditure* (annual), *Statistical Abstract* (annual), *Census of Population Reports* (quinquennial), *Census of Industrial Production Reports* (annual), *Trade and Shipping Statistics* (annual and monthly), *Trend of Employment and Unemployment, Reports on Vital Statistics* (annual and quarterly), *Statistical Bulletin* (quarterly), *Labour Force Surveys* (annual), *Trade Statistics* (monthly), *Economic Series* (monthly).

Ardagh, J., *Ireland and the Irish: a Portrait of a Changing Society.* London, 1994
Chubb, B., *Government and Politics in Ireland.* 3rd ed. London, 1992
Collins, N. (ed.) *Political Issues in Ireland Today.* Manchester Univ. Press, 1994
Cronin, Mike, *A History of Ireland.* Palgrave, Basingstoke, 2001
Delanty, G. and O'Mahony, P., *Rethinking Irish History: Nationalism, Identity and Ideology.* London, 1997
Foster, R. F., *The Oxford Illustrated History of Ireland.* OUP, 1991
Garvin, T., *1922 The Birth of Irish Democracy.* Dublin, 1997
Harkness, D., *Ireland in the Twentieth Century: a Divided Island.* London, 1995
Hussey, G., *Ireland Today: Anatomy of a Changing State.* Dublin, 1993
Institute of Public Administration, *Ireland: a Directory.* Dublin, annual
Kostick, C., *Revolution in Ireland – Popular Militancy 1917–1923.* London, 1997
Munck, R., *The Irish Economy: Results and Prospects.* London, 1993
O'Beirne Ranelagh, J., *A Short History of Ireland.* 2nd ed. CUP, 1999
O'Hagan, J. W. (ed.) *The Economy of Ireland: Policy and Performance of a Small European Country.* London, 1995
Vaughan, W. E. (ed.) *A New History of Ireland*, 6 vols. Oxford, 1996
Wiles, J. L. and Finnegan, R. B., *Aspirations and Realities: a Documentary History of Economic Development Policy in Ireland since 1922.* London, 1992.

National statistical office: Central Statistics Office, Skehard Road, Cork. *Director-General:* Donal Garvey, M.Sc., M.Sc. (Mgt).
Website: http://www.cso.ie/

ISRAEL

Medinat Israel
(State of Israel)

Capital: Jerusalem
Population projection, 2010: 7·27m.
GDP per capita, 2002: (PPP$) 19,530
HDI/world rank: 0·908/22

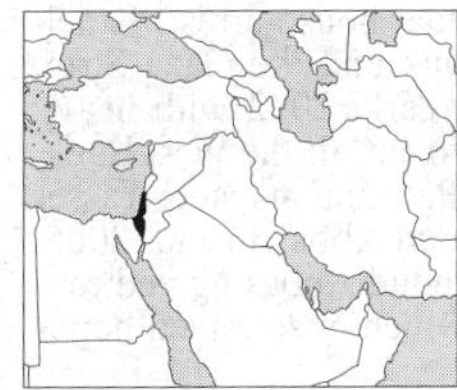

KEY HISTORICAL EVENTS

The area once designated as Palestine, of which Israel forms part, was formerly part of the Ottoman Empire. During the First World War the Arabs under Ottoman rule rebelled and Palestine was occupied by British forces. In 1917 the British Government issued the Balfour Declaration, stating that it viewed 'with favour the establishment in Palestine of a national home for the Jewish people'. In 1922 the League of Nations recognized 'the historical connection of the Jewish people with Palestine' and 'the grounds for reconstituting their national home in that country', and Britain assumed a mandate over Palestine, pending the establishment there of such a national home. In Nov. 1947 the UN General Assembly passed a resolution calling for the establishment of a Jewish and an Arab state in Palestine. On 14 May 1948 the British Government terminated its mandate and the Jewish leaders proclaimed the State of Israel. No independent Arab state was established in Palestine. Instead the neighbouring Arab states invaded Israel on 15 May 1948. The Jewish state defended itself successfully, and the ceasefire in Jan. 1949 left Israel with one-third more land than had been originally assigned by the UN.

In 1967, following some years of uneasy peace, local clashes on the Israeli–Syrian border were followed by Egyptian mass concentration of forces on the borders of Israel. Israel struck out at Egypt on land and in the air on 5–9 June 1967. Jordan joined in the conflict which spread to the Syrian borders. By 11 June the Israelis had occupied the Gaza Strip and the Sinai peninsula as far as the Suez Canal in Egypt, West Jordan as far as the Jordan valley and the heights east of the Sea of Galilee, including Quneitra in Syria.

A further war broke out on 6 Oct. 1973 when Egyptian and Syrian offensives were launched. Following UN Security Council resolutions a ceasefire finally came into being on 24 Oct. In Sept. 1978 Egypt and Israel agreed on frameworks for peace in the Middle East. A treaty was signed in Washington on 26 March 1979 whereby Israel withdrew from the Sinai Desert in two phases; part was achieved on 26 Jan. 1980 and the final withdrawal by 26 April 1982.

In June 1982 Israeli forces invaded the Lebanon. On 16 Feb. 1985 the Israeli forces started a withdrawal, leaving behind an Israeli trained and equipped Christian Lebanese force to act as a control over and buffer against Muslim Shia or Palestinian guerrilla attacks.

In 1993 following declarations by the Prime Minister, Yitzhak Rabin, recognizing the Palestine Liberation Organization (PLO) as representative of the Palestinian people, and by Yasser Arafat, leader of the PLO, renouncing terrorism and recognizing the State of Israel, an agreement was signed in Washington providing for limited Palestinian self-rule in the Gaza Strip and Jericho. Negotiations on the permanent status of the West Bank and Gaza began in 1996. On 4 Nov. 1995 Yitzhak Rabin was assassinated by a Jewish religious extremist. In the subsequent election, a right-wing coalition led by Binyamin Netanyahu took office. Peace talks with the Palestinians then stalled. In Oct. 1998 Israel accepted partial withdrawal from the West Bank on condition that the Palestinians cracked down on terrorism. The following month, 2% of the West Bank was handed over to Palestinian control. Further moves were put on hold after the collapse of the Netanyahu coalition and the announcement of early elections.

In Sept. 1999 Ehud Barak provided the first evidence that the Middle East peace process was back on track by releasing nearly 200 Palestinian prisoners and by handing over 430 sq. km of land on the West Bank. In May 2000 Israel completed its withdrawal from south Lebanon, 22 years after the first invasion. By Oct. 2000 violence had broken out again between Israelis and Palestinians, fuelled by the conflict over control of Jerusalem, with terrorist acts a daily occurrence, leading to heavy casualties on both sides. With peace talks stalled once again, Barak called for a nationwide vote of confidence by putting himself up for re-election as prime minister. Defeated by the right-wing Ariel Sharon in Feb. 2001, he retired from politics. As violence escalated, in Dec. 2001 Israel ended all contact with Yasser Arafat, besieging his compound and putting him under virtual house arrest. Israeli incursions into Palestinian-controlled areas of the West Bank and the Gaza Strip, and suicide attacks by Palestinians, continued unabated in early 2002 with heavy loss of life. In June 2002 Israel began constructing a barrier to cut off the West Bank, with the aim of shielding the country from suicide bombers. Palestinian leader Yasser Arafat died on 11 Nov. 2004. He was succeeded by Mahmoud Abbas in Jan. 2005. In Feb. 2005 Israeli prime minister Ariel Sharon and Mahmoud Abbas agreed to a 'cessation of hostilities' between the two peoples, a move which encouraged hopes of a resumption of the peace process.

TERRITORY AND POPULATION

The area of Israel, including the Golan Heights (1,150 sq. km) and East Jerusalem (70 sq. km), is 21,946 sq. km (8,473 sq. miles), with a population estimated in 2002 to be 6·6m., including East Jerusalem, the Golan Heights and Israeli settlers in the occupied territories. Population density, 252 per sq. km.

The UN gives a projected population for 2010 of 7·27m.

In 2001, 91·8% of the population lived in urban areas.

Population by place of origin as of 1995: Europe and America, 1·8m.; former USSR, 0·66m.; Morocco, 0·5m.; Iraq, 0·25m.; Poland, 0·25m.; Romania, 0·25m.; Yemen, 0·15m.; Iran, 0·13m.; Algeria and Tunisia, 0·12m.

The Jewish Agency, which, in accordance with Article IV of the Palestine Mandate, played a leading role in establishing the State of Israel, continues to organize immigration.

Israel is administratively divided into six districts:

District	*Area (sq. km)*	*Population*[1]	*Chief town*
Northern	4,501	1,127,200	Nazareth
Haifa	854	838,900	Haifa
Central	1,242	1,541,100	Ramla
Tel Aviv	170	1,161,100	Tel Aviv
Jerusalem[2]	627	794,100	Jerusalem
Southern	14,107	948,500	Beersheba

[1]2002. [2]Includes East Jerusalem.

On 23 Jan. 1950 the Knesset proclaimed Jerusalem the capital of the State and on 14 Dec. 1981 extended Israeli law into the Golan Heights. Population of the main towns (2002): Jerusalem, 680,400; Tel Aviv/Jaffa, 360,400; Haifa, 270,800; Rishon le-Ziyyon, 211,600; Ashdod, 187,500; Beersheba, 181,500; Petach Tikva, 172,600; Holon, 165,800; Netanya, 164,800; Bene Berak, 138,900; Bat Yam, 133,900; Ramat Gan, 126,600.

The official languages are Hebrew and Arabic.

SOCIAL STATISTICS

2001 births, 136,638; deaths, 37,173; marriages, 38,924; divorces, 11,164. 2001 crude birth rate per 1,000 population of Jewish population, 18·3; Non-Jewish: Muslims, 36·8; Christians, 20·0; Druzes, 26·2. Crude death rate (2001), Jewish, 6·6; Muslims, 2·8; Christians, 4·7; Druzes, 3·0. Infant mortality rate per 1,000 live births (2001), Jewish, 4·1; Muslims, 8·2; Christians, 4·9 (1996–99); Druzes, 8·7 (1996–99). Life expectancy, 2001, 76·9 years for males and 80·8 for females. Average annual population growth rate, 1992–2002, 2·7%. Fertility rate, 2001, 2·8 births per woman.

Immigration. The following table shows the numbers of immigrants entering Palestine/Israel.

1997	66,221	1999	76,766	2001	43,580
1998	56,730	2000	60,192	2002	33,567

There were 199,516 immigrants in 1990 and 176,100 in 1991 following the fall of communism in eastern Europe and the break-up of the former Soviet Union.

CLIMATE

From April to Oct., the summers are long and hot, and almost rainless. From Nov. to March, the weather is generally mild, though colder in hilly areas, and this is the wet season. Jerusalem, Jan. 12·8°C, July 28·9°C. Annual rainfall, 657 mm. Tel Aviv, Jan. 17·2°C, July 30·2°C. Annual rainfall, 803 mm.

CONSTITUTION AND GOVERNMENT

Israel is an independent sovereign republic, established by proclamation on 14 May 1948.

In 1950 the Knesset (*Parliament*), which in 1949 had passed the Transition Law dealing in general terms with the powers of the Knesset, President and Cabinet, resolved to enact from time to time fundamental laws, which eventually, taken together, would form the Constitution. The nine fundamental laws that have been passed: the Knesset (1958), Israel Lands (1960), the President (1964), the Government (1968), the State Economy (1975), the Army (1976), Jerusalem, capital of Israel (1980), the Judicature (1984) and the Electoral System (1996).

The *President* (head of state) is elected by the Knesset by secret ballot by a simple majority; his term of office is five years. He may be re-elected once.

The Knesset, a one-chamber Parliament, consists of 120 members. It is elected for a four-year term by secret ballot and universal direct suffrage. Under the system of election introduced in 1996, electors vote once for a party and once for a candidate for Prime Minister. To be elected Prime Minister, a candidate must gain more than half the votes cast, and be elected to the Knesset. If there are more than two candidates and none gain half the vote, a second round is held 15 days later. The Prime Minister forms a cabinet (no fewer than eight members and no more than 18) with the approval of the Knesset.

National Anthem. 'Hatikvah' ('The Hope'); words by N. H. Imber.

RECENT ELECTIONS

Ariel Sharon of Likud won the election for *Prime Minister* on 6 Feb. 2001 with 62·4% of the vote, against 37·6% for the incumbent Prime Minister Ehud Barak of Avoda (Labor). In the parliamentary (Knesset) elections on 28 Jan. 2003, Prime Minister Ariel Sharon's Likud party (conservative) won 37 of 120 seats, Labor-Meimad (social democratic) 19, Shinui-Mifleget Merkaz (liberal) 15, Shas 11, National Union 7, Meretz 6, National Religious Party 5, United Torah Judaism 5 and smaller parties 15. Turn-out was 68·5%.

In a parliamentary vote for the presidency on 31 July 2000, Moshe Katzav defeated Shimon Peres in the second round. He claimed 63 votes against 57 for Peres.

CURRENT ADMINISTRATION

President: Moshe Katzav; b. 1945 (Likud; sworn in 1 Aug. 2000).

Following the election of 6 Feb. 2001 Ariel Sharon formed an eight-party coalition. In Oct. 2002 Labour Party ministers resigned from the cabinet following a dispute over the funding of Jewish settlements in the West Bank. Unable to maintain the coalition without support from the Labour Party, Ariel Sharon was forced to call early elections which were held on 28 Jan. 2003. A national unity government was formed after two parties left the previous coalition in late 2004. In March 2005 the new coalition was composed as follows:

Prime Minister and Minister of Science and Technology and Social Welfare: Ariel Sharon; b. 1928 (Likud; sworn in 7 March 2001).

Vice Prime Minister: Shimon Peres (Labor-Meimad). *Vice Prime Minister and Minister of Industry, Trade and Labour:* Ehud Olmert (Likud). *Deputy Prime Minister and Minister of Foreign Affairs:* Silvan Shalom (Likud).

Minister of Agriculture and Rural Development: Yisrael Katz (Likud). *Defence:* Shaul Mofaz (Likud). *Education, Culture and Sport:* Limor Livnat (Likud). *Finance:* Binyamin Netanyahu (Likud). *Health:* Dani Naveh (Likud). *Housing and Construction:* Isaac Herzog (Labor-Meimad). *Immigrant Absorption and Justice:* Tzipi Livni (Likud). *Interior:* Ophir Pines-Paz (Labor-Meimad). *Public Security:* Gideon Ezra (Likud). *Transportation:* Meir Shitrit (Likud). *National Infrastructures:* Binyamin Ben-Eliezer (Labor-Meimad). *Tourism:* Abraham Hirchson (Likud). *Communications:* Dalia Itzik (Labor-Meimad). *Environment:* Shalom Simhon (Labor-Meimad). *Ministers without Portfolio:* Natan Scheransky (Likud-Israel Baaliyah); Tzachi Hanegbi (Likud); Matan Vilnai (Labor-Meimad); Haim Ramon (Labor-Meimad).

Office of the Prime Minister: http://www.pmo.gov.il

DEFENCE

Conscription (for Jews and Druze only) is three years (usually four years for officers; two years for women). The Israel Defence Force is a unified force, in which army, navy and air force are subordinate to a single chief-of-staff. The Minister of Defence is *de facto* C.-in-C.

Defence expenditure in 2003 totalled US$10,325m., representing 9·5% of GDP. Expenditure per capita in 2003 was US$1,544, a figure exceeded only by Qatar and Kuwait.

Nuclear Weapons. Israel has an undeclared nuclear weapons capability. Although known to have a nuclear bomb, it pledges not to introduce nuclear testing to the Middle East. According to the Stockholm International Peace Research Institute, the nuclear arsenal was estimated to have approximately 200 warheads in Jan. 2004. Israel has never admitted possessing biological or chemical weapons, but according to *Deadly Arsenals*, published by the Carnegie Endowment for International Peace, it does have a chemical and biological weapons programme.

Army. Strength (2002) 120,000 (conscripts 85,000). There are also 530,000 reservists available on mobilization. In addition there is a paramilitary border police of 8,500.

Navy. The Navy, tasked primarily for coastal protection and based at Haifa, Ashdod and Eilat, includes three small diesel submarines and three corvettes.

Naval personnel in 2002 totalled 6,500 (including a Naval Commando of 300) of whom 2,500 are conscripts. There are also 11,500 naval reservists available on mobilization.

Air Force. The Air Force (including air defence) has a personnel strength (2002) of 35,000 (20,000 conscripts), with 454 (250 stored) first-line aircraft, all jets, of Israeli and US manufacture including F-4E *Phantoms*, F-15s and F-16s, and 135 armed helicopters. There are 20,000 Air Force reservists.

INTERNATIONAL RELATIONS

Israel is a member of the UN, WTO, Inter-American Development Bank and IOM. It is one of the largest recipients of foreign aid, in 1996 receiving US$2·2bn, representing around US$400 per person—the highest amount per person of any country.

ECONOMY

Services accounted for an estimated 81% of GDP in 1997, industry 17% and agriculture 2%.

Overview. Israel experienced its worst recession in 50 years between 2001–03, owing to high security costs and a sharp decline in tourism. The *intifada* has hampered foreign investment, exports and economic reforms. In 2000 the government opened the telecommunications sector to foreign competition. In 2002 the government introduced emergency measures, including an increase in the budget deficit to 3·9% from the targeted 3%. State expenditures have been cut through a freeze in social benefits and the minimum wage. In early 2002 the Bank of Israel cut interest rates by 2 percentage points and the currency dropped to 4·60 shekel to the US dollar.

Currency. The unit of currency is the *shekel* (ILS) of 100 *agorot.* Foreign exchange reserves were US$24,782m. in June 2002. Gold reserves have been negligible since 1998. There was inflation of 1·1% in both 2000 and 2001, but 2002 saw a steep increase, with inflation of 5·7%. Total money supply in May 2002 was 37,702m. shekels.

Budget. Budget revenue and expenditure (in 1m. shekels), year ending 31 Dec.:

	1996	*1997*	*1998*	*1999*	*2000*	*2001*
Revenue	123,796	145,110	159,911	173,187	194,736	195,376
Expenditure	149,571	165,250	183,046	197,954	208,603	224,287

Performance. There was real GDP growth of 6·4% in 2000, but Israel experienced a recession in 2001, with the economy shrinking by 0·5%. In 2002 there was then an upturn, with real GDP growth of 3·3%. Total GDP was US$110·4bn. in 2001.

Banking and Finance. The Bank of Israel was established by law in 1954 as Israel's central bank. Its Governor is appointed by the President on the recommendation of the Cabinet for a five-year term. He acts as economic adviser to the government and has ministerial status. The *Governor* is Prof. Stanley Fischer. Central bank reserves in Dec. 2002 were US$24·1bn. The government raised some US$4bn. from bank privatizations during the 1990s.

In 2001 there were 23 commercial banks headed by Bank Leumi Le Israel, Bank Hapoalim and Israel Discount Bank, two merchant banks, three foreign banks, eight mortgage banks and nine lending institutions specifically set up to aid industry and agriculture.

There is a stock exchange in Tel Aviv.

Israel was one of 15 countries and territories named in a report in June 2000 as failing to co-operate in the fight against international money laundering. The Financial Action Task Force on Money Laundering was set up by the G7 group of major industrialized nations.

Weights and Measures. The metric system is in general use. The (metrical) *dunam* = 1,000 sq. metres.

ENERGY AND NATURAL RESOURCES

Environment. Carbon dioxide emissions from the consumption and flaring of fossil fuels in 2002 were the equivalent of 9·5 tonnes per capita.

Electricity. Installed capacity in 2000 was 9·1m. kW. Electric power production amounted to 42·92bn. kWh in 2000; consumption per capita was 6,864 kWh in 2000.

Oil and Gas. The only significant hydrocarbon is oil shale. Crude petroleum reserves in 2002 were 4m. bbls.

Water. In the northern Negev farming has been aided by the Yarkon–Negev water pipeline. This has become part of the overall project of the 'National Water Carrier', which is to take water from the Sea of Galilee (Lake Kinnereth) to the south. The plan includes a number of regional projects such as the Lake Kinnereth–Negev pipeline which came into operation in 1964; it has an annual capacity of 320m. cu. metres. Total water production in 2001 amounted to 1,885m. cu. metres, of which 1,800m. cu. metres was consumed.

Minerals. The most valuable natural resources are the potash, bromine and other salt deposits of the Dead Sea. Production figures (2000) in 1,000 tonnes: phosphate rock, 4,110; potash, 1,748; lignite (1999), 944; salt, 526.

Agriculture. In the coastal plain mixed farming, poultry raising, citriculture and vineyards are the main agricultural activities. The Emek (the Valley of Jezreel) is the main agricultural centre of Israel. Mixed farming is to be found throughout the valleys; the sub-tropical Beisan and Jordan plainlands are also centres of banana plantations and fish breeding. In Galilee mixed farming, olive and tobacco plantations prevail. The Hills of Ephraim are a vineyard centre; many parts of the hill country are under afforestation.

There were 338,000 ha of arable land in 2001 and 86,000 ha of permanent crops. Production, 2000 (in 1,000 tonnes): tomatoes, 550; melons and watermelons, 447; grapefruit and pomelos, 370; potatoes, 349; oranges, 300; tangerines and mandarins, 140; bananas, 130; cucumbers and gherkins, 108; chillies and green peppers, 97; onions, 90.

Livestock (2000), 388,000 cattle, 350,000 sheep, 163,000 pigs, 70,000 goats, 28m. poultry.

Types of rural settlement: (1) the *Kibbutz* and *Kvutza* (communal collective settlement), where all property and earnings are collectively owned and work is collectively organized. (115,700 people lived in 268 *Kibbutzim* in 1999.) (2) The *Moshav* (workers' co-operative smallholders' settlement) which is founded on the principles of mutual aid and equality of opportunity between the members, all farms being equal in size (184,500 in 411). (3) The *Moshav Shitufi* (co-operative settlement), which is based on collective ownership and economy as in the *Kibbutz,* but with each family having its own house and being responsible for its own domestic services (18,200 in 43). (4) Other rural settlements in which land and property are privately owned and every resident is responsible for his own well-being. In 1999 there were a total of 259 non-cooperative villages with a population of 314,900.

Forestry. In 2000 forests covered 132,000 ha or 6·4% of the total land area. Timber production was 27,000 cu. metres in 2001.

Fisheries. Catches in 2001 totalled approximately 5,000 tonnes, of which 3,400 tonnes were from marine waters.

INDUSTRY

The leading companies by market capitalization in Israel, excluding banking and finance, in Jan. 2002 were: Teva Pharmaceutical Industries Ltd (40bn. shekels); Check Point Software Technologies Ltd (20bn. shekels); and BEZEQ—The Israel Telecommunications Corporation Ltd (12bn. shekels).

Products include chemicals, metal products, textiles, tyres, diamonds, paper, plastics, leather goods, glass and ceramics, building materials, precision instruments, tobacco, foodstuffs, electrical and electronic equipment.

Labour. The economically active workforce was 2,270,500 in 2001 (1,236,200 males). The principal areas of activity were: manufacturing, mining and quarrying, 394,200; wholesale and retail trade/repair of motor vehicles, motorcycles and personal and household goods, 299,800; education, 283,700; real estate, renting and business activities, 277,200; and health and social work, 225,100. Unemployment was 10·5% in 2002, up from 6·4% in 1996.

Trade Unions. New Histadrut (The New General Federation of Workers), founded in 1920 as Histadrut, had 700,000 members in 2000. Several trades unions also exist representing other political and religious groups.

INTERNATIONAL TRADE

Imports and Exports. External trade, in US$1m., for calendar years:

	1998	*1999*	*2000*	*2001*	*2002*
Imports f.o.b.	26,241	30,041	34,036	30,979	31,212
Exports f.o.b.	23,190	25,827	31,153	27,974	27,653

The main exportable commodities are citrus fruit and by-products, fruit juices, flowers, wines and liquor, sweets, polished diamonds, chemicals, tyres, textiles, metal products, machinery, electronic and transportation equipment. The main exports in 1999 were: machinery and equipment, 32·6% (of which a third was telecommunication equipment); worked diamonds, 24·7%; chemicals and chemical products, 12·8%. In 2000 the main export markets were: USA, 35·5%; UK, 5·5%; Belgium, 5·4%; Germany, 4·5%.

Main imports in 1999 were: machinery and transport equipment, 35·2%; manufactured goods, 30·7% (of which 60% was diamonds); chemicals and related products, 8·9%; mineral fuels, 6·9%; foodstuffs, 4·9%. Main import suppliers in 2000: USA, 20·7%; Belgium, 11·1%; Germany, 8·1%; UK, 7·6%.

COMMUNICATIONS

Roads. There were 16,903 km of paved roads in 2002, including 74 km of motorway. Registered motor vehicles in 2002 totalled 1,522,112 passenger cars, 19,140 buses and coaches and 335,724 lorries and vans. There were 525 fatalities as a result of road accidents in 2002.

Rail. There were 676 km of standard gauge line in 2002. 17·5m. passengers were carried in 2002 and 10·3m. tonnes of freight in 2000. One of the smallest metro systems in the world (1,800 metres) was opened in Haifa in 1959.

Civil Aviation. There are international airports at Tel Aviv (Ben Gurion), Eilat (J. Hozman), Haifa and Ovda. Tel Aviv is the busiest airport, in 2000 handling 9,815,015 passengers (9,283,287 on international flights) and 336,188 tonnes of freight. El Al is the state-owned airline. In 1999 it flew 79·5m. km and carried 2,972,400 passengers (all on international flights). In 2003 services (mainly domestic) were also provided by another Israeli airline, Arkia, and by over 40 international carriers.

Shipping. Israel has three commercial ports—Haifa, Ashdod and Eilat. In 2002, 5,984 ships departed from Israeli ports; 45,810,000 tonnes of freight and 137,000 passengers were handled. The merchant fleet totalled 765,000 GRT in 2002.

Telecommunications. A public company responsible to the Ministry of Communications administers the telecommunications service. In 2002 there were 9,434,000 telephone subscribers (equivalent to 1,421·7 per 1,000 population) and 1·61m. PCs were in use (242·6 for every 1,000 persons). Israel had 6,334,000 mobile phone subscribers in 2002 (954·5 per 1,000 inhabitants—among the highest penetration rates in the world) and 140,000 fax machines were in use in 1999. There were 2·0m. Internet users in 2002.

Postal Services. The Ministry of Communications supervises the postal service. In 1998 there were 664 post offices, or one for every 8,990 persons.

SOCIAL INSTITUTIONS

Justice. *Law.* Under the Law and Administration Ordinance, 5708/1948, the first law passed by the Provisional Council of State, the law of Israel is the law which was obtaining in Palestine on 14 May 1948 in so far as it is not in conflict with that Ordinance or any other law passed by the Israel legislature and with such modifications as result from the establishment of the State and its authorities.

Capital punishment was abolished in 1954, except for support given to the Nazis and for high treason.

The law of Palestine was derived from Ottoman law, English law (Common Law and Equity) and the law enacted by the Palestine legislature, which to a great extent was modelled on English law.

Civil Courts. Municipal courts, established in certain municipal areas, have criminal jurisdiction over offences against municipal regulations and bylaws and certain specified offences committed within a municipal area. Magistrates courts, established in each district and sub-district, have limited jurisdiction in both civil and criminal matters. District courts, sitting at Jerusalem, Tel Aviv and Haifa, have jurisdiction, as courts of first instance, in all civil matters not within the jurisdiction of magistrates courts, and in all criminal matters, and as appellate courts from magistrates courts and municipal courts. The 14-member Supreme Court has jurisdiction as a court of first instance (sitting as a High Court of Justice dealing mainly with administrative matters) and as an appellate court from the district courts (sitting as a Court of Civil or of Criminal Appeal).

In addition, there are various tribunals for special classes of cases. Settlement Officers deal with disputes with regard to the ownership or possession of land in settlement areas constituted under the Land (Settlement of Title) Ordinance.

Religious Courts. The rabbinical courts of the Jewish community have exclusive jurisdiction in matters of marriage and divorce, alimony and confirmation of wills of members of their community and concurrent jurisdiction with the civil courts in all other matters of personal status of all members of their community with the consent of all parties to the action.

The courts of the several recognized Christian communities have a similar jurisdiction over members of their respective communities.

The Muslim religious courts have exclusive jurisdiction in all matters of personal status over Muslims who are not foreigners, and over Muslims who are foreigners, if under the law of their nationality they are subject in such matters to the jurisdiction of Muslim religious courts.

Where any action of personal status involves persons of different religious communities, the President of the Supreme Court will decide which court shall have jurisdiction, and whenever a question arises as to whether or not a case is one of personal status within the exclusive jurisdiction of a religious court, the matter must be referred to a special tribunal composed of two judges of the Supreme Court and the president of the highest court of the religious community concerned in Israel.

In 2001 government expenditure on public security and justice totalled 7,238m. shekels. The population in penal institutions in Jan. 2002 was 10,164 (163 per 100,000 of national population).

Religion. Religious affairs are under the supervision of a special Ministry, with departments for the Christian and Muslim communities. The religious affairs of each community remain under the full control of the ecclesiastical authorities concerned: in the case of the Jews, the Ashkenazi and Sephardi Chief Rabbis, in the case of the Christians, the heads of the various communities, and in the case of the Muslims, the Qadis. The Druze were officially recognized in 1957 as an autonomous religious community.

In 2001 there were: Jews, 4,960,000; Muslims, 930,000; others (mainly Christians and Druze), 360,000.

The Chief Rabbis are Yona Metzger (Ashkenazi) and Shlomo Amar (Sephardi).

Education. The adult literacy rate in 2001 was 95·1% (male, 97·1%; female, 93·1%). There is free and compulsory education from five to 16 years and optional free education until 18. There is a unified state-controlled elementary school system with a provision for special religious schools. The standard curriculum for all elementary schools is issued by the Ministry with a possibility of adding supplementary subjects comprising not more than 25% of the total syllabus. Most schools in towns are maintained by municipalities, a number are private and some are administered by teachers' co-operatives or trustees.

In 2000–01 there were 1,485,000 Hebrew pupils and 353,000 Arab pupils in the education system. In primary schools and kindergartens in 2000–01 there were 800,000 Hebrew children and 247,000 Arab children. There were 45,000 Hebrew teachers and 11,000 Arab teachers in 1999–2000. In secondary education there were 454,000 Hebrew pupils and 106,000 Arab pupils in 2000–01, with 47,000 Hebrew teachers and 7,000 Arab teachers in 1999–2000. In special education there were 31,060 pupils in 1998–99. In post-secondary education, such as colleges, universities and vocational institutions, there were 235,000 pupils, of which 231,000 were Hebrew.

The Hebrew University of Jerusalem, founded in 1925, comprises faculties of the humanities, social sciences, law, science, medicine and agriculture. In 2002–03 it had 22,600 students. The Technion in Haifa had 13,118 students. The Weizmann Institute of Science in Rehovoth, founded in 1949, had 760 students in 1995–96.

Tel Aviv University had 26,100 students in 1995–96. In 2002–03 the religious Bar-Ilan University at Ramat Gan, opened in 1965, had 31,200 students, the Haifa University had about 13,000 students and the Ben Gurion University had more than 15,000 students.

In 2001 government expenditure on education totalled 28,279m. shekels. In 2000–01 total expenditure on education came to 7·6% of GNP.

Health. In 1995 there were 259 hospitals with 61 beds per 10,000 inhabitants. There were 22,345 physicians, 6,733 dentists, 35,579 nurses, 3,511 pharmacists and 1,080 midwives in 1998. In 2001 government expenditure on health totalled 12,960m. shekels.

Welfare. The National Insurance Law of 1954 provides for old-age pensions, survivors' insurance, work-injury insurance, maternity insurance, family allowances and unemployment benefits. In 2001 recipients of allocations from the National

Insurance Institute included (monthly averages): child allowances, 2,154,735; old age pensions, 571,200; general disability allowances, 142,440; income support benefits, 142,011; maternity grants, 129,089; survivors' pensions, 105,818; unemployment benefits, 104,707.

CULTURE

World Heritage Sites. There are three sites under Israeli jurisdiction in the World Heritage List: Masada and the old city of Acre were both inscribed in 2001. Masada was built as a palace complex and fortress by Herod the Great. It was the site of the mass suicide of about 1,000 Jewish patriots in the face of a Roman army in the 1st century AD and is a symbol of the ancient kingdom of Israel. The port city of Acre preserves remains of its medieval Crusader buildings beneath the existing Muslim fortified town dating from the 18th and 19th centuries. The White City of Tel Aviv—the Modern Movement (2003) is an example of early 20th century town planning, based on the plan of Sir Patrick Geddes.

Broadcasting. Television and the state radio station, Kol Israel (Voice of Israel), are controlled by the Israel Broadcasting Authority. There is a national programme, two commercial programmes, a music programme and a service in Arabic. There were 2·15m. TV sets (colour by PAL) in 2001 and 3·21m. radio receivers in 2000.

Press. In 1996 there were 34 daily newspapers. Combined circulation was 1,650,000, at a rate of 291 per 1,000 inhabitants.

Tourism. In 2000 there were 2,400,000 foreign tourists, bringing revenue of US$3·10bn.

Calendar. The Jewish year 5765 corresponds to 16 Sept. 2004–3 Oct. 2005; 5766 corresponds to 4 Oct. 2005–22 Sept. 2006.

Libraries. In 1995 there was one National Library with 3m. volumes and 2,176 registered users. In 1993 there were 1,180 public libraries with 11,242,000 volumes and 737,565 registered users.

DIPLOMATIC REPRESENTATIVES

Of Israel in the United Kingdom (2 Palace Green, Kensington, London, W8 4QB)
Ambassador: Zvi Heifetz.

Of the United Kingdom in Israel (192 Hayarkon St., Tel Aviv 63405)
Ambassador: Simon McDonald.

Of Israel in the USA (3514 International Dr., NW, Washington, D.C., 20008)
Ambassador: Daniel Ayalon.

Of the USA in Israel (71 Hayarkon St., Tel Aviv)
Ambassador: Daniel C. Kurtzer.

Of Israel to the United Nations
Ambassador: Dan Gillerman.

Of Israel to the European Union
Ambassador: Oded Eran.

FURTHER READING

Central Bureau of Statistics. *Statistical Abstract of Israel.* (Annual)—*Statistical Bulletin of Israel.* (Monthly)

Beitlin, Y., *Israel: a Concise History.* London, 1992

Bleaney, C. H., *Israel.* [Bibliography] 2nd ed. ABC-Clio, Oxford and Santa Barbara (CA), 1994

Bregman, Ahron, *History of Israel.* Palgrave Macmillan, Basingstoke, 2002

Freedman, R. (ed.) *Israel Under Rabin.* Boulder (CO), 1995

Garfinkle, A., *Politics and Society in Modern Israel: Myths and Realities.* Armonk (NY), 1997

Gilbert, Martin, *Israel: A History.* New York, 1998

Sachar, H. M., *A History of Israel.* 2 vols. OUP, 1976–87

Schlör, Joachim, *Tel Aviv: From Dream to City.* Reaktion, London, 1999

Segev, T., *1949: The First Israelis.* New York, 1986

Thomas, Baylis, *How Israel Was Won: A Concise History of the Arab–Israeli Conflict (1900–1999).* Lexington Books, Pennsylvania, 2000

Wasserstein, Bernard, *Israel and Palestine: Why They Fight and Can They Stop?* Profile Books, London, 2003

Other more specialized titles are entered under PALESTINIAN-ADMINISTERED TERRITORIES.

National statistical office: Central Bureau of Statistics, Prime Minister's Office, POB 13015, Jerusalem 91130.
Website: http://www.cbs.gov.il/
National library: The Jewish National and University Library, Jerusalem

PALESTINIAN-ADMINISTERED TERRITORIES

KEY HISTORICAL EVENTS

Under the Israeli-Palestinian agreement of 28 Sept. 1995 the Israeli army redeployed from six of the seven largest Palestinian towns in the West Bank and from 460 smaller towns and villages. Following this in April 1996 an 82-member *Palestinian Council* was elected and also a head (*Rais*) of the executive authority of the Council. The rest of the West Bank stayed under Israeli army control with some progressive redeployments at six-month intervals, although Palestinian civil affairs here too were administered by the Palestinian Council. Negotiations on the permanent status of the West Bank and Gaza began in May 1996. Issues to be resolved include the position of 0·17m. Israelis in the West Bank and 0·18m. in East Jerusalem, the status of Jerusalem, military locations and water supplies.

Following the opening of an archaeological tunnel in Jerusalem, armed clashes broke out at the end of Sept. 1996 between demonstrators and Palestinian police on the one hand and Israeli troops. On 18 Nov. 1996 the Israeli Minister of Defence approved plans for an expansion of Jewish settlement in the West Bank. Under an agreement brokered by King Hussein of Jordan and signed by the Prime Minister of Israel and the President of the Palestinian Authority on 15 Jan. 1997 Israeli troop withdrawals from 80% of Hebron and all rural areas of the West Bank were scheduled to take place in three phases between 28 Feb. 1996 and 31 Aug. 1998.

The Israeli decision in Feb. 1997 to continue to promote Jewish settlement in the Jerusalem suburb of Har Homa was perceived by the Palestinian authorities as a hostile move and caused a setback to peace negotiations. In 1998 an American proposal that Israel should withdraw from 13·1% of the West Bank was not agreed on, but at a meeting in the USA in Oct. Israel accepted partial withdrawal on condition that the Palestinians cracked down on terrorism.

President Netanyahu's defeat by Ehud Barak in Israel's 1999 elections led to improved relations with the Palestinian Liberation Organization. Israel and the PLO signed the Sharm el-Shakh Memorandum in Sept. 1999 which established a time-frame for the implementation of outstanding commitments from earlier Palestinian-Israeli agreements. Israel conducted two more phases of redeployment from the West Bank in Sept. 1999 and Jan. 2000. The permanent status negotiations, having commenced in May 1996, began in earnest in Nov. 1999. In March 2000 Yasser Arafat accepted Israel's plan for a further expansion of self-rule in the West Bank, involving the transfer of another 6·1% of the West Bank to the control of the Palestinian Authority. As a result, 39·8% of the West Bank is under full or partial Palestinian control. But violence escalated, and in Dec. 2001 Israel ended all direct contact with Yasser Arafat, besieging his compound and putting him under virtual house arrest. In March 2002 the UN Security Council endorsed a Palestinian state for the first time. Israeli incursions into Palestinian-controlled areas of the West Bank and the Gaza Strip, and suicide attacks by Palestinians, continued unabated in early 2002 with heavy loss of life. In March 2003 the Palestinian parliament approved the creation of the post of prime minister. Mahmoud Abbas was nominated the Palestinian Authority's first premier, resulting in Yasser Arafat losing many of his powers. Yasser Arafat died on 11 Nov. 2004. Mahmoud Abbas was elected president in Jan. 2005. In Feb. 2005 he and Israeli prime minister Ariel Sharon agreed to a 'cessation of hostilities' between the two peoples, a move which encouraged hopes of a resumption of the peace process.

TERRITORY AND POPULATION

The 1997 census population of the Palestinian territory was 2,895,683; 2000 estimate 3,150,000. The UN gives a projected population for 2010 of 4·51m.

The West Bank (preferred Palestinian term, Northern District) has an area of 5,651 sq. km; 1997 census population was 1,873,476. The projected population for 2004 was 2,476,000, in addition to 365,000 Jewish settlers and 10,000 troops deployed there. 97% of the population in 1988 were Palestinian Arabs. In 2001 there were 1,860,000 were Muslims, 230,000 Jews and 200,000 Christians and others. In 2004 there was a Palestinian diaspora of 4·8m. The birth rate in 2004 was estimated at 39·6 per 1,000 population and the death rate 4·8 per 1,000. In 1995–99 the infant mortality rate was 24·4 per 1,000 live births. The fertility rate in 1999 was 5·5 births per woman. In 2003 there were 31,646 private cars and 14,521 commercial vehicles and trucks registered. There were (2003–04) 542,520 pupils in basic stage education and 59,909 in secondary stage. In 1998–99 there were 36,224 students in institutions of higher education. In 2003 there were 54 hospitals.

The Gaza Strip (preferred Palestinian term, Gaza District) has an area of 365 sq. km; 1997 census population was 1,022,207. The population doubled between 1975 and 1995. Crude birth rate in 2004 was 43·7 per 1,000 population. The death rate was estimated at 3·9 per 1,000 population. The fertility rate in 1999 was 6·8 births per woman. Infant mortality, 1995–99, 27·3 per 1,000 live births. Agricultural production, 2002 estimates, in 1,000 tonnes: oranges, 105; tomatoes, 48; potatoes, 35; cucumbers and gherkins, 18; grapefruit and pomelos, 10. Total fish catch in 2001 was 2,144 tonnes. In 2003–04 there were 374,713 students in basic stage education, 41,185 in secondary stage and 30,058 students in higher education (1998–99). In 2003 there were 17 hospitals.

The chief town is Gaza itself. Over 98% of the population are Arabic-speaking Muslims. In 1995 an estimated 94·2% of the population lived in urban areas. Citrus fruits, wheat and olives are grown, with farm land covering 193 sq. km (1980) and occupying most of the active workforce. In 2003 there were 38,677 private cars and 9,392 commercial vehicles and trucks registered. Gaza International Airport, at the southern edge of the Gaza Strip, opened in Nov. 1998. Telecommunications development has been rapid, the number of fixed line telephone subscribers more than trebling between 1997 and 2000. In 2003 there were 243,494 subscribers. In 2003 life expectancy at birth was 71·7 years.

CONSTITUTION AND GOVERNMENT

In April 1996 the Palestinian Council removed from its Charter all clauses contrary to its recognition by Israel, including references to armed struggle as the only means of liberating Palestine, and the elimination of Zionism from Palestine. The *President* is directly elected and heads the executive organ, the Palestinian National Authority, one fifth of whose members he appoints, while four fifths are elected by the *National Council*. The latter comprises 88 members and is directly elected by the first-past-the-post system from 16 electoral districts. The Palestinian Authority was created by agreement of the PLO and Israel as an interim instrument of self-rule for Palestinians living on the West Bank and Gaza Strip. The failure of the PLO and Israel to strike a permanent status agreement has resulted in the Authority retaining its powers. It is entitled to establish ministries and subordinate bodies, as required to fulfil its obligations and responsibilities. It possesses legislative and executive powers within the functional areas transferred to it in the 1995 Interim Agreement. Its territorial jurisdiction is restricted to Areas A and B in the West Bank and approximately two-thirds of the Gaza Strip.

Following an Israeli-Palestinian agreement on customs duties and VAT in Aug. 1994 the Palestinians set up their own customs and immigration points into Gaza and Jericho. Israel collects customs dues on Palestinian imports through Israeli entry points and transfers these to the Palestinian treasury.

A special committee is working on drafting a new Palestinian constitution. In March 2003 parliament approved the creation of the position of prime minister. Yasser Arafat nominated Mahmoud Abbas, the PLO Secretary General, to be the first premier.

There is a Palestinian *Council for Reconstruction and Development.*

RECENT ELECTIONS

Elections for *President* were held on 9 Jan. 2005. Mahmoud Abbas was elected *President* by 67·4% of votes cast, ahead of Mustafa Barghouti with 21·0%. There were five other candidates. In the *National Council* elections of 20 Jan. 1996, 55 seats went to the Liberation Movement of Palestine, 15 to independents, 7 to Independent Fatah, 4 to Independent Islamists, 3 to Independent Christians, 1 to Samaritans and 1 other, with 2 vacant.

CURRENT ADMINISTRATION

President of the Palestinian Authority: Mahmoud Abbas; b. 1935.

Prime Minister: Ahmed Qureia; b. 1937.

Palestinian President's Office: http://www.p-p-o.com

ECONOMY

Currency. Israeli currency is in use.

Banking and Finance. Banking is regulated by the Palestinian Monetary Authority. Palestine's leading bank is Arab Bank. A securities exchange, the Palestine Securities Exchange, opened in Nablus in Feb. 1997.

COMMUNICATIONS

Telecommunications. In 2003 there were 243,494 telephone subscribers, or 71·0 per 1,000 inhabitants. In March 2001 there were 60,000 Internet users.

SOCIAL INSTITUTIONS

Justice. The Palestinian police consists of some 15,000; they are not empowered to arrest Israelis, but may detain them and hand them over to the Israeli authorities.

FURTHER READING

Kimmerling, B. and Migdal J. S., *Palestinians: the Making of a People.* Harvard Univ. Press, 1994.—*The Palestinian People: A History.* Harvard Univ. Press, 2003

Robinson, G. E., *Building a Palestinian State: the Incomplete Revolution.* Indiana Univ. Press, 1997

Rubin, B., *Revolution until Victory? The Politics and History of the PLO.* Harvard Univ. Press, 1994

Segev, T., *One Palestine, Complete.* Metropolitan Books, New York, 2000

Stendel, O., *The Arabs in Israel.* Brighton, 1996

Tessler, M., *A History of the Israeli-Palestinian Conflict.* Indiana Univ. Press, 1994

Wasserstein, Bernard, *Israel and Palestine: Why They Fight and Can They Stop?* Profile Books, London, 2003

Statistical office: Palestinian Central Bureau of Statistics.
Website: http://www.pcbs.gov.ps

ITALY

Repubblica Italiana

Capital: Rome
Population projection, 2010: 56·56m.
GDP per capita, 2002: (PPP$) 26,430
HDI/world rank: 0·920/21

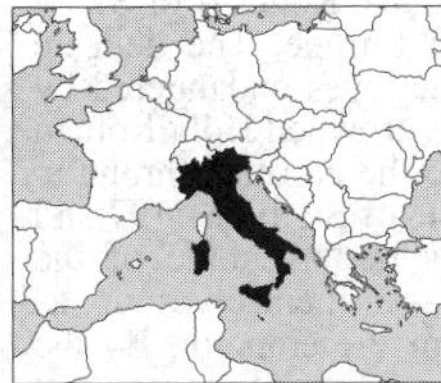

KEY HISTORICAL EVENTS

Excavations at Isernia uncovered remains of Palaeolithic Neanderthal man that date back 70,000 years. Stone Age and Bronze Age settlements have been found across the Italian peninsula. The Etruscans, established in Italy by around 1200 BC, were navigators competing for valuable trade routes with the Phoenicians and Greeks. During the 8th century BC Greek cities established colonies along the southern coast and in Sicily. *Magna Graecia* flourished for about six centuries before succumbing to Rome.

From 264 BC Carthage and Rome fought three Punic Wars for Mediterranean supremacy. In 218 BC Hannibal crossed the Alps to defeat the Romans. However, the destruction of Carthage in 146 BC was total. Rome incorporated Macedonian Greece and Spain into her colonies and became the dominant power in the Mediterranean. Trade brought riches and corruption to Rome. After Spartacus, an escaped slave, led 70,000 of his fellow slaves in a rampage throughout the peninsula, Julius Caesar, the conqueror of Gaul, emerged as leader. When he was assassinated in 44 BC, his rivals fought to gain control. Caesar's nephew Octavian was crowned the first emperor of Rome in 27 BC, assuming the title Augustus.

Augustus reigned for 45 years. With the aid of a professional army and an imperial bureaucracy he established the *Pax Romana* while extending the empire and disseminating its laws and civic culture. Latin developed into an expressive and poetic language that shaped the Romance languages of modern Europe. In 100 BC Rome itself had more than 1·5m. inhabitants. In 14 AD Augustus was succeeded by his stepson, Tiberius, who saw the rise of Christianity. Successive emperors tried to suppress the new religion, which spread quickly throughout the empire. The deranged Emperor Nero, who came to power in 54 AD, persecuted the Christians and was accused of burning Rome. His death in AD 68 ended the Julio-Claudian dynasty.

Elected emperor by the Senate in AD 98, Trajan expanded the empire from the Persian Gulf to Britain, from the Caspian Sea to Morocco and from the Sahara to the Danube. But by the 3rd century AD, Rome was losing control of its empire. After Emperor Constantine converted to Christianity in 313, he established Rome as the headquarters of the Christian religion. Constantine also cultivated the wealthy eastern regions of the Empire and, in 324, he moved his capital to Constantinople (now Istanbul). The Co-emperors Valentinian and Valens divided the empire in 364 for administrative purposes but the west and east gradually became alienated, separated by invaders, language and religious interpretation. 'Rome' endured in the east as the Byzantine Empire, the most powerful medieval state in the Mediterranean.

The western half of the Roman Empire, having embraced Christianity as the state religion, came under repeated pressure from Central European ('Barbarian') tribes. Rome was captured and sacked in 455 by the Vandals and in 476 a Germanic mercenary captain, Odovacar, deposed Romulus Augustus, the last of the emperors in the West. Italy was re-conquered in the 6th century by Emperor Justinian from Constantinople; Byzantium retained parts of southern Italy until the 11th century.

The invasion of Italy by the Lombards in 568 eventually penetrated as far south as Benevento but they were unable to take Rome. The pope invited the Franks under King Pepin to invade, who in 756 overthrew the Lombards and established the Papal States. Pepin's son, Charlemagne, was crowned emperor on Christmas Day 800 by Pope Leo III in Rome. The installation of a 'Roman' emperor in the West—what would become the Holy Roman Empire—furthered the separation between Rome and Byzantium.

After the death of Charlemagne's son, Louis the Pious, the Frankish empire was split in three. Many small independent rival states were established while in Rome the aristocracy fought over the papacy. Meanwhile, southern Italy prospered under Muslim rule. By 831, Muslim Arabs had invaded Sicily and made Palermo their capital. Southern Italy lived under Arab influence for more than 200 years while further north remained unsettled. In 962 Otto I, a Saxon, was crowned Holy Roman Emperor, the first of the German emperors.

At the beginning of the 11th century the Normans arrived in southern Italy, assimilating the culture and coexisting peacefully with the Arabs. Roger II of Sicily left the Hauteville monarchy one of the most powerful in Europe. The delicate relationship between the Holy Roman Empire and the Papacy was endangered by Imperial aspirations in Italy. After Frederick I Barbarossa was crowned Holy Roman Emperor in 1155, he married off his son Henry to the heir to the Norman throne in Sicily. Frederick II, Barbarossa's grandson, came to the throne of Sicily in 1197 and was crowned Holy Roman Emperor in 1220. During this period, some of the northern cities freed themselves from feudal control and set themselves up as autonomous states under the protection of either the pope or the emperor. By the end of the 13th century Venice and Genoa were the dominant maritime powers. Rome had lost her glory and the Papal States began to fall apart. In 1378 the Roman cardinals elected one of their own, Urban VI, as pope. Urban's unpopularity was such that the French cardinals elected their own pope, Clement VII, who set up his rival claim in Avignon. Thus began the Great Schism that separated the papacy from Rome for nearly half a century.

Italy was at the forefront of the Renaissance, a flowering of artistic and intellectual humanist expression. After the Peace of Lodi in 1454, the powerful ruling families such as the Medici in Florence were at leisure to sponsor the Renaissance and Rome became again the centre of Italian political, cultural and intellectual life. This peace was shattered in 1494 by the invasion of Charles VIII, king of France. Encouraged to pursue his claim to the crown of Naples by Ludovico Sforza, duke of Milan, Charles shocked the Italian cities into an alliance to expel his army. The appearance of Spanish power in Naples began the Habsburg-Valois wars that used Italy as a battlefield until the Peace of Cateau-Cambrésis in 1559. These Italian Wars radically altered the political landscape of the peninsula, leaving Spain dominant and nearly destroying the powerful Venetian Republic. The Medici family, having been evicted by Charles VIII, was reinstated by Emperor Charles V, who had sacked Rome in 1527.

In the second half of the 16th century the Church of Rome was obliged to respond to the Protestant Reformation. During the Counter-Reformation, the Inquisition, backed by Catholic Spain, was used to suppress heresy. Spain's hegemony faltered after Charles II (the last of the Spanish Habsburgs) died in 1700. Italy was divided amongst the Austrian Habsburgs, the Spanish Bourbons, Savoy and the independent states.

In 1796 Napoléon Bonaparte invaded Italy and declared an Italian Republic under his personal rule. In creating a single political entity, he laid the basis for modern Italy. The Congress of Vienna, which met after the defeat of Napoléon in 1815, reinstated Italy's former rulers. Secret societies, such as 'Young Italy' led by Giuseppe Mazzini, fought for a new constitution to reunify the country. Giuseppe Garibaldi, whose terrorist activities for Young Italy had obliged him to flee to South America, returned to Italy in 1848. The prime minister of Sardinia-Piedmont, Count Camillo Benso di Cavour, attempted to remove Austria from Italy with French help but it was not until Garibaldi and 1,000 volunteers (the Red Shirts) took Sicily and Naples from the Bourbons in 1860 that unification became a real possibility. Italy was declared a Kingdom in 1861 under the king of Sardinia-Piedmont, Victor Emmanuel II, though Venice was governed by the Habsburgs until 1866 and Rome by the French until 1870. Only the Papal troops resisted the advance of the Italian army in 1870 and Pope Pius IX refused to recognize the Kingdom of Italy. In retaliation, the government stripped the pope of his temporal powers.

When the First World War broke out in 1914, Italy remained neutral. In 1919 Benito Mussolini founded the Italian Fascist Party. He raised a militia of 40,000 'Black Shirts' and marched on Rome in 1922. His Fascist party won the elections of 1924 and Mussolini assumed the title *Il Duce*. In 1929 he signed a pact with Pope Pius XI declaring Catholicism the sole religion of Italy and recognizing the

Vatican as an independent state, in return for papal recognition of the Kingdom of Italy.

In 1935 Italy invaded Abyssinia (Ethiopia). Mussolini and Adolf Hitler's Rome-Berlin Axis took Italy into the Second World War in June 1940. Mussolini's invasion of Greece was a disaster, necessitating the diversion of German troops from the Eastern Front. The Allied armies landed in Sicily in July 1943 and in the face of diminishing support for fascism and Hitler's refusal to assign more troops to the defence of Italy, the king led a coup against Mussolini and had him arrested. In the 45 days that followed, Italy exploded in a series of uprisings against the war. The king signed an armistice with the allies and declared war on Germany but Nazi troops had already overrun northern Italy. The Germans rescued Mussolini from prison and installed him as a puppet ruler. In 1945 Mussolini was recaptured by Italian partisans and shot.

Following the end of the war, Italy became a republic. With more than 300 political factions struggling for power, few governments lasted longer than a year. Despite this instability, the war-damaged Italian economy revived from the early 1950s. The industrialized northern regions thrived while the less industrialized south remained underdeveloped.

In 1957 Italy became a founder member of the European Economic Community (EEC). The rapid growth of the motor industry, most notably Fiat in Turin, saw huge migrations of peasants from the south to work in the factories. By the mid-1960s, the Communist Party had more card-carrying members than the Christian Democrats but was still excluded from government. Social unrest was commonplace and in 1969 a series of strikes, demonstrations and riots followed Europe-wide unrest. Terrorist groups were active including the left-wing Red Brigade. Christian Democrat Aldo Moro, twice prime minister, was held hostage and murdered by the Red Brigade in 1978 while working towards a compromise to allow the Communists to enter government.

The 1990s brought a new wave of political scandals. In 1992 the arrest of a Socialist Party worker on charges of accepting bribes in exchange for public works contracts sparked off Italy's largest ever corruption investigation, implicating thousands of politicians, public officials and businessmen. The old political establishment was driven out of office.

In 1994 a right-wing coalition led by Silvio Berlusconi, a multi-millionaire media tycoon, was elected. Berlusconi lost his majority when the Northern League withdrew after nine months, advocating a 'Northern Republic of Padania', a separation of the rich northern states from the poorer southern ones. The 1996 elections brought to power the centre-left 'Olive Tree' alliance. Prime Minister Romano Prodi balanced the budget with a succession of economic measures in preparation for Italy's entry into EMU. In 2001 Berlusconi formed a new centre-right coalition and introduced the first major constitutional reforms in 55 years, allowing the nation's 20 regions increased responsibility for their own tax, education and environmental programmes.

TERRITORY AND POPULATION

Italy is bounded in the north by Switzerland and Austria, east by Slovenia and the Adriatic Sea, southeast by the Ionian Sea, south by the Mediterranean Sea, southwest by the Tyrrhenian Sea and Ligurian Sea and west by France.

The area is 301,277 sq. km. Populations at successive censuses were as follows:

10 Feb. 1901	33,778	15 Oct. 1961	50,624
10 June 1911	36,921	24 Oct. 1971	54,137
1 Dec. 1921	37,856	25 Oct. 1981	56,557
21 April 1931	41,043	20 Oct. 1991	56,778
21 April 1936	42,399	21 Oct. 2001	56,996
4 Nov. 1951	47,516		

Population estimate, 1 Jan. 2003, 57,321,070 (29,719,809 females). Density: 189 per sq. km.

The UN gives a projected population for 2010 of 56·56m.

In 2001, 67·1% of the population lived in urban areas.

The following table gives area and population of the Autonomous Regions (censuses 1991 and 2001):

Regions	Area in sq. km	Resident pop. census, 1991	Resident pop. census, 2001	Density per sq. km, 2001
Piemonte (Piedmont)	25,399	4,302,565	4,214,677	166
Valle d'Aosta[1]	3,262	115,938	119,548	37
Lombardia (Lombardy)	23,857	8,856,074	9,032,554	379
Trentino-Alto Adige[1]	13,618	890,360	940,016	69
Bolzano-Bozen	7,400	440,508	462,999	63
Trento	6,218	449,852	477,017	77
Veneto	18,364	4,380,797	4,527,694	247
Friuli-Venezia Giulia[1]	7,845	1,197,666	1,183,764	151
Liguria	5,418	1,676,282	1,571,783	290
Emilia Romagna	22,123	3,909,512	3,983,346	180
Toscana (Tuscany)	22,992	3,529,946	3,497,806	152
Umbria	8,456	811,831	825,826	98
Marche	9,693	1,429,205	1,470,581	152
Lazio	17,203	5,140,371	5,112,413	297
Abruzzi	10,794	1,249,054	1,262,392	117
Molise	4,438	330,900	320,601	72
Campania	13,595	5,630,280	5,701,931	419
Puglia	19,348	4,031,885	4,020,707	208
Basilicata	9,992	610,528	597,768	60
Calabria	15,080	2,070,203	2,011,466	133
Sicilica (Sicily)[1]	25,709	4,966,386	4,968,991	193
Sardegna (Sardinia)[1]	24,090	1,648,248	1,631,880	68

[1]With special statute.

Communes of more than 100,000 inhabitants, with population resident at the censuses of 20 Oct. 1991 and 21 Oct. 2001:

	1991	2001		1991	2001
Roma (Rome)	2,775,250	2,733,416	Foggia	156,268	155,203
Milano (Milan)	1,369,231	1,256,211	Salerno	148,932	138,188
Napoli (Naples)	1,067,365	1,004,500	Perugia	144,732	149,125
Torino (Turin)	962,507	865,263	Ferrara	138,015	130,992
Palermo	698,556	686,722	Ravenna	135,844	134,631
Genova (Genoa)	678,771	610,307	Reggio nell'Emilia	132,030	141,877
Bologna	404,376	371,217	Rimini	127,960	128,656
Firenze (Florence)	403,294	356,118	Siracusa (Syracuse)	125,941	123,657
Bari	342,309	316,532	Sassari	122,339	120,729
Catania	333,075	313,110	Pescara	122,236	116,286
Venezia (Venice)	309,422	271,073	Monza	120,651	120,204
Verona	255,824	253,208	Bergamo	114,936	113,143
Taranto	232,334	202,033	Forlì	109,541	108,335
Messina	231,693	252,026	Terni	108,248	105,018
Trieste	213,100	211,184	Vicenza	107,454	107,223
Padova (Padua)	215,137	204,870	Latina	106,203	107,898
Cagliari	204,237	164,249	Piacenza	102,268	95,594
Brescia	194,502	187,567	Trento	101,545	104,946
Reggio di Calabria	177,580	180,353	La Spezia	101,442	91,391
Modena	176,990	175,502	Torre del Greco	101,361	90,607
Parma	170,520	163,457	Ancona	101,285	100,507
Livorno	167,512	156,274	Novara	101,112	100,910
Prato	165,707	172,499	Lecce	100,884	83,303

The official language is Italian, spoken by 94·1% of the population in 1991. There are 0·3m. German-speakers in Bolzano and 30,000 French-speakers in Valle d'Aosta.

In addition to Sicily and Sardinia, there are a number of other Italian islands, the largest being Elba (363 sq. km), and the most distant Lampedusa, which is 205 km from Sicily but only 113 km from Tunisia.

SOCIAL STATISTICS

Vital statistics (and rates per 1,000 population), 2002: births, 535,538 (9·4); deaths, 558,270 (9·8); marriages, 265,635 (4·7). 2000: divorces, 37,573 (0·7). Infant deaths, 2002 (up to one year of age): 2,400 (4·5 per 1,000 live births). Expectation of life, 2001: females, 82·8 years; males, 76·7. At the 2001 population census 18·68% of the population was over 65, the highest percentage of any country in the world.

Annual population growth rate, 1992–2002, 0·1%; fertility rate, 2001, 1·2 births per woman. With only 10·2% of births being to unmarried mothers, Italy has one of the lowest rates of births out of wedlock in Europe.

In 2002 there were 2,947 suicides; 76·6% were men.

In Jan. 2002 there were 1,448,392 legal immigrants living in Italy, up from 1,379,749 a year earlier. In 2000, 56,601 people emigrated from Italy and there were 226,968 immigrants into the country. Italy received 7,281 asylum applications in 2002, equivalent to 0·1 per 1,000 inhabitants. New legislation was introduced in 2002 to tighten up immigration rules.

CLIMATE

The climate varies considerably with latitude. In the south, it is warm temperate, with little rain in the summer months, but the north is cool temperate with rainfall more evenly distributed over the year. Florence, Jan. 47·7°F (8·7°C), July 79·5°F (26·4°C). Annual rainfall 33" (842 mm). Milan, Jan. 38·7°F (3·7°C), July 73·4°F (23·0°C). Annual rainfall 38" (984 mm). Naples, Jan. 50·2°F (10·1°C), July 77·4°F (25·2°C). Annual rainfall 36" (935 mm). Palermo, Jan. 52·5°F (11·4°C), July 78·4°F (25·8°C). Annual rainfall 35" (897 mm). Rome, Jan. 53·4°F (11·9°C), July 76·3°F (24·6°C). Annual rainfall 31" (793 mm). Venice, Jan. 43·3°F (6·3°C), July 70·9°F (21·6°C). Annual rainfall 32" (830 mm).

CONSTITUTION AND GOVERNMENT

The Constitution dates from 1948. Italy is 'a democratic republic founded on work'. Parliament consists of the *Chamber of Deputies* and the *Senate.* The Chamber is elected for five years by universal and direct suffrage and consists of 630 deputies. The Senate is elected for five years on a regional basis by electors over the age of 25, each Region having at least seven senators. The total number of senators is 315. The Valle d'Aosta is represented by one senator only, the Molise by two. The President of the Republic can nominate 11 senators for life from eminent persons in the social, scientific, artistic and literary spheres. The President may become a senator for life. The *President* is elected in a joint session of Chamber and Senate, to which are added three delegates from each Regional Council (one from the Valle d'Aosta). A two-thirds majority is required for the election, but after a third indecisive scrutiny the absolute majority of votes is sufficient. The President must be 50 years or over; term of office, seven years. The Speaker of the Senate acts as the deputy President. The President can dissolve the chambers of parliament, except during the last six months of the presidential term. An attempt to create a new constitution, which had been under consideration for 18 months, collapsed in June 1998.

A *Constitutional Court*, consisting of 15 judges who are appointed, five each by the President, Parliament (in joint session) and the highest law and administrative courts, can decide on the constitutionality of laws and decrees, define the powers of the State and Regions, judge conflicts between the State and Regions and between the Regions, and try the President and Ministers.

The revival of the Fascist Party is forbidden. Direct male descendants of King Victor Emmanuel are excluded from all public offices and have no right to vote or to be elected; their estates are forfeit to the State. For 56 years they were also banned from Italian territory until the constitution was changed in 2002 to allow them to return from exile. Titles of nobility are no longer recognized, but those existing before 28 Oct. 1922 are retained as part of the name.

A referendum was held in June 1991 to decide whether the system of preferential voting by indicating four candidates by their listed number should be changed to a simpler system, less open to abuse, of indicating a single candidate by name. The electorate was 46m. Turn-out was 62·5% (there was a 50% quorum). 95·6% of votes cast were in favour of the change. As a result, an electoral reform of 1993 provides for the replacement of proportional representation by a system in which 475 seats in the Chamber of Deputies are elected by a first-past-the-post single-round vote and 155 seats by proportional representation in a separate single-round vote on the same day. There are 27 electoral regions. There is a 4% threshold for entry to the Chamber of Deputies.

At a further referendum in April 1993, turn-out was 77%. Voters favoured the eight reforms proposed, including a new system of election to the Senate and the abolition of some ministries. 75% of the Senate is now elected by a first-past-the-post system, the remainder by proportional representation; no party may present more than one candidate in each constituency. In July 1997 an all-party parliamentary commission on constitutional reform proposed a directly elected president with responsibility for defence and foreign policy, the devolving of powers to the regions, a reduction in the number of seats in the Senate and in the lower house and the creation of a third chamber to speak on behalf of the regions.

National Anthem. 'Fratelli d'Italia' ('Brothers of Italy'); words by G. Mameli, tune by M. Novaro, 1847.

RECENT ELECTIONS

Parliamentary elections were held on 13 May 2001. The turn-out was 81·4%. The House of Freedoms Alliance (comprised of Forza Italia, the National Alliance and the Northern League) won 368 seats in the Chamber of Deputies and 177 in the Senate, the Olive Tree Alliance (Ulivo; comprised of the Democrats of the Left (DS), La Margherita coalition and the Sunflower coalition) 242 and 125, the New Communist Foundation (RC) 11 and 3. Minor parties won nine seats in the Chamber of Deputies and ten in the Senate. Forza Italia—the leading party of the House of Freedoms Alliance—received the highest percentage of votes of any of the parties contesting the election, with 30%.

European Parliament. Italy has 78 (87 in 1999) representatives. At the June 2004 elections turn-out was 73·1% (70·6% in 1999). Ulivo won 25 seats—the DS, 12 (political affiliation in European Parliament: Party of European Socialists), La Margherita, 7 (Alliance of Liberals and Democrats for Europe), Social Democrats, 2 (Party of European Socialists), the European Republican Movement, 1 (Alliance of Liberals and Democrats for Europe), South Tyrolean People's Party, 1 (European People's Party–European Democrats), ind. 2 (Party of European Socialists)—with 31·1% of votes cast; Forza Italia gained 16 seats with 21·0% of votes cast (European People's Party–European Democrats); the National Alliance, 9 with 11·5% (Union for a Europe of Nations); the RC, 5 with 6·1% (European Unitary Left/Nordic Green Left); the Union of Christian and Centre Democrats, 5 with 5·9% (European People's Party–European Democrats); the Northern League, 4 with 5·0% (Independence and Democracy Group); Federation of Greens, 2 with 2·5% (Greens/European Free Alliance); Italian Communist Party, 2 with 2·4% (European Unitary Left/Nordic Green Left); Lista Bonino (Radicals), 2 with 2·3% (Alliance of Liberals and Democrats for Europe); Società Civile di Pietro, 2 with 2·1% (Alliance of Liberals and Democrats for Europe); United Socialists for Europe, 2 with 2·0% (non-attached); Alleanza Populare Udeur, 1 with 1·3% (European People's Party–European Democrats); Alternativa Sociale-Alessandra Mussolini, 1 with 1·2% (non-attached); the Pensioners Party, 1 with 1·1% (European People's Party–European Democrats); Social Movement Fiamma Tricolore, 1 with 0·7% (non-attached).

CURRENT ADMINISTRATION

President: Carlo Azeglio Ciampi; b. 1920 (elected on 13 May 1999; sworn in on 18 May).

In May 2005 the government comprised (FI = Forza Italia; AN = National Alliance; LN = The Northern League; UDC = Union of Christian and Centre Democrats; Nuovo PSI = Socialist Party; PRI = Italian Republican Party):

Prime Minister: Silvio Berlusconi; b. 1936 (FI; sworn in on 11 June 2001 having previously held office from 11 May 1994–17 Jan. 1995).

First Deputy Prime Minister and Minister of Foreign Affairs: Gianfranco Fini (AN). *Second Deputy Prime Minister:* Marco Giulio Tremonti (FI).

Minister of Interior: Giuseppe Pisanu (FI). *Justice:* Roberto Castelli (LN). *Finance and Economic Affairs:* Domenico Siniscalco (ind.). *Industry and Commerce:* Claudio Scajola (FI). *Education, University and Scientific Research:* Letizia Moratti (ind.). *Labour and Social Affairs:* Roberto Maroni (LN). *Defence:* Antonio Martino (FI). *Agriculture and Forestry:* Giovanni Alemanno (AN). *Environment:* Altero Matteoli (AN). *Transport:* Pietro Lunardi (ind.). *Health:* Francesco Storace (AN). *Culture:* Rocco Buttiglione (UDC). *Communications:* Mario Landolfi (AN). *Regional Affairs:* Enrico La Loggia (FI). *European Affairs:* Giorgio La Malfa (PRI). *Public Administration and Security:* Mario Baccini (UDC). *Implementation of Government Activities:* Stefano Caldoro (Nuovo PSI). *Equal*

Opportunities: Stefania Prestigiacomo (FI). *Relations with Parliament:* Carlo Giovanardi (UDC). *Innovation and Technology:* Lucio Stanca (ind.). *Institutional Reform and Devolution:* Roberto Calderoli (LN). *Development and Territorial Cohesion:* Gianfranco Micciché (FI). *Italians Abroad:* Mirko Tremaglia (AN).

Government Website: http://www.governo.it

DEFENCE

Head of the armed forces is the Defence Chief of Staff. There is conscription for ten months, but the military draft is to be phased out by 2006. In Aug. 1998 the government voted to allow women into the armed forces.

In 2003 defence expenditure totalled US$27,751m. (US$481 per capita), representing 1·9% of GDP.

Army. Strength (2002) 128,600 (57,000 conscripts). Equipment includes 440 *Leopard,* 378 *Centauro* and 200 *Ariete* tanks. First line Army reserves number 11,900 with a further 500,000 personnel available for mobilization.

The paramilitary Carabinieri number 111,800. In addition there were 79,000 public security guards run by the Ministry of the Interior and 63,500 Finance Guards run by the Treasury.

Navy. The principal ships of the Navy are the light aircraft carrier *Giuseppe Garibaldi* and the helicopter-carrying cruiser *Vittorio Veneto*. The combatant forces also include six diesel submarines, four destroyers and 14 frigates. The Naval Air Arm, 2,500 strong, operates 18 combat aircraft and 79 armed helicopters. In addition there is a Special Forces commando of some 600 assault swimmers.

Main naval bases are at La Spezia, Brindisi, Taranto and Augusta. The personnel of the Navy in 2002 numbered 38,000 (5,000 conscripts), including the naval air arm and the marine battalion. There were 23,000 naval reservists.

Air Force. Control is exercised through two regional headquarters near Taranto and Milan.

Air Force strength in 2002 was about 50,800 (8,200 conscripts). There were 261 combat aircraft in operation in 2000 including Tornados and F-104 Starfighters. There were 30,300 Air Force reservists in 2002.

INTERNATIONAL RELATIONS

Italy is a member of the UN, WTO, NATO, BIS, OECD, EU, Council of Europe, WEU, OSCE, CERN, CEI, Inter-American Development Bank, Asian Development Bank, IOM and the Antarctic Treaty. Italy is a signatory to the Schengen Accord of June 1990 which abolishes border controls between Italy, Austria, Belgium, Denmark, Finland, France, Germany, Greece, Iceland, Luxembourg, the Netherlands, Norway, Portugal, Spain and Sweden. On 6 April 2005 Italy ratified the new EU constitution. The Senate approved the treaty by 217 votes to 16; it had already been approved by the Chamber of Deputies in Jan. 2005.

ECONOMY

Agriculture accounted for 2·6% of GDP, industry 27·3% and services 70·1% in 2002.

Overview. Italy ranks among the world's top ten economies. In recent years Italy has suffered from slow growth and fiscal concerns, with average growth of 1% per annum over the last decade. After labour market reforms in the 1990s, employment has been strong and consumption has remained buoyant. However, Italy still suffers from structural weaknesses, such as a large public debt, regional imbalances, higher than euro-area average inflation, low productivity growth, low employment rates and low levels of FDI. Labour reforms have secured increases in hours worked but total factor productivity has remained low. The export sector has suffered more from the appreciation of the euro than that of other euro area countries. At over 100% of GDP, the public debt ratio is one of the highest in the world, tax and spending ratios are high and age-related spending will increase significantly in the future. The EU Stability and Growth Pact requires the debt ratio to be reduced to 60% and the budget to be balanced by 2006, which puts greater pressure on Italy's fiscal policy than on other EU members. New legislation to limit spending has been introduced but policy implementation has fallen short of targets in recent years and a significant decline in the debt ratio requires additional structural measures. The IMF believes that population ageing will increase annual pension spending by approximately 2% of GDP over coming years, and annual health spending will rise by 3% per year. Pension reform in 2004 increased the effective retirement age starting in 2008; the IMF considers this reform to be a significant but insufficient step towards addressing these problems.

Currency. On 1 Jan. 1999 the euro (EUR) became the legal currency in Italy; irrevocable conversion rate 1,936·27 lire to 1 euro. The euro, which consists of 100 cents, has been in circulation since 1 Jan. 2002. There are seven euro notes in different colours and sizes denominated in 500, 200, 100, 50, 20, 10 and 5 euros, and eight coins denominated in 2 and 1 euros, then 50, 20, 10, 5, 2 and 1 cents. On the introduction of the euro there was a 'dual circulation' period before the lira ceased to be legal tender on 28 Feb. 2002. Euro banknotes in circulation on 1 Jan. 2002 had a total value of €97·4bn.

Inflation was 2·2% in 2004, the lowest rate in five years. In June 2002 gold reserves were 78·83m. troy oz and foreign exchange reserves US$20,533m. (US$45,307m. in Dec. 1999). Total money supply in June 2002 was €54,958m.

Budget. In 2000 revenues totalled €444·50bn. (€441·16bn. in 1999) and expenditures €462·35bn. (€454·00bn. in 1999). Principal sources of revenue in 2000: taxes on income, profits and capital gains, €153·60bn.; social security contributions, €144·47bn.; taxes on goods and services, €103·64bn. Main items of expenditure by economic type in 2000: social benefits, €193·61bn.; interest, €73·77bn.; compensation of employees, €72·29bn.

VAT is 20% (reduced rates, 10% and 4%).

The public debt at 31 Dec. 2002 totalled €1,220,956m. Between 1992 and 2002 the public deficit came down from more than 10% to 2·4%, or possibly less, of gross domestic product. Interest rates have also declined significantly.

Performance. Total GDP was US$1,466bn. in 2003. There was real GDP growth of 1·1% in 2004, up from 0·4% in 2003.

According to the Aug. 2003 *OECD Economic Survey*, 'Italy's key challenges are to raise the potential rate of growth and increase resilience to future shocks, to address the issue of competitiveness by closing the inflation gap with the euro-area, and to safeguard the sustainability of public finances while also continuing to provide appropriate fiscal support to the growth process.'

Banking and Finance. The bank of issue is the Bank of Italy (founded 1893). It is owned by public-sector banks. Its *Governor* (Antonio Fazio) is selected without fixed term by the 13 directors of the Bank's non-executive board. In 1991 it received increased responsibility for the supervision of banking and stock exchange affairs, and in 1993 greater independence from the government. Its gold reserve amounted to 40,929bn. lire in Dec. 1998; the foreign credit reserves of the Exchange Bureau (*Ufficio Italiano Cambi*) amounted to 88,611bn. lire.

The number of banks has gradually been declining in recent years, from 1,176 in 1990 to 862 in 2000. Of the 921 banks in 1998, 562 were co-operative banks. Italy's largest bank is Banca Intesa, following its merger with Banca Commerciale Italiana in 1999. In June 2000 it had assets of 643,000bn. lire. Other major banks are San Paolo-IMI and UniCredito Italiano.

The 'Amato' law of July 1990 gave public sector banks the right to become joint stock companies and permitted the placing of up to 49% of their equity with private shareholders. In 1999 the last state-controlled bank was sold off.

On 31 Dec. 2000 the post office savings banks had deposits of 270,011bn. lire. In the same year credit institutions had deposits of 1,005,484bn. lire.

Legislation reforming stock markets came into effect in Dec. 1990. In 1996 local stock exchanges, relics of pre-unification Italy, were closed, and stock exchange activities concentrated in Milan.

ENERGY AND NATURAL RESOURCES

Environment. Italy's carbon dioxide emissions from the consumption and flaring of fossil fuels in 2002 were the equivalent of 7·8 tonnes per capita.

Electricity. In 2001 installed capacity was 78,787 MW and the total power generated was 279·0bn. kWh (19·3% hydro-electric). Consumption in 2001 was

285·5bn. kWh, of which: industry, 151·0bn. kWh; services, 67·8bn. kWh; domestic use, 61·5bn. kWh; agriculture, 5·2bn. kWh. Consumption per capita was 5,554 kWh in 2000. Italy has four nuclear reactors in permanent shutdown, the last having closed in 1990.

Oil and Gas. Oil production, 2002, 5,394,197 tonnes. Proven oil reserves in 2002 were 0·6bn. bbls. In 2002 natural gas production was 15·1bn. cu. metres with proven reserves of 230bn. cu. metres.

Minerals. Fuel and mineral resources fail to meet needs. Only sulphur and mercury yield a substantial surplus for exports.

Production of metals and minerals (in tonnes) was as follows:

	1998	*1999*	*2000*	*2001*	*2002*
Sulphur	3,413,522	3,338,162	3,339,761	—	—
Feldspar	2,503,541	2,493,846	2,851,289	3,240,457	3,159,569
Bentonite	580,209	562,674	636,589	579,029	463,231
Lead	10,102	9,734	5,961	4,016	4,709
Zinc	5,242	—	—	—	—

Agriculture. In 2000, 1,120,000 persons were employed in agriculture, of whom 451,000 were dependent (148,000 female); independently employed were 669,000 (203,000 female). At the fifth agricultural census, held on 22 Oct. 2000, there were 13,212,652 sq. km of agricultural and forest lands, distributed as follows (in 1,000 ha): woods, 4,711; cereals, 4,052; forage and pasture, 3,414; olive trees, 1,081; vines, 676; leguminous plants, 66. In 2001 there were 8·17m. ha of arable land and 2·80m. ha of permanent crops.

At the 2000 census agricultural holdings numbered 2,593,090 and covered 19,607,094 ha. 2,457,960 owners (95·7%) farmed directly 13,868,478 ha (70·3%); 132,935 owners (3·9%) worked with hired labour on 5,706,993 ha (29·1%); the remaining 2,195 holdings (0·4%) of 31,623 ha (0·6%) were operated in other ways. 97,307 share-croppers tilled 1,445,826 ha. Only 13,212,652 sq. km was in active agricultural use.

Agriculture and fishing accounted for 1·5% of exports and 3·4% of imports in 2001.

Figures compiled by the Soil Association, a British organization, show that in 1999 Italy set aside 900,000 ha (5·3% of its agricultural land) for the growth of organic crops.

In 2001, 1,650,000 tractors were in use and 51,000 harvester-threshers.

Output of principal crops (in 1,000 tonnes) in 2002: sugarbeets, 12,726; maize, 10,824; wheat, 7,444; grapes, 7,394; tomatoes, 5,748; olives, 3,079; apples, 2,203; potatoes, 1,961; oranges, 1,687; peaches and nectarines, 1,587; rice, 1,371; barley, 1,177; pears, 924; soybeans, 566; lemons, 501.

Wine production in 2001 totalled 56,005,000 hectolitres. Italy is the second-largest wine producer in the world after France. In 2002 Italy was the leading producer of grapes, but France produced more wine. Wine consumption in Italy has declined dramatically in recent times, from more than 110 litres per person in 1966 to 52·9 litres per person in 2001.

Livestock, 2001: cattle, 6,232,000; sheep and goats, 12,279,000; pigs, 8,766,000; horses, 280,000; buffaloes, 173,000; chickens, 100m.; turkeys, 23m. Livestock products, 2000 (in 1,000 tonnes): cow milk, 11,741; sheep milk, 850; buffalo milk, 158; goat milk, 140; pork, bacon and ham, 1,475; beef and veal, 1,160; poultry meat, 1,140; cheese, 1,011; butter, 101; eggs, 768. Italy is the second largest producer of sheep milk, after China.

Forestry. In 2001 forests covered 6·85m. ha or 22·7% of the total land area. Timber production was 7·45m. cu. metres in 2001.

Fisheries. The fishing fleet comprised, in 2002, 16,045 motor boats of 215,247 gross tonnes. The catch in 2001 was 310,397 tonnes, of which more than 98% were from marine waters.

INDUSTRY

The leading companies by market capitalization in Italy, excluding banking and finance, in May 2004 were: Ente Nazionale Idrocarburi (ENI), an integrated oil company (US$82·1bn.); Enel, an energy service provider (US$49·6bn.); and Telecom Italia Mobile (US$46·5bn.).

The value added at factor cost in 2001 was €1,098,992m. The percentage of industrial value at factor cost by activity sector was: agriculture, forestry and fishing: 2·93%; construction: 4·92%; financial activity, currency and real activities: 26·13%; strictly industry: 22·74%; trade, transport, hotels and restaurants: 24·21%; other services: 19·07%. Main strictly industry items (% of overall total) in 2001 were: metal production and metallic products: 2·69%; machines and mechanical apparatus: 2·50%; textiles and clothing: 2·40%; electric energy—production and distribution: 2·20%; food, beverages and tobacco: 2·10%; electric machines, electric apparatus and optical instruments: 1·74%; chemicals and synthetic fibres: 1·70%.

Production, 2001: cement, 38,965,000 tonnes; crude steel (2002), 26,100,000 tonnes; polyethylene resins, 1,100,114 tonnes; artificial and synthetic fibres (including staple fibre and waste), 627,482 tonnes; motor vehicles, 1,272,000 units; TV sets, 1,208,000 units.

Labour. In 2003 the workforce was 24,150,000 (69·3% males and 42·7% females) of whom 21,829,000 were employed. 2,096,000 were unemployed and looking for work. The unemployment rate over the past four years has been regularly declining; in 2003 it was 8·6%, down from 10·8% in 2000. By June 2004 it had declined further, to 7·7%. In 2002, 63·2% of the workforce were in services, 31·8% in industry and 5·0% in agriculture. There are strong indications of labour markets having become less rigid, especially in the north. In the north-east unemployment was 3·3% in 2003, in the north-west 4·4% and in the centre 6·6%; in the south it was 18·3%. In 1996 the difference in the unemployment rates in the north and in the south was 12%, compared to a difference of just 2% in the 1960s. Nearly 60% of Italy's jobless have been out of work for more than a year, the highest rate in any industrialized country. Pensionable retirement age was 60 for men and 55 for women in 1991, but this is being progressively raised to 65 for both sexes. In 2002 the rate of employment among people aged 55–64 was just 4·1%.

In 1997 parliament approved the so-called 'Treu Package', which involves a large number of institutional changes regarding working hours and apprenticeships, mainly for young people from the south, and the introduction of employment agencies. As a consequence, the share of temporary workers over total employees had grown from 6·2% in 1993 to 9·9% in 2002.

Trade Unions. There are three main groups: the Confederazione Generale Italiana del Lavoro (CGIL; formerly Communist-dominated), the Confederazione Italiana Sindacati Lavoratori (CISL; Catholic) and the Unione Italiana del Lavoro (UIL). Membership: CGIL (1996), 5·2m. (2·9m. retired); CISL (1999), 4·0m. (2·0m. retired); UIL (1996), 1·6m. (0·4m. retired). In referendums held in June 1995 the electorate voted to remove some restrictions on trade union representation, end government involvement in public sector trade unions and end the automatic deduction of trade union dues from wage packets.

INTERNATIONAL TRADE

Imports and Exports. The territory covered by foreign trade statistics includes Italy and the Municipality of Livigno; Campione; San Marino and the Vatican City are excluded.

The following table shows the value of Italy's foreign trade (in US$1bn.):

	1998	*1999*	*2000*	*2001*	*2002*
Imports	206·9	212·4	230·9	229·4	237·2
Exports	242·6	235·9	240·5	244·9	253·7

Percentage of trade with EU countries in 2002: imports, 72·5%; exports, 69·2%. Principal import suppliers, 2002 (% of total trade): Germany, 17·76%; France, 11·28%; UK, 4·94%; USA, 4·87%. Principal export markets: Germany, 13·68%; France, 12·16%; USA, 9·74%; UK, 6·90%.

Imports/exports by category, 2001 (% volume):

	Imports	*Exports*
Chemicals and artificial fibres	12·9	9·5
Electric and precision instruments	14·1	10·1
Food, beverages and tobacco	6·9	5·1
Leather and leather products	2·5	5·4
Machinery and mechanical equipment	7·9	19·8
Metals and metal products	9·8	8·0

	Imports	Exports
Minerals	10·2	0·0
Textiles and clothing	5·3	10·6
Transport equipment	14·3	10·9
Other products	16·1	19·8

COMMUNICATIONS

Roads. Roads totalled 479,688 km in 1999, of which 6,621 km were motorways, 46,009 km were highways and main roads, 114,909 km were secondary roads and 312,149 km other roads. In 2001 there were 40,743,777 motor vehicles, including: passenger cars, 33,239,029 (563 per 1,000 inhabitants); buses and coaches, 89,858; vans and trucks, 3,541,545. There were 6,682 fatalities in road accidents in 2001.

Rail. The length of state-run railway (*Ferrovie dello Stato*) in 2002 was 15,985 km (10,891 km electrified). In 2001 the state railways carried 491·8m. passengers and 83·2m. tonnes of freight. There are metros in Naples (79 km), Milan (68 km), Rome (33·5 km), Genoa (5·0 km) and Catania (3·8 km), and tram/light rail networks in Genoa, Milan (240 km), Naples, Trieste and Turin (119 km).

Civil Aviation. There are major international airports at Bologna (G. Marconi), Genoa (Cristoforo Colombo), Milan (Linate and Malpensa), Naples (Capodichino), Pisa (Galileo Galilei), Rome (Leonardo da Vinci/Fiumicino), Turin (Caselle) and Venice (Marco Polo). A number of other airports have a small selection of international flights. The national carrier, Alitalia, is 62% owned by the state. As a response to severe economic struggles, the company announced plans in 2004 to split into two and reduce the workforce by 2,700. As part of this restructuring, Alitalia received €400m. from the government. In Jan. 2005 the EU Commission launched an investigation into complaints that the finance constituted illegal state aid. In 1997 it flew 297·2m. km and carried 24,551,600 passengers. There are a number of other Italian airlines, most notably Meridiana, which flew 24·4m. km and carried 2,935,400 passengers in 1998. The busiest airport for passenger traffic is Rome (Fiumicino), which in 2001 handled 24,331,558 passengers (12,244,136 on international flights), plus 381,956 passengers in transit and 169,648 tonnes of freight. Milan Malpensa was the second busiest for passengers, handling 18,457,037 (14,169,573 on international flights), plus 109,652 passengers in transit, but the busiest for freight, with 289,382 tonnes. Linate, which handled 7,131,604 passengers in 2001 (4,995,000 on domestic flights), plus 738 passengers in transit, had been the principal Milan airport and for many years Italy's second busiest for passenger traffic, but in 1998 a new terminal was opened at Malpensa with many foreign operators subsequently using it instead of Linate.

Shipping. The mercantile marine in 2000 totalled 9·60m. GRT, including oil tankers 1·10m. GRT. In 2000 vessels totalling 211,242,000 NRT entered ports and vessels totalling 137,864,000 NRT cleared. 2,039,697 passengers embarked and 2,185,645 departed in 1995. The chief ports are Genoa (51,748,000 tonnes of cargo handled in 2002), Trieste, Venice, Livorno, Gioia Tauro and Ravenna.

Telecommunications. There were 79,767,900 telephone subscribers in 2002, or 1,412·7 per 1,000 persons. In May 1999 Olivetti bought a controlling stake in the telephone operator Telecom Italia, and in July 2001 Pirelli, backed by the Benetton clothing empire, in turn paid €7bn. (US$6·1bn.) to take over control of Telecom Italia. In 2002 mobile phone subscribers numbered 53,003,000, equivalent to 938·7 per 1,000 population (among the highest penetration rates in the world). TIM (Telecom Italia Mobile) is the largest operator, with a 45% share of the market, ahead of Omnitel, which has a 35% share. There were 13·0m. PCs in use (230·7 per 1,000 persons) in 2002 and 1·8m. fax machines in 1999. There were 19·9m. Internet users in 2002.

Postal Services. In 1997 there were 13,967 post offices, or one for every 4,120 persons.

SOCIAL INSTITUTIONS

Justice. Italy has one court of cassation, in Rome, and is divided for the administration of justice into 29 appeal court districts, subdivided into 164 tribunal *circondari* (districts). There are also 93 first degree assize courts and 29 assize courts of appeal. For civil business, besides the magistracy above mentioned, *Giudici di pace* have jurisdiction in petty plaints.

2,231,550 crimes were reported in 2002; 768,771 persons were indicted in 2002. On 31 Dec. 2002 there were 55,670 persons in prison (2,469 females). There were 16,788 foreigners in prison (1,008 females). In 1947 the re-established democracy rewrote the Legislative Order; the constitution of the Italian Republic abolished the death penalty sanctioned in 1930 by Codice Penale, commonly known as Codice Rocco. Although the death penalty was abolished for ordinary crimes in 1947, it was not until 1994 that it was abolished for all crimes.

Religion. The treaty between the Holy See and Italy of 11 Feb. 1929, confirmed by article 7 of the Constitution of the republic, lays down that the Catholic Apostolic Roman Religion is the only religion of the State. Other creeds are permitted, provided they do not profess principles, or follow rites, contrary to public order or moral behaviour.

The appointment of archbishops and of bishops is made by the Holy See; but the Holy See submits to the Italian government the name of the person to be appointed in order to obtain an assurance that the latter will not raise objections of a political nature. In March 2004 there were 39 cardinals.

Catholic religious teaching is given in elementary and intermediate schools. Marriages celebrated before a Catholic priest are automatically transferred to the civil register. Marriages celebrated by clergy of other denominations must be made valid before a registrar.

There were 46,260,000 Roman Catholics in 2001, 680,000 Muslims, 1,350,000 adherents of other religions and 9,600,000 non-religious and atheists.

Education. Five years of primary and three years of secondary education are compulsory from the age of six. In 2000–01 there were 25,044 pre-school institutions with 1,576,562 pupils and 128,972 teachers (state and non-state schools); 18,854 primary schools with 2,810,337 pupils and 287,344 teachers (state and non-state schools); 7,908 compulsory secondary schools (*scuole medie*) with 1,776,889 pupils and 209,971 teachers (state and non-state schools); and 6,624 higher secondary schools with 2,570,509 pupils and 307,279 teachers (state and non-state schools).

Higher secondary education is subdivided into classical (*ginnasio* and classical *liceo*), scientific (scientific *liceo*), language lyceum, professional institutes and technical education: agricultural, industrial, commercial, technical, nautical institutes, institutes for surveyors, institutes for girls (five-year course) and teacher-training institutes (four-year course).

In 2001–02 there were 59 universities, of which two are universities of Italian studies for foreigners, three specialized universities (commerce; education; Roman Catholic), three polytechnical university institutes and six Free Universities; seven specialized university institutes (architecture; bio-medicine; modern languages; naval studies; oriental studies; social studies; teacher training). In 2001–02 there were 1,702,575 university students and 56,060 academic staff.

Adult literacy rate, 2001, 98·5% (male 98·9%; female 98·1%).

In 2000–01 total expenditure on education came to 4·7% of GNP and in 1999–2000 accounted for 9·5% of total government spending.

Health. The provision of health services is a regional responsibility, but they are funded by central government. Medical consultations are free, but a portion of prescription costs are payable. In 2000 the National Health Service included 1,425 hospitals of which 785 were public with 212,165 beds and 640 private hospitals with 56,359 beds. In 2000 there were 112,332 doctors and 273,520 auxiliary medical personnel. A survey published by the World Health Organization in June 2000 to measure health systems in all of the sovereign countries and find which country has the best overall health care ranked Italy in second place, behind France. In 2002 Italy spent 8·5% of its GDP on health.

Welfare. Social expenditure is made up of transfers which the central public departments, local departments and social security departments make to families. Payment is principally for pensions, family allowances and health services.

Expenditure on subsidies, public assistance to various classes of people and people injured by political events or national disasters are also included.

In 2001 Italians received a state pension at 56 or after 35 years of work, whichever comes first. However, this is gradually being scaled up, to 62 years of age or 37 years in work by 2006. Public pensions are indexed to prices; 22,210,241 pensions were paid in 2001, with payments totalling €170,779·0m. (including 16,910,061 private sector, with payments totalling €130,169·7m.). Current social security expenditure in 2001 was €381m. Social contributions totalled €154,731m.

CULTURE

World Heritage Sites. Italy has 39 sites that have been included on UNESCO's World Heritage List. They are listed here in the order in which they were designated world heritage sites: the Rock Drawings in Valcamonica near Brescia (1979); Santa Maria delle Grazie with 'The Last Supper' by Leonardo da Vinci (1980); the Historic Centre of Rome, the properties of the Holy See in that city enjoying extraterritorial rights (1980); San Paolo Fuori le Mura Historic Centre of Florence (1982); Venice and its Lagoon (1987); Piazza del Duomo, Pisa (1987); Historic Centre of San Gimignano (1990); I Sassi di Matera (1993); Vicenza, the City of Palladio and the Villas of the Veneto (1994); Historic Center of Siena (1995); Historic Center of Naples (1995); Ferrara (1995); Crespi d'Adda (1995); Castel del Monte (1996); Trulli of Alberobello (1996); Early Christian Monuments and Mosaics of Ravenna (1996); Historic Centre of the City of Pienza (1996); The 18th-Century Royal Palace at Caserta with the Park, the Aqueduct of Vanvitelli and the San Leucio Complex (1997); Residences of the Royal House of Savoy (1997); Botanical Garden (Orto Botanico), Padua (1997); Cathedral, Torre Civica and Piazza Grande, Modena (1997); Archaeological Areas of Pompeii, Ercolano and Torre Annunziata (1997); Villa Romana del Casale (1997); Su Nuraxi di Barumini (1997); Portovenere, Cinque Terre and the Islands (Palmaria, Tino and Tinetto) (1997); The Costiera Amalfitana (1997); Archaeological Area of Agrigento (1997); Cilento and Vallo di Diano National Park (1998); Historic Centre of Urbino (1998); Archaeological Area and the Patriarchal Basilica of Aquileia (1998); Villa Adriana (1999); Aeolian Islands (2000); Assisi (2000); the City of Verona (2000); Villa d'Este, Tivoli (2001); the Late Baroque Towns of the Val di Noto (2002); and Sacri Monti of Piedmont and Lombardy (2003); Val d'Orcia (2004), part of the agricultural hinterland of Siena; and the Etruscan Necropolises of Cerveteri and Tarquinia (2004).

Broadcasting. Broadcasting is regulated by the Public Radio-Television Administration Council.

Questions have been raised over the impartiality of state-owned *Radiotelevisione Italiana* (RAI) but all attempts at privatization have been rejected. RAI, the public television company, broadcasts three public channels, RAI 1, RAI 2 and RAI 3. Mediaset, a private company controlled by Fininvest, produces three commercial channels: Canale 5, Italia 1 and Rete 4. RAI 1 has the highest viewing figures, followed by Canale 5, RAI 2 and Italia 1. There are 15 national and about 820 local private TV networks. There were 50·0m. radio receivers and 28·3m. TV sets (colour by PAL) in 2000. In 2002, 16,216,006 television licences were bought.

Cinema. In 2001 there were 2,243 cinemas and 3,198 screens, and 110m. admissions. In 2001 gross box office receipts came to €589m. and 103 full-length films were made.

Press. There were (1998) 126 dailies and 543 weeklies. Several of the papers are owned or supported by political parties. The church and various economic groups exert strong right of centre influence on editorial opinion. Most newspapers are regional but *Corriere della Sera* (which has the highest circulation of any Italian newspaper), *La Repubblica*, *La Stampa* and *Il Giorno* are the most important of those papers that are nationally circulated. In 2001 a total of 53,131 book titles were published in 275m. copies.

Tourism. In 2002, 36,355,046 foreigners visited Italy; receipts from tourism in 2000 were US$27·44bn.

Festivals. One of the most traditional festivals in Italy is the Carnival di Ivrea which lasts for a week in late Feb. or early March. Among the famous arts festivals is the

Venice Film Festival in Sept. Venice also plays host, in the ten days before Ash Wednesday, to a large carnival. Major music festivals are the Maggio Musicale Fiorentino in Florence (May–June), the Ravenna Festival (June–July), the Spoleto Festival (June–July), the Rossini Opera Festival at Pesaro (Aug.) and the Verona Summer Opera Festival (July–Sept.).

Libraries. In 2002 there were 12,614 public libraries, four National libraries and 1,924 Higher Education libraries; they held a combined 93,629,000 volumes. There were 274,425,000 visits to the public libraries in 1997.

Museums and Galleries. In 2002 there were 192 museums and galleries and 198 archeological sites. There were 31,041,436 visitors, up from 29,543,020 in 2001.

DIPLOMATIC REPRESENTATIVES

Of Italy in the United Kingdom (14 Three Kings Yard, Davies Street, London, W1K 4EH)
Ambassador: Giancarlo Aragona.

Of the United Kingdom in Italy (Via XX Settembre 80A, 00187, Rome)
Ambassador: Sir Ivor Roberts, KCMG.

Of Italy in the USA (3000 Whitehaven Street, NW, Washington, D.C., 20008)
Ambassador: Sergio Vento.

Of the USA in Italy (Via Veneto 119/A, Rome)
Ambassador: Melvin F. Sembler.

Of Italy to the United Nations
Ambassador: Marcello Spatafora.

FURTHER READING

Istituto Nazionale di Statistica. *Annuario Statistico Italiano.—Compendio Statistico Italiano* (Annual).—*Italian Statistical Abstract* (Annual).—*Bollettino Mensile di Statistica* (Monthly).

Absalom, R., *Italy since 1880: a Nation in the Balance?* Harlow, 1995
Baldassarri, M. (ed.) *The Italian Economy: Heaven or Hell?* London, 1993
Bufacchi, Vittorio and Burgess, Simon, *Italy since 1989*. Macmillan, London, 1999
Burnett, Stanton H. and Mantovani, Luca, *The Italian Guillotine: Operation 'Clean Hands' and the Overthrow of Italy's First Republic.* Rowman and Littlefield, Oxford, 1999
Di Scala, S. M., *Italy from Revolution to Republic: 1700 to the Present*. Boulder (CO), 1995
Duggan, Christopher, *A Concise History of Italy.* CUP, 1994
Frei, M., *Italy: the Unfinished Revolution*. London, 1996
Furlong, P., *Modern Italy: Representation and Reform.* London, 1994
Gilbert, M., *Italian Revolution: the Ignominious End of Politics, Italian Style.* Boulder (CO), 1995
Ginsborg, Paul, *Italy and its Discontents, 1980–2001.* Penguin, London, 2002
Gundie, S. and Parker, S. (eds.) *The New Italian Republic: from the Fall of the Berlin Wall to Berlusconi*. London, 1995
McCarthy, P., *The Crisis of the Italian State: from the Origins of the Cold War to the Fall of Berlusconi*. London, 1996
OECD, *OECD Economic Surveys 1998–99: Italy.* Paris, 1998
Plant, Margaret, *Venice: Fragile City 1797–1997.* Yale Univ. Press, 2002
Putnam, R., *et al.*, *Making Democracy Work: Civic Traditions in Modern Italy.* Princeton Univ. Press, 1993
Richards, C., *The New Italians.* London, 1994
Smith, D. M., *Modern Italy: A Political History*. Yale Univ. Press, 1997
Sponza, L. and Zancani, D., *Italy.* [Bibliography] ABC-Clio, Oxford and Santa Barbara (CA), 1995
Turner, Barry, (ed.) *Italy Profiled.* Macmillan, London, 1999
Volcanasek, Mary L., *Constitutional Politics in Italy.* Macmillan, London, 1999

National statistical office: Istituto Nazionale di Statistica (ISTAT), 16 Via Cesare Balbo, 00184 Rome.
Website: http://www.istat.it
National library: Biblioteca Nazionale Centrale, Vittorio Emanuele II, Viale Castro Pretorio, Rome.

JAMAICA

Capital: Kingston
Population projection, 2010: 2·83m.
GDP per capita, 2002: (PPP$) 3,980
HDI/world rank: 0·764/79

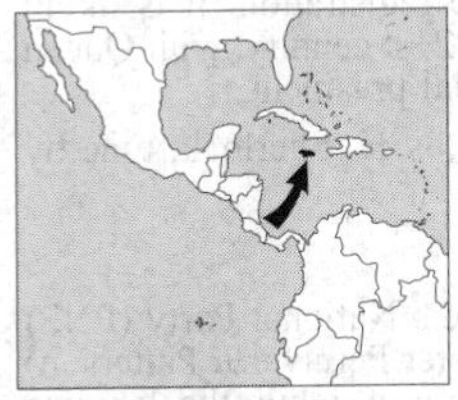

KEY HISTORICAL EVENTS

Jamaica was discovered by Columbus in 1494 and was occupied by the Spaniards from 1509 until 1655 when the island was captured by the English. In 1661 a representative constitution was established consisting of a governor, privy council, legislative council and legislative assembly. The slavery introduced by the Spanish was augmented as sugar production increased in value and extent in the 18th century. The plantation economy collapsed with the abolition of the slave trade in the late 1830s. The 1866 Crown Colony government was introduced with a legislative council. In 1884 a partially elective legislative council was instituted. Women were enfranchised in 1919. By the late 1930s, demands for self-government increased and the constitution of Nov. 1944 stated that the governor was to be assisted by a freely-elected house of representatives of 32 members, a legislative council (the upper house) of 15 members, and an executive council. In 1958 Jamaica joined with Trinidad, Barbados, the Leeward Islands and the Windward Islands to create the West Indies Federation; but Jamaica withdrew in 1961. In 1959 internal self-government was achieved and in 1962 Jamaica became an independent state within the British Commonwealth.

TERRITORY AND POPULATION

Jamaica is an island which lies in the Caribbean Sea about 150 km south of Cuba. The area is 4,244 sq. miles (10,991 sq. km). The population at the census of Sept. 2001 was 2,607,632, distributed on the basis of the 13 parishes of the island as follows: Kingston and St Andrew, 651,878; St Thomas, 91,604; Portland, 80,205; St Mary, 111,466; St Ann, 166,762; Trelawny, 73,066; St James, 175,127; Hanover, 67,037; Westmoreland, 138,947; St Elizabeth, 146,404; Manchester, 185,801; St Catherine, 482,308; Clarendon, 237,024. 2001 density: 237 per sq. km. There is a worldwide Jamaican diaspora of more than 2m.

The UN gives a projected population for 2010 of 2·83m.

Chief towns: Kingston, 655,000 (in 1999), metropolitan area; (1995 figures) Spanish Town, 110,400; Portmore, 93,800; Montego Bay, 82,000; May Pen, 45,900; Mandeville, 39,900.

In 2001, 56·6% of the population were urban. The population is about 75% of African ethnic origin.

SOCIAL STATISTICS

Vital statistics (2002): births, 52,300 (20·0 per 1,000 population); deaths, 16,900 (6·5); marriages (1999), 26,871 (10·4); divorces (1999), 1,131 (0·4). There were 17,669 emigrants in 1995, mainly to the USA. Expectation of life at birth, 2001, 73·5 years for males and 77·5 years for females. Annual population growth rate, 1991–2002, 0·8%; infant mortality, 2001, 17 per 1,000 live births; fertility rate, 2001, 2·4 births per woman.

CLIMATE

A tropical climate but with considerable variation. High temperatures on the coast are usually mitigated by sea breezes, while upland areas enjoy cooler and less humid conditions. Rainfall is plentiful over most of Jamaica, being heaviest in May and from Aug. to Nov. The island lies in the hurricane zone. Kingston, Jan. 76°F (24·4°C), July 81°F (27·2°C). Annual rainfall 32" (800 mm).

CONSTITUTION AND GOVERNMENT

Under the Constitution of Aug. 1962 the Crown is represented by a Governor-General appointed by the Crown on the advice of the Prime Minister. The

Governor-General is assisted by a Privy Council of six appointed members. The Legislature comprises the *House of Representatives* and the *Senate.* The Senate consists of 21 senators appointed by the Governor-General, 13 on the advice of the Prime Minister, eight on the advice of the Leader of the Opposition. The House of Representatives (60 members) is elected by universal adult suffrage for a period not exceeding five years. Electors and elected must be Jamaican or Commonwealth citizens resident in Jamaica for at least 12 months before registration. It is likely that Jamaica will become a republic in the early part of the 21st century, with Queen Elizabeth II being replaced as head of state by a ceremonial president.

National Anthem. 'Eternal Father, bless our land'; words by H. Sherlock, tune by R. Lightbourne.

RECENT ELECTIONS

In parliamentary elections held on 16 Oct. 2002 the People's National Party (PNP) won a fourth consecutive term (the third under Prime Minister Percival J. Patterson) with 34 seats (down from 50 in 1997) and 52·2% of votes cast, while the Jamaica Labour Party (JLP) took 26 (up from 10 in 1997), with 47·2% of the vote. Turn-out was 56·3%.

CURRENT ADMINISTRATION

Governor-General: Sir Howard Felix Cooke.

In March 2005 the cabinet comprised:

Prime Minister and Minister of Defence: Percival J. Patterson, QC; b. 1935 (PNP; elected on 30 March 1992 and re-elected 1997 and 2002).

Minister of Agriculture: Roger Clarke. *Commerce, Science and Technology:* Phillip Paulwell. *Development:* Paul Robertson. *Education, Youth and Culture:* Maxine Henry-Wilson. *Finance and Planning:* Omar Davies. *Foreign Affairs and Foreign Trade:* Keith Desmond Knight. *Health:* John Junor. *Industry and Tourism:* Aloun N'dombet Assamba. *Information:* Burchell Whiteman. *Justice and Attorney General:* A. J. Nicholson. *Labour and Social Security:* Horace Dalley. *Land and the Environment:* Dean Peart. *Local Government, Community Development and Sport:* Portia Simpson-Miller. *National Security:* Peter Phillips. *Transportation and Works:* Robert Pickersgill. *Water and Housing:* Donald Buchanan.

Cabinet Website: http://www.cabinet.gov.jm

DEFENCE

In 2003 defence expenditure totalled US$52m. (US$20 per capita), representing 0·7% of GDP.

Army. The Jamaica Defence Force consists of a Regular and a Reserve Force. Total strength (Army, 2002), 2,500. Reserves, 950.

Navy. The Coast Guard, numbering 190 in 2002, operates seven inshore patrol craft based at Port Royal.

Air Force. The Air Wing of the Jamaica Defence Force was formed in July 1963 and has since been expanded and trained successively by the British Army Air Corps and Canadian Air Force personnel. There are no combat aircraft. Personnel (2002), 140.

INTERNATIONAL RELATIONS

Jamaica is a member of the UN, WTO, the Commonwealth, OAS, Inter-American Development Bank, ACS, CARICOM and is an ACP member state of the ACP-EU relationship.

ECONOMY

Agriculture accounted for 5·5% of GDP in 2002, industry 29·1% and services 65·3%.

Overview. Jamaica, the third largest island of the Caribbean, has a small open economy, chiefly driven by tourism. Leading exports are alumina, bauxite, bananas and sugar. The country suffers from drug trafficking and private sector development is hampered by poor quality infrastructure. Corruption is a serious problem. Jamaica depends on foreign direct investment (FDI) to finance its current account deficit.

Although inflation has been kept in single digits since 1997–98, the tight monetary policy together with high fiscal deficits have led to high interest rates and reduced competitiveness. The unemployment rate is around 15%. The government aims to reduce rigidity in the labour market. Poverty is high, around 24% in rural areas.

Currency. The unit of currency is the *Jamaican dollar* (JMD) of 100 *cents*. The Jamaican dollar was floated in Sept. 1990. Inflation in 2002 was 7·1%. Foreign exchange reserves were US$1,839m. in June 2002 and total money supply was J$52,360m.

Budget. Revenue and expenditure for fiscal years ending 31 March (in J$1m.):

	1997	*1998*	*1999*	*2000*	*2001*
Revenue	75,370	81,695	98,012	118,982	123,004
Expenditure	92,454	101,160	112,506	122,929	135,523

The chief items of current revenue are income taxes, consumption taxes and customs duties. The chief items of current expenditure are public debt, education and health.

Performance. Jamaica has been experiencing major economic difficulties in recent years, with negative growth in 1996, 1997, 1998 and 1999. The economy has recovered slightly in the meantime, with growth of 0·9% in 2000, 1·1% in 2001 and 1·5% in 2002. Total GDP in 2003 was US$7·8bn.

Banking and Finance. The central bank and bank of issue is the Bank of Jamaica. The *Governor* is Derick Milton Latibeaudiere, OJ.

In 2002 there were five commercial banks, three development banks and two other banks (National Export-Import Bank of Jamaica and the National Investment Bank of Jamaica). Total assets of commercial banks in 1995 were J$121,324·9m.; deposits were J$89,135·4m.

There is a stock exchange in Kingston, which participates in the regional Caribbean exchange.

ENERGY AND NATURAL RESOURCES

Environment. In 2002 carbon dioxide emissions from the consumption and flaring of fossil fuels were the equivalent of 4·2 tonnes per capita.

Electricity. The Jamaica Public Service Co. is the public supplier. Total installed capacity, 2000, 1·4m. kW. Production in 2000 was 6·63bn. kWh; consumption per capita in 2000 was 2,518 kWh.

Oil and Gas. There is an oil refinery in Kingston.

Minerals. Jamaica is the third largest producer of bauxite, behind Australia and Guinea. Ceramic clays, marble, silica sand and gypsum are also commercially viable. Production in 2001 (in tonnes): bauxite ore, 12·4m.; limestone, 3·5m.; sand and gravel, 2·2m.; gypsum, 320,323.

Agriculture. In 2001 there were 174,000 ha of arable land and 110,000 ha of permanent crops.

2000 production (in 1,000 tonnes): sugarcane, 2,600; yams, 196; bananas, 130; coconuts, 115; oranges, 72; grapefruit and pomelos, 42; pumpkins and squash, 42; plantains, 34.

Livestock (2000): cattle, 400,000; goats, 440,000; pigs, 180,000; poultry, 11m. Livestock products, 2000 (in 1,000 tonnes): beef and veal, 15; pork, bacon and ham, 7; poultry meat, 73.

Forestry. Forests covered 325,000 ha in 2000, or 30·0% of the total land area. Timber production was 874,000 cu. metres in 2001.

Fisheries. Catches in 2001 totalled approximately 5,700 tonnes, of which 92% were sea fish.

INDUSTRY

Alumina production, 2002, 3·6m. tonnes. Output of other products (in tonnes): cement (2002), 621,831; residual fuel oil (2000), 533,000; distillate fuel oil (2000), 193,000; sugar (2002), 174,949; petrol (2000), 135,000; wheat flour (2000), 130,000; molasses (2003), 72,631; fertilizer (1995), 57,500; cigarettes (2000),

991m. units; rum (2003), 25·5m. litres. In 2001 industry accounted for 30·8% of GDP, with manufacturing contributing 13·0%.

Labour. Total labour force (2000), 1·11m., of whom 933,500 were employed. In 1998, 258,600 were employed in community, social and personal services; 204,400 in wholesale and retail trade, restaurants and hotels; 200,100 in agriculture, hunting, forestry and fishing; and 78,400 in construction. In 2000 the unemployment rate was 15·5% (22·3% for females and 10·2% for males).

INTERNATIONAL TRADE

Foreign debt was US$5,477m. in 2002.

Imports and Exports. Value of imports and domestic exports for calendar years (in US$1m.):

	1998	*1999*	*2000*	*2001*	*2002*
Imports f.o.b.	2,743·9	2,685·6	3,004·3	3,072·6	3,179·6
Exports f.o.b.	1,613·4	1,499·1	1,562·8	1,454·4	1,309·1

Principal imports in 2000 (% of total): machinery and transport equipment 22·6%, mineral fuels, lubricants and related minerals 19·6%, miscellaneous manufactured articles 13·6% and food 13·5%.

Principal domestic exports in 2000 (% of total): crude materials (excluding fuels) 56·9%, food 17·3%, miscellaneous manufactured articles 12·0% and chemicals 5·2%.

Main import suppliers, 2000: USA, 44·8%; Trinidad and Tobago, 10·0%; Japan, 6·0%; France, 5·0%; Venezuela, 3·9%. Main export markets, 2000: USA, 39·1%; UK, 11·5%; Canada, 10·2%; Norway, 9·1%; Japan, 2·3%.

COMMUNICATIONS

Roads. In 1999 the island had about 18,700 km of roads (13,100 km surfaced). In 1996 there were 104,000 passenger cars and 22,000 lorries and vans. There were 292 fatalities in traffic accidents in 2002.

Civil Aviation. International airlines operate through the Norman Manley and Sangster airports at Palisadoes and Montego Bay. In 2000 Sangster International was the busiest for passenger traffic, handling 2,739,000 passengers and 6,400 tonnes of freight. Norman Manley airport is busier for freight, handling 20,680 tonnes of freight but only 1,415,862 passengers. Air Jamaica, originally set up in conjunction with BOAC and BWIA in 1966, became a new company, Air Jamaica (1968) Ltd. In 1969 it began operations as Jamaica's national airline. In 1999 scheduled airline traffic of Jamaica-based carriers flew 35·1m. km and carried 1,670,000 passengers.

Shipping. In 2002 the merchant marine totalled 75,000 GRT, including oil tankers 2,000 GRT. In 2001 there were 3,574 visits to all ports; 15·6m. tonnes of cargo were handled. In 2002 Kingston had 2,520 visits and handled 11·1m. tonnes. In 1997 vessels totalling 12,815,000 NRT entered ports and vessels totalling 6,457,000 NRT cleared.

Telecommunications. In 2002 there were 1,850,000 telephone subscribers (706·6 per 1,000 population) and there were 141,000 PCs in use (53·9 for every 1,000 persons). Mobile phone subscribers numbered 1,400,000 in 2002. In 1995 there were 600 fax machines and in 2002 there were 600,000 Internet users.

Postal Services. In 1998 there were 688 post offices, or one for every 3,690 persons.

SOCIAL INSTITUTIONS

Justice. The Judicature comprises a Supreme Court, a court of appeal, resident magistrates' courts, petty sessional courts, coroners' courts, a traffic court and a family court which was instituted in 1975. The Chief Justice is head of the judiciary. Jamaica was one of ten countries to sign an agreement in Feb. 2001 establishing a Caribbean Court of Justice to replace the British Privy Council as the highest civil and criminal court. In the meantime the number of signatories has risen to twelve. The court was inaugurated at Port-of-Spain, Trinidad on 16 April 2005.

In 1995, 54,595 crimes were reported, of which 33,889 were cleared up. The daily average prison population, 1995, was 3,289. In 2001 there were 1,138 murders. The rate of 43·6 per 100,000 persons is more than seven times that of the USA.

The population in penal institutions in Nov. 2003 was 4,744 (176 per 100,000 of national population).

Police. The Constabulary Force in 1995 stood at approximately 5,861 officers, sub-officers and constables (men and women).

Religion. Freedom of worship is guaranteed under the Constitution. The main Christian denominations are Anglican, Baptist, Roman Catholic, Methodist, Church of God, United Church of Jamaica and Grand Cayman (Presbyterian-Congregational-Disciples of Christ), Moravian, Seventh-Day Adventist, Pentecostal, Salvation Army and Quaker. Pocomania is a mixture of Christianity and African survivals. Non-Christians include Hindus, Jews, Muslims, Bahai followers and Rastafarians.

Education. Adult literacy was 87·3% in 2001 (91·0% among females but only 83·4% among males).

Education is free in government-operated schools. Schools and colleges in 1994–95 (government-operated and grant-aided): basic, 1,694; infant, 29; primary, 792; primary with infant department, 83; all-age, 430; primary and junior high, 20; new secondary, 47; secondary high, 56; comprehensive high, 23; technical high, 12; agricultural/vocational, 6; special, 11; (independent): kindergarten/preparatory, 126; secondary high with preparatory department, 28; high/vocational, 5; business education, 29; (tertiary): teacher-training, 13.

Enrolment in 2002–03 in primary institutions was 332,900, in secondary institutions 226,500, in tertiary institutions 12,500 and in universities 20,700. Numbers of teachers, 1994–95: infant schools, 299; primary, 5,399; all-age and primary and junior high (grades 1 to 9), 6,424; new secondary, 1,852; secondary high, 4,132; technical high, 831; comprehensive high, 2,393; agricultural/vocational, 119.

The University of the West Indies is at Kingston. In 1994–95 it had 12,630 students, 800 external students and about 900 academic staff. The University of Technology in Kingston had 6,374 students, and the College of Agriculture, Science and Education in Portland, 533 students. Large numbers of educated Jamaicans have left the island over the past 30 years, but in the early part of the 21st century there are signs that young professionals are increasingly returning to Jamaica.

In 2000–01 total expenditure on education came to 6·6% of GNP and 11·1% of total government spending.

Health. In 1996 there were 24 hospitals with a provision of 24 beds per 10,000 inhabitants. There were 421 physicians, 57 dentists, 1,241 nurses, 52 pharmacists and 273 midwives in 1996.

Welfare. The official retirement age is 65 years (men) or 60 years (women). The old-age pension is made up of a basic benefit of J$900 a week (reduced to J$675 a week with annual average contributions of between 26 and 38 weeks; J$450 with 13 weeks to 25 weeks), plus an earnings-related benefit of J$0·06 a week for every J$13 of employer-employee contributions paid during the working lifetime.

Jamaica's social welfare projects also cover disability and survivor benefits, sickness and maternity, and work injury. Jamaica has no unemployment programmes.

CULTURE

Broadcasting. There were (1995) seven commercial and one publicly owned broadcasting stations; the latter also operates a television service (colour by NTSC), and there was one commercial television station. In 2000 there were 2·03m. radio and in 2001 there were 510,000 TV sets.

Press. In 1996 there were three daily newspapers with a combined circulation of 158,000, at a rate of 63 per 1,000 inhabitants.

Tourism. In 2000 there were 1,323,000 foreign tourists and (in 1998) 674,000 cruise ship arrivals. Tourism receipts in 2000 totalled US$1,333m.

DIPLOMATIC REPRESENTATIVES

Of Jamaica in the United Kingdom (1–2 Prince Consort Rd, London, SW7 2BZ)
Acting High Commissioner: Sharon Saunders.

Of the United Kingdom in Jamaica (Trafalgar Rd, Kingston 10)
High Commissioner: Peter Mathers, LVO.

Of Jamaica in the USA (1520 New Hampshire Ave., NW, Washington, D.C., 20036)
Ambassador: Gordon Shirley.

Of the USA in Jamaica (2 Oxford Rd, Kingston 5)
Ambassador: Sue McCourt Cobb.

Of Jamaica to the United Nations
Ambassador: Stafford O. Neil.

Of Jamaica to the European Union
Ambassador: Evadne Coye.

FURTHER READING

Planning Institute of Jamaica. *Economic and Social Survey, Jamaica.* Annual.—*Survey of Living Conditions*. Annual

Statistical Institute of Jamaica. *Statistical Abstract.* Annual.—*Demographic Statistics.* Annual.—*Production Statistics.* Annual

Boyd, D., *Economic Management, Income Distribution, and Poverty in Jamaica.* Praeger Publishers, Westport (CT), 1988

Hart, R., *Towards Decolonisation: Political, Labour and Economic Developments in Jamaica 1938–1945.* Univ. of the West Indies Press, Kingston, 1999

Henke, H. W. and Mills, D., *Between Self-Determination and Dependency: Jamaica's Foreign Relations 1972–1989.* Univ. of the West Indies Press, Kingston, 2000

Ingram, K. E., *Jamaica.* [Bibliography] 2nd ed. ABC-Clio, Oxford and Santa Barbara (CA), 1997

National library: National Library of Jamaica, Kingston.
National statistical office: Statistical Institute of Jamaica (STATIN), POB 643, Kingston 5. *Director General*, Sonia Jackson.
Website: http://www.statinja.com

JAPAN

Nihon (or Nippon[1]) Koku
(Land of the Rising Sun)

Capital: Tokyo
Population projection, 2010: 128·00m.
GDP per capita, 2002: (PPP$) 26,940
HDI/world rank: 0·938/9

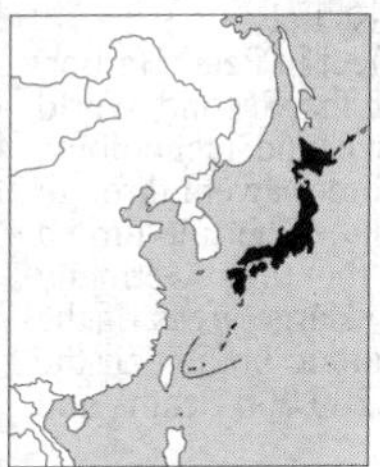

KEY HISTORICAL EVENTS

Hunter-gatherers from the Asian mainland crossed via land bridges to Japan, leaving evidence of Palaeolithic habitation. Rice was introduced by about 400 BC and the use of metals around a century later. Japanese polities are attested first by Chinese sources in AD 57; Japanese armies were active in Korea in the 4th century AD, suggesting a degree of political unity by this period. Chinese script and Confucian works arrived in Japan in the 4th century AD and Buddhism in the 6th century. Indigenous beliefs consolidated into Shintoism, which evolved into a national religion.

As the imperial office became increasingly religious, power passed into the hands of the nobility. Fujiwara Yoshifusa (804–72) was regent of Japan from 857 and by the 11th century the Fujiwaras were unchallenged rulers of the country. In the 12th century, however, Japan fell into anarchy. The nobles, or *daimyo*, exercised power through a warrior class—the *samurai*. When Taira Kiyamori seized power a civil war, the Gempei War, followed (1180–85). Power passed to Minamoto Yoritomo (1147–92), who created a new office, the shogunate. For the next 700 years Japan was ruled by a military dictator, the *shogun*, while the emperor lived reclusively as a religious and national symbol.

In 1334 a brief restoration of power to the emperor was ended by Ashikaga Takauji (1305–58), who established a strong military government. The Ashikaga family ruled as shoguns based in Kyoto. When they fell victim to the ambitions of rival warlords Japan suffered the Fighting Principalities (*Sengokujidai*; 1467–1603).

From 1543 Portuguese traders and missionaries settled on the southern and western coasts. The Portuguese, and later the Dutch, imported western ideas and religion along with firearms, used by warlords to seize power and reunite the country. The last was Tokugawa Ieyasu (1542–1616), who held power from 1600 and diminished the threat of the *daimyo*. The rulers of Japan until 1869, the Tokugawa shogunate saw foreign influences as a danger to their supremacy. Therefore, they decreed that Japan should become a closed society (*sakoku*). In 1636 Japanese were forbidden to emigrate. Europeans were expelled, except for a single Dutch trading post in Nagasaki. Christianity was suppressed and Japan entered 220 years of self-imposed isolation. Cut off from outside influences, Japan gained stability and a strong sense of national identity.

In 1853 an American fleet led by Commodore Matthew C. Perry appeared off the Japanese coast. Faced with the threat of invasion, Japan was forced to open up to international trade. Humiliated by Perry's mission, the Tokugawa shogunate collapsed. Reformers seized Kyoto but they needed a national symbol to legitimize their rule. In 1869 the emperor, Meiji, emerged from the shadows, surprising the country by his zeal for modernization, which led to a period of rapid reform and transformed Japan into a modern nation—the Meiji Restoration. His city, Edo, was renamed Tokyo, meaning 'eastern capital'. While power remained in the hands of the nobility, the peasants were freed from serfdom and priority was given to developing industry and modern technology.

A revitalized Japan defeated China in 1894–95 and gained Taiwan. In 1900 Japan intervened alongside the western powers against the Boxer Rebellion in China. In war with Russia in 1903–04 over Korea and Manchuria, Japan astonished the West by destroying the Russian fleet. Japan annexed Korea (1910) and took control of parts of Manchuria. In 1902 Japan made an alliance with Britain. To emphasise Japan's western credentials, Tokyo entered the First World War, against Germany.

[1]Both forms are valid, and derive from different pronunciations of a Chinese character.

But when territorial gains fell short of expectations, Tokyo's disillusion with the West began. The collapse of world trade at the end of the 1920s brought hardship and helped the rise of political extremism and nationalism. Japan began a phase of aggressive expansionism. In 1931 Japan's Kwantung Army precipitated the annexation of Manchuria, becoming the puppet-state of Manchukuo, and subsequently entered various coastal areas of China. In 1937 there was a full-scale war with China. Japanese forces took Shanghai in 1937, Guangzhou in 1938 and Nanjing in 1940. By the end of 1940, Japan had occupied French Indochina and formed a triple alliance (or Axis) with Nazi Germany and Fascist Italy.

Under Gen. Tojo Hideki (1884–1948), Japan attacked the US fleet in Pearl Harbor, Hawaii in Dec. 1941. This provoked the United States to enter the Second World War and ranged Japan against forces that were superior in size and technology. Nevertheless, the war went initially in Japan's favour. Japanese forces swept through the Pacific and into Malaya and the Dutch East Indies (Indonesia). The tide turned with the American victory at Midway in late 1942 but by the time Germany surrendered in May 1945 Japanese forces were still in control of large areas of the Pacific and Southeast Asia. In Aug. 1945 US planes dropped atomic bombs on the Japanese cities of Hiroshima and Nagasaki, causing more than 200,000 deaths and forcing surrender.

A defeated Japan was reformed by the occupying US forces under Gen. Douglas MacArthur. In 1945 Shintoism, which had become associated with aggressive nationalism, ceased to be the state religion. In the following year, the emperor renounced his divinity and a liberal constitution was introduced in 1946. Japan signed a peace treaty in 1951 at San Francisco and the American occupation of Japan ended in April 1952 when the country regained its independence.

The new Japan remained a monarchy, albeit one in which the emperor was a figurehead. Japan renounced war and the threat or use of force, but retained 'Self Defence Forces'. Japanese cities and industry were rebuilt. An astonishing economic recovery was led by an aggressive export policy. Huge investment in new technology gave the country a dominant position in many industries including motor vehicles, shipbuilding, electrical goods, electronics and computers. From 1955 until 1993 the political scene was dominated by the centre-right pro-business Liberal Democrats (LDP). However, a series of major financial scandals broke the party's monopoly and coalition governments followed. By 2000 the LDP had resumed its dominant role.

TERRITORY AND POPULATION

Japan consists of four major islands, Honshu, Hokkaido, Kyushu and Shikoku, and many small islands, with an area of 377,829 sq. km. Census population (1 Oct. 2000) 126,925,843 (males 62,110,764, females 64,815,079). Oct. 2003 population: 127,619,000; density, 338 per sq. km.

The UN gives a projected population for 2010 of 128·00m.

In 2001, 78·9% of the population lived in urban areas. Foreigners registered on 31 Dec. 2003 were 1,915,030: including 613,791 Koreans, 462,396 Chinese, 274,700 Brazilians, 185,237 Filipinos, 53,649 Peruvians, 47,836 Americans, 34,825 Thais, 23,853 Vietnamese, 22,862 Indonesians, 18,230 British, 14,234 Indians, 11,984 Canadians, 11,582 Australians, 9,707 Bangladeshis, 9,008 Malaysians and 1,846 stateless persons. In 2002 Japan accepted 14 asylum seekers.

Japanese overseas, Oct. 2002, 873,641; of these 315,976 lived in the USA, 72,343 in Brazil, 64,090 in China (26,267 in Hong Kong), 50,864 in the UK, 46,893 in Australia, 36,375 in Canada, 30,384 in France, 27,810 in Germany, 25,329 in Thailand and 20,697 in Singapore.

The official language is Japanese.

A law of May 1997 'on the promotion of Ainu culture' marked the first official recognition of the existence of an ethnic minority in Japan.

The areas, populations and chief cities of the principal islands (and regions) are:

Island/Region	*Sq. km*	*Pop. estimate 2002*	*Chief cities*
Hokkaido	83,454	5,670,000	Sapporo
Honshu/Tohoku	66,889	9,778,000	Sendai
Honshu/Kanto	32,423	40,871,000	Tokyo
Honshu/Chubu	66,790	21,718,000	Nagoya
Honshu/Kinki	33,110	22,754,000	Osaka

Island/Region	*Sq. km*	*Pop. estimate 2002*	*Chief cities*
Honshu/Chugoku	31,915	7,718,000	Hiroshima
Shikoku	18,803	4,137,000	Matsuyama
Kyushu	42,170	13,447,000	Fukuoka
Okinawa	2,272	1,339,000	Naha

The leading cities, with population in 2003 (in 1,000), are:

Akashi	291	Kanazawa	441	Okayama	625
Akita	313	Kashiwa	328	Okazaki	339
Amagasaki	462	Kasugai	291	Osaka	2,490
Aomori	297	Kawagoe	326	Otsu	294
Asahikawa	361	Kawaguchi	468	Sagamihara	605
Chiba	889	Kawasaki	1,259	Saitama	1,038
Fujisawa	386	Kitakyushu	997	Sakai	787
Fukui	250	Kobe	1,484	Sapporo	1,838
Fukuoka	1,315	Kochi	327	Sendai	991
Fukushima	289	Koriyama	332	Shizuoka	469
Fukuyama	407	Koshigaya	311	Suita	344
Funabashi	557	Kumamoto	656	Takamatsu	334
Gifu	402	Kurashiki	434	Takatsuki	352
Hachioji	524	Kyoto	1,386	Tokorozawa	332
Hakodate	283	Machida	392	Tokushima	262
Hamamatsu	576	Maebashi	283	Tokyo	8,083
Higashiosaka	496	Matsudo	466	Toyama	321
Himeji	477	Matsuyama	475	Toyohashi	358
Hirakata	403	Miyazaki	306	Toyonaka	388
Hiratsuka	253	Morioka	281	Toyota	345
Hiroshima	1,119	Nagano	359	Utsunomiya	446
Ibaraki	259	Nagasaki	419	Wakayama	390
Ichihara	281	Nagoya	2,117	Yamagata	251
Ichikawa	450	Naha	306	Yao	267
Ichinomiya	278	Nara	364	Yokkaichi	289
Iwaki	363	Niigata	515	Yokohama	3,467
Kagoshima	546	Nishinomiya	442	Yokosuka	435
Kakogawa	266	Oita	439		

The Tokyo conurbation, with a population in 2000 of 26·44m., is the largest in the world, having overtaken New York around 1970.

SOCIAL STATISTICS

Statistics (in 1,000) for calendar years:

	1996	*1997*	*1998*	*1999*	*2000*	*2001*	*2002*
Births	1,207	1,192	1,203	1,178	1,191	1,171	1,154
Deaths	896	913	936	982	962	970	982

Crude birth rate of Japanese nationals in present area, 2002, was 9·2 per 1,000 population (1947: 34·3); crude death rate, 7·8; marriage rate per 1,000 persons, 6·0; divorce rate per 1,000 persons, 2·3. In 2002 the most popular age for marrying was 30·8 for males and 28·6 for females. The infant mortality rate per 1,000 live births, 3·0 (2002), is one of the lowest in the world. Expectation of life was 78·3 years for men and 85·2 years for women in 2002, the highest rates in the world. A World Health Organization report published in June 2000 put the Japanese in first place in a 'healthy life expectancy' list, with an expected 74·5 years of healthy life for babies born in 1999. Japan had 23,038 centenarians in 2004. Japan has a very fast ageing population, stemming from a sharply declined fertility rate and one of the highest life expectancies in the world. The number of centenarians is increasing by more than 2,000 every year. Annual population growth rate, 1992–2002, 0·2%.

In 2002 the average number of children a Japanese woman bears in her life reached a record low of 1·32.

There were a record 34,427 suicides in 2003 (72·5% males).

CLIMATE

The islands of Japan lie in the temperate zone, northeast of the main monsoon region of South-East Asia. The climate is temperate with warm, humid summers and relatively mild winters except in the island of Hokkaido and northern parts of Honshu facing the Japan Sea. There is a month's rainy season in June–July, but the best seasons are spring and autumn, although Sept. may bring typhoons. Tokyo, Jan.

5·8°C, July 25·4°C. Annual rainfall 1,467 mm. Hiroshima, Jan. 5·3°C, July 26·9°C. Annual rainfall 1,541 mm. Nagasaki, Jan. 6·8°C, July 26·6°C. Annual rainfall 1,960 mm. Osaka, Jan. 5·8°C, July 27·2°C. Annual rainfall 1,306 mm. Sapporo, Jan. –4·1°C, July 20·5°C. Annual rainfall 1,128 mm.

CONSTITUTION AND GOVERNMENT

The Emperor is Akihito (b. 23 Dec. 1933), who succeeded his father, Hirohito on 7 Jan. 1989 (enthroned, 12 Nov. 1990); married 10 April 1959, to Michiko Shoda (b. 20 Oct. 1934). *Offspring:* Crown Prince Naruhito (Hironomiya; b. 23 Feb. 1960); Prince Fumihito (Akishinomiya; b. 30 Nov. 1965); Princess Sayako (Norinomiya; b. 18 April 1969). Prince Naruhito married Masako Owada (b. 9 Dec. 1963) 9 June 1993. *Offspring:* Princess Aiko (b. 1 Dec. 2001). The succession to the throne is fixed upon the male descendants. The 1947 constitution supersedes the Meiji constitution of 1889. In it the Japanese people pledge themselves to uphold the ideas of democracy and peace. The Emperor is the symbol of the unity of the people. Sovereign power rests with the people. The Emperor has no powers related to government. Fundamental human rights are guaranteed.

Legislative power rests with the *Diet*, which consists of the *House of Deputies* (Shugi-in), elected by men and women over 20 years of age for a four-year term, and an upper house, the *House of Councillors* (Sangi-in) of 242 members (96 elected by party list system with proportional representation according to the d'Hondt method and 146 from prefectural districts), one-half of its members being elected every three years. The number of members has been reduced in recent years. There had been 252 members until 2001 and 247 members from 2001 until elections of July 2004.

The number of members in the House of Deputies was reduced from 500 to 480 for the election of June 2000, of whom 300 were to be elected from single-seat constituencies, and 180 by proportional representation on a base of 11 regions. There is a 2% threshold to gain one of the latter seats. Donations to individual politicians are to be supplanted over five years by state subsidies to parties.

A new electoral law passed in Oct. 2000 gives voters a choice between individual candidates and parties when casting ballots for the proportional representation seats in the *House of Councillors*.

On becoming prime minister in April 2001 Junichiro Koizumi established a panel to consider introducing the direct election of prime ministers by popular vote.

National Anthem. 'Kimigayo' ('The Reign of Our Emperor'); words 9th century, tune by Hiromori Hayashi. On 9 Aug. 1999 a law on the national flag and the national anthem was enacted. The law designates the Hinomaru and 'Kimigayo' as the national flag and national anthem of Japan. The 'Kimi' in 'Kimigayo' indicates the Emperor who is the symbol of the State and of the unity of the people, deriving his position from the will of the people with whom resides sovereign power; 'Kimigayo' depicts the state of being of the country as a whole.

RECENT ELECTIONS

Elections to the House of Deputies were held on 8 Nov. 2003. Turn-out was 59·9%. The Liberal Democratic Party (LDP; Jiyu Minshu-to) gained 237 seats (with 34·9% of the vote); Democratic Party (Minshu-to), 177 (37·4%); Clean Government Party (Komei-to), 34 (14·8%); Communist Party of Japan (Nihon Kyosan-to), 9 (7·7%); Social Democratic Party (SDP; Shakai Minshu-to), 6 (5·2%); Conservative Party (Hoshu-to), 4; Independents' Party (Mushozoku-no-kai), 1; Liberal League (Jiyu Rengo), 1. Non-partisans took 11 seats. The ruling LDP relies on its support primarily from rural areas, with only a tenth of urban voters actively supporting it.

Elections to 121 seats of the House of Councillors were held on 11 July 2004. The Democratic Party gained 50 seats, LDP 49, Komeito 11, SDP 2, Communist Party of Japan 4, and ind. 5. As a result the LDP held 115 seats, Democratic Party 82, Komeito 24, Communist Party of Japan 9, Social Democratic Party 5 and ind. 7.

CURRENT ADMINISTRATION

Prime Minister: Junichiro Koizumi; b. 1942 (LDP; appointed 26 April 2001).

In March 2005 the government comprised:

Minister of Justice, Minister of State for Youth Affairs and Measures for Declining Birthrate: Chieko Nohno. *Foreign Affairs:* Nobutaka Machimura. *Finance:*

Sadakazu Tanigaki. *Education, Culture, Sports, Science and Technology:* Nariaki Nakayama. *Health, Labour and Welfare:* Hidehisa Otsuji. *Agriculture, Forestry and Fisheries:* Yoshinobu Shimamura. *Economy, Trade and Industry:* Shoichi Nakagawa. *Land, Infrastructure and Transport:* Kazuo Kitagawa. *Internal Affairs and Communications:* Taro Aso. *Environment, Minister of State for Okinawa and Northern Territories Affairs:* Yuriko Koike.

Chief Cabinet Secretary and Minister of State for Gender Equality: Hiroyuki Hosoda. *Minister of State for Defence:* Yoshinori Ohno. *Chairman of the National Public Safety Commission, Minister of State for Disaster Management and for National Emergency Legislation:* Yoshitaka Murata. *Minister of State for Science and Technology, Food Safety and Information Technology:* Yasufumi Tanahashi. *Minister of State for Economic and Fiscal Policy, and Privatization of the Postal Services:* Heizo Takenaka. *Minister of State for Administrative and Regulatory Reform, Special Zones for Structural Reform, Industrial Revitalization Corporation of Japan and Regional Revitalization:* Seiichiro Murakami. *Minister of State for Financial Services:* Tatsuya Ito.

Office of the Prime Minister: http://www.kantei.go.jp

DEFENCE

Japan has renounced war as a sovereign right and the threat or the use of force as a means of settling disputes with other nations. Its troops had not previously been able to serve abroad, but in 1992 the House of Representatives voted to allow up to 2,000 troops to take part in UN peacekeeping missions. A law of Nov. 1994 authorizes the Self-Defence Force to send aircraft abroad in rescue operations where Japanese citizens are involved. Following the terror attacks on New York and Washington of 11 Sept. 2001, legislation was passed allowing Japan's armed forces to take part in operations in the form of logistical support assisting the US-led war on terror. The legislation permits troops to take part in limited overseas operations but not to engage in combat. In May 2003 parliament passed a series of measures in response to North Korea's nuclear programme. Central government won increased control over the military which now has greater freedom to requisition civilian property in the event of attack.

In Jan. 1991 Japan and the USA signed a renewal agreement under which Japan pays 40% of the costs of stationing US forces and 100% of the associated labour costs. US forces in Japan totalled 38,450 in 2002, nearly half of them on Okinawa. A US-Japanese agreement of Dec. 1996 stipulates that one fifth of the territory on Okinawa occupied by the US military is to be returned to local landowners by 2008.

Total armed forces in 2002 numbered 239,900, including 10,400 women.

Defence expenditure in 2003 totalled US$42,835m. (US$337 per capita), representing 1·0% of GDP.

Army. The 'Ground Self-Defence Force' is organized in five regional commands and in 2002 had a strength of 148,200 and a reserve of 47,000. The USA maintains an army force of 1,800.

Navy. The 'Maritime Self-Defence Force' is tasked with coastal protection and defence of the sea lanes to 1,000 nautical miles range from Japan. The main elements of the fleet are organized into four escort flotillas based at Yokosuka, Kure, Sasebo and Maizuru. The submarines are based at Yokosuka and Kure.

Personnel in 2002 numbered 44,400 including the Naval Air Arm. The combatant fleet, all home-built, includes 16 diesel submarines, 44 destroyers and ten frigates. The Air Arm operated 80 combat aircraft and 91 armed helicopters in 2002. Air Arm personnel was estimated at 9,800 in 2002.

Air Force. An 'Air Self-Defence Force' was inaugurated on 1 July 1954. Its equipment includes (2002) F-15 *Eagles,* F-4E *Phantoms* and Mitsubishi F-1 fighters.

Strength (2002) 45,600 operating 280 combat aircraft.

INTERNATIONAL RELATIONS

In terms of total aid given, Japan was the second most generous country in the world in 2003 after the USA, donating US$8·9bn. in international aid in the course of the year. This represented 0·20% of its GNI.

Japan is a member of the UN, BIS, OECD, Inter-American Development Bank, Asian Development Bank, Colombo Plan, APEC, IOM and the Antarctic Treaty.

ECONOMY

In 2001 services accounted for 71·0% of GDP, industry 27·6% and agriculture, forestry and fisheries 1·4%.

Overview. The world's second largest economy after the USA, Japan recorded growth of 2·7% in 2004 but has had a series of recessions in the past decade. According to the IMF, Japan's longstanding problems of sluggish economic activity, deflation, and financial and corporate sector weaknesses are easing. Recent strong investment has allowed for the upgrading of Japan's ageing capital stock, and strong consumption growth has increased labour market conditions and business confidence. Unemployment has fallen to below 4·5% from the record high of 5·5% in 2003. However, labour market flexibility remains low owing to private sector practices such as the seniority based wage system. Japan's output per capita, measured in purchasing power parity terms, has fallen from 83% of the US level in the early 1990s to less than 75% in 2004. Weak performance during the late 1990s and early 2000s can be attributed to the collapse of the asset price bubble, problems in the banking sector, weak competition and outdated regulations.

Monetary policy has been supportive of recent growth, with short term interest rates of approximately zero. In 2004 public debt stood at 166% GDP, the highest level in the industrialized world. Further use of fiscal instruments is thus constrained. With tax cuts and persistently slow economic growth in the recent past, the share of tax revenue in GDP is the second lowest in the OECD area. The authorities aim to constrain fiscal deficit growth and to achieve a budget surplus by the early 2010s. Financial institutions have made progress in strengthening their positions. However, some weaknesses remain in the banking sector, particularly with respect to non-performing loans, which stood at 7·2% of GDP in 2003. Recent strengthening of the macroeconomic climate has, however, improved the outlook for the repayment of loans and for bank profits.

The ratio of elderly to younger people is increasing more rapidly in Japan than in the other OECD countries. As a consequence pension expenditure has doubled from 6% to 12% of national income, putting greater pressure on public finances.

Currency. The unit of currency is the *yen* (JPY). Inflation in 1997 was 1·8% slowing to 0·6% in 1998. There was then deflation of 0·3% in 1999, 0·7% in both 2000 and 2001, 0·9% in 2002 and 0·3% in 2003. Japan's foreign exchange reserves totalled US$844·5bn. in Dec. 2004 (US$172·4bn. in 1995)—the highest in the world. Gold reserves in June 2002 were 24·60m. troy oz. In Dec. 2003 the currency in circulation consisted of 76,910,000m. yen Bank of Japan notes and 4,423,000m. yen subsidiary coins.

Budget. Ordinary revenue and expenditure for fiscal year ending 31 March 2004 balanced at 81,789,100m. yen.

Of the proposed revenue (in yen) in 2003, 41,786,000m. was to come from taxes and stamps, 36,445,000m. from public bonds. Main items of expenditure: social security, 18,990,700m.; local government, 16,392,600m.; public works, 8,097,100m.; education, 6,471,200m.; defence, 4,953,000m.

The outstanding national debt incurred by public bonds was estimated in March 2002 to be 448,162,000m. yen.

The estimated 2003 budgets of the prefectures and other local authorities forecast a total revenue of 86,211,000m. yen, to be made up partly by local taxes and partly by government grants and local loans.

Performance. The real GDP growth rate for 2003 was 1·4%, rising to 2·7% in 2004, although Japan had negative growth in both the second and third quarters. In 2003 Japan's total GDP was US$4,326·4bn., the second highest in the world after the USA.

The Jan. 2003 *OECD Economic Survey* noted that 'Despite continuing deflation and weakness in the financial sector, the Japanese economy has recovered at a moderate pace since early 2002, led by a sharp increase in exports. The weak yen in early 2002 and the already low level of inventories have supported export growth and increased production, which in turn have led to an improvement in business sentiment. The recovery has been particularly strong in electronics and in other exporting sectors, especially automobiles. Activity in domestic sectors has also started to recover, though at a modest rate.'

Banking and Finance. The Nippon Ginko (Bank of Japan), founded 1882, finances the government and the banks, its function being similar to that of a central bank in other countries. The Bank undertakes the management of Treasury funds and foreign exchange control. Its *Governor* is Toshihiko Fukui (appointed March 2003 for a five-year term). Its gold bullion and cash holdings at 31 Dec. 2002 stood at 638,000m. yen.

There were in Feb. 2004, six city banks, 64 regional banks, 27 trust banks, two long-term credit banks, 50 member banks of the second association of regional banks, 309 Shinkin banks (credit associations), 185 credit co-operatives, 72 foreign banks and six others. There is also a public corporation Japan Post handling postal savings which amounted to 229,938,100m. yen in Sept. 2003. Total savings by individuals, including insurance and securities, stood at 1,209,453,100m. yen on 30 Sept. 2003, and about 61% of these savings were deposited in banks and the post office. In 1999 a number of important mergers were announced in the banking sector, most notably the proposed merger of the Industrial Bank of Japan, Dai-Ichi Kangyo and Fuji Bank, which in Sept. 2000 created Mizuho Financial Group, the world's biggest bank in terms of assets, at over 135,000bn. yen (US$1,283bn.). The second and fourth biggest banks, the Mitsubishi Tokyo Financial Group and UFJ Holdings, announced in Aug. 2004 that they had reached a basic agreement to merge to create the world's largest bank by Oct. 2005.

Japan's banks are in a situation where many of them would be insolvent if they admitted the market value of the loans, shares and property they hold. At 31 March 2003 it was estimated that the banking system's bad loans amounted to 21,441bn. yen.

There are five stock exchanges, the largest being in Tokyo.

ENERGY AND NATURAL RESOURCES

Environment. Japan's carbon dioxide emissions from the consumption and flaring of fossil fuels in 2002 accounted for 4·8% of the world total and were equivalent to 9·3 tonnes per capita. An *Environmental Sustainability Index* compiled for the World Economic Forum meeting in Feb. 2002 ranked Japan 78th in the world out of 142 countries analysed, with 48·6%. The index measured the ability of countries to maintain favourable environmental conditions and examined various factors including pollution levels and the use or abuse of natural resources.

Electricity. Japan is poor in energy resources, and nuclear power generation is important in reducing dependence on foreign supplies. In 2003 Japan had a nuclear generating capacity of 44,153 MW. Total installed generating capacity was 248·4m. kW in 2000. Electricity produced in 2002 was 1,097,167m. kWh. In 2003 there were 53 nuclear reactors; in 2002 nuclear reactors produced approximately 39% of electricity. In 2001, ten regional publicly-held supply companies produced 72·3% of output. There are four plants under construction and plans to construct a further eight nuclear power plants. Consumption per capita in 2001 was an estimated 7,567 kWh.

Oil and Gas. Output of crude petroleum, 2002, was 723,000 kilolitres, almost entirely from oilfields on the island of Honshu, but 241·9m. kilolitres of crude oil had to be imported. Output of natural gas, 2002, 2,571m. cu. metres; with reserves of 40bn. cu. metres.

Minerals. Ore production in tonnes, 2002, of coal (2001), 3,208,000; zinc, 42,851; lead, 5,723; copper (2001), 744; iron (2001), 258; silver, 81,416 kg; gold, 8,615 kg. Gypsum production, 2000, 5,917,000 tonnes; salt production, 2001, 1,358,000 tonnes.

Agriculture. Agricultural workers in 2002 on farms with 0·3 ha or more of cultivated land or 0·5m. yen annual sales were 3·8m. (including 0·22m. subsidiary and seasonal workers), representing 4·5% (2000) of the labour force as opposed to 24·7% in 1962. Land under cultivation in 2002 was 4·8m. ha, down from 6·1m. ha in 1961. In 2001 Japan had 0·35m. ha of permanent crops. Average farm size was

1·6 ha in 2002. In 2001 there were 2,028,000 tractors and 1,042,000 harvester-threshers.

Rice is the staple food, but its consumption is declining. Rice cultivation accounted for 1,689,000 ha in 2002. Output of rice (in 1,000 tonnes) was 10,748 in 1995, 9,490 in 2000 and 8,889 in 2002.

Production in 2002 (in 1,000 tonnes) of sugarbeets was 4,098; potatoes (2001), 2,959; cabbages (2001), 1,435; sugarcane, 1,328; onions (2001), 1,259; wheat, 829; tomatoes (2001), 798; cucumbers (2001), 736; carrots (2001), 691; aubergines (2001), 448; soybeans, 270; pumpkins and squash (2001), 228; taro (2001), 218; yams (2001), 182. Sweet potatoes, which in the past mitigated the effects of rice famines, have, in view of rice over-production, decreased from 4,955,000 tonnes in 1965 to 1,030,000 tonnes in 2002. Domestic sugar production accounted for only 32% of requirement in 2001. In 2002, 1·48m. tonnes were imported, 52·4% of this being imported from Australia, 27·3% from Thailand, 12·6% from South Africa.

Fruit production, 2002 (in 1,000 tonnes): oranges, 1,229; apples, 926; watermelons (2001), 573; pears, 407; persimmons, 269; grapes, 232.

Livestock (2003): 4·52m. cattle (including about 1·72m. milch cows), 9·72m. pigs, 29,000 goats (2000), 27,000 horses (2000), 16,000 sheep (2000), 284m. chickens. Livestock products (in 1,000 tonnes): milk (2003), 8,400; meat (2000), 3,015; eggs (2000), 2,508.

Forestry. Forests covered 25·11m. ha in 2000, or 66·4% of the land area. There was an estimated timber stand of 3,758m. cu. metres in 2001. Timber production was 16·24m. cu. metres in 2001.

Fisheries. The catch in 2001 was 4,719,152 tonnes, excluding whaling. More than 98% of fish caught are from marine waters. Japan's annual catch is the fourth largest in the world after those of China, Peru and the USA. It is also the leading importer of fishery commodities, with imports in 2001 totalling US$13·45bn.

INDUSTRY

The leading companies by market capitalization in Japan, excluding banking and finance, in May 2004 were: the Toyota Motor Corporation (US$130·7bn.); NTT DoCoMo ('anywhere') Incorporated (US$92·2bn.), a wireless voice and data communications company; and the Nippon Telegraph and Telephone Corporation (NTT), (US$79·0bn.).

The industrial structure is dominated by corporate groups (*keiretsu*) either linking companies in different branches or linking individual companies with their suppliers and distributors.

Japan's industrial equipment, 2000, numbered 589,713 plants of all sizes, employing 9·70m. production workers.

Output in 2001 included: watches, 515·3m.; computers, 11·6m.; cameras, 7·91m.; refrigerators, 3·87m.; television sets, 2·86m.; radio sets, 1·9m. The chemical industry ranks fourth in shipment value after machinery, metals and food products. Production, 2001, included (in tonnes): sulphuric acid, 6·7m.; caustic soda, 4·22m.; ammonium sulphate, 1·59m.; calcium superphosphate, 0·25m. A total of 10,257,000 motor vehicles were manufactured in Japan in 2002, making it the second largest producer after the USA. It is the largest producer of passenger cars (8,618,000 in 2002).

Output, in 1,000 tonnes, of crude steel (2002) was 107,745; ordinary rolled steel (2001), 78,927; pig iron (2001), 78,836; cement (2002), 71,828.

In 2001 paper production was 18·39m. tonnes; paperboard, 12·33m. tonnes.

Output of cotton yarn, 2001, 139,000 tonnes, and of cotton cloth, 603m. sq. metres. Output, 2001, 30,000 tonnes of woollen yarns and 95m. sq. metres of woollen fabrics. Output, 2001, of synthetic woven fabrics, 1,484m. sq. metres; rayon woven fabrics, 213m. sq. metres; silk fabrics, 31m. sq. metres.

4,813m. litres of beer were produced in 2001–02; 3,670m. litres of soft drinks and mineral water in 2001.

2000 production (in 1,000 tonnes): distillate fuel oil, 60,032; petrol, 41,776; residual fuel oil, 35,668; kerosene, 22,699.

Shipbuilding orders in 2002 totalled 12,944,000 GRT. In 2001, 11,729,000 GRT were launched, of which 3,092,000 GRT were tankers.

Labour. Total labour force, 2004, was 66·42m., of which 11·50m. were in manufacturing, 11·23m. in wholesale and retail trade, 8·81m. in services, 5·84m. in construction, 5·31m. in health and welfare, 3·47m. in hotels and restaurants, 3·23m. in transport, 2·84m. in education and 2·64m. in agriculture and forestry. Retirement age is being raised progressively from 60 years to reach 65 by 2013. However, in 1995 the average actual retirement age among males was 66.

In Jan. 2003 unemployment stood at 5·5%, the highest rate on record. It had also been 5·5% in Aug. and Oct. 2002. By Dec. 2004, however, it had fallen to 4·4%, the lowest rate in six years. In 2001, 29,000 working days were lost in industrial stoppages. In 2003 the average working week was 38·45 hours.

Trade Unions. In 2002 there were 10,801,000 workers organized in 65,642 unions. In Nov. 1989 the 'Japanese Private Sector Trade Union Confederation' (Rengo), which was organized in 1987, was reorganized into the 'Japan Trade Union Confederation' (Rengo) with the former 'General Council of Japanese Trade Unions' (Sohyo) and other unions, and was the largest federation with 6,829,000 members in 2002. The 'National Confederation of Trade Unions' (Zenroren) had 787,000 members and the 'National Trade Union Council' (Zenrokyo) 169,000 members.

INTERNATIONAL TRADE

Imports and Exports. Trade (in US$1m.):

	1997	*1998*	*1999*	*2000*	*2001*	*2002*
Imports	338,705	280,505	311,246	379,718	349,190	337,833
Exports	420,896	387,958	419,358	479,284	403,227	417,015

In 2001 Japanese imports accounted for 5·8% of the world total imports, and exports 6·9% of the world total exports.

Distribution of trade by countries (customs clearance basis) (US$1m.):

	Exports		*Imports*	
	2001	*2002*	*2001*	*2002*
Africa	4,432	4,918	4,543	5,698
Australia	7,683	8,323	14,451	14,023
Canada	6,563	7,331	7,751	7,163
China	30,941	39,985	57,786	61,863
Germany	15,639	14,135	12,395	12,435
Hong Kong	23,248	25,448	1,457	1,420
Latin America	17,855	16,234	9,700	9,568
ASEAN	54,270	55,796	54,382	51,708
Korea, Republic of	25,285	28,629	17,210	15,502
Taiwan	24,214	26,282	14,195	13,572
UK	12,145	11,969	6,003	5,419
USA	121,146	118,875	63,171	61,863

Principal items in 2002, with value in 1m. yen were:

	Imports, c.i.f.		*Exports, f.o.b.*
Machinery and transport equipment	13,434,000	Machinery and transport equipment	37,542,000
Mineral fuels	8,174,000	Chemicals	4,174,000
Foodstuffs	5,282,000	Metals and metal products	3,227,000
Metal ores and scrap	950,000	Textile products	918,000

The importation of rice was prohibited until the emergency importation of 1m. tonnes from Australia, China, Thailand and the USA in 1993–94 to offset a poor domestic harvest. The prohibition was lifted in line with WTO agreements. Until 2000 rice imports had limited access; the market is now fully open.

COMMUNICATIONS

Roads. The total length of roads (including urban and other local roads) was 1,171,647 km at 1 April 2001. There were 53,866 km of national roads of which 53,303 km were paved. In 2001, 77·1% of all roads were paved. Motor vehicles, at 31 Dec. 2002, numbered 72,254,000, including 54,540,000 passenger cars and 17,480,000 commercial vehicles. In 2001 there were 4,289,700 new car registrations. In 2003 there were 7,702 road deaths (10,679 in 1995).

The world's longest undersea road tunnel, spanning Tokyo Bay, was opened in Dec. 1997. The Tokyo Bay Aqualine, built at a cost of 1·44trn. yen (US$11·3bn.), consists of a 4·4 km (2·7 mile) bridge and a 9·4 km tunnel that allows commuters to cross the bay in about 15 minutes.

Rail. The first railway was completed in 1872, between Tokyo and Yokohama (29 km). Most railways are of 1,067 mm gauge, but the high-speed 'Shinkansen' lines are standard 1,435 mm gauge. In April 1987 the Japanese National Railways was reorganized into seven private companies, the Japanese Railways (JR) Group—six passenger companies and one freight company. Total length of railways in March 2001 was 27,501 km, of which the JR had 20,057 km and other private railways 7,444 km. In 2002 the JR carried 8,585m. passengers (other private, 12,976m.) and 38m. tonnes of freight (other private, 18m.). An undersea tunnel linking Honshu with Hokkaido was opened to rail services in 1988.

There are metros in Tokyo (two systems, total 286 km in 2001), Fukuoka (18 km), Kobe (two systems, total 30 km), Kyoto (26 km), Nagoya (78 km), Osaka (116 km), Sapporo (48 km), Sendai (15 km) and Yokohama (40 km). There are also tram/light rail networks in 19 cities.

Civil Aviation. The main international airports are at Fukuoka, Hiroshima, Kagoshima, Nagoya, Naha, Niigata, Osaka (Kansai International), Sapporo, Sendai and two serving Tokyo—at Narita (New Tokyo International) and Haneda (Tokyo International). The principal airlines are Japan Airlines (JAL), Japan Air System and All Nippon Airways. In the financial year 2002 Japanese companies carried 96·66m. passengers on domestic services and 17·89m. passengers on international services. JAL flew 361·8m. km in 2002 and carried 33,525,752 passengers, All Nippon Airways flew 259·1m. km and carried 43,680,438 passengers, and Japan Air System flew 106·9m. km and carried 21,426,817 passengers.

In 2000 Narita handled 24,813,053 passengers (24,022,075 on international flights) and 1,885,691 tonnes of freight. Osaka (Kansai International) handled 19,499,000 passengers (11,657,000 on international flights) and 966,800 tonnes of freight in 2000. Built on a reclaimed offshore island, it was only opened in Sept. 1994 but in 2000 was the 18th busiest airport in the world for freight, with Narita ranked 3rd. Tokyo Haneda is mainly used for domestic flights, but handled 56,379,000 passengers in 2000 (55,476,000 on domestic flights), making it the 6th busiest airport in the world for overall traffic volume.

Shipping. On 1 July 2001 the merchant fleet consisted of 5,733 vessels of 100 GRT and over; total tonnage 14m. GRT; there were 161 ships for passenger transport (203,000 GRT), 1,602 cargo ships (954,000 GRT) and 727 oil tankers (3,331,000 GRT). In 2000 vessels totalling 461,903,000 net registered tons entered ports. The busiest ports are Chiba (158,929,000 freight tonnes handled in 2002), Nagoya, Yokohama, Osaka and Kitakyushu.

Coastguard. The 'Japan Coast Guard' consists of one headquarters, 11 regional headquarters, 66 offices, one maritime guard and rescue office, 53 stations, six info-communication management centres, seven traffic advisory service centres, 14 air stations, one transnational organized crime strike force station, one special security station, one special rescue station, one national strike team station, five district communications centres, four hydrographic observatories, one Loran navigation system centre and 39 aids-to-navigation offices (with 5,604 aids-to-navigation facilities); and controlled 52 large patrol vessels, 44 medium patrol vessels, 23 small patrol vessels, 233 patrol craft, 13 hydrographic service vessels, five large firefighting boats, four medium firefighting boats, 87 special guard and rescue boats, one aids-to-navigation evaluation vessel, four buoy tenders and 50 aids-to-navigation tenders in the financial year 2003. Personnel numbered 12,258. The 'Japan Coast Guard' aviation service includes 29 fixed-wing aircraft and 46 helicopters.

Telecommunications. Telephone services have been operated by private companies (NTT and others) since 1985. There were 152,267,000 telephone subscribers (equivalent to 1,194·9 per 1,000 population) in 2002. In 2002 Japan had 81,118,400 mobile phone subscribers. There were 48·7m. PCs in use in 2002 (382·2 per 1,000 persons) and 16m. fax machines in 1997. There were 57·2m. Internet users in 2002. Approximately 70% of Internet users are men. Internet commerce, or e-commerce, amounted to US$1·2bn. in 1998 and was forecast to total US$16bn. in 2001.

Postal Services. There were 24,752 post offices in 2002, handling a total of 25,647m. items of domestic mail, and foreign items of mail numbering 80m. out of and 262m. into Japan. Privatization of the post office is set to take place in 2007.

SOCIAL INSTITUTIONS

Justice. The Supreme Court is composed of the Chief Justice and 14 other judges. The Chief Justice is appointed by the Emperor, the other judges by the Cabinet. Every ten years a justice must submit himself to the electorate. All justices and judges of the lower courts serve until they are 70 years of age.

Below the Supreme Court are eight regional higher courts, district courts in each prefecture (four in Hokkaido) and the local courts.

The Supreme Court is authorized to declare unconstitutional any act of the Legislature or the Executive which violates the Constitution.

In 2002, 3,693,928 penal code offences were reported, including 1,396 homicides. The death penalty is authorized; there were two executions in 2004. The average daily population in penal institutions in 2001 was 63,415 (49·81 per 100,000 population).

Religion. State subsidies have ceased for all religions, and all religious teachings are forbidden in public schools. In Dec. 2002 Shintoism claimed 107·78m. adherents, Buddhism 95·56m.; these figures overlap. Christians numbered 1·92m. In Sept. 2003 the Roman Catholic church had two cardinals.

Education. Education is compulsory and free between the ages of six and 15. Almost all national and municipal institutions are co-educational. In May 2003 there were 14,174 kindergartens with 108,822 teachers and 1,760,000 pupils; 23,169 elementary schools with 413,890 teachers and 7,227,000 pupils; 11,060 lower secondary schools with 252,050 teachers and 3,748,000 pupils; 5,331 upper secondary schools with 258,537 teachers and 3,810,000 pupils; 525 junior colleges with 13,534 teachers and 250,000 pupils; and 63 technical colleges with 7,000 teachers and 57,875 pupils. There were also 918 special schools for children with physical disabilities (63,228 teachers, 96,473 pupils).

Japan has seven main state universities: Tokyo University (1877); Kyoto University (1897); Tohoku University, Sendai (1907); Kyushu University, Fukuoka (1910); Hokkaido University, Sapporo (1918); Osaka University (1931); and Nagoya University (1939). In addition, there are various other state and municipal as well as private universities. There are 702 colleges and universities altogether with (May 2003) 2,804,000 students and 310,825 teachers (156,155 full-time).

In 2000–01 total expenditure on education came to 3·5% of GNP and 10·5% of total government spending.

The adult literacy rate in 2001 was at least 99%.

Health. Hospitals on 1 Oct. 2002 numbered 9,187 with 1,642,593 beds. The hospital bed provision of 129 per 10,000 population (2001) was one of the highest in the world. Physicians in 2002 numbered 249,574 (provision of one for every 511 persons); dentists, 90,499. In 2001 Japan spent 7·8% of its GDP on health.

Welfare. There are in force various types of social security schemes, such as health insurance, unemployment insurance and age pensions. The old age pension system in Japan is made up of a two-tiered public benefit. The first tier of the public pension is the basic pension which is payable from age 60 with 25 years' contributions. The normal retirement age will gradually increase to age 65 in 2013 for men and in 2018 for women. To receive the full benefit amount, 40 years' contributions to the system are necessary. There is an earnings floor for contributions at approximately 28% of average earnings. The monthly premium of the National Pension is uniformly fixed (13,300 yen in fiscal year 2002). The full basic pension was a flat amount of 804,200 yen in fiscal year 2002. There were a total of 41m. pensioners in 2000.

14 weeks maternity leave is statutory.

In 2000, 12,866,887 persons and 9,015,632 households received some form of regular public assistance, the total of which came to 1,973,420m. yen. A proposed reform of the pension system involves the public making higher payments for lower benefits.

CULTURE

World Heritage Sites. Japan has 12 sites on the UNESCO World Heritage List (date of inscription on the list in brackets): the Buddhist Monuments in the Horyu-ji Area (1993); Himeji-jo (1993); Yakushima (1993); Shirakami-Sanchi (1993); the Historic Monuments of Ancient Kyoto (Kyoto, Uji and Otsu Cities) (1994), including 13 of Kyoto's Buddhist temples, three Shinto shrines and one castle—temples include Byôdo-in, Daigo-ji, Enryaku-ji, Ginkaku-ji, Kinkaku-ji, Kiyomizu-dera, Kôzan-ji, Ninna-ji, Nishi Hongan-ji, Ryôan-ji, Saihô-ji, Tenryū-ji and Tô-ji; the Historic Villages of Shirakawa-go and Gokayama (1995); Hiroshima Peace Memorial (Genbaku Dome) (1996); Itsukushima Shinto Shrine (1996); the Historic Monuments of Ancient Nara (1998), including five Buddhist temples—Tôdai-ji, Kôfuku-ji, Gango-ji, Yakushi-ji and Tôshôdai-ji—and three listed shrines—Kasuga Taisha, Kasuga Yama Primeval Forest and the remains of Heijô-kyô Palace; Shrines and Temples of Nikko (1999); Gusuku Sites and Related Properties of the Kingdom of Ryukyu (2000); Sacred sites and pilgrimage routes in the Kii mountain range (2004).

Broadcasting. Broadcasting is under the aegis of the public Japan Broadcasting Corporation (Nippon Hoso Kyokai) and the National Association of Commercial Broadcasters (Minporen). The former transmits two national networks and an external service, Radio Japan (22 languages). In 2002 there were 127 commercial television companies operating on terrestrial broadcasting waves. There were 93m. TV sets (colour by NTSC) in 2001 and 121m. radio receivers in 2000. In 2002 there were 23·33m. cable TV subscribers, and in 1998 more than 68,000 cable TV stations.

Cinema. In 2003 cinemas numbered 2,681 with an annual attendance of 162m. (1960: 1,014m.). Of 622 new films shown in 2003, 287 were Japanese.

Press. In 2001 daily newspapers numbered 124 with aggregate circulation of 71·69m. (the highest circulation of daily newspapers in the world) including four major English-language newspapers. The newspapers with the highest circulation are *Yomiuri Shimbun* (daily average of 10·2m. copies in 2002) and *Asahi Shimbun* (daily average of 8·3m. copies in 2002). They are also the two most widely read newspapers in the world.

In 2002, 74,259 book titles were published.

Tourism. In 2002, 5,771,975 foreigners visited Japan, 755,196 of whom came from the USA and 379,832 from the UK. Japanese travelling abroad totalled 16,522,804. Tourism receipts in 2000 totalled US$3·37bn.

Festivals. Japan has a huge number of annual festivals, among the largest of which are the Sapporo Snow Festival (Feb.); Hakata Dontaku, Fukuoka City (May); the Sanja Festival of Asakusa Shrine, Tokyo (May); the Tanabata Festival in Hiratsuka City (July) and Sendai City (Aug.); the Nebuta Festival in Aomori City (Aug.); and Jidai Matsuri, Kyoto (Oct.).

The World Expo is being held in Nagoya from 25 March–25 Sept. 2005.

Libraries. In 2002 public libraries numbered 2,742 (including one National Diet Library), holding 308m. books. In addition the 699 university libraries held 179m. Japanese and 92m. foreign books.

Theatre and Opera. In 2003 there were five National Theatres: National Theatre (traditional Japanese performances); Nogakudo (Noh Theatre); Bunraku Theatre (Japanese puppet show); the New National Theatre (Opera House); and National Theatre Okinawa.

Museums and Galleries. In 2002 there were 1,120 museums. These included 383 historical, 383 fine arts and 141 general museums. There were 113,977,000 visitors in 2001.

DIPLOMATIC REPRESENTATIVES

Of Japan in the United Kingdom (101–104 Piccadilly, London, W1J 7JT)
Ambassador: Yoshiji Nogami.

Of the United Kingdom in Japan (1 Ichiban-cho, Chiyoda-ku, Tokyo 102-8381)
Ambassador: Graham Fry.

Of Japan in the USA (2520 Massachusetts Ave., NW, Washington, D.C., 20008)
Ambassador: Ryozo Kato.

Of the USA in Japan (10–5, Akasaka 1-chome, Minato-ku, Tokyo)
Ambassador: Howard H. Baker.

Of Japan to the United Nations
Ambassador: Kenzo Oshima.

Of Japan to the European Union
Ambassador: Kazuo Asakai.

FURTHER READING

Statistics Bureau of the Prime Minister's Office (up to 2000) and Statistics Bureau of the Ministry of Public Management, Home Affairs, Posts and Telecommunications (from 2001): *Statistical Year-Book* (from 1949).— *Statistical Abstract* (from 1950).—*Monthly Bulletin* (from April 1950)
Economic Planning Agency (up to 2000) and Economic and Social Research Institute (from 2001) of the Cabinet Office: *Economic Survey* (annual), *Economic Statistics* (monthly), *Economic Indicators* (monthly)
Ministry of International Trade and Industry (up to 2000) and the Ministry of Economy, Trade and Industry (from 2001): *Foreign Trade of Japan* (annual)

Allinson, G. D., *Japan's Postwar History*. London, 1997
Argy, V. and Stein, L., *The Japanese Economy*. London, 1996
Bailey, P. J., *Post-war Japan: 1945 to the Present*. Oxford, 1996
Beasley, W. G., *The Rise of Modern Japan: Political, Economic and Social Change Since 1850*. 2nd ed. London, 1995
Buruma, Ian, *Inventing Japan: 1853–1964*. Weidenfeld & Nicolson, London, 2003
The Cambridge Encyclopedia of Japan. CUP, 1993
Cambridge History of Japan. vols. 1–5. CUP, 1990–93
Campbell, A. (ed.) *Japan: an Illustrated Encyclopedia*. Tokyo, 1994
Clesse, A., *et al.* (eds.) *The Vitality of Japan: Sources of National Strength and Weakness*. London, 1997
Eades, J. S., *Tokyo*. [Bibliography] ABC-Clio, Oxford and Santa Barbara (CA), 1998
Gordon, A., *Postwar Japan as History*. Univ. of California Press, 1993
Henshall, K. G., *A History of Japan, From Stone Age to Superpower*. Palgrave, Basingstoke, 2001
Ito, T., *The Japanese Economy*. Boston (Mass.), 1992
Jain, P. and Inoguchi, T., *Japanese Politics Today*. London, 1997
Japan: an Illustrated Encyclopedia. London, 1993
Johnson, C., *Japan: Who Governs? The Rise of the Developmental State*. New York, 1995
McCargo, Duncan, *Contemporary Japan*. 2nd ed. Palgrave Macmillan, Basingstoke, 2004
McClain, James, *Japan: A Modern History*. W. W. Norton, New York, 2001
Nakano, M., *The Policy-making Process in Contemporary Japan*. London, 1996
Okabe, M. (ed.) *The Structure of the Japanese Economy: Changes on the Domestic and International Fronts*. London, 1994
Perren, R., *Japanese Studies From Pre-History to 1990*. Manchester Univ. Press, 1992
Schirokauer, C., *Brief History of Japanese Civilization*. New York, 1993
Woronoff, J., *The Japanese Economic Crisis*. 2nd ed. London, 1996

National statistical office: Statistics Bureau, Prime Minister's Office, Tokyo.
Website: http://www.stat.go.jp/

JORDAN

Al-Mamlaka Al-Urduniya Al-Hashemiyah (Hashemite[1] Kingdom of Jordan)

Capital: Amman
Population estimate, 2010: 6·39m.
GDP per capita, 2002: (PPP$) 4,220
HDI/world rank: 0·750/90

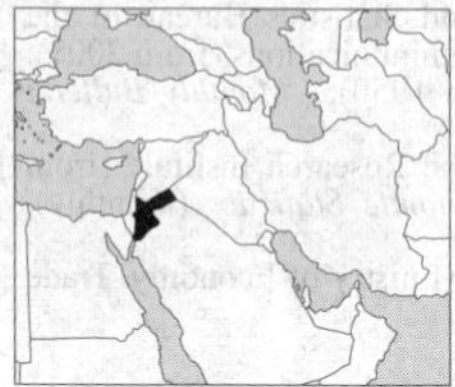

KEY HISTORICAL EVENTS

Egyptian control was established over Semitic Amorite tribes in the Jordan valley in the 16th century BC. However, Egypt's conflict with the Hittite Empire allowed the development of autonomous kingdoms such as Edom, Moab, Gilead and Ammon (centred on modern Amman). The Israelites settled on the east bank of the Jordan in the 13th century and crossed into Canaan. David subjugated Moab, Edom and Ammon in the 10th century but the Assyrians wrested control in the 9th century, remaining until 612 BC. Nabataea expanded in the south during the Babylonian and Persian periods until conquered for Rome by Pompey in the 1st century BC. After Trajan's campaign of 106 AD, the Jordan area was absorbed as Arabia Petraea.

Rome (later Byzantium) and Sassanid Persia clashed over the area but a Muslim army under Khalid ibn al-Walid defeated Byzantium in 636 at the Yarmuk River. After the fall of the Umayyad Caliphate in 750, the centre of power moved from Damascus to Baghdad and Jordan was neglected. The principality of Oultre Jourdain, established by the Christian crusader kingdom of Jerusalem in the early 12th century, was destroyed by Saladin in 1187. The Mamluk Empire held power until the advent of the Turkish Ottoman Empire in the 16th century.

The Arabs of the Ottoman Damascus province rebelled with British support in 1916. The Hashemite Prince Faisal ibn Husayn took Aqaba in 1917 and the British took Amman and Damascus in 1918. The First World War victors decreed two mandates—British Palestine and French Syria. Britain created the Transjordan Emirate in 1922, ruled semi-autonomously by Faisal's brother, Abdullah. Full independence was achieved on 25 May 1946 as the Hashemite Kingdom of Transjordan (Jordan from 1949).

Transjordan declared war on the Israeli state in May 1948, taking the West Bank and East Jerusalem, an occupation supported only by Britain. Palestinian resistance to the annexation culminated in King Abdullah's assassination in 1951. Talal, his son and successor, was deemed mentally unfit in 1952 and Hussein ibn Talal was installed in 1953. After an attempted coup in 1957, instigated by West Bank Palestinians, King Hussein banned political parties and ended Palestinian representation. A brief union with Iraq, ruled by his cousin, ended after an Iraqi republican coup in 1958. Hussein turned to Britain and the USA for military and financial support.

Fatah and the Palestine Liberation Organization (PLO) maintained terrorist attacks on Israel from Jordan, provoking Israeli retaliation in the West Bank. Despite secret co-operation with Israel over containing the Palestinians, Hussein allied with Syria and Egypt in the war of June 1967. Israel repelled Jordanian forces from the West Bank, moving the de facto border to the River Jordan. This devastated the Jordanian economy but removed Palestinian opposition to the Hashemite regime. However, Jordan's relations with the Palestinians deteriorated; in Sept. 1970 four airliners were destroyed by Palestinian extremists in the Jordanian desert. Jordan, with US and British assistance, repelled a Syrian invasion and evicted the PLO. Relations with Israel also worsened from 1977 with the Jewish settlement programme in the West Bank.

On 31 July 1988 Hussein dissolved Jordan's legal and administrative ties with the West Bank in reaction to the *intifada*, which he saw as a threat to his regime. Elections in 1989 led the way to the suspension of martial law—in place from

[1]'Hashemite' denotes a descendant of the prophet Mohammed.

1967–91. Hussein, constrained by Jordan's economic and political ties with Iraq, refused to abandon Saddam Hussein in the 1991 Gulf War, creating a rift with Jordan's Western partners. Multiparty elections were held in 1993, giving Hussein parliamentary support. He signed a peace treaty with Israel in 1994. In Jan. 1999 Hussein replaced as crown prince his brother, Hassan, with his son, Abdullah, who succeeded on his father's death a month later.

TERRITORY AND POPULATION

Jordan is bounded in the north by Syria, east by Iraq, southeast and south by Saudi Arabia and west by Israel. It has an outlet to an arm of the Red Sea at Aqaba. Its area is 89,342 sq. km. The provisional 2004 census population was 5,100,396; density 57·1 per sq. km.

The UN gives a projected population for 2010 of 6·39m. (including immigrant workers).

In 2001, 78·8% of the population lived in urban areas. Estimated population of the 12 governorates:

Governorate	*2003*	*Governorate*	*2003*
Ajloun	121,700	Karak	220,300
Amman	2,085,100	Ma'an	106,700
Aqaba	110,200	Madaba	139,700
Balqa	359,500	Mafraq	252,600
Irbid	977,600	Tafilah	83,300
Jerash	161,100	Zarqa	862,000

The largest towns, with estimated population, 2000: Amman, the capital, 1,147,000; Zarqa, 429,000; Irbid, 247,000.

The official language is Arabic.

SOCIAL STATISTICS

Births, 2003, 148,294; deaths, 16,937. Rates, 2003 per 1,000 population: birth, 27·1; death, 3·1. Annual population growth rate, 1992–2002, 3·9%. Life expectancy at birth in 2001; 69·3 years for men, 72·1 for women. Jordan has a young population: 2003 estimates showed 37·8% aged under 15, 58·7% aged 15–64 and 3·5% aged 65 and over. Infant mortality, 2002, 22 per 1,000 live births; fertility rate, 2002, 3·7 births per woman.

CLIMATE

Predominantly a Mediterranean climate, with hot dry summers and cool wet winters, but in hilly parts summers are cooler and winters colder. Those areas below sea-level are very hot in summer and warm in winter. Eastern parts have a desert climate. Amman, Jan. 46°F (7·5°C), July 77°F (24·9°C). Annual rainfall 13·4" (340·6 mm). Aqaba, Jan. 61°F (16°C), July 89°F (31·5°C). Annual rainfall 1·4" (36·7 mm).

CONSTITUTION AND GOVERNMENT

The Kingdom is a constitutional monarchy headed by H. M. King **Abdullah Bin Al Hussein** II, born 30 Jan. 1962, married H. M. Queen Rania (Rania Al-Yassin, b. 31 Aug. 1970) on 10 June 1993. He succeeded on the death of his father, H. M. King Hussein, on 7 Feb. 1999. *Sons:* Hussein, b. 28 June 1994; Hashem, b. 30 Jan. 2005; *daughters:* Iman, b. 27 Sept. 1996; Salma, b. 26 Sept. 2000.

The Constitution ratified on 8 Dec. 1952 provides that the Cabinet is responsible to Parliament. The legislature consists of a *Senate* of 40 members appointed by the King and a *Chamber of Deputies* of 110 members (six are reserved for women elected by an electoral college) elected by universal suffrage. Nine seats are reserved for Christians, six for Bedouin and three for Circassians. A law of 1993 restricts each elector to a single vote.

The lower house was dissolved in 1976 and elections postponed because no elections could be held in the West Bank under Israeli occupation. Parliament was reconvened on 9 Jan. 1984. By-elections were held in March 1984 and six members were nominated for the West Bank, bringing Parliament to 60 members. Women voted for the first time in 1984. On 9 June 1991 the King and the main political movements endorsed a national charter which legalized political parties in return for the acceptance of the constitution and monarchy. Movements linked to, or financed by, non-Jordanian bodies are not allowed.

National Anthem. 'Asha al Malik' ('Long Live the King'); words by A. Al Rifai, tune by A. Al Tanir.

RECENT ELECTIONS

Elections to the Chamber of Deputies were held on 17 June 2003, having been postponed three times since 2001. 62 of the 110 seats were won by independents loyal to the king. The Islamic Action Front won 18 seats. Turn-out was 59%.

CURRENT ADMINISTRATION

In April 2005 the government consisted of:

Prime Minister and Minister of Defence: Adnan Badran; b. 1935 (in office since 5 April 2005).

Deputy Prime Minister for Parliamentary Affairs and Minister of Political Development: Hesham Al Tal.

Minister of Foreign Affairs: Farouq Al Qasrawi. *Planning and International Co-operation:* Suhair Al Ali. *Justice:* Muhammad Ali Al Alawneh. *Interior:* Awni Yerfas. *Education, Higher Education and Scientific Research:* Khalid Touqan. *Awqaf and Islamic Affairs:* Abdul Salam Al Abadi. *Water and Irrigation:* Raed Abul So'oud. *Finance:* Basem Awadallah. *Labour:* Basem Al Salem. *Tourism and Antiquities:* Alia Hattough-Bouran. *Energy and Mineral Resources:* Azmi Khreisat. *Social Development:* Abdullah Owiadat. *Public Works and Housing:* Yousef Hyasat. *Municipal Affairs:* Tawfiq Krishan. *Culture:* Asma Khader. *Health:* Saeed Darwazeh. *Industry and Trade:* Sharif Al Zu'bi. *Environment:* Khalid Al Irani. *Telecommunications and Information Technology:* Nadia Saeed. *Transport:* Soud Nsairat. *Agriculture:* Yousef Al Shureiqi. *Minister of State for Public Sector Reforms:* Taiseer Al Smadi. *Minister of State for Government Performance:* Salah Din Al Bashir. *Minister of State for Judicial Affairs:* Abed Al Shakhanbeh.

Government Website: http://www.kinghussein.gov.jo/government.html

DEFENCE

Defence expenditure in 2003 totalled US$889m. (US$162 per capita), representing 12·5% of GDP.

Army. Total strength (2002) 84,700. In addition there were 30,000 army reservists, a paramilitary Public Security Directorate of approximately 10,000 and a civil militia 'People's Army' of approximately 35,000.

Navy. The Royal Jordanian Naval Force numbered 540 in 2002 and operates a handful of patrol boats, all based at Aqaba.

Air Force. Strength (2002) 15,000 personnel (including 3,400 Air defence), 101 combat aircraft (including F-5Es, F-16As and Mirage F1s) and 22 armed helicopters.

INTERNATIONAL RELATIONS

A 46-year-old formal state of hostilities with Israel was brought to an end by a peace agreement on 26 Oct. 1994.

Jordan is a member of the UN, WTO, IOM, OIC, Islamic Development Bank and the League of Arab States.

ECONOMY

Services accounted for 71·9% of GDP in 2002, industry 25·9% and agriculture 2·2%.

Overview. Jordan is classified by the World Bank as a small, lower middle-income country. It has no significant natural resources but relies primarily on its human capital for development and growth. Jordan has suffered external shocks related to the situation in Iraq and in the West Bank and Gaza. These have had an impact on exports, tourism and foreign and domestic investment. Despite these difficulties recent growth has been robust with growth of 3·3% in 2003. Reforms have continued and have been accelerated in some areas, including macroeconomic stabilization, private investment and privatization. Despite the strength of recent economic growth, external debt remains high, at 85% of GDP in 2001, with unemployment of around 15% in 2004. The World Bank estimates that the number of Jordanians living in poverty declined by one third between 1997 and 2002, but remains high at 14·2% in 2004. According to the IMF Jordan's main challenges in the medium term concern oil price vulnerability, dependence on foreign loans and the reformation of an incomplete direct tax system.

Currency. The unit of currency is the *Jordan dinar* (JD.) of 1,000 *fils*. Inflation in 2002 was 1·8%. Foreign exchange controls were abolished in July 1997. Foreign exchange reserves were US$3,650m. and gold reserves 408,000 troy oz in June 2002. Total money supply in March 2002 was JD.2,095m.

Budget. Revenue and expenditure over a six-year period (in JD.1m.):

	1998	*1999*	*2000*	*2001*	*2002*	*2003*
Revenue	1,574·9	1,732·1	1,815·9	1,968·0	2,020·8	2,381·2
Expenditure	2,087·7	2,039·5	2,054·1	2,192·3	2,296·7	2,542·6

Performance. Total GDP was US$8·6bn. in 2003. Real GDP growth in 2003 was 3·3% (4·8% in 2002).

Banking and Finance. The Central Bank of Jordan was established in 1964 (*Governor*, Dr Umayya Toukan). In 2002 there were nine national banks, seven foreign banks and 11 specialized credit institutions. Assets and liabilities of the banking system (including the Central Bank, commercial banks, the Housing Bank and investment banks) totalled JD.8,430·4m. in 1995.

There is a stock exchange in Amman (Amman Financial Market).

Weights and Measures. The metric system is in force. Land area is measured in *dunums* (1 dunum = 0·1 ha).

ENERGY AND NATURAL RESOURCES

Environment. Carbon dioxide emissions in 2003 were the equivalent of 3·39 tonnes per capita.

Electricity. Installed capacity was 1·7m. kW in 2000. Production (2003) 7·99bn. kWh; consumption per capita was 1,509 kWh.

Oil and Gas. Natural gas reserves in 2003 totalled 5·83bn. cu. metres, with production (2000) 237m. cu. metres.

Water. 99% of the total population and 100% of the urban population has access to safe drinking water.

Minerals. Phosphate ore production in 2003 was 6·47m. tonnes; potash, 1·96m. tonnes.

Agriculture. The country east of the Hejaz Railway line is largely desert; northwestern Jordan is potentially of agricultural value and an integrated Jordan Valley project began in 1973. In 1993 about 15% of land was given over to agricultural use (including 9% permanent pasture and 4% arable crops). In 2001 there were 73,500 ha of irrigated land. In 2001 there were 256,400 ha of arable land and 87,800 ha of permanent crops. There were 5,770 tractors in 2001 and 168 harvester-threshers.

Production in 2000 (in 1,000 tonnes): tomatoes, 354; olives, 134; cucumbers and gherkins, 133; potatoes, 97; pumpkins and squash, 49; apples, 37; watermelons, 35; lemons and limes, 29; cauliflowers, 26; bananas, 21; cabbages, 12.

Livestock (2003): 1·5m. sheep; 547,000 goats; 66,000 cattle; 18,000 asses (2000); 18,000 camels (2000); 25m. chickens (2000). Total meat production was 130,810 tonnes in 2000; milk, 214,340 tonnes.

Forestry. Forests covered 86,000 ha in 2000, or 1·0% of the land area. In 2001, 234,000 cu. metres of roundwood were cut.

Fisheries. Fish landings in 2001 totalled 520 tonnes, mainly from inland waters.

INDUSTRY

According to the Financial Times Survey (FT 500), the largest company by market capitalization in Jordan on 4 Jan. 2001 was Arab Bank (US$1,970·7m.).

The number of industrial units in 2002 was 17,834, employing 124,421 persons in mining, quarrying, manufacturing and the production and distribution of electricity. The principal industrial concerns are the production or processing of phosphates, potash, fertilizers, cement and oil.

Production in 1,000 tonnes: cement (2001), 3,149; residual fuel oil (2000), 1,496; distillate fuel oil (2000), 895; fertilizers (2000), 619; phosphoric acid (2002), 594.

Labour. The workforce in 1996 was 935,000. In 2002, 692,070 persons worked in social and public administration, 150,922 in commerce, 122,741 in mining and manufacturing, and 31,095 in transport and communications. In 1993, 54,995 persons worked in agriculture. Unemployment was officially 12% in Oct. 2000 but was estimated by economists to be more than 20%. In 2000 Jordan had more than 600,000 foreign workers, many of them Iraqis.

INTERNATIONAL TRADE

Foreign debt was US$8,094m. in 2002. Legislation of 1995 eases restrictions on foreign investment and makes some reductions in taxes and customs duties.

Imports and Exports. Imports (f.o.b.) in 2002 totalled US$5,069·2m. and exports (f.o.b.) US$2,766·1m. Major exports are phosphate, potash, fertilizers, foodstuffs, pharmaceuticals, fruit and vegetables, textiles, cement, plastics, detergent and soap.

Main exports in 1999 were to: Saudi Arabia, 15·9%; India, 12·6%; and Japan, 5·2%. Principal import sources were from: Germany, 9·9%; USA, 8·6%; and Italy, 6·1%. In 2000 Jordan became the first Arab country to sign a free trade agreement with the USA.

COMMUNICATIONS

Roads. Total length of roads, 2003, 7,364 km, of which 2,972 km were main roads. In 2003 there were 422,904 passenger cars (77·1 per 1,000 inhabitants), 686 motorcycles and mopeds, 8,910 coaches and buses, and 113,223 trucks and vans. There were 832 deaths in road accidents in 2003 (388 in 1992).

Rail. The 1,050 mm gauge Hejaz Jordan and Aqaba Railway runs from the Syrian border at Nassib to Ma'an and Naqb Ishtar and Aqaba Port (total, 618 km). The state railway is only minimally operational. Passenger-km travelled in 2000 came to 2m. and freight tonne-km to 671m.

Civil Aviation. The Queen Alia International airport is at Zizya, 30 km south of Amman. There are also international flights from Amman's second airport. Queen Alia International handled 2,384,860 passengers in 2000 (2,350,346 on international flights) and 82,185 tonnes of freight. The national carrier is Royal Jordanian, which flew 36·2m. km and carried 1,252,200 passengers (all on international flights) in 1999.

Shipping. In 2002 sea-going shipping totalled 69,000 GRT. Vessels totalling 2,789,000 NRT entered ports in 2002. The main port is Aqaba.

Telecommunications. There were 1,949,300 telephone subscribers in 2003, or 355·7 per 1,000 persons. In Jan. 2000 the government sold a 40% stake in Jordan Telecommunications Company to France Telecom for US$508m. There were 200,000 PCs (37·5 for every 1,000 persons) in 2002 and 52,000 fax machines in 1998. Jordan had 1,325,000 mobile phone subscribers in 2003. The number of Internet users in 2002 was 307,500.

Postal Services. In 2003 there were 393 post offices.

SOCIAL INSTITUTIONS

Justice. The legal system is based on Islamic law (Shari'a) and civil law, and administers justice in cases of civil, criminal or administrative disputes. The constitution guarantees the independence of the judiciary. Courts are divided into three tiers: regular courts (courts of first instance, magistrate courts, courts of appeal, Court of Cassation/High Court of Justice); religious courts (Shari'a courts and Council of Religious Communities); special courts (e.g. police court, military councils, customs court, state security court).

The death penalty is authorized; there was one confirmed execution in 2004. The murder rate in 2000 stood at two per 100,000 population. The population in penal institutions in Jan. 2002 was 5,448 (106 per 100,000 of national population).

Religion. About 94% of the population are Sunni Muslims.

Education. Adult literacy in 2003 was 90·1% (male, 94·9%; female, 85·1%). Basic primary and secondary education is free and compulsory. In 2002–03 there were 1,366 kindergartens (1,362 private) with 4,871 teachers and 92,244 pupils; 2,789 basic schools (662 private) with 55,911 teachers and 1,222,360 pupils; 1,205 secondary schools (154 private) with 15,213 teachers and 179,842 pupils; and 55 vocational schools with 3,557 teachers and 43,424 pupils. In 1996–97 there were six state and 11 private universities. 19,221 Jordanians were studying abroad in 2003.

In 1999–2000 total expenditure on education came to 5·0% of GNP and 20·6% of total government spending.

Health. There were 7,250 physicians, 2,140 dentists, 12,929 nurses and 3,363 pharmacists in 1997; and 861 midwives in 1995. In 2003 there were a total of 9,743 hospital beds in 97 hospitals.

Welfare. There are numerous government organizations involved in social welfare projects. The General Union of Voluntary Societies finances and supports the Governorate Unions, voluntary societies, and needy individuals through financial and in-kind aid.

CULTURE

World Heritage Sites. There are three sites on the World Heritage List: the rose-red rock-carved city of Petra and Quseir Amra (both entered on the list in 1985) and Um er-Rasas (2004). Petra is over 2,000 years old and contains more than 800 monuments, some built but most carved out of the natural rock. Quseir Amra is the best preserved of Jordan's 'desert castles' and is noted for its frescoes. Um er-Rasas (Kastron Mefa'a) is an archaeological site largely unexcavated, containing remains from the Roman, Byzantine and Early Muslim periods.

Broadcasting. The Jordan Radio and Television Corporation transmits two national radio services (one in English), a Koran service and an external service, Radio Jordan. There are two television services (colour by PAL). There were 1·85m. radio receivers in use in 2000 and 852,000 TV sets in 2001.

Press. In 1998 there were eight daily newspapers with a combined circulation of 352,000.

Tourism. Tourism accounts for 8·5% of GDP. In 2000 there were 1,427,000 foreign tourists; spending by tourists totalled US$723m.

DIPLOMATIC REPRESENTATIVES

Of Jordan in the United Kingdom (6 Upper Phillimore Gdns, Kensington, London, W8 7HA)
Ambassador: Timoor Daghistani.

Of the United Kingdom in Jordan (PO Box 87, Abdoun, Amman)
Ambassador: Christopher Prentice.

Of Jordan in the USA (3504 International Dr., NW, Washington, D.C., 20008)
Ambassador: Karim Tawfiq Kawar.

Of the USA in Jordan (Abdoun, Amman)
Ambassador: Vacant.
Chargé d'Affaires a.i.: David Hale.

Of Jordan to the United Nations
Ambassador: Prince Zeid Raad Al Hussein.

Of Jordan to the European Union
Ambassador: Vacant.
Chargé d'Affaires a.i.: Malek Twal.

FURTHER READING

Department of Statistics. *Statistical Yearbook*
Central Bank of Jordan. *Monthly Statistical Bulletin*
Dallas, R., *King Hussein, The Great Survivor.* Profile Books, London, 1998
Rogan, E. and Tell, T. (eds.) *Village, Steppe and State: the Social Origins of Modern Jordan.* London, 1994
Salibi, Kamal, *The Modern History of Jordan*. I. B. Tauris, London, 1998
Satloff, R. B., *From Abdullah to Hussein: Jordan in Transition.* OUP, 1994
Wilson, M. C., *King Abdullah, Britain and the making of Jordan*. CUP, 1987

National statistical office: National Information Technology Centre, P. O. Box 259 Jubeiha, 11941 Amman.
Website: http://www.nic.gov.jo

KAZAKHSTAN

Qazaqstan Respūblīkasy

Capital: Astana
Population projection, 2010: 15·13m.
GDP per capita, 2002: (PPP$) 5,870
HDI/world rank: 0·766/78

KEY HISTORICAL EVENTS

Turkestan (part of the territory now known as Kazakhstan) was conquered by the Russians in the 1860s. In 1866 Tashkent was occupied, followed in 1868 by Samarkand. Subsequently further territory was conquered and united with Russian Turkestan. In the 1870s Bokhara was subjugated, with the emir, by an agreement of 1873, recognizing Russian suzerainty. In the same year Khiva became a vassal state to Russia. Until 1917 Russian Central Asia was divided politically into the Khanate of Khiva, the Emirate of Bokhara and the Governor-Generalship of Turkestan. In the summer of 1919 the authority of the Soviet Government extended to these regions. The Khan of Khiva was deposed in Feb. 1920, and a People's Soviet Republic was set up, the medieval name of Khorezm being revived. In Aug. 1920 the Emir of Bokhara suffered the same fate and a similar regime was set up in Bokhara. The former Governor-Generalship of Turkestan was constituted an Autonomous Soviet Socialist Republic within the RSFSR on 11 April 1921.

In the autumn of 1924 the Soviets of the Turkestan, Bokhara and Khiva Republics decided to redistribute their territories on a nationality basis; at the same time Bokhara and Khiva became Socialist Republics. The redistribution was completed in May 1925, when the new states of Uzbekistan, Turkmenistan and Tajikistan were accepted into the USSR as Union Republics. The remaining districts of Turkestan populated by Kazakhs were united with Kazakhstan which was established as an Autonomous Soviet Republic in 1925 and became a constituent republic in 1936. Independence was declared on 16 Dec. 1991 when Kazakhstan joined the CIS. Nursultan Nazarbaev became president, and legislation has been introduced to award him privileges for life. Over a million of the country's ethnic Russians and Germans have returned to their homelands in the last ten years. Kazakhstan has been focusing on border disputes with China and Uzbekistan and fighting fundamentalism along with other Central Asian governments.

TERRITORY AND POPULATION

Kazakhstan is bounded in the west by the Caspian Sea and Russia, in the north by Russia, in the east by China and in the south by Uzbekistan, Kyrgyzstan and Turkmenistan. The area is 2,724,900 sq. km (1,052,090 sq. miles). The 1999 census population was 14,952,420 (density of 5·5 per sq. km), of whom Kazakhs accounted for 53·4% and Russians 30·0%. There are also Ukrainians, Uzbeks, Germans, Tatars, Uigurs and smaller minorities. 2002 estimate: 14,862,000. In 1999 the population was 51·8% female; it was 55·9% urban in 2001. During the 1990s some 1·5m. people left Kazakhstan—mostly Russians and Germans returning to their homelands. Approximately 10·8m. Kazakhs live abroad.

The UN gives a projected population for 2010 of 15·13m.

Kazakhstan's administrative divisions consist of 14 provinces and two cities as follows, with area and population:

	Area (sq. km)	*Population (1999)*		*Area (sq. km)*	*Population (1999)*
Almaty[1]	223,900	1,558,500	Ongtüstik Qazaqstan	117,300	1,978,300
Almaty City	300	1,129,400	Pavlodar	124,800	807,000
Aqmola[2]	121,400	836,300	Qaraghandy	428,000	1,410,200
Aqtöbe	300,600	682,600	Qostanay	196,000	1,017,700
Astana City	300	319,300	Qyzylorda	226,000	596,200
Atyraū[3]	118,600	440,300	Shyghys Qazaqstan	283,300	1,531,000
Batys Qazaqstan	151,300	616,800	Soltüstik Qazaqstan	123,200	726,000
Mangghystaū	165,600	314,700	Zhambyl[4]	144,300	988,800

[1]Formerly Alma-Ata. [2]Formerly Tselinograd and then Akmola. [3]Formerly Gurev. [4]Formerly Dzhambul.

In Dec. 1997 the capital was moved from Almaty to Aqmola, which was renamed Astana in May 1998 (the name of the province remained as Aqmola). Astana has a population of 313,000 (2000). Other major cities, with 2000 populations: Almaty (1,129,000); Qaraghandy (437,000); Shymkent (360,000).

The official language is Kazakh.

SOCIAL STATISTICS

2003: births, 247,946; deaths, 155,277; marriages, 110,414. Rates, 2003 (per 1,000 population): births, 16·6; deaths, 10·4. Suicides in 1996 numbered 4,796 (rate of 30·1 per 100,000 population). Expectation of life at birth, 2001, 60·3 years for males and 71·5 years for females. Infant mortality, 2001, 61 per 1,000 live births; fertility rate, 2001, 2·0 births per woman.

CLIMATE

The climate is generally fairly dry. Winters are cold but spring comes earlier in the south than in the far north. Almaty, Jan. –4°C, July 24°C. Annual rainfall 598 mm.

CONSTITUTION AND GOVERNMENT

Relying on a judgement of the Constitutional Court that the 1994 parliamentary elections were invalid, President Nazarbaev dissolved parliament on 11 March 1995 and began to rule by decree. A referendum on the adoption of a new constitution was held on 30 Aug. 1995. The electorate was 8·8m.; turn-out was 80%. 89% of votes cast were in favour. The Constitution thus adopted allows the President to rule by decree and to dissolve parliament if it holds a no-confidence vote or twice rejects his nominee for Prime Minister. It establishes a parliament consisting of a 39-member Senate (two selected by each of the elected assemblies of Kazakhstan's 16 principal administrative divisions plus seven appointed by the president); and a lower house of 77 (67 popularly elected by single mandate districts, with ten members elected by party-list vote). The constitution was amended in Oct. 1998 to provide for a seven-year presidential term.

A Constitutional Court was set up in Dec. 1991 and a new Constitution adopted on 28 Jan. 1993, but President Nazarbaev abolished the Constitutional Court in 1995. In June 2000 a bill to provide President Nazarbaev with life-long powers and privileges was passed into law.

National Anthem. 'Zharalghan namystan qaharman khalyqpyz' ('We are brave people, children of honesty'); words by M. Alimbaev, tune by M. Tulebayev and Y. Brusilovsky.

RECENT ELECTIONS

At the presidential elections of 10 Jan. 1999 Nursultan Nazarbaev was re-elected with 79·8% of votes cast against three other candidates.

National Assembly elections were held on 19 Sept. and 3 Oct. 2004. President Nursultan Nazarbaev's Otan (Fatherland) Party won 42 seats. Aist (Agrarian and Industrial Union of Workers Block) won 11 seats, the Asar (All Together) Party 4, the Ak Zhol (Bright Path) Party 1, the Democratic Party 1 and ind. 18. There were widespread allegations that the elections were fraudulent.

CURRENT ADMINISTRATION

President: Nursultan Nazarbaev; b. 1940 (elected in 1991 and re-elected in 1999).

In March 2005 the government comprised:

Prime Minister: Daniyal Akhmetov; b. 1954 (sworn in 13 June 2003).

First Deputy Prime Minister: Akhmetzhan Yesimov. *Deputy Prime Ministers:* Sauat Mynbayev (also *Minister of Industry and Trade*); Byrganym Aytimova (also *Minister of Education and Science*).

Minister of Agriculture: Serik Umbetov. *Defence:* Col. Gen. Mukhtar Altynbayev. *Economy and Budget Planning:* Kairat Kelimbetov. *Foreign Affairs:* Kasymzhomart Tokayev. *Internal Affairs:* Zautbek Turisbekov. *Energy and Mineral Resources:* Vladimir Shkolnik. *Justice:* Onalsyn Zhumabekov. *Health:* Erbolat Dossayev. *Labour and Social Security:* Gulzhana Karagusova. *Transport and Communications:* Kazhmurat Nagmanov. *Environmental Protection:* Aitkul Samakova. *Culture, Information and Sports:* Esetzhan Kosubaev. *Finance:* Arman Dunayev.

Chairman, Senate (Upper House): Nurtay Abikaev.
Chairman, Majlis (Lower House): Ural Mukhamedzhanov.

Office of the President: http://www.president.kz

DEFENCE

Defence expenditure in 2003 totalled US$1,500m. (US$101 per capita), representing 1·5% of GDP.

Army. Personnel, 2002, 41,000. Paramilitary units: Presidential Guard (2,000), Government Guard (500), Ministry of the Interior Security Troops (20,000), Frontier Guards (12,000).

Navy. A 3,000-strong Maritime Border Guard operates on the Caspian Sea. Kazakhstan hopes to have a fully-fledged navy by 2013.

Air Force. In 2002 there was an Air Force division with about 19,000 personnel with some 164 combat aircraft, including MiG-29 and Su-27 interceptors and MiG-27, Su-24 and Su-25 strike aircraft.

INTERNATIONAL RELATIONS

In Jan. 1995 agreements were reached for closer integration with Russia, including the combining of military forces, currency convertibility and a customs union.

Kazakhstan is a member of the UN, CIS, OSCE, Asian Development Bank, ECO, IOM, OIC, Islamic Development Bank and the NATO Partnership for Peace. Sandwiched between Russia and China, in 1998 President Nazarbaev signed major treaties with both countries in the hope of improving relations with both.

ECONOMY

Agriculture accounted for 8·6% of GDP in 2002, industry 38·6% and services 52·8%.

Currency. The unit of currency is the *tenge* of 100 *tiyn*, which was introduced on 15 Nov. 1993 at 1 tenge = 500 roubles. It became the sole legal tender on 25 Nov. 1993. Inflation was running at nearly 1,880% in 1994, but dropped dramatically and was only 6·4% in 2003. In June 2002 foreign exchange reserves were US$2,280m. and gold reserves amounted to 1·74m. troy oz. Total money supply in May 2002 was 258,470m. tenge.

Budget. Government revenue and expenditure (in 1m. tenge), year ending 31 Dec.:

	1998	*1999*	*2000*	*2001*
Revenue	262,916	207,765	317,747	393,584
Expenditure	318,253	304,150	372,612	475,710

Performance. The break-up of the Soviet Union triggered an economic collapse as orders from Russian factories for Kazakhstan's metals and phosphates, two mainstays of the economy, dried up. Low oil and commodity prices cut revenues by a third in 1998. Real GDP growth was –1·9% in 1998 but there was a slight recovery in 1999, with growth of 2·7%. Growth was an impressive 9·8% in 2000, an even more spectacular 13·5% in 2001 and 9·5% in 2002. Total GDP in 2003 was US$29·7bn. The size of the economy is expected to double between 2004 and 2008, and triple between 2004 and 2015, as a result of increasing oil production.

Banking and Finance. The central bank and bank of issue is the National Bank (*Governor,* Anvar Saydenov). In 2001 there were 44 domestic banks, with assets totalling US$5·3bn. The largest bank is Kazkommertsbank (KKB), with assets of US$1·8bn. in Dec. 2002. There were also 12 branches or representative offices of foreign banks. Foreign direct investment amounted to US$2·8bn. in 2001, more than double the 2000 total.

ENERGY AND NATURAL RESOURCES

Environment. Carbon dioxide emissions from the consumption and flaring of fossil fuels in 2002 were the equivalent of 9·9 tonnes per capita.

Electricity. Installed capacity was 19·0m. kW in 2000. Output in 2003 was 63·9bn. kWh. There is one nuclear power station. Consumption per capita was an estimated 3,666 kWh in 2000.

Oil and Gas. Proven oil reserves in 2002 were 9·0bn. bbls. The onshore Tengiz field has estimated oil reserves between 6bn. and 9bn. bbls.; the onshore Karachaganak field has oil reserves of 2bn. bbls., and gas reserves of 600,000m. cu. metres. Output of crude oil, 2003, 52·2m. tonnes; natural gas, 2002, 12·3bn. cu. metres with proven reserves (2002) of 1,840bn. cu. metres. The first major pipeline for the export of oil from the Tengiz field was opened in March 2001, linking the Caspian port of Atyraū with the Russian Black Sea port of Novorossiisk. In Sept. 1997 Kazakhstan signed oil agreements with China worth US$9·5bn.; these include a 3,000 km pipeline to Xinjiang province in western China. Oil and gas investment by foreign companies is now driving the economy. In 1997 oil production sharing deals were concluded with two international consortia to explore the North Caspian basin and to develop the Karachaganak gas field. A huge new offshore oilfield in the far north of the Caspian Sea, known as East Kashagan, was discovered in early 2000. The field could prove to be the largest find in the last 30 years, and estimates suggest that it may contain 50bn. bbls. of oil. The various recent discoveries have meant that by 2010 Kazakhstan aims to have become the world's sixth largest oil producer. Oil production is expected to triple in the next ten years.

It is believed that there may be as much as 14bn. tonnes of oil and gas reserves under Kazakhstan's portion of the Caspian Sea.

A state-owned national company, Kazmunaigaz, was created in 2002 to manage the oil and natural gas industries.

Minerals. Kazakhstan is extremely rich in mineral resources, including coal, bauxite, cobalt, vanadium, iron ores, chromium, phosphates, borates and other salts, copper, lead, manganese, molybdenum, nickel, tin, gold, silver, tungsten and zinc. Production figures (2003), in tonnes: coal, 80·60m.; iron ore, 19·28m.; bauxite, 4·74m.; lignite, 4·31m.; copper, 485,000; zinc, 394,000; uranium (2002), 2,800; silver, 827·4; gold, 19·3.

Agriculture. Kazakh agriculture has changed from primarily nomad cattle breeding to production of grain, cotton and other industrial crops. In 2002 agriculture accounted for 9% of GDP. There were 21·54m. ha of arable land and 0·14m. ha of permanent crops in 2001. 2·35m. ha were irrigated in 2001. In 1993, 181·3m. ha were under cultivation, of which private subsidiary agriculture accounted for 0·3m. ha and commercial farming 6·3m. ha in 16,300 farms. Around 60,000 private farms have emerged since independence.

Tobacco, rubber plants and mustard are also cultivated. Kazakhstan has rich orchards and vineyards. Kazakhstan is noted for its livestock, particularly its sheep, from which excellent quality wool is obtained. Livestock (2003): 4·56m. cattle (down from 9·57m. in 1993), 9·79m. sheep (down from 33·63m. in 1993), 1·49m. goats, 1·23m. pigs, 1·02m. horses and 23·79m. chickens.

Output of main agricultural products (in 1,000 tonnes) in 2003: wheat, 11,537; potatoes, 2,308; barley, 2,154; watermelons, 604; tomatoes, 448; maize, 438; sugarbeets, 424; cabbages, 328; onions, 320; sunflower seeds, 293; rice, 273. Livestock products, 2002 (in 1,000 tonnes): cow's milk, 4,110; meat, 676; eggs, 117. Kazakhstan is a major exporter of grain to Russia, but in recent years there has been a significant reduction in the quantity exported as a result of low crop yields coupled with the need to meet domestic demand.

Forestry. Forests covered 12·15m. ha in 2000, or 4·5% of the land area. In 1999, 315,000 cu. metres of timber were cut.

Fisheries. Catches in 2001 totalled 30,654 tonnes, exclusively freshwater fish.

INDUSTRY

Kazakhstan was heavily industrialized in the Soviet period, with non-ferrous metallurgy, heavy engineering and the chemical industries prominent. Output was valued at 2,000bn. tenge in current prices in 2001, up from 1,798bn. tenge in 2000. Production, 2003 (in 1,000 tonnes) includes: crude steel, 5,069; pig iron, 4,138; residual fuel oil, 3,069; distillate fuel oil, 2,754; cement, 2,581; wheat flour, 2,123; petrol, 1,841; ferroalloys (2002), 1,241; fabrics (1997), 24·6m. sq. metres; leather footwear (1997), 0·8m. pairs; TV sets (2001), 347,000 units.

Labour. In 2002 the economically active labour force numbered 6,708,900, with the main areas of activity as follows: agriculture, hunting and forestry, 2,366,700;

trade, restaurants and hotels, 1,007,200; industry, 824,000; education, 589,000; transport, storage and communications, 503,700. In 2003 the unemployment rate was 8·8% (down from 13·5% in 1999).

INTERNATIONAL TRADE

In Jan. 1994 an agreement to create a single economic zone was signed with Kyrgyzstan and Uzbekistan. Since Jan. 1992 individuals and enterprises have been able to engage in foreign trade without needing government permission, except for goods 'of national interest' (fuel, minerals, mineral fertilizers, grain, cotton, wool, caviar and pharmaceutical products) which may be exported only by state organizations. Foreign debt was US$17,538m. in 2002.

Imports and Exports. In 2003 imports (c.i.f.) were valued at US$8,408·7m. and exports (f.o.b.) at US$12,926·7m. In 2003, 39·0% of imports came from Russia, 8·7% from Germany, 6·2% from China and 5·6% from the USA. Main export markets in 2003 were Bermuda, 17·0%; Russia, 15·2%; Switzerland, 13·0%; China, 12·8%. Main imports: machinery, mechanical appliances and electrical equipment, transportation equipment, and mineral products. Main exports: mineral products, ferrous and non-ferrous metals, and vegetable products.

COMMUNICATIONS

Roads. In 2002 there were 82,980 km of roads, of which 22,781 were national roads. In 1997 an estimated 1bn. passengers used public transport and 1bn. tonnes of freight were carried. Passenger cars in use in 2003 numbered 1,148,754, and there were also 261,327 trucks and vans and 61,391 buses and coaches. There were 2,147 fatalities as a result of road accidents in 1999.

Rail. In 2000 there were 13,545 km of 1,520 mm gauge railways (3,528 km electrified 1994). Passenger-km travelled in 2003 came to 10·7bn. and freight tonne-km to 147·7bn.

Civil Aviation. The national carrier is Air Kazakhstan. There is an international airport at Almaty. In 1999 scheduled airline traffic of Kazakhstan-based carriers flew 33·2m. km, carrying 667,000 passengers (318,000 on international flights).

Shipping. There is one large port, Aktau. In 1993, 1·2m. passengers and 4m. tonnes of freight were carried on inland waterways. Merchant shipping totalled 11,845 GRT and 20 vessels in 2002.

Telecommunications. Telephone subscribers numbered 2,910,100 in 2002, or 182·2 per 1,000 persons. There were 1,027,000 mobile phone subscribers in 2002 and 2,000 fax machines in 1999. Kazakhstan had 250,000 Internet users in 2002.

Postal Services. In 1998 there were 3,580 post offices.

SOCIAL INSTITUTIONS

Justice. In 1994, 201,796 crimes were reported; in 1996 there were 2,986 murders. The population in penal institutions in April 2001 was 84,000 (522 per 100,000 of national population—one of the highest rates in the world). A moratorium on the death penalty was decreed in Dec. 2003 with a view to eventual abolition.

Religion. There were some 4,000 mosques in 1996 (63 in 1990). An Islamic Institute opened in 1991 to train imams. A Roman Catholic diocese was established in 1991. In 2001 there were 6,988,000 Muslims, 1,216,000 Russian Orthodox and 318,000 Protestants. The remainder of the population followed other religions or were non-religious.

Education. In 2002–03, 147,500 children were attending pre-school institutions, there were 1,120,000 pupils at primary schools, 2,187,700 pupils at secondary schools and 597,500 students at higher education institutions. Adult literacy rate is more than 99%.

Health. In 1996 there were 1,518 hospitals with a provision of 123 beds per 10,000 inhabitants. There were 53,207 physicians, 3,783 dentists, 97,824 nurses, 9,903 pharmacists and 8,456 midwives in 1998.

Welfare. In Jan. 1994 there were 2·1m. age and 0·9m. other pensioners. Pension contributions are 20% of salary and are payable to the State Pension Fund.

CULTURE

World Heritage Sites. Kazakhstan has two sites on the UNESCO World Heritage List: the Mausoleum of Khoja Ahmed Yasawi (inscribed on the list in 2003), an excellent and well preserved example of late 14th century Timurid architecture; and Petroglyphs within the Archaeological Landscape of Tamgaly (2004), a concentration of some 5,000 rock carvings.

Broadcasting. Broadcasting is the responsibility of the Kazakh State Radio and Television Co. There are three national and 13 regional radio programmes, a Radio Moscow relay and a foreign service, Radio Alma-Ata (Kazakh, English). There is one TV channel (colour by SECAM). There were 6·27m. radio receivers in 2000 and 5·44m. television receivers in 2001.

Cinema. In 1997 there were 1,129 cinemas with an annual attendance of 1·0m.

Press. In 1995 there were 472 periodicals in Kazakh, 511 in Russian and 60 in both languages. There is frequent harassment of independent journalists.

Tourism. In 2000 there were 1,471,000 foreign tourists; spending by tourists totalled US$356m.

DIPLOMATIC REPRESENTATIVES

Of Kazakhstan in the United Kingdom (33 Thurloe Sq., London, SW7 2SD)
Ambassador: Erlan Idrissov.

Of the United Kingdom in Kazakhstan (Ul. Furmanova 173, Almaty 480091)
Ambassador: James Lyall Sharp.

Of Kazakhstan in the USA (1401 16th Street, NW, Washington, D.C., 20036)
Ambassador: Kanat B. Saudabayev.

Of the USA in Kazakhstan (Ul. Furmanova 99/97a, Almaty 480091)
Ambassador: John M. Ordway.

Of Kazakhstan to the United Nations
Ambassador: Yerzhan Kazykhanov.

Of Kazakhstan to the European Union
Ambassador: Konstantin Zhigalov.

FURTHER READING

Alexandrov, M., *Uneasy Alliance: Relations Between Russia and Kazakhstan in the Post-Soviet Era, 1992–1997.* Greenwood Publishing Group, Westport (CT), 1999

Nazpary, J., *Post-Soviet Chaos: Violence and Dispossession in Kazakhstan.* Pluto Press, London, 2001

Olcott, Marta Brill, *The Kazakhs*. Stanford, 1987.—*Kazakhstan: Unfilled Promise.* Carnegie Endowment for International Peace, Washington, D.C., 2001

National statistical office: Agency of Kazakhstan on Statistics, 125 Abay Ave., 480008 Almaty, Kazakhstan.
Website: http://www.stat.kz

KENYA

Jamhuri ya Kenya
(Republic of Kenya)

Capital: Nairobi
Population projection, 2010: 34·96m.
GDP per capita, 2002: (PPP$) 1,020
HDI/world rank: 0·488/148

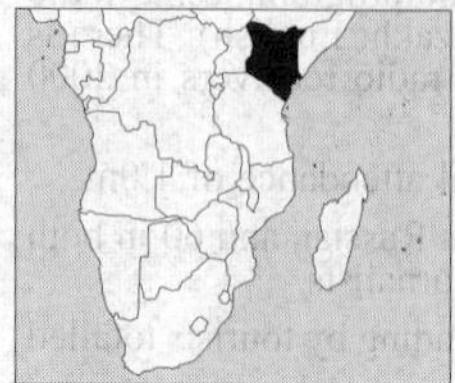

KEY HISTORICAL EVENTS

Prior to colonialism, the area comprised African farming communities, notably the Kikuyu and the Masai. From the 16th century through to the 19th, they were loosely controlled by the Arabic rulers of Oman. In 1895 the British declared part of the region the East Africa Protectorate, which from 1920 was known as the Colony of Kenya. The influx of European settlers was resented by Africans not only for the whites' land holdings but also for their exclusive political representation in the colonial Legislative Council. A state of emergency existed between Oct. 1952 and Jan. 1960 during the period of the Mau Mau uprising. Over 13,000 Africans and 100 Europeans were killed. The Kenya African Union was banned and its president, Jomo Kenyatta, imprisoned. The state of emergency ended in 1960. Full internal self-government was achieved in 1962 and in Dec. 1963 Kenya became an independent member of the Commonwealth. In 1982 Kenya became a one-party state and in 1986 party preliminary elections were instituted to reduce the number of parliamentary candidates at general elections. Only those candidates obtaining over 30% of the preliminary vote were eligible to stand. On the death of Kenyatta in Aug. 1978, Daniel T. arap Moi, the vice-president, became acting president and was elected in 1979, and then re-elected in 1983, 1988, 1992 and 1997. An attempted coup in 1982 was unsuccessful. A multi-party election was permitted in 1992 and again in 1997, the first genuinely competitive elections since 1963.

TERRITORY AND POPULATION

Kenya is bounded by Sudan and Ethiopia in the north, Uganda in the west, Tanzania in the south and Somalia and the Indian Ocean in the east. The total area is 582,646 sq. km, of which 581,677 sq. km is land area. In the 1989 census the population was 21,443,636 (19% urban; up to 34·3% by 2001). The 1999 census gave a population of 28,686,607 (14,481,018 females). 2002 estimate: 31,469,000.

The UN gives a projected population for 2010 of 34·96m.

The land areas, populations and capitals of the provinces are:

Province	*Sq. km*	*Census 1999*	*Capital*	*Census 1999*
Rift Valley	182,539	6,987,036	Nakuru	231,262
Eastern	153,473	4,631,779	Embu	52,446
Nyanza	12,547	4,392,196	Kisumu	322,734
Central	13,220	3,724,159	Nyeri	101,238
Western	8,264	3,358,776	Kakamega	74,115
Coast	82,816	2,487,264	Mombasa	655,018
Nairobi	696	2,143,254		
North-Eastern	128,124	962,143	Garissa	69,203

Other large towns (1999): Eldoret (197,449), Ruiru (109,574), Thika (106,707).

Most of Kenya's 26·44m. people belong to 13 tribes, the main ones including Kikuyu (about 22% of the population), Luhya (14%), Luo (13%), Kalenjin (12%), Kamba (11%), Gusii (6%), Meru (5%) and Mijikenda (5%).

Swahili is the official language, but people belonging to the different tribes have their own language as their mother tongue. English is spoken in commercial centres.

SOCIAL STATISTICS

1995 births, 1,013,000; deaths, 312,000. Birth rate (per 1,000 population), 1995, 37·3; death rate, 11·5. Annual population growth rate, 1992–2002, 2·3%. Expectation of life at birth in 2001 was 44·9 years for males and 47·9 years for females. Infant mortality, 2001, 78 per 1,000 live births. Fertility rate, 2001, 4·3 births per woman, down from 5·8 in 1991. In 2000 more than half of Kenyans lived below the poverty line, up by over 10% in the space of ten years.

CLIMATE

The climate is tropical, with wet and dry seasons, but considerable differences in altitude make for varied conditions between the hot, coastal lowlands and the plateau, where temperatures are very much cooler. Heaviest rains occur in April and May, but in some parts there is a second wet season in Nov. and Dec. Nairobi, Jan. 65°F (18·3°C), July 60°F (15·6°C). Annual rainfall 39" (958 mm). Mombasa, Jan. 81°F (27·2°C), July 76°F (24·4°C). Annual rainfall 47" (1,201 mm).

CONSTITUTION AND GOVERNMENT

There is a unicameral *National Assembly*, which until the Dec. 1997 elections had 200 members, comprising 188 elected by universal suffrage for a five-year term, ten members appointed by the President, and the Speaker and Attorney-General *ex officio*. Following a review of constituency boundaries, the National Assembly now has 210 elected members, 12 members appointed and the two *ex officio* members, making 224 in total. The President is also directly elected for five years; he appoints a Vice-President and other Ministers to a Cabinet over which he presides. A constitutional amendment of Aug. 1992 stipulates that the winning presidential candidate must receive a nationwide majority and also the vote of 25% of electors in at least five of the eight provinces. The sole legal political party had been the Kenya African National Union (KANU), but after demonstrations by the pro-reform lobby which led to extreme violence, KANU agreed to legalize opposition parties. A Constitutional Review Commission was established in 1997 to amend the Constitution before elections that were scheduled for 2002. In Sept. 2002 the Commission recommended changes to Kenya's system of government, including the curbing of presidential powers and the introduction of an executive prime ministerial position. However, in Oct. 2002 President Daniel arap Moi announced the dissolution of parliament before the Commission had completed its task, preventing a new constitution from being in place in time for the elections.

National Anthem. 'Ee Mungu nguvu yetu' ('Oh God of all creation'); words by a collective, tune traditional.

RECENT ELECTIONS

Presidential elections held on 27 Dec. 2002 were won by Mwai Kibaki of the opposition National Rainbow Coalition (NARC) with 62·2% of the vote, against 31·3% for Uhuru Kenyatta, candidate of the ruling Kenya African National Union (KANU), and 5·9% for Simeon Nyachae of the Forum for the Restoration of Democracy-People (FORD-People). Turn-out was 57·2%. Mwai Kibaki's victory ended nearly 40 years of KANU rule since Kenya became independent in 1963.

In parliamentary elections also held on 27 Dec. 2002 NARC won 125 of 210 seats, KANU 64, FORD-People 14, Sisi Kwa Sisi 2, Safina 2, Forum for the Restoration of Democracy-Asili 2 and Shirikisho Party of Kenya 1.

CURRENT ADMINISTRATION

President: Mwai Kibaki; b. 1931 (NARC; sworn in 30 Dec. 2002).

Following the elections of 27 Dec. 2002 a new cabinet was formed, composed in March 2005 as follows:

Vice President: Moodi Awori; b. 1927 (appointed 25 Sept. 2003).

Minister of Agriculture: Kipruto arap Kirwa. *Co-operative Development and Marketing:* Peter Njeru Ndwiga. *East African and Regional Co-operation:* John Koech. *Education, Science and Technology:* George Saitoti. *Energy:* Simeon Nyachae. *Environment and Natural Resources:* Stephen Kalonzo Musyoka. *Finance:* David Mwiraria. *Foreign Affairs:* Chirau Ali Mwakwere. *Gender, Sports, Culture and Social Services:* Ochilo Ayacko. *Health:* Charity Ngilu Kaluki. *Information and Communication, and Tourism and Wildlife (acting):* Raphael Tuju. *Justice and Constitutional Affairs:* Kiraitu Murungi. *Labour and Human Resource Development:* Dr Newton Kulundu. *Lands and Housing:* Amos Kimunya. *Livestock and Fisheries Development:* Joseph Konzolo Munyao. *Local Government:* Musikari Kombo. *Planning and National Development:* Prof. Peter Anyang Nyongo. *Regional*

Development Authorities: Abdi Mohamed. *Roads and Public Works:* Raila Amolo Odinga. *Trade and Industry:* Dr Mukhisa Kituyi. *Transport:* John Njoroge Michuki. *Water:* Martha Wangari Karua.

Office of the President: http://www.officeofthepresident.go.ke

DEFENCE

In 2003 defence expenditure totalled US$237m. (US$7 per capita), representing 1·8% of GDP.

Army. Total strength (2002) 20,000. In addition there is a paramilitary Police General Service Unit of 5,000.

Navy. The Navy, based in Mombasa, consisted in 2002 of 1,400 personnel.

Air Force. An air force, formed on 1 June 1964, was built up with RAF assistance. Equipment includes F-5E/F-5F attack jets. Personnel (2002) 3,000, with 29 combat aircraft and 34 armed helicopters.

INTERNATIONAL RELATIONS

Kenya is a member of the UN, WTO, the Commonwealth, the African Union, African Development Bank, COMESA, EAC, the Intergovernmental Authority on Development, IOM and is an ACP member state of the ACP-EU relationship.

In Nov. 1999 a treaty was signed between Kenya, Tanzania and Uganda to create a new East African Community as a means of developing East African trade, tourism and industry and laying the foundations for a future common market and political federation.

ECONOMY

Agriculture contributed 16·9% of GDP in 2002, industry 19·0% and services 64·1%.

Kenya used to have one of the strongest economies in Africa but years of mismanagement and corruption have had a detrimental effect, made worse in 2000 by one of the longest droughts in living memory. Up to US$1bn. in international aid was frozen during the Moi era because Kenya failed to pass anti-corruption legislation.

Overview. Since a privatization programme was launched in 1992, the government has completed the sale of the majority of the 207 enterprises originally targeted. The government's fiscal programme lost track in 2000–01 owing to failure to privatize Kenya Telkom and loss of foreign aid. In July 2003 the World Bank announced a resumption of loans to the Kenyan government in response to successful anti-corruption reforms.

Currency. The monetary unit is the *Kenya shilling* (KES) of 100 *cents*. The currency became convertible in May 1994. The shilling was devalued by 23% in April 1993. The annual rate of inflation was 2·0% in 2002. Foreign exchange reserves were US$1,120m. in June 2002. Gold reserves have been negligible since 1998. In May 2002 total money supply was K Sh 133,063m.

Budget. In 2002–03 revenues totalled K Sh 210,798m. and expenditures K Sh 304,063m. Tax revenue accounted for 85·0% of revenues; recurrent expenditure accounted for 89·5% of expenditures. The fiscal year ends on 30 June.

Performance. Real GDP growth was 1·8% in 2003 (1·1% in 2002). Total GDP in 2003 was US$12·76bn.

Banking and Finance. The central bank and bank of issue is the Central Bank of Kenya (*Governor*, Dr Andrew Mullei, appointed March 2003). There are 43 banks, 2 non-banking financial institutions and a couple of building societies. In Dec. 2003 their combined assets totalled K Sh 567,600m. In 1998 the government offloaded 25% of its stake in the Kenya Commercial Bank, which lowered its shareholding to 35%. In 2004 it further lowered its shareholding, to 25%.

There is a stock exchange in Nairobi.

ENERGY AND NATURAL RESOURCES

Environment. Kenya's carbon dioxide emissions from the consumption and flaring of fossil fuels in 2002 were the equivalent of 0·3 tonnes per capita.

Electricity. Installed generating capacity was 1·14m. kW in 2003; mostly provided by hydropower from power stations on the Tana river, with some from oil-fired power stations and by geothermal power. Production in 2003 was 4·66bn. kWh, with consumption per capita 142 kWh. In 1999 it was decided to encourage the private sector to take part in electricity generation alongside the state-owned Kenya Electricity Generating Company as a means of bringing to an end the shortage of power and the frequent blackouts. In June 2000 a rationing scheme was introduced in much of the country restricting the power supply to 12 hours a day, and sometimes less.

Oil and Gas. Kenya signed an oil and gas exploration deal in 1997 with Canada's Tornado Resources Ltd, who pledged to commit a minimum of US$7m. over a three-year period.

Minerals. Production, 2001 (in 1,000 tonnes): lime and limestone, 31,631; soda ash (2002), 304; fluorite, 119. Other minerals include gold (1,545 kg in 2001), raw soda, diatomite, garnets, salt and vermiculite.

Agriculture. As agriculture is possible from sea-level to altitudes of over 2,500 metres, tropical, sub-tropical and temperate crops can be grown and mixed farming is pursued. In 2001 there were 4·6m. ha of arable land and 560,000 ha of permanent crop land. 87,000 ha were irrigated in 2001. There were 12,568 tractors in 2001 and 800 harvester-threshers. Four-fifths of the country is range-land which produces mainly livestock products and the wild game which is a major tourist attraction.

Tea, coffee and horticultural products, particularly flowers, are all major foreign exchange earners.

Kenya has about 131,450 ha under tea production, and is the world's fourth largest producer and largest exporter of tea. The production is high quality tea, raised in near-perfect agronomic conditions. It is plucked the whole year round, and almost exclusively by hand. In 2003 production was 294,000 tonnes; exports were worth US$434m.

Coffee output in 2003 was 55,000 tonnes; 170,000 ha is under coffee production. Some 75% of the total hectarage under coffee is cultivated by smallholders, although their production has been in decline in recent years.

Other major agricultural products (2000, in 1,000 tonnes): sugarcane (2003), 4,200; maize (2003), 2,520; potatoes (2003), 1,000; cassava, 950; sweet potatoes, 535; plantains, 370; pineapples, 280; bananas, 210; sorghum, 133; wheat, 105.

Maize is Kenya's most important food crop with about 1·3m. ha under cultivation and annual production of over 2·5m. tonnes. Sisal, pyrethrum, maize and wheat are crops of major importance in the Highlands, while coconuts, cashew nuts, cotton, sugar, sisal and maize are the principal crops grown at the lower altitudes.

Livestock (2003): cattle, 12·8m.; goats, 11·5m.; sheep, 9·5m.; camels, 863,000; pigs, 337,000; chickens, 28·6m.

More than half the agricultural labour force is employed in the livestock sector, accounting for 10% of GDP.

Forestry. Forests covered 17·1m. ha in 2000 (30·0% of the land area), mainly between 1,800 and 3,300 metres above sea-level. There are coniferous, broad-leaved, hardwood and bamboo forests. Timber production was 21·8m. cu. metres in 2001.

Fisheries. Catches in 2003 totalled 147,665 tonnes, of which 139,811 tonnes were freshwater fish. While the aggregate landings from Kenya's inland waters (more than 90% from Lake Victoria) have grown over the past 20 years, marine fishing has not reached its full potential, despite a coastline of 680 km. Fish landed from the sea totals between 5,000 and 78,000 tonnes annually, but there is an estimated potential of 200,000 tonnes in tuna and similar species.

INDUSTRY

In 2001 industry accounted for 18·2% of GDP, with manufacturing contributing 12·5%. In 2003 there were 579 manufacturing firms employing more than 50 persons. The main products are textiles, chemicals, vehicle assembly and transport equipment, leather and footwear, printing and publishing, food and tobacco processing and oil refining. Production (2003) included (in tonnes): cement, 1,658,073; distillate fuel oil, 578,344; sugar, 448,489; residual fuel oil, 338,313;

kerosene, 278,968; petrol, 254,702; wheat flour, 179,866; maize meal, 120,942; cattle feed, 99,616.

Labour. The labour force in 1998–99 was 12,326,000. In 1998–99 the unemployment level was estimated to be 1·8m. The average Kenyan earns US$350 a year.

INTERNATIONAL TRADE

Foreign debt was US$6,031m. in 2002. Foreign investment on the stock exchange has been permitted since 1 Jan. 1995. Export Processing Zones were introduced in 1990, offering foreign companies exemption from taxes and duties for ten years.

Imports and Exports. Imports and exports for calendar years in US$1m.:

	1999	*2000*	*2001*	*2002*	*2003*
Imports f.o.b.	2,731·8	3,044·0	3,176·1	3,277·9	3,708·3
Exports f.o.b.	1,756·7	1,782·2	1,894·0	1,671·2	1,798·7

Principal exports in 2003: horticultural produce, 26·7%; tea, 24·1%; chemicals, 5·2%; coffee, 4·6%. Imports: machinery and transport equipment, 26·1%; petroleum, 23·3%; chemicals, 15·9%; manufactured goods, 13·4%.

Main import suppliers, 2003: United Arab Emirates, 11·3%; Saudi Arabia, 8·6%; South Africa, 8·3%; UK, 7·0%; Japan, 6·6%; India, 5·3%; USA, 5·1%; Indonesia, 4·4%; Germany, 3·9%. Main export markets, 2003: Uganda, 16·7%; UK, 11·6%; Tanzania, 8·0%; Netherlands, 7·7%; Pakistan, 5·0%; Rwanda, 3·3%; Egypt, 3·0%.

The UK is the largest foreign investor in Kenya with over US$1,500m. in more than 60 enterprises.

COMMUNICATIONS

Roads. Of some 63,942 km of roads in 2000, only about 12·1% are paved. In 1996 more than 80,000 km of roads were unclassified. The network has seriously deteriorated since the mid 1980s through poor maintenance. Urban roads comprise around 7,000 km, or about 5% of the total road network, but less than half of them are classified as 'good' or in 'fair' condition. Yet more than 70% of all vehicles in the country use urban roads because of the heavy concentration of economic activities in urban areas. Overall, more than 80% of passengers and freight are carried on the roads. There were, in 2003, 270,000 passenger cars, 47,000 motorcycles, 227,000 vans and trucks and 47,000 buses and coaches. There were 13,400 road accidents in 2003, resulting in 2,800 fatalities.

Rail. In 2002 route length was 2,597 km of metre-gauge. Passenger-km travelled in 2002 came to 288m. and freight tonne-km to 1,538m.

Civil Aviation. There are international airports at Nairobi (Jomo Kenyatta International) and Mombasa (Moi International). The national carrier is the now privatized Kenya Airways. KLM has a 26% share of Kenya Airways. In 1999 Kenya Airways flew 22·5m. km and carried 1,246,000 passengers (807,600 on international flights). In 2000 Jomo Kenyatta International handled 2,734,108 passengers and 135,619 tonnes of freight, and Moi International 853,944 passengers and 2,716 tonnes of freight.

Shipping. The main port is Mombasa, which handled 12·8m. tonnes of cargo in 2002. Container traffic has doubled since 1990 to 246,731 TEUs (twenty-foot equivalent units) in 2001. The merchant marine totalled 19,000 GRT in 2002, including oil tankers 5,000 GRT. In 2001 vessels totalling 10,600,000 NRT entered ports.

Telecommunications. Kenya had 1,653,300 telephone subscribers in 2002, or 51·8 per 1,000 persons. The government aims to improve telephone availability in rural areas from 0·16 lines per 100 persons in 1997 to one line per 100 by 2015, and in urban areas from four lines to 20 lines per 100 persons. In 2002 mobile phone subscribers numbered 1,325,200. There were 204,000 PCs in 2002 (6·4 per 1,000 persons) and 3,800 fax machines in 1999. In 2002 there were 400,000 Internet users.

Postal Services. In 1998 there were 1,033 post offices, or one for every 28,100 persons.

SOCIAL INSTITUTIONS

Justice. The courts of Justice comprises the court of Appeal, the High Court and a large number of subsidiary courts. The court of Appeal is the final Apellant court in the country and is based in Nairobi. It comprises seven Judges of Appeal. In the course of its Appellate duties the court of Appeal visits Mombasa, Kisumu, Nakuru and Nyeri. The High court with full jurisdiction in both civil and criminal matters comprises a total of 28 puisne Judges. Puisne Judges sit in Nairobi (16), Mombasa (two), Nakuru, Kisumu, Nyeri, Eldoret, Meru and Kisii (one each).

The Magistracy consists of approximately 300 magistrates of various cadres based in all provincial, district and some divisional centres. In addition to the above there are the Kadhi courts established in areas of concentrated Muslim populations: Mombasa, Nairobi, Malindi, Lamu, Garissa, Kisumu and Marsabit. They exercise limited jurisdiction in matters governed by Islamic Law.

There were 17,589 criminal convictions in 1993; the prison population was 35,278 in 2002 (111 per 100,000 of national population).

Religion. In 2001 there were 6·78m. Roman Catholics, 6·40m. African Christians, 6·17m. Protestants, 2·90m. Anglicans and 2·24m. Muslims. Traditional beliefs persist.

Education. The adult literacy rate in 2001 was 83·3% (89·5% among males and 77·3% among females). Free primary education was introduced in 2003. In 2002–03 there were 29,465 pre-primary schools with 49,914 teachers and 1,619,401 pupils. 7,185,106 pupils were in primary schools in 2003 with 178,622 teachers. In 2003 there were also 884,950 pupils and 46,445 teachers in secondary schools; 32 teacher training schools with 21,136 students; 24 technical training institutes with 18,611 students. There were three polytechnics with 14,106 students, and six universities (Nairobi, Moi, Kenyatta, Maseno, Egerton and Jomo Kenyatta University College of Agriculture and Technology) with 58,016 students.

In 2003–04 total expenditure on education came to 7·7% of GNP and 20·6% of total government spending.

Health. In 2003 there were 4,813 physicians, 772 dentists, 40,081 nurses and 1,881 pharmacists. There were 526 hospitals (with 63,407 beds), 649 health centres and 3,382 sub-centres and dispensaries in 2003. Free medical service for all children and adult out-patients was launched in 1965.

CULTURE

World Heritage Sites. Kenya has three sites on the UNESCO World Heritage List: Mount Kenya National Park/Natural Forest (1997), including the second highest peak in Africa; Lake Turkana National Parks (1997 and 2001); and Lamu Old Town (2001), the oldest and best-preserved Swahili settlement in East Africa.

Broadcasting. Broadcasting is the responsibility of KBC, which transmits the following services: National (in Swahili), General (English), Central (four languages), Western (six languages), North-Eastern and Coastal (four languages). KBC also provides television programmes, mainly in English and Swahili (colour by PAL). There are several private broadcasting stations, including Kenya Television Network (which broadcasts CNN), Stellavision (which broadcasts Sky News), Capital Radio and Metro FM. The BBC has been awarded a licence to broadcast on the FM frequency. Number of sets: TV (2001), 813,000; radio (2000), 6·76m.

Press. In 1996 there were four daily papers with a total circulation of 263,000. In May 2002 the Kenyan parliament passed a law making it illegal to sell books, newspapers or magazines that had not been submitted to the government for review.

Tourism. In 2003 there were 1,146,100 foreign visitors. Once Kenya's fastest growing source of foreign exchange, receipts from tourism had dropped from US$500m. a year to US$257m. a year by 2000. A European Union grant is helping to revive the industry; in 2003 receipts from tourism amounted to US$338·6m. In 1998 tourism employed approximately 200,000 people and contributed 11% of GDP.

DIPLOMATIC REPRESENTATIVES

Of Kenya in the United Kingdom (45 Portland Pl., London, W1B 1AS)
High Commissioner: Joseph Kirugumi Muchemi.

Of the United Kingdom in Kenya (Upper Hill Road, Nairobi)
High Commissioner: Edward Clay, CMG.

Of Kenya in the USA (2249 R. St., NW, Washington, D.C., 20008)
Ambassador: Leonard Ngaithe.

Of the USA in Kenya (United Nations Avenue, Gigiri, Nairobi)
Ambassador: William M. Bellamy.

Of Kenya to the United Nations
Ambassador: Judith Mbula Bahemuka.

Of Kenya to the European Union
Ambassador: Peter Nkuraiya.

FURTHER READING

Anderson, David, *Histories of the Hanged: The Dirty War in Kenya and the End of Empire.* W. W. Norton, New York and Weidenfeld & Nicolson, London, 2005

Coger, D., *Kenya.* [Bibliography] 2nd ed. ABC-Clio, Oxford and Santa Barbara (CA), 1996

Elkins, Caroline, *Britain's Gulag.* Jonathan Cape, London, 2005; US title: *Imperial Reckoning: The Untold Story of the End of Empire in Kenya.* Henry Holt, New York, 2005

Haugerud, A., *The Culture of Politics in Modern Kenya.* CUP, 1995

Kyle, Keith, *The Politics of the Independence of Kenya.* Macmillan, London, 1999

Miller, N. N., *Kenya: the Quest for Prosperity.* 2nd ed. Boulder (CO), 1994

Ogot, B. A. and Ochieng, W. R. (eds.) *Decolonization and Independence in Kenya, 1940–93.* London, 1995

Throup, David and Hornsby, Charles, *Multiparty Politics in Kenya.* James Currey, Oxford, 1999

Widner, J. A., *The Rise of a Party State in Kenya: from 'Harambee' to 'Nayayo'.* Univ. of California Press, 1993

National statistical office: Central Bureau of Statistics, Ministry of Planning and National Development, POB 30266, Nairobi

KIRIBATI

Ribaberikin Kiribati
(Republic of Kiribati)

Capital: Bairiki (Tarawa)
Population, 2000: 84,000
GDP per capita: not available
GNP per capita: $830

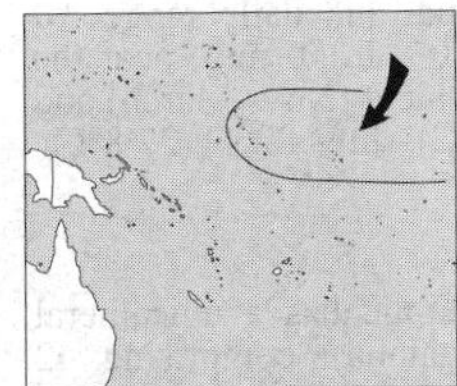

KEY HISTORICAL EVENTS

The islands that now constitute Kiribati were first settled by early Austronesian-speaking peoples long before the 1st century AD. Fijians and Tongans arrived about the 14th century and subsequently merged with the older groups to form the traditional I-Kiribati Micronesian society and culture. The Gilbert and Ellice Islands were proclaimed a British protectorate in 1892 and annexed at the request of the native governments as the Gilbert and Ellice Islands Colony on 10 Nov. 1915. On 1 Oct. 1975 the Ellice Islands severed constitutional links with the Gilbert Islands and took on a new name, Tuvalu. The Gilberts achieved full independence as Kiribati in 1979. Internal self-government was obtained on 1 Nov. 1976 and independence on 12 July 1979 as the Republic of Kiribati.

TERRITORY AND POPULATION

Kiribati (pronounced Kiribahss) consists of three groups of coral atolls and one isolated volcanic island, spread over a large expanse of the Central Pacific with a total land area of 811 sq. km (313 sq. miles). It comprises **Banaba** or Ocean Island (6 sq. km), the 16 **Gilbert Islands** (280 sq. km), the 8 **Phoenix Islands** (29 sq. km), and 8 of the 11 **Line Islands** (496 sq. km), the other 3 Line Islands (Jarvis, Palmyra Atoll and Kingman Reef) being uninhabited dependencies of the USA. The capital is the island of Bairiki in Tarawa. The gradual rise in sea levels in recent years is slowly reducing the area of the islands.

Population, 2000 census, 84,494 (42,848 females); density, 104 per sq. km.

In 1995 an estimated 64·3% of the population lived in rural areas. Between 1995 and 2000 the number of people living in urban areas increased by 6·4%. Between 1988 and 1993, 4,700 people were resettled on Teraina and Tabuaeran atolls because the main island group was overcrowded. Since then the government's programme has been suspended owing to the need to improve the physical infrastructure and housing.

The population distribution at the 2000 census was 49·4% in the Outer Islands, 42·9% in South Tarawa (urban area) and 7·7% in the Line and Phoenix Islands. Banaba, all 16 Gilbert Islands, Kanton (or Abariringa) in the Phoenix Islands and three atolls in the Line Islands (Teraina, Tabuaeran and Kiritimati—formerly Washington, Fanning and Christmas Islands respectively) are inhabited; their populations in 2000 (census) were as follows:

Banaba (Ocean Is.)	276	Abemama	3,142	Nikunau	1,733
Makin	1,691	Kuria	961	Onotoa	1,668
Butaritari	3,464	Aranuka	966	Tamana	962
Marakei	2,544	Nonouti	3,176	Arorae	1,225
Abaiang	5,794	Tabiteuea	4,582	Kanton	61
Tarawa	41,194	North Tabiteuea	3,365	Teraina	1,087
North Tarawa	4,477	South Tabiteuea	1,217	Tabuaeran	1,757
South Tarawa	36,717	Beru	2,732	Kiritimati	3,431
Maiana	2,048				

The remaining 12 atolls have no permanent population; the seven Phoenix Islands comprise Birnie, Rawaki (formerly Phoenix), Enderbury, Manra (formerly Sydney), Orona (formerly Hull), McKean and Nikumaroro (formerly Gardner), while the others are Malden and Starbuck in the Central Line Islands, and Millennium Island (formerly Caroline), Flint and Vostok in the Southern Line Islands. The population is almost entirely Micronesian.

English is the official language; I-Kiribati (Gilbertese) is also spoken.

SOCIAL STATISTICS

1997 births (estimate), 2,200; deaths, 600. 1997 estimated birth rate, 26·8 per 1,000 population; death rate, 7·7 per 1,000; infant mortality rate, 51·5 per 1,000 live births; life expectancy, 62·3 years. Annual population growth rate, 1992–2002, 1·5%; fertility rate, 2001, 4·6 births per woman.

CLIMATE

The Line Islands, Phoenix Islands and Banaba have a maritime equatorial climate, but the islands further north and south are tropical. Annual and daily ranges of temperature are small; mean annual rainfall ranges from 50" (1,250 mm) near the equator to 120" (3,000 mm) in the north. Typhoons are prevalent (Nov.–March) and there are occasional tornadoes. Tarawa, Jan. 83°F (28·3°C), July 82°F (27·8°C). Annual rainfall 79" (1,977 mm).

CONSTITUTION AND GOVERNMENT

Under the constitution founded on 12 July 1979 the republic has a unicameral legislature, the *House of Assembly* (Maneaba ni Maungatabu), comprising 42 members, 40 of whom are elected by popular vote, and two (the Attorney-General *ex officio* and a representative from the Banaban community) appointed for a four-year term. The *President* is directly elected and is both Head of State and government.

National Anthem. 'Teirake kain Kiribati' ('Stand up, Kiribatians'); words and tune by U. Ioteba.

RECENT ELECTIONS

The last House of Assembly elections were held on 9 and 16 May 2003. Maneaban te Mauri (MTM; 'Protect the Maneaba') won 24 seats and Boutokanto Koaava (BK; 'Pillars of Truth') won 16 seats.

On 28 March 2003 President Teburoro Tito (MTM) was defeated in a no-confidence motion. On 4 July 2003 Anote Tong (BK) won the presidential elections with 47·4% of the vote, defeating his brother, Dr Harry Tong (MTM) who took 43·5%. Banuera Berina of the Maurin Kiribati Pati came third with 9·1%.

CURRENT ADMINISTRATION

President and Minister of Foreign Affairs and Immigration: Anote Tong (elected 4 July 2003).

In March 2005 the government comprised:

Vice President and Minister of Education, Youth and Sport Development: Teima Onorio.

Minister of Commerce, Industry and Co-operatives: Ioteba Redfern. *Communications, Transport and Tourism Development:* Naatan Teewe. *Environment, Land and Agricultural Development:* Martin Tofinga. *Finance and Economic Development:* Nabuti Mwemwenikarawa. *Health and Medical Services:* Natanera Kirata. *Internal Affairs and Social Development:* Amberoti Nikora. *Labour and Human Resources Development:* Bauro Tongaai. *Line and Phoenix Islands:* Tawita Temoku. *Fisheries and Marine Resources Development:* Tetabo Nakara. *Public Works and Utilities:* James Tom.

INTERNATIONAL RELATIONS

Kiribati is a member of the UN, Commonwealth, Asian Development Bank, the Pacific Islands Forum and the Pacific Community (formerly the South Pacific Commission) and is an ACP member state of the ACP-EU relationship.

ECONOMY

Agriculture accounted for 14·2% of GDP in 2002, industry 10·9% and services 74·9%.

Currency. The currency in use is the Australian *dollar*. In 2002 the inflation rate was 3·2%, down from 6·0% in 2001.

Budget. Foreign financial aid, mainly from the UK and Japan, has amounted to 25–50% of GDP in recent years. Revenues in 2000 totalled $A107·8m. and expenditures $A90·0m.

Performance. Real GDP growth was 1·8% in 2001 and 1·0% in 2002. Total GDP in 2002 was US$58m.

Banking and Finance. The Bank of Kiribati is 25% government-owned and 75% owned by ANZ Bank. In 1999 it had total assets of $A46·3m. There is also a Development Bank of Kiribati and a network of village lending banks and credit institutions.

ENERGY AND NATURAL RESOURCES

Environment. Carbon dioxide emissions from the consumption and flaring of fossil fuels were the equivalent of 0·3 tonnes per capita in 2002.

Electricity. Installed capacity (2000), 2,000 kW; production (2000), 7m. kWh.

Agriculture. In 2001 there were 2,000 ha of arable land and 37,000 ha of permanent crops. Copra and fish represent the bulk of production and exports. The principal tree is the coconut; other food-bearing trees are the pandanus palm and the breadfruit. The only vegetable which grows in any quantity is a coarse calladium (alocasia) with the local name 'bwabwai', which is cultivated in pits; taro and sweet potatoes are also grown. Coconut production (2000), 77,000 tonnes; copra, 12,000 tonnes; bananas, 5,000 tonnes; taro, 2,000 tonnes. Principal livestock: pigs (12,000 in 2000).

Forestry. Forests covered 28,000 ha in 2000, or 38·4% of the land area.

Fisheries. Tuna fishing is an important industry; licenses are held by the USA, Japan and the Republic of Korea. Catches in 2001 totalled 32,375 tonnes, exclusively from sea fishing.

INDUSTRY

Industry is concentrated on fishing and handicrafts.

Labour. The economically active population in paid employment (not including subsistence farmers) totalled 11,167 in 1990. In 1994, 11% were employed in agriculture, 4% in industry and 85% in services. Some 70% of the labour force are underemployed; 2% unemployed.

INTERNATIONAL TRADE

Imports and Exports. Total exports (1999), $A14·0m.; imports, $A63·7m. Main import sources in 1996: Australia, 46·1%; Fiji Islands, 18·7%; Japan, 8·6%; New Zealand, 8·4%; China, 5·9%. Main export markets in 1994: Japan, 32·9%; USA, 17·1%; Hong Kong, 12·9%; Bangladesh, 8·6%; Germany, 8·6%. Principal exports: copra, seaweed, fish; imports: foodstuffs, machinery and equipment, manufactured goods and fuel.

COMMUNICATIONS

Roads. In 1999 there were 670 km of roads.

Civil Aviation. There were 20 airports in 2002. In 2003 there were scheduled services from Tarawa (Bonriki) to the Marshall Islands, Nauru and the Fiji Islands.

Shipping. The main port is at Betio (Tarawa). Other ports of entry are Banaba, English Harbor and Kanton. There is also a small network of canals in the Line Islands. The merchant marine fleet totalled 4,000 GRT in 2002.

Telecommunications. Main telephone lines numbered 4,500 in 2002, or 51 per 1,000 population. There were 200 fax machines in 1999 and 2,000 PCs in use in 2000 (18·0 per 1,000 persons). Kiribati had 2,000 Internet users in 2002.

Postal Services. In 1997 there were 25 post offices.

SOCIAL INSTITUTIONS

Justice. In 1989 Kiribati had a police force of 232 under the command of a Commissioner of Police. The Commissioner of Police is also responsible for prisons, immigration, fire service (both domestic and airport) and firearms licensing. There is a Court of Appeal and High Court, with judges at all levels appointed by the President.

The population in penal institutions in 2002 was 64 (equivalent to 67 per 100,000 of national population).

Religion. In 2001, 53% of the population were Roman Catholic and 38% Protestant (Congregational); there are also small numbers of Seventh-Day Adventists, Latter-day Saints (Mormons), Baha'i and Church of God.

Education. In 2002 there were 14,823 pupils and 660 teachers at primary schools and 10,334 pupils in general secondary education with 561 teachers. There is also a teachers' training college with 110 students (1995) and a marine training centre offering training for about 100 merchant seamen a year. The Tarawa Technical Institute at Betio offers part-time technical and commercial courses.

Health. The government maintains free medical and other services. In 1998 there were 26 physicians, four dentists and 208 nurses. There was one hospital on Tarawa in 1990 with 283 beds, and dispensaries on other islands.

CULTURE

Broadcasting. *Radio Kiribati*, a division of the Broadcasting and Publications Authority, transmits daily in English and I-Kiribati from Tarawa. A satellite link to Australia was established in 1985. There were 32,600 radio receivers and 3,030 TV receivers in 2000.

Cinema. There are no cinemas. There is a private-owned projector with film shows once a week in every village on South Tarawa.

Press. In 2003 there were two newspapers: the government-owned *Te Uekera* and the independent weekly *Kiribati Newstar.*

Tourism. Tourism is in the early stages of development. In 2000 there were 1,000 foreign tourists, bringing in revenue of US$2m.

DIPLOMATIC REPRESENTATIVES

Of Kiribati in the United Kingdom
Acting High Commissioner: Makurita Baaro (resides in Kiribati).
Honorary Consul: Michael Walsh (The Great House, Llanddewi Rydderch, Monmouthshire, NP7 9UY).

Of the United Kingdom in Kiribati
High Commissioner: Charles Mochan (resides at Suva, Fiji Islands).

Of the USA in Kiribati
Ambassador: David Lyon (resides at Suva, Fiji Islands).

FURTHER READING

Tearo, T., *Coming of Age*. Tarawa, 1989

National statistical office: Kiribati Statistics Office, PO Boz 67, Baikiki.

KOREA

Daehan Minguk
(Republic of Korea)

Capital: Seoul
Population projection, 2010: 49·08m.
GDP per capita, 2002: (PPP$) 16,950
HDI/world rank: 0·888/28

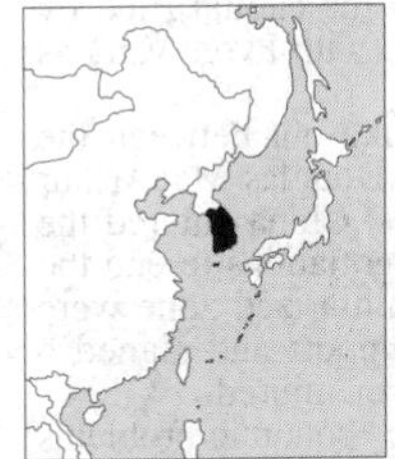

KEY HISTORICAL EVENTS

The Korean peninsula was first settled by tribal peoples from Manchuria and Siberia. Agricultural communities developed into tribal states. Three powerful figures, King T'aejo (AD 53–146) of Koguryo, King Koi (AD 234–86) of Paekche and King Naemul (AD 356–402) of Silla, established hereditary monarchies. With China's support Silla conquered Paekche in 660 and Koguryo in 668. In 676 Silla drove out the Chinese and gained control of the peninsula.

In the 8th century powerful provincial families oversaw the decentralization of power. Two provincial leaders, Kyonhwon and Kungye, established the Later Paekche (892) and Later Koguryo (901) as rivals to Silla. The powerful leader Wang Kon founded Koryo (now Kaesong, North Korea) in 918 and established a unified kingdom in the Korean peninsula in 936. Members of the military, who were not eligible for any hierarchical position above the second of nine levels, led a military coup in 1170, establishing a military regime that held power for the next sixty years.

In 1231 the Mongols invaded Koryo but were resisted for nearly three decades. Under a power-sharing agreement, which came into force in 1258, Koryo retained its identity as a unified state. In 1392 a rebellion, led by General Yi Song-gye, ended the Koryo dynasty. General Yi named the state Choson, and appointed Hanyang (now Seoul) as the capital. Avatamsaka Buddhism was dropped in favour of a new Chinese-influenced Confucian ethical system and the state was governed by a hereditary aristocracy (the *yangban*). In 1443 the Korean phonetic alphabet (*hangul*) was developed under King Sejong.

In 1592 Japan, newly unified under the command of Toyotomi Hideyoshi, sent an army to Korea supposedly as part of an invasion of China. Anti-Japanese sentiment prompted Koreans to fight in the war alongside troops dispatched from Ming China. However, Japanese forces did not withdraw completely until Toyotomi's death in 1598, leaving Korea in ruins. Despite efforts by China and Korea to stem the advances of the Manchu in the early 17th century, Seoul was captured in 1636. During the 17th and 18th centuries, Korea's agriculture developed as irrigation improved and rice, tobacco and ginseng became important crops. By the late 18th century many Korean scholars had turned to Roman Catholicism, leading to government suppression of the religion in a bid to preserve the dominance of Confucianism.

In 1864 Taewon'gun, the father of the child-king Kojong, took power and pursued a programme that isolated Korea from the outside world. When Taewon'gun was eventually forced to step down, foreign influence increased. Radicals staged a coup in 1884 but were quickly defeated by Chinese troops. An agreement to maintain a balance of power in the region was signed by Japan and China the following year. As modernization gained pace, the peasants turned to *Tonghak* ('Eastern Learning'), a new religion based on traditional beliefs. A Tonghak rebellion in 1894 saw China send in troops. Japan responded by sending its own forces and war broke out. By the following year Japan had secured control of the peninsula.

Japan defeated the Russians in 1905 and made Korea a protectorate. After annexation in 1910 there were restrictions on freedom of speech and the language and history of Japan was taught in schools. When the Japanese suppressed a 2m.-strong demonstration in 1919, independence leaders established a provisional government in Shanghai and named Syngman Rhee as president. Tokyo reimposed military rule in 1931 when war broke out between Japan and China. Koreans were forced to support Japan's military efforts during the Second World War. The Shanghai provisional government, having moved to Chungking in southwest China, declared war on Japan in Dec. 1941. It prepared an army of resistance fighters, who joined the Allied forces in China and fought with them until the Japanese surrender in 1945.

Korea was promised independence by China, Britain and the USA at the Cairo conference of 1943 but after Japan's collapse, Korea was divided in two along the 38° Parallel. Initially the USA and the USSR had agreed informally to a four-way power share with Britain and the Republic of China. However, in the north Soviet forces helped to establish a Communist-led provisional government under Kim Il Sung. In 1948 the southern Republic of Korea (with Seoul as the capital), led by Rhee, and the northern Democratic People's Republic of Korea (with Pyongyang as capital) came into being.

After Soviet and US troops had left the peninsula, war broke out between the North and South in June 1950. A US-led UN force under Gen. Douglas MacArthur entered South Korea and pushed back the North Korean forces. China entered the war and contributed 1·2m. troops to the North Korean side. Negotiations to end the war began in 1951 and a new international boundary and demilitarized zone were declared in 1953. The USA offered South Korea financial support and signed a mutual security pact with Rhee. The war left 4m. people dead or injured.

Traditionally an agricultural region, South Korea faced severe economic problems after partition. Rhee's authoritarian rule, marred by corruption, was widely condemned. The elections of 1960 were blighted by violence and fraud and when the police shot 125 students during a demonstration, the government was forced to step down and Rhee was exiled. In May 1961 Gen. Park Chung Hee led a military coup. Park's government revived the economy through the development of manufacturing and increased foreign investment. In 1972 Park proclaimed martial law and abolished the national assembly. In 1979 he was assassinated and the country collapsed into chaos. Chun Doo-hwan became leader in 1980 and revived the national assembly. The economy continued to grow but so did dissatisfaction with the government; a new constitution in 1987 required the president to be elected by popular vote.

In 1992 Kim Young-sam became the first civilian to be elected president since the Korean War. He launched an anti-corruption campaign and pursued closer relations with North Korea. In 1997 Kim Dae-jung was elected president. Kim forged a 'sunshine policy' aimed at closer ties with the North and received the Nobel peace prize. The two Koreas have undertaken a series of joint commercial and infrastructural projects. In 2002 Kim was replaced by Roh Moo-hyun, who continued the 'sunshine policy', despite North Korea's deteriorating relationship with the USA. In Feb. 2003 the land border between the two Koreas was opened for the first time in half a century.

TERRITORY AND POPULATION

South Korea is bounded in the north by the demilitarized zone (separating it from North Korea), east by the East Sea, south by the Korea Strait (separating it from Japan) and west by the Yellow Sea. The area is 99,585 sq. km. The population (census, 1 Nov. 2000) was 46,136,101 (22,977,519 females); density, 463·35 per sq. km (one of the highest in the world). In 2001 the urban population was 82·4%. The population estimate for July 2002 was 47·64m.

The UN gives a projected population for 2010 of 49·08m.

The official language is Korean. In July 2000 the Korean government introduced a new Romanization System for the Korean Language to romanize Korean words into English.

There are nine provinces (*do*) and seven metropolitan cities with provincial status. Area and population in 2000:

Province	*Area (in sq. km)*	*Population (in 1,000)*	*Province*	*Area (in sq. km)*	*Population (in 1,000)*
Gyeonggi	10,135	8,984	Jeju	1,846	513
Gyeongsangnam	10,516	2,909	Seoul (city)	606	9,895
Gyeongsangbuk	19,024	2,725	Busan (city)	760	3,663
Jeollanam	11,987	1,996	Daegu (city)	886	2,481
Jeollabuk	8,050	1,891	Incheon (city)	965	2,475
Chungcheongnam	8,586	1,845	Daejeon (city)	540	1,368
Gangwon	16,502	1,487	Gwangju (city)	501	1,353
Chungcheongbuk	7,432	1,467	Ulsan (city)	1,056	1,014

Cities with over 500,000 inhabitants (census 2000):

Seoul	9,895,217	Ulsan	1,014,428	Cheongju	586,700
Busan	3,662,884	Suwon	946,704	Anyang	580,544
Daegu	2,480,578	Seongnam	914,590	Ansan	562,920
Incheon	2,475,139	Goyang	763,971	Changwon	517,410
Daejeon	1,368,207	Bucheon	761,389	Pohang	515,714
Gwangju	1,352,797	Jeonju	616,468		

SOCIAL STATISTICS

2001: births, 557,228; deaths, 242,730; marriages, 320,063; divorces, 135,014. Rates per 1,000 population in 2001: birth, 11·6; death, 5·1; marriage, 6·9; divorce, 2·8. Suicides numbered 12,277 in 2001. Expectation of life at birth, 2001, 79·0 years for females and 71·4 for males. Life expectancy had been 47 in 1955 and 62 in 1971. Infant mortality, 2001, 5·1 per 1,000 live births; fertility rate, 1·3 births per woman. Annual population growth rate in 2002 was 0·6%. In 2001 the average age of first marriage was 29·6 for men and 26·8 for women, with 28·0 years being the average age that women had their first child. South Korea has one of the most rapidly ageing populations in the world, partly owing to an ever-decreasing birth rate. In 2002, 7·9% of the population were over 65, up from 2·9% in 1960. There were 14·31m. households in 2000, with on average 3·1 members per household. 11,584 South Koreans emigrated in 2001, down from 15,307 in 2000. Between 1962 and 1998 a total of 847,714 Koreans emigrated, 77·8% of them to the USA. 5·65m. Koreans lived abroad in 2001, including 2·1m. in the USA, 1·9m. in China and 640,000 in Japan.

CLIMATE

The country experiences continental temperate conditions. Rainfall is concentrated in the period April to Sept. and ranges from 40" (1,020 mm) to 60" (1,520 mm). Busan, Jan. 36°F (2·2°C), July 76°F (24·4°C). Annual rainfall 56" (1,407 mm). Seoul, Jan. 23°F (–5°C), July 77°F (25°C). Annual rainfall 50" (1,250 mm).

CONSTITUTION AND GOVERNMENT

The 1988 Constitution provides for a *President*, directly elected for a single five-year term, who appoints the members of the *State Council* and heads it, and for a *National Assembly* (*Gukhoe*), currently of 299 members, directly elected for four years (243 from constituencies and 56 from party lists in proportion to the overall vote). The minimum voting age is 20.

National Anthem. 'Aegukga' ('A Song of Love for the Country'); words anonymous, tune by Ahn Eaktay.

RECENT ELECTIONS

Presidential elections were held on 19 Dec. 2002. Roh Moo-hyun of the ruling Millennium Democratic Party won with 48·9% of votes cast, against 46·6% for Lee Hoi-chang of the Grand National Party. Turn-out was 70·2%.

Elections to the National Assembly were held on 15 April 2004. Turn-out was 59·9%. Uri Party (UD) won 152 out of 299 seats with 38·3% of votes cast; the Grand National Party (HD) won 121 with 35·8%; the Democratic Labour Party (MDD) 10 with 13·0%; the Millennium Democratic Party (SMD) 9 with 7·1%; the United Liberal Democrats (JMY) 4 with 2·8%. National Alliance 21 won one seat and two seats went to non-partisans.

CURRENT ADMINISTRATION

President: Roh Moo-hyun; b. 1946 (Uri Party, formerly of the Millennium Democratic Party; sworn in on 25 Feb. 2003, suspended on 12 March 2004, following a vote in the National Assembly to impeach him, but reinstated on 14 May 2004).

In March 2005 the cabinet comprised:

Prime Minister: Lee Hai-chan; b. 1952 (took office on 30 June 2004).

Deputy Prime Minister and Minister of Finance and Economy: Han Duck-soo. *Deputy Prime Minister and Minister of Education and Human Resources Development:* Kim Jin-pyo. *Deputy Prime Minister and Minister of Science and Technology:* Oh Myung.

Minister of Agriculture and Forestry: Park Hong-soo. *Commerce, Industry and Energy:* Lee Hee-beom. *Construction and Transportation:* Kang Dong-suk. *Culture and Tourism:* Chung Dong-chae. *Environment:* Kwak Kyul-ho. *Foreign Affairs and Trade:* Ban Ki-moon. *Health and Welfare:* Kim Geun-tae. *Information and Communication:* Chin Dae-je. *Justice:* Kim Seong-kew. *Planning and Budget:* Byeon Yang-kyoon. *Labour:* Kim Dae-hwan. *Maritime Affairs and Fisheries:* Oh Geo-don. *National Defence:* Yoon Kwang-ung. *Gender Equality:* Jang Ha-jin. *Unification:* Chung Dong-young. *Government Policy Co-ordination:* Vacant. *Government Administration and Home Affairs:* Oh Young-kyo.

National Assembly Speaker: Park Kwan-yong.

Office of the Prime Minister: http://www.opm.go.kr

DEFENCE

Peacetime operational control, which had been transferred to the United Nations Command (UNC) under a US general in July 1950 after the outbreak of the Korean War, was restored to South Korea on 1 Dec. 1994. In the event of a new crisis, operational control over the Korean armed forces will revert to the Combined Forces Command (CFC). Conscription is 26 months in the Army, 28 months in the Navy and 30 months in the Air Force. Conscripts may choose or be required to exchange military service for civilian work. There were 37,140 US personnel based in South Korea in 2002. By 2008 the American combat strength is set to decline by a third. Defence expenditure in 2003 totalled US$14,632m. (US$305 per capita), representing 2·8% of GDP.

Army. Strength (2002) 560,000 (140,000 conscripts). Paramilitary Civilian Defence Corps, 6·28m. The armed forces reserves numbered 3·04m.

Navy. In 2002 the Navy had a substantial force of 63,000 (19,000 conscripts), including 28,000 marine corps troops; it continued its steady modernization programme. Current strength includes 160 surface vessels, 20 support vessels, ten submarines/submersibles and 70 aircraft. The main bases are at Jinhae, Incheon and Busan.

Air Force. In 2002 the Air Force had a strength of 63,000 men and 538 combat aircraft including 560 fighters, 40 special aircraft and 210 support aircraft.

INTERNATIONAL RELATIONS

Defections to South Korea from North Korea totalled 1,281 in 2003 (1,139 in 2002, 583 in 2001, 312 in 2000, 41 in 1995 and 8 in 1993).

South Korea is a member of the UN, WTO, BIS, OECD, Asian Development Bank, Colombo Plan, APEC, IOM and the Antarctic Treaty.

The aim of Korea's foreign policy is to secure international support for peace and stability in Northeast Asia, including a means to reunify the Korean Peninsula without confrontation.

ECONOMY

Agriculture, forestry and fishing accounted for 3·6% of GDP in 2002, industry (including mining, construction and power and water supply) 33·8% and services 62·6%.

Overview. China is set to become Korea's largest trading partner and, in 2004, became Korea's top foreign direct investment destination. Korea has experienced fluctuating growth rates in the last few years; there were high rates of growth in 2002 and 2004, but in 2003 growth was at its slowest in five years. The improved performance in 2004 was partly a result of strong export demand. Employment in manufacturing fell between 1997 and 2001 from 23% to 19% whilst that of the service sector rose from 66% to 70%. Korea's performance is greatly affected by weaknesses in consumer spending, a consequence of high levels of household debt following the credit card crisis of 2002. Between 2000 and 2002 Korea experienced a credit card boom which ended with 3·7m. defaulters by the end of 2003, 10% of the adult population. Progress in resolving the credit card debt problem has been slow. The Korean IT sector has a highly diversified product portfolio, with export receipts from goods such as high-quality mobile phones and flat displays recently surpassing those of semiconductors. In 2004 nearly a fifth of all exports went to

China. The *chaebol* (conglomerates), controlled by their founding families, hold a dominant position in the economy. In 2003 and 2004 the *chaebol* came under increasing pressure from the financial watchdog and government to improve accounting procedures and transparency.

The government owns a third of the commercial banks. Privatizing the commercial banks and developing a market-orientated financial system should be a priority, according to the OECD. The authorities have singled out the education, health care and legal services industries as candidates for deregulation and liberalization.

Currency. The unit of currency is the *won* (KRW). There was inflation in 2002 of 2·8%, rising to 3·4% in 2003. Foreign exchange reserves were US$111,934m. in June 2002 (US$31,928m. in 1995) and gold reserves 442,000 troy oz. Total money supply in May 2002 was 53,335bn. won.

Budget. Revenue and expenditure (in 1,000,000m. won), including bond issuances, at the 2002 budget: 105·8 and 105·8. Sources of revenue: national tax, 93·8; non-tax, 12·0. Expenditure includes: economic development, 27·4; education, 18·5; defence, 17·1; infrastructure, 13·9; general administration, 10·0; contingency, 2·5.

External liabilities in Dec. 2002 were 154,114m. won.

Performance. Total GDP in 2003 was US$605·3bn. GDP growth rate was 7·0% in 2002 but 3·1% in 2003, the lowest rate since 1998. Growth was forecast to rise to 5·0% in 2004.

Banking and Finance. The central bank and bank of issue is the Bank of Korea (*Governor*, Park Seung). In Oct. 2002 bank deposits totalled 498,886bn. won, of which 447,329bn. won were savings and time deposits.

In Dec. 2001 there were 20 national and provincial commercial banks. The largest bank is Kookmin Bank, with assets in Sept. 2002 of 204,337bn. won (US$171·47bn.). Other major banks are the National Agricultural Cooperative Federation (NACF) and Woori (formerly Hanvit) Bank. There were 40 foreign banks in Dec. 2002. In Dec. 2001 non-bank financial institutions included 44 insurance companies, 45 securities companies and three merchant banks. The use of real names in financial dealings has been required since 1994.

South Korea has started to open up once protected industries to foreign ownership, and in 2002 attracted US$9·1bn. in foreign direct investment.

There is a stock exchange in Seoul.

Weights and Measures. The metric system is in use alongside traditional measures. 1 *gwan* = 3·75 kg. 1 *pyeong* = 3·3 sq. metres.

ENERGY AND NATURAL RESOURCES

Environment. South Korea's carbon dioxide emissions from the consumption and flaring of fossil fuels in 2002 were the equivalent of 9·5 tonnes per capita. An *Environmental Sustainability Index* compiled for the World Economic Forum meeting in Feb. 2002 ranked South Korea 135th in the world out of 142 countries analysed, with 35·9%. The index measured the ability of countries to maintain favourable environmental conditions and examined various factors including pollution levels and the use or abuse of natural resources.

Electricity. Installed capacity in 2001 was 51m. kW. Electricity generated (2001) was 285,224m. kWh. Power sources in 2001: nuclear, 39·3%; coal, 38·7%; liquefied natural gas, 10·7%; oil, 9·8%; hydro-electric, 1·5%. There were 18 nuclear reactors in use in 2003. Consumption per capita in 2001 was estimated at 5,444 kWh.

Oil and Gas. In 2001 the imports of petroleum products amounted to 1,099m. bbls., of which crude oil was 859·4m. bbls. The output of petroleum products was 892·8m. bbls., consumption 743·6m. bbls. and the volume of exports 295·0m. bbls. In 2001, 873·4m. bbls. of crude oil were imported. In Sept. 1999 a massive crude oil terminal was opened at Yeosu, Jeollanam-do. It has a capacity to store more than 30m. bbls.

In 2001 imports of natural gas totalled 16·1m. tonnes, consumption 16·0m. tonnes. The total output of city gas in 2001 was 12,657m. cu. metres as was consumption, of which 8,964m. cu. metres was used for household purposes, 3,376m. cu. metres for industrial use and 1,761m. cu. metres for commercial use. In April 1999 a large underwater gas deposit was discovered off the southeastern coast of the country, which was estimated to contain up to 60bn. cu. metres of natural gas.

Water. Water consumption in 2000 was 33,100m. cu. metres, of which 15,800m. cu. metres was for agricultural purposes, 7,300m. cu. metres was supplied to households and 2,900m. cu. metres was for industrial use. Of the total population, 87·8% had tap water in 2001 and per capita supply was 374 litres per day. As of 2001 there were 1,206 dams with walls higher than 15 metres and containing a total of 17·96bn. cu. metres of water.

Minerals. In 2001, 599 mining companies employed 12,103 people. Output, 2001, included (in tonnes): limestone, 82m.; anthracite coal, 3·82m.; iron ore, 0·2m.; zinc ore, 10,259; lead ore, 1,975; gold, 28,595 kg; silver, 664,533 kg. The largest gold deposits in South Korea were discovered in Suryun Mine near Daegu in June 1999. The mine contained an estimated 9·9 tonnes of gold, worth approximately US$81m. Salt production averages 500,000 tonnes a year.

Agriculture. Cultivated land was 1·88m. ha in 2001, of which 1·15m. ha were rice paddies. In 2001 there were 1·70m. ha of arable land and 193,000 ha of permanent crops. In 2001 the farming population was 3·93m. and there were 1·35m. farms. The agricultural workforce was 2·1m. in 2001. There were 201,089 tractors in 2001.

In 2001, 1·08m. ha were sown to rice. Production (2001, in 1,000 tonnes): rice, 5,515; cabbages, 3,450; onions, 1,078; melons and watermelons, 972; tangerines and mandarins, 645; potatoes, 604; barley, 593; grapes, 454; cucumbers and gherkins, 451; pears, 419; chillies and green peppers, 411; garlic, 406; sweet potatoes, 273. Livestock in 2001 (in 1,000): cows, 1,954; pigs, 8,720; sheep, 441; chickens, 102,393.

Forestry. Forest area was 6·42m. ha in 2001 (64% of the land area). Total stock was 428·3m. cu. metres. In 1997, 70% of the total forest area was privately owned. Timber production was 1·5m. cu. metres in 2001.

Fisheries. In 2001 there were a total of 94,835 boats (864,853 gross tonnes). 482 deep-sea fishing vessels were operating overseas as of Dec. 2002. The fish catch was 1,907,925 tonnes in 2001, mainly from marine waters.

INDUSTRY

The leading companies by market capitalization in South Korea, excluding banking and finance, in May 2004 were: Samsung Electronics Company Ltd (US$71·1bn.); SK Telecom Company Ltd (US$13·8bn.); and POSCO, a steel manufacturing company (US$10·7bn.).

Manufacturing industry is concentrated primarily on oil, petro-chemicals, chemical fibres, construction, iron and steel, mobile phones, cement, machinery, chips, shipbuilding, automobiles and electronics. Tobacco manufacture is a semi-government monopoly. Industry is dominated by giant conglomerates (*chaebol*). There were 3·01m. businesses in 2000, of which 261,119 were incorporated. 916,688 businesses were in wholesale and retail trades, 607,718 in dining and accommodation, 329,488 in services, 313,246 in manufacturing and 265,598 in transport and communications. The leading *chaebol* are Samsung, with assets in April 2002 of 72·4trn. won; LG, with assets of 54·5trn. won; and SK, with assets of 46·8trn. won.

Production in 2001: petroleum products, 857·5m. bbls.; cars (2002), 3·15m.; mobile phones, 90m.; TV sets, 9·32m.; refrigerators, 5·13m. Production in 1,000 tonnes: cement, 52,046; crude steel (2002), 45,400; pig iron (2002), 26,600; artificial fertilizers, 3,500; soft drinks (1997), 2,514m. litres; beer, 1,776m. litres; cigarettes, 94·1bn. units.

Shipbuilding orders totalled 6·41m. GT in 2001.

Labour. At Dec. 2001 the population of working age (15 to 59 years) was 36·48m. The economically-active population was 22·18m.; 0·82m. (2001) were registered unemployed. At Nov. 2002, 13·9m. persons were employed in services, 4·2m. in manufacturing, 2·2m. in agriculture, fisheries and forestry, 1·8m. in construction and 19,000 in mining. 6·34m. persons were self-employed in Nov. 2002. Unemployment was 3·8% in Sept. 2004. An annual legal minimum wage is set by the *Minimum Wage Act* (enforced from 1988), which applies to all industries. From Sept. 2002 to Aug. 2003 it was 18,200 won per day and 514,500 won per month. In Dec. 2001 the average monthly wage was 1·75m. won. In 2001 the working week averaged 47 hours (including a half day on Saturdays). In July 2004 the working week in the civil service, for financial and insurance firms, and for employers with 1,000 or more staff was reduced from 44 to 40 hours. A five-day working week for smaller companies is being gradually phased in; employers with fewer than 20 workers do not have to introduce the shorter working week until 2011. Workers in South Korea put in the longest hours of any OECD country. In 2003 full- and part-time workers put in an average of 2,390 hours—nearly 46 hours a week.

Trade Unions. At Dec. 2001 there were 6,150 unions with a total membership of 1,568,723. 877,827 workers belong to the government-recognized Federation of Korean Trade Unions. Since 1997 unions have been permitted to engage in political activities, and the ban on more than one union in a work place has been extended up to 2006. The Korean Confederation of Trade Unions (*President*, Lee Soo-ho), had 644,000 members in 2002.

INTERNATIONAL TRADE

Total external foreign debt was US$110,109m. in 2001. In May 1998 the government removed restrictions on foreign investment in the Korean stock market. It also began to allow foreign businesses to engage in mergers and acquisitions. From July 1998 foreigners were allowed to buy plots of land for both business and non-business purposes. Since Aug. 1990 South Korean businesses and individuals have been permitted to make investments and set up branch offices in North Korea, on an approval basis. According to the Unification Ministry, the overall volume of inter-Korean trade was US$641m. in 2002 (US$342m. in business transactions and US$298m. in non-profit transactions), a 59·3% increase on 2001.

Imports and Exports. Exports in 2002 (provisional figures) were US$162·8bn.; imports, US$152·0bn. Main import suppliers (in US$1bn.): Japan, 28·8; USA, 22·3; China, 16·9. Main export markets: USA, 31·4; China, 22·8; EU, 20·7; Japan, 16·5 (2001).

Major exports in 2002 included (in US$1bn.): semi-conductor chips, 16·6; continuous woven man-made fibres, 15·6; automobiles, 14·8; codeless communication apparatus, 13·6; computers, 12·9; electrical appliances, 10·7; machinery, 9·2; petro-chemicals, 9·1. Major imports (as of 20 Dec. 2002) included: crude oil, 18·6; semi-conductor chips, 17·0; computers, 5·5; petroleum products, 4·9; liquefied natural gas, 4·0. Rice imports were prohibited until 1994, but following the GATT Uruguay Round the rice market opened to foreign imports in 1995.

Trade Fairs. In 2001 there were about 100 trade fairs hosted by COEX and 30 hosted by BEXCO (Busan). 3,187 Korean companies participated in 145 trade fairs held in other countries supported by KOTRA, the Korea Trade-Investment Agency.

COMMUNICATIONS

Roads. In 2001 there were 91,396 km of roads, of which 77% (70,146 km) were paved. 10·7m. passengers (2000) and 535·76m. tonnes of freight were carried in 2001. In Dec. 2001 motor vehicles registered totalled 12,914,115, including 8,889,327 passenger cars. There were 991,590 new car registrations in 2002 (by Nov.). In 2001 there were 8,097 fatalities as a result of road accidents (9,353 in 2000). At 16·9 deaths per 100,000 people, South Korea has among the highest death rates in road accidents of any industrialized country. The first of two planned cross-border roads between the two Koreas opened in Feb. 2003.

Rail. In 2001 the National Railroad totalled 3,127 km of 1,435 mm gauge (667·5 km electrified) and 20 km of 762 mm gauge. In 2001 railways carried 912m. passengers and 45m. tonnes of freight. In June 2000 it was agreed to start consultations to restore the railway from Seoul to Sinuiju, on the North Korean/Chinese border, by rebuilding a 12 km long stretch from Munsan, in South Korea, to Jangdan, on the South Korean/North Korean border, and an 8 km long stretch in North Korea. Work on the restoration began in Sept. 2000 but has been delayed in part because of the diplomatic crisis between North Korea and the USA, which escalated in Oct. 2002.

There are metros in Seoul (287 km), and smaller ones in Busan (70·5 km), Daegu (25·7 km) and Incheon (24·6 km).

Civil Aviation. There are six international airports in South Korea: at Seoul (Incheon), Busan (Gimhae), Daegu, Jeju, Yangyang and Cheongju. The new Incheon airport, 50 km to the west of Seoul, built on reclaimed land made up of four small islands, opened in March 2001 and is the largest airport in Asia. It has replaced Gimpo Airport as Seoul's International Airport. The national carrier is Korean Air. Another Korean carrier, Asiana Airlines, also provides services, as did in 2002 around 57 foreign airlines. In 2001, 28·5m. passengers and 423,692 tonnes of cargo were carried on domestic routes and 19·7m. passengers and 1·8m. tonnes of cargo on international routes.

In 2000 Seoul's Gimpo airport handled 36,639,067 passengers (18,738,579 on domestic flights), making it the 13th busiest airport in the world for passenger traffic. It handled 1,846,896 tonnes of freight, making it the fourth busiest for freight. Busan handled 9,358,152 passengers (8,015,414 on domestic flights) and 182,402 tonnes of freight. Jeju handled 9,125,939 passengers (8,793,142 on domestic flights) and 280,031 tonnes of freight.

Shipping. In 2002 there were 51 ports (28 for international trade), including Busan, Incheon, Gunsan, Mokpo, Yeosu, Pohang, Donghae, Jeju, Masan, Ulsan, Daesan and Kwangyang. In 1997 the merchant marine comprised 562 vessels totalling 25·15m. DWT, representing 3·4% of the world's tonnage. 298 vessels (66·87% of gross tonnage) were registered under foreign flags. Total GRT in 2002, 7·05m., including oil tankers 841,000 GRT. In 2001 vessels totalling 770,284,000 NRT entered ports and vessels totalling 776,250,000 NRT cleared. The busiest port is Busan, which in 1999 was visited by 69,429 vessels of 450,033,000 GRT. It is the world's third busiest container port, after Hong Kong and Singapore.

In 2001, 9,340,000 domestic passengers and 1,075,000 international passengers took ferries and other ocean-going vessels. There were a total of 6,586 registered vessels in 2001.

Telecommunications. There were 22,725,000 main telephone lines in 2001 (480 per 1,000 persons). In 2001 public telephones totalled 516,000. In 2002 the number of mobile phone subscribers was 32,342,000 (68·0% of the population). The largest operator, SK Telecom, has 39·5% of the market share, ahead of KTF, with 33·7%. 60·1% of households had PCs in 2002. There were approximately 25·6m. Internet users in July 2002.

Postal Services. As of 2001 there were 3,688 post offices operating, with each *myon* (administrative unit comprising several villages) having one or more post offices. In 2002 the mail volume totalled 4,498m. items.

SOCIAL INSTITUTIONS

Justice. Judicial power is vested in the Supreme Court, High Courts, District Courts and Family Court, as well as the Administrative Court and Patent Court. The single six-year term Chief Justice is appointed by the President with the consent of the National Assembly. The other 13 Justices of the Supreme Court are appointed by the President with the consent of the National Assembly, upon the recommendation of the Chief Justice, for renewable six-year terms; the Chief Justice appoints other judges. The death penalty is authorized. In Jan. 2002 there were 1,508 judges, 1,134 prosecutors and about 3,800 private practising lawyers.

The population in penal institutions in Oct. 2002 was 60,721 (128 per 100,000 of national population).

Religion. Traditionally, Koreans have lived under the influence of shamanism, Buddhism (introduced AD 372) and Confucianism, which was the official faith from 1392 to 1910. Catholic converts from China introduced Christianity in the 18th century, but a ban on Roman Catholicism was not lifted until 1882. The Anglican Church was introduced in 1890 and became an independent jurisdiction in 1993 under the Archbishop of Korea. In 1998 it had 110 churches, 175 priests and some 65,000 faithful. Religious affiliations of the population in 2001: Buddhism, 23·3%; Protestantism, 19·8%; Roman Catholicism, 6·7%; Confucianism, 0·5%; others, 0·8%; no religion, 49·6%. In Sept. 2003 there was one Roman Catholic cardinal.

Education. The Korean education system consists of a six-year elementary school, a three-year middle school, a three-year high school and college and university (two to four years). Elementary education for 6–11 year olds is compulsory. Mandatory middle school education began in 2002.

The total number of schools has increased sixfold from 3,000 in 1945 to 19,124 in 2002, with 11,957,388 enrolled students. In 2002 there were 8,343 kindergartens with 550,256 pupils and 29,673 teachers; 5,384 elementary schools with 4,138,366 pupils and 147,497 teachers; 1,841,030 pupils and 95,283 teachers at 2,809 middle schools; and 1,995 high schools with 1,795,509 pupils and 44,177 teachers. In 2002 there were 163 colleges and universities with 1,771,738 students and 44,177 teachers; 11 teacher training colleges with 23,259 students and 721 teachers; 945 graduate schools with 262,867 students; and 19 industrial universities with 187,040 students and 2,543 teachers. In 1996, 5·6% of the population was enrolled in tertiary education, up from just 0·6% in 1970. Around 150,000 South Koreans were studying abroad in 2001.

In 2000–01 total expenditure on education came to 3·8% of GNP and 17·4% of total government spending. The adult literacy was 97·9% in 2001 (99·2% of males and 96·6% of females).

Health. In 2000 there were 285 general hospitals (with 113,518 beds), 20,053 other hospitals and clinics (130,162 beds), 7,412 oriental medical hospitals and clinics (8,436 beds) and 10,527 dental hospitals and clinics. In 2000 there were 72,503 physicians (648 people per doctor), 10,108 oriental medical doctors, 18,039 dentists, 8,728 midwives (1992), 160,295 nurses and 50,623 pharmacists. In 2001 South Korea spent 5·9% of its GDP on health. In 1998, 67·6% of all adult men smoked (the highest proportion in any country in the world), but only 6·7% of women were smokers.

Welfare. In Dec. 2001, 16·3m. persons were covered by the National Pension System introduced in 1988. Employers and employees make equal contributions; persons joining by choice or in rural areas pay their own contributions. The System covers age pensions, disability pensions and survivors' pensions.

Under a system of unemployment insurance introduced in July 1995, workers laid off after working at least six months for a member employer are entitled to benefits averaging 50% of their previous wage for a period of 90 up to 240 days.

CULTURE

World Heritage Sites. There are seven sites in the South Korea that appear on the UNESCO World Heritage List. They are (with year entered on list): the Sokkuram Grotto and Pulguksa Temple (1995), the Temple of Haeinsa (1995), Chongmyo Shrine (1995), Changdeokgung Palace, Seoul (1997), Hwasong fort, Suwon (1997), the dolmens of Kanghwa (2000), Gyeongju historic area (2000).

Broadcasting. The Korean Broadcasting System (KBS) is a public corporation which broadcasts seven radio channels, two terrestrial TV channels and two satellite TV channels. KBS maintains a nationwide network that connects the key station in Seoul with 25 local stations. It also maintains ten bureaux overseas. In addition to KBS, there is a semi-public TV broadcaster, Munhwa Broadcasting Corporation (MBC), and one commercial TV network, Education Broadcasting System (EBS). Cable TV was inaugurated in March 1995. It had 3·5m. paying subscribers in 2000 and provided 44 channels. There were 17·0m. TV sets (colour by NTSC) in 2001 and 48·6m. radio receivers in 2000.

Cinema. In 2000 there were 376 cinemas with a seating capacity of 193,775. 48 full-length films were produced in 1999.

Press. There were 123 dailies in 2001 and 6,913 periodicals. The main dailies are *Chosun Ilbo* (average circulation of 2·4m. per issue), *JoongAng Ilbo* (average circulation of 2·1m. per issue) and *Dong-A Ilbo* (average circulation of 2·0m. per issue).

A total of 36,185 book titles and 118m. books were published in 2002.

Tourism. In 2001, 6,084,476 Koreans travelled abroad and 5,147,204 foreign nationals visited South Korea (4,542,159 in 1997). In 2001 tourist revenues from foreign visitors totalled US$6·4bn.; overseas travel expenditure by Koreans going abroad totalled US$6·5bn. On 18 Nov. 1998 the first South Korean tourists to visit North Korea set sail on a cruise and tour organized by the South Korean firm Hyundai.

Libraries. There were 9,337 libraries in 2001, including one national library, one congressional, 420 public, 420 university and 7,918 libraries at primary, middle and high schools. There were also 578 specialized and professional libraries.

Theatre and Opera. There are 316 theatres nationwide. 47 have 1,200 seats that can accommodate large-scale dramas, operas, dances and musicals. The Seoul Arts Centre has an opera house.

Museums and Galleries. In 2001 there were 249 museums, including 25 national museums, 36 public museums, 107 private museums and 81 university museums. There were an estimated 500 art galleries in 2001.

DIPLOMATIC REPRESENTATIVES

Of the Republic of Korea in the United Kingdom (60 Buckingham Gate, London, SW1E 6AJ)
Ambassador: Vacant.
Chargé d'Affaires a.i.: Il-Soo Kim.

Of the United Kingdom in the Republic of Korea (4 Jeong-dong, Jung-gu, Seoul 100–120)
Ambassador: Warwick Morris.

Of the Republic of Korea in the USA (2450 Massachusetts Ave., NW, Washington, D.C., 20008)
Ambassador: Hong Seok-hyun.

Of the USA in the Republic of Korea (82 Sejongno, Jongno-gu, Seoul)
Ambassador: Thomas Hubbard.

Of the Republic of Korea to the United Nations
Ambassador: Kim Sam-hoon.

Of the Republic of Korea to the European Union
Ambassador: Oh Haeng-kyeom.

FURTHER READING

National Bureau of Statistics. *Korea Statistical Yearbook*
Bank of Korea. *Economic Statistics Yearbook*
Castley, R., *Korea's Economic Miracle*. London, 1997
Cumings, B., *Korea's Place in the Sun: A Modern History*. New York, 1997
Hoare, James E., *Korea.* [Bibliography] ABC-Clio, Oxford and Santa Barbara (CA), 1997
Kang, M.-H., *The Korean Business Conglomerate: Chaebol Then and Now*. Univ. of California Press, 1996
Kim, D.-H. and Tat, Y.-K. (eds.) *The Korean Peninsula in Transition*. London, 1997
Simons, G., *Korea: the Search for Sovereignty.* London, 1995
Smith, H., *Industry Policy in Taiwan and Korea in the 1980s*. Edward Elgar, 2000
Song, P.-N., *The Rise of the Korean Economy.* 2nd ed. OUP, 1994
Tennant, R., *A History of Korea*. London, 1996

National statistical office: National Bureau of Statistics, Ministry of Finance and Economy, Seoul.
Website: http://www.nso.go.kr/

NORTH KOREA

Chosun Minchu-chui Inmin Konghwa-guk (Democratic People's Republic of Korea)

Capital: Pyongyang
Population projection, 2010: 23·27m.
GDP per capita: not available

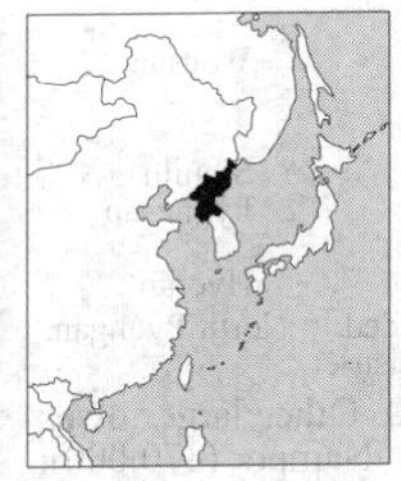

KEY HISTORICAL EVENTS

Korea was ruled by Japan from 1905–45. Although promised independence by China, Britain and the USA, Korea was divided along the 38° Parallel after Japan's defeat in 1945. The north was occupied by Soviet troops, who supported a Communist-led provisional government under Kim Il Sung. In 1948 the southern Republic of Korea, led by Syngman Rhee, and the northern Democratic People's Republic of Korea (with Pyongyang as capital) came into being.

After Soviet and US troops had left the peninsula, war broke out between the North and South in June 1950. A US-led UN force under Gen. Douglas MacArthur entered South Korea and pushed back the North Korean forces. China entered the war and contributed 1·2m. troops to the North Korean side. Negotiations to end the war began in 1951 and a new international boundary and demilitarized zone were declared in 1953. The USA offered South Korea financial support and signed a mutual security pact with Rhee. The war left 4m. people dead or injured. In the aftermath of war, Kim tightened his grip on North Korea, introducing his Marxist-influenced philosophy of *Juche* (self-reliance), rejecting foreign assistance. Industrialization and military spending gathered pace in the later 1950s and the 1960s but economically North Korea fell way behind its southern neighbour.

When the Soviet Union collapsed in 1990–91, North Korea went into an economic crisis that included widespread famine. Attempts to improve relations with South Korea in the early 1990s faltered over the North's nuclear capacity. Kim died in 1994 and power passed to his son, Kim Jong Il. Under the younger Kim the economy has fallen to below subsistence level although spending on the military remains high. In 1997 the UN World Food Programme estimated that 2m. North Koreans faced starvation. More than 5% of the population starved to death during the 1990s. In 2000 Kim received South Korean President Kim Dae-jung as relations between the North and South appeared to be thawing. Relations with the USA worsened during 2002 and 2003 after US president George Bush accused North Korea of forming part of what he called the 'Axis of Evil' along with Iraq and Iran. North Korea re-activated a nuclear plant and announced its withdrawal from the nuclear non-proliferation treaty. In Feb. 2003 the land border between the two Koreas was opened for the first time in half a century when South Korean tourism officials visited a resort in North Korea. In Feb. 2005 North Korea publicly admitted for the first time that it possessed nuclear weapons.

For the early history of North Korea see KOREA: Key Historical Events *on page 1003.*

TERRITORY AND POPULATION

North Korea is bounded in the north by China, east by the sea of Japan, west by the Yellow Sea and south by South Korea, from which it is separated by a demilitarized zone of 1,262 sq. km. Its area is 122,762 sq. km.

The census population in 1993 was 21,213,378; density 172·8 per sq. km. In the elections to the Supreme People's Assembly held on 26 July 1998, 687 deputies were elected, as was the case in 1990. The South Korean weekly NEWSREVIEW stated that North Korea has made it a rule that there should be one deputy per 30,000 people, suggesting that the population has remained stable since 1990. 30,000 multiplied by 687 would give a population of 20·61m., more than 1·5m. less than official estimates. 2002 population estimate: 22,511,000.

The UN gives a projected population for 2010 of 23·27m.

The area, 1987 population (in 1,000) and chief towns of the provinces, special cities and special districts:

	Area in sq. km	Population	Chief Town
Chagang	16,968	1,156	Kanggye
North Hamgyong[1]	17,570	2,003	Chongjin
South Hamgyong	18,970	2,547	Hamhung
North Hwanghae	8,007	1,409	Sariwon
South Hwanghae	8,002	1,914	Haeju
Hyangsan (special district)[2]	...	28	
Kaesong (special city)	1,255	331	
Kangwon	11,152	1,227	Wonsan
Najin Sonbong (special city)[3]	...	...	
Nampo (special city)	753	715	
North Pyongan[4]	12,191	2,380	Sinuiju
South Pyongan	11,577	2,653	Pyongsan
Pyongyang (special city)	2,000	2,355	
Yanggang	14,317	628	Hyesan

[1]Area and population include Najin Sonbong special city. [2]Area included in North Pyongan. [3]Created in 2001. [4]Area includes Hyangsan special district.

Pyongyang, the capital, had a 1999 population of 3,136,000. Other large towns (estimate, 1987): Hamhung (701,000); Chongjin (520,000); Nampo (370,000); Sunchon (356,000).

The official language is Korean.

SOCIAL STATISTICS

1995 births, 477,000; deaths, 122,000. 1995 birth rate, 21·6 per 1,000 population; death rate, 5·5. Annual population growth rate, 1990–99, 1·6%. Marriage is discouraged before the age of 32 for men and 29 for women. Life expectancy at birth, 1997, was 59·8 years for males and 64·5 years for females. Infant mortality, 1990–95, 24 per 1,000 live births; fertility rate, 2001, 2·1 births per woman. It was estimated in 1999 that up to 300,000 North Korean food-seeking refugees had gone to China to escape the famine. 27% of the population is classified as 'hostile' by the regime and 45% as 'unstable'.

CLIMATE

There is a warm temperate climate, though winters can be very cold in the north. Rainfall is concentrated in the summer months. Pyongyang, Jan. 18°F (–7·8°C), July 75°F (23·9°C). Annual rainfall 37" (916 mm).

CONSTITUTION AND GOVERNMENT

The political structure is based upon the Constitution of 27 Dec. 1972. Constitutional amendments of April 1992 delete references to Marxism-Leninism but retain the Communist Party's monopoly of rule. The Constitution provides for a 687-seat *Supreme People's Assembly* elected every five years by universal suffrage. Citizens of 17 years and over can vote and be elected. The government consists of the *Administration Council* directed by the Central People's Committee.

The head of state is the *President*, elected for four-year terms. On the death of Kim Il Sung on 8 July 1994 his son and designated successor, Kim Jong Il (b. 1942), assumed all his father's posts. On 5 Sept. 1998 he took over as President and 'Supreme Leader'.

Party membership was 2m. in 1995. There are also the puppet religious Chongu and Korean Social Democratic Parties and various organizations combined in a Fatherland Front.

National Anthem. 'A chi mun bin na ra i gang san' ('Shine bright, o dawn, on this land so fair'); words by Pak Se Yong, tune by Kim Won Gyun.

RECENT ELECTIONS

Elections to the Supreme People's Assembly were held on 3 Aug. 2003. Only the list of the Democratic Front for the Reunification of the Fatherland was allowed to participate. 687 deputies were elected unopposed.

CURRENT ADMINISTRATION

President: Kim Jong Il. He also holds the posts of *Supreme Commander of the Korean People's Army* and *Chairman of the National Defence Commission*.

In March 2005 the government included:

Prime Minister: Pak Pong-chu (appointed 3 Sept. 2003).

Vice Prime Ministers: Kwak Pom-ki, Chon Sung-hun, No Tu-ch'ol.

Minister of Agriculture: Yi Kyong-sik. *Chemical Industry:* Yi Mu-yong. *City Management:* Ch'oe Chong-kon. *Commerce:* Yi Yong-son. *Construction and Building Materials Industry:* Vacant. *Culture:* Ch'oe Ik-kyu. *Education:* Kim Yong-chin. *Electronic Industry:* O Su-yong. *Crude Oil Industry:* Vacant. *Extractive Industries:* Yi Kwang-nam. *Finance:* Mun Il-Pong. *Fisheries:* Yi Song-ung. *Foreign Affairs:* Paek Nam-sun. *Foreign Trade:* Rim Kyong-man. *Forestry:* Sok Kun-su. *Labour:* Yi Won-il. *Land and Environment Protection:* Chang Il-son. *Land and Marine Transport:* Kim Yong-il. *Light Industry:* Yi Chu-o. *Metal and Machine-Building Industries:* Kim Sung-hyon. *People's Security:* Ju Sang-song. *Post and Telecommunications:* Yi Kum-pom. *Power and Coal Industries:* Chu Tong-il. *Procurement and Food Administration:* Choe Nam-kyun. *Public Health:* Kim Su-hak. *Railways:* Kim Yong-sam. *State Construction Control:* Pae Tal-chun. *State Inspection:* Kim Ui-sun.

President, Supreme People's Assembly Praesidium: Kim Yong-nam. *Vice Presidents:* Yang Hyong-sop, Kim Yong-t'ae.

In practice the country is ruled by the Korean Workers' (*i.e.*, Communist) Party which elects a Central Committee which in turn appoints a Politburo.

Office of the President: http://www.korea-dpr.com/

DEFENCE

The Supreme Commander of the Armed Forces is Kim Jong Il. Military service is compulsory at the age of 16 for periods of 5–8 years in the Army, 5–10 years in the Navy and 3–4 years in the Air Force, followed by obligatory part-time service in the Pacification Corps to age 40. Total armed forces troops were estimated to number 1,082,000 in 2002, up from 840,000 in 1986 although down from 1,160,000 in 1997.

Defence expenditure in 2003 totalled US$5,500m. (US$243 per capita), and represented 25·0% of GDP—the highest percentage of any country in the world.

In 1998 North Korea tested a medium-range nuclear-capable Taepo Dong-1 missile. It has also developed a shorter-range No-Dong ballistic missile in addition to Scud B and Scud C missiles, and is known to be developing a longer-range inter-continental ballistic missile, the two-stage Taepo Dong-2, which experts believe could reach Alaska and the westernmost Hawaiian islands.

Nuclear Weapons. North Korea was for many years suspected of having a secret nuclear-weapons programme, and perhaps enough material to build two warheads. In Oct. 2002 it revealed that it had developed a nuclear bomb in violation of an arms control pact agreed with the USA in 1994. North Korea has not signed the Comprehensive Nuclear-Test-Ban-Treaty, which is intended to bring about a ban on any nuclear explosions. In Feb. 2005 it declared that it had manufactured nuclear weapons—a claim that cannot be verified—and stated that it would not re-enter multilateral negotiations on its disarmament. North Korea is widely suspected of having both biological and chemical weapons.

Army. One of the world's biggest, the Army was estimated at 950,000 personnel in 2002 with around 600,000 reserves. There is also a paramilitary worker-peasant Red Guard of some 3·5m. and a Ministry of Public Security force of 189,000 including border guards.

Equipment includes some 3,500 T-34, T-54/55, T-62 and Type-59 main battle tanks.

Navy. The Navy, principally tasked to coastal patrol and defence, comprises 26 diesel submarines, three small frigates and six corvettes. Personnel in 2002 totalled about 46,000 with 65,000 reserves.

Air Force. The Air Force had a total of 621 combat aircraft and 86,000 personnel in 2002. Combat aircraft include J-5/6/7s (Chinese built versions of MiG-17/19/23s), MiG-29s, Su-7s and Su-25s.

INTERNATIONAL RELATIONS

In Sept. 1999 following negotiations between Pyongyang and Washington in Berlin, Pyongyang agreed to put off its plan to test-fire an advanced long-range missile whilst the USA agreed gradually to lift economic sanctions imposed in 1950. The gesture on the part of the USA was the most significant since the end of the Korean War.

In 2000 North Korea received US$220m. in foreign aid, of which US$114m. came from South Korea.

North Korea is a member of the UN and the Antarctic Treaty.

ECONOMY

Agriculture is estimated to account for approximately 25% of GDP, industry 60% and services 15%.

Overview. In Dec. 1993 it was officially admitted that the third seven-year plan had failed to achieve its industrial targets owing to the disappearance of Communist markets and aid. Policy now concentrates on the development of agriculture, light industry and foreign trade but progress is impeded by an all-powerful bureaucracy and a reluctance to depart from the Marxist-Stalinist line. Changes in the economy in July 2002—the revocation of the rationing system for rice and large increases in prices for food, electricity and housing—prompted hopes of an upturn but food shortages became critical in 2003 after the deterioration of relations with international donors.

Currency. The monetary unit is the *won* (KPW) of 100 *chon*. Banknotes were replaced by a new issue in July 1992. Exchanges of new for old notes were limited to 500 won. In July 2002 the government readjusted the value of the won from an artificially set rate of 2·15 won per dollar to 150 won per dollar, although the black market rate is nearer 800 won to the dollar. Inflation was an estimated 5% in 1998.

Budget. Estimated revenue, 1999, 19,801m. won; expenditure, 20,018m. won.

Performance. The real GDP growth rate was 6·2% in 1999 following a decade of negative growth. This was followed in 2000 by growth of 1·3%, rising in 2001 to 3·7%. GDP per head was put at US$741 in 1997, or about a thirteenth of that of South Korea.

Banking and Finance. The bank of issue is the Central Bank of Korea (*Governor*, Kim Wan-su). In 2002 there were seven state banks, seven joint venture banks and two foreign investment banks.

Weights and Measures. While the metric system is in force traditional measures are in frequent use. The *jungbo* = one ha; the *ri* = 3,927 metres.

ENERGY AND NATURAL RESOURCES

Environment. Carbon dioxide emissions from the consumption and flaring of fossil fuels in 2002 were the equivalent of 3·5 tonnes per capita. An *Environmental Sustainability Index* compiled for the World Economic Forum meeting in Feb. 2002 ranked North Korea 140th in the world out of 142 countries analysed, with 32·3%. The index measured the ability of countries to maintain favourable environmental conditions and examined various factors including pollution levels and the use or abuse of natural resources.

Electricity. There are three thermal power stations and four hydro-electric plants. Installed capacity was 9·5m. kW in 2000. Production in 2000 was 19·4bn. kWh. Consumption per capita was 1,474 kWh in 2000. Hydro-electric potential exceeds 8m. kW. A hydro-electric plant and dam under construction on the Pukhan River near Mount Kumgang has been denounced as a flood threat by the South Koreans, who constructed a defensive 'Peace Dam' in retaliation. American aid to increase energy supply slowed after evidence that North Korea had broken its promise to freeze its nuclear weapons programme. But in Oct. 1998 Japan agreed to contribute US$1bn. towards building two nuclear power stations and the US Congress agreed to funds to supply fuel oil on condition that North Korea abandons its nuclear ambitions. In Aug. 2002 work began on the construction of the two western-designed light-water nuclear reactors. In Feb. 2003 North Korea reactivated its nuclear reactor at Yongbyon that had been dormant since 1994.

Oil and Gas. Oil wells went into production in 1957. An oil pipeline from China came on stream in 1976. China's supplies account for 70% of North Korea's oil consumption. Refinery distillation output amounted to 2·5m. tonnes in 1998.

Minerals. North Korea is rich in minerals. Estimated reserves in tonnes: coal, 11,990m.; manganese, 6,500m.; iron ore, 3,300m.; uranium, 26m.; zinc, 12m.; lead, 6m.; copper, 2·15m. 54m. tonnes of coal and 16m. tonnes of lignite were mined in 2000, 11m. tonnes of iron ore in 1996 and 13,000 tonnes of copper ore in 2002. 2001 production of gold was 2,000 kg; silver (2001 estimate), 40 tonnes; salt (1997 estimate), 590,000 tonnes.

Agriculture. In 2001 there were 2·5m. ha of arable land and 300,000 ha of permanent crop land. In 1995 there were 0·65m. ha of paddy fields. In 2002, 3·32m. persons were economically active in agriculture.

Collectivization took place between 1954 and 1958. 90% of the cultivated land is farmed by co-operatives. Land belongs either to the State or to co-operatives, and it is intended gradually to transform the latter into the former, but small individually-tended plots producing for 'farmers' markets' are tolerated as a 'transition measure'.

There is a large-scale tideland reclamation project. In 2001, 1·46m. ha were under irrigation, making possible two rice harvests a year. There were 70,000 tractors in 2001. The technical revolution in agriculture (nearly 95% of ploughing, etc., is mechanized) has considerably increased the yield of wheat (sown on 103,000 ha). Production (2000, in 1,000 tonnes): rice, 1,690; potatoes, 1,402; maize, 1,041; apples, 650; cabbages, 630; sweet potatoes, 468; soybeans, 350; dry beans, 280; melons and watermelons, 214.

Livestock, 2000: pigs, 2·97m.; goats, 2·10m.; cattle, 600,000; sheep, 190,000; 10m. chickens.

A chronic food shortage has led to repeated efforts by UN agencies to stave off famine. In Jan. 1998 the UN launched an appeal for US$378m. for food for North Korea, the largest ever relief effort mounted by its World Fund Programme.

Forestry. Forest area in 2000 was 8·21m. ha (68·2% of the land area). Timber production was 7·06m. cu. metres in 2001.

Fisheries. In 2001 total catch was approximately 200,000 tonnes, of which 90% were sea fish.

INDUSTRY

Industries were intensively developed by the Japanese occupiers, notably cotton spinning, hydro-electric power, cotton, silk and rayon weaving, and chemical fertilizers. Production: pig iron (2002), 800,000 tonnes; cement (2002), 5·3m. tonnes; crude steel (2000), 1·11m. tonnes; textile fabrics (1994), 350m. metres; TV sets (1995), 240,000 units; motor cars (2000), 6,600 units; ships (1995), 50,000 GRT. Annual steel production capacity was 4·3m. tonnes in 1987. Industrial production is estimated to have halved between 1990 and 2000.

Labour. The labour force totalled 11,881,000 (55% males) in 1996. Nearly 29% of the economically active population in 2002 were engaged in agriculture.

INTERNATIONAL TRADE

Joint ventures with foreign firms have been permitted since 1984. A law of Oct. 1992 revised the 1984 rules: foreign investors may now set up wholly-owned facilities in special economic zones, repatriate part of profits and enjoy tax concessions. In 1996 foreign debt was estimated at US$11,830m. The USA imposed sanctions in Jan. 1988 for alleged terrorist activities. Since June 1995 South Korean businesses and individuals have been permitted to make investments and set up branch offices in North Korea.

Imports and Exports. Exports in 2001 were US$826m.; imports, US$1,847m. In 2001 China was the biggest import supplier (31%), followed by Japan (13%) and South Korea (12%); Japan was the main export destination (27%), ahead of South Korea (21%) and China (20%). The chief exports are metal ores and products, the chief imports machinery and petroleum products.

COMMUNICATIONS

Roads. There were around 31,200 km of road in 1999, of which 2,000 km were paved. There were 262,000 passenger cars in 2000. The first of two planned cross-border roads between the two Koreas opened in Feb. 2003.

Rail. The railway network totalled 8,533 km in 1990, of which 3,250 km were electrified. In 1990, 38·5m. tonnes of freight and 35m. passengers were carried. In June 2000 it was agreed to start consultations to restore the railway from Sinuiju, on the North Korean/Chinese border, to Seoul by rebuilding an 8 km long stretch from Pongdong-ni to Changdan, on the North Korean/South Korean border, and a 12 km long stretch in South Korea. The first two rail links between the two Koreas are currently under construction.

There is a metro and tramway in Pyongyang.

Civil Aviation. There is an international airport at Pyongyang (Sunan). There were flights in 2003 to Bangkok, Beijing, Khabarovsk, Macao, Shenyang and Vladivostok. The national carrier is Air Koryo.

Shipping. The leading ports are Chongjin, Wonsan and Hungnam. Pyongyang is connected to the port of Nampo by railway and river. In 2002 the ocean-going merchant fleet totalled 870,000 GRT, including oil tankers 16,000 GRT.

The biggest navigable river is the Yalu, 698 km up to the Hyesan district.

Telecommunications. An agreement to share in Japan's telecommunications satellites was reached in Sept. 1990. There were 1,100,000 main telephone lines in 2000, or 45·8 per 1,000 population. In 1995 there were 3,000 fax machines. North Korea's first Internet cafe opened in May 2002.

SOCIAL INSTITUTIONS

Justice. The judiciary consists of the Supreme Court, whose judges are elected by the Assembly for three years; provincial courts; and city or county people's courts. The procurator-general, appointed by the Assembly, has supervisory powers over the judiciary and the administration; the Supreme Court controls the judicial administration.

In Jan. 1999 approximately 200,000 political prisoners were being held at ten detention camps in the country.

Religion. The Constitution provides for 'freedom of religion as well as the freedom of anti-religious propaganda'. In 2001 there were 3·0m. Chondoists. Another 3·4m. followed traditional beliefs. There were also significant numbers of Christians and Buddhists.

Education. Free compulsory universal technical education lasts 11 years: one pre-school year, four years primary education starting at the age of six, followed by six years secondary. In 1994–95 there were 37 universities, 31 specialized universities and 108 specialized colleges.

The adult literacy rate is 95%.

Health. Medical treatment is free. In 1995 there were 64,006 physicians, 38,792 nurses and 12,931 midwives. The hospital bed provision in 1989 of 135 per 10,000 population was one of the highest in the world.

North Korea has been one of the least successful countries in the battle against undernourishment in the past 25 years. Between 1980 and 1996 the proportion of undernourished people rose from 16% of the population to 48%. Many people have had to resort to eating twigs, bark and leaves.

CULTURE

World Heritage Sites. There is one UNESCO site in North Korea: the Complex of Koguryo Tombs (2004).

Broadcasting. The government-controlled Korean Central Broadcasting Station and Korean Central Television Station are responsible for radio and TV broadcasting. In 1991 there were 34 radio and 11 TV stations (colour by PAL). There were 3·33m. radio and 1·17m. TV sets in 2000. All radio and television stations being government-run, North Koreans know very little of the outside world. They have been told that the food shortages of recent years were a global catastrophe and that they are comparatively well-off. However, North Korean refugees sheltering with ethnic Koreans in China are learning more about the outside world and word of the South Korean prosperity is filtering back into North Korea.

Press. There were three daily newspapers in 1996. The party newspaper is *Nodong* (or *Rodong*) *Sinmun* (Workers' Daily News). Circulation is about 600,000.

Tourism. A 40-year ban on non-Communist tourists was lifted in 1986. In 1998 there were 130,000 foreign tourists. On 19 Nov. 1998 North Korea received its first tourists from South Korea, on a cruise and tour organized by the South Korean firm Hyundai.

Calendar. A new yearly calendar was announced on 9 July 1997 based on Kim Il Sung's birthday on 15 April 1912. Thus 1912 became *Juche* year 1; 2005 is *Juche* year 95.

DIPLOMATIC REPRESENTATIVES

Of North Korea in the United Kingdom (73 Gunnersbury Avenue, London W5 4LP)
Ambassador: Ri Yong Ho.

Of the United Kingdom in North Korea (Munsu Dong Diplomatic Compound, Pyongyang)
Ambassador: David Slinn, OBE.

Of North Korea to the United Nations
Ambassador: Pak Kil-yon.

Of North Korea to the European Union
Ambassador: Vacant.

FURTHER READING

Cha, Victor D. and Kang, David C., *Nuclear North Korea: A Debate on Engagement Strategies.* Columbia Univ. Press, 2003

Cumings, Bruce, *North Korea: Another Country.* New Press, New York, 2004

Harrison, S., *Korean Endgame: A Strategy for Reunification and US Disengagement.* Princeton Univ. Press, 2002

Hunter, H., *Kim Il-Song's North Korea.* Praeger Publishers, Westport (CT), 1999

Kleiner, J., *Korea: a Century of Change.* World Scientific Publishing Co., Singapore, 2001

Oh, K. and Hassig, R. C., *North Korea Through the Looking Glass.* Brookings Institution Press, Washington (D. C.), 2000

O'Hanlon, Michael E. and Mochizuki, Mike, *Crisis on the Korean Peninsula: How to Deal with a Nuclear North Korea.* McGraw-Hill, New York, 2003

Sigal, L. V., *Disarming Strangers: Nuclear Diplomacy with North Korea.* Princeton Univ. Press, 1999

Smith, H., *et al.* (eds.) *North Korea in the New World Order*. London, 1996

National statistical office: Central Statistics Bureau, Pyongyang.

KUWAIT

Dowlat al Kuwait
(State of Kuwait)

Capital: Kuwait
Population projection, 2010: 3·04m.
GDP per capita, 2002: (PPP$) 16,240
HDI/world rank: 0·838/44

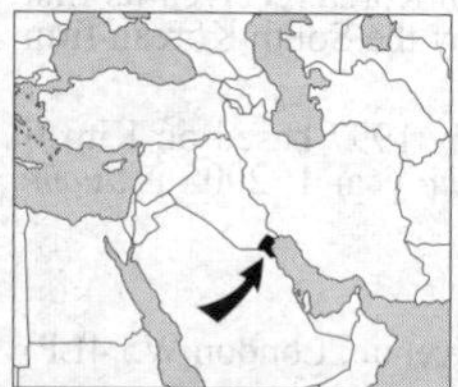

KEY HISTORICAL EVENTS

The ruling dynasty was founded by Shaikh Sabah al-Awwal, who ruled from 1756 to 1772. In 1899 Shaikh Mubarak concluded a treaty with Great Britain wherein, in return for the assurance of British protection, he undertook to support British interests. In 1914 the British Government recognized Kuwait as an independent government under British protection. On 19 June 1961 an agreement reaffirmed the independence and sovereignty of Kuwait and recognized the Government of Kuwait's responsibility for the conduct of internal and external affairs. On 2 Aug. 1990 Iraqi forces invaded the country. Following the expiry of the date set by the UN for the withdrawal of Iraqi forces, an air offensive was launched by coalition forces, followed by a land attack on 24 Feb. 1991. Iraqi forces were routed and Kuwait City was liberated on 26 Feb. On 10 Nov. 1994 Iraq recognized the independence and boundaries of Kuwait.

TERRITORY AND POPULATION

Kuwait is bounded in the east by the Persian Gulf, north and west by Iraq and south and southwest by Saudi Arabia, with an area of 17,818 sq. km. In 1992–93 the UN Boundary Commission redefined Kuwait's border with Iraq, moving it slightly northwards in conformity with an agreement of 1932. The population at the census of 1995 was 1,575,570, of whom about 58·5% were non-Kuwaitis. Official population estimate, 2004: 2,638,579; density, 148 per sq. km. In 2001, 96·1% of the population were urban.

The UN gives a projected population for 2010 of 3·04m.

The country is divided into six governorates: the capital (comprising Kuwait City, Kuwait's nine islands and territorial and shared territorial waters) (2004 population, 439,030); Farwaniya (686,116); Hawalli (565,767); Ahmadi (449,716); Jahra (322,783); Mubarak Al-Kabir (175,167). The capital city is Kuwait, with a population in 1995 of 28,747. Other major cities are (1995 populations): as-Salimiya (129,775), Qalib ash-Shuyukh (102,169), Hawalli (82,154), Hitan-al-Janubiyah (62,241).

The Neutral Zone (Kuwait's share, 2,590 sq. km), jointly owned and administered by Kuwait and Saudi Arabia from 1922 to 1966, was partitioned between the two countries in May 1966, but the exploitation of the oil and other natural resources continues to be shared.

Over 78% speak Arabic, the official language. English is also used as a second language.

SOCIAL STATISTICS

Births, 2003, 43,982; deaths, 4,424. The birth rate was 17·6 per 1,000 population. Kuwait's 2003 death rate, at 1·8 per 1,000 population, was the lowest in the world. Expectation of life at birth, 2002, was 75·7 years for males and 77·6 years for females. Infant mortality, 2003, 8·2 per 1,000 live births. Annual population growth rate, 1992–2002, 2·1%.

Total fertility rate for Kuwaiti females was 4·1 births per woman in 2003. Kuwait has had one of the largest reductions in its fertility rate of any country in the world over the past 25 years, having had a rate of 7·2 births per woman in 1975. Kuwait has a young population, with 40·7% of the population being under 15 in June 2004.

CLIMATE

Kuwait has a dry, desert climate which is cool in winter but very hot and humid in summer. Rainfall is extremely light. Kuwait, Jan. 56°F (13·5°C), July 99°F (36·6°C). Annual rainfall 5" (125 mm).

CONSTITUTION AND GOVERNMENT

The ruler is HH Shaikh Jaber al-Ahmed al-Jaber al-Sabah, the 13th Amir of Kuwait, who succeeded on 31 Dec. 1977.

In 1990 the *National Council* was established, consisting of 50 elected members and 25 appointed by the Amir. It was replaced by a *National Assembly* or *Majlis al-Umma* in 1992, consisting of 50 elected members. The franchise is limited to men over 21 whose families have been of Kuwaiti nationality since before 1920 and the sons of persons naturalized since 1992. In May 1999 the cabinet approved a draft law giving women the right to vote and run for parliament. However, in Dec. 1999 parliament rejected the bill allowing women to vote by a margin of 32 to 20.

Executive authority is vested in the *Council of Ministers.*

National Anthem. 'Watanil Kuwait salemta lilmajdi, wa ala jabeenoka tali ossaadi,' ('Kuwait, my fatherland! May you be safe and glorious! May you always enjoy good fortune!'); words by Moshari al-Adwani, tune by Ibrahim Nassar al-Soula.

RECENT ELECTIONS

At the all-male National Assembly elections on 5 July 2003 Islamist candidates won 21 seats, supporters of the government 14, liberals 3 (down from 14 at the previous election) and independents 12. Turn-out was 80·0%. An alternative election was staged by women, denied the vote. The Amir's decree offering female suffrage in 1999 was opposed by traditionalists.

CURRENT ADMINISTRATION

In April 2005 the government comprised:

Prime Minister: Shaikh Sabah Al-Ahmed Al-Jaber Al-Sabah; b. 1929 (appointed 13 July 2003).

First Deputy Prime Minister and Interior Minister: Shaikh Nawwaf Al-Ahmad Al-Sabah. *Deputy Prime Minister and Defence Minister:* Shaikh Jaber Mubarak Al-Hamad Al-Sabah. *Deputy Prime Minister and State Minister for Cabinet Affairs and National Assembly Affairs:* Mohammad Dayfallah Al-Sharar.

Minister of Foreign Affairs, Social Affairs, Labour, and Information (Acting): Anas Al Rashed. *Commerce and Industry:* Abd Al-Rahman Al-Tawil. *Communications and Planning:* Shaikh Ahmad Abdallah Al-Ahmad Al-Sabah. *Energy:* Shaikh Ahmad Fahd Al-Ahmad Al-Sabah. *Justice:* Ahmad Yaqub Baqr. *Finance, Public Works and Minister of State for Housing Affairs:* Badr Nasir Al-Humaydi. *Religious Endowments (Awqaf) and Islamic Affairs:* Abdallah Al-Matuq. *Education and Higher Education:* Rashid Hamad Mohammad Al-Hamad. *Health:* Dr Mohammad Ahmad Jarallah.

Speaker: Jasim Al-Khurafi.

Council of Ministers (Arabic only): http://www.fatwa.gov.kw

DEFENCE

In Sept. 1991 the USA signed a ten-year agreement with Kuwait to store equipment, use ports and carry out joint training exercises. Conscription is for two years. There were over 8,000 US and UN personnel based in Kuwait in 2002 as well as a UK RAF *Tornado* squadron.

Defence expenditure in 2003 totalled US$3,794m. (US$1,593 per capita), representing 9·4% of GDP. The expenditure per capita in 2003 was the second highest in the world after that of Qatar.

Army. Strength (2002) about 11,000 including 1,600 foreign personnel. In addition there is a National Guard of 6,600.

Navy. Personnel in 2002 numbered 2,000, including 500 Coast Guard personnel.

Air Force. From a small initial combat force the Air Force has grown rapidly, although it suffered heavy losses after the Iraqi invasion of 1990–91. Equipment includes F/A-18 *Hornet* strike aircraft and Mirage F-1s. Personnel strength was estimated (2002) at 2,500, with 81 combat aircraft and 20 armed helicopters.

INTERNATIONAL RELATIONS

Kuwait is a member of the UN, WTO, the League of Arab States, Gulf Co-operation Council, OPEC, OIC and Islamic Development Bank.

ECONOMY

Industry accounted for 59·7% of GDP in 2003 and services 40·3%.

Overview. Kuwait's Planning Ministry released a five-year plan in 2001 calling for the development of information technology and modern education to create a suitable environment for a free economy.

Currency. The unit of currency is the *Kuwaiti dinar* (KD) of 1,000 *fils*. Inflation in 2003 was 1·0%. Foreign exchange reserves were US$10,260m. in June 2002, monetary gold reserves were 2·54m. troy oz and total money supply (M3) was KD 2,156m.

In 2001 the six Gulf Arab states—Kuwait, along with Bahrain, Oman, Qatar, Saudi Arabia and the United Arab Emirates—signed an agreement to establish a single currency by 2010.

Budget. The fiscal year begins on 1 April. Revenues in 2002–03 totalled KD 6,219m. and expenditures KD 4,927m. Oil accounts for 80% of government revenues. Expenditure by function in 2002–03 (in KD 1m.): defence, 1,180; education, 701; public order and safety, 531; social security and welfare, 452; health, 300.

Performance. Real GDP growth was 9·7% in 2003. Total GDP in 2003 was US$32·06bn. In 2003 there was a current account surplus of US$7,566m.

Banking and Finance. The *Governor* of the Central Bank is Sheikh Salem AbdulAziz Al-Sabah. There is also the Kuwait Finance House. In 2002 there were eleven national banks and one Islamic banking firm. The combined assets of banks operating in Kuwait totalled KD 18,818m. in Dec. 2003. Foreign banks are banned.

There is a stock exchange, linked with those of Bahrain and Oman.

ENERGY AND NATURAL RESOURCES

Environment. Kuwait's carbon dioxide emissions from the consumption and flaring of fossil fuels were the equivalent of 25·5 tonnes per capita in 2002. An *Environmental Sustainability Index* compiled for the World Economic Forum meeting in Feb. 2002 ranked Kuwait 142nd in the world out of the 142 countries analysed, with 23·9%. The index measured the ability of countries to maintain favourable environmental conditions and examined various factors including pollution levels and the use or abuse of natural resources.

Electricity. There are six power stations with a total installed capacity of 9·2m. kW in 2002. Production in 2003 was 38·6bn. kWh; consumption per capita was 15,434 kWh.

Oil and Gas. Crude oil production in 2003, 769·3m. bbls. Kuwait produced 2·6% of the world total oil output in 2002 and had reserves amounting to 96·5bn. bbls. Only Saudi Arabia, Iran, Iraq and the United Arab Emirates have greater reserves. Most of the oil is in the Great Burgan area (reserves of approximately 70bn. bbls.), comprising the Burgan, Maqwa and Ahmadi fields located south of Kuwait City. Natural gas production was 11·0bn. cu. metres in 2002 with 1,490bn. cu metres of proven reserves (2002).

Water. The country depends upon desalination plants. In 1993 there were four plants with a daily total capacity of 216m. gallons. Fresh mineral water is pumped and bottled at Rawdhatain. Underground brackish water is used for irrigation, street cleaning and livestock. Production, 2003, 127,185m. gallons (95,174m. gallons fresh, 32,011m. gallons brackish). Consumption, 2003, 119,521m. gallons (94,987m. gallons fresh, 24,534m. gallons brackish).

Agriculture. There were 10,400 ha of arable land in 2003 and 2,100 ha of permanent crops. Production of main crops, 2003 (in 1,000 tonnes): tomatoes, 64; cucumbers and gherkins, 35; potatoes, 21; dates, 16; aubergines, 15; chillies and green peppers, 8; pumpkins and squash, 8; cauliflowers, 7.

Livestock (2003): sheep, 481,000; goats, 194,000; cattle, 27,000; camels, 6,000; poultry, 30m. Milk production (2003), 43,000 tonnes.

Forestry. Forests covered 5,000 ha in 2000, or 0·3% of the land area.

Fisheries. The total catch in 2001 was 5,846 tonnes, exclusively from sea fishing. In the space of a month in 2001 more than 2,000 tonnes of dead fish were washed ashore. Some experts claimed the cause was the alleged pumping of raw sewage into the Gulf while others attributed it to waste from the oil industry. Shrimp fishing was important, but has declined since the 1990–91 war through oil pollution of coastal waters. Before the discovery of oil, pearls were at the centre of Kuwait's economy, but today pearl fishing is only on a small scale.

INDUSTRY

According to the Financial Times Survey (FT 500), the largest companies by market capitalization in Kuwait on 4 Jan. 2001 were: The National Bank of Kuwait (US$3,579·8m.); Mobile Telephone (US$2,466·7m.); and Kuwait Finance House (US$1,489·6m.).

Industries, apart from oil, include boat building, fishing, food production, petrochemicals, gases and construction. Production figures in 2000 (in 1,000 tonnes): distillate fuel oil, 11,626; residual fuel oil, 8,642; kerosene, 5,789; liquefied petroleum gas, 3,003; jet fuel, 1,745; petrol, 1,377; cement, 1,187.

Labour. In June 2004 the labour force totalled 1,551,342 (81·3% non-Kuwaitis). Of the total labour force, 52·1% worked in social, community and personal services, 15·2% in trade, hotels and restaurants, 7·2% in construction and 5·8% in manufacturing. Registered unemployment in June 2004 was 1·7%. Approximately 93% of the workforce are civil servants.

Trade Unions. There is a Kuwaiti Trade Union Federation, but in 2002 only 5·6% of the workforce belonged to a union or labour group.

INTERNATIONAL TRADE

Kuwait, along with Bahrain, Oman, Qatar, Saudi Arabia and the United Arab Emirates began the implementation of a customs union in Jan. 2003.

Imports and Exports. Imports (f.o.b.) were valued at US$16,252m. in 2003 (US$8,117m. in 2002) and exports (f.o.b.) at US$22,427m. (US$15,366m. in 2002). Oil accounts for 91% of revenue from exports, and oil exports account for approximately 46% of GDP. The main non-oil export is chemical fertilizer.

Main export markets, 2003: Saudi Arabia, 13·7%; Iraq, 10·8%; UAE, 10·0%. Main import suppliers, 2003: Germany, 10·3%; Japan, 9·9%; USA, 1·6%.

COMMUNICATIONS

Roads. There were about 5,507 km of roads in 2003, 80·6% of which were paved. Number of vehicles in 2003 was 955,000 (777,000 passenger cars, or 334 per 1,000 inhabitants, and 104,000 trucks and vans). There were 45,376 road accidents in 2003 involving injury with 1,704 fatalities.

Civil Aviation. There is an international airport (Kuwait International). The national carrier is the state-owned Kuwait Airways. In 1999 it flew 36·5m. km and carried 2,130,000 passengers (all on international flights). Kuwait International airport handled 4,260,136 passengers in 2003 and 144,727 tonnes of freight.

Shipping. The port of Kuwait formerly served mainly as an entrepôt, but this function is declining in importance with the development of the oil industry. The largest oil terminal is at Mina Ahmadi. Three small oil ports lie to the south of Mina Ahmadi: Mina Shuaiba, Mina Abdullah and Mina Al-Zor. The merchant fleet totalled 2,256,000 GRT in 2002, of which 1,628,000 GRT were oil tankers. In 2002 vessels totalling 2,052,000 NRT entered ports and vessels totalling 1,178,000 NRT cleared.

Telecommunications. Kuwait had 1,708,900 telephone subscribers in 2002, or 722·9 per 1,000 population, and there were 285,000 PCs (120·6 for every 1,000 persons). In 2002 mobile phone subscribers numbered 1,227,000 and in 1999 there were 60,000 fax machines. The number of Internet users in 2002 was 250,000.

Postal Services. In 2003 there were 113,000 post office boxes, 96,301 rented. There were 31,943 outgoing telegrams and 26,482 incoming.

SOCIAL INSTITUTIONS

Justice. In 1960 Kuwait adopted a unified judicial system covering all levels of courts. These are: Courts of Summary Justice, Courts of the First Instance, Supreme Court of Appeal, Court of Cassation and a Constitutional Court. Islamic Sharia is a major source of legislation. The death penalty is still in use. There were nine confirmed executions in 2004.

The population in penal institutions in 1997 was 1,735 (100 per 100,000 of national population).

Religion. In 2001, 1,020,000 people were Sunni Muslims, 680,000 Shia Muslims, 230,000 other Muslims and 340,000 other (mostly Christian and Hindu).

Education. Education is free and compulsory from six to 14 years. In 2002–03 there were 245 pre-primary schools with 4,675 teachers for 62,724 pupils, 314 primary schools with 11,594 teachers for 153,956 pupils, 281 intermediate schools with 11,826 teachers for 134,742 pupils and 12,279 teachers in 215 secondary schools for 110,041 pupils. There were 17,828 students at Kuwait University in 2002–03. A pan-Arab Open University based in Kuwait and with branches in several other Middle Eastern countries was opened in Nov. 2002 with an initial enrolment of 3,000 students. Adult literacy rate in 2003 was 93·4% (97·7% among men and 89·3% among women). Total expenditure on education in 1995: KD 490,000,000 or 5·7% of GDP.

Health. Medical services are free to all residents. In 2003 there were 15 hospitals and sanatoria, with a provision of 4,712 beds (19 per 10,000 population). There were 3,643 doctors (15 per 10,000 population), 613 dentists, 8,997 nurses and 532 pharmacists in 2003 and 19 midwives in 1995. There were 74 clinics and other health centres and 1,569,549 people were admitted to public hospitals in 2003.

CULTURE

Broadcasting. The government-controlled Radio Kuwait and Kuwait Television broadcast a main and a second radio programme, a Koran programme and a service in English and four TV programmes (colour by PAL). In 2001 there were 950,000 TV receivers and in 2000 there were 1,400,000 radios.

Press. In 1999 there were eight daily newspapers, with a combined circulation of about 535,000. Formal press censorship was lifted in Jan. 1992.

Tourism. There were 94,000 foreign tourists in 2003, bringing revenue of US$98m. There were 38 hotels providing 5,063 beds in 2003.

DIPLOMATIC REPRESENTATIVES

Of Kuwait in the United Kingdom (2 Albert Gate, London, SW1X 7JU)
Ambassador: Khaled Al-Duwaisan, GCVO.

Of the United Kingdom in Kuwait (Arabian Gulf St., Kuwait)
Ambassador: Christopher Wilton, CMG.

Of Kuwait in the USA (2940 Tilden St., NW, Washington, D.C., 20008)
Ambassador: Salem Abdulla Al-Jaber Al-Sabah.

Of the USA in Kuwait (Al-Masjed Al-Aqsa Street, Bayan, Kuwait)
Ambassador: Richard LeBaron.

Of Kuwait to the United Nations
Ambassador: Nabeela Abdulla Al-Mulla.

Of Kuwait to the European Union
Ambassador: Abdulazeez A. Al-Sharikh.

FURTHER READING

Al-Yahya, M.A., *Kuwait: Fall and Rebirth.* London, 1993

Clements, F. A., *Kuwait.* [Bibliography] ABC-Clio, 2nd ed. Oxford and Santa Barbara (CA), 1996

Crystal, J., *Kuwait: the Transformation of an Oil State.* Boulder (Colo.), 1992

Finnie, D. H., *Shifting Lines in the Sand: Kuwait's Elusive Frontier with Iraq.* London, 1992

National statistical office: Statistics and Census Sector, Ministry of Planning
Website: http://www.mop.gov.kw

KYRGYZSTAN

Kyrgyz Respublikasy

Capital: Bishkek
Population projection, 2010: 5·62m.
GDP per capita, 2002: (PPP$) 1,620
HDI/world rank: 0·701/110

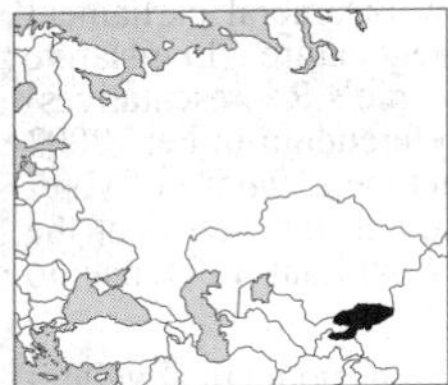

KEY HISTORICAL EVENTS

Kyrgyzstan became part of Soviet Turkestan, which itself became a Soviet Socialist Republic within the Russian Soviet Federal Socialist Republic (RSFSR) in April 1921. In 1924, when Central Asia was reorganized territorially on a national basis, Kyrgyzstan was separated from Turkestan. In Dec. 1936 Kyrgyzstan was proclaimed one of the constituent Soviet Socialist Republics of the USSR. With the collapse of the Soviet Empire, the republic asserted its claim to sovereignty in 1990 and declared independence in Sept. 1991. Askar Akayev became president in 1990 and subsequently expanded presidential powers. Kyrgyzstan became a member of the CIS in Dec. 1991.

Incursions into Kyrgyz territory by Islamic rebels and border skirmishes in the Fergana Valley are a cause for concern for all Central Asian governments. Kyrgyzstan tripled its defence budget for 2001 to combat terrorism. Allegations of widespread government corruption and disputed parliamentary elections in Feb. 2005 led to widespread popular protests. The Supreme Court declared the elections void and Kurmanbek Bakiyev was appointed prime minister and acting president. Akayev, in exile in Russia, resigned as president in April 2005.

TERRITORY AND POPULATION

Kyrgyzstan is situated on the Tien-Shan mountains and bordered in the east by China, west by Kazakhstan and Uzbekistan, north by Kazakhstan and south by Tajikistan. Area, 199,900 sq. km (77,180 sq. miles). Population (census 1999), 4,822,938 (2,442,473 females); density, 24 per sq. km. 2002 estimate: 5,064,000. In 2001, 65·6% of the population lived in rural areas.

The UN gives a projected population for 2010 of 5·62m.

The republic comprises seven provinces (Batken, Djalal-Abad, Issyk-Kul, Naryn, Osh, Talas and Chu) plus the city of Bishkek, the capital (formerly Frunze; 1999 census population, 750,327). Other large towns are Osh (208,520), Djalal-Abad (70,401), Przhevalsk (64,322), Tokmak (59,409), Karabalta (47,159), Balykchy (41,342) and Naryn (40,050).

The Kyrgyz are of Turkic origin and formed 64·9% of the population in 1999; the rest included Uzbeks (13·8%), Russians (12·5%), Dungans (1·1%) and Ukrainians (1·0%).

The official languages are Kyrgyz and Russian. After the break-up of the Soviet Union, Russian was only the official language in provinces where Russians are in a majority. However, in May 2000 parliament voted to make it an official language nationwide, mainly in an attempt to stem the ever-increasing exodus of skilled ethnic Russians. The Roman alphabet (in use 1928–40) was re-introduced in 1992.

SOCIAL STATISTICS

2003 births, 105,490; deaths, 35,941; marriages, 34,266. Rates, 2003 (per 1,000 population): birth, 20·9; death, 7·1; infant mortality (per 1,000 live births), 59. Life expectancy, 2003, 64·5 years for males and 72·2 for females. In 2000 the most popular age for marrying was 20–24 for both males and females. Annual population growth rate, 2000–03, 0·9%; fertility rate, 2003, 2·5 births per woman.

CLIMATE

The climate varies from dry continental to polar in the high Tien-Shan, to sub-tropical in the southwest (Fergana Valley) and temperate in the northern foothills. Bishkek, Jan. 9°F (–13°C), July 70°F (21°C). Annual rainfall 14·8" (375 mm).

CONSTITUTION AND GOVERNMENT

A new Constitution was adopted on 5 May 1993. The Presidency is executive, and directly elected for renewable five-year terms. At a referendum on 30 Jan. 1994, 96% of votes cast favoured President Akayev's serving out the rest of his term of office; turn-out was 95%. At a referendum on 22–23 Oct. 1994 turn-out was 87%. 75% of votes cast were in favour of instituting referendums as a constitutional mechanism, and 73% were in favour of establishing a new bicameral parliament (*Jogorku Kenesh*), with a 35-member directly-elected legislature (Legislative Assembly), and a 70-member upper house (Assembly of People's Representatives) elected on a regional basis and meeting twice a year. At a referendum in Feb. 2003 it was decided to revert to a unicameral parliament of 75 members. 94·5% of votes cast at a referendum on 10 Feb. 1996 were in favour of giving the President the right to appoint all ministers except the Prime Minister without reference to parliament.

National Anthem. 'Ak möngülüü aska yoolor, talaalar' ('High mountains, valleys and fields'); words by Z. Sadikova and Š. Kulueva, tune by N. Davlyesova and K. Moldovasanova.

RECENT ELECTIONS

Parliamentary elections were held on 27 Feb. and 13 March 2005 in which 74 of 75 seats were allocated. However, following protests the Supreme Court annulled the results of the elections and the Upper House of parliament named Kurmanbek Bakiyev acting prime minister and acting president. The new parliament later confirmed Bakiyev as prime minister and the Upper House was dissolved.

Presidential elections were held on 29 Oct. 2000. President Akayev was re-elected for a third term in office by 74·4% of votes cast against two opponents. Independent monitors said the election did not comply with democratic standards. In June 2000 a special commission had been created to test the knowledge of the Kyrgyz language of the candidates for the presidency. Several potential candidates failed the test, and the strongest rival to President Akayev declined to take the test and was barred from standing.

Presidential elections were scheduled to take place on 10 June 2005 after Akayev was forced to resign in April 2005.

CURRENT ADMINISTRATION

President (acting): Kurmanbek Bakiyev.

In April 2005 the government comprised:

Prime Minister (acting): Kurmanbek Bakiyev.

First Deputy Prime Minister: Medetbek Kerimkulov. *Deputy Prime Ministers:* Isengul Boljurova; Adakhan Madumarov; Daniyar Usenov.

Minister of Defence: Ismael Isakov. *Finance:* Akylbek Japarov. *Foreign Affairs:* Roza Otunbayeva. *Economic Development, Industry and Trade:* Armangeldy Muraliev. *Health:* Fnu Aytimbekova. *Internal Affairs:* Myktybek Abdildayev. *Justice (acting):* Erkin Mamirov. *Labour and Social Welfare, and Education, Science and Culture:* Dosbol Nur Uulu. *Agriculture and Water Resources:* Abdimalik Anarbayev. *Ecology and Emergencies:* Janysh Rustenbekov. *Transport and Communications:* Ishenbay Kadyrbekov.

Government Website: http://www.gov.kg/

DEFENCE

Conscription is for 18 months. Defence expenditure in 2003 totalled US$220m. (US$44 per capita), representing 2·6% of GDP. The USA opened a military base in Kyrgyzstan in 2001 to aid the war in Afghanistan against the Taliban. In Sept. 2003 Kyrgyzstan also agreed to allow Russia to open an air force base in the country.

Army. Personnel, 2002, 8,500. In addition there is a combined forces reserve of 57,000 and 5,000 border guards.

Air Force. There is an aviation element with MiG-21 fighters and a variety of other ex-Soviet equipment. Personnel, 2002, 2,400.

INTERNATIONAL RELATIONS

Kyrgyzstan is a member of the UN, WTO, CIS, OSCE, Asian Development Bank, ECO, IOM, OIC, Islamic Development Bank and the NATO Partnership for Peace.

ECONOMY

Agriculture accounted for 37·7% of GDP in 2002, industry 23·3% and services 39·0%.

Currency. On 10 May 1993 Kyrgyzstan introduced its own currency unit, the *som* (KGS), of 100 *tyiyn*, at a rate of 1 som = 200 roubles. Inflation was 5·6% in 2003, falling to 2·8% in 2004. Gold reserves totalled 83,000 troy oz in June 2002 and foreign exchange reserves US$237m. Total money supply in June 2002 was 6,247m. soms.

Budget. Government revenue and expenditure (in 1m. soms), year ending 31 Dec.:

	1998	*1999*	*2000*	*2001*	*2002*	*2003*
Revenue[1]	6,090·7	7,873·7	9,280·1	11,917·7	13,588·1	15,747·9
Expenditure[2]	7,298·3	9,312·0	11,308·2	12,255·7	15,188·6	16,890·6

[1]Without official transfers. [2]Without state investment programmes.

Performance. Real GDP growth was 7·0% in 2003. Total GDP in 2003 was US$1·9bn.

Banking and Finance. The central bank and bank of issue is the National Bank (*Chairman,* Ulan Sarbanov). There were 22 commercial banks, including three foreign banks, in 2002. There is a stock exchange in Bishkek.

ENERGY AND NATURAL RESOURCES

Environment. Kyrgyzstan's carbon dioxide emissions from the consumption and flaring of fossil fuels were the equivalent of 1·5 tonnes per capita in 2002.

Electricity. Installed capacity was 4·0m. kW in 2004. Production in 2003 was 14·02bn. kWh, around 92·7% hydro-electric; consumption per capita was 2,804 kWh.

Oil and Gas. Output of oil, 2003, 69,500 tonnes; natural gas, 2003, 27·1m. cu. metres.

Minerals. In 2003 lignite production totalled 351,700 tonnes and coal production 63,600 tonnes. Some gold is mined.

Agriculture. Kyrgyzstan is famed for its livestock breeding, in particular the small Kyrgyz horse. In 2004 there were 2,882,000 sheep, 1,003,000 cattle, 795,000 goats, 340,000 horses and 2m. chickens. Yaks are bred as meat and dairy cattle, and graze on high altitudes unsuitable for other cattle. Crossed with domestic cattle, hybrids give twice the yield of milk.

There were 1·34m. ha of arable land in 2003 and 67,000 ha of permanent crops. Number of peasant farms (2003), 255,822.

Principal crops include wheat, barley, corn and vegetables. Fodder crops for livestock are grown, particularly lucerne; also sugarbeet, cotton, tobacco and medicinal herbs. Sericulture, fruit, grapes and vegetables are major branches.

Output of main agricultural products (in 1,000 tonnes) in 2003: potatoes, 1,308; wheat, 1,014; sugarbeet, 812; corn for grain, 399; barley, 198; tomatoes, 144; carrots, 126; raw cotton, 106; cabbages, 104; onions, 104; cucumbers, 50. Livestock products, 2003, in 1,000 tonnes: beef and veal, 94; mutton and goat meat, 44; milk, 1,192; eggs, 268m. units.

Forestry. In 2003 forests covered 1,057,000 ha, or 5·3% of the land area. Timber production in 2001 was 26,000 cu. metres.

Fisheries. The catch in 2003 was 93 tonnes, entirely from freshwater fishing.

INDUSTRY

Industrial enterprises include food, timber, textile, engineering, metallurgical, oil and mining. There are also sugar refineries, tanneries, cotton and wool-cleansing works, flour-mills and a tobacco factory. In 2001 industry accounted for 28·3% of GDP, with manufacturing contributing 10·8%. In 2003 output was valued at 48,940·1m. soms at current prices.

Production, 2003: cement, 757,300 tonnes; carpets, 13·4m. sq. metres; woven cotton (2000), 6m. sq. metres; footwear, 238,000 pairs.

Labour. Out of 1,837,000 people in employment in 2003, 951,200 were engaged in agriculture, hunting and forestry; 205,800 in wholesale and retail trade/repair of motor vehicles, motorcycles and personal and household goods; 151,900 in education; and 113,700 in manufacturing. In 2004 the unemployment rate was 2·9%.

INTERNATIONAL TRADE

In Jan. 1994 an agreement to create a single economic zone was signed with Kazakhstan and Uzbekistan. In March 1996 Kyrgyzstan joined a customs union with Russia, Kazakhstan and Belarus. Total external debt was US$1,797m. in 2002.

Imports and Exports. Imports (c.i.f.) were valued at US$717·0m. in 2003 and exports (f.o.b.) at US$581·7m. Principal imports in 2001: petroleum and natural gas, 22·6%; machinery and apparatus, 21·0%; food products, 11·7%; chemicals and chemical products, 9·5%. Principal exports in 2001: nonferrous metals (notably gold), 51·7%; machinery and apparatus, 12·0%; electricity, 9·8%; agricultural products (notably tobacco), 9·5%.

Main import suppliers in 2003: Russia, 24·6%; Kazakhstan, 23·8%; China, 10·8%; USA, 6·7%; Uzbekistan, 5·5%; Germany, 5·3%. Main export markets, 2003: United Arab Emirates, 24·8%; Switzerland, 20·3%; Russia, 16·7%; Kazakhstan, 9·8%; Canada, 5·3%; China, 4·0%.

COMMUNICATIONS

Roads. There were 18,800 km of roads in 2003, including 140 km of motorways. 91·4% of all roads in 2003 were paved. Passenger cars in use in 2003 numbered 188,900 (38 per 1,000 inhabitants). There were 897 road accident fatalities in 2003.

Rail. In the north a railway runs from Lugovaya through Bishkek to Rybachi on Lake Issyk-Kul. Towns in the southern valleys are linked by short lines with the Ursatyevskaya–Andizhan railway in Uzbekistan. Total length of railway, 2000, 417 km. Passenger-km travelled in 2003 came to 49·8m. and freight tonne-km to 562m.

Civil Aviation. There is an international airport at Bishkek (Manas). The national carrier is Kyrgyzstan Airlines. In 2003 Bishkek handled 217,576 passengers (112,487 on international flights) and 1,978 tonnes of freight. In 1999 scheduled airline traffic of Kyrgyzstan-based carriers flew 8·6m. km, carrying 312,000 passengers (136,000 on international flights).

Shipping. The total length of inland waterways was 460 km in 2003. In 2003, 38,700 tonnes of freight were carried.

Telecommunications. There were 539,900 telephone subscribers in 2003, equivalent to 107 for every 1,000 persons, and 65,000 PCs in use in 2002. There were 138,600 mobile phone subscribers in 2003. Internet users numbered 642,300 in 2003.

Postal Services. In 1997 there were 914 post offices.

SOCIAL INSTITUTIONS

Justice. In 2004, 32,616 crimes were reported, including 419 murders and attempted murders. The population in penal institutions in March 2002 was 19,500 (390 per 100,000 of national population). A moratorium on the death penalty, first imposed in 1998, was extended in Jan. 2005 for another year.

Religion. In 2001, 75% of the population was Sunni Muslim. There were some 1,000 mosques, 30 Russian Orthodox, 17 Evangelical, 9 Seventh Day Adventist and 8 Lutheran churches in 1996.

Education. In 2003 there were 417 pre-primary schools for 47,464 pupils; in 2004 there were 143 primary schools with 11,769 pupils, 160 basic schools with 32,192 pupils, 1,778 secondary schools with 1,084,922 pupils and 13,337 university level lecturers for 218,273 students. There were 49 higher educational institutions and 75 secondary professional education establishments in 2004–05. Kyrgyz University had 20,855 students in 2004–05. Adult literacy was 98·7% in 1999.

In 1998–99 total expenditure on education came to 5·7% of GNP.

Health. In 2003 there were 13,608 physicians, 1,076 dentists, 21,120 nurses and 2,663 midwives; in 2003 there were 151 hospitals.

Welfare. In Jan. 1994 there were 443,000 age and 196,000 other pensioners.

CULTURE

Broadcasting. Kyrgyz Radio and Kyrgyz Television are state-controlled. There are two national radio programmes, with some broadcasting in English and German. There is one commercial radio station. In 1993 there were three hours of TV broadcasting a day (colour by SECAM). In 2000 there were 542,000 radio receivers and in 2001 there were 242,000 television receivers.

Cinema. In 1999 there were 293 cinemas with an annual attendance of 0·3m.

Press. There were three daily newspapers in 1996, with a combined circulation of 67,000.

Tourism. In 1999 there were 69,000 foreign tourists; spending by tourists in 2000 totalled US$15m.

DIPLOMATIC REPRESENTATIVES

Of Kyrgyzstan in the United Kingdom (Ascot House, 119 Crawford St., London, W1H 1AF)
Ambassador: Dilde Sarbagysheva.

Of the United Kingdom in Kyrgyzstan
Ambassador: James Lyall Sharp (resides at Almaty, Kazakhstan).

Of Kyrgyzstan in the USA (1732 Wisconsin Ave., NW, Washington, D.C., 20007)
Ambassador: Baktybek Abdrissaev.

Of the USA in Kyrgyzstan (171 Prospekt Mira, Bishkek 720016)
Ambassador: Stephen Young.

Of Kyrgyzstan to the United Nations
Ambassador: Nurbek Jeenbaev.

Of Kyrgyzstan to the European Union
Ambassador: Tchinguiz Aitmatov.

FURTHER READING

Anderson, J., *Kyrgyzstan: Central Asia's Island of Democracy?* Routledge, London, 1999

National statistical office: National Statistical Committee of the Kyrgyz Republic, 374 Frunze Street, Bishkek City 720033.
Website: http://stat-gvc.bishkek.su/

LAOS

Sathalanalath Pasathipatai Pasasonlao (Lao People's Democratic Republic)

Capital: Vientiane
Population projection, 2010: 6·59m.
GDP per capita, 2002: (PPP$) 1,720
HDI/world rank: 0·534/135

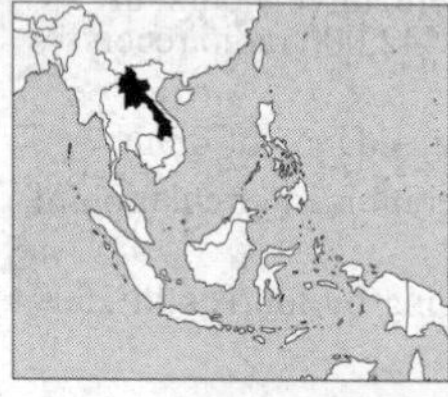

KEY HISTORICAL EVENTS

The Kingdom of Laos, once called Lanxang (the Land of a Million Elephants), was founded in the 14th century. In 1893 Laos became a French protectorate and in 1907 acquired its present frontiers. In 1945, after French authority had been suppressed by the Japanese, an independence movement known as Lao Issara (Free Laos) set up a government which collapsed with the return of the French in 1946. Under a new constitution of 1947 Laos became a constitutional monarchy under the Luang Prabang dynasty and in 1949 became an independent sovereign state within the French Union. An almost continuous state of war began in 1953 between the Royal Lao Government, supported by American bombing and Thai mercenaries, and the Patriotic Front Pathet Lao, supported by North Vietnamese troops. Peace talks resulted in an agreement on 21 Feb. 1973 providing for the formation of a provisional government of national union and the withdrawal of foreign troops. A provisional coalition government was duly formed in 1974. However, after the Communist victories in neighbouring Vietnam and Cambodia in April 1975, the Pathet Lao took over the running of the whole country, maintaining only a façade of a coalition. On 29 Nov. 1975 HM King Savang Vatthana abdicated and the People's Congress proclaimed a People's Democratic Republic of Laos on 2 Dec. 1975. Since then the country has been run by a regime with zero tolerance for dissent and a fierce distrust of foreigners.

TERRITORY AND POPULATION

Laos is a landlocked country of 236,800 sq. km (91,428 sq. miles) bordered on the north by China, the east by Vietnam, the south by Cambodia and the west by Thailand and Myanmar. Apart from the Mekong River plains along the border of Thailand, the country is mountainous, particularly in the north, and in places densely forested.

The population (1995 census) was 4,581,258 (2,315,931 females); density, 19 per sq. km. Population, 2002 estimate; 5,535,000. In 2001, 80·3% of the population lived in rural areas.

The UN gives a projected population for 2010 of 6·59m.

There are 16 provinces and 1 prefecture divided into 133 districts and one special region (*khetphiset*). Area, population and administrative centres in 1996:

Province	*Sq. km*	*Population (in 1,000)*	*Administrative centre*
Attopeu	10,320	87·7	Samakhi Xai
Bokeo	6,196	114·9	Ban Houei Xai
Bolikhamxai	14,863	164·9	Paksan
Champassak	15,415	503·3	Pakse
Houa Phan	16,500	247·3	Xam Neua
Khammouane	16,315	275·4	Thakhek
Luang Namtha	9,325	115·2	Luang Namtha
Luang Prabang	16,875	367·2	Luang Prabang
Oudomxai	15,370	211·3	Muang Xai
Phongsali	16,270	153·4	Phongsali
Salavan	10,691	258·3	Salavan
Savannakhet	21,774	674·9	Shanthabouli
Sayabouri	16,389	293·3	Sayabouri
Sekong	7,665	64·2	Sekong

Province	*Sq. km*	*Population (in 1,000)*	*Administrative centre*
Vientiane	15,927	286·8	Phonghong
Vientiane[1]	3,920	531·8	Vientiane
Xaisomboun[2]	7,105	54·2	Ban Muang Cha
Xieng Khouang	15,880	201·2	Phonsavanh

[1]Prefecture. [2]Special Region (1995 population).

The capital and largest town is Vientiane, with a population of (1999 estimate) 640,000. Other important towns are (census 1985): Savannakhet, 96,652; Luang Prabang, 68,399; Pakse, 47,323.

The population is divided into three groups: about 67% Lao-Lum (Valley-Lao); 17% Lao-Theung (Lao of the mountain sides); and 7·4% Lao-Sung (Lao of the mountain tops), who comprise the Hmong and Yao (or Mien). Lao is the official language. French and English are spoken.

SOCIAL STATISTICS

Estimated 1997 births, 211,000; deaths, 69,000. 1997 rates per 1,000 population, estimate: birth, 41·2 per 1,000 population; death, 13·4; infant mortality, 87 per 1,000 live births (2001). Life expectancy, 2001: 52·7 years for men and 55·2 for women. Annual population growth rate, 1992–2002, 2·4%. Fertility rate, 2001, 5·0 births per woman.

CLIMATE

A tropical monsoon climate, with high temperatures throughout the year and very heavy rains from May to Oct. Vientiane, Jan. 70°F (21·1°C), July 81°F (27·2°C). Annual rainfall 69" (1,715 mm).

CONSTITUTION AND GOVERNMENT

On 15 Aug. 1991 the National Assembly adopted a new constitution. The head of state is the President, elected by the National Assembly, which consists of 109 members (99 prior to the elections of Feb. 2002).

Under the constitution the Lao People's Revolutionary Party (LPRP) remains the 'central nucleus' of the 'people's democracy'; other parties are not permitted. The LPRP's Politburo comprises 11 members, including Khamtay Siphandone (LPRP, *President*).

National Anthem. 'Xatlao tangtae dayma lao thookthuana xeutxoo sootchay' ('For the whole of time the Lao people have glorified their Fatherland'); words by Sisana Sisane, tune by Thongdy Sounthonevichit.

RECENT ELECTIONS

The National Assembly (Fourth Legislature) elected Khamtay Siphandone as president at the first session of the Fourth National Assembly held on 23–26 Feb. 1998.

There were parliamentary elections on 24 Feb. 2002 in which the Revolutionary People's Party of Laos (PPPL) won 108 seats. Only one (approved) non-partisan candidate won a seat.

CURRENT ADMINISTRATION

President: Gen. Khamtay Siphandone; b. 1924 (PPPL; elected 24 Feb. 1998 and re-elected March 2001).

Vice President: Lt.-Gen. Choummali Saignason.

In March 2005 the government consisted of:

Prime Minister: Boungnang Volachit (PPPL; in office since 27 March 2001).

Deputy Prime Ministers: Maj. Gen. Asang Laoli; Thongloun Sisoolit (also *Chairman of State Planning Committee*); Somsavat Lengsavad (also *Minister for Foreign Affairs*).

Minister of Agriculture and Forestry: Sian Saphangthong. *Commerce and Tourism:* Soulivong Daravong. *Communications, Transport, Posts and Construction:* Bouathong Vonglokham. *Defence:* Douangchai Phichit. *Education:* Phimmasone Leuangkhamma. *Finance:* Chansy Phosikham. *Industry and Handicrafts:* Onneua Phommachanh. *Information and Culture:* Phandouangchit

Vongsa. *Interior and Security:* Thongban Sengaphon. *Justice:* Kham Ouane Boupha. *Labour and Social Welfare:* Somphanh Phengkhammi. *Public Health:* Ponemek Daraloy.

DEFENCE

Military service is compulsory for a minimum of 18 months. Defence expenditure in 2003 totalled US$38m. (US$7 per capita), representing 2·0% of GDP.

Army. There are four military regions. Strength (2002) about 26,000. In addition there are local defence forces totalling over 100,000.

Navy. There is a riverine force of about 600 personnel (2002).

Air Force. The Air Force has about 24 combat aircraft, including MiG-21 fighters. Personnel strength, about 3,500 in 2002.

INTERNATIONAL RELATIONS

Laos is a member of the UN, Asian Development Bank, Colombo Plan, ASEAN, Mekong Group and the International Organization of the Francophonie.

ECONOMY

In 2002 agriculture accounted for 50·3% of GDP, industry 23·5% and services 26·2%.

Overview. The fifth five-year plan (2001–05) aims at an annual growth of 7–7·5%.

Currency. The unit of currency is the *kip* (LAK). Inflation was 127·1% in 1999 but fell to 8·6% in 2001 before rising to 10·6% in 2002. Foreign exchange reserves were US$135m. in May 2002 and total money supply 539,490m. kip. Gold reserves were 66,000 troy oz in June 2002.

Budget. Revenues in 2001–02 met 90% of the targeted 2,335·5bn. kip and expenditure was 3,769bn. kip (93·4% of target).

Performance. Real GDP growth was 5·8% in 2001 and 5·9% in 2002. Total GDP in 2003 was US$2·0bn.

Banking and Finance. The central bank and bank of issue is the State Bank (*Governor*, Phoumy Thipphavone). There were 17 commercial banks in 2002 (seven foreign; branches only permitted). Total savings and time deposits in 1991 amounted to 4,075m. kip.

ENERGY AND NATURAL RESOURCES

Environment. In 2002 carbon dioxide emissions from the consumption and flaring of fossil fuels were the equivalent of 0·1 tonnes per capita.

Electricity. Total installed capacity in 2001–02 was 644 MW, of which 627 MW was hydro-electric. In 2001 production was 3,590 GWh, almost exclusively hydro-electric. Consumption was 710 GWh; 2,823 GWh were exported and 182 GWh were repurchased. In 1996, 16% of households had electricity, mainly in Vientiane.

Minerals. 2002 output (in tonnes): gypsum, 160,000; salt, 22,100; tin, 510; coal, 355.

Agriculture. There were 747,000 ha of arable land in 2001 and 81,000 ha of permanent crop land. The chief products (2001 output in tonnes) are: rice, 2,334,500; sugarcane, 320,000; maize, 111,869; cassava (2000), 71,000; sweet potatoes (2000), 52,000; tobacco, 36,000; potatoes (2000), 35,000; pineapples (2000), 34,000; soybeans, 33,200; melons (2000), 33,000; coffee, 25,200; cotton, 12,000. Opium is produced but its manufacture is controlled by the state.

Livestock (2001): cattle, 1·21m.; pigs, 1·36m.; buffaloes, 1·05m.; goats, 123,800; poultry, 13·87m.

Forestry. Forests covered 12·44m. ha in 2002, or 47% of the land area, down from 13·18m. ha in 1990. They produce valuable woods such as teak. Timber production, 2001, 6·46m. cu. metres.

Fisheries. The catch in 2001 was approximately 30,000 tonnes, entirely from inland waters.

INDUSTRY

Production in 2002: cement, 201,000 tonnes; iron bars, 13,000 tonnes; detergent, 650 tonnes; nails, 650 tonnes; corrugated iron, 2·8m. sheets; plywood, 2·1m. sheets; mineral water, 235m. litres; beer, 60·49m. litres; soft drinks, 13·15m. litres; oxygen, 21,500 cylinders; cigarettes, 38·3m. packets; lumber, 155,000 cu. metres.

Labour. The working age is 16–55 for females and 16–60 for males. At the 1995 census there were 1,086,172 females and 1,051,112 males within those age groups. Over 75% of the economically active population in 1995 were engaged in agriculture, fishing and forestry.

INTERNATIONAL TRADE

Since 1988 foreign companies have been permitted to participate in Lao enterprises. Total foreign debt was US$2,665m. in 2002.

Imports and Exports. Imports were estimated at US$534·60m. in 2002 (US$528·27m. in 2001) and exports at US$319·60m. (US$324·89m. in 2001). The main imports in 2000 were: consumption goods, 50·6%; mineral fuels, 13·9%; materials for garment assembly, 10·6%. Main exports: electricity, 32·0%; garments, 26·1%; wood products, 24·8%. Main import suppliers, 2001: Thailand, 52·0%; Vietnam, 26·5%; China, 5·7%; Singapore, 3·3%. Main export markets, 2001: Vietnam, 41·5%; Thailand, 14·8%; France, 6·1%; Germany, 4·6%.

COMMUNICATIONS

Roads. In 1999 there were 21,716 km of roads, of which 44·5% were paved. In 1996 there were 16,320 passenger cars (3·4 per 1,000 inhabitants), 4,200 trucks and vans and 231,000 motorcycles. There were 1,820 traffic accidents with 600 fatalities in 1992. A bridge over the River Mekong, providing an important north-south link, was opened in 1994.

Rail. The Thai railway system extends to Nongkhai, on the Thai bank of the Mekong River.

Civil Aviation. There are two international airports at Vientiane (Wattay) and Luang Prabang. The national carrier is Lao Aviation, which in 2002 operated domestic services and international flights to Bangkok, Chiangmai, Hanoi, Ho Chi Minh City, Kunming, Phnom Penh and Siem Reap (Cambodia). In 1999 scheduled airline traffic of Laos-based carriers flew 2·0m. km, carrying 197,000 passengers (54,000 on international flights).

Shipping. The River Mekong and its tributaries are an important means of transport. 898,000 tonnes of freight were carried on inland waterways in 1995. Merchant shipping totalled 2,000 GRT in 2002.

Telecommunications. In 2002 there were 117,100 telephone subscribers (21·2 per 1,000 persons) and 18,000 PCs in use (3·3 for every 1,000 persons). Laos had 15,000 Internet users in 2002. There were 55,200 mobile phone subscribers in 2002 and 500 fax machines in 1995.

Postal Services. There were 106 post offices in 1998.

SOCIAL INSTITUTIONS

Justice. Criminal legislation of 1990 established a system of courts and a prosecutor's office. Polygamy became an offence.

Religion. In 2001 some 2·75m. were Buddhists (Hinayana), but about 40% of the population follow tribal religions.

Education. In 2000 there were 723 kindergartens with 38,000 pupils and 2,000 teachers, 9,737 primary schools with 891,000 pupils and 27,000 teachers, and 248,000 pupils and 11,400 teachers at general secondary level.

There are eight teacher training institutes (four teacher training colleges and four teacher training schools) and one college of Pali. In June 1995 the National University of Laos (NUOL) was established by merging nine existing higher education institutes and a centre of agriculture. NUOL comprises faculties in agriculture, pedagogy, political science, economics and management, forestry, engineering and architecture, medical science, humanities and social science, science, and literature.

Adult literacy in 2001 was 65·6% (male, 76·8%; female, 54·4%). Laos has only a small educated elite.

In 2000–01 total expenditure on education came to 2·4% of GNP and 8·8% of total government spending.

Health. In 1995 there were 25 hospitals, 131 health centres and 542 dispensaries. In 1996 there were 1,208 physicians, 214 dentists and 5,354 nurses.

CULTURE

World Heritage Sites. Laos has two sites on the UNESCO World Heritage List: the Town of Luang Prabang (inscribed on the list in 1995), a unique blend of Lao and European colonial architecture; and Vat Phou and Associated Ancient Settlements within the Champasak Cultural Landscape (2001), including a Khmer era Hindu temple complex.

Broadcasting. The government-controlled National Radio of Laos broadcasts a national and six regional programmes and an external service (six languages). Lao National TV transmits for three hours daily. There were 781,000 radio sets in 2000 and 280,000 television receivers in 2001 (colour by PAL).

Press. In 1996 there were three dailies (one in English).

Tourism. There were 673,823 foreign visitors in 2001 (270,000 in 1999) and revenue from tourism amounted to US$103·8m.

DIPLOMATIC REPRESENTATIVES

Of Laos in the United Kingdom
Ambassador: Soutsakhone Pathammavong (resides at Paris).

Of the United Kingdom in Laos
Ambassador: David Fall (resides at Bangkok).

Of Laos in the USA (2222 S. St., NW, Washington, D.C., 20008)
Ambassador: Phanethong Phommahaxay.

Of the USA in Laos (Rue Bartholonie, Vientiane)
Ambassador: Douglas Alan Hartwick.

Of Laos to the United Nations
Ambassador: Alounkèo Kittikhoun.

Of Laos to the European Union
Ambassador: Thongphachanh Sonnasinh.

FURTHER READING

National Statistical Centre. *Basic Statistics about the Socio-Economic Development in the Lao P.D.R.* Annual.

Stuart-Fox, M., *Laos: Politics, Economics and Society*. London, 1986—*History of Laos*. Cambridge Univ. Press, 1997

National statistical office: National Statistical Centre, Vientiane.

LATVIA

Latvijas Republika

Capital: Riga
Population projection, 2010: 2·16m.
GDP per capita, 2002: (PPP$) 9,210
HDI/world rank: 0·823/50

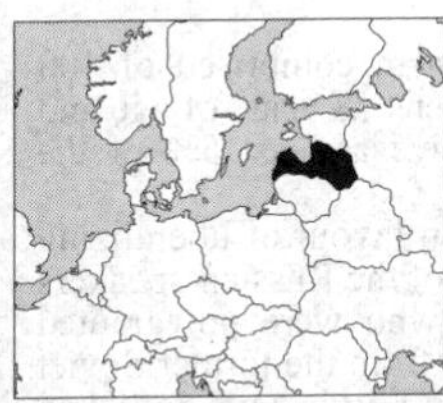

KEY HISTORICAL EVENTS

The territory that is now Latvia was controlled by crusaders, primarily the German Order of Livonian Knights, until 1561 when Latvia fell into Polish and Swedish hands. Between 1721 and 1795 Latvia was absorbed into the Russian empire. Soviet rule was proclaimed in Dec. 1917, but was overthrown when the Germans occupied all Latvia (Feb. 1918). Restored when the Germans withdrew (Dec. 1918), the Soviets were again overthrown, this time by combined British naval and German military forces (May–Dec. 1919), when a democratic government was set up. This regime was in turn replaced by a coup which took place in May 1934. The secret protocol of the Soviet–German agreement of 23 Aug. 1939 assigned Latvia to the Soviet sphere of interest. On 4 May 1990 the Latvian Supreme Soviet declared, by 138 votes to nil with 58 abstentions, that the Soviet occupation of Latvia on 17 June 1940 was illegal, and resolved to re-establish the 1922 Constitution. In a referendum in March 1991 the principle of independence was supported by 73·6%. A fully independent status was conceded by the USSR State Council in Sept. 1991. The large Russian minority was initially disadvantaged by the introduction of citizenship and language laws which have since been repealed. President Vīķe-Freiberga was elected as the former Communist bloc's first female president in June 1999. Latvia became a member of NATO in March 2004 and the European Union in May 2004.

TERRITORY AND POPULATION

Latvia is situated in northeastern Europe. It is bordered by Estonia on the north and by Lithuania on the southwest, while on the east there is a frontier with the Russian Federation and to the southeast with Belarus. Territory, 64,589 sq. km (larger than Denmark, the Netherlands, Belgium and Switzerland). Population (2000 census), 2,377,383; density, 37 per sq. km.

The UN gives a projected population for 2010 of 2·16m.

In 2001, 60·4% of the population were urban. Nationalities in 1997: Latvians 55·3%, Russians 32·5%, Belorussians 4·0%, Ukrainians 2·9%, Poles 2·2%, Lithuanians 1·3%, Jews 0·4%, Roma 0·3%, Estonians 0·1%, Germans 0·1%.

There are 26 counties (*rajons) and* seven municipalities with separate status. The capital is Riga (764,329, or nearly a third of the country's total population, at 2000 census); other principal towns, with 2000 populations, are Daugavpils (115,265), Liepāja (89,448), Jelgava (63,652), Jurmala (55,718) and Ventspils (43,928).

The official language is Latvian.

SOCIAL STATISTICS

2001: births, 19,664 (rate of 8·3 per 1,000 population); deaths, 32,991 (14·0 per 1,000 population); marriages, 9,258 (3·9 per 1,000 population); divorces, 5,740 (2·4 per 1,000 population); infant mortality, 17 per 1,000 live births (2001). In 2001 life expectancy was 65·0 years for males but 75·8 years for females. In 2001 the most popular age range for marrying was 25–29 for males and 20–24 for females. The annual population growth rate in the period 1992–2002 was –1·3%, giving Latvia one of the fastest declining populations of any country. Fertility rate, 2001, 1·1 births per woman (one of the lowest rates in the world). In 2001 there were 1,443 immigrants and 6,602 emigrants.

CLIMATE

The climate is relatively temperate but changeable. Average temperatures in Jan. range from –2·8°C in the western coastal town of Liepāja to –6·6°C in the inland town of Daugavpils. The average summer temperature is 20°C.

CONSTITUTION AND GOVERNMENT

The Declaration of the Renewal of the Independence of the Republic of Latvia dated 4 May 1990, and the 21 Aug. 1991 declaration re-establishing *de facto* independence, proclaimed the authority of the Constitution *(Satversme)*. The Constitution was fully re-instituted as of 6 July 1993, when the fifth Parliament *(Saeima)* was elected.

The head of state in Latvia is the *President*, elected by parliament for a period of four years.

The highest legislative body is the one-chamber parliament comprised of 100 deputies and elected in direct, proportional elections by citizens 18 years of age and over. Deputies serve for four years and parties must receive at least 5% of the national vote to gain seats in parliament.

In a referendum on 3 Oct. 1998, 53% of votes cast were in favour of liberalizing laws on citizenship, which would simplify the naturalization of the Russian-speakers who make up nearly a third of the total population and who were not granted automatic citizenship when Latvia regained its independence from the former Soviet Union in 1991. Around half of the 650,000 ethnic Russians in Latvia have not taken out Latvian citizenship. Ethnic Russians who are not Latvian citizens do not have the right to vote. A seven-member *Constitutional Court* was established in 1996 with powers to invalidate legislation not in conformity with the constitution. Its members are appointed by parliament for ten-year terms.

Executive power is held by the *Cabinet of Ministers*.

National Anthem. 'Dievs, svēti Latviju' ('God bless Latvia'); words and tune by Kārlis Baumanis.

RECENT ELECTIONS

Vaira Vīķe-Freiberga, a Canadian professor who had fled Latvia as a seven-year-old, was elected President of the Republic of Latvia on 17 June 1999. She was re-elected on 20 June 2003.

Parliamentary elections were held on 5 Oct. 2002. Former central bank governor Einars Repše's newly-formed liberal 'New Era' (Jaunais laiks; JL) party won 26 seats with 23·9% of votes cast; For Human Rights in a United Latvia (Par cilvēka tiesībām vienotā Latvijā; PCTVL) won 24 with 18·9%; the People's Party (Tautas partija; TP), 21 with 16·7%; Latvia's First Party (Latvijas Pirmā Partija; LPP), 10 with 9·6%; the Green and Farmers Union (Zaļo un Zemnieku savienība; ZZS), 12 with 9·5%; and Fatherland and Freedom Alliance/LNNK (Apvienība 'Tēvzemei un Brīvībai'; TB/LNNK), 7 with 5·4%. Prime Minister Andris Bērziņš' Latvia's Way party (Savienība 'Latvijas ceļš'; LC) failed to secure a single seat. Turn-out was 71·5%.

European Parliament. Latvia has nine representatives. At the June 2004 elections turn-out was 41·2%. The TB/LNNK won 4 seats with 29·8% of votes cast (political affiliation in European Parliament: Union for a Europe of Nations); JL, 2 with 19·7% (European People's Party–European Democrats); PCTVL, 1 with 10·7% (Greens/European Free Alliance); the TP, 1 with 6·6% (European People's Party–European Democrats); the LC, 1 with 6·5% (Alliance of Liberals and Democrats for Europe).

CURRENT ADMINISTRATION

President: Vaira Vīķe-Freiberga; b. 1937 (sworn in on 8 July 1999).

Prime Minister: Aigars Kalvītis; b. 1966 (TP; took office on 2 Dec. 2004). He formed a new four-party coalition government which in March 2005 comprised:

Minister for Defence: Einars Repše (JL). *Foreign Affairs:* Artis Pabriks (TP). *Economics:* Krišjānis Kariņš (JL). *Finance:* Oskars Spurdziņš (TP). *Interior:* Ēriks Jēkabsons (LPP). *Education and Science:* Ina Druviete (JL). *Culture:* Helēna Demakova (TP). *Justice:* Solvita Āboltiņa (JL). *Environment:* Raimonds Vējonis (ZZS). *Agriculture:* Mārtiņš Roze (ZZS). *Transport:* Ainārs Šlesers (LPP). *Welfare:* Dagnija Staķe (ZZS). *Health:* Gundars Bērziņš (TP). *Regional Development and Local Government:* Māris Kučinskis (TP). *Children and Family Affairs:* Ainars Baštiks (LPP). *Special Assignments for Society Integration Affairs:* Ainars Latkovskis (JL). *Special Assignments for Electronic Government Affairs:* Jānis Reirs (JL).

Office of the President: http://www.president.lv

DEFENCE

Since Latvia gained its independence in Aug. 1991, a renewal process for Latvia's armed forces, including the National Armed forces, the Home Guard and Border Guard, has been under way. Military service is compulsory for male citizens from the age of 19 (women and men 18 years and older can join the national defence forces voluntarily) and the duration of military service is 12 months. Conscientious objectors have the option of serving in non-military service. Latvia has signed a defence co-operation treaty with Lithuania and Estonia to co-ordinate Baltic States' defence and security activities.

In 2003 military expenditure totalled US$194m. (US$84 per capita), representing 1·9% of GDP.

Army. The Army was 4,300 strong in 2002. There is a National Guard reserve of five brigades, and a paramilitary Frontier Guard of 3,200.

Navy. A small coastal protection force, based at Riga and Liepāja, numbered 930 in 2002. Latvia, Estonia and Lithuania have established a joint naval unit 'BALTRON' (Baltic Naval Squadron), with bases at Liepāja, Riga and Ventspils in Latvia, Tallinn in Estonia and Klaipėda in Lithuania.

Air Force. Personnel numbered 270 in 2002. There are no combat aircraft.

INTERNATIONAL RELATIONS

Latvia is a member of the UN, WTO, BIS, NATO, EU, Council of Europe, OSCE, Council of the Baltic Sea States, IOM and an Associate Partner in WEU. Latvia held a referendum on EU membership on 20 Sept. 2003, in which 67·4% of votes cast were in favour of accession, with 32·6% against. It became a member of NATO on 29 March 2004 and the EU on 1 May 2004.

ECONOMY

Agriculture accounted for 4·7% of GDP in 2002, industry 24·7% and services 70·6%.

The Latvian Privatization Agency, established in 1994 to oversee the privatization process, has adopted a case-by-case approach. 97% of all state enterprises have been assigned for privatization. In 2003 the private sector constituted 70% of GDP and 76% of employment.

Overview. Core exports include wood and related products. There is strong export growth in live animals, animal and vegetable products, and metals. Small- and medium-sized enterprises account for over 50% of GDP and employ 70% of the workforce. The private sector accounts for around 67% of GDP. Corruption is still a problem. According to the IMF, the Bank of Latvia has kept monetary developments on track. The currency is pegged to the SDR (Special Drawing Right) and monetary policy has achieved price stability. Inflation has fallen from above 17% in 1996 to under 4%. Unemployment is around 13% and the labour market could be more flexible. Average incomes are low by EU standards but the gap is closing. Riga has the lowest unemployment rate, while the eastern parts of the country have the highest unemployment.

Currency. The unit of currency is the *lats* (LVL) of 100 *santims*. The lats has been pegged to the SDR basket. In 2003 inflation was 3·6%, down from 109·1% in 1993. Gold reserves were 249,000 troy oz in June 2002 and foreign exchange reserves US$1,145m. Total money supply in June 2002 was 924m. lats.

Budget. The financial year is the calendar year. The fiscal deficit, which had reached 4·0% of GDP (mostly as a consequence of the Russian financial crisis) declined to 2·0% in 2000 and 1·7% of GDP in 2001, but increased to 2·7% in 2002 and 3·2% in 2003.

Government revenue and expenditure (in 1m. lats), year ending 31 Dec.:

	2000	*2001*	*2002*	*2003*
Revenue	1,264·5	1,340·5	1,529·2	1,715·5
Expenditure	1,335·8	1,373·2	1,597·1	1,735·7

The standard rate of VAT is 18·0% (reduced rate, 9·0%).

Performance. GDP growth of 6·8% was recorded in 2000, rising to 7·9% in 2001—the highest rate in Europe. Despite further impressive growth rates in 2002 (6·1%)

and 2003 (7·5%), Latvia has the lowest GDP per capita of any of the ten countries that joined the EU in May 2004. Total GDP was US$9·7bn. in 2003.

Banking and Finance. The Bank of Latvia both legally and practically is a completely independent institution. Governor of the Bank and Council members are appointed by Parliament for office for six years (present *Governor*, Ilmars Rimševičs). In 2002 there were 22 banks in Latvia, including the Riga branches of Société Générale and Vereinsbank. In 1999 the transitional period which had been given for banks to ensure they had capital of €5m. ended with 14 banks fulfilling the requirement. Latvia's largest bank is Parex Bank, with deposits in 2001 of 592·5m. lats. Foreign direct investment inflows in 2003 totalled US$360m. The accumulated FDI at the end of 2002 reached US$2·75bn.

There is a stock exchange in Riga.

ENERGY AND NATURAL RESOURCES

Environment. Latvia's carbon dioxide emissions from the consumption and flaring of fossil fuels in 2002 were the equivalent of 4·2 tonnes per capita. An *Environmental Sustainability Index* compiled for the World Economic Forum meeting in Feb. 2002 ranked Latvia tenth in the world, with 63·0%. The index measured the ability of countries to maintain favourable environmental conditions and examined various factors including pollution levels and the use or abuse of natural resources.

Electricity. Electricity production in 2001 totalled 4·16bn. kWh. Consumption per capita in 2000 was 2,434 kWh. 68% of electrical power produced in Latvia is generated in hydro-electric power stations. The largest consumers are industry (34%) and private users (23%). Installed capacity was 2·1m. kW in 2001.

Oil and Gas. Latvia produces virtually no oil and is dependent on imports, although the Latvian Development Agency estimates that there are 733m. bbls. of offshore reserves in the Latvian areas of the Baltic Sea. Oil consumption was 43,000 bbls. per day in 2001. All Latvia's natural gas supplies are imported from Russia. Consumption in 2001 totalled 1·7bn. cu. metres.

Minerals. Peat deposits extend over 645,000 ha or about 10% of the total area, and it is estimated that total deposits are 3bn.–4bn. tonnes. Peat output in 2001 totalled 555,003 tonnes.

Production of other minerals (in 1,000 tonnes): sand and gravel (2002), 700; limestone (1999), 437; gypsum (2001), 125. Clays and dolomite are also produced.

Agriculture. In 2001 there were 1·84m. ha of arable land and 29,000 ha of permanent crops. Cattle and dairy farming are the chief agricultural occupations. Oats, barley, rye, potatoes and flax are the main crops.

In 2001 there were 174,459 farms. 43% of farms have fewer than 5 ha. There were 56,300 tractors and 6,200 harvester-threshers in 2001. Large state and collective farms have been converted into shareholding enterprises; the remainder have been divided into small private holdings for collective farm workers or former owners.

In 2001, 14·7% of the economically active population were employed in agriculture.

Output of crops (in 1,000 tonnes), 2000: grain, 927 (made up of: wheat, 385; barley, 322; oats, 115; rye, 105); potatoes, 747; sugarbeets, 408; cabbages, 66; apples, 24; carrots, 21.

Livestock, 2000: cattle, 378,000; pigs, 405,000; sheep, 27,000; poultry, 3m. Livestock products (2000, in 1,000 tonnes): meat, 61; milk, 825; eggs, 26.

Forestry. In 2000 Latvia's total forest area was 2·9m. ha, or 47·1% of the land area. The overall resources of wood amount to 502m. cu. metres (an increase of 118m. cu. metres since 1984), including 304m. cu. metres of softwood. Private forests account for 44·2% or 1·3m. ha and comprise about 153,000 holdings. Timber production in 2001 was 12·84m. cu. metres.

The share of the forest sector in gross industrial output is between 13 and 15%. Timber and timber products exports account for 37–38% of Latvia's total exports.

To provide the protection of forests there are three forest categories: commercial forests, 70·4%; restricted management forests, 18·6%; protected forests, 11·0%.

Fisheries. In 2001 the total catch was 125,433 tonnes, of which marine fish 124,852 tonnes. The main types of fish caught are sprat, Baltic herring, cod and salmon. The Latvian fishing fleet consists of almost 400 vessels.

INDUSTRY

Industry accounted for 26·1% of GDP in 2001, with manufacturing contributing 14·8%.

Industrial output in 1,000 tonnes: steel products (1999), 520; cement (2001), 500; crude steel (2000), 500; sugar (2002), 77; sawnwood (2002), 3·95m. cu. metres; wood-based panels (2002), 318,000 cu. metres; beer (2003), 246·6m. litres.

Labour. The total labour force in Nov. 2001 numbered 1,105,500. In Nov. 2000 there were 966,800 persons in employment in Latvia (excluding those in compulsory military service). The leading areas of activity were: manufacturing, 171,300; wholesale and retail trade/repair of motor vehicles, motorcycles and personal and household goods, 154,500; agriculture, hunting, forestry and fishing, 128,400. In 1999 women constituted 50% of the workforce, a higher percentage than in any other European country. In 2004 there was a monthly minimum wage of 80 lats. Average monthly salary was 192 lats in 2003. The official unemployment rate in June 2002 was 12·7%. The average monthly salary in the public sector in early 2000 was 168·39 lats.

Trade Unions. The Free Trade Union Federation of Latvia, LBAS (*President:* Pēteris Krīgers) was established in 1990. In 2003 there were 28 branch trade unions and professional employee unions representing more than 250,000 members.

INTERNATIONAL TRADE

State debt, as a proportion of GDP, has increased from 14·7% in 2000 to 15·4% in 2001, 16·6% in 2002 and 19·5% in 2003. Total external debt was US$6,690m. in 2002.

Imports and Exports. Imports (f.o.b.) were valued at US$4,020m. in 2002 (US$3,566m. in 2001) and exports (f.o.b.) at US$2,576m. (US$2,216m. in 2001). The main exports are wood and wood products (38·8%), textiles and textile articles (13·8%), base metals and articles of base metals (13·3%). The leading imports are machinery and mechanical appliances (20·6%), mineral products (12·4%), products of chemical and allied industries (11·1%), metals and products thereof (8·3%). Main export markets (2002): Germany, 15·5%; UK, 14·6%; Sweden, 10·5%, Lithuania, 8·4%; Estonia, 6·0%. Main import suppliers (2002): Germany, 17·2%; Lithuania, 9·8%; Russia, 8·8%; Finland, 8·0%; Sweden, 6·4%. In 1997, 48·9% of exports went to the EU and 53·2% of imports were from the EU. Since 1997 trade with the EU has continued to grow and trade with Russia and other former Soviet republics has declined, with trade between Latvia and Russia halving between 1997 and 2001.

COMMUNICATIONS

Roads. In 2001 there were 60,472 km of roads, including 20,279 km of national roads. In 2002 public road transport totalled 2,361m. passenger-km and freight 6,160m. tonne-km. In 2002 there were 518 fatalities in traffic accidents. With 22·1 deaths per 100,000 population in 2002 Latvia has one of the highest death rates in road accidents of any industrialized country. In 1996, 213·5 km of road was repaired and 13·1 km of new road built. Passenger cars in 2002 numbered 619,081 (266 per 1,000 inhabitants), in addition to which there were 102,734 trucks and vans, 22,157 motorcycles and mopeds and 11,164 buses and coaches.

Rail. In 2000 there were 2,331 km of 1,520 mm gauge route (258 km electrified). In 2003, 48·4m. tonnes of cargo and 23·0m. passengers were carried by rail. The main groups of freight transported are oil and oil products, mineral fertilizers, ferrous metals and ferrous alloys.

Civil Aviation. There is an international airport at Riga. A new national carrier, Air Baltic, assumed control of Latavio and Baltic International Airlines in 1995 and began flying in Oct. 1995. It has since then become eastern Europe's first low-cost airline. In 1998 it flew 4·7m. km, carrying 175,000 passengers. In 2003 it operated scheduled services to Berlin, Copenhagen, Hamburg, Helsinki, Kyiv, Moscow,

Prague, Stockholm, Tallinn, Vilnius and Warsaw. In 2000 Riga handled 574,356 passengers and 3,618 tonnes of freight.

Shipping. There are three large ports (with 51·1m. tonnes of cargo handled, 2002): Ventspils (29m.), Riga (18m.) and Liepāja (4m.). 7,100 ships in all docked at the three ports in 2002. A total of 47·7m. tonnes were loaded at the three ports in 2002 and 3·4m. tonnes unloaded. In 2002 the merchant marine totalled 89,000 GRT, including oil tankers 4,000 GRT (oil tankers 279,000 GRT in 1996 out of a total of 723,000 GRT).

Ventspils can handle up to 100,000 containers a year and it is estimated that it will be able to handle 250,000 a year when the second stage of a US$70m. development project is completed.

Telecommunications. Telecommunications are conducted by companies in which the government has a 51% stake, under the aegis of the state-controlled Lattelekom. In 2002 telephone subscribers numbered 1,618,400 (694·9 per 1,000 inhabitants) and 400,000 PCs were in use (171·7 per 1,000 persons). There were 917,200 mobile phone subscribers in 2002 and 900 fax machines in 1995. The number of Internet users in 2002 was 310,000.

Postal Services. In 1998 there were 978 post offices.

SOCIAL INSTITUTIONS

Justice. A new criminal code came into force in 1998. Judges are appointed for life. There are a Supreme Court, regional and district courts and administrative courts. The death penalty is retained but has been subject to a moratorium since Oct. 1996; it was abolished for peacetime offences in 1999. In 2003, 51,773 crimes were reported, 48·8% of which were solved; 13,586 people were convicted for offences. There were 220 murders in 2003 (a 6·3% increase on 2002). In June 2003 there were 8,156 people in penal institutions, giving a prison population rate of 352 per 100,000 population.

Religion. In order to practise in public, religious organizations must be licensed by the Department of Religious Affairs attached to the Ministry of Justice. New sects are required to demonstrate loyalty to the state and its traditional religions over a three-year period. Traditionally Catholics and Lutherans constitute the largest churches, with about 500,000 and 400,000 members respectively in 2002. Congregations in Feb. 2003: Lutherans, 307; Roman Catholics, 252; Russian Orthodox, 117; Baptists, 90; Old Believers, 67; Adventists, 47; Jews, 13; others, 47. In Sept. 2003 the Roman Catholic church had one cardinal.

Education. Adult literacy rate in 2001 was over 99%. The Soviet education system has been restructured on the UNESCO model. Education may begin in kindergarten. From the age of six or seven education is compulsory for nine years in comprehensive schools. This may be followed by three years in special secondary school or one to six years in art, technical or vocational schools. In 2003–04 there were 1,044 schools with 327,358 pupils.

State-financed education is available in Latvian and eight national minority languages (Russian, Polish, Hebrew, Ukrainian, Estonian, Lithuanian, Roma and Belorussian), although the use of Latvian in the classroom is being increased. A bilingual curriculum had to be implemented by all minority primary schools from the start of the 2002–03 school year. Secondary schools started to implement minority education curricula with an increased Latvian-language component (60% of all teaching) from Sept. 2004. In 2003–04, 230,212 pupils were taught solely in Latvian, 95,841 received instruction in Russian and 1,305 in other minority languages.

In 2002 there were 37 higher education institutions, with 118,944 students. Courses at state-financed universities are conducted in Latvian. A number of private educational institutions have languages of instruction other than Latvian.

Total expenditure on education in 2000–01 came to 5·9% of GNP.

Health. In 2003 there were 7,900 physicians and dentists. In 1998 there were 13,455 nurses and 81 midwives. There were 131 hospitals in 2003 with a provision of 78 beds per 10,000 persons.

Welfare. The official retirement age is age 62 years (men) or age 59 (women). However, the retirement age for women is increasing, by six months each year, so that in 2009 it will also be 62 years. In 2002 the minimum pension was equal to the state social security allowance of 30 lats a month. The minimum pension is increased by 1·1% for an insurance period of at least 20 years, by 1·3% for an insurance period of 20 to 30 years and by 1·5% and for an insurance period of more than 30 years. In 2003 there were 607,000 pension recipients.

The government runs an unemployment benefit scheme in which the amount awarded is determined by the number of insurance contributions and the length of previous employment.

CULTURE

World Heritage Sites. Latvia has one site on the UNESCO World Heritage List: the Historic Centre of Riga (inscribed on the list in 1997), a late-medieval Hanseatic centre.

Broadcasting. Broadcasting is overseen by the nine-member National Radio and Television Council appointed by parliament for four-year terms. There are 26 TV broadcasting companies and 23 radio broadcasting companies. Latvijas Radio broadcasts three programmes and an external service (English, German, Swedish). Latvijas Televizija transmits on two networks (colour by PAL). There were 1·65m. radio receivers in 2000 and 1·97m. television receivers in 2001.

Press. Latvia had 26 daily newspapers in 2000 with a combined circulation of 327,000 (135 per 1,000 inhabitants). 2,178 book titles were published in 1999.

Tourism. In 2000 there were 509,000 foreign tourists; revenue totalled US$131m. In 2003 there were 2·3m. border crossings by Latvian travellers returning from abroad (mainly visitors to neighbouring countries for short-stay shopping trips and visits to friends and relatives). In 2003 there were 326 hotels and other accommodation facilities.

Festivals. There is an annual Riga Opera Festival in June. The National Song Festival (held every five years) will next be held in 2006.

DIPLOMATIC REPRESENTATIVES

Of Latvia in the United Kingdom (45 Nottingham Place, London, W1U 5LY)
Ambassador: Indulis Bērziņš.

Of the United Kingdom in Latvia (5 Alunana ielā, Riga, LV 1010)
Ambassador: Andrew Tesoriere.

Of Latvia in the USA (4325 17th St., NW, Washington, D.C., 20011)
Ambassador: Māris Riekstiņš.

Of the USA in Latvia (7 Raina Boulevard, Riga, LV 1510)
Ambassador: Catherine Todd Bailey.

Of Latvia to the United Nations
Ambassador: Gints Jegermanis.

Of Latvia to the European Union
Ambassador: Andris Ķesteris.

FURTHER READING

Central Statistical Bureau. *Statistical Yearbook of Latvia.—Latvia in Figures.* Annual.
Dreifeld, J., *Latvia in Transition.* Riga, 1997
Lieven, A., *The Baltic Revolution: Estonia, Latvia, Lithuania and the Path to Independence.* 2nd ed. Yale Univ. Press, 1994
Misiunas, R. J. and Taagepera, R., *The Baltic States: the Years of Dependence, 1940–91.* 2nd ed. Farnborough, 1993
Smith, I. A. and Grunts, M. V., *The Baltic States.* [Bibliography] ABC-Clio, Oxford and Santa Barbara (CA), 1993
Who is Who in Latvia. Riga, 1996

National statistical office: Central Statistical Bureau, Lāčplēša ielā 1, 1301 Riga.
Website: http://www.csb.lv/

LEBANON

Jumhouriya al-Lubnaniya
(Republic of Lebanon)

Capital: Beirut
Population projection, 2010: 4·00m.
GDP per capita, 2002: (PPP$) 4,360
HDI/world rank: 0·758/80

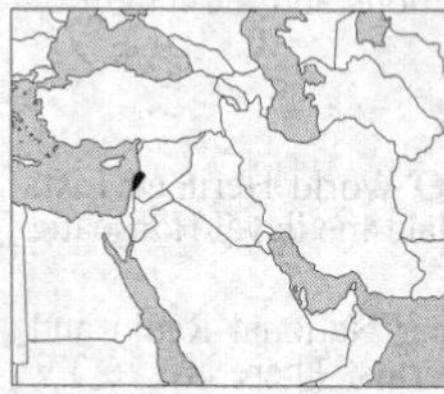

KEY HISTORICAL EVENTS

The Ottomans invaded Lebanon, then part of Syria, in 1516–17 and held nominal control until 1918. After 20 years' French mandatory regime, Lebanon was proclaimed independent on 26 Nov. 1941. In early May 1958 the Muslim opposition to President Chamoun rose in insurrection and for five months the Muslim quarters of Beirut, Tripoli, Sidon and the northern Bekaa were in insurgent hands. On 15 July the US Government landed army and marines who re-established Government authority. Internal problems were exacerbated by the Palestinian problem. An attempt to regulate the activities of Palestinian fighters through the secret Cairo agreement of 1969 was frustrated both by the inability of the Government to enforce its provisions and by an influx of battle-hardened fighters expelled from Jordan in Sept. 1970. From March 1975 Lebanon was beset by civil disorder by which the economy was brought to a virtual standstill.

By Nov. 1976 large-scale fighting had been brought to an end by the intervention of the Syrian-dominated Arab Deterrent Force. Large areas of the country, however, remained outside governmental control, including West Beirut, which was the scene of frequent conflict between opposing militia groups. In March 1978 there was an Israeli invasion following a Palestinian attack inside Israel. Israeli troops eventually withdrew in June, but instead of handing over all their positions to UN Peacekeeping Forces, they installed Israeli-controlled Christian Lebanese militia forces in border areas. In June 1982 Israeli forces once again invaded, this time in massive strength, and swept through the country, eventually laying siege to and bombing Beirut. In Sept. Palestinian forces, together with the PLO leadership, evacuated Beirut. Israeli forces started a withdrawal on 16 Feb. 1985 but it was not until the end of 1990 that the various militias which had held sway in Beirut withdrew. A new Government of National Reconciliation was announced on 24 Dec. 1990. The dissolution of all militias was decreed by the National Assembly in April 1991, but the Shia Muslim militia Hizbollah was allowed to remain active. Following a 17-day Israeli bombardment of Hizbollah positions in April 1996, a US-brokered unsigned 'understanding' of 26 April 1996 guaranteed that Hizbollah guerrillas and Palestinian radical groups would cease attacks on civilians in northern Israel and granted Israel the right to self-defence. Hizbollah maintained the right to resist Israel's occupation of Lebanese soil. In May 2000 Israel completed its withdrawal from south Lebanon, 22 years after the first invasion. On 14 Feb. 2005 former Prime Minister Rafiq al-Hariri was assassinated in a bomb attack on his car, sparking international condemnation of the murder and massive public protests at the continued presence of Syrian soldiers in the country. Soon afterwards Syria began withdrawing and redeploying its 14,000 troops and intelligence agents from Beirut.

TERRITORY AND POPULATION

Lebanon is mountainous, bounded on the north and east by Syria, on the west by the Mediterranean and on the south by Israel. The area is 10,452 sq. km (4,036 sq. miles). Population (2002 estimate), 3·59m.; density, 344 per sq. km. In 2001, 90·0% of the population were urban.

The UN gives a projected population for 2010 of 4·00m.

The principal towns, with estimated population (1998), are: Beirut (the capital), 1·5m.; Tripoli, 160,000; Zahlé, 45,000; Saida (Sidon), 38,000.

The official language is Arabic. French and, increasingly, English are widely spoken in official and commercial circles. Armenian is spoken by a minority group.

SOCIAL STATISTICS

2001 estimates: births, 86,000; deaths, 19,000. Estimated rates, 2001 (per 1,000 population): births, 24·3; deaths, 5·4. Infant mortality was 28 per 1,000 live births in 2001; expectation of life (2001), 71·7 years for males and 74·8 for females. Annual population growth rate, 1992–02, 2·3%; fertility rate, 2001, 2·2 births per woman.

CLIMATE

A Mediterranean climate with short, warm winters and long, hot and rainless summers, with high humidity in coastal areas. Rainfall is largely confined to the winter months and can be torrential, with snow on high ground. Beirut, Jan. 55°F (13°C), July 81°F (27°C). Annual rainfall 35·7" (893 mm).

CONSTITUTION AND GOVERNMENT

The first Constitution was established under the French Mandate on 23 May 1926. It has since been amended in 1927, 1929, 1943 (twice), 1947 and 1990. It is based on a separation of powers, with a President, a single-chamber *National Assembly* elected by universal suffrage at age 21 in 12 electoral constituencies, and an independent judiciary. In Oct. 1995 the National Assembly extended the President's term of office from six to nine years. The executive consists of the President and a Prime Minister and Cabinet appointed after consultation between the President and the National Assembly. The system is adapted to the communal balance on which Lebanese political life depends by an electoral law which allocates deputies according to the religious distribution of the population, and by a series of constitutional conventions whereby, *e.g.,* the President is always a Maronite Christian, the Prime Minister a Sunni Muslim and the Speaker of the Assembly a Shia Muslim. There is no party system. In Aug. 1990, and again in July 1992, the National Assembly voted to increase its membership, and now has 128 deputies with equal numbers of Christians and Muslims.

On 21 Sept. 1990 President Hrawi established the Second Republic by signing constitutional amendments which had been negotiated at Taif (Saudi Arabia) in Oct. 1989. These institute an executive collegium between the President, Prime Minister and Speaker, and remove from the President the right to recall the Prime Minister, dissolve the Assembly and vote in the Council of Ministers.

National Anthem. 'Kulluna lil watan lil 'ula lil 'alam' ('All of us for our country, flag and glory'); words by Rashid Nachleh, tune by W. Sabra.

RECENT ELECTIONS

Elections were held on 27 Aug. and 3 Sept. 2000. Resistance and Development (Amal–Hizbollah alliance) won 23 seats; al-Karamah (Dignity) won 18; Baalbeck–Hermel al Ii'tilafiah (Baalbeck–Hermel Coalition) 9; al-Jabhar al-Nidal al-Watani (National Defence Front) 8; Wahdal al-Jabal (Mountain Union) 7. Non-partisans won 20 seats. A number of smaller parties won 43 seats between them.

On 3 Sept. 2004 parliament voted to extend Presdent Emile Lahoud's term by a further three years.

CURRENT ADMINISTRATION

President: Emile Lahoud; b. 1936 (sworn in 24 Nov. 1998; re-elected for a further three years in Sept. 2004).

In April 2005 the government comprised:

Prime Minister: Najib Mikati; b. 1955 (took office 19 April 2005).

Deputy Prime Minister and Minister of Defence: Élias Murr.

Minister of Foreign Affairs: Mahmoud Hammoud. *Interior:* Hassan Sabeh. *Education and Culture:* Ghassan Salamé. *Information and Tourism:* Charles Rizk. *Justice:* Khaled Kabbani. *Health and Social Affairs:* Mohammed Jawad Khalifé. *Public Works and Displaced Persons:* Adel Hamié. *Environment and Administrative Development:* Tarek Mitri. *Energy and Industry:* Bassam Yammine. *Finance, Economy and Commerce:* Damien Kattar. *Telecommunications, Youth and Sport:* Alain Tabourian. *Labour and Agriculture:* Trad Hamadé.

President's Website: http://www.presidency.gov.lb

DEFENCE

There were 14,000 Syrian troops in the country in early 2005, but in March 2005 Lebanon and Syria agreed that the troops would be redeployed to the Bekaa Valley in the east of the country. They were subsequently all withdrawn from Lebanon. The United Nations Interim Force in Lebanon (UNIFIL), created in 1978, had a strength of 3,638 in 2002.

Conscription is for 12 months.

Defence expenditure in 2003 totalled US$512m. (US$114 per capita), representing 2·8% of GDP.

Army. The strength of the Army was 70,000 in 2002 and includes a Presidential Guard and five special forces regiments. There is an internal security force, run by the Ministry of the Interior, some 13,000 strong.

Navy. A force of 830 personnel (2002) operate a handful of small craft.

Air Force. The Air Force had (2002) about 1,000 personnel. No combat aircraft were operated.

INTERNATIONAL RELATIONS

A Treaty of Brotherhood, Co-operation and Co-ordination with Syria of May 1991 provides for close relations in the fields of foreign policy, the economy, military affairs and security. The treaty stipulates that Lebanese government decisions are subject to review by six joint Syrian-Lebanese bodies.

Lebanon is a member of the UN, the League of Arab States, OIC, Islamic Development Bank and the International Organization of the Francophonie.

ECONOMY

Agriculture accounted for 11·7% of GDP in 2002, industry 21·0% and services 67·3%.

Overview. The semi-autonomous Council of Development and Reconstruction, originally set up in 1977, was revived in 1991 to oversee a post-civil war rehabilitation programme 'Horizon 2000'. In 1995 this programme was revised and extended up to 2007.

Currency. The unit of currency is the *Lebanese pound* (LBP) of 100 *piastres*. There was deflation of 0·4% in both 2000 and 2001, but then inflation of 1·8% in 2002. In June 2002 foreign exchange reserves totalled US$4,604m., gold reserves were 9·22m. troy oz and total money supply was £Leb.2,231·10bn. There is a fluctuating official rate of exchange, fixed monthly; in practice it is used only for the calculation of *ad-valorem* customs duties on Lebanese imports and for import statistics. For other purposes the free market is used.

Budget. The fiscal year is the calendar year.

Government revenue and expenditure (in £Leb.1m.):

	1995	*1996*	*1997*	*1998*	*1999*
Revenue	3,003	3,534	3,753	4,449	4,868
Expenditure	6,342	7,732	9,728	8,385	8,910

Performance. Total GDP was US$19·0bn. in 2003. In both 2001 and 2002 there was real GDP growth of 2·0%.

Banking and Finance. The Bank of Lebanon (*Governor*, Riad Salameh) is the bank of issue. In 1994 there were 52 domestic banks, 14 subsidiaries and 12 foreign banks, with 590 branches in all. Commercial bank deposits in June 1998 totalled £Leb.41,836,800m. There is a stock exchange in Beirut (closed 1983–95).

Lebanon was one of 15 countries and territories named in a report in June 2000 as failing to co-operate in the fight against international money laundering. The Financial Action Task Force on Money Laundering was set up by the G7 group of major industrialized nations.

ENERGY AND NATURAL RESOURCES

Environment. Lebanon's carbon dioxide emissions from the consumption and flaring of fossil fuels in 2002 were the equivalent of 4·5 tonnes per capita.

Electricity. Installed capacity in 2000 was 2·3m. kW. Production in 2000 was 9·24bn. kWh and consumption per capita 3,041 kWh.

Minerals. There are no commercially viable deposits.

Agriculture. In 2001 there were 170,000 ha of arable land and 143,000 ha of permanent crop land. Crop production (in 1,000 tonnes), 2000: tomatoes, 335; sugarbeets, 330; potatoes, 270; grapes, 245; cucumbers and gherkins, 190; oranges, 165; watermelons, 135; apples, 120; lemons and limes, 111; bananas, 110; olives, 105; onions, 85; cabbages, 83.

Livestock (2000): goats, 485,000; sheep, 380,000; cattle, 77,000; pigs, 64,000; chickens, 32m.

Forestry. The forests of the past have been denuded by exploitation and in 2000 covered 36,000 ha, or 3·5% of the total land area. Timber production was 89,000 cu. metres in 2001.

Fisheries. The catch in 2001 was 3,670 tonnes, of which 3,650 tonnes were sea fish.

INDUSTRY

According to the Financial Times Survey (FT 500), the largest company by market capitalization in Lebanon on 4 Jan. 2001 was SOLIDERE (US$1,051·9m.), a Beirut development and reconstruction company.

In 2001 industry accounted for 21·9% of GDP, with manufacturing contributing 10·3%. Industrial production, 2001 (in 1,000 tonnes): cement, 2,890; flour, 420; sulphuric acid, 357; mineral water, 276·8m. litres.

Labour. The workforce was some 650,000 in 1995, of whom 72,000 worked in agriculture. Following considerable labour unrest, an agreement on wage increases and social benefits was concluded between the government and the General Confederation of Lebanese Workers (GCLW) in Dec. 1993.

Trade Unions. The main unions are the General Confederation of Lebanese Workers and the General Confederation of Sectoral Unions.

INTERNATIONAL TRADE

Foreign and domestic trade is the principal source of income. Foreign debt was US$17,077m. in 2002.

Imports and Exports. Imports, 2002: US$6,445m.; exports, US$1,046m. Major imports in 1999 were (in US$1m.): machinery and transport equipment, 1,522·1; manufactured goods, 981·8; foodstuffs, 940·1; chemicals, 666·9; petroleum, 505·6. Major exports were (in US$1m.): foodstuffs, 92·0 (59·1 were vegetables and fruit); chemicals (including phosphoric acids), 91·8; machinery and transport equipment, 80·6; precious metal jewellery, 52·0; gold, 40·3.

In 1999 the main export markets were (in US$1m.): Saudi Arabia, 70·6; UAE, 53·7; France, 52·1; Switzerland, 44·4; USA, 41·9; Syria, 32·1. Main import suppliers (in US$1m.): Italy, 676·0; France, 592·8; Germany, 550·1; USA, 499·1; Switzerland, 440·9; UK, 270·5.

COMMUNICATIONS

Roads. There were about 7,300 km of roads in 1999, of which 84·9% were paved. Passenger cars in 1997 numbered 1,299,400, and there were also 85,240 trucks and vans, 61,470 motorcycles and mopeds and 6,830 buses and coaches. In 1997 there were 3,315 road accidents resulting in 357 deaths.

Rail. Railways are state-owned. There is 222 km of standard gauge track.

Civil Aviation. Beirut International Airport was served in 2003 by nearly 30 airlines. It handled 2,244,788 passengers (all on international flights) in 2000 and 59,243 tonnes of freight. The national airline is the state-owned Middle East Airlines, which in 1999 flew 17·7m. km, carrying 719,400 passengers (all on international flights).

Shipping. Beirut is the largest port, followed by Tripoli, Jounieh and Saida (Sidon). Total GRT in 2002 was 229,000, including oil tankers 1,000 GRT.

Telecommunications. Lebanon had 1,453,900 telephone subscribers in 2002, or 425·8 per 1,000 persons. Mobile phone subscribers numbered 775,100 in 2002 and there were 275,000 PCs in use (80·5 for every 1,000 persons). There were 3,000 fax machines in 1995. The number of Internet users in 2002 was 400,000.

SOCIAL INSTITUTIONS

Justice. The population in penal institutions in March 2003 was 6,382 (172 per 100,000 of national population). The death penalty is still in force. There were three confirmed executions in 2004, the first ones since 1998.

Religion. In 2001 it was estimated that the population was 56·6% Muslim (34·8% Shia and 21·8% Sunni), 36·0% Christian (mainly Maronite) and 7·4% Druze. In 1996 there were 119 Roman Catholic bishops. In Sept. 2003 there was one cardinal.

Education. There are state and private primary and secondary schools. In 1999–2000 there were 384,539 pupils with 20,571 teachers at primary schools; and (2000–01) 322,136 pupils with 43,959 teachers in general secondary education. There are 13 universities, including two American and one French, and ten other institutions of higher education. In 2000–01 there were 134,018 students in tertiary education and 9,459 academic staff. Adult literacy was 86·5% in 2001 (92·4% among males and 81·0% among females). In 2000–01 total expenditure on education came to 2·9% of GNP and 11·1% of total government spending.

There is an Academy of Fine Arts.

Health. There were 153 hospitals in 1995 (provision of 22 beds per 10,000 population), and in 1997 there were 7,203 physicians, 2,744 dentists, 3,430 nurses and 1,715 pharmacists.

CULTURE

World Heritage Sites. There are five sites under Lebanese jurisdiction in the World Heritage List. Four were entered on the list in 1984: the ruins of Anjar, a city founded by the Muslim Arab caliph Walid I at the beginning of the 8th century; Baalbek, the most impressive ancient site in Lebanon and one of the most important Roman ruins in the Middle East; Byblos, the site of multi-layered ruins of one of the most ancient cities of Lebanon, dating back to Neolithic times; and Tyre, which has important archaeological remains, principally from Roman times. The Qadisha Valley and Bcharre district, inscribed in 1998, has been the site of monastic communities since the earliest years of Christianity. Its cedar trees, among the most highly prized building materials of the ancient world, are survivors of a sacred forest.

Broadcasting. The government-controlled Radio Lebanon transmits in Arabic, French, English and Armenian. Télé-Liban, which is government-owned, transmits programmes from 13 stations. Colour is by SECAM H. There were 1·20m. TV sets in 2001 and 2·46m. radio receivers in 2000.

Press. In 1996 there were 15 daily newspapers with a combined circulation of 435,000, at a rate of 141 per 1,000 inhabitants.

Tourism. In 2000 there were 742,000 foreign tourists, spending US$742m. Lebanon has experienced a tourism boom since the attacks on the USA of 11 Sept. 2001, boosted by large numbers of visitors from Arab Gulf countries wary of travelling to Europe and North America.

Festivals. Major annual cultural events are the Al Bustan Festival of music, dance and theatre in Feb.–March; Baalbek International Festival, which reopened in 1997 after an absence of 23 years; Hamra Festival in June; Beiteddine Festival in July–Aug.; Tyre Festival; Byblos Festival; and the Beirut Film Festival.

DIPLOMATIC REPRESENTATIVES

Of Lebanon in the United Kingdom (15–21 Kensington Palace Gdns, London, W8 4QN)

Ambassador: Jihad Mortada.

Of the United Kingdom in Lebanon (Embassies Complex, Army St, Zkak Al-Blat, Serail Hill, PO Box 11–471, Beirut)
Ambassador: James Watt, CVO.

Of Lebanon in the USA (2560 28th St., NW, Washington, D.C., 20008)
Ambassador: Dr Farid Abboud.

Of the USA in Lebanon (P. O. Box 70–840, Antelias, Beirut)
Ambassador: Jeffrey D. Feltman.

Of Lebanon to the United Nations
Ambassador: Sami Kronfol.

Of Lebanon to the European Union
Ambassador: Fawzi Fawaz.

FURTHER READING

Choueiri, Y. M., *State and Society in Syria and Lebanon.* Exeter Univ. Press, 1994
Fisk, R., *Pity the Nation: Lebanon at War.* 2nd ed. OUP, 1992
Gemayel, A., *Rebuilding Lebanon.* New York, 1992
Hiro, D., *Lebanon Fire and Embers: a History of the Lebanese Civil War.* New York, 1993

National library: Dar el Kutub, Parliament Sq., Beirut.
National statistical office: Service de Statistique Générale, Beirut.
Website: http://www.cas.gov.lb

LESOTHO

Kingdom of Lesotho

Capital: Maseru
Population projection, 2010: 1·76m.
GDP per capita, 2002: (PPP$) 2,420
HDI/world rank: 0·493/145

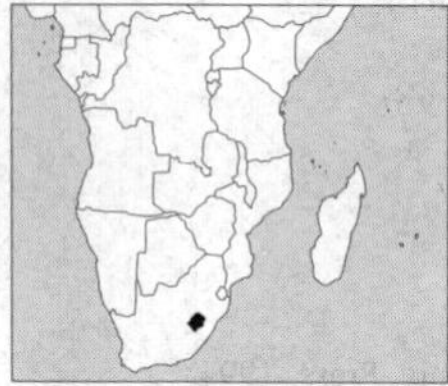

KEY HISTORICAL EVENTS

The Basotho nation was constituted in the 19th century under the leadership of Moshoeshoe I, bringing together refugees from disparate tribes scattered by Zulu expansionism in southern Africa. After war with land-hungry Boer settlers in 1856 (and again in 1886), Moshoeshoe appealed for British protection. This was granted in 1868, and in 1871 the territory was annexed to the Cape Colony (now Republic of South Africa), but in 1883 it was restored to the direct control of the British government through the High Commissioner for South Africa. In 1965 full internal self-government was achieved under King Moshoeshoe II. On 4 Oct. 1966 Basutoland became an independent and sovereign member of the British Commonwealth as the Kingdom of Lesotho. Chief Leabua Jonathan, leader of the Basotho National Party and prime minister from 1965, suspended the constitution when the elections of 1970 were declared invalid. On 20 Jan. 1986, after a border blockade by the Republic of South Africa, Chief Jonathan was deposed in a bloodless military coup led by Maj.-Gen. Justin Lekhanya who granted significant powers to the king. King Moeshoeshoe II was deposed in Nov. 1990 and replaced by King Letsie III. Maj.-Gen. Lekhanya was deposed in May 1991. A democratic constitution was promulgated in April 1993. The elections in May 1998 were won by the ruling Lesotho Congress for Democracy. In Sept. 1998 an army mutiny prompted intervention from South Africa to support the government.

TERRITORY AND POPULATION

Lesotho is an enclave within South Africa. The area is 11,720 sq. miles (30,355 sq. km).

The census in 1996 showed a total population of 1,960,069 persons; density, 64·6 per sq. km. In 2001 the population was 71·3% rural. The United Nations population estimate for 2000 was 1,785,000.

The UN gives a projected population for 2010 of 1·76m.

There are ten districts, all named after their chief towns, except Berea (chief town, Teyateyaneng). Area and population:

Region	*Area (in sq. km.)*	*Population (1986 census, in 1,000)*	*Population (2001 estimate, in 1,000)*
Berea	2,222	194·6	300·6
Butha-Buthe	1,767	100·6	126·9
Leribe	2,828	258·0	362·3
Mafeteng	2,119	195·6	238·9
Maseru	4,279	311·1	477·6
Mohale's Hoek	3,530	164·4	206·8
Mokhotlong	4,075	74·7	89·7
Qacha's Nek	2,349	64·0	80·3
Quthing	2,916	110·4	140·6
Thaba-Tseka	4,270	104·1	133·7

In 1999 the capital, Maseru, had an estimated population of 373,000. Other major towns (with 1986 census population) are: Teyateyaneng, 14,251; Mafeteng, 12,667; Qacha's Nek, 10,000 (1992 estimate); Hlotse, 9,595.

The official languages are Sesotho and English.

The population is more than 98% Basotho. The rest is made up of Xhosas, approximately 3,000 expatriate Europeans and several hundred Asians.

SOCIAL STATISTICS

1995 births, 76,000; deaths, 21,000. Rates, 1995: birth (per 1,000 population), 37; death, 10. Annual population growth rate, 1992–02, 1·1%. Life expectancy at birth in 2001 was 35·4 years for males and 41·7 years for females, largely as a consequence of approximately 31% of all adults being infected with HIV. Infant mortality, 2001, 91 per 1,000 live births; fertility rate, 2001, 4·5 births per woman.

CLIMATE

A healthy and pleasant climate, with variable rainfall, but averaging 29" (725 mm) a year over most of the country. The rain falls mainly in the summer months of Oct. to April, while the winters are dry and may produce heavy frosts in lowland areas and frequent snow in the highlands. Temperatures in the lowlands range from a maximum of 90°F (32·2°C) in summer to a minimum of 20°F (–6·7°C) in winter.

CONSTITUTION AND GOVERNMENT

Lesotho is a constitutional monarchy with the King as Head of State. Following the death of his father, Moshoeshoe II, **Letsie III** succeeded to the throne in Jan. 1996.

The 1993 constitution provided for a *National Assembly* comprising an elected 80-member lower house and a *Senate* of 22 principal chiefs and 11 members nominated by the King. For the elections of May 2002 a new voting system was introduced, increasing the number of seats in the National Assembly to 120, elected for a five-year term as before, but with 80 members in single-seat constituencies and 40 elected by proportional representation.

National Anthem. 'Lesotho fatsela bontat'a rona' ('Lesotho, land of our fathers'); words by F. Coillard, tune by L. Laur.

RECENT ELECTIONS

Following the elections of May 1998 the King swore allegiance to a new constitution and the Military Council was dissolved.

Parliamentary elections were held on 25 May 2002. The ruling Lesotho Congress for Democracy (LCD) won 77 seats with 54·9% of votes cast, the Basotho National Party (BNP) 21 with 22·4%, the Lesotho People's Congress (LPC) 5 with 5·8% and the National Independent Party (NIP) 5 with 5·5%. The remaining seats went to smaller parties with less than 5% of votes cast. Turn-out was 68·1%.

CURRENT ADMINISTRATION

In March 2005 the Council of Ministers comprised:

Prime Minister, Minister of Defence and Public Service: Pakalitha Bethuel Mosisili; b. 1945 (LCD; sworn in 29 May 1998).

Deputy Prime Minister and Minister for Home Affairs and Public Safety: Archibald Lesao Lehola. *Minister for Justice, Human Rights and Rehabilitation, and for Law and Constitutional Affairs:* Refiloe Masemene. *Education:* Mohlabi Tsekoa. *Foreign Affairs:* Monyane Moleleki. *Finance and Development Planning:* Timothy Thahane. *Employment and Labour:* Mpeo Mahase-Moiloa. *Local Government:* Dr Ponts'o Suzan 'Matumelo Sekatle. *Gender, Youth and Sports:* Mathabiso Lepono. *Industry, Trade and Marketing:* Mpho Meli Malie. *Health and Social Welfare:* Dr Motloheloa Phooko. *Tourism and Culture:* Lebohang Ntsinyi. *Communications, Science and Technology:* Motsoahae Thomas Thabane. *Natural Resources:* Manphono Khaketla. *Public Works and Transport:* Popane Lebesa. *Agriculture and Food Safety:* Rakoro Phororo. *Forestry and Land Reclamation:* Ralechate Mokose. *To the Prime Minister:* Rammotsi Lehata.

The *College of Chiefs* settles the recognition and succession of Chiefs and adjudicates cases of inefficiency, criminality and absenteeism among them.

Government Website: http://www.lesotho.gov.ls

DEFENCE

South African and Botswanan troops intervened after a mutiny by Lesotho's armed forces in Sept. 1998. The foreign forces were withdrawn in May 1999.

The Royal Lesotho Defence Force has 2,000 personnel. Defence expenditure totalled US$26m. in 2003 (US$15 per capita), representing 2·3% of GDP.

INTERNATIONAL RELATIONS

Lesotho is a member of the UN, WTO, the Commonwealth, the African Union, African Development Bank, SADC and is an ACP member state of the ACP-EU relationship.

ECONOMY

In 2002 agriculture accounted for 16·3% of GDP, industry 43·1% and services 40·6%.

Overview. The Lesotho National Development Corporation promotes industrial and tourist trade development.

Currency. The unit of currency is the *loti* (plural *maloti*) (LSL) of 100 *lisente*, at par with the South African rand, which is legal tender. Total money supply in June 2002 was 1,471m. maloti. Inflation was 12·3% in 2002. Foreign exchange reserves were US$388m. in June 2002.

Budget. Revenues in 2000–01 were 2,752m. maloti and expenditures 2,898m. maloti.

Performance. Real GDP growth was 3·6% in 2001 and 4·2% in 2002. Total GDP in 2003 was US$1·1bn.

Banking and Finance. The Central Bank of Lesotho (*Governor,* E. M. Matekane) is the bank of issue, founded in 1982 to succeed the Lesotho Monetary Authority. There are three commercial banks (Lesotho Bank, Nedbank Lesotho, Standard Bank Lesotho) and one development bank (Lesotho Building Finance Corp.). Savings deposits totalled 342·8m. maloti in 1993.

ENERGY AND NATURAL RESOURCES

Environment. Lesotho's carbon dioxide emissions from the consumption and flaring of fossil fuels in 2002 were the equivalent of 0·1 tonnes per capita.

Electricity. Capacity (1993) 13,400 kW (98% supplied by South Africa). Consumption in 1996 was 335m. kWh.

Minerals. Diamonds are the main product; 2000–01 output was 1,140 carats. Sandstone production, 16,000 sq. metres (1996).

Agriculture. Agriculture employs two-thirds of the workforce. The chief crops were (2000 production in 1,000 tonnes): maize, 102; sorghum, 25; wheat, 21; dry beans, 9. Peas and other vegetables are also grown. Soil conservation and the improvement of crops and pasture are matters of vital importance. In 2001 there were 330,000 ha of arable land and 4,000 ha of permanent crop land. There were 2,000 tractors in 2001.

Livestock (2000): cattle, 520,000; sheep, 750,000; goats, 580,000; asses, 154,000; horses, 100,000; chickens, 2m.

Forestry. Timber production was 2·03m. cu. metres in 2001.

Fisheries. The catch in 2001 was approximately 24 tonnes, exclusively from inland waters.

INDUSTRY

Important industries are food products, beverages, textiles and chemical products.

Labour. The labour force in 1996 was 847,000 (63% males). In 1998, 76,100 were working in mines in South Africa.

INTERNATIONAL TRADE

Lesotho is a member of the Southern African Customs Union (SACU) with Botswana, Namibia, South Africa and Swaziland. Foreign debt was US$637m. in 2002.

Imports and Exports. In 2002 imports (f.o.b.) were valued at US$736·0m. (US$678·6m. in 2001) and exports (f.o.b.) at US$354·8m. (US$278·6m. in 2001).

Principal exports in 1993 (in 1,000 maloti): machinery and transport equipment, 25,540; wool, 16,853; manufactures, 13,426; cattle, 8,409; mohair, 5,131; canned vegetables, 2,275; wheat flour, 1,717.

The bulk of international trade is with South Africa. In 1998 SACU member countries accounted for 88·7% of imports and 65·5% of exports.

COMMUNICATIONS

Roads. The road network in 1999 totalled 5,940 km, of which 18·3% were paved. In 1996 there were 12,610 passenger cars (5·7 per 1,000 inhabitants) plus 25,000 trucks and vans. In 1999 there were 3,817 traffic accidents with 290 fatalities.

Rail. A branch line built by the South African Railways, one mile long, connects Maseru with the Bloemfontein–Natal line at Marseilles for transport of cargo.

Civil Aviation. There are direct flights from Maseru to Johannesburg. In 2000 Maseru handled 28,613 passengers (28,503 on international flights).

Telecommunications. Lesotho had 126,000 telephone subscribers in 2002, or 58·2 for every 1,000 persons. There were 600 fax machines in 1995. In 2002 there were 21,000 Internet users. Mobile phones have been available since 1996 and in 2002 there were 92,000 subscribers.

Postal Services. In 1998 there were 157 post offices.

SOCIAL INSTITUTIONS

Justice. The legal system is based on Roman-Dutch law. The Lesotho High Court and the Court of Appeal are situated in Maseru, and there are Magistrates' Courts in the districts. 5,888 criminal offences were reported in 1993.

The population in penal institutions in 2002 was 3,000 (143 per 100,000 of national population).

Religion. In 2001 there were 0·82m. Roman Catholics, 0·28m. Protestants, 0·26m. African Christians and the remainder followed other religions.

Education. Education levels: pre-school, 3 to 5 years; first level (elementary), 6 to 12; second level (secondary or teacher training or technical training), 7 to 13; third level (university or teacher training college). Lesotho has the highest proportion of female pupils at primary schools in Africa, with 51% in 2000–01. It also has the highest proportion of female pupils in Africa at secondary level education, with 54% in 2000–01, and at tertiary level education, with 63% in 2000–01. In 2002 there were 418,668 pupils in 1,333 primary schools with 8,908 teachers and 81,130 pupils in 224 secondary schools with 3,384 teachers; in 2002 there were 1,739 students in the National Teacher-Training College with 108 teachers and 1,859 students in 8 technical schools with 172 teachers. The National University of Lesotho was established in 1975 at Roma; enrolment in 2001–02, 3,266 students. The adult literacy rate in 2001 was 83·9% (73·3% among males but 93·9% among females). Lesotho has the biggest difference in literacy rates between the sexes in favour of females of any country in the world, and the highest female literacy rate in Africa.

In 1999–2000 total expenditure on education came to 7·9% of GNP and 18·5% of total government spending.

Health. In 1995 there were 105 physicians, 10 dentists, 1,169 nurses and 914 midwives. There were 22 hospitals in 1987.

CULTURE

Broadcasting. Radio Lesotho transmits daily in English and Sesotho. The broadcasting authority is the Lesotho National Broadcasting Service. In 2000 there were 94,600 radio sets and in 2001 there were 70,000 TV sets (colour by PAL).

Press. There were seven non-daily newspapers and periodicals in 1996. Combined circulation of the two daily papers was 15,000, at a rate of 7·6 per 1,000 inhabitants.

Tourism. In 1999 there were 186,000 foreign tourists; spending by tourists in 2000 totalled US$24m.

DIPLOMATIC REPRESENTATIVES

Of Lesotho in the United Kingdom (7 Chesham Pl., Belgravia, London, SW1 8HN)
High Commissioner: Lebohang Ramohlanka.

Of the United Kingdom in Lesotho (PO Box Ms 521, Maseru 100)
High Commissioner: Frank Martin.

Of Lesotho in the USA (2511 Massachusetts Ave., NW, Washington, D.C., 20008)
Ambassador: Molelekeng Ernestina Rapolaki.

Of the USA in Lesotho (254 Kingsway Avenue, Maseru 100)
Ambassador: June Carter Perry.

Of Lesotho to the United Nations
Ambassador: Lebohang Moleko.

Of Lesotho to the European Union
Ambassador: Moliehi Mathato Adel Matlanyane.

FURTHER READING

Bureau of Statistics. *Statistical Reports.* [Various years]

Haliburton, G. M., *A Historical Dictionary of Lesotho.* Scarecrow Press, Metuchen (NJ), 1977
Johnston, D., *Lesotho.* [Bibliography] 2nd ed. ABC-Clio, Oxford and Santa Barbara (CA), 1996
Machobane, L. B. B. J., *Government and Change in Lesotho, 1880–1966: A Study of Political Institutions.* Macmillan, Basingstoke, 1990

National statistical office: Bureau of Statistics, PO Box 455, Maseru.
Website: http://www.bos.gov.ls/

LIBERIA

Republic of Liberia

Capital: Monrovia
Population projection, 2010: 4·13m.
GDP per capita: not available

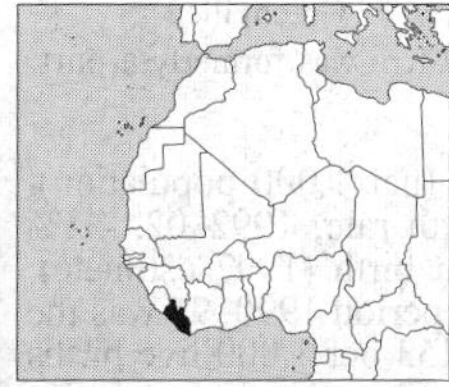

KEY HISTORICAL EVENTS

The Republic of Liberia was created on the Grain Coast for freed American slaves. In 1822 a settlement was formed near the spot where Monrovia now stands. On 26 July 1847 the State was constituted as the Free and Independent Republic of Liberia.

On 12 April 1980 President Tolbert was assassinated and his government overthrown in a coup led by Master-Sergeant Samuel Doe. At the beginning of 1990 rebel forces entered Liberia from the north and fought their way successfully southwards to confront President Doe's forces in Monrovia. The rebels comprised the National Patriotic Front of Liberia (NPFL) led by Charles Taylor, and the hostile breakaway Independent National Patriotic Front led by Prince Johnson. A peacekeeping force dispatched by the Economic Community of West African States (ECOWAS) disembarked at Monrovia on 25 Aug. 1990. On 9 Sept. President Doe was assassinated by Johnson's rebels. ECOWAS installed a provisional government led by Amos Sawyer. Charles Taylor also declared himself president, as did the former vice-president, Harry Moniba. A succession of ceasefires was negotiated and broken. An ECOWAS-sponsored peace agreement was signed on 17 Aug. 1996 in Abuja, providing for the disarmament of all factions by the end of Jan. 1997 and the election of a president on 31 May 1997. By the end of Jan. 1997 some 20,000 out of perhaps 60,000 insurgents had surrendered their arms. The civil war is reckoned to have killed up to 200,000 people and made 1m. homeless. Charles Taylor was elected president in July 1997. In Feb. 2002 Taylor declared a state of emergency after an attack by a group of rebels on the town of Kley, where thousands of refugees from Sierra Leone were encamped.

In Aug. 2003 the UN called for the immediate deployment of an ECOWAS peacekeeping force, to be replaced by a full UN force on 1 Oct. Nigerian peacekeepers arrived on 4 Aug. 2003. Taylor relinquished power to his vice-president, Moses Blah, and to a transitional government on 11 Aug.

TERRITORY AND POPULATION

Liberia is bounded in the northwest by Sierra Leone, north by Guinea, east by Côte d'Ivoire and southwest by the Atlantic ocean. The total area is 99,065 sq. km. At the census (1984) the population was 2,101,628. Estimate (2002) 3,207,000; density, 32 per sq. km.

The UN gives a projected population for 2010 of 4·13m.

In 1995 an estimated 55% of the population were rural. English is the official language spoken by 15% of the population. The rest belong in the main to three linguistic groups: Mande, West Atlantic and the Kwa. These are in turn subdivided into 16 ethnic groups: Bassa, Bella, Gbandi, Mende, Gio, Dey, Mano, Gola, Kpelle, Kissi, Krahn, Kru, Lorma, Mandingo, Vai and Grebo.

Monrovia, the capital, had (1999) a population of 479,000.

There are 15 counties, whose areas, populations (1999 estimate) and capitals were as follows:

County	*Sq. km*	*1999 population*	*Chief town*
Bomi	1,955	114,316	Tubmanburg
Bong	8,099	299,825	Gbarnga
Gbarpolu[1]	...	...	Bepolu
Grand Bassa	8,759	215,338	Buchanan
Grand Cape Mount	5,827	120,141	Robertsport
Grand Gedeh	17,029	94,497	Zwedru
Grand Kru[2]	...	39,062	Barclayville
Lofa	19,360	351,492	Voinjama
Margibi	3,263	219,417	Kakata

County	Sq. km	1999 population	Chief town
Maryland	5,351	71,977	Harper
Montserrado	2,740	843,783	Bensonville
Nimba	12,043	338,887	Saniquillie
River Gee[1]	...	...	Fish Town
Rivercess	4,385	38,167	Rivercess
Sinoe	10,254	79,241	Greenville

[1]Created since 1999. [2]Area included in Maryland, of which Grand Kru was formerly a part.

SOCIAL STATISTICS

1997 births, estimate, 110,000; deaths, 30,000. 1997 rates (per 1,000 population), estimate: birth, 42·3; death, 11·5. Annual population growth rate, 1992–02, 4·3% (the highest of any sovereign country). Life expectancy at birth (1997 estimate): male, 56·4 years; female, 61·7 years. Infant mortality in the period 1990–95 was the highest in the world, at 200 per 1,000 live births, up from 153 per 1,000 live births over the period 1980–85. Fertility rate, 2001, 6·8 births per woman.

CLIMATE

An equatorial climate, with constant high temperatures and plentiful rainfall, although Jan. to May is drier than the rest of the year. Monrovia, Jan. 79°F (26·1°C), July 76°F (24·4°C). Annual rainfall 206" (5,138 mm).

CONSTITUTION AND GOVERNMENT

A Constitution was approved by referendum in July 1984 and came into force on 6 Jan. 1986. Under it the National Assembly consisted of a 26-member Senate and a 64-member House of Representatives.

National Anthem. 'All hail, Liberia, hail!'; words by President Daniel Warner, tune by O. Lucas.

RECENT ELECTIONS

Presidential and parliamentary elections were held on 20 July 1997. The electorate was 700,000; turn-out was 85%. Charles Taylor (National Patriotic Party) was elected president with 75·3% of the vote. His closest rival, Ellen Johnson-Sirleaf (Unity Party), won 9·6% of the vote. There were two other candidates.

In the elections to the House of Representatives on the same day the National Patriotic Party (NPP) won 49 of the 64 seats, and 21 of the 26 Senate seats. The Unity Party (UP) won 7 seats (and 3 in the Senate) and the All Liberia Coalition Party (ALCOP) won 3 seats (and 2 in the Senate).

Parliamentary and presidential elections are scheduled to take place on 14 Oct. 2005.

CURRENT ADMINISTRATION

On 14 Oct. 2003 Gyude Bryant took office as Chairman of the National Transitional Government.

In March 2005 the Transitional Government comprised:

Vice President: Wesley Johnson.

Minister of Agriculture: George Kammie. *Commerce and Industry:* Samuel Wulu. *Defence:* Daniel Chea. *Education:* Evelyne Kandakai. *Finance:* Lusine Kamara. *Foreign Affairs:* Thomas Yaya Nimley. *Gender Development:* Vaba Gayflor. *Health and Social Welfare:* Peter Coleman. *Information, Culture and Tourism:* Vacant. *Internal Affairs:* H. Dan Morias. *Justice:* Kabineh Janneh. *Labour:* Laveli Supuwood. *Land, Mines and Energy:* Willie Mulbah. *National Security:* Vacant. *Planning and Economic Affairs:* Christian Herbert. *Posts and Telecommunications:* Eugene Lenn Nagbe. *Public Works:* Vacant. *Rural Development:* Ermat C. B. Jones. *Transport:* Vamba Kanneh. *Youth and Sports:* Wheatonia Dixon-Barnes. *Minister of State for Presidential Affairs:* Jackson Doe.

Speaker of the Transitional Assembly: George Dweh (LURD; elected Oct. 2003).

DEFENCE

In June 2003 UN Secretary-General Kofi Annan called for an international peacekeeping force to restore peace after fighting broke out between government forces and Liberians United for Reconciliation and Democracy (LURD). An

ECOWAS peacekeeping force of over 3,000 troops was deployed initially, but this has been replaced by the UN Peacekeeping Mission in Liberia (UNIMIL), which with 15,000 troops in early 2004 is the world's largest UN peacekeeping force.

Defence expenditure totalled US$45m. in 2003 (US$13 per capita), representing 11·4% of GDP.

INTERNATIONAL RELATIONS

Liberia is a member of the UN, the African Union, African Development Bank, ECOWAS, IOM and is an ACP member state of the ACP-EU relationship.

ECONOMY

Agriculture accounts for approximately 77% of GDP (the highest proportion of any country), industry 5% and services 18%.

Currency. US currency is legal tender. There is a *Liberian dollar* (LRD), in theory at parity with the US dollar. Between 1993 and March 2000 different notes were in use in government-held Monrovia and the rebel-held country areas, but on 27 March 2000 a set of new notes went into circulation to end the years of trading in dual banknotes. Inflation was an estimated 11% in 1998. Total money supply was L$1,859m. in May 2002.

Budget. Revenue in 2002 was US$72·7m.; expenditure was US$80·1m.

Performance. The economy is estimated to have contracted by 4% in 1998, but there followed a recovery, with growth in 1999 estimated at 15%. In 2003 total GDP was US$0·4bn.

Banking and Finance. The National Bank of Liberia opened on 22 July 1974 to act as a central bank. The *Governor* of the bank is Elias Saleeby. There were only three banks in operation in Jan. 2004.

ENERGY AND NATURAL RESOURCES

Environment. Liberia's carbon dioxide emissions from the consumption and flaring of fossil fuels were the equivalent of 0·1 tonnes per capita in 2002.

Electricity. Installed capacity in 2000 was 0·3m. kW. Production in 2000 was about 524m. kWh. Consumption per capita in 2000 was an estimated 180 kWh.

Minerals. 2001 estimates: gold production 1,000 kg and diamond production 170,000 carats.

Agriculture. In 1995 more than 70% of the labour force were engaged in agriculture. There were 380,000 ha of arable land in 2001 and 220,000 ha of permanent crops. Principal crops (2000) in 1,000 tonnes: cassava, 380; sugarcane, 250; rice, 200; bananas, 95; palm oil, 42. Livestock (2000): cattle, 36,000; pigs, 120,000; sheep, 210,000; goats, 220,000; chickens, 4m.

Forestry. Forest area was 3·48m. ha (31·3% of the land area) in 2000. In 2001, 5·26m. cu. metres of roundwood were cut. There are rubber plantations.

Fisheries. Fish landings in 2001 were 11,286 tonnes, of which approximately 65% from sea fishing.

INDUSTRY

There are a number of small factories. Production of cement, cigarettes, soft drinks, palm oil and beer are the main industries.

Labour. In 1996 the labour force was 977,000 (61% males). In 1995 around 70% of the population were engaged in agriculture, fisheries and forestry.

INTERNATIONAL TRADE

Foreign debt was US$2,324m. in 2002.

Imports and Exports. Imports in 2001 were US$180·9m. and exports US$127·4m. Main import sources in 1999 were South Korea, 27·4%; Japan, 24·8%; Germany, 14·1%; Singapore, 7·1%. Major export destinations in 2001 were Norway, 23·8%; Germany, 10·5%; France, 7·5%; Singapore, 6·5%.

In 1989 iron ore accounted for about 51% of total export earnings, rubber 26% and logs and timber 20%.

COMMUNICATIONS

Roads. There were about 10,600 km of roads in 1999 (only 6·2% of which were paved). In 1996 there were 9,400 cars and 32,000 goods vehicles.

Rail. There is a total of 490 km single track. A 148-km freight line connects iron mines to Monrovia. There is a line from Bong to Monrovia (78 km). All railways have been out of use since 1997 because of the civil war.

Civil Aviation. There are two international airports (Roberts International and Sprigg Payne), both near Monrovia. In 2003 there were services to Abidjan, Accra, Brussels, Freetown and Lagos.

Shipping. There are ports at Buchanan, Greenville, Harper and Monrovia. The government maintains no control over the operation of ships flying the Liberian flag. In 2002 shipping registered totalled 50·40m. GRT (second only to Panama), including oil tankers 18·64m. GRT. In 2000 the fleet consisted of 1,557 vessels of 100 GRT or over, including 585 tankers.

Telecommunications. Telephone main lines numbered 6,700 in 2000, or 2·1 per 1,000 persons. In July 2000 there were 300 Internet users.

SOCIAL INSTITUTIONS

Religion. There were (2001) about 1·27m. Christians and 520,000 Sunni Muslims, plus 1·39m. followers of traditional beliefs.

Education. Schools are classified as: (1) Public schools, maintained and run by the government; (2) Mission schools, supported by foreign Missions and subsidized by the government; (3) Private schools, maintained by endowments and sometimes subsidized by the government. Adult literacy in 1995 was 38·3%; 53·9% among males, 22·4% among females.

Health. In 1997 there were 53 physicians (one for every 43,434 inhabitants), 2 dentists, 136 nurses and 99 midwives. There were 92 hospitals in 1988.

CULTURE

Broadcasting. In 2000 there were 863,000 radio and 78,700 television receivers (colour by PAL).

Press. There were six daily newspapers in 1996 with a combined circulation of 35,000.

DIPLOMATIC REPRESENTATIVES

Of Liberia in the United Kingdom (23 Fitzroy Sq., London, W1 6EW)
Ambassador: Vacant.
Chargé d'Affaires a.i.: Jeff Gongoer Dowana, Sr.

Of the United Kingdom in Liberia
Ambassador: Dr John Mitchiner (resides at Freetown, Sierra Leone).

Of Liberia in the USA (5201 16th St., NW, Washington, D.C., 20011)
Ambassador: Vacant.
Chargé d'Affaires a.i.: Prince Porte.

Of the USA in Liberia (111 United Nations Drive, Mamba Point, Monrovia)
Ambassador: John W. Blaney.

Of Liberia to the United Nations
Ambassador: Lami Kawah.

Of Liberia to the European Union
Ambassador: Vacant.
Chargé d'Affaires a.i.: Youngor Telewoda.

FURTHER READING

Daniels, A., *Monrovia Mon Amour: a Visit to Liberia.* London, 1992
Elwood Dunn, D., *Liberia.* [Bibliography] ABC-Clio, Oxford and Santa Barbara (CA), 1995
Sawyer, A., *The Emergence of Autocracy in Liberia: Tragedy and Challenge.* San Francisco, 1992

LIBYA

Jamahiriya Al-Arabiya Al-Libiya Al-Shabiya Al-Ishtirakiya Al-Uzma (Great Socialist People's Libyan Arab Republic)

Capital: Tripoli
Population projection, 2010: 6·33m.
GDP per capita, 1996: (PPP$) 7,570
HDI/world rank: 0·794/58

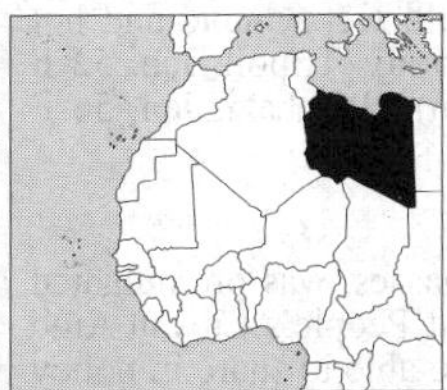

KEY HISTORICAL EVENTS

Tripoli fell under Ottoman domination in the 16th century and although in 1711 the Arab population secured some measure of independence, the country came under the direct rule of Turkey in 1835. In 1911 Italy occupied Tripoli and in 1912, by the Treaty of Ouchy, Turkey recognized the sovereignty of Italy in Tripoli. During the Second World War, the British army expelled the Italians and their German allies, and Tripolitania and Cyrenaica were placed under British, and Fezzan under French, military administration. This continued until 1950 under a UN directive. Libya became an independent, sovereign kingdom with the former Amir of Cyrenaica, Muhammad Idris al Senussi, as king on 24 Dec. 1951. King Idris was deposed in Sept. 1969 by a group of army officers, 12 of whom formed the Revolutionary Command Council which, chaired by Col. Muammar Qadhafi, proclaimed the Libyan Arab Republic. In 1977 the Revolutionary Command Council was superseded by a more democratic People's Congress. Qadhafi remained head of state. Throughout the 1980s Libya had constant disagreements with its neighbours and its relations with the USA and other Western countries deteriorated, culminating in the US bombing of the capital in April 1987 to punish Qadhafi for his alleged support of international terrorism. A US trade embargo was enforced in 1986. In 1992 the UN imposed sanctions after Libya refused to surrender suspects in the 1988 bombing of a Pan Am flight over Lockerbie in Scotland. In April 1999 Libya handed over the two suspects to be tried in the Netherlands but under Scottish law. In Jan. 2001 Abdelbaset Ali Mohmed al Megrahi was sentenced to life imprisonment after being found guilty of murder. The UN had suspended sanctions in 1999, but only formally lifted them in Sept. 2003. In April 2004 the USA eased economic sanctions after Colonel Qadhafi pledged to end his Weapons of Mass Destruction programme. Sanctions were then formally lifted in Sept. 2004.

TERRITORY AND POPULATION

Libya is bounded in the north by the Mediterranean Sea, east by Egypt and Sudan, south by Chad and Niger and west by Algeria and Tunisia. The area is 1,759,540 sq. km. The estimated population at the 2003 census was 5,678,500; density, 3·2 per sq. km. In 2001, 87·9% of the population lived in urban areas. Ethnic composition, 1995: Libyan Arab and Berber, 79%; other (mainly Egyptians, Sudanese and Chadians), 21%.

The UN gives a projected population for 2010 of 6·33m.

The country was formerly divided into 13 administrative regions, but following reforms in 1998 there are now 26 administrative regions (*Shabiyat*). They are Shabiya Al-Batan, Shabiya Jabal Al-Akhdar, Shabiya Al-Wahad, Shabiya Al-Jofra, Shabiya Wadi Al-Hait, Shabiya Al-Morqib, Shabiya Tripoli, Shabiya Sabrata/Sorman, Shabiya Yefrin, Shabiya Derna, Shabiya Al-Marj, Shabiya Al-Kofra, Shabiya Murzaq, Shabiya Wadi Al-Shaati, Shabiya Ben Walid, Shabiya Al-Jafarah, Shabiya Nikat Al-Khams, Shabiya Nalout, Shabiya Al-Qoba, Shabiya Benghazi, Shabiya Sirte, Shabiya Sabah, Shabiya Musrata, Shabiya Tarhouna/Msallata, Shabiya Zawiyah and Shabiya Gharyan.

The two largest cities are Tripoli, the capital (population of 1,773,000 in 1999), and Benghazi (804,000 in 1995).

The official language is Arabic.

SOCIAL STATISTICS

Estimates, 2001: births, 99,000; deaths, 18,000. Estimated rates, 2001 (per 1,000 population): births, 18·6; deaths, 3·4. Life expectancy (2001), 70·4 years for men and 75·0 for women. Annual population growth rate, 1992–02, 2·0%; infant mortality, 2001, 16 per 1,000 live births; fertility rate, 2001, 3·5 births per woman.

CLIMATE

The coastal region has a warm temperate climate, with mild wet winters and hot dry summers, although most of the country suffers from aridity. Tripoli, Jan. 52°F (11·1°C), July 81°F (27·2°C). Annual rainfall 16" (400 mm). Benghazi, Jan. 56°F (13·3°C), July 77°F (25°C). Annual rainfall 11" (267 mm).

CONSTITUTION AND GOVERNMENT

In 1977 a new form of direct democracy, the state of the masses, was promulgated and the name of the country was changed to Great Socialist People's Libyan Arab Jamahiriya. Under this system, every adult is supposed to be able to share in policy making through the Basic People's Congresses of which there are some 2,000. These Congresses appoint People's Committees to execute policy. Provincial and urban affairs are handled by People's Committees responsible to Municipality People's Congresses, of which there are 26, now called *Shabiyat*. Officials of these Congresses and Committees form at national level the 3,000-member General People's Congress which normally meets for about a week early each year (usually in March). This is the highest policy-making body in the country. The General People's Congress appoints its own General Secretariat and the General People's Committee, whose members (the equivalents of ministers elsewhere) head the government departments which execute policy at national level.

Until 1977 Libya was ruled by a Revolutionary Command Council (RCC) headed by Col. Muammar Qadhafi. Upon its abolition in that year the five surviving members of the RCC became the General Secretariat of the General People's Congress, still under Qadhafi's direction. In 1979 they stood down to be replaced by officials elected by the Congress. Since then, Col. Qadhafi has retained his position as Leader of the Revolution. Neither he nor his former RCC colleagues have any formal posts in the present administration, although they continue to wield considerable authority.

National Anthem. 'Allah Akbar' ('God is Great'); words by Abdullah Al-Din, tune by Mahmoud Al-Sharif.

CURRENT ADMINISTRATION

Leader: Col. Muammar Abu Minyar al-Qadhafi; b. 1942 (came to power 1 Sept. 1969).

In March 2005 the Secretariat for the General People's Congress was headed by: *Secretary:* Al-Zanati Muhammad Al-Zanati. *Assistant Secretary:* Ahmed Mohammed Ibrahim.

In March 2005 the General People's Committee comprised:

Secretary: Dr Mohammed Shukri Ghanem. *Deputy Secretary and Secretary for Production:* Dr Ali Baghdadi Al-Mahmudi. *Foreign Liaison and International Co-operation:* Abdul Rahman Mohammed Shalgam. *Energy:* Fethi Omar bin Chetwane. *Employment and Vocational Training:* Ma'tuq Mohammed Ma'tuq. *Planning:* Dr Taher Al-Hadi Al-Jehaimi. *Tourism:* Umar Al-Mabruk Al-Tayyif. *Higher Education:* Abdussalam Abdallah. *Justice:* Ali Omar Abu Bakr. *Public Security:* Naser Al-Mabrouk Abdallah. *Finance:* Mohamed Ali Al-Houeiz. *Economy and Trade:* Abd Al-Qadir Bilkhayr.

DEFENCE

There is selective conscription for one–two years. Defence expenditure in 2003 totalled US$742m. (US$133 per capita), representing 4·2% of GDP.

Nuclear Weapons. In Dec. 2003 Col. Muammar Qadhafi agreed to dismantle his weapons of mass destruction programmes. He also agreed unconditionally to allow inspectors from international organizations to enter Libya.

Army. Strength (2002) 45,000 (25,000 conscripts). In addition there is a People's Militia of 40,000 which acts as a reserve force.

Navy. The fleet, a mixture of Soviet and West European-built ships, includes one diesel submarines, one frigate and one corvette. There is a small Naval Aviation wing operating seven armed helicopters.

Personnel in 2002 totalled 8,000, including coastguard. The main naval bases are at Tripoli, Benghazi, Derna, Tobruk and Al Khums.

Air Force. The Air Force has over 400 combat aircraft, including MiG-21s, MiG-23s, MiG-25s and Mirage 5Ds, but many are in storage. Personnel total (2002) about 23,000.

INTERNATIONAL RELATIONS

Libya is a member of the UN, the African Union, OPEC, Arab Maghreb Union, African Development Bank, OIC, Islamic Development Bank and IOM. Libya has declared its desire to join the WTO.

ECONOMY

Agriculture accounted for an estimated 5·3% of GDP in 2002, industry 64·0% and services 30·6%.

Overview. In Nov. 2003 the government announced a three-part privatization scheme, including mineral and chemical industries, which will run until 2008. The government is aiming to privatize 360 state-owned companies between 2004 and 2008.

Currency. The unit of currency is the *Libyan dinar* (LYD) of 1,000 *millemes*. The dinar was devalued 15% in Nov. 1994, and alongside the official exchange rate a new rate was applied to private sector imports. Foreign exchange reserves were US$13,146m. in June 2002 and total money supply was 7,249m. dinars. Inflation was negative in 2000 (at –2·9%), in 2001 (–8·5%) and again in 2002 (–9·8%).

Budget. In 2001 revenues totalled 5,999m. dinars and expenditures 5,626m. dinars. Oil accounts for 60% of government revenues.

Performance. GDP growth was 0·5% in 2001 but a recession followed, with the economy shrinking by 0·2% in 2002. Total GDP in 2001 was US$34·1bn.

Banking and Finance. A National Bank of Libya was established in 1955; it was renamed the Central Bank of Libya in 1972. The *Governor* is Dr Ahmed M. Menesi. All foreign banks were nationalized by Dec. 1970. In 1972 the government set up the Libyan Arab Foreign Bank whose function is overseas investment and to participate in multinational banking corporations. The National Agricultural Bank has been set up to give loans and subsidies to farmers to develop their land and to assist them in marketing their crops. There are six other banks.

Weights and Measures. Although the metric system has been officially adopted and is obligatory for all contracts, the following weights and measures are still used: *oke* = 1·282 kg; *kantar* = 51·28 kg; *draà* = 46 cm; *handaza* = 68 cm.

ENERGY AND NATURAL RESOURCES

Environment. Libya's carbon dioxide emissions from the consumption and flaring of fossil fuels in 2002 were the equivalent of 8·7 tonnes per capita.

Electricity. Installed capacity in 2000 was 4·6m. kW. Production was about 20·04bn. kWh in 2000 and consumption per capita an estimated 3,789 kWh.

Oil and Gas. Oil accounts for 30% of Libya's GDP. Crude oil production in 2003 totalled 70·0m. tonnes. Reserves (2003) 236·0bn. bbls. Some analysts believe reserves may be as high as 100bn. bbls. The National Oil Corporation (NOC) is the state's organization for the exploitation of oil resources. Libya's first oilfields were discovered in 1959, but the offshore sector remains relatively unexplored although the decision to abandon programmes for developing weapons of mass destruction in 2003 led to greatly increased interest among foreign oil companies. Oil export revenues more than doubled between 1998 and 2003. Production is expected to increase by nearly a third by 2009.

Proven natural gas reserves totalled 1,310bn. cu. metres in 2002. Agip, the Italian oil company, is investing US$3bn. in a project to export natural gas to Europe. Production (2002) 5·7bn. cu. metres.

Water. Since 1984 a US$20bn. project has been under way to bring water from aquifers underlying the Sahara to the inhabited coastal areas of Libya. This scheme, called the 'Great Man-Made River', is intended, on completion, to bring 6,000 cu. metres of water a day along some 4,000 km of pipes. Phase I was completed in Aug. 1991; Phase II of the project (covering the west of Libya) was announced in Sept. 1989. The river is providing Libya's main centres of population with clean water as well as making possible the improvement and expansion of agriculture. The whole project is more than three-quarters complete.

Minerals. Iron ore deposits have been found in the south.

Agriculture. Only the coastal zone, which covers an area of about 17,000 sq. miles, is really suitable for agriculture. Of some 25m. acres of productive land, nearly 20m. are used for grazing and about 1m. for static farming. Agriculture employs around 17% of the workforce. The sub-desert zone produces the alfalfa plant. The desert zone and the Fezzan contain some fertile oases. In 2001 there were 1·82m. ha of arable land and 0·34m. ha of permanent crops. 470,000 ha were irrigated in 2001. There were 34,000 tractors in 2001 and 3,410 harvester-threshers.

Cyrenaica has about 10m. acres of potentially productive land and is suitable for grazing. Certain areas are suitable for dry farming; in addition, grapes, olives and dates are grown. About 143,000 acres are used for settled farming; about 272,000 acres are covered by natural forests. The Agricultural Development Authority plans to reclaim 6,000 ha each year for agriculture. In the Fezzan there are about 6,700 acres of irrigated gardens and about 297,000 acres are planted with date palms.

Production (2000, in 1,000 tonnes): tomatoes, 250; watermelons, 215; potatoes, 210; olives, 190; onions, 180; wheat, 160; dates, 133; barley, 70; oranges, 43.

Livestock (2000): 5·1m. sheep, 1·9m. goats, 143,000 cattle, 71,000 camels, 25m. chickens.

Forestry. Forest area in 2000 was 358,000 ha (0·2% of the land area). In 2001, 652,000 cu. metres of roundwood were cut.

Fisheries. The catch in 2001 was approximately 33,239 tonnes, entirely from marine waters.

INDUSTRY

Industry employs nearly 30% of the workforce. Small scale private sector industrialization in the form of partnerships is permitted. Output (2000, in 1,000 tonnes): distillate fuel oil, 4,662; residual fuel oil, 4,330; cement (1997), 2,524; petrol, 2,030.

Labour. The labour force in 1996 was 1,601,000 (79% males).

INTERNATIONAL TRADE

In1986 the USA applied a trade embargo on the grounds of Libya's alleged complicity in terrorism. Many of the economic sanctions were lifted in April 2004, although Libya remains on Washington's list of state sponsors of terror, as a result of which arms exports are still banned. In 1992 UN sanctions were imposed for Libya's refusal to deliver suspected terrorists for trial in the UK or USA, but these were formally lifted in 2003. In Feb. 1989 Libya signed a treaty of economic co-operation with the four other Maghreb countries; Algeria, Mauritania, Morocco and Tunisia.

Imports and Exports. In 2000 imports were valued at US$7·6bn. and exports at US$13·9bn. Some 80% of GDP derives from trade. Oil accounts for over 95% of exports, worth US$13·4bn. in 2003. Main export markets in 2000 were Italy (33%),

Germany (24%), Spain (10%) and France (5%); main import suppliers were Italy (24%), Germany (12%), Tunisia (9%) and UK (7%).

COMMUNICATIONS

Roads. There were an estimated 83,200 km of roads in 1999 (57·2% paved). Passenger cars numbered 809,500 in 1996 (154·1 per 1,000 inhabitants), in addition to which there were 356,000 trucks and vans. There were 1,080 deaths as a result of road accidents in 1996.

Civil Aviation. The UN ban on air traffic to and from Libya enforced since April 1992 was lifted in April 1999 following the handing over for trial of two suspected Lockerbie bombers. Libyan Arab Airlines provides both international and domestic services. In 1999 scheduled airline traffic of Libya-based carriers flew 3·8m. km, carrying 571,000 passengers.

Shipping. Sea-going vessels totalled 165,000 GRT in 2002, including oil tankers 7,000 GRT.

Telecommunications. In 2001 telephone subscribers numbered 710,000 (127·2 per 1,000 population). The national operator is the state-run General Posts and Telecommunications Company (GPTC). In 2002 there were 70,000 mobile phone subscribers and 130,000 PCs in use. There are two mobile phone companies, Al-Madar and Libyana, both of which are state-owned. Internet users numbered 125,000 in 2002.

Postal Services. In 1998 there were 342 post offices, or one for every 15,600 persons.

SOCIAL INSTITUTIONS

Justice. The Civil, Commercial and Criminal codes are based mainly on the Egyptian model. Matters of personal status of family or succession matters affecting Muslims are dealt with in special courts according to the Muslim law. All other matters, civil, commercial and criminal, are tried in the ordinary courts, which have jurisdiction over everyone.

There are civil and penal courts in Tripoli and Benghazi, with subsidiary courts at Misurata and Derna; courts of assize in Tripoli and Benghazi, and courts of appeal also in Tripoli and Benghazi.

The population in penal institutions in 1998 was approximately 6,750 (127 per 100,000 of national population).

Religion. Islam is declared the State religion, but the right of others to practise their religions is provided for. In 2001, 92% were Sunni Muslims.

Education. In 2001–02 there were 750,204 primary school pupils and 824,538 secondary level pupils. In 1994–95 there were three universities, one medical and one technological university. There were three other institutes of higher education. In 2001–02 there were 359,146 tertiary level students. Adult literacy in 2001 was 80·8% (male, 91·3%; female, 69·3%).

Health. There were 6,092 physicians in 1997 and 619 dentists, 17,136 nurses and 1,095 pharmacists in 1996. Provision of hospital beds in 1991 was 41 per 10,000 population.

CULTURE

World Heritage Sites. Libya has five sites on the UNESCO World Heritage List: the Archaeological Site of Leptis Magna (inscribed on the list in 1982); the Archaeological Site of Sabrata (1982); the Archaeological Site of Cyrene (1982); the Rock-art Sites of Tadrart Acacus (1985); and the Old Town of Ghadames (1988).

Broadcasting. Broadcasting is controlled by the government Libyan Jamihiriya Broadcasting and People's Revolution Broadcasting-Television. Radio has a home service, external services in English, French and Arabic and a Holy Koran programme. In 2000 there were 1·43m. radio and 717,000 TV receivers (colour by SECAM H).

Press. In 1996 there were four daily newspapers with a combined circulation of 71,000.

Tourism. In 2000 there were 174,000 foreign tourists; spending in 1999 was US$28m.

DIPLOMATIC REPRESENTATIVES

Of Libya in the United Kingdom (61–62 Ennismore Gdns, London SW7 1NH)
Ambassador: Mohammed Abdul Qasim Al-Zwai.

Of the United Kingdom in Libya (PO Box 4206, Tripoli)
Ambassador: Anthony Layden.

The USA has established a Liaison Office in Libya (Corinthia Bab Africa Hotel, Souk al-Thulatha, Al-Gadim, Tripoli)
Principal Officer: Gregory Berry.

Of Libya to the United Nations
Ambassador: Ali Abd al-Salam al-Turayki.

Of Libya to the European Union
Ambassador: Hamed Ahmed Elhouderi.

FURTHER READING

Pazzanita, A. G., *The Maghreb.* [Bibliography] ABC-Clio, Oxford and Santa Barbara (CA), 1998

Simons, G., *Libya: the Struggle for Survival.* London, 1993

Vandewalle, D. (ed.) *Qadhafi's Libya, 1969–1994.* London, 1995

LIECHTENSTEIN

Fürstentum Liechtenstein
(Principality of Liechtenstein)

Capital: Vaduz
Population, 2003: 34,000
GDP per capita: not available

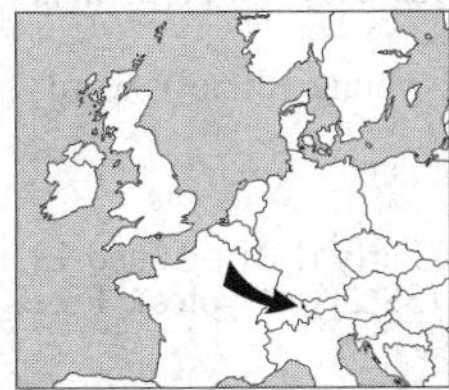

KEY HISTORICAL EVENTS

Liechtenstein is a sovereign state with a history dating back to 1342 when Count Hartmann III became ruler of the county of Vaduz. Additions were later made to the count's domains and by 1434 the territory reached its present boundaries. On 23 Jan. 1719 the Emperor Charles VI constituted the two counties as the Principality of Liechtenstein. In 1862 the constitution established an elected diet. After the First World War, Liechtenstein was represented abroad by Switzerland. Swiss currency was adopted in 1921. On 5 Oct. 1921 a new constitution based on that of Switzerland extended democratic rights, but in March 2003 the people of Liechtenstein voted in a referendum to give their prince the power to govern without reference to elected representatives.

TERRITORY AND POPULATION

Liechtenstein is bounded on the east by Austria and the west by Switzerland. Total area 160 sq. km (61·8 sq. miles). The population (Dec. 2003) was 34,294 (17,413 females), including 11,786 resident foreigners, giving a density of 214 per sq. km.

The population of Liechtenstein is predominantly rural. Population of Vaduz (2003) 5,005. The language is German.

SOCIAL STATISTICS

In 2003 there were 347 births and 217 deaths (rates of 10·2 per 1,000 population and 6·4 respectively). The annual population growth rate was 1·4% over the period 1999–2003.

CLIMATE

There is a distinct difference in climate between the higher mountains and the valleys. In summer the peaks can often be foggy while the valleys remain sunny and warm, while in winter the valleys can often be foggy and cold whilst the peaks remain sunny and comparatively warm. Vaduz, Jan. 0°C, July 20°C. Annual rainfall 1,090 mm.

CONSTITUTION AND GOVERNMENT

Liechtenstein is a constitutional monarchy ruled by the princes of the House of Liechtenstein.

The reigning Prince is **Hans-Adam II,** b. 14 Feb. 1945; he succeeded his father Prince Francis-Joseph, 13 Nov. 1989 (he exercised the prerogatives to which the Sovereign is entitled from 26 Aug. 1984); married on 30 July 1967 to Countess Marie Kinsky von Wchinitz und Tettau. *Offspring:* Hereditary Prince Alois (b. 11 June 1968), married Duchess Sophie of Bavaria on 3 July 1993 (*offspring:* Prince Joseph Wenzel, b. 24 May 1995; Marie Caroline, b. 17 Oct. 1996; Georg Antonius, b. 20 April 1999; Nikolaus Sebastian, b. 6 Dec. 2000); Prince Maximilian (b. 16 May 1969), married Angela Brown on 29 Jan. 2000 (*offspring:* Alfons, b. 18 May 2001); Prince Constantin (b. 15 March 1972), married Countess Marie Kálnoky de Köröspatak on 17 July 1999 (*offspring:* Moritz, b. 27 May 2003); Princess Tatjana (b. 10 April 1973), married Philipp von Lattorff on 5 June 1999 (*offspring:* Lukas, b. 13 May 2000; Elisabeth, b. 25 Jan. 2002; Marie Teresa, b. 18 Jan. 2004). The monarchy is hereditary in the male line.

The present constitution of 5 Oct. 1921 provided for a unicameral parliament (*Landtag*) of 15 members elected for four years, but this was amended to 25 members in 1988. Election is on the basis of proportional representation. The prince can call and dismiss the parliament, and following a referendum held on 16 March 2003, dismiss the government and veto bills. On parliamentary recommendation, he appoints the ministers. According to the constitution, the Government is a collegial body consisting of five ministers including the prime minister. Each minister has an Alternate who takes part in the meetings of the collegial Government if the minister is unavailable. Any group of 1,000 persons or any three communes may propose legislation (initiative). Bills passed by the parliament may be submitted to popular referendum. A law is valid when it receives a majority approval by the parliament and the prince's signed concurrence. The capital is Vaduz.

National Anthem. 'Oben am jungen Rhein' ('Up above the young Rhine'); words by H. H. Jauch; tune, 'God save the Queen'.

RECENT ELECTIONS

At the elections on 13 March 2005 the Progressive Citizens' Party (FBP) gained 12 seats (48·7% of votes cast); the Patriotic Union (VU), 10 (38·2% of votes); Free List (FL), 3 (13·0% of votes). Turn-out was 86·5%.

CURRENT ADMINISTRATION

Head of Government, and Minister for Finance, Construction, Public Works and General Government Affairs: Otmar Hasler; b. 1953 (FBP; sworn in 5 April 2001).

In April 2005 the cabinet comprised:

Deputy Head of Government, and Minister for Economic Affairs, Justice and Sport: Klaus Tschütscher. *Education, Environmental Affairs, Land-Use Planning, Agriculture, Forestry and Social Affairs:* Hugo Quaderer. *Foreign Affairs, Family Affairs and Gender Equality, and Culture:* Rita Kieber-Beck. *Health, Interior, Transportation and Telecommunications:* Martin Meyer.

Princely House Website: http://www.fuerstenhaus.li

INTERNATIONAL RELATIONS

Liechtenstein is a member of the UN, WTO, OSCE, EFTA, EEA and the Council of Europe.

ECONOMY

Liechtenstein is one of the world's richest countries with a well diversified economy. Low taxes and bank secrecy laws have made Liechtenstein a successful financial centre.

Currency. Swiss currency has been in use since 1921.

Budget. Budget (in Swiss francs), 2003: revenue, 739,949,279; expenditure, 745,201,777. There is no public debt.

Performance. Real GDP growth was 6·1% in 2002. Total GDP was US$2,345m. in 2001.

Banking and Finance. There were 16 banks in 2003. Combined total assets were 34,908·3m. Swiss francs in 2003.

Liechtenstein was one of 15 countries and territories named in a report in June 2000 as failing to co-operate in the fight against international money laundering. The Financial Action Task Force on Money Laundering was set up by the G7 group of major industrialized nations.

ENERGY AND NATURAL RESOURCES

Electricity. In 2003 the consumption of electricity was 329,582 MWh (imported 270,333 MWh; produced in Liechtenstein 59,249 MWh).

Agriculture. In 2001 there were 962 ha of arable land (agricultural land 2001: 3,750 ha). In 2001 approximately 1,000 ha (26% of all agricultural land—the highest proportion of any country) was set aside for organic farming. The rearing of cattle on the Alpine pastures is highly developed. In 2003 there were 5,314 cattle (including 2,737 milch cows), 408 horses, 3,070 sheep, 241 goats, 1,979 pigs. Total production of dairy produce in 2003 was 13,499 tonnes.

Forestry. In 2003 there were 6,700 ha of forest (42% of the land area). Timber production in 2001 was 8,000 cu. metres.

INDUSTRY

Liechtenstein has a broadly diversified economic structure with a significant emphasis on industrial production. The most important branches of the heavily export-oriented industry are mechanical engineering, plant construction, manufacturing of precision instruments, dental technology and the food-processing industry.

Labour. The farming population went down from 70% in 1930 to 1·3% in 2003. The rapid change-over has led to the immigration of foreign workers (Austrians, Germans, Italians, Swiss). The workforce was 29,055 in 2003, including employees commuting from abroad (13,413 in 2003).

INTERNATIONAL TRADE

Liechtenstein has been in a customs union with Switzerland since 1923.

Imports and Exports. Exports of home produce in 2003 (in Swiss francs), for member companies affiliated to the Chamber of Industry and Commerce, amounted to 4,646m. Swiss francs: 595m. (12·8%) went to Switzerland, 2,000m. (43·1%) went to EEA countries and 2,051m. (44·1%) went to other countries. Imports in 2000 amounted to 1,456m. Swiss francs.

COMMUNICATIONS

Roads. There are 400 km of roads. Postal buses are the chief means of public transportation within the country and to Austria and Switzerland. There were 23,524 cars in 2003. There were 582 road accidents in 2002 (none fatal).

Rail. The 10 km of main railway passing through the country is operated by Austrian Federal Railways.

Telecommunications. In 2003 there were 19,945 main telephone lines. In 2002 there were 11,400 mobile phone subscribers and Internet users numbered 20,000.

Postal Services. Post and telegraphs are administered by Switzerland. There were 12 post offices in 2004.

SOCIAL INSTITUTIONS

Justice. The principality has its own civil and penal codes. The lowest court is the county court, *Landgericht*, presided over by one judge, which decides minor civil cases and summary criminal offences. The criminal court, *Kriminalgericht*, with a bench of five judges is for major crimes. Another court of mixed jurisdiction is the court of assizes (with three judges) for misdemeanours. Juvenile cases are treated in the Juvenile Court (with a bench of three judges). The superior court, *Obergericht*, and Supreme Court, *Oberster Gerichtshof*, are courts of appeal for civil and criminal cases (both with benches of five judges). An administrative court of appeal from government actions and the State Court determines the constitutionality of laws.

The death penalty was abolished in 1989.

Police. The principality has no army. 2003: police force 103, auxiliary police 35.

Religion. In 2003, 80·4% of the population was Roman Catholic and 7·1% Protestant; 12·5% belonged to other religions.

Education. In 2004 there were 16 primary, 3 upper, 7 secondary and 2 grammar schools, with approximately 4,300 pupils and 550 teachers. Other schools include an evening technical school and a music school.

Health. There is an obligatory sickness insurance scheme. In 2003 there was one hospital, but Liechtenstein has an agreement with the Swiss cantons of St Gallen and Graubünden and the Austrian Federal State of Vorarlberg that her citizens may use certain hospitals. In 2003 there were 64 physicians, 26 dentists and 2 pharmacists.

CULTURE

Broadcasting. In 1997 there were 21,000 radios and 12,000 TV sets.

Cinema. There were three cinemas in 2003.

Press. In 2003 there were two daily newspapers with a total circulation of 17,652, and one weekly with a circulation of 32,658.

Tourism. In 2003, 50,207 tourists visited Liechtenstein.

DIPLOMATIC REPRESENTATIVES

In 1919 Switzerland agreed to represent the interests of Liechtenstein in countries where it has diplomatic missions and where Liechtenstein is not represented in its own right. In so doing Switzerland always acts only on the basis of mandates of a general or specific nature, which it may either accept or refuse, while Liechtenstein is free to enter into direct relations with foreign states or to set up its own additional diplomatic missions.

Of the United Kingdom in Liechtenstein
Ambassador: Simon Featherstone (resides at Berne).

Of Liechtenstein to the USA (1300 Eye St., NW, Suite 550W, Washington, D.C., 20005)
Ambassador: Claudia Fritsche.

Of Liechtenstein to the United Nations
Ambassador: Christian Wenaweser.

Of Liechtenstein to the European Union
Ambassador: Prince Nikolaus of Liechtenstein.

FURTHER READING

Amt für Volkswirtschaft. *Statistisches Jahrbuch.* Vaduz

Rechenschaftsbericht der Fürstlichen Regierung. Vaduz. Annual, from 1922
Jahrbuch des Historischen Vereins. Vaduz. Annual since 1901
National library: Landesbibliothek, Vaduz

Beattie, David, *Liechtenstein: A Modern History.* I. B. Tauris, London, 2004
Meier, Regula A., *Liechtenstein.* [Bibliography] ABC-Clio, Oxford and Santa Barbara (CA), 1993

National statistical office: Amt für Volkswirtschaft, Vaduz
Website (German only): http://www.llv.li/amtsstellen/llv-avw-statistik.htm

LITHUANIA

Lietuvos Respublika

Capital: Vilnius
Population projection, 2010: 3·31m.
GDP per capita, 2002: (PPP$) 10,320
HDI/world rank: 0·842/41

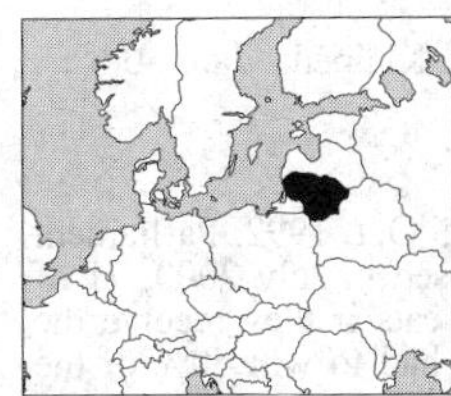

KEY HISTORICAL EVENTS

At the time of Tatar-Mongol domination of Russia, Lithuania annexed Russian lands until by the middle of the 15th century Belorussia, along with those parts of Russia and Ukraine as far as the Black Sea, were under its rule. Lithuania united with Poland dynastically in 1385 and politically in 1569. During the partitions of the Polish-Lithuanian Commonwealth by Russia, Prussia and Austria in the 18th century, Lithuania yielded its Russian territories and was absorbed into the Russian empire in 1795. Following the German occupation during the First World War and the Russian revolution on 16 Feb. 1918, heavy fighting occurred between the Soviet, German, Polish and Lithuanian forces. In April 1919 the Soviets withdrew and the re-formed Lithuanian government established a democratic republic. Lithuanian independence was recognized by the Treaty of Versailles. In Dec. 1926 the democratic regime was overthrown by a coup. The secret protocol of the Soviet-German frontier treaty of 23 Sept. 1939 assigned the greater part of Lithuania to the Soviet sphere of influence. Lithuania became a Soviet Socialist Republic of the USSR on 3 Aug. 1940.

On 11 March 1990 the newly-elected Lithuanian Supreme Soviet proclaimed independence, a decision unacceptable to the USSR government. Initially dispatched to Vilnius to enforce conscription, Soviet army units occupied key buildings in the face of mounting popular unrest. On 13 Jan. 1991 the army fired on demonstrators and there were fatal casualties. A referendum on independence was held in Feb. 1991 at which 90·5% voted in favour. A fully independent status was conceded by the USSR on 6 Sept. 1991. The first presidential elections were held in 1993 and won by Algirdas Brazauskas, who was subsequently elected to be the current prime minister. Lithuania became a member of NATO in March 2004 and the European Union in May 2004.

TERRITORY AND POPULATION

Lithuania is bounded in the north by Latvia, east and south by Belarus, and west by Poland, the Russian enclave of Kaliningrad and the Baltic Sea. The total area is 65,200 sq. km (25,212 sq. miles) and the population (2001 census) 3,483,972 (1,854,824 females; 2,332,098, or 66·9%, urban); density, 53·4 per sq. km. Of the 2001 census population, Lithuanians accounted for 83·5%, Poles 6·7%, Russians 6·3% (9·4% in 1989), Belorussians 1·2%, Ukrainians 0·7% and Jews 0·1%.

The UN gives a projected population for 2010 of 3·31m.

There are ten counties (with capitals of the same name): Alytus; Kaunas; Klaipėda; Marijampolė; Panevėžys; Šiauliai; Tauragė; Telšiai; Utena; Vilnius.

The capital is Vilnius (Jan. 2002 population, 553,373). Other large towns are Kaunas (376,575), Klaipėda (192,498), Šiauliai (133,528) and Panevėžys (119,417).

The official language is Lithuanian, but ethnic minorities have the right to official use of their language where they form a substantial part of the population. All residents who applied by 3 Nov. 1991 received Lithuanian citizenship, requirements for which are ten years' residence and competence in Lithuanian.

SOCIAL STATISTICS

2002: births, 30,014; deaths, 41,072; marriages, 16,151; divorces, 10,579; infant deaths, 238. Rates (per 1,000 population): birth, 8·6; death, 11·8; marriage, 4·7; divorce, 3·1. The population started to decline in 1993, a trend which is set to continue. Annual population growth rate, 1990–2003, –0·6%. In 2002, 8,386 births were registered to unmarried mothers and there were 18,907 legally induced abortions. Life expectancy at birth in 2002 was 66·21 years for males and 77·58 years for females. In 2002 the most popular age range for marrying was 20–24 for both males and females. Infant mortality, 2002, 7·9 per 1,000 live births; fertility rate, 1·24 births per woman. In 2002 there were 7,086 emigrants and 5,110 immigrants.

Lithuania has the world's highest suicide rate, at 44·7 per 100,000 inhabitants in 2002 (a rate of 80·7 among males but only 13·1 among women).

CLIMATE

Vilnius, Jan. –2·8°C, July 20·5°C. Annual rainfall 520 mm. Klaipėda, Jan. –0·6°C, July 19·4°C. Annual rainfall 770 mm.

CONSTITUTION AND GOVERNMENT

A referendum to approve a new constitution was held on 25 Oct. 1992. Parliament is the 141-member *Seimas*. Under a new electoral law passed in July 2000, 71 of the parliament's 141 members will defeat rivals for their seats if they receive the most votes in a single round of balloting. Previously they had to win 50% of the votes or face a run-off against the nearest competitor. The parliament's 70 other seats are distributed according to the proportional popularity of the political parties at the ballot box.

The *Constitutional Court* is empowered to rule on whether proposed laws conflict with the constitution or existing legislation. It comprises nine judges who serve nine-year terms, one third rotating every three years.

National Anthem. 'Lietuva, tėvyne mūsų' ('Lithuania, our fatherland'); words and tune by V. Kurdirka.

RECENT ELECTIONS

Presidential elections were held in two rounds on 13 and 27 June 2004. In the first round former president Valdas Adamkus won 30·7% of the vote, ahead of former prime minister Kazimiera Prunskienė with 21·4%, Petras Auštrevičius 19·3%, Vilija Blinkevičiūtė 16·6% and Česlovas Juršėnas 11·9%. Turn-out was 39·4%. In the second round run-off Adamkus won 52·6% against 47·4% for Prunskienė. Turn-out was 52·4%.

Parliamentary elections were held in two rounds on 10 and 24 Oct. 2004. The Labour Party won 38 of the 141 seats (28·4% of the votes cast), Prime Minister Algirdas Brazauskas' coalition 'For a Working Lithuania' 32 (20·6%), the Homeland Union 25 (14·7%), the Liberal and Centre Union 18 (9·2%), former president Rolandas Paksas' coalition 'For the Order and Justice' 11 (11·4%), the Peasants' and New Democratic Party Union 10 (6·6%), Election Action of Lithuania's Poles 2 (3·8%) and ind. 5 (5·2%). Turn-out for the first round was 46·1% and for the second round 40·2%.

European Parliament. Lithuania has 13 representatives. At the June 2004 elections turn-out was 48·2%. The Labour Party won 5 seats with 30·2% of votes cast (political affiliation in European Parliament: Alliance of Liberals and Democrats for Europe); Lithuanian Social-Democratic Party, 2 with 14·4% (Party of European Socialists); the Homeland Union, 2 with 12·6% (European People's Party–European Democrats); the Liberal and Centre Union, 2 with 11·2% (Alliance of Liberals and Democrats for Europe); the Peasants' and New Democratic Party Union, 1 with 7·4% (Union for a Europe of Nations); the LDP, 1 with 6·8% (Union for a Europe of Nations).

CURRENT ADMINISTRATION

President: Valdas Adamkus; b. 1926 (took office on 12 July 2004; previously held office from Feb. 1998–Feb. 2003).

Prime Minister: Algirdas Mykolas Brazauskas; b. 1932 (A. Brazauskas Social Democratic Coalition; in office since 3 July 2001).

In April 2005 the cabinet comprised:

Minister of Foreign Affairs: Antanas Valionis. *Defence:* Gediminas Kirkilas. *Finance:* Vacant. *Economy:* Viktor Uspaskich. *Social Security and Labour:* Vilija Blinkevičiūtė. *Interior:* Gintaras Jonas Furmanavičius. *Health:* Žilvinas Padaiga. *Justice:* Gintautas Bužinskas. *Agriculture:* Kazimiera Prunskienė. *Environment:* Arūnas Kundrotas. *Transport:* Zigmantas Balčytis. *Culture:* Vladimiras Prudnikovas. *Education and Science:* Remigijus Motuzas.

Seimas Speaker: Artûras Paulauskas.

Government of the Republic of Lithuania: http://www.lrvk.lt

DEFENCE

Conscription is for 12 months. In 2003 military expenditure totalled US$359m., representing 2% of GDP. US$287·7m. went to the ministry of defence with US$71·3m. going to the security agencies, border guard service and anti-terrorism units. In 2002 logistic forces numbered 1,044 and Training and Doctrine Command (TRADOC) numbered 3,353.

Army. The Army numbered 7,332 in 2003 and included one motorized infantry brigade ('Iron Wolf'). First line reserves numbered 25,000 in 2002, including 11,700 in the Volunteer National Defence Service. There is a 784-strong joint Polish/Lithuanian battalion (LITPOLBAT) which is a component of the EU's rapid reaction forces.

Navy. In 2003 Naval Forces numbered 693 personnel and operated several vessels including two corvettes. Lithuania, Estonia and Latvia have established a joint naval unit 'BALTRON' (Baltic Naval Squadron), with bases at Klaipėda in Lithuania, Tallinn in Estonia, and Liepāja, Riga and Ventspils in Latvia.

Air Force. The Air Force consisted of 1,172 personnel in 2003. There are no combat aircraft.

The joint Baltic Regional Air Surveillance Network (BALTNET), established in co-operation between the air forces of Estonia, Latvia and Lithuania, has its co-ordination centre in Karmėlava in Lithuania.

INTERNATIONAL RELATIONS

Lithuania is a member of the UN, WTO, BIS, NATO, EBRD, IMF, UNESCO, FAO, IMO, EU, Council of Europe, OSCE, IAEA, Council of the Baltic Sea States, IOM and EAPC and is an Associate Partner of the WEU. Lithuania held a referendum on EU membership on 10–11 May 2003, in which 91·0% of votes cast were in favour of accession, with 9·0% against. It became a member of NATO on 29 March 2004 and the EU on 1 May 2004. On 11 Nov. 2004 Lithuania became the first European Union member to ratify the new EU constitution. The parliament approved the treaty by 84 votes to four, with three abstentions.

ECONOMY

Agriculture accounted for 7·1% of GDP in 2002, industry 31·2% and services 61·7%.

Overview. Privatization, co-ordinated by the State Property Fund, is close to completion. The third stage of privatization began in Nov. 1997. In 2002, 963 entities were privatized, the biggest of which was the Lithuanian Agricultural Bank.

Currency. The unit of currency is the *litas* (plural: *litai*) of 100 *cents*, which was introduced on 25 June 1993 and became the sole legal tender on 1 Aug. The litas was pegged to the US dollar on 1 April 1994 at US$1 = four litai, but since 2 Feb. 2002 it has been pegged to the euro at 3·4528 litai = one euro. Inflation, which reached a high of 1,161% in the early 1990s, was negative in 2003, at –1·2%. Total money supply was 6,678m. litai in May 2002. Gold reserves were 186,000 troy oz in June 2002 and foreign exchange reserves US$2,230m.

Budget. Total revenue in 2002 amounted to 10,330m. litai and expenditure to 11,466m. litai. Revenue in 2002 included: VAT, 37%; personal income tax, 24%. Expenditure in 2002 included (in 1m. litai): education, 3,073; social welfare, 1,149; public order, 1,009; general public services, 903; defence, 857; transport and communications, 844; health, 613.

VAT is 18% (reduced rates, 9% and 5%).

Performance. Among the wealthiest provinces of the former Soviet Union, Lithuania has weathered the economic crisis overspilling from Russia. 47·8% of exports in 2001 went to the EU compared to just 11% to Russia. In 1999 Lithuania experienced a recession, with the economy shrinking by 1·8%. There was then a recovery in 2000, with growth of 4·0%, rising to 6·5% in 2001 and further to 6·7% in 2002, making Lithuania the fastest-growing economy in Europe in 2002 having been the second fastest-growing in 2001. Total GDP in 2003 was US$18·2bn. At Nov. 2003 total public debt stood at €3·8bn., of which €2·6bn. was foreign debt.

Banking and Finance. The central bank and bank of issue is the Bank of Lithuania (*Governor*, Reinoldijas Šarkinas). A programme to restructure and privatize the state banks was started in 1996. In 2003 there were ten commercial banks, three foreign bank branches, three foreign bank representative offices, the central credit union of Lithuania and 57 credit unions in operation. The largest private bank in Lithuania is JSC Vilniaus Bankas, which controls approximately 37% of the total banking assets in the country. At Dec. 2003 it was estimated that total assets of domestic commercial banks amounted to 22bn. litai.

A stock exchange opened in Vilnius in 1993. In Oct. 1999 its capitalization was US$3·5bn. The trading volume in 1999 was US$575m.

ENERGY AND NATURAL RESOURCES

Environment. According to Lithuania's Ministry of Environment, carbon dioxide emissions were the equivalent of 4·4 tonnes per capita in 2002.

Electricity. Installed capacity was 6·57m. kW in 2002; production was 17·7bn. kWh. A nuclear power station (with two reactors) in Ignalina was responsible for 79·8% of total output in 2002, and there are also two large hydro-electric, five public and five autoproducer thermal plants. No other country has such a high percentage of its electricity generated through nuclear power. However, at the EU's insistence the government is committed to closing down Ignalina. The process to close the first reactor began on 31 Dec. 2004. The whole facility is scheduled to close by the end of 2009. Electricity consumption per capita in 2002 was 2,827 kWh.

Oil and Gas. Oil production started from a small field at Kretinga in 1990. In Jan. 2003 remaining recoverable reserves were estimated at 3·25m. tonnes; potential recoverable resources, 60–80m. tonnes. Production in 2002 from ten oilfields was 432,000 tonnes.

Minerals. Production in 2002 (in 1,000 tonnes): limestone, 984; peat, 491. Quarrying of stone, clay and sand totalled 1·47m. cu. metres in 1998.

Agriculture. In 2002 agriculture employed about 17·2% of the workforce. As of 1 Jan. 2003 the average farm size was 15·2 ha, one of the lowest in eastern Europe; the agricultural land area was 3,956,200 ha. In 2002 there were 2·93m. ha of arable land and 59,000 ha of permanent crops. In 2002, 242,000 persons were employed in agriculture and forestry.

Output of main agricultural products (in 1,000 tonnes) in 2002: potatoes, 1,531; wheat, 1,218; sugarbeets, 1,052; barley, 871; rye, 170; rapeseed, 105; cabbages, 98; oats, 97. Value of agricultural production, 2002 (in 1m. litai), was 4,303·3, of which from individual farm holdings, 3,396·2; and from agricultural partnerships and enterprises, 907·1.

Livestock, Jan. 2003 (in 1,000): cattle, 779·1 (of which milch cows, 443·3); pigs, 1,061·0; sheep and goats, 35·6; horses, 60·7; poultry, 6,848·1. There were 103,000 tractors in use in 2002. Animal products, 2002 (in 1,000 tonnes): meat, 173·6; milk, 770·9; eggs, 779m. units.

Forestry. In 2002 forests covered 2·0m. ha, or 30·6% of Lithuania's territory, and consist of conifers, mostly pine. Timber production in 2002, 5·9m. cu. metres.

Fisheries. In Jan. 2004 the fishing fleet comprised 90 vessels averaging 872 GRT. Total catch in 2002 amounted to 151,530 tonnes (mainly from sea fishing), compared to 57,477 tonnes in 1995.

INDUSTRY

Industrial output included (in 1,000 tonnes): petrol (2000), 1,559; distillate fuel oil (2000), 1,450; residual fuel oil (2000), 798; mineral and chemical fertilizers (2001), 786; cement (2001), 529; sulphuric acid (2001), 465; sugar (2002), 150; cotton fabrics (1998), 63·8m. cu. metres; linen (1998), 15·9m. sq. metres; woollen fabrics (1998), 14·3m. sq. metres; silk (1998), 7·8m. sq. metres; television picture tubes (1998), 1,794,000 units; bicycles (2001), 323,000 units; refrigerators (2001), 260,000 units; TV sets (2001), 143,000 units.

Labour. In 2002 the workforce was 1·6m. (69·9% in private enterprises and 30·1% in the public sector). Employed population by activity (as a percentage): manufacturing, 18·6; wholesale and retail trade, 15·0; education, 9·9; health and social work, 6·7; construction, 6·6; transport and communications, 6·2; real estate, 3·9. Employment skills, 33·2% with tertiary education, 52·5% with upper secondary education, 11·8% with lower secondary. In 2002 the average monthly wage was 1,013·9 litai; legal minimum wage was 450 litai in 2003.

In 2002 old age pension for men started at 62 years and for women at 58. Average number of persons entitled to pensions in 2001 was 636,900. The unemployment rate in Sept. 2003 was 9·3%.

Trade Unions. On 1 Jan. 2001 there were 655 registered unions (339 in operation) affiliated with four federations: the Lithuanian Trade Union Centre (LPSC); the Lithuanian Trade Union Unification (LPSS); the Lithuanian Workers Union (LDS); the Lithuanian Labour Federation (LDF). The LPSC and the LPSS merged on 1 May 2002 to form the Lithuanian Trade Union Confederation (LPSK), now Lithuania's largest trade union organization with 120,000 members.

INTERNATIONAL TRADE

In order to foster export growth, Lithuania maintains a fairly liberal foreign trade regime. There is no quantitative import restriction and the import duties are one of the lowest in central Europe. By the end of 1998 free trade agreements with the European Union, EFTA, neighbouring Latvia and Estonia, as well as with Central European Free Trade Agreement countries (CEFTA) and Ukraine were signed. Meanwhile, most favoured-nation status is applied to trade with Russia.

Foreign investors may purchase up to 100% of the equity companies in Lithuania. By mid-2003, €4·06bn. of foreign capital had been invested. Leading source nations of foreign investment were Denmark, Sweden, Estonia, Germany and the USA.

Total foreign debt was €2·66bn. in 2003.

Individual laws on three free economic zones (namely the laws on Šiauliai, Klaipėda and Kaunas) have been cleared by Lithuania's Parliament, the Seimas.

Imports and Exports. In 2001 imports were valued at €7·1bn. and exports at €5·1bn. Main export markets, 2001: UK, 13·8%; Germany, 12·6%; Latvia, 12·6%; Russia, 11·0%. Main import suppliers: Russia, 25·3%; Germany, 17·2%; Poland, 4·9%; Italy, 4·2%. Main exports are mineral products, textiles and textile articles, electrical equipment, TV sets, chemical products and prepared foodstuffs.

COMMUNICATIONS

Roads. In 2002 there were 77,148 km of roads, of which 89·7% were paved. The Via Baltica, a US$180m. project, will upgrade a 1,000 km (620 mile) international highway linking Finland, Estonia, Latvia, Lithuania and Poland, and there are plans to continue the link to western and southern Europe.

In 2002 there were 1,180,745 passenger cars, 15,376 buses, 466 trolleybuses, 105,545 goods vehicles and 21,017 motorcycles. In 2002 public transport carried 347·8m. passengers. There were 6,091 traffic accidents in 2002, with 697 fatalities.

Rail. There are 1,775 km of railway track in operation in Lithuania. The majority of rail traffic is diesel propelled, although 122 km of track is electrified. In 2003, 6·7m. passengers and 43·5m. tonnes of freight were carried.

Civil Aviation. The main international airport is based in the capital, Vilnius. Other international airports are at Kaunas, Palanga and Šiauliai. The largest airline is Lithuanian Airlines (a state-owned joint stock company, but scheduled to be privatized by the end of 2005), which has regular scheduled flights to most of Europe's main transit hubs. In 2003 a number of other international airlines ran regular scheduled flights. In 2003 Lithuanian Airlines flew 8·8m. km, carrying 312,000 passengers (311,500 on international flights). In 2003 Vilnius was the busiest airport for passenger traffic, handling 719,850 passengers, but Kaunas (which handles approximately 6,700 tonnes per annum) was the busiest for freight.

Shipping. The ice-free port of Klaipėda plays a dominant role in the national economy and Baltic maritime traffic. It has the second largest tonnage in the Baltic region and a cargo capacity of 30m. tonnes per annum. A 205 ha site at the port is dedicated a *Free Economic Zone,* which offers attractive conditions to foreign investors.

In 2003 the merchant fleet numbered 67 ships totalling 362,103 GRT, including eight bulkers, 35 general cargo ships, three tankers and 17 reefers. The turnover of the port in 2003 was 21m. tonnes (up from 12·7m. in 1995).

In 2003 there were 902·3 km of inland waterways, of which 467·7 km were used for carrying freight and passengers. The inland fleet comprised 142 working vessels.

Telecommunications. A majority stake in Lithuanian Telecom (the only fixed telephone service provider) was sold to the Finnish and Swedish consortium SONERA in 1998 and by Jan. 2003 the telecommunications market was fully liberalized. Lithuanian Telecom had 994,000 subscribers in Jan. 2003. In June 2003 there were 1,935,800 mobile phone subscribers (56% penetration). In 2002, 380,000 PCs were in use (109·8 per 1,000 persons). In 1995 there were 6,200 fax machines. The number of Internet users in 2002 was 500,000.

Postal Services. In 2003 there were 945 post offices.

SOCIAL INSTITUTIONS

Justice. The general jurisdiction court system consists of the Supreme Court, the Court of Appeal, five county courts and 54 district courts. Specialized administrative courts were established in 1999. In Jan. 2003 there were 669 judges: 421 in district courts; 139 in county courts; 22 in the Court of Appeal; 33 in the Supreme Court; 41 in the administrative county courts; and 13 in the High Administrative Court.

77,108 crimes were reported in 1999, of which 41·0% were solved. In 2001 there were 378 murders. 2,240 persons were convicted of offences in 1999. Lithuania's murder rate, at 10·8 per 100,000 population in 2001, ranks among the highest in Europe. In Jan. 2003 there were 11,070 prisoners, 8,520 of whom had been convicted. The death penalty was abolished for all crimes in 1998.

Religion. Under the Constitution, the state supports religious groups which have been active in Lithuania for 400 years, i.e., the Roman Catholic, Evangelical Lutheran, Evangelical Reformats and Orthodox Churches. In 2001, 76% of the population were Roman Catholic. As of 1 Jan. 2000 there were 693 Roman Catholic churches with 732 priests, and 43 Orthodox churches with 41 priests. There is an archbishopric of Vilnius and 13 bishops. In 1999 the Lutheran Church had 41 churches, 54 parishes and 23 pastors headed by a bishop. In Sept. 2003 there was one cardinal.

Education. Education is compulsory from seven to 16. In 2002–03 there were 686 pre-school establishments with 90,860 pupils and 2,172 general schools with 49,286 teachers and 594,313 pupils, in the following categories:

Type of School	*No. of Schools*	*No. of Pupils*
Nursery	148	12,219
Primary	683	35,819
Junior	25	2,326
Basic	645	118,415
Special	67	7,212
Secondary	574	400,566
Adult	27	17,318

119,548 students (70,777 females) attended 19 institutions of higher education and 22,367 (13,735 females) attended vocational colleges in 2002–03. The adult literacy rate in 2003 was 99·7%.

In 2002 total expenditure on education represented 27·1% of total government expenditure.

Health. In 2002 there were 13,856 physicians, 2,309 dentists and 26,918 nurses. There were 196 hospitals with 31,031 beds in 2002, and 2,238 pharmacists.

Welfare. The social security system is financed by the State Social Insurance Fund. In 2002, 625,000 persons were eligible for retirement pensions, 188,000 for disability provisions and 219,000 for widow's/widower's pensions. In 2002 the average state social insurance old age pension was 323 litai (monthly).

CULTURE

World Heritage Sites. Lithuania has two sites on the UNESCO World Heritage List: Vilnius Historic Centre (inscribed on the list in 1994) and Kernave Archaeological Site (2004).

Lithuania also shares the Curonian Spit (2000) with the Russian Federation as a UNESCO site. A sand-dune spit between Zelenogradsk, Kaliningrad Region, and Klaipėda, Lithuania, the Spit was subject to massive protective engineering in the 19th century.

Broadcasting. In 2002 there were two national and eight commercial radio networks and 57 local commercial radio stations; two national and three commercial TV networks and 28 local TV stations (colour by PAL). There were 2·1m. radio receivers and 1·41m. television receivers in 2003.

Cinema. There were 68 cinemas in 2003; attendance, 1,342,535; gross box office receipts came to 14·4m. litai.

Press. In 2003 there were 337 newspapers (306 in Lithuanian, 19 in Russian, four in Polish, three in English, three in German, one in Yiddish and one in Belorussian) and 391 magazines. 4,859 book titles were published in 2002.

Tourism. There were 4,195,200 foreign tourists in 2001; tourism receipts amounted to US$391m. in 2000.

DIPLOMATIC REPRESENTATIVES

Of Lithuania in the United Kingdom (84 Gloucester Place, London, W1U 6AU)
Ambassador: Aurimas Taurantas.

Of the United Kingdom in Lithuania (Antakalnio g. 2, 2055 Vilnius)
Ambassador: Colin Roberts.

Of Lithuania in the USA (2622 16th St., NW, Washington, D.C., 20009)
Ambassador: Vygaudas Ušackas.

Of the USA in Lithuania (Akmenu g. 6, 2600 Vilnius)
Ambassador: Stephen D. Mull.

Of Lithuania to the United Nations
Ambassador: Gediminas Šerkšnys.

Of Lithuania to the European Union
Ambassador: Oskaras Jusys.

FURTHER READING

Department of Statistics to the Government. *Statistical Yearbook of Lithuania – Economic and Social Development in Lithuania.* Monthly.

Hood, N., *et al.* (eds.) *Transition in the Baltic States.* 1997

Lieven, A., *The Baltic Revolution: Estonia, Latvia, Lithuania and the Path to Independence.* 2nd ed. Yale Univ. Press, 1994

Misiunas, R. J. and Taagepera, R., *The Baltic States: the Years of Dependence, 1940–91.* 2nd ed. Farnborough, 1993

Smith, I. A. and Grunts, M. V., *The Baltic States.* [Bibliography] ABC-Clio, Oxford and Santa Barbara (CA), 1993

Vardys, V. S. and Sedaitis, J. B., *Lithuania: the Rebel Nation.* Boulder (CO), 1997

National statistical office: Department of Statistics to the Government, Gedimino Pr. 29, LT 01 500 Vilnius. *Director General:* Algirdas Gediminas Semeta.
Website: http://www.std.lt/web/main.php

LUXEMBOURG

Grand-Duché de Luxembourg

Capital: Luxembourg
Population projection, 2010: 494,000
GDP per capita, 2002: (PPP$) 61,190
HDI/world rank: 0·933/15

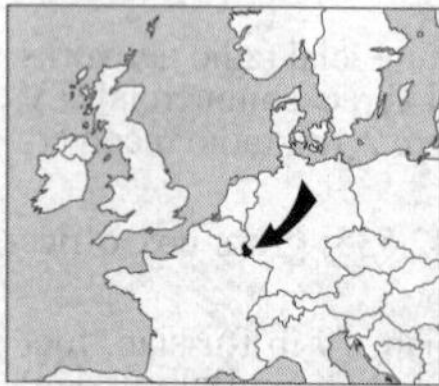

KEY HISTORICAL EVENTS

Lying at the heart of Western Europe between Belgium, France and Germany, the Grand-Duchy of Luxembourg has been an independent State ever since the Treaty of London of 19 April 1839. The origins of Luxembourg stretch back to AD 963 when Count Sigfried founded the castle of Lutzilinburhurch. The House of Luxembourg was most prominent on the European scene during the 14th and 15th centuries, when four Counts of the House of Luxembourg became Emperors of the Holy Roman Empire and Kings of Bohemia. The House of Luxembourg subsequently went into decline and was successively occupied by Burgundy, Spain, Austria and finally by revolutionary France. In 1815 the Vienna Treaty decided that the Grand Duchy of Luxembourg would come under the Netherlands ruling house of Orange-Nassau. In 1839 the Walloon-speaking area was joined to Belgium. The union with the Netherlands ended in 1890. In both world wars (1914–18 and 1939–45) Luxembourg, a neutral country, was invaded and occupied by German forces. In June 1942 Luxembourg became the only Nazi-occupied country to stage a general strike against the occupation. In 1948 a Benelux customs union formed by Belgium, the Netherlands and Luxembourg allowed for standardization of prices, taxes and wages and the free movement of labour among the three countries. Luxembourg was a founder member of the European Union.

TERRITORY AND POPULATION

Luxembourg has an area of 2,586 sq. km (999 sq. miles) and is bounded on the west by Belgium, south by France, east by Germany. A census took place on 15 Feb. 2001; the population was 439,539 (including 162,285 foreigners); density, 170 per sq. km. The percentage of foreigners living in Luxembourg has increased dramatically in recent years, from 26% in 1986 to 36·9% in 2001. The main countries of origin of foreigners living in Luxembourg are Portugal (58,657 in Feb. 2001), France (19,979) and Italy (18,996).

In 2001, 91·8% of the population were urban. The capital, Luxembourg, has (Feb. 2001) 76,688 inhabitants; Esch-sur-Alzette, the centre of the mining district, 27,146; Dudelange, 17,230; Differdange, 10,284; Diekirch, 6,068; and Echternach, 4,610.

The UN gives a projected population for 2010 of 494,000.

Lëtzebuergesch is spoken by most of the population, and since 1984 has been an official language with French and German.

SOCIAL STATISTICS

Statistics (figures in parentheses indicate births and deaths of resident foreigners):

	Births	*Deaths*	*Marriages*	*Divorces*
1998	5,386 (2,439)	3,901 (469)	2,040	1,017
1999	5,582 (2,707)	3,793 (521)	2,090	1,043
2000	5,723 (2,806)	3,754 (547)	2,148	1,030
2001	5,459 (2,736)	3,719 (531)	1,983	1,029

2001 rates per 1,000 population; birth, 12·9; death, 8·4; marriage, 4·5; divorce, 2·3. Nearly half of annual births are to foreigners. In 2001 the most popular age range for marrying was 25–29 for both males and females. Life expectancy at birth in 2001 was 74·8 years for males and 81·2 years for females. Annual population growth rate, 1992–02, 1·5%. Infant mortality, 2001, 5·7 per 1,000 live births; fertility rate, 1·7 births per woman. In 2002 Luxembourg received 1,043 asylum applications.

A UNICEF report published in 2000 showed that only 1·2% of children in Luxembourg live in poverty (in households with incomes below the US official poverty line converted into national currencies), the lowest percentage of any country.

CLIMATE

In general the country resembles Belgium in its climate, with rain evenly distributed throughout the year. Average temperatures are Jan. 0·8°C, July 17·5°C. Annual rainfall 30·8" (782·2 mm).

CONSTITUTION AND GOVERNMENT

The Grand Duchy of Luxembourg is a constitutional monarchy.

The reigning Grand Duke is **Henri**, b. 16 April 1955, son of the former Grand Duke Jean and Princess Joséphine-Charlotte of Belgium; succeeded 7 Oct. 2000 on the abdication of his father; married Maria Teresa Mestre 14 Feb. 1981. (*Offspring:* Prince Guillaume, b. 11 Nov. 1981; Prince Felix, b. 3 June 1984; Prince Louis, b. 3 Aug. 1986; Princess Alexandra, b. 16 Feb. 1991; Prince Sebastian, b. 16 April 1992).

The constitution of 17 Oct. 1868 was revised in 1919, 1948, 1956, 1972, 1983, 1988, 1989, 1994, 1996 and 1998.

The separation of powers between the legislature and the executive is not very strong, resulting in much interaction between the two bodies. Only the judiciary is completely independent.

The 12 cantons are divided into four electoral districts: the South, the East, the Centre and the North. Voters choose between party lists of candidates in multi-member constituencies. The parliament is the *Chamber of Deputies*, which consists of a maximum of 60 members elected for five years. Voting is compulsory and there is universal suffrage. Seats are allocated according to the rules of proportional representation and the principle of the smallest electoral quote. There is a *Council of State* of 21 members appointed by the Sovereign. Membership is for a maximum period of 15 years, with retirement compulsory at the age of 72. It advises on proposed laws and any other question referred to it.

The head of state takes part in the legislative power, exercises executive power and has a part in the judicial power. The constitution leaves to the sovereign the right to organize the government, which consists of a Minister of State, who is Prime Minister, and of at least three Ministers. Direct consultation by referendum is provided for in the Constitution.

National Anthem. 'Ons Hemecht' ('Our Homeland'); words by M. Lentz, tune by J. A. Zinnen.

RECENT ELECTIONS

Elections took place on 13 June 2004. The Christian Social Party (CSV) won 24 seats (with 36·1% of the vote), the Socialist Workers' Party (LSAP) 14 (23·4%), the Democratic Party (DP) 10 (16·1%), the Greens (Déi Gréng) 7 (11·6%) and the Action Committee for Democracy and Pensions Justice (ADR) 7 (9·9%). Turn-out was 91·7%. Following the election a coalition government was formed between the Christian Social Party and the Socialist Workers' Party.

European Parliament. Luxembourg has six representatives. At the June 2004 elections turn-out was 90·0%. CSV won 3 seats with 37·1% of votes cast (political affiliation in European Parliament: European People's Party–European Democrats); LSAP, 1 with 22·1% (Party of European Socialists); the Greens, 1 with 15·0% (Greens/European Free Alliance); the Democratic Party, 1 with 14·9% (Alliance of Liberals and Democrats for Europe).

CURRENT ADMINISTRATION

In March 2005 the Christian Social Party–Socialist Workers' Party coalition comprised:

Prime Minister, Minister of State, Finance and the Exchequer: Jean-Claude Juncker; b. 1954 (CSV; sworn in 20 Jan. 1995). He is currently the European Union's longest-serving prime minister.

Deputy Prime Minister, Minister of Foreign Affairs and Immigration: Jean Asselborn (LSAP). *Agriculture, Viticulture, Rural Development, Middle Classes,*

Housing and Tourism: Fernand Boden (CSV). *Treasury and Budget, Justice and Defence:* Luc Frieden (CSV). *The Family, Integration and Equal Opportunities:* Marie-Josée Jacobs (CSV). *Health and Social Security:* Mars Di Bartolomeo (LSAP). *Environment and Transport:* Lucien Lux (LSAP). *Interior and Land Management:* Jean-Marie Halsdorf (CSV). *Economy, External Commerce and Sport:* Jeannot Krecké (LSAP). *Civil Service and Administrative Reform, and Public Works:* Claude Wiseler (CSV). *Co-operation and Humanitarian Action:* Jean-Louis Schiltz (CSV). *Labour and Employment, Culture, Higher Education and Research, and Religious Affairs:* François Biltgen (CSV). *National Education and Professional Training:* Mady Delvaux-Stehres (LSAP).

The *Speaker* is Lucien Weiler.

Government Website (French only): http://www.gouvernement.lu

DEFENCE

There is a volunteer light infantry battalion of (2001) 842, of which only the career officers are professionals. In recent years Luxembourg soldiers and officers have been actively participating in peacekeeping missions, mainly in the former Yugoslavia. There is also a Gendarmerie of 612. In 2000 the Gendarmerie and the police force merged to form the Police grand-ducale. NATO maintains a squadron of E-3A *Sentries*.

In 2003 military expenditure totalled US$233m. (US$520 per capita), representing 0·9% of GDP.

INTERNATIONAL RELATIONS

Luxembourg is a member of the UN, WTO, NATO, Benelux, the EU, OECD, the Council of Europe, WEU, OSCE, Asian Development Bank, IOM and the International Organization of the Francophonie. The Schengen Accord of June 1990 abolished border controls between Luxembourg, Austria, Belgium, Denmark, Finland, France, Germany, Greece, Iceland, Italy, the Netherlands, Norway, Portugal, Spain and Sweden.

Luxembourg gave US$0·2bn. in international aid in 2003, which at 0·80% of GNI made it the world's fourth most generous country as a percentage of its gross national income.

ECONOMY

Services accounted for 79·4% of GDP in 2002, industry 19·9% and agriculture 0·7%.

According to the anti-corruption organization *Transparency International*, Luxembourg ranked equal 13th in the world in a 2004 survey of the countries with the least corruption in business and government. It received 8·4 out of 10 in the annual index.

Overview. The financial sector is the country's biggest employer. Financial services account for 38% of GDP. Other buoyant sectors of the Luxembourg economy include telecommunications, audio-visual and multimedia, industrial plastics and air transports.

Currency. On 1 Jan. 1999 the euro (EUR) became the legal currency in Luxembourg; irrevocable conversion rate 40·3399 Luxembourg francs to 1 euro. The euro, which consists of 100 cents, has been in circulation since 1 Jan. 2002. There are seven euro notes in different colours and sizes denominated in 500, 200, 100, 50, 20, 10 and 5 euros, and eight coins denominated in 2 and 1 euros, then 50, 20, 10, 5, 2 and 1 cents. On the introduction of the euro there was a 'dual circulation' period before the Luxembourg franc ceased to be legal tender on 28 Feb. 2002. Euro banknotes in circulation on 1 Jan. 2002 had a total value of €5·6bn.

Inflation in 2001 was 2·7%, falling to 2·1% in 2002. Foreign exchange reserves were US$24m. in 1997. Gold reserves were 76,000 troy oz in June 2002 and total money supply €505m.

Budget. Revenue and expenditure for calendar years in €1m.:

	1999	*2000*	*2001*	*2002*
Revenue	4,976	5,687	5,709	5,977
Expenditure	4,855	5,595	5,148	5,999

Public debt in 2002 was €640·11m.

VAT is 15%, with reduced rates of 12%, 6% and 3%. According to government projections, the general government surplus was expected to be €14,930,500 in 2001. Income taxes and business taxes have been reduced to preserve competitiveness in the international environment. The normal tax rate for companies came down to 37·45% in 1998, compared with 40·3% in 1996.

Performance. In terms of GDP per head, Luxembourg is the richest country in the world, with a per capita PPP (purchasing power parity) GDP of €48,700 in 2001.

Real GDP growth was 6·0% in 1999 and 8·9% in 2000, and averaged 6·8% between 1996 and 2000, but was only 1·0% in 2001 and 0·1% in 2002. Total GDP in 2003 was US$26·2bn.

The Sept. 2003 *OECD Economic Survey* forecasts 'medium-term growth that is likely to be lower than in the past, although still considerably higher than in other European countries.'

Banking and Finance. Luxembourg's Central Bank (formerly the Monetary Institute) was established in July 1998 (*Director-General*, Yves Mersch). In Nov. 2002 there were 179 banks. German banks make up nearly a third of all the banks. Total deposits in 1998 were €8,262·9m.; net assets in unit trusts, €482·1bn. (2001); net assets in investment companies, €441·5bn. (2001). There is a stock exchange.

In 2001 the financial sector accounted for 21·5% of gross added value at basic prices and the banks showed a net profit of €3·6bn. The total number of approved insurance companies in 2001 was 93, with reinsurance companies numbering 264; the amount of premiums due was €6,333·9m.

In 2003 Luxembourg received US$87·6bn. worth of foreign direct investment, the highest total of any country.

ENERGY AND NATURAL RESOURCES

Environment. Carbon dioxide emissions from the consumption and flaring of fossil fuels in 2002 were the equivalent of 23·0 tonnes per capita.

Electricity. Apart from hydro-electricity and electricity generated from fossil fuels, Luxembourg has no national energy resources. Installed capacity in 2001 was 1·6m. kW. Net electricity production was 1,592m. kWh in 2001 and consumption per capita 15,654 kWh in 2000.

Agriculture. The contribution of agriculture, viticulture and forestry to the economy has been gradually declining over the years, accounting for only 0·6% of gross added value at basic prices in 2001. However, the actual output of this sector has nearly tripled during the past 30 years, a trend common to many EU countries. There were 5,289 workers engaged in agricultural work (including wine-growing and forestry) in 2001 (726 wage-earners), and 638 farms with an average area of 55·2 ha; 127,942 ha were under cultivation in 2001.

Production, 2001 (in tonnes) of main crops: grassland and pasturage, 450,761; forage crops, 247,858; maize, 129,272; bread crops, 58,825; potatoes, 22,770; colza (rape), 8,780. Production, 2001 (in 1,000 tonnes) of meat, 27·1; milk, 269·7. In 2001, 134,826 hectolitres of wine were produced. In 2001 there were 7,534 tractors, 706 harvester-threshers, 1,553 manure spreaders and 1,721 gatherer-presses.

Livestock (15 May 2001): 3,126 horses, 205,193 cattle, 78,540 pigs, 8,476 sheep.

Forestry. In 2000 there were 88,600 ha of forests, which in 2000 produced 191,716 cu. metres of broadleaved and 163,504 cu. metres of coniferous wood.

INDUSTRY

According to the Financial Times Survey (FT 500), the largest company by market capitalization in Luxembourg on 4 Jan. 2001 was SES (US$4,557·7m.), a global satellite communications company.

In 2001 there were 2,920 industrial enterprises, of which 1,888 were in the building industry. Production, 2001 (in tonnes): rolled steel products, 4,518,537; steel, 2,724,679. The world's largest steel producer, Arcelor, has its headquarters in Luxembourg. Created in Feb. 2002 through the merger of Arbed of Luxembourg, Aceralia of Spain and Usinor of France, it expects to produce in excess of 40m. tonnes of steel annually and to account for approximately 5% of world steel output. The steel industry mainly relies on imported ore.

Labour. In 2001 the estimated total workforce was 277,000. The government fixes a legal minimum wage. Retirement is at 65. Employment creation averaged 3·5% every year between 1985 and 2001, with a total increase in jobs of 58·1% over the period. In Dec. 2004 the standardized unemployment rate was 4·4%. Luxembourg has one of the lowest rates of unemployment of any EU member country. The minimum wage in Jan. 2003 was €7·91 an hour.

Between 1989 and 1998 strikes cost Luxembourg an average of just six days per 1,000 employees a year (the second lowest in the European Union, with Austria having four per 1,000), compared to the EU average of 85 per 1,000.

There was a 5·8% increase in employment in 2001. Of the new jobs created, around two-thirds went to so-called *frontaliers,* workers living in surrounding countries who commute into Luxembourg to work. More than 100,000 people cross into Luxembourg every day from neighbouring France, Germany and Belgium to work, principally in the financial services industry.

Trade Unions. The main trade unions are the OGB-L (Socialist) and the LCGB (Christian-Social). Other sectorial unions include ALEBA (the banking sector), FNCTTFEL (railworkers) and FEP (private employers). In Oct. 1998 union representatives were elected in both the private and public sectors.

INTERNATIONAL TRADE

Luxembourg is in the process of turning itself into a centre for electronic commerce, the world's fastest-growing industry.

Imports and Exports. In 2000 exports reached 156% of GDP. Exports in 2001 (provisional figures) totalled €9,081·9m. and imports €12,335·0m. In 2000, 84·2% of exports went to other EU member countries and 83·1% of imports were from other EU member countries.

Principal imports and exports by standard international trade classification (provisional figures) in €1m.:

	Exports		*Imports*	
	2000	*2001*	*2000*	*2001*
Food and live animals	318·6	382·0	735·2	826·0
Beverages and tobacco	262·1	230·0	420·0	398·6
Crude materials, oils, fats and waxes	100·1	101·8	599·1	665·9
Mineral fuels and lubricants	9·5	9·9	1,064·7	932·3
Chemicals and related products	558·9	576·7	1,110·0	1,244·5
Manufactured goods in metals	2,544·0	2,548·3	1,451·8	1,396·1
Other manufactured goods classified chiefly by material	1,354·7	1,440·1	802·6	934·2
Machinery	2,004·3	2,183·5	2,514·9	2,657·8
Transport equipment	349·6	390·1	1,760·2	1,876·6
Other manufactured goods	1,093·4	1,219·5	1,289·8	1,403·0
Total	8,595·2	9,081·9	11,748·3	12,335·0

Trade with selected countries (provisional figures) in €1m.:

	Exports		*Imports*	
	2000	*2001*	*2000*	*2001*
Austria	120·2	111·0	104·5	121·6
Belgium	1,103·2	1,114·9	4,193·2	4,232·8
France	1,766·2	1,781·4	1,458·4	1,574·8
Germany	2,060·9	2,233·1	2,870·6	3,099·5
Italy	470·8	565·6	224·1	210·3
Netherlands	461·3	407·4	559·0	630·4
Spain	249·5	273·7	92·3	117·1
UK	651·3	744·5	363·5	516·5
Total EU	7,249·8	7,688·4	10,042·5	10,698·9
Non-EU Europe	857·2	875·5	1,251·1	1,256·2
Japan	57·6	55·4	128·7	133·2
NIEA[1]	199·4	188·3	235·3	252·2
USA	347·5	319·0	769·0	711·5
Total	8,595·2	9,081·9	11,748·3	12,335·0

[1]New industrialized economies of Asia (Singapore, South Korea, Taiwan, Indonesia, Malaysia and China).

Trade Fairs. The *Foires Internationales de Luxembourg* occurs twice a year, and there are a growing number of specialized fairs.

COMMUNICATIONS

Roads. On 1 Jan. 2002 there were 2,875 km of roads of which 126 km were motorways. Motor vehicles registered at 1 Jan. 2002 included 341,272 passenger cars, 21,730 trucks, 1,122 coaches and 11,945 motorcycles. In 2001 there were 774 road accidents with 70 fatalities.

Rail. In 2001 there were 274 km of railway (standard gauge) of which 261 km were electrified; 13·6m. passengers were carried.

Civil Aviation. Findel is the airport for Luxembourg. 1,625,323 passengers and 510,965 tonnes of freight were handled in 2001. The national carrier is Luxair, 23·1% state-owned. Cargolux has developed into one of the major international freight carriers. In 1999 scheduled airline traffic of Luxembourg-based carriers flew 57·1m. km, carrying 843,000 passengers (all on international flights).

Shipping. A shipping register was set up in 1990. In 2001 merchant shipping totalled 1,591,281 tonnes. 159 vessels were registered at 25 June 2002.

Telecommunications. Luxembourg had 346,763 main telephone lines in 2001, or 785 for every 1,000 population. There were 265,000 PCs in use in 2002 (590·2 per 1,000 persons) and 473,000 mobile phone subscribers (1,060·5 per 1,000 persons—the highest rate in any sovereign country). There were 25,000 fax machines in use in 2001. In 2002 Luxembourg had 165,000 Internet users.

Postal Services. In 2001 there were 108 post offices. In 2001 a total of 153·2m. items of mail were processed.

SOCIAL INSTITUTIONS

Justice. The Constitution makes the Courts of Law independent in performing their functions, restricting their sphere of activity, defining their limit of jurisdiction and providing a number of procedural guarantees. The Constitution has additionally laid down a number of provisions designed to ensure judges remain independent of persons under their jurisdiction, and to ensure no interference from the executive and legislative organs. All judges are appointed by Grand-Ducal order and are irremovable.

The judicial organization comprises three Justices of the Peace (conciliation and police courts). The country is, in addition, divided into two judicial districts—Luxembourg and Diekirch. District courts deal with matters such as civic and commercial cases. Offences which are punishable under the Penal Code or by specific laws with imprisonment or hard labour fall within the jurisdiction of the criminal chambers of District Courts, as the Assize Court was repealed by law in 1987. The High Court of Justice consists of a Supreme Court of Appeal and a Court of Appeal.

The judicial organization of the Grand-Duchy does not include the jury system. A division of votes between the judges on the issue of guilt/innocence may lead to acquittal. Society before the Courts of Law is represented by the Public Prosecutor Department, composed of members of the judiciary directly answerable to the government.

In 1999 a new Administrative Tribunal, Administrative Court and Constitutional Court were established.

The population in penal institutions in Sept. 2002 was 380.

Religion. The population was 91% Roman Catholic in 2001. There are small Protestant, Jewish, Greek, Russian Orthodox and Muslim communities as well.

Education. The adult literacy rate in 2001 was at least 99%. Education is compulsory for all children between the ages of six and 15. In 2000–01 there were 10,706 children in pre-primary school with 751 teachers; 31,218 pupils in primary schools; 31,278 pupils in secondary schools. In higher education (2001–02) the Higher Institute of Technology (IST) had 360 students and there were 394 students in teacher training. In 2001–02 the University Centre of Luxembourg had 1,778 students. Luxembourg does not have a full-time university, so many students have to go abroad, predominantly to France, Germany and Belgium. In 2000–01, 5,017 students pursued university studies abroad.

In 1999–2000 total expenditure on education came to 4·0% of GNP and 8·5% of total government spending.

Health. In 2001 there were 1,140 doctors (389 GPs and 751 specialists) and 289 dentists. There were 19 hospitals and 3,035 hospital beds in 2000. In 2002 Luxembourg spent 6·2% of its GDP on health.

Welfare. The official retirement age is 65 years for both men and women. To be eligible, a pensioner must have paid 120 months contributions. The maximum old-age pension is €5,130·08 per month. The minimum pension is €1,108·10 per month if insured for 40 years, reduced by 1/40 for each year less than 40. A minimum pension is not payable if the person has been insured for less than 20 years.

Unemployment benefit is 80% (85% if the insured has a dependant child) of the basis salary during the previous three months, up to 2·5 times the social minimum wage. Recent graduates receive 70% of the social minimum wage whereas self-employed persons receive 80% of the social minimum wage.

CULTURE

World Heritage Sites. Luxembourg has one site on the UNESCO World Heritage List: the City of Luxembourg—its Old Quarters and Fortifications (inscribed on the list in 1994).

Broadcasting. The major broadcaster of TV and radio programmes is RTL Group, formerly CLT (*Compagnie Luxembourgeoise de Télédiffusion*), along with local and regional radio stations that have emerged since the 1991 Law on Electronic Media. CLT was set up in 1929 and started broadcasting in 1932. In the same year Radio Luxembourg started broadcasting its multilingual programmes. In 1954 CLT received an exclusive licence for broadcasting radio and TV in the Grand-Duchy, which was extended until the end of 2010 in 1995.

With 24 television and 14 radio stations in eight countries, RTL Group is Europe's largest TV, radio and production company. Listed on the London Stock Exchange, the Luxembourg-based media group operates TV channels and radio stations in Germany, France, Belgium, the Netherlands, UK, Luxembourg, Spain and Hungary. CLT-UFA S.A. also broadcast four TV channels and three radio stations via the ASTRA satellite system. The 1991 Law on Electronic Media allowed the creation of four new radio networks and 15 local radio stations, and thus ended the CLT monopoly.

The commercial *Radio-Télé-Luxembourg* broadcasts one programme in Lëtzebuergesch on FM. There are commercial and religious programmes in French, German, English, Italian, Portuguese and Spanish. More than 40 international TV programmes are broadcast by cable. The country's cable penetration is 90%, while satellite amounts to 15·5% and terrestrial to 2·5%. Luxembourg has over 150 local, independent cable networks and counts four major cable operators.

In 2001 there were 295,000 TV sets in use and in 2000 there were 300,000 radio receivers. Satellite and cable TV is widespread (colour by SECAM V).

Cinema. In 2000 there were 25 cinema screens throughout the country. Cinema attendances in 2000 totalled 1,362,006.

Press. There were six daily newspapers in 2001 with a circulation of 162,934, equivalent to 369 per 1,000 inhabitants. There are a number of weekly titles with a circulation of 124,166.

Tourism. In 2001 there were 858,686 tourists, and 7,568 hotel rooms and 1,221,852 overnight stays. Tourists spent US$391m. in 2000. Camping is widespread, and weekend and short-stay tourism accounts for many tourists. There were 1,015,300 overnight stays at campsites in 2001.

Festivals. The Festival International Echternach (May–June) and the Festival of Wiltz (June–July) are annual events. Both feature a variety of classical music, jazz, theatre and recitals.

Libraries. In 1998 there were 33 libraries (excluding higher education libraries). There were 298,197 library loans in 1997.

Theatre and Opera. There are several theatres in Luxembourg City, including the *Grand Théâtre de la Ville*, *Théâtre des Capucins* and *Théâtre du Centaure*. There are also a number of smaller theatres elsewhere, notably in Esch/Alzette and Echternach.

Museums and Galleries. The main museums in Luxembourg City are the *Musée d'Histoire de la Ville*, the *Villa Vauban*, the *Musée National d'Histoire Naturelle* and the *Musée National d'Histoire et d'Art*. There are smaller museums in the rest of the country. In 2000 there were two national museums, 11 public museums and three private museums, which had 189,403 visitors.

DIPLOMATIC REPRESENTATIVES

Of Luxembourg in the United Kingdom (27 Wilton Crescent, London, SWIX 8SD)
Ambassador: Jean-Louis Wolzfeld.

Of the United Kingdom in Luxembourg (14 Blvd Roosevelt, L-2450 Luxembourg)
Ambassador: James Clark.

Of Luxembourg in the USA (2200 Massachusetts Ave., NW, Washington, D.C., 20008)
Ambassador: Arlette Conzemius.

Of the USA in Luxembourg (22 Blvd. Emmanuel Servais, L-2535 Luxembourg)
Ambassador: Peter Terpeluk, Jr.

Of Luxembourg to the United Nations
Ambassador: Jean-Marc Hoscheit.

FURTHER READING

STATEC. *Annuaire Statistique 2002.*

Christophory, J. and Thoma, E., *Luxembourg.* [Bibliography] 2nd ed. ABC-Clio, Oxford and Santa Barbara (CA), 1997

Newcomer, J., *The Grand Duchy of Luxembourg: The Evolution of Nationhood, 963 AD to 1983.* 2nd ed. Editions Emile Borschette, Luxembourg, 1995

National Library: 37 Boulevard Roosevelt, Luxembourg City.
National statistical office: Service Central de la Statistique et des Etudes Economiques (STATEC), CP 304, Luxembourg City, L-2013 Luxembourg. *Director:* Serge Allegrezza.
Website (French only): http://www.statec.pub.lu

MACEDONIA

Republika Makedonija
The Republic of Macedonia
(Former Yugoslav Republic of Macedonia)

Capital: Skopje
Population projection, 2010: 2·12m.
GDP per capita, 2002: (PPP$) 6,470
HDI/world rank: 0·793/60

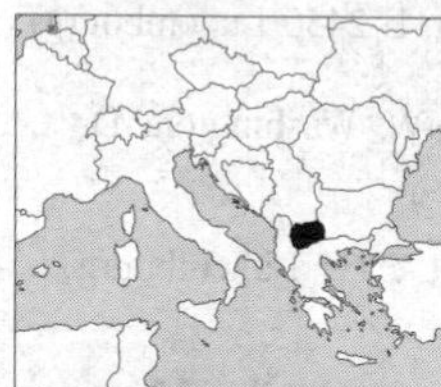

KEY HISTORICAL EVENTS

The history of Macedonia can be traced to the reign of King Karan (808–778 BC), but the country was at its most powerful at the time of Philip II (359–336 BC) and Alexander the Great (336–323 BC). At the end of the 6th century AD Slavs began to settle in Macedonia. There followed a long period of internal fighting but the spread of Christianity led to consolidation and the creation of the first Macedonian Slav state, the Kingdom of Samuel, 976–1018. In the 14th century it fell to Serbia, and in 1355 to the Turks. After the Balkan wars of 1912–13 Turkey was ousted and Serbia received part of the territory, the rest going to Bulgaria and Greece. In 1918 Yugoslav Macedonia was incorporated into Serbia as South Serbia, becoming a republic in the Socialist Federal Republic of Yugoslavia. Claims to the historical Macedonian territory have long been a source of contention with Bulgaria and Greece. Macedonia declared its independence on 18 Sept. 1991. In April 1999 the Kosovo crisis which led to NATO air attacks on Yugoslavian military targets set off a flood of refugees into Macedonia, although most returned home after the end of the crisis.

In March 2001 there were a series of clashes between government forces and ethnic Albanian separatists near the border between Macedonia and Kosovo. As violence escalated Macedonia found itself on the brink of civil war. In May 2001 the new national unity government gave ethnic Albanian rebels a 'final warning' to end their uprising. As the crisis worsened, a stand-off within the government between the Macedonian and the ethnic Albanian parties was only resolved after the intervention of Javier Solana, the EU's foreign and security policy chief. A number of Macedonian soldiers were killed in clashes with the rebels, and following reverses in the military campaign the commander of the Macedonian army, Jovan Andrevski, resigned in June 2001. In Aug. 2001 a peace accord was negotiated.

TERRITORY AND POPULATION

Macedonia is bounded in the north by Serbia and Montenegro, in the east by Bulgaria, in the south by Greece and in the west by Albania. Its area is 25,713 sq. km. According to the 2002 census final results, the population on 1 Nov. 2002 was 2,022,547. The main ethnic groups in 1994 were Macedonians (1,296,000), Albanians (441,000), Turks (78,000), Romas (44,000), Serbs (40,000) and Vlachs (9,000). Ethnic Albanians predominate on the western side of Macedonia. Minorities are represented in the Council for Inter-Ethnic Relations. In Dec. 2000 density was 79 per sq. km. In 2001, 59·5% of the population lived in urban areas.

The UN gives a projected population for 2010 of 2·12m.

Macedonia is divided into 123 municipalities. The major cities (with 2002 census population) are: Skopje, the capital, 467,257; Kumanovo, 103,205; Bitola, 86,408; Prilep, 73,351; Tetovo, 70,841.

The official languages are Macedonian, which uses the Cyrillic alphabet, and Albanian.

SOCIAL STATISTICS

In 2001: births, 27,010; deaths, 19,619; marriages, 13,267; divorces, 1,448; infant deaths (2000), 346. Rates (per 1,000 population): birth, 13·3; death, 8·3; marriage, 7·0; divorce, 0·7. Infant mortality, 2000 (per 1,000 live births), 11·8. Expectation of life at birth in 2001 was 71·2 years for males and 75·5 years for females. Annual population growth rate, 1992–2002, 0·6%. In 2001 the most popular age range for marrying was 25–29 for males and 20–24 for females. Fertility rate, 2000, 1·9 births per woman.

Migration within the Republic of Macedonia, 2000: 12,419. International (external) migration: emigrated persons, 172; immigrated persons 1,199. Net migration in 2000 was 1,027.

CLIMATE

Macedonia has a mixed Mediterranean-continental type climate, with cold moist winters and hot dry summers. Skopje, Jan. –0·4°C, July 23·1°C.

CONSTITUTION AND GOVERNMENT

At a referendum held on 8 Sept. 1991 turn-out was 74%; 99% of votes cast were in favour of a sovereign Macedonia. On 17 Nov. 1991 parliament promulgated a new constitution which officially proclaimed Macedonia's independence. This was replaced by a constitution adopted on 16 Nov. 2001 which for the first time included the recognition of Albanian as an official language. It also increased access for ethnic Albanians to public-sector jobs.

The *President* is directly elected for five-year terms. Candidates must be citizens aged at least 40 years. The parliament is a 120-member single-chamber *Assembly* (*Sobranie*), elected by universal suffrage for four-year terms. There is a *Constitutional Court* whose members are elected by the assembly for non-renewable eight-year terms, and a *National Security Council* chaired by the President. Laws passed by the Assembly must be countersigned by the President, who may return them for reconsideration, but cannot veto them if they gain a two-thirds majority.

Political Parties. The Law on Political Parties makes a distinction between a political party and an association of citizens. The signatures of 500 citizens with the right to vote must be produced for a party to be legally registered. Presently the country has 34 legally registered parties.

National Anthem. 'Denes nad Makedonija se radja novo sonce na slobodata' ('Today a new sun of liberty appears over Macedonia'); words by V. Maleski, tune by T. Škalovski.

RECENT ELECTIONS

Following the death of Boris Trajkovski in a plane crash on 26 Feb. 2004, presidential elections were held on 14 April 2004. Branko Crvenkovski (Social Democratic League of Macedonia), the incumbent prime minister, took 42·5% of the vote, Saško Kedev (Internal Macedonian Revolutionary Organization-Democratic Party for Macedonian National Unity) 34·1%, Gzim Ostreni (Democratic Union for Integration) 14·8% and Zidi Xhelili (Democratic Party of Albanians) 8·6%. In the run-off on 28 April Crvenkovski won with 60·6% against Kedev with 39·4%. Turn-out was 53·4%.

Parliamentary elections were held on 5 Sept. 2002. The Together for Macedonia coalition, comprising the Social Democratic League of Macedonia (SDSM) and the Liberal-Democratic Party (LDP), won 59 seats with 40·5% of votes cast, defeating Prime Minister Ljubčo Georgievski's Internal Macedonian Revolutionary Organization-Democratic Party for Macedonian National Unity (VMRO-DMPNE-LPM) with 34 seats and 24·4%. The Democratic Union for Integration (DUI) won 16 seats with 11·9%; the Democratic Party of Albanians (PDS), 7 with 5·2%; the Democratic Prosperity Party (PDP), 2 with 2·3%; the National-Democratic Party (NDP), 1 with 2·1%; and the Socialist Party of Macedonia (SPM), 1 with 2·1%. Turn-out was 73·5%.

CURRENT ADMINISTRATION

President: Branko Crvenkovski; b. 1962 (SDSM; sworn in 12 May 2004). He was previously prime minister from Aug. 1992–Nov. 1998 and Nov. 2002–May 2004.

Prime Minister: Vlado Buckovski; b. 1962 (SDSM; sworn in 17 Dec. 2004).

Following elections in Sept. 2002, a SDSM-LDP-DUI coalition government was formed, which in March 2005 was composed as follows:

Deputy Prime Minister and Minister of Defence: Jovan Manasievski (LDP). *Deputy Prime Minister for European Integration:* Radmila Shekerinska (SDSM). *Deputy Prime Minister for Political Systems:* Musa Xhaferi (DUI). *Deputy Prime Minister for Economic Systems:* Minco Jordanov (SDSM).

Minister of Agriculture, Forestry and Water Supply: Sadulla Duraku (LDP). *Culture:* Blagoja Stefanovski (SDSM). *Economy:* Fatmir Besimi (DUI). *Education and Science:* Azis Polozani (DUI). *Environment:* Zoran Sapuric (LDP). *Finance:* Nikola Popovski (SDSM). *Foreign Affairs:* Ilinka Mitreva (SDSM). *Health:* Vladimir Dimov (SDSM). *Interior:* Ljubomir Mihajlovski (SDSM). *Justice:* Meri Mladenovska-Gjorgjievska (SDSM). *Local Self-Government:* Rizvan Sulejmani (DUI). *Labour and Social Policy:* Stevco Jakimovski (LDP). *Transport and Communications:* Xhemali Mehazi (DUI). *Minister without Portfolio:* Vlado Popovski (LDP).

Government Website: http://www.gov.mk

DEFENCE

The President is the C.-in-C. of the armed forces. There is conscription for nine months.

Defence expenditure in 2003 totalled US$137m. (US$67 per capita), representing 3·1% of GDP.

The European Union's first ever peacekeeping force (EUFOR) officially started work in Macedonia on 1 April 2003, replacing the NATO-led force that had been in the country since 2001.

Army. Army strength was estimated at 11,300 (8,000 conscripts) in 2002 with potential reserves of 60,000. There is a paramilitary police force of 7,600.

Navy. In 2002 the Marine Wing numbered 400, with five river patrol craft.

Air Force. The Army Air Force numbered 800 in 2002, and had four combat aircraft and 12 armed helicopters.

INTERNATIONAL RELATIONS

On 13 Sept. 1995 under the auspices of the UN, Macedonia and Greece agreed to normalize their relations.

Macedonia is a member of the UN, WTO, BIS, the Council of Europe, OSCE, the Central European Initiative, the NATO Partnership for Peace and the International Organization of the Francophonie.

ECONOMY

Agriculture accounted for 12·3% of GDP in 2002, industry 30·2% and services 57·5%.

Currency. The national currency of Macedonia is the *denar* (MKD), of 100 *deni*.

Gold reserves were 196,000 troy oz in May 2002 and foreign exchange reserves US$825m. Inflation was 1·2% in 2003 (2·4% in 2002). Total money supply was 25,725m. denars in June 2002.

Budget. In 2002 revenues totalled 53,089m. denars and expenditures 59,979m. denars.

Performance. In 2000 real GDP growth was 4·5%, but in 2001 the political turmoil in the country resulted in the economy contracting by 4·5%. There was then a slight recovery in 2002, with a growth rate of 0·7%. Total GDP in 2003 was US$4·7bn.

Banking and Finance. The central bank and bank of issue is the National Bank of Macedonia. Its *Governor* is Petar Goshev (since May 2004). Privatization of the banking sector was completed in 2000. In 2001 there were 20 commercial banks, six of which were majority foreign-owned. As of 31 Dec. 1998 commercial banks' total non-government deposits were 23,136m. denars, and non-government savings deposits were 15,095m. denars. The largest banks are Stopanska Banka, followed by Komercijalna Banka; between them they control more than half the total assets of all banks in Macedonia.

A stock exchange opened in Skopje in 1996.

ENERGY AND NATURAL RESOURCES

Environment. Macedonia's carbon dioxide emissions from the consumption and flaring of fossil fuels were the equivalent of 4·0 tonnes per capita in 2002.

Electricity. Installed capacity in 2000 was 1·5m. kW. Output in 2000: 6·81bn. kWh, of which 1·17bn. kWh were from hydro-electric plants. Consumption per capita was 3,404 kWh in 2000.

Oil and Gas. A 230-km long pipeline bringing crude oil to Macedonia from Thessaloniki in Greece opened in July 2002. Built at a cost of over US$130m., it has the capacity to provide Macedonia with 2·5m. tonnes of crude oil annually.

Minerals. Macedonia is relatively rich in minerals, including lead, zinc, copper, iron, chromium, nickel, antimony, manganese, silver and gold. Output in 2001 (in tonnes): lignite, 8,056,661; copper ore, 2,650,000; lead-zinc ore, 571,802; lead-zinc concentrates, 53,981; copper concentrate, 25,012; chromium concentrate, 1,535 (1997); refined silver, 23.

Agriculture. At the 1994 census the active agricultural population was 91,354. In 2001 there were 611,982 ha of arable land, 629,825 ha of pasture and 46,000 ha of permanent crops. In 2001, 152,887 ha of arable land were owned by agricultural organizations and 459,095 ha by individual farmers.

Crop production, 2001 (in 1,000 tonnes): wheat, 246; grapes, 230; potatoes, 176; watermelons, 130; tomatoes, 126; wine, 119; maize, 117; peppers, 112; lucerne, 104; barley, 92; cabbages, 75; apples, 38; sugarbeets, 38; onions, 31; cucumbers and gherkins, 29; tobacco, 23; plums, 13. In 2001, 119,000 tonnes of wine were produced.

Livestock, 2001 (in 1,000): cattle, 265; sheep, 1,285; pigs, 189; horses, 46; chickens, 2,750. Livestock products, 2001 (in 1,000 tonnes): pork, bacon and ham, 8; beef, 6; mutton, 6; poultry, 5; cow's milk, 248m. litres; sheep's milk, 47m. litres; eggs (total), 395m.

There were 63,280 tractors in use in 2001.

Forestry. Forests covered 997,374 ha in 2001, chiefly oak and beech. 792,000 cu. metres of timber were cut in 2001.

Fisheries. Total catch in 2001 was 1,135 tonnes, entirely from inland waters.

INDUSTRY

In 1999 there were 94,404 enterprises (90,426 private, 1,112 public, 1,257 co-operative, 1,577 mixed and 32 state-owned). 2001 production (in tonnes): cement, 585,000; residual fuel oil (2000), 377,000; distillate fuel oil (2000), 259,000; petrol (2000), 131,000; sulphuric acid, 101,058; ferro-alloys, 27,287; detergents, 19,248.

Labour. In April 2002 there were 561,400 employed persons, including: 133,600 in agriculture, hunting and forestry; 132,400 in manufacturing; 64,200 in wholesale and retail trade/repair of motor vehicles, motorcycles and personal and household goods; and 33,700 in education. The number of unemployed persons in 2002 was 263,483, giving an unemployment rate of 31·9%.

INTERNATIONAL TRADE

The foreign debt of Macedonia, including debt taken over from the former Yugoslavia, was US$1,619m. in 2002.

Imports and Exports. In 2002 imports (f.o.b.) were valued at US$1,878·1m. (US$1,681·8m. in 2001) and exports (f.o.b.) at US$1,110·5m. (US$1,155·4m. in 2001).

Main export markets, 2000: Yugoslavia (25·3%), Germany (19·4%), USA (12·6%), Italy (6·6%), Greece (6·4%). Main import suppliers, 2000: Germany (12·1%), Ukraine (9·9%), Greece (9·6%), Russia (9·2%) and Yugoslavia (9·1%).

COMMUNICATIONS

Roads. In 2001 there were 937 km of main roads, 3,643 km of regional roads and 8,347 km of local roads: 1,176 km of roads were paved and 6,710 km asphalted. 13·7m. passengers and 6·7m. tonnes of freight were transported. There were 309,562 cars, 2,620 buses and 21,727 lorries in 2001. In 1996 there were 2,505 road accidents with 154 fatalities.

Rail. In 2001 there were 697 km of railways (233 km electrified). 1·3m. passengers and 2·8m. tonnes of freight were transported.

Civil Aviation. There are international airports at Skopje and Ohrid. There are two Macedonia-based carriers—Interimpex-Avioimpex, which flew 3·3m. km and carried 215,400 passengers in 1999, and the smaller Macedonian Airlines. In 2000 Skopje handled 864,155 passengers (all on international flights) and 3,046 tonnes of freight. Ohrid handled 63,255 passengers (all on international flights) and 65 tonnes of freight.

Telecommunications. In 2002 there were 560,000 main telephone lines (271·3 per 1,000 inhabitants) and 365,300 mobile phone subscribers. In 1999 there were 3,000 fax machines. There were 100,000 Internet users in 2002. In 2002 the Hungarian firm Matav acquired a 51% stake in MakTel, the state monopoly telecommunications provider, in the most significant economic development in the country's history. The deal, worth €618·2m. (US$568·4m.) over two years, is the biggest foreign investment to date.

Postal Services. In 2001 there were 312 post offices.

SOCIAL INSTITUTIONS

Justice. Courts are autonomous and independent. Judges are tenured and elected for life on the proposal of the *Judicial Council*, whose members are themselves elected for renewable six-year terms. The highest court is the Supreme Court. There are 27 courts of first instance and three higher courts.

The population in penal institutions in Sept. 2002 was 1,248 (61 per 100,000 of national population).

Religion. Macedonia is traditionally Orthodox but the church is not established and there is freedom of religion. In 2001 there were 1·21m. Serbian (Macedonian) Orthodox and 580,000 Sunni Muslims. In 1967 an autocephalous Orthodox church split off from the Serbian. Its head is the Archbishop of Ohrid and Macedonia whose seat is at Skopje. It has five bishoprics in Macedonia and representatives in USA, Canada and Australia. It has some 300 priests.

The Muslim Religious Union has a superiorate at Skopje. The Roman Catholic Church has a seat at Skopje.

Education. Adult literacy was 94·6% in 1998. Education is free and compulsory for eight years. In 2001, 36,502 children attended 52 pre-school institutions and 438 infant schools of elementary education. In 2001–02 there were 244,740 pupils enrolled in 1,007 primary, 92,554 in 95 secondary and 1,123 in higher schools, and 343,587 students in higher education. There are universities at Skopje (Cyril and Methodius, founded in 1949; 35,812 students and 1,350 academic staff in 2001–02) and Bitola (founded 1979; 8,898 students and 211 academic staff in 2001–02).

In 1999–2000 total expenditure on education came to 4·2% of GNP.

Health. In 1998 there were 4,501 doctors, 1,144 dentists, 329 pharmacologists, and 58 hospitals with 10,311 beds. In the villages there were 330 medical units.

Welfare. In 2001 social assistance was paid to 80,334 households. Child care and special supplements went to 63,205 children, and 15,909 underage and 78,298 adults received social benefits. There were 241,221 pensioners in 1998.

CULTURE

World Heritage Sites. The Former Yugoslav Republic of Macedonia has one site on the UNESCO World Heritage List: Ohrid Region with its Cultural and Historic Aspect and its Natural Environment (inscribed on the list in 1979), a rich repository of Byzantine art and architecture.

Broadcasting. The national Macedonian Radio and Television (colour by PAL) is government-funded. It broadcasts on three TV and six radio channels. In 2001 there were also 28 local public broadcasting enterprises (state-owned), 18 of which transmitted only radio programmes while the other ten transmitted radio and TV programmes. In 2001 there were 50 private radio and 42 private TV stations. In 2000 there were 570,000 TV subscribers and 415,000 radio receivers.

Cinema. There were 26 cinemas and 426,666 admissions in 2001; gross box office receipts came to 29m. denars. Five documentary films were made in 2002.

Press. There were eight daily newspapers and 11 weeklies in 2001, and 117 other newspapers and periodicals published in Macedonian, Albanian, Turkish, English and other languages.

There are two news agencies in Macedonia, the Macedonian Information Agency (national) and Makfax (privately owned).

Tourism. In 2000 tourists numbered 632,523 spending 2·43m. nights in Macedonia.

DIPLOMATIC REPRESENTATIVES

Of Macedonia in the United Kingdom (5th floor, 25 James Street, London, W1U 1DU)
Ambassador: Gjorgji Spasov.

Of the United Kingdom in Macedonia (Dimitrija Chupovski 26, 1000 Skopje)
Ambassador: Robert Chatterton Dickson.

Of Macedonia in the USA (1101 30th Street, NW, Suite 302, Washington, D.C., 20007)
Ambassador: Nikola Dimitrov.

Of the USA in Macedonia (Blvd Ilinden, 1000 Skopje)
Ambassador: Lawrence E. Butler.

Of Macedonia to the United Nations
Ambassador: Igor Dzundev.

Of Macedonia to the European Union
Ambassador: Sasko Stefkov.

FURTHER READING

Danforth, L. M., *The Macedonian Conflict: Ethnic Nationalism in a Transnational World.* Princeton Univ. Press, 1996

Poulton, H., *Who Are the Macedonians?* Farnborough, 1996

National statistical office: State Statistical Office, Dame Gruev 4, Skopje. *Director:* Blagica Novkovska.
Website: http://www.stat.gov.mk

MADAGASCAR

Repoblikan'i Madagasikara

Capital: Antananarivo
Population projection, 2010: 21·09m.
GDP per capita, 2002: (PPP$) 740
HDI/world rank: 0·469/150

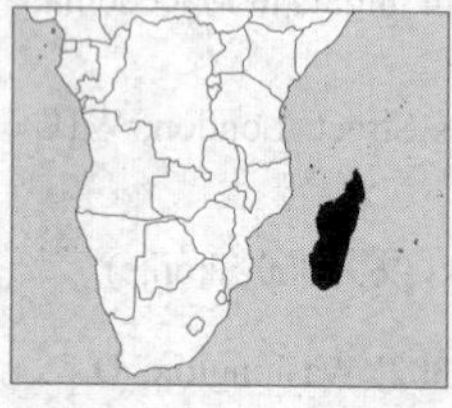

KEY HISTORICAL EVENTS

The island was settled by people of African and Indonesian origin when it was visited by the Portuguese explorer, Diego Diaz, in 1500. The island was unified under the Imérina monarchy between 1797 and 1861, but a French protectorate was established in 1895. Madagascar became a French colony on 6 Aug. 1896 and achieved independence on 26 June 1960.

In Feb. 1975 Col. Richard Ratsimandrava, Head of State, was assassinated. The 1975 Constitution instituted a 'Democratic Republic' in which only a single political party was permitted.

After six months of anti-government unrest an 18-month transitional administration was agreed. A new Constitution instituted the Third Republic in Sept. 1992.

Following the presidential election of Dec. 2001 the opposition candidate Marc Ravalomanana claimed victory, although the High Constitutional Court ruled that a run-off was needed. On 22 Feb. 2002 Ravalomanana declared himself president and imposed a state of emergency. However, incumbent Didier Ratsiraka and his government set up a rival capital in Toamasina. In April 2002 both men agreed to a recount of votes to solve the dispute. Ravalomanana was declared president following the recount.

TERRITORY AND POPULATION

Madagascar is situated 400 km (250 miles) off the southeast coast of Africa, from which it is separated by the Mozambique channel. Its area is 587,041 sq. km (226,658 sq. miles). At the 1993 census the population was 12,092,157 (50·45% female); density, 20·6 per sq. km. Estimate (2002), 18,946,000 (69·9% rural, 2001). Population density, 32 per sq. km.

The UN gives a projected population for 2010 of 21·09m.

Province	*Area in sq. km*	*Population (1993 census)*	*Chief town*	*Population (1993 census)*
Antananarivo	58,283	3,483,236	Antananarivo	1,432,000[1]
Antsiranana	43,046	942,410	Antsiranana	54,418[2]
Fianarantsoa	102,373	2,671,150	Fianarantsoa	99,005
Mahajanga	150,023	1,330,612	Mahajanga	100,807
Toamasina	71,911	1,935,330	Toamasina	127,441
Toliary	161,405	1,729,419	Toliary	61,460[2]

[1]1999 figure. [2]1990 estimate.

The indigenous population is of Malayo-Polynesian stock, divided into 18 ethnic groups of which the principal are Merina (26%) of the central plateau, the Betsimisaraka (15%) of the east coast and the Betsileo (12%) of the southern plateau. Foreign communities include Europeans, mainly French (30,000), Indians (15,000), Chinese (9,000), Comorians and Arabs.

The official language is Malagasy. French is the language of international communication.

SOCIAL STATISTICS

1997 estimated births, 595,000; deaths, 198,000. Rates, 1997 estimates (per 1,000 population): births, 42·3; deaths, 14·1. Infant mortality, 2001 (per 1,000 live births), 84. Expectation of life in 2001 was 51·9 years for males and 54·2 for females. Annual population growth rate, 1992–02, 2·9%. Fertility rate, 2001, 5·8 births per woman.

CLIMATE

A tropical climate, but the mountains cause big variations in rainfall, which is very heavy in the east and very light in the west. Antananarivo, Jan. 70°F (21·1°C), July

59°F (15°C). Annual rainfall 54" (1,350 mm). Toamasina, Jan. 80°F (26·7°C), July 70°F (21·1°C). Annual rainfall 128" (3,256 mm).

CONSTITUTION AND GOVERNMENT

Following a referendum, a Constitution came into force on 30 Dec. 1975 establishing a Democratic Republic. It provided for a National People's Assembly elected by universal suffrage from the single list of the *Front National pour la Défense de la Révolution Socialiste Malgache.* Executive power was vested in the President with the guidance of a Supreme Revolutionary Council.

Under a convention of 31 Oct. 1991 the powers of the National People's Assembly and the Supreme Revolutionary Council were delegated to a High State Authority for a Provisional government. Following a referendum on 19 Aug. 1992 at which turn-out was 77·68% and 75·44% of votes cast were in favour, a new Constitution was adopted on 21 Sept. 1992 establishing the Third Republic. Under this the *National Assembly* has 160 seats (increased from 150 for the 2002 election). There is also a *Senate* of 90 members.

A referendum on 17 Sept. 1995 was in favour of the President appointing and dismissing the Prime Minister, hitherto elected by parliament. The electorate was 6m.; turn-out was 50%.

National Anthem. 'Ry tanindrazanay malala ô!' ('O our beloved Fatherland'); words by Pastor Rahajason, tune by N. Raharisoa.

RECENT ELECTIONS

At the first round of presidential elections on 16 Dec. 2001 there were six candidates. Turn-out was 66·7%. Official results gave Marc Ravalomanana 46·2% of votes cast against 40·9% for Didier Ratsiraka, forcing the two men into a run-off, but Marc Ravalomanana himself claimed to have won the election outright. Ravalomanana declared himself president on 24 Feb. 2002 but with Ratsiraka refusing to accept defeat there were effectively two presidents. On 18 April 2002 the two men signed a deal designed to end the bitter power struggle. Following the announcement by the Supreme Court of a recount of the votes cast in the presidential election, the two candidates agreed that in the event of neither obtaining a majority, a referendum would be held to settle the issue. In the recount the High Constitutional Court declared Marc Ravalomanana the winner with 51·5% of votes against 35·9% for Didier Ratsiraka, with others obtaining 12·6% between them, although the result was not recognized by Ratsiraka. On 6 May 2002 Marc Ravalomanana was sworn in as president. In protest, four of Madagascar's six provinces declared independence. In June 2002 US President George W. Bush gave formal recognition of Ravalomanana's claim to the presidency. On 5 July 2002 Ratsiraka left Madagascar for the Seychelles amidst warnings of arrest from Ravalomanana's government.

In parliamentary elections held on 15 Dec. 2002 President Marc Ravalomanana's I Love Madagascar party won 103 of the 160 seats, his allies within the National Unity coalition 22, ind. also 22 and minor parties 13. Turn-out was 67·6%.

CURRENT ADMINISTRATION

President: Marc Ravalomanana; b. 1949 (ind., sworn in 6 May 2002).

In March 2005 the cabinet was composed as follows:

Prime Minister: Jacques Sylla; b. 1946 (ind.).

Deputy Prime Minister and Minister for Economic Programmes, Transportation, Public Works and Regional Administration: Zazah Ramandimbiarison.

Minister of Foreign Affairs: Gen. Marcel Ranjeva. *Interior:* Gen. André Soja. *Defence:* Behajaina Petera. *Agriculture, Livestock and Fisheries:* Harrison Andriarimanana. *Civil Service, Labour and Social Laws:* Théodore Ranjivason. *Tourism and Culture:* Jean Jacques Rabenirina. *Finance and Budget:* Andriamparany Radavidson. *Energy and Mines:* Olivier Donat Andriamahefaparany. *Environment:* Gen. Charles Sylvain Rabotoarison. *Health:* Jean-Louis Robinson. *Industrialization, Commerce and Development of the Private Sector:* Olivier Andrianarison-Sahobisoa. *Justice:* Henriette Ratsiharivala. *Posts and Telecommunications:* Bruno Ramaroson Andriantavison. *Population, Social Protection and Leisure:* Zafilaza. *Basic and*

Higher Education and Scientific Research: Hajanirina Razafinjatovo. *Youth and Sports:* Henri François Randrianjatovo.

Government Website: http://www.madagascar.gov.mg

DEFENCE

There is conscription (including civilian labour service) for 18 months. Defence expenditure totalled US$81m. in 2003 (US$5 per capita), representing 1·5% of GDP.

Army. Strength (2002) 12,500 and gendarmerie 8,100.

Navy. In 2002 the maritime force had a strength of 500 (including 100 marines).

Air Force. Personnel (2002) 500. There are 12 combat aircraft.

INTERNATIONAL RELATIONS

Madagascar is a member of the UN, WTO, the African Union, African Development Bank, COMESA, IOM, the International Organization of the Francophonie and is an ACP member state of the ACP-EU relationship.

ECONOMY

In 2002 agriculture contributed 31·7% of GDP, industry 14·4% and services 53·8%.

Currency. In July 2003 President Marc Ravalomanana announced that the *Ariary* (MGA) would become the official currency, replacing the *Malagasy franc* (MGFr). The Ariary became legal tender on 1 Aug. 2003 and although the Malagasy franc is no longer legal tender it will remain exchangeable until 2009. The Ariary is subdivided into five *Iraimbilanja*.

In June 2002 foreign exchange reserves were US$393m. Inflation in 2002 was 4·5%. Total money supply in May 2002 was MGFr5,265·55bn.

Budget. Budget revenue and expenditure (in MGFr1bn.), year ending 31 Dec.:

	1997	*1998*	*1999*	*2000*
Revenue	1,746·8	2,077·0	2,666·8	3,067·8
Expenditure	2,879·4	3,477·5	4,068·8	4,477·7

Performance. Total GDP in 2003 was US$5·5bn. There was a recession in 2002 with the economy contracting by 12·7% as a result of the six-month long political crisis, but a recovery followed in 2003 with real GDP growth of 9·8%.

Banking and Finance. A Central Bank, the *Banque Centrale de Madagascar*, was formed in 1973, replacing the former *Institut d'Émission Malgache* as the central bank of issue. The *Governor* is Gaston Ravelojaona. All commercial banking and insurance was nationalized in 1975 and privatized in 1988. Of the six other banks, the largest are the *Bankin'ny Tantsaha Mpamokatra* and the *BNI—Crédit Lyonnais de Madagascar*.

ENERGY AND NATURAL RESOURCES

Environment. Madagascar's carbon dioxide emissions from the consumption and flaring of fossil fuels in 2002 were the equivalent of 0·1 tonnes per capita.

Electricity. Installed capacity was 0·2m. kW in 2000. Production in 2000 was 807m. kWh, with consumption per capita being 51 kWh.

Oil and Gas. Natural gas reserves (2002), 2·8bn. cu. metres.

Minerals. Mining production in 2000 included: chromite, 118,750 tonnes; graphite, 40,328 tonnes; salt, 25,530 tonnes. There have also been discoveries of precious and semi-precious stones in various parts of the country, in particular sapphires, topaz and garnets.

Agriculture. 75–80% of the workforce is employed in agriculture. There were 3·0m. ha of arable land in 2001 and 0·6m. ha of permanent crops. 1·09m. ha were irrigated in 2001. The principal agricultural products in 2000 were (in 1,000 tonnes): rice, 2,300; cassava, 2,228; sugarcane, 2,200; sweet potatoes, 476; potatoes, 293; bananas, 260; mangoes, 204; taro, 155; maize, 150; coconuts, 84; dry beans, 84; oranges, 83. Rice is produced on some 40% of cultivated land.

Cattle breeding and agriculture are the chief occupations. There were, in 2000, 10·36m. cattle, 1·37m. goats, 900,000 pigs, 800,000 sheep and 20m. chickens.

Forestry. In 2000 the area under forests was 11·73m. ha, or 20·2% of the total land area. The forests contain many valuable woods, while gum, resins and plants for tanning, dyeing and medicinal purposes abound. Timber production was 10·01m. cu. metres in 2001.

Fisheries. The catch of fish in 2001 was 135,583 tonnes (78% from marine waters).

INDUSTRY

Industry, hitherto confined mainly to the processing of agricultural products, is now extending to cover other fields.

Labour. In 1996 the workforce was 7,199,000 (55% males). In 1995 approximately 75% of the economically active population were engaged in agriculture, fisheries and forestry.

INTERNATIONAL TRADE

Foreign debt was US$4,518m. in 2002.

Imports and Exports. In 2002 imports (f.o.b.) were valued at US$603m. (US$955m. in 2001) and exports (f.o.b.) at US$486m. (US$928m. in 2001). The principal exports in 1999 were cotton fabrics (13%), cloves (8%), coffee (7%), precious and semi-precious stones (7%) and vanilla (5%). Principal imports in 1999 were machinery and transport equipment (27%), petroleum products (24%), manufactured goods (15%) and foodstuffs (11·5%). Main import suppliers, 1999: France, 20·7%; Iran, 12·4%; Bahrain, 8·7%; China, 6·7%. Main export markets, 1999: France, 37·8%; Singapore, 7·5%; Germany, 6·4%; USA, 5·4%.

COMMUNICATIONS

Roads. In 1999 there were about 49,827 km of roads, 11·6% of which were paved. There were 60,480 passenger cars in 1996, 37,972 trucks and vans and 4,850 buses and coaches. 25 people died in road accidents in 1995.

Rail. In 2000 there were 883 km of railways, all metre gauge. In 2000, 0·2m. passengers and 0·1m. tonnes of freight were transported.

Civil Aviation. There are international airports at Antananarivo (Ivato) and Mahajanga (Amborovy). The national carrier is Air Madagascar, which is 89·5% state-owned. In 1999 it flew 8·7m. km, carrying 317,600 passengers (144,800 on international flights). In 2000 Antananarivo handled 689,210 passengers (350,030 on domestic flights) and 14,914 tonnes of freight.

Shipping. The main ports are Toamasina, Mahajanga, Antsiranana and Toliara. In 2002 the merchant marine totalled 35,000 GRT, including oil tankers 5,000 GRT. In 2000 vessels totalling 4,842,000 NRT entered ports.

Telecommunications. Madagascar had 222,500 telephone subscribers in 2002, equivalent to 14·0 per 1,000 persons, and 46,000 PCs were in use (2·9 per 1,000 persons). In 2002 there were 163,000 mobile phone subscribers. In 2002 there were 55,000 Internet users.

Postal Services. There were 764 post offices in 1998, or one for every 19,700 persons.

SOCIAL INSTITUTIONS

Justice. The Supreme Court and the Court of Appeal are in Antananarivo. In most towns there are Courts of First Instance for civil and commercial cases. For criminal cases there are ordinary criminal courts in most towns. In 1996 government expenditure on public order and safety totalled MGFr59,200m.

The population in penal institutions in July 1999 was 20,109 (130 per 100,000 of national population).

Religion. About 48% of the population practise the traditional religion, 43% are Christians (of whom approximately half are Roman Catholic and half are Protestant, mainly belonging to the Fiangonan'i Jesosy Kristy eto Madagasikara) and 9% are followers of other religions (predominantly Islam). In Sept. 2003 the Roman Catholic church had one cardinal.

Education. Education is compulsory from six to 14 years of age. In 2000–01 there were 46,482 teachers for 2·3m. pupils in primary schools, 382,474 pupils in general programmes at secondary level with 16,795 (1995–96) teachers and 31,386 students at university level. In 1994–95 there were six universities. Adult literacy rate in 2001 was 67·3% (male, 74·2%; female, 60·6%). In 2000–01 total expenditure on education came to 3·2% of GNP.

Health. There were nine hospital beds per 10,000 population in 1990. In 1996 there were 1,470 physicians, 137 dentists, 2,969 nurses and 1,471 midwives. In 1996 government expenditure on health totalled MGFr191,300m.

Welfare. In 1996 government expenditure on social security and welfare totalled MGFr26,000m.

CULTURE

World Heritage Sites. Tsingy de Bemaraha Strict Nature Reserve joined the UNESCO World Heritage List in 1990. The undisturbed forests, lakes and mangrove swamps are the habitat for rare and endangered lemurs and birds. The Royal Hill of Ambohimanga was added in 2001, a royal city and burial site and a symbol of Malagasy identity.

Broadcasting. The government-controlled Radio-Télévision Malagasy is responsible for broadcasting. There are radio programmes in Malagasy and French, and 12 hours TV transmission a day (colour by PAL). In 2000 there were 3·35m. radio sets and in 2001 there were 390,000 TV sets.

Press. In 1996 there were five daily newspapers with a total circulation of 66,000.

Tourism. There were 160,000 tourists in 2000. Receipts totalled US$116m.

DIPLOMATIC REPRESENTATIVES

Of Madagascar in the United Kingdom
Ambassador: Vacant.
Chargé d'Affaires a.i.: Guy Rakotomena (resides at Paris).
Honorary Consul: Stephen Hobbs (16 Lanark Mansions, Pennard Rd, London, W12 8DT).

Of the United Kingdom in Madagascar (Lot II 164 Ter, Alarobia-Amboniloha BP 167, Antananarivo)
Ambassador: Brian Donaldson.

Of Madagascar in the USA (2374 Massachusetts Ave., NW, Washington, D.C., 20008)
Ambassador: Narisoa Rajaonarivony.

Of the USA in Madagascar (14–16 rue Rainitovo, Antsahavola, Antananarivo)
Ambassador: James D. McGee.

Of Madagascar to the United Nations
Ambassador: Zina Andrianarivelo.

Of Madagascar to the European Union
Ambassador: Jean Beriziky.

FURTHER READING

Banque des Données de l'Etat. *Bulletin Mensuel de Statistique*
Allen, P. M., *Madagascar*. Boulder (CO), 1995
Brandt, H. and Brown, M., *Madagascar.* [Bibliography] ABC-Clio, Oxford and Santa Barbara (CA), 1993

National statistical office: Institut National de la Statistique (INSTAT), BP 485 Anosy, Antananarivo 101.
Website (French only): http://www.cite.mg/instat/index.htm

MALAŴI

Dziko la Malaŵi
(Republic of Malaŵi)

Capital: Lilongwe
Population projection, 2010: 13·80m.
GDP per capita, 2002: (PPP$) 580
HDI/world rank: 0·388/165

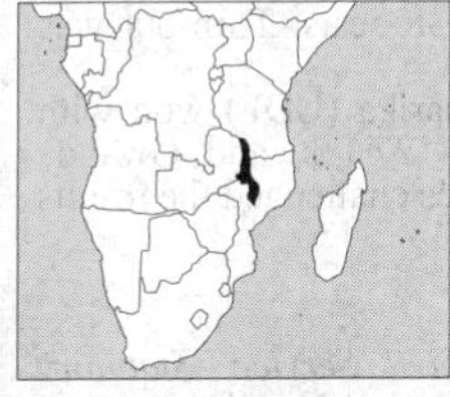

KEY HISTORICAL EVENTS

The explorer David Livingstone reached Lake Nyasa, now Lake Malaŵi, in 1859 and it was the land along the lake's western shore that became, in 1891, the British Protectorate of Nyasaland. In 1884 the British South Africa Company applied for a charter to trade. Pressure on land, the colour bar and other grievances generated Malaŵian resistance. In 1953 Nyasaland was joined with Southern Rhodesia (Zimbabwe) and Northern Rhodesia (Zambia) to form the Federation of Rhodesia and Nyasaland, under British control. This union was dissolved in 1963 when Nyasaland was for a year self-governing, until on 6 July 1964 it became independent, adopting the name of Malaŵi. In 1966 Malaŵi was declared a republic and Dr Hastings Banda became the first president, establishing a one party dictatorship which lasted for 30 years. In 1994 Malaŵi returned to multi-party democracy.

TERRITORY AND POPULATION

Malaŵi lies along the southern and western shores of Lake Malaŵi (the third largest lake in Africa), and is otherwise bounded in the north by Tanzania, south by Mozambique and west by Zambia. Area (including the inland water areas of Lake Malombe, Chilwa, Chiuta and the Malaŵi portion of Lake Malaŵi, which total 24,208 sq. km), 118,484 sq. km (45,747 sq. miles).

Population at census 1998, 9,933,868; density, 83·8 per sq. km. 2002 population estimate: 11,850,000. In 2001, 84·9% of the population was rural.

The UN gives a projected population for 2010 of 13·80m.

Population of main towns (estimated 1998): Blantyre, 2m.; Lilongwe, 1m.; Mzuzu, 100,000; Zomba, 70,000. Population of the regions (1998 census): Northern, 1,233,560; Central, 4,066,340; Southern, 4,633,968.

The official languages are Chichewa, spoken by over 50% of the population, and English.

SOCIAL STATISTICS

2001 estimates: births, 556,000; deaths, 222,000. Estimated rates, 2001 (per 1,000 population): births, 47·8; deaths, 19·1. Annual population growth rate, 1992–02, 1·9%. Expectation of life at birth in 2001 was 37·9 years for males and 39·1 for females. Infant mortality, 2001, 114 per 1,000 live births; fertility rate, 2001, 6·5 births per woman.

CLIMATE

The tropical climate is marked by a dry season from May to Oct. and a wet season for the remaining months. Rainfall amounts are variable, within the range of 29–100" (725–2,500 mm), and maximum temperatures average 75–89°F (24–32°C), and minimum temperatures 58–67°F (14·4–19·4°C). Lilongwe, Jan. 73°F (22·8°C), July 60°F (15·6°C). Annual rainfall 36" (900 mm). Blantyre, Jan. 75°F (23·9°C), July 63°F (17·2°C). Annual rainfall 45" (1,125 mm). Zomba, Jan. 73°F (22·8°C), July 63°F (17·2°C). Annual rainfall 54" (1,344 mm).

CONSTITUTION AND GOVERNMENT

The *President* is also head of government. Malaŵi was a one-party state, but following a referendum on 14 June 1993, in which 63% of votes cast were in favour of reform, a new Constitution was adopted on 17 May 1994 which ended Hastings Banda's life presidency and provided for the holding of multi-party elections. At these Bakili Muluzi was elected president by 47·16% of votes cast against President

Banda and two other opponents. There is a *National Assembly* of 192 members, elected for five-year terms in single-seat constituencies.

National Anthem. 'O God Bless our Land of Malaŵi'; words and tune by M.-F. Sauka.

RECENT ELECTIONS

At parliamentary elections of 18 May 2004 the Malaŵi Congress Party (MCP—formerly the only legal party) won 59 seats; the United Democratic Front (UDF), 49; and the Mgwirizano coalition, 27. Independents took 38 seats. Turn-out was 52%.

At the concurrent presidential elections Bingu wa Mutharika (UDF) won with 35·9% of the vote, ahead of John Tembo (MCP), with 27·1%, and Gwanda Chakuamba (Mgwirizano) with 25·7%. Both losing candidates challenged the results and the fairness of the elections.

CURRENT ADMINISTRATION

President and Minister Responsible for Defence, the Civil Service, Statutory Corporations and Privatization: Dr Bingu wa Mutharika; b. 1934 (Democratic Progressive Party; sworn in on 24 May 2004).

President Mutharika was sworn into office despite protests from his two opponents in the May elections. In Feb. 2005 he left the UDF after a power struggle with its chairman, former president Bakili Muluzi, and launched a new party, the Democratic Progressive Party. The 'National Unity' government consisted of the following in March 2005:

Vice President and Minister of Water Development: Dr Cassim Chilumpha.

Minister of Agriculture, Irrigation and Food Security: Gwanda Chakuamba. *Economic Planning and Development:* David Faiti. *Education and Human Resources:* Yusuf Mwawa. *Industry, Science and Technology:* Khumbo Chirwa. *Finance:* Goodall Gondwe. *Foreign Affairs:* Davis Katsonga. *Health:* Dr Hetherwick Ntaba. *Information, Communications and Tourism:* Dr Kenneth Lipenga. *Home Affairs and Internal Security:* Uladi Mussa. *Justice and Constitutional Affairs:* Henry Phoya. *Labour and Vocational Training:* Jaffalie Mussa. *Lands, Housing and Surveys:* Bazuka Mhango. *Local Government and Rural Development:* Dr George Chaponda. *Mines, Natural Resources and Environment:* Eunice Kazembe. *Social Development and Persons with Disabilities:* Clement Chiwaya. *Trade and Private Sector Development:* Dr Martin Kansichi. *Youth, Sports and Culture:* Henry Chimunthu Banda. *Transport and Public Works:* Henry Mussa. *Women, Child Welfare and Community Services:* Joyce Banda.

Government Website: http://www.malawi.gov.mw

DEFENCE

All services form part of the Army. Defence expenditure totalled US$11m. in 2003 (US$1 per capita), representing 0·7% of GDP.

Army. Personnel (2002) 5,300. In addition there is a paramilitary mobile police force totalling 1,500.

Navy. The Navy, based at Monkey Bay on Lake Nyasa, numbered 220 personnel in 2002.

Air Wing. The Air Wing acts as infantry support and numbered 80 in 1999 with no combat aircraft.

INTERNATIONAL RELATIONS

Malaŵi is a member of the UN, WTO, the Commonwealth, African Development Bank, COMESA (the Common Market for Eastern and Southern Africa), the African Union and SADC and is an ACP member state of the ACP-EU relationship.

ECONOMY

Agriculture accounted for 36·7% of GDP in 2002, industry 14·9% and services 48·4%.

Overview. A privatization programme began in 1996. Of 100 state-owned enterprises, 36 had been privatized by 2002.

Currency. The unit of currency is the *kwacha* (MWK) of 100 *tambala*. Foreign exchange reserves were US$178m. and gold reserves 10,000 troy oz in May 2002. Foreign exchange controls were abolished in Feb. 1994. Inflation has fallen from 83·1% in 1995 to 27·2% in 2001 and further to 14·1% in 2002. Total money supply in Dec. 2001 was K.9,829m.

Budget. Budget (in K.1bn.):

	1998	*1999*	*2000*	*2001*
Revenue	10·84	14·63	20·44	22·60
Expenditure	16·41	23·19	35·82	16·05

Performance. Real GDP growth was negative in 2001, at –4·2%, but there was then a slight recovery, with growth of 1·8% in 2002. Total GDP was US$1·7bn. in 2003.

Banking and Finance. The central bank and bank of issue is the Reserve Bank of Malaŵi (founded 1964). The *Governor* is Dr Elias Ngalande. In 2002 there were four commercial banks, one development bank, three merchant banks and a savings bank.

There is a stock exchange in Blantyre.

ENERGY AND NATURAL RESOURCES

Environment. Carbon dioxide emissions from the consumption and flaring of fossil fuels in 2002 were the equivalent of 0·1 tonnes per capita.

Electricity. The Electricity Supply Commission of Malaŵi is the sole supplier. Installed capacity was 0·2m. kW in 2000. Production was approximately 886m. kWh in 2000; consumption per capita was an estimated 78 kWh. Only 4% of the population has access to electricity.

Oil and Gas. In 1997 Malaŵi and Mozambique came to an agreement on the construction of an oil pipeline between the two countries.

Minerals. Mining operations have been limited to small-scale production of coal, limestone, rubies and sapphires, but companies are now moving in to start exploration programmes. Bauxite reserves are estimated at 29m. tonnes and there are proven reserves of clays, diamonds, glass and silica sands, graphite, limestone, mercurate, phosphates, tanzanite, titanium and uranium. Output: limestone (1999), 171,900 tonnes; gemstones (2000), 16,390 kg.

Agriculture. Malaŵi is predominantly an agricultural country. Agricultural produce contributes 90% of export earnings. There were 2·2m. ha of arable land in 2001 and 140,000 ha of permanent crops. Maize is the main subsistence crop and is grown by over 95% of all smallholders. Tobacco is the chief cash crop, employing 80% of the workforce, generating 35% of GDP and providing 70% of export earnings. Also important are groundnuts, cassava, millet and rice. There are large plantations which produce sugar, tea and coffee. Production (2000, in 1,000 tonnes): maize, 2,300; sugarcane, 2,000; potatoes, 1,700; cassava, 900; plantains, 200; tobacco, 120; groundnuts, 110; bananas, 93; rice, 87; dry beans, 84; sorghum, 55; tea, 50.

Livestock in 2000: cattle, 760,000; goats, 1,270,000; pigs, 240,000; sheep, 115,000; chickens, 15m.

Forestry. In 2000 the area under forests was 2·56m. ha, or 27·2% of the total land area. Timber production in 2001 was 5·52m. cu. metres.

Fisheries. Landings in 2001 were 40,619 tonnes, entirely from inland waters.

INDUSTRY

Index of industrial production in 2001 (1984 = 100): total general industrial production, 101·9; of this goods for the domestic market were at 73·2 and export goods were at 101·5. Electricity and water were at 231·7.

Labour. The labour force in 1996 was 4,807,000 (51% males). Approximately 85% of the economically active population in 1995 were engaged in agriculture, fisheries and forestry.

INTERNATIONAL TRADE

External debt was US$2·91bn. in 2002.

Imports and Exports. In 2001 exports amounted to K.36·22bn. (K.23·63bn. in 2000) and imports K.39·48bn. (K.32·25bn. in 2000). Major exports, 2001 (in K.1bn.): tobacco, 18·36; and sugar, 7·85. Major imports, 2001 (in K.1bn.): fuel oils, 5·32.

Principal destinations for exports in 2001 were South Africa (19·1%), USA (15·4%), Germany (11·2%), Japan (7·6%). Main sources of imports were South Africa (39·7%), Zimbabwe (16·0%), Zambia (10·9%), USA (2·6%).

Trade Fairs. The annual Malaŵi International Trade Fair takes place in Blantyre, the commercial capital.

COMMUNICATIONS

Roads. The road network consisted of an estimated 28,400 km in 1999, of which 18·5% were paved.

Rail. Malaŵi Railways operate 797 km on 1,067 mm gauge, providing links to the Mozambican ports of Beira and Nacala. In 1999–2000 passenger-km travelled came to 19m. and freight tonne-km to 62m.

Civil Aviation. The national carrier is Air Malaŵi. It flies to a number of regional centres in Ethiopia, Kenya, South Africa, Zambia and Zimbabwe. In 1999 scheduled airline traffic of Malaŵi-based carriers flew 2·4m. km, carrying 112,000 passengers (63,000 on international flights). There are international airports at Lilongwe (Lilongwe International Airport) and Blantyre (Chileka). In 2000 Lilongwe handled 175,915 passengers (120,575 on international flights) and 4,182 tonnes of freight, and Blantyre had 101,809 passengers (53,426 on international flights) and 680 tonnes of freight.

Shipping. In 1995 lake ships carried 169,000 passengers and 6,000 tonnes of freight.

Telecommunications. Malaŵi had 159,100 telephone subscribers in 2002, or 15·2 for every 1,000 population, and 14,000 PCs were in use (1·3 per 1,000 persons). Mobile phone subscribers numbered 86,000 in 2002 and there were 1,300 fax machines in 1999. There were 27,000 Internet users in 2002.

Postal Services. In 1998 there were 314 post offices.

SOCIAL INSTITUTIONS

Justice. Justice is administered in the High Court and in the magistrates' courts. Traditional courts were abolished in 1994. Appeals from magistrates' courts lie to the High Court, and appeals from the High Court to Malaŵi's Supreme Court of Appeal.

The population in penal institutions in Nov. 2003 was 8,566 (70 per 100,000 of national population).

Religion. 2001 estimates: 2,600,000 Roman Catholic; 2,070,000 Protestant (mostly Presbyterian); 1,770,000 African Christian; 1,560,000 Muslim; 820,000 traditional beliefs. The remainder follow other religions.

Education. The adult literacy rate in 2001 was 61·0% (75·0% among males and 47·6% among females). Fees for primary education were abolished in 1994. In 2001 the number of pupils in primary schools was 3·19m. (53,444 teachers). The primary school course is of eight years' duration, followed by a four-year secondary course. In 2001 there were 294,638 pupils in secondary schools (7,593 teachers). English is taught from the 1st year and becomes the general medium of instruction from the 4th year.

The University of Malaŵi (consisting of four colleges and one polytechnic) had 4,127 students and 535 academic staff in 2002. A new university at Mzuzu opened in 1998 and provides courses for secondary school teachers.

In 1999–2000 total expenditure on education came to 4·2% of GNP.

Health. In 1989 there were 186 doctors, giving a provision of one doctor for every 49,118 persons—the lowest ratio in the world. In 1989 there were 284 nurses and 5 pharmacists. In 1987 there were 395 hospitals with a provision of 16 beds per 10,000 inhabitants.

CULTURE

The dances of the Malaŵi are a strong part of their culture. The National Dance Troupe (formerly the Kwacha Cultural Troupe) formed in Nov. 1987 as a part of the Department of Arts and Crafts of the Ministry of Education.

World Heritage Sites. Malaŵi has one site on the UNESCO World Heritage List: Lake Malaŵi National Park (inscribed on the list in 1984).

Broadcasting. The Malaŵi Broadcasting Corporation, a statutory body, broadcasts in English, Chichewa, Yao, Tumbuka, Lomwe Sena and Tonga. There were 5·4m. radio sets in 2000, up from 260,000 in 1980. No other country had such a large percentage increase in the number of radio receivers in use over the same period. There is a national radio station in Blantyre providing two channels and five private radio stations have been operating since 1997.

A national television station opened in 1999. There were 40,000 sets in use in 2001.

Press. There are more than 16 newspapers in circulation, the main ones being: *The Daily Times* (English, Monday to Friday), 17,000 copies daily; *The Nation* (English, Monday to Friday), 16,000 copies daily; *Malaŵi News* (English and Chichewa, Saturdays), 23,000 copies weekly; and *Weekend Nation* (English and Chichewa, Saturdays), 16,000 copies weekly. In addition there is *Odini* (English and Chichewa), 8,500 copies fortnightly; *Boma Lathu* (Chichewa), 150,000 copies monthly; *Za Alimi* (English and Chichewa), 10,000 copies monthly.

Tourism. There were 228,000 tourists in 2000 bringing in revenue of US$27m.

Museums and Galleries. The main attraction is the Museum of Malaŵi.

DIPLOMATIC REPRESENTATIVES

Of Malaŵi in the United Kingdom (33 Grosvenor St., London, W1K 4QT)
High Commissioner: Ibrahim Laston Bwanausi Milazi.

Of the United Kingdom in Malaŵi (PO Box 30042, Lilongwe 3)
High Commissioner: Norman Ling.

Of Malaŵi in the USA (1156 15th St, NW, Suite 320, Washington, D.C., 20005)
Ambassador: Bernardo Sande.

Of the USA in Malaŵi (Area 40, Plot 24, Kenyatta Road, Lilongwe 3)
Ambassador: Vacant.
Chargé d'Affaires a.i.: David Gilmour.

Of Malaŵi to the United Nations
Ambassador: Brown Chimphamba.

Of Malaŵi to the European Union
Ambassador: Dr Jerry Aleksander Alikopaga Jana.

FURTHER READING

National Statistical Office. *Monthly Statistical Bulletin*
Ministry of Economic Planning and Development. *Economic Report.* Annual

Decalo, S., *Malaŵi.* [Bibliography] 2nd ed. ABC-Clio, Oxford and Santa Barbara (CA), 1995
Kalinga, O. J. M. and Crosby, C. A., *Historical Dictionary of Malaŵi.* Scarecrow Press, Lanham, Maryland, 1993

National statistical office: National Statistical Office, POB 333, Zomba.
Website: http://www.nso.malawi.net/

MALAYSIA

Persekutuan Tanah Malaysia
(Federation of Malaysia)

Capital: Putrajaya (Administrative), Kuala Lumpur (Financial)
Population projection, 2010: 27·51m.
GDP per capita, 2002: (PPP$) 9,120
HDI/world rank: 0·793/59

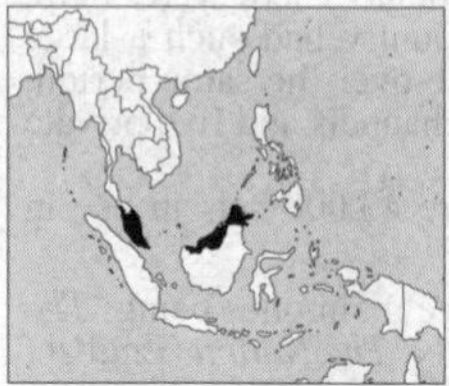

KEY HISTORICAL EVENTS

Excavations at Niah in Sarawak have uncovered evidence of human settlement from 38,000 BC. Indian traders introduced the Sanskrit language. Hinduism and Buddhism gained a foothold and were practised alongside traditional animist beliefs.

The Hinduized Srivijaya empire, centred on Palembang in Sumatra, ruled until the late 13th century when Sumatra fell to a Javan invasion, after which the king of Sukothai sent forces into the Malay Peninsula. The Sumatran kingdom of Melayu next ruled over the southern part of the Peninsula, followed by the Madjapahit, the last Hindu empire of Java. In the mid-15th century Melaka emerged as the key trading port in the region. A pattern of government was established in Melaka that became the basis of Malay identity. Gujarati sailors introduced Islam to the region through Melaka in the 15th century. In 1511 the port was captured by the Portuguese navigator Alfonso de Albuquerque.

The sultanates of Johor and Aceh and the Portuguese vied for control over the Straits of Melaka. The early 17th century saw the arrival of Dutch trading ships. The United Netherlands East India Company formed an alliance with Johor to besiege Melaka. After it was captured in 1641, the Dutch brokered a peace deal between Aceh and Johor.

In the mid-18th century Johor and Melaka became entrepôts for the trade in tea between China and Europe. Ships owned by the British East India Company (EIC) began plying the Melaka straits in greater numbers. The British sought to increase their control over the maritime route to China and Sir Thomas Stamford Raffles was ordered to establish an entrepôt in the southern reaches of the Melaka Straits. In 1819 he signed a treaty with Sultan Husein Syah of Johor and founded Singapore. Five years later the British formally acquired Melaka from the Dutch. From 1826 Penang, Singapore and Melaka were ruled by the British authorities in India under a joint administration known as the Straits Settlements. In 1832 Singapore replaced Penang as the capital of the Straits Settlements.

The discovery of tin deposits at Larut (western Malay Peninsula) in the 1850s led to large-scale immigration by Chinese miners and labourers. With piracy on the increase in the Melaka straits, merchants asked the British to restore order. In 1874 the British Residential system was extended to Perak, Selangor and Sungei Ujung. In each region, a British Resident functioned as an adviser to the Malay Sultan. In 1896 the three states and Pahang were grouped together as the Federated Malay States, presided over by a British resident general at Kuala Lumpur. Tamils from south India and Sri Lanka arrived as indentured labourers. Negotiations between the British and Siamese in the early years of the 20th century led to British control over the northern states of Kedah, Perlis, Kelantan and Terengganu. Between 1905–08 Malaysia experienced a rubber boom, in line with the expansion of the motor car industry in Europe and North America. Rubber plants, originally from the forests of Brazil and introduced to Malaysia in the 1880s, were planted in every state in Malaysia by 1908 and by 1913 rubber had eclipsed tin as the country's chief export.

Rubber, tin and oil made Malaya a focus for Imperial Japan from early in the Second World War. When Pearl Harbor and Hong Kong came under attack from Japanese forces in Dec. 1941, other Japanese divisions came ashore at Kota Bharu and Miri. British forces retreated south to Singapore, which capitulated on 15 Feb. 1942. Thailand allied itself with Japan and was granted control of the northern Malay states in 1943.

When the British returned in 1946 they reorganized the colony into the Malayan Union. The Malay elite, fearing equal rights for Chinese and Indian subjects, demanded the continuation of individual sultanates. Forced to compromise, Britain established the Federation of Malaya in Feb. 1948, administered by a high commissioner in Kuala Lumpur. Within months the Federation was under attack from the Chinese-dominated Malayan Communist Party (MCP). The Communist insurrection hastened the transition to Malayan independence. The first federal-level election was won by the Alliance Party, a loose coalition of Malay, Chinese and Indian parties, led by Tunku (Prince) Abdul Rahman. On 31 Aug. 1957 the Federation of Malaya became independent with Tunku Abdul Rahman as the first prime minister.

The concept of Malaysia, as a broader federation including Sabah, Sarawak, Singapore and the British protectorate of Brunei, took shape in Sept. 1963, though Brunei declined to join. The new nation was opposed by Indonesia and Singapore seceded in 1965. Tension between the Chinese and Malay communities led to inter-ethnic violence, reaching a peak in the riots of May 1969. After parliamentary rule was restored in 1971, Abdul Razak launched a series of five-year plans to eradicate poverty and to restructure the economy.

Mahathir Mohamad won the 1981 elections for the United Malays National Organization (UMNO). Mahathir shifted the economy away from commodities towards manufacturing, services and tourism. A prolonged spell of economic growth and stability was broken by the 1997–98 recession but Mahathir refused to accept financial aid from the International Monetary Fund. In Sept. 1998 Mahathir dismissed Anwar Ibrahim, his finance minister, deputy prime minister and heir apparent. Anwar was found guilty of corruption charges in 1999. Mahathir stepped down as prime minister in Oct. 2003, to be succeeded by Abdullah Ahmad Badawi. Badawi won a landslide victory in the March 2004 general election for the National Front and released Anwar from prison in Sept. 2004.

TERRITORY AND POPULATION

The federal state of Malaysia comprises the 13 states and three federal territories of Peninsular Malaysia, bounded in the north by Thailand, and with the island of Singapore as an enclave on its southern tip; and, on the island of Borneo to the east, the state of Sabah (which includes the federal territory of the island of Labuan), and the state of Sarawak, with Brunei as an enclave, both bounded in the south by Indonesia and in the northwest and northeast by the South China and Sulu Seas.

The area of Malaysia is 329,847 sq. km (127,354 sq. miles) and the population (2000 census) 23,274,690; density, 70·6 per sq. km. Malaysia's national waters cover 515,256 sq. km. In 2001, 58·1% of the population lived in urban areas.

The UN gives a projected population for 2010 of 27·51m.

The growth of the population has been:

Year	*Peninsular Malaysia*	*Sarawak*	*Sabah/Labuan*	*Total Malaysia*
1980	11,426,613	1,307,582	1,011,046	13,745,241
1991	14,797,616	1,718,380	1,863,659	18,379,655
2000	18,523,632	2,071,506	2,679,552	23,274,690

The areas, populations and chief towns of the states and federal territories are:

Peninsular States	*Area (in sq. km)*	*Population (2000 census)*	*Chief Town*	*Population (1991 census)*
Johor	18,987	2,740,625	Johor Bharu	328,436
Kedah	9,425	1,649,756	Alor Setar	124,412
Kelantan	15,024	1,313,014	Kota Bharu	219,582
Kuala Lumpur[1]	243	1,379,310	Kuala Lumpur	1,145,342[1]
Melaka	1,652	635,791	Melaka	75,909
Negeri Sembilan	6,644	859,924	Seremban	182,869
Pahang	35,965	1,288,376	Kuantan	199,484
Perak	21,005	2,051,236	Ipoh	382,853
Perlis	795	204,450	Kangar	14,247
Pulau Pinang	1,031	1,313,449	Penang (Georgetown)	219,603
Putrajaya[1]	50	. . .[2]	Putrajaya	. . .
Selangor	7,910	4,188,876[2]	Shah Alam	102,019
Terengganu	12,955	898,825	Kuala Terengganu	228,119
Other states				
Labuan[1]	92	76,067	Victoria	. . .
Sabah	73,619	2,603,485	Kota Kinabalu	76,120
Sarawak	124,450	2,071,506	Kuching	148,059

[1]Federal territory. [2]Putrajaya figure included in population of Selangor.

Other large cities (1997 estimate): Petaling Jaya (254,350), Kelang (243,355), Taiping (183,261), Sibu (126,381), Sandakan (125,841) and Miri (87,167).

Putrajaya, a planned new city described as an 'intelligent garden city', became the administrative capital of Malaysia in 1999 and was created a federal territory on 1 Feb. 2001.

Malay is the national language of the country—53% of the population are Malays. The government promotes the use of the national language to foster national unity. However, the people are free to use their mother tongue and other languages. English as the second language is widely used in business. In Peninsular Malaysia Chinese dialects and Tamil are also spoken. In Sabah there are numerous tribal dialects and Chinese (Mandarin and Hakka dialects predominate). In Sarawak Mandarin and numerous tribal languages are spoken. In addition to Malays, 26% of the population are Chinese, 12% other indigenous ethnic groups, 8% Indians and 1% others.

SOCIAL STATISTICS

2001 births, 535,500; deaths, 105,700. 2001 rates (per 1,000 population): birth, 22·3; death, 4·4. Life expectancy, 2001: males, 70·4 years; females, 75·3 years. Annual population growth rate, 1992–02, 2·4%. Infant mortality, 2001, seven per 1,000 live births; fertility rate, 2001, 3·0 births per woman. Today only 8% of Malaysians live below the poverty line, compared to 50% in the early 1970s.

CLIMATE

Malaysia lies near the equator between latitudes 1° and 7° North and longitudes 100° and 119° East. Malaysia is subject to maritime influence and the interplay of wind systems which originate in the Indian Ocean and the South China Sea. The year is generally divided into the South-East and the North-East Monsoon seasons. The average daily temperature throughout Malaysia varies from 21°C to 32°C. Humidity is high.

CONSTITUTION AND GOVERNMENT

The Constitution of Malaysia is based on the Constitution of the former Federation of Malaya, but includes safeguards for the special interests of Sabah and Sarawak. It was amended in 1983. The Constitution provides for one of the Rulers of the Malay States to be elected from among themselves to be the *Yang di-Pertuan Agong* (Supreme Head of the Federation). He holds office for a period of five years. The Rulers also elect from among themselves a Deputy Supreme Head of State, also for a period of five years. In Feb. 1993 the Rulers accepted constitutional amendments abolishing their legal immunity.

Supreme Head of State (Yang di-Pertuan Agong). HRH Syed Sirajuddin ibni al-Marhum Syed Putra Jamalullail, b. 1943, acceded 13 Dec. 2001.

Raja of Perlis. HRH Syed Sirajuddin ibni al-Marhum Syed Putra Jamalullail, b. 1943, acceded 17 April 2000.

Sultan of Kedah. HRH Tuanku Haji Abdul Halim Mu'adzam Shah ibni Al-Marhum Sultan Badlishah, b. 1927, acceded 14 July 1958.

Sultan of Johor. HRH Sultan Mahmood Iskandar ibni Al-Marhum Sultan Ismail, b. 1932, acceded 11 May 1981 (Supreme Head of State from 26 April 1984 to 25 April 1989), returned as Sultan of Johor 26 April 1989.

Sultan of Perak. HRH Sultan Azlan Shah Muhibbuddin Shah ibni Al-Marhum Sultan Yussuf Izzuddin Ghafarullahu-luhu Shah, b. 1928, acceded 3 Feb. 1984.

Yang Di-Pertuan Besar Negeri Sembilan. HRH Tuanku Jaafar ibni Al-Marhum Tuanku Abdul Rahman, b. 1922, acceded 18 April 1967.

Sultan of Kelantan. HRH Sultan Ismail Petra ibni Al-Marhum Sultan Yahya Petra, b. 1949, appointed 29 March 1979.

Sultan of Terengganu. HRH Sultan Mizan Zainal Abidin ibni al-Mahrum Sultan Mahmud Al-Muktafi Billah Shah, b. 1962, acceded 15 May 1998.

Sultan of Pahang. Sultan Haji Ahmad Shah Al-Musta'in Billah ibni Al-Marhum Sultan Abu Bakar Ri'Ayatuddin Al-Mu'Adzam Shah, b. 1930, acceded 8 May 1975.

Sultan of Selangor. HRH Sharafuddin Idris Shah ibni al-Marhum Sultan Salehuddin Abdul Aziz Shah, b. 1945, appointed 22 Nov. 2001.

Yang di-Pertua Negeri Pulau Pinang. HE Datuk Abdul Rahman Haji Abbas, b. 1938, appointed 1 May 2001.

Yang di Pertua Negeri Melaka. HE Tan Sri Khalil Yaakob, b. 1937, appointed 4 June 2004.

Yang di-Pertua Negeri Sarawak. HE Tun Datuk Patinggi Abang Mohamad Salaheddin, b. 1921, acceded 4 Dec. 2000.

Yang di-Pertua Negeri Sabah. HE Datuk Ahmad Shah Abdullah, b. 1946, acceded 1 Jan. 2003.

The federal parliament consists of the *Yang di-Pertuan Agong* and two *Majlis* (Houses of Parliament) known as the *Dewan Negara* (Senate) of 69 members (26 elected, two by each state legislature; and 43 appointed by the *Yang di-Pertuan Agong*) and *Dewan Rakyat* (House of Representatives) of 219 members. Appointment to the Senate is for three years. The maximum life of the House of Representatives is five years, subject to its dissolution at any time by the *Yang di-Pertuan Agong* on the advice of his Ministers.

National Anthem. 'Negaraku' ('My Country'); words collective, tune by Pierre de Béranger.

RECENT ELECTIONS

Elections to the *Dewan Rakyat* and 11 state assemblies were held on 21 March 2004. The 14-party National Front Coalition (BN; Barisan Nasional) gained 198 seats, obtaining 64·4% of the votes cast (the predominant partner, the United Malays National Organization (UMNO), won 109 seats). The Democratic Action Party (Parti Tindakan Deomkratik) won 12 seats (9·5%), the Islamic Party of Malaysia (PAS) won seven seats (15·8%) and the People's Justice Party (Parti Keadilan Rakyat) won one seat. One non-partisan was elected. The National Front Coalition also gained a majority in every state assembly except Kelantan, held by PAS, which lost Terengganu. Turn-out was 63·6%.

CURRENT ADMINISTRATION

In March 2005 the government comprised:

Prime Minister, Minister of Finance and Internal Security: Dato' Seri Abdullah bin Haji Ahmad Badawi; b. 1939 (UMNO; took office on 31 Oct. 2003).

Deputy Prime Minister and Minister of Defence: Dato' Sri Haji Mohd Najib bin Tun Haji Abdul Razak. *Minister of Transport:* Datuk Seri Chan Kong Choy. *Energy, Water and Communications:* Datuk Seri Dr Lim Keng Yaik. *Entrepreneurial and Co-operative Development:* Datuk Mohamed Khaled Nordin. *Works:* Dato' Seri S. Samy Vellu. *International Trade and Industry:* Datuk Seri Rafidah binti Aziz. *Education:* Datuk Hishammuddin Tun Hussein. *Rural and Regional Development:* Datuk Abdul Aziz Shamsuddin. *Agriculture and Agro-Based Industry:* Tan Sri Muhyiddin Yassin. *Domestic Trade and Consumer Affairs:* Datuk Shafie Apdal. *Health:* Datuk Dr Chua Soi Lek. *Foreign Affairs:* Datuk Seri Syed Hamid bin Syed Jaafar Albar. *Information:* Datuk Paduka Abdul Kadir Sheikh Fadzir. *Arts, Culture and Tourism:* Datuk Seri Dr Rais Yatim. *Human Resources:* Datuk Dr Fong Chan Onn. *Natural Resources and Environment:* Datuk Seri Adenan Satem. *Housing and Local Government:* Dato' Ong Ka Ting. *Women, Family and Community Development:* Datuk Seri Shahrizat binte Abdul Jalil. *Youth and Sports:* Datuk Azalina Othman Said. *Home Affairs:* Datuk Azmi Khalid. *Higher Education:* Datuk Dr Shafie Mohd Salleh. *Science, Technology and Innovations:* Datuk Dr Jamaluddin Jarjis. *Tourism:* Datuk Leo Michael Toyad. *Plantation Industries and Commodities:* Datuk Peter Chin Fah Kui. *Federal Territories:* Tan Sri Mohamed Isa Abdul Samad. *Second Minister of Finance:* Tan Sri Nor Mohamed Yakcop. *Ministers in Prime Minister's Department:* Tan Sri Datuk Seri Paglima Bernard Giluk Dompok, Dato' Seri Mohamad Nazri bin Abdul Aziz, Datuk Mustapha bin Mohamed, Datuk Seri Mohd Radzi bin Sheik Ahmad, Prof. Datuk Dr Abdullah bin Md. Zin, Datuk Dr Maximus Johnity Ongkili.

Office of the Prime Minister: http://www.pmo.gov.my

DEFENCE

The Constitution provides for the Head of State to be the Supreme Commander of the Armed Forces who exercises his powers in accordance with the advice of the Cabinet. Under their authority, the Armed Forces Council is responsible for all matters relating to the Armed Forces other than those relating to their operational use. The Ministry of Defence has established bilateral defence relations with countries within as well as outside the region. Malaysia is a member of the Five Powers Defence Arrangement with Australia, New Zealand, Singapore and the UK.

The Malaysian Armed Forces has participated in 16 UN peacekeeping missions in Africa, the Middle East, Indo-China and Europe. Five of the operations are military contingents, the remainder are Observer Groups.

In 2003 defence expenditure totalled US$2,412m. (US$97 per capita), representing 2·3% of GDP.

Army. Strength (2002) about 80,000. There is a paramilitary Police General Operations Force of 18,000 and a People's Volunteer Corps of 240,000 of which 17,500 are armed.

Navy. The Royal Malaysian Navy is commanded by the Chief of the Navy from the integrated Ministry of Defence in Kuala Lumpur. There are four operational areas: No. 1, Kuantan Naval Base, covering the eastern peninsular coast; No. 2, Labuan naval Base, covering the East Malaysia coast; No. 3, Lumut Naval Base, covering the western peninsular coast; and No. 4, Kuching Naval Base, covering Sarawak's coast. The peacetime tasks include fishery protection and anti-piracy patrols. The fleet includes four frigates. A Naval aviation squadron operates six armed helicopters.

Navy personnel in 2002 totalled 12,000 including 160 Naval Air personnel. There were 1,000 naval reserves.

Air Force. Formed on 1 June 1958, the Royal Malaysian Air Force is equipped primarily to provide air defence and air support for the Army, Navy and Police. Its secondary role is to render assistance to government departments and civilian organizations.

Personnel (2002) totalled about 8,000, with 95 combat aircraft including F-5Es, MiG-29s and Bae *Hawks*. There were 600 Air Force reserves.

INTERNATIONAL RELATIONS

Malaysia was in dispute with Indonesia over sovereignty of two islands in the Celebes Sea. Both countries agreed to accept the Judgment of the International Court of Justice which decided in favour of Malaysia in Dec. 2002.

Malaysia is a member of the UN, WTO, BIS, the Commonwealth, Asian Development Bank, Colombo Plan, APEC, ASEAN, Mekong Group, Organization of Islamic Conference and Islamic Development Bank.

ECONOMY

In 2002 agriculture accounted for 9·2% of GDP, industry 47·3% and services 43·5%.

Overview. Malaysia is still recovering from the Asian crisis of 1997, when the *ringgit* devalued 48%. In 2002 real GDP grew by 4·1% from the 0·3% growth seen in 2001. Growth was strongest in the services and mining sectors. Growth on the demand side has been helped by low unemployment, lower income taxes, low interest rates and increased access to credit. Fiscal policy has been the main counter-cyclical instrument used by the authorities. The fiscal deficit can be financed domestically owing to a high savings rate (34% of GDP in 2002) and sufficient liquidity in the banking system. The exchange rate is fixed to the US dollar. However, in 2003 and 2004 the continued fall of the dollar raised questions on whether the ringgit is undervalued. Exports grew by 6% in 2002 and have since continued to expand. In 2003 the overall balance of payments improved on account of the large surplus in the current account, larger inflows of long-term capital and a lower net outflow of short-term capital. The Non-Performing Loans ration of the Malaysian banking system has declined steadily to 13·9% in mid-2003, although progress still needs to be made in the merchant banking sector.

Currency. The unit of currency is the Malaysian *ringgit* (RM) of 100 *sen*, which is pegged to the US dollar at 3·8 ringgit = 1 US$. Foreign exchange reserves were US$32,287m. and gold reserves 1·17m. troy oz in June 2002. In 2002 there was inflation of 1·8%. Total money supply in June 2002 was RM85,913m.

Budget. Revenue and expenditure for calendar years, in RM1bn.:

	1999	*2000*	*2001*[1]	*2002*[1]
Revenue	58·7	61·9	79·6	83·6
Operating expenditure	46·7	56·5	63·8	66·7

[1]Estimate.

Sources of revenue in 2000: direct taxes, 47·2% (55·2%—2002 est.); indirect taxes, 29·1% (25·5%—2002 est.); non-tax revenue, 23·7% (19·3%—2002 est.).

Federal government net development (in addition to operating) expenditure in 2000: RM25,032m. Social services accounted for 33·2% of operating expenditure in 2000, general administration 14·9%, security 12·3% and economic services 11·7%.

Performance. Malaysia was badly affected by the Asian financial crisis, with the economy contracting by 7·4% in 1998. However, there was a recovery in 1999, with growth of 6·1%, rising to 8·9% in 2000. There was a recession in the second half of 2001 although the economy still expanded by 0·3% in the year as a whole. 2002 saw growth of 4·1%, rising to 5·3% in 2003. Total GDP in 2003 was US$103·2bn.

Banking and Finance. The central bank and bank of issue is the Bank Negara Malaysia (*Governor*, Dr Zeti Akhtar Aziz). In 2002 there were 47 domestic commercial banks, merchant banks and finance companies. Total deposits with commercial banks at 31 Dec. 1996 were RM194,974m. The largest commercial bank is Malayan Banking Berhad (Maybank), with assets in June 2003 of RM127·6bn. The Islamic Bank of Malaysia began operations in July 1983. In 1998 there were 59 banks with off-shore licences in Labuan.

There is a stock exchange at Kuala Lumpur, known as BSKL.

ENERGY AND NATURAL RESOURCES

Environment. Malaysia's carbon dioxide emissions from the consumption and flaring of fossil fuels in 2002 were the equivalent of 5·9 tonnes per capita.

Electricity. Installed capacity in 2000, 13·8m. kW. In 2000 an estimated 69,280m. kWh were generated. Consumption per capita in 2000 was about 2,977 kWh.

Oil and Gas. Crude petroleum reserves, 2002, 3·0bn. bbls. Oil production, 2003, was 38·8m. tonnes. Natural gas reserves, 2002, 2,120bn. cu. metres. Production of natural gas in 2002 was 50·3bn. cu. metres. In April 1998 Malaysia and Thailand agreed to share equally the natural gas jointly produced in an offshore area which both countries claim as their own territory. It was expected that from 2001 around 18m. cu. metres of natural gas would be produced in the area every day.

Minerals. In 1998 mining contributed 6·9% of GDP. Bauxite production in 2001 was 64,000 tonnes; gold, 3,965 kg. 2000: coal, 382,942 tonnes; iron ore, 259,000 tonnes; tin, 6,307 tonnes.

Agriculture. In 2002 agriculture contributed 9·2% of GDP. There were 1·80m. ha of arable land in 2001 and 5·79m. ha of permanent crops. In 2001 approximately 365,000 ha were irrigated. Production in 2000 (in 1,000 tonnes): palm kernels, 3,163; sugarcane, 1,600; rice, 1,382; rubber, 917; coconuts, 683; bananas, 545; cassava, 380. Livestock (2000): pigs, 1·83m.; cattle, 734,000; goats 238,000; sheep, 145,000; buffaloes, 142,000; chickens, 120m. Malaysia's output of palm kernels is the highest of any country. Only Thailand and Indonesia produce more rubber.

Forestry. In 2000 there were 19·29m. ha of forests, or 58·7% of the total land area. Timber production in 2001 was 16·35m. cu. metres.

Fisheries. Total catch in 2002 amounted to 1,275,555 tonnes, almost entirely from sea fishing.

INDUSTRY

The leading companies by market capitalization in Malaysia, excluding banking and finance, in May 2004 were: Telekom Malaysia (US$8·5bn.); Tenaga Nasional, an electricity company (US$7·9bn.); and Malaysia International Shipping (US$5·8bn.).

In 2001 industry accounted for 48·3% of GDP, with manufacturing contributing 30·5%. Production figures for 2001 (in 1,000 tonnes): cement, 13,820; palm oil, 11,660; distillate fuel oil (2000), 7,935; petrol (2000), 3,744; residual fuel oil (2000),

2,526; refined sugar, 1,210; wheat flour, 664; plywood (2002), 4,341,000 cu. metres; cigarettes, 25·6bn. units; radio sets, 28·8m. units; pneumatic tyres, 13·1m. units; TV sets, 9·5m. units.

Labour. In 2001 the workforce was 9,892,000 (46·7% female in 2000), of whom 9,535,000 were employed (22·6% in manufacturing, 14·2% in agriculture, forestry and fishing, 10·5% in government services and 8·9% in construction). Unemployment was 3·8% in 2002. It is estimated that Malaysia has some 500,000 illegal workers.

Trade Unions. Membership was 784,881 in 2001, of which the Malaysian Trades Union Congress, an umbrella organization of 235 unions, accounted for 0·5m. Number of unions was 578.

INTERNATIONAL TRADE

Privatization policy permits foreign investment of 25–30% generally; total foreign ownership is permitted of export-oriented projects. External debt was US$48,557m. in 2002.

Imports and Exports. In 2002 exports totalled RM354·5bn. and imports RM303·5bn. The trade surplus in 2002 was RM51·0bn., down from RM73·1bn. in 1999.

Chief exports, 2002: microcircuits, transistors and valves, 20·5%; computers, office machines and parts, 18·4%; telecommunications equipment, 5·4%. Main imports, 2002: microcircuits, transistors and valves, 29·2%; computers, office machines and parts, 6·9%; telecommunications equipment, 4·3%.

In 2002 the leading export markets were: USA (20·2%), Singapore (17·1%), Japan (11·2%). Principal import sources in 2002 were: Japan (17·8%), USA (16·4%), Singapore (12·0%).

COMMUNICATIONS

Roads. Total road length in 1999 was 65,877 km, of which 49,605 km were paved and 16,272 km were unpaved. In 2002 there were 5,069,412 passenger cars in use, 51,158 buses and coaches, 713,148 trucks and vans and 5,842,617 motorcycles and mopeds. There were 6,035 deaths as a result of road accidents in 2000, which at 29 per 100,000 people ranks among the highest rates in the world.

Rail. In 1999 there were 1,949 km of railway tracks. Passenger-km travelled in 2000 came to 4,800m. and freight tonne-km to 1,230m. There are two metro systems in Kuala Lumpur with a combined length of 56 km.

Civil Aviation. There are a total of 19 airports of which five are international airports and 14 are domestic airports at which regular public air transport is operated. *International airports;* Kuala Lumpur, Penang, Kota Kinabalu, Kuching and Langkawi. *Domestic airports;* Johor Bharu, Alor Setar, Ipoh, Kota Bharu, Kuala Terengganu, Kuantan, Melaka, Sandakan, Lahad Datu, Tawau, Labuan, Bintulu, Sibu and Miri. There are 39 Malaysian airstrips of which ten are in Sabah, 15 in Sarawak and 14 in peninsular Malaysia.

In 2003, 40 international airlines operated through Kuala Lumpur (KLIA-Sepang). Malaysia Airlines, the national airline, is 39% state-owned, and operates domestic flights within Malaysia and international flights to nearly 40 different countries. In 1999 it flew 206·9m. km, carrying 14,984,600 passengers (6,770,550 on international flights). In 2000 Kuala Lumpur handled 14,353,000 passengers (10,249,000 on international flights) and 510,600 tonnes of freight. Kota Kinabalu handled 2,970,000 passengers in 2000 and Penang 2,682,000.

Shipping. The major ports are Port Kelang, Pulau Pinang, Johor Pasir Gudang, Tanjung Beruas, Miri, Rajang, Pelabuhan Sabah, Port Dickson, Kemaman, Teluk Ewa, Kuantan, Kuching and Bintulu. Port Kelang, the busiest port, handled 82,271,000 freight tonnes of cargo in 2002. In 1996 there were 2,429 marine vessels including 118 oil tankers (0·73m. GRT), 198 passenger carriers (0·03m. GRT) and 426 general cargo ships (0·76m. GRT), with a total GRT of 4·27m. In 1996, 167·9m. tonnes of cargo were loaded and unloaded. Total container throughput in 2002 was 8,716,463 TEUs (twenty-foot equivalent units). In 2002 merchant shipping totalled 5,394,000 GRT, including oil tankers 767,000 GRT.

Telecommunications. In 2002 there were 13,911,300 telephone subscribers, or 567·2 per 1,000 inhabitants, and 3·6m. PCs were in use (146·8 for every 1,000 persons). There were 3,092 telex subscribers in 1999 and 175,000 fax machines in 1998. Malaysia had 7,841,000 Internet users in 2002 and 9,241,400 mobile phone subscribers.

Postal Services. Postal services are the responsibility of the Ministry of Energy, Water and Communications. In 1998 there were 6,036 postal services networks established in Malaysia, including 626 post offices.

SOCIAL INSTITUTIONS

Justice. The judicial power is vested in the Federal Court, the High Court of Malaya, the High Court of Borneo and subordinate courts: Sessions Courts, Magistrates' Courts and *Mukim* chiefs' Courts.

The Federal Court comprises the Lord President—who is also the head of the Judiciary—the Chief Justice of the High Courts and the Judge of the Federal Court. It has jurisdiction to determine the validity of any law made by Parliament or by a State legislature and disputes between States or between the Federation and any State. It also has jurisdiction to hear and determine appeals from the High Courts.

The death penalty is authorized and was used in 2002. The population in penal institutions in 2002 was 28,804 (125 per 100,000 of national population).

Religion. Malaysia has a multi-racial population divided between Islam, Buddhism, Taoism, Hinduism and Christianity. Under the Federal constitution, Islam is the official religion of Malaysia but there is freedom of worship. In 2000 there were an estimated 12·30m. Muslims, 4·02m. Buddhists, 2·70m. adherents of Chinese traditional religions, 1·63m. Hindus and 1·49m. Christians.

Education. School education is free; tertiary education is provided at a nominal fee. There are six years of primary schooling starting at age seven, three years of universal lower secondary, two years of selective upper secondary and two years of pre-university education. During the Seventh Plan period (1996–2000), a number of major changes were introduced to the education and training system with a view to strengthening and improving the system. These efforts are expected to improve the quality of output to meet the manpower needs of the nation, particularly in the fields of science and technology. In addition, continued emphasis will be given to expand educational opportunities for those in the rural and remote areas. Under the Seventh Plan, the Education Ministry allocated RM8,437,200 on this education programme and RM1,661,600 for training purposes.

In 2000–01 there were 3,017,902 pupils at primary schools with 159,375 teachers, 2,205,426 pupils with 120,002 teachers at secondary schools and 549,205 students and 20,473 academic staff at higher education institutions.

Adult literacy was 87·9% in 2001 (91·7% among males and 84·0% among females).

In 2000 total expenditure on education was RM12,923m. (22·9% from the total budget). In 2000–01 total expenditure on education came to 6·8% of GNP and 26·7% of total government spending.

Health. In 2001 there were 15,619 doctors, 2,144 dentists, 31,129 nurses and 2,333 pharmacists. In 2001 the Ministry of Health ran a total of 855 health clinics and 1,744 dental clinics. In 2000 there were 374 hospitals (provision of one bed per 492 inhabitants).

Welfare. The Employment Injury Insurance Scheme (SOCSO) provides medical and cash benefits and the Invalidity Pension Scheme provides protection to employees against invalidity as a result of disease or injury from any cause. Other supplementary measures are the Employees' Provident Fund, the pension scheme for all government employees, free medical benefits for all who are unable to pay and the provision of medical benefits particularly for workers under the Labour Code. In 1998 there were 49 welfare service institutions with capacity for 7,170.

CULTURE

World Heritage Sites. There are two sites in Malaysia that appear on the UNESCO World Heritage List, both entered in 2000. Both are in Eastern Malaysia. They are the Gunung Mulu National Park with its limestone caves; and Kinabalu Park/Mount Kinabalu.

Broadcasting. There are five TV Stations (colour by PAL). The government-controlled Radio Television Malaysia broadcasts radio and TV programmes nationally. The Voice of Malaysia (broadcasting in eight languages) is beamed internationally. System TV Malaysia Berhad transmits from Kuala Lumpur and is also beamed throughout the country. There were 9·76m. radio receivers in 2000 and 4·77m. television receivers in 2001.

Press. The Malaysian Media Agencies are comprised of the press, magazine and press agencies/local media, which are further divided into home and foreign news. In 1999 a total of 5,084 book titles were published.

Tourism. In 2002 there were 13,292,000 foreign tourists, spending US$6,785m.

Festivals. National Day (31 Aug.) is celebrated in Kuala Lumpur at the Dataran Merdeka and marks Malaysia's independence.

Libraries. The National Library of Malaysia is strong on information technology. The 14 state public libraries and 31 ministry and government department libraries are linked in a Common User Scheme called Jaringan Ilmu (Knowledge Network).

Theatre and Opera. Performances by the National Budaya Group include premiere theatre staging, dance drama, national choir concerts, national symphony orchestra, chamber music, and traditional and folk music. Local theatre groups regularly stage contemporary Asian and western dramas, dance dramas and the *bangsawan* (traditional Malay opera).

Museums and Galleries. There is a National Museum for preserving, restoring and imparting knowledge on the historical and cultural heritage of Malaysia. The National Art Gallery promotes Malaysian visual arts through exhibitions, competitions and support programmes which are held locally and abroad.

DIPLOMATIC REPRESENTATIVES

Of Malaysia in the United Kingdom (45 Belgrave Sq., London, SW1X 8QT)
High Commissioner: Dato'Abd Aziz bin Mohammed.

Of the United Kingdom in Malaysia (185 Jalan Ampang, 50450 Kuala Lumpur)
High Commissioner: Bruce Cleghorn, CMG.

Of Malaysia in the USA (3516 International Court, NW, Washington, D.C., 20008)
Ambassador: Dato' Sheikh Abdul Khalid Ghazzali.

Of the USA in Malaysia (376 Jalan Tun Razak, Kuala Lumpur)
Ambassador: Christopher J. LaFleur.

Of Malaysia to the United Nations
Ambassador: Datuk Rastam Mohamed Isa.

Of Malaysia to the European Union
Ambassador: Dato' Mohamed Ridzam Deva bin Abdullah.

FURTHER READING

Department of Statistics: Kuala Lumpur. *Yearbook of Statistics, Malaysia* (2004); *Yearbook of Statistics, Sabah* (2004); *Yearbook of Statistics, Sarawak* (2004); *Vital Statistics, Malaysia* (2003).

Prime Minister's Department: Economic Planning Unit. *Malaysian Economy in Figures.* Annual, 2004.

Andaya, B. W. and Andaya, L. Y., *A History of Malaysia*. 2nd ed. Palgrave, Basingstoke, 2001

Drabble, J., *An Economic History of Malaysia, c. 1800–1990*. Palgrave, Basingstoke, 2001

Kahn, J. S. and Wah, F. L. K., *Fragmented Vision: Culture and Politics in Contemporary Malaysia.* Sydney, 1992

BNM: Kuala Lumpur. *Bank Negara Malaysia, Annual Report.* 1998

National statistical office: Department of Statistics, Block C6, Parcel C, Federal Government Administrative Centre, 62514 Putrajaya.
Website: http://www.statistics.gov.my/

MALDIVES

Divehi Raajjeyge Jumhooriyyaa
(Republic of the Maldives)

Capital: Malé
Population projection, 2010: 391,000
GDP per capita, 2001: (PPP$) 4,798
HDI/world rank: 0·752/84

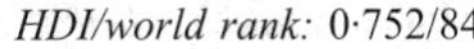

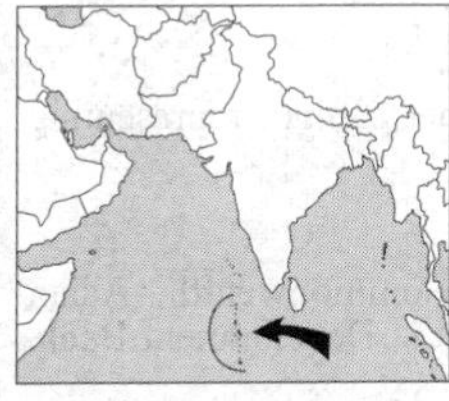

KEY HISTORICAL EVENTS

The islands were under British protection from 1887 until complete independence was achieved on 26 July 1965. The Maldives became a republic on 11 Nov. 1968.

TERRITORY AND POPULATION

The republic, some 400 miles to the southwest of Sri Lanka, consists of 1,192 low-lying (the highest point is 1·8 metres above sea-level) coral islands, grouped into 26 atolls. 199 are inhabited. Area 115 sq. miles (298 sq. km). At the 2000 census the population was 270,101 (137,200 males); density, 906·4 per sq. km.

The UN gives a projected population for 2010 of 391,000.

In 2001, 72·0% of the population lived in rural areas. Capital, Malé (2000 population, 74,000).

The official and spoken language is Divehi.

SOCIAL STATISTICS

2001 births, 4,882; deaths, 1,081. Birth rate, 2001, per 1,000 population, 17·7; death rate, 3·9. Annual population growth rate, 1992–02, 3·0%. Life expectancy at birth in 2002 was 67·7 years for males and 66·8 years for females. Infant mortality, 2002, 58 per 1,000 live births; fertility rate, 2001, 5·5 births per woman.

CLIMATE

The islands are hot and humid, and affected by monsoons. Malé: average temperature 81°F (27°C), annual rainfall 59" (1,500 mm).

CONSTITUTION AND GOVERNMENT

There is a Citizens' *Majlis* (Parliament) which consists of 50 members, 8 of whom are nominated by the President and 42 directly elected (2 each from Malé and the 20 administrative districts) for a term of five years. There are no political parties. The President of the Republic is elected by the Citizens' Majlis.

National Anthem. 'Gavmii mi ekuverikan matii tibegen kuriime salaam' ('In national unity we salute our nation'); words by M. J. Didi, tune by W. Amaradeva.

RECENT ELECTIONS

President Maumoon Abdul Gayoom was re-elected in a referendum held on 17 Oct. 2003. As sole candidate, he won 90·3% of the votes cast. Turn-out was 77%. At the last elections to the *Majlis* on 22 Jan. 2005 only non-partisans were elected, but both the government and the opposition Maldives Democratic Party—which operates in self-imposed exile out of Sri Lanka—claimed victory.

CURRENT ADMINISTRATION

In March 2005 the government consisted of:

President: Maumoon Abdul Gayoom; b. 1937 (in office since 1978; re-elected unopposed for a sixth 5-year term in Oct. 2003).

Minister of Atolls Administration: Abdulla Hameed. *Agriculture, Fisheries and Marine Resources:* Abdulla Kamaaludeen. *Defence and National Security:* Ismail Shafeeu. *Finance and Treasury:* Mohammed Jaleel. *Foreign Affairs:* Fathullah Jameel. *Gender, Family Development and Social Security:* Zahiya Zareer. *Interior and Environment:* Umar Zahir. *Transport and Civil Aviation:* Ilyas Ibrahim. *Planning and National Development:* Hamdoon Hameed. *Employment and Labour:* Abdul Rasheed Hussain. *Tourism:* Mustafa Lutfi. *Education, and Justice (acting):* Mahmood Shaugee. *Information, Arts and Culture:* Ahmed Abdulla. *Trade and Industries:* Abdullah Yameen. *Health:* Aneesa Ahmed. *Science, Technology and Communications:* Midhat Hilmy. *Youth and Sports:* Ibrahim Maniku. *Attorney General:* Hassan Saeed.

Speaker of Citizens' Majlis: Ahmed Zahir.

Office of the President: http://www.presidencymaldives.gov.mv

DEFENCE

In 2003 military expenditure totalled US$40m. (US$138 per capita), representing 6·4% of GDP.

INTERNATIONAL RELATIONS

The Maldives is a member of the UN, WTO, the Commonwealth, Asian Development Bank, Colombo Plan, SAARC, OIC and Islamic Development Bank.

ECONOMY

Fisheries accounts for approximately 7% of GDP, industry 15% and services 78%.

Currency. The unit of currency is the *rufiyaa* (MVR) of 100 *laari*. There was negative inflation in 2003 of 2·9%. Gold reserves were 1,900 troy oz in Oct. 2004. Foreign exchange reserves were US$192·4m in Oct. 2004. Total money supply was 5,581m. rufiyaa in Oct. 2004.

Budget. In 2002 (year ending 31 Dec.) government total revenue was 2,582·4m. rufiyaa; expenditure 3,135·5m. rufiyaa.

Performance. Real GDP growth was 6·5% in 2002, rising to 8·5% in 2003. Total GDP in 2003 was US$644·5m.

Banking and Finance. The Maldives Monetary Authority (*Governor*, Mohamed Jaleel), established in 1981, is endowed with the regular powers of a central bank and bank of issue. There is one domestic commercial bank (Bank of Maldives) and branches of four foreign banks.

ENERGY AND NATURAL RESOURCES

Environment. Carbon dioxide emissions from the consumption and flaring of fossil fuels were the equivalent of 1·7 tonnes per capita in 2002.

Electricity. Installed capacity was 36,000 kW in 2000. Production in 2003 was 157m. kWh; consumption per capita in 2000 was 384 kWh. Utilization in Malé was 97m. kWh in 2003.

Minerals. Inshore coral mining has been banned as a measure against the encroachment of the sea.

Agriculture. There were 4,000 ha of arable land in 2001 and 5,000 ha of permanent crops. Principal crops in 2000 (in 1,000 tonnes): coconuts, 16; copra, 3; tree nuts, 2; bananas, 1.

Fisheries. The total catch in 2003 was 155,415 tonnes. The Maldives has the highest per capita consumption of fish and fishery products of any country in the world. In the period 1999–2001 the average person consumed 187 kg (412 lb) a year, or more than 11 times the average for the world as a whole.

INDUSTRY

The main industries are fishing, tourism, shipping, lacquerwork and garment manufacturing.

Labour. In 2000 the economically active workforce totalled 87,987 (59,279 males) of whom 86,245 were employed.

INTERNATIONAL TRADE

Total foreign debt amounted to US$270m. in 2002.

Imports and Exports. In 2003 imports (f.o.b.) were valued at US$414·3m. (US$344·7m. in 2002) and exports (f.o.b.) at US$152·0m. (US$132·5m. in 2002). Tuna is the main export commodity. It is exported principally to Thailand, Sri Lanka, Japan and some European markets. Main import suppliers in 2003 were Singapore (24·9%), Sri Lanka (13·7%), India (10·1%), Malaysia (7·7%), UAE (7·6%). Leading export destinations were USA (23·3%), Thailand (16·4%), Sri Lanka (13·6%), Japan (10·3%), UK (9·7%).

COMMUNICATIONS

Roads. In 2003 there were 1,751 cars, 14,370 motorbikes/autocycles, 431 lorries, 127 trucks, 92 tractors, 431 vans, 36 buses, 248 jeeps, 704 pickups, 403 other vehicles.

Civil Aviation. The former national carrier Air Maldives collapsed in April 2000 with final losses in excess of US$50m. In 2003 there were 1,833,620 passenger arrivals, 21m. pieces of cargo and 100,352 pieces of mail handled at Malé's international airport. There are four domestic airports. In 1999 scheduled airline traffic of Maldives-based carriers flew 5·1m. km, carrying 344,000 passengers (273,000 on international flights).

Shipping. The Maldives Shipping Line operated (1992) ten vessels. In 2000 merchant shipping totalled 58,000 GRT.

Telecommunications. In Oct. 2004 telephone subscribers numbered 31,300 (108 fixed lines per 1,000 inhabitants) and mobile phone users 98,300. Landline and mobile usage combined gives an overall density of 447 telephones per 1,000 inhabitants. At the end of 2003 the number of PCs in use was estimated at 25,000. There were approximately 15,000 internet users in 2003.

Postal Services. At the end of Nov. 2004 there were 197 agency post offices and nine sub-post offices. There are a total of 300 employees.

SOCIAL INSTITUTIONS

Justice. Justice is based on the Islamic Shari'ah.

Religion. The State religion is Islam.

Education. Adult literacy in 2001 was 97·0% (male, 97·1%; female, 96·9%). Education is not compulsory. In 2004 there were 81 government schools (57,139 pupils), 176 community schools (38,043 pupils) and 337 private schools (104,214 pupils) with a total of 5,239 teachers. In 1998–99 total expenditure on education came to 6·5% of GNP and 11·2% of total government spending.

Health. In 2003 there were 236 beds at the Indira Gandhi Memorial Hospital in Malé, 6 regional hospitals (226 beds) and 27 health centres. In 2003 there were 315 doctors and 785 nurses, 251 pharmacists and 409 midwives.

CULTURE

Broadcasting. Voice of Maldives and Television Maldives are government-controlled. In 2004 there were an estimated 200,000 radio receivers and 10,800 television sets (colour by PAL).

Press. In 1996 there were three daily newspapers, seven weekly and 13 monthly.

Tourism. Tourism is the major foreign currency earner. There were 563,600 visitors in 2003, spending US$401·6m.

Festivals. The Maldives' National Day in May commemorates the victory of Mohammed Thakurufaan over the Portuguese in 1573. Victory Day celebrates the defeat of Sri Lankan mercenaries who tried to overthrow the Maldivian government on 3 Nov. 1988. Republic Day is on 11 Nov.

DIPLOMATIC REPRESENTATIVES

Of the Maldives in the United Kingdom (22 Nottingham Pl., London W1U 5NJ)
High Commissioner: Hassan Sobir.

Of the United Kingdom in the Maldives
High Commissioner: Stephen Evans, CMG, OBE (resides at Colombo, Sri Lanka).

Of the Maldives in the USA (800 2nd Ave., Suite 400E, New York, NY 10017)
Ambassador: Dr Mohamed Latheef.

Of the USA in the Maldives
Ambassador: Jeffrey J. Lunstead (resides at Colombo, Sri Lanka).

Permanent Representative of the Maldives to the United Nations
Ambassador: Dr Mohamed Latheef.

Of the Maldives to the European Union
Ambassador: Vacant.

FURTHER READING

Gayoom, M. A., *The Maldives: A Nation in Peril.* Ministry of Planning, Human Resources and Environment, Republic of Maldives, 1998

Reynolds, Christopher H. B., *Maldives.* [Bibliography] ABC-Clio, Oxford and Santa Barbara (CA), 1993

National Statistics Office: Statistics Section, Ministry of Planning and National Development.
Website: http://www.planning.gov.mv

MALI

République du Mali

Capital: Bamako
Population projection, 2010: 16·21m.
GDP per capita, 2002: (PPP$) 930
HDI/world rank: 0·326/174

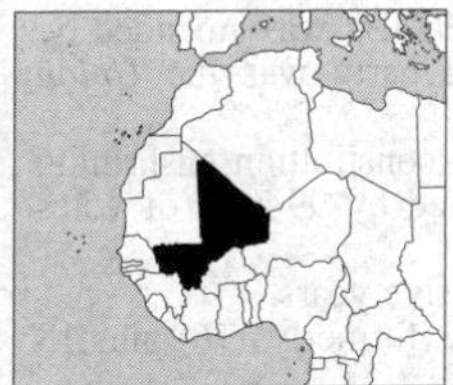

KEY HISTORICAL EVENTS

Mali's power reached its peak between the 11th and 13th centuries when its gold-based empire controlled much of the surrounding area. The country was annexed by France in 1904. The region became the territory of French Sudan as part of French West Africa. The country became an autonomous state within the French Community on 24 Nov. 1958, and on 4 April 1959 joined with Senegal to form the Federation of Mali. The Federation achieved independence on 20 June 1960, but Senegal seceded on 22 Aug. and Mali proclaimed itself an independent republic on 22 Sept. There was an army coup on 19 Nov. 1968, which brought Moussa Traoré to power. Ruling the country for over 22 years, he wrecked the economy. A further coup followed in March 1991.

In Jan. 1991 a ceasefire was signed with Tuareg insurgents in the north and in April 1992 a national pact was concluded providing for a special administration for the Tuareg north.

Under President Alpha Oumar Konaré, two elections for the National Assembly were held. The first (April 1997) was cancelled by the Constitutional Court and the second, in July 1997, was boycotted by opposition parties. Amadou Toumani Touré, a former military ruler, won presidential elections held in April and May 2002.

TERRITORY AND POPULATION

Mali is bounded in the west by Senegal, northwest by Mauritania, northeast by Algeria, east by Niger and south by Burkina Faso, Côte d'Ivoire and Guinea. Its area is 1,248,574 sq. km (482,077 sq. miles) and it had a population of 10,179,170 at the 1998 census (69·2% rural in 2001). Density, 8·2 per sq. km. 2002 population estimate: 12,674,000.

The UN gives a projected population for 2010 of 16·21m.

The areas, populations and chief towns of the regions are:

Region	*Sq. km*	*1998 population*	*Chief town*
Gao	170,572	495,178	Gao
Kayes	119,743	1,424,657	Kayes
Kidal	151,430	65,524	Kidal
Koulikoro	95,848	1,620,811	Koulikoro
Mopti	79,017	1,405,370	Mopti
Ségou	64,821	1,652,594	Ségou
Sikasso	70,280	1,839,747	Sikasso
Tombouctou	496,611	496,312	Tombouctou
Capital District	252	1,178,977	Bamako

In 1999 the capital, Bamako, had an estimated population of 1,083,000.

In 1996 the principal ethnic groups numbered (in 1,000): Bambara, 2,930; Fulani, 1,290; Senufo, 1,100; Soninke, 800; Tuareg, 675; Songhai, 660; Malinke, 610; Dogon, 370. The official language is French; Bambara is spoken by about 60% of the population.

SOCIAL STATISTICS

1997 estimates: births, 492,000; deaths, 191,000. Vital statistics rates, 1997 estimates (per 1,000 population): births, 50·3; deaths, 19·5. Infant mortality, 2001 (per 1,000 live births), 141. Expectation of life in 2001 was 47·8 years for males and 48·9 for females. Annual population growth rate, 1992–02, 2·8%; fertility rate, 2001, 7·0 children per woman.

CLIMATE

A tropical climate, with adequate rain in the south and west, but conditions become increasingly arid towards the north and east. Bamako, Jan. 76°F (24·4°C), July 80°F (26·7°C). Annual rainfall 45" (1,120 mm). Kayes, Jan. 76°F (24·4°C), July 93°F (33·9°C). Annual rainfall 29" (725 mm). Tombouctou, Jan. 71°F (21·7°C), July 90°F (32·2°C). Annual rainfall 9" (231 mm).

CONSTITUTION AND GOVERNMENT

A constitution was approved by a national referendum in 1974; it was amended by the National Assembly on 2 Sept. 1981. The sole legal party was the *Union démocratique du peuple malien* (UDPM).

A national conference of 1,800 delegates agreed a draft constitution enshrining multi-party democracy in Aug. 1991, and this was approved by 99·76% of votes cast at a referendum in Jan. 1992. Turn-out was 43%.

The *President* is elected for not more than two terms of five years.

There is a *National Assembly*, consisting of 147 deputies (formerly 116) plus 13 Malinese living abroad.

A *Constitutional Court* was established in 1994.

National Anthem. 'A ton appel, Mali' ('At your call, Mali'); words by S. Kouyate, tune by B. Sissoko.

RECENT ELECTIONS

Presidential elections were held in two rounds on 28 April and 12 May 2002. In the first round Amadou Toumani Touré won 28·0% of votes cast, against 22·7% for Soumaïla Cissé and 20·7% for Ibrahim Boubacar Keita. Turn-out was 38·6%. In the run-off between Touré and Cissé on 12 May, Touré won with 64·4% of the vote against 35·7% for Cissé.

Parliamentary elections were held in two rounds on 14 and 28 July 2002. Initial results indicated victory for the Alliance for Democracy in Mali (ADEMA) with 67 seats (down from 128 in 1997) and 47 seats for the Hope 2002 coalition. On 10 Aug. 2002 the Constitutional Court ruled these results invalid and released new results giving 66 seats to the Hope Coalition 2002 against 51 for the Alliance for Democracy in Mali. Turn-out was 25·7%.

CURRENT ADMINISTRATION

President: Amadou Toumani Touré; b. 1948 (sworn in 8 June 2002, having previously been president from March 1991–June 1992 following a coup).

In March 2005 the government comprised:

Prime Minister: Ousmane Issoufi Maïga; b. 1945 (sworn in 30 April 2004).

Minister for Environment and Decontamination: Nancouma Kéita. *Planning and National Development:* Marimatia Diarra. *Livestock and Fishing:* Oumar Ibrahima Touré. *Handicrafts and Tourism:* Bah N'Diaye. *Education:* Mohamed Lamine Traoré. *Industry and Commerce:* Choguel Kokala Maïga. *Territorial Administration and Local Collectivities:* Gen. Kafougouna Koné. *Foreign Affairs and International Co-operation:* Moctar Ouane. *Malians Abroad and African Integration:* Oumar Hamadoun Diko. *Agriculture:* Seydou Traoré. *Communications and Information Technology:* Gaoussou Drabo. *Mines, Energy and Water Resources:* Hamed Diane Sémega. *Culture:* Cheick Oumar Sissoko. *Social Development, Solidarity and the Aged:* Djibril Tangara. *Economy and Finance:* Abou-Bacar Traoré. *Civil Service, State Reform and Relations with the Institutions:* Badi Ould Ganfoud. *Employment and Professional Training:* Diallo M'Bodji Sène. *Promotion of Investment and of Small- and Medium-Sized Enterprises:* Ousmane Thiam. *Promotion of Women, Children and the Family:* Berthé Aïssata Bengaly. *Defence and Veterans:* Mamadou Clazié Cissouma. *Justice and Keeper of the Seals:* Fanta Sylla. *State Territories and Land Affairs:* Soumaré Aminata Sidibé. *Health:* Maïga Zeinab Mint Youba. *Equipment and Transport:* Abdoulaye Koïta. *Internal Security and Civil Protection:* Col. Sadio Gassama. *Youth and Sports:* Moussa Balla Diakité. *Housing and Urbanization:* Modibo Sylla.

DEFENCE

There is a selective system of two years' conscription, for civilian or military service. Defence expenditure totalled US$81m. in 2003 (US$7 per capita), representing 1·8% of GDP.

Army. Strength (2002) 7,350. There are also paramilitary forces of 4,800.

Navy. There is a Navy of 50 operating three patrol craft.

Air Force. Personnel (2002) total about 400. There were around 16 combat aircraft.

INTERNATIONAL RELATIONS

Mali is a member of the UN, WTO, the African Union, African Development Bank, ECOWAS, IOM, OIC, Islamic Development Bank, the International Organization of the Francophonie and is an ACP member state of the ACP-EU relationship.

ECONOMY

Agriculture accounted for 34·2% of GDP in 2002, industry 29·7% and services 36·1%.

Currency. The unit of currency is the *franc CFA* (XOF), which replaced the Mali franc in 1984. It has a parity rate of 655·957 francs CFA to one euro. Total money supply in May 2002 was 460,722m. francs CFA and foreign exchange reserves were US$508m. Gold reserves were 19,000 troy oz in June 2000. Inflation was 2·4% in 2002.

Budget. Revenues for 2002 were 379·4bn. francs CFA and expenditures 601·5bn. francs CFA.

Performance. Real GDP growth was 3·5% in 2001, rising to 9·7% in 2002. In 2003 total GDP was US$4·3bn.

Banking and Finance. The bank of issue and the central bank is the regional Central Bank of West African States (BCEAO). The *Governor* is Charles Konan Banny. In 2002 there were eight commercial and two development banks.

There is a stock exchange in Bamako.

ENERGY AND NATURAL RESOURCES

Environment. Carbon dioxide emissions from the consumption and flaring of fossil fuels were the equivalent of 0·1 tonnes per capita in 2002.

Electricity. Installed capacity in 2000 was 0·1m. kW. Production in 2000 totalled about 412m. kWh, approximately 57% of it hydro-electric. Consumption per capita was an estimated 36 kWh in 2000.

Minerals. Gold (56,026 kg in 2002) is the principal mineral produced. There are also deposits of iron ore, uranium, diamonds, bauxite, manganese, copper, salt, limestone, phosphate, gypsum and lithium.

Agriculture. About 80% of the population depends on agriculture, mainly carried on by small peasant holdings. Mali is second only to Egypt among African cotton producers. In 2001 there were 4·66m. ha of arable land and 40,000 ha of permanent cropland. There were 2,600 tractors in 2001 and 650 harvester-threshers. Production in 2000 included (estimates, in 1,000 tonnes): millet, 953; rice, 810; sorghum, 714; seed cotton, 480; maize, 438; sugarcane, 300; cottonseed, 220; cotton lint, 200; groundnuts, 140.

Livestock, 2000: cattle, 6·20m.; sheep, 6·00m.; goats, 8·55m.; asses, 652,000; camels, 292,000; chickens, 25m.

138,000 ha were irrigated in 2001.

Forestry. In 2000 forests covered 13·19m. ha, or 10·8% of the total land area. Timber production in 2001 was 5·20m. cu. metres.

Fisheries. In 2001 approximately 100,000 tonnes of fish were caught, exclusively from inland waters.

INDUSTRY

The main industries are food processing, followed by cotton processing, textiles and clothes. Cement and pharmaceuticals are also produced.

Labour. In 1996 the workforce was estimated to be 5,472,000 (54% males). In 1995 over 80% of the economically active population were engaged in agriculture, fisheries and forestry. Large numbers of Malians emigrate temporarily to work abroad, principally in Côte d'Ivoire.

INTERNATIONAL TRADE

Foreign debt was US$2,803m. in 2002.

Imports and Exports. In 2001 imports (f.o.b.) were valued at US$734·7m. (US$592·1m. in 2000) and exports (f.o.b.) at US$725·2m. (US$545·1m. in 2000). Principal export commodities are cotton and livestock (between them accounting for three-quarters of Mali's annual exports) and gold. The main export markets are France and its former colonies, western Europe and China. Principal import commodities are machinery and equipment, foodstuffs, construction materials, petroleum and textiles. Main import suppliers are also France and its former colonies (in particular Côte d'Ivoire), western Europe and China.

COMMUNICATIONS

Roads. There were (1999 estimate) 15,100 km of classified roads, of which 1,830 km were paved. In 1996 there were 26,190 passenger cars (three per 1,000 inhabitants) and 18,240 trucks and vans. There were 72 road accident deaths in 1994.

Rail. Mali has a railway from Kayes to Koulikoro by way of Bamako, a continuation of the Dakar–Kayes line in Senegal; total length 734 km (metre-gauge). Passenger-km travelled in 2000 came to 204m. and freight tonne-km to 193m.

Civil Aviation. There is an international airport at Bamako (Senou), which handled 315,000 passengers (306,000 on international flights) and 5,400 tonnes of freight in 2000. In 2003 Trans African Airlines operated services to Abidjan, Brazzaville, Cotonou, Dakar, Lomé and Pointe-Noire. There were also international flights to Accra, Addis Ababa, Banjul, Bobo-Dioulasso, Casablanca, Conakry, Douala, Kano, Lagos, Libreville, N'Djaména, Niamey, Nouakchott, Ouagadougou, Paris and Tripoli. In 1999 scheduled airline traffic of Mali-based carriers flew 3·0m. km, carrying 84,000 passengers (all on international flights).

Shipping. For about seven months in the year small steamboats operate a service from Koulikoro to Tombouctou and Gao, and from Bamako to Kouroussa.

Telecommunications. Mali had 102,400 telephone subscribers in 2002, or 9·6 per 1,000 population, and there were 15,000 PCs in use (1·4 per 1,000 persons). In 2002 there were 52,600 mobile phone subscribers. In 2002 Internet users numbered 25,000.

Postal Services. In 1998 there were 124 post offices.

SOCIAL INSTITUTIONS

Justice. The Supreme Court was established at Bamako in 1969 with both judicial and administrative powers. The Court of Appeal is also at Bamako, at the apex of a system of regional tribunals and local *juges de paix*.

The population in penal institutions in Feb. 2002 was 4,040 (34 per 100,000 of national population).

Religion. The state is secular, but predominantly Sunni Muslim. About 15% of the population follow traditional animist beliefs and there is a small Christian minority.

Education. The adult literacy rate in 2001 was 26·4% (36·7% among males and 16·6% among females). In 2000–01 there were 600 teachers for 15,106 children in pre-primary schools, and 17,788 teachers for 1,127,360 pupils in primary schools; in 1998–99 there were 217,700 secondary school pupils and 18,662 students in tertiary education. During the period 1990–95 only 19% of females of primary school age were enrolled in school.

In 1999–2000 total expenditure on education came to 3·0% of GNP.

Health. In 1987 there were four hospital beds per 10,000 inhabitants. In 1994 there were 419 physicians, 9 dentists, 1,167 nurses and 267 midwives.

CULTURE

World Heritage Sites. Mali has four sites on the UNESCO World Heritage List: Old Towns of Djenné (inscribed on the list in 1988), a market centre established in 250 BC and an important Islamic centre in the 16th century—its buildings are all mudbrick, plastered annually with adobe; Tomboctou (1988) an important Islamic centre, containing the Koranic Sankore University and the famous Djingareyber Mosque; the Cliff of Bandiagara (Land of the Dogons) (1989), for its natural and architectural wonders; and the Tomb of Askia (2004).

Broadcasting. Broadcasting is the responsibility of the autonomous Radiodiffusion Télévision du Mali. Number of sets: radio (2000), 597,000; TV (2001), 200,000 (colour by SECAM).

Press. In 1996 there were three daily newspapers with a combined circulation of 12,000.

Tourism. There were 91,000 foreign tourists in 2000, bringing in revenue of US$50m.

DIPLOMATIC REPRESENTATIVES

Of Mali in the United Kingdom (resides at Brussels)
Ambassador: Ibrahim Bocar Ba.

Of the United Kingdom in Mali
Ambassador: Peter Newall (resides at Dakar, Senegal).

Of Mali in the USA (2130 R. St., NW, Washington, D.C., 20008)
Ambassador: Abdoulaye Diop.

Of the USA in Mali (Rue Rochester NY and Rue Mohamed V, Bamako)
Ambassador: Vicki Huddleston.

Of Mali to the United Nations
Ambassador: Cheick Sidi Diarra.

Of Mali to the European Union
Ambassador: Ibrahim Bocar Ba.

FURTHER READING

National statistical office: Direction National de la Statistique et de l'Informatique, BP 12 rue Adunard, Port 233.
Website: http://www.dnsi.gov.ml

MALTA

Repubbblika ta' Malta

Capital: Valletta
Population projection, 2010: 405,000
GDP per capita, 2002: (PPP$) 17,640
HDI/world rank: 0·875/31

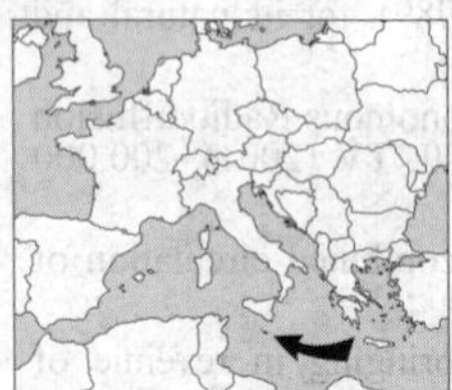

KEY HISTORICAL EVENTS

Malta was held in turn by Phoenicians, Carthaginians and Romans, and was conquered by Arabs in 870. From 1090 it was subject to the same rulers as Sicily until 1530, when it was handed over to the Knights of St John, who ruled until dispersed by Napoléon in 1798. The Maltese rose in rebellion against the French and the island was blockaded by the British aided by the Maltese from 1798 to 1800. The Maltese people freely requested the protection of the British Crown in 1802 on condition that their rights and privileges be preserved. The island was finally annexed to the British Crown by the Treaty of Paris in 1814. Malta became independent on 21 Sept. 1964 and a republic within the Commonwealth on 13 Dec. 1974. On 1 May 2004 Malta became a member of the European Union.

TERRITORY AND POPULATION

The three Maltese islands and minor islets lie in the Mediterranean 93 km (at the nearest point) south of Sicily and 288 km east of Tunisia. The area of Malta is 246 sq. km (94·9 sq. miles); Gozo, 67 sq. km (25·9 sq. miles) and the virtually uninhabited Comino, 3 sq. km (1·1 sq. miles); total area, 316 sq. km (121·9 sq. miles). The census population in 1995 was 376,335. Population, 31 Dec. 2002, 397,296; Malta island, 366,028; Gozo and Comino, 31,268. Density, 1,257 per sq. km.

The UN gives a projected population for 2010 of 405,000.

In 2002, 91·2% of the population were urban. Chief town and port, Valletta, population 7,173 (2002) but the southern harbour district, 85,562. Other towns: Birkirkara, 22,334; Qormi, 18,553; Mosta, 17,936; Zabbar, 15,057; Sliema, 12,575.

The constitution provides that the national language and language of the courts is Maltese, but both Maltese and English are official languages.

SOCIAL STATISTICS

2002: births, 3,805; deaths, 3,031; marriages, 2,240; emigrants, 96; returned emigrants, 382. 2002 rates per 1,000 population: birth, 9·9; death, 7·8; marriage, 5·8. Divorce and abortion are illegal. In 2002 the most popular age range for marrying was 25–29 for males and 20–24 for females. Life expectancy at birth in 2001: 76·1 years for males and 80·9 years for females. Annual population growth rate, 1992–02, 0·7%. Infant mortality in 2002: 6·0 per 1,000 live births; fertility rate, 2002, 1·5 births per woman.

CLIMATE

The climate is Mediterranean, with hot, dry and sunny conditions in summer and very little rain from May to Aug. Rainfall is not excessive and falls mainly between Oct. and March. Average daily sunshine in winter is six hours and in summer over ten hours. Valletta, Jan. 12·8°C (55°F), July 25·6°C (78°F). Annual rainfall 578 mm (23").

CONSTITUTION AND GOVERNMENT

Malta is a parliamentary democracy. The Constitution of 1964 provides for a *President*, a *House of Representatives* of members elected by universal suffrage and a Cabinet consisting of the Prime Minister and such number of Ministers as may be appointed. The Constitution makes provision for the protection of fundamental rights and freedom of the individual, and for freedom of conscience and religious worship, and guarantees the separation of executive, judicial and legislative powers. The House of Representatives currently has 65 members directly elected on a plurality basis.

National Anthem. 'Lil din l'art helwa, l'omm li tatna isimha' ('Guard her, O Lord, as ever Thou hast guarded'); words by Dun Karm Psaila, tune by Dr Robert Samut.

RECENT ELECTIONS

At the elections of 12 April 2003 the electorate was 294,106; turn-out was 96·2%. The Nationalist Party (NP) gained 35 seats with 51·8% of votes cast; the Labour Party (MLP), 30 with 47·5%.

European Parliament. Malta has five representatives. At the June 2004 elections turn-out was 82·4%. The MLP won 3 seats with 49·0% of votes cast (political affiliation in European Parliament: Party of European Socialists); and the NP 2 with 40·0% (European People's Party–European Democrats).

CURRENT ADMINISTRATION

President: Dr Edward Fenech Adami; b. 1934 (NP; sworn in 4 April 2004).

In March 2005 the government comprised:

Prime Minister and Minister of Finance: Dr Lawrence Gonzi; b. 1953 (NP; sworn in 23 March 2004).

Deputy Prime Minister, Minister for Justice and Home Affairs and Leader of the House of Representatives: Dr Tonio Borg. *Education, Youth and Employment:* Dr Louis Galea. *Foreign Affairs and Investment Promotion:* Dr Michael Frendo. *Tourism and Culture:* Dr Francis Zammit Dimech. *Competitiveness and Communications:* Censu Galea. *Resources and Infrastructure:* Ninu Zammit. *Gozo:* Giovanna Debono. *Health, the Elderly and Community Care:* Dr Louis Deguara. *Information Technology and Investment:* Dr Austin Gatt. *Rural Affairs and the Environment:* George Pullicino. *Urban Development and Roads:* Jesmond Mugliett. *Family and Social Solidarity:* Dolores Cristina.

Speaker: Anton Tabone.

Government Website: http://www.gov.mt

DEFENCE

The Armed Forces of Malta (AFM) are made up of a Headquarters and three Regiments. On 1 Jan. 2004 they had a strength of 1,838 uniformed and civilian personnel. An Emergency Volunteer Reserve Force was introduced in 1998 on a small scale. In addition to infantry and light air defence artillery weapons, the AFM are equipped with helicopters, light fixed wing and trainer aircraft. There is no conscription.

Apart from normal military duties, AFM are also responsible for Search and Rescue, airport security, surveillance of Malta's territorial and fishing zones, harbour traffic control and anti-pollution duties.

In 2003 military expenditure totalled US$95m. (US$237 per capita), representing 2·1% of GDP.

Navy. There is a maritime squadron numbering 227 personnel.

Air Force. The Air Squadron operates light aircraft and has a strength of 83 personnel.

INTERNATIONAL RELATIONS

Malta is a member of the UN, WTO, the Commonwealth, EU, the Council of Europe, OSCE, IAEA, the Organization for the Prohibition of Chemical Weapons, the Comprehensive Test-Ban Treaty Organization, IOM and the Inter-Parliamentary Union. Malta held a referendum on EU membership on 9 March 2003, in which 53·6% of votes cast were in favour of accession, with 46·4% against. It became a member of the EU on 1 May 2004.

ECONOMY

Services accounted for 71·0% of GDP in 2002, industry 26·2% and agriculture 2·8%.

Overview. The prime objectives of economic strategy are the achievement of a sustainable rate of economic growth, high employment and low stable inflation. To compete internationally, the private sector must be the prime mover of the economy. In the 1999 budget, the government committed itself to reducing the budget deficit to 4% of GDP by 2004. To maximize the benefits from privatization, the government aims at strategic partnerships with international enterprises.

An Institute for the Promotion of Small Enterprises (IPSE) has been established and a number of supporting incentive schemes are being implemented. A Business Promotion Act (BPA) has been enacted to update the Industrial Development Act (IDA) of 1988. The aim is to promote industries that demonstrate growth and employment potential. To maintain Malta's competitive position as a tourist attraction, the Malta Tourism Authority launched its first Strategic Plan for the period 2000–02. The Malta Financial Services Centre regulates and supervises credit and financial institutions with effect from 1 Jan. 2002.

Currency. The unit of currency is the *Maltese lira* (formerly *pound*) (MTL) of 100 *cents*. Total money supply was Lm644m. in March 2002. Inflation was 2·9% in 2001 and 2·2% in 2002. Gold reserves were 4,000 troy oz in June 2002 and foreign exchange reserves US$1,769m.

Budget. Revenue and expenditure (in Lm1m.):

	1998	*1999*	*2000*	*2001*	*2002*
Revenue	659·1	721·9	642·3	797·4	771·0
Expenditure	666·0	691·0	716·2	766·7	819·3

The most important sources of revenue are Customs and Excise tax, customs and excise duties, income tax, VAT, social security and receipts from the Central Bank of Malta. Also significant in certain years are proceeds from the sale of Government shares, foreign grants and foreign and local loans.

The standard rate of VAT is 18·0%.

Performance. In 2002 the economy expanded by 1·7% in real terms, whilst Jan.–Sept. 2003 data showed that real GDP growth remained subdued at 0·3% when compared to the first three quarters of 2002. Total GDP in 2001 was US$3·6bn.

Banking and Finance. The Central Bank of Malta (*Governor*, Michael C. Bonello) was founded in 1968. In Jan. 2004 there were 16 licensed credit institutions carrying out domestic and international banking activities. In addition thirteen local financial institutions licensed in terms of the Financial Institutions Act 1994 also provide services that range from exchange bureau related business to merchant banking.

There is a stock exchange in Valletta.

ENERGY AND NATURAL RESOURCES

Environment. Malta's carbon dioxide emissions from the consumption and flaring of fossil fuels in 2002 were the equivalent of 7·1 tonnes per capita.

Electricity. Electricity is generated at two interconnected thermal power stations located at Marsa (272 MW) and Delimara (305 MW). The primary transmission voltages are 132,000, 33,000 and 11,000 volts while the low-voltage system is 400/230V, 50Hz with neutral point earthed. Installed capacity was 577,000 kW in 2000. Production in 2003 was 2·23bn. kWh; consumption per capita was 5,220 kWh.

Oil and Gas. Malta enjoys a large offshore area, represent geological extensions of southeast Sicily, east Tunisia and northwest Libya where significant hydrocarbon reserves and production exists. Active exploration is at present being carried out by TGS-Nopec, Pancontinental Oil & Gas and TM Services Ltd in offshore areas. Discussions are also underway with oil companies with a view to awarding new licences. The policy of Malta in the oil and gas sector is to intensify exploration by offering oil companies competitive terms and returns that are commensurate with the risk undertaken.

Water. The demand for water during 2003 was 34m. cu. metres. Seawater desalination (Reverse Osmosis Plants) provides 54% of the total potable water requirements.

Agriculture. Malta is self-sufficient in fresh vegetables, pig meat, poultry, eggs and fresh milk. The main crops are potatoes (the spring crop being the country's primary agricultural export), vegetables and fruits, with some items such as tomatoes serving as the main input in the local canning industry. In 2001 there were about 1,524 full-time farmers and 12,589 part-time. There were around 11,959 agricultural holdings and 943 intensive livestock farm units. In 2001 there were 9,000 ha of arable land and 1,000 ha of permanent crops.

Agriculture contributes around Lm35·8m. annually towards GDP, or 2·6%. 2001 production figures (in 1,000 tonnes): potatoes, 25; tomatoes, 18; melons, 12; wheat, 10; onions, 7; cauliflowers, 6.

Livestock in 2001: cattle, 18,417; pigs, 80,481; sheep, 10,376; chickens, 1·9m. Livestock produce accounted for 60·7% of the total value of agricultural production during 2001.

Fisheries. In 2001 the fishing industry employed 1,747 power-propelled fishing boats, engaging around 365 full time and 1,598 part-time fisherman. The catch for 2001 was 841 tonnes, valued at Lm1,587,044. It is estimated that during 2001 the local aquaculture industry produced a total of about 1,235 tonnes of sea bass and bream. 95% of the local production was exported to EU countries in 2001, especially to Italy.

INDUSTRY

Besides manufacturing (food, clothing, chemicals, electrical machinery parts and electronic components and products), the mainstays of the economy are ship repair and shipbuilding, agriculture, small crafts units, tourism and the provision of other services such as the freeport facilities. The majority of state-aided manufacturing enterprises operating in Malta are foreign-owned or with foreign interests. The Malta Development Corporation is the government agency responsible for promoting investment, while the Malta Export Trade Corporation serves as a catalyst to the export of local products.

Labour. The labour supply in Dec. 2002 was 144,016 (females, 40,185), including 35,571 in private direct production (agriculture and fisheries, 2,203; manufacturing, 28,970; oil drilling, construction and quarrying, 6,398), 50,059 in private market services, 47,992 in the public sector (including government departments, armed forces, revenue security corps, independent statutory bodies and companies with government majority shareholding) and 1,206 in temporary employment. There were 7,188 registered unemployed (5·0% of labour supply).

Trade Unions. In 2003 there were 33 Trade Unions with a total membership of 86,061 and 23 employers' associations with a total membership of 8,960. In 2003 the largest union was the General Workers' Union with a total membership of 47,254.

INTERNATIONAL TRADE

Imports are being liberalized. Marsaxlokk is an all-weather freeport zone for transhipment activities. The Malta Export Trade Corporation promotes local exports. External debt was US$1,531m. in 2001.

Imports and Exports. In 2002 imports (f.o.b.) were valued at Lm1,222·3m. (Lm1,225·1m. in 2001) and exports (f.o.b.) at Lm905·4m. (Lm880·6m. in 2001). In 2002 the principal items of imports were: machinery and transport equipment, Lm596·3m.; semi-manufactures, Lm151·0m.; manufactures, Lm116·8m.; foodstuffs, Lm109·8m.; fuels, Lm103·0m.; chemicals, Lm96·4m. Of domestic exports: machinery and transport equipment, Lm517·7m.; manufactures, Lm166·8m.; semi-manufactures, Lm50·9m.; foodstuffs, Lm21·4m.; chemicals, Lm13·4m.

In 2000 imports valued at Lm281·9m. came from France; Lm249·7m. from Italy; Lm158·5m. from USA; Lm122·1m. from Germany; Lm119·7m. from UK. Main export markets: USA, Lm286·5m.; Singapore, Lm164·7m.; Germany, Lm96·7m.; France, Lm84·1m.; UK, Lm70·0m.; Italy, Lm33·1m.

Trade Fairs. The Malta Trade Fairs Corporation organizes the International Fair of Malta (early July).

COMMUNICATIONS

Roads. In 2002 there were 2,254 km of roads, including 185 km of motorways. About 94% of roads are paved. Motor vehicles licensed up to 31 Dec. 2002 totalled 261,329 including: private cars, 195,055; commercial vehicles, 43,852; motorcycles, 13,097; self drive cars, 5,454. There were 15 deaths as a result of road accidents in 2000.

Civil Aviation. The national carrier is Air Malta, which is 96·4% state-owned. There were scheduled services in 2003 to around 30 different countries. In 2001 there were 32,652 commercial aircraft movements at Malta International Airport. 2,806,013 passengers and 12,925 tonnes of freight/mail were handled. In 1999 Air Malta flew 24·0m. km and carried 1,421,300 passengers.

Shipping. There is a car ferry between Malta and Gozo. The number of vessels registered on 30 Sept. 2003 was 3,365 totalling 26,702,959 GT, a total only exceeded by Panama, Liberia, the Bahamas and Greece. Ships entering harbour in the period Oct. 2002–Sept. 2003 totalled 9,043. 410 cruise vessels put in during the same period.

The Malta Freeport plays an important role in the economy as it is effectively positioned to act as a distribution centre in the Mediterranean. Apart from providing efficient transhipment operations to the major shipping lines, the Freeport offers warehouse facilities and the storage and blending of oil products.

Telecommunications. The Maltacom plc group is Malta's leading telecommunications and ancillary services provider. Malta's national network consist of 12 AXE10 Ericsson Digital Exchanges and one Siemens EWSD Exchange. Maltacom provides various data services including packet switching, frame relay and high-speed leased lines. The company has an optical fibre-based SDH backbone and large companies are connected to the Network. Maltacom's International Network includes two fully digital gateways, two satellite Standard B Earth Stations (one transmitting to the Atlantic Ocean Region and the other to the Indian Ocean Region) and an optic fibre submarine cable linking Malta to Sicily (Italy) and terrestrially extending to Palermo which is the hub of international submarine cables passing through the Mediterranean.

In 2002 telephone subscribers numbered 484,100 (1,222·5 per 1,000 inhabitants) and there were 101,000 PCs (255·1 per 1,000 persons). Mobile phone subscribers numbered 276,900 in 2002 and there were 6,000 fax machines in 1996. In 2002 there were 82,900 Internet users.

Postal Services. In 1994 there were 50 post offices operated by Maltapost plc. Airmail dispatches are forwarded twice daily to the UK, Canada, Australia, USA and Italy. Airmails from most countries are received daily or every other day. There are branch post offices and sub post offices in most towns and villages in Malta and Gozo.

SOCIAL INSTITUTIONS

Justice. The number of persons arrested between 1 Jan. 2001 and 31 Oct. 2001 was 5,451; those found guilty numbered 2,180. 184 persons were committed to prison.

In Jan. 2003 total police strength was 1,841 including 107 officers (92 males and 15 females) and 1,734 other ranks (250 females).

Malta abolished the death penalty for all crimes in 2000.

Religion. 98% of the population belong to the Roman Catholic Church, which is established by law as the religion of the country, although full liberty of conscience and freedom of worship are guaranteed.

Education. Adult literacy rate, 2001, 92·3% (male, 91·5%; female, 93·0%).

Education is compulsory between the ages of 5 and 16 and free in government schools from kindergarten to university. Kindergarten education is provided for three- and four-year old children. The primary school course lasts six years. In 2003 there were 19,300 children enrolled in 77 state primary schools. There are education centres for children with special needs, but they are taught in ordinary schools if possible.

Secondary schools, trade schools and junior lyceums provide secondary education in the state sector. At the end of their primary education, pupils sit the 11+ examination to start a secondary education course. Pupils who qualify are admitted in the junior lyceum, while the others attend secondary schools. In 2003–04, 11 junior lyceums had a total of 9,700 students (5,600 girls and 4,100 boys). About 8,200 pupils attend secondary schools. Five centres providing secondary education for under-performing students have a registered student population of about 900, of which 500 are boys. Secondary schools and junior lyceums offer a five-year course leading to the Secondary Education Certificate and the General Certificate of Education, Ordinary Level.

At the end of the five-year secondary course, students may opt to follow a higher academic or technical or vocational course of from one to four years. The academic courses generally lead to Intermediate and Advanced Level examinations set by the British universities. The Matriculation Certificate, which qualifies students for admission to university, is a broad-based holistic qualification covering—among others—the humanities and the sciences, together with systems of knowledge.

About 35% of the student population attend non-state schools, from kindergarten to higher secondary level. In Oct. 2003 there were about 25,700 pupils attending non-state schools, 800 of whom were at post-compulsory secondary level, 17,100 were in schools run by the Roman Catholic Church, while 8,500 students were attending private schools. Under an agreement between the government and the Church, the government subsidizes Church schools and students attending these schools do not pay any fees. During 2001 the government introduced tax rebates for parents whose children attended independent schools.

More than 9,800 students (including 750 from overseas) were following courses at the University in 2003. University students receive a stipend.

A post-compulsory vocational college, the Malta College of Arts, Science and Technology, provides vocational and technical courses up to degree level. In Oct. 2003 about 9,000 students (47% of which were females) were following post-compulsory education in state colleges and institutes.

In 1999–2000 total expenditure on education came to 4·9% of GNP.

Health. In 2003 there were 1,254 doctors, 169 dentists, 799 pharmacists, 1,060 paramedics, 365 midwives and 5,220 nursing personnel. There were eight hospitals (three private) with 2,122 beds. There are also nine health centres.

Welfare. Legislation provides a national contributory insurance scheme and also for the payment of non-contributory allowances, assistances and pensions. It covers the payment of marriage grants, maternity benefits, child allowances, parental allowances, handicapped child allowance, family bonus, sickness benefit, injury benefits, disablement benefits, unemployment benefit, contributory pensions in respect of retirement, invalidity and widowhood, and non-contributory medical assistance, free medical aids, social assistance, a carers' pension and pensions for the handicapped, the blind and the aged.

Malta's average actual retirement age is just 53 years, compared to the EU average of 57.

CULTURE

World Heritage Sites. Malta has three sites on the UNESCO World Heritage List (all inscribed on the list in 1980): Hal Saflieni Hypogeum, a prehistoric underground necropolis; the City of Valletta, a highly concentrated centre marked by the influences of Romans, Byzantines and Arabs and the Knights of St John; and the Megalithic Temples of Malta, seven temples on Malta and Gozo.

Broadcasting. Radio and TV services are under the control of the Broadcasting Authority, an independent statutory body. The government-owned Public Broadcasting Services Ltd was set up in 1991 and operates three radio stations and a TV station (colour by PAL). Legislation of 1991 introduced private commercial broadcasting. In 2003 there were 11 radio and four TV services and a cable TV network. In 2001 there were 222,000 television sets and in 1997 there were 255,000 radio receivers.

Cinema. In 2004 there were eight cinemas.

Press. In 2004 there were two English and two Maltese dailies, five Maltese and three English weeklies and two financial weeklies in English.

Tourism. Tourism is the major foreign currency earner, and accounts for more than 25% of Malta's GDP.

In 2002, 1·13m. tourists visited Malta, generating earnings of Lm246·3m. Cruise passenger visits totalled 341,632. Over 40% of tourists are from the UK.

Festivals. Major festivals include the Malta Song Festival; Carnival Festivals at Valletta (Feb.); History and Elegance Festival at Valletta (April); National Folk Singing; Malta International Arts Festival; Malta Jazz Festival; International Food and Beer Festival (June/July); Festa Season (June–Sept.); Malta International Choir Festival (Nov.).

Libraries. The National Library, housed in one of Valletta's 18th century buildings, is Malta's foremost research Library, founded in 1763. There is a Central Public Library in Floriana, Branch Libraries in government schools in most towns and villages, and the University of Malta Library.

Theatre and Opera. The Manoel Theatre (built 1731) is Malta's National Theatre. There is also the Mediterranean Conference Centre in Valletta, and the Astra Theatre in Victoria, Gozo.

Museums and Galleries. In Valletta: National Museum of Archaeology, National Museum of Fine Arts, Palace Armoury, War Museum (Fort St. Elmo). Mdina and Rabat: National Museum of Natural History, Museum of Roman Antiquities, St Paul's Catacombs, the Cathedral Museum. Paula: Hal Saflieni Hypoguem. Qrendi: Hagar Qim and Mnajra Megalithic Temples. Birzebbuga: Ghar Dalam Cave and Museum. Vittoriosa: Maritime Museum. Gozo (Victoria): Museum of Archaeology, Natural Science Museum, Folklore Museum. Xaghra: Ggantija Megalithic Temples.

DIPLOMATIC REPRESENTATIVES

Of Malta in the United Kingdom (36–38 Piccadilly, London, W1J 0LE)
Acting High Commissioner: Gawdenz Galea.

Of the United Kingdom in Malta (Whitehall Mansions, Ta'Xbiex Seafront, Msida MSD 11)
High Commissioner: Vincent Fean.

Of Malta in the USA (2017 Connecticut Ave., NW, Washington, D.C., 20008)
Ambassador: John Lowell.

Of the USA in Malta (Development House, St Anne St., Floriana)
Ambassador: Vacant.
Chargé d'Affaires a.i.: William Grant.

Of Malta to the United Nations
Ambassador: Victor Camilleri.

Of Malta to the European Union
Ambassador: Vacant.
Chargé d'Affaires a.i.: Tarcisio Zammit.

FURTHER READING

Central Office of Statistics (Lascaris, Valletta). *Statistical Abstracts of the Maltese Islands*, a quarterly digest of statistics, quarterly and annual trade returns, annual vital statistics and annual publications on shipping and aviation, education, agriculture, industry, National Accounts and Balance of Payments.

Department of Information (3 Castille Place, Valletta). *The Malta Government Gazette, Malta Information, Economic Survey [year], Reports on the Working of Government Departments, The Maltese Economy in Figures, 1986–1995, Business Opportunities on Malta, Acts of Parliament and Subsidiary Legislation, Laws of Malta, Constitution of Malta 1992.*

Central Bank of Malta. *Annual Reports.*

Chamber of Commerce (annual). *Trade Directory.*

Berg, W. G., *Historical Dictionary of Malta*. Metuchen (NJ), 1995

Boswell, D. and Beeley, B., *Malta.* [Bibliography] 2nd ed. ABC-Clio, Oxford and Santa Barbara (CA), 1998.

The Malta Yearbook. Valletta

National statistical office: Central Office of Statistics, Auberge d'Italie, Valletta.
Website: http://www.nso.gov.mt

MARSHALL ISLANDS

Republic of the Marshall Islands

Capital: Majuro Atoll
Population, 1999: 51,000
GDP per capita: not available
GNP per capita: $2,190

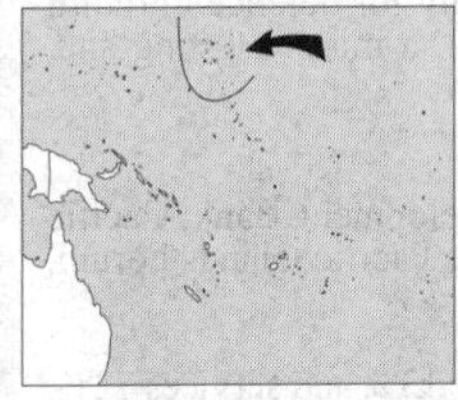

KEY HISTORICAL EVENTS

A German protectorate was formed in 1886 which was occupied at the beginning of the First World War by Japan. Japan was awarded a mandate by the League of Nations in 1919. During the Second World War the Islands were occupied by Allied forces in 1944, and became part of the UN Trust Territory of the Pacific Islands created on 18 July 1947 and administered by the USA. On 21 Oct. 1986 the islands gained independence. A Compact of Free Association with the USA came into force and was extended by 20 years in 2003.

TERRITORY AND POPULATION

The Marshall Islands lie in the North Pacific Ocean north of Kiribati and east of Micronesia, and consist of an archipelago of 31 coral atolls, 5 single islands and 1,152 islets strung out in two chains, eastern and western. Of these, 25 atolls and islands are inhabited. The land area is 181 sq. km (70 sq. miles). The capital is Majuro in the eastern chain (population, 1999 census, 23,682). The principal atoll in the western chain is Kwajalein, containing the only other town, Ebeye (population, 1999 census, 10,903). The two archipelagic island chains of Bikini and Enewetak are former US nuclear test sites; Kwajalein is now used as a US missile test range. The islands lay claim to the US territory of Wake Island. At the census of 1999 the population was 50,840 (26,026 males); density, 281 per sq. km. 2003 estimate: 56,000.

In 1995 some 69% of the population lived in urban areas. About 97% of the population are Marshallese, a Micronesian people.

English is universally spoken and is the official language. Two major Marshallese dialects from the Malayo-Polynesian family, and Japanese, are also spoken.

SOCIAL STATISTICS

2001 births, estimate, 1,511; deaths, 271. 2001 rates per 1,000 population, estimates: birth, 28·0; death, 5·0. Infant mortality rate, 2000, 35 per 1,000 live births; life expectancy, 2000, 68·4 years. Annual population growth rate, 1999–2003, 2·5%; fertility rate, 2001, 5·7 births per woman.

CLIMATE

Hot and humid, with wet season from May to Nov. The islands border the typhoon belt. Jaluit, Jan. 81°F (27·2°C), July 82°F (27·8°C). Annual rainfall 161" (4,034 mm).

CONSTITUTION AND GOVERNMENT

Under the constitution which came into force on 1 May 1979, the Marshall Islands form a republic with a *President* as head of state and government, who is elected for four-year terms by the parliament. The parliament consists of a 33-member *House of Assembly* (Nitijela), directly elected by popular vote for four-year terms. There is also a 12-member appointed *Council of Chiefs* (Iroij) which has a consultative and advisory capacity on matters affecting customary law and practice.

RECENT ELECTIONS

President Kessai Note was re-elected by parliament on 5 Jan. 2004, defeating Justin de Brum. At the House of Assembly elections on 17 Nov. 2003 President Note's United Democratic Party won 20 of the 33 seats.

CURRENT ADMINISTRATION

President: Kessai Note (UDP; elected on 3 Jan. 2000; re-elected 5 Jan. 2004).

In March 2005 the government comprised:

Minister of Assistance to the President: Witten Philippo. *Education:* Wilfred Kendall. *Finance:* Brenson Wase. *Foreign Affairs and Trade:* Gerald Zackios. *Health and Environment:* Alvin Jacklick. *Internal Affairs and Social Welfare:* Rien Morris. *Justice:* Donald Capelle. *Public Works:* Mattlan Zackhras. *Resources, Development and Works:* John Silk. *Transportation and Communications:* Michael Konelios.

DEFENCE

The Compact of Free Association gave the USA responsibility for defence in return for US assistance. In 2003 the US lease of Kwajalein Atoll, a missile testing site, was extended by 50 years.

INTERNATIONAL RELATIONS

The Marshall Islands are a member of the UN, Asian Development Bank, Pacific Community (formerly the South Pacific Commission) and the Pacific Islands Forum.

ECONOMY

Agriculture accounts for approximately 15% of GDP, industry 13% and services 72%.

Currency. US currency is used. The average annual inflation rate during the period 1990–96 was 6·4%.

Budget. Revenue in 1997–98 was US$61·4m.; expenditure was US$50·9m. Under the terms of the Compact of Free Association, the USA provides approximately US$65m. a year in aid.

Performance. Real GDP growth was 0·6% in 2001 (0·7% in 2000). Total GDP in 2003 was US$0·1bn.

Banking and Finance. There are three Banks: the Bank of Marshall Islands, the Marshall Islands Development Bank and the Bank of Guam.

The Marshall Islands were one of 15 countries and territories named in a report in June 2000 as failing to co-operate in the fight against international money laundering. The Financial Action Task Force on Money Laundering was set up by the G7 group of major industrialized nations.

ENERGY AND NATURAL RESOURCES

Electricity. Total installed capacity (1997), 20,200 kW. Production (1999), 63m. kWh.

Minerals. High-grade phosphate deposits are mined on Ailinglaplap Atoll. Deep-seabed minerals are an important natural resource.

Agriculture. A small amount of agricultural produce is exported: coconuts, tomatoes, melons and breadfruit. Other important crops include copra, taro, cassava and sweet potatoes. Pigs and chickens constitute the main livestock. In 2001 there were 3,000 ha of arable land and 7,000 ha of permanent crop land.

Fisheries. Total catch in 2001 amounted to 37,098 tonnes. There is a commercial tuna-fishing industry with a canning factory on Majuro. Seaweed is cultivated. Fisheries offers one of the best opportunities for economic growth.

INDUSTRY

The main industries are copra, fish, tourism, handicrafts (items made from shell, wood and pearl), mining, manufacturing, construction and power.

Labour. The total labour force numbered 11,488 in 1988. An estimated 16% were unemployed in 1991. In 1994 agriculture accounted for 16% of the working population; industry, 14%; services, 70%.

INTERNATIONAL TRADE

The Compact of Free Association with the USA is the major source of income for the Marshall Islands, and accounts for about 70% of total GDP.

Imports and Exports. Imports (mainly oil) were estimated at US$68·2m. in 2000; exports, US$7·3m. Main import suppliers in 1997: USA, 47·2%; Guam, 4·8%;

Australia, 4·0%; Singapore, 3·4%. The USA accounted for approximately 80·0% of exports in 1997. Main exports: coconut oil, copra cake, chilled and frozen fish, pet fish, shells and handicrafts.

COMMUNICATIONS

Roads. There are paved roads on major islands (Majuro, Kwajalein); roads are otherwise stone-, coral- or laterite-surfaced. In 1994 there were 1,418 passenger cars and 193 trucks and buses.

Civil Aviation. There were nine paved and seven unpaved airports in 1996. The main airport is Majuro International. In 2003 there were flights to Guam, Honolulu, Johnston Island, Kiribati and Micronesia as well as domestic services. The national carrier is Air Marshall Islands.

Shipping. Majuro is the main port. In 2000 merchant shipping consisted of 302 vessels totalling 9,745,000 GRT, including oil tankers 5,462,000 GRT. The ship's register of the Marshall Islands is a flag of convenience register.

Telecommunications. In 2002 there were 4,900 telephone subscribers (87·2 per 1,000 persons). There is a US satellite communications system on Kwajalein and two Intelsat satellite earth stations (Pacific Ocean). Mobile phone subscribers numbered 600 in 2002 and there were 3,000 PCs in use (53·0 per 1,000 persons). There were 1,300 Internet users in 2002.

Postal Services. Postal services are available on the main island of Majuro and also in Ebeye.

SOCIAL INSTITUTIONS

Justice. The Supreme Court is situated on Majuro. There is also a High Court, a District Court and 23 Community Courts. A Traditional Court deals with disputes involving land properties and customs.

Religion. The population is mainly Protestant, with Roman Catholics next. Other Churches and denominations include Latter-day Saints (Mormons), Jehovah's Witnesses, Baptists, Baha'i, Seventh Day Adventists and Assembly of God.

Education. In 1998–99 there were 12,421 pupils with 548 teachers in 103 primary schools, and 2,667 pupils with 162 teachers in 16 secondary schools. There is a College of the Marshall Islands, and a subsidiary of the University of the South Pacific, on Majuro. In 1999–2000 total expenditure on education came to 13·8% of GNP.

Health. There were two hospitals in 1997, with a total of 129 beds. There were 34 doctors, 141 nurses and health assistants, 4 dentists and 6 midwives in 1997.

CULTURE

Broadcasting. There are one TV and three radio stations.

Press. There is a publication called Micronitor (The Marshall Islands Journal).

Tourism. In 2000 there were 5,000 foreign tourists; spending by tourists totalled US$4m. Tourism offers one of the best opportunities for economic growth.

Festivals. Custom Day and the Annual Canoe Race are the main festivals.

DIPLOMATIC REPRESENTATIVES

Of the United Kingdom in the Marshall Islands
Ambassador: Ian Powell (resides at Suva, Fiji Islands).

Of the Marshall Islands in the USA (2433 Massachusetts Ave., NW, Washington, D.C., 20008)
Ambassador: Banny de Brum.

Of the USA in the Marshall Islands (Oceanside Mejen Weto, Long Island, Majuro)
Ambassador: Greta N. Morris.

Of the Marshall Islands to the United Nations
Ambassador: Alfred Capelle.

Of the Marshall Islands to the European Union
Ambassador: Vacant.

MAURITANIA

République Islamique Arabe et Africaine de Mauritanie

Capital: Nouakchott
Population projection, 2010: 3·52m.
GDP per capita, 2002: (PPP$) 2,220
HDI/world rank: 0·465/152

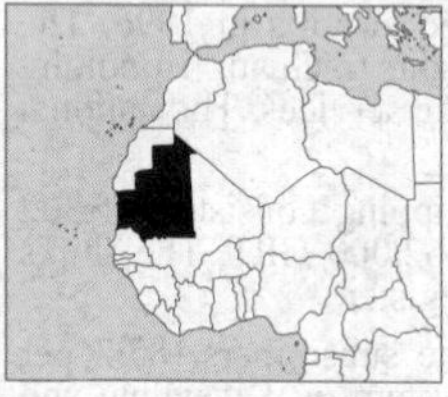

KEY HISTORICAL EVENTS

Mauritania became a French protectorate in 1903 and a colony in 1920. It achieved full independence on 28 Nov. 1960. Mauritania became a one-party state in 1964.

The 1980s were characterized by territorial disputes with Morocco and Senegal. Seizing power in 1984, Lieut.-Col. Maaouya Ould Sid'Ahmed Taya prepared the way for a new constitution allowing for a multi-party political system, which also gave extensive powers to the president. A coup attempt against Ould Taya failed in June 2003.

TERRITORY AND POPULATION

Mauritania is bounded west by the Atlantic Ocean, north by Western Sahara, northeast by Algeria, east and southeast by Mali, and south by Senegal. The total area is 1,030,700 sq. km (398,000 sq. miles) of which 47% is desert, and the population at the census of 2000 was 2,548,157; density, 2·47 per sq. km. In 2001, 59·0% of the population was urban.

The UN gives a projected population for 2010 of 3·52m.

Area (in sq. km), population (at the 2000 census) and chief towns of the Nouakchott Capital District and 12 regions:

Region	*Area*	*Population*	*Chief town*
Açâba	36,600	249,596	Kiffa
Adrar	215,300	60,847	Atâr
Brakna	33,800	240,167	Aleg
Dakhlet Nouâdhibou	22,300	75,976	Nouâdhibou
Gorgol	13,600	248,980	Kaédi
Guidimaka	10,300	186,697	Sélibaby
Hodh ech-Chargui	182,700	275,288	Néma
Hodh el-Gharbi	53,400	219,167	Aïoun el Atrouss
Inchiri	46,800	11,322	Akjoujt
Nouakchott District	1,000	611,883	Nouakchott
Tagant	95,200	61,984	Tidjikdja
Tiris Zemmour	252,900	53,586	Zouérate
Trarza	67,800	252,664	Rosso

Principal towns (1999 population): Nouakchott, 881,000 including the suburbs of Nouâdhibou and Kaédi.

In 1987 there were also 0·43m. nomads.

The major ethnic groups are (with numbers in 1993): Moors (of mixed Arab, Berber and African origin), 1,513,400; Wolof, 147,000; Tukulor, 114,600; Soninke, 60,000.

Arabic is the official language. French no longer has official status. Pulaar, Soninke and Wolof are national languages.

SOCIAL STATISTICS

2000 estimates: births, 109,000; deaths, 34,000. 2000 rates, estimate (per 1,000 population): births, 42·9; deaths, 13·4. Expectation of life at birth in 2001 was 50·3 years for males and 53·5 for females. Annual population growth rate, 1992–02, 2·8%. Infant mortality, 2001, 120 per 1,000 live births; fertility rate, 2001, 6·0 births per woman.

CLIMATE

A tropical climate, but conditions are generally arid, even near the coast, where the only appreciable rains come in July to Sept. Nouakchott, Jan. 71°F (21·7°C), July 82°F (27·8°C). Annual rainfall 6" (158 mm).

CONSTITUTION AND GOVERNMENT

A referendum was held in July 1991 to approve a new constitution instituting multi-party politics. Turn-out was 85·34%; 97·94% of votes cast were in favour.

The new constitution envisages that the President is elected by universal suffrage for renewable six-year terms. There is a 56-member *Senate* and an 81-member *National Assembly*. Parties specifically Islamic are not permitted.

National Anthem. No words, tune by T. Nikiprowetzky.

RECENT ELECTIONS

Presidential elections were held on 7 Nov. 2003. Col. Maaouya Ould Sid'Ahmed Taya was re-elected with 67·0% of votes cast. Mohamed Khouna Ould Haidalla took 18·7% of the vote, Ahmed Ould Daddah 6·9% and Messaoud Ould Boulkheir 5·0%. Turn-out was 60·8%.

Elections for the National Assembly were held on 19 and 26 Oct. 2001. The Democratic and Socialist Republican Party (PRDS) gained 64 seats with 51·0% of votes cast. Turn-out was 54·5%. In the Senate elections of 7 and 14 April 2000 the PRDS obtained 52 of the 56 seats.

CURRENT ADMINISTRATION

President: Maaouya Ould Sid'Ahmed Taya; b. 1943 (PRDS; assumed office 12 Dec. 1984 and re-elected 1992, 1997 and 2003).

Prime Minister: Sghaïr Ould M'Bareck; b. 1954 (PRDS; appointed on 6 July 2003).

In March 2005 the cabinet comprised:

Minister of National Defence: Baba Ould Sidi. *Interior, Posts and Telcommunications:* Lemrabott Sidi Mahmoud Ould Cheikh Ahmed. *Foreign Affairs and Co-operation:* Mohamed Vall Ould Bellal. *Justice:* Diabira Bakary. *Finance:* Sidi Ould Didi. *Economic Affairs and Development:* Mohamed Sidya Ould Mohamed Khaled. *Fisheries and Maritime Economy:* Ba Mamadou Mbare. *Trade, Handicrafts and Tourism:* Mohamed Kaber Ould Khattry. *Mines and Industry:* Kane Moustapha. *Oil and Energy:* Zeïdane Ould H'Meyda. *Health and Social Affairs:* Mohamed Lemine Ould Selmane. *Culture, Youth and Sports:* Ahmedou Ould Ahmedou. *Labour and Civil Service:* Salka Mint Bilal. *Equipment and Transportation:* Moustapha Ould Abdellah. *National Education:* Mohamed Lemine Ould Deidah. *Rural Development, Hydraulics and Environment:* Sidi Mohamed Ould Taleb Amar. *Communications and Relations with Parliament:* Hammoud Ould Abdi. *Literacy and Islamic Orientation:* Mohamed Mahmoud Ould Boye.

Government Website (French and Arabic only): http://www.mauritania.mr

DEFENCE

Conscription is authorized for two years. Defence expenditure in 2003 totalled US$19m. (US$7 per capita), representing 1·7% of GDP.

Army. There are six military regions. Army strength was approximately 15,000 in 2002. In addition there was a Gendarmerie of 3,000 and a National Guard of 2,000.

Navy. The Navy, some 500 strong in 2002, is based at Nouâdhibou.

Air Force. Personnel (2002), 250 with eight combat aircraft.

INTERNATIONAL RELATIONS

Mauritania is a member of the UN, WTO, the African Union, the League of Arab States, Arab Maghreb Union, African Development Bank, IOM, OIC, Islamic Development Bank, International Organization of the Francophonie and is an ACP member state of the ACP-EU relationship.

ECONOMY

In 2002 agriculture accounted for 20·8% of GDP, industry 29·4% and services 49·8%.

Currency. The monetary unit is the *ouguiya* (MRO) which is divided into five *khoums*. In Oct. 1992 the ouguiya was devalued 28%. Foreign exchange reserves were US$284m. in Sept. 2000. Gold reserves were 12,000 troy oz in Jan. 2001. Inflation was 3·9% in 2002. Total money supply in May 2002 was 29,078m. ouguiya.

Budget. Revenues were 51·8bn. ouguiya in 2001 and expenditures 54·4bn. ouguiya.

Performance. Real GDP growth was 4·0% in 2001 and 3·3% in 2002. Mauritania's total GDP in 2003 was US$1·1bn.

Banking and Finance. The Central Bank (created 1973) is the bank of issue (*Governor,* Zeine Ould Zeidane). In 2002 there were seven commercial banks and two Islamic banks. Bank deposits totalled 12,304m. ouguiya in 1992.

ENERGY AND NATURAL RESOURCES

Environment. In 2002 carbon dioxide emissions from the consumption and flaring of fossil fuels were the equivalent of 1·1 tonnes per capita.

Electricity. Installed capacity was 0·1m. kW in 2000. Production in 2000 was around 163m. kWh; consumption per capita was an estimated 61 kWh.

Oil and Gas. Oil was discovered off the coast of Mauritania in 2001. Production is expected to begin during 2005, initially with 75,000 bbls. a day.

Minerals. There are reserves of copper, gold, phosphate, gypsum, platinum and diamonds. Iron ore, 10·3m. tonnes of which were mined in 2001, accounts for about 11% of GNP and 40% of exports. Gold, 1995, 57,900 troy oz. Prospecting licences have also been issued for diamonds.

Agriculture. Only 1% of the country receives enough rain to grow crops, so agriculture is mainly confined to the south, in the Senegal river valley. There were 488,000 ha of arable land in 2001 and 12,000 ha of permanent crops. Production (2000, in 1,000 tonnes): sorghum, 134; rice, 103; dates, 22; millet, 13; maize, 11; watermelons, 8; yams, 3.

Herding is the main occupation of the rural population and accounted for 16% of GDP in 1992. In 2000 there were 6·20m. sheep; 4·14m. goats; 1·43m. cattle; 1·21m. camels (1999); 4m. chickens.

Forestry. There were 317,000 ha of forests in 2000 covering 0·3% of the land area, chiefly in the southern regions, where wild acacias yield the main product, gum arabic. In 2001, 1·47m. cu. metres of roundwood were cut.

Fisheries. Total catch in 2001 was approximately 83,596 tonnes, of which 94% came from marine waters. Mauritania's coastal waters are among the world's most abundant fishing areas, earning it significant amounts of hard currency through licensing agreements. Fishing-related fees account for an estimated 15% of Mauritania's national budget.

INDUSTRY

Output, 2000 (in tonnes): residual fuel oil, 364,000; petrol, 235,000; distillate fuel oil, 153,000; frozen and chilled fish (2001), 27,000; hides and skins (2001), 5,400.

Labour. In 1996 the workforce was 1,072,000 (56% males). In 1994, 430,000 people worked in agriculture, forestry and fishing, 177,000 in services and 80,000 in industry.

INTERNATIONAL TRADE

Total foreign debt was US$2,309m. in 2002. In Feb. 1989 Mauritania signed a treaty of economic co-operation with the four other Maghreb countries—Algeria, Libya, Morocco and Tunisia.

Imports and Exports. In 1998 imports (f.o.b.) were valued at US$318·7m. (US$316·5m. in 1997) and exports (f.o.b.) at US$358·6m. (US$423·6m. in 1997). Main exports are fish and fish products (57% of total exports) and iron ore (40%). Main imports are foodstuffs, consumer goods, petroleum products and capital goods. Principal export markets in 1997 were Japan (23·3%), followed by Italy and France. Main import suppliers were France (25·5%), followed by Spain and Germany.

COMMUNICATIONS

Roads. There were about 7,660 km of roads in 1999, of which 870 km were asphalted. In 1996 there were 18,810 passenger cars and 10,450 commercial vehicles.

Rail. A 704-km railway links Zouérate with the port of Point-Central, 10 km south of Nouâdhibou, and is used primarily for iron ore exports. In 1995 it carried 11·3m. tonnes of freight.

Civil Aviation. There are international airports at Nouakchott, Nouâdhibou and Néma. Air Mauritanie provides domestic services, and in 2003 operated international services to Abidjan, Bamako, Bissau, Casablanca, Cotonou, Dakar, Las Palmas and Paris. In 1997 scheduled airline traffic of Mauritania-based carriers flew 4·3m. km, carrying 245,000 passengers (110,000 on international flights).

Shipping. In 2002 the merchant fleet totalled 48,000 GRT. The major ports are at Point-Central (for mineral exports), Nouakchott and Nouâdhibou.

Telecommunications. In 2002 Mauritania had 278,800 telephone subscribers (103·9 per 1,000 persons) and there were 29,000 PCs in use (10·8 per 1,000 persons). Mobile phone subscribers numbered 247,200 in 2002. There were 3,300 fax machines in 1999. In 2002 there were 10,000 Internet users.

Postal Services. In 1998 there were 61 post offices.

SOCIAL INSTITUTIONS

Justice. There are courts of first instance at Nouakchott, Atâr, Kaédi, Aïoun el Atrouss and Kiffa. The Appeal Court and Supreme Court are situated in Nouakchott. Islamic jurisprudence was adopted in 1980.

The population in penal institutions in 2002 was 1,354 (48 per 100,000 of national population).

Religion. Over 99% of Mauritanians are Sunni Muslim, mainly of the Qadiriyah sect.

Education. Basic education is compulsory for all children between the ages of six and 14. In 2000–01 there were 360,677 pupils and 8,636 teachers in primary schools, 76,658 secondary level pupils with 2,749 teachers and 9,033 tertiary level students with 301 academic staff. The University of Nouakchott had 2,850 students and 70 academic staff in 1994–95. Adult literacy rate in 2001 was 40·7% (male, 51·1%; female, 30·7%).

Total expenditure on education came to 3·6% of GNP in 1999–2000 and 16·6% of total government spending in 1998–99.

Health. In 1990 there were 16 hospitals with a provision of seven beds per 10,000 persons. There were 323 physicians, 47 dentists, 1,461 nurses and 267 midwives in 1995.

In the period 1990–98 only 37% of the population had access to safe drinking water.

CULTURE

World Heritage Sites. Mauritania has two sites on the UNESCO World Heritage List: Banc d'Arguin National Park (inscribed on the list in 1989), a coastal park of dunes and swamps; and the Ancient *Ksour* of Ouadane, Chinguetti, Tichitt and Oualata (1996), Islamic trading and religious centres in the Sahara.

Broadcasting. The government-controlled Office de Radiodiffusion-Télévision de Mauritanie is responsible for broadcasting. There are two radio and one TV networks. There were 260,000 TV sets (colour by SECAM) in 2001 and 360,000 radio sets in 1997.

Press. In 1996 there were two daily newspapers with a circulation of 1,000.

Tourism. There were 30,000 foreign tourists in 2000; spending by tourists in 1999 totalled US$28m.

DIPLOMATIC REPRESENTATIVES

Of Mauritania in the United Kingdom (8 Carlos Place, London, W1K 3AS)
Ambassador: Youssouf Diagana.

Of the United Kingdom in Mauritania
Ambassador: Haydon Warren-Gash (resides at Rabat, Morocco).

Of Mauritania in the USA (2129 Leroy Pl., NW, Washington, D.C., 20008)
Ambassador: Mohamedou Ould Michel.

Of the USA in Mauritania (Rue Abdallaye, Nouakchott)
Ambassador: Joseph LeBaron.

Of Mauritania to the United Nations
Ambassador: Dah Ouid Abdi.

Of Mauritania to the European Union
Ambassador: Aliou Ibra Ba.

FURTHER READING

Belvaud, C., *La Mauritanie.* Paris, 1992

Calderini, S., *et al., Mauritania.* [Bibliography] ABC-Clio, Oxford and Santa Barbara (CA), 1992

Pazzanita, A. G., *The Maghreb.* [Bibliography] ABC-Clio, Oxford and Santa Barbara (CA), 1998

National statistical office: Office National de la Statistique, BP240, Nouakchott.
Website (French only): http://www.ons.mr

MAURITIUS

Republic of Mauritius

Capital: Port Louis
Population projection, 2010: 1·29m.
GDP per capita, 2002: (PPP$) 10,810
HDI/world rank: 0·785/64

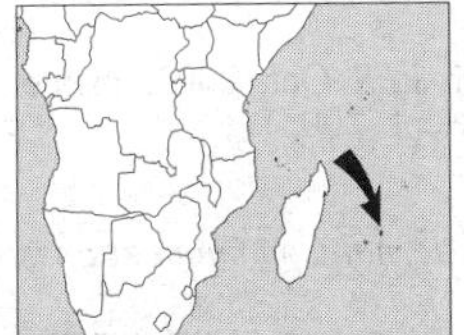

KEY HISTORICAL EVENTS

Mauritius was discovered by the Portuguese between 1507 and 1512. But the Dutch were the first settlers who named it after their stadtholder, Count Maurice. The British occupied the island in 1810 and it was formally ceded to Great Britain by the Treaty of Paris, 1814. Independence was attained within the Commonwealth on 12 March 1968. Mauritius became a republic on 12 March 1992.

TERRITORY AND POPULATION

Mauritius, the main island, lies 500 miles (800 km) east of Madagascar. Rodrigues is 350 miles (560 km) east. The outer islands are Agalega and the St Brandon Group. Area and population:

Island	*Area in sq. km*	*2003 mid-year population*
Mauritius	1,865	1,186,363
Rodrigues	104	36,448
Outer Islands	71	289
Total	2,040	1,223,100

Port Louis is the capital (147,688 inhabitants in 2003). Other towns: Beau Bassin-Rose Hill, 106,978; Vacoas-Phoenix, 103,564; Curepipe, 81,600; and Quatre Bornes, 78,538. In 2003, 57·6% of the population were rural.

The UN gives a projected population for 2010 of 1·29m.

Ethnic composition, 1996: Hindus, 52%; 'General Population' (i.e. European, African, Creole), 33%; Muslims, 10%; Chinese, 5%.

The official language is English, although French is widely used. Creole and Bhojpuri are vernacular languages.

SOCIAL STATISTICS

2003: births, 19,343 (rate of 15·8 per 1,000 population); deaths, 8,520 (7·0 per 1,000); marriages, 10,812 (8·8 per 1,000); divorces, 1,190 (1·0 per 1,000). In 1996 the suicide rate was 20·6 per 100,000 population among men and 6·4 per 100,000 among women. Annual population growth rate, 2000–03, 1·0%. In 2003 the most popular age range for marrying was 25–29 for males and 20–24 for females. Life expectancy at birth in 2002 was 68·6 years for males and 75·3 for females. Infant mortality, 2003, 13 per 1,000 live births; fertility rate, 2003, 1·9 births per woman.

CLIMATE

The sub-tropical climate is humid. Most rain falls in the summer. Rainfall varies between 40" (1,000 mm) on the coast to 200" (5,000 mm) on the central plateau, though the west coast only has 35" (875 mm). Mauritius lies in the cyclone belt, whose season runs from Nov. to April, but is seldom affected by intense storms. Port Louis, Jan. 73°F (22·8°C), July 81°F (27·2°C). Annual rainfall 40" (1,000 mm).

CONSTITUTION AND GOVERNMENT

The head of state is the *President*, elected by a simple majority of members of the National Assembly.

The 70-seat *National Assembly* consists of 62 elected members (three each for the 20 constituencies of Mauritius and two for Rodrigues) and eight additional seats in order to ensure a fair and adequate representation of each community within the Assembly. Elections are held every five years on the basis of universal adult suffrage.

National Anthem. 'Glory to thee, Motherland'; words by J. G. Prosper, tune by P. Gentille.

RECENT ELECTIONS

Parliamentary elections were held on 11 Sept. 2000. The coalition of the Mauritian Socialist Movement (MSM) and the Mauritian Militant Movement (MMM) won 54 seats with 51·7% of votes cast. The coalition of the Mauritius Labour Party and the Mauritian Party of Xavier Duval won 6 with 36·5% and the remaining 2 seats were won by the Rodrigues People's Organization.

CURRENT ADMINISTRATION

President: Sir Anerood Jugnauth (MSM); b. 1930 (sworn in 7 Oct. 2003; prime minister from June 1982 to Dec. 1995 and Sept. 2000 to Sept. 2003).

Vice President: Raouf Bundhun.

In March 2005 the cabinet was composed as follows:

Prime Minister, Minister of Defence, Home Affairs and External Communications: Paul Bérenger (MMM); b. 1945 (took office 30 Sept. 2003).

Deputy Prime Minister and Minister of Finance and Economic Development: Pravind Jugnauth. *Industry and Financial Services:* Khushhal Khushiram. *Housing and Lands, and Fisheries:* Georges Pierre Lesjongard. *Social Security, National Solidarity, Senior Citizen Welfare and Institutional Reform:* Samioullah Lauthan. *Public Utilities:* Alan Ganoo. *Agriculture, Food Technology and Natural Resources:* Nandcoomar Bodha. *Environment and National Development:* Rajesh Bhagwan. *Public Infrastructure and Land Transport:* Ajay Guness. *Civil Service Affairs and Administrative Reforms:* Ahmad Jeewah. *Labour and Industrial Relations:* Showkutally Soodhun. *Tourism and Leisure:* Anil Kumarsingh Gayan. *Women's Rights, Child Development and Family Welfare:* Arianne Navarre-Marie. *Foreign Affairs, International Trade and Regional Co-operation:* Jaya Krishna Cuttaree. *Education and Scientific Research:* Steve Obeegadoo. *Health and Quality of Life:* Ashock Jugnauth. *Arts and Culture:* Leela Devi Dookun. *Commerce and Co-operatives:* Motee Ramdass. *Information Technology and Telecommunications:* Deelchand Jeeha. *Justice, Human Rights and Attorney General:* Emmanuel Leung Shing, QC. *Training, Skills Development and Productivity:* Sangeet Fowdar. *Youth and Sports:* Ravi Yerrigadoo. *Shipping, Rodrigues and Outer Islands:* Prithviraj Auroomooga Putten. *Small and Medium Enterprises, Handicraft and the Informal Sector:* Premdut Koonjoo.

Government Website: http://ncb.intnet.mu/govt/house.htm

DEFENCE

The Police Department is responsible for defence. Its strength was (2004) 10,500. In addition there is a special mobile paramilitary force of approximately 1,900, a Coast Guard of about 800 and a helicopter unit of about 100.

Defence expenditure totalled US$13m. in 2003 (US$10 per capita), representing 0·2% of GDP.

INTERNATIONAL RELATIONS

Mauritius is a member of the UN, WTO, the Commonwealth, the African Union, African Development Bank, COMESA, International Organization of the Francophonie, SADC and is an ACP member state of the ACP-EU relationship. Mauritius is also a founder member of the Indian Ocean Rim Association for Regional Co-operation.

ECONOMY

Agriculture accounted for 6·2% of GDP in 2003, industry 30·2% and services 63·6%.

Currency. The unit of currency is the *Mauritius rupee* (MUR) of 100 *cents*. There are Bank of Mauritius notes, cupro-nickel coins, nickel-plated steel coins and copper-plated steel coins. Inflation was 3·9% in 2003. In June 2002 foreign exchange reserves were US$964m., gold reserves totalled 62,000 troy oz and total money supply was Rs 15,131m.

Budget. For years ending 30 June: government recurrent revenue in 2004 (revised estimates) was Rs 32,155m. (Rs 29,488m. in 2003). Capital revenue in 2004 (revised estimates) was Rs 7,193m. (Rs 3,153m. in 2003). Recurrent and capital expenditure in 2004 were Rs 36,700m. and Rs 8,500m. respectively (Rs 33,529m. and Rs

8,407m. in 2003). Principal sources of recurrent revenue, 2003–04 (revised estimates): direct taxes, Rs 6,310m.; indirect taxes, Rs 22,505m.; receipts from public utilities, Rs 190m.; receipts from public services, Rs 946m.; rental of government property, Rs 130m.; interest and royalties, Rs 1,826m.; reimbursement, Rs 238m.; miscellaneous income, Rs 10m.

Performance. Real GDP growth was 4·6% in 2003 (1·8% in 2002). Total GDP in 2003 was US$5·2bn.

Banking and Finance. The Bank of Mauritius (founded 1967) is the central bank. The *Governor* is Rameswurlall Basant Roi. In 2002 there were eight commercial banks, two offshore banks and one development bank. Non-bank financial intermediaries are the Post Office Savings Bank, the State Investment Corporation Ltd, the Mauritius Leasing Company, the National Mutual Fund, the National Investment Trust and the National Pension Fund. Other financial institutions are the Mauritius Housing Company and the Development Bank of Mauritius. There is also a stock exchange in Port Louis.

ENERGY AND NATURAL RESOURCES

Environment. Carbon dioxide emissions were the equivalent of 2·3 tonnes per capita in 2003.

Electricity. Installed capacity was 0·65m. kW in 2003. Production (2003) was 1·86bn. kWh. Consumption per capita in 2003 was 1,330 kWh.

Agriculture. 74,117 ha were planted with sugarcane in 2003; production in 2003 was 5,199,384 tonnes. Main secondary crops (2003, in 1,000 tonnes): tomatoes, 13; bananas, 12; potatoes, 12; pumpkins and squash, 8; cucumbers, 7; cabbages, 6; onions, 4. In 2001 there were 100,000 ha of arable land and 6,000 ha of permanent cropland. 21,619 ha were irrigated in 2003.

Livestock, 2002: cattle, 28,000; goats, 93,000; pigs, 14,000.

Livestock products (2003) in tonnes: beef and veal, 2,580; pork, bacon and ham, 1,040; milk, 4,000; eggs, 12,500.

Forestry. The total forest area was 16,000 ha in 2000 (7·9% of the land area). In 2003 timber production totalled 14,007 cu. metres.

Fisheries. The catch in 2003 totalled 9,449 tonnes, exclusively sea fish.

INDUSTRY

Manufacturing includes: sugar, textile products, footwear and other leather products, diamond cutting, jewellery, furniture, watches and watchstraps, sunglasses, plastic ware, chemical products, electronic products, pharmaceutical products, electrical appliances, ship models and canned food. There were 11 sugar mills in 2003; sugar production in 2003 was 537,155 tonnes. Production figures for other leading commodities: beer (2003), 38·8m. litres; rum (2003), 7·0m. litres; molasses (2003), 160,041 tonnes; animal feeds (2002), 138,657 tonnes.

Labour. In 2003 the labour force was estimated at 549,500. Manufacturing employed the largest proportion, with 27·1% of total employment; wholesale and retail trade, 14·3%; agriculture, forestry and fishing, 9·4%; construction, 9·3%. In 2003 the unemployment rate was estimated at 10·2%.

Trade Unions. In 1996 there were 330 registered trade unions with a total membership of about 110,000.

INTERNATIONAL TRADE

External debt was US$1,013m. at June 2003.

Imports and Exports. In 2003 imports (c.i.f.) were valued at US$2,301·2m. (US$2,156·5m. in 2002) and exports (f.o.b.) at US$1,850·4m. (US$1,798·8m. in 2002). In 2003 Rs 8,068m. of the imports came from South Africa, Rs 7,841m. from France, Rs 5,539m. from China and Rs 5,438m. from India. In 2003 Rs 15,915m. of the exports went to the UK, Rs 9,403m. to France, Rs 8,772m. to the USA and Rs 3,184m. to Madagascar.

Major exports (2003) included articles of apparel and clothing, Rs 26,759m.; sugar, Rs 8,775m.; fish and fish preparations, Rs 3,167m.; textile yarns, fabrics and make-up articles, Rs 2,055m. Major imports in 2003 included manufactured goods (paper, textiles, iron and steel), Rs 18,863m.; machinery and transport equipment, Rs 14,241m.; food and live animals, Rs 10,308m.

COMMUNICATIONS

Roads. In 2003 there were 75 km of motorway, 950 km of main roads, 990 km of secondary and other roads. In 2003 there were 107,907 cars, 3,418 buses and coaches, 125,602 motorcycles and 33,997 trucks and vans. In 2003 there were 131 deaths as a result of road accidents.

Civil Aviation. In 2000, 1,783,848 passengers and 41,269 tonnes of freight were handled at Sir Seewoosagur Ramgoolam International Airport. The national carrier is Air Mauritius, which is partly state-owned. In 1999 it flew 23·4m. km, carrying 801,700 passengers (743,100 on international flights).

Shipping. A free port was established at Port Louis in Sept. 1991. In 2002 merchant shipping totalled 58,000 GRT. In 2003 vessels totalling 8,309,000 NRT entered ports and vessels totalling 8,843,000 NRT cleared.

Telecommunications. In 2002 there were 677,200 telephone subscribers, equivalent to 559·5 per 1,000 population. Mauritius Telecom, formed in 1992, provided telephone services to 183,902 subscribers in 1996 through 58 exchanges. There were 466,000 mobile phone subscribers in 2003 and 32,000 fax machines in use in 1999. Communication with other parts of the world is by satellite and microwave links. In 2002 there were 141,000 PCs in use (116·5 per 1,000 persons). Mauritius had 120,000 Internet users in 2002.

Postal Services. In 1998 there were 101 post offices.

SOCIAL INSTITUTIONS

Justice. There is an Ombudsman. The death penalty was abolished for all crimes in 1995.

The population in penal institutions in April 2003 was 2,565 (210 per 100,000 of national population).

Religion. In 2001 there were 610,000 Hindus, 330,000 Roman Catholics and 190,000 Muslims. In Sept. 2003 there was one cardinal.

Education. The adult literacy rate in 2001 was 84·8% (88·0% among males and 81·7% among females). Primary and secondary education is free, primary education being compulsory. Almost all children aged 5–11 years attend schools. In 2003 there were 124,933 pupils in 278 primary schools and 100,447 pupils in 169 secondary schools in the island of Mauritius, and 4,683 pupils in 13 primary schools and 3,400 in six secondary schools in Rodrigues. In 2003, 4,922 teachers were enrolled for training at the Mauritius Institute of Education.

In 2003–04 there were 5,745 students and 383 academic staff at the University of Mauritius.

In 2000–01 total expenditure on education came to 3·7% of GNP and 13·3% of total government spending.

Health. In 2003 there were 1,172 physicians, 154 dentists, 2,795 nurses and midwives, and 279 pharmacists. There were 12 hospitals in 2002 with a provision of 29 beds per 10,000 inhabitants.

CULTURE

Broadcasting. Broadcasting is run by the commercial Mauritius Broadcasting Corporation. There were 359,000 television sets (colour by SECAM V) in 2001 and 450,000 radio sets in 2000.

Cinema. In 2004 there were 28 cinemas; in 1997 cinemas had a seating capacity of about 25,000.

Press. There were seven daily papers in French in 2003 (with occasional articles in English), with a combined circulation (2000) of about 138,000.

Tourism. In 2003 there were 702,000 visitors, bringing in US$683m. in tourist revenue.

Festivals. Independence Day is marked by an official celebration at the Champ de Mars racecourse on 12 March. The Hindu festival of Cavadee is celebrated by the Tamil community at the beginning of the year; the major three-day Hindu festival of Maha Shivarati takes place around Feb./March. Other Hindu festivals include Divali and Ganesh Chaturhi, which is celebrated around Aug./Sept. The Spring Festival is celebrated on the eve of the Chinese New Year; Ougadi, the Telegu new year, is celebrated in March; the Tamil new year, Varusha Pirappu, takes place in April. Muslim festivals include Eid El Fitr and Eid El Adha. On 9 Sept. pilgrims visit the grave of the 19th century missionary Père Laval who is regarded as a national saint.

DIPLOMATIC REPRESENTATIVES

Of Mauritius in the United Kingdom (32–33 Elvaston Pl., London, SW7 5NW)
High Commissioner: Jaynarain Meetoo.

Of the United Kingdom in Mauritius (Les Cascades Bldg., Edith Cavell St, Port Louis)
High Commissioner: David Snoxell.

Of Mauritius in the USA (4301 Connecticut Ave., NW, Washington, D.C., 20008)
Ambassador: Dr Usha Jeetah.

Of the USA in Mauritius (Rogers House, John Kennedy St., Port Louis)
Ambassador: John Price.

Of Mauritius to the United Nations
Ambassador: Jagdish Dharamchang Koonjul.

Of Mauritius to the European Union
Ambassador: Sutiawan Gunessee.

FURTHER READING

Central Statistical Information Office. *Bi-annual Digest of Statistics.*
Bennett, Pamela R., *Mauritius.* [Bibliography] ABC-Clio, Oxford and Santa Barbara (CA), 1992
Bowman, L. W., *Mauritius: Democracy and Development in the Indian Ocean.* Aldershot, 1991

National statistical office: Central Statistics Office, LIC Building, President John Kennedy Street, Port Louis.
Website: http://statsmauritius.gov.mu

MEXICO

Estados Unidos Mexicanos (United States of Mexico)

Capital: Mexico City
Population projection, 2010: 113·32m.
GDP per capita, 2002: (PPP$) 8,970
HDI/world rank: 0·802/53

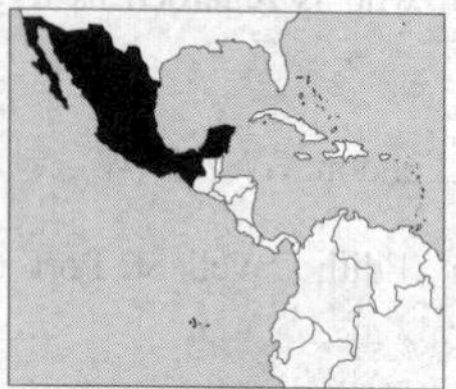

KEY HISTORICAL EVENTS

From about 2000 BC the people of Ancient Mexico began to settle in villages and to cultivate maize and other crops. From about 1000 BC the main cultures included the Olmec on the Gulf Coast, the Maya in the Yucatán peninsula and modern day Chiapas, the Zapotecs and Mixtecs in Oaxaca, the Tarascans in Michoacán and the Toltecs in central Mexico. One of the largest and most powerful cities in ancient Mexico was Teotihuacán, which in the 6th century AD was one of the six most populous cities in the world. By the time the Spanish *conquistadores* arrived in 1519, the dominant people were the Mexica, more commonly known as the Aztecs, whose capital Tenochtitlán became Mexico City after the conquest. Hernán Cortés landed on the Gulf Coast in 1519 and by 1521 had destroyed the Aztec state. The land conquered by Cortés was named New Spain, and was ruled by the Spanish Crown for three centuries. Rich silver mines were discovered and large estates (*haciendas*) were formed. Social dislocation and European diseases caused a collapse of the indigenous population. In 1520 the native population was probably 20m. By 1540 it had fallen to 6·5m. and by 1650 the figure was just over 1m.

Independence from Spain was declared in the Plan of Iguala on 24 Feb. 1821 when Agustín de Iturbide proclaimed himself Emperor of Mexico. He ruled for two years. There followed half a century of coups and counter coups. Spain invaded Tampico in 1829. Texas declared secession in 1836. The Mexican dictator Antonio de Santa Anna marched north but was defeated by the Texans. The 1848 Treaty of Guadalupe ended a two-year war with the USA, forcing Mexico to cede a huge swathe of its territory. In 1860 the conservatives were defeated by the liberal Reform government of Benito Juárez, who abolished the *fueros* (clerical and military privileges). The French Intervention (1862–67) installed the Habsburg Maximilian of Austria as Emperor of Mexico. With the loss of French military support, Maximilian was defeated and executed by Juárez's republicans.

From 1876–1910, a period known as the *porfiriato*, Mexico was ruled (with one interlude from 1880–84) by General Porfirio Díaz. Díaz imposed a degree of stability and order. He encouraged foreign investment that funded an expansion of the railways and an export-led boom. The economy faltered in the first decade of the 20th century. Díaz was deposed in 1911 by Francisco Madero whose Plan of San Luís Potosí launched the Mexican Revolution. Madero was deposed and assassinated in 1913. There followed a civil war fought by the armies of Venustiano Carranza, Pancho Villa and Emiliano Zapata. A new Constitution was written in 1917. Zapata was ambushed and killed in 1919 and Carranza was assassinated in 1920. Villa retired the same year but was assassinated in 1923.

In the 1920s Alvaro Obregón and Plutarco Elías Calles ruled Mexico. Obregón's assassination in 1928 led to the formation of the Natural Revolutionary Party (PRN), later the Institutional Revolutionary Party (PRI), which ruled Mexico for the rest of the century. Lázaro Cárdenas, who was president from 1934–40, nationalized the oil industry and accelerated the distribution of land. The election of Cárdenas' successor, Miguel Alemán, was opposed unsuccessfully by the last military rebellion in Mexico's history. Alemán's pro-business administration began a long period of economic prosperity, the 'Mexican Miracle'. However, by the late 1960s the Mexican economic and political system was under increasing strain. An uprising led by students ended in a bloody massacre in the Tlatelolco district of Mexico City in 1968. Financial and economic problems in the 1980s increased the strain on the political system. In 1988 the PRI candidate, Carlos Salinas de Gortari, defeated

Cuauhtémoc Cárdenas, son of the former president and candidate of the Democratic Revolutionary Party (PRD), in a rigged election. Salinas took Mexico into the North American Free Trade Agreement (NAFTA) with the USA and Canada in 1992. Salinas' choice as the PRI's presidential candidate, Luís Donaldo Colosio, was assassinated in Tijuana on 23 March 1994 and Ernesto Zedillo was hastily chosen in his place. In the same year the Zapatista National Liberation Army (EZLN) led an uprising in Chiapas.

In 2000 Vicente Fox Quesada of the National Action Party (PAN) was elected to the presidency. Fox has attempted to address two key issues: Mexico's economic and financial weakness and illegal migration to the USA.

TERRITORY AND POPULATION

Mexico is bounded in the north by the USA, west and south by the Pacific Ocean, southeast by Guatemala, Belize and the Caribbean Sea, and northeast by the Gulf of Mexico. It comprises 1,967,183 sq. km (759,529 sq. miles), including uninhabited islands (5,127 sq. km) offshore.

Population at recent censuses: 1970, 48,225,238; 1980, 66,846,833; 1990, 81,249,645; 2000, 97,361,711 (50,007,325 females). Population density, 49·5 per sq. km (2000). 74·6% of the population were urban in 2001.

The UN gives a projected population for 2010 of 113·32m.

Area, population and capitals of the Federal District and 31 states:

	Area (Sq. km)	*Population (1995 counting)*	*Population (2000 census)*	*Capital*
Federal District	1,499	8,489,007	8,591,309	Mexico City
Aguascalientes	5,589	862,720	943,506	Aguascalientes
Baja California Norte	70,113	2,112,140	2,487,700	Mexicali
Baja California Sur	73,677	375,494	423,516	La Paz
Campeche	51,833	642,516	689,656	Campeche
Chiapas	73,887	3,584,786	3,920,515	Tuxtla Gutiérrez
Chihuahua	247,087	2,793,537	3,047,867	Chihuahua
Coahuila de Zaragoza	151,571	2,173,775	2,295,808	Saltillo
Colima	5,455	488,028	540,679	Colima
Durango	119,648	1,431,748	1,445,922	Victoria de Durango
Guanajuato	30,589	4,406,568	4,656,761	Guanajuato
Guerrero	63,794	2,916,567	3,075,083	Chilpancingo de los Bravo
Hidalgo	20,987	2,112,473	2,231,392	Pachuca de Soto
Jalisco	80,137	5,991,176	6,321,278	Guadalajara
México	21,461	11,707,964	13,083,359	Toluca de Lerdo
Michoacán de Ocampo	59,864	3,870,604	3,979,177	Morelia
Morelos	4,941	1,442,662	1,552,878	Cuernavaca
Nayarit	27,621	896,702	919,739	Tepic
Nuevo Léon	64,555	3,550,114	3,826,240	Monterrey
Oaxaca	95,364	3,228,895	3,432,180	Oaxaca de Juárez
Puebla	33,919	4,624,365	5,070,346	Heroica Puebla de Zaragoza
Querétaro de Arteaga	11,769	1,250,476	1,402,010	Santiago de Querétaro
Quintana Roo	50,350	703,536	873,804	Chetumal
San Luis Potosí	62,848	2,200,763	2,296,363	San Luis Potosí
Sinaloa	58,092	2,425,675	2,534,835	Culiacán Rosales
Sonora	184,934	2,085,536	2,213,370	Hermosillo
Tabasco	24,661	1,748,769	1,889,367	Villahermosa
Tamaulipas	79,829	2,527,328	2,747,114	Ciudad Victoria
Tlaxcala	3,914	883,924	961,912	Tlaxcala de Xicohténcatl
Veracruz-Llave	72,815	6,737,324	6,901,111	Xalapa-Enríquez
Yucatán	39,340	1,556,622	1,655,707	Mérida
Zacatecas	75,040	1,336,496	1,351,207	Zacatecas
Total	1,967,183	91,158,290	97,361,711	

The official language is Spanish, the mother tongue of over 93% of the population (2000), but there are some indigenous language groups (of which Náhuatl, Maya, Zapotec, Otomi and Mixtec are the most important) spoken by 6,044,547 persons over five years of age (census 2000).

The populations (2000 census) of the largest cities (250,000 and more) were:

Mexico City	8,591,309	Ecatepcec de Morelos	1,621,827	Heroica Puebla de Zaragoza	1,271,673
Guadalajara	1,646,183				

Ciudad Nezahualcoyotl	1,225,083
Juárez	1,187,275
Tijuana	1,148,681
Monterrey	1,110,909
León de los Aldama	1,020,818
Zapopan	910,690
Naucalpan de Juárez	835,053
Tlalnepantla	714,735
Guadalupe	669,842
Mérida	662,530
Chihuahua	657,876
San Luis Potosí	629,208
Acapulco de Juárez	620,656
Aguascalientes	594,092
Saltillo	562,587
Morelia	549,996
Mexicali	549,873
Hermosillo	545,928
Culiacán Rosales	540,823
Santiago de Querétaro	536,463
Torreón	502,964
San Nicolás de los Garza	496,878
Chimalhuacan	482,530
Ciudad López Mateos	467,544
Tlaquepaque	458,674
Toluca de Lerdo	435,125
Cuautitlan Izcalli	433,830
Victoria de Durango	427,135
Tuxtla Gutiérrez	424,579
Veracruz	411,582
Reynosa	403,718
Cancún	397,191
Heroica Matamoros	376,279
Xalapa-Enríquez	373,076
Villahermosa	330,846
Mazatlán	327,989
Cuernavaca	327,162
Xico	322,784
Irapuato	319,148
Tonalá	315,278
Nuevo Laredo	308,828
Tampico	295,442
Celaya	277,750
Apodaca	270,369
Tepic	265,817
San Francisco Coalco	252,291
Oaxaca de Juárez	251,846
Ciudad Obregón	250,790

SOCIAL STATISTICS

Statistics for calendar years:

	Births	*Deaths*	*Marriages*	*Divorces*
1999	2,769,089	443,950	743,856	49,721
2000	2,798,339	437,667	707,442	52,358
2001	2,767,610	443,127	665,434	57,370
2002	2,699,084	459,687	...	...
2003	2,655,894	472,140	...	...

Rates per 1,000 population, 2003: births, 25·6; deaths, 4·6. In 2000 the most popular age range for marrying was 20–24 for both males and females. Infant mortality was 24 per 1,000 live births in 2001. Life expectancy at birth in 2001 was 70·1 years for males and 76·1 years for females. Annual population growth rate, 1992–02, 1·7%. Fertility rate, 2001, 2·6 births per woman. Much of the population still lives in poverty, with the gap between the modern north and the backward south constantly growing.

CLIMATE

Latitude and relief produce a variety of climates. Arid and semi-arid conditions are found in the north, with extreme temperatures, whereas in the south there is a humid tropical climate, with temperatures varying with altitude. Conditions on the shores of the Gulf of Mexico are very warm and humid. In general, the rainy season lasts from May to Nov. Mexico City, Jan. 55°F (12·9°C), July 61°F (16·2°C). Annual rainfall 31" (787·6 mm). Guadalajara, Jan. 63°F (17·0°C), July 72°F (22·1°C). Annual rainfall 39" (987·6 mm). La Paz, Jan. 62°F (16·8°C), July 86°F (29·9°C). Annual rainfall 7" (178·3 mm). Mazatlán, Jan. 68°F (20·0°C), July 84°F (29·0°C). Annual rainfall 32" (822·1 mm). Mérida, Jan. 73°F (23·0°C), July 81°F (27·4°C). Annual rainfall 39" (990·0 mm). Monterrey, Jan. 58°F (14·3°C), July 83°F (28·1°C). Annual rainfall 23" (585·4 mm). Puebla de Zaragoza, Jan. 52°F (11·4°C), July 62°F (16·9°C). Annual rainfall 36" (900·8 mm).

CONSTITUTION AND GOVERNMENT

A new Constitution was promulgated on 5 Feb. 1917 and has been amended from time to time. Mexico is a representative, democratic and federal republic, comprising 31 states and a federal district, each state being free and sovereign in all internal affairs, but united in a federation established according to the principles of the Fundamental Law. The head of state and supreme executive authority is the *President*, directly elected for a non-renewable six-year term. The constitution was amended in April 2001, granting autonomy to 10m. indigenous peoples. The amendment was opposed both by the National Congress of Indigenous Peoples and Zapatista rebels who claimed it would leave many indigenous people worse off.

There is complete separation of legislative, executive and judicial powers (Art. 49). Legislative power is vested in a General Congress of two chambers, a *Chamber of Deputies* and a *Senate*. The Chamber of Deputies consists of 500 members directly elected for three years, 300 of them from single-member constituencies and 200 chosen under a system of proportional representation. In 1990 Congress voted a new Electoral Code. This establishes a body to organize elections (IFE), an electoral court (TFE) to resolve disputes, new electoral rolls and introduce a voter's registration card. Priests were enfranchised in 1991.

The Senate comprises 128 members, four from each state and four from the federal district, directly elected for six years. Members of both chambers are not immediately re-eligible for election. Congress sits from 1 Sept. to 31 Dec. each year; during the recess there is a permanent committee of 15 deputies and 14 senators appointed by the respective chambers.

National Anthem. 'Mexicanos, al grito de guerra' ('Mexicans, at the war-cry'); words by F. González Bocanegra, tune by Jaime Nunó.

RECENT ELECTIONS

At the presidential elections of 2 July 2000—the first in Mexico that were deemed free and fair—Vicente Fox of the Partido Acción Nacional (National Action Party/ Alliance for Change) won 42·5% of the vote, defeating Francisco Labastida of the Partido Revolucionario Institucional (Institutional Revolutionary Party/PRI) who gained 36·1%. There were four other candidates. It was the first time in 71 years that the PRI had lost power.

Elections were held on 2 July 2000 for the Chamber of Senators (and the Chamber of Deputies). Following the election the composition of the Senate was: PRI, 58 of the 128 seats (45·3%); Alliance for Change (consisting of the National Action Party and the Ecologist Green Party of Mexico), 53 (41·4%); Alianza por México (Alliance for Mexico/AM), 17 (13·3%).

In the elections of 6 July 2003 to the Chamber of Deputies, President Vicente Fox's National Action Party (PAN) won 153 seats (23·1% of the vote), losing a quarter of its seats. The main opposition party, the PRI, won 224 seats (30·6%) and its ally, the Ecologist Green Party (PVEM), won 17 seats (4·0%). The PRI-PVEM joint list took 13·4% of the vote. The Party of the Democratic Revolution (PRD) won 95 seats (17·6%), the Labour Party (PT) won 6 seats (2·4%) and the Convergence for Democracy won 5 seats (2·3%). The Partido de la Sociedad Nacionalista, the Partido Alianza Social, the Partido México Posible, the Partido Liberal Mexicano and Fuerza Ciudadana failed to win seats. Turn-out was 41·8%.

CURRENT ADMINISTRATION

President: Vicente Fox Quesada; b. 1942 (Alliance for Change; sworn in 1 Dec. 2000).

In March 2005 the government comprised:

Minister of Government: Santiago Creel Miranda. *Foreign Affairs:* Luis Ernesto Derbéz Bautista. *Defence:* Gen. Gerardo Clemente Ricardo Vega García. *Naval Affairs:* Adm. Marco Antonio Peyrot González. *Finance and Public Credit:* Francisco Gil Díaz. *Social Development:* Josefina Vázquez Mota. *Energy:* Fernando Elizondo Barragán. *Economy:* Fernando Canales Clariond. *Agriculture, Livestock, Rural Development, Fisheries and Food:* Javier Usabiaga Arroyo. *Communication and Transport:* Pedro Cerisola y Weber. *Education:* Reyes Támez Guerra. *Health:* Julio Frenk Mora. *Public Security and Justice Services:* Ramón Martín Huerta. *Labour and Social Welfare:* Carlos Abascal Carranza. *Agrarian Reform:* Florencio Salazar Adame. *Tourism:* Rodolfo Elizondo Torres. *Environment and Natural Resources:* Alberto Cárdenas Jiménez. *Public Service:* Eduardo Romero Ramos. *Attorney General:* Gen. Rafael Macedo de la Concha.

Presidency Website: http://www.presidencia.gob.mx

DEFENCE

In 2003 defence expenditure totalled US$2,938m. (US$29 per capita), representing 0·5% of GDP.

Army. Enlistment into the regular army is voluntary, but there is also one year of conscription (four hours per week) by lottery. Strength of the regular army (2002) 144,000 (60,000 conscripts). There are combined reserve forces of 300,000. In addition there is a rural defence militia of 14,000.

Navy. The Navy is primarily equipped and organized for offshore and coastal patrol duties. It includes three destroyers and eight frigates. The naval air force, 1,100 strong, operates eight combat aircraft.

Naval personnel in 2002 totalled 37,000, including the naval air force and 8,700 marines.

Air Force. The Air Force had (2002) a strength of about 11,770 with 107 combat aircraft, including PC-7s, AT-33s and F-5Es, and 71 armed helicopters.

INTERNATIONAL RELATIONS

Mexico is a member of the UN (and most UN System organizations), WTO, BIS, OECD, OAS, Inter-American Development Bank (IADB), LAIA, ACS, APEC, NAFTA and IOM. A free trade agreement was signed with the European Union in 1999.

ECONOMY

Agriculture accounted for 4·0% of GDP in 2002, industry 26·5% and services 69·5%.

Overview. Mexico is the world's 13th largest economy and the fourth largest oil producer. Economic performance improved in the 1990s—GDP growth was high, inflation decreased and the current account deficit remained moderate. In 2001 Mexico's economy overtook Brazil's to become the largest in Latin America. Trade liberalization and the North American Free Trade Agreement (NAFTA) contributed to the economic transformation. The government's key economic policy instruments have been fiscal and monetary discipline and a flexible exchange rate policy. Privatization has created a leaner public sector. External factors such as high oil prices and strong performance in the USA have also contributed to growth. However, recovery from the economic slowdown in 2001 has been slow. Growth is constrained by poor incentives for labour to work in the formal sector where productivity is higher. Additional resources are required to expand the physical infrastructure and to address acute poverty. The labour market is characterized by a high degree of real wage flexibility, while benefiting from low labour costs and a limited tax wedge. Labour market reforms have increased foreign direct investment.

Currency. The unit of currency is the *Mexican peso* (MXP) of 100 *centavos*. A new peso was introduced on 1 Jan. 1993: 1 new peso = 1,000 old pesos. The peso was devalued by 13·94% in Dec. 1994. Foreign exchange reserves were US$45,147m. and gold reserves 191,000 troy oz in June 2002. The annual inflation rate, which in 1995 was 35·0%, fell to 5·0% in 2002 and further to 4·5% in 2003. Total money supply in June 2002 was 507,075m. new pesos.

Budget. Government revenue and expenditure (in 1m. new pesos), year ending 31 Dec.:

	1995	*1996*	*1997*	*1998*	*1999*	*2000*
Revenue	281,138	384,466	468,187	501,231	634,449	811,431
Expenditure	292,479	387,810	516,230	563,990	712,137	875,775

Performance. In 2001 the economy contracted by 0·2% in the wake of the worldwide economic downturn, but there then followed a slight recovery, with real GDP growth of 0·8% in 2002 and 1·3% in 2003. In 2003 total GDP was US$626·1bn.

Banking and Finance. The Bank of Mexico, established 1 Sept. 1925, is the central bank of issue (*Governor*, Guillermo Ortíz Martínez). It gained autonomy over monetary policy in 1993. Exchange rate policy is determined jointly by the bank and the Finance Ministry. Banks were nationalized in 1982, but in May 1990 the government approved their reprivatization. The state continues to have a majority holding in foreign trade and rural development banks. In 1999 Congress approved the removal of regulations limiting foreign holdings to 49%.

In 2000 there were 34 commercial banks, seven major development banks and one foreign bank. Mexico's largest bank is Banamex. In 2001 the American financial services company Citigroup bought Mexico's largest financial group, Banacci, and its second largest bank, Banamex, for US$12·5bn., but retained the name Banamex. Most of Mexico's leading banks are now foreign-owned.

There is a stock exchange in Mexico City.

ENERGY AND NATURAL RESOURCES

Environment. Mexico's carbon dioxide emissions from the consumption and flaring of fossil fuels in 2002 were the equivalent of 3·6 tonnes per capita.

Electricity. Installed capacity, 2000, 45·7m. kW. Output in 2000 was 228·87bn. kWh and consumption per capita 2,368 kWh. In 2003 there were two nuclear reactors in operation.

Oil and Gas. Crude petroleum production was 178·4m. tonnes in 2002. Mexico produced 5·0% of the world total oil output in 2002, and had reserves amounting to 12·6bn. bbls. Revenues from oil exports provide about a third of all government revenues. Natural gas production was 34·8bn. cu. metres in 2002 with 250bn. cu. metres in proven reserves (2002).

Minerals. Output (in 1,000 tonnes): iron ore (2001), 11,500; lignite (2000), 9,130; salt (2002), 8,700; gypsum (2002), 6,500; coal (2000), 2,214; silica (1998), 1,732; sulphur (1998), 913; fluorite (1998), 620; zinc (2001), 429; aluminium (1999), 426; copper (2001), 367; manganese (1998), 203; feldspar (1998), 198; lead (1998), 176; barite (1998), 161; silver (2001), 2·8; gold (2000), 26,375 kg. Mexico is the biggest producer of silver in the world.

Agriculture. In 2001 Mexico had 24·8m. ha of arable land and 2·5m. ha of permanent cropland. There were 6·32m. ha of irrigated land. There were 324,890 tractors and 22,500 harvester-threshers in 2001. In 2002 agriculture contributed 4·0% of GDP (6·0% in 1997). Some 60% of agricultural land belongs to about 30,000 *ejidos* (with 15m. members), communal lands with each member farming his plot independently. *Ejidos* can now be inherited, sold or rented. A land-titling programme (PROCEDE) is establishing the boundaries of 4·6m. plots of land totalling 102m. ha. Other private farmers may not own more than 100 ha of irrigated land or an equivalent in unirrigated land. There is a theoretical legal minimum of 10 ha for holdings, but some 60% of private farms were less than 5 ha in 1990. Laws abolishing the *ejido* system were passed in 1992.

Sown areas, 2000 (in 1,000 ha) included: maize, 8,661; beans, 2,252; sorghum, 2,170; coffee beans, 757; wheat, 749; sugarcane, 659; barley, 312; chick-peas, 210; chillies and green peppers, 142; safflower seeds, 103; rice, 98.

Production in 2000 (in 1,000 tonnes): sugarcane, 49,275; maize, 18,761; sorghum, 6,400; oranges, 3,390; wheat, 3,300; tomatoes, 2,401; chillies and green peppers, 1,813; bananas, 1,802; potatoes, 1,593; mangoes, 1,529; coconuts, 1,313; lemons and limes, 1,297; beans, 1,219; watermelons, 993; avocados, 939; papayas, 636; barley, 532; melons (excluding watermelons), 500.

Livestock (2000): cattle, 30·29m.; sheep, 5·90m.; pigs, 13·69m.; goats, 9·60m.; horses, 6·25m.; mules, 3·27m.; asses, 3·25m.; chickens, 476m. Meat production, 2000 (in 1,000 tonnes): beef and veal, 1,415; pork, bacon and ham, 1,035; horse, 79; goat, 39; lamb and mutton, 32; poultry meat, 1,896. Dairy production, 2000 (in 1,000 tonnes): cow milk, 9,474; goat milk, 134; eggs, 1,666; cheese, 148; honey, 57.

Forestry. Forests extended over 55·21m. ha in 2000, representing 28·9% of the land area, containing pine, spruce, cedar, mahogany, logwood and rosewood. There are 14 forest reserves (nearly 0·8m. ha) and 47 national park forests of 0·75m. ha. Timber production was 45·16m. cu. metres in 2001.

Fisheries. The total catch in 2001 was 1,398,592 tonnes, of which 1,306,438 tonnes came from sea fishing.

INDUSTRY

The leading companies by market capitalization in Mexico, excluding banking and finance, in May 2004 were: América Móvil SA de CV (a mobile phone company), US$22·2bn.; Teléfonos de México SA de CV (Telemex), US$20·2bn.; and Wal-Mart de México SA de CV (general retailers, formerly Cifra), US$13·4bn.

In 2001 the manufacturing industry provided 19·6% of GDP. Output in 2001 (in 1,000 tonnes): cement, 32,239; residual fuel oil (2000), 25,500; petrol (2000), 15,700; crude steel (2002), 14,100; distillate fuel oil (2000), 12,961; sugar (2002), 5,073; pig iron, 4,363; wheat flour, 2,611; cigarettes, 56·1bn. units; soft drinks, 13,005·0m. litres; beer, 6,163·2m. litres. Car production in particular has benefited from membership of NAFTA. Production has increased from 861,000 in 1993 to 1,273,000 in 2001.

Labour. In the period March–June 2001 the employed population totalled 39,004,300. The principal areas of activity were (in 1,000): wholesale and retail trade/repair of motor vehicles, motorcycles and personal and household goods, 8,839·2; manufacturing, 7,373·0; agriculture, hunting and forestry, 6,920·7; construction, 2,396·9; hotels and restaurants, 1,982·2; education, 1,971·6. Unemployment rate, March–June 2002, 1·9%. The daily minimum wage at Jan. 2004 ranged from 42·11 new pesos to 45·24 new pesos.

Trade Unions. The Mexican Labour Congress (CTM) is incorporated into the Institutional Revolutionary Party, and is an umbrella organization numbering some 5m. A breakaway from CTM took place in 1997 when rebel labour leaders set up the National Union of Workers (UNT) to combat what they saw as a sharp drop in real wages.

INTERNATIONAL TRADE

In Sept. 1991 Mexico signed the free trade Treaty of Santiago with Chile, envisaging an annual 10% tariffs reduction from Jan. 1992. The North American Free Trade Agreement (NAFTA), between Canada, Mexico and the USA, was signed on 7 Oct. 1992 and came into effect on 1 Jan. 1994. A free trade agreement was signed with Costa Rica in March 1994. Some 8,300 products were free from tariffs, with others to follow over ten years. The Group of Three (G3) free trade pact with Colombia and Venezuela came into effect on 1 Jan. 1995. Total foreign debt was US$141,264m. in 2002, a figure exceeded only by Brazil, China and Russia.

Imports and Exports. Trade for calendar years in US$1m.:

	1998	*1999*	*2000*	*2001*	*2002*
Imports f.o.b.	125,374	141,975	174,458	168,397	168,679
Exports f.o.b.	117,459	136,391	166,455	158,443	160,763

Of total imports in 1999, 74·3% came from USA, 3·5% from Germany, 3·3% from Japan, 1·9% from Canada and 1·9% from South Korea. Of total exports in 1999, 88·4% went to USA, 1·7% to Canada, 1·5% to Germany, 0·7% to Spain and 0·6% to Japan. In 1998 exports to the USA accounted for 21% of GDP.

The in-bond (*maquiladora*) assembly plants generate the largest flow of foreign exchange. Although originally located along the US border when the programme was introduced in the 1960s, they are now to be found in almost every state. In 2000 there were over 3,000 'foreign to Mexico' manufacturing companies, employing more than 1m. people. Manufactured goods account for 90% of trade revenues.

COMMUNICATIONS

Roads. The total road length in 1999 was 329,532 km, of which 6,429 km were motorways, 41,765 other main roads, 62,344 km secondary roads and 218,994 km other roads. In 2000 there were 10,443,489 passenger cars, 7,931,590 trucks and vans and 111,756 buses and coaches.

Rail. The National Railway, *Ferrocarriles Nacionales de Mexico*, was split into five companies in 1996 as a preliminary to privatization. It comprises 26,623 km of 1,435 mm gauge (246 km electrified). In 2000 passenger-km travelled came to 91m. and freight tonne-km to 48·9bn. Passenger traffic has declined dramatically over the past ten years and has virtually ceased. There is a 178 km metro in Mexico City with ten lines. There are light rail lines in Guadalajara (48 km) and Monterrey (23 km).

Civil Aviation. There is an international airport at Mexico City (Benito Juárez) and 55 other international and 29 national airports. Each of the larger states has a local airline which links it with main airports. The national carriers are Aeromexico, Mexicana, Aerocalifornia, Aerolíneas Internacionales and Aviacsa; Aeromexico and Mexicana, both privatized in the late 1980s, are the main ones. In 1999 Aeromexico carried 8,672,000 passengers (1,959,300 on international flights) and Mexicana 7,359,700 passengers (2,901,500 international). In 2000 Mexico City handled 21,042,610 passengers (13,878,558 on domestic flights). Cancún was the second busiest airport for passengers in 2000, with 7,572,246 (5,915,439 on international flights). Guadalajara handled 5,021,004 passengers (3,279,602 on domestic flights).

Shipping. Mexico had 90 ocean ports in 1998, of which, on the Gulf coast, the most important include Tampico, Coatzacoalcos, Altamira, Progreso, Tuxpan, Morelos and Cozumel. Those on the Pacific Coast include Lazaro Cardenas, Manzanillo, Guaymas, La Paz-Pichilingue, Ensenada, Topolobampo, Mazatlán and Salina Cruz. Mexico's busiest port is Manzanillo, which handled 13,304,000 tonnes of cargo in 2002. The privatization of port operations has been taking place since the early 1990s.

Merchant shipping loaded 139·5m. tonnes and unloaded 62m. tonnes of cargo in 1996. In 2002 the merchant marine had a total tonnage of 937,000 GRT, including oil tankers 455,000 GRT. In 2002 vessels totalling 51,718,000 NRT entered ports and vessels totalling 130,536,000 NRT cleared.

Telecommunications. Telmex, previously a state-controlled company, was privatized in 1991. It controls about 98% of all the telephone service. There were 40,869,900 telephone subscribers in 2002, or 401·2 for every 1,000 persons, and there were 8,353,000 PCs in use (82·0 per 1,000 population). Mexico had 25,928,300 mobile phone subscribers in 2002 and 10,033,000 Internet users. There were 285,000 fax machines in 1997.

Postal Services. There were 9,149 post offices in 1998 (local administration, offices, agencies), equivalent to one for every 9,950 persons.

SOCIAL INSTITUTIONS

Justice. Magistrates of the Supreme Court are appointed for six years by the President and confirmed by the Senate; they can be removed only on impeachment. The courts include the Supreme Court with 21 magistrates, 12 collegiate circuit courts with three judges each and nine unitary circuit courts with one judge each, and 68 district courts with one judge each.

The penal code of 1 Jan. 1930 abolished the death penalty, except for the armed forces.

There were 15,596 murders in 1995 (a rate of 17·2 per 100,000 population). The population in penal institutions in June 2000 was 154,765 (156 per 100,000 of national population).

Religion. In 2001 an estimated 91% of the population was Roman Catholic, down from 98% in 1950. In Sept. 2003 there were five cardinals. The Church is separated from the State, and the constitution of 1917 provided strict regulation of this and all other religions. In Nov. 1991 Congress approved an amendment to the 1917 constitution permitting the recognition of churches by the state, the possession of property by churches and the enfranchisement of priests. Church buildings remain state property. In 2001 there were estimated to be 3·82m. Protestants, plus followers of various other religions. There were 811,000 Latter-day Saints (Mormons) in 1998.

Education. Adult literacy was 91·4% in 2001 (male, 93·5%; female, 89·5%). Primary and secondary education is free and compulsory, and secular, although religious instruction is permitted in private schools. By 2000 Mexicans were attending school for an average of 7·6 years, almost a year more than in 1994.

In 2002–03 there were:

	Establishments	*Teachers*	*Students (in 1,000)*
Pre-school	74,758	163,282	3,636
Primary	99,463	557,278	14,857
Secondary	29,749	325,233	5,660
Baccalaureate	9,668	202,161	2,936
Vocational training	1,659	31,683	359
Medium/Professional	664	17,280	167
Higher education	2,539	192,593	1,932
Postgraduate education	1,283	21,685	138

In 2000 total expenditure on education came to 6·1% of GDP, including 1,374m. new pesos on the *Programa de Apoyo Federal a Entidades Federativas* (Federal Support Program to the States).

Health. In 1997 there were 4,506 hospitals (1,539 public), with a total provision of 103,530 beds. In 1997 there were 116,047 physicians, 8,926 dentists and 161,303 nurses. In 2001 Mexico spent 6·6% of its GDP on health.

Welfare. As of 1 July 1997 all workers had to join the private insurance system, while the social insurance system was being phased out. At retirement, employees covered by the social insurance system before 1997 can choose to receive benefits from either the social insurance system or the private insurance system. The official retirement age is 65 years but to be eligible, a pensioner must have paid 1,250 weeks of contributions. The guaranteed minimum pension is equal to the minimum salary in July 1997 indexed to prices. On social insurance, the minimum monthly pension is 100% of the minimum monthly salary in Mexico City (1,357·20 new pesos in 2004).

Unemployment benefit exists under a labour law which requires employers to pay a dismissed employee a lump sum equal to three months' pay plus 20 days' pay for each year of service. Social security pays an unemployment benefit of between 75% and 95% of the old-age pension for unemployed persons aged 60 to 64.

CULTURE

World Heritage Sites. Mexico has 24 UNESCO world heritage sites. They are (with year entered on list): the Sian Ka'an nature reserve; the historic centre of Mexico City and the canal and island network of Xochimilco; Puebla's historic centre; the pre-Hispanic city of Teotihuacán, now a major archaeological site; the Historic Centre of Oaxaca and archaeological site of Monte Alban; and Palenque—lying in the foothills of the Altos de Chiapas, the Maya ruins of Palenque are surrounded by waterfalls, rainforest and fauna (all 1987); the historic town of Guanajuato and adjacent disused silver mines; and the pre-Hispanic city of Chichen-Itza, Yucatan (both 1988); the historic centre of Morelia, on the southern Pacific coast (1991); the pre-Hispanic city of El Tajin, Veracruz (1992); the El Vizcaino whale sanctuary; the historic centre of Zacatecas, once a major silver mining centre; and the Sierra de San Francisco rock paintings (all 1993); the 14 early 16th-century monasteries on Popocatepetl, to the southeast of Mexico City (1994); the Maya town of Uxmal, Yucatán, with its preserved pyramids and sculptures; and the historic monuments zone of Querétaro (both 1996); the Hospicio (Hospice) Cabañas, Guadalajara (1997); the historic monuments zone of Tlacotalpan; and the archeological zone of Paquimé, Casas Grandes in Chihuahua (both 1998); the historic fortified town of Campeche; and Xochicalco's archaeological monuments zone, Morelos state (both 1999); the Ancient Maya City of Calakmul, Campeche (2002); the Franciscan Missions in the Sierra Gorda of Queretaro (2003); and Luis Barragán House and Studio in Mexico City (2004).

Broadcasting. In 1997 there were 1,342 radio stations and 580 television stations licensed by the *Dirección General de Concesiones y Permisos de Telecomunicaciones*. Most radio stations carry the 'National Hour' programme. Television services are provided by the Televisa, Televisión Azteca and Multivision. There were 32·3m. radio receivers in 2000 and 28·3m. TV sets (colour by NTSC) in 2001.

Cinema. In 1999 there were 2,320 cinemas and 120m. admissions.

Press. In 2000 there were 311 daily newspapers with a circulation of 9,251,000, equivalent to 94 per 1,000 inhabitants.

Tourism. There were 20·64m. tourists in 2000, putting Mexico eighth in the world list; gross revenue, including border visitors, amounted to US$8,295m. in 2000.

DIPLOMATIC REPRESENTATIVES

Of Mexico in the United Kingdom (16 St George Street, Hanover Sq., London W1S 1LX)
Ambassador: Juan Bremer de Martino.

Of the United Kingdom in Mexico (Rio Lerma 71, Col. Cuauhtémoc, 06500 México, D.F.)
Ambassador: Denise Holt.

Of Mexico in the USA (1911 Pennsylvania Ave., NW, Washington, D.C., 20006)
Ambassador: Carlos Alberto de Icaza.

Of the USA in Mexico (Paseo de la Reforma 305, 06500 México, D.F.)
Ambassador: Antonio O. Garza, Jr.

Of Mexico to the United Nations
Ambassador: Enrique Berruga Filloy.

Of Mexico to the European Union
Ambassador: Porfirio Muñoz Ledo y Lazo de la Vega.

FURTHER READING

Instituto Nacional de Estadística, Geografía e Informática. *Anuario Estadístico de los Estados Unidos Mexicanos. Mexican Bulletin of Statistical Information.* Quarterly.

Aspe, P., *Economic Transformation: the Mexican Way.* Cambridge (MA), 1993
Bartra, R., *Agrarian Structure and Political Power in Mexico.* Johns Hopkins Univ. Press, 1993
Bethell, L. (ed.) *Mexico since Independence.* CUP, 1992
Camp, R. A., *Politics in Mexico.* 2nd ed. OUP, 1996
Hamnett, Brian R., *A Concise History of Mexico.* CUP, 1999
Krauze, E., *Mexico, Biography of Power: A History of Modern Mexico, 1810–1996.* London, 1997
Philip, G. (ed.) *The Presidency in Mexican Politics.* London, 1991.—*Mexico.* [Bibliography] 2nd ed. ABC-Clio, Oxford and Santa Barbara (CA), 1993
Rodríguez, J. E., *The Evolution of the Mexican Political System.* New York, 1993
Ruíz, R. E., *Triumphs and Tragedy: a History of the Mexican People.* New York, 1992
Turner, Barry (ed.) *Latin America Profiled.* Macmillan, London, 2000
Whiting, V. R., *The Political Economy of Foreign Investment in Mexico: Nationalism, Liberalism, Constraints on Choice.* Johns Hopkins Univ. Press, 1992

National statistical office: Instituto Nacional de Estadística, Geografía e Informática (INEGI), Aguascalientes.
Website (Spanish only): http://www.inegi.gob.mx

MICRONESIA

Federated States of Micronesia

Capital: Palikir
Population projection, 2010: 115,000
GDP per capita: not available
GNP per capita: $2,150

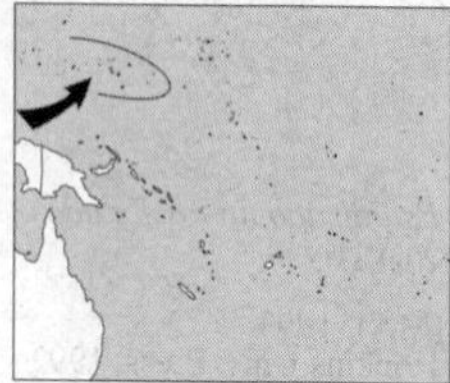

KEY HISTORICAL EVENTS

Spain acquired sovereignty over the Caroline Islands in 1886 but sold the archipelago to Germany in 1899. Japan occupied the Islands at the beginning of the First World War and in 1921 they were mandated to Japan by the League of Nations. Captured by Allied Forces in the Second World War, the Islands became part of the UN Trust Territory of the Pacific Islands created on 18 July 1947 and administered by the USA. The Federated States of Micronesia came into being on 10 May 1979. American trusteeship was terminated on 3 Nov. 1986 by the UN Security Council and on the same day Micronesia entered into a 15-year Free Association with the USA. An amended 20-year Compact of Free Association was signed on 14 May 2003, guaranteeing US$1·8bn. to Micronesia in grants for a government trust fund.

TERRITORY AND POPULATION

The Federated States lie in the North Pacific Ocean between 137° and 163° E, comprising 607 islands with a total land area of 701 sq. km (271 sq. miles). The population (2000 census) was 107,008; density, 153 per sq. km.

The UN gives a projected population for 2010 of 115,000.

In 1995 an estimated 72·3% of the population lived in rural areas.

The areas and populations of the four major groups of island states (east to west) are as follows:

State	*Area (sq. km)*	*Population (2000 census)*	*Headquarters*
Kosrae	110	7,686	Tofol
Pohnpei	345	34,486	Kolonia
Chuuk	127	53,595	Weno
Yap	119	11,241	Colonia

Kosrae consists of a single island. Its main town is Lelu (2,591 inhabitants in 2000). Pohnpei comprises a single island (covering 334 sq. km) and eight scattered coral atolls. Kolonia (5,681 inhabitants in 2000) was the national capital of the Federated States. The new capital, Palikir (6,227 inhabitants in 2000), lies approximately 10 km southwest in the Palikir valley. Chuuk consists of a group of 14 islands within a large reef-fringed lagoon (44,000 inhabitants in 1994); the state also includes 12 coral atolls (8,000 inhabitants), the most important being the Mortlock Islands. The chief town is Weno (16,121 inhabitants in 1994). Yap comprises a main group of four islands (covering 100 sq. km with 7,000 inhabitants in 1994) and 13 coral atolls (4,000 inhabitants), the main ones being Ulithi and Woleai. Colonia is its chief town (3,161 inhabitants in 1994).

English is used in schools and is the official language. Trukese, Pohnpeian, Yapese and Kosrean are also spoken.

SOCIAL STATISTICS

1997 births, estimate, 3,500; deaths, 800. 1997 rates, estimate: birth rate, 27·7 per 1,000 population; death rate, 6·1 per 1,000; infant mortality rate, 35·1 per 1,000 live births. 1997 life expectancy, 68·2 years. Annual population growth rate, 1992–02, 0·7%; fertility rate, 2001, 5·1 births per woman.

CLIMATE

Tropical, with heavy year-round rainfall, especially in the eastern islands, and occasional typhoons (June–Dec.). Kolonia, Jan. 80°F (26·7°C), July 79°F (26·1°C). Annual rainfall 194" (4,859 mm).

CONSTITUTION AND GOVERNMENT

Under the Constitution founded on 10 May 1979, there is an executive presidency and a 14-member National Congress, comprising ten members elected for two-year terms from single-member constituencies of similar electorates, and four members elected one from each State for a four-year term by proportional representation. The Federal President and Vice-President first run for the Congress before they are elected by members of Congress for a four-year term.

RECENT ELECTIONS

The last election for Congress was held on 8 March 2005. Only non-partisans were elected. Joseph Urusemal was elected President and Redley Killion was confirmed as Vice-President (elected on 11 May 1999) by Congress on 11 May 2003.

CURRENT ADMINISTRATION

President: Joseph J. Urusemal; b. 1952 (took office 11 May 2003).

Vice-President: Redley Killion.

In March 2005 the government comprised:

Minister of Foreign Affairs: Sebastian Anefal. *Finance and Administration:* Nick Andon. *Health, Education and Social Affairs:* Dr Jefferson Benjamin. *Economic Affairs (acting):* Ishmael Lebehn. *Justice (acting):* Harry Seymour. *Transportation, Communications and Infrastructure:* Akallino Susaia. *Public Defender:* Beauleen Carl-Worswick. *Postmaster-General:* Bethwel Henry.

Speaker of the Congress: Peter Christian.

Government Website: http://www.fsmgov.org

INTERNATIONAL RELATIONS

Micronesia is a member of the UN, Asian Development Bank, Pacific Community (formerly the South Pacific Commission) and the Pacific Islands Forum.

ECONOMY

Currency. US currency is used. Foreign exchange reserves were US$83m. and total money supply was US$19m. in May 2002.

Budget. US compact funds are an annual US$100m. Revenue (2001–02), US$160m.; expenditure, US$155m.

Performance. Real GDP growth was 2·5% in 2000 and 0·9% in 2001. In 2003 total GDP was US$0·2bn.

Banking and Finance. There are three commercial banks: Bank of Guam, Bank of Hawaii and Bank of the Federated States of Micronesia. There is also a Federated States of Micronesia Development Bank and a regulatory Banking Board.

ENERGY AND NATURAL RESOURCES

Electricity. Capacity (1995), 38,500 kW.

Minerals. The islands have few mineral deposits except for high-grade phosphates.

Agriculture. Agriculture consists mainly of subsistence farming: coconuts, breadfruit, bananas, sweet potatoes and cassava. A small amount of crops are produced for export, including copra, tropical fruits, peppers and taro. Production (2000, in 1,000 tonnes): coconuts, 140; copra, 18; cassava, 12; sweet potatoes, 3; bananas, 2. Livestock (2000): pigs, 32,000; cattle, 14,000; goats, 4,000. In 2001 there were 4,000 ha of arable land and 32,000 ha of permanent crops.

Fisheries. In 2001 the catch amounted to approximately 18,062 tonnes, almost entirely from marine waters. Fishing licence fees were US$20m. in 1993 and are a primary revenue source.

INDUSTRY

The chief industries are construction, fish processing, tourism and handicrafts (items from shell, wood and pearl).

Labour. Two-thirds of the labour force are government employees. In 1994, 8,092 people worked in public administration and 7,375 in agriculture, fisheries and farming out of a total labour force of 27,573. The unemployment rate was 15·2%.

INTERNATIONAL TRADE

Imports and Exports. Total exports (2002), US$14·4m.; imports, US$104·3m. Main import suppliers, 2002: USA (excluding Guam), 42·2%; Guam, 20·2%; Japan, 10·6%. Main export markets, 2002: USA (excluding Guam), 29·0%; Japan, 18·7%; Guam, 7·9%. The main exports are copra, bananas, black pepper, fish and garments. Main imports: foodstuffs and beverages, manufactured goods, machinery and equipment.

COMMUNICATIONS

Roads. In 1999 there were 240 km of roads (42 km paved).

Civil Aviation. There are international airports on Pohnpei, Chuuk, Yap and Kosrae. Services are provided by Continental Airlines. In 2003 there were international flights to Guam, Honolulu, Manila, the Marshall Islands and Palau in addition to domestic services. There were five airports in 1996 (four paved).

Shipping. The main ports are Kolonia (Pohnpei), Colonia (Yap), Lepukos (Chuuk), Okat and Lelu (Kosrae). In 2002 merchant shipping totalled 13,000 GRT.

Telecommunications. Micronesia had 10,100 telephone subscribers in 2001, or 86·7 per 1,000 population. Mobile phone subscribers numbered 1,800 in 2002. There were 500 fax machines in 1998. The islands are interconnected by shortwave radiotelephone. There are four earth stations linked to the Intelsat satellite system. There were 6,000 Internet users in 2002.

Postal Services. All four states have postal services.

SOCIAL INSTITUTIONS

Justice. There is a Supreme Court headed by the Chief Justice with two other judges, and a State Court in each of the four states with 13 judges in total.

Religion. The population is predominantly Christian. Yap is mainly Roman Catholic; Protestantism is prevalent elsewhere.

Education. In 2001–02 there were 26,440 pupils in primary schools; 7,446 pupils in high schools; and 799 students (1999) at the College of Micronesia in Pohnpei. The Micronesia Maritime and Fisheries Academy in Yap (est. 1990) provides education and training in fisheries technology at secondary and tertiary levels.

In 2001–02 total expenditure on education came to 6·7% of GNP.

Health. In 1994 there were four hospitals with 325 beds. There were 76 physicians, 16 dentists and 368 nurses in 1999.

In the period 1990–98 only 22% of the population had access to safe drinking water.

CULTURE

Broadcasting. There were five radio and six TV stations in 1996. In 1996 there were 22,000 radio sets and in 2001 there were 2,450 TV receivers (colour by NTSC).

Tourism. In 2000 there were 33,000 visitors.

DIPLOMATIC REPRESENTATIVES

Of the United Kingdom in Micronesia
Ambassador: Ian Powell (resides at Suva, Fiji Islands).

Of Micronesia in the USA (1725 N St., NW, Washington, D.C., 20036)
Ambassador: Jesse B. Marehalau.

Of the USA in Micronesia (POB 1286, Kolonia, Pohnpei)
Ambassador: Larry Miles Dinger.

Of Micronesia to the United Nations
Ambassador: Masao Nakayama.

FURTHER READING

Wuerch, W. L. and Ballendorf, D. A., *Historical Dictionary of Guam and Micronesia.* Metuchen (NJ), 1995

MOLDOVA

Republica Moldova

Capital: Chişinau
Population projection, 2010: 4·23m.
GDP per capita, 2002: (PPP$) 1,420
HDI/world rank: 0·681/113

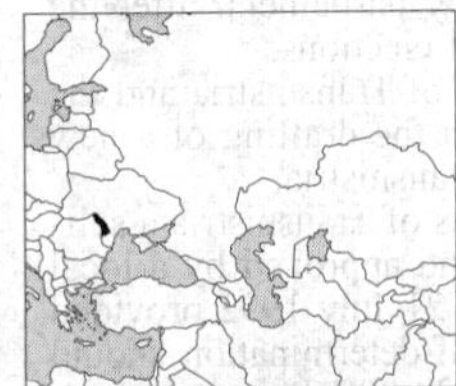

KEY HISTORICAL EVENTS

In Dec. 1991 Moldova became a member of the CIS, a decision ratified by parliament in April 1994. Fighting took place in 1992 between government forces and separatists in the (largely Russian and Ukrainian) area east of the River Nistru (Transnistria). An agreement signed by the presidents of Moldova and Russia on 21 July 1992 brought to an end the armed conflict and established a 'security zone' controlled by peacekeeping forces from Russia, Moldova and Transnistria. On 21 Oct. 1994 a Moldo-Russian agreement obliged Russian troops to withdraw from the territory of Moldova over three years but the agreement was not ratified by the Russian Duma. On 8 May 1997 an agreement between Transnistria and the Moldovan government to end the separatist conflict stipulated that Transnistria would remain part of Moldova as it was territorially constituted in Jan. 1990. In 1997 some 7,000 Russian troops were stationed in Transnistria. In the autumn of 1999 Ion Sturza's centre-right coalition collapsed, along with privatization plans for the wine and tobacco industries. Communist President Vladimir Voronin, who was elected in 2001, has proposed giving the Russian language official status and joining the Russia–Belarus union.

TERRITORY AND POPULATION

Moldova is bounded in the east and south by Ukraine and on the west by Romania. The area is 33,848 sq. km (13,067 sq. miles). In 2000 the estimated population was 4,295,000 (52·2% female).

The UN gives a projected population for 2010 of 4·23m.

In 2001, 58·3% of the population lived in rural areas. The 1989 census population was 4,335,360, of whom Moldovans accounted for 64·5%, Ukrainians 13·9%, Russians 13%, Gagauzi 3·5%, Bulgarians 2% and Jews 1·5%.

Apart from Chişinau, the capital (population of 655,000 in 1999), major towns are Tiraspol (185,000 in 1993), Beltsy (156,000 in 1993) and Bender (133,000 in 1992).

The official Moldovan language (i.e. Romanian) was written in Cyrillic prior to the restoration of the Roman alphabet in 1989. It is spoken by 75% of the population; the use of other languages (Russian, Gagauz) is safeguarded by the Constitution.

SOCIAL STATISTICS

2001: births, 36,448; deaths, 40,075. Rates, 2001 (per 1,000 population): births, 10·0; deaths, 11·0. In 2001 the most popular age range for marrying was 20–24 for both males and females. Life expectancy at birth in 2001 was 64·9 years for males and 71·8 years for females. Annual population growth rate, 1992–02, –0·2%. Infant mortality, 2001, 27 per 1,000 live births; fertility rate, 2001, 1·5 births per woman. By the end of 1998 more than 46% of the population were classified as living in absolute poverty.

CLIMATE

The climate is temperate, with warm summers, crisp, sunny autumns and cold winters with snow. Chişinau, Jan. –7°C, Jul. 20°C. Annual rainfall 677 mm.

CONSTITUTION AND GOVERNMENT

A declaration of republican sovereignty was adopted in June 1990 and in Aug. 1991 the republic declared itself independent. A new Constitution came into effect on 27 Aug. 1994, which defines Moldova as an 'independent, democratic and unitary state'. At a referendum on 6 March 1994 turn-out was 75·1%; 95·4% of votes cast favoured 'an independent Moldova within its 1990 borders'. The referendum (and the Feb. parliamentary elections) were not held by the authorities in Transnistria. In a further referendum on 4 June 1999, on whether to switch from a parliamentary system to a presidential one, turn-out was 58% with the majority of the votes cast being in favour of the change.

Parliament (*Parlamentul*) has 101 seats and is elected for four-year terms. There is a 4% threshold for election; votes falling below this are re-distributed to successful parties. The *President* is now elected for four-year terms by parliament, after the constitution had been amended to abolish direct presidential elections.

The 1994 Constitution makes provision for the autonomy of Transnistria and the Gagauz (Gagauzi Yeri) region. Work began in July 2003 on the drafting of a new constitution to resolve the conflict between Moldova and Transnistria.

Transnistria. In the predominantly Russian-speaking areas of Transnistria a self-styled 'Dniester Republic' was established in Sept. 1991, and approved by a local referendum in Dec. 1991. A Russo-Moldovan agreement of 21 July 1992 provided for a special statute for Transnistria and a guarantee of self-determination should Moldova unite with Romania. The population in 2001 was 634,000. Romanian here is still written in the Cyrillic alphabet. At a referendum on 24 Dec. 1995, 81% of votes cast were in favour of adopting a new constitution proclaiming independence.

On 17 June 1996 the Moldovan government granted Transnistria a special status as 'a state-territorial formation in the form of a republic within Moldova's internationally recognized border'.

Elections for chief regional executive were held on 9 Dec. 2001. Turn-out was 64%. Igor Smirnov (b. 1941) was re-elected for a third five-year term against two opponents winning nearly 82% of votes cast.

Gagauz Yeri. This was created an autonomous territorial unit by Moldovan legislation of 13 Jan. 1995. In 2000 the population was 172,000. There is a 35-member *Popular Assembly* directly elected for four-year terms and headed by a *Governor*, who is a member of the Moldovan cabinet. At the elections of 28 May and 11 June 1995 turn-out was 68%.

Governor. Gheorghe Tabunscic; b. 1939.

National Anthem. The Romanian anthem was replaced in 1994 by a traditional tune, 'Lîmbă noastră' ('Our Tongue'); words by Alexei Mateevici, tune by Alexandru Cristi.

RECENT ELECTIONS

At the parliamentary elections held on 6 March 2005 the Party of Communists of the Republic of Moldova (PCRM) won 56 seats with 46·0% of the votes, the Democratic Moldova bloc 34 with 28·5% and the Christian Democratic People's Party 11 with 9·1%. Turn-out was 63.7%.

Following the parliamentary elections of March 2005 parliament re-elected Vladimir Voronin as president on 4 April 2005. Voronin received 75 votes against 1 for another communist candidate, Gheorghe Duca.

CURRENT ADMINISTRATION

President: Vladimir Voronin; b. 1941 (PCRM; sworn in 7 April 2001 and re-elected 4 April 2005).

In April 2005 the government comprised:

Prime Minister: Vasile Tarlev; b. 1963 (PCRM; sworn in 19 April 2001; reappointed 8 April 2005).

Deputy Prime Ministers: Valerian Cristea; Andrei Stratan (also *Minister of Foreign Affairs*).

Minister of Agriculture and Food Industries: Anatolie Gorodenco. *Culture and Tourism:* Artur Cozma. *Defence:* Valeriu Plesca. *Economy and Commerce:* Valeriu Lazar. *Education, Youth and Sport:* Victor Tvircun. *Environment and Natural Resources:* Constantin Mihailescu. *Finance:* Zinaida Greceanâi. *Health and Social Protection:* Valerian Revenco. *Industry and Infrastructure:* Vladimir Antosii. *Internal Affairs:* Gheorghe Papuc. *Justice:* Victoria Iftodi. *Reintegration:* Vasile Sova. *Information Development*: Vladimir Molojen. *Transport and Roads Management:* Miron Gagauz.

Government Website: http://www.moldova.md

DEFENCE

Conscription is up to 18 months. In 2003 military expenditure totalled US$150m. (US$35 per capita), representing 2·4% of GDP.

Russian troops remained in Transnistria after Moldova gained independence, but in Nov. 1999 the Organization for Security and Co-operation in Europe (OSCE) passed a resolution at its summit requiring Russia to withdraw its troops to Russia by Dec. 2002, unconditionally and under international observation. This deadline was extended to Dec. 2003. Both troops and equipment were withdrawn during the first six months of 2003.

Army. Personnel, 2002, 5,560 (5,200 conscripts). There is also a paramilitary Interior Ministry force of 2,500, riot police numbering 900 and combined forces reserves of some 66,000.

Air Force. Personnel (including air defence), 2002, 1,400.

INTERNATIONAL RELATIONS

Moldova is a member of the UN, WTO, OSCE, CIS, the Council of Europe, CEI, Danube Commission, BSEC, IOM, International Organization of the Francophonie and the NATO Partnership for Peace.

ECONOMY

Agriculture accounted for 24·1% of GDP in 2002, industry 23·2% and services 52·7%.

Overview. A privatization programme started in 1993. By the end of 2000, 92% of housing had been privatized. The sale of Moldtelecom and its stake in the energy sector are priorities.

Currency. A new unit of currency, the *leu* (MDL), replaced the rouble in Nov. 1993. Inflation was 5·3% in 2002, down from a peak of 2,198% in the early 1990s. Foreign exchange reserves were US$219m. in June 2002 and total money supply 2,607m. lei.

Budget. Total revenue and total expenditure (in 1m. lei), years ending 31 Dec.:

	1998	*1999*	*2000*	*2001*	*2002*
Revenue	2,808·8	3,064·0	4,033·5	4,078·5	4,977·6
Expenditure	3,271·6	3,660·2	4,738·6	4,335·9	5,756·5

Performance. Moldova's economy has been in dire straits although it is now making a strong recovery. Economic growth was negative in 1998 at –6·5% and again in 1999, at –3·4%. A limited recovery followed in 2000 with growth of 2·1%. In 2001 there was growth of 6·1%, rising to 7·2% in 2002.

Between 1990 and 1996 the average annual real growth in GNP per capita was –16·8%. Of all the former Soviet republics Moldova's economy, along with that of Georgia, has suffered the most since 1989 when political and economic reforms took place across central and eastern Europe. In 2002 the level of GDP was estimated to be only 38% of that in 1989. Total GDP was US$1·9bn. in 2003.

Banking and Finance. The central bank and bank of issue is the National Bank (*Governor*, Leonid Talmaci). At June 2002 there were 21 commercial banks and one savings bank. There is a stock exchange in Chişinau.

ENERGY AND NATURAL RESOURCES

Environment. Moldova's carbon dioxide emissions from the consumption and flaring of fossil fuels in 2002 were the equivalent of 2·3 tonnes per capita.

Electricity. Installed capacity in 2000 was 1·0m. kW. Production was about 3·31bn. kWh in 2000; consumption per capita in 2000 was an estimated 1,400 kWh.

Minerals. There are deposits of lignite, phosphorites, gypsum and building materials.

Agriculture. Agriculture employs about 700,000 people. Land under cultivation in 1997 was 2·5m. ha, of which 0·3m. ha was accounted for by private subsidiary agriculture and 6,700 ha (in 1993) by commercial agriculture in 3,100 farms. In 2001 there were 1·82m. ha of arable land and 355,000 ha of permanent crops. Agriculture is Moldova's biggest exporter, accounting for 75% of total exports.

Output of main agricultural products (in 1,000 tonnes) in 2000: sugarbeets, 1,800; maize, 1,091; wheat, 770; grapes, 450; potatoes, 342; sunflower seeds, 280; wine, 240. Livestock (2000): 416,000 cattle, 974,000 sheep, 705,000 pigs, 14m. chickens. Livestock products, 2000 (in 1,000 tonnes): milk, 571; meat, 88; eggs, 32.

Forestry. In 2000 forests covered 325,000 ha, or 9·9% of the total land area. Timber production in 2001 was 57,000 cu. metres.

Fisheries. The catch in 2001 (exclusively freshwater fish) was estimated at 387 tonnes.

INDUSTRY

There are canning plants, wine-making plants, woodworking and metallurgical factories, a factory of ferro-concrete building materials, footwear, dairy products and textile plants. Manufacturing accounted for 18·2% of GDP in 2001. Production (in tonnes): crude steel (2000), 909,000; cement (2001), 158,000; raw sugar (2002), 125,000; wheat flour (2001), 122,000; canned fruit and vegetables (2001), 86,300; footwear (2001), 1·1m. pairs; 9·4bn. cigarettes (2001); 25,000 washing machines (2001); wine (2001), 155·0m. litres.

Labour. In 2001 the labour force totalled 1,616,700 (810,100 males). A total of 1,499,000 persons were in employment in 2001, including 763,400 engaged in agriculture, hunting, forestry and fisheries, 144,500 in wholesale and retail trade/repair of motor vehicles, motorcycles and personal and household goods, 136,800 in manufacturing and 100,900 in education. In 2002 the unemployment rate was 6·8%.

INTERNATIONAL TRADE

Foreign debt was US$1,349m. in 2002.

Imports and Exports. In 2002 imports (f.o.b.) were valued at US$1,038·1m. (US$878·6m. in 2001) and exports (f.o.b.) at US$659·8m. (US$567·3m. in 2001). Chief import sources in 2002 were: Ukraine, 20·4%; Russia, 15·3%; Romania, 11·4%; Germany, 9·2%. Main export markets in 2002 were: Russia, 35·4%; Italy, 9·1%; Ukraine, 9·1%; Romania, 8·4%. Moldova's main export commodity is wine, ahead of tobacco. Leading imports are mineral products and fuel, machinery and equipment, chemicals and textiles.

COMMUNICATIONS

Roads. There were 12,719 km of roads in 2002 (86·3% paved). Passenger cars in use in 2002 numbered 268,822 (74·3 per 1,000 inhabitants), there were 46,277 trucks and vans, 15,777 buses and coaches, and 78,814 motorcycles and mopeds. In 1999 there were 2,669 road accidents resulting in 395 deaths.

Rail. Total length in 2000 was 1,139 km of 1,520 mm gauge. Passenger-km travelled in 2000 came to 315m. and freight tonne-km to 1,538m.

Civil Aviation. The main Moldovan-based airline is Air Moldova, which had flights in 2003 to Amman, Amsterdam, Athens, Bucharest, İstanbul, Larnaca, Moscow, Paris, Prague, Rome and Vienna. In 2000 the airport at Chişinau handled 254,234 passengers (all on international flights) and 2,159 tonnes of freight. In 1999 scheduled airline traffic of Moldovan-based carriers flew 2·3m. km, carrying 43,000 passengers (all on international flights).

Shipping. In 1993, 0·3m. passengers and 0·3m. tonnes of freight were carried on inland waterways.

Telecommunications. There were 864,200 telephone subscribers in 2001 (196·8 per 1,000 persons) and 77,000 PCs in use in 2002 (17·5 per 1,000 persons). There were 338,200 mobile phone subscribers in 2002—up from just 2,200 in 1997—and 700 fax machines in use in 1999. In 2002 there were 150,000 Internet users. Privatization of the state-owned telecommunications company, Moldtelecom, is a priority for the government. A majority stake offer from MGTS, Moscow's main telephone company, failed in Nov. 2002.

Postal Services. In 1998 there were 1,276 post offices.

SOCIAL INSTITUTIONS

Justice. 47,515 crimes were reported in 1994. The population in penal institutions in Jan. 2003 was 10,903 (301 per 100,000 of national population). The death penalty was abolished for all crimes in 1995.

Religion. Religious affiliation in 2001: Romanian Orthodox, 1·26m.; Russian (Moldovan) Orthodox, 342,000.

Education. In 2000–01 there were 77,539 children and 8,508 teachers in pre-schools; 236,763 pupils and 11,648 teachers in primary schools; and 413,029 pupils and 30,518 teachers in secondary schools. There were 102,825 students (7,268 academic staff) in tertiary education in 2000–01. In 1996–97 there were 97 vocational secondary schools, 54 technical colleges and nine higher educational institutions including the state university. Adult literacy rate in 2001 was 99·0% (male, 99·6%; female, 98·4%).

In 2000–01 total expenditure on education came to 3·8% of GNP and represented 15·0% of total government expenditure.

Health. In Jan. 1996 there were 312 hospitals with 54,300 beds, a provision of 125 per 10,000 inhabitants. In 1998 there were 14,959 physicians, 1,761 dentists, 37,355 nurses, 2,885 pharmacists and 3,723 midwives.

Welfare. There were 649,000 age pensioners and 267,000 other pensioners in Jan. 1994.

CULTURE

Broadcasting. The government authority Radioteleviziunea Nationala is responsible for broadcasting. There are two national radio programmes, a Radio Moscow relay, and a foreign service, Radio Moldova International. There is a national state TV service and a private TV network. Romanian and Russian channels are also broadcast. There were 1·3m. television receivers in 2001 and 3·3m. radio receivers in 2000.

Press. Moldova has 567 newspapers and magazines. Of these 323 are published in Moldovan, four in English and the rest in Russian.

Tourism. In 2000 there were 17,000 foreign tourists, spending US$4m.

DIPLOMATIC REPRESENTATIVES

Of Moldova in the United Kingdom (resides at Brussels)
Ambassador: Mariana Durleşteanu.

Of the United Kingdom in Moldova (ASITO Building, Office 320, 57/1 Banulescu-Bodoni Str, Chişinau 2005)
Ambassador: Bernard Whiteside, MBE.

Of Moldova in the USA (2101 S St., NW, Washington, D.C., 20008)
Ambassador: Mihail Manoli.

Of the USA in Moldova (103 Strada Alexei Matveevici, Chişinau)
Ambassador: Heather M. Hodges.

Of Moldova to the United Nations
Ambassador: Vsevolod Grigore.

Of Moldova to the European Union
Ambassador: Mihai Popov.

FURTHER READING

Gribincea, M., *Agricultural Collectivization in Moldavia.* East European Monographs, Columbia Univ. Press, 1996

King, C., *Post-Soviet Moldova: A Borderland in Transition.* International Specialized Book Service, Portland, Oregon, 1997.—*The Moldovans: Romania, Russia, and the Politics of Culture.* Hoover Institution Press, Stanford, 2000

Mitrasca, M., *Moldova: A Romanian Province Under Russian Rule: Diplomatic History from the Archives of the Great Powers.* Algora Publishing, New York, 2002

National Statistical Office: Department for Statistics and Sociology, MD-2028, Hîncesti 53, Chişinau.
Website: http://www.statistica.md

MONACO

Principauté de Monaco

Capital: Monaco
Population estimate, 2000: 32,000
GDP per capita: not available

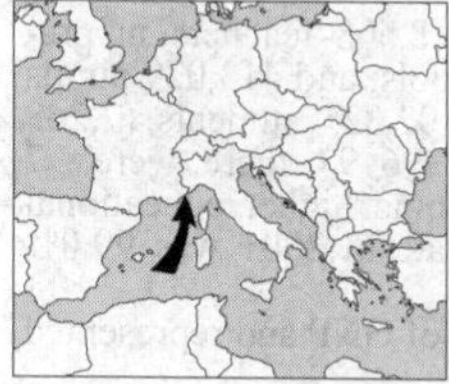

KEY HISTORICAL EVENTS

From 1297 Monaco belonged to the house of Grimaldi. In 1731 it passed to the female line, Louise Hippolyte, daughter of Antoine I, heiress of Monaco, marrying Jacques de Goyon Matignon, Count of Torigni, who took the name and arms of Grimaldi. The Principality was placed under the protection of the Kingdom of Sardinia by the Treaty of Vienna, 1815, and under that of France in 1861.

TERRITORY AND POPULATION

Monaco is bounded in the south by the Mediterranean and elsewhere by France (Department of Alpes Maritimes). The area is 197 ha (1·97 sq. km). The Principality is divided into four districts: Monaco-Ville, la Condamine, Monte-Carlo and Fontvieille. Population (2000 census), 32,020; there were 6,089 Monegasques (19%), 10,229 French (32%) and 6,410 Italian (20%).

The official language is French.

SOCIAL STATISTICS

2001: births, 748; deaths, 636; marriages, 175; divorces, 77. Rates per 1,000 population, 1998: birth, 26·3; death, 17·8; marriage, 6·0; divorce, 2·5. Annual population growth rate, 1992–02, 1·1%; fertility rate, 2001, 1·8 births per woman.

CLIMATE

A Mediterranean climate, with mild moist winters and hot dry summers. Monaco, Jan. 50°F (10°C), July 74°F (23·3°C). Annual rainfall 30" (758 mm).

CONSTITUTION AND GOVERNMENT

On 17 Dec. 1962 a new constitution was promulgated which maintains the hereditary monarchy.

The reigning Prince is **Albert II**, b. 14 March 1958, son of Prince Rainier III, 1923–2005, and Grace Kelly, 1929–1982. Prince Albert succeeded his father Rainier III, who died on 6 April 2005.

Sisters of the Prince. Princess Caroline Louise Marguerite, b. 23 Jan. 1957; married Philippe Junot on 28 June 1978, divorced 9 Oct. 1980; married Stefano Casiraghi on 29 Dec. 1983 (died 3 Oct. 1990); married Prince Ernst of Hanover on 23 Jan 1999. *Offspring:* Andrea, b. 8 June 1984; Charlotte, b. 3 Aug. 1986; Pierre, b. 7 Sept. 1987; Alexandra, b. 20 July 1999. Princess Stéphanie Marie Elisabeth, b. 1 Feb. 1965, married Daniel Ducruet on 1 July 1995, divorced 4 Oct. 1996; married Adans López Peres on 12 Sept. 2003. *Offspring:* Louis, b. 27 Nov. 1992; Pauline, b. 4 May 1994; Camille, b. 15 July 1998.

Prince Rainier III renounced the principle of divine right. Executive power is exercised jointly by the Prince and a four-member *Council of government*, headed by a Minister of State (a French citizen). A 24-member *National Council* is elected for five-year terms.

The constitution can be modified only with the approval of the National Council. A law of 1992 permits Monegasque women to give their nationality to their children.

National Anthem. 'Principauté Monaco ma patrie' ('Principality of Monaco my fatherland'); words by T. Bellando de Castro, tune by C. Albrecht.

RECENT ELECTIONS

In parliamentary elections held on 9 Feb. 2003 the opposition Union for Monaco won 21 of 24 seats against 3 for the ruling National Democratic Union. Turn-out was about 80%.

CURRENT ADMINISTRATION

Chief of State: Prince Albert II.

In March 2005 the cabinet comprised:

Minister of State: Patrick Leclercq; b. 1938 (sworn in 5 Feb. 2000).

Minister of Finance and Economics: Franck Biancheri. *Environmental Affairs and Town Planning:* Gilles Tonelli. *Social Affairs and Health:* Denis Ravera. *Interior:* Philippe Deslandes. *President of the National Council:* Stéphane Valeri.

Government Website: http://www.monaco.gouv.mc

INTERNATIONAL RELATIONS

Monegasque relations with France are based on conventions of 1963. French citizens are treated as if in France. Monaco is a member of the UN, Council of Europe, OSCE and the International Organization of the Francophonie.

ECONOMY

Currency. On 1 Jan. 1999 the euro (EUR) replaced the French franc as the legal currency in Monaco; irrevocable conversion rate 6·55957 French francs to one euro. The euro, which consists of 100 cents, has been in circulation since 1 Jan. 2002. There are seven euro notes in different colours and sizes denominated in 500, 200, 100, 50, 20, 10 and 5 euros, and eight coins denominated in 2 and 1 euros, then 50, 20, 10, 5, 2 and 1 cents. On the introduction of the euro there was a 'dual circulation' period before the franc ceased to be legal tender on 17 Feb. 2002.

Budget. Revenues in 2001 totalled 4,094·84m. francs (€624·25m.) and expenditures 4,073·77m. francs (€621·04m.).

Performance. Monaco does not publish annual income information, but its economy is estimated to have grown by 1·6% in 2001.

Banking and Finance. There were 44 banks in 2001 of which 22 were Monegasque banks.

ENERGY AND NATURAL RESOURCES

Electricity. Electricity is imported from France. 475 GWh were supplied to 24,074 customers in 2001; output capacity, 83 MW.

Oil and Gas. In 2001, 58 GWh of gas were supplied to 4,269 customers; output capacity was 19 MW.

Water. Total consumption (2001), 5·71m. cu. metres.

INDUSTRY

The main industry is tourism. There is some production of cosmetics, pharmaceuticals, glassware, electrical goods and precision instruments.

Labour. There were 39,543 persons employed in Jan. 2001. 36,072 worked in the private sector; 3,471 in the public sector. Some 25,000 French citizens work in Monaco.

Trade Unions. Membership of trade unions was estimated at 2,000 out of a workforce of 25,600 in 1989.

INTERNATIONAL TRADE

Imports and Exports. There is a customs union with France. Exports for 2001 totalled €394m.; imports, €403m. Main imports: pharmaceuticals, perfumes, clothing, paper, synthetic and non-metallic products, and building materials.

COMMUNICATIONS

Roads. There were estimated to be 50 km of roads in 2001 and 32,800 vehicles. Monaco has the densest network of roads of any country in the world. In 2001, 4,065,632 people travelled by bus.

Rail. The 1·7 km of main line passing through the country are operated by the French National Railways (SNCF). In 2001, 3,307,146 people arrived at or departed from Monaco railway station.

Civil Aviation. There are helicopter flights to Nice with Heli Air Monaco and Heli Inter. Helicopter movements (2001) at the Heliport of Monaco (Fontvieille), 49,245; the number of passengers carried was 142,074. The nearest airport is at Nice in France.

Shipping. In 2001 there were 1,052 vessels registered, of which 12 were over 100 tonnes. 1,787 yachts put in to the port of Monaco and 1,029 at Fontvieille in 2001. 119 liners put in to port in Monaco; 2,285 people embarked, 1,692 disembarked and 67,539 were in transit.

Telecommunications. In 2002 there were 33,700 land-based telephone lines and 19,300 mobile phone subscribers. Internet users numbered 16,000 in 2002.

Postal Services. 20m. items were posted and 26m. items were delivered by the Post Office in 2001.

SOCIAL INSTITUTIONS

Justice. There are the following courts: *Tribunal Suprème*, *Cour de Révision*, *Cour d'Appel*, a Correctional Tribunal, a Work Tribunal, a Tribunal of the First Instance, two Arbitration Commissions for Rents (one commercial, one domestic), courts for Work-related Accidents and Supervision, a *Juge de Paix*, and a Police Tribunal. There is no death penalty.

Police. In 1993 the police force (Sûreté Publique) comprised 500 personnel. Monaco has one of the highest number of police per head of population of any country in the world.

Religion. 90% of the resident population are Roman Catholic. There is a Roman Catholic archbishop.

Education. In 2002–03, in the public sector, there were 7 pre-school institutions (*écoles maternelles*) with 713 pupils; 4 elementary schools with 1,374 pupils; 3 secondary schools with 2,430 pupils. There were 142 primary teachers and 286 secondary school teachers in total in 2002–03. In the private sector there were 2 pre-schools and 3 primary schools with 222 and 525 pupils respectively; and 1 secondary school with 710 pupils. In 2000–01 education amounted to 6·7% of total government expenditure.

The University of Southern Europe in Monaco had 112 students in 1996–97.

Health. In 2000, 18·5% of total government expenditure was spent on public health. In 2002 there were 156 doctors, 21 dentists and 19 childcare nurses. Monaco has the highest provision of hospital beds of any country, with 162 per 10,000 population in 2002.

CULTURE

Broadcasting. Radio Monte Carlo broadcasts FM commercial programmes in French (long- and medium-waves). Radio Monte Carlo owns 55% of *Radio Monte Carlo* Relay Station on Cyprus. The foreign service is dedicated exclusively to religious broadcasts and is maintained by voluntary contributions. It operates in 36 languages under the name 'Trans World Radio' and has relay facilities on Bonaire, West Indies; it is planning to build relay facilities in the southern parts of Africa. *Télé Monte-Carlo* broadcasts TV programmes in French, Italian and English (colour by SECAM H). There is a 30-channel cable service. In 1997 there were 34,000 radio receivers and 25,000 television receivers.

Press. Monaco had one newspaper in 1995 with a circulation of 8,000, equivalent to 250 per 1,000 inhabitants.

Tourism. In 2001, 296,925 foreign visitors spent a total of 797,842 nights in Monaco. The main visitors are Italians, followed by French and Americans. 82,241 people attended 674 congresses in 2001. There are three casinos run by the state, including the one at Monte Carlo attracting 0·4m. visitors a year.

Festivals. Residents of Monaco celebrate the Feast of St John on 23 and 24 June each year. One of the highlights of the folk festival is the lighting of a bonfire in Palace Square by the sovereign's footmen. Each July the Monte Carlo International Fireworks Festival attracts pyrotechnic specialists from all over the world, and the famous Monte Carlo rally and historic car rally take place annually in Jan. and Feb.

DIPLOMATIC REPRESENTATIVES

British Consul-General (resident in France)*:* Simon Lever.
British Honorary Consul: Eric J. F. Blair.

Consul-General for Monaco in London: Ivan Bozidar Ivanovic.

Of Monaco to the United Nations
Ambassador: Gilles Noghès.

Of Monaco to the European Union
Ambassador: Jean Pastorelli.

FURTHER READING

Journal de Monaco. Bulletin Officiel. 1858 ff.

Hudson, Grace L., *Monaco.* [Bibliography] ABC-Clio, Oxford and Santa Barbara (CA), 1991

MONGOLIA

Mongol Uls

Capital: Ulan Bator
Population projection, 2010: 2·86m.
GDP per capita, 2002: (PPP$) 1,710
HDI/world rank: 0·668/117

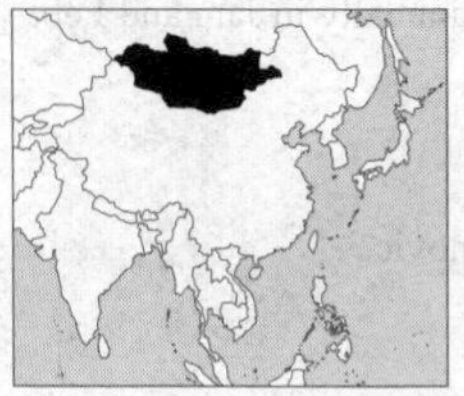

KEY HISTORICAL EVENTS

Temujin became khan of Hamag Mongolia in 1190. Having united by conquest various Tatar and Mongolian tribes he was confirmed as 'Universal' ('Genghis', 'Chingiz') khan in 1206. The expansionist impulse of his nomadic empire (Beijing captured in 1215; Samarkand in 1220) continued after his death in 1227. Tamurlaine (died 1405) was the last of the conquering khans. In 1368 the Chinese drove the Mongols from Beijing, and for the next two centuries Sino-Mongolian relations alternated between war and trade. In 1691 Outer Mongolia accepted Manchu rule. The head of the Lamaist faith became the symbol of national identity, and his seat ('Urga', now Ulan Bator) was made the Mongolian capital. When the Manchu dynasty was overthrown in 1911 Outer Mongolia declared its independence under its spiritual ruler and turned to Russia for support against China. Soviet and Mongolian revolutionary forces set up a provisional government in March 1921. On the death of the spiritual ruler a people's republic and new constitution were proclaimed in May 1924. With Soviet help Japanese invaders were fended off during the Second World War. The Mongols then took part in the successful Soviet campaign against Inner Mongolia and Manchuria. On 5 Jan. 1946 China recognized the independence of Outer Mongolia. Until 1990 sole power was in the hands of the Mongolian People's Revolutionary (Communist) Party (MPRP), but an opposition Mongolian Democratic Party, founded in Dec. 1989, achieved tacit recognition and held its first congress in Feb. 1990. Following demonstrations and hunger-strikes, on 12 March the entire MPRP Politburo resigned and political opposition was legalized.

TERRITORY AND POPULATION

Mongolia is bounded in the north by the Russian Federation, and in the east and south and west by China. Area, 1,565,008 sq. km (604,250 sq. miles). Population (2000 census), 2,373,493 (1,195,512 females). Density, 2000, 1·5 per sq. km. In 2001, 56·7% of the population were urban.

The UN gives a projected population for 2010 of 2·86m.

The population is predominantly made up of Mongolian peoples (81·5% Khalkh). There is a Turkic Kazakh minority (4·3% of the population) and 20 Mongol minorities. The official language is Khalkh Mongol.

The republic is administratively divided into four municipalities—Ulan Bator, the capital (2000 population, 760,077), Darhan-Uul (83,271 in 2000), Orhon (71,525 in 2000) and Govisumber (12,230 in 2000)—and 18 provinces *(aimag)*. The provinces are sub-divided into 334 districts or counties *(suums)*.

SOCIAL STATISTICS

Births, 2001, 49,685; deaths, 15,999. 2001 rates: births, 20·5 per 1,000 population; deaths, 6·6 per 1,000; marriages, 5·1 per 1,000; divorces, 0·3 per 1,000. Annual population growth rate, 1992–02, 1·1%. Infant mortality rate, 2001, 61 per 1,000 live births. Expectation of life in 2001 was 61·3 years for males and 65·3 for females. Fertility rate, 2001, 2·4 births per woman.

CLIMATE

A very extreme climate, with six months of mean temperatures below freezing, but much higher temperatures occur for a month or two in summer. Rainfall is very low and limited to the months mid-May to mid-Sept. Ulan Bator, Jan. –14°F (–25·6°C), July 61°F (16·1°C). Annual rainfall 8" (208 mm).

CONSTITUTION AND GOVERNMENT

The Constitution of 12 Feb. 1992 abolished the 'People's Democracy', introduced democratic institutions and a market economy and guarantees freedom of speech.

The *President* is directly elected for renewable four-year terms.

Since June 1992 the legislature has consisted of a single-chamber 76-seat parliament, the *Great Hural (Ulsyn Ich-Chural)*, which elects the Prime Minister.

National Anthem. 'Darkhan manai khuvsgalt uls' ('Our sacred revolutionary republic'); words by Tsendiyn Damdinsüren, tune by Bilegin Damdinsüren and Luvsanjamts Murjorj.

RECENT ELECTIONS

At the parliamentary elections of 27 June 2004 turn-out was 76·4%. Preliminary results declared that the Revolutionary People's Party of Mongolia (MAKN) gained 36 seats (72 in 2000), the Motherland Democracy (EOA, comprising the Democratic Party, the Civic Will Republican Party and the Mongol Democratic New Socialist Party) 34 seats and the Republican Party one seat. Three seats went to non-partisans. Two seats, initially declared for the EOA, were deemed undecided by the electoral commission and required another ballot. One of these went to MAKN, giving them 37 seats, and the other to an independent, giving them four.

In presidential elections on 20 May 2001, incumbent Natsagiin Bagabandi (MAKN) won with 57·9% of the vote, followed by Radnaasumbereliyn Gonchigdorj (Democratic Party) with 36·6% and Luvsandamba Dashnyam (Civic Will Party) with 3·6%. Turn-out was 82%.

CURRENT ADMINISTRATION

President: Natsagiin Bagabandi; b. 1940 (Revolutionary People's Party of Mongolia; elected May 1997).

In March 2005 the coalition government comprised:

Prime Minister: Tsakhiagiyn Elbegdorj; b. 1963 (Motherland Democracy; since 20 Aug. 2004, having previously been prime minister from April to Dec. 1998).

Deputy Prime Minister: Chultemin Ulaan.

Minister of Defence: Tserenhuugiin Sharavdorj. *Finance:* Norovyn Altankhuyag. *Foreign Affairs:* Tsendiin Munkh-Orgil. *Health:* Togsjargalyn Gandi. *Industry and Commerce:* Sukhbaataryn Batbold. *Education, Culture and Science:* Puntsagiin Tsagaan. *Environment:* Ulambayaryn Barsbold. *Energy:* Tuvdengiin Ochirkhuu. *Food and Agriculture:* Dendeviin Terbishdagva. *Construction and Town Planning:* Nyamjavyn Batbayar. *Justice and Internal Affairs:* Tsendiin Nyamdorj. *Social Welfare and Labour:* Tsevelmaagiin Bayarsaikhan. *Roads, Transport and Tourism:* Gavaagiin Batkhuu. *Secretary General of the Government:* Sangajavyn Bayartsogt. *Ministers without Portfolio:* Ichinkhorlogiin Erdenebaatar; Ukhnaagiin Hurelsukh.

Government Website: http://www.pmis.gov.mn

DEFENCE

Conscription is for one year for males aged 18–28 years. Defence expenditure in 2003 totalled US$15m. (US$6 per capita), representing 1·4% of GDP.

Army. Strength (2002) 7,500 (4,000 conscripts). There is a border guard of 6,000, 1,200 internal security troops and 500 Civil Defence Troops.

Air Force. The Air Force had a strength of 800 in 2002 with 11 armed helicopters and nine aircraft in store.

INTERNATIONAL RELATIONS

Mongolia is a member of the UN, WTO, the Asian Development Bank and the Colombo Plan.

ECONOMY

In 2002 agriculture accounted for 29·7% of GDP, industry 15·9% and services 54·4%.

Overview. Mongolia has for centuries had a traditional nomadic pastoral economy which the government aims to transform into a market economy. An Agency for National Development, headed by a minister of cabinet rank, co-ordinates economic policy. A law of May 1991 introduced privatization by the distribution of vouchers worth 10,000 tugriks to 2m. citizens to acquire holdings or to buy small businesses or livestock. About 45% of state-owned assets had been privatized by 2001.

Currency. The unit of currency is the *tugrik* (MNT) of 100 *möngö*. The tugrik was made convertible in 1993. In June 2002 foreign exchange reserves were US$210m., gold reserves totalled 41,000 troy oz and total money supply was 187,680m. tugriks. Inflation, which stood at 268% in 1993, had been brought down to below 10% by 1998 and in 2002 was 0·9%.

Budget. Total revenue and expenditure (in 1m. tugriks):

	1998	*1999*	*2000*	*2001*
Revenue	183,552	196,561	303,215	358,244
Expenditure	201,279	232,795	306,037	353,580

Main sources of revenue, 2001 (in 1m. tugriks): taxes, 265,384 (including: domestic taxes on goods and services, 145,335; social security contributions, 61,306; income, profits and capital gains tax, 27,875; taxes on foreign trade, 27,018); non-tax revenue, 88,457. Major items of expenditure, 2001 (in 1m. tugriks): social security and welfare, 84,093; economic affairs and services, 49,504; health, 30,192; general public services, 29,317.

Performance. Real GDP growth was 1·0% in 2001 and 3·9% in 2002. Total GDP in 2003 was US$1·2bn.

Banking and Finance. The Mongolian Bank (established 1924) is the bank of issue, being also a commercial, savings and development bank: the *Governor* is Chook O. Chuluunbat. It has 21 main branches. There were 25 other banks in 2002. The largest bank is the state-owned Trade and Development Bank.

A stock exchange opened in Ulan Bator in 1992.

ENERGY AND NATURAL RESOURCES

Environment. In 2002 carbon dioxide emissions from the consumption and flaring of fossil fuels in Mongolia were the equivalent of 2·9 tonnes per capita.

Electricity. Installed capacity was 0·9m. kW in 2000. There are six thermal electric power stations. Production, 2000, 2·93bn. kWh; consumption per capita in 2000 was 1,302 kWh.

Minerals. There are large deposits of copper, nickel, zinc, molybdenum, phosphorites, tin, wolfram and fluorspar; production of the latter in 1996, 565,100 tonnes. There are major coalmines near Ulan Bator and Darhan. In 2000 lignite production was 4·18m. tonnes and coal production was 833,000 tonnes. Copper production, 2001, 133,503 tonnes; gold production, 2001, 13,675 kg.

Agriculture. The prevailing Mongolian style of life is pastoral nomadism. 73% of agricultural production derives from cattle-raising. In 2000 there were 14·0m. sheep, 3·50m. cattle, 3·08m. horses and 360,000 camels. The number of goats rose from 5·5m. to 10m. between 1992 and 2000 as production of cashmere has increased along with the market economy. In late 1999 and early 2000 approximately 3m. animals died as a result of extreme weather and overgrazing, and in late 2000 and early 2001 more than 1·3m. animals died.

The total agricultural area in 1995 was 118·5m. ha. 96% was sown to cereals, 1·6% to fodder and 0·9% to vegetables. In 2001 there were 1·20m. ha of arable land and 1,000 ha of permanent crop land. In 2000 output of major crops was 186,000 tonnes of wheat (down from 607,000 in the period 1989–91); 70,000 tonnes of potatoes (down from 128,000 in 1989–91); 4,000 tonnes of barley (down from 83,000 in 1989–91). Livestock products, 2000 (in 1,000 tonnes): meat, 230; cow's milk, 285; goat's milk, 34; sheep's milk, 22. In 2001 there were 5,000 tractors and 1,150 harvester-threshers.

Collectivized farms, set up in the 1950s under Stalin, have been broken up and the land redistributed.

Forestry. Forests, chiefly larch, cedar, fir and birch, occupied 10·65m. ha in 2000 (6·8% of the land area). Timber production was 631,000 cu. metres in 2001.

Fisheries. The catch in 2001 was 117 tonnes, entirely from inland waters.

INDUSTRY

Industry is still small in scale and local in character. The food industry accounts for 25% of industrial production. The main industrial centre is Ulan Bator; others are at Erdenet and Baga-Nur, and a northern territorial industrial complex is being developed based on Darhan and Erdenet to produce copper and molybdenum concentrates, lime, cement, machinery and wood- and metal-worked products. Production figures: cement (2002), 148,000 tonnes; lime (2002), 41,000 tonnes; bread (2000), 20,000 tonnes; carpets (2000), 705,000 sq. metres; sawnwood (1998), 300,000 cu. metres.

Labour. Out of 870,800 people in employment in Dec. 2002, 381,400 were engaged in agriculture, hunting, fishing and forestry; 104,500 in wholesale and retail trade/repair of motor vehicles, motorcycles and personal and household goods; 59,300 in education; and 55,600 in manufacturing. In July 2003 there were 37,300 registered unemployed persons.

Trade Unions. The Confederation of Mongolian Trade Unions had 450,000 members in 1994.

INTERNATIONAL TRADE

Mongolia is dependent on foreign aid. The largest donor in 1992 was Japan. Foreign debt was US$1,037m. in 2002.

Joint ventures with foreign firms are permitted. Foreign investors may acquire up to 49% of the equity in Mongolian companies. Foreign companies (except in precious metal mining) have a five-year tax holiday and a further five years at 50% of the tax rate.

Imports and Exports. In 2002 imports (f.o.b.) were valued at US$680·2m. (US$623·8m. in 2001) and exports (f.o.b.) at US$524·0m. (US$523·2m. in 2001). Main exports, 2001: copper concentrate, 28·1%; gold, 14·3%; cashmere, 13·4%.

Principal import suppliers in 2002: Russia, 34·1%; China, 24·4%; South Korea, 12·2%; Japan, 6·2%. Main export markets, 2002: China, 42·4%; USA, 31·6%; Russia, 8·6%; South Korea, 4·4%.

COMMUNICATIONS

Roads. The total road network covered 49,250 km in 2002, including 11,121 km of highway. There are 1,185 km of surfaced roads running around Ulan Bator, from Ulan Bator to Darhan, at points on the frontier with the Russian Federation and towards the south. Truck services run where there are no surfaced roads. Vehicles in use in 2002 included 63,224 passenger cars and 26,319 trucks and vans. In 2000 passenger transport totalled 388m. passenger-km and freight 126m. tonne-km. In 2000 there were 5,991 road accidents resulting in 338 fatalities.

Rail. The Trans-Mongolian Railway (1,928 km of 1,524 mm gauge in 1992) connects Ulan Bator with the Russian Federation and China. There are spur lines to Erdenet and to the coalmines at Nalayh and Sharyn Gol. A separate line connects Choybalsan in the east with Borzaya on the Trans-Siberian Railway. Passenger-km travelled in 2000 came to 1,070m. and freight tonne-km to 4,293m.

Civil Aviation. MIAT-Mongolian Airlines operates internal services, and in 2003 flew from Ulan Bator to Beijing, Berlin, Frankfurt, Hohhot, Irkutsk, Moscow, Seoul and Tokyo. In 1999 it flew 6·3m. km, carrying 224,700 passengers (98,300 on international flights). In 1999 Ulan Bator handled 244,939 passengers and 2,556 tonnes of freight.

Shipping. There is a steamer service on the Selenge River and a tug and barge service on Hövsgöl Lake. 70,000 tonnes of freight were carried in 1990.

Telecommunications. Mongolia had 344,000 telephone subscribers in 2002, or 141·6 for every 1,000 persons. There were 216,000 mobile phone subscribers in 2002, up from 2,000 in 1998. There were 69,000 PCs in use (28·4 for every 1,000 persons) in 2002 and 7,900 fax machines in 1999. There were 50,000 Internet users in 2002.

Postal Services. There were 339 post offices in 1997. A total of 1·1m. pieces of mail were processed in 1997.

SOCIAL INSTITUTIONS

Justice. The Procurator-General is appointed, and the Supreme Court elected, by parliament for five years. There are also courts at province, town and district level. Lay assessors sit with professional judges. The death penalty is in force.

The population in penal institutions in 2002 was 7,256 (279 per 100,000 of national population).

Religion. Tibetan Buddhist Lamaism is the prevalent religion; the Dalai Lama is its spiritual head. In 1995 there were about 100 monasteries and 2,500 monks.

Education. Adult literacy was 98·5% in 2001 (male, 98·6%; female, 98·3%). Schooling begins at the age of seven. In 2000–01 there were 79,294 children in pre-primary education; 250,437 pupils and 7,755 teachers in primary education; and 259,888 students and 12,333 teachers in secondary schools. There were 84,970 students in tertiary education in 2000–01. In 1994–95 there were one university and four specialized universities (agricultural; medical; pedagogical; technical). There were also colleges of commerce and business, economics, and railway engineering, and an institute of culture and art.

In 2000–01 total expenditure on education came to 6·6% of GNP.

Health. In 1997 there were 407 hospitals with the equivalent of 78 beds per 10,000 inhabitants. There were 5,676 physicians (provision of one for every 411 persons), 315 dentists and 7,169 nurses in 1998.

Welfare. In 1995, 102·8m. tugriks were spent on maternity benefits.

CULTURE

World Heritage Sites. Mongolia has one site on the UNESCO World Heritage List: the Orkhon Valley Cultural Landscape (inscribed on the list in 2004), an extensive area on both banks of the Orkhon River including the archaeological remains of Kharkhorum, the 13th and 14th century capital of Genghis Khan's vast Empire. A second site falls under joint Mongolian and Russian jurisdiction: Uvs Nuur Basin (2003), an important saline lake system supporting a rich wildlife, especially the snow leopard and Asiatic ibex.

Broadcasting. In 2003 there were four television stations: the government-financed Ulan Bator Broadcasting System (UBS) and Mongol TV and the private Channel 25 and Eagle TV. Ulan Bator Radio (UBS) broadcasts two national programmes and an external service (English, Chinese, Japanese, Russian). Number of sets: TV (2001), 173,000; radio (2000), 368,000.

Press. In 2003 there were five daily newspapers, including *Onoodor* (10,000 regular subscribers) and *Udriin Sonin* (Daily News), and two English-language weeklies, the *UB Post* and the government's *Mongol Messenger*.

Tourism. In 2002 there were 198,000 foreign tourists; spending by tourists totalled US$130m. Of 166,000 tourists in 2001, 80,000 were from elsewhere in Asia, 79,000 from Europe and 6,000 from the Americas.

DIPLOMATIC REPRESENTATIVES

Of Mongolia in the United Kingdom (7 Kensington Ct, London, W8 5DL)
Ambassador: Davaasambuu Dalrain.

Of the United Kingdom in Mongolia (30 Enkh Taivny Gudamzh, Ulan Bator 13)
Ambassador: Richard Austen, MBE.

Of Mongolia in the USA (2833 M Street, NW, Washington, D.C., 20007)
Ambassador: Ravdan Bold.

Of the USA in Mongolia (Micro Region 11, Big Ring Road, Ulan Bator)
Ambassador: Pamela J. Slutz.

Of Mongolia to the United Nations
Ambassador: Baatar Choisuren.

Of Mongolia to the European Union
Ambassador: Sodoviin Onon.

FURTHER READING

State Statistical Office: *Mongolian Economy and Society in [year]: Statistical Yearbook.—National Economy of the MPR, 1924–1984: Anniversary Statistical Collection.* Ulan Bator, 1984

Akiner, S. (ed.) *Mongolia Today.* London, 1992
Becker, J., *The Lost Country.* London, 1992
Bruun, O. and Odgaard, O. (eds.) *Mongolia in Transition.* Richmond, 1996
Griffin, K. (ed.) *Poverty and the Transition to a Market Economy in Mongolia.* London, 1995
Nordby, Judith, *Mongolia in the Twentieth Century.* Farnborough, 1993.—*Mongolia.* [Bibliography] ABC-Clio, Oxford and Santa Barbara (CA), 1993

National statistical office: Government Building 3, Ulan Bator-20A.

MOROCCO

Mamlaka al-Maghrebia
(Kingdom of Morocco)

Capital: Rabat
Population projection, 2010: 34·07m.
GDP per capita, 2002: (PPP$) 3,810
HDI/world rank: 0·620/125

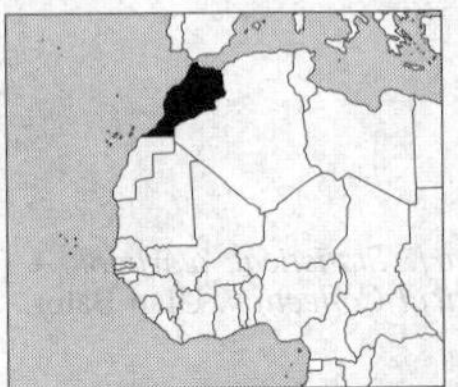

KEY HISTORICAL EVENTS

The native people of Morocco are the Berbers, an ancient race who have suffered the attention of a succession of invaders. When the city of Carthage fell to Rome in the second century BC, the African Mediterranean coast was under Roman dominance for almost six hundred years. When the Roman Empire in turn fell into decline, the area was invaded first by the Vandals in AD 429 and later by Byzantium in AD 533. An Arab invasion of Morocco in AD 682 marked the end of Byzantium dominance and the first Arab rulers, the Idrisid dynasty, ruled for 150 years. Arab and Berber dynasties succeeded the Idrisids until the 13th century when the country was plunged into bitter civil war between Arab and Berber factions. The reign of Ahmed I al-Man-sur in the first Sharifian dynasty stabilized and unified the country between 1579 and 1603. Moors and Jews expelled from Spain settled in Morocco during this time and the country flourished. In 1415 the Moroccan port of Ceuta was captured by Portugal. Moroccan forces defeated the Portuguese in 1578 and by 1700 had regained control of many coastal towns which had previously been in Portuguese hands. During the 18th and early 19th centuries the Barbary Coast became the scene of widespread piracy.

As part of the Entente Cordiale, Britain recognized Morocco as a French sphere of influence and in 1904 Morocco was divided between France and Spain, with the former receiving the larger area. From 1912 to 1956 Morocco was divided into a French protectorate, a Spanish protectorate, and the international zone of Tangier which was established by France, Great Britain and Spain in 1923. On 29 Oct. 1956 the international status of the Tangier Zone was abolished and Morocco became a kingdom on 18 Aug. 1957, with the Sultan taking the title Mohammed V. Succeeding his father on 3 March 1961, King Hassan tried to combine the various parties in government and established an elected House of Representatives but political unrest led him to discard any attempt at a parliamentary government and to rule autocratically from 1965 to 1977. In 1977 a new Chamber of Representatives was elected and under the constitution Morocco became a constitutional monarchy with a single elected chamber.

TERRITORY AND POPULATION

Morocco is bounded by Algeria to the east and southeast, Mauritania to the south, the Atlantic Ocean to the northwest and the Mediterranean to the north. Excluding the Western Saharan territory claimed and retrieved since 1976 by Morocco, the area is 458,730 sq. km . The population at the 2004 census (including Western Sahara) was 29,891,708; density (including Western Sahara), 42·1 per sq. km. At the 2004 census Western Sahara had an area of 252,120 sq. km and a population of about 356,000. The Moroccan superficie is 710,850 sq. km. The population was 56·1% urban in 2001.

The UN gives a projected population for 2010 of 34·07m.

Morocco has 16 states (*wilaya'at*) divided further into 71 prefectures and provincial units. Areas of the states and census populations in 2004:

State	*Area in sq. km*	*Population*	*State*	*Area in sq. km*	*Population*
Chaouia-Ouardigha	16,760	1,655,660	Guelmin-Es Semara	71,970	462,410
Doukkala-Abda	13,285	1,984,039	Laâyoune-Boujdour-Sakia El Hamra[1]	...	256,152
Fès-Boulemane	19,795	1,573,055	Marrakesh-Tensift-Al Haouz	31,160	3,102,652
Gharb-Chrarda-Béni Hssen	8,805	1,859,540	Meknès-Tafilalet	79,210	2,141,527
Grand Casablanca	1,615	3,631,061			

State	Area in sq. km	Population	State	Area in sq. km	Population
Oriental	82,820	1,918,094	Souss Massa-Draâ	70,880	3,113,653
Oued Eddahab-Lagouira[1]	...	99,367	Tadla-Azilal	17,125	1,450,519
Rabat-Salé-Zemmour-Zaer	9,580	2,366,494	Tangier-Tétouan	11,570	2,470,372
			Taza-Al Hoceima-Taounate	24,155	1,807,113

[1]Laâyoune-Boujdour-Sakia El Hamra and Oued Eddahab-Lagouira correspond roughly to Western Sahara.

The chief cities (with populations in 1,000, 2004) are as follows:

Casablanca	2,934	Tangiers	670	Safi	285
Rabat	1,623	Meknès	536	Mohammedia	189
Fès (Fez)	947	Oujda	401	Khouribga	166
Marrakesh	823	Kénitra	359	Béni Mellal	163
Agadir	679	Tétouan	321		

The official language is Arabic, spoken by 75% of the population. Berber languages, including Tachelhit (or Soussi), Tamazight and Tarafit (or Rifia), are spoken by about half the population. French (widely used for business), Spanish (in the north) and English are also spoken.

SOCIAL STATISTICS

2002 estimates: births, 632,000; deaths, 169,000. Estimated rates, 2002 (per 1,000 population): birth, 21·0; death, 5·6. Annual population growth rate, 1992–02, 1·7%. Life expectancy at birth in 2001 was 66·2 years for males and 69·9 years for females. Infant mortality, 2001, 39 per 1,000 live births; fertility rate, 2001, 3·1 births per woman.

CLIMATE

Morocco is dominated by the Mediterranean climate which is made temperate by the influence of the Atlantic Ocean in the northern and southern parts of the country. Central Morocco is continental while the south is desert. Rabat, Jan. 55°F (12·9°C), July 72°F (22·2°C). Annual rainfall 23" (564 mm). Agadir, Jan. 57°F (13·9°C), July 72°F (22·2°C). Annual rainfall 9" (224 mm). Casablanca, Jan. 54°F (12·2°C), July 72°F (22·2°C). Annual rainfall 16" (404 mm). Marrakesh, Jan. 52°F (11·1°C), July 84°F (28·9°C). Annual rainfall 10" (239 mm). Tangiers, Jan. 53°F (11·7°C), July 72°F (22·2°C). Annual rainfall 36" (897 mm).

CONSTITUTION AND GOVERNMENT

The ruling King is **Mohammed VI,** born on 21 Aug. 1963, married to Salma Bennani on 21 March 2002; succeeded on 23 July 1999, on the death of his father Hassan II, who reigned 1961–99. *Son:* Hassan, b. 8 May 2003. The King holds supreme civil and religious authority, the latter in his capacity of Emir-el-Muminin or Commander of the Faithful. He resides usually at Rabat, but occasionally in one of the other traditional capitals, Fès (founded in 808), Marrakesh (founded in 1062), or at Skhirat.

A new Constitution was approved by referendum in March 1972 and amendments were approved by referendum in May 1980 and Sept. 1992. The Kingdom of Morocco is a constitutional monarchy. Parliament consists of a *Chamber of Representatives* composed of 325 deputies directly elected for five-year terms. For the Sept. 2002 elections a series of measures were introduced, including a new proportional representation voting system and a national list reserved for women candidates to ensure that at least 10% of new MPs are females.

A referendum on 13 Sept. 1996 established a second *Chamber of Counsellors,* composed of 270 members serving nine-year terms, of whom 162 are elected by local councils, 81 by chambers of commerce and 27 by trade unions. The Chamber of Counsellors has power to initiate legislation, issue warnings of censure to the government and ultimately to force the government's resignation by a two-thirds majority vote. The electorate was 12·3m. and turn-out was 82·95%. The King, as sovereign head of State, appoints the Prime Minister and other Ministers, has the right to dissolve Parliament and approves legislation.

A new electoral code of March 1997 fixed voting at 20 and made enrolment on the electoral roll compulsory. In Dec. 2002 King Mohammed VI announced that the voting age was to be lowered from 20 to 18.

National Anthem. 'Manbit al Ahrah, mashriq al anwar' ('Fountain of freedom, source of light'); words by Ali Squalli Houssaini, tune by Leo Morgan.

RECENT ELECTIONS

Elections to the Chamber of Representatives took place on 27 Sept. 2002. The USFP (Union Socialiste des Forces Populaires) won 50 seats, down from 57 seats in 1997; the PI (Istiqlal/Parti d'Indépendence) gained 48 seats, up from 32 in 1997; and the PJD (Parti de la Justice et du Développement), the only Islamic party taking part in the elections, trebled its representation from 14 to 42 seats. The Rassemblement National des Indépendants won 41 seats, the Mouvement Populaire 27, the Mouvement Nationale Populaire 18, the Union Constitutionnelle 16, the Parti National-Démocrate 12, the Front des Forces Démocratiques also 12, the Parti du Progrès et du Socialisme 11 and the Union Democratique 10. A further 11 parties obtained fewer than ten seats each. Turn-out was 51·6%.

In elections to the Chamber of Counsellors on 5 Dec. 1997 the centre Rassemblement National des Indépendents gained 42 seats, ahead of a second centre party, the Mouvement Démocratique et Social, with 33 seats.

CURRENT ADMINISTRATION

In March 2005 the six-party coalition government comprised:

Prime Minister: Driss Jettou; b. 1945 (USFP; in office since 9 Oct. 2002).

Minister for Foreign Affairs and Co-operation: Mohamed Benaissa. *Interior:* Al Mustapha Sahel. *Justice:* Mohamed Bouzoubaa. *Finance and Privatization:* Fathallah Oualalou. *'Habous' and Islamic Affairs:* Ahmed Toufiq. *Territorial Development, Water Resources and the Environment:* Mohamed El Yazghi. *Agriculture and Rural Development:* Mohand Laenser. *Employment and Professional Training:* Mustapha Mansouri. *Social Development, Family and Solidarity:* Abderrahim Harouchi. *National Education and Youth Affairs:* Habib El Malki. *Modernization and the Public Sector:* Mohammed Boussaid. *Culture:* Mohammed Achaari. *Equipment and Transport:* Karim Ghellab. *Industry, Commerce and Economic Upgrading:* Salaheddine Mezouar. *Tourism, Handicrafts and Economy:* Adil Douiri. *Health:* Mohammed Cheikh Biadillah. *Relations with Parliament:* Mohammed Saad El Alami. *Energy and Mines:* Mohammed Boutaleb. *Communications and Government Spokesperson:* Nabil Benabdallah. *Foreign Trade:* Mustapha Mechahouri. *Minister of State:* Abbas El Fassi.

Office of the Prime Minister (French only): http://www.pm.gov.ma

DEFENCE

Conscription is authorized for 18 months. Defence expenditure in 2003 totalled US$1,826m. (US$61 per capita), representing 4·2% of GDP.

Army. The Army is deployed in two commands: Northern Zone and Southern Zone. There is also a Royal Guard of 1,500. Strength (2002), 175,000 (100,000 conscripts). There is also a Royal Gendarmerie of 20,000, an Auxiliary Force of 30,000 and reserves of 150,000.

Navy. The Navy includes two frigates, 27 patrol and coastal combatants and four amphibious craft.

Personnel in 2002 numbered 7,800, including a 1,500 strong brigade of Naval Infantry. Bases are located at Casablanca, Agadir, Al Hoceima, Dakhla and Tangiers.

Air Force. Personnel strength (2002) about 13,500, with 95 combat aircraft, including F-5s and Mirage F-1s, and 24 armed helicopters.

INTERNATIONAL RELATIONS

Morocco is a member of the UN, WTO, the League of Arab States, Arab Maghreb Union, African Development Bank, IOM, OIC, Islamic Development Bank and the International Organization of the Francophonie.

ECONOMY

Agriculture accounted for 16·1% of GDP in 2002, industry 30·3% and services 53·6%.

Overview. Per capita income grew 0·9% a year between 1991 and 2001, compared to 2·5% per year between 1984 and 1990. Poverty increased from 13·1% of the population in 1991 to 19% of the population in 1998. Since 2001 macroeconomic stability and growth have improved. The government is undertaking a series of structural reforms to consolidate macroeconomic and financial stability, increase access to basic social services and fight poverty. Morocco's trade is focused on EU countries, which in 2001 accounted for 77% of exports and supplied 56% of imports. The government is abolishing tariffs in preparation for the 2012 implementation of its three-stage free-trade association agreement with the EU, which will completely liberalize the market for industrialized goods by 2012.

Currency. The unit of currency is the *dirham* (MAD) of 100 *centimes*, introduced in 1959. Foreign exchange reserves were US$9,006m. and gold reserves 708,000 troy oz in June 2002. Since 1993 the dirham has been convertible for current account operations. Inflation was 2·8% in 2002. Total money supply in May 2002 was DH248,359m.

Budget. Revenues in 2002 totalled DH98,261m. and expenditures DH118,999m. The main revenue items were VAT (24·4%), taxes on income and profits (16·6%) and excise taxes (16·4%). Current expenditure accounted for 76·2% of total expenditures and capital expenditure 17·8%.

VAT is 20%.

Performance. Real GDP growth was 3·2% in 2002 and 5·5% in 2003. Total GDP in 2003 was US$44·5bn.

Banking and Finance. The central bank is the Bank Al Maghrib (*Governor*, Abdellatif Jouahri) which had assets of DH17,063m. on 31 Dec. 1999. There were 12 other banks in 2002 and three development banks, specializing respectively in industry, housing and agriculture.

There is a stock exchange in Casablanca.

ENERGY AND NATURAL RESOURCES

Environment. Carbon dioxide emissions from the consumption and flaring of fossil fuels in 2002 were the equivalent of 1·0 tonnes per capita.

Electricity. Installed capacity was 4·0m. kW in 2000. Production was 13·27bn. kWh (approximately 95% thermal) in 2000 and consumption per capita 544 kWh.

Oil and Gas. Natural gas reserves in 2002 were 1·3bn. cu. metres; output (2000), 51m. cu. metres.

Minerals. The principal mineral exploited is phosphate (Morocco has the largest reserves in the world), the output of which was 21·98m. tonnes in 2001. Other minerals (in tonnes, 2001) are: barytine, 471,102; salt (2000), 188,000; lead, 110,906; zinc, 89,339; coal (2000), 29,000; manganese, 13,757; copper (2000), 7,125; iron ore (2000), 6,000; silver, 281.

Agriculture. Agricultural production is subject to drought; about 1·35m. ha were irrigated in 2001. 85% of farmland is individually owned. Only 1% of farms are over 50 ha; most are under 3 ha. There were 8·75m. ha of arable land in 2001 and 0·97m. ha of permanent crops. Main land usage, 2000 (in 1,000 ha): wheat, 2,902; barley, 2,251; maize, 238. There were 43,226 tractors in 2001 and 3,763 harvester-threshers.

Production in 2000 (in 1,000 tonnes): sugarbeets, 2,883; wheat, 1,381; sugarcane, 1,326; potatoes, 1,090; melons and watermelons, 874; oranges, 870; tomatoes, 764; tangerines and mandarins, 514; barley, 467; olives, 400.

Livestock, 2000: cattle, 2·67m.; sheep, 17·30m.; goats, 5·12m.; asses, 980,000; chickens, 100m. Livestock products in 2000 included (in 1,000 tonnes): milk, 1,212; meat, 540.

Forestry. Forests covered 3·03m. ha in 2000, or 6·8% of the total land area. Produce includes firewood, building and industrial timber and some cork and charcoal. Timber production was 971,000 cu. metres in 2001.

Fisheries. Total catch in 2001 was 1,083,276 tonnes (sea fish, 1,082,293 tonnes). Morocco's annual catch is the highest of any African country. Total catch value in 1994 was DH3,195m.

INDUSTRY

According to the Financial Times Survey (FT 500), the largest companies in Morocco by market capitalization on 4 Jan. 2001 were: ONA (Omnium Nord Africain), a food and beverages conglomerate, at US$1,805·4m.; and BCM (Banque Commerciale du Maroc), at US$1,100·4m.

In 2001 industry accounted for 31·4% of GDP, with manufacturing contributing 17·3%. Production (in 1,000 tonnes): cement (2001), 8,058; residual fuel oil (2000), 2,365; distillate fuel oil (2000), 2,322; sugar (2000), 556; petrol (2000), 383; paper and paperboard (2002), 129; olive oil (2001), 41.

Labour. Of 9,487,600 persons in employment in 2002, 4,209,300 were engaged in agriculture, hunting, fishing and forestry; 1,371,300 in wholesale and retail trade/repair of motor vehicles, motorcycles and personal and household goods; 1,171,300 in manufacturing; and 871,100 in education, health and social work, and other community, social and personal service activities. The unemployment rate in 2002 was 11·6%. In July 2004 the minimum hourly wage was DH9·66.

Trade Unions. In 1996 there were six trade unions: UMT (Union Marocaine de Travail), CDT (Confédération Démocratique du Travail), UGTM (Union Générale des Travailleurs Marocaine), UNTM (National Union of Moroccan Workers), USP (Union of Popular Workers) and the SNP (National Popular Union).

INTERNATIONAL TRADE

In 1989 Morocco signed a treaty of economic co-operation with the four other Maghreb countries: Algeria, Libya, Mauritania and Tunisia. In 1995 Morocco signed an association agreement with the EU to create a free trade zone in 12 years. Foreign debt was US$18,601m. in 2002.

Imports and Exports. Imports and exports for calendar years in US$1m.:

	1998	*1999*	*2000*	*2001*	*2002*
Imports f.o.b.	9,463	9,957	10,654	10,164	10,900
Exports f.o.b.	7,144	7,509	7,419	7,142	7,839

Imports in 2002 included: machinery and apparatus, 19·3%; mineral fuels, 15·6%; food, beverages and tobacco, 11·8%; cotton fabric and fibres, 6·4%. Exports included: garments, 21·4%; food, beverages and tobacco, 20·5%; knitwear, 10·4%; phosphoric acid, 6·8%.

Main import suppliers in 2001: France, 24·1%; Spain, 10·3%; UK, 6·2%; Italy, 5·0%. Leading export markets in 2001: France, 32·8%; Spain, 15·3%; UK, 8·6%; Italy, 5·7%.

COMMUNICATIONS

Roads. In 2002 there were 57,694 km of classified roads, including 467 km of motorways and 11,288 km of main roads. A motorway links Rabat to Casablanca. In 2000 freight transport totalled 2,952m. tonne-km. In 2000 there were 1,230,068 passenger cars, 315,550 trucks and vans, 15,019 buses and coaches and 20,397 motorcycles and mopeds. There were 48,371 road accidents in 2000 (3,627 fatalities).

Rail. In 2000 there were 1,907 km of railways, of which 1,003 km were electrified. Passenger-km travelled in 2000 came to 1·96bn. and freight tonne-km to 4·58bn. In 2003 the construction of two 40 km-long rail tunnels under the Straits of Gibraltar was agreed with Spain with an estimated cost of US$30m.

Civil Aviation. The national carrier is Royal Air Maroc. The major international airport is Mohammed V at Casablanca; there are eight other airports. Casablanca handled 3,547,130 passengers in 2000 (2,623,244 on international flights) and 43,487 tonnes of freight. Marrakesh (Menara) handled 1,411,725 passengers and 2,353 tonnes of freight and Agadir (Al Massira) handled 1,126,938 passengers and 1,787 tonnes of freight in 2000. In July 1997 Morocco launched its first private air company, Regional Air Lines, to serve the major regions of the kingdom, in addition to southern Spain and the Canary Islands. In 1999 scheduled airline traffic of Moroccan-based carriers flew 63·1m. km, carrying 3,392,000 passengers (2,587,000 on international flights).

Shipping. There are 12 ports, the largest being Casablanca, Tangiers and Jorf Lasfar. 1·56m. passengers and 40·6m. tonnes of freight were handled in 1994. In 2002 sea-going shipping totalled 502,000 GRT, including oil tankers 4,000 GRT.

Telecommunications. In 2002 there were 7,326,100 telephone subscribers (equivalent to 247·1 per 1,000 population) and 457,000 PCs were in use (15·4 per 1,000 persons). In 1997 there were 18,000 fax machines. French media group Vivendi Universal bought a 35% stake in the state-run operator Maroc Telecom in 2000, and in Jan. 2005 increased its holding to 51%. In 2002 there were 6,198,700 mobile phone subscribers, up from just 74,500 in 1997. Morocco had 700,000 Internet users in 2002.

Postal Services. In 1998 there were 1,469 main post offices.

SOCIAL INSTITUTIONS

Justice. The legal system is based on French and Islamic law codes. There are a Supreme Court, 21 courts of appeal, 65 courts of first instance, 196 centres with resident judges and 706 communal jurisdictions for petty offences.

The population in penal institutions in Dec. 2002 was 54,207 (176 per 100,000 of national population). On ascending to the throne in July 1999, King Mohammed VI pardoned and ordered the release of 7,988 prisoners and reduced the terms of 38,224 others.

Religion. Islam is the established state religion. 98% of the population are Sunni Muslims of the Malekite school and 0·2% are Christians, mainly Roman Catholic, and there is a small Jewish community.

Education. The adult literacy rate in 2001 was 49·8% (62·6% among males and 37·2% among females). Education in Berber languages has been permitted since 1994; Berber languages were officially added to the syllabus in 2003. Education is compulsory from the age of seven to 13. In 1993–94 there were 28,335 Koranic schools (33,721 in 1990) with 30,367 teachers and 611,729 pupils. In 2000–01 pre-primary schools had 41,513 teachers for 742,287 pupils and there were 136,558 teachers at primary schools for 3,842,000 pupils. In 1999–2000 there were 90,799 teachers in secondary schools for 1,541,000 pupils. In 1996–97 there were 13 universities with 7,566 teachers and 218,516 students (89,223 women), 8,390 students (1,761 women) in teacher training and (1992–93) 8,967 students and 1,145 teachers in other higher education institutions. An English-language university was opened at Ifrane in Jan. 1995, initially with a staff of 35 and 300 students (scheduled to rise to 3,500).

In 2000–01 total expenditure on education came to 5·6% of GNP.

Health. In 1997 there were 12,534 physicians, 1,090 dentists, 28,610 nurses and 2,997 pharmacists. In 1993 in the public sector there were 98 hospitals with 24,725 beds, 103 health centres with 1,548 beds and 1,220 dispensaries.

CULTURE

World Heritage Sites. Morocco has eight sites on the UNESCO World Heritage List: the Medina of Fès (inscribed on the list in 1981); the Medina of Marrakesh (1985); the Ksar of Ait-Ben-Haddou (1987); the Historic City of Meknès (1996); the Archaeological Site of Volubilis (1997); the Medina of Tétouan (1997); the Medina of Essaouira/Magador (2001); and the Portuguese City of Mazagan, now part of the city of El Jadida (2004).

Broadcasting. The government-controlled Radiodiffusion Télévision Marocaine broadcasts three national (one in French, English and Spanish) and eight regional radio programmes and one TV channel (colour by SECAM V). Broadcasting in Berber languages commenced in 1994. There is also a government commercial radio service and an independent TV channel. There were 4·86m. TV sets in 2001 and 6·92m. radio sets in 2000.

Cinema. There were 175 cinemas in 1997 and a total attendance of 14·3m. Six full-length films were made in 2000.

Press. In 2000 there were 23 daily newspapers, with a combined circulation of 846,000 (equivalent to 28 per 1,000 inhabitants). In 2000 a number of foreign and local newspapers were banned. Some had been accused of trying to destabilize the country's institutions, including the military. In 1997, 1,339 book titles were published.

Tourism. There were 4,113,000 foreign tourists in 2000, bringing revenue of US$2·04bn. The tourism sector employs some 600,000 people, equivalent to 5·8% of the workforce.

DIPLOMATIC REPRESENTATIVES

Of Morocco in the United Kingdom (49 Queen's Gate Gdns, London, SW7 5NE)
Ambassador: Mohammed Belmahi.

Of the United Kingdom in Morocco (17 Blvd de la Tour Hassan, Rabat)
Ambassador: Haydon Warren-Gash.

Of Morocco in the USA (1601 21st St., NW, Washington, D.C., 20009)
Ambassador: Aziz Mekouar.

Of the USA in Morocco (2 Ave. de Mohamed el Fassi, Rabat)
Ambassador: Thomas T. Riley.

Of Morocco to the United Nations
Ambassador: Mohamed Bennouna.

Of Morocco to the European Union
Ambassador: Fath'allah Sijilmassi.

FURTHER READING

Direction de la Statistique. *Annuaire Statistique du Maroc.—Conjoncture Économique.* Quarterly *Bulletin Official*. Rabat.

Bourqia, Rahma and Gilson Miller, Susan (eds.) *In the Shadow of the Sultan: Culture, Power and Politics in Morocco.* Harvard Univ. Press, 2000

Findlay, Anne M. and Allan M., *Morocco.* [Bibliography] 2nd ed. ABC-Clio, Oxford and Santa Barbara (CA), 1995

Pazzanita, A. G., *The Maghreb.* [Bibliography] ABC-Clio, Oxford and Santa Barbara (CA), 1998

Pennell, C. R., *Morocco: From Empire to Independence.* Oneworld Publications, Oxford, 2003

National library: Bibliothèque Générale et Archives, Rabat.

National statistical office: Direction de la Statistique, Haute Commissariat au Plan, BP 178, Rabat.
Website (French only): http://www.statistic-hcp.ma

WESTERN SAHARA

The Western Sahara was designated by The United Nations in 1975, its borders having been marked as a result of agreements made between France, Spain and Morocco in 1900, 1904 and 1912. Sovereignty of the territory is in dispute between Morocco and the Polisario Front (Popular Front for the Liberation of the Saguia el Hamra and Rio de Oro), which formally proclaimed a government-in-exile of the Sahrawi Arab Democratic Republic (SADR) in Feb. 1976. According to a new UN Security Council resolution adopted in July 2003, Western Sahara should be a semi-autonomous region of Morocco for five years. There is then to be a referendum to decide whether it remains part of Morocco or becomes a separate state.

Area 252,120 sq. km (97,346 sq. miles). Around 356,000 inhabitants (2004 estimate) are within Moroccan jurisdiction. Another estimated 196,000 Saharawis live in refugee camps around Tindouf in southwest Algeria. The main towns are El-Aaiún (Laâyoune), the capital (184,000 inhabitants in 2004), Dakhla and Es-Semara.

Life expectancy at birth (1997 est.) male, 46·7 years; female, 50·0 years. Birth rate (1997 est.) per 1,000 population: 46·1; death rate: 17·5. The UN gives a projected population for 2010 of 363,000.

The population is Arabic-speaking, and almost entirely Sunni Muslim.

President: Mohammed Abdelaziz.
Prime Minister: Abdelkader Taleb Oumar.

Rich phosphate deposits were discovered in 1963 at Bu Craa. Morocco holds 65% of the shares of the former Spanish state-controlled company. Production reached 5·6m. tonnes in 1975, but exploitation has been severely reduced by guerrilla activity. After a nearly complete collapse, production and transportation of phosphate resumed in 1978, ceased again, and then resumed in 1982. Installed electrical capacity was 58,000 kW in 2000, with production in 2000 of approximately 88m. kWh. There are about 6,100 km of motorable tracks, but only about 500 km of paved roads. There are airports at El-Aaiún and Dakhla. As most of the land is desert, less than 19% is in agricultural use, with about 2,000 tonnes of grain produced annually. There were 56,000 radio receivers and 6,000 television sets in 1997. In 1989 there were 27 primary schools with 14,794 pupils and 18 secondary schools with 9,218 pupils. In 1994 there were 100 physicians, equivalent to one per 2,504 inhabitants.

FURTHER READING

Sheley, Toby, *Endgame in the Western Sahara: What Future for Africa's Last Colony?* Zed Books, London, 2004

Zoubir, Y. H. and Volman, D. (eds.) *The International Dimensions of the Western Sahara Conflict.* New York, 1993

MOZAMBIQUE

República de Moçambique

Capital: Maputo
Population projection, 2010: 21·01m.
GDP per capita, 2002: (PPP$) 1,050
HDI/world rank: 0·354/171

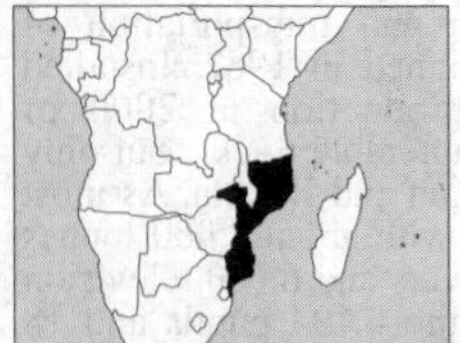

KEY HISTORICAL EVENTS

Mozambique was at first ruled as part of Portuguese India but a separate administration was created in 1752. Following a decade of guerrilla activity, independence was achieved on 25 June 1975. A one-party state dominated by the Liberation Front of Mozambique (FRELIMO) was set up but armed insurgency led by the Mozambique National Resistance (RENAMO) continued until 4 Oct. 1992. The peace treaty provided for all weapons to be handed over to the UN and all armed groups to be disbanded within six months. In 1994 the country held its first multi-party elections. In early 2000 some 700 people died in the floods which made thousands homeless.

TERRITORY AND POPULATION

Mozambique is bounded east by the Indian ocean, south by South Africa, southwest by Swaziland, west by South Africa and Zimbabwe and north by Zambia, Malaŵi and Tanzania. It has an area of 799,380 sq. km (308,642 sq. miles) and a population, according to the 1997 census, of 16,099,246 (7,714,306 males), giving a density of 20 per sq. km. Up to 1·5m. refugees abroad and 5m. internally displaced persons during the Civil War have begun to return home. Official population estimate, 2002: 18,082,523.

The UN gives a projected population for 2010 of 21·01m.

In 2001, 66·8% of the population were rural, but urbanization is increasing rapidly. In the period 1990–95 the annual growth in the urban population was 8·7%, a rate only exceeded by Botswana. The areas, populations and capitals of the provinces are:

Province	*Sq. km*	*Estimate 2002*	*Capital*
Cabo Delgado	82,625	1,525,634	Pemba
Gaza	75,709	1,266,431	Xai-Xai
Inhambane	68,615	1,326,848	Inhambane
Manica	61,661	1,207,332	Chimoio
City of Maputo	602	1,044,618	
Province of Maputo	25,756	1,003,992	Maputo
Nampula	81,606	3,410,141	Nampula
Niassa	129,056	916,672	Lichinga
Sofala	68,018	1,516,166	Beira
Tete	100,724	1,388,205	Tete
Zambézia	105,008	3,476,484	Quelimane

The capital is Maputo (1997 population, 989,386). Other large cities (with 1997 populations) are Matola (440,927), Beira (412,588) and Nampula (314,965).

The main ethnolinguistic groups are the Makua/Lomwe (52% of the population), the Tsonga/Ronga (24%), the Nyanja/Sena (12%) and Shona (6%).

Portuguese remains the official language, but vernaculars are widely spoken throughout the country. English is also widely spoken.

SOCIAL STATISTICS

2001 estimates: births, 753,000; deaths, 331,000. Estimated rates per 1,000 population, 2001: births, 41·7; deaths, 18·3. Infant mortality per 1,000 live births, 2001, 125. Life expectancy at birth, 2001, was 37·4 years for males and 40·9 years for females. Annual population growth rate, 1992–02, 2·6%; fertility rate, 2001, 6·0 births per woman.

CLIMATE

A humid tropical climate, with a dry season from June to Sept. In general, temperatures and rainfall decrease from north to south. Maputo, Jan. 78°F (25·6°C),

July 65°F (18·3°C). Annual rainfall 30" (760 mm). Beira, Jan. 82°F (27·8°C), July 69°F (20·6°C). Annual rainfall 60" (1,522 mm).

CONSTITUTION AND GOVERNMENT

On 2 Nov. 1990 the People's Assembly unanimously voted a new Constitution, which came into force on 30 Nov. This changed the name of the state to 'Republic of Mozambique', legalized opposition parties, provided for universal secret elections and introduced a bill of rights including the right to strike, press freedoms and habeas corpus. The head of state is the *President*, directly elected for a five-year term. Parliament is a 250-member *National Assembly*.

National Anthem. 'Patria Amada' ('Beloved Motherland'); words and tune by J. Sigaulane Chemane.

RECENT ELECTIONS

In the parliamentary elections of 1–2 Dec. 2004 the Liberation Front of Mozambique (FRELIMO) won 160 of the 250 available seats with 62·0% of the vote. The Mozambican National Resistance (RENAMO) won the remaining 90 seats with 29·7%. Turn-out was 36·4%.

In the presidential election, also held on 1–2 Dec. 2004, FRELIMO's Armando Guebuza took 63·7% of the vote against RENAMO's Afonso Marceta Macacho Dhlakama.

CURRENT ADMINISTRATION

President: Armando Guebuza; b. 1943 (FRELIMO; sworn in 2 Feb. 2005).

In March 2005 the government comprised:

Prime Minister: Luísa Dias Diogo; b. 1958 (took office on 17 Feb. 2004).

Minister of Agriculture: Tomás Mandlate. *Defence:* Tobias Dai. *Development and Planning:* Aiuba Cuereneia. *Education:* Aires Bonifácio Ali. *Energy:* Salvador Namburete. *Environmental Action Co-ordinator:* Luciano de Castro. *Finance:* Manuel Chang. *Fisheries:* Cadmiel Muthemba. *Foreign Affairs and Co-operation:* Alcinda Abreu. *Health:* Paulo Ivo Garrido. *Industry and Commerce:* António Fernando. *Interior:* José Pacheco. *Justice:* Esperança Alfredo Machavela. *Labour:* Helena Taipo. *Mineral Resources and Energy:* Esperança Bias. *Public Works and Housing:* Felício Zacarias. *Science and Technology:* Venâncio Massingue. *State Administration:* Lucas Chomera. *Tourism:* Fernando Sumbana. *Transport and Communications:* António Munguambe. *Veterans Affairs:* Feliciano Salomão Gundana. *Women's and Social Affairs:* Virgília Matabele. *Youth and Sport:* David Simango. *Minister of Diplomatic Affairs (President's Office):* Francisco Madeira. *Minister of Parliamentary Affairs (President's Office):* Isabel Manuel Nkavadeka.

Government Website: http://www.mozambique.mz

DEFENCE

The President of the Republic is C.-in-C. of the armed forces. Defence expenditure totalled US$93m. in 2003 (US$5 per capita), representing 2·2% of GDP.

Army. Personnel numbered 9–10,000 in 2002.

Navy. Naval personnel in 2002 were believed to total 150.

Air Force. Personnel (2002) 1,000 (including air defence units). There were four armed helicopters but no combat aircraft.

INTERNATIONAL RELATIONS

Mozambique is a member of the UN, WTO, the Commonwealth, the African Union, African Development Bank, SADC, Non-Aligned Movement, Organization of the Islamic Conference, Islamic Development Bank, Indian Ocean Rim, Organization of the Portuguese Language Countries and is an ACP member state of the ACP-EU relationship.

IMF projections to 2005 indicated the halving of aid inflows from US$1bn. a year in the 1990s to US$500m. Mozambique is very heavily dependent on foreign aid. In 1996 official aid made up 72% of GDP.

ECONOMY

Agriculture accounted for 26·6% of GDP in 2002, industry 28·9% and services 44·5%.

Overview. A privatization programme launched in 1989 resulted in the partial or total privatization of over 1,200 enterprises by 2002. Heavy flooding in 2000 devastated the economy and infrastructure.

Currency. The unit of currency is the *metical* (MZM) of 100 *centavos*. Inflation was 9·0% in 2001, rising to 16·8% in 2002. Foreign exchange reserves were US$706m. in June 2002. Total money supply in May 2002 was 10,364·30bn. meticais.

Budget. In 2001 revenues were 19,253m. meticais and expenditures 23,221m. meticais.

Performance. GDP growth has averaged 8·2% since 1995, making Mozambique one of Africa's fastest expanding economies. Mozambique was forecast to be among the fastest growing economies in the world in 2000 but the disastrous floods of early 2000 caused a major setback, resulting in growth for the year of only 1·6%. However, the economy then grew by 13·9% in 2001, one of the highest rates in the world, and 8·3% in 2002. Total GDP in 2003 was US$4·3bn.

Banking and Finance. Most banks had been nationalized by 1979. The central bank and bank of issue is the Bank of Mozambique (*Governor,* Adriano Afonso Maleiane) which hived off its commercial functions in 1992 to the newly-founded Commercial Bank of Mozambique. In 1998 the Commercial Bank of Mozambique had 35% of deposits. In 2002 there were ten commercial banks, three foreign banks and a credit fund for agricultural and rural development. The new Mozambique Stock Exchange opened in Maputo in Oct. 1999. By the late 1990s financial services had become one of the fastest-growing areas of the economy.

ENERGY AND NATURAL RESOURCES

Environment. Carbon dioxide emissions from the consumption and flaring of fossil fuels in 2002 were the equivalent of 0·1 tonnes per capita.

Electricity. Installed capacity was 2·1m. kW in 2000. Production in 2000 was 6·97m. kWh; consumption per capita was 88 kWh.

Oil and Gas. Natural gas finds are being explored for potential exploitation, and both onshore and offshore foreign companies are prospecting for oil. In 2002 natural gas reserves were 57bn. cu. metres. Some river basins, especially the Rovuma, Zambezi and Limpopo, are of interest to oil prospectors.

Water. Although the country is rich in water resources, the provision of drinking water to rural areas remains a major concern.

Minerals. There are deposits of pegamite, tantalite, graphite, apatite, tin, iron ore and bauxite. Other known reserves are: nepheline, syenite, magnetite, copper, garnet, kaolin, asbestos, bentonite, limestone, gold, titanium and tin.

Output (in 1,000 tonnes): aluminium (2001), 266; salt (1997 estimate), 60; coal (2000), 19; bauxite (2001), 7.

Agriculture. All land is owned by the state but concessions are given. There were 4·0m. ha of arable land in 2001 and 0·24m. ha of permanent crops. 107,000 ha were irrigated in 2001. There were 5,750 tractors in 2001. Production in 1,000 tonnes (2000): cassava, 4,643; maize, 1,019; sugarcane, 440; coconuts, 300; sorghum, 252; rice, 158; groundnuts, 100; seed cotton, 80; copra, 73; bananas, 59; cottonseed, 51; potatoes, 50.

Livestock, 2000: 1·32m. cattle, 392,000 goats, 125,000 sheep, 180,000 pigs, 28m. chickens.

A quarter of all crops and a third of cattle were lost during the flooding which devastated the country in the early part of 2000.

Forestry. In 2000 there were 30·60m. ha of forests, or 39·0% of the land area, including eucalyptus, pine and rare hardwoods. In 2001 timber production was 18·04m. cu. metres.

Fisheries. The catch in 2001 was 32,512 tonnes, of which 24,436 tonnes were from sea fishing. Prawns and shrimps are the major export at 10,000 tonnes per year. The potential sustainable annual catch is estimated at 500,000 tonnes of fish (anchovies 300,000 tonnes, the rest mainly mackerel).

INDUSTRY

Although the country is overwhelmingly rural, there is some substantial industry in and around Maputo (steel, engineering, textiles, processing, docks and railways). A huge aluminium smelter, completed in 2000, is scheduled to produce 250,000 tonnes annually and is a focal point in the country's strategy of attracting foreign investment.

Labour. The labour force in 1996 totalled 9,221,000 (52% males). In 1998, 83% of the economically active population were engaged in agriculture, 8% in industry and 9% in services. Women represent 48% of the total labour force.

Trade Unions. The main trade union confederation is the Organização dos Trabalhadores de Moçambique, but several unions have broken away.

INTERNATIONAL TRADE

Foreign debt was US$4,609m. in 2002.

Imports and Exports. Imports (c.i.f.) totalled US$997·3m. in 2001 (US$1,046·0m. in 2000). Exports (f.o.b.) totalled US$726·0m. in 2001 (US$364·0m. in 2000). Principal imports in 1999 (in US$1m.): machinery and transport equipment, 287·6; foodstuffs, 113·5 (including 76·1 of cereals); manufactured goods, 79·4; chemicals, 73·9; mineral fuels, 73·9. Principal exports in 1999: prawns, 74·8; mineral fuels, 67·8; cashew nuts, 40·2; cotton, 20·0.

Main import suppliers in 1998: Southern African Customs Union, 42·2%; Portugal, 7·9%; USA, 5·3%. Main export markets in 1999: Southern African Customs Union, 28·1%; Zimbabwe, 14·8%; Spain, 12·7%; India, 11·8%; Portugal, 9·0%.

COMMUNICATIONS

Roads. In 1999 there were estimated to be 30,400 km of roads, of which 18·7% were paved. Passenger cars numbered 4,900 in 1996 (0·3 per 1,000 inhabitants), down from 60,000 in 1993. There were 4,748 road accidents in 1997, with 805 fatalities.

The flooding of early 2000 washed away at least one fifth of the country's main road linking the north and the south.

Rail. The state railway consists of five separate networks, with principal routes on 1,067 mm gauge radiating from the ports of Maputo (950 km), Beira (994 km) and Nacala (914 km). Total length in 1995 was 2,983 km of 1,067 mm gauge and 140 km of 762 mm gauge. In 2000, 1·8m. passengers and 2·2m. tonnes of freight were carried.

In early 2000 long sections of the railway line linking Mozambique with Zimbabwe were washed away in the floods.

Civil Aviation. There are international airports at Maputo and Beira. The national carrier is the state-owned Linhas Aéreas de Moçambique (LAM). It provides domestic services and in 2003 operated international routes to Comoros, Dar es Salaam, Durban, Harare, Johannesburg and Lisbon. In 1998 Maputo handled 310,000 passengers (188,000 on international flights) and Beira 63,000 (59,000 on domestic flights). In 1999 scheduled airline traffic of Mozambique-based carriers flew 5·3m. km, carrying 235,000 passengers (87,000 on international flights).

Shipping. The principal ports are Maputo, Beira, Nacala and Quelimane. In 2002 the merchant fleet had a total displacement of 37,000 GRT.

Telecommunications. Telephone subscribers numbered 338,500 in 2002 (18·6 per 1,000 persons) and there were 82,000 PCs in use (4·5 per 1,000 persons). There were 254,800 mobile phone subscribers in 2002 and 7,200 fax machines in 1995. In 2001 there were 30,000 Internet users.

Postal Services. In 1998 there were 353 post offices. Postal services in Mozambique are provided by a public company, Correios de Moçambique, EP (CDM).

SOCIAL INSTITUTIONS

Justice. The 1990 Constitution provides for an independent judiciary, *habeas corpus*, and an entitlement to legal advice on arrest. The death penalty was abolished in Nov. 1990. The judiciary is riddled with bribery and extortion.

The population in penal institutions in Dec. 1999 was 8,812 (50 per 100,000 of national population).

Religion. About 55% of the population follow traditional animist religions. In 2001 there were 6·18m. Christians (mainly Roman Catholic) and 2·04m. Muslims. In Sept. 2003 there was one cardinal.

Education. The adult literacy rate in 2001 was 45·2% (61·2% among males but only 30·0% among females).

In 2003 there were 3,177,586 pupils with 51,912 teachers in 9,027 primary schools; and 160,093 pupils with 4,112 teachers at 154 secondary schools. Private schools and universities were permitted to function in 1990. Eduardo Mondlane University had 3,470 students and 390 academic staff in 1995–96. In the late 1990s a further four institutions of higher education opened: the Higher Institute of International Relations (ISRI), the Pedagogical University (UP), the University and Polytechnic Higher Institute (ISPU) and the Catholic University (UC).

In 1999–2000 total expenditure on education came to 2·5% of GNP and 12·3% of total government spending.

Health. There were (1997) 10 hospitals, 418 health centres and 996 medical posts. There were two psychiatric hospitals. In 1990 there were 387 doctors (equivalent to one for every 36,320 persons), 1,139 midwives, 3,533 nursing personnel, 108 dentists and 353 pharmacists. Private health care was introduced alongside the national health service in 1992.

CULTURE

World Heritage Sites. Mozambique has one site on the UNESCO World Heritage List: the Island of Mozambique (inscribed on the list in 1991), a Portuguese trading post with a style of architecture unchanged since the 16th century.

Broadcasting. Radio Moçambique is part state-owned and part commercial. There are three national programmes in Tsonga and Portuguese and an external service in English. Television is at a trial stage (colour by PAL). There were 230,000 TV receivers in 2001 and 778,000 radio sets in 2000.

TVM is the national television station; RTK (Klint Radio and Television) is privately owned.

Cinema. There is a National Institute of Cinema (INC), set up in 1975 just after Mozambique became independent.

Press. There are two well-established daily newspapers (*Noticias* and *Diário* in Maputo and Beira respectively). Five additional newspapers were registered in 1998: *Savana*, *Mediacoop*, *Demos*, *Metical* and *Domingo*.

Tourism. Tourism is a potential growth area for the country. There are 2,500 km of Indian Ocean beaches, coral reefs, diving, deep-sea fishing, wildlife, game parks, highlands and plains.

Festivals. There are annual culture festivals throughout the country.

Libraries. As well as libraries at the higher education institutes, there is an independent public library in Maputo.

Theatre and Opera. In addition to state-owned theatres and opera houses, Avenida and Matchedge are privately owned.

DIPLOMATIC REPRESENTATIVES

Of Mozambique in the United Kingdom (21 Fitzroy Sq., London, W1T 6EL)
High Commissioner: Antonio Gumende.

Of the United Kingdom in Mozambique (Ave. Vladimir I. Lenine 310, Maputo)
High Commissioner: Howard Parkinson, CVO.

Of Mozambique in the USA (1990 M. St., NW, Washington, D.C., 20036)
Ambassador: Armando Alexandre Panguene.

Of the USA in Mozambique (Ave Kenneth Kaunda 193, Maputo)
Ambassador: Helen R. Meagher La Lime.

Of Mozambique to the United Nations
Ambassador: Filipe Chidumo.

Of Mozambique to the European Union
Ambassador: Maria Manuela dos Santos Lucas.

FURTHER READING

Andersson, H., *Mozambique: a War against the People.* London, 1993
Finnegan, W., *A Complicated War: the Harrowing of Mozambique.* California Univ. Press, 1992
Newitt, M., *A History of Mozambique.* Farnborough, 1996

National statistical office: Instituto Nacional de Estatística, Av. Ahmed Sekou Touré, No. 21
Website (Portuguese only): http://www.ine.gov.mz/

MYANMAR

Myanmar Naingngandaw (Union of Myanmar)

Capital: Yangon (Rangoon)
Population projection, 2010: 53·39m.
GDP per capita, 1996: (PPP$) 1,027
HDI/world rank: 0·551/132

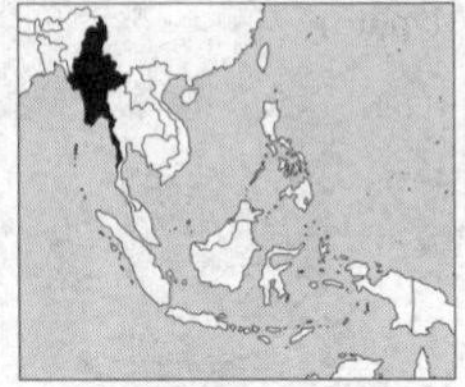

KEY HISTORICAL EVENTS

After Burma's invasion of the kingdom of Assam, the British East India Company retaliated in defence of its Indian interests and in 1826 drove the Burmese out of India. Territory was annexed in south Burma but the kingdom of Upper Burma, ruled from Mandalay, remained independent. A second war with Britain in 1852 ended with the British annexation of the Irrawaddy Delta. In 1885 the British invaded and occupied Upper Burma. In 1886 all Burma became a province of the Indian empire. There were violent uprisings in the 1930s and in 1937 Burma was separated from India and permitted some degree of self-government. Independence was achieved in 1948. In 1958 there was an army coup, and another in 1962 led by Gen. Ne Win, who installed a Revolutionary Council and dissolved parliament.

The Council lasted until March 1974 when the country became a one-party socialist republic. On 18 Sept. 1988 the Armed Forces seized power and set up the State Law and Order Restoration Council (SLORC). Since then civil unrest has cost more than 10,000 lives. On 19 June 1989 the government changed the name of the country in English to the Union of Myanmar. Aung San Suu Kyi, leader of the National League for Democracy, was put under house arrest in July 1989. In spite of her continuing detention, her party won the 1990 election by a landslide, but the military junta refused to accept the results. She was eventually freed in July 1995, only to be placed under house arrest for a second time in Sept. 2000 and again released in May 2002.

TERRITORY AND POPULATION

Myanmar is bounded in the east by China, Laos and Thailand, and west by the Indian Ocean, Bangladesh and India. Three parallel mountain ranges run from north to south; the Western Yama or Rakhine Yama, the Bagu Yama and the Shaun Plateau. The total area of the Union is 261,228 sq. miles (676,577 sq. km). The population in 1983 (census) was 35,313,905. Estimate (2000) 49·01m. (24·66m. female); density, 72 per sq. km. In 2001, 71·8% of the population lived in rural areas.

The UN gives a projected population for 2010 of 53·39m.

The leading towns are: Yangon (Rangoon), the capital (1999 population of 4,101,000); other towns (1983 estimates), Mandalay, 532,985; Moulmein, 219,991; Pegu, 150,447; Bassein, 144,092; Sittwe (Akyab), 107,907; Taunggye, 107,607; Monywa, 106,873.

The population of the seven states and seven administrative divisions (2000 estimates): Irrawaddy Division, 6,779,000; Magwe Division, 4,548,000; Mandalay Division, 6,574,000; Pegu Division, 5,099,000; Sagaing Division, 5,488,000; Tenasserim Division, 1,356,000; Yangon Division, 5,560,000; Chin State, 480,000; Kachin State, 1,272,000; Kayah State, 266,000; Karen State, 1,489,000; Mon State, 2,502,000; Rakhine State, 2,744,000; Shan State, 4,851,000. Myanmar is inhabited by many ethnic nationalities. There are as many as 135 national groups with the Bamars, comprising about 68·96% of the population, forming the largest group.

The official language is Burmese; English is also in use.

SOCIAL STATISTICS

1995 births, 1,263,000; deaths, 465,000. Birth rate (1995), 28·0 per 1,000 population; death rate, 10·3. Annual population growth rate, 1992–02, 1·5%. Life expectancy at birth, 2001, was 54·4 years for males and 59·8 years for females. Infant mortality, 2001, 77 per 1,000 live births; fertility rate, 2001, 3·0 births per woman.

CLIMATE

The climate is equatorial in coastal areas, changing to tropical monsoon over most of the interior, but humid temperate in the extreme north, where there is a more significant range of temperature and a dry season lasting from Nov. to April. In coastal parts, the dry season is shorter. Very heavy rains occur in the monsoon months May to Sept. Rangoon, Jan. 77°F (25°C), July 80°F (26·7°C). Annual rainfall 104" (2,616 mm). Akyab, Jan. 70°F (21·1°C), July 81°F (27·2°C). Annual rainfall 206" (5,154 mm). Mandalay, Jan. 68°F (20°C), July 85°F (29·4°C). Annual rainfall 33" (828 mm).

CONSTITUTION AND GOVERNMENT

Following elections in May 1990, the ruling State Law and Order Restoration Council (SLORC) said it would hand over power after the People's Assembly had agreed on a new constitution, but in July 1990 it stipulated that any such constitution must conform to guidelines which it would itself prescribe.

In May 1991, 48 members of the National League for Democracy (NLD) were given prison sentences on charges of treason. In July 1991 opposition members of the People's Assembly were unseated for alleged offences ranging from treason to illicit foreign exchange dealing. Such members, and unsuccessful candidates in the May 1990 elections, are forbidden to stand in future elections.

On 28 Nov. 1995 the government re-opened a 706-member Constitutional Convention in which the NLD was given 107 places. The NLD withdrew on 29 Nov.

In Nov. 1997 the country's ruling generals changed the name of the government to the State Peace and Development Council (SPDC) and reshuffled the cabinet. In Dec. 1997, following a period when the national currency fell to a record low, there were further changes to the cabinet, while corruption investigations were begun against some former ministers.

National Anthem. 'Gba majay Bma' ('We shall love Burma for ever'); words and tune by Saya Tin.

RECENT ELECTIONS

In elections in May 1990 the opposition National League for Democracy (NLD), led by Aung San Suu Kyi (b. 1945), won 392 of the 485 People's Assembly seats contested with some 60% of the valid vote. Turn-out was 72%, but 12·4% of ballots cast were declared invalid. The military ignored the result and refused to hand over power.

CURRENT ADMINISTRATION

In March 2005 the government comprised:

Chairman of the State Peace and Development Council (SPCD) and Minister of Defence: Senior Gen. Than Shwe; b. 1933 (in office since 23 April 1992).

Prime Minister: Lieut.-Gen. Soe Win; b. 1948 (appointed 19 Oct. 2004).

Secretary-1 of the SPDC: Lieut.-Gen. Thein Sein. *Secretary-2 of the SPDC:* Vacant.

Minister of Agriculture and Irrigation: Maj.-Gen. Htay Oo. *Industry (No. 1):* Aung Thaung. *Industry (No. 2):* Maj.-Gen. Saw Lwin. *Foreign Affairs:* Maj. Gen. Nyan Win. *National Planning and Economic Development:* Soe Tha. *Transport:* Maj.-Gen. Thein Swe. *Culture:* Maj.-Gen. Kyi Aung. *Co-operatives:* Col. Zaw Min. *Rail Transportation:* Maj.-Gen. Aung Min. *Energy:* Brig.-Gen. Lun Thi. *Education:* Than Aung. *Health:* Dr Khaw Myint. *Commerce:* Brig.-Gen. Tin Naing Thein. *Hotels and Tourism, and Communications, Posts and Telegraphs:* Brig.-Gen. Thein Zaw. *Finance and Revenue:* Maj. Gen. Hla Tun. *Religious Affairs:* Brig.-Gen. Thura Myint Maung. *Construction:* Maj.-Gen. Saw Tun. *Immigration and Population:* Maj.-Gen. Sein Htwa. *Labour, and Science and Technology:* U Thaung. *Information:* Brig.-Gen. Kyaw Hsan. *Progress of Border Areas, National Races and Development Affairs:* Col. Thein Nyunt. *Electric Power:* Maj.-Gen. Tin Htut. *Sports:* Brig.-Gen. Thura Aye Myint. *Forestry:* Brig.-Gen. Thein Aung. *Home Affairs:* Maj.-Gen. Maung Oo. *Mines:* Brig.-Gen. Ohn Myint. *Social Welfare, Relief and Resettlement:* Maj.-Gen. Sein Htwa. *Livestock and Fisheries:* Brig.-Gen. Maung Maung Thein. *Office of the Prime Minister:* Brig.-Gen. Pyi Sone, Tin Winn, Than Shwe.

DEFENCE

Military expenditure in 2003 totalled US$6,260m. (US$127 per capita), representing 9·6% of GDP.

Army. The strength of the Army was reported to be about 325,000 in 2002. The Army is organized into 12 regional commands. There are two paramilitary units: People's Police Force (65,000) and People's Militia (35,000).

Navy. Personnel in 2002 totalled about 10,000 including 800 naval infantry.

Air Force. The Air Force is intended primarily for internal security duties. Personnel (2002) 9,000 operating 113 combat aircraft, including F-7s, and 29 armed helicopters.

INTERNATIONAL RELATIONS

Myanmar is a member of the UN, WTO, Asian Development Bank, Colombo Plan, ASEAN and the Mekong Group.

In 2001 tension between Myanmar and neighbouring Thailand escalated amid a series of border skirmishes, in part over the cross-border trade in drugs. In May 2002 the border between the two countries was closed following a diplomatic row. It was re-opened in Oct. 2002.

ECONOMY

Agriculture accounted for 53·2% of GDP in 1998, industry 9·0% and services 37·8%.

Currency. The unit of currency is the *kyat* (MMK) of 100 *pyas*. Total money supply was K.779,984m. in Feb. 2002. Foreign exchange reserves were US$454m. in March 2002 and gold reserves 231,000 troy oz in June 2002. Inflation was 34·5% in 2001, rising to 46·9% in 2002. Since 1 June 1996 import duties have been calculated at a rate US$1 = K.100.

Budget. Budget revenue and expenditure (in K.1m.), year beginning 1 April:

	1996	*1997*	*1998*	*1999*	*2000*
Revenue	54,726	86,690	116,066	122,895	134,308
Expenditure	80,120	98,426	124,064	153,497	221,255

State budget estimates are classified into three parts, *viz.* State Administrative Organizations, State Economic Enterprises and Town and City Development Committees.

Performance. Real GDP growth was 10·5% in 2001 and 5·5% in 2002. In spite of recent impressive growth, Myanmar's per capita GDP fell from US$80 in 1968 to US$70 in 1998.

Banking and Finance. The Central Bank of Myanmar was established in 1990. Its *Governor* is Kyaw Kyaw Maung. In 2002 there were two state banks (Myanma Economic Bank and Myanma Foreign Trade Bank), two development banks (Myanma Agricultural and Rural Development Bank and Myanma Investment and Commercial Bank) and 17 private banks. Since 1996 foreign banks with representative offices (there were 31 in 1996) have been permitted to set up joint ventures with Myanmese banks. The foreign partner must provide at least 35% of the capital. The state insurance company is the Myanmar Insurance Corporation. Deposits in savings banks were K.30,963m. in 1994.

A stock exchange opened in Rangoon in 1996.

Weights and Measures. The British Imperial and metric systems are used but in the markets traditional measurements are common: one *tical* (*kyat-tha*) = 16·33 grams; one *viss* (*peit-tha*) = 100 ticals.

ENERGY AND NATURAL RESOURCES

Environment. Myanmar's carbon dioxide emissions from the consumption and flaring of fossil fuels in 2002 were the equivalent of 0·2 tonnes per capita.

Electricity. Total electricity generated, 2000, 5·08bn. kWh; consumption per capita in 2000 was 106 kWh. Installed capacity was 1·5m. kW in 2000.

Oil and Gas. Production (2000) of crude oil was 411,000 tonnes; natural gas (1999), 4·8bn. cu. metres. There were proven natural gas reserves of 346bn. cu. metres in 2002.

Minerals. Production in 2000 (in tonnes): lignite, 524,000; hard coal, 51,000; copper, 26,711. 1995–96: zinc concentrates, 6,070; refined lead, 4,250; tin, tungsten and scheelite mixed, 1,400; tin concentrates, 492; refined tin metal, 310; antimonial lead, 210; tungsten concentrates, 95; nickel speiss, 60; refined silver, 260,000 fine oz; gold (1999), 267 kg.

Agriculture. In 1995–96, 4·5m. peasant families cultivated 10·1m. ha. In 2001 there were 10·0m. ha of arable land and 635,000 ha of permanent crops.

Liberalization measures of 1990 permit farmers to grow crops of their choice. 1·99m. ha were irrigated in 2001. Production (2000, in 1,000 tonnes): rice, 20,000; sugarcane, 5,147; dry beans, 1,229; groundnuts, 640; onions, 507; plantains, 354; maize, 349; sesame seeds, 302; sunflower seeds, 270; coconuts, 263; potatoes, 245. Opium output was 1,097 tonnes in 2001, 828 tonnes in 2002 and 810 tonnes in 2003. Myanmar overtook Afghanistan as the world's largest producer of opium in 2001, but following the fall of the Taliban, opium production in Afghanistan increased to such an extent that output in 2002 and 2003 was higher in Afghanistan than in Myanmar.

Livestock (2000): cattle, 10·96m.; buffaloes, 2·44m.; pigs, 3·91m.; goats, 1·39m.; sheep, 390,000; chickens, 44m. There were 6·8m. draught cattle in 1997. In 2001 there were 10,304 tractors and 21,562 harvester-threshers.

Forestry. Forest area in 2000 was 34·42m. ha, covering 52·3% of the total land area. Teak resources cover about 6m. ha (15m. acres). In 2001, 39·37m. cu. metres of roundwood were cut.

Fisheries. In 2001 the total catch was 1,166,868 tonnes (931,492 tonnes from sea fishing). Aquacultural fish production was 79,851 tonnes in 1995–96. Cultured pearls and oyster shells are produced.

INDUSTRY

Production in 1,000 tonnes: cement (2001), 384; sawnwood (2002), 381; sugar (2000), 75; fertilizers (2001), 60; paper and paperboard (2002), 42; cigarettes (2001), 2,650m. units; clay bricks (2001), 77m. units; bicycles (1995–96), 35,042 units.

Labour. In 1998 the civilian workforce in employment numbered 18,359,000. The leading areas of activity (in 1,000) were: agriculture, hunting, forestry and fishing, 11,507; wholesale and retail trade/repair of motor vehicles, motorcycles and personal and household goods, 1,781; manufacturing, 1,666. In 2001 there were 398,300 persons aged 18 years and over registered as unemployed.

INTERNATIONAL TRADE

In Aug. 1991 the USA imposed trade sanctions in response to alleged civil rights violations. Foreign debt was US$6,556m. in 2002. A law of 1989 permitted joint ventures, with foreign companies or individuals able to hold 100% of the shares.

Imports and Exports. Since 1990 in line with market-oriented measures firms have been able to participate directly in trade.

Imports in 2001 totalled US$2,587·9m. and exports US$2,316·9m. Main imports, 1997–98: machinery and transport equipment, 28·6%; intermediate raw materials, 19·9%; basic manufactures, 15·8%; capital construction material, 12·3%; consumer durable goods, 4·3%. Leading import suppliers in 1997–98 were Singapore, 31·1%; Japan, 15·3%; Thailand, 9·8%; China, 9·4%. Main exports in 1997–98: pulses and beans, 22·3%; teak, 11·1%; fish and fish products, 4·6%; hardwood, 2·5%; rubber, 2·1%. Main export markets, 1997–98: India, 22·6%; Singapore, 13·2%; Thailand, 11·9%; China, 10·6%.

COMMUNICATIONS

Roads. There were 28,200 km of roads in 1996, of which 3,440 km were surfaced. An estimated 27,000 passenger cars were in use in 1996 (less than one per 1,000 inhabitants). In 1995–96 the state service ran 951 buses, 197 taxis and 1,969 lorries. There were also 155,107 buses and 29,694 lorries in private co-operative ownership. In 1995–96, 121·28m. passengers and 1·19m. tonnes of freight were carried by road.

Rail. In 1995 there were 3,955 km of route on metre gauge. Passenger-km travelled in 2000 came to 4,451m. and freight tonne-km to 1,122m.

Civil Aviation. Myanma Airways International operates domestic services and in 2003 had international flights to Bangkok, Kuala Lumpur and Singapore. In 1999 it flew 4·0m. km, carrying 392,200 passengers.

Shipping. There are nearly 100 km of navigable canals. The Irrawaddy is navigable up to Myitkyina, 1,450 km from the sea, and its tributary, the Chindwin, is navigable for 630 km. The Irrawaddy delta has approximately 3,000 km of navigable water. The Salween, the Attaran and the G'yne provide about 400 km of navigable waters around Moulmein. In 2002 merchant shipping totalled 402,000 GRT.

In 1995–96, 24·5m. passengers and 1·03m. tonnes of freight were carried on inland waterways. The ocean-going fleet of the state-owned Myanma Five Star Line in 1995 comprised 11 liners, 4 short-haul vessels and 3 coastal passenger/cargo vessels. In 1995–96, 60,000 passengers and 1,030,000 tonnes of freight were transported coastally and overseas. In 2000 vessels totalling 4,545,000 NRT entered ports and vessels totalling 2,252,000 NRT cleared. The port is Rangoon.

Telecommunications. Myanmar had 309,000 telephone subscribers in 2001 (6·4 per 1,000 persons) and there were 58,000 PCs in use in 2002 (1·2 for every 1,000 persons). In 2002 mobile phone subscribers numbered 48,000 and in 1999 there were 2,500 fax machines in use. There were 25,000 Internet users in 2002.

Postal Services. In 1998 there were 1,238 post offices.

SOCIAL INSTITUTIONS

Justice. The highest judicial authority is the Chief Judge, appointed by the government. At the end of 1993 there were 53,195 people held in prisons. Amnesty International reported in 2000 that there were more than 2,000 political prisoners in the country's jails.

Religion. About 89·3% of the population—mainly Bamars, Shans, Mons, Rakhines and some Kayins—are Buddhists, while the rest are Christians, Muslims, Hindus and Animists. The Christian population is composed mainly of Kayins, Kachins and Chins. Islam and Hinduism are practised mainly by people of Indian origin.

Education. Education is free in primary, middle and vocational schools; fees are charged in senior secondary schools and universities. In 2000–01 there were 4,781,543 pupils at primary schools with 148,231 teachers; and 2,317,834 pupils at secondary schools with 75,272 teachers. In 1995–96 there were 1,578 monastic primary schools (permitted since 1992) with 80,863 pupils.

In higher education in 1995–96 there were 12 teacher training schools with 315 teachers and 2,067 students, 5 teacher training institutes with 304 teachers and 2,170 students, 17 technical high schools with 498 teachers and 7,145 students, 11 technical institutes with 668 teachers and 12,080 students, 10 agricultural high schools with 100 teachers and 1,053 students, 7 agricultural institutes with 162 teachers and 1,844 students, 41 vocational schools with 369 teachers and 6,532 students, 6 universities with 3,050 teachers and 154,680 students, 6 degree colleges with 705 teachers and 53,362 students, and 10 colleges with 629 teachers and 40,327 students.

There was also a University for the Development of the National Races of the Union and institutes of medicine (3), dentistry, paramedical science, pharmacy, nursing, veterinary science, economics, technology (2), agriculture, education (2), foreign languages, computer science and forestry. An institute of remote education maintains a correspondence course at university level.

The adult literacy rate was 85·0% in 2001 (89·1% among males and 81·0% among females).

In 1999–2000 total expenditure on education came to 0·6% of GNP and 8·7% of total government spending.

Health. In 1996 there were 737 hospitals with a provision of seven beds per 10,000 inhabitants. In 1999 there were 12,313 physicians, 871 dentists, 10,820 nurses and 9,162 midwives. Public spending on health is less than 0·2% of GDP.

Welfare. In 1995–96 contributions to social security totalled (K.1m.) 117·5 (from employers, 73·2; from employees, 43·9). Benefits paid totalled 82·6, and included: sickness, 12·9; maternity, 3·9; disability, 3·7; survivors' pensions, 1·3.

CULTURE

Broadcasting. The government runs a TV and a radio station. There were 365,000 television receivers (colour by NTSC) in 2001 and 2·8m. radio sets in 2000.

Press. There were four daily newspapers in 1998, with a combined circulation of 400,000, at a rate of nine per 1,000 inhabitants.

Tourism. In 2000 there were 208,000 foreign tourists; spending by tourists totalled US$42m.

DIPLOMATIC REPRESENTATIVES

Of Myanmar in the United Kingdom (19A Charles St., London, W1J 5DX)
Ambassador: Vacant.
Chargé d'Affaires a.i.: U Than Htike.

Of the United Kingdom in Myanmar (80 Strand Rd, Rangoon)
Ambassador: Victoria Bowman.

Of Myanmar in the USA (2300 S. St., NW, Washington, D.C., 20008)
Ambassador: Linn Myaing.

Of the USA in Myanmar (581 Merchant St., Rangoon)
Ambassador: Carmen Martinez.

Of Myanmar to the United Nations
Ambassador: Kyaw Tint Swe.

Of Myanmar to the European Union
Ambassador: Wunna Maung Lwin.

FURTHER READING

Aung San Suu Kyi, *Freedom from Fear and Other Writings.* London, 1991
Carey, P. (ed.) *Burma: The Challenge of Change in a Divided Society.* London, 1997
Thant Myint-U, *The Making of Modern Burma.* CUP, 2001

National statistical office: Ministry of National Planning and Economic Development, Rangoon.

NAMIBIA

Republic of Namibia

Capital: Windhoek
Population projection, 2010: 2·12m.
GDP per capita, 2002: (PPP$) 6,210
HDI/world rank: 0·607/126

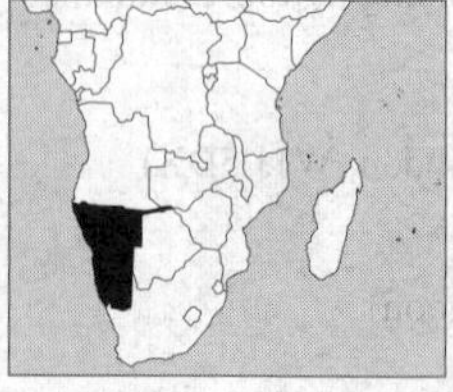

KEY HISTORICAL EVENTS

In 1884 South West Africa was declared a German protectorate. Germany then introduced racial segregation and the exploitation of the diamond mines began. In 1915 the Union of South Africa occupied German South West Africa and on 17 Dec. 1920 the League of Nations entrusted the territory as a Mandate to the Union of South Africa. After World War II South Africa applied for its annexation to the Union and continued to administer the territory in defiance of various UN resolutions. In June 1968 the UN changed the name of the territory to Namibia.

After negotiations between South Africa and the UN, a multi-racial Advisory Council was appointed in 1973 in preparation for independence, but despite several attempts at organizing free elections South Africa remained dominant in the area until the UN Transition Assistance Group supervised elections for the constituent assembly in Nov. 1989. Independence was achieved on 21 March 1990.

TERRITORY AND POPULATION

Namibia is bounded in the north by Angola and Zambia, west by the Atlantic Ocean, south and southeast by South Africa and east by Botswana. The Caprivi Strip (Caprivi Region), about 300 km long, extends eastwards up to the Zambezi river, projecting into Zambia and Botswana and touching Zimbabwe. The area, including the Caprivi Strip and Walvis Bay, is 825,112 sq. km. South Africa transferred Walvis Bay to Namibian jurisdiction on 1 March 1994. Census population, 1991, 1,409,920 (723,593 females; urban, 32·76%). 2001 census population, 1,830,330 (density 2·2 per sq. km). In 2001, 68·6% of the population were rural.

The UN gives a projected population for 2010 of 2·12m.

Population by ethnic group at the censuses of 1970 and 1981 and estimates for 1991:

	1970	*1981*	*1991*
Ovambos	342,455	506,114	665,000
Kavangos	49,577	95,055	124,000
Damaras	64,973	76,179	100,000
Hereros	55,670	76,296	100,000
Whites	90,658	76,430	85,000
Namas	32,853	48,541	64,000
Caprivians	25,009	38,594	50,000
Coloureds	28,275	42,254	. . .
Bushmen	21,909	29,443	. . .
Basters	16,474	25,181	. . .
Tswanas	4,407	6,706	. . .
Other	. . .	12,403	. . .
	732,260	1,033,196	1,401,711

Namibia is administratively divided into 13 regions. Area, population and chief towns in 2001:

Region	*Area (in sq. km)*	*Population*	*Chief town*
Caprivi (Liambezi)	19,532	79,826	Katima Mulilo
Erongo	63,719	107,663	Swakopmund
Hardap	109,888	68,249	Mariental
Karas	161,324	69,329	Keetmanshoop
Khomas	36,804	250,262	Windhoek
Kunene	144,254	68,735	Opuwo
Ohangwena	10,582	228,348	Oshikango

Region	Area (in sq. km)	Population	Chief town
Okavango	43,417	202,694	Rundu
Omaheke	84,731	68,039	Gobabis
Omusati	13,637	228,842	Outapi
Oshana	5,290	161,916	Oshakati
Oshikoto	26,607	161,007	Tsumeb
Otjozondjupa	105,327	135,384	Grootfontein

Towns with populations over 5,000 (2001): Windhoek, 233,529; Rundu, 44,413; Walvis Bay, 42,015; Ondangwa, 29,783 (estimate); Oshakati, 28,255; Swakopmund, 25,442 (estimate); Grootfontein, 21,595 (estimate); Rehoboth, 21,300; Otjiwarongo, 19,614; Okahandja, 18,155 (estimate); Keetmanshoop, 15,543; Gobabis, 13,856; Lüderitz, 13,276 (estimate); Tsumeb, 13,108; Mariental, 11,977 (estimate); Khorixas, 10,906 (estimate).

English is the official language. Afrikaans and German are also spoken.

SOCIAL STATISTICS

1996 births, estimate, 63,000; deaths, 13,000. Rates (1996 estimate) per 1,000 population: birth, 37·3; death, 8·0. Expectation of life, 2001: males, 45·5 years; females, 49·2. Annual population growth rate, 1992–02, 2·7%; infant mortality, 2001, 55 per 1,000 live births; fertility rate, 2001, 5·0 births per woman.

CLIMATE

The rainfall increases steadily from less than 50 mm in the west and southwest up to 600 mm in the Caprivi Strip. The main rainy season is from Jan. to March, with lesser showers from Sept. to Dec. Namibia is the driest African country south of the Sahara.

CONSTITUTION AND GOVERNMENT

On 9 Feb. 1990 with a unanimous vote the Constituent Assembly approved the Constitution which stipulated a multi-party republic, an independent judiciary and an executive *President* who may serve a maximum of two five-year terms. The constitution was amended in 1999 to allow President Sam Nujoma to stand for a third term in office.

The bicameral legislature consists of a 78-seat *National Assembly*, 72 members of which are elected for five-year terms by proportional representation and up to six appointed by the president by virtue of position or special expertise, and a 26-seat *National Council* consisting of two members from each Regional Council elected for six-year terms.

National Anthem. 'Namibia, land of the brave'; words and tune by Axali Doeseb.

RECENT ELECTIONS

Presidential and parliamentary elections were held on 15–16 Nov. 2004. Hifikepunye Pohamba (South West Africa People's Organization/SWAPO) was elected president with 76·4% of votes cast followed by Ben Ulenga (Congress of Democrats/CoD) with 7·3%, Katuutire Kaura (Democratic Turnhalle Alliance/DTA) with 5·2%, Kuaima Riruako (National Unity Democratic Organization/NUDO) with 4·2% and Chief Justus Garoëb (United Democratic Front/UDF) with 3·7%. Turn-out was 85·0%. In the parliamentary elections SWAPO won 55 of the available 72 seats with 75·1% of the vote; the CoD, 5 with 7·2%; DTA, 4 with 5·0%; NUDO, 3 with 4·1%; UDF, 3 with 3·5%; Republican Party, 1 with 1·9%; Monitor Action Group, 1 with 0·8%. Turn-out was 84·4%.

CURRENT ADMINISTRATION

President: Hifikepunye Pohamba; b. 1935 (SWAPO; sworn in 21 March 2005).

In March 2005 the government comprised:

Prime Minister: Nahas Angula; b. 1943 (SWAPO; sworn in 21 March 2005).

Deputy Prime Minister: Libertina Amathila.

Minister of Home Affairs and Immigration: Rosalia Ngidinwa. *Presidential Affairs:* Albert Kawana. *Foreign Affairs:* Marco Hausiku. *Finance:* Saara Kuugongelwa-Amadhila. *Education:* Nangolo Mbumba. *Health and Social Services:* Richard Kamwi. *Mines and Energy:* Erkki Nghimtina. *Justice and Attorney General:* Pendukeni Iivula-Iithana. *Regional and Local Government, Housing and Rural Development:* John Pandeni. *Agriculture, Water and Forests:* Nickey Iyambo. *Trade and Industry:* Immanuel Ngatjizeko. *Environment and Tourism:* Willem Konjore. *Works, Transport and Communications:* Joel Kaapanda. *Lands and Rehabilitation:* Jerry Ekandjo. *Fisheries and Marine Resources:* Dr Abraham Iyambo. *Safety and Security, and Defence (acting):* Peter Tsheehama. *Youth, National Service, Culture and Sport:* John Mutorwa. *Women's Affairs and Child Welfare:* Marlène Mungunda. *Labour and Social Protection:* Alpheus Naruseb. *Information and Broadcasting:* Netumbo Nandi-Ndaitwah. *Minister without Portfolio:* Ngarikutuke Tjiriange.

Office of the Prime Minister: http://www.opm.gov.na

DEFENCE

In 2003 defence expenditure totalled US$105m. (US$52 per capita), representing 2·3% of GDP.

Army. Personnel (2002), 9,000.

Coastguard. A force of 200 (2002) is based at Walvis Bay.

Air Force. The Army has a small air wing.

INTERNATIONAL RELATIONS

Namibia is a member of the UN, WTO, the Commonwealth, the African Union, African Development Bank, SADC and is an ACP member state of the ACP-EU relationship.

ECONOMY

Agriculture accounted for 10·6% of GDP in 2002, industry 31·1% and services 58·3%.

The Namibian economy is heavily dependent on mining and fisheries.

Overview. Although the country is dependent on uranium, diamonds, silver, tin and zinc, the majority of the population is employed in agriculture and few benefit from the mineral wealth. The mining sector accounts for 50% of exports. 80% of the manufacturing industry is in food-related industries. There is strong potential for tourism. Since 1990 the government's role in the economy has expanded. It controls the electricity and water utilities, the national airline and a telecommunications company. Namibia is a member of the Southern African Customs Union, which has a 12% common external tariff. The country promotes foreign investment but favours domestic and foreign partnerships. Trade is closely linked to South Africa, although the EU is the country's core export market. Unemployment (including underemployment) is near 60%. The country's history of apartheid policies has led to unequal income distribution, one of the highest in the world, and a shortage of skilled labour. Agriculture employs nearly half of the workforce. Namibia has one of the highest rates of HIV/AIDS infection in the world.

Currency. The unit of currency is the *Namibia dollar* (NAD) of 100 *cents*, introduced on 14 Sept. 1993 and pegged to the South African rand. The rand is also legal tender at parity. In 2002 inflation was 11·3%. In June 2002 foreign exchange reserves were US$230m. Gold reserves are negligible. Total money supply in June 2002 was N$7,063m.

Budget. The financial year runs from 1 April. In 1999–2000 total government revenue was N$7,184·9m. (N$7,765·3m. estimated for 2000–01) and total expenditure was N$7,831·3m. (2000–01 estimate, N$8,610·0m.).

Performance. Real GDP growth was 2·4% in 2001 and 2·7% in 2002; total GDP in 2003 was US$4·7bn.

Banking and Finance. The Bank of Namibia is the central bank. Its *Governor* is Tom Alweendo. Commercial banks in 2002 included First National Bank of Namibia, Namibia Banking Corporation, StandardBank Namibia, Commercial Bank of Namibia, Bank Windhoek (the only locally-owned bank) and City Savings and Investment Bank. There is a state-owned Agricultural Bank and a merchant bank, UAL-Namibia. Total assets of commercial banks were R2,383·2m. at 31 Dec. 1991.

There are two building societies with total assets (31 March 1990) R424·9m. A Post Office Savings Bank was established in 1916. In March 1991 its total assets were R21·8m. A stock exchange (NSE) is in operation in Windhoek.

ENERGY AND NATURAL RESOURCES

Environment. Carbon dioxide emissions from the consumption and flaring of fossil fuels were the equivalent of 1·2 tonnes per capita in 2002.

Electricity. In 2002 electricity production was 1·4bn. kWh. Namibia also imports electricity from South Africa (1·0bn. kWh in 2002). Consumption per capita in 1995 was 584 kWh.

Oil and Gas. Natural gas reserves in 2002 totalled 85bn. cu. metres.

Water. The 12 most important dams have a total capacity of 589·2m. cu. metres. The Kunene, the Okavango, the Zambezi, the Kwando or Mashi and the Orange River are the only permanently running rivers but water can generally be obtained by sinking shallow wells. Except for a few springs, mostly hot, there is no surface water.

Minerals. There are diamond deposits both inshore and off the coast, with production equally divided between the two. Some 3bn. carats of diamonds are believed to be lying in waters off Namibia's Atlantic coast. Namibia produced 1,611,000 carats in 1999, with 98% of the diamonds being of gem quality. Output (in tonnes): salt (1997), 493,000; lead (1996), 67,760; zinc (2001), 31,803; copper (2001), 12,392; silver (2001), 32; gold (2001), 2,851 kg; diamonds (2000), 1,606,000 carats. Uranium production, 2002, 2,333 tonnes.

Agriculture. Namibia is essentially a stock-raising country, the scarcity of water and poor rainfall rendering crop-farming, except in the northern and northeastern parts, almost impossible. There were 816,000 ha of arable land in 2001 and 4,000 ha of permanent crops. There were 3,150 tractors in 2001. Generally speaking, the southern half is suited for the raising of small stock, while the central and northern parts are more suited for cattle. Guano is harvested from the coast, converted into fertilizer in South Africa and most of it exported to Europe. In 1995, 45% of the active labour force worked in the agricultural sector, and 45% of the population was dependent on agriculture.

Livestock (2000): 2·06m. cattle, 2·10m. sheep, 1·65m. goats, 2m. chickens.

In 2000, 75,000 tonnes of milk and 60,000 tonnes of meat were produced. Principal crops (2000, in tonnes): millet, 79,000; maize, 49,000; sorghum, 7,000; seed cotton, 5,000; wheat, 4,000.

Forestry. Forests covered 8·04m. ha in 2000, or 9·8% of the land area.

Fisheries. Pilchards, mackerel and hake are the principal fish caught. The catch in 2001 was 547,492 tonnes, of which more than 99% came from marine waters. Conservation policies are in place. The policy aims at ensuring that the country's fisheries resources are utilized on a sustainable basis and also aims to ensure their lasting contribution to the country's economy.

INDUSTRY

Of the estimated total of 400 undertakings, the most important branches are food production (accounting for 29·3% of total output), metals (12·7%) and wooden products (7%). The supply of specialized equipment to the mining industry, the assembly of goods from predominantly imported materials and the manufacture of metal products and construction material play an important part. Small industries (including home industries, textile mills, leather and steel goods) have expanded.

Products manufactured locally include chocolates, beer, cement, leather shoes, delicatessen meats and game meat products.

Labour. Of 431,800 people in employment in 2000, 126,500 were engaged in agriculture, hunting and forestry; 46,300 in community, social and personal service activities; 39,300 in real estate, renting and business activities; and 38,900 in wholesale and retail trade/repair of motor vehicles, motorcycles and personal and household goods. In 2000 the unemployment rate was 33·8%.

INTERNATIONAL TRADE

Total foreign debt was US$140m. in 1996. Export Processing Zones were established in 1995 to grant companies with EPZ status some tax exemptions and other incentives. The Offshore Development Company (ODC) is the flagship of the Export Processing Zone regime. The EPZ regime does not restrict; any investor (local or foreign) enjoys the same or equal advantages in engaging themselves in any choice of business (allowed by law).

Imports and Exports. In 2002 imports (f.o.b.) were valued at US$1,250·5m. (US$1,325·5m. in 2001) and exports (f.o.b.) at US$1,071·6m. (US$1,147·0m. in 2001). Exports in 1996 (in US$1m.) included diamonds (542), fish (289), uranium and other minerals (237), meat products (82), cattle (58), small stock (42). The largest import supplier in 1996 was South Africa with 87%; largest export markets: UK, 34%; South Africa, 27%.

COMMUNICATIONS

Roads. In 2002 the total road network covered 42,237 km, including 4,550 km of national roads. In 2002 there were 160,274 registered motor vehicles, including 82,580 passenger cars and 76,080 trucks and vans. There were 340 deaths as a result of road accidents in 2002.

Rail. The Namibia system connects with the main system of the South African railways at Ariamsvlei. The total length of the line inside Namibia was 2,382 km of 1,065 mm gauge in 1996. In 1995–96 railways carried 124,000 passengers and 1·7m. tonnes of freight.

Civil Aviation. The national carrier is the state-owned Air Namibia. In 2000 the major airport, Windhoek's Hosea Kutako International, handled 481,000 passengers (437,000 on international flights). Eros is used mainly for domestic flights. In 1999 scheduled airline traffic of Namibian-based carriers flew 7·1m. km, carrying 201,000 passengers (165,000 on international flights).

Shipping. The main port is Walvis Bay. During 1997–98, 808 ships called and 1,156,143 tonnes of cargo were landed. There is a harbour at Lüderitz which handles mainly fishing vessels. In 2002 merchant shipping totalled 69,000 GRT.

Telecommunications. Telecom Namibia is the responsible corporation. In 2002 telephone subscribers numbered 271,400 (144·8 per 1,000 inhabitants) and there were 133,000 PCs in use (70·9 per 1,000 persons). Mobile phone subscribers numbered 150,000 in 2002. In 2002 there were 50,000 Internet users.

Postal Services. The national postal service is run by Namibia Post. In 1998 there were 115 post offices, or one for every 14,400 persons.

SOCIAL INSTITUTIONS

Justice. There is a Supreme Court, a High Court and a number of magistrates' and lower courts. An Ombudsman is appointed. Judges are appointed by the president on the recommendation of the Judicial Service Commission.

The population in penal institutions in Dec. 2001 was 4,814 (267 per 100,000 of national population).

Religion. About 75% of the population is Christian (mainly Protestants).

Education. Literacy was 82·7% in 2001 (male, 83·4%; female, 81·9%). Primary education is free and compulsory. In 2001–02 there were 398,381 pupils at primary schools, 130,577 at secondary schools and 13,339 students at institutions of higher education (55% female in 1999–2000). The University of Namibia had 3,941 students and 198 academic staff in 2000.

In 1999–2000 total expenditure on education came to 7·7% of GNP.

Health. In 1992 there were 47 hospitals (four private) and 238 clinics and health centres. There were 495 physicians, 67 dentists, 2,817 nurses and 1,954 midwives in 1997.

CULTURE

Broadcasting. The Namibian Broadcasting Corporation operates a national radio service from three stations and vernacular services. It also operates ten TV stations (colour by PAL). In 2001 there were 141,000 TV sets and in 2000 there were 258,000 radios in use. One privately-owned television channel and two privately-owned radio stations operate from Windhoek.

Press. There were four daily and three weekly newspapers in 1997.

Tourism. In 2001 there were 670,000 visitors who spent US$404m. The tourism industry was devastated in 2000 by the Angolan civil war spilling over into the north of Namibia.

DIPLOMATIC REPRESENTATIVES

Of Namibia in the United Kingdom (6 Chandos St., London, W1G 9LU)
High Commissioner: Monica Ndiliawike Nashandi.

Of the United Kingdom in Namibia (116 Robert Mugabe Ave., 9000 Windhoek)
High Commissioner: Alastair MacDermott.

Of Namibia in the USA (1605 New Hampshire Ave., NW, Washington, D.C., 20009)
Ambassador: Leonard Nangolo Iipumbu.

Of the USA in Namibia (14 Lossen St., Private Bag 12029, Windhoek)
Ambassador: Joyce A. Barr.

Of Namibia to the United Nations
Ambassador: Martin Andjaba.

Of Namibia to the European Union
Ambassador: Peter Hitjitevi Katjavivi.

FURTHER READING

Herbstein, D. and Evenston, J., *The Devils are Among Us: the War for Namibia.* London, 1989
Kaela, L. C. W., *The Question of Namibia.* London, 1996
Schoeman, Elna and Stanley, *Namibia.* [Bibliography] 2nd ed. ABC-Clio, Oxford and Santa Barbara (CA), 1997
Sparks, D. L. and Green, D., *Namibia: the Nation after Independence.* Boulder, (CO), 1992

National statistical office: National Planning Commission.
Website: http://www.npc.gov.na/cbs/index.htm

NAURU

Republic of Nauru

Population, 2003: 13,000
GDP per capita: not available

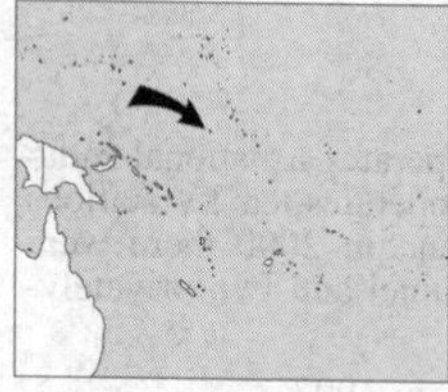

KEY HISTORICAL EVENTS

Nauru was first settled by Melanesians and Polynesians. The island was discovered by Capt. John Fearn in 1798 and was annexed by Germany in Oct. 1888. Phosphates were discovered in 1900 and exploited by the British Pacific Phosphate Company. Nauru was surrendered to Australian forces in 1914. It was administered by the UK under a League of Nations mandate from 1920 and occupied by Japanese forces from 1942–45. In 1947 the UN approved a trusteeship agreement with Australia, New Zealand and the UK and Nauru was granted independence on 31 Jan. 1968. Phosphate mining provided one of the world's highest GDP per capita rates. In 1993 Australia and the UK agreed to out-of-court settlements for environmental damage during mining. Nauru agreed to hold asylum seekers for Australia in 2001. The depletion of phosphates and mismanagement of revenues caused a financial crisis in the early 21st century. Nauru is bankrupt and is almost totally reliant on aid from Australia. In 2003 President Bernard Dowiyogo closed Nauru's offshore banks after US allegations of money-laundering. During 2003 there were six changes of president. In Sept. 2004 a state of emergency was declared after the health minister was suspended and parliament was dismissed for failing to pass the national budget.

TERRITORY AND POPULATION

Nauru is a coral island surrounded by a reef situated 0° 32' S. lat. and 166° 56' E. long. Area, 21·3 sq. km. At the 1992 census the population totalled 9,919, of whom 6,832 were Nauruans. Estimated population in July 2003: 12,570; density, 590 per sq. km.

Nauruan is the official language, although English is widely used for government purposes.

SOCIAL STATISTICS

1995 births, 203; deaths, 49; marriages, 57. Rates, 1995 (per 1,000 population): births, 20·3; deaths, 4·9; marriage, 5·7; infant mortality, 41 (per 1,000 live births). Annual population growth rate, 1992–02, 2·5%; fertility rate, 2001, 4·5 births per woman.

CLIMATE

A tropical climate, tempered by sea breezes, but with a high and irregular rainfall, averaging 82" (2,060 mm). Average temperature, Jan. 81°F (27·2°C), July 82°F (27·8°C). Annual rainfall 75" (1,862 mm).

CONSTITUTION AND GOVERNMENT

A Legislative Council was inaugurated on 31 Jan. 1966. An 18-member Parliament is elected on a three-yearly basis.

National Anthem. 'Nauru bwiema, ngabena ma auwe' ('Nauru our homeland, the country we love'); words by a collective, tune by L. H. Hicks.

RECENT ELECTIONS

At the last elections on 23 Oct. 2004, followers of President Ludwig Scotty won a majority. On 26 Oct. 2004 Scotty was elected president unopposed.

CURRENT ADMINISTRATION

In Aug. 2003 President Ludwig Scotty lost a vote of confidence and left office. His successor, René Harris was also ousted by a confidence vote on 22 June 2004 and Scotty took office again.

In March 2005 the government comprised:

President and Minister of Public Service and Civil Aviation: Ludwig Scotty (since 22 June 2004, having previously served as president from May–Aug. 2003).

Minister assisting the President and Minister for Foreign Affairs, Internal Affairs, Finance and Customs: David Adeang. *Minister of Health, Women's Affairs and Shipping:* Dr Kieren Keke. *Education and Vocational Training, Telecommunications, Youth Affairs and Public Works:* Baron Waqa. *Island Development, Culture and Tourism, and Nauru Phosphate Royalties Trust:* Frederick Pitcher. *Justice, Nauru Fisheries and Marine Resources, Immigration and Sports:* Godfrey Thoma.

Speaker: Russell Kun.

INTERNATIONAL RELATIONS

Nauru is a member of the UN, Asian Development Bank, the Commonwealth, the Pacific Community and the Pacific Islands Forum.

ECONOMY

Currency. The Australian dollar is in use.

Budget. Revenues in 1995–96 were estimated to be US\$23·4m. and expenditures US\$64·8m.

Performance. Real GDP growth was 7·0% in 1995 (4·5% in 1994).

Banking and Finance. The Bank of Nauru is a state bank and there is a commercial bank, Hampshire Bank and Trust Inc.

Nauru was one of 15 countries and territories named in a report in June 2000 as failing to co-operate in the fight against international money laundering. The Financial Action Task Force on Money Laundering was set up by the G7 group of major industrialized nations.

ENERGY AND NATURAL RESOURCES

Environment. Carbon dioxide emissions from the consumption and flaring of fossil fuels were the equivalent of 13·6 tonnes per capita in 2002.

Electricity. Installed capacity in 2000 was 10,000 kW; production was estimated at 33m. kWh in 2000.

Minerals. A central plateau contained high-grade phosphate deposits. The interests in the phosphate deposits were purchased in 1919 from the Pacific Phosphate Company by the UK, Australia and New Zealand. In 1967 the British Phosphate Corporation agreed to hand over the phosphate industry to Nauru for approximately \$A20m. over three years. Nauru took over the industry in July 1969; production in 2001 totalled 266,000 tonnes, compared to 747,000 tonnes in 1992. It is estimated that the deposits will be exhausted by 2008. In May 1989 Nauru filed a claim against Australia for environmental damage caused by the mining. In Aug. 1993 Australia agreed to pay compensation of \$A73m. In March 1994 New Zealand and the UK each agreed to pay compensation of \$A12m.

Agriculture. Livestock (2000): pigs, 3,000. In 2000 the crop of coconuts was an estimated 2,000 tonnes.

Fisheries. The catch in 2001 was approximately 400 tonnes.

INTERNATIONAL TRADE

Imports and Exports. The export trade consists almost entirely of phosphate shipped mainly to New Zealand and Australia. Imports: food, building construction materials, machinery for the phosphate industry and medical supplies. Exports, 1999, US\$40m.; imports, US\$20m. Around half of exports go to New Zealand and half of imports are from Australia.

COMMUNICATIONS

Roads. In 1999 there were 30 km of roads, 24 km of which were paved.

Civil Aviation. There is an airfield on the island capable of accepting medium size jet aircraft. The national carrier, Air Nauru, is a wholly owned government subsidiary. It has one aircraft. In 2003 it flew to Brisbane, Melbourne, Nadi and Tarawa. In 1999 scheduled airline traffic of Nauru-based carriers flew 2·5m. km, carrying 143,000 passengers (all on international flights).

Shipping. Deep offshore moorings can accommodate medium-size vessels. Shipping coming to the island consists of vessels under charter to the phosphate industry or general purpose vessels bringing cargo by way of imports.

Telecommunications. There were 2,200 main telephone lines in operation in 1996. International telephone, telex and fax communications are maintained by satellite. A satellite earth station was commissioned in 1990.

Postal Services. In 1997 there was one post office.

SOCIAL INSTITUTIONS

Justice. The highest Court is the Supreme Court of Nauru. It is the Superior Court of record and has the jurisdiction to deal with constitutional matters in addition to its other jurisdiction. There is also a District Court which is presided over by the Resident Magistrate who is also the Chairman of the Family Court and the Registrar of Supreme Court. The laws applicable in Nauru are its own Acts of Parliament. A large number of British statutes and much common law has been adopted insofar as is compatible with Nauruan custom.

Religion. The population is mainly Roman Catholic or Protestant.

Education. Attendance at school is compulsory between the ages of six and 17. In 2003 there were 588 children in pre-primary schools with 44 teachers, 1,375 pupils in primary schools with 63 teachers and 645 pupils in secondary schools with 34 teachers. There is also a trade school with four instructors and an enrolment of 88 trainees. Scholarships are available for Nauruan children to receive secondary and higher education and vocational training in Australia and New Zealand.

In 2000–01 total expenditure on education came to 7·0% of total government spending.

Health. In 1995 there were 17 physicians and 62 nurses.

CULTURE

Broadcasting. The government-controlled Nauru Broadcasting Service broadcasts a home service in Nauruan and English for three hours daily. There were 7,000 radio sets in use and 500 television sets in 1997. New Zealand television programmes are received.

DIPLOMATIC REPRESENTATIVES

Of Nauru in the United Kingdom
Honorary Consul: Martin Weston (Romshed Courtyard, Underriver, Nr Sevenoaks, Kent, TN15 0SD).

Of the United Kingdom in Nauru
High Commissioner: Charles Mochan (resides at Suva, Fiji Islands).

Of the USA in Nauru
Ambassador: David Lyon (resides at Suva, Fiji Islands).

Of Nauru to the United Nations
Ambassador: Vinci Clodumar.

FURTHER READING

Weeremantry, C., *Nauru: Environmental Damage under International Trusteeship.* OUP, 1992

NEPAL

Nepal Adhirajya
(Kingdom of Nepal)

Capital: Kathmandu
Population projection, 2010: 29·15m.
GDP per capita, 2002: (PPP$) 1,370
HDI/world rank: 0·504/140

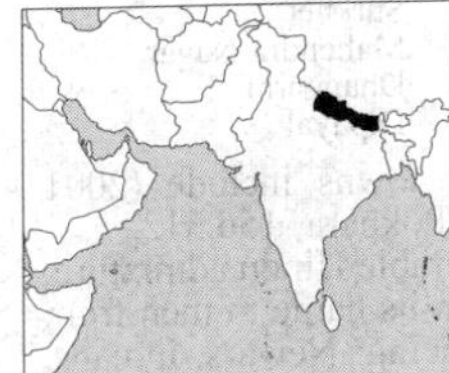

KEY HISTORICAL EVENTS

Nepal is an independent Himalayan Kingdom located between India and the Tibetan region of China. From the 8th to the 11th centuries many Buddhists fled to Nepal from India, which had been invaded by Muslims. In the 18th century Nepal was a collection of small principalities (many of Rajput origin) and the three kingdoms of the Malla dynasty: Kathmandu, Patan and Bhadgaon. In central Nepal lay the principality of Gurkha (or Gorkha); its ruler after 1742 was Prithvi Narayan Shah, who conquered the small neighbouring states. Fearing his ambitions, in 1767 the Mallas brought in forces lent by the British East India Company. In 1769 these forces were withdrawn and Gurkha was then able to conquer the Malla kingdoms and unite Nepal as one state with its capital at Kathmandu. In 1846 the Rana family became the effective rulers of Nepal, establishing the office of prime minister as hereditary. In 1860 Nepal reached agreement with the British in India whereby Nepali independence was preserved and the recruitment of Gurkhas to the British army was sanctioned.

In 1950 the Shah royal family allied itself with Nepalis abroad to end the power of the Ranas. The last Rana prime minister resigned in Nov. 1951, the king having proclaimed a constitutional monarchy in Feb. 1951. A new constitution, approved in 1959, led to confrontation between the king and his ministers; it was replaced by one less liberal in 1962. In Nov. 1990 the king relinquished his absolute power. The Maoists abandoned parliament in 1996 and launched a 'people's war' in the aim of turning the kingdom into a republic. This has resulted in more than 3,500 deaths.

In June 2001 the king and queen, along with six other members of the royal family, were shot dead by their son and heir to the throne, Crown Prince Dipendra, allegedly following a dispute over his choice of bride. Prince Dipendra then shot himself. The former monarch's younger brother, Gyanendra, was crowned king. In Nov. 2001 King Gyanendra declared a state of emergency and ordered troops to contain a fresh outbreak of Maoist violence. The government lifted the state of emergency in Aug. 2002. In Jan. 2003 the government and Maoist rebels reached a ceasefire agreement, seen as a first step towards bringing to an end the rebels' seven-year insurgency. In Feb. 2005 King Gyanendra dismissed his government and once more declared a state of emergency, taking control of the country and suspending democracy for three years.

TERRITORY AND POPULATION

Nepal is bounded in the north by China (Tibet) and the east, south and west by India. Area 147,181 sq. km; population census 2001, 23,151,423 of which 11,587,502 were female; density 157·3 per sq. km. In 2001, 87·8% of the population were rural.

The UN gives a projected population for 2010 of 29·15m.

The country is divided into five regions and subdivided into 14 zones. Area, population and administrative centres:

Zone/Region	*Sq. km*	*Population (2001 census)*	*Administrative centre*
Koshi	9,669	2,110,664	Biratnagar
Mechi	8,196	1,307,669	Ilam
Sagarmatha	10,591	1,926,143	Rajbiraj
East Region	28,456	5,344,476	Dhankuta
Bagmati	9,428	3,008,487	Kathmandu
Janakpur	9,669	2,557,004	Jaleswar
Narayani	8,313	2,466,138	Birganj
Central Region	27,410	8,031,629	Kathmandu

Zone/Region	*Sq. km*	*Population (2001 census)*	*Administrative centre*
Dhanlagiri	8,148	556,191	Baglung
Gandaki	12,275	1,487,954	Pokhara
Lumbini	8,975	2,526,868	Butwal
West Region	29,398	4,571,013	Pokhara
Bheri	10,545	1,417,085	Nepalganj
Karuali	21,351	309,084	Jumla
Rapti	10,482	1,286,806	Tulsipur
Mid-West Region	42,378	3,012,975	Surkhet
Mahakali	6,989	860,475	Mahendra Nagar
Seti	12,550	1,330,855	Dhangarhi
Far West Region	19,539	2,191,330	Dipayal

Capital, Kathmandu; population (2001) 671,846. Other towns include (2001 census population): Biratnagar, 166,674; Lalitpur, 162,991; Pokhara, 156,312.

The indigenous people are of Tibetan origin with a considerable Hindu admixture. The Gurkha clan became predominant in 1559 and has given its name to men from all parts of Nepal. There are 18 ethnic groups, the largest being: Newars, Indians, Tibetans, Gurungs, Mogars, Tamangs, Bhotias, Rais, Limbus and Sherpas. The official language is Nepalese but there are 20 new languages divided into numerous dialects.

SOCIAL STATISTICS

Births, 1995, 815,000; deaths, 257,000. 1995 birth rate per 1,000 population, 38·0; death rate, 12·0. Annual population growth rate, 1992–02, 2·3%. Expectation of life was 59·4 years for males and 58·9 years for females in 2001. Infant mortality, 2001, 66 per 1,000 live births; fertility rate, 2001, 4·6 births per woman.

CLIMATE

Varies from cool summers and severe winters in the north to sub-tropical summers and mild winters in the south. The rainfall is high, with maximum amounts from June to Sept., but conditions are very dry from Nov. to Jan. Kathmandu, Jan. 10°C, July, 25°C. Average annual rainfall, 1,424 mm.

CONSTITUTION AND GOVERNMENT

The sovereign is HM Maharajadhiraja **Gyanendra Bir Bikram Shah Dev** (b. 1947), who succeeded Crown Prince Dipendra on 4 June 2001 on the latter's death two days after he had shot and killed his father, the former king Birendra.

Under the constitution of 9 Nov. 1990 Nepal became a constitutional monarchy based on multi-party democracy. *Parliament* has two chambers: a 205-member House of Representatives (*Pratinidhi Sabha*) elected for five-year terms, and a 60-member National Council (*Rastriya Sabha*), of which ten members are nominated by the king. In Feb. 2005 for the second time since ascending to the throne King Gyanendra dismissed the prime minister and his cabinet and assumed full executive powers.

National Anthem. 'Sri man gumbhira nepali prachanda pratapi bhupati' ('May glory crown our illustrious sovereign, the gallant Nepalese'); words by C. Chalise, tune by B. Budhapirthi.

RECENT ELECTIONS

In parliamentary elections held on 3 and 17 May 1999 the Nepali Congress Party (NCP) won an absolute majority, winning 110 of the 205 seats and bringing an end to a succession of weak coalition governments. The Communist Party/Unified Marxist-Leninists (NKP-EML) won 68 seats, the National Democratic Party (RPP) 11, Nepalese Goodwill Party (NSP) 5, National People's Front (RJM) 5, United People's Front (SJN) 1, Nepalese Workers' and Farmers' Party (NMKP) 1. Four results were unavailable.

CURRENT ADMINISTRATION

On 4 Oct. 2002 King Gyanendra dismissed Prime Minister Sher Bahadur Deuba's government, following the latter's failure to arrange parliamentary elections for Nov. 2002. On 11 Oct. 2002 King Gyanendra appointed a new cabinet with Lokendra

Bahadur Chand of the conservative, royalist RPP as prime minister. However, he resigned on 30 May 2003. His replacement, Surya Bahadur Thapa, resigned on 7 May 2004. Sher Bahadu Deuba was reappointed on 2 June 2004. On 1 Feb. 2005 King Gyanendra again dismissed Prime Minister Sher Bahadur Deuba's government, and assumed power himself.

In March 2005 the cabinet comprised:

Vice Chairmen: Tulsi Giri (also *Minister for Law, Justice and Parliamentary Affairs; Water Resources, Land and Transport Management; Forest and Soil Conservation; Science and Technology*); Kirti Nidhi Bista (also *Minister for Industry, Commerce and Supplies; Agriculture and Co-operatives; Population and Environment; Physical Planning and Works; Health*).

Minister for Foreign Affairs: Ramesh Nath Pandey. *Interior:* Dan Bahadur Shahi. *Finance:* Madhukar Shamsher Jang Bahadur Rana. *Education and Sports:* Radha Krishna Mainali. *General Administration:* Krishna Lal Thakali. *Culture, Tourism and Civil Aviation:* Buddhi Raj Bajracharya. *Women, Children and Social Welfare:* Durga Shrestha. *Information and Communication:* Tanka Dhakal. *Local Development:* Khadga Bahadur. *Labour and Transport Management:* Ram Narayan Singh.

Office of the Council of Ministers: http://www.pmo.gov.np

DEFENCE

The King is commander-in-chief of the armed forces, but shares supreme military authority with the National Defence Council.

Defence expenditure in 2003 totalled US$110m. (US$4 per capita), representing 1·9% of GDP.

Army. Strength (2002) 51,000, and there is also a 40,000-strong paramilitary police force.

Air Force. The Army's air wing has no combat aircraft. Personnel, 2002, 320.

INTERNATIONAL RELATIONS

Nepal is a member of the UN, WTO, the Asian Development Bank, the Colombo Plan, the SAARC and is a founding member of Non-aligned Movement (NAM).

ECONOMY

Agriculture accounted for 40·7% of GDP in 2002, industry 21·7% and services 37·5%.

Overview. In the past 15 years the government has embarked on economic reform—eliminating business licenses and registration requirements—to encourage trade and foreign investment. The production of textiles and carpets accounts for over two-thirds of foreign exchange earnings. Apart from agricultural land and forests, exploitable natural resources are mica, hydropower and tourism.

Currency. The unit of currency is the *Nepalese rupee* (NPR) of 100 *paisas*. 50 *paisas* = 1 *mohur.* Inflation was 2·9% in 2002. Foreign exchange reserves were US$1,034m. in June 2002 and gold reserves totalled 15,000 troy oz (153,000 troy oz in April 2002). Total money supply in Dec. 2001 was NRs 72,161m.

Budget. Revenues and expenditures in NRs 1m. for fiscal years ending 14/15 July:

	1997–98	*1998–99*	*1999–2000*	*2000–01*	*2001–02*[1]
Revenue	31,492	34,809	40,484	46,607	48,384
Expenditure	51,964	54,720	60,794	73,905	75,705

[1]Provisional.

Performance. Real GDP growth was 4·8% in 2001 but there was then a recession in 2002, with the economy shrinking by 0·5%. Nepal's total GDP in 2003 was US$5·8bn.

Banking and Finance. The Central Bank is the bank of issue (*Governor*, Bijaya Nath Bhattarai). In 2002 there were four domestic commercial banks (Kumari Bank; Nepal Bank; Nepal Industrial and Commercial Bank; Rastriya Banijya Bank), ten joint-venture banks and four development finance organizations (Agricultural

Development Bank; Nepal Development Bank; Nepal Housing Development Finance Corporation; Nepal Industrial Development Corporation).

There is a stock exchange in Kathmandu.

ENERGY AND NATURAL RESOURCES

Environment. Nepal's carbon dioxide emissions from the consumption and flaring of fossil fuels in 2002 were the equivalent of 0·1 tonnes per capita.

Electricity. Installed capacity was 0·5m. kW in 2000. Production in 2000 was an estimated 1·43bn. kWh (88% hydro-electric), with consumption per capita about 67 kWh.

Minerals. Production (in tonnes), 2002: limestone, 356,218; coal (2000), 18,000; agricultural lime (2001), 15,587; salt, 5,000; talcum, 2,621; magnesite (2000), 1,640.

Agriculture. Agriculture is the mainstay of the economy, providing a livelihood for over 90% of the population and accounting for 39% of GDP. In 2001 there were 3·1m. ha of arable land and 92,000 ha of permanent crops. Cultivated land accounts for 26·5% of land use; forest and woodland 42·4%. Crop production (2000, in 1,000 tonnes): rice, 4,030; sugarcane, 2,103; maize, 1,445; wheat, 1,184; potatoes, 1,183; millet, 295.

Livestock (2000); cattle, 7·03m.; buffaloes, 3·50m.; sheep, 870,000; goats, 6·50m.; pigs, 900,000; chickens, 18m.

Forestry. In 2000 the area under forests was 3·9m. ha, or 27·3% of the total land area. There are eight national parks, covering 1m. ha, five wildlife reserves (170,490 ha) and two conservation areas (349,000 ha). Timber production was 14·0m. cu. metres in 2001, mainly for use as fuelwood and charcoal. Expansion of agricultural land has led to widespread deforestation.

Fisheries. The catch in 2001 was 16,700 tonnes, entirely from inland waters.

INDUSTRY

In 2002 industry accounted for 20·9% of GDP, with manufacturing contributing 8·1%. Production (2001–02 unless otherwise stated): cement, 215,000 tonnes; sugar, 65,000 tonnes; soap, washing powder and detergents, 55,100 tonnes; animal feed, 22,000 tonnes; paper and paperboard, 13,000 tonnes; tea (1994), 2,351 tonnes; synthetic textiles (1994), 14·7m. metres; electrical cable (1994), 9·3m. metres; cotton woven fabrics, 2·5m. metres; leather (1994), 1,369,750 sq. metres; shoes, 0·71m. pairs; beer (2003), 23·1m. litres; cigarettes, 6,979m. units. Brewing is one of the successes of Nepal's economy, accounting for some 3% of GDP.

Labour. The labour force in 1996 totalled 10,179,000 (60% males). In 1992, 84% of the economically active population were engaged in agriculture, forestry or fisheries.

INTERNATIONAL TRADE

External debt was an estimated US$2,953m. in 2002.

Imports and Exports. In 2001 imports (f.o.b.) amounted to US$1,485·7m. (US$1,590·1m. in 2000); exports (f.o.b.) US$720·5m. (US$776·1m. in 2000). Principal export commodities are carpets, clothing, leather goods, pulses, raw jute and jute goods, and handicrafts. Hand-knotted woollen carpets are the largest overseas export item constituting almost 32% of foreign exchange earnings. Main partners are India, USA, Germany, UK. Principal import commodities are petroleum products, transport equipment and parts, chemical fertilizer and raw wool. Main partners are India, Singapore, Japan, Germany.

COMMUNICATIONS

Roads. In 1999 there were 13,223 km of roads, of which 30·8% were paved.

Rail. 101 km (762 mm gauge) connect Jayanagar on the North Eastern Indian Railway with Janakpur and thence with Bizalpura (54 km). 653,000 passengers and 9,151 tonnes of freight were carried in 1994.

Civil Aviation. There is an international airport (Tribhuvan) at Kathmandu. The national carrier is the state-owned Royal Nepal Airlines. It operates domestic services and in 2003 flew to Bangalore, Bangkok, Bombay, Delhi, Dubai, Hong Kong, Kuala Lumpur, Osaka, Shanghai and Singapore. In 1995 Kathmandu handled 1,357,000 passengers (868,000 on international flights) and 13·9m. tonnes of freight. In 1999 scheduled airline traffic of Nepali-based carriers flew 8·7m. km, carrying 583,000 passengers (452,000 on international flights).

Telecommunications. In 2002 Nepal had 349,600 telephone subscribers (15·1 per 1,000 persons) and there were 85,000 PCs in use (3·7 for every 1,000 persons). There were 8,000 fax machines in 1999. In 2002 Nepal had 80,000 Internet users. Mobile phone subscribers numbered 21,900 in 2002. The mobile phone network was switched off following King Gyanendra's declaration of a state of emergency in Feb. 2005.

Postal Services. In 1998 there were 4,156 post offices.

SOCIAL INSTITUTIONS

Justice. The Supreme Court Act established a uniform judicial system, culminating in a supreme court of a Chief Justice and no more than six judges. Special courts to deal with minor offences may be established at the discretion of the government. The Chief Justice is appointed by the king on recommendation of the Constitutional Council. Other judges are appointed by the king on the recommendation of the Judicial Council.

The death penalty was abolished in 1997. The population in penal institutions in 2002 was 7,132 (29 per 100,000 of national population).

Religion. Nepal is a Hindu state. Hinduism was the religion of 82·8% of the people in 2001. Buddhists comprise 8·9% and Muslims 4·2%. Christian missions are permitted, but conversion is forbidden.

Education. The adult literacy rate in 2001 was 42·9% (60·5% among males and 25·2% among females). Only Yemen has a bigger difference in literacy rates between the sexes. In 1998 there were 22,994 primary schools; 6,023 lower secondary schools; 3,178 secondary schools; and 310 higher secondary schools. In 2000–01 there were 257,968 children (11,785 teachers) in pre-primary schools, 3,623,150 pupils (97,879 teachers) in primary schools and 1,349,909 pupils (45,655 teachers) in secondary schools. There are five universities; the Tribhuvan University had 93,800 students and 4,300 academic staff in 1995–96.

In 2000–01 total expenditure on education came to 3·6% of GNP and 14·1% of total government spending.

Health. There were 874 physicians and 3,845 nurses in 1997. In 1996 there were 82 hospitals with 3,604 beds, 17 health centres and 775 medical posts. In 1997 hospital bed provision was just two for every 10,000 persons.

CULTURE

World Heritage Sites. Nepal has four sites on the UNESCO World Heritage List: Sagarmatha National Park (inscribed on the list in 1979); Kathmandu Valley (1979); Royal Chitwan National Park (1984); and Lumbini, the Birthplace of the Lord Buddha (1997).

Broadcasting. Radio Nepal is part government-owned and part commercial. It broadcasts in Nepali and English from three stations. The government-owned Nepal Television transmits from one station (colour by PAL). In 2000 there were 883,000 radio sets and in 2001 there were 193,000 TV sets.

Press. In 1998 there were 166 daily newspapers, including the official English-language *Rising Nepal*, three bi-weeklies and 814 weeklies. Press censorship was relaxed in June 1991, but following the imposition of a state of emergency in Feb. 2005 the press was subjected to total censorship.

Tourism. Foreign tourists visiting Nepal numbered 298,100 in 2001, down from 376,500 in 2000, largely as a consequence of the massacre of the royal family and an upsurge in Maoist rebel violence. Revenue from tourism totalled US$166·8m. in 2000. In 1998, 27,612 hotel beds were available. Tourism accounts for approximately 4% of GDP.

Festivals. Hindu, Buddhist and traditional festivals crowd the Nepali lunar calendar. Dasain (Sept./Oct.) is the longest and most widely observed festival in Nepal. The 15 days of celebration include Dashami, when family elders are honoured. Tihar (Oct./Nov.) celebrates the Hindu goddess Laxmi. During the first three days crows, dogs and cows are worshipped, followed by the spirit, or self. It concludes with Bhai Tika ('Brother's Day'). Buddha Jayanti (May/June) remembers the birth, enlightenment and death of the Buddha. Sherpas gather at Tengboche Monastery near Mount Everest in May to observe Mani Rimdu with meditation, mask dances and Buddhist ceremonies.

DIPLOMATIC REPRESENTATIVES

Of Nepal in the United Kingdom (12A Kensington Palace Gdns, London, W8 4QU)
Ambassador: Prabal S. J. B. Rana, CVO.

Of the United Kingdom in Nepal (Lainchaur, Kathmandu, POB 106)
Ambassador: Keith Bloomfield.

Of Nepal in the USA (2131 Leroy Pl., NW, Washington, D.C., 20008)
Ambassador: Kedar Bhakta Shrestha.

Of the USA in Nepal (Pani Pokhari, Kathmandu)
Ambassador: James Moriarty.

Of Nepal to the United Nations
Ambassador: Murari Raj Sharma.

Of Nepal to the European Union
Ambassador: Narayan Shumshere Thapa.

FURTHER READING

Central Bureau of Statistics. *Statistical Pocket Book.* [Various years]

Borre, O., *et al.*, *Nepalese Political Behaviour.* Aarhus Univ. Press, 1994
Ghimire, K., *Forest or Farm? The Politics of Poverty and Land Hunger in Nepal.* OUP, 1993
Sanwal, D. B., *Social and Political History of Nepal.* London, 1993

National statistical office: Central Bureau of Statistics, National Planning Commission Secretariat, Kathmandu.
Website: http://www.cbs.gov.np

THE NETHERLANDS

Koninkrijk der Nederlanden
(Kingdom of the Netherlands)

Capital: Amsterdam
Seat of government: The Hague
Population projection, 2010: 16·58m.
GDP per capita, 2002: (PPP$) 29,100
HDI/world rank: 0·942/5

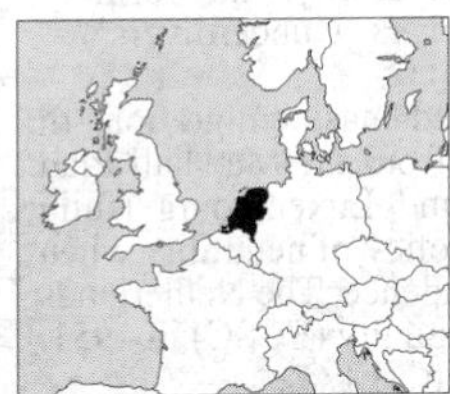

KEY HISTORICAL EVENTS

In the 3rd century AD Germanic tribes, such as the Franks, began to enter Roman territory. With the collapse of Roman government in Gaul and on the Rhine in the 5th century, the Franks extended their power from Austrasia (the central Rhine region). The spread of Christianity in the 7th century assisted Frankish expansion into the northern Low Countries. In the Middle Ages powerful landowners established the large counties (Flanders, Hainault, Namur and Holland) and duchies (Brabant, Limburg and Guelders). Most were under the authority of the German king but with a degree of independence that was to become a defining characteristic of Dutch politics. Dykes were built from Friesland to Flanders to drain the bogs and marshes for pasturage and agrarian use.

The Burgundian era was born of a series of dynastic matches, most importantly that of Duke Philip II (the Bold) of Burgundy and Margaret, Countess of Flanders and Artois in 1369. The summoning of the Estates in 1464 in Brugge (Bruges) represented the first parliamentary assembly in the Low Countries. The reign of Charles the Bold (1467–77) saw the first serious attempt to create a unitary kingdom but when his daughter Mary succeeded she was forced to concede traditional privileges. Her marriage to Maximilian of Habsburg, the future Holy Roman Emperor, brought the Low Countries into personal union with Austria. Mary's son, Philip the Handsome, inherited the Spanish throne through his wife, Juana the Mad.

Philip II of Spain imposed a new ecclesiastical hierarchy as a centralizing force but the Reformation strengthened the traditional independence of the towns and provinces. In 1566 Philip sent the duke of Alba to restore his authority, thereby sparking full-scale revolt and the Eighty Years War (1568–1648). The 1576 Pacification of Ghent brought together Catholic and Protestant provinces in response to Spanish repression and the 'Spanish Fury' massacre in Antwerp. The mainly Catholic southern provinces were largely regained for Philip by the duke of Parma in 1578, forcing a 'closer union'—the Union of Utrecht—in the north in 1579, committed to resisting the Spanish. This marked the birth of the United Provinces of the Netherlands, or the 'Dutch Republic', controlled by the stadtholders. With recognition from England and France, the 1609 Twelve Year Truce with Spain recognized the independence of the United Provinces. Lasting peace with Spain was won at the 1648 Treaty of Münster, which formally recognized the Dutch Republic.

The 17th century has traditionally been called the Dutch Golden Age. From the Twelve Year Truce, the Dutch economy expanded through trade with the Baltic, France, Iberia and the colonies of the West and East Indies. The United East Indies Company, chartered in 1602, held quasi-sovereign authority over its colonies in Sri Lanka, India and Indonesia. Relations with England deteriorated after the execution of Charles I. Competition for trade between the two great maritime powers caused a series of Anglo-Dutch Wars. Opposition in England to the Catholic James II encouraged William III of Orange to invade in 1688 and to claim the English throne with his wife, Mary Stuart.

Revolutionary France's invasion of Belgium (the Spanish Netherlands) in 1794 rapidly extended to the United Provinces. A period of political modernization included an elected national assembly. The republic ended in 1806 when Napoléon installed his brother, Louis, as king. Louis adopted the cause of his new subjects, frequently defying his brother in favour of Dutch interests. Louis was removed but after the defeat of Napoléon the northern provinces were united with Belgium and Luxembourg under the Kingdom of the Netherlands. In 1830 Belgium proclaimed its independence, rejecting a common identity with the predominantly Protestant north.

A policy of neutrality kept the Netherlands out of the First World War but when Adolf Hitler came to power, German control of the Netherlands and Belgium was seen as essential to protect the industrial Ruhr. The Dutch armed forces were overwhelmed within a week in May 1940 and queen and government went into exile in London. The Netherlands suffered greatly during the latter part of the Second World War, with famine and a death toll of 270,000. Persecution of the Jews began in Oct. 1941. The first transports left in July 1942, mostly to Auschwitz. 107,000 Dutch Jews were transported and murdered. Dutch resistance took the form of civilian sabotage and the hiding of Jews and *onkerduikers* ('underdivers')—underground military operatives.

The destruction of the economy and infrastructure caused mass emigration. In 1947 the Netherlands accepted US$1bn. for reconstruction from the Marshall Plan and began the Benelux Economic Union with Belgium and Luxembourg (fully established in 1958). The Dutch government abandoned its policy of neutrality when it joined NATO in 1949, the year it granted Indonesia independence. The Netherlands was a founder member of the European Coal and Steel Community (ECSC) in 1951, which later merged with the European Economic Community (EEC).

Social liberalization has characterized the Netherlands in recent years. Euthanasia and homosexual marriage were legalized in 2000. 2002 was a momentous year in the Netherlands, beginning with the adoption of the euro in Jan. In April, Prime Minister Wim Kok's government resigned over Dutch inaction in preventing the massacre at Srebrenica in 1995. During the subsequent election campaigning, the right-wing politician Pim Fortuyn was assassinated by an animal-rights activist who opposed Fortuyn's anti-immigration policies.

TERRITORY AND POPULATION

The Netherlands is bounded in the north and west by the North Sea, south by Belgium and east by Germany. The area is 41,528 sq. km, of which 33,873 sq. km is land. Projects of sea-flood control and land reclamation (polders) by the construction of dams and drainage schemes have continued since 1920. More than a quarter of the country is below sea level.

The population was 13,060,115 at the census of 1971 and 16,105,000 on 1 Jan. 2002 (8,133,000 females). Population growth in 2001, 0·7%. The population reached 16m. on 8 March 2001.

The UN gives a projected population for 2010 of 16·58m.

On-going 'rolling' censuses have replaced the former decennial counts.

Area, estimated population and density, and chief towns of the 12 provinces on 1 Jan. 2002:

	Area 1995 (in sq. km)	*Population 2002*	*Density 2002 per sq. km land area*	*Provincial capital*
Groningen	2,967·10	570,000	244	Groningen
Friesland	5,740·75	636,000	189	Leeuwarden
Drenthe	2,680·49	479,000	181	Assen
Overijssel	3,420·06	1,094,000	328	Zwolle
Flevoland	2,412·29	342,000	240	Lelystad
Gelderland	5,143·36	1,949,000	391	Arnhem
Utrecht	1,434·24	1,140,000	821	Utrecht
Noord-Holland	4,059·09	2,559,000	958	Haarlem
Zuid-Holland[1]	3,445·75	3,424,000	1,211	The Hague
Zeeland	2,931·91	377,000	209	Middelburg
Noord-Brabant	5,081·83	2,391,000	485	's-Hertogenbosch
Limburg	2,209·29	1,143,000	528	Maastricht
Total	41,526·16	16,105,000	475	

[1]Since 29 Sept. 1994 includes inhabitants of the municipality of The Hague formerly registered in the abolished Central Population Register.

In 2001, 89·6% of the population lived in urban areas.

Population of municipalities with over 50,000 inhabitants on 1 Jan. 2002:

Alkmaar	92,992	Alphen a/d Rijn	70,649	Amsterdam	735,526
Almelo	71,026	Amersfoort	129,720	Apeldoorn	154,859
Almere	158,902	Amstelveen	77,256	Arnhem	140,736

Assen	60,230	Den Helder	60,083	Purmerend	73,476
Bergen op Zoom	65,793	Helmond	82,853	Roosendaal	77,640
Breda	163,427	Hengelo	80,910	Rotterdam	598,660
Capelle a/d Ijssel	65,226	's-Hertogenbosch	131,697	Schiedam	76,576
Delft	96,936	Hilversum	83,096	Sittard-Geleen	97,953
Deventer	86,072	Hoogeveen	53,186	Smallingerland	53,493
Dordrecht	120,222	Hoorn	66,458	Spijkenisse	75,147
Ede	103,708	Kerkrade	50,680	Tilburg	197,358
Eindhoven	204,776	Leeuwarden	90,516	Utrecht	260,625
Emmen	108,367	Leiden	117,170	Veenendaal	60,669
Enschede	151,346	Leidschendam-Voorburg	74,085	Velsen	67,407
Gouda	71,688	Lelystad	66,460	Venlo	91,400
Groningen	175,569	Maastricht	122,005	Vlaardingen	73,935
Haarlem	147,831	Nieuwegein	62,140	Zaanstad	137,669
Haarlemmermeer	118,553	Nijmegen	154,616	Zeist	59,682
The Hague	457,726	Oosterhout	52,968	Zoetermeer	110,500
Hardenberg	57,483	Oss	67,383	Zwolle	109,000
Heerlen	95,004				

Urban agglomerations as at 1 Jan. 2000: Amsterdam, 1,002,868; Rotterdam, 989,956; The Hague, 610,245; Utrecht, 366,186; Eindhoven, 302,274; Leiden, 250,302; Dordrecht, 241,218; Heerlen, 218,078; Tilburg, 215,419; Groningen, 191,722; Haarlem, 191,079; Breda, 160,615; Amersfoort, 154,890; 's-Hertogenbosch, 154,368; Apeldoorn, 153,261; Nijmegen, 152,200; Enschede, 149,505; Arnhem, 139,576; Geleen-Sittard, 127,322; Maastricht, 122,070; Zwolle, 105,801.

The first national language is Dutch and the second is Friesian.

SOCIAL STATISTICS

Vital statistics for calendar years:

	Live births		*Marriages*	*Divorces*	*Deaths*
	Total	*Outside marriage*			
1998	199,408	41,439	86,956	32,459	137,482
1999	200,445	45,592	89,428	33,571	140,487
2000	206,619	51,539	88,074	34,650	140,527
2001	202,603	55,108	82,091	37,104	140,377
2002	202,083	58,857	85,808	33,179	142,355

2002 rates per 1,000 population: birth, 12·5; death, 8·8. Annual population growth rate, 1992–02, 0·6%. In 2000 the suicide rate per 100,000 population was 11·6 (men, 15·8; women, 7·6). In 2001 the average age of marrying was 34·6 years for males and 31·5 for females. Expectation of life, 2001, was 75·5 years for males and 80·9 for females. Infant mortality, 2001, 5·4 per 1,000 live births; fertility rate, 2001, 1·7 births per woman. The annual abortion rate, at under 8 per 1,000 women aged 15–44, is among the lowest in the world. Percentage of population by age in 2001: 0–19 years, 24·5%; 20–64, 61·9%; 65 and over, 13·7%. In 2002 the Netherlands received 18,667 asylum applications, equivalent to 1·2 per 1,000 inhabitants.

CLIMATE

A cool temperate maritime climate, marked by mild winters and cool summers, but with occasional continental influences. Coastal temperatures vary from 37°F (3°C) in winter to 61°F (16°C) in summer, but inland the winters are slightly colder and the summers slightly warmer. Rainfall is least in the months Feb. to May, but inland there is a well-defined summer maximum in July and Aug.

The Hague, Jan. 37°F (2·7°C), July 61°F (16·3°C). Annual rainfall 32·8" (820 mm). Amsterdam, Jan. 36°F (2·3°C), July 62°F (16·5°C). Annual rainfall 34" (850 mm). Rotterdam, Jan. 36·5°F (2·6°C), July 62°F (16·6°C). Annual rainfall 32" (800 mm).

CONSTITUTION AND GOVERNMENT

According to the Constitution (promulgated 1814; last revision, 1983), the Kingdom consists of the Netherlands, Aruba and the Netherlands Antilles. Their relations are regulated by the 'Statute' for the Kingdom, which came into force on 29 Dec. 1954. Each part enjoys full autonomy; they are united, on a footing of equality, for mutual assistance and the protection of their common interests.

The Netherlands is a constitutional and hereditary monarchy. The royal succession is in the direct female or male line in order of birth. The reigning Queen is **Beatrix Wilhelmina Armgard,** born 31 Jan. 1938, daughter of Queen Juliana and Prince Bernhard; married to Claus von Amsberg on 10 March 1966 (born 6 Sept. 1926, died 6 Oct. 2002); succeeded to the crown on 30 April 1980, on the abdication of her mother. *Offspring:* Prince Willem-Alexander, born 27 April 1967, married to Máxima Zorreguieta on 2 Feb. 2002 (*offspring:* Catharina-Amalia, born 7 Dec. 2003); Prince Johan Friso, born 25 Sept. 1968, married to Mabel Wisse Smit on 24 April 2004; Prince Constantijn, born 11 Oct. 1969, married to Laurentien Brinkhorst on 19 May 2001 (*offspring:* Eloise, born 8 June 2002; Claus-Casimir, born 21 March 2004).

The Queen receives an allowance from the civil list. This was €3,966,000 in 2003; and that of Crown Prince Willem-Alexander, €949,000. Princess Máxima also receives allowances from the civil list.

Sisters of the Queen. Princess Irene Emma Elisabeth, born 5 Aug. 1939, married to Prince Charles Hugues de Bourbon-Parma on 29 April 1964, divorced 1981 (*sons:* Prince Carlos Javier Bernardo, born 27 Jan. 1970; Prince Jaime Bernardo, born 13 Oct. 1972; *daughters:* Princess Margarita Maria Beatriz, born 13 Oct. 1972; Princess Maria Carolina Christina, born 23 June 1974); Princess Margriet Francisca, born in Ottawa, 19 Jan. 1943, married to Pieter van Vollenhoven on 10 Jan. 1967 (*sons:* Prince Maurits, born 17 April 1968; Prince Bernhard, born 25 Dec. 1969; Prince Pieter-Christiaan, born 22 March 1972; Prince Floris, born 10 April 1975); Princess Maria Christina, born 18 Feb. 1947, married to Jorge Guillermo on 28 June 1975 (*sons:* Bernardo, born 17 June 1977; Nicolas, born 6 July 1979; *daughter:* Juliana, born 8 Oct. 1981).

The central executive power of the State rests with the Crown, while the central legislative power is vested in the Crown and Parliament (the *States-General*), consisting of two Chambers. The upper *First Chamber* is composed of 75 members, elected by the members of the Provincial States. The 150-member *Second Chamber* is directly elected by proportional representation for four-year terms. Members of the States-General must be Netherlands subjects of 18 years of age or over. The Hague is the seat of the Court, government and Parliament; Amsterdam is the capital.

The *Council of State*, appointed by the Crown, is composed of a vice-president and not more than 28 members. The monarch is president, but the day-to-day running of the Council is in the hands of the vice-president. The Council has to be consulted on all legislative matters. The Sovereign has the power to dissolve either Chambers, subject to the condition that new elections take place within 40 days, and the new Chamber be convoked within three months. Both the government and the Second Chamber may propose Bills; the First Chamber can only approve or reject them without inserting amendments. The meetings of both Chambers are public, although each of them may by a majority vote decide on a secret session. A Minister or Secretary of State cannot be a member of Parliament at the same time.

The Constitution can be revised only by a Bill declaring that there is reason for introducing such revision and containing the proposed alterations. The passing of this Bill is followed by a dissolution of both Chambers and a second confirmation by the new States-General by two-thirds of the votes. Unless it is expressly stated, all laws concern only the realm in Europe, and not the overseas part of the kingdom, Aruba and the Netherlands Antilles.

National Anthem. 'Wilhelmus van Nassaue'; words by Philip Marnix van St Aldegonde, tune anonymous.

RECENT ELECTIONS

Party affiliation in the First Chamber as elected on 25 May 2003: Christian Democrat Appeal (CDA), 23 seats; Labour Party (PvdA), 19; People's Party for Freedom and Democracy (VVD), 15; Green Left, 5; Socialist Party (SP), 4; Democrats '66 (D66), 3; Christian Union (CU), 2; Political Reformed Party (SGP), 2; List Pim Fortuyn party (LPF), 1; Independent Group in the Senate—Frisian National Party, 1.

Elections to the Second Chamber were held on 22 Jan. 2003. The CDA won 44 seats with 28·6% of votes cast (43 seats at the 2002 election); the PvdA, 42 seats and 27·3% (23 in 2002); the VVD, 28 seats and 17·9% (24); SP, 9 seats and 6·3% (9); the List Pim Fortuyn party (LPF), 8 seats and 5·7% (26); the Green Left, 8 seats and 5·1% (10); D66, 6 seats and 4·1% (7); the Christian Union (CU), 3 seats and 2·1% (4); SGP, 2 seats and 1·6% (2). Turn-out was 79·9%.

European Parliament. The Netherlands has 27 (31 in 1999) representatives. At the June 2004 elections turn-out was 39·1% (29·9% in 1999). The CDA won 7 seats with 24·4% of votes cast (political affiliation in European Parliament: European People's Party–European Democrats); the PvdA, 7 with 23·6% (Party of European Socialists); the VVD, 4 with 13·2% (Alliance of Liberals and Democrats for Europe); Green Left, 2 with 7·4% (Greens/European Free Alliance); Europa Transparant, 2 with 7·3% (Greens/European Free Alliance); the SP, 2 with 7·0% (European Unitary Left/Nordic Green Left); CU-SGP, 2 with 5·9% (Independence and Democracy Group); D66, 1 with 4·2% (Alliance of Liberals and Democrats for Europe).

CURRENT ADMINISTRATION

A coalition government of CDA, VVD and D66 was sworn in on 27 May 2003. In March 2005 it comprised:

Prime Minister: Jan Peter Balkenende; b. 1956 (CDA).

Deputy Prime Minister and Minister of Finance: Gerrit Zalm (VVD). *Deputy Prime Minister, Minister for Government Reform and Kingdom Relations:* Thom de Graaf (D66). *Foreign Affairs:* Bernard Bot (CDA). *Justice:* Piet Hein Donner (CDA). *Interior and Kingdom Relations:* Johan Remkes (VVD). *Education, Culture and Science:* Maria van der Hoeven (CDA). *Defence:* Henk Kamp (VVD). *Housing, Spatial Planning and the Environment:* Sybilla Dekker (VVD). *Transport, Public Works and Water Management:* Karla Peijs (CDA). *Economic Affairs:* Laurens Jan Brinkhorst (D66). *Agriculture, Nature Management and Fisheries:* Cees Veerman (CDA). *Health, Welfare and Sport:* Hans Hoogervorst (VVD). *Development Co-operation:* Agnes van Ardenne (CDA). *Immigration and Integration:* Rita Verdonk (VVD). *Social Affairs and Employment:* Aart Jan de Geus (CDA).

Office of the Prime Minister: http://www.minaz.nl

DEFENCE

Conscription ended on 30 Aug. 1996.

The total strength of the armed forces in 2002 was 49,580, including 4,155 women. In 2003 defence expenditure totalled US$8,256m. (US$509 per capita), representing 1·6% of GDP.

Army. The 1st Netherlands Army Corps is assigned to NATO. It consists of ten brigades and Corps troops.

Personnel in 2002 numbered 23,150, including 1,630 women. The National Territorial Command forces consist of territorial brigades, security forces, some logistical units and staffs. Some units in the Netherlands may be assigned to the UN as peacekeeping forces. The army is responsible for the training of these units.

There is a paramilitary Royal Military Constabulary, 3,300 strong. In addition there are 22,200 army reservists.

Navy. The principal headquarters and main base of the Royal Netherlands Navy is at Den Helder, with minor bases at Vlissingen (Flushing), Curaçao (Netherlands Antilles) and Oranjestad (Aruba). Command and control in home waters is exercised jointly with the Belgian Navy (submarines excepted).

The combatant fleet includes four diesel submarines, two destroyers and nine frigates. In 2002 personnel totalled 12,130 (1,150 women), including 950 in the Naval Air Service and 3,100 in the Royal Netherlands Marine Corps.

Air Force. The Royal Netherlands Air Force (RNLAF) had 8,850 personnel in 2002 (975 women). It has a first-line combat force of 143 combat aircraft and 30 attack helicopters. Equipment includes F-16A/Bs. All squadrons are operated by Tactical Air Command.

INTERNATIONAL RELATIONS

The Netherlands is a member of the UN, WTO, NATO, BIS, OECD, EU, Council of Europe, WEU, OSCE, CERN, Inter-American Development Bank, Asian

Development Bank, IOM and the Antarctic Treaty. The Netherlands is a signatory of the Schengen Accord which abolishes border controls between the Netherlands and Austria, Belgium, Denmark, Finland, France, Germany, Greece, Iceland, Italy, Luxembourg, Norway, Portugal, Spain and Sweden.

In 1899 the first International Peace Conference was held in The Hague with the aim of developing mechanisms of interventional law to contribute to disarmament, the prevention of war, and the peaceful settlement of disputes. In 1999 The Hague Appeal for Peace 1999 Conference brought together a wide variety of organizations, activists, citizens and world leaders to discuss new projects and initiatives for the promotion of peace in the 21st century from 11–16 May 1999.

The Hague is the seat of several international organizations, including the International Court of Justice.

The Netherlands gave US$4·1bn. in international aid in 2003, which at 0·81% of GNI made it the world's third most generous country as a percentage of its gross national income.

ECONOMY

Services accounted for 71·4% of GDP in 2002, industry 25·9% and agriculture 2·7%.

According to the anti-corruption organization *Transparency International*, the Netherlands ranked 10th in the world in a 2004 survey of the countries with the least corruption in business and government. It received 8·7 out of 10 in the annual index.

Overview. The economy is characterized by one of the highest levels of average income. The country's geographical position and the small market makes the economy open and outward looking. Multinationals enjoy a favourable tax regime. Government policy is based on free market principles including the introduction of market forces into the public utilities. The Netherlands is a leader in structural and regulatory reform in Europe, but the process has slowed. In 2002 the tax system was reformed to shift the burden from direct taxation to indirect and environmental taxes.

Currency. On 1 Jan. 1999 the euro (EUR) became the legal currency in the Netherlands; irrevocable conversion rate 2·20371 guilders to 1 euro. The euro, which consists of 100 cents, has been in circulation since 1 Jan. 2002. There are seven euro notes in different colours and sizes denominated in 500, 200, 100, 50, 20, 10 and 5 euros, and eight coins denominated in 2 and 1 euros, then 50, 20, 10, 5, 2 and 1 cents. On the introduction of the euro there was a 'dual circulation' period before the guilder ceased to be legal tender on 28 Jan. 2002. Euro banknotes in circulation on 1 Jan. 2002 had a total value of €29·7bn.

Gold reserves were 28·15m. troy oz in June 2002 and foreign exchange reserves US$5,290m. (US$31,060m. in 1995). Inflation was 4·2% in 2001, but has been falling since, to 3·3% in 2002, 2·1% in 2003 and 1·2% in 2004. Total money supply was €16,206m. in June 2002.

Budget. Central government revenues and expenditures in €1m.:

	2001	*2002*	*2003*
Revenue	117,914	181,622	184,341
Expenditure	176,548	185,842	195,666

Principal sources of revenue in 2003: social security contributions, €65·71bn.; taxes on goods and services, €52·04bn.; taxes on income, profits and capital gains, €44·61bn. Main items of expenditure by economic type in 2003: social benefits, €86·14bn.; grants, €58·52bn.; compensation of employees, €16·43bn.

In 2003 the budget deficit exceeded 3%, the target set by the European Stability and Growth Pact, reaching 3·2%.

As from Jan. 2001 VAT is 19·0% (reduced rate, 6·0%).

Performance. There was a recession in 2003, with the economy contracting by 0·9%, but a recovery followed in 2004 with real GDP growth of 1·3%. In 2003 total GDP was US$511·6bn.

The July 2004 *OECD Economic Survey* suggests that: 'The upswing in the world economy will help exports to grow for the first time after two years of stagnation. … All in all, the recovery is likely to be less strong than after previous recessions as a result of both the domestic factors hampering consumption and the loss of competitiveness.'

Banking and Finance. The central bank and bank of issue is the Netherlands Bank (*President*, Arnout Wellink), founded in 1814 and nationalized in 1948. Its Governor is appointed by the government for seven-year terms. The capital amounted to €500m. in 2002. In 2002 there were 18 leading commercial banks. The largest banks are ABN Amro Holding NV (assets in 2003 of US$707·8bn.) and ING Bank NV (assets in 2003 of US$684·0bn.). There is a stock exchange in Amsterdam; it is a component of Euronext, which was created in Sept. 2000 through the merger of the Amsterdam, Brussels and Paris bourses.

ENERGY AND NATURAL RESOURCES

Environment. Carbon dioxide emissions from the consumption and flaring of fossil fuels in 2002 were the equivalent of 15·9 tonnes per capita.

The Netherlands is one of the world leaders in recycling. In 1998, 46% of all household waste was recycled, including 84% of glass.

Electricity. Installed capacity was 21·0m. kW in 2000. Production of electrical energy in 2000 was 92·11bn. kWh (approximately 4% nuclear); consumption per capita was 6,999 kWh. There was one nuclear reactor in operation in 2003.

Oil and Gas. Production of natural gas in 2002, 59·9bn. cu. metres. Reserves in 2002 were 1,760bn. cu. metres. The Groningen gas field in the north of the country is the largest in continental Europe. In 2001 crude oil production was 1·37m. tonnes; reserves were 107m. bbls. in 2002.

Wind. There were 1,472 wind turbines and an installed capacity of 685 MW at the end of 2002.

Minerals. In 2001, 5·0m. tonnes of salt were produced. Aluminium production in 2001 totalled 294,000 tonnes.

Agriculture. The Netherlands is one of the world's largest exporters of agricultural produce. There were 101,500 farms in 2000. Agriculture accounted for 22·8% of exports and 15·1% of imports in 1998. The agricultural sector employs 2·7% of the workforce. In 2001 there were 905,000 ha of arable land and 33,000 ha of permanent crops. The total area of cultivated land in 2001 was 1,931,000 ha: grassland, 993,000 ha; arable crops, 798,000 ha; horticultural crops, 110,000 ha, of which 100,000 ha was in the open and 11,000 ha was under glass; fallow land, 30,000 ha. In 2002, 258,000 people were employed in agriculture (89,700 women).

The yield of the more important arable crops, in 1,000 tonnes, was as follows:

Crop	*2000*	*2001*	*2002*
Potatoes	8,127	7,016	–
Sugarbeets	6,728	5,947	–
Wheat	1,143	991	1,111
Sown onions	821	765	883
Barley	288	387	352

Other major fruit and vegetable production in 2000 included (in 1,000 tonnes): tomatoes, 600; apples, 575; cucumbers and gherkins, 465; cabbages, 284; carrots, 274; mushrooms, 263; chillies and green peppers, 250; pears, 125.

Cultivated areas of main flowers (2002) in 1,000 ha: tulips, 10·6; lilies, 5·1; daffodils, 2·0; gladioli, 1·5; hyacinths, 1·2.

Livestock, 2001 (in 1,000) included: 11,648 pigs; 3,858 cattle; 1,186 sheep; 121 horses and ponies; 102,503 turkeys and chickens.

Animal products in 2000 (in 1,000 tonnes) included: pork, bacon and ham, 1,643; beef and veal, 485; poultry, 713; milk, 10,800; cheese, 690; butter, 126; hens' eggs, 660.

Forestry. Forests covered 375,000 ha in 2000, or 11·1% of the land area. In 2001, 865,000 cu. metres of roundwood were cut.

Fisheries. Total catch in 2001 was 518,162 tonnes (chiefly scad, herring, mackerel and plaice), of which 515,962 tonnes were from marine waters. There were 932 fishing vessels in 2002.

INDUSTRY

The leading companies by market capitalization in the Netherlands, excluding banking and finance, in May 2003 were: Royal Dutch Petroleum Company (US$94·9bn.); Unilever NV (US$33·4bn.), a consumer goods firm; and Koninklijke Philips Electronics NV (US$25·7bn.). At 31 Dec. 1999 there were 6,572 enterprises in the manufacturing industry, of which 3,689 had 20–49 employees and 182 had 500 employees or more; total annual sales for 1997 were 151,229m. euros.

The three largest industrial sectors are chemicals, food processing and metal, mechanical and electrical engineering. The food products and beverages industry employed 168,000 people at 30 Sept. 2000 (annual sales for 2000 in €1m., 45,217); machinery and equipment, 101,000 (15,630); electrical machinery and apparatus, 96,000 (17,805); other fabricated metal products, 111,000 (13,831); publishing, printing and reproduction of recorded media, 93,000 (13,412); chemicals and chemical products, 75,000 (35,779); transport equipment, 59,000 (12,461); rubber and plastic products, 39,000 (5,869).

Labour. The total labour force in 2001 was 7,311,000 persons (2,990,000 women) of whom 248,000 (142,000) were unemployed, with 146,000 (69,000) registered unemployed. By education level, the 2001 labour force included (in 1,000): primary education, 633; junior general secondary, 496; pre-vocational secondary, 1,017; senior general secondary, 429; senior vocational secondary, 2,738; vocational colleges, 1,329; university, 664.

The unemployment rate was 4·7% in Dec. 2004, among the lowest rates in the EU. Although the Netherlands has a very low unemployment rate, for every 100 people below the age of 65 who are active in the labour market, 35 are not. In 1995 the average age for retirement among males was 58.

In 2000 the weekly working hours (excluding overtime) of employees were 35·6 for men and 25·5 for women. In 2000 full-time employees' working hours (excluding overtime) totalled 1,710; part-time 945; and flexible 849. Workers in the Netherlands put in among the shortest hours of any industrialized country. In 1996 only 11% of male workers and 4% of female workers worked more than 40 hours a week. In 2003 part-time work accounted for approximately 34% of all employment in the Netherlands—the highest percentage in any major industrialized country. 76·0% of part-time workers in 2003 were women. Average annual gross earnings of employees in 2000 were €26,500 for men and €14,900 for women. In 2001 gross hourly wage earnings by type of employment ranged from €26·42 in mining and quarrying, €22·01 in public utilities and €21·34 in public administration and social security to €10·64 in hotels and restaurants.

Trade Unions. Trade unions are grouped in three central federations: Christian National Trade Union Confederation (CNV), Trade Union Confederation for Middle and Higher Management (MHP) and General Netherlands Trade Union Confederation (FNV). Total membership was 1·92m. in 2001, approximately 25% of waged employees. In Nov. 1993 an agreement on wage restraint was concluded between the trade unions and the employers' federations, in return for an enhancement of the roles of works committees and professional training for employees.

INTERNATIONAL TRADE

On 5 Sept. 1944 and 14 March 1947 the Netherlands signed agreements with Belgium and Luxembourg for the establishment of a customs union. On 1 Jan. 1948 this union came into force and the existing customs tariffs of the Belgium–Luxembourg Economic Union and of the Netherlands were superseded by the joint Benelux Customs Union Tariff. It applied to imports into the three countries from outside sources, and exempted from customs duties all imports into each of the three countries from the other two.

Imports and Exports. Imports and exports for calendar years (in €1m.):

	1997	*1998*	*1999*	*2000*	*2001*
Imports	157,438	168,445	178,719	216,057	218,330
Exports	171,421	180,725	188,599	231,854	241,339

Value of trade with major partners (in €1m.):

Country	Imports 2001	Exports 2001	Imports (% change on 2000)	Exports (% change on 2000)
Belgium	20,177	28,502	+1	+4
France	12,617	24,944	+3	+2
Germany	40,253	61,697	+5	+3
Ireland	3,809	2,320	–3	+26
Italy	6,173	15,076	+1	+10
Japan	8,696	2,522	–6	+9
Norway	4,504	1,878	–7	+13
Spain	4,742	8,474	+1	+12
Sweden	4,379	4,953	–11	–7
Switzerland	2,379	3,911	–3	–2
UK	19,458	26,884	–6	+7
USA	21,525	10,559	–2	–3

The main imports in 2001 (in €1m.) included machines (including electrical machines), 68,415; chemical products, 24,785; food and live animals, 18,249; road vehicles, 15,046; crude petroleum, 12,245; clothing, 6,348; oil products, 5,367; iron and steel, 4,317; non-ferrous metals, 3,453; paper and paperboard, 3,096. Main exports included machines (including electrical machines), 70,316; chemical products, 36,915; food and live animals, 29,280; oil products, 14,381; raw materials (inedible) except fuels, 11,614; road vehicles, 11,002; fruit and vegetables, 7,633; natural and manufactured gas, 6,864; beverages and tobacco, 5,476; meat, 4,136; iron and steel, 3,879; clothing, 3,608.

COMMUNICATIONS

Roads. In 1999 the length of the Netherlands road network was 116,500 km, including 2,235 km of motorways. 90% of roads are paved. Number of private cars (2002), 6·71m.; trucks and vans, 0·88m.; motorcycles, 461,000. There were 987 fatalities as a result of road accidents in 2002, equivalent to 6·1 fatalities per 100,000 population. Only the UK had a lower death rate from road accidents in 2002.

Rail. All railways are run by the mixed company 'N.V. Nederlandse Spoorwegen'. Route length in 2001 was 2,809 km. Passengers carried (2001), 319m.; goods transported, 26·1m. tonnes. There is a metro (23 km) and tram/light rail network (153 km) in Amsterdam and in Rotterdam (28 km and 141 km). Tram/light rail networks operate in The Hague (122 km) and Utrecht (28 km).

Civil Aviation. There are international airports at Amsterdam (Schiphol), Rotterdam, Maastricht and Eindhoven. The Royal Dutch Airlines (KLM) was founded on 7 Oct. 1919. In Oct. 2003 it merged with Air France to form Air France-KLM, in which the French state owns a 44·0% stake. In 1999 KLM flew 357·9m. km, carrying 15,568,200 passengers (15,437,400 on international flights). Services were provided in 2003 by around 80 foreign airlines. In 2001 Amsterdam handled 39,309,000 passengers (39,100,000 on international flights in 2000 out of a total 39,271,000) and 1,183,000 tonnes of freight. Rotterdam is the second busiest airport, handling 748,000 passengers in 2001, followed by Maastricht, with 360,000 in 2001.

Sea-going Shipping. Survey of the Netherlands mercantile marine as at 1 Jan. (capacity in 1,000 GRT):

Ships under Netherlands flag	*2001 Number*	*2001 Capacity*	*2002 Number*	*2002 Capacity*
Passenger ships	17	644	19	734
Freighters (100 GRT and over)	514	3,225	511	3,444
Tankers	61	517	57	477
	592	4,386	587	4,655

In 2001, 42,372 sea-going ships (including 7,418 Dutch-registered ships) of 605·24m. gross tons entered Netherlands ports.

Total goods traffic by sea-going ships in 2001 (with 2000 figures in brackets), in 1m. tonnes, amounted to 326 (325) unloaded and 98 (99) loaded; total seaborne goods traffic in 2001 (and 2000) at Rotterdam was 313·4 (319·6) and at Amsterdam 48·1 (42·1).

The number of containers (including flats) at Dutch ports in 2001 (and 2000) was: unloaded from ships, 1,982,000 (2,001,000), and 1,893,000 (2,005,000) loaded into ships.

Inland Shipping. The total length of navigable rivers and canals is 5,046 km, of which 2,398 km is for ships with a capacity of 1,000 and more tonnes. On 1 Jan. 2002 the inland fleet used for transport (with carrying capacity in 1,000 tonnes) was composed as follows:

	Number	*Capacity*
Self-propelled barges	3,636	3,879
Dumb barges	549	275
Pushed barges	666	1,347
	4,851	5,501

In 2001, 241·3m. tonnes of goods were transported on rivers and canals, of which 137·7m. tonnes was by international shipping. Goods transport on the Rhine across the Dutch–German frontier near Lobith amounted to 163·3m. tonnes.

Telecommunications. The Netherlands had 22,100,000 telephone subscribers in 2002 (equivalent to 1,364·6 per 1,000 population), and there were 7,557,000 PCs (466·6 per 1,000 persons). Mobile phone subscribers numbered 12,060,000 in 2002 and there were 600,000 fax machines in 1997. There were 9·73m. Internet users in Sept. 2002.

Postal Services. In 1998 there were 2,387 post offices, equivalent to one for every 6,580 persons.

SOCIAL INSTITUTIONS

Justice. Justice is administered by the High Court (Court of Cassation), by five courts of justice (Courts of Appeal), by 19 district courts and by 61 cantonal courts. The Cantonal Court, which deals with minor offences, comprises a single judge; more serious cases are tried by the district courts, comprising as a rule three judges (in some cases one judge is sufficient); the courts of appeal are constituted of three and the High Court of five judges. All judges are appointed for life by the Sovereign (the judges of the High Court from a list prepared by the Second Chamber of the States-General). They can be removed only by a decision of the High Court.

At the district court the juvenile judge is specially appointed to try children's civil cases and at the same time charged with administration of justice for criminal actions committed by young persons between 12 and 18 years old, unless imprisonment of more than six months ought to be inflicted; such cases are tried by three judges.

The population in penal institutions at 30 Sept. 2000 was 11,759, of which 5,223 were convicted. The total number of inmates during the year was 43,210 (40,228 men). 1,357,600 crimes were reported in 2001.

Police. The police force is divided into 25 regions. There is also a National Police Service which includes the Central Criminal Investigation Office, which deals with serious crimes throughout the country, and the International Criminal Investigation Office, which informs foreign countries of international crimes.

Religion. Entire liberty of conscience is granted to the members of all denominations. The royal family belong to the Dutch Reformed Church.

According to estimates of 2001, the population aged 18 years and over was: Roman Catholics, 31%; Dutch Reformed Church, 14%; Calvinist, 7%; other creeds, 9%; no religion, 40%. The government of the Reformed Church is Presbyterian. On 1 July 1992 the Dutch Reformed Church had 1 synod, 9 provincial districts, 75 classes, about 160 districts and about 2,000 parishes. Their clergy numbered 1,735. The Roman Catholic Church had, Jan. 1992, 1 archbishop (of Utrecht), 6 bishops, 4 assistant bishops and about 1,750 parishes and rectorships. In Sept. 2003 there were two Roman Catholic cardinals. The Old Catholics had (1 July 1992) 1 archbishop (Utrecht), 1 bishop and 28 parishes. The Jews had, in 1992, 40 communities. At 1 Jan. 2000 there were an estimated 735,600 Muslims (4·6% of the population) and 86,100 Hindus (0·5%).

Education. Statistics for the scholastic year 2001–02:

	Schools	*Full-time pupils/students (in 1,000) Total*
Primary education	7,036	1,552
Special primary education	361	52
Expertise centres	331	48
Secondary education	795	904
Senior vocational secondary education	70	271
Apprenticeship training	67	162
Vocational colleges	64	258
University education	13	159

Academic Year 2001–02

	Full-time students Total	*% female*
University education:		
Agriculture	3,793	49
Behaviour and Social Sciences	34,191	69
Economics	28,414	29
Education	632	54
Engineering	24,888	18
Health	20,807	62
Language and Culture	23,434	64
Law	25,125	55
Science	12,455	32
Other	564	76
Total	174,303	49

In 2001 there were 123,000 participants in adult basic education; and, in 2002, 19,400 Open University students.

In 1999–2000 total expenditure on education came to 4·8% of GNP and 10·4% of total government spending. The adult literacy rate is at least 99%.

Health. On 1 Jan. 2001 there were 7,763 general practitioners, 12,594 physiotherapists, 7,513 dentists, 3,069 pharmacists and 1,627 midwives; on 1 Jan. 2000, a total of 14,712 specialists. There were 131 hospitals and 55,438 licensed hospital beds (excluding mental hospitals) at 1 Jan. 2000. The 1919 Opium Act (amended in 1928 and 1976) regulates the production and consumption of 'psychoactive' drugs. Personal use of cannabis is effectively decriminalized and the sale of soft drugs through 'coffee shops' is not prosecuted provided certain conditions are met. Euthanasia became legal when the First Chamber (the Senate) gave its formal approval on 10 April 2001 by 46 votes to 28. The Second Chamber had voted to make it legal by 104 votes to 40 in Nov. 2000. The law came into effect on 1 April 2002. During 2000 euthanasia organizations recorded 2,123 instances of doctors helping patients to die. The Netherlands was the first country to legalize euthanasia. In 2002 the Netherlands spent 9·1% of its GDP on health.

Welfare. The General Old Age Pension Act (AOW) entitles everyone to draw an old age pension from the age of 65. At 31 Dec. 2001 there were 2,365,600 persons entitled to receive an old age pension, and 163,100 a pension under the Surviving Relatives Insurance; 1,864,300 parents were receiving benefits under the General Family Allowances Act. In 2001 there were 981,300 persons claiming labour disablement benefits and 166,000 persons claiming benefits under the Unemployment Act.

CULTURE

World Heritage Sites. The Kingdom of the Netherlands has seven sites on the UNESCO World Heritage list: Schokland and its surroundings (inscribed on the list in 1995); the defence line at Amsterdam (1996); the mill network at Kinderdijk-Elshout (1997); the historic area of Willemstad, the inner city and harbour in Curaçao (Netherlands Antilles) (1997); the D. F. Wouda steam pumping station

(1998); Droogmakerij de Beemster (Beemster Polder) (1999); and the Rietveld Schröder house (2000).

Broadcasting. Public broadcasting programmes are provided by broadcasting associations representing clearly identifiable social or religious ideals or groupings. The six associations work together in the Netherlands Broadcasting Corporation, *Nederlandse Omroepprogramma Stichting* (NOS). There are three national television channels (colour by PAL) and five radio stations. In addition, there are regional radio stations in every province, a limited number of regional television stations and 400 local radio stations. Commercial broadcasting was introduced in 1992. Dutch-language commercial companies include RTL 4 and 5 which broadcast in Dutch from Luxembourg, Veronica, SBS6, TV10 and the Music Factory. Public broadcasting revenue is obtained from radio and television licences and from advertising.

There were 8·9m. TV receivers in 2001 and 15·6m. radio receivers in 2000. There were 6·32m. cable TV subscribers in 2001.

Cinema. In 2001 there were 558 cinemas and film houses with a seating capacity of 279,000. Total attendance was 23·72m.

Press. In 1996 there were 38 daily newspapers with a combined circulation of 4·8m., equivalent to 306 per 1,000 inhabitants. The most widely read daily is *De Telegraaf*, with average daily sales of 808,000 copies (2003).

Tourism. Tourism is a major sector of the economy, earning US$6,951m. in revenue in 2000. There were 10,200,000 foreign visitors in that year.

Festivals. Floriade, a world-famous horticultural show, takes place every ten years and is the largest Dutch attraction, being attended by 2·3m. people in 2002. The Maastricht Carnival in April attracts many visitors. The Flower Parade from Noordwijk to Haarlem occurs in late April. Koninginnedag on 30 April is a nationwide celebration of Queen Beatrix's birthday. The Oosterparkfestival, a cultural celebration of that district of Amsterdam, runs for three days in the first week of May. Liberation Day is celebrated every five years on 5 May, with the next occurrence being in 2010. An international music festival, the Holland Festival, is held in Amsterdam throughout June each year and the Early Music Festival is held in Utrecht. The North Sea Jazz Festival, the largest in Europe, takes place in The Hague. Each year the most important Dutch and Flemish theatre productions of the previous season are performed at the Theatre Festival in Amsterdam and Antwerp (Belgium). The Holland Dance Festival is held every other year in The Hague and the Springdance Festival in Utrecht annually. Film festivals include the Rotterdam Film Festival in Feb., the World Wide Video Festival in April, the Dutch Film Festival in Sept. and the International Documentary Film Festival of Amsterdam in Dec.

Libraries. In 1997 there were 1,130 public libraries, 4 National libraries and 856 Higher Education libraries. There were 69,797,000 visits to libraries in 1997.

Theatre and Opera. In 1997–98 there were 56,670 music and theatre performances (including rock and pop concerts) of which 14,530 were plays, 8,240 concerts, 2,390 opera and operetta and 2,900 ballet and dance, with a total attendance of 15,607,000 (excluding rock and pop concerts).

Museums and Galleries. In 1999 there were 902 museums open to the public, to which visits totalled 20,679,000. The Rijksmuseum and Vincent Van Gogh Museums in Amsterdam and the Kröller-Müller Museum in Otterlo attract the most visitors.

DIPLOMATIC REPRESENTATIVES

Of the Netherlands in the United Kingdom (38 Hyde Park Gate, London, SW7 5DP)
Ambassador: Count Jan de Marchant et d'Ansembourg.

Of the United Kingdom in the Netherlands (Lange Voorhout 10, 2514 ED The Hague)
Ambassador: Sir Colin Budd, KCMG.

Of the Netherlands in the USA (4200 Linnean Ave., NW, Washington, D.C., 20008)
Ambassador: Boudewijn van Eenennaam.

Of the USA in the Netherlands (Lange Voorhout 102, The Hague)
Ambassador: Clifford M. Sobel.

Of the Netherlands to the United Nations
Ambassador: Dirk Jan van der Berg.

FURTHER READING

Centraal Bureau voor de Statistiek. *Statistical Yearbook of the Netherlands.* From 1923/24.—*Statistisch Jaarboek.* From 1899/1924.—*CBS Select (Statistical Essays).* From 1980.—*Statistisch Bulletin.* From 1945; weekly.—*Maandschrift.* From 1944; monthly bulletin.—*90 Jaren Statistiek in Tijdreeksen* (historical series of the Netherlands 1899–1989)
Nationale Rekeningen (National Accounts). From 1948–50.—*Statistische onderzoekingen.* From 1977.—*Regionaal Statistisch Zakboek* (Regional Pocket Yearbook). From 1972
Staatsalmanak voor het Koninkrijk der Nederlanden. Annual. The Hague, from 1814
Staatsblad van het Koninkrijk der Nederlanden. The Hague, from 1814
Staatscourant (State Gazette). The Hague, from 1813
Andeweg, Rudy B. and Irwin, Galen A., *Governance and Politics of the Netherlands.* Palgrave Macmillan, Basingstoke, 2005
Cox, R. H., *The Development of the Dutch Welfare State: from Workers' Insurance to Universal Entitlement.* Pittsburgh Univ. Press, 1994
Gladdish, K., *Governing from the Centre: Politics and Policy-Making in the Netherlands.* London, 1991
King, P. K. and Wintle, M., *The Netherlands.* [Bibliography] ABC-Clio, Oxford and Santa Barbara (CA), 1988
van Os, Andre, *Amsterdam.* [Bibliography] ABC-Clio, Oxford and Santa Barbara (CA), 1997

National library: De Koninklijke Bibliotheek, Prinz Willem Alexanderhof 5, The Hague.
National statistical office: Centraal Bureau voor de Statistiek, Netherlands Central Bureau of Statistics, POB 4000, 2270 JM Voorburg.
Statistics Netherlands Website: http://www.cbs.nl

ARUBA

KEY HISTORICAL EVENTS

Discovered by Alonzo de Ojeda in 1499, the island of Aruba was claimed for Spain but not settled. It was acquired by the Dutch in 1634, but apart from garrisons, was left to the indigenous Caiquetious (Arawak) Indians until the 19th century. From 1828 it formed part of the Dutch West Indies and, from 1845, part of the Netherlands Antilles with which, on 29 Dec. 1954, it achieved internal self government. Following a referendum in March 1977, the Dutch government announced on 28 Oct. 1981 that Aruba would proceed to independence separately from the other islands. Aruba was constitutionally separated from the Netherlands Antilles from 1 Jan. 1986, and full independence promised by the Netherlands after a ten-year period. However, an agreement with the Netherlands government in June 1990 deletes, at Aruba's request, references to eventual independence.

TERRITORY AND POPULATION

The island, which lies in the southern Caribbean 32 km north of the Venezuelan coast and 68 km west of Curaçao, has an area of 180 sq. km (75 sq. miles) and a population in Dec. 2000 of 91,065; density 506 inhabitants per sq. km. The chief towns are Oranjestad, the capital (1998 population, 29,000) and San Nicolas. Dutch is the official language, but the language usually spoken is Papiamento, a creole language. Over half the population is of Indian stock, with the balance of Dutch, Spanish and mestizo origin.

SOCIAL STATISTICS

Annual growth rate, 1999, 1·1%. Life expectancy in 2000 was 70 years for males and 76 years for females. Birth rate per 1,000 population (1999), 13·9; death rate, 6·3; infant mortality, 7·2.

CLIMATE

Aruba has a tropical marine climate, with a brief rainy season from Oct. to Dec. Oranjestad (1998), Jan. 28°C (82°F), July 29·4°C (85°F). The annual rainfall in 2000 was 551 mm.

CONSTITUTION AND GOVERNMENT

Under the separate constitution inaugurated on 1 Jan. 1986, Aruba is an autonomous part of the Kingdom of the Netherlands with its own legislature, government, judiciary, civil service and police force. The Netherlands is represented by a Governor appointed by the monarch. The unicameral legislature *(Staten)* consists of 21 members elected for a four-year term of office.

RECENT ELECTIONS

Elections were held on 28 Sept. 2001. The Movimento Electoral di Pueblo (MEP) won with 12 out of 21 seats (52·4% of the vote), against 6 seats (26·7%) for prime minister Henny Eman's Arubaanse Volkspartij (AVP), 2 seats (9·6%) for the Partido Patriótico Arubiano (PPA) and 1 seat (5·7%) for the Organización Liberal Arubianco (OLA). Turn-out was 86·5%. The result gave Aruba its first absolute majority in an election.

CURRENT ADMINISTRATION

Governor: Fredis Refunjol; b. 1950 (took office on 11 May 2004).

In March 2005 the government comprised:

Prime Minister and Minister of General Affairs and Equipment: Nelson O. Oduber; b. 1947 (MEP; sworn in for second term in office 30 Oct. 2001, having previously served 1989–1994).

Deputy Prime Minister, Minister of Social Affairs and Infrastructure: Marisol Tromp. *Education:* Fredis Refunjol. *Finance and Economic Affairs:* Nilo Swaen. *Justice:* Hyacintho Croes. *Health:* Candelario Wever. *Sports, Culture, and Labour:* Ramon Lee. *Tourism and Transportation:* Edison Briesen.

Government Website: http://www.aruba.com

ECONOMY

Currency. Since 1 Jan. 1986 the currency has been the *Aruban florin*, at par with the Netherlands Antilles guilder. Total money supply in 2001 was 1,841m. Aflorins. There were 126m. Aflorins in circulation in 2001. Inflation was 4·2% in 2002. Foreign exchange reserves in June 2002 were US$311m.; gold reserves were 100,000 troy oz. Net foreign assets (including gold and revaluation of gold) in 2000 were 556·3m. Aflorins.

Budget. The 2001 budget totalled 731·8m. Aflorins revenue and grants. Tax revenue was 606·3m. Aflorins in 2001.

Performance. There was a recession in 2002, with negative growth of 3·8%. GDP per capita was 35,966 Aflorins in 2002.

Banking and Finance. There were six domestic and Dutch banks, and one foreign bank, in 2000. There is a special tax regime for offshore banks. The *President* of the Central Bank of Aruba is Robert Henriquez.

ENERGY AND NATURAL RESOURCES

Electricity. In 2001 consumption of electricity was 673,611 MWh.

Fisheries. In 2001 the catch totalled 163 tonnes.

INDUSTRY

The government has established six industrial sites at Oranjestad harbour. The quantity of oil refined in 2001 was 64m. bbls.

Labour. The working age population (15–64 yrs) grew between 1991–2000 from 45,563 to 62,637 persons. The economically active population in 2000 numbered 44,384 persons of which 41,286 were employed and 3,098 unemployed. The employment rate for women grew from 52·8% to 59·2% during the 1990s.

Trade Unions. There are four trade unions: COC, Chambers of Commerce; ATIA, Aruba Trade and Industrial Association; ORMA, Oranjestad Retail and Merchants Association; SNBA, San Nicolas Business Association.

EXTERNAL ECONOMIC RELATIONS

There are two Free Zones at Oranjestad.

Imports and Exports. 2002: exports, US$1,516m.; imports, US$2,050m. Leading import suppliers are USA, Netherlands, Venezuela and Netherlands Antilles. Leading export destinations are USA, Colombia, Netherlands and Netherlands Antilles.

COMMUNICATIONS

Roads. In 1984 there were 380 km of surfaced highways. In 2000 there were 39,995 passenger cars and 5,443 commercial vehicles. There were 439 passenger cars per 1,000 inhabitants.

Civil Aviation. There is an international airport (Aeropuerto Internacional Reina Beatrix). There were flights in 2003 to Amsterdam, Atlanta, Barranquilla, Bogotá, Bonaire, Boston, Caracas, Charlotte, Chicago, Curaçao, Harrisburg, Hartford, Las Piedras, Manchester, Maracaibo, Miami, Minneapolis, New York, Paramaribo, Philadelphia, Pittsburgh, Raleigh/Durham, San Juan, Santo Domingo and Washington, D.C. In Dec. 2003 a new airline, Royal Aruban Airlines was launched, with flights to Curaçao and Fort Lauderdale. In 2002 Aruba handled 13,761 commercial landings and 3,113 non-commercial landings. In total 759,285 passengers arrived by air, 751,106 departed and 153,663 were in transit.

Shipping. Oranjestad has a container terminal and cruise ship port. The port at Barcadera services the offshore and energy sector and a deep-water port at San Nicolas services the oil refinery.

Telecommunications. Aruba had 90,100 telephone subscribers in 2001, or 850·3 per 1,000 inhabitants. There were 10,500 mobile phone subscribers in 1999 and 5,736 Internet subscribers.

Postal Services. In 1998 there were four post offices.

SOCIAL INSTITUTIONS

Justice. There is a Common Court of Justice with the Netherlands Antilles. Final Appeal is to the Supreme Court in the Netherlands. The population in penal institutions in Nov. 1998 was 204 (equivalent to 225 per 100,000 population).

Religion. In 2000, 86·2% of the population were Roman Catholic.

Education. In 2000 there were 28 pre-primary, 40 primary, 15 secondary and four middle-level schools, also a teacher training college and law school. Literacy rate (2000 census), 97·3%. The share of education in the 2000–01 budget was 16·0%.

Health. In 2000 there were 123 doctors, 29 dentists, 18 pharmacists and one hospital with 305 beds.

Welfare. All citizens are entitled to an old age pension at the age of 60.

CULTURE

Broadcasting. In 2000 there were 18 radio stations and three commercial television stations (colour by NTSC). In 2000 there were 51,000 radio and 20,000 TV sets.

Press. In 1997 there were eight daily newspapers with a combined circulation of 52,000. At more than 700 newspapers per 1,000 inhabitants, Aruba has one of the highest rates of circulation in the world.

Tourism. In 2000 there were 721,224 tourists and 490,148 cruise-ship visitors. In 2000 tourist receipts were 1,498·7m. Aflorins. The majority of tourists are from the USA (63·5%), Venezuela (15·5%), Colombia (4·4%) and the Netherlands (4·2%).

FURTHER READING

Schoenhals, K., *Netherlands Antilles and Aruba.* [Bibliography] ABC-Clio, Oxford and Santa Barbara (CA), 1993
Central Bureau of Statistics Website: http://www.aruba.com/extlinks/govs/cbstats.html

THE NETHERLANDS ANTILLES

De Nederlandse Antillen

KEY HISTORICAL EVENTS

With Aruba, the islands formed part of the Dutch West Indies from 1828, and the Netherlands Antilles from 1845, with internal self-government being granted on 29 Dec. 1954.

TERRITORY AND POPULATION

The Netherlands Antilles comprise two groups of islands, the Leeward group (Curaçao and Bonaire) being situated 100 km north of the Venezuelan coast and the

Windward group (Saba, Sint Eustatius and the southern portion of Sint Maarten) situated 800 km away to the northeast, at the northern end of the Lesser Antilles. The total area is 800 sq. km (308 sq. miles) and the population at the 2001 census was 175,653. The UN gives a projected population for 2010 of 233,000. An estimated 69·2% of the population were urban in 1995. Willemstad is the capital and had a 1999 population of 123,000.

The areas, populations and chief towns of the islands are:

Island	*Sq. km*	*2001 population*	*Chief town*
Bonaire	288	10,791	Kralendijk
Curaçao	444	130,627	Willemstad
Saba	13	1,349	The Bottom
Sint Eustatius	21	2,292	Oranjestad
Sint Maarten[1]	43	30,594	Philipsburg

[1]The northern portion (St Martin) belongs to France.

Dutch is the official language, but the languages usually spoken are Papiamento (derived from Dutch, Spanish and Portuguese) on Curaçao and Bonaire, and English in the Windward Islands.

SOCIAL STATISTICS

1999, live births, 2,803; deaths, 1,321; marriages, 956; divorces, 532. Annual growth rate, 1995–99, 1·3%. Expectation of life at birth, 1990–95, was 72·4 years for males and 78·5 for females. Infant mortality, 1990–95, 13 per 1,000 live births; fertility rate, 2·2 births per woman.

CLIMATE

All the islands have a tropical marine climate, with very little difference in temperatures over the year. There is a short rainy season from Oct. to Jan. Willemstad, Feb. 27·7°C, Aug. 29°C. Annual rainfall 499 mm.

CONSTITUTION AND GOVERNMENT

On 29 Dec. 1954 the Netherlands Antilles became an integral part of the Kingdom of the Netherlands but are fully autonomous in internal affairs, and constitutionally equal with the Netherlands and Aruba. The Sovereign of the Kingdom of the Netherlands is Head of State and Government, and is represented by a Governor.

The executive power in internal affairs rests with the Governor and the Council of Ministers. The Ministers are responsible to a unicameral legislature *(States)* consisting of 22 members, elected for a four-year term in three multi-seat constituencies and two single-seat constituencies. The executive power in external affairs is vested in the Council of Ministers of the Kingdom, in which the Antilles is represented by a Minister Plenipotentiary with full voting powers.

At a referendum in Curaçao on 19 Nov. 1993, 73% of votes cast favoured maintaining the status quo of Curaçao as part of the Netherlands Antilles. At a referendum in Oct. 1994 Sint Maarten, Sint Eustatius and Saba voted to remain part of the Netherlands Antilles.

RECENT ELECTIONS

In elections held on 18 Jan. 2002 the Workers' Liberation Front 30th May (FOL) won 5 seats (with 23·0% of votes cast), the Party for the Restructured Antilles (PAR) 4 (20·6%), the National People's Party 3 (13·4%), the Labour Party People's Crusade 2 (12·1%), the Democratic Party Sint Maarten 2, the Bonaire Patriotic Union 2, the Democratic Party 2, with 1 seat each going to four other parties.

CURRENT ADMINISTRATION

Governor: Frits Goedgedrag; b. 1951 (took office on 1 July 2002).

In March 2005 the cabinet was composed as follows:

Prime Minister, and Minister of Foreign Affairs and General Affairs: Etienne Ys; b. 1962 (took office on 3 June 2004; previously held office from June 2002–July 2003).

Deputy Prime Minister, and Minister of Economic Affairs and Labour: Errol Cova. *Education and Cultural Affairs:* Martiza Silberie. *Justice:* Norberto Vieira Ribeiro. *Finance:* Ersilla de Lannooy. *Telecommunications and Transport:* Omayra

Leeflang. *Health and Social Affairs:* Joan Theodora-Brewster. *Constitutional and Interior Affairs:* Richard Gibson. *Minister Plenipotentiary to the Hague:* Paul Comenencia.

ECONOMY

Currency. The unit of currency is the *Netherlands Antilles guilder, gulden* (ANG) or *florin* (NAfl.) divided into 100 *cents.* The NA guilder has been pegged to the US dollar at US$1 = 1·79 NA guilder since 12 Dec. 1971. Gold reserves were 548,000 troy oz in June 2000 and foreign exchange reserves US$373m. in May 2002. In 2002 inflation was 0·5%. Total money supply in April 2002 was 1,233m. NA guilders.

Budget. Central government revenues for 2002 were 616·5m. NA guilders and expenditures 768·9m. NA guilders.

Performance. After a recession in 1999 and 2000 real GDP growth was 0·6% in 2001 and 0·2% in 2002.

Banking and Finance. At 31 Dec. 1994 the Bank of Netherlands Antilles (*President,* Emsley Tromp) had total assets and liabilities of 514·4m. NA guilders; commercial banks, 3,913m. NA guilders.

ENERGY AND NATURAL RESOURCES

Environment. Carbon dioxide emissions from the consumption and flaring of fossil fuels were the equivalent of 52·9 tonnes per capita in 2002.

Electricity. Installed capacity in 2000 was 0·2m. kW. Production in 2000 totalled 1·12bn. kWh and consumption per capita was 5,209 kWh.

Oil and Gas. The economy was formerly based largely on oil refining at the Shell refinery on Curaçao, but following an announcement by Shell that closure was imminent, this was sold to the Netherlands Antilles government in Sept. 1985, and leased to Petróleos de Venezuela to operate on a reduced scale. The refinery has a capacity of 470,000 bbls. a day, but output has not reached this for several years.

Minerals. Calcium carbonate (limestone) has been mined since 1980; production (1991), 0·32m. tonnes. Production of limestone, 1990 (estimate), 0·36m. tonnes; salt, 1996, 0·36m. tonnes.

Agriculture. Livestock (2002): cattle, 1,000; goats, 13,000; pigs, 2,000; sheep, 8,000; asses, 3,000.

Fisheries. Total catch estimate (2001), approximately 950 tonnes.

INDUSTRY

Curaçao has an oil refinery and a large ship-repair dry docks. Bonaire has a textile factory and a modern equipped salt plant. Sint Maarten's industrial activities are primarily based on a rum factory and a fishing factory.

Labour. In 1997 the economically active population numbered 56,200; of which 18,400 were employed in community and social services, 14,600 in trade, 7,300 in financial services and 5,700 in manufacturing. In 1992 the unemployment rate was 15·3% (Curaçao, 1995: 62,236; unemployment rate 13·1%).

EXTERNAL ECONOMIC RELATIONS

Imports and Exports. In 2002 imports totalled US$1,602·7m. and exports US$589·3m. In 1998 crude petroleum made up 54% of imports, aluminium 6% and refined petroleum products 5%. 86% of exports in 1998 was refined petroleum products. Principal import suppliers in 2000: USA, 25·8%; Mexico, 20·7%; Gabon, 6·6%; Italy, 5·8%. Main export markets, 2000: USA, 35·9%; Guatemala, 9·4%; Venezuela, 8·7%; France, 5·4%. There is a Free Zone on Curaçao.

COMMUNICATIONS

Roads. In 1989 the Netherlands Antilles had 845 km of surfaced highway distributed as follows: Curaçao, 590; Bonaire, 226; Sint Maarten, 19. Number of motor vehicles registered in 1994, 166,392.

Civil Aviation. There are international airports on Curaçao (Curaçao-Hato Airport), Bonaire (Flamingo Airport) and Sint Maarten (Princess Juliana Airport). Dutch Caribbean Airways operates on domestic routes, and in 2003 also served Amsterdam, Caracas, Coro, Las Piedras, Maracaibo, Miami, Paramaribo, Port-au-Prince, Port-of-Spain, Santo Domingo and Valencia (Venezuela). In 2000 Sint Maarten handled 1,266,000 passengers and Curaçao 911,000; in 1995 Bonaire handled 286,117, Sint Eustatius 49,369 and Saba (1994) 45,457.

Shipping. 5,152 ships (totalling 31,785,000 GRT) entered the port of Curaçao in 1995; 1,011 ships (15,911,000 GRT) entered the port of Bonaire; 1,400 ships entered the port of Sint Maarten. In 1995 Curaçao handled 171,854 passengers; in 1994 Bonaire handled 12,736 and Sint Maarten 718,550. Merchant shipping in 2002 totalled 1,391,000 GRT.

Telecommunications. Number of telephone main lines in 2000 was 80,000 (371·6 per 1,000 population). The number of Internet users in Dec. 1999 was 2,000. There were 13,000 mobile phone subscribers in 1996.

SOCIAL INSTITUTIONS

Justice. There is a Court of First Instance, which sits in each island, and a Court of Appeal in Willemstad. The population in penal institutions in Nov. 1998 was 780 (365 per 100,000 population).

Religion. In 2001 about 70% of the population were Roman Catholics and 10% were Protestants (Sint Maarten and Sint Eustatius being primarily Protestant).

Education. In 2000–01 there were 22,140 pupils in primary schools, 2,337 pupils in special schools, 12,174 pupils in general secondary schools, 3,710 pupils in junior and senior secondary vocational schools, and 928 students in vocational colleges and universities.

In 2000–01 total expenditure on education came to 13·6% of total government spending.

Health. In 1998 there were 222 hospitals with a provision of 53 beds per 10,000 inhabitants. There were 339 physicians, 62 dentists, 1,198 nurses, 42 pharmacists and 11 midwives in 1998.

CULTURE

World Heritage Sites. The Netherlands Antilles has one site on the UNESCO World Heritage List: the Historic Area of Willemstad, Inner City and Harbour (inscribed on the list in 1997), established on the island of Curaçao in 1634 by Dutch traders.

Broadcasting. In 1995 there were 32 radio transmitters (8 on Bonaire, 17 on Curaçao, 2 on Saba, 1 on Sint Eustatius and 4 on Sint Maarten) and each island had one cable television station, broadcasting in Papiamento, Dutch, English and Spanish. Broadcasting is administered by Landsradio, Telecommunication Administration and Tele Curaçao. In 1997 there were 217,000 radio and 69,000 TV sets (colour by NTSC) in use. In addition, Radio Nederland and Trans World Radio have powerful relay stations operating on medium- and short-waves from Bonaire.

Press. In 1996 there were six daily newspapers (combined circulation of 70,000).

Tourism. In 1998 there were 751,000 tourists and 1,132,000 cruise passengers.

DIPLOMATIC REPRESENTATIVES

US Consul-General: Deborah A. Bolton (J. B. Gorsiraweg 1, Curaçao).

FURTHER READING

Central Bureau of Statistics. *Statistical Yearbook of the Netherlands Antilles*

Bank of the Netherlands Antilles. *Annual Report.*

Schoenhals, K., *Netherlands Antilles and Aruba.* [Bibliography] ABC-Clio, Oxford and Santa Barbara (CA), 1993

Statistical office: Central Bureau of Statistics, Fort Amsterdam Z/N, Curaçao
Website: http://www.central-bureau-of-statistics.an

NEW ZEALAND

Capital: Wellington
Population projection, 2010: 4·06m.
GDP per capita, 2002: (PPP$) 21,740
HDI/world rank: 0·926/18

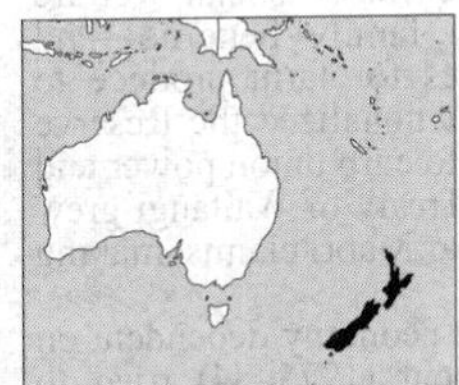

KEY HISTORICAL EVENTS

The earliest settlers of New Zealand are thought to have originated from eastern Polynesia, around the turn of the first millennium. By Capt. James Cook's arrival in 1769, settlements existed throughout the North Island, with smaller settlements in the South Island. The first recorded European contact was Dutch explorer Abel Tasman in 1642. A Dutch cartographer gave the name New Zealand to compliment the larger New Holland (Australia).

Contact between Maori and Europeans, or *Pakeha*, opened the way for sealing and whaling stations. Coastal trade grew in the early 19th century and trade routes were established between Maori and New South Wales as early as the 1820s. With greater contact, both Maori and Pakeha saw the need to regulate Pakeha settlement. In 1833 the Colonial Office in London appointed a Resident, James Busby, who prompted thirty-five chiefs to sign a Declaration of Independence as the 'United Tribes of New Zealand'. The Treaty of Waitangi formalized relations between Maori and Pakeha in 1840. In principle—or at least in the Maori text—this treaty guaranteed Maori chieftainship, or *rangatiratanga*, while granting governorship, or *kawanatanga*, to Queen Victoria. In practice sovereignty was transferred to the Crown.

Established in 1840, Auckland was chosen as the colony's capital by its first governor, Capt. William Hobson. Planned migration occurred through the New Zealand Company with settlements at Wellington and Wanganui (1840), New Plymouth (1841) and Nelson (1842). Scottish immigrants founded Dunedin (1848) and Edward Gibbon Wakefield made plans for a model English settlement at Christchurch (1851). In 1852 representative government was established with a constitution providing for a House of Representatives and Legislative Council. The governor retained the right of veto and was responsible for 'Native' policy. The Legislative Council was disbanded in 1950 leaving New Zealand with a unicameral parliament.

War broke out in the 1840s and 1860s in the central and western North Island between settlers, represented by the British army, and Maori opposed to further settlement. Land belonging to rebellious tribes was confiscated and the Native Land Court, formed in 1865, was charged with determining the ownership of Maori land according to Pakeha law. Where Maori land and user rights existed communally, the Court sought to define parcels of land owned individually, thereby facilitating land sales.

New Zealand provided 8·6% of Britain's wool imports in 1861 and had 8·5m. sheep by 1867. The development of refrigerated shipping in the 1880s boosted meat exports. A Liberal Party was formed in 1889 and, backed by unions and the landless, won the 1890 election. Richard John Seddon took over the Liberal leadership in 1892 and remained premier until his death in 1906. Among Liberal achievements were the Land and Income Tax Act 1891 and the Advance to Settlers Act 1894 which assisted 17,000 people on to the land by 1912. In 1893 New Zealand become the first country to grant female suffrage.

In 1901 New Zealand declined the offer to join the Commonwealth of Australia and remained a British colony until 1907 when it gained Dominion status. Parliament remained subordinate to the British parliament until the adoption in 1947 of the Statute of Westminster under which New Zealand became fully sovereign with the British monarch as head of state. The Australian New Zealand Army Corps fought for Britain in both World Wars. New Zealand contributed around 100,000 soldiers in the First World War from a population of little more than 1m.; 17,000 died. 9,000 New Zealanders died in the influenza epidemic spread by returning soldiers, with a Maori mortality rate six times that of Pakeha. New Zealand's Second World War contribution was even greater: around 200,000 joined allied forces from a population of 1·6m.

Political divisions intensified in the early 20th century. Workers' unions, early supporters of the Liberal Party, rallied around an embryonic Labour movement while farmers and employers favoured William 'Farmer Bill' Massey's Reform Party. Amid industrial unrest in 1912, Reform took power, introducing anti-union legislation and promoting the interests of farmers. Micky Savage's first Labour government (1935–49) reclaimed for New Zealand its title of social laboratory of the world. It introduced one of the world's most comprehensive social welfare systems—incorporating pensions, health, education and family benefits—and increased state housing, introduced state guaranteed prices for farm produce to protect farmers from international price fluctuations, and nationalized the Reserve Bank. The National Party gained power in 1949, promising to curb union power and economic controls. Maori demands for recognition of the Treaty of Waitangi grew in the 1970s. Labour established the Waitangi Tribunal to hear Maori claims, making its powers retrospective to 1840.

Britain's entry into the EEC in 1973 was a setback for an economy dependent on exports to Britain. Robert Muldoon's National government (1975–84) tried to ameliorate the effects through tariff protection, wage and price freezes, and increased borrowing for 'Think Big' public works. The country found a new direction in the free market policies of David Lange's Labour government, which came to power in 1984. In 1973 Australia and New Zealand had tried to halt French nuclear testing in the Pacific through the International Court of Justice. The 1985 bombing of the *Rainbow Warrior* in Auckland harbour by French secret service agents reopened the issue.

Labour lost the 1990 election to a National Party led by Jim Bolger who cut back state intervention, outlawed compulsory union membership and introduced individual contracts, weakening union power. Jenny Shipley led a leadership coup in 1997 and became the country's first female prime minister. The first elected female prime minister was Helen Clark who led the Labour Party to victory in the 1999 election. Electoral reform in the 1990s saw New Zealand move from a first-past-the-post system to proportional representation under the mixed member proportional system (MMP).

TERRITORY AND POPULATION

New Zealand lies southeast of Australia in the south Pacific, Wellington being 1,983 km from Sydney. There are two principal islands, the North and South Islands, besides Stewart Island, Chatham Islands and small outlying islands, as well as the territories overseas.

New Zealand (*i.e.*, North, South and Stewart Islands) extends over 1,750 km from north to south. Area, excluding territories overseas, 270,534 sq. km: comprising North Island, 115,777 sq. km; South Island, 151,215 sq. km; Stewart Island, 1,746 sq. km; Chatham Islands, 963 sq. km. The minor islands (total area, 320 sq. miles or 829 sq. km) included within the geographical boundaries of New Zealand (but not within any local government area) are the following: Kermadec Islands (34 sq. km), Three Kings Islands (8 sq. km), Auckland Islands (606 sq. km), Campbell Island (114 sq. km), Antipodes Islands (62 sq. km), Bounty Islands (1 sq. km), Snares Islands (3 sq. km), Solander Island (1 sq. km). With the exception of meteorological station staff on Raoul Island in the Kermadec Group and Campbell Island there are no inhabitants.

The Kermadec Islands were annexed to New Zealand in 1887, have no separate administration and all New Zealand laws apply to them. Situation, 29° 10' to 31° 30' S. lat., 177° 45' to 179° W. long., 1,600 km NNE of New Zealand. The largest of the group is Raoul or Sunday Island, 29 sq. km, smaller islands being Macaulay and Curtis, while Macaulay Island is 5 km in circuit.

Growth in census population, exclusive of territories overseas:

	Total population	*Average annual increase (%)*		*Total population*	*Average annual increase (%)*
1858	115,462	—	1901[1]	815,853	1·89
1878	458,007	7·33	1906	936,304	2·75
1881	534,030	5·10	1911	1,058,308	2·52
1886	620,451	3·05	1916[1]	1,149,225	1·50
1891	668,632	1·50	1921	1,271,644	2·27
1896	743,207	2·13	1926	1,408,139	2·06

	Total population	*Average annual increase (%)*		*Total population*	*Average annual increase (%)*
1936[2]	1,573,810	1·13	1976[1]	3,129,383	1·71
1945[1, 2]	1,702,298	0·83	1981[1]	3,175,737	0·20
1951[1]	1,939,472	2·37	1986[1]	3,307,084	0·82
1956[1]	2,174,062	2·31	1991[1]	3,434,950	0·77
1961[1]	2,414,984	2·12	1996[1]	3,681,546	1·44
1966[1]	2,676,919	2·10	2001[1]	3,820,749	0·76
1971[1]	2,862,631	1·34			

[1]Excluding members of the Armed Forces overseas.

[2]The census of New Zealand is quinquennial, but the census falling in 1931 was abandoned as an act of national economy, and owing to war conditions the census due in 1941 was not taken until 25 Sept. 1945.

The latest census took place on 6 March 2001. Of the 3,820,749 people counted, 3,737,277 were usually resident in the country and 83,472 were overseas visitors. Estimated population as at 30 June 2003, 4,009,100.

In 2001, 85·4% of the population lived in urban areas. Density, 14·5 per sq. km (2001).

The usually-resident populations of regional councils (all data conforms with boundaries redrawn after the 1989 re-organization of local government) in 1996 and 2001:

Local Government Region	*Total Population 1996 census*	*2001 census*	*Percentage change 1996–2001 (%)*
Northland	137,052	140,133	2·2
Auckland	1,068,657	1,158,891	8·4
Waikato	350,112	357,726	2·2
Bay of Plenty	224,364	239,412	6·7
Gisborne	45,786	43,974	–4·0
Hawke's Bay	142,788	142,947	0·1
Taranaki	106,590	102,858	–3·5
Manawatu-Wanganui	228,771	220,089	–3·8
Wellington	414,048	423,765	2·3
Total North Island	2,718,171	2,829,798	4·1
Tasman	37,971	41,352	8·9
Nelson	40,278	41,568	3·2
Marlborough	38,397	39,558	3·0
West Coast	32,514	30,303	–6·8
Canterbury	468,039	481,431	2·9
Otago	185,082	181,542	–1·9
Southland	97,098	91,005	–6·3
Total South Island	899,385	906,753	0·8
Area outside region	747	726	–2·8
Total New Zealand	*3,618,303*	*3,737,277*	*3·3*

The UN gives a projected population for 2010 of 4·06m.

Between 1991 and 2001 the number of people who identified themselves as being of European ethnicity dropped from 83·2% to 80·0%. Pacific Island people made up 6·5% of the population in 2001 (5·0% in 1991); Asian ethnic groups went from 3·0% in 1996 to 6·6% in 2001. Permanent and long-term arrivals in 2001 totalled 81,094, including 16,844 from the UK, 12,186 from Australia, 11,107 from the People's Republic of China, 4,249 from India and 3,920 from Japan. Permanent and long-term departures in 2001 totalled 71,368, including 36,033 to Australia, 14,852 to the UK, 3,151 to the USA and 1,874 to Japan.

Maori population: 1896, 42,113; 1936, 82,326; 1945, 98,744; 1951, 115,676; 1961, 171,553; 1971, 227,414; 1981, 279,255; 1986, 294,201; 1991, 324,000; 1996, 523,374; 2001, 526,281 (13·8% of the total population, up from 9·4% in 1991). In addition, 604,110 people in 2001 said they have Maori ancestry, compared with 434,847 in 1991. There were estimated in 1995 to be 10,123 fully fluent speakers of Maori and a further 12,153 who were at the medium to high fluency level. In the 1996 census, 153,669 New Zealanders said they could hold a conversation about everyday matters in Maori. In 2001, one in four people of Maori ethnicity claimed to speak the language.

From the 1970s organizations were formed to pursue Maori grievances over loss of land and resources. The Waitangi Tribunal was set up in 1975 as a forum for complaints about breaches of the Treaty of Waitangi, and in 1984 empowered to hear claims against Crown actions since 1840. Direct negotiations with the Crown have been offered to claimants and a range of proposals to resolve historical grievances launched for public discussion in Dec. 1994. These proposals specify that all claims are to be met over ten years with treaty rights being converted to economic assets. There have been four recent major treaty settlements: NZ$170m. each for Tainui and Ngai Tahu, the NZ$150m. Sealord fishing agreement and NZ$40m. for Whakatohea in the Bay of Plenty. The Maori Land Court has jurisdiction over Maori freehold land and some general land owned by Maoris under the Te Ture Whenua Maori Act 1993.

Resident populations of main urban areas at the 2001 census were as follows:

North Island		Wanganui	39,423
Auckland	1,074,510	Wellington	339,747
Gisborne	31,719	Whangarei	46,050
Hamilton	166,128		
Hastings and Napier	113,673	*South Island*	
New Plymouth	47,763	Christchurch	334,107
Palmerston North	72,681	Dunedin	107,088
Rotorua	52,608	Invercargill	46,305
Tauranga	95,697	Nelson	53,688

English and Maori are the official languages.

SOCIAL STATISTICS

Statistics for calendar years:

	Total live births	*Deaths*	*Marriages*	*Divorces (decrees absolute)*
1998	57,818	26,206	20,135	10,037
1999	57,053	28,122	21,085	9,931
2000	56,605	26,660	20,655	9,936
2001	55,799	27,825	19,972	9,700
2002	54,021	28,065	20,690	10,300
2003	56,134	28,010	...	...

Birth rate, 2003, 14·14 per 1,000 population; death rate, 7·54 per 1,000 population; infant mortality, 2003, 6·07 per 1,000 live births. Annual population growth rate, 1992–02, 1·1%. In 2000 there were 458 suicides (516 in 1999). Expectation of life, 2003: males, 75·34 years; females, 81·44. Fertility rate, 2003, 1·79 births per woman.

In the year ending March 2003 there were 97,250 immigrants (69,490 in 2001) and 54,730 emigrants (78,760 in 2001).

CLIMATE

Lying in the cool temperate zone, New Zealand enjoys very mild winters for its latitude owing to its oceanic situation, and only the extreme south has cold winters. The situation of the mountain chain produces much sharper climatic contrasts between east and west than in a north-south direction. Mean daily maximum temperatures and rainfall figures:

	Jan (°C)	*July (°C)*	*Annual rainfall (mm) in 2000*
Auckland	23·3	14·4	1,046
Christchurch	22·5	11·2	706
Dunedin	18·9	9·9	926
Wellington	20·3	11·3	994

The highest extreme temperature recorded in 2000 was 35·0°C, recorded at both Darfield and Culverden on 4 March, and the lowest –12·4°C, at Tekapo on the morning of 24 Aug.

CONSTITUTION AND GOVERNMENT

Definition was given to the status of New Zealand by the (Imperial) Statute of Westminster of Dec. 1931, which had received the antecedent approval of the New Zealand Parliament in July 1931. The Governor-General's assent was given to the Statute of Westminster Adoption Bill on 25 Nov. 1947.

The powers, duties and responsibilities of the Governor-General and the Executive Council are set out in Royal Letters Patent and Instructions thereunder of 11 May 1917. In the execution of the powers vested in him the Governor-General must be guided by the advice of the Executive Council.

At a referendum on 6 Nov. 1993 a change from a first-past-the-post to a proportional representation electoral system was favoured by 53·9% of votes cast.

Parliament is the *House of Representatives*, consisting of 120 members (for the 2002 election 62 were general seats, 51 party list seats and 7 Maori seats), elected by universal adult suffrage on the mixed-member-proportional system (MMP) for three-year terms. The five Maori electoral districts cover the whole country. Maori and people of Maori descent are entitled to register either for a general or a Maori electoral district. As at Sept. 1997 there were 163,310 persons on the Maori electoral roll. There are now six Maori seats at general elections.

Joseph, P. A., *Constitutional Law in New Zealand.* Sydney, 1993.—(ed.) *Essays on the Constitution*. Sydney, 1995

McGee, D. G., *Parliamentary Practice in New Zealand.* 2nd ed. Wellington, 1994

Ringer, J. B., *An Introduction to New Zealand Government.* Christchurch, 1992

Vowles, J. and Aimer, P. (eds.) *Double Decision: the 1993 Election and Referendum in New Zealand.* Victoria (Wellington) Univ. Press, 1994

National Anthem. 'God Defend New Zealand'; words by T. Bracken, tune by J. J. Woods. There is a Maori version, Aotearoa, words by T. H. Smith. The UK national anthem has equal status.

RECENT ELECTIONS

At parliamentary elections on 27 July 2002 turn-out was 75·4%. The Labour Party won 52 seats with 41·3%; the National Party 27 with 20·9%; the right-wing New Zealand First Party 13 with 10·4%; Association of Consumers and Tax Payers 9 with 7·1%; the Green Party 9 with 7·0%; United Future 8 with 6·7%; and Jim Anderton's Progressive Coalition 2 with 1·7%.

CURRENT ADMINISTRATION

Governor-General: Dame Silvia Cartwright, DBE (b. 1943; sworn in 4 April 2001).

The government is formed by a centre-left coalition of the Labour Party and Jim Anderton's Progressive Coalition. In March 2005 the cabinet consisted of:

Prime Minister, Minister of Arts, Culture and Heritage: Helen Clark; b. 1950 (Labour; in office since 10 Dec. 1999).

Deputy Prime Minister, Minister of Finance, and Revenue: Michael Cullen (Labour).

Minister of Economic Development, Industry and Regional Development, and Forestry: James (Jim) Anderton (Progressive Coalition). *Health, and Food Safety:* Annette King (Labour). *Foreign Affairs and Trade, Justice, and Pacific Island Affairs:* Phil Goff (Labour). *Agriculture, Biosecurity, and Trade Negotiations:* James Sutton (Labour). *Education, State Services, Energy, and Sport and Recreation:* Trevor Mallard (Labour). *Environment, and Disarmament and Arms Control:* Marian Hobbs (Labour). *Police, Internal Affairs, Civil Defence, and Veterans' Affairs:* George Hawkins (Labour). *Labour, Immigration, Corrections, and State Owned Enterprises:* Paul Swain (Labour). *Conservation, Local Government, and Building Issues:* Chris Carter (Labour). *Transport, Commerce, Land Information, and Statistics:* Peter Hodgson (Labour). *Defence, and Tourism:* Mark Burton (Labour). *Attorney General, and the Treaty of Waitangi Negotiations:* Margaret Wilson (Labour). *Courts, Customs, and the Community and Voluntary Sector:* Rick Barker (Labour). *Maori Affairs:* Parekura Horomia (Labour). *Housing, Social Development and Employment, Broadcasting, Research, Science and Technology, Crown Research Institutes, and Youth Affairs:* Steven Maharey (Labour). *Accident Compensation Corporation, Women's Affairs, and Senior Citizens:* Ruth Dyson (Labour). *Fisheries:* David Benson-Pope (Labour).

Office of the Prime Minister: http://www.govt.nz

DEFENCE

The control and co-ordination of defence activities is obtained through the Ministry of Defence. New Zealand forces serve abroad in Australia, Iraq and Singapore, and with UN peacekeeping missions.

Defence expenditure in 2003 totalled US$1,171m. (US$292 per capita), representing 1·5% of GDP.

Army. Personnel total in 2003: 4,388, plus reserves numbering 2,718 (2,031 territorial, 687 civilians).

Navy. The Navy includes three frigates. The main base and Fleet headquarters is at Auckland.

The Royal New Zealand Navy personnel totalled 1,978 uniformed plus 354 reserve personnel in 2003.

Air Force. Squadrons are based at RNZAF Base Auckland and RNZAF Base Ohakea. Flying training is conducted at Ohakea and Auckland. Ground training is carried out at RNZAF Base Woodbourne.

The uniform strength in 2003 was 2,200, with six combat aircraft.

INTERNATIONAL RELATIONS

New Zealand is a member of the UN, WTO, the Commonwealth, OECD, Asian Development Bank, the Pacific Community, the Pacific Islands Forum, Colombo Plan, APEC, IOM and the Antarctic Treaty.

ECONOMY

Agriculture accounted for 8% of GDP in 2001, industry 23% and services 69%.

According to the anti-corruption organization *Transparency International*, New Zealand ranked second in the world in a 2004 survey of the countries with the least corruption in business and government. It received 9·6 out of 10 in the annual index.

Overview. The economy has experienced strong performance despite the 1997 Asian crisis, periods of drought and the global slowdown. Real GDP growth averaged 3·75% between 1999 and 2003. Unemployment has been cut and inflation has remained within the 1–3% target range set by the Bank of New Zealand. Public sector debt has been significantly reduced by sizeable and growing budget surpluses. The net public debt to GDP ratio was reduced from 50% in 1994 to 20% in 2000. According to the IMF, the strong economic performance is attributable to the extensive reforms of New Zealand's previously highly regulated and protected economy in the 1980s. However, the Labour government is reversing some of the earlier reforms: trade unions have been given more power in wage negotiations, further privatization has been ruled out and the top rate of the income tax has been raised from 33% to 39%. The main sectors in the economy are agriculture, fishing and forestry; the manufacturing sector is predominantly geared towards exports. Since 2000 exports have benefited from favourable movements in world prices, particularly for dairy and meat products, a trend partly countered by the continued appreciation of the New Zealand dollar, which led to a deterioration in net exports in 2004. Government spending accounts for more than 40% of GDP, in spite of cuts in benefits introduced in the 1990s. The tax system is one of the most neutral and efficient in the OECD area. The pension system is generous compared to international standards.

Currency. The monetary unit is the *New Zealand dollar* (NZD), of 100 *cents*. The total value of notes and coins on issue from the Reserve Bank in Dec. 2000 was NZ$2,069m. Inflation was 1·5% in 2003. In June 2002 foreign exchange reserves were US$1,843m. Gold reserves are negligible. Total money supply in June 2002 was NZ$18,235m.

Budget. Total central government revenue for 2003 was NZ$57,027m. (NZ$49,979m. in 2002). Central government expenditure in 2003 was NZ$55,224m. (NZ$47,653m. in 2002).

2003 tax revenue was NZ$39,785m. and NZ$2,763m. was earned through levies, fees, fines and penalties. In 2000 income tax on individuals amounted to NZ$15,776m.; company tax, NZ$4,158m.; withholding taxes, NZ$1,563m.

The gross public debt at June 2003 was NZ$38,285m., of which NZ$24,380m. was held in New Zealand currency, NZ$6,697m. in foreign currency and NZ$7,208m. in non-sovereign-guaranteed debt.

Performance. The New Zealand economy grew by 4·4% in 2002 and 3·5% in 2003. Total GDP was US$76·3bn. in 2003.

Banking and Finance. The central bank and bank of issue is the Reserve Bank (*Governor*, Dr Alan Bollard).

The financial system comprises a central bank (the Reserve Bank of New Zealand), registered banks and other financial institutions. Registered banks include banks from abroad, which have to satisfy capital adequacy and managerial quality requirements. Other financial institutions include the regional trustee banks, now grouped under Trust Bank, building societies, finance companies, merchant banks and stock and station agents. The number of registered banks was 18 in 2003 of which only four were operating in New Zealand before 1986. Around 99% of the assets of the New Zealand banking system were under the ownership of a foreign bank parent.

The primary functions of the Reserve Bank are the formulation and implementation of monetary policy to achieve the economic objectives set by the government, and the promotion of the efficiency and soundness of the financial system, through the registration of banks, and supervision of financial institutions. Since 1996 supervision has been conducted on a basis of public disclosure by banks of their activities every quarter.

On 30 June 2003 the assets of the Reserve Bank were NZ$11,543m. (including government securities totalling NZ$3,300m. and marketable securities totalling NZ$3,137m.).

The stock exchange in Wellington conducts on-screen trading, unifying the three former trading floors in Auckland, Christchurch and Wellington. There is also a stock exchange in Dunedin.

ENERGY AND NATURAL RESOURCES

Environment. New Zealand's carbon dioxide emissions from the consumption and flaring of fossil fuels were the equivalent of 9·7 tonnes per capita in 2002.

Electricity. On 1 April 1987 the former Electricity Division of the Ministry of Energy became a state-owned enterprise, the Electricity Corporation of N.Z. Ltd, which has since been split into two state-owned enterprises causing a competitive wholesale electricity market to be established. Around 68% of the country's electricity is generated by renewable sources. Hydro-electric plants, mainly based in the South Island, account for some 61% with geothermal power, generated in the North Island, accounting for around 7%. The rest comes from natural gas (25%), coal, wind and landfill gas. Electricity generating capacity, 2000, 8·5m. kW. Consumption per capita was 10,183 kWh in 2000.

Electricity consumption statistics (in GWh) for years ended 31 March are:

	Residential	*Commercial*	*Industrial*	*Total consumption*
1999	11,290	7,334	14,010	32,635
2000	11,057	6,919	14,759	32,735
2001	11,306	6,819	15,142	33,267
2002	11,660	6,965	14,525	33,150

New Zealand also has two wind farms.

Oil and Gas. Crude oil production was estimated at 42,160 bbls. per day in 2001, all from the Taranaki region. Around 75% of production is exported. 119,700 bbls. per day were imported in 2001. Proven reserves were estimated at 90m. bbls. in 2002.

In 2002 gasfields produced 6·1bn. cu. metres. Gas reserves are estimated to last until about 2014, with the Maui field possibly running out in 2006. In 2003 proven natural gas reserves were estimated at 41·77bn. cu. metres.

Minerals. Coal production in 2002 was 4·46m. tonnes. Of the 45 mines operating in 2002, 29 were opencast and 16 underground, responsible for 79·6% and 20·3% of total coal production respectively. Only twelve mines produced over 200,000 tonnes of coal and 14 operations had an output of less than 10,000 tonnes. Around 60% of New Zealand's exported coal goes to India and Japan.

While New Zealand's best known non-fuel mineral is gold (producing about 9·77 tonnes in 2002 worth NZ$212m.) there is also production of silver, ironsand, aggregate, limestone, clay, aluminium, dolomite, pumice, salt, serpentinite, zeolite and bentonite. In addition, there are resources or potential for deposits of titanium (ilmenite beach sands), platinum, sulphur, phosphate, silica and mercury.

Agriculture. Two-thirds of the land area is suitable for agriculture and grazing. The total area of farmland in use in 2002 was 15,640,000 ha. There were 11,967,000 ha of grazing, arable, fodder and fallow land, 110,000 ha of land for horticulture and

1,879,000 ha of plantations of exotic timber. In 2001 there were 1·5m. ha of arable land and 1·87m. ha of permanent crops.

The largest freehold estates are held in the South Island. The number of occupied holdings as at 30 June 2002 were as follows:

Regional Council	*No. of farms*	*Total area of farms (1,000 ha)*	*Regional Council*	*No. of farms*	*Total area of farms (1,000 ha)*
Auckland	5,500	302	Canterbury	10,000	3,151
Bay of Plenty	5,700	600	Marlborough	1,700	723
Gisborne	1,300	653	Nelson	190	21
Hawke's Bay	3,900	962	Otago	4,100	2,368
Manawatu-Wanganui	6,500	1,545	Southland	4,300	1,198
Northland	5,800	836	Tasman	1,900	277
Taranaki	3,900	496	West Coast	830	225
Waikato	12,000	1,730	*Total South Island*	*23,000*	*8,013*
Wellington	2,500	504			
Total North Island	*47,000*	*7,627*	*Total New Zealand*	*70,000*	*15,640*

Production of main crops (2000, in 1,000 tonnes): potatoes, 500; apples, 482; wheat, 360; barley, 281; maize, 174; pumpkins and squash, 155; tomatoes, 85; carrots, 80; grapes, 80; cauliflower, 63.

Livestock, 2002: sheep, 39·54m.; cattle, 9·65m.; pigs, 344,000; goats, 153,000; deer, 1·64m.; chickens, 13m. (2000). Total meat produced in 2002 was 1·40m. tonnes (including 576,000 tonnes of beef and veal, and 521,000 tonnes of lamb and mutton). Meat industry products are New Zealand's second largest export income earner, accounting for about 14% of merchandise exports. New Zealand's main meat exports are lamb, mutton and beef. About 65% of lamb, 61% of beef and 51% of mutton produced in New Zealand in 2001–02 was exported overseas. The domestic market absorbs over 99% of the pigmeat and poultry produced in New Zealand. 54% of the world's exported sheepmeat comes from New Zealand.

Production of wool for the year 2002–03 was 173,000 tonnes. Milk production for 2000–01 totalled a record 12,322m. litres. In 1998–99 butter production totalled 232,948 tonnes and cheese production 238,535 tonnes.

Forestry. Forests covered 8·0m. ha in 2002 (30% of New Zealand's land area), up from 7·67m. ha in 1990. Of this, about 6·2m. ha are indigenous forest and 1·8m. ha planted productive forest. New planting and restocking was 65,900 ha in 2002. Introduced pines form the bulk of the large exotic forest estate and among these radiata pine is the best multi-purpose tree, reaching log size in 25–30 years. Other species planted are Douglas fir and Eucalyptus species. Total roundwood production in 2002–03 was 23·10m. cu. metres. The table below shows production of rough sawn timber in 1,000 cu. metres for years ending 31 March:

	Indigenous			*Exotic*			*All Species*
	Rimu and Miro	*Beech*	*Total*	*Radiata Pine*	*Douglas Fir*	*Total*	*Total*
1997	44	7	56	2,761	122	2,967	3,023
1998	28	5	38	2,995	105	3,157	3,195
1999	30	4	38	2,996	143	3,188	3,226
2000	22	6	30	3,583	134	3,776	3,806
2001	17	8	28	3,625	136	3,820	3,848

In 2002–03 forest industries consisted of approximately 360 sawmills, 7 plywood and 11 veneer plants, 4 particle board mills, 8 wood pulp mills (4 of which also produced paper and paperboard) and 6 fibreboard mills.

The basic products of the pulp and paper mills are mechanical and chemical pulp which are converted into newsprint, kraft and other papers, paperboard and fibreboard. Production of woodpulp in the year ending 31 March 2002 amounted to 1,523,730 tonnes and of paper (including newsprint paper and paperboard) to 846,727 tonnes.

Fisheries. In 2001 the total catch was 561,110 tonnes, almost entirely from sea fishing. The total value of New Zealand fisheries exports during the year ended Dec. 2002 was NZ$1,530m., of which hoki exports constituted NZ$314·7m.

INDUSTRY

The leading companies by market capitalization in New Zealand, excluding banking and finance, in Jan. 2002 were: Telecom Corporation of New Zealand Ltd (TCNZ),

NZ$9bn.; Carter Holt Harvey Ltd (NZ$3bn.), a forest products company; and Lion Nathan Ltd (NZ$3bn.), a brewing company.

Statistics of manufacturing industries (in NZ$1m.):

Production year	*Salaries and wages paid*	*Closing stocks of raw materials*	*Closing stocks of finished goods*	*Operating income*	*Purchases and other operating expenses*
2001–02	8,961	2,618	4,945	63,396	47,163
2002–03	9,523	2,595	6,954	65,146	47,770

The following is a statement of the value of the products (including repairs) of the principal industries for the year 2002–03 (in NZ$1m.):

Industry group	*Salaries and wages paid*	*Closing stocks of raw materials*	*Closing stocks of finished goods*	*Operating income*	*Purchases and other operating expenses*
Dairy and meat products	1,481	261	3,015	16,057	13,777
Other food	869	213	651	6,939	5,063
Beverage, malt and tobacco	292	154	423	2,926	2,060
Textile and apparel	579	205	296	3,069	2,092
Wood products	674	107	381	4,245	3,227
Paper and paper products	407	110	206	2,870	2,002
Printing, publishing and recorded media	796	84	84	3,392	2,001
Petroleum and industrial chemical	267	195	192	3,202	2,154
Rubber, plastic and other chemical products	728	218	513	4,144	2,840
Non-metallic mineral products	295	52	137	2,041	1,364
Basic metal	314	108	161	2,041	1,524
Structural, sheet and fabricated metal products	780	195	214	4,112	2,849
Transport equipment manufacturing	499	212	145	2,244	1,488
Machinery and equipment	1,138	357	429	5,876	4,010
Furniture and other manufacturing	405	124	106	1,984	1,317

Labour. There were an estimated 1,928,300 persons employed in the quarter ending Sept. 2003. The largest number of employed people worked in the community, social and personal services area (27·4%); followed by wholesale and retail trade, restaurants and hotels (22·9%); and manufacturing (14·7%). Unemployment total for the quarter ending Sept. 2003 was estimated to be 86,300. The unemployment rate for the quarter ending Sept. 2004 was 3·8% of the workforce.

The weekly average wage in the quarter ended June 2003 was NZ$857 for men, NZ$685 for women. A minimum wage is set by the government annually. As of 1 April 2004 it was NZ$9·00 an hour; a youth rate of NZ$7·20 per hour applies for 16–17 year-olds. In 2002 there were 46 work stoppages (42 in 2001) with 34,398 person-days of work lost (54,440 in 2001).

Trade Unions. In 2000, 19 industrial unions of workers (representing 80% of all union members) were affiliated to the Council of Trade Unions, NZCTU (*President*, Ross Wilson). Compulsory trade union membership was made illegal in 1991, and the national wage award system was replaced by local wage agreements under the Employment Contracts Act 1991. In Dec. 2002 there were 174 unions in total with a combined membership of 334,783.

INTERNATIONAL TRADE

Total overseas debt was NZ$130,615m. in June 2003. In 1990 New Zealand and Australia completed the Closer Economic Relations Agreement (initiated in 1983), which provides for mutual free trade in goods.

Imports and Exports. Trade in NZ$1m. for recent years ending 30 June:

	Exports, including re-exports (f.o.b.)	*Imports (c.i.f.)*	*Balance of Merchandise Trade*
1999	22,582	24,248	–1,666
2000	26,111	29,193	–3,082

	Exports, including re-exports (f.o.b.)	*Imports (c.i.f.)*	*Balance of Merchandise Trade*
2001	32,000	31,927	73
2002	32,332	31,811	521
2003	29,291	32,161	–2,870

The principal imports for the 12 months ended 30 June 2003 were:

Commodity	*Value (NZ$1m. v.f.d.)*
Vehicles, parts and accessories	4,985
Mechanical machinery and equipment	4,333
Mineral fuels	3,152
Electrical machinery and equipment	2,699
Plastics and plastic articles	1,279
Optical, medical and measuring equipment	967
Paper, paperboard and paper articles	924
Aircraft and parts	804
Pharmaceutical products	747
Iron or steel articles	491
Iron and steel	481
Apparel (not knitted or crocheted)	446

The principal exports for the 12 months ended 30 June 2003 were:

Commodity	*Value (NZ$1m. f.o.b.)*
Dairy produce, eggs and honey	4,714
Meat and edible offal	4,111
Wood and articles of wood	2,386
Machinery and mechanical appliances	1,356
Fish, crustaceans and molluscs	1,215
Albuminoidal substances; modified starches; glues; enzymes	1,148
Fruits and nuts (edible)	1,032
Aluminium and aluminium articles	980
Wool, fine or coarse animal hair	943
Electrical machinery, equipment and parts	938

The leading export destinations in 2002–03 (exports and re-exports f.o.b., in NZ$1m.) were: Australia, 6,050; USA, 4,366; Japan, 3,354; China, 1,457; UK, 1,361; Republic of Korea, 1,178; Germany, 855. The principal import suppliers in 2002–03 (imports v.f.d., in NZ$1m.) were: Australia, 7,278; USA, 4,067; Japan, 3,876; China, 2,687; Germany, 1,713; UK, 1,120; Malaysia, 864.

COMMUNICATIONS

Roads. Total length of roads in 2002 was 92,200 km (62·8% paved), including 190 km of motorways. There were 74 national and provincial state highways comprising 10,570 km of roadway, including the principal arterial traffic routes.

In Feb. 2003 there were 9,830 full-time equivalent persons employed in the provision of road passenger transport and 23,890 persons providing road freight transport.

Total expenditure on roads (including state highways), streets and bridges—by the central government and local authorities combined—amounted to NZ$959m. in 2002.

At 31 March 2003 motor vehicles licensed numbered 2,916,734, of which 2,010,024 were cars. In 2003 there were 7,780 omnibuses/public taxis and 38,447 motorcycles. In 2002 there were 366,918 trucks and 373,940 trailers.

In 2002 there were 404 deaths in road accidents.

Rail. New Zealand Rail was privatized in 1994 but renationalized in 2004. In 1994 a 24-hour freight link was introduced between Auckland and Christchurch. There were, in 2002, 3,898 km of 1,067 mm gauge railway open for traffic (506 km electrified). New Zealand Rail Limited was renamed Tranz Rail Limited in 1995. In 2003 Tranz Rail carried 14·8m. tonnes of freight and 12·3m. passengers. Total revenue in the financial year 1999–2000 was NZ$594·5m.

At 30 June 2003 Tranz Rail track and rolling stock included 322 diesel, electric and shunting locomotives, 4,048 freight wagons, 177 passenger carriages and commuter units, three rail/road ferries (linking the North and South Islands) and plant and support equipment. After renationalization Tranz Rail was renamed Toll NZ.

Civil Aviation. There are international airports at Wellington, Auckland and Christchurch, with Auckland International being the main airport. The national carrier is Air New Zealand, which was privatized in 1989 but then renationalized in 2001. Trans-Tasman air travel is subject to agreement between Air New Zealand and Qantas.

New Zealand has one of the highest ratios of aircraft to population in the world with 3,530 aircraft in the year to March 2003. Since 1992 air transport flights have increased by about 9% per year. In 1999 scheduled airline traffic of New Zealand-based carriers flew 172·2m. km, carrying 8,892,000 passengers (2,829,000 on international flights). In 2002 there were 113 airports, of which 46 had paved runways.

Shipping. In 2002 merchant shipping totalled 180,000 GRT, including oil tankers 50,000 GRT. In 2003 there were 1,069 km of waterway.

Telecommunications. The provision of telecommunication services is the responsibility of the Telecom Corporation of New Zealand, formed in 1987 and privatized in 1990; and CLEAR Communications, which began operations in Dec. 1990. In 2002 there were 4,201,000 telephone subscribers, or 1,066·5 for every 1,000 persons, and 1,630,000 PCs in use (621·7 per 1,000 persons). There were 65,000 fax machines in 1995. New Zealand had 2·06m. Internet users in Aug. 2002.

Postal Services. On 1 April 1998 the Postal Services Act removed New Zealand Post's former statutory monopoly on the carriage of letters and opened the postal market to full competition. To carry out a business involving the carriage of letters, a person or company must be registered as a postal operator with the Ministry of Commerce.

In 2003 there were 315 post shops, 697 post centre franchises and 2,735 stamp resellers.

SOCIAL INSTITUTIONS

Justice. The judiciary consists of the Court of Appeal, the High Court and District Courts. All exercise both civil and criminal jurisdiction. Final appeal lies to the Privy Council in London. Special courts include the Maori Land Court, the Maori Appellate Court, Family Courts, the Youth Court, Environment Court and the Employment Court. In 2003 there were 5,826 sentenced inmates of whom 274 were women. Of male inmates in 2001, 53% (some 2,499) identified themselves as Maori only compared to 29% who identified themselves as European only. There were 170,999 convictions, including 14,537 for violent offences, in 2002. The death penalty for murder was replaced by life imprisonment in 1961.

The Criminal Injuries Compensation Act, 1963, which came into force on 1 Jan. 1964, provided for compensation of persons injured by certain criminal acts and the dependants of persons killed by such acts. However, this has now been phased out in favour of the Accident Compensation Act, 1982, except in the residual area of property damage caused by escapees. The Offenders Legal Aid Act 1954 provides that any person charged or convicted of any offence may apply for legal aid which may be granted depending on the person's means and the gravity of the offence etc. Since 1970 legal aid in civil proceedings (except divorce) has been available for persons of small or moderate means. The Legal Services Act 1991 now brings together in one statute the civil and criminal legal aid schemes.

Police. The police are a national body maintained by the central government. In June 2003 there were 7,257 full-time equivalent sworn officers (16% female).

Ombudsmen. The office of Ombudsman was created in 1962. From 1975 additional Ombudsmen have been authorized. There are currently two. Ombudsmen's functions are to investigate complaints under the Ombudsman Act, the Official Information Act and the Local Government Official Information and Meetings Act from members of the public relating to administrative decisions of central, regional and local government. During the year ended 30 June 2003 a total of 4,418 complaints were received. A total of 27 complaints were sustained during the year and 729 were still under investigation

Religion. No direct state aid is given to any form of religion. For the Church of England the country is divided into seven dioceses, with a separate bishopric

(Aotearoa) for the Maori. The Presbyterian Church is divided into 23 presbyteries and the Maori Synod. The Moderator is elected annually. The Methodist Church is divided into ten districts; the President is elected annually. The Roman Catholic Church is divided into four dioceses, with the Archbishop of Wellington as Metropolitan Archbishop. In Sept. 2003 there was one cardinal.

Adherents of leading religions at the 2001 census were as follows:

Religious denomination	*Adherents*	*Religious denomination*	*Adherents*
Anglican	584,793	Brethren	20,406
Catholic	486,012	Jehovah's Witnesses	17,826
Presbyterian	417,453	Assemblies of God	16,023
Methodist	120,708	Salvation Army	12,618
Baptist	51,426	Seventh-day Adventist	12,600
Ratana	48,975	All other religious affiliations	398,847
Buddhist	41,664	No religion	1,028,052
Latter-day Saints (Mormons)	39,915	Object to state	239,241
Hindu	39,876	Not specified	211,638
Pentecostal	30,222		
Islam/Muslim	23,637	Total	3,841,932[1]

[1]Where a person reported more than one religious affiliation, they have been counted in each applicable group.

Education. Education is compulsory between the ages of 6 and 15. Children aged three and four years may enrol at the 606 free kindergartens maintained by Free Kindergarten Associations, which receive government assistance. There are also 492 play centres which also receive government subsidy. In 2002 there were 45,169 and 14,879 children on the rolls respectively. There were also 1,612 care centres in 2002 with 76,246 children, 545 *te kohanga reo* (providing early childhood education in the Maori language) with 10,389 children, and a number of other smaller providers of early childhood care and education.

In 2002 there were 2,132 state primary schools (including intermediate and state contributing schools), with 411,850 pupils; the number of teachers was 19,329. A correspondence school for children in remote areas and those otherwise unable to attend school had 7,872 primary and secondary pupils and 242 teachers. In 2003 there were 45 registered private primary and intermediate schools with 6,106 pupils. In 2002 there were 534 teachers at private primary and intermediate schools.

In 2002 there were 320 state secondary schools with 14,577 full-time teachers and 212,426 pupils. There were also 58 state composite area schools with 4,831 scholars in the secondary division. In 2003 there were 2,280 full-time secondary pupils taught by 282 secondary teachers at the Correspondence School. There were 17 registered private secondary schools with 615 teachers and 8,498 pupils in 2002.

New Zealand has eight universities—the University of Auckland, Auckland University of Technology, University of Waikato (at Hamilton), Victoria University of Wellington, Massey University (at Palmerston North), the University of Canterbury (at Christchurch), the University of Otago (at Dunedin) and Lincoln University (near Christchurch). The number of equivalent full-time students attending universities in 2002 was 100,772. There were four teachers' training colleges with 6,338 equivalent full-time students in 2002, and 63,741 equivalent full-time students were enrolled in polytechnic courses in 2002.

Total budgeted expenditure estimated in 2003 on education was NZ$8·2bn. (16·8% of government expenses). The universities are autonomous bodies. All state-funded primary and secondary schools are controlled by boards of trustees. Education in state schools is free for children under 19 years of age. All educational institutions are reviewed every three years by teams of educational reviewers.

A series of reforms is being implemented by the government following reports of 18 working groups on tertiary education. These include a new funding system, begun in 1991 and based solely on student numbers.

The adult literacy rate in 2001 was at least 99%.

Health. In 2003 there were 10,355 practising doctors. In 2002 there were 85 public hospitals with 12,484 beds and 360 private hospitals with 11,341 beds. In 2002 New Zealand spent 8·5% of its GDP on health. Total budgeted expenditure on health in 2003–04 was NZ$9·6bn.

Welfare. Non-contributory old-age pensions were introduced in 1898. Large reductions in welfare expenditure were introduced by the government in Dec. 1990.

From 1 Oct. 1998 anyone receiving unemployment benefit, sickness benefit, a training benefit, a 55 plus benefit, or a young job seekers allowance has received a benefit called the Community Wage. In return for receiving the Community Wage, recipients are expected to search for work, meet with Work and Income New Zealand when asked, take a suitable work offer and take part in activities that would improve their chances of finding a job.

In the budget of July 1991 it was announced that current rates of Guaranteed Retirement Income Scheme (GRI) payment would be frozen until 1 April 1993, thereafter to be on the previous year's consumer price index. On 1 April 1992 GRI was replaced by the national superannuation scheme which is income-tested. Eligibility has been gradually increased to 65 years. Universal eligibility is available at 70 years. At 1 April 2003 a married couple received NZ$377·38 per week, a single person living alone NZ$245·30 per week.

Social Welfare Benefits.

Benefits	*Number in force at 30 June 2003*	*Total expenditure 2003 (NZ$1,000)*
Community Wage—Job Seeker	111,906	1,287,730
Community Wage—Training	4,291	37,942
Community Wage—Sickness	39,902	460,209
Invalids' Benefit	68,507	926,515
Domestic Purposes' Benefit	109,295	1,634,477
Orphans' Benefit/ Unsupported Child's Benefit	6,789	47,081
Widows' Benefit	8,659	90,265
Transitional Retirement Benefit	2,110	42,013
New Zealand Superannuation	457,278	5,798,873
Veterans' Pension	7,872	87,625
War Pension	22,271	108,862
Total Income Support	838,880	10,521,592

Reciprocity with Other Countries. New Zealand has overseas social security agreements with the United Kingdom, the Netherlands, Greece, Ireland, Australia, Jersey and Guernsey, Denmark, Canada and Italy. The main purpose of these agreements is to encourage free movement of labour and to ensure that when a person has lived or worked in more than one country, each of those countries takes a fair share of the responsibility for meeting the costs of that person's social security coverage. New Zealand also pays people eligible for New Zealand Superannuation or veterans' pensions who live in the Cook Islands, Niue or Tokelau.

CULTURE

World Heritage Sites. There are three UNESCO World Heritage sites under New Zealand jurisdiction. Te Wahipounamu, on South Island, and the New Zealand Sub-Antarctic Islands were listed in 1990 and 1998 respectively. The Sub-Antarctic Islands consist of the Auckland Islands, Antipodes Islands, Bounty Islands, Campbell Island and the Snares. Tongariro National Park, on North Island, was listed in 1988.

Broadcasting. Legislation of 1995 split the state-owned Radio New Zealand into a government-owned public radio broadcasting company and some 40 commercial stations.

Television New Zealand operates two channels. Two other channels, TV3 and TV4, are commercial. There are also regional TV networks. Pay television was introduced in May 1990—Sky Entertainment operates on more than 70 channels. Maori Television was launched in March 2004. Colour is by PAL. The New Zealand Public Radio Service also includes the Radio New Zealand International, a short-wave which broadcasts to the South Pole. There are 21 regional Maori stations for the promotion of Maori culture. In 2000 there were 3·85m. radio and in 2001 there were 2·13m. television receivers.

Cinema. Cinema admissions totalled 18·3m. in 2003, up from 6·1m. in 1991. Gross box office receipts came to NZ$156·1m. in 2003. In 1999 there were 315 cinema screens.

Press. In 2003 there were 24 daily newspapers with a combined daily average circulation of 740,763, giving a rate of 185 per 1,000 inhabitants. The *New Zealand Herald,* published in Auckland, had the largest daily circulation in 2003, with an average of 210,910 copies. Other major dailies are *The Dominion Post* and *The Press*, with circulations of over 90,000 copies.

There are two Sunday newspapers, *Sunday Star-Times* and *Sunday News*, both published by Fairfax New Zealand Limited and distributed nationwide. The *Sunday Star-Times* is a broadsheet and circulates about 204,000 copies while the *Sunday News* is a tabloid and circulates 115,000 (2000) copies every Sunday.

Tourism. There were 2,062,423 tourists in the year to March 2003 (in 2000, 1,652,000) of whom 638,354 were from Australia, 240,029 were from the UK, 205,796 were from the USA and 172,716 were from Japan. International tourism generated US$3·02bn. in 2002.

Festivals. The biennial New Zealand Festival takes place in Wellington in Feb./March in even-numbered years. The biennial Christchurch Arts Festival takes place in July/Aug. in odd-numbered years.

DIPLOMATIC REPRESENTATIVES

Of New Zealand in the United Kingdom (New Zealand House, Haymarket, London, SW1Y 4TQ)
High Commissioner: Russell Marshall, CNZM.

Of the United Kingdom in New Zealand (44 Hill St., Wellington, 1)
High Commissioner: Richard Fell, CVO.

Of New Zealand in the USA (37 Observatory Cir., NW, Washington, D.C., 20008)
Ambassador: John Wood.

Of the USA in New Zealand (29 Fitzherbert Terr., Wellington)
Ambassador: Charles J. Swindells.

Of New Zealand to the United Nations
Ambassador: Don J. MacKay.

Of New Zealand to the European Union
Ambassador: Wade Armstrong.

FURTHER READING

Statistics New Zealand. *New Zealand Official Yearbook.—Key Statistics: a Monthly Abstract of Statistics.—Profile of New Zealand.*

Belich, James, *Making Peoples: a History of the New Zealanders from Polynesian Settlement to the End of the Nineteenth century.* London, 1997.—*Paradise Reforged: A History of New Zealanders from the 1880s to the Year 2000.* London, 2002

Harland, B., *On Our Own: New Zealand in a Tripolar World.* Victoria Univ. Press, 1992

Harris, P. and Levine, S. (eds.) *The New Zealand Politics Source Book.* 2nd ed. Palmerston North, 1994

Massey, P., *New Zealand: Market Liberalization in a Developed Economy.* London, 1995

Patterson, B. and K., *New Zealand.* [Bibliography] 2nd ed. ABC-Clio, Oxford and Santa Barbara (CA), 1998

Sinclair, K. (ed.) *The Oxford Illustrated History of New Zealand.* 2nd ed. OUP, 1994

For other more specialized titles see under CONSTITUTION AND GOVERNMENT and DEFENCE above.

National statistical office: Statistics New Zealand, POB 2922, Wellington, 1.
Website: http://www.stats.govt.nz/

TERRITORIES OVERSEAS

Territories Overseas coming within the jurisdiction of New Zealand consist of Tokelau and the Ross Dependency.

Tokelau

Tokelau is situated some 500 km to the north of Samoa and comprises three dispersed atolls—Atafu, Fakaofo and Nukunonu. The land area is 12 sq. km and the population at the 1996 census was 1,507, giving a density of 126 per sq. km.

The British government transferred administrative control of Tokelau to New Zealand in 1925. Formal sovereignty was transferred to New Zealand in 1948 by act of the New Zealand Parliament. New Zealand statute law, however, does not apply to Tokelau unless it is expressly extended to Tokelau. In practice New Zealand legislation is extended to Tokelau only with its consent.

Under a programme agreed in 1992, the role of Tokelau's political institutions is being better defined and expanded. The process under way enables the base of Tokelau government to be located within Tokelau's national level institutions rather than as before, within a public service located largely in Samoa. In 1994 the Administrator's powers were delegated to the *General Fono* (the national representative body), and when the *General Fono* is not in session, to the *Council of Faipule*. The Tokelau Amendment Act 1996 conferred on the *General Fono* a power to make rules for Tokelau, including the power to impose taxes.

Coconuts (the source of copra) are the only cash crop. Pulaka, breadfruit, papayas, the screw-pine and bananas are cultivated as food crops. Livestock comprises pigs, poultry and goats.

Tokelau affirmed to the United Nations in 1994 that it had under active consideration both the Constitution of a self-governing Tokelau and an act of self-determination. It also expressed a strong preference for a future status of free association with New Zealand.

Ross Dependency

By Imperial Order in Council, dated 30 July 1923, the territories between 160° E. long. and 150° W. long. and south of 60° S. lat. were brought within the jurisdiction of the New Zealand government. The region was named the Ross Dependency. From time to time laws for the Dependency have been made by regulations promulgated by the Governor-General of New Zealand.

The mainland area is estimated at 400,000–450,000 sq. km and is mostly ice-covered. In Jan. 1957 a New Zealand expedition under Sir Edmund Hillary established a base in the Dependency. In Jan. 1958 Sir Edmund Hillary and four other New Zealanders reached the South Pole.

The main base—Scott Base, at Pram Point, Ross Island—is manned throughout the year, about 12 people being present during winter. The annual activities of 200–300 scientists and support staff are managed by a crown agency, Antarctica New Zealand, based in Christchurch.

SELF-GOVERNING TERRITORIES OVERSEAS

THE COOK ISLANDS

KEY HISTORICAL EVENTS

The Cook Islands, which lie between 8° and 23° S. lat., and 156° and 167° W. long., were made a British protectorate in 1888, and on 11 June 1901 were annexed as part of New Zealand. In 1965 the Cook Islands became a self-governing territory in 'free association' with New Zealand.

TERRITORY AND POPULATION

The islands fall roughly into two groups—the scattered islands towards the north (Northern group) and the islands towards the south (Southern group). The islands with their populations at the census of 1996:

Lower Group—	*Area sq. km*	*Population*	*Lower Group—*	*Area sq. km*	*Population*
Aitutaki	18·3	2,389	Mauke (Parry Is.)	18·4	652
Atiu	26·9	956	Mitiaro	22·3	319
Mangaia	51·8	1,108	Rarotonga	67·1	11,225
Manuae and Te au-o-tu	6·2	—			

Northern Group—	Area sq. km	Population	Northern Group—	Area sq. km	Population
Manihiki (Humphrey)	5·4	668	Rakahanga (Reirson)	4·1	249
Nassau	1·3	99	Suwarrow (Anchorage)	0·4	4
Palmerston (Avarua)	2·1	49			
Penrhyn (Tongareva)	9·8	606	Total	235·4	19,103
Pukapuka (Danger)	1·3	779			

Population density in 1996 was 76 per sq. km. In 1996 an estimated 58·8% of the population lived in urban areas. The 2001 total population (17,700) and the estimated resident population (13,400) have fallen since 1996, the latter by approximately 26%.

SOCIAL STATISTICS

1999: births, 346; deaths, 96. Birth rate (1999, per 1,000 population), 21·1; death rate, 5·9. Life expectancy was estimated (1998) at: males, 62·2 years; females 73·1. Fertility rate, 2001, 3·3 births per woman.

CLIMATE

Oceanic climate where rainfall is moderate to heavy throughout the year, with Nov. to March being particularly wet. Weather can be changeable from day to day and can end in rainfall after an otherwise sunny day. Rarotonga, Jan. 26°C, July 20°C. Annual rainfall 2,060 mm.

CONSTITUTION AND GOVERNMENT

The Cook Islands Constitution of 1965 provides for internal self-government but linked to New Zealand by a common Head of State and a common citizenship, that of New Zealand. It provides for a ministerial system of government with a Cabinet consisting of a Prime Minister and not more than eight nor fewer than six other Ministers. There is also an advisory council composed of hereditary chiefs, the 15-member House of Ariki, without legislative powers. The New Zealand government is represented by a New Zealand Representative and the Queen, as head of state, by the Queen's Representative. The capital is Avarua on Rarotonga.

The unicameral *Parliament* comprises 25 members elected for a term of five years.

RECENT ELECTIONS

At the elections of 7 Sept. 2004 the centrist Democratic Party won 14 of the 24 seats, the Cook Islands Party won 9 seats and ind. 1 seat.

CURRENT ADMINISTRATION

High Commissioner: Kurt Meyer.

Prime Minister: Jim Marurai.

ECONOMY

Overview. A package of economic reforms including privatization and deregulation was initiated in July 1996 to deal with a national debt of US$141m., 120% of GDP.

Currency. The Cook Island *dollar* was at par with the New Zealand *dollar*, but was replaced in 1995 by New Zealand currency.

Budget. Revenue, 1996–97, NZ$45·8m.; expenditure, NZ$44·8m. Grants from New Zealand, mainly for medical, educational and general administrative purposes, totalled NZ$11·3m. in 1996–97.

Performance. Real GDP growth was 1·3% in 1995 (1·5% in 1994).

Banking and Finance. There are four banks in the Cook Islands. The Cook Islands Savings Bank is state-owned and has deposit services throughout the islands. The Cook Islands Development Bank is a state-owned corporation funded in part by loans from the Asian Development Bank. The two remaining banks are subsidiaries of the Australia and New Zealand Banking Group Limited and the Westpac Bank, which are both Australian-owned and major banks in Australasia.

The Cook Islands were one of 15 countries and territories named in a report in June 2000 as failing to co-operate in the fight against international money laundering. The Financial Action Task Force on Money Laundering was set up by the G7 group of major industrialized nations.

ENERGY AND NATURAL RESOURCES

Electricity. Production in 2000 was 25m. kWh. Installed capacity was 8,000 kW in 2000.

Minerals. The islands of the Cook group have no significant mineral resources. However, the seabed, which forms part of the exclusive economic zone, has some of the highest concentrations of manganese nodules in the world. Manganese nodules are rich in cobalt and nickel.

Agriculture. In 2001 there were approximately 4,000 ha of arable land and 3,000 ha of permanent crops. Production estimates (2002, in 1,000 tonnes): coconuts, 5; cassava, 3; mangoes, 3. Livestock (2002): 40,000 pigs, 2,000 goats.

Forestry. Timber production was 5,000 cu. metres in 2001.

Fisheries. In 2001 the total catch was estimated at 700 tonnes, entirely from sea fishing.

INDUSTRY

Labour. In 1996 there were 5,230 persons actively employed in the Cook Islands and 764 unemployed. Of those employed, 3,072 were men and 2,158 were women.

INTERNATIONAL TRADE

Imports and Exports. Exports, mainly to New Zealand, were valued at NZ$6·0m. in 1998. Main items exported were fresh fruit and vegetables and black pearls. Imports totalled NZ$70·7m.

COMMUNICATIONS

Roads. In 1992 there were 320 km of roads and, in 1991, 5,015 vehicles.

Civil Aviation. New Zealand has financed the construction of an international airport at Rarotonga which became operational for jet services in 1973. There are nine useable airports. Domestic services are provided by Air Rarotonga, and in 2003 there were also services to Auckland, Honolulu, Los Angeles, the Fiji Islands, French Polynesia and Vancouver.

Shipping. A fortnightly cargo shipping service is provided between New Zealand, Niue and Rarotonga. In 2002 merchant shipping totalled 8,000 GRT.

Telecommunications. In 2002 there were 6,200 telephone lines in service. There were 1,500 mobile phone subscribers in 2002 and 3,600 Internet users.

Postal Services. A full range of postal services are offered and there are post agents in all inhabited islands.

SOCIAL INSTITUTIONS

Justice. There is a High Court and a Court of Appeal, from which further appeal is to the Privy Council in the UK.

The population in penal institutions in 2002 was 24 (equivalent to 120 per 100,000 population).

Religion. From the census of 1996, 58% of the population belong to the Cook Islands Christian Church; about 17% are Roman Catholics, and the rest are Latter-day Saints and Seventh-Day Adventists and other religions.

Education. In March 1998 there were 28 primary schools with 140 teachers and 2,711 pupils, 23 secondary schools with 129 teachers and 1,779 pupils, and 26 pre-schools with 30 teachers and 460 pupils.

In 1998–99 total expenditure on education came to 13·1% of total government spending.

Health. A user pay scheme was introduced in July 1996 where all Cook Islanders pay a fee of NZ$5·00 for any medical or surgical treatment including consultation. Those under the age of 16 years or over the age of 60 years are exempted from payment of this charge. The dental department is privatized except for the school dental health provision. This service continues to be free to all schools.

The Rarotonga Hospital, which is the referral hospital for the outer islands, consists of 80 beds. The hospital has 8 doctors, 33 registered nurses and 11 hospital aides.

CULTURE

Broadcasting. In 1997 there were approximately 4,000 TV receivers and 14,000 radio receivers.

There are two radio stations (AM and FM) operating in the Cook Islands.

Press. The *Cook Islands News* (circulation 1,800 in 1996) is the sole daily newspaper. The *Cook Islands Star*, which is published fortnightly, is sold in the Cook Islands and in New Zealand.

Tourism. In 2002 there were 81,473 tourist arrivals; revenue in 2002 totalled US$36m.

FURTHER READING

Local statistical office: Ministry of Finance and Economic Management, P.O. Box 41, Rarotonga, Cook Islands.

Statistical office: Cook Islands Statistics Office.
Website: http://www.stats.gov.ck

NIUE

KEY HISTORICAL EVENTS

Captain James Cook sighted Niue in 1774 and called it Savage Island. Christian missionaries arrived in 1846. Niue became a British Protectorate in 1900 and was annexed to New Zealand in 1901. Internal self-government was achieved in free association with New Zealand on 19 Oct. 1974, New Zealand taking responsibility for external affairs and defence. Niue is a member of the South Pacific Forum. In Jan. 2004 Cyclone Heta destroyed the capital, Alofi, and a state of emergency was declared, although it was lifted a month later.

TERRITORY AND POPULATION

Niue is the largest uplifted coral island in the world. Distance from Auckland, New Zealand, 2,161 km; from Rarotonga, 933 km. Area, 258 sq. km; height above sea level, 67 metres. The population has been declining steadily, from around 6,000 in the 1960s to 1,812 recorded in the 2001 census, giving a population density of 7 per sq. km. Migration to New Zealand is the main factor in population change. The capital is Alofi.

SOCIAL STATISTICS

Annual growth rate, 1992–02, –1·2%. In the period 1997–2001 average number of births registered was 29 per year; average number of deaths, 16. Fertility rate, 2001, 2·6 births per woman.

CLIMATE

Oceanic, warm and humid, tempered by trade winds. May to Oct. are cooler months. Temperatures range from 20°C to 28°C.

CONSTITUTION AND GOVERNMENT

There is a Legislative Assembly (*Fono*) of 20 members, 14 elected from 14 constituencies and 6 elected by all constituencies.

RECENT ELECTIONS

Parliamentary elections were held on 30 April 2005. Seven of parliament's 20 seats, including that of Prime Minister Young Vivian, were uncontested. A total of 17 incumbent candidates were re-elected.

CURRENT ADMINISTRATION

High Commissioner: Sandra Lee.

Prime Minister: Young Vivian (Niue People's Party; took office in May 2002).

ECONOMY

Budget. Financial aid from New Zealand, 1995–96, totalled NZ$8·4m.

Banking and Finance. Niue was one of 15 countries and territories named in a report in June 2000 as failing to co-operate in the fight against international money laundering. The Financial Action Task Force on Money Laundering was set up by the G7 group of major industrialized nations.

ENERGY AND NATURAL RESOURCES

Electricity. Production in 2000 was about 3m. kWh; installed capacity was 1,000 kW in 2000.

Agriculture. In 2001 there were approximately 4,000 ha of arable land and 3,000 ha of permanent crops. The main commercial crops of the island are coconuts, taro and yams.

In 2002 there were 2,000 pigs.

Fisheries. In 2001 the total catch was approximately 200 tonnes, exclusively from marine waters.

INTERNATIONAL TRADE

Imports and Exports. Exports, 2002, NZ$0·14m.; imports, NZ$3·25m.

COMMUNICATIONS

Civil Aviation. Weekly commercial air services link Niue with New Zealand, Sydney and Samoa.

Telecommunications. There is a wireless station at Alofi, the port of the island. Telephone main lines (2002) 1,100. Internet users (2002) 900.

SOCIAL INSTITUTIONS

Justice. There is a High Court under a Chief Justice, with a right of appeal to the New Zealand Supreme Court.

Religion. At the 1991 census, 1,487 people belonged to the Congregational (Ekalesia Niue); Latter-day Saints (213), Roman Catholics (90), Jehovah's Witness (47), Seventh Day Adventists (27), other (63), no religion (34), not stated (1).

Education. In 2002 there was one primary school with 17 teachers and 251 pupils, and one secondary school with 29 teachers and 240 pupils. There is also the University of the South Pacific.

Health. In 1992 there were 4 doctors, 1 dentist, 6 midwives and 19 nursing personnel. The 24-bed hospital at Alofi was destroyed by Cyclone Heta in Jan. 2004.

CULTURE

Broadcasting. There were 1,000 radio receivers in 1997. Cable television is available.

Press. A weekly newspaper is published in English and Niuean; circulation about 400.

Tourism. In 2002 there were 3,155 visitors (1,158 on vacation).

NICARAGUA

República de Nicaragua

Capital: Managua
Population projection, 2010: 6·38m.
GDP per capita, 2002: (PPP$) 2,470
HDI/world rank: 0·667/118

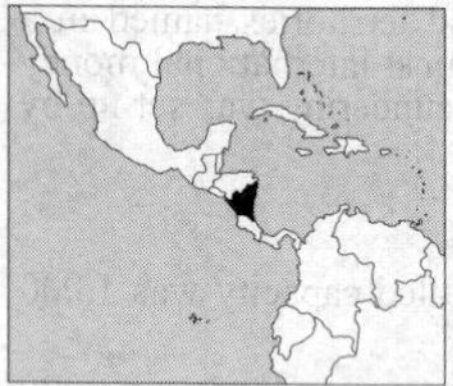

KEY HISTORICAL EVENTS

Colonization of the Nicaraguan Pacific coast was undertaken by Spaniards from Panama, beginning in 1523. France and Britain, however, and later the USA, all tried to play a colonial or semi-colonial role in Nicaragua. Nicaragua became an independent republic in 1838 but its independence was often threatened by US intervention. Between 1910 and 1930 the country was under almost continuous US military occupation.

In 1914 the Bryan-Chamarro Treaty entitled the USA to a permanent option for a canal route through Nicaragua, a 99-year option for a naval base in the Bay of Fonseca on the Pacific coast and occupation of the Corn Islands on the Atlantic coast. The Bryan-Chamarro Treaty was not abrogated until 14 July 1970 when the Corn Islands returned to Nicaragua.

The Somoza family dominated Nicaragua from 1933 to 1979. Imposing a brutal dictatorship, they secured for themselves a large share of the national wealth. In 1962 the radical Sandanista National Liberation Front was formed with the object of overthrowing the Somozas. After 17 years of civil war the Sandanistas triumphed. On 17 July 1979 President Somoza fled into exile. The USA made efforts to unseat the revolutionary government by supporting the Contras (counter-revolutionary forces). It was not until 1988 that the state of emergency was lifted as part of the Central American peace process. Rebel anti-Sandanista activities had ceased by 1990; the last organized insurgent group negotiated an agreement with the government in April 1994.

In Oct. 1998 Hurricane Mitch devastated the country causing 3,800 deaths.

TERRITORY AND POPULATION

Nicaragua is bounded in the north by Honduras, east by the Caribbean, south by Costa Rica and west by the Pacific. Area, 131,812 sq. km (121,428 sq. km dry land). The coastline runs 450 km on the Atlantic and 305 km on the Pacific. The census population in April 1995 was 4,357,099 (density, 33·3 per sq. km). 2002 estimate: 5,335,000. In 2001, 56·5% of the population were urban.

The UN gives a projected population for 2010 of 6·38m.

15 administrative departments and two autonomous regions are grouped in three zones. Areas (in sq. km), populations at the 1995 census and chief towns:

	Area	*Population*	*Chief town*
Pacific Zone	18,429	2,467,742	
Carazo	1,050	149,407	Jinotepe
Chinandega	4,926	350,212	Chinandega
Granada	929	155,683	Granada
León	5,107	336,894	León
Managua	3,672	1,093,760	Managua
Masaya	590	241,354	Masaya
Rivas	2,155	140,432	Rivas
Central-North Zone	35,960	1,354,246	
Boaco	4,244	136,949	Boaco
Chontales	6,378	144,635	Juigalpa
Estelí	2,335	174,894	Estelí
Jinotega	9,755	257,933	Jinotega
Madriz	1,602	107,567	Somoto
Matagalpa	8,523	383,776	Matagalpa
Nueva Segovia	3,123	148,492	Ocotal
Atlantic Zone	67,039	535,111	
Atlántico Norte[1]	32,159	192,716	Puerto Cabezas
Atlántico Sur[1]	27,407	272,252	Bluefields
Río San Juan	7,473	70,143	San Carlos

[1]Autonomous region.

The capital is Managua with (1999 estimate) 930,000 inhabitants. Other cities (1995 populations): León, 123,865; Chinandega, 97,387; Masaya, 88,971; Granada, 71,783; Estelí, 71,550; Tipitapa, 67,925; Matagalpa, 59,397; Juigalpa, 36,999.

The population is of Spanish and Amerindian origins with an admixture of Afro-Americans on the Caribbean coast. Ethnic groups in 1997: Mestizo (mixed Amerindian and white), 69%; white, 17%; black, 9%; Amerindian, 5%. The official language is Spanish.

SOCIAL STATISTICS

2002 estimates: births, 175,000; deaths, 28,000. Estimated rates (per 1,000 population), 2002: births, 32·8; deaths, 5·2. Annual population growth rate, 1992–02, 2·8%. 2001 life expectancy: male 66·8 years, female 71·5. Infant mortality, 2001, 36 per 1,000 live births; fertility rate, 2001, 4·0 births per woman.

CLIMATE

The climate is tropical, with a wet season from May to Jan. Temperatures vary with altitude. Managua, Jan. 81°F (27°C), July 81°F (27°C). Annual rainfall 38" (976 mm).

CONSTITUTION AND GOVERNMENT

A new Constitution was promulgated on 9 Jan. 1987. It provides for a unicameral 93-seat *National Assembly* comprising 90 members directly elected by proportional representation, together with three unsuccessful presidential election candidates.

The *President* and *Vice-President* are directly elected for a five-year term commencing on the 10 Jan. following their date of election. The President may stand for a second term, but not consecutively.

National Anthem. 'Salve a ti Nicaragua' ('Hail to thee, Nicaragua'); words by S. Ibarra Mayorga, tune by L. A. Delgadillo.

RECENT ELECTIONS

Presidential and parliamentary elections took place on 4 Nov. 2001. In the presidential elections Enrique Bolaños Geyer was elected with 56·3% of votes cast, defeating José Daniel Ortega Saavedra (42·3%) and Alberto Saborío (1·4%). At the parliamentary elections the Constitutional Liberal Party gained 47 seats with 53·2% of votes cast; the Sandinista National Liberation Front, 43 (42·1%); and the Conservative Party of Nicaragua, 2 (2·1%).

CURRENT ADMINISTRATION

President: Enrique Bolaños Geyer; b. 1928 (Constitutional Liberal Party; in office since 10 Jan. 2002).

Vice President: José Rizo Castellón.

In March 2005 the government comprised:

Minister of Agriculture and Forestry: José Augusto Navarro Flores. *Transportation and Infrastructure:* Pedro Solórzano Castillo. *Government:* Dr Julio Vega Pasquier. *Education, Sports and Culture:* Miguel Ángel García. *Defence:* Dr José Adán Guerra Pastoras. *Development, Industry and Commerce:* Mario Arana. *Environment and Natural Resources:* Arturo Harding Lacayo. *Finance and Public Credit:* Mario Arana Sevilla. *Foreign Affairs:* Norman José Caldera Cardenal. *Health:* José Antonio Alvarado. *Labour:* Virgilio Gurdián Castellón. *Family:* Carmen Largaespada.

Office of the President (Spanish only): http://www.presidencia.gob.ni/

DEFENCE

In 2003 defence expenditure totalled US$31m. (US$6 per capita), representing 1·2% of GDP.

Army. There are six regional commands. Strength (2002) 12,000.

Navy. The Nicaraguan Navy was some 800 strong in 2002.

Air Force. The Air Force has been semi-independent since 1947. Personnel (2002) 1,200, with no combat aircraft and 15 armed helicopters.

INTERNATIONAL RELATIONS

Nicaragua is a member of the UN, WTO, OAS, Inter-American Development Bank, ACS, IOM, SELA and the Central American Common Market.

ECONOMY

In 2002 agriculture accounted for 18·0% of GDP, industry 25·0% and services 57·0%.

Overview. Nicaragua, one of Latin America's poorest countries, suffers from low productivity, high current account deficit, high unemployment and a severe external debt burden. As a result the economy is dependent on foreign aid, amounting to 20% of GDP. Coffee and meat account for around 40% of exports. The collapse of coffee prices has had serious impact on rural living standards. The country's leading trading partners are the USA, the members of the Central American Common Market and the EU. Corruption is a problem. Structural reforms are focused on government procurement, the reform of social security and privatization. The unemployment rate is 8–10%. Half the population lives in poverty and about 17% fall below the extreme poverty line.

Currency. The monetary unit is the *córdoba* (NIO), of 100 *centavos*, which replaced the córdoba oro in 1991 at par. Inflation was 4·0% in 2002. In May 2002 foreign exchange reserves were US$402m. In March 2002 total money supply was 4,754m. córdobas.

Budget. Total revenue and expenditure (in 1m. córdobas), years ending 31 Dec.:

	1997	*1998*	*1999*	*2000*
Revenue	5,404·8	6,976·5	7,956·2	9,193·4
Expenditure	6,435·3	7,850·5	10,853·5	12,512·1

In 1998 tax revenue accounted for 85·7% of total revenues. Current expenditure accounted for 67·2% of total expenditures and capital expenditure 31·6%.

Performance. Real GDP growth was 1·0% in 2002 (3·0% in 2001). Total GDP in 2003 was US$4·1bn.

Banking and Finance. The Central Bank of Nicaragua came into operation on 1 Jan. 1961 as an autonomous bank of issue, absorbing the issue department of the National Bank. The *President* is Dr Mario Alonso Icabalceta. There were seven private commercial banks in 2000.

There is a stock exchange in Managua.

ENERGY AND NATURAL RESOURCES

Environment. Nicaragua's carbon dioxide emissions from the consumption and flaring of fossil fuels in 2002 were the equivalent of 0·7 tonnes per capita.

Electricity. Installed capacity in 2000 was 0·6m. kW. In 2000, 2·29bn. kWh were produced; consumption per capita in 2000 was 474 kWh.

Minerals. Production of gold in 2001 was 3,745 kg; silver (2001), 2,498 kg; limestone (2001), 580,000 tonnes.

Agriculture. In 2001 there were 1·94m. ha arable land and 236,000 ha permanent cropland. 95,000 ha were irrigated in 2001. Production (in 1,000 tonnes) in 2000: sugarcane, 4,000; maize, 364; rice, 285; dry beans, 114; sorghum, 102; bananas, 92; coffee, 82; oranges, 71; groundnuts, 67; cassava, 52; pineapples, 47; plantains, 40; soybeans, 23.

In 2000 there were 1·66m. cattle, 400,000 pigs, 245,000 horses and 10m. chickens. Animal products (in 1,000 tonnes), 2000: beef and veal, 49; pork, bacon and ham, 6; poultry, 39; milk, 231; eggs, 30.

Forestry. The forest area in 2000 was 3·28m. ha, or 27·0% of the land area. Timber production was 5·88m. cu. metres in 2001.

Fisheries. In 2001 the catch was 22,799 tonnes (21,748 tonnes from sea fishing), up from 4,582 tonnes in 1989.

INDUSTRY

Industry accounted for 26·0% of GDP in 2001, with manufacturing contributing 14·4%. Important industries include chemicals, textiles, metal products, oil refining and food processing. Production in 2000 (in 1,000 tonnes): cement, 568; residual fuel oil, 411; raw sugar, 398; distillate fuel oil, 205; petrol, 102; wheat flour (2001), 60; vegetable oil (2001), 21; rum (1998), 7·7m. litres; sawnwood (2002), 45,000 cu. metres.

Labour. The workforce in 2001 was 1,900,400 (1,315,000 males). In 2001, 1,701,700 persons were in employment, of whom 739,000 were engaged in agriculture, hunting, forestry and fishing; 294,300 in community, social and personal services; 279,800 in wholesale and retail trade, and restaurants and hotels; and 131,600 in manufacturing. There were 178,000 unemployed in 2000, a rate of 9·8%.

INTERNATIONAL TRADE

Foreign debt was US$6,485m. in 2002.

Imports and Exports. Imports and exports in US$1m.:

	1998	*1999*	*2000*	*2001*	*2002*
Imports f.o.b.	1,397·1	1,698·2	1,653·1	1,620·4	1,636·4
Exports f.o.b.	580·1	552·4	649·9	614·6	605·1

Main imports in 1999 were: machinery and transport equipment, 29·8%; chemicals, 15·2%; foodstuffs, 14·7%; petroleum and related products, 7·7%. Principal exports were: coffee, 27·8%; seafood, 13·5%; meat, 8·8%; gold, 5·9%.

Main import suppliers, 1999: USA, 33·2%; Costa Rica, 12·1%; Guatemala, 7·8%; Panama, 7·1%; El Salvador, 5·8%; Japan, 5·3%. Main export markets, 1999: USA, 36·3%; El Salvador, 13·4%; Germany, 10·5%; Honduras, 6·8%; Costa Rica, 5·4%; Belgium, 4·0%.

COMMUNICATIONS

Roads. Road length in 2002 was 18,712 km, of which 11·4% were asphalted. In 2002 there were 83,168 passenger cars (15·6 per 1,000 inhabitants), 6,947 buses and coaches, 106,115 trucks and vans and 28,973 motorcycles and mopeds.

Civil Aviation. In 1999 scheduled airline traffic of Nicaragua-based carriers flew 0·8m. km, carrying 59,000 passengers (all on international flights). The Augusto Sandino international airport at Managua handled 758,000 passengers in 2000 (612,000 on international flights) and 19,900 tonnes of freight.

Shipping. The merchant marine totalled 4,000 GRT in 2002. The Pacific ports are Corinto (the largest), San Juan del Sur and Puerto Sandino through which pass most of the external trade. The chief eastern ports are El Bluff (for Bluefields) and Puerto Cabezas.

Telecommunications. In 2002 there were 411,600 telephone subscribers, or 76·6 per 1,000 population, and 150,000 PCs in use (27·9 for every 1,000 persons). Mobile phone subscribers numbered 202,800 in 2002. Nicaragua had 90,000 Internet users in 2002.

Postal Services. In 1998 there were 183 post offices.

SOCIAL INSTITUTIONS

Justice. The judicial power is vested in a Supreme Court of Justice at Managua, 5 chambers of second instance and 153 judges of lower courts.

The population in penal institutions in June 1999 was 7,198 (143 per 100,000 of national population).

Religion. The prevailing form of religion is Roman Catholicism (3·59m. adherents in 2001), but religious liberty is guaranteed by the Constitution. There were also 810,000 Protestants in 2001. There is one arch-bishopric, seven bishoprics and one cardinal.

Education. Adult literacy rate in 2001 was 66·8% (male, 66·5%; female, 67·1%). In 2002 there were 8,251 primary schools with 923,391 pupils, 364,012 secondary school pupils and (2001) 70,925 students at university level.

In 1994–95 there were two universities and three specialized universities (agriculture; engineering; polytechnic) with 1,260 academic staff.

In 2000–01 total expenditure on education came to 13·8% of total government expenditure. A 15-year National Plan for Education is under way which aims to transform education by means of expanding provision in rural areas, providing greater access to pre-school and adult education, improving the quality of teacher training, modernizing the curriculum and investing in materials and infrastructure.

Health. In 1994 there were 56 hospitals, with a provision of 11 beds per 10,000 population. There were 4,551 physicians, 1,099 dentists and 2,577 nurses in 1995.

CULTURE

World Heritage Sites. Nicaragua has one site on the UNESCO World Heritage List: the Ruins of León Viejo (inscribed on the list in 2000), a 16th century Spanish settlement.

Broadcasting. Broadcasting is administered by the Instituto Nicaraguense de Telecomunicaciones y Correos (Telcor). There were 640,000 television sets (colour by NTSC) in 2001 and 1·37m. radio receivers in 2000.

Press. In 1996 there were four daily newspapers in Managua, with a total circulation of 135,000.

Tourism. In 2000 there were 486,000 foreign tourists, spending US$116m. Tourist numbers grew by nearly 500% between 1990 and 1998.

DIPLOMATIC REPRESENTATIVES

Of Nicaragua in the United Kingdom (Suite 31, Vicarage House, 58–60 Kensington Church St., London, W8 4DP)
Ambassador: Vacant.
Chargé d'Affaires a.i.: Andrés Gómez.

Of the United Kingdom in Nicaragua (embassy in Managua closed in March 2004)
Ambassador: Georgina Butler (resides at San José, Costa Rica).

Of Nicaragua in the USA (1627 New Hampshire Ave., NW, Washington, D.C., 20009)
Ambassador: Salvador Stadthagen.

Of the USA in Nicaragua (Km. 4½ Carretera Sur, Managua)
Ambassador: Barbara C. Moore.

Of Nicaragua to the United Nations
Ambassador: Eduardo J. Sevilla Somoza.

Of Nicaragua to the European Union
Ambassador: Vacant.
Chargé d'Affaires a.i.: Ricardo Paúl Lira.

FURTHER READING

Dijkstra, G., *Industrialization in Sandinista Nicaragua: Policy and Party in a Mixed Economy.* Boulder (CO), 1992

Jones, Adam, *Beyond the Barricades: Nicaragua and the Struggle for the Sandinista Press, 1979–1998.* Ohio Univ. Press, Athens (OH), 2002

Woodward, R. L., *Nicaragua.* [Bibliography] 2nd ed. ABC-Clio, Oxford and Santa Barbara (CA), 1994

National statistical office: Dirección General de Estadística y Censos, Managua.
Website (Spanish only): http://www.inec.gob.ni/

NIGER

République du Niger

Capital: Niamey
Population projection, 2010: 15·39m.
GDP per capita, 2002: (PPP$) 800
HDI/world rank: 0·292/176

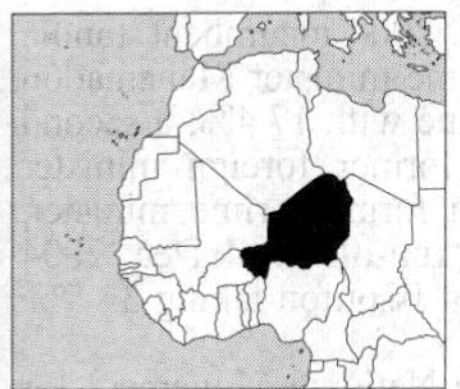

KEY HISTORICAL EVENTS

Niger was occupied by France after 1883. It achieved full independence on 3 Aug. 1960. Guerrilla activity by Tuaregs of the Armed Resistance Organization (ORA) seeking local autonomy in the north continued into 1995. On 27 Jan. 1996 the army chief of staff Gen. (then Col.) Barré Maïnassara deposed President Ousmane Mahamane and dissolved parliament. In April 1999 President Maïnassara was assassinated by bodyguards at Niamey airport, prompting troops and tanks onto the streets of the capital. A week after the President's assassination, Daouda Mallam Wanké, leader of the presidential guard and the officer widely suspected of being behind the killing, was named as Maïnassara's successor.

TERRITORY AND POPULATION

Niger is bounded in the north by Algeria and Libya, east by Chad, south by Nigeria, southwest by Benin and Burkina Faso, and west by Mali. Area, 1,186,408 sq. km, with a population at the 2001 census (provisional) of 10,790,352; density, 9 per sq. km. In 2001, 79·0% of the population were rural.

The UN gives a projected population for 2010 of 15·39m.

The country is divided into the capital, Niamey, an autonomous district, and seven departments. Area, population and chief towns at the 2001 census (provisional):

Department	*Sq. km*	*Population*	*Chief town*	*Population*
Agadez	634,209	313,274	Agadez	76,957
Diffa	140,216	329,658	Diffa	23,233
Dosso	31,002	1,479,095	Dosso	43,293
Maradi	38,581	2,202,035	Maradi	147,038
Niamey	670	674,950	Niamey	674,950
Tahoua	106,677	1,908,100	Tahoua	72,446
Tillabéry	89,623	1,858,342	Tillabéry	16,181
Zinder	145,430	2,024,898	Zinder	170,574

The population is composed chiefly of Hausa (53%), Songhai and Djerma (21%), Tuareg (10·5%), Fulani (10%) and Kanuri-Manga (4·5%). The official language is French. Hausa, Djerma and Fulani are national languages.

SOCIAL STATISTICS

1997 estimates: births, 504,000; deaths, 225,000. Rates, 1997 estimates, per 1,000 population: birth rate, 53·7 (the highest birth rate in the world); death rate, 24·0; infant mortality, 156 per 1,000 live births (2001). Annual population growth rate, 1992–02, 3·5%. Expectation of life at birth, 2001: 45·3 years for males and 45·9 for females. Fertility rate, 2001, 8·0 children per woman (the highest anywhere in the world).

CLIMATE

Precipitation determines the geographical division into a southern zone of agriculture, a central zone of pasturage and a desert-like northern zone. The country lacks water, with the exception of the southwestern districts, which are watered by the Niger and its tributaries, and the southern zone, where there are a number of wells. Niamey, 95°F (35°C). Annual rainfall varies from 22" (560 mm) in the south to 7" (180 mm) in the Sahara zone. The rainy season lasts from May until Sept., but there are periodic droughts.

CONSTITUTION AND GOVERNMENT

Theoretically, Niger is a unitary multi-party democracy. The *President* is directly elected for a five-year term renewable once. There is an 83-member *National Assembly* elected for a five-year term by proportional representation.

At a referendum on 12 May 1996, 90% of votes cast were in favour of a new constitution; turn-out was 33%.

National Anthem. 'Auprès du grand Niger puissant' ('By the banks of the mighty great Niger'); words by M. Thiriet, tune by R. Jacquet and N. Frionnet.

RECENT ELECTIONS

In the first round of presidential elections held on 16 Nov. 2004 incumbent Tandja Mamadou won 40·7% of the votes followed by former prime minister Mahamadou Issoufou with 24·6%; former president Mahamane Ousmane with 17·4%; a second former prime minister, Amadou Cheiffou, with 6·4%; former foreign minister Moumouni Adamou Djermakoye with 6·1%; and a third former prime minister, Hamid Algabid, with 4·9%. Turn-out was 48·3%. In the run-off on 4 Dec. 2004 Tandja Mamadou won 65·5% of the vote with Mahamadou Issoufou taking 34·5%. Turn-out was 45·0%.

Parliamentary elections were held on 4 Dec. 2004. The National Movement for the Development Society (MNSD) won 38 seats; the Democratic and Social Convention, 22; the Nigerien Party for Democracy and Socialism, 17; the Social Democratic Rally, 7; the Rally for Democracy and Progress, 6; the Alliance for Democracy and Progress, 5; and the Party for Socialism and Democracy in Niger, 1. Turn-out was 44·7%.

CURRENT ADMINISTRATION

President: Tandja Mamadou; b. 1938 (MNSD; sworn in 22 Dec. 1999 and re-elected in Dec. 2004).

In March 2005 the government comprised:

Prime Minister: Hama Amadou; b. 1950 (MNSD; sworn in 3 Jan. 2000, having previously held office Feb. 1995–Jan. 1996).

Minister of Animal Resources: Abdoulaye Jina. *Defence:* Hassane Souley 'Bonto'. *Basic Education and Literacy:* Hamani Arouna. *Finance and Economy:* Ali Lamine Zène. *Foreign Affairs and Co-operation:* Aïchatou Mindaoudou. *Health and Disease Control:* Ary Ibrahim. *Secondary and Higher Education, Research and Technology:* Ousmane Galidama. *Interior and Decentralization:* Mounkaïla Mody. *Justice and Keeper of the Seals:* Matty Elhadji Salissou. *Mines and Energy:* Mohamed Abdoulahi. *Privatization and Restructuring of Enterprises:* Gazoli Laouali Rahamou. *Civil Service and Labour:* Kanda Siptey. *Transport:* Souleymane Kane. *Agricultural Development:* Labo Moussa. *Youth, Sports and Francophonie:* Abdouramane Seydou. *Promotion of Women and Protection of Children:* Ousmane Zeinalou Mouley. *Territorial and Community Development:* Mahamane Moussa. *Commerce, Industry and Promotion of Private Sector:* Sala Habi Mahamadou Salissou. *Urban Development, Housing and Public Property:* Diallo Aissa Abdoulaye. *Culture, Arts and Communication:* Oumarou Adari. *Population and Social Work:* Boukari Zila Mohamadou. *Tourism and Handicrafts:* Amadou Nouhou. *Professional and Technical Training, Responsible for Youth Employment:* Abdou Daouda. *Minister of State Responsible for Water Resources, Environment and Desertification Control:* Abdou Labo. *Minister of State Responsible for Equipment:* Seyni Oumarou. *Minister Responsible for Institutions and Government Spokesman:* Mohamed Ben Omar.

DEFENCE

Selective conscription for two years operates. Defence expenditure totalled US$25m. in 2003 (US$2 per capita), representing 1·0% of GDP.

Army. There are three military districts. Strength (2002) 5,200. There are additional paramilitary forces of some 5,400.

Air Force. In 2002 the Air Force had 100 personnel. There are no combat aircraft.

INTERNATIONAL RELATIONS

Niger is a member of the UN, WTO, the African Union, African Development Bank, ECOWAS, the Lake Chad Basin Commission, OIC, Islamic Development Bank,

IOM, International Organization of the Francophonie, and is an ACP member state of the ACP-EU relationship.

ECONOMY

Agriculture accounted for 39·6% of GDP in 2002, industry 17·0% and services 43·4%.

Currency. The unit of currency is the *franc CFA* (XOF) with a parity of 655·957 francs CFA to one euro. In May 2002 total money supply was 84,319m. francs CFA and foreign exchange reserves were US$85m. Gold reserves were 11,000 troy oz in June 2000. Inflation in 2002 was 2·7%.

Budget. In 2000 revenue (in 1,000m. francs CFA) was 162·2 and expenditure 204·8. Taxes accounted for 63·4% of revenues, and external aids and gifts 32·1%. Current expenditures accounted for 67·6% of expenditure.

Performance. Real GDP growth was 7·1% in 2001 and 3·0% in 2002; total GDP in 2003 was US$2·7bn.

Banking and Finance. The regional Central Bank of West African States (BCEAO)—*Governor,* Charles Konan Banny—functions as the bank of issue. There were six commercial banks in 2002, three development banks and a savings bank.

There is a stock exchange in Niamey.

ENERGY AND NATURAL RESOURCES

Environment. In 2002 Niger's carbon dioxide emissions from the consumption and flaring of fossil fuels were the equivalent of 0·1 tonnes per capita.

Electricity. Installed capacity was 0·1m. kW in 2000. Production in 2000 amounted to about 238m. kWh, with consumption per capita an estimated 42 kWh.

Minerals. Large uranium deposits are mined at Arlit and Akouta. Uranium production (2002), 3,075 tonnes. Niger's uranium production is exceeded only by those of Canada and Australia. Phosphates are mined in the Niger valley, and coal reserves are being exploited by open-cast mining (production of hard coal in 2000 was an estimated 175,000 tonnes). Salt production in 1997 was 3,000 tonnes.

Agriculture. Production is dependent upon adequate rainfall. There were 4·49m. ha of arable land in 2001 and 11,000 ha of permanent crops. 66,000 ha were irrigated in 2001. There were 128 tractors in 2001. Production estimates in 2000 (in 1,000 tonnes): millet, 2,250; sorghum, 400; onions, 180; sugarcane, 140; cassava, 120; groundnuts, 110; rice, 73; tomatoes, 65; sweet potatoes, 35.

Livestock (2000): cattle, 2·22m.; goats, 6·60m.; sheep, 4·30m.; asses, 530,000; camels, 410,000; chickens, 20m. Livestock products (in 1,000 tonnes), 2000: milk, 168; meat, 125; cheese, 14; eggs, 9.

Forestry. There is a government programme of afforestation as a protection from desert encroachment. There were 1·33m. ha of forests in 2000 (1·0% of the land area). Timber production in 2001 was 3·27m. cu. metres, mainly for fuel.

Fisheries. There are fisheries on the River Niger and along the shores of Lake Chad. In 2001 the catch was 20,800 tonnes, exclusively from inland waters.

INDUSTRY

Some small manufacturing industries, mainly in Niamey, produce textiles, food products, furniture and chemicals. Output of cement in 2000 (estimate), 30,000 tonnes.

Labour. The labour force in 1996 totalled 4,497,000 (56% males). Nearly 90% of the economically active population in 1994 were engaged in agriculture, fisheries and forestry.

Trade Unions. The national confederation is the *Union Syndicale des Travailleurs du Niger,* which has 15,000 members in 31 unions.

INTERNATIONAL TRADE

Foreign debt was US$1,797m. in 2002.

Imports and Exports. In 1999 imports were valued at US$316·2m. (US$420·0m. in 1998) and exports at US$179·7m. (US$336·8m. in 1998). In 1998 the main imports were (in US$1m.): foodstuffs, 120·6; refined petroleum, 56·4; machinery and transport equipment, 55·5; manufactured goods, 52·8; and chemicals, 41·0. The main exports in 1988 were: uranium, 133·0; road vehicles, 37·2; cigarettes, 34·6; vegetables (especially onions), 29·7; textiles, 27·2; and livestock, 26·2.

The main import suppliers in 1999 were France (22·4%), Côte d'Ivoire (15·1%), China (8·3%) and Nigeria (8·0%). The main export destinations in 1999 were France (44·5%), Nigeria (27·0%), Japan (17·9%) and Spain (4·2%).

COMMUNICATIONS

Roads. In 1999 there were approximately 10,100 km of roads including 800 km of paved roads. Niamey and Zinder are the termini of two trans-Sahara motor routes; the Hoggar–Aïr–Zinder road extends to Kano and the Tanezrouft–Gao–Niamey road to Benin. A 648-km 'uranium road' runs from Arlit to Tahoua. There were, in 1996, 38,220 passenger cars (3·8 per 1,000 inhabitants) and 15,200 trucks and vans.

Civil Aviation. There is an international airport at Niamey (Diori Hamani Airport), which handled 83,000 passengers in 2000 (81,000 on international flights). In 2003 there were international flights to Abidjan, Bamako, Casablanca, Dakar, Khartoum, Libreville, Ouagadougou, Paris and Tripoli. In 1999 scheduled airline traffic of Niger-based carriers flew 3·0m. km, carrying 84,000 passengers (all on international flights).

Shipping. Sea-going vessels can reach Niamey (300 km inside the country) between Sept. and March.

Telecommunications. Niger had 23,800 telephone subscribers in 2001 (2·1 per 1,000 population)—the lowest penetration rate of any country in the world. In 2002 there were 7,000 PCs in use (0·6 per 1,000 persons) and 16,600 mobile phone subscribers. Internet users numbered 15,000 in 2002.

Postal Services. In 1998 there were 53 post offices, or one for every 190,000 persons.

SOCIAL INSTITUTIONS

Justice. There are Magistrates' and Assize Courts at Niamey, Zinder and Maradi, and justices of the peace in smaller centres. The Court of Appeal is at Niamey.

The population in penal institutions in 2002 was approximately 6,000 (52 per 100,000 of national population).

Religion. In 2001 there were 9·39m. Sunni Muslims. There are some Roman Catholics, and traditional animist beliefs are widespread.

Education. In 2000–01 there were 578 teachers for 12,300 children in pre-primary schools and 15,668 teachers for 656,589 pupils in primary schools. During the period 1990–95 only 18% of females of primary school age were enrolled in school. In 2001–02 there were 112,033 pupils in secondary schools. There were 13,400 students in tertiary education (806 academic staff) in 2000–01. There is a university and an Islamic university.

Adult literacy in 2001 was 16·5% (male, 24·4%; female, 8·9%). The rates for both males and females are the lowest in the world.

In 2000–01 total expenditure on education came to 2·8% of GNP.

Health. In 1987 there were five hospital beds per 10,000 inhabitants. There were 325 physicians, 19 dentists, 2,126 nurses and 511 midwives in 1997.

CULTURE

World Heritage Sites. Niger has three sites on the UNESCO World Heritage List: the Aïr and Ténéré Natural Reserves (inscribed on the list in 1991), part of the largest protected area in Africa (7·7m. ha); and the 'W' National Park of Niger (1996), a savannah and forested area of biodiversity.

Broadcasting. La Voix du Sahel and Télé-Sahel under the government's Office de Radiodiffusion Télévision du Niger are responsible for radio and TV broadcasting (colour by PAL). In 2000 there were 1·27m. radio sets and in 2001 there were 110,000 TV sets.

Press. In 1998 there were two daily newspapers with a combined circulation of 4,000.

Tourism. In 2000 there were 50,000 foreign tourists; spending by tourists in 1999 totalled US$24m.

DIPLOMATIC REPRESENTATIVES

Of Niger in the United Kingdom
Ambassador: Adamou Seydou (resides at Paris).

Of the United Kingdom in Niger
Ambassador: David Coates (resides at Abidjan, Côte d'Ivoire).

Of Niger in the USA (2204 R. St., NW, Washington, D.C., 20008)
Ambassador: Joseph Diatta.

Of the USA in Niger (BP 11201, Rue des Ambassades, Niamey)
Ambassador: Dennise G. Mathieu.

Of Niger to the United Nations
Ambassador: Ousmane Moutari.

Of Niger to the European Union
Ambassador: Abdou Agbarry.

FURTHER READING

Miles, W. F. S., *Hausaland Divided: Colonialism and Independence in Nigeria and Niger.* Cornell University Press, 1994

Zamponi, Lynda F., *Niger.* [Bibliography] ABC-Clio, Oxford and Santa Barbara (CA), 1994

National statistical office: Direction de la Statistique et de l'Informatique, Ministère du Plan, Niamey.

NIGERIA

Federal Republic of Nigeria

Capital: Abuja
Population projection, 2010: 145·92m.
GDP per capita, 2002: (PPP$) 860
HDI/world rank: 0·466/151

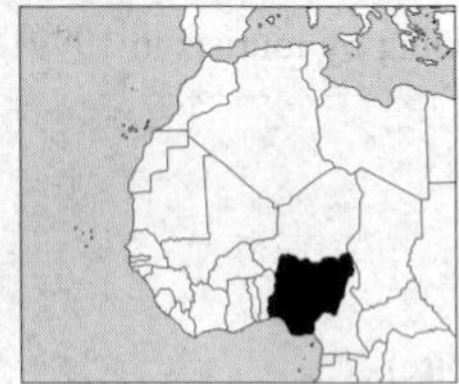

KEY HISTORICAL EVENTS

The earliest evidence of human settlement dates from 9000 BC. The Nok culture, traces of which are visible in Nigerian art today, prevailed from around 800 BC to AD 200. By 1000 the state of Kanem was flourishing, thanks to the trans-Saharan trade route that ran from West Africa to the Mediterranean. In the 11th century northern Nigeria split into seven independent Hausa city-states. By the 14th century, two states had developed in the south, Oyo and Benin, with the Igbo people of the southeast living in village communities. West of the Niger, the Ife flourished between the 11th and 15th centuries. The importance of the Ife civilization is evident today; all Yoruba states claim that their leaders are descended from the Ife as a way of establishing legitimacy. At the end of the 18th century, Fulani religious groups waged war in the north, merging states to create the single Islamic state of the Sokoto Caliphate.

In the late 15th century Portuguese navigators began to purchase slaves in the region. They were followed by British, French and Dutch traders. From the 1650s until the 1860s, slave trading caused a forced migration of around 3·5m. people. After the abolition of the slave trade in Britain in 1807, attempts to find a lucrative alternative led to the production of palm oil for export. An internal slave trade developed.

In 1804 Usuman dan Fodio began a reformist 'Holy war', conquering the Hausa city-states, though Kanem-Bornu retained its independence. However, by the late 19th century Kanem-Bornu's power was in steep decline. Usuman's son, Muhammed Bello, established a state centred at Sokoto, controlling most of northern Nigeria for the rest of the century. In the south, the Oyo region was troubled by civil wars, brought to an end when the British intervened. Britain took Lagos as its colony in 1861. By 1906 Britain controlled Nigeria as the Colony (Lagos), the Protectorate of Southern Nigeria and the Protectorate of Northern Nigeria, amalgamating the regions in 1914 to establish the Colony and Protectorate of Nigeria. British dominance was resisted in the south by the Ijebu (a Yoruba tribe), by the Aro (Igbo) in the east and by the Aniocha (Igbo) in the west.

British colonial rule brought development in the transportation and communications systems and a shift towards cash crops. Western and Christian influence prevailed, spreading far more rapidly in the south—where British control had been secure over a longer period. This added to the growing disparity between north and south. Nigerian forces helped to defeat the German army in Cameroon in the First World War. In the 1920s demands increased for African representation. In 1923 Herbert Macaulay founded the Nigerian National Democratic Party. In 1944 he joined with others to form the National Council of Nigeria and the Cameroon (NCNC). In 1951 Britain agreed a new constitution that would provide for elected representation on a regional basis. When the constitution failed in 1952, Nigeria was divided into three regions, Eastern, Western and Northern, plus the federal territory of Lagos. In 1956 the Western and Eastern regions became self-governing, as did the Northern region in 1959.

In 1960 Nigeria declared independence. A coalition government was formed, with Abukar Tafawa Balewa as prime minister. Continuing conflict between north and south undermined the new republic. In 1966 a military coup installed Maj.-Gen. Aguiyi-Ironsi, an Igbo, as head of a military government. Another coup later in the year placed Lieut.-Col. Yakubu Gowon in power and saw many northern Igbo massacred. In May 1967 the Igbo people of the south declared their region independent from the rest of the country, naming the breakaway republic Biafra. Civil war raged for three years until federal Nigeria triumphed at the price of 1m. dead and widespread famine and destruction. A period of relative prosperity, based on oil, was accompanied by government overspending, corruption and crime. In the

1980s recession sent oil prices down and Nigeria found itself struggling with debt, inflation and mass unemployment.

Gen. Murtala Muhammad, who overthrew Gowon's regime in 1975, was assassinated a year later. He was succeeded by Gen. Olusegun Obasanjo, who oversaw the transition to civilian rule, while juggling the need for Western aid with his support for African nationalist movements. A bloodless coup in 1985 brought to power Maj.-Gen. Ibrahim Babangida, who reneged on his promise to restore civilian government. When unrest eventually forced his resignation, Gen. Sani Abacha became president and closed down all unions and political institutions. After the execution of writer Ken Saro-Wiwa and eight other human rights activists in 1995 Nigeria was suspended from the Commonwealth.

Abacha died in office in 1998. He was succeeded by Maj.-Gen. Abdusalam Abubakar, who brought about a return to civilian rule. In Feb. 1999 Nigeria chose as president Olusegun Obasanjo, who had retired from the army. The country was readmitted to the Commonwealth. However, tribal and religious conflict continued and fighting between the Igbo Christians and Hausa Muslims over the implementation of Islamic law has left thousands dead.

TERRITORY AND POPULATION

Nigeria is bounded in the north by Niger, east by Chad and Cameroon, south by the Gulf of Guinea and west by Benin. It has an area of 356,667 sq. miles (923,768 sq. km). For sovereignty over the Bakassi Peninsula *see* CAMEROON: Territory and Population. Census population, 1991, 88,244,581 (43,969,970 females; urban, 36%); population density, 95·8 per sq. km. Estimate, 2002, 120,942,000; density, 131 per sq. km. In 2001, 55·2% of the population were rural.

The UN gives a projected population for 2010 of 145·92m.

There were 30 states and a Federal Capital Territory (Abuja) in 1991.

Area, population and capitals of these states:

State	*Area (in sq. km)*	*Population (1991 census)*	*Capital*
Adamawa	36,917	2,124,049	Yola
Bauchi	64,605	4,294,413	Bauchi
Benue	34,059	2,780,398	Makurdi
Borno	70,898	2,596,589	Maiduguri
Jigawa	23,154	2,829,929	Dutse
Kaduna	46,053	3,969,252	Kaduna
Kano	20,131	5,362,040	Kano
Katsina	24,192	3,878,344	Katsina
Kebbi	36,800	2,062,226	Birnin-Kebbi
Kogi	29,833	2,099,046	Lokoja
Kwara	36,825	1,566,469	Ilorin
Niger	76,363	2,482,367	Minna
Plateau	58,030	3,283,784	Jos
Sokoto	65,735	4,392,391	Sokoto
Taraba	54,473	1,480,590	Jalingo
Yobe	45,502	1,411,481	Damaturu
Federal Capital Territory	7,315	378,671	Abuja
Total North	*730,885*	*46,992,039*	

State	*Area (in sq. km)*	*Population (1991 census)*	*Capital*
Abia	6,320	2,297,978	Umuahia
Akwa Ibom	7,081	2,359,736	Uyo
Anambra	4,844	2,767,903	Awka
Cross River	20,156	1,865,604	Calabar
Delta	17,698	2,570,181	Asaba
Edo	17,802	2,159,848	Benin City
Enugu	12,831	3,161,295	Enugu
Imo	5,530	2,485,499	Owerri
Lagos	3,345	5,685,781	Ikeja
Ogun	16,762	2,338,570	Abeokuta
Ondo	20,959	3,884,485	Akure
Osun	9,251	2,203,016	Oshogbo

State	Area (in sq. km)	Population (1991 census)	Capital
Oyo	28,454	3,488,789	Ibadan
Rivers	21,850	3,983,857	Port-Harcourt
Total South	*192,883*	*41,252,542*	

Six new states were created in 1996, three in the north and three in the south. In the north, Zamfara State was created from Sokoto, with its headquarters at Gusau; Nassarawa State was created from Plateau, with its headquarters at Lafia; and Gombe State was created from Bauchi, with its headquarters at Gombe. In the south, Ekiti State was created from Ondo, with its capital at Ado-Ekiti; Bayelsa State was created from Rivers, with its headquarters at Yenagoa; and Ebonyi State was created by merging Abia and Enugu, with its headquarters at Abakaliki.

Abuja replaced Lagos as the federal capital and seat of government in Dec. 1991.

Estimated population of the largest cities, 1995:

Lagos	1,484,000[1]	Ila	257,400	Kumo	144,400
Ibadan	1,365,000	Oyo	250,100	Shomolu	144,100
Ogbomosho	711,900	Ikerre	238,500	Oka	139,600
Kano	657,300	Benin City	223,900	Ikare	137,300
Oshogbo	465,000	Iseyin	211,800	Sapele	135,800
Ilorin	464,000	Katsina	201,500	Deba Habe	135,400
Abeokuta	416,800	Jos	201,200	Minna	133,600
Port Harcourt	399,700	Sokoto	199,900	Warri	122,900
Zaria	369,800	Ilobu	194,400	Bida	122,500
Ilesha	369,000	Offa	192,300	Ikire	120,200
Onitsha	362,700	Ikorodu	180,300	Makurdi	120,100
Iwo	353,000	Ilawe-Ekiti	179,900	Lafia	119,500
Ado-Ekiti	350,500	Owo	178,900	Inisa	116,800
Abuja (capital)	339,100	Ikirun	177,000	Shagamu	114,300
Kaduna	333,600	Calabar	170,000	Awka	108,400
Mushin	324,900	Shaki	169,700	Gombe	105,200
Maiduguri	312,100	Ondo	165,400	Igboho	103,300
Enugu	308,200	Akure	158,200	Ejigbo	103,300
Ede	299,500	Gusau	154,000	Agege	100,300
Aba	291,600	Ijebu-Ode	152,500	Ugep	100,000
Ife	289,500	Effon-Alaiye	149,300		

[1]Greater Lagos had a population of 12,763,000 in 1999.

There are about 250 ethnic groups. The largest linguistic groups are the Hausa (21·4% of the total) and the Yoruba (also 21·4%), followed by Igbo (18·0%), Fulani (11·3%), Ibibio (5·6%), Kanuri (4·1%), Edo (3·4%), Tiv (2·2%), Ijaw (1·8%), Bura (1·5%) and Nupe (1·3%). The official languages are English and (since 1997) French, but 50% of the population speak Hausa as a *lingua franca*.

SOCIAL STATISTICS

1995 births, estimate, 4,760,000; deaths, 1,360,000. Rates, 1995: birth, 49 (per 1,000 population); death, 14. Infant mortality, 2001, 110 (per 1,000 live births). Annual population growth rate, 1992–02, 2·8%. Life expectancy at birth, 2001, was 51·3 years for males and 52·3 years for females. Fertility rate, 2001, 5·6 children per woman.

CLIMATE

Lying wholly within the tropics, temperatures everywhere are high. Rainfall varies greatly, but decreases from the coast to the interior. The main rains occur from April to Oct. Lagos, Jan. 81°F (27·2°C), July 78°F (25·6°C). Annual rainfall 72" (1,836 mm). Ibadan, Jan. 80°F (26·7°C), July 76°F (24·4°C). Annual rainfall 45" (1,120 mm). Kano, Jan. 70°F (21·1°C), July 79°F (26·1°C). Annual rainfall 35" (869 mm). Port Harcourt, Jan. 79°F (26·1°C), July 77°F (25°C). Annual rainfall 100" (2,497 mm).

CONSTITUTION AND GOVERNMENT

The constitution was promulgated on 5 May 1999, and entered into force on 29 May. Nigeria is a federation, comprising 36 states and a federal capital territory. The constitution includes provisions for the creation of new states and for boundary adjustments of existing states. The legislative powers are vested in a *National*

Assembly, comprising a *Senate* and a *House of Representatives.* The 109-member Senate consists of three senators from each state and one from the federal capital territory, who are elected for a term of four years. The House of Representatives comprises 360 members, representing constituencies of nearly equal population as far as possible, who are elected for a four-year term. The president is elected for a term of four years and must receive not less than one-quarter of the votes cast at the federal capital territory.

National Anthem. 'Arise, O compatriots, Nigeria's call obey'; words by a collective, tune by B. Odiase.

RECENT ELECTIONS

The preliminary results of the elections to the House of Representatives on 12 April 2003 were: the People's Democratic Party (PDP) 213 seats with 54·5% of the vote, the All Nigeria People's Party (ANPP) 95 seats (27·4%), the Alliance for Democracy (AD) 31 seats (9·3%), the United Nigeria People's Party (UNPP) 2 seats (2·7%), the All Progressives Grand Alliance (APGA) 2 seats (1·4%), the National Democratic Party (NDP) 1 seat (1·9%) and the People's Redemption Party (PRP) 1 seat (0·8%). Turn-out was 50%.

In the Senate elections (preliminary results) on the same days 73 seats went to the PDP, 28 to the ANPP and 6 to the AD. Turn-out was 49%.

Presidential elections were held on 19 April 2003. President Olusegun Obasanjo (PDP) won against 19 opponents with 61·9% of the votes cast. His main opponent, Muhammadu Buhari (ANPP), received 32·2%, and Chukwuemeka Ojukwu (APGA) 3·3%. Buhari refused to accept the result, claiming serious irregularities. International observers witnessed evidence of widespread fraud. Turn-out was 69%.

CURRENT ADMINISTRATION

President: Olusegun Obasanjo; b. 1937 (PDP; inaugurated 29 May 1999 and re-elected 19 April 2003).

Vice President: Atiku Abubakar.

In March 2005 the government comprised:

Minister of Agriculture: Malam Adamu Bello. *Aviation:* Isa Yuguda. *Commerce:* Idris Waziri. *Communications:* Chief Cornelius Adebayo. *Co-operation and Integration:* Lawan Gana Guba. *Culture and Tourism:* Chief Franklin Ogbuewu. *Defence:* Dr Rabiu Kwankaso. *Education:* Prof. Fabian Osuji. *Environment:* Col. Bala Mande. *Federal Capital Territory:* Mallam Nasir El-Rufai. *Finance:* Ngozi Okonjo-Iweala. *Foreign Affairs:* Oluyemi Adeniji. *Health:* Prof. Eyitayo Lambo. *Housing:* Mobolaji Osomo. *Industries:* Alhaji Magaji Mohammed. *Information:* Chukwuemeka Chikelu. *Internal Affairs:* Dr Iyorcha Ayu. *Justice and Attorney General:* Chief Akinlolu Olujimi. *Labour and Productivity:* Dr Hassan Lawal. *Police Affairs:* Broderick Bozimo. *Power and Steel:* Liyel Imoke. *Science and Technology:* Prof. Turner Isoun. *Solid Minerals:* Mangu Odion Ugbesa. *Sports and Social Development:* Col. Musa Mohammed. *Transport:* Dr Abiye Sekibo. *Water Resources:* Muktar Shagari. *Women and Youth:* Rita Akpan. *Works:* Adeseye Ogunlewe. *Minister of Presidency (Inter-Governmental Affairs and Special Duties):* Frank Nweke.

Nigerian Parliament: http://www.nigeriacongress.org

DEFENCE

In 2003 defence expenditure totalled US$853m., equivalent to US$6 per capita and representing 1·8% of GDP.

Army. Strength (2002) 62,000.

Navy. The Navy includes one frigate with a helicopter and two corvettes. The Navy has a small aviation element. Naval personnel in 2002 totalled 7,000, including Coastguard. The main bases are at Apapa (Lagos) and Calabar.

Air Force. The Air Force has been built up with the aid of a German mission; much first-line equipment was received from the former Soviet Union. Personnel (2002) total about 9,500, with about 86 combat aircraft including MiG-21s, Jaguars and Alpha Jets. In addition there were about 16 armed helicopters. Serviceability of both combat aircraft and helicopters is about 50%.

INTERNATIONAL RELATIONS

Nigeria is a member of the UN, WTO, the African Union, African Development Bank, ECOWAS, the Lake Chad Basin Commission, OIC, OPEC, IOM and is an ACP member state of the ACP-EU relationship.

ECONOMY

Agriculture accounted for 31·2% of GDP in 2002, industry 43·8% and services 25·0%.

Overview. Nigeria's economy is highly dependent on the oil sector, which accounts for 46% of GDP and for 85% of the country's foreign exchange earnings. Nigeria's level of GNP per capita, approximately US$260, is below the level at independence 40 years ago and below the level achieved in 1985. Despite the country's relative oil wealth, approximately 66% of the population live in poverty, compared to 43% in 1985. Nigeria's poor economic performance can be attributed to economic mismanagement, corruption, excessive dependence on oil, poor infrastructure, lack of transparency in the business environment and a heavy handed government. The 'shadow' (black market) economy constitutes 77% of the country's official GDP—one of the highest percentages in the world. The middle-income oil-producing economy of 5m. people has a per capita income of approximately US$2,200. The non-oil producing economy of 115m. people has an average per capita income of US$200. A ten-year rift with the IMF ended with an agreement (Jan. 1999) on a Fund-monitored economic reform programme, including abolishing the dual exchange rate, ending the subsidy on local fuel and increasing privatization.

Currency. The unit of currency is the *naira* (NGN) of 100 *kobo*. Foreign exchange reserves were US$9,226m. in May 2002 (US$1,443m. in 1995). A dual exchange rate, abolished in Oct. 1999, allowed the government to purchase US dollars for 25% of the market price. Gold reserves were 687,000 troy oz in May 2002. Inflation was 18·0% in 2001 and 13·7% in 2002. In March 2002 total money supply was ₦835,923m.

Budget. The financial year is the calendar year. 2000 revenue, ₦1,927,087m. (tax revenue 33·1%; non-tax revenue 66·9%); expenditure, ₦1,834,305m. In 1999 recurrent expenditure accounted for 75·6% of total expenditures and capital expenditure 24·4%.

Performance. Real GDP growth was 10·2% in 2003, partly owing to increased oil prices but also a result of a strengthened non-oil sector. Before the discovery of oil in the early 1970s Nigeria's GDP per head was around US$200. By the early 1980s it had reached around US$800, but has now declined to some US$300. Total GDP in 2003 was US$50·2bn.

Banking and Finance. The Central Bank of Nigeria is the bank of issue (*Governor*, Prof. Charles C. Soludo).

A banking crisis resulted in a decline in the number of banks to 74 at March 1999. Of these, 17 had missed the deadline for increasing their capital to US$5·75m. by the end of 1998 and faced closure if they did not recapitalize, merge or get taken over by the end of the first quarter of 1999. In banking surveys for 1998, 26 banks were classed as 'distressed' and only 25 as 'acceptable risks or better'. There are three main banks—Union Bank of Nigeria, First Bank of Nigeria and Union Bank for Africa. In Jan. 2005 United Bank for Africa and Standard Trust Bank, Nigeria's fifth-biggest bank, agreed to merge and create the largest bank in west Africa. In 2002 there were 12 merchant banks and two development banks. Total assets of commercial banks, 1995, ₦463,671m.; merchant banks, ₦91,803m. Total saving deposits, Dec. 1995, ₦121,026m.

The Nigerian Stock Exchange is in Lagos.

ENERGY AND NATURAL RESOURCES

Environment. Nigeria's carbon dioxide emissions from the consumption and flaring of fossil fuels were the equivalent of 0·8 tonnes per capita in 2002. An *Environmental Sustainability Index* compiled for the World Economic Forum meeting in Feb. 2002 ranked Nigeria 133rd in the world out of 142 countries analysed, with 36·7%. The index measured the ability of countries to maintain favourable environmental conditions and examined various factors including pollution levels and the use or abuse of natural resources.

Electricity. Installed capacity, 2000, 5·9m. kW. Production, 2000, 15·76bn. kWh (37% kWh hydro-electric); consumption per capita was 137 kWh in 2000.

Oil and Gas. Oil accounts for around 97% of Nigeria's exports. The cumulative income from oil over more than 30 years exceeds US$330,000m. Nigeria's oil production amounted to 98·6m. tonnes in 2002. Reserves in 2002 totalled 24·0bn. bbls. There are four refineries. Oil income in 1998 was around US$1bn. a month, representing more than 75% of government revenue, but unrest which threatened to escalate into civil war caused production to be cut by around a third. Most of Nigeria's oil wealth comes from onshore wells, but there are also large untapped offshore deposits.

Natural gas reserves, 2002, were 3,510bn. cu. metres; production, 2002, 17·7bn. cu. metres. Nigeria has signed an agreement for a US$430m., 600-km pipeline to supply natural gas to Benin, Ghana and Togo. It is expected to come into operation in late 2006 moving around 1,415,000 cu. metres per day in the first instance, in the process helping to reduce Nigeria's dependence on oil for government revenue. In Dec. 2002 the African Development Bank, six Nigerian banks and 19 international banks announced plans to invest US$1bn. in the Nigeria Liquefied Natural Gas company (NLNG) to exploit exports to the USA and Europe. Ownership of the NLNG is shared between the Nigerian National Petroleum Corporation, Total Fina Elf, Royal Dutch/Shell and AGIP.

Minerals. Production, 1998 (in tonnes): limestone, 3·66m.; coal (2000), 61,000; marble, 22,460. There are large deposits of iron ore, coal (reserves estimate 245m. tonnes), lead and zinc. There are small quantities of gold and uranium. Lead production was 5,000 tonnes in 2002. Tin is also mined.

Agriculture. Of the total land mass, 75% is suitable for agriculture, including arable farming, forestry, livestock husbandry and fisheries. In 2001, 28·5m. ha were arable and 2·7m. ha permanent cropland. 0·23m. ha were irrigated in 2001. 90% of production was by smallholders with less than 3 ha in 2000, and less than 1% of farmers had access to mechanized tractors. Main food crops are millet and sorghum in the north, plantains and oil palms in the south, and maize, yams, cassava and rice in much of the country. The north is, however, the main food producing area. Cocoa is the crop that contributes most to foreign exchange earnings. Output, 2000 (in 1,000 tonnes): cassava, 32,697; yams, 25,873; sorghum, 7,520; millet, 5,960; maize, 5,476; taro, 3,835; rice, 3,277; groundnuts, 2,783; plantains, 1,902; sweet potatoes, 1,662; palm oil, 896; pineapples, 881; tomatoes, 879. Nigeria is the biggest producer of yams, accounting for more than two-thirds of the annual world output. It is also the leading cassava and taro producer and the second largest millet producer.

Livestock, 2000: cattle, 19·83m.; sheep, 20·50m.; goats, 24·30m.; pigs, 4·86m.; chickens, 126m. Products (in 1,000 tonnes), 2000: beef and veal, 298; goat meat, 154; mutton and lamb, 91; pork, bacon and ham, 78; poultry meat, 172; milk, 386; eggs, 435.

Forestry. There were 13·52m. ha of forests in 2000, or 14·8% of the land area. Timber production in 2001 was 69·12m. cu. metres.

Fisheries. The total catch in 2001 was 452,146 tonnes, of which 297,971 tonnes came from sea fishing.

INDUSTRY

In 2001 industry accounted for 35·5% of GDP, with manufacturing contributing 4·2%. 2000 production (in 1,000 tonnes) included: cement (2001), 3,000; residual fuel oil, 1,410; distillate fuel oil, 1,076; petrol, 1,041; palm oil (2001), 903; kerosene, 670; paper and products (1998), 57; cigarettes (1995), 256m. units. Also plywood (2001), 55,000 cu. metres.

Labour. The labour force in 1996 totalled 45,565,000 (64% males). There were 196 work stoppages in 1995 with 235·1m. working days lost. Unemployment in 1999 was approximately 40%.

Trade Unions. All trade unions are affiliated to the Nigerian Labour Congress.

INTERNATIONAL TRADE

Nigeria's external debt was US$30,476m. in 2002. President Obasanjo failed to settle with the IMF in March 2002, preventing rescheduling and debt relief.

Imports and Exports. Exports in 2000 totalled an estimated US$20·4bn.; imports US$13·7bn. In 1999 crude oil amounted to 98·9% of exports by value. Other exports included ships and boats, and cocoa. Principal imports in 1999 were: machinery and transport equipment, 27·7%; foodstuffs, 26·1%; manufactured goods, 19·9%; chemicals, 15·7%.

In 2000 the main export markets were: USA, 46·1%; Spain, 10·7%; India, 6·1%; France, 5·2%; Portugal, 3·6%. Main import suppliers, 2000: UK, 10·9%; USA, 9·2%; France, 8·9%; Germany, 7·4%; China, 6·3%.

COMMUNICATIONS

Roads. The road network covered 194,394 km in 1999, including 1,194 km of motorways. In 1996 there were 885,080 motor cars and 912,579 trucks and vans. There were 16,793 road accidents with 6,364 fatalities in 1996.

Rail. In 1995 there were 3,505 route-km of track (1,067 mm gauge). Passenger-km travelled in 1997 came to 179m. and freight tonne-km to 120m.

Civil Aviation. Lagos (Murtala Muhammed) is the major airport, and there are also international airports at Port Harcourt and Kano (Mallam Aminu Kano Airport). The national carrier is Nigeria Airways. The government sold a 49% stake to a UK leasing company, Airwing Aerospace, in 2002. In 2000 Lagos handled 2,489,000 passengers (1,435,000 on domestic flights) and, in 1998, 15,100 tonnes of freight. Nigeria Airways flew 2·7m. km in 1999, carrying 109,200 passengers (30,300 on international flights).

Shipping. In 2002 the merchant marine totalled 411,000 GRT, including oil tankers 285,000 GRT. In 1997 vessels totalling 2,464,000 NRT entered ports and vessels totalling 2,510,000 NRT cleared. The principal ports are Lagos and Port Harcourt. There is an extensive network of inland waterways.

Telecommunications. In 2002 there were 2,335,100 telephone subscribers (19·4 per 1,000 persons) and 853,000 PCs in use (7·1 per 1,000 persons). A 51% stake in the state-run telecommunications company Nitel was sold for more than US$1bn. to a consortium of Nigerian investors, European fund managers and Portugal Telecommunications in Nov. 2001 in what was described as Africa's biggest privatization. Mobile phone subscribers numbered 1,633,000 in 2002. The largest mobile phone company is MTN Nigeria Communications. Nigeria had 420,000 Internet users in 2002.

Postal Services. In 1998 there were 3,971 post offices. A total of 391m. pieces of mail were processed in 1998.

SOCIAL INSTITUTIONS

Justice. The highest court is the Federal Supreme Court, which consists of the Chief Justice of the Republic, and up to 15 Justices appointed by the government. It has original jurisdiction in any dispute between the Federal Republic and any State or between States; and to hear and determine appeals from the Federal Court of Appeal, which acts as an intermediate appellate Court to consider appeals from the High Court.

High Courts, presided over by a Chief Justice, are established in each state. All judges are appointed by the government. Magistrates' courts are established throughout the Republic, and customary law courts in southern Nigeria. In each of the northern States of Nigeria there are the Sharia Court of Appeal and the Court of Resolution. Muslim Law has been codified in a Penal Code and is applied through Alkali courts. In Oct. 1999 *sharia*, or Islamic law, was introduced in the northern province of Zamfara. The death penalty is in force and was last used in Jan. 2002.

The population in penal institutions in March 2002 was 39,368 (33 per 100,000 of national population).

Religion. Muslims and Christians both constitute about 45% of the population; traditional animist beliefs are also widespread. Northern Nigeria is mainly Muslim; southern Nigeria is predominantly Christian and western Nigeria is evenly divided between Christians, Muslims and animists. In Sept. 2003 the Roman Catholic church had two cardinals.

Education. The adult literacy rate was 65·4% in 2001 (73·3% among males and 57·7% among females). Under the new Universal Basic Education scheme it was hoped that this would rise to 70% by 2003. Free, compulsory education is to be provided for all children aged between six and 15 under the terms of the scheme. In 2002 there were 49,343 primary schools with 29·58m. pupils and 537,741 teachers; 10,000 secondary schools with 7·49m. pupils and 187,126 teachers; and 1·25m. students at 158 tertiary education institutions.

In 1995 there were 13 universities, 2 agricultural and 5 technological universities, 21 polytechnics, 7 colleges and 2 institutes. There were 150,072 university students and 10,742 academic staff.

Health. Health provision, 1995: one doctor per 3,707 people; one nurse per 605; one hospital bed per 1,477.

Nigeria has made significant progress in the reduction of undernourishment in the past 25 years. By 2000 only 9% of the population was undernourished, one of the lowest rates in sub-Saharan Africa; but only 50% of Nigerians have access to clean drinking water.

CULTURE

World Heritage Sites. The Sukur Cultural Landscape, a hilly area in Adamawa State (northeastern Nigeria), was entered on the UNESCO World Heritage list in 1999.

Broadcasting. In 2003 the Federal Radio Corporation of Nigeria, a statutory body, was broadcasting from five national radio stations in English, Yoruba, Hausa and Igbo, and an international service, Voice of Nigeria (eight languages in 2003). In 2001 there were six private radio stations in operation. The government Nigerian Television Authority transmits a national service (colour by PAL, in English only), and over 30 states have their own stations. In 2001 there were nine private stations and two private satellite stations. In 2000 there were 23m. radio sets and in 2001 there were 12m. TV sets.

Press. In 1996 there were 25 daily newspapers with a combined circulation of 2,740,000.

Tourism. In 2000 there were 813,000 foreign visitors; spending by tourists totalled US$200m.

DIPLOMATIC REPRESENTATIVES

Of Nigeria in the United Kingdom (Nigeria House, 9 Northumberland Ave., London, WC2N 5BX)
High Commissioner: Dr Christopher Kolade.

Of the United Kingdom in Nigeria (Shehu Shangari Way North, Maitama, Abuja)
High Commissioner: Richard Gozney, CMG.

Of Nigeria in the USA (3519 International Court, NW, Washington, D.C., 20008)
Ambassador: George A. Obiozor.

Of the USA in Nigeria (7 Mambilla St., Abuja)
Ambassador: John Campbell.

Of Nigeria to the United Nations
Ambassador: Aminu Wali.

Of Nigeria to the European Union
Ambassador: Vacant.
Chargé d'Affaires a.i.: V. A. Okoedion.

FURTHER READING

Forrest, T., *Politics and Economic Development in Nigeria*. Boulder (CO), 1993
Maier, K., *This House Has Fallen: Midnight in Nigeria*. Penguin Press, London and PublicAffairs, New York, 2000
Miles, W. F. S., *Hausaland Divided: Colonialism and Independence in Nigeria and Niger.* Cornell Univ. Press, 1994

National statistical office: Federal Office of Statistics, Plot 205, Bacita Close, Gakki, Area 2, P.M.B. 127, Abuja.
Website: http://www.nigeriabusinessinfo.com/fos.htm

NORWAY

Kongeriket Norge
(Kingdom of Norway)

Capital: Oslo
Population projection, 2010: 4·65m.
GDP per capita, 2002: (PPP$) 36,600
HDI/world rank: 0·956/1

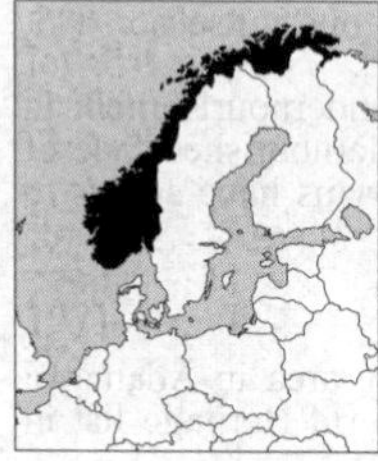

KEY HISTORICAL EVENTS

The first settlers arrived at the end of the Ice Age. Archaeological remains of hunting-fishing communities in Finnmark and Rogaland date from 9500–8000 BC. By 2500 BC a new influx of settlers brought cattle and crop farming. Links with Roman-occupied Gaul in the first four centuries AD were strong. By 800 AD tribal groups had established their own legislative assemblies, the *things*.

In the 9th century communities from the Vik, an area between the south coasts of Norway and Sweden, gave their name to the people collectively known as Vikings. The Norwegian Vikings sailed to the Atlantic islands, England, France, Scotland and Ireland, and also colonized Iceland. The saga writers recorded their exploits, including Eric the Red's discovery of Greenland. His son, Leif Erikson, voyaged across the Davis Strait, to America, probably the first European to do so.

Harald Fairhair took the first steps towards centralized rule. Battles with rival chieftains culminated in about 900 when Harald was proclaimed king of the Norwegians. His successors were less assertive and by the mid-10th century the country was under the suzerainty of Harald Bluetooth, king of Denmark. Bluetooth's grandson, Canute the Great, incorporated England into his North Sea Empire before turning to Sweden. However, on the death of Canute the English chose their own king while the Danish and Norwegian nobles decided to unite, resulting in a Norwegian ruler for Denmark. The Viking's territorial expansion came to an end with King Harald Hardrada's defeat at the battle of Stamford Bridge in England in 1066. Supported by the English church, the Norwegian monarchy gained strength. By the 12th century the balance of power between the church and monarchy had become a source of civil conflict, which was only resolved when Håkon IV became king in 1217. Håkon presided over Norway's 'Golden Age'; both Greenland and Iceland ceded control to Norway. Håkon's son, Magnus VI, oversaw the codification of national law.

Between 1349–50, during union with Sweden, the Black Death killed around two-thirds of the population. The cohesion of government was undermined as many official positions were taken by Danes and Swedes. Vulnerable to German encroachment, the incentive for all three Scandinavian kingdoms to unite was strong. When the Danish king died in 1375 his widow, Margaret, became regent of Denmark and, on the death of Håkon, regent of Norway. Defeating the German claimant to the Swedish throne, she cleared the way to a Nordic union. With the death of her son Olav in 1387 and unable to take the triple crown for herself, she nominated her five-year-old nephew, Erik of Pomerania, as king of all three countries. His election was formalized at Kalmar in 1397. From 1450 the Norwegian government was based in Copenhagen; Danes and Germans took many administrative positions. Norway remained a province of Denmark, with limited control over internal affairs, until the 19th century.

In the Napoleonic Wars, Denmark and Norway were allied with France. Napoléon's defeat at the battle of Leipzig in 1813 was followed by a successful attack on Denmark from Sweden. By the Treaty of Kiel (1814), Norway was ceded to Sweden but a new constitution gave Norway control over internal affairs. In the second half of the century, the merchant navy grew to become the third largest after the United States and Great Britain. In a 1905 referendum the overwhelming majority of Norwegians voted for separation. A Danish prince was installed as Håkon VII of Norway.

Norway declared its neutrality in the First World War. This did not prevent the loss of almost half of its merchant navy. In the Second World War, Norway was invaded by Germany and an occupation government with Vidkun Quisling as its front man was set up. Apart from this wartime episode, the social democrats held office, and the majority in the Storting (parliament), from 1935–65.

Post-war recovery was based on an agreement with the trade unions. In return for price controls, food subsidies and full employment guarantees, the unions accepted compulsory arbitration for all wage disputes and virtually forswore the use of the strike. By 1949 productivity and living standards were higher than most other Western countries. But the rise in world prices triggered by the Korean War increased the price of essential imports. The use of subsidies to counteract the adverse balance of trade reached its limit when they became the largest item in the national budget. In 1950 food prices were allowed to get closer to their market level and the cost of living increased by 30% over three years.

A referendum held in 1972 rejected membership of the European Economic Community (EEC). Norway agreed to a series of bilateral free-trade treaties with EEC members but opposition to joining remained strong. On the inception of the EU in 1992, the government renewed the campaign for membership, which was again rejected by referendum. Since the 1960s and the discovery of vast off-shore deposits, the oil and gas export industry has made Norway one of the world's richest economies. Norway is one of the world's most generous international aid donors in proportion to national wealth.

TERRITORY AND POPULATION

Norway is bounded in the north by the Arctic Ocean, east by Russia, Finland and Sweden, south by the Skagerrak Straits and west by the North Sea. The total area of mainland Norway is 323,758 sq. km, including 17,506 sq. km of fresh water. Total coastline, including fjords, 21,340 km. There are more than 50,000 islands along the coastline. Exposed mountain (either bare rock or thin vegetation) makes up over 70% of the country. 25% of the land area is woodland and 4% tilled land.

Population (2001 census) was 4,520,947 (2,240,281 males; 2,280,666 females); population density per sq. km, 14·8. Estimated population, 1 Jan. 2003, 4,552,252; population density, 14·9. With the exception of Iceland, Norway is the most sparsely populated country in Europe.

The UN gives a projected population for 2010 of 4·65m.

There are 19 counties (*fylke*). Land area, population and densities:

	Land area (sq. km)	*Population (1990 census)*	*Population (2003 estimate)*	*Density per sq. km 2003*
Østfold	3,889	238,296	255,122	66
Akershus	4,587	417,653	483,283	105
Oslo (City)	427	461,190	517,401	1,212
Hedmark	26,120	187,276	188,281	7
Oppland	23,827	182,578	183,582	8
Buskerud	13,856	225,172	241,371	17
Vestfold	2,140	198,399	218,171	102
Telemark	14,186	162,907	165,855	12
Aust-Agder	8,485	97,333	103,195	12
Vest-Agder	6,817	144,917	159,219	23
Rogaland	8,553	337,504	385,020	44
Hordaland	14,962	410,567	441,660	30
Sogn og Fjordane	17,864	106,659	107,274	6
Møre og Romsdal	14,596	238,409	244,309	17
Sør-Trøndelag	17,839	250,978	268,188	15
Nord-Trøndelag	20,777	127,157	127,610	6
Nordland	36,302	239,311	236,950	7
Troms	25,147	146,716	152,247	6
Finnmark	45,879	74,524	73,514	2
Mainland total	306,253[1]	4,247,546	4,552,252	15

[1]118,244 sq. miles.

The Arctic territories of Svalbard and Jan Mayen have an area of 61,606 sq. km. Persons staying on Svalbard and Jan Mayen are registered as residents of their home Norwegian municipality.

In 2001, 75·0% of the population lived in urban areas.

Population of the principal urban settlements on 1 Jan. 2002:

Oslo	783,829	Kristiansand	62,546	Moss	33,960
Bergen	209,375	Tromsø	50,754	Bodø	32,700
Stavanger/Sandnes	166,703	Tønsberg	43,991	Arendal	30,916
Trondheim	142,891	Ålesund	43,302	Hamar	28,045
Frederikstad/Sarpsborg	95,077	Haugesund	39,729	Larvik	22,650
Drammen	88,481	Sandefjord	38,366	Halden	21,668
Porsgrunn/Skien	84,049				

The official language is Norwegian, which has two versions: Bokmål (or Riksmål) and Nynorsk (or Landsmål).

The Sami, the indigenous people of the far north, number some 40,000 and form a distinct ethnic minority with their own culture and language.

SOCIAL STATISTICS

Statistics for calendar years:

	Marriages	Divorces	Births	Still-born	Outside marriage[1]	Deaths
1998	22,349	9,213	58,352	247	28,573	44,112
1999	23,456	9,124	59,298	241	29,100	45,170
2000	25,356	10,053	59,234	225	29,368	44,002
2001	22,967	10,308	56,696	241	28,194	43,981
2002	24,069	10,450	55,434	197	27,890	44,465

[1]Excluding still-born.

Rates per 1,000 population, 2002, birth, 12·2; death, 9·8; marriage, 5·3; divorce, 2·3. Average annual population growth rate, 1992–2002, 0·54% (2002, 0·62%). In 2000 there were 541 suicides, giving a rate of 12·1 per 100,000 population (men, 18·4 per 100,000; women, 5·8).

Expectation of life at birth, 2001, was 75·8 years for males and 81·7 years for females. Infant mortality, 2002, 3·5 per 1,000 live births; fertility rate, 2002, 1·75 births per woman. 50% of births are to unmarried mothers. In 2001 the average age at marriage was 35·3 years for males and 32·1 years for females (32·0 years and 29·3 years respectively for first marriages).

At 1 Jan. 2002 the immigrant population totalled 310,704, including 24,565 from Pakistan, 22,772 from Sweden, 19,169 from Denmark and 16,386 from Vietnam. In 2002 Norway received 17,480 asylum applications. Most were from Yugoslavia (2,460), Russia (1,718), Iraq (1,624) and Somalia (1,534).

A UNICEF report published in 2000 showed that 3·9% of children in Norway live in poverty (in households with income below 50% of the national median), the second lowest percentage of any country behind Sweden.

In the Human Development Index, or HDI (measuring progress in countries in longevity, knowledge and standard of living), Norway ranked first in the world in the list published in the Human Development Report for both 2001 and 2002, having been second behind Canada for the previous two years.

CLIMATE

There is considerable variation in the climate because of the extent of latitude, the topography and the varying effectiveness of prevailing westerly winds and the Gulf Stream. Winters along the whole west coast are exceptionally mild but precipitation is considerable. Oslo, Jan. 24·3°F (–4·3°C), July 61·5°F (16·4°C). Annual rainfall 30·0" (763 mm). Bergen, Jan. 34·7°F (1·5°C), July 58·1°F (14·5°C). Annual rainfall 88·6" (2,250 mm). Trondheim, Jan. 26°F (–3·5°C), July 57°F (14°C). Annual rainfall 32·1" (870 mm). Bergen has one of the highest rainfall figures of any European city. The sun never fully sets in the northern area of the country in the summer and even in the south, the sun rises at around 3 a.m. and sets at around 11 p.m.

CONSTITUTION AND GOVERNMENT

Norway is a constitutional and hereditary monarchy.

The reigning King is **Harald V**, born 21 Feb. 1937, married on 29 Aug. 1968 to Sonja Haraldsen. He succeeded on the death of his father, King Olav V, on 21 Jan. 1991. *Offspring:* Princess Märtha Louise, born 22 Sept. 1971 (married Ari Behn, b. 30 Sept. 1972, on 24 May 2002; *offspring*, Maud Angelica, b. 29 April 2003; Leah Isadora, b. 8 April 2005); Crown Prince Haakon Magnus, born 20 July 1973 (married Mette-Marit Tjessem Høiby, b. 19 Aug. 1973, on 25 Aug. 2001; *offspring*, Ingrid Alexandra, b. 21 Jan. 2004; *offspring* of Crown Princess Mette-Marit from previous relationship, Marius, b. 13 Jan. 1997). The king and queen together receive an annual personal allowance of 7·0m. kroner from the civil list, and the Crown Prince and Crown Princess together 4·7m. kroner. Princess Märtha Louise relinquished her allowance in 2002. Women have been eligible to succeed to the throne since 1990. There is no coronation ceremony. The royal succession is in direct male line in the order of primogeniture. In default of male heirs the King may propose a successor to the Storting, but this assembly has the right to nominate another, if it does not agree with the proposal.

The Constitution, voted by a constituent assembly on 17 May 1814 and modified at various times, vests the legislative power of the realm in the *Storting* (Parliament). The royal veto may be exercised; but if the same Bill passes two Stortings formed by separate and subsequent elections it becomes the law of the land without the assent of the sovereign. The King has the command of the land, sea and air forces, and makes all appointments.

The 165-member Storting is directly elected by proportional representation. The country is divided into 19 districts, each electing from 4 to 15 representatives.

The Storting, when assembled, divides itself by election into the *Lagting* and the *Odelsting*. The former is composed of one-fourth of the members of the Storting, and the other of the remaining three-fourths. Each Ting (the Storting, the Odelsting and the Lagting) nominates its own president. Most questions are decided by the Storting, but questions relating to legislation must be considered and decided by the Odelsting and the Lagting separately. Only when the Odelsting and the Lagting disagree, the Bill has to be considered by the Storting in plenary sitting, and a new law can then only be decided by a majority of two-thirds of the voters. The same majority is required for alterations of the Constitution, which can only be decided by the Storting in plenary sitting. The Storting elects five delegates, whose duty it is to revise the public accounts. The Lagting and the ordinary members of the Supreme Court of Justice (the *Høyesterett*) form a High Court of the Realm (the *Riksrett*) for the trial of ministers, members of the *Høyesterett* and members of the Storting. The impeachment before the *Riksrett* can only be decided by the Odelsting.

The executive is represented by the King, who exercises his authority through the Cabinet. Cabinet ministers are entitled to be present in the Storting and to take part in the discussions, but without a vote.

National Anthem. 'Ja, vi elsker dette landet' ('Yes, we love this land'); words by B. Bjørnson, tune by R. Nordraak.

RECENT ELECTIONS

At the elections for the Storting held on 10 Sept. 2001 the following parties were elected: Labour Party (DNA), winning 43 out of 165 seats (with 24·3% of the vote); Conservative Party (H), 38 (21·2%); Progress Party (FrP), 26 (14·7%); Socialist Left Party (SV), 23 (12·4%); Christian People's Party (KrF), 22 (12·5%); Centre Party (Sp), 10 (5·6%); Liberal Party (V), 2 (3·9%); Coastal Party (KYST), 1 (1·7%). Turnout was 74·5%. The governing Labour Party suffered its worst election result in nearly a century and was unable to form a government. The new government comprised the Christian People's Party, the Conservative Party and the Liberal Party.

Parliamentary elections are scheduled to take place on 12 Sept. 2005.

CURRENT ADMINISTRATION

In March 2005 the minority coalition government comprised:

Prime Minister: Kjell Magne Bondevik; b. 1947 (Christian People's Party; sworn in 19 Oct. 2001, having previously held office from Oct. 1997 to March 2000).

Minister of Local Government and Regional Development: Erna Solberg (H). *Culture and Church Affairs:* Valgerd Svarstad Haugland (KrF). *Children and Family Affairs:* Laila Dåvøy (KrF). *Industry and Trade:* Børge Brende (H). *Foreign Affairs:* Jan Petersen (H). *Fisheries and Coastal Affairs:* Svein Ludvigsen (H). *Finance:* Per-Kristian Foss (H). *International Development:* Hilde Frafjord Johnson (KrF). *Labour and Social Affairs:* Dagfinn Høybråten (KrF). *Agriculture and Food:* Lars Sponheim (V). *Justice and Police:* Odd Einar Dørum (V). *Modernization:* Morten Andreas Meyer (H). *National Defence:* Kristin Krohn Devold (H). *Transport and*

Communication: Torild Skogsholm (V). *Education and Research:* Kristin Clemet (H). *Health and Care Services:* Ansgar Gabrielsen (H). *Petroleum and Energy:* Thorhild Widvey (H). *Environment:* Knut Arild Hareide (KrF).

Office of the Prime Minister: http://odin.dep.no

DEFENCE

Conscription is for 12 months, with four to five refresher training periods.

In 2003 defence spending totalled US$4,387m. (US$962 per capita), representing 2·0% of GDP. Expenditure per capita was the highest of any European country in 2003.

Army. There are a Northern and a Southern command, and within these the Army is organized in two joint commands, four land commands and 14 territorial regiments.

Strength (2002) 14,700 (including 8,700 conscripts). The fast mobilization reserve numbers 89,000.

Navy. The Royal Norwegian Navy has three components: the Navy, Coast Guard and Coastal Artillery. Main Naval combatants include six new German-built Ula class submarines and three frigates.

The personnel of the navy totalled 6,100 in 2002, of whom 3,300 were conscripts. 160 served in Coastal Defence and 270 in the Coast Guard. The main naval base is at Bergen (Håkonsvern), with subsidiary bases at Horten and Tromsø.

The naval elements of the Home Guard on mobilization can muster some 4,900 personnel.

Air Force. The Royal Norwegian Air Force comprises the Air Force and the Anti-air Artillery.

Total strength (2002) is about 5,000 personnel, including 3,200 conscripts. There were 61 combat aircraft in operation including F-16A/Bs.

Home Guard. The Home Guard is organized in small units equipped and trained for special tasks. Service after basic training is one week a year. The Home Guard consists of the Land Home Guard (strength, 2002, 73,000), Sea Home Guard and Anti-Air Home Guard. *See under* Navy *above.*

INTERNATIONAL RELATIONS

Norway is a member of the UN, WTO, BIS, NATO, EFTA, OECD, Council of Europe, OSCE, CERN, Council of the Baltic Sea States, Nordic Council, Inter-American Development Bank, Asian Development Bank, IOM and the Antarctic Treaty, and an Associate Member of the WEU. Norway has acceded to the Schengen Accord abolishing border controls between Norway, Austria, Belgium, Denmark, Finland, France, Germany, Greece, Iceland, Italy, Luxembourg, the Netherlands, Portugal, Spain and Sweden.

In a referendum on 27–28 Nov. 1994, 52·2% of votes cast were against joining the EU. The electorate was 3,266,182; turn-out was 88·88%.

Norway gave US$2·0bn. in international aid in 2002, which at 0·92% of GNI made it the world's most generous country as a percentage of its gross national income.

ECONOMY

Services accounted for 59·9% of GDP in 2002, industry 38·3% and agriculture 1·8%.

Transparency International, the anti-corruption organization, ranked Norway 8th in the world in a survey of the countries with the least corruption in business and government in 2004. It received 8·9 out of 10 in the annual index.

Overview. Although a small economy, in terms of GDP per capita Norway is one of the world's wealthiest nations. As the central government budget represents a large share of the economy, fiscal policy is a vital component of economic stability. Labour market tensions and high oil revenues have meant that fiscal policies have not met their objectives, which places a heavy burden on monetary policy. In 2002 passenger tax on air travel was abolished, property taxes reduced and duties on alcohol were lowered. Monetary policy aims at a stable exchange rate.

Currency. The unit of currency is the *Norwegian krone* (NOK) of 100 *øre*. After Oct. 1990 the krone was fixed to the ecu in the EMS of the EU in the narrow band of 2·25%, but it was freed in Dec. 1992. Annualized inflation was 1·3% in 2002 and 2·5% in 2003. Foreign exchange reserves were US$16,048m. and gold reserves 1·18m. troy oz in June 2002. In May 2002 total money supply was 658,812m. kroner.

Budget. Central government current revenue and expenditure (in 1m. kroner) for years ending 31 Dec.:

	1999	*2000*	*2001*[1]	*2002*[1]
Revenue	495,283	643,173	712,019	698,126
Expenditure	429,055	462,555	488,351	563,191

[1]Provisional.

The standard rate of VAT is 24·0%.

Performance. The strong performance of the Norwegian economy in 1993–98 lifted mainland GDP by 20%, but there was a significant slowdown in 1998 when the oil price collapsed at a time when the labour market was overheated. Real GDP growth, which averaged 5·1% between 1994–97, was 2·7% in 2001 but only 1·1% in 2002 and 0·4% in 2003. There was a strong recovery in 2004, with growth provisionally estimated at about 3%. Norway's total GDP in 2003 was US$221·6bn.

The OECD reported in Sept. 2002 that 'Strong growth through the five years to 1998 was induced by a strong expansion in the private sector due to the improvement in competitiveness in the early 1990s, a significant fall in interest rates in 1993 and higher oil investments. It necessitated a fiscal and monetary policy tightening, which, together with a drop in oil investment, has damped activity since then. Despite moderate output growth in recent years, the labour market has remained tight, causing a sharp deterioration in competitiveness. Furthermore, as Norway is the world's third largest oil exporter…, the high oil price since 2000 has led to very large current account and government surpluses.'

Banking and Finance. Norges Bank is the central bank and bank of issue. Supreme authority is vested in the Executive Board consisting of seven members appointed by the King and the Supervisory Council consisting of 15 members elected by the Storting. The *Governor* is Svein Gjedrem. Total assets and liabilities at 31 Dec. 2001 were 987,693m. kroner. This was estimated to have risen to 1,078,787m. kroner by 31 Dec. 2002.

There are three major commercial banks: Nordea Bank Norge ASA, DNB Holding ASA and Fokus. Total assets and liabilities of the 22 commercial banks at 31 Dec. 2001 were 826,250m. kroner. The number of savings banks at 31 Dec. 2001 was 130; total assets and liabilities on 31 Dec. 2001 were 625,183m. kroner.

There is a stock exchange in Oslo.

ENERGY AND NATURAL RESOURCES

Environment. Norway's carbon dioxide emissions from the consumption and flaring of fossil fuels in 2002 were the equivalent of 10·1 tonnes per capita. An *Environmental Sustainability Index* compiled for the World Economic Forum meeting in Feb. 2002 ranked Norway second in the world behind Finland, with 73·0%. The index measured the ability of countries to maintain favourable environmental conditions and examined various factors including pollution levels and the use or abuse of natural resources.

In 2002 there were 19 national parks (total area, 1,702,200 ha), 1,615 nature reserves (322,000 ha), 126 landscape protected areas (1,139,300 ha) and 79 other areas with protected flora and fauna (9,700 ha).

Norway is one of the world leaders in recycling. In 1999, 38% of all household waste was recycled, including 81% of glass.

Electricity. Norway is the sixth largest producer of hydropower in the world and the largest in Europe. The potential total hydro-electric power was estimated at 180,199m. kWh in 1999. Installed electrical capacity in 2000 was 30·0m. kW, more than 99% of it hydro-electric. Production, 2002 estimate, was 130,598m. kWh (over 99% hydro-electric). Consumption per capita in 2000, at 27,595 kWh, was one of the highest in the world. In 1991 Norway became the first country in Europe to deregulate its energy market. Norway is a net importer of electricity.

Oil and Gas. There are enormous oil reserves in the Norwegian continental shelf. In 1966 the first exploration well was drilled. Production of crude oil, 2002, 157,262,000 tonnes. Norway is the world's third biggest oil exporter after Saudi Arabia and Russia, producing around 3·1m. bbls. a day in 2000. It had proven reserves of 10·3bn. bbls. in 2002. In March 1998 Norway announced that it would reduce its output for the year by 100,000 bbls. per day as part of a plan to cut global crude production. In June 2001 the Norwegian government sold a 17·5% stake in Statoil, the last major state-owned oil company in western Europe. The privatization was the largest in Norway's history.

Output of natural gas, 2002, 65·4bn. cu. metres with proven reserves of 2,190bn. cu. metres.

Minerals. Production (in tonnes): aluminium (2001), 1,068,000; ferrotitanium ore (1996), 758,711; coal (2000), 629,000; iron ore (1999), 520,000; copper concentrates (1996), 31,736; zinc ore (1996), 8,619; lead ore (1995), 3,721.

Agriculture. Norway is barren and mountainous. The arable area is in strips in valleys and around fjords and lakes.

In 2001 the agricultural area was 1,031,200 ha, of which 639,300 ha were meadow and pasture, 172,600 ha were sown to barley, 82,700 ha to oats, 63,100 ha to wheat and 15,100 ha to potatoes. Production (in 1,000 tonnes) in 2001: hay, 2,940; barley, 612; potatoes, 388; oats, 333; wheat, 252.

Livestock, 2001, 973,123 cattle (334,981 milch cows), 983,367 sheep (one year and over), 47,784 dairy goats, 696,822 pigs, 3,126,944 hens, 100,000 silver and platinum fox, 370,000 blue fox, 450,000 mink and 168,100 reindeer.

Forestry. In 2000 the total area under forests was 8·87m. ha, or 28·9% of the total land area. Productive forest area, 2000, approximately 7·45m. ha. About 80% of the productive area consists of conifers and 20% of broadleaves. In 2001, 8·40m. cu. metres of roundwood were cut.

Fisheries. The total number of fishermen in 2002 was 18,648, of whom 4,735 had another chief occupation. In 2002 the number of registered fishing vessels (all with motor) was 7,802, and of these 2,847 were open boats.

The catch in 2002 totalled 2,743,299 tonnes, almost entirely from sea fishing. The catch of herring in 2002 totalled 577,275 tonnes, capelin 522,349 tonnes and cod 228,750 tonnes. 10,691 seals were caught in 2002 (of which 3,575 harp and 7,116 hooded seals). Commercial whaling was prohibited in 1988, but recommenced in 1993: 671 whales were caught in 2002. Norway is the third largest exporter of fishery commodities, after Thailand and China. In 2001 exports were valued at US$3·64bn.

INDUSTRY

The leading companies by market capitalization in Norway, excluding banking and finance, in May 2004 were: Den Norske Stats Oljeselskap AS (Statoil), US$27·6bn.; Norsk Hydro ASA (US$16·5bn.), an oil, metals and chemicals producer; and Telenor ASA (US$13·0bn.), a telecommunications company.

Industry is chiefly based on raw materials. Paper and paper products, industrial chemicals and basic metals are important export manufactures. In the following table figures are given for industrial establishments in 2000. The values are given in 1m. kroner.

Industries	*Establish-ments*	*Number of employees*	*Gross value of production*	*Value added*
Coal and peat	10	240	233	–113
Metal ores	5	346	543	224
Other mining and quarrying	346	3,194	5,390	2,250
Food products	1,655	53,252	116,495	32,097
Beverages and tobacco	49	6,247	17,872	12,141
Textiles	329	4,764	4,043	1,475
Clothing, etc.	131	1,530	1,158	425
Leather and leather products	35	523	510	142
Wood and wood products	998	14,634	17,846	5,221
Pulp, paper and paper products	98	8,855	20,342	6,338
Printing and publishing	1,927	34,476	34,891	14,146

Industries	*Establish-ments*	*Number of employees*	*Gross value of production*	*Value added*
Refined petroleum products and basic chemicals	93	8,737	58,136	8,972
Other chemical products	106	5,767	13,965	4,339
Rubber and plastic products	357	6,714	7,656	2,568
Other non-metallic mineral products	603	9,422	13,920	4,910
Basic metals	131	13,818	48,233	12,467
Metal products, except machinery/ equipment	1,251	20,355	20,032	7,961
Machinery and equipment	1,267	23,684	30,010	10,051
Office machinery and computers	16	580	1,380	199
Electrical machinery and apparatus	359	9,138	11,993	4,095
Radio, television, communication equipment	78	5,352	11,423	3,856
Medical, precision and optical instruments	324	6,320	9,278	3,166
Oil platforms	105	19,658	25,895	9,018
Motor vehicles and trailers	118	5,631	6,505	2,128
Other transport equipment	565	14,689	21,213	5,898
Other manufacturing industries	856	14,800	15,404	5,612
Total (including other industries)	121,763	286,479	496,494	147,444

Labour. Norway has a tradition of centralized wage bargaining. Since the early 1960s the contract period has been for two years with intermediate bargaining after 12 months, to take into consideration such changes as the rate of inflation.

The labour force averaged 2,378,000 in 2002 (1,116,000 females). The total number of employed persons in 2002 averaged 2,286,000 (1,076,000 females), of whom 2,118,000 were salaried employees and wage earners, 154,000 self-employed and 7,000 family workers. Distribution of employed persons by occupation in 2002 showed 440,000 in health and social work; 401,000 in trade; 293,000 in manufacturing and mining; 272,000 in finance; 161,000 in transport and communications; 157,000 in construction; 145,000 in public administration, services and defence; 86,000 in agriculture; 31,000 in oil and gas extraction; 14,000 in public utilities.

There were 92,000 registered unemployed in 2002, giving a rate of 3·9%. Unemployment then rose, and was 4·4% of the workforce in Oct. 2004.

There were 16 work stoppages in 2002 (3 in 2001): 150,775 working days were lost (619 in 2001).

Trade Unions. There were 1,485,065 union members at the end of 1999.

INTERNATIONAL TRADE

Imports and Exports. Total imports and exports in calendar years (in 1m. kroner):

	1998	*1999*	*2000*	*2001*	*2002*
Imports	282,638	266,677	302,852	296,135	276,563
Exports	304,653	355,171	529,836	532,041	473,265

Major import suppliers in 2002 (value in 1m. kroner): Sweden, 42,434·6; Germany, 36,106·7; Denmark, 21,778·5; UK, 20,129·4; USA, 16,902·9; China, 14,680·5; France, 12,869·3; Netherlands, 12,858·2; Italy, 10,653·1; Finland, 9,117·0. Imports from economic areas: EU, 184,373·2; Nordic countries, 74,349·3; OECD, 230,835·0.

Major export markets in 2002 (value in 1m. kroner): UK, 91,350·4; Germany, 59,983·0; Netherlands, 45,222·7; USA, 41,178·4; France, 39,972·4; Sweden, 35,685·9; Denmark, 19,002·7; Italy, 17,735·5; Canada, 17,266·5; Belgium, 14,242·1. Exports to economic areas: EU, 351,773·2; Nordic countries, 65,434·0; OECD, 437,898·9.

Principal imports in 2002 (in 1m. kroner): motor vehicles, 25,424·0; transport equipment except motor vehicles, 17,553·2; electrical machinery, 14,723·5; general industrial machinery and equipment, 14,143·9; passenger cars including station wagons, 14,079·4; office machines and computers, 13,504·7; clothing and accessories, 10,789·0; telecommunications and sound apparatus and equipment, 10,296·8; metalliferous ores and metal scrap, 10,046·8; manufactures of metals, 9,728·3; specialized machinery for particular industries, 9,588·9; automatic data processing machines, 7,753·3; iron and steel, 7,568·6; petroleum and petroleum products, 7,481·3. Principal exports in 2002 (in 1m. kroner): petroleum, petroleum products and related materials, 217,882·3 (including crude petroleum, 204,972·2); natural and manufactured gas, 66,255·8 (including natural gas, 59,409·1); fish, crustaceans and molluscs, and preparations thereof, 27,387·6; non-ferrous metals, 26,225·9 (including aluminium, 18,698·3); transport equipment excluding road vehicles, 16,906·7; general industrial machinery and equipment, 9,085·7; paper, paperboard and products, 8,618·7; ships over 100 tonnes, 8,127·4; electrical machinery, apparatus and appliances, 7,063·5.

COMMUNICATIONS

Roads. In 2002 the length of public roads (including roads in towns) totalled 91,852 km. Total road length in 2002 included: national roads, 26,964 km; provincial roads, 27,162 km; local roads, 37,726 km. Number of registered motor vehicles, 2002, included: 1,899,767 passenger cars (including station wagons and ambulances), 258,133 vans, 234,991 tractors and special purpose vehicles, 130,528 mopeds, 95,453 combined vehicles, 94,645 motorcycles, 77,442 goods vehicles (including lorries) and 34,110 buses. In 2002 there were 8,724 road accidents with 272 fatalities.

Rail. The length of state railways in 2001 was 4,178 km (2,519 km electrified). Operating receipts of the state railways in 1998 were 3,958m. kroner; operating expenses, 4,180m. kroner. The state railways carried 8,190,000 tonnes of freight and 49,396,000 passengers in 2001. As recently as 1995, 20,909,000 tonnes of freight had been carried in the year.

There is a metro (98 km) and tram/light rail line (54 km) in Oslo.

Civil Aviation. The main international airports are at Oslo (Gardermoen), Bergen (Flesland), Trondheim (Værnes) and Stavanger (Sola). Kristiansand (Kjevik) and Torp also have a few international flights. The Scandinavian Airlines System (SAS) resulted from the 1950 merger of the three former Scandinavian airlines. SAS Norge ASA is the Norwegian partner (SAS Denmark A/S and SAS Sverige AB being the other two). Norway and Denmark each hold two-sevenths of the capital of SAS and Sweden three-sevenths. Braathens is the major airline after SAS, carrying 5,936,600 passengers in 1999 (648,700 on international flights).

In 2000 Oslo (Gardermoen) handled 14,194,334 passengers (7,480,800 on domestic flights) and 56,686 tonnes of freight. Bergen is the second busiest airport for passenger traffic, with 3,725,633 in 2000 (3,017,449 on domestic flights), and Trondheim second busiest for freight, with 7,784 tonnes (and 2,829,448 passengers) in 2000. Oslo Fornebu, which had for many years been the busiest airport, closed down in 1998 to be replaced by Gardermoen as the country's main international airport.

Shipping. The Norwegian International Ship Register was set up in 1987. At 31 Dec. 2002, 786 ships were registered (510 Norwegian) totalling 20,625,000 GRT. 208 tankers accounted for 8,514,000 GRT. There were also 810 ships totalling 2,685,000 GRT on the Norwegian Ordinary Register. These figures do not include fishing boats, tugs, salvage vessels, icebreakers and similar special types of vessels. Norway's merchant fleet represents 4·3% of total world tonnage. In 1999, 46,037,000 passengers were carried by coastwise shipping on long distance, local and ferry services. The warm Gulf Stream ensures ice-free harbours throughout the year. The busiest port, Narvik, handled 13·0m. tonnes of cargo in 2002.

Telecommunications. There were 7,167,000 telephone subscribers in 2002 (1,573·1 per 1,000 inhabitants) and 2,405,000 PCs (527·9 for every 1,000 persons). Norway had 3,840,400 mobile phone subscribers in 2002 and in 1997 there were 220,000 fax machines. Internet users numbered 2·68m. in July 2002, approximately 59% of the population.

In Dec. 2000 the government sold off a 21% stake in Telenor, the country's largest telecommunications operator.

Postal Services. In 2001 post offices began to be converted to Post in Shops. 452 post offices were replaced by 519 Post in Shops. In addition, 29 post offices were upgraded to Post Shops and five Business Centres and five Call Centres were established. The final target is a minimum of 1,150 Post in Shops, 300 Post Shops and 20 Business Centres. In 1997 a total of 2,524m. items of mail were processed, or 555 per person.

SOCIAL INSTITUTIONS

Justice. The judicature is common to civil and criminal cases; the same professional judges preside over both. These judges are state officials. The participation of lay judges and jurors, both summoned for the individual case, varies according to the kind of court and kind of case.

The 96 city or district courts of first instance are in criminal cases composed of one professional judge and two lay judges, chosen by ballot from a panel elected by the local authority. In civil cases two lay judges may participate. These courts are competent in all cases except criminal cases where the maximum penalty exceeds six years imprisonment. In every community there is a Conciliation Board composed of three lay persons elected by the district council. A civil lawsuit usually begins with mediation by the Board which can pronounce judgement in certain cases.

The five high courts, or courts of second instance, are composed of three professional judges. Additionally, in civil cases two or four lay judges may be summoned. In serious criminal cases, which are brought before high courts in the first instance, a jury of ten lay persons is summoned to determine whether the defendant is guilty according to the charge. In less serious criminal cases the court is composed of two professional and three lay judges. In civil cases, the court of second instance is an ordinary court of appeal. In criminal cases in which the lower court does not have judicial authority, it is itself the court of first instance. In other criminal cases it is an appeal court as far as the appeal is based on an attack against the lower court's assessment of the facts when determining the guilt of the defendant. An appeal based on any other alleged mistakes is brought directly before the Supreme Court.

The Supreme Court *(Høyesterett)* is the court of last resort. There are 18 Supreme Court judges. Each individual case is heard by five judges. Some major cases are determined in plenary session. The Supreme Court may in general examine every aspect of the case and the handling of it by the lower courts. However, in criminal cases the Court may not overrule the lower court's assessment of the facts as far as the guilt of the defendant is concerned.

The Court of Impeachment *(Riksretten)* is composed of five judges of the Supreme Court and ten members of Parliament.

The population in penal institutions in Sept. 2002 was 2,662 (59 per 100,000 of national population).

Religion. There is freedom of religion, the Church of Norway (Evangelical Lutheran), however, being the national church, endowed by the State. Its clergy are nominated by the King. Ecclesiastically Norway is divided into 11 bishoprics, 96 archdeaconries and 626 clerical districts. There were 304,000 members of registered and unregistered religious communities outside the Evangelical Lutheran Church, subsidized by central government and local authorities in 2002. There were also 109 Muslim congregations with 70,487 members. The Roman Catholics are under a Bishop at Oslo, a Vicar Apostolic at Trondheim and a Vicar Apostolic at Tromsø.

Education. Free compulsory schooling in primary and lower secondary schools was extended to 10 years from 9, and the starting age lowered to 6 from 7, in July 1997. All young people between the ages of 16 and 19 have the statutory right to three years of upper secondary education. In 2001 there were 5,776 kindergartens (children up to six years old) with 192,649 children and 53,816 staff. In 2001–02 there were 3,248 primary and lower secondary schools with 599,468 pupils and 44,925 teachers; 685 upper secondary schools with 185,824 pupils and 19,375 teachers; and 60 colleges, with 116,356 students and 4,946 teachers.

There are four universities: Oslo (founded 1811), with 31,426 students in Oct. 2001; Bergen (1946), with 16,579 students; Tromsø (1968), with 6,171 students; and the Norwegian University of Science and Technology (1996, formerly the University of Trondheim and the Norwegian Institute of Technology), with 19,403 students. There are also six university colleges and 26 state colleges. In 2001–02 the universities and university colleges had 81,358 students, and the state colleges 116,256 students. The University of Tromsø is responsible for Sami language and studies.

In 2000–01 total expenditure on education came to 6·9% of GNP and 16·2% of total government spending. The adult literacy rate in 2001 was at least 99%.

Health. The health care system, which is predominantly publicly financed (mainly by a national insurance tax), is run on both county and municipal levels. Persons who fall ill are guaranteed medical treatment, and health services are distributed according to need. In 2001 there were the equivalent of 7,323 full-time doctors, 21,733 nurses and 5,385 auxiliary nursing personnel. In 1994 provision of hospital beds was 51 per 10,000 population. In 2002 Norway spent 8·7% of its GDP on health. In 2002, 30% of men and 30% of women smoked. The rate among women is one of the highest in the world.

Welfare. In 2002 there were 624,054 old age pensioners who received a total of 72,685m. kroner, 292,224 disability pensioners who received 35,662m. kroner, 25,914 widows and widowers who received 1,935m. kroner and 25,470 single parents who received 2,078m. kroner. In 2002, 1,061,460 children received family allowances. Maternity leave is for one year on 80% of previous salary; unused portions may pass to a husband. In 2002 sickness benefits totalling 46,659·1m. kroner were paid: 26,117·0m. kroner in sickness allowances and 20,542·1m. kroner in medical benefits. Expenditure on benefits at childbirth and adoption totalled 8,511·4m. kroner to 125,177 recipients in 2002.

CULTURE

World Heritage Sites. Norway's UNESCO heritage sites (with year listed) are: the 12–13th century wooden church in Sogn og Fjordane on the west coast, the Urnes Stave Church (1979); the 58 wooden buildings in Bergen's wharf of Bryggen (1979); the wooden houses of the copper mining village of Røros (1980), active between the 17–20th centuries; the pre-historic Rock Drawings of Alta (1995) in the Alta Fjord; and Vegaøyan—the Vega Archipelago (2004), a cluster of dozens of islands centred on Vega, just south of the Arctic Circle.

Broadcasting. The Norwegian Broadcasting Corporation is a non-commercial enterprise operated by an independent state organization and broadcasts one programme (P1) on long, medium, and short-waves and on FM and one programme (P2) on FM. Local programmes are also broadcast. It broadcasts one TV programme from 2,259 transmitters. Colour programmes are broadcast by the PAL system. In 2000 there were 4·1m. radio and 3·0m. television receivers.

Cinema. There were 394 cinemas in 2001, with a seating capacity of 84,854. Attendances totalled 12·5m.

Press. There were 61 daily newspapers with a combined average net circulation of 2·20m. in 2002, and 91 weeklies and semi-weeklies with 689,000. Norway has one of the highest circulation rates of daily newspapers in Europe, at 596 per 1,000 inhabitants in 2000. In 1999 a total of 4,985 book titles were published.

Tourism. In 2000 there were 4,348,000 foreign tourists. In 2002 there were 1,124 hotels and 847 camping sites. Receipts from foreign tourism totalled US$1·94bn. in 2000.

Libraries. In 2001 there were 947 public libraries, 3,397 school libraries and (2002) 342 special and research libraries (three national).

Theatre and Opera. There were 7,808 theatre and opera performances attended by 1,420,146 people at 22 theatres in 2001.

Museums and Galleries. There were 508 museums in 2001 (35 art, 417 social history, 9 natural history and 47 mixed social and natural history), with 8,535,245 visitors.

DIPLOMATIC REPRESENTATIVES

Of Norway in the United Kingdom (25 Belgrave Sq., London, SW1X 8QD)
Ambassador: Tarald Osnes Brautaset.

Of the United Kingdom in Norway (Thomas Heftyesgate 8, 0244 Oslo)
Ambassador: Mariot Leslie.

Of Norway in the USA (2720 34th St., NW, Washington, D.C., 20008)
Ambassador: Knut Vollebaek.

Of the USA in Norway (Drammensveien 18, 0244 Oslo)
Ambassador: John D. Ong.

Of Norway to the United Nations
Ambassador: Johan L. Løvald.

Of Norway to the European Union
Ambassador: Bjørn T. Grydeland.

FURTHER READING

Statistics Norway (formerly Central Bureau of Statistics). *Statistisk Årbok; Statistical Yearbook of Norway.—Economic survey* (annual, from 1935; with English summary from 1952, now published in *Økonomiske Analyser*, annual).—*Historisk Statistikk; Historical Statistics.—Statistisk Månedshefte* (with English index)

Norges Statskalender. From 1816; annual from 1877

Petersson, O., *The Government and Politics of the Nordic Countries*. Stockholm, 1994

Turner, Barry, (ed.) *Scandinavia Profiled*. Macmillan, London, 2000

National library: The National Library of Norway, Drammensveien 42b, 0255 Oslo.
National statistical office: Statistics Norway, PB 8131 Dep., N-0033 Oslo.
Website: http://www.ssb.no/

SVALBARD

An archipelago situated between 10° and 35° E. long. and between 74° and 81° N. lat. Total area, 61,229 sq. km (23,640 sq. miles). The main islands are Spitsbergen, Nordaustlandet, Edgeøya, Barentsøya, Prins Karls Forland, Bjørnøya, Hopen, Kong Karls Land and Kvitøya. The Arctic climate is tempered by mild winds from the Atlantic.

The archipelago was probably discovered by Norsemen in 1194 and rediscovered by the Dutch navigator Barents in 1596. In the 17th century whale-hunting gave rise to rival Dutch, British and Danish-Norwegian claims to sovereignty; but when in the 18th century the whale-hunting ended, the question of the sovereignty of Svalbard lost its significance. It was again raised in the 20th century, owing to the discovery and exploitation of coalfields. By a treaty, signed on 9 Feb. 1920 in Paris, Norway's sovereignty over the archipelago was recognized. On 14 Aug. 1925 the archipelago was officially incorporated in Norway.

Total population on 1 Jan. 1999 was 2,423, of whom 1,476 were Norwegians, 939 Russians and 8 Poles. Coal is the principal product. There are 2 Norwegian and 2 Russian mining camps. 399,940 tonnes of coal were produced from Norwegian mines in 1999 valued at 72,208,000 kroner.

There were 2,413 motor vehicles and trailers registered at 31 Dec. 1999, including 1,145 snow scooters. There are research and radio stations, and an airport near Longyearbyen (Svalbard Lufthavn) opened in 1975.

Greve, T., *Svalbard: Norway in the Arctic*. Oslo, 1975
Hisdal, V., *Geography of Svalbard*. Norsk Polarinstitutt, Oslo, rev. ed., 1984

JAN MAYEN

This bleak, desolate and mountainous island of volcanic origin and partly covered by glaciers is situated at 71° N. lat. and 8° 30' W. long., 300 miles north-northeast of Iceland. The total area is 377 sq. km (146 sq. miles). Beerenberg, its highest peak, reaches a height of 2,277 metres. Volcanic activity, which had been dormant, reactivated in Sept. 1970.

The island was possibly discovered by Henry Hudson in 1608, and it was first named Hudson's Tutches (Touches). It was again and again rediscovered and renamed. Its present name derives from the Dutch whaling captain Jan Jacobsz May, who indisputably discovered the island in 1614. It was uninhabited, but occasionally visited by seal hunters and trappers, until 1921 when Norway established a radio and meteorological station. On 8 May 1929 Jan Mayen was officially proclaimed as incorporated into the Kingdom of Norway. Its relation to Norway was finally settled by law of 27 Feb. 1930. A LORAN station (1959) and a CONSOL station (1968) have been established.

BOUVET ISLAND

Bouvetøya

This uninhabited volcanic island, mostly covered by glaciers and situated at 54° 25' S. lat. and 3° 21' E. long., was discovered in 1739 by a French naval officer, Jean Baptiste Loziert Bouvet, but no flag was hoisted till, in 1825, Capt. Norris raised the Union Jack. In 1928 Great Britain waived its claim to the island in favour of Norway, which in Dec. 1927 had occupied it. A law of 27 Feb. 1930 declared Bouvetøya a Norwegian dependency. The area is 59 sq. km (23 sq. miles). Since 1977 Norway has had an automatic meteorological station on the island.

PETER I ISLAND

Peter I Øy

This uninhabited island, situated at 68° 48' S. lat. and 90° 35' W. long., was sighted in 1821 by the Russian explorer, Admiral von Bellingshausen. The first landing was made in 1929 by a Norwegian expedition which hoisted the Norwegian flag. On 1 May 1931 Peter I Island was placed under Norwegian sovereignty, and on 24 March 1933 it was incorporated as a dependency. The area is 249 sq. km (96 sq. miles).

QUEEN MAUD LAND

Dronning Maud Land

On 14 Jan. 1939 the Norwegian Cabinet placed that part of the Antarctic Continent from the border of Falkland Islands dependencies in the west to the border of the Australian Antarctic Dependency in the east (between 20° W. and 45° E.) under Norwegian sovereignty. The territory had been explored only by Norwegians and hitherto been ownerless. In 1957 it was given the status of a dependency.

OMAN

Saltanat 'Uman
(Sultanate of Oman)

Capital: Muscat
Population projection, 2010: 3·46m.
GDP per capita, 2002: (PPP$) 13,340
HDI/world rank: 0·770/74

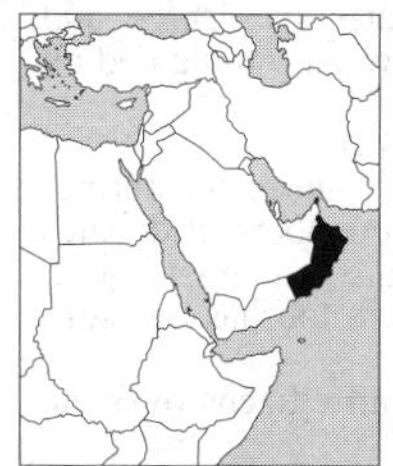

KEY HISTORICAL EVENTS

The ancestors of present day Oman are believed to have arrived in two waves of migration, the first from the Yemen and the second from northern Arabia. In the 9th century maritime trade flourished and Sohar became the greatest sea port in the Islamic world. In the early 16th century the Portuguese occupied Muscat. The Ya'aruba dynasty introduced a period of renaissance in Omani fortunes both at home and abroad, uniting the country and bringing prosperity; but, on the death in 1718 of Sultan bin Saif II, civil war broke out over the election of his successor. Persian troops occupied Muttrah and Muscat but failed to take Sohar which was defended by Ahmad bin Said who expelled the Persians from Oman after the civil war had ended. In 1744 the Al bu Said family assumed power and has ruled to the present day. Oman remained largely isolated from the rest of the world until 1970 when Said bin Taimur was deposed by his son Qaboos in a bloodless coup.

TERRITORY AND POPULATION

Situated at the southeast corner of the Arabian peninsula, Oman is bounded in the northeast by the Gulf of Oman and southeast by the Arabian Sea, southwest by Yemen and northwest by Saudi Arabia and the United Arab Emirates. There is an enclave at the northern tip of the Musandam Peninsula. An agreement of April 1992 completed the demarcation of the border with Yemen, and an agreement of March 1990 finalized the border with Saudi Arabia.

With a coastline of 1,700 sq. km from the Strait of Hormuz in the north to the borders of the Republic of Yemen, the Sultanate is strategically located overlooking ancient maritime trade routes linking the Far East and Africa with the Mediterranean.

The Sultanate of Oman occupies a total area of 309,500 sq. km and includes different terrains that vary from plain to highlands and mountains. The coastal plain overlooking the Gulf of Oman and the Arabian Sea forms the most important and fertile plain in Oman.

The **Kuria Muria** islands were ceded to the UK in 1854 by the Sultan of Muscat and Oman. On 30 Nov. 1967 the islands were retroceded to the Sultan of Muscat and Oman, in accordance with the wishes of the population. They are now known as the **Halaniyat Islands**.

In 2003 the census population was 2,340,815 (density 7·6 per sq. km.), chiefly Arabs, and including 0·6m. foreign workers.

The UN gives a projected population for 2010 of 3·46m.

In 2001, 76·5% of the population lived in urban areas. In the period 1990–95 the annual growth in the urban population was 8·2%, a rate only exceeded by Botswana and Mozambique. The census population of the capital, Muscat, in 2003 was 632,073.

The official language is Arabic; English is in commercial use.

SOCIAL STATISTICS

2002 estimates: births, 71,000; deaths, 10,000. Estimated rates, 2002 (per 1,000 population): births, 25·7; deaths, 3·5. Consequently Oman has a very young population, with approximately 41% of the population under the age of 15. Expectation of life at birth, 2001, was 70·8 years for males and 74·1 years for females. Average annual population growth rate, 1992–2002, 3·3%. Fertility rate, 2001, 5·6 births per woman, down from 7·8 in 1988. Oman has achieved some of the most rapid advances ever recorded. Infant mortality declined from 200 per 1,000 live births in 1960 to 12 per 1,000 live births in 2001, and as recently as 1970 life expectancy was just 40.

CLIMATE

Oman has a desert climate, with exceptionally hot and humid months from April to Oct., when temperatures may reach 47°C. Light monsoon rains fall in the south from June to Sept., with highest amounts in the western highland region. Muscat, Jan. 28°C, July 46°C. Annual rainfall 101 mm. Salalah, Jan. 29°C, July 32°C. Annual rainfall 98 mm.

CONSTITUTION AND GOVERNMENT

Oman is a hereditary absolute monarchy. The Sultan legislates by decree and appoints a Cabinet to assist him. The Basic Statute of the State was promulgated on 6 Nov. 1996.

The present Sultan is **Qaboos bin Said Al Said** (b. Nov. 1940).

In 1991 a new consultative assembly, the *Majlis al-Shura*, replaced the former State Consultative Chamber. The Majlis consists of 83 elected members. It debates domestic issues, but has no legislative or veto powers. There is also an upper house, the *Majlis al Dawla*, which consists of 53 appointed members; it too has advisory powers only.

In Dec. 2002 the Sultan of Oman extended voting rights to all citizens over the age of 21.

National Anthem. 'Ya Rabbana elifidh lana jalalat al Saltan' ('O Lord, protect for us his majesty the Sultan'); words and tune anonymous.

RECENT ELECTIONS

The last elections to the *Majlis al Shura* were on 4 Oct. 2003. No parties are allowed. 83 legislators were chosen for three-year terms from among 506 candidates (including 15 women). Two women were elected.

CURRENT ADMINISTRATION

The Sultan is nominally Prime Minister and Minister of Foreign Affairs, Defence and Finance.

In March 2005 the other Ministers were:

Special Representative of the Sultan: Thuwayni bin Shihab Al Said.

Deputy Prime Minister for Cabinet Affairs: Fahd bin Mahmud Al Said. *Minister Responsible for Foreign Affairs:* Yusuf bin Alawi bin Abdallah. *Agriculture and Fisheries:* Salim bin Hilal bin Ali al-Khalili. *Civil Service:* Hilal bin Khalid al-Ma'awali. *Commerce and Industry:* Maqbul bin Ali bin Sultan. *Defence Affairs:* Badr bin Saud bin Harib Al Busaidi. *Transportation and Communications:* Mohammed bin Abdullah bin Isa Al Harthi. *Education:* Yahya bin Saud bin Mansour Al Suleimi. *Housing, Electricity and Water:* Khamis bin Mubarak bin Issa Al Alawi. *Regional Municipalities, Environment and Water Resources:* Abdullah bin Salem bin Amer Al Rawas. *National Economy:* Ahmad bin Abd al-Nabi al-Makki. *Health:* Dr Ali bin Muhammad bin Musa. *Information:* Hamad bin Mohammed bin Mohsin al Rashdi. *Interior:* Saud bin Ibrahim bin Saud Al Busaidi. *Justice:* Muhammad bin Abdallah bin Zahir al-Hinai. *National Heritage and Culture:* Sayyid Haitham bin Tariq Al Said. *Oil and Gas:* Muhammad bin Hamad bin Seif al-Rumhi. *Social Development:* Amir bin Shuwayn al-Husni. *Awqaf and Religious Affairs:* Abdallah bin Muhammad bin Abdallah al-Salimi. *Diwan of the Royal Court:* Said Ali bin Hamoud al-Busaidi. *Royal Office:* Gen. Ali bin Majid al-Mamari. *Higher Education:* Rawya bint Saud Al-Bussaidi. *Legal Affairs:* Muhammad bin Ali bin Nasir al-Alawi. *Labour:* Jama bin Ali bin Juma. *Tourism:* Rajiha bint Abdul Amir ibn Ali. *Minister of State and Governor of the Capital:* Sayyid Al-Mutassim bin Hamoud al-Busaidi. *Minister of State and Governor of Dhofar:* Muhammad bin Ali al-Qutaybi.

Government Website: http://www.omanet.com

DEFENCE

Military expenditure in 2003 totalled US$2,468m. (US$950 per capita), representing 11·6% of GDP.

Army. Strength (2002) about 25,000. In addition there are 6,400 Royal Household troops. A paramilitary tribal home guard numbers 4,000.

Navy. The Navy is based principally at Seeb (HQ) and Wudam. Naval personnel in 2002 totalled 4,200.

The wholly separate Royal Yacht Squadron consists of a yacht and support ship with helicopter and troop-carrying capability.

Air Force. The Air Force, formed in 1959, has 40 combat aircraft including in 2002 two strike/interceptor squadrons of Jaguars and a ground attack squadron of Hawks.

Personnel (2002) about 4,100.

INTERNATIONAL RELATIONS

A 1982 Memorandum of Understanding with the UK provided for regular consultations on international and bilateral issues.

Oman is a member of the UN, WTO, the League of Arab States, the Organization of the Islamic Conference, Islamic Development Bank and the Gulf Co-operation Council.

ECONOMY

Industry accounted for 53·2% of GDP in 2002, services 44·7% and agriculture 2·1%.

Currency. The unit of currency is the *Rial Omani* (OMR). It is divided into 1,000 *baiza*. The rial is pegged to the US dollar. In June 2002 foreign exchange reserves were US$3,133m., total money supply was RO 813m. and gold reserves totalled 1,000 troy oz (291,000 troy oz in April 2002). Inflation was negative in 2000, 2001 and 2002, at –1·2%, –1·0% and –0·7% respectively.

In 2001 the six Gulf Arab states—Oman, along with Bahrain, Kuwait, Qatar, Saudi Arabia and the United Arab Emirates—signed an agreement to establish a single currency by 2010.

Budget. Budget revenue and expenditure (in RO 1m.):

	1997	*1998*	*1999*	*2000*	*2001*
Revenue	1,867·4	1,426·6	1,401·8	1,831·2	2,077·2
Expenditure	1,848·0	1,820·1	1,859·4	2,179·5	2,295·1

In 1999 approximately 70% of total revenue came from oil.

Performance. Real GDP growth was 9·3% in 2001 and 2·3% in 2002. Total GDP in 2002 was US$20·1bn.

Banking and Finance. The bank of issue is the Central Bank of Oman, which commenced operations in 1975 (*President*, Hamood Sangour Al Zadjali). All banks must comply with BIS capital adequacy ratios and have a minimum capital of RO 20m. (minimum capital requirement for foreign banks established in Oman is RO 3m.). In 2002 there were 15 commercial banks (of which nine were foreign) and three specialized banks. The largest bank is BankMuscat SAOG, with assets of RO 1·3bn. It was created in 2000 following a merger between BankMuscat and the Commercial Bank of Oman.

There is a stock exchange in Muscat, which is linked with those in Bahrain and Kuwait.

ENERGY AND NATURAL RESOURCES

Environment. Oman's carbon dioxide emissions from the consumption and flaring of fossil fuels in 2002 were the equivalent of 8·2 tonnes per capita.

Electricity. Installed capacity was 2·4m. kW in 2000. Production in 2000 was 12·06bn. kWh, with consumption per capita 5,021 kWh (2000).

Oil and Gas. The economy is dominated by the oil industry. Oil in commercial quantities was discovered in 1964 and production began in 1967. Production in 2003 was 40·7m. tonnes. In 2000 exports of oil stood at 29·5m. tonnes. Total proven reserves were estimated in 2002 to be 5·5bn. bbls. It was announced in Aug. 2000 that two new oilfields in the south of the country had been discovered, with a potential combined daily production capacity of 12,200 bbls. a day. Earlier in 2000 oil began to be pumped from two further recently-discovered oilfields.

Gas is likely to become the second major source of income for the country. Oman's proven gas reserves were 864bn. cu. metres in 2002. The discovery in 2000 of two new fields could yield a daily production of 1·78m. cu. metres. Natural gas production was 14·8bn. cu. metres in 2002.

Water. Oman relies on a combination of aquifers and desalination plants for its water, augmented by a construction programme of some 60 recharge dams.

Desalination plants at Ghubriah and Wadi Adai provide most of the water needs of the capital area. In 1999 water production was 20,136m. gallons.

Minerals. Production in 1998 (in 1,000 tonnes): limestone, 1,902; marble, 166; gypsum, 165; chromite, 30; salt, 14; silver (2001), 3 tonnes; gold (2000), 1,029 kg. The mountains of the Sultanate of Oman are rich in mineral deposits; these include chromite, coal, asbestos, manganese, gypsum, limestone and marble. The government is studying the exploitation of gold, platinum and sulphide.

Agriculture. Agriculture and fisheries are the traditional occupations of Omanis and remain important to the people and economy of Oman to this day. The country now produces a wide variety of fresh fruit, vegetables and field crops. The country is rapidly moving towards its goal of self-sufficiency in agriculture with the total area under cultivation standing at over 70,000 ha and total output more than 1m. tonnes. This has not been achieved without effort. In a country where water is a scarce commodity it has meant educating farmers on efficient methods of irrigation and building recharge dams to make the most of infrequent rainfall. In 2001 there were 38,000 ha of arable land and 43,000 ha of permanent crops. 62,000 ha were irrigated in 2001. According to a census of 1992–93, about 103,000 people were employed in agriculture of whom a third were women.

The coastal plain (Batinah) northwest of Muscat is fertile, as are the Dhofar highlands in the south. In the valleys of the interior, as well as on the Batinah coastal plain, date cultivation has reached a high level, and there are possibilities of agricultural development. Agricultural products, 2000 estimates (in 1,000 tonnes): dates, 135; tomatoes, 34; watermelons, 32; lemons and limes, 31; bananas, 28. Vegetable and fruit production are also important, and livestock are raised in the south where there are monsoon rains. Camels (98,000 in 2000) are bred by the inland tribes. Other livestock, 2000: sheep, 180,000; cattle, 213,000; goats, 729,000; chickens, 3m. Live animals and meat constitute more than 25% of the country's non-oil exports.

Fisheries. The catch was 126,531 tonnes in 2001, exclusively sea fish. More than 80% is taken by some 85,000 self-employed fishermen.

INDUSTRY

Apart from oil production, copper smelting and cement production, there are light industries, mainly food processing and chemical products. The government gives priority to import substitute industries.

Labour. Males constituted 84% of the labour force in 1999. In 1995 there were 619,351 employees in the private sector and 110,529 persons in government service. The employment of foreign labour is being discouraged following 'Omanization' regulations of 1994.

INTERNATIONAL TRADE

Total foreign debt was US$4,639m. in 2002. A royal decree of 1994 permits up to 65% foreign ownership of Omani companies with a five-year tax and customs duties exemption.

Oman, along with Bahrain, Kuwait, Qatar, Saudi Arabia and the United Arab Emirates began the implementation of a customs union in Jan. 2003.

Imports and Exports. Imports and exports in US$1m.:

	1997	*1998*	*1999*	*2000*	*2001*
Imports f.o.b.	4,645	5,215	4,300	4,593	5,311
Exports f.o.b.	7,657	5,521	7,239	11,319	11,074

In 1999 crude oil exports made up approximately 74% of total exports; the main non-oil exports were road vehicles (7%). Main export markets in 2000 were: United Arab Emirates, 40·1%; Saudi Arabia, 8·4%; Iran, 7·8%; Yemen, 7·8%; USA, 5·5%; UK, 3·8%. Main import suppliers, 2000: United Arab Emirates, 29·5%; Japan, 18·1%; UK, 5·8%; USA, 5·4%; Germany, 3·7%; South Korea, 3·4%.

In 2000 the value of Oman's exports rose 56·4% compared to 1999. Over the same period oil exports rose by 61·1%.

COMMUNICATIONS

Roads. A network of adequate graded roads links all the main sectors of population, and only a few mountain villages are not accessible by motor vehicles. In 1999 there were about 32,800 km of roads including 550 km of motorways and 2,160 km of main roads. In 1996 there were 211,000 passenger cars and 97,000 vans and lorries. The estimated average distance travelled by a passenger car in the year 1996 was 36,200 km.

In 1999 there were 8,947 road accidents and 473 deaths.

Civil Aviation. Oman has a 25% share in Gulf Air with Bahrain, Qatar and the UAE. In 2003 Gulf Air ran services in and out of Seeb International Airport (20 miles from Muscat) to Abu Dhabi, Amman, Bahrain, Bangkok, Bombay, Cairo, Dar es Salaam, Delhi, Dubai, Frankfurt, Kuwait, London, Madras, Manila, Nairobi, Riyadh and Thiruvananthapuram. Oman Air also flies on some international routes. In 2000 Seeb International Airport (Muscat) handled 2,622,000 passengers and 68,600 tonnes of freight.

Oman's two major airports, Seeb International and Salalah (mainly domestic flights), have been privatized as part of a project to develop Seeb as a regional hub. It will be rebuilt by a consortium (British Airports Authority, Oman's Bahwan Trading Company and ABB Equity Ventures) that was awarded a 25-year concession to operate the airports in Jan. 2002.

Shipping. In Mutrah a deep-water port (named Mina Qaboos) was completed in 1974. The annual handling capacity is 1·5m. tonnes. Mina Salalah, the port of Salalah, has a capacity of 1m. tonnes per year. Sea-going shipping totalled 19,000 GRT in 2002.

Telecommunications. The General Telecommunications Organization maintains a telegraph office at Muscat and an automatic telephone exchange. In 2002 there were 692,500 telephone subscribers (255·4 per 1,000 persons) and 95,000 PCs in use (35·0 for every 1,000 persons). Mobile phone subscribers numbered 464,900 in 2002 and there were 6,400 fax machines in 1997. In 2002 there were 18,000 Internet users.

Postal Services. In 1999 there were 94 post offices. 16m. items of mail were exchanged between Oman and the rest of the world in 1999.

SOCIAL INSTITUTIONS

Justice. The population in penal institutions in 2000 was 2,020 (81 per 100,000 of national population).

Religion. In 2001, 83·5% of the population were Muslim. There were also Hindu and Christian minorities.

Education. Adult literacy was 73·0% in 2001 (male, 80·9%; female, 63·5%). In 2003–04 there were 1,022 schools. The total number of pupils in state education in 2003–04 was 576,472 (139,082 in basic education and 437,390 in general education) with 32,345 teachers (13,939 in basic education and 18,406 in general education). Oman's first university, the Sultan Qaboos University, opened in 1986 and in 2003–04 there were 12,437 students.

In 2001–02 total expenditure on education came to 4·4% of GNP.

Health. In 1998 there were 47 hospitals (13 of which are considered referral hospitals) with 4,443 beds. There were also 117 health centres. In 1999 there were 3,143 doctors, 237 dentists, 395 pharmacists and 7,525 nursing staff.

CULTURE

World Heritage Sites. The four sites under Omani jurisdiction are (with the year entered on the list): Bahla Fort (1987); the archaeological sites of Bat, Al-Khutm and Al-Ayn, a collection of settlements and necropolises of the 3rd millennium BC (1988); the Arabian Oryx Sanctuary, a protected area for endangered species (1994); and the Frankincense Trail, a group of archaeological sites representing the production and distribution of frankincense (2000).

Broadcasting. The government-owned Radio Oman broadcasts in Arabic and English. A colour (PAL) television service, the government-owned Oman Television, covering Muscat and the surrounding area, started transmission in 1974. A television service for Dhofar opened in 1975. In 1991 there were seven television stations. Total number of radios (2000), 1·49m.; and televisions (2000), 1·35m. (563 per

1,000 inhabitants). Television usage has increased dramatically since 1980, when there were just 35,000 TV receivers in Oman (31 per 1,000 inhabitants). Oman had both the greatest percentage increase in the number of TV receivers of any country in the world between 1980 and 2000 and the greatest numerical increase in the number of receivers per 1,000 inhabitants.

Press. In 1996 there were four daily newspapers with a combined circulation of 63,000.

Tourism. Foreign visitors numbered 571,000 in 2000. In 1999 there were 102 hotels with a total of over 5,138 rooms. Tourism accounts for 1% of GDP.

Festivals. National Day (18 Nov.); Spring Festival in Salalah (July–Aug.); Ramadan (Dec.).

Libraries. Three public libraries are run by the Royal Court of Diwan, the Islamic Institute and the Ministry of National Heritage.

Theatre and Opera. There is one national theatre.

Museums and Galleries. The main attractions are the Omani Museum (est. 1974) at Medinat al-Alam; the Omani-French Museum, Children's Museum and Bait al-Zubair (a historic house) at Muscat; the Natural History Museum at the Ministry of National Heritage and Culture; the National Museum; Salalah Museum; the Sultan's Armed Forces museum at Bait al-Falaj; the Oil & Gas Exhibition at Mina al-Fahal. There is also a museum in the historic fort at Sohar.

In 1998 total museum attendance was 96,000.

DIPLOMATIC REPRESENTATIVES

Of Oman in the United Kingdom (167 Queen's Gate, London, SW7 5HE)
Ambassador: Hussain bin Ali bin Abdullatif.

Of the United Kingdom in Oman (PO Box 185, Mina Al Fahal, Postal Code 116, Muscat)
Ambassador: Stuart Laing.

Of Oman in the USA (2535 Belmont Rd, NW, Washington, D.C., 20008)
Ambassador: Mohamed Ali Al-Khusaiby.

Of the USA in Oman (PO Box 202, Medinat Qaboos, Muscat)
Ambassador: Richard L. Baltimore.

Of Oman to the United Nations
Ambassador: Fuad Mubarak Al-Hinai.

Of Oman to the European Union
Ambassador: Khadija bint Hassan Salman Al-Lawati.

FURTHER READING

Clements, F. A., *Oman.* [Bibliography] 2nd ed. ABC-Clio, Oxford and Santa Barbara (CA), 1994

Owtram, Francis, *A Modern History of Oman: Formation of the State since 1920.* I. B. Tauris, London, 2002

Skeet, I., *Oman: Politics and Development.* London, 1992

National statistical office: Ministry of National Economy, Information and Documentation Centre, POB 881, Muscat 113.
Website: http://www.moneoman.gov.om

PAKISTAN

Islami Jamhuriya e Pakistan (Islamic Republic of Pakistan)

Capital: Islamabad
Population projection, 2010: 181·75m.
GDP per capita, 2002: (PPP$) 1,940
HDI/world rank: 0·497/142

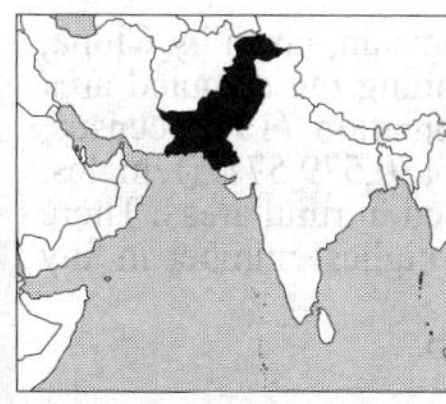

KEY HISTORICAL EVENTS

The State of Pakistan was created on 14 Aug. 1947 to provide Indian Muslims with their own state. Pakistan's status was that of a Dominion within the Commonwealth; it became a republic in 1956 and left the Commonwealth in 1972. Efforts to rejoin were opposed by India until 1989 when Pakistan once more became a full member of the Commonwealth.

The first of several periods of martial law began in 1958, followed by the rule of Field Marshal Mohammad Ayub Khan (until 1969) and Gen. Agha Mohammad Yahya Khan (until 1971). During the latter's term, differences between East and West Pakistan came to a head. Civil war broke out in March 1971 and ended in Dec. 1971 with the creation of Bangladesh. A new constitution came into force on 14 Aug. 1973, providing a federal parliamentary government with a president as head of state and a prime minister as head of the government. Zulfiquar Ali Bhutto became prime minister. His government was thought by traditionalists to be not sufficiently Islamic. There was an army coup led by Gen. Mohammad Zia ul-Haq in July 1977. Zulfiquar Ali Bhutto was hanged for conspiring to murder. His daughter, Benazir, held power twice in the 1990s but was eventually overthrown in 1996 when the President, Farooq Leghari, dismissed the government for corruption and mismanaging the economy.

Relations between Pakistan and India have foundered on the issue of Kashmir, a disputed territory divided by a ceasefire line negotiated by the UN in 1949. On 28 May 1998 Pakistan carried out five nuclear tests in the deserts of Balochistan in response to India's tests earlier in the month. US President Bill Clinton invoked sanctions but Pakistan subsequently carried out a sixth test. With first steps towards a nuclear agreement, the USA lifted most sanctions. On 11 June, following India's example, Pakistan announced a unilateral moratorium on nuclear tests. On 12 Oct. 1999 the military chief, Gen. Pervez Musharraf, seized power in a coup, overthrowing the democratically-elected government of prime minister Nawaz Sharif. The coup, which lasted less than three hours, was launched after the prime minister had tried to dismiss Gen. Musharraf from his position as army chief of staff. The former prime minister and his senior allies were placed under house arrest and subsequently put on trial. Nawaz Sharif was found guilty of corruption and sentenced to life imprisonment. The coup marked the first time in history that a military regime had taken over an affirmed nuclear power.

There have been some 35,000 deaths since the outbreak of the Kashmir insurgency in 1988. Negotiations with India over the future of the disputed territory of Kashmir began in July 1999. In May 2001 India ended its six-month long ceasefire. It then invited Pakistan's government to enter talks about the dispute, which ended with hopes of avoiding further violence. Following the terror attacks on New York and Washington of 11 Sept. 2001 Pakistan found itself in a central role in the war against terrorism. With neighbouring Afghanistan believed to be sheltering Osama bin Laden, the USA persuaded President Musharraf to allow American forces access to Pakistani air bases. In return the USA lifted the remaining sanctions imposed on Pakistan after it carried out a series of nuclear tests in 1998. In Dec. 2001 an attack was made on the Indian parliament by suicide bombers. Although no group claimed responsibility, the Indian authorities suspected Kashmiri separatists, leading to increasing tension between Pakistan and India. However, President Musharraf's subsequent crackdown on militants helped to bring the two countries back from the brink of war. Tension between Pakistan and India increased following an attack on an Indian army base in Indian-occupied Kashmir on 14 May 2002. The attack, which killed 31 people, was linked to Islamic terrorists infiltrating into the Kashmir valley from Pakistan. It drew widespread criticism of Pakistani President Pervez Musharraf for failing to combat terrorism in the disputed region. Between 25 and 28 May Pakistan carried out three tests of short-range ballistic missiles. In Nov. 2003 Pakistan and India agreed to observe a further ceasefire along the Line of Control in Kashmir.

TERRITORY AND POPULATION

Pakistan is bounded in the west by Iran, northwest by Afghanistan, north by China, east by India and south by the Arabian Sea. The area (excluding the disputed area of Kashmir) is 307,374 sq. miles (796,095 sq. km); population (1998 census, excluding Azad, Kashmir, Baltistan, Diamir and Gilgit), 130,579,571 (females, 62,739,434). 2002 estimate: 150,213,000. In 2001, 66·6% lived in rural areas. There were 2·2m. refugees in 2001, mostly from Afghanistan, the highest number in any country in the world.

The UN gives a projected population for 2010 of 181·75m.

The population of the principal cities is as follows:

		1998 census			
Karachi	9,269,265	Rawalpindi	1,406,214	Peshawar	988,005
Lahore	5,063,499	Hyderabad	1,151,274	Islamabad	791,085
Faisalabad	1,977,246	Gujranwala	1,124,799	Quetta	560,307

Population of the provinces (census of 1998):

	Area (sq. km)	*1998 census population (in 1,000)* Total	*Male*	*Female*	*Urban*	*1998 density per sq. km*
North-West Frontier Province	74,521	17,555	8,963	8,592	2,973	236
Federally administered Tribal Areas	27,219	3,138	1,635	1,503	83	115
Federal Capital Territory Islamabad	907	799	430	369	524	881
Punjab	205,344	72,585	37,509	35,076	22,699	353
Sind	140,914	29,991	15,823	14,168	14,662	213
Balochistan	347,190	6,511	3,481	3,030	1,516	19

Urdu is the national language and the *lingua franca*, although only spoken by about 10% of the population; English is used in business, higher education and in central government. Around 60% of the population speak Punjabi.

SOCIAL STATISTICS

1997 estimates: births, 4,950,000; deaths, 1,240,000. Rates, 1997 (per 1,000 population): birth, 36; death, 9; infant mortality (per 1,000 live births), 84 (2001). Formal registration of marriages and divorces has not been required since 1992. Expectation of life in 2001 was 60·6 years for men and 60·3 years for women. Annual population growth rate, 1992–2002, 2·5%. Fertility rate, 2001, 5·2 births per woman.

CLIMATE

A weak form of tropical monsoon climate occurs over much of the country, with arid conditions in the north and west, where the wet season is only from Dec. to March. Elsewhere, rain comes mainly in the summer. Summer temperatures are high everywhere, but winters can be cold in the mountainous north. Islamabad, Jan. 50°F (10°C), July 90°F (32·2°C). Annual rainfall 36" (900 mm). Karachi, Jan. 61°F (16·1°C), July 86°F (30°C). Annual rainfall 8" (196 mm). Lahore, Jan. 53°F (11·7°C), July 89°F (31·7°C). Annual rainfall 18" (452 mm). Multan, Jan. 51°F (10·6°C), July 93°F (33·9°C). Annual rainfall 7" (170 mm). Quetta, Jan. 38°F (3·3°C), July 80°F (26·7°C). Annual rainfall 10" (239 mm).

CONSTITUTION AND GOVERNMENT

Under the 1973 Constitution, the *President* was elected for a five-year term by a college of parliamentary deputies, senators and members of the Provincial

Assemblies. Parliament is bicameral, comprising a *Senate* of 100 members and a *National Assembly* of 342. In the *Senate*, each of the four provinces is allocated 14 seats, while the federally administered tribal areas and the federal capital are assigned eight and two seats respectively. In addition, each province is conferred four seats for technocrats and four for women. Two seats, one for technocrats and another for women, are reserved for the federal capital. The *National Assembly* is directly elected for five-year terms. 272 members are elected in single-seat constituencies, there are 10 seats for non-Muslim minorities and 60 seats for women.

Following the 1999 coup Gen. Musharraf announced that the Constitution was to be held 'in abeyance' and issued a 'Provisional Constitution Order No. 1' in its place. In Aug. 2002 he unilaterally amended the constitution to grant himself the right to dissolve parliament.

During the period of martial law from 1977–85 the Constitution was also in abeyance, but not abrogated. In 1985 it was amended to extend the powers of the President, including those of appointing and dismissing ministers and vetoing new legislation until 1990. Legislation of 1 April 1997 abolished the President's right to dissolve parliament, appoint provincial governors and nominate the heads of the armed services.

Gen. Pervez Musharraf, Chief of the Army Staff, assumed the responsibilities of the chief executive of the country following the removal of Prime Minister Nawaz Sharif on 12 Oct. 1999. He formed a National Security Council consisting of six members belonging to the armed forces and a number of civilians with expertise in various fields. A Federal Cabinet of Ministers was also installed working under the guidance of the National Security Council. Also formed was the National Reconstruction Bureau, a think tank providing institutional advice and input on economic, social and institutional matters. The administration declared that it intended to first restore economic order before holding general elections to install a civilian government. The Supreme Court of Pakistan allowed the administration a three-year period, which expired on 12 Oct. 2002, to accomplish this task. Elections were held on 10 Oct. 2002. On 30 April 2002 a referendum was held in which 97·7% voted in favour of extending Musharraf's rule by a further five years. Turn-out was around 50%. He amended the constitution in Aug. 2002 to formally extend his mandate by five years.

The Constitution obliges the government to enable the people to order their lives in accordance with Islam.

National Anthem. 'Pak sarzamin shadbad' ('Blessed be the sacred land'); words by Abul Asr Hafeez Jaulandhari, tune by Ahmad G. Chaagla.

RECENT ELECTIONS

Pakistan's first general elections since the military coup in 1999 took place on 10 Oct. 2002. The former prime minister Benazir Bhutto's Pakistan People's Party won 71 of 272 seats with 25·8% of votes cast; pro-Musharraf Pakistan Muslim League (Quaid-e-Azam) took 69 with 25·7%; while a coalition of six hardline Islamic parties, Muttahida Majlis-e-Amal, won 53 with 11·3%. Despite winning 9·4% of the vote, the Pakistan Muslim League (Nawaz Sharif) of exiled former prime minister Nawaz Sharif took only 19 seats. The remaining seats went to smaller parties and non-partisans. After the election, allocation of seats to women and minority representatives was carried out in accordance with the constitution resulting in the Pakistan Muslim League (Quaid-e-Azam) having 117 seats, the Pakistan People's Party 81, the Muttahida Majlis-e-Amal 60 and Pakistan Muslim League (Nawaz Sharif) 19. Turn-out was 42%.

CURRENT ADMINISTRATION

President: Gen. Pervez Musharraf; b. 1943 (since 20 June 2001).

Following the overthrow of prime minister Nawaz Sharif in Oct. 1999, Gen. Pervez Musharraf assumed power. He appointed a National Security Council to function as the country's supreme governing body and subsequently a full cabinet of ministers. In June 2001 he declared himself president. Following the elections of Oct. 2002 a coalition government was formed. In March 2005 it comprised:

Prime Minister and Minister of Finance: Shaukat Aziz; b. 1949 (PML-Q; sworn in 28 Aug. 2004).

Senior Federal Minister for Defence: Rao Sikandar Iqbal. *Minister for Commerce:* Humayoon Akhtar Khan. *Communication:* Muhammad Shamim Siddiqui. *Culture, Sports and Youth Affairs:* Muhammad Ajmal Khan. *Defence Production:* Habibullah Khan Warriach. *Education:* Javed Ashraf Qazi. *Environment:* Tahir Iqbal. *Food, Agriculture and Livestock:* Sikandar Hayat Khan Bosan. *Foreign Affairs:* Mian Khursheed Mehmood Kasuri. *Frontier Affairs:* Sardar Yar Muhammad Rind. *Health:* Mohammad Nasir Khan. *Housing and Works:* Safwanullah Syed. *Industries and Production:* Jehangir Khan Tareen. *Information and Broadcasting:* Sheikh Rashid Ahmad. *Information Technology:* Awais Ahmad Khan Leghari. *Interior:* Aftab Ahmed Khan Sherpao. *Kashmir Affairs and Northern Areas:* Makhdoom Faisal Saleh Hayat. *Labour, Manpower and Overseas Pakistanis:* Ghulam Sarwar Khan. *Law, Justice and Human Rights:* Muhammad Wasi Zafar. *Local Government and Rural Development:* Abdul Razzaq Thahim. *Narcotics Control:* Ghaus Bux Khan Maher. *Parliamentary Affairs:* Sher Afghan Khan Niazi. *Petroleum and Natural Resources:* Amanullah Khan Jadoon. *Population Welfare:* Chaudhry Shahbaz Hussain. *Ports and Shipping:* Babar Khan Ghauri. *Privatization and Investment:* Abdul Hafeez Shaikh. *Railways:* Mian Shamim Haider. *Religious Affairs:* Muhammad Ijaz-ul-Haq. *Science and Technology:* Nouraiz Shakoor. *Social Welfare and Special Education:* Zobaida Jalal. *Textiles Industry:* Mushtaq Ali Cheema. *Tourism:* Syed Ghazi Ghulb Jamal. *Water and Power:* Liaquat Ali Jatoi.

Government Website: http://www.pakistan.gov.pk

DEFENCE

A *Council for Defence and National Security* was set up in Jan. 1997, comprising the President, the Prime Minister, the Ministers of Defence, Foreign Affairs, Interior, Finance and the military chiefs of staff. The Council advised the government on the determination of national strategy and security priorities, but was disbanded in Feb. 1997. The Council was revived in Oct. 1999 following the change of government but was to have a wider scope and not restrict itself to defence matters.

Defence expenditure in 2003 totalled US$3,129m. (US$21 per capita), representing 4·5% of GDP.

Nuclear Weapons. Pakistan began a secret weapons programme in 1972 to reach parity with India, but was restricted for some years by US sanctions. The Stockholm International Peace Research Institute estimates that Pakistan has manufactured between 30 and 50 nuclear weapons. In May 1998 Pakistan carried out six nuclear tests in response to India's tests earlier in the month. Pakistan, known to have a nuclear weapons programme, has not signed the Comprehensive Nuclear-Test-Ban-Treaty, which is intended to bring about a ban on any nuclear explosions. According to *Deadly Arsenals*, published by the Carnegie Endowment for International Peace, Pakistan has both chemical and biological weapon research programmes.

Army. Strength (2002) 520,000. There were also 292,000 personnel in paramilitary units: National Guard, Frontier Corps and Pakistan Rangers. Army reserves number around 500,000. In April 2004 the army announced a cut-back of 50,000 soldiers.

Most armoured equipment is of Chinese origin including over 2,350 main battle tanks. There is an air wing with fixed-wing aircraft and 20 attack helicopters.

Navy. The combatant fleet includes seven French-built diesel submarines, three midget submarines for swimmer delivery and eight ex-British frigates. The Naval Air wing operates six combat aircraft and nine armed helicopters.

The principal naval base and dockyard are at Karachi. Naval personnel in 2002 totalled 25,000. There is a marine force estimated at 1,200 personnel and naval reserves of 5,000.

Air Force. The Pakistan Air Force came into being on 14 Aug. 1947. It has its headquarters at Peshawar and is organized within three air defence sectors, in the northern, central and southern areas of the country. There is a flying college at Risalpur and an aeronautical engineering college at Korangi Creek.

Total strength in 2002 was 366 combat aircraft and 45,000 personnel. Equipment included Mirage IIIs, Mirage 5s, F-16s, Q-5s and J-7s. There were 8,000 Air Force reservists.

INTERNATIONAL RELATIONS

Pakistan is a member of the UN, WTO, the Commonwealth (not 1972–89), Asian Development Bank, Economic Co-operation Organisation (ECO), South Asian Association for Regional Co-operation (SAARC), IOM, Organisation of Islamic Conference (OIC), Islamic Development Bank, Non-Aligned Movement (NAM), Inter-Parliamentary Union (IPU), IMCO, International Atomic Energy Agency (IAEA), D-8, Conference on Disarmament, United Nations Commission on Human Rights, International Narcotics Control Board, United Nations Environment Programme and the Colombo Plan. Following Gen. Musharraf's coup in Oct. 1999, Pakistan was suspended from the Commonwealth's councils. The suspension was ended in May 2004.

ECONOMY

Agriculture accounted for 23·6% of GDP in 2002, industry 22·9% and services 53·4%. In Jan. 1999 the IMF approved a loan of US$575m. to Pakistan.

Overview. Supported by the IMF's Poverty Reduction and Growth Facility (PRGF), totalling US$1·3bn, Pakistan has established sound macroeconomic management and implemented structural reforms. GDP growth in 2002 was 4·4% but was forecast to increase, boosted by increased government expenditure. The government is reforming the social services and government accounting and auditing practices, and plans to restructure and privatize public enterprises, reduce the government's role in agricultural marketing and liberalize the financial sector and inter-bank foreign exchange markets. Poverty rates began to rise in the late 1990s. The quality of education and health services is low compared to other developing countries. Cotton is crucial for the economy, as it determines the cost and availability of the main raw material for the yarn-spinning industry (concentrated around the city of Karachi). Pakistan is one of the world's largest producers of raw cotton but value-adding is minimal; most of the yarn is exported.

Currency. The monetary unit is the *Pakistan rupee* (PKR) of 100 *paisas.* Gold reserves in June 2002 were 2·09m. troy oz; foreign exchange reserves, US$4,822m. Inflation was 2·9% in 2002 (3·1% in 2001). The rupee was devalued by 3·65% in Sept. 1996 and 8% in Oct. 1997, and by 4·2% in June 1998 in response to the financial problems in Asia. In May 2002 total money supply was Rs978,848m.

Budget. The financial year ends on 30 June. Revenue and expenditure (in Rs1m.):

	1997–98	*1998–99*	*1999–2000*	*2000–01*	*2001–02*[1]
Revenue	433,636	464,372	531,300	535,091	632,799
Expenditure	584,624	627,147	725,642	739,662	843,081

[1]Provisional.

Performance. Real GDP growth was 4·4% in 2002 and 6·2% in 2003. Pakistan's total GDP in 2003 was US$68·8bn.

Banking and Finance. The State Bank of Pakistan is the central bank (*Governor*, Dr Ishrat Hussain); it came into operation as the Central Bank on 1 July 1948 and was nationalized in 1974 with other banks. Private commercial bank licences were re-introduced in 1991.

The State Bank of Pakistan is the issuing authority of domestic currency, custodian of foreign exchange reserves and bankers for the federal and provincial governments and for scheduled banks. It also manages the rupee public debt of the federal and provincial governments. The National Bank of Pakistan acts as an agent of the State Bank where the State Bank has no offices of its own.

In Feb. 1994 the State Bank of Pakistan was granted more autonomy to regulate the monetary sector of the economy.

In Dec. 1999 the Supreme Court ruled that Islamic banking methods, whereby interest is not permitted, had to be used from 1 July 2001. However, the decision was rescinded in June 2002. The State Bank offered three options for the implementation of Islamic banking practices: i) banks to establish an independent Islamic bank; ii) the opening of subsidiaries of existing commercial banks; iii) the establishment of new branches to execute Islamic banking procedures.

In June 1998 total assets of the issue department of the State Bank of Pakistan amounted to Rs238,999m. and those of the banking department Rs254,670m.; total deposits, Rs170,769m.

In June 1998 there were 56 banks (21 foreign) with total assets of Rs1,654,094m. In 2002 there were 45 leasing banks, operating in accordance with Sharia demands. There is a Federal Bank for Co-operatives.

Foreign direct investment was a record high US$1,405m. in 2003, up from US$823m. in 2002 and US$385m. in 2001.

There are stock exchanges in Islamabad, Karachi and Lahore. The Karachi Stock Exchange was the world's best performing bourse in 2002, recording a 112% rise.

ENERGY AND NATURAL RESOURCES

Environment. Pakistan's carbon dioxide emissions from the consumption and flaring of fossil fuels were the equivalent of 0·7 tonnes per capita in 2002.

Electricity. Installed capacity of the State Power System in 2000 was 17·4m. kW, of which 4·83m. kW was hydro-electric, 12·44m. kW was thermal and 0·14 kW was nuclear. In 2003 there were two nuclear reactors in use. Production in 2000 was 65·75bn. kWh, of which 70% was thermal and 29% was hydro-electric. Consumption per capita in 2000 was 478 kWh. By 1999, 10·55m. consumers had access to electric power including 66,949 villages (of a total of 125,083).

Oil and Gas. Crude petroleum production in 2000 was 2·7m. tonnes. Reserves in 2002 were 298m. bbls. Exploitation is mainly through government incentives and concessions to foreign private sector companies. Natural gas production in 2002 was 20·9bn. cu. metres with 750bn. cu. metres of proven reserves (2002). The French oil company Total agreed a US$3bn. deal with the government in July 2003 for exploration in the Arabian Sea.

Water. Pakistan's Indus Basin irrigation system is the largest and oldest in the world. It includes a network of 43 independent canal systems and two storage reservoirs. Total length of main canals is 58,000 km which serve 35m. acres of cultivatable land.

Currently three major surface water projects are under way, as are flood control schemes and programmes to check the problems of waterlogging and salinity.

Minerals. Production (tonnes, 1998–99): limestone, 8·72m.; coal (2000), 3·17m.; rock salt, 870,000; gypsum (2000), 377,000; dolomite, 102,859; china clay, 66,000; fire clay, 61,000; chromite, 22,000; barytes, 20,000; fullers earth, 11,000; bauxite (2001), 4,000. Other minerals of which useful deposits have been found are magnesite, sulphur, marble, antimony ore, bentonite, celestite, fluorite, phosphate rock, silica sand and soapstone.

Agriculture. The north and west are covered by mountain ranges. The rest of the country consists of a fertile plain watered by five big rivers and their tributaries. Agriculture is dependent almost entirely on the irrigation system based on these rivers. Area irrigated, 2001, 17·82m. ha. Agriculture employs around half of the workforce. In 1998–99 it provided 24·5% of GDP. In 2001 there were 21·49m. ha of arable land and 672,000 ha of permanent crops.

Pakistan is self-sufficient in wheat, rice and sugar. Areas harvested, 2000: wheat, 8·46m. ha; seed cotton, 2·95m. ha; rice, 2·31m. ha; sugarcane, 1·01m. ha; chick-peas, 0·97m. ha; maize, 0·89m. ha. Production, 2000 (1,000 tonnes): sugarcane, 46,333; wheat, 21,079; rice, 7,000; seed cotton, 5,735; cottonseed, 3,824; cotton lint, 1,912; potatoes, 1,868; onions, 1,648; maize, 1,351; oranges, 1,310; mangoes, 938; apples, 600; dates, 580; chick-peas, 565.

A Land Reforms Act of 1977 reduced the upper limit of land holding to 100 irrigated or 200 non-irrigated acres. A new agricultural income tax was introduced in 1995, from which holders of up to 25 irrigated or 50 unirrigated acres are exempt. Of about 5m. farms, 12% are of less than 10 ha. In 1998–99, 21·92m. ha were arable land; 23·04m. ha were cropland; 4·20m. ha were forest.

Livestock, 2000 (in 1m.): goats, 47·4; sheep, 24·1; buffaloes, 22·7; cattle, 22·0; asses, 4·5; camels, 1·2; poultry, 148·0.

Livestock products, 2000 (in 1,000 tonnes): beef and veal, 357; poultry, 327; goat, 323; mutton and lamb, 190; buffalo milk, 16,910; cow milk, 8,039; goat milk, 586; eggs, 331; wool, 62.

Forestry. The area under forests in 2000 was 2·36m. ha, some 3·1% of the total land area. Timber production in 2001 totalled 33·23m. cu. metres.

Fisheries. In 2001 the catch totalled 607,020 tonnes, approximately 70% from marine waters and the rest from inland waters.

INDUSTRY

Industry is based largely on agricultural processing, with engineering and electronics. Government policy is to encourage private industry, particularly small businesses. The public sector, however, is still dominant in large industries. Steel, cement, fertilizer and vegetable ghee are the most valuable public sector industries.

Production in tonnes (in 1998–99 unless otherwise stated): cement (2000–01), 9,674,000; sugar (2002), 3,334,000; residual fuel oil (2000), 1,991,000; distillate fuel oil (2000), 1,744,000; cotton yarn, 895,000; pig iron, 735,000; vegetable ghee, 615,000; coke, 443,000; paper and board, 256,000; steel billets, 212,000; soda ash, 186,000; caustic soda, 82,000; jute textiles, 63,000; sulphuric acid (2001), 57,000; cotton cloth, 443m. sq. metres; bicycles, 409,000 items; jeeps and cars, 28,815 items.

Labour. Out of 36·85m. people in employment in 1999–2000, 31·69m. were males. A total of 17·84m. persons were engaged in agriculture, hunting, forestry and fishing, 5·23m. in community, social and personal services, 4·98m. in wholesale and retail trade, restaurants and hotels, and 4·23m. in manufacturing.

In 2001 there were four industrial disputes and 7,078 working days were lost.

Trade Unions. In 1997 there were 7,355 trade unions with a membership of 1,022,275.

INTERNATIONAL TRADE

Foreign debt was US$33,672m. in 2002. Most foreign exchange controls were removed in Feb. 1991. Foreign investors may repatriate both capital and profits, and tax exemptions are available for companies set up before 30 June 1995.

Imports and Exports. Trade in US$1m.:

	1998	*1999*	*2000*	*2001*	*2002*
Imports f.o.b.	9,834	9,520	9,896	9,741	10,406
Exports f.o.b.	7,850	7,673	8,739	9,131	9,792

Major exports in 1998–99 (in Rs1m.): cotton cloth, 40,295; cotton yarns, 33,928; rice, 19,439; carpets, 6,723; leather, 6,346. Major imports in 1998–99 (in Rs1m.): machinery, 52,759; petroleum and petroleum products, 44,867; chemicals, 40,329; edible oils, 31,892; transport equipment, 18,247; grains, pulses and flour, 14,948; dyes and colours, 4,770.

Major export markets in 1998–99 (in Rs1m.): USA, 60,890; Hong Kong, 20,654; Germany, 18,929; UK, 18,537; UAE, 14,421; Japan, 9,696. Major import suppliers in 1998–99 (in Rs1m.): USA, 26,737; Japan, 26,597; Saudi Arabia, 21,825; Kuwait, 17,478; UK, 14,395; Germany, 13,413.

COMMUNICATIONS

Roads. In 2001 there were 257,683 km of roads, of which 367 km were motorway and 8,413 km highways or national roads. In 2002 there were 1,008,927 passenger cars, 111,931 trucks, 72,819 buses, and 1,545,133 motorcycles. There were 12,440 road accidents involving injury in 1998, with 5,290 fatalities.

A US$1bn. 333-km motorway linking Islamabad and Lahore was opened in 1998, and a new Karachi to Peshawar highway is under construction. Work is also in progress on Islamabad-Peshawar, Karachi-Hyderabad and Pindi Bhattian-Faisalabad links.

All traffic in Pakistan drives on the left. All cars must be insured and registered. Minimum age for driving: 18 years.

Rail. In 2000 Pakistan Railways had a route length of 7,791 km (of which 293 km electrified) mainly on 1,676mm gauge, with some metre gauge line. Passenger-km travelled in 2002–03 came to 19·8bn. and freight tonne-km to 4·6bn.

Civil Aviation. There are international airports at Karachi, Islamabad, Lahore, Peshawar and Quetta.

The national carrier is Pakistan International Airlines, or PIA (founded 1955; 56% of shares are held by the government). It covers 55 international and 37 domestic stations. During 1998–99, 59,097,000 revenue km were flown, compared with 78,796,000 during 1996–97. The revenue passengers carried totalled 3·86m. during 1998–99 and revenue tonne km came to 1,001m. Operating revenues of the corporation stood at Rs16,745bn. and operating expenditure at Rs19,603bn. during 1997–98. PIA resumed flights to Delhi in Jan. 2004.

Shipping. In 2002 ocean-going shipping totalled 247,000 GRT, including oil tankers 50,000 GRT. The busiest port is Karachi. In 2001–02 cargo traffic totalled 25,852,000 tonnes (6,244,000 tonnes loaded and 19,608,000 tonnes discharged). In 1998–99, 1,262 international vessels were handled at the port of Karachi. There is also a port at Port Qasim.

Telecommunications. The telegraph and telephone system is government-owned. Telephone subscribers numbered 4,893,600 in 2002, or 33·5 per 1,000 inhabitants, and in 2001 there were 600,000 PCs in use (4·2 for every 1,000 persons). In March 1999 there were 401 telegraph offices and 155 customer service centres working in the country. There were 1,238,600 mobile phone subscribers in 2002 and 268,000 fax machines in use in 1999. Pakistan had 1·5m. Internet users in 2002.

Postal Services. In 1998–99 there were 13,294 post offices.

SOCIAL INSTITUTIONS

Justice. The Federal Judiciary consists of the Supreme Court of Pakistan, which is a court of record and has three-fold jurisdiction; original, appellate and advisory. There are four High Courts in Lahore, Peshawar, Quetta and Karachi. Under the Constitution, each has power to issue directions of writs of *Habeas Corpus, Mandamus, Certiorari* and others. Under them are district and sessions courts of first instance in each district; they have also some appellate jurisdiction. Criminal cases not being sessions cases are tried by judicial magistrates. There are subordinate civil courts also.

The Constitution provides for an independent judiciary, as the greatest safeguard of citizens' rights. There is an Attorney-General, appointed by the President, who has right of audience in all courts and the Parliament, and a Federal Ombudsman.

A Federal Shariat Court at the High Court level has been established to decide whether any law is wholly or partially un-Islamic. In Aug. 1990 a presidential ordinance decreed that the criminal code must conform to Islamic law (Shariah), and in May 1991 parliament passed a law incorporating it into the legal system.

378,301 crimes were reported in 2001. Execution of the death penalty for murder, in abeyance since 1986, was resumed in 1992. In 2004 there were 23 confirmed executions. There were 9,528 murders in 2001. The population in penal institutions in 2002 was 87,000 (59 per 100,000 of national population).

Religion. Pakistan was created as a Muslim state. The Muslims are mainly Sunni, with an admixture of 15–20% Shia. Religious groups: Muslims, 93%; Christians, 2%; Hindus, Parsees, Buddhists, Qadianis and others. There is a Minorities Wing at the Religious Affairs Ministry to safeguard the constitutional rights of religious minorities.

Education. The National Education Policy (1998–2010) was launched in March 1998. The major aim was the eradication of illiteracy and the spread of a basic education. The policy stresses vocational and technical education, disseminating a common culture based on Islamic ideology. The principle of free and compulsory primary education has been accepted as the responsibility of the state. The adult literacy rate in 2001 was 44·0% (58·2% among males and 28·8% among females). Pakistan has the lowest literacy rate among males outside of Africa. Adult literacy programmes are being strengthened.

About 77% of children aged 5–9 are enrolled at school. Figures for 2000–01:

	Students (in 1,000)	*Teachers (in 1,000)*	*Institutions*
Primary	17,135	408·9	147,700
Middle	3,759	209·6	25,500
Secondary	1,565	260·2	14,800
Secondary vocational	83	9·4	630

	Students (in 1,000)	*Teachers (in 1,000)*	*Institutions*
Arts and Science Colleges	763	27·5	916
Professional Colleges	159	9·1	352
Universities	125	6·0	26

There are also more than 4,000 seminary schools. In 2000–01 total expenditure on education came to 1·8% of GNP and 7·8% of total government spending.

Health. In 1998 there were 872 hospitals and 4,551 dispensaries (with a total of 90,659 beds) and 852 maternity and child welfare centres. There were 82,682 doctors, 32,938 nurses, 22,103 midwives and 3,444 dentists.

Welfare. The official retirement age is 60 (men) or 55 (women and miners). To qualify for a pension, 15 years of contributions are needed. The minimum old age and survivor pension is Rs700 per month (as of Nov. 2001).

Medical services, provided mainly through social security facilities, cover cash and medical benefits such as general medical care, specialist care, medicines, hospitalization, maternity care and transportation.

CULTURE

There is a Pakistan National Council of the Arts, a cultural organization to promote art and culture in Pakistan and abroad.

World Heritage Sites. There are six sites under Pakistani jurisdiction which appear on the UNESCO World Heritage List. They are (with year entered on list): the archaeological ruins at Moenjodaro (1980), Taxila (1980), the Buddhist ruins at Tahkt-i-Bahi and the neighbouring city remains at Sahr-i-Bahlol (1980), Thatta (1981), the Fort and Shalamar Gardens in Lahore (1981) and Rohtas Fort (1997). The Fort and Shalamar Gardens in Lahore are among the 35 sites included in the World Heritage in Danger List.

Broadcasting. The Pakistan Broadcasting Corporation is an autonomous body operating 24 stations for 19 regional languages and 16 foreign languages. Five of its major stations have three channels (two AM and one FM). The second AM is generally reserved for sports, educational and entertainment broadcasting whilst FM channels cater mostly for music lovers. There is a school channel broadcasting on FM.

The network of PBC transmitters consists of 28 medium wave transmitters with a radiating power of 2,261 kW, 13 short wave transmitters of 1,131 kW and 5 FM transmitters of 12 kW. It covers 95% of the population and 80% of the total area of the country. A separate government authority, Azad Kashmir Radio, broadcasts in Kashmir.

The commercial Pakistan Television Corporation transmits on 13 VHF/UHF channels (colour by PAL). PTV's signal is also uplinked through Asiasat Transponder. There are six PTV centres in the major cities—Islamabad, Lahore, Karachi, Peshawar and Quetta—and 36 rebroadcast centres. Its headquarters is in Islamabad. Its transmissions reach 88% of the population. Number of sets in use: TV (2001), 21·4m.; radio (2000), 14·7m.

Cinema. There were 600 screens in 1999. 49 full-length films were made in 1999 in Urdu, Punjabi, Pushto and Sindhi. There were seven film studios.

Press. In 1999 there were 352 dailies and 560 non-daily newspapers. Average combined circulation of all dailies in 1999 was 3,558,750.

Tourism. In 2000 there were 543,000 foreign tourists. More than half of foreign tourist arrivals in 1997 were for the purpose of visiting friends and relatives, followed by business (18·3%), holidays and recreation (13·4%) and religion (2·5%). Tourist revenue in 2000 was US$86m.

Festivals. Pakistan is rich in culture. Famous festivals include the Eid Festival, Eid-e-Milad un Nabi (Birthday of Prophet Muhammad), the Basnat Festival, Shab-e-Baraat Festival and the Independence Day Festival.

Libraries. The Liaqat National Library is in Karachi, and the library of the National Archives is in Islamabad. Baitul Quran at Lahore is exclusively devoted to the manuscripts of the Holy Quran. The libraries of the Punjab University, Karachi

University and the Quaid-i-Azam library in Lahore hold a combined 700,000 volumes. The Islamic Research Institute Library at Islamabad has an important collection on Islam.

Theatre and Opera. There are regular theatrical productions in the major cities. There are 15 fully equipped theatre halls in Rawalpindi, Lahore, Karachi and Peshawar, and traditional street theatre is still prominent.

Museums and Galleries. There are dozens of galleries and museums in Islamabad, Lahore, Karachi, Peshawar and Quetta. Amongst the most famous are the National Art Gallery, Shakir Ali Museum, Choukandi Art Gallery, Karachi Art Council, Tasneen Art Gallery, the Lahore Art Museum, the National Heritage Museum and the National Archives. There are also dozens of archaeological sites in Pakistan dating back to 3,000 BC including Moenjodaro, Harppa, Taxila, Kot Diji and Dir.

DIPLOMATIC REPRESENTATIVES

Of Pakistan in the United Kingdom (35–36 Lowndes Sq., London, SW1X 9JN)
High Commissioner: Maleeha Lodhi.

Of the United Kingdom in Pakistan (Diplomatic Enclave, Ramna 5, Islamabad)
High Commissioner: Mark J. Lyall Grant, CMG.

Of Pakistan in the USA (3517 International Court, NW, Washington, D.C., 20008)
Ambassador: Jehangir Karamat.

Of the USA in Pakistan (Diplomatic Enclave, Ramna, 5, Islamabad)
Ambassador: Nancy J. Powell.

Of Pakistan to the United Nations
Ambassador: Munir Akram.

Of Pakistan to the European Union
Ambassador: Tariq Fatemi.

FURTHER READING

Government Planning Commission. *Ninth Five Year Plan, 1998–2003*. Karachi, 1998
Federal Bureau of Statistics.—*Pakistan Statistical Yearbook.—Statistical Pocket Book of Pakistan.* (Annual)
Ahmed, A. S., *Jinnah, Pakistan and Islamic Identity: The Search for Saladin*. London, 1997
Ahsan, A., *The Indus Saga and the Making of Pakistan*. Oxford, 1997
Akhtar, R., *Pakistan Year Book.* Karachi/Lahore
Bhutto, B., *Daughter of the East.* London, 1988
Burki, S. J., *Pakistan: the Continuing Search for Nationhood.* 2nd ed. Boulder (Colo.), 1992
James, W. E. and Roy, S. (eds.) *The Foundations of Pakistan's Political Economy: Towards an Agenda for the 1990s*. London, 1992
Joshi, V. T., *Pakistan: Zia to Benazir*. Delhi, 1995
Malik, I. H., *State and Civil Society in Pakistan: the Politics of Authority, Ideology and Ethnicity*. London, 1996

National library: National Library of Pakistan, Islamabad.

National statistical office: Federal Bureau of Statistics, Statistics Division, Islamabad.
Website: http://www.statpak.gov.pk/

PALAU

Republic of Palau

Capital: Koror
Population estimate, 2000: 19,000
GDP per capita: not available

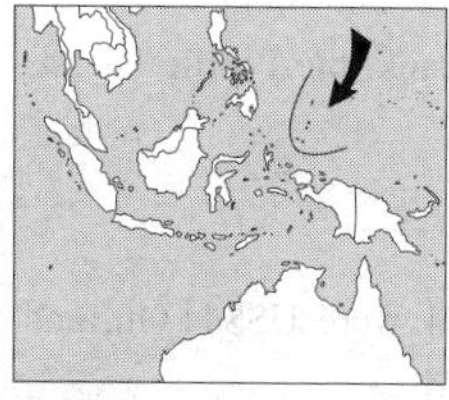

KEY HISTORICAL EVENTS

Spain acquired sovereignty over the Palau Islands in 1886 but sold the archipelago to Germany in 1899. Japan occupied the islands in 1914 and in 1921 they were mandated to Japan by the League of Nations. Captured by Allied Forces in 1944, the islands became part of the UN Trust Territory of the Pacific Islands created on 18 July 1947 and administered by the USA. Following a referendum in July 1978 in which Palauans voted against joining the new Federated States of Micronesia, the islands became autonomous from 1 Jan. 1981. A referendum in Nov. 1993 favoured a Compact of Free Association with the USA. Palau became an independent republic on 1 Oct. 1994.

TERRITORY AND POPULATION

The archipelago lies in the western Pacific and has a total land area of 490 sq. km (189 sq. miles). It comprises 26 islands and over 300 islets. Only nine of the islands are inhabited, the largest being Babelthuap (396 sq. km), but most inhabitants live on the small island of Koror (18 sq. km) to the south, containing the present headquarters (a new capital is being built in eastern Babelthuap). The total population of Palau at the time of the 2000 census was 19,129, giving a density of 37·7 per sq. km. Koror's population according to the 2000 census was 13,303. In 1995 approximately 73% of the population were Palauans.

In 1995 an estimated 71·2% of the population lived in urban areas. Some 6,000 Palauans live abroad. The local language is Palauan; both Palauan and English are official.

SOCIAL STATISTICS

2001 births, 300; deaths, 138. Rates, 2001 (per 1,000 population): births, 15·3; deaths, 7·0; infant mortality, 17 per 1,000 live births. Annual population growth rate, 1992–2002, 2·3%. Expectation of life: males, 69 years; females, 73. Fertility rate, 2001, 2·8 births per woman.

CLIMATE

Palau has a pleasantly warm climate throughout the year with temperatures averaging 81°F (27°C). The heaviest rainfall is between July and Oct.

CONSTITUTION AND GOVERNMENT

The Constitution was adopted on 2 April 1979 and took effect from 1 Jan. 1981. The Republic has a bicameral legislature, the *Olbiil era Kelulau* (National Congress), comprising a 9-member *Senate* and a 16-member *House of Delegates* (one from each of the Republic's 16 states), both elected for a term of four years as are the *President* and *Vice-President.* Customary social roles and land and sea rights are allocated by a matriarchal 16-clan system.

RECENT ELECTIONS

At the elections on 2 Nov. 2004 Tommy Remengesau, Jr was re-elected president with 66·5% of votes cast against 33·5% for Polycarp Basilius. At the legislative elections which were also held on 2 Nov. 2004 only non-partisans were elected.

CURRENT ADMINISTRATION

President: Tommy Remengesau, Jr; b. 1956 (in office since 1 Jan. 2001).

Vice-President and Minister of Justice: Elias Camsek Chin.

In March 2005 the cabinet consisted of:

Minister of Finance: Elbuchel Sadang. *Commerce and Trade:* Otoichi Besebes. *Community and Cultural Affairs:* Alexander Merep. *Education:* Mario Katosang. *Resources and Development:* Fritz Koshiba. *State:* Temmy Shmull. *Health:* Victor Yano.

INTERNATIONAL RELATIONS

Palau is a member of the UN, IMF, Asian Development Bank, the Pacific Islands Forum and the Pacific Community.

ECONOMY

Currency. US currency is used.

Budget. Central government revenues for fiscal year 2001 were US$44·0m. and expenditures US$78·0m.

Performance. Real GDP growth was 1·1% in 2001, following negative growth in 2000, of –0·7%. Total GDP in 2003 was US$0·1bn.

Banking and Finance. The National Development Bank of Palau is situated in Koror. Other banks include the Bank of Guam, the Bank of Hawaii, Bank Pacific, Melekeok Government Bank and the Pacific Savings Bank.

ENERGY AND NATURAL RESOURCES

Environment. Palau's carbon dioxide emissions in 1999 were the equivalent of 12·9 tonnes per capita.

Electricity. Electricity production was about 210m. kWh in 2000; installed capacity was 62,000 kW in 2000.

Agriculture. The main agricultural products are bananas, coconuts, copra, cassava and sweet potatoes. In 1997 agriculture contributed 7% of GDP. In 2001 there were 4,000 ha of arable land and 2,000 ha of permanent crop land.

Forestry. Forests covered 35,000 ha in 2000, or 76·1% of the land area.

Fisheries. In 2001 the catch totalled approximately 2,000 tonnes, mainly tuna.

INDUSTRY

There is little industry, but the principal activities are food-processing and boat-building.

Labour. The economically active population totalled 10,686 in 1995, of whom 2,630 worked in government services, 1,896 in agriculture and 1,005 in tourism.

INTERNATIONAL TRADE

Imports and Exports. Imports (2001) US$105·3m.; exports (2001) US$23·4m. The main trading partner is Japan for exports and the USA for imports.

COMMUNICATIONS

Roads. There were 61 km of roads in 1996 of which 36 km are paved.

Civil Aviation. The main airport is on Koror (Airai). In 2003 there were scheduled flights to Guam, Manila, Yap (Micronesia) and Taipei.

Shipping. There is a port at Malakal. In 1995 over 280 vessels called there, delivering cargo totalling in excess of 70,000 tonnes.

Telecommunications. In 2001 there were 6,600 telephone access lines.

SOCIAL INSTITUTIONS

Justice. There is a Supreme Court and various subsidiary courts.

Religion. The majority of the population is Roman Catholic.

Education. In 2002–03 there were 3,048 pupils at primary schools and 1,231 at secondary schools. In 2004 there were 23 primary schools and 6 secondary schools. There were 727 students at Palau Community College in 2002–03. The adult literacy rate is 92%.

In 1999–2000 total expenditure on education came to 20·0% of total government spending.

Health. In 1998 there was one hospital, 20 physicians, 2 dentists, 26 nurses and 1 midwife.

CULTURE

Broadcasting. There is a radio station (WSZB) which broadcasts daily on AM and FM, and ICTV Cable TV presents 12 channels with CNN. In 1997 there were an estimated 11,000 televisions and 12,000 radios.

Press. The local newspaper *Tia Belau* is published bi-weekly.

Tourism. Tourism is a major industry, particularly marine-based. There were 54,000 foreign tourists in 2001.

DIPLOMATIC REPRESENTATIVES

Of the United Kingdom in Palau
Ambassador: Ian Powell (resides at Suva, Fiji Islands).

Of Palau in the USA (1800 K St., Suite 714, Washington, D.C., 20036)
Ambassador: Hersey Kyota.

Of the USA in Palau
Ambassador: Francis J. Ricciardone, Jr. (resides at Manila).

Of Palau to the United Nations
Ambassador: Stuart Beck.

PANAMA

República de Panamá

Capital: Panama City
Population projection, 2010: 3·52m.
GDP per capita, 2002: (PPP$) 6,170
HDI/world rank: 0·791/61

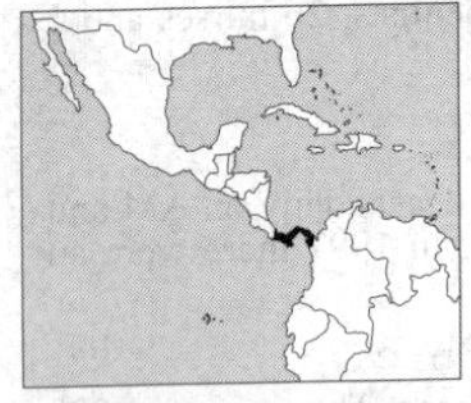

KEY HISTORICAL EVENTS

A revolution, inspired by the USA, led to the separation of Panama from the United States of Colombia and the declaration of its independence on 3 Nov. 1903. This was followed by an agreement making it possible for the USA to build and operate a canal connecting the Atlantic and Pacific oceans through the Isthmus of Panama. The treaty granted the USA in perpetuity the use, occupation and control of a Canal Zone, in which the USA would possess full sovereign rights. In return the USA guaranteed the independence of the republic. The Canal was opened on 15 Aug. 1914.

The US domination of Panama has provoked frequent anti-American protests. In 1968 Col. Omar Torrijos Herrera took power in a coup and attempted to negotiate a more advantageous treaty with the USA. Two new treaties between Panama and the USA were agreed on 10 Aug. and signed on 7 Sept. 1977. One dealt with the operation and defence of the Canal until the end of 1999 and the other guarantees permanent neutrality.

Torrijos vacated the presidency in 1978 but maintained his power as head of the National Guard until his death in an air crash in 1981. Subsequently Gen. Manuel Noriega, Torrijos' successor as head of the National Guard, became the strong man of the regime. His position was threatened by some internal political opposition and economic pressure applied by the USA but in Oct. 1989 a US-backed coup attempt failed. On 15 Dec. Gen. Noriega declared a 'state of war' with the USA. On 20 Dec. the USA invaded. Gen. Noriega surrendered on 3 Jan. 1990. Accused of drug dealing he was convicted by a court in Miami and is now serving a 40-year jail sentence. All remaining US troops left the country when the Panama Canal was handed back to Panama at the end of 1999.

TERRITORY AND POPULATION

Panama is bounded in the north by the Caribbean Sea, east by Colombia, south by the Pacific Ocean and west by Costa Rica. The area is 75,001 sq. km. Population at the census of 2000 was 2,839,177 (1,432,566 males); density, 37·6 per sq. km. The population was 56·6% urban in 2001.

The UN gives a projected population for 2010 of 3·52m.

The largest towns (2000) are Panama City, the capital, on the Pacific coast (469,307); its suburb San Miguelito (293,745); Tocumen (82,419); and David (77,057).

The areas and populations of the nine provinces and the five indigenous districts were:

Province	*Sq. km*	*Census 2000*	*Capital*
Bocas del Toro	4,601	89,269	Bocas del Toro
Chiriquí	6,477	368,790	David
Coclé	4,927	202,461	Penonomé
Colón	4,891	204,208	Colón
Darién	11,091	39,151	La Palma
Emberá[1]	4,398	8,246	Cirilo Guainora
Herrera	2,341	102,465	Chitré
Kuna de Madungandí[1]	2,319	3,305	...
Kuna de Wargandí[1]	775	1,133	...
Kuna Yala[1]	2,393	32,446	El Porvenir
Los Santos	3,805	83,495	Las Tablas
Ngöbe-Buglé[1]	6,673	110,080	Chichica
Panamá	9,633	1,385,052	Panama City
Veraguas	10,677	209,076	Santiago

[1]Indigenous district.

The population is a mix of African, American, Arab, Chinese, European and Indian immigrants. The official language is Spanish.

SOCIAL STATISTICS

2003 births, 61,753; deaths, 13,248; marriages, 10,310; divorces, 2,732. Birth rate, 2003 (per 1,000 population): 19·8; death rate: 4·3. Annual population growth rate, 1992–2002, 2·0%. Expectation of life at birth, 2001, was 72·0 years for males and 77·1 years for females. In 1999 the most popular age range for marrying was 25–29 for both males and females. Infant mortality, 2003, 15 per 1,000 live births; fertility rate, 2001, 2·5 births per woman.

CLIMATE

Panama has a tropical climate, unvaryingly with high temperatures and only a short dry season from Jan. to April. Rainfall amounts are much higher on the north side of the isthmus. Panama City, Jan. 79°F (26·1°C), July 81°F (27·2°C). Annual rainfall 70" (1,770 mm). Colón, Jan. 80°F (26·7°C), July 80°F (26·7°C). Annual rainfall 127" (3,175 mm). Balboa Heights, Jan. 80°F (26·7°C), July 81°F (27·2°C). Annual rainfall 70" (1,759 mm). Cristóbal, Jan. 80°F (26·7°C), July 81°F (27·2°C). Annual rainfall 130" (3,255 mm).

CONSTITUTION AND GOVERNMENT

The 1972 Constitution, as amended in 1978 and 1983, provides for a *President*, elected for five years, two *Vice-Presidents* and a 72-seat *Legislative Assembly* to be elected for five-year terms by a direct vote. To remain registered, parties must have attained at least 50,000 votes at the last election. A referendum held on 15 Nov. 1992 rejected constitutional reforms by 64% of votes cast. Turn-out was 40%. In a referendum on 30 Aug. 1998 voters rejected proposed changes to the constitution which would allow for a President to serve a second consecutive term.

National Anthem. 'Alcanzamos por fin la victoria' ('We achieve victory in the end'); words by J. de la Ossa, tune by Santos Jorge.

RECENT ELECTIONS

In the presidential election on 2 May 2004 Martín Torrijos Espino of the Revolutionary Democratic Party (PRD) won 47·5% of the vote. Guillermo Endara Galimany (Solidarity Party) won 30·6%, José Miguel Alemán (Arnulfist Party; PA) 17·0% and Ricardo Martinelli (Democratic Change; CD) 4·9%.

In the Legislative Assembly elections, also held on 2 May 2004, the PRD won 41 seats, with 37·9% of the vote. The PA won 17 seats with 19·3%; Solidarity Party, 8, with 15·7%; the Nationalist Republican Liberal Movement (Molirena), 3, with 8·6%; CD, 2, with 7·4%; the People's Party, 2, with 6·0%; and the National Liberal Party, 1, with 5·2%. Five seats were undeclared. Turn-out for both elections was 76·9%.

CURRENT ADMINISTRATION

President: Martín Torrijos Espino; b. 1963 (Revolutionary Democratic Party; sworn in 1 Sept. 2004). His father, Omar Torrijos Herrera, was the military ruler of Panama from 1968 to 1981.

First Vice-President and Minister of Foreign Affairs: Samuel Lewis Navarro. *Second Vice-President:* Rubén Arosemana Valdés.

In March 2005 the government comprised:

Minister of Government and Justice: Héctor Alemán. *Public Works:* Carlos Vallarino. *Economy and Finance:* Ricaurte Vásquez. *Agricultural Development:* Laurentino Cortizo. *Commerce and Industry:* Alejandro Ferrer. *Health:* Camilo Alleyne. *Labour and Work Development:* Reynaldo Rivera. *Education:* Juan Bosco Bernal. *Housing:* Balbina Herrera. *Youth, Women, Childhood and Family:* Leonor Calderón. *Minister of the Presidency:* Ubaldino Real.

Panamanian Parliament (Spanish only): http://www.asamblea.gob.pa

DEFENCE

The armed forces were disbanded in 1990 and constitutionally abolished in 1994. Divided between both coasts, the National Maritime Service, a coast guard rather than a navy, numbered around 400 personnel in 2002. In addition there is a paramilitary police force of 11,000 and a paramilitary air force of 400 with no combat aircraft. In 2003 defence expenditure totalled US$100m. (US$34 per capita), representing 0·9% of GDP. For Police *see* Justice *below*.

INTERNATIONAL RELATIONS

Panama is a member of the UN, WTO, OAS, Inter-American Development Bank, ACS, IOM, Non-aligned Movement and WTO.

ECONOMY

Agriculture accounted for 5·7% of GDP in 2002, industry 13·8% and services 80·5%.

Currency. The monetary unit is the *balboa* (PAB) of 100 *centésimos*, at parity with the US dollar. The only paper currency used is that of the USA. US coinage is also legal tender. Inflation in 2002 was 1·0%. In June 2002 foreign exchange reserves were US$1,055m. In March 2002 total money supply was 1,121m. balboas.

Budget. Budget revenue and expenditure (in 1m. balboas), year ending 31 Dec.:

	1996	*1997*	*1998*	*1999*	*2000*
Revenue	2,140·3	2,202·8	2,331·2	2,664·5	2,688·4
Expenditure	2,255·3	2,341·3	2,606·8	2,650·9	2,803·9

Performance. Real GDP growth was 0·3% in 2001 and 0·8% in 2002. Total GDP in 2003 was US$12·9bn.

Banking and Finance. There is no statutory central bank. Banking is supervised and promoted by the Superintendency of Banks (formerly the National Banking Commission); the *Superintendente* is Delia Cárdenas. Government accounts are handled through the state-owned *Banco Nacional de Panama*. In 2002 there were two other state banks, 47 banks operating under general licence, 29 under international licence and six as representative offices. Total assets of commercial banks, June 1996, US$33,400m., total deposits, US$25,000m. (including offshore, US$15,900m.).

Panama was one of 15 countries and territories named in a report in June 2000 as failing to co-operate in the fight against international money laundering. The Financial Action Task Force on Money Laundering was set up by the G7 group of major industrialized nations.

There is a stock exchange in Panama City.

Weights and Measures. The US and metric system are used.

ENERGY AND NATURAL RESOURCES

Environment. Panama's carbon dioxide emissions from the consumption and flaring of fossil fuels in 2002 were the equivalent of 4·5 tonnes per capita.

Electricity. In 2000 capacity was 1·3m. kW. Production was 5·00bn. kWh in 2002, with consumption per capita 1,734 kWh (2000).

Minerals. Limestone, clay and salt are produced. There are known to be copper deposits.

Agriculture. In 2001 there were 548,000 ha of arable land and 147,000 ha of permanent crops. Production in 2000 (in 1,000 tonnes): sugarcane, 2,000; bananas, 807; rice, 319; plantains, 111; melons and watermelons, 102; oranges, 85; maize, 80; cassava, 32; pineapples, 29; potatoes, 22; yams, 20. Livestock (2000): 1,360,000 cattle, 280,000 pigs, 166,000 horses and 12m. chickens.

Forestry. Forests covered 2·88m. ha in 2000 (38·6% of the land area). There are great timber resources, notably mahogany. Production in 2001 totalled 1·34m. cu. metres.

Fisheries. In 2001 the catch totalled approximately 235,000 tonnes, almost entirely from sea fishing. Shrimps are the principal species caught.

INDUSTRY

The main industry is agricultural produce processing. Other areas include oil refining, chemicals and paper-making. Residual fuel oil production (2000), 1,194,000 tonnes; cement (2001), 760,000 tonnes; distillate fuel oil (2000), 516,000 tonnes; petrol (2000), 274,000 tonnes; sugar (2002), 152,000 tonnes.

Labour. In Aug. 2003 a total of 1,145,982 persons were in employment, with principal areas of activity as follows: wholesale and retail trade/repair of motor vehicles, motorcycles and personal and household goods, 196,418; agriculture, hunting and forestry, 228,305; manufacturing, 105,830; transport, storage and communications, 85,883. In Aug. 2003 the unemployment rate was 13·1%.

Trade Unions. 77,500 workers belonged to trade unions in 1994, of whom 27,000 were members of the *Confederación de Trabajadores de la República de Panamá*.

INTERNATIONAL TRADE

The Colón Free Zone is an autonomous institution set up in 1953. 1,556 companies were operating there in 1997. Factories in export zones are granted tax exemption on profits for 10–20 years and exemption from the provisions of the labour code. Foreign debt was US$8,298m. in 2002.

Imports and Exports. Imports and exports in US$1m.:

	1998	*1999*	*2000*	*2001*	*2002*
Imports f.o.b.	7,714·6	6,689·4	6,981·4	6,671·7	6,460·2
Exports f.o.b.	6,350·1	5,303·3	5,838·5	5,996·4	5,283·8

Main exports: bananas, shellfish, sugar. Main imports: machinery and apparatus, transport equipment, mineral fuels. Chief export markets, 1999: USA, 45%; Germany, 11%; Costa Rica, 5%; Belgium, 4%. Chief import suppliers, 1999: USA, 36%; Japan, 7%; Ecuador, 5%; Mexico, 5%.

COMMUNICATIONS

Roads. In 2002 there were 11,978 km of roads, of which 35·9% were paved. The road from Panama City westward to the cities of David and Concepción and to the Costa Rican frontier, with several branches, is part of the Pan-American Highway. The Trans-Isthmian Highway connects Panama City and Colón. In 2003 there were 251,500 passenger cars, 77,400 lorries and vans and 17,000 buses and coaches. There were 401 road accident fatalities in 2002.

Rail. The 1,524 mm gauge *Ferrocarril de Panama*, which connects Ancón on the Pacific with Cristóbal on the Atlantic along the bank of the Panama Canal, is the principal railway. The United Brands Company runs 376 km of railway, and the Chiriquí National Railroad 171 km.

Civil Aviation. There is an international airport at Panama City (Tocumén International). The national carrier is COPA, which flew to 15 different countries in 2003. In 1999 it flew 23·9m. km and carried 932,500 passengers. In 2002 Tocumén International handled 1,938,933 passengers and 84,362 tonnes of freight.

Shipping. Panama, a nation with a transcendental maritime career and a strategic geographic position, is the shipping world's preferred flag for ship registry. The Ship Registry System equally accepts vessels of local or international ownership, as long as they comply with all legal parameters. Ship owners also favour Panamanian registry because fees are low. Today, the Panamanian fleet is the largest in the world with 6,222 ships registered and 103,581,459 net tons in 2001.

All the international maritime traffic for Colón and Panama runs through the Canal ports of Cristóbal, Balboa and Manzanillo International.

Panama Canal. The Panama Canal Commission is concerned primarily with the operation of the Canal. In Oct. 2002 a new toll structure was adopted based on ship size and type.

At present some 90% of the world's shipping fleet can use the Canal, but this is set to drop as many new ships are too wide for the Canal. Feasibility studies for an additional set of locks that could take today's largest ships are under way.

Administrator of the Panama Canal Authority. Alberto Alemán Zubieta.

Particulars of the ocean-going commercial traffic through the Canal are given as follows:

Fiscal year ending 30 Sept.	*No. of vessels transiting*	*Cargo in long tons*	*Tolls revenue (in US$1)*
2002	11,790	187,815,000	587,567,000
2003	11,634	188,273,000	664,667,000

Most numerous transits by flag (2003): Panama, 2,740; Liberia, 1,347; Bahamas, 922; Cyprus, 697; Malta, 565.

Statistical Information: The Panama Canal Authority Corporate Communications Division

Annual Reports on the Panama Canal, by the Administrator of the Panama Canal

Rules and Regulations Governing Navigation of the Panama Canal. The Panama Canal Authority

Major, J., *Prize Possession: the United States and the Panama Canal, 1903–1979.* CUP, 1994

Telecommunications. Panama had 936,400 telephone subscribers in 2002, or 311·5 per 1,000 persons, and there were 115,000 PCs in use (38·3 for every 1,000 persons). There were 525,800 mobile phone subscribers in 2002 and 268,000 fax machines in 1999. There were 120,000 Internet users in 2001.

Postal Services. In 2002 there were 127 post and telegraph offices.

SOCIAL INSTITUTIONS

Justice. The Supreme Court consists of nine justices appointed by the executive. There is no death penalty. The police force numbered 13,000 in 1999, and includes a Presidential Guard.

The population in penal institutions in March 2003 was 10,630 (354 per 100,000 of national population).

Religion. 80% of the population is Roman Catholic, 14% Protestant. The remainder of the population follow other religions (notably Islam). There is freedom of religious worship and separation of Church and State. Clergymen may teach in the schools but may not hold public office.

Education. Adult literacy was 92·1% in 2001 (male, 92·7%; female, 91·4%). Elementary education is compulsory for all children from seven to 15 years of age. In 2002 there were 408,249 pupils at 3,116 primary schools and 244,097 pupils with 15,181 teachers at secondary schools. There were four universities and twenty specialist institutions with 117,624 students and 8,444 academic staff. There were also a nautical school, a business school and institutes of teacher training and tourism.

In 2000–01 total expenditure on education came to 6·2% of GNP.

Health. In 2002 there were 61 hospitals with a provision of 25 beds per 10,000 persons. There were 4,203 physicians, 897 dentists, 3,451 nurses and 612 pharmacists.

CULTURE

World Heritage Sites. Panama has three sites on the UNESCO World Heritage List: the Fortifications on the Caribbean side of Panama: Portobelo-San Lorenzo (inscribed on the list in 1980); Darien National Park (1981); and the Archaeological Site of Panamá Viejo and the Historic District of Panamá (1997, 2003).

Broadcasting. There are about 60 broadcasting stations, mostly commercial, grouped in the Asociación Panameña de Radiodifusión. There are four television channels (colour by NTSC) and an educational channel. In 2000 there were 884,000 radio sets and in 2001 there were 560,000 TV sets in use.

Press. In 1996 there were seven dailies with a combined circulation of 166,000, equivalent to 62 per 1,000 inhabitants.

Tourism. In 2000 there were 479,000 foreign tourists, bringing revenue of US$576m.

DIPLOMATIC REPRESENTATIVES

Of Panama in the United Kingdom (40 Hertford Street, London, W1J 7SH)
Ambassador: Vacant.
Chargé d'Affaires a.i.: Miguel Angel González.

Of the United Kingdom in Panama (Torre Swiss Bank, Calle 53, Apartado 889, Panama City 1)
Ambassador: Jim Malcolm, OBE.

Of Panama in the USA (2862 McGill Terr., NW, Washington, D.C., 20008)
Ambassador: Federico Antonio Humbert Arias.

Of the USA in Panama (37 Street and Balboa Avenida, Panama City 5)
Ambassador: Linda Watt.

Of Panama to the United Nations
Ambassador: Ricardo Alberto Arias.

Of Panama to the European Union
Ambassador: Rolando A. Guevara Alvarado.

FURTHER READING

Statistical Information: The Controller-General of the Republic (Contraloria General de la República, Calle 35 y Avenida 6, Panama City) publishes an annual report and other statistical publications.

McCullough, D. G., *The Path Between the Seas: The Creation of the Panama Canal, 1870–1914.* Simon and Schuster, New York, 1999

Sahota, G. S., *Poverty Theory and Policy: a Study of Panama.* Johns Hopkins Univ. Press, 1990

Other titles are listed under Panama Canal, *above.*

National library: Biblioteca Nacional, Departamento de Información, Av. Balboa y Federico Boyd, Ciudad de Panama.
Website (Spanish only): http://www.contraloria.gob.pa

PAPUA NEW GUINEA

Capital: Port Moresby
Population projection, 2010: 6·57m.
GDP per capita, 2002: (PPP$) 2,270
HDI/world rank: 0·542/133

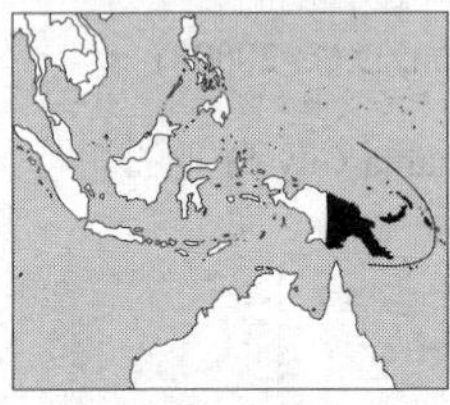

KEY HISTORICAL EVENTS

The Spanish first claimed the island in 1545 but the first attempt at colonization was made in 1793 by the British. The Dutch, however, claimed the west half of the island as part of the Dutch East Indies in 1828. On 6 Nov. 1884 a British Protectorate was proclaimed over the southern portion of the eastern half of New Guinea and in 1888 the territory was annexed. On 1 Sept. 1906 the Governor-General of Australia declared that British New Guinea was to be known henceforth as the Territory of Papua. The northern portion of New Guinea was a German colony until 1914 when Australian armed forces occupied it and it remained under their administration until becoming a League of Nations mandated territory in 1921, administered by Australia, and later a UN Trust Territory (of New Guinea). Australia granted Papua New Guinea self-government on 1 Dec. 1973, and on 16 Sept. 1975 Papua New Guinea became a fully independent state.

What began in 1988 as an armed campaign by tribes claiming traditional land rights against the Australian owner of the massive Panguna copper field soon escalated into a civil war for the secession of the island of Bougainville. Fighting between the government and the Bougainville Revolutionary Army (BRA) continued until 3 Sept. 1994 when a peace agreement set up a provisional Bougainville government. The ceasefire was broken by the rebels in mid-1995. In April 1998 the government of Papua New Guinea signed a 'permanent' truce with the secessionists. The nine-year rebellion claimed 20,000 lives. In Jan. 2001 the government and Bougainville signed a peace agreement that sets Bougainville on course to an autonomous government and a referendum on independence.

TERRITORY AND POPULATION

Papua New Guinea extends from the equator to Cape Baganowa in the Louisiade Archipelago to 11° 40' S. lat. and from the border of West Irian to 160° E. long. with a total area of 462,840 sq. km. According to the 2000 census the population was 5,190,786 (2,691,744 males); density, 11·2 per sq. km.

The UN gives a projected population for 2010 of 6·57m.

In 2001, 82·4% of the population lived in rural areas. In 1999 population of Port Moresby (National Capital District) was 293,000. Population of other main towns (1990 census): Lae, 80,655; Madang, 27,057; Wewak, 23,224; Goroka, 17,855; Mount Hagen, 17,392; Rabaul, 17,022. Area and population of the provinces:

Provinces	*Sq. km*	*Census 2000*	*Capital*
Bougainville	9,300	175,160	Arawa
Central	29,500	183,983	Port Moresby
Chimbu	6,100	259,703	Kundiawa
East New Britain	15,500	220,133	Rabaul
East Sepik	42,800	343,181	Wewak
Eastern Highlands	11,200	432,972	Goroka
Enga	12,800	295,031	Wabag
Gulf	34,500	106,898	Kerema
Madang	29,000	365,106	Madang
Manus	2,100	43,387	Lorengau
Milne Bay	14,000	210,412	Alotau
Morobe	34,500	539,404	Lae
National Capital District	240	254,158	—
New Ireland	9,600	118,350	Kavieng
Oro	22,800	133,065	Popondetta
Sandaun	36,300	185,741	Vanimo
Southern Highlands	23,800	546,265	Mendi
West New Britain	21,000	184,508	Kimbe
Western	99,300	153,304	Daru
Western Highlands	8,500	440,025	Mount Hagen

The principal local languages are Neo-Melanesian (or Pidgin, a creole of English) and Hiri Motu. English is in official use.

SOCIAL STATISTICS

1995 births, 142,000; deaths, 44,000. 1995 birth rate, 32·9 per 1,000 population; death rate, 10·3. Expectation of life at birth in 2001 was 56·2 years for males and 58·1 years for females. Annual population growth rate, 1992–2002, 2·6%. Infant mortality, 2001, 70 per 1,000 live births; fertility rate, 2001, 4·4 births per woman.

CLIMATE

There is a monsoon climate, with high temperatures and humidity the year round. Port Moresby is in a rain shadow and is not typical of the rest of Papua New Guinea. Jan. 82°F (27·8°C), July 78°F (25·6°C). Annual rainfall 40" (1,011 mm).

CONSTITUTION AND GOVERNMENT

The head of state is the British sovereign, who is represented by a *Governor-General*, nominated by parliament for six-year terms. A single legislative house, known as the *National Parliament*, is made up of 109 members: 89 district representatives and 20 provincial representatives (MPs). The members are elected by universal suffrage; elections are held every five years. All citizens over the age of 18 are eligible to vote and stand for election. Voting is by secret ballot and follows the limited preferential system. The *Prime Minister*, nominated by parliament and appointed by the Governor-General, selects ministers for the National Executive Council. The government cannot be subjected to a vote of no confidence in the first 18 months of office. The 20 provincial assemblies, comprising elected national MPs, appointed members and elected local government representatives, are headed by a Governor, normally the provincial representative in the National Parliament.

National Anthem. 'Arise, all you sons of this land'; words and tune by T. Shacklady.

RECENT ELECTIONS

Parliamentary elections were scheduled to take place between 15 June and 29 July 2002 but a troubled electoral process meant that results in some areas were left undeclared. Sir Michael Somare's National Alliance Party won 19 out of 109 seats; Sir Mekere Morautu's People's Democratic Movement, 12 seats; the People's Progress Party, 8; the Papua and Niugini Union Pati, 6; the People's Action Party, 5; the People's Labour Party, 4; ind., 17.

Sir Paulias Matane was elected governor-general by parliament on 27 May 2004.

CURRENT ADMINISTRATION

Governor-General: Sir Paulias Matane; b. 1931 (took office on 29 June 2004).

In March 2005 the government comprised:

Prime Minister: Sir Michael Somare, GCMG, CH; b. 1936 (National Alliance Party; sworn in on 5 Aug. 2002 for the third time, having previously been prime minister from 1975 to 1980 and from 1982 to 1985).

Minister of Agriculture and Livestock: Matthew Siune. *Correctional Institutional Services:* Posi Menai. *Culture and Tourism:* David Basua. *Defence:* Matthew Gubag. *Education:* Michael Laimo. *Environment and Conservation:* William Duma. *Finance and Treasury:* Bart Philemon. *Fisheries:* Ben Semri. *Foreign Affairs:* Sir Rabbie Namaliu. *Forestry:* Patrick Pruaitch. *Health:* Melchior Pep. *Higher Education, Research, Science and Technology:* Brian Pulayasi. *Housing:* Atimeng Buhupe. *Lands:* Petrus Thomas. *State Enterprises and Information:* Puka Temu. *Inter-Governmental Relations and Bougainville Affairs:* Sir Peter Barter. *Internal Security:* Bire Kimisopa. *Justice:* Mark Maipakai. *Labour and Industrial Relations:* Roy Biyama. *Mining:* Sam Akoitai. *National Planning and Monitoring:* Moses Maladina. *Public Services:* Sinai Brown. *Oil and Energy:* Sir Moi Avei. *Trade and Industry:* Paul Tiensten. *Transport and Civil Aviation:* Don Poyle. *Welfare and Social Development:* Lady Carol Kidu. *Works:* Gabriel Kapris.

Speaker of Parliament: Jeffery Nape.

Government Website: http://www.pngonline.gov.pg

DEFENCE

The Papua New Guinea Defence Force had a total strength of 3,100 in 2002 consisting of land, maritime and air elements. The Navy is based at Port Moresby and Manus. Personnel numbered 400 in 2002. There is an air force, 250 strong in 2002, but it does not possess any combat aircraft.

Defence expenditure in 2003 totalled US$19m. (US$3 per capita), representing 0·5% of GDP.

INTERNATIONAL RELATIONS

Papua New Guinea is a member of the UN, WTO, the Commonwealth, Asian Development Bank, Colombo Plan, APEC, Antarctic Treaty, the South Pacific Commission and the Pacific Community and is an observer at ASEAN and an ACP member state of the ACP-EU relationship.

ECONOMY

Agriculture accounted for 27·2% of GDP in 2002, industry 39·4% and services 33·4%.

Currency. The unit of currency is the *kina* (PGK) of 100 *toea*. The kina was floated in Oct. 1994. Foreign exchange reserves were US$457m. and gold reserves 63,000 troy oz in April 2002. Inflation was 11·8% in 2002. In March 2002 total money supply was K1,663m.

Budget. Budget revenue and expenditure (in K1m.):

	1995	*1996*	*1997*	*1998*	*1999*
Revenue	1,497·8	1,728·7	1,783·6	1,717·6	2,045·7
Expenditure	1,719·9	1,855·3	2,075·4	2,158·3	2,753·0

In 1999, 97% of total revenue came from taxation.

Performance. Papua New Guinea has been experiencing a recession, with the economy shrinking by 1·3% in 2000, 3·4% in 2001 and 3·3% in 2002. There were signs in 2003 that a slight recovery in the economic situation was under way. Total GDP in 2003 was US$3·4bn.

Banking and Finance. The Bank of Papua New Guinea (*Governor*, L. Wilson Kamit, CBE) assumed the central banking functions formerly undertaken by the Reserve Bank of Australia on 1 Nov. 1973. A national banking institution, the Papua New Guinea Banking Corporation, has been established. This bank has assumed the Papua New Guinea business of the Commonwealth Trading Bank of Australia.

In 2002 there were seven commercial banks (Australia and New Zealand Banking Group; Bank of Hawaii; Bank of South Pacific; Maybank; MBf Finance; Papua New Guinea Banking Corporation; Westpac Bank) and a Rural Development Bank.

Total commercial bank deposits, 1992, K1,318·2m. Total savings account deposits, 1992, K226·8m. In addition, the Agriculture Bank of Papua New Guinea had assets of K82·6m. in 1992, and finance companies and merchant banks had total assets of K198·4m.

There is a stock exchange in Port Moresby.

ENERGY AND NATURAL RESOURCES

Environment. Carbon dioxide emissions from the consumption and flaring of fossil fuels in 2002 were the equivalent of 0·5 tonnes per capita.

Electricity. Installed capacity was 0·5m. kW in 2000. Production in 2000 was 2·18bn. kWh, around 51% of it hydro-electric. Consumption per capita was 453 kWh.

Oil and Gas. Natural gas reserves in 2002 were 350bn. cu. metres; output in 1998 was 83m. cu. metres. Crude oil production (1999), 29m. bbls. Oil predominantly comes from the Iagifu field in the Southern Highlands. There were 238m. bbls. of proven oil reserves in 2002.

Minerals. In 2001 mining produced 15·5% of GDP. Copper is the main mineral product. Gold, copper and silver are the only minerals produced in quantity. The Misima open-pit gold mine was opened in 1989 but its resources were depleted by the end of 2001. The Porgera gold mine opened in 1990 with an expected life of

20 years. Major copper deposits in Bougainville have proven reserves of about 800m. tonnes; mining was halted by secessionist rebel activity. Copper and gold deposits in the Star Mountains of the Western Province are being developed by Ok Tedi Mining Ltd at the Mt Fubilan mine. Production of gold commenced in 1984 and of copper concentrates in 1987. In 2000 Ok Tedi Mining Ltd produced 200,900 tonnes of copper; and in 1996, 47 tonnes of gold and 39m. bbls. of crude oil. Gold mining also began at Lihir in 1997. In 2001 total gold production was 67 tonnes; silver production in 1999 was 67 tonnes.

Agriculture. In 1995 agriculture employed nearly 78% of the workforce. In 2001 there were 210,000 ha of arable land and 650,000 ha of permanent cropland. Minor commercial crops include pyrethrum, tea, peanuts and spices. Locally consumed food crops include sweet potatoes, maize, taro, bananas, rice and sago. Tropical fruits grow abundantly. There is extensive grassland. The sugar industry has made the country self-sufficient in this commodity while a beef-cattle industry is being developed.

Production (2000, in 1,000 tonnes): coconuts, 826; bananas, 700; sweet potatoes, 480; sugarcane, 430; palm oil, 299; yams, 220; copra, 170; taro, 170; cassava, 120; coffee, 83.

Livestock (2000): pigs, 1·55m.; cattle, 87,000; chickens, 4m.

Forestry. The forest area totalled 30·60m. ha in 2000 (67·6% of the land area). In 1995 about 15m. ha of high quality tropical hardwoods were considered suitable for development. Timber production is important for both local consumption and export. Timber production was 8·60m. cu. metres in 2001.

Fisheries. Tuna is the major resource. In 2001 the fish catch was an estimated 122,419 tonnes (89% sea fish).

INDUSTRY

Secondary and service industries are expanding for the local market. The main industries are food processing, beverages, tobacco, timber products, wood and fabricated metal products. Industry accounted for 42·7% of GDP in 2001, with manufacturing contributing 8·1%. Production (2002): palm oil, 370,000 tonnes; copra, 110,000 tonnes; wood-based panels, 79,000 cu. metres; sawnwood, 70,000 cu. metres.

Labour. The labour force in 1996 totalled 2,160,000 (58% males). In 1996 formal employment in the building and construction industries rose by 27·5%, but around 85% of the population is dependent on non-monetarized agriculture.

INTERNATIONAL TRADE

Australian aid amounts to an annual $A300m. The 'Pactra II' agreement of 1991 establishes a free trade zone with Australia and protects Australian investments. Foreign debt was US$2,485m. in 2002.

Imports and Exports. Exports in 2001 were US$1,812·9m. (US$2,094·1m. in 2000); imports, US$932·4m. (US$998·8m. in 2000). The main imports in terms of value are machinery and transport equipment, manufactured goods, and food and live animals; and the main exports crude petroleum, gold and logs.

Of exports in 1999, Australia took 38·1%; Japan, 16·9%; Germany, 9·6%; USA, 6·6%; South Korea, 5·8%; of imports, Australia furnished 53·5%; Singapore, 12·9%; Japan, 5·6%; New Zealand, 4·1%; USA, 3·6%.

COMMUNICATIONS

Roads. In 1999 there were 19,600 km of roads, only about 690 km of which were paved. Motor vehicles numbered 116,000 in 1996 (31,000 passenger cars and 85,000 trucks and vans).

Civil Aviation. Jacksons International Airport is at Port Moresby. The state-owned national carrier is Air Niugini. In 2003 there were scheduled international flights to Brisbane, Cairns, Honiara, Manila, Singapore, Sydney and Tokyo. There are a total of 177 airports and airstrips with scheduled services.

Shipping. There are 12 entry and four other main ports served by five major shipping lines; the Papua New Guinea Shipping Corporation is state-owned. Seagoing shipping totalled 72,000 GRT in 2002, including oil tankers 2,000 GRT.

Telecommunications. In 2001 there were 72,700 telephone subscribers, or 13·7 for every 1,000 inhabitants. In 2002, 321,000 PCs were in use (58·7 for every 1,000 persons). There were 15,000 mobile phone subscribers in 2002 and 800 fax machines in 1995. Internet users numbered 75,000 in 2002. A 51% stake in the state-owned telecommunications company Telikom PNG is scheduled to be sold to Zimbabwean-based Econet, but in Sept. 2004 the deal was put on hold.

Postal Services. The 1996 Postal Service Act created the government-owned Post PNG Limited. In 2004 its network consisted of 31 post offices, 26 agency post offices and two international mail exchange centres.

SOCIAL INSTITUTIONS

Justice. In 1983 over 1,500 criminal and civil cases were heard in the National Court and an estimated 120,000 cases in district and local courts. The discretionary use of the death penalty for murder and rape was introduced in 1991.

The population in penal institutions in 2002 was 3,302 (66 per 100,000 of national population).

Religion. At the 2000 census there were 4·93m. Christians: Roman Catholics made up 27·0%; Lutherans, 19·5%; United Church, 11·5%; Anglicans, 3·2%. In 1998 the Catholic Church had four archdioceses (Madang, Mount Hagen, Port Moresby and Rabaul), 14 dioceses, 340 parishes and 540 priests.

Education. Obligatory universal primary education is a government objective. In 1990 about two-thirds of eligible children were attending school. In 2001 there were 3,055 elementary and primary schools with 395,129 pupils and 11,307 teachers, 77,451 pupils in secondary schools (2,187 teachers) and 14,333 students in institutes of higher education. There are six universities: the University of Papua New Guinea (UPNG), Port Moresby; the Papua New Guinea University of Technology, Lae; Divine Word University, Madang; Pacific Adventist University, Boroko; the University of Goroka; and the University of Vudal, Rabaul. UPNG, founded in 1965, has two campuses in the capital, five provincial open campuses and 13 study centres. In 2002 there were also ten colleges, eight nursing schools and three academic institutes.

Adult literacy rate was 64·6% in 2001 (71·1% among males and 57·7% among females).

In 2000–01 total expenditure on education came to 2·4% of GNP and 17·5% of total government spending.

Health. In 1998 there were 342 physicians, 127 dentists and 3,141 nurses. Provision of hospital beds in 1993 was 34 per 10,000 persons.

CULTURE

Broadcasting. The National Broadcasting Commission operates three networks: national, provincial and commercial. A national service is relayed throughout the country. Each province has a broadcasting service, while the larger urban centres are also covered by a commercial network relayed from Port Moresby. Two commercial television stations broadcast from Port Moresby (colour by PAL). In 2001 there were 110,000 television receivers and in 2000 there were 446,000 radio receivers.

Press. In 2004 there were two daily newspapers (the *Post-Courier* and the *National*) and a number of weeklies and monthlies. The *Post-Courier* is the oldest (1969) and most widely read, with a daily circulation of 29,000.

Tourism. In 2002 there were 54,000 (58,000 in 2000) visitors; spending by tourists totalled US$92m. in 2000.

Festivals. Alongside the major Christian festivals several cultural shows are held, in Enga (late July), at Mount Hagen (Western Highlands; late Aug.) and at Goroka (Eastern Highlands; mid-Sept.). Independence Day is celebrated on 16 Sept.

Libraries. The National Library Service was created in 1975 and the National Library opened in 1978. The University of Papua New Guinea's Michael Somare Library has over 450,000 volumes. The National Archives were established in 1957 at Waigani, National Capital District.

DIPLOMATIC REPRESENTATIVES

Of Papua New Guinea in the United Kingdom (3rd Floor, 14 Waterloo Pl., London, SW1Y 4AR)
High Commissioner: Jean Kekedo, OBE.

Of the United Kingdom in Papua New Guinea (PO Box 212, Waigani NCD 131)
High Commissioner: David Gordon-Macleod.

Of Papua New Guinea in the USA (1779 Massachusetts Ave., NW, Washington, D.C., 20036)
Ambassador: Evan Paki.

Of the USA in Papua New Guinea (Douglas St., Port Moresby)
Ambassador: Robert W. Fitts.

Of Papua New Guinea to the United Nations
Ambassador: Robert Aisi.

Of Papua New Guinea to the European Union
Ambassador: Vacant.
Chargé d'Affaires a.i.: Kapi Maro.

FURTHER READING

National Statistical Office. *Summary of Statistics.* Annual.—*Abstract of Statistics.* Quarterly.
Bank of Papua New Guinea. *Quarterly Economic Bulletin.*
Turner, A., *Historical Dictionary of Papua New Guinea.* Metuchen (NJ), 1995
Waiko, J. D., *Short History of Papua New Guinea.* OUP, 1993

National statistical office: National Statistical Office, PO Box 337, Waigani, National Capital District, Port Moresby.
Website: http://www.nso.gov.pg

PARAGUAY

República del Paraguay

Capital: Asunción
Population projection, 2010: 6·89m.
GDP per capita, 2002: (PPP$) 4,610
HDI/world rank: 0·751/89

KEY HISTORICAL EVENTS

Paraguay was occupied by the Spanish in 1537 and became a Spanish colony as part of the viceroyalty of Peru. The area gained its independence, as the Republic of Paraguay, on 14 May 1811. Paraguay was then ruled by a succession of dictators. During a devastating war fought from 1865 to 1870 between Paraguay and a coalition of Argentina, Brazil and Uruguay, Paraguay's population was reduced from about 600,000 to 233,000. Further severe losses were incurred during the war with Bolivia (1932–35) over territorial claims in the Chaco inspired by the unfounded belief that minerals existed in the territory. A peace treaty by which Paraguay obtained most of the area her troops had conquered was signed in July 1938.

A new constitution took effect in Feb. 1968 under which executive power is discharged by an executive president. Gen. Alfredo Stroessner Mattiauda was re-elected seven times between 1958 and 1988. Since then, Paraguay has been under more or less democratic government. On 23 March 1999 Paraguay's vice-president Luis Maria Argaña was assassinated. The following day, Congress voted to impeach President Cubas who was said to be implicated in the murder. He then resigned.

TERRITORY AND POPULATION

Paraguay is bounded in the northwest by Bolivia, northeast and east by Brazil and southeast, south and southwest by Argentina. The area is 406,752 sq. km (157,042 sq. miles).

The 2002 census population was 5,163,198 (2,603,242 males), giving a density of 12·7 per sq. km. In 2002, 56·7% lived in urban areas.

The UN gives a projected population for 2010 of 6·89m.

In 2002 the capital, Asunción, had a population of 512,112. Other major cities (2002 census populations) are: Ciudad del Este, 222,274; San Lorenzo, 204,356; Luque, 185,127.

There are 17 departments and the capital city. Area and population at the 2002 census:

Department	*Area in sq. km*	*Population*	*Department*	*Area in sq. km*	*Population*
Asunción (city)	117	512,112	Canendiyú	14,667	140,137
Central	2,465	1,362,893	Caazapá	9,496	139,517
Alto Paraná	14,895	558,672	Amambay	12,933	114,917
Itapúa	16,525	453,692	Misiones	9,556	101,783
Caaguazú	11,474	435,357	Neembucú	12,147	76,348
San Pedro	20,002	318,698	*Oriental*	*159,827*	*5,028,012*
Cordillera	4,948	233,854	Presidente Hayes	72,907	82,493
Paraguari	8,705	221,932	Boquerón[1]	91,669	41,106
Concepción	18,051	179,450	Alto Paraguay[2]	82,349	11,587
Guairá	3,846	178,650	*Occidental*	*246,925*	*135,186*

[1]Incorporates former department of Nueva Asunción.
[2]Incorporates former department of Chaco.

The population is mixed Spanish and Guaraní Indian. There are 89,000 unassimilated Indians of other tribal origin, in the Chaco and the forests of eastern Paraguay. 24·8% of the population speak only Guaraní; 51·5% are bilingual (Spanish/Guaraní); and 7·6% speak only Spanish.

Mennonites, who arrived in three groups (1927, 1930 and 1947), are settled in the Chaco and eastern Paraguay. There are also Korean and Japanese settlers.

SOCIAL STATISTICS

2002 births, 123,674; deaths, 19,416. Rates, 2002 (per 1,000 population): birth, 24·0; death, 3·8. Annual population growth rate, 1990–2002, 2·2%. Expectation of life,

2001: 68·3 years for males and 72·8 for females. Infant mortality, 2001, 26 per 1,000 live births; fertility rate, 2001, 3·9 births per woman.

CLIMATE

A tropical climate, with abundant rainfall and only a short dry season from July to Sept., when temperatures are lowest. Asunción, Jan. 81°F (27°C), July 64°F (17·8°C). Annual rainfall 53" (1,316 mm).

CONSTITUTION AND GOVERNMENT

On 18 June 1992 a Constituent Assembly approved a new constitution. The head of state is the *President,* elected for a non-renewable five-year term. Parliament consists of an 80-member *Chamber of Deputies,* elected from departmental constituencies, and a 45-member *Senate,* elected from a single national constituency.

National Anthem. 'Paraguayos, república o muerte!' ('Paraguayans, republic or death!'); words by F. Acuña de Figueroa, tune by F. Dupuy.

RECENT ELECTIONS

Parliamentary and presidential elections were held on 27 April 2003. Nicanor Duarte Frutos of the ruling Republican National Alliance–Colorado Party (ANR) was elected president with 37·1% of votes cast. Julio César Franco Gómez of the Authentic Radical Liberal Party (PLRA) won 24·0%, Pedro Fadul Niella of the Movement Fatherland of the Best (MPQ) 21·3% and Guillermo Sánchez Guffanti of the National Union of Ethical Citizens (UNACE) 13·5%. Turn-out was 64·2%. As a result of the election the Colorado Party maintained its status as the longest-ruling party in the world.

In the Chamber of Deputies the ANR won 37 seats with 35·3% of votes cast, the PLRA won 21 seats (25·7%), the MPQ won 10 seats (15·3%), the UNACE won 10 seats (14·7%) and the Party for a Country of Solidarity (PPS) won 2 seats (3·3%). Turn-out was 64%. In the Senate the ANR won 16 seats, the PLRA won 12, the MPQ won 8, the UNACE won 7 and the PPS won 2. Turn-out was 58·8%.

CURRENT ADMINISTRATION

President: Nicanor Duarte Frutos; b. 1956 (ANR; sworn in 15 Aug. 2003).

Vice-President: Luis Alberto Castiglioni.

In March 2005 the cabinet comprised:

Minister of Agriculture and Livestock: Antonio Ibañez. *Education and Culture:* Blanca Ovelar de Duarte. *Finance and Economy:* Dionisio Borda. *Foreign Affairs:* Leila Rachid de Cowles. *Industry and Commerce:* Ernst Bergen. *Interior:* Rogelio Benítez. *Justice and Labour:* Juan Dario Monges. *National Defence:* Roberto González. *Public Health and Social Welfare:* Julio Cesar Velasquez. *Public Works and Communications:* José Alberto Alderete.

DEFENCE

The army, navy and air forces are separate services under a single command. The President of the Republic is the active C.-in-C. Conscription is for 12 months (two years in the navy).

In 2003 defence expenditure totalled US$44m. (US$8 per capita), representing 0·8% of GDP.

Army. Strength (2002) 14,900 (10,400 conscripts). In addition there is a paramilitary Special Police Force numbering 14,800.

Navy. Personnel in 2002 totalled 2,000 including 900 marines (of which 200 conscripts) and 100 naval aviation.

Air Force. The Air Force had a strength of 1,700 in 2002 (600 conscripts). There are 28 combat aircraft including F-5E/Fs.

INTERNATIONAL RELATIONS

Paraguay is a member of the UN, WTO, OAS, Inter-American Development Bank, Mercosur, LAIA and IOM.

ECONOMY

In 2002 agriculture accounted for 22·0% of GDP, industry 28·4% and services 49·6%.

Currency. The unit of currency is the *guaraní* (PYG), notionally divided into 100 *céntimos*. In May 2002 total money supply was 2,373·85bn. guaranís. Foreign exchange reserves were US$450m. in June 2002 and gold reserves 35,000 troy oz. Inflation was 10·5% in 2002.

Budget. In 2001 (in 1m. guaranís) budgetary central government revenue was 4,838,720 and expenditure 5,201,422.

Revenue items, 2001 (in 1m. guaranís): tax revenue, 2,851,461; non-tax revenue, 1,984,721. Expenditure items, 2001 (in 1m. guaranís): current expenditure, 4,370,383 (including expenditure on goods and services, 2,718,080); capital expenditure, 831,038 (including acquisition of fixed capital assets, 667,958).

Performance. In 2001 real GDP growth was 2·7% but Paraguay then went into recession, with the economy shrinking by 3·9% in 2002. GDP per capita has fallen from US$1,930 in 1996 to approximately US$1,125 in 2000. Total GDP in 2003 was US$5·8bn.

Banking and Finance. The Central Bank is a state-owned autonomous agency with the sole right of note issue, control over foreign exchange and the supervision of commercial banks (*Governor*, Gilberto Rodríguez Garcete). There is a Superintendencia de Bancos under Rodrigo Fernando Ortiz Frutos. In 2002 there were five commercial banks and 11 foreign banks.

There is a stock exchange in Asunción.

ENERGY AND NATURAL RESOURCES

Environment. Paraguay's carbon dioxide emissions from the consumption and flaring of fossil fuels were the equivalent of 0·6 tonnes per capita in 2002.

Electricity. Installed capacity was 8·1m. kW in 2000. Output (2000), 53·52bn. kWh (almost exclusively hydro-electric); consumption per capita in 2000 was 1,116 kWh.

Minerals. The country is poor in minerals. Limestone, gypsum, kaolin and salt are extracted. Deposits of bauxite, iron ore, copper, manganese and uranium exist. 2001 output: limestone, 16,320 tonnes; kaolin, 66,500 tonnes.

Agriculture. In 1999 agriculture employed 35% of the workforce and produced 90% of the country's exports. In 2001 there were approximately 3·02m. ha of arable land and 90,000 ha of permanent crops.

At the agrarian census of 1991 there were 307,221 farms working 23,799,737 ha. 122,750 farms had fewer than 5 ha; 884 had over 5,000 ha.

Output (in 1,000 tonnes), 2000: cassava, 3,500; sugarcane, 2,850; soybeans, 2,750; maize, 900; wheat, 250; oranges, 209; seed cotton, 205; cottonseed, 123; watermelons, 110; rice, 93. *Yerba maté*, or strongly flavoured Paraguayan tea, continues to be produced but is declining in importance.

Livestock (2000); 9·91m. cattle, 2·70m. pigs, 413,000 sheep, 400,000 horses and 25m. chickens.

Forestry. The area under forests in 2000 was 23·37m. ha, or 58·8% of the total land area. Timber production was 9·69m. cu. metres in 2001.

Fisheries. In 2001 the catch totalled approximately 25,000 tonnes, exclusively from inland waters.

INDUSTRY

Paraguay is one of the least industrialized countries in Latin America. Industries include meat packing, sugar processing, cement, textiles, brewing, wood products and consumer goods. In 2001 industry accounted for 27·5% of GDP, with manufacturing contributing 14·1%.

Labour. The labour force in 2002 totalled 1,980,492 (67·9% males). In 2002, 27% of the economically active population were engaged in agriculture, fisheries, hunting and forestry.

Trade Unions. Trade unionists number about 30,000 (*Confederación Paraguaya de Trabajadores* and *Confederación Cristiana de Trabajadores*).

INTERNATIONAL TRADE

Foreign debt was US$2,967m. in 2002.

Imports and Exports. Trade in US$1m.:

	1998	*1999*	*2000*	*2001*	*2002*
Imports f.o.b.	3,941·5	2,752·9	2,904·0	2,507·0	2,390·9
Exports f.o.b.	3,548·6	2,312·4	2,225·8	1,951·8	2,319·3

Main imports in 1999: machinery, 36·0%; chemicals, 11·9%; manufactured goods, 11·9%; petroleum and related products, 11·0%; tobacco, 8·7%. Main exports: soybeans, 41·5%; cotton, 8·4%; soy oilcake, 7·1%; timber, 5·0%; soybean oil, 4·9%.

Main import suppliers in 1999: Brazil, 28·6%; Argentina, 17·8%; USA, 13·7%; Japan, 6·1%; Germany, 3·8%; Spain, 3·1%. Main export markets, 1999: Brazil, 31·7%; Netherlands, 18·5%; UK, 12·9%; USA, 7·8%; Argentina, 7·2%; Chile, 3·1%.

COMMUNICATIONS

Roads. In 1999 there were around 29,500 km of roads, of which 50·8% were paved. Passenger cars numbered 268,000 in 1999, and there were 175,000 trucks and vans and 9,000 buses and coaches. There were 1,949 road accidents in 1999 resulting in 160 fatalities.

Rail. The President Carlos Antonio López (formerly Paraguay Central) Railway runs from Asunción to Encarnación, on the Río Alto Paraná, with a length of 441 km (1,435 mm gauge), and connects with Argentine Railways over the Encarnación-Posadas bridge opened in 1989. In 1994 traffic amounted to 182,000 tonnes and 24,000 passengers.

Civil Aviation. There is an international airport at Asunción (Silvio Pettirossi). The main Paraguay-based carrier is Transportes Aereos del Mercosur, which flew 4·3m. km and carried 195,000 passengers (all on international flights) in 1999. In 2000 Asunción handled 466,000 passengers (422,000 on international flights) and 6,600 tonnes of freight.

Shipping. Asunción, the chief port, is 1,500 km from the sea. In 2002 ocean-going shipping totalled 47,000 GRT, including oil tankers 4,000 GRT.

Telecommunications. In 2002 telephone subscribers numbered 1,940,200 (335·6 per 1,000 population) and 200,000 PCs were in use (34·6 for every 1,000 persons). There were 1,667,000 mobile phone subscribers in 2002 and 1,700 fax machines in 1995. Paraguay had approximately 100,000 Internet users in 2002.

Postal Services. In 1998 there were 326 post offices.

SOCIAL INSTITUTIONS

Justice. The 1992 constitution confers a large measure of judicial autonomy. The highest court is the Supreme Court with nine members. Nominations for membership must be backed by six of the eight members of the Magistracy Council, which appoints all judges, magistrates and the electoral tribunal. The Council comprises elected representatives of the Presidency, Congress and the bar. There are special Chambers of Appeal for civil and commercial cases, and criminal cases. Judges of first instance deal with civil, commercial and criminal cases in six departments. Minor cases are dealt with by Justices of the Peace.

The Attorney-General represents the State in all jurisdictions, with representatives in each judicial department and in every jurisdiction.

The population in penal institutions in 1999 was 4,088 (75 per 100,000 of national population). The death penalty was abolished for all crimes in 1992.

Religion. Religious liberty was guaranteed by the 1967 constitution. Article 6 recognized Roman Catholicism as the official religion of the country. It had 3·5m. adherents in 2002. There are Mennonite, Anglican and other communities as well. In 2002 followers of other religions (mostly Protestants) totalled 322,000.

Education. Adult literacy was 93·5% in 2001 (male, 94·5%; female, 92·5%). Education is free and nominally compulsory. In 2000–01 there were 966,476 pupils at primary schools and 459,260 at secondary level. In 2001 there were 14 universities (one Roman Catholic) and one institute. There were 83,041 students in tertiary education in 2000–01.

In 2000–01 total public expenditure on education came to 5·0% of GNP and 11·2% of total government spending.

Health. Provision of hospital beds in 1995 was 14 per 10,000 population. There were 3,730 physicians, 1,279 dentists, 1,875 nurses, 433 pharmacists and 1,547 midwives in 1995.

CULTURE

World Heritage Sites. Paraguay has one site on the UNESCO World Heritage List: the Jesuit Missions of La Santísima Trinidad de Paraná and Jesús de Tavarangue (inscribed on the list in 1993).

Broadcasting. In 1993 there were 30 commercial radio stations and in 1999 there were four TV stations (colour by PAL M) and two cable TV stations. In 2000 there were 1·2m. television receivers and 961,000 radio receivers.

Cinema. There are 15 cinemas in Asunción.

Press. In 1996 there were five daily newspapers with a combined circulation of 213,000, at a rate of 43 per 1,000 inhabitants.

Tourism. In 2000 there were 221,000 foreign tourists, bringing revenue of US$66m.

DIPLOMATIC REPRESENTATIVES

Of Paraguay in the United Kingdom (3rd Floor, 344 High Street Kensington, London, W14 8NS)
Ambassador: Vacant.
Chargé d'Affaires a.i.: María Cristina Acosta.

Of the United Kingdom in Paraguay (Avda. Boggiani 5848, C/R16 Boqueron, Asunción)
Ambassador: Anthony Cantor.

Of Paraguay in the USA (2400 Massachusetts Ave., NW, Washington, D.C., 20008)
Ambassador: James Spalding Hellmers.

Of the USA in Paraguay (1776 Mariscal López Ave., Asunción)
Ambassador: John F. Keane.

Of Paraguay to the United Nations
Ambassador: Eladio Loizaga.

Of Paraguay to the European Union
Ambassador: Emilio Gimenez Franco.

FURTHER READING

Gaceta Official, published by Imprenta Nacional, Estrella y Estero Bellaco, Asunción
Anuario Daumas. Asunción
Anuario Estadístico de la República del Paraguay. Asunción. Annual
Nickson, R. A. and Lambert, P. (eds.) *The Transition to Democracy in Paraguay.* Macmillan, London and St Martin's Press, New York, 1997

National library: Biblioteca Nacional, Calle de la Residenta, 820 c/ Perú, Asunción.
National statistical office: Dirección General de Estadísticas, Enuestas y Censos.
Website (Spanish only): http://www.dgeec.gov.py

PERU

República del Perú

Capital: Lima
Population projection, 2010: 29·99m.
GDP per capita, 2002: (PPP$) 5,010
HDI/world rank: 0·752/85

KEY HISTORICAL EVENTS

The Incas of Peru were conquered by the Spanish in the 16th century and subsequent Spanish colonial settlement made Peru the most important of the Spanish viceroyalties in South America. On 28 July 1821 Peru declared its independence, but it was not until after a war which ended in 1824 that the country gained its freedom. In a war with Chile (1879–83) Peru's capital, Lima, was captured and she lost some of her southern territory. Tacna, in the far south of the country, remained in Chilean control from 1880 until 1929. In 1924 Dr Victor Raúl Haya de la Torre founded the *Alianza Popular Revolucionaria Americana* to oppose the dictatorial government then in power. The party was banned between 1931 and 1945 and between 1948 and 1956 its leader failed regularly in the presidential elections but it was at times the largest party in Congress. The closeness of the 1962 elections led Gen. Ricardo Pérez Godoy, Chairman of the Joint Chiefs-of-Staff, to seize power. A coup led by Gen. Nicolás Lindley López deposed him in 1963. There followed, after elections, a period of civilian rule but the military staged yet another coup in 1968. In 1978–79 a constituent assembly drew up a new constitution, after which a civilian government was installed. However, Peru was plagued by political violence for nearly 20 years between the early 1980s and the late 1990s with 69,000 people killed by Maoist Shining Path insurgents, the smaller Tupac Amaru Revolutionary Movement and government forces. On 5 April 1992 President Alberto Fujimori suspended the constitution and dissolved the parliament. A new constitution was promulgated on 29 Dec. 1993. But while Peru has enjoyed stability and economic growth, there was still rule by autocracy which put some politicians above the law. Embroiled in a bribery and corruption scandal, President Fujimori's discredited administration came to an end in Nov. 2000 with his resignation while out of the country.

TERRITORY AND POPULATION

Peru is bounded in the north by Ecuador and Colombia, east by Brazil and Bolivia, south by Chile and west by the Pacific Ocean. Area, 1,285,216 sq. km (including the area of the Peruvian part of Lake Titicaca).

For an account of the border dispute with Ecuador, *see* ECUADOR: Territory and Population.

Census population, 1993, 22,639,443. 2002 official estimate, 26,748,972 (73·1% urban, 2001); density, 21 per sq. km.

The UN gives a projected population for 2010 of 29·99m.

Area and population estimate of the 24 departments and the constitutional province of Callao, together with their capitals:

Department	*Area (in sq. km)*	*Population 2002*	*Capital*	*Population 1998*
Amazonas	39,249	428,095	Chachapoyas	17,527
Ancash	35,865	1,107,828	Huaraz	79,012
Apurímac	20,896	463,131	Abancay	49,513
Arequipa	63,344	1,101,005	Arequipa	710,103
Ayacucho	43,815	550,751	Ayacucho	118,960
Cajamarca	33,318	1,498,567	Cajamarca	108,009
Callao[1]	147	787,154	Callao	424,294
Cusco	72,104	1,208,689	Cusco	278,590
Huancavelica	22,131	443,213	Huancavelica	35,123
Huánuco	36,887	811,865	Huánuco	129,688
Ica	21,306	687,334	Ica	194,820
Junín	44,197	1,246,663	Huancayo	305,039
La Libertad	25,495	1,506,122	Trujillo	603,657
Lambayeque	14,213	1,121,358	Chiclayo	375,058
Lima	34,797	7,748,528	Lima	6,464,693

Department	*Area (in sq. km)*	*Population 2002*	*Capital*	*Population 1998*
Loreto	368,852	907,341	Iquitos	334,013
Madre de Dios	85,183	99,452	Puerto Maldonado	27,407
Moquegua	15,734	156,750	Moquegua	44,824
Pasco	25,320	264,702	Cerro de Pasco	70,058
Piura	35,892	1,636,047	Piura	308,155
Puno	66,988	1,263,995	Puno	101,578
San Martín	51,253	757,740	Moyobamba	31,256
Tacna	16,076	294,214	Tacna	215,683
Tumbes	4,657	202,088	Tumbes	87,557
Ucayali	102,411	456,340	Pucallpa	220,866

[1]Constitutional province.

In 1991 there were some 100,000 Peruvians of Japanese origin. Indigenous peoples account for 47% of the population.

The official languages are Spanish (spoken by 80·3% of the population in 1993), Quechua (16·5%) and Aymara (3%).

SOCIAL STATISTICS

2001: births, 630,947; deaths, 164,296; (1999) infant deaths (under 1 year), 40,900. Rates per 1,000 population (2001): birth, 23·9; death, 6·2. Annual population growth rate, 1992–2002, 1·7%; infant mortality, 2001, 30 per 1,000 live births. Life expectancy, 2001: males, 66·9 years; females, 72·0. Fertility rate, 2001, 2·7 births per woman.

CLIMATE

There is a very wide variety of climate, ranging from equatorial to desert (or perpetual snow on the high mountains). In coastal areas, temperatures vary very little, either daily or annually, though humidity and cloudiness show considerable variation, with highest humidity from May to Sept. Little rain is experienced in that period. In the Sierra, temperatures remain fairly constant over the year, but the daily range is considerable. There the dry season is from April to Nov. Desert conditions occur in the extreme south, where the climate is uniformly dry, with a few heavy showers falling between Jan. and March. Lima, Jan. 74°F (23·3°C), July 62°F (16·7°C). Annual rainfall 2" (48 mm). Cusco, Jan. 56°F (13·3°C), July 50°F (10°C). Annual rainfall 32" (804 mm). El Niño is the annual warm Pacific current which moves to the coasts of Peru and Ecuador. El Niño in 1982–83 resulted in agricultural production down by 8·5% and fishing output down by 40%. El Niño in 1991–94 was unusually long. El Niño in 1997–98 resulted in a sudden rise in the surface temperature of the Pacific by 9°F (5°C) and caused widespread damage and loss of life.

CONSTITUTION AND GOVERNMENT

The 1980 Constitution provided for a legislative *Congress* consisting of a *Senate* and a *Chamber of Deputies*, and an Executive formed of the President and a Council of Ministers appointed by him. Elections were to be every five years with the President and Congress elected, at the same time, by separate ballots.

On 5 April 1992 President Fujimori suspended the 1980 constitution and dissolved Congress.

A referendum was held on 31 Oct. 1993 to approve the twelfth constitution, including a provision for the president to serve a consecutive second term. 52·24% of votes cast were in favour. The constitution was promulgated on 29 Dec. 1993. In Aug. 1996 Congress voted for the eligibility of the President to serve a third consecutive term of office.

Congress has 120 members, elected for a five-year term by proportional representation. In March 2003 it voted to re-establish the Senate, which had been dissolved by former president Alberto Fujimori in 1992.

All citizens over the age of 18 are eligible to vote. Voting is compulsory.

National Anthem. 'Somos libres, seámoslo siempre' ('We are free, let us always be so'); words by J. De La Torre Ugarte, tune by J. B. Alcedo.

RECENT ELECTIONS

Elections were held on 8 April and 3 June 2001 for president and 8 April for the 120-member, single-chamber congress. There were eight presidential candidates in the first round of voting. Alejandro Toledo Manrique of the personalist Peru Posible Party (36·5%) and Alan Gabriel Ludwig García Pérez of the American Revolutionary People's Alliance (25·8%) met in a run-off, which Toledo won with 53·1%. Toledo had withdrawn from presidential elections in 2000 amidst complaints made against the electoral process. He is Peru's first democratically-elected president of indigenous descent.

In the congressional elections of 8 April 2001 the Peru Posible party gained 45 seats with 26·3% of votes cast. The American Revolutionary People's Alliance gained 26 seats (19·7%), the National Unity Party 17 (13·8%), the Moralizing Independent Front 11 (11·0%), Union for Peru 6 (4·1%) and We Are Peru 4 (5·8%). Other parties received less than 5% of votes and won three seats or fewer.

CURRENT ADMINISTRATION

President: Alejandro Toledo Manrique; b. 1946 (Peru Posible; sworn in 28 July 2001).

First Vice-President: Vacant. *Second Vice-President:* David Waisman.

In March 2005 the government comprised:

President of the Council of Ministers (Prime Minister): Dr Carlos Ferrero Costa; b. 1941 (sworn in 15 Dec. 2003).

Minister of Foreign Affairs: Manuel Rodríguez Cuadros. *Defence:* Roberto Chiabra León. *Economy and Finance:* Pedro Pablo Kuczynski. *Interior:* Felix Murazzo. *Justice:* Eduardo Salhuana. *Education and Culture:* Javier Sota Nadal. *Health:* Pilar Mazzetti Soler. *Agriculture:* Manuel Manrique. *Labour:* Juan Sheput. *Foreign Trade and Tourism:* Alfredo Ferrero Diez Canseco. *Energy and Mines:* Glodomiro Sánchez Mejía. *Transport and Communications:* José Ortiz Rivera. *Production:* David Lemor. *Housing, Construction and Sanitation:* Carlos Bruce Montes de Oca. *Women's Affairs and Social Development:* Ana María Romero-Lozada.

President of the Council of Ministers (Spanish only): http://www.pcm.gob.pe

DEFENCE

There is selective conscription for two years. In 2003 defence expenditure totalled US$893m. (US$33 per capita), representing 1·4% of GDP.

Army. There are six military regions. In 2002 the Army comprised approximately 70,000 personnel (52,000 conscripts) and 188,000 reserves. In addition there is a paramilitary national police force of 77,000 personnel.

Navy. The principal ship of the Navy is the former Netherlands cruiser *Almirante Grau*, built in 1953. Other combatants include six diesel submarines and four Italian-built frigates.

The Naval Aviation branch operates seven combat aircraft and 13 armed helicopters.

Callao is the main base, where the dockyard is located and most training takes place. Smaller ocean bases exist at Paita and Talara.

Naval personnel in 2002 totalled 25,000 (10,000 conscripts) including 800 Naval Air Arm and 4,000 Marines.

Air Force. The operational force consists of five combat groups. There are military airfields at Talara, Chiclayo, Piura, Pisco, Lima (2), Iquitos and La Joya, and a floatplane base at Iquitos.

In 2002 there were some 15,000 personnel (2,000 conscripts) and 116 combat aircraft (including Su-22s, Su-25s, Mirage 2000s, Mirage 5s and MiG-29s) and 19 armed helicopters.

INTERNATIONAL RELATIONS

Peru is a member of the UN, WTO, OAS, Inter-American Development Bank, the Andean Group, LAIA, APEC, IOM and Antarctic Treaty.

ECONOMY

Agriculture produced 7·1% of GDP in 1998, industry 36·8% and services 56·1%.

Overview. The Peruvian economy has undergone a significant transformation since 1990—the authorities ended hyperinflation and a debt crisis, implemented tax and pension reforms, and liberalized and privatized the economy. Inflation fell steadily through to 2000 and has since been kept low under the central bank's inflation targeting framework, permitting a gradual reduction of interest rates. In 2004 real per capita GDP was 30% higher than in 1990. The economy suffered a prolonged recession between 1997 and 2001 owing to spillover from crises in emerging markets but has since responded favourably to a policy of fiscal responsibility, targeted social programmes to provide assistance to the poor and job creation programmes. Private investment has been concentrated in the natural resource sector, leading to limited employment creation. According to the IMF the Peruvian investment climate is relatively hostile. Despite positive overall macroeconomic performance the percentage of Peruvians living in poverty reached 54·8% in 2001 owing to increasingly unequal income distribution. The authorities have undertaken structural reforms to open the economy, reduce labour costs in the formal sector and to improve the climate for private investment; however, according to the IMF these reforms are being undertaken with uneven progress.

Currency. The monetary unit is the *nuevo sol* (PES), of 100 *céntimos*, which replaced the inti in 1990 at a rate of 1m. intis = 1 nuevo sol. Inflation, which had been over 7,000% in 1990, was down to 2·0% in 2001 and just 0·2% in 2002, the lowest rate in more than 30 years. Foreign exchange reserves were US$8,053m. in June 2002, gold reserves totalled 1·10m. troy oz and total money supply was 21,506m. sols.

Budget. Budget revenue and expenditure (in 1m. sols), year ending 31 Dec:

	1997	*1998*	*1999*	*2000*	*2001*
Revenue	27,693	29,287	28,706	30,807	29,788
Expenditure	27,264	30,123	34,203	36,053	34,754

In 1997 the World Bank approved a US$150m. loan to help Peru overcome expected problems associated with El Niño.

Performance. Real GDP growth was just 0·6% in 2001 but then 5·3% in 2002, the highest rate in Latin America. Total GDP in 2003 was US$61·0bn.

Banking and Finance. The bank of issue is the Banco Central de Reserva (*President*, Javier Silva Ruete), which was established in 1922. The government's fiscal agent is the Banco de la Nación. In 2002 there were three other government banks (Banco Central Hipotecario del Perú; Banco de la Nación; Corporación Financiera de Desarrollo), ten commercial banks, one regional bank and three foreign banks. Legislation of April 1991 permitted financial institutions to fix their own interest rates and reopened the country to foreign banks. The Central Reserve Bank sets the upper limit.

There are stock exchanges in Lima and Arequipa.

ENERGY AND NATURAL RESOURCES

Peru lays claim to 84 of the world's 114 ecosystems; 28 of its climate types; 19% of all bird species; 20% of all plant species; and 25 conservation areas (seven national parks, eight national reserves, seven national sanctuaries and three historic sanctuaries).

Environment. Peru's carbon dioxide emissions from the consumption and flaring of fossil fuels in 2002 were the equivalent of 1·1 tonnes per capita.

Electricity. In 2001 output was 20·6bn. kWh. Total generating capacity was 6·1m. kW in 2003. 66·1% of the population were supplied with electricity in 1996. Consumption per capita in 2000 was 776 kWh. Peru's reliance on hydro-generated electricity means that electricity production was affected by the drought brought on by the 1997–98 El Niño.

Oil and Gas. Proven oil reserves in Jan. 2003 amounted to 323m. bbls. Output, 2003, 4·5m. tonnes. Natural gas reserves in 2003 were 246bn. cu. metres; output in 2001 was 370m. cu. metres. Commercial development of the huge Camisea gas field began in late 2004.

Minerals. Mining accounted for some 8·4% of GDP in 1996. Lead, copper, iron, silver, zinc and petroleum are the chief minerals exploited. Mineral production (in

1,000 tonnes): iron (1996), 2,876; zinc (2001), 1,057; copper (2001), 722; lead (1996), 249; silver (2001), 2·4; gold (2001), 0·14. 12,000 tonnes of coal were produced in 2000. Early in 1998 Southern Peru Copper, the country's largest mining company, estimated that 3,000 tonnes of copper production had been lost as a result of flooding caused by El Niño.

Agriculture. There are four natural zones: the Coast strip, with an average width of 80 km; the Sierra or Uplands, formed by the coast range of mountains and the Andes proper; the Montaña or high wooded region which lies on the eastern slopes of the Andes; and the jungle in the Amazon Basin, known as the Selva. Legislation of 1991 permits the unrestricted sale of agricultural land. Workers in co-operatives may elect to form limited liability companies and become shareholders.

Production in 2000 (in 1,000 tonnes): sugarcane, 7,750; potatoes, 3,187; rice, 1,665; plantains, 1,415; maize, 1,271; cassava, 986; onions, 367; oranges, 318; lemons and limes, 310; sweet potatoes, 230; tomatoes, 197; mangoes, 180; barley, 175; seed cotton, 175.

Livestock, 2000: sheep, 14·4m.; cattle, 4·9m.; pigs, 2·8m.; alpacas, 2·6m. (1996); poultry, 81m. Livestock products (in 1,000 tonnes), 2000: poultry meat, 580; beef and veal, 136; pork, bacon and ham, 95; mutton and lamb, 31; milk, 1,048.

In 2001 there were 3·70m. ha of arable land and 0·51 ha of permanent crops. 1·2m. ha were irrigated in 2001.

Coca was cultivated in 2000 on approximately 34,000 ha, down from 115,000 ha in 1995.

Forestry. In 2000 the area covered by forests was 65·22m. ha, or 50·9% of the total land area. The forests contain valuable hardwoods; oak and cedar account for about 40%. In 2001 roundwood removals totalled 8·37m. cu. metres.

Fisheries. Sardines and anchovies are caught offshore to be processed into fishmeal, of which Peru is a major producer. Fishing in deeper waters is being developed, subject to government conservation by the imposition of quotas and fishing bans. Total catch in 2001 was 7,986,103 tonnes, almost entirely from sea fishing. In 1999 the catch had a value of US$801·5m. Peru's annual catch is the second largest in the world after that of China. In the first nine months of 1997, 1·3m tonnes of fishmeal was produced, up 3·4% over the same period for 1996.

INDUSTRY

About 70% of industries are located in the Lima/Callao metropolitan area. Industry accounted for 29·7% of GDP in 2001, with manufacturing contributing 15·3%. Production, 2000 (in 1,000 tonnes): cement, 3,265; residual fuel oil, 2,915; distillate fuel oil, 1,700; prepared animal feeds (2001), 1,508; petrol, 1,411; kerosene, 1,099; sugar (2001), 755; soft drinks, 1,110·8m. litres; beer, 570·6m. litres; cigarettes, 3·6bn. units.

Labour. The labour force in 1996 totalled 8,652,000 (71% males). In 1993, 1,852,800 people worked in agriculture, 1,167,000 in commerce, 783,900 in manufacturing, 599,700 in services, 347,500 in transport, 255,000 in building, 72,200 in mining and 18,700 in electricity production. In 2002 an estimated 8·4% of the workforce was unemployed, up from 5·9% in 1991.

Trade Unions. Trade unions have about 2m. members (approximately 1·5m. in peasant organizations and 500,000 in industrial). The major trade union organization is the *Confederación de Trabajadores del Perú*, which was reconstituted in 1959 after being in abeyance for some years. The other labour organizations recognized by the government are the *Confederación General de Trabajadores del Perú*, the *Confederación Nacional de Trabajadores* and the *Central de Trabajadores de la Revolución Peruana*.

INTERNATIONAL TRADE

An agreement of 1992 gives Bolivia duty-free transit for imports and exports through a corridor leading to the Peruvian Pacific port of Ilo from the Bolivian frontier town of Desaguadero, in return for Peruvian access to the Atlantic via Bolivia's roads and railways. Foreign debt was US$28,167m. in 2002.

Imports and Exports. Trade in US$1m.:

	1998	*1999*	*2000*	*2001*	*2002*
Imports f.o.b.	8,262	6,793	7,407	7,273	7,440
Exports f.o.b.	5,757	6,088	6,951	7,007	7,647

In 2001 the main export markets were: USA, 24·8%; UK, 13·5%; China, 6·2%; Japan, 5·6%. Main import suppliers, 2001: USA, 23·1%; Argentina, 6·2%; Chile, 5·9%; Japan, 5·9%. Main imports in 1998 were raw and intermediate materials (41·3%), machinery (24·9%) and consumer goods (23·0%). Leading exports in 1998 were gold (16·2%), copper and copper products (13·6%) and zinc products (7·8%).

COMMUNICATIONS

Roads. In 2000 there were 78,294 km of roads, of which 13·4% were paved. By the end of March 1998, 700 km of road had been affected by El Niño. In 2002 there were 791,862 cars, 400,015 lorries and vans and 45,089 buses and coaches. There were 74,221 road accidents involving injury in 2002 with 2,929 fatalities.

Rail. Total length (1996), 1,992 km on 1,435- and 914-mm gauges. Passenger-km travelled in 2002 came to 98m. and freight tonne-km to 1,008m.

Civil Aviation. There is an international airport at Lima (Jorge Chávez International). In 1996 there were 32 airports. The main Peruvian airlines are Lan Perú and Aero Continente. In 2003 services were also provided by the domestic airlines Aero Cóndor, AVIANDINA and Transportes Aereos Nacionales de Selva, and by more than 20 international carriers. In 1999 scheduled airline traffic of Peruvian-based carriers flew 27·2m. km, carrying 1,900,000 passengers (150,000 on international flights). In 2000 Jorge Chávez International handled 4,506,000 passengers (2,258,000 on international flights) and 105,400 tonnes of freight.

Shipping. In 1994 there were 30 sea-going vessels and 519 lake and river craft. In 2002 sea-going shipping totalled 240,000 GRT (including oil tankers 15,000 GRT). In 2002 vessels totalling 8,260,000 net registered tons entered ports and vessels totalling 6,112,000 NRT cleared. Callao is the busiest port, handling 11,609,000 tonnes of cargo in 2002. There are also ports at Chimbote, Paita and Talara.

Telecommunications. Peru had 4,073,100 telephone subscribers in 2002, or 152·3 per 1,000 population, and there were 1,488,000 PCs in use (55·6 for every 1,000 persons). There were 2,306,900 mobile phone subscribers in 2002 and 15,000 fax machines in 1995. In 2002 there were 2,500,000 Internet users.

Postal Services. In 1998 there were 963 post offices.

SOCIAL INSTITUTIONS

Justice. The judicial system is a pyramid at the base of which are the justices of the peace who decide minor criminal cases and civil cases involving small sums of money. The apex is the Supreme Court with a president and 12 members; in between are the judges of first instance, who usually sit in the provincial capitals, and the superior courts.

The police had some 85,000 personnel in 1991. The population in penal institutions in June 2002 was 27,493 (104 per 100,000 of national population).

Religion. Religious liberty exists, but the Roman Catholic religion is protected by the State, and since 1929 only Roman Catholic religious instruction is permitted in schools, state or private. There were 23·17m. Catholics in 2001 as well as 1·73m. Protestants and 1·19m. with other beliefs (mostly non-religious). In Sept. 2003 there was one cardinal.

Education. Adult literacy was 90·2% in 2001 (male, 94·8%; female, 85·7%). Elementary education is compulsory and free between the ages of 7 and 16; secondary education is also free. In 2003 there were 1,095,665 children in pre-school education, 4,237,378 pupils in primary and 2,567,896 in secondary schools. In 1993 the number of students at the 28 state and 23 private universities was 727,200. There were 251,700 students in other forms of further education.

In 1999–2000 total expenditure on education came to 3·5% of GNP and 21·1% of total government spending.

Health. There were 472 hospitals with a provision of 13 beds per 10,000 inhabitants in 1996. There were 23,349 physicians, 1,197 dentists, 16,043 nurses, 4,789 pharmacists and 3,832 midwives in 1997.

Peru made the greatest progress of any country in the reduction of undernourishment during the 1990s. Between 1990–92 and 2000–02 the proportion of undernourished people declined from 42% of the population to 13%.

Welfare. An option to transfer from state social security (IPSS) to privately-managed funds was introduced in 1993.

CULTURE

World Heritage Sites. There are ten sites in Peru appearing on the UNESCO World Heritage List. They are (with year entered on list) the City of Cusco (1983), the Historic Sanctuary of Machu Picchu (1983), Chavin (Archaeological site) (1985), Huascaran National Park (1985), Chan Chan Archaeological Zone (1986), Manu National Park (1987), Historic Centre of Lima (1988), Rio Abiseo National Park (1990), Lines and Geoglyphs of Nasca and Pampas de Jumana (1994) and the Historical Centre of the City of Arequipa (2000).

Broadcasting. Radio broadcasting is conducted by hundreds of national, provincial and local stations grouped in the Asociación de Radiodifusores del Perú and the Unión de Radioemisores de Provincias del Perú. There are 59 TV companies (colour by NTSC). There were 3·9m. TV sets in use in 2001 and 7·1m. radio receivers in 1997.

Press. There were 74 dailies in 1996 with a combined circulation of 2m.

Tourism. There were 1,027,000 foreign visitors in 2000 (485,000 in 1995), bringing foreign exchange earnings of US$1,001m.

DIPLOMATIC REPRESENTATIVES

Of Peru in the United Kingdom (52 Sloane St., London, SW1X 9SP)
Ambassador: Luis Solari Tudela.

Of the United Kingdom in Peru (Torre Parque Mar, Piso 22, Avenida Jose Larco 1301, Miraflores, Lima)
Ambassador: Richard Ralph, CVO, CMG.

Of Peru in the USA (1700 Massachusetts Ave., NW, Washington, D.C., 20036)
Ambassador: Eduardo Ferrero Costa.

Of the USA in Peru (Avenida La Encalada Cdra 17-Monterrico, Lima)
Ambassador: J. Curtis Struble.

Of Peru to the United Nations
Ambassador: Oswaldo de Rivero Barreto.

Of Peru to the European Union
Ambassador: José Urrutia Ceruti.

FURTHER READING

Instituto Nacional de Estadística e Informática.—*Anuario Estadistico del Perú.—Perú: Compendio Estadístico*. Annual.—*Boletin de Estadistica Peruana*. Quarterly
Banco Central de Reserva. Monthly Bulletin.—*Renta Nacional del Perú*. Annual, Lima

Cameron, M. A., *Democracy and Authoritarianism in Peru: Political Coalitions and Social Change*. London, 1995
Daeschner, J., *The War of the End of Democracy: Mario Vargas Llosa vs. Alberto Fujimori*. Lima, 1993
Gorriti, Gustavo, (trans. Robin Kirk) *The Shining Path: A History of the Millenarian War in Peru*. Univ. of North Carolina Press, 1999
Stokes, S. C., *Cultures in Conflict: Social Movements and the State in Peru*. California Univ. Press, 1995
Strong, S., *Shining Path*. London, 1993
Vargas Llosa, A., *The Madness of Things Peruvian: Democracy under Siege*. Brunswick (NJ), 1994

National statistical office: Instituto Nacional de Estadística e Informática, Av. Gral. Garzón 654–658, Jesús María, Lima.
Website (Spanish only): http://www.inei.gob.pe

PHILIPPINES

Republika ng Pilipinas

Capital: Manila
Population projection, 2010: 89·67m.
GDP per capita, 2002: (PPP$) 4,170
HDI/world rank: 0·753/83

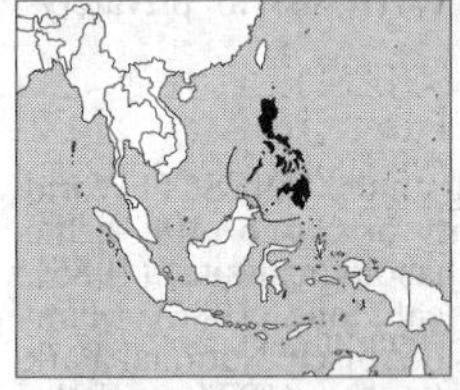

KEY HISTORICAL EVENTS

Discovered by Magellan in 1521, the Philippine islands were conquered by Spain in 1565 and named after the Spanish king, Philip. In Dec. 1898, following the Spanish-American War, the Philippines were ceded to the USA. The Philippines acquired self-government as a Commonwealth of the USA in March 1934. The islands were occupied by the Japanese from 1942 to 1945. Independence was achieved in July 1946. From independence until 1972 the Philippines were governed under a constitution based largely on the US pattern. In Sept. 1972 President Ferdinand Marcos declared martial law. In May 1980 Benigno Aquino, Jr, the leading opponent of Marcos, was released from prison to go to the USA for medical treatment. He was killed when he returned to the Philippines after three years in exile. At the presidential elections of Feb. 1986 Ferdinand Marcos was opposed by Aquino's widow, Corazón. Aquino became president, Marcos fled the country and a new constitution limiting the president to a single, six-year term in office was ratified in Feb. 1987. Insurgent activities carried out since 1972 by the Moro National Liberation Front (Muslims) were ended by a peace agreement of 2 Sept. 1996 which provides for a Muslim autonomous region in an area of Mindanao island in southern Philippines. The rebellion left more than 120,000 people dead. In Oct. 2000 impeachment proceedings began against President Estrada who was alleged to have received more than US$10·8m. from gambling kickbacks. His impeachment trial collapsed in Jan. 2001 when he was forced from office by mass protests. Subsequently Estrada's supporters tried to overthrow his successor, Gloria Macapagal-Arroyo. In Nov. 2001 the fragile peace between the government and Islamic militants was shattered. Since then violence has frequently erupted, the latest episode in early 2005 when fighting on the southern island of Jolo left 90 dead on both sides and caused 12,000 people to flee. On 14 Feb. 2005 three bombs were detonated killing nine and injuring 130.

TERRITORY AND POPULATION

The Philippines is situated between 21° 25' and 4° 23' N. lat. and between 116° and 127° E. long. It is composed of 7,107 islands and islets, 2,773 of which are named. Approximate land area, 300,076 sq. km (115,859 sq. miles). The largest islands (in sq. km) are Luzon (104,688), Mindanao (94,630), Samar (13,080), Negros (12,710), Palawan (11,785), Panay (11,515), Mindoro (9,735), Leyte (7,214), Cebu (4,422), Bohol (3,865) and Masbate (3,269).

The census population in May 2000 was 76,498,735; density, 255·0 per sq. km. In 2001, 59·3% of the population lived in urban areas.

The UN gives a projected population for 2010 of 89·67m.

The area (in 1,000) and population of the 16 regions (from north to south):

Region	*Sq. km*	*2000*	*Region*	*Sq. km*	*2000*
Ilocos	12,840	4,200,478	Central Visayas	14,951	5,701,064
Cordillera[1]	18,294	1,365,220	Eastern Visayas	21,432	3,610,355
Cagayan Valley	26,838	2,813,159	Northern Mindanao	14,033	2,747,585
Central Luzon	18,231	8,030,945	Southern Mindanao	27,141	5,189,335
National Capital	636	9,932,560	Central Mindanao	14,373	2,598,210
Southern Tagalog	46,924	11,793,655	Western Mindanao	16,042	3,091,208
Bicol	17,633	4,674,855	Muslim Mindanao[2]	11,638	2,412,159
Western Visayas	20,223	6,208,733	Caraga	18,847	2,095,367

[1]Administrative region. [2]Autonomous region.

Since the 2000 census Southern Tagalog has been divided into two new regions, Calabarzon and Mimaropa. Southern Mindanao has become Davao, Central Mindanao is now Soccsksargen and Western Mindanao is Zamboanga.

City populations (2000 census, in 1,000) are as follows; all on Luzon unless indicated in parenthesis.

Quezon City[1]	2,160	Iloilo (Panay)	366
Manila (the capital)[1]	1,673	Pasay[1]	363
Caloocan[1]	1,233	Malabon[2]	356
Davao (Mindanao)	1,147	Mandaluyong[1]	304
Cebu (Cebu)	662	Iligan (Mindanao)	285
Zamboanga (Mindanao)	600	Butuan (Mindanao)	267
Pasig[1]	582	Mandaue (Cebu)	256
Makati[1]	524	Navotas[2]	254
Valenzuela[2]	521	Baguio[1]	250
Taguig[2]	510	Batangas	245
Las Piñas[2]	499	Angeles	243
Parañaque[2]	489	Lipa City	219
Cagayan de Oro (Mindanao)	462	Cabanatuan	218
Marikina[2]	437	San Pablo	205
Bacolod (Negros)	429	Lapu-Lapu (Cebu)	200
General Santos (Mindanao)	412	Lucena City	196
Muntilupa[1]	393	Olongapo	194

[1]City within Metropolitan Manila. Population of Metro Manila in 1999, 10,546,000.
[2]Municipality within Metropolitan Manila.

Filipino (based on Tagalog) is spoken by 55% of the population, but as a mother tongue by only 27·9%; among the 76 other indigenous languages spoken, Cebuano is spoken as a mother tongue by 24·3% and Ilocano by 9·8%. English is widely spoken. In 2000 some 5·5m. Filipinos were living and working abroad, including 2m. in the USA, 850,000 in Saudi Arabia and 620,000 in Malaysia.

SOCIAL STATISTICS

Registered births, 2000 (provisional), 1,699,380; deaths, 364,751; marriages, 572,955. Divorce is illegal. Birth rate per 1,000 population (2000), 26·8; death rate, 5·9. Expectation of life at birth, 2001, was 67·6 years for males and 71·6 years for females. Annual population growth rate, 1992–2002, 2·1%. Infant mortality, 2001, 29 per 1,000 live births; fertility rate, 2001, 3·4 births per woman.

CLIMATE

Some areas have an equatorial climate while others experience tropical monsoon conditions, with a wet season extending from June to Nov. Mean temperatures are high all year, with very little variation. Manila. Jan. 77°F (25°C), July 82°F (27·8°C). Annual rainfall 83·3" (2,115·9 mm).

CONSTITUTION AND GOVERNMENT

A new Constitution was ratified by referendum in 1987 with the approval of 78·5% of voters. The head of state is the executive *President*, directly elected for a non-renewable six-year term.

Congress consists of a 24-member upper house, the *Senate* (elected for a six-year term by proportional representation, half of them renewed every three years), and a *House of Representatives* of not more than 250 members (214 directly elected and the rest from party and minority-group lists, for a three-year term).

A campaign led by the president at the time, Fidel Ramos, to amend the constitution to allow him to stand for a second term was voted down by the Senate by 23 to one in Dec. 1996.

National Anthem. 'Land of the Morning', lyric in English by M. A. Sane and C. Osias, tune by Julian Felipe; 'Lupang Hinirang', Tagalog lyric by the Institute of National Language.

RECENT ELECTIONS

The presidential elections of 10 May 2004 were won by President Gloria Macapagal-Arroyo (Lakas-Christian Muslim Democrats) with 40·0% of the votes cast, ahead of Fernando Poe, Jr (Coalition of United Filipinos) with 36·5% of the vote and Panfilo Morena Lacson (Struggle of Democratic Filipinos) with 10·9%. There were two other candidates.

Elections to the House of Representatives were also held on 10 May 2004. Out of a total of 211 seats, 93 went to Lakas-Christian Muslim Democrats, 53 to the National People's Coalition, 34 to the Liberal Party and 11 to the Laban ng Demokratikong Pilipino (Philippine Democratic Party). The remaining seats were shared among party list representatives, non-partisans and others or were vacant.

Senate elections were also most recently held on 10 May 2004, following which Lakas-Christian Muslim Democrats had 7 seats, Coalition of United Filipinos 3, the Liberal Party 3 and non-partisans and others 10 with 1 vacant.

CURRENT ADMINISTRATION

President: Gloria Macapagal-Arroyo; b. 1947 (Lakas-Christian Muslim Democrats; sworn in 20 Jan. 2001 and elected on 10 May 2004). Her father, Diosdado Macapagal, had been president from 1961–65.

Vice-President: Noli de Castro (elected on 10 May 2004).

In March 2005 the government comprised:

Minister of Justice: Raul Gonzalez. *Trade and Industry:* Juan Santos. *Finance:* Cesar Purisima. *National Defence:* Avelino Cruz. *Agriculture:* Arthur Yap. *Foreign Affairs:* Alberto Romulo. *Public Works and Highways:* Hermogenes Ebdane, Jr. *Energy:* Raphael Perpetuo Lotilla. *Education, Culture and Sports:* Florencio Abad. *Labour and Employment:* Patricia Santo Thomas. *Health:* Manuel Dayrit. *Agrarian Reform:* Rene Villa. *Tourism:* Joseph Durano. *Budget and Management:* Emilia Boncodin. *Transport and Communications:* Leandro Mendoza. *Science and Technology:* Estrella Alabastro. *Environment and Natural Resources:* Michael Defensor. *Social Welfare and Development:* Corazon Soliman. *Socio-Economic Planning:* Romulo Neri. *Interior and Local Government:* Angelo Reyes.

Executive Secretary: Eduardo Ermita.

Speaker of the House of Representatives: Jose de Venecia.

Government Website: http://www.gov.ph

DEFENCE

An extension of the 1947 agreement granting the USA the use of several army, navy and air force bases was rejected by the Senate in Sept. 1991. An agreement of Dec. 1994 authorizes US naval vessels to be repaired in Philippine ports. The Philippines is a signatory of the South-East Asia Collective Defence Treaty.

Defence expenditure in 2003 totalled US$783m. (US$10 per capita), representing 1·0% of GDP.

Army. The Army is organized into five area joint-service commands.

Strength (2002) 66,000, with reserves totalling 100,000. The paramilitary Philippines National Police numbered 40,500 in 2002 with a further 62,000 auxiliaries.

Navy. The Navy consists principally of ex-US ships completed in 1944 and 1945, and serviceability and spares are a problem. The modernization programme in progress has been revised and delayed, but the first 30 inshore patrol craft of US and Korean design have been delivered. The present fleet includes one ex-US frigate.

Navy personnel in 2002 was estimated at 24,000 including 7,500 marines.

Air Force. The Air Force had a strength of 16,000 in 2002, with 49 combat aircraft and about 67 armed helicopters. Its fighter-bomber wing is equipped with one squadron of F-5As (only three or four operational).

INTERNATIONAL RELATIONS

The Philippines is a member of the UN, WTO, Asian Development Bank, ASEAN, APEC, the Colombo Plan and IOM.

ECONOMY

Agriculture accounted for 14·7% of GDP in 2002, industry 32·5% and services 52·8%.

Overview. Over the past fifteen years significant progress has been made on establishing a market-orientated economy in the Philippines. Economic growth has been fairly robust, inflation limited, the exchange rate relatively stable and access to foreign markets maintained. The economic environment has been overhauled, foreign investment and trade barriers dismantled and seminal industries deregulated. In 1992–95 most state industrial assets were privatized. Monopolies were dismantled in the telecommunication, oil, civil aviation, shipping, water and power industries. Until the mid-1990s tax revenue steadily expanded allowing the fiscal position to shift from a large deficit into a small surplus. However, in the last few years revenue collections have declined leading to fiscal deficits and compromising the fiscal position. The IMF has urged steps to address the deterioration of fiscal performance and to strengthen the banking system.

Currency. The unit of currency is the *peso* (PHP) of 100 *centavos.* Inflation was 3·1% in 2002. Foreign exchange reserves were US$14,163m. in June 2002 and gold reserves 8·22m. troy oz (3·58m. troy oz in 1995). Total money supply in April 2002 was 410,581m. pesos.

Budget. Total government revenue and expenditure (in 1m. pesos), year ending 31 Dec.:

	1996	*1997*	*1998*	*1999*	*2000*	*2001*
Revenue	409,880	470,105	462,119	478,210	513,386	561,741
Expenditure	401,017	467,319	511,398	585,435	645,804	706,327

Expenditure (2001) included (in 1,000m. pesos): education, 121·4; economic affairs and services, 90·8; transport and communications, 53·1; public order and safety, 47·7.

Total internal public debt was 809,900m. pesos in 1998.

Performance. Total GDP in 2003 was US$80·6bn. Real GDP growth was 4·3% in 2002 and 4·7% in 2003.

Banking and Finance. The Central Bank (*Chairman*, Rafael Buenaventura) issues the currency, manages foreign exchange reserves and supervises the banking system. At 30 June 2003 there were 42 commercial banks (24 regular commercial banks and 18 universal banks), 93 thrift banks and 771 rural and co-operative banks. In June 2003 the total number of banking institutions was 6,414, with total assets of 3,529,128m. pesos.

There is a stock exchange in Manila.

The financial crisis that struck southeast Asia in 1997 led to the floating of the peso in July. It subsequently lost 36% of its value against the dollar.

The Philippines was one of 15 countries and territories named in a report in June 2000 as failing to co-operate in the fight against international money laundering. The Financial Action Task Force on Money Laundering was set up by the G7 group of major industrialized nations.

Weights and Measures. The metric system is used but with some local units, including the *picul* (63·25 kg) for sugar and fibres, and the *cavan* (16·5 gallons) for cereals.

ENERGY AND NATURAL RESOURCES

Environment. Carbon dioxide emissions from the consumption and flaring of fossil fuels in 2002 were the equivalent of 0·8 tonnes per capita.

Electricity. Total installed capacity was 12·3m. kW in 2000. Production was estimated at 45·29bn. kWh in 2000. Consumption per capita was 593 kWh in 2000.

Oil and Gas. The largest natural gas field is the Camago-Malampaya gas field, discovered off the island of Palawan in 1992, with reserves initially put at 76bn. cu. metres but now increased to 85bn. cu. metres. The Philippines' total natural gas reserves in 2002 were 105bn. cu. metres.

Crude petroleum reserves were 178m. bbls. in 2002.

Water. Water production in 1997 was 997m. cu. metres and water consumption 230m. cu. metres. Breakdown of water consumption: industrial, 89m. cu. metres; residential, 82m. cu. metres; and commercial, 59m. cu. metres.

Minerals. Mineral production in 2000 (in tonnes): coal, 1,300,000; salt, 589,528; copper, 129,768; silica sand, 70,000; chromite refractory ore (chromium content), 20,920; nickel bearing ore (2002) 26,532 (nickel content); gold (2001), 33,840 kg; silver, 23,534 kg. Other minerals include rock asphalt, sand and gravel. Total value of mineral production, 1998, 36,829m. pesos.

Agriculture. Agriculture is a mainstay of the economy, contributing up to 30% of national output. In 2001 there were 5·65m. ha of arable land and 5·0m. ha of permanent crops. In 2001, 37·4% of the working population was employed in agriculture. In the period 1990–97 agriculture grew on average by 1·9% a year, but in 1998 contracted by 6·6%.

Output (in 1,000 tonnes) in 2000: sugarcane, 33,732; rice, 12,415; coconuts, 5,761; maize, 4,486; bananas, 4,156; copra, 2,000; cassava, 1,771; pineapples, 1,524. The output of copra is the highest of any country in the world. Minor crops are fruits, nuts, vegetables, coffee, cacao, peanuts, ramie, rubber, maguey, kapok, abaca and tobacco.

Livestock, 2000: buffaloes, 3·02m.; cattle, 2·55m.; pigs, 10·40m.; goats, 6·78m.; poultry, 142m.

Forestry. Forests covered 5·79m. ha (19·4% of the land area) in 2000. Approximately two-thirds of the total forest area was timberland in 1995. Timber production was 44·38m. cu. metres in 2001.

Fisheries. The catch in 2001 was 1,945,217 tonnes (93% from marine waters).

INDUSTRY

Leading sectors are foodstuffs, oil refining and chemicals. Production (in 1,000 tonnes): cement (2001), 11,378; residual fuel oil (2000), 5,067; distillate fuel oil (2000), 4,832; petrol (2000), 2,035; sugar (2002), 1,988; paper and paperboard (2002), 1,056; plywood (2002), 409,000 cu. metres.

Labour. In 2000 the total workforce was 30,911,000, of whom 27,453,000 were employed (17,271,000 in non-agricultural work). Employees by sector, 2000: 12·8m. in services, 10·2m. in agriculture, forestry and fisheries, 2·7m. in manufacturing, 2·0m. in transport and communications and 1·5m. in construction. 3·5m. persons were registered unemployed in 2000. 669,188 persons worked overseas as of Sept. 2000.

The unemployment rate in Oct. 2001 was 9·8%.

Trade Unions. In the third quarter of 2000 there were 10,217 unions with a total membership of 3,778,000.

INTERNATIONAL TRADE

Foreign debt totalled US$59,342m. in 2002. A law of June 1991 gave foreign nationals the right to full ownership of export and other firms, considered strategic for the economy.

Imports and Exports. Values of imports and exports in US$1m.:

	1998	*1999*	*2000*	*2001*	*2002*
Imports f.o.b.	29,524	29,252	33,481	31,986	33,975
Exports f.o.b.	29,496	34,211	37,295	31,243	34,383

Main imports: electronics and components, mineral fuels, lubricants and related materials, industrial machinery and equipment, telecommunications equipment, transport equipment.

Principal exports: electronics, garments, machinery, transport equipment and apparatus, and processed foods. In 2001 electronics exports were worth US$21·6bn. and constituted 67% of all exports. In 1992 they had been worth just US$3bn.

Main sources of import in 2001: Japan, 20·3%; USA, 18·5%; Singapore, 6·6%; South Korea, 6·3%. Main export markets, 2001: USA, 27·5%; Japan, 15·7%; the Netherlands, 9·2%; Singapore, 7·2%.

COMMUNICATIONS

Roads. In 2002 roads totalled 202,124 km; of these, 30,329 km were national roads and 49,805 km were regional roads. In 2002, 4,163,939 motor vehicles were registered, including 749,553 passenger cars, 1,686,229 buses and coaches, and 1,470,383 motorcycles. In 2000 there were 859 fatalities in road accidents (645 in 1996).

Rail. In 1995 the National Railways totalled 429 km (1,067 mm gauge). In 2000 passenger-km totalled 123m. There is a light metro railway in Manila.

Civil Aviation. There are international airports at Manila (Ninoy Aquino) and Cebu (Mactan International). In Sept. 1998 the Asian economic crisis forced the closure of the national carrier, Philippine Airlines, after it had suffered huge losses. However, it has in the meantime resumed its operations both internally and externally. In 1999 scheduled airline traffic of Philippine-based carriers flew 53·0m. km, carrying 5,004,000 passengers (1,922,000 on international flights). In 2000 Manila handled 12,668,000 passengers (7,130,000 on international flights) and 399,500 tonnes of freight.

Shipping. The main ports are Cagayan de Oro, Cebu, Davao, Iloilo, Manila and Zamboanga. Manila, the leading port, handled 43,820,000 tonnes of cargo in 2002. In 2002 merchant shipping totalled 5,320,000 GRT, including oil tankers 146,000 GRT.

Telecommunications. Telephone subscribers numbered 18,511,900 in 2002, or 232·9 per 1,000 inhabitants, and there were 2·2m. PCs in use (equivalent to 27·7 for every 1,000 persons). Mobile phone subscribers numbered 15,201,000 in 2002 and there were 50,000 fax machines in 1998. In 2002 there were approximately 3·5m. Internet users.

Postal Services. In 1995 there were 1,948 post offices.

SOCIAL INSTITUTIONS

Justice. There is a Supreme Court which is composed of a chief justice and 14 associate justices; it can declare a law or treaty unconstitutional by the concurrent votes of the majority sitting. There is a Court of Appeals, which consists of a presiding justice and 50 associate justices. There are 15 regional trial courts, one for each judicial region, with a presiding regional trial judge in its 720 branches. There is a metropolitan trial court in the Metropolitan Manila Area, a municipal trial court in each of the other cities or municipalities and a municipal circuit trial court in each area defined as a municipal circuit comprising one or more cities and/or one or more municipalities.

The Supreme Court may designate certain branches of the regional trial courts to handle exclusively criminal cases, juvenile and domestic relations cases, agrarian cases, urban land reform cases which do not fall under the jurisdiction of quasijudicial bodies and agencies and/or such other special cases as the Supreme Court may determine. The death penalty, abolished in 1987, was restored in 1993 for 13 offences. No-one can be executed until a year after final appeal. In Feb. 1999 a rapist was executed, ending the *de facto* ban on capital punishment which had been in place since 1976. In Dec. 2003 President Arroyo lifted a moratorium on executions imposed in Jan. 2000.

In 1994 there were 96,365 police. Local police forces are supplemented by the Philippine Constabulary, which is part of the armed forces.

In 2003 the prison population was 24,381.

Constabulary. Since 1990 public order has been maintained completely by the Philippine National Police. Qualified Philippine Constabulary personnel were absorbed by the PNP or were transferred to branches or services of the Armed Forces of the Philippines.

Religion. 82% of the population are Roman Catholics, 5% Protestants, 5% Muslims and 7% Buddhists or other religions. There were 398,000 Latter-day Saints (Mormons) in 1998.

The Roman Catholics are organized with three cardinals, 23 archbishoprics, 91 bishoprics, 79 diocese, 2,328 parishes and some 20,873 chapels or missions.

Education. Public elementary education is free and schools are established almost everywhere. The majority of secondary and post-secondary schools are private.

Formal education consists of an optional one to two years of pre-school education; six years of elementary education; four years of secondary education; and four to five years of tertiary or college education leading to academic degrees. Three-year post-secondary non-degree technical/vocational education is also considered formal education. In 1998–99 there were 8,647 pre-school institutions (3,183 private) with (2000–01) 19,678 teachers. In 2001–02 there were 40,763 elementary schools (4,529 private) with 331,448 teachers; 7,683 secondary schools (3,261 private) with 112,210 teachers. In 1998–99 there were 1,383 tertiary schools (1,118 private). In 2000–01 there were 592,289 children in pre-school; in 2001–02 there were 12,826,218 pupils in elementary schools, 5,813,879 in secondary schools and 2,466,056 students in tertiary education.

Non-formal education consists of adult literacy classes, agricultural and farming training programmes, occupation skills training, youth clubs, and community programmes of instructions in health, nutrition, family planning and co-operatives.

In 1994–95 in the public sector there were 20 universities, 1 technological university, 1 polytechnic and 1 technological institute, and 123 other institutions of higher education. In the private sector there were 49 universities, four specialized universities (one Christian; one Roman Catholic; one medical; one for women) and 405 other institutions of higher education.

The adult literacy rate in 2001 was 95·1% (95·3% among males and 95·0% among females).

Total expenditure on education in 2001–02 came to 3·1% of GNP and was equivalent to 14·0% of total government spending.

Health. In 1998 there were 1,713 hospitals (1,097 private) with 81,200 beds (1·1 beds per 1,000 inhabitants). In 1997 there were 1,370 dentists, 4,096 nurses and 13,275 midwives. In 1996 there were 36,375 physicians (provision of one for every 1,923 persons).

Welfare. The Social Security System (SSS) is a contributory scheme for employees. Disbursements in 2001 (in 1m. pesos): social security, 37,813 (1,775,996 recipients); employees' compensation, 1,201 (90,356 recipients).

CULTURE

World Heritage Sites. The Philippines has five sites on the UNESCO World Heritage List: Tubbataha Reef Marine Park (inscribed on the list in 1993); the Baroque Churches of the Philippines (1993); the Rice Terraces of the Philippine Cordilleras (1995); the Historic Town of Vigan (1999); and Puerto-Princesa Subterranean River National Park (1999).

Broadcasting. In 1998 there were 539 AM and FM radio stations and 137 television stations (colour by NTSC). There were 13·5m. TV sets in use in 2001 and 12·4m. radio receivers in 2000.

Cinema. In 1998 there were 1,046 cinemas with a seating capacity of 611,214. 103 feature films were produced in 2000.

Press. There were 47 daily newspapers in 1996, with a combined circulation of 5,700,000, equivalent to 82 per 1,000 inhabitants. In 1999 a total of 1,380 book titles were published (including 631 in social sciences, 227 in literature and 117 in applied sciences).

Tourism. In 2001 there were 1,797,000 foreign visitors; tourist spending totalled US$1,773m. (down from 2,149,000 foreign visitors and receipts of US$2,413m. in 1998). Tourists in 2001 were mainly from other Asian countries and Australasia (1,024,000) and the Americas (451,000).

DIPLOMATIC REPRESENTATIVES

Of the Philippines in the United Kingdom (9A Palace Green, London, W8 4QE)
Ambassador: Edgardo B. Espiritu.

Of the United Kingdom in the Philippines (Floors 15–17, LV Locsin Building, 6752 Ayala Ave., Makati, Metro Manila)
Ambassador: Paul Dimond.

Of the Philippines in the USA (1600 Massachusetts Ave., NW, Washington, D.C., 20036)
Ambassador: Albert F. del Rosario.

Of the USA in the Philippines (1201 Roxas Blvd., Manila)
Ambassador: Vacant.
Chargé d'Affaires a.i.: Joseph A. Mussomeli.

Of the Philippines to the United Nations
Ambassador: Lauro L. Baja, Jr.

Of the Philippines to the European Union
Ambassador: Clemencio Montesa.

FURTHER READING

National Statistics Office. *Philippine Statistical Yearbook.*
Boyce, J. K., *The Political Economy of Growth and Impoverishment in the Marcos Era.* London, 1993
Hamilton-Paterson, J., *America's Boy: The Marcoses and the Philippines.* Granta, London, 1998
Kerkvliet, B. J. and Mojares, R. B. (eds.) *From Marcos to Aquino: Local Perspectives on Political Transition in the Philippines.* Hawaii Univ. Press, 1992
Larkin, J. A., *Sugar and the Origins of Modern Philippine Society.* California Univ. Press, 1993
Vob, R. and Yap, J. T., *The Philippine Economy: East Asia's Stray Cat? Structure, Finance and Adjustment.* London and The Hague, 1996

National statistical office: National Statistics Office, POB 779, Manila.
Website: http://www.census.gov.ph

POLAND

Rzeczpospolita Polska

Capital: Warsaw
Population projection, 2010: 38·37m.
GDP per capita, 2002: (PPP$) 10,560
HDI/world rank: 0·850/37

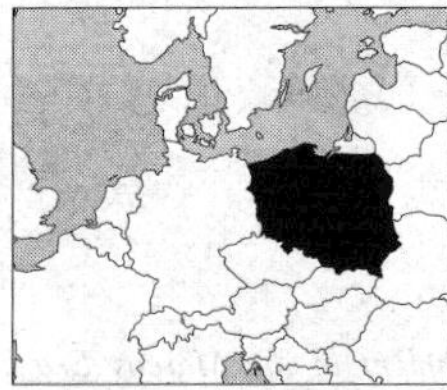

KEY HISTORICAL EVENTS

In the 7th and 8th centuries Slavic peoples settled on the forested plains between the Odra and Vistula rivers. In 966 a Polanie ('plain dwellers') state was founded by Mieszko I, of the Piast dynasty, who placed Poland under the Holy Roman See in 991. Mongol invasions in 1241–42 laid waste much of Poland and in 1308 the Teutonic Knights captured Gdańsk (Danzig), cutting off Poland's access to the sea. In 1386 the marriage of Jagiełło, grand duke of Lithuania, and Jadwiga, daughter of King Louis, brought Lithuania and Poland into personal union. The Jagiełłonian period was an economic and cultural golden age. The Accord of Lublin in 1569 created a political federation, the Commonwealth of Poland–Lithuania, to protect the alliance against an aggressive Russia under Ivan the Terrible. The death in 1572 of the last Jagiełłonian, Sigismund (Zygmunt) II, introduced a non-hereditary elective monarchy. Many foreigners were elected, including Prince István Báthory of Transylvania, who defeated Ivan the Terrible and won back territories lost to Russia.

Sigismund III Vasa was elected king in 1587. His deposition as king of Sweden led to the Polish–Swedish war of 1655–60, in which the Poles won a major battle at Częstochowa. The Great Northern War of 1700–21 saw Poland as the battleground for fighting between Russia, Prussia and Denmark against Sweden. Frederick II of Prussia proposed the division of Poland between Russia, Prussia and Austria—the first Partition of Poland, in 1772. In 1791 Stanisław II, the last king of the remaining Poland–Lithuania, made a bid for independence, which led to a second partition in 1793. A peasant uprising against Russian rule was crushed and Poland was entirely dismembered by Austria, Prussia and Russia in the third partition (1795).

In 1815 Russia took control of the 'Congress' Kingdom of Poland, with the tsar as its hereditary king. Uprisings were savagely suppressed. Widespread Russianization followed the January Uprising (1863–65), though serfdom was abolished. In German Poland Bismarck introduced German as the official language, as part of *Kulturkampf* (struggle with the Catholic Church). Habsburg-controlled Galicia was more tolerant of Polish nationalism and Poles rose to senior government positions. Józef Piłsudski's Socialists led an anti-Russian uprising in 1905 and Piłsudski worked with the Austrian government to expel the Russians during the First World War. However, independence only became achievable with international recognition of Polish self-determination, championed by US President Woodrow Wilson.

Poland regained its independence under Piłsudski's leadership on 11 Nov. 1918. Gdańsk was awarded the status of a free city, and the Polish Corridor was formed between East Prussia and the rest of Germany. Lithuanian Vilnius was seized by Poland in 1919 and annexed in 1922. Fighting also took place with Ukraine over Galicia. Poland narrowly won a war with Russia and signed the Soviet–Polish Peace Treaty in Riga in 1921. Factionalism allowed Piłsudski to mount a coup in May 1926, ruling as dictator until his death in 1935.

A non-aggression pact with Germany was signed in 1934. However, the Russo-German non-aggression pact of Aug. 1939 agreed to partition Poland in the event of war. British and French guarantees of Polish independence obliged them to declare war on Nazi Germany two days after Hitler's troops marched into Poland on 1 Sept. 1939. The German army annexed over half of the country within three weeks; Stalin's troops invaded on 17 Sept., leaving the country occupied for most of the war. The Nazis undertook a policy of liquidation, not only of Jews and ethnic 'undesirables' but also of the intelligentsia to eliminate the Polish leadership class. Over 6m. Poles, or 17% of the population, were killed in the war, half of them Jewish.

Polish forces regrouped under a government-in-exile headed by Gen. Władysław Sikorski and an underground national army, the AK, was formed in Poland. After Germany's invasion of the USSR in 1941, many of the largest concentration camps, and most of the extermination camps, were built on Polish soil, including Auschwitz and Treblinka. In 1943 a Jewish uprising in the Warsaw ghetto was crushed and in 1944 there was a second rebellion against Nazi occupation. The Red Army was on the threshold of Warsaw, but did not intervene. 150,000 civilians and 18,000 members of the AK died. The Soviets recognized the Communist-led 'Lublin Committee', which proclaimed itself the sole legal government when Lublin was liberated in July 1944.

The Potsdam conference set Poland's Western border along the Oder–Neisse line, resulting in Polish and German migration. A Communist-dominated coalition under Władysław Gomułka triumphed in the 1947 elections. Bolesław Beirut, leader of the USSR-backed Polish Communist Party, was named president. An independently minded politician, Gomułka opposed agricultural collectivization. He was removed as secretary general of the Polish Workers' Party (PPR) in Sept. 1948. The nationalization of industry, land expropriation and the restructuring of the economy to favour heavy industry, were accompanied in 1952 by a Soviet-style constitution and the renaming of the country as the People's Republic of Poland.

As food prices spiralled, workers' strikes in Poznań in 1956 were suppressed. Gomułka was reinstated and gained support for a 'Polish way' to socialism. He cut the power of the secret police and ended agricultural collectivization and attacks on the Church. However, when the economy failed to improve, Edward Gierek replaced him and launched a reform programme financed by Western banks. Increased meat prices in July 1980 led to more waves of strikes, culminating in the Lenin shipyards in Gdańsk, where the Solidarity movement was born. Its leader, Lech Wałęsa, demanded independent trade unions, the abolition of censorship and the release of political prisoners. In Feb. 1981 Gen. Wojciech Jaruzelski imposed martial law. When the government proposed unpopular economic reforms in 1987, support for Solidarity led to nationwide strikes. Jaruzelski was forced into negotiations with Wałęsa and the Catholic Church. Solidarity was given legal status and in return agreed to compete for only 35% of the seats in the Sejm. In July 1989 Solidarity won virtually all the seats they contested but refused to join the communists in a grand coalition. Solidarity's Tadeusz Mazowiecki was appointed Poland's first non-communist premier in over 40 years.

Wałęsa won the presidential election of Nov. 1990 and free parliamentary elections took place in Oct. 1991. Solidarity's loyalties as a trade union were often incompatible with its responsibilities as a political party. As the Polish economy grew, Wałęsa's popularity declined. He lost the presidential elections of 1995 to Aleksander Kwaśniewski. In 1997 a new constitution reduced the powers of the president and committed the country to a social market economy. Poland joined NATO in 1999 and on 1 May 2004 became a member of the European Union.

TERRITORY AND POPULATION

Poland is bounded in the north by the Baltic Sea and Russia, east by Lithuania, Belarus and Ukraine, south by the Czech Republic and Slovakia and west by Germany. Poland comprises an area of 312,685 sq. km (120,728 sq. miles).

At the census of 7 Dec. 1988 the population was 37,879,000 (18·47m. males; 63·7% urban). Population in 2002, 38,230,080 (51·4% female in 1999 and 62·6% urban in 2001); density, 122·2 per sq. km.

The UN gives a projected population for 2010 of 38·37m.

The country is divided into 16 regions or voivodships (*wojewodztwo*), created from the previous 49 on 1 Jan. 1999 following administrative reform. Area (in sq. km) and population (in 1,000) in 2002 (density per sq. km in brackets).

Voivodship	*Area*	*Population*	
Dolnośląskie	19,948	2,907	(146)
Kujawsko-Pomorskie	17,970	2,069	(115)
Lubelskie	25,114	2,199	(88)
Lubuskie	13,984	1,009	(72)
Łódzkie	18,219	2,613	(143)
Małopolskie	15,144	3,232	(213)
Mazowieckie	35,598	5,124	(144)
Opolskie	9,412	1,065	(113)
Podkarpackie	17,926	2,104	(117)
Podlaskie	20,180	1,209	(60)

Voivodship	*Area*	*Population*	
Pomorskie	18,293	2,180	(119)
Śląskie	12,294	4,743	(386)
Świętokrzyskie	11,672	1,297	(111)
Warmińsko-Mazurskie	24,203	1,428	(59)
Wielkopolskie	29,826	3,352	(112)
Zachodniopomorskie	22,902	1,698	(74)

Population (in 1,000) of the largest towns and cities (2002):

Warszawa (Warsaw)	1,671·7	Lublin	357·1	Toruń	211·2
Łódź	789·3	Katowice	327·2	Gliwice	203·8
Kraków (Cracow)	758·6	Białystok	291·4	Zabrze	195·2
Wrocław (Breslau)	640·4	Gdynia	253·5	Bytom	193·5
Poznań	578·9	Częstochowa	251·4	Bielsko-Biała	178·0
Gdańsk (Danzig)	461·3	Sosnowiec	232·6	Olsztyn	173·1
Szczecin (Stettin)	415·4	Radom	229·7	Rzeszów	160·4
Bydgoszcz	373·8	Kielce	212·4	Ruda Śląska	150·6

The population is 96·7% Polish. Minorities at the 2002 census included 173,153 Silesians, 152,987 Germans, 48,737 Belorussians and 30,957 Ukrainians. A movement for Silesian autonomy has attracted sufficient support to suggest that further moves towards decentralization may soon be considered. A Council of National Minorities was set up in March 1991. There is a large Polish diaspora, some 65% in the USA.

The national language is Polish.

SOCIAL STATISTICS

2001 (in 1,000): births, 368·2; deaths, 363·2; marriages, 195·1; divorces, 45·3; infant deaths, 2·8. Rates (per 1,000 population): birth, 9·5; death, 9·4; marriage (per 1,000 population), 5·0; divorce, 1·2; infant mortality (per 1,000 live births), 7·7. A law prohibiting abortion was passed in 1993, but an amendment of Aug. 1996 permits it in cases of hardship or difficult personal situation. The most popular age range for marrying in 1999 was 20–24 for both males and females. Expectation of life at birth, 2001, was 69·4 years for males and 77·8 years for females. In 1998 there were 22,200 emigrants (including 16,100 to Germany) and 8,900 immigrants. 71% of Polish emigrants between 1990 and 1998 settled in Germany. Number of suicides, 1997, 4,936; in 1996 the suicide rate per 100,000 population was 24·1 among males and 4·6 among females. Annual population growth rate, 1992–2002, 0·1%; fertility rate, 2001, 1·3 births per woman.

CLIMATE

Climate is continental, marked by long and severe winters. Rainfall amounts are moderate, with a marked summer maximum. Warsaw, Jan. 24°F (–4·3°C), July 64°F (17·9°C). Annual rainfall 18·3" (465 mm). Gdańsk, Jan. 29°F (–1·7°C), July 63°F (17·2°C). Annual rainfall 22·0" (559 mm). Kraków, Jan. 27°F (–2·8°C), July 67°F (19·4°C). Annual rainfall 28·7" (729 mm). Poznań, Jan. 26°F (–3·3°C), July 64°F (17·9°C). Annual rainfall 21·0" (534 mm). Szczecin, Jan. 27°F (–3·0°C), July 64°F (17·7°C). Annual rainfall 18·4" (467 mm). Wrocław, Jan. 24°F (–4·3°C), July 64°F (17·9°C). Annual rainfall 20·7" (525 mm).

CONSTITUTION AND GOVERNMENT

The present Constitution was adopted on 2 April 1997. The head of state is the *President*, who is directly elected for a five-year term (renewable once). The President may appoint, but may not dismiss, cabinets.

The authority of the republic is vested in the *Sejm* (Parliament of 460 members), elected by proportional representation for four years by all citizens over 18. There is a 5% threshold for parties and 8% for coalitions, but seats are reserved for representatives of ethnic minorities even if their vote falls below 5%. 69 of the Sejm seats are awarded from the national lists of parties polling more than 7% of the vote. The Sejm elects a *Council of State* and a *Council of Ministers.* There is also an elected 100-member upper house, the *Senate.* The President and the Senate each has a power of veto which only a two-thirds majority of the Sejm can override. The President does not, however, have a veto over the annual budget. The *Prime Minister* is chosen by the President with the approval of the Sejm.

A *Political Council* consultative to the presidency consisting of representatives of all the major political tendencies was set up in Jan. 1991.

National Anthem. 'Jeszcze Polska nie zginęła' ('Poland has not yet perished'); words by J. Wybicki, tune by M. Ogiński.

RECENT ELECTIONS

At the presidential elections on 8 Oct. 2000, 12 candidates stood; the electorate was 29,122,304 and turn-out was 61·0%. President Aleksander Kwaśniewski of the former communist Democratic Left Alliance (SLD) gained 53·9% of votes cast, Andrzej Olechowski (independent) 17·3% and Marian Krzaklewski of Solidarity Electoral Action (AWS) 15·6%. Other candidates obtained 6% or less.

Parliamentary elections were held on 23 Sept. 2001. The coalition of the Democratic Left Alliance (SLD) and the Union of Labour (UP) won 216 out of 460 seats with 41·0% of the votes. Other parties winning seats were: Citizen's Platform (PO), with 65 seats (12·7%); Self-Defense of the Polish Republic (SRP), 53 (10·2%); Law and Justice Party (PiS), 44 (9·5%); Polish People's Party (PSL), 42 (9·0%); League of Polish Families (LPR), 38 (7·9%); German Minority (MN), 2 (0·4%). In the Senate, the coalition of the Democratic Left Alliance and the Union of Labour won 75 seats, with the Blok Senat 2001 winning 15. The remaining eight seats were taken by other parties. Turn-out was 46·3%.

European Parliament. Poland has 54 representatives. At the June 2004 elections turn-out was 20·4%. The PO won 15 seats with 24·1% of votes cast (political affiliation in European Parliament: European People's Party–European Democrats); the LPR, 10 with 15·9% (Independence and Democracy Group); the PiS, 7 with 12·7% (Union for a Europe of Nations); the SRP, 6 with 10·8% (non-attached); the SLD-UP, 5 with 9·3% (Party of European Socialists); the Freedom Union, 4 with 7·3% (Alliance of Liberals and Democrats for Europe); the PSL, 4 with 6·3% (European People's Party–European Democrats); the Social Democratic Poland Party, 3 with 5·3% (Party of European Socialists).

CURRENT ADMINISTRATION

President: Aleksander Kwaśniewski; b. 1954 (SLD; elected Nov. 1995 and re-elected Oct. 2000).

In March 2004 Prime Minister Leszek Miller announced that he would resign after Poland joined the European Union on 1 May 2004. His successor, Marek Belka, was rejected by the Sejm on 14 May. President Kwaśniewski renominated Belka in June and he was confirmed by the Sejm on 24 June.

In March 2005 the coalition of SLD and UP consisted of:

Prime Minister: Marek Belka; b. 1952 (SLD; sworn in 2 May 2004).

Deputy Prime Minister, Minister of Economy and Labour: Jerzy Hausner. *Deputy Prime Minister, Member of Council of Ministers:* Izabela Jaruga-Nowacka. *Foreign Affairs:* Adam Rotfeld. *Culture:* Waldemar Dąbrowski. *Interior and Administration:* Ryszard Kalisz. *Science:* Michał Kleiber. *Agriculture and Rural Development:* Wojciech Olejniczak. *Infrastructure:* Krzysztof Opawski. *Social Policy:* Krzysztof Pater. *Finance:* Mirosław Gronicki. *Health:* Marek Balicki. *Justice:* Marek Sadowski. *National Education:* Mirosław Sawicki. *Treasury:* Jacek Socha. *National Defence:* Jerzy Szmajdziński. *Environment:* Jerzy Swatoń. *Minister and Member of Council of Ministers:* Sławomir Cytrycki.

Speaker of the Sejm: Włodzimierz Cimoszewicz (SLD).

Office of the Prime Minister: http://www.kprm.gov.pl

DEFENCE

Poland is divided into four military districts: Warsaw, Pomerania, Kraków and Silesia. In 2003 military expenditure totalled US$4,095m. (US$107 per capita), representing 2·0% of GDP.

Three-year civilian duty as a conscientious alternative to conscription of 12 months was introduced in 1988.

Army. Strength (2002) 104,050 (including 58,700 conscripts). In accordance with a programme of modernization of the armed forces, the strength has been gradually declining, from 230,000 in the socialist era in 1988 to 186,000 in 1995 and further to the current figure of just over 104,000. In addition there were 188,000 Army reservists in 2002 and 14,100 border guards.

Navy. The fleet comprises three ex-Soviet and one ex-Norwegian diesel submarines, one ex-Soviet destroyer, three frigates and four corvettes. Naval Aviation operated 26 combat aircraft (including MiG-21s) and 12 armed helicopters.

Personnel in 2002 totalled 14,300 including 7,500 conscripts and 2,000 in Naval Aviation. Bases are at Gdynia, Hel, Świnoujście and Kolobrzeg.

Air Force. The Air Force had a strength (2002) of 36,450 (14,800 conscripts). There are two air defence corps (North and South) with 201 combat aircraft (including MiG-21/29s and Su-22s).

INTERNATIONAL RELATIONS

A treaty of friendship with Germany signed on 17 June 1991 renounced the use of force, recognized Poland's western border as laid down at the Potsdam conference of 1945 (the 'Oder-Neisse line') and guaranteed minority rights in both countries.

Poland is a member of the UN, WTO, NATO, BIS, EU, the Council of Europe, OECD, OSCE, CEFTA, CERN, CEI, Council of the Baltic Sea States, IOM, the Antarctic Treaty and is an associate partner of the WEU. A referendum held on 8 June 2003 approved accession to the EU, with 77·4% of votes cast for membership and 22·6% against. Poland became a member of the EU on 1 May 2004.

ECONOMY

Agriculture accounted for 3·1% of GDP in 2002, industry 30·5% and services 66·4%.

Overview. Poland was the first former Soviet bloc country to embrace economic change. External shocks, tightening of fiscal policies and rising unemployment led to weak demand and output growth. The private sector accounted for 18% of GDP in 1989 and 70% of GDP in 1999, in spite of slow privatization in the manufacturing sector. In the early 1990s the informal market increased, employing around 2m. people. The industrial sector declined from 35% of GDP in 1992, to 27·8% in 1999 and the service sector expanded to 60% of GDP in 2000. The agricultural sector represents a large share of employment but accounted for only 3·3% of GDP in 2000. With EU membership, decline in farm employment is inevitable, and could cause social problems. Most of the banking sector has been privatized, as have many large industries. The economic environment is friendly, with transparent rules for investment and equal treatment for domestic and foreign firms. The high unemployment rate (above 19%) indicates that there are rigidities in the labour market.

Poland is fast becoming two nations, one of well-off city dwellers and one of poor villagers, many working on family farms. An east–west divide has also been emerging, the west benefiting from its close ties to Germany.

Currency. The currency unit is the *złoty* (PLN) of 100 *groszy*. A new złoty was introduced on 1 Jan. 1995 at 1 new złoty = 10,000 old złotys. Inflation dropped from 249% in 1990 to 14·9% in 1997, and further to 0·8% in 2003. The złoty became convertible on 1 Jan. 1990. In 1995 the złoty was subject to a creeping devaluation of 1·2% per month; it was allowed to float in a 14% (+/–7%) band from 16 May 1995. In April 2000 Poland introduced a floating exchange rate. Foreign exchange reserves were US$26,557m. and gold reserves 3·31m. troy oz in June 2002 (0·47m. troy oz in 1996). In Feb. 2002 total money supply was 88,109m. złotys.

Budget. Budget revenue and expenditure (in 1m. złotys):

	1997	*1998*	*1999*	*2000*	*2001*
Revenue	172,507	196,952	201,131	213,865	223,758
Expenditure	185,431	207,370	216,912	236,865	263,580

VAT is 22·0% (reduced rates, 7% and 3%). Taxes accounted for 87·9% of state revenues in 2001. Social security and welfare accounted for 51·5% of expenditures.

Performance. Real GDP growth was 1·4% in 2002, 3·8% in 2003 and 5·4% in 2004, making Poland the fastest growing economy in the EU in 2004. Total GDP in 2003 was US$209·6bn. Real GDP in 2002 was 30% higher than in 1989. No other ex-communist country has seen such consistent progress since 1989. The private sector accounts for more than 70% of GDP.

Banking and Finance. The National Bank of Poland (established 1945) is the central bank and bank of issue (*Governor*, Dr Leszek Balcerowicz). There were 73 banks operating at the end of 2000, of which only seven were controlled—directly or indirectly—by the Polish government through its state treasury. The largest bank is PKO Bank Polski, Poland's major savings bank, which had assets in 2002 of US$21·4bn. Other leading banks are Bank Pekao and BPH PBK.

In 2003 Poland received US$4,225m. of foreign direct investment, down from US$9,341m. in 2000 although up from just US$89m. in 1990. It receives the most foreign direct investment of any of the former socialist countries of central and eastern Europe. The total stock of FDI at the end of 2002 was US$47·9bn.

There is a stock exchange in Warsaw.

ENERGY AND NATURAL RESOURCES

Environment. Poland's carbon dioxide emissions from the consumption and flaring of fossil fuels in 2002 were the equivalent of 7·0 tonnes per capita.

Electricity. Installed capacity was 33·3m. kW in 2000. Production (2001) 142·76bn. kWh; consumption per capita was 3,592 kWh in 2000.

Oil and Gas. Total oil reserves (2002) amount to some 115m. bbls.; natural gas reserves (2002), 170bn. cu. metres. Crude oil production was 767,000 tonnes in 2001; natural gas (2002), 4·0m. cu. metres. The largest oil distributor is Polski Koncern Naftowy ORLEN SA, created by the merger of Petrochemia Płock and Centrala Produktów Naftowych.

Minerals. Poland is a major producer of coal (reserves of some 120,000m. tonnes), copper (56m. tonnes) and sulphur. Production in 2001 (in tonnes): coal, 103·9m.; brown coal, 59·5m.; salt (2002), 4·2m.; copper, 474,000; silver, 1,193.

Agriculture. Poland's agriculture sector employed 18·8% of the working population in 2000. In 2001 there were 13·97m. ha of arable land and 0·34m. ha of permanent crops. In 2001 private farms accounted for 84·5% of the total area of agricultural land, state-owned farms for 12·5% and collective farms 3·0%. There were 2m. farms in 2000. In 2001 agriculture, hunting and forestry contributed 3·8% of GDP.

Output in 2000 (in 1,000 tonnes): potatoes, 24,232; sugarbeets, 13,134; wheat, 8,503; rye, 4,003; barley, 2,783; cabbages, 1,899; apples, 1,450; oats, 1,070.

Livestock, 2001: cattle, 5·73m. (including cows, 3·01m.); pigs, 17·11m.; sheep, 340,000; horses, 550,000; chickens, 48m. Milk production (2001) was 7,025m. litres; meat (2000), 2·85m. tonnes; eggs (2000), 425,000 tonnes.

In 2001 there were 1,308,500 tractors and 97,000 harvester-threshers in use.

Forestry. In 2000 forest area was 9·05m. ha (predominantly coniferous), or 29·7% of the land area. State-owned forests account for 82% of Poland's forests, with the balance being private or municipal. Timber production in 2001 was 25·27m. cu. metres.

Fisheries. The catch was 225,916 tonnes in 2001; 208,127 tonnes were sea fish. In 2001 there were 7,100 people employed in the fishing industry.

INDUSTRY

The leading companies by market capitalization in Poland, excluding banking and finance, in Jan. 2002 were: Telekomunikacja Polska SA (TPSA), 21bn. złotys; Polski Koncern Naftowy Orlen SA (PKN), an oil company (9bn. złotys); and Agora SA, a media company (3bn. złotys).

In 2001 there were 2,054 state firms, 161,049 limited liability companies, 252,608 other companies and 18,812 co-operatives. Production in 2001 (in 1,000 tonnes): cement, 11,918; crude steel, 8,814; distillate fuel oil (2000), 7,219; pig iron (2002), 5,300; petrol (2000), 4,257; residual fuel oil (2000), 3,558; fertilizers, 2,280; paper and paperboard (2002), 2,230; ammonia, 2,070; nitrogenous acid, 2,060; sugar (2002), 2,038; sulphuric acid, 1,945; soda ash, 1,130; sulphur, 1,066; paints and lacquers, 696; plastics in primary forms, 656; vodka, 575; beer, 2,516·3m. litres; soft drinks, 2,185·2m. litres; mineral water, 1,392·5m. litres; cigarettes, 81·7bn. units; bricks, 779m. units; television receivers, 7,481,000 units; tractors, 5,667,000 units; washing machines, 685,000 units; refrigerators and freezers, 589,000 units; telephone sets, 496,000 units; cars, 364,000 units; buses, 1,643 units.

Output of light industry: cotton woven fabrics (2001), 285·0m. sq. metres; silk fabrics (2001), 25·0m. sq. metres; woollen woven fabrics (2001), 10·0m. sq. metres; synthetic fibres (1999), 74,100 tonnes; shoes (2002), 52·5m. pairs.

Restructuring plans were announced in June 1998 aimed at halving within five years the 330,000 workforce employed in the coal and steel industries, with 24 out of 65 coal-mines due to be closed. There has been some privatization in the steel industry.

Labour. In 2001 a total of 14,207,000 persons were in employment. In Dec. 2001, 3,008,000 persons worked in industry, 2,096,000 in trade and repairs, 916,000 in education, 865,000 in health and social services, 841,000 in property, renting and business activities, 772,000 in construction, and 734,000 in transport, storage and communications. The unemployment rate increased steadily for several years peaking at 19·8% in 2002, compared to the EU average of 7·7%. It has declined slightly since then, and in Dec. 2004 stood at 18·3%. Workers made redundant are entitled to one month's wages after one year's service, two months after two years' service and three months after three or more years' service. A five-day working week was introduced in May 2001. The number of hours worked was reduced to 40 in 2003. Retirement age is 60 for women and 65 for men.

Trade Unions. In 1980 under Lech Wałęsa, Solidarity was an engine of political reform. Dissolved in 1982 it was re-legalized in 1989 and successfully contested the parliamentary elections, but was defeated in 1993. It had 2·3m. members in 1991 and 1·2m. in 1998. The official union in the 1980s, OPZZ, had 5m. members in 1990; there were also about 4,000 small unions not affiliated to it. In 1998 OPZZ had 3m. members, and there were some 340 registered unions nationwide. As 22% of members of parliament belong to the two leading unions, they constitute a significant political influence.

INTERNATIONAL TRADE

There were over 30,000 joint ventures in Dec. 1998. Legislation of 1991 removed limits on the repatriation of profits, reduced the number of cases needing licences and ended a 10% ceiling on share purchases. Licenses are required for investment in ports, airports, arms manufacture, estate agency and legal services. Foreign debt was US$69,521m. in 2002.

An agreement of Dec. 1992 with the Czech Republic, Hungary and Slovakia abolished tariffs on raw materials and goods where exports do not compete directly with locally-produced items, and envisaged tariff reductions on agricultural and industrial goods in 1995–97.

Imports and Exports. Trade in US$1m.:

	1998	*1999*	*2000*	*2001*	*2002*
Imports f.o.b.	45,303	45,132	48,210	49,324	53,991
Exports f.o.b.	32,467	30,060	35,902	41,664	46,742

The main exports in 2001 were machinery and apparatus (20·4%); road vehicles (8·9%); food (7·1%); furniture and furniture parts (6·9%); chemicals and chemical products (5·9%). Leading imports were machinery and apparatus (26·1%); chemicals and chemical products (13·9%); road vehicles (7·8%); crude petroleum (5·7%); food (5·3%).

Main export markets, 2001: Germany, 34·4%; France, 5·4%; Italy, 5·4%; United Kingdom, 5·0%; Netherlands, 4·7%. Main import suppliers, 2001: Germany, 24·0%; Russia, 8·8%; Italy, 8·3%; France, 6·8%; UK, 4·2%. In 2000 trade with the European Union accounted for 70·0% of Polish exports and 61·2% of Polish imports.

COMMUNICATIONS

Roads. In 2001 there were 364,697 km of roads, including 399 km of motorways. In 2000 there were 9,991,260 passenger cars, 1,783,008 lorries and vans, 82,356 buses and 802,618 motorcycles and mopeds. In 2000 public transport totalled 31,735m. passenger-km and freight 72,843m. tonne-km. There were 5,534 road accident fatalities in 2001.

Rail. In 1999 Poland had 22,891 km of railways in use (11,614 km electrified). Over 95% is standard 1,435 mm gauge with the rest narrow gauge. By 2000 PKP, the country's train operator, was 6bn. złotys (US$1·3bn.) in debt. In 2001 railways carried 332·2m. passengers and 166·9m. tonnes of freight. Passenger-km travelled in 2001 came to 22·5bn. and freight tonne-km to 47·9bn. Some regional railways are operated by local authorities. A 12 km metro opened in Warsaw in 1995, and there are tram/light rail networks in 13 cities.

Civil Aviation. The main international airport is at Warsaw (Okęcie), with some international flights from Kraków (John Paul II Balice International), Gdańsk, Katowice, Poznań, Szczecin and Wrocław. The national carrier is LOT-Polish Airlines (68% state-owned). It flew 49·0m. km in 1999, carrying 2,140,700 passengers (1,791,100 on international flights). In 2000 Warsaw handled 4,325,815 passengers (3,820,330 on international flights) and 39,600 tonnes of freight.

Shipping. The principal ports are Gdańsk, Szczecin, Świnoujście and Gdynia. 47·75m. tonnes of cargo were handled in 2001. Ocean-going services are grouped into Polish Ocean Lines based on Gdynia and operating regular liner services, and the Polish Shipping Company based on Szczecin and operating cargo services. Poland also has a share in the Gdynia America Line. In 2001, 22·43m. tonnes of freight and 581,000 passengers were carried. In 2002 the merchant marine totalled 586,000 GRT. 524,000 GRT of shipping completed building in 1995. In 2001 vessels totalling 26,568,000 NRT entered ports and vessels totalling 31,730,000 NRT cleared. In 1999 there were 3,813 km of navigable inland waterways. In 2001 inland barges carried 10·3m. tonnes of freight (including coastal traffic).

Telecommunications. There were 21,404,700 telephone subscribers in 2001, or 554·1 per 1,000 persons. There were 14·0m. mobile phone subscribers in 2002. The privatization of *Telekomunikacja Polska* (TP SA), the former state telecom operator, was completed in 2001. It is 34% owned by France Télécom, the biggest foreign investor in Poland. In 2002 there were 4,079,000 PCs (105·6 per 1,000 persons), and in 1995, 55,000 fax machines. The number of Internet users in 2002 was 8·8m.

Postal Services. In 1999 there were 7,888 post offices. A total of 1,217m. pieces of mail were handled in 1995, or 32 items per person.

SOCIAL INSTITUTIONS

Justice. The penal code was adopted in 1969. Espionage and treason carry the severest penalties. For minor crimes there is provision for probation sentences and fines. In 1995 the death penalty was suspended for five years; it had not been applied since 1988. A new penal code abolishing the death penalty was adopted in June 1997.

There exist the following courts: one Supreme Court, one high administrative court, 10 appeal courts, 44 voivodship courts, 288 district courts, 66 family consultative centres and 34 juvenile courts. Judges and lay assessors are appointed. Judges for higher courts are appointed by the President of the Republic from candidatures proposed by the National Council of the Judiciary. Assessors are nominated by the Minister of Justice. Judges have life tenure. An ombudsman's office was established in 1987.

Family consultative centres were established in 1977 for cases involving divorce and domestic relations, but divorce suits were transferred to ordinary courts in 1990. 238,391 criminal sentences were passed in 1997. There were 1,093 convictions for murder in 1997. The population in penal institutions in March 2003 was 83,113 (218 per 100,000 of national population).

Religion. Church-State relations are regulated by laws of 1989 which guarantee religious freedom, grant the Church radio and TV programmes and permit it to run schools, hospitals and old age homes. The Church has a university (Lublin), an Academy of Catholic Theology and seminaries. The archbishop of Warsaw is the primate of Poland (since 1981, Cardinal Józef Glemp; b. 1929). The religious capital is Gniezno, whose archbishop will be the future primate. In Oct. 1978 Cardinal Karol Wojtyła, archbishop of Cracow, was elected Pope as John Paul II. In Sept. 2003 there were seven cardinals.

Statistics of major churches as at Dec. 1997:

Church	*Congregations*	*Places of Worship*[1]	*Clergy*	*Adherents*
Roman Catholic	9,941	17,188	26,911	34,841,893
Uniate	63	101	72	110,380
Old Catholics	149	148	145	50,918

Church	*Congregations*	*Places of Worship*[1]	*Clergy*	*Adherents*
Polish Orthodox	249	3250	292	555,765
Protestant (30 sects)	1,189	865	1,882	159,906
Muslim	10	12	10	5,227
Jewish	24	17	3	1,402
Jehovah's Witnesses	1,692	–	–	122,982

[1]Dec. 1994.

Education. Basic education from seven to 16 is free and compulsory. Free secondary education is then optional in general or vocational schools. Primary schools are organized in complexes based on wards under one director ('ward collective schools'). In 2000–01 there were: pre-primary schools, 18,003 with 885,400 pupils and 73,700 teachers; primary schools, 16,766 with 3,220,600 pupils and 226,400 teachers; lower secondary schools, 6,295 with 1,189,900 pupils and 70,100 teachers; upper secondary schools, 10,573 with 2,452,100 pupils and 135,300 teachers; tertiary institutions, 310 with 1,584,800 students and 79,900 academic staff. In 1997–98 institutions of higher education included 13 universities, 30 polytechnics, 10 agricultural schools, 93 schools of economics, 19 teachers' training colleges, 16 theological colleges and 11 medical schools. In the 15 years from 1980 to 1995 the number of university students in Poland more than trebled. During the 1990s there was a boom in private higher education—by 1998 a quarter of all students in higher education were at private colleges.

The adult literacy rate in 2001 was 99·7%.

Religious (Catholic) instruction was introduced in all schools in 1990; for children of dissenting parents there are classes in ethics.

In 2000–01 total expenditure on education came to 5·3% of GNP and 12·2% of total government spending.

Health. Medical treatment is free and funded from the state budget. Medical care is also available in private clinics. In 2000 there were 767 hospitals with a total of 214,680 beds. There were 85,031 physicians, 11,758 dentists, 189,632 nurses, 22,161 pharmacists and 21,997 midwives in 2000. In Jan. 1999 reform of the health care system was inaugurated. All citizens can now choose their own doctor, who is paid by one of the health-maintenance organizations which are financed directly from the state budget. The share of income tax paid by employers, equalling 7·5% of the amount earned by them, is assigned for the financing of the health care system. In 2001 Poland spent 6·3% of its GDP on health.

Welfare. Social security benefits are administered by the State Insurance Office and funded 45% by a payroll tax and 55% from the state budget. Pensions, disability payments, child allowances, survivor benefits, maternity benefits, funeral subsidies, sickness compensation and alimony supplements are provided. In 2000 social benefits totalling 108,597·7m. złotys were paid (including 92,680·0m. złotys in retirement pay and pensions). There were a total of 9,412,000 pensioners in 2000. Unemployment benefits are paid from a fund financed by a 3% payroll tax. It is indexed in various categories to the average wage and payable for 12 months.

CULTURE

World Heritage Sites. The ten sites under Polish jurisdiction included on the UNESCO world heritage list (with year entered) are: Kraków's Historic Centre (1978), Poland's former capital; Wieliczka Salt Mine (1978), a mine since the 13th century; Auschwitz Concentration Camp (1979), the German concentration camp and nearby Birkenau death camp; Historic Centre of Warsaw (1980), celebrating the 20th century reconstruction of the city's 18th century heart decimated during World War II; Old City of Zamosc (1992), a 16th century town; Medieval Town of Toruń (1997); Castle of the Teutonic Order in Malbork (1997), a medieval brick castle; Kalwaria Zebrzydowska: the Mannerist Architectural and Park Landscape Complex and Pilgrimage Park (1999); Churches of Peace in Jawor and Świdnica (2001), Europe's biggest timber-framed religious buildings; Wooden Churches of Southern Little Poland (2003).

In addition, Poland and Belarus are jointly responsible for Belovezhskaya Pushcha/Bialowieza Forest (1979), in the Baltic/Black Sea region; and Poland and Germany are jointly responsible for Muzkauer Park/Park Muzakowski (2004), a landscaped park astride the Neisse river.

Broadcasting. The public *Polskie Radio i Telewizja* broadcasts three radio programmes and two TV programmes. There are also four commercial TV channels, *Polsat*, *TVN*, *RTL7* and *Nasza TV*. Colour programmes are transmitted by the PAL system. A direct-to-home satellite pay television service was launched in 1998. A digital TV platform *Wizja TV* started broadcasting in Sept. 1998, followed by *Canal Plus'* digital platform. Links with the West are provided through the Eutelstat satellite. Some cable programmes are broadcast in Polish from abroad. In 1992 independent radio and TV broadcasting were introduced under the aegis of a nine-member National Council of Broadcasting and Television. Radio sets in use in 2000, 20·2m.; TV sets in 2001, 15·5m.

Press. In 2000 there were 42 daily newspapers with a combined daily circulation of 3,928,000 (102 per 1,000 inhabitants). The most popular newspapers are *Gazeta Wyborcza, Rzeczpospolita* and the tabloid *Super Express.* 19,192 book titles were published in 1999 (including 4,176 literature, 3,829 social sciences and 3,304 applied sciences).

Tourism. There were 17·4m. foreign visitors in 2000 bringing in revenue of US$6·1bn. Germans account for about 60% of all tourists to Poland.

Festivals. The most significant festivals are the International Chopin Festival at Duszniki Zdrój, held in Aug., and the Warsaw Autumn Festival, held in Sept. The Kraków 2000 Festival had four main themes—Images of God, Sounds of Eternity, Places of Mystery and Magical Words.

DIPLOMATIC REPRESENTATIVES

Of Poland in the United Kingdom (47 Portland Pl., London, W1B 1JH)
Ambassador: Zbigniew Matuszewski.

Of the United Kingdom in Poland (Aleje Róż 1, 00-556 Warsaw)
Ambassador: Charles Crawford, CMG.

Of Poland in the USA (2640 16th St., NW, Washington, D.C., 20009)
Ambassador: Przemysław Grudziński.

Of the USA in Poland (Aleje Ujazdowskie 29/31, 00-540 Warsaw)
Ambassador: Victor Ashe.

Of Poland to the United Nations
Ambassador: Andrzej Towpik.

Of Poland to the European Union
Ambassador: Marek Grela.

FURTHER READING

Central Statistical Office, *Rocznik Statystyczny*. Annual.—*Concise Statistical Yearbook of Poland.—Statistical Bulletin*. Monthly.

Lukowski, Jerzy and Zawadzki, Hubert, *A Concise History of Poland.* CUP, 2001
Mitchell, K. D. (ed.) *Political Pluralism in Hungary and Poland: Perspectives on the Reforms.* New York, 1992
Prazmowska, Anita J., *History of Poland.* Palgrave Macmillan, Basingstoke, 2004
Sanford, G. and Gozdecka-Sanford, A., *Poland.* [Bibliography] 2nd ed. ABC-Clio, Oxford and Santa Barbara (CA), 1993
Sikorski, R., *The Polish House: An Intimate History of Poland.* London, 1997; US title: *Full Circle.* New York, 1997
Slay, B., *The Polish Economy: Crisis, Reform and Transformation.* Princeton Univ. Press, 1994
Staar, R. F. (ed.) *Transition to Democracy in Poland.* New York, 1993
Turner, Barry, (ed.) *Central Europe Profiled.* Macmillan, London, 2000
Wedel, J., *The Unplanned Society: Poland During and After Communism.* Columbia Univ. Press, 1992

National library: Biblioteka Narodowa, Rakowiecka 6, Warsaw.
National statistical office: Central Statistical Office, Aleje Niepodległości 208, 00-925 Warsaw.
Website: http://www.stat.gov.pl

PORTUGAL

República Portuguesa

Capital: Lisbon
Population projection, 2010: 10·08m.
GDP per capita, 2002: (PPP$) 18,280
HDI/world rank: 0·897/26

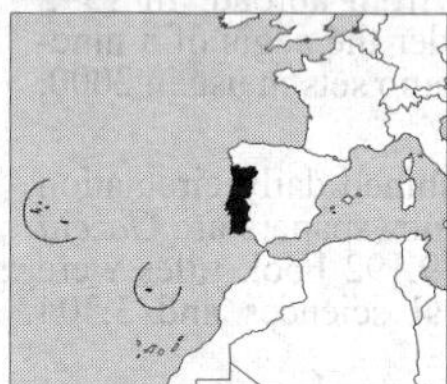

KEY HISTORICAL EVENTS

Western Iberia was inhabited from 8000 BC by Neolithic peoples known as Iberians; Celtic tribes arrived in the north and west in the first millennium BC. Phoenicians colonized the southwest around Cádiz from around 800 BC. After the expulsion of Carthage from Spain in 206 BC, Roman power extended throughout the peninsula. The Lusitani, possibly a Celtic federation, were defeated in 139 BC. From AD 409, with the Roman Empire in decline, the Iberian Peninsula was invaded by Germanic tribes from central Europe, including the Suevi and Visigoths, who established Christian kingdoms. Following the arrival of Muslim armies in Iberia in 711, the southern part of what is now Portugal became part of the Muslim dominion of al-Andalus. The northern and western fringes of Iberia remained largely agrarian, poor and Christian.

Northern Portugal was liberated by Asturias and León; the first king of Portugal, Afonso Henriques, was crowned in 1139. Afonso fought southwards through the Muslim strongholds, capturing Lisbon in 1147. However, the Portuguese reconquest was not completed for 150 years, when Afonso III finally took Algarve in the far south. Afonso III established the first Cortes (assembly) at Leiria in 1254.

Fernando (1367–83) became involved in the Castilian conflict between King Pedro the Cruel and his half brother Enrique de Trastámara, who became Enrique II of Castile in 1369. Fernando's heiress, Beatriz, married Enrique's son, Juan I of Castile, but commoners in Portugal's coastal towns rejected Castilian rule and chose João of Aviz, half brother of Fernando, as king in 1384. A year later, assisted by English archers, the Portuguese won a famous victory over Juan I's Castilian army at the battle of Aljbarrota, securing Portuguese independence.

The capture of Ceuta on the North African coast in 1415 was the beginning of a remarkable era of discovery by Portuguese mariners, spearheaded by João's third son, Henry the Navigator. Madeira and the Azores were rediscovered, though not settled until 1445. In 1487 Bartolomeu Dias rounded the southern cape of the African continent but Christopher Columbus' Spanish patronage resulted in the 1493 Treaty of Tordesillas, which gave Spain all lands west of a vertical line drawn 370 degrees west of the Cape Verde islands. Land to the east was to be the property of Portugal, which included Brazil. In 1497 Vasco da Gama set out from Lisbon to chart a sea route to India. The Portuguese built an administrative capital at Goa and by 1550 it was considered the nation's second city. Fortified trading posts were later established along the coast of East Africa and India. The vast profits generated by the spice trade made Manuel I, the Fortunate, one of the wealthiest rulers in Europe. When King Sebastião inherited the throne in 1557, he launched a disastrous crusade to eradicate Islam in the Maghreb. More than 10,000 Portuguese troops were killed, including Sebastião himself by superior Moroccan forces.

The extinction of the Aviz line in 1580 allowed Felipe II of Spain to claim and annex Portugal. In 1621 a rebellion in Catalonia spurred the Portuguese to rally around the duke of Bragança, who was crowned João IV in 1640. Spain's peace with France, in the 1659 Treaty of the Pyrenees, made João's successor, Afonso VI, anxious to strengthen Portugal's alliance with England. Thus Catherine of Bragança was married to King Charles II in 1662. Her dowry included the right to trade with the Portuguese colonies and the cession of Bombay and Tangier. In return, England agreed to defend Portugal and its colonies.

In 1796 Republican France forced an alliance on a weakened Spain. In 1801 Napoléon and Spain demanded that Portugal abandon its alliance with Britain and open its ports to French and Spanish shipping. When Portugal refused, a French army marched into Lisbon in 1807. The royal family escaped to Brazil with the help of the British, who drove the French out of Portugal in 1811. João VI returned from Brazil in 1822 and accepted a new constitution. Brazil declared its independence, with Pedro IV (João's elder son) as emperor. Following João's death in 1826, Pedro also became king of Portugal but abdicated in favour of his daughter, Maria II, on condition that she accept a new charter limiting royal authority and marry Miguel, his brother. Miguel instead seized the throne and defeated the liberals. Incensed, Pedro IV returned to Portugal in 1832 and Maria was restored to the throne.

Exploration in Africa strengthened Portugal's hold on Angola and Mozambique but the British refused to give up territory that would have linked the two colonies. Amidst growing public discontent, Carlos and his eldest son, Prince Luís Filipe, were assassinated in 1908. Manuel II succeeded to the throne but in 1910 a republican revolution forced his abdication and flight to Britain. In the First World War Portugal was at first neutral, then joined the Allies in 1916. António de Oliveira Salazar became prime minister in 1932. His *Estado Novo* (New State) was nationalist and dictatorial. Political parties, unions and strikes were abolished and dissent was crushed by the notorious PIDE secret police. Portugal was neutral in the Second World War but allowed the Allies to establish naval and air bases. Goa was seized by India in 1961 but Salazar was determined to cling on to Angola, Guinea-Bissau and Mozambique. By 1968 over 100,000 Portuguese were fighting in Africa.

In 1968 Salazar was replaced by Marcello Caetano. In 1974, amid mounting public discontent, a group of officers toppled the government in a bloodless coup known as 'the Revolution of the Carnations'. Gen. António de Spínola was appointed head of the ruling military junta. The secret police force was abolished, all political prisoners were released and full civil liberties were restored. In 1975 Angola, Mozambique, São Tomé e Príncipe and Cape Verde were granted independence but East Timor was seized by Indonesia. In late 1975 the military junta was dissolved, giving way to moderate, socialist governments, which tried unsuccessfully to stabilize the country. In 1982 a centre-right coalition revised the constitution, reducing presidential power and the right of the military to intervene in politics. From 1983–85 a coalition government under the Socialist party leader, Mário Soares, began dismantling the legacy of Salazar's long dictatorship.

In 1986 Soares was elected to the presidency and Portugal was admitted to the European Community. Political stability and economic reforms created a favourable business climate and Portugal became one of the fastest growing economies in Europe. Macao, Portugal's colony on the south coast of China, was handed back to China in 1999. Portugal joined the single European currency in 2001, and in 2002 José Manuel Durão Barroso of the centre-right Social Democratic Party was elected prime minister.

TERRITORY AND POPULATION

Mainland Portugal is bounded in the north and east by Spain and south and west by the Atlantic Ocean. The Atlantic archipelagoes of the Azores and of Madeira form autonomous but integral parts of the republic, which has a total area of 91,905 sq. km. Population (2001 census), 10,356,117 (5,355,976 females).

Mainland Portugal is divided into five regions. At the time of the 2001 census the regions, with their populations, were: North (3,687,293); Central (1,783,596); Lisbon and Tagus Valley (3,467,483); Alentejo (535,753); Algarve (395,218). Population of the Azores, 241,763; Madeira, 245,011. Density (2001), 113 per sq. km (North, 173; Central, 75; Lisbon and Tagus Valley, 291; Alentejo, 20; Algarve, 79; Azores, 104; Madeira, 315). In 2002 Lisbon and Tagus Valley became a smaller Lisbon province, with Central and Alentejo increasing in size. The United Nations population estimate for 2000 was 10,016,000.

The UN gives a projected population for 2010 of 10·08m.

In 2001, 65·6% of the population lived in urban areas. The populations of the districts and Autonomous Regions (2001 census):

Areas	*Population*	*Areas*	*Population*
North	*3,687,293*	Tâmega	551,309
Alto Trás os Montes	223,333	*Central*	*1,783,596*
Ave	509,968	Baixo Mondego	340,309
Cávado	393,063	Baixo Vouga	385,724
Douro	221,853	Beira Interior Norte	115,325
Entre Douro e Vouga	276,812	Beira Interior Sul	78,123
Grande Porto	1,260,680	Cova da Beira	93,579
Minho-Lima	250,275	Dão Lafões	286,313

Areas	*Population*	*Areas*	*Population*
Pinhal Interior Norte	138,535	Oeste[1]	338,711
Pinhal Interior Sul	44,803	Península de Setúbal	714,589
Pinhal Litoral	250,990	*Alentejo*	*535,753*
Serra da Estrela	49,895	Alentejo Central	173,646
Lisbon and Tagus Valley[2]	*3,467,483*	Alentejo Litoral	99,976
		Alto Alentejo	127,026
Grande Lisboa	1,947,261	Baixo Alentejo	135,105
Lezíria do Tejo[3]	240,832	*Algarve*	*395,218*
Médio Tejo[1]	226,090		

[1]Now part of Central. [2]Lisbon since 2002. [3]Now part of Alentejo.

In 1999, 190,896 foreigners were legally registered: 89,516 African; 20,887 Brazilian; 13,344 British; 11,152 Spanish; 7,975 American. 200,000 immigrants have come to Portugal from eastern Europe since 1999.

The chief cities are Lisbon (the capital; 2001 metropolitan area population, 2,683,000), Oporto (2001 metropolitan area population, 1,261,000), Amadora, Braga, Coimbra, Funchal and Setúbal.

The national language is Portuguese.

The Azores islands lie in the mid-Atlantic Ocean, between 1,200 and 1,600 km west of Lisbon. They are divided into three widely separated groups with clear channels between, São Miguel (759 sq. km) together with Santa Maria (97 sq. km) being the most easterly; about 160 km northwest of them lies the central cluster of Terceira (382 sq. km), Graciosa (62 sq. km), São Jorge (246 sq. km), Pico (446 sq. km) and Faial (173 sq. km); still another 240 km to the northwest are Flores (143 sq. km) and Corvo (17 sq. km), the latter being the most isolated and undeveloped of the islands. São Miguel contains over half the total population of the archipelago.

Madeira comprises the island of Madeira (745 sq. km), containing the capital, Funchal; the smaller island of Porto Santo (40 sq. km), lying 46 km to the northeast of Madeira; and two groups of uninhabited islets, Ilhas Desertas (15 sq. km), being 20 km southeast of Funchal and Ilhas Selvagens (4 sq. km), near the Canaries.

SOCIAL STATISTICS

Statistics for calendar years:

	Marriages	*Live births*	*Still births*	*Deaths*	*Divorces*
1997	65,770	112,933	506	104,778	14,078
1998	66,598	113,384	454	106,198	15,278
1999	68,710	116,002	437	107,871	17,676
2000	63,752	120,008	445	105,364	19,104
2001	58,390	112,774	390	105,092	18,851

Vital statistics rates, 2000 (per 1,000 population): birth, 10·9; death, 10·2. Annual population growth rate, 1992–2002, 0·2%. In 2001 the most popular age range for marrying was 25–29 for both males and females. Expectation of life at birth, 2001, was 72·3 years for males and 79·4 years for females. Infant mortality in 2001 was 5 per 1,000 live births, down from 77 per 1,000 live births in 1960, representing the greatest reduction in infant mortality rates in Europe over the past 40 years. Around one in five babies are born outside marriage, up from one in 14 in 1970. Fertility rate, 2001, 1·5 births per woman.

In 2002 Portugal received 245 asylum applications.

CLIMATE

Because of westerly winds and the effect of the Gulf Stream, the climate ranges from the cool, damp Atlantic type in the north to a warmer and drier Mediterranean type in the south. July and Aug. are virtually rainless everywhere. Inland areas in the north have greater temperature variation, with continental winds blowing from the interior. Lisbon, Jan. 52°F (11°C), July 72°F (22°C). Annual rainfall 27·4" (686 mm). Oporto, Jan. 48°F (8·9°C), July 67°F (19·4°C). Annual rainfall 46" (1,151 mm).

CONSTITUTION AND GOVERNMENT

A new Constitution, replacing that of 1976, was approved by the Assembly of the Republic (by 197 votes to 40) on 12 Aug. 1982 and promulgated in Sept. It abolished the (military) Council of the Revolution and reduced the role of the President under it. Portugal is a sovereign, unitary republic. Executive power is vested in the *President*, directly elected for a five-year term (for a maximum of two consecutive terms). The President appoints a Prime Minister and, upon the latter's nomination, other members of the Council of Ministers.

The 230-member *National Assembly* is a unicameral legislature elected for four-year terms by universal adult suffrage under a system of proportional representation. Women did not have the vote until 1976.

Portugal's first referendum, on whether to ease abortion restrictions, was held on 28 June 1998. Turn-out was just 32%, but the result would have had legal force only if more than half the electorate had voted. 51% of voters favoured keeping most abortions a crime, against 49% in favour of permitting the procedure on demand.

National Anthem. 'Herois do mar, nobre povo' ('Heroes of the sea, noble breed'); words by Lopes de Mendonça, tune by Alfredo Keil.

RECENT ELECTIONS

At the presidential elections of 14 Jan. 2001, Jorge Fernando Branco de Sampãio was re-elected President by 55·8% of votes cast against Joaquim Ferreira do Amaral (Social Democrat) who gained 34·5%.

At the parliamentary elections of 20 Feb. 2005 the Socialist Party (PS) won 121 seats (45·1% of votes cast); the Social Democratic Party (PSD), 75 (28·7%); the Communist Party/Green Party coalition (Unitarian Democratic Coalition; UDC), 14 (7·6%); the Popular Party (PP), 12 (7·3%); and the Left Bloc (BE), 8 (6·4%). Turn-out was 65·0%.

European Parliament. Portugal has 24 (25 in 1999) representatives. At the June 2004 elections turn-out was 38·7% (40·4% in 1999). The PS won 12 seats with 45·0% of votes cast (political affiliation in European Parliament: Party of European Socialists); the PSD 7 and the PP 2, with a combined vote of 34·0% (European People's Party–European Democrats); the UDC, 2 with 9·0% (European Unitary Left/Nordic Green Left); the BE, 1 with 5·0% (European Unitary Left/Nordic Green Left).

CURRENT ADMINISTRATION

President: Jorge Sampãio; b. 1939 (PS; first sworn in 9 March 1996 and re-elected Jan. 2001).

In March 2005 the Socialist Party government was composed as follows:

Prime Minister: José Sócrates; b. 1957 (PS; sworn in 12 March 2005).

Ministers of State: Luís Campos e Cunha (also *Minister of Finance*); Diogo Freitas do Amaral (also *Minister of Foreign Affairs*); António Costa (also *Minister of Internal Affairs*).

Minister of Agriculture, Rural Development and Fisheries: Jaime Silva. *Culture:* Isabel Pires de Lima. *Economy and Innovation:* Manuel Pinho. *Education:* Maria de Lurdes Rodrigues. *Environment, Territorial Planning and Regional Development:* Francisco Nunes Correia. *Health:* António Correia de Campos. *Justice:* Alberto Costa. *Labour and Social Security:* José Vieira da Silva. *National Defence:* Luís Amado. *Parliamentary Affairs:* Augusto Santos Silva. *Public Works, Transportation and Communications:* Mário Lino. *Science, Technology and Higher Education:* Mariano Gago. *Minister for the Presidency:* Pedro Silva Pereira.

Government Website: http://www.portugal.gov.pt

DEFENCE

Conscription was abolished in Nov. 2004. Portugal now has a purely professional army.

In 2003 defence expenditure totalled US$3,173m. (US$311 per capita), representing 2·1% of GDP.

Army. Strength (2002) 25,400. There are Army reserves totalling 210,000. Paramilitary forces include the National Republican Guard (25,600) and the Public Security Police (20,800).

Navy. The combatant fleet comprises two French-built diesel submarines and six frigates. Naval personnel in 2002 totalled 10,800 (360 conscripts) including 1,580 marines. There were 930 naval reserves.

Air Force. The Air Force in 2002 had a strength of about 7,000. There were 50 combat plus 15 in store.

INTERNATIONAL RELATIONS

Portugal is a member of the UN, WTO, BIS, EU, OECD, NATO, WEU, the Council of Europe, OSCE, CERN, Inter-American Development Bank and IOM. Portugal is a signatory to the Schengen Accord abolishing border controls between Portugal, Austria, Belgium, Denmark, Finland, France, Germany, Greece, Iceland, Italy, Luxembourg, the Netherlands, Norway, Spain and Sweden.

The Community of Portuguese-speaking Countries (CPLP, comprising Angola, Brazil, Cape Verde, Guinea-Bissau, Mozambique, Portugal and São Tomé e Príncipe) was founded in July 1996 with headquarters in Lisbon, primarily as a cultural and linguistic organization.

ECONOMY

Services account for about 68% of GDP, industry 28% and agriculture 4%.

Overview. A reform of the tax system is a priority. Tax evasion is high but there are low and lightly enforced penalties. Portugal needs more public investment to close its development gap with the rest of the EU but also needs to cut its budget deficit. This will require increased tax revenues. Low interest rates have encouraged domestic companies to invest abroad. With low-cost manufacturing locations in central and eastern Europe, Portugal can no longer rely on low wages to attract foreign investment. The privatization programme has been ambitious, although no major enterprises have been privatized since 1999.

Currency. On 1 Jan. 1999 the euro (EUR) became the legal currency in Portugal; irrevocable conversion rate 200·482 escudos to 1 euro. The euro, which consists of 100 cents, has been in circulation since 1 Jan. 2002. There are seven euro notes in different colours and sizes denominated in 500, 200, 100, 50, 20, 10 and 5 euros, and eight coins denominated in 2 and 1 euros, then 50, 20, 10, 5, 2 and 1 cents. On the introduction of the euro there was a 'dual circulation' period before the escudo ceased to be legal tender on 28 Feb. 2002. Euro banknotes in circulation on 1 Jan. 2002 had a total value of €10·6bn.

Inflation was 3·7% in 2002 and 3·3% in 2003. Gold reserves were 19·51m. troy oz in June 2002 and foreign exchange reserves US$10,125m. Total money supply was €7,091m. in June 2002.

Budget. In 2000 revenues totalled €44·9bn. (€42·0bn. in 1999) and expenditures €47·3bn. (€44·1bn. in 1999). Principal sources of revenue in 2000: taxes on goods and services, €14·2bn.; social security contributions, €12·6bn.; taxes on income, profits and capital gains, €11·1bn. Main items of expenditure by economic type in 2000: social benefits, €16·1bn.; compensation of employees, €15·2bn.; use of goods and services, €3·7bn.

The standard rate of VAT is 19·0% (reduced rates, 12% and 5%).

Performance. In 2001 GDP growth was 1·7%, falling to 0·4% in 2002. There was then a recession in 2003, with the economy shrinking by 1·3%. In the years since Portugal joined the European Union its GDP per head has risen from being 53% of the EU average to being 71% in 2001. Portugal's total GDP in 2003 was US$149·5bn.

Banking and Finance. The central bank and bank of issue is the Bank of Portugal, founded in 1846 and nationalized in 1974. Its *Governor* is Vítor Manuel Ribeiro Constâncio.

On 31 Dec. 1998 there were 81 banks, 6 savings institutions and 160 mutual agricultural credit institutions. The largest Portuguese bank is the state-owned Caixa Geral de Depósitos, which held 21% of all deposits at the end of 1998. There were 19 branches of foreign credit institutions operating in Portugal in 1998.

There are stock exchanges in Lisbon and Oporto.

ENERGY AND NATURAL RESOURCES

Environment. Portugal's carbon dioxide emissions from the consumption and flaring of fossil fuels in 2002 were the equivalent of 6·7 tonnes per capita.

Electricity. Installed capacity was 10·9m. kW in 2000. Production in 2000 was 47·46bn. kWh; consumption per capita was 4,835 kWh. Portugal's electricity market is in the process of being fully liberalized.

Minerals. Portugal possesses considerable mineral wealth. Production in tonnes (2001): limestone, marl and calcite, 37,654,000; granite, 30,155,000; marble, 835,000; salt, 625,785; kaolin, 146,436; copper, 82,965; tin, 1,174; tungsten, 698.

Agriculture. There were 416,000 farms in 2000. The agricultural sector employs 11·5% of the workforce. In 2001 there were 1·99m. ha of arable land and 715,000 ha of permanent crops.

The following figures show the production (in 1,000 tonnes) of the chief crops:

Crop	*1997*	*1998*	*1999*	*Crop*	*1997*	*1998*	*1999*
Cabbages[1]	140	140	140	Olive oil[2]	424	361	512
Carrots	116	145	174	Olives	278	286	262
Fruits				Onions	105	101	121
oranges	204	262	204	Potatoes	1,049	1,225	947
apples	283	162	292	Rice	164	162	152
grapes	843	500	1,041	Sugarbeets	150	183	507
pears	173	19	131	Tomatoes	793	1,089	1,010
Maize	913	1,024	935	Wheat	329	151	352
Oats	44	29	100	Wine[2]	5,914	3,580	7,602

[1]Estimates. [2]In hectolitres.

Livestock (1,000 head):

	1997	*1998*	*1999*
Cattle	1,386	1,409	1,421
Pigs	2,394	2,385	2,350
Sheep	3,432	3,590	3,584
Goats	673	676	630
Poultry[1]	28,000	28,000	28,000

[1]Estimates.

Animal products (mainland) in 1999 (1,000 tonnes): meat, 763·5; milk, 1,636·6; eggs, 90·2; cheese, 51·1.

Forestry. Forests covered 3·67m. ha (40·1% of the land area) in 2000. Portugal is a major producer of cork. Estimated production, 1998, 193,000 tonnes, production of resin (1999), 20,000 tonnes. Timber production was 11·26m. cu. metres in 2001.

Fisheries. The fishing industry is important, although less so than in the past, and the Portuguese eat more fish per person than in any other European Union member country (more than twice the EU average). In 1999 there were 10,933 registered fishing vessels (8,556 with motors) and 26,638 registered fishermen. The catch was 191,214 tonnes in 2001 (almost exclusively from marine waters), down from 410,000 tonnes in 1986.

The 1999 fishing catch consisted of:

Species	*Tonnes*	*Escudos (1m.)*
Sardine	69,448	7,835
Mackerel	30,200	4,623
Shellfish	23,570	18,258
Other	64,804	33,314
Total	188,022	64,030

INDUSTRY

The leading companies by market capitalization in Portugal in May 2004 were: Portugal Telecom SGPS SA (US$12·9bn.); EDP—Electricidade de Portugal (US$8·1bn.); and BCP—Banco Comercial Português (US$7·6bn.).

Output of major industrial products (in tonnes unless otherwise specified):

Product	*1998*	*1999*
Ready-mix concrete	16,358,158	21,025,065
Portland cement	9,784,058	10,078,694
Refined sugar	381,200	359,662
Preparation of animal food feeds	3,883,029	3,737,917
Beer (hectolitres)	7,072,383	6,944,028
Discontinuous synthetic fibre fabric[1]	71,706	66,453
Footwear with leather uppers (1,000 pairs)	61,813	69,900

Product	*1998*	*1999*
Wood pulp	1,688,263	1,741,803
Paper and cardboard	1,122,417	1,142,804
Petrol	2,792,796	2,651,908
Diesel fuel	4,339,836	4,278,908
Glass bottles (1,000)	2,943,432	3,366,832

[1]In 1,000 sq. metres.

Labour. The maximum working week was reduced to 40 hours in 1997. A minimum wage is fixed by the government. In 2004 the minimum wage was €365·60 a month. Retirement is at 65 years for men and 62 for women. In 2000, out of a working population of 5,113,100 (2,782,700 male), 4,908,500 (2,694,800 male) were employed. Unemployment has been gradually increasing, from 4·1% in 2001 to 5·1% in 2002 and further to 6·4% in 2003. By Jan. 2004 it was up to 6·7%. Employment (in 1,000) by sector, 2000 (males in parentheses): services, 2,572·5 (1,187·1); industry, construction, energy and water, 1,719·6 (1,205·3); agriculture, forestry and fishing, 616·3 (302·3). The immigrant population makes up 10% of the labour force.

Trade Unions. In 1999 there were 380 unions. An agreement between trade unions, employers and the government for 1997 involved employment, social security, investment, tax reform and education.

INTERNATIONAL TRADE

Imports and Exports. In 2003 imports (c.i.f.) totalled US$43·71bn. (US$36·94bn. in 2002); exports (f.o.b.), US$30·49bn. (US$24·96bn. in 2002).

In 2003 chemicals, manufactured goods classified chiefly by material and miscellaneous manufactured articles accounted for 40·6% of Portugal's imports and 50·2% of exports; machinery and transport equipment 33·9% of imports and 36·7% of exports; food, live animals, beverages and tobacco 11·3% of imports and 6·8% of exports; mineral fuels, lubricants and related materials 10·4% of imports and 2·5% of exports; and crude materials, inedible, animal and vegetable oil and fats 3·8% of imports and 3·8% of exports.

Imports and exports to main trading partners, 2002 and 2003 (in US$1m.):

	Imports		*Exports*	
From or to	*2002*	*2003*	*2002*	*2003*
Spain	10,266·4	12,505·4	5,058·1	6,782·0
Germany	5,515·4	6,429·2	4,650·8	4,668·4
France	3,755·9	4,307·6	3,045·7	3,884·4
UK	1,917·5	2,131·4	2,628·0	3,322·2
Italy	2,346·0	2,765·5	1,179·8	1,472·8
Netherlands	1,697·9	1,963·6	944·2	1,151·2
Belgium/Luxembourg	1,202·0	1,418·5	1,159·3	1,434·6
USA	853·4	874·3	1,445·0	1,800·8

In 2003 fellow European Union members accounted for 76·0% of Portugal's imports and 78·5% of exports.

COMMUNICATIONS

Roads. In 2001 there were 1,659 km of motorways, 7,510 km of national roads and 4,500 km of secondary roads. In 2001 the number of vehicles registered included 4,416,557 passenger cars, 572,082 motorcycles and mopeds, 334,379 vans and lorries and 18,280 buses and coaches. In 2002 there were 1,655 deaths in road accidents. With 16·0 deaths per 100,000 population in 2002, Portugal has among the highest death rates in road accidents of any industrialized country.

Rail. In 1999 total railway length was 3,579 km. Passenger-km travelled in 2000 came to 3·63bn. and freight tonne-km to 2·18bn. There is a metro (19 km) and tramway (94 km) in Lisbon. A new metro was opened in Oporto in 2002.

Civil Aviation. There are international airports at Portela (Lisbon), Pedras Rubras (Oporto), Faro (Algarve) and Funchal (Madeira). The national carrier is the state-owned TAP-Air Portugal, with some domestic and international flights being provided by Portugália. In 1998 TAP flew 77·7m. km, carrying 4,680,900 passengers; Portugália flew 18·4m. km, carrying 841,600 passengers (472,300 international). In 2000 Lisbon handled 9,213,724 passengers (7,040,503 on international flights) and 104,254 tonnes of freight. Faro was the second busiest in terms of passenger traffic, with 4,571,022 passengers, and Oporto was the second busiest for freight, with 40,755 tonnes.

Shipping. In 1999, 21,296 vessels of 229·06m. tonnes entered the mainland ports. 213,402 passengers embarked and 210,315 disembarked at all Portuguese ports during 1999; 13·88m. tonnes of cargo were loaded and 47·08m. tonnes unloaded. In 2002 merchant ships totalled 1,100,000 GRT, including oil tankers 424,000 GRT.

Telecommunications. Portugal Telecom (PT) was formed from a merger of three state-owned utilities in 1994. It is now fully privatized. Telephone subscribers numbered 12,889,900 in 2002 (1,238·3 per 1,000 population) and there were 1,394,000 PCs in use (133·9 per 1,000 persons). There were 8,528,900 mobile phone subscribers in 2002 and 70,000 fax machines in 1999. Portugal had 4·4m. Internet users in June 2002.

Postal Services. The number of post offices was 1,060 in 1999; a total of 1,221m. pieces of mail were processed during 1999.

SOCIAL INSTITUTIONS

Justice. There are four judicial districts (Lisbon, Oporto, Coimbra and Evora) divided into 47 circuits. In 1999 there were 353 common courts, including 319 of the first instance. There are also 29 administration and fiscal courts.

There are four courts of appeal in each district, and a Supreme Court in Lisbon.

Capital punishment was abolished completely in the Constitution of 1976.

In 1999 there were 53 prisons with an inmate capacity of 11,185. The population in penal institutions in May 2003 was 14,300 (137 per 100,000 of national population).

Religion. There is freedom of worship, both in public and private, with the exception of creeds incompatible with morals and the life and physical integrity of the people. There were 9·52m. Roman Catholics in 2001. In Sept. 2003 there were two cardinals.

Education. Adult literacy rate was 92·5% in 2001 (male 95·0%; female 90·3%). Compulsory education has been in force since 1911, but only 9·8% of the population goes on to further education, compared to the EU average of 21·2%.

In 2000–01 there were 6,233 pre-school establishments (3–6 years) with 224,575 pupils, and 13,859 compulsory basic school establishments (6–10 years) with 1,139,402 pupils. There were 378,691 pupils in secondary schools in 2000–01. There were 35,949 teachers on the mainland in the 1st cycle of basic school, and 113,267 in the 2nd and 3rd cycles of basic school and in secondary schools.

The state university system consists of 14 universities in the public sector and one institute, the Higher Institute of Employment and Business Sciences. There are also ten universities in the private sector and a Roman Catholic university. In 1997–98 there were a total of 204 higher education institutes altogether with a total of 351,784 students. Females account for 64% of Portugal's university graduates.

Total expenditure on education came to 6·1% of GNP in 2001–02 (12·7% of total government expenditure).

Health. In 1998 there were 215 hospitals; and in 1999, 39 clinics and 512 medical centres. In 1999 there were 31,758 doctors, 2,676 dentists, 7,114 pharmacists and 32,984 nurses. In 2002 Portugal spent 9·3% of its GDP on health. Portugal has one of the highest alcohol consumption rates in Europe. Among EU countries only the French drink more. The average Portuguese adult drinks 13·6 litres of alcohol a year, compared to the EU average of 11·1 litres.

Welfare. In 1999, 4,278,479m. escudos were paid in social security benefits. Cash payments in escudos (and types) were: 1,560,983m. (old age), 1,433,485m. (sickness), 517,389m. (disability), 309,051m. (survivors), 223,117m. (family), 159,571m. (unemployment), 74,281m. (social exclusion), 602m. (housing).

CULTURE

World Heritage Sites. (With year entered on list). In the Central Zone of the Town of Angra do Heroísmo in the Azores (1983) are the fortresses of San Sebastião and

San Filipe, the latter built around 1590 on the orders of King Phillip II of Spain. The Monastery of the Hieronymites was built at the turn of the 16th century in Belém, Lisbon, while the capital's Tower of Belém was constructed as a monument to Vasco da Gama's explorations (both 1983). The Monastery of Batalha (1983) near Leiria was built from 1388. The Convent of Christ in Tomar (1983) was originally built in 1160 as the centre of the Templar order. It was taken over by the Order of Christ in 1360 of which Henry the Navigator was made governor in 1418, and was greatly enriched in the 16th century. Other sites are the medieval walled Historic Centre of Evora (1988), the Gothic Cistercian 12th century Monastery of Alcobaça, north of Lisbon (1989), the Cultural Landscape of Sintra (1995), the Historic Centre of Oporto (1996), the Upper Palaeolitic Rock-Art Sites in the Côa Valley (1998) and the Laurisilva of Madeira (1999), an area of biodiverse laurel forest. In 2001 two more sites were added: the Alto Douro Wine Region, famous for its port wine since the 18th century, and the Historic Centre of Guimarães, a town closely associated with the formation of Portuguese identity. The Landscape of the Pico Island Vineyard Culture followed in 2004.

Broadcasting. *Radiodifusão Portuguesa* broadcasts three programmes on medium wave and on FM as well as three regional services and an external service, Radio Portugal (English, French, Italian). There are two state-owned TV channels (Canal 1 and Radiotelevisão Portuguesa 2) and two independent channels, including one religious (colour by PAL). Radio Trans Europe is a high-powered short-wave station, retransmitting programmes of different broadcasting organizations. Number of receivers: TV (2001), 4·27m.; radio (2000), 3·08m. In 2001 there were 1·12m. cable TV subscribers.

Press. In 1999 there were 35 daily newspapers (morning and evening editions) including seven in the Azores and two on Madeira, with a combined annual circulation of 545,092,479. In addition there were 845 periodicals in 1999 with a combined circulation of 219,376,189. In 1998 a total of 9,196 book titles were published.

Tourism. In 2000 tourist revenue increased to US$5,206m. In 1999 there were (in 1,000) 27,016 foreign visitors (26,560 in 1998), including from Spain, 20,507; UK, 1,970; Germany, 980; France, 763; the Netherlands, 483; Italy, 307. There were 1,722 hotel establishments with 216,828 accommodation capacity in 1999. Tourism accounts for 8% of GDP.

DIPLOMATIC REPRESENTATIVES

Of Portugal in the United Kingdom (11 Belgrave Sq., London, SW1X 8PP)
Ambassador: Fernando Andresen Guimarães.

Of the United Kingdom in Portugal (Rua de São Bernardo 33, 1200 Lisbon)
Ambassador: Dame Glynne Evans, DBE, CMG.

Of Portugal in the USA (2125 Kalorama Rd, NW, Washington, D.C., 20008)
Ambassador: Pedro Manuel Dos Reis Alves Catarino.

Of the USA in Portugal (Ave. das Forcas Armadas, 1600 Lisbon)
Ambassador: John N. Palmer.

Of Portugal to the United Nations
Ambassador: João Manuel Guerra Salgueiro.

FURTHER READING

Instituto Nacional de Estatística. *Anuário Estatístico de Portugal/Statistics Year-Book.—Estatísticas do Comércio Externo.* 2 vols. Annual from 1967

Birmingham, David, *A Concise History of Portugal.* CUP, 1993
Laidlar, John, *Lisbon.* [Bibliography] ABC-Clio, Oxford and Santa Barbara (CA), 1997
Maxwell, K., *The Making of Portuguese Democracy.* CUP, 1995
Page, Martin, *The First Global Village: How Portugal Changed the World.* Editorial Notícias, Lisbon, 2002
Saraiva, J. H., *Portugal: A Companion History.* Manchester, 1997
Wheeler, D. L., *Historical Dictionary of Portugal.* Metuchen (NJ), 1994
National library: Biblioteca Nacional de Lisboa, Campo Grande, Lisbon.

National statistical office: Instituto Nacional de Estatística (INE), Avenida António José de Almeida, 1000–043 Lisbon.
Website: http://www.ine.pt

QATAR

Dawlat Qatar
(State of Qatar)

Capital: Doha
Population projection, 2010: 670,000
GDP per capita, 1996: (PPP$) 18,789
HDI/world rank: 0·833/47

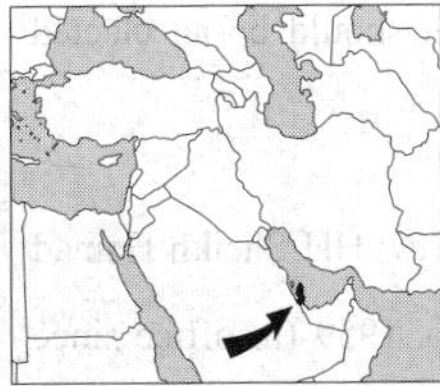

KEY HISTORICAL EVENTS

Qatar embraced Islam in the 7th century AD. As with the rest of the Middle East, Qatar came under Turkish rule for several centuries. Ottoman power was nominal, with real power being in the hands of local sheikhs and tribal leaders. In 1915 the Turks withdrew, and on 3 Nov. 1916 Qatar signed a protection treaty with Britain. The dominant economic activity had traditionally been pearl diving, but around 1930 the pearl market collapsed. In 1939 oil was discovered. Although the Second World War delayed progress, exporting began in 1949. This was to change Qatar dramatically. Qatar declared its independence from Britain on 3 Sept. 1971, ending the Treaty of 1916 which was replaced by a treaty of friendship between the two countries.

TERRITORY AND POPULATION

Qatar is a peninsula running north into the Persian Gulf. It is bounded in the south by the United Arab Emirates. The territory includes a number of islands in the coastal waters of the peninsula, the most important of which is Halul, the storage and export terminal for the offshore oilfields. Area, 11,493 sq. km; population (2004 census), 744,029 (496,382 males); density 64·7 per sq. km. In 2001, 92·9% of the population lived in urban areas.

The UN gives a projected population for 2010 of 670,000.

In 2004 there were ten municipalities:

	2004 census population		*2004 census population*
Doha	339,847	Al Jumayliyah	10,303
Al Rayyan	272,860	Al Shamal	4,915
Al Wakra	31,441	Jarian Al Batnah	6,678
Umm Salal	31,605	Al Ghwayriyah	2,159
Al Khour	31,547	Mesaieed	12,674

The capital is Doha, which is the main port, and had an estimated population in 1999 of 391,000. Other towns are Dukhan (the centre of oil production), Umm Said (the oil-terminal of Qatar), Ruwais, Wakra, Al-Khour, Umm Salal Mohammad and Umm-Bab.

About 40% of the population are Arabs, 18% Indian, 18% Pakistani and 10% Iranian. Other nationalities make up the remaining 14%.

The official language is Arabic.

SOCIAL STATISTICS

Births, 2002, 12,200; deaths, 1,220; marriages, 2,351; divorces, 732. 2002 rates per 1,000 population: births, 20·3; deaths, 2·0. Qatar's 2002 death rate was the second lowest in the world (only Kuwait's was lower). Infant mortality, 2001 (per 1,000 live births), 11. Expectation of life in 2001 was 70·1 years for males and 75·0 for females. Annual population growth rate, 1992–2002, 2·0%. Fertility rate, 2001, 3·4 births per woman.

CLIMATE

The climate is hot and humid. Doha, Jan. 62°F (16·7°C), July 98°F (36·7°C). Annual rainfall 2·5" (62 mm).

CONSTITUTION AND GOVERNMENT

Qatar is ruled by an *Amir.* HH Sheikh Hamad bin Khalifa Al Thani, KCMG (b. 1950) assumed power after deposing his father on 27 June 1995. The heir apparent was Sheikh Hamad's third son, Sheikh Jasim bin Hamad Al Thani (b. 1978), but in

Aug. 2003 he named his fourth son, Sheikh Tamim bin Hamad Al Thani (b. 1979), as heir apparent instead.

Qatar's first written constitution was approved in June 2004 and was set to come into force in June 2005. It allows for a 45-member *Consultative Council* or *Majlis al-Shura*, with 30 members directly elected and 15 appointed by the Amir.

A *Council of Ministers* is assisted by a 35-member nominated Advisory Council.

RECENT ELECTIONS

It was decided in 1998 that the Central Municipal Council should be an elected Assembly.

CURRENT ADMINISTRATION

In March 2005 the government comprised:

Amir, Minister of Defence and C.-in-C. of the Armed Forces: HH Sheikh Hamad bin Khalifa Al Thani; b. 1952.

Prime Minister: Sheikh Abdallah bin Khalifa Al Thani; b. 1959 (in office since 29 Oct. 1996).

First Deputy Prime Minister and Minister of Foreign Affairs: Sheikh Hamad bin Jasim bin Jabir Al Thani. *Second Deputy Prime Minister and Minister of Energy and Industry:* Abdallah bin Hamad al-Attiyah. *Deputy Prime Minister:* Muhammad bin Khalifa Al Thani. *Economy and Commerce:* Sheikh Mohammed bin Ahmed bin Jassim Al Thani. *Finance:* Yusif Husayn al-Kamal. *Education:* Sheikha Ahmad Al-Mahmoud. *Justice:* Hasan bin Abdallah al-Ghanim. *Endowments and Islamic Affairs:* Mohammed bin Abdulatif bin Abdulrahman Almani. *Municipal Affairs and Agriculture:* Hassan Dhabit al-Dousari. *Public Health:* Dr Hajar bin Ahmad al-Hajar. *Housing and Civil Service Affairs:* Sheikh Falah bin Jasim bin Jabir Al Thani. *Minister of State for Interior Affairs:* Sheikh Hamad Bin Nassir Bin Jassim Al-Thani.

DEFENCE

Defence expenditure in 2003 totalled US$1,923m. (US$3,082 per capita), representing 10·0% of GDP. The expenditure per capita in 2003 was the highest in the world.

Army. Personnel (2002) 8,500.

Navy. Personnel in 2002 totalled 1,800; the base is at Doha.

Air Force. The Air Force operates 18 combat aircraft including Mirage 2000 fighters and 19 armed helicopters. Personnel (2002) 2,100.

INTERNATIONAL RELATIONS

Qatar is a member of the UN, WTO, the League of Arab States, OPEC, the Gulf Co-operation Council, OIC and Islamic Development Bank.

In March 2001 the International Court of Justice ruled on a long-standing dispute between Bahrain and Qatar over the boundary between the two countries and ownership of certain islands. Both countries accepted the decision.

ECONOMY

Industry accounted for 70·7% of GDP in 2002, services 28·9% and agriculture 0·4%.

Currency. The unit of currency is the *Qatari riyal* (QAR) of 100 *dirhams*, introduced in 1973. Foreign exchange reserves were US$1,184m. in April 2002 and gold reserves 169,000 troy oz. Total money supply in April 2002 was 5,685m. riyals. There was inflation of 1·0% in 2002.

In 2001 the six Gulf Arab states—Qatar, along with Bahrain, Kuwait, Oman, Saudi Arabia and the United Arab Emirates—signed an agreement to establish a single currency by 2010.

Budget. Revenue (2001–02) 22,754m. riyals; expenditure, 20,504m. riyals. Crude oil accounts for about 90% of revenues.

Performance. Real GDP growth was 11·6% in 2000, 7·2% in 2001 and 3·0% in 2002. Qatar's total GDP in 2001 was US$16·5bn.

Banking and Finance. The Qatar Monetary Agency, which functioned as a bank of issue, became the Central Bank in 1995 (*Governor*, Abdullah Atiyya). In 2003 there were eight commercial domestic banks and seven foreign banks. The largest bank is the Qatar National Bank, with assets in 2003 of 34·8bn. riyals.

A stock exchange was established in Doha by the Amir's decree in 1995, initially to trade only in Qatari stocks.

Heavy investment in energy development increased foreign debt from US$1,300bn. in 1991 to US$10,400bn. in 1997.

ENERGY AND NATURAL RESOURCES

Environment. Qatar's carbon dioxide emissions from the consumption and flaring of fossil fuels in 2002 were the equivalent of 46·1 tonnes per capita, the highest of any sovereign country.

Electricity. Installed capacity was 1·9m. kW in 2000. Production was 9·17bn. kWh in 2000; consumption per capita was 16,227 kWh.

Oil and Gas. Proven reserves of oil (2002) 15·2bn. bbls. Output, 2002, 34·7m. tonnes. Oil accounted for 59% of GDP in 2002.

The North Field, the world's biggest single reservoir of gas and containing 12% of the known world gas reserves, is half the size of Qatar itself. Development cost is estimated at US$25bn. In 2002 natural gas reserves were 14,400bn. cu. metres (the third largest after Russia and Iran); output in 2002 was 29·3bn. cu. metres.

Water. Two main desalination stations have a daily capacity of 167·6m. gallons of drinkable water. A third station is planned, with a capacity of 40m. gallons a day.

Agriculture. 10% of the working population is engaged in agriculture. Percentage of total agricultural area under various crops in 1993: vegetables, 28%; green fodder, 23%; cereals, 22%; palm dates, 20%; and fruits, 7%. Government policy aims at ensuring self-sufficiency in agricultural products. In 2001, 13,000 ha were irrigated. There were 18,000 ha of arable land in 2001 and 3,000 ha of permanent crops. Production (2000) in 1,000 tonnes: dates, 17; tomatoes, 11; pumpkins and squash, 9; aubergines, 5; barley, 5; cucumbers and gherkins, 5; melons and watermelons, 5; onions, 4.

Livestock (2000): sheep, 215,000; goats, 179,000; camels, 50,000; cattle, 14,000; chickens, 4m. Livestock products, 2000 (in 1,000 tonnes): meat, 13; milk, 11; eggs, 4.

Fisheries. The catch in 2001 totalled 8,606 tonnes, entirely from sea fishing. The state-owned Qatar National Fishing Company has three trawlers and its refrigeration unit processes 10 tonnes of shrimps a day.

INDUSTRY

According to the Financial Times Survey (FT 500), the largest companies in Qatar by market capitalization on 4 Jan. 2001 were Qatar Telecom Company (US$1,642·7m.) and Qatar National Bank (US$1,283·4m.).

2001 output (in 1,000 tonnes): ammonia, 1,408; cement, 1,209; residual fuel oil (2000), 940; steel billets, 891; urea (1998), 875; propane (2002), 743; steel bars, 714; butane (2002), 618; distillate fuel oil (2000), 602; ethylene, 535; polyethylene (2002), 379. There is an industrial zone at Umm Said.

Labour. In 1998 the labour force totalled 293,000. In 1999 males constituted 85% of the labour force—only the United Arab Emirates had a lower percentage of females in its workforce.

INTERNATIONAL TRADE

Qatar, along with Bahrain, Kuwait, Oman, Saudi Arabia and the United Arab Emirates began the implementation of a customs union in Jan. 2003.

Imports and Exports. Total imports and exports in calendar years (in 1m. riyals):

	1999	*2000*	*2001*	*2002*
Imports	8,196	10,664	12,323	13,287
Exports	26,258	42,202	39,571	39,960

The main exports are petroleum products (75%), steel and fertilizers. Main imports are machinery and equipment, consumer goods, food and chemicals. Main export markets in 2002: Japan, 46·7%; South Korea, 15·8%; Singapore, 9·3%; United Arab Emirates, 4·0%; Thailand, 3·4%. Main import suppliers, 2002: USA, 14·5%; Japan, 11·7%; Italy, 10·0%; UK, 8·5%; United Arab Emirates, 7·8%.

COMMUNICATIONS

Roads. In 1999 there were about 1,230 km of roads, of which 1,100 km were paved. Passenger cars in 2002 numbered 230,155 (374 per 1,000 inhabitants); there were 14,344 trucks and vans and 104,341 buses and coaches. In 2002 there were 68,550 road traffic accidents resulting in 148 fatalities.

Civil Aviation. Gulf Air is owned equally by Qatar, Bahrain, Oman and the UAE. In 2003 it operated services from Doha International to Abu Dhabi and Bahrain. A Qatari airline, Qatar Airways, operates on the same routes, and in 2003 additionally flew to Amman, Bangkok, Beirut, Bombay, Cairo, Casablanca, Colombo, Damascus, Damman, Dhaka, Dubai, Frankfurt, Hyderabad, Islamabad, Jakarta, Jeddah, Karachi, Kathmandu, Khartoum, Kochi, Kuala Lumpur, Kuwait, Lahore, London, Malé, Manchester, Manila, Milan, Munich, Muscat, Paris, Peshawar, Riyadh, Salalah, Sana'a, Sharjah and Thiruvananthapuram. In June 2003 Qatar Airways commissioned 32 aircraft worth US$5·1bn. from Airbus SAS. Doha handled 2,642,000 passengers (all on international flights) and 67,600 tonnes of freight in 2000.

Shipping. In 2002 sea-going vessels totalled 623,000 GRT, including oil tankers 210,000 GRT. In 1993, 1,383 vessels with a total tonnage of 66,255,841 GRT and 2,697,629 tonnage of cargo was discharged.

Telecommunications. Qatar had 443,200 telephone subscribers in 2002, or 726·6 per 1,000 persons, and there were 110,000 PCs in use. There were 267,200 mobile phone subscribers in 2002 and 10,000 fax machines in 1998. In 2002 there were approximately 70,000 Internet users.

Postal Services. There were 26 post offices in 1999.

SOCIAL INSTITUTIONS

Justice. The Judiciary System is administered by the Ministry of Justice which comprises three main departments: legal affairs, courts of justice and land and real estate register. There are five Courts of Justice proclaiming sentences in the name of HH the Amir: the Court of Appeal, the Labour Court, the Higher Criminal Court, the Civil Court and the Lower Criminal Court. The death penalty is in force. In 2003 there was one execution. The population in penal institutions in 2000 was 570 (95 per 100,000 of national population).

All issues related to personal affairs of Muslims under Islamic Law embodied in the Holy Quran and Sunna are decided by Sharia Courts.

Religion. The population is almost entirely Muslim.

Education. Adult literacy rate was 81·7% in 2001 (80·8% among males and 83·7% among females). There were, in 2002–03, 56,821 pupils and 5,460 teachers at 162 primary schools, 15,825 pupils and 1,784 teachers at secondary schools and, in 2000–01, 7,808 students and 595 teachers at higher education institutions. There were 265 Arab and foreign private schools with 56,183 pupils and 4,092 teachers in 2002–03. The University of Qatar had 7,867 students and 676 academic staff in 2003–04.

Students abroad (2003–04) numbered 374. In 2002–03, 2,009 men and 940 women attended night schools and literacy centres.

Health. There were three government and two private hospitals in 2002. In 2002 there were 1,204 government-employed doctors, 145 government-employed dentists, 279 government-employed pharmacists and 3,139 government-employed nurses.

CULTURE

Broadcasting. The government ministry of information operates the Qatar Broadcasting Service and the Qatar Television Service. The Qatar Television Service transmits in Arabic (Qatar Television One, on channels 9 and 11) and in English

(Qatar Television Two, on channel 37). Transmissions are received from Bahrain, the United Arab Emirates or Saudi Arabia. There are also satellite and cable broadcasters (Al-Jazeera Satellite Channel and Qatar Cable Vision). Al-Jazeera has a reputation for outspoken, independent reporting and has become increasingly high-profile since the attacks on the USA on 11 Sept. 2001. There were 530,000 television receivers in use (colour by PAL) in 2001 and 256,000 radios in 1997.

Press. There are three Arabic language daily newspapers—*Al-Rayah*, *Al-Sharq* and *Al-Watan*. The *Gulf Times* and *Al-Jazeera* (The Peninsula) are English dailies. In 1996 the combined circulation was 90,000.

Tourism. In 1998 there were 451,000 foreign tourists.

DIPLOMATIC REPRESENTATIVES

Of Qatar in the United Kingdom (1 South Audley St., London, WIK 1NB)
Ambassador: Nasser Bin Hamid M. Al-Khalifa.

Of the United Kingdom in Qatar (PO Box 3, Doha, Qatar)
Ambassador: David MacLennan.

Of Qatar in the USA (4200 Wisconsin Ave., NW, Washington, D.C., 20016)
Ambassador: Bader Omar Al Dafa.

Of the USA in Qatar (22 February Street, Doha)
Ambassador: Chase Untermeyer.

Of Qatar to the United Nations
Ambassador: Nassir Abdulaziz Al-Nasser.

Of Qatar to the European Union
Ambassador: Vacant.
Chargé d'Affaires a.i.: Khamis B. Al-Sahoti.

FURTHER READING

Central Statistical Organization. *Annual Statistical Abstract.*
El-Nawawy, Mohammed and Iskandar, Adel, *Al-Jazeera: How the Free Arab News Network Scooped the World and Changed the Middle East.* Westview Press, Boulder (CO), 2002
Unwin, P. T. H., *Qatar.* [Bibliography] ABC-Clio, Oxford and Santa Barbara (CA), 1982

National statistical office: Central Statistical Organization, Presidency of the Council of Ministers, Doha.

ROMANIA

România

Capital: Bucharest
Population projection, 2010: 21·97m.
GDP per capita, 2002: (PPP$) 6,560
HDI/world rank: 0·778/69

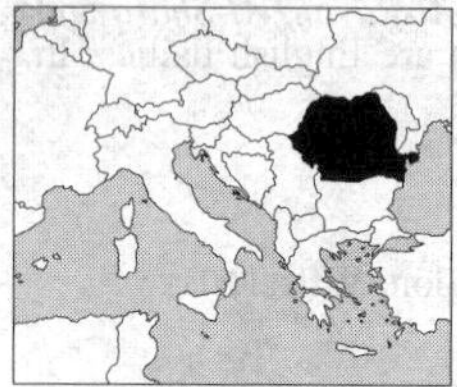

KEY HISTORICAL EVENTS

The foundation of the feudal 'Danubian Principalities' of Wallachia and Moldavia in the late 13th and early 14th centuries marks the beginning of modern Romania. The nobility acted as the Turks' agents until 1711 when, suspected of pro-Russian sentiments, they were replaced by Greek merchant adventurers, the Phanariots. The Phanariot period of ruthless extortion and corruption was ameliorated by Russian influence. Between 1829 and 1834 the foundations of the modern state were laid but Russian interference soon became repressive. The Moldavian and Wallachian assemblies were fused in 1862. In 1866 Carol of Hohenzollern came to the throne and a constitution adopted based on that of Belgium of 1831. Romania was formally declared independent by the Treaty of Berlin of 1878.

This was a period of expansion for an economy controlled by land-owners and nascent industrialists. The condition of the peasantry remained miserable and the rebellion of 1907 was an expression of their discontent. Romania joined the First World War on the allied side in 1916. The spoils of victory brought Transylvania (with large Hungarian and German populations), Bessarabia, Bukovina and Dobrudja into the union with the 'Old Kingdom'. Hit by the world recession, Romania was drawn into Germany's economic orbit. Against this background the fascist Iron Guard assassinated the Liberal leader in 1934. Carol II adopted an increasingly totalitarian rule. Following Nazi and Soviet annexations of Romanian territory in 1940, he abdicated in favour of his son Michael. The government of the fascist Ion Antonescu declared war on the USSR on 22 June 1941. On 23 Aug. 1944 Michael, with the backing of a bloc of opposition parties, deposed Antonescu and switched sides.

The armistice of Sept. 1944 gave the Soviet army control of Romania's territory. This, and the 'spheres of influence' diplomacy of the Allies, predetermined the establishment of communism in Romania. Transylvania was restored to Romania (although it lost Bessarabia and Southern Dobrudja), and large estates were broken up for the benefit of the peasantry. Elections in Nov. 1946 were held in an atmosphere of intimidation and fraudulence. Michael was forced to abdicate and a people's republic was proclaimed. The communist leader, Gheorghe Gheorghiu-Dej, purged himself of his fellow leaders in the early 1950s. Under his successor, Nicolae Ceauşescu, Romania took a relatively independent stand in foreign affairs while becoming increasingly repressive and impoverished domestically.

An attempt by the authorities on 16 Dec. 1989 to evict a Protestant pastor, László Tökés, from his home in Timişoara, provoked a popular protest which escalated into a mass demonstration against the government. A state of emergency was declared but the Army went over to the rebels and Nicolae and Elena Ceauşescu fled the capital. A dissident group which had been active before the uprising, the National Salvation Front (NSF), proclaimed itself the provisional government. The Ceauşescus were captured and after a secret two hour trial by military tribunal, summarily executed on 25 Dec. The following day Ion Iliescu, leader of the National Salvation Front, was sworn in as President. But the Iliescu-led administration, while committed to reform, was inhibited by its communist origins. The economy stalled and the debts piled up. Iliescu was voted out of office and his government replaced by a four-party coalition led by President Emil Constantinescu. Iliescu returned as president in 2000. The economy continued to struggle but in 2004 Romania joined NATO and was given a target date of 2007 for EU membership.

TERRITORY AND POPULATION

Romania is bounded in the north by Ukraine, in the east by Moldova, Ukraine and the Black Sea, south by Bulgaria, southwest by Serbia and Montenegro and northwest by Hungary. The area is 238,391 sq. km. Population (2002 census), 21,698,181; density, 91·0 per sq. km. In 2001, 55·3% of the population lived in urban areas.

The UN gives a projected population for 2010 of 21·97m.

Romania is divided into 41 counties (*județ*) and the municipality of Bucharest (Bucuresti).

County	Area in sq. km	Population (2002 census)	Capital	Population (in 1,000) (2002)
Bucharest[1]	238	1,921,751		
Alba	6,242	382,999	Alba Iulia	66
Arad	7,754	461,730	Arad	173
Argeş	6,826	653,903	Piteşti	169
Bacău	6,621	708,751	Bacău	176
Bihor	7,544	600,223	Oradea	206
Bistriţa-Năsăud	5,355	312,325	Bistriţa	81
Botoşani	4,986	454,023	Botoşani	115
Brăila	4,766	373,897	Brăila	217
Braşov	5,363	588,366	Braşov	284
Buzău	6,103	494,982	Buzău	133
Călăraşi	5,088	324,629	Călărasi	70
Caraş-Severin	8,520	333,396	Reşiţa	84
Cluj	6,674	703,269	Cluj-Napoca	318
Constanţa	7,071	715,172	Constanţa	310
Covasna	3,710	222,274	Sf. Gheorghe	61
Dâmboviţa	4,054	541,326	Tîrgovişte	89
Dolj	7,414	734,823	Craiova	303
Galaţi	4,466	619,522	Galaţi	299
Giurgiu	3,526	298,022	Giurgiu	70
Gorj	5,602	387,409	Tîrgu Jiu	97
Harghita	6,639	326,020	Miercurea-Ciuc	42
Hunedoara	7,063	487,115	Deva	69
Ialomiţa	4,453	296,486	Slobozia	53
Iaşi	5,476	819,044	Iaşi	322
Ilfov[1]	1,583	300,109	—	—
Maramureş	6,304	510,688	Baia Mare	138
Mehedinţi	4,933	306,118	Drobeta-Turnu Severin	104
Mureş	6,714	579,862	Tîrgu Mureş	150
Neamţ	5,896	557,084	Piatra-Neamţ	105
Olt	5,498	490,276	Slatina	79
Prahova	4,716	829,224	Ploieşti	232
Sălaj	3,864	248,407	Zalău	63
Satu Mare	4,418	369,096	Satu Mare	116
Sibiu	5,432	422,224	Sibiu	155
Suceava	8,553	690,941	Suceava	106
Teleorman	5,790	436,926	Alexandria	51
Timiş	8,697	677,744	Timişoara	318
Tulcea	8,499	258,639	Tulcea	93
Vâlcea	5,765	413,570	Râmnicu Vâlcea	108
Vaslui	5,318	455,550	Vaslui	70
Vrancea	4,867	390,268	Focşani	103

[1]Bucharest municipality and surrounding localities of Ilfov cover 1,821 sq. km.

At the 2002 census the following ethnic minorities numbered over 50,000: Hungarians, 1,431,807 (mainly in Transylvania); Roma (Gypsies), 535,140; Ukrainians, 61,098; Germans, 59,764. A *Council of National Minorities* made up of representatives of the government and ethnic groups was set up in 1993. The actual number of Roma is estimated to be nearer 2m. Romania has the largest Roma population of any country.

The official language is Romanian.

SOCIAL STATISTICS

2001: births, 220,368; deaths, 259,603; infant deaths, 4,057; marriages, 129,930; divorces, 31,135. Rates, 2001 (per 1,000 population): live births, 9·8; deaths, 11·6; marriages, 5·8; divorces, 1·4. Infant mortality, 2001 (per 1,000 live births), 19. Expectation of life at birth, 2001, was 67·0 years for males and 74·2 years for females. In 2001 the most popular age range for marrying was 25–29 for males and

20–24 for females. Measures designed to raise the birth rate were abolished in 1990, and abortion and contraception legalized. The annual abortion rate, at nearly 80 per 1,000 women aged 15–44, ranks among the highest in the world. Annual population growth rate, 1992–02, –0·3%; fertility rate, 2001, 1·3 births per woman.

CLIMATE

A continental climate with an annual average temperature varying between 8°C in the north and 11°C in the south. Bucharest, Jan. 27°F (–2·7°C), July 74°F (23·5°C). Annual rainfall 23·1" (579 mm). Constanța, Jan. 31°F (–0·6°C), July 71°F (21·7°C). Annual rainfall 15" (371 mm).

CONSTITUTION AND GOVERNMENT

A new Constitution was approved by a referendum on 18–19 Oct. 2003. Turn-out was 55·7%, and 89·7% of votes cast were in favour. The Constitution, which replaces the previous one from 1991, defines Romania as a republic where the rule of law prevails in a social and democratic state. Private property rights and a market economy are guaranteed. The new pro-European constitution is aimed at helping Romania achieve EU membership.

The head of state is the *President*, elected by direct vote for a maximum of two five-year terms. The president is not allowed to be affiliated with any political party while in office. The President appoints the *Prime Minister*, who then has to be approved by a vote in parliament. The President is empowered to veto legislation unless it is upheld by a two-thirds parliamentary majority. The National Assembly consists of a 332-member *Chamber of Deputies* and a 137-member *Senate*; both are elected for four-year terms from 42 constituencies by modified proportional representation, the number of seats won in each constituency being determined by the proportion of the total vote. 18 seats in the Chamber of Deputies are reserved for ethnic minorities. There is a 3% threshold for admission to either house. Votes for parties not reaching this threshold are redistributed.

There is a *Constitutional Court*.

National Anthem. 'Desteaptăte, Române, din somnul cel de moarte' ('Wake up, Romanians, from your deadly slumber'); words by A. Muresianu, tune by A. Pann.

RECENT ELECTIONS

Presidential elections were held in two rounds on 28 Nov. and 12 Dec. 2004. In the first round Prime Minister Adrian Năstase of the National Union (alliance of Social Democratic Party and Humanist Party) received 40·9% of votes cast, Traian Băsescu of the Justice and Truth Alliance (alliance of Democratic Party and National Liberal Party) 33·9%, Corneliu Vadim Tudor of the Greater Romania Party 12·6% and Markó Béla of the Hungarian Democratic Federation of Romania 5·1%. There were eight other candidates. In the second round run-off Traian Băsescu was elected president with 51·2% of the vote against 48·8% for Adrian Năstase.

In parliamentary elections held on 28 Nov. 2004 the National Union took 132 seats (36·8% of the vote) in the lower house and 57 seats (37·2% of the vote) in the Senate, the Justice and Truth Alliance 113 seats (31·5%) in the lower house and 49 (31·8%) in the Senate, the Greater Romania Party 47 seats (13·0%) and 21 (13·6%) and the Hungarian Democratic Federation of Romania 22 seats (6·2%) and 10 (6·2%).

CURRENT ADMINISTRATION

President: Traian Băsescu; b. 1951 (Justice and Truth Alliance; sworn in 20 Dec. 2004).

In March 2005 the coalition government of the Justice and Truth Alliance, Hungarian Democratic Federation of Romania and Humanist Party comprised:

Prime Minister: Călin Popescu-Tăriceanu; b. 1952 (Justice and Truth Alliance; sworn in 29 Dec. 2004).

Minister of Defence: Teodor Athanasiu. *Foreign Affairs:* Mihai-Răzvan Ungureanu. *Public Finance:* Ionut Popescu. *Administration and Interior:* Vasile Blaga. *Justice:* Monica Luisa Macovei. *Labour, Social Solidarity and the Family:* Gheorghe Barbu. *Economy and Commerce:* Ioan-Codruț Șereș. *Agriculture, Forests and Rural Development:* Gheorghe Flutur. *Transport, Construction and Tourism:*

Gheorghe Dobre. *Education and Research:* Mircea Miclea. *European Integration:* Ene Dinga. *Health:* Mircea Cinteză. *Culture and Religious Affairs:* Monica Octavia Muscă. *Communications and Information Technology:* Zsolt Nagy. *Environment and Water Resources:* Sulfina Barbu.

Government Website: http://www.gov.ro

DEFENCE

Military service is compulsory for 12 months.

In 2003 military expenditure totalled US$1,313m. (US$59 per capita), representing 2·3% of GDP.

Army. Strength (2002) 66,000 (21,000 conscripts) and 130,000 reservists. The Ministry of the Interior operates a paramilitary Frontier Guard (22,900 strong) and a Gendarmerie (57,000).

Navy. The fleet includes one destroyer and six frigates. There is also a naval infantry force.

The headquarters of the Navy is at Mangalia with the main base at Constanța. The Danube flotilla is based at Brăila. Personnel in 2002 totalled 6,200.

Air Force. The Air Force numbered some 17,000 in 2002, with 202 combat aircraft and 21 attack helicopters. These included MiG-21, MiG-23 and MiG-29 fighters.

INTERNATIONAL RELATIONS

Romania is a member of the UN, WTO, BIS, NATO, the Council of Europe, the Central European Initiative, OSCE, BSEC, Danube Commission, IOM, Antarctic Treaty, the International Organization of the Francophonie and is an Associate Partner of the WEU and an Associate Member of the EU. At the European Union's Helsinki Summit in Dec. 1999 Romania, along with five other countries, was invited to begin full negotiations for membership in Feb. 2000, but entry into the EU is likely to be in 2007 at the earliest. Romania became a member of NATO on 29 March 2004.

ECONOMY

Agriculture accounted for 13·1% of GDP in 2002, industry 38·1% and services 48·8%.

Overview. Since the transition to a market economy began in 1989, industry and agriculture have been overtaken by the service sector. There has been privatization in a number of sectors, from telecommunications to the motor industry, steel to banking. But the country has been slower than other Eastern European countries in transforming its economy. The extent to which the state is still involved in the economy hampers the creation of new private enterprises. Corruption is widespread.

Currency. The monetary unit is the *leu*, pl. *lei* (ROL) notionally of 100 *bani*. Foreign exchange reserves were US$6,352m. and gold reserves 3·38m. troy oz in May 2002. Inflation was 154·8% in 1997, but was brought down to 15·3% in 2003. Total money supply was 57,213·9bn. lei in May 2002.

Budget. Total revenue and expenditure (in 1bn. lei) for calendar years:

	1997	*1998*	*1999*	*2000*	*2001*
Revenue	68,394	107,051	171,135	237,161	311,320
Expenditure	79,734	124,595	191,341	273,990	354,837

VAT, introduced in July 1993, is 19%.

Performance. Romania experienced a recession from 1997 to 1999. However, this was followed in 2000 by growth of 2·1%. Strong economic performance since then has resulted in growth of 5·7%, 5·0% and 4·9% in 2001, 2002 and 2003 respectively. Total GDP in 2003 was US$60·4bn.

Banking and Finance. The National Bank of Romania (founded 1880; nationalized 1946) is the central bank and bank of issue under the Minister of Finance. Its *Governor* is Dr Mugur Isărescu. In 2002 there were 31 banks, plus eight branches of foreign banks. Only three banks remain state-owned. The largest bank is Romanian Commercial Bank (Banca Comerciala Romana), with a market share of 31% and assets in 2002 of US$4·5bn. The size of the government's share in the banking sector fell from over 80% in the mid-1990s to just over 40% in 2002.

A stock exchange re-opened in Bucharest in 1995.

ENERGY AND NATURAL RESOURCES

Environment. Romania's carbon dioxide emissions from the consumption and flaring of fossil fuels were the equivalent of 4·5 tonnes per capita in 2002.

Electricity. Installed electric power 2000: 21·9m. kW; output, 2000, 51·94bn. kWh (28% hydro-electric). Consumption per capita was 2,284 kWh. A nuclear power plant at Cernavoda began working in 1996.

Oil and Gas. Oil production in 2002 was 6·1m. tonnes, but with annual consumption of nearly twice as much a large amount has to be imported. There were 1·0bn. bbls. of proven oil reserves in 2002. Romania was the first country to start oil exploration, and in the late 1850s was the world's leading oil producer, with an output of 200 tonnes a year. Natural gas production in 2002 totalled 10·8bn. cu. metres with 100bn. cu. metres in proven reserves (2002).

The oil company Petrom, Romania's largest company, was privatized in 2004 when the government sold a 51% stake to the Austrian oil and gas group ÖMV.

Minerals. The principal minerals are oil and natural gas, salt, lignite, iron and copper ores, bauxite, chromium, manganese and uranium. Output, 2000 (in 1,000 tonnes): lignite, 29,004; salt (2001), 2,224; coal, 281; iron ore (1999), 131; zinc, 27.

Agriculture. Romania has the biggest agricultural area in eastern Europe after Poland. In 2000, 42·8% of the workforce was employed in agriculture. There were 13·94m. ha of agricultural land in 2002 including 8·96m. ha of arable land and 4·63m. ha of permanent pasture. There were 3,081,000 ha of irrigated land in 2001. There were 164,221 tractors and 27,051 harvester-threshers in 2001.

Production (2000, in 1,000 tonnes): wheat, 4,320; maize, 4,200; potatoes, 3,650; sugarbeets, 1,500; cabbages, 1,000; grapes, 981; sunflower seeds, 900; melons and watermelons, 900; tomatoes, 758; barley, 750.

Livestock, 2002 (in 1,000): cattle, 2,865; sheep, 7,221; pigs, 8,229; horses, 909; goats, 737; poultry, 82,000.

A law of Feb. 1991 provided for the restitution of collectivized land to its former owners or their heirs up to a limit of 10 ha. Land could be resold, but there was a limit of 100 ha on total holdings. In 2000 a law was passed allowing the restitution of state farm land for the first time (up to 50 ha of farmland and 10 ha of forest land per family).

Forestry. Total forest area was 6·45m. ha in 2000 (28·0% of the land area); natural forest covered 6·36m. ha and forest plantations 0·09m. ha. Timber production in 2001 was 12·42m. cu. metres.

Fisheries. The catch in 2001 totalled 7,637 tonnes (216,938 tonnes in 1988), of which 5,206 tonnes were from inland waters.

INDUSTRY

In 2001 industry accounted for 37·0% of GDP. Industrial output grew by 7·5% in 2001.

Output of main products (in 1,000 tonnes): cement (2001), 5,668; crude steel (2002), 5,500; distillate fuel oil (2000), 3,839; rolled steel (2000), 3,685; petrol (2000), 2,625; pig iron (2002), 2,500; fertilizers (2000), 1,931; lime (2001), 1,790; wheat flour (2001), 1,597; residual fuel oil (2000), 1,433; ammonia (2001), 1,155; steel tubes (2001), 665; caustic soda (2001), 661; soda ash (2001), 451; paper and paperboard (2002), 370.

Labour. The labour force in 2002 totalled 10·08m.; the employed population was 9·23m., of whom 3·36m. worked in agriculture and 2·38m. in manufacturing and construction. In 2002, 41% of the total workforce were women. The average retirement ages of 50 for women and 54 for men are among the lowest in the world. A minimum monthly wage was set in 1993; it is 2·8m. lei for full-time adult employees from 1 Jan. 2004. The average monthly wage was 5,498,528 lei in Nov. 2002. Unemployment was 8·4% in 2002 (6·7% in 2001).

Trade Unions. In 2002 the National Confederation of Free Trade Unions-Fratia had 44 professional federations, 41 regional branches and 800,000 members; the other major confederations were the National Trade Union Bloc (375,000), Democratic

Trade Union Confederation of Romania (345,000), Alfa Cartel (325,000 members) and Meridien (170,000).

INTERNATIONAL TRADE

Foreign debt was US$14,683m. in 2002. In Nov. 1993 the USA granted Romania most-favoured-nation status.

Foreign investors may establish joint ventures or 100%-owned domestic companies in all but a few strategic industries. After an initial two-year exemption, profits are taxed at 30%, dividends at 10%. The 1991 constitution prohibits foreign nationals from owning real estate.

Imports and Exports. Trade in US$1m.:

	1998	*1999*	*2000*	*2001*	*2002*
Imports f.o.b.	10,927	9,595	12,050	14,354	16,487
Exports f.o.b.	8,302	8,503	10,366	11,385	13,876

Main export commodities are textiles, mineral products and chemicals; principal imports are mineral fuels, machinery and transport equipment, and textiles.

In 2001 Romania's main export markets were: Italy (25·1%); Germany (15·6%); France (8·1%); UK (5·2%). Romania's main import sources in 2001 were: Italy (20·0%); Germany (15·2%); Russia (7·6%); France (6·3%). The EU accounts for approximately 65% of Romanian exports and 59% of imports.

COMMUNICATIONS

Roads. There were 78,492 km of roads in 2001: 113 km of motorways, 14,822 km of national roads, 35,853 km of country roads and 27,817 km of communal roads. In addition there were 119,988 km of urban roads in 2000. At least two-thirds of the main roads are in urgent need of repair. Passenger cars in 2001 numbered 3,225,512 (144 per 1,000 inhabitants). In 2002 there were 7,047 road accidents involving injury resulting in 2,398 deaths.

Rail. Length of standard-gauge route in 2001 was 10,958 km, of which 3,950 km were electrified; there were 378 km of narrow-gauge lines and 57 km of 1,524 mm gauge. Freight carried in 2001, 72·6m. tonnes; passengers, 113·7m. There is a metro (76·5 km) and tram/light rail network (353 km) in Bucharest, and tramways in 13 other cities.

Civil Aviation. Tarom (*Transporturi Aeriene Române*) is the 92·6%-state-owned airline. In 2002 it provided domestic services and international flights to Amman, Amsterdam, Ancona, Athens, Beijing, Beirut, Berlin, Bologna, Brussels, Budapest, Cairo, Chişinau, Copenhagen, Damascus, Dubai, Düsseldorf, Frankfurt, İstanbul, Larnaca, London, Luxembourg, Madrid, Milan, Moscow, Munich, New York, Paris, Prague, Rome, Sofia, Stuttgart, Tel Aviv, Thessaloniki, Treviso, Verona, Vienna, Warsaw and Zürich. In 1999 it flew 23·7m. km, carrying 978,600 passengers (842,700 on international flights). Other Romanian airlines which operated international flights in 2001 were Romavia, Jaro International, Grivco Air, Acvila Air, Carpat Air and Tiriac Air.

Bucharest's airports are at Baneasa (mainly domestic flights) and Otopeni (international flights). Constanța, Cluj-Napoca, Oradea, Arad, Sibiu and Timişoara also have some international flights. Otopeni handled 1,981,000 passengers in 2001 (all on international flights) and 11,475 tonnes of freight in 2000; Timişoara handled 173,000 passengers in 2001 and Banaesa 73,000.

Shipping. In 2001 the merchant marine comprised 163 vessels totalling 1·45m. DWT. The total GRT was 403,974, including oil tankers and container ships, in 2000. In 2001 vessels totalling 12,646,000 NRT entered ports and vessels totalling 13,817,000 NRT cleared. The main ports are Constanța and Constanța South Agigea on the Black Sea and Galați, Brăila and Tulcea on the Danube. In 2001 sea-going transport carried 0·38m. tonnes of freight. In 2001 the length of navigable inland waterways was 1,779 km including: Danube River, 1,075 km; Black Sea Canal, 64 km; Poarta Alba–Midia Navodari Canal, 28 km. The Romanian inland waterway fleet comprised 169 tugs and pushers and 1,695 dumb and pushed vessels with a carrying capacity of 2·23m. tonnes. The freight carried by Romanian vessels was 383,700 tonnes. The traffic of goods in the Romanian inland ports amounted to 18·7m. tonnes.

Telecommunications. Telephone subscribers numbered 7,961,100 in 2001, or 355·6 per 1,000 population, and there were 898,000 PCs in use (40·2 per 1,000 persons). The telecommunications sector was fully liberalized on 1 Jan. 2003, ending the monopoly of the Greek-controlled operator Romtelecom. OTE, the major shareholder, increased its stake in Romtelecom to 54% in Jan. 2003, with the government retaining 46% of shares. There were 5,110,600 mobile phone subscribers in 2002 and 21,000 fax machines in 1995. The number of Internet users in 2002 was 1·8m.

Postal Services. There were 6,324 post offices in 1998.

SOCIAL INSTITUTIONS

Justice. Justice is administered by the Supreme Court, the 41 county courts, 81 courts of first instance and 15 courts of appeal. Lay assessors (elected for four years) participate in most court trials, collaborating with the judges. In 1994 there were 2,471 judges. The *Procurator-General* exercises 'supreme supervisory power to ensure the observance of the law'. The Procurator's Office and its organs are independent of any organs of justice or administration, and only responsible to the Grand National Assembly, which appoints the Procurator-General for four years. The death penalty was abolished in Jan. 1990 and is forbidden by the 1991 constitution. The population in penal institutions in Nov. 2003 was 43,489 (200 per 100,000 of national population).

Religion. The government officially recognizes 17 religions (which receive various forms of state support); the predominant one is the Romanian Orthodox Church. It is autocephalous, but retains dogmatic unity with the Eastern Orthodox Church. It is made up of five metropolitan sees, with 10 archdioceses and 13 dioceses, 158 deaneries and 10,987 parishes. There were 12,320 priests and deacons in 2003.

Religious affiliation at the 2002 census included: Romanian Orthodox, 18,817,975 (about 87% of the population); Roman Catholic, 1,026,429; Protestant Reformed Church, 701,077; Pentecostal, 324,462; Greek Catholics or Uniates, 191,556; Baptist, 126,639; Seventh Day Adventist, 93,670; Muslim, 67,257.

Education. Education is free and compulsory from the age of six. There is compulsory school attendance for ten years. Primary education comprises four years of study, secondary education comprises lower secondary education (organized in two cycles: grades 5th–8th in elementary schools and grades 9th–10th in high schools or vocational schools) and upper secondary education includes further education in high schools. Further secondary education is also available at *lycées*, professional schools or advanced technical schools.

In 2002–03 there were 9,547 kindergartens with 34,300 teachers and 630,000 children; 12,456 primary and secondary schools with 154,000 teachers and 2,198,000 pupils; 1,388 *lycées* (upper secondary schools) with 61,000 teachers and 740,000 pupils; in post-secondary vocational schools there were 6,100 teachers and 270,000 pupils. In 2002–03 primary and secondary education in Hungarian was given to 106,515 pupils, in German to 10,019 pupils and in other national minority languages to 1,536 pupils.

In 2002–03 there were 125 higher education institutions with 742 faculties, 30,000 teaching staff and 596,297 students (545,405 for long-term studies and 50,892 for short-term studies). The distribution of pupils and subjects studied was as follows: pedagogy, 30·3%; economics, 26·5%; technical subjects, 25·6%; law, 10·6%; medicine and pharmacy, 5·4%; arts, 1·5%.

Adult literacy rate in 2001 was 98·2% (male 99·1%; female 97·4%).

In 2000 total expenditure on education came to 3·6% of GNP and represented 12·2% of total government expenditure.

Health. In 2000 there were 439 hospitals, 166,817 hospital beds and 47,354 doctors (including 4,983 dentists).

Welfare. In Dec. 2002 pensioners comprised 3,096,000 old age and retirement, 1,620,000 retired farmers, 719,900 disability, 650,300 survivor allowance and 5,800 social assistance. These drew average monthly pensions ranging from 565,631 lei to 2,060,203 lei. The social security spending in 2002 was 10·4% of GDP.

CULTURE

World Heritage Sites. Romania has seven sites on the UNESCO World Heritage List: the Danube Delta (inscribed on the list in 1991); the Villages with Fortified Churches in Transylvania (1993); the Monastery of Horezu (1993); the Churches of Modavia (1993); the Historic Centre of Sighisoara (1999); the Dacian Fortresses of the Orastie Mountains (1999); and the Wooden Churches of Maramures (1999).

Broadcasting. A National Audiovisual Council was established in 1992, and is the only authority which is permitted to grant broadcasting audiovisual licences to private stations. By 2003 it had granted 3,318 cable licences, 260 television broadcasting licences, 422 radio broadcasting licences, 62 licences for satellite television stations and 15 licences for satellite radio stations. The public radio and TV stations have broadcasts in Romanian, and in Hungarian and German as well as other minority languages in Romania. The public television station also broadcasts by satellite in its programme *TVR International*. The public radio stations broadcast three radio programmes on medium wave and FM. Radio receivers, 2000, 7·3m.; TV (colour by SECAM H), 2001, 8·5m.

Cinema. In 1999 there were 306 cinemas (excluding private ones), with 109,000 seats.

Press. There were, in 1999, 100 daily papers and 2,200 periodicals, including 200 periodicals in minority languages. 8,000 book titles were published in 1999.

Tourism. In 2000 there were 3,274,000 foreign tourists, bringing revenue of US$364m.

Libraries. In 1997 there were 3,246 public libraries, 48 National libraries and 339 Higher Education libraries; they held a combined 92,382,000 volumes. There were 1,994,000 registered public library users in 1997.

DIPLOMATIC REPRESENTATIVES

Of Romania in the United Kingdom (Arundel House, 4 Palace Green, London, W8 4QD)
Ambassador: Dan Ghibernea.

Of the United Kingdom in Romania (24 Strada Jules Michelet, 70154 Bucharest)
Ambassador: Quinton Quayle.

Of Romania in the USA (1607 23rd St., NW, Washington, D.C., 20008)
Ambassador: Sorin Dumitru Ducaru.

Of the USA in Romania (7–9 Strada Tudor Arghezi, Bucharest)
Ambassador: Jack D. Crouch, II.

Of Romania to the United Nations
Ambassador: Mihnea Ioan Motoc.

Of Romania to the European Union
Ambassador: Lazar Comanescu.

FURTHER READING

Comisia Nationala pentru Statistica. *Anuarul Statistic al României/Romanian Statistical Yearbook.* Bucharest, annual.—*Revista de Statistica.* Monthly

Gallagher, T., *Romania after Ceauşescu; the Politics of Intolerance.* Edinburgh Univ. Press, 1995

Rady, M., *Romania in Turmoil: a Contemporary History.* London, 1992

Siani-Davies, M. and P., *Romania.* [Bibliography] 2nd ed. ABC-Clio, Oxford and Santa Barbara (CA), (rev. ed.) 1998

National statistical office: Comisia Nationala pentru Statistica, 16 Libertatii Ave., sector 5, Bucharest.
Website: http://www.insse.ro

RUSSIA

Rossiiskaya Federatsiya

Capital: Moscow
Population projection, 2010: 137·50m.
GDP per capita, 2002: (PPP$) 8,230
HDI/world rank: 0·795/57

KEY HISTORICAL EVENTS

Avar, Goth, Hun and Magyar invasions punctuated the development of the East Slavs from the 4th century AD, while trade with Germanic, Scandinavian and Middle Eastern regions began in the 8th century. In 882 the Varangian prince Oleg of Novgorod took Kyiv and made it the capital of Kievan Rus, the first unified state of the East Slavs, uniting Finnish and Slavic tribes. In the 13th century the area was invaded from the west by Teutonic Knights, Lithuanians and Swedes, and from the south by Mongol and Tartar tribes. In 1223 Genghis Khan's grandson, Batu Khan, conquered Kievan Rus and established the Golden Horde. The Mongols and Tatars made Itil (near modern Astrakhan) the capital. Their dominance lasted until the 15th century when internal struggles finally forced the break up of the empire.

Ivan III (ruled 1462–1505), grand duke of Muscovy, annexed the East Slavic regions, as well as Belarus and the Ukraine, conquered Novgorod in 1478 and opened up contacts with Western Europe. Muscovy, the nucleus of the Russian state, was reformed by the volatile Ivan IV, the 'Terrible' (the first tsar of Russia, from 1547–84). Ivan extended Russia's territory towards Siberia and the Caspian Sea but the costly war with Livonia (1558–82) drained Russia's resources. Ivan's reign was followed by a period of instability, worsened by Polish and Swedish interference. A peace treaty signed with Sweden in 1617 lost Russia Novgorod in exchange for Baltic control. With the Polish occupiers ejected from Moscow, Mikhail Fyodorovich Romanov became tsar of a country ruined by war. Avoiding involvement in the Thirty Years' War, he managed to restore some stability to Russia and strengthen its holdings in the southern regions. However, Russia lost the Baltic coast to Sweden in 1661 and later Belarus and parts of the Ukraine to Poland.

The reign of Peter the Great (1689–1725) signalled the birth of modern Russia. The capital was transferred from Moscow to the newly built St Petersburg (1712). Administrative reforms divided Russia into eight main provinces, put the church under state control and introduced compulsory secular education for the nobility, although the peasantry was forced into serfdom. Peter expanded industry, created the navy and introduced army conscription. An alliance with Denmark, Poland and Saxony against Sweden resulted in the Great Northern War (1700–21) making Russia the leading Baltic power. After the death of Peter the Great, much of the 18th century was marked by disputed succession. Peter I's daughter, Elizabeth, came to power in 1741 in a bloodless coup. During her 21-year reign, her father's reforms were consolidated and European culture and literature flourished. At the end of her reign Russia was involved in the Seven Years' War, occupying Berlin briefly in 1760.

Catherine the Great (ruled 1762–96) combined domestic reforms with an aggressive foreign policy aimed at making Russia the leading European power at the expense of the Turks and Tatars. But in two wars with Turkey she failed to take Constantinople. War with France in 1805 led to a crushing defeat at Austerlitz but when Napoléon invaded Russia in 1812 his army fell victim to the Russian winter. Russia was defeated by Britain, France and Turkey in the Crimean War (1853–56). Alexander II (ruled 1855–81) introduced reforms to modernize Russia, including the partial emancipation of the serfs in 1861. He was assassinated in 1881 and was succeeded by Alexander III (1881–94), whose policies were harsh and reactionary. Widespread famine followed a crop failure in 1891. The Russian empire had expanded to the far reaches of Asia, to Afghanistan and into Central Europe. By the end of Alexander III's reign, only half the population spoke Russian or were members of the Orthodox Church.

Nicholas II's reign (1894–1917) marked the end of Tsarist Russia. Like his father, he did little to improve social conditions for the masses, concentrating instead on military power. In 1904 he embarked on an unpopular war with Japan, exacerbating public discontent. In Jan. 1905 a priest, Georgy Gapon, led a protest of factory workers to St Petersburg's Winter Palace. Troops opened fire killing over 100 people. A general strike broke out paralysing most of Russia and leading to violence between monarchists and insurgents well into 1907. The 1905 revolution saw the establishment of the first *Duma* (parliament), which was, however, soon dissolved.

In 1912 the two strands of the Social Democratic Workers' Party—the Bolsheviks ('majority') led by Vladimir Ilich Ulianov (Lenin), and the Mensheviks ('minority')—split, the Bolsheviks pursuing revolution, the Mensheviks evolutionary change. With the outbreak of the First World War the tsar took command of the armed forces, leaving the tsarina in charge of government. Her influential and much-resented adviser, Grigori Rasputin, was assassinated in 1916. After a mass protest in St Petersburg, soldiers deserted, allying themselves with the workers, a pattern repeated in other cities. A provisional government, led by liberals and including Mensheviks and Bolsheviks, was established and Tsar Nicholas abdicated on 2 March 1917. The Royal Family was executed in July 1918.

In Oct. 1917 the Bolsheviks led by Lenin, newly returned from exile, seized control. Russia was declared a Soviet Republic and the capital was moved back to Moscow. Between 1918–21 a civil war raged between the Bolshevik Red Army, led by Lenin's close ally Leon Trotsky, and the White Army, formed by former imperial officers, Cossacks, anti-communists and anarchists. Lenin instituted the New Economic Policy (NEP) in 1921 to replace War Communism, reintroducing a monetary system and private ownership of small-scale industry and agriculture. In 1922 the Union of Soviet Socialist Republics was established comprising Russia, the Ukraine, Belarus and Transcaucasia. The Turkmen and Uzbek republics were added two years later, and the Tadzhik republic joined in 1929.

On Lenin's death in 1924, Joseph Stalin (Ioseb Dzhugashvili) became general secretary of the Communist Party. Stalin rejected the 'state capitalism' of the NEP, which had failed to provide enough food for the urban workforce. From 1928 Stalin pursued a programme of industrialization and from 1933 agricultural collectivization, which cost the lives of 10m. peasants through famine or persecution. Constructing a personality cult for Lenin and himself, Stalin reasserted his absolute authority in massive purges; in 1934 and 1937 the NKVD (political police) eliminated millions of political dissidents.

Despite a non-aggression pact signed with Germany in Aug. 1939, the USSR was forced into the Second World War in 1941 when Germany invaded. Up to 20m. Soviet lives were lost, almost a million in the battle of Stalingrad alone (1942–43). Expansion before and during the war created 15 aligned republics. Transcaucasia was divided into Armenia, Georgia and Azerbaijan, Kazakh and Kirghiz Soviet Socialist Republics were formed, and, along with Latvia, Lithuania, Estonia and Moldavia, were incorporated into the USSR. Following the war, Stalin managed to gain Western acceptance of a Soviet sphere of influence in Eastern Europe. The Baltic States and large tracts of land from neighbouring countries were annexed, while puppet regimes established Poland, Czechoslovakia, East Germany, Hungary, Bulgaria and Romania as satellites of Moscow.

The blockade of West Berlin (1948–49) and the Soviet detonation of an atomic bomb in Aug. 1949 were major factors in the escalation of the Cold War, waged indirectly in the Korean War (1950–53). On Stalin's death, his successor Nikita Khrushchev condemned the Stalinist regime. Relaxing control in the Eastern Bloc allowed for some liberalization although the Hungarian Uprising and the Poznań Riots in Poland (both 1956) were brutally suppressed and the Berlin Wall built in 1961. Relations with the Soviet Union's ideological ally, China, collapsed over differences in interpretation of Marxist doctrine and Chinese opposition to Khrushchev's attempts at détente with the West. The Cuban Missile Crisis of 1962 intensified hostilities with the West to the brink of nuclear war. Khrushchev's climbdown, coupled with food shortages, led to widespread discontent. He was forced out of office in a 1964 coup led by Leonid Brezhnev, who ruled until 1982.

In Aug. 1968 the USSR invaded Czechoslovakia to suppress an increasingly liberal regime. Relations with the West were further strained when the Soviets invaded Afghanistan in 1979. By the end of his tenure Brezhnev's failing health mirrored the country's economic decline. The domestic price of Brezhnev's obsessive pursuit of prominence in the space race was the failure of the agricultural and consumer-goods sectors and the decline of living standards. From his death in 1982, the country was led by his aides Yuri Andropov, a short-lived reformer, then Konstantin Chernenko.

When the latter died in 1985, Mikhail Gorbachev became general secretary of the Communist Party. He launched *perestroika*, a policy of economic and structural reform. *Glasnost* ('openness') extended civil liberties, including freedom of the press, and led to official rejection of Stalinist-style totalitarianism. The political system was overhauled, with electoral processes made more democratic and some free-market principles introduced. Gorbachev sought warmer relations with both Communist and Western governments and withdrew troops from Afghanistan in 1989. In a rejection of the 'Brezhnev Doctrine', throughout 1989 and 1990 Gorbachev refused to intervene as one Communist regime after another fell in the Eastern Bloc. Within the USSR, the republics began demanding independence. An attempted coup by Communist diehards was frustrated by the intervention of Russian president Boris Yeltsin. On Christmas Day 1991 Gorbachev resigned as Soviet president and the Soviet Union was dissolved.

Confrontation in 1992–93 between President Yeltsin and the Russian Duma climaxed when thousands of armed anti-Yeltsin demonstrators tried to seize the Kremlin. On 4 Oct. 1993 troops took the parliament building by storm after a ten-hour assault in which 140 people died. Yeltsin was re-elected president in 1996. In Aug. 1999 Boris Yeltsin appointed as prime minister Vladimir Putin, a former KGB colonel, who won the presidential election of March 2000.

Under Putin, the war with separatist Chechnya that began in Dec. 1994 intensified. One of his primary aims has been to reduce the power of the business oligarchs and to fight corruption. Tax cuts have been introduced, and in 2000 a programme of regional reform divided Russia's 89 regions into seven new districts run by Kremlin representatives. Following the terror attacks on the USA in Sept. 2001, Putin declared his support for the war on terrorism. In Oct. 2002 a group of Chechen rebels took control of a Moscow theatre and held hostage 800 people for three days. Russian troops stormed the building using an anaesthetic gas, which killed many of the hostages. The new relationship with the USA faltered as a result of the war with Iraq, which Russia opposed. Russia's vulnerability to terrorism was highlighted in Sept. 2004 when hostage takers seized a school in Beslan, in the Russian republic of North Ossetia. A three-day standoff ended with more than 350 people killed, nearly half of them children. Chechen rebels claimed responsibility for the siege.

TERRITORY AND POPULATION

Russia is bounded in the north by various seas (Barents, Kara, Laptev, East Siberian) which join the Arctic Ocean, and in which is a fringe of islands, some of them large. In the east Russia is separated from the USA (Alaska) by the Bering Strait; the Kamchatka peninsula separates the coastal Bering and Okhotsk Seas. Sakhalin Island, north of Japan, is Russian territory. Russia is bounded in the south by North Korea, China, Mongolia, Kazakhstan, the Caspian Sea, Azerbaijan, Georgia, the Black Sea and Ukraine, and in the west by Belarus, Latvia, Estonia, the Baltic Sea and Finland. Kaliningrad (the former East Prussia) is an exclave on the Baltic Sea between Lithuania and Poland in the west. Russia's area is 17,075,400 sq. km and it has 11 time zones. The 2002 census population was 145,166,731 (53·5% females); density, 8·6 per sq. km. Ethnicity in 1989 showed 81·5% were Russians, 3·8% Tatars, 3·0% Ukrainians, 1·2% Chuvash, 0·9% Bashkir, 0·8% Belorussians and 0·7% Mordovians. Chechens, Germans, Udmurts, Mari, Kazakhs, Avars, Jews and Armenians all numbered 0·5m. or more.

In 2001, 72·9% of the population lived in urban areas.

The UN gives a projected population for 2010 of 137·50m.

Russia's population has been declining since the break-up of the Soviet Union and will continue to do so in the future. By 2050 its population is projected to be the same as it was in the early 1950s.

The two principal cities are Moscow, the capital, with a 2002 census population of 10·13m. and St Petersburg (formerly Leningrad), with 4·16m. Other major cities (with 2002 populations) are: Novosibirsk (1·43m.), Nizhny Novgorod (1·31m.), Yekaterinburg (1·29m.), Samara (1·16m.) and Omsk (1·13m.). In May 2000 President Putin signed a decree dividing Russia into seven federal districts, replacing the previous structure of 89 regions. The new districts, with their administrative centres and 2002 populations in brackets, are: Central (Moscow, 38·00m.), North-Western (St Petersburg, 13·97m.), Southern (Rostov-on-Don, 22·91m.), Volga (Nizhny Novgorod, 31·15m.), Ural (Yekaterinburg, 12·37m.), Siberian (Novosibirsk, 20·06m.) and Far-Eastern (Khaborovsk, 6·69m.).

The national language is Russian.

SOCIAL STATISTICS

2001 births, 1,311,604; deaths, 2,251,814; marriages, 1,001,130; divorces, 763,493. Rates, 2001 (per 1,000 population): birth, 9·0; death, 15·5; marriage, 6·9; divorce, 5·3. At the beginning of the 1970s the death rate had been just 9·4 per 1,000 population. Infant mortality, 2001 (per 1,000 live births), 18. There were 2,014,710 legal abortions in 2001. The annual abortion rate, at approximately 70 per 1,000 women aged 15–44, ranks among the highest in the world. The divorce rate is also among the highest in the world. The most popular age range for marrying in 1999 was 18–24 for both males and females. Expectation of life at birth, 2001, was 58·9 years for males and 72·3 years for females. With a difference of 13·4 years, no other country has a life expectancy for females so high compared to that for males. The low life expectancy (down from 64·6 years for males and 74 years for females in the USSR as a whole in 1989) and the low birth rate (down from 17·6 per 1,000 population in the USSR in 1989) is causing a demographic crisis, with the population declining by approximately 750,000 a year. If current trends continue, the population could fall by nearly 40m. in the first half of the 21st century. Disease, pollution, poor health care and alcoholism are all contributing to the dramatic decline in the population. More than 40,000 Russians died of alcohol poisoning in 2002. In 2000, 35% of Russians were living below the poverty line, up from 21% in 1997. Annual population growth rate, 1992–02, –0·3%; fertility rate, 2001, 1·2 births per woman. The suicide rate, at 35·3 per 100,000 population in 1998, is one of the highest in the world. Among males it was 62·6 per 100,000 population in 1998.

CLIMATE

Moscow, Jan. –9·4°C, July 18·3°C. Annual rainfall 630 mm. Arkhangelsk, Jan. –15°C, July 13·9°C. Annual rainfall 503 mm. St Petersburg, Jan. –8·3°C, July 17·8°C. Annual rainfall 488 mm. Vladivostok, Jan. –14·4°C, July 18·3°C. Annual rainfall 599 mm.

CONSTITUTION AND GOVERNMENT

The Russian Soviet Federative Socialist Republic (RSFSR) adopted a declaration of republican sovereignty by 544 votes to 271 in June 1990. It became a founding member of the Commonwealth of Independent States (CIS) in Dec. 1991, and adopted the name 'Russian Federation'. A law of Nov. 1991 extended citizenship to all who lived in Russia at the time of its adoption and to those in other Soviet republics who requested it.

According to the 1993 Constitution the Russian Federation is a 'democratic federal legally-based state with a republican form of government'. The Federation is made up of 21 republics, one autonomous region, ten autonomous areas, six territories, 49 regions and two federal cities. The state is secular. Individuals have freedom of movement within or across the boundaries of the Federation; there is freedom of assembly and association, and freedom to engage in any entrepreneurial activity not forbidden by law. The state itself is based upon a separation of powers and upon federal principles, including a Constitutional Court. The most important matters of state are reserved for the federal government, including socio-economic policy, the budget, taxation, energy, foreign affairs and defence. Other matters, including the use of land and water, education and culture, health and social security, are for the joint management of the federal and local governments, which also have the right to legislate within their spheres of competence. A central role is accorded to the *President*, who defines the 'basic directions of domestic and foreign policy' and represents the state internationally. The President is directly elected for a four-year term, and for not more than two consecutive terms; he must be at least 35 years old, a Russian citizen, and a resident in Russia for the previous ten years. 1m. signatures are needed to validate a presidential candidate, no more than 7% of which may come from any one region or republic. The President has the right to appoint the prime minister, and (on his nomination) to appoint and dismiss deputy prime ministers and ministers, and may dismiss the government as a whole. In the event of the death or incapacity of the President, the Prime Minister becomes head of state.

Parliament is known as the *Federal Assembly* (Federalnoe Sobranie). The 'representative and legislative organ of the Russian Federation', it consists of two chambers: the *Federation Council* (Sovet Federatsii) and the *State Duma* (Gosudarstvennaya Duma). The Federation Council, or upper house, consists of 178 deputies. The State Duma, or lower house, consists of 450 deputies elected for a four-year term. 225 of these are elected from single-member constituencies on the first-past-the-post system, the remainder from party lists by proportional representation. To qualify for candidacy an individual must obtain signatures from at least 1% of voters in the constituency; a party or electoral alliance must obtain a minimum of 100,000 supporting signatures from at least seven regions, but not more than 15% from any one region. There is a 5% threshold for the party-list seats. Parties which gain at least 35 seats may register as a faction, which gives them the right to join the Duma Council and chair committees. Any citizen aged over 21 may be elected to the State Duma, but may not at the same time be a member of the upper house or of other representative bodies. The Federation Council considers all matters that apply to the Federation as a whole, including state boundaries, martial law, and the deployment of Russian forces elsewhere. The Duma approves nominations for Prime Minister, and adopts federal laws (they are also considered by the Federation Council but any objection may be overridden by a two-thirds majority; objections on the part of the President may be overridden by both houses on the same basis). The Duma can reject nominations for Prime Minister but after the third rejection it is automatically dissolved. It is also dissolved if it twice votes a lack of confidence in the government, or if it refuses to express confidence in the government when the matter is raised by the Prime Minister.

A new law was enacted in July 2001 to reduce the proliferation of political parties (then numbering some 200) by introducing stricter registration criteria and obliging existing parties to re-register within two years. In order to register, political parties were required to have at least 10,000 members, with no fewer than 100 members in at least half of Russia's 89 territorial entities. Multiple party membership is banned.

There is a 19-member *Constitutional Court*, whose functions under the 1993 Constitution include making decisions on the constitutionality of federal laws, presidential and government decrees, and the constitutions and laws of the subjects of the Federation. It is governed by a Law on the Constitutional Court, adopted in July 1994. Judges are elected for non-renewable 12-year terms.

National Anthem. In Dec. 2000 the Russian parliament, on President Putin's initiative, decided that the tune of the anthem of the former Soviet Union should be reintroduced as the Russian national anthem. Written by Alexander Alexandrov in 1943, the anthem was composed for Stalin. New words were written by Sergei Mikhalkov, who had written the original words for the Soviet anthem in 1943. The new anthem is 'Rossiya—svyashennaya nasha derzhava, Rossiya—lyubimaya nasha strana' ('Russia—our holy country, Russia—our beloved country'). Boris Yeltsin had introduced a new anthem during his presidency—'Patriotic Song', from an opera by Mikhail Glinka and arranged by Andrei Petrov.

RECENT ELECTIONS

Vladimir Putin was re-elected for a four-year term in presidential elections on 14 March 2004, gaining 71·2% of the votes cast. Nikolai Kharitonov (Communist Party of the Russian Federation; KPRF) won 13·7% of the vote; Sergei Glazyev (Rodina) 4·1%; Irina Khakamada 3·9%; Oleg Malyshkin (Liberal Democratic Party; LDPR) 2·0%; and Sergei Mironov 0·8%. Turn-out was 64·3%.

Elections for the State Duma were held on 7 Dec. 2003: United Russia won 222 seats (with 37·6% of the votes); the KPRF 51 seats (12·6%); Rodina

(Motherland)–National Patriotic Union 37 seats (9·0%); the LDPR 36 seats (11·5%); the People's Party of the Russian Federation 16 seats (1·2%); Jabloko (Apple)–Russian Democratic Party 4 seats (4·3%); and the Agrarian Party of Russia 3 seats (3·6%). 67 other party representatives were elected and 11 non-partisans. Turn-out was 55·8%.

CURRENT ADMINISTRATION

President: Vladimir Putin; b. 1952 (sworn in 7 May 2000 having been acting President since 31 Dec. 1999).

In March 2005 the government comprised:

Prime Minister: Mikhail Fradkov; b. 1950 (sworn in 5 March 2004).

Deputy Prime Minister: Alexander Zhukov.

Minister of Agriculture and Food: Alexei Gordeyev. *Civil Defence, Emergencies and Natural Disasters:* Sergei Shoigu. *Communications:* Leonid Reiman. *Culture and Information:* Alexander Sokolov. *Defence:* Sergei Ivanov. *Economic Development and Trade:* German Gref. *Education and Science:* Andrei Fursenko. *Finance:* Alexei Kudrin. *Foreign Affairs:* Sergei Lavrov. *Health and Social Development:* Mikhail Zurabov. *Industry and Energy:* Viktor Khristenko. *Internal Affairs (MVD):* Rashid Nurgaliev. *Justice:* Yuri Chaika. *Nationalities Affairs:* Vladimir Yakovlev. *Natural Resources:* Yuri Trutnev. *Transportation and Communications:* Igor Levitin. *Head of the Ministerial Apparatus:* Dimitri Kozak.

Chairman of the State Duma: Guennadi N. Seleznev.

Government Website: http://www.gov.ru

DEFENCE

The President of the Republic is C.-in-C. of the armed forces. Conscription was raised from 18 months to two years in April 1995.

The START 2 nuclear arms cutting treaty was ratified by the Duma in April 2000, seven years after it had been signed. This obliged both Russia and the USA to reduce their stocks of strategic weapons from some 6,000 nuclear warheads to 3,500. At the height of the Cold War each side had possessed over 10,000.

A presidential decree of Feb. 1997 ordered a cut in the armed forces of 200,000 men, reducing them to an authorized strength of 1,004,100 in 1999. This figure included 200,000 staff at the Ministry of Defence and 478,000 paramilitary troops (including 196,000 border troops).

Military expenditure totalled US$65,200m. in 2003 (US$455 per capita), representing 4·9% of GDP. Only the USA spent more on defence in 2003.

Nuclear Weapons. Russia's strategic warhead count is now shrinking and stood at 4,422 in Jan. 2004 according to the Stockholm International Peace Research Institute. Shortfalls in planned investments to replace current systems as they reach the end of their service lives means the number of strategic warheads will decline rapidly over the next decade. Current plans are to cut stockpiles to between 2,000 and 2,500, but President Putin has proposed that the target for both Russia and the USA should be 1,500, with even further reductions to follow. On 24 May 2002 the USA and Russia signed an arms control treaty to reduce the number of US and Russian warheads, from between 6,000 and 7,000 each to between 1,700 and 2,200 each, over the next ten years. Russia has pledged to dismantle its biological and chemical weapons programme and to destroy its stockpiles of such weapons, believed to be the largest in the world.

Arms Trade. Russia was the world's third largest exporter after the USA and the UK in 2003, with sales worth US$3,400m., or 11·8% of the world total.

Army. A Russian Army was created by presidential decree in March 1992. In 2002 forces numbered 321,000 (190,000 conscripts). There were estimated to be around 20,000,000 reserves (all armed forces) of whom 2,400,000 had seen service within the previous five years. There were around 17,000 Russian troops stationed outside Russia (including 7,800 in Tajikistan and 4,000 in Georgia) in 2002, the majority in various states of the former USSR. In April 2003 plans were announced to increase military presence in Tajikistan following intelligence reports of increased activity by the Taliban and the al-Qaeda terrorist network in neighbouring Afghanistan.

The Army is deployed in six military districts and one Operational Strategic Group. Equipment includes some 13,870 main battle tanks (including T-55s, T-62s, T-64A/-Bs, T-72L/-Ms, T-80/-U/UD/UMs and T-90s) plus 150 light tanks (PT-76). In addition 8,000 main battle tanks were in store.

The Army air element has some 2,300 attack helicopters in the inventory (of which 600 in store) including Mi-24s and Ka-50s. Funding shortages have reduced serviceability drastically.

Strategic Nuclear Ground Forces. In 2002 there were four rocket armies, each with launcher groups, ten silos and one control centre. Inter-continental ballistic missiles numbered 735. Personnel, 100,000 (50,000 conscripts).

Navy. The Russian Navy continues to reduce steadily and levels of sea-going activity remain very low with activity concentrated on a few operational units in each fleet. The safe deployment and protection of the reduced force of strategic missile-firing submarines remains its first priority; and the defence of the Russian homeland its second. The strategic missile submarine force operates under command of the Strategic Nuclear Force commander whilst the remainder come under the Main Naval Staff in Moscow, through the Commanders of the fleets.

The Northern and Pacific fleets count the entirety of the ballistic missile submarine force, all nuclear-powered submarines, the sole operational aircraft carrier and most major surface warships. The Baltic Fleet organization is based in the St Petersburg area and in the Kaliningrad exclave. Some minor war vessels have been ceded to the Baltic republics. The Black Sea Fleet was for some years the object of wrangling between Russia and Ukraine. Russia eventually received four-fifths of the Black Sea Fleet's warships, with Ukraine receiving about half of the facilities. It was agreed that Russia would rent three harbours for warships and two airfields for a period of 20 years, for a payment of approximately US$100m. annually. The small Caspian Sea flotilla, formerly a sub-unit of the Black Sea Fleet, has been divided between Azerbaijan (25%), and Russia, Kazakhstan and Turkmenistan, the littoral republics (75%). In May 2003 Russia held joint exercises with the Indian fleet in the Arabian Sea for the first time since the collapse of the USSR.

The material state of all the fleets is suffering from continued inactivity and lack of spares and fuel. The nuclear submarine refitting and refuelling operations in the Northern and Pacific Fleets remain in disarray, given the large numbers of nuclear submarines awaiting defuelling and disposal. The strength of the submarine force has now essentially stabilized, but there are still large numbers of decommissioned vessels awaiting their turn for scrapping in a steadily deteriorating state. In Jan. 2003 it was announced that up to a fifth of the fleet was to be scrapped.

The aircraft carrier *Admiral Kuznetsov* is now operational, albeit with a limited aviation capability, and she deployed to the Mediterranean in Dec. 1995.

In 2002 there were 13 operational nuclear-fuelled ballistic-missile submarines, constituted as follows:

Class	*No.*	*Missiles*	*Total no. of missiles*
Delta-IV	6	16 SS-N-23	96
Delta-III	5	16 SS-N-18	80
Typhoon	2	20 SS-N-20	40
			216

The attack submarine fleet comprises a wide range of classes, from the enormous 16,250 tonne 'Oscar' nuclear-powered missile submarine to diesel boats of around 2,000 tonnes. The inventory of tactical nuclear-fuelled submarines comprises six 'Oscar II', one former strategic 'Yankee'-class, nine 'Akula'-class, one 'Sierra'-class and five 'Victor III'-class submarines.

The diesel-powered 'Kilo' class, of which the Navy operates nine, is still building at a reduced rate mostly for export. There are a further four diesel submarines on the active list.

Cruisers are divided into two categories; those optimized for anti-submarine warfare (ASW) are classified as 'Large Anti-Submarine Ships' and those primarily configured for anti-surface ship operations are classified 'Rocket Cruisers'. The principal surface ships of the Russian Navy include the following classes:

Aircraft Carrier. The *Admiral Kuznetsov* of 67,500 tonnes was completed in 1989. It is capable of embarking 20 aircraft and 15–17 helicopters. All other aircraft carriers have been decommissioned or scrapped.

Cruisers. The ships of this classification are headed by the two ships of the Kirov-class, the largest combatant warships, apart from aircraft carriers, to be built since the Second World War. There are, in addition, three Slava-class, one of the Nikolaev ('Kara') class and one Kynda class ship in operation.

Destroyers. There are seven Udaloy-class, the first of which entered service in 1981, one Udaloy II-class and four Sovremenny-class guided missile destroyers in operation. In addition there is a single remaining 'modified Kashin'-class ship and a further one unmodified 'Kashin' also in operation.

Frigates. There are ten frigates in operation including the first of a new class, the 'Neustrashimy', seven Krivak I-class and two Krivak II-class ships.

The Russian Naval Air Force operates some 217 combat aircraft including 45 Tu-22M bombers and 52 Su-24, 10 Su-25 and 52 Su-27 fighters. There were an additional 102 armed helicopters in operation.

Total Naval personnel in 2002 numbered 171,500, of whom an estimated 16,000 were conscripts. Some 11,000 serve in the strategic submarine force, 35,000 in naval aviation, 9,500 naval infantry/coastal defence troops.

Air Force. The Air Force (VVS) and Air Defence Troops (PVO) amalgamated in March 1998 under one Air Force command. Personnel is estimated at 185,000 and comprises some 1,736 combat aircraft but no aircraft.

The Air Force is organized into three main Commands: Long-Range Aviation, Tactical Aviation and Military Transport Aviation. An air force base opened in Kyrgyzstan in Oct. 2003.

Long-Range Aviation comprised in 2002 (numbers in brackets) Tu-160 (15), Tu-22M (117) and Tu-95 (63) bombers, some equipped to carry nuclear weapons.

Tactical Aviation comprised in 2002 (numbers in brackets) Su-24 (371) and Su-25 (235) fighter-bombers and MiG-29 (255), MiG-31 (256) and Su-27 (392) fighters. In addition MiG-25 and Su-24s are used for reconnaissance missions.

INTERNATIONAL RELATIONS

Russia is a member of the UN (Security Council), BIS, the NATO Partnership for Peace, CIS, the Council of Europe, OSCE, Council of the Baltic Sea States, BSEC, Danube Commission, APEC and the Antarctic Treaty. On 16 May 1997 NATO ratified a 'Fundamental Act on Relations, Co-operation and Mutual Security' with Russia. Although not a member of the World Trade Organization, President Putin has made it a stated goal. However, membership is unlikely before the end of 2005 at the earliest.

ECONOMY

Agriculture accounted for 5·7% of GDP in 2002, industry 34·0% and services 60·3%.

In Oct. 1991 a programme was launched to create a 'healthy mixed economy with a powerful private sector'. The prices of most commodities were freed on 2 Jan. 1992.

Privatization, overseen by the State Committee on the Management of State Property, began with small and medium-sized enterprises. A state programme of privatization of state and municipal enterprises was approved by parliament in June 1992, and vouchers worth 10,000 roubles each began to be distributed to all citizens in Oct. 1992. These could be sold or exchanged for shares. Employees had the right to purchase 51% of the equity of their enterprises. 25 categories of industry (including raw materials and arms) remained in state ownership. The voucher phase of privatization ended on 30 June 1994. A post-voucher stage authorized by presidential decree of 22 July 1994 provides for firms to be auctioned for cash following the completion of the sale of up to 70% of manufacturing industry for vouchers. By Dec. 1997 a total of 127,000 enterprises had been privatized; 59% of these were in trade, public catering and personal services, 33% in manufacturing, construction, transport and communications and 2·4% in agriculture. The Ministry of Property Relations was established in 2000 with the mandate of overall federal policies on property issues and the management of state property, and in Dec. 2001 a new Federal Law on Privatization of State and Municipal Property was adopted. By that time a total of 129,811 enterprises had been sold.

Overview. Since the 1998 economic crisis, growth rates have averaged over 6%, just below the target rate of 7·25% required to double GDP in a decade. This economic success is attributed to high oil prices and the devaluation of the rouble. Economic reform has been a primary government objective, and significant progress has been made in recent years. The government has gained recognition for its reform efforts on an international level—in 2002 both the EU and the USA granted market status to the Russian economy. Russia aims to join the World Trade Organization by the end of 2005, a move that requires the reform of the financial and banking sector, a non-discriminatory environment for foreign businesses and the protection of intellectual property rights. Russia's risk status in international financial markets has also improved, marking an increase in investor confidence in the economy. In 2003 short-term new capital flows were positive for the first time since the early 1990s. Public debt has fallen from 80% of GDP in 1998 to approximately 30% today. In 2001 Russia significantly cut its higher rates of personal income tax to a single marginal rate of 13%; this policy manoeuvre increased revenues by 26%. Since 2002 progress on structural reforms has been limited—reforms to pensions and the electricity sector have been scaled down, whilst reforms of the public administration and the social and military sectors have stalled.

Currency. The unit of currency is the *rouble* (RUR), of 100 *kopeks.* In Jan. 1998 the rouble was redenominated by a factor of a thousand. Foreign exchange reserves were US$60,710m. in July 2003 and gold reserves 12·44m. troy oz in June 2002. In 1997 the rouble was tied to the US dollar on a sliding scale ranging from US$1 = 5,500–6,100 roubles on 1 Jan. 1997 to six roubles on 31 Jan. 1998. Inflation, which was 2,510% in 1992, stood at 13·7% in 2003. Total money supply in June 2003 was 2,604·5bn. roubles. In Nov. 2000 President Putin and President Lukashenka of Belarus agreed the introduction of a single currency. The Russian rouble was introduced into Belarus on a non-cash basis on 1 July 2003 with a single currency unit scheduled for introduction in Jan. 2008.

Budget. In 2002 federal budget revenues totalled 2,202bn. roubles (of which tax revenues 1,696bn. roubles) and expenditures 1,714bn. roubles. There was a budget surplus of 1·4% of GDP in 2002. The federal budget has remained in surplus since 2000.

Performance. GDP grew by 1·4% in 1997, the first expansion since the Soviet Union's collapse in 1991; but many economists believed that the booming informal economy added over 25% to the value of GDP. With oil revenues well down and a collapse of the rouble in 1998, Russia defaulted on its debt. In 1998 real GDP growth was –5·3%. There was then a highly impressive turnaround, with growth of 6·3% in 1999 and a record 10·0% in 2000. In 2001 there was growth of 5·1%, in spite of the world economic slowdown and the effects of the attacks on the USA of 11 Sept. 2001, followed by 4·7% in 2002, 7·3% in 2003 and (provisional) 6·9% in 2004. Total GDP was US$433·5bn. in 2003. In May 2003 President Vladimir Putin announced a target of doubling GDP by 2010. In June 2002 Russia was acknowledged as a market economy under United States trade law, symbolically underscoring the country's transformation from a state-planned economy.

Banking and Finance. The central bank and bank of issue is the State Bank of Russia (*Governor*, Sergey Mikhailovich Ignatiev). The Russian Bank for Reconstruction and Development and the State Investment Company were created in 1993 to channel foreign and domestic investment. Foreign bank branches have been operating since Nov. 1992.

By 1995 the number of registered commercial banks had increased to around 5,000 but following the Aug. 1997 liquidity crisis, owing to the ensuing bankruptcies, mergers and the Central Bank's revoking of licences, the number fell to 2,500. This has since fallen to 1,300. Approximately 80% of the commercial banks were state-owned through ministries or state enterprises. In 2001 the leading banks were Sberbank (assets of 771·5bn. roubles), Vneshtorgbank (146·5bn. roubles) and Gazprombank (104·3bn. roubles). In 2001 there were around 1,300 credit institutions.

In the wake of one of the worst financial crises which Russia's market economy had experienced, the central bank tripled interest rates to 150% in May 1998 in an effort to restore stability to the financial system. In 2002 the banking sector in Russia was healthier than at any time since the collapse of the former Soviet Union.

There are stock exchanges in Moscow, Novosibirsk, St Petersburg and Vladivostok.

Russia was one of 15 countries and territories named in a report in June 2000 by the Financial Action Task Force (FATF—set up by the G7 group of major industrialized nations) as failing to co-operate in the fight against international money laundering. In Feb. 2002 Russia implemented an anti-money laundering law, as a result of which the FATF removed it from the list of non-cooperative countries and territories in Oct. 2002.

ENERGY AND NATURAL RESOURCES

Environment. Russia's carbon dioxide emissions from the consumption and flaring of fossil fuels in 2002 accounted for 6·2% of the world total (the third highest after the USA and China), and were equivalent to 10·6 tonnes per capita. An *Environmental Sustainability Index* compiled for the World Economic Forum meeting in Feb. 2002 ranked Russia 72nd in the world, with 49·1%. The index measured the ability of countries to maintain favourable environmental conditions and examined various factors including pollution levels and the use or abuse of natural resources.

Electricity. In 2002 installed capacity was 214·5m. kW and electricity production 889·6bn. kWh. Consumption per capita was 4,181 kWh in 2001. The dominant electricity company is Unified Energy System of Russia (52% state-owned). It generated 617·4bn. kWh in 2002 (69% of all electricity produced in Russia). It is set to be broken up and its generating capacity sold off, although market liberalization is unlikely before 2006. There were 30 nuclear reactors in use in 2003.

Oil and Gas. Russia is the second largest oil producer (after Saudi Arabia) and the second largest exporter (again, after Saudi Arabia). Oil and gas account for 50% of Russia's export revenues. In 2002 there were proven crude petroleum reserves of 60·0bn. bbls. 2002 production of crude petroleum was 379·6m. tonnes (10·7% of the world total and the second highest after Saudi Arabia). There is an extensive domestic oil pipeline system. The main export pipeline to Europe is the Druzhba pipeline (crossing Belarus before splitting into northern and southern routes). The main export terminal is at Novorossiisk on the Black Sea. Other export pipeline developments include the Baltic Pipeline System (the first stage of which became operational in Dec. 2001 with the opening of a new terminal at Primorsk) and the Caspian Pipeline Consortium's pipeline from Tengiz (Kazakhstan) to Novorossiisk, which was commissioned in March 2001.

Output of natural gas in 2002 was 554·9bn. cu. metres, making Russia the world's largest producer. It also has the largest reserves of natural gas—in 2002 it had proven reserves of 47,570bn. cu. metres. There is a comprehensive domestic distribution system (run by Gazprom, a joint-stock company 38%-owned by the Russian government), as well as gas pipelines linking Russia with former Soviet republics. The main export pipelines run from western Siberia through Ukraine and Belarus to European markets. Russia is seeking to diversify its gas export routes and a number of pipeline projects are under development, including the Blue Stream pipeline to Turkey (completed in Oct. 2002). Russia is also looking to export its natural gas to Asian markets.

Minerals. Russia contains great mineral resources: iron ore, coal, gold, platinum, copper, zinc, lead, tin and rare metals. Output, 2001 (in tonnes): coal, 168m.; iron ore, 83m.; lignite, 79m.; bauxite, 4m.; aluminium (2000), 3·25m.; copper, 620,000; nickel (2002), 310,000; zinc (2000), 136,000; chrome ore (2000), 100,000; tin (2000), 5,000; molybdenum (2000), 2,400; gold, 152. Salt production, 1999 estimate: 2m. tonnes. Diamond production, 2002: 23·0m. carats. Only Australia and Botswana produce more diamonds. Annual uranium production is nearly 3,000 tonnes.

Agriculture. A presidential decree of Dec. 1991 authorized the private ownership of land on a general basis, but excluded farmland. Nevertheless, large state and collective farms, inherited from the Soviet era, were forced officially to reorganize, with most becoming joint-stock companies. Farm workers could branch off as private farmers by obtaining a grant of land from their parent farm, although they lacked full ownership rights. In 2002 over 90% of Russia's 400m. ha of farmland remained under the control of the state or former collectives. In Jan. 2003 a new law came into force regulating the possession, use and disposal of land plots designated as agricultural land. The law provides that: the authorities may confiscate farmland if its owners are using it for non-agricultural purposes; regional authorities will have the first option to purchase farmland from its owners; and farmland can only be sold to third parties if authorities refuse their option to buy. The law also deprives foreigners of the right to own agricultural land, although they may lease it for up to 49 years. In 2001 there were 123·86m. ha of arable land and 1·86m. ha of permanent crops. There were 4·6m. ha of irrigated land in 2001.

Output in 2000 (in 1,000 tonnes) included: wheat, 36,000; potatoes, 35,297; sugarbeets, 14,041; barley, 13,266; oats, 5,500; rye, 5,300; cabbages, 4,500; sunflower seeds, 3,900; tomatoes, 1,985; maize, 1,800; carrots, 1,605; onions, 1,320; apples, 1,200. Russia is the world's largest producer of oats and the second largest producer of potatoes and sunflower seeds.

Livestock, 2000: cattle, 27·5m.; pigs, 18·3m; sheep, 14·0m.; poultry, 342m. Livestock products in 2000 (in tonnes): meat, 4·3m.; milk, 31·8m.; eggs, 1·9m.; cheese, 364,000.

Forestry. Russia has the largest area covered by forests of any country in the world, with 851·39m. ha in 2000 (50·4% of the land area). In 2001 timber production was 162·30m. cu. metres, down from 228·52m. in 1992. In 2001 Russia was the world's largest exporter of roundwood with 31·9% of the world total.

Fisheries. Total catch in 2001 was 3,628,323 tonnes (down from 8,211,516 tonnes in 1989). Approximately 94% of the fish caught are from marine waters.

INDUSTRY

As a result of Soviet central planning, Russian industry remains dominated by heavy industries, such as energy and metals. In 2001 fuels and energy production accounted for almost 20% of industrial output and metallurgy for 17%. Machine building and metalworking remained the largest processing industry, accounting for almost 20% of industrial production, followed by chemical manufacture. Light industry accounted for less than 2% of industrial output in 2001. Russia had fewer than 1m. small- and medium-sized enterprises at the end of 2001. Small- and medium-sized enterprises account for only 10–15% of GDP.

The leading companies by market capitalization in Russia in May 2004 were: Gazprom (US$70·8bn.), a gas company; Surgutneftegas (US$25·9bn.), an oil and gas field construction company; and Lukoil Holding (US$23·7bn.), an oil production company.

Output (in tonnes) includes: crude steel (2002), 59·8m.; residual fuel oil (2000), 53·3m.; distillate fuel oil (2000), 49·2m.; rolled steel (2000), 46·7m.; pig iron (2002), 46·2m.; cement (2001), 35·3m.; petrol (2000), 27·2m.; jet fuels (2000), 8·7m.; bread (2001), 8·6m.; sulphuric acid (2001), 8·2m.; paper and paperboard (2002), 5·9m.; steel pipe (2001), 5·4m.; cellulose (2000), 5·0m.; sugar (2002), 1·8m.; caustic soda (2000), 1·2m.; biscuits, pastry and cakes (2001), 1·0m.; soap, washing powder and detergents (2000), 436,000; synthetic fibre (2000), 164,000; (in sq. metres) glass (2001), 33·8m.; (in units) bricks (2000), 10,700m.; motor vehicles (1999), 1·2m.; tractors (1999), 15,417; combine harvesters (2001), 9,063; watches (2000), 6·5m.; refrigerators (2001), 1·5m.; televisions (2001), 1·0m.; washing machines (2001), 1·0m.; cigarettes (2001), 355·6bn.; beer (2001), 6,370m. litres.; soft drinks (2001), 2,730·0m. litres; vodka and liquors (2000), 1,230m. litres; mineral water (2001), 1,220m. litres.

Labour. In 2002 the economically active population numbered 71·7m., of whom 66m. were in employment (8·0% unemployed). Average monthly wages were 4,413·6 roubles in 2002 (compared to 3,240·4 roubles in 2001 and 2,223·4 in 2000; the minimum wage from Oct. 2003 was 600 roubles (compared to 250 roubles in 2001 and 107·8 in 2000). In 2001, 39·9m. people, or 27·6% of the population, had an average per capita money income lower than the subsistence minimum. The state

Federal Employment Service was set up in 1992. Unemployment benefits are paid by the Service for 12 months, payable at: 75% of the average monthly wage during the last two months preceding unemployment for the first three months; 60% for the next four months; and 45% for the last five months. Annual paid leave is 24 working days. The workforce was 72·52m. in 1998, of which 16·76m. worked in services, 14·15m. in mining, manufacturing and public utilities, 8·90m. in trade, 8·28m. in agriculture, 5·41m. in construction, 5·04m. in transport and communications, and 2·57m. in public administration and defence. In 2001, 47,100 working days were lost through strikes (6,000,500 in 1996). Retirement age is 55 years for women, 60 for men.

Trade Unions. The Federation of Independent Trade Unions (founded 1990) is the successor to the former Communist official union organization. In 2002 it comprised 78 regional and 48 sectoral trade unions, with a total membership of 40m. There are also free trade unions.

INTERNATIONAL TRADE

Foreign debt was US$147,541m. in 2002 (much of it inherited from the Soviet Union). Most CIS republics have given up claims on Soviet assets in return for Russia assuming their portion of foreign debt. A Foreign Investment Agency was set up in Dec. 1992. The level of foreign direct investment in Russia is very low relative to other transition economies; the cumulative investment figure from 1991–2001 was US$18,200m. The largest investors in Russia are the USA, Germany, Netherlands and Cyprus. The main areas of investment are pipeline transport, trade and fuel industry. Following an agreement to supply oil to the US West Coast in 2002, Russia is looking to secure American investment in its oil industry.

Imports and Exports. Trade in US$1m.:

	1998	*1999*	*2000*	*2001*	*2002*
Imports f.o.b.	58,014	39,537	44,862	53,764	60,966
Exports f.o.b.	74,443	75,549	105,034	101,884	107,247

In 2000 Germany accounted for 9·0% of exports, USA 7·7%, Italy 7·0%, Belarus 5·4% and China 5·1%. Germany provided 11·5% of imports in 2000, Belarus 11·1%, Ukraine 10·8%, the USA 8·0% and Kazakhstan 6·5%. In 1999, of exports, 18·0% by value was petroleum, 15·4% natural gas, 6·8% machinery and transport equipment, 6·4% iron and steel, 5·6% aluminium and 5·2% chemicals. Of imports, 18·7% by value was machinery and transport equipment, 14·5% foodstuffs, 9·8% manufactured goods and 7·2% chemical products.

COMMUNICATIONS

Roads. In 2002 there were 952,000 km of roads, of which 752,000 were hard surfaced. In 2002, 23,269m. passengers were carried by automotive services, 8,176m. by trolleybuses and 6,987m. by trams. There were 20,353,000 passenger cars in use in 2000 plus 4,400,600 trucks and vans and 640,100 buses and coaches. There were 30,916 road deaths in 2001.

Rail. Length of railways in 2002 was 86,200 km of 1,520 mm gauge (of which 40,300 km electrified), and 957 km of 1,067 mm gauge on Sakhalin island. In 2002, 1,270·9m. passengers and 1,084·2m. tonnes of freight were carried by rail; passenger-km travelled came to 153bn. and freight tonne-km to 1,508bn. There are metro services in Moscow (265 km), St Petersburg (110 km), Nizhny Novgorod (17 km), Novosibirsk (13 km), Samara (9 km) and Yekaterinburg (8 km).

Civil Aviation. The main international airports are at Moscow (Sheremetevo) and St Petersburg (Pulkovo). The national carrier is Aeroflot International Russian Airlines, which is 51% state- and 49% employee-owned. Pulkovo, Siberia, Transaero and Vnukovo Airlines also operate internationally.

In 1999 Aeroflot carried 4,438,900 passengers (3,275,800 on international flights) and flew 164·2m. km; Pulkovo Airlines carried 1,337,800 passengers (464,900 on international flights) and flew 29·1m. km. Moscow Sheremetevo handled 10,764,000 passengers in 2000 (7,825,000 on international flights) and 102,100 tonnes of freight. Moscow Vnukovo is mainly used for internal flights and was the second busiest airport in 2000, handling 3,451,000 passengers (2,802,000 on domestic flights) and 44,000 tonnes of freight. St Petersburg was the third busiest in 2000 for passengers (2,568,304) and for freight (19,101 tonnes).

Shipping. At the end of 2001 the merchant fleet comprised 4,727 vessels totalling 10,247,803 GRT. In 1995, 236 vessels (24% of tonnage) were registered under foreign flags. Vessels totalling 117,306,000 NRT entered ports in 2002 and vessels totalling 100,620,000 NRT cleared. In 2002, 31·1m. passengers and 115·7m. tonnes of freight were carried on 95,900 km of inland waterways. The busiest ports are Novorossiisk (which handled 63,291,000 tonnes in 2002) and St Petersburg (42,680,000 tonnes in 2002).

Telecommunications. Russia had 53,168,100 telephone subscribers in 2002, or 362·7 for every 1,000 persons, but in 1999 there were 6·53m. people on the waiting list for a line—the largest number of any country in the world. There were 17,608,800 mobile phone subscribers in 2002 and 13·0m. PCs in use (88·7 per 1,000 persons), and 53,000 fax machines in 1998. Internet users numbered 18·0m. in Dec. 2001.

Postal Services. In 1997 there were 43,900 post offices (one for every 3,350 persons).

SOCIAL INSTITUTIONS

Justice. The Supreme Court is the highest judicial body on civil, criminal and administrative law. The Supreme Arbitration Court deals with economic cases. The KGB, and the Federal Security Bureau which succeeded it, were replaced in Dec. 1992 by the Federal Counter-Intelligence Service. The legal system is, however, crippled by corruption.

A new civil code was introduced in 1993 to replace the former Soviet code. It guarantees the inviolability of private property and includes provisions for the freedom of movement of capital and goods.

12-member juries were introduced in a number of courts after Nov. 1993, but in the years that followed jury trials were not widely used. However, on 1 Jan. 2003 jury trials began to be phased in nationwide. A new criminal code came into force on 1 Jan. 1997, based on respect for the rights and freedoms of the individual and the sanctity of private property. A further new code that entered force on 1 July 2002 introduced new levels of protection for defendants and restrictions on law enforcement officials. The death penalty is retained for five crimes against the person. It is not applied to minors, women or men over 65.

In 2000, 2,952,400 crimes were recorded, including 28,904 murders, 132,393 robberies and 6,978 rapes. Russia's murder rate, at 19·9 per 100,000 population in 2000, ranks among the highest in the world. In 1996 there were 140 executions (86 in 1995; 1 in 1992). President Yeltsin placed a moratorium on capital punishment in 1996 when Russia joined the Council of Europe, but parliament has refused to abolish the death penalty. The prison population in Aug. 2003 was 865,000. Russia's prison population rate (606 per 100,000 population in Aug. 2003) is the second highest in the world after the USA. In 2003 there were 1,010 prison establishments and institutions.

Religion. The Russian Orthodox Church is the largest religious association in the country. In early 2003 it had 128 dioceses (compared with 67 in 1989), over 19,000 parishes (6,893 in 1988) and about 480 monasteries (18 in 1980). There are also five theological academies, 26 seminaries, 29 pre-seminaries, two Orthodox universities, a theological institute, a women's pre-seminary and 28 icon-painting schools. In 2001 there were 23·6m. adherents. The total number of theological students is around 6,000. There are still many Old Believers, whose schism from the Orthodox Church dates from the 17th century. The Russian Church is headed by the Patriarch of Moscow and All Russia (Metropolitan Aleksi II of St Petersburg and Novgorod, b. 1929; elected June 1990), assisted by the Holy Synod, which has seven members—the Patriarch himself and the Metropolitans of Krutitsy and Kolomna (Moscow), St Petersburg and Kyiv *ex officio*, and three bishops alternating for six months in order of seniority from the three regions forming the Moscow Patriarchate. The Patriarchate of Moscow maintains jurisdiction over 119 eparchies, of which 59 are in Russia; there are parishes of Russian Orthodox abroad, in Belarus, Ukraine, Kazakhstan, Moldova, Uzbekistan, the Baltic states, and in Damascus, Geneva, Prague, New York and Japan. There is a spiritual mission in Jerusalem, and a monastery at Mt Athos in Greece. A Russian Orthodox church was consecrated in Dublin in Ireland in Feb. 2003. Muslims represent the second largest religious community in Russia, numbering 19m. There are an estimated 2m. Protestants, and Jewish communities, primarily in Moscow and St Petersburg, numbered 590,000 in 2001. The *Grand Mufti* is Talgat Tadschuddin.

Education. Adult literacy rate in 2001 was 99·6% (male, 99·7%; female, 99·4%). In 1998 there were 23·97m. pupils in 72,169 primary and secondary day schools; 3·60m. students in 914 higher educational establishments (including correspondence students); and in 1995, 3·6m. students in 6,800 technical colleges of all kinds (including correspondence students); and 5·6m. children in 68,600 pre-school institutions. In 1994–95 there were 822 grammar schools and 505 *lycées* with a combined total of 1m. students. In addition there were 447 private schools with 40,000 pupils.

The Russian Academy of Sciences, founded in 1724 and reorganized in 1925 as the Academy of Sciences of the Union of Soviet Socialist Republics, was restored under its present name in 1991. It is the highest scientific self-governing institution in Russia and has 18 divisions on particular areas of science. The Academy also has three regional branches: the Urals Branch, the Siberian Branch and the Far East Branch. In Jan. 1995 there were 3,968 scientific institutes, of which 2,166 were independent research institutes.

In 2000–01 total expenditure on education came to 3·1% of GNP and 10·6% of total government spending.

A survey for the 1999 *World Competitiveness Yearbook* showed that well-educated people in Russia are the most likely of any country in the world to emigrate—87 out of every 100 well-educated Russians go abroad to live and work.

Health. Doctors in 1998 numbered 682,000, and hospital beds 1·73m. The doctor/inhabitant ratio in 1998 was 1:237 and hospital bed provision in 1998 was 12·1 per 1,000 persons. There were 47,322 dentists, 1,615,000 nurses, 9,122 pharmacists and 91,853 midwives. Expenditure on health in 2000 was 5·3% of GDP. In 1999 and 2000 Russia experienced the highest rate of growth of HIV cases in the world; by March 2003 there were 237,000 registered cases. In 2001 there were 93 cases of tuberculosis per 100,000 people. In 1998, 48% of Russians aged 15 and over smoked—the highest percentage of any country. The annual average cigarette consumption per adult between 1992–2000 was 2,690.

Welfare. Russia is in the process of implementing a reform of its pensions system, the focus of which is to move away from a distributive system to an accumulating (funded) scheme. Instead of citizens paying 28% of their monthly salary into the state pension fund, since 2004 it has been possible to pay between 2% and 6% to private asset managers.

State welfare provision in 1999 included: old age, disability and survivor pensions; sickness and maternity benefits; work injury payments; unemployment benefits; and family allowances. In the period April–June 2002 the average monthly pension was 1,337 roubles. The subsistence level for pensioners was 1,383 roubles a month.

CULTURE

World Heritage Sites. Russia's heritage sites as classified by UNESCO (with year entered on list) are: the Historic Centre of St Petersburg (1990); the Kremlin and Red Square in Moscow (1990); Khizi Pogost (1990); the Historic Monuments of Novgorod and surroundings (1992); Cultural and Historic Ensemble of the Solovetsky Islands (1992); the White Monuments of Vladimir and Suzdal (1992); Architectural Ensemble of the Trinity Sergius Lavra in Sergiev Posad (1993); the Church of the Ascension, Kolomenskoye (1994); Virgin Komi Forests (1995); Lake Baikal (1996); Volcanoes of Kamchatka (1996, 2001); Golden Mountains of Altai (1998); Western Caucasus (1999); the Ensemble of Ferapontov Monastery (2000);

Historic and Architectural Complex of the Kazan Kremlin (2000); Central Sikhote-Alin (2001); the Citadel, Ancient City and Fortress Buildings of Derbent (2003); Ensemble of the Novodevichy Convent in south-west Moscow (2004); Natural System of Wrangel Island Reserve (2004).

The Russian Federation also shares two UNESCO sites, with Lithuania (Curonian Spit) and Mongolia (Uvs Nuur Basin).

Broadcasting. In 2000 there were 79·0m. television receivers. Television broadcasting is still largely state-controlled. In Nov. 2001 a court ordered that the parent company of TV6, the last independent station, be liquidated. It was closed down in Jan. 2002. There are two major channels, ORT (Russian Public Television) and RTR (Russian Television). Colour is by SECAM H. In 1994, 98·8% of the population could receive TV broadcasts. There are also local city channels. Access to cable TV varies with locality; satellite TV reached about 5% of the population in 1993. As well as state radio, 24% of the population in 1995 could receive commercial broadcasts. In 2000 there were 61·1m. radio receivers.

Press. In 1996 there were 285 daily newspapers with a combined circulation of 15,517,000 (105 per 1,000 population). In the same year there were 4,596 non-daily newspapers with a combined circulation of 98,558,000 (665 per 1,000 population). A presidential decree of 22 Dec. 1993 brought the press agencies ITAR-TASS and RIA-Novosti under state control. In 2000, 56,180 titles were published. Russia's media is becoming relatively independent, but press freedom has suffered setbacks since Vladimir Putin became president.

Tourism. There were 7,943,000 foreign visitors in 2002; revenue from foreign tourists amounted to US$4·19bn.

DIPLOMATIC REPRESENTATIVES

Of Russia in the United Kingdom (13 Kensington Palace Gdns, London, W8 4QX)
Ambassador: Grigory B. Karasin.

Of the United Kingdom in Russia (Smolenskaya Naberezhnaya 10, 121099 Moscow)
Ambassador: Sir Roderic Lyne, KBE, CMG.

Of Russia in the USA (2650 Wisconsin Ave., NW, Washington, D.C., 20007)
Ambassador: Yury Ushakov.

Of the USA in Russia (8 Bolshoy Devyatinskiy Pereuulok, 121099 Moscow)
Ambassador: Alexander R. Vershbow.

Of Russia to the United Nations
Ambassador: Andrey I. Denisov.

Of Russia to the European Union
Ambassador: Vacant.

FURTHER READING

Rossiiskii Statisticheskii Ezhegodnik. Moscow, annual (title varies)

Acton, E., *et al.*, *Critical Companion to the Russian Revolution.* Indiana Univ. Press, 1997
Aron, Leon, *Boris Yeltsin: A Revolutionary Life.* HarperCollins, London, 2000
Aslund, Anders (ed.) *Economic Transformation in Russia.* New York, 1994.—*Building Capitalism: the Transformation of the Former Soviet Bloc.* CUP, 2002
Brady, Rose, *Kapitalizm: Russia's Struggle to Free its Economy.* Yale Univ. Press, 2000
Cambridge Encyclopedia of Russia and the Former Soviet Union. CUP, 1995
Dunlop, J., *Russia Confronts Chechnya: Roots of a Separatist Conflict, Vol. 1.* CUP, 1998
Fowkes, B. (ed.) *Russia and Chechnia: The Permanent Crisis, Essays on Russo-Chechen Relations.* St Martin's Press, New York, 1998
Freeze, G. (ed.) *Russia: A History.* OUP, 1997
Gall, C. and de Waal, T., *Chechnya: Calamity in the Caucasus.* New York, 1998
Gorbachev, Mikhail, *On My Country and the World*; translated from Russian. Columbia Univ. Press, New York, 2000
Granville, Brigitte and Oppenheimer, Peter (eds.) *Russia's Post-Community Economy.* OUP, 2001
Gustafson, Thane, *Capitalism Russian-Style.* Cambridge Univ. Press, 2000

Hollander, Paul, *Political Will and Personal Belief: The Decline and Fall of Soviet Communism.* Yale Univ. Press, 2000
Hosking, Geoffrey, *Russia and the Russians, A History from Rus to the Russian Federation.* Allen Lane/The Penguin Press, London, 2001
Kochan, L., *The Making of Modern Russia.* 2nd ed., revised by R. Abraham. London, 1994
Kotkin, Stephen, *Armageddon Averted: the Soviet Collapse 1970–2000.* OUP, 2001
Lieven, A., *Chechnya: Tombstone of Russian Power.* Yale Univ. Press, 1998
Lloyd, J., *Rebirth of a Nation.* London, 1998
Marks, Steven, *How Russia Shaped the Modern World: From Art to Anti-Semitism, Ballet to Bolshevism.* Princeton Univ. Press, 2002
Paxton, J., *Encyclopedia of Russian History.* Denver (CO), 1993.—*Leaders of Russia and the Soviet Union.* Fitzroy Dearborn, London, 2004
Pitman, L., *Russia/USSR.* [Bibliography] 2nd ed. ABC-Clio, Oxford and Santa Barbara (CA), 1994
Putin, Vladimir, *First Person*; interviews, translated from Russian. Hutchinson, London, 2000
Remnick, D., *Resurrection: The Struggle for a New Russia.* Picador, London, 1998
Riasanovsky, N. V., *A History of Russia.* 5th ed. OUP, 1993
Sakwa, R., *Russian Politics and Society.* 2nd ed. London, 1996
Service, Robert, *A History of Twentieth-Century Russia.* Harvard Univ. Press, 1997.—*Lenin: A Biography.* Macmillan, London, 2000.—*Russia: Experiment with a People.* Pan Macmillan, London, 2002
Shevtsova, Lilia, *Putin's Russia.* Carnegie Endowment for International Peace, Washington, D.C., 2003
Shriver, G. (ed. and transl.) *Post-Soviet Russia, A Journey Through the Yeltsin Era.* Columbia Univ. Press, 2000
Westwood, J. N., *Endurance and Endeavour: Russian History, 1812–1992.* 4th ed. OUP, 1993
White, Stephen, *et al.*, *How Russia Votes.* Chatham House (NJ), 1997
White, Stephen, Sakwa, Richard and Gitelman, Zvi, (eds.) *Developments in Russian Politics 6.* Palgrave Macmillan, Basingstoke, 2005
Woodruff, David, *Money Unmade: Barter and the Fate of Russian Capitalism.* Cornell Univ. Press, 2000
Yeltsin, B., *The View from the Kremlin* (in USA *The Struggle for Russia*). London and New York, 1994

National statistical office: Gosudarstvennyi Komitet po Statistike (*Goskomstat*), Moscow.
Website: http://www.gks.ru

THE REPUBLICS

Status

The 21 republics that with Russia itself constitute the Russian Federation were part of the RSFSR in the Soviet period. On 31 March 1992 the federal government concluded treaties with the then 20 republics, except Checheno-Ingushetia and Tatarstan, defining their mutual responsibilities. The *Council of the Heads of the Republics* is chaired by the Russian President and includes the Russian Prime Minister. Its function is to provide an interaction between the federal government and the republican authorities.

ADYGEYA

Part of Krasnodar Territory. Area, 7,600 sq. km (2,934 sq. miles); population (2002 census), 477,000. Capital, Maikop (1996 population, 165,500). Established 27 July 1922; granted republican status in 1991.

President: Hazret Sovmen, b. 1937 (took office on 8 Feb. 2002).

Prime Minister: Asfar Khagur (took office on 30 Dec. 2004).

Chief industries are timber, woodworking, food processing and there is some engineering and gas production. Agriculture consists primarily of crops (beets, wheat, maize), on partly irrigated land. Industrial output was valued in 1993 at 112,000m. roubles, agricultural output at 68,000m. roubles.

In 1994–95 there were 174 schools with 67,000 pupils, three technical colleges with 5,200 students and two higher educational institutions with 6,200 students.

In 1995 the rates of doctors and hospital beds per 10,000 population were 32·7 and 113 respectively.

ALTAI

Part of Altai Territory. Area, 92,600 sq. km (35,740 sq. miles); population (2002 census), 202,900. Capital, Gorno-Altaisk (estimated 2001 population, 53,100). Established 1 June 1922 as Oirot Autonomous Region; renamed 7 Jan. 1948; granted republican status in 1991 and renamed in 1992.

Chairman of the Government: Mikhail Lapshin (since 19 Jan. 2002).

Chief industries are clothing and footwear, foodstuffs, gold mining, timber, chemicals and dairying. Cattle breeding predominates; pasturages and hay meadows cover over 1m. ha, but 142,000 ha are under crops. Industrial output was valued at 19,900m. roubles in 1993, agricultural output at 43,000m. roubles. In 2000, 91,200 people were economically active, of whom 72,000 were in employment.

In 1994–95 there were 39,000 pupils in 194 schools; four technical colleges had 3,100 students and 3,700 students were attending a pedagogical institute.

The rates of doctors and hospital beds per 10,000 population in 1995 were 32·7 and 153 respectively.

BASHKORTOSTAN

Area 143,600 sq. km (55,430 sq. miles), population (2002 census), 4,102,900. Capital, Ufa (1996 population, 1,096,400). Bashkiria was annexed to Russia in 1557. It was constituted as an Autonomous Soviet Republic on 23 March 1919. A declaration of republican sovereignty was adopted in 1990, and a declaration of independence on 28 March 1992. A treaty of Aug. 1994 with Russia preserves the common legislative framework of the Russian Federation while defining mutual areas of competence. The population, census 1989, was 39·3% Russian, 28·4% Tatar, 21·9% Bashkir, 3·0% Chuvash and 2·7% Mari.

A constitution was adopted on 24 Dec. 1993. It states that Bashkiria conducts its own domestic and foreign policy, that its laws take precedence in Bashkiria, and that it forms part of the Russian Federation on a voluntary and equal basis.

President: Murtaza Gubaidullovich Rakhimov (since 7 April 1990).

Prime Minister: Rafael Baidavletov (since 12 Jan. 1999).

Industrial production was valued at 4,188,000m. roubles in 1993, agricultural output at 617,000m. roubles. The most important industries are oil and oil products; there are also engineering, glass and building materials enterprises. Agriculture specializes in wheat, barley, oats and livestock.

In 1994–95 there were 658,000 pupils in 3,317 schools. There is a state university and a branch of the Academy of Sciences with eight learned institutions (511 research workers). There were 59,800 students in 75 technical colleges and 49,800 in 11 higher educational establishments.

In 1995 the rates of doctors and hospital beds per 10,000 population were 40·1 and 131 respectively.

BURYATIA

Area is 351,300 sq. km (135,650 sq. miles). The Buryat Republic, situated to the south of Sakha, adopted the Soviet system on 1 March 1920. This area was penetrated by the Russians in the 17th century and finally annexed from China by the treaties of Nerchinsk (1689) and Kyakhta (1727). Population (2002 census), 981,000. Capital, Ulan-Ude (1996 population, 368,100). The population (1989 census) was 69·9% Russian, 24·0% Buryat, 2·2% Ukrainian, 1·0% Tatar and 0·5% Belorussian.

There is a 65-member parliament, the *People's Hural.*

President: Leonid Potapov (in power since 21 Oct. 1991).

The main industries are engineering, brown coal and graphite, timber, building materials, sheep and cattle farming. Industrial production was valued at 384,000m. roubles in 1993, agricultural output at 181,000m. roubles.

In 1994–95 there were 615 schools with 196,000 pupils, 20 technical colleges with 13,400 students and four higher educational institutions with 19,300 students. A branch of the Siberian Department of the Academy of Sciences had four institutions with 281 research workers.

In 1995 the rates of doctors and hospital beds per 10,000 population were 37·4 and 114 respectively.

CHECHNYA

The area of the Republic of Chechnya is 15,000 sq. km (5,800 sq. miles). The population at the 2002 census was 1,100,300. Capital, Dzhohar (since March 1998; previously known as Grozny). The Chechens and Ingushes were conquered by Russia in the late 1850s. In 1920 each nationality were constituted areas within the Soviet Mountain Republic and the Chechens became an Autonomous Region on 30 Nov. 1922. In Jan. 1934 the two regions were united, and on 5 Dec. 1936 constituted as the Checheno-Ingush Autonomous Republic. This was dissolved in 1944 and the population was deported en masse, allegedly for collaboration with the German occupation forces. It was reconstituted on 9 Jan. 1957: 232,000 Chechens and Ingushes returned to their homes in the next two years.

In 1991 rebel leader Jokhar Dudayev seized control of Chechnya and won elections. In Nov. he declared an independent Chechen Republic. Ingush desire to separate from Chechnya led to fighting along the Chechen-Ingush border and a deployment of Russian troops. An agreement to withdraw was reached between Russia and Chechnya on 15 Nov. 1992. The separation of Chechnya and Ingushetia was formalized in Dec. 1992. In April 1993 President Dudayev dissolved parliament. Hostilities continued throughout 1994 between the government and forces loosely grouped under the 'Provisional Chechen Council'. The Russian government, which had never recognized the Chechen declaration of independence of Nov. 1991, moved troops and armour into Chechnya on 11 Dec. 1994. Grozny was bombed and attacked by Russian ground forces at the end of Dec. 1994 and the presidential palace was captured on 19 Jan. 1995, but fighting continued. On 30 July 1995 the Russian and Chechen authorities signed a ceasefire. However, hostilities, raids and hostage-taking continued; Dudayev was killed in April 1996 and a ceasefire was agreed on 30 Aug. 1996.

Fighting broke out again, however, in Sept. 1999 as Russian forces launched attacks on 'rebel bases'. Fighting intensified and more than 200,000 civilians were forced to flee, mostly to neighbouring Ingushetia. By Feb. 2000 much of Grozny had been destroyed and was closed by the Russians. In June 2000 Vladimir Putin declared direct rule. The war continues, with estimates of the number of deaths varying from 6,500 to 15,000. Over 4,000 Russian soldiers have been killed. However, on 18 Nov. 2001 the first official meeting between negotiators for the Russian government and Chechen separatists took place. In Oct. 2002 a group of Chechen rebels took control of a Moscow theatre and held hostage 800 people for three days, before Russian troops stormed the building. An anaesthetic gas, used to combat the rebels, also killed many of the hostages.

On 23 March 2003 a referendum was held on a new constitution that would keep Chechnya within Russia but give it greater autonomy, and provide a new president and parliament for the republic. Although 96% of votes cast were in favour of the new constitution there was criticism of the conduct of the referendum. Presidential elections held on 5 Oct. 2003 were won by the Kremlin-backed candidate Akhmad Kadyrov, with 80·8% of the vote, but there was widespread condemnation of the electoral process. President Kadyrov was assassinated on 9 May 2004. Presidential elections held on 29 Aug. 2004, widely seen as rigged, were won by the Kremiln-backed Alu Alkhanov with 73·5% of the vote, against 5·9% for Movsur Khamidov, head of the Chechen department of the Federal Security Service. There were five other candidates. Turn-out was 85·2%.

Separatist President Aslan Maskhadov was killed by Russian troops on 8 March 2005.

Moscow-backed President: Alu Alkhanov; b. 1957. *Prime Minister:* Sergey Abramov; b. 1972. *Separatist President (acting):* Abdul-Khalim Sadulayev; b. 1967.

Checheno-Ingushetia had a major oilfield, and a number of engineering works, chemical factories, building materials works and food canneries. There was a timber, woodworking and furniture industry. Industrial output in the two republics was valued at 213,000m. roubles in 1993, agricultural output at 79,000m. roubles.

There were, in the Chechen and Ingush republics in 1993–94, 548 schools with 251,000 pupils, 12 technical colleges with 8,700 students and three places of higher education with 13,100 students. In 1995 the rates of doctors and hospital beds per 10,000 population were 21·1 and 91 respectively.

FURTHER READING

Lieven, A. and Bradner, H., *Chechnya: Tombstone of Russian Power.* Yale Univ. Press, 1999

CHUVASHIA

Area, 18,300 sq. km (7,064 sq. miles); population (2002 census), 1,313,900. Capital, Cheboksary (1996 population, 461,600). The territory was annexed by Russia in the middle of the 16th century. On 24 June 1920 it was constituted as an Autonomous Region, and on 21 April 1925 as an Autonomous Republic. The population (1989 census) was 67·8% Chuvash, 26·7% Russian, 2·7% Tatar and 1·4% Mordovian. Republican sovereignty was declared in Sept. 1990.

President: Nikolai Fedorov (took office on 21 Jan. 1994).

The timber industry antedates the Soviet period. Other industries include railway repair works, electrical and other engineering industries, building materials, chemicals, textiles and food industries. Grain crops account for nearly two-thirds of all sowings and fodder crops for nearly a quarter. Industrial output was valued at 641,000m. roubles in 1993, agricultural output at 224,000m. roubles.

In 1994–95 there were 218,000 pupils at 719 schools, 20,000 students at 27 technical colleges and 18,900 students at three higher educational establishments.

In 1995 the rates of doctors and hospital beds per 10,000 population were 37·9 and 124 respectively.

DAGESTAN

Area, 50,300 sq. km (19,416 sq. miles); population (2002 census), 2,584,200. Capital, Makhachkala (1995 population, 340,200). Over 30 nationalities inhabit this republic apart from Russians (9·2% at 1989 census); the most numerous are Dagestani nationalities (80·2%), Azerbaijanis (4·2%), Chechens (3·2%) and Jews (0·5%). Annexed from Persia in 1723, Dagestan was constituted an Autonomous Republic on 20 Jan. 1921. In 1991 the Supreme Soviet declared the area of republican, rather than autonomous republican, status. Many of the nationalities who live in Dagestan have organized armed militias, and in May 1998 rebels stormed the government building in Makhachkala. In Aug. 1999 Dagestan faced attacks from Islamic militants who invaded from Chechnya. Although Russian troops tried to restore order and discipline, the guerrilla campaign continued.

Chairman of the State Council: Magomedali Magomedov (in power since 1987).

Prime Minister: Atay Aliyev (in office since 14 Oct. 2004).

There are engineering, oil, chemical, woodworking, textile, food and other light industries. Agriculture is varied, ranging from wheat to grapes, with sheep farming and cattle breeding. Industrial output was valued at 136,000m. roubles in 1993, agricultural output at 155,000m. roubles.

In 1994–95 there were 1,609 schools with 413,000 pupils, 17,700 students at 27 technical colleges and six higher education establishments with 28,400 students.

In 1995 the rates of doctors and hospital beds per 10,000 population were 36·5 and 88 respectively.

INGUSHETIA

The history of Ingushetia is interwoven with that of Chechnya (*see above*). Ingush desire to separate from Chechnya led to fighting along the Chechen-Ingush border and a deployment of Russian troops. The separation of Ingushetia from Chechnya was formalized by an amendment of Dec. 1992 to the Russian Constitution. On 15 May 1993 an extraordinary congress of the peoples of Ingushetia adopted a declaration of state sovereignty within the Russian Federation. Skirmishes between Ingush refugees and local police broke out in Aug. 1999 and tensions remained high with the danger of further outbreaks of fighting. The Russian attacks on neighbouring Chechnya in Sept. 1999 led to thousands of Chechen refugees fleeing to Ingushetia.

The capital is Magas (since 1999; formerly Nazran).

Area, 4,300 sq. km (1,700 sq. miles); population (2002 census), 468,900.

There is a 27-member parliament. On 27 Feb. 1994 presidential elections and a constitutional referendum were held. Turn-out was 70%. At the referendum 97% of votes cast approved a new constitution stating that Ingushetia is a democratic law-based secular republic forming part of the Russian Federation on a treaty basis.

President: Murat Zyazikov. *Prime Minister:* Timur Mogushkov.

A special economic zone for Russian residents was set up in 1994, and an 'offshore' banking tax haven in 1996. In 1995 the rates of doctors and hospital beds per 10,000 population were 19·6 and 59 respectively.

KABARDINO-BALKARIA

Area, 12,500 sq. km (4,825 sq. miles); population (2002 census), 900,500. Capital, Nalchik (1996 population, 237,100). Kabarda was annexed to Russia in 1557. The republic was constituted on 5 Dec. 1936. Population (1989 census) included Kabardinians (48·2%), Balkars (9·4%), Russians (31·9%), Ukrainians (1·7%), Ossetians (1·3%) and Germans (1·1%).

A treaty with Russia of 1 July 1994 defines their mutual areas of competence within the legislative framework of the Russian Federation.

President: Valeri Kokov (took office on 9 Jan. 1992).

Main industries are ore-mining, timber, engineering, coal, food processing, timber and light industries, building materials. Grain, livestock breeding, dairy farming and wine-growing are the principal branches of agriculture. Industrial output was valued at 176,000m. roubles in 1993, agricultural output at 113,000m. roubles.

In 1994–95 there were 252 schools with 139,000 pupils, 6,900 students in eight technical colleges and 12,900 students at three higher educational establishments.

In 1995 the rates of doctors and hospital beds per 10,000 population were 44·8 and 120 respectively.

KALMYKIA

Area, 76,100 sq. km (29,382 sq. miles); population (2002 census), 292,400. Capital, Elista (1996 population, 96,200). The population (1989 census) was 45·4% Kalmyk, 37·7% Russian, 2·6% Chechen, 1·9% Kazakh and 1·7% German.

The Kalmyks migrated from western China to Russia (Nogai Steppe) in the early 17th century. The territory was constituted an Autonomous Region on 4 Nov. 1920, and an Autonomous Republic on 22 Oct. 1935; this was dissolved in 1943. On 9 Jan. 1957 it was reconstituted as an Autonomous Region and on 29 July 1958 as an Autonomous Republic once more. In Oct. 1990 the republic was renamed the Kalmyk Soviet Socialist Republic; it was given its present name in Feb. 1992.

President: Kirsan Nikolaevich Ilyumzhinov (since April 1993).

In April 1993 the Supreme Soviet was dissolved and replaced by a professional parliament consisting of 25 of the former deputies. On 5 April 1994 a specially-constituted 300-member constituent assembly adopted a 'Steppe Code' as

Kalmykia's basic law. This is not a constitution and renounces the declaration of republican sovereignty of 18 Oct. 1990. It provides for a *President* elected for five-year terms with the power to dissolve parliament, and a 27-member parliament, the *People's Hural*, elected every four years. It stipulates that Kalmykia is an equal member and integral part of the Russian Federation, functioning in accordance with the Russian constitution.

Main industries are fishing, canning and building materials. Cattle breeding and irrigated farming (mainly fodder crops) are the principal branches of agriculture. Industrial output was valued at 35,600m. roubles in 1993, agricultural output at 89,000m. roubles.

In 1994–95 there were 59,000 pupils in 252 schools, 4,200 students in six technical colleges and 5,100 in higher education. In 1995 the rates of doctors and hospital beds per 10,000 population were 48·8 and 151 respectively.

KARACHAI-CHERKESSIA

Area, 14,300 sq. km (5,521 sq. miles); population (2002 census), 439,700. Capital, Cherkessk (1996 population, 119,900). A Karachai Autonomous Region was established on 26 April 1926 (out of a previously united Karachaevo-Cherkess Autonomous Region created in 1922), and dissolved in 1943. A Cherkess Autonomous Region was established on 30 April 1928. The present Autonomous Region was re-established on 9 Jan. 1957. The Region declared itself a Soviet Socialist Republic in Dec. 1990. Tension between the two ethnic groups increased after the first free presidential election in April 1999 was won by Vladimir Semyonov, an ethnic Karchayev. Despite numerous allegations of fraud the result was upheld by the Supreme Court. There were subsequently fears that the ethnic Cherkess opposition would attempt to set up breakaway government bodies.

President: Mustafa Batdyev, b. 1950 (took office on 4 Sept. 2003).

There are ore-mining, engineering, chemical and woodworking industries. The Kuban-Kalaussi irrigation scheme irrigates 200,000 ha. Livestock breeding and grain growing predominate in agriculture. Industrial output was valued at 114,000m. roubles in 1993, agricultural output at 92,000m. roubles.

In 1994–95 there were 74,000 pupils in 188 secondary schools, six technical colleges with 4,800 students and two institutes with 6,200 students.

In 1995 the rates of doctors and hospital beds per 10,000 population were 29 and 102 respectively.

KARELIA

The Karelian Republic, capital Petrozavodsk (1996 population, 282,200), covers an area of 172,400 sq. km, with a 2002 census population of 716,700. Karelians represent 10% of the population, Russians 73·6%, Belorussians 7% and Ukrainians 3·6% (1989 census).

Karelia (formerly Olonets Province) became part of the RSFSR after 1917. In June 1920 a Karelian Labour Commune was formed and in July 1923 this was transformed into the Karelian Autonomous Soviet Socialist Republic (one of the autonomous republics of the RSFSR). On 31 March 1940, after the Soviet-Finnish war, practically all the territory (with the exception of a small section in the neighbourhood of the Leningrad area) which had been ceded by Finland to the USSR was added to Karelia, and the Karelian Autonomous Republic was transformed into the Karelo-Finnish Soviet Socialist Republic as the 12th republic of the USSR. In 1946, however, the southern part of the republic, including its whole seaboard and the towns of Viipuri (Vyborg) and Keksholm, was attached to the RSFSR, reverting in 1956 to autonomous republican status within the RSFSR. In Nov. 1991 it declared itself the 'Republic of Karelia'.

Head of the Republic: Sergei Katanandov (in power since May 1998).

Karelia has a wealth of timber, some 70% of its territory being forest land. It is also rich in other natural resources, having large deposits of mica, diabase, spar, quartz, marble, granite, zinc, lead, silver, copper, molybdenum, tin, baryta and iron ore. Its lakes and rivers are rich in fish.

There are timber mills, paper-cellulose works, mica, chemical plants, power stations and furniture factories. Industrial output was valued at 520,000m. roubles in 1993, agricultural output at 97,000m. roubles.

In 1994–95 there were 0·12m. pupils in 341 schools. There were 9,700 students in three institutions of higher education and 11,300 in 16 technical colleges.

In 1995 the rates of doctors and hospital beds per 10,000 population were 47·2 and 135 respectively.

KHAKASSIA

Area, 61,900 sq. km (23,855 sq. miles); population (2002 census), 546,100. Capital, Abakan (1996 population, 163,100). Established 20 Oct. 1930; granted republican status in 1991.

Chairman of the Government: Aleksei Lebed (since 9 Jan. 1997).

There are coal- and ore-mining, timber and woodworking industries. The region is linked by rail with the Trans-Siberian line. Industrial output was valued at 545,000m. roubles in 1993, agricultural output at 83,000m. roubles.

In 1994–95 there were 97,000 pupils in 282 secondary schools, 6,200 students in seven technical colleges and 5,600 students at a higher education institution.

In 1995 the rates of doctors and hospital beds per 10,000 population were 36 and 132 respectively.

KOMI

Area, 415,900 sq. km (160,540 sq. miles); population (2002 census), 1,019,000. Capital, Syktyvkar (1995 population, 228,800). Annexed by the princes of Moscow in the 14th century, the territory was constituted as an Autonomous Region on 22 Aug. 1921 and as an Autonomous Republic on 5 Dec. 1936. The population (1989 census) was 57·7% Russian, 23·3% Komi, 8·3% Ukrainian and 2·1% Belorussian.

A declaration of sovereignty was adopted by the republican parliament in Sept. 1990, and the designation 'Autonomous' dropped from the republic's official name.

Head of the Republic: Vladimir Torlopov (since 15 Jan. 2002).

There are coal, oil, timber, gas, asphalt and building materials industries, and light industry is expanding. Livestock breeding (including dairy farming) is the main branch of agriculture. Crop area, 92,000 ha. Industrial output was valued at 1,038,000m. roubles in 1993, agricultural output at 134,000m. roubles.

In 1994–95 there were 196,000 pupils in 595 schools, 11,300 students in three higher educational establishments, 14,200 students in 20 technical colleges; and a branch of the Academy of Sciences with four institutions (297 research workers). In 1995 the rates of doctors and hospital beds per 10,000 population were 39·6 and 134 respectively.

MARI-EL

Area, 23,200 sq. km (8,955 sq. miles); population (2002 census), 728,000. Capital, Yoshkar-Ola (1996 population, 250,900). The Mari people were annexed to Russia, with other peoples of the Kazan Tatar Khanate, when the latter was overthrown in 1552. On 4 Nov. 1920 the territory was constituted as an Autonomous Region, and on 5 Dec. 1936 as an Autonomous Republic. The republic renamed itself the Mari Soviet Socialist Republic in Oct. 1990, and adopted a new constitution in June 1995.

In Dec. 1991 Vladislav Zotin was elected the first president. The population (1989 census) was 47·5% Russian, 43·3% Mari and 5·9% Tatar.

President: Leonid Markelov (since 14 Jan. 2001).

Coal is mined. The main industries are metalworking, timber, paper, woodworking and food processing. Crops include grain, flax, potatoes, fruit and vegetables. Industrial output was valued at 257,000m. roubles in 1993, agricultural output at 153,000m. roubles.

In 1994–95 there were 432 schools with 128,000 pupils; 14 technical colleges and three higher education establishments had 8,900 and 13,100 students respectively.

In 1995 the rates of doctors and hospital beds per 10,000 population were 38 and 126 respectively.

MORDOVIA

Area, 26,200 sq. km (10,110 sq. miles); population (2002 census), 888,700. Capital, Saransk (1996 population, 319,700). By the 13th century the Mordovian tribes had been subjugated by Russian princes. In 1928 the territory was constituted as a Mordovian Area within the Middle-Volga Territory, on 10 Jan. 1930 as an Autonomous Region and on 20 Dec. 1934 as an Autonomous Republic. The population (1989 census) was 60·8% Russian, 32·5% Mordovian and 4·9% Tatar.

President: Nikolai Merkushkin (in power since Jan. 1995).

Industries include wood-processing and the production of building materials, furniture, textiles and leather goods. Agriculture is devoted chiefly to grain, sugarbeet, sheep and dairy farming. Industrial output was valued at 457,000m. roubles in 1993, agricultural output at 185,000m. roubles.

In 1994–95 there were 139,000 pupils in 828 schools, 12,600 students in 21 technical colleges and 22,900 attending two higher educational institutions.

In 1995 the rates of doctors and hospital beds per 10,000 population were 45·2 and 155 respectively.

NORTH OSSETIA (ALANIA)

Area, 8,000 sq. km (3,088 sq. miles); population (2002 census), 709,900. Capital, Vladikavkaz (1996 population, 313,300). North Ossetia was annexed by Russia from Turkey and named the Terek region in 1861. On 4 March 1918 it was proclaimed an Autonomous Soviet Republic, and on 20 Jan. 1921 set up with others as the Mountain Autonomous Republic, with North Ossetia as the Ossetian (Vladikavkaz) Area within it. On 7 July 1924 the latter was constituted as an Autonomous Region and on 5 Dec. 1936 as an Autonomous Republic. In the early 1990s there was a conflict with neighbouring Ingushetia to the east, and to the south the decision of the Georgian government to disband the republic of South Ossetia led to ethnic war, with North Ossetia supporting the South Ossetians. Pressure for Ossetian reunification continues. In Sept. 2004 hostage takers seized a school in the town of Beslan. A three-day standoff ended with more than 350 people killed, nearly half of them children. Chechen rebels claimed responsibility for the siege.

A new Constitution was adopted on 12 Nov. 1994 under which the republic reverted to its former name, Alania. The population (1989 census) was 53% Ossetian, 29% Russian, 5·2% Chechen, 1·9% Armenian and 1·6% Ukrainian.

President: Aleksandr Dzasokhov (since 30 Jan. 1998).

The main industries are non-ferrous metals (mining and metallurgy), maize processing, timber and woodworking, textiles, building materials, distilleries and food processing. There is also a varied agriculture. Industrial output was valued at 167,000m. roubles in 1993, agricultural output at 175,000m. roubles.

There were, in 1994–95, 104,000 children in 214 schools, 10,800 students in 14 technical colleges and 18,100 students in five higher educational establishments.

In 1995 the rates of doctors and hospital beds per 10,000 population were 68·3 and 127 respectively.

SAKHA

The area is 3,103,200 sq. km (1,197,760 sq. miles), making Sakha the largest republic in the Russian Federation; population (2002 census), 948,100. Capital, Yakutsk (1996 population, 196,400). The Yakuts were subjugated by the Russians in the 17th century. The territory was constituted an Autonomous Republic on 27 April 1922. The population (1989 census) was 50·3% Russian, 33·4% Yakut, 7% Ukrainian and 1·6% Tatar.

President: Vyacheslav Shtyrov (since 27 Jan. 2002).

The principal industries are mining (gold, tin, mica, coal) and livestock-breeding. Silver- and lead-bearing ores and coal are worked. Large diamond fields have been opened up; Sakha produces most of the Russian Federation's output. Timber and food industries are developing. Trapping and breeding of fur-bearing animals (sable, squirrel, silver fox) are an important source of income. Industrial production was valued at 1,771,000m. roubles in 1993, agricultural output at 373,000m. roubles.

In 1994–95 there were 193,000 pupils in 715 secondary schools, 10,400 students at 19 technical colleges and 9,700 attending three higher education institutions.

In 1995 the rates of doctors and hospital beds per 10,000 population were 41·3 and 156 respectively.

TATARSTAN

Area, 68,000 sq. km (26,250 sq. miles); population (2002 census), 3,779,800. Capital, Kazan (1999 population, 1,101,500). From the 10th to the 13th centuries this was the territory of the Volga-Kama Bulgar State; conquered by the Mongols, it became the seat of the Kazan (Tatar) Khans when the Mongol Empire broke up in the 15th century, and in 1552 was conquered again by Russia. On 27 May 1920 it was constituted as an Autonomous Republic. The population (1989 census) was 48·5% Tatar, 43·3% Russian, 3·7% Chuvash, 0·9% Ukrainian and 0·8% Mordovian.

In Oct. 1991 the Supreme Soviet adopted a declaration of independence. At a referendum in March 1992, 61·4% of votes cast were in favour of increased autonomy. A Constitution was adopted in April 1992, which proclaims Tatarstan a sovereign state which conducts its relations with the Russian Federation on an equal basis. On 15 Feb. 1994 the Russian and Tatar presidents signed a treaty defining Tatarstan as a state united with Russia on the basis of the constitutions of both, but the Russian parliament has not ratified it.

President: Mintimer Sharipovich Shaimiyev (since June 1991).

The republic has engineering, oil and chemical, timber, building materials, textiles, clothing and food industries. Industrial production was valued at 2,955,000m. roubles in 1993, agricultural output at 532,000m. roubles.

In 1994–95 there were 2,463 schools with 0·56m. pupils, 65 technical colleges with 52,500 students and 16 higher educational establishments with 63,000 students (including a state university). There is a branch of the USSR Academy of Sciences with five institutions (512 research workers). In 1995 the rates of doctors and hospital beds per 10,000 population were 42·3 and 124 respectively.

TUVA

Area, 170,500 sq. km (65,810 sq. miles); population (2002 census), 305,500. Capital, Kyzyl (1996 population, 95,400). Tuva was incorporated in the USSR as an autonomous region on 11 Oct. 1944 and elevated to an Autonomous Republic on 10 Oct. 1961. The population (1989 census) was 64·3% Tuvans and 32% Russian. Tuva renamed itself the 'Republic of Tuva' in Oct. 1991.

A new constitution was promulgated on 22 Oct. 1993 which adopts the name 'Tyva' for the republic. This constitution provides for a 32-member parliament

(*Supreme Hural*), and a *Grand Hural* alone empowered to change the constitution, asserts the precedence of Tuvan law and adopts powers to conduct foreign policy. It was approved by 62·2% of votes cast at a referendum on 12 Dec. 1993.

Chairman of the Government: Sherig-ool Dizizhikovich Oorzhak.

Tuva is well-watered and hydro-electric resources are important. The Tuvans are mainly herdsmen and cattle farmers and there is much good pastoral land. There are deposits of gold, cobalt and asbestos. The main exports are hair, hides and wool. There are mining, woodworking, garment, leather, food and other industries. Industrial production was valued at 25,800m. roubles in 1993, agricultural output at 44,000m. roubles.

In 1994–95 there were 167 schools with 62,000 pupils; six technical colleges with 3,800 students, and one higher education institution with 2,800 students.

In 1995 the rates of doctors and hospital beds per 10,000 population were 36·7 and 187 respectively.

UDMURTIA

Area, 42,100 sq. km (16,250 sq. miles); population (2002 census), 1,570,500. Capital, Izhevsk (1995 population, 654,400). The Udmurts (formerly known as 'Votyaks') were annexed by the Russians in the 15th and 16th centuries. On 4 Nov. 1920 the Votyak Autonomous Region was constituted (the name was changed to Udmurt in 1932), and on 28 Dec. 1934 was raised to the status of an Autonomous Republic. The population (1989 census) was 58·9% Russian, 30·9% Udmurt, 6·9% Tatar, 0·9% Ukrainian and 0·6% Mari. A declaration of sovereignty and the present state title were adopted in Sept. 1990.

A new parliament was established in Dec. 1993 consisting of a 50-member upper house, the *Council of Representatives*, and a full-time 35-member lower house.

President: Alexander Alexandrovich Volkov (in power since April 1995).

Heavy industry includes the manufacture of locomotives, machine tools and other engineering products, most of them for the defence industries, as well as timber and building materials. There are also light industries: clothing, leather, furniture and food. Industrial production was valued at 958,000m. roubles in 1993, agricultural output at 368,000m. roubles.

In 1994–95 there were 902 schools with 263,000 pupils; there were 19,900 students at 30 technical colleges and 24,800 at five higher educational institutions.

In 1995 the rates of doctors and hospital beds per 10,000 population were 48·1 and 129 respectively.

AUTONOMOUS DISTRICTS AND PROVINCES

Agin-Buryat

Situated in Chita region (Eastern Siberia); area, 19,000 sq. km, population (2002 census), 72,200. Capital, Aginskoe. Formed 1937, its economy is basically pastoral.

Chukot

Situated in Magadan region (Far East); area, 737,700 sq. km. Population (2002 census), 53,600. Capital, Anadyr. Formed 1930. Population chiefly Russian, also Chukchi, Koryak, Yakut, Even. Minerals are extracted in the north, including gold, tin, mercury and tungsten.

Evenki

Situated in Krasnoyarsk territory (Eastern Siberia); area, 767,600 sq. km, population, (2002 census) 17,700, chiefly Evenks. Capital, Tura. Formed 1930.

Khanty-Mansi

Situated in Tyumen region (western Siberia); area, 523,100 sq. km, population (2002 census), 1,433,100, chiefly Russians but also Khants and Mansi. Capital, Khanty-Mansiisk. Formed 1930.

Komi-Permyak

Situated in Perm region (Northern Russia); area, 32,900 sq. km, population (2002 census), 135,900, chiefly Komi-Permyaks. Formed 1925. Capital, Kudymkar. Forestry is the main occupation.

Koryak

Situated in Kamchatka; area, 301,500 sq. km, population (2002 census), 25,000. Capital, Palana. Formed 1930.

Nenets

Situated in Archangel region (Northern Russia); area, 176,700 sq. km, population (2002 census), 41,500. Capital, Naryan-Mar. Formed 1929.

Taimyr

Situated in Krasnoyarsk territory, this most northerly part of Siberia comprises the Taimyr peninsula and the Arctic islands of Severnaya Zemlya. Area, 862,100 sq. km, population (2002 census), 39,800, excluding the mining city of Norilsk which is separately administered. Capital, Dudinka. Formed 1930.

Ust-Ordyn-Buryat

Situated in Irkutsk region (Eastern Siberia); area, 22,400 sq. km, population (1996), 135,300. Capital, Ust-Ordynsk. Formed 1937.

Yamalo-Nenets

Situated in Tyumen region (western Siberia); area, 750,300 sq. km, population (2002 census), 507,400. Capital, Salekhard. Formed 1930.

Yevreyskaya (Jewish) Autonomous Oblast (Province)

Part of Khabarovsk Territory. Area, 36,000 sq. km (13,895 sq. miles); population (2002 census), 109,900 (1989 census, Russians, 83·2%; Ukrainians, 7·4%; Jews, 4·2%). Capital, Birobijan (1994 population, 86,000). Established as Jewish National District in 1928. There are a Yiddish national theatre, newspaper and broadcasting service.

RWANDA

Republika y'u Rwanda

Capital: Kigali
Population projection, 2010: 9·56m.
GDP per capita, 2002: (PPP$) 1,270
HDI/world rank: 0·431/159

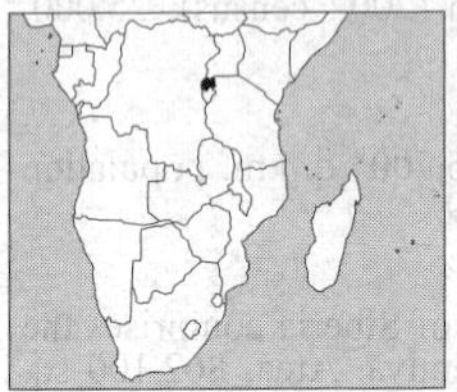

KEY HISTORICAL EVENTS

The Twa—hunter-gatherer pygmies—were the first people to inhabit Rwanda. They were followed by the Hutu, who arrived at some point between AD 500 and 1100. The final group to migrate to Rwanda was the Tutsi around 1400. Their ownership of cattle and combat skills gave them social, economic and political control of the country. A feudalistic system developed: the Tutsi lent cows to the Hutu in return for labour and military service. At the apex was the Tutsi king, the *mwami* (pl., *abami*), who was believed to be of divine origin. The *abami* consolidated their power by reducing the power of neighbouring chiefs. Kigeri IV (reigned 1853–95) established the borders of Rwanda in the 19th century.

The Conference of Berlin in 1885 placed Rwanda under German control. A consequence of German control of Rwanda was the arrival of the Catholic Church through the White Fathers, who established schools and missions from 1899. In the First World War Rwanda was occupied by Belgian forces in 1916 and was declared a Belgian mandate in Aug. 1923 by the League of Nations. The Belgians ruled more directly than the Germans, curtailing the mwami's power and favouring the Tutsi minority on more explicitly racial grounds. From 1952 the UN urged Belgium to integrate Rwandans into the political system. The Belgians continued their policy of favouring the fairer skinned Tutsi, placing them in positions of power over the Hutu majority. By 1959 civil unrest had erupted into civil war. A state of Ruanda-Urundi was established in 1960, under Belgian trusteeship. In 1961 Mwami Kigeli V was exiled by the Belgians, who refused to allow him to return despite pressure from the United Nations. On 27 June 1962 parliament voted to terminate the trusteeship and on 1 July 1962 Rwanda became independent.

The independent state of Rwanda was first governed by the Parmehutu party (representing the 85% Hutu population) but some Tutsis did not accept this. An attempted invasion in 1963 by Tutsis who had fled to Uganda and Burundi was repelled. In retaliation the Hutu massacred over 12,000 Tutsis in Rwanda. The next massacre in 1972–73 was partly in response to massacres of Hutus in neighbouring Tutsi-dominated Burundi. In 1975 Maj.-Gen. Juvénal Habyarimana formed a party, *le Mouvement Révolutionaire National pour le Développement* (MRND), and turned Rwanda into a one-party police state.

In 1990 the Rwandan Patriotic Front (RPF), comprised of between 5,000 and 10,000 Tutsis, invaded Rwanda from Uganda, starting a civil war. A ceasefire on 29 March 1991 led to the Arusha Accords, which allowed other political parties to stand for election and share power. This led to the rise of far-right Hutu power groups, who believed that the only solution to Hutu-Tutsi problems was the extermination of the Tutsi. The assassination of the first legitimately elected Hutu president of Burundi, on 21 Oct. 1993, by Tutsi army officers was followed by the massacre of over 150,000 Hutus in Burundi. The assassination of Habyarimana in a plane crash on 6 April 1994, probably shot down by Hutu extremists, was the first step in a premeditated genocide that killed over 1m. Rwandans in three months and forced over 2m. to flee to neighbouring countries. Gangs of *interahamwe* (civilian death squads) roamed Kigali, killing, looting and raping Tutsis and politically moderate Hutus. When the RPF, led by Paul Kagame, reached Kigali the killings spread to other parts of the county. France dispatched 2,000 troops on a humanitarian mission on 22 June 1994 to maintain a 'safe zone'. The RPF declared the war over on 17 July 1994 and was quickly recognized as the new government.

Genocide trials began in Arusha, Tanzania in Dec. 1996. In Sept. 1998 Jean Kambanda, the former prime minister (April–July 1994), was sentenced to life imprisonment. In April 2000 Paul Kagame (the Tutsi vice-president and defence minister) was elected president by parliament, replacing Pasteur Bizimungu, a Hutu who had been appointed by the RPF, in July 1994. Kagame was re-elected president in Aug. 2003 in Rwanda's first democratic elections since the atrocities.

TERRITORY AND POPULATION

Rwanda is bounded south by Burundi, west by the Democratic Republic of the Congo, north by Uganda and east by Tanzania. A mountainous state of 25,314 sq. km (9,774 sq. miles), its western third drains to Lake Kivu on the border with the Democratic Republic of the Congo and thence to the Congo river, while the rest is drained by the Kagera river into the Nile system.

The population was 7,164,994 at the 1991 census, of whom over 90% were Hutu, 9% Tutsi and 1% Twa (pygmy). 2002 census population, 8,128,553; density, 321·1 per sq. km.

The UN gives a projected population for 2010 of 9·56m.

In 2001 the percentage of the population considered as urban was the lowest of any country in the world, at 6·3% (93·7% rural).

The areas and populations of the 12 administrative divisions (11 provinces and Kigali City) are:

Province	*Area (in sq. km)*	*Population (2002 census)*	*Province*	*Area (in sq. km)*	*Population (2002 census)*
Butare	1,872	725,914	Kibungo	2,964	702,248
Byumba	1,694	707,786	Kibuye	1,748	469,016
Cyangugu	1,894	607,495	Kigali City	313	603,049
Gikongoro	1,974	489,729	Kigali-Ngali	2,780	789,330
Gisenyi	2,047	864,377	Ruhengeri	1,657	891,498
Gitarama	2,141	856,488	Umutara	4,230	421,623

Kigali, the capital, had 603,049 inhabitants in 2002; other towns are Butare, Gisenyi, Gitarama and Ruhengeri.

Kinyarwanda, the language of the entire population, French and English (since 1996) are the official languages. Swahili is spoken in the commercial centres.

SOCIAL STATISTICS

1998 estimates: births, 260,000; deaths, 127,000. Estimated birth rate (per 1,000 population, 1998), 39; estimated death rate (per 1,000 population, 1998), 19. Annual population growth rate, 1992–02, 3·2%. Life expectancy at birth in 2001 was 38·7 years for females and 37·6 for males, up from 23·1 years for females and 22·1 years for males during the period 1990–95 (at the height of the civil war). Infant mortality, 2001, 96 per 1,000 live births; fertility rate, 2001, 5·9 births per woman.

CLIMATE

Despite the equatorial situation, there is a highland tropical climate. The wet seasons are from Oct. to Dec. and March to May. Highest rainfall occurs in the west, at around 70" (1,770 mm), decreasing to 40–55" (1,020–1,400 mm) in the central uplands and to 30" (760 mm) in the north and east. Kigali, Jan. 67°F (19·4°C), July 70°F (21·1°C). Annual rainfall 40" (1,000 mm).

CONSTITUTION AND GOVERNMENT

Under the 1978 Constitution the MRND was the sole political organization.

A new Constitution was promulgated in June 1991 permitting multi-party democracy.

The Arusha Agreement of Aug. 1994 provided for a transitional 70-member National Assembly, which began functioning in Nov. 1994. The seats won by the MRNDD (formerly MRND) were taken over by other parties on the grounds that the MRNDD was culpable of genocide.

A referendum was held on 26 May 2003 which approved a draft constitution by 93·4% (turn-out was 87%). The new constitution, subsequently approved by the Supreme Court, provides for an 80-member *Chamber of Deputies* and a 26-member *Senate*, with the provision that no party may hold more than half of cabinet positions. 53 members of the Chamber of Deputies are directly elected, 24 women are elected by provincial councils, two members are elected by the National Youth Council and one is elected by a disabilities organization. The president, prime minister and parliamentary leader must not be from the same party. These provisions aim to prevent the ethnic divisions that caused genocidal fighting in Rwanda.

National Anthem. 'Rwanda Nziza' ('Beautiful Rwanda'); words by F. Murigo, tune by Capt. J.-B. Hashakaimana.

RECENT ELECTIONS

In a popular election on 25 Aug. 2003 Paul Kagame was re-elected president for a seven-year term with 95·1% of the vote. Faustin Twagiramungu won 3·6% and Népomuscène Nayinzira won 1·3%. Turn-out was 96·6%.

In the first democratic parliamentary elections since the 1994 genocide, held on 30 Sept. 2003, President Kagame's Rwandan Patriotic Front (RPF) and its coalition won 73·8% of the vote. The RPF took 33 seats, the Christian-Democratic Party 3 seats and the Islamic Democratic Party 2 seats; the Rwandese Socialist Party and the Democratic Union of the Rwandese People took one seat each. The Social Democratic Party (SDP) won 12·3% (7 seats), the Liberal Party, 10·6% (6 seats). The Party for Progress and Concord won 2·2% but no seats. Turn-out was 96·5%. Following the Sept. 2003 election, of the 80 Members of Parliament there were 41 men (51·2%) and 39 women (48·8%), the highest percentage of women in a parliament of any country in the world.

CURRENT ADMINISTRATION

President: Paul Kagame; b. 1957 (RPF—Tutsis; sworn in 22 April 2000 having been acting president since 24 March 2000 and re-elected in Aug. 2003).

In March 2005 the government comprised:

Prime Minister: Bernard Makuza; b. 1961 (MDR/Republican Democratic Movement—Hutus; sworn in 8 March 2000).

Minister of Agriculture and Livestock: Patrick Habamenshi. *Defence and National Security:* Maj. Gen. Marcel Gatsinzi. *Lands, Environment, Forestry, Water and Natural Resources:* Drocella Mugorewera. *Commerce, Industry, Investment Promotion, Tourism and Co-operatives:* Manassé Nshuti. *Education, Science, Technology and Research:* Romain Murenzi. *Gender and Family Promotion:* Valérie Nyirahabineza. *Finance and Planning:* Donald Kaberuka. *Foreign Affairs and Regional Co-operation:* Charles Murigande. *Health:* Jean Ntawukuriryayo Damascène. *Justice:* Edda Mukabagwiza. *Internal Affairs:* Christophe Bazivamo. *Youth, Culture and Sports:* Joseph Habineza. *Local Government, Good Governance, Rural Development and Social Affairs:* Protais Musoni. *Infrastructure:* Evariste Bizimana. *Public Service, Skills Development, Vocational Training and Labour:* Andre Habib Bumaya. *Minister to the President's Office:* Solina Nyirahabimana.

Government Website: http://www.gov.rw

DEFENCE

In 2003 defence expenditure totalled US$69m. (US$8 per capita), representing 4·1% of GDP.

Army. Strength (2002) about 49,000–64,000. There was a national police of some 10,000.

INTERNATIONAL RELATIONS

Rwanda is a member of the UN, WTO, the African Union, African Development Bank, COMESA, IOM, the International Organization of the Francophonie and is an ACP member state of the ACP-EU relationship.

ECONOMY

Agriculture accounted for 41·9% of GDP in 2002, industry 21·5% and services 36·6%.

Currency. The unit of currency is the *Rwanda franc* (RWF) notionally of 100 *centimes*. On 3 Jan. 1995, 500-, 1,000- and 5,000-Rwanda franc notes were replaced by new issues, demonetarizing the currency taken abroad by exiles. The currency is not convertible. Foreign exchange reserves were US$180m. in June 2002. Gold reserves are negligible. Inflation was 2·0% in 2002. Total money supply in Dec. 2001 was 63,606m. Rwanda francs.

Budget. In 2000 revenues were 132·4bn. Rwanda francs and expenditures 131·7bn. Rwanda francs.

Performance. Real GDP growth was 35·2% in 1995, following five years of negative growth peaking in a rate of –50·2% in 1994 at the height of the civil war. By 2000 the growth had slowed, but was still 6·0%. In 2001 it rose again to 6·7%, and further in 2002 to 9·4%. Total GDP in 2003 was US$1·6bn.

Banking and Finance. The central bank is the National Bank of Rwanda (founded 1960; *Governor*, François Kanimba), the bank of issue since 1964. There are seven commercial banks (Banque de Kigali, Banque de Commerce et de Développement Industriel, Banque Continentale Africaine au Rwanda, Banque à la Confiance d'Or, Banque Commerciale du Rwanda, Caisse Hypothécaire du Rwanda and Compagnie Générale de Banque), one development bank (Rwandan Development Bank) and one credit union system (Rwandan Union of Popular Banks).

ENERGY AND NATURAL RESOURCES

Environment. Carbon dioxide emissions from the consumption and flaring of fossil fuels in 2002 were the equivalent of 0·1 tonnes per capita.

Electricity. Installed capacity was 43,000 kW in 2000. Production was estimated at 169m. kWh in 2000 and consumption per capita an estimated 24 kWh.

Oil and Gas. In 2002 proven natural gas reserves were 57bn. cu. metres.

Minerals. Production (2002): cassiterite, 197 tonnes; wolfram, 153 tonnes.

Agriculture. There were 1·0m. ha of arable land in 2001 and 300,000 ha of permanent crops. Production (2000 estimates, in 1,000 tonnes): plantains, 2,212; sweet potatoes, 1,033; cassava, 821; dry beans, 215; pumpkins and squash, 206; potatoes, 175; sorghum, 155; taro, 91; maize, 63; sugarcane, 40.

Long-horned Ankole cattle play an important traditional role. Efforts are being made to improve their present negligible economic value. There were, in 2000, 725,000 cattle, 700,000 goats, 320,000 sheep, 160,000 pigs and 1m. chickens.

Forestry. Forests covered 307,000 ha (12·4% of the land area) in 2000. Timber production in 2001 was 7·84m. cu. metres.

Fisheries. The catch in 2001 totalled 6,828 tonnes, entirely from inland waters.

INDUSTRY

There are about 100 small-sized modern manufacturing enterprises in the country. Food manufacturing is the dominant industrial activity (64%) followed by construction (15·3%) and mining (9%). There is a large modern brewery.

Labour. The labour force in 1996 totalled 3,021,000 (51% males). Over 90% of the economically active population in 1995 were engaged in agriculture, fisheries and forestry.

INTERNATIONAL TRADE

Rwanda, Burundi and the Democratic Republic of the Congo make up the Economic Community of the Great Lakes. Foreign debt was US$1,435m. in 2002.

Imports and Exports. In 2002 imports (f.o.b.) amounted to US$233·3m.; exports (f.o.b.) US$67·2m. Major exports are coffee, tea and tin; leading imports are capital goods, food and energy products. Main export markets, 1999: Kenya, 62·4%; Tanzania, 13·9%; Germany, 7·9%; Belgium, 6·5%. Main import suppliers, 1999: Japan, 13·1%; Belgium, 12·8%; Kenya, 12·5%; Saudi Arabia, 8·0%.

COMMUNICATIONS

Roads. There were an estimated 12,000 km of roads in 1999, of which 8·3% were paved. There are road links with Burundi, Uganda, Tanzania and the Democratic Republic of the Congo. In 1996 there were 13,000 passenger cars and 17,100 trucks and vans.

Civil Aviation. There is an international airport at Kigali (Gregoire Kayibanda), which handled 101,000 passengers (96,000 on international flights) in 2000. In 2003 there were scheduled flights to Addis Ababa, Brussels, Bujumbura, Douala, Entebbe, Johannesburg and Nairobi. A national carrier, Rwandair Express, began operations in 2003 flying to Entebbe and Johannesburg.

Telecommunications. Rwanda had 134,000 telephone subscribers in 2002 (equivalent to 16·4 per 1,000 persons) including 110,800 mobile phone subscribers. Internet users numbered 25,000 in 2002. In 1995 there were 500 fax machines.

Postal Services. In 1998 there were 39 post offices, or one for every 169,000 persons.

SOCIAL INSTITUTIONS

Justice. A system of Courts of First Instance and provincial courts refer appeals to Courts of Appeal and a Court of Cassation situated in Kigali. In 1998 a number of people were executed for genocide in the civil war in 1994, including 22 at five different locations throughout the country on 24 April 1998.

Religion. In 2001 approximately 47% of the population were Roman Catholics, 19% Protestants and 7% Muslims. Some of the population follow traditional animist religions. Before the civil war there were nine Roman Catholic bishops and 370 priests. By the end of 1994, three bishops had been killed and three reached retiring age; 106 priests had been killed and 130 had sought refuge abroad.

Education. In 2003–04 there were 2,262 primary schools with 28,254 teachers for 1·8m. pupils; 230,909 secondary pupils with 7,750 teachers; and 15,353 (2001–02) students at university level. Adult literacy rate in 2001 was 68·0% (male, 74·5%; female, 61·9%).

In 2000–01 total expenditure on education came to 2·8% of GNP.

Health. In 1992 there were 150 doctors, and in 1989, seven dentists, 25 pharmacists and 835 nursing personnel. Hospital bed provision in 1990 was one per 588 people.

There were 10,706 reported cases of AIDS by Dec. 1996, and 1·38m. reported of malaria in 1992.

CULTURE

Broadcasting. Colour transmission is on the SECAM V system. There were about 601,000 radio sets and 600 television sets in 1997.

Press. In 1996 there was one daily newspaper with a circulation of 500, equivalent to a rate of one per 10,000 population.

Tourism. In 2001 there were 113,000 foreign tourists; spending by tourists totalled US$25m.

DIPLOMATIC REPRESENTATIVES

Of Rwanda in the United Kingdom (120–122 Seymour Place, London, W1H 1NR)
Ambassador: Rosemary K. Museminali.

Of the United Kingdom in Rwanda (Parcelle No. 1131, Blvd. de l'Umuganda, Kacyira-Sud, POB 576, Kigali)
Ambassador: Sue Hogwood, MBE.

Of Rwanda in the USA (1714 New Hampshire Ave., NW, Washington, D.C., 20009)
Ambassador: Dr Zac Nsenga.

Of the USA in Rwanda (Blvd. de la Révolution, Kigali, POB 28)
Ambassador: Vacant.
Chargé d'Affaires a.i.: Henderson M. Patrick.

Of Rwanda to the United Nations
Ambassador: Stanislas Kamanzi.

Of Rwanda to the European Union
Ambassador: Emmanuel Kayitana Imanzi.

FURTHER READING

Braeckman, C., *Rwanda: Histoire d'un Génocide.* Paris, 1994
Dorsey, L., *Historical Dictionary of Rwanda.* Metuchen (NJ), 1995
Fegley, Randall, *Rwanda.* [Bibliography] ABC-Clio, Oxford and Santa Barbara (CA), 1993
Gourevitch, P., *We Wish to Inform You That Tomorrow We Will Be Killed With Our Families.* Picador, London, 1998
Prunier, G., *The Rwanda Crisis: History of a Genocide.* Farnborough, 1995

ST KITTS AND NEVIS

Federation of St Kitts and Nevis

Capital: Basseterre
Population, 2001: 46,000
GDP per capita, 2002: (PPP$) 12,420
HDI/world rank: 0·844/39

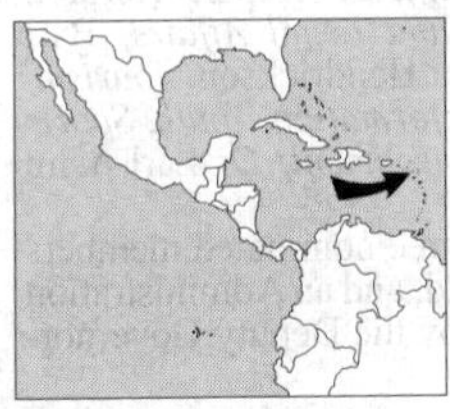

KEY HISTORICAL EVENTS

The islands of St Kitts (formerly St Christopher) and Nevis were discovered and named by Columbus in 1493. They were settled by Britain in 1623 and 1628, but ownership was disputed with France until 1783. In Feb. 1967 colonial status was replaced by an 'association' with Britain, giving the islands full internal self-government. St Kitts and Nevis became fully independent on 19 Sept. 1983. In Oct. 1997 the five-person Nevis legislature voted to end the federation with St Kitts. However, in a referendum held on 10 Aug. 1998 voters rejected independence, only 62% voting for secession when a two-thirds vote in favour was needed. In Sept. 1998 Hurricane Georges caused devastation, leaving 25,000 people homeless, with some 80% of the houses in the islands damaged.

TERRITORY AND POPULATION

The two islands of St Kitts and Nevis are situated at the northern end of the Leeward Islands in the eastern Caribbean. Nevis lies 3 km to the southeast of St Kitts. Population, 2001 census (provisional), 46,111. In 2001, 65·7% of the population were rural.

	Sq. km	*Census 1991*	*Census 2001 (provisional)*	*Chief town*	*Census 2001 (provisional)*
St Kitts	176·1	31,824	34,930	Basseterre	13,220
Nevis	93·3	8,794	11,181	Charlestown	1,820
	269·4	40,618	46,111		

In 1991, 94·9% of the population were Black. English is the official and spoken language.

SOCIAL STATISTICS

Births, 2001, 803; deaths, 352. Rates, 2001 (per 1,000 population): births, 17·4; deaths, 7·6. Infant mortality, 2001 (per 1,000 live births), 20. Expectation of life in 1999 was 68·0 years for males and 71·8 for females. Annual population growth rate, 1991–2001, 1·4%; fertility rate, 2001, 2·4 births per woman.

CLIMATE

Temperature varies between 21·4–30·7°C, with a sea breeze throughout the year and low humidity. Rainfall in 1999 was 1,706·9 mm.

CONSTITUTION AND GOVERNMENT

The British sovereign is the head of state, represented by a Governor-General. The 1983 Constitution described the country as 'a sovereign democratic federal state'. It allowed for a unicameral Parliament consisting of 11 elected Members (eight from St Kitts and three from Nevis) and three appointed Senators. Nevis was given its own Island Assembly and the right to secession from St Kitts.

National Anthem. 'O Land of beauty! Our country where peace abounds'; words and tune by K. A. Georges.

RECENT ELECTIONS

At the National Assembly elections on 25 Oct. 2004 the Labour Party gained 7 seats, the Concerned Citizens Movement 2, the People's Action Movement 1 and the Nevis Reformation Party 1. Turn-out was just over 67%.

CURRENT ADMINISTRATION

Governor-General: Sir Cuthbert Montraville Sebastian, GCMG, OBE; b. 1921 (appointed 1 Jan. 1996).

In March 2005 the government comprised:

Prime Minister, Minister of Finance, Development and Planning, National Security: Dr Denzil L. Douglas; b. 1936 (Labour Party; sworn in 7 July 1995).

Deputy Prime Minister, Minister of International Trade, Labour, Social Security, Telecommunications and Technology, and CARICOM Affairs: Sam Condor.

Minister of Agriculture, Fisheries, Co-operatives, Lands and Housing: Cedric Liburd. *Community, Social Development and Gender Affairs:* Rupert Herbert. *Foreign Affairs and Education:* Timothy Harris. *Justice and Legal Affairs:* Bart Delano. *Public Works, Utilities, Transport and Posts:* Halva Hendrickson. *Tourism, Commerce and Consumer Affairs:* G. A. Dwyer Astaphan. *Information, Youth, Sports and Culture:* Jacinth Lorna Henry-Martin. *Health and Environment:* Dr Earl Asim Martin.

The *Nevis Island* legislature comprises an Assembly of three nominated members and elected members from each electoral district on the Island, and an Administration consisting of the Premier and two other persons appointed by the Deputy Governor-General.

The Premier of *Nevis* is Vance Amory.

Government Website: http://www.stkittsnevis.net

INTERNATIONAL RELATIONS

St Kitts and Nevis is a member of the UN, WTO, the Commonwealth, OAS, ACS, CARICOM, OECS and is an ACP member state of the ACP-EU relationship.

ECONOMY

Agriculture accounted for 3·2% of GDP in 2002, industry 29·7% and services 67·1%.

Currency. The East Caribbean *dollar* (XCD) (of 100 *cents*) is in use. Inflation was 2·1% in 2002. In May 2002 foreign exchange reserves were US$65m. Total money supply was XC$106m. in May 2002.

Budget. In 1999 recurrent revenues were XC$191·4m. (US$70·9m.) and recurrent expenditures XC$236·8m. (US$87·7m.). In 2000 revenues were estimated to be XC$237·8m. (US$88·1m.) and expenditures XC$243·7m. (US$90·3m.). Estimates for 2001 were: revenues, XC$231·4m. (US$85·7m.); expenditure, XC$268·8m. (US$99·6m.).

Performance. Real GDP growth was 2·3% in 2001, but only 0·8% in 2002. Total GDP was US$0·4bn. in 2003.

Banking and Finance. The East Caribbean Central Bank (*Governor*, Sir Dwight Venner) is located in St Kitts. It is a regional bank that serves the OECS countries. In 2002 there were four domestic commercial banks (Bank of Nevis, Caribbean Banking Corporation, Nevis Co-operative Bank and St Kitts-Nevis-Anguilla National Bank), three foreign banks and one development bank. Nevis has some 9,000 offshore businesses registered.

St Kitts and Nevis is a member of the Eastern Caribbean Securities Exchange, based in Basseterre.

St Kitts and Nevis was one of 15 countries and territories named in a report in June 2000 as failing to co-operate in the fight against international money laundering. The Financial Action Task Force on Money Laundering was set up by the G7 group of major industrialized nations.

ENERGY AND NATURAL RESOURCES

Environment. Carbon dioxide emissions from the consumption and flaring of fossil fuels in 2002 were the equivalent of 2·6 tonnes per capita.

Electricity. Installed capacity was 20,000 kW in 2000. Production in 2000 was about 100m. kWh.

Agriculture. The main crops are sugar, coconut, copra and cotton. In 1995, 3,327 ha were sown to sugarcane. In 2001 there were 7,000 ha of arable land and 1,000 ha of permanent crops. Most of the farms are small-holdings and there are a number of coconut estates amounting to some 400 ha under public and private ownership. Production, 2000 (in 1,000 tonnes): sugarcane, 188; coconuts, 1.

Livestock (2000): goats, 15,000; sheep, 7,000; cattle, 4,000; pigs, 3,000.

Forestry. The area under forests in 2000 was 4,000 ha, or 11·1% of the total land area.

Fisheries. The catch in 2001 was 591 tonnes.

INDUSTRY

There are three industrial estates on St Kitts and one on Nevis. Export products include electronics and data processing equipment, and garments for the US market. Other small enterprises include food and drink processing, particularly sugar and cane spirit, and construction. Production of raw sugar (2001), 20,000 tonnes; molasses (1994), 6,000 tonnes.

Labour. In 1994 the economically active population numbered 16,608, of which 22·3% worked in services, finance and real estate, 20·3% in trade and restaurants, 16·5% in public administration and defence, and 10·5% in construction.

INTERNATIONAL TRADE

Foreign debt in 2002 amounted to US$255m.

Imports and Exports. Exports, 2001, US$55·0m.; imports, US$166·7m. Main trading partners are the USA, the UK and other CARICOM members. In 1997, 45·5% of imports were from the USA and 54·0% of exports went to the ISA. The chief export is sugar. Other significant exports are machinery, food, electronics, beverages and tobacco. Main imports include machinery, manufactures, food and fuels.

COMMUNICATIONS

Roads. In 1999 there were about 250 km of roads, of which 200 km were surfaced (124 km paved); and 5,326 passenger cars and 3,742 commercial vehicles.

Rail. There are 58 km of railway operated by the sugar industry.

Civil Aviation. The main airport is the Robert Llewelyn Bradshaw International Airport (just over 3 km from Basseterre). In 2003 there were flights to Anguilla, Antigua, Barbados, British Virgin Islands, Dominica, Grenada, Jamaica, Netherlands Antilles, Nevis (Newcastle), Philadelphia, Puerto Rico, St Lucia, St Vincent, Trinidad and the US Virgin Islands.

Shipping. There is a deep-water port at Bird Rock (Basseterre). 202,000 tons of cargo were unloaded in 1999 and 24,000 tons loaded. The government maintains a commercial motor boat service between the islands.

Telecommunications. In 2002 there were 28,500 telephone subscribers, or 606·4 per 1,000 inhabitants, and 9,000 PCs in use (191·5 for every 1,000 persons). Mobile phone subscribers numbered 5,000 in 2002. In 2002 there were 10,000 Internet users.

Postal Services. In 1998 there were seven post offices.

SOCIAL INSTITUTIONS

Justice. Justice is administered by the Supreme Court and by Magistrates' Courts. They have both civil and criminal jurisdiction. St Kitts and Nevis was one of ten countries to sign an agreement in Feb. 2001 establishing a Caribbean Court of Justice to replace the British Privy Council as the highest civil and criminal court. In the meantime the number of signatories has risen to twelve. The court was inaugurated at Port-of-Spain, Trinidad on 16 April 2005.

The population in penal institutions in June 1999 was 135 (equivalent to 338 per 100,000 of national population).

Religion. In 1991, 27·5% of the population were Anglican, 25·3% Methodist, 6·9% Roman Catholic, 5·5% Pentecostal, 3·9% Baptist and 3·9% Church of God.

Education. Adult literacy was 98% in 1998–99. Education is compulsory between the ages of 5 and 17. In 1998–99 there were 2,490 pupils in 71 pre-primary schools and 28 nurseries with 196 pre-primary teachers. In 1998–99 there were 5,947 pupils (3,556 male) and 293 teachers (57 male) in 23 primary schools, 4,528 pupils and 345 teachers in 7 secondary schools, and 1,153 pupils (555 male) and 70 teachers (13 male) in 9 private schools. There is an Extra-Mural Department of the University of the West Indies, a Non-formal Youth Skills Training Centre (with 55 students) and a Teachers' Training College. Clarence Fitzroy Bryant College has a Sixth Form Division (with 234 students), a Nursing Division (34 students), a Teaching Education Division (61 students), a Division of Technical and Vocational Studies (145 students) and an Adult Education Division (500 students).

In 2000–01 total expenditure on education came to 3·3% of GNP and 16·0% of total government spending.

Health. In 1999 there were 46 doctors, 14 dentists, 184 nurses and 17 pharmacists; and four hospitals, with a provision of 49 beds per 10,000 population.

CULTURE

World Heritage Sites. There is one site on the UNESCO World Heritage List: Brimstone Hill Fortress National Park (inscribed on the list in 1999), a well-preserved example of 17th and 18th century British military architecture.

Broadcasting. There are three AM radio stations and two TV stations. Cable television is also available. In 1997 there were 10,000 television (colour by NTSC) and 28,000 radio receivers.

Press. In 2000 there were two weekly and one twice weekly newspapers.

Tourism. In 1999 an estimated 84,000 tourists visited out of a total of 224,397 arrivals including 137,389 by yacht. In 1999, 40·9% of visitors came from the USA and 15·5% from the UK. There were 30 hotels in 1999 (20 on St Kitts and 10 on Nevis) with 1,508 rooms. Receipts from tourism in 2000 totalled US$58m.

DIPLOMATIC REPRESENTATIVES

Of St Kitts and Nevis in the United Kingdom (2nd Floor, 10 Kensington Ct, London, W8 5DL)
High Commissioner: James Williams.

Of the United Kingdom in St Kitts and Nevis
High Commissioner: John White (resides at Bridgetown, Barbados).

Of St Kitts and Nevis in the USA (OECS Building, 3216 New Mexico Ave., NW, 3rd Floor, Washington, D.C., 20016)
Ambassador: Izben Cordinal Williams.

Of the USA in St Kitts and Nevis
Ambassador: Mary E. Kramer (resides at Bridgetown).

Of St Kitts and Nevis to the United Nations
Ambassador: Joseph Christmas.

Of St Kitts and Nevis to the European Union
Ambassador: George Bullen.

FURTHER READING

Statistics Division. *National Accounts.* Annual.—*St Kitts and Nevis Quarterly.*
Moll, Verna Penn, *St Kitts and Nevis.* [Bibliography] ABC-Clio, Oxford and Santa Barbara (CA), 1995

National library: Public Library, Burdon St., Basseterre.
National statistical office: Statistics Division, Ministry of Finance, Planning and Development, Church St., Basseterre.

ST LUCIA

Capital: Castries
Population projection, 2010: 157,000
GDP per capita, 2002: (PPP$) 5,300
HDI/world rank: 0·777/71

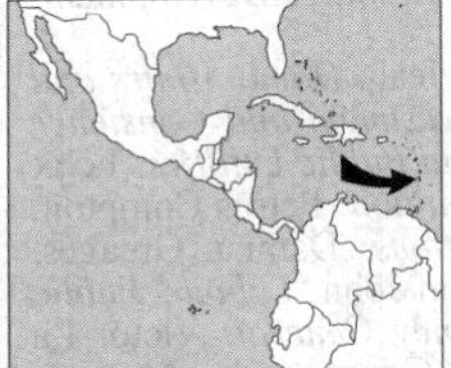

KEY HISTORICAL EVENTS

The island was probably discovered by Columbus in 1502. An unsuccessful attempt to colonize by the British took place in 1605 and again in 1638 when settlers were soon murdered by the Caribs who inhabited the island. France claimed the right of sovereignty and ceded it to the French West India Company in 1642. St Lucia regularly and constantly changed hands between Britain and France, until it was finally ceded to Britain in 1814 by the Treaty of Paris. Since 1924 the island has had representative government. In March 1967 St Lucia gained full control of its internal affairs while Britain remained responsible for foreign affairs and defence. On 22 Feb. 1979 St Lucia achieved independence, opting to remain in the British Commonwealth.

TERRITORY AND POPULATION

St Lucia is an island of the Lesser Antilles in the eastern Caribbean between Martinique and St Vincent, with an area of 238 sq. miles (617 sq. km). Population (2001 census, provisional) 157,775 (79,712 females); density, 255·7 per sq. km. In 2001 the population was 62·0% rural.

Area and provisional populations of the ten administrative districts at the 2001 census were:

Districts	*Sq. km*	*Population*	*Districts*	*Sq. km*	*Population*
Anse-la-Raye	47	6,060	Gros Inlet	101	20,872
Canaries		1,788	Laborie	38	7,363
Castries	79	64,344	Micoud	78	16,041
Choiseul	31	6,128	Soufrière	51	7,656
Dennery	70	12,767	Vieux Fort	44	14,754

The UN gives a projected population for 2010 of 157,000.

The official language is English, but 80% of the population speak a French Creole.

In 1990 over 90% of the population was Black, 6% were of mixed race and 3% of south Asian ethnic origin.

The capital is Castries (population, 1999, 57,000).

SOCIAL STATISTICS

2001 births, 2,919; deaths, 960. Rates, 2001 (per 1,000 population): births, 18·5; deaths, 6·1. Infant mortality, 2001 (per 1,000 live births), 17. Expectation of life in 2001 was 70·5 years for males and 73·8 for females. Annual population growth rate, 1992–02, 0·9%; fertility rate, 2001, 2·6 births per woman.

CLIMATE

The climate is tropical, with a dry season from Jan. to April. Most rain falls in Nov.–Dec.; annual amount varies from 60" (1,500 mm) to 138" (3,450 mm). The average annual temperature is about 80°F (26·7°C).

CONSTITUTION AND GOVERNMENT

The head of state is the British sovereign, represented by an appointed Governor-General. There is a 17-seat *House of Assembly* elected for five years and an 11-seat *Senate* appointed by the Governor-General.

National Anthem. 'Sons and daughters of St Lucia'; words by C. Jesse, tune by L. F. Thomas.

RECENT ELECTIONS

At the elections of 3 Dec. 2001 the St Lucia Labour Party gained 14 seats and the United Workers' Party 3.

CURRENT ADMINISTRATION

Governor-General: Dame Perlette Louisy; b. 1946 (appointed 17 Sept. 1997).

In March 2005 the government comprised:

Prime Minister and Minister of Finance, Economic Affairs, International Financial Services and Information: Dr Kenny Davis Anthony; b. 1951 (appointed 24 May 1997).

Deputy Prime Minister and Minister of Education, Human Resource Development, Youth and Sports: Mario Michel.

Minister of Agriculture, Forestry and Fisheries: Ignatius Jean. *Home Affairs and Internal Security:* Calixte George. *Commerce, Tourism, Investment and Consumer Affairs:* Philip Pierre. *Communications, Works, Transport and Public Utilities:* Felix Finisterre. *Foreign Affairs, International Trade and Civil Aviation:* Petrus Compton. *Health, Human Services, Family Affair and Gender Relations:* Damian Greaves. *Physical Development, Environment and Housing:* Ferguson John. *Labour, Public Service and Co-operatives:* Velon John. *Justice and Attorney General:* Victor La Corbiniere. *Social Transformation, Culture and Local Government:* Menissa Rambally.

Government Website: http://www.stlucia.gov.lc

INTERNATIONAL RELATIONS

St Lucia is a member of the UN, WTO, OAS, ACS, CARICOM, OECS, the Commonwealth, the International Organization of the Francophonie and is an ACP member state of the ACP-EU relationship.

ECONOMY

In 2002 agriculture contributed 6·4% of GDP, industry 18·5% and services 75·1%.

Currency. The East Caribbean *dollar* (XCD) (of 100 *cents*) is in use. US dollars are also normally accepted. Inflation was 0·9% in 2002. Foreign exchange reserves were US$90m. in May 2002. Total money supply was EC$320m. in May 2002.

Budget. Revenues were EC$469·9m. in the fiscal year 1998–99 and expenditures EC$496·6m.

Performance. There was a recession in both 2001 and 2002, with the economy contracting by 5·2% and 0·5% respectively. Total GDP in 2003 was US$0·7bn.

Banking and Finance. The East Caribbean Central Bank based in St Kitts and Nevis functions as a central bank. The *Governor* is Sir Dwight Venner. There are three domestic banks (Caribbean Banking Corporation, St Lucia Co-operative Bank, East Caribbean Financial Holding Company) and three foreign banks.

St Lucia is a member of the Eastern Caribbean Securities Exchange, based in Basseterre.

ENERGY AND NATURAL RESOURCES

Environment. Carbon dioxide emissions from the consumption and flaring of fossil fuels in 2002 were the equivalent of 2·4 tonnes per capita.

Electricity. Installed capacity in 2000 was 66,000 kW. Production in 2000 was 275m. kWh; consumption per capita in 2000 was 1,858 kWh.

Agriculture. In 2001 St Lucia had 4,000 ha of arable land and 14,000 ha of permanent crops. Bananas, cocoa, breadfruit and mango are the principal crops, but changes in the world's trading rules and changes in taste are combining to depress the banana trade. Farmers are experimenting with okra, tomatoes and avocados to help make up for the loss. Production, 2000 (in 1,000 tonnes): bananas, 92; mangoes, 28; coconuts, 12; yams, 5; copra, 2.

Livestock (2000): pigs, 15,000; sheep, 13,000; cattle, 12,000; goats, 10,000.

Forestry. In 2000 the area under forests was 9,000 ha (14·8% of the total land area).

Fisheries. In 2001 the total catch was 1,983 tonnes.

INDUSTRY

The main areas of activity are clothing, assembly of electronic components, beverages, corrugated cardboard boxes, tourism, lime processing and coconut processing.

Labour. In 1993 the economically active population totalled 81,000, around a quarter of whom were engaged in agriculture, fisheries and forestry.

INTERNATIONAL TRADE

Foreign debt in 2002 amounted to US$415m.

Imports and Exports. Imports and exports for calendar years in US$1m.:

	1997	*1998*	*1999*	*2000*	*2001*
Imports	292·4	295·1	312·0	312·5	258·7
Exports	70·3	70·4	60·9	63·0	51·8

Main imports in 2001: food products, 23·0%; machinery and apparatus, 14·9%; refined petroleum, 9·8%. Main exports, 2001: bananas, 46·9%; beer, 18·1%; clothing, 7·1%. Main import suppliers, 2001: USA, 41·8%; Trinidad and Tobago, 15·8%; UK, 9·0%; Japan, 4·2%. Main export markets, 2001: UK, 47·3%; USA, 17·6%; Barbados, 13·4%; Antigua and Barbuda, 3·1%.

COMMUNICATIONS

Roads. The island had about 1,210 km of roads in 1999, of which 150 km were main roads and a further 150 km secondary roads. Passenger cars numbered 14,550 in 1996.

Civil Aviation. There are international airports at Hewanorra (near Vieux-Fort) and Vigie (near Castries). In 2000 Vigie handled 376,000 (370,000 on international flights) and Hewanorra 350,000 passengers (343,000 on international flights).

Shipping. There are two ports, Castries and Vieux Fort. Merchant shipping in 1995 totalled 1,000 GRT. In 1997 vessels totalling 6,803,000 net registered tons entered the ports.

Telecommunications. Main telephone lines numbered 48,900 in 2000 (313·5 per 1,000 persons), and there were 22,000 PCs (141 for every 1,000 persons). There were 14,300 mobile phone subscribers in 2002. Internet users numbered 13,000 in 2001. In 1994 there were 560 fax machines.

Postal Services. There were 63 post offices in 1998.

SOCIAL INSTITUTIONS

Justice. The island is divided into two judicial districts, and there are nine magistrates' courts. Appeals lie to the Eastern Caribbean Supreme Court of Appeal. St Lucia was one of ten countries to sign an agreement in Feb. 2001 establishing a Caribbean Court of Justice to replace the British Privy Council as the highest civil and criminal court. In the meantime the number of signatories has risen to twelve. The court was inaugurated at Port-of-Spain, Trinidad on 16 April 2005.

The population in penal institutions in June 1999 was 365 (243 per 100,000 of national population).

Religion. In 2001, 79% of the population was Roman Catholic.

Education. Primary education is free and compulsory. In 2002–03 there were 81 primary schools with 1,057 teachers for 27,175 pupils; and (1999–2000) 12,817 pupils and 645 teachers at secondary level. There is a community college. Adult literacy rate is 82%.

In 2000–01 total expenditure on education came to 6·1% of GNP and 16·9% of total government spending.

Health. In 1998 there were six hospitals with a provision of 14 beds per 10,000 inhabitants. In 1997 there were 81 physicians, 13 dentists, 312 nurses and 13 pharmacists.

CULTURE

World Heritage Sites. There is one UNESCO site in St Lucia: Pitons Management Area (inscribed on the list in 2004). The site near the town of Soufrière includes the Pitons, two volcanic spires rising side by side from the sea, linked by the Piton Mitan ridge.

Broadcasting. There were 32,000 TV (colour by PAL) and 111,000 radio receivers in 1997. In 2003 there were three television stations broadcasting locally and on satellite and a satellite network, Cablevision. The government-owned Radio St Lucia broadcasts in English and Creole. There were two other radio stations in 2003.

Press. In 2003 there were seven newspapers. The weekly *One Caribbean* had the highest circulation (7,500). *The Voice*, founded in 1885, has a thrice-weekly combined circulation of 15,000.

Tourism. The total number of visitors during 2000 was 270,000. In 1998 there were 372,000 cruise ship arrivals. Receipts in 2000 totalled US$277m.

DIPLOMATIC REPRESENTATIVES

Of St Lucia in the United Kingdom (1 Collingham Gdns, Earls Court, London, SW5 0HW)
High Commissioner: Emmanuel H. Cotter, MBE.

Of the United Kingdom in St Lucia (NIS Waterfront Building, 2nd Floor, Castries)
High Commissioner: John White (resides at Bridgetown, Barbados).

Of St Lucia in the USA (3216 New Mexico Ave., NW, Washington, D.C., 20016)
Ambassador: Sonia Merlyn Johnny.

Of the USA in St Lucia
Ambassador: Mary E. Kramer (resides at Bridgetown).

Of St Lucia to the United Nations
Ambassador: Julian Hunte.

Of St Lucia to the European Union
Ambassador: George Bullen.

FURTHER READING

Momsen, Janet Henshall, *St Lucia.* [Bibliography] ABC-Clio, Oxford and Santa Barbara (CA), 1996

National statistical office: Central Statistical Office, Chreiki Building, Micoud Street, Castries.
Website: http://www.stats.gov.lc/

ST VINCENT AND THE GRENADINES

Capital: Kingstown
Population projection, 2010: 124,000
GDP per capita, 2002: (PPP$) 5,460
HDI/world rank: 0·751/87

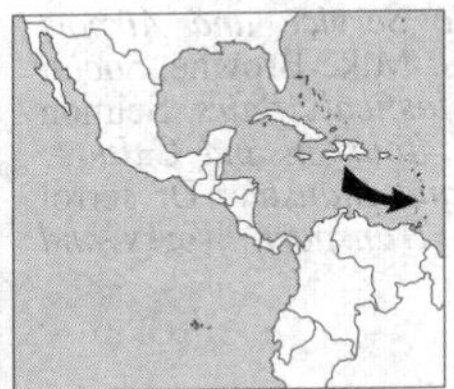

KEY HISTORICAL EVENTS

St Vincent was discovered by Columbus on 22 Jan. (St Vincent's Day) 1498. British and French settlers occupied parts of the islands after 1627. In 1773 the Caribs recognized British sovereignty and agreed to a division of territory between themselves and the British. Resentful of British rule, the Caribs rebelled in 1795, aided by the French, but the revolt was subdued within a year. On 27 Oct. 1969 St Vincent became an Associated State with the UK responsible only for foreign policy and defence, while the islands were given full internal self-government. On 27 Oct. 1979 the colony gained full independence as St Vincent and the Grenadines.

TERRITORY AND POPULATION

St Vincent is an island of the Lesser Antilles, situated in the eastern Caribbean between St Lucia and Grenada, from which latter it is separated by a chain of small islands known as the Grenadines. The total area of 389 sq. km (150 sq. miles) comprises the island of St Vincent itself (345 sq. km) and those of the Grenadines attached to it, of which the largest are Bequia, Mustique, Canouan, Mayreau and Union.

The population at the 1991 census was 106,499, of whom 8,367 lived in the St Vincent Grenadines. 2003 official estimate, 116,812 (55·8% urban in 2001); density 300 per sq. km.

The UN gives a projected population for 2010 of 124,000.

The capital, Kingstown, had 28,000 inhabitants in 1999 (including suburbs). The population is mainly of black (82%) and mixed (13·9%) origin, with small white, Asian and American minorities.

English and French patois are spoken.

SOCIAL STATISTICS

Births, 2001, 1,967; deaths, 720. 2001 birth rate, 18·0 per 1,000 population; death rate, 6·6. Infant mortality, 2001, 22 per 1,000 live births. Life expectancy, 2001, was 72·4 years for males and 75·3 years for females. Annual population growth rate, 1992–02, 0·6%; fertility rate, 2001, 1·9 births per woman.

CLIMATE

The climate is tropical marine, with northeast Trades predominating and rainfall ranging from 150" (3,750 mm) a year in the mountains to 60" (1,500 mm) on the southeast coast. The rainy season is from June to Dec., and temperatures are equable throughout the year.

CONSTITUTION AND GOVERNMENT

The head of state is Queen Elizabeth II, represented by a Governor-General. Parliament is unicameral and consists of a 21-member *House of Assembly,* 15 of which are directly elected for a five-year term from single-member constituencies. The remaining six are senators appointed by the Governor-General (four on the advice of the Prime Minister and two on the advice of the Leader of the Opposition).

National Anthem. 'St Vincent, land so beautiful'; words by Phyllis Punnett, tune by J. B. Miguel.

RECENT ELECTIONS

At the elections to the House of Assembly on 28 March 2001 the opposition Unity Labour Party (ULP, social-democratic) won 12 of the 15 elected seats, against 3 for the ruling New Democratic Party (NDP, conservative).

CURRENT ADMINISTRATION

Governor-General: Sir Frederick Ballantyne (since 2 Sept. 2002).

In March 2005 the government comprised:

Prime Minister, Minister for Finance, Planning, Economic Development, Labour, Information, Grenadine Affairs and Legal Affairs: Dr Ralph E. Gonsalves; b. 1946 (ULP; sworn in 29 March 2001).

Deputy Prime Minister and Minister of Foreign Affairs, Commerce and Trade: Louis Straker. *Minister of National Security, the Public Service and Airport Development:* Vincent Beache. *Education, Youth and Sports:* Mike Browne. *Social Development, Co-operatives, the Family, Gender and Ecclesiastical Affairs:* Selmon Walters. *Agriculture, Lands and Fisheries:* Girlyn Miguel. *Tourism and Culture:* Rene Baptiste. *Telecommunications, Science, Technology and Industry:* Dr Jerrol Thompson. *Health and Environment:* Dr Douglas Slater. *Transport, Works and Housing:* Julian Francis.

INTERNATIONAL RELATIONS

St Vincent and the Grenadines is a member of UN, WTO, OAS, ACS, CARICOM, OECS, the Commonwealth and is an ACP member state of the ACP-EU relationship.

ECONOMY

Agriculture accounted for 10·5% of GDP in 2002, industry 25·2% and services 64·3%.

Currency. The currency in use is the *East Caribbean dollar* (XCD). In 2002 inflation was 1·0%. Foreign exchange reserves were US$60m. in May 2002, and total money supply was EC$272m.

Budget. Total revenue and expenditure in XC$1m. for calendar years:

	1997	*1998*	*1999*	*2000*	*2001*
Revenue	240·5	260·3	276·1	278·9	294·0
Expenditure	337·0	320·9	315·1	309·0	353·2

Performance. Real GDP growth was 0·9% in 2002 (1·1% in 2001). In 2003 total GDP was US$0·4bn.

Banking and Finance. The East Caribbean Central Bank is the bank of issue. The *Governor* is Sir Dwight Venner. There are branches of Barclays Bank PLC, the Caribbean Banking Corporation, FirstCaribbean International, the Canadian Imperial Bank of Commerce and the Bank of Nova Scotia. Locally-owned banks: First St Vincent Bank, Owens Bank, New Bank, the National Commercial Bank and St Vincent Co-operative Bank. The 'offshore' sector numbered over 11,000 organizations in 2001.

St Vincent and the Grenadines was one of 15 countries and territories named in a report in June 2000 as failing to co-operate in the fight against international money laundering. The Financial Action Task Force on Money Laundering was set up by the G7 group of major industrialized nations.

St Vincent and the Grenadines is a member of the Eastern Caribbean Securities Exchange, based in Basseterre.

ENERGY AND NATURAL RESOURCES

Environment. Carbon dioxide emissions from the consumption and flaring of fossil fuels were the equivalent of 1·5 tonnes per capita in 2002.

Electricity. Installed capacity was 16,000 kW in 2000. Production in 2000 was estimated at 85m. kWh; consumption per capita in 2000 was about 752 kWh.

Agriculture. According to the 1985–86 census of agriculture, 29,649 acres of the total acreage of 85,120 were classified as agricultural lands; 5,500 acres were under forest and woodland and all other lands accounted for 1,030 acres. The total arable land was about 8,932 acres, of which 4,016 acres were under temporary crops, 2,256 acres under temporary pasture, 2,289 acres under temporary fallow and other arable land covering 371 acres. 16,062 acres were under permanent crops, of which approximately 5,500 acres were under coconuts and 7,224 acres under bananas; the remainder produce cocoa, citrus, mangoes, avocado pears, guavas and miscellaneous crops. In 2001 there were 7,000 ha of arable land and 7,000 ha of permanent crops. The sugar industry was closed down in 1985 although some sugarcane is grown for rum production. Production (2000, in 1,000 tonnes): bananas, 43; coconuts, 24; sugarcane, 20; copra, 2; maize, 2; sweet potatoes, 2.

Livestock (2000, in 1,000): sheep, 13; pigs, 10; cattle, 6; goats, 6.

Forestry. Forests covered 6,000 ha in 2000, or 15·4% of the land area.

Fisheries. Total catch, 2001, 45,778 tonnes (all from sea fishing).

INDUSTRY

Industries include assembly of electronic equipment, manufacture of garments, electrical products, animal feeds and flour, corrugated galvanized sheets, exhaust systems, industrial gases, concrete blocks, plastics, soft drinks, beer and rum, wood products and furniture, and processing of milk, fruit juices and food items. Rum production, 1994, 0·4m. litres.

Labour. The Department of Labour is charged with looking after the interest and welfare of all categories of workers, including providing advice and guidance to employers and employees and their organizations and enforcing the labour laws. In 1991 the total labour force was 41,682, of whom 33,355 (11,699 females) were employed.

INTERNATIONAL TRADE

Foreign debt was US$206m. in 2002.

Imports and Exports. Imports and exports for calendar years in US$1m.:

	1997	*1998*	*1999*	*2000*	*2001*
Imports	152·6	170·0	177·0	144·3	152·0
Exports	47·3	50·1	49·6	51·7	45·7

Principal exports are bananas, packaged flour and packaged rice. Principal imports are basic manufactures, machinery and transport equipment, and food products.

Main export markets, 1998: CARICOM countries, 51·6%; UK, 40·3%. Main import suppliers, 1999: USA, 37·5%; CARICOM countries, 23·2%; UK, 12·0%.

COMMUNICATIONS

Roads. In 2002 there were 829 km of roads, of which 70% were paved. Vehicles in use (2002): 10,504 passenger cars; 3,019 commercial vehicles.

Civil Aviation. There is an airport (E. T. Joshua) on mainland St Vincent at Arnos Vale. An airport on Union also has regular scheduled services. In 1995 E. T. Joshua handled 185,000 passengers and 1,200 tonnes of freight.

Shipping. In 2000 the merchant navy had 1,366 vessels. Merchant shipping in 2002 totalled 6,584,000 GRT, including oil tankers 313,000 GRT. In 2001 vessels totalling 1,790,000 net registered tons entered and cleared ports.

Telecommunications. There is a fully digital automatic telephone system with 37,300 telephone subscribers in 2002, equivalent to 318·8 for every 1,000 inhabitants. In 2000 there were 17,500 stations and digital radio provide links to Bequia, Mustique, Union, Petit St Vincent and Palm Island. The telephone network has almost 100% geographical coverage. There were 10,000 mobile phone subscribers in 2002 and 14,000 PCs in use (119·7 for every 1,000 persons). In 2002 there were 7,000 Internet users.

Postal Services. There were 41 post offices in 1997.

SOCIAL INSTITUTIONS

Justice. Law is based on UK common law as exercised by the Eastern Caribbean Supreme Court on St Lucia. Final appeal lies to the UK Privy Council. In 1995 there were 4,700 criminal matters disposed of in the three magisterial districts which comprise 11 courts. 62 cases were dealt with in the Criminal Assizes in the High Court. St Vincent and the Grenadines was one of twelve countries to sign an agreement establishing a Caribbean Court of Justice to replace the British Privy

Council as the highest civil and criminal court. The court was inaugurated at Port-of-Spain, Trinidad on 16 April 2005. Strength of police force (1995), 663 (including 19 gazetted officers).

The population in penal institutions in Oct. 2001 was 302 (270 per 100,000 of national population).

Religion. In 2001 there were estimated to be 20,000 Anglicans, 17,000 Pentecostalists, 12,000 Methodists, 12,000 Roman Catholics and 52,000 followers of other religions.

Education. In 2000–01 there were 162 teachers for 2,537 children in pre-primary schools, 761 teachers for 18,200 pupils in primary schools and 405 teachers for 9,756 pupils in secondary schools. In 1989 there were 677 students at university level. Adult literacy in 1998 was 82%.

In 2000–01 total expenditure on education came to 9·9% of GNP and 13·4% of total government spending.

Health. In 1997 there were 11 hospitals with a provision of 19 beds per 10,000 persons. In 1998 there were 59 physicians, 6 dentists and 267 nurses, and in 1991 there were 27 pharmacists.

CULTURE

Broadcasting. The National Broadcasting Corporation (NBC) is part government-owned and part commercial. In 2003 NBC Radio was broadcasting on three FM frequencies. In 1997 there were 77,000 radio and 18,000 TV sets (colour by NTSC).

Press. In 1996 there was one daily newspaper, *The Herald*, with a circulation of 1,000, at a rate of 9 per 1,000 inhabitants.

Tourism. There were 73,000 visitors in 2000, and 35,000 cruise ship arrivals in 1998. Tourism receipts in 2000 totalled US$79m.

Libraries. The St Vincent Public Library is in Kingstown.

DIPLOMATIC REPRESENTATIVES

Of St Vincent and the Grenadines in the United Kingdom (10 Kensington Ct, London, W8 5DL)
High Commissioner: Cenio Elwin Lewis.

Of the United Kingdom in St Vincent and the Grenadines (POB 132, Granby St., Kingstown)
High Commissioner: John White (resides at Bridgetown, Barbados).

Of St Vincent and the Grenadines in the USA (3216 New Mexico Ave., NW, Washington, D.C., 20016)
Ambassador: Ellsworth I. A. John.

Of the USA in St Vincent and the Grenadines
Ambassador: Mary E. Kramer (resides at Bridgetown).

Of St Vincent and the Grenadines to the United Nations
Ambassador: Margaret Hughes Ferrari.

Of St Vincent and the Grenadines to the European Union
Ambassador: George Bullen.

FURTHER READING

Potter, Robert B., *St Vincent and the Grenadines.* [Bibliography] ABC-Clio, Oxford and Santa Barbara (CA), 1992

Sutty, L., *St Vincent and the Grenadines.* London, 1993

SAMOA

O le Malo Tutoatasi o Samoa
(Independent State of Samoa)

Capital: Apia
Population projection, 2010: 192,000
GDP per capita, 2002: (PPP$) 5,600
HDI/world rank: 0·769/75

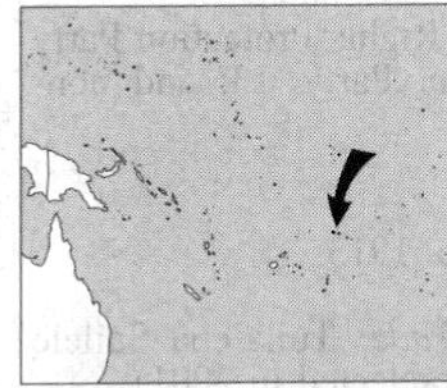

KEY HISTORICAL EVENTS

Polynesians settled in the Samoan group of islands in the southern Pacific from about 1000 BC. Although probably sighted by the Dutch in 1722, the first European visitor was French in 1768. Treaties were signed between the Chiefs and European nations in 1838–39. Continuing strife among the chiefs was compounded by British, German and US rivalry for influence. In the Treaty of Berlin 1889 the three powers agreed to Western Samoa's independence and neutrality. When unrest continued, the treaty was annulled and Western Samoa became a German protectorate until in 1914 it was occupied by a New Zealand expeditionary force. The island was administered by New Zealand from 1920 to 1961. On 1 Jan. 1962 Western Samoa gained independence. In July 1997 the country renamed itself the Independent State of Samoa.

TERRITORY AND POPULATION

Samoa lies between 13° and 15° S. lat. and 171° and 173° W. long. It comprises the two large islands of Savai'i and Upolu, the small islands of Manono and Apolima, and several uninhabited islets lying off the coast. The total land area is 1,093 sq. miles (2,830·8 sq. km), of which 659·4 sq. miles (1,707·8 sq. km) are in Savai'i, and 431·5 sq. miles (1,117·6 sq. km) in Upolu; other islands, 2·1 sq. miles (5·4 sq. km). The islands are of volcanic origin, and the coasts are surrounded by coral reefs. Rugged mountain ranges form the core of both main islands. The large area laid waste by lava-flows in Savai'i is a primary cause of that island supporting less than one-third of the population of the islands despite its greater size than Upolu.

Population at the 2001 census, 176,848. The population at the 2001 census was 134,024 in Upolu (including Manono and Apolima) and 42,824 in Savai'i. The capital and chief port is Apia in Upolu (population 38,836 in 2001). In 2001, 77·7% of the population lived in rural areas.

The UN gives a projected population for 2010 of 192,000.

The official languages are Samoan and English.

SOCIAL STATISTICS

Births, 1995, 4,400; deaths, 1,000. 1995 birth rate per 1,000 population, 25·8; death rate, 6·1. Expectation of life in 2001 was 66·5 years for males and 73·0 for females. Annual population growth rate, 1992–02, was 0·8%. Infant mortality, 2001, 20 per 1,000 live births; fertility rate, 2001, 4·3 births per woman.

CLIMATE

A tropical marine climate, with cooler conditions from May to Nov. and a rainy season from Dec. to April. The rainfall is unevenly distributed, with south and east coasts having the greater quantities. Average annual rainfall is about 100" (2,500 mm) in the drier areas. Apia, Jan. 80°F (26·7°C), July 78°F (25·6°C). Annual rainfall 112" (2,800 mm).

CONSTITUTION AND GOVERNMENT

HH Malietoa Tanumafili II is the sole Head of State for life. Future Heads of State will be elected by the Legislative Assembly and hold office for five-year terms.

The executive power is vested in the *Head of State*, who swears in the *Prime Minister* (who is elected by the Legislative Assembly) and, on the Prime Minister's advice, the Ministers to form the Cabinet. The Constitution also provides for a *Council of Deputies* of three members, of whom the chairman is the Deputy Head of State.

Before 1991 the 49-member *Legislative Assembly* was elected exclusively by *matai* (customary family heads). At the elections of April 1991 the suffrage was universal, but only the approximately 20,000 *matai* could stand as candidates. The electorate was 56,000.

National Anthem. 'Samoa, tula'i ma sisi ia laufu'a ('Samoa, Arise and Raise your Banner'); words and tune by S. I. Kuresa.

RECENT ELECTIONS

At the most recent elections, on 4 March 2001, the Human Rights Protection Party (HRPP) won 23 seats; the Samoan National Development Party, 13; and non-partisans, 13.

CURRENT ADMINISTRATION

Head of State: HH Malietoa Tanumafili II, GCMG, CBE; b. 1913.

In March 2005 the cabinet was composed as follows:

Prime Minister and Minister of Foreign Affairs and Trade: Tuila'epa Sailele Malielegaoi; b. 1945 (HRPP; sworn in 23 Nov. 1998 and re-elected in 2001).

Deputy Prime Minister and Minister of Finance: Misa Telefoni Retzlaff. *Agriculture, Forestry, Fisheries and Meteorological Services:* Tuisugaletaua Sofara Aveau. *Education, Sports and Culture:* Fiame Naomi Mata'afa. *Health:* Mulitalo Siafausa. *Lands, Survey and Environment:* Tuala Sale Tagaloa Kerslake. *Justice:* Vacant. *Women's Affairs:* Tuala Ainiu Iusitino. *Communication and Information Technology:* Palusalue Faapo II. *Commerce, Industry and Labour:* Hans Joachim Keil. *Police:* Ulu Vaomalo Ulu Kini. *Revenue:* Gaina Tino. *Works, Transportation and Infrastructure:* Faumuina Liuga.

Government Website: http://www.samoa.net.ws/govtsamoapress

INTERNATIONAL RELATIONS

Samoa, as an independent state, deals directly with other governments and international organizations. It has diplomatic relations with a number of countries.

Samoa is a member of the UN, the Commonwealth, Asian Development Bank, the Pacific Community, the Pacific Islands Forum and is an ACP member state of the ACP-EU relationship.

ECONOMY

Agriculture accounts for approximately 40% of GDP, industry 25% and services 35%.

Currency. The unit of currency is the *tala* (WST) of 100 *sene.* In 2002 there was inflation of 8·1%. Foreign exchange reserves were US$61m. in June 2002. Total money supply was 92m. tala in June 2002.

Budget. For 2000–01 revenue was SA$262·4m. (tax revenue, 66·6%); expenditure, SA$281·7m. (current expenditure, 58·4%).

Performance. Real GDP growth was 6·2% in 2001 but only 1·8% in 2002. Total GDP in 2003 was US$0·3bn.

Banking and Finance. The Central Bank of Samoa (founded 1984) is the bank of issue. The *Governor* is Papali'i Tommy Scanlan. There is one development bank. Commercial banks include: ANZ, Industrial Bank, International Business Bank Corporation, National Bank of Samoa, Samoa Commercial Bank and Westpac Bank Samoa.

ENERGY AND NATURAL RESOURCES

Environment. Samoa's carbon dioxide emissions from the consumption and flaring of fossil fuels in 2002 were the equivalent of 0·8 tonnes per capita.

Electricity. Installed capacity in 2000 was 20,000 kW. Production was about 66m. kWh. in 2000 and consumption per capita an estimated 386 kWh.

Agriculture. In 2001 there were 60,000 ha of arable land and 69,000 ha of permanent cropland. The main products (2000 estimates, in 1,000 tonnes) are coconuts (130), taro (37), copra (11), bananas (10), papayas (10), pineapples (6) and mangoes (5).

Livestock (2000): cattle, 26,000; pigs, 179,000; asses, 7,000.

Forestry. Forests covered 105,000 ha (37·2% of the land area) in 2000. Timber production was 131,000 cu. metres in 2001.

Fisheries. Fish landings in 2001 totalled approximately 12,966 tonnes.

INDUSTRY

Some industrial activity is being developed associated with agricultural products and forestry.

Labour. In 1991 the total labour force numbered 57,142 (39,839 males).

INTERNATIONAL TRADE

Total external debt was US$234m. in 2002.

Imports and Exports. In 1999 exports (f.o.b.) were valued at US$18·15m. (US$20·40m. in 1998) and imports (f.o.b.) at US$115·66m. (US$96·91m. in 1998). Principal exports are coconuts, palm oil, taro and taamu, coffee and beer. Main imports are machinery and transport equipment, foodstuffs and basic manufactures. New Zealand is the principal trading partner, in 1997 accounting for 48·1% of exports and 37·9% of imports. Australia is the second biggest supplier of imports and American Samoa the second biggest export market.

COMMUNICATIONS

Roads. In 1999 the road network covered 790 km, of which 240 km were main roads. In 1993 there were 1,269 private cars, 1,936 pick-up trucks, 472 trucks, 334 buses, 936 taxis and 67 motorcycles.

Civil Aviation. There is an international airport at Apia (Faleolo), which handled 153,000 passengers (152,000 on international flights) in 2000. The national carrier is Polynesian Airlines. In 2003 it operated domestic services and international flights to American Samoa, Auckland, the Fiji Islands, Honolulu, Los Angeles, Niue, Sydney and Tonga.

Shipping. Sea-going shipping totalled 10,000 GRT in 2002. Samoa is linked to Japan, USA, Europe, the Fiji Islands, Australia and New Zealand by regular shipping services.

Telecommunications. There are three radio communication stations at Apia. Radio telephone service connects Samoa with American Samoa, the Fiji Islands, New Zealand, Australia, Canada, USA and UK. Telephone subscribers numbered 13,000 in 2002 (72·0 per 1,000 population) and there were 1,000 PCs in use (6·7 per 1,000 persons). There were 2,700 mobile phone subscribers in 2002 and 500 fax machines in 1998. Samoa had 4,000 Internet users in 2002.

Postal Services. In 1998 there were 38 post offices.

SOCIAL INSTITUTIONS

Justice. The population in penal institutions in Nov. 2003 was 281 (158 per 100,000 of national population). The death penalty, not used in more than 50 years, was abolished in 2004.

Religion. In 2001 there were 46,200 Latter-day Saints (Mormons), 44,000 Congregationalists, 38,100 Roman Catholics, 21,800 Methodists, and the remainder of the population follow other beliefs. In Sept. 2003 the Roman Catholic church had one cardinal.

Education. In 2002 there were 38,946 pupils at primary schools with 1,446 teachers, and 14,159 pupils and 749 teachers at secondary schools. The University of the South Pacific has a School of Agriculture in Samoa, at Apia. A National University was established in 1984. In 1994–95 it had 614 students and 30 academic staff. There is also a Polytechnic Institute which provides mainly vocational and training courses.

The adult literacy in 2001 was 98·7% (98·9% among males and 98·4% among females).

In 1999–2000 total expenditure on education came to 3·9% of GNP and 13·3% of total government spending.

Health. In 1994 there were two national hospitals, 14 district hospitals, nine health centres and 22 subcentres. In 1996 there were 62 physicians, seven dentists, 281 nurses and 65 midwives.

CULTURE

Broadcasting. Samoa has a state-run commercial TV station, *Televise Samoa* and, since 2001, *Pro-Com Sky Cable TV*. There are four radio stations, three on FM and one on AM. In 2001 there were 26,000 television sets (colour by NTSC) and in 1997 there were 178,000 radio receivers.

Press. There are two dailies, plus a weekly, a fortnightly and a monthly. The most widely read newspaper is the independent *Samoa Observer*.

Tourism. In 2000 there were 88,000 foreign tourists, bringing revenue of US$40m.

DIPLOMATIC REPRESENTATIVES

Of Samoa in the United Kingdom and to the European Union
High Commissioner: Tauiliili Uili Meredith (resides at Brussels).
Honorary Consul: Prunella Scarlett, LVO (Church Cottage, Pedlinge, Nr Hythe, Kent, CT21 4JL).

Of the United Kingdom in Samoa
High Commissioner: Richard Fell, CVO (resides at Wellington).
Honorary Consul: c/o Kruse Enari and Barlow, 2nd Floor, NPF Building, Beach Road, PO Box 2029, Apia.

Of the USA in Samoa
Ambassador: Charles J. Swindells (resides at Wellington).

Of Samoa in the USA and to the United Nations (800 Second Ave., Suite 400D, New York, NY, 10017)
Ambassador: Ali'ioaiga Feturi Elisaia.

Of Samoa to the European Union
Ambassador: Tauiliili Uili Meredith.

FURTHER READING

Hughes, H. G. A., *American Samoa, Western Samoa, Samoans Abroad.* [Bibliography] ABC-Clio, Oxford and Santa Barbara (CA), 1997

SAN MARINO

Repubblica di San Marino

Capital: San Marino
Population projection, 2000: 27,000
GDP per capita: not available

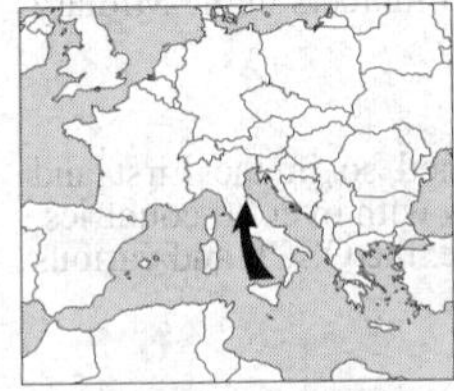

KEY HISTORICAL EVENTS

San Marino is a small republic situated on the Adriatic side of central Italy. According to tradition, St Marinus and a group of Christians settled there to escape persecution. By the 12th century San Marino had developed into a commune ruled by its own statutes and consul. Unsuccessful attempts were made to annex the republic to the papal states in the 18th century and when Napoléon invaded Italy in 1797 he respected the rights of the republic and even offered to extend its territories. In 1815 the Congress of Vienna recognized the independence of the republic. On 22 March 1862 San Marino concluded a treaty of friendship and co-operation, including a *de facto* customs union, with Italy, thus preserving its independence although completely surrounded by Italian territory.

TERRITORY AND POPULATION

San Marino is a land-locked state in central Italy, 20 km from the Adriatic. Area is 61·19 sq. km (23·6 sq. miles) and the population (2000), 26,941; at Dec. 1999 some 13,104 citizens lived abroad.

In 1998 an estimated 90% of the population were urban. Population density, 440·5 per sq. km. The capital, San Marino, has 4,429 inhabitants (2000); the largest town is Serravalle (8,547 in 2000), an industrial centre in the north.

SOCIAL STATISTICS

Births, 2000, 290; deaths, 188; marriages, 193; divorces, 38. Birth rate, 2000 (per 1,000 population), 10·8; death rate, 7·0. Annual population growth rate, 1992–02, 1·4%; fertility rate, 2001, 1·3 births per woman.

CLIMATE

Temperate climate with cold, dry winters and warm summers.

CONSTITUTION AND GOVERNMENT

The legislative power is vested in the *Great and General Council* of 60 members elected every five years by popular vote, two of whom are appointed every six months to act as *Captains Regent*, who are the heads of state.

Executive power is exercised by the ten-member *Congress of State*, presided over by the Captains Regent. The *Council of Twelve*, also presided over by the Captains Regent, is appointed by the Great and General Council to perform administrative functions and is a court of third instance.

National Anthem. No words, tune monastic, transcribed by F. Consolo.

RECENT ELECTIONS

In parliamentary elections on 10 June 2001 the Christian Democratic Party won 25 of 60 seats, with 41·4% of the vote; the Socialist Party 15 with 24·2%; the Progressive Democratic Party 12 with 20·8%; the Popular Democratic Alliance 5 with 8.2%; the Communist Refoundation 2 with 3·4%; and the National Alliance 1 with 1·9%.

CURRENT ADMINISTRATION

In March 2005 the Congress of State comprised:

Minister of Foreign and Political Affairs, Economic Planning and Justice: Fabio Berardi. *Internal Affairs and Civil Protection:* Loris Francini. *Finance, Budget and Transport:* Pier Marino Mularoni. *Industry, Craftsmanship, Commerce, Telecommunications and Economic Co-operation:* Claudio Felici. *Public Education, Universities, Cultural Institutions and Information:* Rosa Zafferani. *Territory,*

Agriculture and Environment: Gian Carlo Venturini. *Health, Social Security and Social Affairs:* Massimo Roberto Rossini. *Labour and Co-operation, Tourism, Sport and Post:* Paride Andreoli.

DEFENCE

Military service is not obligatory, but all citizens between the ages of 16 and 55 can be called upon to defend the State. They may also serve as volunteers in the Military Corps. There is a military Gendarmerie.

INTERNATIONAL RELATIONS

San Marino maintains a traditional neutrality, and remained so in the First and Second World Wars. It has diplomatic and consular relations with over 70 countries.

San Marino is a member of the UN, the Council of Europe, the OSCE and various UN specialized agencies.

ECONOMY

Currency. Since 1 Jan. 2002 San Marino has been using the euro. Italy has agreed that San Marino may mint a small part of the total Italian euro coin contingent with their own motifs. Inflation in 2001 was 3·3%.

Budget. The budget (ordinary and extraordinary) for the financial year ending 31 Dec. 2000 balanced at €452m.

Performance. Real GDP growth was 7·5% in 2001.

Banking and Finance. The Instituto di Credito Sammarinese (*President*, Antonio Valentini), the central bank and bank of issue, was set up in 1986 with public and private resources. Commercial banks include: Banca di San Marino, Credito Industriale Sammarinese, Cassa di Risparmio della Repubblica di San Marino and the Banca Agricola Commerciale della Repubblica di San Marino.

ENERGY AND NATURAL RESOURCES

Electricity. Electricity is supplied by Italy.

Agriculture. There were 1,000 ha of arable land in 2001. Wheat, barley, maize and vines are grown.

INDUSTRY

Labour. Out of 18,077 people in employment in 2000, 5,867 worked in manufacturing and 3,509 in wholesale and retail trade. In Dec. 2000 there were 428 registered unemployed persons.

Trade Unions. There are two Confederations of Trade Unions: the Democratic Confederation of Sammarinese Workers and the Sammarinese Confederation of Labour.

INTERNATIONAL TRADE

Imports and Exports. Export commodities are building stone, lime, wine, baked goods, textiles, varnishes and ceramics. Import commodities are a wide range of consumer manufactures and foodstuffs. San Marino maintains a customs union with Italy.

COMMUNICATIONS

Roads. A bus service connects San Marino with Rimini. There are 252 km of public roads and 40 km of private roads, and (1999) 26,320 passenger cars and 2,763 commercial vehicles.

Civil Aviation. The nearest airport is Rimini, 10 km to the east, which had scheduled flights in 2003 to Berlin, Düsseldorf, Frankfurt, Hamburg, Helsinki, Munich, Naples and Rome.

Telecommunications. San Marino had 20,600 main telephone lines in 2002 and 16,800 mobile phone subscribers. Internet users numbered 14,300 in 2002.

Postal Services. In 1999 there were ten post offices.

SOCIAL INSTITUTIONS

Justice. Judges are appointed permanently by the Great and General Council; they may not be San Marino citizens. Petty civil cases are dealt with by a justice of the peace; legal commissioners deal with more serious civil cases, and all criminal cases and appeals lie to them from the justice of the peace. Appeals against the legal commissioners lie to an appeals judge, and the Council of the Twelve functions as a court of third instance.

Religion. The great majority of the population are Roman Catholic.

Education. Education is compulsory up to 16 years of age. In 2000 there were 15 nursery schools with 991 pupils and 119 teachers, 14 elementary schools with 1,894 pupils and 240 teachers, 3 junior high schools with 729 pupils and 140 teachers, and 1 high school with 1,348 pupils and 87 teachers. The University of San Marino began operating in 1988.

Health. In 2000 there were 141 hospital beds and 117 doctors. A survey published by the World Health Organization in June 2000 to measure health systems in all of the sovereign countries and find which country has the best overall health care ranked San Marino in third place.

CULTURE

Broadcasting. San Marino RTV (colour by PAL) is the state broadcasting company.
In 1999 there were 8,932 television receivers. There were 16,000 radio receivers in 1998.

Cinema. In 1998 there were four cinemas with a seating capacity of 1,800.

Press. San Marino had three daily newspapers in 1999 with a combined daily circulation of 1,800.

Tourism. By the end of Nov. 2000, 3·07m. tourists had visited San Marino during the year.

DIPLOMATIC REPRESENTATIVES

Of the United Kingdom to San Marino
Ambassador: Sir Ivor Roberts, KCMG (resides at Rome).

Of San Marino to the United Nations
Ambassador: Gian Nicola Filippi Balestra.

Of San Marino to the European Union
Ambassador: Savina Zafferani.

FURTHER READING

Edwards, Adrian and Michaelides, Chris, *San Marino.* [Bibliography] ABC-Clio, Oxford and Santa Barbara (CA), 1996

Information: Office of Cultural Affairs and Information of the Department of Foreign Affairs.

SÃO TOMÉ E PRÍNCIPE

República Democrática de São Tomé e Príncipe

Capital: São Tomé
Population projection, 2010: 190,000
GDP per capita, 1997: (PPP$) 1,792
HDI/world rank: 0·645/123

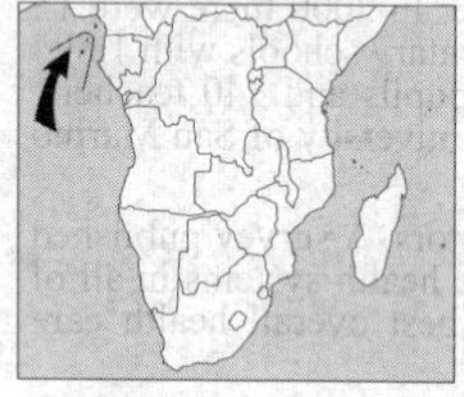

KEY HISTORICAL EVENTS

The islands of São Tomé and Príncipe off the west coast of Africa were colonized by Portugal in the fifteenth century. There may have been a few African inhabitants or visitors earlier but most of the population arrived during the centuries when the islands served as an important slave-trading depot for South America. In the 19th century the islands became the first parts of Africa to grow cocoa. In 1876 Portugal abolished slavery but in practice it continued thereafter with many Angolans, Mozambicans and Cape Verdians being transported to work on the cocoa plantations. Because the slave-descended population was cut off from African culture, São Tomé had a higher proportion than other Portuguese colonies of *assimilados* (Africans acquiring full Portuguese culture and certain rights). São Tomé saw serious riots against Portuguese rule in 1953. From 1960 a Movement for the Liberation of São Tomé e Príncipe operated from neighbouring African territories. In 1970 Portugal formed a 16-member legislative council and a provincial consultative council. Following the Portuguese revolution of 1974 a transitional government was formed. Independence came on 12 July 1975. Independent São Tomé e Príncipe officially proclaimed Marxist-Leninist policies but maintained a non-aligned foreign policy and has received aid from Portugal.

The government was surprised by a coup on 16 July 2003 while President Fradique de Menezes and his foreign minister were abroad. The coup leader, Major Fernando Pereira, installed a junta but accepted a general amnesty from parliament on 24 July after agreeing to allow the ousted president to form a government of national unity.

TERRITORY AND POPULATION

The republic, which lies about 200 km off the west coast of Gabon, in the Gulf of Guinea, comprises the main islands of São Tomé (845 sq. km) and Príncipe and several smaller islets including Pedras Tinhosas and Rolas. It has a total area of 1,001 sq. km (387 sq. miles). Population (census, 2001) 137,599; density, 163 per sq. km. In 2001, 52·4% of the population were rural.

The UN gives a projected population for 2010 of 190,000.

Areas and populations of the two provinces:

Province	*Sq. km*	*Census 2001*	*Chief town*	*Census 2001*
São Tomé	859	131,633	São Tomé	51,886
Príncipe	142	5,966	São António	1,040

The official language is Portuguese. Lungwa São Tomé, a Portuguese Creole, and Fang, a Bantu language, are the spoken languages.

SOCIAL STATISTICS

1997 births, 5,000 (estimate); deaths, 1,200. Rates (1997 estimate): birth rate per 1,000 population, 33·8; death rate, 8·4; infant mortality (per 1,000 live births), 57 (2001). Expectation of life, 2001, 66·6 years for males and 72·4 years for females. Annual population growth rate, 1992–02, 2·6%; fertility rate, 2001, 6·0 births per woman.

CLIMATE

The tropical climate is modified by altitude and the effect of the cool Benguela current. The wet season is generally from Oct. to May, but rainfall varies considerably, from 40" (1,000 mm) in the hot and humid northeast to 150–200"

(3,800–5,000 mm) on the plateau. São Tomé, Jan. 79°F (26·1°C), July 75°F (23·9°C). Annual rainfall 38" (951 mm).

CONSTITUTION AND GOVERNMENT

The 1990 constitution was approved by 72% of votes at a referendum of Aug. 1990. It abolished the monopoly of the Movement for the Liberation of São Tomé e Príncipe (MLSTP). The *President* must be over 34 years old, and is elected by universal suffrage for one or two (only) five-year terms. He or she is also head of government and appoints a Council of Ministers. The 55-member *National Assembly* is elected for four years.

Since April 1995 **Príncipe** has enjoyed internal self-government, with a five-member regional government and an elected assembly.

National Anthem. 'Independência total, glorioso canto do povo' ('Total independence, glorious song of the people'); words by A. N. do Espírito Santo, tune by M. de Sousa e Almeida.

RECENT ELECTIONS

At the presidential election on 29 July 2001 Fradique de Menezes (Independent Democratic Action) was elected by 56·3% of votes cast against Manuel Pinto da Costa (Liberation Movement of São Tomé e Príncipe) with 38·4% and three other opponents. Turn-out was 62·4%.

At the National Assembly elections on 3 March 2002 the Liberation Movement of São Tomé e Príncipe (MLSTP) won 24 seats with 39·6% of votes cast, the coalition of the Force for Change Democratic Movement (MDFM) and the Democratic Convergence Party (PCD) 23 (39·4%), and the Uê Kédadji (UK) 8 (16·2%).

CURRENT ADMINISTRATION

President, C.-in-C: Fradique Bandeira Melo de Menezes; b. 1942 (Independent Democratic Action; sworn in 23 July 2003, having previously held office from 3 Sept. 2001 to 16 July 2003).

In March 2005 the government comprised:

Prime Minister: Damião Vaz de Almeida; b. 1951 (MLSTP; in office since 18 Sept. 2004).

Minister of Agriculture and Fisheries: Hélder Pinto. *Defence and Internal Order:* Óscar Sacramento e Sousa. *Education and Culture:* Álvaro Santiago. *Foreign Affairs, Co-operation and Communities:* Ovídio Manuel Barbosa Pequeno. *Health:* Aberto dos Santos. *Commerce, Industry and Tourism:* Hélder Paquete. *Justice, Public Administration and Relations with Parliament:* Elsa Maria Neto d'Alva Teixeira de Barros Pinto. *Labour, Employment and Solidarity:* Fernando Maquengo. *Planning and Finance:* Adelino Castelo David. *Public Works and Land Management:* Diolindo Costa de Boa Esperança. *Natural Resources and Environment:* Arlindo Carvalho. *Youth, Sport and Professional Training:* José Santiago Viegas. *Secretary of State for Public Administration and State Reform:* Célia Maria Gentil da Costa Pereira.

INTERNATIONAL RELATIONS

São Tomé e Príncipe is a member of the UN, the African Union, African Development Bank, the International Organization of the Francophonie and is an ACP member state of the ACP-EU relationship.

ECONOMY

In 2002 agriculture accounted for 20·0% of GDP, industry 17·0% and services 63·0%.

Overview. Most branches of the economy were nationalized after independence, but economic liberalization began in 1985 and accelerated in the 1990s.

Currency. The unit of currency is the *dobra* (STD) of 100 *centimos*. From a rate of 69·0% in 1997 inflation had fallen to 9·2% by 2002. In Dec. 1997 foreign exchange reserves were US$12m. Total money supply in April 2002 was 98,789m. dobras (up from 23,683m. dobras in Dec. 1996).

Budget. In 2000 revenues totalled 183·4bn. dobras and expenditures 244·4bn. dobras.

Performance. Real GDP growth was 4·1% in 2002 (4·0% in 2001). In 2003 total GDP was US$54m.

Banking and Finance. In 1991 the Banco Central de São Tomé e Príncipe (*Governor*, Maria do Carmo Silveira) replaced the Banco Nacional as the central bank and bank of issue. A private commercial bank, the Banco Internacional de São Tomé e Príncipe, began operations in 1993.

ENERGY AND NATURAL RESOURCES

Environment. In 2002 carbon dioxide emissions from the consumption and flaring of fossil fuels were the equivalent of 0·7 tonnes per capita.

Electricity. Installed capacity, 2000, 6,000 kW. Production was about 18m. kWh in 2000, with consumption per capita being an estimated 130 kWh.

Oil and Gas. There are large oil reserves around São Tomé e Príncipe that could greatly add to the country's wealth; the Joint Development Zone was set up with Nigeria to administer the exploitation because the reserves are located in shared waters. The first license to begin exploration was granted in April 2004.

Agriculture. After independence all landholdings over 200 ha were nationalized into 15 state farms. These were partially privatized in 1985 by granting management contracts to foreign companies, and distributing some state land as small private plots. There were 6,000 ha of arable land in 2001 and 47,000 ha of permanent crops. Production (2000 in 1,000 tonnes): coconuts, 29; bananas, 19; cassava, 5; palm kernels, 4; cocoa beans, 3; maize, 2. There were 4,000 cattle, 3,000 sheep, 2,000 pigs and 5,000 goats in 2000.

Forestry. In 2000 forests covered 27,000 ha, or 31·9% of the land area. In 2001, 9,000 cu. metres of timber were cut.

Fisheries. There are rich tuna shoals. The total catch in 2001 came to approximately 3,500 tonnes.

INDUSTRY

Manufacturing contributed 4·2% of GDP in 2001. There are a few small factories in agricultural processing (including beer and palm oil production), timber processing, bricks, ceramics, printing, textiles and soap-making.

Labour. In 1994 the economically active population was 54,000. There were 15,000 registered unemployed.

INTERNATIONAL TRADE

Foreign debt was US$333m. in 2002. In 1999 São Tomé e Príncipe was the most heavily indebted country in the world in relation to the GNP, owing 615% of its GNP.

Imports and Exports. Trade figures for 2002: imports, US$28·0m.; exports, US$5·1m. Cocoa accounts for two-thirds of all exports.

In 2000 the main export markets were the Netherlands (57·7%) and Portugal (10·9%); main import suppliers were Portugal (41·7%), Angola (13·0%) and Japan (10·8%).

COMMUNICATIONS

Roads. There were an estimated 320 km of roads in 1999, 218 km of which were asphalted. Approximately 4,000 passenger cars were in use in 1996 (30 per 1,000 inhabitants), plus 1,540 trucks and vans.

Civil Aviation. São Tomé airport had flights in 2003 to Cape Verde, Libreville, Lisbon and Luanda. In 1999 São Tomé handled 32,298 passengers and 1,877 tonnes of freight. There is a light aircraft service to Príncipe.

Shipping. São Tomé is the main port, but it lacks a deep water harbour. Neves handles oil imports and is the main fishing port. Portuguese shipping lines run routes to Lisbon, Oporto, Rotterdam and Antwerp. In 2002 merchant shipping totalled 86,000 GRT.

Telecommunications. There were 8,200 telephone subscribers in 2002, or 54·4 per 1,000 population, including 2,000 mobile phone subscribers. Internet users numbered 11,000 in 2002. In 1995 there were 200 fax machines.

Postal Services. In 1998 there were 18 post offices.

SOCIAL INSTITUTIONS

Justice. Members of the Supreme Court are appointed by the National Assembly. There is no death penalty. The population in penal institutions in April 2002 was 130 (79 per 100,000 of national population).

Religion. In 2001, 81% of the population were Roman Catholic. There is a small Protestant church and a Seventh Day Adventist school.

Education. Adult literacy was 57·0% in 1998. Education is free and compulsory. In 1999–2000 there were 71 primary schools and 20,258 pupils, and 10 secondary schools and 10,672 pupils; more than 90% of primary age children were attending school in 1995. There is a vocational centre, a school of agriculture and a pre-university *lycée.*

Health. In 1996 there were 61 physicians, 7 dentists, 167 nurses and 39 midwives.

CULTURE

Broadcasting. Radio broadcasting is conducted by the government-controlled Rádio Nacional. There is a Voice of America radio station, a religious station and a private German station. There were 38,000 radio receivers and 23,000 TV receivers in 1997.

Press. There are four weekly newspapers.

Tourism. In 2001 there were 8,000 foreign tourists, bringing revenue of US$10m.

DIPLOMATIC REPRESENTATIVES

Of São Tomé e Príncipe in the United Kingdom (resides at Brussels)
Ambassador: Vacant.
Chargé d'Affaires a.i.: Armindo de Brito Fernandes.

Of the United Kingdom in São Tomé e Príncipe
Ambassador: John Thompson, MBE (resides at Luanda, Angola).

Of São Tomé e Príncipe in the USA
Ambassador: Vacant.

Of the USA in São Tomé e Príncipe
Ambassador: Barrie R. Walkley (resides at Libreville, Gabon).

Of São Tomé e Príncipe to the United Nations
Ambassador: Vacant.
Chargé d'Affaires a.i.: Domingos Augusto Ferreira.

Of São Tomé e Príncipe to the European Union
Ambassador: Vacant.
Chargé d'Affaires a.i.: António de Lima Viegas.

FURTHER READING

Shaw, Caroline S., *São Tomé e Príncipe.* [Bibliography] ABC-Clio, Oxford and Santa Barbara (CA), 1994

SAUDI ARABIA

Al-Mamlaka al-Arabiya as-Saudiya
(Kingdom of Saudi Arabia)

Capital: Riyadh
Population projection, 2010: 29·18m.
GDP per capita, 2002: (PPP$) 12,650
HDI/world rank: 0·768/77

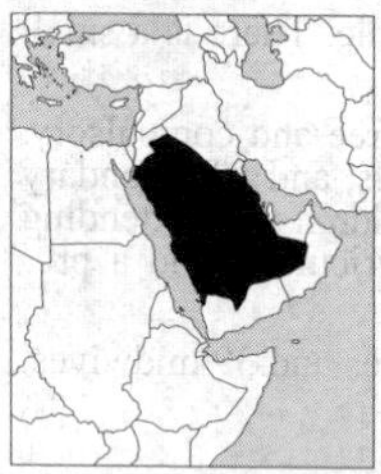

KEY HISTORICAL EVENTS

The pre-Islamic period saw the development of civilizations based on trade in frankincense and spices. The Sabaean and Himyarite kingdoms flourished from around 650 BC and 115 BC respectively, their loose federations of city states lasting until the 6th century AD. They remained for the most part independent despite trading contact with the Roman and Persian empires.

By the 6th century AD the Hejaz region in northwestern Arabia was an important link in the overland trade route from Egypt and the Byzantine Empire to the wider East. The Prophet Muhammad, born in 570, took control of Makkah (Mecca), an important trade-route city of the Hejaz, in 630. He had declared himself a prophetic reformer, destroying the city's pagan idols and declaring it a centre of Muslim pilgrimage dedicated to the worship of Allah (God) alone. Muhammad died in AD 632, by then commanding the loyalty of almost all of Arabia.

Arabia began to fragment and after 1269 most of the Hejaz region came under the suzerainty of the Egyptian Mameluks. The Ottoman Turks conquered Egypt in 1517 and, to counter the influence of the Christian Portuguese in the Gulf region, extended control over the Arabian Peninsula. Portuguese traders were followed by British, Dutch and French merchants in the 17th and 18th centuries, the British gradually securing political and commercial supremacy in the Gulf and southern Arabia.

Saudi Arabia's origins as a political entity lay in the rise of the puritanical Wahhabi movement of the 18th century that called for a return to the original principles of Islam and gained the allegiance of the powerful Al-Saud dynasty in the Nejd region of central Arabia. After a long period of tribal warfare, the Al-Saud family was exiled to Kuwait but Abdulaziz Ibn Abdul Rahman (known to Europeans as Ibn Saud) restored Wahhabi fortunes, recapturing Riyadh in 1902 and reasserting Al-Saud control over Nejd by 1906. After further territorial gains, Britain recognized Abdulaziz as ruler of the Kingdom of Saudi Arabia, an absolute monarchy under Islamic law.

Oil was discovered in 1938 and its commercial exploitation was developed with the support of the USA after the Second World War. Crown Prince Saud succeeded his father in 1953 and ruled until 1964, when he was effectively deposed by his brother Faisal. As king and prime minister, Faisal instituted a programme of economic expansion using the kingdom's increasing oil revenues. Financial support was given to other Arab states in their conflict with Israel. The Oct. 1973 Arab-Israeli war heralded an oil crisis in which Arab producers, including Saudi Arabia, cut supplies to the USA and other Western countries, leading to a fourfold increase in oil prices. However, Faisal subsequently adopted a more conciliatory stance and the close Saudi economic relationship with the USA was reinforced by a co-operation agreement in 1974. In March 1975 Faisal was assassinated by a nephew and his half-brother Khalid became king.

Khalid announced that he would continue Faisal's policies, promoting Islamic solidarity and Arab unity in the wake of hostilities with Israel. Domestically he maintained royal power and the conservative Islamic character of the country. Crown Prince Fahd (Khalid's younger half-brother) succeeded on 13 June 1982. Like his predecessors he exercised absolute power but with the advice of a Consultative Council (*Majlis Al-Shura*) of royal appointees. Fahd was a key participant in diplomatic efforts to end the Iran-Iraq war in 1988 and in the 1989 Taif reconciliation accord, bringing the 14-year Lebanese civil war to a close. His pro-Western stance in the 1990–91 Gulf crisis was crucial to the deployment of the USA-led multinational force raised against Iraq following its invasion of Kuwait.

Anti-Western disaffection has become more overt in recent years. In 1996 a bomb exploded at a US military complex at Dhahran, killing 19. Up to 15 Saudi nationals were believed to have been involved in the terrorist attacks on New York and Washington, D.C. on 11 Sept. 2001, which were co-ordinated by Saudi dissident Osama bin Laden. In May 2003 suicide bombers killed ten US citizens and many others at housing compounds for Western expatriate workers in Riyadh. With King Fahd's poor health, Crown Prince Abdullah, his half-brother, assumed day-to-day responsibilities for running the government in 1996.

TERRITORY AND POPULATION

Saudi Arabia, which occupies nearly 80% of the Arabian peninsula, is bounded in the west by the Red Sea, east by the Persian Gulf and the United Arab Emirates, north by Jordan, Iraq and Kuwait and south by Yemen and Oman. For the border dispute with Yemen *see* YEMEN: Territory and Population. The total area is 2,149,690 sq. km (829,995 sq. miles). Riyadh is the political, and Makkah (Mecca) the religious, capital.

The total population at the 1992 census was 16,948,388. 2001 estimate, 22·84m.; density, 10·6 per sq. km. Approximately 76% of the population are Saudi nationals. In 2001, 86·6% of the population lived in urban areas.

The UN gives a projected population for 2010 of 29·18m.

Principal cities with 1995 population estimates (in 1m.): Riyadh, 3·18 (in 1999); Jeddah, 1·49; Makkah, 0·77; Taif, 0·41 (1991); Madinah, 0·40 (1991); Dammam, 0·35 (1991).

The Neutral Zone (3,560 sq. miles, 5,700 sq. km), jointly owned and administered by Kuwait and Saudi Arabia from 1922 to 1966, was partitioned between the two countries in 1966, but the exploitation of the oil and other natural resources continues to be shared.

The official language is Arabic.

SOCIAL STATISTICS

2001 estimates: births, 715,000; deaths, 84,000. Birth rate (2001) was approximately 34 per 1,000 population; death rate, 4. 75% of the population is under the age of 30. Expectation of life at birth, 2001, was 70·7 years for males and 73·3 years for females, up from 61·4 for males and 64·1 for females over the period 1980–85. No other country had such a large increase in its life expectancy over the same period. Annual population growth rate, 1992–02, 3·0%. Infant mortality, 2001, was 23 per 1,000 live births, down from 58 in the years 1980–85. Fertility rate, 2001, 5·7 births per woman.

CLIMATE

A desert climate, with very little rain and none at all from June to Dec. The months May to Sept. are very hot and humid, but winter temperatures are quite pleasant. Riyadh, Jan. 58°F (14·4°C), July 108°F (42°C). Annual rainfall 4" (100 mm). Jeddah, Jan. 73°F (22·8°C), July 87°F (30·6°C). Annual rainfall 3" (81 mm).

CONSTITUTION AND GOVERNMENT

The reigning King, **Fahd Ibn Abdulaziz Al-Saud** (b. 1923), Custodian of the two Holy Mosques, succeeded in May 1982, after King Khalid's death. In 1995 King Fahd suffered a stroke, since when he has been incapacitated. *Crown Prince:* Prince Abdullah Ibn Abdulaziz Al-Saud (b. 1923), half-brother of the King, is the *de facto* leader. Prince Sultan (b. 1927), a brother of the king, is considered to be next in line after Crown Prince Abdullah. The Saudi royal family is around 7,000-strong.

Constitutional practice derives from Sharia law. There is no formal Constitution, but three royal decrees of 1 March 1992 established a Basic Law which defines the systems of central and municipal government, and set up a 60-man Consultative Council (*Majlis Al-Shura*) of royal nominees in Aug. 1993. The *Chairman* is Muhammad Ibn Ibrahim Ibn Uthman Ibn Jubair. In July 1997 the King decreed an increase of the Consultative Council to a chairman plus 90 members, selected from men of science and experience; and in May 2001 it was increased again to a chairman plus 120 members. The Council does not have legislative powers.

Saudi Arabia is an absolute monarchy; executive power is discharged through a *Council of Ministers*, consisting of the King, Deputy Prime Minister, Second Deputy Prime Minister and Cabinet Ministers.

The King has the post of *Prime Minister* and can veto any decision of the Council of Ministers within 30 days.

In Oct. 2003 the government announced that municipal elections would be held in 2004 for the first time, followed by city elections and partial elections to the *Majlis Al-Shura* in the following years.

National Anthem. 'Sarei lil majd walaya' ('Onward towards the glory and the heights'); words by Ibrahim Khafaji, tune by Abdul Rahman al Katib.

RECENT ELECTIONS

Saudi Arabia's first ever elections were held in three phases between Feb.–April 2005 to create 178 local municipal councils. Half of the 1,184 seats were elected by the people and the other half appointed. Women were not permitted to stand for election or to vote. There are no political parties, but most seats were won by candidates backed by conservative Muslim clerics.

CURRENT ADMINISTRATION

In March 2005 the Council of Ministers comprised:

Prime Minister: King Fahd Ibn Abdulaziz Al-Saud; b. 1923.

First Deputy Prime Minister and Commander of the National Guard: Crown Prince Abdullah Ibn Abdulaziz Al-Saud. *Second Deputy Prime Minister, Minister of Defence and Aviation and Inspector-General:* Prince Sultan Ibn Abdulaziz Al-Saud.

Minister of Municipal and Rural Affairs: Prince Meta'ab Ibn Abdul Aziz Al-Saud. *Interior:* Prince Nayef Ibn Abdulaziz Al-Saud. *Foreign Affairs:* Prince Saud Al-Faisal Ibn Abdulaziz Al-Saud. *Agriculture:* Dr Fahd Ibn Abdulrahman Balghanaim. *Water and Electricity:* Abdul Rahman Al-Hussayen. *Civil Service:* Muhammad Ibn Ali Al-Fayez. *Education:* Abdullah Ibn Saleh Al-Obeid. *Finance:* Dr Ibrahim Ibn Abdulaziz Al-Assaf. *Health:* Dr Hamad Ibn Abdullah Al-Manie. *Higher Education:* Dr Khalid Ibn Mohammed Al-Angary. *Commerce and Industry:* Dr Hashim Ibn Abdullah Al-Yamani. *Culture and Information:* Iyad Ibn Amin Madani. *Islamic Affairs, Endowments, Call and Guidance:* Shaikh Saleh Ibn Abdulaziz Al-Ashaikh. *Justice:* Dr Abdullah Ibn Mohammed Ibn Ibrahim Al-Ashaikh. *Labour:* Dr Ghazi Ibn Abdulrahman Al-Qusaibi. *Social Affairs:* Abdulmohsen Al-Akkas. *Petroleum and Mineral Resources:* Ali Ibn Ibrahim Al-Naimi. *Pilgrimage:* Fouad Ibn Abdul-Salam Al-Farsi. *National Economy and Planning:* Khalid Ibn Muhammad Al-Qusaibi. *Communications and Information Technology:* Muhammad Ibn Jameel Mulla. *Transport:* Dr Jubarah Ibn Eid Al-Suraiseri.

Majlis Website: http://www.shura.gov.sa

DEFENCE

Defence expenditure in 2003 totalled US$18,747m. (US$832 per capita), representing 8·9% of GDP.

5,000 US troops were stationed in Saudi Arabia after the 1991 Gulf War and were joined by a further 20,000 during the 2003 conflict. However, virtually all US troops have now been withdrawn. The Peninsular Shield Force of about 7,000 comprises units from all Gulf Co-operation Council countries.

Army. Strength (2002) was approximately 75,000. There is a paramilitary Frontier Force (approximately 10,500) and a National Guard (see below).

Navy. The Royal Saudi Naval Forces fleet includes four frigates and four corvettes. Naval Aviation forces operate 21 armed helicopters, both ship and shore based.

The main naval bases are at Riyadh (HQ Naval Forces), Jeddah (Western Fleet) and Jubail (Eastern Fleet). Naval personnel in 2002 totalled 15,500, including 3,000 marines.

Air Force. Current combat units include F-15s, F-5Bs, F-5Fs, Tornado strike aircraft and Tornado interceptors. The Air Force operates 432 combat aircraft in all and numbered about 18,000 personnel in 2002.

Air Defence Force. This separate Command was formerly part of the Army. In 2002 it operated surface-to-air missile batteries and had a strength of 16,000.

National Guard. The total strength of the National Guard amounted to approximately 100,000 (75,000 active, 25,000 tribal levies) in 2002. The National

Guard's primary role is the protection of the Royal Family and vital points in the Kingdom. It is directly under royal command. The UK provides small advisory teams to the National Guard in the fields of general training and communications.

INTERNATIONAL RELATIONS

Saudi Arabia is a member of the UN, BIS, the League of Arab States, the Gulf Co-operation Council, OPEC, OIC and Islamic Development Bank.

In April 2001 Saudi Arabia and Iran signed a security pact to fight drug trafficking and terrorism, 13 years after the two countries had broken off relations.

ECONOMY

The oil sector accounts for 45% of GDP. Agriculture accounted for 5·2% of GDP in 2002, industry 52·0% and services 42·8%.

Overview. Saudi Arabia is the world's leading oil producer and exporter (25% of world supply). Oil accounts for 35% of GDP, 75% of government revenue and 85% of exports. Oil revenues are used to develop agriculture, construction, engineering, food processing and metal fabrication. Telecommunications is the fastest growing industry. The government consumes about 30% of GDP; it aims to cut spending to reduce budget deficits. Domestic debt is 100% of GDP. Structural reforms were introduced in 1999 to attract foreign investment. The stock market was opened to foreign investors and tax and customs administrations were reformed.

Saudi Arabia is negotiating for entry into the World Trade Organization. This will require tariff reductions, liberalized financial services and increased competition. A recent reform allows foreigners to own property without a Saudi partner. In 1998, for the first time, American and European oil companies were allowed to invest in the energy sector. However, elsewhere in the economy regulations are opaque and corruption is a problem. Slow moving privatization programmes leave the economy dominated by large state corporations. Economic growth has fallen behind population growth, which has led to a sharp drop in real per capita incomes and high unemployment. There is excessive hiring of foreigners in unproductive service jobs.

Currency. The unit of currency is the *rial* (SAR) of 100 *halalah*. Foreign exchange reserves totalled US$14,859m. in June 2002 and gold reserves were 4·60m. troy oz. There was deflation of 0·7% in 2002, the sixth consecutive year in which Saudi Arabia had experienced deflation. Total money supply in June 2002 was SAR193,002m.

In 2001 the six Gulf Arab states—Saudi Arabia, along with Bahrain, Kuwait, Oman, Qatar and the United Arab Emirates—signed an agreement to establish a single currency by 2010.

Budget. In 1986 the financial year became the calendar year. 2002 budget: revenue, SAR157bn.; expenditure, SAR202bn.

Oil sales account for 80% of state income. Expenditure in 2002: defence and security, SAR69bn.; human resource development, SAR47bn.; public administration, SAR45bn.; health and social development, SAR19bn.

Performance. Real GDP growth was 0·1% in 2002 but then 7·2% in 2003 thanks largely to a surge in oil prices. Total GDP in 2001 was US$186·5bn. Per capita GDP is now around half the level of 1980.

Banking and Finance. The Saudi Arabian Monetary Agency (*Governor*, Hamad Saud Al-Sayari, appointed 1983), established in 1953, functions as the central bank and the government's fiscal agent. In 2002 there were three national banks (the National Commercial Bank, the Al-Rajhi Banking and Investment Corporation and the Riyad Bank), five specialist banks, eight foreign banks and three government specialized credit institutions. The leading banks are National Commercial Bank (assets in 1999 of US$22,895m.), Saudi-American (US$20,520m.) and Riyad Bank (US$17,167m.). Sharia (the religious law of Islam) forbids the charging of interest; Islamic banking is based on sharing clients' profits and losses and imposing service charges. In 1999 total assets of commercial banks were 415,227m. rials.

A number of industry sectors are closed to foreign investors, including petroleum exploration, defence-related activities and financial services.

There is a stock exchange.

ENERGY AND NATURAL RESOURCES

Environment. Saudi Arabia's carbon dioxide emissions from the consumption and flaring of fossil fuels in 2002 were the equivalent of 14·0 tonnes per capita. An *Environmental Sustainability Index* compiled for the World Economic Forum meeting in Feb. 2002 ranked Saudi Arabia 138th in the world out of the 142 countries analysed, with 34·2%. The index measured the ability of countries to maintain favourable environmental conditions and examined various factors including pollution levels and the use or abuse of natural resources.

Electricity. By 1995 over 100 electricity producers had been amalgamated into four companies. Installed capacity was 23·8m. kW in 2000. All electricity is thermally generated. Production was 126·4bn. kWh in 2000; consumption per capita in 2000 was 5,908 kWh.

Oil and Gas. Proven oil reserves (2003) 262·7bn. bbls. (the highest of any country and around 23% of world resources). Oil production began in 1938 by Aramco, which is now 100% state-owned and accounts for about 99% of total crude oil production. Saudi crude output in 2002 totalled 418·1m. tonnes (434·1m. tonnes in 2001) and accounted for 11·7% of the world total oil output. In 1998 oil export revenues were US$33bn., rising to US$41bn. in 1999 and US$70bn. in 2000, before falling to US$56bn. in 2001.

Production comes from 14 major oilfields, mostly in the Eastern Province and offshore, and including production from the Neutral Zone. The Ghawar oilfield, located between Riyadh and the Persian gulf, is the largest in the world, with estimated reserves of 70bn. bbls. Oil reserves are expected to run out in approximately 2085.

In 2002 natural gas reserves were 6,360bn. cu. metres; output in 2002 was 56·4bn. cu. metres. The gas sector has been opened up to foreign investment.

Water. Efforts are under way to provide adequate supplies of water for urban, industrial, rural and agricultural use. Most investment has gone into sea-water desalination. In 1996, 33 plants produced 1·9m. cu. metres a day, meeting 70% of drinking water needs. Total annual consumption was 18,200m. cu. metres in 1995. Irrigation for agriculture consumes the largest amount, from fossil reserves (the country's principal water source), and from surface water collected during seasonal floods. In 1996 there were 183 dams with a holding capacity of 450m. cu. metres. Treated urban waste water is an increasing resource for domestic purposes; in 1996 there were two recycling plants in operation.

Minerals. Production began in 1988 at Mahd Al-Dahab gold mine, the largest in the country. In 1999 total gold production was 4,570 kg. Deposits of iron, phosphate, bauxite, uranium, silver, tin, tungsten, nickel, chrome, zinc, lead, potassium ore and copper have also been found.

Agriculture. Land ownership is under the jurisdiction of the Ministry of Municipal and Rural Affairs.

Since 1970 the government has spent substantially on desert reclamation, irrigation schemes, drainage and control of surface water and of moving sands. Undeveloped land has been distributed to farmers and there are research and extension programmes. Large scale private investment has concentrated on wheat, poultry and dairy production.

In 2001 there were 3·60m. ha of arable land and 194,000 ha of permanent cropland. Approximately 1·62m. ha were irrigated in 2001. In 2002, 8·5% of the economically active population were engaged in agriculture (19·1% in 1990).

About 200,000 tonnes of barley are produced annually as animal fodder. Production of other crops, 2000 (in 1,000 tonnes): wheat, 2,046; dates, 712; melons and watermelons, 426; potatoes, 394; tomatoes, 277; sorghum, 204; cucumbers and gherkins, 125; grapes, 116; onions, 95.

Livestock (2000): 297,000 cattle, 7,576,000 sheep, 4,305,000 goats, 400,000 camels and 130m. chickens. Livestock products (2000, in 1,000 tonnes): milk, 747; meat, 579; eggs, 136.

Forestry. The area under forests was 1·5m. ha (0·7% of the land area) in 2000.

Fisheries. In 2001 the total catch was 49,167 tonnes, entirely from sea fishing.

INDUSTRY

According to the Financial Times Survey (FT 500), the largest companies in Saudi Arabia by market capitalization on 25 March 2004 were Saudi Telecom (US$37·5bn.), SABIC (Saudi Basic Industries), at US$35·1bn., and Saudi Electricity (US$23·1bn.).

In 2001 industry accounted for 51·8% of GDP, with manufacturing contributing 10·2%. The government encourages the establishment of manufacturing industries. Its policy focuses on establishing industries that use petroleum products, petrochemicals and minerals. Petrochemical and oil-based industries have been concentrated at eight new industrial cities, with the two principal cities at Jubail and Yanbu. Products include chemicals, plastics, industrial gases, steel and other metals. In 2004 there were 3,657 factories employing 340,000 workers.

Labour. The labour force in 2001 totalled 6,338,000. In 1999 females constituted 15% of the labour force—only the United Arab Emirates had a lower percentage of females in its workforce. In 2001, 35·7% of the economically active population were engaged in wholesale and retail trade, 18·7% in manufacturing, 15·7% in construction, 6·7% in research, consultancy and recruitment. In 1995 less than 1% worked in the oil sector. There are 6m. foreign workers, including over 1m. Egyptians and over 1m. Indians. Unemployment, which was less than 8% in 1999, reached 12% in 2002. Young people in particular are affected by unemployment.

INTERNATIONAL TRADE

In 1999 foreign debt totalled US$9bn.

Saudi Arabia, along with Bahrain, Kuwait, Oman, Qatar and the United Arab Emirates began the implementation of a customs union in Jan. 2003.

Imports and Exports. Trade in SAR1m.:

	1998	*1999*	*2000*	*2001*	*2002*
Imports f.o.b.	103,117	96,312	103,890	107,276	111,009
Exports f.o.b.	145,023	189,579	289,756	254,225	267,716

The principal export is crude oil; refined oil, petro-chemicals, fertilizers, plastic products and wheat are other major exports. Saudi Arabia is the world's largest exporter of oil, accounting for over 87% of all the country's exports in 2002. Main export destinations, 1999: USA, 18·8%; Japan, 17·5%; South Korea, 9·2%; Singapore, 5·9%. Imports, 1999: USA, 20·8%; Japan, 9·1%; UK, 7·4%; South Korea, 3·5%.

COMMUNICATIONS

Roads. In 2000 there was a total road network of 152,044 km. The total length of all asphalted roads was 45,461 km. A causeway links Saudi Arabia with Bahrain. Passenger cars in use in 1996 numbered 1,744,000 (100 per 1,000 inhabitants) and there were 1,169,000 trucks and vans. Women are not allowed to drive. In 1998 there were 153,727 road accidents resulting in 3,474 deaths.

Rail. 1,435 mm gauge lines of 1,392 km link Riyadh and Dammam with stops at Hofuf and Abqaiq. The network is to be extended by 2,000 km at an estimated cost of US$2·6bn., in four phases, consisting of links to Jeddah, the Jordanian border, Jubail, and Makkah and Madinah. In 1999 railways carried 770,400 passengers and 1·8m. tonnes of freight.

Civil Aviation. The national carrier is the state-owned Saudia. In 1999 Saudia carried 12·7m. passengers, 260,300 tonnes of air cargo and operated 115,300 flights. At the end of 1999 Saudia owned 125 aircraft. There are four major international airports, at Jeddah (King Abdulaziz), Dhahran, Riyadh (King Khaled), and the newly constructed King Fahd International Airport at Dammam. There are also 22 domestic airports. In 2000 Jeddah handled 10,465,147 passengers (5,747,916 on international flights) and 204,581 tonnes of freight. Riyadh was the second busiest airport in 2000, handling 8,379,573 passengers (5,194,469 on domestic flights) and 165,879 tonnes of freight. In 1999, 26·1m. passengers travelled through the country's airports. The volume of air cargo carried was 463,000 tonnes.

Shipping. The ports of Dammam and Jubail are on the Persian Gulf and Jeddah, Yanbu and Jizan on the Red Sea. There is a deepwater oil terminal at Ras Tanura, and 16 minor ports. In 2002 the ports handled 104·2m. tonnes of cargo. In 1995 the merchant marine comprised 110 vessels totalling 8·2m. DWT. In 2002 shipping totalled 1·47m. GRT, including oil tankers 664,000 GRT.

Telecommunications. Saudi Arabia had 8,325,500 telephone subscribers in 2002 or 361·0 per 1,000 inhabitants, and there were 3·0m. PCs in use (130·2 per 1,000 population). There were 5,008,000 mobile phone subscribers in 2002, and 150,000 fax machines in 1995. The number of Internet users in 2002 was 1,418,900. The government sold a 30% stake in Saudi Telecom Company in Dec. 2002.

Postal Services. In 1999 there were 461 main post offices, 185 branch offices, 85 express mail centres and 69 private sector postal agencies.

SOCIAL INSTITUTIONS

Justice. The religious law of Islam (Sharia) is the common law of the land, and is administered by religious courts, at the head of which is a chief judge, who is responsible for the Department of Sharia Affairs. Sharia courts are concerned primarily with family inheritance and property matters. The Committee for the Settlement of Commercial Disputes is the commercial court. Other specialized courts or committees include one dealing exclusively with labour and employment matters; the Negotiable Instruments Committee, which deals with cases relating to cheques, bills of exchange and promissory notes; and the Board of Grievances, whose preserve is disputes with the government or its agencies and which also has jurisdiction in trademark-infringement cases and is the authority for enforcing foreign court judgements.

The death penalty is in force for murder, rape, sodomy, armed robbery, sabotage, drug trafficking, adultery and apostasy; executions may be held in public. There were 36 confirmed executions in 2004. The population in penal institutions in 2000 was 23,720 (110 per 100,000 of national population).

Religion. In 2001, 90% of the total population were Sunni Muslims, 4% Shias, 4% Christians and 1% Hindus. The *Grand Mufti*, Sheikh Abdul Aziz bin Abdullah bin Mohammed Al-Sheikh, has cabinet rank. A special police force, the Mutaween, exists to enforce religious norms.

The annual *Hajj*, the pilgrimage to Makkah, takes place from the 8th to the 13th day of Dhu al Hijjah, the last month of the Islamic year. It attracts more than 1·8m. pilgrims annually. In the current Islamic year, 1426, the *Hajj* will begin on 8 Jan. 2006 in the Gregorian calendar.

Education. The educational system provides students with free education, books and health services. General education consists of kindergarten, six years of primary school and three years each of intermediate and high school. In 1996–97 there were 893 pre-primary schools with 7,703 teachers and 85,484 pupils. In 1998–99 there were 12,234 primary schools with 189,008 teachers and 2,259,849 pupils; 5,901 intermediate schools with 86,630 teachers and 1,035,363 pupils; 3,117 secondary schools with 53,618 teachers and 704,566 pupils. At teacher training colleges there were 1,438 teachers and 21,366 students and at vocational schools 2,536 teachers and 21,551 students. Students can attend either high schools offering programmes in arts and sciences, or vocational schools. Girls' education is administered separately. In 1996 there were more than 30 special schools for the handicapped with about 4,550 students. The adult literacy rate in 2001 was 77·1% (83·5% among males and 68·2% among females). Although Saudi girls were not even allowed to attend school until 1964 women now make up 55% of Saudi Arabia's university students.

In 1996 there were 2,343 adult education centres. In 1997–98 there were seven universities, two Islamic universities and one university of petroleum and minerals. In 1999 there were 120,666 students in higher education institutions with 18,925 teachers. In 1998–99 total expenditure on education came to 9·3% of GNP.

Health. In 1999 there were 1,756 health care centres and clinics, 706 private dispensaries; and, in 2001, 324 hospitals with 46,622 beds. 31,983 doctors, 67,421 nursing and (1999) 37,077 technical staff were employed at these facilities. At Jeddah there is a quarantine centre for pilgrims.

Welfare. The retirement age is 60 (men) or 55 (women), with eligibility based on 120 months of contributions. The minimum monthly old-age pension is SAR1,500, calculated as 2·5% of the average monthly wage during the previous two years multiplied by the number of years of contributions. A 1969 law requires employers with more than 20 employees to pay 100% of wages for the first 30 days of sick leave and 75% of wages for the next 60 days.

Workers' medical benefits include medical, dental and diagnostic treatment, hospitalization, medicines, appliances, transportation and rehabilitation.

CULTURE

Broadcasting. The government-controlled Broadcasting Service of the Kingdom of Saudi Arabia and Saudi Arabian Television are responsible for broadcasting. Radio programmes include two home services, two religious services, services in English and French and an external service. Aramco Oil has a private station. There are TV programmes in Arabic and English; Channel 3 TV is a non-commercial independent. Colour is by SECAM H. In 2000 there were 7·2m. radio sets and in 2001 there were 5·9m. TV sets.

Press. In 1996 there were 13 daily newspapers with a combined circulation of 1,105,000, equivalent to 59 per 1,000 inhabitants. In 1995 there were 168 non-daily newspapers with a combined circulation of 2,150,000 (or 117 per 1,000). The most widely read newspaper is *Asharq Al-Awsat* ('Middle East'), with an average daily circulation of 248,482 in Jan.–June 1998. In 1997 a total of 3,780 book titles were published.

Tourism. There were 6,727,000 foreign tourists in 2001; spending by tourists totalled US$3·42bn.

Calendar. Saudi Arabia follows the Islamic *hegira* (AD 622, when Mohammed left Makkah for Madinah), which is based upon the lunar year of 354 days. The Islamic year 1426 corresponds to 10 Feb. 2005–30 Jan. 2006, and is the current lunar year.

DIPLOMATIC REPRESENTATIVES

Of Saudi Arabia in the United Kingdom (30 Charles St., London, W1J 5DZ)
Ambassador: HRH Prince Turki Al-Faisal.

Of the United Kingdom in Saudi Arabia (PO Box 94351, Riyadh 11693)
Ambassador: Sherard Cowper-Coles, CMG, LVO.

Of Saudi Arabia in the USA (601 New Hampshire Ave., NW, Washington, D.C., 20037)
Ambassador: HRH Prince Bandar Bin Sultan.

Of the USA in Saudi Arabia (PO Box 94309, Riyadh)
Ambassador: James C. Oberwetter.

Of Saudi Arabia to the United Nations
Ambassador: Fawzi Bin Abdul Majeed Shobokshi.

Of Saudi Arabia to the European Union
Ambassador: Nassir Alassaf.

FURTHER READING

Al-Rasheed, Madawi, *A History of Saudi Arabia.* CUP, 2002
Azzam, H., *Saudi Arabia: Economic Trends, Business Environment and Investment Opportunities.* London, 1993
Kostiner, J., *The Making of Saudi Arabia: from Chieftaincy to Monarchical State.* OUP, 1994
Mackey, Sandra, *The Saudis: Inside the Desert Kingdom.* Revised ed. W. W. Norton, New York, 2003
Peterson, J. E., *Historical Dictionary of Saudi Arabia.* Metuchen (NJ), 1994
Wright, J. W. (ed.) *Business and Economic Development in Saudi Arabia: Essays with Saudi Scholars.* London, 1996

National statistical office: Ministry of Finance and National Economy, Department of Statistics, Riyadh.
Website: http://www.saudinf.com/

SENEGAL

République du Sénégal

Capital: Dakar
Population projection, 2010: 11·87m.
GDP per capita, 2002: (PPP$) 1,580
HDI/world rank: 0·437/157

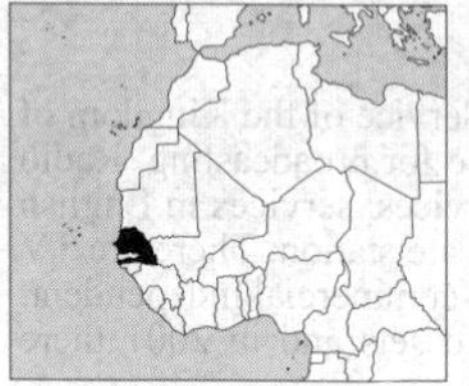

KEY HISTORICAL EVENTS

For much of the 1st millennium AD Senegal was under the influence of the gold-rich Ghana Empire of the Soninke people. In western Senegal the Takrur state was established in the 9th century. Islam was brought in the 11th century by the Zenega Berbers of southern Mauritania, who gave their name to the region, and the Moroccan Almoravids embarked on a proselytizing campaign. The power of the Malinke (Madingo) in present-day Mali expanded in the 13th and 14th centuries, especially under Mansa Musa, who subjugated Takrur and the Tukulor in Senegal. The west was dominated by the Jolof empire, which fragmented into four kingdoms in the 16th century.

Portuguese trading colonies were established on Gorée Island and at Rufisque in around 1444, encouraging the growth of the slave trade. The Dutch took control of Senegalese trade in the 17th century, only to be evicted in 1677 by the French, based at Saint-Louis at the mouth of the Sénégal River. Inland, the Tukolor created a Muslim theocracy in Fouta Toro, usurping the Denianké Dynasty in 1776. Tukolor power grew in the 1850s under al-Hajj Umar Tal, whose *jihad* was contained by treaty with the French in 1857. Britain accepted French hegemony in the region in 1814 after half a century of colonial rivalry, while retaining the Gambia River. Railway construction in 1879 cemented French control over western Senegal and Dakar became the capital of French West Africa in 1904. Casamance and eastern Senegal were conquered in the 1890s.

Senegalese service in the French army in the First World War secured representation in Paris and French citizenship for Africans in certain communes. The colonial administration followed a moderate liberalization programme, including the right to form political parties and trade unions. However, the decline in the groundnut trade in the 1930s increased poverty in Senegal. The expansion of the vote after the Second World War gave support to the Democratic Bloc (BDS), which joined the Socialist Party to become the Progressive Union (UPS), dominating the 1959 elections in the newly-autonomous Senegal. Membership of the French Community lasted until independence on 20 June 1960 as part of the Federation of Mali with French Soudan (Mali); the Federation was dissolved on 20 Aug. 1960.

Léopold Sédar Senghor, the BDS founder and leader of the UPS, was elected president on 5 Sept. 1960. Relations with his prime minister, Mamadou Dia, deteriorated and Senghor had him arrested in Dec. 1962 after an attempted coup. Presidential power was augmented by referendum in 1963, allowing Senghor to ban all other parties in 1966. Senghor appointed Abdou Diouf prime minister in 1973 and began relaxing political restrictions. Abdoulaye Wade founded the Democratic Party (PDS) and a Marxist-Leninist party was formed. Recession and political agitation forced Senghor's resignation in Dec. 1980; Diouf succeeded him and was confirmed by elections in 1983, 1988 and 1993.

Diouf pursued a vigorous foreign policy via the Organization of African Unity and the Economic Community of West African States. He reinstated the Gambian president, Sir Dawda Jawara, in 1981, creating the Senegambian confederation, which lasted until 1989. Unrest in the southern Casamance region escalated into secessionist civil war in the early 1990s. A skirmish on the Mauritanian border in 1989 resulted in the death of Senegalese and Mauritanians expatriates and the closing of the border, a dispute not resolved until 1994. The deterioration of the economy and the Casamance crisis led to electoral defeat in 2000. He conceded peacefully, handing power to his long-term rival, PDS leader Abdoulaye Wade. The coalition with Moustapha Niasse, his prime minister and key electoral ally, broke down in March 2001.

TERRITORY AND POPULATION

Senegal is bounded by Mauritania to the north and northeast, Mali to the east, Guinea and Guinea-Bissau to the south and the Atlantic to the west with The Gambia forming an enclave along that shore. Area, 196,722 sq. km. Population (2002 census, provisional), 9,956,202; estimate, 2003: 10·13m. Population density, 51·5 per sq. km. In 2001 the population was 48·1% urban.

The UN gives a projected population for 2010 of 11·87m.

The areas, populations and capitals of the eleven regions:

Region	*Area (in sq. km)*	*2002 estimate (in 1,000)*	*Capital*
Dakar	550	2,267	Dakar
Diourbel	4,359	1,050	Diourbel
Fatick	7,935	613	Fatick
Kaolack	16,010	1,066	Kaolack
Kolda	21,011	836	Kolda
Louga	29,188	678	Louga
Matam	25,083	423	Matam
Saint-Louis	19,044	689	Saint-Louis
Tambacounda	59,602	606	Tambacounda
Thiès	6,601	1,290	Thiès
Ziguinchor	7,339	438	Ziguinchor

Dakar, the capital, had a provisional census population in 2002 of 1,983,093. Other large cities (with 2002 provisional census population) are: Thiès (237,849), Rufisque (179,797), Kaolack (172,305), Ziguinchor (156,388), Saint-Louis (154,555) and Mbour (153,503).

Ethnic groups are the Wolof (36% of the population), Fulani (16%), Serer (16%), Diola (9%), Tukulor (9%), Bambara (6%), Malinké (6%) and Sarakole (2%).

The official language is French; Wolof is widely spoken.

SOCIAL STATISTICS

Births, 1995, 349,000; deaths, 126,000. Birth rate (1995) per 1,000 population, 42; death rate (1997), 18. Annual population growth rate, 1992–02, 2·4%; infant mortality (2001), 79 per 1,000 live births. Life expectancy in 2001 was 50·2 years for men and 54·5 for women. Fertility rate, 2001, 5·2 births per woman.

CLIMATE

A tropical climate with wet and dry seasons. The rains fall almost exclusively in the hot season, from June to Oct., with high humidity. Dakar, Jan. 72°F (22·2°C), July 82°F (27·8°C). Annual rainfall 22" (541 mm).

CONSTITUTION AND GOVERNMENT

A new constitution was approved by a referendum held on 7 Jan. 2001. The head of state is the *President*, elected by universal suffrage for not more than two five-year terms (previously two seven-year terms). The *President* has the power to dissolve the National Assembly, without the agreement, as had been the case, of a two-thirds majority. The new constitution also abolished the upper house (the Senate), confirmed the status of the prime minister and for the first time gave women the right to own land. For the unicameral, 120-member *National Assembly*, 65 members are elected by simple majority vote in single or multi-member constituencies with 55 elected by a system of party-list proportional representation.

National Anthem. 'Pincez tous vos koras, frappez les balafos' ('All pluck the koras, strike the balafos'); words by Léopold Sédar Senghor, tune by Herbert Pepper.

RECENT ELECTIONS

Presidential elections took place on 27 Feb. and 19 March 2000. In the first round of voting, incumbent Abdou Diouf won 41·3% of the vote, Abdoulaye Wade of the Senegalese Democratic Party received 31·0%, Moustapha Niasse 16·8% and Djibo Ka 7·1%. In the run-off between Diouf and Wade, Wade won, in his fifth attempt to become President, with 58·5% of the vote, ending 40 years of uninterrupted rule by the Socialist Party. Wade is the last president to be elected to a seven-year term. 'Some commentators seized upon the peaceful transition as evidence of Africa's maturing democratic tradition. But while Senegal's success story is worth celebrating it remains an exception'. (*Time*, 10 July 2000).

Parliamentary elections were held on 27 April 2001. Turn-out was 67·4%. Coalition 'Sopi', a coalition led by President Abdoulaye Wade's Senegalese Democratic Party, took 89 seats with 49·6% of votes cast, the Alliance of Progressive Forces 11 with 16·1%, the Socialists 10 with 17·4% and the Union for Democratic Renewal 3 with 3·7%. Six other parties claimed two seats or fewer.

CURRENT ADMINISTRATION

President: Abdoulaye Wade; b. 1926 (PDS; sworn in 1 April 2000).

In March 2005 the government was composed as follows:

Prime Minister: Macky Sall; b. 1961 (PDS; sworn in 21 April 2004).

Minister of State, Minister for Local Communities and Decentralization: Aminata Tall. *Minister of State, Minister for Industry and Handicrafts:* Landing Savané. *Minister of State, Minister for Foreign Affairs:* Cheikh Tidiane Gadio. *Minister of State, Minister of Justice:* Serigne Diop. *Minister of State, Minister for Maritime Economy:* Djibo Leïty Kâ. *Minister of State, Minister for Sports:* Youssoupha Ndiaye. *Minister of State, Agriculture and Water Supply:* Habib Sy.

Minister for Armed Forces: Bécaye Diop. *Economy and Finance:* Abdoulaye Diop. *Interior:* Ousmane Ngom. *Education:* Moustapha Sourang. *Tourism and Civil Aviation:* Ousmane Masseck Ndiaye. *Energy and Mines:* Madické Niang. *Civil Service, Labour and Employment:* Yéro Deh. *Infrastructure, Equipment and Transport:* Mamadou Seck. *Health:* Issa Mbaye Samb. *Information and Government Spokesperson:* Bacar Dia. *Urban and Rural Development:* Seydou Sy Sall. *Family Affairs, Social Development and National Solidarity:* Aïda Mbodj. *Post and Telecommunications, and Promotion of Information Technology:* Joseph Ndong. *Prevention, Public Health and Sanitation:* Lamine Bâ. *Environment and Protection of Nature:* Modou Fada Diagne. *Culture and Historical Heritage:* Safiétou Ndiaye Diop. *NEPAD, African Economic Integration and Good Governance:* Aziz Sow. *Historical Buildings, Housing and Construction:* Salif Ba. *Commerce:* Mamadou Diop. *Small- and Medium-Sized Enterprises, Female Enterprise and Micro-finance:* Maïmouna Sourang Ndir. *Planning and Sustainable Development:* Mamadou Sidibé. *Youth Affairs:* Aliou Sow. *Senegalese Abroad:* Abdou Malal Diop. *Scientific Research:* Christian Sina Diatta. *Decentralization and Regional Planning:* Soukeyna Ndiaye Ba. *Livestock:* Oumy Khairy Gueye Seck. *Relations with National and Regional Governments, and the African Union:* Bineta Samb Ba.

Government Website (French only): http://www.gouv.sn

DEFENCE

There is selective conscription for two years. Defence expenditure totalled US$86m. in 2003 (US$9 per capita), representing 1·4% of GDP.

Army. There are four military zones. The Army had a strength of 8,000 (3,500 conscripts) in 2002. There is also a paramilitary force of gendarmerie and customs of about 5,800.

Navy. Personnel (2002) totalled 600, and bases are at Dakar and Casamance.

Air Force. The Air Force, formed with French assistance, has eight combat aircraft but serviceability is low. Personnel (2002) 800.

INTERNATIONAL RELATIONS

Senegal is a member of the UN, WTO, the African Union, African Development Bank, ECOWAS, OIC, Islamic Development Bank, IOM, International Organization of the Francophonie and is an ACP member state of the ACP-EU relationship.

A short section of the boundary with The Gambia is indefinite.

ECONOMY

Agriculture accounted for 15·0% of GDP in 2002, industry 21·6% and services 63·4%.

Currency. Senegal is a member of the Union Economique et Monétaire Ouest-Africaine (UEMOA). The unit of currency is the *franc CFA* (XOF) with a parity of 655·957 francs CFA to one euro. In May 2002 total money supply was 567,374m. francs CFA. and foreign exchange reserves totalled US$507m. In June 2000 gold reserves were 29,000 troy oz. Inflation was 2·2% in 2002.

Budget. In 2001 the government's total revenue was 602·1bn. francs CFA and total expenditure was 737·6bn. francs CFA.

Performance. Real GDP growth was 1·1% in 2002, rising to 6·5% in 2003. It was estimated to have been about 6% in 2004. Senegal's total GDP in 2003 was US$6·5bn.

Banking and Finance. The Banque Centrale des États de l'Afrique de l'Ouest is the bank of issue of the franc CFA for all the countries of the West African Economic and Monetary Union (Benin, Burkina Faso, Côte d'Ivoire, Mali, Niger, Senegal and Togo) but has had its headquarters in Dakar, the Senegalese capital, since 1973. Its *Governor* is Charles Konan Banny. There are eight commercial banks, the largest including Banque Internationale pour le Commerce et l'Industrie and Banque de l'Habitat (25% state-owned). There are also four development banks and an Islamic bank.

Senegal is affiliated to the regional BRVM stock exchange (serving the member states of the West African Economic and Monetary Union), based in Abidjan, Côte d'Ivoire.

ENERGY AND NATURAL RESOURCES

Environment. Senegal's carbon dioxide emissions from the consumption and flaring of fossil fuels in 2002 were the equivalent of 0·5 tonnes per capita.

Electricity. In 2000 installed capacity was 0·2m. kW. Production in 2000 was 1·47bn. kWh and consumption per capita 155 kWh.

Minerals. In 2002, 2m. tonnes of calcium phosphate were produced. Limestone production in 2002 totalled 1,461,000 tonnes. In 2002 the Sabodala mine in eastern Senegal had proven gold ore reserves of 2·6m. tonnes; annual gold production is approximately 600 kg. Exploration of further gold reserves increased greatly throughout the 1990s. While only three research permits were issued in 1994 this figure had risen to 35 by 1998, with South African, British, American, Canadian and Australian companies all active in the country.

Agriculture. Because of erratic rainfall 25% of agricultural land needs irrigation. Most land is owned under customary rights and holdings tend to be small. In 2001, 2·46m. ha were used as arable land and 40,000 ha for permanent crops. 71,000 ha were irrigated in 2001. There were 700 tractors in 2001 and 155 harvester-threshers. Production, 2000 (in 1,000 tonnes): sugarcane, 889; groundnuts, 828; millet, 506; watermelons, 260; rice, 240; sorghum, 147; mangoes, 75; maize, 66; onions, 65.

Livestock (2000): 4·30m. sheep, 3·59m. goats, 2·96m. cattle, 510,000 horses, 384,000 asses, 330,000 pigs. Animal products (2000, in 1,000 tonnes): meat, 162; milk, 135.

Forestry. Forests covered 6·21m. ha in 2000 (32·2% of the land area). Roundwood production in 2001 amounted to 5·94m. cu. metres.

Fisheries. The fishing fleet comprises 167 vessels totalling 40,600 GRT. In 2001 the total catch was 405,409 tonnes (385,409 tonnes from sea fishing).

INDUSTRY

Predominantly agricultural and fish processing, phosphate mining, petroleum refining and construction materials.

Labour. The workforce (10 years and over) in 1996 was 2,509,000, of whom 77% were engaged in subsistence farming; 60% of the workforce is in the public sector.

Trade Unions. There are two major unions, the *Union Nationale des Travailleurs Sénégalais* (government-controlled) and the *Conféderation Nationale des Travailleurs Sénégalais* (independent) which broke away from the former in 1969 and in 1994 comprised 75% of salaried workers.

INTERNATIONAL TRADE

Foreign debt was US$3,918m. in 2002.

Imports and Exports. In 2001 imports totalled US$1,730m. and exports US$785m. Chief exports: fish, groundnuts, petroleum products, phosphates and cotton. Chief imports: food and beverages, capital goods. Main import suppliers, 1999: France, 30·2%; Nigeria, 7·1%; Italy, 5·9%; Thailand, 5·2%; Germany, 4·3%; USA, 4·1%; Spain, 4·0%. Main export markets, 1999: India, 27·9%; France, 14·8%; Mali, 9·1%; Mauritania, 5·2%; Benin, 4·2%; Côte d'Ivoire, 4·1%; Gambia, 4·0%.

COMMUNICATIONS

Roads. The length of roads in 1999 was estimated to be 14,576 km, of which 4,270 km were paved. There were 98,260 passenger cars (11 per 1,000 inhabitants), 25,276 trucks and vans and 10,477 buses and coaches in 1999. There were 646 deaths as a result of road accidents in 1999.

Rail. There are four railway lines: Dakar-Kidira (continuing in Mali), Thiès-Saint-Louis (193 km), Diourbel-Touba (46 km) and Guinguinéo-Kaolack (22 km). Total length (2000), 906 km (metre gauge). In 2000 railways carried 4·3m. passengers and 1·7m. tonnes of freight, much of which was for export.

Civil Aviation. The international airport is at Dakar/Yoff (Léopold Sédar Senghor), which handled 1,074,000 passengers (1,042,000 on international flights) and 27,800 tonnes of freight in 2000. Air Sénégal is 50% state-owned; in 2003 it flew to Abidjan, Bamako, Banjul, Bissau, Casablanca, Conakry, Cotonou, Las Palmas, Lomé, Lyon, Marseille, Niamey, Nouakchott, Ouagadougou, Paris and Praia in addition to operating on domestic routes. Trans African Airlines flew to Abidjan, Bamako, Brazzaville, Cotonou, Lomé and Pointe-Noire. In 1999 scheduled airline traffic of Senegal-based carriers flew 3·3m. km, carrying 103,000 passengers (84,000 on international flights).

Shipping. In 2002 the merchant marine totalled 47,000 GRT. 5·5m. tonnes of freight were handled in the port of Dakar in 1995. There is a river service on the Senegal from Saint-Louis to Podor (363 km) open throughout the year, and to Kayes (924 km) open from July to Oct. The Senegal River is closed to foreign flags. The Saloum River is navigable as far as Kaolack, the Casamance River as far as Ziguinchor.

Telecommunications. In 2002 telephone subscribers numbered 778,000 (79·4 for every 1,000 persons) and there were 200,000 PCs in use (20·4 per 1,000 persons). Senegal had 553,400 mobile phone subscribers in 2002. Internet users numbered 105,000 in 2002.

Postal Services. There were 134 post offices in 1998.

SOCIAL INSTITUTIONS

Justice. There are *juges de paix* in each *département* and a court of first instance in each region. Assize courts are situated in Dakar, Kaolack, Saint-Louis and Ziguinchor, while the Court of Appeal resides in Dakar. The death penalty, last used in 1967, was abolished in Dec. 2004.

The population in penal institutions in Sept. 2002 was 5,360 (54 per 100,000 of national population).

Religion. The population was 93% Sunni Muslim in 2001, the remainder being Christian (mainly Roman Catholic) or animist. In Sept. 2003 the Roman Catholic church had one cardinal.

Education. The adult literacy rate in 2001 was 38·3% (48·1% among males and 28·7% among females). In 2003–04 there were 1,382,749 pupils and 32,010 teachers in 6,060 primary schools; 355,732 pupils in secondary schools; and (1998–99), 29,303 students in tertiary education. There are four universities (Cheikh Anta Diop, Gaston Berger, Dakar Bourguiba and Sahel). In 1995–96 there were a further 19 institutions of higher education.

In 2000–01 total expenditure on education came to 3·2% of GNP.

Health. In 1996 there were 17 government hospitals, 646 maternity homes, 53 health centres and 768 clinics. There were 649 doctors (266 in government service), 93 dentists, 588 midwives (547 government) and 1,876 other medical personnel (1,630 government). There were 322 pharmacists (16 in government service). Senegal has been one of the most successful countries in Africa in the prevention of AIDS. Levels of infection have remained low, with the anti-AIDS programme having started as far back as 1986. The infection rate has been kept below 2%.

CULTURE

World Heritage Sites. Gorée Island, off the coast of Senegal, was added to the UNESCO World Heritage List in 1978. It was formerly the largest slave trading centre on the African coast. The Djoudj Sanctuary in the Senegal River delta (added in 1981), protects 1·5m. birds. Niokolo-Koba National Park, along the banks of the Gambia River (added in 1981), is home to the Derby eland (largest of the antelopes). The Island of Saint-Louis joined the UNESCO list in 2000, as a reminder of its status as capital between 1872 to 1957.

Broadcasting. The government-owned *Office de Radio-Télévision du Sénégal* broadcasts a national and an international radio service from ten main transmitters. There are also regional services. There is also a TV service (colour by SECAM V). In 2000 there were 1·32m. radio receivers (141 per 1,000 inhabitants) and 376,000 TV receivers (40 per 1,000 inhabitants). As recently as 1980 there had been just 8,000 TV receivers, or only 1·4 per 1,000. The percentage rise in the proportion of the population having TV receivers, at more than 2,700%, was the highest anywhere in the world over the same period.

Press. In 1996 there was one daily newspaper with a circulation of 45,000, equivalent to 5·3 per 1,000 inhabitants.

Tourism. 369,000 foreign tourists visited in 1999. Revenue in 1999 amounted to US$166m.

DIPLOMATIC REPRESENTATIVES

Of Senegal in the United Kingdom (39 Marloes Rd, London, W8 6LA)
Ambassador: Mamadou Niang.

Of the United Kingdom in Senegal (20 Rue du Docteur Guillet, Dakar)
Ambassador: Peter Newall.

Of Senegal in the USA (2112 Wyoming Ave., NW, Washington, D.C., 20008)
Ambassador: Amadou Lamine Ba.

Of the USA in Senegal (Ave. Jean XXIII, Dakar)
Ambassador: Richard Roth.

Of Senegal to the United Nations
Ambassador: Paul Badji.

Of Senegal to the European Union
Ambassador: Saliou Cisse.

FURTHER READING

Centre Français du Commerce Extérieur. *Sénégal: un Marché.* Paris, 1993

Adams, A. and So, J., *A Claim in Senegal, 1720–1994.* Paris, 1996
Dilley, Roy M. and Eades, Jerry S., *Senegal.* [Bibliography] ABC-Clio, Oxford and Santa Barbara (CA), 1994
Phillips, L. C., *Historical Dictionary of Senegal.* 2nd ed, revised by A. F. Clark. Metuchen (NJ), 1995

National statistical office: Direction de la Prévision et de la Statistique, BP 116, Dakar.
Website (French only): http://www.ansd.org

SERBIA AND MONTENEGRO

Capital: Belgrade
Population projection, 2010: 10·50m.
GDP per capita: not available
GNI per capita: $930

Državna Zajednica Srbija i Crna Gora
(State Community of Serbia and Montenegro)

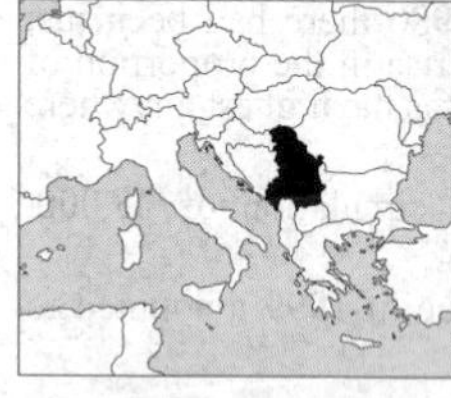

KEY HISTORICAL EVENTS

The assassination of Archduke Franz Ferdinand of Austria in Sarajevo on 28 June 1914 precipitated the First World War. In the winter of 1915–16 the Serbian army was forced to retreat to Corfu, where the government aimed at a centralized, Serb-run state. But exiles from Croatia and Slovenia wanted a South Slav federation. This was accepted by the victorious Allies as the basis for the new state. The Croats were forced by the pressure of events to join Serbia and Montenegro on 1 Dec. 1918. From 1918–29 the country was known as the Kingdom of the Serbs, Croats and Slovenes.

A constitution of 1921 established an assembly but the trappings of parliamentarianism could not bridge the gulf between Serbs and Croats. The Croat peasant leader Radić was assassinated in 1928; his successor, Vlatko Maček, set up a separatist assembly in Zagreb. On 6 Jan. 1929 the king suspended the constitution and established a royal dictatorship, redrawing provincial boundaries without regard for ethnicity. In Oct. 1934 he was murdered by a Croat extremist while on an official visit to France.

During the regency of Prince Paul, the government pursued a pro-fascist line. On 25 March 1941 Paul was induced to adhere to the Axis Tripartite Pact. On 27 March he was overthrown by military officers in favour of the boy king Peter. Germany invaded on 6 April. Within ten days Yugoslavia surrendered; king and government fled to London. Resistance was led by a royalist group and the communist-dominated partisans of Josip Broz, nicknamed Tito. Having succeeded in liberating Yugoslavia, Tito instituted a Soviet-type constitution. He was too independent for Stalin, who sought to topple him. But Tito made a *rapprochement* with the west and it was the Soviet Union under Khrushchev which had to extend the olive branch in 1956. Yugoslavia evolved its 'own road to socialism'. Collectivization of agriculture was abandoned; and Yugoslavia became a champion of international 'non-alignment'. A collective presidency came into being with the death of Tito in 1980.

Dissensions in Kosovo between Albanians and Serbs, and in parts of Croatia between Serbs and Croats, reached crisis point after 1988. On 25 June 1991 Croatia and Slovenia declared independence. Fighting began in Croatia between Croatian forces and Serb irregulars from Serb-majority areas of Croatia. On 25 Sept. the UN Security Council imposed a mandatory arms embargo on Yugoslavia. Slovenia and Croatia declared their independence from the Yugoslav federation on 8 Oct, after a three-month moratorium agreed at EU peace talks on 30 June had expired. After 13 ceasefires had failed, a fourteenth was signed on 23 Nov. under UN auspices. Fighting, however, continued. On 15 Jan. 1992 the EU recognized Croatia and Slovenia as independent states. Bosnia-Herzegovina was recognized on 7 April 1992 and the former Yugoslav Republic of Macedonia on 8 April 1993. A UN delegation began monitoring the ceasefire on 17 Jan. and the UN Security Council on 21 Feb. voted to send a 14,000-strong peace-keeping force to Croatia and Yugoslavia. On 27 April 1992 Serbia and Montenegro created a new federal republic of Yugoslavia. On 30 May, responding to further Serbian military activities in Bosnia and Croatia, the UN Security Council voted to impose sanctions. In mid-1992 NATO committed air, sea and eventually land forces to enforce sanctions and protect humanitarian relief operations in Bosnia. Following the Bosnian-Croatian-Yugoslav (Dayton) agreement all UN sanctions were lifted in Nov. 1995.

In 1998 unrest in Kosovo, with its largely Albanian population, led to a bid for outright independence. Violence flared resulting in what a US official described as 'horrendous human rights violations', including massive shelling of civilians and destruction of villages. A US-mediated agreement, accepted in principle by President Slobodan Milošević, allowed negotiations to proceed and lifted the immediate threat of NATO air strikes. The sticking point on the Serbian side was the international insistence on having 28,000 NATO-led peacemakers in Kosovo to keep apart the warring factions. Meanwhile, the scale of Serbian repression in Kosovo persuaded the NATO allies to take direct action. On the night of 24 March 1999 NATO aircraft began bombing Yugoslav military targets. Further Serbian provocation in Kosovo caused hundreds of thousands of ethnic Albanians to seek refuge in neighbouring countries. On 9 June after 78 days of air attacks NATO and Yugoslavia signed an accord on the Serb withdrawal from Kosovo, and on 11 June NATO's peacekeeping force, KFOR, entered Kosovo.

The general election held on 24 Sept. 2000 resulted in a victory for the opposition democratic leader Vojislav Koštunica, but President Milošević demanded a second round of voting. A strike by miners at the Kolubara coal mine on 29 Sept. led to a relatively peaceful revolution centred on Belgrade on 5 Oct. On 6 Oct. Slobodan Milošević accepted defeat. He was arrested on 1 April 2001 and on 28 June he was handed over to the United Nations War Crimes Tribunal in The Hague.

On 14 March 2002 Serbia and Montenegro agreed to remain part of a single entity called Serbia and Montenegro, thus relegating the name Yugoslavia to history. The agreement was ratified in principle by the federal parliament and the republican parliaments of Serbia and Montenegro on 9 April 2002. The new union came into force on 4 Feb. 2003. Most powers in this loose confederation are divided between the two republics. After 4 Feb. 2006 Serbia and Montenegro will have the right to vote for independence. The final status of Kosovo, which is legally part of Serbia, remains unresolved.

For the early history of Serbia and Montenegro see SERBIA: Key Historical Events on page 1427 and MONTENEGRO: Key Historical Events on page 1425.

TERRITORY AND POPULATION

Serbia and Montenegro is bounded in the north by Hungary, northeast by Romania, east by Bulgaria, south by Macedonia and Albania, and west by the Adriatic Sea, Bosnia-Herzegovina and Croatia. Area, 102,173 sq. km. Population (mid-2001), 10,651,690 (5,370,754 females). Population density (2001), 104·2 per sq. km. In 2001 an estimated 51·6% of the population lived in urban areas.

The UN gives a projected population for 2010 of 10·50m.

In Feb. 2003 the new confederation of Serbia and Montenegro came into being: this comprised the two republics of Montenegro and Serbia, and the two provinces of Kosovo and Metohija, and Vojvodina within Serbia. The confederal capital is Belgrade (Beograd); some capital functions, including the Supreme Court, will be sited in Podgorica. Populations (2001 estimates) of principal towns:

Belgrade	1,581,129	Subotica	142,166
Novi Sad	266,176	Zrenjanin	130,070
Niš	248,561	Pančevo	122,435
Kragujevac	180,192	Smederevo	116,592
Podgorica	168,069	Čačak	114,794

The 1991 census was not carried out in Kosovo and Metohija. 1991 estimated population: Priština, 155,499; Prizren, 92,303; Peć, 68,163; Kosovska Mitrovica, 64,323.

Ethnic groups at the 1991 census: Serbs, 6,504,048; Albanians, 1,714,768; Montenegrins, 519,766; Hungarians, 344,147; Muslims, 336,025; Gypsies, 143,519; Croats, 111,650; Slovaks, 66,863; Macedonians, 47,118; Romanians, 42,364; Bulgarians, 26,922; Valachians, 17,810; Turks, 11,263. At the 1991 census, 361,452 nationals worked abroad.

Refugees and internally displaced persons are estimated at about 600,000.

The official language is Serbian, the eastern variant (Croatian is the western) of Serbo-Croat. Serbian is written in the Cyrillic alphabet.

SOCIAL STATISTICS

2001 (including Kosovo and Metohija): live births, 130,194; deaths, 113,063; marriages, 57,165; divorces, 8,723. 2001 rates (per 1,000 population): birth, 12·2; death, 10·6; marriage, 5·4; infant mortality, 13·1 (per 1,000 live births). In 2001 the most popular age for marrying was 24 for males and 20 for females. Expectation of life in 2001: males, 70·1 years; females, 75·2. Annual population growth rate, 1992–02, 0·2%. Fertility rate, 2001, 1·71 births per woman.

CLIMATE

Most parts have a central European type of climate, with cold winters and hot summers. 2000, Belgrade, Jan. –1·0°C, July 23·5°C. Annual rainfall 367·7 mm. Podgorica, Jan. 2·8°C, July 26·5°C. Annual rainfall 1,499 mm.

CONSTITUTION AND GOVERNMENT

The head of state is the *President*, elected by the members of the federal parliament for a non-renewable four-year term.

The union parliament, the *Assembly of Serbia and Montenegro*, has 126 members, 91 elected from the assembly of Serbia and 35 elected from the assembly of Montenegro for a term of four years. Its assent is necessary to all legislation. The Assembly elects the President and the five-member Cabinet, which has responsibility for foreign affairs, defence, human and minority rights, international economic relations and internal economic affairs.

National Anthem. 'Hej, Slaveni, jošte živi reč naših dedova' ('O Slavs, our ancestors' words will live'), with words by S. Tomašik and tune anonymous, is the provisional anthem of Serbia and Montenegro. A new anthem (and other national symbols including a new flag) may be introduced during 2005.

RECENT ELECTIONS

Svetozar Marović, a Montenegrin and deputy leader of the Democratic Party of Socialists, was elected president by the members of the Union Assembly on 7 March 2003, receiving 65 votes, with 47 against.

On 25 Feb. 2003 the assemblies of Serbia and Montenegro elected deputies from their own number to serve concurrently as members of the Union Assembly. In these elections the Democratic Opposition of Serbia (DOS) gained 37 seats, the Democratic List for European Montenegro (DLECG) (including the Democratic Party of Socialists/DPS) 19, the Democratic Party of Serbia (DSS) 17, (Montenegrin) Together for Changes (ZP) 14, the Serb Socialist Party (SPS) 12, the Serb Radical Party (SRS) 8, the Social Democratic Party (SDP) 5, the Party of Serb Unity (SSJ) 5, the Christian Democratic Party of Serbia (DHSS) 2, the (Serb) Democratic Alternative (DA) 2, others 5.

CURRENT ADMINISTRATION

In March 2005 the government comprised the following:

Union President: Svetozar Marović; b. 1955 (Democratic Party of Socialists/DPS; sworn in 7 March 2003).

Minister for Foreign Affairs: Vuk Drašković. *Defence:* Prvoslav Davinić. *Human and Minority Rights:* Rasim Ljajić. *International Economic Relations:* Prof. Predrag Ivanović. *Internal Economic Affairs:* Amir Nurković.

Government Website: http://www.gov.yu

DEFENCE

Military service is for nine months. Military expenditure totalled US$642m. in 2003 (US$79 per capita), representing 3·0% of GDP. In 1985 expenditure had been US$2,904m.

Army. Personnel (2002) were about 60,000 (37,000 conscripts). In addition there are Ministry of Interior troops numbering about 40,000.

Navy. The Navy comprises four diesel submarines and three frigates. A Marine force of 900 is divided into two 'brigades'.

Personnel in 2002 totalled 3,500 including Marines. The force is based at Kotor.

Air Force. Personnel (2002) 11,000 (3,000 conscripts), with 103 combat aircraft and 442 armed helicopters.

INTERNATIONAL RELATIONS

The former Yugoslavia (SFRY) was a member of the UN and its self-proclaimed successor state (Federal Republic of Yugoslavia) was excluded during the Milošević era from the General Assembly and related bodies such as the IMF and World Bank. However, after Vojislav Koštunica became president in Oct. 2000 Yugoslavia was admitted both to the UN and the IMF. Serbia and Montenegro has succeeded the former Yugoslavia in membership of the UN. It is also a member of the Council of Europe, Danube Commission, BIS and IOM.

ECONOMY

Overview. Once the strongest economy in the Balkans, Serbia and Montenegro is now suffering for the years of state socialism, a devastating war and associated economic sanctions. The USA, EU and World Bank have pledged US$1·28bn. to rebuild the economy following the handing over of Slobodan Milošević to the international war crimes tribunal. However, much of the money is going to international creditors, who are owed US$12·2bn., more than the entire GDP for 2001. A reform programme is in progress to create a market economy but, despite a change of regime, foreign investors have proved reluctant to enter the market. It is estimated that the sale of the most valuable state-owned assets—such as the arms and car manufacturer Zastava—will raise US$150m. to pay off the companies' foreign debts. A quarter of the population are jobless and about 70% live below or at the poverty line. The average household income is US$150 a month. There are 600,000 refugees from the Balkan wars in the country.

Currency. The unit of currency of Serbia is the *dinar* (YUD) of 100 *paras*. On 1 Jan. 2001 Yugoslavia adopted a managed float regime. The National Bank of Yugoslavia began setting the exchange rate of the dinar daily in the foreign exchange market on the previous day. Montenegro adopted the euro as its sole legal currency on 1 Jan. 2002, having made the Deutsche Mark legal tender alongside the dinar on 2 Nov. 1999. In the new Serbia and Montenegro there is a National Bank of Serbia and a Central Bank of Montenegro. In Kosovo both the dinar and the euro are legal tender. Inflation declined from 89·2% in 2001 to 16·5% in 2002, and further to 9·4% in 2003. In Dec. 2000 total foreign exchange reserves were US$890m. and in Dec. 2001 foreign exchange reserves reached US$1,808m. Total money supply was 101·7bn. dinars in Nov. 2001.

Budget. The federal budget for 2001 was set at US$4·3bn.

Performance. In 2001 there was real GDP growth of 5·5% and in 2002 growth of 4·0%, but economic activity is recovering from a very low base. Total GDP in 2003 was US$19·1bn.

Banking and Finance. The banking system of Serbia and Montenegro consists of the central bank, commercial banks and other financial organizations, such as the Post Office Savings Bank, savings and credit organizations and savings and loan associations. The National Bank is the bank of issue responsible for the monetary policy, stability of the currency of Serbia, the dinar, control of the money supply and prescribing the method of maintaining internal and external liquidity. The dinar became fully convertible in May 2002. The present *Governor* of the National Bank of Serbia is Radovan Jelašić. The National Bank of Montenegro is also recognized under the constitution.

There is a stock exchange in Belgrade.

ENERGY AND NATURAL RESOURCES

Environment. Serbia and Montenegro's carbon dioxide emissions from the consumption and flaring of fossil fuels were the equivalent of 4·2 tonnes per capita in 2002.

Electricity. Installed capacity in 2000 was 11·8m. kW. Output in 2000 (without Kosovo and Metohija), was 34,360m. kWh, of which 22,330m. kWh were thermal and 12,030m. kWh hydro-electric. Consumption per capita was 1,942 kWh in 2000 (without Kosovo and Metohija).

Oil and Gas. Crude oil production (2001, without Kosovo and Metohija), 805,000 tonnes; natural gas, 160m. cu. metres.

Minerals. Lignite production (2000, without Kosovo and Metohija), 33,638,000 tonnes; copper ore, 12,896,000 tonnes; bauxite (2001), 610,000 tonnes.

Agriculture. In 2001 (without Kosovo and Metohija) there were 5,629,000 ha of agricultural land, of which 3,402,000 ha were arable (2,128,000 ha cereals; 323,000 ha industrial crops), 717,000 ha meadow and 1,147,000 ha pasture. 4,403,000 ha were in private farms and 1,226,000 ha in agricultural organizations. In 2001 there were 326,000 ha of permanent crops. The economically active agricultural population was 1,061,488 in 1991.

Crop production, 2001 (without Kosovo and Metohija, in 1,000 tonnes): maize, 5,921; wheat, 2,534; sugarbeets, 1,806; potatoes, 1,097; grapes, 416; plums, 338; soybeans, 207.

Livestock, 2001 (without Kosovo and Metohija, in 1,000): cattle, 1,366; pigs, 3,634; sheep, 1,783; horses, 41; poultry, 20,081.

Livestock products, 2001 (without Kosovo and Metohija): meat, 474,000 tonnes; milk, 1,789,000 litres; eggs, 1,419m. In 2001, 130,327,000 litres of wine were produced.

Forestry. The forest area is 2,858,000 ha, of which 1,341,000 ha are in private hands. Timber production in 2001 (without Kosovo and Metohija) was 2·62m. cu. metres.

Fisheries. In 2001 total catch was 1,088 tonnes (672 tonnes from inland waters).

INDUSTRY

In Dec. 2000 there were 211,195 enterprises and institutions, including 122,789 private enterprises, 439 public enterprises, 166 co-operatives and 1,983 social enterprises. In 2000 industrial production was only 39% of the 1989 total.

Industrial output (in 1,000 tonnes) in 2001 (without data for Kosovo and Metohija): cement, 2,418; crude steel, 598; pig iron, 461; residual fuel oil (2000), 461; artificial fertilizers, 368; distillate fuel oil (2000), 253; sugar, 209; petrol (2000), 158; plastics, 157; sulphuric acid, 68; refrigerators, 19,967 units; passenger cars, 7,197 units; TV sets, 5,256 units; tractors, 1,757 units; lorries, 590 units.

Labour. In 2001 there were 2,242,788 workers in the social sector, including 744,016 in industry, 230,231 in trade, 141,844 in transport and communications, 128,899 in education and culture; and, in 2000, 92,000 in communities and organizations, 90,000 in commercial services, 85,000 in catering and tourism and 79,000 in agriculture. In Oct. 2001 in the private sector there were 360,772 self-employed and employed people. Average monthly wage in 2001 (without Kosovo and Metohija) was 5,458 dinars. Unemployment in 2001 was officially 30%.

INTERNATIONAL TRADE

According to the law on foreign investments that was in force in 2000, foreign investors were allowed to make investments in all activities except those in the field of production and turnover of armaments, public information and communications systems, and restricted zones, where they could own up to 49% of capital. In 2000 there were 373 contracts on foreign investments registered. UN sanctions against Yugoslavia were lifted in Nov. 1995 following the Bosnian-Croatian-Yugoslav (Dayton) agreement on Bosnia. External debt was US$12,688m. in 2002.

Imports and Exports. Foreign trade, in US$1m., for calendar year:

	1998	*1999*	*2000*	*2001*
Imports	4,849	3,296	3,711	4,837
Exports	2,858	1,498	1,723	1,903

Breakdown by Standard International Trade Classification categories (value in US$1m.):

	Imports		*Exports*	
	2000	*2001*	*2000*	*2001*
0. Food and live animals	279	441	255	275
1. Beverages and tobacco	53	99	15	17
2. Crude materials	221	188	123	101
3. Fuels and lubricants	745	1,001	4	50
4. Animal and vegetable oils	9	10	17	18
5. Chemicals	556	698	145	132

	Imports		*Exports*	
	2000	*2001*	*2000*	*2001*
6. Manufactured goods	772	948	632	652
7. Machinery and transport equipment	820	1,029	215	243
8. Miscellaneous manufactured items	237	355	270	363
9. Other	19	68	47	50

Main trading partners, 2001 (imports and exports in US$1m.): Russia, 685 and 797; Germany, 589 and 231; Italy, 500 and 312; Bosnia-Herzegovina, 135 and 249; Bulgaria, 324 and 23; Macedonia, 130 and 176.

COMMUNICATIONS

Roads. In 2002 (without data for Kosovo and Metohija) there were 45,290 km of roads comprising 5,602 km of main roads, 11,351 km of regional roads and 28,337 km of other roads. In 2001 there were 1,498,802 passenger cars, 130,293 trucks and vans, and 9,895 buses and coaches. Passenger-km in 2001, without Kosovo and Metohija, were 5,769m. (public transport); tonne-km of freight carried, 553m. There were 1,048 deaths in road accidents in 2000.

Rail. In 2001 there were 4,058 km of railway, of which 1,385 km were electrified. 10,985,000 passengers and 3,376,000 tonnes of freight were carried.

Civil Aviation. There are five airports, the chief ones being at Belgrade and Tivat. The national carrier is JAT (Jugoslovenski Aero Transport) which operates internal flights and in 2003 flew to most major centres in Europe and the Middle East. In March 2003 the airline stated it would retain its name despite the change of name of the country.

Shipping. In 2000 Serbia and Montenegro possessed one sea-going passenger vessel and five cargo vessels totalling 205,000 GRT.

Length of navigable waterways (2001), 1,419 km. In 2001 there were 437 cargo vessels and 3,609,000 tonnes of freight were transported.

Telecommunications. Telephone subscribers numbered 5,243,400 in 2002 (489·1 for every 1,000 persons) and there were 290,000 PCs in use (27·1 per 1,000 persons). There were 2,750,400 mobile phone subscribers in 2002 and 20,000 fax machines in 1999. In 2002 there were 640,000 Internet users.

Postal Services. There were 1,646 post offices in 2001.

SOCIAL INSTITUTIONS

Justice. In 2000 there were two supreme courts, 32 district courts and 153 communal courts, with 2,607 judges and 8,196 lay assessors (without data for Montenegro). There were also 19 economic courts with 287 judges.

In 2000, 34,379 criminal sentences were passed.

The death penalty was abolished for all crimes in 2001.

Religion. Religious communities are separate from the State and are free to perform religious affairs. All religious communities recognized by law enjoy the same rights. Religious breakdown, 2001: Serbian Orthodox, 6·7m.; Muslims, 2·0m.; Roman Catholics, 0·6m.

Serbia has been traditionally Orthodox. Muslims are found in the south as a result of the Turkish occupation. The Serbian Orthodox Church with its seat in Belgrade has 27 bishoprics within the boundaries of former Yugoslavia and 12 abroad (five in the USA and Canada, five in Europe and two in Australia). The Serbian Orthodox Church numbers about 2,000 priests. Its *Patriarch* is Pavle (enthroned 2 Dec. 1990).

As well as in Serbia, the Serbian Orthodox Church is the official church in Montenegro. The Montenegrin church was banned in 1922, but in Oct. 1993 a breakaway Montenegrin church was set up under its own patriarch.

Relations with the Vatican are regulated by a 'Protocol' of 1966.

The Jewish religion has nine communities making up a common league of Jewish Communities with its seat in Belgrade.

Education. Compulsory primary education lasts eight years, secondary 3–4 years. In 2001 (without data for Kosovo and Metohija) there were 1,798 nursery schools with 180,662 pupils and 18,211 employees of which 9,082 were teachers. In

2000–01 there were 4,087 primary schools with 782,559 pupils and 48,770 teachers, and 519 secondary schools with 345,939 pupils and 26,891 teachers. There were 52 institutions of tertiary education with 49,350 students and 1,577 teachers, and 90 institutions of higher education with 141,469 full-time students and 10,356 academic staff.

Adult literacy rate, 1995, 97·9% (male, 98·6%; female, 97·3%).

In 1999–2000 total expenditure on education came to 5·1% of GNP.

Health. In 2000 there were 23,141 doctors, 4,107 dentists, 1,383 pharmacists and 56,933 hospital beds.

Welfare. In 2000 there were 1,349,252 pensioners, of whom 557,754 were old age, 431,527 disability and 339,971 survivors' pensioners. 7,229,004 working days were lost through sickness. In 1999 pensions and disability insurance totalled 25,534,514,000 dinars; old age pension, 8,511,079,000 dinars; and disability, 4,866,896,000 dinars. In 1999, 1,353m. dinars were paid in child allowances.

CULTURE

World Heritage Sites. There are five sites on the UNESCO World Heritage List: the Natural and Culturo-Historical Region of Kotor (inscribed on the list in 1979); Stari Ras and Sopoćani (1979); Durmitor National Park (1980); Studenica Monastery (1986); Dečani Monastery (2004).

Broadcasting. In 2001 (without data for Kosovo and Metohija) there were 70 TV centres (24 private) with 291,324 hours of programme, of which information and documentary 66,990 hours; and 184 broadcasting radio stations (80 private) with 1,004,000 hours of programme, of which 150,000 information and documentary. There were 2,282,000 TV (colour by PAL) and 1,143,000 radio receivers in use in 2001.

Cinema. In 2001 (without data for Kosovo and Metohija) there were 167 cinemas. Cinema attendances were 4,017,000; in 2000, three full-length films were made.

Press. In 2001 there were 27 dailies, 580 other newspapers and 491 periodicals. 4,643 book titles (840 by foreign authors) were published in 2001 in a total of 6,189,000 copies.

Tourism. There were 1,281,029 foreign tourists in 2001 (without data for Kosovo and Metohija). Tourist receipts totalled US$39·9m.

Libraries. In 1998 (without data for Kosovo and Metohija) there were three National, 689 public, 143 Higher Education and 11 non-specialized libraries with a combined 33,681,000 volumes and 8,332,811 registered users.

Museums and Galleries. In 2000 (without data for Kosovo and Metohija) there were 32 art galleries with 1,055 exhibitions and 142 museums with 1,361,000 visitors.

DIPLOMATIC REPRESENTATIVES

Of Serbia and Montenegro in the United Kingdom (28 Belgrave Square, London, SW1X 8QB)
Ambassador: Dragiša Burzan.

Of the United Kingdom in Serbia and Montenegro (Resavska 46, 11000 Belgrade)
Ambassador: David Gowan.

Of Serbia and Montenegro in the USA (2134 Kalorama Rd, NW, Washington, D.C., 20008)
Ambassador: Ivan Vujacić.

Of the USA in Serbia and Montenegro (Kneza Miloša, 50, 11000 Belgrade)
Ambassador: Michael C. Polt.

Of Serbia and Montenegro to the United Nations
Ambassador: Nebojša Kaludjerović.

Of Serbia and Montenegro to the European Union
Ambassador: Pavle Jevremović.

FURTHER READING

Federal Statistical Office. *Statistical Yearbook.*

Allcock, J. B., *Explaining Yugoslavia*. Columbia Univ. Press, 2000
Anzulovic, Branimir, *Heavenly Serbia: From Myth to Genocide.* Hurst, London, 1999
Bennett, C., *Yugoslavia's Bloody Collapse: Causes, Course and Consequences*. Farnborough, 1995
Bokovoy, M. K., *et al*., (eds.) *State-Society Relations in Yugoslavia 1945–1992*. London, 1997
Carpenter, Ted Galen, (ed.) *Nato's Empty Victory.* Cato Institute, Washington, D.C., 2000
Cohen, L. J., *Broken Bonds: the Disintegration of Yugoslavia.* Boulder (CO), 1993
Dyker, D. and Vejvoda, I. (eds.) *Yugoslavia and After: a Study in Fragmentation, Despair and Rebirth*. Harlow, 1996
Friedman, F. (ed.) *Yugoslavia: a Comprehensive English-Language Bibliography.* London, 1993
Glenny, M., *The Fall of Yugoslavia.* London, 1992
Gow, J., *Triumph of the Lack of Will: International Diplomacy and the Yugoslav War*. London and Columbia Univ. Press, 1997
Judah, Tim, *The Serbs: History, Myth and the Destruction of Yugoslavia*. Yale Univ. Press, 1997.—*Kosovo: War and Revenge.* Yale Univ. Press, 2000
Magaš, B., *The Destruction of Yugoslavia: Tracking the Break-up, 1980–92*. London, 1993
Thomas, Robert, *Serbia Under Milosevic: Politics in the 1990s.* Hurst, London, 1999
Udovicki, J., and Ridgeway, J. (eds.) *Burn This House: The Making and Unmaking of Yugoslavia*. Duke, 1997
Woodward, S. L., *Balkan Tragedy: Chaos and Dissolution after the Cold War*. Brookings Institution (Washington), 1995

National statistical office: Federal Statistical Office, Kneza Miloša 20, 11000 Belgrade. *Director:* Dr Ranko Nedeljković.
Website: http://www.szs.sv.gov.yu

REPUBLICS AND PROVINCES

In Feb. 2003 the new Union of Serbia and Montenegro comprised the two republics of Montenegro and Serbia, and the two provinces of Kosovo and Metohija, and Vojvodina within Serbia.

MONTENEGRO

KEY HISTORICAL EVENTS

Montenegro emerged as a separate entity on the break-up of the Serbian Empire in 1355. Owing to its mountainous terrain, it was never effectively subdued by Turkey. It was ruled by Bishop Princes until 1851, when a royal house was founded. The Treaty of Berlin (1828) recognized the independence of Montenegro and doubled the size of the territory. The remains of King Nicholas I, who was deposed in 1918, were returned to Montenegro for reburial in Oct. 1989. As part of Serbia and Montenegro, Montenegro holds jealously to its independence and tries to keep its political distance from Serbia.

On 14 March 2002 Montenegro and Serbia agreed to a new structure for the Yugoslav federation. Following European Union-brokered talks it was agreed that they would remain part of a single entity called Serbia and Montenegro. The parliaments of both Montenegro and Serbia ratified the agreement on 9 April 2002. The new entity came into being on 4 Feb. 2003.

TERRITORY AND POPULATION

Montenegro is a mountainous region which opens to the Adriatic in the southwest. It is bounded in the west by Croatia, northwest by Bosnia-Herzegovina, in the northeast by Serbia and in the southeast by Albania. The capital is Podgorica (population, 1997 estimate, 162,172). Some capital functions are to be transferred to Cetinje, the historic capital of the former kingdom of Montenegro. Its area is 13,812 sq. km. Population at the 2003 census was 672,656, of which the predominating ethnic groups were Montenegrins (273,366), Serbs (201,892) and Albanians (47,682). Population density per sq. km (2003), 48·7.

SOCIAL STATISTICS

Statistics for calendar years:

	Live births	Marriages	Deaths	Growth rate per 1,000
1994	8,887	3,753	4,660	6·7
1995	9,477	3,791	4,921	7·2
1996	9,193	3,869	5,029	6·5
1997	8,758	3,993	5,153	5·6

CONSTITUTION AND GOVERNMENT

There is a 75-member single-chamber National Assembly.

A referendum was held on 29 Feb.–1 March 1992 to determine whether Montenegro should remain within a common state, Yugoslavia, as a sovereign republic. The electorate was 412,000, of whom 66% were in favour. President Milo Djukanović had pledged a referendum on independence in May 2002, but this was postponed with the announcement of the creation of the new entity of Serbia and Montenegro, which came into being on 4 Feb. 2003. After 4 Feb. 2006 Montenegro will be empowered to hold a referendum on independence.

RECENT ELECTIONS

Parliamentary elections were held on 20–21 Oct. 2002. President Milo Djukanović's pro-independence Democratic List for a European Montenegro (including the Democratic Socialist Party) won 39 out of 75 seats with 44·8% of votes cast; the 'Together for Changes' coalition won 30 with 35·9%; the Liberal Alliance, 4 with 5·4%; and the 'Albanians Together' Democratic Coalition, 2 with 2·3%. Turn-out was 77·5%.

In presidential elections held on 22 Dec. 2002 acting president Filip Vujanović won 83·9% of the vote but the result was not valid because the turn-out was less than the required 50%. A follow-up election on 9 Feb. 2003 also failed with a turn-out of 47·7%. Parliament's subsequent amendment of the law on turn-out allowed Vujanović to claim victory on 11 May 2003 with 63·3% against Miodrag Zivković with 30·8% and Dragan Hajduković with 3·9%. Turn-out was 48·5%.

CURRENT ADMINISTRATION

President: Filip Vujanović; b. 1954 (sworn in on 22 May 2003).

Prime Minister: Milo Djukanović; b. 1962 (sworn in on 8 Jan. 2003).

Government Website: http://www.montenegro.yu

ECONOMY

Currency. On 2 Nov. 1999 the pro-Western government decided to make the Deutsche Mark legal tender alongside the dinar. Subsequently it was made the sole official currency, and consequently the euro became the currency of Montenegro on 1 Jan. 2002.

Budget. In 1997 the budget was set at 1,999,000,000 dinars.

Banking and Finance. The Central Bank of Montenegro (*President of the Council*, Ljubisa Krgović) was established in Nov. 2000. Montenegro has 11 commercial banks.

ENERGY AND NATURAL RESOURCES

Electricity. Electricity production in 1997 was 2·27m. kWh.

Minerals. Bauxite production in 1998 totalled 900,000 tonnes. Lignite production in 1997 was 1,282,194 tonnes.

Agriculture. In 1998 the cultivated area was 189,000 ha. Yields (in 1,000 tonnes): potatoes, 51; maize, 9; wheat, 5. Livestock (1,000 head): sheep, 439; cattle, 180; pigs, 22.

Forestry. Timber cut in 1997: 232,000 cu. metres.

INDUSTRY

Production (1997): heavy semi-manufactures, 24,807 tonnes; cotton carded yarn, 166 tonnes.

Labour. In 1997 there were 123,011 workers in the public sector, including 37,491 in industry, 18,589 in trade, catering and tourism, 13,827 in education and culture, 12,003 in transport and communications, 9,020 in communities and organizations and 3,400 in commercial services. In Oct. 1997 in the private sector there were 41,941 self-employed and employed, including 15,150 in trade, 5,774 in catering and tourism and 3,466 in transport and communications. Average monthly salary in Dec. 1998 was 1,556 dinars. Unemployment was running at 33%.

SOCIAL INSTITUTIONS

Justice. In 1997 there were two District Courts, 15 Communal Courts and two Economic courts of law with 222 judges.

Education. In 1997 there were: 69 nurseries with 10,269 pupils; 485 primary schools with 9,129 pupils; 43 secondary schools with 27,747 pupils; one high school with 79 students; 12 higher schools with 7,266 students.

FURTHER READING

Treadway, J. D., *The Falcon and the Eagle: Montenegro and Austria-Hungary, 1908–1914.* Purdue University Press, 1998

SERBIA

KEY HISTORICAL EVENTS

The Serbs received Orthodox Christianity from the Byzantines in 891, but shook off the latter's suzerainty to form a prosperous state, firmly established under Stevan Nemanja (1167–96). A Serbian Patriarchate was established at Peć during the reign of Stevan Dušan (1331–55). Dušan planned the conquest of Constantinople, but he was forestalled by incursions of Turks. After he died many Serbian nobles accepted Turkish vassalage; the reduced Serbian state under Prince Lazar received the coup de grace at Kosovo on St Vitus day, 1389. Turkish preoccupations with a Mongol invasion and wars with Hungary, however, postponed the total incorporation of Serbia into the Ottoman Empire until 1459.

The Turks permitted the Orthodox church to practise, though the Patriarchate was abolished in 1776. The native aristocracy was eliminated and replaced by a system of fiefdoms held in return for military or civil service. Local self-government based on rural extended family units (*zadruga*) continued. In its heyday the Ottoman system probably bore no harder on the peasantry than the Christian feudalism it had replaced, but with the gradual decline of Ottoman power, corruption, oppression and reprisals led to economic deterioration and social unrest.

In 1804 murders carried out by mutinous Turkish infantry provoked a Serbian rising under Djordje Karadjordje. The Sultan's army disciplined the mutineers, but was then defeated by the intransigent Serbs. By the Treaty of Bucharest (1812), however, Russia agreed that Serbia, known as Servia until 1918, should remain Turkish. The Turks reoccupied Serbia with ferocious reprisals. A new rebellion broke out in 1815 under Miloš Obrenović which, this time with Russian support, won autonomy for Serbia within the Ottoman empire. Obrenović had Karadjordje murdered in 1817. In 1838 he was forced to grant a constitution establishing an appointed state council, and abdicated in 1839. In 1842 a coup overthrew the Obrenovićs and Alexander Karadjordjević was elected as ruler. He was deposed in 1858.

During the reign of the western-educated Michael Obrenović (1860 until his assassination in 1868) the foundations of a modern centralized and militarized state were laid, and the idea of a 'Great Serbia', first enunciated in Prime Minister Garašanin's *Draft Programme* of 1844, took root. Milan Obrenović, adopting the title of king, proclaimed formal independence in 1882. He suffered defeats against Turkey (1876) and Bulgaria (1885) and abdicated in 1889. Alexander Obrenović was assassinated in 1903, and replaced by Peter Karadjordjević, who brought in a period of stable constitutional rule.

In its foreign policy, Serbia's striving for an outlet to the sea was consistently thwarted by Austria. Annexing Bosnia in 1908, Austria forced the Serbs to withdraw from the Adriatic after the first Balkan war (1912).

Following the break-up of Yugoslavia, in March 1998 a coalition government was formed between the Socialist Party of Slobodan Milošević and the ultra-nationalist Radical Party.

On 14 March 2002 Serbia and Montenegro agreed to a new structure for the Yugoslav federation. Following European Union-brokered talks it was agreed that they would remain part of a single entity called Serbia and Montenegro, thus relegating the name Yugoslavia to history. The parliaments of both Serbia and Montenegro ratified the agreement on 9 April 2002. The new entity came into being on 4 Feb. 2003. On 12 March 2003 Serb prime minister Zoran Djindjić was assassinated.

TERRITORY AND POPULATION

Serbia is bounded in the northwest by Croatia, in the north by Hungary, in the northeast by Romania, in the east by Bulgaria, in the south by Macedonia and in the west by Albania, Montenegro and Bosnia-Herzegovina. It includes the two provinces (formerly autonomous) of Kosovo and Metohija in the south and Vojvodina in the north. With these Serbia's area is 88,361 sq. km; without, 55,968 sq. km. The capital is Belgrade (population estimate, 1997, 1,597,599). Population at the 1991 census was (with Kosovo and Vojvodina) 9,778,991, of which the predominating ethnic group was Serbs (6,446,595). Population density per sq. km, 110·7; (without Kosovo and Vojvodina), population estimate 5,808,906, of which the predominating ethnic group was Serbs (5,108,682). Population density per sq. km, 103·8. 1997 estimate (with Kosovo and Vojvodina), 9,956,662; density, 112·7 per sq. km; (without) 5,791,643; density, 103·5 per sq. km.

SOCIAL STATISTICS

Statistics for calendar years (without Kosovo and Vojvodina):

	Live births	*Marriages*	*Deaths*	*Growth rate per 1,000*
1995	63,737	32,295	66,756	–0·5
1996	60,924	29,703	69,218	–1·4
1997	59,071	29,638	69,422	–1·8

CONSTITUTION AND GOVERNMENT

There is a 250-member single-chamber National Assembly. The *President* is elected by universal suffrage for not more than two five-year terms.

In Sept. 1990 a new constitution was adopted by the National Assembly. It defined Serbia as a 'democratic' instead of a 'socialist' republic, laid down a framework for multi-party elections, and described Serbia as 'united and sovereign on all its territory', thus stripping Kosovo and Vojvodina of the attributes of autonomy granted by the 1974 federal constitution.

RECENT ELECTIONS

Elections to the Serbian National Assembly were held on 28 Dec. 2003. The Srpska Radikalna Stranka (SRS; Serb Radical Party) won 82 seats (27·7% of the vote); the Demokratska Stranka Srbije (DSS; Democratic Party of Serbia), 53 (18·0%); the Demokratska Stranka (DS; Democratic Party), 37 (12·6%); G17 Plus, 34 (11·7%); SPO-NS, 23 (7·7%); and the Socijalisticka Partija Srbije (SPS; Serb Socialist Party), 21 (7·7%). Five other parties or coalitions failed to win seats. Turn-out was 59·3%. Following the election a coalition government was formed between DSS, G17 Plus and SPO-NS.

In the first round of presidential elections held on 29 Sept. 2002 Yugoslav President Vojislav Koštunica won 30·9% of votes cast, with 27·4% of the vote going to Miroljub Labus and 23·2% for Vojislav Seselj, the favoured candidate of former premier Slobodan Milošević. Turn-out was 55·5%. A run-off between Koštunica and Labus took place on 13 Oct. 2002 but was declared invalid owing to a turn-out of 45·5%—less than the legally-required 50%. A further attempt to hold a new election on 8 Dec. 2002 again failed when fewer than 50% of the electorate voted. A third attempt on 16 Nov. 2003 also failed for the same reason. In Feb. 2004 parliament abolished the 50% turn-out requirement. Another round of elections was held in June 2004. In the first round, on 13 June, Tomislav Nikolić (SRS) took

30·4% of the vote, followed by Boris Tadić (DS) with 27·6%, Bogoljub Karić with 18·2% and Dragan Maršićanin (DSS) with 13·3%. Turn-out was 47·6%. In the run-off on 27 June Tadić took 53·7%, defeating Nicolić with 45·0%. Turn-out was 48·7%.

CURRENT ADMINISTRATION

President: Boris Tadić; b. 1958 (DS; took office on 11 July 2004).

Prime Minister: Vojislav Koštunica; b. 1944 (DSS; took office on 3 March 2004).

Government Website: http://www.serbia.sr.gov.yu

ECONOMY

Budget. In 1997 the budget was set at 13,820,000,000 dinars. VAT at 18% (reduced rate 8%) was introduced on 1 Jan. 2005.

ENERGY AND NATURAL RESOURCES

Electricity. Electricity production in 1997 was 32·77m. kWh.

Minerals. (Excluding Kosovo and Vojvodina). 1997: lignite, 32,608,711 tonnes; copper ore, 20,507,148 tonnes.

Agriculture. (Excluding Kosovo and Vojvodina). In 1997 the cultivated area was an estimated 2,614,000 ha. Yields in 1997 (in 1,000 tonnes): maize, 6,855; wheat, 2,920; sugarbeet, 2,037; potatoes, 918; plums, 489; grapes, 397. Livestock estimates (in 1,000): cattle, 402; sheep, 369; pigs, 74; poultry, 2,577.

Forestry. Timber cut in 1997: 1,614,000 cu. metres.

INDUSTRY

(Excluding Kosovo and Vojvodina). 1997: steel, 862,944 tonnes; lorries, 1,269 units; cars, 9,512 units; sulphuric acid, 150,371 tonnes; plastics, 27,220 tonnes; cement, 924,308 tonnes; sugar, 14,682 tonnes; cotton fabrics, 17,228,000 sq. metres; woollen fabrics, 10,097,000 sq. metres. By late 2000 industry had virtually come to a standstill.

Labour. In 1997 there were 1,921,763 workers in the public sector, including 782,676 in industry and 196,149 in trade, catering and tourism, 165,585 in education and culture, 128,458 in transport and communications, 84,035 in communities and organizations and 71,225 in commercial services. In Oct. 1997 in the private sector there were 486,183 self-employed and employed, including 136,443 in trade, 51,553 in arts and crafts, 36,771 in catering and tourism and 18,468 in transport and communications. Average monthly salary in Dec. 1998 was 1,313 dinars. Unemployment was running at 25%, but by late 2000 had increased to around 50%.

SOCIAL INSTITUTIONS

Justice. In 1997 there were 30 District Courts, 138 Communal Courts and 16 Economic Courts of Law with 1,997 judges.

Education. In 1997 there were: 1,730 nurseries with 174,621 pupils; 3,975 primary schools with 816,059 pupils; 523 secondary schools with 323,781 pupils; 53 high schools with 37,366 students; 83 higher schools with 144,330 students.

FURTHER READING

Judah, T., *The Serbs: History, Myth and the Destruction of Yugoslavia.* Yale Univ. Press, 1997

KOSOVO AND METOHIJA

KEY HISTORICAL EVENTS

Kosovo has a large ethnic Albanian majority. Following Albanian-Serb conflicts, the Kosovo and Serbian parliaments adopted constitutional amendments in March 1989 surrendering much of Kosovo's autonomy to Serbia. Renewed Albanian rioting broke out in 1990. The Prime Minister and six other ministers resigned in April

1990 over ethnic conflicts. In July 1990, 114 of the 130 Albanian members of the National Assembly voted for full republican status for Kosovo but the Serbian National Assembly declared this vote invalid and unanimously voted to dissolve the Kosovo Assembly. Direct Serbian rule was imposed causing widespread violence. Western demands for negotiations in granting Kosovo some kind of special status were rejected. Ibrahim Rugova, the leader of the main Albanian party, the Democratic League of Kosovo (LDK), declared himself 'president' demanding talks on independence. In 1998 armed conflict between Yugoslavia and the Kosovo Liberation Army led to 200,000 people, or a tenth of the population of the whole province, fleeing the fighting. Further repression by Serbian forces led to the threat of NATO direct action. Air strikes against Yugoslavian military targets began on 24 March 1999. Retaliation against Albanian Kosovars led to a massive exodus of refugees. On 9 June after 78 days of air attacks NATO and Yugoslavia signed an accord on the Serb withdrawal from Kosovo, and on 11 June NATO's peacekeeping force, KFOR, entered Kosovo. In Nov. 2001 the Organization for Security and Co-operation in Europe mounted elections for a provincial assembly that were deemed fair and democratic.

TERRITORY AND POPULATION

Area: 10,887 sq. km. The capital is Priština. The 1991 census was not taken. Population estimate of Kosovo and Metohija, 1991, 1,956,196 (1,596,072 Albanians, 194,190 Serbs); density, 179·7 per sq. km. The population in 1998 was 2,190,000 (84% Albanians, 9% Serbs and 7% others). By Sept. 1999 the population had declined to 1,506,000. Although the number of Albanians had dropped by over 430,000, the breakdown of the population had changed to 93% Albanians, 5% Serbs and 2% others. Population estimate of Priština, 1997, 242,000.

SOCIAL STATISTICS

Statistics for calendar years:

	Live births	*Marriages*	*Deaths*	*Growth rate per 1,000*
1994	43,450	11,959	7,667	17·2
1995	44,776	12,979	8,671	17·1
1996	45,343	12,309	8,142	17·3
1997	42,920	11,866	8,624	15·7

CONSTITUTION AND GOVERNMENT

Kosovo is presently under interim international administration, sanctioned by the UN Security Council resolution 1244 of 10 June 1999. The United Nations Interim Administration Mission in Kosovo (UNMIK) has administered Kosovo since the arrival of KFOR (NATO-led peacekeeping force).

There is a 120-member multi-ethnic parliamentary assembly, which first convened on 10 Dec. 2001. The new assembly brought together representatives of Kosovo's ethnic Albanian majority and its Serbian minority for the first time in more than a decade.

RECENT ELECTIONS

Parliamentary elections held on 23 Oct. 2004; turn-out was 51%. The Democratic League of Kosovo won 49 seats with 45·3% of the vote, the Democratic Party of Kosovo 31 with 28·7%, the Alliance for the Future of Kosovo 9 with 8·3%, the Ora Party 9 with 6·3%, the Albanian Christian Democratic Party of Kosovo 2 with 1·8%, the Turkish Democratic Party of Kosovo 2 with 1·4% and the Justice Party 2 with 1·0%. Following the election the Democratic League of Kosovo formed a coalition government with the Alliance for the Future of Kosovo.

Ibrahim Rugova was re-elected president by parliament on 3 Dec. 2004. He received 64 votes with 32 against. On the same day parliament elected Ramush Haradinaj prime minister by 72 votes to 3 against.

CURRENT ADMINISTRATION

President: Ibrahim Rugova; b. 1944 (Democratic League of Kosovo; sworn in 4 March 2002 and re-elected 3 Dec. 2004).

Prime Minister: Bajram Kosumi; b. 1960 (Alliance for the Future of Kosovo; since 23 March 2005).

Special Representative and Head of the United Nations Interim Administration in Kosovo (UNMIK): Søren Jessen-Petersen (Denmark; took office on 16 Aug. 2004).

UNMIK Website: http://www.unmikonline.org

ECONOMY

Budget. In 1997 the budget was set at 13,000,000 dinars.

Banking and Finance. In Aug. 1999 the Deutsche Mark became legal tender alongside the Yugoslav dinar, and on 1 Jan. 2002 the euro became the official currency of Kosovo. The Serb dinar is also legal tender in Kosovo but is used only by ethnic Serbs.

ENERGY AND NATURAL RESOURCES

Electricity. Electricity production in 1997 was 4·87m. kWh.

Minerals. Production (1997): lignite, 8,421,991 tonnes.

Agriculture. The cultivated area in 1997 was an estimated 398,000 ha. Yields in 1997 (in 1,000 tonnes): maize, 296; wheat, 272; potatoes, 92; grapes, 69; plums, 15. Livestock (in 1,000): cattle, 402; sheep, 369; pigs, 74; poultry, 2,577.

Forestry. Timber cut in 1997: 130,000 cu. metres.

INDUSTRY

Production (1997): cement, 89,528 tonnes; sulphuric acid, 26,900 tonnes.

Labour. In 1997 there were 120,763 workers in the public sector, including 54,223 in industry, 10,471 in education and culture, 9,245 in trade, catering and tourism, 8,933 in transport and communications, 7,880 in communities and organizations and 1,526 in commercial services. In Oct. 1997 in the private sector there were 35,869 self-employed and employed, including 15,113 in trade, 5,023 in catering and tourism, 4,364 in arts and crafts and 2,006 in transport and communications. Average monthly salary in Dec. 1998 was 1,066 dinars.

SOCIAL INSTITUTIONS

Education. In 1997 there were: 111 nurseries with 8,179 pupils; 335 primary schools with 42,114 pupils; 55 secondary schools with 14,092 pupils; 4 high schools with 1,621 students; 15 higher schools with 12,725 students.

FURTHER READING

Malcolm, N., *Kosovo: a Short History.* New York Univ. Press, 1998
Vickers, M., *Between Serb and Albanian: A History of Kosovo.* Hurst, London, 1998

VOJVODINA

KEY HISTORICAL EVENTS

After the Battle of Kosovo in 1389 Turkish attacks on the Balkans led to mass migrations of Serbian people to Vojvodina. Turkish rule ended after their 1716–18 war with Austria and the Požarevac peace agreement. In exchange for acting as frontier protectors, the Austrians granted the people of Vojvodina freedom of confession and religious autonomy. However, by 1848 discontent had brewed and a short-lived revolution occurred, in which the Serbs formed an alliance with the Croats, and Vojvodina was briefly declared as an independent dukedom. After the First World War Vojvodina became part of the first Yugoslav state. In 1974 President Tito granted autonomy to Vojvodina, but this status was brought into question after Vojvodina's largely anti-Milošević provincial assembly resigned their positions in 1988. In 1989 the Serbian government, led by Slobodan Milošević, stripped Vojvodina of most of its autonomous rights and secured Serbian control. Since the fall of Milošević in Oct. 2000 there have again been demands for increased autonomy. However, the Assembly of Vojvodina has now only very limited powers.

TERRITORY AND POPULATION

Area: 21,506 sq. km. The capital is Novi Sad. Population of Vojvodina at the 1991 census, 2,013,889 (1,143,723 Serbs, 339,491 Hungarians). Estimate, 1997, 1,976,936; density, 91·9 per sq. km. Population of Novi Sad, 1997, 266,808.

SOCIAL STATISTICS

Statistics for calendar years:

	Live births	*Marriages*	*Deaths*	*Growth rate per 1,000*
1994	21,595	11,048	27,518	–3·0
1995	22,499	11,260	27,177	–2·4
1996	20,483	11,112	28,832	–4·2
1997	20,645	10,706	28,646	–4·0

CONSTITUTION AND GOVERNMENT

The 1990 Serbian constitution deprived Vojvodina of its autonomy. Serbo-Croat was declared the only official language in 1991.

RECENT ELECTIONS

In March 2003 the Assembly of Vojvodina comprised 120 deputies, of which the Democratic Opposition of Serbia had 117 seats and the coalition of the Socialist Party of Serbia and Yugoslav Left two.

CURRENT ADMINISTRATION

President of the Assembly: Bojan Kostreš; b. 1974 (in office since 30 Oct. 2004).

Chairman of the Executive Council: Bojan Pajtić; b. 1970 (in office since 30 Oct. 2004).

Government Website: http://www.vojvodina.sr.gov.yu

ECONOMY

Budget. In 1997 the budget was set at 68,000,000 dinars.

ENERGY AND NATURAL RESOURCES

Electricity. Electricity production in 1997 was 387m. kWh.

Agriculture. The cultivated area in 1997 was an estimated 1,649,000 ha. Yields (in 1,000 tonnes): maize, 3,847; sugarbeet, 1,805; wheat, 1,423; potatoes, 255. Livestock estimates (in 1,000): cattle, 231; sheep, 267; pigs, 1,691; poultry, 7,863.

Forestry. Timber cut in 1997: 548,000 cu. metres.

INDUSTRY

Production (1997): cement, 997,491 tonnes; crude petroleum, 965,655 tonnes; plastics, 212,352 tonnes.

Labour. In 1997 there were 452,005 workers in the public sector, including 181,672 in industry, 38,382 in trade, catering and tourism, 38,000 in education and culture, 26,876 in transport and communications, 18,543 in communities and organizations and 16,901 in commercial services. In Oct. 1997 in the private sector there were 86,320 self-employed and employed including 39,612 in trade, 13,053 in arts and crafts, 5,436 in catering and tourism and 3,985 in transport and communications. Average monthly salary in Dec. 1998 was 1,493 dinars.

SOCIAL INSTITUTIONS

Education. In 1997 there were: 604 nurseries with 48,024 pupils; 535 primary schools with 212,453 pupils; 122 secondary schools with 81,893 pupils; 9 high schools with 7,790 students; and 15 higher schools with 25,505 students.

SEYCHELLES

Republic of Seychelles

Capital: Victoria
Population, 2001: 81,000
GDP per capita, 2001: (PPP$) 18,232
HDI/world rank: 0·853/35

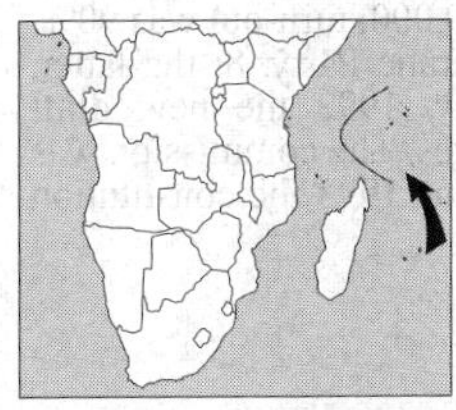

KEY HISTORICAL EVENTS

The Seychelles were colonized by the French in 1756 to establish spice plantations to compete with the Dutch monopoly. The islands were captured by the English in 1794. Subsequently, Britain offered to return Mauritius and its dependencies which included the Seychelles to France if that country would renounce all claims to her possessions in India. France refused and the Seychelles were formally ceded to Britain as a dependency of Mauritius. In Nov. 1903 the Seychelles archipelago became a separate British Crown Colony. Internal self-government was achieved on 1 Oct. 1975 and independence as a republic within the British Commonwealth on 29 June 1976.

The first president, James Mancham, was deposed in a coup on 5 June 1977. Under the new constitution, the Seychelles People's Progressive Front became the sole legal party. There were several attempts to overthrow the regime, but in 1979 and 1984 Albert René was the only candidate in the presidential elections. Under the new constitution approved in June 1993, President René was re-elected against two opponents.

TERRITORY AND POPULATION

The Seychelles consists of 115 islands in the Indian Ocean, north of Madagascar, with a combined area of 175 sq. miles (455 sq. km) in two distinct groups and a population (2002 census, provisional) of 81,177. The Granitic group of 40 islands cover 90 sq. miles (232 sq. km); the principal island is Mahé, with 59 sq. miles (153 sq. km) and 70,828 inhabitants at the 2002 census, the other inhabited islands of the group being Praslin, La Digue, Silhouette, Fregate and North, which together had 8,538 inhabitants in 1997.

The Outer or Coralline group comprises 75 islands spread over a wide area of ocean between the Mahé group and Madagascar, with a total land area of 86 sq. miles (223 sq. km). The main islands are the Amirante Isles (including Desroches, Poivre, Daros and Alphonse), Coetivy Island and Platte Island, all lying south of the Mahé group; the Farquhar, St Pierre and Providence Islands, north of Madagascar; and Aldabra, Astove, Assumption and the Cosmoledo Islands, about 1,000 km southwest of the Mahé group. Aldabra (whose lagoon covers 55 sq. miles), Farquhar and Desroches were transferred to the new British Indian Ocean Territory in 1965, but were returned by Britain to the Seychelles on the latter's independence in 1976.

Victoria, the chief town, had a census population of 24,970 in 2002. In 2001, 64·5% of the population was urban.

The official languages are Creole, English and French but 95% of the population speak Creole.

SOCIAL STATISTICS

2001 births, 1,440; deaths, 554. 2001 rates per 1,000 population, birth, 17·7; death, 6·8; infant mortality (2001), 13 per 1,000 births. Annual population growth rate, 1992–02, 1·0%. Life expectancy at birth in 1997 was estimated to be 70 years (65 for males and 74 for females). Fertility rate, 2001, 1·8 births per woman.

CLIMATE

Though close to the equator, the climate is tropical. The hot, wet season is from Dec. to May, when conditions are humid, but southeast trades bring cooler conditions from June to Nov. Temperatures are high throughout the year, but the islands lie outside the cyclone belt. Victoria, Jan. 80°F (26·7°C), July 78°F (25·6°C). Annual rainfall 95" (2,287 mm).

CONSTITUTION AND GOVERNMENT

Under the 1979 Constitution the Seychelles People's Progressive Front (SPPF) was the sole legal Party. There is a unicameral People's Assembly consisting of 34 seats, of which 25 are directly elected and nine are allocated on a proportional basis, and an executive president directly elected for a five-year term. A constitutional amendment of Dec. 1991 legalized other parties. A commission was elected in July 1992 to draft a new constitution. The electorate was some 50,000; turn-out was 90%. The SPPF gained 14 seats on the commission, the Democratic Party, 8; the latter, however, eventually withdrew. At a referendum in Nov. 1992 the new draft constitution failed to obtain the necessary 60% approval votes. The commission was reconvened in Jan. 1993. At a further referendum on 18 June 1993 the constitution was approved by 73·6% of votes cast.

National Anthem. 'Koste Seselwa' ('Seychelles, Unite').

RECENT ELECTIONS

In parliamentary elections held on 4–6 Dec. 2002 President France-Albert René's Seychelles People's Progressive Front won 23 of the 34 seats with 54·3% of the vote, against 11 for the Seychelles National Party (42·6%). Turn-out was 87%. In presidential elections held between 31 Aug.–2 Sept. 2001 France Albert René was re-elected for a sixth term, obtaining 54·2% of the votes, with his nearest rival, Wavel Ramkalawan of the Seychelles National Party, polling 44·9%.

CURRENT ADMINISTRATION

On 14 April 2004 France-Albert René stepped down as president, a post he had held since 1977.

President: James Alix Michel; b. 1944 (SPPF; took office on 14 April 2004). The President is *Minister of Internal Affairs, Defence, Police, Finance and Legal Affairs*.

Vice-President, Minister of Tourism and Transport, Public Administration, Information Technology and Communications: Joseph Belmont.

In March 2005 the government comprised:

Minister of Administration and Manpower Development: Noellie Alexander. *Education:* Danny Faure. *Environment and Natural Resources:* Ronny Jumeau. *Foreign Affairs:* Patrick Pillay. *Health and Social Services:* Vincent Meriton. *Economic Planning and Employment:* Jacqueline Dugasse. *Land Use and Habitat:* Joel Morgan. *Local Government, Sports and Culture:* Sylvette Pool.

DEFENCE

The Defence Force comprises all services. Personnel (2002) Army, 200; Paramilitary, 250; Coastguard-naval, 200; Air Wing, 20.

Defence expenditure totalled US$12m. in 2003 (US$141 per capita), representing 1·6% of GDP.

Coastguard. There is no longer a navy or air force in the Seychelles. Instead, the Seychelles Coast Guard has superseded these former forces. Based at Port Victoria it includes a small air wing with no combat aircraft.

INTERNATIONAL RELATIONS

Seychelles is a member of the UN, the Commonwealth, the African Union, African Development Bank, COMESA and the International Organization of the Francophonie and is an ACP member state of the ACP-EU relationship.

ECONOMY

Services accounted for 67·1% of GDP in 2002, industry 30·0% and agriculture 2·9%.

Overview. Since the early 1990s the government has attempted to create a free market economy. Tourism forms the backbone of the economy followed by the fisheries sector. In recent years the Seychelles has undertaken efforts to develop an offshore sector as the third pillar of the economy and to position itself as a provider of business and financial services.

Currency. The unit of currency is the *Seychelles rupee* (SCR) divided into 100 *cents*. In June 2002 foreign exchange reserves were US$39m. In April 2002 total money supply was 1,384m. rupees. In 2002 inflation was 0·2%.

Budget. Fiscal budget in 1m. rupees, for calendar years:

	1996	*1997*	*1998*	*1999*	*2000*
Total revenue	1,151·1	1,273·5	1,372·9	1,491·9	1,377·1
Total expenditure	1,495·2	1,680·9	1,879·7	1,905·0	1,969·8

Performance. Total GDP was US$0·7bn. in 2003. Seychelles was in recession in 2001, with the economy contracting by 2·2%, but 2002 saw a very slight recovery, with growth of 0·3%.

Banking and Finance. The Central Bank of Seychelles (established in 1983; *Governor*, Francis Chang Leng), which is the bank of issue, and the Development Bank of Seychelles provide long-term lending for development purposes. There are also six commercial banks, including two local banks (the Seychelles Savings Bank and the Seychelles International Mercantile Banking Co-operation or NOUVOBANQ), and four branches of foreign banks (Barclays Bank, Banque Française Commerciale, Habib Bank and Bank of Baroda).

ENERGY AND NATURAL RESOURCES

Environment. Carbon dioxide emissions from the consumption and flaring of fossil fuels were the equivalent of 7·6 tonnes per capita in 2002.

Electricity. Installed capacity on Mahé and Praslin combined was 28,000 kW in 2000. Production in 2000 was 164m. kWh and consumption per capita 2,025 kWh.

Water. There are two raw water reservoirs, the Rochon Dam and La Gogue Dam, which have a combined holding capacity of 1·05bn. litres.

Treated water consumption in 1998 was 5·5bn. litres.

Agriculture. The main cash crop in 1998 was cinnamon bark, of which 289 tonnes were exported, followed by tea production with exports of 250 tonnes (green leaf). Crops grown for local consumption include bananas, cassava, sweet potatoes, yams, oranges, paw-paw and vegetables. The staple food crop, rice, is imported from Asia. Livestock, 2000: 18,000 pigs, 5,000 goats, 1,000 cattle and 1m. chickens. In 2001 there were 1,000 ha of arable land and 6,000 ha of permanent crop land.

Forestry. In 2000 forests covered 30,000 ha, or 66·7% of the total land area. The Ministry of Environment has a number of ongoing forestry projects which aim at preserving and upgrading the local system. There are also a number of terrestrial nature reserves including three national parks, four special reserves and an area of outstanding natural beauty.

Fisheries. The fisheries sector is the Seychelles' second largest foreign exchange earner. In 1998 it accounted for at least 93% of export revenue. Total catch in 2001 was 47,550 tonnes, exclusively from sea fishing. 1998 fisheries exports amounted to 457·7m. rupees, of which: canned tuna, 412·2m.; fresh/frozen fish, 11·9m.; frozen prawns, 33·6m. Total 1998 fish production (in tonnes) was as follows: canned tuna, 18,939; fresh/frozen fish, 3,334; frozen prawns, 642.

INDUSTRY

Local industry is expanding, the major development in recent years being in tuna canning; in 2000 output totalled 28,781 tonnes, up from 7,500 tonnes in 1995. This is followed by brewing, with 7·1m. litres in 2003. Other main activities include production of cigarettes (40m. in 2000), dairy production, prawn production, paints and processing of cinnamon barks.

Labour. Some 71% of the workforce is employed in services. In 1999, 3,791 people worked in hotels and restaurants and 1,217 in other tourism related jobs. 15,700 are formally employed in the private sector, 6,800 in the public sector and 4,200 in the parastatal sector.

Trade Unions. There are two major trade unions, the National Workers' Union and the Forum for Progress.

INTERNATIONAL TRADE

Foreign debt totalled US$253m. in 2002.

Imports and Exports. Total trade, in US$1m., for calendar years:

	1998	*1999*	*2000*	*2001*	*2002*
Exports (f.o.b.)	122·8	145·7	194·8	216·4	236·7
Imports (f.o.b.)	334·6	369·8	311·6	421·9	376·3

Principal imports: machinery and transport equipment; manufactured goods; food, beverages and tobacco; mineral fuel; chemicals. Principal origins of import, 2000: South Africa (13·6%), France (11·5%), Italy (10·6%), UK (10·6%). Principal exports: canned tuna; frozen prawns; fresh and frozen fish; cinnamon bark. Main export markets, 1998: UK (23·1%), Yemen (21·2%), Germany (19·4%), France (13·2%), Italy (12·9%).

COMMUNICATIONS

Roads. In 1998 there were 343 km of surfaced roads and 54 km of unsurfaced roads. There were 9,068 vehicles registered in 1998.

Rail. There are no railways in the Seychelles.

Civil Aviation. Seychelles International airport is on Mahé. In 2003 Air Seychelles flew on domestic routes and to Bombay, Comoros, Dubai, Frankfurt, Johannesburg, London, Malé, Mauritius, Munich, Paris, Réunion, Rome, Singapore and Zürich. In 1999 it flew 8·8m. km, carrying 347,200 passengers (109,500 on international flights). In 2000 Seychelles International handled 604,415 passengers (315,024 on international flights) and 6,259 tonnes of freight.

Shipping. The main port is Victoria, which is also a tuna-fishing and fuel and services supply centre. In 2002 merchant shipping totalled 65,000 GRT. In 1999 vessels totalling 1,139,000 net registered tons entered ports. Sea freight (1998) included: imports, 636,000 tonnes; exports, 47,000 tonnes; transhipments (fish), 39,000 tonnes.

Telecommunications. There were 65,500 telephone subscribers in 2001, or 799·7 per 1,000 population, and 13,000 PCs were in use in 2002 (156·6 per 1,000 persons). Mobile phone subscribers numbered 44,700 in 2002 and there were 600 fax machines in 1999. Internet users numbered 11,700 in 2002.

Postal Services. In 1998 there were five post offices. The central post office is in Victoria.

SOCIAL INSTITUTIONS

Justice. In 1998, 3,951 criminal and other offences were recorded by the police. The death penalty was abolished for all crimes in 1993.

Religion. 87% of the inhabitants are Roman Catholic, the remainder of the population being followers of other religions (mainly Anglicans, with some 7th Day Adventists, Bahai, Muslim, Hindu, Pentecostal, Jehovah's Witnesses, Buddhist or followers of the Grace and Peace church).

Education. Adult literacy was 84% in 1998. Education is free from five to 12 years in primary schools, and 13 to 17 in secondary schools. There are three private schools providing primary and secondary education and one dealing only with secondary learning. Education beyond 18 years of age is funded jointly by the government and parents. In 2003 there were 9,477 pupils and 675 teachers in primary schools, 7,551 pupils and 552 teachers in secondary schools and 1,652 students and 193 teachers at polytechnic level.

Expenditure on education came to 7·9% of GNP in 1999–2000 and 10·7% of total government spending in 1998–99.

Health. In 1999 there were 108 doctors, 15 dentists and 406 nurses. In 1998 there were 426 hospital beds. The health service is free.

Welfare. Social security is provided for people of 63 years and over, for the disabled and for families needing financial assistance. There is also assistance via means testing for those medically unfit to work and for mothers who remain out of work for longer than their designated maternity leave. Orphanages are also subsidized by the government.

CULTURE

World Heritage Sites. Entered on the UNESCO World Heritage List in 1982, the four coral islands of Aldabra Atoll protect a shallow lagoon. A heritage site since 1983, the Vallée de Mai Nature Reserve is a natural palm forest on the small island of Praslin.

Broadcasting. Broadcasting is under the auspices of the Seychelles Broadcasting Corporation (SBC), an independent body. The SBC owns two radio stations; the AM station which hosts most programmes in Creole with frequent use of English and French; and Paradise FM which broadcasts mainly in English. There is also a religious station, FEBA. The RFI and BBC also transmit programmes locally.

There is only one local TV station directed by the SBC. International TV channels can be reached through Cable TV. TV colour is by PAL. In 1997 there were 42,000 radio receivers and in 2001 there were 16,550 TV sets.

Cinema. There is one cinema, based in Victoria.

Press. There are one daily and two weekly newspapers, as well as two monthly magazines.

Tourism. Tourism is the main foreign exchange earner. Visitor numbers were 130,000 in 2000, spending US$110m.

Festivals. There are numerous religious festivals including Kavadi, an annual procession organized by the Hindu Association of Seychelles. Secular festivals include the annual Youth Festival, Jazz Festival, Creole Festival, Kite Festival and the Subios Festival, a celebration of the underwater world.

Libraries. There is a national library in Victoria with branches on Praslin and La Digue Islands. It also provides a mobile service, and there are libraries in all educational institutions.

Theatre and Opera. There are three national theatres, all located on Mahé. The Mont Fleuri Theatre and the International Conference Centre serve central Mahé while the Anse Royale Theatre caters for the southern region of the island.

Museums and Galleries. There are four museums: the Historical Museum, the Natural History Museum, the National Heritage Museum and the Eco Musée, a museum of the country's economic activities. There is also a National Art Gallery, located in the National Library, and a number of smaller galleries exhibiting mostly local artists.

DIPLOMATIC REPRESENTATIVES

Of Seychelles in the United Kingdom (Box 4PE, 2nd Floor, Eros House, 111 Baker Street, London, W1M 1FE)
High Commissioner: Callixte d'Offay (resides at Paris).

Of the United Kingdom in Seychelles (Victoria House, 3rd Floor, PO Box 161, Victoria, Mahé)
High Commissioner: Diana Skingle.

Of Seychelles in the USA (800 2nd Avenue, Suite 400C, New York, NY 10017)
Ambassador: Claude Morel.

Of the USA in Seychelles
Ambassador: John Price (resides at Port Louis, Mauritius).

Of Seychelles to the United Nations
Ambassador: Claude Morel.

Of Seychelles to the European Union
Ambassador: Callixte d'Offay.

FURTHER READING

Bennett, G. and Bennett, P. R., *Seychelles.* [Bibliography] ABC-Clio, Oxford and Santa Barbara (CA), 1993

Scarr, D., *Seychelles Since 1970: History of a Slave and Post-Slavery Society.* Africa World Press, Lawrenceville (NJ), 2000

National statistical office: Statistics and Database Administration Section (MISD), P. O. Box 206, Victoria, Mahé. *Seychelles in Figures*
Website: http://www.seychelles.net/misdstat/

SIERRA LEONE

Republic of Sierra Leone

Capital: Freetown
Population projection, 2010: 5·86m.
GDP per capita, 2002: (PPP$) 520
HDI/world rank: 0·273/177

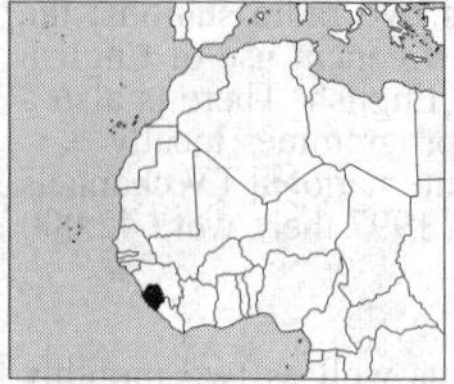

KEY HISTORICAL EVENTS

The Colony of Sierra Leone originated in 1787 when English settlers bought a piece of land intended as a home for natives of Africa who were waifs in London. The land was later used as a settlement for Africans rescued from slave-ships. The hinterland was declared a British protectorate on 21 Aug. 1896. Sierra Leone became independent as a member state of the British Commonwealth on 27 April 1961. In a general election in March 1967, Dr Siaka Stevens' All People's Congress came to power and was installed despite a military coup to prevent his taking office. Sierra Leone became a republic on 19 April 1971 with Dr Siaka Stevens as executive president. Following a referendum in June 1978, a new constitution was instituted under which the ruling All People's Congress became the sole legal party.

A military coup on 29 April 1992 deposed the president and set up a National Provisional Ruling Council whose chairman was in turn deposed in a military coup on 16 Jan. 1996. Presidential and parliamentary elections in Feb.–March 1996 resulted in a new government led by President Ahmed Tejan Kabbah. He was ousted in May 1997 by a group of junior officers. In Feb. 1998 a Nigerian-led intervention force launched an air and artillery offensive against the military junta. For the first time a group of African states joined together to restore a democratically-elected president. On 10 March President Kabbah returned from exile in Guinea, promising a 'new beginning'. But in Jan. 1999 the country again erupted into civil war. Nigeria sent troops to support President Kabbah but having lost control of the diamond fields and with no other resources, the government was powerless. The war, which continued for nearly ten years, has reduced Sierra Leone to one of the poorest countries in the world.

The government reached an agreement with the rebel movement in July 1999 to bring the civil war to an end. Under the terms of the accord the Revolutionary United Front (RUF) was to gain four key government posts along with effective control of the country's mineral resources. In return the RUF was to surrender its weapons. However, civil war broke out again in early 2000. Responding to a government appeal British forces were sent to back up the UN peacekeeping force (UNMASIL). Foday Sankoh, rebel leader of the RUF, was captured and handed over to UN forces in May 2000. In July 2001 the RUF announced that it was formally recognizing the civil government under President Ahmed Tejan Kabbah. By Sept. 2001 there were signs that the civil war might be at an end, and in Jan. 2002 President Kabbah declared the war over. He was re-elected in a presidential election in May 2002 and has been at the forefront of the fight against corruption. Both the UN and the International Monetary Fund have praised the 'remarkable progress' made in Sierra Leone.

TERRITORY AND POPULATION

Sierra Leone is bounded on the northwest, north and northeast by Guinea, on the southeast by Liberia and on the southwest by the Atlantic Ocean. The area is 27,699 sq. miles (71,740 sq. km). Population (census 1985), 3,517,530, of whom about 2,000 were Europeans, 3,500 Asiatics and 30,000 non-native Africans. Estimate (2002), 4,785,000; density, 67 per sq. km. In 2001, 62·7% of the population were rural.

The UN gives a projected population for 2010 of 5·86m.

The capital is Freetown, with 822,000 inhabitants in 1999.

Sierra Leone is divided into four provinces:

	Sq. km	*Census 1985*	*Capital*	*Estimate 1988*
Eastern Province	15,553	960,551	Kenema	13,000
Northern Province	35,936	1,262,226	Makeni	12,000
Southern Province	19,694	740,510	Bo	26,000
Western Province	557	554,243	Freetown	469,776

The provinces are divided into districts as follows: Bo, Bonthe, Moyamba, Pujehun (Southern Province); Kailahun, Kenema, Kono (Eastern Province); Bombali, Kambia, Koinaduga, Port Loko, Toukolili (Northern Province).

The principal peoples are the Mendes (34% of the total) in the south, the Temnes (31%) in the north and centre, the Konos, Fulanis, Bulloms, Korankos, Limbas and Kissis. English is the official language; a Creole (Krio) is spoken.

SOCIAL STATISTICS

Births, 1995, 201,000; deaths, 116,000. Rates (1995, per 1,000 population); birth, 47·8; death, 27·7. Annual population growth rate, 1992–02, 1·5%. Expectation of life at birth in 2001 was 35·8 years for females and 33·2 years for males, the lowest life expectancy for males of any country in the world. A World Health Organization report published in June 2000 ranked Sierra Leone in last place of all 191 sovereign countries in a 'healthy life expectancy' list, with an expected 25·9 years of healthy life for babies born in 1999. Infant mortality was 182 per 1,000 live births in 2001 (the highest in the world). Fertility rate, 2001, 6·5 births per woman.

CLIMATE

A tropical climate, with marked wet and dry seasons and high temperatures throughout the year. The rainy season lasts from about April to Nov., when humidity can be very high. Thunderstorms are common from April to June and in Sept. and Oct. Rainfall is particularly heavy in Freetown because of the effect of neighbouring relief. Freetown, Jan. 80°F (26·7°C), July 78°F (25·6°C). Annual rainfall 135" (3,434 mm).

CONSTITUTION AND GOVERNMENT

In a referendum in Sept. 1991 some 60% of the 2·5m. electorate voted for the introduction of a new constitution instituting multi-party democracy. There is a 124-seat *National Assembly* (112 members elected by popular vote and 12 filled by paramount chiefs).

There is a *Supreme Council of State (SCS)*, and a *Council of State Secretaries.*

National Anthem. 'High We Exalt Thee, Realm of the Free'; words by C. Nelson Fyle, tune by J. J. Akar.

RECENT ELECTIONS

Presidential and parliamentary elections were held on 14 May 2002. In the presidential election, incumbent Ahmad Tejan Kabbah won with 70·6% of the vote ahead of Ernest Koroma with 22·4% and Alimany Paolo Bangura with 1·7%. There were six other candidates. In parliamentary elections, Kabbah's Sierra Leone People's Party (SLPP) won 83 of the 112 seats with Koroma's All People's Congress taking 27 seats.

CURRENT ADMINISTRATION

President and Minister of Defence: Ahmed Tejan Kabbah; b. 1931 (SLPP; elected 17 March 1996 and re-elected in May 2002).

Vice-President: Solomon Berewa.

In March 2005 the government comprised:

Minister of Agriculture and Food Security: Sama Sahr Mondeh. *Country Planning, Forestry, Environment and Social Welfare:* Alfred Bobson Sesay. *Development and Economic Planning:* Mohamed Daramy. *Education, Science and Technology:* Alpha Wurie. *Energy and Power:* Emmanuel Grant. *Finance:* Joseph Dauda. *Foreign Affairs and International Co-operation:* Momodu Koroma. *Health and Sanitation:* Agnes Taylor-Lewis. *Information and Broadcasting:* Septimus Kaikai. *Internal Affairs:* Sam Hinga Norman. *Justice:* Eke Ahmed Halloway. *Labour, Industrial Relations and Social Security:* Alpha Timbo. *Local Government and Community Development:* Sidikie Brima. *Marine Resources:* Okere Adams. *Mineral Resources:* Mohamed Swarray Alhaji Deen. *Political and Parliamentary Affairs:* George Banda Thomas. *Social Welfare, Gender and Children's Affairs:* Shirley Yema Gbujama. *Trade and Industry:* Kadi Sesay. *Transport and Communications:* Prince Harding. *Works, Housing and Technical Maintenance:* Caiser Boima. *Youth and Sport:* Dennis Bright.

Government Website: http://www.sierra-leone.org/govt.html

DEFENCE

In 2003 military expenditure totalled US$17m. (US$3 per capita), representing 2·2% of GDP.

The UN peacekeeping force (UNAMSIL) numbered 11,278 troops and 241 military observers in Nov. 2003, making it one of the largest peacekeeping operation in the world at the time.

Army. Following the civil war, the Army has disbanded and a new National Army has been formed with a strength of some 13,000.

Navy. Based in Freetown there is a small naval force of 200 operating five patrol and coastal combatants.

INTERNATIONAL RELATIONS

Sierra Leone is a member of the UN, WTO, the African Union, African Development Bank, ECOWAS, IOM, OIC, Islamic Development Bank and the Commonwealth and is an ACP member state of the ACP-EU relationship.

ECONOMY

Agriculture accounted for 52·6% of GDP in 2002, industry 31·6% and services 15·7%.

Currency. The unit of currency is the *leone* (SLL) of 100 *cents*. Foreign exchange reserves were US$28m. in June 2002. Inflation was 2·2% in 2001, down from 36·0% in 1998, and there was then deflation in 2002, of 3·1%. Exchange controls were liberalized in 1993. Total money supply in June 2002 was 191,105m. leones.

Budget. In 1999 (year ending 31 Dec.) the government's total revenue was 85,819m. leones (77,199m. leones in 1998) and total expenditure was 252,884m. leones (147,052m. leones in 1998).

Performance. GNP per capita was US$200 in 1996 compared to US$390 in 1982. Real GDP growth was –0·8% in 1998, but the civil war resulted in the economy shrinking by 8·1% in 1999. There was positive growth in 2000 for the first time since 1994, with a rate of 3·8%, rising to 5·4% in 2001 and further to 6·3% in 2002. Total GDP in 2003 was US$0·8bn. Sierra Leone is among the world's bottom five countries in income and life expectancy.

Banking and Finance. The bank of issue is the Bank of Sierra Leone which was established 1964 (*Governor*, James Rogers). There are four commercial banks (two foreign).

ENERGY AND NATURAL RESOURCES

Environment. Carbon dioxide emissions from the consumption and flaring of fossil fuels in 2002 were the equivalent of 0·2 tonnes per capita. An *Environmental Sustainability Index* compiled for the World Economic Forum meeting in Feb. 2002 ranked Sierra Leone 134th in the world out of 142 countries analysed, with 36·5%. The index measured the ability of countries to maintain favourable environmental conditions and examined various factors including pollution levels and the use or abuse of natural resources.

Electricity. Installed capacity was 0·1m. kW in 2000. Production in 2000 was around 246m. kWh; consumption per capita in 2000 was an estimated 56 kWh.

Minerals. The chief minerals mined are diamonds (352,000 carats in 2002) and rutile (203,000 tonnes in 1994–95). There are also deposits of gold, iron ore and bauxite. The presence of rich diamond deposits partly explains the close interest of neighbouring countries in the politics of Sierra Leone.

Agriculture. Agriculture engaged 61% of the workforce in 2002, mainly in small-scale peasant production. Cattle production is important in the north. Production (2000 estimates, in 1,000 tonnes): cassava, 241; rice, 199; palm oil, 36; plantains, 28; sweet potatoes, 28; sugarcane, 21. In 2001 there were 500,000 ha of arable land and 64,000 ha of permanent crops.

Livestock (2000): cattle, 420,000; goats, 200,000; sheep, 365,000; pigs, 52,000; chickens, 6m.

Forestry. In 2000 forests covered 1,055,000 ha, or 14·7% of the total land area. Timber production in 2001 was 5·49m. cu. metres.

Fisheries. In 2001, 75,210 tonnes of fish were caught (61,210 tonnes from marine waters).

INDUSTRY

There are palm oil and rice mills; sawn timber, joinery products and furniture are produced.

Labour. The workforce was 1,610,000 in 1996 (64% males). In 1995 around two-thirds of the economically active population were engaged in agriculture, fisheries and forestry. 14,800 persons were registered unemployed in 1992.

INTERNATIONAL TRADE

Foreign debt was US$1,448m. in 2002.

Imports and Exports. Total trade for 2001: imports, 371·5bn. leones; exports, 57·9bn. leones. Main exports are bauxite, diamonds, gold, coffee and cocoa. A UN-mandated diamond export certification scheme is in force. The Security Council has commended Sierra Leone's government for its efforts in monitoring trade to prevent diamonds from becoming a future source of conflict.

The main import suppliers in 2001 were UK (25·3%), Netherlands (10·1%), USA (7·9%), Germany (6·3%). Principal export markets in 2001 were Belgium (40·6%), USA (9·1%), UK (8·5%), Germany (7·8%).

COMMUNICATIONS

Roads. There were 11,300 km of roads in 2002, of which 8·0% were surfaced. In 2002 there were 11,353 passenger cars and 3,565 vans and trucks. There were 66 deaths as a result of road accidents in 1999.

Civil Aviation. Freetown Airport (Lungi) is the international airport. In 2003 Sierra National Airlines flew to Banjul and London. Other international carriers operated flights to Abidjan, Accra, Brussels, Conakry, Dakar, Lagos and Monrovia. In 1999 scheduled airline traffic of Sierra Leone-based carriers flew 0·3m. km, carrying 19,000 passengers (all on international flights).

Shipping. The port of Freetown has a very large natural harbour. Iron ore is exported through Pepel, and there is a small port at Bonthe. In 2002 the merchant fleet totalled 23,000 GRT. 2·31m. tonnes of cargo were loaded in 1993 and 0·59m. tonnes discharged.

Telecommunications. In 2001 Sierra Leone had 49,600 telephone subscribers (10·1 per 1,000 population) and in 1999 there were 2,500 fax machines. The country's telecommunications network was virtually destroyed during the civil war, and reconstruction and modernization is regarded as a matter of extreme urgency. In 2002 Sierra Leone had 8,000 Internet users. In 2002 there were 66,300 mobile phone subscribers.

Postal Services. In 1995 there were 54 post offices.

SOCIAL INSTITUTIONS

Justice. The High Court has jurisdiction in civil and criminal matters. Subordinate courts are held by magistrates in the various districts. Native Courts, headed by court Chairmen, apply native law and custom under a criminal and civil jurisdiction. Appeals from the decisions of magistrates' courts are heard by the High Court. Appeals from the decisions of the High Court are heard by the Sierra Leone Court of Appeal. Appeal lies from the Sierra Leone Court of Appeal to the Supreme Court which is the highest court.

The death penalty is in force, and 24 soldiers were executed on 19 Oct. 1998 for their part in the May 1997 coup.

Religion. There were 2·49m. Muslims in 2001. Traditional animist beliefs persist; there is also a Christian minority.

Education. The adult literacy rate in 1998 was 31·0%. Primary education is partially free but not compulsory. In 2001–02 there were 2,704 primary schools with 554,308 pupils and 14,932 teachers. In 2000–01 there were 246 secondary schools with 107,776 pupils and 5,264 teachers, and 9,660 students and 1,321 staff at teacher training institutions. There were also 174 technical/vocational establishments with 49,488 pupils and 2,514 staff. There were five institutes of higher education in 1992–93 with 4,742 students and 600 teachers. Fourah Bay College and Njala University College are the two constituent colleges of the University of Sierra Leone. They had 2,571 students and 257 academic staff in 1990–91.

In 1998–99 total expenditure on education came to 1·0% of GNP.

Health. In 1996 there were 339 physicians, 19 dentists, 1,532 nurses and 218 midwives. In 1998 there were 218 hospitals, with the equivalent of eight beds per 10,000 population. In the period 1990–98 only 34% of the population had access to safe drinking water.

CULTURE

Broadcasting. Broadcasting is under the auspices of the government-controlled Sierra Leone Broadcasting Service and Sierra Leone Television, which is part commercial. There were 65,000 TV sets (colour by PAL) in 2001 and 1·14m. radio sets in 2000.

Press. In Jan. 2001 there were 2 daily newspapers (*Concord Times* and *For di People*), 13 weekly papers, 11 twice weekly newspapers and 6 other newspapers. Many published irregularly. The state-owned *Sierra News* had the highest circulation (5,000), followed by *For di People* (4,500). Most newspapers were founded in the 1990s.

Tourism. In 2000 there were 10,000 foreign tourists, bringing revenue of US$12m.

DIPLOMATIC REPRESENTATIVES

Of Sierra Leone in the United Kingdom (Oxford Circus House, 245 Oxford Street, London, W1R 1LF)
High Commissioner: Sulaiman Tejan-Jalloh.

Of the United Kingdom in Sierra Leone (Spur Rd, Freetown)
High Commissioner: Dr John Mitchiner.

Of Sierra Leone in the USA (1701 19th St., NW, Washington, D.C., 20009)
Ambassador: Ibrahim M. Kamara.

Of the USA in Sierra Leone (Corner Walpole and Siaka Stevens St., Freetown)
Ambassador: Thomas N. Hull.

Of Sierra Leone to the United Nations
Ambassador: Joe Robert Pemagbi.

Of Sierra Leone to the European Union
Ambassador: Fode Maclean Dabor.

FURTHER READING

Binns, Margaret and J. Anthony, *Sierra Leone.* [Bibliography] ABC-Clio, Oxford and Santa Barbara (CA), 1992

Conteh-Morgan, E. and Dixon-Fyle, M., *Sierra Leone at the End of the Twentieth Century: History, Politics, and Society.* Peter Lang Publishing, Berne, 1999

Ferme, M., *The Underneath of Things: Violence, History, and the Everyday in Sierra Leone.* Univ. of California Press, 2001

National statistical office: Statistics Sierra Leone, A. J. Momoh Street, Tower Hill, P.M.B. 595, Freetown.
Website: http://www.statistics-sierra-leone.org

SINGAPORE

Republic of Singapore

Population projection, 2010: 4·57m.
GDP per capita, 2002: (PPP$) 24,040
HDI/world rank: 0·902/25

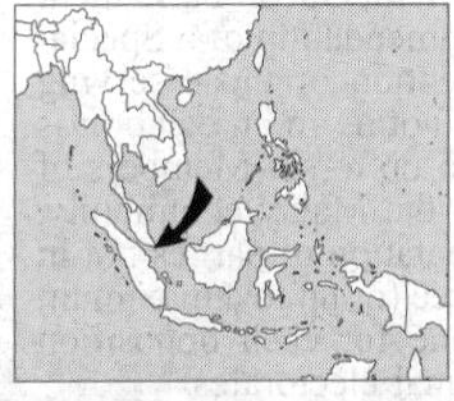

KEY HISTORICAL EVENTS

Singapore Island became part of the Javanese Majapahit Empire in the 14th century. The Portuguese took control of the area in the 16th century, followed by the Dutch a hundred years later. In 1819 Sir Thomas Stamford Raffles, the British East India Administrator, established a trading settlement. The lease to the British East India Company by the Sultan of Johore was followed by the treaty of 2 Aug. 1824 ceding the entire island in perpetuity to the company. In 1826 Penang, Melaka and Singapore were combined as the Straits Settlements. With the opening of the Suez Canal in 1869 and the advent of the steamship, an era of prosperity began for Singapore. Growth continued with the export of tin and rubber from the Malay peninsula.

Singapore fell to the Japanese in 1942 whose occupation continued until the end of the Second World War. In 1945 Singapore became a Crown Colony, being separated from Penang and Melaka. In June 1959 the state was granted internal self-government. When the Federation of Malaysia was formed in Sept. 1963, Singapore became one of the 14 states of the newly created country. On 7 Aug. 1965, by agreement with the Malaysian government, Singapore left the Federation of Malaysia and became an independent sovereign state.

TERRITORY AND POPULATION

The Republic of Singapore consists of Singapore Island and some 63 smaller islands. Singapore Island is situated off the southern extremity of the Malay peninsula, to which it is joined by a 1·1 km causeway carrying a road, railway and water pipeline across the Strait of Johor and by a 1·9 km bridge at Tuas, opened on 2 Jan. 1998. The Straits of Johor between the island and the mainland are 914 metres wide. The island is 682·3 sq. km in area, including the offshore islands.

Census of population (2000): Chinese residents 2,505,379 (76·8%), Malays 453,633 (13·9%), Indians 257,791 (7·9%) and others 46,406 (1·4%); resident population, 3,263,209. Total population in June 2001 was 4,131,200. The population is 100% urban. Population density, 6,055 per sq. km.

The UN gives a projected resident population for 2010 of 4·57m.

Malay, Chinese (Mandarin), Tamil and English are the official languages; Malay is the national language and English is the language of administration.

SOCIAL STATISTICS

2002 births, 40,864; deaths, 15,815. Birth rate per 1,000 population, 2002, 11·4; death rate, 4·4. Annual population growth rate, 1992–02, 2·8%; infant mortality, 2000, 3·3 per 1,000 live births (one of the lowest in the world); life expectancy, 2001, 75·7 years for males and 80·0 years for females. Fertility rate, 2001, 1·5 births per woman. In 1998 the most popular age for marrying was 25–29 for both men and women.

CLIMATE

The climate is equatorial, with relatively uniform temperature, abundant rainfall and high humidity. Rain falls throughout the year but tends to be heaviest from Nov. to Jan. Average daily temperature is 26·8°C with a maximum daily average of 30·9°C and a minimum daily average of 23·9°C. Mean annual rainfall is 2,345 mm.

CONSTITUTION AND GOVERNMENT

Singapore is a republic with a parliamentary system of government. The organs of state—the executive, the legislature and the judiciary—are provided for by a written constitution. The Constitution is the supreme law of Singapore and any law enacted after the date of its commencement, which is inconsistent with its provisions, is void.

The Head of State is the *President*. The administration of the government is vested in the Cabinet headed by the *Prime Minister*. The Prime Minister and the other Cabinet Members are appointed by the President from among the Members of Parliament (MPs). The Cabinet is collectively responsible to Parliament.

Parliament is unicameral consisting of 84 elected members and one Non-Constituency MP (NCMP), elected by secret ballot from single-member and group representation constituencies as well as nine Nominated Members of Parliament (NMPs) who are appointed for a two-year term on the recommendation of a Special Select Committee of Parliament. With the customary exception of those serving criminal sentences, all citizens over 21 are eligible to vote. Voting in an election is compulsory. Group representation constituencies may return up to six Members of Parliament (four before 1996), one of whom must be from the Malay community, the Indian or other minority communities. To ensure representation of parties not in the government, provision is made for the appointment of three (or up to a maximum of six) NCMPs. The number of NCMPs is reduced by one for each opposition candidate returned. There is a common roll without communal electorates.

A Presidential Council to consider and report on minorities' rights was established in 1970. The particular function of this council is to draw attention to any Bill or to any subsidiary legislation which, in its opinion, discriminates against any racial or religious community.

National Anthem. 'Majulah Singapura' ('Onward Singapore'); words and tune by Zubir Said.

RECENT ELECTIONS

A parliamentary election was scheduled to take place on 3 Nov. 2001, but the ruling People's Action Party (PAP) won by default as it was unopposed in 55 of the 84 seats when nominations for the election closed. Nevertheless, voting did take place as a formality, and following the election and the appointment of members by the president the PAP held 82 of the 90 seats.

Presidential elections were scheduled for 24 Aug. 1999. However, these were cancelled after S. R. Nathan emerged as the only candidate who satisfied the requirements of the certificate of eligibility. He thus gained the presidency unopposed.

CURRENT ADMINISTRATION

President: S. R. Nathan; b. 1924 (sworn in 1 Sept. 1999).

In March 2005 the cabinet comprised:

Prime Minister: Lee Hsien Loong; b. 1952 (PAP; sworn in 12 Aug. 2004).

Senior Minister, Prime Minister's Office: Lee Kuan Yew, GCMG, CH. *Deputy Prime Ministers:* Prof. Shunmugam Jayakumar (*Minister of Law*); Dr Tony Tan Keng Yam (*Co-ordinating Minister for Security and Defence*).

Minister of Health: Khaw Boon Wan. *Information, Communications and the Arts:* Dr Lee Boon Yang. *Education:* Tharman Shanmugaratnam. *Foreign Affairs:* BG (NS) George Yong-Boon Yeo. *Manpower:* Dr Ng Eng Hen (also *Second Minister for Education*). *Defence:* RAdm (NS) Teo Chee Hean. *Home Affairs:* Wong Kan Seng. *Community Development and Sports (acting):* Vivian Balakrishnan. *Environment and Water Resources:* Dr Yaacob Ibrahim (also *in Charge of Muslim Affairs*). *Transport:* Yeo Cheow Tong. *National Development:* Mah Bow Tan. *Trade and Industry:* Lim Hng Kiang. *Ministers in Prime Minister's Office:* Lim Boon Heng, Lim Swee Say (also *Second Minister for National Development*).

Government Website: http://www.gov.sg

DEFENCE

Compulsory military service in peacetime for all male citizens and permanent residents was introduced in 1967. The period of service for officers and non-commissioned officers is 30 months, other ranks 24 months. Reserve liability continues to age 50 for officers, 40 for other ranks. In 2000 the SAF (Singapore Armed Forces) comprised 350,000 Operationally Ready National Servicemen and an estimated 60,000 regulars and full-time National Servicemen.

An agreement with the USA in Nov. 1990 provided for an increase in US use of naval and air force facilities.

Singapore is a member of the Five Powers Defence Arrangement, with Australia, New Zealand, Malaysia and the UK.

In 2003 defence expenditure totalled US$4,741m. (US$1,116 per capita), representing 5·2% of GDP.

Army. Strength (2000) 50,000 (including 35,000 conscripts) plus 260,000 reserves. In addition there is a Civil Defence Force totalling over 87,000 including 3,720 conscripts, 23,000 Operationally Ready National Servicemen and 55,146 civil defence volunteers.

Navy. The Republic of Singapore Navy comprises four commands: Fleet, Coastal Command (COSCOM), Naval Logistics Command and Training Command. The fleet includes four diesel submarines. The Navy numbers an estimated 9,600 personnel including approximately 6,000 conscripts and 3,600 regulars. There are two naval bases: Tuas Naval Base and Changi Naval Base, the first phase of which was completed in 2000 and replaces Brani Naval Base.

Air Force. The Republic of Singapore Air Force (RSAF) has fighter squadrons comprising the F16 Falcon and the F5S/F Tiger.

Personnel strength (2000) about 13,500 (3,000 conscripts), with 165 combat aircraft and 20 armed helicopters.

INTERNATIONAL RELATIONS

Singapore is a member of the UN, BIS, WTO, the Commonwealth, Asian Development Bank, Colombo Plan and ASEAN and has ratified the Convention on the Prohibition of the Development, Production, Stockpiling and Use of Chemical Weapons and on their Destruction (CWC), and the UN Framework Convention on Climate Change (UNFCCC).

ECONOMY

Manufacturing (14%), transport and communications (7%), and wholesale and trade (7%) were the main engines for growth in 1999. Services accounted for 64% of GDP in 2000, goods producing industries 33% and owner-occupied dwellings 3·2%.

According to the anti-corruption organization *Transparency International*, Singapore ranked 5th in the world in a 2004 survey of the countries with the least corruption in business and government. It received 9·3 out of 10 in the annual index.

Overview. The central objective is to build up a strong science and technology base to support high-tech industries and to exploit new products and processes, with special emphasis on the life sciences. The government recognizes the need for Singapore to adopt information technology (IT) to remain competitive.

The Economic Development Board (EDB) is the leading government agency responsible for the implementation of economic and industrial development strategies. Its purpose is to develop Singapore into a global city with total business capabilities by attracting foreign investments and developing local enterprise as well as promoting outward investments into the region. Under its Industry 21 plan, the EDB's focus will be on developing Singapore into a global hub of knowledge-driven industries.

Currency. The unit of currency is the *Singapore dollar* (SGD) of 100 *cents*. Total money supply in June 2002 was S$34,888m. There was inflation in 2001 of 1·0%, deflation of 0·4% in 2002 and then inflation of 0·5% in 2003. Total foreign reserves at June 2002 were S$79,668m.

Budget. The fiscal year begins on 1 April. Budgetary central government revenue and expenditure for financial years (in S$1m.):

	1998	*1999*	*2000*	*2001*
Revenue	42,137	43,046	47,427	41,694
Expenditure	24,562	25,203	26,610	30,183

Singapore has the largest current account surplus of any country in relation to the size of its economy, standing at S$36·4bn. in 1999, representing 24% of GNP.

Performance. Real GDP growth was 9·7% in 2000. A recession followed in 2001 as Singapore was hit by the worldwide economic downturn, with the economy contracting by 1·9%. There was then a recovery, with real GDP growth in 2002 of 2·2% and 2003 of 1·1%. Total GDP was US$91·3bn. in 2003. Singapore was placed seventh in the world in the Growth Competitiveness Index in the World Economic Forum's *Global Competitiveness Report 2004–05*. It had been first in 1999. In the 2004 *World Competitiveness Yearbook*, compiled by the International Institute for Management Development, Singapore came top in the ranking for countries with a population of less than 20m.

Banking and Finance. The Monetary Authority of Singapore (*Governor*, Goh Chok Tong) performs the functions of a central bank, except the issuing of currency which is the responsibility of the Board of the Commissioners of Currency.

The Development Bank of Singapore and the Post Office Savings Bank were merged in 1998 to become the largest bank in South-East Asia and one of the leading banks in Asia, with a customer base of more that 3·3m. and a total deposit base of about S$71bn. Together, their total asset value is approximately S$94·5bn.

In April 2004 there were 115 commercial banks in Singapore, of which five were local. There were 49 representative offices, 23 foreign banks with full licences, 37 with 'wholesale' licences and 50 with 'offshore' licences. The total assets/liabilities amounted to S$384,600m. in Dec. 2001. Total deposits of non-bank customers in Dec. 1999 amounted to S$174,454·1m. and advances including bills financing totalled S$147,185·5m. in 1999. There were 66 merchant banks as at 31 Dec. 1999.

The Singapore Exchange (SGX), a merger of the Stock Exchange of Singapore and the Singapore International Monetary Exchange, was officially launched on 1 Dec. 1999.

ENERGY AND NATURAL RESOURCES

Environment. Singapore's carbon dioxide emissions from the consumption and flaring of fossil fuels in 2002 were the equivalent of 27·2 tonnes per capita.

Electricity. In 1995 Singapore Power Pte. Ltd. took over from the Public Utilities Board the responsibility for the provision of electricity and gas. Electrical power is generated by five gas and oil-fired power stations, with a total generating capacity of 7,657m. kW (2001). Production (2001) 33,061m. kWh. Consumption per capita (2000) 8,800 kWh.

Oil and Gas. Replacing the Kallang Gasworks, the Senoko Gasworks started operations in Oct. 1996. It had a total gas production capacity of 1·6m. cu. metres per day. In Jan. 2001 a 640-km gas pipeline linking Indonesia's West Natuna field with Singapore came on stream. It is expected to provide Singapore with US$8bn. worth of natural gas over a 20-year period.

Water. Singapore uses an average of 1·25m. cu. metres of water per day. Singapore's water supply comes from local sources and sources in Johor, Malaysia. The total water supply system comprises 19 raw water reservoirs, nine treatment works, 15 storage or service reservoirs and 5,150 km of pipelines.

Agriculture. Only about 1·49% of the total area is used for farming. Local farms provide only about 35% of hen eggs, 1·6% of chickens and 2·4% of ducks. 18,928 tonnes of vegetables and fruits were produced for domestic consumption in 1999. In 2001 alone Singapore imported 44·1m. chickens, 7m. ducks, 722m. hen eggs, 210,077 tonnes of meat and meat products, 226,126 tonnes of fish and fish products, 352,919 tonnes of vegetables and 358,595 tonnes of fruits for local consumption.

Agro-technology parks house large-scale intensive farms to improve production of fresh food. As of the end of 2000, a total of 1,465 ha of land in Murai, Sungei Tengah, Nee Soon, Loyang, Mandai and Lim Chu Kang had been developed into Agro-technology Parks. Through open tenders, auctions and direct allocations, 247 farms have been allocated 777 ha of land for the production of livestock, eggs, milk, aquarium fish, food fish (fish for consumption), fruits, vegetables, orchids and ornamental and aquatic plants, as well as for the breeding of birds and dogs. When the Agro-technology Parks are fully developed, their output is expected to reach S$450m.

Forestry. In 2000 forests covered 2,000 ha, or 3·3% of the total land area.

Fisheries. The total local supply of fish in 2001 was 3,342 tonnes. Singapore imported 241,000 tonnes of fish and fish products. There are 93 fish processing establishments supplying products for the domestic market, nine establishments for the EU export market and 88 licensed marine farms.

INDUSTRY

The leading companies by market capitalization in Singapore in May 2004 were: Singapore Telecommunications (US$23·4bn.); DBS Group Holdings (US$12·2bn.), a banking group; and the United Overseas Bank (US$11·9bn.).

The largest industrial area is at Jurong, with 35 modern industrial estates housing over 4,036 establishments (engaging ten people or more) in 1999, and 340,907 workers.

Production, 1999 (in S$1m.), totalled 134,533: including electronic products, 70,140·4; chemicals and chemical products, 13,684·1; petroleum, 13,621·6; fabricated metal products, 6,253·9; transport equipment, 5,772·8; food, beverages and tobacco, 3,407·2; publishing, printing and reproduction of recorded media, 2,997·0.

Labour. In 2001 Singapore's labour force comprised 2,119,700 people, of whom 72,900 were unemployed. The majority were employed in community, social and personal services, (436,300 in 1999); manufacturing, 395,600; wholesale and retail trade, 278,900; transport, storage and communications, 203,700; business and real estate, 196,800. In 1998, 25% of the active workforce were foreign workers, up from 12% in 1992. The economic crisis, which started in late 1997, saw a net job loss of approximately 23,400 in 1998. However, in 1999 total employment registered a positive gain of 41,900, which occurred in all major sectors, including the service industries (55,400) and manufacturing (4,600), except for the construction sector which lost 18,300. The unemployment rate averaged 3·3% throughout 2001, compared to the 9-year steady of 2% from 1988–97.

Legislation regulates the principal terms and conditions of employment such as hours of work, sick leave and other fringe benefits. Young people of 14–16 years may work in industrial establishments, and children of 12–14 years may be employed in approved apprenticeship schemes. A trade dispute may be referred to the Industrial Arbitration Court.

The Ministry of Manpower operates an employment service and provides the handicapped with specialized on-the-job training. The Central Provident Fund was established in 1955 to make provision for employees in their old age. At the end of 1999 there were 2,828,000 members with S$88,397m. standing to their credit in the fund. The legal retirement age is 62.

Trade Unions. In 2001 there were 71 registered employee trade unions, three employer unions and one federation of trade unions—the National Trades Union Congress (NTUC). The total membership of the trade unions increased from 272,769 in 1998 to 338,311 in 2001. The vast majority (99%) of the total union membership belonged to the 69 NTUC-affiliated unions. The largest union, the United Workers of Electronic Industries (UWEEI), had 39,508 members in 2000.

INTERNATIONAL TRADE

Foreign investment of up to 40% of the equity of domestic banks is permitted. Total external trade in 2001 was S$425·7bn.

Imports and Exports. Total imports declined from S$232,175m. in 2000 to S$207,692m. in 2001. Exports also declined, from S$237,826m. in 2000 to S$218,026m. in 2001. In 2000 exports reached over 150% of GDP, with exports to Malaysia worth around 27% of GDP.

Imports and exports (in S$1m.), by country, 1999:

	Imports (c.i.f.)	*Exports (f.o.b.)*
Australia	2,464	5,373
China	9,649	6,643
France	4,397	3,709
Germany	6,111	5,522
Hong Kong	5,400	14,915
Italy	2,026	734
Japan	31,325	14,421
Korea (South)	7,063	6,027
Malaysia	29,283	32,164
Saudi Arabia	5,536	547

	Imports (c.i.f.)	*Exports (f.o.b.)*
Taiwan	7,540	9,477
Thailand	8,889	8,536
UK	4,623	7,247
USA	32,044	37,215

The major export markets for 2000 were Malaysia (18%), USA (17%), European Union (13%), Hong Kong (8%) and Japan (7%).

Exports (1999, in S$1m.): machinery and transport equipment, 128,807; mineral fuels, 15,335; chemicals and chemical products, 15,326; manufactured goods, 8,445; food, beverages and tobacco, 4,934; crude materials, 1,562; animal and vegetable oils, 483; miscellaneous manufactured articles, 16,414; miscellaneous transactions necessary, 2,984.

Imports (1999, in S$1m.): machinery and transport equipment, 113,365; mineral fuels, 17,075; manufactured goods, 14,973; chemicals and chemical products, 11,212; food, beverages and tobacco, 6,948; crude materials, 1,471; animal and vegetable oils, 504; miscellaneous manufactured articles, 19,575; miscellaneous transactions necessary, 3,019.

In May 2003 the US and Singapore signed a free trade agreement removing tariffs on trade worth an estimated US$33bn. per annum.

Trade Fairs. Singapore ranked as the world's 5th most important convention city in 2002, and the leading convention city in Asia, according to the Union des Associations Internationales (UAI). In 1999 Singapore hosted 140 meetings recognized by UAI, 2,314 incentive groups, 880 conventions and CommunicAsia, Asia Pacific's largest communications and IT event. The number of conferences with more than 1,000 delegates had doubled in 2000 over the previous year to ten.

COMMUNICATIONS

Roads. In 2002 there were 3,130 km of public roads (100% asphalt-paved). Singapore has one of the densest road networks in the world. In 2002 there were 404,274 private cars, 12,707 buses and 131,437 motorcycles and scooters.

Rail. A 25·8-km main line runs through Singapore, connecting with the States of Malaysia and as far as Bangkok. Branch lines serve the port of Singapore and the industrial estates at Jurong. The total rail length of the Mass Rapid Transit (SMRT) metro is 89·4 km. The 20 km North-East Line (operated by SBS Transit), the world's first fully automated heavy metro, became operational in 2003. In late 1999 the Light Rapid Transit System (LRT) began operations, linking the Bukit Panjang Estate with Choa Chu Kang in the North West region.

Civil Aviation. As of Dec. 2001 Singapore Changi Airport was served by 61 airlines with more than 3,200 weekly flights to and from 138 cities in 50 countries. The national airline is Singapore Airlines, which in 1999 carried 14,527,200 passengers and flew 313·6m. km. Its subsidiary, Silk Air, serves Asian destinations. A total of 28,093,759 passengers were handled in 2001, and 1,507,062 tonnes of freight.

Shipping. Singapore has a large container port, the world's busiest in terms of shipping tonnage in 2001 and second only to Hong Kong in terms of containers handled. The economy is dependent on shipping and entrepôt trade. A total of 146,265 vessels of 960m. gross tonnes (GT) entered Singapore during 2001. In 2001, 3,353 vessels with a total of 23·2m. GT were registered in Singapore. The Singapore merchant fleet ranked 7th among the principal merchant fleets of the world in 2001. Total cargo handled in 2000 was 326·11m. tonnes, and total container throughput in 2001 was 15,570,000 TEUs (twenty-foot equivalent units), ranking Singapore second behind Hong Kong on container traffic.

Telecommunications. In Dec. 2001 there were 1,948,500 telephone lines (penetration rate of 485 per 1,000 population), 2,858,800 mobile phone subscribers and 481,600 pager subscribers. In 1997 Singapore Telecom, one of the largest companies in Asia, lost its monopoly with the entry of a new mobile phone operator and three new paging operators. Singapore had three mobile phone operators, six Internet service providers, and three paging operators as of Feb. 2001. In April 2002 there were 2·31m. Internet users, or 51·84% of the population. In Aug. 2000, 42% of households were Internet subscribers. The Telecommunication Authority of

Singapore (TAS) is the national regulator and promoter of the telecommunication and postal industries. As of Nov. 1999 PC penetration in homes had reached 59% of the population. In 2001 there were 2·1m. PCs or 508·3 per 1,000 inhabitants.

Postal Services. In 1999 there were various postal outlets in operation, comprising 62 main branches and 90 smaller branches. Various services included stamp vendors, postage label vending machines and Self-Service Automated Machines (SAM). A total of 1,487m. postal articles were handled in 1999. During the late 1990s mail volume increased by about 30m. items per year.

SOCIAL INSTITUTIONS

Justice. There is a Supreme Court in Singapore which consists of the High Court and the Court of Appeal. The Supreme Court is composed of a Chief Justice and 11 Judges. The High Court has unlimited original jurisdiction in both civil and criminal cases. The Court of Appeal is the final appellate court. It hears appeals from any judgement or order of the High Court in any civil matter. The Subordinate Courts consist of a total of 47 District and Magistrates' Courts, the Civil, the Family and Crime Registries, the Primary Dispute Resolution Centre, and the Small Claims Tribunal. The right of appeal to the UK Privy Council was abolished in 1994.

Penalties for drug trafficking and abuse are severe, including a mandatory death penalty. In 1994 there were 76 executions, although since then the average annual number has generally been declining—there were five confirmed executions in 2004.

The Technology Court was introduced in 1995 where documents were filed electronically. This process was implemented in Aug. 1998 in the Magistrates appeal and the Court of Appeal.

The population in penal institutions in 2002 (excluding those in drug rehabilitation centres) was 16,310 (388 per 100,000 of national population).

Religion. In 2001, 41·0% of the population were Buddhists and Taoists, 12·0% Muslims, 11·7% Christians and 3·2% Hindus; 0·5% belonged to other religions.

Education. The general literacy rate rose from 84% in 1980 to 92·5% in 2001 (male 96·4%; female 88·7%). Kindergartens are private and fee-paying. Compulsory primary state education starts at six years and culminates at 11 or 12 years with an examination which influences choice of secondary schooling. There are 17 autonomous and eight private fee-paying secondary schools. Tertiary education at 16 years is divided into three branches: junior colleges leading to university; four polytechnics; and ten technical institutes.

Statistics of schools in 2001.

	Schools	*Pupils*	*Teachers*
Primary schools	194	302,733	12,011
Secondary schools	162	187,858	9,491
Junior colleges and Centralized institutes	17	24,582	1,869

There are three universities: the National University of Singapore (established 1905) with 32,028 students in 2001–02, the Nanyang Technological University (established 1991) with 23,025 in 2001–02, and the Singapore Management University (established in 2000).

In 2000–01 total expenditure on education came to 3·5% of GNP and accounted for 23·6% of total government expenditure.

Health. There are 27 hospitals (five general hospitals, one community hospital, seven specialist hospitals/centres and 14 private), with 11,897 beds in 2001. In 2000 there were 5,577 doctors, 1,028 dentists, 16,611 registered nurses and midwives and 1,098 pharmacists.

The leading causes of death are cancer (4,238 deaths in 2000), heart disease (3,940) and pneumonia (1,794).

Welfare. The Central Provident Fund (CPF) was set up in 1955 to provide financial security for workers upon retirement or when they are no longer able to work. In 2001 there were 2,922,673 members with S$92,221m. standing to their credit in the Fund.

CULTURE

The National Arts Council (NAC) was established in 1991 to spearhead the development of the arts.

Broadcasting. The Television Corporation of Singapore broadcasts mainly English and Chinese programmes. Malay and Tamil programmes are offered on Suria and Central, two channels launched in Jan. 2000. A sports-only channel, Sportscity, was also launched in Jan. 2000. Colour is by PAL. There were 816,000 TV licences in 2001 and 2·70m. radio receivers in 2000. Cable subscribers numbered 302,000 in 2001.

Press. In 2001 there were ten daily newspapers, in four languages, with a total daily circulation of about 1·59m. copies. In 2000 a new newspaper, *Project Eyeball*, and two free commuter tabloids, *Streats* and *Today,* were launched. *Project Eyeball* was suspended in June 2001.

Tourism. There were 7,522,200 visitors in 2001. Most came from Indonesia, Japan, Malaysia, Australia, the UK, China, the USA and Taiwan. The total tourism receipts for 2001 came to S$9·16bn. The total number of gazetted hotels increased from 94 in 1997 to 101 in 2000, providing 30,700 rooms.

Festivals. Every Jan. or Feb. the Lunar New Year is celebrated. Other Chinese festivals include Qing Ming (a time for the remembrance of ancestors), Yu Lan Jie (Feast of the Hungry Ghosts) and the Mid-Autumn Festival (Mooncake or Lantern festival).

Muslims in Singapore celebrate Hari Raya Puasa (to celebrate the end of a month-long fast) and Hari Raya Haji (a day of prayer and commemoration of the annual Mecca pilgrimage). There are also Muharram (a New Year celebration) and Maulud (Prophet Muhammad's birthday).

Hindus celebrate the Tamil New Year in mid-April. Thaipusam is a penitential Hindu festival popular with Tamils; and Deepavali, the Festival of Lights, is celebrated by Hindus and Sikhs. Other festivals include Thimithi (a fire-walking ceremony) and Navarathiri (nine nights' prayer).

Buddhists observe Vesak Day, which commemorates the birth, enlightenment and Nirvana of the Buddha, and falls on the full moon day in May.

Christmas, Good Friday and Easter Sunday are also recognized.

DIPLOMATIC REPRESENTATIVES

Of Singapore in the United Kingdom (9 Wilton Crescent, London, SW1X 8SP)
High Commissioner: Michael Eng Cheng Teo.

Of the United Kingdom in Singapore (100 Tanglin Rd, Singapore 247919)
High Commissioner: Alan Collins, CMG.

Of Singapore in the USA (3501 International Pl., NW, Washington, D.C., 20008)
Ambassador: Chan Heng Chee.

Of the USA in Singapore (27 Napier Rd, Singapore 258508)
Ambassador: Franklin L. Lavin.

Of Singapore to the United Nations
Ambassador: Vanu Gopala Menon.

Of Singapore to the European Union
Ambassador: Walter Woon.

FURTHER READING

Department of Statistics. *Monthly Digest of Statistics.—Yearbook of Statistics.*
The Constitution of Singapore. Singapore, 1992
Information Division, Ministry of Information and the Arts. *Singapore* [*year*]: a Review of [*the previous year*].
Ministry of Trade and Industry, *Economic Survey of Singapore.* (Quarterly and Annual)

Chew, E. C. T., *A History of Singapore.* Singapore, 1992
Huff, W. G., *Economic Growth of Singapore: Trade and Development in the Twentieth Century.* CUP, 1994
Myint, S., *The Principles of Singapore Law.* 2nd ed. Singapore, 1992
Tan, C. H., *Financial Markets and Institutions in Singapore.* 7th ed. Singapore, 1992
Vasil, R. K., *Governing Singapore.* Singapore, 1992

National library: National Library, Stamford Rd, Singapore 178896.
National statistical office: Department of Statistics, Minister of Trade and Industry, Singapore 179434.
Website: http://www.singstat.gov.sg

SLOVAKIA

Slovenská Republika

Capital: Bratislava
Population projection, 2010: 5·43m.
GDP per capita, 2002: (PPP$) 12,840
HDI/world rank: 0·842/42

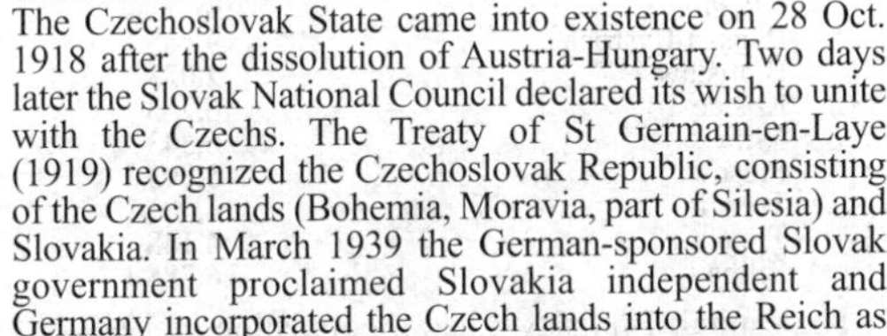

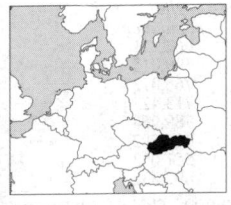

KEY HISTORICAL EVENTS

The Czechoslovak State came into existence on 28 Oct. 1918 after the dissolution of Austria-Hungary. Two days later the Slovak National Council declared its wish to unite with the Czechs. The Treaty of St Germain-en-Laye (1919) recognized the Czechoslovak Republic, consisting of the Czech lands (Bohemia, Moravia, part of Silesia) and Slovakia. In March 1939 the German-sponsored Slovak government proclaimed Slovakia independent and Germany incorporated the Czech lands into the Reich as the 'Protectorate of Bohemia and Moravia'. A government-in-exile, headed by Dr Edvard Beneš, was set up in London. Liberation by the Soviet Army and US Forces was completed by May 1945. Territories taken by the Germans, Poles and Hungarians were restored to Czechoslovak sovereignty. Elections were held in May 1946 following which a coalition government under a Communist Prime Minister, Klement Gottwald, remained in power until 20 Feb. 1948, when 12 of the non-Communist ministers resigned in protest against infiltration of Communists into the police. In Feb. a predominantly Communist government was formed by Gottwald. In May 1948 elections resulted in an 89% majority for the government and President Beneš resigned.

In 1968 pressure for liberalization culminated in the overthrow of the Stalinist leader, Antonín Novotný, and his associates. Under Alexander Dubček's leadership the 'Prague Spring' began to take shape and the outlines of a new political system described as 'socialism with a human face' began to appear as the Communist Party introduced an 'Action Programme' of far-reaching reforms. Soviet pressure to abandon this programme was exerted between May and Aug. 1968 and finally Warsaw Pact forces occupied Czechoslovakia on 21 Aug. The Czechoslovak government was compelled to accept a policy of 'normalization' (*i.e.*, abandonment of most reforms) and the stationing of Soviet forces.

Mass demonstrations demanding political reform began in Nov. 1989. After the authorities' use of violence to break up a demonstration on 17 Nov., the Communist leader resigned. On 30 Nov. the Federal Assembly abolished the Communist Party's sole right to govern, and a new Government was formed on 3 Dec. The protest movement continued to grow and on 10 Dec. another Government was formed. Gustáv Husák resigned as President and was replaced by Václav Havel on the unanimous vote of 323 members of the Federal Assembly on 29 Dec.

At the June 1992 elections the Movement for Democratic Slovakia led by Vladimír Mečiar campaigned on the issue of Slovak independence, and on 17 July the Slovak National Council adopted a declaration of sovereignty by 113 to 24 votes. President Havel resigned as Federal president on 20 July. On 1 Sept. 1992 the Slovak National Council adopted, by 114 votes to 16 with 4 abstentions (and a boycott by the Hungarian deputies), a Constitution for an independent Slovakia to come into being on 1 Jan. 1993. Economic property was divided between Slovakia and the Czech Republic in accordance with a Czechoslovakian law of 13 Nov. 1992. Government real estate became the property of the republic in which it was located. Other property was divided by specially-constituted commissions in the proportion of two (Czech Republic) to one (Slovakia) on the basis of population size. Military material was divided on the two:one principle. Regular military personnel were invited to choose which armed force they would serve in.

Slovakia became a member of NATO in March 2004 and the European Union in May 2004.

TERRITORY AND POPULATION

Slovakia is bounded in the northwest by the Czech Republic, north by Poland, east by Ukraine, south by Hungary and southwest by Austria. Its area is 49,034 sq. km

(18,932 sq. miles). Census population in 2001 was 5,379,455 (2,612,515 male, 2,766,940 female); density, 109·7 per sq. km.

The UN gives a projected population for 2010 of 5·43m.

In 2001, 57·6% of the population lived in urban areas. There are eight administrative regions *(Kraj)*, one of which is the capital, Bratislava. They have the same name as the main city of the region.

Region	*Area in sq. km*	*2001 population*
Banská Bystrica	9,455	662,121
Bratislava	2,053	599,015
Košice	6,753	766,012
Nitra	6,343	713,422
Prešov	8,993	789,968
Trenčin	4,501	605,582
Trnava	4,148	551,003
Žilina	6,788	692,332

The capital, Bratislava, had a population in 1999 of 460,000. The population of other principal towns (1997, in 1,000): Košice, 242; Prešov, 93; Nitra, 88; Žilina, 87; Banská Bystrica, 85; Trnava, 70; Trenčin, 61; Martin, 59.

The population is 85·8% Slovak, 9·7% Hungarian, 1·6% Roma and 0·8% Czech, with some Ruthenians, Ukrainians, Germans and Poles.

A law of Nov. 1995 makes Slovak the sole official language.

SOCIAL STATISTICS

Births, 2001, 51,136; deaths, 51,980; marriages, 23,795; divorces, 9,817. Rates (per 1,000 population), 2000: birth, 10·2; death, 9·8; marriage, 4·8; divorce, 1·7. Expectation of life, 2001, was 69·3 years for males and 77·2 for females. In 2001 the most popular age range for marrying was 25–29 for males and 20–24 for females. Annual population growth rate, 1992–02, 0·2%. Infant mortality, 2001 (per 1,000 live births), 8. Fertility rate, 2001, 1·3 births per woman.

CLIMATE

A humid continental climate, with warm summers and cold winters. Precipitation is generally greater in summer, with thunderstorms. Autumn, with dry, clear weather and spring, which is damp, are each of short duration. Bratislava, Jan. –0·7°C. June 19·1°C. Annual rainfall 649 mm.

CONSTITUTION AND GOVERNMENT

The constitution became effective on 1 Jan. 1993, creating a parliamentary democracy with universal suffrage from the age of 18. Parliament is the unicameral *National Council*. It has 150 members elected by proportional representation to serve four-year terms. The constitution was amended in Sept. 1998 to allow for the direct election of the *President*, who serves for a five-year term. The President may serve a maximum of two consecutive terms.

The Judicial Branch consists of a *Supreme Court*, whose judges are elected by the National Council, and a *Constitutional Court*, whose judges are appointed by the President from a group of nominees approved by the National Council.

Citizenship belongs to all citizens of the former federal Slovak Republic; other residents of five years standing may apply for citizenship. Slovakia grants dual citizenship.

National Anthem. 'Nad Tatrou sa blýska' ('Over the Tatras lightning flashes'); words by J. Matúška, tune anonymous.

RECENT ELECTIONS

Elections to the National Council were held on 20 and 21 Sept. 2002. Former prime minister Vladimír Mečiar's Movement for a Democratic Slovakia (HZDS) won 36 seats with 19·5% of votes cast—the HZDS became the LS-HZDS when it added the prefix 'The People's Party' in June 2003. The Slovak Democratic and Christian Union (SDKÚ) won 28 seats with 15·1%; the Direction Party (Smer), 25 with 13·5%; the Party of the Hungarian Coalition (SMK), 20 with 11·2%; the Christian Democratic Movement (KDH), 15 with 8·3%; the New Civic Alliance (ANO), 15 with 8·0%; and the Slovak Communist Party (KSS), 11 with 6·3%. Turn-out was 70·0%.

In the first round of presidential elections on 3 April 2004, former prime minister Vladimír Mečiar of the LS-HZDS won 32·7% of the vote, against 22·3% for Ivan Gašparovič (Movement for Democracy; HZD) and 22·1% for Eduard Kukan (SDKÚ). There were three other candidates. Turn-out was 47·9%. In the run-off held on 17 April Gašparovič won 59·9% against 40·1% for Mečiar.

European Parliament. Slovakia has 14 representatives. At the June 2004 elections turn-out was 16·7% (the lowest in the EU). The SDKÚ won 3 seats with 17·1% of votes cast (political affiliation in European Parliament: European People's Party–European Democrats); the LS-HZDS, 3 with 17·1% (non-attached); the Smer, 3 with 16·9% (Party of European Socialists); the KDH, 3 with 16·2% (European People's Party–European Democrats); the SMK, 2 with 13·2% (European People's Party–European Democrats).

CURRENT ADMINISTRATION

President: Ivan Gašparovič; b. 1941 (HZD; sworn in on 15 June 2004).

A coalition government was appointed on 15 Oct. 2002 composed of members of the Slovak Democratic and Christian Union (SDKÚ), the Party of the Hungarian Coalition (SMK), the Christian Democratic Movement (KDH) and the New Civic Alliance (ANO). In March 2005 the cabinet was composed as follows:

Prime Minister: Mikuláš Dzurinda; b. 1955 (SDKÚ; sworn in 30 Oct. 1998; re-appointed 15 Oct. 2002).

Deputy Prime Ministers: Daniel Lipšic (KDH; also *Minister of Justice*); Ivan Mikloš (SDKÚ; also *Minister of Finance*); Pavol Rusko (ANO; also *Minister of Economy*); Pál Csáky (SMK; *Responsible for European Integration, Human Rights and Minorities*).

Minister of Foreign Affairs: Eduard Kukan (SDKÚ). *Interior:* Vladimír Palko (KDH). *Defence:* Juraj Liška (SDKÚ). *Culture:* Rudolf Chmel (ANO). *Healthcare:* Rudolf Zajac (ANO). *Education:* Martin Fronc (KDH). *Labour, Social Affairs and Family Affairs:* Ľudovít Kaník (SDKÚ). *Environment:* László Miklós (SMK). *Agriculture:* Zsolt Simon (SMK). *Transport, Post and Telecommunications:* Pavol Prokopovič (SDKÚ). *Construction and Public Works:* László Gyurovszky (SMK).

The *Speaker* is Jozef Migas.

Office of the Prime Minister: http://www.government.gov.sk

DEFENCE

Conscription is for 12 months. In 2003 military expenditure totalled US$627m. (US$117 per capita), representing 1·9% of GDP.

Army. Personnel (2002), 13,000 (including 10,400 conscripts). In addition there are a border police of 1,700, 1,350 civil defence troops and 250 guard troops.

Air Force. There are 60 combat aircraft, including Su-22, Su-25, MiG-21 and MiG-29 fighters and 19 attack helicopters. Personnel (2002), 10,200.

INTERNATIONAL RELATIONS

Slovakia is a member of the UN, WTO, BIS, NATO, EU, Council of Europe, OSCE, OECD, CEFTA, CERN, CEI, Danube Commission, IOM and an associate partner of the WEU. A referendum held on 16–17 May 2003 approved accession to the EU, with 92·5% of votes cast for membership and 7·5% against. Turn-out was 52·2%. Slovakia became a member of NATO on 29 March 2004 and the EU on 1 May 2004.

Slovakia has had a long-standing dispute with Hungary over the Gabčíkovo-Nagymaros Project, involving the building of dam structures in both countries for the production of electric power, flood control and improvement of navigation on the Danube as agreed in a treaty signed in 1977 between Czechoslovakia and Hungary. In late 1998 Slovakia and Hungary signed a protocol easing tensions between the two nations and settling differences over the dam.

ECONOMY

Agriculture accounted for 4·0% of GDP in 2002, industry 28·6% and services 67·4%.

Overview. The economy has experienced high growth rates since 1998, driven by growing foreign direct investment (FDI). Real GDP is growing at approximately 4% per annum, private demand is strong and the export sector is expanding steadily. Membership of the EU since May 2004 is expected to reinforce this trend. Inflation remains high at 6–7% in 2004. Fiscal policy has been less successful; the fiscal deficit in 2002 reached 7·2% of GDP. In 2003 the new government was committed to fiscal consolidation and has resolved to reduce the government deficit below the Maastricht ceiling of 3% by 2006. The unemployment rate is high, at 17·1% in 2003. During the first years after independence in 1993, economic policies in Slovakia were misdirected—structural reforms were postponed and expansionary fiscal policies supported domestic consumption and employment. In 1998 economic policy shifted from state intervention to a policy of pro-market reforms. Following economic transition, the heavy industry and agriculture sectors shrank while the service sector increased its share of GDP to 61·4% in 2000.

Currency. The unit of currency is the *Slovak koruna* or crown (SKK) of 100 *haliers*, introduced on 8 Feb. 1993. The koruna was revalued 4% in May 1995. Foreign exchange reserves were US$4,420m. and gold reserves 1·13m. troy oz in June 2002. Inflation was 8·5% in 2003, up from 3·3% in 2002. Total money supply in Dec. 2001 was 225,566m. koruny.

Budget. Government revenue and expenditure (in 1m. koruny):

	1997	*1998*	*1999*	*2000*	*2001*
Revenue	265,146	274,677	315,436	325,402	331,649
Expenditure	290,026	303,952	317,447	368,407	386,901

VAT, personal and company income tax, real estate taxes and inheritance taxes came into force in Jan. 1993. VAT is 19% (since 1 Jan. 2004).

Performance. There was real GDP growth of 4·5% in 2003 and (provisional) 5·3% in 2004. Slovakia's total GDP in 2003 was US$31·9bn.

Banking and Finance. The central bank and bank of issue is the Slovak National Bank, founded in 1993 (*Governor,* Ivan Šramko). It has an autonomous statute modelled on the German Bundesbank, with the duties of maintaining control over monetary policy and inflation, ensuring the stability of the currency, and supervising commercial banks. However, it is now proposed to amend the central bank law to allow the government to appoint half the members of the board and force the bank to increase its financing of the budget deficit.

In Oct. 1998 the Slovak National Bank abandoned its fixed exchange rate system, whereby the crown's value was fixed within a fluctuation band against a number of currencies, and chose to float the currency.

Decentralization of the banking system began in 1991, and private banks began to operate. The two largest Slovak banks were both privatized in 2001. Erste BankÖsterreich bought an 87·18% stake in Slovenská Sporitel'ňa (Slovak Savings Bank) and the Italian bank IntesaBci bought a 94·47% stake in Všeobecná úverová banka (General Credit Bank). In 2000 Slovenská Sporitel'ňa had assets of US$3·3bn. and Všeobecná úverová banka US$2·8bn. In 2003 there were 13 commercial banks and 2 savings banks.

Foreign direct investment in Slovakia in 2000 totalled US$1,986·9m., more than the total amount in the previous seven years of the country's existence.

There is a stock exchange in Bratislava.

ENERGY AND NATURAL RESOURCES

Environment. Slovakia's carbon dioxide emissions from the consumption and flaring of fossil fuels in 2002 were the equivalent of 7·2 tonnes per capita.

Electricity. Installed capacity in 2002 was 7·4m. kW, of which 2·3m. kW is hydro-electric and 2·2m. kW nuclear. Production in 2000 was 31·99bn. kWh, with consumption per capita 5,425 kWh. There were six nuclear reactors in use in 2003. In 2002 about 65% of electricity was nuclear-generated, a percentage exceeded only in Lithuania and France.

Oil and Gas. In 2002 natural gas reserves were 14bn. cu. metres and oil reserves 9m. bbls. Natural gas production in 2000 amounted to 163m. cu. metres. Slovakia is a net energy importer, relying heavily on Russia for its oil and gas.

Minerals. In 2000, 3·65m. tonnes of lignite were produced. 477,000 tonnes of iron ore were extracted in 2000. There are also reserves of copper, lead, zinc, limestone, dolomite, rock salt and others.

Agriculture. In 2001 there were 1·45m. ha of arable land and 126,000 ha of permanent crops. In 1998 agriculture employed 6·4% of the workforce.

A federal law of May 1991 returned land seized by the Communist regime to its original owners, to a maximum of 150 ha of arable to a single owner.

Production, 2000 (in 1,000 tonnes): wheat, 1,254; sugarbeets, 961; maize, 440; potatoes, 419; barley, 397; rapeseed, 134; sunflower seeds, 117; cabbages, 99; apples, 81; tomatoes, 73; rye, 64; grapes, 61.

Livestock, 2000: cattle, 665,000; pigs, 1·56m.; sheep, 340,000; chickens, 12m. Livestock products, 2000 (in 1,000 tonnes): meat, 303; milk, 1,116; eggs, 65; cheese, 54.

Forestry. The area under forests in 2000 was 2·18m. ha, or 45·3% of the total land area. In 2001 timber production was 5·24m. cu. metres.

Fisheries. In 2001 the total catch was 1,531 tonnes, exclusively freshwater fish.

INDUSTRY

The main industries in Slovakia are chemical products, machinery, electrical apparatus, textiles, clothing and footwear, metal and metal products, food and beverages, paper, earthenware and ceramics. Industry accounted for 31·8% of GDP in 2001, with manufacturing contributing 23·3%. 2002 output included (in 1m. tonnes): crude steel, 4·3; pig iron, 3·5; cement (2001), 3·1; distillate fuel oil (2000), 2·1; coke (1999), 1·6; residual fuel oil (2000), 0·5. Motor vehicle production (2002), 226,000 units. The car-manufacturing sector accounts for a quarter of Slovakia's economy.

Labour. Out of 2,123,700 people in employment in 2001, 553,600 were in manufacturing, 255,700 in wholesale and retail trade/repair of motor vehicles, motorcycles and personal and household goods, 169,500 in construction and 168,900 in education. Workers in Slovakia put in among the longest hours of any country in the industrialized world. In 2002 the average worker put in 1,979 hours. The average monthly salary in 2001 was 12,365 koruny. Slovakia has the cheapest labour force in the EU. In Oct. 2003 the monthly minimum wage was increased to 6,080 koruny. Unemployment is among the highest in Europe, but has been declining slightly in recent years. It stood at 19·4% in 2001, but then declined to 18·7% in 2002 and still further to 16·9% in Dec. 2004. Youth unemployment is particularly high—in 2001 it was in excess of 39%.

INTERNATIONAL TRADE

Foreign debt was US$13,013m. in 2002.

Imports and Exports. Imports and exports in US$1bn.:

	1997	*1998*	*1999*	*2000*	*2001*
Imports f.o.b.	11·7	13·1	11·3	12·8	14·8
Exports f.o.b.	8·8	10·7	10·2	11·9	12·6

In 2000 the leading export markets were: Germany, 27%; Czech Republic, 15%; Italy, 9%; Austria, 8%; Poland, 6%; France, 5%; Hungary, 5%; and Netherlands 3%. Principal import sources in 2000 were: Germany, 27%; Russia, 18%; Czech Republic, 15%; Italy, 6%; Austria, 4%; Poland, 4%; and France, 3%. Main exports are: machinery and transport equipment; manufactured goods; chemicals and chemical products. Main imports are: machinery and transport equipment; semi-manufactured products; mineral fuels.

COMMUNICATIONS

Roads. In 2002 there were 42,970 km of roads, including 302 km of motorways. In 2002 there were 1,326,891 passenger cars, 164,484 trucks and lorries, 10,589 buses and coaches and 47,900 motorcycles and mopeds. In 2002 there were 7,866 road accidents resulting in 626 fatalities.

Rail. In 2000 the length of railway routes was 3,665 km. Most of the network is 1,435 mm gauge with short sections on three other gauges. Passenger-km travelled in 2000 came to 2,870m. and freight tonne-km to 11,234m. There are tram/light rail networks in Bratislava and Košice.

Civil Aviation. The main international airport is at Bratislava (M. R. Stefánik), with some international flights from Košice. There are three Slovakia-based airlines. In 2003 Air Slovakia had flights to Kuwait, Larnaca and Tel Aviv; Slovak Airlines operated domestic services and also flew to Moscow; and SkyEurope (central Europe's first low-cost airline) operated domestic services and also flew to Berlin, Dubrovnik, Mahé, Milan, Munich, Split, Stuttgart and Zürich. In 2000 Bratislava handled 278,654 passengers (264,470 on international flights) and 2,608 tonnes of freight.

Shipping. Merchant shipping in 2002 totalled 7,000 GRT. In 1999 vessels totalling 336,000 NRT entered ports.

Telecommunications. There were 4,326,100 telephone subscribers in 2002, or 804·4 per 1,000 persons, and 970,000 PCs in use (180·4 per 1,000 persons). In 2000 Deutsche Telekom bought a 51% stake in the state-owned Slovakia Telecom. There were 2,923,400 mobile phone subscribers in 2002 and 54,000 fax machines in 1998. Slovakia had 862,800 Internet users in 2002.

Postal Services. In 1998 there were 1,728 post offices.

SOCIAL INSTITUTIONS

Justice. The post-Communist judicial system was established by a federal law of July 1991. This provided for a unified system of four types of court: civil, criminal, commercial and administrative. Commercial courts arbitrate in disputes arising from business activities. Administrative courts examine the legality of the decisions of state institutions when appealed by citizens. In addition, there are military courts which operate under the jurisdiction of the Ministry of Defence. There is a Supreme Court, and a hierarchy of courts under the Ministry of Justice at republic, region and district level. District courts are courts of first instance. Cases are usually decided by senates comprising a judge and two associate judges, although occasionally by a single judge. (Associate judges are citizens in good standing over the age of 25 who are elected for four-year terms). Regional courts are courts of first instance in more serious cases and also courts of appeal for district courts. Cases are usually decided by a senate of two judges and three associate judges, although again occasionally by a single judge. The Supreme Court interprets law as a guide to other courts and functions also as a court of appeal. Decisions are made by senates of three judges. The judges of the Supreme Court are nominated by the President; other judges are appointed by the National Council.

The population in penal institutions in Sept. 2003 was 8,829 (164 per 100,000 of national population).

Religion. A federal Czechoslovakian law of July 1991 provides the basis for church-state relations and guarantees the religious and civic rights of citizens and churches. Churches must register to become legal entities but operate independently of the state. A law of 1993 restored confiscated property to churches and religious communities unless it had passed into private hands, co-operative farms or trading companies. In 2001, 68·9% of the population were Roman Catholic, 6·9% members of the Evangelical Church of the Augsburg Confession, 4·1% Greek Catholic and 2·0% Calvinist. In Sept. 2003 there were two cardinals.

Education. In 1996–97 there were 3,396 pre-school institutions with 170,138 children and 15,633 teachers. In 1995–96 there were 2,485 primary schools with 661,082 pupils and 39,224 teachers, 190 grammar schools with 76,380 students and 5,457 teachers, and 364 vocational schools with 119,853 pupils and 9,558 teachers. There were 357 secondary vocational apprentice training centres with 139,688 pupils and 6,056 teachers; and 400 special schools with 29,914 children and 3,862 teachers. There were 14 universities or university-type institutions with 74,322 students.

In 2000–01 expenditure on education came to 4·2% of GNP. In 1999–2000 total education expenditure was 13·8% of total government spending.

The adult literacy rate in 2001 was at least 99%.

Health. In 1998 there were 19,030 physicians, 2,598 dentists, 38,168 nurses and 1,822 pharmacists. In 1995 there were 62,634 beds in health establishments in total, of which 41,727 were in hospitals. In 2001 Slovakia spent 5·7% of its GDP on health.

Welfare. The age of retirement is 62 for both men and women. To qualify for an old-age pension an employment period of 25 years, for both men and women, is mandatory. The social insurance system has set the minimum pension (with full career) at 550 koruny a month and the maximum pension at 8,282 koruny a month for all pensions. State unemployment benefit is 50% of previous earnings during the first three months, thereafter 45% of previous earnings.

CULTURE

World Heritage Sites. Slovakia has four sites on the UNESCO World Heritage List: Vlkolínec (inscribed on the list in 1993), a group of 45 traditional log houses; Banská Štiavnica (1993), a medieval mining town; Spišský Hrad and its Associated Cultural Monuments (1993)—13th century Spiš Castle is one of the largest castle complexes in central Europe; Bardejov Town Conservation Reserve (2000), a medieval fortified town. Slovakia also shares a UNESCO site with Hungary: the Caves of Aggtelek and Slovak Karst.

Broadcasting. Broadcasting is the responsibility of the government-controlled Slovak Broadcasting Council. The state-run Slovak Radio broadcasts on four wavelengths, and there are 12 private regional stations. Slovak Television is a public corporation. It transmits on two channels (colour by PAL), the second being shared with a commercial station. There are several independent local TV stations, and two cable networks. Number of sets: TV (2001), 2·2m.; radio (2000), 5·2m.

Press. Slovakia had 16 daily newspapers in 2000 with a combined average daily circulation of 705,000. In 1999 a total of 3,153 book titles were published.

Tourism. In 2000 there were 1,053,000 foreign tourists, spending US$432m.

Festivals. The Bratislava Rock Festival takes place in June and the Bratislava Music Festival and Interpodium is in Oct. The Myjava Folklore Festival is held each June, the Zvolen Castle Games in June–July, Theatrical Nitra is in Sept., and there is an annual Spring Music Festival in Košice.

DIPLOMATIC REPRESENTATIVES

Of Slovakia in the United Kingdom (25 Kensington Palace Gdns, London, W8 4QY)
Ambassador: František Dlhopolček.

Of the United Kingdom in Slovakia (Panska 16, 81101 Bratislava)
Ambassador: Judith Macgregor.

Of Slovakia in the USA (3523 International Court, NW, Washington, D.C., 20008)
Ambassador: Rastislav Kacer.

Of the USA in Slovakia (4 Hviezdoslavovo Namestie, 81102 Bratislava)
Ambassador: Ronald Weiser.

Of Slovakia to the United Nations
Ambassador: Peter Burian.

Of Slovakia to the European Union
Ambassador: Miroslav Adamis.

FURTHER READING

Kirschbaum, S. J., *A History of Slovakia: the Struggle for Survival.* London and New York, 1995

Krejcí, Jaroslav and Machonin, Pavel, *Czechoslovakia 1918–1992: A Laboratory for Social Change*. Macmillan, London, 1996

Wheaton, B. and Kavan, Z., *Velvet Revolution: Czechoslovakia 1988–91.* Boulder (CO), 1992

National statistical office: Statistical Office of the Slovak Republic, Miletičova 3, 82467 Bratislava.
Website: http://www.statistics.sk/

SLOVENIA

Republika Slovenija

Capital: Ljubljana
Population projection, 2010: 1·96m.
GDP per capita, 2001: (PPP$) 18,540
HDI/world rank: 0·895/27

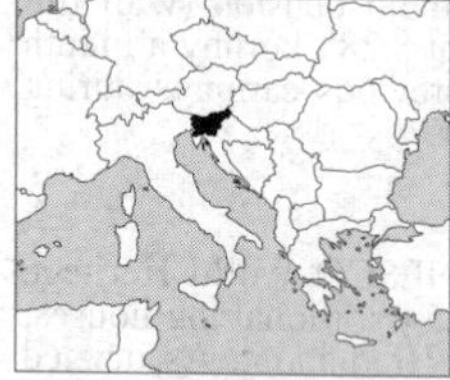

KEY HISTORICAL EVENTS

The lands originally settled by Slovenes in the 6th century were steadily encroached upon by Germans. Slovenia developed as part of Austria-Hungary, after the defeat of the latter in the First World War becoming part of the Kingdom of the Serbs, Croats and Slovenes (Yugoslavia) on 1 Dec. 1918.

In Oct. 1989 the Slovene Assembly voted a constitutional amendment giving it the right to secede from Yugoslavia. On 2 July 1990 the Assembly adopted a 'declaration of sovereignty' and a referendum was held on 23 Dec. 1990 in which 88·5% of participants voted for independence. On 25 June 1991 Slovenia declared independence but agreed to suspend this for three months at peace talks sponsored by the EU. Federal troops moved into Slovenia on 27 June to secure Yugoslavia's external borders, but after some fighting withdrew by the end of July. After the agreed three-month moratorium Slovenia (and Croatia) declared their independence from the Yugoslav Federation on 8 Oct. 1991. Slovenia became a member of NATO in March 2004 and the European Union in May 2004.

TERRITORY AND POPULATION

Slovenia is bounded in the north by Austria, in the northeast by Hungary, in the southeast and south by Croatia and in the west by Italy. The length of coastline is 47 km. Its area is 20,273 sq. km. The capital is Ljubljana: June 2002 population, 253,785. Maribor (population of 95,875 in 2002) is the other major city. In 2002 the census population was 1,964,036. Population (30 June 2003), 1,996,773 (females, 1,019,337); density per sq. km, 98·5. In 2001, 50·8% of the population lived in rural areas.

The UN gives a projected population for 2010 of 1·96m.

The official language is Slovene.

In April 2004 voters rejected plans to restore the civil rights of Slovenia's ethnic minorities, mainly nationals of other former Yugoslav republics, which were 'erased' in 1992.

SOCIAL STATISTICS

Statistics for calendar years:

	Live births	*Deaths*	*Growth rate per 1,000*	*Marriages*	*Divorces*
1998	17,856	19,039	–0·6	7,528	2,074
1999	17,533	18,885	–0·7	7,716	2,074
2000	18,180	18,588	–0·2	7,201	2,125
2001	17,477	18,508	–0·5	6,935	2,274
2002	17,501	18,701	–0·6	7,064	2,457

Rates, 2002 (per 1,000 population): birth, 8·8; death, 9·4. Infant mortality, 2001: 4·2 (per 1,000 live births). There were 581 suicides in 2001 (31 suicides per 1,000 deaths).

In 2001 the most popular age range for marrying was 25–29 years for both males and females. Expectation of life, 2001, was 72·2 years for males and 79·5 for females. Annual population growth rate, 1991–2002, 0·3%. Fertility rate, 2001, 1·2 births per woman.

CLIMATE

Summers are warm, winters are cold with frequent snow. Ljubljana, Jan. –4°C, July 22°C. Annual rainfall 1,383 mm.

CONSTITUTION AND GOVERNMENT

The constitution became effective on 23 Dec.1991. Slovenia is a parliamentary democratic republic with an executive that consists of a directly-elected president, aided by a council of ministers, and a prime minister. It has a bicameral parliament (*Skupščina Slovenije*), consisting of a 90-member *National Assembly* (*Državni Zbor*), 88 members elected for four-year terms by proportional representation with a 4% threshold and two members elected by ethnic minorities; and a 40-member, advisory *State Council* (*Državni Svet*), elected for five-year terms by interest groups and regions. It has veto powers over the National Assembly. Administratively the country is divided into 136 municipalities and 11 urban municipalities.

The Judicial branch consists of a *Supreme Court*, whose judges are elected by the National Assembly, and a *Constitutional Court*, whose judges are elected for nine-year terms by the National Assembly and nominated by the president.

National Anthem. 'Zdravljica' ('A Toast'); words by Dr France Prešeren, tune by Stanko Premrl.

RECENT ELECTIONS

Elections were held for the National Assembly on 3 Oct. 2004; turn-out was 60·5%. The centre-right Slovenian Democratic Party (SDS) won 29 seats with 29·1% of votes cast; the ruling Liberal Democracy of Slovenia (LDS), 23 with 22·8%; United List of Social Democrats of Slovenia (ZLSD; former Communists), 10 with 10·2%; New Slovenia Christian People's Party (NSi), 9 with 9·0%; Slovene People's Party (SLS), 7 with 6·8%; Slovenian National Party (SNS), 6 with 6·3%; Democratic Party of Retired People of Slovenia (DeSUS), 4 with 4·0%.

Presidential elections were held on 10 Nov. 2002. The turn-out was 70·8%. Prime Minister Janez Drnovšek (LDS) received 44·4% of votes cast against 30·8% for Barbara Brezigar, his nearest rival. In the run-off held on 1 Dec. 2002 Janez Drnovšek received 56·6% of votes cast against 43·4% for Barbara Brezigar.

European Parliament. Slovenia has seven representatives. At the June 2004 elections turn-out was 28·3%. The NSi won 2 seats with 23·5% of votes cast (political affiliation in European Parliament: European People's Party–European Democrats); the LDS-DeSUS, 2 with 21·9% (Alliance of Liberals and Democrats for Europe); the SDS, 2 with 17·7% (European People's Party–European Democrats); the ZLSD, 1 with 14·2% (Party of European Socialists).

CURRENT ADMINISTRATION

President: Janez Drnovšek; b. 1950 (LDS; sworn in 22 Dec. 2002).

In March 2005 the coalition government of the Slovenian Democratic Party (SDS), New Slovenia Christian People's Party (NSi), Slovene People's Party (SLS) and Democratic Party of Retired People of Slovenia (DeSUS) comprised:

Prime Minister: Janez Janša; b. 1958 (SDS; sworn in 6 Dec. 2004).

Minister of Agriculture, Food and Forestry: Marija Lukačič (SDS). *Culture:* Vasko Simoniti (SDS). *Defence:* Karl Erjavec (DeSUS). *Economy:* Andrej Vizjak (SDS). *Education and Sport:* Milan Zver (SDS). *Environment and Spatial Planning:* Janez Podobnik (SLS). *Finance:* Andrej Bajuk (NSi). *Foreign Affairs:* Dimitrij Rupel (SDS). *Health:* Andrej Bručan (SDS). *Higher Education, Science and Technology:* Jure Zupan (NSi). *Interior:* Dragutin Mate (SDS). *Justice:* Lovro Šturm (NSi). *Labour, Family and Social Affairs:* Janez Drobnič (NSi). *Public Administration:* Gregor Virant (SDS). *Transport:* Janez Božič (SLS). *Minister without Portfolio Responsible for Local Self-Government and Regional Development:* Ivan Žagar (SLS).

Office of the Prime Minister: http://www.sigov.si

DEFENCE

Compulsory military service for seven months ended in Sept. 2003. The Army is expected to be fully professional by 2010.

In 2003 military expenditure totalled US$378m. (US$192 per capita), representing 1·4% of GDP.

Army. There are six military districts. Personnel (2002), 9,000 (4,000 conscripts) and an army reserve of 20,000. There is a paramilitary police force of 4,500 with 5,000 reserves.

Navy. There is an Army Maritime element numbering 100 personnel.

Air Force. The Army Air element numbers 250 with eight armed helicopters.

INTERNATIONAL RELATIONS

Slovenia is a member of the UN, WTO, BIS, NATO, EU, Council of Europe, OSCE, CEFTA, CEI, the Inter-American Development Bank and IOM, and is an Associate Partner of the WEU. Slovenia held a referendum on EU membership on 23 March 2003, in which 89·6% of votes cast were in favour of accession. It became a member of NATO on 29 March 2004 and the EU on 1 May 2004. On 1 Feb. 2005 Slovenia became the third European Union member to ratify the new EU constitution. The parliament approved the treaty by 79 votes to four, with seven abstentions.

ECONOMY

Agriculture accounted for 3·1% of GDP in 2002, industry 36·2% and services 60·7%.

Overview. Slovenia ranks amongst the most developed of the ten EU accession members that joined in May 2004. Slovenia has a GDP per capita in purchasing power standards of 70% of current EU members, higher than that of Greece and Portugal. The country has achieved an average growth rate of 4% since 1996. Tight monetary and fiscal policies have contributed to macroeconomic stability, balanced fiscal budgets and open foreign trade. The country attracts low levels of foreign direct investment (FDI), partly owing to a reluctance to allow foreign participation in key industries. The authorities aim to adopt the euro in Jan. 2007; by 2004 Slovenia had already met the Maastricht criteria for long-term interest rates and the fiscal deficit and debt ratios. According to the IMF, Slovenia must still allow for policy challenges before the successful adoption of the euro; these challenges include reducing the inflation rate, making wage-setting mechanisms more flexible and enhancing the flexibility of fiscal policy. Since 1996 Slovenia has had single-digit inflation. The inflation rate has declined from 8·9% in 2000 to 3·7% in 2004. The pace of privatization has been slower than in most other Central and Eastern European countries, with enterprises in key sectors remaining under state ownership. The authorities are currently preparing for the liberalization of the natural gas sector, road transport and railways.

Currency. The unit of currency is the *tolar* (SLT) of 100 *stotinas*, which replaced the Yugoslav dinar. Since 28 June 2004 the tolar has been pegged to the euro at a rate of 239·640 tolars = one euro. Inflation was 7·5% in 2002 and 5·6% in 2003. Foreign exchange reserves were US$5,268m. and gold reserves 243,000 troy oz in June 2002. Total money supply in June 2002 was 495,309m. tolars.

Budget. In 2001 total revenues were 1,772·1bn. tolars (1,559·9bn. tolars in 2000) and expenditures 1,843·5bn. tolars (1,621·7bn. tolars in 2000).

Tax revenues in 2001 totalled 1,659·7bn. tolars (including: domestic taxes on goods and services, 659·3bn. tolars; social security contributions, 627·4bn. tolars; tax on income, profits and capital gains, 256·7bn. tolars). Items of expenditure in 2001 included: social security and welfare, 802·4bn. tolars; health, 267·1bn. tolars; education, 197·9bn. tolars.

VAT is 20·0% (reduced rate, 8·5%).

Performance. The GDP growth rate was 3·3% in 2002, 2·5% in 2003 and (provisional) 4·0% in 2004. Of all the central and eastern European countries which joined the European Union in May 2004, Slovenia has the highest per capita GDP. Real GDP in 2002 was 21% higher than in 1989—only Poland among the ex-socialist countries has seen greater progress since 1989. Total GDP in 2003 was US$26·3bn.

Banking and Finance. The central bank and bank of issue, the Bank of Slovenia, was founded on 25 June 1991 upon independence. Its current *Governor* is Mitja Gaspari, appointed on 1 April 2001 for a term of six years. In 2003 there were 20 commercial banks (five subsidiaries of foreign banks and one branch office of a foreign bank) and two savings banks. The largest bank is Nova Ljubljanska banka (NLB), which has a market share of around one third and had assets in 2003 of US$9·1bn. Other large banks are Nova Kreditna Banka Maribor (NKBM) and Abanka Vipa. In 2002 Slovenia received a record US$1·64bn. of foreign direct investment.

There is a stock exchange in Ljubljana (LSE).

ENERGY AND NATURAL RESOURCES

Environment. Slovenia's carbon dioxide emissions from the consumption and flaring of fossil fuels were the equivalent of 8·4 tonnes per capita in 2002.

Electricity. Installed capacity was 2·5m. kW in 2000. There was one nuclear power station in operation in 2003. In 2001, 5,257m. kWh were nuclear-produced, 5,413m. kWh thermal and 3,796m. kWh hydro-electric. The total amount of electricity produced in 2001 was 14,466m. kWh. Consumption per capita in 2001 was 5,568 kWh.

Minerals. Brown coal production was 685,000 tonnes in 2001.

Agriculture. Only around 11% of the population work in agriculture. Output (in 1,000 tonnes) in 2001: maize, 258; sugarbeets, 186; wheat, 180; potatoes, 148; grapes, 107.

Livestock in 2001: pigs, 599,895; cattle, 477,075; sheep, 94,068; poultry, 5,217,000 (2000). Livestock products, 2000: meat, 170,000 tonnes; milk (2001), 633,820 tonnes.

In 2001 there were 173,000 ha of arable land and 30,000 ha of permanent crops.

Forestry. In 2001 the area under forests was 1·14m. ha, or 56·5% of the total land area. Timber production in 2001 was 2·26m. cu. metres.

Fisheries. Total marine fish catch in 2001 was 1,774 tonnes. Freshwater catch was 1,314 tonnes.

INDUSTRY

Industry contributed 31·0% of GDP in 2001. Traditional industries are metallurgy, furniture-making and textiles. The manufacture of electric goods and transport equipment is being developed.

Production (in 1,000 tonnes): cement (2000), 1,252; paper and paperboard (2000), 582; crude steel (2000), 519; passenger cars (2000), 124,843 units; refrigerators for household use (2000), 841,000 units; washing machines (2000), 488,000 units.

Labour. Registered labour force was 880,897 in 2001. In 2001, 427,553 people worked in services, 309,629 in industry, and 41,860 in agriculture and forestry. In Dec. 2003 there were 98,129 registered unemployed; in the fourth quarter of 2003 the unemployment rate was 6·7%. In 2001 the average monthly gross wage per employee was 214,561 tolar.

INTERNATIONAL TRADE

Foreign debt amounted to US$8,799m. in 2002. In 1997 Slovenia accepted 18% of the US$4,400m. commercial bank debt of the former Yugoslavia.

Imports and Exports. Exports (f.o.b.) in 2002 were worth US$10,472·6m. (US$9,342·8m. in 2001) and imports (f.o.b.) US$10,715·7m. (US$9,962·3m. in 2001). Exports accounted for 57·8% of GDP in 2002.

Major exports are road vehicles and parts (11·6%), electrical machinery, apparatus and appliances (11·5%) and furniture (6·9%). Major imports are road vehicles, electrical machinery, industrial machinery, petroleum and petroleum products, and iron and steel.

Share of exports to principal markets in 2002: Germany, 24·8%; Italy, 12·1%; Croatia, 8·7%; Austria, 7·1%; France, 6·7%. Imports: Germany, 19·2%; Italy, 17·9%; France, 10·3%; Austria, 8·3%; Croatia, 3·6%. Nearly 65% of trade is with EU countries.

COMMUNICATIONS

Roads. In 2002 there were 20,250 km of road including 456 km of motorways. There were in 2002: 873,962 passenger cars; 2,189 buses; 83,042 trucks; and 50,779 motorcycles and mopeds. 72·5m. passengers and 4·6m. tonnes of freight were carried by road in 2001. There were 9,199 traffic accidents in 2001 in which 278 persons were killed.

Rail. In 2001 there were 1,229 km of 1,435 mm gauge, of which 504 km were electrified. In 2001, 14·5m. passengers and 15·0m. tonnes of freight were carried.

Civil Aviation. There is an international airport at Ljubljana (Brnik), which handled 986,000 passengers (all on international flights) and 5,800 tonnes of freight in 2000. The national carrier, Adria Airways, has flights to most major European cities and Tel Aviv. In 2000 Ljubljana handled 986,000 passengers (all on international flights) and 5,800 tonnes of freight. In 1999 scheduled airline traffic of Slovenia-based carriers flew 9·1m. km, carrying 556,000 passengers.

Shipping. The biggest port is at Koper. Sea-going shipping totalled 9,146 GRT in 2001. In 2002 vessels totalling 6,825,000 NRT entered ports and vessels totalling 4,430,000 NRT cleared.

Telecommunications. In 2002 Slovenia had 2,677,400 telephone subscribers (1,341·4 per 1,000 inhabitants), including 1,667,200 mobile phone subscribers. The leading telecommunications operator is the state-owned Telekom Slovenije. In 2001 there were 11,072 fax machines in use. The number of Internet users in 2002 was 750,000. There were 600,000 PCs in use (300·6 per 1,000 persons) in 2002.

Postal Services. In 2001 there were 545 post offices.

SOCIAL INSTITUTIONS

Justice. There are 44 district courts, 11 regional courts, four higher courts and a supreme court. There are also four labour courts, one social court and a higher labour and social court. The population in penal institutions in Sept. 2002 was 1,120 (56 per 100,000 of national population).

Religion. 57·8% of the population were Roman Catholic according to the 2002 census.

Education. Adult literacy rate in 2001 was 99·6% (99·7% male; 99·6% female). In 2000–01 there were 816 primary schools with 181,390 pupils and 15,287 teachers; and 149 secondary schools with 104,845 pupils and 9,351 teachers. In 2001–02 there were 46 institutions of higher education with 72,320 students and 6,894 teaching staff. There are two universities, at Ljubljana and Maribor.

In 1995 total expenditure on education came to 5·7% of GNP and represented 12·6% of total government expenditure.

Health. In 2000 there were 4,483 doctors and 10,745 hospital beds. In 1998 there were 1,201 dentists, 3,125 nurses and 887 pharmacists.

Welfare. There were 485,895 people receiving pensions in 2001, of which 296,160 were old-age pensioners. Disability and pension insurance expenses were 655,233m. tolar in 2001.

CULTURE

World Heritage Sites. Slovenia has one site on the UNESCO World Heritage List: Škocjan Caves (inscribed on the list in 1988), consisting of limestone caves, passages and waterfalls more than 200 metres deep.

Broadcasting. The government-controlled Radiotelevizija Slovenija broadcasts three national radio programmes, and also programmes in Hungarian and Italian. There are six nationwide radio networks as well as regional and local stations. Public television transmission is carried out by the two stations of Televizija Slovenija (colour by PAL). There are also national independent TV networks, a network serving Ljubljana and district and several local stations.

There were 730,000 TV receivers in 2001 and 792,000 radio sets in 2000.

Cinema. There were 78 cinemas with a total of 22,400 seats in 2000, and an annual attendance of 2·2m. Nine full-length films were made in 2000.

Press. In 2001 there were seven national daily newspapers, 57 weeklies and three published twice a week. In 2001 a total of 3,598 book titles were published.

Tourism. 1,090,000 foreign tourists came to Slovenia in 2000; receipts from tourism in 2000 totalled US$957m. Tourism accounts for 5% of GDP.

Libraries. In 2000 there were one national library, 54 higher education libraries, 138 special libraries, 60 public libraries and 648 school libraries; they held a combined 25,554,000 volumes.

Theatre and Opera. In 2002 there were nine professional theatres and two operas.

Museums and Galleries. Museums totalled 85 in 1996, with 2·0m. visitors that year.

DIPLOMATIC REPRESENTATIVES

Of Slovenia in the United Kingdom (10 Little College Street, London, SW1P 3SH)
Ambassador: Iztok Mirošič.

Of the United Kingdom in Slovenia (4th Floor, 3 Trg Republike, 1000 Ljubljana)
Ambassador: Hugh Mortimer, LVO.

Of Slovenia in the USA (1525 New Hampshire Ave., NW, Washington, D.C., 20036)
Ambassador: Samuel Žbogar.

Of the USA in Slovenia (Presernova 31, 1000 Ljubljana)
Ambassador: Thomas B. Robertson.

Of Slovenia to the United Nations
Ambassador: Roman Kirn.

Of Slovenia to the European Union
Ambassador: Ciril Stokelj.

FURTHER READING

Benderly, J. and Kraft, E. (eds.) *Independent Slovenia: Origins, Movements, Prospects.* London, 1995

Carmichael, Cathie, *Slovenia.* [Bibliography] ABC-Clio, Oxford and Santa Barbara (CA), 1996

National statistical office: National Statistical Office, Vožarski Pot 12, 1000 Ljubljana.
Website: http://www.sigov.si/zrs/

SOLOMON ISLANDS

Capital: Honiara
Population projection, 2010: 574,000
GDP per capita, 2002: (PPP$) 1,590
HDI/world rank: 0·624/124

KEY HISTORICAL EVENTS

The Solomon Islands were discovered by Europeans in 1568 but 200 years passed before contact was made again. The southern Solomon Islands were placed under British protection in 1893; the eastern and southern outliers were added in 1898 and 1899. Santa Isabel and the other islands to the north were ceded by Germany in 1900. Full internal self-government was achieved on 2 Jan. 1976 and independence on 7 July 1978.

In June 2000 there was a coup by rebels from the island of Malaita. Prime Minister Bartholomew Ulufa'alu was held at gunpoint for two days. As conflict between the so-called Malaita Eagles and the Isatabu Freedom Movement escalated during 2003, an Australian-led peacekeeping force landed to restore order.

TERRITORY AND POPULATION

The Solomon Islands lie within the area 5° to 12° 30' S. lat. and 155° 30' to 169° 45' E. long. The group includes the main islands of Guadalcanal, Malaita, New Georgia, San Cristobal (now Makira), Santa Isabel and Choiseul; the smaller Florida and Russell groups; the Shortland, Mono (or Treasury), Vella La Vella, Kolombangara, Ranongga, Gizo and Rendova Islands; to the east, Santa Cruz, Tikopia, the Reef and Duff groups; Rennell and Bellona in the south; Ontong Java or Lord Howe to the north; and many smaller islands. The land area is estimated at 10,954 sq. miles (28,370 sq. km). The larger islands are mountainous and forest clad, with flood-prone rivers of considerable energy potential. Guadalcanal has the largest land area and the greatest amount of flat coastal plain. Population (1999 census), 409,042; density, 14·4 per sq. km. 2002 population estimate: 464,000. In 2001, 79·8% of the population lived in rural areas.

The UN gives a projected population for 2010 of 574,000.

The islands are administratively divided into a Capital Territory and nine provinces. Area and population:

Province	*Sq. km*	*Census 1999*	*Capital*
Central Islands	615	21,577	Tulagi
Rennell and Bellona	671	2,377	Tigoa
Guadalcanal	5,336	60,275	Honiara
Isabel	4,136	20,421	Buala
Makira and Ulawa	3,188	31,006	Kirakira
Malaita	4,225	122,620	Auki
Temotu	895	18,912	Lata (Santa Cruz)
Western	5,475	62,739	Gizo
Choiseul	3,837	20,008	Taro
Capital Territory	22	49,107	...

The capital, Honiara, on Guadalcanal, is the largest urban area, with an estimated population in 1999 of 68,000. 93% of the population are Melanesian; other ethnic groups include Polynesian, Micronesian, European and Chinese.

English is the official language, and is spoken by 1–2% of the population. In all 120 indigenous languages are spoken; Melanesian languages are spoken by 85% of the population.

SOCIAL STATISTICS

Births, 1997, 15,900; deaths, 1,800. 1997 birth rate (per 1,000 population), 37·3; death rate, 4·3. Life expectancy, 2001, 70·1 years for women and 67·5 for men. Annual population growth rate, 1992–02, 3·2%. Infant mortality, 2001, 20 per 1,000 live births; fertility rate, 2001, 5·4 births per woman.

CLIMATE

An equatorial climate with only small seasonal variations. Southeast winds cause cooler conditions from April to Nov., but northwest winds for the rest of the year bring higher temperatures and greater rainfall, with annual totals ranging between 80" (2,000 mm) and 120" (3,000 mm).

CONSTITUTION AND GOVERNMENT

The Solomon Islands is a constitutional monarchy with the British Sovereign (represented locally by a Governor-General, who must be a Solomon Island citizen) as Head of State. Legislative power is vested in the single-chamber *National Parliament* composed of 50 members, elected by universal adult suffrage for five years. Parliamentary democracy is based on a multi-party system. Executive authority is effectively held by the Cabinet, led by the Prime Minister.

The Governor-General is appointed for up to five years, on the advice of Parliament, and acts in almost all matters on the advice of the Cabinet. The Prime Minister is elected by and from members of Parliament. Other Ministers are appointed by the Governor-General on the Prime Minister's recommendation, from members of Parliament. The Cabinet is responsible to Parliament. Emphasis is laid on the devolution of power to provincial governments, and traditional chiefs and leaders have a special role within the arrangement.

National Anthem. 'God save our Solomon Islands from shore to shore'; words and tune by P. Balekana.

RECENT ELECTIONS

National elections were held on 5 Dec. 2001. The People's Action Party won 20 seats, the Association of Independent Members 13, the Solomon Islands Alliance for Change 12, the People's Progressive Party 3 and the Labour Party 1.

A run-off vote for the premiership was held on 17 Dec. 2001. The former deputy prime minister, Sir Allan Kemakeza, who had been dismissed two months prior to the national elections, defeated Mannasseh Sogavare and Bartholomew Ulafu'alu, both former prime ministers.

Nathaniel Waena was elected governor-general by parliament on 15 June 2004. He defeated Sir Peter Kenilorea and the incumbent, Sir John Lapli.

CURRENT ADMINISTRATION

Governor-General: Nathaniel Waena (since 7 July 2004).

In March 2005 the government comprised:

Prime Minister: Sir Allan Kemakeza; b. 1951 (sworn in 17 Dec. 2001).

Deputy Prime Minister and Minister of Education and Training: Snyder Rini.

Minister of Agriculture and Livestock: Alfred Sasako. *Commerce, Employment and Trade:* Walton Naezon. *Communications, Aviation and Meteorology:* Siméon Bouro. *Culture and Tourism:* Trevor Olavae. *Finance:* Peter Boyers. *Fisheries and Marine Resources:* Paul Maenu'u. *Foreign Affairs:* Laurie Chan. *Forests, Environment and Conservation:* David Holosivi. *Health and Medical Services:* Benjamin Una. *Home Affairs:* Nelson Kile. *Infrastructure Development:* Bernard Giro. *Lands and Surveys:* Siriako Usa. *Mines and Energy:* Stephen Paeni. *Development Planning:* Fred Fono. *National Unity, Reconciliation and Peace:* Augustine Taneko. *Police, National Security and Justice:* Michael Maina. *Provincial Government and Constituency Development:* Clement Rojumana.

DEFENCE

The marine wing of the Royal Solomon Islands Police operates three patrol boats and a number of fast crafts for surveillance of fisheries and maritime boundaries. There is also an RSI Police Field Force stationed at the border with Papua New Guinea.

In July 2003 an Australian-led peacekeeping force landed to restore stability after years of ethnic fighting and high-level corruption. The force included troops from Fiji Islands, New Zealand, Papua New Guinea and Tonga.

INTERNATIONAL RELATIONS

The Solomon Islands is a member of the UN, WTO, the Commonwealth, the Asian Development Bank, the Pacific Community, the Pacific Islands Forum and is an ACP member state of the ACP-EU relationship. The Solomon Islands is also a member of the World Trade Organization and other organizations for regional technical co-operation.

ECONOMY

Overview. The Solomon Islands Alliance for Change (SIAC) coalition embarked on a reform programme in 1997 to encourage private enterprise, including a reduction of the civil service and a tightening of government revenue collection.

Currency. The *Solomon Island dollar* (SBD) of 100 *cents* was introduced in 1977. It was devalued by 20% in Dec. 1997 and 25% in March 2002. Inflation in 2002 was 9·8%. In Jan. 2002 foreign exchange reserves were US$28m. Total money supply was SI$243m. in Sept. 2000.

Budget. The budget estimate for 1998 was for expenditure of SI$631·8m.; total revenue forecast, SI$482m. plus SI$149m. to be secured through concessionary loans.

Performance. Real GDP growth was negative in 2000, 2001 and 2002, at –14·2%, –9·0% and –2·0% respectively. Total GDP in 2003 was US$0·3bn.

Banking and Finance. The Central Bank of Solomon Islands is the bank of issue; its *Governor* is Rick N. Houenipwela ('Hou'). There are three commercial banks and a development bank.

ENERGY AND NATURAL RESOURCES

Environment. Carbon dioxide emissions from the consumption and flaring of fossil fuels in 2002 were the equivalent of 0·4 tonnes per capita.

Electricity. Installed capacity in 2000 was 12,000 kW. Production in 2000 was about 33m. kWh and consumption per capita an estimated 74 kWh. The Solomon Islands Electricity Authority is undertaking projects to increase power generation capacity including the construction of a major hydro-electricity power plant.

Oil and Gas. The potential for oil, petroleum and gas production has yet to be tapped.

Minerals. In 1999 gold output from mining totalled 3,456 kg and silver output 2,138 kg. The only mine in the Solomon Islands closed in 2000 owing to the civil unrest, but it is hoped that production will resume in the future. The value of gold exports in 1999 was SI$113·7m.

Agriculture. Land is held either as customary land (88% of holdings) or registered land. Customary land rights depend on clan membership or kinship. Only Solomon Islanders own customary land; only Islanders or government members may hold perpetual estates of registered land. Coconuts, cocoa, rice and other minor crops are grown. Production, 2000 (in 1,000 tonnes): coconuts, 318; sweet potatoes, 75; taro, 32; palm oil, 28; yams, 25; copra, 23; palm kernels, 7. Agricultural produce earned SI$104·7m. in exports in 1997. In 2000 there were 42,000 ha of arable land and 18,000 ha of permanent crops.

Livestock (2000): pigs, 59,000; cattle, 12,000.

Forestry. Forests covered 2·54m. ha in 2000 (88·8% of the land area). Earnings from forest resources increased from SI$266·6m. in 1994 to SI$309·9m. in 1995 and SI$349·3m. in 1996 but then slumped in 1997 to SI$309·4m. owing to a fall in prices and a government moratorium on the issue of new logging licences. Timber production was 692,000 cu. metres in 2001.

Fisheries. Solomon Islands' waters are among the richest in tuna. Catches have remained well below the maximum sustainable catch limits. Previously closed areas within its territorial waters have been opened to American fishing interests but sustainable harvest rates will not be at risk. The total catch in 2001 was an estimated 30,075 tonnes.

INDUSTRY

Industries include palm oil manufacture (35,000 tonnes in 2002), processed fish production (13,700 tonnes in 2000), rice milling, fish canning, fish freezing, saw milling, food, tobacco and soft drinks. Other products include wood and rattan furniture, fibreglass articles, boats, clothing and spices.

Labour. The Labour Division of the Ministry of Commerce, Employment and Tourism monitors and regulates the domestic labour market. The labour force in

1996 totalled 202,000 (54% males). Around 38% of the economically active population in 1993 were engaged in community, social and personal services and 27% in agriculture, fisheries and forestry.

Trade Unions. Trade Unions exist by virtue of the Trade Unions Act of 1976. The Solomon Islands Council of Trade Unions (SICTU) is the central body. Affiliated members of the SICTU are Solomon Islands National Union of Workers and the Solomon Islands Public Employees Union (SIPEU). SIPEU, which represents employees of the public sector, is the largest single trade union.

INTERNATIONAL TRADE

The Solomon Islands is a member of the World Trade Organization. The government recognizes the private sector as an engine for growth. Through encouraging the private sector the government hopes that the base for a broad diversification of tradeable goods and services can be established.

Total foreign debt in 2002 was US$180m.

Imports and Exports. Imports 2002, SI$436·3m.; exports, SI$390·0m. Main imports, 2002: food and live animals, 24·9%; mineral fuels and lubricants, 17·3%; machinery and transport equipment, 13·2%. Main exports: timber, 65·2%; fish products, 18·1%; cocoa beans, 7·1%. Principal import suppliers (2002): Australia, 31·5%; Singapore, 19·8%; New Zealand, 5·2%. Principal export markets (2002): Japan, 17·1%; South Korea, 16·7%; Philippines, 6·8%.

Trade Fairs. An annual National Cultural and Trade Show/Fair is held in July to coincide with the anniversary of independence.

COMMUNICATIONS

Roads. In 1999 there was estimated to be a total of 1,360 km of roads, of which 34 km were paved. The unpaved roads included 800 km of private plantation roads.

Civil Aviation. A new terminal has been opened at Henderson International Airport in Honiara. The national carrier is Solomon Airlines. In 1999 scheduled airline traffic of Solomon Islands-based carriers flew 4·1m. km, carrying 98,000 passengers (23,000 on international flights).

Shipping. There are international ports at Honiara, Yandina in the Russell Islands and Noro in New Georgia, Western Province. In 2002 the merchant marine totalled 8,000 GRT.

Telecommunications. Telecommunications are operated by Solomon Telekom, a joint venture between the government of Solomon Islands and Cable & Wireless (UK). Telecommunications between Honiara and provincial centres are facilitated by modern satellite communication systems. Telephone subscribers numbered 7,600 in 2002 (17·1 per 1,000 inhabitants) and there were 18,000 PCs in use (40·5 per 1,000 inhabitants). There were approximately 1,000 mobile phone subscribers in 2002 and 800 fax machines in 1999. Internet users numbered 2,200 in 2002.

Postal Services. The Solomon Islands Postal Corporation, a statutory company established in 1996, administers postal services. In 1998 there were 127 post offices.

SOCIAL INSTITUTIONS

Justice. Civil and criminal jurisdiction is exercised by the High Court of Solomon Islands, constituted 1975. A Solomon Islands Court of Appeal was established in 1982. Jurisdiction is based on the principles of English law (as applying on 1 Jan. 1981). Magistrates' courts can try civil cases on claims not exceeding SI$2,000, and criminal cases with penalties not exceeding 14 years' imprisonment. Certain crimes, such as burglary and arson, where the maximum sentence is for life, may also be tried by magistrates. There are also local courts, which decide matters concerning customary titles to land; decisions may be put to the Customary Land Appeal Court. There is no capital punishment.

The population in penal institutions in 1999 was 134 (31 per 100,000 of national population).

Religion. 92% of the population were Christians in 2001.

Education. In 2002 there were 82,330 pupils at primary and 21,700 pupils at secondary level. The adult literacy rate in 1998 was 62·0%.

Training of teachers and trade and vocational training is carried out at the College of Higher Education. The University of the South Pacific Centre is at Honiara. Other rural training centres run by churches are also involved in vocational training.

In 2000–01 total expenditure on education came to 3·6% of GNP and in 1999–2000 accounted for 15·4% of total government spending.

Health. A free medical service is supplemented by the private sector. An international standard immunization programme is conducted in conjunction with the WHO for infants. Tuberculosis has been eradicated but malaria remains a problem. In 1997 there were 11 hospitals, 31 doctors and 464 registered nurses and 283 nursing aides.

CULTURE

Broadcasting. The Solomon Islands Broadcasting Corporation (SIBC) operates a national service and an FM service for Honiara. The other FM station—FM100—is privately operated and broadcasts news and entertainment on a 24-hour basis. There were 12,000 TV receivers in 2001 and 57,000 radio receivers in 1997.

Press. There are two main newspapers in circulation. *The Solomon Star* is daily and the *Solomon Voice* is weekly. The Government Information Service publishes a monthly issue of the *Solomon Nius* which exclusively disseminates news of government activities. Non-government organizations such as the Solomon Islands Development Trust (SIDT) also publish monthly papers on environmental issues.

Tourism. Tourism in the Solomon Islands is still in a development stage. The emphasis is on establishing major hotels in the capital and provincial centres, to be supplemented by satellite Eco-tourism projects in the rural areas. The Solomon Islands Visitors Bureau is the statutory institution for domestic co-ordination and international marketing. In 1999 there were 21,000 foreign tourists, bringing revenue of US$6m.

Festivals. Festivities and parades in the capital and provincial centres normally mark the National Day of Independence. The highlight is the annual National Trade and Cultural Show.

Museums and Galleries. There is a National Museum which has a display of traditional artefacts. Early government and public records are kept at the National Archives and a National Art Gallery displays a number of fine arts and works by Solomon Islands artists.

DIPLOMATIC REPRESENTATIVES

Of the Solomon Islands in the United Kingdom (resides at Brussels)
High Commissioner: Robert Sisilo.

Of the United Kingdom in the Solomon Islands (Telekom House, Mendana Ave., Honiara)
High Commissioner: Brian Baldwin.

Of the USA in the Solomon Islands
Ambassador: Robert W. Fitts (resides at Port Moresby, Papua New Guinea).

Of the Solomon Islands in the USA and to the United Nations (800 2nd Ave, Suite 400L, New York, NY 10017)
Ambassador: Collin Beck.

Of the Solomon Islands to the European Union
Ambassador: Robert Sisilo.

FURTHER READING

Bennett, J. A., *Wealth of the Solomons: A History of a Pacific Archipelago, 1800–1978.* Univ. of Hawaii Press, 1987

National statistical office: Solomon Islands National Statistical Office, PO Box G6, Department of Finance, Honiara.

SOMALIA

Capital: Mogadishu
Population projection, 2010: 12·95m.
GDP per capita: not available

Jamhuriyadda Dimugradiga ee Soomaaliya
(Somali Democratic Republic)

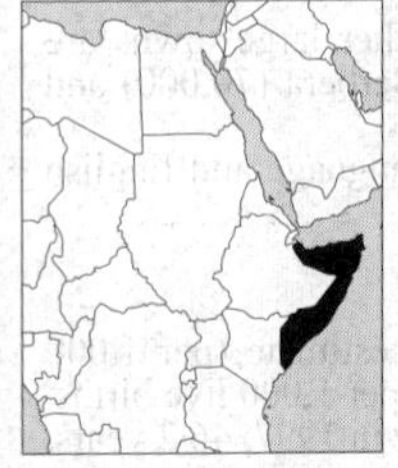

KEY HISTORICAL EVENTS

The origins of the Somali people can be traced back 2,000 years when they displaced an earlier Arabic people. They converted to Islam in the 10th century and were organized in loose Islamic states by the 19th century. The northern part of Somaliland was created a British protectorate in 1884. The southern part belonged to two local rulers who, in 1889, accepted Italian protection for their lands. The Italian invasion of Ethiopia in 1935 was launched from Somaliland and in 1936 Somaliland was incorporated with Eritrea and Ethiopia to become Italian East Africa. In 1940 Italian forces invaded British Somaliland but in 1941 the British, with South African and Indian troops, recaptured this territory as well as occupying Italian Somaliland. After the Second World War British Somaliland reverted to its colonial status and ex-Italian Somaliland became the UN Trust Territory of Somaliland, administered by Italy.

The independent Somali Republic came into being on 1 July 1960 as a result of the merger of the British Somaliland Protectorate, which first became independent on 26 June 1960, and the Italian Trusteeship Territory of Somaliland. On 21 Oct. 1969 Maj.-Gen. Mohammed Siyad Barre took power in a coup. Various insurgent forces combined to oppose the Barre regime in a bloody civil war. Barre fled on 27 Jan. 1991 but interfactional fighting continued. In Aug. 1992 a new coalition government agreed a UN military presence to back up relief efforts to help the estimated 1·5–2m. victims of famine. On 11 Dec. 1992 the leaders of the two most prominent of the warring factions, Ali Mahdi Muhammad and Muhammad Farah Aidid, agreed to a peace plan under the aegis of the UN and a pact was signed on 15 Jan. 1993. At the end of March, the warring factions agreed to disarm and form a 74-member National Transitional Council. On 4 Nov. 1994 the UN Security Council unanimously decided to withdraw UN forces; the last of these left on 2 March 1995.

The principal insurgent group in the north of the country, the Somali National Movement, declared the secession of an independent **'Somaliland Republic'** on 17 May 1991. The Somalian government rejected the secession and Muhammad Aidid's forces launched a campaign to reoccupy the 'Republic' in Jan. 1996. Muhammad Farah Aidid was assassinated in July 1996 and succeeded by his son Hussein Aidid. In July 1998 leaders in the northeast of Somalia proclaimed an 'autonomous state' named **Puntland.**

Peace efforts in neighbouring Djibouti culminated in July 2000 in the establishment of a power-sharing agreement and a national constitution to see Somalia through a three-year transitional period. The election of members of parliament and a civilian government followed in Aug. 2000, and in Oct. the new government moved from Djibouti back to Somalia.

In April 2002 **'Southwestern Somalia'** broke away from Mogadishu, thereby creating a third autonomous Somali state.

TERRITORY AND POPULATION

Somalia is bounded north by the Gulf of Aden, east and south by the Indian ocean, and west by Kenya, Ethiopia and Djibouti. Total area 637,657 sq. km (246,201 sq. miles). In 1987 the census population was 7,114,431. Estimated population (2002): 9,529,000; density, 15 per sq. km. Population counting is complicated owing to large numbers of nomads and refugee movements as a result of famine and clan warfare.

The UN gives a projected population for 2010 of 12·95m.

In 1995 an estimated 74·4% of the population were rural.

The country is administratively divided into 18 regions (with chief cities): Awdal (Saylac), Bakol (Xuddur), Bay (Baydhabo), Benadir (Mogadishu), Bari (Boosaso), Galgudug (Duusa Marreeb), Gedo (Garbahaarrey), Hiran (Beledweyne), Jubbada Dexe (Jilib), Jubbada Hoose (Kismayo), Mudug (Gaalkacyo), Nogal (Garowe), Woqooyi Galbeed (Hargeisa), Sanaag (Ceerigabo), Shabeellaha Dhexe (Jawhar), Shabeellaha Hoose (Marka), Sol (Las Anod), Togder (Burao). Somaliland comprises the regions of Awdal, Woqooyi Galbeed, Togder, Sanaag and Sol. Puntland consists of Bari, Nogal and northern Mudug. Southwestern Somalia consists of Bay, Bakol, Gedo, Jubbada Hoose and Shabeellaha Dhexe.

The capital is Mogadishu (1999 population, 1,162,000). Other large towns are (with 1990 estimates) Hargeisa (90,000), Kismayo (90,000), Berbera (70,000) and Marka (62,000).

The national language is Somali. Arabic is also an official language and English and Italian are spoken extensively.

SOCIAL STATISTICS

Births, 1997 estimate, 300,000; deaths, 121,000. Rates, 1997 estimate (per 1,000 population): birth, 45·5; death, 18·3. Infant mortality, 1997, 126 per 1,000 live births. Annual population growth rate, 1992–02, 2·8%. Life expectancy in 1997, 46·2 years. Fertility rate, 2001, 7·3 births per woman.

CLIMATE

Much of the country is arid, although rainfall is more adequate towards the south. Temperatures are very high on the northern coasts. Mogadishu, Jan. 79°F (26·1°C), July 78°F (25·6°C). Annual rainfall 17" (429 mm). Berbera, Jan. 76°F (24·4°C), July 97°F (36·1°C). Annual rainfall 2" (51 mm).

CONSTITUTION AND GOVERNMENT

The Constitution of 1984 authorized a sole legal party, the Somali Revolutionary Socialist Party. There was an elected President and People's Assembly.

A conference of national reconciliation in July 1991 and again in March 1993 allowed for the setting up of a transitional government charged with reorganizing free elections, but inter-factional fighting and anarchy have replaced settled government.

In Aug. 2000 a transitional parliament with a three-year mandate was inaugurated, at the time in neighbouring Djibouti but subsequently in Mogadishu. There was a 245-member *Transitional National Assembly* appointed by clan chiefs.

Under an agreed charter the transitional assembly was to elect a president who in turn was to form a government. However, ongoing wrangling between Somalia's rival factions continues. In Nov. 2002 leaders of the Somali factions met in order to begin the process of drawing up a new federal constitution. In Jan. 2004 the country's leaders signed an agreement to form a new government based along clan lines. In Aug. 2004 a new 275-member Somali Transitional Federal Parliament was inaugurated in Nairobi, Kenya. The newly-formed government has begun the process of returning from Kenya to Somalia, but is doing so in stages.

Puntland. Puntland, in the northeast region of Somalia, declared itself an 'autonomous state' in July 1998 under the leadership of Abdullahi Yusuf. Since its creation, Puntland has been locked in dispute with Somaliland over control of the Sanaag and Sol areas.

Puntland covers 300,000 sq. km and had a population in 2000 of 2m. The capital is Garowe. Somali is the official language and the Somali shilling is the official currency. Puntland has not received international recognition.

Somaliland. An independent 'Somaliland Republic', based on the territory of the former British protectorate which ran from 1884 until Somali independence in 1960, was established on 17 May 1991 by the principal insurgent group in the north of the country, the Somali National Movement. The Somali government rejected the secession and Muhammad Aidid's forces launched an unsuccessful campaign to reoccupy Somaliland in Jan. 1996. Somaliland is also engaged in a long-running dispute with Puntland over control of the Sanaag and Sol regions. The Republic has failed to secure international recognition but has developed close relations with Ethiopia.

Somaliland covers 137,600 sq. km. The capital is Hargeisa and there is a port at Berbera. There is a population of around 3·5m. Somali is the official language and Arabic and English are also widely used.

There is a bicameral government with a house of representatives and one of elected elders. Dahir Riyale Kahin became *President* in May 2002 and was re-elected in April 2004. The judiciary is independent. The official currency is the Somaliland shilling. The Bank of Somaliland, the central bank, was founded in 1994. The economy is reliant on livestock farming.

Southwestern Somalia. In April 2002 Southwestern Somalia broke away from Mogadishu and was declared an autonomous state by the Rahanwein Resistance Army. Hassan Muhammad Nur 'Shatigadud' was named president but fighting between Shatigadud and several of his deputies ensued, notably around the capital, Baydhabo.

National Anthem. No words, tune by G. Blanc.

RECENT ELECTIONS

Somalia's Transitional Federal Parliament elected Abdullahi Yusuf Ahmed president on 10 Oct. 2004 in Nairobi, Kenya. In the first round Abdullahi Yusuf Ahmed won 80 votes, followed by Abdullahi Ahmed Addou with 35 and Mohamed Qanyare Afrah with 33. There were 23 other candidates. In the second round Ahmed won 147 votes, Addou 83 and Afrah 38, ahead of three other candidates. A third round run-off was required in which Ahmed won 189 against 79 for Addou.

CURRENT ADMINISTRATION

President: Abdullahi Yusuf Ahmed; b. 1934 (sworn in 14 Oct. 2004).

In March 2005 the Transitional Federal Government comprised:

Prime Minister: Ali Muhammad Ghedi; b. 1952 (in office since 3 Nov. 2004).

Vice-Prime Minister, Minister of Finance: Salim Aliyow Ibroow. *Vice-Prime Minister, Minister of Information:* Mohamuud Abdullahi 'Sifir' Jama. *Vice-Prime Minister, Minister of Internal Affairs:* Hussein M. Farah Aidid.

Minister of Agriculture: Hassan Mohamed 'Shatiguduud' Nuur. *Commerce:* Musse Suddi Yalahow. *Constitutional Affairs:* Abdalla Derow Isaaq. *Culture and Heritage:* Abdi Hashi Abdullahl. *Defence:* Gen. Abdirahman Mohamud Ali. *Development of Co-operatives:* Mohamed Abdullahl Kaamil. *Disabled and Orphanages:* Hussein Elaabe Fahiye. *Education:* Ali Abdullahi Osoble. *Energy:* Mohamednuraani Bakar. *Environment and Disaster Management:* Mohamed Osman Maye. *Family and Women's Affairs:* Fowsiiya Mohamed Sheikh Hussein. *Fisheries and Marine Resources:* Hassan Abshir Farah. *Foreign Affairs:* Abdullahi Sheikh Ismail. *Health:* Abdiaziz Sheikh Yussuf. *Higher Education:* Hussein M. Shiekh Hussein. *Industry:* Abdi Mohamed Tarah. *Justice:* Sheikh Adan Mohamed 'Madobe' Nur. *Labour and Human Resources:* Saalah Ali Saalah. *Lands and Settlements:* Moulid Ma'ane Mohamud. *Livestock and Forest Management:* Ibrahim Mohamed Isaaq. *Military Training and Reintegration:* Botaan Isse Alim. *Monetary Affairs:* Abdikanin Ahmed Ali. *National Security:* Mohamed Qanyare Afrah. *Oil:* Yussuf Mohamed Ali. *Planning and International Co-operation:* Abdirisaaq Osman Hassan. *Ports and Marine Affairs:* Ali Ismail Abdi. *Public Works and Housing:* Osman Hassan Ali Ato. *Regional Co-operation:* Ismail Hure Buubaa. *Reconciliation and Diaspora Affairs:* Sheikh Adan Sheikh Mohamed. *Reconstruction and Resettlement:* Barre Adan Shire. *Religious Affairs:* Omar M. Mohamud Filish. *Rural Development:* Mohamed Mohamuud 'Gamadhere' Guleed. *Science and Technology:* Ismail Hassan Jama. *Sports and Youth Affairs:* Ahmed Abdullahl Jama Daakir. *State Goods and Public Markets:* Mohamuud Sayid Adaan. *Surface and Air Transport:* Ibrahim Adan Hassan. *Transport, Post and Telecommunications:* Ali Ahmed Jama. *Tourism and Wildlife:* Mohamed Mohamud Heyd. *Water and Natural Resources:* Mohamud Salaad Nuur.

DEFENCE

With the breakdown of government following the 1991 revolution armed forces broke up into clan groupings, four of them in the north and six in the south.

Defence expenditure totalled US$38m. in 2002 (US$4 per capita), representing 4·0% of GDP.

Army. Following the 1991 revolution there are no national armed forces. In Northern Somalia the Somali National Movement controls an armed clan of 5–6,000 out of a total of 7,000 armed forces in the area. In the rest of the country several local groups control forces of which the Ali Mahdi Faction controls the largest, an armed clan of 10,000.

INTERNATIONAL RELATIONS

Somalia is a member of the UN, the African Union, African Development Bank, OIC, Islamic Development Bank, the League of Arab States and the Intergovernmental Authority on Development and is an ACP member state of the ACP-EU relationship.

ECONOMY

Agriculture accounts for approximately 59% of GDP, industry 10% and services 31%.

Overview. 'Scientific Socialism' was implemented by the military government of Muhammad Siad Barre in the 1970s. In the 1980s exports and manufacturing declined rapidly. In 1983 Saudi Arabia banned the import of Somali livestock, which earned about 80% of foreign currency. An IMF-backed Five Year Plan was instituted in 1987, which included privatization schemes and the reduction of the budget deficit. Civil war from 1988 precipitated the collapse of the national economy, government and banking system. Somalis became dependent on remittances, estimated at US$800m. annually, from the overseas diaspora in the 1990s.

Currency. The unit of currency is the *Somali shilling* (SOS) of 100 *cents*.

Budget. Budget for 1991: revenue, Som.Sh. 151,453m.; expenditure, Som.Sh. 141,141m.

Performance. Real GDP growth was 0·0% in both 1997 and 1998. Total GDP in 1998 was estimated to be US$4bn.

Banking and Finance. Prior to the collapse of central government in 1990, the bank of issue, now inactive, was the Central Bank of Somalia (*Governor*, Dr Mahmamud Mohamed Ulusow). The separatist Somaliland Republic has its own functioning central bank in Hargeisa, the Bank of Somaliland (*Governor*, Abdourahman Dualeh Mohamoud). Remittance companies (*hawala*) took the place of banks in the 1990s, channelling approximately US$800m. a year. Al-Barakaat, the largest *hawala*, was shut down in Nov. 2001. All national banks were bankrupted by 1990. The Universal Bank of Somalia, the first commercial bank in Mogadishu since 1990, opened with European backing in Jan. 2002.

ENERGY AND NATURAL RESOURCES

Environment. Carbon dioxide emissions from the consumption and flaring of fossil fuels in 2002 were the equivalent of 0·1 tonnes per capita.

Electricity. In 2000 installed capacity was 80,000 kW. Production (2000, estimate): 282m. kWh.

Oil and Gas. Natural gas reserves were 5·7bn. cu. metres in 2002.

Minerals. There are deposits of chromium, coal, copper, gold, gypsum, lead, limestone, manganese, nickel, sepiolite, silver, titanium, tungsten, uranium and zinc.

Agriculture. Somalia is essentially a pastoral country, and about 80% of the inhabitants depend on livestock-rearing (cattle, sheep, goats and camels). Half the population is nomadic. In 2001 there were 1·05m. ha of arable land and 26,000 ha of permanent cropland. 200,000 ha were irrigated in 2001. There were 1,700 tractors in 2001. Estimated production, 2000 (in 1,000 tonnes): sugarcane, 220; maize, 210; sorghum, 100; cassava, 70; bananas, 55.

Livestock (2000): 13·1m. sheep; 12·3m. goats; 6·1m. camels; 5·1m. cattle. Somalia has the greatest number of camels of any country in the world.

Forestry. In 2000 the area under forests was 7·52m. ha, or 12·0% of the total land area. In 2001, 9·63m. cu. metres of roundwood were cut. Wood and charcoal are the main energy sources. Frankincense and myrrh are produced.

Fisheries. Approximately 20,000 tonnes of fish were caught in 2001, almost entirely from marine waters.

INDUSTRY

A few small industries exist including sugar refining (production was 20,000 tonnes in 2001), food processing and textiles.

Labour. The labour force totalled 4,291,000 in 1996 (57% males). Approximately 74% of the economically active population in 1995 were engaged in agriculture, fisheries and forestry.

INTERNATIONAL TRADE

Foreign debt was US$2,688m. in 2002.

Imports and Exports. Exports in 1999 were estimated at US$150m. and imports at US$180m.

Principal exports: livestock, hides and skins, bananas. Main export markets in 1999: Yemen, 29%; Saudi Arabia, 28%; United Arab Emirates, 28%; Oman, 6%. Main import suppliers, 1999: Djibouti, 27%; Kenya, 12%; India, 9%; Thailand, 5%.

COMMUNICATIONS

Roads. In 1999 there were an estimated 22,100 km of roads, of which 2,600 km were paved. Passenger cars numbered 1,020 in 1996, and there were 6,440 trucks and vans.

Civil Aviation. There are international airports at Mogadishu and Hargeisa. In 2003 there were flights to Addis Ababa, Dire Dawa, Djibouti, Jeddah and Nairobi in addition to internal services.

Shipping. There are deep-water harbours at Kismayo, Berbera, Marka and Mogadishu. The merchant fleet (2002) totalled 6,000 GRT.

Telecommunications. Somalia had 100,000 main telephone lines in 2002, equivalent to 10 for every 1,000 persons. There were 35,000 mobile phone subscribers in 2002. In 2002 there were 89,000 Internet users. In the absence of a government-controlled telecommunications monopoly three companies—Telcom, Nationlink and Hormuud—compete for both landline and mobile customers.

SOCIAL INSTITUTIONS

Justice. There are 84 district courts, each with a civil and a criminal section. There are eight regional courts and two Courts of Appeal (at Mogadishu and Hargeisa), each with a general section and an assize section. The Supreme Court is in Mogadishu. The death penalty is in force and was used in 2000.

Religion. The population is almost entirely Sunni Muslims.

Education. The nomadic life of a large percentage of the population inhibits education progress. In 1990 adult literacy was estimated at 24%. In 1985 there were 194,335 pupils and 9,676 teachers in primary schools, there were 37,181 pupils and 2,320 teachers in secondary schools, and in 1984, 613 students with 30 teachers at teacher-training establishments. The National University of Somalia in Mogadishu (founded 1959) had 4,650 students and 550 academic staff in 1994–95.

Health. In 1997 Somalia had 265 physicians, 13 dentists, 1,327 nurses and 70 pharmacists. In 1988 there were seven hospital beds per 10,000 inhabitants.

Somalia has among the highest percentages of undernourished people of any country—73% in 1996, up from fewer than 60% in the early 1980s. In the period 1990–98 only 31% of the population had access to safe drinking water.

CULTURE

Broadcasting. The state television station was destroyed in fighting in 1991. Mogadishu-based HornAfrik was launched in 1999 as the first independent radio and television broadcaster. The National Transitional Government runs Radio Mogadishu–Voice of the Somali Republic. The Somali Broadcasting Corporation, based in Boosaso, was shut down by the government of Puntland in May 2002. The Somaliland government banned all private radio stations in June 2002, giving Radio Hargeisa a monopoly. In 1997 there were estimated to be 470,000 radio and 135,000 TV receivers (colour by PAL).

Press. The Somali press collapsed in 1991, with most of its facilities destroyed. Since 2000 several independent newspapers have emerged, including the daily *Wartire* in Hargeisa (Somaliland) and the weeklies *Yamayska* and *Bulsho* in Puntland. There were six daily newspapers in Mogadishu in Oct. 2002. In 1996 average daily circulation of newspapers totalled 10,000.

Tourism. In 1998 there were 10,000 foreign tourists.

DIPLOMATIC REPRESENTATIVES

The Embassy of Somalia in the United Kingdom closed on 2 Jan. 1992.

Of the United Kingdom in Somalia (Waddada Xasan Geedd Abtoow 7–8, Mogadishu)
Staff temporarily withdrawn.

The Embassy of Somalia in the USA closed on 8 May 1991. A liaison office opened in March 1994, and withdrew to Nairobi in Sept. 1994.

Of Somalia to the United Nations
Ambassador: Ahmed Abdo Hashi.

Of Somalia to the European Union
Ambassador: Vacant.

FURTHER READING

Abdisalam, M. I.-S., *The Collapse of the Somali State*. London, 1995
Ghalib, J. M., *The Cost of Dictatorship: the Somali Experience*. New York, 1995
Lewis, I. M., *Blood and Bone: the Call of Kinship in Somali Society*. Lawrenceville (NJ), 1995.—*Understanding Somalia: a Guide to Culture, History and Social Institutions*. 2nd ed. London, 1995
Omar, M. O., *The Road to Zero: Somalia's Self-Destruction*. London, 1995
Samatar, A. I. (ed.) *The Somali Challenge: from Catastrophe to Renewal?* Boulder (CO), 1994

National statistical office: Central Statistical Department, State Planning Commission, Mogadishu.

SOUTH AFRICA

Republic of South Africa

Capital: Pretoria/Tshwane (Administrative), Cape Town (Legislative), Bloemfontein (Judicial)
Seat of Parliament: Cape Town
Seats of Government: Cape Town, Pretoria
Population projection, 2010: 44·94m.
GDP per capita, 2002: (PPP$) 10,070
HDI/world rank: 0·666/119

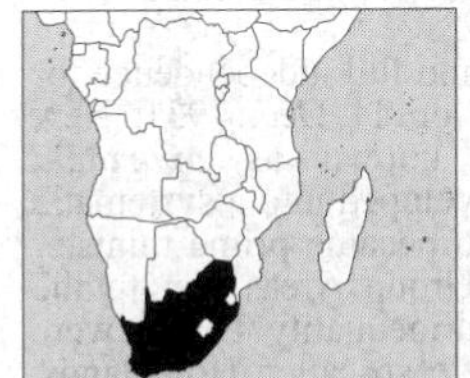

KEY HISTORICAL EVENTS

The San (Bushmen), nomadic hunter-gatherers, lived at the edge of the Kalahari Desert for thousands of years. The Khoikhoi shared customs with the San and spoke related languages but lived in more settled communities, mostly along the Orange River valley and around the Cape. From the fourth century AD, Bantu-speaking farmers settled the east.

Portuguese mariners first rounded the Cape peninsula in 1487, opening a trade route into the Indian Ocean, and were followed by Spanish, English, Dutch and French seafarers. Landing on the Cape peninsula, they bartered sheep and cattle with Khoikhoi pastoralists in return for iron and copper goods. In 1652 the Dutch East India Company established a trading post in the Cape. Relations between the Dutch and the Khoikhoi soon deteriorated: quarrels over rights to graze cattle escalated into warfare as early as 1659. Over the next century the Dutch established large farms, cultivating vines and grain in the fertile Cape valleys. The Khoikhoi, devastated by smallpox, were unable to hold back the *trekboers* (Dutch pastoral farmers), who by 1770 were grazing their cattle as far east as the Fish River. There they came into contact with the Xhosa. More numerous than the Khoikhoi and with greater resistance to European diseases, the Xhosa fought the Dutch settlers in a series of 'Frontier Wars'.

By the late 18th century, Dutch maritime power had declined. Having seized Cape Town in 1795, British sovereignty over the colony was confirmed in 1815. In the early 19th century the Zulu people of the north-eastern region (Natal) strengthened their power-base under their leader, Shaka. Native wars caused havoc and destruction, known as the *Mfecane*. New kingdoms emerged, notably Gaza and Swaziland. The Sotho, under King Moshoshoe, formed the mountain territory now known as Lesotho. The Mfecane led to the migration of thousands of Basotho and Batswana from the High veld and Xhosa from the coastal plains into the Cape Colony. In the 1830s some Boer settlers, who resented British rule, began the 'Great Trek' into the land to the north and east. There they founded the Orange Free State and Transvaal.

The British strengthened their hold over the Cape Colony and Natal by bringing in new settlers, including Indians from Madras and Calcutta, to work as indentured labourers on the new sugar plantations. The population included many Afrikaners as well as the 'coloured' community (descendants of Khoikhoi, white settlers and Malay slaves). Britain annexed the Transvaal in 1877 and in 1879 fought the Zulus, who were victorious at Isandhlwana under King Ketshwayo but were then defeated at Ulundi. Britain restored independence to the Transvaal (the South African Republic) in 1884 and annexed Zululand in 1887. Both the British and the Boers fought African resistance, the last major rising being in Natal in 1906. After the discovery of diamonds at Kimberley in 1867 and of gold in the Transvaal in 1884, Cecil Rhodes, owner of the De Beers Company and for a time prime minister of the Cape, hoped to extend British rule. The Afrikaners, led by Paul Kruger, declared war on Britain in late 1899 to maintain their independence. The Boers suffered a heavy defeat at Paardeberg in 1900 but then switched to guerrilla warfare. The British army, led by Gen. Kitchener, responded by destroying crops and farmsteads. The 'scorched earth' policy was strongly criticized in Europe but in 1902 the Boer republics signed the Treaty of Vereeniging and accepted British rule. They were given self-government in 1907 and on 31 May 1910 the Cape Colony, Natal, the

Transvaal and the Orange Free State combined to form the Union of South Africa, a self-governing dominion under the British Crown.

In the first general election, in 1910, the South African party won 67 seats against 39 seats for the mainly English-speaking Unionist Party. The Union's economy was based on gold and diamond mining, for which there was organized recruitment of migrant African labourers. Pass Laws were in operation, controlling Africans' movements in the towns and industrial areas, where they were regarded officially as temporary residents and segregated in 'townships'. Following the Land Act of 1913, 87% of the land was reserved for white ownership while Africans farmed as tenants or squatters. African protests at segregation and the absence of political rights were led by the South African Native National Congress (SANNC), founded in 1912 and renamed the African National Congress (ANC) in 1923.

The Afrikaner Nationalist Party came to power in 1924 and full independence for South Africa was granted by the Statute of Westminster on 11 Dec. 1931. New segregation measures were enforced that became known as *apartheid* ('separateness'). After the Second World War apartheid developed into a systematic programme of social engineering. Hendrik Verwoerd, who became prime minister in 1958, introduced a plethora of new laws from the Group Areas Act to the Prohibition of Mixed Marriages Act, which hardened racial inequality. Blacks were divided into one of ten tribal groups and forced to move to so-called Homelands, which were intended to become self-sufficient, self-governing states. The massacre by police of 69 protesters against the Pass Laws at Sharpeville on 21 March 1960 led to a major crisis from which, however, the government emerged even stronger. The ANC and the Pan African Congress were banned and the leaders, including Nelson Mandela, were jailed in 1964. After withdrawing from the Commonwealth in 1961, South Africa became increasingly isolated.

On 16 June 1976 many students died when police broke up a demonstration in Soweto, an African township outside Johannesburg. When P. W. Botha became prime minister in 1978, elements of the apartheid system were modified and a new constitution created a three-part parliament, with a House of Assembly for the whites, a House of Representatives for the coloureds and a House of Delegates for the Indians. Africans remained without representation. After large-scale protests, a state of emergency was imposed. Foreign condemnation led to the first economic sanctions against South Africa.

By 1989 a start had been made on dismantling apartheid and in 1990 President F. W. de Klerk lifted a 30-year ban on the ANC and released Nelson Mandela from prison. A whites-only referendum on 17 March 1992 gave nearly 70% support for granting constitutional equality to all races. A new multi-racial parliament was elected on 29 April 1994. The ANC were victorious and on 9 May Nelson Mandela was elected president. In 1997 the Truth and Reconciliation Commission, chaired by Archbishop Desmond Tutu, promised amnesty to those who confessed their crimes under the apartheid system. Mandela retired in 1999. His deputy, Thabo Mbeki, who was elected president in a landslide vote, has since wrestled with a developing economy, continuing inequality, a high crime rate and an AIDS epidemic.

TERRITORY AND POPULATION

South Africa is bounded in the north by Namibia, Botswana and Zimbabwe, northeast by Mozambique and Swaziland, east by the Indian Ocean, and south and west by the South Atlantic, with Lesotho forming an enclave. Area: 1,219,090 sq. km. This area includes the uninhabited Prince Edward Island (41 sq. km) and Marion Island (388 sq. km), lying 1,900 km southeast of Cape Town. The islands were handed over to South Africa in Dec. 1947 to prevent their falling into hostile hands. In 1994 Walvis Bay was ceded to Namibia, and Transkei, Bophuthatswana, Venda and Ciskei were re-integrated into South Africa.

At the census of 2001 the population was 44,819,782 (23,385,739 females), consisting of: Black African, 35,416,167 (79·0% of total population); White, 4,293,641 (9·6%); Coloured, 3,994,506 (8·9%); Indian, 1,115,468 (2·5%).

The UN gives a projected population for 2010 of 44·94m.

57·6% of the population was urban in 2001. In 1999 cities with the largest populations were (estimate in 1,000): Johannesburg (Gauteng), 4,074·6; Durban (KwaZulu-Natal), 2,554·4; Cape Town (Western Cape), 2,522·5; Port Elizabeth

(Eastern Cape), 1,327·7; Pretoria—renamed Tshwane in 2005 (Gauteng), 1,411·9; Bloemfontein (Free State), 584; East London (Eastern Cape), 332.

There were 3,053 immigrants in 2000 and 10,262 emigrants (8,402 in 1999).

Population by province, according to the 2001 census:

Province	*Total (including unspecified)*	*African*	*White*	*Coloured*	*Indian/ Asian*
Eastern Cape	6,436,764	5,635,079	304,506	478,807	18,372
Free State	2,706,776	2,381,073	238,791	83,193	3,719
Gauteng	8,837,179	6,522,792	1,758,398	337,974	218,015
KwaZulu-Natal	9,426,017	8,002,407	483,448	141,887	798,275
Mpumalanga	3,122,991	2,886,345	203,244	22,158	11,244
Northern Cape	822,727	293,976	102,042	424,389	2,320
Northern Province (now Limpopo)	5,273,642	5,128,616	126,276	10,163	8,587
NorthWest	3,669,350	3,358,450	244,035	56,959	9,906
Western Cape	4,524,336	1,207,429	832,901	2,438,976	45,030

There are 11 official languages. Numbers of home speakers at the 2001 census: IsiZulu, 10,677,305 (23·8% of population); IsiXhosa, 7,907,153 (17·6%); Afrikaans, 5,983,426 (13·3%); Sepedi, 4,208,980 (9·4%); English, 3,673,203 (8·6%); Setswana, 3,677,016 (8·2%); Sesotho, 3,555,186 (8·2%); Xitsonga, 1,992,207 (4·4%); Siswati, 1,194,430 (2·75%); Tshivenda, 1,021,757 (2·3%); IsiNdebele, 711,821 (1·6%). The use of any of these languages is a constitutional right 'wherever practicable'. Each province may adopt any of these as its official language. English is the sole language of command and instruction in the armed forces.

SOCIAL STATISTICS

Births: the number of recorded births decreased from 720,988 in 1991 to 409,359 in 2001. Total number of births in 2000 was estimated at 1,408,000.

Officially recorded marriages: the following statistics reflect marriages contracted and divorces granted during 1999, as registered by the civil registration system. (From 1998, under a new bill, customary and traditional marriages are recognized in law.) The total number of marriages officially recorded in 1999 was 155,807. The crude marriage rate was 355 per 100,000 of the population. Western Cape had the highest rate (596 per 100,000), Gauteng the second highest (523 per 100,000) followed by Free State (481 per 100,000). KwaZulu-Natal had the lowest rate (166 per 100,000), in part owing to unregistered customary and traditional marriages occurring mostly in this largely rural province. Of the total marriages officially recorded in 1999, 70,544 (45·3%) were solemnized in magistrates' courts and 52,630 in religious ceremonies. 32,633 were classed under 'unspecified'. In 1999 the median age for marrying was 33·7 years for men and 29·5 years for women. Divorces granted in 1999 totalled 37,098; the modified divorce rate was 660 per 100,000 of the population. Gauteng had the highest rate (1,253 per 100,000); Western Cape (1,140); and Northern Cape (797).

Deaths: the number of deaths increased from 318,287 in 1997 to 454,603 in 2003. Deaths from AIDS are likely to result in life expectancy being just 38 by 2010. A Statistics South Africa report published in Feb. 2005 concluded that the average number of deaths rose from 870 a day in 1997 to 1,370 a day in 2002, with AIDS as the factor underlying much of the increase in mortality. The annual number of deaths in South Africa has increased by 57% since 1997. According to the State of SA's Population Report 2000 the annual population growth rate 1996–2001 was 2·2% and the fertility rate 2·9 births per woman. Life expectancy at birth, 2001, was 47·7 years for males and 54·4 for females. Infant mortality, 2001, 56 per 1,000 live births.

CLIMATE

There is abundant sunshine and relatively low rainfall. The southwest has a Mediterranean climate, with rain mainly in winter, but most of the country has a summer maximum, although quantities show a decrease from east to west. Pretoria, Jan. 73·4°F (23·0°C), July 53·6°F (12·0°C). Annual rainfall 26·5" (674 mm). Bloemfontein, Jan. 73·4°F (23·0°C), July 45·9°F (7·7°C). Annual rainfall 22" (559 mm). Cape Town, Jan. 69·6°F (20·9°C), July 54·0°F (12·2°C). Annual rainfall 20·3"

(515 mm). Johannesburg, Jan. 68·2°F (20·1°C), July 50·7°F (10·4°C). Annual rainfall 28·1" (713 mm).

CONSTITUTION AND GOVERNMENT

An Interim *Constitution* came into effect on 27 April 1994 and was in force until 3 Feb. 1997. Under it, the National Assembly and Senate formed a Constitutional Assembly, which had the task of drafting a definitive Constitution. This was signed into law in Dec. 1996 and took effect on 4 Feb. 1997. The 1996 Constitution defines the powers of the President, Parliament (consisting of the National Assembly and the National Council of Provinces—NCOP), the national executive, the judiciary, public administration, the security services and the relationship between the three spheres of government. It incorporates a Bill of Rights pertaining to, *inter alia*, education, housing, food and water supply, and security, in addition to political rights. All legislation must conform to the Constitution and the Bill of Rights. The Constitution was amended in 2001 to provide that Constitutional Court judges are appointed for a non-renewable 12-year term of office, or until they reach the age of 70 years, except where an Act of Parliament extends the term of office of a Constitutional Court judge. This Constitution Amendment Act also made the head of the Constitutional Court the Chief Justice. The head of the Supreme Court of Appeal is now the President of that Court.

A *Constitutional Court*, consisting of a president, a deputy president and nine other judges, was inaugurated in Feb. 1995. The Court's judges are appointed by the President of the Republic from a list provided by the Judicial Service Commission, after consulting the President of the Constitutional Court (now the Chief Justice) and the leaders of parties represented in the National Assembly.

Parliament is the legislative authority and has the power to make laws for the country in accordance with the Constitution. It consists of the National Assembly and the NCOP. Parliamentary sittings are open to the public.

The *National Assembly* consists of no fewer than 350 and no more than 400 members directly elected for five years, 200 from a national list and 200 from provincial lists in the following proportions: Eastern Cape, 28; Free State, 14; Gauteng, 44; KwaZulu-Natal, 42; Limpopo, 25; Mpumalanga, 11; Northern Cape, 4; North-West, 12; Western Cape, 20. In terms of the 1993 Constitution, which still regulated the 1999 elections, the nine provincial legislatures are elected at the same time and candidates may stand for both. If elected to both, they have to choose between sitting in the national or provincial assembly. In the former case, the runner-up is elected to the Provincial Assembly.

From 21 March 2003, for a period of two weeks, members of the National Assembly and provincial legislatures were allowed to defect to other political parties without losing their seats in both houses, in accordance with a constitutional amendment of 2003. The Act provided for three 'window' periods. The first one was a transitional arrangement consisting of a 15-day period starting on 21 March 2003. The second and third periods were to be for 15 days each, from 1 to 15 Sept. in the second and fourth years following the date of a national and provincial election.

The *National Council of Provinces* (NCOP) consists of 54 permanent members and 36 special delegates and aims to represent provincial interests in the national sphere of government. Delegations from each province consist of ten representatives. Bills (except finance bills) may be introduced in either house but must be passed by both. A finance bill may only be introduced in the National Assembly. If a bill is rejected by one house it is referred back to both after consideration by a joint National Assembly-NCOP committee called the Mediation Committee. Bills relating to the provinces must be passed by the NCOP. By Aug. 2003 more than 780 pieces of legislation had been passed since 1994.

The Constitution mandates the establishment of *Traditional Leaders* by means of either provincial or national legislation. The National House of Traditional Leaders was established in April 1997. Each provincial House of Traditional Leaders nominated three members to be represented in the National House. The National House advises national government on the role of traditional leaders and on customary law.

National Anthem. A combination of shortened forms of 'Die Stem van Suid-Afrika'/'The Call of South Africa' (words by C. J. Langenhoven; tune by M. L. de

Villiers) and the ANC anthem 'Nkosi sikelel' iAfrika'/'God bless Africa' (words and tune by Enos Santonga).

RECENT ELECTIONS

Parliamentary elections were held on 14 April 2004. Turn-out was 89·3%. The African National Congress (ANC) won 279 seats in Parliament's National Assembly with 69·7% of votes cast, the Democratic Alliance (DA) 50 with 12·4%, the Inkatha Freedom Party (IFP) 28 with 7·0%, the United Democratic Movement (UDM) 9 with 2·3%, the New National Party (NNP) 7 with 1·7%, the Independent Democrats (ID) 7 with 1·7%, the African Christian Democratic Party (ACDP) 6 with 1·6%, Freedom Front Plus (VF+) 4 with 0·9%, United Christian-Democratic Party (UCDP) 3 with 0·8%, Pan African Congress of Azania (PAC) 3 with 0·7%, Minority Front (MF) 2 with 0·4% and the Azanian People's Organisation (AZAPO) 2 with 0·3%.

CURRENT ADMINISTRATION

President: Thabo M. Mbeki; b. 1942 (ANC; sworn in 16 June 1999; re-elected 23 April 2004).

In March 2005 the government comprised:

Deputy President: Jacob G. Zuma. *Minister of Agriculture and Land Affairs:* Angela Thoko Didiza. *Arts and Culture:* Zweledinga Pallo Jordan. *Communications:* Dr Ivy F. Matsepe-Cassaburri. *Correctional Services:* Ngconde Balfour. *Defence:* M. G. Patrick Lekota. *Education:* Naledi Pandor. *Environmental Affairs and Tourism:* Marthinus van Schalkwyk. *Finance:* Trevor A. Manuel. *Foreign Affairs:* Dr Nkosazana C. Dlamini-Zuma. *Health:* Dr Manto E. Tshabalala-Msimang. *Home Affairs:* Nosiviwe Mapisa-Nqakula. *Housing:* Dr Lindiwe N. Sisulu. *Intelligence:* Ronald Kasrils. *Justice and Constitutional Development:* Brigitte Sylvia Mabandla. *Labour:* Membathisi M. S. Mdladlana. *Minerals and Energy:* Phumzile Mlambo-Ngcuka. *Provincial and Local Government:* F. Sydney Mufamadi. *Public Enterprises:* Alexander Erwin. *Public Service and Administration:* Geraldine J. Fraser-Moleketi. *Public Works:* Stella N. Sigcau. *Safety and Security:* Charles Nqakula. *Science and Technology:* Mosibudi Mangena. *Social Development and Welfare:* Zola S. T. Skweyiya. *Sport and Recreation:* Mankenkisi Stofile. *Trade and Industry:* Mandisi Bongani Mabuto Mpahlwa. *Transport:* Jeffrey Thamsanqa Radebe. *Water Affairs and Forestry:* Buyelwa Patience Sonjica. *Minister in the Presidency:* Essop G. Pahad.

Government Website: http://www.gov.za

DEFENCE

The South African National Defence Force (SANDF) comprises four services, namely the SA Army, the SA Air Force, the SA Navy and the SA Military Health Service (SAMHS). SAMHS personnel at the end of 2000 totalled 7,328 (3,900 women). South Africa ended conscription in 1994. In July 2002 the SANDF consisted of 76,000 members.

Defence expenditure totalled US$2,633m. in 2003 (equivalent to US$58 per capita), and represented 1·6% of GDP. Defence expenditure in 1985 was US$3,252m. (US$97 per capita and 3·8% of GDP).

Army. Personnel of the South African National Defence Force totalled 60,000 in 2002 (excluding 16,716 civilian employees). Regular army reserves numbered 14,615 in 2002, and the territorial army had a strength of 56,334.

Navy. Navy personnel in 2002 totalled 5,000, with 1,330 reserves. The fleet is based at the naval bases at Simon's Town on the west coast and Durban on the east and includes four *Warrior* class fast attack craft (missile) and two *Daphné* class submarines (to be supplemented from 2005 with three submarines on order from the German Submarine Consortium). The *SAS Amatola*, the first of four corvettes from Germany, arrived in Nov. 2003.

Air Force. Strength (2002) 9,250, with 434 reserves. The Air Force has 84 combat aircraft (*Cheetah* Cs, *Cheetah* Ds, *Impala* Mk1s and *Impala* Mk2s) and 12 attack helicopters.

INTERNATIONAL RELATIONS

South Africa is a member of the UN, BIS, the Commonwealth (except during 1961–94), the African Union, the Southern African Development Community, the

Non-Aligned Movement, the African Development Bank, the Antarctic Treaty and is an ACP member state of the ACP-EU relationship.

ECONOMY

Agriculture accounted for 4·1% of GDP in 2002, industry 32·2% and services 63·7%.

Overview. Since the end of apartheid South Africa has managed to contain inflation and to achieve budgetary discipline. In the early 1990s the removal of international sanctions and the adoption of structural reforms opened the economy to international competition, leading to productivity gains and greater penetration in international markets. These structural reforms have contributed to the sustained increase in growth rates witnessed since 1994—growth increased from an average of 1·2% during 1980–84 to 2·8% since 1994. Employment creation has, however, remained slow. Investment levels in South Africa are low compared to those in other emerging economies. To control inflation the South African Reserve Bank has adopted tight macroeconomic policies. The service sector leads in the economy, surpassing mineral and energy resources. Strong public finances sustain a competitive exchange rate and low interest rates, while monetary policy contains inflationary pressures. Since the end of apartheid the government has focused on controlling the deficit while increasing spending on social programmes to combat inequality. According to the World Bank, South Africa suffers from the highest income disparities in the world, with 53% of the population living in third world conditions. South Africa has one of highest HIV/AIDS infection rates. In a review released by the government in 2003 to evaluate the progress and shortcomings of the last ten years, the government pledged to focus on improving social inclusion, encouraging skill development and improving health care.

Currency. The unit of currency is the rand (ZAR) of 100 cents. A single free-floating exchange rate replaced the former two-tier system on 13 March 1995. The year-on-year rate of increase in the Consumer Price Inflation (CPIX)—the new measure of consumer price inflation for inflation targeting purposes, which excludes home mortgage rates from the overall consumer price index for metropolitan and other urban areas—was 6·6% in 2001, 10·0% in 2002 and reached 11·2% in March 2003.

Foreign exchange reserves were US$5,673m. and gold reserves 5·72m. troy oz in June 2002. Total money supply was R339,233m. in June 2002.

Budget. The central government's State Revenue Account in R1bn.:

	1998–99	*1999–2000*	*2000–01*	*2001–02*	*2002–03*
Revenue	184·0	198·2	215·6	248·1	265·2
Expenditure	201·4	214·8	233·9	262·6	287·9

The 2002 budget provided for expenditure of 26·6% of GDP; revenue, 24·5% of GDP. South Africa's deficit was revised to 2·1% in 2002–03 and is projected to decline to 1·7% by 2004–05. About R47·5bn. or 4·4% of GDP, is spent on debt servicing.

Income tax is the Government's main source of income. As of 2001, South Africa's source-based income tax system was replaced with a residence-based system. With effect from the years of assessment commencing on or after 1 Jan. 2001, residents are (subject to certain exclusions) taxed on their worldwide income, irrespective of where their income is earned. Foreign taxes are credited against South African tax payable on foreign income. Foreign income and taxes are translated into the South African monetary unit, the Rand.

Value-added Tax (VAT) has remained at 14% since 1993. Corporate taxes were reduced to 30% in 1999. A tiered corporate tax was introduced in 2000 with taxes for small businesses reduced by half. R9·9bn. was returned to taxpayers in reduced personal income tax for all income groups but particularly for lower and middle income groups. The marginal tax rate for high-income earners was cut to 42% from 45%. A capital gains tax was introduced from 1 April 2001 and became effective on 1 Oct. 2001.

Performance. Total GDP in 2003 was US$159·9bn. The economy grew by 3·7% in 2004, up from 2·8% in 2003. Average annual growth was 3·2% in the period 2001–04. Gross international reserves were about US$7·9bn. in Dec. 2002.

Banking and Finance. The central bank and bank of issue is the South African Reserve Bank (SARB; established 1920), which functions independently. Its *Governor* is Tito Mboweni. The Banks Act, 1990 governs the operations and prudential requirements of banks.

At the end of Dec. 2002, 42 banks, including 14 branches of foreign banks and two mutual banks, were registered with the Office of the Registrar of Banks. Furthermore, 52 foreign banks had authorized representative offices in South Africa. The banking institutions collectively employed 115,734 workers at 8,438 branches and agencies; their combined assets amounted to R970·9bn. (31 Oct. 2001). Banking in South Africa is dominated by five banks: Standard Bank, FirstRand, Absa and Nedcor, which are commercial banks, and Investec, an investment bank.

The stock exchange, the JSE Securities Exchange, is based in Johannesburg. Foreign nationals have been eligible for membership since Nov. 1995.

ENERGY AND NATURAL RESOURCES

Environment. In 1998 the Committee for Environmental Co-ordination was established to harmonize the work of government departments on environmental issues, and to co-ordinate environmental implementation and national management plans at provincial level.

SANParks manages a system of 20 national parks and there are some 9,000 privately owned game ranches in South Africa, expanding at a rate of 300,000 ha per annum.

South Africa's carbon dioxide emissions from the consumption and flaring of fossil fuels in 2002 were the equivalent of 8·4 tonnes per capita.

Electricity. South African households use over 25% of the country's energy. Coal supplies 75% of primary energy requirements, followed by oil (20·7%), nuclear (3·0%) and natural gas (1·3%). There is one nuclear power station (Koeberg) with two reactors, two gas turbine generators, two conventional hydroelectric plants and two pumped storage stations. Nuclear energy is being investigated as a future potential energy source and alternative to coal. The government has announced it is to sell off Eskom, the parastatal or government-related organization. Eskom generates 95% of the country's electricity (as well as two-thirds of the electricity for the African continent) and owns and operates the national transmission system.

During 2002 Eskom electrified 211,628 homes against the government target of 205,371. Between 1994 and 2003 a total of 3·8m. households were connected to the extended national electricity grid. According to the census of 2001, the percentage of households using electricity had increased from 57·6% to 69·7%. An estimated 7·12m. of South Africa's 10·77m. households had electricity at the end of 2001.

The energy sector contributes about 15% to GDP and employs about 250,000 people. Because of South Africa's large coal deposits, the country is one of the four cheapest electricity suppliers in the world. Residential use is characterized by poor access to facilities and inefficient or hazardous energy sources, such as fuel wood and paraffin.

The first wind-energy farm in Africa was opened at Klipheuwel in the Western Cape on 21 Feb. 2003.

Oil and Gas. South Africa has no significant oil reserves and relies on coal for most of its oil production. It has a highly developed synthetic fuels industry, as well as small deposits of oil and natural gas. Sasol Oil and Petro SA are the two major players in the synthetic fuel market. Synfuels meet approximately 40% of local demand. Natural gas production in 1998 amounted to 1·4bn. cu. metres; however, the prospects for natural gas production have increased by the discovery of offshore reserves close to the Namibian border in 2000. Production is scheduled to commence in 2006 and will be channelled to regulate electricity production.

Petro SA is responsible for exploration of both offshore natural gas and onshore coal-bed methane. The EM gas-field complex off Mossel Bay in the Western Cape started production in the third quarter of 2000, and will ensure sufficient feedstock to PetroSA to maintain current liquid fuel production levels at 36,000 bbls. of petroleum products a day until 2009. The oilfield, Sable, situated about 150 km south off the coast of Mossel Bay, is expected to produce 17% of South Africa's oil needs. Coming into operation in Aug. 2003, it was initially projected to produce 30,000 to 40,000 bbls. of crude oil a day. PetroSA's gas-to-liquid plant supplies about 7% of South Africa's liquid fuel needs.

South Africa is one of the major oil refining nations in Africa with a crude refining capacity of 543,000 bbls. per day.

Minerals. Total value of all minerals sold, 1999: R76,387·1m.

Preliminary 2002 figures indicated that mining contributed R30·6bn. or 8·5% of gross value added, an improvement of R13·86bn. on 2001. The preliminary figures also indicated a 1·5% rise in employment in the mining sector from 407,154 in 2001 to 413,087 in 2002. There were 749 mines and quarries. Sales of primary mineral products accounted for 34·3% of South Africa's total export revenue during 2001.

Mineral production (in tonnes), 2001: coal, 223·5m.; silver, 109·6; iron ore, 34·8m.; limestone, 18·8m.; chrome ore, 5·5m.; manganese, 3·3m.; aluminium, 662,000; copper, 141,000; zinc, 61,221; nickel, 36,443; platinum-group metals, 28,747; gold, 395; diamonds, 11,162,630 carats. In 2001 earnings from platinum surpassed gold for the first time in 100 years. Total revenue from platinum-group metals (PGMs) was US$3·88bn. compared with gold revenue of US$3·37bn. South Africa is the world's leading producer of both platinum and gold.

Agriculture. South Africa has a dual agricultural economy, comprising a well-developed commercial sector and a predominantly subsistence-orientated sector. Much of the land suitable for mechanized farming has unreliable rainfall. Of the total farming area, natural pasture occupies 81% (69·6m. ha) and planted pasture 2·3% (2m. ha). About 13% of South Africa's surface area can be used for crop production. High potential arable land comprises only 22% of the total arable land. Annual crops and orchards are cultivated on 9·9m. ha of dry land and 1·5m. ha under irrigation. There were 72,300 tractors in 2001 and 11,200 harvester-threshers. Primary agriculture contributes about 2·9% to GDP and almost 9% of formal employment. The agricultural sector grew by 4% in 2002, following a decline of 1·7% in 2001. The net income of the farming sector increased from R10,591m. in 2001 to R20,277m. in 2002.

Production (2002, in 1,000 tonnes):

(*Field crops*): maize 13,906; wheat 4,213; sugarcane 3,284; sunflower seed 2,160; hay 1,778; tobacco 529; grain sorghum 382; ground-nuts 322; cotton 155; other 1,237. Total 27,966. South Africa is the main maize producer in the SADC.

(*Horticulture*): deciduous and other fruit 4,396; vegetables 3,522; citrus 2,915; potatoes 2,438; viticulture 2,088; subtropical fruit 941; other 1,124. Total 17,424.

(*Animal products*): poultry and poultry products 10,767; cattle and cattle slaughtered 5,289; sheep and goats slaughtered 1,413; pigs slaughtered 1,090; fresh milk 2,794; milk for dairy products 1,391; wool 1,269.

The value of agricultural imports increased by 13·9% and the value of exports increased by 37·6% for 2001 compared to 2000. In 2002 agricultural exports contributed 8·3% of total exports. Based on 2001 export values, sugar (R2,703m.), wine (R1,963m.), citrus fruit (R1,799m.), grapes (R1,327m.) and preserved fruit and nuts (R990m.) were the most important export products. Rice (R954m.), oil-cake (R762m.), undenatured ethyl alcohol (R602m.), tobacco (R456m.) and palm oil (R455m.) were the most important import products. During 2001 the UK, the Netherlands, Japan and Mozambique were the largest export destinations.

South Africa is one of the largest exporters in the world of avocados, grapes, sugar, citrus and deciduous fruit. According to the South African Wine and Spirits Export Association, the export of white wine increased from 20m. litres in 1992 to 218m. litres in 2002.

Forestry. Africa has developed one of the largest man-made forestry resources in the world. Production from these plantations approached 15·1m. cu. metres, valued at almost R11·86m. in 2001. Together with processed products, the total industry turnover was approximately R2·7bn. in 2001, including R2·0bn. worth of wood-pulp. More than 11·8m. tons (pulpwood, mining timber, matchwood and charcoal) and 3·2m. cu. metres (sawlogs, veneer and poles) were sold in this period. Collectively, the forestry sector employs about 151,000 people. An equivalent of about 60,000 full-time staff are employed in the primary sector (growing and harvesting), while the balance are employed in the processing industries (sawmilling, pulp and paper, mining timber and poles, and board products). In 2001 the forestry industry contributed 1·2% to the entire South African GDP.

Indigenous high forest covers only about 534,000 ha or 0·4% of the country's surface. The private sector owns 971,098 ha (or 72%) of the total plantation area of 1,351,176 ha as well as 161 of the 167 processing plants in the country. The remaining 28% (380,663 ha) is under public ownership. The department of water affairs and forestry is pursuing a reform programme in the forestry sector which will eventually see the government leasing all State-owned forest land to private-sector operators. In 2000–01 there were 1,280 registered private timber growers and more than 14,000 unregistered growers.

The industry was a net exporter to the value of over R5·7bn. in 2002, more than 97% of which was in the form of converted value-added products. The forest-products industry contributed 3·58% of total exports and 1·99% of total imports in 2002. In 2002 paper exports were the most important (R4·25bn. or 38% of the total), followed by solid wood products (R3·78bn. or 34% of the total), pulp (R2·89bn. or 26% of the total), and other products (R0·28bn. or 2% of the total). Woodchip exports, mainly to Japan, accounted for 52% (R1·96bn.) of the total solid wood products exports.

Fisheries. The commercial marine fishing industry is valued at more than R3bn. annually and employs 28,000 people directly. It is an important employer because it pays a relatively high average wage (approximately R36,000) to its employees, of whom the majority are semi-skilled. In 2000 the commercial fishing fleet consisted of 4,477 vessels licensed by the department of environmental affairs and tourism.

The total number of fishing rights allocated stands at 2,200, 1,700 of which are small, medium and micro enterprises. The total catch in 1999 was 588,001 tonnes, 99% of which came from marine fishing. Deep sea hake amounts to over half of the total catch and an estimated 35% of fish is exported.

INDUSTRY

The leading companies by market capitalization in South Africa, excluding banking and finance, in May 2004 were: Anglo American Platinum Corp. Ltd (US$31·3bn.), the world's primary platinum group metals producer; Sasol Ltd (US$10·4bn.), a coal, oil and gas producer; and AngloGold Ashanti Ltd (US$9·3bn.), the world's leading gold producer.

Net value of sales of the principal groups of industries (in R1m.) in 1999: food and food products, 57,136; chemicals and products, 45,353; vehicles and vehicle parts, 42,719; basic iron and steel products, 25,867; fabricated metal products except machinery, 23,536; beverages, 20,653; petroleum products, 20,464; paper and products, 20,400. Total net value including other groups, R397,320m. Manufacturing contributed R108,470m. towards GDP of R544,654m. in 1999, and thus accounted for 20% of the total.

Labour. The Employment Equity Act, 1998 signalled the beginning of the final phase of transformation in the job market, which began with the implementation of the Labour Relations Act. It aims to avoid all discrimination in employment. The Basic Conditions of Employment Act, 1997 applies to all workers except for the South African National Defence Force (SANDF), the South African Secret Service (SASS) and the National Intelligence Agency (NIA). The new provisions include a reduction in the maximum hours of work from 46 to 45 hours per week (however, the Act allows for the progressive reduction of working hours to 40 per week).

The number of those who are economically active—both the employed and the unemployed—was 16·8m. in March 2003. The number of unemployed rose from 2·2m. in 1996 to 5·2m. in March 2003. In March 2003 the unemployment rate was 31·2% (29·4% in Feb. 2002).

The Unemployment Insurance Fund (UIF), providing benefits to unemployed workers, increased its income from R2·1bn. in 2001 to R3·8bn. in 2002–03. By June 2003 more than 530,000 employers had registered their employees with the UIF, while the number of employer declarations stood at 413,111, with a total of R8·2m.

received in contributions. This translates to more than 67% of employers having registered.

Trade Unions. By mid-2003 there were 362 trade unions and 240 registered employer organizations operating in South Africa. In 2000 there were 3·6m. members of trade unions. The most important trade union groups or federations are Federation of Trade Unions of South Africa (FEDUSA), National Council of Trade Unions (NACTU) and Congress of South African Trade Unions (COSATU). The three largest trade unions are the National Union of Mineworkers (NUM), the National Union of Metalworkers of South Africa (NUMSA), both COSATU affiliates, and the Public Servants Association, an affiliate of FEDUSA. Employers also have the right to form associations and to register them with the Department of Labour. The Labour Court has been operating since Nov. 1996.

INTERNATIONAL TRADE

Since 1994 the (rand) value of both exports and imports in manufactured goods has more than doubled. South Africa's four main trading partners in 1999 were the UK, USA, Germany and Japan. In 1999 merchandise exports represented 86% (R148·9bn.) of total exports (merchandise plus net gold exports and excluding receipts for services). The balance of payments on current account reverted from a deficit of R2·9bn. in 2001 to a surplus of R3·3bn. in 2002. This was the first time since 1994 that a surplus was recorded for a full calendar year. Total foreign debt in 2002 was US$25,041m. Total net gold exports in 1999 amounted to R24·2bn. During 1999 the value of merchandise imports was R150·3bn.

The USA is South Africa's number one trading partner in terms of total trade (the sum of exports and imports) recorded in 2002 and the first six months of 2003. Exports to the USA rose in nominal terms from R30bn. in 2001 to R35bn. in 2002. Imports from the USA increased in nominal terms from R25bn. to R31bn. from 2001 to 2002.

Europe accounts for almost half of South Africa's total foreign trade. Seven of South Africa's top ten trading partners are European countries. In 2001–02 South African manufactured exports to Europe grew by 19·8%. A trade, co-operation and development agreement was provisionally implemented on 1 Jan. 2000, under the terms of which South Africa will grant duty-free access to 86% of EU imports over a period of 12 years, while the EU will liberalize 95% of South Africa's imports over a ten-year period. The Agreement provides for ongoing EU financial assistance in grants and loans for development co-operation, which amounts to some R900m. per annum.

In 2002 approximately 16% of South Africa's exports were destined for Africa while imports accounted for only 4% of South Africa's total imports. Within the Southern African Development Community (SADC), a smaller group of countries including South Africa, Botswana, Lesotho, Namibia and Swaziland, have organized themselves into the Southern African Customs Union (SACU), sharing a common tariff regime without any internal barriers. Trade with SADC countries increased from R16bn. to approximately R32bn. during the period 1998 to 2002. However, in 2002, there was a significant increase in the amount of imports from the region, to approximately R4·2bn.

Japan is South Africa's largest trading partner in Asia. It became South Africa's third-largest export destination during 2002. At the end of 2002 total trade between the two countries stood at R43·9bn.

Imports and Exports. Trade in US$1m.:

	1998	*1999*	*2000*	*2001*	*2002*
Imports f.o.b.	27,208	24,554	27,320	25,856	26,713
Exports f.o.b.	29,264	28,627	31,636	30,716	31,085

Main imports (in R1bn.):

	1997	*1998*	*1999*
Machinery and mechanical appliances	40,555	52,057	45,629
Mineral products	16,782	12,943	15,507
Chemicals or allied industries	13,836	15,667	16,959
Vehicles, aircraft, vessels and associated transport equipment	7,116	8,914	10,689
Plastics and articles thereof	5,349	5,871	6,100

Main exports (in R1bn.):

	1997	*1998*	*1999*
Natural or cultured pearls	32,345	33,538	35,173
Base metals and articles thereof	20,859	22,461	24,619
Mineral products	18,418	19,037	21,512
Products of chemicals or allied industries	8,908	9,218	9,987
Vehicles, aircraft, vessels and associated transport equipment	6,604	7,933	12,217
Machinery and mechanical appliances	8,278	9,916	12,008

In Oct. 1998 a transshipment facility for containers opened at Kidatu, southwest of Dar es Salaam, Tanzania, providing a link between the 1,067 mm gauge railways of the southern part of Africa and the 1,000 mm gauge lines of the north. With the opening up of new markets for South Africa elsewhere in the continent, it will help to boost trade and facilitate the shipment of cargo to countries to the north.

COMMUNICATIONS

The public company Transnet Limited was established on 1 April 1990. It handles 176m. tonnes of rail freight per year, 2·8m. tonnes road freight and 194m. tonnes of freight through the harbours, while 13·8m. litres are pumped through its petrol pipelines annually. For the financial year ended 31 March 2001 Transnet reported a profit of R3,287m. (compared to a net loss of R779m. for 2000).

The company, through South African Airways (SAA), flies 6·1m. domestic, regional and international passengers per year. In total, Transnet is worth R72bn. in fixed assets and has a workforce of some 80,000 employees.

Transnet Limited consists of nine main divisions, a number of subsidiaries and related businesses—Spoornet, the National Ports Authority (NPA), South African Port Operations (SAPO), Petronet, Freightdynamics, Propnet, Metrorail, Transtel and Transwerk.

Roads. In 2003 the South African road network comprised some 534,076 km of roads and streets. There is a primary roads network of 9,400 km, with plans to extend it to 20,000 km. Toll roads, which are serviced by 31 mainline toll plazas, cover about 2,200 km. The network includes 1,437 km of dual-carriage freeway, 440 km of single-carriage freeway and 56,967 km of single-carriage main road with unlimited access. South Africa has the longest road network in Africa. As at 31 Dec. 2002 there were 6·99m. registered motor vehicles, more than 4m. of which were motor cars. In 1999 there were 452,915 road accidents with 10,523 fatalities.

Rail. The South African Rail Commuter Corporation Limited (SARCC), an agency of the department of transport, is responsible for commuter rail services. It owns all commuter rail assets and property worth R5bn. SARCC contracts Metrorail (a division of Transnet) to provide services on its behalf. Metrorail carries more than 2·2m. passengers daily, serves 473 stations and operates tracks covering 2,400 km through five metropolitan areas. Metrorail is responsible for some 17% of all public transport in South Africa.

Spoornet provides freight transport and some long-distance passenger transport, including the luxurious Blue Train. Total route length (SARCC and Spoornet) was 22,657 km in 2000.

Civil Aviation. Responsibility for civil aviation safety and security lies with the South African Civil Aviation Authority (SACAA). The Airports Company South Africa (ACSA) owns and operates South Africa's principal airports. The main international airports are: Johannesburg, Cape Town, Durban, Bloemfontein, Port Elizabeth, Pilanesberg, Lanseria and Upington. In April 2003 the Cabinet approved the status of the Kruger Mpumalanga Airport, near Nelspruit, as an international airport. ACSA also has a 35-year concession to operate Pilanesberg International Airport near Sun City in North-West Province.

South African Airways (SAA), Comair, SA Express and SA Airlink operate scheduled international air services. 13 independent operators provide internal flights which link up with the internal network of SAA, Comair and SA Express.

In 2000 Johannesburg handled 11,187,948 passengers (5,981,562 on domestic flights) and 439,994 tonnes of freight. Johannesburg is expected to deal with 13·5m. passengers a year by 2005. Cape Town handled 4,654,000 passengers (3,645,000 on domestic flights). Durban handled 2,501,999 passengers (2,440,929 on domestic flights) and 14,737 tonnes of freight.

The new R750m. domestic terminal at Johannesburg International Airport (JIA) was opened in March 2003. It is the largest terminal in Africa and will increase the airport's total capacity to more than 18m. passengers annually.

Shipping. The South African Maritime Safety Authority (SAMSA) was established on 1 April 1998 as the authority responsible for ensuring the safety of life at sea and the prevention of sea pollution from ships. Approximately 98% of South Africa's exports are conveyed by sea.

The National Ports Authority supervises 16 of South Africa's ports. The largest ports include the deep water ports of Richards Bay, with its multi-product dry bulk handling facilities, multi-purpose terminal and the world's largest bulk coal terminal, and Saldanah featuring a bulk ore terminal adjacent to a bulk oil jetty with extensive storage facilities. Durban, Cape Town and Port Elizabeth provide large container terminals for deep-sea and coastal container traffic. The Port of Durban handles 1·2m. containers per annum. East London, the only river port, has a multi-purpose terminal and dry dock facilities. Mossel Bay is a specialized port serving the south coast fishing industry and offshore gas fields. Trade at the sea ports increased by 74% between 1994–2004, with container throughput more than doubling.

In 2002 the merchant fleet totalled 144,000 GRT, including oil tankers 3,000 GRT. During 1998 the major ports handled a total of 187,008,889 tonnes of cargo, and a total of 13,559 ships' calls were registered.

Telecommunications. According to a study by World Wide Worx, 2·89m. South Africans (one out of every 15) had access to the Internet by the end of 2001. The number was estimated to be 3·1m. by the end of 2002. In July 2000 there were 150,000 fax machines. South Africa has approximately 5·3m. installed telephones and 4·3m. installed exchange lines, representing 39% of total lines installed in Africa.

Telkom SA, the national operator, was awarded a five-year licence in May 1997 giving the company the exclusive right to provide telecommunications services. It was required to install 2·8m. new lines, including 120,000 payphones in the five years to March 2002. Over the same period it was required to provide first-time telephone services for over 3,000 villages, install more than 20,000 new lines for priority customers such as schools and hospitals and replace around 1,200m. analogue lines with digital technology. The transmission network is almost wholly digital. The initial public offering of Telkom on the Johannesburg Securities Exchange and the New York Stock Exchange in March 2003 realized R3·9bn. on the first day.

South Africa, with the operators Vodacom and MTN, is the fourth fastest-growing GSM (Global Systems for Mobile Communications) market in the world. By Oct. 2003 there were 15m. cellular users in the country and the figure is expected to grow to 21m. by 2006. The sector was predicted to be worth R20bn. by 2004.

Postal Services. The South African Post Office handles an average of 6m. letters a day, 70% of which are prepaid mass-mailed letters sent by companies using franking machines. SAPO services over 40m. South Africans and numerous public and private institutions. It delivers mail items to over 7·5m. delivery points. SAPO has 2,760 postal outlets countrywide and 30 mail processing centres.

Public Information Terminals (PiTs) offer government information and an e-mail service, Internet browsing, business sections and educational services. By Sept. 2001, 100 kiosks had been installed in post offices.

SOCIAL INSTITUTIONS

Justice. All law must be consistent with the Constitution and its Bill of Rights. Judgments of courts declaring legislation, executive action, or conduct to be invalid are binding on all organs of state and all persons. The common law of the Republic is based on Roman-Dutch law—that is the uncodified law of Holland as it was at the date of the cession of the Cape to the United Kingdom in 1806. South African law has, however, developed its own unique characteristics.

Judges hold office until they attain the age of 70 or, if they have not served for 15 years, until they have completed 15 years of service or have reached the age of 75, when they are discharged from active service. A judge discharged from active service must be ready to perform service for an aggregate of three months a year until the age of 75. The Chief Justice of South Africa, the Deputy Chief Justice, the President of the Supreme Court of Appeal and the Deputy President of the Supreme Court of Appeal are appointed by the President after consulting the Judicial Service Commission. In the case of the Chief Justice and Deputy Chief Justice, the President must also consult the leaders of parties represented in the National Assembly. The President on the advice of the Judicial Service Commission (JSC) appoints all other judges. No judge may be removed from office unless the JSC finds that the judge suffers from incapacity, is grossly incompetent or is guilty of gross misconduct, and the National Assembly calls for that judge to be removed by a resolution supported by at least two thirds of its members.

The higher courts include: 1) *The Constitutional Court* (CC), which consists of the Chief Justice of South Africa, the Deputy Chief Justice of South Africa and nine other judges. It is the highest court in all matters in which the interpretation of the Constitution or its application to any law, including the common law, is relevant; 2) *The Supreme Court of Appeal*, consisting of a President, a Deputy President and the number of judges of appeal determined by an Act of Parliament. It is the highest court of appeal in all other matters; 3) *The High Courts*, which may decide constitutional matters other than those which are within the exclusive jurisdiction of the Constitutional Court, and any other matter other than one assigned by Parliament to a court of a status similar to that of a High Court. Each High Court is presided over by a Judge President who may divide the area under his jurisdiction into circuit districts. In each such district there shall be held at least twice in every year and at such times and places determined by the Judge President, a court which shall be presided over by a judge of the High Court. Such a court is known as the circuit court for the district in question; 4) *The Land Claims Court*, established under the Restitution of Land Rights Act of 1994 deals with claims for restitution of rights in land to persons or communities dispossessed of such rights after 1913 as a result of past racially discriminatory laws or practices. It has jurisdiction throughout the Republic and the power to determine such claims and related matters such as compensation and rights of occupation; 5) *The Labour Court*, established under the Labour Relations Act, 1995 deals with labour disputes. It is a superior court that has authority, inherent powers and standing in relation to matters under its jurisdiction, equal to that the High Court has in relation to matters under its jurisdiction. Appeals from decisions of the Labour Court lie to the Labour Appeal Court which has authority in labour matters equivalent to that of the Supreme Court of Appeal in other matters.

The lower courts are called Magistrates' Courts. Magisterial districts have been grouped into 13 clusters headed by chief magistrates. From the magistrates court there is an appeal to the High Court having jurisdiction in that area, and then to the Supreme Court of Appeal. In cases involving constitutional matters there is a further appeal to the Constitutional Court. Sentences imposed by district magistrates above a prescribed limit are in most cases subject to automatic review by a judge.

The death penalty was abolished in June 1995 and no executions have taken place since 1989. In 1999 there were 24,210 murders, a rate of 56·2 per 100,000 persons (1994: 26,832 murders, representing a rate of 69·5 per 100,000 persons). South Africa has one of the highest murder rates in the world. Spending on police, prisons and justice services amounted to R23·5bn. in 1999. The population in penal institutions in Oct. 2003 was 180,952 (402 per 100,000 of national population).

Religion. South Africa is a secular state and freedom of worship is guaranteed by the Constitution. Almost 80% of the population professes the Christian faith. Other major religious groups are Hindus, Muslims and Jews. A sizeable minority of the population subscribe to traditional African faiths. In 1992 the Anglican Church of Southern Africa voted by 79% of votes cast for the ordination of women.

Education. The South African Schools Act, 1996 became effective on 1 Jan. 1997 and provides for: compulsory education for students between the ages of seven and 15 years of age, or students reaching the ninth grade, whichever occurs first. Pupils normally enrol for Grade 1 education at the beginning of the year in which they turn seven years of age although earlier entry at the age of six is allowed if the child meets specified criteria indicating that they have reached a stage of school readiness.

In 2003 the South African public education system accommodated 11·7m. school pupils, 448,868 university students, 216,499 technikon students and over 356,000 further education and training college students. There were 27,458 primary, secondary, combined and intermediate schools with 354,201 educators.

In the 2003–04 financial year R69,063m. was allocated to education. In 1999–2000 total expenditure on education came to 5·8% of GNP and 18·1% of total government spending.

There were 22 universities in 2002, two of which are mainly non-residential institutions offering distance tuition; and 15 technikons. The University of South Africa (UNISA) is the oldest and largest university in South Africa and one of the largest distance education institutions in the world. There were 130,347 students and 1,168 teaching and research staff in 2001. In 2000 Vista University (eight campuses) had 26,063 students, the University of Pretoria 25,865, the University of Port Elizabeth 22,366, Rand Afrikaans University (Johannesburg) 20,798 and the University of Stellenbosch 17,532.

According to the *State of South Africa's Population Report 2000,* 18·3% of the population over 20 years of age has had no schooling. The adult literacy rate in 1999 was 84·9% (85·7% for males and 84·2%, females).

Health. Some 40% of South Africans live in poverty and 75% of these live in rural areas where they are deprived of access to health services. By April 2003 free public health services were provided at about 3,500 public health clinics nationwide. There is also a network of mobile clinics run by the government to provide primary and preventive health care.

30,153 doctors were registered with the Health Profession Council of South Africa (HPCSA) at the end of 2002. These include doctors working for the state, doctors in private practice and specialists. Doctors train at the medical schools of eight universities and the majority go on to practise privately. At the end of 2002, 4,499 dentists and 172,869 registered and enrolled nurses and enrolled nursing auxiliaries were registered with the HPCSA. At the end of 2001, 849 oral hygienists and 347 dental therapists were registered. In Dec. 2001, 10,782 pharmacists were registered with the South African Pharmacy Council. Chris Hani Baragwanath Hospital, situated to the southwest of Johannesburg, with its 2,964 beds, is the largest hospital in the world.

In Oct. 1998 the first traditional hospital was opened in Mpumalanga—the Samuel Traditional Hospital. There are about 350,000 traditional healers in South Africa providing services to between 60% and 80% of their communities.

Approximately 4·7m. South Africans are HIV-infected, the highest number in the world (equivalent to nearly 11% of the population of South Africa and nearly 12% of all the people believed to be infected worldwide). In Aug. 2003 the government announced plans to roll out the provision of anti-retrovirals (ARVs) in the public health sector. Under plans to enhance comprehensive care for HIV/AIDS patients in the public sector, it is hoped a universal provision of the drugs will see 1·2m. people on treatment by 2008. It is also envisaged that there will be at least one service point in every local municipality across the country by 2008 for the treatment and care of HIV and AIDS sufferers.

Welfare. At Sept. 2003 the department of social development was disbursing grants through its provincial offices to 6·5m. beneficiaries at a monthly cost of R2·5bn. Recipients are means-tested to determine their eligibility. 3·8m. people received the child support grant (CSG) of R160 per month and 2m. (women aged 60 and above, men aged 65 and above) received old-age grants of R700 per month. The age of children eligible for the CSG will be progressively increased to include children up to the age of 14 years.

Other benefits paid are the disability, foster child, care dependency and war veterans' grants as well as institutional grants and grants in aid.

The total budget allocation for the payment of social assistance by the provincial departments of social development was R18,798bn. in 2000–01.

CULTURE

World Heritage Sites. UNESCO world heritage sites under South African jurisdiction (with year entered on list) are: Greater St Lucia Wetland Park (1999), encompassing marine, wetland and savannah environments; Robben Island (1999), used since the 17th century as a prison, hospital and military base—it was the location for Nelson Mandela's incarceration. Fossil Hominid Sites of Sterkfontein, Swartkrans, Kromdraai and Environs (1999), offering evidence of human evolution over 3·5m. years; uKhahlamba/Drakensberg Park (2000), including caves with 4,000-year old paintings; Mapungubwe Cultural Landscape (2003), a savannah landscape at the confluence of the Limpopo and Shashe rivers and the site of the largest kingdom in Africa in the 14th century; Cape Floral Region Protected Areas (2004).

Broadcasting. Television and radio are regulated by an independent regulatory authority, ICASA. The South African Broadcasting Corporation (SABC), the country's public broadcaster, comprises four full-spectrum free-to-air channels, two satellite pay-TV channels aimed at audiences in Africa, and Bop-TV, which the SABC runs on behalf of the State. Combined, the free-to-air channels are licensed to broadcast in 11 languages and reach a daily adult audience of almost 17m. via the terrestrial signal distribution network and a satellite signal.

M-Net, South Africa's first private subscription television service, was launched in 1986. Today, it has over 1·23m. subscribers in 49 countries across the African continent. In March 1998 the consortium Midi Television was awarded the first privately owned free-to-air television licence.

The SABC's national radio network comprises 20 stations which, combined, reach an average daily adult audience of 20m. Between 1994 and 2003, 94 community radio broadcasting and 10 commercial licences were awarded by ICASA.

In Sept. 1999, 85% of the population was able to receive a television signal (colour by PAL). There are more than 4m. licensed television households. About 50% of all programmes transmitted are produced in South Africa. It is estimated that 88% of the rural population listens to the radio in a seven-day period, compared to 79% in 1994.

Press. The major press groups are Independent Newspapers (Pty) Ltd, Media24 Ltd, CTP/Caxton Publishers and Printers Ltd, and Johnnic Publishing Ltd.

Other important media players include Primedia, Nail (New Africa Investments Limited) and Kagiso Media. Nail has unbundled into a commercial company (New Africa Capital) and a media company (New Africa Media).

The only truly national newspapers are: *Sunday Times* (circulation, July–Dec. 2002, 504,295), *Rapport* (338,702), *The Sunday Independent* (40,151) and the weekly newspaper *City Press*. *Die Burger Saterdag* (Cape Town) is the largest Afrikaans daily (116,370). There are 16 dailies and 11 weekly newspapers.

Tourism. South Africa has one of the fastest-growing tourist industries, contributing R25bn. to the economy in 2000. It contributed 7·1% of gross domestic product in 2002. 6·4m. tourists travelled to the country in 2002. Tourism employs an estimated 3% of South Africa's workforce. It is projected that by 2010 the tourism economy will employ more than 1·2m. people (directly and indirectly). Tourism is the fourth-largest industry in South Africa, supporting some 6,500 accommodation establishments.

Festivals. Best-known arts festivals: the Klein Karoo Festival (Oudtshoorn, Western Cape), which has a strong Afrikaans component, is held in April; the Grahamstown Arts Festival in the Eastern Cape is held in June/July; the Mangaung African Cultural Festival (Macufe) is held in Sept. in Bloemfontein; and the Aardklop Arts Festival, in Potchefstroom in the North-West province, is held in Sept. The Encounters South African International Documentary Festival has been held since 1999.

DIPLOMATIC REPRESENTATIVES

Of South Africa in the United Kingdom (South Africa House, Trafalgar Square, London, WC2N 5DP)
High Commissioner: Lindiwe Mabuza.

Of the United Kingdom in South Africa (255 Hill St., Arcadia, Pretoria 0001)
High Commissioner: Ann Grant.

Of South Africa in the USA (3051 Massachusetts Ave., NW, Washington, D.C., 20008)
Ambassador: Barbara Joyce Mosima Masekela.

Of the USA in South Africa (877 Pretorius St., Arcadia, Pretoria 0083)
Ambassador: Jendayi Frazer.

Of South Africa to the United Nations
Ambassador: Dumisana Shadrack Kumalo.

Of South Africa to the European Union
Ambassador: Jeremy Matthews Matjila.

FURTHER READING

Government Communication and Information System (GCIS), including extracts from the *South Africa Yearbook 2003/04*, compiled and published by GCIS.

Beinart, W., *Twentieth Century South Africa.* OUP, 1994
Brewer, J. (ed.) *Restructuring South Africa.* London, 1994
Butler, Anthony, *Contemporary South Africa.* Palgrave Macmillan, Basingstoke, 2003
Davenport, T. R. H., *South Africa: a Modern History.* 5th ed. Macmillan, Basingstoke, 2000
Davis, G. V., *South Africa.* [Bibliography] 2nd ed. ABC-Clio, Oxford and Santa Barbara (CA), 1994
De Klerk, F. W., *The Last Trek—A New Beginning*. Macmillan, London, 1999
Giliomee, Hermann, *The Afrikaners: Biography of a People.* Univ. of Virginia Press, Charlottesville, 2003
Guelke, Adrian, *Rethinking the Rise of Apartheid.* Palgrave Macmillan, Basingstoke, 2004
Fine, B and Rustomjee Z., *The Political Economy of South Africa.* London, 1996
Hough, M. and Du Plessis, A. (eds.) *Selected Documents and Commentaries on Negotiations and Constitutional Development in the RSA, 1989–1994.* Pretoria Univ., 1994
Johnson, R. W. and Schlemmer, L. (eds.) *Launching Democracy in South Africa: the First Open Election, 1994.* Yale Univ. Press, 1996
Mandela, N., *Long Walk to Freedom: the Autobiography of Nelson Mandela.* Abacus, London, 1994
Meredith, M., *South Africa's New Era: the 1994 Election.* London, 1994
Mostert, N., *Frontiers: the Epic of South Africa's Creation and the Tragedy of the Xhosa People.* London, 1992
Nattrass, N. and Ardington, E. (eds.) *The Political Economy of South Africa.* Cape Town and OUP, 1990
Thompson, L., *A History of South Africa.* 2nd ed. Yale Univ. Press, 1996
The Truth and Reconciliation Commission of South Africa Report, 5 vols. Macmillan, London, 1999
Turner, Barry, (ed.) *Southern Africa Profiled.* Macmillan, London, 2000
Waldmeir, P., *Anatomy of a Miracle: the End of Apartheid and the Birth of the New South Africa.* London, 1997
Who's Who in South African Politics. 5th ed. London, 1995

National statistical office: Statistics South Africa, Private Bag X44, Pretoria 0001.
Website: http://www.statssa.gov.za/

SOUTH AFRICAN PROVINCES

In 1994 the former provinces of the Cape of Good Hope, Natal, the Orange Free State and the Transvaal, together with the former 'homelands' or 'TBVC countries' of Transkei, Bophuthatswana, Venda and Ciskei, were replaced by nine new provinces. Transkei and Ciskei were integrated into Eastern Cape, Venda into Northern Province (now Limpopo), and Bophuthatswana into Free State, Mpumalanga and North-West.

The administrative powers of the provincial governments in relation to the central government are set out in the 1999 Constitution after a revision of the original text demanded by the Constitutional Court in 1996.

EASTERN CAPE

TERRITORY AND POPULATION

The area is 169,580 sq. km and the population at the 2001 census was 6,436,764, the third largest population in South Africa. Of that number: female, 3,461,251;

African/Black, 5,635,079 (87% of the population); Coloured, 478,807 (7%); White, 304,506 (5%); Indian/Asian, 18,372 (0·3%). 37% of the population lived in urban areas in 1996. Density (2001), 38 per sq. km. Life expectancy at birth, 1996, was 60·4 years. At the 2001 census 83·2% spoke IsiXhosa as their home language, 9·3% Afrikaans, 3·6% English and 2·4% Sesotho.

Eastern Cape comprises 77 administrative districts (including Umzimkulu district, an enclave within KwaZulu-Natal).

CONSTITUTION AND GOVERNMENT

The provincial capital is Bisho. There is a 63-seat provincial legislature.

RECENT ELECTIONS

At the provincial elections held on 14 April 2004, 51 seats were won by the ANC, 6 by the UDM, 5 by the DA and 1 by the PAC.

CURRENT ADMINISTRATION

In Feb. 2005 the ANC Executive Council comprised:

Premier: Nosimo Balindlela; b. 1949 (took office on 26 April 2004).

Minister of Agriculture: Gugile Nkwinti. *Education:* Mkhangeli Matomela. *Economic Affairs, Environment and Tourism:* Andre de Wet. *Finance:* Billy Nel. *Health:* Dr M. Bevan Goqwana. *Housing, Local Government and Traditional Affairs:* Neo Moerane-Mamase. *Safety, Security, Liaison and Transport:* Thobile Mhlahlo. *Roads and Public Works:* Sam Kwelita. *Social Development:* Christian Martin. *Sports, Recreation, Arts and Culture:* Nomsa Lizzie Jajula.

Speaker: Noxolo Kiviet. *Director-General:* Dr M. E. Tom (ANC).

Government Website: http://www.ecprov.gov.za

ENERGY AND NATURAL RESOURCES

Electricity. In 1998, 6,818 GWh of electricity were consumed. Approximately 42% of households have electricity.

Water. An estimated 48% of the population do not have access to basic supplies.

Minerals. Total output of mining and quarrying in 1999 was valued at R57m. with 7,154 persons employed.

Agriculture. There are around 6,000 commercial farms with an average area of 1,500 ha. Of this area only 7% is arable land with 45% not farmed at present owing to land ownership disputes in the former homelands (Transkei and Ciskei). Livestock accounts for 77% of commercial agricultural production; 18% comprises horticulture. Total value of agriculture, forestry and fishing output for 1999 was R2,063m.

Forestry. Forestry activities are found in the northeast area of the former Transkei, in Stutterheim and in the northwest of the province. In 1999 there were 169,484 ha of plantation forests.

Fisheries. There is a relatively small sea-fishing industry based on squid, sardines, hake, kinglip and crayfish. Aquaculture produces abalone for export to the Far East.

INDUSTRY

Manufacturing is based mainly in Port Elizabeth and East London with motor manufacturing as the prime industry. Wool, mohair and hides are an important area of the province's agro-industry. Value of manufacturing output in 1999 totalled R14,783m. with 97,035 persons employed.

Labour. As at Oct. 1999 the economically active population numbered 1,419,000, of whom 423,000 were unemployed (29·8%).

COMMUNICATIONS

Roads. Total road network at Dec. 2000 was 38,000 km. Between Dec. 1999 and April 2000 the province's roads were severely damaged by floods. A R40m. reconstruction programme commenced in Oct. 2000. In 1995 there were 31,750 road accidents with 724 fatalities.

Civil Aviation. The province has four airports (Port Elizabeth, East London, Umtata and Bulembu).

Shipping. There are two deep-water ports—Port Elizabeth and East London—with a third planned at Coega.

Telecommunications. Large areas of the province have fewer than four telephones per 1,000 people. A total of R400m. was invested in a new telecommunications infrastructure for the Eastern Cape during the 1997–98 financial year.

SOCIAL INSTITUTIONS

Education. In 1998 there were 2,301,930 enrolled in schools and a total of 68,033 teaching staff. In that year a total of 37,349 students attended the Province's four universities and three technikons. At Oct. 1999 more than 20·9% of people aged 20 years and above had no schooling at all, while 4·7% had completed higher education.

Health. In 1998 there were 108 hospitals (including 42 private hospitals) and 20,538 hospital beds. In the 1997–98 financial year a total of R112m. was allocated to the Primary School Nutrition Programme.

Welfare. The budget allocated for welfare in 2000–01 was R3,950,911, an increase of 7·5% on 1999–2000.

CULTURE

Broadcasting. In 1996 there were 243,662 TV licence holders.

FREE STATE

TERRITORY AND POPULATION

The Free State lies in the centre of South Africa and is situated between the Vaal River in the north and the Orange River in the south. It borders on the Northern Cape, Eastern Cape, North-West, Mpumalanga, KwaZulu-Natal and Gauteng Province and shares a border with Lesotho. The area is 129,480 sq. km, 10·62% of South Africa's total surface area. The province is the third largest in South Africa but has the second smallest population and the second lowest population density. The population at the 2001 census was 2,706,776. Of that number: female, 1,409,171; African/Black, 2,381,073 (88% of the population); White, 238,791 (9%); Coloured, 83,193 (3%); Indian/Asian, 3,719 (0·1%). 63% of the population were between 15 and 64 and at least 69% of the population lived in urban areas in 1996 (in 1911, 80% lived in rural areas). Annual population growth rate: 1–2%. Density (2001), 21 per sq. km. Life expectancy at birth, 1996, was 52·8 years. At the 2001 census, 64·3% (1,742,939) of the population spoke Sesotho as their home language, 11·9% (323,082) Afrikaans, 9·1% (246,192) IsiXhosa, 6·8% (185,389) Setswana, 5·1% (138,091) IsiZulu and 1·2% (31,246) English.

Free State comprises 52 administrative districts. The provincial capital is Bloemfontein (meaning 'fountain of flowers'). Bloemfontein's indigenous name is Mangaung, which means 'place of the big cats'.

CLIMATE

Temperatures are mild with averages ranging from 19·5°C in the west to 15°C in the east. Maximum temperatures in the west can reach 36°C in summer. Winter temperatures in the high-lying areas of the eastern Free State can drop as low as –15°C. The western and southern areas are semi-desert.

CONSTITUTION AND GOVERNMENT

There is a 30-seat provincial legislature. The Free State Executive Council, headed by the *Premier*, administers the province through ten Departments.

The Free State House of Traditional Leaders advises the Legislature on matters pertaining to traditional authorities and tribal matters.

RECENT ELECTIONS

In the election held on 14 April 2004 the ANC retained its majority and won 25 of the 30 seats; the DA three; the ACDP one; and VF+ one.

CURRENT ADMINISTRATION

In Feb. 2005 the ANC Executive Council comprised:

Premier: Beatrice Marshoff; b. 1957 (took office on 26 April 2004).

Minister of Agriculture: 'Ace' Magashule. *Education:* Mantsheng Tsopo. *Finance:* France Morule. *Health:* Sakhiwo Belot. *Local Government and Housing:* Itumeleng Kotsoane. *Public Works, Roads and Transport:* Seiso Mohai. *Public Safety, Security and Liaison:* Pule Makgoe. *Social Development:* Zanele Dlungwana. *Sports, Arts, Culture, Science and Technology:* Malefetsane Mafereka. *Tourism, Environment and Economic Affairs:* Benjamin Malakoane.

Speaker: Mxolisi Dukwane. *Director-General:* Khotso de Wee.

Government Website: http://www.fs.gov.za

ENERGY AND NATURAL RESOURCES

Electricity. In the Free State, Eskom distributes electricity through 3,000 km of distribution lines, 9,000 km of reticulation (network) lines; and has an installed capacity of 1,200,740 MVA. Mining (60% of sales) and local governments (30% of sales) are Eskom's biggest Free State's customers.

In 1998, 9,110 GWh of electricity were consumed.

Water. The largest storage dams are the Gariep and Vanderkloof dams, both of which have hydro-electric stations.

According to the 1996 census, piped water was available in the homes of 41% of the population while a further 19% was supplied by communal village standpipes.

Minerals. The province contributes about 16·5% of South Africa's total mineral output. Apart from rich gold and diamond deposits, the Free State is the source of numerous other minerals and is the founding home of South Africa's famous oil-from-coal industry centred on Sasolburg. Bentonite clays, gypsum, salt and phosphates are to be found while large concentrates of thorium-ilminite-zircon also occur. In 1999, 69,547 people were employed in mining.

Agriculture. Good agricultural conditions allow for a wide variety of farming industries. Of the total 12·7m. ha, 90% (11·5m. ha) is utilized as farmland. Of this, 63·9% is natural grazing; 2·1% is for nature conservation; and 1·1% is used for other purposes. Dryland cultivation is practised on 97% of the arable land, while the remaining 3% is under irrigation.

In 1998 there were a total of 11,647 commercial farmers working 48,420 farming units in the province. The eastern region is the major producer of small grains; the northern region, maize and beef; and the southern region, mutton and wool. The province produces about 40% of total maize and 50% of total wheat production in South Africa.

INDUSTRY

Labour. As at Oct. 1999 the economically active population numbered 965,000, of whom 225,000 were unemployed (23·3%).

COMMUNICATIONS

Roads. The Free State Department of Public Works, Roads and Transport is responsible for maintenance of a rural network, which consists of 20,452 km tertiary gravel roads, 21,470 km secondary gravel roads, 6,965 km primary paved roads, and 910 km national roads, of which 25 km are not tarred. In 1995 there were 26,163 road accidents with 997 fatalities.

Rail. Spoornet is one of the biggest companies in the Free State with 4,217 employees. Spoornet transports most of the province's maize, wheat, gold ore, petroleum and fertilizer. The Spoornet infrastructure consists of approximately 4,000 km of tracks, of which 1,300 km are electrified.

Postal Services. In 1998 there were 330 post offices, 29 part-time post offices, seven Postpoints (situated in locations such as chainstores, etc.) and 144 retail postal agencies.

SOCIAL INSTITUTIONS

Justice. Small claims courts operate in 11 centres, providing informal forums where citizens appear in person before a commissioner. The decision of the commissioner is final and the parties cannot appeal to a higher court. Civil claims can be instituted in the magistrates' court, there being 67 magistrate's offices in the province. The Free State provincial division of the Supreme Court is in Bloemfontein. The Circuit Court is a local division of the provincial division of the Supreme Court which visits certain areas. The Circuit Court tries criminal cases only. In 1998, 523 attorneys and 42 advocates practised in the province.

Education. In 1998 there were 810,000 pupils and 24,078 teachers. More than 2,000 farm schools cater for 95,000 pupils. Nine technical colleges provide vocational training for school leavers. Technikon Free State has 8,000 students on the main campus in Bloemfontein and four campuses for distance education situated in Welkom, Kimberley, Kroonstad and Qwaqwa. There are eight teacher training colleges with 4,600 students. The University of the Orange Free State is the only fully fledged residential university and, in 1998, had a student population of 9,787. 1998 literacy rate: 84·42%. According to the 1996 census, 16% of those aged 20 and over had no schooling; 33% had some secondary education.

Health. In 1999 there were 33 public hospitals, 26 private hospitals and 234 clinics. Total hospital beds (1999), 2,277.

CULTURE

Broadcasting. Apart from the national broadcaster, SABC, several private and community radio stations exist, catering for the three primary language groups in the province. In 1996 there were 164,092 TV licence holders.

Press. There is one daily newspaper, *Di Volksblad*, which is published in Afrikaans. Several 'knockanddrop'-type weekly newspapers are produced on a regional basis.

FURTHER READING

Free State: The Winning Province. Chris van Rensburg Publications, Johannesburg, 1997

GAUTENG

TERRITORY AND POPULATION

Gauteng is the smallest province in South Africa, covering an area of 18,810 sq. km (approximately 1·4% of the total land surface of South Africa). The population at the 2001 census was 8,837,179. Of that number: female, 4,392,500; African/Black, 6,522,792 (74%); White, 1,758,398 (20%); Coloured, 337,974 (3·8%); Indian/Asian, 218,015 (2·5%). 97% of the population lived in urban areas in 1996. Density (2001), 470 per sq. km. Life expectancy at birth, 1996, was 59·6 years. At the 2001 census, 21·5% spoke IsiZulu as their home language, 14·3% Afrikaans, 13·1% Sesotho, 12·4% English, 10·7% Sepedi, 8·4% Setswana, 7·6% IsiXhosa, 5·7% Xitsonga, 1·9% IsiNdebele, 1·7% Tshivenda and 1·4% SiSwati.

The province of Gauteng, at first called Pretoria-Witwatersrand-Vereeniging (PWV), comprises 23 administrative districts. The provincial capital is Johannesburg. In the Sesotho language, Gauteng means 'Place of Gold'.

CONSTITUTION AND GOVERNMENT

There is a 73-seat provincial legislature.

RECENT ELECTIONS

At the provincial elections held on 14 April 2004, 51 seats were won by the ANC, 15 by the DA, two by the IFP and one each by ACDP, ID, UDM, VF+ and the PAC.

CURRENT ADMINISTRATION

In Feb. 2005 the ANC Executive Council comprised:

Premier: Mbhazima Sam Shilowa; b. 1958 (took office on 15 June 1999, reinaugurated on 29 April 2004).

Minister of Agriculture, Conservation and the Environment: Khabisi Mosunkutu. *Community Safety:* Firoz Cachalia. *Education:* Angelina Motshekga. *Finance and Economic Affairs:* Paul Mashatile. *Health:* Gwendoline M. Ramokgopa. *Housing:* Nomvula Mokonyane. *Local Government:* Dorothy Mahlangu. *Public Transport,*

Roads and Works: Ignatius Jacobs. *Social Development:* Bob Mabaso. *Sport, Arts, Culture and Recreation:* Barbara Creecy.

Speaker: Richard Mdakane. *Director-General:* Mogopodi Mokoena.

Government Website: http://www.gpg.gov.za

ENERGY AND NATURAL RESOURCES

Electricity. In 1998, 56,548 GWh of electricity were consumed (30% of South Africa's total consumption).

Water. The largest storage dam on the southern edge of the province is the Vaal Dam. In 1996 piped water was available in the homes of about 68% of the population while 15% was supplied by communal village standpipes.

Minerals. In 1999, 104,017 people were employed in mining.

Agriculture. In 1996 there were 2,342 farms with 339,295 agricultural workers; gross farming income amounted to R2,283·3m.

INDUSTRY

Labour. As at Oct. 1999 the economically active population numbered 3,416,000, of whom 705,000 were unemployed (20·6%).

COMMUNICATIONS

Roads. In 1995 there were 202,583 road accidents with 2,318 fatalities.

Civil Aviation. Johannesburg International Airport is the main airport in the province.

Telecommunications. In 1996 at least 45% of the population had telephones or mobile phones; 4% had no access at all to a telephone.

SOCIAL INSTITUTIONS

Education. In 1998 there were 1·6m. children enrolled in schools with a total of 44,324 teaching staff. In that year a total of 336,004 students attended the Province's six universities and five technikons. According to the 1996 census, 40% of the population had some secondary education—the highest rate in any of South Africa's provinces.

Health. In 1998 there were 137 hospitals (including 108 private hospitals) and 32,852 hospital beds.

CULTURE

Broadcasting. There were 978,762 TV licence holders in 1996.

KWAZULU-NATAL

TERRITORY AND POPULATION

The area is 92,180 sq. km and the population at the 2001 census was 9,426,017. Of that number: female, 5,016,926; African/Black, 8,002,407 (84·8% of the population); Indian/Asian, 798,275 (8·5%); White, 483,448 (5·1%); Coloured, 141,887 (1·5%). 43% lived in urban areas in 1996. Density (2001), 102 per sq. km. Life expectancy at birth, 1996, was 53·0 years. At the 2001 census, 80·8% spoke IsiZulu as their home language, 13·6% English, 2·3% IsiXhosa and 1·5% Afrikaans.

KwaZulu-Natal comprises 66 administrative districts. The provincial capital is Pietermaritzburg, chosen by referendum in 1995.

CONSTITUTION AND GOVERNMENT

There is an 80-seat provincial legislature.

RECENT ELECTIONS

At the provincial elections held on 14 April 2004, 38 seats were won by the ANC, 30 by the IFP, seven by DA, two by ACDP, two by the Minority Front and one by UDM.

CURRENT ADMINISTRATION

In Feb. 2005 the ANC-led coalition government comprised:

Premier: J. S. 'S'bu' Ndebele; b. 1948 (ANC; took office on 23 April 2004).

Minister of Agriculture and Environmental Affairs: Prof. Gabriel Ndabandaba (ANC). *Culture and Tourism:* Narend Singh (IFP). *Education:* Ina Cronje (ANC). *Finance and Economic Development:* Dr Zweli Mkhize (ANC). *Health:* Peggy Nkonyeni (ANC). *Housing, Local Government and Traditional Affairs:* Mike Mabuyakhula (ANC). *Public Works:* Blessed Gwala (IFP). *Social Affairs:* Inkosi Nyanga Ngubane (IFP). *Sports and Recreation:* Amichand Rajbansi (Minority Front). *Transport, Community Safety and Liaison:* Bheki Cele (ANC).

Speaker: Willis Mchunu (ANC). *Director-General:* Adv. R. K. Sizani.

Government Website: http://www.kwazulunatal.gov.za

ENERGY AND NATURAL RESOURCES

Electricity. 37,344 GWh of electricity were consumed in 1999.

Water. In 1996 piped water was available in the homes of 39% of the population.

Minerals. Coal is mined in the north of the province. In 1999, 6,888 people were employed in mining.

Agriculture. In 1996 there were 5,037 farms with 115,496 agricultural workers; gross farming income amounted to R4,490·3m. Sugarcane production is the main agricultural activity.

INDUSTRY

Labour. As at Oct. 1999 the economically active population numbered 2,635,000, of whom 682,000 were unemployed (25·9%).

COMMUNICATIONS

Roads. In 2000 the road network totalled 42,000 km. There were 1,575 fatalities as a result of road traffic accidents in 1997.

Civil Aviation. Durban International Airport is the main airport in the province.

Shipping. Durban harbour is the busiest in South Africa and one of the ten largest harbours in the world. Coal is exported from Richards Bay.

SOCIAL INSTITUTIONS

Education. Since 1995 education has been provided by a unified KwaZulu-Natal Education Department (KZNED). In 1998 there were 2,725,371 children enrolled in schools with a total of 74,834 teaching staff. In that year a total of 30,684 students attended the Province's three universities and three technikons. According to the 1996 census, 23% of the population aged 20 and above had no schooling; 32% had some secondary education.

Health. In 1998 there were 114 hospitals (including 48 private hospitals) and 31,673 hospital beds.

CULTURE

Broadcasting. There were 392,573 TV licence holders in 1996.

LIMPOPO

TERRITORY AND POPULATION

The area is 123,280 sq. km and the population at the 2001 census was 5,273,642. Of that number: female, 2,878,858; African/Black, 5,128,616 (97% of the population); White, 126,276 (2·4%); Coloured, 10,163 (0·2%); Indian/Asian, 8,587 (0·2%). 11·9% lived in urban areas in 1996. Density (2001), 43 per sq. km. Life expectancy at birth, 1996, was 60·1 years. At the 2001 census 52·0% spoke Sepedi as their home language, 22·3% Xitsonga, 15·9% Tshivenda, 2·3% Afrikaans and 1·5% IsiNdebele.

Limpopo (Northern Province until March 2003) comprises 32 administrative districts. The provincial capital is Pietersburg.

CONSTITUTION AND GOVERNMENT
There is a 49-seat provincial legislature.

RECENT ELECTIONS
At the provincial elections held on 14 April 2004, 45 seats were won by the ANC, two by the DA and one each by ACDP and UDM.

CURRENT ADMINISTRATION
In Feb. 2005 the ANC Executive Council comprised:

Premier: Sello Moloto; b. 1965 (sworn in on 26 April 2004).

Minister of Agriculture: Dikeledi Magadzi. *Education:* Dr P. Aaron Motsoaledi. *Health and Social Development:* Charles Sekoeti. *Local Government and Housing:* Maite Mashabane. *Public Works:* Thumba Mufamadi. *Safety, Security and Liaison:* Rosina Semenya. *Sports, Recreation, Arts and Culture:* Joe Maswanganyi. *Roads and Transport:* Stan Motimele. *Economic Development, Environment and Tourism:* Collins Chabane. *Provincial Treasury:* Happy Joyce Mashamba.

Speaker: Tshenwani Farasani. *Director-General:* Ms M. B. Monama.

Government Website: http://www.limpopo.gov.za

ENERGY AND NATURAL RESOURCES
Electricity. In 1998, 7,234 GWh of electricity were consumed.

Water. In 1996 piped water was available in the homes of 17% of the population, with 40% relying on public taps.

Minerals. In 1999, 39,805 people were employed in mining.

Agriculture. In 1996 (excluding the former Venda now within the province) there were 7,273 farms with 121,757 agricultural workers; gross farming income amounted to R3,934·5m.

INDUSTRY
Labour. As at Oct. 1999 the economically active population numbered 1,050,000, of whom 357,000 were unemployed (34·0%).

COMMUNICATIONS
Roads. In 1995 there were 15,841 road accidents with 693 fatalities.

SOCIAL INSTITUTIONS
Education. In 1998 there were 1,810,603 children enrolled in schools with a total of 57,155 teaching staff. 17,933 students attended the Province's two universities in the same year. According to the 1996 census, almost 37% of the population aged 20 years and over had no schooling.

Health. In 1998 there were 49 hospitals (including two private hospitals) and 13,342 hospital beds.

CULTURE
Broadcasting. There were 99,362 TV licence holders in 1996.

MPUMALANGA

TERRITORY AND POPULATION
The area is 78,370 sq. km and the population at the 2001 census was 3,122,991. Of that number: female, 1,625,658; African/Black, 2,886,345 (92·4% of the population); White, 203,244 (6·5%); Coloured, 22,158 (0·7%); Indian/Asian, 11,244 (0·4%).

39·1% lived in urban areas in 1996. Density (2001), 40 per sq. km. Life expectancy at birth, 1996, was 53·5 years. At the 2001 census, 30·8% spoke SiSwati as their home language, 26·3% IsiZulu, 12·1% IsiNdebele, 10·8% Sepedi, 6·1% Afrikaans, 3·8% Xitsonga, 3·7% Sesotho, 2·7% Setswana, 1·7% English and 1·5% IsiXhosa.

Mpumalanga comprises 28 administrative districts. The provincial capital is Nelspruit.

CONSTITUTION AND GOVERNMENT

There is a 30-seat provincial legislature.

RECENT ELECTIONS

At the provincial elections held on 14 April 2004, 27 seats were won by the ANC, two by the DA and one by VF+.

CURRENT ADMINISTRATION

In Feb. 2005 the ANC government comprised:

Premier: Thabang Makwetla; b. 1957 (took office on 30 April 2004).

Minister of Agriculture, Conservation, Environment and Land Administration: Madala Masuku. *Culture, Sports and Recreation:* Nomsa Mtsweni. *Economic Development and Planning:* S. William Lubisi. *Education:* Siphosezwe Masango. *Finance:* Mmathulare Coleman. *Health and Social Development:* Pogisho Phasha. *Local Government and Housing:* Jabu Mahlangu. *Public Works:* K. Candith Mashego-Dlamini. *Roads and Transport:* Fish Mahlalela. *Safety and Security:* Dinah Pule.

Speaker: Yvonne 'Pinky' Phosa. *Director-General:* Adv. M. Stanley Soko.

Government Website: http://www.mpumalanga.gov.za

ENERGY AND NATURAL RESOURCES

Electricity. In 1998, 24,200 GWh of electricity were consumed.

Water. Currently about 65% of the population receive water from house connections, with 20% relying on communal taps.

Minerals. In 1999, 61,826 people were employed in mining.

Agriculture. In 1996 (excluding that part of the former Bophuthatswana now within the province) there were 4,675 farms with 101,051 agricultural workers; gross farming income amounted to R3,972·8m.

INDUSTRY

Labour. As at Oct. 1999 the economically active population numbered 916,000, of whom 224,000 were unemployed (24·4%).

COMMUNICATIONS

Roads. In 1995 there were 22,744 road accidents with 1,191 fatalities.

SOCIAL INSTITUTIONS

Education. In 1998 there were 935,528 children enrolled in schools with a total of 1,967 teaching staff. According to the 1996 census, 28% of those aged 20 years and over had no schooling; 38% had some secondary education.

Health. In 1998 there were 36 hospitals (including 11 private hospitals) and 5,506 hospital beds. In Oct. 1998 the first traditional hospital was opened in Mpumalanga—the Samuel Traditional Hospital.

CULTURE

Broadcasting. There were 138,085 TV licence holders in 1996.

NORTHERN CAPE

TERRITORY AND POPULATION

The area is 361,800 sq. km and the population at the 2001 census was 822,727. Of that number: female, 421,559; Coloured, 424,389 (51·6% of the population);

African/Black, 293,976 (35·7%); White, 102,042 (12·4%); Indian/Asian, 2,320 (0·3%). At least 70% lived in urban areas in 1996. Density (2001), 2 per sq. km. Life expectancy at birth, 1996, was 55·6 years. At the 2001 census, 68·0% spoke Afrikaans as their home language, 20·8% Setswana, 6·2% IsiXhosa and 2·5% English.

Northern Cape comprises six administrative districts: Diamond Fields with Kimberley as the provincial and economic capital; Kalahari, which is the second richest and densely populated area in the province and includes the magisterial districts of Kuruman and Postmasburg; Hantam (North-West) with the towns of Calvinia, Sutherland, Williston, Fraserburg and Carnavon; Benede-Orange with Upington as the agricultural, economic and cultural capital of the region; Bo-Karoo with De Aar as the capital of the area; and Namaqualand which is strong in mining.

CONSTITUTION AND GOVERNMENT

There is a 30-seat provincial legislature.

RECENT ELECTIONS

At the provincial elections held on 14 April 2004, 21 seats were won by the ANC, three by the DA, two by ID, two by the NNP and one each by VF+ and ACDP.

CURRENT ADMINISTRATION

In Feb. 2005 the ANC Executive Council comprised:

Premier: E. Dipuo Peters (took office on 30 April 2004).

Minister of Agriculture and Land Affairs: Tina M. Joemat-Petterson. *Education:* Archie Lucas. *Finance and Economic Affairs:* Penene Pakes Dikgetsi. *Health:* Kagisho Molusi. *Local Government and Housing:* Eunice Silao. *Provincial Safety and Liaison:* Boeboe van Wyk. *Social Services and Population Development:* Goolam H. Akharawaray. *Sport, Arts and Culture:* Temsi Madikane. *Tourism, Environmental Affairs and Conservation:* Pieter Saaiman. *Transport, Roads and Public Works:* Fred Wyngaardt.

Speaker: Connie Seoposengwe. *Director-General:* M. Hendry Hendricks (ANC).

Government Website: http://www.northern-cape.gov.za

ENERGY AND NATURAL RESOURCES

Electricity. In 1998, 3,034 GWh of electricity were consumed.

Water. In 1996 piped water was available in the homes of almost 49% of the population with 21% supplied by communal stand pipes.

Minerals. The province is well endowed with a variety of mineral deposits. Diamonds are found in shallow water at Port Nolloth, Hondeklipbaai and Lamberts Bay, and also mined inland along the entire coastal strip from the Orange river mouth in the north to Lamberts Bay in the south. Copper is mined in Namaqualand. Iron and manganese occur in two parallel north-south belts from Postmasburg in the south to Sishen/Kathu/Hotazel in the north. Limestone, asbestos and gypsum salt are also mined. In 1999, 19,235 people were employed in mining.

Agriculture. Intensive irrigation takes place along the Orange River which supports vineyards and agribusiness. Stock farming predominates in the Bo-Karoo and Hantam areas. In 1996 there were 6,730 farms with 58,198 agricultural workers; gross farming income amounted to R1,418·9m.

INDUSTRY

Labour. As at Oct. 1999 the economically active population numbered 298,000, of whom 54,000 were unemployed (18·1%).

COMMUNICATIONS

Roads. In 1995 there were 7,273 road accidents with 326 fatalities.

Rail. The main rail link is between Cape Town and Johannesburg, via Kimberley. Other main lines link the Northern Cape with Port Elizabeth via De Aar while another links Upington with Namibia.

Civil Aviation. Five airports are used for scheduled flights—Kimberley, Upington, Aggeneys, Springbok and Alexander Bay.

SOCIAL INSTITUTIONS

Education. In 1998 there were 206,597 children enrolled in schools with a total of 7,142 teaching staff. According to the 1996 census, almost 21% of those aged 20 years and over had no schooling; 31% had some secondary education.

Health. In 1998 there were 48 hospitals (including 29 private hospitals) and 2,966 hospital beds.

CULTURE

Broadcasting. There were 85,140 TV licence holders in 1996.

Tourism. Parks are a major tourism asset with the total area under protection being 1,080,200 ha. Provincial nature reserves occupy 50,240 ha. Hunting is a growing activity in the province.

NORTH-WEST

TERRITORY AND POPULATION

The area is 116,190 sq. km and the population at the 2001 census was 3,669,350. Of that number: female, 1,847,802; African/Black, 3,358,450 (91·3% of the total population); White, 244,035 (6·6%); Coloured, 56,959 (1·5%); Indian/Asian, 9,906 (0·3%). Density (2001), 32 per sq. km. Life expectancy at birth, 1996, was 53·3 years. At the 2001 census 65·2% spoke Setswana as their home language, 7·5% Afrikaans, 5·8% IsiXhosa, 5·7% Sesotho, 4·7% Xitsonga, 4·2% Sepedi, 2·5% IsiZulu, 1·3% IsiNdebele, 1·2% English and 0·6% SiSwati.

North-West Province comprises 32 administrative districts. The provincial capital is Mmabatho.

CONSTITUTION AND GOVERNMENT

There is a 33-seat provincial legislature.

RECENT ELECTIONS

At the provincial elections held on 14 April 2004 the ANC won 27 seats, UCDP three, DA two and VF+ one.

CURRENT ADMINISTRATION

In Feb. 2005 the ANC Executive Council comprised:

Premier: Ednah Molewa; b. 1957 (took office on 30 April 2004).

Minister of Agriculture, Conservation, Environment and Tourism: Ndleleni Duma. *Education:* Rev. Johannes Tselapedi. *Finance and Economic Development:* Darkey Afrika. *Health:* Mandlenkosi Eliot Mayisela. *Local Government and Housing:* F. Phenye Vilakazi. *Public Works:* Howard D. Yawa. *Safety and Security:* Maureen Modiselle. *Social Development:* R. Nomende Rasmeni. *Sports, Arts and Culture:* Nikiwe Num. *Transport and Roads:* Jerry D. Thibedi.

Speaker: Thandie Modise. *Director-General:* Dr M. A. Bakane-Tuoane.

Government Website: http://www.nwpg.gov.za

ENERGY AND NATURAL RESOURCES

Electricity. In 1998, 27,920 GWh of electricity were consumed.

Water. In 1996 piped water was available in the homes of almost 30% of the population. The most-used source of water was the public tap, used by more than 31% of the population.

Minerals. In 1999, 132,499 people were employed in mining.

Agriculture. In 1996 (excluding the TBVC countries of Transkei, Bophuthatswana, Venda and Ciskei now within the province) there were 7,512 farms with 98,349 agricultural workers; gross farming income amounted to R3,038·3m.

INDUSTRY

Labour. As at Oct. 1999 the economically active population numbered 1,018,000, of whom 240,000 were unemployed (23·5%).

COMMUNICATIONS

Roads. In 1995 there were 13,453 road accidents with 624 fatalities.

Telecommunications. Around 17% of the population had telephones or mobile phones in 1996; 19% had no access at all to a telephone.

SOCIAL INSTITUTIONS

Education. In 1998 there were 953,737 children enrolled in schools with a total of 31,962 teaching staff. In the same year, 24,296 students attended the Province's two universities and one technikon. According to the 1996 census, almost 22% of those aged 20 or over had no schooling.

Health. In 1998 there were 49 hospitals (including 17 private hospitals) and 10,012 hospital beds.

CULTURE

Broadcasting. In 1996 there were 116,680 TV licence holders.

Tourism. In 1999 there was a total of 343,915 international visitors (5·5% of total international visitors to South Africa) with 114,639 jobs created as a result.

WESTERN CAPE

TERRITORY AND POPULATION

The area is 129,386 sq. km. Population, 2001 census, 4,524,336. Of that number: females, 2,332,014; Coloured, 2,438,976 (53·9%); African/Black, 1,207,429 (26·7%); White, 832,901 (18·4%); Indian/Asian, 45,030 (1·0%). Density (2001), 35 per sq. km. Life expectancy at birth, 1996, was 60·8 years. At the 2001 census, 55·3% spoke Afrikaans as their home language, 23·7% IsiXhosa and 19·3% English. In 1996, 3·5m. (85% of total population) lived in urban areas.

There are 41 administrative districts. The capital is Cape Town.

CONSTITUTION AND GOVERNMENT

There is a 42-seat provincial parliament.

RECENT ELECTIONS

At the provincial elections held on 14 April 2004, 19 seats were won by the ANC, 12 by the DA, five by the NNP, three by ID, two by ACDP and one by the UDM.

CURRENT ADMINISTRATION

In Feb. 2005 the ANC/NNP provincial cabinet comprised:

Premier: Ebrahim Rasool; b. 1962 (ANC; took office on 30 April 2004).

Minister of Agriculture: Kobus Dowry (NNP). *Community Safety:* Leonard Ramatlakane (ANC). *Education:* Cameron Dugmore (ANC). *Environmental Affairs and Development Planning:* Tasneem Essop (ANC). *Finance, Economic Development and Tourism:* Lynne Brown (ANC). *Health:* Pierre Uys (NNP). *Local Government and Housing:* Marius Fransman (ANC). *Public Works and Transport:* Mcebisi Skwatsha (ANC). *Social Services and Poverty Alleviation:* Kholeka Mqulwana (ANC). *Sport and Culture:* Chris Stali (ANC).

Speaker: Shaun Byneveldt (ANC). *Director-General:* Dr Gilbert Lawrence.

Government Website: http://www.westerncape.gov.za

ENERGY AND NATURAL RESOURCES

Electricity. In 1998, 15,305 GWh of electricity were consumed.

Water. Many small rural towns and farming communities rely on groundwater for domestic water supplies. In comparison with the rest of the country relatively few people in the province do not have access to adequate water supplies.

Minerals. In 1999, 2,561 people were employed in mining.

Agriculture. There were 9,759 farms with 198,378 agricultural workers in 1996; gross farming income amounted to R7,533·6m.

INDUSTRY

Labour. As at Oct. 1999 the economically active population numbered 1,811,000, of whom 248,000 were unemployed (13·7%).

COMMUNICATIONS

Roads. Motor vehicles registered (1996) totalled 1,102,226, including 679,977 passenger cars, 238,087 light commercial vehicles, 35,478 heavy commercial vehicles and 28,153 motorcycles. In 1995 there were 87,117 road accidents with 1,286 fatalities.

Civil Aviation. Cape Town International Airport is the main airport in the province.

Telecommunications. In 1996, 55·2% of the population had a telephone or mobile phone; 3% had no access at all to a telephone.

SOCIAL INSTITUTIONS

Education. In 1998 there were 902,879 children enrolled in schools with a total of 25,393 teaching staff. In that year, 60,330 students attended the Province's three universities and two technikons. According to the 1996 census, 10·6% of people aged 20 years and over had higher education qualifications.

Health. In 1998 there were 114 hospitals (including 69 private hospitals) and 18,533 hospital beds.

CULTURE

Broadcasting. There were 681,644 TV licence holders in 1996.

Tourism. Overseas visitors to the province in 2002 totalled 976,000 (excluding Africa); domestic visitor trips, 4,326,000.

SPAIN

Reino de España
(Kingdom of Spain)

Capital: Madrid
Population projection, 2010: 41·28m.
GDP per capita, 2002: (PPP$) 21,460
HDI/world rank: 0·922/20

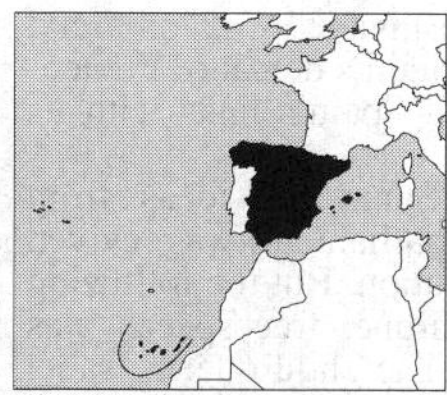

KEY HISTORICAL EVENTS

The first known inhabitants were a mix of Iberians, who spoke a non Indo-European language, and Celtic peoples, who were mainly in the north and west of the peninsula. From the 8th century BC the Phoenicians established trading colonies such as Gades (Cádiz), importing metalworking, music and literacy in the form of a semi-syllabic script. From around 215 BC the Iberian Peninsula was a battleground for the Romans and the Carthaginians. Fighting between the two powers continued until the Carthaginians were forced off the peninsula in 206 BC, after which Roman laws and customs were gradually adopted.

In AD 409 Visigoths, Suevi and Vandals crossed the Pyrenees and by 470 most of the leading families were of Germanic origin. Toledo became the capital and seat of the Visigothic monarchs. Muslim armies, triumphant in North Africa, crossed to the Iberian Peninsula in 711. Toledo fell to Arab and Berber forces and the death of King Roderic marked the end of Visigothic hegemony.

The Muslim conquerors brought a new language, religion and culture, which dominated large parts of Iberia. The Umayyad dynasty used Córdoba as the administrative centre of al-Andalus until 1031. New trade links with Egypt, Persia and the Islamic world fostered Córdoba and Seville as beacons of modernity and creativity. From about 900 there was a gradual expansion of the Christian principalities, known as the *Reconquista*, or reconquest of Spain by the Christians. Norman knights fought in Catalonia and French settlers arrived in towns along the pilgrimage route to Santiago de Compostela. The most powerful Christian kingdoms—Aragon, Castile and Portugal—pushed south and east and by 1300 Granada was the last remaining Islamic dominion, though in rural areas the Islamic faith and the Arabic language survived for centuries. While Córdoba declined, Barcelona emerged as an economic success story on a par with Genoa and Venice.

By the early 14th century Castile and Aragon were the dominant kingdoms, though both were racked by infighting and rebellion. King Pedro the Cruel of Castile was challenged by his half-brother Enrique de Trastámara. The English supported Pedro and his heirs but Enrique eventually prevailed, with French assistance, establishing the Trastámara dynasty in 1369.

The Spanish monarchy was founded in 1469 following the marriage of Isabel (Isabella), princess of Castile, and Fernando (Ferdinand), heir to the throne of Aragon. Under their joint reign, they laid the foundations for a unified Spain. In 1478 they established the Spanish Inquisition, expelling and executing tens of thousands of Jews and other non-Christians. Granada, the last Islamic territory, surrendered in 1492. The Spanish crowns passed to Juana *la loca* (the Mad) and her husband, Philip (Felipe) the Handsome, heir to the Habsburg domains in Germany and Flanders. When Fernando died in 1516, Juana and Felipe's son, Charles of Ghent, inherited Spain, its colonies in the New World, Naples and, following the death of Maximilian I in 1519, the Habsburg territories. Shortly afterwards, he was elected Holy Roman Emperor, a title he held as Charles V (Carlos I of Spain).

Christopher Columbus paved the way for the Spanish colonies in the New World. In 1521 the conquistador Hernando Cortés overthrew the Aztecs. After 1540 gold and silver began pouring into Spanish coffers from mines in Peru and Mexico while sugar plantations were established in the Caribbean. The rise of Spain as a military power began in the 1560s in the reign of Felipe II. He built a powerful navy and annexed Portugal in 1580. The new fleet defended the American supply routes from English attacks and set up new colonies in the Philippines and at Buenos Aires.

Spain's Golden Age faltered in the late 16th century following a popular uprising in the Netherlands under William of Orange. The Dutch established their own colonies in Asia and started making inroads in Brazil. Spain was weakened by the cost of defending its empire against France and England and in 1640 Catalonia and Portugal rebelled. The crowning of Carlos II, a disabled child, in 1665 symbolized Spain's growing vulnerability and isolation from the rest of Europe.

Carlos II died childless in 1700, leaving the throne to Philippe, duke of Anjou and grandson of King Louis XIV of France. Under Felipe (Philippe) V, the first in a line of five Bourbon monarchs, Spain restored its influence in Italy, where Naples and Sicily were recovered from Austria in 1734. The 1780s were a period of stability and prosperity before the French Revolution, when France invaded Catalonia and the Basque provinces, forcing an alliance with Carlos IV. Britain's defeat of Franco-Spanish naval forces at the Battle of Trafalgar undermined Spain's links with its colonies.

In 1813 French forces were finally expelled from Spain but ideas from revolutionary France had taken root. The medieval Cortes (parliament) was revived and a liberal reformist group brought in Spain's first constitution. But the following year, when Fernando VII was restored to the Spanish throne, free speech was repressed and Spain entered a severe economic recession. The child queen, Isabel II, inherited the throne in 1833. During her reign there were attempts to reinstate a constitution but her support for neo-catholic reactionaries in her governments of the 1860s fanned the flames of revolution. In 1873 the Cortes proclaimed a republic but it was marked by instability and a coup restored the Bourbon monarchy less than a year later. Spain was defeated by the USA in the Spanish-American War of 1898, resulting in the loss of Cuba, Puerto Rico, Guam and the Philippines.

Spain was neutral during the First World War, which led to a boom in trade and industry. However, this prosperity did not filter through society and workers were faced with inflation and high food prices. In 1923 Gen. Miguel Primo de Rivera led a coup, abolished the 1876 constitution and dismissed the Cortes. Primo de Rivera's alternative to the constitutional monarchy was the National Political Union but it attracted only right wing enthusiasts. A financial crisis forced Primo de Rivera's resignation in 1930. The following year a republican-socialist coalition proclaimed the Second Republic. The 1936 elections saw the country split between the Republicans (an uneasy alliance of communists, socialists and anarchists) and the Nationalists (the army, the Catholic church, monarchists and the fascist-style Falange Party).

The assassination of the opposition leader José Calvo Sotelo by Republican police officers in July 1936 gave the army, led by Gen. Francisco Franco, an excuse to stage a coup. His failure to overthrow the government led to a protracted civil war, in which the Nationalists received military and financial support from Nazi Germany and Fascist Italy, while the elected Republican government received support from the Soviet Union and, to a lesser degree, from the International Brigades, consisting of left wing volunteers from across Europe.

By 1939 the Nationalists had prevailed. More than 350,000 Spaniards died in the fighting, while some 100,000 Republicans were executed or died in prison after the civil war. Franco withdrew the economy from world markets and established a self-sufficient autarky. Spain benefited from neutrality in the Second World War but by the late 1940s the economy was lagging. There was growing unrest in the 1950s, with nationwide strikes and open opposition to the Franco regime from university students and intellectuals.

Franco died in 1975, having earlier named Juan Carlos, the grandson of Alfonso XIII, his successor. Under King Juan Carlos, Spain returned to democracy. The first elections were held in 1977 and a new constitution was approved by referendum in 1978. In Feb. 1981 there was an attempted fascist coup but order was restored after 18 hours. The following year saw a spectacular victory for the socialist party, which presided over a rapid expansion in the economy during its 14 years in power. In 1986 Spain joined the European Economic Community.

The campaign waged by ETA, the Basque separatist terrorist group, is still far from a resolution. In 1996 Spain elected a conservative party under the leadership of José María Aznar. In March 2000 he was re-elected with an absolute majority. Madrid suffered Spain's worst terrorist attack on 11 March 2004 when four commuter trains were bombed, killing 191 and injuring over 1,800 people. The government initially blamed ETA but suspicion quickly moved to al-Qaeda. On 14 March the Socialists defeated the People's Party in general elections. Prime minister-elect José Luis

Rodríguez Zapatero vowed to withdraw Spanish troops from Iraq and instead bolster operations in Afghanistan. The last Spanish troops left Iraq in May 2004.

TERRITORY AND POPULATION

Spain is bounded in the north by the Bay of Biscay, France and Andorra, east and south by the Mediterranean and the Straits of Gibraltar, southwest by the Atlantic and west by Portugal and the Atlantic. Continental Spain has an area of 492,592 sq. km, and including the Balearic and Canary Islands and the towns of Ceuta and Melilla on the northern coast of Africa, 506,030 sq. km (195,378 sq. miles). Population (census, 2001), 40,847,371 (20,825,521 females). In 2001, 77·8% of the population lived in urban areas; population density in 2001 was 83 per sq. km. In 2002 foreigners resident in Spain numbered 1,977,944, including 307,458 from Morocco, 259,522 from Ecuador, 191,018 from Colombia, 128,121 from the UK and 113,308 from Germany. Foreigners constitute 4·7% of the population.

The UN gives a projected population for 2010 of 41·28m.

The growth of the population has been as follows:

Census year	*Population*	*Rate of annual increase*	*Census year*	*Population*	*Rate of annual increase*
1860	15,655,467	0·34	1960	30,903,137	1·05
1910	19,927,150	0·72	1970	33,823,918	0·95
1920	21,303,162	0·69	1981	37,746,260	1·05
1930	23,563,867	1·06	1991	38,872,268	0·30
1940	25,877,971	0·98	2001	40,847,371	0·51
1950	27,976,755	0·81			

Area and population of the autonomous communities (in italics) and provinces at the 2001 census:

Autonomous community/ Province	*Area (sq. km)*	*Population*	*Per sq. km*
Andalusia	*87,595*	*7,357,558*	*84*
Almería	8,775	536,731	61
Cádiz	7,436	1,116,491	150
Córdoba	13,771	761,657	55
Granada	12,647	821,660	65
Huelva	10,128	462,579	45
Jaén	13,496	643,820	46
Málaga	7,306	1,287,017	176
Sevilla	14,036	1,727,603	123
Aragón	*47,720*	*1,204,215*	*25*
Huesca	15,636	206,502	13
Teruel	14,810	135,858	9
Zaragoza	17,274	861,855	50
Asturias	*10,604*	*1,062,998*	*100*
Baleares	*4,992*	*841,669*	*169*
Basque Country	*7,234*	*2,082,587*	*288*
Álava	3,037	286,387	94
Guipúzcoa	1,980	673,563	340
Vizcaya	2,217	1,122,637	506
Canary Islands	*7,492*	*1,694,477*	*226*
Palmas, Las	4,111	887,676	216
Santa Cruz de Tenerife	3,381	806,801	239
Cantabria	*5,321*	*535,131*	*101*
Castilla-La Mancha	*79,461*	*1,760,516*	*22*
Albacete	14,924	364,835	24
Ciudad Real	19,813	478,957	24
Cuenca	17,140	200,346	12
Guadalajara	12,214	174,999	14
Toledo	15,370	541,379	35
Castilla y León	*94,224*	*2,456,474*	*26*
Ávila	8,050	163,442	20
Burgos	14,292	348,934	24
León	15,581	488,751	31
Palencia	8,052	174,143	22
Salamanca	12,350	345,609	28
Segovia	6,921	147,694	21
Soria	10,306	90,717	9
Valladolid	8,111	498,094	61
Zamora	10,561	199,090	19
Catalonia	*32,113*	*6,343,110*	*198*
Barcelona	7,728	4,805,927	622
Gerona	5,910	565,304	96
Lérida	12,172	362,206	30
Tarragona	6,303	609,673	97
Extremadura	*41,634*	*1,058,503*	*25*
Badajoz	21,766	654,882	30
Cáceres	19,868	403,621	20
Galicia	*29,575*	*2,695,880*	*91*
Coruña, La	7,951	1,096,027	138
Lugo	9,856	357,648	36
Orense	7,273	338,446	47
Pontevedra	4,495	903,759	201
Madrid	*8,028*	*5,423,384*	*676*
Murcia	*11,314*	*1,197,646*	*106*
Navarra	*10,391*	*555,829*	*53*
Rioja, La	*5,045*	*276,702*	*55*
Valencian Community	*23,255*	*4,162,776*	*175*
Alicante	5,817	1,461,925	251
Castellón	6,632	484,566	73
Valencia	10,806	2,216,285	205
Ceuta[1]	*20*	*71,505*	*3,575*
Melilla[1]	*12*	*66,411*	*5,534*
Total	*506,030*	*40,847,371*	*81*

[1]Ceuta and Melilla gained limited autonomous status in 1994.

The capitals of the autonomous communities are: *Andalusia*: Sevilla (Seville); *Aragón*: Zaragoza (Saragossa); *Asturias*: Oviedo; *Baleares*: Palma de Mallorca; *Basque Country*: Vitoria; *Canary Islands*, dual capitals, Las Palmas and Santa Cruz de Tenerife; *Cantabria*: Santander; *Castilla-La Mancha*: Toledo; *Castilla y León*: Valladolid; *Catalonia*: Barcelona; *Extremadura:* Mérida; *Galicia*: Santiago de Compostela; *Madrid*: Madrid; *Murcia*: Murcia (but regional parliament in Cartagena); *Navarra*: Pamplona; *La Rioja*: Logroño; *Valencian Community*: Valencia.

The capitals of the provinces are the towns from which they take the name, except in the cases of Álava (capital, Vitoria), Guipúzcoa (San Sebastián) and Vizcaya (Bilbao).

The islands which form the Balearics include Majorca, Minorca, Ibiza and Formentera. Those which form the Canary Archipelago are divided into two provinces, under the name of their respective capitals: Santa Cruz de Tenerife and Las Palmas de Gran Canaria. The province of Santa Cruz de Tenerife is constituted by the islands of Tenerife, La Palma, Gomera and Hierro; that of Las Palmas by Gran Canaria, Lanzarote and Fuerteventura, with the small barren islands of Alegranza, Roque del Este, Roque del Oeste, Graciosa, Montaña Clara and Lobos.

Places under Spanish sovereignty in Africa (Alhucemas, Ceuta, Chafarinas, Melilla and Peñón de Vélez) constitute the two provinces of Ceuta and Melilla.

Populations of principal towns in 2001:

Town	*Population*	*Town*	*Population*	*Town*	*Population*
Albacete	152,155	Getafe	153,868	Pamplona	189,364
Alcalá de Henares	179,602	Gijón	270,211	Parla	80,545
Alcobendas	95,104	Granada	240,522	Reus	91,616
Alcorcón	149,594	Guecho	84,024	Sabadell	187,201
Algeciras	106,710	Hermanas, Dos	103,282	Salamanca	156,006
Alicante	293,629	Hospitalet	244,323	San Baudilio del Llobregat	80,041
Almería	173,338	Huelva	140,862	San Fernando	84,014
Avilés	83,511	Jaén	112,921	San Sebastián	181,700
Badajoz	136,851	Jerez de la Frontera	187,087	Santa Coloma de Grammanet	115,568
Badalona	210,370	Laguna, La	135,004	Santa Cruz de Tenerife	217,415
Baracaldo	95,515	Leganés	173,163	Santander	184,661
Barcelona	1,527,190	León	135,794	Santiago de Compostela	93,273
Bilbao	353,950	Lérida	115,000	Sevilla	704,114
Burgos	167,962	Logroño	136,841	Tarragona	117,184
Cáceres	84,439	Lorca	79,481	Tarrasa	179,300
Cádiz	136,236	Lugo	89,509	Telde	91,160
Cartagena	188,003	Madrid	3,016,788	Torrejón de Ardoz	101,056
Castellón de la Plana	153,225	Málaga	535,686	Valencia	761,871
Córdoba	314,805	Marbella	115,871	Valladolid	318,576
Cornellá de Llobregat	81,881	Mataró	109,298	Vigo	288,324
Coruña, La	242,458	Móstoles	198,819	Vitoria	221,270
Coslada	79,862	Murcia	377,888	Zaragoza	620,419
Elche	201,731	Orense	109,011		
Ferrol, El	79,520	Oviedo	202,938		
Fuenlabrada	179,735	Palencia	80,801		
		Palma de Mallorca	358,462		
		Palmas, Las	370,649		

Languages. The Constitution states that 'Castilian is the Spanish official language of the State', but also that 'All other Spanish languages will also be official in the corresponding Autonomous Communities'. At the last linguistic census (2001) Catalan (an official EU language since 1990) was spoken in Catalonia by 74·5% of people and understood by 94·5%. It is also spoken in Baleares, Valencian Community (where it is frequently called Valencian), and in Aragón, a narrow strip close to the Catalonian and Valencian Community boundaries. Galician, a language very close to Portuguese, was understood in 1998 by 98·4% of people in Galicia and spoken by 89·2%; Basque by a significant and increasing minority in the Basque Country, and by a small minority in northwest Navarra. It is estimated that one-third of all Spaniards speaks one of the other three official languages as well as standard Castilian. In bilingual communities, both Castilian and the regional language are taught in schools and universities.

SOCIAL STATISTICS

Statistics for calendar years:

	Marriages	*Divorces*	*Births*	*Deaths*
1999	208,129	36,900	380,130	371,102
2000	216,451	38,973	397,632	360,391
2001	208,057	37,630	406,380	360,131
2002[1]	209,065	...	416,518	366,528
2003[1]	210,155	...	439,863	383,729

[1]Provisional.

Rate per 1,000 population, 2001: births, 10·0; deaths, 8·9; marriages, 5·1. In 1998 the most popular age range for marrying was 25–29 for both males and females. Annual population growth rate, 1992–02, 0·4%. Suicide rate (per 100,000 population), 1998: 6·6. Expectation of life, 2001, was 75·6 years for males and 82·6 for females. Infant mortality, 2001, four per 1,000 live births; fertility rate, 2001, 1·1 births per woman (one of the lowest rates in the world). In 2002 Spain received 6,179 asylum applications, equivalent to 0·2 per 1,000 inhabitants.

CLIMATE

Most of Spain has a form of Mediterranean climate with mild, moist winters and hot, dry summers, but the northern coastal region has a moist, equable climate, with rainfall well distributed throughout the year, mild winters and warm summers, and less sunshine than the rest of Spain. The south, in particular Andalusia, is dry and prone to drought.

Madrid, Jan. 41°F (5°C), July 77°F (25°C). Annual rainfall 16·8" (419 mm). Barcelona, Jan. 46°F (8°C), July 74°F (23·5°C). Annual rainfall 21" (525 mm). Cartagena, Jan. 51°F (10·5°C), July 75°F (24°C). Annual rainfall 14·9" (373 mm). La Coruña, Jan. 51°F (10·5°C), July 66°F (19°C). Annual rainfall 32" (800 mm). Sevilla, Jan. 51°F (10·5°C), July 85°F (29·5°C). Annual rainfall 19·5" (486 mm). Palma de Mallorca, Jan. 51°F (11°C), July 77°F (25°C). Annual rainfall 13·6" (347 mm). Santa Cruz de Tenerife, Jan. 64°F (17·9°C), July 76°F (24·4°C). Annual rainfall 7·72" (196 mm).

CONSTITUTION AND GOVERNMENT

Following the death of General Franco in 1975 and the transition to a democracy, the first democratic elections were held on 15 June 1977. A new Constitution was approved by referendum on 6 Dec. 1978, and came into force 29 Dec. 1978. It established a parliamentary monarchy.

The reigning king is **Juan Carlos I**, born 5 Jan. 1938. The eldest son of Don Juan, Conde de Barcelona, Juan Carlos was given precedence over his father as pretender to the Spanish throne in an agreement in 1954 between Don Juan and General Franco. Don Juan, who resigned his claims to the throne in May 1977, died on 1 April 1993. King (then Prince) Juan Carlos married, in 1962, Princess Sophia of Greece, daughter of the late King Paul of the Hellenes and Queen Frederika. *Offspring:* Elena, born 20 Dec. 1963, married 18 March 1995 Jaime de Marichalar (*Offspring:* Felipe, b. 17 July 1998; Victoria, b. 9 Sept. 2000); Cristina, born 13 June 1965, married 4 Oct. 1997 Iñaki Urdangarín (*Offspring:* Juan, b. 29 Sept. 1999; Pablo, b. 6 Dec. 2000; Miguel, b. 30 Apr. 2002); Felipe, Prince of Asturias, heir to the throne, born 30 Jan. 1968, married 22 May 2004 Letizia Ortiz Rocasolano.

The King receives an allowance, part of which is taxable, approved by parliament each year. In 2005 this was €7·8m. There is no formal court; the (private) *Diputación de la Grandeza* represents the interests of the aristocracy.

Legislative power is vested in the *Cortes Generales*, a bicameral parliament composed of the Congress of Deputies (lower house) and the Senate (upper house). The *Congress of Deputies* has not less than 300 nor more than 400 members (350 in the general election of 2004) elected in a proportional system under which electors choose between party lists of candidates in multi-member constituencies.

The *Senate* has 259 members of whom 208 are elected by a majority system: the 47 mainland provinces elect four senators each, regardless of population; the larger islands (Gran Canaria, Mallorca and Tenerife) elect three senators and each of the smaller islands or groups of islands (Ibiza-Formentera, Minorca, Fuerteventura, Gomera, Hierro, Lanzarote and La Palma) elect one senator. To these each self-governing community appoints one senator, and an additional senator for every million inhabitants in their respective territories. Currently 51 senators are appointed by the self-governing communities. Deputies and senators are elected by universal secret suffrage for four-year terms. The Prime Minister is elected by the Congress of Deputies.

The *Constitutional Court* is empowered to solve conflicts between the State and the Autonomous Communities; to determine if legislation passed by the Cortes is contrary to the Constitution; and to protect the constitutional rights of individuals violated by any authority. Its 12 members are appointed by the monarch. It has a nine-year term, with a third of the membership being renewed every three years.

National Anthem. 'Marcha Real' ('Royal March'); no words, tune anonymous.

RECENT ELECTIONS

A general election took place on 14 March 2004. Turn-out was 77·2%. In the *Congress of Deputies* the Spanish Socialist Workers' Party (PSOE) won 164 seats with 42·6% of votes cast; the Popular Party (PP), 148 with 37·6%; Convergence and Union (CiU; Catalan nationalists), 10 with 3·2%; the Catalan separatist Republican Left of Catalunya (ERC), 8 with 2·5%; Basque Nationalist Party (PNV), 7 with 1·6%; the Communist-led United Left Coalition (IU), 5 with 5·0%; Canarian Coalition (CC), 3 with 0·9%; Galician Nationalist Bloc (BNG), 2 with 0·8%; the Aragonese Junta, 1 with 0·4%; the non-radical separatist Basque Solidarity Party (EA), 1 with 0·3%; Navarra Yes, 1 with 0·2%. The Andalusian Party (PA) won no seats with 0·7%. In the *Senate*, the PP won 102 seats; PSOE, 81; Entesa Catalana de Progrés, 12; CiU, 4; PNV, 4; CC, 3.

European Parliament. Spain has 54 (64 in 1999) representatives. At the June 2004 elections turn-out was 45·9% (64·3% in 1999). The PSOE (political affiliation in European Parliament: Party of European Socialists) won 24 seats and the Greens (Greens/European Free Alliance) 1 seat, with a combined 43·3% of votes cast; the PP, 23 with 41·3% (European People's Party–European Democrats); Galeuzca (a coalition of the PNV, BNG and the Democratic Convergence of Catalunya), 3 with 5·2% (PNV and the Democratic Convergence of Catalunya have affiliated themselves with the Alliance of Liberals and Democrats for Europe and BNG with Greens/European Free Alliance); the IU (a coalition of United Left Coalition and Initiative for Catalonia-Greens, 2 with 4·2% (one European Unitary Left/Nordic Green Left; one Greens/European Free Alliance); Europa de los Pueblos, 1 with 2·5% (Greens/European Free Alliance).

CURRENT ADMINISTRATION

In March 2005 the government comprised:

President of the Council and Prime Minister: José Luis Rodríguez Zapatero; b. 1960 (PSOE; elected 14 March 2004 and sworn in 17 April 2004).

First Vice President and Minister for the Presidency: María Teresa Fernandez de la Vega. *Second Vice President and Minister for the Economy:* Pedro Solbes. *Foreign Affairs and Co-operation:* Miguel Ángel Moratinos. *Justice:* Juan Fernando López Aguilar. *Interior:* José Antonio Alonso. *Defence:* José Bono. *Education and Science:* María Jesús San Segundo. *Labour, Social Affairs and Immigration:* Jesús Caldera. *Agriculture and Fisheries:* Elena Espinosa. *Public Administration:* Jordi Sevilla. *Environment:* Cristina Narbona. *Health and Consumer Affairs:* Elena Salgado. *Development:* Magdalena Álvarez. *Industry, Commerce and Tourism:* José Montilla. *Culture:* Carmen Calvo. *Housing:* María Antonia Trujillo.

Government Website: http://www.la-moncloa.es

DEFENCE

Conscription was abolished in 2001. The government had begun the phased abolition of conscription in 1996. In 2002 the armed forces became fully professional. However, a shortfall in recruitment in Spain has meant that descendants of Spanish migrants, many of whom have never been to Europe, are now joining. Since 1989 women have been accepted in all sections of the armed forces.

In 2003 defence expenditure totalled US$9,944m. (US$242 per capita), representing 1·2% of GDP.

Army. A Rapid Reaction Force is formed from the Spanish Legion and the airborne and air-portable brigades. There is also an Army Aviation Brigade consisting of 153 helicopters (28 attack).

Strength (2002) 118,000 (including 6,600 women). Of these 4,450 are stationed on the Balearic Islands, 8,600 on the Canary Islands and 8,100 in Ceuta and Melilla. There were 265,000 army reservists in 2002.

Guardia Civil. The paramilitary *Guardia Civil* numbers 72,600.

Navy. The principal ship of the Navy is the *Príncipe de Asturias*, a light vertical/short take-off and landing aircraft carrier. Her air group includes AV-8S Matador (Harrier) combat aircraft. There are also eight French-designed submarines and 15 frigates.

The Naval Air Service operates 17 combat aircraft and 37 armed helicopters. Personnel numbered 700 in 2002. There are 5,600 marines.

Main naval bases are at Ferrol, Rota, Cádiz, Cartagena, Palma de Mallorca, Mahón and Las Palmas (Canary Islands).

In 2002 personnel totalled 26,950 (1,600 women) including the marines and naval air arm. There were 18,500 naval reservists in 2002.

Air Force. The Air Force is organized as an independent service, dating from 1939. It is administered through four operational commands. These are geographically oriented following a reorganization in 1991 and comprise Central Air Command, Strait Air Command, Eastern Air Command and Air Command of the Canaries.

There were 198 combat aircraft in 2002 including 91 EF/A-18s, 23 F-5Bs and 65 Mirage F-1s.

Strength (2002) 22,750 (including 1,200 women). There were 45,000 air force reservists in 2002.

INTERNATIONAL RELATIONS

Spain is a member of the UN, WTO, BIS, the Council of Europe, NATO, OECD, WEU, the EU, OSCE, CERN, Inter-American Development Bank, Asian Development Bank and the Antarctic Treaty, and is a signatory to the Schengen Accord, which abolishes border controls between Spain, Austria, Belgium, Denmark, Finland, France, Germany, Greece, Iceland, Italy, Luxembourg, the Netherlands, Norway, Portugal and Sweden.

On 20 Feb. 2005 Spain became the first European Union member to ratify the new EU constitution through a referendum. Voters approved the constitution with 76·7% of votes cast in favour and 17·2% against, although turn-out was only 42·3%.

ECONOMY

Agriculture accounted for 3·4% of GDP in 2002, industry 30·1% and services 66·5%.

Overview. Since the implementation of structural reforms in the mid 1990s Spain's macroeconomic performance has been consistently strong, with average growth in excess of 4% between 1995 and 2004. Despite the global economic slowdown, growth in Spain in 2002 was more than one percentage point above the euro area average. Since 1999 Spain has experienced a persistent inflation rate differential of approximately 1·25% with the euro area, driven in part by overvaluation in the housing sector. According to the OECD, wage and price rigidities need to fall to see a reduction in this differential. Fiscal consolidation, started in the mid 1990s, led to the elimination of the government deficit in 2001. The government has followed a neutral fiscal stance since 2003, aiming to maintain a balanced budget. Spain suffers from comparatively high unemployment and low female employment rates, as well as low productivity gains. Only Poland and Slovakia among the EU member countries have higher unemployment, although the rate did begin to decline in 2004. The OECD states that structural reforms are required to raise the employment rate and to boost productivity growth. Despite recent reforms to reduce employment rigidities, major distortions remain in the labour market, which is segmented and suffers from high regional dispersion.

Currency. On 1 Jan. 1999 the euro (EUR) became the legal currency in Spain; irrevocable conversion rate 166·386 pesetas to 1 euro. The euro, which consists of 100 cents, has been in circulation since 1 Jan. 2002. There are seven euro notes in different colours and sizes denominated in 500, 200, 100, 50, 20, 10 and 5 euros, and eight coins denominated in 2 and 1 euros, then 50, 20, 10, 5, 2 and 1 cents. On the introduction of the euro there was a 'dual circulation' period before the peseta ceased to be legal tender on 28 Feb. 2002. Euro banknotes in circulation on 1 Jan. 2002 had a total value of €68·6bn.

Foreign exchange reserves were US$28,939m. in June 2002 (US$65,773m. in Feb. 1998) and gold reserves 16·83m. troy oz. Inflation was 3·5% in 2002 and 3·0% in both 2003 and 2004. Total money supply was €34,255m. in June 2002.

Budget. In 2001 revenues totalled €212,571m. (€197,510m. in 2000) and expenditures €209,402m. (€199,791m. in 2000). Principal sources of revenue in 2001: social security contributions, €81,985m.; taxes on income, profits and capital gains, €54,829m.; taxes on goods and services, €49,737m. Main items of expenditure in 2001: social protection, €83,052m.; general public services, €60,492m.; health, €32,308m.

VAT is normally 16%, with a rate of 7% on certain services (catering and hospitality), and 4% on basic foodstuffs.

Performance. Real GDP growth was 2·8% in 2001 and 2·2% in 2002 and 2·5% in 2003. Total GDP (2003): US$836·1bn.

The *OECD Economic Survey* of May 2003 reported: 'Output growth has remained strong for a number of years, with robust job creation, despite the recent slowdown. But inflation has been higher than the euro area average, raising competitiveness concerns while—partly as a result of strong job creation—productivity has been weak. The prudent fiscal account of recent years has resulted in balanced public accounts. Any cyclical slippage can thus be tolerated if the economic upturn in 2003 is weaker than expected, though a structural deficit needs to be avoided.'

Banking and Finance. The central bank is the Bank of Spain (*Governor*, Jaime Caruana) which gained autonomy under an ordinance of 1994. Its Governor is appointed for a six-year term. The Banking Corporation of Spain, *Argentaria*, groups together the shares of all state-owned banks, and competes in the financial market with private banks. In 1993 the government sold 49·9% of the capital of Argentaria; the remainder in two flotations ending on 13 Feb. 1998.

Spanish banking is dominated by two main banks—BSCH (Banco Santander Central Hispano) and BBVA (Banco Bilbao Vizcaya Argentaria). BSCH had assets of €335·5bn in Sept. 2002 and BBVA assets of €309·2bn. in March 2003.

There are stock exchanges in Madrid, Barcelona, Bilbao and Valencia.

ENERGY AND NATURAL RESOURCES

Environment. In 2002 Spain's carbon dioxide emissions from the consumption and flaring of fossil fuels were the equivalent of 8·3 tonnes per capita.

Electricity. Installed capacity was 52·9m. kW in 2000. The total electricity output in 2000 amounted to 224·74bn. kWh, of which 28% was nuclear, 14% hydro-electric and 58% other (carbon, natural gas, petroleum). Consumption per capita in 2000 was 5,807 kWh.

In Oct. 2000 Endesa SA and Iberdrola SA, the country's two largest electricity companies, announced merger plans. The new company would have been in charge of 80% of Spain's electricity output. However, in Feb. 2001 the two companies shelved the proposed merger. In 2003 there were nine nuclear reactors in operation.

Oil and Gas. Spain is heavily dependent on imported oil; Mexico is its largest supplier. Crude oil production (2000), 227,000 tonnes.

The government sold its remaining stake in the oil, gas and chemicals group Repsol in 1997. Natural gas production (2001) totalled 509m. cu. metres. Ever increasing consumption means that Spain has to import large quantities of natural gas, primarily from Algeria.

Wind. Spain is one of the world's largest wind-power producers, with 7,814 turbines and an installed capacity of 4,635 MW at the end of 2002.

Minerals. Coal production (2000), 11·32m. tonnes; other principal minerals (in 1,000 tonnes): lignite (2000), 12,154; gypsum and anhydrite (2001), 7,500; anthracite (2001), 4,694; salt (2000), 3,869; potash (2001), 570; aluminium (2001), 376; zinc (2001), 184; pyrites (2001), 152; fluorspar (2001), 134; lead (2001), 49.

In 1995 a large mercury deposit was found in southern Spain which could raise mercury levels to within a quarter of proven world reserves. Gold production, 2001, 3,300 kg; silver production, 2000, 66,000 kg.

Agriculture. There were 1,287,000 farms in Spain in 2000. Agriculture employed about 5·9% of the workforce in 2002. It accounts for 15·8% of exports and 15·6% of imports.

There were 13·02m. ha of arable land in 2001 and 4·93m. ha of permanent crops. In 2002 there were 914,000 tractors and 52,000 harvester-threshers; in 2001 there were 132,000 milking machines in use.

Principal	*Area (in 1,000 ha)*			*Yield (in 1,000 tonnes)*		
crops	*2000*	*2001*	*2002*	*2000*	*2001*	*2002*
Barley	3,278	2,992	3,100	11,063	6,249	8,333
Sugarbeets	125	107	115	7,930	6,755	8,040
Wheat	2,353	2,177	2,402	7,294	5,008	6,783
Maize	433	513	463	3,992	4,982	4,463
Potatoes	119	115	114	3,078	2,992	3,104
Oats	432	446	473	954	665	916
Rice	117	116	113	827	876	815
Sunflower seeds	839	858	754	919	871	757

Spain has more land dedicated to the grape than any other country in the world and is ranked third among wine producers (behind Italy and France). Production of wine (2001), 30,951,000 hectolitres; of grapes, 5,272,000 tonnes.

The area planted with tomatoes in 2002 was 60,000 ha, yielding 3,878,000 tonnes; with onions, 23,000 ha, yielding 992,000 tonnes; peppers, 23,000 ha, yielding 980,000 tonnes.

Fruit production (2002, in tonnes): oranges, 2,867,000; tangerines, 1,952,000; peaches, 1,247,000; lemons, 920,000; apples, 653,000; pears, 603,000.

Production of olives, 2001–02, 6,983,000 tonnes; olive oil, 1,422,000 tonnes. Spain is the world's leading producer both of olives and olive oil.

Livestock (2000): cattle, 6·20m.; sheep, 23·70m.; goats, 2·87m.; pigs, 23·68m.; chickens, 128·0m.; asses and mules, 0·26m.; horses, 0·25m. Livestock products (2000, in 1,000 tonnes): pork, bacon and ham, 2,962; beef and veal, 697; mutton and lamb, 222; poultry meat, 891; milk, 6,526; cheese, 175; eggs, 522.

Forestry. In 2000 the area under forests was 14·37m. ha, or 28·8% of the total land area. In 2001 timber production was 15·13m. cu. metres.

Fisheries. Spain is the second largest fishing country in the EU after Denmark; it is also the EU's leading importer of fishery commodities. Fishing vessels had a total tonnage of 519,867 tonnes in 2002, the highest in the EU (596,441 GRT in 1994); fleets have been gradually reduced from 20,558 boats in 1991 to 14,887 in 2002. Total catch in 2001 amounted to 1,084,820 tonnes, almost exclusively sea fish.

INDUSTRY

The leading companies by market capitalization in Spain, excluding banking and finance, in May 2004 were: Telefónica SA (US$72·1bn.); Telefónica Móviles SA (US$44·6bn.); and Repsol YPF (US$25·9bn.), an oil and gas company.

Industrial products (in tonnes): cement (2000), 38·2m.; distillate fuel oil (2000), 20·1m.; crude steel (2002), 16·4m.; residual fuel oil (2000), 13·1m.; petrol (2000), 9·6m.; paper and paperboard (2002), 5·4m.; plastics (1999), 4·1m.; pig iron (2002), 4·0m.; jet fuels (2000), 3·7m.; sulphuric acid (1999), 3·3m.; nitrogenous fertilizers (2000), 951,000; cigarettes (2001), 74·8bn. units.

The number of vehicles manufactured in 2002 was 2,855,000. In 2000, 2·15m. refrigerators were manufactured; and (in 1998) 2·6m. cookers, hotplates and microwaves, and 2·3m. washing machines; number of TV sets (1995), 5·39m. In 2001, 4,730·5m. litres of soft drinks, 4,072·3m. litres of mineral water and 2,680·2m. litres of beer were produced.

Labour. The economically active population numbered 15,945,600 in 2001, with the principal areas of activity as follows: manufacturing, 3,005,600; wholesale and retail trade/repair of motor vehicles, motorcycles and personal and household goods, 2,555,900; construction, 1,850,200; real estate, renting and business activities, 1,238,300; public administration and defence/compulsory social security, 1,008,100.

The monthly minimum wage for adults (2004) was €460·50. The average working week in 2003 was 35·4 hours. The retirement age is 65 years. In 1999 part-time work accounted for less than 9% of all employment in Spain—the lowest percentage in any major industrialized country.

Spain's unemployment rate reached a peak of nearly 25% in 1994 but went down to 10·6% in 2001 before rising slightly to 11·3% in 2002. In Dec. 2004 it was 10·4%. The unemployment rate among women is double that among men. Between 1996 and early 2000 Spain created as many new jobs as were created in the rest of the EU put together. In spite of the high unemployment rate, by 2000 there were labour shortages in agriculture and construction, as a result of which the government reached an agreement with Morocco to import temporary contract labour.

Between 1993 and 2002 strikes cost Spain an average of 248 days per 1,000 employees a year, compared to the EU average of 64 per 1,000. Spain's figure was the highest in the EU.

Trade Unions. The Constitution guarantees the establishment and activities of trade unions provided they have a democratic structure. The most important trade unions are *Comisiones Obreras* (CO), with 790,000 members in 1997, and *Unión General de Trabajadores* (UGT), which had 775,000 members in 1997.

INTERNATIONAL TRADE

Imports and Exports. Trade in US$1m.:

	1998	*1999*	*2000*	*2001*	*2002*
Imports f.o.b.	132,744	143,002	151,025	150,474	158,893
Exports f.o.b.	111,986	112,664	116,205	117,935	125,795

Main exports in 2001: road vehicles, 23·0%; machinery, 16·0%; food, 12·0% (of which fruits and vegetables, 6·3%); chemicals and chemical products, 9·7%.

Principal imports in 2001: road vehicles, 15·6%; nonelectrical machinery, 13·3%; chemicals and chemical products, 11·2%; electrical machinery, 8·7%; crude and refined petroleum, 8·6%.

Leading export markets in 2002 were: France (18·9%), Germany (11·4%), Portugal (9·5%), United Kingdom (9·5%), Italy (9·3%); leading import sources in 2002 were France (16·9%), Germany (16·5%), Italy (8·6%), United Kingdom (6·4%), the Netherlands (4·8%). In 2000 the EU accounted for 63·1% of Spain's imports and 69·6% of exports.

COMMUNICATIONS

Roads. In 2001 the total length of roads was 664,852 km; the network included 11,152 km of motorways, 24,458 km of highways/national roads and 139,341 km of secondary roads. 99% of all roads in Spain were paved in 2001. In 2001 private road transport totalled 359,667m. passenger-km and public road transport 51,712m. passenger-km; freight transport totalled 114,011m. tonne-km in 2001. Number of cars (2001), 18,150,880; trucks and vans, 3,949,001; buses, 56,146; motorcycles and mopeds, 3,291,200. In 2002, 5,347 persons were killed in road accidents.

Rail. The total length of the state railways in 2000 was 13,868 km, mostly broad (1,668-mm) gauge (7,525 km electrified). State railways are run by the National Spanish Railway Network (RENFE). There is a high-speed standard-gauge (1,435-mm) railway from Madrid to Sevilla, opened in 1992. The line has been extended northwards from Madrid to Lérida, with passenger services beginning in Oct. 2003. Passenger-km travelled in 2000 came to 19·9bn. and freight tonne-km to 12·1bn. There are metros in Madrid (121 km), Valencia (118 km), Barcelona (81 km) and Bilbao (28 km). In 2003 the construction of two 40 km-long rail tunnels under the Straits of Gibraltar was agreed with Morocco with an estimated cost of US$30m.

Civil Aviation. There are international airports at Madrid (Barajas), Barcelona (Prat del Llobregat), Alicante, Almería, Bilbao, Gerona, Las Palmas de Gran Canaria, Ibiza, Lanzarote, Málaga, Palma de Mallorca, Santiago de Compostela, Sevilla, Tenerife (Los Rodeos and Reina Sofía), Valencia, Valladolid and Zaragoza. There are 43 airports open to civil traffic. A small airport in Seo de Urgel operates in Andorra. The national carrier is Iberia Airlines. Iberia Airlines, which was 99·8% state-owned, went through the first stage of privatization in 1999 before the second phase was indefinitely postponed in Nov. 1999. Of other airlines, the largest are Air Europa and Spanair. Services are also provided by about 70 foreign airlines. In 1999 Iberia flew 258·8m. km, carrying 22,203,700 passengers (8,447,600 on international flights). Madrid was the busiest airport in 2000, handling 32,566,066 passengers (16,517,059 on domestic flights) and 305,499 tonnes of freight. Barcelona was the second busiest in 2000, with 19,375,338 (9,988,206 on domestic flights) and 87,300 tonnes of freight. Palma de Mallorca was the third busiest for passengers, with 19,296,722 (14,460,592 on international flights). Las Palmas was the third busiest for freight, with 43,568 tonnes in 2000.

Shipping. In 2000 the merchant fleet comprised 1,554 vessels (of 100 gross tons or more) totalling 2·03m. GRT (including oil tankers 600,000 GRT); shipyards launched 219,673 GRT in 1996. In 2001 vessels totalling 198,696,000 NRT entered ports and vessels totalling 59,267,000 NRT cleared. The leading ports are Algeciras-La Linea (51,251,000 tonnes of cargo in 2002), Barcelona, Bilbao, Ceuta, Las Palmas, Santa Cruz de Tenerife, Tarragona and Valencia.

Telecommunications. In 2002 there were 52,180,600 telephone subscribers (1,282·6 per 1,000 persons) and 7,972,000 PCs were in use (196·0 per 1,000 persons). The government disposed of its remaining 21% stake in Telefónica in Feb. 1997, bringing 1·4m. shareholders into the company's equity base. A second operator, Retevisión, accounts for 3% of the domestic market, which was wholly deregulated in 1998. The mobile phone business was deregulated in 1995; the market is shared by Telefónica (with a 56% share of the market), Airtel and Amena (Retevisión).

Spain had 33,531,000 mobile phone subscribers in 2002 (824 for every 1,000 persons) and 7·89m. Internet users in May 2002. In 1996 fax machines numbered 700,000.

Postal Services. In 1998 there were 4,093 post offices; a total of 4,574m. pieces of mail were processed during the year, or 115 items per person.

SOCIAL INSTITUTIONS

Justice. Justice is administered by Tribunals and Courts, which jointly form the Judicial Power. Judges and magistrates cannot be removed, suspended or transferred except as set forth by law. The Constitution of 1978 established the *General Council of the Judicial Power*, consisting of a President and 20 magistrates, judges, attorneys and lawyers, governing the Judicial Power in full independence from the state's legislative and executive organs. Its members are appointed by the *Cortes Generales*. Its President is that of the Supreme Court (*Tribunal Supremo*), who is appointed by the monarch on the proposal of the General Council of the Judicial.

The Judicature is composed of the Supreme Court; 17 Higher Courts of Justice, one for each autonomous community; 52 Provincial High Courts; Courts of First Instance; Courts of Judicial Proceedings, not passing sentences; and Penal Courts, passing sentences.

The Supreme Court consists of a President, and various judges distributed among seven chambers: one for civil matters, three for administrative purposes, one for criminal trials, one for social matters and one for military cases. The Supreme Court has disciplinary faculties; is court of appeal in all criminal trials; for administrative purposes decides in first and second instance disputes arising between private individuals and the State; and in social matters makes final decisions.

A new penal code came into force in May 1996, replacing the code of 1848. It provides for a maximum of 30 years imprisonment in specified exceptional cases, with a normal maximum of 20 years. Sanctions with a rehabilitative intent include fines adjusted to means, community service and weekend imprisonment. The death penalty was abolished by the 1978 Constitution. The prison population in Nov. 2003 was 56,140 (138 per 100,000 of national population); 110,844 criminal sentences were passed in 1996. A jury system commenced operating in Nov. 1995 in criminal cases (first trials in May 1996). Juries consist of nine members.

A juvenile criminal law of 1995 lays emphasis on rehabilitation. It raised the age of responsibility from 12 to 14 years. Criminal conduct on the part of children under 14 is a matter for legal protection and custody. 14- and 15-year-olds are classified as 'minors'; 16- and 17-year-olds as 'young persons'; and the legal majority for criminal offences is set at 18 years. Persons up to the age of 21 may, at the courts' discretion, be dealt with as juveniles.

The *Audiencia Nacional* deals with terrorism, monetary offences and drug-trafficking where more than one province is involved. Its president is appointed by the General Council of the Judicial Power.

There is an Ombudsman (*Defensor del Pueblo*), who is elected for a five-year term (currently Enrique Múgica Herzog; b. 1932).

Religion. There is no official religion. Roman Catholicism is the religion of the majority. In Sept. 2003 there were nine cardinals. There are 11 metropolitan sees and 52 suffragan sees, the chief being Toledo, where the Primate resides. The archdioceses of Madrid-Alcalá and Barcelona depend directly from the Vatican. There are about 0·25m. other Christians, including several Protestant denominations, about 60,000 Jehovah's Witnesses and 29,000 Latter-day Saints (Mormons), and 0·45m. Muslims, including Spanish Muslims in Ceuta and Melilla. The first synagogue since the expulsion of the Jews in 1492 was opened in Madrid on 2 Oct. 1959. The number of people of Judaist faith is estimated at about 15,000.

Education. In 1991 the General Regulation of the Educational System Act came into force. This Act gradually extends the school-leaving age to 16 years and determines the following levels of education: infants (3–5 years of age), primary (6–11), secondary (12–15) and baccalaureate or vocational and technical (16–17). Primary and secondary levels of education are now compulsory and free. Religious instruction is optional.

In Sept. 1997 a joint declaration with trade unions, parents' and schools' associations was signed in support of a new finance law guaranteeing that spending on education will reach 6% of GDP within five years, thus protecting it from changes in the political sphere. In 2004 total expenditure on education came to 5·4% of GNP.

A new compulsory secondary education programme has replaced the Basic General Education programme which was in force since 1970. In addition, university entrance exams underwent reform in 1997, resulting in greater emphasis now being placed on the teaching of Humanities at secondary level.

In 2004–05 pre-primary education (under six years) was undertaken by 1,419,307 pupils; primary or basic education (6–14 years): 2,494,598 pupils. In 200–01 there were 75,040 teachers in pre-primary and 175,135 teachers in primary schools. Secondary education (14–17 years), including high schools and technical schools, was conducted at 6,276 schools, with 3,054,263 pupils and 167,182 teachers in 2004–05.

In 2003 there were 71 universities: 50 public state universities and 21 private universities (including Catholic establishments). In 2004–05 there were 1,330,574 students at state universities; 132,197 at private universities.

Adult literacy rate, 2001, 97·7% (male 98·6%; female 96·9%).

Health. In 2003 there were 190,665 doctors, 56,501 pharmacists and 220,769 nurses (including 6,764 midwives). There were 16,133 dentists in 1998. Number of hospitals (2001), 767, with 146,367 beds. In 2002 Spain spent 7·6% of its GDP on health.

Welfare. The social security budget was €82,425,871,000 in 2004, including €66·1bn. for pensions, €5·3bn. for temporary incapacity, €1·4bn. for health and €620m. for social services. The minimum pension in 2001 was the equivalent of just over €5,000 per year, made in 14 payments.

In 1997 the system of contributions to the social security and employment scheme was: for pensions, sickness, invalidity, maternity and children, a contribution of 28·3% of the basic wage (23·6% paid by the employer, 4·7% by the employee); for unemployment benefit, a contribution of 7·8% (6·2% paid by the employer, 1·6% by the employee). There are also minor contributions for a Fund of Guaranteed Salaries, working accidents and professional sicknesses, and for vocational training.

CULTURE

World Heritage Sites. There are 37 sites under Spanish jurisdiction that appear on the UNESCO World Heritage List. They are (with year entered on list): Historic Centre of Córdoba (1984), Alhambra, Generalife and Albayzin, Granada (1984), Burgos Cathedral (1984), Monastery and site of the Escurial, Madrid (1984), Parque

Güell, Palacio Güell and Casa Mila in Barcelona (1984), Altamira Cave (1985), Old Town of Segovia and its Aqueduct (1985), Monuments of Oviedo and the Kingdom of the Asturias (1985), Santiago de Compostela (Old town) (1985), Old Town of Ávila, with its Extra-Muros churches (1985), Mudejar Architecture of Teruel (1986), Historic City of Toledo (1986), Garajonay National Park (1986), Old Town of Cáceres (1986), Cathedral, Alcazar and Archivo de Indias in Sevilla (1987), Old City of Salamanca (1988), Poblet Monastery (1991), Archaeological Ensemble of Mérida (1993), Royal Monastery of Santa Maria de Guadalupe (1993), Route of Santiago de Compostela (1993), Doñana National Park (1994), Historic Walled Town of Cuenca (1996), La Lonja de la Seda de Valencia (1996), Las Médulas (1997), the Palau de la Música Catalana and the Hospital de Sant Pau, Barcelona (1997), San Millán Yuso and Suso Monasteries (1997), University and Historic Precinct of Alcalá de Henares (1998), Rock-Art of the Mediterranean Basin on the Iberian Peninsula (1998), Ibiza, Biodiversity and Culture (1999), San Cristóbal de La Laguna (1999), the Archaeological Ensemble of Tarraco (2000), The Palmeral of Elche (2000), the Roman Walls of Lugo (2000), Catalan Romanesque Churches of the Vall de Boí (2000), Archaeological Site of Atapuerca (2000), Úbeda-Baeza: Urban duality, cultural unity (2003), and for France and Spain: Pyrénées—Mount Perdu (1997).

Broadcasting. *Radio Nacional de España* broadcasts five programmes on medium-wave and FM, as well as many regional programmes; it has one commercial programme. The most successful domestic network is that of an independent, Cadena SER (*Sociedad Española de Radiodifusión*); *Cadena de Ondas Populares Españolas* (COPE) is owned by the Roman Catholic church. Two independent radio networks cover the whole of Spain. They are *Antena 3* and *Radio 80* (taken over by SER in 1992). *Radio Exterior* broadcasts abroad.

Televisión Española broadcasts two channels (TVE1 and TVE2) and also has an international channel. There are three nationwide commercial TV networks: *Antena 3*, *Tele 5* and the pay-TV channel *Canal Plus*, which had 1·4m. subscribers in 1997. There were in 1999 the following regional TV networks: *TV3* (launched in 1983) and *Canal 33* (1989), both broadcasting in Catalan; *ETB1* (1983) and *ETB2* (1987), both broadcasting in Basque—*ETB1* exclusively so and *ETB2* partly so, but additionally with much output in Castilian; *Televisión de Galicia* (1985), in Galician; *TM3* (1989), in Castilian, for the area of Madrid; *Canal 9* (1989), mostly in Valencian (Catalan); and *Tele-Sur* (1989), in Castilian, for Andalusia. There are two digital TV channels, *Vía Digital* and *Canal Satélite Digital*, both launched in 1997. Colour transmissions are carried by PAL.

Number of receivers: radios (2000), 13·5m.; TV (2001), 22·8m.

Cinema. There were 1,112 cinemas (4,348 screens) in 2004 with an audience of 141·5m. (18·8m. for Spanish films and 122·6m. for foreign films). In Nov. 1997 the Madrid School of Cinema was established. In 2004 gross box office receipts came to €680m.

Press. In 2003–04 there were 91 daily newspapers with a total daily circulation of 4·10m. copies. Eight publishing groups controlled around 80% of the daily press, with another 100 or so independents accounting for the other 20%. The main titles are: *El País* (average daily circulation 462,000), *El Mundo* (300,000) and *ABC* (276,000), along with the dedicated sports paper, *Marca* (386,000).

In 2003, 72,048 book titles were published of which 21,661 were categorized as literature, history and literary criticism.

Tourism. In 2003 Spain was behind only France in the number of foreign visitor arrivals, and behind only the USA for tourism receipts. In 2003 tourism accounted for 11·4% of GDP; receipts for 2003 amounted to US$41·8m. In 2003, 51·8m. tourists visited Spain. Overnight stays in hotels in 2004 (provisional) totalled 235m. of which 48·8% were between June and Sept.; there were 1·1m. places available in hotels. Average occupancy rate was 53·6% in 2004.

Festivals. Religious Festivals: Epiphany (6 Jan.), the Feast of the Assumption (15 Aug.), All Saints Day (1 Nov.) and Immaculate Conception (8 Dec.) are all public holidays. Cultural Festivals: Day of Andalusia (28 Feb.), the Feast of San José in Valencia (19 March) is the culmination of a 13-day festival; the Festival of the Sardine in Murcia is an end of Easter parade in which a huge papier mâché sardine is burned; Feria de Abril is a huge festival in Sevilla at the end of April which features flamenco dancing and bull-fighting; the San Fermines Festival, which takes place in mid-July, is most famous for the running of the bulls in the streets of Pamplona; La Tomatina, a battle of revellers armed with 50 tonnes of tomatoes, takes place on the last Wednesday in Aug. and is the highlight of the annual fiesta in Buñol, Valencia; National Day of Catalonia (11 Sept.); Spanish National Day (12 Oct.).

Libraries. In 2002 there were 3,832 public libraries, one National library, 1,762 specialized libraries, 410 for specific user groups, 355 Higher Education libraries and 11 central libraries of Autonomous Communities; they held a combined 117·6m. volumes. There were 153m. visits to libraries by more than 12·6m. users in 2002. 62·7% of libraries had Internet access in 2002.

Museums and Galleries. Spain had 1,438 museums in 2000 with 3·7m. visitors. The Museu del Prado in Madrid received 1·8m. visitors in 2000.

DIPLOMATIC REPRESENTATIVES

Of Spain in the United Kingdom (39 Chesham Pl., London, SW1X 8SB)
Ambassador: Carlos Miranda.

Of the United Kingdom in Spain (Calle de Fernando el Santo, 16, 28010 Madrid)
Ambassador: Stephen J. L. Wright, CMG.

Of Spain in the USA (2375 Pennsylvania Ave., NW, Washington, D.C., 20037)
Ambassador: Carlos Westendorp y Cabeza.

Of the USA in Spain (Serrano 75, 28006 Madrid)
Ambassador: Vacant.
Chargé d'Affaires a.i.: J. Robert Manzanares.

Of Spain to the United Nations
Ambassador: Juan Antonio Yáñez-Barnuevo.

FURTHER READING

Barton, Simon, *A History of Spain.* Palgrave Macmillan, Basingstoke, 2004
Carr, Raymond (ed.) *Spain: A History.* OUP, 2000
Closa, Carlos and Heywood, Paul, *Spain and the European Union.* Palgrave Macmillan, Basingstoke, 2004
Conversi, D., *The Basques, The Catalans and Spain.* Hurst, London, 1997
Harrison, Joseph and Corkhill, David, *Spain: A Modern European Economy.* Ashgate Publishing, Aldershot, 2004
Heywood, P., *The Government and Politics of Spain.* London, 1995
Hooper, J., *The New Spaniards.* 2nd ed. [of *The Spaniards*] London, 1995
Peréz-Díaz, V. M., *The Return of Civil Society: the Emergence of Democratic Spain.* Harvard Univ. Press, 1993
Powell, C., *Juan Carlos of Spain: Self-Made Monarch.* London and New York, 1996
Shields, Graham J., *Spain.* [Bibliography] 2nd ed. ABC-Clio, Oxford and Santa Barbara (CA), 1994.—*Madrid.* [Bibliography] ABC-Clio, Oxford and Santa Barbara (CA), 1996

National library: Biblioteca Nacional, Madrid.
National statistical office: Instituto Nacional de Estadística (INE), Paseo de la Castellana, 183, Madrid.
Website: http://www.ine.es

SRI LANKA

Sri Lanka Prajathanthrika Samajavadi Janarajaya (Democratic Socialist Republic of Sri Lanka)

Capital: Sri Jayewardenepura Kotte (Administrative and Legislative), Colombo (Commercial)
Population projection, 2010: 20·05m.
GDP per capita, 2002: (PPP$) 3,570
HDI/world rank: 0·740/96

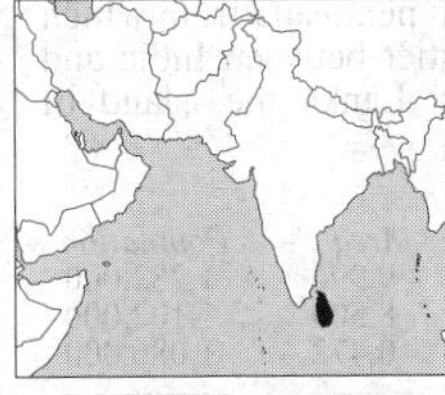

KEY HISTORICAL EVENTS

In the 18th century the central kingdom, Kandy, was the only surviving independent state on the island of Ceylon. The Dutch, who had obtained their first coastal possessions in 1636, had driven out the Portuguese to become the dominant power in the island. In 1796 the British East India Company sent a naval force to Ceylon (as the British then called it). The Dutch surrendered their possessions, which left the British in control of the maritime areas surrounding Kandy. These areas were at first attached to the Madras Presidency of India but in 1802 they were constituted a separate colony under the Crown. Once the British began to develop their new territory they came to see Kandy as a threat. The Kandyan Convention of 1815 annexed Kandy to British Ceylon while recognizing most of the traditional rights of the chiefs. However, in 1817 the chiefs rebelled. The rebellion was suppressed and the rights established by the Convention were abolished.

Ceylon was then united for the first time since the 12th century. The British built up a plantation economy. Coffee was dominant until an outbreak of *Hoemilia vastatrix* fungus destroyed the plants in 1870. Spices, cocoa and rice all followed but tea became the main cash crop after successful experiments in the 1880s. Foreign rule served to subdue the traditional hostility between northern Tamils and southern Sinhalese. The Ceylon National Congress, formed in 1919, contained both Sinhalese and Ceylon Tamil groups. (The Indian Tamils brought in as a labour force for the tea estates were a separate community.) Tamil national feeling, however, was expressed over the issue of the use of Tamil languages in schools. As early as 1931 a general election took place under universal suffrage, just two years after the first one in the UK. On 4 Feb. 1948 Ceylon became a Dominion of the Commonwealth. In 1956 Solomon Bandaranaike became prime minister at the head of the People's United Front, advocating neutral foreign policy and the promotion of Sinhalese national culture at home. In Sept. 1959 he was murdered; his widow Sirimavo Bandaranaike succeeded him in July 1960 at the head of an increasingly socialist government. In May 1972 Ceylon became a republic and adopted the name Sri Lanka. In July 1977 the United National Party (dominant until 1956) returned to power and in 1978 a new constitution set up a presidential system. The problem of communal unrest remained unsolved and Tamil separatists were active. In 1983 the Tamil United Liberation Front members of parliament were asked to renounce their objective for a separate Tamil state in the north and the east of the country. They refused and withdrew from parliament. Militant Tamils then began armed action which developed into civil war. A state of emergency ended on 11 Jan. 1989, but violence continued.

President Ranasinghe Premadasa was assassinated on 1 May 1993. A ceasefire was signed on 3 Jan. 1995, but fighting broke out again in April. The 'Liberation Tigers of the Tamil Eelam' stronghold of Jaffna in the far north of the country was captured by government forces in Dec. 1995 and by mid-1997 was under government control. In April 2000 the Tamil Tigers captured a military garrison at Elephant Pass, the isthmus that links Jaffna to the rest of Sri Lanka, increasing the possibility that they might re-take the Jaffna peninsula. A month-long ceasefire began in Dec. 2001 amid signs that the Tigers might be willing to engage in peace talks, and on 22 Feb. 2002 the government and Tamil Tiger leaders agreed to an internationally-monitored ceasefire, paving the way to the first full-scale peace talks for seven years. An estimated 61,000 people died during the 19-year long conflict. In late 2002 the Tamil Tigers abandoned their ambitions for a separate state, settling instead for regional autonomy. However, in Nov. 2003 President Kumaratunga declared a state of emergency after dismissing three ministers, suspending parliament and sending troops on to the streets. She had accused the government of making too many concessions to Tamil Tiger rebels.

On 26 Dec. 2004 Sri Lanka, along with a number of other south Asian countries, was hit by a devastating tsunami following an undersea earthquake. The death toll in Sri Lanka alone was put at 31,000.

TERRITORY AND POPULATION

Sri Lanka is an island in the Indian Ocean, south of the Indian peninsula from which it is separated by the Palk Strait. On 28 June 1974 the frontier between India and Sri Lanka in the Palk Strait was redefined, giving to Sri Lanka the island of Kachchativu.

Area (in sq. km) and population (1994 estimates):

Provinces	*Area*	*Population*	*Provinces*	*Area*	*Population*
Western	3,684	4,599,000	Eastern	9,996	1,282,000
Southern	5,544	2,330,000	Uva	8,500	1,102,000
Central	5,674	2,261,000	North-Central	10,472	1,086,000
North-Western	7,888	2,107,000			
Sabaragamuwa	4,968	1,735,000	Total	65,610	17,865,000
Northern	8,884	1,363,000			

Population (in 1,000) according to ethnic group and nationality at the 1981 census: 10,980 Sinhalese, 1,887 Sri Lanka Tamils, 1,047 Sri Lanka Moors, 819 Indian Tamils, 47 Malays, 39 Burghers, 28 others. Non-nationals of Sri Lanka totalled 635,150.

Population, 2001 (census, provisional), 18,732,255 (in some areas experiencing civil war estimates were used and combined with actual totals for other districts); density, 286 per sq. km. In 2001, 76·9% of the population lived in rural areas. Ethnic mix, 74% Sinhalese, 18% Tamil.

The UN gives a projected population for 2010 of 20·05m.

Between the mid-1980s and the mid-1990s approximately 0·3m. Tamils left the country, one-third as refugees to India and two-thirds to seek political asylum in the West.

Colombo (the largest city) had 690,000 inhabitants in 1999. Other major towns and their populations (1990 estimates) are: Dehiwela-Mt Lavinia, 196,000; Moratuwa, 170,000; Jaffna, 129,000; Sri Jayewardenepura Kotte (now the administrative and legislative capital), 109,000; Kandy, 104,000; Galle, 84,000.

Sinhala and Tamil are the official languages; English is in use.

SOCIAL STATISTICS

Births, 1999, 329,121; deaths, 114,392. 1999 birth rate (per 1,000 population), 17·3; death rate, 6·0; infant mortality rate, 1999 (per 1,000 live births), 17. Life expectancy, 2001, 75·5 years for females and 69·6 for males. Annual population growth rate, 1992–02, 0·9%. Infant mortality, 2001, 17 per 1,000 live births; fertility rate, 2001, 2·1 births per woman. Sri Lanka has the third oldest population in Asia, after Japan and Singapore, thanks largely to relatively good health and a low fertility rate.

CLIMATE

Sri Lanka, which has an equatorial climate, is affected by the North-east Monsoon (Dec. to Feb.), the South-west Monsoon (May to July) and two inter-monsoons (March to April and Aug. to Nov.). Rainfall is heaviest in the southwest highlands while the northwest and southeast are relatively dry. Colombo, Jan. 79·9°F (26·6°C), July 81·7°F (27·6°C). Annual rainfall 95·4" (2,424 mm). Trincomalee, Jan. 78·8°F (26°C), July 86·2°F (30·1°C). Annual rainfall 62·2" (1,580 mm). Kandy, Jan. 73·9°F (23·3°C), July 76·1°F (24·5°C). Annual rainfall 72·4" (1,840 mm). Nuwara Eliya, Jan. 58·5°F (14·7°C), July 60·3°F (15·7°C). Annual rainfall 75" (1,905 mm).

On 26 Dec. 2004 an undersea earthquake centred off the Indonesian island of Sumatra caused a huge tsunami that flooded large areas along the southern and eastern coasts of Sri Lanka resulting in 31,000 deaths. In total there were 290,000 deaths in twelve countries.

CONSTITUTION AND GOVERNMENT

A new constitution for the Democratic Socialist Republic of Sri Lanka was promulgated in Sept. 1978.

The Executive *President* is directly elected for a seven-year term renewable once.

Parliament consists of one chamber, composed of 225 members (196 elected and 29 from the National List). Election is by proportional representation by universal suffrage at 18 years. The term of Parliament is six years. The Prime Minister and other Ministers, who must be members of Parliament, are appointed by the President.

National Anthem. 'Sri Lanka Matha, Apa Sri Lanka' ('Mother Sri Lanka, thee Sri Lanka'); words and tune by A. Samarakone. There is a Tamil version, 'Sri Lanka thaaya, nam Sri Lanka'; words anonymous.

RECENT ELECTIONS

Presidential elections were held on 21 Dec. 1999. Incumbent Chandrika Bandaranaike Kumaratunga was re-elected against two opponents by 51·1% of votes cast. Turn-out was around 73%.

In Feb. 2004 President Kumaratunga dissolved parliament, dismissed the cabinet of Prime Minister Ranil Wickremasinghe and called for new elections. At the election of 2 April 2004 the United People's Freedom Alliance (made up of six parties including the Sri Lanka Freedom Party) gained 105 seats with 45·6% of the vote; the United National Party 82 with 37·8%; the Sri Lanka Tamil Government Party/Tamil National Alliance 22 with 6·8%; the National Heritage Party 9 with 6·0%; and the Sri Lanka Muslim Congress 5 with 2·0%. Other parties received less than 1% of votes cast. Turn-out was 76·0%.

CURRENT ADMINISTRATION

In March 2005 the government comprised:

President and Minister of Defence, Education, and Relief, Rehabilitation and Reconciliation: Chandrika Bandaranaike Kumaratunga; b. 1945 (Sri Lanka Freedom Party; sworn in 12 Nov. 1994, re-elected 21 Dec. 1999).

Prime Minister, Minister of Highways: Mahinda Rajapaksa; b. 1945 (Sri Lanka Freedom Party; sworn in 6 April 2004).

Minister of Agriculture, Livestock, Land and Irrigation: Anura Kumara Dissanayake. *Agricultural Marketing Development, Hindu Affairs and Tamil Language Schools and Vocational Training (North):* Douglas Devananda. *Christian and Parliamentary Affairs:* Milroy Fernando. *Constitutional Affairs:* D. E. W. Gunasekera. *Cultural Affairs and National Heritages:* Vijitha Herath. *Environment and Natural Resources:* A. H. M. Fowzie. *Estate Community Infrastructure:* C. B. Ratnayake. *Finance:* Dr Sarath Amunugama. *Fisheries and Aquatic Resources:* Chandrasena Wijesinghe. *Foreign Affairs:* Lakshman Kadirgamar. *Healthcare, Nutrition and Uva Wellassa Development:* Nimal Siripala de Silva. *Housing and Construction Industry, Eastern Province Education and Irrigation Development:* Ferial Ashraff. *Indigenous Medicine:* Tissa Karaliyadde. *Industry, Tourism and Investment Promotion:* Anura Bandaranaike. *Infrastructure Development in the Eastern Province:* A. L. M. Athaulla. *Justice and Judicial Reforms:* John Senaviratne. *Labour Relations and Foreign Employment:* Athauda Senaviratne. *Plantation Industries:* Anura Priyadharshana Yapa. *Ports and Aviation, Information and Media:* Mangala Samaraweera. *Post and Telecommunications and Upcountry Development:* D. M. Jayaratne. *Power and Energy:* Susil Premajayantha. *Provincial Councils and Local Government:* Janaka Bandara Tennakoon. *Public Administration and Home Affairs:* Amarasiri Dodangoda. *Public Security, Law and Order:* Ratnasiri Wickremanayake. *Regional Infrastructure Development:* S. B. Nawinna. *River Basin Development and Rajarata Development:* Maithripala Sirisena. *Samurdhi and Poverty Alleviation:* Pavithra Wanniarachchi. *Science and Technology:* Tissa Vitharana. *Skills Development, Vocational and Technical Education:* Piyasena Gamage. *Small and Rural Industries:* K. D. Lal Kantha. *Sports and Youth Affairs:* Jeewan Kumaranatunga. *Trade, Commerce and Consumer Affairs:* Jeyaraj Fernandopulle. *Transport:* Felix Perera. *Urban Development and Water Supply:* Dinesh Gunawardene. *Women's Empowerment and Social Welfare:* Sumedha Jayasena.

Government Website: http://www.priu.gov.lk

DEFENCE

Defence expenditure in 2003 totalled US$515m. (US$27 per capita), representing 2·8% of GDP.

Army. Strength (2002), 118,000. In addition there were 1,100 reserves. Paramilitary forces consist of the Ministry of Defence Police (60,600, including 1,000 women and a 3,000-strong anti-guerrilla force), the Home Guard (13,000) and the National Guard (some 15,000).

Navy. The main naval base is at Trincomalee. Personnel in 2002 numbered 20,600, including a reserve of about 2,400.

Air Force. Air Force bases are at Anuradhapura, Katunayake, Ratmalana, Vavuniya and China Bay, Trincomalee. Total strength (2002) about 19,300 with 22 combat aircraft and 24 armed helicopters. Main attack aircraft types included *Kfirs* and MiG-27s.

INTERNATIONAL RELATIONS

Sri Lanka is a member of the UN, WTO, the Commonwealth, the Asian Development Bank, the Colombo Plan, SAARC and IOM.

ECONOMY

Agriculture accounted for 20·5% of GDP in 2002, industry 26·3% and services 53·2%.

The conflict with the minority separatists, the Tamil Tigers, is estimated to have cost the country between 1 and 1·5% in growth per year.

Overview. 20 years of civil war and conflict have disrupted inter-regional commerce, deepened poverty, damaged infrastructure and weakened public finances. Since the commencement of the peace process in Feb. 2002, the government has embarked upon reforms to invigorate and revive the economy. Reforms that have played a key role in economic development include the floatation of the exchange rate, privatization, the introduction of a VAT system, the amendment of banking laws and the restructuring of financial markets. In June 2003 the international community promised aid worth US$4·5bn. over the following four years conditional on the continuation of the peace process. In 2002 the main sources of growth were consumption and tourism and in 2003 exports and private investment added further impetus to growth. In 2003 heightened political instability had adverse implications for financial markets and foreign private investment. The tsunami of Dec. 2004 has had an adverse effect on the economy, particularly in relation to tourism.

Currency. The unit of currency is the *Sri Lankan rupee* (LKR) of 100 *cents*. Foreign exchange reserves were US$884m. and gold reserves 626,000 troy oz in Dec. 2001. Inflation was 9·6% in 2002, down from 14·2% in 2001. Total money supply in March 2002 was Rs 125,695m.

Budget. Revenue and expenditure of central government in Rs 1m. for financial years ending 31 Dec.:

	1996	*1997*	*1998*	*1999*	*2000*	*2001*[1]
Revenue	146,280	165,036	175,032	195,905	211,282	231,463
Expenditure	212,787	228,732	253,808	267,611	322,048	367,966

[1]Provisional.

The principal sources of revenue in 2001 were: general sales tax, 21%; excise taxes, 19%; national security levy, 18%; import duties, 13%; income tax, 13%; non-tax revenue, 11%.

The principal items of recurrent expenditure in 2001 were: public debt interest, 32%; defence, 22%; public service, 15%; provincial councils, 10%; pensions, 9%; welfare, 8%.

Performance. The economy contracted by 1·5% in 2001, but recovered in 2002, with growth of 4·0%. Total GDP in 2003 was US$18·5bn.

Banking and Finance. The Central Bank of Sri Lanka is the bank of issue (*Governor*, Sunil Mendis). Two state-owned commercial banks, the Bank of Ceylon and the People's Bank, account for about 70% of bank lending. There are also 21 private banks (17 foreign). There are four development banks and two merchant banks. Total assets of commercial banks at 31 Dec. 1994, Rs 286,933m. Assets of the Sri Lanka National Savings Bank at 31 Dec. 1999 were Rs 100,813m. In the five years to Sept. 2000 Sri Lanka attracted US$715m. in foreign direct investment, including more than US$200m. in 1999.

There is a stock exchange in Colombo.

ENERGY AND NATURAL RESOURCES

Environment. Carbon dioxide emissions from the consumption and flaring of fossil fuels in 2002 were the equivalent of 0·6 tonnes per capita.

Electricity. Installed capacity (2000), 2·1m. kW. Production, 2000, 6·84bn. kWh (47% hydro-electric). Consumption per capita in 2000 was 354 kWh.

Oil and Gas. Construction of a US$1·6bn. oil refinery at Hambantota in the south of the island began in 1999.

Water. The Mahaweli Authority scheme, which began in 1978, had led to the irrigation of 354,000 ha of land by 2001.

Minerals. Gems are among the chief minerals mined and exported. Graphite is also important; production in 2001 was 4,895 tonnes. Production of ilmenite, 1998, 34,118 tonnes. Some rutile is also produced (1,930 tonnes in 1998). Salt extraction is the oldest industry. The method is solar evaporation of sea-water. Production, 2001, 130,272 tonnes.

Agriculture. There were 896,000 ha of arable land in 2001 and 1·02m. ha of permanent crops. Agriculture engages 47·5% of the labour force. Main crops in 2000 (in 1,000 tonnes): rice, 2,767; coconuts, 1,950; sugarcane, 1,114; plantains, 600; tea, 285; cassava, 260; rubber, 99; mangoes, 86. Tea plantations are being returned to the private sector after nationalization in 1975. Sri Lanka ranks third in the world for tea production, behind India and China.

Livestock in 2000: 1,617,000 cattle; 728,000 buffaloes; 514,000 goats; 10m. chickens.

Forestry. The area under forests in 2000 was 1·94m. ha, or 30·0% of the land area. In 2001, 6·52m. cu. metres of roundwood were cut.

Fisheries. Total catch in 2001 was 279,640 tonnes (89% from sea fishing).

INDUSTRY

The main industries are the processing of rubber, tea, coconuts and other agricultural commodities, tobacco, textiles, clothing and leather goods, chemicals, plastics, cement and petroleum refining. Industrial production fell by 2·1% in 2001.

Labour. The labour force in the period Oct.–Dec. 2000 totalled 6,708,620 (66% males). In the period Jan.–March 1998 (excluding Northern and Eastern provinces), the economically active workforce numbered 5,946,150, of which 2,472,290 worked in agriculture, hunting, forestry and fishing, 1,006,730 in community, social and personal services, 914,700 in manufacturing and 593,740 in wholesale and retail trade, restaurants and hotels.

In the period Oct.–Dec. 2000 the unemployment rate was 11·3% (excluding Northern and Eastern provinces).

Trade Unions. In 1994 there were 1,304 registered trade unions.

INTERNATIONAL TRADE

Foreign debt in 2002 was US$9,611m.

Imports and Exports. Trade in US$1m.:

	1999	*2000*	*2001*	*2002*	*2003*
Imports f.o.b.	5,365·5	6,483·6	5,376·9	5,495·0	6,004·8
Exports f.o.b.	4,596·2	5,439·6	4,816·9	4,699·2	5,133·2

Principal exports in 1999: clothing, 51·3%; tea, 13·7%; yarn and fabrics, 4·6%. Principal imports: manufactured goods, 39·2%; machinery and transport equipment, 23·2%; foodstuffs, 12·7%; chemicals, 8·4%; petroleum, 5·1%.

In 1999 the main export markets were the USA (39·6%), the UK (13·3%), Germany (4·8%) and Japan (3·5%). The main import suppliers were Japan (10·4%), India (9·5%), Singapore (8·4%) and UK (4·7%).

COMMUNICATIONS

Roads. In 2000 the road network totalled 74,828 km in length, including 11,462 km of national roads and 10,404 of secondary roads. Number of motor vehicles, 2002, 1,573,529, comprising 253,447 passenger cars, 67,702 buses and coaches, 328,913 trucks and vans and 923,467 motorcycles and mopeds. There were 2,029 fatalities in road accidents in 2002.

Rail. In 1996 there were 1,463 km of railway (1,676 mm gauge). Passenger-km travelled in 2001–02 came to 4,079m. and freight tonne-km to 131m.

Civil Aviation. There is an international airport at Colombo (Bandaranaike). The national carrier is SriLankan Airlines (formerly Air Lanka), which has been part-owned and managed by Emirates since 1998. In 1999 SriLankan Airlines flew 28·1m. km and carried 1,421,500 passengers (all on international flights). Colombo handled 2,880,387 passengers and 127,116 tonnes of freight in 2000.

Shipping. In 2002 the merchant marine totalled 81,000 GRT, including oil tankers 6,000 GRT. Colombo is a modern container port; Trincomalee and Galle are natural harbours. In 1994, 3,568 merchant vessels totalling 55m. GRT entered the ports: 9,588,000 tonnes of goods were unloaded and 5,892,000 tonnes loaded. In 2002 vessels totalling 39,336,000 NRT entered ports.

Telecommunications. Sri Lanka had 1,814,700 telephone subscribers in 2002 (95·8 per 1,000 population) and there were 250,000 PCs in use (13·2 for every 1,000 persons). There were 931,600 mobile phone subscribers in 2002 and 11,000 fax machines in 1995. There were approximately 200,000 Internet users in 2002.

Postal Services. In 1998 there were 4,282 post offices, or one for every 4,380 persons.

SOCIAL INSTITUTIONS

Justice. The systems of law which are valid are Roman-Dutch, English, Tesawalamai, Islamic and Kandyan.

Kandyan law applies in matters relating to inheritance, matrimonial rights and donations; Tesawalamai law applies in Jaffna as above and in sales of land. Islamic law is applied to all Muslims in respect of succession, donations, marriage, divorce and maintenance. These customary and religious laws have been modified by local enactments.

The courts of original jurisdiction are the High Court, Provincial Courts, District Courts, Magistrates' Courts and Primary Courts. District Courts have unlimited civil jurisdiction. The Magistrates' Courts exercise criminal jurisdiction. The Primary Courts exercise civil jurisdiction in petty disputes and criminal jurisdiction in respect of certain offences.

The Constitution of 1978 provided for the establishment of two superior courts, the Supreme Court and the Court of Appeal.

The Supreme Court is the highest and final superior court of record and exercises jurisdiction in respect of constitutional matters, jurisdiction for the protection of fundamental rights, final appellate jurisdiction in election petitions and jurisdiction in respect of any breach of the privileges of Parliament. The Court of Appeal has appellate jurisdiction to correct all errors in fact or law committed by any court, tribunal or institution.

The population in penal institutions in 2002 was 17,485 (91 per 100,000 of national population). The death penalty, last used in 1976, was reinstated in Nov. 2004.

Police. The strength of the police service in 1994 was 30,236.

Religion. In 2001 the population was 71% Buddhist, 12% Hindu, 9% Muslim and 7% Roman Catholic.

Education. Education is free and is compulsory from age five to 14 years. The literacy rate in 2001 was 91·9% (male, 94·5%; female, 89·3%). Sri Lanka's rate compares very favourably with the rates of 58·0% in India and 44·0% in Pakistan.

In 1995 there were 9,657 primary schools with 70,537 teachers for 1·9m. pupils. There were 2·3m. secondary pupils with 103,572 teachers and 63,660 students in higher education with 2,636 staff. There are nine universities, one open (distance) university and one Buddhist and Pali university.

In 1998–99 total expenditure on education came to 3·1% of GNP.

Health. In 1993 there were 426 hospitals, including 84 maternity homes, and 350 central dispensaries. The hospitals had 48,948 beds. In 1999 there were 6,881 physicians, 471 dentists, 19,362 nurses, 848 pharmacists and 7,899 midwives. Total state budget expenditure on health, 1993, Rs 7,160m.

Welfare. To qualify for an old-age pension an individual must be above the age of 55 for men or 50 for women. However, a grant is payable at any age if the person is emigrating permanently. Old-age benefits are made up of a lump sum equal to total employee and employer contributions, plus interest.

The family allowances programme is being implemented in stages. Families earning below Rs1,000 a month are entitled to Rs500 a month benefit.

CULTURE

World Heritage Sites. Sri Lanka has seven sites on the UNESCO World Heritage List: Sacred City of Anuradhapura (inscribed on the list in 1982); Ancient City of Polonnaruwa (1982); Ancient City of Sigiriya (1982); Sinharaja Forest Reserve (1988); Sacred City of Kandy (1988); Old Town of Galle and its Fortifications (1988); and the Golden Temple of Dambulla (1991).

Broadcasting. Broadcasting is provided by the Sri Lanka Broadcasting Corporation. There were 2·2m. TV sets (colour by PAL) in 2001 and 3·9m. radio receivers in 2000.

Press. In 1996 there were six daily newspapers with a combined circulation of 530,000, at a rate of 29 per 1,000 inhabitants.

Tourism. In 2000 there were 400,000 foreign tourists, bringing revenue of US$253m.

DIPLOMATIC REPRESENTATIVES

Of Sri Lanka in the United Kingdom (13 Hyde Park Gdns, London, W2 2LU)
High Commissioner: Kshenuka Senewiratne.

Of the United Kingdom in Sri Lanka (190 Galle Rd, Kollupitiya, Colombo 3)
High Commissioner: Stephen Evans, CMG, OBE.

Of Sri Lanka in the USA (2148 Wyoming Ave., NW, Washington, D.C., 20008)
Ambassador: Devinda Rohan Subasinghe.

Of the USA in Sri Lanka (210 Galle Rd, Kollupitiya, Colombo 3)
Ambassador: Jeffrey J. Lunstead.

Of Sri Lanka to the United Nations
Ambassador: Vacant.
Chargé d'Affaires a.i.: Bernard Goonetilleke.

Of Sri Lanka to the European Union
Ambassador: Chrysantha Romesh Jayasinghe.

FURTHER READING

De Silva, C. R., *Sri Lanka: a History.* Delhi, 1991
McGowan, W., *Only Man is Vile: the Tragedy of Sri Lanka.* New York, 1992

National statistical office: Department of Census and Statistics, POB 563, Colombo 7
Website: http://www.statistics.gov.lk

SUDAN

Jamhuryat es-Sudan
(The Republic of The Sudan)

Capital: Khartoum
Population projection, 2010: 38·32m.
GDP per capita, 2002: (PPP$) 1,820
HDI/world rank: 0·505/139

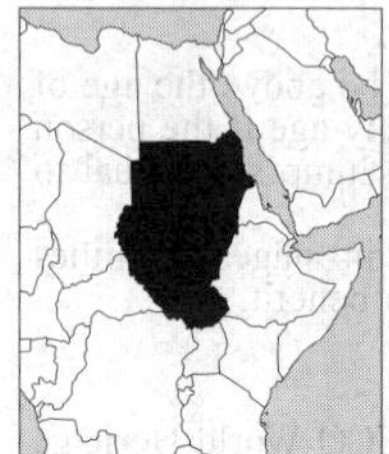

KEY HISTORICAL EVENTS

Egyptian influences were felt in Nubia (north-eastern Sudan) from around 3,000 BC. When Egypt's power waned in the 11th century BC, Kush (based at Nepata, modern Marawi) became a powerful kingdom on trade routes linking the Nile to the Red Sea. Under King Piantkhi in 750 BC, the whole of Egypt was brought under Kushite control. However, the invasion of Egypt by Assyrian forces in 671 BC forced a retreat to Nepata. By AD 200 Kush was in decline and was finally overthrown in 350 by the king of Aksum (Ethiopia).

Sudan was brought back into contact with the Mediterranean world in the 6th century by the arrival of Coptic Christian missionaries. They established churches in three middle-Nile kingdoms: Nobatia in the north and Maqurrah and 'Alwah in the south. Muslim Arabs, in control of Egypt from 639, sent raiding parties up the Nile and absorbed Nobatia. In 1250 Egypt came under the control of Mamluk sultans, who devastated Maqurrah, opening it up to Arab immigrants. 'Alwah retained its Christian traditions until 1500. The Arabs were repulsed by the Funj kingdom from the upper Blue Nile, which conquered Al Jazirah region by 1607 and expanded northwards in the 17th century.

In 1820 Muhammad 'Ali, the Ottoman viceroy of Egypt, sent an army to conquer the Funj kingdom. Ismail Pasha, viceroy of Egypt from 1863, enlisted the help of the European powers to make productive use of the Nile river system in return for the end of the slave trade. In 1879, amid rising discontent, Ismail's financial backing collapsed, ending the project. Declaring himself the Mahdi ('divinely guided one') in 1881, Muhammad Ahmad led a movement to end Ottoman Egyptian influence. The British organized a disastrous evacuation of Egyptians and foreigners from Khartoum in 1885. In a series of attacks between 1896–98, an Anglo-Egyptian force destroyed the Mahdist state, creating a joint government of Sudan.

In 1911 the irrigation of Al Jazirah region established cotton as mainstay of the economy. In the 1920s 'Ali 'Abd al Latif, inspired by Egyptian nationalists, founded the White Flag League. In 1924 after the British governor-general was assassinated in Cairo, all Egyptian troops were expelled from Sudan. In 1948 a predominantly elective legislative assembly was established. The Independence Front gained a majority over the National Front, which aimed for union with Egypt. Following the 1952 revolution in Egypt, Britain and Egypt agreed to prepare Sudan for independence. It became a parliamentary republic in 1956 but in 1958 Gen. Ibrahim Abboud led a military coup. He re-established civilian government in 1964.

In 1969 Col. Muhammad Gaafur al-Nimeiry staged a coup and banned all political parties. A civil war was ended by agreement between the government and the Southern Sudan Liberation Front in 1972. In the late 1970s Nimeiry dismissed his cabinet and closed universities in an attempt to quell opposition. In the 1980s conflict increased with the largely Christian and animist Sudan People's Liberation Army (SPLA) in southern Sudan. Nimeiry imposed Sharia law in 1983, further inflaming the south. He was overthrown in 1985.

Following elections in 1986 a civilian government led by Sadiq al-Mahdi ruled until he was ousted three years later by Lieut.-Gen. Omar Ahmed al-Bashir, who reinforced Islamic law, banned opposition parties and pursued the war with the south. Opposition from the fundamentalist National Islamic Front, led by Hassan al-Turabi, prompted al-Bashir to declare a state of emergency. Al-Turabi was placed under house-arrest.

In Jan. 2002 a ceasefire in the civil war allowed relief aid to be distributed in the drought-stricken south-central region but fighting continued elsewhere. Over 2m. died in the civil conflict and 4m. became refugees. The government and the SPLA agreed a framework for peace in July 2002 that called for southern autonomy and a referendum on independence after six years. In Sept. 2003 an accord between the two sides called for the withdrawal of government troops from the south and rebel forces from the north but new fighting was sparked off in the Darfur region of western Sudan. In May 2004 the government and the SPLA signed a peace deal that called for shared power in a bid to end the civil war. However, continued fighting between the government and black Muslims in Darfur has raised fears of ethnic cleansing. More than 1m. people in Darfur have been displaced since rebels took up arms. In Dec. 2004 the final details of the peace deal were agreed, with the SPLA being given a share of political power and oil wealth during a six-year transition period, at the end of which the south will be able to hold a referendum on whether to secede.

TERRITORY AND POPULATION

Sudan is bounded in the north by Egypt, northeast by the Red Sea, east by Eritrea and Ethiopia, south by Kenya, Uganda and the Democratic Republic of the Congo, west by the Central African Republic and Chad, and northwest by Libya. Its area, including inland waters, is 2,505,810 sq. km. In 1993 the census population was 25·6m. Population estimate (2000), 31·08m., giving a density of 12·4 per sq. km. In 2001, 63·0% of the population were rural.

The UN gives a projected population for 2010 of 38·32m.

In Feb. 1994 the former nine regions were subdivided to form 26 federal states as follows:

Former region	*New states*
Khartoum	Khartoum
Bahr al-Ghazal	Western Bahr al-Ghazal; Northern Bahr al-Ghazal; Warab
Central	Gezira; White Nile; Sinnar; Blue Nile
Darfur	Northern Darfur; Southern Darfur; Western Darfur
Eastern	Red Sea; Gedaref; Kassala
Equatoria	Eastern Equatoria; Western Equatoria; Bahr al-Jabal
Kurdufan	Northern Kurdufan; Southern Kurdufan; Western Kurdufan
Northern	Nile; Northern State
Upper Nile	Upper Nile; Unity State; Jonglei; Buheyrat

The capital, Khartoum, had a population of 2,628,000 in 1999. Other major cities, with 1993 populations, are Port Sudan (305,385), Kassala (234,270), Nyala (228,778), al-Obeid (228,096), Wadi Medani (218,714) and al-Qadarif (189,384).

The northern and central thirds of the country are populated by Arab and Nubian peoples, while the southern third is inhabited by Nilotic and Bantu peoples. Sudan has more internally displaced people (4m. in 2000) than any other country.

Arabic, the official language, is spoken by 60% of inhabitants. English is the second language.

SOCIAL STATISTICS

1997 births, 1,323,000; deaths, 365,000. Rates, 1997 estimates (per 1,000 population); births, 40·6; deaths, 11·2. Infant mortality, 2001 (per 1,000 live births), 65. Expectation of life in 2001 was 56·9 years for females and 54·0 for males. Annual population growth rate, 1992–02, 2·3%. Fertility rate, 2001, 4·6 births per woman.

CLIMATE

Lying wholly within the tropics, the country has a continental climate and only the Red Sea coast experiences maritime influences. Temperatures are generally high for most of the year, with May and June the hottest months. Winters are virtually cloudless and night temperatures are consequently cool. Summer is the rainy season inland, with amounts increasing from north to south, but the northern areas are virtually a desert region. On the Red Sea coast, most rain falls in winter. Khartoum, Jan. 64°F (18·0°C), July 89°F (31·7°C). Annual rainfall 6" (157 mm). Juba, Jan. 83°F (28·3°C), July 78°F (25·6°C). Annual rainfall 39" (968 mm). Port Sudan, Jan.

74°F (23·3°C), July 94°F (34·4°C). Annual rainfall 4" (94 mm). Wadi Halfa, Jan. 50°F (10·0°C), July 90°F (32·2°C). Annual rainfall 0·1" (2·5 mm).

CONSTITUTION AND GOVERNMENT

The constitution was suspended after the 1989 coup and a 12-member Revolutionary Council then ruled. A 300-member Provisional National Assembly was appointed in Feb. 1992 as a transitional legislature pending elections. These were held in March 1996. The President is elected for a five-year term by the people. The National Assembly (*Majlis Watani*), has 360 members, 270 of whom are directly elected for four years in single-seat constituencies with 90 nominated to represent specific groups.

On 26 May 1998 President Omar Hassan Ahmad al-Bashir approved a new constitution. Notably this lifted the ban on opposition political parties, although the government continued to monitor and control criticism until the constitution legally came into effect.

National Anthem. 'Nahnu Jundullah, Jundu Al-Watlan' ('We are the defenders of our homeland, blessed by Allah'); words by A. M. Salih, tune by A. Murjan.

RECENT ELECTIONS

Presidential elections were held from 13–22 Dec. 2000. President Omar Hassan Ahmed al-Bashir was re-elected by 86·5% of votes cast, with his nearest rival, former president Gaafar Nimeiry, gaining 9·6%. The main opposition groups and most of the electorate boycotted the polls. At the National Assembly elections held at the same time the ruling National Congress Party (NCP) won 355 of the 360 seats.

CURRENT ADMINISTRATION

President: Lieut.-Gen. Omar Hassan Ahmad al-Bashir; b. 1944 (NCP; appointed 1989, re-elected March 1996 and Dec. 2000).

First Vice-President: Ali Osman Mohammed Taha. *Second Vice-President:* Moses Machar.

In March 2005 the government comprised:

Minister of the Interior: Abdulraheem Mohammed Hussein. *Foreign Affairs:* Mustafa Osman Ismail. *Defence:* Maj. Gen. Bakri Hassan Salih. *Justice and Attorney General:* Ali Muhammad Osman Yasin. *Finance and Planning:* al-Zubeir Ahmed al-Hassan. *Culture, and National Heritage and Tourism:* Abdulbasit Abdulmajid. *Agriculture and Forestry:* Majzoub el Khalifa Ahmed. *Animal and Fish Resources:* Galwak Deng. *Humanitarian Affairs:* Ibrahim Mahmoud Hamed. *Irrigation:* Kamal Mohamed Ali. *Energy and Mining:* Awad Ahmed al-Jaz. *Industry:* Jalal Yousif el Degair. *Investment:* al-Cherif Ahmad Omar Badr. *External Trade:* Abdulhameed Musa Kasha. *Welfare and Social Planning:* Samya Ahmed Mohammed. *Higher Education:* Mubarak Mohammed Al Maghzoub. *Urban Development and Environment:* Tigani Adam Tahir. *Education:* Ahmed Babikir Nahar. *Electricity:* Ali Tameem Fartak. *Aviation:* Joseph Malwal. *Roads and Bridges:* Mohamed Tahir Aela. *Federal Rule:* Nafie Ali Nafie. *Health:* Dr Ahmed Ballal Osman. *Labour:* Alison Manani Magaya. *Science and Technology:* El Zubair Taha. *Youth and Sports:* Hassan Osman Rizig. *Parliamentary Affairs, and Information and Communication (acting):* Abdulbasit Sabdarat. *Religious Guidance and Endowments:* Isam Ahmed el Bashir. *International Co-operation:* Yusuf Suleiman Takana. *Transport:* Sammani al-Cheikh al-Waseilah. *Minister of the Presidency:* Altayeb Ibrahim Mohamed Kheir. *Ministers of the Cabinet:* Al-Hadi Abdallah Mohammed al-Awad; Abdella Ali Safi al-Nur; Martin Malwal Arop.

DEFENCE

There is conscription for three years. Defence expenditure totalled US$426m. in 2003 (US$13 per capita), representing 2·7% of GDP. According to *Deadly Arsenals*, published by the Carnegie Endowment for International Peace, Sudan has both biological and chemical weapons research programmes.

Army. Strength (2002) 112,500 (20,000 conscripts). There is a paramilitary People's Defence Force of about 7,000 and additional army reserves of 85,000.

Navy. The Navy operates in the Red Sea and also on the River Nile. The flotilla suffers from lack of maintenance and spares. Personnel in 2002 were believed to number 1,500. Major bases are at Port Sudan (HQ), Flamingo Bay and Khartoum.

Air Force. Personnel totalled (2002) about 3,000, with over 40 combat aircraft including F-5s, J-6s (Chinese-built versions of MiG-19s), F-7s (Chinese-built versions of MiG-21s) and MiG-23s.

INTERNATIONAL RELATIONS

Sudan is a member of the UN, the African Union, African Development Bank, COMESA, the Intergovernmental Authority on Development, IOM, OIC, Islamic Development Bank, the League of Arab States and is an ACP member state of the ACP-EU relationship.

Following the attacks on New York and Washington on 11 Sept. 2001 Sudan sought to distance itself from fundamentalism and international terrorism.

ECONOMY

Agriculture accounted for 39·2% of GDP, industry 18·3% and services 42·5% in 2002.

Overview. Since 1997 the Sudanese authorities have undertaken economic reforms that have contributed to broad based growth. In 1997 Sudan began implementing IMF macroeconomic reforms that have successfully stabilized inflation. Sudan began exporting crude oil in 1999 and recorded its first trade surplus in 1999. Current oil production stands at 220,000 bbls. per day, of which 70% is exported. In 2002 and 2003 Sudan adopted a further economic reform programme in which the authorities switched to indirect monetary management and broad money targeting, introduced a managed float exchange rate regime and began strengthening the fiscal regime. Sudan's primary resources are agricultural, but oil production and exports have been increasing in importance since Oct. 2000. Sudan's trade regime is considered by the IMF to be fairly open, with few non-tariff trade barriers and a simple average tariff rate of 22·7%. However, exports other than oil are stagnant owing to foreign currency constraints, inadequate infrastructure and a small industrial sector.

Currency. Until 1992 the monetary unit was the *Sudanese pound* (SDP) of 100 *piastres* and 1,000 *milliemes*. This was replaced in May 1992 by the *dinar* at a rate of 1 dinar = £S10. Sudanese pounds remain legal tender. Inflation was 8·3% in 2002. Foreign exchange reserves were US$224m. in June 2002 and total money supply was 307,763m. dinars.

Budget. In 1999 total revenues were 215,562m. dinars (162,143m. dinars in 1998) and total expenditure 227,265m. dinars (171,129m. dinars in 1998).

Performance. Real GDP growth was 5·3% in 2001 and 5·0% in 2002. Sudan's total GDP in 2003 was US$17·8bn.

Banking and Finance. The Bank of Sudan (*Governor:* Sabir Mohammed Hassan) opened in Feb. 1960 with an authorized capital of £S1·5m. as the central bank and bank of issue. Banks were nationalized in 1970 but in 1974 foreign banks were allowed to open branches. The application of Islamic law from 1 Jan. 1991 put an end to the charging of interest in official banking transactions, and seven banks are run on Islamic principles. Mergers of seven local banks in 1993 resulted in the formation of the Khartoum Bank, the Industrial Development Bank and the Savings Bank. In 2000 there were 25 commercial and private banks. In May 2000 the government announced plans for the banks to merge into six groups to consolidate the national economy but the restructure was yet to be implemented by 2004.

A stock exchange opened in Khartoum in 1995.

ENERGY AND NATURAL RESOURCES

Environment. Sudan's carbon dioxide emissions from the consumption and flaring of fossil fuels in 2002 were the equivalent of 0·3 tonnes per capita.

Electricity. Installed capacity was 0·8m. kW in 2000. Production in 2000 was 2·26bn. kWh, with consumption per capita 73 kWh.

Oil and Gas. In 2002 oil reserves totalled 563m. bbls. In June 1998 Sudan began exploiting its reserves and on 31 Aug. 1999 it officially became an oil producing country; production in 2000 totalled 9·3m. tonnes. An oil refinery at Al-Jayli, with a capacity of 2·5m. tonnes, opened in 2000. Natural gas reserves in 2002 were 113bn. cu. metres.

Minerals. Mineral deposits include graphite, sulphur, chromium, iron, manganese, copper, zinc, fluorspar, natron, gypsum and anhydrite, magnesite, asbestos, talc, halite, kaolin, white mica, coal, diatomite (kieselguhr), limestone and dolomite, pumice, lead, wollastonite, black sands and vermiculite pyrites. Chromite and gold are mined. Production of salt, 2001: 77,783 tonnes; chromium ore (metal content), 2002: 14,000 tonnes; gold, 2001: 5,417 kg.

Agriculture. 80% of the population depends on agriculture. Land tenure is based on customary rights; land is ultimately owned by the government. There were 16·23m. ha of arable land in 2001 and 420,000 ha of permanent crops. 1·95m. ha were irrigated in 2001. There were 11,856 tractors in 2001 and 1,590 harvester-threshers.

Production (2000 estimates) in 1,000 tonnes: sugarcane, 4,982; sorghum, 2,521; groundnuts, 990; millet, 496; sesame seed, 305; seed cotton, 245; tomatoes, 242; wheat, 214; mangoes, 192; dates, 176; melons and watermelons, 169; cottonseed, 157. Livestock (2000): cattle, 37·09m.; sheep, 42·80m.; goats, 37·80m.; chickens, 42m.; camels, 3·8m.

Forestry. Forests covered 61·63m. ha in 2000, or 25·9% of the total land area. The annual loss of 959,000 ha of forests between 1990 and 2000 was exceeded only in Brazil and Indonesia. In 2001, 19·04m. cu. metres of roundwood were cut.

Fisheries. In 2001 the total catch was 58,000 tonnes, of which 53,000 tonnes were freshwater fish.

INDUSTRY

Production figures (in 1,000 tonnes): distillate fuel oil (2000), 835; sugar (2002), 744; wheat flour (1999), 532; residual fuel oil (2000), 305; cement (2001), 146; vegetable oils (2001), 32. In 2000 an industrial complex assembling 12,000 vehicles a year opened.

Labour. The total workforce in 1996 was 10,652,000 (71% males). 68% of the economically active population in 1995 were engaged in agriculture, fisheries and forestry.

INTERNATIONAL TRADE

Foreign debt was US$16,389m. in 2002.

Imports and Exports. In 2002 imports (f.o.b.) amounted to US$2,152·8m. (US$1,395·1m. in 2001); exports (f.o.b.) US$1,949·1m. (US$1,698·7m. in 2001). The main exports are oil, cotton, gum arabic, oil seeds, sorghum, livestock, sesame, gold and sugar. Main imports are petroleum products, machinery and equipment, foodstuffs, manufactured goods, medicines and chemicals. The main import sources in 2000 were Saudi Arabia (11·8%), France (8·6%), Italy (6·3%), United Arab Emirates (5·5%) and Germany (5·4%). Principal export markets in 2000 were Saudi Arabia (18·1%), Japan (15·7%), UK (9·2%), South Korea (7·9%) and Italy (7·1%).

COMMUNICATIONS

Roads. In 1999 there were estimated to be 11,900 km of roads, of which 4,320 km were paved. There were an estimated 285,000 passenger cars and 53,000 trucks and vans in 1996.

Rail. The total length of the railways is 4,599 km. In 2000 the railways carried 0·4m. passengers and 1·4m. tonnes of freight.

Civil Aviation. There is an international airport at Khartoum. The national carrier is the government-owned Sudan Airways, which operates domestic and international services. In 1999 scheduled airline traffic of Sudan-based carriers flew 6·7m. km, carrying 390,000 passengers (245,000 on international flights).

Shipping. Supplementing the railways are regular steamer services of the Sudan Railways. Port Sudan is the major seaport; Suakin port opened in 1991. Sea-going shipping totalled 33,000 GRT in 2002, including oil tankers 1,000 GRT.

Telecommunications. In 2002 Sudan had 862,600 telephone subscribers (26·5 per 1,000 persons) and 200,000 PCs were in use (6·1 per 1,000 persons). There were 25,000 fax machines in 1999 and 190,800 mobile phone subscribers in 2002. The number of Internet users in 2002 was 84,000.

Postal Services. In 1998 there were 491 post offices.

SOCIAL INSTITUTIONS

Justice. The judiciary is a separate independent department of state, directly and solely responsible to the President of the Republic. The general administrative supervision and control of the judiciary is vested in the High Judicial Council.

Civil Justice is administered by the courts constituted under the Civil Justice Ordinance, namely the High Court of Justice—consisting of the Court of Appeal and Judges of the High Court, sitting as courts of original jurisdiction—and Province Courts—consisting of the Courts of Province and District Judges. The law administered is 'justice, equity and good conscience' in all cases where there is no special enactment. Procedure is governed by the Civil Justice Ordinance.

Justice for the Muslim population is administered by the Islamic law courts, which form the Sharia Divisions of the Court of Appeal, High Courts and Kadis Courts; President of the Sharia Division is the Grand Kadi. In Dec. 1990 the government announced that Sharia would be applied in the non-Muslim southern parts of the country as well.

Criminal Justice is administered by the courts constituted under the Code of Criminal Procedure, namely major courts, minor courts and magistrates' courts. Serious crimes are tried by major courts, which are composed of a President and two members and have the power to pass the death sentence. Major Courts are, as a rule, presided over by a Judge of the High Court appointed to a Provincial Circuit or a Province Judge. There is a right of appeal to the Chief Justice against any decision or order of a Major Court, and all its findings and sentences are subject to confirmation by him.

Lesser crimes are tried by Minor Courts consisting of three Magistrates and presided over by a Second Class Magistrate, and by Magistrates' Courts.

The population in penal institutions in March 2003 was approximately 12,000 (36 per 100,000 of national population).

Religion. Islam is the state religion. In 2001, 70% of the population were Sunni Muslims, concentrated in the north; Christians (17%) and traditional animists (12%) are concentrated in the south. In Sept. 2003 the Roman Catholic church had one cardinal.

Education. In 2000–01 there were 12,985 teachers for 349,306 pupils at pre-primary schools; 96,050 teachers (1999–2000) for 2·8m. pupils at primary schools; and (1999–2000) 42,513 secondary school teachers for 979,514 pupils. In 1996 there were 17 universities, two Islamic universities, one university of science and technology, and an institute of advanced banking. There were also 14 other higher education institutions. Adult literacy rate in 2001 was 58·8% (male, 70·0%; female, 47·7%).

Health. In 1996 there were 2,818 physicians, 219 dentists, 18,158 nurses and 344 pharmacists. Hospital bed provision in 1986 was eight per 10,000 population.

CULTURE

World Heritage Sites. Sudan has one site on the UNESCO World Heritage List: Gebel Barkal and the Sites of the Napatan Region (inscribed on the list in 2003), a collection of tombs, pyramids and palaces of the Second Kingdom of Kush (900 BC to AD 350).

Broadcasting. Broadcasting is controlled by the Sudan National Broadcasting Corporation and Sudan Television (colour by PAL). There are also two regional TV stations, in the centre and in the north of the country. There were 12·27m. TV sets in 2001 and 7·55m. radio receivers in 1997.

Press. In 1999 there were around 20 daily newspapers. Opposition newspapers are permitted although they are vetted by an official censor.

Tourism. In 2000 there were 50,000 foreign tourists. There were seven National Parks and ten protected areas in 2000.

DIPLOMATIC REPRESENTATIVES

Of Sudan in the United Kingdom (3 Cleveland Row, London, SW1A 1DD)
Ambassador: Dr Hassan Abdin Mohammad Osman.

Of the United Kingdom in Sudan (off Sharia Al Baladia, Khartoum East)
Ambassador: William Patey.

Of Sudan in the USA (2210 Massachusetts Ave., NW, Washington, D.C., 20008)
Ambassador: Vacant.
Chargé d'Affaires a.i.: Khidir Haroun Ahmed.

Of the USA in Sudan (Sharia Ali Abdul Latif, POB 699, Khartoum)
Ambassador: Vacant.
Chargé d'Affaires a.i.: David Kaeuper.

Of Sudan to the United Nations
Ambassador: Elfatih Mohamed Ahmed Erwa.

Of Sudan to the European Union
Ambassador: Ali Youssif Ahmed.

FURTHER READING

Daly, M. W., *Sudan.* [Bibliography] 2nd ed. ABC-Clio, Oxford and Santa Barbara (CA), 1992

Daly, M. W. and Sikainga, A. A. (eds.) *Civil War in the Sudan.* I. B. Tauris, London, 1993

Deng, F. M., *War of Visions: Conflict of Identities in the Sudan.* The Brookings Institution, Washington (D.C.), 1995

SURINAME

Republic of Suriname

Capital: Paramaribo
Population projection, 2010: 458,000
GDP per capita, 2002: (PPP$) 6,590
HDI/world rank: 0·780/67

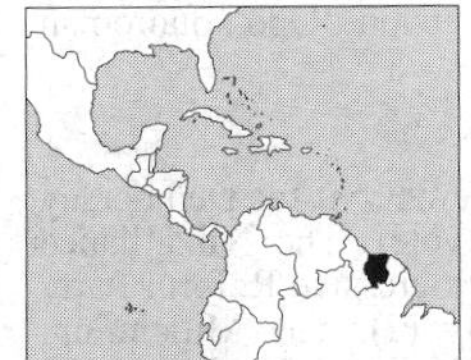

KEY HISTORICAL EVENTS

The first Europeans to reach the area were the Spanish in 1499 but it was the British who established a colony in 1650. At the peace of Breda (1667), Suriname was assigned to the Netherlands in exchange for the colony of New Netherland in North America. Suriname was twice in British possession during the Napoleonic Wars, in 1799–1802 and 1804–16, when it was returned to the Netherlands.

On 25 Nov. 1975 Suriname gained full independence. On 25 Feb. 1980 the government was ousted in a coup and a National Military Council (NMC) established. A further coup on 13 Aug. replaced several members of the NMC and the State President. Other attempted coups took place in 1981 and 1982, with the NMC retaining control. In Oct. 1987 a new constitution was approved by referendum. Following elections in Nov. Suriname returned to democracy in Jan. 1988 but on 24 Dec. 1990 a further military coup deposed the government. There was a peace agreement with rebel groups in Aug. 1992 and elections were held in May 1996.

TERRITORY AND POPULATION

Suriname is located on the northern coast of South America between 2–6° North latitude and 54–59° West longitude. It is bounded in the north by the Atlantic Ocean, east by French Guiana, west by Guyana, and south by Brazil. Area, 163,820 sq. km. Estimate, 2002, 423,000; density, 2·6 per sq. km.

The UN gives a projected population for 2010 of 458,000.

The capital, Paramaribo, had (2000 estimate) 294,000 inhabitants.

Suriname is divided into ten districts. They are (with 2000 population estimate and chief town): Brokopondo, population 7,663 (Brokopondo); Commewijne, 22,134 (Nieuw Amsterdam); Coronie, 3,092 (Totness); Marowijne, 13,351 (Albina); Nickerie, 35,577 (Nieuw Nickerie); Para, 15,190 (Onverwacht); Paramaribo, 225,218—representing 52% of Suriname's total population (Paramaribo); Saramacca, 13,250 (Groningen); Sipaliwini, 24,823 (local authority in Paramaribo); Wanica, 73,219 (Lelydorp).

Major ethnic groups in percentages of the population in 1991: Creole, 35%; Indian, 33%; Javanese, 16%; Bushnegroes (Blacks), 10%; Amerindian, 3%. 74·7% of the population lived in urban areas in 2001.

The official language is Dutch. English is widely spoken next to Hindi, Javanese and Chinese as inter-group communication. A vernacular, called 'Sranan' or 'Surinamese', is used as a *lingua franca*. In 1976 it was decided that Spanish was to become the nation's principal working language.

SOCIAL STATISTICS

Births, 2000, 9,804; deaths, 3,090. 2000 rates per 1,000 population: birth rate, 22·5; death rate, 7·1. The population growth rate in 1999 was 1·5%. Expectation of life, 2001, was 68·2 years for males and 73·4 for females. Annual population growth rate, 1992–02, 0·7%. Infant mortality, 2001, 26 per 1,000 live births; fertility rate, 2001, 2·1 births per woman.

CLIMATE

The climate is equatorial, with uniformly high temperatures and rainfall. The temperature is an average of 27°C throughout the year; there are two rainy seasons (May–July and Nov.–Jan.) and two dry seasons (Aug.–Oct. and Feb.–April). Paramaribo, Jan. 21°C, July 32·4°C. Average rainfall 182·3 mm.

CONSTITUTION AND GOVERNMENT

Parliament is a 51-member *National Assembly*. The head of state is the *President*, elected for a five-year term by a two-thirds majority by the National Assembly, or, failing that, by an electoral college, the United People's Conference (UPC) enlarged by the inclusion of regional and local councillors, by a simple majority.

National Anthem. 'God zij met ons Suriname' ('God be with our Suriname'); words by C. A. Hoekstra, tune by J. C. de Puy. There is a Sranan version, 'Opo kondreman oen opo'; words by H. de Ziel.

RECENT ELECTIONS

Parliamentary elections were held on 25 May 2000. The New Front for Democracy (NF) won 32 of the available 51 seats (47·3% of the vote). The NF alliance comprises the National Party of Suriname (14 seats), the Progressive Reform Party (9), Pertjajah Luhur (7) and the Suriname Labour Party (2). The Millennium Combination alliance won 10 seats (15·1%), Democratic National Platform 2000 alliance won 3 seats (10%), Democratic Alternative '91 alliance won 2 seats (6·1%) and the Political Wing of the FAL won 2 seats (4·1%). Nine other groupings received 3·2% of the vote or less, with the Progressive Workers' and Farmers' Union claiming 1 seat with 0·7%.

On 4 Aug. 2000 Ronald Venetiaan was elected *President* by the National Assembly, claiming 37 out of 51 votes. Jules Ajodhia was elected *Vice-President* and *Prime Minister*.

Parliamentary elections were scheduled to take place on 25 May 2005.

CURRENT ADMINISTRATION

President: Runaldo Ronald Venetiaan; b. 1936 (National Party of Suriname; sworn in 12 Aug. 2000 for a second time, having previously held office from Sept. 1991 to Sept. 1996).

Vice-President and Prime Minister: Jules Ajodhia (Progressive Reform Party; sworn in 12 Aug. 2000 for a second time, also having previously held office from Sept. 1991 to Sept. 1996).

In March 2005 the government comprised:

Minister of Foreign Affairs: Marie Levens. *Defence:* Ronald Assen. *Finance:* Humphrey Hildenberg. *Natural Resources:* Franco Rudy Demon. *Justice and Police:* Siegfried Gilds. *Regional Development:* Romeo van Russel. *Education and Human Development:* Walter Sandriman. *Transport, Communication and Tourism:* Guno Castelen. *Planning and Development Co-operation:* Keremchand Raghoebarsingh. *Public Works:* Dewanand Balesar. *Health:* Mohamed Rakieb Khudabux. *Social Affairs:* Samuel Pawironadi. *Labour:* Clifford Marica. *Agriculture and Fisheries:* Geetapersad Gangaram Panday. *Interior:* Urmila Joella-Sewnundum. *Trade and Industry:* Michael Jong Tjien Fa.

DEFENCE

In 2003 defence expenditure totalled US$8m. (US$18 per capita), representing 0·7% of GDP.

Army. Total strength was estimated at 1,400 in 2002.

Navy. In 2002 personnel, based at Paramaribo, totalled 240.

Air Force. Personnel (2002): 200. There were seven combat aircraft.

INTERNATIONAL RELATIONS

In June 2000 a maritime dispute arose between Suriname and Guyana over offshore oil exploration.

Suriname is a member of the UN, WTO, OAS, Inter-American Development Bank, ACS, CARICOM, OIC, Islamic Development Bank and is an ACP member state of the ACP-EU relationship.

ECONOMY

In 2002 agriculture contributed 11·1% of GDP, industry 19·6% and services 69·3%.

Currency. The unit of currency is the *Suriname guilder* (SRG; written as Sf[lorin]) of 100 *cents*. Foreign exchange reserves totalled US$114m. and gold reserves were 263,000 troy oz in June 2002. Total money supply in April 2002 was 417,896m. Sf. Inflation in 2002 was 28·3%.

Budget. 1999 revenue (in 1m. Sf) was 301,495·5, made up of: direct taxes, 84,360·0; indirect taxes, 117,902·0; bauxite levy and other revenues, 31,641·5; aid, 67,592·0.

Total expenditure in 1999 (in 1m. Sf) was 139,071·1, made up of: wages and salaries, 72,116·2; grants and contributions, 16,701·8; other current expenditures, 32,979·0; capital expenditure, 17,274·1.

Performance. After two years of recession in 1999 and 2000 real GDP growth was 4·9% in 2001 and 2·7% in 2002. In 2002 total GDP was US$0·9bn.

Banking and Finance. The Central Bank of Suriname (*Governor,* Andre Telting) is a bankers' bank and also the bank of issue. There are three commercial banks; the Suriname People's Credit Bank operates under the auspices of the government. There is a post office savings bank, a mortgage bank, an investment bank, a long-term investments agency, a National Development Bank and an Agrarian Bank.

ENERGY AND NATURAL RESOURCES

Environment. Suriname's carbon dioxide emissions from the consumption and flaring of fossil fuels in 2002 were the equivalent of 4·0 tonnes per capita.

Electricity. Installed capacity in 1999 was 0·4m. kW. Production (1999) 1·64bn. kWh; consumption per capita in 1999 was 3,814 kWh.

Oil and Gas. Crude petroleum production (2000), 602,000 tonnes. Reserves in 2002 were 74m. bbls.

Minerals. Bauxite is the most important mineral. Suriname is the seventh largest bauxite producer in the world. Production (2001), 4,512,000 tonnes.

Agriculture. Agriculture is restricted to the alluvial coastal zone; in 2001 there were 57,000 ha of arable land and 10,000 ha of permanent crops . The staple food crop is rice. Production (in 1,000 tonnes), 180 in 1999; 164 in 2000. Other crops (2000 in 1,000 tonnes): sugarcane, 90; bananas, 49; plantains, 11; oranges, 10; coconuts, 9; groundnuts, 9; cassava, 3. Livestock in 2000: cattle, 128,727; sheep, 7,360; goats, 6,930; pigs, 22,280; poultry, 2·0m.

Forestry. Forests covered 14·11m. ha in 2000, or 90·5% of the land area. In terms of percentage coverage, Suriname was the world's most heavily forested sovereign country in 2000. Production of roundwood in 2001 was 199,000 cu. metres.

Fisheries. The catch in 2001 amounted to an estimated 18,915 tonnes, almost entirely from marine waters.

INDUSTRY

There is no longer any aluminium smelting, but there are food-processing and wood-using industries. Production: alumina (2001), 1,900,000 tonnes; cement (2001), 60,000 tonnes; prepared animal feeds (1996), 14,000 tonnes; wheat flour (1996), 14,000 tonnes; sawnwood (2002), 47,000 cu. metres.

Labour. Out of 88,200 people in employment in 1998, 32,000 were in community, social and personal services, 16,500 in trade, restaurants and hotels and 9,900 in construction. In 1998 there were 10,500 unemployed persons, or 10·6% of the workforce.

INTERNATIONAL TRADE

Imports and Exports. In 2002 imports (f.o.b.) amounted to US$321·9m. (US$297·2m. in 2001); exports (f.o.b.) US$369·3m. (US$437·0m. in 2001).

Principal imports, 2000: nonelectrical machinery, 22·5%; food products, 13·4%; road vehicles, 13·2%. Principal exports, 2000: alumina, 62·1%; gold, 11·4%; crustaceans and molluscs, 7·0%.

In 1998 exports (in US$1m.) were mainly to Netherlands (97·97), Norway (90·49), USA (84·50), Canada (44·82) and France (35·92); imports were mainly from the USA (231·9), Netherlands (141·4), Trinidad and Tobago (57·4), Netherlands Antilles (32·3) and Japan (30·69).

COMMUNICATIONS

Roads. The road network covered 4,492 km in 2000, of which 26·0% were paved. In 2000 there were 61,000 passenger cars, 21,000 trucks and vans, 2,000 buses and coaches and 31,000 motorcycles and mopeds. There were 68 fatalities in road accidents in 2000.

Rail. There are two single-track railways.

Civil Aviation. There is an international airport at Paramaribo (Johan Adolf Pengel). The national carrier is Surinam Airways, which in 2003 had flights to Amsterdam, Belem, Cayenne, Curaçao, Georgetown, Haiti, Miami and Port of Spain. In 1999 scheduled airline traffic of Suriname-based carriers flew 5·6m. km, carrying 194,000 passengers (190,000 on international flights). In 1998 there were 131,014 passenger arrivals and 131,012 departures.

Shipping. The Royal Netherlands Steamship Co. operates services to the Netherlands, the USA, and regionally. The Suriname Navigation Co. maintains services from Paramaribo to Georgetown, Cayenne and the Caribbean area. Merchant shipping in 2002 totalled 5,000 GRT. In 2000 vessels totalling 1,120,000 NRT entered ports and vessels totalling 2,186,000 NRT cleared.

Telecommunications. Telephone subscribers numbered 164,400 in 2001, equivalent to 373·6 for every 1,000 persons, and 20,000 PCs were in use (45·5 per 1,000 inhabitants). There were 108,400 mobile phone subscribers in 2002 and 800 fax machines in 1996. In 2002 there were 20,000 Internet users.

SOCIAL INSTITUTIONS

Justice. Members of the court of justice are nominated by the President. There are three cantonal courts. Suriname was one of ten countries to sign an agreement in Feb. 2001 establishing a Caribbean Court of Justice to replace the British Privy Council as the highest civil and criminal court. In the meantime the number of signatories has risen to twelve. The court was inaugurated at Port-of-Spain, Trinidad on 16 April 2005.

The population in penal institutions in June 1999 was 1,933 (437 per 100,000 of national population).

Religion. In 2001 there were estimated to be 162,000 Christians of varying denominations, 119,000 Hindus and 85,000 Muslims.

Education. Adult literacy was 93·0% in 1998. In 1999–2000, 269 primary schools out of a total of 306 had 2,845 teachers and 61,418 pupils. 107 secondary schools had 1,744 teachers and 27,930 pupils. In 2000–01 the university had 2,745 students. There is a teacher training college with (2000–01) 1,942 students.

Health. In 2000 there were 1,683 general hospital beds and 224 physicians.

CULTURE

World Heritage Sites. Suriname has two sites on the UNESCO World Heritage List: Central Suriname Nature Reserve (inscribed on the list in 2000); and the Historic Inner City of Paramaribo (2002).

Broadcasting. The government controls the partly commercial Stichting Radio Omroep Suriname and Radio Suriname Internationaal, and Surinaamse Televisie Stichting. There were 115,000 TV sets (colour by NTSC) in 2001 and 300,000 radio receivers in 1997. There were 41 radio and nine television stations in 1999.

Cinema. There were two cinemas in Paramaribo in 1999.

Press. There were two daily newspapers in 1998 with a combined average circulation of 28,000, equivalent to 68 per 1,000 inhabitants.

Tourism. In 1999 there were 130,686 foreign tourist arrivals; in 1998 receipts totalled US$45m.

Festivals. The people of Suriname celebrate Chinese New Year (Jan.); Phagwa, a Hindu celebration (March–April); Id-Ul-Fitre, the sugar feast at the end of Ramadan (May); Avondvierdaagse, a carnival (during the Easter holidays); Suriflora, a celebration of plants and flowers (April–May); Keti koti, an Afro-Surinamese holiday to commemorate the abolition of slavery (1 July); Suri-pop, a popular music festival (July); Nationale Kunstbeurs, arts and crafts (Oct.–Nov.); Divali, the Hindu ceremony of light (Nov.); Djaran Kepang, a Javanese dance held on feast days; Winti-prey, a ceremony for the Winti gods.

Museums and Galleries. The main museums (1998) were: Surinaams Museum and Fort Zeelandia in Paramaribo; the Open Air Museum at Nieuw Amsterdam. Art Galleries include: Suriname Art 2000; the Academy for Higher Arts and Cultural Education; and the Ready Tex Art Boutique, all in Paramaribo; and Nola Hatterman Instituut at Fort Zeelandia.

DIPLOMATIC REPRESENTATIVES

Of Suriname in the United Kingdom
Ambassador: Vacant.
Chargé d'Affaires a.i.: Nell J. Stadwisk-Kappel (resides at The Hague).

Of the United Kingdom in Suriname
Ambassador: Stephen Hiscock (resides at Georgetown, Guyana).

Of Suriname in the USA (4301 Connecticut Ave., NW, Washington, D.C., 20008)
Ambassador: Henry Lothar Illes.

Of the USA in Suriname (Dr Sophie Redmondstraat 129, Paramaribo)
Ambassador: Marsha E. Barnes.

Of Suriname to the United Nations
Ambassador: Ewald Wensley Limon.

Of Suriname to the European Union
Ambassador: Gerhard Otmar Hiwat.

FURTHER READING

Dew, E. M., *Trouble in Suriname, 1975–1993.* New York, 1995

National statistical office: Algemeen Bureau voor de Statistiek, POB 244, Paramaribo.

SWAZILAND

Umbuso weSwatini
(Kingdom of Swaziland)

Capital: Mbabane (Administrative), Lobamba (Legislative)
Population projection, 2010: 1·08m.
GDP per capita, 2002: (PPP$) 4,550
HDI/world rank: 0·519/137

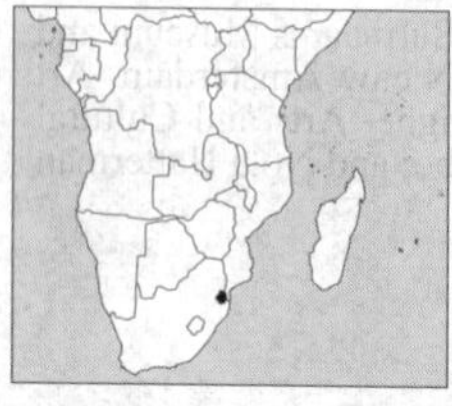

KEY HISTORICAL EVENTS

The Swazi migrated into the country to which they have given their name in the last half of the 18th century. The independence of the Swazis was guaranteed in the conventions of 1881 and 1884 between the British Government and the Government of the South African Republic. In 1894 the South African Republic was given powers of protection and administration. In 1902, after the conclusion of the Boer War, a special commissioner took charge, and under an order-in-council in 1903 the Governor of the Transvaal administered the territory. Swaziland became independent on 6 Sept. 1968. A state of emergency imposed in 1973 is still in force. On 25 April 1986 King Mswati III was installed as King of Swaziland.

TERRITORY AND POPULATION

Swaziland is bounded in the north, west and south by South Africa, and in the east by Mozambique. The area is 6,704 sq. miles (17,363 sq. km). *De facto* population (census 1997), 929,718 (489,564 females); density, 53·5 per sq. km. 2002 population estimate: 1,061,000. More than 50% of the population is under 18 years of age.

The UN gives a projected population for 2010 of 1·08m.

In 2001, 73·3% of the population were rural. The country is divided into four districts: Hhohho, Lubombo, Manzini and Shiselweni.

Main urban areas: Mbabane, the administrative capital (73,000 inhabitants in 1999); Manzini; Big Bend; Mhlume; Nhlangano.

The population is 84% Swazi and 10% Zulu. The official languages are Swazi and English.

SOCIAL STATISTICS

1997 estimates: births, 31,000; deaths, 8,000. Estimated rates, 1997 (per 1,000 population): births, 35·5; deaths, 8·6. As a result of the impact of AIDS, expectation of life has gradually been declining. It was 58 years in 1995, but by 2001 was down to 36·5 years for males and 39·9 years for females. In 2002, 38·6% of all adults were infected with HIV. In Sept. 2001 King Mswati III told the teenage girls of the country to stop having sex for five years as part of the country's drive to reduce the spread of HIV. Annual population growth rate, 1992–02, 1·9%. Infant mortality, 2001, 106 per 1,000 live births; fertility rate, 2001, 4·5 births per woman.

CLIMATE

A temperate climate with two seasons. Nov. to March is the wet season, when temperatures range from mild to hot, with frequent thunderstorms. The cool, dry season from May to Sept. is characterized by clear, bright sunny days. Mbabane, Jan. 68°F (20°C), July 54°F (12·2°C). Annual rainfall 56" (1,402 mm).

CONSTITUTION AND GOVERNMENT

The reigning King is **Mswati III** (b. 1968; crowned 25 April 1986), who succeeded his father, King Sobhuza II (reigned 1921–82). The King rules in conjunction with the Queen Mother (his mother, or a senior wife). Critics of the King or his mother run the risk of arrest.

A new constitution was adopted in Nov. 2003. There is a *House of Assembly* of 65 members, 55 of whom are elected each from one constituency (*inkhundla*), and 10 appointed by the King; and a *House of Senators* of 30 members, 10 of whom are elected by the House of Assembly and 20 appointed by the King. Elections are held in two rounds, the second being a run-off between the five candidates who come first in each constituency.

There is also a traditional *Swazi National Council* headed by the King and Queen Mother at which all Swazi men are entitled to be heard.

National Anthem. 'Nkulunkulu mnikati wetibusiso temaSwati' ('O Lord our God bestower of blessings upon the Swazi'); words by A. E. Simelane, tune by D. K. Rycroft.

RECENT ELECTIONS

At the elections of 18 Oct. 2003 only non-partisans were elected. Political parties are illegal and advocates of multi-party politics are considered to be troublemakers.

CURRENT ADMINISTRATION

In March 2005 the cabinet comprised:

Prime Minister: Absalom Themba Dlamini (sworn in on 26 Nov. 2003).

Deputy Prime Minister: Albert H. Shabangu.

Minister for Agriculture and Co-operatives: Mtiti Fakudze. *Economic Planning and Development:* Rev. Absalom Muntu Dlamini. *Education:* Constance Simelane. *Enterprise and Employment:* Lutfo Dlamini. *Finance:* Majozi Sithole. *Foreign Affairs:* Mabili Dlamini. *Health and Social Welfare:* Sipho Shongwe. *Housing and Urban Development:* Dumsile Sukati. *Interior:* Prince Gabheni Dlamini. *Justice and Constitutional Affairs:* Prince David Dlamini. *Natural Resources:* Mfomfo Nkambule. *Public Service and Information:* Themba Msibi. *Public Works and Transport:* Elijah Shongwe. *Tourism, Environment and Communication:* Thandie Shongwe.

Government Website: http://www.gov.sz

DEFENCE

Army Air Wing. There are two Israeli-built Arava transports with weapon attachments for light attack duties.

INTERNATIONAL RELATIONS

Swaziland is a member of the UN, WTO, the African Union, African Development Bank, COMESA, SADC, the Commonwealth and is an ACP member state of the ACP-EU relationship.

ECONOMY

Agriculture accounted for 15·7% of GDP in 2002, industry 49·8% and services 34·5%.

Currency. The unit of currency is the *lilangeni* (plural *emalangeni*) (SZL) of 100 *cents* but Swaziland remains in the Common Monetary Area and the South African rand is legal tender. In 2002 inflation was 11·8%. In June 2002 foreign exchange reserves were US$253m. and total money supply was 832m. emalangeni.

Budget. The fiscal year begins on 1 April. Total revenue in financial year 2000 totalled 2,708·2m. emalangeni and total expenditure 2,899·7m. emalangeni.

Performance. Real GDP growth was 1·6% in 2002 (1·8% in 2001). Total GDP in 2003 was US$1·8bn.

Banking and Finance. The central bank and bank of issue is the Central Bank of Swaziland (*Governor,* Martin Dlamini), established in 1974. In 2004 there were four banking institutions, three foreign (South African-owned) private banks, Swazibank (state-owned) and a housing bank. In 2003 there were 178 credit and saving unions.

In 1990 Swaziland Stock Brokers was established to trade in stocks and shares for institutional and private clients.

ENERGY AND NATURAL RESOURCES

Environment. Swaziland's carbon dioxide emissions from the consumption and flaring of fossil fuels were the equivalent of 0·8 tonnes per capita in 2002.

Electricity. Installed capacity was 50,000 kW in 1993. Production was about 348m. kWh in 2001; total consumption was an estimated 963m. kWh. Swaziland imports about two-thirds of its electricity needs from South Africa.

Minerals. Output (in tonnes) in 2002: coal, 313,272; asbestos (2000), 12,690; quarry stone (2001), 350,000 cu. metres. Diamond production was 64,000 carats in 1994. The diamond mine closed down in 1996 and the asbestos mine in 2000.

The oldest known mine (iron ore) in the world, dating back to 41,000 BC, was located at the Lion Cavern Site on Ngwenya Mountain.

Agriculture. In 2001 there were 178,000 ha of arable land and 12,000 ha of permanent cropland. Production (2000, in 1,000 tonnes): sugarcane, 4,436; maize, 72; grapefruit and pomelos, 47; oranges, 36; seed cotton, 23; cottonseed, 15; pineapples, 11; groundnuts, 8; cotton lint, 7.

Livestock (2000): cattle, 610,000; goats, 440,000; pigs, 33,000; chickens, 3m.

Forestry. Forests covered 522,000 ha in 2000, or 30·3% of the land area. In 2001 timber production was 890,000 cu. metres.

Fisheries. Estimated total catch, 2001, approximately 70 tonnes, exclusively from inland waters.

INDUSTRY

Most industries are based on processing agricultural products and timber. Footwear and textiles are also manufactured, and some engineering products.

Labour. In June 1996, 89,860 persons were in formal employment; 15,892 Swazis worked in gold mines in South Africa in 1994. Unemployment rose to 30% in 1999.

Trade Unions. In 1998 there were 21 affiliated trade unions grouped in the Swaziland Federation of Trade Unions with a combined membership of 83,000, and four unions grouped in the Swaziland Federation of Labour.

INTERNATIONAL TRADE

Swaziland has a customs union with South Africa and receives a pro rata share of the dues collected. External debt was US$342m. in 2002.

Imports and Exports. In 2002 imports (f.o.b.) amounted to US$1,034·6m. (US$1,116·4m. in 2001); exports (f.o.b.) US$955·2m. (US$1,039·7m. in 2001). Main export commodities are soft drink concentrates, sugar, wood pulp and cotton yarn; main import products are motor vehicles, machinery, transport equipment, foodstuffs, petroleum products and chemicals. By far the most significant trading partner is South Africa. In 2001, 94·5% of imports came from South Africa; 78·0% of exports went to South Africa in 2001.

COMMUNICATIONS

Roads. The total length of roads in 2000 was 3,107 km, of which 1,420 km were main roads. There were 40,544 passenger cars in 2001 plus 38,090 trucks and vans and 5,737 buses and coaches. There were 5,352 road accidents involving injury in 2001 with 255 fatalities.

Rail. In 1997 the system comprised 301 km of route (1,067 mm gauge). Freight tonne-km in 2000 came to 875m.

Civil Aviation. There is an international airport at Manzini (Matsapha). Swazi Express Airways had flights in 2003 to Durban and Maputo. In 1999 scheduled airline traffic of Swaziland-based carriers flew 0·6m. km, carrying 12,000 passengers (all on international flights).

Telecommunications. Swaziland had 98,100 telephone subscribers in 2002, or 95·0 for every 1,000 persons, and 25,000 PCs were in use. In 1996 there were 1,200 fax machines. There were around 20,000 Internet users and 63,000 mobile phone subscribers in 2002.

Postal Services. There were 60 post offices in 1997, or one for every 15,200 persons.

SOCIAL INSTITUTIONS

Justice. The constitutional courts practice Roman-Dutch law. The judiciary is headed by the Chief Justice. There is a High Court and various Magistrates and Courts. A Court of Appeal with a President and three Judges deals with appeals from the High Court. There are 16 courts of first instance. There are also traditional Swazi National Courts.

The population in penal institutions in Aug. 2002 was 3,400 (359 per 100,000 of national population).

Religion. In 2001 there were 480,000 African Christians, 160,000 Protestants and the remainder of the population followed other religions (including traditional beliefs).

Education. In 2001 there were 541 primary schools with 212,064 children and 6,594 teachers. The teacher/pupil ratio has decreased from 40/1 in the 1970s to 32/1. About half the children of secondary school age attend school. There are also private schools. In 2001 there were 61,335 children (3,647 teachers) in secondary and high school classes. Many secondary and high schools teach agricultural activities.

The University of Swaziland, at Matsapha, had 3,692 students in 2000. There are three teacher training colleges (total enrolment in 1994–95, 857) and eight vocational institutions (1,150 students and 147 teachers in 1991). There is also an institute of management.

Rural education centres offer formal education for children and adult education geared towards vocational training. The adult literacy rate in 2001 was 80·3% (81·3% among males and 79·4% among females).

In 1999–2000 total expenditure on education came to 6·0% of GNP.

Health. In 1998 there were 176 hospitals, clinics and health centres. There were 149 physicians in 1996.

CULTURE

Broadcasting. The Broadcasting Corporation and Swaziland Television Authority are government-owned. Swaziland Broadcasting Services run on a semi-commercial basis. In 2000 there were 169,000 radio receivers and in 2001 there were 32,000 television receivers (colour by PAL).

Press. In 2003 there were three daily newspapers: *The Swazi Observer* (English-language with a circulation of 3,000 in 1999), *The Times of Swaziland* (English, 15,000), founded in 1897, and *Tikhatsi* (siSwati, 7,500).

Tourism. There were 281,000 foreign tourists in 2000, bringing revenue of US$34m.

Libraries. There is a government-subsidized National Library Service, which comprises two libraries at Mbabane and Manzini with 11 branches throughout the country.

DIPLOMATIC REPRESENTATIVES

Of Swaziland in the United Kingdom (20 Buckingham Gate, London, SW1E 6LB)
High Commissioner: Vacant.
Acting High Commissioner: Zwelethu Mnisi.

Of the United Kingdom in Swaziland (2nd Floor, Lilunga House, Gifillan Street, Mbabane)
High Commissioner: David Reader.

Of Swaziland in the USA (1712 New Hampshire Ave., NW, Washington, D.C., 20009)
Ambassador: Mary M. Kanya.

Of the USA in Swaziland (2350 Mbabane Place, Dulles, Mbabane)
Ambassador: Lewis W. Lucke.

Of Swaziland to the United Nations
Ambassador: Clifford Sibusiso Mamba.

Of Swaziland to the European Union
Ambassador: Thembayena Annastasia Dlamini.

FURTHER READING

Matsebula, J. S. M., *A History of Swaziland.* 3rd ed. London, 1992
Nyeko, B., *Swaziland.* [Bibliography] 2nd ed. ABC-Clio, Oxford and Santa Barbara (CA), 1994

National statistical office: Central Statistical Office, POB 456, Mbabane.
Website: http://www.gov.sz/home.asp?pid=75

SWEDEN

Konungariket Sverige
(Kingdom of Sweden)

Capital: Stockholm
Population projection, 2010: 8·94m.
GDP per capita, 2002: (PPP$) 26,050
HDI/world rank: 0·946/2

KEY HISTORICAL EVENTS

Sweden was covered by an ice cap until 14,000 years ago. The first inhabitants (from 10,000 BC) were hunters and fishermen but from 500 BC agriculture predominated. Swedish Vikings set up trading stations in Russia in the 9th century AD, travelled to the Black and Caspian Seas and developed trading links with the Byzantine Empire and the Caliphate. Paganism was dominant until the end of the 11th century when the country was fully Christianized.

By 1200 Sweden had developed into a kingdom with much the same borders as it has today, except that Skåne, Halland and Blekinge in the south formed part of Denmark, and Jämtland, Härjedalen and Bohuslän in the west belonged to Norway. There was a struggle for power between the Sverker and Erik families, who ruled alternately between 1160–1250. Central authority was established by the mid-13th century. Hanseatic merchants traded in Sweden and German immigrants controlled Kalmar and Gotland. The Hanseatic trading posts to the east included Finland, which was brought into the Swedish kingdom. In 1340 Valdemar Atterdag, king of Denmark, fought with Sweden over the southern provinces of Skåne, Halland and Blekinge. In 1361 he attacked Gotland in one of the bloodiest battles in Nordic history. In 1350 the Black Death killed over a third of the population.

Inheritance and marriage ties united the crowns of Denmark, Norway and Sweden in 1389, under the rule of Queen Margaret of Denmark. In 1397 the loose association known as the Union of Kalmar confirmed her five-year old nephew, Erik of Pomerania, as king of the three countries. The Swedish nationalist Sten Sture defeated the Danes at the Battle of Brunkeberg in Stockholm. The union, which lasted until 1521, was weakened by rebellions and reprisals that culminated in the Stockholm Bloodbath in 1520, when eighty dignitaries were executed on the orders of the Danish king, Christian II. In 1521 Christian II was overthrown by Gustav Vasa, a Swedish nobleman, who was elected king in 1523.

Gustav Vasa's reign (1523–60) laid the foundations of the Swedish state, which was converted to Lutheranism from the 1520s. Power was concentrated in the hands of the king and in 1544 a hereditary monarchy was established. Swedish foreign policy focused on controlling the Baltic Sea, and this led to wars with Denmark from the 1560s. In 1629 Gustavus Adolphus (Gustaf II Adolf) consolidated Sweden's position on the Russian side of the Baltic, gaining Livonia. Sweden defeated Denmark in two wars (1643 and 1657) to take control of the previously Danish provinces of Skåne, Halland, Blekinge and Gotland and the Norwegian provinces of Bohuslän, Jämtland and Härjedalen. Gustavus Adolphus took his troops into northern Europe to counter the Catholic forces in the Thirty Years War. This cost him his life but gave Sweden large possessions in northern Germany.

Following the death of Karl XII in 1718, the Swedish Parliament (Riksdag) established a new constitution that abolished royal absolutism and placed power in the hands of parliament. But royal authority was soon reasserted. After defeat in the Great Northern War (1700–21) against Denmark, Poland and Russia, Sweden lost most of its Baltic territories, including a part of Finland and all its north-German possessions except west Pomerania. During the Napoleonic Wars, Sweden lost Finland to Russia and withdrew from its remaining German provinces. In 1810 Napoléon's marshall, Jean-Baptiste Bernadotte, assumed power as Karl XIV Johan. He tried to win back Finland from Russia, but had to make do with a union of Sweden and Norway, confirmed by the treaty of Kiel in 1814. The short war against Norway in 1814 was Sweden's last military adventure. Since then, Sweden has favoured neutrality.

After the Napoleonic Wars, Sweden suffered economic stagnation. Of a population of 5m., over 1m. emigrated between 1866 and 1914, mostly to North America. Industry did not start to grow until the 1890s. However, it then developed rapidly and after the Second World War Sweden was transformed into one of the leading industrial nations in Europe. In the six years to 1951 the country's GNP rose by 20%. Economic success was partly thanks to the early utilization of hydroelectric power, which supported the pulp and paper industries of the northern forests.

Social democracy began as the political offshoot of the trade unions. The working class was supported by intellectuals, such as Hjalmar Branting, the first Scandinavian socialist prime minister. In the 1930s reforms included restrictions on child and female labour, free elementary education and old-age pensions. Sweden was a founder member of EFTA (European Free Trade Agreement) in 1959. From the mid-1970s the improvements in living standards slowed and in 1976 a non-socialist coalition was formed under Centre Party chairman Thorbjörn Fälldin. In 1982 the Social Democrats resumed office with Olof Palme as prime minister. The assassination of Palme in 1986 shook the country, which had been spared political violence for nearly 200 years.

In the 1990s industrial production fell and unemployment rose, which led to a high budget deficit and increased national debt. Popular dissatisfaction showed in the 1991 election, when a non-socialist coalition government was formed with Carl Bildt as prime minister. Launching a programme of deregulation and privatization, Bildt did much to prepare the economy for closer involvement with Europe. But the government did not manage to reduce unemployment, the budget deficit or the national debt. Hence, the 1994 election put the Social Democrats back in power, with Ingvar Carlsson as prime minister. Sweden became a member of the European Union in 1995. In 1996 Göran Persson replaced Carlsson. Despite economic problems, the country still boasts one of the highest standards of living and one of the most advanced welfare systems.

TERRITORY AND POPULATION

Sweden is bounded in the west and northwest by Norway, east by Finland and the Gulf of Bothnia, southeast by the Baltic Sea and southwest by the Kattegat. The area is 449,964 sq. km, including water (96,000 lakes) totalling 39,030 sq. km. At the 1990 census the population was 8,587,353. Estimate, Dec. 2002, 8,940,788; density 19·9 per sq. km. In 2001, 83·3% of the population lived in urban areas.

The UN gives a projected population for 2010 of 8·94m.

Area, population and population density of the counties (*län*):

	Land area (in sq. km)	*Population (1990 census)*	*Population (31 Dec. 2002)*	*Density per sq. km (31 Dec. 2002)*
Stockholm	6,490	1,640,389	1,850,467	284
Uppsala	6,989	268,503	298,655	42
Södermanland	6,062	255,546	259,006	42
Östergötland	10,562	402,849	413,438	39
Jönköping	10,475	308,294	327,971	31
Kronoberg	8,458	177,880	176,978	21
Kalmar	11,171	241,149	234,627	21
Gotland	3,140	57,132	57,381	18
Blekinge	2,941	150,615	149,875	51
Skåne	11,027	1,068,587	1,145,090	104
Halland	5,454	254,568	278,551	51
Västra Götaland	23,942	1,458,166	1,508,230	63
Värmland	17,586	283,148	273,419	16
Örebro	8,517	272,474	273,412	32
Västmanland	6,302	258,544	258,912	41
Dalarna	28,193	288,919	276,636	10
Gävleborg	18,192	289,346	277,012	15
Västernorrland	21,678	261,099	244,319	11
Jämtland	49,443	135,724	127,947	3
Västerbotten	55,401	251,846	255,230	5
Norrbotten	98,911	263,546	253,632	3

There are some 17,000 Sami (Lapps).

On 31 Dec. 2002 aliens in Sweden numbered 399,469. Of these, 120,825 were from Nordic countries; 121,454 from the rest of Europe; 22,279 from Africa; 12,846 from North America; 16,120 from South America; 102,131 from Asian countries; 1,260 from the former USSR; 2,329 from Oceania; and 225 country unknown. The main individual countries of origin of aliens were: Finland, 71,266; Iraq, 37,873; Norway, 25,975.

Immigration: 2000, 58,659; 2001, 60,795; 2002, 64,087. Emigration: 2000, 34,091; 2001, 32,141; 2002, 33,009.

More than 11% of the population of Sweden is foreign-born, the highest proportion in any of the Nordic countries.

Population of the 50 largest communities, 1 Jan. 2003:

Stockholm	758,148	Huddinge	86,457	Solna	57,585
Göteborg	474,921	Karlstad	80,934	Gotland	57,381
Malmö	265,481	Södertälje	79,613	Mölndal	57,079
Uppsala	179,673	Nacka	76,624	Örnsköldsvik	55,047
Linköping	135,066	Botkyrka	75,216	Falun	54,841
Västerås	128,902	Växjö	75,036	Norrtälje	53,702
Örebro	125,520	Kristianstad	74,951	Varberg	53,346
Norrköping	123,303	Luleå	72,139	Trollhättan	52,937
Helsingborg	119,406	Skellefteå	71,813	Uddevalla	49,683
Jönköping	118,581	Haninge	70,902	Skövde	49,405
Umeå	106,525	Kungsbacka	66,573	Nyköping	49,310
Lund	100,402	Järfälla	61,290	Hässleholm	48,536
Borås	98,150	Karlskrona	60,676	Borlänge	47,049
Sundsvall	93,252	Täby	60,198	Motala	42,078
Gävle	91,276	Kalmar	60,066	Lidingö	41,192
Eskilstuna	90,089	Sollentuna	58,515	Piteå	40,531
Halmstad	86,585	Östersund	58,156		

A 16-km long fixed link with Denmark was opened in July 2000 when the Öresund motorway and railway bridge between Malmö and Copenhagen was completed.

The official language is Swedish.

SOCIAL STATISTICS

Statistics for calendar years:

	Total living births	*To mothers single, divorced or widowed*	*Stillborn*	*Marriages*	*Divorces*	*Deaths exclusive of still-born*
1998	89,028	48,658	306	31,598	20,761	93,271
1999	88,173	48,751	339	35,628	21,000	94,726
2000	90,441	50,037	355	39,895	21,502	93,461
2001	91,466	50,756	349	35,778	21,022	93,752
2002	95,815	53,678	352	38,012	21,322	95,009

Rates, 2002, per 1,000 population: births, 10·7; deaths, 10·6; marriages, 4·3; divorces, 2·4. Sweden has one of the highest rate of births outside marriage in Europe, at 56% in 2002. In 2002 the most popular age range for marrying was 25–29 for women and 30–34 for men. Expectation of life in 2001: males, 77·4 years; females, 82·4. Annual population growth rate, 1993–2002, 0·2%. Infant mortality, 2002, 3·3 per 1,000 live births (one of the lowest rates in the world). Fertility rate, 2000, 1·5 births per woman. In 2002 Sweden received 33,016 asylum applications (16,303 in 2000), equivalent to 3·7 per 1,000 inhabitants.

A UNICEF report published in 2000 showed that 2·6% of children in Sweden live in poverty (in households with income below 50% of the national median), the lowest percentage of any country. The report also showed that the poverty rate of children in lone-parent families was 6·7%, compared to 1·5% in two-parent families.

CLIMATE

The north has severe winters, with snow lying for 4–7 months. Summers are fine but cool, with long daylight hours. Further south, winters are less cold, summers are warm and rainfall well distributed throughout the year, although slightly higher in the summer. Stockholm, Jan. 0·4°C, July 17·2°C. Annual rainfall 385 mm.

CONSTITUTION AND GOVERNMENT

The reigning King is **Carl XVI Gustaf**, b. 30 April 1946, succeeded on the death of his grandfather Gustaf VI Adolf, 15 Sept. 1973, married 19 June 1976 to Silvia

Renate Sommerlath, b. 23 Dec. 1943 (Queen of Sweden). *Daughter* and *Heir Apparent:* Crown Princess Victoria Ingrid Alice Désirée, Duchess of Västergötland, b. 14 July 1977; *son:* Prince Carl Philip Edmund Bertil, Duke of Värmland, b. 13 May 1979; *daughter:* Princess Madeleine Thérèse Amelie Josephine, Duchess of Hälsingland and Gästrikland, b. 10 June 1982. *Sisters of the King.* Princess Margaretha, b. 31 Oct. 1934, married 30 June 1964 to John Ambler; Princess Birgitta (Princess of Sweden), b. 19 Jan. 1937, married 25 May 1961 (civil marriage) and 30 May 1961 (religious ceremony) to Johann Georg, Prince of Hohenzollern; Princess Désirée, b. 2 June 1938, married 5 June 1964 to Baron Niclas Silfverschiöld; Princess Christina, b. 3 Aug. 1943, married 15 June 1974 to Tord Magnuson. *Uncles of the King.* Count Sigvard Bernadotte of Wisborg, b. 7 June 1907, died 4 Feb. 2002; Count Carl Johan Bernadotte of Wisborg, b. 31 Oct. 1916.

Under the 1975 Constitution Sweden is a representative and parliamentary democracy. The King is Head of State, but does not participate in government. Parliament is the single-chamber *Riksdag* of 349 members elected for a period of four years in direct, general elections.

The manner of election to the *Riksdag* is proportional. The country is divided into 29 constituencies. In these constituencies 310 members are elected. The remaining 39 seats constitute a nationwide pool intended to give absolute proportionality to parties that receive at least 4% of the votes. A party receiving less than 4% of the votes in the country is, however, entitled to participate in the distribution of seats in a constituency, if it has obtained at least 12% of the votes cast there.

A parliament, the *Sameting*, was instituted for the Sami (Lapps) in 1993.

National Anthem. 'Du gamla, du fria' ('Thou ancient, thou free'); words by R. Dybeck; folk-tune.

RECENT ELECTIONS

In parliamentary elections held on 15 Sept. 2002 Prime Minister Göran Persson's Swedish Social Democratic Labour Party (SAP) won 144 seats with 39·8% of votes cast (131 with 36·4% in 1998), the Moderate Alliance Party 55 with 15·2% (82 with 22·9%), the Liberal Party 48 with 13·3% (17 with 4·7%), the Christian Democratic Party 33 with 9·1% (42 with 11·8%), the Left Party 30 with 8·3% (43 with 12·0%), the Centre Party 22 with 6·1% (18 with 5·1%) and the Green Party 17 with 4·6% (16 with 4·5%). Turn-out was 80·1%. Following the 2002 election, of the 349 Members of Parliament there were 191 men (54·7%) and 158 women (45·3%). Only Rwanda has a higher percentage of women in its parliament.

European Parliament. Sweden has 19 (22 in 1999) representatives. At the June 2004 elections turn-out was 37·2% (38·3% in 1999). The SAP won 5 seats with 24·8% of votes cast (political affiliation in European Parliament: Party of European Socialists); the Moderate Party, 4 with 18·2% (European People's Party–European Democrats); June List, 3 with 14·4% (Independence and Democracy Group); Vänsterpartiet (Far Left), 2 with 9·8% (European Unitary Left/Nordic Green Left); the Liberal Party, 2 with 9·8% (Alliance of Liberals and Democrats for Europe); the Centre Party, 1 with 6·3% (Alliance of Liberals and Democrats for Europe); the Green Party, 1 with 5·9% (Greens/European Free Alliance); the Christian Democratic Party, 1 with 5·7% (European People's Party–European Democrats).

CURRENT ADMINISTRATION

A minority Social Democratic government was formed in Oct. 1998. Following parliamentary elections in Sept. 2002 a new Social Democratic government was formed. In March 2005 the government comprised:

Prime Minister: Göran Persson; b. 1949 (SAP; sworn in 21 March 1996).

Deputy Prime Minister: Bosse Ringholm.

Minister of Agriculture, Food and Consumer Affairs: Ann-Christin Nykvist. *Communications and Regional Policy:* Ulrica Messing. *Defence:* Leni Björklund. *Education and Culture:* Leif Pagrotsky. *Employment:* Hans Karlsson. *Environment:* Lena Sommestad. *Finance:* Pär Nuder. *Foreign Affairs:* Laila Freivalds. *Health and Elderly Care:* Ylva Johansson. *Housing:* Mona Sahlin. *Industry and Trade:* Thomas Östros. *Integration, Metropolitan and Gender Equality Issues:* Jens Orback. *International Development Co-operation:* Carin Jämtin. *Justice:* Thomas Bodström. *Local Government Finances and Financial Market Issues:* Sven-Erik Österberg.

Migration and Asylum Policy: Barbro Holmberg. *Pre-School Education, Youth Affairs and Adult Learning:* Lena Hallengren. *Public Health and Social Services:* Morgan Johansson. *Schools:* Ibrahim Baylan. *Social Affairs:* Berit Andnor.

The *Speaker* is Björn von Sydow.

Office of the Prime Minister: http://www.sweden.gov.se

DEFENCE

The Supreme Commander is, under the government, in command of the three services. The Supreme Commander is assisted by the Swedish Armed Forces HQ. There is also a Swedish Armed Forces Logistics Organization.

The conscription system consists of 7½–18 months of military service for males. Females have the possibility to serve on a voluntary basis.

In 2003 military expenditure totalled US$5,532m. (US$618 per capita), representing 1·8% of GDP. Sweden's national security policy is currently undergoing a shift in emphasis. Beginning with the decommissioning of obsolete units and structures, the main thrust of policy is the creation of contingency forces adaptable to a variety of situations.

The government stressed that Sweden's membership of the EU (in 1995) did not imply any change in Sweden's traditional policy of non-participation in military alliances, with the option of staying neutral in the event of war in its vicinity.

Sweden has modern air raid shelters with capacity for some 7m. people. Since this falls short of providing protection for the whole population, evacuation and relocation operations would be necessary in the event of war.

The National Board of Psychological Defence, whose main task is to safeguard the free, undisrupted transmission of news, has also made preparations for 'psychological defence' in wartime. This is regarded as the best possible antidote against enemy propaganda, disinformation and rumour-mongering of the kind that can be expected in times of war.

Army. The Army consists of one division HQ and divisional units, six army brigade command and control elements, and 54 battalions. Army strength, Jan. 2003, 20,000 (10,769 conscripts). The Army can mobilize a reserve of approximately 200,000 of whom 85,000 are Home Guard and 11,100 reservists.

The Home Guard is part of the Army. Its main task is to protect important local installations against sabotage.

Navy. The Navy has two surface warfare flotillas, one mine warfare flotilla, one submarine flotilla and one amphibious brigade.

The personnel of the Navy in Jan. 2003 totalled 5,600 (active manpower, including 2,600 conscripts). Strength available for mobilization, 20,000 (includes 2,500 reservists).

Air Force. The Air Force consists of three fighter control and air surveillance battalions, eight air-base battalions, eight fighter squadrons, two air transport squadrons (central) and two air transport squadrons (regional).

Strength (Jan. 2003) 6,500 (2,000 conscripts), plus 16,000 available for mobilization (including 1,670 reservists).

During peacetime all the helicopters of the Swedish Armed Forces are organized into a detached organization directly under the Swedish Armed Forces Headquarters.

INTERNATIONAL RELATIONS

Sweden is a member of the UN, WTO, BIS, NATO Partnership for Peace, BIS, OECD, EU, Council of Europe, OSCE, CERN, Nordic Council, Council of the Baltic Sea States, Inter-American Development Bank, Asian Development Bank, IOM and the Antarctic Treaty. Sweden is a signatory to the Schengen Accord, which abolishes border controls between Sweden, Austria, Belgium, Denmark, Finland, France, Germany, Greece, Iceland, Italy, Luxembourg, the Netherlands, Norway, Portugal and Spain.

Sweden gave US$2·1bn. in international aid in 2003, which at 0·70% of GNI made it the world's fifth most generous country as a percentage of its gross national income.

In a referendum held on 14 Sept. 2003 Swedish voters rejected their country's entry into the common European currency, 56·1% opposing membership of the euro against 41·8% voting in favour. Turn-out was 81·2%.

ECONOMY

Services accounted for 70·0% of GDP in 2002, industry 28·2% and agriculture 1·8%.

According to the anti-corruption organization *Transparency International*, in 2004 Sweden ranked 6th in the world in a survey of the countries with the least corruption in business and government. It received 9·2 out of 10 in the annual index.

Overview. Sweden combines an extensive welfare state with a market economy. Expenditure ceilings and a target for the cyclically adjusted budget surplus have governed fiscal policy since 1997. In 2002 an expansionary fiscal policy and competitive exports contributed to sound economic developments. Fiscal stimulus for 2002 has targeted household expenditure. Monetary policy has targeted a 2% inflation rate since 1993. GDP per capita has growth faster than the OECD average in recent years, after a long period of slower than average growth. In Sept. 2003 a referendum rejected adopting the euro. The working age population in Sweden will start to diminish towards 2010 unless it can be bolstered by net immigration. Raising productivity growth is a key strategy in the management of demographic trends and in the maintenance of living standards. The authorities have deregulated a number of sectors, including electricity, telecommunications and part of transport. The OECD suggests that further efficiency gains could be made by addressing anti-competitive behaviour, exposing the public sector to competition, removing regulator obstacles and reducing high marginal tax rates.

Currency. The unit of currency is the *krona* (SEK), of 100 *öre*. The annual inflation rate was 2·2% in 2002, 1·9% in 2003 and 0·4% in 2004. Foreign exchange reserves were US$14,967m. and gold reserves 5·96m. troy oz in June 2002.

Budget. Revenue of 684·5bn. kr. and expenditure of 717·7bn. kr. was estimated for the total budget (Current and Capital) for financial year 2003.

Revenue and expenditure for 2002 (1m. kr.):

Revenue	
Tax revenues	659,389
—Taxes on income	65,103
—Social security contribution	249,825
—Taxes on property	40,243
—Taxes on goods and services	290,125
—Reallocation fee	23,705
—Cash difference account	–4,196
—Tax reductions	–5,414
From government activities	49,113
From sale of property	93
Loans repaid	2,720
Computed revenues	9,865
Contributions, etc., from the EU	9,307
Total revenue	730,488

Expenditure	
The Swedish political system	7,333
Economy and fiscal administration	8,838
Tax administration and collection	8,049
Justice	24,052
Foreign policy administration and international co-operation	1,137
Total defence	44,588
International development assistance	15,684
Immigrants and refugees	6,695
Health care, medical care, social services	31,040
Financial security in the event of illness and disability	112,889
Financial security in old age	33,794
Financial security for families and children	50,197
The labour market	60,968
Working life	1,066
Study support	20,668
Education and university research	40,871
Culture, the media, religious organizations and leisure	8,095
Community planning, housing supply and construction	8,736
Regional balance and development	3,388
General environment and conservation	2,934
Energy	2,253
Communications	24,361
Agriculture and forestry, fisheries, etc.	13,922
Business sector	3,453
General grants to municipalities	102,333
Interest on Central Government Debt, etc.	67,340
Contribution to the European Community	20,648
Other expenditure	3,978
	729,309

VAT is 25% (reduced rates, 12% and 6%). In 2002 tax revenues were 50·6% of GDP (the highest percentage of any developed country).

Performance. Real GDP growth was 4·3% in 2000, but only 1·0% in 2001 as a consequence of world economic slump. There was growth of 2·0% in 2002 and 1·5% in 2003 before a strong upturn in the economy led to growth of 3·8% in 2004. Sweden's total GDP in 2003 was US$300·8bn.

The OECD reported in Aug. 2002 that 'Sweden's economic performance has remained robust despite the slowdown last year and its prospects are bright.

Macroeconomic policies may need to adjust as the economy picks up, while structural reforms are needed to assure better medium-term growth prospects. However, the momentum of structural reform has slackened and further progress is needed across a wide range of policy areas to maintain growth in living standards and to meet the costs of a generous social welfare system and coming demographic challenges.'

Sweden was ranked third in the Growth Competitiveness Index in the World Economic Forum's *Global Competitiveness Report 2004–05*.

In 2002 the state debt amounted to 1,160bn. kr.

Banking and Finance. The central bank and bank of issue is the *Sveriges Riksbank*. The bank has 11 trustees, elected by parliament, and is managed by a directorate, including the governor, appointed by the trustees. In Jan. 2003 a new *Governor*, Lars Heikensten, was appointed for a six-year term. In 2001 there were 52 commercial banks. Their total deposits in 2000 amounted to 1,104,570m. kr.; advances to the public in 2000 amounted to 975,212m. kr. In April 2003 there were 77 savings banks and 20 branches of foreign banks. The largest banks are Nordea Bank AB (previously MeritaNorbanken, formed in 1997 when Nordbanken of Sweden merged with Merita of Finland), Svenska Handelsbanken, Skandinavska Enskilda Banken and FöreningsSparbanken. In April 2000 MeritaNordbanken acquired Denmark's Unidanmark, thereby becoming the Nordic region's biggest bank in terms of assets. It became Nordea Bank AB in Dec. 2001. By Oct. 2000 approximately 27% of the Swedish population were using e-banking.

There is a stock exchange in Stockholm.

ENERGY AND NATURAL RESOURCES

Environment. Sweden's carbon dioxide emissions from the consumption and flaring of fossil fuels in 2002 were the equivalent of 6·2 tonnes per capita. An *Environmental Sustainability Index* compiled for the World Economic Forum meeting in Feb. 2002 ranked Sweden third in the world, with 72·6%. The index measured the ability of countries to maintain favourable environmental conditions and examined various factors including pollution levels and the use or abuse of natural resources.

Electricity. Sweden is rich in hydro-power resources. Installed capacity was 33,835 MW in 2001, of which 16,568 MW was in hydro-electric plants, 9,436 MW in nuclear plants and 7,536 MW in thermal plants. Electricity production in 2001 was 161,615m. kWh; consumption was 168,770 kWh. In 2000 consumption per capita was 17,154 kWh. A referendum of 1980 called for the phasing out of nuclear power by 2010. In Feb. 1997 the government began denuclearization by designating one of the 12 reactors for decommissioning. The state corporation Vattenfall was given the responsibility of financing and overseeing the transition to the use of non-fossil fuel alternatives. In 2003 there were 11 nuclear reactors in operation.

Minerals. Sweden is a leading producer of iron ore with around 2% of the world's total output. It is the largest iron ore exporter in Europe. There are also deposits of copper, gold, lead, zinc and alum shale containing oil and uranium. Iron ore produced, 2001, 19·5m. tonnes; zinc (mine output, zinc content), 156,334 tonnes; copper (mine output, copper content), 74,269 tonnes.

The mining industry accounts for 1·0% of the market value of Sweden's total industrial production and employs 0·5% of the total industrial labour force.

Agriculture. In 1999 the total area of land given over to farms of 2 ha or more was 7,630,720 ha, of which 2,746,929 ha was arable land; 447,149 was natural pasture; 3,734,193 was forest; and 702,449 other. Of the land used for arable farming in 2002, 2–5 ha holdings covered a total area of 41,110 ha; 5·1–10 ha holdings covered 91,570 ha; 10·1–20 ha, 200,735; 20·1–30 ha, 193,279; 30·1–50 ha, 376,113; 50·1–100 ha, 717,112 and holdings larger than 100 ha covered 1,060,022 ha. There were 70,950 agricultural enterprises in 2002 compared to 150,014 in 1971 and 282,187 in 1951. Around 37% of the enterprises were between 5 and 20 ha. Figures compiled by the Soil Association, a British organization, show that in 1999 Sweden set aside 268,000 ha (11·2% of its agricultural land—one of the highest proportions in the world) for the growth of organic crops.

Agriculture accounts for 5·8% of exports and 7·9% of imports. The agricultural sector employs 3% of the workforce.

	Area (1,000 ha)			Production (1,000 tonnes)		
Chief crops	*2000*	*2001*	*2002*	*2000*	*2001*	*2002*
Ley	917·3	929·6	941·0	. . .	. . .	2,737·0
Sugarbeet	55·5	54·8	54·8	2,602·2	2,659·4	2,664·3
Wheat	401·6	399·2	339·6	2,399·9	2,344·8	2,112·6
Barley	411·2	397·5	416·8	1,634·4	1,642·1	1,777·9
Oats	295·5	278·2	295·0	1,151·1	963·7	1,180·7
Potatoes	32·9	32·2	31·7	980·1	916·0	913·6
Rye	34·5	34·4	24·4	187·3	180·0	128·2

Milk production (in 1,000 tonnes) 2001, 3,339; meat, 424; cheese, 125; butter, 49.

Livestock, 2002: cattle, 1,637,465; sheep and lambs, 426,772; pigs, 1,881,743; poultry, 6,268,656. There were 121,367 reindeer in Sami villages in 2001. Harvest of moose during open season 2002: 102,853.

Forestry. Forests form one of the country's greatest natural assets. The growing stock includes 43% spruce, 39% pine and 16% broad-leaved. In 2000 forests covered 27·13m. ha (65·9% of the land area). The state owns only 5% of productive forest lands. During 1993 most government-owned timberland was transferred to a forest production corporation (AssiDomän) in which the state owns 51% of shares, and the remaining 49% are quoted on the stock exchange. Public ownership accounts for 8% of the forests, limited companies own 37%, the state 5% and the remaining 50% is in private hands. Of the 63·0m. cu. metres of wood felled in 2001, 32·7m. cu. metres were sawlogs, 23·6m. cu. metres pulpwood, 5·9m. cu. metres fuelwood and 1·0m. cu. metres other.

Fisheries. In 2001 the total catch was 305,700 tonnes, worth 1,191·3m. kr. In 2002 the fishing fleet comprised 1,820 vessels of 45,371 gross tonnes.

INDUSTRY

The leading companies by market capitalization in Sweden, excluding banking and finance, in May 2004 were: Telefonaktiebolaget LM Ericsson (US$45·2bn.); H & M—Hennes & Mauritz AB (US$20·5bn.), a clothing and cosmetics company; and TeliaSonera (US$19·8bn.), a telecommunications company.

Manufacturing is mainly based on metals and forest resources. Chemicals (especially petro-chemicals), building materials and decorative glass and china are also important.

Industry groups	*Sales value of production (gross) in 1m. kr. 2001*
Manufacturing industry	*1,264,988*
Food products, beverages and tobacco	114,915
Textiles and textile products, leather and leather products	12,963
Wood and wood products	62,354
Pulp, paper and paper products, publishers and printers	168,881
Coke, refined petroleum products and nuclear fuel	8,212
Chemicals, chemical products and man-made fibres	96,826
Rubber and plastic products	31,482
Other non-metallic mineral products	22,587
Basic metals	78,329
Fabricated metal products, machinery and equipment	633,719
Other manufacturing industries	34,720
Mines and quarries	*11,623*

In 2001 industry accounted for 27·4% of GDP, with industrial production growing by 0·3%.

Labour. In 2002 there were 4,244,000 persons in the labour force, employed as follows: 800,000 in trade and communication; 792,000 in health and social work;

747,000 in manufacturing, mining, quarrying, electricity and water services; 611,000 in financial services and business activities; 391,000 in education, research and development; 330,000 in personal services and cultural activities, and sanitation; 241,000 in public administration; 235,000 in construction; 91,000 in agriculture, forestry and fishing. The unemployment rate in Dec. 2004 was 6·4%. In 2002, 76·3% of men and 73·4% of women between the ages of 15 and 64 were in employment. No other major industrialized nation has such a small gap between the employment rates of the sexes. The average monthly salary in 2001 was 21,300 kr. (23,300 kr. for men and 19,200 kr. for women).

In 2002 a total of 838 working days were lost through strikes, compared to 733,284 in 1995.

Trade Unions. At 31 Dec. 2002 the Swedish Trade Union Confederation (LO) had 16 member unions with a total membership of 1,918,800; the Central Government Organization of Salaried Employees (TCO) had 19, with 1,276,027; the Swedish Confederation of Professional Associations (SACO) had 26, with 537,488; the Central Organization of Swedish Workers (SAC) had 7,664 members.

INTERNATIONAL TRADE

Imports and Exports. Imports and exports (in 1m. kr.):

	1998	*1999*	*2000*	*2001*[1]	*2002*[1]
Imports	544,984	568,008	669,182	657,489	646,941
Exports	675,209	700,960	796,941	787,764	789,409

[1]Provisional.

Breakdown by Standard International Trade Classification (SITC, revision 3) categories (value in 1m. kr.; 2001 figures are estimates):

	Imports		*Exports*	
	2000	*2001*	*2000*	*2001*
0. Food and live animals	35,217	39,823	16,447	18,995
1. Beverages and tobacco	5,245	6,037	3,517	4,737
2. Crude materials	22,288	22,434	48,136	45,726
3. Fuels and lubricants	60,166	57,508	26,744	26,462
4. Animal and vegetable oils	1,111	1,200	985	1,161
5. Chemicals	63,934	71,779	74,939	86,752
6. Manufactured goods	92,977	94,800	160,020	168,668
7. Machinery and transport equipment	301,855	272,356	399,763	361,293
8. Miscellaneous manufactured items	86,230	91,419	65,582	72,592
9. Other	158	132	808	1,378

Principal exports in 2001 (in 1m. kr.): road vehicles, 100,342; telecommunications, sound recording and similar appliances, 72,684; paper, paperboard and manufactures thereof, 66,830; medical and pharmaceutical preparations, 43,170. The engineering industry accounts for some 55% of Swedish exports. This includes mobile telephony, which is the largest product group in the Swedish export market. The telecommunications company Ericsson is now the leading export company, ahead of Volvo.

Imports and exports by countries (value in 1m. kr.; 2001 figures are estimates):

	Imports from		*Exports to*	
	2000	*2001*	*2000*	*2001*
Denmark	50,457	56,261	46,164	47,914
Finland	37,893	35,625	44,340	43,919
France	39,246	42,555	41,710	39,954
Germany	117,977	116,263	87,386	83,130
Netherlands	51,072	46,811	39,714	39,346
Norway	54,649	55,182	60,146	67,329
UK	63,935	58,668	74,781	69,640
USA	44,797	35,616	75,360	87,806

In 2001 other EU member countries accounted for 54·2% of exports and 66·8% of imports. Exports were equivalent to 44% of Sweden's GDP in 1999.

COMMUNICATIONS

Roads. In 2003 there were 212,000 km of roads open to the public of which 98,256 km were state-administered roads (main roads, 15,341 km; secondary roads, 82,915 km). There were also 1,544 km of motorway. 79% of all roads in 2003 were surfaced. Motor vehicles in 2002 included 4,043,000 passenger cars, 409,000 lorries, 14,000 buses and 373,000 motorcycles and mopeds. There were 979,000 Volvos, 402,000 Volkswagens, 373,000 Saabs and 344,000 Fords registered in 2002. Sweden has one of the lowest death rates in road accidents of any industrialized country, at 6·3 deaths per 100,000 people. 560 people were killed in traffic accidents in 2002.

Rail. Total length of railways at 31 Dec. 2002 was 11,079 km (7,709 km electrified). In 2001, 139m. passengers and 54·0m. tonnes of freight were carried. There is a metro in Stockholm (108 km), and tram/light rail networks in Stockholm, Göteborg (81 km) and Norrköping.

Civil Aviation. The main international airports are at Stockholm (Arlanda), Göteborg (Landvetter) and Malmö (Sturup). The principal carrier is Scandinavian Airlines System (SAS), which resulted from the 1950 merger of the three former Scandinavian airlines. SAS Sverige AB is the Swedish partner (SAS Denmark A/S and SAS Norge ASA being the other two). Sweden holds three-sevenths of the capital of SAS and Denmark and Norway each two-sevenths. SAS has a joint paid-up capital of 14,241m. Sw. kr. Capitalization of SAS Sverige AB, 5,560m. Sw. kr., of which 50% is owned by the government and 50% by private enterprises.

Malmö Aviation and Skyways AB, both Sweden-based carriers, operate some international as well as domestic flights.

In 2002 Stockholm (Arlanda) handled 16,431,207 passengers (10,401,495 on international flights) and (2001) 112,775 tonnes of freight. Göteborg (Landvetter) was the second busiest airport, handling 3,908,462 passengers (2,698,088 on international flights) and (2001) 51,814 tonnes of freight. Malmö handled 1,913,834 passengers in 2002 (1,139,931 on domestic flights).

Shipping. The mercantile marine consisted on 31 Dec. 2002 of 399 vessels of 3·10m. GRT. Cargo vessels entering Swedish ports in 2002 numbered 20,044 (106·92m. GRT) while passenger ferries numbered 75,182 (879·09m. GRT). The number of cargo vessels leaving Swedish ports in 2002 totalled 20,140 (103·01m. GRT) and the number of passenger ferries leaving was 75,194 (878·78m. GRT).

The busiest port is Göteborg. In 2002 a total of 32·29m. tonnes of goods were loaded and unloaded there (28·68m. tonnes unloaded from and loaded to foreign ports). Other major ports are Brofjorden, Trelleborg, Helsingborg and Malmö.

Telecommunications. There were 14,528,000 telephone subscribers in 2002, or 1,624·5 per 1,000 population. In June 2000 the state sold off a 30% stake in the Swedish telecommunications operator Telia. In Dec. 2002 Telia and the Finnish telecommunications operator Sonera merged to become TeliaSonera. The Swedish state owns 46% and the Finnish state 19%. In 2002 there were 7,949,000 mobile phone subscribers in use. More than 88% of Swedes are mobile phone subscribers—among the highest penetration rates in the world. There were 5,556,000 PCs in 2002, equivalent to 621·3 per 1,000 population—the second highest rate in the world behind the USA. In 1996 there were 450,000 fax machines in use. In Sept. 2002 there were 6·02m. Internet users, or 67·81% of the total population (the second highest percentage in the world, after Iceland).

Sweden has been one of the most active countries in the adoption of information technology. Kista Science Park, in the northwest of Stockholm, was ranked second equal in the world behind Silicon Valley by *Wired Magazine* in 2000 in a listing of the most significant locations for IT research and development.

Postal Services. There were 1,740 post offices at the end of 2001. In the meantime many traditional post offices have closed down and have been replaced by up to 3,000 new postal service outlets in locations such as shops and petrol stations. A total of 5,555m. pieces of mail were processed in 1999, equivalent to 627 per person.

SOCIAL INSTITUTIONS

Justice. Sweden has two parallel types of courts—general courts that deal with criminal and civil cases and general administrative courts that deal with cases related to public administration. The general courts have three instances: 23 county administrative courts, four administrative courts of appeal and the Supreme Administrative Court. There are 72 district courts, of which 25 also serve as real estate courts. In addition, a number of special courts and tribunals have been established to hear specific kinds of cases and matters.

Every district court, court of appeal, county administrative court and administrative court of appeal has a number of lay judges. These take part in the adjudication of both specific concrete issues and matter of law; each has the right to vote.

Criminal cases are normally tried by one judge and three lay judges. Civil disputes are normally heard by a single judge or three judges. In the courts of appeal, criminal cases are determined by three judges and two lay judges. Civil cases are tried by three or four judges. In the settlement of family cases, lay judges take part in the proceedings in both the district court and in the court of appeal. Proceedings in the general administrative courts are in writing; i.e. the court determines the case on the basis of correspondences between the parties. Nevertheless, it is also possible to hold a hearing. The cases are determined by a single judge or one judge and three lay judges. In the administrative court of appeal, cases are normally heard by three judges or three judges and two lay judges.

Those who lack the means to take advantage of their rights are entitled to legal aid. Everyone suspected of a serious crime or taken into custody has the right to a public counsel (advocate). The title advocate can only be used by accredited members of the Swedish Bar Association. Qualifying as an advocate requires extensive theoretical and practical training. All advocates in Sweden are employed in the private sector.

The control over the way in which public authorities fulfil their commitments is exercised by the Parliamentary Ombudsmen and the Chancellor of Justice. In 2000–01 the Ombudsmen received 4,664 cases altogether, of which 133 were instituted on their own initiative. Sweden has no constitutional court. However, in each particular case the courts do have a certain right to ascertain whether a statute meets the standards set out by superordinate provisions.

The population in penal institutions in Oct. 2002 was 6,506 (73 per 100,000 of national population). There are 55 prisons spread throughout the country.

There were 166 reported murders in 2001 (121 in 1990 and 175 in 2000).

In June 2003 Sweden agreed to accommodate the prison term of Blijana Plavšić, the ex-president of the Republika Srpska in Bosnia-Herzegovina, who was sentenced to 11 years for crimes against humanity by the International War Crimes Tribunal at the Hague.

Religion. The Swedish Lutheran Church was disestablished in 2000. It is headed by Archbishop Karl Gustav Hammar (b. 1943) and has its metropolitan see at Uppsala. In 1996 there were 13 bishoprics and 2,544 parishes. The clergy are chiefly supported from the parishes and the proceeds of the church lands. Around 87% of the population, equivalent to 7·7m. people, belong to the Church of Sweden. Other denominations, in 2001: Pentecostal Movement, 89,482 members; The Mission Covenant Church of Sweden, 65,299; InterAct, 28,955; Salvation Army, 19,745; Örebro Missionary Society (1996), 22,801; The Baptist Union of Sweden, 18,003; Swedish Evangelical Mission, 17,283; Swedish Alliance Missionary Society, 12,868; Holiness Mission (1996), 6,393. There were also 95,000 Roman Catholics (under a Bishop resident at Stockholm). The Orthodox and Oriental churches number around 98,500 members.

There were around 250,000 Muslims and 18,000 Jews in Sweden in 1998, making Islam Sweden's second largest religion.

Education. In 2002–03 there were 710,140 pupils in primary education (grades 1–6 in compulsory comprehensive schools); secondary education at the lower stage (grades 7–9 in compulsory comprehensive schools) comprised 347,085 pupils. In secondary education at the higher stage (the integrated upper secondary school) there were 322,587 pupils in Oct. 2002 (excluding pupils in the fourth year of the technical course regarded as third-level education). The folk high schools, 'people's colleges', had 26,573 pupils on courses of more than 15 weeks in the autumn of 2002.

In municipal adult education there were 287,584 students in 2001–02.

There are also special schools for pupils with visual and hearing handicaps (757 pupils in 2002) and for those who are intellectually disabled (20,941 pupils).

In 2001–02 there were in integrated institutions for higher education 354,636 students enrolled for undergraduate studies. The number of students enrolled for postgraduate studies in 2001 was 18,564.

In 1999–2000 total expenditure on education came to 7·9% of GNP and accounted for 13·6% of total government expenditure. The adult literacy rate in 2001 was at least 99%. In an OECD literacy survey carried out between 1994 and 1999, analysing prose literacy, document literacy and quantitative literacy, Sweden led the world, ahead of Denmark and Norway.

Health. In 2002 there were 25,700 doctors, 4,300 dentists, 78,800 nurses and midwives and 27,925 hospital beds. In 2002 Sweden spent 9·2% of its GDP on health.

In 1998, 19% of Swedes were smokers (males, 22%; females, 17%).

Welfare. Social insurance benefits are granted mainly according to uniform statutory principles. All persons resident in Sweden are covered, regardless of citizenship. All schemes are compulsory, except for unemployment insurance. Benefits are usually income-related. Most social security schemes are at present undergoing extensive discussion and changes.

Type of social insurance scheme	*Payments 2002 (in 1m. kr.)*
Old-age pension	161,228
Sickness insurance	98,734
Unemployment insurance	22,689
Child allowance	21,018
Parental insurance	19,630
Survivor's pension	14,421
Housing supplement	10,514
Attendance allowance	9,767
Work injury insurance	7,273

Under a Pension Reform Plan Sweden is one of the world's leaders in the shift to private pension systems. In the new system each worker's future pension will be based on the amount of money accumulated in two separate individual accounts. The bulk of retirement income will come from a notional account maintained by the government on behalf of the individual, but a significant portion of retirement income will come from a completely private individual account. There are two types of pension—the income pension and the premium pension. The income pension comes under a pay-as-you-go system, with the premium pension being a scheme where contributions are invested in a fund chosen by the insured person.

CULTURE

World Heritage Sites. Sweden has 13 sites on the UNESCO World Heritage List, as follows: the royal palace of Drottningholm (1991); the Viking settlements of Birka and Hovgården (1993); the Engelsberg ironworks (1993); the Bronze Age rock carvings in Tanum (1994); Skogskyrkogården cemetery (1994); the Hanseatic town of Visby (1995); the Lapponian area (home of the Sami people in the Arctic circle) (1996); the church town of Gammelstad in Luleå (1996); the naval port of Karlskrona (1998); the High Coast (located on the west coast of the southern Gulf of Bothnia) (2000); the agricultural landscape of Southern Öland (2000); the Mining Area of the Great Copper Mountain in Falun (2001); and the Varberg Radio Station (2004) at Grimeton in southern Sweden.

Broadcasting. 3,397,000 combined radio and TV reception fees were paid in 2002. There were 8·3m. radio receivers and 5·1m. television sets in 2000. There were 2·0m. cable TV subscribers in 2001. *Sveriges Radio AB* is a non-commercial semi-governmental corporation, transmitting three national programmes and regional programmes. It also broadcasts two TV programmes (colour by PAL). One channel, TV4, is commercial but semi public service, and there are five fully commercial satellite channels, TV3, Kanal 5, TV6, ZTV and TV8.

Cinema. In 2002 there were 1,176 cinemas. Total attendance was 18m. A total of 180 new foreign films and 21 new Swedish films were shown during 2002. In 2002 gross box office receipts came to 1,335m. kr.

Press. In 2002 there were 168 daily newspapers with an average weekday net circulation of 4,064,000. More than 80% of people in Sweden read a daily newspaper. The leading papers in terms of circulation are the tabloid Social Democratic *Aftonbladet*, with average daily sales of 412,000 in 1998; the independent *Dagens Nyheter*, with average daily sales of 361,000 in 1998; the liberal tabloid *Expressen*, with average daily sales of 328,000 in 1998; and the liberal *Göteborgs-Posten*, with average daily sales of 258,000 in 1998. In 2002 a total of 10,092 book titles were published.

Tourism. There were 2,746,000 foreign tourists in 2000, bringing revenue of US$4·11bn. In 2001 foreign visitors stayed 4,926,857 nights in hotels and 964,052 in holiday villages and youth hostels. In 2001 there were 2,618 accommodation establishments with 261,160 beds.

Libraries. In 2002 there were one national library, 329 public libraries, 38 university libraries and 31 special libraries.

Theatre and Opera. State-subsidized theatres gave 13,505 performances for audiences totalling 2,790,232 during 2002. The National Theatre (Kungliga Dramatiska Teatern) and the National Opera (Operan) are both located in Stockholm.

Museums and Galleries. Sweden had 241 public museums and art galleries in 2002 with a combined total of 16,142,330 visits.

DIPLOMATIC REPRESENTATIVES

Of Sweden in the United Kingdom (11 Montagu Pl., London, W1H 2AL)
Ambassador: Staffan Carlsson.

Of the United Kingdom in Sweden (Skarpögatan 6–8, S-115 93 Stockholm)
Ambassador: Anthony Cary, CMG.

Of Sweden in the USA (1501 M Street, NW, Suite 900, Washington, D.C., 20005-1702)
Ambassador: Jan Eliasson.

Of the USA in Sweden (Dag Hammarskjölds Väg 31, S-115 89 Stockholm)
Ambassador: Teel Bivins.

Of Sweden to the United Nations
Ambassador: Anders Lidén.

FURTHER READING

Statistics Sweden. *Statistik Årsbok/Statistical Yearbook of Sweden.—Historisk statistik för Sverige* (Historical Statistics of Sweden). 1955 ff.—*Allmän månadsstatistik* (Monthly Digest of Swedish Statistics).—*Statistiska meddelanden* (Statistical Reports). From 1963

Henrekson, M., *An Economic Analysis of Swedish Government Expenditure*. Aldershot, 1992
Petersson, O., *Swedish Government and Politics*. Stockholm, 1994
Sveriges statskalender. Published by Vetenskapsakademien. Annual, from 1813
Turner, Barry, (ed.) *Scandinavia Profiled.* Macmillan, London, 2000

National library: Kungliga Biblioteket, Stockholm.
National statistical office: Statistics Sweden, PO Box 24300, SE–104 51 Stockholm.
Website: http://www.scb.se/
Swedish Institute Website: http://www.si.se

SWITZERLAND

Schweizerische Eidtgenossenschaft—Confédération Suisse—Confederazione Svizzera[1]

Capital: Berne
Population projection, 2010: 7·09m.
GDP per capita, 2002: (PPP$) 30,010
HDI/world rank: 0·936/11

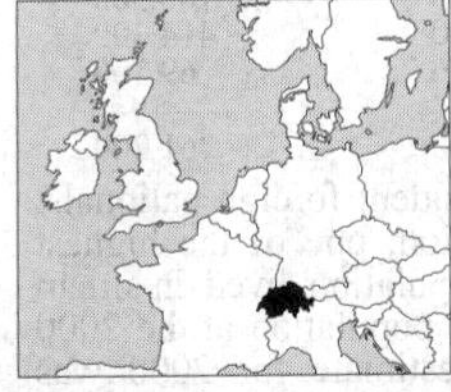

KEY HISTORICAL EVENTS

The history of Switzerland can be traced back to Aug. 1291 when the Uri, Schwyz and Unterwalden entered into a defensive league. In 1353 the league included eight members and in 1515, 13. In 1648 the league became formally independent of the Holy Roman Empire. No addition was made to the number of cantons until 1798 in which year, under the influence of France, the unified Helvetic Republic was formed. This failed to satisfy the Swiss and in 1803 Napoléon granted a new constitution and increased the number of cantons to 19. In 1815 the perpetual neutrality of Switzerland and the inviolability of her territory were guaranteed by Austria, France, Great Britain, Portugal, Prussia, Spain and Sweden, and the Federal Pact, which included three new cantons, was accepted by the Congress of Vienna. In 1848 a new constitution was approved. The 22 cantons set up a federal government (consisting of a federal parliament and a federal council) and a federal tribunal. This constitution, in turn, was on 29 May 1874 superseded by the present constitution, which also combines the federal principle with a national and local use of referendums. Female franchise dates only from Feb. 1971. In a national referendum held in Sept. 1978, 69·9% voted in favour of the establishment of a new canton, Jura, which was established on 1 Jan. 1979.

Switzerland was neutral in both world wars. After the First World War, it joined the League of Nations, which was based in Geneva. But after the Second World War neutrality was thought to conflict with membership of the UN, though Switzerland participates in its agencies, and since 1948 has been a contracting party to the Statute of the International Court of Justice. In March 2001 a referendum on whether to begin immediate talks on joining the European Union was rejected, with 76·7% of voters against. But in a referendum in March 2002 Switzerland did vote to join the UN, with 54·6% of voters in favour of membership.

TERRITORY AND POPULATION

Switzerland is bounded in the west and northwest by France, north by Germany, east by Austria and south by Italy. Area and population by canton (with date of establishment):

Canton	*Area (sq. km) (31 Dec. 1997)*	*Census Population (1 Dec. 1980)*	*Population Estimate (31 Dec. 2001)*
Uri (1291)	1,077	33,883	35,000
Schwyz (1291)	908	97,354	131,400
Obwalden (1291)	491	25,865	32,700
Nidwalden (1291)	276	28,617	38,600
Lucerne (1332)	1,494	296,159	350,600
Zürich (1351)	1,729	1,122,839	1,228,600
Glarus (Glaris) (1352)	685	36,718	38,300
Zug (1352)	239	75,930	100,900
Fribourg (Freiburg) (1481)	1,671	185,246	239,100
Solothurn (Soleure) (1481)	791	218,102	245,500
Basel-Town (Bâle-V.) (1501)	37	203,915	186,700
Basel-Country (Bâle-C.) (1501)	518	219,822	261,400
Schaffhausen (Schaffhouse) (1501)	298	69,413	73,400
Appenzell-Outer Rhoden (1513)	243	47,611	53,200

[1]The Latin 'Confoederatio Helvetica' is also in use.

Canton	*Area (sq. km) (31 Dec. 1997)*	*Census Population (1 Dec. 1980)*	*Population Estimate (31 Dec. 2001)*
Appenzell-Inner Rhoden (1513)	173	12,844	15,000
Berne (1553)	5,959	912,022	947,100
St Gallen (St Gall) (1803)	2,026	391,995	452,600
Graubünden (Grisons) (1803)	7,105	164,641	185,700
Aargau (Argovie) (1803)	1,404	453,442	550,900
Thurgau (Thurgovie) (1803)	991	183,795	228,200
Ticino (Tessin) (1803)	2,812	265,899	311,900
Vaud (Waadt) (1803)	3,212	528,747	626,200
Valais (Wallis) (1815)	5,224	218,707	278,200
Neuchâtel (Neuenburg) (1815)	803	158,368	166,500
Geneva (1815)	282	349,040	414,300
Jura (1979)	838	64,986	69,100
Total	41,284	6,365,960	7,261,200

In 1999 there were 3,663,700 females and 1,406,600 resident foreign nationals. In 2000 foreign nationals made up 19·3% of the population, one of the highest proportions in western Europe. In 2001, 67·5% of the population lived in urban areas. Population density in 1997 was 172 per sq. km. The population at the 2000 census was 7,288,010. The United Nations population estimate for 2000 was 7,173,000.

The UN gives a projected population for 2010 of 7·09m.

German, French and Italian are the official languages; Romansch (spoken mostly in Graubünden), hitherto a national language, was upgraded to 'semi-official' in 1996. German is spoken by the majority of inhabitants in 19 of the 26 cantons, French in Fribourg, Vaud, Valais, Neuchâtel, Jura and Geneva, and Italian in Ticino. At the 1990 census 63·6% of the population gave German as their mother tongue, 19·2% French, 7·6% Italian, 0·6% Romansch and 8·9% other languages. 1997 statistics were 65·0% German, 18·4% French, 9·8% Italian and 0·8% Romansch.

At the end of 2001 the five largest cities were Zürich (340,900); Geneva (176,000); Basle (164,900); Berne (122,500); Lausanne (115,600). At the end of 1999 the population figures of conurbations were: Zürich, 943,400; Geneva, 457,500; Basle, 401,600; Berne, 319,100; Lausanne, 288,100; other towns, 1999 (and their conurbations), Winterthur, 88,000 (119,700); St Gallen, 69,800 (132,500); Lucerne, 57,000 (181,400); Biel, 48,800 (84,200).

SOCIAL STATISTICS

Statistics for calendar years:

	Live births	*Marriages*	*Divorces*	*Deaths*
1997	80,584	39,102	17,073	62,839
1998	78,949	38,683	17,868	62,569
1999	78,408	40,646	20,768	62,503
2000	78,458	39,758	10,511	62,528
2001	73,509	35,987	15,778	61,287

Rates (2001, per 1,000 population): birth, 10·1; death, 8·4; marriage, 4·9; divorce, 2·1. In 2001 the most popular age range for marrying was 30–34 for males and 25–29 for females. Expectation of life, 2001: males, 75·8 years; females, 82·2. Over the period 1990–95 the suicide rate per 100,000 population was 22·7 (men, 34·3; women, 11·6). Annual population growth rate, 1992–02, 0·3%. Infant mortality, 2001, 5 per 1,000 live births; fertility rate, 2001, 1·4 births per woman. In 2002 Switzerland received 26,217 asylum applications, equivalent to 3·7 per 1,000 inhabitants (one of the highest rates of any European country).

CLIMATE

The climate is largely dictated by relief and altitude, and includes continental and mountain types. Summers are generally warm, with quite considerable rainfall; winters are fine, with clear, cold air. Berne, Jan. 32°F (0°C), July, 65°F (18·5°C). Annual rainfall 39·4" (986 mm).

CONSTITUTION AND GOVERNMENT

A new Constitution was accepted on 18 April 1999 in a popular vote and came into effect on 1 Jan. 2000, replacing the constitution dating from 1874. Switzerland is a republic. The highest authority is vested in the electorate, i.e., all Swiss citizens over 18. This electorate, besides electing its representatives to the Parliament, has the voting power on amendments to, or on the revision of, the Constitution as well as on Switzerland joining international organizations for collective security or supranational communities (mandatory referendum). It also takes decisions on laws and certain international treaties if requested by 50,000 voters or eight cantons (facultative referendum), and it has the right of initiating constitutional amendments, the support required for such demands being 100,000 voters (popular initiative). The Swiss vote in more referendums—three or four a year—than any other nation. A mandatory referendum and a Constitutional amendment demanded by popular initiative require a double majority (a majority of the voters and a majority of the cantons voting in favour of the proposal) to be accepted while a facultative referendum is accepted if a majority of the voters vote in favour of the proposal. Between 1971 and 2003, 104 initiatives were put to the vote but only six were adopted. Turn-out dropped from a peak of 64·0% in the 1930s to a low of 40·6% in the 1980s.

The Federal government is responsible for legislating matters of foreign relations, defence (within the framework of its powers), professional education and technical universities, protection of the environment, water, public works, road traffic, nuclear energy, foreign trade, social security, residence and domicile of foreigners, civil law, banking and insurance, monetary policy and economic development. It is also responsible for formulating policy concerning statistics gathering, sport, forests, fishery and hunting, post and telecommunications, radio and television, private economic activity, competition policy, alcohol and gambling.

The legislative authority is vested in a parliament of two chambers: the Council of States (*Ständerat/Conseil des États*) and the National Council (*Nationalrat/Conseil National*). The Council of States is composed of 46 members, chosen and paid by the 23 cantons of the Confederation, two for each canton. The mode of their election and the term of membership depend on the canton. Three of the cantons are politically divided—Basle into Town and Country, Appenzell into Outer-Rhoden and Inner-Rhoden, and Unterwalden into Obwalden and Nidwalden. Each of these 'half-cantons' sends one member to the State Council. The Swiss parliament is a militia/semi-professional parliament.

The National Council has 200 members directly elected for four years, in proportion to the population of the cantons, with the proviso that each canton or half-canton is represented by at least one member. The members are paid from federal funds. The parliament sits for at least four ordinary three-week sessions annually. Extraordinary sessions can be held if necessary and if demanded by the Federal Council, 25% of the National Council or five cantons.

The 200 seats are distributed among the cantons according to population size:

Zürich	34	Basel-Town (Bâle-V.)	5
Berne	26	Graubünden (Grisons)	5
Vaud (Waadt)	18	Neuchâtel (Neuenburg)	5
Aargau (Argovie)	15	Schwyz	4
St Gallen (St Gall)	12	Zug	3
Geneva	11	Jura	2
Lucerne	10	Schaffhausen (Schaffhouse)	2
Ticino (Tessin)	8	Appenzell Inner-Rhoden	1
Basel-Country (Bâle-C.)	7	Appenzell Outer-Rhoden	1
Fribourg (Freiburg)	7	Glarus	1
Solothurn (Soleure)	7	Nidwalden	1
Valais (Wallis)	7	Obwalden	1
Thurgau (Thurgovie)	6	Uri	1

A general election takes place by ballot every four years. Every citizen of the republic who has entered on his 18th year is entitled to a vote, and any voter may be elected a deputy. Laws passed by both chambers may be submitted to direct popular vote, when 50,000 citizens or eight cantons demand it; the vote can be only 'Yes' or 'No'. This principle, called the *referendum*, is frequently acted on.

The chief executive authority is deputed to the *Bundesrat*, or Federal Council, consisting of seven members, elected for four years by the *United Federal Assembly*, i.e., joint sessions of both chambers, such as to represent both the different geographical regions and language communities. The members of this council must not hold any other office in the Confederation or cantons, nor engage in any calling or business. In the Federal Parliament legislation may be introduced either by a member, or by either chamber, or by the Federal Council (but not by the people). Every citizen who has a vote for the National Council is eligible to become a member of the executive.

The *President* of the Federal Council (called President of the Confederation) and the Vice-President are the first magistrates of the Confederation. Both are elected by the United Federal Assembly for one calendar year from among the Federal Councillors, and are not immediately re-eligible to the same offices. The Vice-President, however, may be, and usually is, elected to succeed the outgoing President.

The seven members of the Federal Council act as ministers, or chiefs of the seven administrative departments of the republic. The city of Berne is the seat of the Federal Council and the central administrative authorities.

National Anthem. 'Trittst im Morgenrot daher'/'Sur nos monts quand le soleil'/'Quando il ciel' di porpora' ('Step into the rosy dawn'); German words by Leonard Widmer, French by C. Chatelanat, Italian by C. Valsangiacomo, tune by Alberik Zwyssig.

RECENT ELECTIONS

In elections to the *National Council* on 19 Oct. 2003 the Swiss People's Party/Democratic Centre Union (SPPDCU) took 26·6% of the vote (55 seats), the Social Democratic Party of Switzerland (SPS) took 23·4% (52), the Radicals (FDP) took 17·3% (36), the Christian Democratic People's Party (CVP) took 14·4% (28), the Greens took 7·4% (13), the Protestant People's Party took 2·3% (3), the Liberal Party took 2·2% (4), the Federal Democratic Union took 1·3% (2) and the Swiss Labour Party took 0·7% (2 seats). The following parties won one seat each: the Swiss Democrats, the League of Ticinesians, Solidarities, the Christian Social Party and the Socialist Green Alternative of Zug. Turn-out was 45·6%.

In the Council of States the CVP hold 15 seats, the FDP 14, the SPS 9 and the SPPDCU 8.

At an election held in the United Federal Assembly on 9 Dec. 2004 Samuel Schmid was elected president and Moritz Leuenberger was elected vice-president.

CURRENT ADMINISTRATION

In March 2005 the Federal Council comprised:

President of the Confederation and Chief of the Department of Defence, Civil Protection and Sports: Samuel Schmid; b. 1947 (SPPDCU; sworn in 1 Jan. 2005).

Vice President and Chief of the Department of Transport, Communications and Energy: Moritz Leuenberger; b. 1946 (SPS; sworn in 1 Jan. 2005).

Minister of Economic Affairs: Joseph Deiss. *Foreign Affairs:* Micheline Calmy-Rey (SPS). *Home Affairs:* Pascal Couchepin (FDP). *Justice and Police:* Christoph Blocher (SVP). *Finance:* Hans-Rudolf Merz (FDP).

Federal Authorities Website: http://www.admin.ch

DEFENCE

There are fortifications in all entrances to the Alps and on the important passes crossing the Alps and the Jura. Large-scale destruction of bridges, tunnels and defiles are prepared for an emergency.

In 2003 military expenditure totalled US$3,486m. (US$475 per capita), representing 1·1% of GDP.

Army. There are about 2,000 regular soldiers, but some 380,000 conscripts undergo training annually (15 weeks recruit training at 20; 10 refresher courses of 19 days every two years between 21 and 42). Proposals ('Army 95') implemented in 1995 envisaged an Armed Forces based on the three areas of promoting peace, defence and general civil affairs support. Troop levels will gradually be cut to 120,000.

The administration of the Swiss Army is partly in the hands of the Cantonal authorities, who can promote officers up to the rank of captain. In peacetime the Army has no general; in time of war the Federal Assembly in joint session of both Houses appoints a general.

In 1999 for the first time a small Swiss contingent was deployed outside the country, in Kosovo, but without arms and under the protection of Austrian troops.

Navy. The Army includes a Marine force with patrol boats.

Air Force. The Air Force has three flying regiments. The fighter squadrons are equipped with Swiss-built F-5E Tiger IIs and Mirage IIIS/RS. Personnel (2002), 30,600 on mobilization, with 138 combat aircraft.

INTERNATIONAL RELATIONS

Switzerland is a member of the UN, WTO, BIS, OECD, the Council of Europe and the NATO Partnership for Peace, OSCE, EFTA, CERN, Inter-American Development Bank, Asian Development Bank, IOM, Antarctic Treaty and the International Organization of the Francophonie. In a referendum in 1986 the electorate voted against UN membership, but in a further referendum on 4 March 2002, 54·6% of votes cast were in favour of joining. Switzerland officially became a member at the UN's General Assembly in Sept. 2002. An official application for membership of the EU was made in May 1992, but in Dec. 1992 the electorate voted against joining the European Economic Area. At a referendum in March 2001, 76·7% of voters rejected membership talks with the EU, with just 23·3% in favour; turn-out was 55·1%. However, the government reaffirmed plans to begin entry talks by 2007.

ECONOMY

Services account for about 64% of GDP, industry 34% and agriculture 2%.

According to the anti-corruption organization *Transparency International*, Switzerland ranked 7th in the world in a 2004 survey of the countries with the least corruption in business and government. It received 9·1 out of 10 in the annual index.

Overview. Switzerland is a small but open economy with one of the highest living standards in the world. Owing to a lack of raw materials, prosperity is built on labour skills and technological expertise. Earnings from services include tourism and banking. High labour costs and product market rigidities in the sheltered economy pose problems of competitiveness. In 2000 the National Bank introduced a monetary policy framework, aiming at keeping inflation below 2%. Monetary independence is crucial to Switzerland, as it permits lower interest rates than those prevailing in the euro zone to give Swiss companies a competitive advantage.

Currency. The unit of currency is the *Swiss franc* (CHF) of 100 *centimes* or *Rappen*. Foreign exchange reserves were US$33,309m. and gold reserves 66·24m. troy oz in June 2002 (83·28m. troy oz in March 2000). Inflation was 0·6% in 2002 and 2003, and 0·8% in 2004. Total money supply in June 2002 was 171,584m. Swiss francs.

Budget. Revenue and expenditure of the Confederation, in 1m. Swiss francs, for calendar years:

	1999	*2000*	*2001*	*2002*	*2003*
Revenue	45,656	47,132	50,215	50,722	49,962
Expenditure	43,016	51,683	49,114	47,405	47,161

VAT is 7·6%, with reduced rates of 3·6% and 2·4%.

Performance. Total GDP was US$309·5bn. in 2003. Real GDP growth in 1999 was 1·3%, but in 2000 growth reached 3·6%, the highest for ten years. For 2001 growth of 1·0% was recorded. In 2002 growth was just 0·4%, followed by a recession with the economy contracting by 0·4% in 2003.

Banking and Finance. The National Bank, with headquarters divided between Berne and Zürich, opened on 20 June 1907. It has the exclusive right to issue banknotes. The *Chairman* is Jean-Pierre Roth.

On 31 Dec. 2000 there were 375 banks with total assets of 2,124,880m. Swiss francs. They included 24 cantonal banks, three big banks, 103 regional and saving banks, one *Raiffeisen* (consisting of 537 member banks) and 244 other banks. The number of banks has come down from over 495 in 1990. In 2004 the largest banks in order of market capitalization were UBS (US$79·2bn.) and Crédit Suisse Groupe (US$37·2bn.). UBS ranks third in Europe by market capitalization. Banking and finance is one of Switzerland's most successful industries, and contributes 7·1%

of the country's GDP and 11·2% of the GDP's added values (1998). Switzerland is the capital of the offshore private banking industry. It is reckoned that a third of the internationally invested private assets worldwide are managed by Swiss banks.

Money laundering was made a criminal offence in Aug. 1990. Complete secrecy about clients' accounts remains intact, but anonymity was abolished in July 1991.

The stock exchange system has been reformed under federal legislation of 1990 on securities trading and capital market services. The four smaller exchanges have been closed and activity concentrated on the major exchanges of Zürich, Basle and Geneva, which harmonized their operations with the introduction of the Swiss Electronic Exchange (EBS) in Dec. 1995. Zürich is a major international insurance centre.

In Aug. 1998 Crédit Suisse and UBS AG agreed a deal to pay US$1·25bn. (£750m.) to Holocaust survivors over a three-year-period in an out-of-court settlement. The deal brought to an end the issue of money left in Holocaust victims' Swiss Bank accounts which were allowed to remain dormant after the war.

ENERGY AND NATURAL RESOURCES

Environment. In 2002 carbon dioxide emissions from the consumption and flaring of fossil fuels were the equivalent of 6·2 tonnes per capita. An *Environmental Sustainability Index* compiled for the World Economic Forum meeting in Feb. 2002 ranked Switzerland fifth in the world, with 66·5%. The index measured the ability of countries to maintain favourable environmental conditions and examined various factors including pollution levels and the use or abuse of natural resources.

Switzerland is the world leader in recycling. In 1998, 52% of all household waste was recycled, including 91% of glass and 89% of aluminium cans (in both cases the highest percentage of any country).

Electricity. The Energy 2000 programme aims to stabilize consumption. Installed capacity was 18·0m. kW in 2000. Production was 68·7bn. kWh in 2000. 35·9% of energy produced in 1999 was hydro-electric from storage power stations, 35·6% nuclear, 35·9% hydro-electric from storage power stations, 25·6% hydro-electric from turbine power stations and 3·8% from conventional thermal. In Sept. 1990, 54% of citizens voted for a ten-year moratorium on the construction of new nuclear plants. There are currently five nuclear reactors in use. Consumption per capita in 2000 was 8,504 kWh.

Minerals. Approximately 6,000 people work in mining and quarrying. Salt production, 1997: 400,000 tonnes.

Agriculture. The country is self-sufficient in wheat and meat. Agriculture is protected by subsidies, price guarantees and import controls. Farmers are guaranteed an income equal to industrial workers. Agriculture occupied 4·0% of the total workforce in 2002. In 1999 there were 293,949 ha of open arable land, 115,933 ha of cultivated grassland and 608,798 ha of natural grassland and pastures. In 1999 there were 12,921 ha of vineyards. In 1999 there were 73,591 farms (41% in mountain or hill regions), of which 5,258 were under 1 ha, 18,154 over 20 ha, and 23,300 in part-time use (1996). In 2001 there were 412,000 ha of arable land and 24,000 ha of permanent crops. Approximately 7·8% of all agricultural land is used for organic farming—one of the highest proportions in the world.

Area harvested, 1999 (in 1,000 ha): cereals, 182; coarse grains, 89; sugarbeets, 17; potatoes, 14. Production, 2000 (in 1,000 tonnes): sugarbeets, 1,410; potatoes, 584; wheat, 548; barley, 273; maize, 209; carrots, 56; rapeseed, 39. Fruit production (in 1,000 tonnes) in 2000 was: apples, 380; grapes, 165; pears, 130. Wine is produced in 25 of the cantons. In 2000 vineyards produced 128,000 tonnes of wine.

Livestock, 2000: cattle, 1,600,000; pigs, 1,450,000; horses, 45,000; sheep, 450,000; goats, 65,000; chickens, 7m. Livestock products, 2000 (in 1,000 tonnes): meat, 415; milk, 3,910; cheese, 155.

Forestry. The forest area was 1·20m. ha in 2000 (30·3% of the land area). In 2001, 5·0m. cu. metres of roundwood were cut.

Fisheries. Total catch, 2001, 1,715 tonnes, exclusively freshwater fish.

INDUSTRY

The leading companies by market capitalization in Switzerland, excluding banking and finance, in May 2004 were: Novartis AG (US$125·5bn.), a pharmaceuticals company; Nestlé SA (US$104·9bn.), a world leader in food and beverages; and Roche AG (US$95·9bn.), a healthcare company.

The chief food producing industries, based on Swiss agriculture, are the manufacture of cheese, butter, sugar and meat. Among the other industries, the manufacture of textiles, clothing and footwear, chemicals and pharmaceutical products, the production of machinery (including electrical machinery and scientific and optical instruments) and watch and clock making are the most important. The leading industries in 1998 in terms of value added (in 1m. Swiss francs) were: non-electrical machinery and transport equipment, 20,757; chemicals and chemical products, 13,026; fabricated metal products, 8,143; food, 5,667; electrical machinery, 4,883.

Labour. In 2002 the total working population was 3,634,000, of whom 690,000 people were in manufacturing, 624,000 in trade, 398,000 in property, renting and business activities, and 397,000 in health and social services. In Feb. 2004 the unemployment rate stood at 4·2%; in the canton of Uri the rate was just 1·4%. In 1997, 86% of men and 69% of women between the ages of 15 and 64 were in employment. No other major industrialized nation had such a high percentage of men in employment.

The foreign labour force with permit of temporary residence was 939,000 in Aug. 1995 (326,600 women). Of these 261,400 were Italian, 146,700 Yugoslav, 108,600 French, 103,400 Portuguese and 89,600 German. In 1997 approximately 800,000 EU citizens worked in Switzerland.

Trade Unions. The Swiss Federation of Trade Unions had about 419,000 members in 1996.

INTERNATIONAL TRADE

Legislation of 1991 increased the possibilities of foreign ownership of domestic companies.

Imports and Exports. Imports and exports, excluding gold (bullion and coins) and silver (coins), were (in 1m. Swiss francs):

	1997	*1998*	*1999*	*2000*	*2001*
Imports	110,087	115,847	120,057	139,402	141,889
Exports	110,417	114,055	120,725	136,015	138,492

In 2001 the EU accounted for 76·2% of imports (108·2bn. Swiss francs) and 60·0% of exports (83·1bn. Swiss francs). Main import suppliers in 2001 (share of total trade): Germany, 30·1%; France, 10·3%; Italy, 9·4%; USA, 5·9%; UK, 5·8%. Main export markets: Germany, 21·7%; USA, 11·3%; France, 8·9%; Italy, 8·0%; UK, 5·5%.

Main imports in 2001 (in 1m. Swiss francs): consumer goods, 51,805; equipment goods, 36,435; raw materials and semi-manufactures, 35,392.

Main exports in 2001 (in 1m. Swiss francs): chemicals, 41,833; machinery and electronics, 36,022; precision instruments, clocks and watches and jewellery, 21,641.

COMMUNICATIONS

Roads. In 2002 there were 71,212 km of roads, comprising 1,706 km of motorways, 18,109 km of cantonal roads and 51,397 km of local roads. Motor vehicles in 2002 (in 1,000): passenger cars, 3,701; commercial vehicles, 290; buses, 17; motorcycles and mopeds, 745. Goods transport by road, 2001, totalled 23,500m. tonne-km. There were 75,351 road accidents (23,737 accidents involving personal injury) in 2000 with 592 fatalities. In 1990 there had been 954 fatalities.

Rail. In 2000 the length of the general traffic railways was 5,057 km, of which the Swiss Federal Railways (SBB) 2,973 km. In 2002 the Federal Railway carried 320·3m. passengers and 54·9m. tonnes of freight. In 2000 work began on what is set to be the world's longest rail tunnel—the 58-km long tunnel under the Gotthard mountain range in the Alps linking Erstfeld and Bodio. The tunnel is scheduled to open in 2015. There are tram/light rail networks in Basle, Berne, Geneva, Lausanne, Neuchâtel and Zürich. There are many other lines, the most important of which are the Berne–Lötschberg–Simplon (114 km) and Rhaetian (377 km) networks.

Civil Aviation. There are international airports at Basle (Euroairport, which also serves Mulhouse in France), Berne (Belp), Geneva (Cointrin), Lugano and Zürich. Swissair, the former national carrier, faced collapse and grounded flights in Oct. 2001. In 1998 it flew 218·8m. km, carrying 12,144,500 passengers (11,163,200 on international flights). In April 2002 a successor airline, swiss, took over as the national carrier. Services were also provided in 2003 by over 80 foreign airlines. Zürich is the busiest airport, handling 22,446,000 passengers in 2000 (21,192,000 on international flights) and 395,100 tonnes of freight. Geneva handled 7,677,000 passengers (6,604,000 on international flights) and 36,300 tonnes of freight in 2000.

Shipping. In 1997 there were 1,214 km of navigable waterways. 12·3m. tonnes of freight were transported. A merchant marine was created in 1941, the place of registry of its vessels being Basle. In 2002 it totalled 559,000 GRT.

Telecommunications. Switzerland had 11,069,000 telephone subscribers in 2002 (1,520·2 per 1,000 persons) and there were 4,225,000 PCs in use, equivalent to 580·3 per 1,000 population—one of the highest rates in the world. Mobile phone subscribers numbered 5,747,000 in 2002 and there were 207,000 fax machines in 1996. There were 3·85m. Internet users in June 2002.

Postal Services. In 1996 there were 3,630 post offices, or one for every 1,950 persons.

SOCIAL INSTITUTIONS

Justice. The Federal Court, which sits at Lausanne, consists of 30 judges and 30 supplementary judges, elected by the Federal Assembly for six years and eligible for re-election; the President and Vice-President serve for two years and re-election is not practised. The Tribunal has original and final jurisdiction in suits between the Confederation and cantons; between different cantons; between the Confederation or cantons and corporations or individuals; between parties who refer their case to it; or in suits which the constitution or legislation of cantons places within its authority. It is a court of appeal against decisions of other federal authorities, and of cantonal authorities applying federal laws. The Tribunal comprises two courts of public law, two civil courts, a chamber of bankruptcy, a chamber of prosecution, a court of criminal appeal, a court of extraordinary appeal and a federal criminal court.

A Federal Insurance Court sits in Lucerne, and comprises nine judges and nine supplementary judges elected for six years by the Federal Assembly.

A federal penal code replaced cantonal codes in 1942. It abolished capital punishment except for offences in wartime; this latter proviso was abolished in 1992.

The population in penal institutions in Sept. 2002 was 4,987 (68 per 100,000 of national population).

Religion. There is liberty of conscience and of creed. At the 2000 census 41·8% of the population were Roman Catholic, 35·3% Protestant and 11·1% without religion. In 2000 the figures were estimated to be: Roman Catholics, 3,048,000; Protestants, 2,569,000; other, 1,671,000. In Sept. 2003 the Roman Catholic church had three cardinals.

Education. Education is administered by the confederation, cantons and communes and is free and compulsory for nine years. Compulsory education consists of four years (Basel-Town and Vaud), five years (Aargau, Basel-Country, Neuchâtel and Ticino) or six years (other cantons) of primary education, and the balance in Stage I secondary education. This is followed by three to five years of Stage II secondary education in general or vocational schools. Tertiary education is at universities, universities of applied science, higher vocational schools and advanced vocational training institutes.

In 1999–2000 there were 157,751 children in pre-primary schools. There were 807,101 pupils in compulsory education (475,044 at primary, 283,317 at lower secondary and 48,740 at special schools), 94,481 in Stage II general secondary education and 208,497 in Stage II vocational education, and 116,511 students in higher education, including 95,657 students at universities and 16,749 at universities of applied sciences.

There are ten universities (date of foundation and students in 1999–2000): Basle (1460, 7,783), Berne (1528, 10,127), Fribourg (1889, 8,900), Geneva (1559, 12,873), Lausanne (1537, 9,762), Lucerne (16th century, 251); Neuchâtel (1866, 3,256), St Gallen (1899, 4,549), Ticino (1996, 1,191), Zürich (1523, 20,360); and three institutions of equivalent status: St Gallen PHS (1867, 312), Federal Institute of Technology Lausanne (1853, 4,841), Federal Institute of Technology Zürich (1854, 11,492). The seven universities of applied sciences were founded in 1997. Enrolment figures for 1999–2000 were: Berne, 2,416; Western Switzerland, 4,236; Northwestern Switzerland, 2,266; Central Switzerland, 1,009; Ticino, 658; Eastern Switzerland, 1,748; Zürich, 4,416.

In 1998 total expenditure on education came to 20,759m. Swiss francs. In 1999–2000 total expenditure on education came to 5·2% of GNP and accounted for 15·2% of total government expenditure. The adult literacy rate in 2001 was at least 99%.

Health. In 1998 there were an estimated 23,700 doctors (one for every 301 persons) and there were 1,651 pharmacies. There were 3,470 dentists in 1998. Hospital bed provision in 1998 was 64 for every 10,000 persons. In 1998 the Swiss smoked an average 2,734 cigarettes per person. In 2002 Switzerland spent 11·2% of its GDP on health—the highest percentage of any European country. Although active euthanasia is illegal in Switzerland, doctors may help patients die if they have given specific consent.

Welfare. The Federal Insurance Law against accident and illness, of 13 June 1911, entitled all citizens to insurance against illness; foreigners could also be admitted to the benefits. Major reform of the law was ratified in 1994 and came into effect in 1996, making it compulsory for all citizens. Subsidies are paid by the Confederation and the Cantons only for insured persons with low incomes. Also compulsory are the Old-Age and Survivors' Insurance (OASI, since 1948), Invalidity Insurance (II, since 1960) and Accident Insurance (1984/1996). Unemployment Insurance (1984) and Occupational benefit plans (Second Pillar, 1985) are compulsory for employees only.

The following amounts (in 1m. Swiss francs) were paid in social security benefits:

	1996	*1997*	*1998*
Federal Old-Age Pensions	24,817	25,803	26,731
Federal Invalidity Insurance	7,313	7,652	7,965
Supplementary Benefits (OASI/II)	1,326	1,376	1,420
Occupational benefit plans	26,110[1]	27,300	28,688[1]
Loss of Earnings Insurance	621	582	558
Unemployment Insurance	6,124	8,028[2]	6,208[2]
Family Allowances	4,100	4,263	4,316
Sickness Insurance	17,192	17,672	18,403
Accident Insurance for employees	5,887	6,060	5,975

[1]Federal Office for Social Insurances estimate. [2]Provisional.

CULTURE

World Heritage Sites. There are six sites in Switzerland that appear on the UNESCO World Heritage List. They are (with the year entered on list): the Abbey-Cathedral of St Gallen (1983), the 9th-century Benedictine convent of St John at Müstair (1983), the Old City of Berne (1983), the three castles and city walls of Bellinzona (2000), the Jungfrau-Aletsch-Bietschhorn mountain region (2001) and Monte San Giorgio (2003).

Broadcasting. Schweizerische Radio- und Fernsehgesellschaft/Société Suisse de Radiodiffusion et Télévision/Società Svizzera di Radiotelevisione is a non-profit-making company responsible for radio and television services. There are German, French and Italian radio and TV networks (colour by PAL). The German radio service has three programmes, local programmes and also broadcasts in Romansch; the French service ('Suisse Romande') has three programmes, as does the Italian. There is an external service, Swiss Radio International (Arabic, English, Spanish) and four city-based private stations. The UN and the Red Cross have radio stations. There were 4·0m. TV sets in use in 2001 and 7·2m. radio receivers in 2000. More than 90% of households have cable TV—in 1999 there were 2·62m. TV licences altogether and 2·39m. cable TV subscribers.

Cinema. There were 482 cinemas in 1999; total attendance for the year was 15·4m. 75 films were produced in 1999.

Press. There were 78 daily newspapers in 2000 with a total circulation of 2,628,600 (365 per 1,000 population). There were 120 non-daily papers with a combined circulation of 1,196,000 in 1999 (168 per 1,000 population). 13,694 book titles were published in 1999.

Tourism. Tourism is an important industry. In 2000 there were 11,400,000 foreign tourists staying in hotels and health establishments, bringing revenue of US$7·3bn. In 1999 overnight stays by tourists totalled 67,772,000. 12·01m. Swiss citizens travelled abroad in 1999.

Festivals. The Lucerne Festival is one of Europe's leading cultural events and since 2001 has been split into three festivals: Ostern during Lent, Sommer in Aug.–Sept. and Piano in Nov. The 2002 festivals were attended by a total of 102,800 people.

Libraries. In 1999 there was one National library with 3,109,000 volumes and 12,466 registered users, and 34 non-specialized libraries with 8,886,000 volumes and 472,217 users. In 1998 there were nine higher education libraries with 23,090,000 volumes and 186,232 users; and in 1998 approximately 6,000 libraries in total.

Museums and Galleries. In 1999 there were 929 museums.

DIPLOMATIC REPRESENTATIVES

Of Switzerland in the United Kingdom (16–18 Montagu Pl., London, W1H 2BQ)
Ambassador: Alexis P. Lautenberg.

Of the United Kingdom in Switzerland (Thunstrasse 50, 3005 Berne)
Ambassador: Simon Featherstone.

Of Switzerland in the USA (2900 Cathedral Ave., NW, Washington, D.C., 20008)
Ambassador: Christian Blickenstorfer.

Of the USA in Switzerland (Jubilaeumstrasse 93, 3005, Berne)
Ambassador: Pamela P. Willeford.

Of Switzerland to the United Nations
Ambassador: Peter Maurer.

Of Switzerland to the European Union
Ambassador: Dante Martinelli.

FURTHER READING

Office Fédéral de la Statistique. *Annuaire Statistique de la Suisse.*

Butler, Michael, Pender, Malcolm and Charnley, Joy, *Making of Modern Switzerland, 1848–1998.* Macmillan, Basingstoke, 2000

Church, Clive, *Politics and Government of Switzerland.* Palgrave Macmillan, Basingstoke, 2003

Kriesi, Hanspeter, Farago, Peter, Kohli, Martin and Zarin-Nejadan, Milad, *Contemporary Switzerland.* Palgrave Macmillan, Basingstoke, 2005

New, M., *Switzerland Unwrapped: Exposing the Myths.* London, 1997

National library: Bibliothèque Nationale Suisse, Hallwylstr. 15, 3003 Berne.
National statistical office: Office Fédéral de la Statistique, Espace de l'Europe 10, 2010 Neuchâtel.
SFSO Information Service e-mail: *information@bfs.admin.ch*
Website: http://www.statistik.admin.ch

SYRIA

Jumhuriya al-Arabya as-Suriya (Syrian Arab Republic)

Capital: Damascus
Population projection, 2010: 20·84m.
GDP per capita, 2002: (PPP$) 3,620
HDI/world rank: 0·710/106

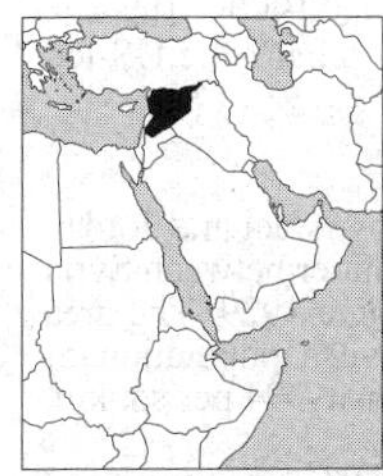

KEY HISTORICAL EVENTS

Ancient Syria, an area including modern Israel, Lebanon and Jordan, witnessed some of the world's earliest civilizations, such as Semitic Ebla, which flourished in the 25th century BC near Aleppo. Subsequent centuries brought Mesopotamian influences and empires, including the Akkadians and Ur. The Amorite cities were overrun by the Hittites in the mid-2nd millennium BC before the establishment of the Hurrian kingdom of Mitanni, destroyed by Hittite and Egyptian conflict over the Fertile Crescent. Aramaean kingdoms were harried by warfare with Assyria, which extended its empire from the northeast in the 9th century BC. Immigration of Cimmerians and Scythians in the 7th century broke Assyrian hegemony, which was followed by Babylonian rule.

The Persian King Cyrus defeated Babylon in 539 BC, returning the enslaved Israelites to Jerusalem. Persian rule in turn fell to the onslaught of Alexander the Great in the 4th century BC. His Greek successors—Seleucids and Ptolomies—ruled Syria until the expansion of Rome in the early 2nd century BC. Syria became a Roman province in 64 BC. The Greek cities of the interior (the Decapolis) were rebuilt, including Damascus. Palmyra (Tadmur), an important city on the trade routes to the Euphrates, rose against Rome under Queen Zenobia but was defeated in 272 AD. Syria became an important frontier zone under Diocletian, who established lines of defences (*limes*) against eastern invaders. Syria's cities, such as Edessa, contained the earliest Christian communities; Antioch, where St Peter preached, was made a patriarchate in 451.

Syria continued to prosper under Byzantium until the Persian invasions of the 6th century. Emperor Heraclius' victory over the Persians in the 620s was short-lived as Muslim Arab forces triumphed at the Battle of the Yarmuk River in 636. Damascus became the capital of the Umayyad Caliphate in 661, though Christians and Jews were tolerated. The collapse of the Umayyads led to the establishment of the Abbasid Caliphate in Baghdad in 750. The Abbasids' successors were defeated by a resurgent Byzantium in 969 and the Seljuk Turks in 1085. However, in 1098 Edessa and Antioch were taken by Christian crusaders and Jerusalem in 1099. Zengi of Mosul recovered much of Syria in the 12th century, paving the way for the empire-building of Saladin. Mongol invasions from 1260 were repelled by the Egyptian Mamluks, who removed the last crusaders from the Holy Land in 1302. The Mamluk state survived until defeat at the hands of the Ottoman Turks in 1516 and Syria became part of a Levantine empire.

An Egyptian insurrection in Syria was defeated in 1840 with European intervention. Turko-Arab relations deteriorated in the early 20th century until the British and French defeated the Ottomans in 1918. Faisal ibn Husayn of Mecca became king of Syria in March 1920 but was evicted by France, who took control of the Syrian mandate. The separation of Lebanon, Palestine and Transjordan reduced Syria to its modern borders. During the Second World War the French Vichy government's forces were defeated by the British and Free French and elections were held in 1943. The nationalist Shukri al-Kuwatli was elected president and European forces withdrew in 1946.

A series of military coups between 1949–54 interrupted civilian government. A pact with the USSR in 1956 took second place to the Pan-Arabism that led to union with Egypt in Feb. 1958. However, Syrian discontent led to secession in Sept. 1961. The 1963 coup brought the Ba'athists (Arab Renaissance Party) to power. The Syrian Ba'athists split from the Iraqi Ba'athists, creating serious tensions between the two countries and Syrian support for Iran. War with Israel in 1967 resulted in the loss of the Golan Heights. Lieut.-Gen. Hafez al-Assad seized power in 1970. He was elected president in 1971 and embarked on a 'corrective movement' to crack down on corruption. Domestic opposition to the Alawite (Shia sect) regime was suppressed; the Sunni fundamentalist Muslim Brotherhood was brutally destroyed along with the city of Hamah in 1982. Syrian forces invaded Lebanon in 1976 to prevent a Palestinian victory over the Maronite Christians. Syrian influence remained strong in Lebanon despite Israeli victories in the country.

Assad joined the international coalition against the Iraqi occupation of Kuwait in 1991 and engaged in unsuccessful direct talks with Israel in the 1990s. He was succeeded on his death in 2000 by his son, Bashar, who refused to back the US-led invasion of Iraq in 2003.

TERRITORY AND POPULATION

Syria is bounded by the Mediterranean and Lebanon in the west, by Israel and Jordan in the south, by Iraq in the east and by Turkey in the north. The frontier between Syria and Turkey was settled by the Franco-Turkish agreement of 22 June 1929. The area is 185,180 sq. km (71,498 sq. miles). The census of 1994 gave a population of 13,782,000. Estimate (2002), 17,396,000 (51·8% urban, 2001); density, 94 per sq. km.

The UN gives a projected population for 2010 of 20·84m.

Area and population (1996 estimate, in 1,000) of the 14 districts *(mohafaza)*:

	Sq. km	*Population*		*Sq. km*	*Population*
Aleppo (Halab)	18,500	3,694	Homs (Hims)	42,223	1,471
Damascus City	105	1,347	Idlib	6,097	1,270
Damascus District	18,032	1,237	Lattakia (Ladhiqiyah)	2,297	936
Dará	3,730	689	Qunaytirah	1,861	330
Deir Ez-Zor	33,060	994	Raqqah	19,616	592
Hamah	8,883	1,415	Suwaydá	5,550	380
Hasakah	23,334	1,013	Tartous	1,892	730

The capital is Damascus (Dimashq), with a 1999 population of 2,270,000. Other principal towns (population, 1994 in 1,000): Aleppo, 1,840 (1995); Homs, 558; Lattakia, 303; Hamah, 273; Al-Kamishli, 165; Raqqah, 138; Deir Ez-Zor, 133.

Arabic is the official language, spoken by 89% of the population, while 6% speak Kurdish (chiefly Hasakah governorate), 3% Armenian and 2% other languages.

SOCIAL STATISTICS

2001 births, estimate, 524,000; deaths, 88,000. Rates, 2001 estimate (per 1,000 population): birth, 30·9; death, 5·2. Infant mortality, 2001 (per 1,000 live births), 23. Expectation of life, 2001, was 70·2 years for males and 72·7 for females. Annual population growth rate, 1992–02, 2·6%. Fertility rate, 2001, 3·8 births per woman.

CLIMATE

The climate is Mediterranean in type, with mild wet winters and dry, hot summers, though there are variations in temperatures and rainfall between the coastal regions and the interior, which even includes desert conditions. The more mountainous parts are subject to snowfall. Damascus, Jan. 38·1°F (3·4°C), July 77·4°F (25·2°C). Annual rainfall 8·8" (217 mm). Aleppo, Jan. 36·7°F (2·6°C), July 80·4°F (26·9°C). Annual rainfall 10·2" (258 mm). Homs, Jan. 38·7°F (3·7°C), July 82·4°F (28°C). Annual rainfall 3·4" (86·7 mm).

CONSTITUTION AND GOVERNMENT

A new Constitution was approved by plebiscite on 12 March 1973 and promulgated on 14 March. It confirmed the Arab Socialist Renaissance *(Ba'ath)* Party, in power since 1963, as the 'leading party in the State and society'. Legislative power is held by a 250-member People's Assembly *(Majlis al-Sha'ab)*, renewed every four years in 15 multi-seat constituencies, in which 167 seats are guaranteed for the Al Jabha al Watniyah at Wahdwamiyah (JWW/National Progressive Front) alliance of parties (i.e. the Ba'ath party and partners). The government is formed by the Ba'ath.

The president is appointed by the Parliament and is confirmed for a seven-year term in a referendum. At a referendum on 10 July 2000 Bashar Al-Assad (b. 1965) was confirmed as *President* following the death of his father, who had been president since 1971.

National Anthem. 'Humata al Diyari al aykum salaam' ('Defenders of the Realm, on you be peace'); words by Khalil Mardam Bey, tune by M. S. and A. S. Flayfel.

RECENT ELECTIONS

Elections were held on 5 March 2003. The ruling National Progressive Front (led by the Ba'ath Party) won 167 of 250 seats and non-partisan candidates the remaining 83. Turn-out was 63%.

CURRENT ADMINISTRATION

Following the death of Lieut.-Gen. Hafiz al-Assad on 10 June 2000, a presidential referendum was held on 10 July 2000. The former president's son Bashar al-Assad won 97·3% of the vote.

President: Bashar al-Assad; b. 1965 (Ba'ath; sworn in 17 July 2000).

Vice-Presidents: Abd al-Halim ibn Said Khaddam, Mohammad Zuhayr Mashariqa.

Prime Minister: Mohammed Naji Al-Otari; b. 1944 (Ba'ath; sworn in 10 Sept. 2003). In March 2005 the government comprised:

Minister of Agriculture: Adel Safar. *Awqaf:* Muhammad Ziyad Al-Ayyoubi. *Communications and Technology:* Bashir al-Munajjed. *Culture:* Mahmoud al-Sayed. *Defence:* Lieut.-Gen. Hassan Turkmani. *Economy and Trade:* Amer Hassan Loutfi. *Education:* Ali Saad. *Electricity:* Munib Sa'm al-Daher. *Expatriates:* Butheina Shaaban. *Finance:* Mohammed al-Hussein. *Foreign Affairs:* Farouk al-Shara. *Health:* Maher Houssami. *Higher Education:* Hani Mortada. *Housing and Building:* Nehad Mushantat. *Industry:* Ghassan Tayyara. *Information:* Mahdi Dakhlallah. *Interior:* Ghazi Kanaan. *Irrigation:* Nader al-Boni. *Justice:* Mohammed Al-Ghafari. *Local Administration and Environment:* Helal al-Atrash. *Oil:* Ibrahim Haddad. *Presidential Affairs:* Ghassan al-Laham. *Social Affairs and Labour:* Diala Al-Hajj Aref. *Tourism:* Saadallah Agha al-Qalaa. *Transport:* Makram Obied.

The President's Website: http://www.assad.org

DEFENCE

Military service is compulsory for a period of 30 months. Defence expenditure in 2003 totalled US$1,522m. (US$88 per capita), representing 7·0% of GDP. According to *Deadly Arsenals*, published by the Carnegie Endowment for International Peace, Syria has a chemical weapons programme and a biological weapons research programme. Syria had 14,000 troops based in Lebanon in early 2005, but in March 2005 the two countries agreed that Syria would begin to redeploy the troops to the Bekaa Valley in the east of the country. They were subsequently all withdrawn from Lebanon.

Army. Strength (2002) about 215,000 (including conscripts) with an additional 280,000 available reservists. In addition there is a gendarmerie of 8,000 and a Workers Militia of approximately 100,000.

Navy. The Navy includes three diesel submarines and two small frigates. A small naval aviation branch of the Air Force operates anti-submarine helicopters. Personnel in 2002 numbered approximately 4,000. The main base is at Tartous.

Air Force. The Air Force, including Air Defence Command, had (2002) about 40,000 personnel, 611 combat aircraft and 90 armed helicopters, including 170 MiG-21, 134 MiG-23, 30 MiG-25 and 22 MiG-29 supersonic interceptors. In addition there were 90 Su-22 and 20 Su-24 fighter-bombers, as well as some MiG-25 reconnaissance aircraft.

INTERNATIONAL RELATIONS

A Treaty of Brotherhood, Co-operation and Co-ordination with Lebanon of May 1991 provides for close relations in the fields of foreign policy, the economy, military affairs and security. By the treaty the Lebanese government's decisions are subject to review by six joint Syrian-Lebanese bodies.

Syria is a member of the UN, the League of Arab States, OIC and Islamic Development Bank.

ECONOMY

In 2002 agriculture accounted for 23·5% of GDP, industry 29·3% and services 47·1%.

Overview. Between 1990–95 economic growth was strong at 5–7%, owing to reform measures taken in the early 1990s and a major oil discovery. Since 1995 economic growth has slowed significantly. Since 2000 growth rates have been low, between 1·5 and 3·5%, which are relatively low given Syria's rate of population growth of 2·6% per annum. The agricultural sector generates 30% of GDP and over half of Syria's export earnings come from crude petroleum. The weak performance of the economy is attributed to an inefficient state-owned banking system and other state-owned enterprises, multiple exchange rates and exchange controls, restrictions on private sector activity, large agricultural subsidies and the pressures of rapid population growth.

Currency. The monetary unit is the *Syrian pound* (SYP) of 100 *piastres*. Inflation was 1·5% in 2002. Gold reserves were 833,000 troy oz in April 2002. Total money supply in Dec. 2001 was £Syr.419,916m.

Budget. Budget revenue and expenditure (in £Syr.1m.):

	1995	*1996*	*1997*	*1998*	*1999*
Revenue	131,002	152,231	179,202	180,437	196,127
Expenditure	141,957	155,596	181,723	185,973	190,300

Performance. There was real GDP growth of 2·7% in 2002; total GDP in 2003 was US$21·5bn.

Banking and Finance. The Central Bank is the bank of issue. Commercial banks were nationalized in 1963. The *Governor* of the Central Bank is Mohammed Bashar Kabarra. In Aug. 2000 it was announced that private banks were to be established for the first time in nearly 40 years and that a stock exchange would be set up for the first time ever. In 2004 there were six foreign private banks.

ENERGY AND NATURAL RESOURCES

Environment. Syria's carbon dioxide emissions from the consumption and flaring of fossil fuels in 2002 were the equivalent of 2·9 tonnes per capita.

Electricity. Installed capacity was 6·0m. kW in 2000. Production in 2000 was approximately 22·63bn. kWh, with consumption per capita an estimated 1,386 kWh.

Oil and Gas. Crude oil production (2003), 29·5m. tonnes. Reserves in 2002 were 2,500m. bbls. Gas reserves (2002), 240bn. cu. metres. Natural gas production (2002), 4·1bn. cu. metres.

Water. In 1992 there were five main dams and 127 surface dams. Production of drinking water, 1995, 608·86m. cu. metres.

Minerals. Phosphate deposits have been discovered. Production, 2001, 2,043,000 tonnes; other minerals are gypsum (345,000 tonnes in 2001) and salt (106,000 tonnes in 2001). There are indications of lead, copper, antimony, nickel, chrome and other minerals widely distributed. Sodium chloride and bitumen deposits are being worked.

Agriculture. The arable area in 2001 was 4·64m. ha and there were 815,000 ha of permanent cropland. 1·27m. ha were irrigated in 2001. In 2001 there were 100,347 tractors and 4,500 harvester-threshers in use.

Production of principal crops, 2001 (in 1,000 tonnes): wheat, 4,745; sugarbeets, 1,175; seed cotton, 1,010; olives, 866; tomatoes, 732; cottonseed, 656; potatoes, 480; oranges, 465; grapes, 389; apples, 263; watermelons, 218; maize, 216; barley, 196.

Production of animal products, 2000 (in 1,000 tonnes): milk, 1,696; meat, 350; eggs, 120; cheese, 89.

Livestock (2000, in 1,000): sheep, 14,500; goats, 1,100; cattle, 920; asses, 198; chickens, 22,000.

Forestry. In 2000 there were 461,000 ha of forest (2·5% of the land area). Timber production in 2001 was 50,000 cu. metres.

Fisheries. The total catch in 2001 was 8,291 tonnes (72% freshwater fish).

INDUSTRY

Public-sector industrial production in 2001 included (in tonnes): cement, 5,428,000; residual fuel oil (2000), 4,906,000; distillate fuel oil (2000), 4,307,000; petrol

(2000), 1,294,000; fertilizers (2000), 330,000; vegetable oil, 89,000; cotton yarn, 83,000; refrigerators (2000), 96,000 units; washing machines (2000), 66,000 units; cigarettes, 12·0bn. units; woollen carpets (2000), 1·7m. sq. metres.

Labour. In 1996 the labour force totalled 4,396,000 (74% males). Unemployment was nearly 20% in 2000.

Trade Unions. In 1995 there were 199 trade unions with 460,967 members.

INTERNATIONAL TRADE

Foreign debt was US$21,504m. in 2002.

Imports and Exports. Trade in US$1m.:

	1996	*1997*	*1998*	*1999*	*2000*
Imports f.o.b.	4,516	3,603	3,320	3,590	3,723
Exports f.o.b.	4,178	4,057	3,142	3,806	5,146

Main imports, 1999 included: machinery and transport equipment, 19·7%; foodstuffs, 17·8%; iron and steel, 11·5%; chemicals, 9·9%; textile yarn, 9·1%. Main exports included: petroleum and products, 68·4%; vegetables and fruit, 11·0%; cotton, 4·1%.

In 1999 imports came mainly from Germany (7·0%), France (5·7%), Italy (5·6%), Turkey (4·7%) and USA (4·6%). Exports went mainly to Italy (26·6%), France (20·6%), Turkey (9·2%), Saudi Arabia (8·3%) and Spain (6·9%).

COMMUNICATIONS

Roads. In 2002 there were 46,698 km of roads, including 6,807 km of main roads and 27,073 km of secondary roads. There were in 2002 a total of 181,017 passenger cars, 46,560 buses and coaches and 367,048 vans and lorries. In 2002 there were 7,154 road accidents involving injury resulting in 1,653 deaths.

Rail. In 1995 the network totalled 2,423 km of 1,435 mm gauge (Syrian Railways) and 327 km of 1,050 mm gauge (Hedjaz-Syrian Railway). Passenger-km travelled in 2000 came to 196m. and freight tonne-km to 1,568m.

Civil Aviation. The main international airport is at Damascus, with some international traffic at Aleppo and Lattakia. The national carrier is the state-owned Syrian Arab Airlines. In 1998 it flew 12·8m. km, carrying 665,300 passengers (642,800 on international flights). Damascus handled 1,656,184 passengers in 1999 (1,560,200 on international flights) and 26,296 tonnes of freight. Aleppo was the second busiest airport in 1999, handling 222,674 passengers (156,440 on international flights) and 2,489 tonnes of freight.

Shipping. In 2002 the merchant marine totalled 472,000 GRT. Vessels totalling 2,827,000 NRT entered ports in 2001 and vessels totalling 2,794,000 NRT cleared.

Telecommunications. There were 2,499,300 telephone subscribers in 2002 (146·7 per 1,000 inhabitants), but in 2000 a total of 3·03m. people had been on the waiting list for a line. Mobile phone subscribers numbered 400,000 in 2002. There were 330,000 PCs in use (19·4 for every 1,000 persons) in 2002 and 22,000 fax machines in 1999. The number of Internet users in 2002 was 220,000.

Postal Services. There were 619 post offices in 1998.

SOCIAL INSTITUTIONS

Justice. Syrian law is based on both Islamic and French jurisprudence. There are two courts of first instance in each district, one for civil and one for criminal cases. There is also a Summary Court in each sub-district, under Justices of the Peace. There is a Court of Appeal in the capital of each governorate, with a Court of Cassation in Damascus. The death penalty is in force, and executions may be held in public.

The population in penal institutions in 1997 was 14,000 (93 per 100,000 of national population).

Religion. In 2001 there were an estimated 14·39m. Muslims (namely Sunni with some Shias and Ismailis). There are also Druzes and Alawites. Christians (920,000 in 2001) include Greek Orthodox, Greek Catholics, Armenian Orthodox, Syrian

Orthodox, Armenian Catholics, Protestants, Maronites, Syrian Catholics, Latins, Nestorians and Assyrians. There are also Jews and Yezides. In Sept. 2003 the Roman Catholic church had one cardinal.

Education. In 1995 there were 1,037 kindergartens with 90,681 children; 10,420 primary schools with 113,384 teachers and 2,651,247 pupils; 2,526 intermediate and secondary schools with 50,779 teachers and 841,964 pupils. In 1995, 14 teacher colleges had 766 teachers and 4,989 students; 292 schools for technical education had 10,105 teachers and 72,859 students. Adult literacy in 2001 was 75·3% (male, 88·8%; female, 61·6%).

In 1995–96 there were four universities and one higher institution of political science, with 161,185 students and 4,806 academic staff.

In 2000–01 total expenditure on education came to 4·4% of GNP and accounted for 11·1% of total government expenditure.

Health. In 1995 there were 17,623 beds in 294 hospitals, and 795 health centres. There were 22,293 physicians, 11,456 dentists, 29,259 nurses and 8,205 pharmacists in 1998 and 6,063 midwives in 1995.

CULTURE

World Heritage Sites. There are four sites under Syrian jurisdiction that appear in the UNESCO World Heritage List. They are (with year entered on the list): the old city of Damascus, dating from the 3rd millennium BC (1979); the old city of Bosra, once the capital of the Roman province of Arabia (1980); Palmyra (Tadmur), a desert oasis northeast of Damascus (1980); and the old city of Aleppo, located at the crossroads of various trade routes since the 2nd millennium BC (1986).

Broadcasting. Broadcasting is controlled by the government-owned Syrian Broadcasting and Television Organization. There are two national radio programmes and an external service and two TV programmes (colour by SECAM H). In 2000 there were 4·50m. radio sets and in 2001 there were 2·86m. TV sets.

Press. In 1996 there were eight national daily newspapers with a combined circulation of 287,000.

Tourism. In 2000 there were 1,416,000 foreign tourists; revenue totalled US$1·08bn.

DIPLOMATIC REPRESENTATIVES

Of Syria in the United Kingdom (8 Belgrave Sq., London, SW1X 8PH)
Ambassador: Sami M. Khiyami.

Of the United Kingdom in Syria (Kotob Building, 11 Mohammad Kurd Ali St., Malki, Damascus POB 37)
Ambassador: Peter Ford.

Of Syria in the USA (2215 Wyoming Ave., NW, Washington, D.C., 20008)
Ambassador: Imad Mustafa.

Of the USA in Syria (Abu Rumaneh, Al Mansur St. No. 2, Damascus)
Ambassador: Margaret Scobey.

Of Syria to the United Nations
Ambassador: Fayssal Mekdad.

Of Syria to the European Union
Ambassador: Toufic Salloum.

FURTHER READING

Choueiri, Y., *State and Society in Syria and Lebanon.* Exeter Univ. Press, 1994
George, Alan, *Syria: Neither Bread nor Freedom.* Zed Books, London, 2003
Kienle, Eberhard, *Contemporary Syria: Liberalization Between Cold War and Peace.* I. B. Tauris, London, 1997

National statistical office: Central Bureau of Statistics, Office of the Prime Minister, Damascus.

TAJIKISTAN

Jumkhurii Tojikiston

Capital: Dushanbe
Population projection, 2010: 6·74m.
GDP per capita, 2002: (PPP$) 980
HDI/world rank: 0·671/116

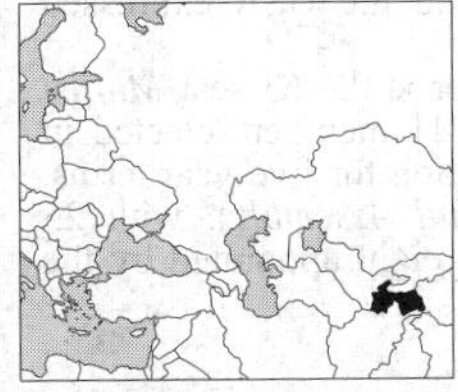

KEY HISTORICAL EVENTS

The Tajik Soviet Socialist Republic was formed from those regions of Bokhara and Turkestan where the population consisted mainly of Tajiks. It was admitted as a constituent republic of the Soviet Union on 5 Dec. 1929. In Aug. 1990 the Tajik Supreme Soviet adopted a declaration of republican sovereignty and in Dec. 1991 the republic became a member of the CIS. After demonstrations and fighting, the Communist government was replaced by a Revolutionary Coalition Council on 7 May 1992. Following further demonstrations, President Nabiev was ousted on 7 Sept. Civil war broke out, and the government resigned on 10 Nov. On 30 Nov. it was announced that a CIS peacekeeping force would be sent to Tajikistan. A state of emergency was imposed in Jan. 1993. On 23 Dec. 1996 a ceasefire was signed. A further agreement on 8 March 1997 provided for the disarmament of the Islamic-led insurgents, the United Tajik Opposition, and their eventual integration into the regular armed forces. A peace agreement brokered by Iran and Russia was signed in Moscow on 27 June 1997 stipulating that the opposition should have 30% of ministerial posts in a Commission of National Reconciliation. The country's first multi-party parliamentary election was held in Feb. 2000, although it was criticized by observers for failing to meet democratic standards. President Rakhmonov, first elected in 1994, won a second term in 1999.

Ethnic conflict and terrorist attacks continue to plague Tajikistan, with Russia offering military support. Fighting in the Fergana Valley, particularly by the Islamist Movement of Uzbekistan, is a cause for concern for all Central Asian governments.

TERRITORY AND POPULATION

Tajikistan is bordered in the north and west by Uzbekistan and Kyrgyzstan, in the east by China and in the south by Afghanistan. Area, 143,100 sq. km (55,240 sq. miles). It includes two regions (Sughd and Khatlon), one autonomous region (Gorno-Badakhshan Autonomous Region), the city of Dushanbe and regions of republican subordination. 2000 census population, 6,127,000 (3,082,000 males); density, 42·8 per sq. km. 80% of the population in 2000 were Tajiks, 15% Uzbeks and 1% Russians.

The UN gives a projected population for 2010 of 6·74m.

In 2001, 73·4% of the population lived in rural areas, making it the most rural of the former Soviet republics.

The capital is Dushanbe (2000 population, 562,000). Other large towns are Khujand (formerly Leninabad), Kulyab and Kurgan-Tyube.

The official language is Tajik, written in Arabic script until 1930 and after 1992 (the Roman alphabet was used 1930–40; the Cyrillic, 1940–92).

SOCIAL STATISTICS

1999 births, estimate, 110,300; deaths, 24,900. Rates, 1999 estimate (per 1,000 population): births, 17·7; deaths, 4·0. Life expectancy, 2001, 65·6 years for men and 71·0 for women. Annual growth, 1992–02, 1·2%. Infant mortality, 2001, 53 per 1,000 live births; fertility rate, 2001, 3·1 births per woman.

CLIMATE

Considering its altitude, Tajikistan is a comparatively dry country. July to Sept. are particularly dry months. Winters are cold but spring comes earlier than farther north. Dushanbe, Jan. –10°C, July 25°C. Annual rainfall 375 mm.

CONSTITUTION AND GOVERNMENT

In Nov. 1994 a new Constitution was approved by a 90% favourable vote by the electorate, which enhanced the President's powers. The head of state is the

President, elected by universal suffrage. When the 1994 Constitution took effect the term of office was five years. However, an amendment to the Constitution prior to the 1999 election extended the presidential term to seven years, although a president could only serve one term. A further referendum approved in June 2003 allows President Rakhmonov to serve two additional terms after his current one expires in 2006, theoretically enabling him to remain in office until 2020. The Organization for Security and Co-operation in Europe and the USA expressed concerns at the result.

Tajikistan has a bicameral legislature. The lower chamber is the 63-seat *Majlisi Namoyandagon* (*Assembly of Representatives*), which has 41 members elected in single-seat constituencies and 22 by proportional representation for five-year terms. The upper chamber is the 33-seat *Majlisi Milliy* (*National Assembly*), with 25 members chosen for five-year terms by local deputies and eight appointed by the president.

RECENT ELECTIONS

At presidential elections on 6 Nov. 1999 President Rakhmonov was re-elected with around 97% of votes cast. His opponent, Davlat Ismonov, received around 2%. Turn-out was 98%.

The country's first multi-party elections to the Assembly of Representatives were held on 27 Feb. and 12 March 2000. Turn-out in the first round was put at 93·2%. The People's Democratic Party of Tajikistan (HDKT) won 64·5% of the vote and 30 of the 63 available seats, the Communist Party (CP) 20·6% and 13, the Islamic Renaissance Party (IRP) 7·5% and 2. Three other parties won 3·5% of the vote or less. 15 seats went to non-partisans and 3 were left vacant or unavailable. Elections to the National Assembly were held on 12 March 2000. 25 of the 33 seats were voted for by local majlisi deputies and 8 were appointed by the president.

In parliamentary elections held on 27 Feb. 2005 the People's Democratic Party of Tajikistan won 52 of 63 seats (74% of the vote), the Communist Party 4 (13%), the Islamic Renaissance Party of Tajikistan 2 (8%), and ind. 5. Turn-out was 92·6%. With one party having secured more than two-thirds support, a second round of voting scheduled for 13 March was cancelled.

CURRENT ADMINISTRATION

President: Emomali Rakhmonov; b. 1952 (HDKT; as Speaker elected by the former Supreme Soviet 19 Nov. 1992, re-elected 6 Nov. 1994 and 6 Nov. 1999).

In March 2005 the government comprised:

Prime Minister: Akil Akilov; b. 1944 (HDKT; sworn in 20 Dec. 1999).

First Deputy Prime Minister: Hajji Akbar Turajonzoda. *Deputy Prime Minister:* Khayrinisso Mavlonova.

Minister of Agriculture: Voris Madaminov. *Communications:* Saidmahmad Zubaidov. *Culture:* Radjabmat Amirov. *Defence:* Col.-Gen. Sherali Khairullaev. *Economy and Trade:* Hakim Soliyev. *Education:* Abdujabbor Rahmonov. *Emergency Situations:* Mirzo Ziyoyev. *Finance:* Safarali Najmuddinov. *Internal Affairs:* Khomiddin Sharipov. *Justice:* Halifabobo Hamidov. *Foreign Affairs:* Talbak Nasarov. *Transport:* Abdurahim Ashurov. *Energy:* Jurabek Nurmahmadov. *Grain Products:* Bekmurod Urokov. *Health:* Nusratullo Faizulloev. *Labour and Social Sevices:* Zokir Vazirov. *Land Improvement and Water Resources:* Abduqohir Nazirov. *Security:* Khayriddin Abdurahimov. *Industry:* Zayd Saidov. *State Revenue:* Ghulomjon Babaev.

DEFENCE

In 2002 the Army had a strength of 6,000. There is a paramilitary Border Guard of 1,200. An estimated 12,000 Russian Federal Border Guards, 7,800 Russian Army personnel and some Air Force units are stationed in the country.

Defence expenditure in 2003 totalled US$150m. (US$24 per capita), representing 2·1% of GDP.

In April 2003 Russia announced plans to increase its military presence in Tajikistan in response to intelligence reports of increased activity by the Taliban and al-Qaeda in neighbouring Afghanistan.

Army. Personnel strength approximately 6,000.

INTERNATIONAL RELATIONS

Tajikistan is a member of the UN, the NATO Partnership for Peace, CIS, OSCE, ECO, IOM, OIC and Islamic Development Bank.

ECONOMY

In 2002 agriculture accounted for 24·3% of GDP, industry 24·0% and services 51·7%.

Overview. The economy is mainly agrarian; the sector employs two-thirds of the labour force and contributes 11% to export revenues, despite under 10% of land being arable. Economic growth averaged 7·5% between 1999–2001 and improved inflation management has aided the implementation of macroeconomic policies. Civil war and repeated changes of political leadership in the 1990s prevented the government from establishing a coherent economic policy to address the challenges of independence from the Soviet Union. As a result, the economy deteriorated more rapidly than in other ex-Soviet countries. In 1995 GDP per capita had been reduced to 40% of the 1991 level; during this period the economy reverted to subsistence agriculture as food and labour markets collapsed. In 1996 a reform programme began, supported by the IMF and the World Bank. Despite a slow start and the Russian financial crisis in 1998, the focus on economic reconstruction has enabled the economy to make significant progress in the transition toward a market economy. Reforms have included small-scale privatization, land reform, the restructuring of the banking system and the legal system and the development of market-based institutions.

Currency. The unit of currency is the *somoni* (TJS) of 100 *dirams*, which replaced the Tajik rouble on 30 Oct. 2000 at 1 somoni = 1,000 Tajik roubles. The introduction of the new currency was intended to strengthen the national banking system. The IMF voiced their support for the new currency, which it believes will contribute to macroeconomic stability and expedite the transition to a market economy. Inflation in 1993 was 2,195%, declining to 418% in 1996 and still further to 32·9% in 2000, the reduction being helped by a US$22m. IMF loan in 1996 and maintenance of a tighter monetary regime. By 2002 the rate had fallen to 12·2%.

Budget. Total revenue in 2001 was 288·7m. somoni and total expenditure was 292·5m. somoni.

Performance. Annual real GDP growth was negative for four consecutive years in the mid-1990s. However, the economy slowly recovered and in 2000 growth was 8·3%, rising to 10·2% in 2001. There was growth of 9·1% in 2002 and 10·2% in 2003. Total GDP in 2003 was US$1·3bn.

Banking and Finance. The central bank and bank of issue is the National Bank (*Chairman*, Murotali Alimardonov). In 1998 there were 27 commercial and private banks but the number had fallen to 14 by 2002 after a process of consolidation.

ENERGY AND NATURAL RESOURCES

Environment. In 2002 Tajikistan's carbon dioxide emissions from the consumption and flaring of fossil fuels were the equivalent of 0·8 tonnes per capita.

Electricity. Installed capacity in 2000 was 4·4m. kW. Production was 14·2bn. kWh in 2000 and consumption per capita 2,517 kWh.

Oil and Gas. In 2000 oil production was 18,000 tonnes; natural gas output in 2000 was 40m. cu. metres.

Minerals. There are deposits of brown coal, lead, zinc, iron ore, antimony, mercury, gold, silver, tungsten and uranium. Lignite production, 2000, 20,000 tonnes. Aluminium production, 2001, 289,000 tonnes.

Agriculture. Area under cultivation in 1997 was 9·6m. ha, mainly in the hands of state and collective farms. In 2001 there were 930,000 ha of arable land and 130,000 ha of permanent crops. Cotton is the major cash crop, with various fruits, sugarcane, jute, silk, rice and millet also being grown.

Output of main agricultural products (in 1,000 tonnes) in 2000: wheat, 358; seed cotton, 294; potatoes, 250; cottonseed, 210; tomatoes, 185; onions, 128. Livestock,

2000: 1·59m. sheep; 1·04m. cattle; 590,000 goats; 1m. chickens. Livestock products, 2000 (in 1,000 tonnes): meat, 31; milk, 331.

Forestry. Forests covered 400,000 ha in 2000, or 2·8% of the land area.

Fisheries. Total catch in 2001 was 137 tonnes, exclusively from inland waters.

INDUSTRY

Major industries: aluminium, electro-chemical plants, textile machinery, carpet weaving, silk mills, refrigerators, hydro-electric power. Output: cement (2001), 69,000 tonnes; mineral nitrogenous fertilizer (2000), 4,000 tonnes; cotton woven fabrics (2001), 14m. sq. metres; carpets and rugs (1999), 1m. sq. metres; silk fabrics (2001), 248,000 sq. metres; footwear (2001), 100,000 pairs.

Labour. The economically active force in 1997 totalled 1,143,000. The principal areas of activity were: agriculture, hunting and forestry, 528,000; education, 160,000; manufacturing, 137,000; and health and social work, 82,000. In 2000 the unemployment rate was 3·0%.

INTERNATIONAL TRADE

Total external debt was US$1,153m. in 2002.

Imports and Exports. In 2002 imports were valued at US$822·9m. and exports at US$699·1m. Main imports: petroleum products, grain, manufactured consumer goods; main exports: cotton and aluminium. Principal import suppliers, 2000: Uzbekistan, 28·8%; Russia, 16·1%; Ukraine, 13·1%; Kazakhstan, 12·8%. Principal export markets in 2000: Russia, 37·4%; Netherlands, 25·7%; Uzbekistan, 14·1%; Switzerland, 10·4%.

COMMUNICATIONS

Roads. In 2000 there were 27,767 km of roads. There were an estimated 8,820 passenger cars, buses, lorries and vans in 1996. In 2000 there were 1,333 road accidents, resulting in 406 fatalities.

Rail. Length of railways, 2000, 533 km. Passenger-km travelled in 2000 came to 83m. and freight tonne-km to 1·33bn.

Civil Aviation. There are international airports at Dushanbe and Khujand. The national carrier is Tajikistan Airlines, which in 2003 flew to İstanbul, Moscow, Munich and a variety of Asian cities. In 2003 there were flights with other airlines to Bishkek, Ekaterinburg, Samara and St Petersburg. In 1999 scheduled airline traffic of Tajikistan-based carriers flew 4·1m. km, carrying 156,000 passengers (79,000 on international flights).

Telecommunications. Tajikistan had 250,800 telephone subscribers in 2002, or 39·3 for every 1,000 persons. Mobile phone subscribers numbered 13,200 in 2002 and there were 2,100 fax machines in 1999. There were 3,500 Internet users in 2002.

Postal Services. In 1997 there were 706 post offices.

SOCIAL INSTITUTIONS

Justice. In 1994, 14,279 crimes were reported, including 636 murders or attempted murders. The population in penal institutions in Sept. 2003 was approximately 10,000 (159 per 100,000 of national population). The death penalty is in force.

Religion. The Tajiks are predominantly Sunni Muslims (80%); Shia Muslims, 5%.

Education. The adult literacy rate in 2001 was 99·3% (99·6% among males and 98·9% among females). In 2000–01 there were 680,100 pupils and 31,216 teachers at primary schools; 847,445 pupils and 54,593 teachers at secondary schools; and 78,540 students at higher education institutions.

There is one university, which had 7,220 students in 1994–95.

In 2001–02 total expenditure on education came to 2·5% of GNP.

Health. There were 449 hospitals in 1994. In 1998 there were 12,291 physicians, 1,125 dentists, 29,597 nurses, 734 pharmacists and 3,999 midwives.

Welfare. In Jan. 1994 there were 0·41m. old age pensioners and 0·2m. other pensioners.

CULTURE

Broadcasting. Broadcasting is controlled by the State Teleradio Broadcasting Company. Tajik Radio broadcasts three national programmes, a Radio Moscow relay and a foreign service (Dari, Iranian). In 2000 there were 870,000 radio receivers and in 2001 there were 2·2m. TV receivers.

Press. There were two daily newspapers in 1996 with a combined circulation of 120,000, equivalent to 21 per 1,000 inhabitants.

Tourism. In 1998, 511,000 foreign tourists visited Tajikistan.

DIPLOMATIC REPRESENTATIVES

Of Tajikistan in the United Kingdom
Honorary Consul: Benjamin Brahms (33 Ovington Square, London, SW3 1LJ).

Of the United Kingdom in Tajikistan (Lufti 43, Dushanbe)
Ambassador: Graeme Loten.

Of Tajikistan in the USA (1005 New Hampshire Ave., NW, Washington, D.C., 20037)
Ambassador: Khamrokhon Zaripov.

Of the USA in Tajikistan (10 Pavlov St., Dushanbe)
Ambassador: Richard E. Hoagland.

Of Tajikistan to the United Nations
Ambassador: Rashid Alimov.

Of Tajikistan to the European Union
Ambassador: Sharif Rahimov.

FURTHER READING

Abdullaev, K. and Akbarzadeh, S., *Historical Dictionary of Tajikistan.* Rowman and Littlefield Publishing, Lanham, Maryland, 2002

Akiner, S., *Tajikistan: Disintegration or Reconciliation?* Royal Institute of International Affairs, London, 2001

Djalili, M. R. (ed.) *Tajikistan: The Trials of Independence.* Macmillan, Basingstoke, 1998

GORNO-BADAKHSHAN AUTONOMOUS REGION

Comprising the Pamir massif along the borders of Afghanistan and China, the province was set up on 2 Jan. 1925, initially as the Special Pamir Province. Area, 63,700 sq. km (24,590 sq. miles). The population at the 2000 census was 206,000 (1989: 89·5% Tajik, 6·7% Kirghiz). Capital, Khorog (30,000). The inhabitants are predominantly Ismaili Muslims.

Mining industries are developed (gold, rock-crystal, mica, coal, salt). Wheat, fruit and fodder crops are grown, and cattle and sheep are bred in the western parts. In 1990 there were 74,200 cattle and 329,500 sheep and goats. Total area under cultivation, 18,400 ha.

In 1990–91 there were 47,600 students at all levels of education. There were 140 doctors and 1,400 junior medical personnel in 1991.

TANZANIA

Jamhuri ya Muungano wa Tanzania
(United Republic of Tanzania)

Capital: Dodoma
Population projection, 2010: 41·93m.
GDP per capita, 2002: (PPP$) 580
HDI/world rank: 0·407/162

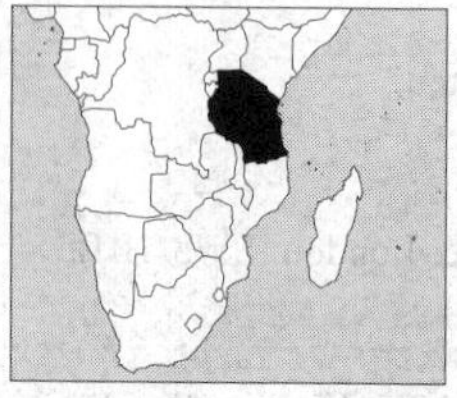

KEY HISTORICAL EVENTS

At the end of the 17th century the inhabitants of Zanzibar drove out the Portuguese with the assistance of the Arabs of Oman. In 1887 the Sultan of Zanzibar handed over the administration of his possessions to the north of Vanga on the African continent to the British East Africa Association. These territories eventually passed to the British government and are now part of Kenya. In 1888 a similar concession was granted to the German East Africa Association of the Sultan's mainland territories between the River Umba and Cape Delgado. German East Africa was conquered by the Allies in the First World War and subsequently divided between the Belgians, the Portuguese and the British. The country was administered as a League of Nations mandate until 1946, and then as a UN trusteeship territory until 9 Dec. 1961.

Tanganyika (Tanzania) achieved responsible government in Sept. 1960 and full self-government on 1 May 1961. On 9 Dec. 1961 Tanganyika became a sovereign independent member state of the Commonwealth of Nations. On 9 Dec 1962 the country adopted a republican form of government (still within the British Commonwealth) and Dr Nyerere was elected as the first president.

On 24 June 1963 Zanzibar gained internal self-government followed by full independence on 9 Dec. 1963. On 12 Jan. 1964 the sultanate was overthrown by a revolt of the Afro-Shirazi Party leaders who established the People's Republic of Zanzibar. Also in Jan. 1964 there was an attempted coup against Nyerere who had to seek British military help. On 26 April 1964 Tanganyika, Zanzibar and Pemba combined to form the United Republic of Tanzania. The first multi-party elections were held in 1995.

TERRITORY AND POPULATION

Tanzania is bounded in the northeast by Kenya, north by Lake Victoria and Uganda, northwest by Rwanda and Burundi, west by Lake Tanganyika, southwest by Zambia and Malaŵi, and south by Mozambique. Total area 942,799 sq. km (364,881 sq. miles), including the offshore islands of Zanzibar (1,554 sq. km) and Pemba (906 sq. km) and inland water surfaces (59,050 sq. km). 2002 census population, 34,569,232 (17,658,911 females); density, 39·1 per sq. km.

The UN gives a projected population for 2010 of 41·93m.

In 2001, 68·8% of the population lived in rural areas. 0·5m. Hutu refugees were forcibly repatriated to Rwanda in Dec. 1996. Tanzania has the highest refugee population in Africa, with 650,000 at the end of 2001.

The chief towns (1988 census populations) are Dar es Salaam, the chief port and former capital (2,115,000 in 2000), Tanga (187,634), Mwanza (172,287) and Zanzibar Town (157,634). Dodoma, the capital, had a population of 83,205 in 1988.

The United Republic is divided into 26 administrative regions of which 21 are in mainland Tanzania, three in Zanzibar and two in Pemba. Areas and 2002 populations of the regions:

Region	*Sq. km*	*Population*	*Region*	*Sq. km*	*Population*
Arusha	36,486	1,292,973	Lindi	66,046	791,306
Dar es Salaam	1,393	2,497,940	Manyara	45,820	1,040,461
Dodoma	41,311	1,686,996	Mara	19,566	1,368,602
Iringa	56,864	1,495,333	Mbeya	60,350	2,070,046
Kagera	28,388	2,033,888	Morogoro	70,799	1,759,809
Kigoma	37,037	1,679,109	Mtwara	16,707	1,128,523
Kilimanjaro	13,309	1,381,149	Mwanza	19,592	2,942,148

Region	Sq. km	Population	Region	Sq. km	Population
Pwani (Coast)	32,407	889,154	*Zanzibar and Pemba*	*2,460*	*984,625*
Rukwa	68,635	1,141,743	Pemba North	574	186,013
Ruvuma	63,498	1,117,166	Pemba South	332	176,153
Shinyanga	50,781	2,805,580	Zanzibar North	470	136,953
Singida	49,341	1,090,758	Zanzibar South	854	94,504
Tabora	76,151	1,717,908	Zanzibar West	230	391,002
Tanga	26,808	1,642,015			

The official languages are English and Swahili (spoken as a mother tongue by only 8·8% of the population, but used as a *lingua franca* by 90%).

SOCIAL STATISTICS

1997 births, estimate, 1,208,000; deaths, 583,000. 1997 rates per 1,000 population: birth, 41·0; death, 19·8. Annual population growth rate, 1992–2002, 2·6%. Life expectancy in 2001 was 43·0 years for men and 45·0 for women. 45% of the population was below 15 years old in 1997. Infant mortality, 2001, 104 per 1,000 live births; fertility rate, 2001, 5·2 births per woman.

CLIMATE

The climate is very varied and is controlled largely by altitude and distance from the sea. There are three climatic zones: the hot and humid coast, the drier central plateau with seasonal variations of temperature, and the semi-temperate mountains. Dodoma, Jan. 75°F (23·9°C), July 67°F (19·4°C). Annual rainfall 23" (572 mm). Dar es Salaam, Jan. 82°F (27·8°C), July 74°F (23·3°C). Annual rainfall 43" (1,064 mm).

CONSTITUTION AND GOVERNMENT

The *President* is head of state, chairman of the party and commander-in-chief of the armed forces. The second Vice-President is head of the executive in Zanzibar. The Prime Minister and first Vice-President is also the leader of government business in the National Assembly.

The *Bunge (National Assembly)* is composed of 232 Members of Parliament elected from the Constituencies, five delegates from the Zanzibar House of Representatives, the Attorney General and 37 women, making 274 in total.

In Dec. 1979 a separate Constitution for Zanzibar was approved. Although at present under the same Constitution as Tanzania, Zanzibar has, in fact, been ruled by decree since 1964.

National Anthem. 'God Bless Africa/Mungu ibariki Afrika'; words collective, tune by M. E. Sontonga and V. E. Webster.

RECENT ELECTIONS

Presidential and parliamentary elections were held on 29 Oct. 2000, in many places postponed or extended because of administrative problems or faults. International observers described the elections in the semi-autonomous island of Zanzibar as chaotic. Benjamin Mkapa was elected President with 71·7% of votes cast. His party, Chama Cha Mapinduzi (Revolutionary State Party), gained 244 seats, the Civic United Front gained 15, Chama Cha Democracia na Maendeleo (Party for Democracy and Progress) 4, the Tanzania Labour Party 3 and the United Democratic Party 2.

Presidential and parliamentary elections are scheduled to take place on 30 Oct. 2005.

CURRENT ADMINISTRATION

President: Benjamin Mkapa; b. 1938 (Chama Cha Mapinduzi/CCM; sworn in 30 Nov. 1995 and re-elected in Oct. 2000).

Vice-President: Dr Ali Mohamed Sheni.

In March 2005 the government consisted of:

Prime Minister: Frederick Sumaye; b. 1950 (CCM; sworn in 28 Nov. 1995).

President of Zanzibar: Amani Abeid Karume.

Minister of Home Affairs: Omar Ramadhani Mapuri. *Finance:* Basil Mramba. *Justice and Constitutional Affairs:* Bakari Mwapachu. *Defence:* Philemon Sarungi. *Industries and Trade:* Juma Ngasongwa. *Communications and Transport:* Mark

Mwandosya. *Agriculture and Food:* Charles Kennja. *Health:* Anna Abdalla. *Foreign Affairs and International Co-operation:* Jakaya Kikwete. *Education:* James Mungai. *Energy and Mineral Resources:* Daniel Yona. *Water and Livestock Development:* Edward Lowassa. *Tourism, Natural Resources and Environment:* Zakhia Meghji. *Lands and Human Settlements:* Gideon Cheyo. *Science, Technology and Higher Education:* Ng'wandu Pius. *Works:* John Magufuli. *Labour, Youth Development and Sports:* Juma Kapuya. *Community Development, Women's Affairs and Children:* Asha Rose Migiro. *Co-operatives and Marketing:* George Kahama. *Regional Affairs and Local Government:* Hassan Nigwilizi.

Government Website: http://www.tanzania.go.tz

DEFENCE

Conscription is for two years, which may include civilian service. Defence expenditure totalled US$301m. in 2003 (US$8 per capita), representing 3·1% of GDP.

Army. Strength (2002), 23,000. There is also a Citizen's Militia of 80,000 and a paramilitary Police Field Force of 1,400.

Navy. Personnel in 2002 totalled about 1,000. The principal bases are at Dar es Salaam, Zanzibar and Mwanza.

Air Force. The Tanzanian People's Defence Force Air Wing was built up initially with the help of Canada, but combat equipment has been acquired from China. Personnel totalled 3,000 in 2002 (including some 2,000 air defence troops), with J-7 (MiG-21), J-6 (MiG-19) and J-5 (MiG-17) combat aircraft, mostly in store.

INTERNATIONAL RELATIONS

Tanzania is a member of the UN, WTO, the African Union, the Commonwealth, African Development Bank, COMESA, SADC, EAC, IOM and is an ACP member state of the ACP-EU relationship.

In Nov. 1999 a treaty was signed between Tanzania, Kenya and Uganda to create a new East African Community as a means of developing East African trade, tourism and industry and laying the foundations for a future common market and political federation.

ECONOMY

Agriculture accounted for 44·7% of GDP in 2002, industry 16·1% and services 39·2%.

Overview. Since the mid-1990s Tanzania has undertaken IMF structural reforms and has made major progress towards restoring macroeconomic stability and promoting private sector-led growth. Between 1993 and 2002, 66% of all state-owned enterprises were privatized. The majority of companies privatized were small and medium sized companies; the privatization of the larger more strategic enterprises is continuing.

Currency. The monetary unit is the *Tanzanian shilling* (TZS) of 100 *cents*. Foreign exchange reserves were US$1,199m. in June 2002. Inflation, which was 26·5% in 1995, had fallen to 4·6% in 2002, the lowest rate for more than 20 years. Total money supply in May 2002 was Sh. 792,213m.

Budget. The fiscal year ends 30 June. Total revenues in 2001–02 were an estimated US$764m. and government expenditure totalled US$989m. Tax revenues accounted for 91% of total revenues.

Performance. Real GDP growth was 6·1% in 2001 and 6·3% in 2002. Total GDP in 2003 was US$9·9bn.

Banking and Finance. The central bank is the Bank of Tanzania (*Governor*, Daudi Ballali).

On 6 Feb. 1967 all commercial banks with the exception of National Co-operative Banks were nationalized, and their interests vested in the National Bank of Commerce on the mainland (fully privatized in March 2000) and the Peoples' Bank in Zanzibar. However, in 1993 private-sector commercial banks were allowed to open. In 1997 the National Bank of Commerce, which controls 70% of the country's banking and has 34 branches, was split into a trade bank, a regional rural bank and a micro-finance bank. It was privatized in 2000, with the South African concern Absa Group Limited purchasing a 55% stake. The government retained 30% with the International Finance Corporation holding 15%. In 2000 there were 17 banks operating in Tanzania.

Foreign direct investment totalled US$224·2m. in 2001.

A stock exchange opened in Dar es Salaam in 1996.

ENERGY AND NATURAL RESOURCES

Environment. Tanzania's carbon dioxide emissions from the consumption and flaring of fossil fuels in 2002 were the equivalent of 0·1 tonnes per capita.

Electricity. Installed capacity was 0·5m. kW in 2000. Production in 2000 was 2·55bn. kWh, with consumption per capita estimated at 74 kWh. In 1998 only 10% of the population had access to electricity. By 2015 the government aims to have increased this to 40% under a new structure principally managed by the private sector.

Oil and Gas. A number of international companies are exploring for both gas and oil. In 2002 natural gas reserves were 28bn. cu. metres.

Minerals. Tanzania's mineral resources include gold, nickel, cobalt, silver and diamonds. International funds injected to improve Tanzania's economy have resulted in notable increases, particularly in gold production. The first commercial gold mine began operating in Mwanza in 1998. By 2000 production revenue had reached US$184m., up from US$3·3m. in 1998. Gold production in 2001 totalled 30,088 kg. Large deposits of coal and tin exist but mining is on a small scale. Diamond production in 2001 totalled 191,000 carats, worth US$27·7m.

Agriculture. About 80% of the workforce are engaged in agriculture, chiefly in subsistence farming. Agricultural produce contributes around 85% of exports. There were 4·0m. ha of arable land in 2001 and 950,000 ha of permanent crops. 170,000 ha were irrigated in 2001. There were 7,600 tractors in 2001. Production of main agricultural crops in 2000 (in 1,000 tonnes) was: cassava, 5,758; maize, 2,551; sugarcane, 1,355; bananas and plantains, 1,304; sweet potatoes, 480; rice, 379; coconuts, 350; sorghum, 335; dry beans, 260; potatoes, 250. Zanzibar is a major producer of cloves.

Livestock (2000): 14·38m. cattle; 4·20m. sheep; 9·95m. goats; 28m. chickens. Livestock products (2000, in 1,000 tonnes): milk, 781; meat, 326; eggs, 58; honey, 25.

Forestry. Forests covered 38·81m. ha in 2000 (43·9% of the total land area). In 2001, 23·26m. cu. metres of roundwood were cut.

Fisheries. Catch (2001) 335,900 tonnes, of which 283,000 tonnes were from inland waters.

INDUSTRY

Industry is limited, and is mainly textiles, petroleum and chemical products, food processing, tobacco, brewing and paper manufacturing.

INTERNATIONAL TRADE

Foreign debt was US$7,244m. in 2002.

Imports and Exports. In 2002 imports (f.o.b.) amounted to US$1,511·3m. (US$1,560·3m. in 2001); exports (f.o.b.) US$902·5m. (US$776·4m. in 2001). Principal exports, 1999: coffee, 17·1%; cashew nuts, 16·8%; fish, 10·3%; tobacco, 8·9%; cotton, 7·4%; tea, 4·7%. Principal imports, 1999: machinery and transport equipment, 39·4%; manufactured goods, 15·4%; chemicals, 10·4%; petroleum, 8·0%; cereals, 5·7%. Main export markets, 1999: India, 19·5%; UK, 17·0%; Japan, 8·0%; Netherlands, 5·7%; Singapore, 4·5%. Main import suppliers, 1999: Japan, 10·9%; UK, 7·8%; USA, 6·0%; Kenya, 5·8%; India, 5·6%.

COMMUNICATIONS

Roads. In 1999 there were about 88,200 km of roads, of which 3,700 km were paved. Passenger cars in use in 1996 numbered 23,760; and there were 86,000 buses and coaches, and 29,700 trucks and vans.

Rail. In 1977 the independent Tanzanian Railway Corporation was formed. The network totals 2,722 km (metre-gauge), excluding the joint Tanzanian Zambian (Tazara) railway's 969 km in Tanzania (1,067 mm gauge) operated by a separate administration. In 2000 the state railway carried 0·6m. passengers and 1·2m. tonnes of freight, and in 1994 the Tazara carried 1·8m. passengers and 0·6m. tonnes of freight.

In Oct. 1998 a transhipment facility for containers opened at Kidatu, southwest of Dar es Salaam, providing a link between the 1,067 mm gauge railways of the southern part of Africa and the 1,000 mm gauge lines of the north.

Civil Aviation. There are three international airports: Dar es Salaam, Zanzibar and Kilimanjaro (Moshi/Arusha). Air Tanzania, the national carrier, provides domestic services and in 2003 had flights to Abu Dhabi, Blantyre, Johannesburg, Lilongwe, Mombasa, Muscat and Nairobi. In 1999 Air Tanzania Corporation flew 3·1m. km, carrying 190,000 passengers (75,400 on international flights). Dar es Salaam is the busiest airport, handling 556,785 passengers in 2000 (348,558 on international flights) and 11,048 tonnes of freight.

Shipping. In 2002 the merchant marine totalled 47,000 GRT, including oil tankers 8,000 GRT. The main seaports are Dar es Salaam, Mtwara, Tanga and Zanzibar. There are also ports on the lakes. In 1991, 1m. tonnes of freight were loaded, and 2·9m. unloaded.

Telecommunications. Tanzania had 831,600 telephone subscribers in 2002 (24·1 per 1,000 inhabitants) and there were 144,000 PCs in use (4·2 per 1,000 inhabitants). There were 670,000 mobile phone subscribers in 2002 and 100 fax machines in 1995. Tanzania had 80,000 Internet users in 2002.

Postal Services. In 1998 there were 612 post offices.

SOCIAL INSTITUTIONS

Justice. The Judiciary is independent in both judicial and administrative matters and is composed of a four-tier system of Courts: Primary Courts; District and Resident Magistrates' Courts; the High Court and the Court of Appeal. The Chief Justice is head of the Court of Appeal and the Judiciary Department. The Court's main registry is at Dar es Salaam; its jurisdiction includes Zanzibar. The Principal Judge is head of the High Court, also headquartered at Dar es Salaam, which has resident judges at seven regional centres.

The population in penal institutions in June 2002 was 44,063 (120 per 100,000 of national population).

Religion. In 2001 there were 18·3m. Christians (including Roman Catholics, Anglicans and Lutherans) and 11·5m. Muslims. Muslims are concentrated in the coastal towns; Zanzibar is 99% Muslim. The remainder of the population follow traditional religions. In Sept. 2003 the Roman Catholic church had one cardinal.

Education. In 1999–2000 there were 11,409 primary schools with 103,731 teachers for 4·19m. pupils. At secondary level there were 247,579 pupils with 12,496 (1997) teachers in 826 schools, and at university level in 2000–01 there were 21,960 students with 2,192 academic staff. Primary school fees were abolished in Jan. 2002.

Technical and vocational education is provided at several secondary and technical schools, and at the Dar es Salaam Technical College. There are 42 teacher training colleges, including the college at Chang'ombe for secondary-school teachers.

There is one university, one university of agriculture and one open university. There are also nine other institutions of higher education.

Adult literacy rate in 2001 was 76·0% (male, 84·5%; female, 67·9%). In 1998–99 total expenditure on education came to 2·2% of GNP.

Health. In 1995 there were 1,277 physicians, 218 dentists, 26,536 nurses and 13,953 midwives. In 1991 there were 173 hospitals with 24,130 beds.

CULTURE

World Heritage Sites. Tanzania has six sites on the UNESCO World Heritage List: Ngorongoro Conservation Area (inscribed on the list in 1979); the Ruins of Kilwa Kisiwani and of Songo Mnara (1981); Serengeti National Park (1981); Selous Game

Reserve (1982); Kilimanjaro National Park (1987); and the Stone Town of Zanzibar (2000).

Broadcasting. The government-controlled Radio Tanzania and Sauti ya Tanzania Zanzibar are responsible for radio broadcasting on the mainland and on Zanzibar respectively. On the mainland there is a national service and a commercial programme in Swahili and an external service in English. There is television only on Zanzibar provided by the government-run Television Zanzibar (colour by PAL). There were 1·5m. TV sets in 2001 and 9·1m. radio receivers in 2000.

Press. In 1996 there were three dailies (one in English), with a combined circulation of 120,000.

Tourism. Tourism contributes approximately 16% of GDP, but it is hoped that by 2010 the share will exceed 25%. There were, in 2001, 12 national parks in Tanzania. In 2000 there were 459,000 foreign tourists, bringing revenue of US$739m., compared to 153,000 visitors in 1990. Tourism is the country's second largest foreign exchange earner after agriculture.

DIPLOMATIC REPRESENTATIVES

Of Tanzania in the United Kingdom (3 Stratford Pl., London, W1C 1AS)
High Commissioner: Hassan Omar Gumbo Kibelloh.

Of the United Kingdom in Tanzania (Umoja House, Garden Ave., PO Box 9200 Dar es Salaam)
High Commissioner: Dr Andrew Pocock.

Of Tanzania in the USA (2139 R. St., NW, Washington, D.C., 20008)
Ambassador: Andrew Mhando Daraja.

Of the USA in Tanzania (686 Old Bagamoyo Rd, Msasani, PO Box 9123, Dar es Salaam)
Ambassador: Vacant.
Chargé d'Affaires a.i.: Michael Owen.

Of Tanzania to the United Nations
Ambassador: Augustine Philip Mahiga.

Of Tanzania to the European Union
Ambassador: Ali Abeid Aman Karume.

FURTHER READING

Darch, C., *Tanzania.* [Bibliography] 2nd ed. ABC-Clio, Oxford and Santa Barbara (CA), 1996

National statistical office: National Bureau of Statistics, Box 796, Dar es Salaam.
Website: http://www.tanzania.gov.tz/statistics.html

THAILAND

Prathet Thai
(Kingdom of Thailand)

Capital: Bangkok
Population projection, 2010: 66·95m.
GDP per capita, 2002: (PPP$) 7,010
HDI/world rank: 0·768/76

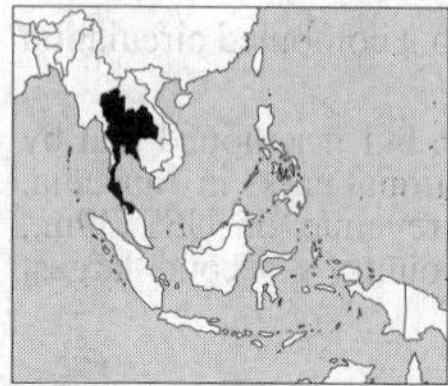

KEY HISTORICAL EVENTS

The Thais migrated to the present territory from Nan Chao in the Yunnan area of China in the 8th and 9th centuries. Thailand's leading general, Chao Phraya Chakkri, assumed the throne in 1782, thus establishing the dynasty which still heads the Thai state. Siam, as Thailand was called until 1939, remained an independent state ruled by an absolute monarchy until 24 June 1932. Discontented with the social, political and economic stagnation of the country, a group of rebels calling themselves the People's Party precipitated a bloodless coup. The rebels seized control of the army and persuaded the king to accept the introduction of constitutional monarchy. When, the following year, the king tried to dissolve the newly appointed General Assembly, the army moved to prevent him, thus becoming the dominant force behind the government, which they have remained ever since. Nationalism dominated political life through the 1930s. In 1939 Field Marshal Pibul Songgram became premier and embarked on a pro-Japanese policy that brought Thailand into the Second World War on Japan's side.

After 1945 political life was characterized by periods of military rule interspersed with short attempts at democratic, civilian government. Democratic government was reintroduced for a short time after 1963 and again from 1969 to 1971 when another successful military coup was staged, aimed at checking the high crime rate and the growth of Communist insurgence. A new, moderately democratic constitution was introduced in 1978.

On 23 Feb. 1991 a military junta seized power in the most recent of 17 coups since 1932. Following the appointment of Gen. Suchinda Kraprayoon as prime minister on 17 April 1992 there were massive anti-government demonstrations over several weeks in the course of which many demonstrators were killed. Gen. Suchinda resigned and in May the legislative assembly voted that future prime ministers should be elected by its members rather than appointed by the military. The 1995 election was fought against a background of political and financial corruption. After the 1996 election a new constitution was drafted allowing for the separation of the executive, legislative and judicial branches of government.

On 26 Dec. 2004 Thailand, along with a number of other south Asian countries, was hit by a devastating tsunami following an undersea earthquake. The death toll in Thailand was put at 5,000.

TERRITORY AND POPULATION

Thailand is bounded in the west by Myanmar, north and east by Laos and southeast by Cambodia. In the south it becomes a peninsula bounded in the west by the Indian Ocean, south by Malaysia and east by the Gulf of Thailand. The area is 513,115 sq. km (198,114 sq. miles).

At the 2000 census the population was 60,916,441 (30,901,208 females); density, 118·7 per sq. km. 20,825,262 lived in the Northeastern region, 11,433,061 in the Northern region, 14,215,503 in the Central region, 8,087,471 in the Southern region and 6,355,144 in Bangkok. In 2001, 80·0% of the population lived in rural areas.

The UN gives a projected population for 2010 of 66·95m.

Thailand is divided into four regions, 76 provinces and Bangkok, the capital. Population of Bangkok (2000 provisional census figure), 6,320,174. Other towns (2000 provisional census figures): Samut Prakan (378,694), Nonthaburi (291,307), Udon Thani (220,493), Nakhon Ratchasima (204,391), Hat Yai (185,557).

Thai is the official language, spoken by 53% of the population as their mother tongue. 27% speak Lao (mainly in the northeast), 12% Chinese (mainly in urban areas), 3·7% Malay (mainly in the south) and 2·7% Khmer (along the Cambodian border).

SOCIAL STATISTICS

2000 births, 773,009; deaths, 365,741. 2000 birth rate per 1,000 population, 12·5; death rate, 5·9. Annual population growth rate, 1992–2002, 1·1%. Of the total population in 2002, 22% were under 15 years, 72% between 15 and 64 years, and 6% aged 65 and over. Expectation of life (2001): 64·9 years for men; 73·2 years for women. Infant mortality, 2001, 24 per 1,000 live births; fertility rate, 2001, 2·0 births per woman.

CLIMATE

The climate is tropical, with high temperatures and humidity. Over most of the country, three seasons may be recognized. The rainy season is June to Oct., the cool season from Nov. to Feb. and the hot season is March to May. Rainfall is generally heaviest in the south and lightest in the northeast. Bangkok, Jan. 78°F (25·6°C), July 83°F (28·3°C). Annual rainfall 56" (1,400 mm).

On 26 Dec. 2004 an undersea earthquake centred off the Indonesian island of Sumatra caused a huge tsunami that flooded coastal areas in western Thailand resulting in 5,000 deaths. In total there were 290,000 deaths in twelve countries.

CONSTITUTION AND GOVERNMENT

The reigning King is **Bhumibol Adulyadej,** born 5 Dec. 1927. King Bhumibol married on 28 April 1950 Princess Sirikit, and was crowned 5 May 1950 (making him currently the world's longest-reigning monarch). *Offspring:* Princess Ubol Ratana (born 5 April 1951, married Aug. 1972 Peter Ladd Jensen); Crown Prince Vajiralongkorn (born 28 July 1952, married 3 Jan. 1977 Soamsawali Kitiyakra); Princess Maha Chakri Sirindhorn (born 2 April 1955); Princess Chulabhorn (born 4 July 1957, married 7 Jan. 1982 Virayudth Didyasarin).

Parliament consists of a 200-member *Senate*, fully elected for the first time in 2000, and a 500-member *House of Representatives*, elected for four-year terms by universal suffrage of citizens over 17 years, with 400 constituency MPs and 100 from party lists. The present constitution dates from 1997. It is Thailand's 16th since 1932 and the first to emerge from public consultation rather than a military coup. It particularly tries to eradicate vote-buying. It introduced proportional representation for some seats, established an independent election commission, and required that votes be counted away from the polling stations. The constitution further required all cabinet members to resign their parliamentary seats.

The *Prime Minister* is elected by the House of Representatives.

National Anthem. 'Prathet Thai ruam nua chat chua Thai' ('Thailand, cradle of Thais wherever they may be'); words by Luang Saranuprapan, tune by Phrachen Duriyang.

RECENT ELECTIONS

At the elections to the House of Representatives of 6 Feb. 2005 the Thai Rak Thai Party (TRT) gained 375 seats; the Democratic Party (PP), 96; Thai Nation (PCT), 27; Great People's Party (PM), 2.

There were elections to the Senate on 4 March, 29 April, 4 June and 9 July 2000. 200 members were elected in single-seat constituencies. Only non-partisans were allowed to stand. A number of members were disqualified amid allegations of vote fraud.

CURRENT ADMINISTRATION

Following the 2001 election a coalition was formed between the TRT, PCT and PKWM. It was renewed following the Feb. 2005 election and in March 2005 comprised:

Prime Minister: Thaksin Shinawatra; b. 1949 (TRT; sworn in 9 Feb. 2001).

Deputy Prime Ministers: Somkid Jatusripitak (also *Minister of Finance*), Chitchai Wannasathit (also *Minister of Interior*), Chaturon Chaisang, Surakiart Sathirathai, Phinij Jarusombat, Wissanu Krea-Ngam.

Minister of Defence: Gen. Thammarak Isarangura Na Ayutthaya. *Foreign Affairs:* Kantathi Suphamongkhon. *Tourism and Sports:* Somsak Thepsuthin. *Social Development and Human Security:* Pracha Maleenont. *Agriculture and Co-operatives:* Sudarat Keyuraphan. *Transport:* Suriya Jungrungreangkit. *Natural Resources and*

Environment: Yongyut Tiyapairat. *Information and Communications Technology:* Suwit Khunkitti. *Energy:* Wiset Jupibal. *Commerce:* Thanong Bidaya. *Justice:* Suwat Liptapanlop. *Labour:* Sora-at Klinpratoom. *Culture:* Uraiwan Thienthong. *Education:* Adisai Bodharamik. *Public Health:* Suchai Charoenratanakul. *Industry:* Watana Muangsook. *Science and Technology:* Korn Thapparansi.

Office of the Prime Minister: http://www.spokesman.go.th/

DEFENCE

Conscription is for two years. In 2003 defence expenditure totalled US$1,931m. (US$31 per capita), representing 1·3% of GDP.

Army. Strength (2002) 190,000. In addition there were 50,000 National Security Volunteer Corps, 20,000 *Thahan Phran* (a volunteer irregular force), 40,000 Border Police and a 50,000 strong paramilitary provincial police force.

Navy. The Royal Thai Navy is, next to the Chinese, the most significant naval force in the South China Sea. The fleet includes a small Spanish-built vertical/short-take-off-and-land carrier *Chakrinaruebet,* which entered service in 1997 and operates 13 ex-Spanish AV-8A Harrier aircraft and helicopters, and 12 frigates. Manpower was 68,000 (2002) including 18,000 marines and a naval air wing of 1,700.

The main bases are at Bangkok, Sattahip, Songkla and Phang Nga, with the riverine forces based at Nakhon Phanom.

Air Force. The Royal Thai Air Force had a strength (2002) of 48,000 personnel and 194 combat aircraft, including F-16s and F-5Es. The RTAF is made up of a headquarters and Combat, Logistics Support, Training and Special Services Groups.

INTERNATIONAL RELATIONS

Thailand is a member of the UN, WTO, BIS, Asian Development Bank, ASEAN, the Colombo Plan, APEC, the Mekong Group and IOM.

In 2001 tension between Thailand and neighbouring Myanmar escalated amid a series of border skirmishes, in part over the cross-border trade in drugs. In May 2002 the border between the two countries was closed following a diplomatic row. It was re-opened in Oct. 2002.

ECONOMY

In 2002 agriculture accounted for 9·3% of GDP, industry 42·7% and services 48·0%.

Thailand's 'shadow' (black market) economy is estimated to constitute approximately 70% of the country's official GDP, one of the highest percentages of any country in the world.

Overview. In the 25 years to 1998 an agricultural base was transformed into a diverse industrialized economy. An export oriented, labour-intensive manufacturing sector has developed through the promotion of foreign investment. During the 1990s the fastest growth was seen in the high technology goods sector, such as computer accessories, and motor vehicle parts. The 1998 Asian crisis had a severe impact on Thailand, with GDP contracting by 10·5% in 1998, increased inflation and high unemployment. Domestic and external demand dropped and poverty rose. However, the Thai economy recovered quickly; in 1999 the economy was growing at over 4%. Following the crisis Thailand began to implement reform of the financial sector, corporate governance and competition policy. National Economic and Social Development Plans (NESD) have been the backbone of policy making for 35 years. The Ninth NESD (2002–06) is geared towards an integrated approach, with policy focusing on promoting the tourist industry and the property sector. Emphasis will also be put on restructuring bad debts, addressing overleveraged firms and privatizing state enterprises. The tsunami of Dec. 2004 has had an adverse effect on the economy, particularly in relation to tourism.

Currency. The unit of currency is the *baht* (THB) of 100 *satang*. After being pegged to the US dollar, the baht was devalued and allowed to float on 2 July 1997. It was the devaluation of the baht that sparked the financial turmoil that spread throughout the world over the next year. Foreign exchange reserves were US$35,985m. and gold reserves 2·50m. troy oz in June 2002. Inflation was 0·6% in 2002. Total money supply in May 2002 was 598,378m. baht.

Budget. The fiscal year starts on 1 Oct. Total revenues and expenditures (in 1m. baht):

	1995–96	*1996–97*	*1997–98*	*1998–99*	*1999–2000*
Revenue	872,967	870,421	753,347	739,136	789,518
Expenditure	757,961	957,707	1,051,667	1,160,241	884,796

Principal expenditure in 1999–2000 (in 1m. baht) was on: education (198,514), transportation and communication (99,335), agriculture, forestry, fishing and hunting (78,132), health (74,427) and defence (73,571).

Performance. Following the financial crisis in the second half of 1997 the economy contracted by 10·5% in 1998. Growth recovered to 4·4% in 1999 and in 2000 was 4·8%, but 2001 saw growth of only 2·1% in the wake of the general downturn in the world economy. In 2002 there was real GDP growth of 5·4%, rising to 6·3% in 2003. Growth in 2004 was also estimated to have been above 6%. Thailand's total GDP in 2003 was US$143·2bn.

Banking and Finance. The Bank of Thailand (founded in 1942) is the central bank and bank of issue, an independent body although its capital is government-owned. Its assets and liabilities in 2002 were 2,853,897m. baht. Its *Governor* is Pridiyathorn Devakula. In 2002 there were 30 commercial banks, 13 domestic banks and 21 foreign banks. In addition the Thai government controlled four banks in 2002: the Bank of Agriculture and Agricultural Co-operatives, the Government Housing Bank, the Government Savings Bank and the Export-Import Bank of Thailand. Total assets of commercial banks, 2002, 6,900,947m. baht. Deposits, 2001, 5,109,973m. baht.

There is a stock exchange (SET) in Bangkok.

Weights and Measures. The metric system is official but traditional units are still employed: one *catty* = 600 grams; one *picul* = 100 catty; one *wah* = 2 metres; one *sen* = 20 wah; one *rai* = 1 sq. sen.

ENERGY AND NATURAL RESOURCES

Environment. Thailand's carbon dioxide emissions from the consumption and flaring of fossil fuels were the equivalent of 3·0 tonnes per capita in 1999.

Electricity. Installed capacity, 2000, was 27·6m. kW. Output, 2000, 101·58bn. kWh, with consumption per capita 1,674 kWh.

Oil and Gas. Proven crude petroleum reserves in 2002 were 600m. bbls. Production of crude petroleum (2003), 9·0m. tonnes. Thailand and Vietnam settled an offshore dispute in 1997 which stretched back to 1973. Demarcation allowed for petroleum exploration in the Gulf of Thailand, with each side required to give the other some revenue if an underground reservoir is discovered which straddles the border.

Production of natural gas (2002), 18·9bn. cu. metres. Estimated reserves, 2002, 380bn. cu. metres. In April 1998 Thailand and Malaysia agreed to share equally the natural gas jointly produced in an offshore area which both countries claim as their own territory.

Minerals. The mineral resources include cassiterite (tin ore), wolfram, scheelite, antimony, lignite, copper, gold, manganese, molybdenum, rubies, sapphires, silver, zinc and zircons. Production, 2002 (in tonnes): limestone, 53·67m.; lignite, 19·60m.; gypsum, 6·33m.; salt (2001), 952,265; feldspar, 710,543; zinc ore, 151,575; kaolin clay, 127,182; fluorite, 2,270.

Agriculture. In 2001 there were 15·0m. ha of arable land and 3·3m. ha of permanent cropland. 4·92m. ha were irrigated in 2001. The chief produce is rice, a staple of the national diet. Output of the major crops in 2000 was (in 1,000 tonnes): sugarcane, 51,210; rice, 23,403; cassava, 18,509; maize, 4,571; pineapples, 2,281; natural rubber, 2,236; bananas, 1,720; coconuts, 1,373; mangoes, 1,350; tangerines, mandarins and satsumas, 640; palm oil, 520; watermelons, 400; soybeans, 346; oranges, 320; onions, 300; sorghum, 250. Thailand is the world's leading producer of both natural rubber and pineapples.

Livestock, 2000: cattle, 6,100,000; pigs, 7,682,000; buffaloes, 2,100,000; goats, 130,000; sheep, 42,000; chickens, 172m.; ducks, 22m.

Forestry. Forests covered 14·76m. ha in 2000, or 28·9% of the land area. Teak and other hardwoods grow in the deciduous forests of the north; elsewhere tropical evergreen forests are found, with the timber yang the main crop (a source of yang oil). In 2001, 27·50m. cu. metres of roundwood were cut.

Fisheries. In 2001 the total catch came to 2,881,316 tonnes with marine fishing accounting for over 92% of all fish caught. Thailand is the leading exporter of fishery commodities in the world, with exports in 2001 totalling US$4·04bn.

INDUSTRY

The leading companies by market capitalization in Thailand in May 2004 were: PTT, a petroleum exploration and production company (US$10·9bn.); Advanced Info Service (AIS), a mobile phone provider (US$6·5bn.); and the Siam Cement Group (US$6·4bn.).

Production of manufactured goods in 2002 included 31·68m. tonnes of cement, 13·39m. tonnes of distillate fuel oil (2000), 6·87m. tonnes of residual fuel oil (2000), 5·95m. tonnes of sugar, 5·59m. tonnes of petrol (2000), 2·5m. tonnes of crude steel, 768,098 tonnes of synthetic fibre, 519,006 tonnes of galvanized iron sheets, 208,000 tonnes of tin plate (2001), 1,636·0m. litres of soft drinks (2001), 1,238·0m. litres of beer (2001), 30·8bn. cigarettes, 169,304 automobiles and 415,593 commercial vehicles, and 6,096,000 televisions.

Labour. In the period Sept.–Dec. 2003 the total labour force was 35·5m.; 14·2m. persons were employed in agriculture, hunting and forestry, 5·3m. in manufacturing, 5·2m. in wholesale and retail trade and 2·1m. in hotels and restaurants. The unemployment rate was 2·4% in June 2002. A minimum wage is set by the National Wages Committee. It varied between 133 baht and 170 baht per day in Jan. 2004.

INTERNATIONAL TRADE

Foreign debt was US$59,211m. in 2002.

Imports and Exports. Trade in US$1m.:

	1998	*1999*	*2000*	*2001*	*2002*
Imports f.o.b.	36,515	42,762	56,193	54,620	57,020
Exports f.o.b.	52,753	56,775	67,894	63,202	66,795

In 1999 main exports by category: machinery and transport equipment, 41·9%; manufactured goods, 11·8%; fish and seafood, 7·0%; clothing, 6·0%; chemicals, 5·0%; rice, 3·3%. Imports: machinery and transport equipment, 43·1%; chemicals, 10·8%; petroleum, 9·5%; iron and steel, 5·4%.

In 1999 the main import sources were Japan (24·4%), USA (12·8%), Singapore (5·9%), China (5·0%), Malaysia (5·0%) and South Korea (3·5%). Principal export destinations were USA (21·7%), Japan (14·1%), Singapore (8·7%), Hong Kong (5·1%), Netherlands (3·8%), Malaysia (3·6%) and the UK (3·6%).

COMMUNICATIONS

Roads. In 2000 there were 57,403 km of roads, of which 98·5% were paved. Vehicles in use in 2002 included: 2·66m. passenger cars, 3·54m. commercial vehicles and 16·58m. motorcycles.

Rail. The State Railway totals 4,623 km. Passenger-km travelled in 1999–2000 came to 10·0bn. and freight tonne-km to 3·3bn. A metro (‘Skytrain’), or elevated transit system, was opened in Bangkok in 1999. A second (underground) mass transit system in Bangkok, the Bangkok Subway, was opened in 2004.

Civil Aviation. There are international airports at Bangkok (Don Muang), Chiangmai, Phuket and Hat Yai. The national carrier, Thai Airways International, is 53·98% state-owned. In 1999 it flew 163·4m. km, carrying 15,950,500 passengers (10,100,400 on international flights). Bangkok handled 28,323,474 passengers in 2000 (20,965,985 on international flights) and 873,792 tonnes of freight. Phuket is the second busiest airport for passenger traffic, with 3,562,636 passengers in 2000 (2,213,874 on domestic flights), and Chiangmai the second busiest for freight, with 23,804 tonnes in 2000. Work on a new Bangkok airport (Suvarnabhumi) is scheduled for completion in late 2005.

Shipping. In 2002 merchant shipping totalled 1,880,000 GRT, including oil tankers 209,000 GRT. Vessels totalling 68,079,000 NRT entered ports in 2000 and vessels totalling 33,154,000 NRT cleared.

Telecommunications. In 2002 telephone subscribers numbered 22,616,800 (365·5 per 1,000 population) and 2,461,000 PCs were in use (39·8 for every 1,000 inhabitants). There were 16,117,000 mobile phone subscribers in 2002 and 150,000 fax machines in 1997. Thailand had 4·8m. Internet users in 2002.

Postal Services. There were 4,265 post offices in 1998, or one for every 14,300 persons.

SOCIAL INSTITUTIONS

Justice. The judicial power is exercised in the name of the King, by *(a)* courts of first instance, *(b)* the court of appeal *(Uthorn)* and *(c)* the Supreme Court *(Dika)*. The King appoints, transfers and dismisses judges, who are independent in conducting trials and giving judgment in accordance with the law.

Courts of first instance are subdivided into 20 magistrates' courts *(Kwaeng)* with limited civil and minor criminal jurisdiction; 85 provincial courts *(Changwad)* with unlimited civil and criminal jurisdiction; the criminal and civil courts with exclusive jurisdiction in Bangkok; the central juvenile courts for persons under 18 years of age in Bangkok.

The court of appeal exercises appellate jurisdiction in civil and criminal cases from all courts of first instance. From it appeals lie to Dika Court on any point of law and, in certain cases, on questions of fact.

The Supreme Court is the supreme tribunal of the land. Besides its normal appellate jurisdiction in civil and criminal matters, it has semi-original jurisdiction over general election petitions. The decisions of Dika Court are final. Every person has the right to present a petition to the government who will deal with all matters of grievance.

The death penalty is still in force and there were four executions in 2003. The population in penal institutions in mid-2002 was 258,076 (401 per 100,000 of national population).

Religion. At the 2000 census 94·6% of the population were Buddhists and 4·6% Muslims. In Sept. 2003 the Roman Catholic church had one cardinal.

Education. Education is compulsory for children for nine years and is free in local municipal schools. In 2002 there were 6,096,208 pupils with (in 1999) 293,391 teachers. There were 4,068,188 secondary school pupils in 2002 with (in 1999) 242,892 teachers. There were 946,187 students in vocational education in 2001. In higher education there were 1,984,843 students in 2002. In 1996 there were 13 universities, two open (distance) universities, four institutes of technology and one institute of development administration in the public sector, and nine universities and one institute of technology in the private sector.

The adult literacy rate in 2001 was 95·7% (97·3% among males and 94·1% among females).

In 2000–01 total expenditure on education came to 5·5% of GNP.

Health. In 2000 there were 1,293 hospitals, with a provision of 21 beds per 10,000 population in 1996. In 2000 there were 18,025 doctors, 4,141 dentists, 6,384 pharmacists, 70,978 nurses and (in 1995) 9,713 midwives. Thailand has been one of the most successful countries in the developing world in the fight against AIDS. By the mid-1990s the government was spending US$80m. a year on AIDS education, and the number of sexually transmitted diseases reported from government clinics fell from some 400,000 in 1986 to below 50,000 in 1995. However, since 1996 AIDS expenditure has been declining rapidly. As a result, HIV infections are now increasing among several risk groups after a period of overall decline.

CULTURE

World Heritage Sites. There are four sites in Thailand that appear on the UNESCO World Heritage List. They are (with the year entered on list): the Thung Yai-Huai Kha Khaeng wildlife sanctuaries (1991); the palace, temples, Buddhas, etc. of the historic town of Sukhothai (1991); the 15th–18th century historic town of Ayutthaya (1991); and the Bronze Age Ba Chiang archaeological site (1992).

Broadcasting. The Radio and Television Executive Committee controls the administrative, legal, technical and programming aspects of broadcasting, and consists of representatives of various government bodies. All radio stations are operated by, or under the supervision of, government agencies. Radio Thailand broadcasts three national programmes, provincial programmes, an educational service and an external service (nine languages), and the Voice of Free Asia. Television of Thailand is the state service (colour by PAL). There are three commercial channels and an Army service. At the 2000 census 91·5% of households had televisions and 77·2% had radios. In 2001 there were 18·4m. TV receivers.

Press. In 1996 there were 30 daily newspapers, with a combined circulation of about 3·8m.

Tourism. In 2002, 10·87m. foreign tourists visited Thailand. Tourist revenue in 2000 was US$7·12bn.

DIPLOMATIC REPRESENTATIVES

Of Thailand in the United Kingdom (29–30 Queen's Gate, London, SW7 5JB)
Ambassador: Vikrom Koompirochana.

Of the United Kingdom in Thailand (Wireless Rd, Bangkok 10330)
Ambassador: David Fall.

Of Thailand in the USA (1024 Wisconsin Ave., NW, Washington, D.C., 20007)
Ambassador: Kasit Piromya.

Of the USA in Thailand (120 Wireless Rd, Bangkok 10330)
Ambassador: Darryl Norman Johnson.

Of Thailand to the United Nations
Ambassador: Laxanachantorn Laohaphan.

Of Thailand to the European Union
Ambassador: Vacant.

FURTHER READING

National Statistical Office *Thailand Statistical Yearbook.*

Krongkaew, M. (ed.) *Thailand's Industrialization and its Consequences*. London, 1995
Kulick, E. and Wilson, D., *Thailand's Turn: Profile of a New Dragon.* London and New York, 1993 (NY, 1994)
Smyth, David, *Thailand.* [Bibliography] 2nd ed. ABC-Clio, Oxford and Santa Barbara (CA), 1998

National statistical office: National Statistical Office, Thanon Lan Luang, Bangkok 10100.
Website: http://www.nso.go.th

TOGO

République Togolaise

Capital: Lomé
Population projection, 2010: 5·73m.
GDP per capita, 2002: (PPP$) 1,480
HDI/world rank: 0·495/143

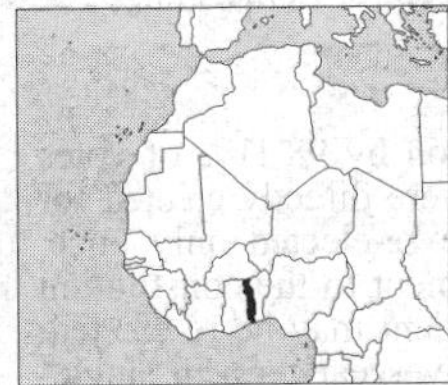

KEY HISTORICAL EVENTS

Europeans, beginning with the Portuguese who first visited the area in 1471–72, traded on the coast for centuries, especially in slaves. In the 19th century palm oil exports flourished at Anecho, Agoue and Porto Seguro, where British, French and German traders operated. Several prominent Togolese families of partly Brazilian or Portuguese origin, still important among the coastal African élite, arose at that time. Despite the important rival influences of Britain and France in the area, it was Germany that established colonial rule on the coast in 1884. German control was then extended inland but only in 1912 was the colony fully subdued.

German Togo was overrun by the Allies in 1914. It was partitioned in 1919 into British and French Mandated Territories under the League of Nations. After the Second World War French Togo and British Togoland became Trust Territories under the United Nations. In British Togoland a referendum was held on 9 May 1956, in which a majority voted for union with Gold Coast, although most people in the south voted for union with French Togo. The whole territory was merged with what soon afterwards became independent Ghana, but many Togolese objected. In French Togo partial self-government was granted in 1956. On 27 April 1960 the country became independent.

On 13 Jan. 1963 President Olympio was murdered by soldiers. His successor was deposed in a bloodless military coup in Jan. 1967 and on 14 April 1967 Gen. (then Col.) Gnassingbé Eyadéma assumed the Presidency. A new constitution was approved in 1992. On Gnassingbé Eyadéma's death on 5 Feb. 2005 the military installed his son, Faure Gnassingbé, as his successor. The next day parliament changed the constitution to legalize his succession. Under international pressure he stepped down on 25 Feb. 2005, with parliament speaker Abass Bonfoh becoming interim president.

TERRITORY AND POPULATION

Togo is bounded in the west by Ghana, north by Burkina Faso, east by Benin and south by the Gulf of Guinea. The area is 56,785 sq. km. The population of Togo in 1981 (census) was 2,700,982; 2002 estimate, 4·79m.; density, 84 per sq. km.

The UN gives a projected population for 2010 of 5·73m.

In 2001, 66·1% of the population lived in rural areas. In 1997, 46% were below the age of 15. The capital is Lomé (population in 1999, 790,000), other towns being Sokodé (51,000), Lama-Kara (35,000), Atakpamé (30,000), Kpalimé (30,000), Bassar (22,000), Dapaong (22,000) and Mango (20,000).

Area, population and chief town of the five regions:

Region	*Area in sq. km*	*Population (1981 census)*	*Population (1989 estimate)*	*Chief town*
Centrale	13,182	269,174	339,000	Sokodé
De La Kara	11,630	432,626	531,500	Lama-Kara
Des Plateaux	16,975	561,656	810,500	Atakpamé
Des Savanes	8,602	326,826	410,500	Dapaong
Maritime	6,396	1,039,700	1,147,800[1]	Lomé

[1]1984 figure.

There are 37 ethnic groups. The south is largely populated by Ewe-speaking peoples (forming 44% of the population) and related groups, while the north is mainly inhabited by Hamitic groups speaking Kabre (27%), Gurma (14%) and Tem (4%). The official language is French but Ewe and Kabre are also taught in schools.

SOCIAL STATISTICS

Births, 1996, 197,000; deaths, 55,000. 1996 birth rate (per 1,000 population), 45·5; death rate, 12·8. Expectation of life (2001) was 48·6 years for males and 52·0 for females. Annual population growth rate, 1992–2002, 2·9%. Infant mortality, 2001, 79 per 1,000 live births; fertility rate, 2001, 5·5 births per woman.

CLIMATE

The tropical climate produces wet seasons from March to July and from Oct. to Nov. in the south. The north has one wet season, from April to July. The heaviest rainfall occurs in the mountains of the west, southwest and centre. Lomé, Jan. 81°F (27·2°C), July 76°F (24·4°C). Annual rainfall 35" (875 mm).

CONSTITUTION AND GOVERNMENT

A referendum on 27 Sept. 1992 approved a new constitution by 98·11% of votes cast. Under this the *President* and the *National Assembly* were directly elected for five-year terms. Initially the president was allowed to be re-elected only once. However, on 30 Dec. 2002 parliament approved an amendment to the constitution lifting the restriction on the number of times that the president may be re-elected. The National Assembly has 81 seats and is elected for a five-year term in single-seat constituencies.

National Anthem. 'Terre de nos aïeux' ('Land of our forefathers').

RECENT ELECTIONS

In presidential elections held on 24 April 2005 Faure Gnassingbé (son of former president Gnassingbé Eyadéma) of the Togolese People's Assembly (Rassemblement du Peuple Togolais; RPT) won with 60·2% of the vote. Emmanuel Bob Akitani of the Union des Forces de Changement (UFC) took 38·2%. Nicolas Lawson of the Renewal and Redemption Party won 1·0% and Harry Olympio of the Rally for Support of Democracy 0·6%. Turn-out was 63·6%. The UFC claimed the results were rigged and there were widespread protests in Lomé. Gnassingbé was confirmed as president by the constitutional court on 3 May 2005.

At the parliamentary elections on 27 Oct. 2002 the main opposition parties to the RPT, the former sole party, boycotted the election, protesting a lack of transparency in the voting process. Turn-out was put at around 60% and preliminary results showed the RPT had won 72 of the available 81 seats, down 7 on its 1999 showing.

CURRENT ADMINISTRATION

President: Faure Gnassingbé; b. 1966 (RPT; sworn in 4 May 2005).

In March 2005 the government comprised:

Prime Minister: Koffi Sama; b. 1944 (RPT; sworn in 29 June 2002).

Minister of Agriculture, Animal Breeding and Fisheries: Komikpine Bamenante. *Civil Service, Labour and Employment:* Rodolphe Kossivi Osseyi. *Communication and Civic Education:* Pitang Tchalla. *Culture:* Angèle Aguigah. *Economy, Finance and Privatization:* Débaba Bale. *Energy and Water Resources:* Issifou Okoulou-Kantchati. *Environment and Forest Resources:* Gen. Zoumaro Gnofame. *Foreign Affairs and Co-operation:* Kokou Tozoun. *Health:* Suzanne Aho Assouma. *Higher Education and Research:* Charles Kondi Agba. *Industry, Commerce, Transport and the Development of the Franc Zone:* Takpandja Lalle. *Interior, Security and Decentralization:* Akila Esso Boco. *Justice, Human Rights and Keeper of the Seals:* Katari Foli-Bazi. *Democracy and Rule of Law Promotion:* Roland Yao Kpotsra. *National Defence and War Veterans:* Gen. Assani Tidjani. *Primary and Secondary Education:* Komi Klassou. *Public Works, Mines, Posts and Telecommunications:* Vacant. *Relations with the National Assembly:* Comlangan Mawutoè d'Almeida. *Social Affairs, Promotion of Women and Protection of Children:* Sayo Boyoti. *Technical Education and Professional Training:* Edo Kodjo Agbobli. *Tourism, Leisure and Handicrafts:* Ebina Dorothée Iloudjè. *Town Planning and Housing:* Dovi Kavégué. *Youth and Sports:* Agouta Ouyenga.

Government Website (French only): http://www.republicoftogo.com/

DEFENCE

There is selective conscription which lasts for two years. Defence expenditure totalled US$31m. in 2003 (US$6 per capita), representing 1·7% of GDP.

Army. Strength (2002) 9,000, with a further 750 in a paramilitary gendarmerie.

Navy. In 2002 the Naval wing of the armed forces numbered 200 and was based at Lomé.

Air Force. The Air Force—established with French assistance—numbered (2002) 250, with 16 combat aircraft.

INTERNATIONAL RELATIONS

Togo is a member of the UN, WTO, the African Union, African Development Bank, ECOWAS and the International Organization of the Francophonie, OIC, Islamic Development Bank and is an ACP member state of the ACP-EU relationship.

ECONOMY

Agriculture contributed 38·1% of GDP in 2002, industry 18·5% and services 43·3%.

Overview. After civil and economic turmoil in the early 1990s, a structural redevelopment programme, launched in 1994, resulted in positive growth. Privatization began in the 1980s and resumed in 1996 with World Bank support.

Currency. The unit of currency is the *franc CFA* (XOF) with a parity of 655·957 francs CFA to one euro. Foreign exchange reserves were US$201m. in May 2002 and total money supply was 173,247m. francs CFA. Gold reserves were 13,000 troy oz in June 2000. Inflation in 2002 was 3·1%.

Budget. In 1999 revenues were 140·4bn. francs CFA and expenditures 173·7bn. francs CFA.

Performance. Real GDP growth was 0·6% in 2001, rising to 2·9% in 2002. Total GDP in 2003 was US$1·8bn.

Banking and Finance. The bank of issue is the Central Bank of West African States (BCEAO). The *Governor* is Charles Konan Banny. In 2003 there were six commercial banks, three development banks, a savings bank and a credit institution.

ENERGY AND NATURAL RESOURCES

Environment. Togo's carbon dioxide emissions from the consumption and flaring of fossil fuels in 2002 were the equivalent of 0·2 tonnes per capita.

Electricity. Installed capacity in 2000 was 38,000 kW. In 2000 production totalled around 68m. kWh. Additional electricity is imported from Ghana. Consumption per capita in 2000 was 128 kWh.

Minerals. Output of phosphate rock in 2002 was 1·1m. tonnes. Other minerals are limestone, iron ore and marble.

Agriculture. Agriculture supports about 80% of the population. Most food production comes from individual holdings under 3 ha. Inland, the country is hilly; dry plains alternate with arable land. There were 2·51m. ha of arable land in 2001 and 0·12m. ha of permanent crops. There are considerable plantations of oil and cocoa palms, coffee, cacao, kola, cassava and cotton. Production, 2000 (in 1,000 tonnes): cassava, 694; yams, 666; maize, 494; seed cotton, 162; sorghum, 142; cottonseed, 91; rice, 81; cotton lint, 65; dry beans, 45; millet, 39; groundnuts, 35.

Livestock (2000, in 1,000): cattle, 215; sheep, 740; pigs, 850; goats, 1,110; chickens, 8,000.

Forestry. Forests covered 510,000 ha in 2000, or 9·4% of the land area. Teak plantations covered 8,600 ha. In 2001, 5·78m. cu. metres of roundwood were cut.

Fisheries. The catch in 2001 totalled 23,163 tonnes (78% from marine waters).

INDUSTRY

Industry is small-scale. Cement and textiles are produced and food processed. In 2001 industry accounted for 21·1% of GDP, with manufacturing contributing 9·7%.

Labour. In 1996 the workforce was 1,739,000 (60% males). Around 62% of the economically active population in 1995 were engaged in agriculture, fisheries and forestry. In 2002 the statutory minimum wage was 125·16 francs CFA per hour.

Trade Unions. With the abandonment of single-party politics, the former monolithic Togo National Workers Confederation (CNTT) has split into several federations and independent trade unions.

INTERNATIONAL TRADE

A free trade zone was established in 1990. Foreign debt was US$1,581m. in 2002.

Imports and Exports. In 2001 imports (f.o.b.) amounted to US$516·1m. (US$484·6m. in 2000); exports (f.o.b.) US$357·2m. (US$361·8m. in 2000). The main import suppliers in 1999 were France (17·5%), Côte d'Ivoire (11·6%), Benin (6·0%), Italy (4·1%) and the Netherlands (4·1%). Principal export destinations were Benin (16·6%), Ghana (10·9%), Canada (5·1%), Brazil (4·8%) and Nigeria (4·1%).

COMMUNICATIONS

Roads. There were an estimated 7,520 km of roads in 1999, of which 2,380 km were paved. In 1996 there were 79,200 passenger cars, 59,000 motorcycles and 33,660 commercial vehicles.

Rail. There are four metre-gauge railways connecting Lomé, with Aného (continuing to Cotonou in Benin), Kpalimé, Tabligbo and (via Atakpamé) Blitta; total length 525 km. In 1994 the railways carried 5·7 tonne-km and 0·6m. passengers.

Civil Aviation. In 2003 Trans African Airlines flew from Tokoin airport, near Lomé, to Abidjan, Bamako, Brazzaville, Cotonou, Dakar and Pointe-Noire. There were also international flights with other airlines to Addis Ababa, Brussels, Douala, Kinshasa, Lagos, Libreville, Ouagadougou and Paris. In 2000 Tokoin handled 166,000 passengers (all on international flights) and 5,400 tonnes of freight. In 1999 scheduled airline traffic of Togo-based carriers flew 3·0m. km, carrying 84,000 passengers (all on international flights).

Shipping. In 2002 merchant shipping totalled 13,000 GRT.

Telecommunications. Togo had 221,200 telephone subscribers in 2002 (44·1 per 1,000 population) and there were 150,000 PCs in use (29·9 per 1,000 persons). There were 18,000 fax machines in 1999 and 170,000 mobile phone subscribers in 2002. Togo had 200,000 Internet users in 2002.

Postal Services. In 1995 there were 50 post offices.

SOCIAL INSTITUTIONS

Justice. The Supreme Court and two Appeal Courts are in Lomé, one for criminal cases and one for civil and commercial cases. Each receives appeal from a series of local tribunals.

The population in penal institutions in 1998 was 2,043 (46 per 100,000 of national population).

Religion. In 2001, 38% of the population followed traditional animist religions; 35% were Christian and 19% Muslim.

Education. The adult literacy rate in 2001 was 58·4% (73·4% among males and 44·0% among females). In 2000–01 there were 945,103 pupils and 27,523 teachers in primary schools, and 288,764 pupils in secondary schools; in 1999–2000 there were 15,171 students in higher education institutions. In 1990 about 50% of children of school age were attending school. The University of Benin at Lomé (founded in 1970) had 9,139 students and 134 academic staff in 1994–95.

In 2000–01 total expenditure on education came to 4·9% of GNP and accounted for 23·2% of total government expenditure.

Health. In 1990 hospital bed provision was 16 per 10,000 population. In 1995 there were 320 physicians, 29 dentists, 1,252 nurses and 438 midwives. Government expenditure on health in 1995 was estimated at 5,900m. francs CFA.

CULTURE

World Heritage Sites. There is one UNESCO site in Togo: Koutammakou, the land of the Batammariba (inscribed on the list in 2004).

Broadcasting. Broadcasting is provided by the government-controlled Radiodiffusion-Télévision Togolaise. There were 170,000 TV receivers (colour by SECAM V) in 2001 and 1·33m. radio sets in 2000.

Press. There is one government-controlled daily newspaper (circulation 10,000).

Tourism. In 2000 there were 60,000 foreign tourists; spending by tourists totalled US$5m.

DIPLOMATIC REPRESENTATIVES

Of Togo in the United Kingdom (resides in Paris)
Ambassador: Tchao Sotou Bere.

Of the United Kingdom in Togo
Ambassador: Gordon Wetherell (resides at Accra, Ghana).

Of Togo in the USA (2208 Massachusetts Ave., NW, Washington, D.C., 20008)
Ambassador: Akoussouleou Bodjona.

Of the USA in Togo (Rue Kouenou and Beniglato 15, BP 852, Lomé)
Ambassador: Gregory W. Engle.

Of Togo to the United Nations
Ambassador: Vacant.

Of Togo to the European Union
Ambassador: Ohara Kati Korga.

FURTHER READING

Decalo, Samuel, *Togo.* [Bibliography] ABC-Clio, Oxford and Santa Barbara (CA), 1995

TONGA

Kingdom of Tonga

Capital: Nuku'alofa
Population projection, 2010: 110,000
GDP per capita, 2002: (PPP$) 6,850
HDI/world rank: 0·787/63

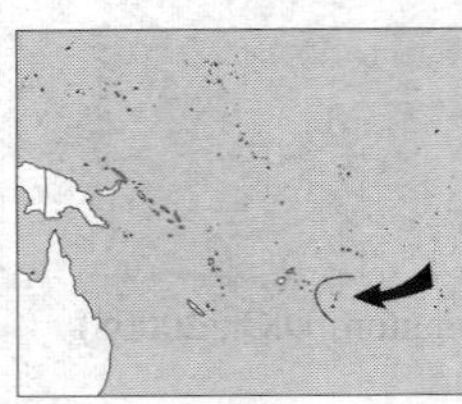

KEY HISTORICAL EVENTS

The Tongatapu group of islands in the south western Pacific Ocean were discovered by Tasman in 1643. The Kingdom of Tonga attained unity under Taufa'ahau Tupou (George I) who became ruler of his native Ha'apai in 1820, of Vava'u in 1833 and of Tongatapu in 1845. By 1860 the kingdom had become converted to Christianity. In 1862 the king granted freedom to the people from arbitrary rule of minor chiefs and gave them the right to the allocation of land for their own needs. These institutional changes, together with the establishment of a parliament of chiefs, paved the way towards a democratic constitution. By the Anglo-German Agreement of 14 Nov. 1899, the Tonga Islands became a British protectorate. The protectorate was dissolved on 4 June 1970 when Tonga, the only ancient kingdom surviving from the pre-European period in Polynesia, achieved independence within the Commonwealth.

TERRITORY AND POPULATION

The Kingdom consists of some 169 islands and islets with a total area, including inland waters and uninhabited islands, of 748 sq. km (289 sq. miles), and lies between 15° and 23° 30' S. lat and 173° and 177° W. long, its western boundary being the eastern boundary of the Fiji Islands. The islands are split up into the following groups (reading from north to south): the Niuas, Vava'u, Ha'apai, Tongatapu and 'Eua. The three main groups, both from historical and administrative significance, are Tongatapu in the south, Ha'apai in the centre and Vava'u in the north. Census population (1996) 97,784; density, 131 per sq. km. 2002 population estimate: 103,000. In 1995, 59% of the population lived in rural areas.

The UN gives a projected population for 2010 of 110,000.

The capital is Nuku'alofa on Tongatapu, population (1999) 37,000.

There are five divisions comprising 23 districts:

Division	*Sq. km*	*Census 1996*	*Capital*
Niuas	72	2,018	Hihifo
Vava'u	119	15,715	Neiafu
Ha'apai	110	8,138	Pangai
Tongatapu	261	66,979	Nuku'alofa
'Eua	87	4,934	Ohonua

Tongan and English are both spoken.

SOCIAL STATISTICS

Births, 2000, 2,471; deaths, 653; marriages, 747; divorces, 75. Annual population growth rate, 1992–2002, 0·3%. Infant mortality, 1999 estimate, 38 per 1,000 live births. Fertility rate, 2001, 3·8 births per woman.

CLIMATE

Generally a healthy climate, although Jan. to March hot and humid, with temperatures of 90°F (32·2°C). Rainfall amounts are comparatively high, being greatest from Dec. to March. Nuku'alofa, Jan. 25·8°C, July 21·3°C. Annual rainfall 1,643 mm. Vava'u, Jan. 27·3°C, July 23·4°C. Annual rainfall 2,034 mm.

CONSTITUTION AND GOVERNMENT

The reigning King is **Taufa'ahau Tupou IV**, GCVO, GCMG, KBE, born 4 July 1918, succeeded on 16 Dec. 1965 on the death of his mother, Queen Salote Tupou III.

The present Constitution is almost identical with that granted in 1875 by King George Tupou I. There is a Privy Council, Cabinet, Legislative Assembly and

Judiciary. The 30-member *Legislative Assembly*, which meets annually, is composed of the King, nine nobles elected by their peers, nine elected representatives of the people and the Privy Councillors (numbering 11); the King appoints one of the nine nobles to be the Speaker. The elections are held triennially.

National Anthem. 'E 'Otua, Mafimafi, ko ho mau 'eiki Koe' ('Oh Almighty God above, thou art our Lord and sure defence'); words by Prince Uelingtoni Ngu Tupoumalohi, tune by K. G. Schmitt.

RECENT ELECTIONS

Elections were held on 16 March 2005 for the nine elected seats. Seven seats were won by the Human Rights and Democracy Movement in Tonga.

CURRENT ADMINISTRATION

In April 2005 the government comprised:

Prime Minister, Minister of Communications, Civil Aviation, Marine Affairs and Ports: Prince Lavaka ata Ulukalala (one of the King's sons).

Deputy Prime Minister, Minister of Environment and Tourism: Cecil James Cocker.

Minister of Agriculture, Fisheries and Food: Siosaia Ma'Ulupekotofa Tuita. *Education:* Tevita Hala Palefau. *Finance:* Siosiua Utoikamanu. *Foreign Affairs, and Defence (acting):* Sonatane Tu'a Taumoepeau Tupou. *Health:* Dr Viliami Tangi. *Justice and Attorney General:* Siaosi Taimani 'Aho. *Lands, Surveys and Natural Resources:* Fielakepa. *Forestry:* Peauafi Haukinima. *Labour, Commerce and Industry:* Fred Sevele. *Police, Fire Services and Prisons:* Nuku. *Works and Disaster Relief Activities:* Tu'Ivakano.

Government Website: http://www.pmo.gov.to

DEFENCE

Navy. A naval force, some 125-strong in 1999, was based at Touliki, Nuku'alofa.

Air Force. An Air Force was created in 1996 and operates three Beech 18s for maritime patrol.

INTERNATIONAL RELATIONS

Tonga is a member of the UN, the Commonwealth, the Asian Development Bank, the Pacific Community and the Pacific Islands Forum, and is an ACP member state of the ACP-EU relationship.

ECONOMY

In 2002 agriculture accounted for 28·5% of GDP, industry 15·1% and services 56·3%.

Currency. The unit of currency is the *pa'anga* (TOP) of 100 *seniti*. In 2002 there was inflation of 15·0%. In June 2002 foreign exchange reserves were US$22m. Total money supply in June 2002 was T$42m.

Budget. Revenues were T$77·5m. in 2000–01, with expenditures T$84·7m.

Performance. In 2001 real GDP growth was 0·5%, rising to 1·6% in 2002. Total GDP in 2003 was US$163m.

Banking and Finance. The National Reserve Bank of Tonga (*Governor,* Siosi Cocker Mafi) was established in 1989 as a bank of issue and to manage foreign reserves. The Bank of Tonga and the Tonga Development Bank are both situated in Nuku'alofa with branches in the main islands. Other commercial banks in Nuku'alofa are ANZ Banking Group Ltd, the MBF Bank Ltd, the National Reserve Bank of Tonga and the Westpac Banking Corp.

ENERGY AND NATURAL RESOURCES

Environment. Tonga's carbon dioxide emissions from the consumption and flaring of fossil fuels in 2002 were the equivalent of 1·4 tonnes per capita.

Electricity. Production (2000 estimate) 35m. kWh. Installed capacity (2000) 8,000 kW.

Agriculture. In 2001 there were 17,000 ha of arable land and 31,000 ha of permanent crops. Production (2000 estimates, in 1,000 tonnes): yams, 31; cassava, 28; taro, 27; coconuts, 25; sweet potatoes, 5; plantains, 4; lemons and limes, 3; oranges, 3.

Livestock (2000): pigs, 81,000; goats, 14,000; horses, 11,000; cattle, 9,000.

Forestry. Timber production in 2001 was 2,000 cu. metres.

Fisheries. In 2001 the catch totalled 4,673 tonnes.

INDUSTRY

The main industries produce food and beverages, paper, chemicals, metals and textiles.

INTERNATIONAL TRADE

Foreign debt in 2002 amounted to US$74m.

Imports and Exports. In 2001 imports were valued at US$63·7m. and exports at US$6·7m. Main exports are coconut oil, vanilla beans, root crops, desiccated coconut and watermelons; main imports are food and live animals, basic manufactures, machinery and transport equipment, and mineral fuels and lubricants. The leading import suppliers in 1999–2000 were USA (35·2%), Australia (23·0%), New Zealand (12·3%) and Fiji Islands (10·3%). Principal export markets were Japan (57·5%), USA (18·5%), New Zealand (7·6%) and Australia (2·6%).

COMMUNICATIONS

Roads. In 1999 there were 680 km of roads (184 km paved). Vehicles in use in 1996 numbered approximately 1,140 passenger cars, 740 trucks and vans, and 40 buses and coaches.

Civil Aviation. There is an international airport at Nuku'alofa on Tongatapu. The national carrier was the state-owned Royal Tongan Airlines, but it ceased operations in May 2004 owing to financial difficulties. In 1998 Nuku'alofa handled 129,000 passengers (88,000 on international flights) and 1,100 tonnes of freight.

Shipping. In 2002 sea-going shipping totalled 291,000 GRT, including oil tankers 41,000 GRT. Two shipping lanes provide monthly services to American Samoa, Australia, the Fiji Islands, Kiribati, New Caledonia, New Zealand, Samoa and Tuvalu.

Telecommunications. The operation and development of the National Telecommunication Network and Services are the responsibilities of the Tonga Telecommunication Commission (TCC). There were 14,600 telephone subscribers in 2002, or 147·0 per 1,000 population. In 2002 mobile phone subscribers numbered 3,400 and there were 2,000 PCs in use, and there were approximately 200 fax machines in 1995. In 2002 there were 2,900 Internet users. Ucall mobile GSM digital has been in operation in Tonga since Dec. 2001.

SOCIAL INSTITUTIONS

Justice. The judiciary is presided over by the Chief Justice. The enforcement of justice is the responsibility of the Attorney-General and the Minister of Police. In 1994 the UK ceased appointing Tongan judges and subsidizing their salaries.

Religion. In 2001 there were 44,000 adherents of the Free Wesleyan Church and 16,000 Roman Catholics, with the remainder of the population being followers of other religions (notably Latter-day Saints).

Education. In 2002 there were a total of 17,105 pupils with 773 teachers in primary schools and 14,567 pupils with 1,012 teachers in secondary schools. There is an extension centre of the University of the South Pacific at Nuku'alofa, a teacher training college and three technical institutes.

Adult literacy in 1996 was estimated at 98·5%. In 2000–01 total expenditure on education came to 5·3% of GNP and accounted for 17·8% of total government expenditure.

Health. There were four hospitals in 1993 with a provision of 28 beds per 10,000 inhabitants. In 1997 there were 43 physicians, nine dentists, 309 nurses and 30 midwives.

CULTURE

Broadcasting. The Tonga Broadcasting Commission is an independent statutory board which operates two programmes. There is also a religious service. There were 61,000 radio sets in 1997. There are two television channels, and in 1997 an estimated 2,000 TV receivers.

Press. In 1996 there was one daily newspaper with a circulation of 7,000.

Tourism. There were 35,000 visitors in 2000. Receipts totalled US$9m.

DIPLOMATIC REPRESENTATIVES

Of Tonga in the United Kingdom (36 Molyneux St., London, W1H 5BQ)
Acting High Commissioner: Viela Tupou.

Of the United Kingdom in Tonga (POB 56 Nuku'alofa)
High Commissioner: Paul Nessling.

Of Tonga in the USA (250 E. 51st St., New York, NY 10022)
Ambassador: Sonatane Tu'a Taumoepeau Tupou.

Of the USA in Tonga
Ambassador: David Lyon (resides at Suva, Fiji Islands).

Of Tonga to the United Nations
Ambassador: Fekitamoeloa 'Utoikamanu.

Of Tonga to the European Union
Ambassador: Col. Fetu'utolu Tupou.

FURTHER READING

Campbell, I. C., *Island Kingdom: Tonga, Ancient and Modern.* Canterbury (NZ) Univ. Press, 1994

Wood-Ellem, E., *Queen Salote of Tonga, The Story of an Era 1900–1965.* Auckland Univ. Press, 2000

TRINIDAD AND TOBAGO

Capital: Port-of-Spain
Population projection, 2010: 1·33m.
GDP per capita, 2002: (PPP$) 9,430
HDI/world rank: 0·801/54

Republic of Trinidad and Tobago

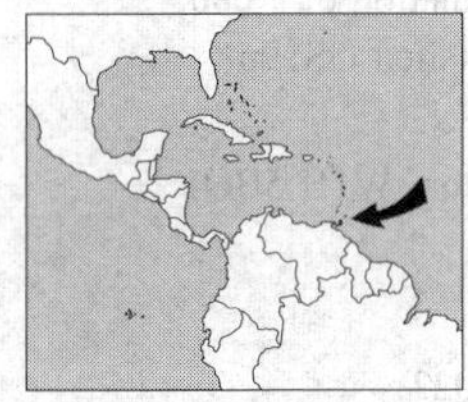

KEY HISTORICAL EVENTS

When Columbus visited Trinidad in 1498 the island was inhabited by Arawak Indians. Tobago was occupied by the Caribs. Trinidad remained a neglected Spanish possession for almost 300 years until it was surrendered to a British naval expedition in 1797. The British first attempted to settle Tobago in 1721 but the French captured the island in 1781 and transformed it into a sugar-producing colony. In 1802 the British acquired Tobago and in 1899 it was administratively combined with Trinidad. When slavery was abolished in the late 1830s, the British subsidized immigration from India to replace plantation labourers. Sugar and cocoa declined towards the end of the 19th century. Oil and asphalt became the dominant sources of income. On 31 Aug. 1962 Trinidad and Tobago became an independent member of the Commonwealth. A Republican Constitution was adopted on 1 Aug. 1976.

TERRITORY AND POPULATION

The island of Trinidad is situated in the Caribbean Sea, about 12 km off the northeast coast of Venezuela; several islets, the largest being Chacachacare, Huevos, Monos and Gaspar Grande, lie in the Gulf of Paria which separates Trinidad from Venezuela. The smaller island of Tobago lies 30·7 km further to the northeast. Altogether, the islands cover 5,128 sq. km (1,980 sq. miles), of which Trinidad (including the islets) has 4,828 sq. km (1,864 sq. miles) and Tobago 300 sq. km (116 sq. miles). In 2000 the census population was 1,262,366 (Trinidad, 1,208,282; Tobago, 54,084); density, 246 per sq. km.

The UN gives a projected population for 2010 of 1·33m.

In 2001, 74·5% of the population were urban. Capital, Port-of-Spain (2000 census, 49,031); other important towns, San Fernando (55,419), Arima (32,278) and Point Fortin (19,056). The main town on Tobago is Scarborough. Those of African descent are (1990 census) 39·6% of the population; East Indians, 40·3%; mixed races, 18·4%; European, Chinese and others, 1·6%.

English is generally spoken.

SOCIAL STATISTICS

Births, 1999, 18,600; deaths, 9,400. 1999 birth rate (per 1,000 population), 14·5; death rate, 7·3; growth rate, 0·6%. Expectation of life, 2001, was 68·6 years for males and 74·6 for females. Annual population growth rate, 1992–2002, 0·5%. Infant mortality, 2001, 17 per 1,000 live births; fertility rate, 2001, 1·6 births per woman.

CLIMATE

A tropical climate cooled by the northeast trade winds. The dry season runs from Jan. to June, with a wet season for the rest of the year. Temperatures are uniformly high the year round. Port-of-Spain, Jan. 76·3°F (24·6°C), July 79·2°F (26·2°C). Annual rainfall 1,869·8 mm.

CONSTITUTION AND GOVERNMENT

The 1976 Constitution provides for a bicameral legislature of a *Senate* and a *House of Representatives*, who elect the *President*, who is head of state. The *Senate* consists of 31 members, 16 being appointed by the President on the advice of the Prime Minister, six on the advice of the Leader of the Opposition and nine at the discretion of the President.

The *House of Representatives* consists of 36 (34 for Trinidad and two for Tobago) elected members and a Speaker elected from within or outside the House.

Executive power is vested in the Prime Minister, who is appointed by the President, and the Cabinet.

National Anthem. 'Forged from the love of liberty'; words and music by P. Castagne.

RECENT ELECTIONS

In parliamentary elections held on 7 Oct. 2002 the People's National Movement (PNP) won 20 out of 36 seats with 50·7% of votes cast, against 16 seats with 46·5% for the United National Congress (UNC). Turn-out was 69·8%. As a result Patrick Manning of the People's National Movement was returned to power. The elections ended a year-long deadlock between Manning and opposition leader, Basdeo Panday. Panday, who previously served as the country's first prime minister of East Indian descent between 1995–2001, refused to accept Manning's appointment as prime minister following the election of Dec. 2001, in which both parties had taken 18 seats.

CURRENT ADMINISTRATION

President: Maxwell Richards; b. 1931 (PNM; sworn in 17 March 2003).

In March 2005 the cabinet comprised:

Prime Minister, Minister for Finance: Patrick Manning; b. 1946 (PNM; sworn in 24 Dec. 2001).

Minister for Agriculture, Land and Marine Resources: Jarrette Narine. *Community Development and Culture:* Joan Yuille-Williams. *Education:* Hazel Manning. *Energy and Energy Industries:* Eric Williams. *Foreign Affairs:* Knowlson Gift. *Health:* John Rahael. *Housing:* Dr Keith Rowley. *Labour, and Small and Micro Enterprise Development:* Anthony Roberts. *Legal Affairs:* Danny Montano. *Local Government:* Rennie Dumas. *National Security:* Martin Joseph. *Planning and Development:* Camille Robinson-Regis. *Public Administration and Information:* Lenny Saith. *Public Utilities:* Penelope Beckles. *Science, Technology and Tertiary Education:* Colm Imbert. *Social Development:* Mustapha Abdul-Hamid. *Sports and Youth Affairs:* Roger Boynes. *Tourism:* Howard Chin Lee. *Trade, Industry and Consumer Affairs:* Ken Valley. *Works and Transport:* Franklin Khan. *Attorney General:* John Jeremie.

Government Website: http://www.gov.tt/

DEFENCE

The Defence Force has one infantry battalion, one engineer and one service battalion. The small air element is under the control of the Coast Guard. Personnel in 2002 totalled 2,700.

The police force has 4,294 personnel.

In 2003 defence expenditure totalled US$29m. (US$22 per capita), representing 0·3% of GDP. In the 1999–2000 budget the Ministry of National Security received a total allocation of $1,154m.

Navy. In 2002 there was a coastguard of 700 including an air wing of 50.

INTERNATIONAL RELATIONS

Trinidad and Tobago is a member of the UN and many of its specialized agencies including WIPO, IMF, the World Bank, IDA, IFC, IOB and ILO; and of WTO, the Commonwealth, OAS, Inter-American Development Bank, CARICOM, Association of Caribbean States (ACS), Caribbean Development Bank, Andean Development Bank and is an ACP member state of the ACP-EU relationship.

ECONOMY

Services accounted for 53·0% of GDP in 2002, industry 45·7% and agriculture 1·3%.

Currency. The unit of currency is the *Trinidad and Tobago dollar* (TTD) of 100 *cents*. Inflation in 2002 was 4·2%. In April 1994 the TT dollar was floated and managed by the Central Bank at TT$6·06 to US$1·00. Foreign exchange reserves in April 2002 were US$1,875m. and gold reserves 61,000 troy oz. Total money supply in March 2002 was TT$6,697m.

Budget. The fiscal year for the budget is 1 Oct. to 30 Sept. In 1999–2000 total government revenue was TT$12,028·5m. (TT$10,263·6m. in 1998–99) and total expenditure was TT$12,308·5m. (TT$10,526·3m. in 1998–99). The 2000–01 budget envisaged total recurrent revenue of TT$12,539·0m. (TT$9,998·2m. in 1998–99) and total capital expenditure of TT$1,027·0m. (TT$1,033·8m. in 1999–2000).

Performance. Real GDP growth was 3·3% in 2001 and 2·7% in 2002. Total GDP in 2003 was US$10·2bn.

Banking and Finance. The Central Bank of Trinidad and Tobago began operations in 1964 (*Governor*, Ewart Williams). Its net reserves were US$1,281·1m. in Aug. 2000. There are seven commercial banks. Government savings banks are established in 69 offices, with a head office in Port-of-Spain. The stock exchange in Port-of-Spain participates in the regional Caribbean exchange.

ENERGY AND NATURAL RESOURCES

Environment. Carbon dioxide emissions from the consumption and flaring of fossil fuels were the equivalent of 23·7 tonnes per capita in 2002.

Electricity. In 2000 installed capacity was 1·47m. kW, electricity production was 5·46bn. kWh and consumption per capita 4,233 kWh.

Oil and Gas. Oil production is one of Trinidad's leading industries. Commercial production began in 1908; production of crude oil in 2003 was 7·9m. tonnes. Reserves in 2002 totalled 700m. bbls. Crude oil is also imported for refining. Oil accounted for 30% of GDP and 75% of revenues in 1996, but dependence on the oil industry is declining. In 2002 production of natural gas was 16·8bn. cu. metres. Proven reserves of natural gas were 660bn. cu. metres in 2002. A major discovery of approximately 50bn. cu. metres was made by BP in 2000, followed by a further discovery of approximately 30bn. cu. metres in 2002.

Agriculture. Production of main crops (2000 estimates, in 1,000 tonnes): sugarcane, 1,500; coconuts, 23; oranges, 20; grapefruit and pomelos, 8; pumpkins and squash, 8; rice, 7; bananas, 6; maize, 5; plantains, 4. There were 75,000 ha of arable land and 47,000 ha of permanent cropland in 2001, and 11,000 ha of pasture in 1999.

Livestock (2000): goats, 59,000; pigs, 41,000; cattle, 35,000; sheep, 12,000; chickens, 10m. Livestock products, 2000 estimates: meat, 30,000 tonnes (including poultry, 26,000 tonnes); milk, 10,000 tonnes.

Forestry. Forests covered 259,000 ha in 2000, or 50·5% of the land area. Timber production for 2001 was 92,000 cu. metres.

Fisheries. The catch in 2001 totalled 11,408 tonnes.

INDUSTRY

Industrial production includes: ammonia and urea (production, 1998, 3,946,700 tonnes), iron and steel (2001, 3,550,800 tonnes), residual fuel oil (2000, 3,294,000 tonnes), methanol (1999, 2,149,800 tonnes), distillate fuel oil (2000, 1,697,000 tonnes), petrol (2000, 1,345,000 tonnes), cement (2001, 697,000 tonnes), sugar (2002, 104,000 tonnes), rum (1998, 3,916,000 proof gallons), beer (2000, 62·5m. litres), cigarettes (2000, 2,050,000 units). Trinidad and Tobago ranks among the world's largest producers of ammonia and methanol.

Labour. The working population in the first quarter of 2003 was 588,300. The number of unemployed was 65,000. 77,300 people worked in construction (including electricity and water); 55,500 in manufacturing (including other mining and quarrying); 38,600 in transport storage and communication; 37,800 in agriculture; 17,500 in petroleum and gas; other services, 295,300. Total employment: 523,300. The unemployment rate in the first quarter of 2003 was 11·0%.

Trade Unions. About 30% of the labour force belong to unions, which are grouped under the National Trade Union Centre.

INTERNATIONAL TRADE

The Foreign Investment Act of 1990 permits foreign investors to acquire land and shares in local companies, and to form companies. External debt was US$2,672m. in 2002.

Imports and Exports. In 2001 exports totalled US$4,304·2m. and imports US$3,586·1m. Mineral fuels and products account for 54% of exports, and machinery and transport equipment 34% of imports. The principal import sources in 1999 were USA (40·0%), Venezuela (11·9%), Colombia (5·2%) and Canada (5·2%). The main export markets in 1999 were USA (39·8%), Jamaica (8·4%), Barbados (5·2%) and the Netherlands Antilles (3·6%).

COMMUNICATIONS

Roads. In 1999 there were about 8,320 km of roads, of which 51·1% were paved. Motor vehicles registered in 1997 totalled 237,299.

Civil Aviation. There is an international airport at Port-of-Spain (Piarco) and in Tobago (Crown Point). In 2000 Piarco handled 1,768,932 passengers (1,329,879 on international flights) and 32,057 tonnes of freight. The national carrier is BWIA West Indies Airways, which was privatized in March 1995 by the Acker group of companies. In 2003 it flew to Antigua, Barbados, Caracas, Georgetown, Grenada, Kingston, London, Manchester, Miami, Nassau, New York, Paramaribo, St Kitts, St Maarten, San Jose, Santo Domingo, Toronto and Washington. In 1999 it carried 1,111,700 passengers (1,045,900 on international flights).

Shipping. Sea-going shipping totalled 27,000 GRT in 2002; 3,687,328 tonnes of cargo were handled at Port-of-Spain in 1999. There is a deep-water harbour at Scarborough (Tobago). The other main harbour is Point Lisas.

Telecommunications. International and domestic communications are provided by Telecommunications Services of Trinidad and Tobago (TSTT) by means of a satellite earth station and various high-quality radio circuits. The marine radio service is also maintained by TSTT. There were 687,000 telephone subscribers in 2002, or 527·8 per 1,000 inhabitants, and 104,000 PCs (79·5 for every 1,000 persons). There were 361,900 mobile phone subscribers in 2002 and 5,000 fax machines in 1998. Internet users numbered 138,000 in 2002.

Postal Services. Number of post offices (1998), 75; postal agencies, 167.

SOCIAL INSTITUTIONS

Justice. The High Court consists of the Chief Justice and 11 puisne judges. In criminal cases a judge of the High Court sits with a jury of 12 in cases of treason and murder, and with nine jurors in other cases. The Court of Appeal consists of the Chief Justice and seven Justices of Appeal. In hearing appeals, the Court is comprised of three judges sitting together except when the appeal is from a Summary Court or from a decision of a High Court judge in chambers. In such cases two judges would comprise the Court. There is a limited right of appeal from it to the Privy Council. There are three High Courts and 12 magistrates' courts. There is an *Ombudsman*. Trinidad and Tobago was one of ten countries to sign an agreement in Feb. 2001 establishing a Caribbean Court of Justice to replace the British Privy Council as the highest civil and criminal court. In the meantime the number of signatories has risen to twelve. The court was inaugurated at Port-of-Spain on 16 April 2005.

The death penalty is authorized and still used. There were ten executions in 1999.

The population in penal institutions in June 1999 was 4,794 (351 per 100,000 of national population).

Religion. In 2001, 29·9% of the population were Roman Catholics (under the Archbishop of Port-of-Spain), 24·2% Hindus, 19·2% Protestants, 11·2% Anglicans (under the Bishop of Trinidad and Tobago) and 6·0% Muslims.

Education. In 1999–2000 there were 162,736 pupils enrolled in 481 primary schools, 17,715 in government secondary schools, 21,068 in assisted secondary schools, 33,053 in junior secondary schools, 21,930 in senior comprehensive schools, 3,057 in senior secondary schools, 8,677 in composite schools and 3,935 in technical and vocational schools. There were 4,121 pupils enrolled in the three Technical and Vocational schools for the period 1998–99. The University of the West Indies campus in St Augustine (1999–2000) had 7,585 students and 477 academic staff. 1,307 of the students were from other countries.

Adult literacy was 98·4% in 2001 (male, 99·0%; female, 97·8%).

In 2000–01 total expenditure on education came to 4·3% of GNP and accounted for 16·7% of total government expenditure.

Health. In 1999 there were 1,171 physicians, 189 dentists, 500 pharmacists and 71 hospitals and nursing homes with 4,384 beds. There were 1,936 nurses and midwives and 1,486 nursing assistants in government institutions.

CULTURE

Broadcasting. Radio programmes are overseen by the Telecommunications Authority. There are 16 commercial stations. There are three TV stations, as well as community and cable services. There were 449,000 television receivers (colour by NTSC) in 2001 and 672,000 radio sets in 2000.

Press. There are three daily newspapers (*Trinidad Express, Trinidad Guardian* and *Newsday*), with a total daily circulation of 195,692 in Dec. 1999, and three Sunday newspapers, with a total circulation of 165,646. Weekly newspapers include *Punch, The Catholic News, The Probe, The Bomb, Show Time, The Independent* and *The Chutney Star. The Mirror* is published three times a week.

Tourism. There were 358,836 visitors in 1999, plus 57,230 cruise ship visitors. Revenue from tourism in 1999 was US$210m.

Festivals. Religious festivals: the Feast of La Divina Pastora, or Sipari Mai, a Catholic and Hindu celebration of the Holy Mother Mary; Saint Peter's Day Celebration, the Patron Saint of Fishermen; Hosein, or Hosay, a Shia Muslim festival; Phagwah, a Hindu spring festival; Santa Rosa, a Caribbean Amerindian festival; Eid-ul-Fitr, the Muslim festival at the end of Ramadan; Divali, the Hindu festival of light; Christmas. Cultural festivals: Carnival (on 27 and 28 Feb. in 2006); Spiritual Baptist Shouter Liberation Day, a recognition of the Baptist religion; Indian Arrival Day, commemorating the arrival of the first East Indian labourers; Sugar and Energy Festival; Pan Ramajay, a music festival of all types; Emancipation, a recognition of the period of slavery; Tobago Heritage Festival, celebrating Tobago's traditions and customs; Parang Festival, traditional folk music of Christmas; Pan Jazz Festival; Music Festival, predominantly classical music but Indian and Calypso are included.

When a public holiday falls on a Sunday, the holiday is celebrated on the Monday immediately following.

DIPLOMATIC REPRESENTATIVES

Of Trinidad and Tobago in the United Kingdom (42 Belgrave Sq., London, SW1X 8NT)
High Commissioner: Glenda Morean-Phillip.

Of the United Kingdom in Trinidad and Tobago (19 St Clair Ave., Port-of-Spain)
High Commissioner: Ronald Nash, CMG, LVO.

Of Trinidad and Tobago in the USA (1708 Massachusetts Ave., NW, Washington, D.C., 20036)
Ambassador: Marina Annette Valere.

Of the USA in Trinidad and Tobago (15 Queen's Park West, Port-of-Spain)
Ambassador: Roy L. Austin.

Of Trinidad and Tobago to the United Nations
Ambassador: Philip Sealy.

Of Trinidad and Tobago to the European Union
Ambassador: Learie Edgar Rousseau.

FURTHER READING

Chambers, F., *Trinidad and Tobago.* [Bibliography] ABC-Clio, Oxford and Santa Barbara (CA), 1986

Williams, E., *History of the People of Trinidad and Tobago.* Africa World Press, Lawrenceville (NJ), 1993

Central library: The Central Library of Trinidad and Tobago, Queen's Park East, Port-of-Spain.
National statistical office: Central Statistical Office, 80 Independence Square, Port-of-Spain.
Website: http://cso.gov.tt

TUNISIA

Jumhuriya at-Tunisiya
(Republic of Tunisia)

Capital: Tunis
Population projection, 2010: 10·58m.
GDP per capita, 2002: (PPP$) 6,760
HDI/world rank: 0·745/92

KEY HISTORICAL EVENTS

Settled by the Phoenicians, the area became a powerful state under the dynasty of the Berber Hafsids (1207–1574). Tunisia was nominally a part of the Ottoman Empire from the end of the 17th century and descendants of the original Ottoman ruler remained Beys of Tunis until the modern state of Tunisia was established. A French protectorate since 1883, Tunisia saw anti-French activity in the late 1930s. However, Tunisia supported the Allies in the Second World War and was the scene of heavy fighting. France granted internal self-government in 1955 and Tunisia became fully independent on 20 March 1956. A constitutional assembly was established and Habib Bourguiba became prime minister. A republic was established in 1957, the Bey deposed and the monarchy was abolished; Bourguiba became president. In 1975 the constitution was changed so that Bourguiba could be made President-for-life. Bourguiba was overthrown in a bloodless coup in 1987. His successor as president, Zine El Abidine Ben Ali, introduced democratic reforms but a long running struggle with Islamic fundamentalists has been marked by sporadic violence and the suspension of political rights.

TERRITORY AND POPULATION

Tunisia is bounded in the north and east by the Mediterranean Sea, west by Algeria and south by Libya. The area is 164,150 sq. km, including inland waters. In 2004 the census population was 9,910,872; density, 60 per sq. km. In 2001, 66·1% of the population were urban.

The UN gives a projected population for 2010 of 10·58m.

The areas and populations (2004 census) of the 24 governorates:

	Land area in sq. km	*Population*		*Land area in sq. km*	*Population*
Aryanah (Ariana)	498	382,600[1]	Qasrayn (Kassérine)	8,066	412,278
Bajah (Béja)	3,558	304,501	Qayrawan (Kairouan)	6,712	546,209
Banzart (Bizerta)	3,685	524,128	Qibili (Kebili)	22,084	143,218
Bin Arus (Bin Arous)	761	505,773	Safaqis (Sfax)	7,545	855,256
Jundubah (Jendouba)	3,102	416,608	Sidi Bu Zayd (Sidi Bouzid)	6,994	395,506
Kaf (Le Kef)	4,965	258,790	Silyanah (Siliana)	4,631	233,985
Madaniyin (Médénine)	8,588	432,503	Susah (Sousse)	2,621	544,413
Mahdiyah (Mahdia)	2,966	377,853	Tatawin (Tataouine)	38,889	143,524
Manubah (Manouba)	1,060	327,000[1]	Tawzar (Tozeur)	4,719	97,526
Munastir (Monastir)	1,019	455,590	Tunis	346	983,861
Nabul (Nabeul)	2,788	693,890	Zaghwan (Zaghouan)	2,768	160,963
Qabis (Gabès)	7,175	342,630			
Qafsah (Gafsa)	8,990	323,709			

[1]2002 estimates.

Tunis, the capital, had (2001 census estimate in 1,000) 690·9 inhabitants. Other main cities (2001 census estimate in 1,000): Sfax, 263·8; Ariana, 205·9; Sousse, 149·4; Kairouan, a holy city of the Muslims, 115·5; Bizerta, 110·8; Ettadhamen, 110·0; Gabès, 108·2.

The official language is Arabic but French is the main language in the media, commercial enterprise and government departments. Berber-speaking people form less than 1% of the population.

SOCIAL STATISTICS

Births, 2002 estimate, 163,000; deaths, 2002 estimate, 57,000; marriages (2001), 61,800. Rates (2002): birth, 16·7 per 1,000 population; death, 5·8. Annual population growth rate, 1992–2002, 1·3%. In 1998 the most popular age range for marrying was 30–34 for males and 20–24 for females. Expectation of life, 2001, was 70·5 years for males and 74·5 for females. Infant mortality, 2002, 22 per 1,000 live births; fertility rate, 2001, 2·2 births per woman.

CLIMATE

The climate ranges from warm temperate in the north, where winters are mild and wet and the summers hot and dry, to desert in the south. Tunis, Jan. 48°F (8·9°C), July 78°F (25·6°C). Annual rainfall 16" (400 mm). Bizerta, Jan. 52°F (11·1°C), July 77°F (25°C). Annual rainfall 25" (622 mm). Sfax, Jan. 52°F (11·1°C), July 78°F (25·6°C). Annual rainfall 8" (196 mm).

CONSTITUTION AND GOVERNMENT

The Constitution was promulgated on 1 June 1959 and reformed in 1988. The office of President-for-life was abolished and Presidential elections were to be held every five years. The *President* and the *National Assembly* are elected simultaneously by direct universal suffrage for a period of five years. On 27 May 2002 a referendum was held in which 99% of votes cast were in favour of abolishing the three-term limit on the presidency and of raising the age limit for incumbent presidents from 70 to 75 years. The results were viewed with scepticism by human rights groups and opposition figures, who saw the referendum as an attempt by President Zine El Abidine Ben Ali to retain power. Ben Ali was due to retire in 2004 after his third presidential term.

The *Majlis al-Nuwaab* (*National Assembly*) has 182 seats, with members elected from single-seat constituencies.

National Anthem. 'Humata al Hima' ('Defenders of the Homeland'); words by Mustapha al Rafi, tune by M. A. Wahab.

RECENT ELECTIONS

Presidential and parliamentary elections were held on 24 Oct. 2004; turn-out was 91·5%. President Zine El Abidine Ben Ali (Constitutional Democratic Assembly) was re-elected by 94·4% of votes cast against 3·8% for Mohamed Bouchiha (Popular Unity Party), 0·9% for Mohamed Ali Halouani (Ettajdid Movement) and 0·8% for Mounir Béji (Social Liberal Party). In the parliamentary elections the ruling Constitutional Democratic Assembly (CDA) won 152 of 189 available National Assembly seats with 87·6% of votes cast, the Movement of Social Democrats 14 with 4·6%, the Popular Unity Party 11 with 3·6%, the Unionist Democratic Union 7 with 2·2%, the Democratic Initiative Movement 3 with 1·0% and the Social Liberal Party 2 with 0·6%. The main opposition party, the Progressive Democratic Party, boycotted the elections, claiming that they were rigged.

CURRENT ADMINISTRATION

President: Zine El Abidine Ben Ali; b. 1936 (CDA; sworn in 7 Nov. 1987, re-elected March 1994, Oct. 1999 and Oct. 2004).

In March 2005 the cabinet comprised:

Prime Minister: Mohamed Ghannouchi; b. 1941 (CDA; sworn in 17 Nov. 1999).

Special Adviser to the President and Spokesman for the President: Abdelaziz Ben Dhia. *Minister of Defence:* Hédi M'henni. *State Property and Property Affairs:* Ridha Grira. *Justice and Human Rights:* Béchir Tekkari. *Foreign Affairs:* Abdelbaki Hermassi. *Interior and Local Development:* Rafik Belhaj Kacem. *Development and International Co-operation:* Mohamed Nouri Jouini. *Environment and Sustainable Development:* Nadhir Hamada. *Equipment, Housing and Land Development:* Samira Khayach Belhaj. *Social Affairs, Solidarity and Tunisians Abroad:* Rafaa Dekhil. *Finance:* Mohamed Rachid Kechiche. *Trade and Handicrafts:* Mondher Zenaïdi. *Tourism:* Tijani Haddad. *Education and Training:* Mohamed Raouf Najjar. *Higher Education:* Lazhar Bououni. *Scientific Research, Technology and Expertise Development:* Sadok Korbi. *Employment and Vocational Integration of Youth:* Chadli Laroussi. *Public Health:* Kechrid Ridha. *Culture and Protection of National Heritage:* Mohamed Aziz Ben Achour. *Religious Affairs:* Boubaker El Akhzouri. *Industry, Energy and Small and Medium-Sized Enterprises:* Afif Chelbi. *Family, Children, Seniors' and Women's Affairs:* Saloua Ayachi Labben. *Youth, Sport and*

Physical Education: Abdallah Kaâbi. *Agriculture and Water Resources:* Mohamed Habib Haddad. *Communications Technology:* Montassar Ouaili. *Transport:* Abderrahim Zouari. *Minister Director of the Presidential Office:* Ahmed Iyadh Ouederni.

Government Website (French only): http://www.ministeres.tn

DEFENCE

Selective conscription is for one year. Defence expenditure in 2003 totalled US$494m. (US$50 per capita), representing 2·0% of GDP.

Army. Strength (2002) 27,000 (22,000 conscripts). There is also a National Guard numbering 12,000.

Navy. In 1999 naval personnel totalled 4,500. Forces are based at Bizerta, Sfax and Kelibia.

Air Force. The Air Force operated 29 combat aircraft in 2002, including 15 F-5E/F Tiger II fighters, and 15 armed helicopters. Personnel (2002) about 3,500 (700 conscripts).

INTERNATIONAL RELATIONS

Tunisia is a member of the UN, WTO, the African Union, the Islamic Conference, the League of Arab States, Arab Maghreb Union, African Development Bank, IOM, Islamic Development Bank and the International Organization of the Francophonie.

ECONOMY

In 2002 agriculture accounted for 10·3% of GDP, industry 29·3% and services 60·4%.

Overview. Between 1997–2002 economic growth averaged 4·6% per annum. Inflation remained low and stable and the government deficit was reduced from 4·3% to 3·0% of GDP. Economic success since the mid-1990s is due to well-paced and co-ordinated policy, including appropriate macroeconomic policies, a gradual opening of the economy and well targeted social policies. Capital flows abroad were restricted in order to channel savings to domestic investment projects. The authorities have made significant progress in privatizing state enterprises, strengthening the banking sector, improving the investment climate, opening the economy under the Association Agreement with the EU and enhancing competitiveness. However, unemployment remains high at 15% and growth has not been high enough for real incomes to be raised to lower-tier OECD country levels. Significant structural impediments remain in the economy including high trade protection, a heavily regulated onshore sector alongside a dynamic export-orientated offshore sector, state control over a substantial part of the economy, financial sector vulnerabilities and labour market rigidities.

Currency. The unit of currency is the *Tunisian dinar* (TND) of 1,000 *millimes*. The currency was made convertible on 6 Jan. 1993. Foreign exchange reserves were US$2,195m. and gold reserves 218,000 troy oz in June 2002. Inflation was 2·8% in 2002. Total money supply was 6,687m. dinars in April 2002.

Budget. The fiscal year is the calendar year. Revenue and expenditure in 1m. dinars:

	1997	*1998*	*1999*	*2000*
Revenue	6,012·8	7,058·2	7,179·3	7,625·0
Expenditure	6,677·4	7,160·2	7,864·8	8,544·1

Performance. Real GDP growth was 1·7% in 2002 (4·9% in 2001). Tunisia's total GDP in 2003 was US$24·3bn.

Banking and Finance. The Central Bank of Tunisia (*Governor*, Taoufik Baccar) is the bank of issue. In 2003 there were twelve commercial banks, six development banks, two merchant banks and five 'offshore' banks.

There is a small stock exchange (42 companies trading in 2002).

ENERGY AND NATURAL RESOURCES

Environment. Tunisia's carbon dioxide emissions from the consumption and flaring of fossil fuels in 2002 were the equivalent of 2·2 tonnes per capita.

Electricity. Installed capacity was 2·3m. kW in 2000. Production in 2000 was about 10·07bn. kWh; consumption per capita was an estimated 1,040 kWh.

Oil and Gas. Crude petroleum production (2003) was 3·1m. tonnes with 0·3m. bbls. in proven reserves (2002). Natural gas production (2000), 2·1bn. cu. metres with 76bn. cu metres in proven reserves (2002).

Water. In 1993 there were 20 large dams, 250 hillside dams and some 1,000 artificial lakes.

Minerals. Mineral production (in 1,000 tonnes) in 2001: phosphate rock, 8,144; salt, 654; iron ore, 294; zinc ore (concentrated), 73; lead ore (concentrated), 7 (2000).

Agriculture. There are five agricultural regions: the *north*, mountainous with large fertile valleys; the *northeast*, with the peninsula of Cap Bon, suited for the cultivation of oranges, lemons and tangerines; the *Sahel*, where olive trees abound; the *centre*, a region of high tablelands and pastures; and the *desert* of the south, where dates are grown.

Some 23% of the population are employed in agriculture. Large estates predominate; smallholdings are tending to fragment, partly owing to inheritance laws. There were some 0·4m. farms in 1990 (0·32m. in 1960). Of the total area of 15,583,000 ha, about 9m. ha are productive, including 2m. under cereals, 3·6m. used as pasturage, 0·9m. forests and 1·3m. uncultivated. In 2001, 381,000 ha were irrigated. There were 2·77m. ha of arable land in 2001 and 2·13m. ha of permanent crops. There were 35,100 tractors in 2001 and 2,850 harvester-threshers. The main crops are cereals, citrus fruits, tomatoes, melons, olives, dates, grapes and olive oil. Production, 2000 (in 1,000 tonnes): olives, 1,000; tomatoes, 905; wheat, 842; melons, including watermelons, 475; potatoes, 290; barley, 242; chillies and green peppers, 190; grapes, 150; onions, 133; oranges, 115; apples, 108; dates, 103; sugarbeets, 76; peaches and nectarines, 73; tree nuts, 61; almonds, 60.

Livestock, 2000 (in 1,000): sheep, 6,600; goats, 1,400; cattle, 790; camels, 231; asses, 230; mules, 81; horses, 56. Livestock products, 2000 (in 1,000 tonnes): meat, 219; milk, 919; eggs, 80.

Forestry. In 2000 there were 510,000 ha of forests (3·1% of the land area). Timber production in 2001 was 2·32m. cu. metres.

Fisheries. In 2001 the catch amounted to 98,482 tonnes, almost exclusively from marine waters.

INDUSTRY

Production (in 1,000 tonnes): cement (2000), 5,647; sulphuric acid (1999), 4,858; residual fuel oil (2000), 653; phosphoric acid (2000), 607; distillate fuel oil (2000), 537; lime (2001), 467; crude steel (2002), 220. Industry accounted for 28·8% of GDP in 2001, with manufacturing contributing 18·5%.

Labour. The labour force in 2002 totalled 3,375,700 (71·8% males), of which 2,852,000 were employed. Unemployment was 14·9% in 2002.

Trade Unions. The Union Générale des Travailleurs Tunisiens won 27 seats in the parliamentary elections of 1 Nov. 1981. There are also the Union Tunisienne de l'Industrie, du Commerce et de l'Artisanat (UTICA, the employers' union) and the Union National des Agriculteurs (UNA, farmers' union).

INTERNATIONAL TRADE

In Feb. 1989 Tunisia signed a treaty of economic co-operation with the other countries of Maghreb: Algeria, Libya, Mauritania and Morocco. Foreign debt was US$12,625m. in 2002.

Tunisia was the first country to sign a partnership agreement with the European Union. The agreement aims at creating a non-agricultural free trade zone by 2008.

Imports and Exports. Trade in US$1m.:

	1998	*1999*	*2000*	*2001*	*2002*
Imports f.o.b.	7,875	8,014	8,093	8,997	8,981
Exports f.o.b.	5,724	5,873	5,840	6,606	6,857

Main exports in 1999: clothing and accessories, 41·0%; manufactured goods, 10·1%; electric machinery, 9·5%; petroleum, 7·2%; olive oil, 5·5%; fertilizers, 5·0%;

phosphorous pentoxide and phosphoric acids, 4·0%. Main imports in 1999: machinery and transport equipment, 34·2%; textile yarn and fabrics, 16·0%; chemicals and related products, 8·1%; foodstuffs, 6·1%; clothing, 5·7%; petroleum, 5·3%; iron and steel, 3·2%.

The main import suppliers in 2000 were France (26·3%), Italy (19·1%) and Germany (9·6%). Main export markets in 2000 were France (26·8%), Italy (23·0%) and Germany (12·5%).

COMMUNICATIONS

Roads. In 2001 there were 18,997 km of roads, including 142 km of motorways and 4,750 km of national roads. 65·4% of all roads in 2001 were paved. Vehicles in 2002 numbered 869,931 (585,194 passenger cars, 266,499 trucks and vans, 12,181 buses and coaches and 6,057 motorcycles). In 2000 there were 12,652 road accidents which resulted in 1,499 fatalities.

Rail. In 1994 there were 2,152 km of railways (468 km of 1,435 mm gauge and 1,684 km of metre-gauge), of which 110 km were electrified. Passenger-km travelled in 2000 came to 1,243m. and freight tonne-km to 2,279m. There is a light rail network in Tunis (33 km).

Civil Aviation. The national carrier, Tunis Air, is 84·86% state-owned. It carried 1,922,600 passengers in 1999 (all on international flights) and flew 27·3m. km. There are six international airports. In 2000 Monastir (Habib Bourguiba) handled 3,887,000 passengers (3,878,000 on international flights) and 1,300 tonnes of freight. Tunis-Carthage handled 3,331,000 (3,062,000 on international flights) and 24,000 tonnes of freight. Djerba handled 2,100,000 passengers (1,870,000 on international flights) and 2,412 tonnes of freight.

Shipping. There are ports at Tunis, its outer port Tunis-Goulette, Sfax, Sousse and Bizerta, all of which are directly accessible to ocean-going vessels. The ports of La Skhirra and Gabès are used for the shipping of Algerian and Tunisian oil. In 2002 sea-going shipping totalled 186,000 GRT, including oil tankers 20,000 GRT. In 2001 vessels totalling 58,610,000 GRT entered ports and vessels totalling 58,595,000 GRT cleared.

Telecommunications. There were 1,651,900 telephone subscribers (168·3 per 1,000 persons) in 2002, and 300,000 PCs in use (30·6 per 1,000 persons). Tunisia had 503,900 mobile phone subscribers in 2002 and there were 31,000 fax machines in 1997. Internet users numbered 505,500 in 2002.

Postal Services. In 1995 there were 947 post offices. A total of 117m. pieces of mail were processed in 1995.

SOCIAL INSTITUTIONS

Justice. There are 51 magistrates' courts, 13 courts of first instance, three courts of appeal (in Tunis, Sfax and Sousse) and the High Court in Tunis.

A Personal Status Code was promulgated on 13 Aug. 1956 and applied to Tunisians from 1 Jan. 1957. This raised the status of women, made divorce subject to a court decision, abolished polygamy and decreed a minimum marriage age.

The population in penal institutions in Dec. 1996 was 23,165 (252 per 100,000 of national population).

Religion. The constitution recognizes Islam as the state religion. In 2001 there were 9·72m. Sunni Muslims. The remainder of the population follow other religions, including Roman Catholicism.

Education. The adult literacy rate in 2001 was 72·1% (82·3% among males and 61·9% among females). All education is free from primary schools to university. In 2002–03 there were 4,486 state primary schools with 59,245 teachers and 1,265,462 pupils; and 51,738 teachers and 1,057,233 pupils at 1,117 state secondary schools.

Higher education includes six universities, three of them being specialized by faculty, a teacher training college, a school of law, two centres of economic studies, two schools of engineering, two medical schools, a faculty of agriculture, two institutes of business administration and one school of dentistry.

In 2000–01 total expenditure on education came to 7·2% of GNP and accounted for 17·4% of total government expenditure.

Health. There were 169 hospitals and specialized institutes and centres in 2000. In 1994 provision of beds was 18 per 10,000 population. In 2000 there were 7,339 doctors, 1,319 dentists, 26,409 nurses (1997) and 1,841 pharmacists.

Welfare. A system of social security was set up in 1950 (amended 1963, 1964 and 1970).

CULTURE

World Heritage Sites. Tunisia has eight sites on the UNESCO World Heritage List: the Amphitheatre of El Jem (inscribed on the list in 1979); the Site of Carthage (1979); the Medina of Tunis (1979); Ichkeul National Park (1980); the Punic Town of Kerkuane and its Necropolis (1985); the Medina of Sousse (1988); Kairouan (1988); and Dougga/Thugga (1997).

Broadcasting. The government-controlled Radiodiffusion-Télévision Tunisienne provides a national radio programme, an international service—Radio Tunisie Internationale (French and Italian)—and two regional programmes. There are Arabic and French TV networks (colour by SECAM V). Number of sets: TV (2001), 2·00m.; radio (1997), 2·06m.

Press. In 2000 there were seven daily newspapers with a total average circulation of 179,963, giving a rate of 19 per 1,000 inhabitants. Press freedom is severely limited.

Tourism. In 2000 there were 5,057,000 foreign tourists, bringing revenue of US$1·5bn. Revenues doubled between 1991 (US$685m.) and 1996, and tourism now accounts for 10% of GDP.

DIPLOMATIC REPRESENTATIVES

Of Tunisia in the United Kingdom (29 Prince's Gate, London, SW7 1QG)
Ambassador: Mohamed Ghariani.

Of the United Kingdom in Tunisia (5 Place de la Victoire, Tunis)
Ambassador: Robin Kealy, CMG.

Of Tunisia in the USA (1515 Massachusetts Ave., NW, Washington, D.C., 20005)
Ambassador: Hatem Atallah.

Of the USA in Tunisia (Les Berges du Lac, 1053 Tunis)
Ambassador: William J. Hudson.

Of Tunisia to the United Nations
Ambassador: Ali Hachani.

Of Tunisia to the European Union
Ambassador: Tahar Sioud.

FURTHER READING

Pazzanita, A. G., *The Maghreb.* [Bibliography] ABC-Clio, Oxford and Santa Barbara (CA), 1998

National statistical office: Institut National de la Statistique, 27 Rue de Liban, Tunis.
Website (French only): http://www.ins.nat.tn

TURKEY

Türkiye Cumhuriyeti
(Republic of Turkey)

Capital: Ankara
Population projection, 2010: 77·97m.
GDP per capita, 2002: (PPP$) 6,390
HDI/world rank: 0·751/88

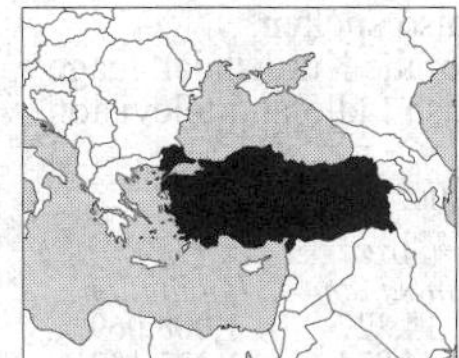

KEY HISTORICAL EVENTS

The area of modern Turkey equates to the ancient region of Anatolia (Asia Minor). There is evidence of human habitation in Anatolia around 7500 BC. Between 1900 and 1600 BC the area came under Hittite rule, vying for power with Egypt and eventually extending into Syria. Anatolia was regularly invaded by forces from the Greek islands and was overrun by invading Persians in the 6th century BC.

Alexander the Great defeated the Persians around 330 BC. After his death there was a long civil war between the Seleucids and the Ptolemies, while the kingdoms of Galatia, Armenia, Pergamum, Cappadocia, Bithynia and Pontus all established footholds in the region. Rome gained dominance around the 2nd century BC and brought stability and prosperity. Turkey was home to some of the earliest centres of Christianity, such as Antioch (modern Antakya) and Ephesus. In AD 324 the Emperor Constantine began the construction of a new capital, Constantinople, at Byzantium. Constantinople became the centre of the Byzantine (Eastern Roman) Empire, which reached its pinnacle under Justinian in the mid-6th century.

Islamic troops attacked Constantinople in the 670s initiating centuries of warfare and rivalry between Islamic forces and Byzantium. The Great Seljuk Empire established dominance over an area that encompassed modern Turkey during the 11th century. They came under threat during the Crusades and from the Mongols but fell to the Ottomans (an alliance of Turkish warriors who emerged in the 13th century). The Ottomans, under Mehmet, seized Constantinople in 1453. Under the rule of Suleiman the Magnificent (1494–1566) the empire expanded to its fullest extent (including an area from Morocco to Persia and westwards into the Balkans) and Constantinople developed into a centre of cultural and intellectual excellence.

From the late 16th century, however, the Empire began to decline, its power weakening rapidly in the 19th century. The Kingdom of Greece broke away from Ottoman rule in 1832, with Serbs, Romanians, Armenians, Albanians, Bulgarians and Arabs demanding independence soon afterwards. Attempts by Turkey to re-define itself were further hindered in the 20th century by World War I, during which it sided with Germany. In fighting with Greece over disputed territory from 1920–22, the Turkish National Movement was led by Mustafa Kemal (Atatürk: 'Father of the Turks'), who wanted a republic based on a modern secular society. Turkey became a republic on 29 Oct. 1923. Islam ceased to be the official state religion in 1928 and women were given the franchise.

On 27 May 1960 the Turkish Army overthrew the government and party activities were suspended. A new constitution was approved in a referendum held on 9 July 1961 and general elections held the same year. On 12 Sept. 1980 the Turkish armed forces again drove the government from office. A new constitution was enforced after a national referendum on 7 Nov. 1982. In the face of mounting Islamicization of government policy, the Supreme National Security Council reaffirmed its commitment to the secularity of the state. On 6 March 1997 Prime Minister Neçmettin Erbakan, leader of the pro-Islamist Welfare Party, promised to combat Muslim fundamentalism but in June he was forced to resign by a campaign led by the Army.

There are quarrels with Greece over the division of Cyprus, oil rights under the Aegean and ownership of uninhabited islands close to the Turkish coast. Kurdish rebels have for many years been active in the southeast, occupying a large part of the Turkish army. However, in Feb. 2000 the Kurdish Workers' party (PKK) formally abandoned its 15-year rebellion and adopted the democratic programme urged by its imprisoned leader, Abdullah Öçalan. The conflict has cost 40,000 lives.

TERRITORY AND POPULATION

Turkey is bounded in the west by the Aegean Sea and Greece, north by Bulgaria and the Black Sea, east by Georgia, Armenia and Iran, and south by Iraq, Syria and the Mediterranean. The area (including lakes) is 780,580 sq. km (301,382 sq. miles). At the 1990 census the population was 56,473,035. The most recent census took place in Oct. 2000, by when the population had increased to 67,844,903. In 2001, 66·2% of the population lived in urban areas.

The UN gives a projected population for 2010 of 77·97m.

Turkish is the official language. Kurdish and Arabic are also spoken.

Some 12m. Kurds live in Turkey. In Feb. 1991 limited use of the Kurdish language was sanctioned, and in Aug. 2002 parliament legalized Kurdish radio and television broadcasts.

Area and population of the 81 provinces at the 2000 census:

	Area in sq. km	*Population*		*Area in sq. km*	*Population*
Adana	12,788	1,854,270	Kahramanmaraş	14,327	1,008,069
Adıyaman	7,614	623,811	Karabük	4,074	225,102
Afyon	14,230	812,416	Karaman	9,163	243,399
Ağri	11,376	528,744	Kars	9,442	327,056
Aksaray	7,626	400,145	Kastamonu	13,108	376,725
Amasya	5,520	365,231	Kayseri	16,917	1,049,659
Ankara	25,706	4,007,860	Kilis	1,338	114,724
Antalya	20,591	1,726,205	Kırıkkale	4,365	383,508
Ardahan	5,576	133,756	Kırklareli	6,550	328,461
Artvin	7,436	191,934	Kırşehir	6,570	253,239
Aydin	8,007	953,006	Kocaeli	3,626	1,203,335
Balıkesir	14,292	1,076,347	Konya	38,157	2,217,969
Bartın	2,140	184,178	Kütahya	11,875	656,716
Batman	4,694	446,719	Malatya	12,313	853,658
Bayburt	3,652	97,358	Manisa	13,810	1,260,169
Bilecik	4,307	194,326	Mardin	8,891	705,098
Bingöl	8,125	255,395	Mersin	15,853	1,668,007
Bitlis	6,707	388,678	Muğla	13,338	717,384
Bolu	10,037	270,654	Muş	8,196	453,654
Burdur	6,887	256,803	Nevşehir	5,467	309,914
Bursa	10,963	2,106,687	Niğde	7,312	348,081
Çanakkale	9,737	464,975	Ordu	6,001	887,765
Çankırı	7,388	269,579	Osmaniye	3,320	463,196
Çorum	12,820	597,065	Rize	3,920	365,938
Denizli	11,868	843,122	Sakarya	4,817	746,060
Diyarbakır	15,355	1,364,209	Samsun	9,579	1,203,681
Düzce	1,014	314,266	Şanliurfa	18,584	1,436,956
Edirne	6,276	402,606	Siirt	5,406	264,778
Elazığ	9,153	572,933	Sinop	5,862	225,574
Erzincan	11,903	315,806	Şırnak	7,172	354,061
Erzurum	25,066	942,340	Sivas	28,488	752,828
Eskişehir	13,652	706,009	Tekirdağ	6,218	626,549
Gaziantep	6,207	1,293,849	Tokat	9,958	828,027
Giresun	6,934	524,010	Trabzon	4,685	979,295
Gümüşhane	6,575	186,953	Tunceli	7,774	93,584
Hakkâri	7,121	235,841	Uşak	5,341	322,654
Hatay	5,403	1,232,910	Van	19,069	877,524
Iğdir	3,539	168,634	Yalova	674	168,593
Isparta	8,933	514,379	Yozgat	14,123	682,919
İstanbul	5,220	10,033,478	Zonguldak	3,481	615,599
İzmir	11,973	3,387,908			

Population of cities of over 200,000 inhabitants in 2000:

İstanbul	9,119,315	Urfa	839,817
Ankara	3,540,522	Diyarbakır	818,396
İzmir	2,750,273	Kayseri	721,211
Bursa	1,616,649	Manisa	714,760
Adana	1,400,523	Samsun	633,118
Konya	1,314,146	Balikesir	577,595
Mersin	1,021,086	Erzurum	565,516
Gaziantep	1,018,700	Eskişehir	557,028
Antalya	933,847	Malatya	499,713

Trabzon	485,081	Denizli	410,776
Sakarya	450,146	Elazığ	366,839
Van	446,976	Batman	305,475
Sivas	419,897	Kırıkkale	285,294

SOCIAL STATISTICS

Births, 2001, 1,507,000; deaths, 463,000. 2001 birth rate per 1,000 population, 21·8; death rate, 6·7. 2001 marriages, 453,213 (rate of 6·5 per 1,000 population); divorces (2000), 34,862 (rate of 0·5 per 1,000 population). Annual population growth rate, 1990–2002, 1·6%. Expectation of life, 2002, was 66·2 years for males and 70·9 for females. Infant mortality, 1990–95, was 53 per 1,000 live births, down from 102 in 1980–85. The rate dropped more in Turkey than in any other country over the same period. By 2001 it had declined to 36 per 1,000 live births. Fertility rate, 2001, 2·4 births per woman. In 1999 the most popular age for marrying was 25–29 for males and 20–24 for females.

CLIMATE

Coastal regions have a Mediterranean climate, with mild, moist winters and hot, dry summers. The interior plateau has more extreme conditions, with low and irregular rainfall, cold and snowy winters, and hot, almost rainless summers. Ankara, Jan. 32·5°F (0·3°C), July 73°F (23°C). Annual rainfall 14·7" (367 mm). İstanbul, Jan. 41°F (5°C), July 73°F (23°C). Annual rainfall 28·9" (723 mm). İzmir, Jan. 46°F (8°C), July 81°F (27°C). Annual rainfall 28" (700 mm).

CONSTITUTION AND GOVERNMENT

On 7 Nov. 1982 a referendum established that 98% of the electorate were in favour of a new Constitution. The *President* is elected for seven-year terms. The Presidency is not an executive position, and the President may not be linked to a political party. There is a 550-member *Turkish Grand National Assembly*, elected by universal suffrage (at 18 years and over) for five-year terms by proportional representation. There is a *Constitutional Court* consisting of 15 regular and five alternating members.

National Anthem. 'Korkma! Sönmez bu şafaklarda yüzen al sancak' ('Be not afraid! Our flag will never fade'); words by Mehmed Akif Ersoy, tune by Zeki Güngör.

RECENT ELECTIONS

Parliamentary elections were held on 3 Nov. 2002. The Justice and Development Party (AKP)—former Islamists—won 363 of the 550 seats with 34·3% of votes cast, against 178 seats and 19·4% for the Republican People's Party (CHP). Remaining seats went to independents. Parties which failed to secure the 10% of votes needed to gain parliamentary representation included the True Path Party (DYP) with 9·6%; the Nationalist Action Party (MHP), 8·3%; the Youth Party (GP), 7·2%; the Democratic People's Party (DEHAP), 6·2%; the Motherland Party (ANAP), 5·1%; the Saadet Party (SP), 2·5%; the Democratic Left Party (DSP) of outgoing Prime Minister Bülent Ecevit, 1·2%; the Grand Unity Party (BBP), 1·1%; and the New Turkey Party (YTP), 1·0%. Turn-out was 78·9%. An absolute majority was achieved in a Turkish parliamentary election for the first time in 15 years.

Voting for president took place on 1 May 2000 in parliament. Ahmet Necdet Sezer failed to get the required two-thirds majority in the first two rounds. However, in the third round only a simple majority is required, which he received gaining 330 of the 550 available votes.

CURRENT ADMINISTRATION

President: Ahmet Necdet Sezer; b. 1941 (sworn in 16 May 2000).

In March 2005 the government comprised:

Prime Minister: Recep Tayyip Erdoğan; b. 1954 (AKP; sworn in 14 March 2003).

Deputy Prime Ministers: Abdullah Gül (also *Foreign Minister*); Abdüllatif Şener (also *Minister of State*); Mehmet Ali Şahin (also *Minister of State*).

Minister of Defence: Vecdi Gönül. *Development and Public Works:* Zeki Ergezen. *Interior:* Abdülkadir Aksu. *Justice:* Cemil Çiçek. *Finance:* Kemal Unakıtan.

Education: Hüseyin Çelik. *Health:* Recep Akdağ. *Transport:* Binalı Yıldırım. *Agriculture:* Sami Güçlü. *Labour:* Murat Başesgioğlu. *Trade and Industry:* Ali Coşkun. *Energy:* Hilmi Güler. *Culture and Tourism:* Atilla Koç. *Environment and Forestry:* Osman Pepe. *Ministers of State:* Güldal Akşit; Mehmet Aydın; Beşir Atalay; Ali Babacan; Kürşad Tüzmen.

The *Speaker* is Bülent Arınç.

Office of the Prime Minister (Turkish only): http://www.basbakanlik.gov.tr

DEFENCE

The *National Security Council*, chaired by the Prime Minister and comprising military leaders and the ministers of defence and the economy, also functions as a *de facto* constitutional watchdog. Reforms passed in July 2003 in preparation for EU membership aimed to reduce the influence of the military in the political system. In Oct. 2003 the Turkish parliament voted to send 10,000 troops to Iraq, which would have made it the third largest force in the country after the USA and the UK, but the Iraqi Governing Council rejected the plan.

Conscription is 18 months.

In 2003 defence expenditure totalled US$11,649m., up from US$3,489m. in 1985. Spending per capita in 2003 was US$165, up from US$69 per capita in 1985. The 2003 expenditure represented 4·9% of GDP.

Army. Strength (2002) 402,000 (325,000 conscripts) with a potential reserve of 258,700. There is also a paramilitary gendarmerie-cum-national guard of 150,000. In addition 36,000 Turkish troops are stationed in Northern Cyprus.

Navy. The fleet includes 13 diesel submarines and 19 frigates. The main naval base is at Gölcük in the Gulf of İzmit. There are five others, at Aksaz-Karaağaç, Eregli, İskenderun, İzmir and Mersin. There are three naval shipyards: Gölcük, İzmir and Taşkizak.

The naval air component operates 16 armed helicopters. There is a Marine Regiment some 3,100-strong.

Personnel in 2002 totalled 52,750 (34,500 conscripts) including marines.

Air Force. The Air Force is organized as two tactical air forces, with headquarters at Eskisehir and Diyarbakır. There were 485 combat aircraft in operation in 2002 including F-5A/Bs, F-4E Phantoms and F-16C/Ds.

Personnel strength (2002), 60,100 (31,500 conscripts).

INTERNATIONAL RELATIONS

In Oct. 1998 Turkish troops mobilized on the border with Syria in protest against Syrian support for Kurdish rebels operating from its territory.

Following the terror attacks on New York and Washington of 11 Sept. 2001 Turkey expressed support for the USA, later becoming the first Muslim country to send soldiers to Afghanistan, to help train anti-Taliban fighters and to administer aid.

Turkey is a member of the UN, WTO, BIS, OECD, NATO, Council of Europe, OSCE, BSEC, Asian Development Bank, ECO, OIC, Islamic Development Bank, IOM and an Associate Member of the WEU, and has applied to join the EU. At the European Union's Helsinki Summit in Dec. 1999 Turkey was awarded candidate status. Talks on membership are set to begin in late 2005 but Turkey is unlikely to join the EU before 2015 at the earliest.

ECONOMY

Agriculture accounted for 13·4% of GDP in 2002, industry 29·1% and services 57·5%.

Overview. The strongest sectors in the economy are services and manufacturing. The share of agriculture is approximately 13% of GDP and 46% of the workforce. In 2000 Turkey committed to a programme of wide ranging structural reforms, strong fiscal adjustment and a pre-announced exchange rate crawl. In 2001 the economy was hit by a financial and currency crisis that caused the collapse of the three-year exchange rate based stabilization programme. In May 2001 a strengthened programme was introduced with the aim of additional IMF support.

Key structural reforms emphasize public sector reform, liberalizing markets and building a strong banking sector. Banking sector distortions affect both public and private banks and have been linked to poor economic performance through the crowding out of private investment and inefficient credit allocation by the banking system. Despite these problems the reforms are proving to be successful—in 2004 GDP growth was nearly 9% and inflation was at its lowest level in more than a quarter of a century.

Currency. The unit of currency is the *new Turkish lira* (YTL) of 100 *kuruş*. It was introduced on 1 Jan. 2005, replacing the Turkish lira (TRL) at 1 new Turkish lira = 1m. Turkish lira. Gold reserves were 3·73m. troy oz in June 2002 and foreign exchange reserves US$22,238m. Inflation has fallen every year since 1997, when it was 85·7%. It was 45·0% in 2002, 25·3% in 2003 and 10·6% in 2004. Total money supply in Dec. 2001 was TRL5,188,070bn.

Budget. The fiscal year is the calendar year. Revenue and expenditure in TRL1trn.:

	1999	*2000*	*2001*	*2002*
Revenue	19,798·3	35,425·8	51,090·0	73,569·0
Expenditure	29,467·3	49,134·2	79,856·0	111,512·0

Tax revenues were TRL66,105trn. in 2002.

Performance. Real GDP growth was negative in 1999, at –4·7%, but in 2000 there was growth of 7·4%. In 2001, however, the economy shrank again, by 7·5%—the worst performance since the Second World War—before recovering again in 2002, with growth of 7·9%. In 2003 there was real GDP growth of 5·8%, rising in 2004 to 8·9%. Total GDP was US$237·9bn. in 2003.

Banking and Finance. The Central Bank (Merkez Bankası; *Governor*, Süreyya Serdengeçti) is the bank of issue. In 2003 there were 36 commercial banks (three state-owned, two under the Deposit Insurance Fund, 18 private, 13 foreign), and 14 development and investment banks. The Central Bank's assets were US$51·66bn. in 2003. The assets and liabilities of deposit money banks were US$25·8bn. Turkey's largest bank is the state-owned Ziraat Bankası, with assets in 1999 of TRL10,202,000,000m. At the end of 1998 it held nearly 18% of all bank deposits. Foreign direct investment in 2003 was US$575m. In Sept. 2000 a Banking Regulation and Supervision Board was established to serve as an independent banking regulator. In Dec. 2000 the IMF gave Turkey an emergency loan of US$7·5bn. as the country experienced a financial crisis after ten banks were placed in receivership. The economic crisis continued as the *lira* was floated on the international market and lost 30% of its value against the US dollar in the space of 12 hours in Feb. 2001. Within a week the lira had been devalued by approximately 40%. In April 2001 Turkey secured a further US$10bn. loan from the IMF and the World Bank. This was followed in Feb. 2002 with a three-year US$16bn. loan from the IMF, taking total loans paid or pledged to USS$31bn.

There is a stock exchange in İstanbul (ISE).

ENERGY AND NATURAL RESOURCES

Environment. In 2002 Turkey's carbon dioxide emissions from the consumption and flaring of fossil fuels were the equivalent of 2·7 tonnes per capita.

Electricity. In 2003 installed capacity was 31·28m. kW (10·6m. kW hydro-electric); gross production in 2002 was 129·4bn. kWh and consumption per capita 1,904 kWh.

Oil and Gas. Crude oil production (2002) was 2,541,000 tonnes. Reserves in 2002 were 296m. bbls. Refinery distillation output in 2000 amounted to 23·7m. tonnes. In 2000, 21,583,000 tonnes of crude petroleum were imported. Natural gas output was 370m. cu. metres in 2002.

Accords for the construction of an oil pipeline from Azerbaijan through Georgia to the Mediterranean port of Ceyhan in southern Turkey, and a gas pipeline from Turkmenistan through Azerbaijan and Georgia, to Erzurum in northeastern Turkey, were signed in Nov. 1999. Work on the oil pipeline, which is expected to become operational before the end of 2005, began in Sept. 2002.

Minerals. Turkey is rich in minerals, and is a major producer of chrome.

Production of principal minerals (in 1,000 tonnes) in 2002 was: lignite, 49,627; iron, 3,433; coal, 3,313; magnesite, 3,044; copper (gross weight), 2,940; boron, 2,214; salt, 2,197; chrome, 327.

Agriculture. In 2002 there were 6,745,000 households engaged in farming, of which 148,190 were engaged purely in animal farming. Holdings are increasingly fragmented by the custom of dividing land equally amongst sons. Agriculture accounts for 46% of the workforce but only 13·4% of GDP. In 2001 Turkey had 23·81m. ha of arable land and 2·55m. ha of permanent crops. Approximately 4·5m. ha were irrigated in 2001. Vineyards, orchards and olive groves occupied 2,530,000 ha in 1998.

Production (2000, in 1,000 tonnes) of principal crops: sugarbeets, 16,854; wheat, 16,500; barley, 6,800; tomatoes, 6,800; melons and watermelons, 5,800; potatoes, 5,475; grapes, 3,400; apples, 2,500; maize, 2,500; onions, 2,300; seed cotton, 2,151; cucumbers and gherkins, 1,550; chillies and green peppers, 1,400; cottonseed, 1,360; oranges, 1,100; aubergines, 850; tree nuts, 831; sunflower seeds, 800; cotton lint, 791; cabbages, 732; olives, 600; hazelnuts, 550; lemons and limes, 520; apricots, 500; chick-peas, 500; tangerines and mandarins, 500. Turkey is the largest producer of apricots and hazelnuts.

Livestock, 2000 (in 1,000): sheep, 29,435; cattle, 11,031; goats, 8,057; asses, 603; horses, 330; buffaloes, 176; mules, 133; chickens, 27,000. Livestock products, 2000 (in 1,000 tonnes): milk, 9,876; meat, 1,386; eggs, 660; cheese, 131; honey, 71.

Forestry. There were 20·7m. ha of forests in 2000. Timber production was 16·16m. cu. metres in 2001.

Fisheries. The catch in 2001 totalled 527,730 tonnes (484,407 tonnes from marine waters). Aquaculture production, 1995, 21,607 tonnes (mainly carp and trout).

INDUSTRY

Production in 2001 (in 1,000 tonnes unless otherwise stated): cement, 30,125; crude steel (2002), 16,500; residual fuel oil (2000), 8,022; distillate fuel oil (2000), 6,646; coke (1999), 2,802; petrol (2000), 2,744; sugar (2002), 2,128; paper and paperboard (2002), 1,643; iron and steel bars (1997), 1,193; nitrogenous fertilizers, 748; cotton yarn, 557; ethylene, 400; polyethylene, 263; sulphuric acid, 234; olive oil (2002), 206; pig iron, 158; PVC, 147; cotton woven fabrics (2000), 567m. sq. metres; woollen woven fabrics (2000), 91m. sq. metres; carpets, 12,974,000 sq. metres; TV sets, 8,025,000 units; refrigerators, 2,245,000 units; motor cars, 277,000 units; lorries, 30,112 assembled units; tractors, 15,020 units; cigarettes, 77·2bn. units.

Labour. In 2001 there were 20,367,000 people in employment (5,463,000 women): 7,184,000 were engaged in agriculture, hunting and forestry, 3,548,000 in manufacturing, 2,883,000 in wholesale and retail trade/repair of motor vehicles, motorcycles and personal and household goods and 1,118,000 in public administration and defence/compulsory social security. In 2002 the unemployment rate stood at 9·9%. In 1996, 93% of male workers and 80% of female workers worked more than 40 hours a week. The proportion of adults between the ages of 15 and 64 in employment has gradually fallen, from 69% in 1975 to only 50% in 1997. Although the population of working age has been growing at an average of 3% a year, total employment has grown at only 1·5% a year. The monthly minimum wage has been YTL489 since 1 Jan. 2005.

Trade Unions. There are four national confederations (including Türk-İş and Disk) and six federations. There are 35 unions affiliated to Türk-İş and 17 employers' federations affiliated to Disk, whose activities were banned on 12 Sept. 1980. In 2001 labour unions totalled 104 and employers' unions 49. Some 2·75m. workers belonged to unions in 2003. Membership is forbidden to civil servants (including schoolteachers). There were 52 strikes in 2000 involving 18,705 workers, with 368,475 working days lost.

INTERNATIONAL TRADE

Total foreign debt in June 2002 was US$125,700m. A customs union with the EU came into force on 1 Jan. 1996.

Imports and Exports. Trade in US$1m.:

	1998	*1999*	*2000*	*2001*	*2002*
Imports f.o.b.	45,440	39,768	54,041	41,399	51,203
Exports f.o.b.	31,220	29,325	31,664	31,334	35,761

Chief exports (2002) in US$1m.: machinery and automotive industry products, 8,587; ready-made garments, 8,057; textile products, 4,244; food products, 3,627; iron and steel, 1,824. Chief imports: machinery and automotive industry products, 15,539; minerals and oil, 9,026; chemicals, 7,873; food and agricultural raw materials, 3,981; iron and steel, 2,162.

The main export markets in 2002 (in US$1m.) were: Germany, 5,811; USA, 3,229; UK, 2,987; Italy, 2,237; France, 2,108; Russia, 1,168. Main import suppliers: Germany, 6,967; Italy, 4,102; Russia, 3,863; USA, 3,050; France, 3,007; UK, 2,416; Japan, 1,445. By 2001 the EU was accounting for 50·5% of exports and 45·2% of imports.

COMMUNICATIONS

Roads. In 2002 there were 354,421 km of roads, including 1,851 km of motorway. In 2002 the total number of road vehicles was 7,283,250 (4,600,140 cars, 1,274,406 trucks and vans, 361,797 buses and coaches and 1,046,907 motorcycles and mopeds). There were 2,954 fatalities from road accidents in 2001.

Rail. Total length of railway lines in 2000 was 8,671 km (1,435 mm gauge), of which 1,752 km were electrified. Passenger-km travelled in 2000 came to 5·81bn. and freight tonne-km to 9·73bn. There are metro systems operating in Ankara, Bursa, İstanbul and İzmir.

Civil Aviation. There are international airports at İstanbul (Atatürk), Dalaman (Muğla), Ankara (Esenboga), İzmir (Adnan Menderes), Adana and Antalya. The national carrier is Turkish Airlines, which is 98·2% state-owned. In 2000 it flew 144·1m. km and carried 11,951,493 passengers (5,514,007 on international flights).

In 2000 İstanbul handled 14,647,818 passengers (9,465,965 on international flights) and 219,244 tonnes of freight. Antalya was the second busiest airport for passenger traffic, with 7,456,658 passengers (6,779,733 on international flights), and Ankara third with 4,027,928 passengers (2,800,943 on domestic flights).

Shipping. In 2000 the merchant shipping fleet consisted of 1,153 vessels totalling 5,833,000 GRT, including oil tankers 625,000 GRT. The main ports are: İskenderun, İstanbul, İzmir, Mersin, Samsun and Trabzon.

In 2001 vessels totalling 125,997,000 GRT entered ports and vessels totalling 96,867,000 GRT cleared.

Telecommunications. In 2002 telephone subscribers numbered 42,289,200 (628·6 for every 1,000 persons) and there were 3·0m. PCs in use (44·6 per 1,000 persons). In 1998 there were 119,000 fax machines. Turkey had 4·9m. Internet users in 2002 and 23,374,400 mobile phone subscribers.

Postal Services. In 2002 there were 4,471 post offices. A total of 1,088m. pieces of mail were processed in 1998.

SOCIAL INSTITUTIONS

Justice. The unified legal system consists of: (1) justices of the peace (single judges with limited but summary penal and civil jurisdiction); (2) courts of first instance (single judges, dealing with cases outside the jurisdiction of (3) and (4)); (3) central criminal courts (a president and two judges, dealing with cases where the crime is punishable by imprisonment over five years); (4) commercial courts (three judges); (5) state security courts, to prosecute offences against the integrity of the state (a president and two judges).

The civil and military High Courts of Appeal sit at Ankara. The Council of State is the highest administrative tribunal; it consists of five chambers. Its 31 judges are nominated from among high-ranking personalities in politics, economy, law, the army, etc. The Military Administrative Court deals with the judicial control of administrative acts and deeds concerning military personnel. The Court of Jurisdictional Disputes is empowered to resolve disputes between civil, administrative and military courts. The Supreme Council of Judges and Public Prosecutors appoints judges and prosecutors to the profession and has disciplinary powers.

The Civil Code and the Code of Obligations have been adapted from the corresponding Swiss codes. The Penal Code is largely based upon the Italian Penal

Code, and the Code of Civil Procedure closely resembles that of the Canton of Neuchâtel. The Commercial Code is based on the German.

The population in penal institutions in Sept. 2003 was 64,051 (92 per 100,000 of national population).

The death penalty, not used since 1984, was abolished in peacetime in Aug. 2002. The government signed a European Convention protocol abolishing the death penalty entirely in Jan. 2004.

Religion. Islam ceased to be the official religion in 1928. The Constitution guarantees freedom of religion but forbids its political exploitation or any impairment of the secular character of the republic.

In 2001 there were 64·36m. Muslims, two-thirds Sunni and one-third Shia (Alevis). The Greek Orthodox, Gregorian Armenian, Armenian Apostolic and Roman Catholic Churches are represented in İstanbul, and there are small Uniate, Protestant and Jewish communities.

Education. Adult literacy in 2002 was 93·5% (male, 94·4%; female, 86·5%). The Basic Education Law of 1997 extended the duration of compulsory schooling from five to eight years. Primary education is compulsory and co-educational from the age of six to 14 and, in state schools, free. There are plans to raise the duration of compulsory schooling to 12 years. Religious instruction (Sunni Muslim) in state schools is now compulsory. In Aug. 2002 parliament legalized education in Kurdish. In 1991 there were 5,197 religious secondary schools with 0·29m. pupils up to 14 years.

Statistics for 2001–02	*Number*	*Teachers*	*Students*
Pre-school institutions	10,554	14,520	256,392
Primary schools	34,993	375,511	10,310,844
High schools	2,637	72,609	1,490,376
Vocational and technical high schools	3,428	66,176	821,893

In 2003 there were 76 universities. In 2002–03 a total of 1,894,000 students enrolled at 1,379 establishments of higher education (including the universities); teaching staff numbered 74,134. In 2001, 41,867 students were studying abroad.

In 2000–01 total expenditure on education came to 3·4% of GNP. Only 18% of Turkey's workforce has completed secondary education and only 8% has higher education qualifications.

Health. In 1999 there were 81,988 physicians, 14,226 dentists, 70,270 nurses, 22,065 pharmacists and 41,271 midwives. There were 1,184 hospitals with 156,549 beds (including maternity hospitals) in 1998 and 151 health centres. In 1998, 39% of the population aged 15 and over smoked—a rate only exceeded in Russia and the Fiji Islands.

Welfare. In 2000, 1,349,151 beneficiaries received TRL2,273,278,239m. from the Government Employees Retirement Fund. Of these, 820,167 persons were retired and 376,131 were widows, widowers or orphans of retired persons. There were 3,339,327 beneficiaries from the Social Insurance Institution in 2000 (3,216,445 through disability, old age and death insurance).

CULTURE

World Heritage Sites. UNESCO world heritage sites under Turkish jurisdiction (with year entered on list) are: Historic Areas of İstanbul (1985), including the ancient Hippodrome of Constantine, the 6th-century Hagia Sophia and the 16th-century Suleymaniye Mosque; Göreme National Park and the Rock Sites of Cappadocia (1985); Great Mosque and Hospital of Divriği (1985), founded in the early 13th century; Hattusha (1986), the former capital of the Hittite Empire; Nemrut Dag (1987), including the 1st century BC mausoleum of Antiochus I; Xanthos-Letoon (1988), the capital of Lycia; Hierapolis-Pamukkale (1988), including mineral forests, petrified waterfalls and the ruins of ancient baths, temples and other Greek monuments; City of Safranbolu (1994), a caravan station from the 13th century; Archaeological Site of Troy (1998).

Broadcasting. Broadcasting is regulated by the nine-member Radio and Television Supreme Council. The government monopoly of broadcasting was abolished in 1994 and in 2002 there were 36 national, 108 regional and 1,054 local radio stations; and

15 national, 16 regional and 229 local TV stations (colour by PAL). The Turkish Radio Television Corporation (TRT) broadcasts tourist radio programmes and a foreign service, Voice of Turkey. Number of receivers in use: TV (2001), 21·2m.; radio (1998), 12·9m.

Press. In 2002 there were 26 daily newspapers with a combined average daily circulation of 3·5m. In 2002, 3,450 periodicals were published. The most widely read newspapers are *Hürriyet* and *Sabah*, with average daily circulations of 640,000 and 470,000 respectively. In 1998, 9,383 book titles were published.

Tourism. In 2002 there were 13,247,000 foreign visitors. Revenue totalled US$7·64bn. in 2000. Tourism accounts for 4·7% of the country's GDP.

DIPLOMATIC REPRESENTATIVES

Of Turkey in the United Kingdom (43 Belgrave Sq., London, SW1X 8PA)
Ambassador: Akin Alptuna.

Of the United Kingdom in Turkey (Sehit Ersan Caddesi 46/A, Cankaya, Ankara)
Ambassador: Sir Peter Westmacott, KCMG, LVO.

Of Turkey in the USA (2525 Massachusetts Ave., NW, Washington, D.C., 20008)
Ambassador: Osman Faruk Loğoğlu.

Of the USA in Turkey (110 Atatürk Blvd, Ankara)
Ambassador: Eric S. Edelman.

Of Turkey to the United Nations
Ambassador: Baki İlkin.

Of Turkey to the European Union
Ambassador: Oğuz Demiralp.

FURTHER READING

State Institute of Statistics. *Türkiye İstatistik Yilliği/Statistical Yearbook of Turkey.—Diş Ticaret İstatistikleri/Foreign Trade Statistics* (Annual).—*Aylik İstatistik Bülten* (Monthly).

Abramowitz, Morton, (ed.) *Turkey's Transformation and American Policy.* Century Foundation, New York, 2000
Ahmad, F., *The Making of Modern Turkey.* London, 1993
Barkey, Henri J. and Fuller, Graham E., *Turkey's Kurdish Question.* Rowman and Littlefield, Lanham (MD), 1999
Goodwin, Jason, *Lords of the Horizons: a History of the Ottoman Empire.* Henry Holt, New York, USA, 1999
Howe, Marvin, *Turkey Today: A Nation Divided over Islam's Revival.* Westview, Oxford, 2000
İnalcık, H., Faroqhi, S., McGowan, B., Quataert, D. and Pamuk, Ş., *An Economic and Social History of the Ottoman Empire.* Cambridge Univ. Press, 1994
Kedourie, S., *Turkey: Identity, Democracy, Politics.* London, 1996
Mango, Andrew, *Ataturk.* John Murray, London and Overlook, New York, 1999
McDowall, David, *A Modern History of the Kurds.* I. B. Tauris, London, 1996
Pettifer, J., *The Turkish Labyrinth: Atatürk and the New Islam.* London, 1997
Pope, N. and Pope, H., *Turkey Unveiled: Atatürk and After.* London, 1997
Zürcher, E. J., *Turkey: a Modern History.* London and New York, 1993 (NY, 1994)

National statistical office: State Institute of Statistics Prime Ministry, Necatibey Caddesi no. 114, 06100 Ankara.
Website: http://www.die.gov.tr/ENGLISH/index.html

TURKMENISTAN

Capital: Ashgabat
Population projection, 2010: 5·41m.
GDP per capita, 2001: (PPP$) 4,320
HDI/world rank: 0·752/86

KEY HISTORICAL EVENTS

Until 1917 Russian Central Asia was divided politically into the Khanate of Khiva, the Emirate of Bokhara and the Governor-Generalship of Turkestan. The Khan of Khiva was deposed in Feb. 1920 and a People's Soviet Republic was set up. In Aug. 1920 the Emir of Bokhara suffered the same fate. The former Governor-Generalship of Turkestan was constituted an Autonomous Soviet Socialist Republic within the RSFSR on 11 April 1921. In the autumn of 1924 the Soviets of the Turkestan, Bokhara and Khiva Republics decided to redistribute their territories on a nationality basis. The redistribution was completed in May 1925 when the new states of Uzbekistan, Turkmenistan and Tadzhikistan were accepted into the USSR as Union Republics. Following the break-up of the Soviet Union, Turkmenistan declared independence in Oct. 1991. Saparmurad Niyazov was elected president and founded the Democratic Party of Turkmenistan, the country's only legal party. Also prime minister and Supreme Commander of the armed forces, parliament proclaimed him head of state for life in Dec. 1999. He holds the official title of 'Turkmenbashi', leader of all Turkmen. In July 2000 President Niyazov introduced a law requiring all officials to speak Turkmen.

TERRITORY AND POPULATION

Turkmenistan is bounded in the north by Kazakhstan, in the north and northeast by Uzbekistan, in the southeast by Afghanistan, in the southwest by Iran and in the west by the Caspian Sea. Area, 448,100 sq. km (186,400 sq. miles). The 1995 census population was 4,483,251; density 10·0 per sq. km. In 1999, 85% of the population were Turkmen, 7% Russian, 5% Uzbek and 3% other. Since then the Russian population has declined dramatically as the rights of Russians living in Turkmenistan deteriorated considerably. A dual-citizenship treaty between Turkmenistan and Russia has been rescinded. 2002 population estimate: 4,792,000. In 2001, 55·0% of the population lived in rural areas.

The UN gives a projected population for 2010 of 5·41m.

There are five administrative regions (*velayaty*): Ahal, Balkan, Dashoguz, Lebap and Mary, comprising 42 rural districts, 15 towns and 74 urban settlements. The capital is Ashgabat (formerly Ashkhabad; 1999 population, 525,000); other large towns are Turkmenabat (formerly Chardzhou), Mary (Merv), Balkanabad (Nebit-Dag) and Dashoguz.

Languages spoken include Turkmen, 72%; Russian, 12%; Uzbek, 9%; other, 7%.

SOCIAL STATISTICS

1998 births, 98,461; deaths, 29,628. Rates per 1,000 population, 1998: birth, 20·3; death, 6·1. Annual population growth rate, 1992–2002, 2·1%. Life expectancy, 2001: 63·3 years for males and 70·0 for females. Infant mortality, 2001, 76 per 1,000 live births; fertility rate, 2001, 3·3 births per woman.

CLIMATE

The summers are warm to hot but the humidity is relatively low. The winters are cold but generally dry and sunny over most of the country. Ashgabat, Jan. –1°C, July 25°C. Annual rainfall 375 mm.

CONSTITUTION AND GOVERNMENT

A new constitution was adopted on 18 May 1992. It provides for an executive head of state. The 50-member *Majlis* (Assembly) serves as the main legislative body. The 2,507-member *Khalk Maslakhaty* (People's Council) is the highest representative body. It is composed of the 50 Majlis members, 10 appointees, 50 directly elected representatives, the Council of Ministers, the Supreme Court chairman, the Procurator General and the heads of local councils. It is charged with constitutional and legislative review and may pass a motion of no-confidence in the president.

At a referendum on 16 Jan. 1994, 99·99% of votes cast were in favour of prolonging President Niyazov's term of office to 2002. In 1999 the *Khalk Maslakhaty* declared him president for life.

National Anthem. 'Turkmenbasyn guran beyik binasy' ('The country which Turkmenbashi has built'); composed by Veli Muhatov.

RECENT ELECTIONS

At the presidential elections of June 1992, the electorate was 1·86m. Saparmurad Niyazov was re-elected unopposed by 99·5% of votes cast.

Majlis elections were held on 19 Dec. 2004 and 9 Jan. 2005. The only party standing was the Democratic Party (DP; former Communists). All 50 seats were filled; turn-out was 76·9%. Elections to the *Khalk Maslakhaty* took place on 7 April 2003 under the same system.

CURRENT ADMINISTRATION

In March 2005 the government comprised:

President and Prime Minister: Saparmurad Niyazov (Saparmurad Turkmenbashi since 1993); b. 1940 (DP; sworn in 27 Oct. 1990).

Deputy Prime Ministers: Begench Atamuradov (also *Minister of Agriculture*); Rejepdurdy Ataev (also *Minister of Industry and Construction Materials*); Dortguly Aydogdiyev (also *Minister of Textile Industry*).

Minister of Communications: Resulberdi Khozhagurbanov. *Culture, Television and Radio Broadcasting:* Maral Byashimova. *Defence:* Maj.-Gen. Agageldy Mamedgeldiev. *Economy and Finance:* Jumaniyaz Annaorazov. *Education:* Khydr Saparlyev. *Environmental Protection:* Magtymguly Akmuradov. *Justice:* Asyrgeldi Gulgaraev. *Foreign Affairs:* Rashid Meredov. *Health and Medical Industry:* Gurganguly Berdimukhamedov. *Internal Affairs:* Akmamet Rakhmanov. *Motor Transport and Roads:* Baymuhammet Kelov. *National Security:* Geldymukhamet Ashirmukhamedov. *Oil and Gas Industries and Mineral Resources:* Amangeldy Pudakov. *Power Engineering and Industry:* Atamurad Berdyev. *Railways:* Orazberdy Hudayberdiev. *Social Security:* Orazmurat Begmuradov. *Trade and Foreign Economic Relations:* Gurbangeldi Melekeyev. *Water Resources:* Byashimklych Kalandarov.

Chairman, Supreme Council (Majlis): Ovezgeldi Atayev.

DEFENCE

Defence expenditure in 2003 totalled US$350m. (US$72 per capita), representing 1·2% of GDP.

Army. In 2002 the Army was 14,500-strong.

Navy. The government has announced its intention to form a Navy/Coast Guard. The Caspian Sea Flotilla is operating as a joint Russian, Kazakhstani and Turkmenistani flotilla under Russian command. It is based at Astrakhan.

Air Force. The Air Force, with 3,000 personnel, had 89 combat aircraft in 2002 (with an additional 200 in store) including Su-17s and MiG-29s.

INTERNATIONAL RELATIONS

Turkmenistan is a member of the UN, the NATO Partnership for Peace, OSCE, CIS, Asian Development Bank, ECO, OIC and Islamic Development Bank.

ECONOMY

In 2002 agriculture accounted for 21·3% of GDP, industry 41·0% and services 37·7%. In 1999 an estimated 25% of economic output was being produced by the private sector.

Overview. The economy is dependent on the gas and cotton industries. Export of Turkmenistan's large gas reserves has been hindered by reliance on Russian pipelines. A privatization programme was launched on 1 June 1994.

Currency. The unit of currency is the *manat* (TMM) of 100 *tenesi.* Foreign exchange reserves were US$300m. in 1993. Inflation was 11·6% in 2001. The manat was devalued in 1994 to an official rate of US$1 = 230 manat.

Budget. Revenues were 3,693bn. manat in 1999 and expenditures 3,894bn. manat.

Performance. Total GDP in 2003 was US$6·0bn. Annual real GDP growth averaged –10·6% between 1994 and 1997. However, a revival in the economy led to growth of 7·0% in 1998, followed by a spectacular 16·4% in 1999, 18·6% in 2000, 20·4% in 2001, 19·8% in 2002 and 16·9% in 2003 (the highest rate in the world). The rapid growth of recent years is largely down to large-scale gas exports to Russia.

Banking and Finance. There are two types of bank in Turkmenistan—state commercial banks and joint stock open-end commercial banks. The central bank is the State Central Bank of Turkmenistan (*Chairman*, Shekersoltan Mukhammedova). A government-led restructuring of the banking sector in 1999 saw the total number of banks reduced from 67 to 12 by 2002.

ENERGY AND NATURAL RESOURCES

Environment. Carbon dioxide emissions from the consumption and flaring of fossil fuels in 2002 were the equivalent of 7·4 tonnes per capita.

Electricity. Installed capacity in 2000 was 3·9m. kW. Production was 9·85bn. kWh in 2000, with consumption per capita 1,853 kWh in 2000.

Oil and Gas. Turkmenistan possesses the world's fifth largest reserves of natural gas and substantial oil resources, but disputes with Russia have held up development. Expansion and development of the Garashsyzlyk area could lead to oil production approaching 500,000 bbls. a day by 2007. Oil production in 2003 was 10·4m. tonnes. Accords for the construction of a gas pipeline from Turkmenbashi on the Caspian Sea coast through Azerbaijan and Georgia, to Ceyhan on the Mediterranean in Turkey, were signed in Nov. 1999. It is scheduled for completion during 2005.

In 2002 gas reserves were estimated at 2,010bn. cu. metres and oil reserves at 500m. bbls. In 2003 crude petroleum production was 10·0m. tonnes and natural gas 59·1bn. cu. metres.

Minerals. There are reserves of coal, sulphur, magnesium, potassium, lead, barite, viterite, bromine, iodine and salt.

Agriculture. Cotton and wheat account for two-thirds of agricultural production. Barley, maize, corn, rice, wool, silk and fruit are also produced. 2000 produced a bumper wheat harvest. Production of main crops (2000, in 1,000 tonnes): wheat, 1,700; seed cotton, 1,040; cottonseed, 625; cotton lint, 187; grapes, 152; tomatoes, 145; watermelons, 65. There were 1·75m. ha of arable land in 2001 and 65,000 ha of permanent crops.

Livestock, 2000: sheep, 5·60m.; cattle, 850,000; goats, 368,000; pigs, 46,000; chickens, 4m.

Forestry. There were 3·76m. ha of forests (8·0% of the land area) in 2000.

Fisheries. There are fisheries in the Caspian Sea. The total catch in 2001 was 12,749 tonnes, exclusively freshwater fish.

INDUSTRY

Main industries: oil refining, gas extraction, chemicals, manufacture of machinery, fertilizers, textiles and clothing. Output, 2000 (in tonnes): residual fuel oil, 2,365,000; distillate fuel oil, 2,247,000; petrol, 1,132,000; cement (2001), 448,000; cotton woven fabrics (2001), 61·0m. sq. metres; footwear (2001), 375,000 pairs.

Labour. The labour force in 1996 totalled 1,750,000 (55% males). Of the total workforce, 44% were engaged in agriculture, 21% in services and 10% in mining, manufacturing and public utilities. Average monthly wage in 1994 was 1,000 manat.

INTERNATIONAL TRADE

External debt was US$1,771m. in 2001.

Imports and Exports. Exports, 2000, US$2,506m.; imports, US$1,785m. Main imports: light manufactured goods, processed food, metalwork, machinery and parts. Main exports: gas, oil and cotton. The main import suppliers in 1998 were Ukraine (16·1%), Turkey (13·1%), Russia (11·6%), Germany (6·9%) and USA (6·4%). The leading export markets were Iran (24·1%), Turkey (18·3%), Azerbaijan (6·9%), UK (4·9%) and Russia (4·7%).

COMMUNICATIONS

Roads. Estimated length of roads in 1999, 24,000 km (of which 81·2% were paved). In 1998 there were 492 fatalities as a result of road accidents.

Rail. Length of railways in 2000, 2,521 km of 1,520 mm gauge. A rail link to Iran was opened in May 1996, and there are plans to build a further 2,000 km of rail network. In 2000, 3·5m. passengers and 18·0m. tonnes of freight were carried.

Civil Aviation. In 2003 Avia Company Turkmenistan operated flights from Ashgabat to Abu Dhabi, Almaty, Amritsar, Bangkok, Birmingham, Delhi, Dubai, Frankfurt, İstanbul, Kyiv, London, Moscow and Tashkent. In 1999 scheduled airline traffic of Turkmenistan-based carriers flew 8·6m. km, carrying 220,000 passengers (all on international flights).

Shipping. In 2002 sea-going shipping totalled 46,000 GRT (including oil tankers, 6,000 GRT). In 1993, 1·1m. tonnes of freight were carried by inland waterways.

Telecommunications. Telephone subscribers numbered 382,200 in 2002 (78·8 per 1,000 population), including 8,200 mobile phone subscribers. There were 8,000 Internet users in 2001.

Postal Services. There were 1,673 post offices in 1996.

SOCIAL INSTITUTIONS

Justice. In 1994, 14,824 crimes were reported, including 308 murders and attempted murders. The death penalty was abolished in 1999 (there were over 100 executions in 1996). The population in penal institutions in Oct. 2000 was approximately 22,000 (489 per 100,000 of national population).

Religion. Around 87% of the population in 2001 were Muslims (mostly Sunni).

Education. There is compulsory education until the age of 14. In 1994–95 there were 1,900 primary and secondary schools with 940,600 pupils; and in 1993–94 there were 11 higher educational institutions with 38,900 students, 41 technical colleges with 29,000 students, and 11 music and art schools.

In Jan. 1994, 0·2m. children (29·5% of those eligible) were attending pre-school institutions. In 1999 adult literacy was over 98%.

Health. There were 368 hospitals in 1995 with 46,000 beds. In 1997 there were 14,022 physicians, 1,010 dentists, 21,436 nurses, 1,566 pharmacists and 3,664 midwives.

Welfare. In Jan. 1994 there were 0·3m. old-age, and 0·16m. other, pensioners.

CULTURE

World Heritage Sites. Turkmenistan has one site on the UNESCO World Heritage List: the State Historical and Cultural Park 'Ancient Merv' (inscribed on the list in 1999), the oldest and best-preserved Central Asian Silk Route city, dominated by Seljuk architecture.

Broadcasting. Turkmen Radio is government-controlled. It broadcasts two national programmes and one regional, a Moscow Radio relay and a foreign service, Voice of Turkmen. There is one state-run TV station broadcasting on three channels. In 2000 there were 1·2m. radio receivers and in 2001 there were 880,000 television sets.

Press. In 2000 there were two daily newspapers with a combined average circulation of 31,512.

Tourism. In 1998 there were 300,000 foreign tourists. Receipts totalled US$192m.

Calendar. In Aug. 2002 President Saparmurat Niyazov renamed the days of the week and the months, for example with Jan. becoming 'Turkmenbashi' after the president's official name, meaning 'head of all the Turkmen'. April has been renamed in honour of the president's mother. Tuesday is now 'Young Day' and Saturday 'Spiritual Day'.

DIPLOMATIC REPRESENTATIVES

Of Turkmenistan in the United Kingdom (2nd Floor, St George's House, 14–17 Wells St., London, W1T 3PD)
Ambassador: Yazmurad N. Seryaev.

Of the United Kingdom in Turkmenistan (3rd Floor, Office Building, Ak Atin Plaza Hotel, Ashgabat)
Ambassador: Paul Brummell.

Of Turkmenistan in the USA (2207 Massachusetts Ave., NW, Washington, D.C., 20008)
Ambassador: Meret Bairamovich Orazov.

Of the USA in Turkmenistan (9 Puskin St., Ashgabat)
Ambassador: Tracey Jacobson.

Of Turkmenistan to the United Nations
Ambassador: Aksoltan T. Ataeva.

Of Turkmenistan to the European Union
Ambassador: Niyazklych Nurklychev.

TUVALU

Capital: Fongafale
Population, 2000: 11,000
GDP per capita: not available

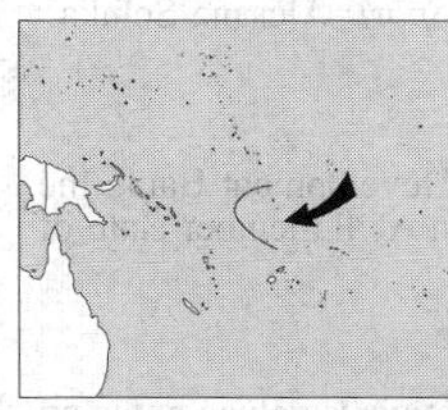

KEY HISTORICAL EVENTS

Formerly known as the Ellice Islands, Tuvalu is a group of nine islands in the western central Pacific. Joining the British controlled Gilbert Islands Protectorate in 1916, they became the Gilbert and Ellice Islands colony.

After the Japanese occupied the Gilbert Islands in 1942, US forces occupied the Ellice Islands. A referendum held in 1974 produced a large majority in favour of separation from the Ellice Islands. Independence was achieved on 1 Oct. 1978. Early in 1979 the USA signed a treaty of friendship with Tuvalu and relinquished its claim to the four southern islands in return for the right to veto any other nation's request to use any of Tuvalu's islands for military purposes.

TERRITORY AND POPULATION

Tuvalu lies between 5° 30' and 11° S. lat. and 176° and 180° E. long. and comprises Nanumea, Nanumaga, Niutao, Nui, Vaitupu, Nukufetau, Funafuti (administrative centre; 2002 estimated population, 4,492), Nukulaelae and Niulakita. Population (census 2002) 9,561, excluding an estimated 1,500 who were working abroad, mainly in Nauru and Kiribati. Area approximately 10 sq. miles (26 sq. km). Density, 2002, 373 per sq. km.

In 2002 an estimated 52·9% of the population lived in rural areas. The population is of a Polynesian race.

Both Tuvaluan and English are spoken.

SOCIAL STATISTICS

2000 births, 229; deaths, 109. Rates (per 1,000 population): births, 21; deaths, 10; infant mortality (per 1,000 live births), 35. Expectation of life: males, 64 years; females, 71. Annual population growth rate, 1992–2002, 1·4%; fertility rate, 2000, 2·9 births per woman.

CLIMATE

A pleasant but monotonous climate with temperatures averaging 86°F (30°C), though trade winds from the east moderate conditions for much of the year. Rainfall ranges from 120" (3,000 mm) to over 160" (4,000 mm). Funafuti, Jan. 84°F (28·9°C), July 81°F (27·2°C). Annual rainfall 160" (4,003 mm). Although the islands are north of the recognized hurricane belt they were badly hit by hurricanes in the 1990s, raising fears for the long-term future of Tuvalu as the sea level continues to rise.

CONSTITUTION AND GOVERNMENT

The Head of State is the British sovereign, represented by an appointed Governor-General. The Constitution provides for a Prime Minister and the cabinet ministers to be elected from among the 15 members of the *Fale I Fono* (*Parliament*).

National Anthem. 'Tuvalu mote Atua' ('Tuvalu for the Almighty'); words and tune by A. Manoa.

RECENT ELECTIONS

Elections were held on 2 Aug. 2002. Only non-partisans were elected as there are no political parties. Maatia Toafa was elected prime minister by parliament on 11 Oct. 2004 by eight votes to seven against Elisala Pita.

CURRENT ADMINISTRATION

Governor-General: Filoimea Telito (sworn in 15 April 2005).

In March 2005 the cabinet comprised:

Prime Minister and Minister of Foreign Affairs and Labour: Maatia Toafa (sworn in 11 Oct. 2004; acting prime minister from 27 Aug. 2004 to 10 Oct. 2004).

Deputy Prime Minister and Minister of Works and Energy, Communications and Transport: Saufatu Sopoanga. *Finance, Economic Planning and Industries:* Bikenibeu Paeniu. *Natural Resources:* Samuelu P. Teo. *Home Affairs, Rural and Urban Development:* Leti Pelesala. *Health, Education and Sport:* Alesana Seluka.

Speaker: Otinielu Tausi.

INTERNATIONAL RELATIONS

Tuvalu is a member of the UN, the Commonwealth, Asian Development Bank, the Pacific Community and the Pacific Islands Forum, and is an ACP member state of the ACP-EU relationship.

ECONOMY

Currency. The unit of currency is the Australian *dollar* although Tuvaluan coins up to $A1 are in local circulation.

Budget. In 2001 the budget envisaged revenue of $A26·7m. and expenditure of $A35·3m.

Performance. Real GDP growth was 5·2% in 2001.

Banking and Finance. The Tuvalu National Bank was established at Funafuti in 1980, and is a joint venture between the Tuvalu government and Wespac International. There is also a development bank.

ENERGY AND NATURAL RESOURCES

Electricity. Installed capacity was 2·6 MW in 2002; production was 4,355 MWh.

Agriculture. Coconut palms are the main crop. Production of coconuts (2000 estimate), 2,000 tonnes. Fruit and vegetables are grown for local consumption. Livestock, 2000: pigs, 13,000.

Fisheries. Sea fishing is excellent, particularly for tuna. Total catch, 2001, approximately 500 tonnes. A seamount was discovered in Tuvaluan waters in 1991 and is a good location for deep-sea fish. The sale of fishing licences to American and Japanese fleets provides a significant source of income.

INDUSTRY

Small amounts of copra, handicrafts and garments are produced.

INTERNATIONAL TRADE

Imports and Exports. Commerce is dominated by co-operative societies, the Tuvalu Co-operative Wholesale Society being the main importer. Main sources of income are copra, stamps, handicrafts and remittances from Tuvaluans abroad. 1999 imports, US$10·7m.; 1999 exports, US$1·4m. The leading import suppliers are Australia, the Fiji Islands, New Zealand and Japan. The main export destination is Australia.

COMMUNICATIONS

Roads. In 2002 there were 20 km of roads.

Civil Aviation. In 2002 Air Kiribati operated four flights a week from Funafuti International to Suva.

Shipping. Funafuti is the only port and a deep-water wharf was opened in 1980. In 2002 merchant shipping totalled 49,000 GRT.

Telecommunications. In 2002 there were approximately 700 main telephone lines in operation. There were 1,300 Internet users in 2002.

SOCIAL INSTITUTIONS

Justice. There is a High Court presided over by the Chief Justice of the Fiji Islands. A Court of Appeal is constituted if required. There are also eight Island Courts with limited jurisdiction.

Religion. The majority of the population are Christians, mainly Protestant, but with small groups of Roman Catholics, Seventh Day Adventists, Jehovah's Witnesses and Baha'is. There are some Muslims and Latter-day Saints (Mormons).

Education. There were 1,798 pupils at nine primary schools in 2001, and 558 pupils at Motufoua Secondary School in 2001. The Fetuvalu High School reopened in 2002 with Form 3 only. Education is free and compulsory from the ages of six to 13. There is a Maritime Training School at Funafuti, and the University of the South Pacific, based in the Fiji Islands, has an extension centre at Funafuti.

In 1999–2000 total expenditure on education came to 16·8% of total government expenditure.

Health. In 2002 there was one central hospital situated at Funafuti and clinics on each of the other eight islands; there were seven doctors and 34 nurses.

CULTURE

Broadcasting. The Tuvalu Broadcasting Service transmits daily, and all islands have daily radio communication with Funafuti. There were about 4,000 radio receivers in 1997 and 100 TV sets in 1996.

Press. The Government Broadcasting and Information Division produces *Tuvalu Echoes*, a fortnightly publication, and *Te Lama*, a monthly religious publication.

Tourism. There were 1,304 visitor arrivals in 2002 (639 in 1995).

DIPLOMATIC REPRESENTATIVES

Of Tuvalu in the United Kingdom (Tuvalu House, 230 Worple Road, London, SW20 8RH)
Honorary Consul: Vacant.

Of the United Kingdom in Tuvalu
High Commissioner: Charles Mochan (resides at Suva, Fiji Islands).

Of Tuvalu in the USA
Ambassador: Vacant.

Of the USA in Tuvalu
Ambassador: David Lyon (resides at Suva, Fiji Islands).

Of Tuvalu to the United Nations
Ambassador: Enele S. Sopoaga.

FURTHER READING

Bennetts, P. and Wheeler, T., *Time and Tide: The Islands of Tuvalu.* Lonely Planet Publications, Melbourne, 2001

National statistical office: Ministry of Finance, Economic Planning and Industries, Private Bag, Vaiaku, Funafuti.

UGANDA

Republic of Uganda

Capital: Kampala
Population projection, 2010: 33·00m.
GDP per capita, 2003: (PPP$) 1,390
HDI/world rank: 0·493/146

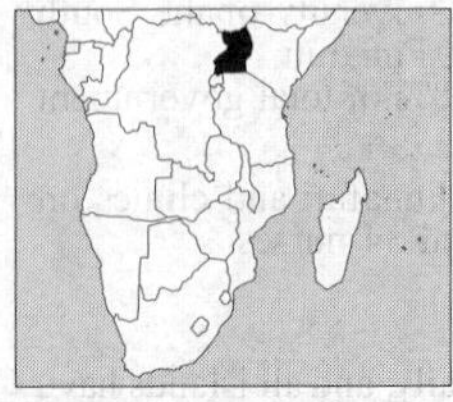

KEY HISTORICAL EVENTS

Bantu-speaking mixed farmers migrated into southwest Uganda around 500 BC. In the following centuries Nilotic-speaking pastoralists entered northern Uganda. By AD 1300 the Chwezi states were established in southern Uganda. In 1500 Nilotic-speaking Luo people invaded the Chwezi states and established the kingdoms of Buganda, Bunyoro and Ankole. Northern Uganda became home to the Alur and Acholi ethnic groups. During the 17th century Bunyoro was southern Uganda's most powerful state but from about 1700 Buganda superseded Bunyoro and a century later it dominated a large territory bordering Lake Victoria from the Victoria Nile to the Kagera River. The king (*kabaka*) maintained a large court and a powerful army and traded in cattle, ivory and slaves.

Arab traders from Zanzibar reached Lake Victoria by 1844, bringing Islam. In 1862 John Speke, a British explorer, became the first European to visit Buganda, by then a highly developed state. He met with Kabaka Mutesa I, as did Henry Stanley, who reached Buganda in 1875, persuading Mutesa to welcome Christian missionaries. In 1884 Mutesa was succeeded by Mwanga, who attempted to halt the spread of the new religions but was deposed by Christian and Muslim converts in 1888. In 1889 the reinstated Mwanga signed a treaty of friendship with Germany. However, in 1890 Britain and Germany signed a treaty giving Britain rights to what was to become Uganda and Germany control over what is now Tanzania. In 1894 Britain made Uganda a protectorate.

In 1901 a railway from Mombasa on the Indian Ocean to Kisumu, on Lake Victoria, allowed for the export of cotton, coffee and sugar, produced by African smallholders rather than plantations as in other colonies. Many south Asians were encouraged to settle in Uganda, where they played a leading role in the country's commerce. In 1921 a legislative council for the protectorate was established (although its first African member was admitted only in 1945). When the British and Asians rejected African attempts to break into cotton ginning, the Baganda rioted and burned down the houses of pro-government chiefs in Kampala.

Appointed governor in 1952, Sir Andrew Cohen set about economic and political reforms: removing obstacles to African cotton ginning, encouraging co-operatives, establishing the Uganda Development Corporation and reorganizing the Legislative Council to include Africans. Kabaka Mutesa II refused to co-operate with Cohen's plan for a fully integrated Buganda. Cohen deported him to London, which set off a storm of protest. Two year later Mutesa II was reinstated, officially as a 'constitutional monarch' but in reality having considerable political clout. In 1960 Milton Obote formed the Uganda People's Congress (UPC) as a coalition opposed to Buganda dominance.

On 9 Oct. 1962 Uganda became independent, with Obote as prime minister. Buganda was given considerable autonomy. In 1963 Uganda became a republic and Mutesa II was elected president. The first years of independence were dominated by a struggle between the central government and Buganda. In 1966 Obote introduced a new constitution that ended Buganda's autonomy. Obote forced the kabaka to flee the country. In 1967 a new constitution increased the power of the president and divided Buganda into four districts. The traditional kingships were also abolished.

In Jan. 1971 Obote, at the time out of the country, was deposed in a coup by Maj.-Gen. Idi Amin Dada. In 1972 he ordered Asians who were not citizens of Uganda to leave the country and within three months all 60,000 had left, most of them for Britain. Their expulsion hit the Ugandan economy hard. Amin's rule became increasingly dictatorial and brutal; it is estimated that over 300,000 Ugandans were killed during the 1970s. Divisions in the military led to a number of coup attempts.

In 1976 Amin declared himself president for life and two years later he invaded Tanzania in an attempt to annex the Kagera region. The following year Tanzania launched a successful counter-invasion and unified anti-Amin forces under the Uganda National Liberation Front (UNLF). Amin's forces were driven out and he fled to exile in Saudi Arabia. Tanzania left an occupation force in Uganda. A military coup on 10 May 1980 was headed by Paolo Muwanga, who governed Uganda until national elections in Dec. 1980. Obote made a triumphant return from Tanzania and rallied his former UPC supporters. The Democratic Party (DP), led by Paul Kawanga Ssemogerere, were announced as winners but Muwanga seized control of the Electoral Commission and announced a UPC victory 18 hours later, which was verified by the Commonwealth Observer Group.

In Feb. 1981 a former Military Commission member, Yoweri Museveni, declared a National Resistance Army (NRA). Museveni vowed to overthrow Obote by means of a popular rebellion, and what became known as the 'war in the bush' began. Approximately 200,000 Ugandans sought refuge in neighbouring Rwanda, Zaïre and Sudan. In 1985 a military coup deposed Obote and Lieut.-Gen. Tito Okello became head of state. When it was not given a role in the new regime, the NRA continued its guerrilla campaign. It took Kampala in 1986 and Museveni became the new president. He concentrated on rebuilding the ruined economy by cutting back the army and civil service and reforming agriculture and industry. In 1993 Museveni permitted the restoration of traditional kings, including Ronald Muwenda Mutebi II as kabaka. In May 1996 Museveni was returned to office in the country's first direct presidential elections. Museveni supporters dominated a new parliament, chosen in elections in June.

Museveni was re-elected in 2001, following a period of relative stability and economic growth. However, his popularity was diminished by discontent with Uganda's intervention in the Democratic Republic of the Congo's (formerly Zaïre) civil war and signs of corruption in the government. Uganda's forces were largely withdrawn from the Democratic Republic of the Congo by the end of 2002 but fighting continues with the Lord's Resistance Army in the north of the country.

TERRITORY AND POPULATION

Uganda is bounded in the north by Sudan, in the east by Kenya, in the south by Tanzania and Rwanda, and the west by the Democratic Republic of the Congo. Total area 241,548 sq. km, including inland waters.

The 2002 census population was 24,748,977 (12,124,761 males, 12,624,216 females); density, 102 per sq. km. The largest city is Kampala, the capital (population of 1,208,544 in 2002). Other major towns are Jinja, Mbale, Masaka, Gulu, Entebbe, Soroti and Mbarara. In 2001, 85·5% of the population lived in rural areas.

The projected population for 2010 is 33·00m.

The country is administratively divided into 56 districts, which are grouped in four geographical regions (which do not have administrative status). Area and estimated population of the regions in 2002:

Region	*Area in sq. km*	*Population in 1,000*
Central Region	61,352	6,683·9
Eastern Region	39,525	6,301·7
Northern Region	85,392	5,346·0
Western Region	55,278	6,417·4

The official language is English, but Kiswahili is used as a *lingua franca*. About 70% of the population speak Bantu languages; Nilotic languages are spoken in the north and east.

Uganda is host to around 500,000 refugees from a number of neighbouring countries, and internally displaced people. Probably in excess of 100,000 southern Sudanese fled to Uganda during 1996.

SOCIAL STATISTICS

Births, 1995, 1,004,000; deaths, 421,000. Rates per 1,000 population, 1995: birth, 51·0; death, 21·4. Uganda's life expectancy at birth in 2001 was 43·9 years for males and 45·4 years for females. Life expectancy declined dramatically until the late 1990s, largely owing to the huge number of people in the country with HIV.

However, for both males and females expectation of life is now starting to rise again. Annual population growth rate, 1992–2002, 3·0%. Infant mortality, 2001, 79 per 1,000 live births; fertility rate, 2001, 7·1 births per woman.

CLIMATE

Although in equatorial latitudes, the climate is more tropical, because of its elevation, and is characterized by two distinct rainy seasons, March–May and Sept.–Nov. June–Aug. and Dec.–Feb. are comparatively dry. Temperatures vary little over the year. Kampala, Jan. 74°F (23·3°C), July 70°F (21·1°C). Annual rainfall 46·5" (1,180 mm). Entebbe, Jan. 72°F (22·2°C), July 69°F (20·6°C). Annual rainfall 63·9" (1,624 mm).

CONSTITUTION AND GOVERNMENT

The *President* is head of state and head of government, and is elected for a five-year term by adult suffrage. The constitution allows the incumbent no more than two consecutive terms. Having lapsed in 1966, the kabakaship was revived as a ceremonial office in 1993. Ronald Muwenda Mutebi (b. 13 April 1955) was crowned Mutebi II, 36th Kabaka, on 31 July 1993.

Until 1994 the national legislature was the 278-member National Resistance Council, but this was replaced by a 284-member *Constituent Assembly* in March 1994. A new constitution was adopted on 8 Oct. 1995 and the Constituent Assembly dissolved. Since 1996 Uganda's parliament has been the 303-seat *National Assembly.* A referendum on the return of multiparty democracy was held on 29 June 2000, but 88% of voters supported President Museveni's 'no-party' Movement system of government. Turn-out was 51%. In Feb. 2003 President Museveni pledged to lift the ban on political parties.

National Anthem. 'Oh, Uganda, may God uphold thee'; words and tune by G. W. Kakoma.

RECENT ELECTIONS

Presidential elections were held on 12 March 2001. President Museveni was re-elected by 69·3% of votes cast, with his main rival, Kizza Besigye, receiving 27·8% of the vote. Turn-out was 70·3%. Local non-government monitors described the election as flawed.

Parliamentary elections were held on 26 June 2001. 214 non-partisan members were directly elected in single-seat constituencies. 78 other members had been elected earlier in the month from special interest groups (53 District Women Representatives, ten army representatives, and five each to represent the disabled, the trade unions and youth). Turn-out was 70·3%.

CURRENT ADMINISTRATION

President: Yoweri K. Museveni; b. 1945 (sworn in 27 Jan. 1986; re-elected 1996 and 2001).

In March 2005 the government comprised:

Vice-President: Prof. Gilbert Bukenya (sworn in 6 June 2003).

Prime Minister: Apollo Nsibambi; b. 1938 (sworn in 5 April 1999).

First Deputy Prime Minister and Minister of Disaster Preparedness and Refugees: Brig. Gen. Moses Ali. *Deputy Prime Minister and Minister of Public Service:* Henry Muganwa Kajura.

Minister of Defence: Amama Mbabazi. *Education and Sports:* Namirembe Bitamazire. *Foreign Affairs:* Sam Kutesa. *Trade, Industry, Tourism, Wildlife and Antiquities:* Daudi Migereko. *Energy and Mineral Development:* Syda Bbumba. *Health:* Jim Katugugu Muhwezi. *Gender, Labour and Social Development:* Zoe Bakoko Bakoru. *Justice, Constitutional Affairs and Attorney General:* Kiddu Makubuya. *Local Government:* Prof. Tarsis Barana Kabwegyere. *Internal Affairs:* Ruhakana Ruganda. *Water, Lands and Environment:* Col. Kahinda Otafiire. *Public Works, Transport, Housing and Communications:* John Nasasira. *Finance, Planning and Economic Development:* Ezra Suruma. *Agriculture, Animal Industry and Fisheries:* Janat Mukwaya. *Security:* Betty Akech. *Minister without Portfolio:* Crispus Kiyonga. *Office of the President:* Beatrice Wabudeya. *Office of the Prime Minister:* Mondo George Kagonyera.

Speaker of Parliament: Edward Ssekandi.

Ugandan Parliament: http://www.parliament.go.ug

DEFENCE

In 2003 defence expenditure totalled US$154m. (US$6 per capita), representing 2·4% of GDP.

Army. The Uganda People's Defence Forces had a strength estimated at 50–60,000 in 2002. There is a Border Defence Unit about 600-strong and local defence units estimated at 15,000.

Navy. There is a Marine unit of the police (400-strong in 2002).

Air Force. The Army's aviation wing operated 16 combat aircraft and two armed helicopters in 2002.

INTERNATIONAL RELATIONS

Uganda is a member of UN, WTO, the African Union, African Development Bank, COMESA, EAC, IOM, Islamic Conference Organization, Islamic Development Bank, the Commonwealth, the Intergovernmental Authority on Development and is an ACP member state of the ACP-EU relationship.

In Nov. 1999 Uganda, Tanzania and Kenya created a new East African Community to develop East African trade, tourism and industry and to lay the foundations for a future common market and political federation.

ECONOMY

In 2002 agriculture accounted for 31·0% of GDP, industry 21·5% and services 47·5%.

Overview. In the early 1990s the economy achieved high GDP growth rates, annual inflation was reduced to under 10% and the incidence of poverty fell considerably. However, since the late 1990s growth has decreased, partly owing to the collapse in coffee prices. The economy grew at 6% per year between 1998 and 2003, while average underlying inflation stayed fairly constant at approximately 5%. The political climate in Uganda stabilized in the early 1980s, allowing ambitious economic reforms. Under the Poverty Eradication Action Plan (PEAP), launched in 1997, the authorities pursued a strategy to reduce poverty to less than 10% of the population by 2017. Whilst the long term growth rate has fallen short of achieving this target, the incidence of poverty has been greatly reduced from 44% of the population in 1997 to 35% in 2000. Uganda's fiscal and external stability indicators have worsened in recent years; the government has set out a plan to achieve fiscal consolidation to improve stability which includes increasing revenue collection and decreasing public administration expenditure.

Currency. The monetary unit is the *Uganda shilling* (UGS) notionally divided into 100 *cents*. In 1987 the currency was devalued by 77% and a new 'heavy' shilling was introduced worth 100 old shillings. Inflation was negative in 2002, at –2·0%. Foreign exchange reserves in May 2002 were US$893m. Total money supply in April 2002 was Shs 966,075m.

Budget. The provisional total expenditure for the financial year 2001 (year ending 30 June) was Shs 1,516bn. In 2000 total revenue (provisional) was Shs 1,105bn. Expenditures (in Shs) in 2000–01 included: education, 401bn.; defence, 212bn.; roads, 138bn.; health, 111bn.; agriculture, 22bn.

Performance. Real GDP growth was 5·5% in 2001, rising to 6·6% in 2002. In recent times Uganda has consistently been among Africa's best performers. In spite of growth rates which averaged 6·4% over ten years to 1998, per capita income is only just around the level of 1971, when Gen. Idi Amin came to power. Uganda's total GDP in 2003 was US$6·2bn.

Banking and Finance. The Bank of Uganda (*Governor,* Emmanuel Tumusiime Mutebile) was established in 1966 and is the central bank and bank of issue. In addition there are five foreign, six commercial and two development banks. There is also the state-owned Uganda Development Bank, which is scheduled for eventual privatization.

In 2003 foreign direct investment totalled a record high US$283m.

ENERGY AND NATURAL RESOURCES

Environment. Uganda's carbon dioxide emissions from the consumption and flaring of fossil fuels were the equivalent of 0·1 tonnes per capita in 2002.

Electricity. Installed capacity in 2000 was 0·3m. kW, about 95% of which was provided by the Owen Falls Extension Project (a hydro-electric scheme). Production (2000) 1·57bn. kWh. Per capita consumption (2000) 64 kWh. Only 5% of the population has access to electricity and less than 1% of the rural population.

Oil and Gas. Oil was discovered in north-west Uganda in 1999. A Canadian company Heritage Oil Corporation and Energy Africa are exploring the potential for commercial exploitation.

Minerals. In Nov. 1997 extraction started on the first of an estimated US$400m. worth of cobalt from pyrites. Tungsten and tin concentrates are also mined. There are also significant quantities of clay and gypsum.

Agriculture. 80% of the workforce is involved with agriculture. In 2001 the agricultural area included 5·10m. ha of arable land and 2·10m. ha of permanent crops. Agriculture is one of the priority areas for increased production, with many projects funded both locally and externally. It contributes 90% of exports. Production (2000 estimates) in 1,000 tonnes: plantains, 9,533; cassava, 4,966; sweet potatoes, 2,398; sugarcane, 1,550; maize, 1,096; bananas, 610; millet, 534; potatoes, 478; dry beans, 420; sorghum, 361; coffee, 205. Coffee is the mainstay of the economy, accounting for more than 50% of the annual commodity export revenue. Uganda is the world's leading producer of plantains.

Livestock (2000): cattle, 5·97m.; goats, 3·70m.; sheep, 1·98m.; pigs, 0·97m.; chickens, 25m. Livestock products, 2000 (in 1,000 tonnes): milk, 511; meat, 234.

Forestry. In 2000 the area under forests was 4·19m. ha, or 21·0% of the total land area. Exploitable forests consist almost entirely of hardwoods. Timber production in 2001 totalled 37·79m. cu. metres. Uganda has great potential for timber-processing for export, manufacture of high-quality furniture and wood products, and various packaging materials.

Fisheries. In 2001 fish landings totalled 220,726 tonnes, entirely from inland waters. Fish farming (especially carp and tilapia) is a growing industry. Uganda's fish-processing industry has greatly expanded in recent years, and fisheries exports, valued at US$87m. in 2002, now rival coffee and tourism as the major foreign currency earners.

INDUSTRY

Production (in 1,000 tonnes): cement (2001), 416; sugar (2002), 160; soap (1999), 84; beer (1999), 117·8m. litres. In 2001 industry accounted for 20·9% of GDP, with manufacturing contributing 9·8%. Industrial production grew by 5·4% in 2001.

Labour. The labour force in 1996 totalled 10,084,000 (52% males). Around 80% of the workforce are involved in the coffee business.

INTERNATIONAL TRADE

Foreign debt was US$4,100m. in 2002.

Imports and Exports. In 2002 imports (f.o.b.) amounted to US$1,113·5m. (US$1,026·6m. in 2001); exports (f.o.b.) US$480·7m. (US$451·6m. in 2001). Coffee, cotton, tea and tobacco are the principal exports. Coffee accounts for nearly 70% of exports—in 1998–99 coffee exports were worth US$282·2m. Timber, tea and fish exports are increasingly important. In 2001 the main export markets were Germany (12·0%), Netherlands (10·2%) and the USA (8·7%). Main import suppliers in 2001 were Kenya (41·0%), UK (7·6%) and India (6·8%). During the 1990s exports grew by an average of 30% every year.

COMMUNICATIONS

Roads. In 1999 there were an estimated 27,000 km of roads, of which 6·7% were paved. There were 46,930 passenger cars in 1998, 48,650 lorries and vans and 15,829 buses and coaches. In 1999 there were 4,986 road accidents resulting in 1,527 deaths.

In 1997 the government embarked upon a ten-year road-improvement programme, costing US$1·5bn., funded by international loans.

Rail. The Uganda Railways network totals 1,241 km (metre gauge). In 1996 passenger services were suspended and have not been reinstated in the meantime. Freight tonne-km in 2000 came to 210m.

A US$20m. project is under way to establish a direct rail link between Kampala and Johannesburg, South Africa.

Civil Aviation. There is an international airport at Entebbe, 40 km from Kampala. The main Ugandan carrier is East African Airlines, which in 2003 flew to Bujumbura, Johannesburg and Nairobi. In 1999 scheduled airline traffic of Uganda-based carriers flew 4·6m. km, carrying 179,000 passengers (36,000 on international flights). In 2000 Entebbe handled 373,064 passengers (343,746 on international flights) and 26,048 tonnes of freight.

Telecommunications. There were 448,300 telephone subscribers in 2002 (18·1 per 1,000 persons) and 82,000 PCs in use (3·3 per 1,000 persons). Mobile phone subscribers numbered 393,300 in 2002 and there were 3,000 fax machines in 1996. In 2002 Uganda had 100,000 Internet users.

Postal Services. In 1998 there were 313 post offices.

SOCIAL INSTITUTIONS

Justice. The Supreme Court of Uganda, presided over by the Chief Justice, is the highest court. There is a Court of Appeal and a High Court below that. Subordinate courts, presided over by Chief Magistrates and Magistrates of the first, second and third grade, are established in all areas: jurisdiction varies with the grade of Magistrate. Chief and first-grade Magistrates are professionally qualified; second- and third-grade Magistrates are trained to diploma level at the Law Development Centre, Kampala. Chief Magistrates exercise supervision over and hear appeals from second- and third-grade courts, and village courts.

The population in penal institutions in May 2002 was approximately 21,900 (89 per 100,000 of national population). The death penalty is still in force. In 2003 there were three executions.

Religion. In 2001 there were 10·05m. Roman Catholics, 9·45m. Anglicans and 1·25m. Muslims. In Sept. 2003 there was one Roman Catholic cardinal. Traditional beliefs are also widespread.

Education. In 2003 there were 7,633,314 pupils and 145,587 teachers at 13,353 primary schools. In 1995, 93·9% of primary schools were government-aided and 6·1% private. There were 683,609 students and 38,549 teachers at 2,055 secondary schools in 2003. In 1995 there were 13,174 students in 94 primary teacher training colleges; 13,360 students in 24 technical institutes and colleges; 22,703 students in 10 national teachers' colleges; 1,628 students in 5 colleges of commerce; 504 students in the Uganda Polytechnic, Kyambogo; 800 students in the National College of Business Studies, Nakawa. In 1995–96 there was one university and one university of science and technology in the public sector, and one Christian, one Roman Catholic and one Islamic university in the private sector. In 1995–96 there were 30,266 students in tertiary education. The adult literacy rate was 68·0% in 2001 (78·1% among males and 58·0% among females).

School attendance has trebled since Yoweri Museveni became president in 1986. In 1997 free primary education was introduced, initially for four children in every family but from 2003 for all children. In 1999–2000 total expenditure on education came to 2·3% of GNP.

Health. In 1988 there were 980 health centres (217 private), and in 1989 there were 81 hospitals and 20,136 hospital beds. In 1996 there were 42 dentists, 3,897 nurses and 2,835 midwives and there were 840 physicians in 1993. Uganda has been one of the most successful African countries in the fight against AIDS. A climate of free debate, with President Museveni recognizing the threat as early as 1986 and making every government department take the problem seriously, resulted in HIV prevalence among adults declining from approximately 30% in 1992 to 11% in 2000.

CULTURE

World Heritage Sites. Uganda has three sites on the UNESCO World Heritage List: Bwindi Impenetrable National Park (inscribed on the list in 1994); Rwenzori Mountains National Park (1994); and the Tombs of the Buganda Kings at Kasubi (2001).

Broadcasting. The government runs Radio Uganda, which has ten stations and transmits three regional programmes, and Uganda Television with nine stations and one programme. Colour is by PAL. There were about 2·9m. radio receivers and 620,000 television sets in 2000. There are three private television operators.

Press. There were two daily newspapers in 1996 with a combined circulation of 40,000, and four non-daily newspapers and periodicals.

Tourism. In 2002 there were 254,000 foreign tourists; spending by tourists totalled US$185m.

Festivals. The main festivals are for Islamic holidays (March and June), Martyrs' Day (3 June), Heroes' Day (9 June) and Independence Day (9 Oct.).

Theatre and Opera. There is a National Theatre at Kampala.

Museums and Galleries. The Nommo Gallery houses famous works of art, and is involved in educational and other cultural programmes.

DIPLOMATIC REPRESENTATIVES

Of Uganda in the United Kingdom (Uganda House, 58/59 Trafalgar Square, London, WC2N 5DX)
High Commissioner: Tomasi Sisye Kiryapawo.

Of the United Kingdom in Uganda (10/12 Parliament Ave., Kampala)
High Commissioner: Adam Wood.

Of Uganda in the USA (5911 16th St., NW, Washington, D.C., 20011)
Ambassador: Edith Ssempala.

Of the USA in Uganda (1577 Ggaba Road, Kampala)
Ambassador: Jimmy Kolker.

Of Uganda to the United Nations
Ambassador: Francis Butagira.

Of Uganda to the European Union
Ambassador: Vacant.
Chargé d'Affaires a.i.: Lewis Balinda.

FURTHER READING

Museveni, Y., *What is Africa's Problem?* London, 1993.—*The Mustard Seed.* London, 1997
Mutibwa, P., *Uganda since Independence: a Story of Unfulfilled Hopes.* London, 1992
Nyeko, B., *Uganda.* [Bibliography] 2nd ed. ABC-Clio, Oxford and Santa Barbara (CA), 1996

National statistical office: Uganda Bureau of Statistics, P. O. Box 13, Entebbe.
Website: http://www.ubos.org

UKRAINE

Ukraina

Capital: Kyiv (formerly Kiev)
Population projection, 2010: 46·04m.
GDP per capita, 2002: (PPP$) 4,870
HDI/world rank: 0·777/70

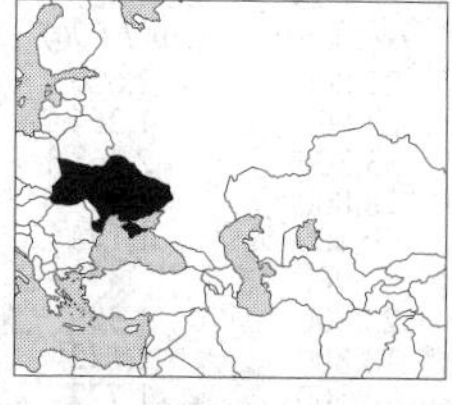

KEY HISTORICAL EVENTS

Kyiv (formerly Kiev) was the centre of the Rus principality in the 11th and 12th centuries and is still known as the Mother of Russian cities. The western Ukraine principality of Galicia was annexed by Poland in the 14th century. At about the same time, Kyiv and the Ukrainian principality of Volhynia were conquered by Lithuania before being absorbed by Poland. Poland, however, could not subjugate the Ukrainian cossacks, who allied themselves with Russia. Ukraine, except for Galicia (part of the Austrian Empire, 1772–1919), was incorporated into the Russian Empire after the second partition of Poland in 1793.

In 1917, following the Bolshevik revolution, the Ukrainians in Russia established an independent republic. Austrian Ukraine proclaimed itself a republic in 1918 and was federated with its Russian counterpart. The Allies ignored Ukrainian claims to Galicia, however, and in 1918 awarded that area to Poland. From 1922 to 1932, drastic efforts were made by the USSR to suppress Ukrainian nationalism. Ukraine suffered from the forced collectivization of agriculture and the expropriation of foodstuffs; the result was the famine of 1932–33 when more than 7m. people died. Following the Soviet seizure of eastern Poland in Sept. 1939, Polish Galicia was incorporated into the Ukrainian SSR. When the Germans invaded Ukraine in 1941 hopes that an autonomous or independent Ukrainian republic would be set up under German protection were disappointed. Ukraine was re-taken by the USSR in 1944. The Crimean region was joined to Ukraine in 1954.

On 5 Dec. 1991 the Supreme Soviet declared Ukraine's independence. Ukraine was one of the founder members of the CIS in Dec. 1991. After independence Crimea, which was part of Russia until 1954, became a source of contention between Moscow and Kyiv. The Russian Supreme Soviet laid claim to the Crimean port city of Sevastopol, the home port of the 350-ship Black Sea Fleet, despite an agreement to divide the fleet. There was also conflict between Ukraine and Russia over possession and transfer of nuclear weapons, delivery of Russian fuel to Ukraine and military and political integration within the CIS. Leonid Kuchma was elected president in 1994 and re-elected in 1999. Support for him fell after public demonstrations against maladministration including the accusation that he was responsible for the murder of a radical journalist. Conflicts between the presidential administration and government led to the sacking of reform-minded prime minister Viktor Yushchenko in April 2001, who was replaced by Kuchma loyalist Anatolii Kinakh at the end of May. The Pope's historic visit to Ukraine in June 2001 was accompanied by disturbances, particularly in the capital. Presidential elections in Oct. and Nov. 2004 were won by Kuchma's chosen successor, Viktor Yanukovich, who defeated Viktor Yushchenko in the second round run-off. But observers claimed the election failed to meet democratic standards. Widespread protests followed in Kyiv. After the poll was declared invalid Yushchenko was elected president in the repeat of the run-off.

TERRITORY AND POPULATION

Ukraine is bounded in the east by the Russian Federation, north by Belarus, west by Poland, Slovakia, Hungary, Romania and Moldova, and south by the Black Sea and Sea of Azov. Area, 603,700 sq. km (233,090 sq. miles). The 1995 census population was 51·7m., of whom 73% were Ukrainians, 22% Russians, 1% Jews and 4% other—Belorussians, Moldovans, Hungarians, Bulgarians, Poles and Crimean Tatars (most of the Tatars were forcibly transported to Central Asia in 1944 for anti-Soviet activities during the Second World War). In 2001 the census population was 48,416,000, of whom 25,941,000 were female (67·0% urban in 2001); density, 80 per sq. km.

The UN gives a projected population for 2010 of 46·04m.

Ukraine is divided into 24 provinces, two municipalities (Kyiv and Simferopol) and the Autonomous Republic of Crimea. Area and populations at the census of 2001:

	Area (sq. km)	Population (in 1,000)		Area (sq. km)	Population (in 1,000)
Cherkaska	20,900	1,402	Lvivska	21,800	2,626
Chernihivska	31,900	1,236	Mykolaïvska	24,600	1,264
Chernivetska	8,100	923	Odeska	33,300	2,468
Crimea	26,100	2,031	Poltavska	28,800	1,630
Dnipropetrovska	31,900	3,560	Rivnenska	20,100	1,173
Donetska	26,500	4,843	Sevastopol	900	378
Ivano-Frankivska	13,900	1,409	Sumska	23,800	1,300
Kharkivska	31,400	2,910	Ternopilska	13,800	1,142
Khersonska	28,500	1,174	Vinnytska	26,500	1,772
Khmelnitska	20,600	1,431	Volynska	20,200	1,061
Kirovohradska	24,600	1,129	Zakarpatska	12,800	1,258
Kyiv	800	2,607	Zaporizhska	27,200	1,926
Kyivska	28,100	1,828	Zhytomyrska	29,900	1,389
Luhanska	26,700	2,546			

The capital is Kyiv (population 2,602,000 in 2001). Other towns with 2001 populations over 0·2m. are:

	Population (in 1,000)		Population (in 1,000)		Population (in 1,000)
Kharkiv	1,470	Vinnytsya	357	Dniprodzerzhynsk	256
Dnipropetrovsk	1,064	Simferopol	343	Khmelnitsky	254
Odesa	1,029	Sevastopol	341	Kirovohrad	253
Donetsk	1,016	Kherson	328	Rivne	249
Zaporizhzhya	814	Poltava	318	Chernivtsi	240
Lviv	732	Chernihiv	301	Kremenchuk	234
Kryvy Rih	667	Cherkasy	295	Ternopil	228
Mykolaïv	514	Sumy	293	Ivano-Frankivsk	218
Mariupol	492	Horlivka	292	Lutsk	209
Luhansk	463	Zhytomyr	284	Bila Tserkva	200
Makiïvka	390				

The 1996 Constitution made Ukrainian the sole official language. Russian (the language of 22% of the population), Romanian, Polish and Hungarian are also spoken. Additionally, the 1996 Constitution abolished dual citizenship, previously available if there was a treaty with the other country (there was no such treaty with Russia). Anyone resident in Ukraine since 1991 may be naturalized.

SOCIAL STATISTICS

2001 births, 376,478; deaths, 745,952; marriages, 309,602; divorces, 181,334. Rates (per 1,000 population), 2000: births, 7·8; deaths, 15·4. Average annual population growth rate, 1992–2002, –0·6%. Expectation of life at birth in 2001 was 64·1 years for males and 74·4 years for females. In 2001 the most popular age range for marrying was 20–24 for both males and females. Infant mortality, 2001, 17 per 1,000 live births; fertility rate, 2001, 1·1 births per woman (one of the lowest rates in the world).

CLIMATE

Temperate continental with a subtropical Mediterranean climate prevalent on the southern portions of the Crimean Peninsula. The average monthly temperature in winter ranges from 17·6°F to 35·6°F (–8°C to 2°C), while summer temperatures average 62·6°F to 77°F (17°C to 25°C). The Black Sea coast is subject to freezing, and no Ukrainian port is permanently ice-free. Precipitation generally decreases from north to south; it is greatest in the Carpathians where it exceeds more than 58·5" (1,500 mm) per year, and least in the coastal lowlands of the Black Sea where it averages less than 11·7" (300 mm) per year.

CONSTITUTION AND GOVERNMENT

In a referendum on 1 Dec. 1991, 90·3% of votes cast were in favour of independence. Turn-out was 83·7%.

A new Constitution was adopted on 28 June 1996. It defines Ukraine as a sovereign, democratic, unitary state governed by the rule of law and guaranteeing civil rights. The head of state is the *President*, elected directly by the people for a five-year term.

Parliament is the 450-member unicameral *Supreme Council*, elected for four-year terms. Half of the members are elected according to party and electoral bloc lists in a single, nationwide electoral district (proportional representation). The other 225 are elected from lists of candidates in 225 electoral districts. For an election to be valid, turn-out in an electoral district must reach 50%. The Prime Minister is nominated by the President with the agreement of more than half the Supreme Council. There is an 18-member *Constitutional Court*, six members being appointed by the President, six by parliament and six by a panel of judges. Constitutional amendments may be initiated at the President's request to parliament, or by at least one third of parliamentary deputies. The Communist Party was officially banned in the country in 1991, but was renamed the Socialist Party of Ukraine. Hard-line Communists protested against the ban, which was rescinded by the Supreme Council in May 1993.

National Anthem. 'Shche ne vmerla, Ukraïny i slava, i volya' ('Ukraine's freedom and glory has not yet perished'); words by P. Chubynsky, tune by M. Verbytsky.

RECENT ELECTIONS

Parliamentary elections were held on 30 March 2002. Former prime minister Viktor Yushchenko's Our Ukraine Party won 112 of 450 seats with 23·6% of votes cast, For United Ukraine 102 (11·8%), the Communist Party of Ukraine 66 (20·0%), the Socialist Party of Ukraine 24 (6·9%), the United Social-Democratic Party of Ukraine 24 (6·3%) and the Yuliya Tymoshenko Election Bloc 21 (7·2%). Other parties and non-partisans accounted for the remainder. There were widespread accusations of vote-rigging.

Presidential elections were held in two rounds on 31 Oct. and 21 Nov. 2004. In the first round former prime minister Viktor Yushchenko won 39·9% of the vote against 39·3% for Prime Minister Viktor Yanukovich, 5·8% for Oleksandr Moroz and 5·0% for Petro Symonenko. Western observers claimed the election failed to meet democratic standards. In the second round Viktor Yanukovich won 51·5% of the vote and Viktor Yushchenko 48·5%. Again the election was deemed to be flawed, leading to widespread protests in the capital, Kyiv. On 27 Nov. 2004 parliament passed a resolution declaring the poll invalid. On 1 Dec. parliament dismissed Prime Minister Viktor Yanukovich's government in a no-confidence vote and on 3 Dec. the Supreme Court annulled the second round of the election. When it was held again on 26 Dec. Viktor Yushchenko received 54·1% of the vote and Viktor Yanukovich 45·9%.

CURRENT ADMINISTRATION

President: Viktor Yushchenko; b. 1954 (sworn in 23 Jan. 2005).

In March 2005 the coalition government comprised:

Prime Minister: Yuliya Tymoshenko; b. 1960 (sworn in 24 Jan. 2005).

First Deputy Prime Minister: Anatoliy Kinakh. *Deputy Prime Ministers:* Roman Bezsmertny (also *Minister of Territorial Administrative Reform*); Oleh Rybachuk (also *Minister of Eurointegration*); Mykola Tomenko (also *Minister of Humanitarian Policy*).

Minister of Agrarian Policy: Oleksandr Baranivsky. *Culture and Arts:* Oksana Bilozir. *Defence:* Anatoliy Hrytsenko. *Economy:* Serhij Terjokhin. *Education and Science:* Stanislav Nikolayenko. *Emergencies:* David Zhvaniya. *Environmental Protection:* Pavlo Ihnatenko. *Family, Children and Youth Affairs:* Yuriy Pavlenko. *Finance:* Victor Pynzenyk. *Foreign Affairs:* Borys Tarasyuk. *Fuel and Energy:* Ivan Plachkov. *Health:* Mykola Polishchuk. *Industrial Policy:* Volodymyr Shandra. *Interior:* Yurii Lutsenko. *Justice:* Roman Zvarych. *Labour and Social Policy:* Vyacheslav Kyrylenko. *Transport and Communications:* Yevhen Chervonenko.

Government Website: http://www.kmu.gov.ua

DEFENCE

The 1996 Constitution bans the stationing of foreign troops on Ukrainian soil, but permits Russia to retain naval bases. Conscription is for 18 months (army and air force) or two years (navy). On 31 May 1997 the presidents of Ukraine and Russia signed a Treaty of Friendship and Co-operation which provided *inter alia* for the division of the former Soviet Black Sea Fleet and shore installations. There were around 1m. armed forces reserves in 1999.

Military expenditure in 2003 totalled US$5,500m. (US$114 per capita), representing 2·1% of GDP.

Army. In 2002 ground forces numbered about 150,700. There were three Operational Commands (North, South and West). Equipment included 3,905 main battle tanks (T-55s, T-64s, T-72s, T-80s and T-84s) and 205 attack helicopters.

In addition there were 44,000 Ministry of Internal Affairs troops, 45,000 Border Guards and 9,500 civil defence troops.

Navy. In 2002 the Ukrainian elements of the former Soviet Black Sea Fleet numbered 13,500, including 2,500 Naval Aviation and an estimated 3,000 naval infantry, with fleet units based at Sevastopol and Odesa. The operational forces include two frigates and one cruiser (*Ukraina)* in refit.

The aviation forces of the former Soviet Black Sea Fleet under Ukrainian command include anti-submarine and maritime reconnaissance aircraft. The personnel of the Ukrainian Naval Aviation Force numbered (2002) about 2,500.

Air Force. Ukraine is limited to 1,090 combat aircraft and 330 armed helicopters under the Conventional Forces in Europe Agreement, and will have to dispose of some material.

Equipment includes 449 combat aircraft. Active aircraft type include Tu-22Ms, MiG-29s, Su-24s, Su-25s and Su-27s.

Personnel (including Air Defence), 2002, 49,100.

INTERNATIONAL RELATIONS

Ukraine is a member of the UN, CIS, the Council of Europe, OSCE, CEI, BSEC, Danube Commission, the NATO Partnership for Peace and IOM.

Ukraine has received over US$2bn. in US assistance, more than any other former Soviet republic.

ECONOMY

In 2002 agriculture accounted for 15·3% of GDP, industry 38·2% and services 46·5%.

Overview. Ukraine's economy experienced a revival in 2000 and 2001 after eight years of steep decline. This was partly as a result of home market driven growth including expansion of domestic demand, in particular increased household consumption and in-country investment, which was up by more than 20% in 2001, and partly thanks to the rise of export-oriented industries and the expansion of foreign, notably Russian, export markets for Ukrainian products.

Currency. The unit of currency is the *hryvnia* of 100 *kopiykas*, which replaced karbovanets on 2 Sept. 1996 at 100,000 karbovanets = 1 hryvnia. 2000 saw the introduction of a floating exchange rate for the hryvnia. Inflation had been as high as 4,735% in 1993 but declined to just 0·8% in 2002, before rising in 2003 to 5·2%. Foreign exchange reserves in June 2002 were US$3,105m.; gold reserves were 494,000 troy oz (negligible in 1992). Total money supply in June 2002 was 32,530m. hryvnias.

Budget. 2001 budget (in 1m. hryvnias): revenue, 54,569·3; expenditure, 58,973·6.

Tax revenue in 2001 (in 1m. hryvnias) totalled 44,265·8 (including social security contributions, 19,637·7; and domestic taxes on goods and services, 15,871·6). Expenditure included (in 1m. hryvnias): social security and welfare, 25,466·9; general public services, 4,327·8; and education, 3,651·0.

Performance. Ukraine's economy has seen some progress in the last few years. Between 1994 and 1998 average annual real GDP growth was –10·0%, and it was still negative in 1999, at –0·2%. In 2000, however, the economy expanded by 5·9% and in 2001 real GDP growth was 9·2%. 2002 saw growth of 4·8%. In 2003 total GDP was US$49·5bn.

Banking and Finance. A National Bank was founded in March 1991. It operates under government control, its Governor being appointed by the President with the approval of parliament. Its *Governor* is Volodymyr Stelmakh. There were 176 banks in all in 2003, with assets totalling 85,232m. hryvnias.

There is a stock exchange in Kyiv.

ENERGY AND NATURAL RESOURCES

Environment. Carbon dioxide emissions from the consumption and flaring of fossil fuels in 2002 were the equivalent of 7·9 tonnes per capita. An *Environmental Sustainability Index* compiled for the World Economic Forum meeting in Feb. 2002 ranked Ukraine 136th in the world out of the 142 countries analysed, with 35·0%. The index measured the ability of countries to maintain favourable environmental conditions and examined various factors including pollution levels and the use or abuse of natural resources.

Electricity. Installed capacity was 53·9m. kW in 2000. In 2000 production was 171·45bn. kWh; consumption per capita was 3,381 kWh. A Soviet programme to greatly expand nuclear power-generating capacity in the country was abandoned in the wake of the 1986 accident at Chernobyl. Chernobyl was closed down on 15 Dec. 2000. It is planned that two new reactors will be built to replace it. In 2003 there were 13 nuclear reactors in use; in 2002 they supplied 46% of output.

Oil and Gas. In 2000 output of crude petroleum was 3·8m. tonnes; in 2002 production of natural gas was 17·2bn. cu. metres with 1,120bn. cu. metres of proven gas reserves.

Water. In 1997 water consumption totalled 15,623m. cu. metres.

Minerals. Ukraine's industrial economy, accounting for more than a quarter of total employment, is based largely on the republic's vast mineral resources. The Donetsk Basin contains huge reserves of coal, and the nearby iron-ore reserves of Kryvy Rih are equally rich. Among Ukraine's other mineral resources are manganese, bauxite, nickel, titanium and salt. Coal accounts for roughly 30% of the country's energy production. Coal production, 2000, 79·92m. tonnes; iron ore production, 2001, 54·7m. tonnes; manganese production, 1997, 3·2m. tonnes; salt production, 1997 estimate, 2·5m. tonnes.

Agriculture. Ukraine has extremely fertile black-earth soils in the central and southern portions, totalling nearly two-thirds of the territory. The original vegetation of the area formed three broad belts that crossed the territory of Ukraine latitudinally. Mixed forest vegetation occupied the northern third of the country, forest-steppe the middle portion and steppe the southern third of the country. Now, however, much of the original vegetation has been cleared and replaced by cultivated crops. In 2001 there were 32·56m. ha of arable land and 0·93m. ha of permanent crops.

Output (in 1,000 tonnes) in 2000: sugarbeets, 13,185; potatoes, 13,037; wheat, 10,159; barley, 6,873; maize, 3,840; sunflower seeds, 3,460; apples, 1,325; tomatoes, 1,320; pumpkins and squash, 1,100; cabbages, 1,070. Livestock, 2000: 10,627,000 cattle, 10,073,000 pigs, 10,060,000 sheep, 825,000 goats, 698,000 horses, 94m. chickens, 22m. ducks. Livestock products, 2000 (in 1,000 tonnes): meat, 1,720; milk, 12,562; eggs, 477.

Forestry. The area under forests in Ukraine in 2000 was 9·58m. ha (16·5% of the total land area). In 2001, 9·86m. cu. metres of timber were produced.

Fisheries. In 2001 the catch totalled 351,260 tonnes, of which 346,917 tonnes were from sea fishing. The total catch in 1988 had been 1,048,157 tonnes.

INDUSTRY

In 2001 industry accounted for 39·0% of GDP, with manufacturing contributing 23·3%. Industrial production grew by 8·6% in 2001. Output, 2002 (in tonnes unless otherwise stated): crude steel, 33·4m.; pig iron, 27·1m.; rolled ferrous metals,

26·4m.; cement (2001), 5·8m.; residual fuel oil (2000), 3·2m.; distillate fuel oil (2000), 2·7m.; mineral fertilizer, 2·3m.; petrol (2000), 2·1m.; sugar (2001), 1·8m.; sulphuric acid (2001), 1·0m.; milk products (1997), 661,000; processed meats (1997), 558,000; paper and paperboard, 532,000; butter, 131,000; fabrics, 90m. sq. metres; footwear (2001), 14·6m. pairs; refrigerators, 583,000 units; washing machines (2001), 166,000 units, cigarettes (2001), 69·7bn. units.

Labour. In 2000 a total of 18,063,000 persons were in employment. The principal areas of activity were (in 1,000): agriculture, hunting, forestry and fishing, 4,977; manufacturing, 2,914; wholesale and retail trade, and restaurants and hotels, 1,406; transport, storage and communication, 1,228. In April 2001 there were 1,149,200 unemployed and the registered level of unemployment was 4·2%.

Trade Unions. There are 13 trade unions grouped in a Federation of Ukrainian Trade Unions (*Chair*, Oleksandr Stoyan).

INTERNATIONAL TRADE

In 2002 total foreign debt was US$13,555m.

Imports and Exports. Trade in US$1m.:

	1998	*1999*	*2000*	*2001*	*2002*
Imports f.o.b.	16,283	12,945	14,943	16,893	17,959
Exports f.o.b.	13,699	13,189	15,722	17,091	18,669

Main import suppliers in 1999: Russia, 47·9%; Germany, 7·3%; Turkmenistan, 3·7%; USA, 3·1%. Main exports markets in 1999: Russia, 19·2%; China, 5·9%; Turkey, 5·4%; Germany, 4·5%.

Main exports, 2002: ferrous and nonferrous metals, 39·3%; wood and wood products, 14·5%; food and raw materials, 13·2%. Main imports, 2002: fuel and energy products, 41·0%; machinery, 22·4%; chemicals and chemical products, 13·1%.

COMMUNICATIONS

Roads. In 2002 there were 169,679 km of roads, including 12,202 km of national roads. There were 5,399,967 passenger cars in 2002 and 1,744,359 motorcycles and mopeds. There were 34,488 road accidents involving injury in 2002 (5,982 fatalities).

Rail. Total length was 22,302 km in 2000, of which 9,170 km were electrified. Passenger-km travelled in 2000 came to 51·8bn. and freight tonne-km to 172·8bn. There are metros in Kyiv, Kharkiv, Kryvy Rih and Dnipropetrovsk.

Civil Aviation. The main international airport is Kyiv (Boryspil), and there are international flights from seven other airports. The largest Ukrainian carrier is Air Ukraine, which in 1998 flew 13·0m. km and carried 313,100 passengers. Air Ukraine operates domestic services and had international flights in 2003 to Amman, Baku, Beijing, Dubai, Helsinki, Moscow, New York, Novosibirsk, St Petersburg, Tashkent, Tbilisi, Tripoli, Tunis and Yerevan. Ukraine International Airlines also operated on some domestic routes, with international flights in 2003 to Amsterdam, Barcelona, Berlin, Brussels, Dubai, Frankfurt, Helsinki, Lisbon, London, Madrid, Paris, Rome, Vienna and Zürich.

In 2000 Kyiv handled 1,359,303 passengers (1,309,872 on international flights) and 12,015 tonnes of freight. Simferopol was the second busiest airport for passenger traffic in 1999, with 298,235 passengers (230,048 on international flights), and Odesa the second busiest for freight, with 3,839 tonnes.

Shipping. In 1997, 2m. passengers and 9m. tonnes of freight were carried by inland waterways. In 1995 there were 649 ocean-going vessels, totalling 5·83m. DWT. 38 vessels (5·09% of total tonnage) were registered under foreign flags. In 2002 GRT totalled 1,350,000, including oil tankers 39,000 GRT. The main seaports are Mariupol, Odesa, Kherson and Mykolaïv. Odesa is the leading port, and takes 30m. tonnes of cargo annually. In 2001 vessels totalling 7,404,000 NRT entered ports and vessels totalling 49,310,000 NRT cleared.

Telecommunications. In 2001 telephone subscribers numbered 12,894,200 (256·4 per 1,000 persons), but in 1999 a total of 2·65m. people had been on the waiting list for a line. There were 4,200,000 mobile phone subscribers in 2002 and 951,000 PCs in use (19·0 per 1,000 persons). There were 48,000 fax machines in 1999. In 2002 Ukraine had 900,000 Internet users.

Postal Services. In 1998 there were 15,227 post offices. In 1997, 359m. letters, 17m. telegrams and 2m. packages were handled.

SOCIAL INSTITUTIONS

Justice. A new civil code was voted into law in June 1997. Justice is administered by the Constitutional Court of Ukraine and by courts of general jurisdiction. The Supreme Court of Ukraine is the highest judicial organ of general jurisdiction. The death penalty was abolished in 1999. Over the period 1991–95, 642 death sentences were awarded and 442 carried out; there were 169 executions in 1996. In March 1997 death penalties were still being awarded but not carried out. 553,994 crimes were reported in 2000.

The population in penal institutions in April 2003 was 198,858 (415 per 100,000 of national population).

Religion. The majority faith is the Orthodox Church, which is split into three factions. The largest is the Ukrainian Orthodox Church, Moscow Patriarchate (the former exarchate of the Russian Orthodox Church), headed by Volodymyr (Sabodan), Metropolitan of Kyiv and All Ukraine, which recognizes Aleksi II (Aleksey Mikhailovich Ridiger) as Patriarch of Moscow and All Russia and insists that all Ukrainian churches should be under Moscow's jurisdiction. There were 9·5m. adherents in 2001. The second largest is the Ukrainian Orthodox Church, Kyivan Patriarchate, headed by Metropolitan Filaret, Patriarch of Kyiv and All Rus-Ukraine, which was created in June 1992. It had 4·8m. adherents in 2001. Metropolitan Filaret was excommunicated by the Ukrainian Orthodox Church, Moscow Patriarchate in Feb. 1997. The third faction is the Ukrainian Autocephalous Orthodox Church, headed by Metropolitan Mefodiy (Kudryakov) of Ternopil, which favours the unification of the three bodies. Only the Ukrainian Orthodox Church, Moscow Patriarchate is in communion with world Orthodoxy.

The hierarchy of the Roman Catholic Church (*Primate*, Cardinal Marian Jaworski, Archbishop Metropolitan of Lviv) was restored by the Pope's confirmation of ten bishops in Jan. 1991. In Sept. 2003 there were two cardinals. The Ukrainian Greek Catholic Church (*Head*, Cardinal Lubomyr Husar, Major Archbishop, Metropolitan of Lviv and Galicia) is a Church of the Byzantine rite, which is in full communion with the Roman Church. Catholicism is strong in the western half of the country.

Education. In 2003–04 the number of pupils in 21,900 primary and secondary schools was 5·9m.; 339 further education establishments had 1,843,800 students, and 670 technical colleges, 592,900 students; 977,000 children were attending pre-school institutions.

In 1995–96 there were seven universities and an international university of science and technology.

Adult literacy rate in 2001 was 99·6% (male, 99·8%; female, 99·5%).

In 2000–01 total expenditure on education came to 4·4% of GNP.

Health. In 1998 there were 150,382 physicians, 19,615 dentists, 370,171 nurses, 23,488 pharmacists and 29,523 midwives. There were 503,000 beds in 3,400 hospitals in 1997.

Welfare. There were 10·3m. old-age pensioners in 2002 and 3·5m. other pensioners. The total included 821,000 Chernobyl victims. In 2002 social insurance and pension security programmes totalled 27·4bn. hryvnias, representing 12·4% of GDP.

CULTURE

World Heritage Sites. Ukraine has two sites on the UNESCO World Heritage List: Kyiv—Saint Sophia Cathedral and Related Monastic Buildings, Kyiv-Pechersk Lavra (inscribed on the list in 1990); and Lviv—the Ensemble of the Historic Centre (1998).

Broadcasting. Broadcasting is administered by the government State Teleradio Company of Ukraine. The state-controlled Ukrainian Radio broadcasts three national and various regional programmes, a shared relay with Radio Moscow, and a foreign service (Ukrainian, English, German and Romanian). There were four independent stations in 1993 and 44m. radio receivers in 2000. The state-controlled Ukrainian Television broadcasts on two channels (colour by SECAM H). In 2001 there were 23m. television receivers.

Cinema. In 1999 there were 7,795 cinemas with a total attendance of 5,138,000. Three full-length films were made in 1999.

Press. In 2000 there were 61 daily newspapers with an average combined circulation of 8,683,100 (175 per 1,000 inhabitants). In 1999 a total of 6,282 book titles were published (2,690 in social sciences, 1,086 in applied sciences and 1,011 in literature).

Tourism. There were 4,232,000 foreign tourists in 2000; total receipts were US$2,207m.

Libraries. In 1999 there were 19,079 libraries with 301·8m. volumes of books and 17·3 m. registered users.

DIPLOMATIC REPRESENTATIVES

Of Ukraine in the United Kingdom (60 Holland Park, London, W11 3SJ)
Ambassador: Ihor Mitiukov.

Of the United Kingdom in Ukraine (01025 Kyiv, Desyatinna 9)
Ambassador: Robert Brinkley.

Of Ukraine in the USA (3350 M St., NW, Washington, D.C., 20007)
Ambassador: Mykhailo Reznik.

Of the USA in Ukraine (10 Yurii Kotsiubynskyi St., Kyiv 01901)
Ambassador: John Herbst.

Of Ukraine to the United Nations
Ambassador: Valeriy P. Kuchynsky.

Of Ukraine to the European Union
Ambassador: Roman Vasyliovych Shpek.

FURTHER READING

Encyclopedia of Ukraine, 5 vols. Toronto, 1984–93

D'Anieri, Paul, *Economic Interdependence in Ukrainian–Russian Relations*. State Univ. of New York Press, 2000

Koropeckyj, I. S., *The Ukrainian Economy: Achievements, Problems, Challenges.* Harvard Univ. Press, 1993

Kuzio, Taras, *Ukraine under Kuchma: Political Reform, Economic Transformation and Security Policy in Independent Ukraine.* London, 1997

Kuzio, Taras, Kravchuk, Robert and D'Anieri, Paul, *State and Institution Building in Ukraine.* St Martin's Press, New York, 2000

Kuzio, T. and Wilson, A., *Ukraine: Perestroika to Independence.* London, 1994

Lieven, Anatol, *Ukraine and Russia: A Fraternal Rivalry.* United States Institute of Peace Press, 2000

Magocsi, P. R., *A History of Ukraine.* Toronto Univ. Press, 1997

Motyl, A. J., *Dilemmas of Independence: Ukraine after Totalitarianism.* New York, 1993

Nahaylo, B., *Ukrainian Resurgence.* 2nd ed. Univ. of Toronto Press, 2000

Reid, A., *Borderland: A Journey Through the History of Ukraine.* Weidenfeld & Nicolson, London, 1997

Wilson, Andrew, *The Ukrainians: Unexpected Nation.* Yale University Press, 2000

National statistical office: State Committee of Statistics of Ukraine.
Website: http://www.ukrstat.gov.ua/

CRIMEA

The Crimea is a peninsula extending southwards into the Black Sea with an area of 26,100 sq. km. Population (2001 estimate), 2,033,700 (Ethnic groups, Sept. 1993: Russians, 61·6%; Ukrainians, 23·6%; Tatars, 9·6%). The capital is Simferopol.

It was occupied by Tatars in 1239, conquered by Ottoman Turks in 1475 and retaken by Russia in 1783. In 1921 after the Communist revolution it became an autonomous republic, but was transformed into a province (*oblast*) of the Russian Federation in 1945, after the deportation of the Tatar population in 1944 for alleged collaboration with the German invaders in the Second World War. 46% of the total Tatar population perished during the deportation. Crimea was transferred to Ukraine in 1954 and became an autonomous republic in 1991. About half the surviving Tatar population of 0·4m. had returned from exile by mid-1992.

At elections held in two rounds on 16 and 30 Jan. 1994 Yuri Meshkov was elected *President*. The post of president was abolished by Ukraine after calls for a referendum on Crimean independence.

Parliamentary elections were held on 31 March 2002. Turn-out was around 63%. The Serhii Kunitsyn Block obtained 39 seats, the Leonid Hrach Block 28, Crimean Tatars 5, the Russian Block 5, SDPUo 3 and ind. 20. The *Prime Minister* is Anatolii Serhiiovych Matvienko and the *Chairman of Parliament* Boris Deich.

On 2 Nov. 1995 parliament adopted a new constitution which defines the Crimea as 'an autonomous republic forming an integral part of Ukraine'. The status of 'autonomous republic' was confirmed by the 1996 Ukrainian Constitution, which provides for Crimea to have its own constitution as approved by its parliament. The Prime Minister is appointed by the Crimean parliament with the approval of the Ukrainian parliament.

The Tatar National Kurultay (Parliament) elects an executive board (*Mejlis*). The *Chairman* is Mustafa Jemilev. In 1993 the Kurultay decided to participate in Ukrainian elections.

UNITED ARAB EMIRATES

(UAE)

Imarat al-Arabiya al-Muttahida

Capital: Abu Dhabi
Population projection, 2010: 3·36m.
GDP per capita, 1998: (PPP$) 17,935
HDI/world rank: 0·824/49

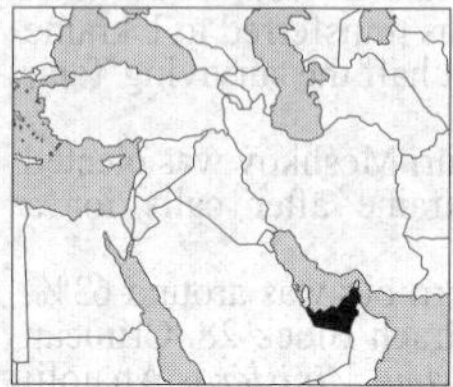

KEY HISTORICAL EVENTS

In the 3rd millennium BC a culture known as Umm al-Nar developed in modern-day Abu Dhabi, its influence spreading inland and along the coast of Oman. There was trade with the Mesopotamian civilization and the Indus culture, centring on the export of copper from the Hajar mountains. The coastal areas of the United Arab Emirates (UAE) and Oman came under Sassanian (Persian) influence from the 4th century AD until the early 7th century when the Islamic era began. After the death of the Prophet Muhammad, tribes in the Dibba region along the eastern coast rebelled before Islamic forces won a decisive battle in AD 632.

In the Middle Ages much of the region was part of the Persian Kingdom of Hormuz, which controlled the approach to the Gulf and most of the trade. European intervention in the Gulf began in the early 16th century when the Portuguese established a commercial monopoly, building a number of forts including Julfar (in modern-day Ras al-Khaimah), a major medieval trading centre. Portuguese ascendancy was later challenged by the Dutch and then by the British, who used their naval power to protect trade with India.

By that time two major tribal confederations had grown powerful along the coast of the lower Gulf. The largest tribal grouping, the Bani Yas, was established on the coast by the late 16th century, while the Qawasim, a maritime people, emerged as a serious challenge to British shipping. Piracy was rife until the early 19th century when the British sent naval expeditions to the Gulf ports to suppress the raiders. In 1820 Britain signed the General Treaty of Peace against piracy and the slave trade with the principal Arab sheikhdoms. Britain took responsibility for the defence of the territory and for external relations but the sheikhdoms were otherwise autonomous and followed the traditional, absolute form of Arab monarchy.

Economic transformation began with the discovery of oil off the coast of Abu Dhabi. Sheikh Shakhbut bin Sultan al-Nahyan, the ruler of Abu Dhabi from 1928–66, granted the first of several oil exploration concessions to foreign companies in 1939. The Second World War delayed exploration and the first commercial discovery was not made until the late 1950s. Sheikh Shakhbut, perceived as an obstacle to the development of the industry, was deposed in 1966 in favour of his younger brother Sheikh Zayed bin Sultan al-Nahyan, who was elected president of the UAE in 1971 by the rulers of the other emirates. In the late 1960s oil was discovered in Dubai, in Sharjah, and then in Ras al-Khaimah in the 1980s.

In Jan. 1968 Britain announced the withdrawal of its military forces from the area now known as the Federation of Arab Emirates. Bahrain and Qatar seceded from the Federation in 1971. Abu Dhabi, Dubai, Sharjah, Umm al Qaiwain, Ajman and Fujairah agreed a federal constitution for the United Arab Emirates. The British accordingly terminated its special treaty relationship and the UAE became independent on 2 Dec. 1971. The remaining sheikhdom, Ras al-Khaimah, joined the UAE in Feb. 1972. In June 1996 the Federal National Council approved a permanent constitution replacing the provisional document that had been renewed every five years since 1971. At the same time, Abu Dhabi City was designated the UAE's capital.

UAE forces joined the USA-led international coalition against Iraq after the invasion of Kuwait in 1990. Following the Sept. 2001 terrorist attacks in the USA, the UAE's banking sector was subject to international scrutiny, and the government consequently ordered financial institutions to freeze the assets of 62 organizations and individuals suspected of funding terrorist movements. The USA stationed forces in the UAE during the invasion of Iraq in March 2003.

TERRITORY AND POPULATION

The Emirates are bounded in the north by the Persian Gulf, northeast by Oman, east by the Gulf of Oman and Oman, south and west by Saudi Arabia, and northwest by Qatar. Their area is approximately 32,300 sq. miles (83,657 sq. km), excluding over 100 offshore islands. The total population at the 1995 census was 2,377,453 (797,710 females). 2002 population estimate, 2,934,000; density, 35 per sq. km. About one-tenth are nomads. In 2001, 87·1% of the population lived in urban areas. Approximately 88% of the population are foreigners, the highest percentage of any country.

The UN gives a projected population for 2010 of 3·36m.

Populations of the seven Emirates, 2003 estimates (in 1,000): Abu Dhabi, 1,591; Ajman, 235; Dubai, 1,204; Fujairah, 118; Ras al-Khaimah, 195; Sharjah, 636; Umm al Qaiwain, 62. The chief cities are Abu Dhabi, the federal capital (population of 904,000 in 1999), Dubai, Sharjah and Ras al-Khaimah. In addition to being the most populous Emirate, Abu Dhabi is also the wealthiest, ahead of Dubai.

The official language is Arabic; English is widely spoken.

SOCIAL STATISTICS

2002 births, 58,070; deaths, 5,994. 2002 birth rate (per 1,000 population), 19·8; death rate, 2·0; infant mortality rate (per 1,000 live births), 8 (2001). The UAE's 2002 death rate was the second lowest in the world (only Kuwait's was lower). Life expectancy, 2001, 73·0 years for men and 77·1 years for women. Annual population growth rate, 1992–2002, 2·8%; fertility rate, 2001, 3·0 births per woman.

CLIMATE

The country experiences desert conditions, with rainfall both limited and erratic. The period May to Sept. is generally rainless. Dubai, Jan. 74°F (23·4°C), July 108°F (42·3°C). Annual rainfall 2·4" (60 mm). Sharjah, Jan. 64°F (17·8°C), July 91°F (32°C). Annual rainfall 4·2" (105 mm).

CONSTITUTION AND GOVERNMENT

The Emirates is a federation, headed by a *Supreme Council of Rulers* which is composed of the seven rulers which elects from among its members a *President* and *Vice-President* for five-year terms, and appoints a *Council of Ministers*. The Council of Ministers drafts legislation and a federal budget; its proposals are submitted to a *Federal National Council* of 40 elected members which may propose amendments but has no executive power. There is a *National Consultative Council* made up of citizens.

National Anthem. There are no words, tune by M. A. Wahab.

CURRENT ADMINISTRATION

President: HH Sheikh Khalifa bin Zayed al-Nahyan, Ruler of Abu Dhabi (b. 1948; appointed 3 Nov. 2004).

Members of the Supreme Council of Rulers:

President: HH Sheikh Khalifa bin Zayed al-Nahyan.

Vice-President and Prime Minister: HH Sheikh Maktoum bin Rashid al-Maktoum, Ruler of Dubai.

HH Dr Sheikh Sultan bin Mohammed al-Qassimi, Ruler of Sharjah.

HH Sheikh Saqr bin Mohammed al-Qassimi, Ruler of Ras al-Khaimah.

HH Sheikh Hamad bin Mohammed al-Sharqi, Ruler of Fujairah.

HH Sheikh Humaid bin Rashid al-Nuaimi, Ruler of Ajman.

HH Sheikh Rashid bin Ahmed al-Mualla, Ruler of Umm al Qaiwain.

In March 2005 the cabinet comprised:

Prime Minister: HH Sheikh Maktoum bin Rashid al-Maktoum; b. 1946 (sworn in for second time 20 Nov. 1990, having held office from 1971–79).

Deputy Prime Ministers: HH Sheikh Sultan bin Zayed al-Nahyan; HH Sheikh Hamdan bin Zayed al-Nahyan.

Minister of the Interior: Maj.-Gen. Sheikh Saif bin Zayed al-Nahyan. *Finance and Industry:* HH Sheikh Hamdan bin Rashid al-Maktoum. *Defence:* Gen. Sheikh Mohammed bin Rashid al-Maktoum. *Economy and Planning:* Sheikha Lubna al-Qasimi. *Information and Culture:* Sheikh Abdullah bin Zayed al-Nahyan. *Communications:* Sultan bin Saeed al Mansouri. *Public Works:* Sheikh Hamdan bin Mubarak al-Nahyan. *Education:* Sheikh Nahyan bin Mubarak Al Nahyan. *Energy:* Mohammed bin Dha'en Al Hamili. *Labour and Social Affairs:* Dr Ali bin Abdullah Al Ka'abi. *Agriculture and Fisheries:* Saeed Mohammed al-Ragabani. *Justice, Islamic Affairs and Endowments:* Mohammed Nakhira al-Dhahiri. *Foreign Affairs:* Rashid Abdullah al-Nuaimi. *Health:* Hamad Abdul Rahman al-Madfa. *Presidential Affairs:* Sheikh Mansour bin Zayed Al Nahyan. *Supreme Council and Gulf Co-operation Council Affairs*: Sheikh Fahim bin Sultan Al Qasimi.

Government Website: http://www.uae.gov.ae

DEFENCE

In 2003 defence expenditure totalled US$1,642m. (US$406 per capita), representing 2·1% of GDP.

Army. The strength was (2002) 35,000.

Navy. The combined naval flotilla of the Emirates includes two frigates. Personnel in 2002 numbered 2,500. The main base is at Abu Dhabi, with minor bases in the other Emirates.

Air Force. Personnel (2002) 4,000, with 101 combat aircraft (including Mirage 2000s and *Hawks*), and 49 armed helicopters.

The USA maintains 1,300 Air Force personnel in the UAE.

INTERNATIONAL RELATIONS

The UAE is a member of the UN, WTO, OPEC, the Gulf Co-operation Council, the League of Arab States and Islamic Development Bank.

ECONOMY

In 2002 agriculture accounted for 3·5% of GDP, industry 51·0% and services 45·5%.

Overview. The UAE is the sixth largest oil exporter in the world. Despite volatile oil prices, the economy has performed reasonably well over the last five years. The economy is relatively diversified, including petrochemicals, aluminium, tourism and banking. During this period the authorities pursued a market-orientated growth strategy, an open trade system and liberal capital flow regime. The combination of an increase in spending of approximately 50% between 1998 and 2001 and lower oil revenue and investment income has resulted in a deterioration in the consolidated fiscal balance, which shifted from a surplus of 6% in 2000 to a deficit of 5% in 2001.

Currency. The unit of currency is the *dirham* (AED) of 100 *fils*. Gold reserves were 397,000 troy oz in May 2002 and foreign exchange reserves US$13,428m. Inflation was 1·4% in 2002. Total money supply in May 2002 was DH 44,564m.

In 2001 the six Gulf Arab states—the United Arab Emirates, along with Bahrain, Kuwait, Oman, Qatar and Saudi Arabia—signed an agreement to establish a single currency by 2010.

Budget. The fiscal year is the calendar year. Revenue in 2001 totalled DH 82,480m. and expenditure DH 96,083m.

Revenue is principally derived from oil-concession payments. Defence, education, and public order and safety are the main items of expenditure.

Performance. In 1998 total GDP was US$47·2bn. There was real GDP growth of 3·8% in 2001 and 1·5% in 2002.

Banking and Finance. The UAE Central Bank was established in 1980 (*Governor*, Sultan bin Nasser Al-Suweidi). The largest banks are National Bank of Abu Dhabi, National Bank of Dubai, Emirates Bank International, MashreqBank and Abu Dhabi Commercial Bank. Foreign banks are restricted to eight branches each.

ENERGY AND NATURAL RESOURCES

Environment. In 2002 carbon dioxide emissions from the consumption and flaring of fossil fuels were the equivalent of 43·5 tonnes per capita, among the highest in the world. An *Environmental Sustainability Index* compiled for the World Economic Forum meeting in Feb. 2002 ranked the United Arab Emirates 141st in the world out of 142 countries analysed, with 25·7%. Only Kuwait was ranked lower. The index measured the ability of countries to maintain favourable environmental conditions and examined various factors including pollution levels and the use or abuse of natural resources.

Electricity. Installed capacity was 5·8m. kW in 2000. Production in 2000 was approximately 31·89bn. kWh, with consumption per capita an estimated 12,237 kWh.

Oil and Gas. Oil and gas provided about 33·7% of GDP in 2002. Oil production, 2002, 105·6m. tonnes. The UAE produced 3·0% of the world total oil output in 2002, and had reserves in 2003 amounting to 97·8bn. bbls. Only Saudi Arabia, Iran and Iraq have greater reserves. Oil production in Abu Dhabi is 85% of the UAE's total.

Abu Dhabi has reserves of natural gas, nationalized in 1976. There is a gas liquefaction plant on Das Island. Gas proven reserves (2002) were 6,010bn. cu. metres. Natural gas production, 2002, 46·0bn. cu. metres.

Water. Production of drinking water by desalination of sea water (1994) was 117,000m. gallons.

Minerals. Sulphur, gypsum, chromite and lime are mined.

Agriculture. The fertile Buraimi Oasis, known as Al Ain, is largely in Abu Dhabi territory. By 1994, 21,194 farms had been set up on land reclaimed from sand dunes. A lack of water and good soil means few natural opportunities for agriculture but there is a programme of fostering agriculture by desalination, dam-building and tree-planting; strawberries, flowers and dates are now cultivated for export. 72,370 ha were under cultivation in 1994. In 2001 there were 50,000 ha of arable land and 188,000 ha of permanent cropland. Output, 2000 (estimates, in 1,000 tonnes): tomatoes, 780; dates, 318; melons and watermelons, 78; cabbages, 58; pumpkins and squash, 31; aubergines, 28; lemons and limes, 18. Livestock products, 2000 (in 1,000 tonnes): meat, 89; milk, 45; eggs, 13.

Livestock (2000): goats, 1·2m.; sheep, 467,000; camels, 200,000; cattle, 110,000; chickens, 15m.

Forestry. 321,000 ha were under forests in 2000 (3·8% of the total land area).

Fisheries. Catch, 2001, approximately 110,000 tonnes (exclusively marine fish).

INDUSTRY

According to the Financial Times Survey (FT 500), the largest companies in the United Arab Emirates by market capitalization on 4 Jan. 2001 were Etisalat (market capitalization of US$6,164·2m.), National Bank of Dubai (market capitalization of US$1,689·3m.) and Emaar Properties (market capitalization of US$1,594·5m.).

In 2001 industry accounted for 52·4% of GDP, with manufacturing contributing 13·8%. Products include aluminium, cable, cement, chemicals, fertilizers (Abu Dhabi), rolled steel and plastics (Dubai, Sharjah), and tools and clothing (Dubai). The diamond business is becoming increasingly important in Dubai.

Labour. Males constituted 87% of the economically active labour force in 2000 (the highest percentage of any country in the world). A total of 1,779,000 persons were in employment in 2000, with the leading areas of activity as follows: construction, 340,100; wholesale and retail trade/repair of motor vehicles, motorcycles and personal and household goods, 246,700; public administration and defence/compulsory social security, 235,400; manufacturing, 195,000. In 2000 the unemployment rate was 2·3%.

INTERNATIONAL TRADE

There are free trade zones at Jebel Ali (administered by Dubai), Sharjah and Fujairah. Foreign companies may set up wholly owned subsidiaries. In 1994 there were 650 companies in the Jebel Ali zone.

The United Arab Emirates, along with Bahrain, Kuwait, Oman, Qatar and Saudi Arabia began the implementation of a customs union in Jan. 2003.

Imports and Exports. Imports in 2001 totalled DH 120·6bn.; exports DH 176·9bn. Principal imports: machinery and transport equipment, food and textiles. Crude petroleum and natural gas are the main exports.

Main import suppliers, 2001: Japan (10·2%), USA (9·6%), UK (8·8%), China (8·6%), Germany (6·7%), India (6·7%). Main export markets: Japan (36·4%), India (7·5%), South Korea (7·1%), Singapore (6·3%), Iran (3·8%), Oman (3·4%).

COMMUNICATIONS

Roads. In 1999 there were 1,088 km of roads. In 1996 there were 252,000 motor vehicles (excluding bikes and mopeds).

Civil Aviation. There are international airports at Abu Dhabi, Al Ain, Dubai, Fujairah, Ras al-Khaimah and Sharjah. Dubai is the busiest airport, handling 11,117,000 passengers and 562,700 tonnes of freight in 2000. Abu Dhabi handled 2,894,000 passengers and Sharjah 196,200 tonnes of freight. Gulf Air is owned equally by Abu Dhabi, Bahrain, Oman and Qatar. Dubai set up its own airline, Emirates, in 1985. It now operates internationally, and in 1997 carried 3,555,700 passengers (all on international flights). In 2003 two budget airlines inaugurated scheduled services out of the UAE—Gulf Traveller, the low cost branch of Gulf Air, and Air Arabia. Etihad Airways, the national airline of the United Arab Emirates, began operations in March 2004.

Shipping. There are 15 commercial seaports, of which five major ports are on the Persian Gulf (Zayed in Abu Dhabi, Rashid and Jebel Ali in Dubai, Khalid in Sharjah, and Saqr in Ras al-Khaimah) and two on the Gulf of Oman: Fujairah and Khor Fakkan. Rashid and Fujairah are important container terminals. In 2002 the merchant marine totalled 703,000 GRT, including oil tankers 221,000 GRT.

Telecommunications. Telephone subscribers numbered 3,521,700 in 2002 (1,100·5 per 1,000 persons) and there were 450,000 PCs in use (140·6 for every 1,000 persons). There were 2,428,100 mobile phone subscribers in 2002 and 18,000 fax machines in use in 1999. There were 1,175,600 Internet users in 2002.

Postal Services. In 1998 there were 243 post offices.

SOCIAL INSTITUTIONS

Justice. The basic principles of the law are Islamic. Legislation seeks to promote the harmonious functioning of society's multi-national components while protecting the interests of the indigenous population. Each Emirate has its own penal code. A federal code takes precedence and ensures compatibility. There are federal courts with appellate powers, which function under federal laws. Emirates have the option to merge their courts with the federal judiciary.

The death penalty for drug smuggling was introduced in April 1995.

Religion. Most inhabitants are Sunni Muslims, with a small Shia minority.

Education. In 2000–01 there were 67,749 pre-primary pupils with 3,691 teachers, 280,248 primary pupils with 17,573 teachers, and 220,134 secondary pupils with 16,950 teachers. In 2002–03 there were 16,128 students at the Emirates University and 14,265 students in higher colleges. There were 2,245 students at the four faculties of Zayed University in 2002–03. The adult literacy rate in 2001 was 76·7% (75·2% among males and 79·8% among females). In 1998–99 total expenditure on education came to 1·8% of GNP.

Health. In 1996 there were 36 government hospitals with 4,344 beds. In 1994 there were 14 private hospitals, 128 government health centres, a herbal medicine centre and 752 private clinics. There were 4,749 physicians in 1997 and 644 dentists, 8,450 nurses and 2,007 pharmacists in 1996.

CULTURE

Broadcasting. There are several government authorities providing broadcasting nationally (Voice of the United Arab Emirates, Capital Radio, which is partly commercial, and United Arab Emirates Television Service), and regionally (UAE Radio and Television-Dubai, Ras al-Khaimah Broadcasting, Umm al Qaiwain Broadcasting and Sharjah TV). The major satellite news channels are Al-Arabiya, based in Dubai, and Abu Dhabi TV. Both came to prominence at the time of the war in Iraq in March–April 2003. There were 780,000 TV sets (colour by PAL) in 2001 and 1·03m. radio receivers in 2000.

Press. In 1996 there were nine daily newspapers (five Arabic and four English) with a combined circulation of 0·3m.

Tourism. In 1999 there were 2,481,000 foreign tourists bringing in a total revenue of US$607m.

DIPLOMATIC REPRESENTATIVES

Of the UAE in the United Kingdom (30 Prince's Gate, London, SW7 1PT)
Ambassador: Easa Saleh Al Gurg, CBE.

Of the United Kingdom in the UAE (POB 248, Abu Dhabi)
Ambassador: Richard Makepeace.

Of the UAE in the USA (3522 International Court, NW, Washington, D.C., 20008)
Ambassador: Alasari Saeed Aldhahri.

Of the USA in the UAE (POB 4009, Abu Dhabi)
Ambassador: Michele J. Sison.

Of the UAE to the United Nations
Ambassador: Abdulaziz Nasser Al-Shamsi.

Of the UAE to the European Union
Ambassador: Abdel Hadi Abdel Wahid Al-Khajah.

FURTHER READING

Clements, F. A., *United Arab Emirates.* [Bibliography] ABC-Clio, Oxford and Santa Barbara (CA), (rev. ed.) 1998

Vine, P. and Al Abed, I., *United Arab Emirates: A New Perspective.* Trident Press, Naples, Florida, 2001

UNITED KINGDOM OF GREAT BRITAIN AND NORTHERN IRELAND

Capital: London
Population projection, 2010: 60·39m.
GDP per capita, 2002: (PPP$) 26,150
HDI/world rank: 0·936/12

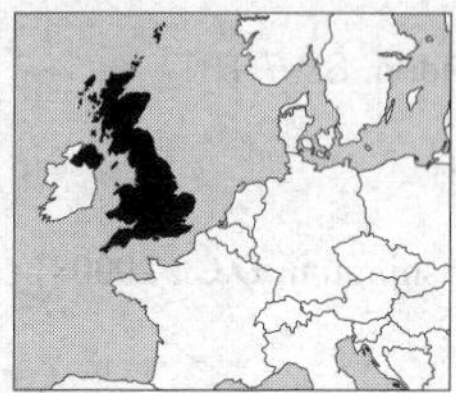

KEY HISTORICAL EVENTS

Remains of Stone Age settlements of hunters and fishermen suggest that the first inhabitants crossed from the European low countries on causeways. By the time their successors had turned to subsistence farming, the land links to the continent had disappeared. The first Britons to use bronze and iron tools were Celts, the dominant force of Western Europe before the Romans.

Emperor Claudius' invasion in AD 43 established Roman rule in southern England. Scotland resisted the Roman legions and Hadrian's Wall was built as a northern frontier between the Tyne and Solway Firth in the early 2nd century. After the Roman withdrawal in the early 5th century, the Romano-British were pushed back to higher land in the west by waves of invading Saxons, Angles and Jutes. Danish invasions in 865 established the Danelaw in northern England. Alfred the Great of Wessex resisted Danish expansion, strengthening Anglo-Saxon unity.

William, duke of Normandy led the Norman Conquest and was crowned king in 1066. Henry II, the founder of the Plantagenet dynasty, was feudatory lord of half of France but Henry's son John lost most of the French possessions. The Hundred Years War (1338–1453) with France ended with the loss of all remaining French possessions except Calais. In 1387 and in later outbreaks, the Black Death reduced the population by over a third. A dynastic struggle between the rival houses of York and Lancaster was concluded by the invasion of Henry Tudor in 1485. His son, Henry VIII, asserted royal authority over the church and rejected papal supremacy. Protestantism became firmly established under Elizabeth I.

The accession of James VI of Scotland to the English throne in 1603 brought the two countries into dynastic union. A struggle for supremacy between Crown and Parliament sparked off the Civil War in 1642. Charles I was executed by Parliament in 1649, beginning the republican rule of Protector Oliver Cromwell. The Stuart monarchy was restored in 1660, on terms which conceded financial authority and thus decision-making power to Parliament. The attempt of the Catholic James II to restore the royal prerogative led to the intervention of William of Orange. James fled the country and the crown was taken by William with his wife Mary Stuart as queen regnant.

The parliaments of England and Scotland were united in 1707 under Queen Anne. With the accession of the Hanoverian George I in 1714, the system of Parliamentary party government took hold. Steam power allowed industry to thrive in the north of England, Scotland and South Wales where there were large reserves of coal. The demand for raw materials and the pursuit of markets for finished goods opened up trade throughout the civilized world. Britain's first successful colonies in North America were established in the reign of James I (1603–25) and, soon afterwards, Bermuda, St Kitts, Barbados and Nevis were colonized. By the mid-17th century, Britain controlled the American east coast and had strong bases in India and in the West Indies, where the sugar economy was dependent on slave labour imported from West Africa. Britain emerged much strengthened from the War of the League of Augsburg (1689–97) and the War of the Spanish Succession (1702–13) while French ambitions in Europe and beyond were severely curtailed. But it was the Seven Years' War (1756–63), in which France and Prussia were the chief contenders, that deprived France of her remaining territorial claims in North America and India and confirmed Britain as the world's leading maritime power.

Relations between Parliament and Crown went through an unsettled period in the reign of George III, who was blamed for the loss of the American colonies in the War of Independence. Britain recognized America's right to self-government in 1783. In 1793 revolutionary France declared war, and was not finally defeated until 1815. The demands of war further stimulated the new, steam-powered industries. But there was unrest as an increasingly urban society found its interests poorly represented by a parliament composed chiefly of landowners. The Reform Act of 1832 extended representation in Parliament, and further acts (1867, 1884, 1918 and 1928) led gradually to universal adult suffrage.

Ireland was brought under direct rule from Westminster in 1801, creating the United Kingdom of Great Britain and Ireland. The Victorian empire included India, Canada, Australasia and vast territories in Africa and Eastern Asia. After the Boer Wars of 1881 and 1899–1902 against the Dutch settlers in South Africa, Britain negotiated a Union of South Africa, by which South Africa enjoyed the same autonomy agreed for Canada (1867), Australia (1901) and later New Zealand (1907). The 'dominion' status of these countries was clarified by the Statute of Westminster (1931). With the spread of trade unionism and the emergence of the Labour Party, the gap between right- and left-wing politics widened after 1900. Labour had to wait until 1924 to form its first government but the Liberal landslide of 1906 carried forward the programme of social reform, including free basic health care, school meals and non-contributory old age pensions.

On 3 Aug. 1914 Germany invaded Belgium, obliging Britain by treaty to retaliate. Four years of bloody trench warfare ensued in Northern France and Belgium, with American intervention in 1917 helping to break the stalemate. The United Kingdom alone lost 715,000 soldiers and another 200,000 from the empire. Rebellions in Ireland led in 1920 to partition with the northern six counties remaining British while the southern 26 counties moved to independence as the Irish Free State in 1922.

A post-war boom was followed by a lengthy recession and heavy unemployment. When Germany invaded Poland on 1 Sept. 1939 Britain, bound once more by treaty, declared war. Although British military casualties were less than the 1914–18 war, the civilian population was hit much worse during the Second World War; over 90,000 died, many as a result of German bombing in the Battle of Britain in 1940.

The United Kingdom ended the Second World War virtually bankrupt. With the independence of India, the centrepiece of the British Empire, in 1947, decolonization took root, reaching its climax in the 1960s. In the 1945 election a Labour government was returned with a large majority, having pledged to establish a free National Health Service, an ambitious housing programme and the state control of major industries. The US Marshall Plan, providing massive investment to rebuild Europe, was conditional on the participating nations putting their economies in order. But when continental leaders made the first tentative moves towards European unity, the UK remained aloof. Britain looked instead to a Commonwealth of former colonies, recognizing the British monarch as its symbolic head, and to the 'special' relationship with the United States. It was not until 1973 that Britain joined the European Community. On the wider international scene, the limits of independent military action were made clear by the Suez crisis of 1956 when the UK, in collusion with France and Israel, failed to stop Egypt nationalizing the Suez Canal.

In 1979 a Conservative government led by Margaret Thatcher came to power, committed to a free market economy. State industry was returned to private enterprise and the trade unions were stripped of much of their power. Despite rising living standards, there was concern about the quality of essential services such as education and health. In 1997 a Labour government, committed to a free market, was returned with a large Commons majority. Reforms to the system of government included the abolition of voting rights of hereditary peers in the House of Lords and the setting up of directly elected assemblies for Scotland, Wales and Northern Ireland. Prime Minister Tony Blair has shown greater enthusiasm for involvement in Europe, arguing for entry into the single currency, should certain economic criteria be met. Conversely, war in Iraq and its aftermath have gone a long way to re-cementing the 'special' relationship with the USA.

TERRITORY AND POPULATION

Area (in sq. km) and population at the census taken on 29 April 2001:

Divisions	*Area*	*Population*
England	130,281	49,138,831
Wales	20,732	2,903,085
Scotland	77,925	5,062,011
Northern Ireland	14,135	1,685,267
	243,073	58,789,194

Population of the United Kingdom (present on census night) at the four previous decennial censuses:

Divisions	*1961*	*1971*	*1981*	*1991*
England[1]	43,460,525	46,018,371	46,226,100[2]	46,382,050
Wales	2,644,023	2,731,204	2,790,500[2]	2,811,865
Scotland	5,179,344	5,228,963	5,130,700	4,998,567
Northern Ireland	1,425,042	1,536,065	1,532,196[3]	1,577,836
United Kingdom	52,708,934	55,514,603	55,679,496[2]	55,770,318

[1]Areas now included in Wales formed the English county of Monmouthshire until 1974.
[2]The final counts for England and Wales are believed to be over-stated as a result of an error in processing. The preliminary counts presented here rounded to the nearest hundred are thought to be more accurate.
[3]There was a high level of non-enumeration in Northern Ireland during the 1981 census mainly as a result of protests in Catholic areas about the Republican hunger strikes.

UK population estimate, mid-2004, 59,787,000 (30,544,000 females and 29,243,000 males); density, 246 per sq. km. In 2001, 89·5% of the population lived in urban areas.

The projected population for 2010 is 60·82m.

Population of the United Kingdom by sex at census day 2001:

Divisions	*Males*	*Females*
England	23,923,390	25,215,441
Wales	1,403,900	1,499,185
Scotland	2,432,494	2,629,517
Northern Ireland	821,449	863,818
United Kingdom	28,581,233	30,207,961

Households in the United Kingdom at the 2001 census: England, 21,262,000; Wales, 1,276,000; Scotland, 2,192,000; Northern Ireland, 627,000.

The age distribution in the United Kingdom at census day in 2001 was as follows (in 1,000):

Age-group	*England and Wales*	*Scotland*	*Northern Ireland*	*United Kingdom*
Under 5	3,094	277	115	3,486
5 and under 10	3,308	307	123	3,738
10 „ 15	3,425	323	133	3,881
15 „ 20	3,217	317	129	3,663
20 „ 25	3,122	314	109	3,545
25 „ 35	7,419	699	242	8,360
35 „ 45	7,749	781	247	8,777
45 „ 55	6,887	689	199	7,775
55 „ 65	5,507	550	162	6,219
65 „ 70	2,292	239	65	2,596
70 „ 75	2,074	207	58	2,339
75 „ 85	2,933	271	77	3,281
85 and upwards	1,012	88	23	1,123

In 2001, 18·85% of the population of the UK were under the age of 14, 60·35% between 15 and 59, 13·29% between 60 and 74, and 7·51% aged 75 and over. In 1951 only 3·54% of the population had been 75 and over.

England and Wales. The census population (present on census night) of England and Wales 1801 to 2001:

Date of enumeration	*Population*	*Pop. per sq. mile*	*Date of enumeration*	*Population*	*Pop. per sq. mile*
1801	8,892,536	152	1831	13,896,797	238
1811	10,164,256	174	1841	15,914,148	273
1821	12,000,236	206	1851	17,927,609	307

Date of enumeration	*Population*	*Pop. per sq. mile*	*Date of enumeration*	*Population*	*Pop. per sq. mile*[1]
1861	20,066,224	344	1931	39,952,377	685
1871	22,712,266	389	1951	43,757,888	750
1881	25,974,439	445	1961	46,104,548	791
1891	29,002,525	497	1971	48,749,575	323
1901	32,527,843	558	1981	49,016,600	325
1911	36,070,492	618	1991	49,193,915	330
1921	37,886,699	649	2001	52,041,916	345

[1]Per sq. km from 1971.

Estimated population of England and Wales, mid-2004, 53,017,000 (27,046,000 females and 25,971,000 males).

The birthplaces of the population of Great Britain at census day 2001 were: England, 43,967,372; Wales, 2,815,088; Scotland, 5,229,366; Northern Ireland, 256,503; Ireland, 494,154; other European Union countries, 763,171; elsewhere, 3,578,273.

Ethnic Groups. The 1991 census was the first to include a question on ethnic status.

Percentage figures from the 2001 census relating to ethnicity in England and Wales:

	England and Wales (%)	*England (%)*	*Wales (%)*
White			
British	87·5	87·0	96·0
Irish	1·2	1·3	0·6
Other	2·6	2·7	1·3
Mixed			
White and Black Caribbean	0·5	0·5	0·2
White and Black African	0·2	0·2	0·1
White and Asian	0·4	0·4	0·2
Other Mixed	0·3	0·3	0·1
Asian or Asian British			
Indian	2·0	2·1	0·3
Pakistani	1·4	1·4	0·3
Bangladeshi	0·5	0·6	0·2
Other Asian	0·5	0·5	0·1
Black or Black British			
Caribbean	1·1	1·1	0·1
African	0·9	1·0	0·1
Other Black	0·2	0·2	0·0
Chinese	0·4	0·4	0·2
Other ethnic groups	0·4	0·4	0·2

In Scotland about 2% of the population in 2001 were from a minority (non-White) ethnic group, compared with 1·3% in 1991. Pakistanis formed the largest such group, constituting 0·3%.

11 'Standard Regions' (also classified as 'level 1 regions' for EU purposes) are identified in the UK as economic planning regions. They have no administrative significance. They are: Northern Ireland, Scotland, Wales, and eight regions of England (East Anglia, East Midlands, North, North West, South East, South West, West Midlands, Yorkshire and Humberside).

The following table shows the distribution of the urban and rural population of England and Wales (persons present) in 1951, 1961, 1971 and 1981:

	England and Wales	*Population Urban districts*[1]	*Rural districts*[1]	*Percentage Urban*	*Rural*
1951	43,757,888	35,335,721	8,422,167	80·8	19·2
1961	46,071,604	36,838,442	9,233,162	80·0	20·0
1971	48,755,000	38,151,000	10,598,000	78·2	21·5
1981	49,011,417	37,686,863	11,324,554	76·9	23·1

[1]As existing at each census.

Urban and rural areas were re-defined for the 1981 and 1991 censuses on a land use basis. In Scotland 'localities' correspond to urban areas. The 1981 census gave the usually resident population of England and Wales as 48,521,596, of which 43,599,431 were in urban areas; and of Scotland as 5,035,315, of which 4,486,140 were in localities.

British Citizenship. Under the British Nationality Act 1981 there are three main forms of citizenship: citizenship for persons closely connected with the UK; British

Dependent Territories citizenship; British Overseas citizenship. British citizenship is acquired automatically at birth by a child born in the UK if his or her mother or father is a British citizen or is settled in the UK. A child born abroad to a British citizen is a British citizen by descent. British citizenship may be acquired by registration for stateless persons, and for children not automatically acquiring such citizenship or born abroad to parents who are citizens by descent; and, for other adults, by naturalization. Requirements for the latter include five years' residence (three years for applicants married to a British citizen). The Hong Kong (British Nationality) Order 1986 created the status of British National (Overseas) for citizens connected with Hong Kong before 1997, and the British Nationality (Hong Kong) Act 1990 made provision for up to 50,000 selected persons to register as British citizens.

Emigration and Immigration. Immigration is mainly governed by the Immigration Act 1970 and Immigration Rules made under it. British and Commonwealth citizens with the right of abode before 1983 are not subject to immigration control, nor are citizens of European Economic Area countries. Other persons seeking to work or settle in the UK must obtain a visa or entry clearance.

Total international migration estimates for recent years are as follows.

Inflows:

	Total	*British*	*Non-British*
1999	453,800	116,400	337,400
2000	483,400	104,100	379,300
2001	479,600	106,300	373,300
2002	512,800	94,600	418,200

Outflows:

	Total	*British*	*Non-British*
1999	290,800	139,200	151,600
2000	320,700	161,100	159,600
2001	307,700	159,200	148,500
2002	359,400	185,700	173,700

The number of immigrants into the UK in 2002, at 512,800, was the highest on record for a calendar year, as was the number of emigrants from the UK in 2002, at 359,400.

In 2002 there were 115,965 acceptances for settlement in the UK (108,410 in 2001), including from: Asia, 46,585; Africa, 39,165; Europe, 11,740. Main individual countries were: Pakistan, 11,935; Somalia, 10,000; India, 8,005; South Africa, 6,135; Nigeria, 5,325; Bangladesh, 4,725; USA, 4,355; Zimbabwe, 3,530; Australia, 3,500.

Asylum. In 2003 there were 49,405 applications for asylum (compared to a record 84,130 applications in 2002, 71,025 in 2001, 29,640 in 1996 and 2,905 in 1984). The main countries of origin in 2002 were Iraq, Zimbabwe, Afghanistan and Somalia. The 2002 figure was the highest in Europe. Applications, including dependants, were an estimated 110,700 in 2002. While respecting its obligations to political refugees under the UN Convention and Protocol relating to the status of Refugees, the government has powers under the Asylum and Immigration Act 1996 to weed out applicants seeking entry for non-political reasons and to designate certain countries as not giving risk of persecution. In the period 1990–99 the UK accepted 12·1% of asylum applicants as genuine refugees.

Coleman, D. and Salt, J., *The British Population: Patterns, Trends and Processes.* OUP, 1992

See also ENGLAND, SCOTLAND, WALES *and* NORTHERN IRELAND: Territory and Population.

SOCIAL STATISTICS

UK statistics, 2003: births, 695,525 (288,500 outside marriage); deaths, 612,033; marriages, 306,214; divorces, 166,737; abortions (2002), 197,119. Great Britain statistics, 2003: births, 673,877; deaths, 597,571; marriages, 298,457; divorces, 164,418. The number of births in 2003 was the highest since 1999, but prior to that the lowest since 1975. In 1976, uniquely in British history, deaths in the UK (680,800) exceeded births (675,500). In 2002 cancer caused 159,000 deaths (26%

of all deaths in the UK, making it the biggest killer, ahead of coronary heart disease, at 117,000 (19%) and respiratory diseases, at 79,000 (13%). UK life expectancy, 2001: males, 75·4 years; females, 80·4. A World Health Organization report published in June 2000 put Britons in 14th place in a 'healthy life expectancy' list, with an expected 71·7 years of healthy life for babies born in 1999. Annual population growth rate, 1992–2002, 0·3%. In 2001 there were 5,910 suicides (4,446 among men and 1,464 among women), giving a suicide rate of 10 per 100,000 population. The average rate in the European Union as a whole in 1998 was 12 per 100,000. Infant mortality, 2001, 5·5 per 1,000 live births. Fertility rate, 2001, 1·6 births per woman. Of the 695,525 live births in the UK in 2003, 41·5% were to unmarried women, up from 6% in 1961 and 20% in 1986. In 1999 for the first time there were more births to women in the 30–34 age group than in the 25–29 bracket. UK birth rate (per 1,000 population), 2003, 11·7; death rate, 2003, 10·3. The average age of first marriage in England and Wales in 2001 was 30·6 years for men and 28·4 years for women, up from 24·6 years for men and 22·6 years for women in 1971. 40% of marriages in 1999 were religious and 60% civil, compared to 52% religious and 48% civil in 1981.

In 2001, 15·9% of the total population was over 65, up from 11·7% in 1960. As the ageing population continues to grow, it has been estimated that by 2010 there will be 350,000 more people over the age of 80 than there were at the end of the 20th century. The first decade of the new century is also expected to see a rise of 1·4m., or 23%, in the number of people between 55 and 64. By 2000 the number of centenarians had surpassed 8,000.

In 2000 the average household in Great Britain consisted of 2·4 people, down from 3·1 in 1961. There were more than 1·5m. single parents in 2001, comprising 6·5% of all households.

England and Wales statistics (in 1,000), 2003 (and 2002): births, 621 (596); deaths, 539 (535); marriages, 268 (256); divorces, 153 (148). In 2002 there was a rise in the number of births for the first time since 1996.

Britain has one of the highest rates of drug usage in Europe. Figures released in Nov. 1999 showed that approaching 40% of schoolchildren aged 15 and 16 have tried cannabis, and 9% of adults did so in the previous 12 months. Use of ecstasy, amphetamines and LSD in England and Wales was the highest in the European Union. Drug-related deaths increased by 70% between 1992 and 1999.

A UNICEF report published in 2000 showed that 19·8% of children in Great Britain live in poverty (in households with income below 50% of the national median), compared to just 2·6% in Sweden. The report also showed that the poverty rate of children in lone-parent families was 45·6%, compared to 13·3% in two-parent families.

See also NORTHERN IRELAND: Social Statistics.

CLIMATE

The climate is cool temperate oceanic, with mild conditions and rainfall evenly distributed over the year, though the weather is very changeable because of cyclonic influences. In general, temperatures are higher in the west and lower in the east in winter and rather the reverse in summer. Rainfall amounts are greatest in the west, where most of the high ground occurs.

London, Jan. 39°F (3·9°C), July 64°F (17·8°C). Annual rainfall 25" (635 mm). Aberdeen, Jan. 38°F (3·3°C), July 57°F (13·9°C). Annual rainfall 32" (813 mm). Belfast, Jan. 40°F (4·5°C), July 59°F (15·0°C). Annual rainfall 37·4" (950 mm). Birmingham, Jan. 38°F (3·3°C), July 61°F (16·1°C). Annual rainfall 30" (749 mm). Cardiff, Jan. 40°F (4·4°C), July 61°F (16·1°C). Annual rainfall 42·6" (1,065 mm). Edinburgh, Jan. 38°F (3·3°C), July 58°F (14·5°C). Annual rainfall 27" (686 mm). Glasgow, Jan. 39°F (3·9°C), July 59°F (15·0°C). Annual rainfall 38" (965 mm). Manchester, Jan. 39°F (3·9°C), July 61°F (16·1°C). Annual rainfall 34·5" (876 mm).

CONSTITUTION AND GOVERNMENT

The reigning Queen, Head of the Commonwealth, is **Elizabeth II** Alexandra Mary, b. 21 April 1926, daughter of King George VI and Queen Elizabeth; married on 20 Nov. 1947 Lieut. Philip Mountbatten (formerly Prince Philip of Greece), created Duke of Edinburgh, Earl of Merioneth and Baron Greenwich on the same day and created Prince Philip, Duke of Edinburgh, 22 Feb. 1957; succeeded to the crown on the death of her father, on 6 Feb. 1952.

Offspring. Prince Charles Philip Arthur George, Prince of Wales (Heir Apparent), b. 14 Nov. 1948; married Lady Diana Frances Spencer on 29 July 1981; after divorce, 28 Aug. 1996, Diana, Princess of Wales. She died in Paris in a road accident on 31 Aug. 1997; married Camilla Parker Bowles on 9 April 2005. *Offspring of first marriage:* William Arthur Philip Louis, b. 21 June 1982; Henry Charles Albert David, b. 15 Sept. 1984. Princess Anne Elizabeth Alice Louise, the Princess Royal, b. 15 Aug. 1950; married Mark Anthony Peter Phillips on 14 Nov. 1973; divorced, 1992; married Cdr Timothy Laurence on 12 Dec. 1992. *Offspring of first marriage:* Peter Mark Andrew, b. 15 Nov. 1977; Zara Anne Elizabeth, b. 15 May 1981. Prince Andrew Albert Christian Edward, created Duke of York, 23 July 1986, b. 19 Feb. 1960; married Sarah Margaret Ferguson on 23 July 1986; after divorce, 30 May 1996, Sarah, Duchess of York. *Offspring:* Princess Beatrice Mary, b. 8 Aug. 1988; Princess Eugenie Victoria Helena, b. 23 March 1990. Prince Edward Antony Richard Louis, created Earl of Wessex and Viscount Severn, 19 June 1999, b. 10 March 1964; married Sophie Rhys-Jones, Countess of Wessex, on 19 June 1999. *Offspring:* Lady Louise Alice Elizabeth Mary, b. 8 Nov. 2003.

Sister of the Queen. Princess Margaret Rose, Countess of Snowdon, b. 12 Aug. 1930; married Antony Armstrong-Jones (created Earl of Snowdon, 3 Oct. 1961) on 6 May 1960; divorced, 1978; died 9 Feb. 2002. *Offspring:* David Albert Charles (Viscount Linley), b. 3 Nov. 1961, married Serena Alleyne Stanhope on 8 Oct. 1993. *Offspring:* Charles Patrick Inigo Armstrong Jones, b. 1 July 1999. Lady Sarah Frances Elizabeth Chatto, b. 1 May 1964; married Daniel Chatto on 14 July 1994. *Offspring:* Samuel David Benedict Chatto, b. 28 July 1996; Arthur Robert Nathaniel Chatto, b. 5 Feb. 1999.

The Queen's legal title rests on the statute of 12 and 13 Will. III, ch. 3, by which the succession to the Crown of Great Britain and Ireland was settled on the Princess Sophia of Hanover and the 'heirs of her body being Protestants'. By proclamation of 17 July 1917 the royal family became known as the House and Family of Windsor. On 8 Feb. 1960 the Queen issued a declaration varying her confirmatory declaration of 9 April 1952 to the effect that while the Queen and her children should continue to be known as the House of Windsor, her descendants, other than descendants entitled to the style of Royal Highness and the title of Prince or Princess, and female descendants who marry and their descendants should bear the name of Mountbatten-Windsor.

Lineage to the throne. 1) Prince of Wales. 2) Prince William of Wales. 3) Prince Henry of Wales. 4) Duke of York. 5) Princess Beatrice of York. 6) Princess Eugenie of York.

By letters patent of 30 Nov. 1917 the titles of Royal Highness and Prince or Princess are restricted to the Sovereign's children, the children of the Sovereign's sons and the eldest living son of the eldest son of the Prince of Wales.

Provision is made for the support of the royal household, after the surrender of hereditary revenues, by the settlement of the Civil List soon after the beginning of each reign. The Civil List Act of 1 Jan. 1972 provided for a decennial, and the Civil List (Increase of Financial Provision) Order 1975 for an annual review of the List, but in July 1990 it was again fixed for one decade.

The Civil List of 2001–10 provides for an annuity of £7,900,000 to the Queen; and £359,000 to Prince Philip. These amounts are the same as for the period 1991–2000. The income of the Prince of Wales derives from the Duchy of Cornwall. The Civil List was exempted from taxation in 1910. The Queen has paid income tax on her private income since April 1993.

The supreme legislative power is vested in Parliament, which consists of the Crown, the House of Lords and the House of Commons, and dates in its present form from the middle of the 14th century. A Bill which is passed by both Houses and receives Royal Assent becomes an Act of Parliament and part of statute law.

Parliament is summoned, and a General Election is called, by the sovereign on the advice of the Prime Minister. A Parliament may last up to five years, normally divided into annual sessions. A session is ended by prorogation, and most Public Bills which have not been passed by both Houses then lapse, unless they are subject to a carry over motion. A Parliament ends by dissolution, either by will of the sovereign or by lapse of the five-year period.

Under the Parliament Acts 1911 and 1949, all Money Bills (so certified by the Speaker of the House of Commons), if not passed by the Lords without amendment, may become law without their concurrence within one month of introduction in the Lords. Public Bills, other than Money Bills or a Bill extending the maximum duration of Parliament, if passed by the Commons in two successive sessions and rejected each time by the Lords, may become law without being passed by the Lords provided that one year has elapsed between Commons second reading in the first session and third reading in the second session, and that the Bill reaches the Lords at least one month before the end of the second session. The Parliament Acts have been used three times since 1949: in 1991 for the War Crimes Act, in 1999 for the European Parliamentary Elections Act and for the Sexual Offences (Amendment) Act in 2000.

Peerages are created by the sovereign, on the advice of the prime minister, with no limits on their number. The following are the main categories of membership (composition at 5 Jan. 2004, excluding 13 peers who were on leave of absence):

Party	*Life Peers*	*Hereditary: Elected by Party*	*Hereditary: Elected Office Holders*	*Hereditary: Royal Office Holders*	*Bishops*	*Total*
Conservative	161	41	8	–	–	210
Labour	177	2	2	–	–	181
Liberal Democrat	59	3	2	–	–	64
Crossbench	145	29	2	2	–	178
Archbishops and Bishops	–	–	–	–	25	25
Other	6	–	–	–	–	6
Total	548	75	14	2[1]	25	664

[1]The Duke of Norfolk, Earl Marshal and the Marquess of Cholmondeley, Lord Great Chamberlain.

Composition by type:

Archbishops and bishops	25
Life Peers under the Appellate Jurisdiction Act 1876	27
Life Peers under the Life Peerages Act 1958	533 (109 women)
Peers under the House of Lords Act 1999	92 (4 women)
Total	677

The House of Commons consists of members (of both sexes) representing constituencies determined by the Boundary Commissions. Persons under 21 years of age, Clergy of the Church of England and of the Scottish Episcopal Church, Ministers of the Church of Scotland, Roman Catholic clergymen, civil servants, members of the regular armed forces, policemen, most judicial officers and other office-holders named in the House of Commons (Disqualification) Act are disqualified from sitting in the House of Commons. No peer eligible to sit in the House of Lords can be elected to the House of Commons unless he has disclaimed his title, but Irish peers and holders of courtesy titles, who are not members of the House of Lords, are eligible.

The Representation of the People Act 1948 abolished the business premises and University franchises, and the only persons entitled to vote at Parliamentary elections are those registered as residents or as service voters. No person may vote in more than one constituency at a general election. All persons may apply to vote by post if they are unable to vote in person, or if they fulfil certain legal requirements they may also be entitled to vote by proxy. Elections are held on the first-past-the-post system, in which the candidate who receives the most votes is elected.

All persons over 18 years old and not subject to any legal incapacity to vote and who are either British subjects or citizens of Ireland are entitled to be included in the register of electors for the constituency containing the address at which they were residing on the qualifying date for the register, and are entitled to vote at elections held during the period for which the register remains in force.

Members of the armed forces, Crown servants employed abroad, and the wives accompanying their husbands, are entitled, if otherwise qualified, to be registered as 'service voters' provided they make a 'service declaration'. To be effective for a particular register, the declaration must be made on or before the qualifying date for that register. In certain circumstances, British subjects living abroad may also vote.

The Parliamentary Constituencies Act 1986, as amended by the Boundary Commissions Act 1992, provided for the setting up of Boundary Commissions for England, Wales, Scotland and Northern Ireland. The Commissions' last reports were made in 1995, and thereafter reports are due at intervals of not less than eight and not more than 12 years; and may be submitted from time to time with respect to the area comprised in any particular constituency or constituencies where some change appears necessary. Any changes giving effect to reports of the Commissions are to be made by Orders in Council laid before Parliament for approval by resolution of each House. The Parliamentary electorate of the United Kingdom and Northern Ireland in the register in Dec. 2004 numbered 44,180,243 (37,043,608 in England, 2,233,467 in Wales, 3,857,631 in Scotland and 1,045,537 in Northern Ireland).

At the UK general election held on 5 May 2005, 645 out of 646 members were returned, 528 from England, 59 from Scotland, 40 from Wales and 18 from Northern Ireland. Every constituency returns a single member. Voting was postponed in Staffordshire South owing to the death of a candidate shortly before the election. This constituency was previously a Conservative seat.

One of the main aspects of the Labour government's programme of constitutional reform is Scottish and Welsh devolution. In the referendum on Scottish devolution on 11 Sept. 1997, 1,775,045 votes (74·3%) were cast in favour of a Scottish parliament and 614,400 against (25·7%). The turn-out was 60·4%, so around 44·8% of the total electorate voted in favour. For the second question, on the Parliament's tax-raising powers, 1,512,889 votes were cast in favour (63·5%) and 870,263 against (36·5%). This represented 38·4% of the total electorate.

On 18 Sept. 1997 in Wales there were 559,419 votes cast in favour of a Welsh assembly (50·3%) and 552,698 against (49·7%). The turn-out was 51·3%.

For current MPs' salaries *see below*. Members of the House of Lords are unsalaried but may recover expenses incurred in attending sittings of the House within maxima for each day's attendance of £64·00 for day subsistence, £128·00 for night subsistence and £53·50 for secretarial and research assistance and office expenses. Additionally, Members of the House who are disabled may recover the extra cost of attending the House incurred by reason of their disablement. In connection with attendance at the House and parliamentary duties within the UK, Lords may also recover the cost of travelling to and from home.

The executive government is vested nominally in the Crown, but practically in a committee of Ministers, called the Cabinet, which is dependent on the support of a majority in the House of Commons. The head of the Cabinet is the *Prime Minister*, a position first constitutionally recognized in 1905. The Prime Minister's colleagues in the Cabinet are appointed on his recommendation.

Governments and Prime Ministers since the Second World War (Con = Conservative Party; Lab = Labour Party):

1945–51	Lab	Clement Attlee	1970–74	Con	Edward Heath
1951–55	Con	Winston Churchill	1974–76	Lab	Harold Wilson
1955–57	Con	Sir Anthony Eden	1976–79	Lab	James Callaghan
1957–63	Con	Harold Macmillan	1979–90	Con	Margaret Thatcher
1963–64	Con	Sir Alec Douglas-Home	1990–97	Con	John Major
1964–70	Lab	Harold Wilson	1997–	Lab	Tony Blair

Salaries. Members of Parliament receive an annual parliamentary salary of £59,095 (2005–06). Ministers who are MPs receive this in addition to their ministerial salary. Total salaries accepted for 2005–06 (including parliamentary salaries where applicable): Prime Minister, £183,932 (£124,837 ministerial salary); Cabinet Ministers, £74,902 or £133,997 if also members of the House of Commons (Cabinet Ministers in the House of Lords, £101,668); Ministers of State, £97,949 (in the Lords £79,382); Parliamentary Under-Secretaries, £88,586 (in the Lords, £69,138); Government Chief Whip, £133,997 (in the Lords, £79,382); Leader of the Opposition, £127,757 (in the Lords, £69,138); Speaker, £133,997; Attorney-General, £106,358; Lord Advocate, £99,682 (2004–05); Solicitor-General for Scotland, £86,007 (2004–05). Cabinet ministers in the Commons receive the parliamentary salary but those in the Lords do not. In addition to pay, MPs are entitled to Office Costs, Supplementary London, Additional Costs, Mileage, Temporary Assistance and Winding Up Allowances, reimbursement of costs owing to recall during a recess and a Resettlement Grant. Ministers receive a severance payment of three months' salary.

The Privy Council. Before the development of the Cabinet System, the Privy Council was the chief source of executive power, but now its functions are largely formal. It advises the monarch to approve Orders in Council and on the issue of royal proclamations, and has some independent powers such as the supervision of the registration of the medical profession. It consists of all Cabinet members, the Archbishops of Canterbury and York, the Speaker of the House of Commons and senior British and Commonwealth statesmen. There are a number of advisory Privy Council committees. The Judicial Committee is the final court of appeal from courts of the UK dependencies, the Channel Islands and the Isle of Man, and some Commonwealth countries.

Freedom of Information Act. The Freedom of Information Act 2000 was implemented gradually between Nov. 2002 and Jan. 2005 when the General Right of Access to all information became law. Not to be confused with the Data Protection Act of 1998, the FOIA allows individuals to gain access to information held by public authorities in England, Wales and Northern Ireland. A separate Act applies in Scotland. Some information is exempted from release, for example security-related documents. An independent Commissioner for Information oversees the process.

Bogdanor, V., *Devolution in the United Kingdom*. OPUS, 1999
Bruce, A., *et al. The House of Lords: 1,000 Years of British Tradition*. London, 1994
Butler, D. and Butler, G., *British Political Facts, 1900–1994*. London, 1994
Dod's Parliamentary Companion. London [published after elections]
Harrison, B., *The Transformation of British Politics, 1860–1995*. OUP, 1996
Norris, P., *Electoral Change in Britain since 1945*. Oxford, 1996
Shell, D., *The House of Lords*. 2nd ed. Hemel Hempstead, 1992
The Times Guide to the House of Commons. London, [published after elections]
Waller, R., *The Almanac of British Politics*. 4th ed. London, 1991

See also NORTHERN IRELAND.

Local Government. Administration is carried out by four types of bodies: (i) local branches of some central ministries, such as the Departments of Health and Social Security; (ii) local sub-managements of nationalized industries; (iii) specialist authorities such as the National Rivers Authority; and (iv) the system of local government described below. The phrase 'local government' has come to mean that part of the local administration conducted by elected councils. There are separate systems for England, Wales and Scotland.

The Local Government Act 1992 provided for the establishment of new unitary councils (authorities) in England, responsible for all services in their areas, though the two-tier structure of district and county councils remained for much of the country. In 1996 all of Wales and Scotland was given unitary local government systems.

Local authorities have statutory powers and claims on public funds. Relations with central government are maintained through the Department of the Environment, Transport and the Regions in England, and through the Welsh and Scottish Executives. In England the Home Office and the Department of Education and Skills are also concerned with some local government functions. (These are performed by departments within the Welsh and Scottish Offices.) Ministers have powers of intervention to protect individuals' rights and safeguard public health, and the government has power to cap (i.e. limit) local authority budgets.

The chair of the council is one of the councillors elected by the rest. In boroughs and cities his or her title is Mayor. Mayors of cities may have the title of Lord Mayor conferred on them. 53 towns in England and Wales and five in Scotland have the status of city. Brighton and Hove, Wolverhampton and Inverness were awarded city status in 2000. In 2002 Preston, Newport, Stirling, Lisburn and Newry were given city status to mark Queen Elizabeth II's golden jubilee. This status is granted by the personal command of the monarch and confers no special privileges or powers. In Scotland, the chair of city councils is deemed Lord Provost, and is elsewhere known as Convenor or Provost. In Wales, the chair is called Chairman in counties and Mayor in county boroughs. Any parish or community council can by simple resolution adopt the style 'town council' and the status of town for the parish or community. Basic and other allowances are payable to councillors (except Scottish community councillors).

Functions. Legislation in the 1980s initiated a trend for local authorities to provide services by, or in collaboration with, commercial or voluntary bodies rather than provide them directly. Savings are encouraged by compulsory competitive tendering. In England, county councils are responsible for strategic planning, transport planning, non-trunk roads and regulation of traffic, personal social services, consumer protection, disposal of waste, the fire and library services and, partially, for education. District councils are responsible for environmental health, housing, local planning applications (in the first instance) and refuse collection. Unitary authorities combine the functions of both levels.

Finance. Revenue is derived from the Council Tax, which supports about one-fifth of current expenditure, the remainder being funded by central government grants and by the redistribution of revenue from the national non-domestic rate (property tax). Capital expenditure is financed by borrowing within government-set limits and sales of real estate.

Elections. England: The 36 metropolitan districts are divided into wards, each represented by three councillors. One-third of the councillors are elected each year for three years out of four. All metropolitan districts had an election on 1 May 2003. The 238 district councils and the 47 English unitary authorities are divided into wards. Each chooses either to follow the metropolitan district system, or to have all seats contested once every four years, or to elect by halves every two years. 232 district councils had an election on 1 May 2003. The 34 county councils have one councillor for each electoral division, elected every four years, with elections scheduled for 5 May 2005.

In London there are 33 councils (including the City of London), the whole of which are elected every four years. London borough elections will next be held in 2006. The Greater London Authority has a 25-member Assembly, elected using AMS (Additional Member System), and a directly elected mayor, elected by the SV (Supplementary Vote) system. For the election of London Assembly members London is divided into 14 constituencies. Each constituency elects one member, in addition to which there are 11 'London Member' seats. Elections take place every four years. Ken Livingstone (ind.) was elected mayor on 4 May 2000, and re-elected as the Labour candidate on 10 June 2004.

Wales: The 22 unitary authorities are split between single and multi-member wards, elected every four years. Elections were last held on 10 June 2004.

Scotland: The 32 unitary authorities hold elections every four years. The last elections were held on 1 May 2003.

Resident citizens of the UK, Ireland, a Commonwealth country or an EU country may (at age 18) vote and (at age 21) stand for election.

Election Results. Local government elections for 37 councils on 5 May 2005 resulted in the Conservative control of 24 councils, Labour 6, the Liberal Democrats 3, with no overall control in 4. The Conservatives gained 152 seats (bringing their total to 1,193), Labour lost 114 (total 612), the Liberal Democrats gained 40 (total 493), the Greens gained 6 (total 8), Residents' Associations gained 3 (total 8) and others lost 35 (total 78).

Local government elections for 166 councils on 10 June 2004 resulted in the Conservative control of 51 councils, Labour 39, the Liberal Democrats 9, Plaid Cymru 1, Residents' Associations 1 and others 3, with no overall control in 62. The Conservatives gained 283 seats (bringing their total to 1,714), Labour lost 479 (total 2,250), the Liberal Democrats gained 137 (total 1,283), Plaid Cymru lost 28 (total 172) and others gained 27 (total 660).

The election to provide London with an elected Mayor and a 25-member London Assembly took place on 10 June 2004. Ken Livingstone (Lab.) won with 55·39% of the vote after counting second preferences. He gained 828,380 first and second votes (685,541 as first votes), beating Steve Norris (Conservative) into second place.

National Anthem. 'God Save the Queen' (King) (words and tune anonymous; earliest known printed source, 1744).

RECENT ELECTIONS

At the general election of 5 May 2005, 27,132,327 votes were cast. The Labour Party won 356 seats with 35·2% of votes cast (413 seats with 42·0% in 2001); the Conservative Party 197 with 32·3% (166 with 32·7%); the Liberal Democratic Party 62 with 22·1% (52 with 18·8%); others 3 (1). Regional parties (Scotland): the Scottish National Party won 6 seats (5 in 2001); (Wales): Plaid Cymru 3 (4); (Northern Ireland): the Democratic Unionist Party 9 (5); Sinn Féin 5 (4); the Social and Democratic Labour Party 3 (3); the Ulster Unionist Party 1 (6). Labour gained no seats and lost 47; the Conservatives gained 36 seats and lost 3; the Liberal Democrats gained 16 seats and lost 5. Turn-out was 61·3%.

In April 2005 at the dissolution of parliament, 119 of 659 seats were held by women, approximately 18·1%; Rwanda has the highest proportion of women MPs, with 48·8% following the election of Sept. 2003.

Pensioners represent 24% of the voting age but at the 2001 general election accounted for 35% of the votes cast.

European Parliament. The United Kingdom has 78 (87 in 1999) representatives. At the June 2004 elections turn-out was 38·9% (24·0% in 1999—the lowest in any of the EU member countries). The Conservative Party won 27 seats with 27·4% of votes cast (political affiliation in European Parliament: European People's Party–European Democrats); the Labour Party, 19 with 22·3% (Party of European Socialists); UK Independence Party, 12 with 16·8% (11 Independence and Democracy Group, one non-attached); the Liberal Democrats, 12 with 15·1% (Alliance of Liberals and Democrats for Europe); the Green Party, 2 with 6·2% (Greens/European Free Alliance); the Scottish National Party, 2 with 3·0% (Greens/European Free Alliance); Plaid Cymru, 1 with 1·1% (Greens/European Free Alliance). Voting for these parties was on a proportional system, used for the first time in Britain in 1999. Voting in Northern Ireland was by the transferable vote system: the Democratic Unionist Party (non-attached), the Ulster Unionist Party (European People's Party–European Democrats) and Sinn Féin (European Unitary Left/Nordic Green Left) gained 1 seat each.

CURRENT ADMINISTRATION

In May 2005 the government consisted of the following:

(a) 23 MEMBERS OF THE CABINET

Prime Minister, First Lord of the Treasury and Minister for the Civil Service: Tony Blair, b. 1953.

Deputy Prime Minister and First Secretary of State: John Prescott, b. 1938.

Chancellor of the Exchequer: Gordon Brown, b. 1951.

Secretary of State for Foreign and Commonwealth Affairs: Jack Straw, b. 1946.

Secretary of State for the Home Department: Charles Clarke, b. 1950.

Secretary of State for the Environment, Food and Rural Affairs: Margaret Beckett, b. 1943.

Secretary of State for Transport and for Scotland: Alistair Darling, b. 1953.

Secretary of State for Health: Patricia Hewitt, b. 1948.

Chancellor of the Duchy of Lancaster and Minister for the Cabinet Office: John Hutton, b. 1955.

Secretary of State for Northern Ireland and for Wales: Peter Hain, b. 1950.

Secretary of State for Defence: Dr John Reid, b. 1947.

Secretary of State for Culture, Media and Sport: Tessa Jowell, b. 1947.

Parliamentary Secretary to the Treasury and Chief Whip: Hilary Armstrong, b. 1945.

Secretary of State for Education and Skills: Ruth Kelly, b. 1968.

Chief Secretary to the Treasury: Des Browne, b. 1955.

Lord Privy Seal and Leader of the House of Commons: Geoff Hoon, b. 1953.

Minister without Portfolio: Ian McCartney, b. 1951.

Leader of the House of Lords and Lord President of the Council: Baroness Amos, b. 1954.

Secretary of State for Constitutional Affairs and Lord Chancellor: Lord Falconer of Thoroton, QC, b. 1951.

Secretary of State for International Development: Hilary Benn, b. 1953.

Secretary of State for Work and Pensions: David Blunkett, b. 1947.

Secretary of State for Trade and Industry: Alan Johnson, b. 1950.

Minister of Communities and Local Government: David Miliband, b. 1965.

(Non-cabinet member but attends cabinet meetings): Lord Grocott, b. 1940, *Lords Chief Whip and Captain of the Honourable Corps of Gentlemen at Arms.*

(b) LAW OFFICERS

Attorney General: Lord Goldsmith, QC, b. 1950.

Solicitor General: Mike O'Brien, b. 1954.

Advocate General for Scotland: Dr Lynda Clark, QC, b. 1949.

(c) MINISTERS OF STATE (BY DEPARTMENT)

Office of the Deputy Prime Minister: Yvette Cooper, b. 1969; Phil Woolas, b. 1959.

Department of Culture, Media and Sport: Richard Caborn, b. 1943, *Minister for Sport and Tourism.*

Department for Constitutional Affairs: Harriet Harman, b. 1950.

Ministry of Defence: Adam Ingram, b. 1947, *Minister for Armed Forces.*

Department for of Education and Skills: Jacqui Smith, b. 1962, *Minister for Schools;* Beverley Hughes, b. 1950, *Minister for Children and Families;* Bill Rammell, b. 1959, *Minister for Higher Education and Lifelong Learning.*

Department of the Environment, Food and Rural Affairs: Elliot Morley, b. 1952, *Minister for Climate Change and Environment.*

Foreign and Commonwealth Office: Douglas Alexander, b. 1967, *Minister for Europe;* Ian Pearson, b. 1959, *Minister for Trade;* Dr Kim Howells, b. 1946, *Minister for the Middle East.*

Department of Health: Rosie Winterton, b. 1958; Jane Kennedy, b. 1958; Lord Warner of Brockley, b. 1940.

Home Office: Tony McNulty, b. 1958, *Minister for Immigration, Citizenship and Nationality;* Baroness Scotland of Asthal, b. 1965, *Minister for Criminal Justice System and Law Reform;* Hazel Blears, b. 1956, *Minister for Crime Reduction, Policing and Community Safety.*

Northern Ireland Office: Lord Rooker, b. 1941; David Hanson, b. 1957.

Department for Trade and Industry: Alun Michael, b. 1943, *Minister for Industry and the Regions (Responsible for Supporting Successful Enterprise);* Malcolm Wicks, b. 1947, *Minister for Energy;* Ian Pearson, b. 1959, *Minister for Trade.*

Department of Transport: Dr Stephen Ladyman, b. 1952.

Treasury: John Healey, b. 1960, *Financial Secretary;* Ivan Lewis, b. 1967, *Economic Secretary;* Dawn Primarolo, b. 1954, *Paymaster-General.*

Department for Work and Pensions: Margaret Hodge, MBE, b. 1944, *Minister for Work;* Stephen Timms, b. 1955, *Minister for Pensions.*

(d) PARLIAMENTARY SECRETARIES AND UNDER-SECRETARIES (BY DEPARTMENT)

Cabinet Office: Jim Murphy, b. 1967.

Office of the Deputy Prime Minister: Jim Fitzpatrick, b. 1952; Baroness Andrews, OBE, b. 1943.

Department of Culture, Media and Sport: David Lammy, b. 1972; James Purnell, b. 1970.

Ministry of Defence: Don Touhig, b. 1947; Lord Drayson, b. 1960.

Department for Education and Skills: Maria Eagle, b. 1961; Phil Hope, b. 1955; Dr Andrew Adonis, b. 1963.

Department for the Environment, Food and Rural Affairs: Ben Bradshaw, b. 1960; Lord Bach of Lutterworth, b. 1946; Jim Knight, b. 1965.

Foreign and Commonwealth Office: Lord Triesman, b. 1943.

Department of Health: Caroline Flint, b. 1961; Liam Byrne, b. 1970.

Home Office: Paul Goggins, b. 1953; Fiona Mactaggart, b. 1953; Andy Burnham, b. 1970.

Department for Constitutional Affairs: Baroness Ashton of Upholland, b. 1956; Bridget Prentice, b. 1952.

Department for Trade and Industry: Lord Sainsbury of Turville, b. 1940; Gerry Sutcliffe, b. 1953; Barry Gardiner, b. 1957; Meg Munn, b. 1959 (also reports to Secretary of State for Culture, Media and Sport on equality issues).

Department for Transport: Derek Twigg, b. 1959; Karen Buck, b. 1958.

Department for International Development: Gareth Thomas, b. 1967.

Department for Work and Pensions: Lord Hunt of Kingsheath, OBE, b. 1949; Anne McGuire, b. 1949; James Plaskitt, b. 1954.

Northern Ireland Office: Angela Smith, b. 1959; Shaun Woodward, b. 1958.

Scotland Office: David Cairns, b. 1966.

Wales Office: Nick Ainger, b. 1949.

Leader of the House of Commons: Nigel Griffiths, b. 1953, *Deputy Leader of the House of Commons.*

(e) OPPOSITION FRONT BENCH

Leader of the Opposition: Michael Howard, b. 1941.

Shadow leader of the House of Lords: Lord Strathclyde, b. 1960.

The *Speaker* of the House of Commons is Michael Martin (Labour), elected on 23 Oct. 2000.

Government Website: http://www.direct.gov.uk

DEFENCE

The Defence Council was established on 1 April 1964 under the chairmanship of the Secretary of State for Defence, who is responsible to the Sovereign and Parliament for the defence of the realm. Vested in the Defence Council are the functions of commanding and administering the Armed Forces. The Secretary of State heads the Department of Defence.

Defence policy decision-making is a collective governmental responsibility. Important matters of policy are considered by the full Cabinet or, more frequently, by the Defence and Overseas Policy Committee under the chairmanship of the Prime Minister.

Total full-time trained strength in 2003 numbered 188,600, untrained regulars 24,500 and reserve personnel 259,300. In 2003 UK armed forces abroad included 22,000 personnel based in Germany, about 11,000 in Iraq, 3,275 based in Cyprus, about 3,000 in Kuwait, 1,400 serving as part of SFOR II in Bosnia-Herzegovina, 1,200 based in the Falkland Islands, 1,120 based in Brunei and 575 based in Gibraltar.

The ban on homosexuals serving in the armed forces, which had been upheld by a House of Commons vote in May 1996, was suspended in Sept. 1999 after the European Court of Human Rights ruled that the current ban was unlawful.

Defence Budget. The defence budget for 2004–05 was £29,710m. (US$57,239m.), rising to £30,888m. (US$59,509m.) for 2005–06. Defence spending in 2003 represented 2·4% of GDP, down from 5·2% in 1985. Per capita defence expenditure in 2003 totalled £438 (US$722). It was announced in July 2002 that the defence budget would rise by £3·5bn. (US$5·4bn.) over three years, the largest sustained increase in planned defence spending in 20 years.

Nuclear Weapons. Having carried out its first test in 1952, there have been 45 tests in all. The nuclear arsenal consisted of approximately 185 warheads in Jan. 2004 according to the Stockholm International Peace Research Institute.

Arms Trade. The UK is a net-exporter of arms and in 2003 was the world's second largest exporter after the USA (with sales worth US$4·7bn., or 16·3% of the world total). In 2002 BAE SYSTEMS was the UK's largest arms producing company and the 5th largest in the OECD. It accounted for US$14·1bn. of arms sales. Rolls Royce was the 14th largest producer, accounting for US$2·8bn. of sales. The UK was the 9th largest recipient of major conventional weapons in the world during the period 1998–2002, spending US$575m. in 2002 (US$1,217m. in 2001).

Army. The Field Army is run from Headquarters Land Command, based at Wilton. The Ministry of Defence retains direct control of units in Northern Ireland, although day-to-day military responsibility is given to the Chief of the General Staff. The

Permanent Joint Headquarters, recently formed at Northwood, is responsible for overseas garrisons, which include the Falkland Islands, Cyprus and Brunei.

The established strength of the Regular Army in 2004 was 116,760 which includes soldiers under training and Gurkhas. In addition there were some 3,390 Royal Irish Home Service soldiers. There were 3,700 Gurkhas in 2004. The strength of the Regular Reserves was 160,800. There were 10,700 soldiers based in Northern Ireland in 2004 in addition to the 3,390 Royal Irish Home Service soldiers.

The role of the Territorial Army (TA) is to act as a general Reserve for the Army by reinforcing it as required, with individuals, sub-units and other units, either in the UK or overseas; and by providing the framework and basis for regeneration and reconstruction to cater for the unforeseen in times of national emergency. The TA also provides a nationwide link between the military and civil communities. Strength, 2004, 40,350. In addition, men who have completed service in the Regular Army normally have some liability to serve in the Regular Reserve. All members of the TA and Regular Reserve may be called out by a Queen's Order in time of emergency of imminent national danger, and most of the TA and a large proportion of the Regular Reserve may be called out by a Queen's Order when warlike operations are in preparation or in progress. The Home Service Battalions of the Royal Irish Regiment are only liable for service in Northern Ireland.

Equipment includes 543 main battle tanks (156 Challenger 1s, 386 Challenger 2s and 1 Chieftain).

Women serve throughout the Army in the same regiments and corps as men. There are only a few roles in which they are not employed such as the Infantry and Royal Armoured Corps.

The Oxford Illustrated History of the British Army. OUP, 1995

Navy. Control of the Royal Navy is vested in the Defence Council and is exercised through the Admiralty Board, chaired by the Secretary of State for Defence.

The C.-in-C. Fleet, headquartered at Northwood, is responsible for the command of the fleet, while command of naval establishments in the UK is exercised by the C.-in-C. Naval Home Command from Portsmouth. Main naval bases are at Devonport, Portsmouth and Faslane, with a minor base overseas at Gibraltar.

The Royal Naval Reserve (RNR) and the Royal Marines Reserve (RMR) are volunteer forces which together in 2004 numbered 3,500. The RNR provides trained personnel in war to supplement regular forces.

The roles of the Royal Navy are first, to deploy the national strategic nuclear deterrent, second to provide maritime defence of the UK and its dependent territories, third to contribute to the maritime elements of NATO's force structure and fourth to meet national maritime objectives outside the NATO area. Personnel strength was about 40,950 (including Royal Marines) in 2004.

The strategic deterrent is borne by four Trident submarines—*Vanguard, Victorious, Vigilant* and *Vengeance*. They are each capable of deploying 16 US-built Trident II D5 missiles.

The strength of the fleet's major units in the respective years:

	1999	*2000*	*2001*	*2002*	*2003*	*2004*
Strategic Submarines	3	4	4	4	4	4
Nuclear Submarines	11	11	11	11	11	11
Diesel Submarines	nil	nil	nil	nil	nil	nil
Aircraft Carriers	2[1]	2[1]	2[1]	2[1]	2[1]	2[1]
Destroyers	11	11	11	11	11	11
Frigates	20	20	20	21	20	20

[1]Following government policy, of the three Carriers held, only two are kept in operational status.

The principal surface ships are the Light vertical/short take-off and landing Aircraft Carriers of the Invincible class (*Invincible, Illustrious* and *Ark Royal*) completed 1980–85, embarking an air group including Sea Harrier vertical/short take-off and landing fighters. Two of these ships are maintained in the operational fleet, with the third (currently *Ark Royal*) either in refit or reserve. These ships are to be replaced with a new class of two large aircraft carriers due in service in 2012 and 2015. A Helicopter Carrier, specifically designed for amphibious operations, *HMS Ocean*, entered service in 1998 and was joined by two amphibious Landing Platform Docks (LPD), *HMS Albion* and *HMS Bulwark*, in 2003 and 2004 respectively.

The Fleet Air Arm (6,200-strong in 2003) had 188 aircraft in 2004, of which 26 were combat aircraft (Sea Harrier vertical/short take-off and landing fighter aircraft) and 162 were armed helicopters.

The Royal Marines Command, 7,000-strong in 2004, provides a commando brigade comprising three commando groups. The Special Boat Squadron and specialist defence units complete the operational strength.

The total number of trained naval service personnel was 36,300 in April 2004 (down from 45,600 in April 1996).

Jane's Fighting Ships. London, annual
The Oxford Illustrated History of the Royal Navy. OUP, 1996

Air Force. The Royal Flying Corps was established in May 1912, with military and naval wings, of which the latter became the independent Royal Naval Air Service in July 1914. On 2 Jan. 1918 an Air Ministry was formed, and on 1 April 1918 the Royal Flying Corps and the Royal Naval Air Service were amalgamated, under the Air Ministry, as the Royal Air Force (RAF).

In 1937 the units based on aircraft carriers and naval shore stations again passed to the operational and administrative control of the Admiralty, as the Fleet Air Arm. In 1964 control of the RAF became a responsibility of the Ministry of Defence.

The RAF is administered by the Air Force Board, of which the Secretary of State for Defence is Chairman. Following recommendations in the 1998 Strategic Defence Review, which placed increased emphasis on Joint and Expeditionary operations, the RAF has experienced considerable restructuring. The creation of the tri-service Defence Logistics Organisation (DLO) resulted in the closure of Logistics Command on 31 Oct. 1999 with most of the logistics support functions previously carried out by the Command now subsumed into the new organization. However, those former Logistics Command Units responsible for tasks falling to the RAF rather than DLO have now been passed to the two remaining RAF Commands: Strike Command and Personnel and Training Command.

Strike Command's mission is to deliver and develop air power in the most effective manner to meet the UK's foreign and security policy. It is responsible for all of the RAF's frontline forces. It operates 427 combat aircraft (plus 121 in store) including 217 Tornados, 53 Jaguars and 60 Harriers (used for battlefield support).

As an expeditionary force, the RAF, on an increasing basis, exercises and operates overseas. Current and recent basing/deployments include the Falklands, Cyprus, Italy and the Balkans, Scandinavia, North America, the Middle East and the Far East. Headquarters RAF Strike Command is based at RAF High Wycombe.

Personnel and Training Command, which is based at RAF Innsworth in Gloucestershire, was established in 1994, and exercises responsibility for the RAF Personnel Management Agency (RAF PMA) and Training Group Defence Agency (TGDA). RAF PMA handles career management of RAF Regular and Reserve Forces, whilst the TGDA is responsible for recruitment and training. HQ PTC also provides department of state functions, such as defence policy-making and service to ministers and Parliament, and the career management of civilian personnel worldwide.

RAF personnel, 1 Dec. 2002, 53,040 (including 5,844 women); total trained personnel, 48,493. Since Dec. 1991 women have been eligible to fly combat aircraft. There were also 14,000 Air Force reserves in 2002 including 1,900 volunteers. In addition there were 28,000 ex-RAF personnel with a recall liability, having left the RAF with a service pension.

INTERNATIONAL RELATIONS

The UK is a member of the UN, WTO, NATO, BIS, OECD, EU, the Council of Europe, WEU, OSCE, CERN, the Commonwealth, Inter-American Development Bank, Asian Development Bank, the Pacific Community, IOM and the Antarctic Treaty.

In 2003 the UK gave US$6·2bn. in international aid, representing 0·34% of its GDP. In actual terms this made the UK the 5th most generous country in the world, but as a percentage of GDP only the 10th most generous.

ECONOMY

In 2002 services accounted for 72·6% of GDP, industry 26·4% and agriculture 1·0%.

According to the anti-corruption organization *Transparency International*, in 2004 the United Kingdom ranked 11th in the world in a survey of the countries with the least corruption in business and government. It received 8·6 out of 10 in the annual index.

Overview. The UK ranks among the world's top five economies. Economic growth has been relatively immune to global conditions in recent years and the economy has gained momentum relative to the euro area. Between 1993 and 2001 the UK enjoyed sustained non-inflationary output growth, the longest period of expansion in 30 years. Inflation has been stabilized close to its target of 2·5% and unemployment rates are amongst the lowest in the OECD. The strong performance has been driven by a healthy services sector and strong domestic demand, whilst weaknesses in the manufacturing sector and in exports have been a hindrance to the economy. Since 1995 consumption has grown significantly faster than output. Private consumption accounts for nearly 70% of GDP. Despite almost closing the GDP per capita gap with other European countries, the disparity with the most successful OECD countries—Canada, the USA and Australia—remains, partly owing to weaker productivity levels in the UK.

The service sector accounts for more than two-thirds of GDP. The financial services sector represents 20% of GDP thanks to the strength of the City of London and the rapid growth in business services. The manufacturing sector has declined more than in other industrialized countries and accounts for 20% of GDP. The decline is partly owing to the strong value of the currency and low productivity. As imports have outpaced exports, the trade deficit has widened. From 1979–97 the Conservative government introduced reforms that made the UK one of Europe's freest economies. The Labour government has since continued with privatization, deregulation and competition reforms. The country is open to foreign investment and there are more non-EU businesses in the UK than in other European nations.

The Code for Fiscal Stability, introduced in 1998, stipulates that the government may borrow only to invest, not to support current spending. The 'sustainable investment rule' aims at maintaining the public sector net debt below 40% of GDP over the economic cycle. Spending on health care and education are low compared to those in other OECD counties, with the result that public services are overstretched.

Currency. The unit of currency is the *pound sterling* (£; GBP) of 100 *pence* (p.). Before decimalization on 15 Feb. 1971 £1 = 20 shillings (*s*) of 12 pence (*d*). A gold standard was adopted in 1816, the sovereign, a £1, or twenty-shilling gold coin, weighing 7·98805 grams. It is eleven-twelfths pure gold and one-twelfth alloy. Currency notes for £1 and 10*s*. were first issued by the Treasury in 1914, replacing the circulation of sovereigns. The issue of £1 and 10*s*. notes was taken over by the Bank of England in 1928. 10*s*. notes ceased to be legal tender in 1970 and £1 notes (in England and Wales) in 1988. Sterling was a member of the exchange rate mechanism of the European Monetary System from 8 Oct. 1990 until 16 Sept. 1992 ('Black Wednesday').

Inflation. Consumer Price Index (CPI) inflation was 1·3% in 2004 (1·3% in 2002 and 1·4% in 2003).

Coinage. Estimated number of coins in circulation at 31 Dec. 2002: £2, 205m.; £1, 1,341m.; 50p, 666m.; 20p, 1,955m.; 10p, 1,490m.; 5p, 3,360m.; 2p, 5,940m.; 1p, 9,800m.

Banknotes. The Bank of England issues notes in denominations of £5, £10, £20 and £50 up to the amount of the fiduciary issue. Under the provisions of the Currency Act 1983 the amount of the fiduciary issue is limited, but can be altered by direction of HM Treasury on the advice of the Bank of England. Since Nov. 1998 the limit has been £34,300m., although this was temporarily raised to £50,000m. over the millennium period.

All current series Bank of England notes are legal tender in England and Wales. Some banks in Scotland (Bank of Scotland, Clydesdale Bank and the Royal Bank of Scotland) and Northern Ireland (Bank of Ireland, First Trust Bank, Northern Bank and Ulster Bank) have note-issuing powers.

The total amount of Bank of England notes issued at 31 Dec. 2002 was £33,900m., of which £33,897m. represented notes with other banks and the public, and £3m. notes in the Banking Department of the Bank of England.

Foreign exchange reserves were US$34,583m. and gold reserves 10·10m. troy oz in June 2002 (22·98m. troy oz in April 1999).

Budget. The March 2005 budget forecast public sector borrowing for 2004–05 at £34·4bn., falling to £32bn. in 2005–06, £29bn. in 2006–07, £27bn. in 2007–08, £24bn. in 2008–09 and £22bn. in 2009–10. Public sector net debt as a proportion of GDP was put at 34·4% for 2004–05, rising to 37·1% by 2009–10.

Current spending for 2004–05 was set at £451·1bn., increasing to £581bn. by 2009–10. Net investment was to rise from £18·3bn. in 2004–05 to £34bn. by 2009–10.

Among the budget's provisions was the raising of the starting rate for paying stamp duty on property from £60,000 to £120,000 and an increase in the inheritance tax threshold to £275,000. As part of the on-going scheme to reduce expenditure on government departments, 7,800 jobs are to be relocated out of London and the southeast. Other measures saw an extra £400m. allocated to defence expenditure. Pension credits are to increase by 13% over a three-year period to achieve a minimum weekly pensioner income of £119 and single parents are to receive a £2,000 bonus for returning to work.

'Mr Brown's lengthy list of pledges and handouts, prudently matched by tax rises invisible to voters, has given the opposition a hard target to shoot at. It was, indeed, a political Budget.' (*Financial Times*, 17 March 2005).

Current Budget (in £1bn.).	*2003–04 Outturn*	*2004–05 Estimate*	*2005–06 Projection*
Current Receipts	418·9	449·7	486·7
Current Expenditure	425·3	451·1	476·9

Surplus on Current Budget (in £1bn.).	*2003–04 Outturn*	*2004–05 Estimate*	*2005–06 Projection*
	–20·4	–16·1	–6

Current Receipts (in £1bn.).	*2003–04 Outturn*	*2004–05 Estimate*	*2005–06 Projection*
Total Inland Revenue (net of tax credits)	228·0	249·6	277·5
Total Customs and Excise	115·7	120·4	126·5
Net Taxes and National Insurance Contributions	396·8	425·6	461·9
Current Receipts	418·9	449·7	486·7

Departmental Expenditure Limits (Resource Budget, in £1bn.).	*2003–04 Outturn*	*2004–05 Estimate*	*2005–06 Planned*
Education and Skills	23·1	24·6	26·3
Health	62·7	69·1	75·1
of which: NHS	60·9	66·9	72·8
Transport	7·8	8·3	8·8
Office of the Deputy Prime Minister	6·0	6·2	6·4
Local Government	40·9	43·4	46·2
Home Office	11·7	12·3	12·8
Departments for Constitutional Affairs	3·2	3·4	3·7
Attorney General's Departments	0·6	0·7	0·7
Defence	31·3	32·6	32·7
Foreign and Commonwealth Office	1·6	1·8	1·8
International Development	3·8	3·9	4·5
Trade and Industry	4·4	5·3	5·9
Environment, Food and Rural Affairs	2·7	3·2	3·1
Culture, Media and Sport	1·3	1·5	1·5
Work and Pensions	8·3	8·4	8·4
Scotland[1]	18·8	20·0	21·4
Wales[1]	9·8	10·7	11·3
Northern Ireland Executive[1]	6·4	7·0	7·3
Northern Ireland Office	1·0	1·2	1·2
Chancellor's Departments	4·5	5·0	5·2
Cabinet Office	1·9	2·0	2·0

[1]For Scotland, Wales and Northern Ireland, the split between current and capital budgets is decided by the respective executives.

VAT, introduced on 1 April 1973, is 17·5% (reduced rate, 5·0%). In 2004–05 tax revenues were estimated at 36·3% of GDP (35·6% in 2003–04).

In 2003–04 the budget deficit exceeded 3%, the target set by the European Stability and Growth Pact, reaching 3·2%, although it fell to 2·9% in 2004–05.

Performance. In 2003 total GDP was £1,088,650m. (US$1,794,858m.), the fourth highest in the world after the USA, Japan and Germany.

Economic growth was 3·9% in 2000 and was 2·3% in 2001 (the fastest rate of any of the Group of Seven leading industrialized countries during the year). In 2002 the growth rate of 1·8% was the lowest in a decade, but growth was then 2·2% in 2003, rising to 3·1% in 2004.

The March 2004 *OECD Economic Survey* reported: 'The performance of the UK economy has been impressive in recent years, underpinned by wide-ranging structural reforms and sound macroeconomic policy frameworks. The OECD projects growth above potential in 2004 and 2005, with unemployment remaining low, but instability stemming from the housing market is a risk. ... Ensuring macroeconomic stability, while addressing the remaining weaknesses through further structural reforms offers the prospect of continuing strong economic performance.'

In the 2005 budget the estimated growth rate for the year was put at 3·0–3·5%. Growth for 2006 was forecast to be 2·5–3·0%.

In the World Economic Forum's *Global Competitiveness Report 2004–5* the UK was placed 11th in the world in the Growth Competitiveness Ranking and 6th in the Business Competitiveness Ranking.

Banking and Finance. The Bank of England is the government's banker and the 'banker's bank'. It has the sole right of note issue in England and Wales. It was founded by Royal Charter in 1694 and nationalized in 1946. The capital stock has, since 1 March 1946, been held by HM Treasury. The *Governor* (appointed for five-year terms) is Mervyn King (b. 1948; took office 2003).

The statutory Bank Return is published weekly. End-Dec. figures are as follows (in £1m.):

	Notes in circulation	*Notes and coins in Banking Department*	*Public deposits (government)*	*Other deposits*[1]
1998	25,722	8	229	8,022
1999	30,281	9	164	12,605
2000	30,690	10	382	10,062
2001	32,895	5	452	11,317
2002	33,897	3	690	14,049

[1]Including Special Deposits.

Major British Banking Groups' statistics at end Dec. 2002: total deposits (sterling and currency), £1,318,734m.; sterling market loans, £263,544m.; market loans (sterling and currency), £420,703m.; advances (sterling and currency), £1,031,825m.; sterling investments, £97,060m.

Britain's largest bank is HSBC, both by assets and market capitalization. It had assets in Dec. 2003 of US$1,034bn. The Royal Bank of Scotland is the second largest, both by assets and market capitalization.

In May 1997 the power to set base interest rates was transferred from the Treasury to the Bank of England. The government continues to set the inflation target but the Bank has responsibility for setting interest rates to meet the target. Base rates are now set by a nine-member Monetary Policy Committee at the Bank; members include the Governor. Membership of the Court (the governing body) was widened. The 1998 Act provides for Court to consist of the Governor, two Deputy Governors and 16 Directors. Responsibility for supervising banks was transferred from the Bank to the Financial Services Authority (FSA). The base rate was raised from 4·50% to 4·75% on 5 Aug. 2004.

National Savings Bank. Statistics for 2001 and 2002:

	Ordinary accounts		*Investment accounts*	
	2001	*2002*	*2001*	*2002*
Amounts—	*in £1,000*	*in £1,000*	*in £1,000*	*in £1,000*
Received	668,522	651,513	909,592	927,439
Interest credited	23,007	11,567	374,261	282,162
Paid	(672,908)	(654,082)	(1,605,234)	(1,414,741)
Due to depositors at 31 March	1,368,686	1,377,684	7,638,055	7,432,915

There are stock exchanges in Belfast, Birmingham, Glasgow and Manchester which function mainly as representative offices for the London Stock Exchange (called International Stock Exchange until May 1991). In July 1991 the 91 shareholders voted unanimously for a new memorandum and articles of association which devolves power to a wider range of participants in the securities industry, and replaces the Stock Exchange Council with a 14-member board. The FTSE 100 ended 2004 at 4,814·4, up from 4,476·9 at the end of 2003 (gaining 7·5% during the year—the second consecutive annual rise).

In 2000 the UK received a record total of US$118·76bn. worth of foreign direct investment. In 2001 the total declined by more than half to US$52·62bn., and in 2003 it was only US$14·52bn. By the end of 2002 the UK had attracted foreign direct investment totalling US$568bn.—a figure exceeded only by the USA.

Roberts, R. and Kynaston, D. (eds.) *The Bank of England: Money, Power and Influence, 1694–1994*. OUP, 1995

Weights and Measures. Conversion to the metric system, which replaced the imperial system, became obligatory on 1 Oct. 1995. The use of the pint for milk deliveries and bar sales, and use of miles and yards in road signs, is exempt indefinitely, and the use of the pound (weight) in selling greengrocery was exempt until 1999.

ENERGY AND NATURAL RESOURCES

Environment. The UK's carbon dioxide emissions from the consumption and flaring of fossil fuels in 2002 were the equivalent of 9·4 tonnes per capita. The UK's total emission of greenhouse gases is estimated to have fallen from 777m. tonnes in 1990 to 696m. tonnes in 2002. An *Environmental Sustainability Index* compiled for the World Economic Forum meeting in Feb. 2002 ranked the UK 91st in the world out of 142 countries analysed, with 46·1%. The index measured the ability of countries to maintain favourable environmental conditions and examined various factors including pollution levels and the use or abuse of natural resources.

In England and Wales 8% of household waste was recycled in 1998, compared to 52% in Switzerland. The rate in Scotland was under 6%.

Electricity. The Electricity Act of 1989 implemented the restructuring and transfer to the private sector of the electricity supply industry.

(England and Wales)

Generators. Under the 1989 Act, National Power and Powergen took over the fossil fuel and hydro-electric power stations previously owned by the Central Electricity Generating Board, and were privatized in 1991. National Power was split into two companies in 2000, International Power plc and Innogy plc. Nuclear Electric, responsible for operating the 12 nuclear power stations, and Scottish Nuclear were merged as a single holding company in 1996 with two new operating subsidiaries, Magnox Electric and British Energy. Both were privatized in 1996. Under licence, generating companies may also be involved in electricity supply. There were a total of 31 nuclear reactors in use in the UK at 15 nuclear power stations in the UK in Sept. 2002. The UK generation market is now very diverse, with 42 major power producers compared to seven in 1990.

Transmission. The privatized National Grid Transco is responsible for operating the transmission system and for co-ordinating the operation of power stations connected to it. The company also operates the Cross-Channel link with France and the interconnection with the Scottish power system.

Distribution and Supply. The 12 Area Boards were replaced under the 1989 Act by 12 successor companies, which were privatized in 1990. These were: East Midlands Electricity (now Powergen Energy); Eastern Electricity (now part of Powergen); London Electricity (now LE Group); Manweb (now part of ScottishPower); Midlands Electricity (now Aquila Networks Services); Northern Electric (supply business now owned by Innogy); Norweb (now part TXU Europe, part United Utilities); SEEBOARD (now part of LE Group); Southern Electric (now part of Scottish and Southern Energy); SWALEC (renamed Hyder, and now part of Western Power Distribution); South Western Electricity (now part of Western Power Distribution); and Yorkshire Electricity (supply business owned by Innogy, distribution business owned by Northern Electric). The companies are in the main responsible for maintaining their local distribution networks, and have a statutory duty to supply electricity to their tariff customers. However, following a number of mergers and takeovers in the industry, some companies are now responsible only for distribution or supply in their areas. Some of the companies are also involved in the retailing of electrical goods and electrical contracting, and some have diversified into other business activities.

See also SCOTLAND.

The Electricity Association. The Electricity Association is the trade association of the UK electricity companies, providing a forum for members to discuss matters of common interest, a collective voice for the electricity industry when needed, and specialist research and professional services. It publishes an annual *Electricity Industry Review*, which contains detailed information on the development of the industry during the previous year.

Regulation. The Office of Electricity Regulation *('Offer')* was set up under the 1989 Act to protect consumer interests following privatization. In 1999 it was merged with the Office of Gas Supply ('*Ofgas*') to form the Office of Gas and Electricity Markets ('*Ofgem*'), reflecting the opening up of all markets for electricity and gas supply to full competition from May that year, with many suppliers now offering both gas and electricity to customers.

Statistics. The electricity industry contributes about 1·3% of the UK's Gross Domestic Product. The installed capacity of all UK power stations in 2001 was 67,965 MW. In 2000 the fuel generation mix was: coal-fired 34%, nuclear 25%, gas 38%, hydro and renewables 2%, and oil 1%. 314,586 GWh were supplied to 28m. customers, of which domestic users took 29%, industrial users 29% and commercial and other users the remaining 42%. The average domestic consumption per capita in 2000 was 4,256 kWh.

Electricity Association. *Electricity Industry Review*. Annual

Surrey, J. (ed.) *The British Electricity Experience: Privatization—the Record, the Issues, the Lessons*. London, 1996

Oil and Gas. Production in 1,000 tonnes, in 2003: throughput of crude and process oils, 84,515; refinery use, 5,390. Refinery output: gas/diesel oil, 27,579; motor spirit, 22,627; fuel oil, 9,513; aviation turbine fuel, 5,277; burning oil, 3,521; naphtha, 3,516; propane, butane and other petroleum gases, 2,976; bitumen, 1,925; lubricating oils, 576. Total output of petroleum products, 79,139. Crude oil production (2003), 106·1m. tonnes. The UK's oil production is the second highest in Europe after that of Norway, and is the eleventh highest in the world, greater than that of either Kuwait or Libya. The UK had proven oil reserves of 4·5bn. bbls. at the end of 2003 and is a net exporter of oil.

In 2003 the total income from sales of oil produced was £14·5bn., with the value of net exports of oil and oil products £4·5bn.

The first significant offshore gas discovery was made in 1965 in the North Sea, followed in 1969 by the first commercial oil offshore. Offshore production of gas began in 1967 and oil in 1975.

Oil and gas have played an important part in providing the UK's energy needs. In 2003, either through direct use or as a source of energy to produce electricity, oil and gas accounted for some 74% of total UK energy consumption, with UK-based production supplying some 92% of the gas consumed.

Oil products also provide important contributions to other industries, such as feedstocks for the petro-chemical industry and lubricants for various uses. While the importance of oil as a source of energy for electrical generation and use by industry and commercial operations has declined with the increasing use of gas, oil still makes up around 20% of total industrial uses of energy. Its prime importance is in the transport sector, where it provides 99% of the total energy used.

The United Kingdom usually exports around two-thirds of the oil it produces, with the key export markets being the USA and other EU countries.

The reform of the old nationalized gas industry began with the Gas Act of 1986, which paved the way for the privatization later that year of the British Gas Corporation, and established the Director General of Gas Supply (DGSS) as the independent regulator. This had a limited effect on competition, as British Gas retained a monopoly on tariff (domestic) supply. Competition progressively developed in the industrial and commercial (non-tariff) market.

The Gas Act 1995 amended the 1986 Act to prepare the way for full competition, including the domestic market. It created three separate licences—for Public Gas Transporters who operate pipelines, for Shippers (wholesalers) who contract for gas to be transported through the pipelines, and for Suppliers (retailers) who then market gas to consumers. It also placed the DGSS under a statutory duty to secure effective competition.

The domestic market was progressively opened to full competition from 1996 until May 1998.

In 1997 British Gas took a commercial decision to de-merge its trading business. Centrica plc (a new company) was formed to handle the gas sales, gas trading, services and retail businesses of BG, together with the gas production businesses of the North and South Morecambe Field. The remaining parts of the business, including transportation and storage and the international downstream activities, were contained in BG plc. As a result of subsequent changes, Transco (owner and operator of the UK's National Gas Transmission System) is now owned by National Grid Transco (NGT). NGT is also the owner and operator of the National Electricity Grid.

The regulator for Britain's gas and electricity industries is *Ofgem* (Office of the Gas and Electricity Markets), created in 1999 through the merger of *Ofgas* (Office of Gas Supply) and *Offer* (Office of Electricity Regulation). Its role is to protect and advance the interests of consumers by promoting competition where possible.

A second European Directive was published in June 2003 with rules for the internal market in natural gas. Member states were allowed one year to execute its provisions; the UK implemented the directive in July 2004.

The UK became a net importer of gas during 2004. In preparation for increasing import dependency, several gas infrastructure projects are scheduled to come on stream over the next few years, supplying the UK with gas from a number of sources, including Norway, Continental Europe, Qatar and Algeria. There is already a pipeline (the Interconnector) linking the UK and European gas grids. This link to Continental Europe opened in Oct. 1998 and has an export capacity of 20bn. cu. metres a year and an import capacity of 8·5bn. cu. metres a year.

Proven gas reserves in 2003 were some 630bn. cu. metres. Production was 102·7bn. cu. metres in 2003. In 2003, 35% of gas produced was used by domestic users and 29% by electricity generators.

Wind. In 2003 there were 84 wind farms and 1,043 turbines with a capacity of 649·4 MW for electricity generation.

Minerals. Legislation to privatize the coal industry was introduced in 1994 and established the Coal Authority to take over from British Coal Corporation. The Coal Authority is the owner of almost all the UK's coal reserves; it licenses private coal-mining, deals with subsidence claims in former mining areas and disposes of property not required for operational purposes. In 2004 there were nine former British Coal collieries, six additional deep mines and 45 opencast mines, employing some 7,630 mineworkers.

Total production from deep mines was 16·4m. tonnes in 2002 (83·8m. tonnes in 1988). Output from opencast sites, 2002, 13·1m. tonnes (1988, 17·9m. tonnes). In 2002 inland coal consumption was 58·6m. tonnes (113·3m. tonnes in 1988).

Output of non-fuel minerals in Great Britain, 2002 (in 1,000 tonnes): limestone, 88,013; sand and gravel, 82,721; igneous rock, 44,544; dolomite, 12,946; sandstone, 11,788; clay and shale, 10,306; chalk, 8,587; salt, 5,800; industrial sand, 3,833; china clay, 2,467.

Steel and metals. Steel production in recent years (in 1m. tonnes):

1998	17·3
1999	16·3
2000	15·2
2001	13·5
2002	11·7

Deliveries of finished steel products from UK mills in 2001 were worth £6bn. in product sales and comprised 6·7m. tonnes to the UK domestic market and 6·3m.

tonnes for export. About three-quarters of UK steel exports went to other EU countries. UK steel imports in 2001 were about 6·8m. tonnes. The UK steel industry's main markets are construction (22%), automotive (17%), mechanical engineering (24%) and metal goods (14%). Corus Group (formerly British Steel) is the UK's largest steel producer (and the third largest steel company in the world) and produces about 85% of UK crude steel. The UK steel industry has improved productivity nearly 5-fold over the past 20 years.

Agriculture. Land use in 1996: agriculture, 77%; urban, 10%; forests, 10%; other, 3%. In 2002 agricultural land in the UK totalled (in 1,000 ha) 18,388, comprising agricultural holdings, 17,154; and common grazing, 1,234. Land use of the former (in 1,000 ha): all grasses, 6,652; crops, 4,573; rough grazing, 4,484; bare fallow, 33; other, 1,412. Area sown to crops (in 1,000 ha): cereals, 3,245; other arable crops, 993; horticultural crops, 176; fruit, 35.

In 2001 there were 5·70m. ha of arable land and 51,000 ha of permanent crops.

Figures compiled by the Soil Association show that in April 2003 the area of fully organic farmland in the UK was 534,300 ha. Including land in conversion, 4·3% of the agricultural land was managed organically in April 2002. Organic food sales for the UK in 2001–02 totalled £920m., up from £805m. in 2000–01.

Farmers receiving financial support under the EU's Common Agricultural Policy are obliged to 'set-aside' land in order to control production. In 2002 such set-aside totalled 611,000 ha. There were 500,000 tractors and 47,000 harvester-threshers in 2001.

The number of workers employed in agriculture was, in 2002, 193,900 (47,900 female) of whom 64,200 were seasonal or casual workers. Of the 116,300 regular workers, 40,100 were part-time. In 1990 the number of workers employed in agriculture had been 273,800. There were some 303,100 farm holdings in 2002. Average size of holdings, 56·6 ha.

Total farm incomes dropped from £5·3bn. to £1·7bn. between 1995 and 2000, before rising to £2·4bn. in 2002. Food and live animals accounted for 3·0% of exports and 6·4% of imports in 2002, down from 4·5% of exports and 8·6% of imports in 1991.

Area given over to principal crops in the UK:

	Wheat	*Sugarbeets*	*Potatoes*	*Barley*	*Oilseed rape*	*Oats*
			Area (1,000 ha)			
1998	2,045	189	164	1,253	507	98
1999	1,847	183	178	1,179	417	92
2000	2,086	173	166	1,128	332	109
2001	1,635	177	165	1,245	404	112
2002	1,996	169	158	1,101	357	126

Production of principal crops in the UK:

	Wheat	*Sugarbeets*	*Potatoes*	*Barley*	*Oilseed rape*	*Oats*
			Total product (1,000 tonnes)			
1998	15,450	10,002	6,417	6,620	1,566	585
1999	14,870	10,584	7,100	6,580	1,737	540
2000	16,700	9,335	6,635	6,490	1,129	640
2001	11,580	8,335	6,649	6,660	1,157	621
2002	15,973	9,557	6,967	6,128	1,468	753

Horticultural crops. 2002 output (in 1,000 tonnes): carrots, 755; onions, 283; cabbage, 244; apples, 177; peas, 177; turnips and swedes, 119; cauliflowers, 116; lettuce, 110; parsnips, 101; tomatoes, 101.

Livestock in the UK as at June in each year (in 1,000):

	1998	*1999*	*2000*	*2001*	*2002*
Cattle	11,519	11,423	11,135	10,602	10,345
(dairy)	(2,439)	(2,440)	(2,336)	(2,251)	(2,227)
(beef)	(1,947)	(1,924)	(1,842)	(1,708)	(1,657)
Sheep	44,471	44,656	42,264	36,716	35,834
Pigs	8,146	7,284	6,482	5,845	5,588
Poultry	152,906	153,621	157,051	166,896	155,745[1]

[1]Provisional.

Livestock products, 2002 (1,000 tonnes): beef and veal, 995; pork, 940; bacon and ham, 493; mutton and lamb, 423; poultry meat, 1,696; hens' eggs, 982; cheese, 396. Milk production in 2002 totalled 14·92m. tonnes.

In March 1996 the government acknowledged the possibility that bovine spongiform encephalopathy (BSE) might be transmitted to humans as a form of Creutzfeldt-Jakob disease via the food chain. Confirmed cases of BSE in cattle in the UK: 1988, 2,180; 1989, 7,133; 1990, 14,181; 1991, 25,026; 1992, 36,680; 1993, 34,370; 1994, 23,943; 1995, 14,301; 1996, 8,013; 1997, 4,310; 1998, 3,179; 1999, 2,256; 2000, 1,311; 2001, 781; 2002, 445; 2003, 173; 2004, 82. Confirmed deaths attributed to nvCJD (new variant Creutzfeldt-Jakob Disease, the form of the disease thought to be linked to BSE): 1995, 3; 1996, 10; 1997, 10; 1998, 18; 1999, 15; 2000, 28; 2001, 20; 2002, 17; 2003, 18; 2004, 9.

British beef was widely banned overseas and in March 1996 the European Commission introduced a ban on the export of bovine animals, semen and embryos, beef and beef products and mammalian meat and bonemeal from the UK. The government introduced a number of preventive measures including bans on sales of older meat and the use of meat in animal feed and fertilizer, and compensation schemes. Following inspections, the European Commission allowed for the export of deboned beef and beef products beginning 1 Aug. 1999.

In Feb. 2001 the UK was hit by a major foot-and-mouth disease epidemic for the first time since 1967–68, with 2,030 confirmed cases and 4,050,000 animals being slaughtered during the months which followed. The last confirmed case was on 30 Sept. 2001. In the 1967–68 epidemic there had been 2,364 cases with approximately 434,000 animals slaughtered.

Forestry. In March 2003 the area of woodland in Britain was 2,722,000 ha, of which the Forestry Commission managed 787,000 ha. There were approximately 29,500 full-time equivalent jobs in the forestry industry and wood-processing industries in 1998–99, of which 11,200 were in wood processing, 5,900 in forest establishment and maintenance, 5,800 in harvesting and haulage, 4,600 in other non-forest activities such as office work research, and 2,000 in other forest activities such as nurseries and road construction. In 2002 a total of 7·05m. cu. metres of roundwood was produced.

New planting (2002–03), 12,950 ha (816 ha, Forestry Commission; 12,134 ha, private woodlands).

Forestry Commission (*Website:* http://www.forestry.gov.uk). *Forestry Facts and Figures.* Annual

Fisheries. Quantity (in 1,000 tonnes) and value (in £1,000) of fish of British taking, landed in Great Britain (excluding salmon and sea-trout):

Quantity	*1998*	*1999*	*2000*	*2001*	*2002*
Wet fish	428·3	389·8	337·6	332·1	334·9
Shell fish	124·2	116·7	127·0	136·2	130·7
	552·5	506·5	464·7	458·3	465·6
Value					
Wet fish	323,297	297,831	268,816	256,364	250,845
Shell fish	160,708	166,299	153,247	167,323	163,844
	484,005	464,131	422,063	423,687	414,689

In Dec. 2002 the fishing fleet comprised 7,033 registered vessels. Major fishing ports: (England) Brixham, Newlyn, Plymouth; (Scotland) Aberdeen, Fraserburgh, Kinlochbervie, Lerwick, Lochinver, Mallaig, Peterhead, Scrabster.

In the period 1999–2001 the average person in the UK consumed 20 kg of fish and fishery products a year, compared to the European Union average of 24 kg.

INDUSTRY

The largest companies by market capitalization in the UK on 6 March 2005 were: BP, at £123,329m. (US$237,199m.), compared to £98,257m. (US$177,216m.) in March 2004; HSBC, at £96,049m. (US$184,731m.), compared to £93,522m. (US$168,676m.); and Vodafone, at £91,411m. (US$175,811m.), compared to £90,552m. (US$163,320m.).

In 2003 there were 162,585 manufacturing firms, of which 185 employed 1,000 or over persons, and 84,285 employed nine or fewer.

Chemicals and chemical products. Manufacturers' sales, (in £1m.) in 2001: primary plastics and other plastic products, 17,023; pharmaceutical preparations and basic pharmaceutical products, 8,691; organic basic chemicals, 5,740; perfumes and toilet products, 2,584; paints, etc., 2,512; rubber products, 2,492; soap, polish and detergents, 1,941; inorganic basic chemicals, 1,159; pesticides, etc., 1,129; dyes, 1,067.

Construction. Total value (in £1m.) of constructional work in Great Britain in 2002 was 83,593, including new work, 45,370 (of which housing, 12,072). Cement production, 2002, 11,089,000 tonnes; brick production, 2002, 2,070m. units.

Electrical Goods. Manufacturers' sales (in £1m.) for 2001: computers, etc., 9,391; telephone and telegraph equipment, 4,231; electronic valves and tubes and other electronic components, 3,647; radio and electronic capital goods (2000), 3,600; television and radio receivers, sound or video recording, 3,087.

Engineering, machinery and instruments. Manufacturers' sales (in £1m.) for 2001: motor vehicles, 20,040; aircraft and spacecraft, 11,738; parts and accessories for motor vehicles and engines, 8,358; appliances for measuring, checking and testing, 5,722; non-domestic cooling and ventilation equipment, 3,280; lifting and handling equipment, 2,771; medical and surgical equipment and orthopaedic appliances, 1,876. Car production, 2002, 1,629,744 units.

Foodstuffs, etc. Manufacturers' sales (in £1m.) for 2001: operation of dairies, 5,726; bread, fresh pastry goods and cakes, 3,916; beer, 3,627; cocoa, chocolate and sugar confectionery, 3,356; biscuits, rusks, preserved pastry goods and cakes, 3,107; meat production and preservation, 3,082; mineral water and soft drinks, 2,973; grain mill products, 2,478; fruit and vegetable processing and preservation, 2,383; poultry production and preservation, 1,996; prepared feeds for farm animals, 1,947; distilled alcoholic beverages, 1,898; tobacco products, 1,796. Alcoholic beverage production, 2002: beer, 5,667·2m. litres (5,955·2m. litres in 1991); wine, 1,122·2m. litres (658·3m. litres in 1991); spirits, 450·8m. litres (447·6m. litres in 1991).

Metals. Manufacturers' sales (in £1m.) for 2001: metal structures and parts of structures, 5,140; general mechanical engineering, 2,862; forging, pressing, stamping and roll forming of metal, 1,962; treatment and coating of metals, 1,116; steel tubes, 1,081.

Textiles and clothing. Manufacturers' sales (in £1m.) in 2001: women's outerwear and underwear, 1,416; carpets and rugs, 898; household textiles, 893; textile weaving, 831; preparation and spinning of textile fibres, 668; men's outerwear and underwear, 573.

Wood products, furniture, paper and printing. Manufacturers' sales (in £1m.) in 2001: furniture of whatever construction, 7,045; journals and periodicals, 7,028; wood products except furniture, 5,159; newspapers, 3,951; cartons, boxes and cases, 3,399; publishing of books, 3,362; paper and paperboard, 3,140.

Labour. In 2003 the UK's total economically active population (i.e. all persons in employment plus the claimant unemployed) was (in 1,000) 29,595 (13,473 females), of whom 28,110 (12,889 females) were in employment, including 24,598 (11,887 females) as employees and 3,338 (911 females) as self-employed. In 1993 only 25,304,000 people had been in employment, representing an increase of 2,806,000 in ten years. UK employees by form of employment in 2003 (in 1,000): wholesale and retail trade, repair of motor vehicles, motorcycles and household goods, 4,451; real estate renting and business activities, 3,965; manufacturing industry, 3,501; health and social work, 2,850; education, 2,234; hotels and restaurants, 1,818; transport, storage and communications, 1,549; public administration and defence, compulsory social security, 1,477; construction, 1,145; financial intermediation, 1,050; agriculture, hunting, forestry and fishing, 233. Between 1998 and 2003 employment in service industries increased by 1,969,000 while employment in manufacturing declined by 696,000 over the same period.

Registered unemployed in UK as at spring (in 1,000; figures seasonally adjusted): 1998, 1,779 (6·2%); 1999, 1,762 (6·1%); 2000, 1,641 (5·6%); 2001, 1,435 (4·9%)—the lowest rate in more than 20 years; 2002, 1,533 (5·2%); 2003, 1,484 (5·0%). Of the 1,484,000 unemployed people, 900,000 were men and 584,000 women. The number of unemployed people on benefits was 813,200 in Jan. 2005 (giving a rate of 2·6%), the lowest since records began in 1975. The unemployment rate on the

International Labour Organization (ILO) definition, which includes all those who are looking for work whether or not claiming unemployment benefits, was 4·7% in Oct.–Dec. 2004.

In 2001 there were 3·7m. businesses in the UK of which 1·6m. were registered at Companies House. Approximately 99% of UK businesses have fewer than 50 employees. There were an estimated 342,000 business start-ups in 2001, with business closures numbering 410,000.

Workers (in 1,000) involved in industrial stoppages (and working days lost): 1998, 93 (0·28m.); 1999, 141 (0·24m.); 2000, 183 (0·50m.); 2001, 180 (0·52m.); 2002, 943 (1·32m.). In 1975, 6m. working days had been lost through stoppages. Between 1996 and 2002 strikes cost Britain an average of 25 working days per 1,000 employees a year.

The Wages Councils set up in 1909 to establish minimum rates of pay (in 1992 of 2·5m. workers) were abolished in 1993. The Labour government, elected in May 1997, was committed to the introduction of a National Minimum Wage and established a Low Pay Commission to advise on its implementation. It is currently £4·85 an hour for adults and £4·10 for 18–21 year olds. In April 2003 the average gross salary in Britain for full-time employees was £25,170 (£28,065 for men and £20,314 for women). Average hourly pay for full-time employees excluding overtime in April 2003 in Britain was £12·03 (£12·88 for males and £10·56 for females). Average weekly earnings were highest in London, at £636·90, and lowest in the northeast, at £402·10.

Britons in full-time employment worked an average of 43·5 hours a week in 2001, compared to the EU average of 40·1 hours. Both men and women in full-time employment put in longer hours than in any other European country.

Trade Unions. In 2003 there were 71 unions affiliated to the Trades Union Congress (TUC) with a total membership of 6·7m. (2·7m. of them women), down from a peak of 12·2m. in 1980. The unions affiliated to the TUC in 2003 ranged in size from UNISON with 1·29m. members to the Sheffield Wool Shear Workers' Union with 15 members. The four largest unions, however, account for more than half the total membership. In 1998, 60% of public-sector employees and 19% of private-sector employees were unionized.

The TUC's executive body, the General Council, is elected at the annual Congress. Congress consists of representatives of all unions according to the size of the organization, and is the principal policy-making body.

The General Secretary (Brendan Barber, b. 1951) is elected from nominations submitted by the unions. The TUC draws up policies and promotes and publicizes them. It makes representations to government, employers and international bodies. The TUC also carries out research and campaigns, and provides a range of services to unions including courses for union representatives.

The TUC is affiliated to the International Confederation of Free Trade Unions, the Trade Union Advisory Committee of OECD, the Commonwealth Trade Union Council and the European Trade Union Confederation. The TUC provides a service of trade union education. It provides members to serve, with representatives of employers, on the managing boards of such bodies as the Health and Safety Commission and the Advisory, Conciliation and Arbitration Service.

Clegg, H. A., *A History of British Trade Unions since 1889* [until 1951]. 3 vols. Oxford, 1994
Pelling, H., *A History of British Trade Unionism*. 5th ed. London, 1992.
Taylor, R., *The TUC From the General Strike to New Unionism.* Palgrave, Basingstoke, 2000
Willman, P. *et al., Union Business: Trade Union Organization and Financial Reform in the Thatcher Years.* CUP, 1993

INTERNATIONAL TRADE

Imports and Exports. Value of the imports and exports of merchandise, excluding bullion and specie (in US$1m.):

	Total imports	*Total exports*
2003	382,213·2	304,669·2
2004	457,131·6	346,546·8

Until 1992 all overseas trade statistics were compiled from Customs declarations. With the inception of the Single Market on 1 Jan. 1993, however, the requirement for Customs declarations in intra-EU trade was removed.

In 2004 the UK's trade with non-EU-15 countries was: imports, US$217,678·8m.; exports, US$155,084·4m. (2003 figures were imports US$178,982·4m. and exports US$136,588·8m.).

In 2004 other EU-15 members accounted for 53·6% of the UK's foreign trade, compared with 25·2% in 1956. The USA accounted for 11·8%, up from 9·1% in 1956, and the rest of the world 34·6%, down from 65·7% in 1956.

Figures for trade by countries and groups of countries (in US$1m.):

	Imports from		*Exports to*	
EU-15 countries	*2003*	*2004*	*2003*	*2004*
EU	203,230·8	239,452·8	168,080·4	191,462·4
Austria	4,317·6	4,194·0	2,011·2	1,964·4
Belgium and Luxembourg	20,535·6	24,588·0	17,840·4	18,985·2
Denmark	4,768·8	5,505·6	3,504·2	3,648·0
Finland	4,306·8	4,268·4	2,400·0	2,449·2
France and Monaco	31,670·4	35,760·0	29,641·2	33,476·4
Germany	53,124·0	62,854·8	32,814·0	39,172·8
Greece	1,008·0	1,186·8	2,004·0	2,526·0
Ireland	15,753·6	18,410·4	20,416·8	25,239·6
Italy	18,660·0	21,592·8	13,610·4	15,156·0
Netherlands	25,042·8	32,558·4	21,424·8	21,730·8
Portugal, Azores and Madeira	3,126·0	3,477·6	2,335·2	2,838·0
Spain	13,490·4	15,835·2	13,964·4	16,429·2
Sweden	7,425·6	9,222·0	6,112·8	7,846·8
Other foreign countries				
Europe—				
Baltic States	1,742·4	2,379·6	646·8	614·4
Czech Republic	2,343·6	2,352·0	1,635·6	1,762·8
Hungary	1,863·6	2,866·8	1,393·2	1,692·0
Iceland	507·6	674·4	238·8	314·4
Norway	10,768·8	16,130·4	3,183·6	3,663·6
Poland	2,566·8	3,303·6	2,379·6	2,562·0
Romania	1,130·4	1,446·0	831·6	1,118·4
Russia	4,059·6	6,501·6	2,318·4	2,691·6
Slovakia	428·4	474·0	387·6	402·0
Switzerland and Liechtenstein	6,446·4	6,576·0	4,758·0	5,415·6
Turkey	4,471·2	6,174·0	2,786·4	3,619·2
Other in Europe	2,101·2	2,236·8	3,116·4	3,788·4
Africa—				
Algeria	427·2	686·4	310·8	307·2
Egypt	723·6	932·4	756·0	1,227·6
Morocco	745·2	954·0	584·4	625·2
Nigeria	145·2	207·6	1,227·6	1,420·8
South Africa and Namibia	5,122·8	6,540·0	2,925·6	3,483·6
Tunisia	230·4	352·8	238·8	277·2
Other in Africa	4,209·6	4,957·2	2,643·6	2,874·0
Asia and Oceania—				
Australia	2,984·4	3,480·0	3,754·8	4,407·6
China	14,023·2	19,471·2	3,162·0	4,359·6
Hong Kong	9,235·2	10,794·0	4,087·2	4,846·8
India	3,508·8	4,286·4	3,740·4	4,116·0
Indonesia	1,568·4	1,761·6	736·8	729·6
Japan	13,479·6	15,081·6	6,109·2	6,943·2
Korea (South)	4,282·8	5,732·4	2,389·2	2,661·6
Malaysia	3,134·4	3,783·6	1,696·8	1,826·4
New Zealand	922·8	1,084·8	612·0	766·8
Pakistan	870·0	1,035·6	480·0	634·8
Philippines	1,196·4	1,230·0	628·8	579·6
Singapore	4,489·2	6,331·2	2,598·0	3,148·8
Taiwan	3,686·4	4,383·6	1,478·4	1,746·0
Thailand	2,760·0	3,297·6	937·2	1,173·6
Other in Asia and Oceania	3,292·8	4,178·4	846·0	872·4
Middle East—				
Iran	50·4	80·4	778·8	816·0
Israel	1,440·0	1,726·8	2,248·8	2,558·4
Kuwait	558·0	764·4	620·4	654·0
Saudi Arabia	1,280·4	2,223·6	3,007·2	2,961·6
United Arab Emirates	1,567·2	1,569·6	2,827·2	4,189·2
Other Middle East	529·2	685·2	2,317·2	2,647·2

	Imports from 2003	Imports from 2004	Exports to 2003	Exports to 2004
America—				
Argentina	421·2	499·2	222·0	327·6
Brazil	2,476·8	2,895·6	1,356·0	1,452·0
Canada	6,217·2	7,832·4	5,365·2	6,116·4
Chile	692·4	885·6	200·4	248·4
Colombia	373·2	518·4	174·0	213·6
Mexico	830·4	771·6	1,135·2	1,148·4
USA	39,453·6	42,068·4	47,936·4	52,494·0
Venezuela	190·8	390·0	237·6	344·4
Other in America	2,139·6	2,620·8	1,442·4	1,464·0
Total, foreign countries (including some not specified above)	382,213·2	457,131·6	304,669·2	346,546·8

In 2003 chemicals, manufactured goods classified chiefly by material and miscellaneous manufactured articles accounted for 41·4% of imports and 42·3% of exports; machinery and transport equipment 40·7% of the UK's imports and 41·3% of exports; mineral fuels, lubricants and related materials 6·5% of imports and 8·8% of exports; food, live animals, beverages and tobacco 8·6% of imports and 5·6% of exports; and crude materials, inedible, animal and vegetable oil and fats 2·8% of imports and 2·0% of exports.

Trade Fairs. London ranks as the third most popular convention city behind Paris and Brussels according to the Union des Associations Internationales (UAI), hosting 1·9% of all international meetings held in 2002.

COMMUNICATIONS

Roads. Responsibility for the construction and maintenance of trunk roads belongs to central government. Roads not classified as trunk roads are the responsibility of county or unitary councils.

In 2002 there were 391,653 km of public roads, classified as: motorways, 3,477 km; trunk roads, 11,692 km; other major roads, 34,973 km; minor roads, 341,511 km.

In 2002 journeys by car, vans and taxis totalled 634bn. passenger km (less than 60bn. in the early 1950s). Even in the early 1950s passenger km in cars, vans and taxis exceeded the annual total at the end of the 20th century by rail. Motor vehicles in 2002 included 24,543,000 passenger cars, 941,000 mopeds, scooters and motorcycles, 92,000 public transport vehicles and 2,622,000 other private and light goods vehicles. In 2001, 73% of households had regular use of a car with 28% of households having use of two or more cars. New vehicle registrations in 2002, 3,229,400. Driving tests, 2002–03 (in 1,000): applications, 1,468; tests held, 1,344; tests passed, 583; pass rate, 43%. The driving test was extended in 1996 to include a written examination.

Road casualties in Great Britain in 2003, 290,607 including 3,508 killed. Britain has the lowest death rates in road accidents of any industrialized country, at 5·8 deaths per 100,000 people.

Inter- and intra-urban bus and coach journeys average 46bn. passenger-km annually. Passenger journeys by local bus services, 2001–02, 4,347m. For London buses *see* Transport for London *under* Rail, *below*.

Rail. In 1994 the nationalized railway network was restructured to allow for privatization. Ownership of the track, stations and infrastructure was vested in a government-owned company, Railtrack, which was privatized in May 1996.

Passenger operations were reorganized into 25 train-operating companies, which were transferred to the private sector by Feb. 1997. By March 1997 all freight operations were also privatized. On 3 Oct. 2002 a new private sector not-for-profit company limited by guarantee, Network Rail, took over from Railtrack plc as network owner and operator. The train-operating companies pay Network Rail for access to the rail network, and lease their rolling stock from three private-sector companies.

The rail network comprises around 16,700 route km (a third electrified). Annual passenger-km have increased from 32·1bn. in 1996–97 to 39·7bn. in 2002–03, an increase of almost 24%. Passenger journeys have increased by 22% from 801m. in 1996–97 to 976m. in 2002–03. The amount of freight moved declined gradually over many years to 13·0bn. tonne-km in 1995–96. Following privatization it has risen sharply to 18·7bn. tonne-km in 2002–03. In 2002–03 a total of 50 people (excluding trespassers and suicides) were fatally injured on the railways (compared to 3,431 deaths in road accidents in 2002).

Eurotunnel PLC holds a concession from the government to operate the Channel Tunnel (49·4 km), through which vehicle-carrying and Eurostar passenger trains are run in conjunction with French and Belgian railways. A new dedicated high-speed line is planned to connect the Channel Tunnel to London St Pancras. This line will be used by both international and domestic trains. Construction is being undertaken in two sections with the first section having opened in Sept. 2003. The entire line should open in 2007.

Transport *for* London (T*f*L) is accountable to the Mayor of London and is responsible for implementing his Transport Strategy as well as planning and delivering a range of transport facilities. T*f*L's remit covers London Underground (since July 2003), London Buses, the Docklands Light Railway and Croydon Tramlink. It is also responsible for London River Services, Victoria Coach Station and London's Transport Museum, and provides transport for users with reduced mobility via Dial-a-Ride. As well as running the central London congestion charging scheme, T*f*L manages a 580 km network of London's main roads, all 4,600 traffic lights and the private hire trade. It also provides grants to London Boroughs to fund local transport improvements.

Every weekday in Greater London, 5·4m. journeys are made on London's buses, 3m. on the underground, 7m. on foot, 0·3m. by bicycle, 0·2m. by taxi, 160,000 on the Docklands Light Railway and 60,000 on Croydon Tramlink.

The privately franchised Docklands Light Railway is operated in east inner London.

There are metros in Glasgow and Newcastle, and light rail systems in Birmingham/Wolverhampton, Blackpool, Manchester, Nottingham and Sheffield.

Civil Aviation. All UK airports handled a total of 188·8m. passengers during 2002. Of those, 116·7m. were handled by London area airports (Heathrow, Gatwick, London City, Luton and Stansted).

Busiest airports in 2002:

	Passengers	*International*		*Freight (tonnes)*
Heathrow	63,362,097	56,361,161	Heathrow	1,234,940
Gatwick	29,627,420	26,090,738	Gatwick	242,510
Manchester	18,809,185	15,874,818	East Midlands	219,252
Stansted	16,054,522	13,587,995	Stansted	184,449
Birmingham	8,027,730	6,689,631	Manchester	113,279

Heathrow is Europe's busiest airport for passenger traffic, ahead of Paris Charles de Gaulle, Frankfurt, Amsterdam, Madrid and Gatwick, the sixth busiest (in 2001). More international passengers use Heathrow than any other airport in the world.

Following the Civil Aviation Act 1971, the Civil Aviation Authority (CAA) was established as an independent public body responsible for the economic and safety regulation of British civil aviation. A CAA wholly owned subsidiary, National Air Traffic Services, operates air traffic control. Highlands and Islands Airports Ltd is owned by the Scottish Office and operates ten airports.

There were 16,662 civil aircraft registered in the UK at 1 Jan. 2003.

British Airways is the largest UK airline, with a total of 270 aircraft in service at 31 Dec. 2001, including 35 aircraft used by British Airways (European Operations at Gatwick) Limited. British airways operates long- and short-haul international services, as well as an extensive domestic network. British Airways also has franchise agreements with other UK operators: British Mediterranean Airways, Comair, GB Airways, Loganair, Regional Air and Sun-Air of Scandinavia. Other major airlines in 2001 (with numbers of aircraft): Air 2000 (29); Airtours International Airways Ltd (31); Britannia Airways (31); British Midland (46); Flybe British European (31), formerly Jersey European Airways (UK); KLM UK (37); Manx and British Regional (50); Virgin Atlantic (34). According to CAA airline statistics, in 2001 British Airways flew 538·1m. km and carried 27,471,994 passengers (23,383,377 on international flights). Virgin Atlantic ranked second on the basis of aircraft-km flown (115·1m. km) and Britannia Airways second on the basis of passengers carried (7,905,269). In April 2003 British Airways announced that Concorde, the world's first supersonic jet which began commercial service in 1976, would be permanently grounded from Oct. 2003. In recent years low-cost airlines such as Ryanair and easyJet have become increasingly popular. Serving only domestic and European destinations, they recovered quickly from the slump of the airline business following the attacks on New York and Washington on 11 Sept. 2001.

The most frequently flown route into and out of the UK in 2002 was Heathrow–New York John F. Kennedy and vice-versa (2,513,629 passengers), followed by Heathrow–Paris Charles de Gaulle and vice-versa (2,150,791) and Heathrow–Dublin and vice-versa (2,108,291).

Shipping. The UK-owned merchant fleet (trading vessels over 100 GT) in June 2001 totalled 612 ships of 12·0m. DWT and 9·4m. GT. The UK-owned and registered fleet totalled 369 ships of 3·2m. DWT.

The average age (DWT) of the UK-owned fleet was 10·2 years, while that of the world fleet was 13·3 years. Total gross international revenue in 2000 was £5,122m. The net direct contribution to the UK balance of payments was £1,435m.; there were import savings of £1,830m., giving a total contribution of £3,266m.

The principal ports are (with 1m. tonnes of cargo handled in 2002): Grimsby and Immingham (55·7), London (51·2), Tees and Hartlepool (50·4), Forth (42·2), Milford Haven (34·5). Total traffic in 2002 was 558·3m. tonnes.

Inland Waterways. There are approximately 3,500 miles (5,630 km) of navigable canals and river navigations in Great Britain. Of these, the publicly-owned British Waterways (BW) is responsible for some 385 miles (620 km) of commercial waterways (maintained for freight traffic) and some 1,160 miles (1,868 km) of cruising waterways (maintained for pleasure cruising, fishing and amenity). BW is also responsible for a further 450 miles (732 km) of canals, some of which are not navigable. BW's trading income for the year to 31 March 2003 was £81·7m. Third party-funding principally for restoration schemes contributed £27·9m. Additionally, British Waterways was in receipt of Government grants of £82·0m.

River navigations and canals managed by other authorities include the Thames, Great Ouse and Nene, Norfolk Broads and Manchester Ship Canal.

The Association of Inland Navigation Authorities (AINA) represents some 30 navigation authorities providing an almost complete UK coverage.

Telecommunications. In 2004 there were around 120 operators offering fixed telecommunication services, including six mobile phone operators. Fixed-link telephone services were offered by BT, Mercury Communications, Kingston Communications (Hull), most of the cable operators and the public telecommunications operators. BT (then British Telecom) was established in 1981 to take over the management of telecommunications from the Post Office. In 1984 it was privatized as British Telecommunications plc, changing its trading name from British Telecom to BT in 1991.

By 1998 all of the BT system was served by digital exchanges. There are almost 3·5m. km of optical fibre in place. In 2002 there were 85,066,000 telephone subscribers (equivalent to 1,439·6 per 1,000 population). 91% of UK households had a fixed telephone in 2004, a fall from a peak of 94% in 2000 as increasingly UK consumers began using mobile telephones as their main form of telecommunication. In March 2002, 70% of the lines were residential and 30% business. There were 146,300 public payphones in 2002. BT handles a daily average of 103m. telephone calls a day and 22m. calls to emergency fire, police or ambulance services a year. Total estimated UK retail telecommunications expenditure in the year to Sept. 2004 was £37·7bn., an increase of 4% on the previous year.

In 1996 there were 1·99m. fax receivers. Electronic services include electronic mail ('e-mail') and a complete corporate global messaging network. BT telephone, television and business services are carried by 15–20 satellites. In 2002 BT employed 108,600 persons worldwide.

In 2002 there were 49,677,000 mobile telephone subscribers in the UK (840·78 per 1,000 persons), up from 8,841,000 in 1997. The leading operators are O2 (with an estimated 24·4% share of the market), Orange (23·8%), Vodafone (22·7%), T-Mobile (18·7%), Virgin (7·9%) and 3 (2·4%). 3 was launched by Hutchison on 3 March 2003 and is the UK's first mainland third generation mobile network.

Telecommunications services are regulated by the Office of Communications (*'Ofcom'*) in the interests of consumers.

Internet. In Sept. 2002 there were 34·3m. Internet users in the UK (more than in any other country in Europe), just over 57% of the total population. According to a survey published in Dec. 1999, 3·6m. children between the ages of seven and 16 used the Internet, with 52% of users being boys, compared to 61% in March 1999. In Oct. 1998, 42% of users were at home and 38% at work. In 2000, 45% of households had a home computer; there were 24·0m. PCs in total in 2002 (405·7 per 1,000 inhabitants). By the end of 2004 around 30% of fixed lines were either ISDN or broadband enabled and there were over 6m. UK broadband subscribers (38% of all Internet connections).

Postal Services. Royal Mail Group plc operates three distinct businesses: Royal Mail (letter delivery), Parcelforce Worldwide (parcel delivery) and Post Office Ltd (retailing and agency services). Every area of the country is served by regional offices for each of the businesses. Royal Mail collects and delivers 82m. letters a day to the 27m. UK addresses. Other services include electronic mail, guaranteed mail deliveries (same-day and overnight to UK addresses), and Swiftair deliveries to 140 other countries and territories. The British Postal Consultancy Service provides advice to administrations abroad.

In 2002 there were almost 17,500 post offices, around 600 operated directly by Post Office Ltd, the remainder (sub-post offices) on a franchise or agency basis, and 120,000 posting points. Staff numbered 200,000 in 2001–02.

SOCIAL INSTITUTIONS

Justice. *England and Wales.* The legal system of England and Wales, divided into civil and criminal courts, has at the head of the superior courts, as the ultimate court of appeal, the House of Lords, which hears each year appeals in civil matters, including a certain number from Scotland and Northern Ireland, as well as some appeals in criminal cases. In order that civil cases may go from the Court of Appeal to the House of Lords, it is necessary to obtain the leave of either the Court of Appeal or the House itself, although in certain cases an appeal may lie direct to the House of Lords from the decision of the High Court. An appeal can be brought from a decision of the Court of Appeal or the Divisional Court of the Queen's Bench Division of the High Court in a criminal case provided that the Court is satisfied that a point of law 'of general public importance' is involved, and either the Court or the House of Lords is of the opinion that it is in the public interest that a further appeal should be brought. As a judicial body, the House of Lords consists of the Lord Chancellor (although the present Lord Chancellor, Lord Falconer of Thoroton, has chosen not to sit judicially), the Lords of Appeal in Ordinary, commonly called Law Lords, and such other members of the House as hold or have held high judicial office. The final court of appeal for certain of the Commonwealth countries is the Judicial Committee of the Privy Council which, in addition to Privy Counsellors who are or have held high judicial office in the UK, includes others who are or have been Chief Justices or Judges of the Superior Courts of Commonwealth countries.

The Government published proposals in 2003 to set up a new Supreme Court, separate from the House of Lords, which would take over responsibility for the cases heard by the House of Lords and the devolution cases presently heard by the Judicial Committee of the Privy Council. Provisions to give effect to this were included in the Constitutional Reform Bill introduced in 2004, which is expected to complete its parliamentary passage during 2005.

Civil Law. The main courts of original civil jurisdiction are the High Court and county courts.

The High Court has exclusive jurisdiction to deal with specialist classes of case e.g. judicial review. It has concurrent jurisdiction with county courts in cases involving contract and tort although it will only hear those cases where the issues are complex or important. The High Court also has appellate jurisdiction to hear appeals from lower tribunals.

The judges of the High Court are attached to one of its three divisions: Chancery, Queen's Bench and Family; each with its separate field of jurisdiction. The Heads of the three divisions are the Lord Chief Justice (Queen's Bench), the

Vice-Chancellor (Chancery) and the President of the Family Division. In addition there are 107 High Court judges (100 men and seven women). For the hearing of cases at first instance, High Court judges sit singly. Appellate jurisdiction is usually exercised by Divisional Courts consisting of two (sometimes three) judges, though in certain circumstances a judge sitting alone may hear the appeal. High Court business is dealt with in the Royal Courts of Justice and by over 130 District Registries outside London.

County courts can deal with all contract and tort cases, and recovery of land actions, regardless of value. They have upper financial limits to deal with specialist classes of business such as equity and Admiralty cases. Certain county courts have been designated to deal with family, bankruptcy, patents and discrimination cases.

There are about 220 county courts located throughout the country, each with its own district. A case may be heard by a circuit judge or by a district judge. Defended claims are allocated to one of three tracks—the small claims track, the fast track and the multi-track. The small claims track provides a simple and informal procedure for resolving disputes, mainly in claims for debt, where the value of the claim is no more than £5,000. Parties should be able to do this without the need for a solicitor. Other claims valued between £5,000 and £15,000 will generally be allocated to the fast track, and higher valued claims which could not be dealt with justly in the fast track may be allocated to the multi-track.

Specialist courts include the Patents Court, which deals only with matters concerning patents, registered designs and appeals against the decision of the Comptroller General of Patents. Cases suitable to be heard by a county court are dealt with at Central London County Court.

The Court of Appeal (Civil Division) hears appeals in civil actions from the High Court and county courts, and tribunals. Its President is the Master of the Rolls, aided by up to 37 Lords Justices of Appeal (as at 1 Jan. 2004) sitting in six or seven divisions of two or three judges each.

Civil proceedings are instituted by the aggrieved person, but as they are a private matter, they are frequently settled by the parties through their lawyers before the matter comes to trial. In very limited classes of dispute (e.g. libel and slander), a party may request a jury to sit to decide questions of fact and the award of damages.

Criminal Law. At the base of the system of criminal courts in England and Wales are the magistrates' courts which deal with over 96% of criminal cases. In general, in exercising their summary jurisdiction, they have power to pass a sentence of up to six months imprisonment and to impose a fine of up to £5,000 on any one offence. They also deal with the preliminary hearing of cases triable at the Crown Court. In addition to dealing summarily with over 2·0m. cases, which include thefts, assaults, drug abuse, etc., they also have a limited civil and family jurisdiction.

Magistrates' courts normally sit with a bench of three lay justices. Although unpaid they are entitled to loss of earnings and travel and subsistence allowance. They undergo training after appointment and they are advised by a professional legal adviser. In central London and in some provincial areas full-time District Judges (formerly known as stipendiary magistrates) have been appointed. Generally they possess the same powers as the lay bench, but they sit alone. On 31 March 2004 the total strength of the lay magistracy was 28,029 including 13,846 women. Justices are appointed on behalf of the Queen by the Lord Chancellor.

Justices are selected and trained specially to sit in Youth and Family Proceedings Courts. Youth Courts deal with cases involving children and young persons up to and including the age of 17 charged with criminal offences (other than homicide and other grave offences). These courts normally sit with three justices, including at least one man and one woman, and are accommodated separately from other courts.

Family Proceedings Courts deal with matrimonial applications and Children Act matters, including care, residence and contact and adoption. These courts normally sit with three justices including at least one man and one woman.

Above the magistrates' courts is the Crown Court. This was set up by the Courts Act 1971 to replace quarter sessions and assizes. Unlike quarter sessions and assizes, which were individual courts, the Crown Court is a single court which is capable of sitting anywhere in England and Wales. It has power to deal with all trials on indictment and has inherited the jurisdiction of quarter sessions to hear appeals, proceedings on committal of persons from the magistrates' courts for sentence, and certain original proceedings on civil matters under individual statutes.

The jurisdiction of the Crown Court is exercisable by a High Court judge, a Circuit judge or a Recorder or Assistant Recorder (part-time judges) sitting alone, or, in specified circumstances, with justices of the peace. The Lord Chief Justice has given directions as to the types of case to be allocated to High Court judges (the more serious cases) and to Circuit judges or Recorders respectively.

Appeals from magistrates' courts go either to a Divisional Court of the High Court (when a point of law alone is involved) or to the Crown Court where there is a complete re-hearing on appeals against conviction and/or sentence. Appeals from the Crown Court in cases tried on indictment lie to the Court of Appeal (Criminal Division). Appeals on questions of law go by right, and appeals on other matters by leave. The Lord Chief Justice or a Lord Justice sits with judges of the High Court to constitute this court. Thereafter, appeals in England and Wales can be made to the House of Lords.

There remains as a last resort the invocation of the royal prerogative exercised on the advice of the Home Secretary. In 1965 the death penalty was abolished for murder and abolished for all crimes in 1998.

All contested criminal trials, except those which come before the magistrates' courts, are tried by a judge and a jury consisting of 12 members. The prosecution or defence may challenge any potential juror for cause. The jury decides whether the accused is guilty or not. The judge is responsible for summing up on the facts and directing the jury on the relevant law. He sentences offenders who have been convicted by the jury (or who have pleaded guilty). If, after at least two hours and ten minutes of deliberation, a jury is unable to reach a unanimous verdict it may, on the judge's direction, provided that in a full jury of 12 at least ten of its members are agreed, bring in a majority verdict. The failure of a jury to agree on a unanimous verdict or to bring in a majority verdict may involve the retrial of the case before a new jury.

The Employment Appeal Tribunal. The Employment Appeal Tribunal, which is a superior Court of Record with the like powers, rights, privileges and authority of the High Court, was set up in 1976 to hear appeals on questions of law against decisions of employment tribunals and of the Certification Officer. The appeals are heard by a High Court Judge sitting with two members (in exceptional cases four) appointed for their special knowledge or experience of industrial relations either on the employer or the trade union side, with always an equal number on each side. The great bulk of their work is concerned with the problems which can arise between employees and their employers.

Military Courts. Offences committed by persons subject to service law under the Army Act 1955, the Air Force Act 1955 or the Naval Discipline Act 1957 may be dealt with either summarily or by courts-martial.

The Personnel of the Law. All judicial officers are independent of Parliament and the Executive. They are appointed by the Crown on the advice of the Prime Minister or the Lord Chancellor or directly by the Lord Chancellor himself, and hold office until retiring age. Under the Judicial Pensions and Retirement Act 1993 judges normally retire by age 70 years.

The legal profession is divided; barristers, who advise on legal problems and can conduct cases before all courts, usually act for the public only through solicitors, who deal directly with the legal business brought to them by the public and have rights to present cases before certain courts. The distinction between the two branches of the profession has been weakened since the passing of the Courts and Legal Services Act 1990, which has enabled solicitors to obtain the right to appear as advocates before all courts. Long-standing members of both professions are eligible for appointment to most judicial offices.

For all judicial appointments up to and including the level of Circuit Judge (except for Recordership, which is achieved on promotion from assistant Recordership), it is necessary to apply in writing to be considered for appointment. Vacancies are advertised. A panel consisting of a judge, an official and a lay member decide whom to invite for interview and also interview the shortlisted applicants. They make recommendations to the Lord Chancellor, who retains the right of final recommendation to the Sovereign or appointment, as appropriate.

Legal Services. The system of legal aid in England and Wales was established after the Second World War under the Legal Aid and Advice Act 1949. The Legal Aid Board was then set up under the Legal Aid Act 1988, and took over the administration of legal aid from the Law Society in 1989. The Legal Services Commission (LSC) was set up under the Access to Justice Act 1999 and replaced the Legal Aid Board on 1 April 2000. The LSC is an executive non-departmental public body. It comprises a Chair and eight members, all appointed by the Lord Chancellor. It is responsible for the development and administration of two schemes in England and Wales: the *Community Legal Service*, which from 1 April 2000 replaced the old civil scheme of legal aid, bringing together networks of funders and suppliers into partnerships to provide the widest possible access to information and advice; and the *Criminal Defence Service*, which from 2 April 2001 replaced the old system of criminal legal aid and provides criminal services to people accused of crimes. Only organizations with a contract with the LSC are able to provide advice or representation funded by the LSC.

Under the Community Legal Service, which improves access to justice for those most in need, the LSC directly funds legal services for eligible clients. Some solicitors are prepared to give a free or low-cost initial interview whether or not the client qualifies for funding. The different levels of service in civil matters are *Legal Help, Help at Court, Approved Family Help, Family Mediation, Legal Representation* and *Support Funding.* Approved Family Help is available in two forms (*Help with Mediation* and *General Family Help*), as are Legal Representation (*Investigative Help* and *Full Representation*) and Support Funding (*Investigative Support* and *Litigation Support*).

The purpose of the Criminal Defence Service is to ensure that people suspected or accused of a crime have access to advice, assistance and representation, as the interests of justice require. The different levels of service are: *Police Station Advice and Assistance* (covers support for individuals questioned by police about an offence, whether or not they have been arrested); *Advice and Assistance* (covers help from a solicitor with general advice, writing letters, negotiating, obtaining a barrister's opinion and preparing a written case); *Advocacy Assistance* (covers the cost of a solicitor to prepare a client's case and initial representation in certain proceedings in both the magistrates' and the crown court); *Representation* (covers the cost of a solicitor to prepare a client's defence before a court appearance and to represent the client there, plus dealing with issues such as bail).

In 2001–02 the Commission received funding of £1·2bn. with which to fund the provision of services and spent £71·6m. on administration costs. Community Legal Services payments in 2001–02 came to £734·5m. (1,005,000 acts of assistance) and net Criminal Defence Services payments to £508·3m. (1,697,200 acts of assistance), giving net Legal Services Commission payments of £1,242·8m. and a total of 2,702,200 acts of assistance.

See also SCOTLAND.

CIVIL JUDICIAL STATISTICS

ENGLAND AND WALES	*2002*
Appellate Courts	
Judicial Committee of the Privy Council	89
House of Lords	45
Court of Appeal	1,088
High Court of Justice (appeals and special cases from inferior courts)	5,413
Courts of First Instance (excluding Magistrates' Courts and Tribunals)	
High Court of Justice:	
Chancery Division	35,919
Queen's Bench Division	18,624
County courts: Matrimonial suits	171,054
County courts: Other	1,626,779
Restrictive Practices Court	—

CRIMINAL STATISTICS

ENGLAND AND WALES	*Total number of offenders*[1]		*Indictable offences*[1]	
	2002	*2003*	*2002*	*2003*
Aged 10 and over				
Proceeded against in magistrates' courts	1,924,828	2,000,822	517,065	509,179
Found guilty at magistrates' courts	1,361,637	1,431,520	281,188	278,089

	Total number of offenders[1] 2002	2003	Indictable offences[1] 2002	2003
Aged 10 and over				
Found guilty at the Crown Court	59,648	59,690	57,093	56,998
Cautioned	225,355	241,803	142,931	150,748
Aged 10 and under 18				
Proceeded against in magistrates' courts	146,568	140,790	81,025	74,671
Found guilty at magistrates' courts	90,725	89,658	45,397	43,166
Found guilty at the Crown Court	3,821	2,883	3,713	2,787
Cautioned[2]	86,588	91,933	56,649	58,646

[1]On the principal offence basis. [2]From 1 June 2000 the Crime and Disorder Act 1998 came into force nationally and removed the use of cautions for persons under 18 and replaced them with reprimands and final warnings.

British Crime Survey (BCS) interviews in 2002–03 estimate there were approximately 12·3m. crimes. This represents a decrease of 2% compared with the estimate for 2001–02. In the year to March 2003 crimes recorded by the police in England and Wales totalled 5·9m. which, once the impact of the National Crime Recording Standard has been taken into account, suggests an underlying fall of 3% compared to the year to March 2002. 80% of all crimes were against property. In the 12 months ending March 2002 a total of 5·5m. offences were recorded by the police in England and Wales.

In Sept. 2003 the prison population in England and Wales was 73,741 (72,097 in Sept. 2002). In 2001 the incarceration rate of 137 people per 100,000 inhabitants was the highest in western Europe. The annual average prison population rose 58% between 1992 and 2002, but the recorded crime level went up by only 18%. During this time the female prison population rose by 175%, from 1,562 to 4,299, but the male prison population only rose by 54%. These figures do not include prisoners held in police cells.

See also SCOTLAND *and* NORTHERN IRELAND.

Police. In England and Wales there are 43 police forces, each maintained by a police authority typically comprising nine local councillors, three magistrates and five independent members. London is policed by the Metropolitan Police Service (responsible to the 23-member Metropolitan Police Authority, 12 of whom are members of the Greater London Assembly) and the City of London Police (whose police authority is the City of London Corporation). A tripartite arrangement (Secretary of State for Scotland, Chief Constable and Police Authority) exists for the accountability of the police service in Scotland.

Figures show that the total strength of the police service in England and Wales at 31 March 2003 was 133,366 (including 25,390 women). Police officers are supported by police staff and at the end of March 2003 there were 63,105 police staff (43,948 female). In addition there were 11,037 special constables (including 3,319 women). Total provision for policing in England and Wales to be supported by grant in 2004–05 was £10·1bn. This is a cash increase of £400m. over 2003–04, or 4·2%, and builds on substantial government investment in the Police Service over the past three years.

Religion. The Anglican Communion has originated from the Church of England and parallels in its fellowship of autonomous churches the evolution of British influence beyond the seas from colonies to dominions and independent nations. The Archbishop of Canterbury presides as *primus inter pares* at the decennial meetings of the bishops of the Anglican Communion at the Lambeth Conference and at the biennial meetings of the Primates and the Anglican Consultative Council. The last Conference was held in Canterbury in 1998 and was attended by 743 bishops. Average attendance at Sunday worship in 2001 numbered 1·6m., compared to 3·5m. in 1950.

The Anglican Communion consists of 38 self-governing Churches. These are: The Anglican Church of Aotearoa, New Zealand and Polynesia; The Anglican Church of Australia; The Church of Bangladesh; The Episcopal Anglican Church of Brazil; The Church of the Province of Burundi; The Anglican Church of Canada; The Church of the Province of Central Africa; The Anglican Church of the Central America Region; The Province of the Anglican Church of the Congo; The Church of England; Hong Kong Sheng Kung Hui; The Church of the Province of the Indian

Ocean; The Church of Ireland; Nippon Sei Ko Kai; The Episcopal Church in Jerusalem and the Middle East; The Church of the Province of Kenya; The Anglican Church of Korea; The Church of the Province of Melanesia; The Anglican Church of Mexico; The Church of the Province of Myanmar (Burma); The Church of the Province of Nigeria; The Church of North India; The Church of Pakistan; The Anglican Church of Papua New Guinea; The Philippine Episcopal Church; The Province of the Episcopal Church of Rwanda; The Scottish Episcopal Church; The Church of the Province of South East Asia; The Church of the Province of Southern Africa; The Anglican Church of the Southern Cone of America; The Church of South India; The Episcopal Church of the Sudan; The Church of the Province of Tanzania; The Church of the Province of Uganda; The Episcopal Church in the United States of America; The Church in Wales; The Church of the Province of West Africa; and The Church in the Province of the West Indies. There are Extra Provincial Dioceses of Bermuda, Cuba, Portugal, Puerto Rico, Spain, Sri Lanka and Venezuela, and new provinces are also currently in formation. Churches in Communion include the Mar Thoma Syrian Church, the Philippine Independent Church, and some Lutheran and Old Catholic Churches in Europe. The Church in China is known as a 'post denominational' Church whose formation included Anglicans in the Holy Catholic Church in China.

England and Wales. The established Church of England, which baptizes about 20% of the children born in England (i.e. excluding Wales but including the Isle of Man and the Channel Islands), is Anglican. Civil disabilities on account of religion do not attach to any class of British subject. Under the Welsh Church Acts, 1914 and 1919, the Church in Wales and Monmouthshire was disestablished as from 1 April 1920, and Wales was formed into a separate Province.

The Queen is, under God, the supreme governor of the Church of England, with the right, regulated by statute, to nominate to the vacant archbishoprics and bishoprics. The Queen, on the advice of the First Lord of the Treasury, also appoints to such deaneries, prebendaries and canonries as are in the gift of the Crown, while a large number of livings and also some canonries are in the gift of the Lord Chancellor.

There are two archbishops (at the head of the two Provinces of Canterbury and York), and 42 diocesan bishops including the bishop of the diocese in Europe, which is part of the Province of Canterbury. Dr Rowan Williams was enthroned as *Archbishop of Canterbury* in Feb. 2003. Each archbishop has also his own particular diocese, wherein he exercises episcopal, as in his Province he exercises metropolitan, jurisdiction. In Dec. 2002 there were 62 suffragan and assistant bishops, 41 deans and provosts of cathedrals and 114 archdeacons. The *General Synod*, which replaced the Church Assembly in 1970 in England, consists of a House of Bishops, a House of Clergy and a House of Laity, and has power to frame legislation regarding Church matters. The first two Houses consist of the members of the Convocations of Canterbury and York, each of which consists of the diocesan bishops and elected representatives of the suffragan bishops, six for Canterbury province and three for York (forming an Upper House); deans and archdeacons, and a certain number of proctors elected as the representatives of the priests and deacons in each diocese, together with, in the case of Canterbury Convocation, four representatives of the Universities of Oxford, Cambridge, London and the Southern Universities, and in the case of York two representatives of the Universities of Durham and Newcastle and the other Northern Universities, and three archdeacons to the Armed Forces, the Chaplain General of Prisons and two representatives of the Religious Communities (forming the Lower House). The House of Laity is elected by the lay members of the Deanery Synods but also includes three representatives of the Religious Communities. The Houses of Clergy and Laity also include a small number of *ex officio* members. Every Measure passed by the General Synod must be submitted to the Ecclesiastical Committee, consisting of 15 members of the House of Lords nominated by the Lord Chancellor and 15 members of the House of Commons nominated by the Speaker. This committee reports on each Measure to Parliament, and the Measure receives the Royal Assent and becomes law if each House of Parliament resolves that the Measure be presented to the Queen.

Parochial affairs are managed by annual parochial church meetings and parochial church councils. In 2002 there were 12,900 ecclesiastical parishes, inclusive of the

Isle of Man and the Channel Islands. These parishes do not, in many cases, coincide with civil parishes. Although most parishes have their own churches, not every parish nowadays can have its own incumbent or priest. About 2,000 non-stipendiary clergy hold a bishop's licence to officiate at services.

In 2002 there were 5,060 incumbents excluding dignitaries, 1,935 other clergy of incumbent status and 1,502 assistant curates working in the parishes.

Women have been admitted to Holy Orders (but not the Episcopate) as deacons since 1987 and as priests since 1994. At 31 Dec. 2002 there were 1,247 full-time stipendiary women clergy, 1,197 of whom were in the parochial ministry. Between 1993 and 2002, 495 clergymen resigned because they disagreed with the ordination of women. 67 clergymen subsequently re-entered the Church of England ministry and of the 495 who resigned, 258 are known to have joined the Roman Catholic Church and 29 the Orthodox Church.

Private persons possess the right of presentation to over 2,000 benefices; the patronage of the others belongs mainly to the Queen, the bishops and cathedrals, the Lord Chancellor, and the colleges of the universities of Oxford and Cambridge. In addition to the dignitaries and parochial clergy already identified there were, in 2002, 112 cathedral and 309 full-time non-parochial clergy working within the diocesan framework, giving a total of 9,182 full-time stipendiary clergy working within the diocesan framework as at Dec. 2002. In addition there were 249 part-time stipendiary clergy. Although these figures account for the majority of active clergy in England, there are many others serving in parishes and institutions who cannot be quantified with any certainty. They include 1,159 full-time hospital, Forces, prison, industrial, and school and college chaplains.

Of the 40,609 buildings registered for the solemnization of marriages at 30 June 2000 (statistics from the Office of National Statistics), 16,481 belonged to the Church of England and the Church in Wales, and 24,128 to other religious denominations (Methodist, 6,641; Roman Catholic, 3,342; Baptist, 3,109; United Reformed, 1,675; Congregational, 1,257; Calvinistic Methodist, 1,084; Jehovah's Witnesses, 817; Salvation Army, 751; Brethren, 742; Unitarians, 165; other Christian, 4,095; Sikhs, 147; Muslims, 127; other non-Christian, 176). Of the 249,227 marriages celebrated in 2001 (331,150 in 1990), 60,878 were in the Established Church and the Church in Wales (115,328 in 1990), 28,111 in other denominations (43,837 in 1990) and 160,238 were civil marriages in Register Offices (156,875 in 1990).

Roman Catholics in England and Wales were estimated at 4,121,004 in 2000. There are 22 dioceses in five provinces and one Bishopric of the Forces (also covers Scotland). Cormac Murphy O'Connor was installed as *Archbishop of Westminster* in March 2000. He was created a cardinal in Feb. 2001. In Sept. 2003 there were two Roman Catholic cardinals. There are five archbishops, 17 other diocesan bishops and seven auxiliary or assistant bishops. There are 5,429 priests in active ministry and 2,814 parish churches. There are 1,260 convents of female religious, who number 8,656.

Membership of other denominations in the UK in 1991 (and 1975): Presbyterians, 1,291,672 (1·65m.); Methodists, 483,387 (0·61m.); Baptists, 241,842 (0·27m.); other Protestants, 123,677; independent churches, 408,999; Orthodox, 265,258 (0·2m.); Afro-Caribbean churches, 69,658; Latter-day Saints (Mormons) (1998), 173,800; Jehovah's Witnesses, 0·12m.; Spiritualists, 60,000; Muslims, 0·99m. (0·4m.); Sikhs, 0·39m. (0·12m.); Hindus, 0·14m. (0·1m.); Jews, 108,400 (0·11m.).

In 2001 for the first time the census asked an optional question about religion. In England and Wales 37·3m. people described themselves as Christian. In England, 3·1% of the population stated their religion as Muslim, 1·1% Hindu, 0·7% Sikh, 0·5% Jewish and 0·3% Buddhist. In Wales, 0·7% of the population stated their religion as Muslim, 0·2% Buddhist, 0·2% Hindu, 0·1% Jewish and 0·1% Sikh. In England and Wales 7·7m. people said they had no religion (14·6% in England and 18·5% in Wales). Just over 4m. people chose not to answer the religion question.

In Scotland the 2001 census asked two questions on religion—religion of upbringing and current religion. For religion of upbringing, the largest groups were Church of Scotland (47%), no religion (18%) and Roman Catholic (17%). The equivalent percentages for current religion were 42%, 28% and 16%.

Across all denominations, adult church attendance in the UK was less than 8% of the population in 2000.

The Salvation Army is an international Christian church working in 109 countries. In 2004 in the UK it had 821 local church centres and 92 social service centres with 4,545 employees and 1,507 active Salvation Army officers (ministers).

There is a 400-member Board of Deputies of British Jews.

In 2002 there were approximately 1·57m. visits to York Minster, 1·11m. to Canterbury Cathedral, 1·06m. to Westminster Abbey, London and 781,000 to St Paul's Cathedral, London.

See also SCOTLAND *and* NORTHERN IRELAND.

Bradley, I., *Marching to the Promised Land: Has the Church a Future?* London, 1992.
De La Noy, M., *The Church of England: a Portrait.* London, 1993.

Education. *Adult Literacy and Numeracy.* The government published the *Skills for Life Strategy* in 2001 in response to the recommendations in the 1999 Moser report (*A Fresh Start. Improving Literacy and Numeracy).* The strategy covers adults aged 16 and above at skills levels of pre-entry up to and including Level 2. The results of the 2003 *Skills for Life Needs and Impact Survey* showed that in England 5·2m. adults aged 16–65 have literacy levels below Level 1 (equivalent to the level expected of an average 11 year old) and 15m. have numeracy skills below Level 1. By July 2003, 470,000 adults had achieved a first literacy, language or numeracy qualification. Ultimately, the strategy aims to help 2·25m. adults improve their literacy, language and numeracy skills by 2010, with an interim target of 1·5m. adults by 2007.

The Publicly Maintained System of Education. Compulsory schooling begins at the age of five (four in Northern Ireland) and the minimum leaving age for all pupils is 16. No tuition fees are payable in any publicly maintained school (but it is open to parents, if they choose, to pay for their children to attend independent schools run by individuals, companies or charitable institutions). The post-school or tertiary stage, which is voluntary, includes universities, further education establishments and other higher education establishments (including those which provide courses for the training of teachers), as well as adult education and the youth service. Financial assistance (grants and loans) is generally available to students in higher education and to some students on other courses in further education.

National Curriculum. The National Curriculum was introduced in 1988 and revised in 1999. It determines the content of what will be taught, sets attainment targets for learning and determines how performance will be assessed and reported.

The National Curriculum comprises the core subjects of English, maths and science; and foundation subjects of information communication technology, design and technology, history, geography, modern foreign languages, art and design, music, PE and citizenship.

At key stage 4 (ages 14–16) schools must provide access for each pupil to a minimum of one course in the arts (art and design, music, dance, drama and media arts), one course in the humanities (history and geography), at least one modern foreign language, and design and technology. However, since Sept. 2004 these subject areas are no longer compulsory for key stage 4 pupils.

In addition, pupils must be taught religious education, sex education (though parents have the right to withdraw their children from either) and, for pupils aged over 14, careers education. Every school must also provide a form of daily collective worship, but with the right to withdraw.

Early Years Education. Early years education services include: state nursery schools, nursery classes in primary schools and reception classes; private, voluntary and independent sector nursery schools; and childminder networks. There are 35,000 settings in the state private and voluntary sectors delivering the government's early education curriculum. Since March 2004 all three and four year-olds have been provided with a free, part-time, early education place available at any of these settings.

Primary Schools. These provide compulsory education for pupils from the age of five up to the age of 11 (12 in Scotland). Most public sector primary schools take boys and girls in mixed classes. Some pre-compulsory age pupils attend nursery classes within primary schools, however, and in England some middle schools cater for pupils at either side of the secondary education transition age. There are 22,509 public sector mainstream primary schools with an average of 22 pupils per teacher.

Middle Schools. A number of local education authorities operate a middle school system. These provide for pupils from the age of 8, 9 or 10 up to the age of 12, 13 or 14, and are deemed either primary or secondary according to the age range of the pupils.

Secondary Schools. There are 4,225 secondary schools in Great Britain providing for pupils from the age of 11 upwards. Some local authorities have retained selection at age 11 for entry to grammar schools, of which there are 234. There are 130 secondary modern schools providing a general education up to the minimum school leaving age of 16, although exceptionally some pupils stay on beyond that age. In public sector mainstream secondary schools in Great Britain there are an average 16 pupils per teacher.

Almost all local education authorities operate a system of comprehensive schools to which pupils are admitted without reference to ability or aptitude. There are 3,420 such schools in Great Britain with over 3·4m. pupils. With the development of comprehensive education, various patterns of secondary schools have come into operation. Principally these are: 1) All-through schools with pupils aged 11 to 18 or 11 to 16; pupils over 16 being able to transfer to an 11 to 18 school or a sixth form college providing for pupils aged 16 to 19. (Since 1 April 1993, sixth form colleges have been part of the further education sector—there are 102 sixth form colleges). 2) Local education authorities operating a three-tier system involving middle schools where transfer to secondary school is at ages 12, 13 or 14. These correspond to 12 to 18, 13 to 18 and 14 to 18 comprehensive schools respectively. 3) In areas where there are no middle schools a two-tier system of junior and senior comprehensive schools for pupils aged 11 to 18, with optional transfer to these schools at age 13 or 14.

Specialist Schools. These include Business and Enterprise Colleges, Mathematics and Computing Colleges, Science Colleges, Engineering Colleges, Technology Colleges, Language Colleges, Art Colleges, Music Colleges, Humanities Colleges and Sports Colleges. There is a programme to help existing maintained secondary schools to specialize in a particular area of the curriculum, while continuing to cover the full National Curriculum. To be included in the programme, schools must raise sponsorship and then prepare development plans, in competition with other schools, to seek extra government funding. They must also demonstrate how they will share their resources and expertise with local schools and the wider community. The first Technology Colleges operated from Sept. 1994. By Sept. 2001 there were 685 Specialist Schools in England. In 2004 there were 1,956 Specialist Schools.

City Technology Colleges. Established in partnership between government and business sponsors under the Education Reform Act 1988, there are 14 independent all-ability secondary schools. They teach the full National Curriculum but give special emphasis to technology, science and mathematics. Government meets all recurrent costs. Sponsors are required to provide a 20% contribution towards the cost of all capital projects.

Music and Dance Scheme (formerly the Music and Ballet Scheme). The 'Aided Pupil Scheme' for boys and girls with outstanding talent in music or dance (principally ballet) helps parents with the fees and boarding costs at eight specialist private schools in England. Since Sept. 2004 a national grants scheme has been piloted.

Special Education. It is estimated that, nationally, some 20% of the school population will have special educational needs at some time during their school career. In just over 2% of cases the Local Education Authority will need to make a statutory assessment of special educational needs under the Education Act 1996. (In Scotland pupils are assessed for a Record of Needs.)

Maintained schools must use their best endeavours to make provision for such pupils. The Special Educational Needs Code of Practice, a revised version of which came into force on 1 Jan. 2002, gives practical guidance.

Further Education (Non-University). In April 2001 the Learning and Skills Council (LSC) took over the responsibility for funding the Further Education (FE) sector in

England. The LSC is primarily responsible for funding full- and part-time education and training provision for people aged 16 to 19 in FE colleges, sixth form colleges, work-based and LEA maintained institutions. It also funds some higher education in FE sector colleges and since April 2002 has had responsibility for school sixth form funding. It also makes provision for learning basic skills and adult and community learning for those aged 19 and over.

Further education is the largest sector providing educational opportunities for the over 16s. There are 415 FE colleges in England, with 3·9m. students. Of the students on Council funded provision, 18% were under 19 and 82% were adults.

In Wales, the National Council for Education and Training (CETW) funds FE provision. The Scottish FEFC (SFEFC) funds FE colleges in Scotland, while the Department for Employment and Learning funds FE colleges in Northern Ireland.

The Youth Service. The priority age group for the service is 13–19 year olds, but the target age group may extend to 11–25 year olds. Provision is usually in the form of youth clubs and centres, or through ‘detached’ or outreach work aimed at young people at risk from alcohol or drug misuse, or of drifting into crime. There is an increasing emphasis on youth workers working with disaffected, and socially excluded, young people.

The Learning and Skills Act, 2000 gives the Secretary of State power to secure the provision of support for all 13–19 year olds for the purpose of encouraging and enabling young people to stay on and to participate in education and training.

Local Authority youth services are required to provide adequate facilities for further education including social, physical and recreational training and organized leisure time. The Youth Service provides a key contribution to the Connexions Service (a free information, guidance, advice and job placement service to all young people under the age of 21 years), which began operating in England in April 2001. In 2004–05, £460m. was invested. There are currently 88 national voluntary youth organizations running a total of 98 projects. This includes nine joint projects involving two or more organizations.

Independent/State School Partnerships Grant Scheme. The aim is to promote collaborative working between the independent and state school sectors to raise standards in education. A total of 47 one, two, and three year projects are receiving £1·6m. of funding which commenced in 2003.

Higher Education (HE) Student Support. Students are expected to make a contribution towards their tuition fees. The maximum that a student was expected to pay towards their tuition in 2004–05 was £1,150. The annual income threshold at which fees start to be payable is set at £21,475. It is expected that about 60% of all students will not have to pay fees. Students on teacher training courses (other than first degrees), in the fifth or later years of medical and dental courses, and on NHS-funded courses in professions allied to medicine, pay no fees.

Loans are available to help with students’ living costs. All students are entitled to 75% of the maximum loan, with the remaining quarter subject to income assessment. The maximum loans available in 2002–03 were: £5,050 (living away from home and studying in London); £4,095 (living away from home and studying outside London); and £3,240 (living at home). These loans do not have to be repaid until the student has left university or college and is earning over £10,000 a year. They are repaid on an income contingent basis, set at 9% of gross income over £10,000 a year.

In 2004–05 part-time students were eligible for a fee grant of up to £575 and a course grant of up to £250 for help with other costs.

Applications for support in HE are made through Local Education Authorities. Students’ loan accounts are managed by the Student Loans Company (SLC).

Extra, non-repayable, help is targeted at: those with disabilities; those with dependants; and those entering HE from low-income families in inner city areas. Help is also available from universities and colleges for students who get into financial difficulties. In 2004–05 the amount available to be distributed by universities and colleges to students in financial difficulties was £70m.

Postgraduate studentships and research grants are available from the Research Councils and the Arts and Humanities Research Board (AHRB). There are six grant-awarding Research Councils which each report to the Office of Science and

Technology in the Department for Trade and Industry. They offer awards to students studying within the broad spectrum of economics, engineering, astronomy, and medical, biological and physical sciences. There are three types of funding: advanced course studentships which are for masters level taught courses, usually of one year's duration, research masters training awards and standard research studentships, which are for PhD or MPhil students on programmes of up to three years full-time or five years part-time.

The AHRB also makes awards for postgraduate study and research. It funds studentships in the humanities for Masters and Doctoral programmes, as well as awards for students undertaking a range of professional or vocational training in these subject areas. Both Research Council and AHRB funding is awarded on a competitive basis. In 2002–03 the six Research Councils granted 6,538 awards, while in the same year the AHRB made 1,809 awards. The British Academy complements the work of the AHRB and the Economic and Social Research Council by supporting individual scholars with personal research grants, for amounts up to £5,000; postdoctoral fellowships; research readerships and professorships; grants with international programmes, including overseas exchange schemes; and support for conferences.

Career Development Loans (CDLs). Introduced in 1988, CDLs are specifically designed to help individuals acquire and improve vocational skills, and are aimed at those who would otherwise not have reasonable or adequate access to the funds. Loans of between £300 and £8,000 can be applied for to support up to two years of education or learning (plus up to one year's practical work experience where it forms part of the course). The Department for Education and Skills operates the programme in partnership with three high street banks (Barclays, The Co-operative and the Royal Bank of Scotland). The Department for Education and Skills pays the interest on the loan for the period of supported learning and for up to one month afterwards. The individual then repays the loan to the bank in accordance with their loan agreement. Subject to certain conditions it may be possible for individuals to defer their loan re-payments for up to 17 months.

By Oct. 2004 over £750m. had been advanced to over 208,000 applicants.

Teachers. Qualified teacher status (QTS) is linked to an undergraduate or postgraduate course of teacher training. Computerized skills tests in numeracy and literacy now form part of the requirements for QTS. Newly qualified teachers are then required to complete an induction programme during their first year of teaching.

Those who are recognized as qualified teachers in Scotland or Northern Ireland are also entitled to apply to the General Teaching Council for England or the General Teaching Council for Wales for qualified teacher status. Teachers who are nationals of participating member states of the European Economic Area who are recognized as qualified in their own countries may also be entitled to apply for qualified teacher status if they meet the requirements on the mutual recognition of qualifications.

Those who have trained overseas in a country outside of the European Economic Area with at least two years' teaching experience may be eligible for assessment against the induction and qualified teacher status standards without further training. Those who are successful are exempted from serving an induction period.

From Sept. 2000 a new, flexible, modular postgraduate route was introduced to allow trainees to receive more individualized teacher training. This takes account of any prior learning and experience, and is broken up into flexible modules which trainees can undertake when convenient to them.

In 2003–04 there were about 33,930 new entrants to conventional initial teacher training courses.

In Jan. 2004, 472,500 (provisional) full-time equivalent teachers were employed in maintained schools in the UK.

Finance. Total managed education and training expenditure by central and local government in the UK for 2004–05 was £52·0bn. (£49·4bn. in 2001–02 and £35·4bn. in 1994–95). This equates to 5·4% of GDP (4·9% in 2001–02 and 5·1% in 1994–95).

Independent Schools. Independent schools which belong to an association affiliated to the Independent Schools Council (accounting for 80% of pupils) are subject to an inspection regime agreed between the government and the ISC. Non-association schools are inspected by HM inspectors from OFSTED on a five–six year cycle.

The earliest of the independent schools were founded by medieval churches. Many were founded as 'grammar' (classical) schools in the 16th century, receiving charters from the reigning sovereign. Reformed mainly in the middle of the 19th century, among the best-known are Eton College, founded in 1440 by Henry VI; Winchester College (1394), founded by William of Wykeham, Bishop of Winchester; Harrow School, founded in 1560 as a grammar school by John Lyon, a yeoman; and Charterhouse (1611). Among the earliest foundations are King's School, Canterbury, founded 600; King's School, Rochester (604) and St Peter's, York (627).

Higher Education. In 2003–04 there were almost 2·1m. higher education students in the UK at some 90 universities, 60 higher education colleges or on higher education courses in further education colleges. The number of male and female students is roughly equal, although female students do now outnumber males. 25% of the UK population between the ages of 25 and 64 have been through tertiary education, compared to an OECD average of 22%.

Total funding for higher education institutions in England was around £12·7bn. in 2002–03. Approximately 60% of this comes from UK or European Union governments in the form of grants via the funding councils, public contributions to standard tuition fees and research grants and contracts. Higher education institutions are funded by four UK bodies, one each for England, Scotland, Wales and Northern Ireland. Their roles include: allocating funds for teaching and research; promoting high-quality education and research; advising government on the needs of higher education; informing students about the quality of higher education available; and ensuring the proper use of public funds.

The *Open University* received its Royal Charter on 1 June 1969 and is an independent, self-governing institution, awarding its own degrees at undergraduate and postgraduate level. It is financed by the government through the Higher Education Funding Council for England for all its students in England, Wales and Northern Ireland and through the Scottish HEFC for the teaching of its students in Scotland, and by the receipt of students' fees. At the heart of most courses is a series of specially produced textbooks or 'course units' (which are also widely used in the rest of the HE sector). They are closely integrated with a varying mix of set books, recommended reading, television programmes, audio and video tapes, home experiment kits, computer-based learning programmes, multimedia resources and network services. There are also 339 local tutorial centres where face-to-face tutorials may be offered. No formal qualifications are required for entry to undergraduate courses. Residents from most countries of Western Europe aged 18 or over may apply (though some courses are not available outside the UK). There are over 200 undergraduate courses; many are available on a one-off basis. In 2003–04 there were over 149,700 undergraduates and over 20,700 postgraduate level students. The university has 4,784 full-time staff working at Milton Keynes and in 13 Regional Centres throughout the country. There are almost 8,000 part-time associate lecturers.

The only university independent of the state system is the *University of Buckingham*, which opened in 1976 and received a Royal charter in 1983. It offers two-year honours degrees, the academic year commencing in Jan., July or Oct., and consisting of four ten-week terms. There are four areas of study: Business; Humanities; Law; and Sciences. In 2003 there were 578 full-time and 43 part-time undergraduate students and 105 postgraduate students. There were 58 teachers (seven part-time).

All universities charge fees, but financial help is available to students from several sources, and the majority of students receive some form of financial assistance.

See also SCOTLAND *and* NORTHERN IRELAND.

British Council. The purpose of the British Council is to build mutually beneficial relationships between people in the UK and other countries, and to increase appreciation of the UK's creative ideas and achievements. Established in 1934 and incorporated by Royal Charter in 1940, it is the UK's international organization for educational and cultural relations. Its headquarters are in London and Manchester, with further centres in Belfast, Cardiff and Edinburgh. Independent and non-political, it is represented in 110 countries, running a mix of offices, libraries, information centres, Knowledge and Learning Centres and English-teaching operations. Its main areas of activity are in education and training, examination administration, English language teaching, learning and capacity building, the arts and sciences, sport, governance and civil society. The British Council's total income in 2003–04 was £473m. This was made up of government grants (£171m.), revenues from English-language teaching and client-funded education services (£199m.) and development programmes, principally in education and training, which are managed on behalf of the British government and other clients (£103m.).

Chair: Lord Kinnock.

Director-General: David Green, KCMG.

Headquarters: 10 Spring Gdns, London, SW1A 2BN.

Website: http://www.britishcouncil.org

Health. The National Health Service (NHS) in England and Wales started on 5 July 1948. There is a separate Act for Scotland.

The NHS is a charge on the national income in the same way, for example, as the armed forces. Every person normally resident in the UK is entitled to use any part of the service, and no insurance qualification is necessary.

Since its inception, the NHS has been funded from general taxation and national insurance (NI) contributions, and the present government has maintained the original principle that the NHS should be a service provided to all those who need it, regardless of their ability to pay or where they live. In 2003–04 the NHS in England was funded 20·4% by NI contributions, 73·5% by general taxation and 2·1% by charges for drugs and dental treatment, and the rest from other receipts. Health authorities may raise funds from voluntary sources; hospitals may take private, paying patients.

In 2003–04 the planned total expenditure on health as a percentage of GDP in the UK was 8·1%; the planned UK net NHS expenditure for 2003–04 was £74·8bn.

Organization. The National Health Service and Community Care Act, 1990, provided for a major restructuring of the NHS. From 1 April 1991 health authorities became the purchasers of healthcare, concentrating on their responsibilities to plan and obtain services for their local residents by the placement of health service contracts with the appropriate units. Day-to-day management tasks became the responsibility of hospitals and other units, with whom the contracts are placed, in their capacity as providers of care.

In April 1996 the Regional Health Authorities were replaced by eight regional offices of the NHS Executive. The District Health Authorities and Family Health Service Authorities were replaced by comprehensive Health Authorities directly financed by central government's Hospital and Community Health Services funds. The budget for 1996–97 was £2,260m.

The key responsibility of Health Authorities is to ensure that the health needs of their local communities are met. They have the purchasing power to commission hospital and community health services for their residents. In doing so they have a duty to ensure that high standards are maintained and that they are securing the best possible value for money.

The Health Authorities manage the Family Doctor (or General Medical) Service and also organize the general dental, pharmaceutical and ophthalmic services for their areas. Doctors may take part in the Family Doctor Service, and are paid for their NHS work; they may also take private fee-paying patients.

NHS Trusts are established as self-governing units within the NHS. Trusts are responsible for the ownership and management of the hospitals or other establishments or facilities vested in them, and for carrying out the individual functions set out in their establishment orders. In April 1996 there were 520 Trusts, representing most hospitals.

General practitioners (GPs) may apply for fundholding status, responsible for their own NHS budget for a specified range of goods and services. There are two types of fundholder: Standard fundholders for practices with at least 5,000 patients in England and 4,000 in Wales and Scotland, who purchase the full range of in- and out-patient services; and Community fundholders, for smaller practices of at least 3,000 patients, who purchase only community nursing services and diagnostic tests. In 1996 there were some 14,000 fundholding GPs in 3,300 practices, covering 47% of the population.

Services. The NHS broadly consists of hospital and specialist services, general medical, dental and ophthalmic services, pharmaceutical services, community health services and school health services. In general these services are free of charge; the main exceptions are prescriptions, spectacles, dental and optical examination, dentures and dental treatment, amenity beds in hospitals, and some community services, for which contributory charges are made with certain exemptions.

In 2002 there were 28,031 Unrestricted Principals and Equivalents (UPEs) in England each with an average of 1,838 patients. There were 1,782 in Wales with an average of 1,704 patients each and 3,765 in Scotland with an average of 1,392. There were 18,400 general dental practitioners including their assistants in England, 1,015 in Wales and 2,123 in Scotland. In Great Britain in 2002 there were 78,580 hospital medical staff and 367,520 (headcount) qualified nursing, midwifery and health visiting staff (an increase of 68,554 from 1990) excluding agency staff. In 2002–03 provision of beds in England was 38 per 10,000 population. There were 186,290 hospital beds in England in 2002–03 (232,201 in 1992–93).

Private. In recent years increasing numbers of people have turned to private medical insurance. This covers the costs of private medical treatment (PMI) for curable short-term medical conditions. PMI includes the costs of surgery, specialists, nursing and accommodation at a private hospital or in a private ward of an NHS hospital. Approximately 11% of the UK population have private medical insurance. The leading companies are BUPA Healthcare, AXA PPP healthcare and Norwich Union Healthcare Ltd.

In 2001, 27% of the population of the UK aged 15 and over smoked. In 1974 the percentage had been 45%, with 51% of males and 41% of females smoking. Over the years the difference between the percentage of men and of women who smoke has been declining; in 2001, 28% of men and 26% of women smoked. Among 11-to-15-year-olds 12% of girls but only 9% of boys smoked in 2000. The overall percentage of the UK population who are smokers is similar to the average for the EU as a whole, but among men the percentage of smokers in the UK is lower than in the EU as a whole whereas among women it is higher. Alcohol consumption has increased in recent years. Whereas in 1961 the average Briton consumed the equivalent of 4·5 litres of pure alcohol a year, by 2003 this figure had risen to 9·1 litres. By 2000, 21·0% of the population were considered obese (having a body mass index over 30), compared to 14·0% in 1991 and 7·0% in 1980.

The UK's AIDS rate stands at 24·1 cases per 100,000 population.

A survey published by the World Health Organization in June 2000 to measure health systems in all of the sovereign countries and find which country has the best overall health care ranked the UK in 18th place.

See also NORTHERN IRELAND.

Personal Social Services. Under the Local Authority Social Services Act, 1970, and in Scotland the Social Work (Scotland) Act, 1968, the welfare and social work services provided by local authorities were made the responsibility of a new local authority department—the Social Services Department in England and Wales, and Social Work Departments in Scotland headed by a Director of Social Work, responsibility in Scotland passing in 1975 to the local authorities. The social services thus administered include: the fostering, care and adoption of children, welfare services and social workers for people with learning difficulties and the mentally ill, the disabled and the aged, and accommodation for those needing residential care services. Legislation of 1996 permits local authorities to make cash payments as an alternative to community care. In Scotland the Social Work Departments' functions also include the supervision of persons on probation, of adult offenders and of persons released from penal institutions or subject to fine supervision orders.

Personal Social Services staff numbered 208,300 in 2002. The total cost of these services was £13,598m. for 2001–02. Expenditure is reviewed by the Social Services Inspectorate and the Audit Commission (in Scotland by the Social Work Services Inspectorate and the Accounts Commission).

Welfare. The National Insurance Act 1965 now operates under the Social Security Contributions and Benefits Act 1992 and the Social Security Administration Act 1992.

Since 1975 Class 1 contributions have been related to the employee's earnings and are collected with PAYE income tax. Class 2 and Class 3 contributions remain flat-rate, but, in addition to Class 2 contributions, those who are self-employed may be liable to pay Class 4 contributions, which for the year 2005–06 are at the rate of 8% on profits or gains between £4,896 and £32,760 (with a further 1% contribution on any profit exceeding the upper limit), which are assessable for income tax under Schedule D. The non-employed and others whose contribution record is not sufficient to give entitlement to benefits are able to pay a Class 3 contribution of £7·35 per week in 2005–06 voluntarily, to qualify for a limited range of benefits. Class 2 weekly contributions for 2005–06 for men and women are £2·10. Class 1A contributions are paid by employers who provide employees with a car and fuel for their private use.

The Social Security Pensions Act 1975 introduced earnings-related retirement, invalidity and widows' pensions. Members of occupational pension schemes may be contracted out of the earnings-related part of the state scheme relating to retirement and widows' benefits. Employee's national insurance contribution liability depends on whether he/she is in contracted-out or not contracted-out employment.

Full-rate contributions for non-contracted-out employment in 2005–06:

Weekly Earnings (in £1)	*Employee pays*	*Employer pays*
Below 82 (Lower Earnings Limit)	Nil	Nil
82–94 (Primary Threshold/Secondary Threshold)	Nil	Nil
94–630 (Upper Earnings Limit)	11%	12·8%
Over 630 (Upper Earnings Limit)	See footnote[1]	12·8%

[1]£58·96 plus 1% on earnings over £630 per week.

For contracted-out employment, the contracted-out rebate for primary contributions (employee's contribution) is 1·6% of earnings between the lower earnings limit and the upper earnings limit for all forms of contracting-out; the contracted-out rebate for secondary contributions (employer's contributions) is 3·5% of earnings between the lower earnings limit and the upper earnings limit.

Contributions together with interest on investments form the income of the *National Insurance Fund* from which benefits are paid. 28,350,000 persons (12,590,000 women) paid contributions in 2001–02, including 25,620,000 employees at standard rate.

Receipts, 2001–02 (in £1m.), 79,972, including: contributions, 58,050; investment income, 1,146; compensation from Consolidated Fund for recoveries, 710. Disbursements (in £1m.), 55,795, including: Retirement Pensions, 45,677; Widow's Pensions, 1,132; administration, 873; Jobseekers' Allowance (Contributory), 478; Redundancy Payments, 232; Pensioners' Lump Sums, 131; transfers to Northern Ireland, 110; Maternity Allowances, 57.

Statutory Sick Pay (SSP). Employers are responsible for paying statutory sick pay (SSP) to their employees who are absent from work through illness or injury for up to 28 weeks in any three-year period. All employees aged between 16 and 65 (60 for women) with earnings above the Lower Earnings Limit are covered by the scheme whenever they are sick for four or more days consecutively. The weekly rate is £68·20. For most employees SSP completely replaces their entitlement to state incapacity benefit which is not payable as long as any employer's responsibility for SSP remains.

Contributory benefits. Qualification for these depends upon fulfilment of the appropriate contribution conditions, except that persons who are incapable of work as the result of an industrial accident may receive incapacity benefit followed by invalidity benefit without having to satisfy the contributions conditions.

Jobseekers' Allowance. Unemployed persons claiming the allowance must sign a 'Jobseekers' Agreement' setting out a plan of action to find work. The allowance is not payable to persons who left their job voluntarily or through misconduct. Claimants with sufficient National Insurance contributions are entitled to the allowance for six months regardless of their means; otherwise, recipients qualify through a means test and the allowance is fixed according to family circumstances, at a rate corresponding to Income Support for an indefinite period. In May 2003 there were 832,300 people receiving the Jobseekers' Allowance (631,700 males). Payments start at £33·85 per week.

Incapacity benefit. Entitlement begins when entitlement to SSP (if any) ends. There are three rates: a lower rate for the first 28 weeks; a higher rate between the 29th and 52nd week; and a long-term rate from the 53rd week of incapacity. It also comprises certain age additions and increases for adult and child dependants. A more objective medical test of incapacity for work was introduced for incapacity benefit as well as for other social security benefits paid on the basis of incapacity for work. This test applies after 28 weeks' incapacity for work and assesses ability to perform a range of work-related activities rather than the ability to perform a specific job. Benefit is taxable after 28 weeks. Some 1,506,500 claims were being made in Feb. 2003.

Statutory Maternity Pay. Pregnant working women may be eligible to receive statutory maternity pay directly from their employer for a maximum of 26 weeks if average gross earnings are £82 a week or more (2005–06). There are two rates: a higher rate (90% of average earnings for the first six weeks), and a lower rate of £106·00 or 90% of earnings (whichever is less) for up to 20 weeks. For women who do not qualify for Statutory Maternity Pay, including self-employed women, there is a Maternity Allowance.

A payment of £500 from the Social Fund (Sure Start Maternity Grant) may be available if the mother or her partner are receiving income support, income-based Jobseeker's Allowance, Working Families' Tax Credit or Disabled Person's Tax Credit. It is also available if a woman adopts a baby.

Statutory Paternity Pay. From 6 April 2003 working fathers have the right to two weeks paid paternity leave providing average gross earnings are £82 a week or more (2005–06). This will be paid at the same rate as the lower rate of Statutory Maternity Pay (£106 a week or 90% of average weekly earnings if this is less than £106).

Bereavement Benefits. There are three main types of Bereavement Benefits available to men and women widowed on or after 9 April 2001: bereavement payment, widowed parent's allowance, bereavement allowance. *Bereavement Payment* is a single tax-free lump sum of £2,000 payable immediately on bereavement. A widower/widow may be able to get this benefit if their late spouse has paid enough National Insurance Contributions (NIC) and was under 60 at death; or was not getting a Category A State Retirement Pension at death. *Widowed Parent's Allowance* is a weekly benefit payable when the widower/widow is receiving Child Benefit. The amount of Widowed Parent's Allowance is based on the late spouse's NIC record. He/she may also get benefit for the eldest dependent child and further higher benefit for each subsequent child; also an additional pension based on their late spouse's earnings. If the late spouse was a member of a contracted-out occupational scheme or a personal pension scheme, that scheme is responsible for paying the whole or part of the additional pensions. Widowed Parent's Allowance is taxable. *Bereavement Allowance* is a weekly benefit payable to widows and widowers without dependent children and is payable between age 45 and State Pension age. The amount of Bereavement Allowance payable to a widower/widower between 45 and 54 is related to their age at the date of entitlement. Their weekly rate is reduced by 7% for each year they are aged under 55 so that they get 93% rate at age 54, falling to 30% at age 45. Those aged 55 or over at the date of entitlement will get the full rate of Bereavement Allowance. The amount of Bereavement Allowance is based on the late spouse's NIC record and is payable for a maximum of 52 weeks from the date of bereavement. A widower/widow cannot get a Bereavement Allowance at the same time as a Widowed Parent's Allowance. There were some 196,100 recipients of widows' benefits in March 2003.

Retirement Pension. The state retirement ('old-age') pension scheme has two components: a basic pension and an earnings-related pension (State Earnings Related Pension—SERPS). The amount of the first is subject to National Insurance contributions made; SERPS is 1·25% of average earnings between the lower weekly earnings limit for Class I contribution liability and the upper earnings limit for each year of such earnings, building up to 25% in 20 years. For individuals reaching pensionable age after 6 April 1999, changes in the way pensions are calculated will be phased in over ten years to include a lifetime's earnings with an accrual rate of 20%. Pensions are payable to women at 60 years of age and men at 65, but the age differential will be progressively phased out starting in April 2010. There are standard rates for single persons and for married couples, the latter being 159% of two single-person rates. Proportionately reduced pensions are payable where contribution records are deficient.

Employees in an occupational scheme may contract out of SERPS provided that the occupational scheme provides a pension not less than the 'guaranteed minimum pension'. Self-employed persons, and also employees, may substitute personal pension schemes for SERPS.

Self- and non-employed persons may contribute voluntarily for retirement pension.

Persons who defer claiming their pension during the five years following retirement age are paid an increased amount, as do men and women who had paid graduated contributions. In March 2003 some 11,242,500 persons were receiving National Insurance retirement pensions (7,037,000 women and 4,205,500 men). The basic state pension in 2005–06 is £82·05 per week for a single person and £131·20 per week for a married couple. Since 1 Oct. 1989 the pension for which a person has qualified may be paid in full whether a person continues in work or not irrespective of the amount of earnings. Although for males the official retirement age is 65, in 1995 the average actual retirement age among males was 62.

At the age of 80 a small age addition is payable. In addition non-contributory pensions are now payable, subject to residence conditions, to persons aged 80 and over who do not qualify for a retirement pension or qualify for one at a low rate.

Pensioners whose pension is insufficient to live on may qualify for Income Support.

Non-Contributory Benefits.

Child Benefit. Child benefit is a tax-free cash allowance normally paid to the mother. The weekly rates are highest for the eldest qualifying child (£17·00 weekly in 2005–06) and less for each other child (£11·40 weekly in 2005–06). Child benefit is payable for children under 16, for 16- and 17-year-olds registered for work or training, and for those under 19 receiving full-time non-advanced education. Some 7,342,000 families received benefit in Aug. 2003.

Child Support Agency. The Child Support Agency is responsible for calculating, collecting and enforcing child maintenance payments. The non-resident parent pays 15% of their net income if they have one child, 20% for two and 30% for three or more children. The agency currently deals with around 1·3m. child support cases.

Working Tax Credit. This tackles poor work incentives and persistent poverty among working people. For families with children, credit is available for those with incomes up to a maximum of around £14,000. It also extends support to low-income working people without children aged 25 or over working 30 hours or more a week. The Working Tax Credit is not just restricted to those with children; the amount of the award varies considerably depending on the prevailing circumstances. Both single persons and couples may be eligible.

Child Tax Credit. The Child Tax Credit aims at creating a single system of support for families with children, payable irrespective of the work status of the adults in the household. This means that the Child Tax Credit forms a stable and secure income bridge as families move off welfare and into work. It also provides a common framework of assessment, so that all families are part of the same inclusive system. The Child Tax Credit provides a family element of up to £545 per year and a child element of up to £1,690 per child per year in addition to Child Benefit. The amount paid varies depending on the number of children and the gross annual joint income.

Guardian's Allowance. A person responsible for an orphan child may be entitled to a guardian's allowance in addition to child benefit. Normally, both the child's parents must be dead but when they never married or were divorced, or one is missing, or serving a long sentence of imprisonment, the allowance may be paid on the death of one parent only. In May 2002 there were 2,300 recipients.

Attendance Allowance. This is a tax-free Social Security benefit for disabled people over 65 who need help with personal care. The rates are increased for the terminally ill. There were some 1,340,700 recipients in May 2003.

Carers' Allowance. This is a taxable benefit which may be paid to those who forgo the opportunity of full-time work to care for a person who is receiving attendance allowance, constant attendance allowance or the highest or middle-core component of Disability Living Allowance. There is a weekly rate, with increases for dependants. In March 2002 there were 387,000 recipients.

Disability Living Allowance. This is a non-taxable benefit available to people disabled before the age of 65, who need help with getting around or with personal care for at least three months. The mobility component has two weekly rates, the care component has three. There were some 2,497,600 recipients in May 2003.

Industrial Injuries Disablement and Death Benefits. The scheme provides a system of insurance against 'personal injury by accident arising out of and in the course of employment' and against certain prescribed diseases and injuries owing to the nature of the employment. There are no contribution conditions for the payment of benefit. There were 280,400 recipients in 2001 at any one time. Two types of benefit are provided:

—*Disablement benefit.* This is payable where, as the result of an industrial accident or prescribed disease, there is a loss of physical or mental faculty. The loss of faculty will be assessed as a percentage by comparison with a person of the same age and sex whose condition is normal. If the assessment is between 14–100% benefit will be paid as weekly pension. The rates vary from 20% disabled to 100% disablement. Assessments of less than 14% do not normally attract basic benefit except for certain progressive chest diseases. Pensions for persons under 18 are at a reduced rate. When injury benefit was abolished for industrial accidents occurring and prescribed diseases commencing on or after 6 April 1983, a common start date was introduced for the payment of disablement benefit 90 days (excluding Sundays) after the date of the relevant accident or onset of the disease.

—*Death Benefit.* This is payable to the widow of a person who died before 11 April 1988 as the result of an industrial accident or a prescribed disease. For deaths which occurred on or after 11 April 1988, a widow is entitled to full widow's benefits. Allowances may be paid to people who are suffering from pneumoconiosis or byssinosis or certain other slowly developing diseases due to employment before 5 July 1948. They must not at any time have been entitled to benefit under the Industrial Injuries provision of the Social Security Act, or compensation under Workmen's Compensation Acts, or have received damages through the courts.

War Pensions. Pensions are payable for disablement or death as a result of service in the armed forces. Similar schemes exist for other groups such as merchant seaman injured as a result of war or for civilians injured by enemy action in the Second World War. The amount depends on the degree of disablement. There were some 260,700 recipients in March 2003.

Housing Benefit. The housing benefit scheme assists persons who need help to pay their rent, using general assessment rules and benefit levels similar to those for the income support scheme. The scheme sets a limit of £16,000 on the amount of capital a person may have and still remain entitled. Restrictions on the granting of benefit to persons under 25 were introduced in 1995. In 2003 some 1,838,100 claims for rent rebate and 1,958,300 for rent allowance were being made at any one time.

Income Support. Income Support is a non-contributory benefit for people aged 16 or over, not working 16 hours or more a week or with a partner not working more than 24 hours or more per week, and not required to be available for employment. These include single parents, long-term sick or disabled persons, and those caring for them who qualify for Invalid Care Allowance. Income Support is not payable if the claimant (or claimant and partner together) has capital assets that total more than £8,000. These include savings, investments or property other than their home. Savings/capital assets worth under £3,000 are ignored. Savings between £3,000 and £8,000 are treated as if each £250 or part of £250 brings in an income of £1 per week. Income Support claimants whose partners are of pensionable age may have up to £12,000 and still be entitled to Income Support. Claimants in residential care and nursing homes are allowed to have up to £16,000 and still be entitled to Income Support. From 6 Oct. 2003 a new Pension Credit replaced Minimum Income Guarantee (Income Support for people aged 60 and over). In 2003 there were

3,982,200 Income Support claimants at any one time. The average weekly award was £73·40 in May 2003.

Council Tax Benefit. Subject to rules broadly similar to those governing the provision of income support and housing benefit, people may receive rebates of up to 100% of their council tax. In 2003 some 4,627,800 households received such help. A person who is liable for the council tax may also claim benefit (called 'second adult rebate') for a second adult who is not liable to pay the council tax and who is living in the home on a non-commercial basis.

The Social Fund. This comprises: *Sure Start Maternity Grant* (a payment of up to £500 for each baby expected, born or adopted, payable to persons receiving Income Support, Income-based Jobseekers' Allowance, Child Tax Credit, Working Tax Credit or Pension Credit); *Funeral Payments* (a payment of fees levied by the burial authorities and crematoria, plus up to £700 for other funeral expenses, to persons receiving Income Support, Income-based Jobseekers' Allowance, Housing Benefit, Child Tax Credit, Working Tax Credit or Pension Credit); *Cold Weather Payments* (a payment of £8·50 for any consecutive seven days when the temperature is below freezing to persons receiving income support who are pensioners, disabled or have a child under five); *Winter Fuel Payments* (a payment of £200 to every household with a person aged 60 or over providing they do not live permanently in a hospital, residential care or nursing home, or £300 if the household has someone aged 80 years old or over). The Discretionary Social Fund comprises: *Community Care Grants* (payments to help persons receiving income support to move into the community or avoid institutional care); *Budgeting Loans* (interest-free loans to persons receiving income support for expenses difficult to budget for); *Crisis Loans* (interest-free loans to anyone without resources in an emergency where there is no other means of preventing serious risk to health or safety). Savings over £500 (£1,000 for persons aged 60 or over) are taken into account before payments are made.

Hill, M., *The Welfare State in Britain: a Political History since 1945.* Aldershot, 1993
Timmins, N., *The Five Giants: a Biography of the Welfare State.* London, 1995

CULTURE

World Heritage Sites. Sites under UK jurisdiction which appear on UNESCO's world heritage list are (with year entered on list): Giant's Causeway and Causeway Coast (1986), rock formations on the Antrim Plateau in Northern Ireland; Durham Castle and Cathedral (1986), the largest example of a Norman cathedral; Ironbridge Gorge (1986), built in the 18th century and considered the emblem of the industrial revolution; Studley Royal Park, including the Ruins of Fountains Abbey (1986), developed from the 18th century on the site of a former Cistercian abbey in Yorkshire; Stonehenge, Avebury and Associated Sites (1986), among the world's most famous pre-historic monoliths; Castles and Town Walls of King Edward in Gwynedd (1986), a testament to the early period of English colonization in the late 13th century; St Kilda (1986), a volcanic archipelago on the coast of the Hebrides; Blenheim Palace (1987), seat of the Dukes of Marlborough near Oxford and birthplace of Sir Winston Churchill; City of Bath (1987), with remains from its time as a Roman spa town, and home to many examples of neo-classical Georgian architecture; Hadrian's Wall (1987), built in the second century on the border between England and Scotland; Westminster Palace, Westminster Abbey and Saint Margaret's Church (1987)—the palace is the medieval seat of parliament re-built in the 19th century, the abbey the site of all coronations since the 11th century and Saint Margaret's is a small medieval gothic church; Henderson Island (1988), a South Pacific atoll; Tower of London (1988), a Norman fortress built to guard London; Canterbury Cathedral, St Augustine's Abbey and St Martin's Church (1988), the spiritual seat of the Church of England; Old and New Towns of Edinburgh (1995), the Scottish capital; Gough Island Wildlife Reserve (1995), one of the least disturbed island and marine eco-systems in the region; Maritime Greenwich (1997), including Britain's first Palladian building, designed by Inigo Jones, Christopher Wren's Royal Naval College and the Royal Observatory; Heart of Neolithic Orkney (1999), comprising several important neolithic monuments; Historic Town of St George's and Related Fortifications, Bermuda (2000), an example of early English New World colonialism; Blaenavon Industrial Landscape (2000), a symbol of South Wales' role as a coal and iron provider in the 19th century; Dorset and East Devon Coast (2001), which demonstrate rock formations and fossil remains from the Mesozoic Era; Derwent Valley Mills (2001), 18th-century cotton mills at the forefront of the Industrial Revolution; New Lanark (2001), Robert Owen's model industrial community and cotton mills of the early 19th century; Saltaire (2001), a mid-19th century planned industrial community for the textile industry; Royal Botanical Gardens, Kew (2003), containing important botanical collections in a historic landscape; Liverpool—Maritime Mercantile City (2004).

Broadcasting. Radio and television services are provided by the British Broadcasting Corporation (BBC), by licensees of the Office of Communications (*'Ofcom'*) and by the Welsh-language Sianel Pedwar Cymru (S4C, Channel 4 Wales). The BBC, constituted by Royal Charter until 31 Dec. 1996, has responsibility for providing domestic and external broadcast services, the former financed from the television licence revenue, the latter by government grant. The domestic services provided by the BBC include eight national television services, ten national radio network services and a network of local radio stations. Government proposals for the future of the BBC after 2006 were published in March 2005.

Ofcom is responsible for licensing and regulating all non-BBC TV services (except S4C), provided in and from the UK whether analogue or digital. These include ITV1 (regional and breakfast-time licensees), Channel 4, Channel 5, cable and satellite and additional services, such as teletext. Ofcom is also responsible for licensing and regulating independent and national, local and community radio services. S4C is transmitted in Wales, and is funded by the government. The Welsh Authority is the regulator and board of management of S4C.

The BBC's domestic radio services are available on Long Wave, Medium Wave and VHF/FM; those licensed by Ofcom on Medium Wave and VHF/FM. Television services other than those only on cable and satellite are broadcast at UHF in 625-line definition and in colour (by PAL). The BBC World Service, which started life in 1932 as the Empire Service, broadcast in 43 languages to an audience estimated at 150m. in 2002–03. As the self-financed BBC Worldwide TV, the BBC is also involved in commercial joint ventures to provide international television services.

The broadcasting authorities are independent of government and are publicly accountable to Parliament for the discharge of their responsibilities. Their duties and powers are laid down in the BBC Royal Charter and the Communications Act 2003.

All independent (non-BBC) radio and television services other than S4C are financed by the sale of broadcasting advertising time, commercial sponsorship, subscription (in the case of cable and satellite services) and ancillary services, such as sales of goods and products, interactive services and pay-per-view revenues.

Ofcom became the new communications sector regulator at the end of 2003, taking over from the Broadcasting Standards Commission (BSC), the Independent Television Commission (ITC), Oftel, the Radio Authority and the Radiocommunications Agency. The aims of Ofcom are: to balance the promotion of choice and competition with the duty to foster plurality, informed citizenship, protect viewers, listeners and customers and promote cultural diversity; serve the interests of the citizen-consumer as the communications industry enters the digital age; support the need for innovators, creators and investors to flourish within markets driven by full and fair competition between all providers; and to encourage the evolution of electronic media and communications networks to the greater benefit of all who live in the UK.

The number of television receiving licences in force on 31 March 2003 was 23,486,000, of which 23,392,000 were for colour. There were 10·5m. satellite and cable TV subscribers in late 2004 (7·1m. with BSkyB, 2·1m. with NTL and 1·3m. with Telewest). In 2000 there were 84·5m. radio receivers, or 1,432 per 1,000 inhabitants—a figure only exceeded in the USA, with 2,118 per 1,000 inhabitants.

Cinema. In 2002 there were 668 cinemas in the UK with 3,258 screens. Admissions were 175·9m. in 2002. Admissions had totalled 500m. in 1960, but had fallen as low as 54m. in 1984. Gross box office takings in 2002 amounted to £755m. In 2002,

369 films were released in the UK, of which 76 were UK films (including USA/UK films and UK co-productions).

Press. In 2005 there were ten national dailies with a combined average daily circulation in Jan. 2005 of 11,687,194, and 11 national Sunday newspapers (12,849,508). There were also about 100 morning, evening and Sunday regional newspapers and 2,000 weeklies (about 1,000 of these for free distribution). There were about 6,500 other commercial periodicals and 4,000 professional and business journals. In 2000 the number of daily newspapers sold per annum was 4bn., down 20% from 5bn. in 1962. The most widely read daily is the tabloid *The Sun*, with an average daily circulation of 3,382,409 in Jan. 2005. The most widely read Sunday paper is the tabloid *News of the World*, which had an average circulation of 3,823,217 in Jan. 2005.

In Jan. 1991 the Press Complaints Commission replaced the former Press Council. It has 15 members and a chair (Sir Christopher Meyer), including seven editors. It is funded by the newspaper industry.

In 2002 a record 125,390 book titles were published (119,001 in 2001), including 11,810 fiction and 10,519 children's books.

Tourism. In 2001 UK residents made 163·1m. trips within the UK, passing 529·6m. nights in accommodation and spending £26,094m. Of these, 101·2m. were holiday-makers spending £17,016m. There were 22·8m. overseas visitors in 2001 staying 189·5m. nights in accommodation and spending £11,306m. UK residents made 58·3m. trips abroad in 2001. The main countries of origin for foreign visitors in 2001 were: USA (3·6m.), France (2·9m.), Germany (2·3m.), Ireland (2·0m.) and the Netherlands (1·4m.). Between 1997 and 2001 visits by USA residents to the UK increased by 148,000, the largest increase for any single country. Over the same period visits by French residents of the UK fell by the greatest number. The UK is the fifth most popular tourist destination in the world.

The leading attraction in 2001 was Blackpool Pleasure Beach, Lancs, with an estimated 6·5m. visits. The leading tourist attractions charging admission in 2001 were: the British Airways London Eye, with 3,850,000 visits; the Tower of London, with 2,019,210; Eden Project in St Austell, with 1,700,000; Natural History Museum in London, with 1,696,176; and Legoland Windsor, with 1,632,000.

In Sept. 2001 there were 2·1m. (not seasonally adjusted) people working in tourism-related industries.

France is the most popular destination for Britons travelling abroad (12·0m. British visitors in 2001), followed by Spain (11·7m.) and USA (4m.). There were 58·3m. trips abroad made by British residents in 2001, up from 13·4m. in 1978.

Festivals. Among the most famous music festivals are the Promenade Concerts or 'Proms', which take place at the Royal Albert Hall in London every year from July to Sept; the Glyndebourne season in Sussex (May to Aug.); the Aldeburgh Festival in Suffolk (June); the Glastonbury Festival in Somerset (June); and the Buxton Festival in Derbyshire (July). The annual London Film Festival takes place in Nov. Literary festivals include the Hay Festival in Herefordshire (late May/early June) and Cheltenham Festival of Literature in Gloucestershire (Oct.). The Edinburgh Festival and the Fringe Festival both take place in Aug./early Sept. and are major international festivals of culture. The Brighton Festival in May is England's largest arts festival. The multicultural Notting Hill Carnival in London takes place at the end of Aug. Other major events in the annual calendar are the New Year's Parade in London, the Crufts Dog Show at the Birmingham National Exhibition Centre (March), the Ideal Home Exhibition in London (March–April), the London Marathon (April), the Chelsea Flower Show (May), Royal Ascot (horse racing, in June), Wimbledon (tennis, in June–July), Henley Royal Regatta (July), Cowes (yachting, in Aug.) and the Lord Mayor's Show in London (Nov.).

Libraries. In 2001–02 there were 4,614 public libraries, 6 National libraries and 875 Higher Education libraries; they held a combined 284,900,000 volumes. There were 36,111,642 registered library users in 2001–02.

Museums and Galleries. The museums with the highest number of visitors are all in London. In 2001 there were 4,918,985 visits to the National Gallery, 4,800,938 to the British Museum, 3,551,885 to the Tate Modern, 1,696,176 to the Natural History Museum and 1,446,344 to the Victoria and Albert Museum.

DIPLOMATIC REPRESENTATIVES

Of the USA in Great Britain (24/31 Grosvenor Sq., London, W1A 1AE)
Ambassador: Vacant.
Chargé d'Affaires a.i.: David T. Johnson.

Of Great Britain in the USA (3100 Massachusetts Ave., NW, Washington, D.C., 20008)
Ambassador: Sir David Manning, KCMG.

Of Great Britain to the United Nations
Ambassador: Sir Emyr Jones Parry, KCMG.

Great Britain's permanent representative to the European Union
Ambassador: John Grant, CMG.

FURTHER READING

Office for National Statistics titles are published by Palgrave Macmillan. The Stationery Office (TSO) publishes most other government publications.
Palgrave Macmillan, Basingstoke. *UK 20xx.* Palgrave Macmillan.—*Annual Abstract of Statistics.* Palgrave Macmillan.—*Monthly Digest of Statistics.* Palgrave Macmillan.—*Social Trends.* Palgrave Macmillan.—*Regional Trends.* Palgrave Macmillan
Central Office of Information. *The Monarchy.* 1992
Directory of British Associations. Beckenham, annual
Beloff, M., *Britain and the European Union: Dialogue of the Deaf.* London, 1997
Black, Jeremy, *A History of the British Isles.* 2nd ed. Palgrave Macmillan, Basingstoke, 2002
Bogdanor, Vernon, *Devolution in the United Kingdom.* OUP, 1999
Bourke, Richard, *Peace in Ireland: The War of Ideas.* Random House, London, 2003
Cairncross, A., *The British Economy Since 1945: Economic Policy and Performance, 1945–1995.* 2nd ed. London, 1995
Creaton, Heather, *London.* [Bibliography] ABC-Clio, Oxford and Santa Barbara (CA), 1996
Dunleavy, Patrick, Gamble, Andrew, Heffernan, Richard and Peele, Gillian (eds.) *Developments in British Politics 7.* Palgrave Macmillan, Basingstoke, 2003
Gascoigne, B. (ed.) *Encyclopedia of Britain.* London, 1994
Harbury, C. D. and Lipsey, R. G., *Introduction to the UK Economy.* 4th ed. Oxford, 1993
Irwin, J. L., *Modern Britain: an Introduction.* 3rd ed. London, 1994
Leventhal, F. M. (ed.) *20th-Century Britain: an Encyclopedia.* New York, 1995
Marr, A., *Ruling Britannia: the Failure and Future of British Democracy.* London, 1995
McCormick, John, *Contemporary Britain.* Palgrave Macmillan, Basingstoke, 2003
Neumann, Peter R., *Britain's Long War: British Strategy in the Northern Ireland Conflict, 1969–98.* Palgrave Macmillan, Basingstoke, 2003
Oakland, J., *British Civilization: an Introduction.* 3rd ed. London, 1995
Oxford History of the British Empire. 2 vols. OUP, Oxford, 1999
Palmer, A. and Palmer, V., *The Chronology of British History.* London, 1995
Penguin History of Britain. 9 vols. London, 1996
Sked, A. and Cook, C., *Post-War Britain: a Political History.* 4th ed. London, 1993
Speck, W. A., *A Concise History of Britain, 1707–1975.* CUP, 1993
Strong, R., *The Story of Britain.* London, 1996
Turner, Barry, (ed.) *UK Today.* Macmillan, London, 2000

Other more specialized titles are listed under TERRITORY AND POPULATION; CONSTITUTION AND GOVERNMENT; ARMY; NAVY; BANKING AND FINANCE; ELECTRICITY; TRADE UNIONS; RELIGION; *and* WELFARE, *above. See also Further Reading in England, Scotland, Wales and Northern Ireland.*

National Statistical Office: National Statistics, 1 Drummond Gate, London, SW1V 2QQ.
Website: http://www.statistics.gov.uk/

ENGLAND

KEY HISTORICAL EVENTS

Emperor Claudius' invasion in AD 43 established Roman rule in southern England. After the failed rebellions in 60 of Queen Boudicca of the Iceni and the suppression of Wales by 78, there was a long period of peaceful settlement, during which the Romans established new towns such as Londinium (London) and Eboracum (York). After the withdrawal of the Roman legions in the early 5th century, Pictish and Saxon raiders harassed the British towns. Defensive Saxon settlements were at first encouraged by the authorities but their rebellion soon threatened the Roman way of life. The Romano-British were pushed back to higher land in the west by waves of invading Saxons, Angles and Jutes. After a period of Mercian supremacy under Offa in the 8th century, the West Saxons (Wessex) dominated southern England. Danish invasions in 865 established the Danelaw in northern England. Alfred the Great of Wessex and his son Edward resisted Danish expansion, strengthening Anglo-Saxon unity under Alfred's successors—Athelstan became the first king of all England in 927.

Danish rule over England was reasserted by Sweyn in 994 and his son, Canute. The Anglo-Saxon restoration was short-lived; William, duke of Normandy led the Norman Conquest in 1066, defeating Harold II at the Battle of Hastings. When William died in 1087, he left Normandy to his eldest son Robert, thus separating it from England. Henry II, the founder of the Plantagenet dynasty, was feudatory lord of half of France but Henry's son John lost most of the French possessions. The barons forced John to sign the Magna Carta in 1215, later interpreted as the source of English civil liberties. Thereafter, the Norman baronage came to regard themselves as English.

The Hundred Years War (1338–1453) with France ended with the loss of all remaining French possessions except Calais. In 1387 and in later outbreaks, the Black Death reduced the population by over a third. A dynastic struggle between the rival houses of York and Lancaster was concluded by the invasion of Henry Tudor in 1485. His son, Henry VIII, asserted royal authority over the church, breaking with Rome. Tudor power reached its zenith with Elizabeth I. Philip II's Spanish Armada, destroyed in 1588, was sent to turn back the Protestant tide in England and to counter English ambitions in the New World.

The accession of James VI of Scotland to the English throne in 1603 brought the two countries into personal union. Charles I's defeat in the Civil War resulted in a republican Commonwealth but the Stuart monarchy was restored in 1660. England and Scotland were united in 1707 under Anne, queen of Great Britain.

TERRITORY AND POPULATION

At the census taken on 29 April 2001 the area of England was 130,281 sq. km and the population 49,138,831, giving a density of 377 per sq. km. England covers 53·7% of the total area of the United Kingdom. Households at the 2001 census: 21,262,000. Estimated population of England, mid-2004, 50,065,000.

Population (present on census night) at the four previous decennial censuses:

1961	*1971*	*1981*	*1991*
43,460,525[1]	46,018,371[1]	46,226,100[2]	46,382,050

[1]Area now included in Wales formed the English county of Monmouthshire until 1974.
[2]The final count is believed to be over-stated as a result of an error in processing. The preliminary counts presented here rounded to the nearest hundred are thought to be more accurate.

Population at census day 2001:

Males	*Females*	*Total*
23,923,390	25,215,441	49,138,831

For further statistical information, see under Territory and Population, United Kingdom.

Eight 'Standard Regions' (also classified as 'level 1 regions' for EU purposes) are identified in England as economic planning regions. They have no administrative significance. Estimated population of the regions of England (in 1,000), 2001, East Anglia, 2,177; East Midlands, 4,175; West Midlands, 5,267; North, 3,004; North West, 6,244; South East, 18,412 (including Greater London, 7,188); South West, 4,934; Yorkshire and Humberside, 4,967. Although the populations of most of the regions increased during the 1990s, the North, North West, and Yorkshire and Humberside saw their populations decline, by 88,000, 148,000 and 16,000 respectively between 1991 and 2001. The population on census day in 2001 in the nine English Government Office regions was as follows: East, 5,388,154; East Midlands, 4,172,179; London, 7,172,036; North East, 2,515,479; North West, 6,730,800; South East, 8,000,550; South West, 4,928,458; West Midlands, 5,267,337; Yorkshire and the Humber, 4,965,838.

Following the local government reorganization in the mid-1990s, there is a mixed pattern to local government in England. Apart from Greater London, England is divided into 34 counties with two tiers of administration; a county council and district councils. There are six metropolitan county areas containing 36 single-tier metropolitan districts.

In addition, there are 46 single-tier unitary authorities which, with the exception of the Isle of Wight, were formerly district councils in the shire counties of England. The Isle of Wight is a unitary county council.

As a consequence of the establishment of the 46 unitary authorities, a number of county areas were abolished. These were Avon, Cleveland and Humberside. Berkshire County Council was also abolished but the county itself is retained for ceremonial purposes. Greater London comprises 32 boroughs and the City of London.

Area in sq. km of English counties and unitary authorities, and population at census day 2001:

	Area (sq. km)	*Population*
Metropolitan counties		
Greater Manchester	1,276	2,482,352
Merseyside	645	1,362,034
South Yorkshire	1,552	1,266,337
Tyne and Wear	540	1,075,979
West Midlands	902	2,555,596
West Yorkshire	2,029	2,079,217
Non-metropolitan counties		
Bedfordshire (Beds)	1,192	381,571
Buckinghamshire (Bucks)	1,565	479,028
Cambridgeshire (Camb)	3,046	552,655
Cheshire	2,083	673,777
Cornwall and Isles of Scilly	3,563	501,267
Cumbria	6,768	487,607
Derbyshire	2,547	734,581
Devon	6,564	704,499
Dorset	2,542	390,986
Durham	2,226	493,470
East Sussex	1,709	492,324
Essex	3,465	1,310,922
Gloucestershire (Gloucs)	2,653	564,559
Hampshire (Hants)	3,679	1,240,032
Hertfordshire (Herts)	1,643	1,033,977
Kent	3,544	1,329,653
Lancashire (Lancs)	2,903	1,134,976
Leicestershire (Leics)	2,083	609,579
Lincolnshire (Lincs)	5,921	646,646
Norfolk	5,371	796,733
Northamptonshire (Northants)	2,364	629,676
Northumberland	5,013	307,186
North Yorkshire (N. Yorks)	8,038	569,660
Nottinghamshire (Notts)	2,085	748,503
Oxfordshire (Oxon)	2,605	605,492
Shropshire (Salop)	3,197	283,240
Somerset (Som)	3,451	498,093
Staffordshire (Staffs)	2,620	806,737
Suffolk	3,801	668,548
Surrey	1,663	1,059,015
Warwickshire	1,975	505,885
West Sussex	1,991	753,612
Wiltshire (Wilts)	3,255	432,973
Worcestershire	1,741	542,107

	Area (sq. km)	*Population*
Unitary Authorities		
Bath and North East Somerset	346	169,045
Blackburn with Darwen	137	137,471
Blackpool	35	142,284
Bournemouth	46	163,441
Bracknell Forest	109	109,606
Brighton and Hove	83	247,820
Bristol, City of	110	380,615
Darlington	197	97,822
Derby	78	221,716
East Riding of Yorkshire	2,408	314,076
Halton	79	118,215
Hartlepool	94	88,629
Herefordshire, County of	2,180	174,844
Isle of Wight	380	132,719
Kingston upon Hull, City of	71	243,595
Leicester	73	279,923
Luton	43	184,390
Medway	192	249,502
Middlesbrough	54	134,847
Milton Keynes	309	207,063
North East Lincolnshire	192	157,983
North Lincolnshire	846	152,839
North Somerset	374	188,556
Nottingham	75	266,995
Peterborough	343	156,060
Plymouth	80	240,718
Poole	65	138,299
Portsmouth	40	186,704
Reading	40	143,214
Redcar and Cleveland	245	139,141
Rutland	382	34,560
Slough	33	119,070
Southampton	50	217,478
Southend-on-Sea	42	160,256
South Gloucestershire	497	245,644
Stockton-on-Tees	204	178,405
Stoke-on-Trent	93	240,643
Swindon	230	180,061
Telford and Wrekin	290	158,285
Thurrock	163	143,042
Torbay	63	129,702
Warrington	181	191,084
West Berkshire	704	144,445
Windsor and Maidenhead	197	133,606
Wokingham	179	150,257
York	272	181,131

Source: Office of National Statistics

In 2003 London had a population of 7,388,000. Populations of next largest cities were: Birmingham (2003), 992,000; Leeds (2003), 715,000; Sheffield (2003), 513,000; Bradford (2001), 468,000; Liverpool (2003), 442,000; Manchester (2003), 432,000; Bristol (2003), 392,000.

Greater London Boroughs. Total area 1,572 sq. km. Population at census day 2001: 7,172,036 (inner London, 2,765,975). Population by borough (census day 2001):

Borough	Population	Borough	Population	Borough	Population
Barking and Dagenham	163,944	Hammersmith and Fulham[1]	165,243	Lewisham[1]	248,924
Barnet	314,561	Haringey[1]	216,510	Merton	187,908
Bexley	218,307	Harrow	207,389	Newham[1]	243,737
Brent	263,463	Havering	224,248	Redbridge	238,628
Bromley	295,530	Hillingdon	242,435	Richmond upon Thames	172,327
Camden[1]	198,027	Hounslow	212,344	Southwark[1]	244,867
Croydon	330,688	Islington[1]	175,787	Sutton	179,667
Ealing	300,947	Kensington and Chelsea[1]	158,922	Tower Hamlets[1]	196,121
Enfield	273,563	Kingston upon Thames	147,295	Waltham Forest	218,277
Greenwich	214,540	Lambeth[1]	266,170	Wandsworth[1]	260,383
Hackney[1]	202,819			Westminster, City of[1]	181,279

[1]Inner London borough.

Source: Office of National Statistics

The City of London (677 acres) is administered by its Corporation which retains some independent powers. Population at census day 2001: 7,186.

CLIMATE

For more detailed information, see under Climate, United Kingdom.

London, Jan. 39°F (3·9°C), July 64°F (17·8°C). Annual rainfall 25" (635 mm). Birmingham, Jan. 38°F (3·3°C), July 61°F (16·1°C). Annual rainfall 30" (749 mm). Manchester, Jan. 39°F (3·9°C), July 61°F (16·1°C). Annual rainfall 34·5" (876 mm).

RECENT ELECTIONS

At the UK general election held in May 2005, 528 members were returned from England. Voting in Staffordshire South was postponed owing to the death of a candidate shortly before the election.

See also Constitution and Government, Recent Elections and Current Administration in United Kingdom.

DEFENCE

For information on defence, see United Kingdom.

ECONOMY

For information on the economy, see United Kingdom.

ENERGY AND NATURAL RESOURCES

For information on energy and natural resources, see United Kingdom.

Water. The Water Act of Sept. 1989 privatized the nine water and sewerage authorities in England: Anglian; North West (now United Utilities Water plc); Northumbrian; Severn Trent; South West; Southern; Thames; Wessex; Yorkshire. There are also 16 water only companies in England and Wales. The Act also inaugurated the National Rivers Authority, with environmental and resource management responsibilities, and the 'regulator' *Office of Water Services (Ofwat)*, charged with protecting consumer interests.

INDUSTRY

Labour. The unemployment rate in the spring of 2001 was 4·6%, compared to 4·8% for the UK as a whole. Unemployment was lowest in the southeast (3·0%) and highest in the northeast (7·4%).

INTERNATIONAL TRADE

For information on international trade, see United Kingdom.

COMMUNICATIONS

For information on communications, see United Kingdom.

SOCIAL INSTITUTIONS

Education. For details on the nature and types of school, see under Education, United Kingdom.

In 2004–05 education and skills expenditure by Central and Local government in England was expected to top £52bn. In Jan. 2001 there were 506 public-sector nursery and primary schools with nursery classes in England; in addition, there were 2,300 independent schools with provision for children under five (including direct grant nurseries). In 2001 there were 44,990 pupils under five attending nursery schools and pupils under five in nursery and infant classes in primary schools. Some of these children were attending part-time.

In Jan. 2001 there were 4,406,215 pupils at 18,069 primary schools in England, of which 2,070 were infant schools providing for pupils up to the age of about seven, the remainder mainly taking pupils from age five through to 11. Nearly all primary schools take both boys and girls. 15% of primary schools had 100 full-time pupils or fewer.

In Jan. 2001 there were 463 middle schools in England deemed either primary or secondary according to the age range of the school concerned.

In Jan. 2001 there were 3,481 secondary schools in England. Some local authorities have retained selection at age 11 for entry to grammar schools, of which there were 159 in 2001. There were a small number of technical schools in 2001 which specialize in technical studies. There were 145 secondary modern schools in 2001, providing a general education up to the minimum school leaving age of 16, although exceptionally some pupils stay on beyond that age.

Almost all local education authorities operate a system of comprehensive schools to which pupils are admitted without reference to ability or aptitude. In Jan. 2004 there were 2,807 such schools in England with over 2·9m. pupils. With the development of comprehensive education, various patterns of secondary schools have come into operation. Principally these are: 1) All-through schools with pupils aged 11 to 18 or 11 to 16; pupils over 16 being able to transfer to an 11 to 18 school or a sixth form college providing for pupils aged 16 to 19. (There are currently 102 sixth form colleges in England). 2) Local education authorities operating a three-tier system involving middle schools where transfer to secondary school is at ages 12, 13 or 14. These correspond to 12 to 18, 13 to 18 and 14 to 18 comprehensive schools respectively; or 3) In areas where there are no middle schools a two-tier system of junior and senior comprehensive schools for pupils aged 11 to 18 with optional transfer to these schools at age 13 or 14.

Under the Education Act 1996 children have special educational needs if they have a learning difficulty which calls for special educational provision to be made for them. In some cases the Local Education Authority will need to make a statutory assessment of special educational needs under the Education Act 1996, which may ultimately lead to a 'statement'. In England the total number of pupils with statements in 2004 was 261,100. In 2004 there were 1,078 maintained special schools and 70 non-maintained special schools.

Outside the state system of education there were in England about 2,302 independent schools in Jan. 2004, ranging from large prestigious schools to small local ones. Some provide boarding facilities but the majority include non-resident day pupils. There are about 586,940 pupils in these schools, which represent about 7% of the total pupil population in England.

Further Education (Non-University). In 2002–03, 3·9m. students were enrolled at FE colleges in England. Those on Learning and Skills Council funded provision were studying for 6·6m. qualifications. Total funding for the FE sector in 2001–02 was £4,029m.

Higher Education. In England in 2003–04 there were 131 institutions of higher education directly funded by the HEFCE (Higher Education Funding Council for England), of which 77 were universities. The HEFCE distributes public money for teaching and research to universities and colleges. It works in partnership with the higher education sector and advises the government on higher education policy. In 2003–04 the HEFCE was set to distribute £5·5bn. in funding, including £3,399m. for teaching and £1,042m. for research.

a) *Universities*

Name (Location)	*No. of students (2001–02)*	*No. of academic staff (2001–02)*
Anglia Polytechnic University (Chelmsford)	26,735	830
Aston University (Birmingham)	7,200	460
University of Bath	12,685	900
Birkbeck, University of London[1]	17,840	470
University of Birmingham	29,245	2,745
Bournemouth University (Poole)	14,275	685
University of Bradford	11,755	655
University of Brighton	17,830	880
University of Bristol	21,195	2,265
Brunel University (Uxbridge)	14,480	875
University of Cambridge	24,910	4,580
University of Central England in Birmingham	23,150	1,205
University of Central Lancashire (Preston)	33,630	910
City University (London)	18,720	735
Courtauld Institute of Art[1]	373	—
Coventry University	17,655	830
De Montfort University (Leicester)	24,575	1,320
University of Derby	24,145	775
University of Durham	14,230	1,115
University of East Anglia (Norwich)	13,210	1,065
University of East London (London)	13,515	690
University of Essex (Colchester)	9,335	650
University of Exeter	12,520	965
University of Gloucestershire (Cheltenham)	9,785	490
Goldsmiths College[1]	7,595	590
University of Greenwich (London)	18,785	860
University of Hertfordshire (Hatfield)	20,965	1,210
Heythrop College[1]	546	
University of Huddersfield	18,525	680
University of Hull	21,695	955
Imperial College London[1]	11,495	3,795
Institute of Cancer Research[1]	540	—
Institute of Education[1]	4,860	—
Keele University (Newcastle-under-Lyme)	12,180	610
University of Kent at Canterbury	12,785	700
King's College London[1]	19,020	3,255
Kingston University (Kingston-upon-Thames)	17,055	960
Lancaster University	15,790	900
University of Leeds	32,770	2,970
Leeds Metropolitan University	46,110	1,140
University of Leicester	16,875	1,425
University of Lincoln	16,515	565
University of Liverpool	22,200	2,015
Liverpool John Moores University	21,585	1,090
London Business School[1]	1,630	—
London Guildhall University[2]	15,360	615
London School of Economics and Political Science[1]	7,695	—
London School of Hygiene and Tropical Medicine[1]	895	—
London South Bank University	21,125	1,045
Loughborough University of Technology	13,855	1,150
University of Luton	11,430	570
University of Manchester[3]	27,145	3,340
University of Manchester Institute of Science and Technology[3]	7,025	9,580
Manchester Metropolitan University	31,590	1,445
Middlesex University (London)	24,860	1,035
University of Newcastle upon Tyne	19,395	2,285
University of North London[2]	17,335	750
University of Northumbria at Newcastle	23,110	1,300
University of Nottingham	27,800	2,605
Nottingham Trent University	25,015	1,300
Open University	156,425	1,310
University of Oxford	22,695	4,270
Oxford Brookes University	16,530	1,030
University of Plymouth	25,235	1,390
University of Portsmouth	19,755	1,040
Queen Mary, University of London[1]	9,610	1,530

a) *Universities (cont.)*

Name (Location)	No. of students (2001–02)	No. of academic staff (2001–02)
University of Reading	15,850	1,260
Royal Academy of Music[1]	620	—
Royal Holloway, University of London[1]	5,775	685
Royal Veterinary College[1]	950	—
St George's Hospital Medical School[1]	3,470	—
University of Salford	21,490	1,100
School of Oriental and African Studies[1]	3,690	—
School of Pharmacy[1]	1,120	—
University of Sheffield	24,510	2,485
Sheffield Hallam University	26,510	1,455
University of Southampton	22,305	2,410
Staffordshire University (Stoke-on-Trent)	16,165	760
University of Sunderland	14,710	1,170
University of Surrey (Guildford)	14,530	1,105
University of Sussex (Brighton)	12,180	990
University of Teesside (Middlesbrough)	18,525	630
Thames Valley University (London)	23,075	510
University College London[1]	17,805	4,635
University of Warwick (Coventry)	27,510	1,475
University of the West of England, Bristol	24,570	1,285
University of Westminster (London)	24,605	1,145
University of Wolverhampton	21,280	1,050
University of York	10,640	1,120

[1]Part of the University of London, which in 2001–02 had 115,445 internal students plus 30,000 external students. [2]In Aug. 2002 London Guildhall University and University of North London merged to form London Metropolitan University. [3]In Oct. 2004 University of Manchester and University of Manchester Institute of Science and Technology merged to form University of Manchester.

b) *Other Institutions*

Bath Spa University College; Bishop Grosseteste College (Lincoln); Bolton Institute of Higher Education; Arts Institute at Bournemouth; Buckinghamshire Chilterns University College (High Wycombe); Canterbury Christ Church University College; Central School of Speech and Drama (London); Chester College of Higher Education; University College Chichester; Conservatoire for Dance and Drama (London); Cranfield University; Cumbria Institute of the Arts; Dartington College of Arts (Totnes); Edge Hill College of Higher Education (Ormskirk); Falmouth College of Arts; Harper Adams University College (Newport); Homerton College, Cambridge; Institute of Advanced Nursing Education (London); Kent Institute of Art and Design (Maidstone); King Alfred's College, Winchester; Liverpool Hope; University of London (Institutes and Activities); The London Institute; Newman College (Birmingham); University College Northampton; Northern School of Contemporary Dance (Leeds); Norwich School of Art and Design; Ravensbourne College of Design and Communication (Bromley); University of Surrey Roehampton; Rose Bruford College of Speech and Drama (Sidcup); Royal Agricultural College (Cirencester); Royal College of Art (London); Royal College of Music (London); Royal Northern College of Music (Manchester); College of St Mark and St John (Plymouth); St Martin's College (Lancaster); St Mary's College (Twickenham); Southampton Institute; The Surrey Institute of Art and Design, University College (Farnham); Trinity and All Saints College (Leeds); Trinity College of Music (London); Wimbledon School of Art; University College, Worcester; Writtle College (Chelmsford); York St John College.

The Teaching and Higher Education Act 1998 made provision for colleges of higher education with degree-awarding powers to adopt the title 'university college'.

CULTURE

Tourism. The leading attraction in 2001 was Blackpool Pleasure Beach, Lancs, with an estimated 6·5m. visits. The leading tourist attractions charging admission in 2001 were: the British Airways London Eye, with 3,850,000 visits; the Tower of London, with 2,019,210; Eden Project in St Austell, with 1,700,000; Natural History Museum in London, with 1,696,176; and Legoland Windsor, with 1,632,000.

FURTHER READING

Day, Alan, *England.* [Bibliography] ABC-Clio, Oxford and Santa Barbara (CA), 1993

Lloyd, T. O., *Empire, Welfare State, Europe: English History, 1906–1992.* 4th ed. OUP, 1993

Heffer, Simon, *Nor Shall My Sword: The Reinvention of England.* Weidenfeld & Nicolson, London, 1999

Oxford History of England. 16 vols. OUP, 1936–91

SCOTLAND

KEY HISTORICAL EVENTS

Earliest evidence of human settlement in Scotland dates from the Middle Stone Age. Hunters and fishermen on the west coast were succeeded by farming communities as far north as Shetland. The Romans, who were active in the first century AD, built Hadrian's Wall between the Tyne and Solway Firth as their northern frontier. At this time, the Picts formed two kingdoms north of the Firth of Clyde. From the 6th century, the Celtic Scots from Dalriada, northern Ireland, fought with Angles and Britons for control of southern Scotland.

In 843 Kenneth MacAlpine united the Scots and the Picts to found the kingdom of Scotland. A legal and administrative uniformity was established by David I (reigned 1124–53). William the Lion abandoned claims to Northumbria in 1209 but began the alliance with France. In 1286 Edward I of England asserted his claim as overlord of Scotland and appointed his son to succeed to the crown. Resistance to English rule was led by William Wallace and, later, by Robert Bruce, who defeated the English at Bannockburn in 1314. His grandson, Robert II, became the first Stewart (Stuart) king in 1371.

Royal minorities undermined the authority of the crown in the 15th century until the accession of James IV in 1488. Relations with England improved after his marriage to Margaret Tudor in 1503 but when Henry VIII invaded France, James attacked England and was killed at the Battle of Flodden in 1513. The young James V was assailed by conflicting pressures from pro-French and pro-English factions but having secured his personal rule, he entered into two successive French marriages. His daughter, Mary Queen of Scots, married the French Dauphin in 1558. Protestant opposition to French influence was bolstered by Elizabeth I of England, who sent troops. Mary was in France when the Scottish parliament renounced papal authority, bolstering the reformist movement, led by John Knox. Returning to Scotland after her husband's death in 1561, Mary was forced to take refuge in England. Her son, James VI, survived the animosity between his own and his mother's followers to make an alliance with England. Deemed a threat because of her claim to the English throne, Mary was executed on Elizabeth's orders in 1587.

Elizabeth died without issue in 1603 and was succeeded by James. Although he styled himself 'king of Great Britain', England and Scotland remained independent. Charles I alienated much of the Scottish nobility and was defeated in the Bishops' Wars by the Covenanters, who rejected English interference in the Scottish church. Scottish armies fought for both sides in the English Civil War, which led to the execution of Charles I in 1649. However, the Scots soon united to accept Charles II as their king. Having established dominance in England, Cromwell moved against Scotland forcing Charles II into exile. His restoration in 1660 was welcomed in both kingdoms. His successor, James VII (James II of England), was less astute in managing religious and political differences. The collapse of his regime in 1688 and the arrival of William of Orange confirmed the Protestant ascendancy in Scotland and England.

The union of parliament in 1707 brought Scotland more directly under English authority. However, Scotland retained its own legal and ecclesiastical systems. The remaining supporters of James VII, the Jacobites, led two abortive risings on behalf of James's son and grandson (the old and new Pretenders) but were defeated decisively at Culloden in 1746.

TERRITORY AND POPULATION

The total area of Scotland is 77,925 sq. km (2001), including its islands, 186 in number, and inland water 1,580 sq. km. Scotland covers 32·1% of the total area of the United Kingdom.

Population (including military in the barracks and seamen on board vessels in the harbours) at the dates of each census:

Date of enumeration	*Population*	*Pop. per sq. mile*	*Date of enumeration*	*Population*	*Pop. per sq. mile*
1801	1,608,420	53	1841	2,620,184	88
1811	1,805,864	60	1851	2,888,742	97
1821	2,091,521	70	1861	3,062,294	100
1831	2,364,386	79	1871	3,360,018	113

SCOTLAND

Date of enumeration	*Population*	*Pop. per sq. mile*[1]	*Date of enumeration*	*Population*	*Pop. per sq. mile*[1]
1881	3,735,573	125	1951	5,096,415	171
1891	4,025,647	135	1961	5,179,344	174
1901	4,472,103	150	1971	5,228,963	67
1911	4,760,904	160	1981	5,130,735	66
1921	4,882,497	164	1991	4,998,567	60
1931	4,842,980	163	2001	5,062,011	65

[1]Per sq. km from 1971.

Population at census day 2001:

Males	*Females*	*Total*
2,432,494	2,629,517	5,062,011

In 2001, 58,652 people aged three and over spoke Gaelic (65,978 in 1991). Households at the 2001 census: 2,192,000.

The age distribution in Scotland at census day on 2001 was as follows (in 1,000):

Age-group	
Under 5	277
5 and under 10	307
10 ,, 15	323
15 ,, 20	317
20 ,, 25	314
25 ,, 35	699
35 ,, 45	781
45 ,, 55	689
55 ,, 65	550
65 ,, 70	239
70 ,, 75	207
75 ,, 85	271
85 and upwards	88

Land area and population by administrative area (30 June 2002):

Council Area	*Area (sq. km)*	*Population*
Aberdeen City	186	209,270
Aberdeenshire	6,313	227,280
Angus	2,182	108,130
Argyll and Bute	6,909	91,030
Clackmannanshire	159	47,930
Dumfries and Galloway	6,426	147,310
Dundee City	60	144,180
East Ayrshire	1,262	119,740
East Dunbartonshire	175	107,310
East Lothian	679	90,750
East Renfrewshire	174	89,630
Edinburgh, City of	264	448,080
Eilean Siar[1]	3,071	26,200
Falkirk	297	145,560
Fife	1,325	350,700
Glasgow City	175	577,350
Highland	25,659	208,140
Inverclyde	160	83,600
Midlothian	354	80,500
Moray	2,238	86,740
North Ayrshire	885	135,650
North Lanarkshire	470	321,350
Orkney Islands	990	19,210
Perth and Kinross	5,286	135,160
Renfrewshire	261	171,940
Scottish Borders	4,732	107,400
Shetland Islands	1,466	21,940
South Ayrshire	1,222	111,670
South Lanarkshire	1,772	302,110
Stirling	2,187	86,150
West Dunbartonshire	159	92,830
West Lothian	427	159,960
Total	77,925	5,054,800

[1]Formerly Western Isles.

Estimated population of Scotland, mid-2004, 5,061,000 (2,624,000 females and 2,437,000 males), giving a density of 65 per sq. km.

Glasgow is Scotland's largest city, with an estimated population of 577,350 in 2002, followed by Edinburgh, the capital (estimated 2002 population, 448,080), and Aberdeen, with 209,270.

The birthplaces of the 2001 census day population in Scotland were: Scotland, 4,410,400; England, 408,948; Wales, 16,623; Northern Ireland, 33,528; Ireland 21,774; other European Union countries, 44,432; elsewhere, 126,306.

SOCIAL STATISTICS

	Estimated resident population at 30 June[1]	*Total births*	*Live births outside marriage*	*Deaths*	*Marriages*	*Divorces, annulments and dissolutions*
1998	5,120,000	57,319	22,319	59,164	29,668	12,384
1999	5,119,200	55,147	22,722	60,281	29,940	11,864
2000	5,114,600	53,076	22,625	57,799	30,367	11,143
2001	5,064,200	52,527	22,760	57,382	29,621	10,631
2002	5,054,800	51,270	22,534	58,103	29,826	10,826

[1]Includes merchant navy at home and forces stationed in Scotland.

Birth rate, 2002, per 1,000 population, 10·1; death rate, 11·5; marriage, 5·9; infant mortality per 1,000 live births, 5·3; sex ratio, 1,047 male births to 1,000 female. Average age of marriage in 2002: males, 35·2, females, 32·8. Expectation of life, 2002: males, 73·3 years, females, 78·8.

CLIMATE

For more detailed information, see under Climate, United Kingdom.

Aberdeen, Jan. 38°F (3·3°C), July 57°F (13·9°C). Annual rainfall 32" (813 mm). Edinburgh, Jan. 38°F (3·3°C), July 58°F (14·5°C). Annual rainfall 27" (686 mm). Glasgow, Jan. 39°F (3·9°C), July 59°F (15°C). Annual rainfall 38" (965 mm).

CONSTITUTION AND GOVERNMENT

In a referendum on devolution on 11 Sept. 1997, Scotland's voters opted for devolved government, calling for the reinstatement of a separate parliament in Scotland, the first since union with England in 1707. 1,775,045 votes (74·3%) were cast in favour of a Scottish parliament and 614,400 against (25·7%). On a turn-out of 60·4%, around 44·8% of the total electorate voted in favour. For the second question, on the Parliament's tax-raising powers, 1,512,889 votes were cast in favour (63·5%) and 870,263 against (36·5%). This represented 38·4% of the total electorate.

The Scottish Parliament is made up of 129 members and manages a budget of £20bn., set to rise to £26bn. in 2005–06. The parliament may pass laws and has limited tax raising powers; it is also responsible for devolved issues, including health, education, police and fire services; however, 'reserved issues' (foreign policy, constitutional matters, and many domestic areas including social security, trade and industry, and employment legislation) remain the responsibility of the British Parliament in Westminster.

RECENT ELECTIONS

At the UK general election held in May 2005, 59 members were returned from Scotland. Labour won 41 seats; the Liberal Democrats, 11; the Scottish National Party, 6; Conservative, 1. At the June 2004 European Parliament elections Labour won 2 seats, the Scottish National Party 2, the Conservatives 2 and Liberal Democrats 1.

In elections to the Scottish Parliament on 1 May 2003, Labour won 50 seats (4 by regional list), against 27 (18 by regional list) for the Scottish National Party, 18 (15 by regional list) for the Conservatives, 17 (4 by regional list) for the Liberal Democrats, 7 (all by regional list) for the Greens, 6 (all by regional list) for the Scottish Socialist Party (SSP) and 4 ind. Of the 129 seats, 73 were won on a first-past-the-post basis and 56 through proportional representation (regional list). Turn-out was 49%. Donald Dewar was elected as *First Minister* on 13 May 1999. He died on 11 Oct. 2000. Jim Wallace was acting first minister until the election of Henry McLeish on 26 Oct. 2000. McLeish resigned on 8 Nov. 2001 and Wallace again assumed the post temporarily. Jack McConnell was elected first minister on 23 Nov. 2001 and re-elected on 15 May 2003.

See also Constitution and Government, Recent Elections and Current Administration in United Kingdom.

CURRENT ADMINISTRATION

First Minister: Jack McConnell; b. 1960 (Labour).

Presiding Officer: George Reid.

Scottish Executive: http://www.scotland.gov.uk

DEFENCE

For information on defence, see United Kingdom.

ECONOMY

Currency. The Bank of Scotland, Clydesdale Bank and the Royal Bank of Scotland have note-issuing powers.

Budget. Government expenditure in Scotland came to £38·6bn. in 2002–03 (including social security £13·4bn., health £6·4bn. and education £5·2bn.). Revenues totalled £31·6bn. (including income tax £7·9bn., social security receipts £5·2bn. and VAT £5·2bn.).

Performance. GDP rose by 0·9% in the third quarter of 2004 and 1·8% in the year ending the third quarter of 2004.

Banking and Finance. There is a stock exchange in Glasgow.

ENERGY AND NATURAL RESOURCES

Electricity. The Electricity Act 1989 created three new companies in Scotland. ScottishPower and Scottish Hydro-Electric (now renamed Scottish and Southern Energy) are vertically integrated companies carrying out generation, transmission, distribution and supply of electricity within their areas. They were privatized in 1990. Scottish Nuclear, responsible for operating the two Scottish nuclear power stations, was merged with Nuclear Electric in 1996. ScottishPower now owns Manweb in England, and Scottish Hydro-Electric has merged with Southern Electric under its new group name.

Water. Water supply is the responsibility of the Regional and Island local authorities. Seven river purification boards are responsible for environmental management.

Agriculture. In 2000 total agricultural area was 5,492,000 ha, of which 3,392,000 ha were used for rough grazing and 1,839,000 ha for crops and grass.

Selected crop production, 2000 (1,000 tonnes): barley, 1,729; potatoes, 1,114; wheat, 829; oats, 116.

Livestock, 2000 (in 1,000): cattle, 2,028; sheep, 9,184; pigs, 558; poultry, 14,296.

Forestry. Total forest area in 2003 was 1,327,000 ha, of which 470,000 ha was owned by the Forestry Commission.

Fisheries. The major fishing ports are Aberdeen, Mallaig, Lerwick and Peterhead. In 2001 there were 2,595 fishing vessels that landed 289,700 tonnes of fish worth £256·7m.

INDUSTRY

Labour. In 2002 the economically active population numbered 2,549,000 (1,181,000 females), of whom 173,000 (66,000 females) were unemployed. This equates to an unemployment rate of 6·8% (7·8% for men and 5·6% for women). By Sept. 2001 employment in Scotland was at its highest in 40 years. In June 2002, 26·9% of the active workforce were in public administration, education and health, 23·7% in distribution, hotels and catering and repairs, 17·0% in banking, finance and insurance, and 12·6% in manufacturing.

COMMUNICATIONS

Roads. Responsibility for the construction and maintenance of trunk roads belongs to the Scottish Office. Roads not classified as trunk roads are the responsibility of county or unitary councils. In 2003 there were 54,500 km of public roads, of which 383 km were motorways. There were 2,104,000 licensed private and light goods vehicles.

Rail. Total railway length in 2003 was 2,698 km. In 2002–2003 a total of 62·2m. passengers travelled by rail and 8·9m. tonnes of freight were carried. There is a metro in Glasgow.

Civil Aviation. There are major airports at Aberdeen, Edinburgh, Glasgow and Prestwick. In 2002 Glasgow was the sixth busiest for passenger traffic in the UK, with 7,768,590 passengers (4,297,116 on domestic flights). Prestwick was the sixth busiest UK airport for freight in 2002, handling 39,500 tonnes. In 2002, 19,783,479 passengers and 68,516 tonnes of freight were carried by Scottish airports.

Shipping. The principal Scottish port is Forth, which handled 41·6m. tonnes of cargo in 2001.

SOCIAL INSTITUTIONS

Justice. The High Court of Justiciary is the supreme criminal court in Scotland and has jurisdiction in all cases of crime committed in any part of Scotland, unless expressly excluded by statute. It consists of the Lord Justice General, the Lord Justice Clerk and 30 other Judges, who are the same Judges who preside in the Court of Session, the Scottish Supreme Civil Court. One Judge is seconded to the Scottish Law Commission. The Court is presided over by the Lord Justice General, whom failing, by the Lord Justice Clerk, and exercises an appellate jurisdiction as well as being a court of first instance. The home of the High Court is Edinburgh, but the court visits other towns and cities in Scotland on circuit and indeed the busiest High Court sitting is in Glasgow. The court sits in Edinburgh both as a Court of Appeal (the *quorum* being two judges if the appeal is against sentence or other disposals, and three in all other cases) and on circuit as a court of first instance. Although the decisions of the High Court are not subject to review by the House of Lords, with the Scotland Act 1998 coming into force on 20 May 1999, there is a limited right of appeal against the termination of a devolution issue to the Judicial Committee of the Privy Council. One Judge sitting with a Jury of 15 persons can, and usually does, try cases, but two or more Judges (with a Jury) may do so in important or complex cases. The court has a privative jurisdiction over cases of treason, murder, rape, breach of duty by Magistrates and certain statutory offences under the Official Secrets Act 1911 and the Geneva Conventions Act 1957. It also tries the most serious crimes against person or property and those cases in which a sentence greater than imprisonment for three years is likely to be imposed.

The appellate jurisdiction of the High Court of Justiciary extends to all cases tried on indictment, whether in the High Court or the Sheriff Court, and persons so convicted may appeal to the court against conviction or sentence, or both, except where the sentence is fixed by law. In such an appeal, a person may bring under review any alleged miscarriage of justice including an alleged miscarriage of justice based on the existence and significance of evidence not heard at the original proceedings provided there is reasonable explanation of why it was not heard and an alleged miscarriage of justice where the Jury returned a verdict which no reasonable Jury, properly directed, could have returned. It is also a court of review from courts of summary jurisdiction, and on the final termination of any summary prosecution the convicted person may appeal to the court by way of stated case on questions of law, but not on questions of fact, except in relation to a miscarriage of justice alleged by the person accused on the basis of the existence and significance of additional evidence not heard at the original proceedings provided that there is a reasonable explanation of why it was not heard. Before cases proceed to a full hearing, leave of appeal must first be granted. Grounds of appeal and any relevant reports are sifted by a Judge sitting alone in chambers, who will decide if there are arguable grounds of appeal. Should leave of appeal be refused, this decision may be appealed to the High Court within 14 days, when the matter will be reviewed by three Judges. The Lord Advocate is entitled to appeal to the High Court against any sentence passed on indictment on the ground that it is unduly lenient, or on a point of law. Both the prosecution and defence, at any time in solemn and summary proceedings, may appeal by way of Bill of Advocation in order to correct irregularities in the preliminary stages of a case. In summary proceedings the accused may appeal by Bill of Suspension, where he desires to bring under review a warrant, conviction or judgement issued by an inferior Judge. In summary proceedings the accused can also appeal against sentence alone by way of Stated Case. In summary proceedings the Crown can appeal against a sentence on the grounds that it is unduly lenient. The court also hears appeals under the Courts-Martial (Appeals) Act 1951.

The Sheriff Court has an inherent universal criminal jurisdiction (as well as an extensive civil one), limited in general to crimes and offences committed within a sheriffdom (a specifically defined region), which has, however, been curtailed by statute or practice under which the High Court of Justiciary has exclusive jurisdiction in relation to the crimes mentioned above. The Sheriff Court is presided over by a Sheriff Principal or a Sheriff, who when trying cases on indictment sits with a Jury of 15 people. His powers of awarding punishment involving imprisonment are restricted to a maximum of three years, but he may under certain statutory powers remit the prisoner to the High Court for sentence if this is felt to be insufficient. The Sheriff also exercises a wide summary criminal jurisdiction and when doing so sits without a Jury; and he has concurrent jurisdiction with every other court within his Sheriff Court district in regard to all offences competent for trial in summary courts. The great majority of offences which come before courts are of a more minor nature and as such are disposed of in the Sheriff Summary Courts or in the District Courts (*see* below). Where a case is to be tried on indictment either in the High Court of Justiciary or in the Sheriff Court, the Judge may, before the trial, hold a preliminary or first diet to decide questions of a preliminary nature, whether relating to the competency or relevancy of proceedings or otherwise. Any decision at a preliminary diet (other than a decision to adjourn the first or preliminary diet or discharge trial diet) can be the subject of an appeal to the High Court of Justiciary prior to the trial. The High Court also has the exclusive power to provide a remedy for all extraordinary occurrences in the course of criminal business where there is no other mode of appeal available. This is known as the Nobile Officium powers of the High Court and all petitions to the High Court as the Nobile Officium must be heard before at least three judges.

In cases to be tried on indictment in the Sheriff Court a first diet is mandatory before the trial diet to decide questions of a preliminary nature and to identify cases which are unlikely to go to trial on the date programmed. Likewise in summary proceedings, an intermediate diet is again mandatory before trial. In High Court cases such matters may be dealt with at a preliminary diet.

District Courts have jurisdiction in more minor offences occurring within a district which before recent local government reorganization corresponded to district council boundaries. These courts are presided over by Lay Magistrates, known as Justices, who have limited powers for fine and imprisonment. In Glasgow District there are also Stipendiary Magistrates, who are legally qualified, and who have the same sentencing powers as Sheriffs.

The Court of Session, presided over by the Lord President (the Lord Justice General in criminal cases), is divided into an inner-house comprising two divisions of five judges each with a mainly appellate function, and an outer-house comprising 22 single Judges sitting individually at first instance; it exercises the highest civil jurisdiction in Scotland, with the House of Lords as a Court of Appeal.

CIVIL JUDICIAL STATISTICS

	2001	*2002*
House of Lords (Appeals from Court of Session)	2	7
Court of Session—		
General Department	4,187	3,563
Petition Department	1,119	1,292
Sheriff Courts—Ordinary Cause	49,001	46,605
Sheriff Courts—Summary Cause	40,931	36,465
Small Claims	39,193	32,256

CRIMINAL STATISTICS

(Persons proceeded against in Scottish courts)

All Crimes and Offences	*2000*	*2001*	*2002*
Persons proceeded against	137,169	139,823	142,900[1]
Persons with a charge proved			
Total	118,147	120,289	124,950
Crimes	39,950	41,853	42,046
Persons aged 8–15[2]	64	81	128

[1]Estimate. [2]Except for serious offences which qualify for solemn proceedings, children aged 8–15 are not proceeded against in Scottish courts. Children within this age group that commit crime are generally referred to the reporter of the children's panel or are given a police warning.

In 2002 there were 427,000 crimes reported, of which 16,000 were violent. The average prison population in Scotland in Nov. 2003 was 6,569.

Police. In Scotland, the unitary councils have the role of police authorities. Establishment levels were abolished in Scotland on 1 April 1996. The actual strength at 31 March 2002 was 12,513 men and 2,738 women. There were 1,119 special constables. The total police net expenditure in Scotland for 2003–2004 was £888·8m.

Religion. The Church of Scotland, which was reformed in 1560, subsequently developed a presbyterian system of church government which was established in 1690 and has continued to the present day.

The supreme court is the General Assembly, which now consists of some 800 members, ministers and elders in equal numbers, together with members of the diaconate commissioned by presbyteries. It meets annually in May, under the presidency of a Moderator appointed by the Assembly. The Queen is normally represented by a Lord High Commissioner, but has occasionally attended in person. The royal presence in a special throne gallery in the hall but outside the Assembly symbolizes the independence from state control of what is nevertheless recognized as the national Church in Scotland.

There are also 46 presbyteries in Scotland, together with one presbytery of England, one presbytery of Europe, and one presbytery of Jerusalem. At the base of this conciliar structure of Church courts are the kirk sessions, of which there were 1,543 on 31 Dec. 2001. The total communicant membership of the Church at that date was 590,503.

The Episcopal Church of Scotland is a province of the Anglican Church and is one of the historic Scottish churches. It consists of seven dioceses. As at 31 Dec. 2002 it had 304 churches and missions, 483 clergy and 45,077 members, of whom 29,831 were communicants.

There are in Scotland some small outstanding Presbyterian bodies and also Baptists, Congregationalists, Methodists and Unitarians.

The Roman Catholic Church which celebrated the centenary of the restoration of the Hierarchy in 1978, had in Scotland (1998) one cardinal archbishop, one archbishop, five bishops, 20 permanent deacons, 907 clergy, 463 parishes and 705,650 adherents.

The proportion of marriages in Scotland according to the rites of the various Churches in 2002 was: Church of Scotland, 37·3%; Roman Catholic, 6·8%; United Free Church of Scotland, 1·5%; Baptist Union of Scotland, 1·2%; others, 14·8%; civil, 38·4%.

Education. In Sept. 2002 there were 2,833 publicly funded (local authority, grant-aided and self-governing) primary, secondary and special schools. All teachers employed in these schools require to be qualified.

Pre-school Education. In Jan. 2003 there were 2,782 pre-school centres that were in partnership with their local authority and 105,078 pupils enrolled in these centres.

Primary Education. In Sept. 2002 there were 2,258 publicly funded primary schools with 413,713 pupils and 22,980 full-time equivalent teachers.

Secondary Education. In Sept. 2002 there were 386 publicly funded secondary schools with 316,903 pupils and 578 adults. All but 21 schools provided a full range of Scottish Certificate of Education courses and non-certificate courses. Pupils who start their secondary education in schools which do not cater for a full range of courses may be transferred at the end of their second or fourth year to schools where a full range of courses is provided. There were 25,040 full-time equivalent teachers in secondary schools.

Independent schools. There were 151 independent schools in Sept. 2002, with a total of 30,370 pupils. A small number of the Scottish independent schools are of the 'public school' type, but they are not known as 'public schools' since in Scotland this term is used to denote education authority (i.e., state) schools.

Special Education. In Sept. 2002 there were 189 publicly funded special schools with 7,981 pupils.

Further Education. Under the Further and Higher Education (Scotland) Act 1992 funding of the Further Education colleges was transferred to central government in 1993. With effect from 1 July 1999 Scotland's FE colleges are funded by the Scottish Further Education Funding Council, a new executive Non Departmental Public Body established by the Secretary of State for Scotland on 1 Jan. 1999.

There are 42 incorporated FE colleges as well as the FE colleges in Orkney and Shetland, which are run by the local education authorities, and two privately managed colleges, Sabhal Mor Ostaig and Newbattle Abbey College. The colleges offer training in a wide range of vocational areas and co-operate with the Scottish Qualifications Authority, the Enterprise, Transport and Lifelong Learning Department and the Education Department of the Scottish Executive in the development of new courses. The qualifications offered by colleges aim to improve the skills of the nation's workforce and increase the country's competitiveness. The colleges benefit from co-operation with industry, through involvement with Industry Lead Bodies and National Training Organizations whose responsibility it is to identify education, training and skills needs at sectoral level. Industry is also represented on college boards of management. Colleges and schools in Scotland are directly involved in providing the new national qualifications introduced in 1999 as a result of the Higher Still development programme.

In 2001–02 there were 453,933 enrolments on vocational courses at Scotland's 46 further education institutions; the full-time equivalent staff number in the colleges was 12,500.

Full-time students resident in Scotland (and EU students) undertaking non-advanced (further education) courses are mainly supported through discretionary further education bursaries which are administered locally by further education colleges within National Policy Guidelines issued by the Scottish Further Education Funding Council. The Colleges have delegated discretionary powers for some aspects of the bursary support award.

In May 2000 the Scottish Executive announced the abolition of tuition fees for all eligible Scottish (and EU) full-time further education students from autumn 2000. The Executive also made a commitment to take steps to align, from autumn 2001, the levels of support available on a weekly basis for FE students with those that will apply for HE students and to begin to align the systems of assessment of parental/family contributions.

Higher Education. In Scotland in 2002 there were 21 institutions of higher education funded by the Scottish Higher Education Funding Council (SHEFC), with the exception of the Scottish Agricultural College which is funded by the Scottish Executive Rural Affairs Department. Included in this total is the Open University. SHEFC took over the responsibility for funding the Open University in Scotland at the start of the 2000–01 academic session. University education in Scotland has a long history. Four universities—St Andrews, Glasgow, Aberdeen and Edinburgh, known collectively as the 'ancient Scottish universities'—were founded in the 15th and 16th centuries. Four further universities—Strathclyde, Heriot-Watt, Stirling and Dundee—were formally established as independent universities between 1964 and 1967, and four others—Napier, Paisley, Robert Gordon and Glasgow Caledonian—were granted the title of university in 1992, with a fifth, the University of Abertay, Dundee, being added in 1994.

Of the remaining higher education institutions, which all offer courses at degree level (although not themselves universities), five were formerly Central Institutions: Edinburgh College of Art, Glasgow School of Art, Queen Margaret University College (Edinburgh), Royal Scottish Academy of Music and Drama (Glasgow) and Scottish Agricultural College (Perth).

Two additional higher education institutions were established in 2001. UHI Millennium Institute was designated as a higher education institution on 1 April when it took over from the local colleges of further education and other non-SHEFC funded institutions responsibility for all HE provision and all students on courses of HE in the Academic Partner institutions. Bell College of Technology became a higher education institution on 1 Aug. when its transfer from the further to the higher education sector was completed.

Further education colleges may also provide higher education courses.

University and HE student and staff figures:

Name (and Location)	*Full-time and sandwich students (2001–02)*	*Full-time academic staff (2001–02)*
Aberdeen Univ.	10,816	1,307
Abertay Dundee Univ.	3,898	250
Bell College of Technology (Hamilton)	2,619	176
Dundee Univ.	9,362	1,310
Edinburgh College of Art	1,623	81
Edinburgh Univ.	19,278	2,723
Glasgow School of Art	1,387	69
Glasgow Caledonian Univ.	11,699	730
Glasgow Univ.	16,651	2,368
Heriot-Watt Univ. (Edinburgh)	5,729	684
Napier Univ. (Edinburgh)	9,550	622
Paisley Univ.	6,532	460
Queen Margaret University College (Edinburgh)	3,241	196
Robert Gordon Univ. (Aberdeen)	7,501	507
Royal Scottish Academy of Music and Drama (Glasgow)	650	28
St Andrews Univ.	6,975	723
Scottish Agricultural College (Perth)	691	257
Stirling Univ.	6,853	563
Strathclyde Univ. (Glasgow)	14,892	1,361
UHI Millennium Institute (Inverness)	2,763	—

In 2001–02 there were 72,809 full-time students in further education colleges (27,610 studying at higher education level and 45,199 studying at further education level) of which 37,672 were female (14,687 HE and 22,985 FE).

All the higher education institutions are independent and self-governing. In addition to funding through the higher education funding councils, they receive tuition fees from the Students Awards Agency for Scotland for students domiciled in Scotland, and through local education authorities for students domiciled in England and Wales. Institutions which carry out research may also receive funding through the five Research Councils administered by the Office of Science and Technology.

Health. In 2002 there were 3,765 GPs with average patient list size of 1,392, and 1,891 dental practitioners.

Welfare. In 2000 there were 904,900 retirement pensioners, 397,700 claimants of income support, 237,300 recipients of disability living allowance, 192,500 beneficiaries of incapacity benefit, 127,900 recipients of attendance allowance, 120,600 claimants of Jobseekers' Allowance and 101,800 recipients of family credit/working family tax credit.

CULTURE

Press. Average daily circulation in Jan. 2005 for the daily *Scotsman* was 69,771 and the *Daily Record* 471,708; and for *Scotland on Sunday* 81,475 and the *Sunday Mail* 585,657.

Tourism. There were 1,589,000 overseas visitors to Scotland in 2001, spending £757m. Overall tourism receipts totalled £4·17bn. The tourist attraction receiving the most visitors is Edinburgh Castle, with 1,127,000 visits in 2001. In 2001 around 9% of the workforce was employed in the tourism industry.

Festivals. The Edinburgh Festival and the Fringe Festival both take place in Aug./early Sept. and are major international festivals of culture.

Museums and Galleries. The most visited museum is Kelvingrove Art Gallery and Museum in Glasgow, with 1,031,138 visits in 2001.

FURTHER READING

Scottish Executive. Scottish Economic Report. TSO (twice yearly).—*Scottish Abstract of Statistics.* TSO (annual)

Brown, A., *et al., Politics and Society in Scotland.* London, 1996

Bruce, D., *The Mark of the Scots.* Birch Lane Press, 1997

Dennistoun, R. and Linklater, M. (eds.) *Anatomy of Scotland.* Edinburgh, 1992

Devine, T. M. and Finlay, R. J. (eds.) *Scotland in the 20th Century*. Edinburgh Univ. Press, 1996
Harvie, C., *Scotland and Nationalism: Scottish Society and Politics, 1707–1994*. 2nd ed. London, 1994
Hunter, J., *A Dance Called America*. Edinburgh, 1997
Keay, J. and J., *Collins Encyclopedia of Scotland: The Story of a Nation*. London, 2000
Macleod, J., *Highlanders: A History of the Gaels*. London, 1997
Magnusson, M., *Scotland: The Story of a Nation*. London, 2000
McCaffrey, J. F., *Scotland in the Nineteenth Century*. London, 1998
Mitchell, James, *Governing Scotland*. Palgrave Macmillan, Basingstoke, 2003

WALES

KEY HISTORICAL EVENTS

After the Roman evacuation, Wales divided into tribal kingdoms. Cunedda Wledig, a prince from southern Scotland, founded a dynasty in the northwest region of Gwynedd—to become the focus for Welsh unity—while the Irish exerted an influence in the kingdom of Dyfed. Offa's Dyke, a defensive earthwork, was the dividing line between England and Wales. In the late 9th century the kings of southern Wales swore fealty to Alfred of Wessex, a relationship assumed by the English crown. Gruffudd ap Llywelyn of Gwynedd briefly united Wales from 1055–63. His death was followed by Norman expansion into southern Wales, where the Marcher lordships were created.

With the accession of Llywelyn the Great (1194–1240), the house of Gwynedd overcame rival claims from Powys and Deheubarth to forge a stable political state under English suzerainty. His grandson, Llywelyn ap Gruffydd (1246–82), was recognized as prince of Wales by Henry III but Llywelyn intrigued against Edward I, who reduced Gwynedd's hegemony. Wales was annexed and subdued by a network of castles. Edward's infant son, born at Caernarvon, was made prince of Wales.

Loyalty to Henry VIII, who was of Welsh descent, was rewarded with political influence. The Act of Union in 1536 made English law general, admitted Welsh representatives to Parliament and established the Council of Wales and the Marches.

TERRITORY AND POPULATION

At the census taken on 29 April 2001 the population was 2,903,085. The area of Wales is 20,732 sq. km. Population density, 2001 census: 140 per sq. km. Wales covers 8·5% of the total area of the United Kingdom.

Population at census day 2001:

Males	*Females*	*Total*
1,403,900	1,499,185	2,903,085

Population (present on census night) at the four previous decennial censuses:

1961	*1971*	*1981*	*1991*
2,644,023[1]	2,731,204[1]	2,790,500[2]	2,811,865

[1]Areas now recognized as Monmouthshire and small sections of various other counties formed the county of Monmouthshire in England until 1974. [2]The final count is believed to be over-stated as a result of an error in processing. The preliminary counts presented here rounded to the nearest hundred are thought to be more accurate.

Estimated population, mid-2004, 2,952,000. Cardiff, the capital and largest city, had a population in 2001 of 305,340; Swansea, the second largest city, had a population of 223,293 in 2001.

In 2001, 457,950 people aged three and over were able to speak, read and write Welsh. Households at the 2001 census: 1,276,000.

For further statistical information, see under Territory and Population, United Kingdom.

Wales is divided into 22 unitary authorities (cities and counties, counties and county boroughs).

Designations, areas and populations of the unitary authority areas at census day 2001:

Unitary Authority	*Designation*	*Area (sq. km)*	*Population*
Blaenau Gwent	County Borough	109	70,058
Bridgend	County Borough	251	128,650
Caerphilly	County Borough	278	169,521
Cardiff	City and County	139	305,340
Carmarthenshire	County	2,394	173,635
Ceredigion	County	1,792	75,384
Conwy	County Borough	1,126	109,597
Denbighshire	County	837	93,092
Flintshire	County	438	148,565
Gwynedd	County	2,535	116,838
Isle of Anglesey	County	711	66,828
Merthyr Tydfil	County Borough	111	55,983
Monmouthshire	County	849	84,879
Neath and Port Talbot	County Borough	441	134,471
Newport	County Borough	190	137,017
Pembrokeshire	County	1,589	112,901
Powys	County	5,181	126,344
Rhondda Cynon Taff	County Borough	424	231,952
Swansea	City and County	378	223,293
The Vale of Glamorgan	County Borough	331	119,500
Torfaen	County Borough	126	90,967
Wrexham	County Borough	504	128,477

SOCIAL STATISTICS

2002: births, 30,205 (10·4 per 1,000 population); deaths, 33,172 (11·4 per 1,000 population); marriages (2000), 14,125 (4·9 per 1,000 population); divorces (2000), 7,704; still births, 164 (5 per 1,000 births); infant mortality, 142 (5 per 1,000 live births).

CLIMATE

For more detailed information, see under Climate, United Kingdom.

Cardiff, Jan. 40°F (4·4°C), July 61°F (16·1°C). Annual rainfall 42·6" (1,065 mm).

CONSTITUTION AND GOVERNMENT

One of the main aspects of the British Labour government's programme of constitutional reform is devolution. On 18 Sept. 1997 in the referendum there were 559,419 votes cast in favour of a Welsh assembly (50·3%) and 552,698 against (49·7%). The turn-out was 51·3%.

RECENT ELECTIONS

At the UK general election in May 2005, 40 members were returned from Wales. Labour won 29 seats (34 in 2001), Liberal Democrats 4 seats (2), Plaid Cymru 3 seats (4), Conservatives 3 seats (0), others 1 seat.

At the 2004 European Parliamentary elections, 2 Labour candidates were elected, 1 Conservative and 1 Plaid Cymru.

In the elections to the Welsh Assembly on 1 May 2003, Labour won 30 seats (all constituencies), followed by Plaid Cymru with 12 (7 by regional list), the Conservatives with 11 (10 by regional list), the Liberal Democrats with 6 (3 by regional list) and 1 independent constituency. Of the 60 seats, 40 seats were won on a first-past-the-post basis and 20 through proportional representation (regional list). 30 seats were won by women. Turn-out was 38%.

See also Constitution and Government, Recent Elections and Current Administration in United Kingdom.

CURRENT ADMINISTRATION

First Secretary: Rhodri Morgan; b. 1939 (Labour).

Presiding Officer: Dafydd Elis-Thomas.

National Assembly for Wales: http://www.wales.gov.uk

DEFENCE

For information on defence, see United Kingdom.

ECONOMY

For information on the economy, see United Kingdom.

ENERGY AND NATURAL RESOURCES

For information on energy and natural resources, see United Kingdom.

Water. The Water Act of Sept. 1989 privatized Welsh Water (Dŵr Cymru Cyfyngedig), along with the nine water authorities in England.

Agriculture. In 2002 there were 36,743 agricultural holdings. Of these, 4,584 were under 2 ha, 11,448 were between 2 and 19 ha, 4,254 were between 20 and 39 ha and 10,527 were over 40 ha. 5,660 were rough-grazing holdings.

The area of tillage in 2002 was 64,800 ha (64,100 ha for crops and 700 ha bare fallow). Major crops, 2001 provisional (1,000 tonnes): barley, 152; wheat, 80; potatoes, 73; oats, 19.

Livestock, 2002: sheep and lambs, 10,050,100; cattle, 1,195,100; pigs, 44,300; poultry, 6,072,000.

Forestry. In 2003 there were 110,000 ha of Forestry Commission woodland and 176,000 ha of non-Forestry Commission woodland.

Fisheries. The major fishing port is Milford Haven. In 2002, in all ports, 17,395 tonnes of fish worth £11,479,000 were landed. There were 500 fishing vessels registered in Wales in 2002.

INDUSTRY

Selected industrial production (gross value added), 2000, provisional (£1m.): textiles and textile products, 1,819; basic metals and fabricated metal products, 1,358; electrical and optical equipment, 1,308; chemicals, chemical products and man-made fibres, 819; food products, beverages and tobacco, 791; transport equipment, 786.

Labour. At Dec. 2002 the workforce numbered 1,291,100. There were 45,500 people claiming unemployment benefit and 162,000 people were self-employed. The largest employment sectors in 2001 were: public administration, education and health, 341,800; distribution, hotels and restaurants, 259,400; manufacturing, 189,000. As a proportion of total employees, 75·9% of the active workforce were in service industries. The unemployment rate in 2002 was 5·6%, compared to 5·1% for the UK as a whole. In 2002, 80,100 working days were lost due to industrial disputes.

INTERNATIONAL TRADE

For information on international trade, see United Kingdom.

COMMUNICATIONS

Roads. Responsibility for the construction and maintenance of trunk roads belongs to the Welsh Office. Roads not classified as trunk roads are the responsibility of county or unitary councils. In 2003 there were 133 km of motorway, 1,576 km of trunk roads and 2,711 km of principal roads. 1,433,300 vehicles were registered in 2001, including 1,288,000 private and light goods vehicles. In 2002 there were 9,700 reported accidents which led to 14,336 casualties and 147 deaths.

Civil Aviation. Cardiff Airport handled 1,499,824 passengers in 2000 (1,405,057 on international flights) and 982 tonnes of freight. A new airline, Air Wales, began services from Cardiff to Cork in 2000 and now flies from Cardiff and Swansea to destinations in England, the Republic of Ireland, Belgium and the Netherlands.

Shipping. The principal ports are (with 1m. tonnes of cargo handled in 2001): Milford Haven (33·8) and Port Talbot (8·3).

Postal Services. Royal Mail employs 6,500 people in Wales and delivers to 1·5m. addresses. In 2000–01 the Post Office handled 490·8m. letters and 0·7m. parcels.

SOCIAL INSTITUTIONS

Justice. In March 2002 police strength amounted to 7,194. During the financial year 2000–01 there were 238,445 notable offences, including 38,230 violent and 1,698 sexual offences. The clear-up rate was 40·8%. 17,643 people were found guilty of indictable offences in Magistrates' Courts in 2001 and 4,106 in Crown Courts.

Religion. Under the Welsh Church Acts, 1914 and 1919, the Church in Wales and Monmouthshire was disestablished as from 1 April 1920, and Wales was formed into a separate Province.

Education. There were 37 maintained nursery schools in Jan. 2003, and 65,199 pupils under five years provided for in nursery schools and in nursery or infants classes in primary schools.

In Jan. 2003 there were 278,613 pupils at 1,602 primary schools. Within these figures, 451 primary schools use Welsh as the sole or main medium of instruction. Such schools are to be found in all parts of Wales but are mainly concentrated in the predominantly Welsh-speaking areas of west and northwest Wales. Generally, children transfer from primary to secondary schools at 11 years of age.

In Jan. 2003 there were 227 secondary schools. All maintained secondary schools are classified as comprehensive; there are no middle schools in Wales. In 2002–03, 53 of the secondary schools were classed as Welsh-speaking as defined in section 354(b) of the Education Act 1996.

Since Sept. 1999, in accordance with the Schools Standards and Framework Act 1998, all maintained schools, including grant maintained schools, in Wales had to change category to one of the following: Community, Community Special, Foundation, Voluntary Controlled, Voluntary Aided. These categories continue to remain in place with the introduction of the Education Act 2002.

Under the Education Act 1996, children have special educational needs if they have a learning difficulty which calls for special educational provision to be made for them. In a minority of cases the local education authority will need to make a statutory assessment of special educational needs under the Education Act 1996, which may ultimately lead to a 'statement of Special Educational Needs'. The total number of pupils with statements in Jan. 2003 was 17,251. From April 2002 Special Educational Needs (SEN) guidance for Wales is set out in the SEN Code of Practice for Wales.

In Jan. 2003, 9,603 full-time pupils attended 61 independent schools.

Post-16 Learning. The National Council for Education and Training Wales (ELWa) was formed from the merger of the four TECs (training and enterprise councils), the Council of Welsh TECs and Further Education Funding Council for Wales (FEFCW) and has been operational since April 2001. It is responsible for the planning and promoting of further, adult and continuing education, work-based training and school sixth forms. The cash grant in aid allocation for 2002–03 was £488·9m. In 2001–02 the FEFCW supported 42,923 full-time and sandwich students and 217,036 students studying part-time in the further education sector at 26 further education institutions and ten higher education institutions. In addition, in 2001–02 ELWa supported 35,520 starts in work-based training or with training to return to the workplace. In 2001, 12% of 16- to 18-year-olds did not have a qualification; five percentage points lower than in 1996. The percentage of adults with no qualification fell from 23% in 1996 to 21% in 2001; and 40% of adults had an NVQ level three or equivalent, up from 35% in 1996. Between 1996 and 1999 it was estimated that around seven in ten adults had functional basis skills in either literacy or numeracy.

Higher Education. In 2000–01 there were 13 institutions of higher education funded directly by the Higher Education Funding Council for Wales (HEFCW), including the University of Glamorgan and the colleges of the University of Wales. In 2002–03 the total budget was £327·44m. There were 110,546 students in the higher education sector in 2000–01, excluding those registered with the Open University, of which 68,491 were full-time and 42,055 part-time students, including those enrolled on higher education provision at further education colleges.

Higher Education Institutes (HEIs)	*Full-time/sandwich HE students at HEIs (2001–02)*	*No. of academic staff (2000–01)*[1]
Univ. of Glamorgan (Pontypridd)	10,112	689
Univ. of Wales, Aberystwyth	6,832	621
Univ. of Wales, Bangor	7,038	688

Higher Education Institutes (HEIs)	*Full-time/sandwich HE students at HEIs (2001–02)*	*No. of academic staff (2000–01)*[1]
Cardiff University[2]	16,068	1,749
Univ. of Wales, Lampeter	966	101
Univ. of Wales, Swansea	8,402	852
Univ. of Wales College of Medicine	2,445	676
Univ. of Wales Institute, Cardiff	6,283	387
Univ. of Wales College, Newport	2,832	183
North East Wales Institute of Higher Education (Wrexham)	2,577	208
Swansea Institute of Higher Education	3,351	196
Trinity College Carmarthen	1,236	81[3]
Welsh College of Music and Drama	527	99

[1]Staff who meet the 25% full-time equivalent threshold.
[2]The public name of the University of Wales, Cardiff.
[3]Excludes part-time staff meeting 25% threshold.

Health. In 2000–01 there were 1,903 GPs, 1,015 dentists and 24,314 nurses, midwives and health visitors. The average daily number of hospital beds available in 2000–01 was 14,600, of which 11,700 were occupied. 514,700 in-patient cases were reported, with stays lasting an average 8·3 days. 61,100 people were on hospital waiting lists.

Welfare. In 2001, 569,000 people received retirement pensions and contributory old-age pensions; 359,000 families received child benefit; and 236,000 people received some form of income support.

CULTURE

Broadcasting. Radio and television services are provided by the Welsh-language Sianel Pedwar Cymru (S4C, Channel 4 Wales). S4C is funded by the government. It acts as both broadcaster and regulator. In 2000–01 there were 1,150,100 television licenses, of which 1,143,500 were colour.

Tourism. In 2001 there were 11·6m. domestic trips (from elsewhere in the UK) into Wales. Visitors stayed 44·6m. nights and spent £1·7bn.

Festivals. Every year there are local and national *eisteddfods* (festivals for musical competitions, etc.). The national *eisteddfod* is held every Aug. in a different location (Y Felinheli, Gwynedd in 2005).

Libraries. In 2001–02 there were 913 libraries with 5,068,000 books. 1,161,000 items were borrowed. The National Library is in Aberystwyth.

Theatre and Opera. There is a Welsh National Opera and the BBC National Orchestra of Wales.

Museums and Galleries. The leading museum is the Museum of Welsh Life in Cardiff, which received 694,899 visits in 2001–02.

FURTHER READING

National Assembly. Digest of Welsh Statistics. National Statistics. Great Britain (annual)

Andrews, Leighton, *Wales Says Yes. The Inside Story of the Yes for Wales Referendum Campaign.* Seren, Bridgend, 1999

Davies, J., *History of Wales.* London, 1993

History of Wales. vols. 3, 4 (1415–1780). 2nd ed. OUP, 1993

Jenkins, G. H., *The Foundations of Modern Wales 1642–1780.* Oxford, 1988.—*The Welsh Language and its Social Domains 1801–1911: A Social History of the Welsh Language.* Univ. of Wales Press, 2000

Jones, G. E., *Modern Wales: a Concise History.* 2nd ed. CUP, 1994

May, J. (ed.) *Reference Wales.* Wales Univ. Press, 1994

Morgan, K. and Mungham, G., *Redesigning Democracy. The Making of the Welsh Assembly.* Seren, Bridgend, 2000

NORTHERN IRELAND

KEY HISTORICAL EVENTS

The Government of Ireland Act 1920 granted Northern Ireland its own bicameral parliament (Stormont). The rejection of home rule by the rest of Ireland (which pursued independence) forced a separation along primarily religious lines, with a large Catholic minority in the six northern counties. Between 1921–72 Stormont had full responsibility for local affairs except for taxation and customs; Northern Ireland was on the whole neglected by Westminster, allowing the virtual exclusion of Catholics from political office. The (predominantly Protestant) Unionist government ignored demands from London and the Catholic community to end communal discrimination.

In the late 1960s a Civil Rights campaign and reactions to it escalated into serious rioting and sectarian violence involving the Irish Republican Army (IRA, a terrorist organization aiming to unify Northern Ireland with the Republic of Ireland) and loyalist paramilitary organizations, such as the Ulster Defence Association. The British Army was deployed to protect civilians and was at first welcomed by the Catholic community. However, British soldiers shot dead 13 Catholic civil rights protesters in (London)Derry on 30 Jan. 1972—'Bloody Sunday'—prompting the Republic of Ireland's foreign minister to demand United Nations intervention. 467 people died in 1972, on account of 'the Troubles', and nearly 1,800 between 1971–77. The Northern Ireland government resigned and direct rule from Westminster was imposed.

Attempts have been made by successive governments to find a means of restoring greater power to Northern Ireland's political representatives on a widely acceptable basis, including a Constitutional Convention (1975–76), a Constitutional Conference (1979–80) and 78-member Northern Ireland Assembly elected by proportional representation in 1982. This was dissolved in 1986, partly in response to Unionist reaction to the Anglo-Irish Agreement signed on 15 Nov. 1985, which established an Intergovernmental Conference of British and Irish ministers to monitor issues of concern to the nationalist community. The Provisional IRA bombing of a Remembrance Day service in Enniskillen in 1987 killed 11. Universally condemned, it galvanized the anti-violence campaign.

On 15 Dec. 1993 the British and Irish prime ministers, John Major and Albert Reynolds, issued a joint declaration as a basis for all-party talks to achieve a political settlement. They invited Sinn Féin, the political wing of the IRA, to join the talks in an All-Ireland Forum after the cessation of terrorist violence. The IRA announced 'a complete cessation of military operations' on 31 Aug. 1994. On 13 Oct. 1994 the anti-IRA Combined Loyalist Military Command also announced a ceasefire 'dependent upon the continued cessation of all nationalist republican violence'.

Elections were held on 30 May 1996 to constitute a 110-member forum to take part in talks with the British and Irish governments. The Ulster Unionist Party won 30 seats, the Social Democratic and Labour Party 21 seats, the Democratic Unionist Party 24 seats and Sinn Féin 17 seats. Opening plenary talks, excluding Sinn Féin, began under the chairmanship of US Senator George Mitchell on 12 June 1996. A marathon negotiating struggle on 9–10 April 1998 led to agreement on a framework for sharing power designed to satisfy Protestant demands for a reaffirmation of their national identity as British, Catholic desires for a closer relationship with the Republic of Ireland and Britain's wish to return to Northern Ireland the powers London assumed in 1972.

Under the Good Friday Agreement, there was to be a democratically elected legislature in Belfast, a ministerial council giving the governments of Northern Ireland and Ireland joint responsibilities in areas like tourism, transportation and the environment, and a consultative council meeting twice a year to bring together ministers from the British and Irish parliaments, and the three assemblies being created in Northern Ireland and in Scotland and Wales. The Irish government eliminated from its constitution its territorial claim on Northern Ireland.

In the referendum on 22 May 1998, 71·1% of votes in Northern Ireland were cast in favour of the Good Friday peace agreement and 94·4% in the Republic of Ireland. As a consequence, in June, Northern Ireland's 1·2m. voters elected the first power-sharing administration since the collapse of the Sunningdale Agreement in 1974. But IRA blockage on the decommissioning of arms continues to hold up the transfer of powers from London to Belfast.

On 15 Aug. 1998 a 200 kg bomb exploded in the centre of Omagh. The dissident republican group the 'Real IRA' claimed responsibility. 29 people died and over 200 were injured, making it the single bloodiest incident of the Troubles—about 3,300 deaths were recorded by the end of 1998.

In Nov. 1999 the Mitchell talks finally produced an agreement between the Ulster Unionists and Sinn Féin, paving the way for devolved government. The new Northern Ireland Assembly met on 29 Nov. 1999 and on 2 Dec. legislative powers were fully devolved from London to Belfast. However, on 11 Feb. 2000 the Assembly was suspended following a breakdown in negotiations on the decommissioning of IRA weapons. Direct rule from London was restored. Devolved government resumed on 30 May after the IRA agreed to open their arms dumps to independent inspection. First Minister David Trimble resigned on 30 June 2001 to pressure republicans over decommissioning but on 22 Oct. Sinn Féin president Gerry Adams announced that he had recommended a 'ground-breaking' step on the arms issue. The IRA made a start on decommissioning arms, ammunition and explosives. David Trimble was re-elected first minister on 6 Nov. 2001.

On 15 Oct. 2002 the Assembly executive was again suspended over allegations of IRA spying at the Northern Ireland Office. Direct rule from London was re-imposed and on 30 Oct. the IRA cut off its links with the weapons decommissioning body. The Ulster Volunteer Force followed suit on 17 Jan. 2003. Elections for the Northern Ireland Assembly took place on 26 Nov. 2003. The theft of £26·5m. from the Northern Bank in Belfast in Dec. 2004 suggests closer than acknowledged associations between Sinn Féin and the IRA. Controversy surrounding the raid has put the peace process on hold.

TERRITORY AND POPULATION

Area (revised by Ordnance Survey of Northern Ireland) and population were as follows:

District	*Mid-year population estimates 2002*	*Area in ha. (including inland water)*
Antrim	48,877	57,686
Ards	74,079	37,619
Armagh	54,958	67,060
Ballymena	58,953	63,202
Ballymoney	27,478	41,820
Banbridge	42,356	45,263
Belfast	274,114	11,488
Carrickfergus	38,109	8,184
Castlereagh	66,329	8,514
Coleraine	56,181	48,551
Cookstown	33,039	62,244
Craigavon	81,500	37,842
Derry (Londonderry)	106,193	38,731
Down	64,836	64,670
Dungannon	48,232	78,360
Fermanagh	58,148	187,582
Larne	30,944	33,567
Limavady	33,210	58,558
Lisburn	109,384	44,684
Magherafelt	40,400	57,280
Moyle	16,244	47,976
Newry and Mourne	88,549	90,243
Newtownabbey	80,218	15,056
North Down	76,984	8,149
Omagh	48,919	113,045
Strabane	38,407	86,165
Northern Ireland	*1,696,641*	*1,413,540*

Northern Ireland's area of 14,135 sq. km represents 5·8% of the total area of the United Kingdom. Chief town (mid-year estimate, 2002): Belfast, 274,114.

Population by gender at the 2002 mid-year estimate was: females, 51·26%; males, 48·74%.

SOCIAL STATISTICS

In 2002 there were 21,385 births and 14,586 deaths, 7,599 marriages and 2,165 divorces.

CLIMATE

For more detailed information, see under Climate, United Kingdom.

Belfast. Jan. 40°F (4·5°C), July 59°F (15·0°C). Annual rainfall 37·4" (950 mm).

CONSTITUTION AND GOVERNMENT

Under the Northern Ireland Act 1998 power that was previously exercised by the NI Departments was devolved to the Northern Ireland Assembly and its Executive Committee of Ministers. The Secretary of State remains responsible for those matters specified in Schedules 2 and 3 of the Act. These broadly equate to policing, security policing, criminal justice, and international relations.

The Parliamentary electorate of Northern Ireland in the register in Dec. 2004 numbered 1,045,537.

Secretary of State for Northern Ireland. Paul Murphy.

RECENT ELECTIONS

At the general election of 5 May 2005, 18 members were returned from Northern Ireland. The Democratic Unionist Party won 9 seats (5 in 2001); Sinn Féin 5 (4); the Social and Democratic Labour Party 3 (3); the Ulster Unionist Party 1 (6).

In the Northern Ireland Assembly elections on 26 Nov. 2003 the Democratic Unionist Party won 30 of the 108 seats, the Ulster Unionist Party 27, Sinn Féin 24, the Social Democratic and Labour Party 18, Alliance Party of Northern Ireland 6, Progressive Unionist Party 1, United Kingdom Unionist Party 1, ind. 1. Turn-out was 63·1%.

At the June 2004 European Parliament elections, voting was by the single transferable vote system: the Democratic Ulster Unionist Party (32·0%), Sinn Féin (26·3%) and the Ulster Unionist Party (Popular European Party) (16·6%) gained 1 seat each. Turn-out was 51·2%.

CURRENT ADMINISTRATION

David Trimble (Ulster Unionist Party) was elected as the Northern Ireland Assembly's 'First Minister' on 6 Nov. 2001 at a special meeting of the Assembly, having resigned from the post on 30 June 2001. Mark Durkan (Social Democratic and Labour Party) was elected deputy first minister. They are joint leaders of the administration. The Assembly has been suspended since Oct. 2002.

Northern Ireland Executive: http://www.nics.gov.uk

ECONOMY

Overview. The Northern Ireland government Department of Enterprise, Trade and Investment (DETI) is responsible for economic policy development, energy, tourism, mineral development, health and safety at work, Companies Registry, Insolvency Service, consumer affairs, and labour market and economic statistics services. DETI has four agencies: Invest Northern Ireland (Invest NI), the Northern Ireland Tourist Board (NITB), the Health and Safety Executive for Northern Ireland (HSENI) and the General Consumer Council for Northern Ireland (GCCNI).

Currency. Banknotes are issued by Allied Irish Banks, Bank of Ireland, First Trust Bank, Northern Bank and Ulster Bank.

Banking and Finance. The Department of Finance and Personnel is responsible for control of the expenditure of Northern Ireland departments, involving liaison with HM Treasury, the European Commission and the Northern Ireland Office on financial matters, economic and social research and analysis; to review and develop rating policy and legislation; procurement for the Northern Ireland public sector; formulation of policy for central personnel management, and legal services, including law reform. The Department's Agencies are: Business Development Service; Land Registers NI; Northern Ireland Statistics and Research Agency; Rate Collection Agency and Valuation and Lands Agency.

Income of the Northern Ireland Consolidated Fund (in £1,000 sterling):

	2000–01	*2001–02*	*2002–03*
Attributed share of UK taxes Grant in Aid from UK government	7,405,400[1]	7,998,998[1]	7,799,000[1]
Regional and district rates	544,600	568,184	609,163
Other receipts	547,028	404,257	385,400
Total	8,497,028	8,971,439	8,793,563

[1]In 2000–01 the funding mechanism was changed to replace the 'Grant in Aid' and 'Attributed share of UK taxation' with a 'Block Grant'.

The public debt at 31 March 2003 was as follows: Ulster Savings Certificates, £13,926,000; Ulster Development Bonds, £12,239,000; borrowing from UK government, £1,380,424,832; borrowing from Northern Ireland government funds, £206,410,359. Excess of public income over public expenditure at 31 March 2003: £453,391,609. Net assets available for debt repayment: £517,176,241.

The above amount of public debt is offset by equal assets in the form of loans from government to public and local bodies, and of cash balances.

ENERGY AND NATURAL RESOURCES

Electricity. There are three power stations with an installed capacity of some 2,100 MW.

In addition, electricity is also supplied through a 500 MW interconnector linking the Northern Ireland Electricity (NIE) and Scottish Power networks and a number of interconnectors linking the NIE network with the Electricity Supply Board (ESB) network in the Republic of Ireland.

Oil and Gas. In Sept. 2001 the Northern Ireland executive approved grant support for the development of the gas network outside the Greater Belfast area, to the North/North West region and for the construction of a South/North pipeline. The North West gas pipeline will make gas available for the new Combined Cycle Turbine power station at Coolkeeragh outside Londonderry during 2005. The South/North pipeline is scheduled to be laid in 2006. Negotiations are ongoing to grant a license to supply gas to the major towns along the route of both these.

Minerals. Output of minerals (in 1,000 tonnes), 2002: basalt and igneous rock (other than granite), 6,681; sandstone, 6,574; sand and gravel, 5,512; limestone, 4,514; other minerals (rocksalt, fireclay, diatomite, granite, chalk, clay and shale), 242. There are lignite deposits of 1,000m. tonnes which have not yet been developed.

Agriculture. Provisional gross output in 2001:

	Quantity	*Value (£1m.)*		*Quantity*	*Value (£1m.)*
Cattle and calves	547,500	371·4	Vegetables (1,000 tonnes)	49·0	14·9
Sheep and lambs	864,000	59·3	Mushrooms (1,000 tonnes)	24·0	27·6
Pigs	940,500	58·7	Other crops	. . .	6·9
Poultry (1,000 tonnes)	184·3	115·4	Flowers, ornamentals and nurserystock	. . .	13·1
Eggs (m. dozen)	64·9	24·2	Capital formation	. . .	48·8
Milk (1m. litres)	1,780·0	292·3	Contract work	. . .	35·8
Other livestock products	. . .	8·0	Other items	. . .	18·0
Cereals (1,000 tonnes)	181·9	20·7			
Potatoes (1,000 tonnes)	254·4	23·9			
Fruit (1,000 tonnes)	37·1	3·0	Gross output	. . .	1,141·9

Area (in 1,000 ha) on farms:

	2001	*2002*	*2003*		*2001*	*2002*	*2003*
Cereals	40	38	38	Grass	840	844	848
Potatoes	7	7	6	Rough grazing	154	152	153
Horticulture	3	3	3	Other land	20	19	20
Other crops	5	5	6				
				Total area	1,068	1,067	1,074

Livestock (in 1,000 heads) on farms at June census:

	2001	*2002*	*2003*		*2001*	*2002*	*2003*
Dairy cows	295	298	290	Sows	41	39	43
Beef cows	312	307	295	Laying hens	2,143	2,099	2,203
Other cattle	1,072	1,080	1,100	Broilers	8,864	11,273	12,811
Ewes	1,232	1,129	1,106				

INDUSTRY

Labour. The main sources of employment statistics are the Census of Employment, conducted every two years, and the Quarterly Employment Survey. In Dec. 1999 there were 625,030 employees, of whom 309,010 were males. Employment in manufacturing and construction amounted to 137,340, 22% of the total employees in employment. 19,400 of these jobs were in the food, drink and tobacco industries, 9,360 in the manufacture of wearing apparel, 9,100 in textiles, 30,840 in construction and 68,640 in other sectors of manufacturing. Unemployment in the spring of 2003, at 5·2%, was the lowest in more than 25 years.

COMMUNICATIONS

Roads. In April 2003 the total length of public roads was 24,825 km, graded for administrative purposes as follows: motorway, 133 km (including 19 km slip roads); Class '1' dual carriageway, 150 km; Class '1' single carriageway, 2,113 km; Class '2', 2,869 km; Class '3', 4,705 km; unclassified, 14,874 km.

The Northern Ireland Transport Holding Company (NITHC) oversees the provision of public transport services in Northern Ireland. Its subsidiary companies, Ulsterbus, Citybus and Northern Ireland Railways, are responsible for the delivery of most bus and rail services under the brand name of Translink.

At 31 March 2000 there were 1,963 professional hauliers and 5,322 vehicles licensed to engage in road haulage.

The number of motor vehicles licensed at 31 Dec. 2002 was 794,477, including private light goods, 666,731; goods vehicles, 20,244; motorcycles, scooters and mopeds, 17,598.

Rail. Northern Ireland Railways, a subsidiary of the Northern Ireland Transport Holding Company, provides rail services within Northern Ireland and cross-border services to Dublin, jointly with Irish Rail. The number of track km operated is 340. In 2002–03 railways carried 6·3m. passengers, generating passenger receipts of £15·4m.

Civil Aviation. There are scheduled air services to three airports in Northern Ireland: Belfast International, Belfast City and City of Derry. Scheduled services are provided by easyJet, bmibaby (British Midland), British Airways' franchise partners and British European (Flybe), Eastern Airways, My Travel Lite, Cityexpress, Jetmagic and Flykeen. In 2002–03 the airports collectively handled approximately 6m. passengers. Belfast International, the busiest airport, is Northern Ireland's main charter airport with holiday flights operated direct to European destinations by a wide range of local and UK tour operators. Belfast International handled 3·7m. passengers in 2003.

Belfast City Airport offers commuter services to 16 regional airports in Great Britain including services to London Heathrow. The City of Derry Airport is situated 14 km from Londonderry and provides services from the northwest of Ireland to Dublin and to two United Kingdom destinations (Glasgow and London Stansted). There are two other licensed airfields at St Angelo and Newtownards. They are used principally by flying clubs, private owners and air taxi businesses.

Shipping. There are five commercial ports in Northern Ireland. Belfast is the largest port, competing with Larne for the majority of the passenger and Roll-on Roll-off services that operate to and from Northern Ireland. Passenger services are currently available to Liverpool, Stranraer, Cairnryan and Troon. In addition, Belfast, Londonderry and Warrenpoint ports offer bulk cargo services mostly for British and European markets. They also occasionally service other international destinations direct.

Total tonnage of goods through the principal ports in Northern Ireland in 2001 was 21·2m. tonnes. Belfast handled 13·3m. tonnes of cargo in 2001.

SOCIAL INSTITUTIONS

Justice. The Lord Chancellor has responsibility for the administration of all courts through the Northern Ireland Court Service and for the appointment of judges and magistrates. The court structure has three tiers: the Supreme Court of Judicature of Northern Ireland (comprising the Court of Appeal, the High Court and the Crown Court), the County Courts and the Magistrates' Courts. There are 20 Petty Sessions districts which when grouped together for administration purposes form seven County Court Divisions and four Crown Court Circuits.

The County Court has general civil jurisdiction subject to an upper monetary limit. Appeals from the Magistrates' Courts lie to the County Court, or to the Court of Appeal on a point of law, while appeals from the County Court lie to the High Court or, on a point of law, to the Court of Appeal.

Police. Following legislation introduced in the House of Commons in May 2000, the Royal Ulster Constabulary has now been replaced by the Police Service of Northern Ireland (PSNI). The Police Authority for Northern Ireland has been replaced by the newly formed Northern Ireland Policing Board. The Police Service continues to undergo significant changes arising from the recommendations of the Commission into the future of policing in Northern Ireland published in 1999. In 2003 the PSNI comprised 7,336 regular officers including those student officers undergoing training, 1,645 full-time reserve officers and 888 part-time reserves. The proportion of Catholic regular officers, which was around 8% in Sept. 1999, had increased to 13·9% by Dec. 2003.

The population in penal institutions in Nov. 2003 was 1,220 (70 per 100,000 population).

Religion. According to the 2001 census there were: Roman Catholics, 678,462; Presbyterians, 348,742; Church of Ireland, 257,788; Methodists, 59,173; other Christian, 102,221; other religions and philosophies, 5,028. There were also 233,853 persons with no religion or religion was not stated.

Education. Public education, other than university education, is presently administered by the Department of Education, the Department of Employment and Learning, and locally by five Education and Library Boards. The Department of Education is concerned with the range of education from nursery education through to secondary, youth services and for the development of community relations within and between schools. The Department of Employment and Learning is responsible for higher education, further education, student support, postgraduate awards, and the funding of teacher training.

Each Education and Library Board is the local education authority for its area. Boards were first appointed in 1973, the year of local government reorganization, and are normally reappointed every four years following the District Council elections. The membership of each Board consists of District councillors, representatives of transferors of schools, representatives of trustees of maintained schools and other persons who are interested in the service for which the Board is responsible. Boards have a duty, amongst other things, to ensure that there are sufficient schools of all kinds to meet the needs of their areas. The Boards are responsible for costs associated with capital works at controlled schools. Voluntary schools, including maintained and voluntary grammar schools, can receive grant-aid from the Department of Education toward capital works of up to 85%, or 100% if they have opted to change their management structures so that no single interest group has a majority of nominees. Most voluntary grammar schools can receive the same rate of grant on the purchase of equipment. The Boards award university and other scholarships; they provide school milk and meals; free books and assisted transport for certain pupils; they enforce school attendance; provide a curriculum advisory and support service to all schools in their area; regulate the employment of children and young people; and secure the provision of youth and recreational facilities. They are also required to develop a comprehensive and efficient library service for their area. Board expenditure is funded at 100% by the Department of Education. Integrated schools receive 100% funding for recurrent costs from the Department of Education, and, where long-term viability has been established, for capital works.

The Education Reform (NI) Order 1989 made provision for the setting up of a Council for Catholic Maintained Schools with effect from April 1990. The Council has responsibility for all maintained schools under Roman Catholic Management which are under the auspices of the diocesan authorities and of religious orders. The main objective of the Council is to promote high standards of education in the schools for which it is responsible. Its functions include providing advice on matters relating to its schools, the employment of teaching staff and administration of appointment procedures, the promotion of effective management, and the promotion and co-ordination of effective planning and rationalization of school provision in the Catholic Maintained sector. The membership of the Council consists of trustee representatives appointed by the Northern Roman Catholic Bishops, parents, teachers, and persons appointed by the Head of the Department of Education in consultation with the Bishops.

There is a Council for the Curriculum, Examinations and Assessment which conducts public examinations and oversees the selection procedure and arrangements for pupil assessment. There is also the Northern Ireland Council for Integrated Education, both of which are grant-aided by the Department of Education.

Integrated Schools. The Department of Education has a statutory duty to encourage and facilitate the development of integrated education. It does not seek to impose integration but responds to parental demand for new integrated schools where this does not involve unreasonable public expenditure. The emphasis for future development of the integrated sector has increasingly been on the transformation of existing schools to integrated status. In Dec. 2003 there were 50 grant-aided integrated schools, with a total enrolment of 16,494 pupils, about 5% of all pupils.

Irish Medium Education. Following a commitment in the Belfast Agreement, the 1998 Education Order placed a statutory duty on the Department to encourage and facilitate the development of Irish-medium education. It also provided for the funding of an Irish-medium promotional body, and funding of Irish-medium schools on the same basis as integrated schools. In Dec. 2003 there were 14 Irish-medium primary schools, one post-primary and twelve units, two of which are post-primary catering for 2,455 pupils.

Pre-school Education is provided in nursery schools or nursery classes in primary schools, reception classes and in funded places in voluntary and private settings. There were 100 nursery schools in 2002–03 with 6,269 pupils, and 7,823 nursery pupils in primary schools. A further 1,180 reception pupils were enrolled in primary schools. In addition there were 5,804 children in funded places in voluntary and private pre-school centres.

Primary Education is from four to 11 years. In 2002–03 there were 897 primary schools with 165,179 pupils. There were also 20 preparatory departments of grammar schools with 2,620 pupils. In 2002–03 there were 8,753 FTE primary school teachers and 154 FTE preparatory department teachers.

Secondary Education is from 11 to 18 years. In 2002–03 there were 71 grammar schools with 63,102 pupils and 164 secondary schools with 92,645 pupils. In 2002–03 there were 6,722 FTE secondary school teachers and 4,118 FTE grammar school teachers.

Further Education. There are 16 institutions of further education. In 2001–02 there were 1,815 full-time and 3,113 part-time teachers, approximately 25,000 full-time enrolments, approximately 36,000 part-time enrolments and approximately 31,000 evening students on vocational courses. There were about 75,000 students on non-vocational (mostly evening) courses.

Special Education. The Education and Library Boards provide for children with special educational needs up to the age of 19. This provision may be made in ordinary classes in primary or secondary schools or in special units attached to those schools, or in special schools. In 1999–2000 there were 53 special schools with 4,861 pupils. This includes three hospital schools.

Universities. There are two universities: the Queen's University of Belfast (founded in 1849 as a college of the Queen's University of Ireland and reconstituted as a separate university in 1908) had 20,912 students, 1,514 full-time and 113 part-time academic staff in 2001–02. The University of Ulster, formed on 1 Oct. 1984, has campuses in Belfast, Coleraine, Jordanstown and Londonderry. In the 2001–02 academic year it had 21,223 students, 1,309 full-time and 93 part-time academic staff.

Full-Time Initial Teacher Education takes place at both universities and at two university colleges of education—Stranmillis and St Mary's—the latter mainly for the primary school sector, in respect of which four-year (Hons) BEd courses are available. The training of teachers for secondary schools is provided, in the main, in the education departments of the two universities, but four-year (Hons) BEd courses are also available in the colleges for intending secondary teachers of religious education, business studies and craft, design and technology. There were a total of 1,840 students (1,479 women) in training at the two university colleges and the two universities during 2001–02.

Health. The Department of Health and Social Services is responsible for the provision of integrated health and personal social services. Four Health and Social Services Boards are responsible for assessing the requirements of their resident populations and for purchasing appropriate services. Since 1 April 1996 services have been delivered exclusively by HSS Trusts (similar to NHS Trusts in the rest of the UK) established under the Health and Personal Social Services (NI) Order 1991.

A total of 19 HSS Trusts are fully operational. Seven HSS Trusts based on acute hospitals and the regional Northern Ireland Ambulance Service are identical in structure and management to NHS Trusts in Great Britain. Of the remaining 12, five provide community-based health and personal social services and six provide both hospital and community-based health and personal social services, reflecting the integrated nature of these services in Northern Ireland. In 2003 there were 1,083 doctors (principals), with an average of 1,647 patients each.

Welfare. The Social Security Agency's remit is now part of the Department for Social Development, and social security schemes are similar to those in Great Britain.

National Insurance. During the year ended 31 March 1999 the expenditure of the National Insurance Fund at £1,251·1m. exceeded contributions by £163·7m. The shortfall in income was made up by a Treasury Grant, investment income and a transfer from the Great Britain Fund. Total benefit expenditure was £1,177·9m., excluding £4·1m. which was subsequently recovered from damages paid to recipients of National Insurance Fund Benefits. Employers received £1m. reimbursement in respect of Statutory Sick Pay paid to their employees. £14·6m. was paid in Jobseekers' Allowance contributions. Widows Benefit amounted to £33·2m. and Retirement Pensions to £802·2m. Incapacity Benefits totalled £323·7m. Maternity Allowance of £1·1m. was paid and employers were reimbursed £17·6m. in respect of Statutory Maternity Pay. £39·3m. was given to personal pension plan providers.

Child Benefit. During the year ended 31 March 1999, £261·4m. was paid. *Income Support:* In 1998–99, £513·6m. was paid. *Family Credit:* In 1998–99, £98·0m. was paid.

CULTURE

Tourism. There were an estimated 1·74m. visits to Northern Ireland in 2002, contributing £274m. to the economy. Domestic holiday makers contributed a further £12m. The Northern Ireland Tourist Board is responsible for encouraging tourism. Nine Areas of Outstanding Natural Beauty and 47 Statutory Nature Reserves have been declared, and there are many country and regional parks.

FURTHER READING

Aughey, A. and Morrow, D. (eds.) *Northern Ireland Politics*. Harlow, 1996

Bardon, Jonathan, *A History of Ulster*. Blackstaff Press, Belfast, 1992

Bloomfield, D., *Peacemaking Strategies in Northern Ireland.* London, 1998

Bourke, Richard, *Peace in Ireland: The War of Ideas.* Random House, London, 2003

Bow, P. and Gillespie, G., *Northern Ireland: a Chronology of the Troubles, 1968–1993.* Dublin, 1993

Dixon, Paul, *Northern Ireland: The Politics of War and Peace*. Palgrave, Basingstoke, 2001

Fay, Marie-Thérèse, Morrisey, Mike and Smyth, Marie, *Northern Ireland's Troubles*. Pluto Press, London, 1999

Fletcher, Martin, *Silver Linings: Travels Around Northern Ireland*. Little, Brown, London, 2000

Hennessey, T., *A History of Northern Ireland 1920–96*. London, 1998

Kennedy-Pipe, C., *The Origins of the Present Troubles in Northern Ireland*. Harlow, 1997

Keogh, D. and Haltzel, M. (eds.) *Northern Ireland and the Politics of Reconciliation.* CUP, 1994

Loughlin, James, *The Ulster Question Since 1945*. Macmillan, London, 1998

McDonald, Henry, *Trimble.* Bloomsbury, London, 2000

McGarry, J. and O'Leary, B. (eds.) *Explaining Northern Ireland: Broken Images*. Oxford, 1995

Neumann, Peter R., *Britain's Long War: British Strategy in the Northern Ireland Conflict, 1969–98*. Palgrave Macmillan, Basingstoke, 2003

Rose, Peter, *How the Troubles Came to Northern Ireland.* Macmillan, London, 1999

Ruane, J. and Todd, J., *The Dynamics of Conflict in Northern Ireland: Power, Conflict and Emancipation*. CUP, 1997

Statistical office: Northern Ireland Statistics and Research Agency (NISRA).
Website: http://www.nisra.gov.uk

ISLE OF MAN

KEY HISTORICAL EVENTS

The Isle of Man was first inhabited approximately 10,000 years ago and the Island became attached to Norway in the 9th century. In 1266 it was ceded to Scotland, but it came under English control in 1333.

The Isle of Man has been a British Crown dependency since 1765, with the British government responsible for its defence and foreign policy. Otherwise it has extensive right of self-government.

A special relationship exists between the Isle of Man and the European Union providing for free trade, and adoption by the Isle of Man of the EU's external trade policies with third countries. The Island remains free to levy its own system of taxes.

TERRITORY AND POPULATION

Area, 221 sq. miles (572 sq. km); resident population census April 2001, 76,315, giving a density of 134 per sq. km. In 2001 an estimated 73% of the population lived in urban areas. The principal towns are Douglas (population, 25,308), Onchan (adjoining Douglas; 8,706), Ramsey (7,626), Peel (3,779) and Castletown (3,082). The Island is divided into six sheadings—Ayre, Garff, Glenfaba, Michael, Middle and Rushen. Garff is further subdivided into two parishes and the others each have three parishes.

SOCIAL STATISTICS

2003: births, 860; deaths, 852; marriages (2002), 430. Annual growth rate, 1996–2001, 1·3%.

CLIMATE

Lying in the Irish Sea, the Island's climate is temperate and lacking in extremes. Thunderstorms, snow and frost are infrequent, although the Island tends to be windy. July and Aug. are the warmest months with an average daily maximum temperature of around 17·6°C (63°F).

CONSTITUTION AND GOVERNMENT

As a result of Revestment in 1765, the Isle of Man became a dependency of the British Crown. The UK government is responsible for the external relations of the Island, including its defence and international affairs, and the Island makes a financial contribution to the cost of these services. The Isle of Man has a special relationship with the European Union. It neither contributes funds to, nor receives money from, the EU. The Isle of Man is not represented in either the UK or European Parliaments.

The Island is administered in accordance with its own laws by the High Court of *Tynwald*, consisting of the President of Tynwald, the *Legislative Council* and the *House of Keys*. The Legislative Council is composed of the Lord Bishop of Sodor and Man, eight members selected by the House of Keys and the Attorney General, who has no vote. The House of Keys is an assembly of 24 members chosen by adult suffrage. The President of Tynwald is chosen by the Legislative Council and the House of Keys, sitting together as Tynwald. An open-air Tynwald ceremony is held in early July each year at St Johns. Until 1990 the Lieut.-Governor, appointed by the UK government, presided over Tynwald.

A Council of Ministers was instituted in 1990, replacing the Executive Council which had acted as an advisory body to the Lieut.-Governor. The Council of Ministers consists of the Chief Minister (elected for a five-year term) and the ministers of the nine major departments, being the Treasury; Agriculture, Fisheries and Forestry; Education; Health and Social Security; Home Affairs; Local Government and the Environment; Tourism and Leisure; Trade and Industry; and Transport.

RECENT ELECTIONS

Elections to the House of Keys were held on 22 Nov. 2001. The Alliance for Progressive Government won 3 seats with 14·6% of the vote; the Manx Labour Party 2 seats (17·3% of the vote); while non-partisans won 17 seats. The Manx Nationalist Party boycotted the elections. Turn-out was 57·6%.

CURRENT ADMINISTRATION

Lieut.-Governor: Ian Macfadyen.

President: Noel Cringle (elected April 2000).

In March 2005 the *Chief Minister* was Donald Gelling. *Finance Minister:* Alan Bell.

Website: http://www.gov.im

ECONOMY

Currency. The Isle of Man government issues its own notes and coins on a par with £ sterling. Various commemorative coins have been minted. Inflation was around 3% at the end of 2003.

Budget. The Isle of Man is statutorily required to budget for a surplus of revenue over expenditure. Revenue is raised from income tax, taxes on expenditure, health and social security contributions, and fees and charges for services.

The standard rate of tax is 10% for personal income, and there is a higher rate of 18%. Companies are liable at 10% on their first £100m. of taxable income and 18% on the balance.

There is a Customs and Excise Agreement with the UK, and rates of tax on expenditure are the same as those in the UK with very few exceptions. In addition, there is a reciprocal agreement on social security with the UK, and the rates of health and social security (National Insurance) contributions are the same as in the UK.

In 2003–04 the Isle of Man government budgeted for expenditure of £700m. and revenue of £705m.

Performance. In 2001–02 GNP was £1,179m. and GDP was £1,128m. Real GDP growth in 2001–02 was 5·4%. Just over 80% of national income is generated from services with the finance sector being the single largest contributor (37%).

Banking and Finance. The banking sector is regulated by the Financial Supervision Commission which is responsible for the licensing and supervision of banks, deposit-takers and financial intermediaries giving financial advice, and receiving client monies for investment and management. A compensation fund to protect investors was set up in 1991 under the Commission.

In Sept. 2003 the deposit base was £29bn., and there were 57 licensed banks, 86 investment businesses and two building societies with Isle of Man licences.

The insurance industry is regulated by the Insurance and Pensions Authority. In June 2003 there were 188 insurance companies.

ENERGY AND NATURAL RESOURCES

Electricity. The Manx Electricity Authority generates most of the Island's electricity by oil-fired power stations although there is a small hydro-electric plant. A cable link with the UK power grid came into operation in Nov. 2000. In 2002, 345m. kWh were sold.

Oil and Gas. All oil and gas needs are met from imports, with gas being imported via a link to the Scotland–Eire gas pipeline. The Island's gas suppliers and distributors are in the private sector.

Minerals. Although lead and tin mining industries were major employers in the past, they have long since shut down and the only mining activity in the Island is now for aggregates. The Lady Isabella, built in 1854 to drain the mines above Laxey, is one of the largest waterwheels in Europe.

Agriculture. The area farmed is about 113,000 acres, being 80% of a total land area of around 141,500 acres. 66,000 acres are grassland with a further 35,000 acres for rough grazing. There are approximately 171,000 sheep, 34,000 cattle, 11,000 poultry and 3,000 pigs on the Island's 726 farms. Agriculture now contributes less than 2% of the Island's GDP.

Forestry. The Department of Agriculture, Fisheries and Forestry has a forestry estate of some 6,800 acres. Commercial forestry is directed towards softwood production. The Manx National Glens and other amenity areas are maintained for public use by the Department, which owns some 18,000 acres of the Island's hills and uplands open for public use.

Fisheries. The Isle of Man is noted for the Manx kipper, a gutted smoked herring. Scallops and the related queen scallops (queenies) are the economic mainstay of the Manx fishing fleet. In 2002 the total catch was 2,923 tonnes.

INDUSTRY

Labour. The economically active population in 2001 was 39,685, of whom 5,703 were self-employed and 635 were unemployed. Employment by sector: finance, 23%; professional services, 20%; distributive services, 11%; manufacturing, 8%; construction, 6%.

At the end of 2003 there were 334 persons on the unemployment register, giving an unemployment rate of 0·8%.

Trade Unions. There were 49 registered trade unions in 2003.

INTERNATIONAL TRADE

The Isle of Man forms part of the customs union of the European Union, although the Island is not part of the EU itself. The relationship with the EU provides for free trade and the adoption of the EU's external trade policies and tariffs with non-EU countries.

Imports and Exports. The Isle of Man is in customs and excise union with the United Kingdom, which is also its main trading partner.

COMMUNICATIONS

Roads. There are 800 km of good roads. At the end of March 2003 there were 63,233 licensed vehicles, with 50,596 of these being private cars. Omnibus services operate to all parts of the Island. The TT (Tourist Trophy) motorcycle races take place annually on the 60·75-km Mountain Circuit.

Rail. Several novel transport systems operate on the Island during the summer season from May to Sept. Horse-drawn trams run along Douglas promenade, and the Manx Electric Railway links Douglas, Laxey, Ramsey and Snaefell Mountain (621 metres) in the north. The Isle of Man Steam Railway also operates between Douglas and Port Erin in the south.

Civil Aviation. Ronaldsway Airport in the south handles scheduled services linking the Island with Belfast, Birmingham, Blackpool, Bristol, Brussels, Dublin, East Midlands, Edinburgh, Glasgow, Jersey, Leeds, Liverpool, London, Manchester, Prestwick and Southampton. Air taxi services also operate.

Shipping. Car ferries run between Douglas and the UK and the Irish Republic. In 2003 there were 272 merchant vessels on the Island's shipping register.

Telecommunications. Manx Telecom Limited, a wholly owned subsidiary of O2, holds the telecommunications licence issued by the Communications Commission for the Isle of Man.

Postal Services. The Isle of Man Post Office Authority operates the Island's mail system and issues various commemorative stamps.

SOCIAL INSTITUTIONS

Justice. The First Deemster is the head of the Isle of Man's judiciary. The Isle of Man Constabulary numbered 246 all ranks in 2003.

The average size of the prison population during 2003 was 69·5, equivalent to 104 per 100,000 of national population. A further 13 persons are serving their sentences in the United Kingdom.

Religion. The Island has a rich heritage of Christian associations, and the Diocese of Sodor and Man, one of the oldest in the British Isles, has existed since 476.

Education. Education is compulsory between the ages of five and 16. In 2003 there were 6,744 pupils in the 35 primary schools and 5,566 pupils in the five secondary schools operated by the Department of Education. The Department also runs a college of further education and a special school. Government expenditure on education totalled £78m. in 2003–04. The Island has a private primary school, a private secondary school and an international business school.

Health. The Island has had its own National Health Service since 1948, providing medical, dental and ophthalmic services. In 2003–04 government expenditure on the NHS was £108m. There are two hospitals, one of which opened in 2003. In 1998 there were 117 physicians, 26 dentists and 25 pharmacists.

Welfare. Numbers receiving certain benefits at Dec. 2003: Retirement Pension, 15,702; Child Benefit, 9,313; Sick and Disablement Benefits, 5,680; Income Support, 2,589; Jobseekers' Allowance, 163. Total government expenditure on the social security system in 2003–04 was £155·4m.

CULTURE

Broadcasting. Manx Radio is a commercial broadcaster operated by the government from Douglas.

Press. In 2003 there were three weekly newspapers, one bi-weekly newspaper and one monthly newspaper. There are also various magazines concentrating on Manx issues.

Tourism. During the late 19th century through to the middle of the 20th century, tourism was one of the Island's main sources of income and employment. Tourism now contributes around 5% of the Island's GDP. There were 239,000 visitors during 2002.

FURTHER READING

Additional information is available from: Economic Affairs Division, Illiam Dhone House, 2 Circular Rd, Douglas, Isle of Man, IM1 1PQ. *e-mail: economics@gov.im*

Isle of Man Digest of Economic and Social Statistics, Isle of Man Government, annual

Belchem, J. (ed.) *A New History of the Isle of Man, Volume V—The Modern Period 1830–1999*. Liverpool Univ. Press, 2000

Kermode, D. G., *Offshore Island Politics: The Constitutional and Political Development of the Isle of Man in the Twentieth Century*. Liverpool Univ. Press, 2001

Moore, A. W., *A History of the Isle of Man*. London, 1900; reprinted Manx National Heritage, 1992

Solly, M., *Government and Law in the Isle of Man*. London, 1994

Manx National Heritage publishes a series of booklets including *Early Maps of the Isle of Man*, *The Art of the Manx Crosses*, *The Ancient & Historic Monuments of the Isle of Man*, *Prehistoric Sites of the Isle of Man*.

CHANNEL ISLANDS

KEY HISTORICAL EVENTS

The Channel Islands consist of Jersey, Guernsey and the following dependencies of Guernsey: Alderney, Brechou, Great Sark, Little Sark, Herm, Jethou and Lihou. They were an integral part of the Duchy of Normandy at the time of the Norman Conquest of England in 1066. Since then they have belonged to the British Crown and are not part of the UK. The islands have created their own form of self-government, with the British government at Westminster being responsible for defence and foreign policy. The Lieut.-Governors of Jersey and Guernsey, appointed by the Crown, are the personal representatives of the Sovereign as well as being the commanders of the armed forces. The legislature of Jersey is 'The States of Jersey', and that of Guernsey is 'The States of Deliberation'.

Left undefended from 1940 to 1945 the islands were the only British territory to fall to Germany.

TERRITORY AND POPULATION

The Channel Islands cover a total of 75 sq. miles (194 sq. km), and in 2001 had a population of approximately 150,000.

The official languages are French and English, but English is now the main language.

CLIMATE

The climate is mild, with an average temperature for the year of 11·5°C. Average yearly rainfall totals: Jersey, 862·9 mm; Guernsey, 858·9 mm. The wettest months are in the winter. Highest temperatures recorded: Jersey (St Helier), 36·0°C; Guernsey (airport), 33·7°C. Maximum temperatures usually occur in July and Aug. (daily maximum 20·8°C in Jersey, slightly lower in Guernsey). Lowest temperatures recorded: Jersey, –10·3°C; Guernsey, –7·4°C. Jan. and Feb. are the coldest months (mean temperature approximately 6°C).

CONSTITUTION AND GOVERNMENT
The Lieut.-Governors and Cs.-in-C. of Jersey and Guernsey are the personal representatives of the Sovereign, the Commanders of the Armed Forces of the Crown, and the channel of communication between the Crown and the insular governments. They are appointed by the Crown and have a voice but no vote in the islands' legislatures. The Secretaries to the Lieut.-Governors are their staff officers.

ENERGY AND NATURAL RESOURCES
Fisheries. Total catch in 2001 was 3,927 tonnes, exclusively from sea fishing.

EXTERNAL ECONOMIC RELATIONS
The Channel Islands are not members of the EU, but participate in ERM through their monetary union with the UK. Trade with the UK is classed as domestic.

COMMUNICATIONS
Civil Aviation. Scheduled air services are maintained by Aer Lingus, Aurigny Air Services, bmibaby, British Airways, British Midland, Cathay Pacific Airways, Flybe British European, Scot Airways, Twin Jet and VLM Airlines.

Shipping. Passenger and cargo services between Jersey, Guernsey and England (Poole) are maintained by Condor Ltd hydrofoil; between Guernsey, Jersey and England and St Malo by the Commodore Shipping Co. Emeraude Ferries connect Jersey and Guernsey with St Malo; local companies run between Guernsey, Alderney and England, and between Guernsey and Sark. In 1998 the merchant marine totalled 2,000 GRT.

SOCIAL INSTITUTIONS
Justice. Justice is administered by the Royal Courts of Jersey and Guernsey, each of which consists of the Bailiff and 12 Jurats, the latter being elected by an electoral college. There is an appeal from the Royal Courts to the Courts of Appeal of Jersey and of Guernsey. A final appeal lies to the Privy Council in certain cases. A stipendiary magistrate in each, Jersey and Guernsey, deals with minor civil and criminal cases.

Religion. Jersey and Guernsey each constitutes a deanery under the jurisdiction of the Bishop of Winchester. The rectories (12 in Jersey; 10 in Guernsey) are in the gift of the Crown. The Roman Catholic and various Nonconformist Churches are represented.

FURTHER READING
Lemprière, R., *History of the Channel Islands.* Rev. ed. London, 1980

JERSEY

TERRITORY AND POPULATION
The area is 116·2 sq. km (44·9 sq. miles). Resident population (2001 census), 87,186 (44,701 females); density, 750 per sq. km. The chief town is St Helier on the south coast. It had a population of 28,310 in 2001. The official language is English (French until 1960). The island has its own language, known as Jersey French, or Jérriaise. French and Portuguese are also spoken.

SOCIAL STATISTICS
In 2002 there were 1,023 births and 841 deaths. Infant mortality rate, 1995 (per 1,000 live births), 6·5. In 2002 there were 641 marriages and 309 division petitions for divorce. Life expectancy, 1999: males, 75 years; females, 81 years.

CONSTITUTION AND GOVERNMENT

The island parliament is the *States of Jersey*. The States comprises the Bailiff, the Lieut.-Governor, the Dean of Jersey, the Attorney-General and the Solicitor-General, and 53 members elected by universal suffrage: 12 Senators (elected for six years, six retiring every third year), the Constables of the 12 parishes (every third year) and 29 Deputies (every third year). They all have the right to speak in the Assembly, but only the 53 elected members have the right to vote; the Bailiff has a casting vote. Except in specific instances, enactments passed by the States require the sanction of The Queen-in-Council. The Lieut.-Governor has the power of veto on certain forms of legislation.

Administration is carried out by Committees of the States.

CURRENT ADMINISTRATION

Lieut.-Governor and C.-in-C. of Jersey: Air Chief Marshal Sir John Cheshire, KBE, CBE.

Secretary and Aide-de-Camp to the Lieut.-Governor: Lieut.-Col. C. Woodrow, OBE, MC, QGM.

Bailiff of Jersey and President of the States: Sir Philip Bailhache.

Government Website: http://www.gov.je

ECONOMY

Currency. The States issue banknotes in denominations of £50, £20, £10, £5 and £1. Coinage from 1p to 50p is struck in the same denominations as the UK. There were £61,016,580 worth of States of Jersey banknotes in 2003 and £4,997,000 worth of coinage in circulation in 2002. Inflation in Sept. 2003 was 3·8%.

Budget. 2003 forecast: revenue, £440m.; expenditure, £394m. Income from taxation was forecast to be £375m.

Parochial rates are payable by owners and occupiers.

Performance. From 1999–2001 GDP grew by 3·35%.

Banking and Finance. In 2002 there were 59 banks; combined deposits were £139·3bn. There were 2,829 registered companies in 2002.

The rate of company tax is currently 20%, but a 0% rate of tax is to be introduced by 2009.

ENERGY AND NATURAL RESOURCES

Agriculture. 2002 total agricultural exports, £34,031,576. Jersey Royal New Potatoes account for 68% of the agricultural exports to the UK. 49·6% of the island's land area was farmed commercially in 2002. In 2001 there were 352 commercial farms. In 2002 there were 6,350 cattle (3,970 milch cows).

Fisheries. There were 212 fishing vessels in 2002. The total catch in 2000 was 1,851 tonnes. The value of the fishing industry in 2002 was estimated at £8,707,335.

INDUSTRY

Principal activities: light industry, mainly electrical goods, textiles and clothing.

Labour. At the 2001 census 46,590 persons were economically active, and 150 persons were registered unemployed. Financial services was the largest employment sector, followed by distributive trades, construction, and then hotels and restaurants. Nearly a quarter of all jobs are in the financial and legal sector. By Oct. 2001 there was full employment and over 3,310 unfilled vacancies.

EXTERNAL ECONOMIC RELATIONS

Imports and Exports. Since 1980 the Customs have ceased recording imports and exports. Principal imports: machinery and transport equipment, manufactured goods, food, mineral fuels, and chemicals. Principal exports: machinery and transport equipment, food, and manufactured goods.

COMMUNICATIONS

Roads. In 2002 there were 74,007 private cars, 3,599 hire cars, 7,899 vans, 4,211 lorries, 847 buses and coaches, and 8,505 motorcycles and scooters.

Civil Aviation. Jersey airport is situated at St Peter. It covers approximately 375 acres. In 2002 the airport handled 1,534,808 passengers.

Shipping. All vessels arriving in Jersey from outside Jersey waters report at St Helier or Gorey on first arrival. There is a harbour of minor importance at St Aubin. Number of commercial vessels entering St Helier in 2002, 3,346; number of visiting yachts, 6,741. There were 459,594 passenger arrivals and 459,348 passenger departures in 2002.

Telecommunications. Postal, and overseas telephone and telegraph services, are maintained by the Postal Administration of Jersey. The local telephone service is maintained by the Insular Authority. In 2002 main telephone lines numbered 74,273. There were 71,500 mobile phone subscribers.

Postal Services. In 2001 there were 20 post offices; a total of 74·3m. letters were processed.

SOCIAL INSTITUTIONS

Justice. Justice is administered by the Royal Court, consisting of the Bailiff and 12 Jurats (magistrates). There is a final appeal in certain cases to the Sovereign in Council. There is also a Court of Appeal, consisting of the Bailiff and two judges. Minor civil and criminal cases are dealt with by a stipendiary magistrate.

In 2002 there were 15,201 telephone calls requiring operational response; there were 5,427 crime offences, 1,134 disorder offences and 716 road traffic accidents. In Dec. 2003 the daily average prison population was 170.

Education. In 2002 there were seven States secondary schools, one high school and three special needs secondary schools. There were 25 States primary schools. 4,936 pupils attended secondary schools and 7,386 attended primary schools. There were 613 full-time students at the further education college. Expenditure on public education amounted to £81m. in 2001.

Health. Expenditure on public health in 1999 was £79,829,619. In 2000 there were five hospitals with 651 beds. In 2001 there were 94 doctors (general practitioners).

Welfare. A contributory Health Insurance Scheme is administered by the Social Security Department. In 2002 state expenditure for supplementation on the Social Security Fund was £48,136,000. £4,925,000 was paid out in Family Allowance, £5,823,000 on Disability Transport Allowance, £2,910,000 on Non-native Welfare, £3,094,000 on Attendance Allowance and £1,151,000 on the administration of community benefits.

CULTURE

Tourism. In 2002 there were 872,000 visitors to the island, spending £238m.

FURTHER READING

Balleine, G. R., *A History of the Island of Jersey.* Rev. ed. Chichester, 1981

States of Jersey Library: Halkett Place, St Helier.

GUERNSEY

TERRITORY AND POPULATION

The area is 63·1 sq. km. Census population (2001) 59,807. The main town is St Peter Port.

English is spoken, as is a Norman-French dialect in country areas.

SOCIAL STATISTICS

Births during 2001 were 593; deaths, 564.

CONSTITUTION AND GOVERNMENT

The States of Deliberation, the Parliament of Guernsey, is composed of the following members: the Bailiff, who is President *ex officio*; H.M. Procureur and H.M. Comptroller (Law Officers of the Crown), who have a voice but no vote; 45 People's Deputies elected by popular franchise; ten Douzaine Representatives elected by their

Parochial Douzaines; two representatives of the States of Alderney. Since May 2004 there has been a slimmed-down States of Deliberation, and an executive form of government has been introduced. For the first time a chief minister has been appointed. There are also ministers, a deputy chief minister, members of departmental committees, chairmen and members of committees.

The States of Election, an electoral college, elects the Jurats. It is composed of the following members: the Bailiff (President *ex officio*); the 12 Jurats or 'Jurés-Justiciers'; H.M. Procureur and H.M. Comptroller; the 45 People's Deputies and 34 representatives from the 10 Parochial Douzaines.

Since Jan. 1949 all legislative powers and functions (with minor exceptions) formerly exercised by the Royal Court have been vested in the States of Deliberation. Projets de Loi (Bills) require the sanction of The Queen-in-Council.

RECENT ELECTIONS

Elections for People's Deputies were held on 21 April 2004.

CURRENT ADMINISTRATION

Lieut.-Governor and C.-in-C. of Guernsey and its Dependencies: Lieut.-Gen. Sir John Foley, KCB, OBE, MC.

Secretary and Aide-de-Camp to the Lieut.-Governor: Colonel R. H. Graham, MBE.

Bailiff of Guernsey and President of the States: Sir de Vic Carey.

Chief Minister: Laurie Morgan.

Government Website: http://www.gov.gg

ECONOMY

Budget. Year ended 31 Dec. 2001: revenue, including Alderney, £280,165,000; expenditure, including Alderney, £222,901,000. The standard rate of income tax is 20p in the pound. States and parochial rates are very moderate. No super-tax or death duties are levied.

Banking and Finance. There were 67 banks in 2002. Financial services account for about 66% of the export economy.

The general rate of income tax payable by Guernsey companies, currently 20%, is to be reduced to 0% for the tax year 2008.

INDUSTRY

Trade Unions. There is a Transport & General Workers' Union.

EXTERNAL ECONOMIC RELATIONS

Imports and Exports. Horticulture exports (2001) in £1m.: plant production, 20·28; cut flowers, 11·68; postal flowers, 6·10; food, 3·65; seeds, 0·26. In 2002, 74,066,580 litres of petrol and oils were imported.

Trade Fairs. There are several trade fairs each year.

COMMUNICATIONS

Civil Aviation. The airport is situated at La Villiaze. There were direct flights in 2003 to Alderney, Belfast, Birmingham, Bristol, Brussels, Dinard, Dublin, East Midlands, Edinburgh, Exeter, Geneva, Glasgow, Jersey, London (Gatwick and Stansted), Manchester, Milan, Rotterdam, Southampton and Toulouse. In 2002 passenger movements totalled 837,916.

Shipping. The principal port is St Peter Port. There is also a harbour at St Sampson's (mainly for commercial shipping). In 2002 passenger movements totalled 463,530. Ships registered at 31 Dec. 2002 numbered 2,223 and 250 fishing vessels. In 2002, 9,644 yachts visited Guernsey.

Telecommunications. There were 55,000 main telephone lines in 2002, or 874 per 1,000 population. Mobile phone subscribers numbered 37,000 in 2002 and there were 700 fax machines in 1995. Guernsey Telecom was sold to Cable and Wireless in May 2002 and now trades as C & W Guernsey.

SOCIAL INSTITUTIONS

Justice. The population in penal institutions in Nov. 2003 was 83 (equivalent to 128 per 100,000 population).

Education. There are two public schools, one grammar school, a number of modern secondary and primary schools, and a College of Further Education. The total number of schoolchildren in Sept. 2002 was 8,993. Facilities are available for the study of art, domestic science and many other subjects of a technical nature.

Health. Guernsey is not covered by the UK National Health Service. Public health is overseen by the States of Guernsey Insurance Authority and Board of Health. A private medical insurance scheme to provide specialist cover for all residents was implemented by the States on 1 Jan. 1996. In 1993 there was one hospital and 79 physicians.

CULTURE

Broadcasting. Guernsey is served by BBC Radio Guernsey, Island FM and Channel Television.

Press. The *Guernsey Evening Press* is published daily except Sundays.

Tourism. There were 405,000 visitors in 2001; tourism contributed 12% of the economy.

FURTHER READING

Marr, L. J., *A History of Guernsey.* Chichester, 1982

Statistical office: Policy and Research Unit, P. O. Box 43, Sir Charles Frossard House, La Charroterie, St. Peter Port, GY4 6EF.
Website: http://www.gov.gg/esu

ALDERNEY

GENERAL DETAILS

Population (2001 estimate, 2,400). The main town is St Anne's. The island has an airport.

The Constitution of the island (reformed 1987) provides for its own popularly elected President and States (10 members), and its own Court. Elections were held for the five members of the States in Dec. 2004. Alderney levies its taxes at Guernsey rates and passes the revenue to Guernsey, which charges for the services it provides.

President of the States. Sir Norman Browse.
Chief Executive. David Jeremiah, OBE.
Greffier. Sarah Kelly.

FURTHER READING

Coysh, V., *Alderney.* Newton Abbot, 1974

SARK

GENERAL DETAILS

2001 population estimate, 580. The Constitution is a mixture of feudal and popular government with its Chief Pleas (parliament), consisting of 40 tenants and 12 popularly elected deputies, presided over by the Seneschal. The head of the island is the Seigneur. Sark has no income tax. Motor vehicles, except tractors, are not allowed.

Seigneur. J. M. Beaumont.
Seneschal. R. J. Guille.

FURTHER READING

Hathaway, S., *Dame of Sark: An Autobiography.* London, 1961

UNITED KINGDOM OVERSEAS TERRITORIES

There are 14 British Overseas Territories: Anguilla, Bermuda, British Antarctic Territory, British Indian Ocean Territory, British Virgin Islands, Cayman Islands, Falkland Islands, Gibraltar, Montserrat, Pitcairn Islands, St Helena and its Dependencies (Ascension Island and Tristan da Cunha), South Georgia and the South Sandwich Islands, the Sovereign Base Areas of Akrotiri and Dhekelia in Cyprus, and the Turks and Caicos Islands. Three (British Antarctic Territory, British Indian Ocean Territory and South Georgia and the South Sandwich Islands) have no resident populations and are administered by a commissioner instead of a governor.

Gibraltar is a peninsula bordering the south coast of Spain; the Sovereign Base Areas are in Cyprus and the remainder are islands in the Caribbean, Pacific, Indian Ocean and South Atlantic. Gibraltar and the Falkland Islands are the subjects of territorial claims by Spain and Argentina respectively.

The Overseas Territories are constitutionally not part of the United Kingdom. They have separate constitutions, and most of them have elected governments with varying degrees of responsibilities for domestic matters. The Governor, who is appointed by, and represents, HM the Queen, retains responsibility for external affairs, internal security, defence, and in most cases the public service.

At the launch of the White Paper 'Partnership for Progress and Prosperity', in March 1999, the Foreign Secretary of the time, Robin Cook, outlined four underlying principles for the relationship between Britain and the Overseas Territories: self-determination for the Territories; mutual obligations and responsibilities; freedom for the Territories to run their own affairs to the greatest degree possible; and Britain's firm commitment to help the territories develop economically and to assist them in emergencies. He also offered British citizenship, with the right of abode in the UK, to those citizens of the Overseas Territories who did not already enjoy it. The Overseas Territories Consultative Council was established in 1999. The Council, which meets annually, is a forum for discussion of key policy issues between British government ministers and heads of territory governments. On 21 May 2002 the citizenship provisions of the British Overseas Territories Act came into force. It granted British citizenship to the citizens of all Britain's Overseas Territories (except those who derived their British nationality by virtue only of a connection with the Sovereign Base Areas of Akrotiri and Dhekelia in Cyprus).

ANGUILLA

KEY HISTORICAL EVENTS

Anguilla was probably given its name by the Spaniards or the French because of its eel-like shape. It was inhabited by Arawaks for several centuries before the arrival of Europeans. Anguilla was colonized in 1650 by English settlers from neighbouring St Kitts. In 1688 the island was attacked by a party of Irishmen who then settled. Anguilla was subsequently administered as part of the Leeward Islands, and from 1825 became even more closely associated with St Kitts. In 1875 a petition sent to London requesting separate status and direct rule from Britain met with a negative response. Again in 1958 the islanders formally petitioned the Governor requesting a dissolution of the political and administrative association with St Kitts, but this too failed. From 1958 to 1962 Anguilla was part of the Federation of the West Indies.

Opposition to rule from St Kitts erupted on 30 May 1967 when St Kitts policemen were evicted from the island and Anguilla refused to recognize the authority of the State government any longer. During 1968–69 the British government maintained a 'Senior British Official' to advise the local Anguilla Council and devise some solution to the problem. In March 1969, following the ejection from the island of a high-ranking British civil servant, British security forces occupied Anguilla. A Commissioner was installed, and in 1969 Anguilla became *de facto* a separate dependency of Britain, a situation rendered *de jure* on 19 Dec. 1980 under the Anguilla Act 1980 when Anguilla formally separated from the state of St Kitts,

Anguilla-Nevis. A new constitution came into effect in 1982 providing for a large measure of autonomy under the Crown.

TERRITORY AND POPULATION

Anguilla is the most northerly of the Leeward Islands, some 70 miles (112 km) to the northwest of St Kitts and 5 miles (8 km) to the north of St Martin/Sint Maarten. The territory also comprises the island of Sombrero and several other off-shore islets or cays. The total area of the territory is about 60 sq. miles (155 sq. km). *De jure* census population (2001) was 11,561; density of 74·6 per sq. km. Average annual population increase between 1992 and 2001 was 3·2%. People of African descent make up 90% of the population, mixed origins 5% and white 4%. The capital is The Valley. In 1995 an estimated 89% of the population lived in rural areas.

The official language is English.

SOCIAL STATISTICS

Births, 2001, 183; deaths, 66. In 2001 life expectancy at birth for females was 78·0 years and for males 77·9 years. Households numbered 3,788 in 2001.

CLIMATE

Tropical oceanic climate with rain throughout the year, particularly between May and Dec. Tropical storms and hurricanes may occur between July and Nov. Generally summers are hotter than winters although there is little variation in temperatures.

CONSTITUTION AND GOVERNMENT

A set of amendments to the constitution came into effect in 1990, providing for a Deputy Governor, a Parliamentary Secretary and an Opposition Leader. The *House of Assembly* consists of a Speaker, Deputy Speaker, seven directly elected members for five-year terms, two nominated members and two *ex officio* members: the Deputy Governor and the Attorney-General. The Governor discharges his executive powers on the advice of an Executive Council comprising a Chief Minister, three Ministers and two *ex officio* members: the Deputy Governor, Attorney-General and the Secretary to the Executive Council.

RECENT ELECTIONS

In parliamentary elections held on 21 Feb. 2005 the United Front (Anguilla National Alliance and Anguilla Democratic Party) won four of seven seats, the Anguilla National Strategic Alliance two and the Anguilla United Movement one. Turn-out was 74·6%. A coalition of Anguilla National Alliance and Anguilla Democratic Party was formed following the election to serve a second term.

CURRENT ADMINISTRATION

Governor: Alan Huckle; b. 1948 (took office on 28 May 2004).

Chief Minister: Osbourne Fleming; b. 1940 (Anguilla National Alliance; sworn in 6 March 2000).

Government Website: http://www.gov.ai

ECONOMY

Currency. The *Eastern Caribbean dollar* (*see* ANTIGUA AND BARBUDA).

Budget. In 1998 government revenue was EC$72·3m. and expenditure EC$71·0m. The main sources of revenue are custom duties, tourism and bank licence fees. There is little taxation. A ‘Policy Plan’ with the UK provided for £10·5m. of aid in 1994–97.

Performance. Real GDP growth was –4·3% in 1995 and 7·0% in 1994.

Banking and Finance. The East Caribbean Central Bank based in St Kitts-Nevis functions as a central bank. The *Governor* is Sir Dwight Venner. There is a small offshore banking sector. In 1996 there were two domestic and two foreign commercial banks.

ENERGY AND NATURAL RESOURCES

Electricity. Production (2000) 45·8m. kWh.

Agriculture. Because of low rainfall, agriculture potential is limited. About 1,200 ha are cultivable. Main crops are pigeon peas, maize and sweet potatoes. Livestock consists of sheep, goats, pigs and poultry. The island relies on imports for food.

Fisheries. Fishing is a thriving industry (mainly lobster). The estimated total catch in 2001 was 250 tonnes.

INDUSTRY

Labour. The unemployment rate was 7·8% in July 2002.

EXTERNAL ECONOMIC RELATIONS

Imports and Exports. Merchandise exports in 2002 (and 2001) were US$4·8m. (US$3·6m.); imports in 2002 (and 2001) were US$61·5m. (US$68·5m.)

COMMUNICATIONS

Roads. There are about 40 miles of tarred roads and 25 miles of secondary roads. In 1991 there were 2,450 passenger cars and 733 commercial vehicles.

Civil Aviation. Wallblake is the airport for The Valley. Anguilla is linked to neighbouring islands by services operated by American Airlines, Caribbean Star Airlines, Coastal Air Transport, LIAT and WINAIR.

Shipping. The main seaports are Sandy Ground and Blowing Point, the latter serving passenger and cargo traffic to and from St Martin. In 2002 merchant shipping totalled 1,000 GRT.

Telecommunications. There is a modern internal telephone service with (1997) 5,422 main lines in operation; and international telegraph, telex, fax and Internet services. In Dec. 1998 there were 800 mobile phone subscribers.

SOCIAL INSTITUTIONS

Justice. Justice is based on UK common law as exercised by the Eastern Caribbean Supreme Court on St Lucia. Final appeal lies to the UK Privy Council.

Religion. There were in 2001 Anglicans (29%), Methodists (24%), plus Seventh Day Adventists, Pentecostals, Church of God, Baptists and Roman Catholics as significant minorities.

Education. Adult literacy was 80% in 1995. Education is free and compulsory between the ages of five and 17 years. There are six government primary schools with (1996) 1,540 pupils and one comprehensive school with (1996) 1,060 pupils. Higher education is provided at regional universities and similar institutions.

In 1998–99 expenditure on education came to 14·4% of total expenditure.

Health. In 1996 there was one hospital with a total of 60 beds, four health centres and a government dental clinic. There were five government-employed and three private doctors.

Welfare. A social security system was instituted in 1982 to provide age and disability pensions, and sickness and maternity benefits.

CULTURE

Broadcasting. There is one government (Radio Anguilla) and two other radio broadcasters. TV is privately owned; there are two channels and a cable system. In 1997 there were 3,000 radio and 1,000 television receivers.

Press. In 1995 there were one daily, two weeklies and a quarterly periodical.

Tourism. Tourism accounts for 50% of GDP. In 2000 there were 44,000 visitor arrivals (around two-thirds from the USA); revenue totalled US$55m.

FURTHER READING

Petty, C. L., *Anguilla: Where there's a Will, there's a Way.* Anguilla, 1984.—*A Handbook History of Anguilla.* Anguilla, 1991.

Statistical office: Anguilla Statistics Department, PO Box 60, The Valley, Anguilla.
Website: http://www.gov.ai/statistics

BERMUDA

KEY HISTORICAL EVENTS

The islands were discovered by Juan Bermúdez, probably in 1503, but were uninhabited until British colonists were wrecked there in 1609. A plantation company was formed; in 1684 the Crown took over the government. A referendum in Aug. 1995 rejected independence from the UK.

TERRITORY AND POPULATION

Bermuda consists of a group of 138 islands and islets (about 20 inhabited), situated in the western Atlantic (32° 18' N. lat., 64° 46' W. long.); the nearest point of the mainland, 940 km distant, is Cape Hatteras (North Carolina). The area is 20·59 sq. miles (53·3 sq. km). In June 1995 the USA surrendered its lease on land used since 1941 for naval and air force bases. At the 2000 census the population numbered 62,059; density, 1,164 per sq. km. Capital, Hamilton; population, 2000, 969. Population of St George's, 2000, 1,752.

Ethnic composition, 2000: black, 54·8%; white, 34·0%.

The official language is English. Portuguese is also used.

SOCIAL STATISTICS

In 2001 there were 831 live births, 923 marriages and 442 deaths. Average annual growth rate, 1991–2000, 0·7%. Life expectancy at birth, 2001: 70 years (male); 78 years (female).

CLIMATE

A pleasantly warm and humid climate, with up to 60" (1,500 mm) of rain spread evenly throughout the year. Hamilton, Jan. 63°F (17·2°C), July 79°F (26·1°C). Annual rainfall 58" (1,463 mm).

CONSTITUTION AND GOVERNMENT

Under the 1968 constitution the *Governor*, appointed by the Crown, is normally bound to accept the advice of the Cabinet in matters other than external affairs, defence, internal security and the police, for which he retains special responsibility. The legislature consists of a Senate of 11 members, five appointed by the Governor on the recommendation of the Premier, three by the Governor on the recommendation of the Opposition Leader and three by the Governor in his own discretion. The members of the *House of Assembly* are elected, one from each of 36 constituencies (as of 2003) by universal suffrage.

At a referendum on 17 Aug. 1995, 16,369 votes were cast against the option of independence, and 5,714 were in favour. The electorate was 38,000; turn-out was 58%.

RECENT ELECTIONS

A general election was held on 24 July 2003. Turn-out was 74·9%. The Progressive Labour Party (PLP) won 22 of the 36 seats in parliament, with 51·6% of votes cast. The United Bermuda Party (UBP), which had been in government for 35 years until 1998, won 14 seats, with 48·0%. The PLP is largely representative of the black population, while the UBP membership is mostly white.

CURRENT ADMINISTRATION

Governor: Sir John Vereker; b. 1944 (took office on 11 April 2002).

Premier: Alex Scott; b. 1940 (took office on 29 July 2003).

Government Website: http://www.gov.bm

DEFENCE

The Bermuda Regiment numbered 684 in 1996.

ECONOMY

Bermuda is the world's third largest insurance market after London and New York. Reserves of insurance companies total BD$39bn.

Currency. The unit of currency is the *Bermuda dollar* (BMD) of 100 *cents* at parity with the US dollar. Inflation was 2·9% in 2001, up from 2·7% in 2000.

Budget. The fiscal year ends on 31 March. The 2002–03 budget envisaged revenue of BD$609m. and current expenditure of BD$571m. Estimated chief sources of revenue (in BD$1m.) in 2002–03: customs duties, 177; companies fees, 48; land tax, 37; passenger tax, 22; vehicle licences, 22.

Performance. Real GDP growth was 1·5% in 2002. GDP in 2001 was $2·2bn.

Banking and Finance. Bermuda is an offshore financial centre with tax exemption facilities. In 2002 there were 13,318 international companies registered in Bermuda, with insurers the most important category. There are three commercial banks, with total assets of BD$17,974m. in 2001. HSBC bought the Bank of Bermuda in 2003 for US$1·3bn. At the end of 2001 there were 12,101 exempted companies, 578 exempted partnership companies, 639 non-resident companies and 14 non-resident insurance companies on the Bermuda register. Bermuda is now the world's third largest insurance market after London and New York. The Bermuda Monetary Authority (*Chairman,* Cheryl-Ann Lister) acts as a central bank. There is a stock exchange, the BSX.

Weights and Measures. Metric, except that US and Imperial (British) measures are used in certain fields.

ENERGY AND NATURAL RESOURCES

Environment. Bermuda's carbon dioxide emissions from the consumption and flaring of fossil fuels in 2002 were the equivalent of 8·9 tonnes per capita.

Electricity. Installed capacity was 0·1m. kW in 2000. Production in 2000 was 603m. kWh, with consumption per capita 9,571 kWh.

Minerals. Bermuda is rich in limestone.

Agriculture. The chief products are fresh vegetables, bananas and citrus fruit. In 1995, 839 acres were being used for production of vegetables, fruit and flowers as well as for pasture, forage and fallow. In 2001, 613 persons were employed in agriculture. In 2001 the total value of agricultural products was BD$354,000. Livestock, 2002: 1,000 cattle, 1,000 horses, 1,000 pigs.

Forestry. Approximately 20% of land is woodland.

Fisheries. In 1998 there were 153 registered commercial fishing vessels and 276 registered fishermen. The total catch in 2001 was 315 tonnes. Fishing is centred on reef-dwelling species such as groupers and lobsters.

INDUSTRY

Bermuda's leading industry is tourism, with annual revenue in excess of US$350m.

Labour. The labour force numbered 37,597 in 2001.

Trade Unions. There are nine trade unions with a total membership (1995) of 8,728.

EXTERNAL ECONOMIC RELATIONS

Foreign firms conducting business overseas only are not subject to a 60% Bermuda ownership requirement. In 2002, 10,328 international companies had a physical presence in Bermuda.

Imports and Exports. The visible adverse balance of trade is more than compensated for by invisible exports, including tourism and off-shore insurance business.

Merchandise imports in 2001 (and 2000) were US$750m. (US$719m.); exports in 2001 (and 2000) were US$45m. (US$51m.). In 1999 the USA accounted for 17·8% of imports and 9·8% of exports, and the UK 15·4% of imports and 6·9% of exports. The EU (excluding the UK) accounted for 77·9% of exports and 35·4% of imports.

Principal imports are food, beverages and tobacco, machinery, chemicals, clothing, fuels and transport equipment. The bulk of exports comprise sales of fuel to aircraft and ships, and re-exports of pharmaceuticals.

COMMUNICATIONS

Roads. There are 225 km of public highway and 222 km of private roads. In 2001 there were a total of 45,342 vehicles including: 20,334 private cars; 856 buses, taxis and limousines; 3,676 trucks; 7,724 auxiliary cycles; and 11,918 motorcycles and scooters. There are heavy fines for breaking the speed limit of 35 km/h (22 mph). Bermuda limits cars to one per household and bans hire vehicles.

Civil Aviation. The Bermuda International Airport is 19 km from Hamilton. It handled 833,511 passengers and 5,771 tonnes of freight in 2001. Air Canada, American Airlines, British Airways, Continental Airlines, Delta Airlines and US Airways serve Bermuda with regular scheduled services.

Shipping. There are three ports: Hamilton, St George's and Dockyard. There is an open shipping registry. In 2002 ships registered totalled 4·80m. GRT, including oil tankers 898,000 GRT. In 2001, 1,566 overseas ships called in Bermuda.

Telecommunications. Telephone subscribers numbered 86,000 in 2002, equivalent to 1,323·1 for every 1,000 inhabitants, and there were 34,000 PCs in use (523·1 per 1,000 inhabitants). In 2002 there were 30,000 mobile phone subscribers. Bermuda had 25,000 Internet users in April 2000.

Postal Services. There were 15 post offices in 1995.

SOCIAL INSTITUTIONS

Justice. There are four magistrates' courts, three Supreme Courts and a Court of Appeal. The police had a strength of about 433 men and women in 2003.

Bermuda is the only country in the world where McDonald's restaurants are banned by law.

Religion. Many religions are represented, but the larger number of worshippers are attracted to the Anglican, Methodist, Roman Catholic, Seventh Day Adventist, African Methodist Episcopal and Baptist faiths.

Education. Education is compulsory between the ages of five and 16, and government assistance is given by the payment of grants and, where necessary, school fees. In 2001 there were 6,284 pupils in government schools and 3,606 in private schools. There were 714 full-time students attending the Bermuda College in 2001. A restructuring of secondary school education has resulted in the construction of two new state-of-the-art secondary schools, Cedarbridge Academy and the Berkeley Institute.

In 2002 the adult literacy rate was 98%. In 1998–99 total expenditure on education came to 17·0% of total government spending.

Health. In 2001 there were two hospitals, 120 physicians and surgeons, 62 dentists and hygienists, eight optometrists, 36 pharmacists, 14 dieticians and 528 nurses.

CULTURE

Broadcasting. Radio and television broadcasting are commercial; there are two broadcasting companies which offer a choice of five AM and three FM radio stations, and three TV channels. A cable TV service also offers some 40 channels (colour by NTSC). In 1997 there were 82,000 radio and 66,000 TV receivers, or 1,042 TVs per 1,000 inhabitants—more than anywhere else in the world.

Press. In 2003 there was one daily newspaper with a circulation of about 17,000 and two weeklies with a combined circulation of about 15,000.

Tourism. In 2002, 283,967 tourists visited Bermuda by air and sea. Visitor expenditure in 2002 was US$274·2m.

FURTHER READING

Government Department of Statistics. *Bermuda Facts and Figures.* Annual.
Ministry of Finance. *Economic Review.* Annual.

Boultbee, P. and Raine, D., *Bermuda.* [Bibliography] ABC-Clio, Oxford and Santa Barbara (CA), 1998
Zuill, W. S., *The Story of Bermuda and Her People.* 2nd ed. London, 1992

National library: The Bermuda National Library, Hamilton.
Statistical office: Government Department of Statistics, Hamilton.

BRITISH ANTARCTIC TERRITORY

KEY HISTORICAL EVENTS

The British Antarctic Territory was established on 3 March 1962, as a consequence of the entry into force of the Antarctic Treaty, to separate those areas of the then Falkland Islands Dependencies which lay within the Treaty area from those which did not (i.e. South Georgia and the South Sandwich Islands).

TERRITORY AND POPULATION

The territory encompasses the lands and islands within the area south of 60°S latitude lying between 20°W and 80°W longitude (approximately due south of the Falkland Islands and the Dependencies). It covers an area of some 1,700,000 sq. km, and its principal components are the South Orkney and South Shetland Islands, the Antarctic Peninsula (Palmer Land and Graham Land), the Filchner and Ronne Ice Shelves and Coats Land.

There is no indigenous or permanently resident population. There is, however, an itinerant population of scientists and logistics staff of about 300, manning a number of research stations.

CURRENT ADMINISTRATION

Commissioner: Tony Crombie (non-resident).

Administrator: Dr Michael Richardson.

BRITISH INDIAN OCEAN TERRITORY

KEY HISTORICAL EVENTS

This territory was established to meet UK and US defence requirements by an Order in Council on 8 Nov. 1965, consisting then of the Chagos Archipelago (formerly administered from Mauritius) and the islands of Aldabra, Desroches and Farquhar (all formerly administered from Seychelles). The latter islands became part of Seychelles when that country achieved independence on 29 June 1976. In Nov. 2000 the High Court ruled that the 2,000 Ilois people deported between 1967 and 1973 had been removed unlawfully. However, Chagos islanders lost a UK High Court case for compensation and the right to return in 2003.

TERRITORY AND POPULATION

The group, with a total land area of 23 sq. miles (60 sq. km), comprises five coral atolls (Diego Garcia, Peros Banhos, Salomon, Eagle and Egmont), of which the largest and southernmost, Diego Garcia, covers 17 sq. miles (44 sq. km) and lies 450 miles (724 km) south of the Maldives. A US Navy support facility has been established on Diego Garcia. There is no permanent population.

CURRENT ADMINISTRATION

Commissioner: Tony Crombie (non-resident).

Administrator: Tony Humphries.

Commissioner's Representative: Cdr Adam Peters.

BRITISH VIRGIN ISLANDS

KEY HISTORICAL EVENTS

Discovered by Columbus on his second voyage in 1493, British Virgin Islands were first settled by the Dutch in 1648 and taken over in 1666 by a group of English planters. The islands were annexed to the British Crown in 1672. Constitutional government was granted in 1773, but was later surrendered in 1867. A Legislative Council formed in that year was abolished in 1902. In 1950 a partly nominated and partly elected Legislative Council was restored. A ministerial system of government was introduced in 1967.

TERRITORY AND POPULATION

The Islands form the eastern extremity of the Greater Antilles and number 60, of which 16 are inhabited. The largest, with estimated populations (2000), are Tortola,

16,630; Virgin Gorda, 3,063; Anegada, 204; and Jost Van Dyke, 176. Other islands had a total population (estimate 2000) of 181; marine population (estimate 1989), 124. Total area 59·3 sq. miles (130 sq. km); total population (1991 census), 16,749. The most recent estimate of the population of the British Virgin Islands was 20,254 in 2000. In 1995 an estimated 56% of the population were urban. The capital, Road Town, on the southeast of Tortola, is a port of entry; population (estimate 2000), 7,974.

The official language is English. Spanish and Creole are also spoken.

SOCIAL STATISTICS

Birth rate, 2001, was 15·4 per 1,000 population; death rate, 4·9 per 1,000. Life expectancy in 2001 was an estimated 75·5 years. Annual growth rate, 1·96% in 2000.

CLIMATE

A pleasant healthy sub-tropical climate with summer temperatures lowered by sea breezes and cool nights. Road Town (1999), Jan. 21°C, July 27°C; rainfall (1998), 1471 mm.

CONSTITUTION AND GOVERNMENT

The Constitution dates from 1967 but was amended in 1977 and 1994. The Executive Council consists of the Governor, the Chief Minister, the Attorney-General *ex officio* and four ministers. The ministers are appointed by the Governor from among the elected members of the Legislative Council. The *Legislative Council* consists of the five ministers, five directly elected members from constituencies and four members from 'at large' seats covering the territory as a whole. The Speaker is elected from outside the Council.

RECENT ELECTIONS

In parliamentary elections on 16 June 2003 the National Democratic Party (NDP) won eight of the 13 seats, ahead of the governing Virgin Islands Party (VIP) with five seats. Turn-out was 72%.

CURRENT ADMINISTRATION

Governor: Tom Macan.

Chief Minister: Dr Orlando Smith (NDP; sworn in 17 June 2003).

INTERNATIONAL RELATIONS

The Islands are an associate member of CARICOM, OECS, UNESCO and ECLAC.

The UK government is responsible for the international relations of the Territory. Through this link, the Territory is party to a large number of treaties and international covenants.

ECONOMY

The economy is based on tourism and international financial services.

Currency. The official unit of currency is the US dollar.

Budget. In 2000 revenue was US$183·1m. and expenditure US$134·6m. (goods and services, US$63·7m.; wages and salaries, US$50·1m.; subsidies and transfers, US$19·7m.; interest payments, US$1·2m.) Outstanding debt, in 2000, US$37·1m.

Performance. Real GDP growth was 8·7% in 2001 following growth of 4·4% in 2000. In 2001 the GDP per capita was US$35,954.

Banking and Finance. In 2003 there were 13 banks and in 1999 there were 189 trust companies. As of Sept. 2001 total deposits were US$1,143·8m. Financial Services has surpassed the performance of the tourism industry to become the largest contributor to the GDP. As of 30 June 2001, 448,767 International Business Companies were registered in the British Virgin Islands.

ENERGY AND NATURAL RESOURCES

Electricity. Production, 2000, 260·1m. kWh. In 2000 installed capacity was 13,000 kW.

Agriculture. The value of agricultural production in 1997 was US$1·52m. despite three destructive hurricanes in the course of the year. In 1994: total land suitable for agriculture, 5,324 acres; crops, 1,767 acres; and pastures, 3,557 acres. Agricultural production is limited, with the chief products being livestock (including poultry), fish, fruit and vegetables.

Livestock (2002): cattle, 2,000; pigs, 2,000; sheep, 6,000; goats, 10,000.

Forestry. The area under forests in 2000 was 3,000 ha, or 20·0% of the total land area.

Fisheries. The total catch was approximately 50 tonnes in 2001.

INDUSTRY

The construction industry is a significant employer. There are a rum distillery, ice-making plants and cottage industries producing tourist items.

Labour. In 1997, of the 11,996 strong labour force, 21·4% were employed in the public sector, 3·6% in industry, 0·2% in agriculture and 74·8% in other areas. In 1991 the unemployment rate was 3·6%.

EXTERNAL ECONOMIC RELATIONS

Imports and Exports. There is a very small export trade, almost entirely with the Virgin Islands of the USA. In 2000 imports were US$237·6m. and exports US$26·6m.

COMMUNICATIONS

Roads. In 2000 there were 362·09 km of paved roads and 10,631 registered vehicles.

Civil Aviation. Beef Island Airport, about 16 km from Road Town, is capable of receiving 80-seat short-take-off-and-landing jet aircraft. Several airlines serve the British Virgin Islands, notably LIAT and Caribbean Star Airlines. There are scheduled flights to Puerto Rico and a number of islands in the Eastern Caribbean.

Shipping. There are two deep-water harbours: Port Purcell and Road Town. There are services to the Netherlands, UK, USA and other Caribbean islands. Merchant shipping totalled 23,000 GRT in 2002.

Telecommunications. In 2002 there were 11,700 main telephone lines and 8,000 mobile phone subscribers. Internet users numbered 4,000 in 2002. An external telephone service links Tortola with Bermuda and the rest of the world.

SOCIAL INSTITUTIONS

Justice. Law is based on UK common law. There are courts of first instance. The appeal court is in the UK.

Religion. There are Anglican, Methodist, Seventh-Day Adventist, Roman Catholic, Baptist, Pentecostal and other Christian churches in the Territory. There are also Jehovah's Witness and Hindu congregations.

Education. In 1997 adult literacy was 98·2%. Primary education is provided in 15 government schools, three secondary divisions, 16 private schools and one school for children with special needs. Total number of pupils in primary schools (1997) 2,633.

Secondary education to GCSE level and Caribbean Examination Council level is provided by the BVI High School, and the secondary divisions of the schools on Virgin Gorda and Anegada. Total number of secondary level pupils (1997), 1,424. In 1996 the total number of classroom teachers in all government schools was 116.

In 1986 a branch of the Hull University (England) School of Education was established.

Government expenditure, 1995 (estimate), US$4·3m.

Health. As of 31 Dec. 2000 there were 19 doctors, 74 nurses, 44 public hospital beds and one private hospital with ten beds. Expenditure, 2000 (estimate) was US$7·6m.

CULTURE

Broadcasting. Radio ZBVI transmits 10,000 watts; and British Virgin Islands Cable TV operates a cable system of 43 television channels and one pay-per-view channel (colour by NTSC). In 2000 there were 9,000 radio sets and 6,200 TV receivers.

Press. In 2000 there were three weekly newspapers.

Tourism. Tourism is the most important industry and in 2000 accounted for some 14·1% of economic activity. There were 519,409 foreign tourists in 2000 of which 281,119 were overnight visitors, 188,522 were cruise ship arrivals and 49,768 day-trippers. Total tourist expenditure for 2000 was US$315m. In 1999 the tourism industry employed 12,509 people.

FURTHER READING

Moll, V. P., *Virgin Islands.* [Bibliography] ABC-Clio, Oxford and Santa Barbara (CA), 1991

CAYMAN ISLANDS

KEY HISTORICAL EVENTS

The islands were discovered by Columbus on 10 May 1503 and (with Jamaica) were recognized as British possessions by the Treaty of Madrid in 1670. Grand Cayman was settled in 1734 and the other islands in 1833. They were administered by Jamaica from 1863, but remained under British sovereignty when Jamaica became independent on 6 Aug. 1962.

TERRITORY AND POPULATION

The Islands consist of Grand Cayman, Cayman Brac and Little Cayman. Situated in the Caribbean Sea, about 200 miles (320 km) northwest of Jamaica. Area, 100 sq. miles (260 sq. km). Census population of 1999, 39,410 (52·5% Caymanians by birth). Estimated density, 1996, 135 per sq. km. Estimated population 2001, 41,400. The spoken language is English. The chief town is George Town with a population of 20,626.

The areas and populations of the islands are:

	Sq. km	*1979*	*1989*	*1999*
Grand Cayman	197	15,000	23,881	37,473
Cayman Brac	39	1,607	1,441	1,822
Little Cayman	26	70	33	115

SOCIAL STATISTICS

2001: births, 622; deaths, 133. 2000: resident marriages, 397. Annual growth rate, 1989–99, 4·5%.

CLIMATE

The climate is tropical maritime, with a cool season from Nov. to March. The average yearly temperature is 27°C, and rainfall averages 57" (1,400 mm) a year at George Town. Hurricanes may be experienced between July and Nov.

CONSTITUTION AND GOVERNMENT

The 1972 Constitution provides for a *Legislative Assembly* consisting of the Speaker (who may be an elected member), three official members (the Chief Secretary, the Attorney General and the Financial Secretary) and 15 elected members. The *Executive Council* consists of the Governor (as Chairman), the three official members and five ministers elected by the elected members of the Legislative Assembly. The Islands are a self-governing overseas territory of the United Kingdom.

RECENT ELECTIONS

At the Legislative Assembly elections on 8 Nov. 2000, no national teams were formed. Eight seats were won by teams formed at district level. The new assembly has eight incumbents, six new legislators and one re-elected member (prior service 1988–96). In Nov. 2001, ten members of the Legislative Assembly formed the United Democratic Party. In 2002 the opposition formed the People's Progressive Movement.

CURRENT ADMINISTRATION

Governor: Bruce Dinwiddy.

Government Website: http://www.gov.ky

ECONOMY

Currency. The unit of currency is the *Cayman Island dollar* (KYD/CI$) of 100 *cents.*

Budget. 31 Dec. 2001: revenue, CI$273·2m.; expenditure, CI$288·8m. Public debt, CI$92·5m.; total reserves, CI$10·2m.

Performance. Real GDP growth in 2002 was an estimated 1·9%; in 2000 growth slowed to an estimated 3·2%, down from a five-year average of 5%.

Banking and Finance. Financial services, the Island's chief industry, are monitored by the Cayman Islands Monetary Authority (*Chairman,* Timothy Ridley). At Dec. 2001, 545 commercial banks and trust companies held licenses that permit the holders to offer services to the public, 31 domestically. Most of the world's leading banks have branches or subsidiaries in the Cayman Islands. At the end of 2001, 64,495 companies, almost all offshore, were registered as well as 2,937 mutual funds and 542 insurance companies. Assets of Cayman-registered banks exceeded US$1trn. in 2004.

ENERGY AND NATURAL RESOURCES

Electricity. Installed capacity was 115 MW in 2000, and an all-time peak demand of 70·18 MW occurred in Oct. 2000. Production in 2000 was about 330m. kWh; consumption per capita was an estimated 8,684 kWh.

Agriculture. Mangoes, bananas, citrus fruits, yams, cassava, breadfruit, tomatoes, honey, beef, pork and goatmeat are produced for local consumption.

Fisheries. In 2001 the total catch was 125 tonnes.

INDUSTRY

Labour. Unemployment rate: 7·5% of workforce in Oct. 2002 (10% Oct. 2001).

EXTERNAL ECONOMIC RELATIONS

Imports and Exports. Exports, 1998, totalled US$1·44m.; imports, US$505·56m.

COMMUNICATIONS

Roads. There were (2000) about 461 miles of road on Grand Cayman; 25 miles on Cayman Brac and on the three islands 25,061 licensed motor vehicles.

Civil Aviation. George Town (O. Roberts) on Grand Cayman and Cayman Brac have international airports. George Town handled 901,000 passengers (834,000 on international flights) and 3,900 tonnes of freight in 2000. Cayman Airways and Island Air provide a regular inter-island service. Cayman Airways also flies to Miami, Houston, Tampa, Cuba and Jamaica. Eight additional international airlines provide services to London, Toronto, Jamaica, the Bahamas, Honduras and five US cities, including New York and Atlanta.

Shipping. Motor vessels ply regularly between the Cayman Islands, Jamaica, Cuba and Florida. In 2001, 192,303 tonnes of cargo were offloaded at the port on Grand Cayman, 13,552 on Cayman Brac and, in 2000, 1,845 at Little Cayman.

Telecommunications. At the end of 2001 there were 31,926 direct telephone lines and over 17,000 mobile customers.

SOCIAL INSTITUTIONS

Justice. There is a Grand Court, sitting six times a year for criminal sessions at George Town under a Chief Justice and two puisne judges. There are three Magistrates presiding over the Summary Court.

The population in penal institutions in Nov. 2003 was 210 (equivalent to 501 per 100,000 population, one of the highest rates in the world).

Religion. The residents are primarily Christian (85%) and over 12 denominations meet regularly; Church of God, Presbyterian/United, Roman Catholic, Baptist and Seventh-Day Adventists are the largest. Other religions, including Ba'hai, Buddhism, Hinduism, Islam and Judaism, have representation in the community.

Education. In 2002 there were ten government primary schools with 2,212 pupils, and 1,913 pupils attended the three government high schools. In 2001 about 2,240 students were enrolled in ten private schools. There are two government facilities for special educational needs: a school for children and a training centre for adults. Four institutions—a private four-year college, a private medical college, the government community college and law school—provide tertiary education.

Health. The government's health services complex in George Town includes a 124-bed hospital, a dental clinic and an eye clinic. On Grand Cayman there are four district health centres. There is a hospital on Cayman Brac (18 beds) and a health centre on Little Cayman. In 2001 there were 38 doctors in government service (including four on Cayman Brac) and 37 in private practice.

CULTURE

Broadcasting. There are seven radio stations (one Christian), four broadcast television channels (two Christian) and a 38-channel microwave relay cable system.

Press. There are two newspapers, both printed on weekdays. News and opinion are also available on at least seven Internet sites.

Tourism. Tourism is the chief industry after financial services, and in 2000 there were 3,756 beds in hotels and 2,341 rooms in apartments, guest houses and cottages. There were 334,071 tourist arrivals by air and 1,214,757 cruise ship arrivals. Tourism receipts in 1999 totalled US$439m.

FURTHER READING

Compendium of Statistics of the Cayman Islands, 2003. Cayman Islands Government Statistics Office, 2004
Cayman Islands Annual Report 2003. Cayman Islands Government Information Services, 2004
Boultbee, Paul G., *Cayman Islands.* [Bibliography] ABC-Clio, Oxford and Santa Barbara (CA), 1996

FALKLAND ISLANDS

KEY HISTORICAL EVENTS

France established a settlement in 1764 and Britain a second settlement in 1765. In 1770 Spain bought out the French and drove off the British. This action on the part of Spain brought that country and Britain to the verge of war. The Spanish restored the settlement to the British in 1771, but the settlement was withdrawn on economic grounds in 1774. In 1806 Spanish rule was overthrown in Argentina, and the Argentine claimed to succeed Spain in the French and British settlements in 1820. The British objected and reclaimed their settlement in 1832 as a Crown Colony.

On 2 April 1982 Argentine forces occupied the Falkland Islands. On 3 April the UN Security Council called, by 10 votes to 1, for Argentina's withdrawal. After a military campaign, but without a formal declaration of war, the UK regained possession on 14–15 June when Argentina surrendered. In April 1990 Argentina's Congress declared the Falkland and other British-held South Atlantic islands part of the new Argentine province of Tierra del Fuego though the threat of hostilities has been lifted.

TERRITORY AND POPULATION

The Territory comprises numerous islands situated in the South Atlantic Ocean about 480 miles northeast of Cape Horn covering 12,200 sq. km. The main East Falkland Island, 6,760 sq. km; the West Falkland, 5,410 sq. km, including the adjacent small islands. The population at the census of 2001 was 2,379. The only town is Stanley, in East Falkland, with a 2001 population of 1,989. The population is nearly all of British descent, with 1,326 born in the Islands (2001 census figures) and 925 in the UK. In 1995, 84·1% lived in urban areas. A British garrison of about 2,000 servicemen, stationed in East Falkland in 1991, is not included in the 2001 census figures, but the 534 civilians employed there are.

The official language is English.

SOCIAL STATISTICS

In 2000 there were 27 births and 11 deaths on the islands.

CLIMATE

A cool temperate climate, much affected by strong winds, particularly in spring. Stanley, Jan. 49°F (9·4°C), July 35°F (1·7°C). Annual rainfall 24" (625 mm).

CONSTITUTION AND GOVERNMENT

A new Constitution came into force in 1997, updating the previous constitution of 1985 which incorporated a chapter protecting fundamental human rights, and in the preamble recalled the provisions on the right of self-determination contained in international covenants.

Executive power is vested in the Governor who must consult the Executive Council except on urgent or trivial matters. He must consult the Commander British Forces on matters relating to defence and internal security (except police).

There is a *Legislative Council* consisting of eight members (five from Stanley and three from Camp, elected every four years) and two *ex officio* members, the Chief Executive and Financial Secretary. Only elected members have a vote.

British citizenship was withdrawn by the British Nationality Act 1981, but restored after the Argentine invasion of 1982.

RECENT ELECTIONS

Elections to the Legislative Assembly were held on 22 Nov. 2001. Only non-partisans were elected.

CURRENT ADMINISTRATION

Governor: Howard Pearce.

Chief Executive: Chris Simpkins.

Government Website: http://www.falklands.gov.fk

DEFENCE

Since 1982 the Islands have been defended by a 2,000-strong garrison of British servicemen. In addition there is a local volunteer defence force.

ECONOMY

The GNP of the Islands is estimated to have tripled from 1985–87 as a result of the expansion of the fishing industry. In 1998–99 the GNP was estimated at £53m.

Overview. In 2001 the Falklands Islands government published the Islands Plan, a three-year rolling programme aimed at achieving sustainable economic growth whilst preserving the natural environment. Policy-making is also influenced by the Falkland Islands Development Corporation (FIDC), established in 1984.

Currency. The unit of currency is the *Falkland Islands pound* (FKP) of 100 *pence*, at parity with £1 sterling.

Budget. Revenue and expenditure (in £ sterling) for fiscal year ending 30 June 2000 was: revenue, 52·3m.; expenditure, 40·4m.

Banking and Finance. The only bank is Standard Chartered Bank, which had assets of £31m. in 1997.

ENERGY AND NATURAL RESOURCES

Electricity. Electricity production in 2000 totalled about 15m. kWh. Installed capacity in 2000 was 9,000 kW.

Oil and Gas. In 1996 the Falkland Islands government awarded production licences to Shell, Amerada Hess, Desire Petroleum and International Petroleum Corporation (Sodra), allowing them to begin oil exploration. The licensed areas are situated 150 km north of the Islands over the North Falkland Basin. Six exploration wells were drilled in 1998 and analysis of the findings suggested that in excess of 60bn. bbls. of oil have been generated in the basin.

Agriculture. The economy was formerly based solely on agriculture, principally sheep farming. Following a programme of sub-division, much of the land is divided into family-size units. There were 100 farms in 1997, averaging 33,600 acres and 8,200 sheep. Wool is the principal product; 1,870,000 tonnes worth £2,292,000 was exported to the UK in 1998.

Livestock: in April 2000 there were over 700,000 sheep. 2002 estimates: cattle, 4,000; horses, 1,000.

Fisheries. Since the establishment of a 150-mile interim conservation and management zone around the Islands in 1986 and the consequent introduction, on 1 Feb. 1987, of a licensing regime for vessels fishing within the zone, income from the associated fishing activities is now the largest source of revenue. Licences raised £25m. in 1992 but this figure had fallen to £20m. by 1998–99. In 2000 the fish catch (1,000 tonnes) was: illex, 190; loligo, 64; blue whiting, 23; hoki, 20; hake, 3; others, 19. The growth in the annual fish catch since the mid 1980s has been one of the fastest in the world.

On 26 Dec. 1990 the Falklands outer conservation zone was introduced which extends beyond the 150-mile zone out to 200 miles from baselines. In Nov. 1992 commercial fishing in the outer zone was banned, the zone was reopened to fishing in 1994. A UK-Argentine South Atlantic Fisheries Commission was set up in 1990; it meets at least twice a year. In 2001 there were 27 registered fishing vessels.

INDUSTRY

Labour. In 2001 there were 2,025 people employed full-time, including 358 in construction and 326 in agriculture, hunting and fishing. The growth of the fishing industry has ensured practically zero unemployment.

EXTERNAL ECONOMIC RELATIONS

Around 85% of trade is with the UK, the rest with Latin America, mainly Chile. In 1998 imports totalled £23·5m.; exports (mainly wool), £3·5m. (1995).

COMMUNICATIONS

Roads. There are over 50 km of surfaced roads and another 400 km of unsurfaced road. This includes the 80 km between Stanley and Mount Pleasant Airport. Other settlements outside Stanley are linked by tracks. There were about 1,100 private cars in 1996.

Civil Aviation. Air communication is currently via Ascension Island. An airport, completed in 1986, is sited at Mount Pleasant on East Falkland. RAF Tristar aircraft operate a twice-weekly service between the Falklands and the UK. A Chilean airline, LanChile, runs a weekly service to Puerto Montt, Punta Arenas, Rio Gallegos and Santiago. Aircraft movements at Stanley Airport in 1998 amounted to 4,264 with 7,715 passengers moving through the airport.

Shipping. A charter vessel calls four or five times a year to/from the UK. Vessels of the Royal Fleet Auxiliary run regularly to South Georgia. Sea links with Chile and Uruguay began in 1989. In 2002 merchant shipping totalled 54,000 GRT.

Telecommunications. Number of telephone main lines in 2002 was 2,400. International direct dialling is available, as are international facsimile links. In 2002 there were 1,900 Internet users.

Postal Services. In 1998 there were two post offices and 740 post boxes. Airmail is generally received and dispatched twice weekly and surface post is airlifted out about once every two weeks. Surface mail is received approximately once every three weeks.

SOCIAL INSTITUTIONS

Justice. There is a Supreme Court, and a Court of Appeal sits in the UK; appeals may go from that court to the judicial committee of the Privy Council. The senior resident judicial officer is the Senior Magistrate. There is an Attorney General and a Senior Crown Counsel.

Education. Education is compulsory between the ages of five and 16 years. In Stanley in 2002 there were 30 pre-school pupils, 190 primary pupils (18 teachers) and 160 pupils in the 11–16 age range (18 teachers). In rural areas students attend small settlement schools or are visited by one of seven travelling teachers. Lessons may also be carried out over the radio or telephone.

Health. The Government Medical Department is responsible for all medical services to civilians. Primary and secondary health care facilities are based at the King Edward VII Memorial Hospital, the only hospital on the islands. It has 28 beds. It is staffed by five doctors, six sisters (including four midwives), eight staff nurses, a health visitor, counsellor, physiotherapist, social worker and an auxiliary nursing staff. The Royal Army Medical Corps staff the surgical facilities. There are two dentists on the island. Estimated expenditure (1994–95), £2,092,490.

Welfare. In 1998 total amount spent on old age pension payments was £504,075. Total amount spent on family allowance payments was £336,365.

CULTURE

Broadcasting. The Falkland Islands Broadcasting Station (FIBS), in conjunction with British Forces Broadcasting Service (BFBS), broadcasts 24 hours a day on FM and MW. Some BBC World Service programmes are also available.

BFBS also provides a single channel TV service (UKPAL) to Stanley, Mount Pleasant and most outlying camp settlements and a cable TV service is also in operation. In 1997 there were 1,000 TV and 1,000 radio sets.

Tourism. In the 1999–2000 season there were estimated to be 30,000 cruise ship visitors, representing a 400% increase over three seasons. There are tourist lodges at Port Howard, San Carlos, Sea Lion Island and Pebble Island. Stanley has two hotels.

FURTHER READING

Day, Alan, *The Falkland Islands, South Georgia and the South Sandwich Islands.* [Bibliography] ABC-Clio, Oxford and Santa Barbara (CA), 1996

Gough, B., *The Falkland Islands/Malvinas: the Contest for Empire in the South Atlantic.* London, 1992

GIBRALTAR

KEY HISTORICAL EVENTS

The Rock of Gibraltar was settled by Moors in 711. In 1462 it was taken by the Spaniards, from Granada. It was captured by Admiral Sir George Rooke on 24 July 1704, and ceded to Great Britain by the Treaty of Utrecht, 1713. The cession was confirmed by the treaties of Paris (1763) and Versailles (1783). In 1830 Gibraltar became a British crown colony.

On 10 Sept. 1967 a UN resolution on the decolonization of Gibraltar led to a referendum to ascertain whether the people of Gibraltar wished to retain their link with the UK. Out of an electorate of 12,762, an overwhelming majority voted to retain the British connection.

The border was closed by Spain in 1969, opened to pedestrians in 1982 and fully opened in 1985. In 1973 Gibraltar joined the European Community as a dependent territory of the United Kingdom. In 2001 talks were held between Britain and Spain over the colony's sovereignty. In a joint statement, the British and Spanish foreign ministers said they would work towards a comprehensive agreement by the summer of 2002. Gibraltar's government held an unofficial referendum on sharing sovereignty with Spain on 7 Nov. 2002 in which 98·97% of votes cast were against joint sovereignty. While Britain sees the principle of shared sovereignty as the definitive solution, Spain maintains its historic claim to outright control.

TERRITORY AND POPULATION

Gibraltar is situated in latitude 36°07' N and longitude 05°21' W. Area, 2½ sq. miles (6·5 sq. km) including port and harbour. Total population, (2003), 28,605 (of whom 23,069 were British Gibraltarian, 3,270 Other British and 2,266 Non-British); density, 4,400 per sq. km. The population is mostly of Genoese, Portuguese and Maltese and Spanish descent.

The official language is English. Spanish, Italian and Portuguese are also spoken.

SOCIAL STATISTICS

Statistics (2003): births, 363; deaths, 234; marriages, 829. Rates per 1,000 population, 2000: birth, 15·1; death, 9·7; marriage, 26·7 (the highest in Europe and one of the highest in the world).

CLIMATE

The climate is warm temperate, with westerly winds in winter bringing rain. Summers are pleasantly warm and rainfall is low. Mean maximum temperatures: Jan. 16°C, July 28°C. Annual rainfall 722 mm.

CONSTITUTION AND GOVERNMENT

A new Constitution was introduced in 1969. The Legislative and City Councils were merged to produce an enlarged legislature known as the *Gibraltar House of Assembly*. Executive authority is exercised by the Governor, who is also Commander-in-Chief. The Governor retains direct responsibility for matters relating to defence, external affairs and internal security. However, he is normally required to act in accordance with the advice of the Gibraltar Council, which consists of four *ex officio* members (the Deputy Governor, the Deputy Fortress Commander, the Attorney-General and the Financial and Development Secretary) together with five elected members of the House of Assembly appointed by the Governor after consultation with the Chief Minister. There is a Council of Ministers presided over by the Chief Minister.

The House of Assembly consists of a Speaker appointed by the Governor, 15 elected and two *ex officio* members (the Attorney-General and the Financial and Development Secretary).

Gibraltarians have full UK citizenship.

RECENT ELECTIONS

At the elections of 27 Nov. 2003 the electorate was 10,317 and turnout was 57·73%. The ruling Gibraltar Social Democratic Party (GSD) gained eight seats with 51% of votes cast. The opposition alliance of the Gibraltar Socialist Labour Party and the Liberal Party took 40% of the vote, gaining five and two seats respectively.

CURRENT ADMINISTRATION

Governor and C.-in-C: Sir Francis Richards, KCMG, CVO, b. 1945 (sworn in on 27 May 2003).

Chief Minister: Peter Caruana; b. 1956 (GSD; elected in 1996, re-elected in 2000 and 2003).

Deputy Chief Minister and Minister for Trade and Industry and Communications: Joe Holliday. *Education, Employment and Training:* Dr Bernard Linares. *Health:* Lt. Col. Ernest Britto. *Housing:* Jaime Netto. *Social Affairs:* Yvette Del Agua. *Heritage, Culture, Youth and Sport:* Clive Beltran. *Environment, Roads and Utilities:* Fabian Vinet.

Speaker (House of Assembly): John E. Alcantara.

Government Website: http://www.gibraltar.gov.gi

DEFENCE

The Ministry of Defence presence consists of a tri-service garrison numbering approximately 900 uniformed personnel. Supporting the garrison are approximately 1,100 locally-employed civilian personnel. The garrison supports a NATO Headquarters.

ECONOMY

Overview. The economy is primarily dependent on service industries and port facilities, with income derived from tourism, transhipment and, perhaps most importantly in terms of growth, the provision of financial services.

Currency. The legal tender currency is UK sterling. Also legal tender are Government of Gibraltar Currency notes and coins. The *Gibraltar pound* (GIP) of 100 *pence* is at parity with the UK £1 sterling. The total of Government of Gibraltar notes in circulation at 31 March 2004 was £14·3m. The annual rate of inflation was 2·5% in 2003.

Budget. Departmental revenue credited to the Consolidated Fund for the year ending 31 March 2003 totalled £166·3m. whilst expenditure amounted to £135·3m. The main sources of Consolidated Fund revenues were Income Tax (£65·5m.), import duties (£29·2m.), Corporation Tax (£16·9m.) and General Rates (£12m.). Main items of Consolidation Fund expenditure: Education, Culture and Training (£19·8m.); Social Affairs (£13·3m.); Electricity (£12·5m.); Technical Services (£12·2m.); contributions to the Gibraltar Health Authority (£11·9m.); Police (£8m.); Housing (£7·5m.); Tourism and Transport (£7·2m.).

Performance. In 2000–01 Gibraltar's provisional GDP was £433·6m., equivalent to £15,863 per head.

Banking and Finance. At March 2004 there were 17 authorized banks. The majority of these are either subsidiaries or branches of major UK or other European Economic Area (EEA) banks. In 1989 the Financial Services Commission was established to regulate financial activities. The banking sector provides services to both local and non-resident customers. Many of these banks specialize in providing private banking to high net worth individuals who are not resident in Gibraltar.

ENERGY AND NATURAL RESOURCES

Environment. Gibraltar's carbon dioxide emissions from the consumption and flaring of fossil fuels in 2002 were the equivalent of 144·1 tonnes per capita, the highest in the world.

Electricity. Production in 2001 amounted to 126m. kWh.

Oil and Gas. Gibraltar is dependent on imported petroleum for its energy supplies.

Agriculture. Gibraltar lacks agricultural land and natural resources; the territory is dependent on imports of foodstuffs and fuels.

INDUSTRY

The industrial sector (including manufacturing, construction and power) employed around 17% of the working population in 1999.

Labour. The total insured labour force at Oct. 1998 was 12,774. Principal areas of employment (Oct. 1998): community, social and personal services, 5,937; trade, restaurants and hotels, 3,739; manufacturing, 402; electricity and water, 232; other, 1,511. (Figures cover only non-agricultural activities, excluding mining and quarrying). An estimated 2% of the labour force were unemployed in 2002.

Trade Unions. In 1991 there were eight registered trade unions.

EXTERNAL ECONOMIC RELATIONS

Gibraltar has a special status within the EU which exempts it from the latter's fiscal policy.

Imports and Exports. Imports in 2003 totalled £286·1m. and exports £90·1m (excluding petroleum products).

Britain provided 28% of imports in 2003 and is the largest source. Other major trade partners include the Netherlands, Spain and Japan. Foodstuffs accounted for 7% of total imports in 2003. Value of non-fuel imports, 2003, £286·1m. Mineral fuels comprised about 60% of the value of total imports in 2003. Exports are mainly re-exports of petroleum and petroleum products supplied to shipping, and include manufactured goods, wines, spirits, malt and tobacco. Gibraltar depends largely on tourism, offshore banking and other financial sector activity, the entrepôt trade and the provision of supplies to visiting ships. In 2003 Gibraltar recorded a visible trade deficit of £196·0m.

COMMUNICATIONS

Roads. There are 56 km of roads including 6·8 km of pedestrian way. In 2004 there were 12,395 private vehicles, 5,358 motorcycles, 1,065 goods vehicles and 98 omnibuses and 103 taxis.

Civil Aviation. There is an international airport, Gibraltar North Front. Scheduled flights were operated in 2003 by British Airways to London (Gatwick), and by

Monarch Airlines to London (Luton) and Manchester. In 2003, 133,005 passengers arrived by air and 132,852 departed; 66 tonnes of freight were loaded and 325 tonnes were unloaded (figures exclude military freight). The airport was designed to accommodate 1m. passengers a year, but is underutilized owing to Spain's exclusion of Gibraltar as a European regional airport.

Shipping. The Strait of Gibraltar is a principal ocean route between the Mediterranean and Black Sea areas and the rest of the world. A total of 6,751 merchant ships of 147·7m. GRT entered port during 2003, including 5,758 deep-sea ships of 146·1m. GRT. In 2003, 4,387 calls were made by yachts of 147,510 GRT. 167 cruise liners called during 2003 involving 137,979 passengers.

Telecommunications. Gibtelecom and its two wholly owned subsidiaries Gibraltar Telecommunications International Limited (Gibtel) and Gibconnect are responsible for the provision of most of the telecommunications and internet services and the supply of communications equipment in Gibraltar.

As at 31 Dec. 2003 the Group's fixed exchange lines stood at 25,657. By the end of 2003 there were 15,709 mobile GSM phone customers.

Postal Services. Airmail is dispatched to London, and via London to destinations worldwide, six times a week in direct flights. Surface letter mail and parcel mail to and from the United Kingdom is dispatched and received via the land frontier five times a week.

SOCIAL INSTITUTIONS

Justice. The judicial system is based on the English system. There is a Court of Appeal, a Supreme Court, presided over by the Chief Justice, a Court of First Instance and a Magistrates' Court.

The population in penal institutions in Nov. 2003 was 31 (equivalent to 112 per 100,000 population).

Religion. According to the 1991 census 76·9% of the population were Roman Catholic, 6·9% Muslim, 6·9% Church of England and 2·3% Jewish. In 2000 there were 7 Roman Catholic and 3 Anglican churches (including 1 Catholic and 1 Anglican cathedral), 1 Presbyterian and 1 Methodist church, 4 synagogues and 1 mosque.

Education. Free compulsory education is provided between ages four and 15 years. The medium of instruction is English. The comprehensive system was introduced in Sept. 1972 and all schools currently follow a locally adapted version of the National Curriculum for England and Wales. In the 2003–04 academic year there were 11 primary and two secondary schools. Primary schools are divided into first schools for children aged 4–8 years and middle schools for children aged 8–12 years. All primary schools are mixed though secondary schools are single-sex.

Vocational education and training is available at the Gibraltar College (a post-15 institution), the Construction Training Centre and the Cammel Laird Training Centre; the former two are managed by the Gibraltar government and the latter by Cammel Laird (and part-funded by the Government). In Sept. 2003 there were 3,082 pupils at government primary schools, 305 at private primary schools and 198 at the Services school. 970 pupils were enrolled at the boys' comprehensive school and 954 at the girls' comprehensive. There were 309 students in the Gibraltar College. Government expenditure on education in the year ended 31 March 2004 was £19m.

Health. The Gibraltar Health Authority is the organization responsible for providing health care in Gibraltar. The Authority operates a Group Practice Medical Scheme which is a contributory scheme and enables registered persons to access free medical treatment. In 2002 there were two hospitals with 226 beds. Total expenditure on medical and health services during year ended 31 March 2002 was £31·4m.

Welfare. The social security system consists of: the Social Security (Employment Injuries Insurance) Scheme which only applies to employed persons; the Social Security (Short-Term Benefits) Scheme which provides for payments of maternity grants. maternity allowance, death grants and unemployment benefit; and the Social Security (Open Long-Term Benefits) Scheme which provides for pensions and widows' allowances.

CULTURE

Broadcasting. Radio Gibraltar broadcasts for 24 hours daily, 22 hours in English and two hours in Spanish; and GBC Television operates for 24 hours daily in English (colour by PAL). At 31 Dec. 2003 there were 7,500 TV licences.

Press. In 2003 there were two daily and one weekly papers.

Tourism. In 2000 more than 7·3m. tourists visited Gibraltar (including day-visitors) bringing in revenue of £162m. There are around 2,000 hotel beds in Gibraltar. Tourism accounts for an estimated 35% of GDP.

FURTHER READING

Gibraltar Year Book. Gibraltar (Annual)
Morris, D. S. and Haigh, R. H., *Britain, Spain and Gibraltar, 1940–90: the Eternal Triangle.* London, 1992

MONTSERRAT

KEY HISTORICAL EVENTS

Montserrat was discovered by Columbus in 1493 and colonized by Britain in 1632, who brought Irish settlers to the island. Montserrat formed part of the federal colony of the Leeward Islands from 1871 until 1958, when it became a separate colony following the dissolution of the Federation.

On 18 July 1995 the Soufriere Hills volcano erupted for the first time in recorded history, which led to over half the inhabitants being evacuated to the north of the island, and the relocation of the chief town, Plymouth. Another major eruption on 25 June 1997 caused a number of deaths and led to further evacuation.

TERRITORY AND POPULATION

Montserrat is situated in the Caribbean Sea, 43 km southwest of Antigua. The area is 39·5 sq. miles (102 sq. km). Census population, 1991, 10,639; estimate, 2002, 4,500. What was previously the capital, Plymouth, is now deserted as a result of the continuing activity of the Soufriere Hills volcano. The safe area is in the north of the island.

The official language is English.

CLIMATE

A tropical climate with an average annual rainfall of 60" (1,500 mm) the wettest months being Sept.–Dec., with a hurricane season June–Nov. Plymouth, Jan. 76°F (24·4°C), July 81°F (27·2°C).

CONSTITUTION AND GOVERNMENT

Montserrat is a British Overseas Territory. The Constitution dates from the 1989 Montserrat Constitutional Order. The head of state is Queen Elizabeth II, represented by a *Governor* who heads an Executive Council, comprising also the Chief Minister, the Financial Secretary, the Attorney-General and three other ministers. The *Legislative Council* consists of seven elected members, two civil service officials (the Attorney-General and Financial Secretary) and two nominated members; it sits for five-year terms.

RECENT ELECTIONS

In elections to the Legislative Council on 2 April 2001 the New People's Liberation Movement won seven of the nine seats against two for the National Progressive Party.

CURRENT ADMINISTRATION

Governor: Deborah Barnes Jones; b. 1956 (since 10 May 2004).

Chief Minister: John Osborne; b. 1936 (since 5 April 2001, having previously been in office from 1978 to 1991).

INTERNATIONAL RELATIONS

Montserrat is a member of CARICOM and the OECS.

ECONOMY

Currency. Montserrat's currency is the *Eastern Caribbean dollar* (*see* ANTIGUA AND BARBUDA: Currency).

Budget. In 1998 the estimated expenditure was EC$60·6m. compared with actual expenditure of EC$63·5m. in 1997, a reduction of 5%.

Performance. Real GDP growth was –2·9% in 1995 and 0·8% in 1994.

Banking and Finance. The East Caribbean Central Bank based in St Kitts and Nevis functions as a central bank. The *Governor* is Sir Dwight Venner. In 2003 there were four commercial banks and in 1996 there were 21 offshore banks. Responsibility for overseeing offshore banking rests with the Governor.

ENERGY AND NATURAL RESOURCES

Electricity. Production (2000) 12m. kWh. Installed capacity (2000): 4,000 kW.

Agriculture. 3,700 ha are normally suitable for agriculture, with about half in use, but only 1,000 ha were available in 1996 because of the volcanic crisis. In 1998 there were 2,000 ha of arable and permanent crop land. Potatoes, tomatoes, onions, mangoes and limes were produced in recent times. Meat production began in 1994 and the island soon became self-sufficient in chicken, mutton and beef.

Livestock (2002); cattle, 10,000; pigs, 1,000; sheep, 5,000; goats, 7,000.

Forestry. The area under forests in 2000 was 3,000 ha, or 27·3% of the total land area.

Fisheries. The total catch in 2001 was estimated at 50 tonnes.

INDUSTRY

Manufacturing has in recent years contributed about 6% to GDP and accounted for 10% of employment, but has been responsible for about 80% of exports. It has been limited to rice milling and the production of light consumer goods such as electronic components, light fittings, plastic bags and leather goods. The volcanic activity has put a halt to the milling of rice in the exclusion zone and curtailed the production of light consumer goods.

Trade Unions. There is one trade union, the Montserrat Allied Workers Union (MAWU).

EXTERNAL ECONOMIC RELATIONS

Imports and Exports. Imports in 2002 totalled US$25·4m.; exports, US$1·5m. The USA was the main trading partner.

COMMUNICATIONS

Roads. In 1995 there were 205 km of paved roads, 25 km of unsurfaced roads and 50 km of tracks. In 1995 there were 2,700 cars and 400 commercial vehicles registered. These figures changed as a result of the volcanic eruptions of 1995 and 1997 but since then the government, through the Ministry of Communications and Works, has been focusing its road developments in the north of the island, and a number of road work projects are under way.

Civil Aviation. At the W. H. Bramble airport LIAT used to provide services to Antigua with onward connections to the rest of the eastern Caribbean, but it was closed in June 1997 as volcanic activity increased. A new airport is scheduled to open during 2005.

Shipping. Plymouth is the port of entry, but alternative anchorage was provided at Old Bay Road during the volcanic crisis.

Telecommunications. Number of telephone main lines, 1997, 3,800. With the migration of people to the north and overseas, and the subsequent destruction of the southern part of the island, the number of telephones has since shrunk to 2,100. There were 300 mobile phone subscribers in 1997.

SOCIAL INSTITUTIONS

Justice. Law is based on UK common law as exercised by the Eastern Caribbean Supreme Court. Final appeal lies to the UK Privy Council. Law is administered by the West Indies Associated States Court, a Court of Summary Jurisdiction and Magistrate's Courts.

Religion. In 1997, 25% of the population were Anglican, 20% Methodist, 15% Pentecostal, 10% Adventist and 10% Roman Catholic.

Education. In 1996–97 there were 11 primary schools (only four open), a comprehensive secondary school with three campuses, and a technical college. Schools are run by the government, the churches and the private sector. There is a medical school, the American University of the Caribbean.

In 2000–01 total expenditure on education came to 7·9% of total government spending.

Health. In 1996 there were four medical officers, one surgeon, one dentist and one hospital with 69 beds.

CULTURE

Broadcasting. There is a government-owned radio station (ZJB) and two commercial stations (Radio Antilles and GEM Radio). There is a commercial cable TV company (colour by NTSC).

Press. In 1996 there was one weekly newspaper.

Tourism. Tourism at one time contributed about 30% of GDP. There were 36,077 visitors including 11,636 cruise ship arrivals in 1994. However, after the volcanic eruptions the tourist industry declined dramatically; over half the island is closed. There were 10,000 visitors in 2000.

FURTHER READING

Fergus, H. A., *Montserrat: History of a Caribbean Colony.* London, 1994

PITCAIRN ISLAND

KEY HISTORICAL EVENTS

Pitcairn was discovered by Carteret in 1767, but remained uninhabited until 1790, when it was occupied by nine mutineers of HMS *Bounty*, with 12 women and six men from Tahiti. Nothing was known of their existence until the island was visited in 1808.

TERRITORY AND POPULATION

Pitcairn Island (1·75 sq. miles; 4·6 sq. km) is situated in the Pacific Ocean, nearly equidistant from New Zealand and Panama (25° 04' S. lat., 130° 06' W. long.). Adamstown is the only settlement. The population in 2003 was 48. The uninhabited islands of Henderson (31 sq. km), Ducie (3·9 sq. km) and Oeno (5·2 sq. km) were annexed in 1902. Henderson is a World Heritage Site.

CLIMATE

An equable climate, with average annual rainfall of 80" (2,000 mm) spread evenly throughout the year. Mean monthly temperatures range from 75°F (24°C) in Jan. to 66°F (19°C) in July.

CONSTITUTION AND GOVERNMENT

The Local Government Ordinance of 1964 constitutes a *Council* of ten members, of whom six are elected annually, three are nominated (one by the six elected members and two by the Governor), and the Island Secretary is an *ex officio* member. No political parties exist. The Island Magistrate, who is elected triennially, presides over the Council; other members hold office for only one year. Liaison between Governor and Council is through a Commissioner in the Auckland, New Zealand, office of the British Consulate-General.

CURRENT ADMINISTRATION

Governor: Richard Fell.

Mayor: Jay Warren.

Government Website: http://www.government.pn

ECONOMY

Currency. New Zealand currency is used.

Budget. For the year to 31 March 1997 revenue was NZ$604,234 and expenditure NZ$601,665.

ENERGY AND NATURAL RESOURCES

Fisheries. The catch in 2001 was approximately eight tonnes.

COMMUNICATIONS

Roads. There were (1997) 6 km of roads. In 1997 there were 29 motorcycles.

SOCIAL INSTITUTIONS

Justice. The Island Court consists of the Island Magistrate and two assessors.

Education. In 2004 there was one teacher and nine pupils.

FURTHER READING

Murray, S., *Pitcairn Island: the First 200 Years.* La Canada (CA), 1992

ST HELENA

KEY HISTORICAL EVENTS

The island was uninhabited when discovered by the Portuguese in 1502. It was administered by the East India Company from 1659 and became a British colony in 1834. Napoléon died there in exile in 1821.

Public demonstrations took place in April 1997 against government spending cuts and the Governor's imposition of his own head of social services.

TERRITORY AND POPULATION

St Helena, of volcanic origin, is 3,100 km from the west coast of Africa. Area, 47 sq. miles (121·7 sq. km), with a cultivable area of 243 ha. The population at the 1998 census was 5,157. In 1995 an estimated 62·6% of the population were urban. The capital and port is Jamestown, population (1998) 1,300.

The official language is English.

Ascension is a small island of volcanic origin, of 34 sq. miles (88 sq. km), 700 miles northwest of St Helena. There are 120 ha providing fresh meat, vegetables and fruit. The estimated population in 1999 was 1,050.

The island is the resort of sea turtles, rabbits, the sooty tern or 'wideawake', and feral donkeys.

A cable station connects the island with St Helena, Sierra Leone, St Vincent, Rio de Janeiro and Buenos Aires. There is an airstrip (Miracle Mile) near the settlement of Georgetown; the Royal Air Force maintains an air link with the Falkland Islands.

Administrator: Andrew Kettlewell.

Tristan da Cunha is the largest of a small group of islands in the South Atlantic, lying 1,320 miles (2,124 km) southwest of St Helena, of which they became dependencies on 12 Jan. 1938. Tristan da Cunha has an area of 98 sq. km and a population (2002) of 284, all living in the settlement of Edinburgh. Inaccessible Island (10 sq. km) lies 20 miles west, and the three Nightingale Islands (2 sq. km) lie 20 miles south of Tristan da Cunha; they are uninhabited. Gough Island (90 sq. km) is 220 miles south of Tristan and has a meteorological station.

Tristan consists of a volcano rising to a height of 2,060 metres, with a circumference at its base of 34 km. The volcano, believed to be extinct, erupted unexpectedly early in Oct. 1961. The whole population was evacuated without loss and settled temporarily in the UK; in 1963 they returned to Tristan. Potatoes remain the chief crop. Cattle, sheep and pigs are now reared, and fish are plentiful.

Population in 1996, 292. The original inhabitants were shipwrecked sailors and soldiers who remained behind when the garrison from St Helena was withdrawn in 1817.

At the end of April 1942 Tristan da Cunha was commissioned as HMS *Atlantic Isle*, and became an important meteorological and radio station. In Jan. 1949 a South African company commenced crawfishing operations. An Administrator was appointed at the end of 1948 and a body of basic law brought into operation. The Island Council, which was set up in 1932, consists of a Chief Islander, three nominated and eight elected members (including one woman), under the chairmanship of the Administrator.

Administrator: Bill Dickson.

SOCIAL STATISTICS

2001 figures for St Helena: births, 36; deaths, 41; marriages, 20; divorces (2000), 9. Annual growth rate, 1990–95, 0·6%.

CLIMATE

A mild climate, with little variation. Temperatures range from 75–85°F (24–29°C) in summer to 65–75°F (18–24°C) in winter. Rainfall varies between 13" (325 mm) and 37" (925 mm) according to altitude and situation.

CONSTITUTION AND GOVERNMENT

The St Helena Constitution Order of 1988 entered into force on 1 Jan. 1989. The *Legislative Council* consists of the Governor, two *ex officio* members (the Government Secretary and the Treasurer) and 12 elected members. The Governor is assisted by an *Executive Council* consisting of the two *ex officio* members and the chairs of the six Council Committees.

RECENT ELECTIONS

The last Legislative Council elections were on 27 June 2001. Only non-partisans were elected.

CURRENT ADMINISTRATION

Governor and C.-in-C: Michael Clancy.

Government Website: http://www.sainthelena.gov.sh

ENERGY AND NATURAL RESOURCES

Electricity. Production in 2000 totalled 7m. kWh. Installed capacity in 2000 was 4,000 kW.

Agriculture. In 2001 there were 4,000 ha of arable land.

Fisheries. The total catch in 2001 was 866 tonnes.

INDUSTRY

Labour. In 2000 there were 270 registered unemployed persons.

COMMUNICATIONS

Roads. There were (1988) 94 km of all-weather motor roads. There were 1,301 vehicles in 1987.

Shipping. There is a service from Cardiff (UK) six times a year, and links with South Africa and neighbouring islands. In 1995 vessels entered totalling 55,000 net registered tons.

Telecommunications. In 2002 there were 2,200 main telephone lines in operation. There were 500 Internet users in 2002.

SOCIAL INSTITUTIONS

Justice. Police force, 32; cases are dealt with by a police magistrate.

Religion. There are ten Anglican churches, four Baptist chapels, three Salvation Army halls, one Seventh Day Adventist church and one Roman Catholic church.

Education. Three pre-school playgroups, seven primary and one comprehensive school controlled by the government had 1,188 pupils in 1987. The Prince Andrew School (opened in 1989) offers vocational courses leading to British qualifications.

Health. There were three doctors, one dentist and one hospital in 1992.

CULTURE

Broadcasting. The Cable & Wireless Ltd cable connects St Helena with Cape Town and Ascension Island. The government-run Radio St Helena broadcasts daily and relays BBC programmes. Number of radio receivers (1997), approximately 3,000. Television reception was introduced in 1996 from the BBC World Service, South African M-Net and a US Satellite channel. There were some 2,000 TV receivers in 1997.

FURTHER READING

Day, A., *St. Helena, Ascension and Tristan da Cunha.* [Bibliography] ABC-Clio, Oxford and Santa Barbara (CA), 1997

SOUTH GEORGIA AND THE SOUTH SANDWICH ISLANDS

KEY HISTORICAL EVENTS

The first landing and exploration was undertaken by Captain James Cook, who formally took possession in the name of George III on 17 Jan. 1775. British sealers arrived in 1788 and American sealers in 1791. Sealing reached its peak in 1800. A German team was the first to carry out scientific studies there in 1882–83. Whaling began in 1904 and ceased in 1966, and the civil administration was withdrawn. Argentine forces invaded South Georgia on 3 April 1982. A British naval task force recovered the Island on 25 April 1982.

TERRITORY AND POPULATION

South Georgia lies 1,300 km southeast of the Falkland Islands and has an area of 3,760 sq. km. The South Sandwich Islands are 760 km southeast of South Georgia and have an area of 340 sq. km. In 1993 crown sovereignty and jurisdiction were extended from 12 miles (19 km) to 200 miles (322 km) around the islands. There is no permanent population. There is a small military garrison. The British Antarctic Survey have a biological station on Bird Island. The South Sandwich Islands are uninhabited.

CLIMATE

The climate is wet and cold, with strong winds and little seasonal variation. 15°C is occasionally reached on a windless day. Temperatures below –15°C at sea level are unusual.

CONSTITUTION AND GOVERNMENT

Under the new Constitution which came into force on 3 Oct. 1985 the Territories ceased to be dependencies of the Falkland Islands. Executive power is vested in a Commissioner who is the officer for the time being administering the government of the Falkland Islands. The Commissioner is obliged to consult the officer for the time being commanding Her Majesty's British Forces in the South Atlantic on matters relating to defence and internal security (except police). The Commissioner, whenever practicable, consults the Executive Council of the Falkland Islands on the exercise of functions that in his opinion might affect the Falkland Islands. There is no Legislative Council. Laws are made by the Commissioner (Howard Pearce, resident in the Falkland Islands).

ECONOMY

Budget. The total revenue of the Territories (estimate, 1988–89) £268,240, mainly from philatelic sales and investment income. Expenditure (estimate), £194,260.

COMMUNICATIONS

There is occasional communication by sea with the Falkland Islands by means of research and ice patrol ships. Royal Fleet Auxiliary ships, which serve the garrison, run regularly to South Georgia. Mail is dropped from military aircraft.

SOCIAL INSTITUTIONS

Justice. There is a Supreme Court for the Territories and a Court of Appeal in the United Kingdom. Appeals may go from that court to the Judicial Committee of the Privy Council. There is no magistrate permanently in residence. The Officer Commanding the garrison is usually appointed a magistrate.

FURTHER READING

Day, Alan, *The Falkland Islands, South Georgia and the South Sandwich Islands.* [Bibliography] ABC-Clio, Oxford and Santa Barbara (CA), 1996

SOVEREIGN BASE AREAS OF AKROTIRI AND DHEKELIA IN CYPRUS

KEY HISTORICAL EVENTS

The Sovereign Base Areas (SBAs) are those parts of the island of Cyprus that stayed under British jurisdiction and remained British sovereign territory when the 1960 Treaty of Establishment created the independent Republic of Cyprus. The Akrotiri facility formed a strategic part of the West's nuclear capacity during the Cold War. The SBAs were used for the deployment of troops in the Gulf War in 1991. Military intelligence is now the key role of the SBAs. The construction of massive antennae at the RAF communications base at Akrotiri sparked violent riots in 2001 and 2002, led by a Greek Cypriot MP. In Feb. 2003 the British Government offered to surrender approximately half the area of the SBAs as an incentive for a settlement between the Greek and Turkish administrations in Cyprus.

TERRITORY AND POPULATION

The Sovereign Base Areas (SBAs), with a total land area of 254 sq. km (98 sq. miles), comprise the Western SBA (123 sq. km), including Episkopi Garrison and RAF Akrotiri (opened 1956), and the Eastern SBA (131 sq. km), including Dhekelia Garrison. The SBAs cover 3% of the land area of the island of Cyprus. There are approximately 3,000 military personnel and approximately 5,000 civilians. The British Government has declared that it will not develop the SBAs other than for military purposes. Citizens and residents of the Republic of Cyprus are guaranteed freedom of access and communications to and through the SBAs.

The SBAs are administered as military bases reporting to the Ministry of Defence in London. The Administrator is the Commander, British Forces Cyprus. The joint force headquarters are at Episkopi. Greek and English are spoken.

CURRENT ADMINISTRATION

Administrator: Maj.-Gen. Peter Thomas Clayton Pearson (appointed Sept. 2003).

THE TURKS AND CAICOS ISLANDS

KEY HISTORICAL EVENTS

After a long period of rival French and Spanish claims the islands were eventually secured to the British Crown in 1766, and became a separate colony in 1973 after association at various times with the colonies of the Bahamas and Jamaica.

TERRITORY AND POPULATION

The Islands are situated between 21° and 22°N. lat. and 71° and 72°W. long., about 80 km east of the Bahamas, of which they are geographically an extension. There are over 40 islands, covering an estimated area of 192 sq. miles (497 sq. km). Only eight are inhabited: Grand Caicos, the largest, is 48 km long by 3 to 5 km broad; Grand Turk, the capital and main political and administrative centre, is 11 km long by 2 km broad. Population, 1990 census, 12,350; Grand Turk, 3,761; Providenciales,

5,586; South Caicos, 1,220; Middle Caicos, 275; North Caicos, 1,305; Salt Cay, 213. The estimated population for 2000 was 19,350. An estimated 56·4% of the population were rural in 1995.

The official language is English.

SOCIAL STATISTICS

Vital statistics (1997): births, 160; deaths, 58. Annual growth rate, 1995–99, 3·3%.

CLIMATE

An equable and healthy climate as a result of regular trade winds, though hurricanes are sometimes experienced. Grand Turk, Jan. 76°F (24·4°C), July 83°F (28·3°C). Annual rainfall 21".

CONSTITUTION AND GOVERNMENT

A new Constitution was introduced in 1988 and amended in 1992. The Executive Council comprises two official members: the Chief Secretary and the Attorney-General; a Chief Minister and five other ministers from among the elected members of the Legislative Council; and is presided over by the Governor. The Legislative Council consists of a Speaker, the two official members of the Executive Council, 13 elected members and three appointed members.

RECENT ELECTIONS

At general elections held on 24 April 2003 for the 13 elective seats on the Legislative Council, the People's Democratic Movement (PDM) won seven seats and the People's National Party (PNP) won six. By-elections on 7 Aug. 2003 gave the PNP a majority and a total of eight seats on the Council.

CURRENT ADMINISTRATION

Governor: Jim Poston; b. 1945 (took office on 16 Dec. 2002).

Chief Minister: Michael Misick; b. 1966 (PNP; took office on 15 Aug. 2003).

INTERNATIONAL RELATIONS

The Islands are a member of CARICOM.

ECONOMY

Overview. The economy is based on free-market private sector-led development. The focus is on the service sector, but tourism and finance are still the dominant industries.

Currency. The US dollar is the official currency. Inflation was 3·5% in 1999.

Budget. In 1999 current revenues were US$61·8m. and current expenditures US$62·0m.

Performance. GDP growth was 8·6% in 1999 (11·4% in 1998).

Banking and Finance. There were five commercial banks in 2003. Offshore finance is a major industry.

Weights and Measures. The Imperial system is generally in use.

ENERGY AND NATURAL RESOURCES

Electricity. Electrical services are provided to all of the inhabited islands. Total electricity production for 2000 was about 5m. kWh. Installed capacity in 2000 was 4,000 kW. For all US appliances, 110 volts, 60 cycles, are suitable.

Oil and Gas. Both oil and gas are imported.

Agriculture. Farming is done on a small scale mainly for subsistence.

Fisheries. In 2001 the total catch was estimated at 1,300 tonnes. Conch and lobster are the traditional catches.

INDUSTRY

Labour. In 1989, out of a total population of 4,885 aged 14 or over, 4,043 were working, 573 unemployed and 269 economically inactive.

EXTERNAL ECONOMIC RELATIONS

Imports and Exports. Exports, 1999, US$137·0m.; imports, US$175·6m. The main export is dried, frozen and processed fish.

COMMUNICATIONS

Civil Aviation. The international airports are on Grand Turk and Providenciales. International services are provided by Air Canada, Air Jamaica, American Airlines, Bahamasair, British Airways, Delta Airlines, TCI Skyking, Tropical Airways d'Haiti and US Airways. An internal air service provides regular daily flights between the inhabited islands.

Shipping. The main ports are at Grand Turk, Cockburn Harbour and Providenciales. There is a service to Miami. In 2002 the merchant fleet totalled 1,000 GRT.

Telecommunications. There are internal and international cable, telephone, telegraph and fax services.

Postal Services. Postal services are provided on all of the inhabited islands by the government. Postal agencies such as UPS and Federal Express also exist.

SOCIAL INSTITUTIONS

Justice. Laws are a mixture of Statute and Common Law. There is a Magistrates Court and a Supreme Court. Appeals lie from the Supreme Court to the Court of Appeal which sits in Nassau, Bahamas. There is a further appeal in certain cases to the Privy Council in London.

Religion. There are Anglican, Methodist, Baptist and Evangelist groups.

Education. The adult literacy rate is 98%. Education is free between the ages of five and 14 in the ten government primary schools; there are also four private primary schools. In March 1993 the average number of pupils in the four government secondary schools was 1,075.

In 2000–01 total expenditure on education came to 16·8% of total government expenditure.

Health. In 1995 there were six doctors, one dentist, 56 nurses and midwives, and 36 hospital beds.

CULTURE

Broadcasting. The government operates the semi-commercial Radio Turks and Caicos. There are also two commercial stations and one religious. In 1997 there were about 8,000 radio sets. There is cable and satellite TV.

Press. There is one weekly and one bi-weekly newspaper.

Tourism. Number of visitors, 2000, 152,000. Tourism receipts totalled US$285m. in 2000. In 1999 tourism accounted for 9% of GDP.

FURTHER READING

Boultbee, P. G., *Turks & Caicos Islands.* [Bibliography] ABC-Clio, Oxford and Santa Barbara (CA), 1991

UNITED STATES OF AMERICA

Capital: Washington, D.C.
Population projection, 2010: 314·92m.
GDP per capita, 2002: (PPP$) 35,750
HDI/world rank: 0·939/8

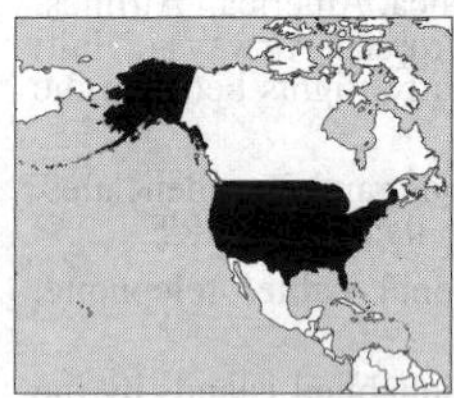

KEY HISTORICAL EVENTS

The earliest inhabitants of the North American continent can be traced back to Palaeolithic times. The Pueblo culture in modern-day Colorado and New Mexico flourished from the 11th to the 14th century AD. In the 12th century permanent settlements appeared in the east where cultivation and fishing supported major fortified towns. The first Europeans to make their presence felt were the Spanish, based in Florida before venturing north and west. Santa Fe in New Mexico was founded in 1610. By the mid-17th century there was competition from the French centred on Quebec.

In 1607 an English colony was established at Jamestown, southern Virginia. After a perilous start Virginia's population grew rapidly to meet the European demand for tobacco. Maryland, originally a refuge for persecuted Catholics, also thrived on the tobacco trade. To make up for the shortage of labour, slaves were imported from Africa.

In 1620 a hundred pilgrims landed at Plymouth Rock to found a Puritan enclave, which became the colony of Massachusetts. Other settlements of Christian radicals fleeing persecution soon followed. Not all were tolerant of beliefs that differed from their own. Pennsylvania, the colony named after the Quaker William Penn, was exceptional in offering freedom of worship to 'all persons who confess and acknowledge the one almighty and eternal God'. In 1664 the British took control of Dutch interests, including New Amsterdam, renamed New York. Almost all of the eastern seaboard was now claimed by British settlers who were also venturing inland. Their main European rivals were the French, who claimed an area around and to the southwest of the Great Lakes. With American Indian tribes allied to both sides, there was heavy fighting in 1744 and 1748. Within a decade British forces had captured most of the French strongholds. After the Treaty of Paris in 1763, Britain commanded the whole of North America east of the Mississippi while Spain, having surrendered Florida, gained Louisiana from France.

For a brief period colonization was restricted to the area east of the Appalachians, the rest of the territory being reserved for Indian tribes. This soon became a point of issue between the settlers who were intent on expansion and the government in London, which wanted a settled, self-supporting community benefiting British trade. Having disposed of the French threat, the colonists felt confident enough to defy orders that ignored their interests. In particular, they objected to the Navigation Acts, which required goods to be carried in British vessels, and to various taxes imposed without consultation. The centre of opposition was Boston, scene of the infamous 'tea party' when, in 1763, militants destroyed a cargo of East India tea. In 1775 the arrest of rebel ringleaders provoked the 13 colonies to set up a *de facto* government that appointed George Washington commander of American forces.

The War of Independence lasted seven years from 1776. The decisive moment came at last with the surrender of General Burgoyne and his 8,000 troops in upper New York State in Oct. 1777, a defeat that persuaded a cautious France to enter the war. Under the peace terms secured in 1783, Britain kept Canada leaving the new United States with territory stretching from the Atlantic to the Mississippi. A constitution based on democratic principles came into force in 1789. It allowed for a federal government headed by a president and executive, a legislature with a House of Representatives and a Senate, and a judiciary, with ultimate authority on constitutional matters exercised by a Supreme Court. The first president was George Washington, elected in 1789. In 1800 Washington, D.C. was declared the national capital.

Hostilities with Britain resumed in 1812 when an attempted invasion of Canada was repulsed. Louisiana, having reverted to French rule and subsequently sold to the USA, was secured for the Union. In 1836 Texas broke away from Mexico, surviving as an independent republic until 1845 when it was annexed by the USA. This provoked war with Mexico that ended in 1848 with the USA taking over what are now the states of California, Arizona, Colorado, Utah, Nevada and New Mexico. In 1846 a long-running dispute with Britain confirming US title to Oregon acted as a spur to western migration, as did the Californian gold rush of 1848. By the 1850s the railroad was bringing economic prosperity to the Midwest. In 1862 the Homestead Act allocated 160 acres to anyone who was ready to farm it and Alaska was purchased from Russia in 1867. The settlement of the west was deemed complete in 1890, the year that Idaho and Wyoming became states, leaving only Utah, Oklahoma and New Mexico to complete the contiguous states.

The transition from a rural society to an industrial power created tensions between the slave-owning southern states and the rest of the Union; the North resented the advantage cheap labour gave to the South, especially in the cotton industry. The southern states seceded from the Union in 1860–61 and formed a Confederacy. When Confederate troops fired on the US flag at Fort Sumter, President Abraham Lincoln ordered a blockade of the South. More American lives were lost in the Civil War than in the two world wars combined. The military balance was maintained until 1863 when the North secured a crushing victory at the Battle of Gettysburg. However, the war continued until April 1865 when Robert E. Lee surrendered to Ulysses S. Grant at Appomattox Courthouse in Virginia. A few days later Lincoln was assassinated. Contrary to Lincoln's hopes, the South was rushed into a social revolution. This in turn led to terrorist violence and the emergence of the Ku Klux Klan as the standard bearer of lynch law. While the 13th amendment prohibited slavery, political freedom was denied to the black community by state imposed literacy tests and discriminatory property taxes.

By 1900 the USA rivalled Britain and Germany as the world's dominant power. With vast natural resources and a manufacturing capacity that secured 11% of world trade, rapid growth was supported by European labour. Between 1881–1920, 23m. immigrants entered the US, the largest population movement ever recorded. The USA remained neutral at the beginning of the First World War but in 1917 the arrival of the American Expeditionary Force was critical to the Allied breakthrough. Post-war America, relatively unscathed by the European conflict, was able to dictate terms at the Versailles peace conference. But President Wilson's 'fourteen points', which set out a plan for collective security policed by a League of Nations, was rejected by the Senate in 1920 and America retreated once again into isolationism.

The 1929 Stock Market Crash started a succession of bank failures, which led to widespread bankruptcies and mass unemployment. With the election of Franklin D. Roosevelt as president, a series of radical measures, known collectively as the New Deal, aimed at revitalizing the nation. Cheap loans to restart factories and farms and huge investment in public works proved to be the key to recovery though unemployment remained high until production was boosted by the demands of another world war. As in 1914, there was opposition to direct involvement in a European war. Roosevelt compromised by supplying Britain with much needed armaments on favourable terms. However, opposition to Japanese expansion into China and South East Asia brought unexpected retaliation at Pearl Harbor, when much of the US fleet was destroyed. America declared war on Japan while Germany declared war on America. The US military effort focused initially on the Pacific but after 1942 American forces were also committed to the campaign in North Africa and Europe. With the D-Day landings in June 1944, US troops led the attack on Germany and in May 1945, within a month of Roosevelt's death, Germany surrendered. President Harry Truman forced a Japanese surrender by sacrificing Hiroshima and Nagasaki to the atomic bomb.

The threat of a Soviet takeover in Europe was countered by the formation of NATO in 1949 and the provision of dollar aid under the 1947 Marshall Plan to kick start European economic recovery. The risk of a return to isolationism receded still further when China fell to communism. In 1950 American troops went to the aid of South Korea when it was invaded by the communist North. A ceasefire was negotiated after Dwight Eisenhower was elected president in 1953. In the early 1960s civil rights were high on the political agenda. Foremost among the campaigners for racial equality was Martin Luther King, Jr. who was awarded the Nobel Peace Prize in 1964. He was assassinated four years later.

Social tensions were exacerbated by the Cold War confrontation. In his first year of office President John F. Kennedy was embarrassed by the failed Bay of Pigs invasion when anti-Castro Cubans, trained and supported by the CIA, attempted to overthrow the country's communist regime. The building of the Berlin Wall in Aug. 1961 symbolized a hardening of the Cold War. In 1962 Kennedy had to confront the prospect of the Soviets placing missiles in Cuba. World war was averted by an agreement between the two nations allowing for a withdrawal of the missiles on condition of a US promise not to invade Cuba. The incident prompted a thawing in East–West relations and in 1963 the USA, UK and USSR signed the Nuclear Test Ban Treaty which, for the first time, put a brake on the spread of nuclear weapons.

Kennedy was assassinated in Dallas in Nov. 1963. He was succeeded by his vice-president, Lyndon Johnson, who implemented civil rights legislation, including the Voting Rights Act, and introduced Medicare (health insurance for the elderly). By 1966 over 350,000 American troops were in Vietnam and by the following year almost 80,000 Americans had been killed or wounded. Johnson's successor, Richard Nixon, reduced the number of troops in Vietnam from 550,000 in 1969 to 30,000 three years later but authorized military operations in North Vietnam, Laos and Cambodia in the hope of forcing North Vietnam to the negotiating table. Elsewhere, he signed the Strategic Arms Limitation Treaty (SALT) with Moscow in 1972 and relaxed trade restrictions against China.

Nixon agreed a ceasefire with North Vietnam. However, his second term of office was cut short by the Watergate scandal, involving a break-in at the Democratic Party headquarters. Threatened with Congressional impeachment, Nixon resigned in Aug. 1974. Gerald Ford, who replaced Nixon, lost the 1976 presidential election to Democrat Jimmy Carter, who secured the neutrality of the Panama Canal and brokered the Camp David talks between Egypt and Israel. He also re-established diplomatic ties with China. Henry Kissinger, who was secretary of state under Nixon and Carter, oversaw America's withdrawal from Southeast Asia. Attempts at further improving US–Soviet relations were scuppered when the signing of the Strategic Arms Limitation Treaty (SALT II) was postponed because of the Soviet invasion of Afghanistan in 1979. Radical Iranian students stormed the US embassy in Tehran in late 1979 and seized over 50 US hostages. After a year of negotiations, a failed US military rescue mission contributed to Republican Ronald Reagan's landslide victory at the 1980 presidential polls.

Reagan's economic policies redefined American society in the 1980s. He introduced a 25% tax cut for individuals and corporations, slashing welfare but increasing military expenditure. In 1986 he reduced the number of tax rates, abolishing tax altogether for many low-income earners. Relations between the USA and USSR improved in the mid-eighties after successful negotiations on the destruction of a range of intermediate-range nuclear weapons. George Bush took over the presidency in 1989. The collapse of the Soviet empire in 1990 extended US economic aid to Eastern Europe and Bush signed a non-aggression pact with Soviet leader Mikhail Gorbachev, effectively ending the Cold War. In 1990–91 Bush led a coalition of European and Arab states to repel the Iraqi invasion of Kuwait.

The Democrats regained control of the White House with the election of Bill Clinton in 1992. Clinton combined economic recovery at home with an active foreign policy, which underlined America's role as the only superpower. He secured the passage of the North American Free Trade Agreement, which created a free-trade zone between the United States, Canada and Mexico. Unemployment reached its lowest levels since the late-1960s and in 1998 there was a federal budget surplus for the first time in almost 30 years. On the international scene Clinton brokered talks between the Palestinian leader Yasser Arafat and Israeli Prime Minister Yitzhak Rabin that resulted in limited Palestinian self-rule. In 1995 he was instrumental in securing the Dayton accords that offered peace between Yugoslavia, Croatia and Bosnia-Herzegovina. Sudan and Afghanistan were attacked in 1998, having been linked with the al-Qaeda terrorist network held responsible for the bombing of US embassies in Tanzania and Kenya. In 1999 there was an American-led NATO campaign of air strikes against Yugoslavia when the country's leaders refused to end a campaign of violence against ethnic Albanians in Kosovo.

Clinton's second term of office was dominated by scandal, most damagingly an affair with Monica Lewinsky, a White House intern. He was impeached for perjury and obstruction of justice although the senate trial ended when neither motion gained a simple majority. In 2000 Clinton's vice president, Al Gore, lost the presidential election to George W. Bush, whose first budget included a $1·25trn. tax cut. Following talks with Russian President Vladimir Putin in June 2001 the two leaders signed an anti-nuclear deal to reduce their respective strategic nuclear warheads by two-thirds over the next ten years.

On 11 Sept. 2001 the heart of New York City was devastated after hijackers flew two jet airliners into the World Trade Center. A plane also crashed into the Pentagon, in Washington, D.C., and a fourth hijacked plane crashed near the town of Shanksville, Pennsylvania. The death toll for New York was 2,749, with 67 countries reporting dead or missing citizens. Osama bin Laden, the leader of the al-Qaeda terrorist network believed to be living in Afghanistan at the invitation of the ruling Taliban, was held responsible. Military action against Afghanistan followed, with air strikes beginning on 7 Oct. 2001. In early 2002 Bush declared North Korea, Iran and Iraq 'an axis of evil' and by Sept. 2002 was pressing the UN to act against Iraq. On 20 March 2003 US forces, supported by the UK, initiated a war aimed at 'liberating Iraq'. On 9 April 2003 American forces took control of central Baghdad, effectively bringing an end to the rule of Saddam Hussein.

In Nov. 2004 George W. Bush won re-election for a second term and pledged to continue the war on global terrorism.

TERRITORY AND POPULATION

The United States is bounded in the north by Canada, east by the North Atlantic, south by the Gulf of Mexico and Mexico, and west by the North Pacific Ocean. The area of the USA is 3,794,083 sq. miles (9,826,629 sq. km), of which 3,537,438 sq. miles (9,161,922 sq. km) are land and 256,645 sq. miles (664,707 sq. km) are water (comprising Great Lakes, inland and coastal water).

Population at each census from 1790 to 2000 (including Alaska and Hawaii from 1960). Figures do not include Puerto Rico, Guam, American Samoa or other Pacific islands, or the US population abroad. Residents of Indian reservations not included before 1890.

	White	*Black*	*Other races*	*Total*
1790	3,172,464	757,208	—	3,929,672
1800	4,306,446	1,002,037	—	5,308,483
1810	5,862,073	1,377,808	—	7,239,881
1820	7,866,797	1,771,562	—	9,638,359
1830	10,537,378	2,328,642	—	12,866,020
1840	14,195,805	2,873,648	—	17,069,453
1850	19,553,068	3,638,808	—	23,191,876
1860	26,922,537	4,441,830	78,954	31,443,321
1870	34,337,292	5,392,172	88,985	39,818,449
1880	43,402,970	6,580,793	172,020	50,155,783
1890	55,101,258	7,488,676	357,780	62,947,714
1900	66,868,508	8,834,395	509,265	76,212,168
1910	81,812,405	9,828,667	587,459	92,228,531
1920	94,903,540	10,463,607	654,421	106,021,568
1930	110,395,753	11,891,842	915,065	123,202,660
1940	118,357,831	12,865,914	941,384	132,165,129
1950	135,149,629	15,044,937	1,131,232	151,325,798
1960	158,831,732	18,871,831	1,619,612	179,323,175
1970	177,748,975	22,580,289	2,882,662	203,211,926
1980	188,371,622	26,495,025	11,679,158	226,545,805
1990	199,686,070	29,986,060	19,037,743	248,709,873
2000	211,460,626	34,658,190	35,303,090	281,421,906

The mid-year population estimate for 2004 was 293,655,404.

The UN gives a projected population for 2010 of 314·92m.

2000 density, 30·7 per sq. km (79·6 per sq. mile). Urban population (persons living in places with at least 2,500 inhabitants) at the 2000 census was 222,358,309 (79·0%); rural, 59,063,597. In 1990 it was 75·2%; in 1980, 73·7%; in 1970, 73·6%.

Sex distribution by race of the population at the 2000 census:

	Males	*Females*
White	103,773,194	107,687,432
Black or African American	16,465,185	18,193,005
American Indian and Alaska Native	1,233,982	1,241,974
Asian	4,948,741	5,294,257
Native Hawaiian and Other Pacific Islander	202,629	196,206
Other Race	8,009,214	7,349,859
Two or More Races	3,420,618	3,405,610
Total	138,053,563	143,368,343

Alongside these racial groups, and applicable to all of them, a category of 'Hispanic origin' comprised 35,305,818 persons (including 20,640,711 of Mexican ancestry), up 12,927,277 from 22,378,541 in 1990. Hispanics are now the largest ethnic minority in the USA.

Among ten-year age groups the 35–44 age group contained most people according to the 2000 census, with a total of 45,148,527 (16·0% of the population).

At the 2000 census there were 104,705,000 households, up from 93,347,000 in 1990.

At the 2000 census there were 50,454 people aged 100 or over, compared to 36,000 in 1990. Of the 50,454 centenarians in 2002, 40,397 were female, and of the 36,000 in 1990, 28,000 were female.

The 2000 census showed that 47·0m. persons five years and over spoke a language other than English in the home, including Spanish or Spanish Creole by 28·1m.; French or French Creole by 2·1m.; Chinese by 2·0m.; German by 1·4m.; Tagalog by 1·2m.; Italian by 1·0m.; Vietnamese by 1·0m.

The following table includes population statistics, the year in which each of the original 13 states (Connecticut, Delaware, Georgia, Maryland, Massachusetts, New Hampshire, New Jersey, New York, North Carolina, Pennsylvania, Rhode Island, South Carolina, Virginia) ratified the constitution, and the year when each of the other states was admitted into the Union. Traditional abbreviations for the names of the states are shown in brackets with postal codes for use in addresses.

The USA is divided into four geographic regions comprised of nine divisions. These are, with their 2000 census populations: Northeast (comprised of the New England and Middle Atlantic divisions), 53,594,378; Midwest (East North Central, West North Central), 64,392,776; South (South Atlantic, East South Central, West South Central), 100,236,820; West (Mountain, Pacific), 63,197,932.

Geographic divisions and states		*Land area: sq. miles, 2000*	*Census population 1 April 2000*	*Pop. per sq. mile, 2000*
United States		3,537,438	281,421,906	79·6
New England		62,810	13,922,517	221·7
Connecticut (1788)	*(Conn./CT)*	4,845	3,405,565	702·9
Maine (1820)	*(Me./ME)*	30,862	1,274,923	41·3
Massachusetts (1788)	*(Mass./MA)*	7,840	6,349,097	809·8
New Hampshire (1788)	*(N.H./NH)*	8,968	1,235,786	137·8
Rhode Island (1790)	*(R.I./RI)*	1,045	1,048,319	1,003·2
Vermont (1791)	*(Vt./VT)*	9,250	608,827	65·8
Middle Atlantic		99,448	39,671,861	398·9
New Jersey (1787)	*(N.J./NJ)*	7,417	8,414,350	1,134·4
New York (1788)	*(N.Y./NY)*	47,214	18,976,457	401·9
Pennsylvania (1787)	*(Pa./PA)*	44,817	12,281,054	274·0
East North Central		243,513	45,155,037	185·4
Illinois (1818)	*(Ill./IL)*	55,584	12,419,293	223·4
Indiana (1816)	*(Ind./IN)*	35,867	6,080,485	169·5
Michigan (1837)	*(Mich./MI)*	56,804	9,938,444	175·0
Ohio (1803)	*(Oh./OH)*	40,948	11,353,140	277·3
Wisconsin (1848)	*(Wis./WI)*	54,310	5,363,675	98·8

Geographic divisions and states		Land area: sq. miles, 2000	Census population 1 April 2000	Pop. per sq. mile, 2000
West North Central		507,913	19,237,739	37·9
Iowa (1846)	*(Ia./IA)*	55,869	2,926,324	52·4
Kansas (1861)	*(Kans./KS)*	81,815	2,688,418	32·9
Minnesota (1858)	*(Minn./MN)*	79,610	4,919,479	61·8
Missouri (1821)	*(Mo./MO)*	68,886	5,595,211	81·2
Nebraska (1867)	*(Nebr./NE)*	76,872	1,711,263	22·3
North Dakota (1889)	*(N.D./ND)*	68,976	642,200	9·3
South Dakota (1889)	*(S.D./SD)*	75,885	754,844	9·9
South Atlantic		266,115	51,769,160	194·5
Delaware (1787)	*(Del./DE)*	1,954	783,600	401·0
Dist. of Columbia (1791)	*(D.C./DC)*	61	572,059	9,378·0
Florida (1845)	*(Fla./FL)*	53,927	15,982,378	296·4
Georgia (1788)	*(Ga./GA)*	57,906	8,186,453	141·4
Maryland (1788)	*(Md./MD)*	9,774	5,296,486	541·9
North Carolina (1789)	*(N.C./NC)*	48,711	8,049,313	165·2
South Carolina (1788)	*(S.C./SC)*	30,110	4,012,012	133·2
Virginia (1788)	*(Va./VA)*	39,594	7,078,515	178·8
West Virginia (1863)	*(W. Va./WV)*	24,078	1,808,344	75·1
East South Central		178,596	17,022,810	95·3
Alabama (1819)	*(Al./AL)*	50,744	4,447,100	87·6
Kentucky (1792)	*(Ky./KY)*	39,728	4,041,769	101·7
Mississippi (1817)	*(Miss./MS)*	46,907	2,844,658	60·6
Tennessee (1796)	*(Tenn./TN)*	41,217	5,689,283	138·0
West South Central		426,094	31,444,850	73·8
Arkansas (1836)	*(Ark./AR)*	52,068	2,673,400	51·3
Louisiana (1812)	*(La./LA)*	43,562	4,468,976	102·6
Oklahoma (1907)	*(Okla./OK)*	68,667	3,450,654	50·3
Texas (1845)	*(Tex./TX)*	261,797	20,851,820	79·7
Mountain		856,078	18,172,295	21·2
Arizona (1912)	*(Ariz./AZ)*	113,635	5,130,632	45·2
Colorado (1876)	*(Colo./CO)*	103,718	4,301,261	41·5
Idaho (1890)	*(Id./ID)*	82,747	1,293,953	15·6
Montana (1889)	*(Mont./MT)*	145,552	902,195	6·2
Nevada (1864)	*(Nev./NV)*	109,826	1,998,257	18·2
New Mexico (1912)	*(N. Mex./NM)*	121,356	1,819,046	15·0
Utah (1896)	*(Ut./UT)*	82,144	2,233,169	27·2
Wyoming (1890)	*(Wyo./WY)*	97,100	493,782	5·1
Pacific		896,874	45,025,637	50·2
Alaska (1959)	*(Ak./AK)*	571,951	626,932	1·1
California (1850)	*(Calif./CA)*	155,959	33,871,648	217·2
Hawaii (1960)	*(Hi./HI)*	6,423	1,211,537	188·6
Oregon (1859)	*(Oreg./OR)*	95,997	3,421,399	35·6
Washington (1889)	*(Wash./WA)*	66,544	5,894,121	88·6
Outlying Territories, total		4,033	4,199,913[1]	1,041·4[1]
American Samoa (1900)		77	57,291	744
Guam (1898)		212	154,805	737
Johnston Atoll (1858)		1	1,100[2]	1,100[2]
Midway Islands (1867)		2	150[2]	75[2]
Northern Marianas (1947)		179	69,221	387
Puerto Rico (1898)		3,425	3,808,610	1,112
Virgin Islands (1917)		134	108,612	811
Wake Island (1898)		3	124[2]	41[2]

[1]Based on a combination of 2000 census figures and estimates for the minor outlying islands as indicated. [2]2000 estimate.

The 2000 census showed 31,107,889 foreign-born persons. The ten countries contributing the largest numbers who were foreign-born were: Mexico, 9,177,487; Philippines, 1,369,070; India, 1,022,552; China, 988,857; Vietnam, 988,174; Cuba, 872,716; Korea, 864,125; Canada, 820,771; El Salvador, 817,336; Germany, 706,704; Dominican Republic, 687,677. A total of 849,807 immigrants were admitted in 2000 (1,536,483 in 1990).

Population of cities with over 100,000 inhabitants at the censuses of 1990 and 2000:

Cities	*Census 1990*	*Census 2000*
New York, NY	7,322,564	8,008,278
Los Angeles, CA	3,485,398	3,694,820
Chicago, IL	2,783,726	2,896,016
Houston, TX	1,630,553	1,953,631
Philadelphia, PA	1,585,577	1,517,550
Phoenix, AZ	983,403	1,321,045
San Diego, CA	1,110,549	1,223,400
Dallas, TX	1,006,877	1,188,580
San Antonio, TX	935,933	1,144,646
Detroit, MI	1,027,974	951,270
San Jose, CA	782,248	894,943
Indianapolis, IN	741,952	791,926
San Francisco, CA	723,959	776,733
Jacksonville, FL	635,230	735,617
Columbus, OH	632,910	711,470
Austin, TX	465,622	656,562
Baltimore, MD	736,014	651,154
Memphis, TN	610,337	650,100
Milwaukee, WI	628,088	596,974
Boston, MA	574,283	589,141
Washington, DC	606,900	572,059
Nashville-Davidson, TN	510,784	569,891
El Paso, TX	515,342	563,662
Seattle, WA	516,259	563,374
Denver, CO	467,610	554,636
Charlotte, NC	395,934	540,828
Fort Worth, TX	447,619	534,694
Portland, OR	437,319	529,121
Oklahoma City, OK	444,719	506,132
Tucson, AZ	405,390	486,699
New Orleans, LA	496,938	484,674
Las Vegas, NV	258,295	478,434
Cleveland, OH	505,616	478,403
Long Beach, CA	429,433	461,522
Albuquerque, NM	384,736	448,607
Kansas City, MO	435,146	441,545
Fresno, CA	354,202	427,652
Virginia Beach, VA	393,069	425,257
Atlanta, GA	394,017	416,474
Sacramento, CA	369,365	407,018
Oakland, CA	372,242	399,484
Mesa, AZ	288,091	396,375
Tulsa, OK	367,302	393,049
Omaha, NE	335,795	390,007
Minneapolis, MN	368,383	382,618
Honolulu, HI	365,272	371,657
Miami, FL	358,548	362,470
Colorado Springs, CO	281,140	360,890
St Louis, MO	396,685	348,189
Wichita, KS	304,011	344,284
Santa Ana, CA	293,742	337,977
Pittsburgh, PA	369,879	334,563
Arlington, TX	261,721	332,969
Cincinnati, OH	364,040	331,285
Anaheim, CA	266,406	328,014
Toledo, OH	332,943	313,619
Tampa, FL	280,015	303,447
Buffalo, NY	328,123	292,648
St Paul, MN	272,235	287,151
Corpus Christi, TX	257,453	277,454
Aurora, CO	222,103	276,393
Raleigh, NC	207,951	276,093
Newark, NJ	275,221	273,546
Lexington-Fayette, KY	225,366	260,512
Anchorage, AK	226,338	260,283
Louisville, KY	269,063	256,231
Riverside, CA	226,505	255,166
St Petersburg, FL	238,629	248,232
Bakersfield, CA	174,280	247,057
Stockton, CA	210,943	243,771
Birmingham, AL	265,968	242,820
Jersey City, NJ	228,537	240,055
Norfolk, VA	261,229	234,403
Baton Rouge, LA	219,531	227,818
Hialeah, FL	188,004	226,419
Lincoln, NE	191,972	225,581
Greensboro, NC	183,521	223,891
Plano, TX	128,713	222,030
Rochester, NY	231,636	219,773
Glendale, AZ	148,134	218,812
Garland, TX	180,650	215,768
Madison, WI	191,262	208,054
Fort Wayne, IN	173,072	205,727
Fremont, CA	173,339	203,413
Scottsdale, AZ	130,069	202,705
Montgomery, AL	187,106	201,568
Shreveport, LA	198,525	200,145
Augusta-Richmond County, GA	44,639	199,775
Lubbock, TX	186,206	199,564
Chesapeake, VA	151,976	199,184
Mobile, AL	196,278	198,915
Des Moines, IA	193,187	198,682
Grand Rapids, MI	189,126	197,800
Richmond, VA	203,056	197,790
Yonkers, NY	188,082	196,086
Spokane, WA	177,196	195,629
Glendale, CA	180,038	194,973
Tacoma, WA	176,664	193,556
Irving, TX	155,037	191,615
Huntington Beach, CA	181,519	189,594
Arlington, VA[1]	170,897	189,453
Modesto, CA	164,730	188,856
Durham, NC	136,611	187,035
Columbus, GA	179,278	186,291
Orlando, FL	164,693	185,951
Boise City, ID	125,738	185,787
Winston-Salem, NC	143,485	185,776
San Bernardino, CA	164,164	185,401
Jackson, MS	196,637	184,256
Little Rock, AR	175,795	183,133
Salt Lake City, UT	159,936	181,743
Reno, NV	133,850	180,480
Newport News, VA	170,045	180,150

Cities	Census 1990	Census 2000	Cities	Census 1990	Census 2000
Chandler, AZ	90,533	176,581	Concord, CA	111,348	121,780
Laredo, TX	122,899	176,576	Evansville, IN	126,272	121,582
Henderson, NV	64,942	175,381	Hartford, CT	139,739	121,578
Knoxville, TN	165,121	173,890	Fayetteville, NC	75,695	121,015
Amarillo, TX	157,615	173,627	Cedar Rapids, IA	108,751	120,758
Providence, RI	160,728	173,618	Elizabeth, NJ	110,002	120,568
Chula Vista, CA	135,163	173,556	Lansing, MI	127,321	119,128
Worcester, MA	169,759	172,648	Lancaster, CA	97,291	118,718
Oxnard, CA	142,216	170,358	Fort Collins, CO	87,758	118,652
Dayton, OH	182,044	166,179	Coral Springs, FL	79,443	117,549
Garden Grove, CA	143,050	165,196	Stamford, CT	108,056	117,083
Oceanside, CA	128,398	161,029	Thousand Oaks, CA	104,352	117,005
Tempe, AZ	141,865	158,625	Vallejo, CA	109,199	116,760
Huntsville, AL	159,789	158,216	Palmdale, CA	68,842	116,670
Ontario, CA	133,179	158,007	Columbia, SC	98,052	116,278
Chattanooga, TN	152,466	155,554	El Monte, CA	106,209	115,965
Fort Lauderdale, FL	149,377	152,397	Abilene, TX	106,654	115,930
Springfield, MA	156,983	152,082	North Las Vegas, NV	47,707	115,488
Springfield, MO	140,494	151,580	Beaumont, TX	114,323	113,866
Santa Clarita, CA	110,642	151,088	Waco, TX	103,590	113,726
Salinas, CA	108,777	151,060	Independence, MO	112,301	113,288
Tallahassee, FL	124,773	150,624	Peoria, IL	113,504	112,936
Rockford, IL	139,426	150,115	Inglewood, CA	109,602	112,580
Pomona, CA	131,723	149,473	Springfield, IL	105,227	111,454
Paterson, NJ	140,891	149,222	Simi Valley, CA	100,217	111,351
Overland Park, KS	111,790	149,080	Lafayette, LA	94,440	110,257
Santa Rosa, CA	113,313	147,595	Gilbert, AZ	29,188	109,697
Syracuse, NY	163,860	147,306	Carrollton, TX	82,169	109,576
Kansas City, KS	149,767	146,866	Bellevue, WA	86,874	109,569
Hampton, VA	133,793	146,437	West Valley City, UT	86,976	108,896
Lakewood, CO	126,481	144,126	Clearwater, FL	98,784	108,787
Vancouver, WA	46,380	143,560	Costa Mesa, CA	96,357	108,724
Irvine, CA	110,330	143,072	Peoria, AZ	50,618	108,364
Aurora, IL	99,581	142,990	South Bend, IN	105,511	107,789
Moreno Valley, CA	118,779	142,381	Downey, CA	91,444	107,323
Pasadena, TX	119,363	141,674	Waterbury, CT	108,961	107,271
Hayward, CA	111,498	140,030	Manchester, NH	99,567	107,006
Brownsville, TX	98,962	139,722	Allentown, PA	105,090	106,632
Bridgeport, CT	141,686	139,529	McAllen, TX	84,021	106,414
Hollywood, FL	121,697	139,357	Joliet, IL	76,836	106,221
Warren, MI	144,864	138,247	Lowell, MA	103,439	105,167
Torrance, CA	133,107	137,946	Provo, UT	86,835	105,166
Eugene, OR	112,669	137,893	West Covina, CA	96,086	105,080
Pembroke Pines, FL	65,452	137,427	Wichita Falls, TX	96,259	104,197
Salem, OR	107,786	136,924	Erie, PA	108,718	103,717
Pasadena, CA	131,591	133,936	Daly City, CA	92,311	103,621
Escondido, CA	108,635	133,559	Clarksville, TN	75,494	103,445
Sunnyvale, CA	117,229	131,760	Norwalk, CA	94,279	103,298
Savannah, GA	137,560	131,510	Gary, IN	116,646	102,746
Fontana, CA	87,535	128,929	Berkeley, CA	102,724	102,743
Orange, CA	110,658	128,821	Santa Clara, CA	93,613	102,361
Naperville, IL	85,351	128,358	Green Bay, WI	96,466	102,313
Alexandria, VA	111,183	128,283	Cape Coral, FL	74,991	102,286
Rancho Cucamonga, CA	101,409	127,743	Arvada, CO	89,235	102,153
Grand Prairie, TX	99,616	127,427	Pueblo, CO	98,640	102,121
Fullerton, CA	114,144	126,003	Athens-Clarke County, GA	45,734	101,489
Corona, CA	76,095	124,966	Cambridge, MA	95,802	101,355
Flint, MI	140,761	124,943	Westminster, CO	74,625	100,940
Mesquite, TX	101,484	124,523	San Buenaventura (Ventura), CA	92,575	100,916
Sterling Heights, MI	117,810	124,471	Portsmouth, VA	103,907	100,565
Sioux Falls, SD	100,814	123,975	Livonia, MI	100,850	100,545
New Haven, CT	130,474	123,626	Burbank, CA	93,643	100,316
Topeka, KS	119,883	122,377			

[1]Arlington CDP (census designated place) is not incorporated as a city.

Immigration and naturalization. The Immigration and Nationality Act, as amended, provides for the numerical limitation of most immigration. The Immigration Act of

1990 established major revisions in the numerical limits and preference system regulating legal immigration. The numerical limits are imposed on visas issued and not admissions. The maximum number of visas allowed to be issued under the preference categories in 2003 was 397,532: 226,000 for family-sponsored immigrants and 171,532 for employment-based immigrants. Within the overall limitations the per-country limit for independent countries is set to 7% of the total family and employment limits, while dependent areas are limited to 2% of the total.

Immigrant aliens admitted to the USA for permanent residence, by country or region of birth, for fiscal years:

	Immigrants admitted			
Country or region of birth	*2000*	*2001*	*2002*	*2003*
All countries	849,807	1,064,318	1,063,732	705,827
Europe	132,480	175,371	174,209	100,769
Bosnia-Herzegovina	11,828	23,640	25,373	6,168
Germany	7,638	9,886	8,961	5,101
Poland	10,114	11,818	12,746	10,526
Russia	17,110	20,413	20,833	13,951
Ukraine	15,810	20,975	12,217	11,666
UK	13,385	18,436	16,421	9,601
Other Europe	56,595	70,203	68,658	43,759
Asia	265,400	349,776	342,099	244,759
China and Taiwan	54,692	68,597	71,118	47,606
Hong Kong	5,419	8,321	6,090	3,582
India	42,046	70,290	71,105	50,372
Japan	7,094	9,619	8,301	5,993
Korea (North and South)	15,830	20,742	21,021	12,512
Philippines	42,474	53,154	51,308	45,397
Thailand	3,785	4,291	4,175	3,158
Vietnam	26,747	35,531	33,627	22,133
Other Asia	67,313	79,231	75,354	54,006
North and Central America	344,805	407,888	404,437	250,726
Canada	16,210	21,933	19,519	11,446
Mexico	173,919	206,426	219,380	115,864
Cuba	20,831	27,703	28,272	9,304
Dominican Republic	17,536	21,313	22,604	26,205
El Salvador	14,606	31,272	31,168	28,296
Haiti	22,364	27,120	20,268	12,314
Jamaica	16,000	15,393	14,898	13,384
Trinidad and Tobago	6,660	6,665	5,771	4,153
Other Caribbean	4,807	5,352	4,676	3,455
Other Central America	51,837	44,642	37,811	26,269
Other North America	35	69	70	36
South America	56,074	68,888	74,506	55,247
Colombia	14,498	16,730	18,845	14,777
Ecuador	7,685	9,706	10,602	7,083
Other South America	33,891	42,452	45,059	33,387
Africa	44,731	53,948	60,269	48,738
Australia and New Zealand	3,031	4,044	3,705	2,731
Other countries	3,286	4,403	4,507	2,857

The total number of immigrants admitted from 1820 up to 30 Sept. 2003 was 68,923,308; this included 7,227,324 from Germany, 6,675,296 from Mexico and 5,443,948 from Italy.

The number of immigrants admitted for legal permanent residence in the United States in the fiscal year 2003 was 705,827. Included in this total were 358,411 aliens previously living abroad who obtained immigrant visas through the US Department of State and became legal permanent residents upon entry into the United States. The remaining 347,416 legal immigrants, including former undocumented immigrants, refugees and asylees, had adjusted status through the Citizenship and Immigration Services (USCIS).

A total of 463,204 persons were naturalized in fiscal year 2003 (including 56,093 persons born in Mexico).

The refugee admissions ceiling for the fiscal year 2003 was fixed at 70,000, including 20,000 from Africa and 16,500 from Europe.

SOCIAL STATISTICS

Figures include Alaska beginning with 1959 and Hawaii beginning with 1960.

	Live births	*Deaths*	*Marriages*	*Divorces*	*Deaths under 1 year*
1900	—	343,217	709,000	56,000	—
1910	2,777,000	696,856	948,000	83,000	—
1920	2,950,000	1,118,070	1,274,476	170,505	170,911
1930	2,618,000	1,327,240	1,126,856	195,961	143,201
1940	2,559,000	1,417,269	1,595,879	264,000	110,984
1950	3,632,000	1,452,454	1,667,231	385,144	103,825
1960	4,257,850	1,711,982	1,523,000	393,000	110,873
1970	3,731,386	1,921,031	2,158,802	708,000	74,667
1980	3,612,258	1,989,841	2,390,252	1,189,000	45,526
1990	4,158,212	2,148,463	2,448,000	1,182,000	38,351
1994	3,952,767	2,278,994	2,362,000	1,191,000	31,000
1995	3,899,589	2,312,132	2,336,000	1,169,000	30,000
1996	3,891,494	2,314,690	2,344,000	1,150,000	28,000
1997	3,880,894	2,314,245	2,384,000	1,163,000	28,000
1998	3,941,553	2,337,256	2,244,000	—	28,000
1999	3,959,417	2,391,399	2,358,000	—	28,000
2000	4,058,814	2,403,351	2,329,000	—	27,000
2001	4,025,933	2,416,425	2,345,000	—	28,000
2002	4,021,726	2,443,387	2,254,000	—	28,000
2003	4,091,063[1]	2,443,908[1]	2,187,000[1]	—	—

[1]Preliminary.

Rates (per 1,000 population):

	Birth	*Death*	*Marriage*	*Divorce*
1994	15·0	8·7	9·1	4·6
1995	14·6	8·7	8·9	4·4
1996	14·4	8·6	8·8	4·3
1997	14·2	8·5	8·9	4·3
1998	14·3	8·5	8·4	—
1999	14·2	8·6	8·6	—
2000	14·4	8·5	8·2	—
2001	14·1	8·5	8·2	—
2002	13·9	8·5	7·8	—
2003	14·1[1]	8·4[1]	7·5[1]	

[1]Preliminary.

Rate of natural increase per 1,000 population: 7·7 in 1991; 5·4 in 2002. Annual population growth rate, 1990–2000, 1·3%.

Even though the marriage rate shows a gradual decline, it remains much higher than in most other industrial countries. The most popular age range for marrying is 25–29 for males and 20–24 for females. Estimated number of births to unmarried women in 2001 was 1,349,000 (33·0% of all births), compared to 666,000 in 1980. The USA has the highest rate of births to teenage women in the industrialized world, at 46·1 per 1,000 women in 2001. Between 1970 and 1998 the annual number of births rose by 5·7%. The number of births within marriage declined by 19·2% whereas the number outside of marriage rose by 223·6%. The number of lone-parent families rose by 190·2% over the same period. Whereas in 1970 as many as 83·4% of children lived with both biological parents, by 2000 only 60·4% were living with married biological parents and 2·1% with unmarried biological parents.

Infant mortality rates, per 1,000 live births: 29·2 in 1950; 12·9 in 1980; 6·8 in 2001. Fertility rate, 2001, 2·0 births per woman (3·6 in 1960).

There were 1·31m. abortions in 2000 (1·61m. in 1990), giving a rate of 21·3 for every 1,000 women aged 15–44, compared to a high of 29·3 per 1,000 in 1980 and 1981.

Expectation of life, 1970: males, 67·1 years; females, 74·7 years. 2001: males, 74·0 years; females, 79·7 years.

Numbers of deaths by principal causes, 2001 (and as a percentage of all deaths): heart disease, 700,100 (29·0%); cancer, 553,800 (22·9%); stroke, 163,500 (6·8%); chronic lower respiratory disease, 123,000 (5·1%); accidents, 101,500 (4·2%); diabetes mellitus, 71,400 (3·0%); pneumonia and influenza, 62,000 (2·6%); Alzheimer's disease, 53,900 (2·2%); kidney diseases, 39,500 (1·6%); septicemia, 32,200 (1·3%); suicide, 30,600 (1·3%); liver diseases, 27,000 (1·1%).

The number of Americans living in poverty in 2002 was 34·6m. or 12·1% of the total population, down from 15·1% in 1993.

A UNICEF report published in 2000 showed that 22·4% of children in the USA live in poverty (in households with income below 50% of the national median), compared to just 2·6% in Sweden. The report also showed that the poverty rate of children in lone-parent families was 55·4%, compared to 15·8% in two-parent families.

CLIMATE

For temperature and rainfall figures, *see* entries on individual states as indicated by regions, below, of mainland USA.

Pacific Coast. The climate varies with latitude, distance from the sea and the effect of relief, ranging from polar conditions in North Alaska through cool to warm temperate climates further south. The extreme south is temperate desert. Rainfall everywhere is moderate. *See* Alaska, California, Oregon, Washington.

Mountain States. Very varied, with relief exerting the main control; very cold in the north in winter, with considerable snowfall. In the south, much higher temperatures and aridity produce desert conditions. Rainfall everywhere is very variable as a result of rain-shadow influences. *See* Arizona, Colorado, Idaho, Montana, Nevada, New Mexico, Utah, Wyoming.

High Plains. A continental climate with a large annual range of temperature and moderate rainfall, mainly in summer, although unreliable. Dust storms are common in summer and blizzards in winter. *See* Nebraska, North Dakota, South Dakota.

Central Plains. A temperate continental climate, with hot summers and cold winters, except in the extreme south. Rainfall is plentiful and comes at all seasons, but there is a summer maximum in western parts. *See* Mississippi, Missouri, Oklahoma, Texas.

Mid-West. Continental, with hot summers and cold winters. Rainfall is moderate, with a summer maximum in most parts. *See* Indiana, Iowa, Kansas.

Great Lakes. Continental, resembling that of the Central Plains, with hot summers but very cold winters because of the freezing of the lakes. Rainfall is moderate with a slight summer maximum. *See* Illinois, Michigan, Minnesota, Ohio, Wisconsin.

Appalachian Mountains. The north is cool temperate with cold winters, the south warm temperate with milder winters. Precipitation is heavy, increasing to the south but evenly distributed over the year. *See* Kentucky, Pennsylvania, Tennessee, West Virginia.

Gulf Coast. Conditions vary from warm temperate to sub-tropical, with plentiful rainfall, decreasing towards the west but evenly distributed over the year. *See* Alabama, Arkansas, Florida, Louisiana.

Atlantic Coast. Temperate maritime climate but with great differences in temperature according to latitude. Rainfall is ample at all seasons; snowfall in the north can be heavy. *See* Delaware, District of Columbia, Georgia, Maryland, New Jersey, New York State, North Carolina, South Carolina, Virginia.

New England. Cool temperate, with severe winters and warm summers. Precipitation is well distributed with a slight winter maximum. Snowfall is heavy in winter. *See* Connecticut, Maine, Massachusetts, New Hampshire, Rhode Island, Vermont. *See* also Hawaii and Outlying Territories.

CONSTITUTION AND GOVERNMENT

The form of government of the USA is based on the constitution adopted on 17 Sept. 1787 and effective from 4 March 1789.

By the constitution the government of the nation is composed of three co-ordinate branches, the executive, the legislative and the judicial.

The Federal government has authority in matters of general taxation, treaties and other dealings with foreign countries, foreign and inter-state commerce, bankruptcy, postal service, coinage, weights and measures, patents and copyright, the armed forces (including, to a certain extent, the militia), and crimes against the USA; it has sole legislative authority over the District of Columbia and the possessions of the USA.

The 5th article of the constitution provides that Congress may, on a two-thirds vote of both houses, propose amendments to the constitution, or, on the application of the legislatures of two-thirds of all the states, call a convention for proposing amendments, which in either case shall be valid as part of the constitution when ratified by the legislatures of three-fourths of the several states, or by conventions in three-fourths thereof, whichever mode of ratification may be proposed by Congress. Ten amendments (called collectively 'the Bill of Rights') to the constitution were added 15 Dec. 1791; two in 1795 and 1804; a 13th amendment, 6 Dec. 1865, abolishing slavery; a 14th in 1868, including the important 'due process' clause; a 15th, 3 Feb. 1870, establishing equal voting rights for white and black; a 16th, 3 Feb. 1913, authorizing the income tax; a 17th, 8 April 1913, providing for popular election of senators; an 18th, 16 Jan. 1919, prohibiting alcoholic liquors; a 19th, 18 Aug. 1920, establishing woman suffrage; a 20th, 23 Jan. 1933, advancing the date of the President's and Vice-President's inauguration and abolishing the 'lameduck' sessions of Congress; a 21st, 5 Dec. 1933, repealing the 18th amendment; a 22nd, 27 Feb. 1951, limiting a President's tenure of office to two terms, or two full terms in the case of a Vice-President who has succeeded to the office of President and has served two years or less of another President's term, or one full term in the case of a Vice-President who has succeeded to the office of President and has served more than two years of another President's term; a 23rd, 30 March 1961, granting citizens of the District of Columbia the right to vote in national elections; a 24th, 4 Feb. 1964, banning the use of the poll-tax in federal elections; a 25th, 10 Feb. 1967, dealing with Presidential disability and succession; a 26th, 22 June 1970, establishing the right of citizens who are 18 years of age and older to vote; a 27th, 7 May 1992, providing that no law varying the compensation of Senators or Representatives shall take effect until an election has taken place.

National motto. 'In God we trust'; formally adopted by Congress 30 July 1956.

Presidency. The executive power is vested in a president, who holds office for four years, and is elected, together with a vice-president chosen for the same term, by electors from each state, equal to the whole number of senators and representatives to which the state may be entitled in the Congress. The President must be a natural-born citizen, resident in the country for 14 years, and at least 35 years old.

The presidential election is held every fourth (leap) year on the Tuesday after the first Monday in Nov. Technically, this is an election of presidential electors, not of a president directly; the electors thus chosen meet and give their votes (for the candidate to whom they are pledged, in some states by law, but in most states by custom and prudent politics) at their respective state capitals on the first Monday after the second Wednesday in Dec. next following their election; and the votes of the electors of all the states are opened and counted in the presence of both Houses of Congress on the sixth day of Jan. The total electorate vote is one for each senator and representative. Electors may not be a member of Congress or hold federal office. If no candidate secures the minimum 270 college votes needed for outright victory, the 12th Amendment to the Constitution applies, and the House of Representatives chooses a president from among the first three finishers in the electoral college. (This last happened in 1824).

If the successful candidate for President dies before taking office the Vice-President-elect becomes President; if no candidate has a majority or if the successful candidate fails to qualify, then, by the 20th amendment, the Vice-President acts as President until a president qualifies. The duties of the Presidency, in absence of the President and Vice-President by reason of death, resignation, removal, inability or failure to qualify, devolve upon the Speaker of the House under legislation enacted on 18 July 1947. In case of absence of a Speaker for like reason, the presidential duties devolve upon the President *pro tem.* of the Senate and successively upon those members of the cabinet in order of precedence, who have the constitutional qualifications for President.

The presidential term, by the 20th amendment to the constitution, begins at noon on 20 Jan. of the inaugural year. This amendment also installs the newly elected Congress in office on 3 Jan. instead of—as formerly—in the following Dec. The President's salary is $400,000 per year (taxable), with an additional $50,000 to assist in defraying expenses resulting from official duties. Also he may spend up to $100,000 non-taxable for travel and $19,000 for official entertainment. In 1999 the presidential salary was increased for the president taking office in Jan. 2001, having remained at $200,000 a year since 1969. The office of Vice-President carries a salary of $208,100 and $10,000 allowance for expenses, all taxable. The Vice-President is *ex officio* President of the Senate, and in the case of 'the removal of the President, or of his death, resignation, or inability to discharge the powers and duties of his office', he becomes the President for the remainder of the term.

PRESIDENTS OF THE USA

Name	*From state*	*Term of service*	*Born*	*Died*
George Washington	Virginia	1789–97	1732	1799
John Adams	Massachusetts	1797–1801	1735	1826
Thomas Jefferson	Virginia	1801–09	1743	1826
James Madison	Virginia	1809–17	1751	1836
James Monroe	Virginia	1817–25	1759	1831
John Quincy Adams	Massachusetts	1825–29	1767	1848
Andrew Jackson	Tennessee	1829–37	1767	1845
Martin Van Buren	New York	1837–41	1782	1862
William H. Harrison	Ohio	Mar.–Apr. 1841	1773	1841
John Tyler	Virginia	1841–45	1790	1862
James K. Polk	Tennessee	1845–49	1795	1849
Zachary Taylor	Louisiana	1849–July 1850	1784	1850
Millard Fillmore	New York	1850–53	1800	1874
Franklin Pierce	New Hampshire	1853–57	1804	1869
James Buchanan	Pennsylvania	1857–61	1791	1868
Abraham Lincoln	Illinois	1861–Apr. 1865	1809	1865
Andrew Johnson	Tennessee	1865–69	1808	1875
Ulysses S. Grant	Illinois	1869–77	1822	1885
Rutherford B. Hayes	Ohio	1877–81	1822	1893
James A. Garfield	Ohio	Mar.–Sept. 1881	1831	1881
Chester A. Arthur	New York	1881–85	1830	1886
Grover Cleveland	New York	1885–89	1837	1908
Benjamin Harrison	Indiana	1889–93	1833	1901
Grover Cleveland	New York	1893–97	1837	1908
William McKinley	Ohio	1897–Sept. 1901	1843	1901
Theodore Roosevelt	New York	1901–09	1858	1919
William H. Taft	Ohio	1909–13	1857	1930
Woodrow Wilson	New Jersey	1913–21	1856	1924
Warren Gamaliel Harding	Ohio	1921–Aug. 1923	1865	1923
Calvin Coolidge	Massachusetts	1923–29	1872	1933
Herbert C. Hoover	California	1929–33	1874	1964
Franklin D. Roosevelt	New York	1933–Apr. 1945	1882	1945
Harry S Truman	Missouri	1945–53	1884	1972
Dwight D. Eisenhower	New York	1953–61	1890	1969
John F. Kennedy	Massachusetts	1961–Nov. 1963	1917	1963
Lyndon B. Johnson	Texas	1963–69	1908	1973
Richard M. Nixon	California	1969–74	1913	1994
Gerald R. Ford	Michigan	1974–77	1913	—
James Earl Carter	Georgia	1977–81	1924	—
Ronald W. Reagan	California	1981–89	1911	2004
George H. Bush	Texas	1989–93	1924	—
Bill (William J.) Clinton	Arkansas	1993–2001	1946	—
George W. Bush	Texas	2001–	1946	—

VICE-PRESIDENTS OF THE USA

Name	*From state*	*Term of service*	*Born*	*Died*
John Adams	Massachusetts	1789–97	1735	1826
Thomas Jefferson	Virginia	1797–1801	1743	1826
Aaron Burr	New York	1801–05	1756	1836
George Clinton	New York	1805–12[1]	1739	1812
Elbridge Gerry	Massachusetts	1813–14[1]	1744	1814
Daniel D. Tompkins	New York	1817–25	1774	1825
John C. Calhoun	South Carolina	1825–32[1]	1782	1850
Martin Van Buren	New York	1833–37	1782	1862
Richard M. Johnson	Kentucky	1837–41	1780	1850
John Tyler	Virginia	Mar.–Apr.1841[1]	1790	1862
George M. Dallas	Pennsylvania	1845–49	1792	1864
Millard Fillmore	New York	1849–50[1]	1800	1874
William R. King	Alabama	Mar.–Apr. 1853[1]	1786	1853

Name	*From state*	*Term of service*	*Born*	*Died*
John C. Breckinridge	Kentucky	1857–61	1821	1875
Hannibal Hamlin	Maine	1861–65	1809	1891
Andrew Johnson	Tennessee	Mar.–Apr. 1865[1]	1808	1875
Schuyler Colfax	Indiana	1869–73	1823	1885
Henry Wilson	Massachusetts	1873–75[1]	1812	1875
William A. Wheeler	New York	1877–81	1819	1887
Chester A. Arthur	New York	Mar.–Sept. 1881[1]	1830	1886
Thomas A. Hendricks	Indiana	Mar.–Nov. 1885[1]	1819	1885
Levi P. Morton	New York	1889–93	1824	1920
Adlai Stevenson	Illinois	1893–97	1835	1914
Garret A. Hobart	New Jersey	1897–99[1]	1844	1899
Theodore Roosevelt	New York	Mar.–Sept. 1901[1]	1858	1919
Charles W. Fairbanks	Indiana	1905–09	1855	1920
James S. Sherman	New York	1909–12[1]	1855	1912
Thomas R. Marshall	Indiana	1913–21	1854	1925
Calvin Coolidge	Massachusetts	1921–Aug. 1923[1]	1872	1933
Charles G. Dawes	Illinois	1925–29	1865	1951
Charles Curtis	Kansas	1929–33	1860	1935
John N. Garner	Texas	1933–41	1868	1967
Henry A. Wallace	Iowa	1941–45	1888	1965
Harry S Truman	Missouri	1945–Apr. 1945[1]	1884	1972
Alben W. Barkley	Kentucky	1949–53	1877	1956
Richard M. Nixon	California	1953–61	1913	1994
Lyndon B. Johnson	Texas	1961–Nov. 1963[1]	1908	1973
Hubert H. Humphrey	Minnesota	1965–69	1911	1978
Spiro T. Agnew	Maryland	1969–73	1918	1996
Gerald R. Ford	Michigan	1973–74	1913	—
Nelson Rockefeller	New York	1974–77	1908	1979
Walter Mondale	Minnesota	1977–81	1928	—
George H. Bush	Texas	1981–89	1924	—
Danforth Quayle	Indiana	1989–93	1947	—
Albert Gore	Tennessee	1993–2001	1948	—
Richard B. Cheney	Wyoming	2001–	1941	—

[1]Position vacant thereafter until commencement of the next presidential term.

Cabinet. The administrative business of the nation has been traditionally vested in several executive departments, the heads of which, unofficially and *ex officio*, formed the President's cabinet. Beginning with the Interstate Commerce Commission in 1887, however, an increasing amount of executive business has been entrusted to some 60 so-called independent agencies, such as the Housing and Home Finance Agency, Tariff Commission, etc.

All heads of departments and of the 60 or more administrative agencies are appointed by the President, but must be confirmed by the Senate.

Congress. The legislative power is vested by the Constitution in a Congress, consisting of a Senate and House of Representatives.

Electorate. By amendments of the constitution, disqualification of voters on the ground of race, colour or sex is forbidden. The electorate consists of all citizens over 18 years of age. Literacy tests have been banned since 1970. In 1972 durational residency requirements were held to violate the constitution. In 1973 US citizens abroad were enfranchised.

With limitations imposed by the constitution, it is the states which determine voter eligibility. In general states exclude from voting: persons who have not established residency in the jurisdiction in which they wish to vote; persons who have been convicted of felonies whose civil rights have not been restored; persons declared mentally incompetent by a court.

Illiterate voters are entitled to receive assistance in marking their ballots. Minority-language voters in jurisdictions with statutorily prescribed minority concentrations are entitled to have elections conducted in the minority language as well as English. Disabled voters are entitled to accessible polling places. Voters absent on election days or unable to go to the polls are generally entitled under state law to vote by absentee ballot.

The Constitution guarantees citizens that their votes will be of equal value under the 'one person, one vote' rule.

Senate. The Senate consists of two members from each state (but not from the District of Columbia), chosen by popular vote for six years, approximately one-third retiring or seeking re-election every two years. Senators must be no less than 30 years of age; must have been citizens of the USA for nine years, and be residents in the states for which they are chosen. The Senate has complete freedom to initiate legislation, except revenue bills (which must originate in the House of Representatives); it may, however, amend or reject any legislation originating in the lower house. The Senate is also entrusted with the power of giving or withholding its 'advice and consent' to the ratification of all treaties initiated by the President with foreign powers, a two-thirds majority of senators present being required for approval. (However, it has no control over 'international executive agreements' made by the President with foreign governments; such 'agreements' cover a wide range and are more numerous than formal treaties.)

The Senate has 21 Standing Committees to which all bills are referred for study, revision or rejection. The House of Representatives has 20 such committees. In both Houses each Standing Committee has a chairman and a majority representing the majority party of the whole House; each has numerous sub-committees. The jurisdictions of these Committees correspond largely to those of the appropriate executive departments and agencies. Both Houses also have a few select or special Committees with limited duration.

House of Representatives. The House of Representatives consists of 435 members elected every second year. The number of each state's representatives is determined by the decennial census, in the absence of specific Congressional legislation affecting the basis. The number of representatives for each state in the 109th congress, which began in Jan. 2005 (based on the 2000 census), is given below:

Alabama	7	Indiana	9	Nebraska	3	South Carolina	6
Alaska	1	Iowa	5	Nevada	3	South Dakota	1
Arizona	8	Kansas	4	New Hampshire	2	Tennessee	9
Arkansas	4	Kentucky	6	New Jersey	13	Texas	32
California	53	Louisiana	7	New Mexico	3	Utah	3
Colorado	7	Maine	2	New York	29	Vermont	1
Connecticut	5	Maryland	8	North Carolina	13	Virginia	11
Delaware	1	Massachusetts	10	North Dakota	1	Washington	9
Florida	25	Michigan	15	Ohio	18	West Virginia	3
Georgia	13	Minnesota	8	Oklahoma	5	Wisconsin	8
Hawaii	2	Mississippi	4	Oregon	5	Wyoming	1
Idaho	2	Missouri	9	Pennsylvania	19		
Illinois	19	Montana	1	Rhode Island	2		

The constitution requires congressional districts within each state to be substantially equal in population. Final decisions on congressional district boundaries are taken by the state legislatures and governors. By custom the representative lives in the district from which he is elected. Representatives must be not less than 25 years of age, citizens of the USA for seven years and residents in the state from which they are chosen.

In addition, five delegates (one each from the District of Columbia, American Samoa, Guam, the US Virgin Islands and Puerto Rico) are also members of Congress. They have a voice but no vote, except in committees. The delegate from Puerto Rico is the resident commissioner. Puerto Ricans vote at primaries, but not at national elections. Each of the two Houses of Congress is sole 'judge of the elections, returns and qualifications of its own members'; and each of the Houses may, with the concurrence of two-thirds, expel a member. The period usually termed 'a Congress' in legislative language continues for two years, terminating at noon on 3 Jan.

The salary of a senator is $162,100 per annum, with tax-free expense allowance and allowances for travelling expenses and for clerical hire. The salary of the Speaker of the House of Representatives is $208,100 per annum, with a taxable allowance. The salary of a Member of the House is $162,100 ($180,100 for the Majority Leader and Minority Leader).

No senator or representative can, during the time for which he is elected, be appointed to any *civil* office under authority of the USA which shall have been created or the emoluments of which shall have been increased during such time; and no person holding *any* office under the USA can be a member of either House during his continuance in office. No religious text may be required as a qualification to any office or public trust under the USA or in any state.

Indians. By an Act passed on 2 June 1924 full citizenship was granted to all Indians born in the USA, though those remaining in tribal units were still under special federal jurisdiction. The Indian Reorganization Act of 1934 gave the tribal Indians, at their own option, substantial opportunities of self-government and the establishment of self-controlled corporate enterprises empowered to borrow money and buy land, machinery and equipment; these corporations are controlled by democratically elected tribal councils. Recently a trend towards releasing Indians from federal supervision has resulted in legislation terminating supervision over specific tribes. In 1988 the federal government recognized that it had a special relationship with, and a trust responsibility for, federally recognized Indian entities in continental USA and tribal entities in Alaska. In 2003 the Bureau of Indian Affairs listed 562 'Indian Entities Recognized and Eligible to Receive Services'. Indian lands (1991) amounted to 52,092,247 acres, of which 41,868,582 was tribally owned and 10,233,665 in trust allotments. Indian lands are held free of taxes. Total Indian population at the 2000 census was 2,475,956, of which California (333,346), Oklahoma (273,230), Arizona (255,879) and New Mexico (173,483) accounted for more than 40%.

The **District of Columbia,** ceded by the State of Maryland for the purposes of government in 1791, is the seat of the US government. It includes the city of Washington, and embraces a land area of 61 sq. miles. The Reorganization Plan No. 3 of 1967 instituted a Mayor Council form of government with appointed officers. In 1973 an elected Mayor and elected councillors were introduced; in 1974 they received power to legislate in local matters. Congress retains power to enact legislation and to veto or supersede the Council's acts. Since 1961 citizens have had the right to vote in national elections. On 23 Aug. 1978 the Senate approved a constitutional amendment giving the District full voting representation in Congress. This has still to be ratified.

The Commonwealth of Puerto Rico, American Samoa, Guam and the Virgin Islands each have a local legislature, whose acts may be modified or annulled by Congress, though in practice this has seldom been done. Puerto Rico, since its attainment of commonwealth status on 25 July 1952, enjoys practically complete self-government, including the election of its governor and other officials. The conduct of foreign relations, however, is still a federal function and federal bureaux and agencies still operate in the island.

General supervision of territorial administration is exercised by the Office of Territories in the Department of Interior.

Local Government. The Union comprises 13 original states, seven states which were admitted without having been previously organized as territories, and 30 states which had been territories—50 states in all. Each state has its own constitution (which the USA guarantees shall be republican in form), deriving its authority, not from Congress, but from the people of the state. Admission of states into the Union has been granted by special Acts of Congress, either (1) in the form of 'enabling Acts' providing for the drafting and ratification of a state constitution by the people, in which case the territory becomes a state as soon as the conditions are fulfilled, or (2) accepting a constitution already framed, and at once granting admission.

Each state is provided with a legislature of two Houses (except Nebraska, which since 1937 has had a single-chamber legislature), a governor and other executive officials, and a judicial system. Both Houses of the legislature are elective, but the senators (having larger electoral districts usually covering two or three counties compared with the single county or, in some states, the town, which sends one representative to the Lower House) are less numerous than the representatives, while in 38 states their terms are four years; in 12 states the term is two years. Of the four-year senates, Illinois, Montana and New Jersey provide for two four-year terms and one two-year term in each decade. Terms of the lower houses are usually shorter; in 45 states, two years. The trend is towards annual sessions of state legislatures; most meet annually now whereas in 1939 only four did.

The Governor is elected by direct vote of the people over the whole state for a term of office ranging in the various states from two to four years, and with a salary ranging from $70,000 (Maine) to $179,000 (New York). His duty is to see to the faithful administration of the law, and he has command of the military forces of the state. He may recommend measures but does not present bills to the legislature. In some states he presents estimates. In all but one of the states (North Carolina) the

Governor has a veto upon legislation, which may, however, be overridden by the two Houses, in some states by a simple majority, in others by a three-fifths or two-thirds majority. In some states the Governor, on his death or resignation, is succeeded by a Lieut.-Governor who was elected at the same time and has been presiding over the state Senate. In several states the Speaker of the Lower House succeeds the Governor.

National Anthem. The Star-spangled Banner, 'Oh say, can you see by the dawn's early light'; words by F. S. Key, 1814, tune by J. S. Smith; formally adopted by Congress 3 March 1931.

RECENT ELECTIONS

At the presidential election on 2 Nov. 2004 turn-out at 53·6% (51·2% in 2000). Certified results gave George W. Bush (R.) 62,028,285 votes (50·73%), John Kerry (D.) 59,028,109 (48·27%), Ralph Nader (ind.) 463,647 (0·38%), Michael Badnarik (Libertarian Party) 397,234 (0·32%), Michael Peroutka (Constitution Party) 143,609 (0·12%), David Cobb (Green Party) 119,862 (0·10%). Electoral college votes: Bush, 286; Kerry, 251; John Edwards, 1.

Voting percentages and electoral college votes by state in 2004:

a) Majority for Bush

State	*Bush (%)*	*Kerry (%)*	*3rd Place (%)*	*Electoral College (votes)*
Alabama	62·5	36·8	0·4[1]	9
Alaska	61·1	35·5	1·6[1]	3
Arizona	54·9	44·4	0·6[2]	10
Arkansas	54·3	44.5	0·6[1]	6
Colorado	51·7	47·0	0·6[1]	9
Florida	52·1	47·1	0·4[1]	27
Georgia	58·0	41·4	0·6[2]	15
Idaho	68·4	30·3	0·6[2]	4
Indiana	59·9	39·3	0·7[2]	11
Iowa	49·9	49·2	0·4[1]	7
Kansas	62·0	36·6	0·8[1]	6
Kentucky	59·6	39·7	0·5[1]	8
Louisiana	56·7	42·2	0·4[1]	9
Mississippi	59·0	40·2	0·3[1]	6
Missouri	53·3	46·1	0·4[2]	11
Montana	59·1	38·6	1·4[1]	3
Nebraska	65·9	32·7	0·7[1]	5
Nevada	50·5	47·9	0·6[1]	5
New Mexico	49·8	49·0	0·5[1]	5
North Carolina	56·0	43·6	0·3[2]	15
North Dakota	62·9	35·5	1·2[1]	3
Ohio	50·8	48·7	0·3[2]	20
Oklahoma	65·6	34·4	—	7
South Carolina	58·0	40·9	0·3[1]	8
South Dakota	59·9	38·4	1·1[1]	3
Tennessee	56·8	42·5	0·4[1]	11
Texas	61·1	38·2	0·5[2]	34
Utah	71·5	26·0	1·2[1]	5
Virginia	53·7	45·5	0·3[2]	13
West Virginia	56·1	43·2	0·5[1]	5
Wyoming	68·9	29·1	1·1[1]	3

b) Majority for Kerry

	Kerry	*Bush*	*3rd Place*	
California	54·3	44·4	0·4[2]	55
Connecticut	54·3	43·9	0·8[1]	7
Delaware	53·3	45·8	0·6[1]	3
D.C.	89·2	9·3	0·7[1]	3
Hawaii	54·0	45·3	0·4[3]	4
Illinois	54·8	44·5	0·6[2]	21
Maine	53·6	44·6	1·1[1]	4
Maryland	55·9	42·9	0·5[1]	10
Massachusetts	61·9	36·8	0·5[2]	12
Michigan	51·2	47·8	0·5[1]	17
Minnesota	51·1	47·6	0·7[1]	9

	Kerry	*Bush*	*3rd Place*	
New Hampshire	50·2	48·9	0·7[1]	4
New Jersey	52·9	46·2	0·5[1]	15
New York	58·4	40·1	1·4[1]	31
Oregon	51·3	47·2	0·4[2]	7
Pennsylvania	50·9	48·4	0·4[2]	21
Rhode Island	59·4	38·7	1·1[1]	4
Vermont	58·9	38·8	1·4[1]	3
Washington	52·8	45·6	0·8[1]	11
Wisconsin	49·7	49·3	0·5[1]	10

[1]Nader. [2]Badnarik. [3]Cobb.

Following the elections of 2 Nov. 2004 the 109th Congress (2005–06) is constituted as follows: Senate—55 Republicans, 44 Democrats and 1 ind. (51 Democrats, 48 Republicans and 1 ind. for the 108th Congress); House of Representatives—232 Republicans, 202 Democrats, 1 ind. (229 Republicans, 204 Democrats, 1 ind. and 1 vacancy for the 108th Congress).

The Speaker of the House of Representatives is Dennis Hastert (R.). The Majority Leader of the Senate is Bill Frist (R.).

CURRENT ADMINISTRATION

President of the United States: George W. Bush, of Texas; b. 1946. Majored in History at Yale (1968); MA in Business Administration (1975); unsuccessfully ran for Congress (1977); became shareholder in Texas Rangers baseball team (1988); governor of Texas (1994–2000).

Vice President: Richard ‘Dick’ Cheney, b. Wyoming, 1941. Deputy White House counselor in Nixon administration (1970); assistant to the president and White House chief of staff during the Ford administration (1974); House of Representatives (1979–89); Secretary of Defense (1989–93). Vice President since 2001.

In March 2005 the cabinet consisted of the following:

1. *Secretary of State* (created 1789). Condoleezza Rice, b. Alabama, 1954. Fellow of Stanford University Center for International Security and Arms Control (1981–89); Soviet affairs adviser to George H. Bush (1989–91); Provost of Stanford University (1993–99); National security adviser (2001–05).

2. *Secretary of the Treasury* (1789). John Snow, b. Ohio, 1939. PhD in Economics (1965) and LLB (1967). Entered Department of Transportation in 1972; Deputy Undersecretary of Transportation in Ford administration (1975–76). Joined Chessie System Inc. in 1977; President and CEO (1989) of CSX Corp. and Chairman (1991); Secretary of the Treasury since 2003.

3. *Secretary of Defense* (1947). Donald Rumsfeld, b. Illinois, 1932. Elected to the House of Representatives (1962–69); Ambassador to the North Atlantic Treaty Organisation (1973–74); Secretary of Defense to President Ford (1975–77); Special US negotiator for Middle Eastern problems (1983–84); Secretary of Defense since 2001.

4. *Attorney General* (Department of Justice, 1870). Alberto ‘Al’ Gonzales, b. Texas, 1955. Joined Vinson & Elkins law firm in Houston in 1982; Legal adviser to Governor Bush in Texas (1994–97); Texas Secretary of State (1997–99); Judge of Supreme Court of Texas (1999–2000); White House counsel (2001–05).

5. *Secretary of the Interior* (1849). Gale Norton, b. Kansas, 1954. Associate solicitor at the Department of the Interior (1985–90); Colorado attorney general and chair of the Environment Committee for the National Association of Attorneys General (1991–99); Environment Committee chair for the Republican National Lawyers Association (1999–2001); Secretary of the Interior since 2001.

6. *Secretary of Agriculture* (1889). Michael Johanns, b. Iowa, 1950. Lancaster county board of commissioners (1982–86); Lincoln city council (1989–91); Mayor of Lincoln (1991–99); Governor of Nebraska (1999–2005).

7. *Secretary of Commerce* (1903). Carlos Gutierrez, b. Cuba, 1954. Career with Kellogg Company began in 1975 in Mexico City; General Manager Kellogg operations in Mexico (1985); Chairman of the board and Chief Executive Officer of the Kellogg Company (1999–2005).

8. *Secretary of Labor* (1913). Elaine Chao, b. Taiwan, 1953. White House Fellow (1983–84); Deputy Secretary of the US Department of Transportation in Washington (1989–91); Director of the Peace Corps (1992); President of United Way of America

(1992–96); Chairman of Heritage Foundation's Asian Studies Center Advisory Council (1998); Secretary of Labor since 2001.

9. *Secretary of Health and Human Services* (1953). Michael O. Leavitt, b. Utah, 1951. Former president and chief executive of the Leavitt Group; Governor of Utah for three terms (1992–2003); Chief of the Environmental Protection Agency (2003–05).

10. *Secretary of Housing and Urban Development* (1966). Alphonso Jackson, b. Texas. Director of Public Safety, St Louis (1977); President and CEO of the Texas Housing Authority (1989–96); President of American Electric Power-TEXAS (1996–2001); deputy secretary and chief operating officer of Housing and Urban Development (2001–04). Secretary of Housing and Urban Development since 2004.

11. *Secretary of Transportation* (1967). Norman Mineta, b. California, 1931. Congressman for Silicon Valley (1974–95); Chairman, US House of Representatives Committee on Public Works and Transportation (1993); Chairman, Federal Aviation Administration's National Civil Aviation Review Commission (1997). He is the only Democrat in the cabinet. Secretary of Transportation since 2001.

12. *Secretary of Energy* (1977). Samuel W. Bodman, b. Chicago, 1938. Member of the American Academy of Arts and Sciences; Chairman, CEO, and Director (variously) of Cabot Corporation (1987–2001); Deputy commerce secretary (2001–03); Deputy treasury secretary (2003–05).

13. *Secretary of Education* (1979). Margaret Spellings, b. Michigan, 1958. Political director of George W. Bush's first gubernatorial campaign (1994); Senior adviser to Governor Bush on Education in Texas (1994–2000); Assistant to president for domestic policy (2000–05).

14. *Secretary of Veterans' Affairs* (1989). R. James 'Jim' Nicholson, b. Iowa, 1938. Westpoint Graduate (1961); 30 years service in Army; retired as a Colonel (1991); Chair of Republican National Committee (1997–2001); US Ambassador to the Vatican (2001–05).

15. *Secretary of Homeland Security* (2002). Michael Chertoff, b. New Jersey, 1953. Special counsel US Senate Whitewater Commission (1994–96); Director of the Justice Department's criminal division (2001–03); Federal judge on the 3rd US Circuit Court of Appeals (2003–05).

Each of the above cabinet officers receives an annual salary of $180,100 and holds office during the pleasure of the President.

A number of administrators also have honorary cabinet status.

Key White House Posts: White House Chief of Staff: Andrew Card; National Security Adviser: Stephen Hadley; White House Counsel: Harriet Miers; Press Secretary: Scott McClellan; Assistant for Economic Affairs: Stephen Friedman; Office of Management and Budget: Joshua Bolten; Council of Economic Advisors: Dr N. Gregory Mankiw; Office of the US Trade Representative: Robert Zoellick.

Office of the President: http://www.whitehouse.gov

DEFENCE

The President is C.-in-C. of the Army, Navy and Air Force.

The National Security Act of 1947 provides for the unification of the Army, Navy and Air Forces under a single Secretary of Defense with cabinet rank. The President is also advised by a National Security Council and the Office of Civil and Defense Mobilization.

Defence expenditure in 2003 totalled US$404,920m. (US$1,391 per capita), representing 3·7% of GDP (down from 6·1% of GDP in 1985). The USA spent more on defence in 2003 than the next thirteen biggest spenders combined. US expenditure was 41% of the world total. In 1997 the Quadrennial Defense Review (QDR) was implemented—a plan to transform US defence strategy and military forces.

The estimated number of active military personnel in 2003 was 1,427,000.

The USA is the world's largest exporter of arms, with sales in 2003 worth $13·6bn., or 47·5% of the world total. In 2002 Boeing and Lockheed Martin were the two largest arms producing companies in the USA, accounting for $20·5bn. and $18·9bn. worth of sales respectively.

The USA's last nuclear test was in 1993. In accordance with START I—the treaty signed by the US and USSR in 1991 to reduce strategic offensive nuclear capability—the number of nuclear warheads (intercontinental ballistic missiles, submarine-launched ballistic missiles and bombers) in Jan. 2004 was approximately 5,886. In 1990 the number of warheads had been 12,718. Strategic nuclear delivery vehicles were made up as follows:

Intercontinental ballistic missiles: 500 Minuteman III; 29 Peacekeeper (MX).

Submarine-launched ballistic missiles: 72 Trident I (C-4); 288 Trident II (D-5).

Bombers: 93 B-52H; 21 B-2.

In May 2001 President Bush called for the development of an anti-missile shield to move beyond the constraints of the Anti-Ballistic Missile Treaty. In Dec. 2001 he announced that the USA was unilaterally abandoning the Treaty. As the relationship with Russian president Vladimir Putin strengthened following the events of 11 Sept. 2001 he proposed a reduction of operational nuclear warheads to between 1,700 and 2,200 by 2010. On 24 May 2002 the USA and Russia signed an arms control treaty to reduce the number of US and Russian warheads, from between 6,000 and 7,000 each to between 1,700 and 2,200 each, over the next ten years.

Army. *Secretary of the Army.* Francis J. Harvey.

The Secretary of the Army is the head of the Department of the Army. Subject to the authority of the President as C.-in-C. and of the Secretary of Defense, he is responsible for all affairs of the Department.

The Army consists of the Active Army, the Army National Guard of the US, the Army Reserve and civilian workforce; and all persons appointed to or enlisted into the Army without component; and all persons serving under call or conscription, including members of the National Guard of the States, etc., when in the service of the US. The strength of the Active Army was (2003) 485,000 (including 71,400 women).

The Army budget for fiscal years 2003–05 is as follows: 2003, $90,933m.; 2004, $93,903m; 2005, $98,376m.

The US Army Forces Command, with headquarters at Fort McPherson, Georgia, commands the Third US Army; four continental US Armies, and all assigned Active Army and US Army Reserve troop units in the continental US, the Commonwealth of Puerto Rico, and the Virgin Islands of the USA. The headquarters of the continental US Armies are: First US Army, Fort George G. Meade, Maryland; Second US Army, Fort Gillem, Georgia; Fifth US Army, Fort Sam Houston, Texas; Sixth US Army, Presidio of San Francisco, California. The US Army Space Command, with headquarters in Colorado Springs (CO), is the Army component to the US Space Command.

Approximately 32% of the Active Army is deployed outside the continental USA. Several divisions, which are located in the USA, keep equipment in Germany and can be flown there in 48–72 hours. Headquarters of US Seventh and Eighth Armies are in Europe and Korea respectively.

Combat vehicles of the US Army are the tank, armoured personnel carrier, infantry fighting vehicle, and the armoured command vehicle. The first-line tanks are the M1A1 Abrams tank, and the M1 Abrams. The standard armoured infantry personnel carrier is the M2 Bradley Fighting Vehicle (BFV), which is replacing the older M113.

The Army has nearly 4,900 aircraft, all but about 300 of them helicopters, including AH-1 Cobra and AH-64 Apache attack helicopters.

Over 95% of recruits enlisting in the Army have a high-school education and over 50% of the Army is married. Women serve in both combat support and combat service support units.

The National Guard is a reserve military component with both a state and a federal role. Enlistment is voluntary. The members are recruited by each state, but are equipped and paid by the federal government (except when performing state missions). As the organized militia of the several states, the District of Columbia, Puerto Rico and the Territories of the Virgin Islands and Guam, the Guard may be called into service for local emergencies by the chief executives in those jurisdictions; and may be called into federal service by the President to thwart invasion or rebellion or to enforce federal law. In its role as a reserve component of the Army, the Guard is subject to the order of the President in the event of national emergency. In 2003 it numbered 472,200 (Army, 352,000; Air Force, 110,200).

The Army Reserve is designed to supply qualified and experienced units and individuals in an emergency. Members of units are assigned to the Ready Reserve, which is subject to call by the President in case of national emergency without declaration of war by Congress. The Standby Reserve and the Retired Reserve may be called only after declaration of war or national emergency by Congress. In 2003 the Army Reserve numbered 346,000.

Navy. *Secretary of the Navy.* Gordon R. England.

The Navy's Operating Forces include the Atlantic Fleet, divided between the 2nd fleet (home waters) and 6th fleet (Mediterranean) and the Pacific Fleet, similarly divided between the 3rd fleet (home waters), the 7th fleet (West Pacific) and the 5th fleet (Indian Ocean), which was formally activated in 1995 and maintained by units from both Pacific and Atlantic.

The authorized budget for the Department of the Navy (which includes funding both for the Navy and Marine Corps) for fiscal years 2003–05 is as follows: 2003, $111,184m.; 2004, $114,720m.; 2005, $119,114m.

Personnel and fleet strength declined during the mid-1990s but are now stabilizing. The '600-ship battle force' planned in the late 1980s has reduced to a current figure of 317. The Navy personnel total in 2003 was 400,000.

The operational strength of the Navy in the year indicated:

Category	*1992*	*1997*	*2002*	*2003*
Strategic Submarines	23	18	18	16
Nuclear Attack Submarines	87	67	54	56
Aircraft Carriers	12	11[1]	12[1]	12[1]
Amphibious Carriers	13	11	11	11
Cruisers	46	30	27	27
Destroyers	51	56	55	49
Frigates	90	31	28	30

[1]Includes the USS *John F. Kennedy* as 'operational and training reserve carrier' in the Naval Reserve Force.

Ships in the inactive reserve are not included in the table, but those serving as Naval Reserve Force training ships are.

Submarine Forces. A principal part of the US naval task is to deploy the seaborne strategic deterrent from nuclear-powered ballistic missile-carrying submarines (SSBN), of which there were 16 in 2003, all of the Ohio class. The listed total of 56 nuclear-powered attack submarines includes two of three new Seawolf class and 51 of the Los Angeles class. There is also one of the Sturgeon class and two converted submarines of the Ohio class.

Surface Combatant Forces. The surface combatant forces are comprised of modern cruisers, destroyers and frigates. These ships provide multi-mission capabilities to achieve maritime dominance in the crowded and complex littoral warfare environment.

The cruiser force consists of 27 Ticonderoga class ships. There are 39 guided-missile Arleigh Burke Aegis class destroyers, ten Spruance class destroyers and 30 (22 active and eight in the reserve force) Oliver Hazard Perry class guided missile frigates.

Aircraft carriers. There are eight nuclear-powered Nimitz class carriers. The USS *Enterprise,* completed in 1961, was the prototype nuclear-powered carrier. The two ships of the Kitty Hawk and one of the John F. Kennedy classes were completed between 1961 and 1968, and represent the last oil-fuelled carriers built by the US Navy. All carriers deploy an air group which comprises on average two squadrons each of F-14 Tomcat fighters and three squadrons each of F/A-18 Hornet fighter/ground attack aircraft.

Naval Aviation. The principal function of the naval aviation organization (strength in 2003 of 10,506) is to train and provide combat ready aviation forces. The main carrier-borne combat aircraft in the current inventory are 877 F/A-18 Hornet dual-purpose fighter/attack aircraft out of a total of 1,705 combat aircraft.

The Marine Corps. While administratively part of the Department of the Navy, the Corps ranks as a separate armed service, with the Commandant serving in his own right as a member of the Joint Chiefs of Staff, and responsible directly to the Secretary of the Navy. Its strength had stabilized at 174,400 by 2003.

The role of the Marine Corps is to provide specially trained and equipped amphibious expeditionary forces. The Corps includes an autonomous aviation element numbering 34,686 in 2003.

The US Coast Guard. The Coast Guard operates under the Department of Transportation in time of peace and as part of the Navy in time of war or when directed by the President. The act of establishment stated the Coast Guard 'shall be a military service and branch of the armed forces of the United States at all times'.

The Coast Guard is the country's oldest continuous sea-going service and its missions include maintenance of aids to navigation, icebreaking, environmental response (oil spills), maritime law enforcement, marine licensing, port security, search and rescue and waterways management.

The workforce in 2003 was made up of approximately 37,582 military personnel augmented by 6,750 civilians. On an average Coast Guard day, the service saves 14 lives, conducts 120 law enforcement boardings, seizes 209 pounds of marijuana and 170 pounds of cocaine, boards 90 large vessels for port safety checks, processes 120 seaman's documents, investigates 17 marine accidents, inspects 64 commercial vessels, assists 328 people in distress, saves $2,490,000 in property, services 150 aids to navigation and interdicts 176 illegal immigrants.

Air Force. *Secretary of the Air Force (acting).* Michael L. Dominguez.

The Department of the Air Force was activated within the Department of Defense on 18 Sept. 1947, under the terms of the National Security Act of 1947.

The USAF has the mission to defend the USA through control and exploitation of air and space. For operational purposes the service is divided into eight major commands, 37 field operating agencies and three direct-reporting units.

The bulk of the combat forces are grouped under the Air Combat Command, which controls strategic bombing, tactical strike, air defence and reconnaissance assets in the USA.

Air Force bombers include the B-1B Lancer, the B-2A and the B-52G/H Stratofortress, which has been the primary manned strategic bomber for over 35 years. In the fighter category are the F-15 Eagle, the F-16 Fighting Falcon and the F-117A, the world's first operational aircraft to exploit low-observable stealth technology.

The Air Force budget for fiscal years 2003–05 is as follows: 2003, $108,451m.; 2004, $113,805m.; 2005, $120,679m.

In 2003 the Air Force had approximately 367,600 military personnel. Since 1991 women have been authorized to fly combat aircraft, but not until 1993 were they allowed to fly fighters.

INTERNATIONAL RELATIONS

The USA is a member of the UN, WTO, NATO, BIS, OECD, OSCE, OAS, Inter-American Development Bank, Asian Development Bank, Pacific Community, Colombo Plan, IOM and the Antarctic Treaty.

In 2003 the USA gave US$15·8bn. in international aid, the highest figure of any country. In terms of a percentage of GNI, however, the USA was the least generous major industrialized country, giving just 0·14% (compared to more than 0·6% in the early 1960s).

ECONOMY

Services accounted for approximately 72% of GDP in 2003, industry 26% and agriculture 2%.

According to the anti-corruption organization *Transparency International*, in 2004 the USA ranked equal 17th in the world in a survey of the countries with the least corruption in business and government. It received 7·5 out of 10 in the annual index.

Per capita income in 2002 was $30,832, up from $19,572 in 1990.

Overview. The US economy has experienced the highest real GDP growth of the G7 countries since the early 1980s, well above the OECD average. Per capita real income in the USA ranks amongst the highest in the OECD. Economic growth has varied widely since 2001, with quarterly growth moving between 0·7% and 7·4%. Productivity growth increased in the mid-1990s adding momentum to growth. In both the first and third quarters of 2001 the economy contracted. In the third quarter of 2003 the economy experienced a growth rate of 7·4%, the highest rate in nearly two decades; growth since mid-2003 has been strong. Recent growth has been fuelled by tax cuts, low interest rates and an increase in consumer and business spending. Consumer spending has been strong since 2002. Spending has been strengthened by low interest rates, a boom in house prices and strong growth in disposable incomes owing to tax cuts. Confidence in the US corporate market declined after the collapse of energy giant Enron in Dec. 2002. $62·8bn. of assets were frozen, making this the largest bankruptcy case in US history. In response, widespread reforms of corporate governance were put in place, which have been largely successful at restoring confidence.

Economic policies have moved from short-term stabilization to strengthening the base for durable growth. Interest rates fell during the early 2000s, when the interest rate was cut for the first time since 1992, reaching a rate of 1% in 2003, the lowest rate since 1958. Interest rates have risen since 2003 in an attempt to pre-empt inflation.

The volume of trade is the largest in the world, although the value of the country's external sector as a percentage of GDP is relatively low. The USA is self-sufficient in most raw materials. Core industries include motor vehicles, steel, aerospace, chemicals, telecommunications, and electronics and computers. The current account has been in a position of deficit since the early 1980s. The deficit reached a record high of –5·25% in the first quarter of 2003. US residents have net external claims of 25% of GDP, a figure which continues to grow.

Since 2001 the economy has benefited from three major rounds of tax cuts. In June 2001 tax cuts worth $1·35trn. over ten years were legislated. In March 2002 reforms increased investment incentives and extended unemployment benefits. In Jan. 2003 the government announced a $670bn. package to boost share prices and attract business investment. The federal budget has moved from a position of surplus in the early 2000s to a deficit in excess of 4%. The deterioration of the accounts is attributed to lower tax receipts following the recession, the termination of the stock market bubble and an expansion of defence and homeland security. According to the OECD, recent tax and spending changes imply that the deficit will remain substantial over the next decade unless the tax base is broadened and recent reductions in marginal tax rates are reversed. Further fiscal pressures are emerging from the retirement of the baby-boom generation and rising life expectancy, which will put further strain on entitlement programmes. Spending on Social Security, Medicare and Medicaid is projected to rise from 8% of GDP to 18% by 2050. The programmes' unfunded liability is estimated by the IMF to be 180% of GDP if measured over a 75-year horizon.

Currency. The unit of currency is the *dollar* (USD) of 100 *cents*. Notes are issued by the 12 Federal Reserve Banks, which are denoted by a branch letter (A = Boston, MA; B = New York, NY; C = Philadelphia, PA; D = Cleveland, OH; E = Richmond, VA; F = Atlanta, GA; G = Chicago, IL; H = St Louis, MO; I = Minneapolis, MN; J = Kansas City, MO; K = Dallas, TX; L = San Francisco, CA).

Inflation was 1·6% in 2001, 2·4% in 2002, 1·9% in 2003 and 3·3% in 2004. Foreign exchange reserves in June 2002 were US$32,166m. Gold reserves in June 2002 were 262·0m. troy oz. The USA has the most gold reserves of any country, and more than the combined reserves of the next two (Germany and France). Total money supply in March 2002 was $1,552bn.

Budget. The budget covers virtually all the programmes of federal government, including those financed through trust funds, such as for social security, Medicare and highway construction. Receipts of the government include all income from its sovereign or compulsory powers; income from business-type or market-orientated activities of the government is offset against outlays. The fiscal year ends on 30 Sept. (before 1977 on 30 June). Budget receipts and outlays, including off-budget receipts and outlays (in $1m.):

Fiscal year ending in	*Receipts*	*Outlays*	*Surplus* (+) *or deficit* (–)
1950	39,443	42,562	–3,119
1960	92,492	92,191	+301
1970	192,807	195,649	–2,842
1980	517,112	590,941	–73,829
1990	1,031,969	1,253,116	–221,147
2000	2,025,218	1,789,067	+236,151
2003	1,782,342	2,159,917	–377,575
2004	1,880,071	2,292,215	–412,144
2005[1]	2,052,845	2,479,404	–426,559
2006[1]	2,177,550	2,567,617	–390,067

[1]Estimates.

President George W. Bush unveiled his toughest budget proposals to date in Feb. 2005. The budget submitted to Congress involves cutting spending in 150 domestic programmes in an attempt to reduce the massive budget deficit, but spending on defence was set to increase by 4·8% and homeland security by 6·8%.

Budget and off-budget receipts, by source, for fiscal years (in $1m.):

Source	*2004*	*2005*[1]	*2006*[1]
Individual income taxes	808,959	893,704	966,877
Corporation income taxes	189,371	226,526	220,258
Social insurance and retirement receipts	733,407	773,731	818,834
Excise taxes	69,855	74,013	75,566
Other	78,479	84,871	96,015
Total	1,880,071	2,052,845	2,177,550

[1]Estimates.

Budget and off-budget outlays, by function, for fiscal years (in $1m.):

Function	*2004*	*2005*[1]	*2006*[1]
National defence	455,908	465,871	447,398
Education, training, employment and social service	87,945	96,254	88,703
Health	240,134	257,532	268,396
Medicare	269,360	295,432	345,746
Income security	332,837	350,918	359,535
Social security	495,548	519,686	544,821
Veterans' benefits and services	59,779	68,161	68,390
Energy	–166	1,441	2,121
Natural resources and environment	30,725	30,960	31,163
Commerce and housing credit	5,273	10,653	6,816
Transportation	64,626	68,486	70,673
Community and regional development	15,797	20,141	19,097
Net interest	160,245	177,948	211,076
International affairs	26,891	31,961	38,447
General science, space and technology	23,053	24,021	23,967
Agriculture	15,440	30,504	26,020
Administration of justice	45,535	40,657	43,099
General government	21,822	18,855	17,754
Allowances	—	34,899	24,168
Undistributed offsetting receipts	–58,537	–64,976	–69,773
Total	2,292,215	2,479,404	2,567,617

[1]Estimates.

Budget and off-budget outlays, by agency, for fiscal years (in $1m.):

Agency	*2004*	*2005*[1]	*2006*[1]
Legislative Branch	3,885	4,083	4,356
The Judiciary	5,392	5,741	6,145
Agriculture	71,769	94,912	94,590
Commerce	5,850	6,278	6,500
Defence—Military	437,116	444,068	426,315
Education	62,816	70,953	64,272
Energy	19,972	22,178	21,969
Health and Human Services	543,389	585,772	643,886
Homeland Security	26,537	33,259	33,284
Housing and Urban Development	45,019	42,614	40,185
Interior	8,914	9,433	9,812
Justice	28,954	21,171	23,380
Labor	56,706	50,034	51,713
State	10,934	11,934	14,109
Transportation	54,547	58,215	60,585
Treasury	374,817	402,972	441,198
Veterans Affairs	59,554	68,046	68,281
Corps of Engineers	4,838	4,891	4,643
Defence—Civil	41,730	43,460	44,489
Environmental Protection Agency	8,334	7,862	8,202
Executive Office of the President	3,308	5,765	7,192
General Services Administration	–403	459	54
International Assistance Programmes	13,737	14,754	17,022
National Aeronautics and Space Administration	15,189	15,719	15,744
National Science Foundation	5,118	5,641	5,666
Office of Personnel Management	56,535	60,964	64,259

Agency	*2004*	*2005*[1]	*2006*[1]
Small Business Administration	4,075	3,036	790
Social Security Administration	530,205	559,048	583,492
Other independent agencies	5,904	19,671	22,607
Allowances	—	34,899	24,168
Undistributed Offsetting Receipts	–212,526	–228,428	–241,291
Total	2,292,215	2,479,404	2,567,617

[1]Estimates.

National Debt. Federal debt held by the public (in $1m.), and per capita debt (in $1) on 30 June to 1976 and on 30 Sept. since then:

	Public debt	*Per capita*		*Public debt*	*Per capita*
1920	24,299	229	1990	2,411,558	9,696
1930	16,185	132	2000	3,409,804	12,083
1940	42,772	324	2001	3,319,615	11,644
1950	219,023	1,447	2002	3,540,427	12,296
1960	236,840	1,321	2003	3,913,443	13,458
1970	283,198	1,394	2004	4,295,544	14,628
1980	711,923	3,143			

National Income. The Bureau of Economic Analysis of the Department of Commerce prepares detailed estimates on the national income and product. In Dec. 2003 the Bureau revised these accounts back to 1929. The principal tables are published monthly in *Survey of Current Business;* the complete set of national income and product tables are published in the *Survey* normally each Aug., showing data for recent years.

Gross Domestic Product

(in $1,000m.)

	1999	*2000*	*2001*	*2002*	*2003*
Gross Domestic Product	9,268·4	9,817·0	10,128·0	10,487·0	11,004·0
Personal consumption expenditures	6,282·5	6,739·4	7,055·0	7,376·1	7,760·9
Durable goods	817·6	863·3	883·7	916·2	950·7
Nondurable goods	1,804·8	1,947·2	2,017·1	2,080·1	2,200·1
Services	3,660·0	3,928·8	4,154·3	4,379·8	4,610·1
Gross private domestic investment	1,625·7	1,735·5	1,614·3	1,579·2	1,665·8
Fixed investment	1,558·8	1,679·0	1,646·1	1,568·0	1,667·0
Nonresidential	1,133·9	1,232·1	1,176·8	1,063·9	1,094·7
Structures	282·2	313·2	322·6	271·6	261·6
Equipment and software	851·7	918·9	854·2	792·4	833·1
Residential	424·9	446·9	469·3	504·1	572·3
Change in private inventories	66·9	56·5	–31·7	11·2	–1·2
Net exports of goods and services	–260·5	–379·5	–367·0	–424·9	–498·1
Exports	991·2	1,096·3	1,032·8	1,005·0	1,046·2
Goods	697·2	784·3	731·2	697·0	726·4
Services	294·0	311·9	301·6	308·0	319·8
Imports	1,251·7	1,475·8	1,399·8	1,429·9	1,544·3
Goods	1,045·5	1,243·5	1,167·9	1,189·6	1,282·0
Services	206·3	232·3	231·9	240·2	262·3
Government consumption expenditures and gross investment	1,620·8	1,721·6	1,825·6	1,956·6	2,075·5
Federal	555·8	578·8	612·9	680·8	752·2
National defence	360·6	370·3	392·6	437·4	496·4
Nondefence	195·2	208·5	220·3	243·4	255·7
State and local	1,065·0	1,142·8	1,212·8	1,275·8	1,323·3

Relation of Gross Domestic Product, Gross National Product, Net National Product, National Income and Personal Income

(in $1,000m.)

	1999	*2000*	*2001*	*2002*	*2003*
Gross domestic product	9,268·4	9,817·0	10,128·0	10,487·0	11,004·0
Plus: Income receipts from the rest of the world	320·8	382·7	322·4	301·8	329·0
Less: Income payments to the rest of the world	287·0	343·7	278·8	274·7	273·9
Equals: Gross national product	9,302·2	9,855·9	10,171·6	10,514·1	11,059·2

Relation of Gross Domestic Product, Gross National Product, Net National Product, National Income and Personal Income

(in $1,000m.)

	1999	*2000*	*2001*	*2002*	*2003*
Less: Consumption of fixed capital	1,101·3	1,187·8	1,281·5	1,303·9	1,353·9
Private	914·3	990·8	1,075·5	1,092·8	1,135·9
Domestic business	769·8	836·1	903·7	912·6	942·6
Capital consumption allowances	883·6	943·9	1,028·7	1,126·3	1,225·6
Less: Capital consumption adjustment	113·7	107·8	124·9	213·6	283·0
Households and institutions	144·5	154·8	171·7	180·2	193·3
Government	187·0	197·0	206·0	211·2	218·1
General government	158·4	166·4	172·7	178·0	183·6
Government enterprises	28·6	30·6	33·3	33·2	34·5
Equals: Net national product	8,200·9	8,668·1	8,890·2	9,210·1	9,705·2
Less: Statistical discrepancy	–35·7	–127·2	–89·6	–15·3	25·6
Equals: National income	8,236·7	8,795·2	8,979·8	9,225·4	9,679·6
Less: Corporate profits with inventory valuation and capital consumption adjustment	851·3	817·9	767·3	874·6	1,021·1
Taxes on production and imports less subsidies	629·8	664·6	673·3	724·4	751·3
Contributions for government social insurance	661·4	702·7	731·1	748·3	773·2
Net interest and miscellaneous payment on assets	495·4	559·0	566·3	532·9	543·0
Business current transfer payments (net)	67·4	87·1	92·8	80·9	77·7
Current surplus of government enterprises	10·1	5·3	–1·4	2·8	9·5
Wage accruals less disbursements	5·2	0	0	0	0
Plus: Personal income receipts on assets	1,264·2	1,387·0	1,380·0	1,334·6	1,322·7
Personal current transfer receipts	1,022·1	1,084·0	1,193·9	1,282·7	1,335·4
Equals: Personal income	7,802·4	8,429·7	8,724·1	8,878·9	9,161·8
Addenda:					
Gross domestic income	9,304·1	9,944·1	10,217·6	10,502·3	10,978·5
Gross national income	9,337·9	9,983·1	10,261·3	10,529·4	11,033·6
Gross national factor income	8,630·6	9,226·1	9,496·5	9,721·3	10,195·1
Net domestic product	8,167·1	8,629·1	8,846·5	9,183·1	9,650·1
Net domestic income	8,202·9	8,756·3	8,936·2	9,198·4	9,624·5
Net national factor income	7,529·4	8,038·3	8,215·0	8,417·4	8,841·1

National Income by Type of Income

(in $1,000m.)

	1999	*2000*	*2001*	*2002*	*2003*
National income	8,236·7	8,795·2	8,979·8	9,225·4	9,679·6
Compensation of employees	5,357·1	5,782·7	5,942·1	6,069·5	6,289·0
Wage and salary accruals	4,471·4	4,829·2	4,942·8	4,976·3	5,103·6
Government	729·3	774·7	815·9	862·6	897·9
Other	3,742·1	4,054·5	4,126·9	4,113·7	4,205·6
Supplements to wages and salaries	885·7	953·4	999·3	1,093·2	1,185·5
Employer contributions for employee pension and insurance funds	562·4	609·9	642·7	729·6	808·9
Employer contributions for government social insurance	323·3	343·5	356·9	363·6	376·6
Proprietors' income with inventory valuation and capital consumption adjustment	678·3	728·4	771·9	769·6	834·1
Farm	28·6	22·7	19·7	9·7	21·8
Nonfarm	649·7	705·7	752·2	759·9	812·3
Rental income of persons with capital consumption adjustment	147·3	150·3	167·4	170·9	153·8
Corporate profits with inventory valuation and capital consumption adjustment	851·3	817·9	767·3	874·6	1,021·1
Taxes on corporate income	258·6	265·2	204·1	183·8	234·9
Profits after tax with inventory valuation and capital consumption adjustment	592·6	552·7	563·2	690·7	786·2
Net dividends	337·4	377·9	370·9	390·0	395·3

National Income by Type of Income
(in $1,000m.)

	1999	2000	2001	2002	2003
Undistributed profits with inventory valuation and capital consumption adjustment	255·3	174·8	192·3	300·7	390·9
Net interest and miscellaneous payments	495·4	559·0	566·3	532·9	543·0
Taxes on production and imports	674·0	708·9	728·6	762·6	798·1
Less: Subsidies	44·2	44·3	55·3	38·2	46·7
Business current transfer payments (net)	67·4	87·1	92·8	80·9	77·7
To persons (net)	34·1	42·4	50·0	33·7	28·9
To government (net)	35·9	43·7	47·5	46·7	46·6
To the rest of the world (net)	–2·6	1·0	–4·7	0·4	2·2
Current surplus of government enterprises	10·1	5·3	–1·4	2·8	9·5
Cash flow:					
Net cash flow with inventory valuation and capital consumption adjustment	887·2	864·8	944·8	1,058·5	1,173·4
Undistributed profits with inventory valuation and capital consumption adjustment	255·3	174·8	192·3	300·7	390·9
Consumption of fixed capital	632·0	690·0	752·5	757·8	782·5
Less: Inventory valuation adjustment	1·0	–14·1	11·3	–1·2	–14·1
Equals: Net cash flow	886·3	878·9	933·5	1,059·8	1,187·5
Addenda:					
Proprietors' income with inventory valuation and capital consumption adjustment	678·3	728·4	771·9	769·6	834·1
Farm	28·6	22·7	19·7	9·7	21·8
Proprietors' income with inventory valuation adjustment	34·4	28·5	25·5	15·4	27·8
Capital consumption adjustment	–5·8	–5·8	–5·9	–5·8	–5·9
Nonfarm	649·7	705·7	752·2	759·9	812·3
Proprietors' income (without inventory valuation and capital consumption adjustment)	595·2	641·8	657·0	647·5	673·9
Inventory valuation adjustment	–0·5	–1·6	1·4	–0·6	–1·9
Capital consumption adjustment	54·9	65·5	93·8	113·0	140·2
Rental income of persons with capital consumption adjustment	147·3	150·3	167·4	170·9	153·8
Rental income of persons (without capital consumption adjustment)	157·2	160·8	178·5	182·3	165·9
Capital consumption adjustment	–9·9	–10·5	–11·1	–11·4	–12·1
Corporate profits with inventory valuation and capital consumption adjustment	851·3	817·9	767·3	874·6	1,021·1
Corporate profits with inventory valuation adjustment	776·8	759·3	719·2	756·8	860·4
Profits before tax (without inventory valuation and capital consumption adjustment)	775·9	773·4	707·9	758·0	874·5
Taxes on corporate income	258·6	265·2	204·1	183·8	234·9
Profits after tax (without inventory valuation and capital consumption adjustment)	517·2	508·2	503·8	574·2	639·6
Net dividends	337·4	377·9	370·9	390·0	395·3
Undistributed profits (without inventory valuation and capital consumption adjustment)	179·9	130·3	132·9	184·1	244·2
Inventory valuation adjustment	1·0	–14·1	11·3	–1·2	–14·1
Capital consumption adjustment	74·5	58·6	48·1	117·8	160·8

Real Gross Domestic Product
(in 1,000m. chained [2000] dollars[1])

	1999	2000	2001	2002	2003
Gross domestic product	9,470·3	9,817·0	9,890·7	10,074·8	10,381·3
Personal consumption expenditures	6,438·6	6,739·4	6,910·4	7,123·4	7,355·6
Durable goods	804·6	863·3	900·7	959·6	1,030·6
Nondurable goods	1,876·6	1,947·2	1,986·7	2,037·4	2,112·4
Services	3,758·0	3,928·8	4,023·2	4,128·6	4,220·3

Real Gross Domestic Product
(in 1,000m. chained [2000] dollars[1])

	1999	*2000*	*2001*	*2002*	*2003*
Gross private domestic investment	1,642·6	1,735·5	1,598·4	1,560·7	1,628·8
Fixed investment	1,576·3	1,679·0	1,629·4	1,548·9	1,627·3
Nonresidential	1,133·3	1,232·1	1,180·5	1,075·6	1,110·8
Structures	293·2	313·2	306·1	251·6	237·4
Equipment and software	840·2	918·9	874·2	826·5	879·2
Residential	443·6	446·9	448·5	470·0	511·2
Change in private inventories	68·9	56·5	–31·7	11·7	–0·8
Net exports of goods and services	–296·2	–379·5	–399·1	–472·1	–518·5
Exports	1,008·2	1,096·3	1,036·7	1,012·3	1,031·8
Goods	705·2	784·3	736·3	706·4	721·7
Services	303·2	311·9	300·4	305·7	309·9
Imports	1,304·4	1,475·8	1,435·8	1,484·4	1,550·3
Goods	1,095·2	1,243·5	1,204·1	1,248·5	1,307·3
Services	209·1	232·3	231·6	235·9	243·3
Government consumption expenditures and gross investment	1,686·9	1,721·6	1,780·3	1,857·9	1,909·4
Federal	573·7	578·8	601·4	646·6	689·6
National defence	372·2	370·3	384·9	414·6	451·8
Non-defence	201·5	208·5	216·5	232·0	237·6
State and local	1,113·2	1,142·8	1,179·0	1,211·4	1,219·8
Residual	–5·8	0·2	1·6	3·7	0·8

[1]In 1996 the chain-weighted method of estimating GDP replaced that of constant base-year prices. In chain-weighting the weights used to value different sectors of the economy are continually updated to reflect changes in relative prices.

Performance. Total GDP in 2003 was US$10,881·6bn., representing approximately 30% of the world's total GDP. Real GDP growth was 3·7% in 2000. The economy contracted in the first and third quarters of 2001, but recovery in the final quarter was sufficient to give an overall growth rate of 0·8% in 2001. In 2002 there was growth of 1·9%, rising to 3·0% in 2003 and 4·4% in 2004. In the 2004 *World Competitiveness Yearbook*, compiled by the International Institute for Management Development, the USA came top in the world ranking for countries with more than 20m. people. The USA was first in the Business Competitiveness Index and second behind Finland in the Growth Competitiveness Index in the World Economic Forum's *Global Competitiveness Report 2004–05*.

According to the Nov. 2002 *OECD Economic Survey* 'The recession that followed the longest expansion on record was surprisingly mild, despite the disruptive effects of the terrorist attacks in September 2001. This owed a great deal to monetary and fiscal stimulus. But it also reflected firms' ability to maintain productivity gains. While this bodes well for a renewed period of economic expansion, the recovery that began early this year is still fragile.'

Banking and Finance. The Federal Reserve System, established under The Federal Reserve Act of 1913, comprises the Board of seven Governors, the 12 regional Federal Reserve Banks with their 25 branches, and the Federal Open Market Committee. The seven members of the Board of Governors are appointed by the President with the consent of the Senate. Each Governor is appointed to a full term of 14 years or an unexpired portion of a term, one term expiring every two years. The Board exercises broad supervisory authority over the operations of the 12 Federal Reserve Banks, including approval of their budgets and of the appointments of their presidents and first vice presidents; it designates three of the nine directors of each Reserve Bank including the Chairman and Deputy Chairman. The Chairman of the Federal Reserve Board is appointed by the President for four-year terms. The *Chairman* is Alan Greenspan. The Board has supervisory and regulatory responsibilities over banks that are members of the Federal Reserve System, bank holding companies, bank mergers, Edge Act and agreement corporations, foreign activities of member banks, international banking facilities in the USA, and activities of the US branches and agencies of foreign banks. Legislation of 1991 requires foreign banks to prove that they are subject to comprehensive consolidated supervision by a regulator at home, and have the Board's approval to establish branches, agencies and representative offices. The Board also assures the smooth functioning and continued development of the nation's vast payments system. Another area of the Board's responsibilities involves the implementation by regulation of major federal laws governing consumer credit.

In 2004, three of the four largest banks in the world in terms of market value were US banks. Citigroup was the largest ($240·9bn.). The second and fourth largest were Bank of America ($183·4bn.) and J. P. Morgan Chase ($141·0bn.). Citigroup had assets in March 2004 of $1·26trn. (ranking it second in the world behind Japan's Mizuho Financial Group). Bank of America's market capitalization figure reflects its merger in April 2004 with FleetBoston Financial; J. P. Morgan Chase's market capitalization figure reflects its merger in July 2004 with Bank One.

The key stock exchanges are the New York Stock Exchange (NYSE), the Nasdaq Stock Exchange (NASDAQ) and the American Stock Exchange (ASE). There are several other stock exchanges, in Philadelphia, Boston, San Francisco (Pacific Stock Exchange) and Chicago, although trading is very limited in them.

In 2000 the USA received a record $314·01bn. worth of foreign direct investment, but in 2003 this fell to just $29·77m. By the end of 2002 it had attracted foreign direct investment totalling $1,505bn.—more than twice as much as any other country.

By Oct. 2000 approximately 18% of the population were using e-banking.

Weights and Measures. The US Customary System derives from the British Imperial System. It differs in respect of the *gallon* (= 0·83268 Imperial gallon); *bushel* (= 0·969 Imperial bushel); *hundredweight* (= 100 lb); and the *short* or *net ton* (= 2,000 lb).

ENERGY AND NATURAL RESOURCES

Environment. The USA's carbon dioxide emissions from the consumption and flaring of fossil fuels in 2002 accounted for 23·4% of the world total, higher than any other country, and were equivalent to 20·0 tonnes per capita. The population of the USA is only 4·6% of the world total. An *Environmental Sustainability Index* compiled for the World Economic Forum meeting in Feb. 2002 ranked the USA 45th in the world, with 53·2%. The index measured the ability of countries to maintain favourable environmental conditions and examined various factors including pollution levels and the use or abuse of natural resources.

In March 2001 President Bush rejected the 1997 Kyoto Protocol, which aims to combat the rise in the earth's temperature through the reduction of industrialized nations' carbon dioxide emissions from the consumption and flaring of fossil fuels by an average 5·2% below 1990 levels by 2012. In Feb. 2002 he unveiled an alternative climate-change plan to the Kyoto Protocol, calling for voluntary measures to reduce the rate of increase of US carbon dioxide emissions from the consumption and flaring of fossil fuels.

The USA recycled 31·5% of its household waste in 1998, ranking it seventh in the world.

Electricity. Net capacity in 2001 was 848·2m. kW. Fossil fuel accounts for approximately 70% of electricity generation. In 2002, 20% of electricity was produced by 104 nuclear reactors. (The last one to begin commercial operation was in 1996.) The USA has more nuclear reactors in use than any other country in the world. In 2003 the USA had a nuclear generating capacity of 98,622 MW at the 104 nuclear reactors. Electricity production in 2001 was the highest in the world, at 3,733,521m. kWh. Consumption per capita in 2000 was 14,684 kWh.

Oil and Gas. Crude oil production (2002), 2,097m. bbls. Production has been gradually declining since the mid-1980s, when annual production was 3,274m. bbls. Only Saudi Arabia and Russia produce more crude oil. Proven reserves were 30·4bn. bbls. in 2002, but they are expected to be exhausted by 2011. Output (2001) was valued at $46·25bn. Imported supplies account for approximately half of US oil consumption, with Saudi Arabia supplying a sixth of US oil imports. In Oct. 2002 the USA took its first delivery of Russian oil for its Strategic Petroleum Reserve as a consequence of an energy dialogue declared by Presidents George W. Bush and Vladimir Putin at their summit in May 2002.

The USA is by far the largest single consumer of natural gas, and the second largest producer after Russia. Natural gas production, 2002, was 19·34trn. cu. ft. Proven gas reserves in 2002 totalled 184trn. cu. ft.

Wind. The USA is one of the largest producers of wind-power. By the end of 2002 total installed capacity amounted to 4,685 MW.

Water. The total area covered by water is 256,645 sq. miles. Americans' average annual water usage is nearly 67,000 cu. ft per person—more than twice the average for an industrialized nation.

Non-Fuel Minerals. The USA is wholly dependent upon imports for columbium, bauxite, mica sheet, manganese, strontium and graphite, and imports over 80% of its requirements of industrial diamonds, fluorspar, platinum, tantalum, tungsten, chromium and tin.

Total value of non-fuel minerals produced in 2002 was $38,000m. ($33,445m. in 1990). Details of some of the main minerals produced are given in the following tables.

Production of metals:

	Unit	*Quantity 2001*	*Value ($1m.) 1997*
Copper	1,000 tonnes	1,340	4,580
Gold	tonnes	335	3,850
Iron ore	1m. tonnes	46	1,890
Lead	1,000 tonnes	466	460
Magnesium metal	1,000 tonnes	45	400
Silver	tonnes	1,740	338
Zinc	1,000 tonnes	842	860
Total metals			*13,074*

Precious metals are mined mainly in California and Utah (gold); and Nevada, Arizona and Idaho (silver).

Production of non-metals:

	Unit	*Quantity 2001*	*Value ($1m.) 1997*
Barite	1,000 tonnes	400	16
Boron	1,000 tonnes	1,070[1]	580
Bromine	1,000 tonnes	212	198
Cement	1m. short tons	84[1]	5,710
Clays	1,000 tonnes	40,000	1,670
Diatomite	1,000 tonnes	644	184
Feldspar	1,000 tonnes	800	43
Garnet (industrial)	1,000 tonnes	53	6
Gypsum	1m. tonnes	16	132
Lime	1m. short tons	19	1,200
Phosphate rock	1m. tonnes	32	1,076
Pumice	1,000 tonnes	920	16
Salt	1m. tonnes	45	993
Sand and gravel	1m. tonnes	1,158	4,778
Sodium sulphate	1,000 tonnes	512	35
Stone (crushed)	1m. tonnes	1,600	8,070

[1]2000.

Aluminium production for 2001, 2·64m. tonnes; uranium production for 2002, 919 tonnes. The USA is the world's leading producer of salt.

Coal. Proven coal reserves were 275,627m. short tons in 2002, more than a quarter of the world total. Output in 2001 (in 1m. short tons): 1,127·7 including bituminous coal, 611·3; sub-bituminous coal, 434·4; lignite, 80·0; anthracite, 1·9. 2000 output from opencast workings, 700m. short tons; underground mines, 374m. short tons. Value of total output, 2000, $18·02bn.

Agriculture. Agriculture in the USA is characterized by its ability to adapt to widely varying conditions, and still produce an abundance and variety of agricultural products. From colonial times to about 1920 the major increases in farm production were brought about by adding to the number of farms and the amount of land under cultivation. During this period nearly 320m. acres of virgin forest were converted to crop land or pasture, and extensive areas of grasslands were ploughed. Improvident use of soil and water resources was evident in many areas.

During the next 20 years the number of farms reached a plateau of about 6·5m., and the acreage planted to crops held relatively stable around 330m. acres. The major source of increase in farm output arose from the substitution of power-driven machines for horses and mules. Greater emphasis was placed on development and improvement of land, and the need for conservation of basic agricultural resources was recognized. A successful conservation programme, highly co-ordinated and on a national scale—to prevent further erosion, to restore the native fertility of damaged land and to adjust land uses to production capabilities and needs—has been in operation since early in the 1930s.

Since the Second World War the uptrend in farm output has been greatly accelerated by increased production per acre and per farm animal. These increases are associated with a higher degree of mechanization; greater use of lime and fertilizer; improved varieties, including hybrid maize and grain sorghums; more effective control of insects and disease; improved strains of livestock and poultry; and wider use of good husbandry practices, such as nutritionally balanced feeds, use of superior sites and better housing. During this period land included in farms decreased slowly, crop land harvested declined somewhat more rapidly, but the number of farms declined sharply.

All land in farms totalled less than 500m. acres in 1870, rose to a peak of over 1,200m. acres in the 1950s and declined to 938m. acres in 2002, even with the addition of the new States of Alaska and Hawaii in 1960. The number of farms declined from 6·35m. in 1940 to 2·13m. in 2002, as the average size of farms doubled. The average size of farms in 2002 was 441 acres, but ranged from a few acres to many thousand acres. In 2002 the total value of land and buildings was $1,144,906m. The average value of land and buildings per acre in 2002 was $1,213.

At the 2000 census 59,063,597 persons (21·0% of the population) were rural, of whom 2,987,531 (just over 1% of the total population) lived on farms. In 2002 there were 1,909,598 farms managed by families or individuals (89·7% of all farms); 1,428,136 farms (67·1% of all farms) were managed by full owners (farmers who own all the land they operate). Hired farmworkers numbered 793,000 in 2002. There were 4·8m. tractors in 2001 and 662,000 harvester-threshers. In 2001 there were 175·21m. ha of arable land and 2·05m. ha of permanent crops. 22·5m. ha were irrigated in 2001.

Cash receipts from farm marketings and government payments (in $1bn.):

	Crops	*Livestock and livestock products*	*Total*
1999	91·9	95·6	187·4
2000	94·1	99·6	193·7
2001	96·4	106·4	202·8

Net farm income was $45·7bn. in 2001.

The harvest area and production of the principal crops for 2001 and 2002 were:

	2001			*2002*		
	Harvested 1m. acres	*Production 1m.*	*Yield per acre*	*Harvested 1m. acres*	*Production 1m.*	*Yield per acre*
Corn for grain (bu.)	68·8	9,507	138	69·3	9,008	130
Soybeans (bu.)	73·0	2,891	39·6	72·2	2,730	37·8
Wheat (bu.)	48·6	1,957	40·2	45·8	1,616	35·3
Cotton (bales)[1]	13·8	20·3	705	12·4	17·1	663
Potatoes (cwt.)	1·2	438	358	1·3	463	363
Hay (sh. tons)	63·5	157	2·47	64·5	151	2·34

[1]Yield in lb.

The USA is the world's leading producer of maize, soybeans, sorghum and tree nuts and the second largest producer of tomatoes, carrots, seed cotton, cottonseed, sugarbeets and apples.

Fruit. Utilized production, in 1,000 tons:

	2000	*2001*	*2002*
Apples	5,161	4,607	4,203
Grapefruit	2,763	2,462	2,427
Grapes	7,687	6,568	7,362
Oranges	12,997	12,221	12,543
Peaches	1,244	1,168	1,236

The farm value of the above crops in 2002 was: apples, $1,571m.; grapefruit, $286m.; grapes, $2,853m.; oranges, $1,834m.; peaches, $504m.

Figures compiled by the Soil Association, a British organization, show that in 1999 the USA set aside 2·2m. acres (0·2% of its agricultural land) for the growth of organic crops. The projected figure of organic food sales for the USA in 2005 was $20bn. (the highest in the world).

Dairy produce. In 2002 production of milk was 170,000m. lb; cheese, 8,599m. lb; butter, 1,355m. lb; ice cream, 989m. gallons; non-fat dry milk, 1,577m. lb; yoghurt, 2,135m. lb. The USA is the world's largest producer of both cheese and milk.

Livestock. In 2002 there were 8,590m. broilers and 272m. turkeys. Eggs produced, 2002, 86·7bn.

Value of production (in $1m.) was:

	2000	*2001*	*2002*
Cattle and calves	28,392	29,293	26,915
Hogs and pigs	10,818	11,430	8,679
Broilers	13,989	16,694	13,435
Turkeys	2,823	2,790	2,700
Eggs	4,345	4,446	4,263

Livestock numbered, in 2003 (1m.): cattle and calves (including milch cows), 96·1; sheep and lambs, 6·4; hogs and pigs, 58·9. Approximate value of livestock (in $1bn.), 2003: cattle, 69·8; hogs and pigs, 4·2; sheep and lambs (in $1m.), 658.

Forestry. Forests covered a total area of 749m. acres (303m. ha) in 2002, or 33% of the land area. Between 1990 and 2000 new planting resulted in the total area under forests increasing by an average of 959,000 acres annually (388,000 ha), a total exceeded only in China. The national forests had an area of 148,456,000 acres in 2002. In 1996 there were 518m. acres of timberland (124m. acres federally owned or managed, 35m. acres state, county or municipality owned, 357m. acres private). Timber production was 16,990m. cu. ft in 2001. The USA is the world's largest producer of roundwood (14·4% of the world total in 2001). It is also the highest consumer of roundwood; timber consumption in 2001 totalled 16·84bn. cu. ft.

There are 662 designated wilderness areas throughout the USA, covering a total of 105·7m. acres (42·8m. ha). More than half of the areas are in Alaska (54%), followed by California (13%), Arizona, Washington and Idaho.

Fisheries. In 2001 the domestic catch was 9,492m. lb, valued at $3,228·3m. (including 1,139m. lb of shellfish valued at $1,711·4m.). Main species landed in terms of value ($1m.): shrimp, 568·5; crab, 381·7; American lobster, 254·3; Alaska pollock, 230·7; salmon, 208·9. Disposition of the domestic catch in 2000 (1m. lb): fresh or frozen, 6,657; tinned, 530; cured, 119; reduced to meal or oil, 1,763. The USA's imports of fishery commodities in 2001 ($10·29bn.) were exceeded only by those of Japan.

In the period 1997–99 the average American citizen consumed 46·5 lb (21·1 kg) of fish and fishery products a year, compared to an average 34·8 lb (15·8 kg) for the world as a whole.

Tennessee Valley Authority. Established by Act of Congress, 1933, the TVA is a multiple-purpose federal agency which carries out its duties in an area embracing some 41,000 sq. miles in the seven Tennessee River Valley states: Tennessee, Kentucky, Mississippi, Alabama, North Carolina, Georgia and Virginia. In addition, 76 counties outside the Valley are served by TVA power distributors. It is the largest public power company in the USA. Its three directors are appointed by the President, with the consent of the Senate; headquarters are in Knoxville (TN).

INDUSTRY

The largest companies in the USA—and the world—by market capitalization in March 2005 were: The Exxon Mobil Corporation (US$402·3bn.), the world's largest integrated oil company; The General Electric Company (US$383·0bn.); and The Microsoft Corporation (US$277·1bn.), the world's leading software company. According to a survey published by the New York-based Interbrand in July 2004, Coca-Cola is the most valuable brand, worth US$67·4bn.

The following table presents industry statistics of manufactures as reported at various censuses from 1909 to 1980 and from the Annual Survey of Manufactures for years in which no census was taken.

The annual Surveys of Manufactures carry forward the key measures of manufacturing activity which are covered in detail by the Census of Manufactures. The large plants in the surveys account for approximately two-thirds of the total employment in operating manufacturing establishments in the USA.

	Number of establishments	*Production workers (average for year)*	*Production workers' wages total ($1,000)*	*Value added by manufacture ($1,000)*
1909	264,810	3,261,736	3,205,213	8,160,075
1919	270,231	9,464,916	9,664,009	23,841,624
1929	206,663	8,369,705	10,884,919	30,591,435
1933	139,325	5,787,611	4,940,146	14,007,540
1939	173,802	7,808,205	8,997,515	24,487,304
1950	260,000	11,778,803	34,600,025	89,749,765
1960	. . .	12,209,514	55,555,452	163,998,531
1970	. . .	13,528,000	91,609,000	300,227,600
1980	. . .	13,900,100	198,164,000	773,831,300
1990	. . .	12,232,700	275,208,400	1,346,970,100
2000	. . .	11,943,646	363,380,819	1,973,622,421
2001	. . .	11,235,111	342,990,489	1,853,929,431

The total number of employees in the manufacturing industry in 2001 was approximately 15,879,000. Manufacturing employment has been steadily declining since the turn of the millennium. Much of the decline reflects the recession that began in 2001 and the relatively weak recovery in demand that followed. In 2000 manufacturing contributed 17% of GDP and provided 14% of jobs, down from 27% of GDP and 31% of jobs in 1960. Industrial production grew far faster during the 1990s than in any other major economy, output expanding by 34% during the period 1990–98. Employees worked an average of 41·5 hours per week in 2000 for an average weekly income of $597.

The leading industries in 2001 in terms of value added by manufacture (in $1m.) were: transportation equipment, 227,675; chemicals and allied products, 226,615; computer and electronic products, 223,718; food, 193,224; fabricated metal products, 138,793. In 2002 a total of 12,272,000 motor vehicles were made in the USA, making it the world's leading vehicle producer.

In 2001 principal commodities produced (by value of shipments, in $1m.) were: transportation equipment, 602,496; food, 451,386; chemicals and allied products, 438,410; computer and electronic products, 429,471; machinery, 266,553.

Net profits (2002) for manufacturing corporations were $207bn. before tax ($146bn. after tax).

The USA is the second largest beer producer after China, with 6,135m. gallons in 2003; and second after China for cigarette production, with 565bn. units in 2002.

Iron and Steel. Output of the iron and steel industries (in 1m. net tons of 2,000 lb), according to figures supplied by the American Iron and Steel Institute, was:

	Pig iron (including ferro-alloys)	*Raw steel*	*Steel by method of production*[1]	
			Electric	*Basic Oxygen*
1995	56·1	104·9	42·4	62·5
1996	54·5	105·3	44·9	60·4
1997	54·7	108·6	47·5	61·1
1998	53·2	108·8	49·1	59·7
1999	51·0	107·4	49·7	57·7
2000	52·8	112·2	52·8	59·5

[1]The sum of these two items should equal the total in the preceding column; any difference is due to rounding.

In 1997 companies comprising 65% of raw steel production employed 83,466 wage-earners who worked an average of 42·7 hours per week and earned an average of $23·90 per hour: total employment costs were $6,465m. and total employment costs for 28,359 salaried employees were $2,378m.

Labour. The Bureau of Labor Statistics estimated that in 2004 the civilian labour force was 147,401,000 (66·0% of those 16 years and over), of whom 139,252,000 were employed and 8,149,000 (5·5%) were unemployed. The unemployment rate has declined from its recent high of 6·3% in June 2003; it was 5·2% in Jan. 2005. Total non-farm payroll employment rose by 2,172,000 in the 12 months ending Dec. 2004. Employment by industry in 2004:

Industry Group	*Male*	*Female*	*Total*	*Percentage distribution*
Employed (1,000 persons):	74,524	64,728	139,252	100·0
Agriculture, forestry, fisheries, and hunting	1,687	546	2,232	1·6

Industry Group	*Male*	*Female*	*Total*	*Percentage distribution*
Mining	483	55	539	0·4
Construction	9,727	1,041	10,768	7·7
Manufacturing: Durable goods	7,600	2,728	10,329	7·4
Manufacturing: Non-durable	3,885	2,270	6,155	4·4
Wholesale and retail trade	11,580	9,289	20,869	15·0
Transportation and utilities	5,342	1,671	7,013	5·0
Information	1,962	1,501	3,463	2·5
Finance activities	4,396	5,572	9,969	7·2
Professional and business services	8,068	6,039	14,108	10·1
Education and health services	7,222	21,497	28,719	20·6
Leisure and hospitality	5,783	6,037	11,820	8·5
Other services	3,330	3,573	6,903	5.0
Public administration	3,458	2,908	6,365	4·6

A total of 14 strikes and lockouts of 1,000 workers or more occurred in 2003, involving 129,200 workers and 4,091,200 idle days; the number of idle days was about one out of every 10,000 available workdays.

On 1 Sept. 1997 the federal hourly minimum wage was raised from $4·75 to $5·15 an hour. On 1 Oct. 1996 it had been raised from $4·25 to $4·75 an hour, the first time it had been raised since 1991. Americans work among the longest hours in the industrialized world, averaging 1,815 hours in 2002.

Labour relations are legally regulated by the National Labor Relations Act, amended by the Labor–Management Relations (Taft–Hartley) Act, 1947 as amended by the Labor–Management Reporting and Disclosure Act, 1959, again amended in 1974, and the Railway Labor Act of 1926, as amended in 1934 and 1936.

A survey for the World Economic Forum's *1999 Global Competitiveness Report* showed that the USA was the easiest country in the world in which to set up a business.

Trade Unions. The labour movement comprises 78 national and international labour organizations plus a large number of small independent local or single-firm labour organizations. The American Federation of Labor and the Congress of Industrial Organizations merged into one organization, the AFL–CIO, in 1955, with 13m. members in 2000. Its president is John Sweeney, elected 1995. There were 16,258,200 union members in total in 2000.

Unaffiliated or independent labour organizations, inter-state in scope, had an estimated total membership excluding all foreign members (1993) of about 3m.

Labour organizations represented 13·8% (17·1m.) of wage and salary workers in 2004; a newly developing 'associative unionism' is not based on the workplace, but provides representation for employees which is portable throughout their work history; 12·5% (15·5m.) were actual members of unions. 36·4% of employees in the public sector, and 7·9% in the private sector, were members of unions in 2004. Strongholds of organized labour are, industry-wise, iron and steel, railways, coal mining and car building; region-wise, East coast cities and the mid-West industrial belt.

INTERNATIONAL TRADE

The North American Free Trade Agreement (NAFTA) between the USA, Canada and Mexico was signed on 7 Oct. 1992 and came into effect on 1 Jan. 1994. The UK has had 'most-favoured-nation' status since 1815.

Imports and Exports. Total value of exports and imports of goods (in $1bn.):

	Exports	*Imports*
2000	781·9	1,218·0
2001	729·1	1,141·0
2002	693·1	1,164·7
2003	724·0	1,263·2

The USA is both the world's leading importer and the leading trading nation, although only the second largest exporter after Germany. In 2002 its trade accounted for 14·7% of the world's exports and 23·4% of imports.

Principal exports and imports (in $1m.), 2002:

	Exports	*Imports*
Agricultural commodities		
Animal feeds	3,824	605
Coffee	8	1,369
Corn	5,108	137

	Exports	*Imports*
Cotton, raw and linters	2,031	25
Hides and skins	1,594	84
Meat and preparations	6,356	4,269
Soybeans	5,734	28
Sugar	13	495
Tobacco, unmanufactured	1,050	701
Vegetables and fruits	7,607	10,194
Wheat	3,630	266
Manufactured goods		
ADP equipment, office machinery	30,368	76,877
Airplane parts	14,309	4,986
Airplanes	27,115	12,329
Alcoholic beverages	505	3,273
Aluminium	2,947	6,757
Artwork/antiques	977	5,194
Basketware, etc.	3,842	6,564
Chemicals – cosmetics	5,870	4,195
Chemicals – dyeing	3,860	2,357
Chemicals – fertilizers	2,106	1,619
Chemicals – inorganic	5,464	6,018
Chemicals – medicinal	15,732	24,748
Chemicals – organic	16,406	30,366
Chemicals – plastics	19,380	10,760
Chemicals – other	12,348	6,168
Clothing	5,485	63,803
Cork, wood, lumber	3,364	7,872
Electrical machinery	66,948	81,158
Fish and preparations	2,976	10,000
Footwear	518	15,387
Furniture and parts	3,814	21,577
Gem diamonds	1,182	12,088
General industrial machinery	30,075	35,200
Gold, non-monetary	3,244	2,428
Iron and steel mill products	5,252	12,951
Lighting, plumbing	1,333	5,566
Metal manufactures, misc.	11,170	16,681
Metal ores; scrap	4,626	3,101
Metalworking machinery	4,140	5,104
Optical goods	2,132	2,836
Paper and paperboard	9,551	14,435
Photographic equipment	3,529	5,325
Plastic articles	6,820	9,138
Platinum	723	2,830
Power generating machinery	32,430	33,922
Printed materials	4,429	3,960
Pulp and waste paper	3,842	2,363
Records/magnetic media	4,414	5,279
Rubber articles	1,423	2,139
Rubber tyres and tubes	2,232	4,765
Scientific instruments	27,087	20,884
Specialized industrial machinery	23,532	18,401
Television, VCR, etc.	19,374	66,212
Textile yarn, fabric	10,263	16,097
Toys/games/sporting goods	2,985	22,067
Travel goods	277	4,402
Vehicles	57,698	168,073
Watches/clocks/parts	236	3,203
Wood manufactures	1,564	7,853
Mineral fuel		
Coal	1,673	966
Crude oil	92	79,252
Petroleum preparations	6,009	20,748
Natural gas	995	10,974

Imports and exports by selected countries for the calendar years 2001 and 2002 (in $1m.):

	General imports		*Exports incl. re-exports*	
Country	*2001*	*2002*	*2001*	*2002*
Australia	6,478	6,479	10,930	13,085
Belgium	10,158	9,807	13,502	13,326

Country	General imports 2001	General imports 2002	Exports incl. re-exports 2001	Exports incl. re-exports 2002
Brazil	14,466	15,781	15,879	12,376
Canada	216,268	209,088	163,424	160,923
China	102,278	125,192	19,182	22,128
France	30,408	28,240	19,864	19,016
Germany	59,077	62,506	29,995	26,630
Hong Kong	9,646	9,328	14,027	12,594
Ireland	18,499	22,438	7,144	6,745
Israel	11,959	12,416	7,475	7,027
Italy	23,790	24,220	9,916	10,057
Japan	126,473	121,429	57,452	51,449
South Korea	35,181	35,572	22,181	22,576
Malaysia	22,340	24,009	9,358	10,344
Mexico	131,338	134,616	101,296	97,470
Netherlands	9,515	9,848	19,485	18,311
Singapore	15,000	14,802	17,652	16,218
Taiwan	33,374	32,148	18,122	18,382
Thailand	14,727	14,793	5,989	4,860
UK	41,369	40,745	40,714	33,205
Venezuela	15,250	15,093	5,642	4,430

COMMUNICATIONS

Roads. On 31 Dec. 2001 the total public road mileage was 3,948,335 miles (urban, 877,004; rural, 3,071,331). Of the urban roads, 12% were state controlled and 87% under local control. 22% of rural roads were controlled by the states, 74% of rural roads were under local control and the remainder were federal park and forest roads. State highway funds were $94,513m. in 2001.

Motor vehicles registered in 2001: 230,428,000, of which 137,633,000 automobiles, 92,045,000 trucks and 750,000 buses. There were 191,276,000 licensed drivers in 2001 and 4,862,000 motorcycle registrations. The average distance travelled by a passenger car in the year 1999 was 11,900 miles. There were 42,116 fatalities in road accidents in 2001.

Rail. Freight service is provided by 12 major independent railroad companies and several hundred smaller operators. Long-distance passenger trains are run by the National Railroad Passenger Corporation (Amtrak), which is federally assisted. Amtrak was set up in 1971 to maintain a basic network of long-distance passenger trains, and is responsible for almost all non-commuter services over some 38,000 route-km, of which it owns only 1,256 km (555 km electrified). Outside the major conurbations, there are almost no regular passenger services other than those of Amtrak, which carried 23,444,000 passengers in 2001. Passenger revenue for Amtrak (2001) was $1,299·9m.; revenue passenger miles, 5,571m.

Civil Aviation. The busiest airport in 2002 was Atlanta (Hartsfield International), which handled 37,720,556 passenger enplanements (34,610,400 on domestic flights). The second busiest was Chicago (O'Hare) with 31,706,328 passenger enplanements (27,347,895 on domestic flights), followed by Los Angeles International, with 26,911,570 passenger enplanements (19,814,818 on domestic flights). As well as being the three busiest airports in the USA for passenger traffic in 2002, they are also three of the five busiest in the world. The five busiest in the world in 2002 were Atlanta, Chicago O'Hare, London Heathrow, Tokyo Haneda and Los Angeles. New York (John F. Kennedy) was the busiest airport in the USA for international passenger enplanements in 2002, with 7,278,793, ahead of Los Angeles International, with 7,096,752.

The leading airports in 2002 on the basis of aircraft departures completed were Chicago, O'Hare (461,394); Atlanta, Hartsfield International (445,461); Dallas/Fort Worth (388,643).

There were 42 airports with more than 100,000 international enplanements in 2002. These were, in descending order: New York (John F. Kennedy); Los Angeles; Miami; Chicago (O'Hare); New York (Newark); San Francisco; Atlanta (Hartsfield); Houston (George Bush); Honolulu; Dallas/Fort Worth; Washington, D.C. (Dulles International); Boston; Detroit (Metropolitan-Wayne County); Philadelphia; Guam; Minneapolis/St Paul; Seattle; San Juan (Luis Muñoz Marin International); Orlando International; New York (LaGuardia); Denver; Phoenix; Charlotte; Cincinnati

(Northern Kentucky International); Fort Lauderdale (Hollywood International); Las Vegas (McCarran); Orlando (Sanfort); Saipan; Pittsburgh; Baltimore; St Louis (Lambert); Tampa; San Diego (Lindbergh Field); Memphis; Cleveland-Hopkins; San Jose; Oakland; San Antonio; Portland; Raleigh-Durham; Washington, D.C. (Ronald Reagan Washington National); Chicago (Midway).

In 2002 Delta Air Lines carried the most passengers of any airline in the world with 86,854,120 (around 4% on international flights), ahead of American Airlines, with 85,710,781 (around 10% on international flights), and Southwest Airlines, with 72,517,787 (all on domestic flights). American Airlines carried the most international passengers of any US carrier, ahead of United Airlines, with 8% of their passengers on international flights.

In 2002 US flag carriers in scheduled service enplaned 614m. revenue passengers.

Shipping. In Oct. 2001 the cargo-carrying US flag fleet consisted of 31,387 vessels, of which 3,835 were of 1,000 GRT and over (2,148 liquid carriers, 760 dry bulk carriers, 126 containerships and 801 other freighters). Of 27,552 vessels of less than 1,000 GRT, 1,767 were liquid carriers, 21,705 dry bulk carriers, four containerships and 4,076 other freighters. Shipping capacity in Oct. 2001 was 72,816,000 GRT, of which the vessels of 1,000 GRT and over totalled 31,877,000 GRT while those of less than 1,000 GRT totalled 40,939,000 GRT. On 1 Jan. 2002 the US merchant marine included 443 ocean-going self-propelled merchant vessels of 1,000 gross tons or over, with an aggregate 15·0m. DWT. This included 130 tankers of 7·5m. DWT.

In 2001 vessels totalling 451,929,000 NRT entered, and 310,973,000 NRT cleared, all US ports. The busiest port is South Louisiana, which handled 235,053,000 tonnes of cargo in 2002 and ranks fourth in the world. Other major ports are Houston, Los Angeles, Long Beach, Corpus Christi, New York-New Jersey and Philadelphia.

Telecommunications. Regional private companies formed from the American Telephone and Telegraph Co. after its dissolution in 1995 ('Baby Bells') operate the telephone, telegraph, telex and electronic transmission services system at the national and local levels. In 2002 telephone subscribers numbered 330,766,800 (or 1,147·0 per 1,000 persons). There were 140,766,800 cellphone subscribers in 2002 (488·1 per 1,000 persons). The leading cellphone operators are Cingular (with more than 46m. subscribers), Verizon, Sprint-Nexel and T-Mobile. There were 190m. PCs in 2002 (658·9 for every 1,000 persons—the highest rate in the world) and in 1997 there were 21m. fax machines. The number of Internet users in April 2002 was estimated to be 165·75m., or 59·1% of the population (among the highest percentages in the world).

Legislation on the media and telecommunications of 1996 coming into force on 31 March 1999 aimed at deregulating the market while preserving safeguards against over-concentration of individual ownership: a single company may not control a network reaching more than 35% of TV viewers, or produce a newspaper and a television service in the same market. Local companies are now permitted to operate long-distance telephone services and also cable TV services.

Postal Services. The US Postal Service superseded the Post Office Department on 1 July 1971.

Postal business for the years ended in Sept. included the following items:

	1999	*2000*	*2001*	*2002*
Number of post offices, stations and branches	38,169	38,060	38,123	37,683
Operating revenue ($1m.)	62,755	64,540	65,834	66,463
Operating expenditures ($1m.)	60,642	62,992	65,640	65,234

SOCIAL INSTITUTIONS

Justice. Legal controversies may be decided in two systems of courts: the federal courts, with jurisdiction confined to certain matters enumerated in Article III of the Constitution, and the state courts, with jurisdiction in all other proceedings. The federal courts have jurisdiction exclusive of the state courts in criminal prosecutions for the violation of federal statutes, in civil cases involving the government, in bankruptcy cases and in admiralty proceedings, and have jurisdiction concurrent with the state courts over suits between parties from different states, and certain suits involving questions of federal law.

The highest court is the Supreme Court of the US, which reviews cases from the lower federal courts and certain cases originating in state courts involving questions of federal law. It is the final arbiter of all questions involving federal statutes and the Constitution; and it has the power to invalidate any federal or state law or executive action which it finds repugnant to the Constitution. This court, consisting of nine justices appointed by the President who receive salaries of $199,200 a year (the Chief Justice, $208,100), meets from Oct. until June every year. For the term ended Sept. 2003 it disposed of 9,406 cases, deciding 84 on their merits. In the remainder of cases it either summarily affirms lower court decisions or declines to review. A few suits, usually brought by state governments, originate in the Supreme Court, but issues of fact are mostly referred to a master.

The US courts of appeals number 13 (in 11 circuits composed of three or more states and one circuit for the District of Columbia and one Court of Appeals for the Federal Circuit); the 179 circuit judges receive salaries of $171,800 a year. Any party to a suit in a lower federal court usually has a right of appeal to one of these courts. In addition, there are direct appeals to these courts from many federal administrative agencies. In the year ending 30 Sept. 2003, 62,390 appeals were filed in the courts of appeals, including 1,543 in the Federal Circuit.

The trial courts in the federal system are the US district courts, of which there are 94 in the 50 states, one in the District of Columbia and one each in the Commonwealth of Puerto Rico and the Territories of the Virgin Islands, Guam and the Northern Marianas. Each state has at least one US district court, and three states have four apiece. Each district court has from one to 28 judgeships. There are 680 US district judges ($162,100 a year), who received 252,962 civil cases in 2002–03.

In addition to these courts of general jurisdiction, there are special federal courts of limited jurisdiction. The US Court of Federal Claims (16 judges at $162,100 a year) decides claims for money damages against the federal government in a wide variety of matters; the Court of International Trade (nine judges at $162,100) determines controversies concerning the classification and valuation of imported merchandise.

The judges of all these courts are appointed by the President with the approval of the Senate; to assure their independence, they hold office during good behaviour and cannot have their salaries reduced. This does not apply to judges in the Territories, who hold their offices for a term of ten years or to judges of the US Court of Federal Claims. The judges may retire with full pay at the age of 70 years if they have served a period of ten years, or at 65 if they have 15 years of service, but they are subject to call for such judicial duties as they are willing to undertake.

In 2001–02, of the 268,071 civil cases filed in the district courts, 166,920 arose under various federal statutes (such as labour, social security, tax, patent, securities, antitrust and civil rights laws); 56,565 involved personal injury or property damage claims; 36,845 dealt with contracts; and 7,731 were actions concerning real property.

In 2000 the number of lawyers in the USA passed the 1m. mark, equivalent to 363 per 100,000 people.

Among the 68,156 offenders convicted in 2000 in the district courts, 24,206 persons were charged with alleged infractions of drug laws, 19,906 with public order offences, 12,454 with property offences and 2,557 with violent offences. All other people convicted were charged with miscellaneous general offences.

Persons convicted of federal crimes may be fined, released on probation under the supervision of the probation officers of the federal courts, confined in prison, or confined in prison with a period of supervised release to follow, also under the supervision of probation officers of the federal courts. Federal prisoners are confined in 87 institutions incorporating various security levels that are operated by the Bureau of Prisons. On 31 Dec. 2002 the total number of prisoners under the jurisdiction of Federal or State adult correctional authorities was 1,440,655. A record 2,033,331 inmates were held in Federal or State prisons or local jails at the end of 2002, giving a rate of 701 per 100,000 population (the highest of any country).

The state courts have jurisdiction over all civil and criminal cases arising under state laws, but decisions of the state courts of last resort as to the validity of treaties or of laws of the USA, or on other questions arising under the Constitution, are subject to review by the Supreme Court of the US. The state court systems are generally similar to the federal system, to the extent that they generally have a number of trial courts and intermediate appellate courts, and a single court of last resort. The highest court in each state is usually called the Supreme Court or Court of Appeals with a Chief Justice and Associate Justices, usually elected but sometimes appointed by the Governor with the advice and consent of the State Senate or other advisory body; they usually hold office for a term of years, but in some instances for life or during good behaviour. The lowest tribunals are usually those of Justices of the Peace; many towns and cities have municipal and police courts, with power to commit for trial in criminal matters and to determine misdemeanours for violation of the municipal ordinances.

There were no executions from 1968 to 1976. The US Supreme Court had held the death penalty, as applied in general criminal statutes, to contravene the eighth and fourteenth amendments of the US constitution, as a cruel and unusual punishment when used so irregularly and rarely as to destroy its deterrent value. The death penalty was reinstated by the Supreme Court in 1976, but has not been authorized in Alaska, the District of Columbia, Hawaii, Iowa, Kansas, Maine, Massachusetts, Michigan, Minnesota, North Dakota, Rhode Island, Vermont, West Virginia and Wisconsin. There were, in Oct. 2004, 3,471 (including 50 women) prisoners under sentence of death. In 2004 there were 59 executions (65 in 2003 but only 14 in 1991). From 1977–2004 there were 944 executions of which 336 were in Texas and 95 in Virginia. The death penalty for offenders under the age of 18 was abolished in March 2005. For the first time since 1963, there were two executions under federal jurisdiction in 2001. In Sept. 2003 the federal Court of Appeals in San Francisco overturned over 100 death sentences in Arizona, Idaho and Montana on the grounds that judges, not juries, had passed sentence, contravening a Supreme Court ruling of 2002.

There were 16,503 murders in 2003, the fourth consecutive year of increase but prior to 1999 the lowest total since 1970. The murder rate in 2003 was 5·7 per 100,000 persons, down from 10·5 per 100,000 in 1980 although up slightly on the previous three years. 63·4% of all murders in 2001 were carried out with firearms.

Religion. *The Yearbook of American and Canadian Churches,* published by the National Council of the Churches of Christ in the USA, New York, gave the following figures available from official statisticians of church bodies: the principal religions (numerically or historically) or groups of religious bodies (in 2001 unless otherwise stated) are shown below:

	No. of churches	*Membership (in 1,000)*
Baptist bodies		
Southern Baptist Convention	42,334	16,053
National Baptist Convention, USA (not available)	9,000	5,000
National Baptist Convention of America, Inc. (2000)	2,500[1]	3,500
American Baptist Churches in the USA	5,786	1,443
American Baptist Association (1998)	1,760	275
Conservative Baptist Association of America (1998)	1,200	200
Baptist Missionary Association of America (1999)	1,334	235
Christian Church (Disciples of Christ)	3,717	805
Christian Churches and Churches of Christ (1998)	5,579	1,072
Church of the Nazarene (2000)	5,070	637
Churches of Christ (1999)	15,000	1,500
Progressive National Baptist Convention, Inc. (1995)	2,000	2,500
The Episcopal Church (2000)	7,364	2,333
Jehovah's Witnesses	11,706	989
Latter-day Saints		
Church of Jesus Christ of Latter-day Saints (Mormons)	11,731	5,210
Reorganized Church of Jesus Christ of Latter-day Saints (1999)	1,236	137
Lutheran bodies		
Evangelical Lutheran Church in America	10,766	5,100
The Lutheran Church–Missouri Synod	6,187	2,540
Wisconsin Evangelical Lutheran Synod (2000)	1,241	722
Mennonite churches		
Mennonite Church (2000)	1,063	120
Old Order Amish Church (1993)	898	81
Methodist bodies		
United Methodist Church	35,275	8,298
African Methodist Episcopal Church (2000)	6,200	2,500
African Methodist Episcopal Zion Church	3,226	1,448
Wesleyan Church (USA) (2000)	1,602	123

	No. of churches	*Membership (in 1,000)*
Pentecostal bodies		
The Church of God in Christ (1991)	15,300	5,500
Assemblies of God (2000)	12,084	2,578
Church of God (Cleveland, Tenn.)	6,605	932
Pentecostal Assemblies of the World, Inc. (1998)	1,750	1,500
Presbyterian bodies		
Presbyterian Church (USA)	11,142	3,456
Presbyterian Church in America (2000)	1,458	306
Reformed Churches		
Reformed Church in America (2000)	898	289
Christian Reformed Church in North America (1999)	739	197
The Salvation Army (1999)	1,410	473
United Church of Christ	5,888	1,359
Seventh-day Adventist Church	4,594	901
Roman Catholic Church[2]	19,496	65,270
Orthodox Churches		
Greek Orthodox Archdiocese of America (2000)	508	1,500
Orthodox Church in America (2000)	721	1,000
Oriental Orthodox Churches		
Armenian Apostolic Church of America (2000)	36	360
Armenian Apostolic Church, Diocese of America (1991)	72	414
Coptic Orthodox Church (2000)	100	300
Non-Christian Religions		
Hindus	—	766
Islam	—	1,104
Jews	—	2,831
Buddhist	—	1,082

[1]1987. [2]In Sept. 2003 there were 14 cardinals.

Education. The adult literacy rate is at least 99%.

Elementary and secondary education is mainly a state responsibility. Each state and the District of Columbia has a system of free public schools, established by law, with courses covering 12 years plus kindergarten. There are three structural patterns in common use; the K8-4 plan, meaning kindergarten plus eight elementary grades followed by four high school grades; the K6-3-3 plan, or kindergarten plus six elementary grades followed by a three-year junior high school and a three-year senior high school; and the K5-3-4 plan, kindergarten plus five elementary grades followed by a three-year middle school and a four-year high school. All plans lead to high-school graduation, usually at age 17 or 18. Vocational education is an integral part of secondary education. Many states also have two-year colleges in which education is provided at a nominal cost. Each state has delegated a large degree of control of the educational programme to local school districts (numbering 14,891 in school year 1998–99), each with a board of education (usually three to nine members) selected locally and serving mostly without pay. The school policies of the local school districts must be in accord with the laws and the regulations of their state Departments of Education. While regulations differ from one jurisdiction to another, in general it may be said that school attendance is compulsory from age seven to 16.

'Charter schools' are legal entities outside the school boards administration. They retain the basics of public school education, but may offer unconventional curricula and hours of attendance. Founders may be parents, teachers, public bodies or commercial firms. Organization and conditions depend upon individual states' legislation. The first charter schools were set up in Minnesota in 1991. By Sept. 1999, 1,484 charter schools were operating in 31 states and Washington, D.C.

In 1940 a new category was established—the 'functionally illiterate', meaning those who had completed fewer than five years of elementary schooling; for persons 25 years of age or over this percentage was 1·6 in March 1999 (for the Black population it was 1·9%); it was 0·6% for white and 0·4% for Blacks in the 25–29-year-old group. It was reported in March 1999 that 83·4% of all persons 25 years old and over had completed four years of high school or more, and that 25·2% had completed a bachelor's degree or more. In the age group 25 to 29, 87·8% had completed four years of high school or more, and 28·2% had completed a bachelor's degree or more. However, according to a report published in 2001 nearly a third of American fourth graders (aged 9–10) are unable to read.

In the autumn of 2000, 15,312,000 students (9,010,000 full-time and 8,591,000 women) were enrolled in 4,182 colleges and universities; 2,428,000 were first-time students. It is projected that in 2010 the student population will number 17,490,000.

In 2001–02 expenditure for public elementary and secondary education totalled $414,708m., comprising $365,053m. for current operating expenses, $38,627m. for capital outlay and $11,029m. for interest on school debt. The current expenditure per pupil in average daily attendance was $7,548.

In 2000–01 total expenditure on education came to 4·9% of GNP and accounted for 15·5% of total government expenditure.

Estimated total expenditures for private elementary and secondary schools in 1998–99 were about $27,700m. In 1998–99 college and university spending totalled about $246,300m., of which about $152,400m. was spent by institutions under public control. The federal government contributed about 12% of total current-fund revenue; state governments, 23%; student tuition and fees, 28%; and all other sources, 37%. Federal support for vocational education in 1998–99 amounted to about $1,128m.

Summary of statistics of regular schools (public and private), teachers and pupils for 2001–02 (compiled by the US National Center for Education Statistics):

Schools by level	*Number of schools*	*Teachers (in 1,000)*[1]	*Enrolment (in 1,000)*
Elementary schools:			
Public	65,228	1,602	33,952
Private	16,530[1]	261	4,765[1]
Secondary schools:			
Public	27,468[2]	1,401	13,736
Private	10,693[1, 2]	188	1,254[1]
Higher education:			
Public	1,713	713	12,233
Private	2,484	315	3,695
Total	110,673	4,480	69,818

[1]Data from 1999–2000. [2]Secondary and Combined.

In the autumn of 1999 there were 20·9 pupils per teacher in public elementary schools in the USA and 9·5 pupils per teacher in public secondary schools.

Most of the private elementary and secondary schools are affiliated with religious denominations. In 1999–2000 there were 6,707 Roman Catholic elementary schools with 1,815,000 pupils and 101,000 teachers, and 1,114 secondary schools with 608,000 pupils and 41,000 teachers.

During the school year 2000–01 high-school graduates numbered about 2,852,000 (of whom about 2,569,000 were from public schools). Institutions of higher education conferred about 1,292,000 bachelor's degrees during the year 2001–02; 595,000 associate's degrees; 482,000 master's degrees; 44,000 doctorates; and 81,000 first professional degrees. In 1998–99 the US Department of Education provided $11,685m. in grants, loans, work-study programmes and other financial assistance to post-secondary students. Other agencies of the Federal Government provided about $2,945m. in additional assistance.

During the academic year 1999–2000, 515,000 foreign students were enrolled in American colleges and universities. The countries with the largest numbers of students in American colleges were: China, 54,500; Japan, 46,900; India, 42,300; South Korea, 41,200; Taiwan, 29,200; Canada, 23,500.

In 1998–99, 130,000 US students were enrolled at colleges and universities abroad. The country attracting the most students from the USA was the United Kingdom, with 27,700.

School enrolment, Oct. 1999, embraced 96·0% of the children who were 5 and 6 years old; 98·7% of the children aged 7–13 years; 98·2% of those aged 14–15; 93·6% of those aged 16–17; and 60·6% of those aged 18–19.

The US National Center for Education Statistics estimates the total enrolment in the autumn of 2000 at all of the country's elementary, secondary and higher educational institutions (public and private) at 68·5m. (67·7m. in the autumn of 1999).

The number of teachers in regular public and private elementary and secondary schools in 2000 increased slightly to about 3,343,000. The average annual salary of public school teachers was $41,800 in 2000.

A survey for the 1999 *World Competitiveness Yearbook* showed that well-educated people in the USA are the least likely of any country in the world to emigrate.

Health. Admission to the practice of medicine (for both doctors of medicine and doctors of osteopathic medicine) is controlled in each state by examining boards directly representing the profession and acting with authority conferred by state law. Although there are a number of variations, the usual time now required to complete training is eight years beyond the secondary school with up to three or more years of additional graduate training. Certification as a specialist may require between three and five more years of graduate training plus experience in practice. In Jan. 2001 the estimated number of physicians (MD and DO—in all forms of practice) in the USA, Puerto Rico and outlying US areas was 836,200 (615,400 in 1990 and 467,700 in 1980).

Dental employment in 2000 numbered 152,000.

Number of hospitals listed by the American Hospital Association in 2001 was 5,801, with 987,000 beds (equivalent to 3·5 beds per 1,000 population). Of the total, 243 hospitals with 53,000 beds were operated by the federal government; 1,156 with 136,000 beds by state and local government; 2,998 with 585,000 beds by non-profit organizations (including church groups); 754 with 109,000 beds were investor-owned. The categories of non-federal hospitals were (2001): 4,908 short-term general and special hospitals with 826,000 beds; 136 non-federal long-term general and special hospitals with 19,000 beds; 491 psychiatric hospitals with 89,000 beds; four tuberculosis hospitals with fewer than 500 beds.

Patient admissions to community hospitals (2001) was 32,813,000; average daily census was 532,000. There were 538·5m. outpatient visits.

Personal health-care costs in 2001 totalled $1,236,400m., distributed as follows: hospital care, $451,200m.; physicians and clinical services, $313,600m.; prescription drugs, $140,600m.; nursing-home care, $98,900m.; dentists, $65,600m.; home health care, $33,200m.; medical durables, $18,400m.; other personal health care, $115,000m. Total national health expenditure in 2001 amounted to $1,424·5bn. In 2002 the USA spent 14·6% of its GDP on health—3% more than any other leading industrialized nation. Public spending on health amounted to 44·9% of total health spending in 2002 (the lowest percentage of any major industrialized nation). A survey published by the World Health Organization in June 2000 to measure health systems in all of the sovereign countries and find which country has the best overall health care ranked the USA in 37th place.

In 2001, 22·7% of Americans (24·7% of males and 20·8% of females) were smokers, down from a peak of over 40% in 1964. By 2000, 30·9% of the adult population were considered obese (having a body mass index over 30), compared to 14·5% in 1971.

Welfare. Social welfare legislation was chiefly the province of the various states until the adoption of the Social Security Act of 14 Aug. 1935. This as amended provides for a federal system of old-age, survivors and disability insurance; health insurance for the aged and disabled; supplemental security income for the aged, blind and disabled; federal state unemployment insurance; and federal grants to states for public assistance (medical assistance for the aged and aid to families with dependent children generally and for maternal and child health and child welfare services).

Legislation of Aug. 1996 began the transfer of aid administration back to the states, restricted the provision of aid to a maximum period of five years, and abolished benefits to immigrants (both legal and illegal) for the first five years of their residence in the USA. The Social Security Administration (formerly part of the Department of Health and Human Services but an independent agency since March 1995) has responsibility for a number of programmes covering retirement, disability, Medicare, Supplemental Security Income and survivors. The Administration for Children and Families (ACF), an agency of the Department of Health and Human Services, is responsible for federal programmes which promote the economic and social wellbeing of families, children, individuals and communities. ACF has federal responsibility for the following programmes: Temporary Assistance for Needy Families; low income energy assistance; Head Start; child care; child protective services; and a community services block grant. The ACF also has federal responsibility for social service programmes for children, youth, native Americans and persons with developmental disabilities.

The Administration on Aging (AoA), an agency in the US Department of Health and Human Services, is one of the nation's largest providers of home- and community-based care for older persons and their caregivers. Created in 1965 with the passage of the Older Americans Act (OAA), AoA is part of a federal, state, tribal and local partnership called the National Network on Aging. It serves about 7m. older persons and their caregivers, and consists of 56 State Units on Aging, 655 Area Agencies on Aging, 236 Tribal and Native organizations, two organizations that serve Native Hawaiians, 29,000 service providers and thousands of volunteers. These organizations provide assistance and services to older individuals and their families in urban, suburban, and rural areas throughout the USA.

The Health Care Financing Administration, an agency of the Health and Human Services Department, has federal responsibility for health insurance for the aged and disabled. Unemployment insurance is the responsibility of the Department of Labor.

In 2002 an average of 2,047,000 families (5,066,000 recipients) were receiving payments under Temporary Assistance for Needy Families. Total payments under Temporary Assistance for Needy Families were $23,590m. in 2000. The role of Child Support Enforcement is to ensure that children are supported by their parents. Money collected is for children who live with only one parent because of divorce, separation or out-of-wedlock birth. In 2001, $18,958m. was collected on behalf of these children.

The Social Security Act provides for protection against the cost of medical care through Medicare, a two-part programme of health insurance for people age 65 and over, people of any age with permanent kidney failure, and for certain disabled people under age 65 who receive Social Security disability benefits. In 2001 payments totalling $141,723m. were made under the hospital portion of Medicare. During the same period, $99,452m. was paid under the voluntary medical insurance portion of Medicare. Medicare enrolment in July 2002 totalled 40·4m.

In 2002 about 45·3m. beneficiaries were on the rolls; the average paid to a retired worker (not counting any benefits paid to his/her dependants) in 2000 was $895 per month. Full retirement benefits are now payable at age 65, with reduced benefits available as early as age 62. Beginning in 2000, the age for full retirement benefits will gradually increase until it reaches 67 in 2027. In 1995 the average actual retirement age for males was 63.

Medicaid is a jointly-funded, Federal-State health insurance programme for certain low-income and needy people. It covers 43m. individuals including children, the aged, blind, and/or disabled, and people who are eligible to receive federally-assisted income maintenance payments.

In Dec. 2001, 6·69m. persons were receiving Supplementary Security Income payments. 1,264,000 old-age persons received $4,664m. in benefits; 78,000 blind people received $398m.; and 5,345,000 disabled people received $27,103m. Payments, including supplemental amounts from various states, totalled $32,165m. in 2001.

In 2000 a total of $436,985m. was spent on cash and non-cash benefits (such as food stamps) for persons with limited incomes. In 2002 the food stamp programme helped 19,100,000 persons at a cost of $18,243m.; and 28·0m. persons received help from the national school lunch programme at a cost of $6,051m.

CULTURE

World Heritage Sites. There are 23 sites under American jurisdiction that appear on the UNESCO World Heritage List. They are (with year entered on list): Mesa Verde National Park, Colorado (1978); Yellowstone National Park, Wyoming/Idaho/Montana (1978); Wrangell-St Elias National Park and Preserve, Alaska (1979); Everglades National Park, Florida (1979); Grand Canyon National Park, Arizona (1979); Independence Hall, Pennsylvania (1979); Redwood National Park, California (1980); Mammoth Cave National Park, Kentucky (1981); Olympic National Park, Washington State (1981); Cahokia Mounds State Historic Site, Illinois (1982); Great Smoky Mountains National Park, North Carolina/Tennessee (1983); San Juan National Historic Site and La Fortaleza, Puerto Rico (1983); the Statue of Liberty, New York (1984); Yosemite National Park, California (1984); Monticello and the University of Virginia, Charlottesville, Virginia (1987); Chaco Culture National Historic Park, New Mexico (1987); Aztec Ruins National

Monument, New Mexico (1987); Hawaii Volcanoes National Park, including Mauna Loa, Hawaii (1987); Glacier Bay National Park and Preserve, Alaska (1992); Pueblo de Taos, New Mexico (1992); Carlsbad Caverns National Park, New Mexico (1995); Waterton-Glacier International Peace Park, Montana (1995).

Broadcasting. The licensing agency for broadcasting stations is the Federal Communications Commission, an independent federal body composed of five Commissioners appointed by the President. Its regulatory activities comprise: allocation of spectrum space; consideration of applications to operate individual stations; and regulation of their operations. In 2001 there were 10,778 commercial radio stations, 1,309 commercial TV stations, 377 non-commercial TV stations and 9,926 cable TV systems. Programming is targeted to appeal to a given segment of the population or audience taste. There are five national TV networks (three commercial; colour by NTSC) with 46 national cable networks. All major cities have network affiliates and additional commercial stations.

Legislation on the media and telecommunications of 1996 came into force on 31 March 1999 deregulating the market while preserving safeguards against over-concentration of individual ownership: a single company may not control a network reaching more than 35% of TV viewers, or produce a newspaper and a television service in the same market. Local companies are now permitted to operate long-distance telephone services and also cable TV services.

Broadcasting to countries abroad is conducted by The Voice of America, which functions under a seven-member council nominated by the President and reviewed by Congress. Voice of America has an annual audience of 94m. and broadcasts in over 50 languages.

In 2000 there were 598m. radio receivers in use, equivalent to 2,118 per 1,000 inhabitants. No other country averaged more than 1,500 radios per 1,000. There were 241m. TV receivers in use in 2000, equivalent to 854 per 1,000 inhabitants (a rate exceeded only in Bermuda). In 2001 there were 66·9m. cable TV subscribers.

Cinema. In 2002 there were 35,170 screens, including 634 drive-ins. Attendance in 2001 totalled 1,487m.; gross box office receipts came to $8·41bn. 628 full-length films were made in 1999.

Press. In 2002 there were 1,457 daily newspapers with a combined daily circulation of 55·2m., the second highest in the world behind Japan. There were 776 morning papers and 704 evening papers, plus 913 Sunday papers (circulation, 58·8m.). Unlike Japan, where circulation is rising, in the USA it has fallen since 1985, when daily circulation was 62·8m. The most widely read newspapers are *USA Today* (average daily circulation in March 2001 of 1·85m.), followed by the *Wall Street Journal* (1·82m.) and the *New York Times* (1·16m.).

Books published in 2001 totalled a record high 141,703, of which 17,349 were fiction, 16,555 sociology and economics, 9,582 juvenile and 9,359 technology. In 2001 US book sales totalled a record $25,463m.

Tourism. In 2001 the USA received 44,898,000 foreign visitors (50,945,000 in 2000), of whom 13,507,000 were from Canada and 9,558,000 from Mexico. 21% of all tourists were from Europe. Only France and Spain received more tourists than the USA in 2001.

In 2000 visitors to the USA spent approximately $85,153m. (excluding transportation paid to US international carriers). The USA has the highest annual revenue from tourists of any country (more than twice as much as Spain, which received the second most in 2000). Expenditure by US travellers in foreign countries for 2001 was an estimated $60,117m. (excluding transportation paid to foreign flag international carriers).

Festivals. There are major opera festivals at Cooperstown (Glimmerglass), New York State (July–Aug.); Santa Fe, New Mexico (June–Aug.); and Seattle, Washington (Aug.). Among the many famous film festivals are the Sundance Film Festival in Jan. and the New York Film Festival in late Sept./early Oct.

Museums and Galleries. Among the most famous museums are the National Gallery in Washington, D.C., the Museum of Fine Arts in Boston, the Metropolitan Museum, the Guggenheim Museum, and the Museum of Modern Art, all in New York, and the Museum of Art in Philadelphia. In 1997, 35% of US adults visited an art museum at least once.

DIPLOMATIC REPRESENTATIVES

Of the USA in the United Kingdom (24 Grosvenor Sq., London, W1A 1AE)
Ambassador: Vacant.
Chargé d'Affaires a.i.: David T. Johnson.

Of the United Kingdom in the USA (3100 Massachusetts Ave., NW, Washington, D.C., 20008)
Ambassador: Sir David Manning.

Of the United States to the United Nations
Ambassador: Vacant.
Chargé d'Affaires a.i.: Anne W. Patterson.

Of the United States to the European Union
Ambassador: Rockwell A. Schnabel.

FURTHER READING

OFFICIAL STATISTICAL INFORMATION

The Office of Management and Budget, Washington, D.C., 20503 is part of the Executive Office of the President; it is responsible for co-ordinating all the statistical work of the different Federal government agencies. The Office does not collect or publish data itself. The main statistical agencies are as follows:

(1) Data User Services Division, Bureau of the Census, Department of Commerce, Washington, D.C., 20233. Responsible for decennial censuses of population and housing, quinquennial census of agriculture, manufactures and business; current statistics on population and the labour force, manufacturing activity and commodity production, trade and services, foreign trade, state and local government finances and operations. (*Statistical Abstract of the United States*, annual, and others).

(2) Bureau of Labor Statistics, Department of Labor, 441 G Street NW, Washington, D.C., 20212. (*Monthly Labor Review* and others).

(3) Information Division, Economic Research Service, Department of Agriculture, Washington, D.C., 20250. (*Agricultural Statistics*, annual, and others).

(4) National Center for Health Statistics, Department of Health and Human Services, 3700 East-West Highway, Hyattsville, MD 20782. (*Vital Statistics of the United States*, monthly and annual, and others).

(5) Bureau of Mines Office of Technical Information, Department of the Interior, Washington, D.C., 20241. (*Minerals Yearbook*, annual, and others).

(6) Office of Energy Information Services, Energy Information Administration, Department of Energy, Washington, D.C., 20461.

(7) Statistical Publications, Department of Commerce, Room 5062 Main Commerce, 14th St and Constitution Avenue NW, Washington, D.C., 20230; the Department's Bureau of Economic Analysis and its Office of Industry and Trade Information are the main collectors of data.

(8) Center for Education Statistics, Department of Education, 555 New Jersey Avenue NW, Washington, D.C., 20208.

(9) Public Correspondence Division, Office of the Assistant Secretary of Defense (Public Affairs P.C.), The Pentagon, Washington, D.C., 20301-1400.

(10) Bureau of Justice Statistics, Department of Justice, 633 Indiana Avenue NW, Washington, D.C., 20531.

(11) Public Inquiry, APA 200, Federal Aviation Administration, Department of Transportation, 800 Independence Avenue SW, Washington, D.C., 20591.

(12) Office of Public Affairs, Federal Highway Administration, Department of Transportation, 400 7th St. SW, Washington, D.C., 20590.

(13) Statistics Division, Internal Revenue Service, Department of the Treasury, 1201 E St. NW, Washington, D.C., 20224.

Statistics on the economy are also published by the Division of Research and Statistics, Federal Reserve Board, Washington, D.C., 20551; the Congressional Joint Committee on the Economy, Capitol; the Office of the Secretary, Department of the Treasury, 1500 Pennsylvania Avenue NW, Washington, D.C., 20220.

OTHER OFFICIAL PUBLICATIONS

Economic Report of the President. Annual. Bureau of the Census. *Statistical Abstract of the United States*. Annual. *Historical Statistics of the United States, Colonial Times to 1970*.

United States Government Manual. Washington. Annual.

The official publications of the USA are issued by the US Government Printing Office and are distributed by the Superintendent of Documents, who issued in 1940 a cumulative *Catalogue of Public Documents of the Congress and of All Departments of the Government of the United States.* This *Catalog* is kept up to date by *United States Government Publications, Monthly Catalog* with annual index and supplemented by *Price Lists*. Each *Price List* is devoted to a special subject or type of material.

Treaties and other International Acts of the United States of America (Edited by Hunter Miller), 8 vols. Washington, 1929–48. This edition stops in 1863. It may be supplemented by *Treaties, Conventions, International Acts, Protocols and Agreements Between the US and Other Powers, 1776–1937* (Edited by William M. Malloy and others). 4 vols. 1909–38. A new Treaty Series, *US Treaties and Other International Agreements,* was started in 1950.

Writings on American History. Washington, annual from 1902 (except 1904–5 and 1941–47).

NON-OFFICIAL PUBLICATIONS

The Cambridge Economic History of the United States. vol. 1. CUP, 1996; vol. 2. CUP, 2000; vol. 3. CUP, 2000

Bacevich, Andrew J., *American Empire: The Realities and Consequences of US Diplomacy.* Harvard Univ. Press, 2002

Brogan, H., *The Longman History of the United States of America.* 2nd ed. Longman, London and New York, 1999

Daalder, Ivo H. and Lindsay, James M., *America Unbound: the Bush Revolution in Foreign Policy.* Brookings Institution Press, Washington, D.C., 2003

Duncan, Russell and Goddard, Joe, *Contemporary America.* 2nd ed. Palgrave Macmillan, Basingstoke, 2005

Fawcett, E. and Thomas, T., *America and the Americans.* London, 1983

Foner, E. and Garraty, J. A. (eds.) *The Reader's Companion to American History.* New York, 1992

Haass, Richard, *The Reluctant Sheriff: The United States After the Cold War.* New York, 1998

Herstein, S. R. and Robbins, N., *United States of America.* [Bibliography] ABC-Clio, Oxford and Santa Barbara (CA), 1982

Jenkins, Philip, *A History of the United States.* 2nd ed. Palgrave Macmillan, Basingstoke, 2002

Jennings, F., *The Creation of America*. CUP, 2000

Jentleson, B. W. and Paterson, T. G. (eds.) *Encyclopedia of US Foreign Relations*. 4 vols. OUP, 1997

Little, Douglas, *American Orientalism: The United States and the Middle East since 1945.* Univ. of North Carolina Press, 2002

Lord, C. L. and E. H., *Historical Atlas of the US.* Rev. ed. New York, 1969

Merriam, L. A. and Oberly, J. (eds.) *United States History: an Annotated Bibliography.* Manchester Univ. Press, 1995

Morison, S. E. with Commager, H. S., *The Growth of the American Republic.* 2 vols. 5th ed. OUP, 1962–63

Norton, M. B., *People and Nation: the History of the United States.* 4th ed. 2 vols. New York, 1994

Peele, Gillian, Bailey, Christopher, J., Cain, Bruce and Peters, B. Guy (eds.) *Developments in American Politics 4.* Palgrave Macmillan, Basingstoke, 2002

Pfucha, F. P., *Handbook for Research in American History: a Guide to Bibliographies and Other Reference Works.* 2nd ed. Nebraska Univ. Press, 1994

Prestowitz, Clyde, *Rogue Nation: American Unilateralism and the Failure of Good Intentions.* Basic Books, New York, 2003

Zunz, Oliver, *Why the American Century?* Univ. of Chicago Press, 1999

Who's Who in America. Annual

National library: The Library of Congress, Independence Ave. SE, Washington, D.C., 20540. *Librarian:* James H. Billington.

National statistical office: Bureau of the Census, Washington, D.C., 20233. *Director:* Louis Kincannon.

Website: http://www.census.gov

STATES AND TERRITORIES

GENERAL DETAILS

Against the names of the Governors, Lieut.-Governors and the Secretaries of State, (D.) stands for Democrat and (R.) for Republican.

See also Local Government on page 1777.

FURTHER READING

Official publications of the various states and insular possessions are listed in the *Monthly Check-List of State Publications*, issued by the Library of Congress since 1910.

The Book of the States. Biennial. Council of State Governments, Lexington, 1953 ff.

State Government Finances. Annual. Dept. of Commerce, 1966 ff.
Bureau of the Census. *State and Metropolitan Area Data Book*. Irregular.—*County and City Data Book*. Irregular.
Hill, K. Q., *Democracy in the 50 States*. Nebraska Univ. Press, 1995

ALABAMA

KEY HISTORICAL EVENTS

The early European explorers were Spanish, but the first permanent European settlement was French, as part of French Louisiana after 1699. During the 17th and 18th centuries the British, Spanish and French all fought for control of the territory; it passed to Britain in 1763 and thence to the USA in 1783, except for a Spanish enclave on Mobile Bay, which lasted until 1813. Alabama was organized as a Territory in 1817 and was admitted to the Union as a state on 14 Dec. 1819.

The economy was then based on cotton, grown in white-owned plantations by black slave labour imported since 1719. Alabama seceded from the Union at the beginning of the Civil War (1861) and joined the Confederate States of America; its capital Montgomery became the Confederate capital. After the defeat of the Confederacy the state was re-admitted to the Union in 1878. Attempts made during the reconstruction period to find a role for the newly freed black slaves—who made up about 50% of the population—largely failed, and when whites regained political control in the 1870s a strict policy of segregation came into force. At the same time Birmingham began to develop as an important centre of iron- and steel-making. Most of the state was still rural. In 1915 a boll-weevil epidemic attacked the cotton and forced diversification into other farm produce. More industries developed from the power schemes of the Tennessee Valley Authority in the 1930s. The black population remained mainly rural, poor and without political power, until the 1960s when confrontations on the issue of civil rights produced reforms.

TERRITORY AND POPULATION

Alabama is bounded in the north by Tennessee, east by Georgia, south by Florida and the Gulf of Mexico and west by Mississippi. Land area, 50,744 sq. miles (131,426 sq. km). Census population, 1 April 2000, 4,447,100 (55·4% urban), an increase of 10·1% since 1990; July 2004 estimate, 4,530,182.

Population in five census years was:

	White	*Black*	*Indian*	*Asiatic*	*Total*	*Per sq. mile*
1930	1,700,844	944,834	465	105	2,646,248	51·3
			All others			
1970	2,533,831	903,467	6,867		3,444,165	66·7
1980	2,872,621	996,335	24,932		3,893,888	74·9
1990	2,975,797	1,020,705	44,085		4,040,587	79·6
2000	3,162,808	1,155,930	128,362		4,447,100	87·6

Of the total population in 2000, 2,300,596 were female, 3,323,678 were 18 years old or older and 2,462,673 were urban. In 2000 the Hispanic population was 75,830, up from 24,629 in 1990 (an increase of 207·9%).

The large cities (2000 census) were: Birmingham, 242,820 (metropolitan area, 921,106); Montgomery (the capital), 201,568 (333,055); Mobile, 198,905 (540,258); Huntsville, 158,216 (342,376); Tuscaloosa, 77,906 (164,875).

SOCIAL STATISTICS

Births, 2002, 58,967 (13·1 per 1,000 population); deaths, 46,069 (10·3); infant deaths, 2001, 9·4 per 1,000 live births; marriages, 2002, 44,158 (9·8); divorces, 24,059 (5·3).

CLIMATE

Birmingham, Jan. 46°F (7·8°C), July 80°F (26·7°C). Annual rainfall 54" (1,372 mm). Mobile, Jan. 52°F (11·1°C), July 82°F (27·8°C). Annual rainfall 62" (1,575 mm). Montgomery, Jan. 49°F (9·4°C), July 81°F (27·2°C). Annual rainfall 52" (1,321 mm). The growing season ranges from 190 days (north) to 270 days (south). Alabama belongs to the Gulf Coast climate zone (*see* UNITED STATES: Climate).

CONSTITUTION AND GOVERNMENT

The present constitution dates from 1901; it has had 742 amendments (as at April 2005). The legislature consists of a Senate of 35 members and a House of

Representatives of 105 members, all elected for four years. The Governor and Lieut.-Governor are elected for four years.

For the 109th Congress, which convened in Jan. 2005, Alabama sends seven members to the House of Representatives. It is represented in the Senate by Richard Shelby (D. 1987–94; R. 1994–2011) and Jeff Sessions (R. 1997–2009).

Applicants for registration must take an oath of allegiance to the United States and fill out an application showing evidence that they meet State voter registration requirements.

Montgomery is the capital.

RECENT ELECTIONS

In the 2004 presidential election Bush polled 1,176,394 votes; Kerry, 693,933; Nader, 6,701.

CURRENT ADMINISTRATION

Governor: Bob Riley (R.), 2003–07 (salary: $96,361).

Lieut.-Governor: Lucy Baxley (D.), 2003–07 ($48,870).

Secretary of State: Nancy Worley (D.), 2003–07 ($72,000).

Government Website: http://www.alabama.gov

ECONOMY

Per capita income (2002) was $25,096.

Budget. In 2002 total state revenue was $14,942m. Total expenditure was $17,996m. (education, $6,811m.; public welfare, $4,110m.; highways, $1,256m.; hospitals, $1,118m.; health, $718m.) Outstanding debt, in 2002, $6,405m.

Performance. Gross State Product was $125,567m. in 2002, ranking Alabama 25th in the United States.

ENERGY AND NATURAL RESOURCES

Oil and Gas. In 2001 Alabama produced 9·3m. bbls. of crude petroleum.

Water. The total area covered by water is approximately 1,675 sq. miles.

Minerals. Principal minerals, 1999–2000 (in net 1,000 tons): limestone, 41,766; coal, 20,317; sand and gravel, 7,846. Value of non-fuel mineral production (2002) was $968m.

Agriculture. The number of farms in 2002 was 47,000, covering 8·9m. acres; the average farm had 189 acres and was valued at $1,698 per acre.

Cash receipts from farm marketings, 2002: crops, $584m.; livestock and poultry products, $2,378m.; total, $2,962m. The net farm income in 2001 was $1,581m. Principal sources: broilers, cattle and calves, eggs, hogs, dairy products, greenhouse and nursery products, peanuts, soybeans, cotton and vegetables. In 2002 broilers accounted for the largest percentage of cash receipts from farm marketings; cattle and calves were second, eggs third, cotton fourth.

Forestry. Alabama had 22·99m. acres of forested land in 2002 of which 647,000 acres were national forest. Area of commercial timberland, 2002, 22,325,022 acres, of which 629,022 acres were public forests and 21,696,000 acres private forests. Harvest volumes in 1995, 294·12m. cu. ft softwood saw timber, 78·63m. cu. ft hardwood saw timber, 744·47m. cu. ft paper fibre and 11·74m. cu. ft poles. Total harvest, 1994, was 1,128·9m. cu. ft. The estimated delivered timber value of forest products in 1994 was $1,359m.

INDUSTRY

In 2001 the state's 5,200 manufacturing establishments had 312,000 employees, earning $10,202m. Alabama is both an industrial and service-oriented state. The chief industries are lumber and wood products, food and kindred products, textiles and apparel, non-electrical machinery, transportation equipment and primary metals.

Labour. In 2002, 1,895,200 were employed in non-agricultural sectors, of whom 481,800 were in services; 434,700 in trade; 353,500 in government; 328,800 in manufacturing; 104,300 in construction; 92,600 in transport and public utilities. In

2003 the total labour force numbered 2,147,400, of whom 5·8% (124,700) were unemployed. A seasonally adjusted calculation for Dec. 2003 numbered the labour force at 2,163,000, with 126,100 (5·8%) unemployed. Average weekly earnings were $547·69 in Dec. 2002.

COMMUNICATIONS

Roads. Total road length in 2002 was 94,435 miles, comprising 73,466 miles of rural road and 20,969 miles of urban road. Registered motor vehicles, 2002, 4,427,999.

Rail. In 2001 the railways had a length of 4,728 miles including side and yard tracks.

Civil Aviation. In 1997 the state had 98 public-use airports. Eight airports are for commercial service, three are relief airports for Birmingham and the rest general aviation. There were 2,492,179 passenger enplanements in 2000.

Shipping. There are 1,600 miles of navigable inland water and 50 miles of Gulf Coast. The only deep-water port is Mobile, with a large ocean-going trade; total tonnage (1997), 36·3m. tons. The Alabama State Docks also operates a system of ten inland docks; there are several privately run inland docks.

SOCIAL INSTITUTIONS

Justice. In 2003 there were 385 law enforcement agencies and six state agencies employing 10,414 sworn and 5,306 civilian people. There were 194,334 offences reported in 2003 of which 18% were cleared by arrest. Total property value stolen in 2003 was $251,864,387 of which 18% was recovered. In total, for past and present felony and misdemeanour crimes, there were 27,156 people arrested for Part I offences, 183,012 for Part II offences, 16,524 for drug violations and 30,905 for alcohol violations. There were 297 homicides in 2003. As of 30 Sept. 2003 there were 27,727 people in prison or community-based facilities of which 190 were on death row awaiting execution. There were also 39,265 people on probation and/or parole. Following the reinstatement of the death penalty by the US Supreme Court in 1976 death sentences have been awarded since 1983. There were three executions in 2003 and two in 2004.

In 41 counties the sale of alcoholic beverage is permitted, and in 26 counties it is prohibited; but it is permitted in eight cities within those 26 counties. Draught beverages are permitted in 22 counties.

Religion. Membership in selected religious bodies (in 1993): Southern Baptist Convention (1,049,441), Black Baptist (estimated 315,331), United Methodist Church (264,968), African Methodist Episcopal Zion Church (134,305), Roman Catholic (137,834 adherents), Churches of Christ (91,660), Assemblies of God (38,442).

Education. In the school year 1996–97 the 1,333 public elementary and high schools required 44,942 teachers to teach 717,284 students enrolled in grades K-12. In 1995–96 there were 16 public senior institutions with 127,465 students and 4,887 faculty members. As of autumn 1998–99 the 19 community colleges had 73,432 students and 4,811 faculty members; two public junior colleges had 3,465 students and 257 faculty members; nine public technical colleges had 8,686 students and 652 faculty members.

Health. In 2001 there were 107 community hospitals with 16,600 beds. A total of 684,000 patients were admitted during the year.

Welfare. Medicare enrolment in July 2002 totalled 705,555. In 2000 a total of 619,480 people in Alabama received Medicaid. In Dec. 2003 there were 867,601 Old-Age, Survivors, and Disability Insurance (OASDI) beneficiaries. A total of 42,052 people were receiving payments under Temporary Assistance for Needy Families (TANF) in Sept. 2002.

CULTURE

Tourism. In 2001 tourists spent approximately $6·1bn. in Alabama, representing an increase of 1% over 2000 spending.

FURTHER READING

Alabama Official and Statistical Register. Montgomery. Quadrennial
Alabama County Data Book. Alabama Dept. of Economic and Community Affairs. Annual
Directory of Health Care Facilities. Alabama State Board of Health
Economic Abstract of Alabama. Center for Business and Economic Research, Univ. of Alabama, 2000

ALASKA

KEY HISTORICAL EVENTS

Discovered in 1741 by Vitus Bering, Alaska's first settlement, on Kodiak Island, was in 1784. The area known as Russian America with its capital (1806) at Sitka was ruled by a Russo-American fur company and vaguely claimed as a Russian colony. Alaska was purchased by the United States from Russia under the treaty of 30 March 1867 for $7·2m. Settlement was boosted by gold workers in the 1880s. In 1884 Alaska became a 'district' governed by the code of the state of Oregon. By Act of Congress approved 24 Aug. 1912 Alaska became an incorporated Territory; its first legislature in 1913 granted votes to women, seven years in advance of the Constitutional Amendment.

During the Second World War the Federal government acquired large areas for defence purposes and for the construction of the strategic Alaska Highway. In the 1950s oil was found. Alaska became the 49th state of the Union on 3 Jan. 1959. In the 1970s new oilfields were discovered and the Trans-Alaska pipeline was opened in 1977. The state obtained most of its income from petroleum by 1985.

Questions of land-use predominate; there are large areas with valuable mineral resources, other large areas held for the native peoples and some still held by the Federal government. The population increased by over 400% between 1940 and 1980.

TERRITORY AND POPULATION

Alaska is bounded north by the Beaufort Sea, west and south by the Pacific and east by Canada. The total area is 663,267 sq. miles (1,717,854 sq. km), making it the largest state of the USA; 571,951 sq. miles (1,481,346 sq. km) are land and 91,316 sq. miles (236,507 sq. km) are water. It is also the least densely populated state. Census population, 1 April 2000, was 626,932, an increase of 14·0% over 1990; July 2004 estimate, 655,435.

Population in five census years was:

	White	*Black*	*All Others*	*Total*	*Per sq. mile*
1950	92,808	...	35,835	128,643	0·23
1970	236,767	8,911	54,704	300,382	0·53
1980	309,728	13,643	78,480	401,851	1·00
1990	415,492	22,451	112,100	550,043	1·00
2000	434,534	21,787	170,611	626,932	1·10

Of the total population in 2000, 324,1212 were male, 436,215 were 18 years old or older and 411,257 were urban. Alaska's Hispanic population was 24,795 in 2000, up from 17,803 in 1990. As of July 2003, 19% of Alaska's population was identified as Alaska Native or American Indian.

The largest county equivalent and city is in the borough of Anchorage, which had a 2000 census population of 260,283. Census populations of the other 14 county equivalents, 2000: Fairbanks North Star, 82,840; Matanuska-Susitna, 59,322; Kenai Peninsula, 49,691; Juneau, 30,711; Bethel, 16,006; Ketchikan Gateway, 14,070; Kodiak Island, 13,913; Valdez-Cordova, 10,195; Nome, 9,196; Sitka, 8,835; North Slope, 7,385; Northwest Arctic, 7,208; Wade Hampton, 7,028; Wrangell-Petersburg, 6,684. Largest incorporated places in 2000 were: Anchorage, 260,683; Juneau, 30,711; Fairbanks, 30,224; Sitka, 8,335; Ketchikan, 7,922; Kenai, 6,942; Kodiak, 6,334; Bethel, 5,471; Wasilla, 5,469; Barrow, 4,581.

SOCIAL STATISTICS

Births, 2002, 9,938 (15·4 per 1,000 population); deaths, 3,030 (4·7—the lowest rate in any US state). 2001: infant mortality rate, 8·1 per 1,000 live births. 2001: marriages, 5,100; divorces, 2,600.

CLIMATE

Anchorage, Jan. 12°F (–11·1°C), July 57°F (13·9°C). Annual rainfall 15" (371 mm). Fairbanks, Jan. –11°F (–23·9°C), July 60°F (15·6°C). Annual rainfall 12" (300 mm). Sitka, Jan. 33°F (0·6°C), July 55°F (12·8°C). Annual rainfall 87" (2,175 mm). Alaska belongs to the Pacific Coast climate zone (*see* UNITED STATES: Climate).

CONSTITUTION AND GOVERNMENT

The state has the right to select 103·55m. acres of vacant and unappropriated public lands in order to establish 'a tax basis'; it can open these lands to prospectors for minerals, and the state is to derive the principal advantage in all gains resulting from the discovery of minerals. In addition, certain federally administered lands reserved for conservation of fisheries and wild life have been transferred to the state. Special provision is made for federal control of land for defence in areas of high strategic importance.

The constitution of Alaska was adopted by public vote, 24 April 1956. The state legislature consists of a Senate of 20 members (elected for four years) and a House of Representatives of 40 members (elected for two years).

For the 109th Congress, which convened in Jan. 2005, Alaska sends one member to the House of Representatives. It is represented in the Senate by Ted Stevens (R. 1968–2009) and Lisa Murkowski (R. 2002–11). The franchise may be exercised by all citizens over 18.

The capital is Juneau.

RECENT ELECTIONS

In the 2004 presidential election Bush polled 190,889 votes; Kerry, 111,025; Nader, 5,069.

CURRENT ADMINISTRATION

Governor: Frank Murkowski (R.), Dec. 2002–Dec. 2006 (salary: $85,776).

Lieut.-Governor: Loren Leman (R.), 2003–07 ($80,040).

Government Website: http://www.state.ak.us

ECONOMY

Per capita personal income (2002) was $31,792.

Budget. In 2002 total state revenue was $5,019m. Total expenditure was $7,402m. (education, $1,567m.; public welfare, $1,151m.; highways, $687m.; government administration, $365m.; natural resources, $240m.) Outstanding debt, in 2002, $5,308m.

Performance. 2002 Gross State Product was $29,708m., ranking Alaska 46th in the United States.

ENERGY AND NATURAL RESOURCES

Oil and Gas. Alaska ranks second behind Texas among the leading oil producers in the USA, with 18% of the national total. Commercial production of crude petroleum began in 1959 and by 1961 had become the most important mineral by value. Production: 2001, 351m. bbls. Proven reserves in 2000 were 4,861m. bbls. Oil comes mainly from Prudhoe Bay, the Kuparuk River field and several Cook Inlet fields. Revenue to the state from petroleum in 2003 was $1,947·6m. (84% of general fund revenues). General fund unrestricted oil revenue collections in 2003: royalty and bonus, $840·3m.; severance tax, $599·0m.; corporate income tax, $151·1m.; property tax, $48·7m. In 2001, 471bn. cu. ft of natural gas was produced. Natural gas (liquid) production, 1997, 35m. bbls. Proven reserves as at 31 Dec. 1997, 631m. bbls.

Oil from the Prudhoe Bay Arctic field is now carried by the Trans-Alaska pipeline to Prince William Sound on the south coast, where a tanker terminal has been built at Valdez.

Water. The total area covered by water is approximately 44,856 sq. miles.

Minerals. Estimated value of production, 2003, in $1,000: zinc, 486,916; gold, 191,986; industrial minerals (including sand, gravel and building stone), 100,000;

silver, 90,773; lead, 70,094; coal, 37,975; peat, 175. Total 2003 value, $980·3m. Value of non-fuel mineral production (2002), $1,030m.

Agriculture. In some parts of the state the climate during the brief spring and summer (about 100 days in major areas and 152 days in the southeastern coastal area) is suitable for agricultural operations, thanks to the long hours of sunlight, but Alaska is a food-importing area. In 2002 there were 590 farms covering a total of 920,000 acres. The average farm had 1,559 acres in 2002 and was valued at $367 per acre.

Farm income, 2001: crops, $24m.; livestock and products, $28m. The net farm income in 2001 was $10m.

In 2002 there were 12,609 cattle and calves, 530 sheep and lambs, 1,200 hogs and pigs, and 2,900 poultry. There were about 15,000 reindeer in Alaska in 2002. Sales of reindeer meat and by-products in 2002 were valued at $453,000.

Forestry. Of the 126·87m. forested acres of Alaska, 10·46m. acres are national forest land. The interior forest covers 115m. acres; more than 13m. acres are considered commercial forest, of which 3·4m. acres are in designated parks or wilderness and unavailable for harvest. The coastal rain forests provide the bulk of commercial timber volume; of their 13·6m. acres, 7·6m. acres support commercial stands, of which 1·9m. acres are in parks or wilderness and unavailable for harvest. In 1992, 590m. bd ft of timber were harvested from private land for a total value of $548·9m., and in 1993, 9·38m. bd ft from state land for $342·6m.

There are 662 designated wilderness areas throughout the USA, covering a total of 105·7m. acres (42·8m. ha). More than 55% of the system is in Alaska (58·2m. acres or 23·5m. ha).

Fisheries. In 2002 commercial fishing landed 5,066m. lb of fish and shellfish at a value of $811·5m. The most important species are salmon, crab, herring, halibut and pollock.

INDUSTRY

In 2003 the state's 549 manufacturing establishments had 11,000 employees, earning $339m. The largest manufacturing sectors are wood processing, seafood products and printing and publishing.

Labour. Total non-agricultural employment, 2001, 290,000. Employees by branch, 2001: government, 79,000; services, 73,000; wholesale and retail trade, 58,000. With a rate of 7·7%, Alaska had the highest unemployment rate in the USA in 2002.

COMMUNICATIONS

Roads. Alaska's highway and road system, 2002, totalled 14,117 miles comprising 1,844 miles of urban road and 12,273 miles of rural road. Registered motor vehicles, 2002, 620,415.

The Alaska Highway extends 1,523 miles from Dawson Creek, British Columbia, to Fairbanks, Alaska. It was built by the US Army in 1942, at a cost of $138m. The greater portion of it, because it lies in Canada, is maintained by Canada.

Rail. There is a railway from Skagway to the town of Whitehorse, the White Pass and Yukon route, in the Canadian Yukon region (this service operates seasonally, although only the section between Skagway and Carcross is in service). The government-owned Alaska Railroad runs from Seward to Fairbanks. This is a freight service with only occasional passenger use. In 2003 there were 466 miles of main line and 59 miles of branch line.

Civil Aviation. Alaska's largest international airports are Anchorage and Fairbanks. In 1999 Alaska Airlines flew 209·2m. km, carrying 13,604,000 passengers (1,530,300 on international flights). There were 2,748,019 passenger enplanements statewide in 2000. General aviation aircraft in the state per 1,000 population is about ten times the US average.

Shipping. Regular shipping services to and from the USA are furnished by two steamship and several barge lines operating out of Seattle and other Pacific coast ports. A Canadian company also furnishes a regular service from Vancouver, BC. Anchorage is the main port.

A 1,435 nautical-mile ferry system for motor cars and passengers (the 'Alaska Marine Highway') operates from Bellingham, Washington and Prince Rupert

(British Columbia) to Juneau, Haines (for access to the Alaska Highway) and Skagway. A second system extends throughout the south-central region of Alaska linking the Cook Inlet area with Kodiak Island and Prince William Sound.

SOCIAL INSTITUTIONS

Justice. The death penalty was abolished in Alaska in 1957. In Oct. 2004 the prison population totalled 4,886.

Religion. Many religions are represented, including Roman Catholic, Southern Baptist, Mormon, Lutheran and other denominations.

Education. Total expenditure on public schools in 2003 was $1·4bn. In 2003 there were 8,100 public school teachers; average salary, 2002–03, $49,694. In 2003 there were 133,000 pupils enrolled at public schools. The University of Alaska (founded in 1922) main campuses had (autumn 1993) 33,087 students. Other colleges had 2,718 students in autumn 1993.

Health. In 2001 there were 19 community hospitals with 1,400 beds. A total of 49,000 patients were admitted during the year.

Welfare. Medicare enrolment in July 2002 totalled 45,788. In 2000 a total of 96,432 people in Alaska received Medicaid. In Dec. 2003 there were 60,860 Old-Age, Survivors, and Disability Insurance (OASDI) beneficiaries. A total of 15,940 people were receiving payments under Temporary Assistance for Needy Families (TANF) in Sept. 2002.

CULTURE

Tourism. About 1·35m. non-residents visited the state in 1997–98, spending nearly $1bn.

FURTHER READING

Statistical Information: Department of Commerce and Economic Development, Economic Analysis Section, POB 110804, Juneau 99811. Publishes *The Alaska Economy Performance Report.*

Alaska Industry–Occupation Outlook to 1995. Department of Labor, Juneau, 1992.
Annual Financial Report. Department of Administration, Juneau.
Falk, Marvin W., *Alaska.* [Bibliography] ABC-Clio, Oxford and Santa Barbara (CA), 1995
Naske, C.-M. and Slotnick, H. E., *Alaska: a History of the 49th State.* 2nd ed. Univ. of Oklahoma Press, 1995

State library: POB 110571, Juneau, Alaska 99811-0571.

ARIZONA

KEY HISTORICAL EVENTS

Spaniards looking for sources of gold or silver entered Arizona in the 16th century, finding there people from several Native American groups, including Tohono O'odham, Navajo, Hopi and Apache. The first Spanish Catholic mission was founded in the early 1690s by Father Eusebio Kino, settlements were made in 1752 and a Spanish army headquarters was set up at Tucson in 1776. The area was governed by Mexico after the collapse of Spanish colonial power. Mexico ceded it to the USA in the Treaty of Guadelupe Hidalgo after the Mexican-American war (1848). Arizona was then part of New Mexico; the Gadsen Purchase (of land south of the Gila River) was added to it in 1853. The whole was organized as the Arizona Territory on 24 Feb. 1863.

Miners and ranchers began settling in the 1850s. Conflicts between Indian and immigrant populations intensified when troops were withdrawn to serve in the Civil War. The Navajo surrendered in 1865, but the Apache continued to fight, under Geronimo and other leaders, until 1886. Arizona was admitted to the Union as the 48th state in 1912.

Large areas of the state have been retained as Indian reservations and as parks to protect the exceptional desert and mountain landscape. In recent years this landscape and the Indian traditions have been used to attract tourist income.

TERRITORY AND POPULATION

Arizona is bounded north by Utah, east by New Mexico, south by Mexico, west by California and Nevada. Land area, 113,634 sq. miles (294,313 sq. km). Of the total area in 1992, 28% was Indian Reservation, 17% was in individual or corporate ownership, 19% was held by the US Bureau of Land Management, 15% by the US Forest Service, 13% by the State and 8% by others. Census population on 1 April 2000 was 5,130,632, an increase of 40·0% over 1990. July 2004 estimate, 5,743,834. The rate of Arizona's population increase during the 1990s was the second fastest in the USA, at 40%. Nevada is the only state to have had faster growth.

Population in six census years:

	White	*Black*	*American Indian*	*Chinese*	*Japanese*	*Total*	*Per sq. mile*
1910	171,468	2,009	29,201	1,305	371	204,354	1·8
1930	378,551	10,749	43,726	1,110	879	435,573	3·8
1960	1,169,517	43,403	83,387	2,937	1,501	1,302,161	11·3
				All others			
1980	2,260,288	74,159	162,854	383,768		2,718,215	23·9
1990	2,963,186	110,524	203,527	387,991		3,665,228	32·3
2000	3,873,611	158,873	255,879	842,269		5,130,632	45·2

Of the total population in 2000, 2,561,057 were female, 3,763,685 were 18 years old or older and 4,523,535 were urban. Arizona's Hispanic population was 1,295,617 in 2000 (25·3%) up from 739,861 in 1990 (an increase of 88·2%).

In 2000 the population of Phoenix was 1,321,045; Tucson, 486,699; Mesa, 396,375; Glendale, 218,812; Scottsdale, 202,705; Chandler, 176,581; Tempe, 158,625; Gilbert, 109,697; Peoria, 108,364; Yuma, 77,515. The Phoenix–Mesa metropolitan area had a 2000 census population of 3,251,876.

SOCIAL STATISTICS

In 2002: births, 87,837 (16·1 per 1,000); deaths, 42,816 (7·8 per 1,000); infant deaths, 2001, 6·9 per 1,000 live births; marriages, 2000, 40,630; dissolutions of marriages, 23,440.

CLIMATE

Phoenix, Jan. 53·6°F (12°C), July 93·5°F (34°C). Annual rainfall 7·66" (194 mm). Yuma, Jan. 56·5°F (13·6°C), July 93·7°F (34·3°C). Annual rainfall 3·17" (80 mm). Flagstaff, Jan. 28·7°F (–1·8°C), July 66·3°F (19·1°C). Annual rainfall 22·8" (579 mm). Arizona belongs to the Mountain States climate zone (*see* UNITED STATES: Climate).

CONSTITUTION AND GOVERNMENT

The state constitution (1911, with 129 amendments) placed the government under direct control of the people through the initiative, referendum and the recall provisions. The state Senate consists of 30 members, and the House of Representatives consists of 60, all elected for two years.

For the 109th Congress, which convened in Jan. 2005, Arizona sends eight members to the House of Representatives. It is represented in the Senate by John McCain (R. 1987–2011) and Jon Kyl (R. 1995–2007).

The state capital is Phoenix. The state is divided into 15 counties.

RECENT ELECTIONS

In the 2004 presidential election Bush polled 1,104,294 votes; Kerry, 893,524; Badnarik, 11,856.

CURRENT ADMINISTRATION

Governor: Janet Napolitano (D.), 2003–07 (salary: $95,000).

Secretary of State: Janice K. Brewer (R.), 2003–07 ($70,000).

Government Website: http://www.az.gov

ECONOMY

Per capita income in 2002 was $26,157.

Budget. In 2002 total state revenue was $17,298m. Total expenditure was $18,119m. (education, $6,327m.; public welfare, $3,437m.; highways, $1,680m.; correction, $734m.; health, $656m.) Outstanding debt, in 2002, $4,348m.

Performance. Gross State Product was $171,781m. in 2002, ranking Arizona 22nd in the United States.

ENERGY AND NATURAL RESOURCES

Primary energy sources are coal (43%), nuclear (41%) and hydropower (13%).

Electricity. As of 1998, 34 power generating plants were located in Arizona, 14 in Maricopa County. The plants are operated by eight public power entities.

Oil and Gas. In 2000 oil production totalled 57,483 bbls. from 21 producing wells. Gas totalled 368m. cu. ft from nine producing wells.

Water. The total area covered by water is approximately 364 sq. miles.

Minerals. The mining industry historically has been and continues to be a significant part of the economy. By value the most important mineral produced is copper. Production in 1999 was 1,213,000 tons. Most of the state's silver and gold are recovered from copper ore. Other minerals include sand and gravel, molybdenum, coal and gemstones. Value of non-fuel mineral production in 2002 was $1,920m.

Agriculture. Arizona, despite its dry climate, is well suited for agriculture along the water-courses and where irrigation is practised on a large scale from great reservoirs constructed by the USA as well as by the state government and private interests. Irrigated area in 2002 was 931,735 acres. The wide pasture lands are favourable for the rearing of cattle and sheep, but numbers are either stationary or declining compared with 1920.

In 2002 Arizona contained 7,300 farms and ranches and the total farm and pastoral area was 26·5m. acres; in 2000 there were 1,344,091 acres of crop land. In 2002 the average farm was 3,630 acres (the second largest average size in the USA after Wyoming) and was valued at $398 per acre. Farming is highly commercialized and mechanized and concentrated largely on cotton picked by machines.

Area under cotton in 2000: upland cotton, 280,000 acres (791,000 bales harvested); American Pima cotton, 5,000 acres (7,200 bales harvested).

In 2001 the cash income from crops was $1,409m., and from livestock and products $1,166m. The net farm income in 2001 was $1,004m. Most important cereals are wheat, corn and barley; most important crops include cotton, citrus fruit, lettuce, broccoli, grapes, cauliflower, melons, onions, potatoes and carrots. In 2001 there were 850,000 cattle, 132,000 sheep, 90,000 hogs and 34,000 goats.

Forestry. The state had a forested area of 19,427,000 acres in 2002, of which 8,223,000 acres were national forest.

INDUSTRY

In 2001 the state's 4,937 manufacturing establishments had 194,000 employees, earning $7,917m. Total value added by manufacturing in 2001 was $28,430m.

Labour. In the first quarter of 2001 (preliminary data) the state had 117,318 employers with an average of 2,258,199 employees earning an average quarterly wage of $8,260. The unemployment rate in 2002 was 6·2%.

COMMUNICATIONS

Roads. In 2002 there were 57,165 miles of roads comprising 19,590 miles of urban road and 37,575 miles of rural road; there were 3,939,581 registered vehicles.

Civil Aviation. In 2001 there were 6,194 registered aircraft and 318 landing facilities of which 218 were airports (including 87 for public use) and 100 were heliports. There were 19,056,204 passenger enplanements statewide in 2000.

SOCIAL INSTITUTIONS

Justice. A 'right-to-work' amendment to the constitution, adopted 5 Nov. 1946, makes illegal any concessions to trade-union demands for a 'closed shop'.

At 30 Sept. 2001 the Arizona state prison held 25,374 male and 2,077 female prisoners. Chain gangs were reintroduced into prisons in 1995. The death penalty is authorized. There were three executions in 2000 but none since then.

Religion. The leading religious bodies are Roman Catholics and Latter-day Saints (Mormons); others include United Methodists, Presbyterians, Baptists, Lutherans, Episcopalians, Eastern Orthodox, Jews and Muslims.

Education. School attendance is compulsory between the ages of six and 16. In 1999–2000, K-12 enrolment numbered 835,404 students. There are 222 school districts containing 1,024 elementary schools and 195 high schools. Charter schools first opened their doors in 1995. There are 261 charter schools providing parents and students with expanded educational choices. In 1999–2000 the total funds appropriated by the state legislature for all education, including the Board of Regents and community colleges, was $3,304,468,400. The state maintains three universities: the University of Arizona (Tucson) with an enrolment of 35,000 in 2001; Arizona State University (three campuses) with 50,000; Northern Arizona University (Flagstaff) with 19,728.

Health. In 2001 there were 78 hospitals; capacity 10,798 beds; 15,258 licensed physicians; 3,062 dentists; 47,213 registered nurses and 9,237 licensed practical nurses.

Welfare. Old-age assistance (maximum depending on the programme) is given to needy citizens 65 years of age or older through the federal supplemental security income (SSI) programme. In Dec. 2000 SSI payments went to 13,196 aged, and 68,297 disabled and blind (average of $387·11 each). In Sept. 2001, 100,618 individuals received Cash Assistance for an average $110·03 each. Cash Assistance cases numbering 39,059 received an average of $283·45 each.

CULTURE

Tourism. In 1999 Arizona had 28m. visitors and 368,045 tourism-related jobs. The state's tourism industry generates about $30bn. in economic activity each year.

FURTHER READING

Statistical information: College of Business and Public Administration, Univ. of Arizona, Tucson 85721. Publishes *Arizona Statistical Abstract.*

Alexander, David V., *Arizona Frontier Military Place Names: 1846–1912.* Las Cruces, NM, 1998

Arizona Commission of Indian Affairs. *Resource Directory, 1997/98.* Phoenix, 1998

Arizona Department of Commerce. *Community Profiles.* Phoenix, 1999

Arizona Department of Health Services, Center for Health Statistics. *Arizona Health Status and Vital Statistics, 1998.* Phoenix, 2000

Arizona Historical Society. *1999/2000 Official Directory, Arizona Historical Museums and Related Support Organizations.* Tucson, 1999

August, Jack L., *Vision in the Desert: Carl Hayden and the Hydropolitics in the American Southwest.* Texas Christian Univ. Press, Fort Worth, 1999

Leavengood, Betty, *Lives Shaped by Landscape: Grand Canyon Women.* Pruett Co., Boulder, 1999

Office of the Secretary of State. *Arizona Blue Book, 1997–98.* 1998

Shillingberg, William B., *Tombstone, A. T.: A History of Early Mining, Milling and Mayhem.* Arthur H. Clark Co., Spokane, 1999

State Government Website: http://www.az.gov/webapp/portal/

Arizona State Library, Archives & Public Records (ASLAPR) Website: http://www.lib.az.us

ARKANSAS

KEY HISTORICAL EVENTS

In the 16th and 17th centuries French and Spanish explorers entered Arkansas, finding there tribes of Chaddo, Osage and Quapaw. The first European settlement was French, at Arkansas Post in 1686, and the area became part of French Louisiana. The USA bought Arkansas from France as part of the Louisiana Purchase in 1803, it was organized as a Territory in 1819 and entered the Union on 15 June 1836 as the 25th state.

The eastern plains by the Mississippi were settled by white plantation-owners who grew cotton with black slave labour. The rest of the state attracted a scattered population of small farmers. The plantations were the centre of political power.

Arkansas seceded from the Union in 1861 and joined the Confederate States of America. At that time the slave population was about 25% of the total.

In 1868 the state was re-admitted to the Union. Attempts to integrate the black population into state life achieved little, and a policy of segregation was rigidly adhered to until the 1950s. In 1957 federal authorities ordered that high school segregation must end. The state governor called on the state militia to prevent desegregation; there was rioting, and federal troops entered Little Rock, the capital, to restore order. It was another ten years before school segregation finally ended.

The main industrial development followed the discovery of large reserves of bauxite.

TERRITORY AND POPULATION

Arkansas is bounded north by Missouri, east by Tennessee and Mississippi, south by Louisiana, southwest by Texas and west by Oklahoma. Land area, 52,068 sq. miles (134,855 sq. km). Census population on 1 April 2000 was 2,673,400, an increase of 13·7% from that of 1990. July 2004 estimate, 2,752,629.

Population in five census years was:

	White	*Black*	*Indian*	*Asiatic*	*Total*	*Per sq. mile*
1910	1,131,026	442,891	460	472	1,574,449	30·0
1960	1,395,703	388,787	580	1,202	1,786,272	34·0
			All others			
1980	1,890,332	373,768	22,335		2,286,435	43·9
1990	1,944,744	373,912	32,069		2,350,725	45·1
2000	2,138,598	418,950	115,852		2,673,400	51·3

Of the total population in 2000, 1,368,707 were female, 1,993,031 were 18 years old or older and 1,404,179 were urban. In 2000 the Hispanic population of Arkansas was 86,866, up from 19,876 in 1990. The increase of 337% was the second largest increase in the USA over the same period.

Little Rock (capital) had a population of 183,183 in 2000; Fort Smith, 80,268; North Little Rock, 60,433; Fayetteville, 58,047; Jonesboro, 55,515; Pine Bluff, 55,085; Springdale, 45,798; Conway, 43,167. The population of the largest metropolitan statistical areas in 2000 was: Little Rock–North Little Rock, 583,845; Fayetteville–Springdale–Rogers, 311,121; Fort Smith, 207,290; Texarkana, 129,749; Pine Bluff, 84,278.

SOCIAL STATISTICS

Births, 2002, were 37,437 (13·8 per 1,000); deaths, 28,513 (10·5 per 1,000). 2001: infant mortality rate (per 1,000 live births), 8·3. 2001: marriages, 38,400; divorces, 17,100.

CLIMATE

Little Rock, Jan. 39·9°F, July 84°F. Annual rainfall 52·4". Arkansas belongs to the Gulf Coast climate zone (*see* UNITED STATES: Climate).

CONSTITUTION AND GOVERNMENT

The General Assembly consists of a Senate of 35 members elected for four years, partially renewed every two years, and a House of Representatives of 100 members elected for two years. The sessions are biennial and usually limited to 60 days. The Governor and Lieut.-Governor are elected for four years.

For the 109th Congress, which convened in Jan. 2005, Arkansas sends four members to the House of Representatives. It is represented in the Senate by Blanche Lincoln (D. 1999–2011) and Mark Pryor (D. 2003–09).

The state is divided into 75 counties; the capital is Little Rock.

RECENT ELECTIONS

In the 2004 presidential election Bush polled 572,898 votes; Kerry, 469,953; Nader, 6,171.

CURRENT ADMINISTRATION

Governor: Mike Huckabee (R.), 2003–07 (salary 2005–06: $78,915).

Lieut.-Governor: Winthrop Rockefeller (R.), 2003–07 ($38,141).

Secretary of State: Charlie Daniels (D.), 2003–07 ($49,321).

Government Website: http://www.state.ar.us

ECONOMY

Per capita personal income (2002) was $23,417.

Budget. In 2002 total revenue was $10,297m. Total expenditure was $11,521m. (education, $4,375m.; public welfare, $2,578m.; highways, $1,079m.; hospitals, $455m.; government administration, $411m.) Outstanding debt, in 2002, $3,002m.

Performance. 2002 Gross State Product was $71,929m., ranking Arkansas 34th in the United States.

Banking and Finance. In 1993–94 total bank deposits were $22,107·8m.

ENERGY AND NATURAL RESOURCES

Oil and Gas. 2001 production of crude oil was 8m. bbls.; natural gas, 467bn. cu. ft.

Water. The total area covered by water is approximately 1,107 sq. miles.

Minerals. The U.S. Bureau of Mines estimated Arkansas' mineral value in 1992 at $287m. Mining employment totalled 3,600 in Oct. 1992. Crushed stone was the leading mineral commodity produced, in terms of value, followed by bromine. Value of domestic non-fuel mineral production in 2002 was $543m.

Agriculture. In 2002, 48,500 farms had a total area of 14·6m. acres; average farm was 301 acres and was valued at $1,469 per acre. 7·46m. acres were harvested cropland. Arkansas ranked first in the production of broilers in 2002 (1,182m. birds) and in the acreage and production of rice (46·2% of US total production) and third in turkeys (28·5m. birds).

Farm income, 2001: crops, $1,625m.; livestock and products, $3,507m. The net farm income in 2001 was $1,400m.

Forestry. In 2002 the state had a forested area of 18,771,000 acres, of which 2,483,000 acres were national forest.

INDUSTRY

In 2001 the state's 3,226 manufacturing establishments had 229,000 employees, earning $6,462m. Total value added by manufacturing in 2001 was $19,868m.

Labour. Total non-agricultural employment, 2001, 1,156,000. Employees by branch, 2001 (in 1,000): services, 280; wholesale and retail trade, 267; manufacturing, 241; government, 194. The unemployment rate in 2002 was 5·4%.

COMMUNICATIONS

Roads. Total road mileage (2002), 98,482 miles—urban, 10,801; rural, 87,681; there were 1,872,750 registered motor vehicles.

Rail. In 2003 there were in the state 2,750 miles of commercial railway. In 2002 rail service was provided by three Class I (1,893 miles) and 23 short-line (Class III) railways (857 miles).

Civil Aviation. In Oct. 1994, seven air carriers and two commuter airlines served the state; there were 175 airports (96 public-use and 79 private). There were 1,676,235 passenger enplanements statewide in 2000.

Shipping. There are about 1,000 miles of navigable rivers, including the Mississippi, Arkansas, Red, White and Ouachita Rivers. The Arkansas River/Kerr-McClellan Channel flows diagonally eastward across the state and gives access to the sea via the Mississippi River.

SOCIAL INSTITUTIONS

Justice. In June 2002 there were 12,655 federal and state prisoners. In 1996, 524,000 violent crimes were committed and a total of 4,175,000 property crimes. The death penalty is authorized. There was one execution in 2003 and one in 2004.

Religion. Main Protestant churches in 1990: Southern Baptist (617,524), United Methodist (197,402), Church of Christ (86,502), Assembly of God (55,438). Roman Catholics (1990), 72,952.

Education. In the school year 1992–93 public elementary and secondary schools had 440,682 enrolled pupils and 25,771 classroom teachers. Average salary of teachers in elementary schools was $25,771, junior high $27,492 and high $27,760.

Higher education is provided at 34 institutions: nine state universities, one medical college, 12 private or church colleges, 12 community or two-year branch colleges and 12 technical colleges. Total enrolment in institutions of higher education in the autumn of 1993 was 99,344.

In the autumn of 1993 there were two vocational-training schools and nine technical institutes with 28,261 students.

Health. In 2001 there were 83 community hospitals with 9,500 beds. A total of 371,000 patients were admitted during the year.

Welfare. Medicare enrolment in July 2002 totalled 446,152. In 2000 a total of 489,325 people in Arkansas received Medicaid. In Dec. 2003 there were 543,727 Old-Age, Survivors, and Disability Insurance (OASDI) beneficiaries. A total of 27,032 people were receiving payments under Temporary Assistance for Needy Families (TANF) in Sept. 2002.

CULTURE

Broadcasting. An educational TV network provides 24-hour a day telecasting; it had five transmitters in 2000.

FURTHER READING

Statistical information: Arkansas Institute for Economic Advancement, Univ. of Arkansas at Little Rock, Little Rock 72204. Publishes *Arkansas State and County Economic Data.*
Agricultural Statistics for Arkansas. Arkansas Agricultural Statistics Service, Little Rock. Annual
Current Employment Developments. Dept. of Labor, Little Rock. Monthly
Statistical Summary for the Public Schools of Arkansas. Dept. of Education, Little Rock. Annual

CALIFORNIA

KEY HISTORICAL EVENTS

There were many small Indian tribes, but no central power, when the area was discovered in 1542 by the Spanish navigator Juan Cabrillo. The Spaniards did not begin to establish missions until the 18th century, when the Franciscan friar Junipero Serra settled at San Diego in 1769. The missions became farming and ranching villages with large Indian populations. When the Spanish empire collapsed in 1821, the area was governed from newly independent Mexico.

The first wagon-train of American settlers arrived from Missouri in 1841. In 1846, during the war between Mexico and the USA, Americans in California proclaimed it to be part of the USA. The territory was ceded by Mexico on 2 Feb. 1848 and became the 31st state of the Union on 9 Sept. 1850.

Gold was discovered in 1848–49 and there was an immediate influx of population. The state remained isolated, however, until the development of railways in the 1860s. From then on the population doubled on average every 20 years. The sunny climate attracted fruit-growers, market-gardeners and wine producers. In the early 20th century the bright lights and cheap labour attracted film-makers to Hollywood, Los Angeles.

Southern California remained mainly agricultural with an Indian or Spanish-speaking labour force until after the Second World War. Now more than 90% of the population is urban, with the main manufacture being hi-technology equipment, much of it for the aerospace, computer and office equipment industries.

TERRITORY AND POPULATION

Land area, 155,959 sq. miles (403,932 sq. km). Census population, 1 April 2000, 33,871,648, an increase of 4,111,627, or 13·8%, over 1990. July 2004 estimate, 35,893,799. The growth rate reflects continued high though somewhat reduced natural increase (excess of births over deaths) as well as substantial net immigration.

Population in five census years was:

	White	*Black*	*Japanese*	*Chinese*	*Total (incl. all others)*	*Per sq. mile*
1910	2,259,672	21,645	41,356	36,248	2,377,549	15·2
1930	5,408,260	81,048	97,456	37,361	5,677,251	36·4
1960	14,455,230	883,861	157,317	95,600	15,717,204	100·8
	White	*Black*	*Asian/other*	*Hispanic*	*Total*	*Per sq. mile*
1990	20,524,327	2,208,801	7,026,893	7,687,938	29,760,021	190·8
2000	20,170,059	2,263,882	11,437,707	10,966,556	33,871,648	217·2

Of the total population in 2000, 16,996,756 (50·2%) were female, 24,621,819 were 18 years old or older and 31,989,663 were urban (94·44%, the highest of the states).

In addition to having the highest population of any state in the USA, California has the largest Hispanic population of any state in terms of numbers and the second largest in terms of percentage of population. In 2000 there were 10,966,556 Hispanics living in California (32·4% of the overall population), representing a rise of 3,278,618 since 1990, the largest numeric rise of any state over the same period. By 2020 Hispanics are projected to form a majority.

The 50 largest cities with 2004 population estimates are:

Los Angeles	3,912,200	Huntington Beach	198,800	Corona	141,800
San Diego	1,294,000	San Bernardino	196,300	Escondido	140,500
San Jose	926,200	Oxnard	186,100	Orange	136,700
San Francisco	792,700	Oceanside	173,300	Fullerton	134,200
Long Beach	487,100	Irvine	171,800	Sunnyvale	131,700
Fresno	456,100	Garden Grove	171,000	Palmdale	131,300
Sacramento	441,000	Ontario	167,900	Lancaster	129,200
Oakland	411,600	Santa Clarita	164,900	Thousand Oaks	126,100
Santa Ana	349,100	Pomona	158,400	Concord	124,900
Anaheim	343,000	Moreno Valley	155,100	El Monte	123,500
Bakersfield	279,700	Fontana	154,800	Vallejo	121,100
Riverside	277,000	Rancho Cucamonga	154,800	Simi Valley	118,800
Stockton	269,100	Santa Rosa	154,400	Inglewood	117,600
Chula Vista	209,100	Salinas	152,200	Costa Mesa	113,000
Fremont	209,100	Torrance	146,200	Downey	112,800
Modesto	206,200	Hayward	144,600	West Covina	111,400
Glendale	205,300	Pasadena	144,000		

Metropolitan areas (2000 census): Los Angeles–Riverside–Orange County, 16,373,645; San Francisco–Oakland–San Jose, 7,039,362; San Diego, 2,813,833; Sacramento–Yolo, 1,796,857; Fresno, 922,516.

SOCIAL STATISTICS

Births in 2002, 529,357 (15·1 per 1,000 population); deaths, 234,565 (6·7 per 1,000 population); infant deaths 2001, 5·4 per 1,000 live births. Marriages (2003), 194,914.

CLIMATE

Los Angeles, Jan. 58°F (14·4°C), July 74°F (23·3°C). Annual rainfall 15" (381 mm). Sacramento, Jan. 45°F (7·2°C), July 76°F (24·4°C). Annual rainfall 18" (457 mm). San Diego, Jan. 57°F (13·9°C), July 71°F (21·7°C). Annual rainfall 10" (259 mm). San Francisco, Jan. 51°F (10·6°C), July 59°F (15°C). Annual rainfall 20" (508 mm). Death Valley, Jan. 52°F (11°C), July 100°F (38°C). Annual rainfall 1·6" (40 mm). California belongs to the Pacific Coast climate zone (*see* UNITED STATES: Climate).

CONSTITUTION AND GOVERNMENT

The present constitution became effective from 4 July 1879; it has had numerous amendments since 1962. The Senate is composed of 40 members elected for four years—half being elected every two years—and the Assembly, of 80 members, elected for two years. Two-year regular sessions convene in Dec. of each even numbered year. The Governor and Lieut.-Governor are elected for four years.

For the 109th Congress, which convened in Jan. 2005, California sends 53 members to the House of Representatives. It is represented in the Senate by Dianne Feinstein (D. 1993–2007) and Barbara Boxer (D. 1993–2011).

The capital is Sacramento. The state is divided into 58 counties.

RECENT ELECTIONS

In the 2004 presidential election Kerry polled 6,745,485 votes and Bush 5,509,826 votes. Badnarik came third with 50,165.

In the 2003 special election Arnold Schwarzenegger polled 4,206,284 votes and Cruz Bustamante polled 2,724,874.

Governor Gray Davis was the first statewide officeholder to be recalled in California. In the Statewide Special Election held on 7 Oct. 2003, 55·4% of Californians voted to remove Davis from the office, while 44·6% voted against the recall. With this outcome, Davis became only the second governor in United States history to be recalled from office. Republican Arnold Schwarzenegger won the replacement vote by a wide margin. The election results were certified on 14 Nov. 2003 and Governor Schwarzenegger was sworn into office on 17 Nov.

CURRENT ADMINISTRATION

Governor: Arnold Schwarzenegger (R.), Nov. 2003–Jan. 2007 (salary: $175,000).

Lieut.-Governor: Cruz Bustamante (D.), 2003–07 ($131,250).

Secretary of State: Bruce McPherson (R.), 2005–07 ($131,250).

Attorney General: Bill Lockyer (D.), 2003–07 ($148,750).

Government Website: http://www.ca.gov

ECONOMY

Per capita personal income (2002) was $32,898.

Budget. For the year ending 30 June 2004, total state revenues were $96·2bn. Total expenditures were $97·2bn. (education, $39·2bn.; health and human services, $26·8bn.; youth and adult corrections, $5·4bn.) Debt outstanding (2004) $33·0bn.

Performance. California's economy, the largest among the 50 states and one of the largest in the world, has major components in high technology, trade, entertainment, agriculture, manufacturing, tourism, construction and services. California experienced an economic recession in 2001 and a sluggish recovery in 2002, with greatest impacts in the high technology sector. The economic recovery, however, broadened and strengthened in 2003 and improved considerably in 2004. Personal income was up 5·4% from a year earlier in the first half of 2004. Made-in-California merchandise exports began to turn around in the fourth quarter of 2003 after falling by 26% in the preceding three years. In the first three quarters of 2004 exports were 20% higher than a year earlier. If California were a country in its own right it would be the world's seventh largest economy, after the USA, Japan, Germany, the United Kingdom, France and Italy. 2003 Gross State Product was $1,446,430m., the highest in the United States and representing more than 13% of the USA's total GDP. Taxable sales in 2003 totalled $460,097m.

Banking and Finance. In 1997 there were 9,796 establishments of depository institutions which included 5,740 commercial banks, 2,626 savings institutions and 1,306 credit unions.

In 2003 savings and loan associations had deposits of $231,071m. Total mortgage loans were $340,861m. On 31 Dec. 2003 all insured commercial banks had demand deposits of $37,844m. and time and savings deposits of $302,404m. Total loans reached $344,729m., of which real-estate loans were $248,152m. Credit unions had assets totalling $95,935m. and total loans outstanding were $58,066m.

ENERGY AND NATURAL RESOURCES

Electricity. Californians spent $20bn. on electricity in 1999. Total consumption amounted to 260,936m. kWh. 75% of electricity is derived from in-state resources. In Jan. 2001 Governor Gray Davis announced a state of emergency after power shortages led to a series of blackouts.

Oil and Gas. California is the nation's third largest oil producing state. Total onshore and offshore production was 257m. bbls. in 2002. California ranks tenth out of US states for the production of natural gas. Net natural gas production in 2002 was 322bn. cu. ft.

Water. The total area covered by water is approximately 2,895 sq. miles. Water quality is judged to be good along 83% of the 960 miles of assessed coastal shoreline.

Minerals. Gold output was 5,284 kg in 2003. Asbestos, boron minerals, diatomite, sand and gravel, lime, salt, magnesium compounds, clays, cement, silver, gypsum and iron ore are also produced.

In 2003 California ranked first among the states in non-fuel mineral production, accounting for more than 9% of the US total. The value of non-fuel minerals produced (2003) was $3·2bn.; the mining industry employed around 22,000 persons in 2003 (compared to 48,000 in the early 1980s).

Agriculture. California is the most diversified agricultural economy in the world, producing more than 350 agricultural commodities. It is by far the largest agricultural producer and exporter in the United States. The state grows more than half of the nation's total of fruits, nuts and vegetables. Many of these commodities are specialty crops and almost solely produced in California. There were, in 2003, 78,500 farms, comprising 27·1m. acres; average farm, 345 acres, valued at $3,526 per acre (2002). The net farm income in 2001 was $3,769m. In 2003 income from marketings reached $27·8bn. Fruit and nut cash receipts, at $7·84bn., were 1% above the previous year and comprised 27% of the total. Vegetable receipts increased 6% from $6·58bn. in 2002 to $6·96bn. in 2003 and comprised 24% of the total. Livestock and poultry receipts jumped 12% and also comprised 24% of the total. California's three leading commodities in cash receipts are milk with $4·03bn., nursery products with $2·44bn. and grapes with $2·30bn.

Production of cotton lint, 2000, was 578,200 short tons; other field and seed crops included (in 1m. short tons): hay and alfalfa, 9; sugarbeet, 2; rice, 2; wheat, 1. Principal fruit, nut and vegetable crops in 2001 (in 1,000 short tons): tomatoes, 9,183; wine, table and raisin grapes, 5,962; lettuce, 3,623; oranges, 2,044; lemons, 859; almonds, 415; grapefruit, 211.

In 2001 there were 1·6m. milch cows; 5·2m. all cattle and calves; 0·84m. sheep and lambs; and 0·15m. hogs and pigs.

Forestry. In 2002 California had 40·23m. acres of forested land, of which 18,515,000 acres were national forest. There are about 16·6m. acres of productive forest land, from which about 2,900m. bd ft are harvested annually. Total value of timber harvest, 2002, $452m. ($576m. in 2001). Lumber production, 2002, 1,690m. bd ft.

Fisheries. The catch in 2003 was 274m. lb; leading species in landings were squid, sardine, crab, urchin, mackerel, sole, salmon, tuna, herring and whiting.

INDUSTRY

In 2003 the fastest-growing industries were in public and private education, retail trade, health services, social services, management consulting and engineering. California achieved better employment levels in 2004. The improvement was primarily as a result of better job growth in construction, trade, transportation and utilities, and information. Limiting the improvement in job growth in 2004 were larger declines in government employment and smaller gains in employment in the financial sector.

Labour. In 2003 the civilian labour force was 17·5m., of whom 16·3m. were employed. A total of 47,600 jobs were lost during 2003, led by computer and electronic product manufacturing, information and management of companies and enterprises. Unemployment rate held steady at 6·7% in 2003.

INTERNATIONAL TRADE

Imports and Exports. Estimated foreign trade through Californian ports totalled $350bn. in 2003. Exports of made-in-California goods increased in 2003 after falling by 23% in the preceding two years. High technology goods dominate California's exports, comprising almost three-quarters of all made-in-California exports. Electronic components and computers account for almost half of total exports.

Total agricultural exports for 2002 were $6·5bn. California's top markets are Canada, European Union, Japan, Hong Kong, Mexico, South Korea, Taiwan, Indonesia, India and Malaysia.

COMMUNICATIONS

Roads. In 2003 California had 71,260 miles of roads inside cities and 98,320 miles outside. There were about 20·5m. registered cars and about 6·8m. commercial vehicles. Motor vehicle collision fatalities in 2003 were 5,714.

Rail. In addition to Amtrak's long-distance trains, local and medium-distance passenger trains run in the San Francisco Bay area sponsored by the California Department of Transportation, and a network of commuter trains around Los Angeles opened in 1992. There are metro and light rail systems in San Francisco and Los Angeles, and light rail lines in Sacramento, San Diego and San Jose.

Civil Aviation. In 2003 there were a total of 939 public and private airports, heliports, stolports and seaplane bases.

A total of 54,970,030 passengers (14,623,903 international; 40,346,127 domestic) embarked/disembarked at Los Angeles airport in 2003. It handled approximately 2,022,076 tonnes of freight (987,864 international; 1,034,212 domestic). At San Francisco airport, in 2003, 28,786,385 passengers (6,695,151 international; 22,091,234 domestic) embarked/disembarked, and 483,413 tonnes of freight (282,574 tonnes international; 200,839 tonnes domestic) were handled. There were 69,396,153 passenger enplanements in 2003.

Shipping. The chief ports are San Francisco and Los Angeles.

SOCIAL INSTITUTIONS

Justice. A 'three strikes law', making 25-years-to-life sentences mandatory for third felony offences, was adopted in 1994 after an initiative (i.e. referendum) was 72% in favour. However, the state's Supreme Court ruled in June 1996 that judges may disregard previous convictions in awarding sentences. In 2004 there were 32 adult prisons. State prisons, 30 June 2004, had 152,859 male and 10,641 female inmates. In June 2004 there were some 3,932 juveniles in custody. As of 30 Nov. 2004 there were 7,527 adults serving 'three strikes' sentences. The death penalty has been authorized following its reinstatement by the US Supreme Court in 1976. Death sentences have been passed since 1980. The first execution since 2002 was carried out in Jan. 2005.

Religion. There is a strong Roman Catholic presence. There were 739,000 Latter-day Saints (Mormons) in 1998.

Education. Full-time attendance at school is compulsory for children from six to 18 years of age for a minimum of 175 days per annum. In autumn 2003 there were 6·9m. pupils enrolled in both public and private elementary and secondary schools. Total state expenditure on public education, 2002–03, was $39·2bn.

Community colleges had 1,631,629 students in autumn 2003.

California has two publicly-supported higher education systems: the University of California (1868) and the California State University and Colleges. In autumn 2003 the University of California, with campuses for resident instruction and research at Berkeley, Los Angeles (UCLA), San Francisco and six other centres, had 208,391 students. California State University and Colleges with campuses at Sacramento, Long Beach, Los Angeles, San Francisco and 15 other cities had 407,530 students. In addition to the 28 publicly-supported institutions for higher education there are 117 private colleges and universities which had a total estimated enrolment of 322,018 in the autumn of 2003.

Health. In 2001 there were 384 community hospitals; capacity, 73,200 beds. A total of 3,332,000 patients were admitted in 2001. On 30 June 2001 state hospitals for the mentally disabled had 4,814 patients.

Welfare. On 1 Jan. 1974 the federal government (Social Security Administration) assumed responsibility for the Supplemental Security Income/State Supplemental Program which replaced the State Old-Age Security. The SSI/SSP provides financial assistance for needy aged (65 years or older), blind or disabled persons. An individual recipient may own assets up to $2,000; a couple up to $3,000, subject to specific exclusions. In 2002–03 fiscal year an average of 95,477 cases per month were receiving an average of $230 in assistance in the general relief programme.

CULTURE

Tourism. The travel and tourism industry provides 5·4% of the state's $1·4trn. economy. Visitors in 2003 spent $78·2bn. generating $3·2bn. in state and local tax revenues. California was the state most visited by overseas travellers in 2003, with

3·9m. overseas visitors—25% of the market share. In 2002 there were 316m. person trips, 309m. from within the United States and 8m. from abroad.

FURTHER READING

California Government and Politics. Hoeber, T. R., *et al*, (eds.) Sacramento, Annual
California Statistical Abstract. 45th ed. Dept. of Finance, Sacramento, 2004
Economic Report of the Governor. Dept. of Finance, Sacramento, Annual
Bean, W. and Rawls, J. J., *California: an Interpretive History.* 6th ed. New York, 1993
Gerston, L. N. and Christensen, T., *California Politics and Government: a Practical Approach.* 3rd ed. New York, 1995

State Library: The California State Library, Library-Courts Bldg, Sacramento 95814.

COLORADO

KEY HISTORICAL EVENTS

Spanish explorers claimed the area for Spain in 1706; it was then the territory of the Arapaho, Cheyenne, Ute and other Plains and Great Basin Indians. Eastern Colorado, the hot, dry plains, passed to France in 1802 and then to the USA as part of the Louisiana Purchase in 1803. The rest remained Spanish, becoming Mexican when Spanish power in the Americas ended. In 1848, after war between Mexico and the USA, Mexican Colorado was ceded to the USA. A gold rush in 1859 brought a great influx of population, and in 1861 Colorado was organized as a Territory. The Territory officially supported the Union in the Civil War of 1861–65, but its settlers were divided and served on both sides.

Colorado became a state in 1876. Mining and ranching were the mainstays of the economy. In the 1920s the first large projects were undertaken to exploit the Colorado River. The Colorado River Compact was agreed in 1922, and the Boulder Dam (now Hoover Dam) was authorized in 1928. Since then irrigated agriculture has overtaken mining as an industry and is as important as ranching. In 1945 the Colorado-Big Thompson project diverted water by tunnel beneath the Rocky Mountains to irrigate 700,000 acres (284,000 ha) of northern Colorado. Now more than 80% of the population is urban, with the majority engaged in telecommunications, aerospace and computer technology.

TERRITORY AND POPULATION

Colorado is bounded north by Wyoming, northeast by Nebraska, east by Kansas, southeast by Oklahoma, south by New Mexico and west by Utah. Land area, 103,718 sq. miles (268,628 sq. km).

Census population, 1 April 2000, 4,301,261, an increase of 30·6% over 1990. In July 2004 the Census Bureau estimate was 4,601,403.

Population in five census years was:

	White	*Black*	*Indian*	*Asiatic*	*Total*	*Per sq. mile*
1910	783,415	11,453	1,482	2,674	799,024	7·7
1950	1,296,653	20,177	1,567	5,870	1,325,089	12·7
			All others			
1980	2,571,498	101,703	216,763		2,889,964	27·9
1990	2,905,474	133,146	255,774		3,294,394	31·8
2000	3,560,005	165,063	576,193		4,301,261	41·5

Of the total population in 2000, 2,165,983 were male, 3,200,466 were 18 years old or older and 3,633,185 were urban. The Hispanic population in 2000 was 735,601, up from 424,302 in 1990 (an increase of 73·4%). Large cities, with 2001 populations: Denver City, 560,365; Colorado Springs, 369,853; Aurora, 283,650; Lakewood, 144,426; Fort Collins, 122,521; Pueblo, 103,030; Westminster, 102,905; Arvada, 102,470.

Main metropolitan areas (2001): Denver–Boulder–Greeley, 2,660,666; Colorado Springs, 533,526; Fort Collins–Loveland, 259,707; Pueblo, 144,383.

SOCIAL STATISTICS

Births, 2002, were 68,418 (15·2 per 1,000 population); deaths, 29,210 (6·5); infant deaths, 2001, 5·8 per 1,000 live births; marriages, 2000, 36,104 (8·4 per 1,000 population); divorces, 20,063.

CLIMATE

Denver, Jan. 31°F (–0·6°C), July 73°F (22·8°C). Annual rainfall 14" (358 mm). Pueblo, Jan. 30°F (–1·1°C), July 83°F (28·3°C). Annual rainfall 12" (312 mm). Colorado belongs to the Mountain States climate zone (*see* UNITED STATES: Climate).

CONSTITUTION AND GOVERNMENT

The constitution adopted in 1876 is still in effect with (1989) 115 amendments. The General Assembly consists of a Senate of 35 members elected for four years, one-half retiring every two years, and of a House of Representatives of 65 members elected for two years. Sessions are annual, beginning 1951. Qualified as electors are all citizens, male and female (except convicted, incarcerated criminals), 18 years of age, who have resided in the state and the precinct for 32 days immediately preceding the election. There is a seven-member State Supreme Court.

For the 109th Congress, which convened in Jan. 2005, Colorado sends seven members to the House of Representatives. It is represented in the Senate by Wayne Allard (R. 1997–2009) and Ken Salazar (D. 2005–11).

The capital is Denver. There are 64 counties.

RECENT ELECTIONS

In the 2004 presidential election Bush polled 1,101,255 votes; Kerry, 1,001,732; Nader, 12,718.

CURRENT ADMINISTRATION

Governor: Bill Owens (R.), 2003–07 (salary: $90,000).

Lieut.-Governor: Jane Norton (R.), 2003–07 ($68,500).

Secretary of State: Donetta Davidson (R.), 2003–07 ($68,500).

Government Website: http://www.colorado.gov

ECONOMY

Per capita personal income (2002) was $33,170.

Budget. In 2002 total revenue was $11,809m. and total expenditure $16,823m. Major areas of expenditure were: education, $5,798m.; public welfare, $3,132m.; highways, $1,421m.; health, $793m; correction, $734m. Debt outstanding, in 2002, was $5,419m.

Performance. 2002 Gross State Product was $179,410m., ranking Colorado 21st in the United States.

Banking and Finance. There are 180 commercial banks insured with the Federal Deposit Insurance Corporation, with $47,631m. in total assets.

ENERGY AND NATURAL RESOURCES

Oil and Gas. In 2001 Colorado produced 803bn. cu. ft of natural gas and 19·2m. bbls. of crude oil. It ranked sixth in the USA for daily gas production, and eleventh in crude oil production. Total production value of all hydrocarbons was $3·05bn.

Water. The Rocky Mountains of Colorado form the headwaters for four major American rivers: the Colorado, Rio Grande, Arkansas and Platte. The total area covered by water is approximately 371 sq. miles.

Minerals. Coal (2001): 33·4m. short tons were produced. In 2001 there were 14,000 people employed in mining, including 8,300 in extracting oil and natural gas. Value of non-fuel minerals, $576m.

Agriculture. In 2002 farms and ranches numbered 30,000, with a total of 31·3m. acres of agricultural land. 5,748,610 acres were harvested crop land; average farm, 1,043 acres. Average value of farmland and buildings per acre in 2002 was $756. Farm income 2001: from crops, $1,354m.; from livestock and products, $3,374m. The net farm income in 2001 was $990m.

Production of principal crops in 2001: corn for grain, 149·8m. bu.; wheat for grain, 69·2m. bu.; barley for grain, 8·6m. bu.; hay, 4,780,000 tons; dry beans, 1,785,000 cwt; oats and sorghum, 11·4m. bu.; sugarbeets, 824,000 tons; potatoes, 23,274,000 cwt; vegetables, 9,523 tons; fruits, 21,900 tons.

In 2001 the number of farm animals was: 3,050,000 cattle, 91,000 milch cows, 780,000 swine and 370,000 sheep.

Forestry. The state had a forested area of 21,637,000 acres in 2002, of which 10,561,000 acres were national forest.

INDUSTRY

In 2001, 2,233,400 were employed in non-agricultural sectors, of which 692,400 were in services; 527,300 in trade; 346,800 in government; 198,500 in manufacturing; 145,800 in construction; 144,500 in finance and insurance; 144,000 in transportation and communications; 14,000 in mining. In manufacturing in 2002 the biggest sub-sectors were: non-electrical machinery, 28,800; food products, 25,400; printing and publishing, 24,900; instruments, 20,500; and electrical machinery, 16,700.

Labour. In 2002 the total labour force was estimated at 2,369,600 of which 2,243,400 were employed. The unemployment rate stood at 5·3%.

Trade Unions. In 2000, 9% of all wage and salary workers were members of unions, compared to a national average of 13·5%. Among manufacturing workers, only 6·6% belonged to labour unions.

INTERNATIONAL TRADE

Imports and Exports. In 2001 Colorado exported $6·1bn. in goods. The largest trading partners were Canada, Japan, Germany, United Kingdom, China (including Hong Kong), Mexico and France. Largest export categories are electronic integrated circuits and microassemblies, automatic data processing machines, components for office machines, measuring instruments and medical devices.

Trade Fairs. The National Western Stock Show and Rodeo is the largest event of its kind in the USA, drawing over 600,000 visitors.

COMMUNICATIONS

Roads. In 2002 there were 86,310 miles of road (9,100 miles state highway agency), of which 15,044 miles were urban roads and 71,266 miles rural roads. There were 2,150,556 motor vehicle registrations in 2002.

Rail. There were 2,747 miles of railway in 2002.

Civil Aviation. In 2000 there were 79 airports open to the public; 17 with commercial service, 62 public non-commercial (general aviation) and 14 private non-commercial. There were 19,475,488 passenger enplanements statewide in 2000.

Telecommunications. Colorado is headquarters to Qwest Communications and AT&T Broadband and Internet Services. Other major communications employers are Level 3 Communications, Avaya and MCIWorldCom.

SOCIAL INSTITUTIONS

Justice. In 2002 there were 18,382 federal and state prisoners. The death penalty is authorized but has not been used since 1997.

Religion. In 1984 the Roman Catholic Church had 550,300 members; the ten main Protestant denominations had 350,900 members; the Jewish community had 45,000 members. Buddhism is among other religions represented.

Education. In 2001 the public elementary and secondary schools had 742,145 pupils, 41,104 teachers (1999); teachers' salaries averaged $36,291. Enrolments in four-year state universities and colleges in 2000 were: University of Colorado at Boulder, 25,458 students; University of Colorado at Denver, 11,328; University of Colorado at Colorado Springs, 6,581; University of Colorado Health Sciences Centre, 2,358; Colorado State University (Fort Collins), 22,939; University of Northern Colorado (Greeley), 10,926; Colorado School of Mines (Golden), 3,287; Metropolitan State College of Denver, 16,773; Colorado State University-Pueblo (was University of Southern Colorado), 4,085; Mesa State College (Grand Junction), 4,893; Fort Lewis College (Durango), 4,260; Adams State College (Alamosa), 2,511; Western State College of Colorado (Gunnison), 2,456.

2000 total enrolments: private four-year universities and colleges, 23,000; two-year colleges, 80,168; all universities and colleges, 221,023.

Health. In 2001 there were 66 community hospitals with 9,400 beds. A total of 413,000 patients were admitted during the year.

Welfare. Medicare enrolment in July 2002 totalled 483,706. In 2000 a total of 380,964 people in Colorado received Medicaid. In Dec. 2003 there were 557,253 Old-Age, Survivors, and Disability Insurance (OASDI) beneficiaries. A total of 32,458 people were receiving payments under Temporary Assistance for Needy Families (TANF) in Sept. 2002.

CULTURE

Broadcasting. There are 97 commercial and public radio stations, broadcasting on both AM and FM frequencies. There are also 14 commercial and four public television stations.

Press. There are 27 daily newspapers. In addition there are 41 weekly newspapers including seven regional business journals.

Tourism. Skiing is a major tourist attraction. Colorado is particularly renowned for the Rocky Mountain National Park and the Mesa Verde National Park, a World Heritage Site.

FURTHER READING

Statistical information: Business Research Division, Univ. of Colorado, Boulder 80309. Publishes *Statistical Abstract of Colorado.*

Griffiths, M. and Rubright, L., *Colorado: a Geography.* Boulder, 1983

State Government Website: http://www.colorado.gov

State Library: Colorado State Library, 201 E. Colfax, Rm. 314, Denver 80203.

CONNECTICUT

KEY HISTORICAL EVENTS

Formerly territory of Algonquian-speaking Indians, Connecticut was first colonized by Europeans during the 1630s, when English Puritans moved there from Massachusetts Bay. Settlements were founded in the Connecticut River Valley at Hartford, Saybrook, Wethersfield and Windsor in 1635. They formed an organized commonwealth in 1637. A further settlement was made at New Haven in 1638 and was united to the commonwealth under a royal charter in 1662. The charter confirmed the commonwealth constitution, drawn up by mutual agreement in 1639 and called the Fundamental Orders of Connecticut.

The area was agricultural and its population of largely English descent until the early 19th century. After the War of Independence Connecticut was one of the original 13 states of the Union. Its state constitution came into force in 1818 and survived with amendment until 1965 when a new one was adopted.

In the early 1800s a textile industry was established using local water power. By 1850 the state had more employment in industry than in agriculture, and immigration from the continent of Europe (and especially from southern and eastern Europe) grew rapidly throughout the 19th century. Some immigrants worked in whaling and iron-mining, but most sought industrial employment. Settlement was spread over a large number of small towns, with no single dominant culture.

Yale University was founded at New Haven in 1701. The US Coastguard Academy was founded in 1876 at New London, a former whaling port.

TERRITORY AND POPULATION

Connecticut is bounded in the north by Massachusetts, east by Rhode Island, south by the Atlantic and west by New York. Land area, 4,845 sq. miles (12,548 sq. km).

Census population, 1 April 2000, 3,405,565, an increase of 3·6% since 1990. July 2004 estimate, 3,503,604.

Population in five census years was:

	White	*Black*	*Indian*	*Asian*	*Total*	*Per sq. mile*
1910	1,098,897	15,174	152	533	1,114,756	231·3
1930	1,576,700	29,354	162	687	1,606,903	328·0
1980	2,799,420	217,433	4,533	18,970	3,107,576	634·3

	White	*Black*	*Indian*	*Asian*	*Others*	*Total*	*Per sq. mile*
1990	2,859,353	274,269	6,654	50,078	96,762	3,287,116	678·6
2000	2,780,355	309,843	9,639	82,313	148,567	3,405,565	702·9

Of the total population in 2000, there were 320,323 persons of Hispanic origin, up from 213,116 in 1990 (an increase of 50·3%). Of the total population in 2000, 1,756,246 were female, 2,563,877 were 18 years old or older and 2,988,057 were urban. There were 183 residents in five Indian Reservations.

The chief cities and towns are (2000 census populations):

Bridgeport	139,529	Waterbury	107,271	West Hartford	63,589
New Haven	123,626	Norwalk	82,951	Greenwich	61,101
Hartford	121,578	Danbury	74,848	Bristol	60,062
Stamford	117,083	New Britain	71,538	Meriden	58,244

SOCIAL STATISTICS

Births (2002) were 42,001 (12·1 per 1,000 population); deaths, 30,122 (8·7); 2001: infant mortality rate (per 1,000 live births), 6·1. 2001: marriages, 18,600; divorces, 9,700.

CLIMATE

New Haven: Jan. 25°F (–3·8°C), July 74°F (23·4°C). Annual rainfall 45" (1,143 mm). Connecticut belongs to the New England climate zone (*see* UNITED STATES: Climate).

CONSTITUTION AND GOVERNMENT

The 1818 Constitution was revised in 1955. On 30 Dec. 1965 a new constitution went into effect, having been framed by a constitutional convention in the summer of 1965 and approved by the voters in Dec. 1965.

The General Assembly consists of a Senate of 36 members and a House of Representatives of 151 members. Members of each House are elected for the term of two years. Legislative sessions are annual.

For the 109th Congress, which convened in Jan. 2005, Connecticut sends five members to the House of Representatives. It is represented in the Senate by Christopher Dodd (D. 1981–2011) and Joseph Lieberman (D. 1989–2007).

There are eight counties. The state capital is Hartford.

RECENT ELECTIONS

In the 2004 presidential election Kerry polled 857,488 votes; Bush, 693,826; Nader, 12,969.

CURRENT ADMINISTRATION

Governor: M. Jodi Rell (R.), July 2004–Jan. 2007 (salary: $150,000).

Lieut.-Governor: Kevin Sullivan (D.), July 2004–Jan. 2007 ($110,000).

Secretary of State: Susan Bysiewicz (D.), 2003–07 ($110,000).

Government Website: http://www.ct.gov

ECONOMY

Per capita personal income (2002) was $42,829, the second highest in the country.

Budget. In 2002 total state revenue was $16,993m. Total expenditure was $20,117m. (education, $4,786m.; public welfare, $3,599m.; hospitals, $1,355m.; government administration, $913m.; highways, $851m.) Outstanding debt, in 2002, $20,784m.

Performance. Gross State Product in 2002 was $165,744m., ranking Connecticut 23rd in the United States.

ENERGY AND NATURAL RESOURCES

Water. The total area covered by water is approximately 698 sq. miles.

Minerals. The state has some mineral resources: crushed stone, sand, gravel, clay, dimension stone, feldspar and quartz. Total non-fuel mineral production in 2002 was valued at $142m.

Agriculture. In 2002 the state had 3,900 farms with a total area of 360,000 acres; the average farm size was 92 acres, valued at $9,491 per acre in 2002 (the highest of any state). Farm income (2001): crops $299m., and livestock and products $177m. The net farm income in 2001 was $144m. Principal crops are grains, hay, tobacco, vegetables, maize, melons, fruit, nuts, berries and greenhouse and nursery products. Livestock (2002): 61,000 all cattle (value $59·8m.), 5,580 sheep, 3,232 swine and 3·8m. poultry ($8·7m.).

Forestry. Total forested area was 1,859,000 acres in 2002.

INDUSTRY

In 2001 the state's 5,413 manufacturing establishments had 233,000 employees, earning $11,202m. Total value added by manufacturing in 2001 was $27,595m.

Labour. Total non-agricultural employment, 2001, 1,682,000. Employees by branch, 2001 (in 1,000): services, 540; wholesale and retail trade, 358; manufacturing, 254; government, 244. The unemployment rate in 2002 was 4·3%.

COMMUNICATIONS

Roads. The total length of highways in 2002 was 21,042 miles comprising 14,933 miles of urban road and 6,109 miles of rural road. Motor vehicles registered in 2002 numbered 2,914,831.

Rail. In 2002 there were 555 miles of railway route miles.

Civil Aviation. In 1995 there were 61 airports (20 commercial, six state-owned and 35 private), 63 heliports and eight seaplane bases. There were 3,508,140 passenger enplanements statewide in 2000.

SOCIAL INSTITUTIONS

Justice. In June 2002 there were 20,243 federal and state prisoners. The death penalty for murder is authorized, and was used in May 2005 for the first time since 1960.

Religion. The leading religious denominations (1990) in the state are the Roman Catholic (1,374,000 members), United Churches of Christ (135,000), Protestant Episcopal (78,000), Jewish (115,000), Methodist (56,000), Black Baptist (64,000), Presbyterian and Greek Orthodox.

Education. Instruction is free for all children and young people between the ages of four and 21 years, and compulsory for all children between the ages of seven and 16 years. In 2000 there were 971 public local schools, three academies, 17 state vocational-technical schools, 30 state or state-aided schools, six regional educational service centres and 335 non-public schools. In 1999 there were 545,500 public school pupils and in 1998–99 there were 36,012 full-time, professional public teachers. Expenditure of the state on public schools, 1999–2000, $5,300m. Average salary of teachers in public schools, 1999, $51,000 (the highest in the United States). In 1999–2000 expenditure per pupil (public elementary and secondary) was $9,365. There were an estimated 28,200 public high-school graduates in 1999.

In 2000 Connecticut had 42 colleges, of which one state university, one external degree college, four state colleges, 12 community-technical colleges and a US Coast Guard Academy were state funded. The University of Connecticut at Storrs, founded 1881, had 21,398 students in 1998. Yale University, New Haven, founded in 1701, had 11,032 students; Wesleyan University, Middletown, founded 1831, 3,204 students; Trinity College, Hartford, founded 1823, 2,258 students; Connecticut College, New London, founded 1915, 1,800 students; The University of Hartford, founded 1877, 6,892 students. The state colleges had 39,354 students in 1998. The US Coast Guard Academy had 795 students in 1998. There were 19 independent (four-year course) colleges and four independent (two-year course) colleges as well as two seminaries, a College of Hospitality Management and a Learning Collaborative.

Health. In 2001 there were 35 community hospitals with 8,000 beds. A total of 360,000 patients were admitted during the year.

Welfare. Medicare enrolment in July 2002 totalled 518,344. In 2000 a total of 419,890 people in Connecticut received Medicaid. In Dec. 2003 there were 582,877 Old-Age, Survivors, and Disability Insurance (OASDI) beneficiaries. A total of 50,243 people were receiving payments under Temporary Assistance for Needy Families (TANF) in Sept. 2002.

CULTURE

Broadcasting. In 1994 there were 75 broadcasting stations and 11 television stations.

Press. In 1994 there were 141 newspapers.

FURTHER READING

State Register and Manual. Secretary of State. Hartford (CT). Annual
Halliburton, W. J., *The People of Connecticut.* Norwalk, 1985

State Library: Connecticut State Library, 231 Capitol Avenue, Hartford (CT) 06105.
State Book Store: Dept. of Environmental Protection, 79 Elm St., Hartford (CT) 06106.
Business Incentives: Connecticut Economic Resource Center, 805 Brook St., Rocky Hill (CT) 06067.
Connecticut Tourism: Dept. of Economic and Community Development, 865 Brook St., Rocky Hill (CT) 06067.

DELAWARE

KEY HISTORICAL EVENTS

Delaware was the territory of Algonquian-speaking Indians who were displaced by European settlement in the 17th century. The first settlers were Swedes who came in 1638 to build Fort Christina (now Wilmington), and colonize what they called New Sweden. Their colony was taken by the Dutch from New Amsterdam in 1655. In 1664 the British took the whole New Amsterdam colony, including Delaware, and called it New York.

In 1682 Delaware was granted to William Penn, who wanted access to the coast for his Pennsylvania colony. Union of the two colonies was unpopular, and Delaware gained its own government in 1704, although it continued to share a royal governor with Pennsylvania until the War of Independence. Delaware then became one of the 13 original states of the Union and the first to ratify the federal constitution (on 7 Dec. 1787).

The population was of Swedish, Finnish, British and Irish extraction. The land was low-lying and fertile, and the use of slave labour was legal. There was a significant number of black slaves, but Delaware was a border state during the Civil War (1861–65) and did not leave the Union.

19th-century immigrants were mostly European Jews, Poles, Germans and Italians. The north became industrial and densely populated, more so after the Second World War with the rise of the petrochemical industry. Industry in general profited from the opening of the Chesapeake and Delaware Canal in 1829; it was converted to a toll-free deep channel for ocean-going ships in 1919.

TERRITORY AND POPULATION

Delaware is bounded in the north by Pennsylvania, northeast by New Jersey, east by Delaware Bay, south and west by Maryland. Land area 1,954 sq. miles (5,061 sq. km). Census population, 1 April 2000, was 783,600, an increase of 17·6% since 1990. July 2004 estimate, 830,364.

Population in five census years was:

	White	*Black*	*Indian*	*Asiatic*	*Total*	*Per sq. mile*
1910	171,102	31,181	5	34	202,322	103·0
1960	384,327	60,688	597	410	446,292	224·0
			All others			
1980	488,002	96,157	10,179		594,338	290·8
1990	535,094	112,460	18,614		666,168	325·9
2000	584,773	150,666	48,161		783,600	401·0

Of the total population in 2000, 403,059 were female, 589,013 were 18 years old or older and 627,758 were urban. The Hispanic population in 2000 was 37,277, up from 15,824 in 1990 (an increase of 135·6%).

The 2000 census figures show Wilmington with a population of 72,664; Dover, 32,135; Newark, 28,547; Milford City, 6,732; Seaford City, 6,699; Middletown, 6,161.

SOCIAL STATISTICS

Births in 2002, 11,090 (13·7 per 1,000 population); deaths, 6,861 (8·5 per 1,000 population); 2001: infant deaths, 10·7 per 1,000 live births; 2001: marriages, 5,200 (6·7 per 1,000 population); divorces, 3,100 (4·0).

CLIMATE

Wilmington, Jan. 31°F (–0·6°C), July 76°F (24·4°C). Annual rainfall 43" (1,076 mm). Delaware belongs to the Atlantic Coast climate zone (*see* UNITED STATES: Climate).

CONSTITUTION AND GOVERNMENT

The present constitution (the fourth) dates from 1897, and has had 51 amendments; it was not ratified by the electorate but promulgated by the Constitutional Convention. The General Assembly consists of a Senate of 21 members elected for four years and a House of Representatives of 41 members elected for two years.

For the 109th Congress, which convened in Jan. 2005, Delaware sends one member to the House of Representatives. It is represented in the Senate by Joseph Biden (D. 1973–2009) and Thomas Carper (D. 2001–07).

The state capital is Dover. Delaware is divided into three counties.

RECENT ELECTIONS

In the 2004 presidential election Kerry polled 200,152 votes; Bush, 171,660; Nader, 2,153.

CURRENT ADMINISTRATION

Governor: Ruth Ann Minner (D.), 2005–09 (salary: $132,500).

Lieut.-Governor: John C. Carney, Jr (D.), 2005–09 ($73,027).

Secretary of State: Dr Harriet Smith Windsor (D.), appointed 2001 ($119,682).

Government Website: http://www.delaware.gov

ECONOMY

Per capita personal income (2002) was $32,307.

Budget. In 2002 total revenue was $4,842m. Total expenditure was $4,646m. (education, $1,434m.; public welfare, $660m.; highways, $370m.; government administration, $351m.; correction, $245m.) Debt outstanding, in 2002, $4,038m.

Performance. 2002 Gross State Product was $47,150m., ranking Delaware 39th in the United States.

Banking and Finance. Delaware National Bank has branches statewide. Also based in Delaware, MBNA is the world's largest independent credit card issuer, with managed loans of $97·5bn.

ENERGY AND NATURAL RESOURCES

Electricity. Net generation of electric energy, 2001, 1·9bn. kWh.

Water. The total area covered by water is approximately 442 sq. miles.

Minerals. The mineral resources of Delaware are not extensive, consisting chiefly of clay products, stone, sand and gravel and magnesium compounds. Total non-fuel mineral production in 2002 was valued at $17m. (includes production for District of Columbia).

Agriculture. Delaware is mainly an industrial state, with agriculture as its principal industry. There were 560,000 acres in 2,400 farms in 2002. The average farm was 233 acres and was valued (land and buildings) at $4,054 per acre in

2002. Farm income (2002): crops $178m., and livestock and products $550m. The net farm income in 2001 was $218m. The major product is broilers, accounting for $494·2m. in cash receipts, out of total farm cash receipts of $727·7m. in 2002.

The chief crops are soybeans, greenhouse products, and corn for feed.

Forestry. Total forested area was 383,000 acres in 2002.

INDUSTRY

In 2001 the state's 694 manufacturing establishments had 42,000 employees, earning $1,745m. Total value added by manufacturing in 2001 was $6,621m. Main manufactures are chemicals, transport equipment and food.

Labour. Total non-agricultural employment, 2001, 419,000. Employees by branch, 2001 (in 1,000): services, 122; wholesale and retail trade, 91; government, 57; manufacturing, 56; finance, insurance and property, 52. The unemployment rate in 2002 was 4·2%.

COMMUNICATIONS

Roads. In 2002 there were 5,845 miles of roads comprising 2,017 miles of urban road and 3,828 miles of rural road; total vehicles registered numbered 674,143.

Rail. In 1999 the state had 271 miles of active rail line, 23 miles of which is part of Amtrak's high-speed Northeast corridor. In 1999 there were 710,245 passenger trips beginning or ending in Delaware—645,808 of which were commuter trips. An important component of Delaware's freight infrastructure is the rail access to the Port of Wilmington.

Civil Aviation. In 1998 Delaware had 11 public use airports and one helistop. There were 596 passenger enplanements statewide in 2000.

SOCIAL INSTITUTIONS

Justice. In June 2002 there were 6,957 federal and state prisoners. The death penalty is authorized. There were two executions in 2001 but there have been none since then.

Religion. The leading religious denominations are Roman Catholics, Methodists, Episcopalians and Lutherans.

Education. The state has free public schools and compulsory school attendance. In Sept. 1999 the elementary and secondary public schools had 113,598 enrolled pupils and 7,023 classroom teachers. Another 26,584 children were enrolled in private and parochial schools. State appropriation for public schools (financial year 1998–99) was about $615m. Average salary of classroom teachers (financial year 1998–99), $43,164. The state supports the University of Delaware at Newark (1834) which had 930 full-time faculty members and 21,346 students in Sept. 1998, Delaware State University, Dover (1892), with 177 full-time faculty members and 3,155 students, and the four campuses of Delaware Technical and Community College (Wilmington, Stanton, Dover and Georgetown) with 301 full-time faculty members and 45,535 students.

Health. In 2001 there were five community hospitals with 1,900 beds. A total of 83,000 patients were admitted during the year.

Welfare. Medicare enrolment in July 2002 totalled 116,363. In 2000 a total of 115,267 people in Delaware received Medicaid. In Dec. 2003 there were 141,488 Old-Age, Survivors, and Disability Insurance (OASDI) beneficiaries. A total of 12,712 people were receiving payments under Temporary Assistance for Needy Families (TANF) in Sept. 2002.

FURTHER READING

Statistical information: Delaware Economic Development Office, Dover, DE 19901. Publishes *Delaware Statistical Overview.*

State Manual, Containing Official List of Officers, Commissions and County Officers. Secretary of State, Dover. Annual

Smeal, L., *Delaware Historical and Biographical Index.* New York, 1984

DISTRICT OF COLUMBIA

KEY HISTORICAL EVENTS

The District of Columbia, organized in 1790, is the seat of the government of the USA, for which the land was ceded by the states of Maryland and Virginia to the USA as a site for the national capital. It was established under Acts of Congress in 1790 and 1791. Congress first met in it in 1800 and federal authority over it became vested in 1801. In 1846 the land ceded by Virginia (about 33 sq. miles) was given back.

TERRITORY AND POPULATION

The District forms an enclave on the Potomac River, where the river forms the southwest boundary of Maryland. The land area of the District of Columbia is 61 sq. miles (159 sq. km).

Census population, 1 April 2000, was 572,059 (100% urban), a decrease of 5·72% from that of 1990. July 2004 estimate, 553,523. Metropolitan area of Washington, D.C.–Baltimore (2000), 7,608,070. The Hispanic population in 2000 was 44,953, up from 32,710 in 1990 (an increase of 37·4%). Of the total population in 2000, 302,693 were female and 457,067 were 18 years old or older.

Population in five census years was:

	White	*Black*	*Indian*	*Chinese and Japanese*	*Total*	*Per sq. mile*
1910	236,128	94,446	68	427	331,069	5,517·8
1960	345,263	411,737	587	3,532	763,956	12,523·9
				All others		
1980	171,768	448,906		17,659	638,333	10,464·4
1990	179,667	339,604		87,629	606,900	9,949·2
2000	176,101	343,312		52,646	572,059	9,378·0

SOCIAL STATISTICS

Births, 2002, were 7,498 (13·1 per 1,000 population); deaths, 5,851 (10·2); 2001: infant mortality rate (per 1,000 live births), 10·6. 2001: marriages, 3,500 (6·8 per 1,000 population); divorces, 1,200 (2·3). The abortion rate, at 68·1 for every 1,000 women in 2000, is the highest of any US state.

CLIMATE

Washington, Jan. 34°F (1·1°C), July 77°F (25°C). Annual rainfall 43" (1,064 mm). The District of Columbia belongs to the Atlantic Coast climate zone (*see* UNITED STATES: Climate).

CONSTITUTION AND GOVERNMENT

Local government, from 1 July 1878 until Aug. 1967, was that of a municipal corporation administered by a board of three commissioners, of whom two were appointed from civil life by the President, and confirmed by the Senate, for a term of three years each. The other commissioner was detailed by the President from the Engineer Corps of the Army. The Commission form of government was abolished in 1967 and a new Mayor Council instituted with officers appointed by the President with the advice and consent of the Senate. On 24 Dec. 1973 the appointed officers were replaced by an elected Mayor and councillors, with full legislative powers in local matters as from 1974. Congress retains the right to legislate, to veto or supersede the Council's acts. The 23rd amendment to the federal constitution (1961) conferred the right to vote in national elections. The District has one delegate and one shadow delegate to the House of Representatives and two shadow senators. The Congressman may participate but not vote on the House floor.

RECENT ELECTIONS

In the 2004 presidential election Kerry polled 202,970 votes (89·2% of the vote—Kerry's best result); Bush, 21,256; Nader, 1,485.

CURRENT ADMINISTRATION

Mayor: Anthony A. Williams (D.), 2003–07 (salary: $145,600).

Secretary of the District: Sherryl Hobbs Newman (D.), appointed April 2003 (salary: $128,619).

Government Website: http://www.dc.gov

ECONOMY

Per capita personal income (2002) was $43,371, the highest in the country.

Budget. The District's revenues are derived from a tax on real and personal property, sales taxes, taxes on corporations and companies, licences for conducting various businesses and from federal payments. The District of Columbia has no bonded debt not covered by its accumulated sinking fund.

Performance. Gross State Product was $66,440m. in 2002.

ENERGY AND NATURAL RESOURCES

Water. The total area covered by water is approximately 7 sq. miles.

Minerals. Non-fuel mineral production is included in figures for Delaware.

INDUSTRY

In 2001 the state's 162 manufacturing establishments had 3,000 employees, earning $92m. Total value added by manufacturing in 2001 was $93m. The main industries are government service, service, wholesale and retail trade, finance, real estate, insurance, communications, transport and utilities.

Labour. Total non-agricultural employment, 2001, 651,000. Employees by branch, 2001 (in 1,000): services, 305; government, 222; wholesale and retail trade, 51. The unemployment rate in 2002 was 6·4%.

COMMUNICATIONS

Roads. In 2002 there were 1,535 miles of roads (1,427 miles state highway agency); there were 237,549 registered vehicles.

Rail. There is a metro in Washington extending to 130 km, and two commuter rail networks.

Civil Aviation. The District is served by three general airports; across the Potomac River in Arlington, Va., is National Airport; in Chantilly, Va., is Dulles International Airport; and in Maryland is Baltimore–Washington International Airport. There were 13,632,535 passenger enplanements in 2000.

SOCIAL INSTITUTIONS

Justice. The death penalty was declared unconstitutional in the District of Columbia on 14 Nov. 1973. In June 2002 there were 3,023 federal and state prisoners.

The District's Court system is the Judicial Branch of the District of Columbia. It is the only completely unified court system in the United States, possibly because of the District's unique city-state jurisdiction. Until the District of Columbia Court Reform and Criminal Procedure Act of 1970, the judicial system was almost entirely in the hands of Federal government. Since that time, the system has been similar in most respects to the autonomous systems of the states.

Religion. The largest churches are the Protestant and Roman Catholic Christian churches; there are also Jewish, Eastern Orthodox and Islamic congregations.

Education. In 1996 there were an estimated 105,700 pupils enrolled at elementary and secondary public schools. Average expenditure per pupil in 1997 was $8,167.

Higher education is given through the Consortium of Universities of the Metropolitan Washington Area, which consists of six universities and three colleges: Georgetown University, founded in 1795 by the Jesuit Order; George Washington University, non-sectarian founded in 1821; Howard University, founded in 1867; Catholic University of America, founded in 1887; American University (Methodist), founded in 1893; University of District of Columbia, founded 1976; Gallaudet College, founded 1864; Trinity College in Washington, D.C. (women's college), founded 1897. There are 18 institutes of higher education altogether.

Health. In 2001 there were ten community hospitals with 3,400 beds. A total of 131,000 patients were admitted during the year.

Welfare. Medicare enrolment in July 2002 totalled 74,175. In 2000 a total of 138,677 people in the District of Columbia received Medicaid. In Dec. 2003 there were 72,209 Old-Age, Survivors, and Disability Insurance (OASDI) beneficiaries.

A total of 41,503 people were receiving payments under Temporary Assistance for Needy Families (TANF) in Sept. 2002.

CULTURE

Tourism. About 20m. visitors stay in the District every year and spend about $1,000m.

FURTHER READING

Statistical Information: The Metropolitan Washington Board of Trade publications.
Reports of the Commissioners of the District of Columbia. Annual. Washington
Bowling, K. R., *The Creation of Washington D.C.: the Idea and the Location of the American Capital.* Washington (D.C.), 1991

FLORIDA

KEY HISTORICAL EVENTS

There were French and Spanish settlements in Florida in the 16th century, of which the Spanish, at St Augustine in 1565, proved permanent. Florida was claimed by Spain until 1763 when it passed to Britain. Although regained by Spain in 1783, the British used it as a base for attacks on American forces during the war of 1812. Gen. Andrew Jackson captured Pensacola for the USA in 1818. In 1819 a treaty was signed which ceded Florida to the USA with effect from 1821 and it became a Territory of the USA in 1822.

Florida had been the home of the Apalachee and Timucua Indians. After 1770 groups of Creek Indians began to arrive as refugees from the European-Indian wars. These 'Seminoles' or runaways attracted other refugees including slaves, the recapture of whom was the motive for the first Seminole War of 1817–18. A second war followed in 1835–42, when the Seminoles retreated to the Everglades swamps. After a third war in 1855–58 most Seminoles were forced or persuaded to move to reserves in Oklahoma.

Florida became a state in 1845. About half of the population were black slaves. At the outbreak of Civil War in 1861 the state seceded from the Union.

During the 20th century Florida continued to grow fruit and vegetables, but real-estate development (often for retirement) and the growth of tourism and the aerospace industry set it apart from other ex-plantation states.

TERRITORY AND POPULATION

Florida is a peninsula bounded in the west by the Gulf of Mexico, south by the Straits of Florida, east by the Atlantic, north by Georgia and northwest by Alabama. Land area, 53,927 sq. miles (139,670 sq. km). Census population, 1 April 2000, 15,982,378, an increase of 23·5% since 1990. July 2004 estimate, 17,397,161.

Population in five federal census years was:

	White	*Black*	*All Others*	*Total*	*Per sq. mile*
1950	2,166,051	603,101	2,153	2,771,305	51·1
1970	5,719,343	1,041,651	28,449	6,789,443	125·6
1980	8,319,448	1,342,478	84,398	9,746,324	180·1
1990	10,749,285	1,759,534	429,107	12,937,926	238·9
2000	12,465,029	2,335,505	1,181,844	15,982,378	296·4

Of the total population in 2000, 8,184,663 were female, 12,336,038 were 18 years old or older and 14,270,020 were urban. The Hispanic population in 2000 was 2,682,715, up from 1,574,143 in 1990 (a rise of 70·4%, the third largest numeric increase of any state in the USA).

The largest cities in the state, 2000 census (and 1990) are: Jacksonville, 735,617 (635,230); Miami, 362,470 (358,548); Tampa, 303,447 (280,015); St Petersburg, 248,232 (238,629); Hialeah, 226,419 (188,004); Orlando, 185,951 (164,693); Fort Lauderdale, 152,397 (149,377); Tallahassee, 150,624 (124,773); Hollywood, 139,357 (121,697); Pembroke Pines, 137,427 (65,452); Coral Springs, 117,549 (79,443); Clearwater, 108,787 (98,784); Cape Coral, 102,286 (74,991); Gainesville, 95,447 (84,770); Port St Lucie, 88,769 (55,759); Miami Beach, 87,933 (92,639); Sunrise, 85,779 (65,683); Plantation, 82,934 (66,814); West Palm Beach, 82,103

(67,764); Palm Bay, 79,413 (62,543); Lakeland, 78,452 (70,576); Pompano Beach, 78,191 (72,411).

Population of the largest metropolitan areas (2000): Miami–Fort Lauderdale, 3,876,380; Tampa-St Petersburg-Clearwater, 2,395,997; Orlando, 1,644,561.

SOCIAL STATISTICS

Births in 2002 were 205,579 (12·3 per 1,000 population); deaths, 167,814 (10·0 per 1,000); infant deaths, 2001, 7·3 (per 1,000); marriages, 2001, 151,300; divorces and other dissolutions, 84,600.

CLIMATE

Jacksonville, Jan. 55°F (12·8°C), July 81°F (27·2°C). Annual rainfall 54" (1,353 mm). Key West, Jan. 70°F (21·1°C), July 83°F (28·3°C). Annual rainfall 39" (968 mm). Miami, Jan. 67°F (19·4°C), July 82°F (27·8°C). Annual rainfall 60" (1,516 mm). Tampa, Jan. 61°F (16·1°C), July 81°F (27·2°C). Annual rainfall 51" (1,285 mm). Florida belongs to the Gulf Coast climate zone (*see* UNITED STATES: Climate).

CONSTITUTION AND GOVERNMENT

The 1968 Legislature revised the constitution of 1885. The state legislature comprises the Senate and House of Representatives. The Senate has 40 members elected for four years. Half of the membership is elected every two years. The House has 120 members, all of whom are elected every two years during elections held in even-numbered years. Sessions of the legislature are held annually, and are limited to 60 days. Senate and House districts are based on population, with each senator and member representing approximately the same number of residents. The Senate and House are reapportioned every ten years when the federal census is released. In addition to the Governor and Lieut.-Governor (who are elected for four years), the constitution provides for a cabinet composed of an attorney general, a chief financial officer and a commissioner of agriculture.

For the 109th Congress, which convened in Jan. 2005, Florida sends 25 members to the House of Representatives. It is represented in the Senate by Bill Nelson (D. 2001–07) and Mel Martinez (R. 2005–11).

The state capital is Tallahassee. The state is divided into 67 counties.

RECENT ELECTIONS

In the 2004 presidential election Bush polled 3,964,522 votes; Kerry, 3,583,544; Nader, 32,971.

CURRENT ADMINISTRATION

Governor: John Ellis 'Jeb' Bush (R.), 2003–07 (salary: $123,175).

Lieut.-Governor: Toni Jennings (R.), 2003–07 ($117,990).

Secretary of State: Glenda E. Hood (R.), appointed Feb. 2003 ($121,931).

Government Website: http://www.myflorida.com

ECONOMY

Per capita personal income (2002) was $29,559.

Budget. In 2002 total state revenue was $47,890m. Total expenditure was $51,834m. (education, $15,643m.; public welfare, $11,879m.; highways, $4,826m.; health, $2,667m.; correction, $2,200m.) Outstanding debt, in 2002, $20,266m.

Performance. 2002 Gross State Product was $520,500m., ranking Florida 4th in the United States.

Banking and Finance. In 2002 there were 301 financial institutions in Florida insured by the US Federal Deposit Insurance Corporation, with assets worth $99,900m. They had 4,626 offices with total deposits of $242,800m.

ENERGY AND NATURAL RESOURCES

Electricity. Electricity production in 2000 totalled 169·9bn. kWh.

Oil and Gas. In 2001, 4m. bbls. of crude oil was produced; natural gas production was 6bn. cu. ft.

Water. The total area covered by water is approximately 5,991 sq. miles.

Minerals. The chief mineral is phosphate rock, of which marketable production in 2002 was 27m. tonnes. This was approximately 75% of US and 25% of the world supply of phosphate in 2002. Other important non-fuel minerals include crushed stone, cement, and sand and gravel. Total non-fuel mineral production for 2002 was valued at $2,020m.

Agriculture. In 2002 there were 10·2m. acres of farmland; 44,000 farms with an average of 232 acres per farm. The total value of land and buildings was $29,330m. in 2002; average value (2002) of land and buildings per acre, $2,836.

Farm income from crops and livestock (2001) was $6,416m., of which crops provided $4,958m. and livestock $1,458m. Major crop contributors are oranges, grapefruit, tomatoes, peppers, other winter vegetables, indoor and landscaping plants and sugarcane. The net farm income in 2001 was $2,166m. In 2003 poultry farms produced 106m. chickens, 2,804m. eggs and 511m. lb of broilers. In 2002 the state had 1·74m. cattle, including 144,800 milch cows, and 33,500 swine.

Forestry. In 2002 Florida had 16·29m. acres of forested land, including 1·13m. acres of national forests. Florida's 31 state forests covered 1·40m. acres in 2002.

Fisheries. Florida has extensive fisheries with shrimp the highest value fishery. Other important catches are spiny lobster, snapper, crabs, hard clams, swordfish and tuna. Commercial catch (2002) totalled 115·6m. lb of fish at a value of $184·6m.

INDUSTRY

In 2001 the state's 15,392 manufacturing establishments had 413,000 employees, earning $14,578m. Total value added by manufacturing in 2001 was $39,974m. Main industries include: printing and publishing, machinery and computer equipment, apparel and finished products, fabricated metal products, and lumber and wood products.

Labour. Total non-agricultural employment, 2001, 7,198,000. Employees by branch, 2001 (in 1,000): services, 2,686; wholesale and retail trade, 1,782; government, 1,029; manufacturing, 469; finance, insurance and property, 458; construction, 403. In 2002 the unemployment rate was 5·5%.

INTERNATIONAL TRADE

Imports and Exports. Export sales of merchandise in 2000 totalled $24·2bn. Florida exported to 213 foreign markets in 2000: Canada was the biggest (10·3% of exports), followed by Brazil (8·4%) and Mexico (8·1%). Other important markets include Japan, Venezuela, Dominican Republic, UK, Colombia, Germany, Argentina and China. The leading export category is computers and electronic products (accounting for 33% of total exports in 2000). Other manufactured exports include transportation equipment, machinery, chemicals, electrical equipment, appliances and parts, and miscellaneous manufactures. The state also exports significant quantities of farm products and other non-manufactured commodities. Total agricultural exports were worth $1·2bn. in 2001.

COMMUNICATIONS

Roads. The state (2002) had 119,785 miles of highways, roads and streets (68,852 miles being urban roads); there were 13,963,596 vehicle registrations. In 2003 there were 3,169 traffic accident fatalities.

Rail. In 2002 there were 2,871 miles of railway and 13 rail companies. There is a metro of 22 miles, a peoplemover and a commuter rail route in Miami.

Civil Aviation. In 2002 Florida had 475 public and private airports (12 international and 20 scheduled commercial service airports), 280 heliports, 13 stolports and 45 seaplane bases. Annual economic activity at Florida airports is responsible for more than 4·7% of Gross State Product. More than 50% of tourists arrive in the state by air each year. There were 56,540,488 passenger enplanements at Florida airports in 2001: the busiest were Miami International (14,941,663), Orlando International (13,622,397), Fort Lauderdale/Hollywood International (8,015,055) and Tampa International (7,901,725).

Shipping. There are 14 deepwater ports: those on the Gulf coast handle mainly domestic trade and those on the Atlantic coast primarily international trade and cruise ship traffic. In 2002–03 the tonnage of total waterborne trade by port was 118·2m. tons (including Tampa: 48·5m. tons; Everglades: 23·3m. tons; Jacksonville: 18·7m. tons; Miami: 9·0m. tons; and Manatee: 7·0m. tons). Almost 14m. cruise passengers embarked and disembarked from Florida ports in 2002–03, principally from Canaveral (4·1m.), Miami (4·0m.) and Everglades (3·4m.). There were 1,540 miles of inland waterways in 2000.

SOCIAL INSTITUTIONS

Justice. The state resumed the use of the death penalty in 1979. There have been 58 executions since 1976, including two in 2004. In June 2002 there were 73,553 federal and state prisoners. Chain gangs were introduced in 1995.

Religion. The main Christian churches are Roman Catholic, Baptist, Methodist, Presbyterian and Episcopalian. There were 107,000 Latter-day Saints (Mormons) in 1998.

Education. Attendance at school is compulsory between seven and 16. In the 2001–02 school year there were 3,314 public elementary and secondary schools with 2,500,478 enrolled pupils. According to the National Center for Education Statistics, Florida's public schools have the highest average enrolment in the country: in the 1999–2000 school year there were 768 pupils per elementary school (compared to a national average of 477) and 1,396 pupils per secondary school (national average 706). Total expenditure on public schools in 2000–01 was $15,024m. The state maintains 28 public community colleges; in 2002–03 there were 880,000 students, about 35% of whom were full-time.

There are 11 state universities with a total of 258,874 students in 2002: the University of Florida at Gainesville (founded 1853) with 46,850 students; the Florida State University at Tallahassee (founded in 1857) with 36,651; the University of South Florida at Tampa (founded 1960) with 37,764; Florida A. & M. (Agricultural and Mechanical) University at Tallahassee (founded 1887) with 12,467; Florida Atlantic University (founded 1964) at Boca Raton with 23,996; the University of West Florida at Pensacola with 9,206; the University of Central Florida at Orlando with 38,795; the University of North Florida at Jacksonville with 13,460; Florida International University at Miami with 33,799; Florida Gulf Coast University (founded 1997) at Fort Myers with 5,236; and New College of Florida (founded 2001) at Sarasota with 650. There are 28 private colleges and universities belonging to the Independent Colleges and Universities of Florida (ICUF) association. Their enrolments vary from fewer than 100 to more than 22,000 students.

Health. In 2001 there were 202 community hospitals with 51,800 beds. A total of 2,207,000 patients were admitted during the year.

Welfare. Medicare enrolment in July 2002 totalled 2,876,168. In 2000 a total of 2,360,417 people in Florida received Medicaid. In Dec. 2003 there were 3,330,425 Old-Age, Survivors, and Disability Insurance (OASDI) beneficiaries. A total of 120,867 people were receiving payments under Temporary Assistance for Needy Families (TANF) in Sept. 2002.

CULTURE

Tourism. During 2002, 73·9m. tourists visited Florida (67·9m. domestic visitors, 4·4m. overseas visitors and 1·6m. from Canada). They generated $48·7bn. in taxable sales and $2·9bn. in state sales tax revenues, making tourism the state's biggest industry.

There are 156 state parks, three national parks, three national forests, 31 state forests, and five national monuments and memorials. In 2002 there were 17·7m. visitors to state parks, raising $31·9m. in revenue.

FURTHER READING

Statistical information: Bureau of Economic and Business Research, Univ. of Florida, Gainesville 32611. Publishes *Florida Statistical Abstract.*

Huckshorn, R. J. (ed.) *Government and Politics in Florida.* Florida Univ. Press, 1991

Morris, A., *The Florida Handbook*. Tallahassee. Biennial
Shermyen, A. H. (ed.) *1991 Florida Statistical Abstract*. Florida Univ. Press, 1991

State Library: 500 S Bronough Street, Tallahassee 32399.

GEORGIA

KEY HISTORICAL EVENTS

Originally the territory of Creek and Cherokee tribes, Georgia was first settled by Europeans in the 18th century. James Oglethorpe founded Savannah in 1733, intending it as a colony which offered a new start to debtors, convicts and the poor. Settlement was slow until 1783, when growth began in the cotton-growing areas west of Augusta. The Indian population was cleared off the rich cotton land and moved beyond the Mississippi. Georgia became one of the original 13 states of the Union.

A plantation economy developed rapidly, using slave labour. In 1861 Georgia seceded from the Union and became an important source of supplies for the Confederate cause, although some northern areas never accepted secession and continued in sympathy with the Union during the Civil War. At the beginning of the war 56% of the population were white, descendants of British, Austrian and New England immigrants; the remaining 44% were black slaves.

The city of Atlanta, which grew as a railway junction, was destroyed during the war but revived to become the centre of southern states during the reconstruction period. Atlanta was confirmed as state capital in 1877. Also in Atlanta were developed successive movements for black freedom in social, economic and political life. The Southern Christian Leadership Conference, led by Martin Luther King (assassinated in 1968), was based in King's native city of Atlanta.

TERRITORY AND POPULATION

Georgia is bounded north by Tennessee and North Carolina, northeast by South Carolina, east by the Atlantic, south by Florida and west by Alabama. Land area, 57,906 sq. miles (149,976 sq. km). Census population, 1 April 2000, was 8,186,453, an increase of 26·4% since 1990. July 2004 estimate, 8,829,383.

Population in five census years was:

	White	*Black*	*Indian*	*Asiatic*	*Total*	*Per sq. mile*
1910	1,431,802	1,176,987	95	237	2,609,121	44·4
1930	1,837,021	1,071,125	43	317	2,908,506	49·7
			All others			
1980	3,948,007	1,465,457	50,801		5,464,265	92·7
1990	4,600,148	1,746,565	131,503		6,478,216	110·0
2000	5,327,281	2,349,542	509,630		8,186,453	141·4

Of the total population in 2000, 4,159,340 were female, 6,017,219 were 18 years old or older and 5,864,163 were urban. The estimated Hispanic population was 435,277 in 2000, up from 108,933 in 1990 (an increase of 299·6%).

The largest cities are: Atlanta (capital), with a population (2000 census) of 416,474; Augusta-Richmond County, 199,775; Columbus, 186,291; Savannah, 131,510; Athens-Clarke County, 101,489. The Atlanta metropolitan area had a 2000 census population of 4,112,198.

SOCIAL STATISTICS

Births, 2002, were 133,300 (15·6 per 1,000 population); deaths, 65,449 (7·6); 2001: infant deaths, 8·6 per 1,000 live births. 2001: marriages, 51,300 (6·3 per 1,000 population); divorces and annulments, 30,600 (3·8).

CLIMATE

Atlanta, Jan. 43°F (6·1°C), July 78°F (25·6°C). Annual rainfall 49" (1,234 mm). Georgia belongs to the Atlantic Coast climate zone (*see* UNITED STATES: Climate).

CONSTITUTION AND GOVERNMENT

A new constitution was ratified in the general election of 2 Nov. 1976, proclaimed on 22 Dec. 1976 and became effective on 1 Jan. 1977. The General Assembly consists of a Senate of 56 members and a House of Representatives of 180 members, both elected for two years. Legislative sessions are annual, beginning the 2nd Monday in Jan. and lasting for 40 days.

Georgia was the first state to extend the franchise to all citizens 18 years old and above.

For the 109th Congress, which convened in Jan. 2005, Georgia sends 13 members to the House of Representatives. It is represented in the Senate by Saxby Chambliss (R. 2003–09) and Johnny Isakson (R. 2005–11).

The state capital is Atlanta. Georgia is divided into 159 counties.

RECENT ELECTIONS

In the 2004 presidential election Bush polled 1,914,254 votes; Kerry, 1,366,149; Badnarik, 18,387.

CURRENT ADMINISTRATION

Governor: Sonny Perdue (R.), 2003–07 (salary: $128,903).

Lieut.-Governor: Mark Taylor (D.), 2003–07 ($83,148).

Secretary of State: Cathy Cox (D.), 2003–07 ($116,743).

Government Website: http://www.georgia.gov

ECONOMY

Per capita personal income (2002) was $28,703.

Budget. In 2002 total state revenue was $24,847m. Total expenditure was $30,053m. (education, $12,155m.; public welfare, $6,525m.; highways, $2,005m.; correction, $1,272m.; health, $809m.) Outstanding debt, in 2002, $8,243m.

Performance. Gross State Product was $305,829m. in 2002, ranking Georgia 10th in the United States.

ENERGY AND NATURAL RESOURCES

Water. The total area covered by water is approximately 1,058 sq. miles.

Minerals. Georgia is the leading producer of kaolin. The state ranks first in production of crushed and dimensional granite, and second in production of fuller's earth and marble (crushed and dimensional). Total value of non-fuel mineral production for 2002 was $1,450m.

Agriculture. In 2002, 50,000 farms covered 11m. acres; the average farm was of 220 acres. In 2002 the average value of farmland and buildings was $2,112 per acre. For 2002 cotton output was 1·6m. bales (of 480 lb). Other major crops include tobacco, corn, wheat, soybeans, peanuts and pecans. Cash income, 2001, $5,515m.: from crops, $1,975m.; from livestock and products, $3,540m. The net farm income in 2001 was $2,299m.

In 2002 farm animals included 1·27m. cattle, 347,816 swine and 2,546m. (2003) poultry.

Forestry. The forested area in 2002 was 24·41m. acres with 855,000 acres of national forest.

INDUSTRY

In 2001 the state's 8,688 manufacturing establishments had 492,000 employees, earning $16,141m. Total value added by manufacturing in 2001 was $57,578m.

Labour. Total non-agricultural employment, 2001, 3,954,000. Employees by branch, 2001 (in 1,000): services, 1,150; wholesale and retail trade, 966; government, 605; manufacturing, 550. Georgia's unemployment rate in 2002 was 5·1%.

COMMUNICATIONS

Roads. In 2002 there were 115,778 miles of roads comprising 28,320 miles of urban road and 87,458 miles of rural road. There were 7,647,523 motor vehicles registered.

Rail. In 2002 there were 4,679 miles of railways and a metro in Atlanta.

Civil Aviation. In 1997 there were 106 public airports, nine with scheduled commercial services. There were 39,394,307 passenger enplanements statewide in 2000.

Shipping. There are deepwater ports at Savannah, the principal port, and Brunswick.

SOCIAL INSTITUTIONS

Justice. In June 2002 there were 46,417 federal and state prisoners. The death penalty is authorized for capital offences. There were two executions in 2004.

Under a Local Option Act, the sale of alcoholic beverages is prohibited in some counties.

Religion. An estimated 57·6% of the population are church members. Of the total population, 45·6% are Protestant, 3·2% are Roman Catholic and 1·1% are Jewish.

Education. Since 1945 education has been compulsory; tuition is free for pupils between the ages of six and 18 years. In 1996 there were 1,799 public elementary and public secondary schools with 1·3m. pupils and 81,058 teachers. Teachers' salaries averaged $33,869 in 1996. Expenditure on public schools (1995–96), $7,781m. or $1,080 per capita and $4,589 per pupil.

The University of Georgia (Athens) was founded in 1785 and was the first chartered State University in the USA (29,404 students in 1996–97). Other institutions of higher learning include Georgia Institute of Technology, Atlanta (12,985); Emory University, Atlanta (11,308); Georgia State University, Atlanta (23,410); and Georgia Southern University, Statesboro (14,312). The Atlanta University Center, devoted primarily to Black education, includes Clark Atlanta University (5,230) and Morris Brown College (2,169) co-educational; Morehouse College (2,884), a liberal arts college for men; Interdenominational Theological Center (419), a co-educational theological school; and Spelman College (1,961), the first liberal arts college for Black women in the USA. Atlanta University serves as the graduate school centre for the complex. Wesleyan College (445) near Macon is the oldest chartered women's college in the world.

Health. In 2001 there were 147 community hospitals with 24,100 beds. A total of 903,000 patients were admitted during the year.

Welfare. Medicare enrolment in July 2002 totalled 951,439. In 2000 a total of 1,289,795 people in Georgia received Medicaid. In Dec. 2003 there were 1,168,095 Old-Age, Survivors, and Disability Insurance (OASDI) beneficiaries. A total of 131,557 people were receiving payments under Temporary Assistance for Needy Families (TANF) in Sept. 2002.

CULTURE

Tourism. In the fiscal year beginning July 1998 visitors to Georgia spent nearly $16bn., an increase of over 81% for the previous year. There are 44 state parks.

FURTHER READING

Statistical information: Selig Center for Economic Growth, Univ. of Georgia, Athens 30602. Publishes *Georgia Statistical Abstract.*

Rowland, A. R., *A Bibliography of the Writings on Georgia History.* Hamden, Conn., 1978

State Law Library: Judicial Building, Capital Sq., Atlanta.

HAWAII

KEY HISTORICAL EVENTS

The islands of Hawaii were settled by Polynesian immigrants, probably from the Marquesas Islands, about AD 400. A second major immigration, from Tahiti, occurred around 800–900. In the late 18th century all the islands of the group were united into one kingdom by Kamehameha I. Western exploration began in 1778, and Christian missions were established after 1820. Europeans called Hawaii the Sandwich Islands. The main foreign states interested were the USA, Britain and France. Because of the threat imposed by their rivalry, Kamehameha III placed Hawaii under US protection in 1851. US sugar-growing companies became dominant in the economy and in 1887 the USA obtained a naval base at Pearl

Harbour. A struggle developed between forces for and against annexation by the USA. In 1893 the monarchy was overthrown. The republican government agreed to be annexed to the USA in 1898, and Hawaii became a US Territory in 1900.

The islands and the naval base were of great strategic importance during the Second World War, when the Japanese attack on Pearl Harbour brought the USA into the war.

Hawaii became the 50th state of the Union in 1959. The 19th-century plantation economy encouraged the immigration of workers, especially from China and Japan. Hawaiian laws, religions and culture were gradually adapted to the needs of the immigrant community.

TERRITORY AND POPULATION

The Hawaiian Islands lie in the North Pacific Ocean, between 18° 54' and 28° 15' N. lat. and 154° 40' and 178° 25' W. long., about 2,090 nautical miles southwest of San Francisco. There are 137 named islands and islets in the group, of which seven major and five minor islands are inhabited. Land area, 6,423 sq. miles (16,636 sq. km). Census population, 1 April 2000, 1,211,537, an increase of 9·3% since 1990; density was 188·6 per sq. mile in 1990. July 2004 population estimate, 1,262,840. Of the total population in 2000, 608,671 were male, 915,770 were 18 years old or older, and 1,108,225 were urban (91·47%, the fourth most urban state).

The principal islands are Hawaii, 4,028 sq. miles, population 1990, 120,317; Maui, 727 sq. miles, population 91,361; Oahu, 600 sq. miles, population 836,231; Kauai, 552 sq. miles, population 50,947; Molokai, 260 sq. miles, population 6,717; Lanai, 141 sq. miles, population 2,426; Niihau, 70 sq. miles, population 230; Kahoolawe, 45 sq. miles (uninhabited). The capital Honolulu—on the island of Oahu—had a population in 2000 of 371,657, and Hilo—on the island of Hawaii—40,759.

Estimated figures in 1999 for racial groups (excluding persons in institutions or military barracks) were: 252,742 white; 223,193 Hawaiian; 219,855 Japanese; 145,248 Filipinos; 44,787 Chinese; 17,430 black (1998); 13,693 Samoan and Tongan; 11,737 Korean; 95,456 Hispanic; 128,144 all others (1998).

SOCIAL STATISTICS

Births, 2002, were 17,477 (14·0 per 1,000 population); deaths, 8,801 (7·1); 2001: infant deaths were at a rate of 6·2 per 1,000 live births. There were 24,000 resident marriages (20·4 per 1,000 population) in 2001, and divorces and annulments numbered 4,500 (3·8 per 1,000 population). Inter-marriage between the races is common. In 1998, 46·3% of marriages were inter-racial. 58·3% were non-resident marriages.

CLIMATE

All the islands have a tropical climate, with an abrupt change in conditions between windward and leeward sides, most marked in rainfall. Temperatures vary little. Average temperatures in Honolulu in 1999: warmest month 81·4°F, coolest month 72·9°F. Annual rainfall in Honolulu (1997) 22·02".

CONSTITUTION AND GOVERNMENT

Hawaii was officially admitted into the United States on 21 Aug. 1959. However, the constitution of the State of Hawaii was created by the 1950 Constitutional Convention, ratified by the voters of the Territory on 7 Nov. 1950, and amended on 27 June 1959. There have been two constitutional conventions since 1950, in 1968 and 1978. In addition to amendments proposed by these conventions the Legislature is able to propose amendments to voters during the general election. This has resulted in numerous amendments.

For the 109th Congress, which convened in Jan. 2005, Hawaii sends two members to the House of Representatives. It is represented in the Senate by Daniel Inouye (D. 1963–2011) and Daniel Akaka (D. 1990–2007).

The state capital is Honolulu. There are five counties.

RECENT ELECTIONS

In the 2004 presidential election Kerry polled 231,708 votes; Bush, 194,191; Cobb, 1,737.

CURRENT ADMINISTRATION

Governor: Linda Lingle (R.), Dec. 2002–Dec. 2006 (salary: $94,780).
  Lieut.-Governor: James R. 'Duke' Aiona, Jr (R.), Dec. 2002–Dec. 2006 ($90,041).

Government Website: http://www.ehawaiigov.org

ECONOMY

Per capita personal income (2002) was $30,040.

Budget. Revenue is derived mainly from taxation of sales and gross receipts, real property, corporate and personal income, and inheritance taxes, licences, public land sales and leases.

In 2002 total state revenue was $5,869m. Total expenditure was $7,446m. (education, $2,257m.; public welfare, $1,126m.; health, $454m.; government administration, $376m.; highways, $236m.) Outstanding debt, in 2002, $5,656m.

Performance. 2002 Gross State Product was $43,998m., ranking Hawaii 42nd in the United States.

Banking and Finance. In 1999 there were five state-chartered banks with assets of $22,705m., and one federal bank.

ENERGY AND NATURAL RESOURCES

Electricity. Installed capacity in 1999 was 1,669,000 kW; total power consumed was 9,380m. kWh.

Oil and Gas. In 1999, $48m. was generated by gas sales.

Water. The total area covered by water is approximately 36 sq. miles. Water consumption in 1999 amounted to 77,610m. gallons.

Minerals. Total value of non-fuel mineral production, 2002, $75m.; mainly crushed stone (6·6m. tonnes in 2001, value $64m.) and cement (300,000 tonnes in 1999, value $26m.).

Agriculture. Farming is highly commercialized and highly mechanized. In 2002 there were about 5,300 farms covering an area of 1·44m. acres; average number of acres per farm, 272, valued at $3,507 per acre. Paid workforce totalled 11,600 in 2002.

Sugar, pineapples and greenhouse products are the staple crops. Farm income, 2001, from crop sales was $419m., and from livestock $91m. The net farm income in 2001 was $94m.

Forestry. Hawaii had 1·75m. acres of forested land in 2002. In 1997 conservation district forest land amounted to 971,876 acres (of which 328,742 was privately owned); there were 46,191 acres of planted forest; and 109,164 acres of natural area.

Fisheries. In 2002 the commercial fish catch was 23·84m. lb with a value of $52·1m. There were 3,798 commercial fishermen in 1999.

INDUSTRY

In 2001 the state's 940 manufacturing establishments had 15,000 employees, earning $463m. Total value added by manufacturing in 2001 was $907m.

Labour. Total non-agricultural employment amounted to 554,000 in 2001; 4·2% (24,732) were unemployed in 2002. Employees by branch, 2001 (in 1,000): services, 186; wholesale and retail trade, 136; government, 115.

Trade Unions. In 1999 there were 115 trade unions with a combined membership of 206,189. In 1998, 19·4% of workers in the private sector belonged to a union: 53·7% in the public sector.

INTERNATIONAL TRADE

Imports and Exports. Sugar exports brought in $168·8m. in 1996; pineapple exports, $147m.

COMMUNICATIONS

Roads. In 2002 there were 4,299 miles of roads comprising 2,119 miles of urban road and 2,180 miles of rural road. There were 892,553 registered motor vehicles.

Civil Aviation. There were nine commercial airports in 1999. Passengers arriving from overseas numbered 7·73m., and there were 10·17m. passengers between the islands. In 1999 Hawaiian Airlines flew 34·8m. km, carrying 5,409,700 passengers (19,100 on international flights). There were 15,054,470 passenger enplanements in 2000.

Shipping. Several lines of steamers connect the islands with the mainland USA, Canada, Australia, the Philippines, China and Japan. In 1999, 1,262 overseas and 2,249 inter-island vessels entered the port of Honolulu carrying a total of 45,494 overseas and 47,950 inter-island passengers as well as 5,721,503 tonnes of overseas and 1,730,662 tonnes inter-island cargo.

Telecommunications. There were 737,653 telephone access lines in 1999.

SOCIAL INSTITUTIONS

Justice. There is no capital punishment in Hawaii. In June 2002 there were 5,541 prisoners in federal and state prisons.

Religion. 1999 estimated membership of leading religious denominations: Roman Catholic Church, 215,000; Buddhism, 100,000; Church of Jesus Christ of Latter-day Saints, 56,000; United Church of Christ, 19,000; Southern Baptists, 17,000; Assembly of God, 11,000; Judaism, 10,000; Episcopal Church, 10,000.

Education. Education is free, and compulsory for children between the ages of six and 18. The language in the schools is English. In 1997–98 there were 251 public schools and 126 private schools. In 1999 there were 185,860 pupils in public schools and 36,226 pupils in private schools. In 1997–98 there were 11,400 teachers in public schools and 2,658 teachers in private schools. In 1997–98, $1,636m. was spent on education and the average annual salary for teachers was $36,598. In 1999 the number of students to enrol at college or university was 60,081.

Health. In 2001 there were 23 community hospitals with 3,200 beds. A total of 108,000 patients were admitted during the year.

Welfare. Medicare enrolment in July 2002 totalled 171,259. In Dec. 2003 there were 194,019 Old-Age, Survivors, and Disability Insurance (OASDI) beneficiaries. A total of 27,743 people were receiving payments under Temporary Assistance for Needy Families (TANF) in Sept. 2002.

CULTURE

Broadcasting. There were (1998) 48 radio and television stations. There were, in addition, two cable television companies (colour by NTSC).

Press. A total of 22 newspapers were in circulation in 1999.

Tourism. Tourism is outstanding in Hawaii's economy. Tourist arrivals numbered only 687,000 in 1965, but were 6·7m. in 1999. Tourist expenditure ($380m. in 1967) contributed $10,279·7m. to the state's economy in 1999.

FURTHER READING

Statistical information: Hawaii State Department of Business, POB 2359, Honolulu 96804. Publishes *The State of Hawaii Data Book.*

Atlas of Hawaii. 3rd ed. Hawaii Univ. Press, 1998

Morris, Nancy J. and Dean, Love, *Hawai'i.* [Bibliography] ABC-Clio, Oxford and Santa Barbara (CA), 1992

Oliver, Anthony M., *Hawaii Facts and Reference Book: Recent Historical Facts and Events in the Fiftieth State.* Honolulu, 1995

IDAHO

KEY HISTORICAL EVENTS

The original people of Idaho were Kutenai, Kalispel, Nez Percé and other tribes, living on the Pacific watershed of the northern Rocky Mountains. European exploration began in 1805, and after 1809 there were trading posts and small settlements, with fur-trapping as the primary economic activity. The area was disputed between Britain and the USA until 1846 when British claims were dropped.

In 1860 gold and silver were found, and there was a rush of immigrant prospectors. The newly enlarged population needed organized government. An area including that which is now Montana was created a Territory in March 1863. Montana was separated from it in 1864. Population growth continued, stimulated by refugees from the Confederate states after the Civil War and by settlements of Mormons from Utah.

Fur-trapping and mining gave way to farming, especially of grains, as the main economic activity. Idaho became a state in 1890, with its capital at Boise. The Territory capital, Idaho City, had been a gold-mining boom town in the 1860s whose population (about 40,000 at its height) was the largest in the Pacific Northwest. The population declined to 1,000 by 1869.

During the 20th century the Indian population shrunk to nearly 1%. The Mormon community has grown to include much of southeastern Idaho and more than half the church-going population of the state.

Industrial history has been influenced by the development of the Snake River of southern Idaho for hydro-electricity and irrigation, especially at the American Falls and reservoir. Processing food, minerals and timber are important to the economy. Much of the state, however, remains sparsely populated and rural. Rapid growth of high technology companies in Idaho's metropolitan areas has prompted economic diversification and rapid population growth.

TERRITORY AND POPULATION

Idaho is within the Rocky Mountains and bounded north by Canada, east by Montana and Wyoming, south by Nevada and Utah, west by Oregon and Washington. Land area, 82,747 sq. miles (214,314 sq. km). Census population, 1 April 2000, 1,293,953, an increase of 28·5% since 1990. July 2004 estimate, 1,393,262.

Population in five census years was:

	White	*Black*	*American Indian*	*Asiatic*	*Total*	*Per sq. mile*
1910	319,221	651	3,488	2,234	325,594	3·9
1930	438,840	668	3,638	1,886	445,032	5·4
1980	901,641	2,716	10,521	5,948	943,935	11·3
1990	950,451	3,370	13,780	9,365	1,006,749	12·2
2000	1,177,304	5,456	17,645	13,197	1,293,953	15·6

Of the total population in 2000, 648,660 were male, 924,923 were 18 years old or older and 859,497 were urban. In 2000 Idaho's Hispanic population was 101,690, up from 52,927 in 1990 (an increase of 92·1%).

The largest cities are: Boise City, with a 2003 population of 190,117; Nampa, 64,269; Idaho Falls, 51,507; Pocatello, 51,009; Meridian, 41,127; Coeur d'Alene, 37,262; Twin Falls, 36,742; Caldwell, 31,041; Lewiston, 30,937.

SOCIAL STATISTICS

Births (2002), 20,970 (15·6 per 1,000 population); deaths, 9,923 (7·4); infant mortality rate, 2001, 6·2 per 1,000 live births; marriages, 2001, 14,867 (10·9 per 1,000 population); divorces, 7,080 (5·2).

CLIMATE

Boise City, Jan. 29°F (–1·7°C), July 74°F (23·3°C). Annual rainfall 12" (303 mm). Idaho belongs to the Mountain States climate zone (*see* UNITED STATES: Climate).

CONSTITUTION AND GOVERNMENT

The constitution adopted in 1890 is still in force; it has had 105 amendments. The Legislature consists of a Senate of 35 members and a House of Representatives of 70 members, all the legislators being elected for two years. It meets annually.

For the 109th Congress, which convened in Jan. 2005, Idaho sends two members to the House of Representatives. It is represented in the Senate by Larry Craig (R. 1991–2009) and Michael Crapo (R. 1999–2011).

The state is divided into 44 counties. The capital is Boise City.

RECENT ELECTIONS

In the 2004 presidential election Bush polled 409,235 votes; Kerry, 181,098; Badnarik, 3,844.

CURRENT ADMINISTRATION

Governor: Dirk Kempthorne (R.), 2003–07 (salary: $101,500).
Lieut.-Governor: Jim Risch (R.), 2003–07 ($26,750).
Secretary of State: Ben Ysursa (R.), 2003–07 ($82,500).

Government Website: http://www.accessidaho.org

ECONOMY

Per capita personal income (2002) was $25,042, ranking Idaho 45th among the 50 states.

Budget. In fiscal year 2002 total state revenue was $4,488m. Total expenditure was $5,234m. (education, $1,830m.; public welfare, $1,003m.; highways, $500m.; government administration, $222m.; correction, $172m.; health and hospitals, $158m.) Outstanding debt, in fiscal year 2002, $2,545m.

Performance. Gross State Product (GSP) in 2002 was $38,558m., ranking Idaho 44th in the United States.

ENERGY AND NATURAL RESOURCES

Electricity. Idaho's rivers provide dependable and low-cost electrical power. Almost two-thirds of Idaho's electrical needs come from this resource, resulting in electricity rates much lower than those found in the East and Midwest.

Water. The total area covered by water is approximately 821 sq. miles. Idaho is second only to California in the amount of water used for irrigating crops.

Minerals. Principal non-fuel minerals are processed phosphate rock, silver, gold, molybdenum and sand and gravel. The estimated value of total mineral output for 2003 was $269m., with an additional value-added through processing of phosphate rock of approximately $211m.

Agriculture. Agriculture is the second largest industry, despite a great part of the state being naturally arid. Extensive irrigation works have been carried out, bringing an estimated 3·5m. acres under irrigation, and there are over 50 soil conservation districts.

In 2003 there were 25,000 farms with a total area of 11·8m. acres; average value per acre (2002), $1,270. In 2003 the average farm was 472 acres.

Farm income, 2003, from crops, $1,848m., and livestock, $2,190m. The most important crops are potatoes and wheat. Other crops are sugarbeet, hay, barley, field peas and beans, onions and apples. The net farm income in 2003 was $1,210m. In 2003 there were 2·0m. cattle, 260,000 sheep, 26,000 hogs and 1·2m. poultry. There were 34m. food-sized trout produced on fish farms. The dairy industry is the fastest growing sector in Idaho agriculture.

Forestry. In 2002 there was a total of 21·65m. acres of forest, of which 16·16m. were national forest.

Fisheries. 74% of the commercial trout processed in the USA was produced in Idaho in 2002. Idaho ranked first in state trout production by producing fish to a value of $30·5m.

INDUSTRY

In 2002 Idaho's 1,763 manufacturing establishments had approximately 60,000 employees, with a payroll of $2,056m. Manufacturing is the leading industry, with value added in 2002 of $5,528m. Electronics and computer equipment made up the largest manufacturing component with value added of $2,718m.

Labour. In 2003, 113,033 people were employed in government, 95,817 in trade, 67,787 in professional and business services, 61,990 in educational and health services, 61,655 in manufacturing and 54,245 in leisure and hospitality. The workforce totalled 692,500 in 2003; state unemployment averaged 5·4%.

Trade Unions. Idaho has a right-to-work law. In 1997, 43,400 people were union members.

COMMUNICATIONS

Roads. In 2003 there were 46,929 miles of public roads (42,519 miles rural, 4,410 urban). Of these, 3,196 were on Native American reservations. There were 1,316,136 registered motor vehicles in 2003.

Rail. The state had (2001) approximately 1,700 miles of railways (including one Amtrak route).

Civil Aviation. There were 68 municipally-owned airports in 2003. There were 1,603,650 passenger enplanements statewide in 2003.

Shipping. Water transport is provided from the Pacific to the port of Lewiston, by way of the Columbia and Snake rivers, a distance of 464 miles.

Postal Services. Idaho is served by the United States Postal Service. Major private carriers, including UPS, Federal Express, and DHL Worldwide Express, provide Idaho residents with global shipping access. There are numerous local mailing and shipping services available in Idaho's larger cities.

SOCIAL INSTITUTIONS

Justice. The death penalty may be imposed for first degree murder or aggravated kidnapping, but the judge must consider mitigating circumstances before imposing a sentence of death. The only execution since 1976 was in 1994. In Nov. 2004 there were 6,309 incarcerated law offenders.

Religion. The leading religious denominations are the Church of Jesus Christ of Latter-day Saints (Mormons; 311,425 adherents in 2000), Roman Catholics, Methodists, Presbyterians, Episcopalians and Lutherans.

Education. In 2003–04 public elementary schools (grades K to 6) had 135,216 pupils and 8,048 teachers; secondary schools had 116,821 pupils and 7,387 classroom teachers. Average salary (2003–04) of teachers was $40,301 (elementary) and $41,422 (secondary).

The University of Idaho, founded at Moscow in 1889, had 559 full-time instructional faculty in 2003, and a total enrolment of 12,895. Boise State University had 278 full-time instructional faculty in 2003 and a total enrolment of 18,332. Idaho State University had 401 full-time instructional faculty in 2003 and a total enrolment of 13,621. There were seven other higher education institutions, three of them public institutions. College and university enrolment in the autumn of 2003 was 73,275.

Health. In 2003 there were 3,282 hospital beds in 48 licensed facilities.

Welfare. Old-age survivor disability insurance (OASDI) is granted to persons if they paid sufficiently into the system or meet other qualifications. 2002: total Idaho beneficiaries, 204,970 with total annual benefit payment of $1,951m.

CULTURE

Broadcasting. In 2003 there were 112 radio stations and 23 television stations.

Press. Idaho has 15 daily newspapers and 52 weekly papers.

Tourism. Money spent by travellers in 1997 was about $1,700m.

FURTHER READING

Statistical information: Idaho Commerce and Labor, 700 West State St., Boise 83720. Publishes *County Profiles of Idaho*, *Community Profiles of Idaho* and *Profile of Rural Idaho* on the Internet.

Schwantes, C. A., *In Mountain Shadows: a History of Idaho*. Nebraska Univ. Press, 1996

Website: http://www.cl.idaho.gov

ILLINOIS

KEY HISTORICAL EVENTS

Territory of a group of Algonquian-speaking tribes, Illinois was explored first by the French in 1673. France claimed the area until 1763 when, after the French and Indian War, it was ceded to Britain along with all the French land east of the Mississippi. In 1783 Britain recognized the US' title to Illinois, which became part of the North West Territory of the USA in 1787, and of Indiana Territory in 1800. Illinois became a Territory in its own right in 1809, and a state in 1818.

Settlers from the eastern states moved on to the fertile farmland, immigration increasing greatly with the opening in 1825 of the Erie Canal from New York along which settlers could move west and their produce back east for sale. Chicago was incorporated as a city in 1837 and quickly became the transport, trading and distribution centre of the middle west. Once industrial growth had begun there, a further wave of immigration took place in the 1840s, mainly of European refugees looking for work. This movement continued with varying force until the 1920s, when it was largely replaced by immigration of black work-seekers from the southern states.

During the 20th century the population became largely urban and heavy industry was established along an intensive network of rail and waterway routes. Chicago recovered from a destructive fire in 1871 to become the hub of this network and at one time the second largest American city.

TERRITORY AND POPULATION

Illinois is bounded north by Wisconsin, northeast by Lake Michigan, east by Indiana, southeast by the Ohio River (forming the boundary with Kentucky), and west by the Mississippi River (forming the boundary with Missouri and Iowa). Land area in 2000: 55,584 sq. miles (143,962 sq. km). Census population, 2000, 12,419,293, an increase of 8·6% since 1990. July 2004 estimate, 12,713,634.

Population in five census years was:

	White	*Black*	*Indian*	*All others*	*Total*	*Per sq. mile*
1910	5,526,962	109,049	188	2,392	5,638,591	100·6
1930	7,266,361	328,972	469	35,321	7,630,654	136·4
			All others			
1980	9,233,327	1,675,398	517,793		11,426,518	203·0

	White	*Black*	*American Indian, or Alaska Native*	*Asian or Pacific Islander*	*Other*	*Total*	*Per sq. mile*
1990	8,957,923	1,690,855	24,077	284,944	472,803	11,430,602	205·6
2000	9,125,471	1,876,875	31,006	428,213	957,728	12,419,293	223·4

Of the total population in 2000, 6,338,957 were female, 9,173,842 were 18 years old or older and 10,909,520 were urban. In 2000 the Hispanic population was 1,527,573 (904,449 in 1990).

The most populous cities (2000 census population) are: Chicago, 2,896,016; Rockford, 150,115; Aurora, 142,990; Naperville, 128,358; Peoria, 112,936; Springfield, 111,454; Joliet, 106,221; Elgin, 94,487; Waukegan, 87,901; Cicero, 85,616.

Metropolitan area populations, 2000 census: Chicago–Gary–Kenosha, 9,157,540; Rockford, 371,236; Peoria–Pekin, 347,387; Springfield, 201,437; Champaign–Urbana, 179,669.

SOCIAL STATISTICS

Births in 2002 were 180,622 (14·3 per 1,000); deaths, 106,667 (8·5 per 1,000); infant mortality rate (2001) 7·7 per 1,000 live births; marriages (2000), 89,469; divorces and annulments (2000), 39,429.

CLIMATE

2001 statistics: Jan. 24·6°F (–4·1°C), July 74·6°F (23·6°C) average mean (O'Hare International Airport). Average annual rainfall 35·55". In 2000 total rainfall was 31·43". Illinois belongs to the Great Lakes climate zone (*see* UNITED STATES: Climate).

CONSTITUTION AND GOVERNMENT

The present constitution became effective on 1 July 1971. The General Assembly consists of a House of Representatives of 118 members elected for two years, and a Senate of 59 members who are divided into three groups; in one, they are elected for terms of four years, four years, and two years; in the next, for terms of four years, two years, and four years; and in the last, for terms of two years, four years, and four years. Sessions are annual. The state is divided into legislative districts, in each of which one senator is chosen; each district is divided into two representative districts, in each of which one representative is chosen.

For the 109th Congress, which convened in Jan. 2005, Illinois sends 19 members to the House of Representatives. It is represented in the Senate by Richard Durbin (D. 1997–2009) and Barack Obama (D. 2005–11).

The capital is Springfield.

RECENT ELECTIONS

In the 2004 presidential election Kerry polled 2,891,550 votes; Bush, 2,345,946; Badnarik, 32,442.

CURRENT ADMINISTRATION

Governor: Rod Blagojevich (D.), 2003–07 (salary: $150,691).

Lieut.-Governor: Patrick Quinn (D.), 2003–07 ($115,235).

Secretary of State: Jesse White (D.), 2003–07 ($132,963).

Government Website: http://www.illinois.gov

ECONOMY

Important industries include financial services, manufacturing, retail and transportation. *Per capita* personal income (2002) was $33,320 in Illinois.

Budget. In 2002 total state revenues $41,095m. Total expenditure was $49,131m. (education, $14,098m.; public welfare, $10,940m.; highways, $3,656m.; health, $2,574m.; correction, $1,359m.) Debt outstanding, in 2002, $34,761m.

Performance. Gross State Product in 2002 was $486,139m., ranking Illinois 5th in the United States.

Banking and Finance. In 2000 there were 526 state-chartered banks, 32 foreign banks and 245 national banks. The assets of banks in Illinois totalled $435,669,401,000 in 2000.

ENERGY AND NATURAL RESOURCES

Electricity. Electricity production 2000, 113·6bn. kWh. There were 11 nuclear plants, with net production of 81·4bn. kWh.

Oil and Gas. Natural gas consumption in 1999 was 1,035bn. cu. ft; total petroleum consumption was 250,369,000 bbls.

Water. The total area covered by water is approximately 2,531 sq. miles. In 1999 there were 26,443 miles of streams.

Minerals. The chief mineral product is coal; in 2001 there were 19 operative mines; the coal output was 33,793,509 tons. Mineral production also includes sand, gravel and limestone. Value of non-fuel mineral production in 2002 was $950m.

Agriculture. In 2002 there were 76,000 farms in Illinois that contained 27·7m. acres of land. The average size of farms was 364 acres and was valued at $2,425 per acre. In 2002 cash receipts from farm marketings in Illinois totalled $7·53bn. Cash receipts: for corn totalled $2·9bn.; for soybeans, $2·1bn.; for livestock and products, $1·8bn.; for hogs, $920m.; for cattle, $528m.; for dairy products, $301m.; for wheat, $111m. The net farm income in 2001 was $1,419m. In 2000 Illinois was the second largest producer among US states of corn and soybeans. There were 4·25m. hogs and pigs in 2001. On 1 Jan. 2000 there were 1·51m. cattle including 445,000 beef cows and 125,000 milch cows.

Forestry. In 2000 there were six state forests and 27 conservation areas. The gross forest area within unit boundaries in 2002 was 856,686 acres of which 270,000 acres was National Forest Land. Total forested area in 2002 was 4·33m. acres.

Fisheries. In 2001 four hatcheries in Illinois had 75m. fish.

INDUSTRY

In 2001 the state's 17,134 manufacturing establishments had 820,000 employees, earning $32,832m. Total value added by manufacturing in 2001 was $94,124m.

Labour. Selected employee sectors, 12 March 2000: manufacturing, 852,646; retail trade, 636,996; healthcare and social assistance, 631,926; accommodation and food services, 406,601; finance and insurance, 344,564; wholesale trade, 344,027;

construction, 265,481; transportation and warehousing, 215,439; arts, entertainment and recreation, 72,105; utilities, 31,173; mining, 8,939. The unemployment rate in 2002 was 6·5%.

Trade Unions. Labour union membership in 2000 was 1,046,300. Approximately 18·9% of workers in Illinois were members of unions in 1998.

INTERNATIONAL TRADE

Imports and Exports. In 2001 exports from Illinois totalled approximately $31·8bn. Exports included computer equipment, industrial machinery, chemicals and agricultural products.

Trade Fairs. Through the Illinois Department of Commerce and Community Affairs (Illinois Trade Office), activities are held to promote trade. Between Aug. 2000 and July 2001 approximately 20 major events (catalogue shows and trade missions including Canada, Mexico, South America, the Middle East, Africa and Asia Pacific) were held.

COMMUNICATIONS

Roads. In 2002 there were 138,337 miles of roads comprising 36,833 miles of urban road and 101,504 miles of rural road. There were 7,524,909 passenger cars in 2001, 1,249,505 pickup trucks, 290,299 recreational vehicles, buses and trucks, 222,607 motorcycles and 176,870 Interstate Registration Plan vehicles.

Rail. Union Station, Chicago is the home of Amtrak's national hub. Amtrak trains provide service to cities in Illinois to many destinations in the US. Illinois is also served by a metro (CTA) system, and by seven groups of commuter railways controlled by METRA, which has many stations and serves several Illinois counties. Total passengers using Amtrak stations in 2000 were 3,583,707. State system mileage, Dec. 2001: Federal aid interstate non-toll, 1,890 miles; other marked non-toll, 11,422 miles; state supplementary non-toll, 2,638 miles; total length, 15,950 miles. There is also a metro system in Chicago (108 miles).

Civil Aviation. In 2001 there were 134 public airports, 496 restricted landing areas and 272 heliports. There were 38,865,020 passenger enplanements statewide in 2000.

Shipping. In 2000 total cargo handled by Chicago's ports was 23,929,489 tons.

Telecommunications. In March 2000, 48,395 employees were on a payroll of $3,000·5m.

Postal Services. In 2001 there were more than 1,000 postal stations.

SOCIAL INSTITUTIONS

Justice. In fiscal year 2001 there were 27 adult correctional centers with an adult inmate population of 45,629. The total number of adult admissions in 2000 was 28,045 and the total number of exits 27,636.

Executions began in 1990 following the US Supreme Court's reinstatement of capital punishment in 1976, with the most recent execution being on 17 March 1999. However, on 31 Jan. 2000 the death penalty was suspended.

A Civil Rights Act (1941), as amended, bans all forms of discrimination by places of public accommodation, including inns, restaurants, retail stores, railroads, aeroplanes, buses, etc., against persons on account of 'race, religion, colour, national ancestry or physical or mental handicap'; another section similarly mentions 'race or colour'.

The Fair Employment Practices Act of 1961, as amended, prohibits discrimination in employment based on race, colour, sex, religion, national origin or ancestry, by employers, employment agencies, labour organizations and others. These principles are embodied in the 1971 constitution.

The Illinois Human Rights Act (1979) prevents unlawful discrimination in employment, real property transactions, access to financial credit and public accommodations, by authorizing the creation of a Department of Human Rights to enforce, and a Human Rights Commission to adjudicate, allegations of unlawful discrimination.

Religion. In 1997 there were 6,579,000 Christians and 269,000 Jews in Illinois. Among the larger Christian denominations are: Roman Catholic (3·6m.), Presbyterian Church, USA (0·2m.), Lutheran Church in America (0·2m.), Lutheran Church Missouri Synod (325,000), American Baptist (105,000), Disciples of Christ (75,000), United Methodist (505,000), Southern Baptist (265,000), United Church of Christ (192,000), Assembly of God (63,000) and Church of Nazarene (50,000).

Education. Education is free and compulsory for children between seven and 16 years of age. In 2000–01 pre K-8 enrolment (public) was 1,471,360; pre K-8 (non-public), 254,817; grades 9–12 enrolment (public), 577,432; grades 9–12 (non-public), 68,559. The total number of elementary teachers (public) was 70,023; elementary teachers (non-public), 11,104; secondary teachers (public), 31,726; secondary teachers (non-public), 4,415. The median salary for all classroom (pre K-12) teachers was $44,977. In autumn 2001 higher education institutions had a total enrolment of 752,753 at nine public universities, 48 community colleges, 97 not-for-profit and 25 for-profit independent colleges and universities.

Major colleges and universities (autumn 2001):

Founded	*Name*	*Place*	*Control*	*Enrolment*
1851	Northwestern University	Evanston	Independent	17,000
1857	Illinois State University	Normal	Public	21,240
1867	University of Illinois	Urbana/Champaign	Public	39,291
		Springfield (1969)		4,288
		Chicago (1946)		24,955
1867	Chicago State University	Chicago	Public	7,079
1869	Southern Illinois University	Carbondale	Public	21,598
		Edwardsville (1957)		12,442
1890	Loyola University of Chicago	Chicago	Roman Catholic	13,019
1891	University of Chicago	Chicago	Independent	12,883
1895	Eastern Illinois University	Charleston	Public	10,531
1895	Northern Illinois University	DeKalb	Public	23,783
1897	Bradley University	Peoria	Independent	5,996
1899	Western Illinois University	Macomb	Public	13,206
1940	Illinois Institute of Technology	Chicago	Independent	6,050
1945	Roosevelt University	Chicago	Independent	7,490
1961	Northeastern Illinois University	Chicago	Public	10,999
1969	Governors State University	University Park	Public	5,860

Health. In 2001 there were 192 community hospitals, with 36,800 beds. Total admissions in 2001 were 1,559,000.

Welfare. In fiscal year 2002 the estimated amount spent on medical assistance programmes was $7·66bn.; child support enforcement, $233m.; Office of the Inspector General, $22m.; Public Aid Recoveries, $19m.; administration, $113m.

In 1999 there were 42,300 participating providers in the state and 24,540,000 medical claims processed.

CULTURE

Broadcasting. In 1999 there were 219 radio stations, nine radio networks and 67 television broadcasting establishments. In 1997 there were 184 cable and other pay TV services establishments.

Press. In 1999 there were 983 newspapers, periodicals, book and database publisher establishments.

Tourism. Visitors spent over $22bn. yielding $15bn. in tax revenue in 1999. The recommended appropriations for tourism for fiscal year 2002 were $69,091,300.

FURTHER READING

Statistical information: Department of Commerce and Community Affairs, 620 Adams St., Springfield 62701. Publishes *Illinois State and Regional Economic Data Book.* Bureau of Economic and Business Research, Univ. of Illinois, 1206 South 6th St., Champaign 61820. Publishes *Illinois Statistical Abstract.*

Blue Book of the State of Illinois. Edited by Secretary of State. Springfield. Biennial

Miller, D. L., *City of the Century: The Epic of Chicago and the Making of America.* Simon and Schuster, New York, 1996

The Illinois State Library: Springfield, IL 62756.

INDIANA

KEY HISTORICAL EVENTS

The area was inhabited by Algonquian-speaking tribes when the first European explorers (French) laid claim to it in the 17th century. They established some fortified trading posts but there was little settlement. In 1763 the area passed to Britain, with other French-claimed territory east of the Mississippi. In 1783 Indiana became part of the North West Territory of the USA; it became a separate territory in 1800 and a state in 1816. Until 1811 there had been continuing conflict with the Indian inhabitants, who were then defeated at Tippecanoe.

Early farming settlement was by families of British and German descent, including Amish and Mennonite communities. Later industrial development offered an incentive for more immigration from Europe, and, later, from the southern states. In 1906 the town of Gary was laid out by the United States Steel Corporation and named after its chairman, Elbert H. Gary. The industry flourished on navigable water midway between supplies of iron ore and of coal. Trade and distribution in general benefited from Indiana Port on Lake Michigan, especially after the opening of the St Lawrence Seaway in 1959. The Ohio River was also exploited for carrying freight.

Indianapolis was built after 1821 and became the state capital in 1825. Natural gas was discovered in the neighbourhood in the late 19th century. This stimulated the growth of a motor industry, celebrated by the Indianapolis 500 race, held annually since 1911.

TERRITORY AND POPULATION

Indiana is bounded west by Illinois, north by Michigan and Lake Michigan, east by Ohio and south by Kentucky across the Ohio River. Land area, 35,867 sq. miles (92,895 sq. km). Census population, 1 April 2000, was 6,080,485, an increase of 9·7% since 1990. July 2004 estimate, 6,237,569.

Population in five census years was:

	White	*Black*	*Indian*	*Asiatic*	*Other*	*Total*	*Per sq. mile*
1930	3,125,778	111,982	285	458	....	3,238,503	89·4
1960	4,388,554	269,275	948	2,447	....	4,662,498	128·9
1980	5,004,394	414,785	7,836	20,557	42,652	5,490,224	152·8
1990	5,020,700	432,092	12,720	37,617	41,030	5,544,159	154·6
2000	5,320,022	510,034	15,815	61,131	173,483	6,080,485	169·5

Of the total population in 2000, 3,098,011 were female, 4,506,089 were 18 years old or older and 4,304,011 were urban. Indiana's Hispanic population was 214,536 in 2000, a 117·2% increase on the 1990 total of 98,789.

The largest cities with census population, 2000, are: Indianapolis (capital), 761,296; Fort Wayne, 205,727; Evansville, 121,582; South Bend, 107,789; Gary, 102,746; Hammond, 83,048; Bloomington, 69,291; Muncie, 67,430; Anderson, 59,734; Terre Haute, 59,614.

SOCIAL STATISTICS

2002 statistics: births, 85,081 (13·8 per 1,000 population); deaths, 55,396 (9·0); infant mortality rate, 2001, 7·5 (per 1,000 live births). Marriages (2001), 34,100.

CLIMATE

Indianapolis, Jan. 29°F (–1·7°C), July 76°F (24·4°C). Annual rainfall 41" (1,034 mm). Indiana belongs to the Mid-West climate zone (*see* UNITED STATES: Climate).

CONSTITUTION AND GOVERNMENT

The present constitution (the second) dates from 1851; it has had (as of Aug. 1999) 41 amendments. The General Assembly consists of a Senate of 50 members elected for four years, and a House of Representatives of 100 members elected for two years. It meets annually.

For the 109th Congress, which convened in Jan. 2005, Indiana sends nine members to the House of Representatives. It is represented in the Senate by Richard Lugar (R. 1977–2007) and Evan Bayh (D. 1999–2011).

The state capital is Indianapolis. The state is divided into 92 counties and 1,008 townships.

RECENT ELECTIONS

In the 2004 presidential election Bush polled 1,479,438 votes; Kerry, 969,011; Badnarik, 18,058.

CURRENT ADMINISTRATION

Governor: Mitch Daniels (R.), 2005–09 (salary: $95,000).
Lieut.-Governor: Becky Skillman (R.), 2005–09 ($76,000).
Secretary of State: Todd Rokita (R.), 2003–07 ($66,000).

Government Website: http://www.in.gov

ECONOMY

Per capita personal income (2002) was $28,233.

Budget. In 2002 total state revenue was $20,116m. Total expenditure was $22,205m. (education, $7,931m.; public welfare, $5,125m.; highways, $1,570m.; government administration, $768m.; correction, $641m.) Outstanding debt, in 2002, $9,456m.

Performance. In 2002 Gross State Product was $204,946m., ranking Indiana 15th in the United States.

ENERGY AND NATURAL RESOURCES

Oil and Gas. Production of crude oil in 2003 was 1,865,000 bbls.; 1,309m. cu. ft of natural gas was produced in 2002.

Water. The total area covered by water is approximately 550 sq. miles.

Minerals. The state produced 53,500,000 tonnes of crushed stone and 257m. tonnes of dimension stone in 2003. Production of coal (2001) was 18bn. short tons. Value of domestic non-fuel mineral production, in 2003, $734m.

Agriculture. Indiana is largely agricultural, about 75% of its total area being in farms. In 2003, 59,500 farms had 15·0m. acres (average, 253 acres). The average value of land and buildings per acre was $2,750 in 2003. Acreage harvested in 2003 was 12·0m., with a market value of $3,462m. for the top two crops (corn and soybeans).

Farm income 2002, $4,800m.: crops were $3,249m.; livestock and products, $1,551m. The net farm income in 2001 was $964m. The four most important products were corn, soybeans, hogs and dairy products. The livestock on 1 Jan. 2004 included 830,000 all cattle, 153,000 milch cows, 45,000 sheep and lambs, 3·1m. hogs and pigs, 22·7m. chickens and 13·1m. turkeys. In 2003 the wool clip yielded 270,000 lb of wool from 40,000 sheep and lambs.

Forestry. In 2002 there were 4·50m. acres of forest including 191,000 acres of national forest.

INDUSTRY

In 2001 Indiana's 9,131 manufacturing establishments had 604,000 employees, earning $23,471m. Total value added by manufacturing in 2001 was $72,122m. The steel industry is the largest in the country.

Labour. Total non-agricultural employment, 2002, 3,523,234. Employees by branch, 2002 (in 1,000): services, 1,562; manufacturing, 601; wholesale and retail trade, 552; government, 429. The unemployment rate in 2003 was 5·1%.

INTERNATIONAL TRADE

Imports and Exports. Exports valued $16·4bn. in 2003.

COMMUNICATIONS

Roads. In 2002 there were 94,288 miles of road (73,893 miles rural) and 5,664,726 registered motor vehicles.

Rail. In 2002 there were 4,255 miles of mainline railway of which 3,872 miles were Class I.

Civil Aviation. Of airports in 2003, 115 were for public use and 581 were for private use. There were 4,915,996 passenger enplanements statewide in 2003.

SOCIAL INSTITUTIONS

Justice. Following the US Supreme Court's reinstatement of the death penalty in 1976, death sentences have been awarded since 1980. There were two executions in 2003 but none in 2004. In June 2002, 21,425 prisoners were under the jurisdiction of state and federal correctional authorities.

The Civil Rights Act of 1885 forbids places of public accommodation to bar any persons on grounds not applicable to all citizens alike; no citizen may be disqualified for jury service 'on account of race or colour'. An Act of 1947 makes it an offence to spread religious or racial hatred.

A 1961 Act provided 'all of its citizens equal opportunity for education, employment and access to public conveniences and accommodations' and created a Civil Rights Commission.

Religion. Religious denominations include Methodists, Roman Catholics, Disciples of Christ, Baptists, Lutherans, Presbyterian churches, Society of Friends, Episcopalians.

Education. School attendance is compulsory from seven to 16 years. In 2003–04 there were an estimated 551,398 pupils attending elementary schools and 459,290 at secondary schools. The average expenditure per pupil was $8,582. Teachers' salaries averaged $45,791 (2003–04). Total expenditure for public schools, 2001–02, $7,988m.

Some leading institutions for higher education were (2003):

Founded	*Institution*	*Control*	*Students (full-time)*
1801	Vincennes University	State	8,185[1]
1824	Indiana University, Bloomington	State	29,768
1832	Wabash College, Crawfordsville	Independent	858
1837	De Pauw University, Greencastle	Methodist	2,319
1842	University of Notre Dame	R.C.	8,303
1847	Earlham College, Richmond	Quaker	1,125
1850	Butler University, Indianapolis	Independent	4,424
1859	Valparaiso University, Valparaiso	Evangelical Lutheran Church	3,003
1870	Indiana State University, Terre Haute	State	9,394
1874	Purdue University, Lafayette	State	30,424
1898	Ball State University, Muncie	State	17,411
1902	University of Indianapolis, Indianapolis	Methodist	2,916
1963	Ivy Tech State College, Indianapolis	State	9,054
1969	Indiana University-Purdue University, Indianapolis	State	21,015
1985	University of Southern Indiana, Evansville	State	8,813

[1]2001.

Health. In 2002 there were 112 community hospitals with 18,961 beds. A total of 715,936 patients were admitted during the year.

Welfare. Medicare enrolment in July 2002 totalled 865,366. In 2002 a total of 686,712 people in Indiana received Medicaid. In Dec. 2003 there were 1,032,417 Old-Age, Survivors, and Disability Insurance (OASDI) beneficiaries. A total of 120,319 people were receiving payments under Temporary Assistance for Needy Families (TANF) in June 2004.

CULTURE

Broadcasting. In 2004 there were 81 television stations and 301 radio stations.

Press. There were 332 newspapers in circulation in 2004.

Tourism. Tourists—65% of whom travelled from outside the state—spent $6·5bn. in 2001.

FURTHER READING

Statistical information: Indiana Business Research Center, Indiana Univ., Indianapolis 46202. Publishes *Indiana Factbook.*

Gray, R. D. (ed.) *Indiana History: a Book of Readings.* Indiana Univ. Press, 1994

Martin, J. B., *Indiana: an Interpretation.* Indiana Univ. Press, 1992

State Library: Indiana State Library, 140 North Senate, Indianapolis 46204.

IOWA

KEY HISTORICAL EVENTS

Originally the territory of the Iowa Indians, the area was explored by the Frenchmen Marquette and Joliet in 1673. French trading posts were set up, but there was little other settlement. In 1803 the French sold their claim to Iowa to the USA as part of the Louisiana Purchase. The land was still occupied by Indians but, in the 1830s, the tribes sold their land to the US government and migrated to reservations. Iowa became a US Territory in 1838 and a state in 1846.

The state was settled by immigrants drawn mainly from neighbouring states to the east. Later there was more immigration from Protestant states of northern Europe. The land was extremely fertile and most immigrants came to farm. Not all the Indian population had accepted the cession and there were some violent confrontations, notably the murder of settlers at Spirit Lake in 1857. The capital, Des Moines, was founded in 1843 as a fort to protect Indian rights. It expanded rapidly with the growth of a local coal field after 1910.

TERRITORY AND POPULATION

Iowa is bounded east by the Mississippi River (forming the boundary with Wisconsin and Illinois), south by Missouri, west by the Missouri River (forming the boundary with Nebraska), northwest by the Big Sioux River (forming the boundary with South Dakota) and north by Minnesota. Land area, 55,869 sq. miles (144,700 sq. km). Census population, 1 April 2000, 2,926,324, an increase of 5·4% since 1990. July 2004 estimate, 2,954,451.

Population in five census years was:

	White	*Black*	*Indian*	*Asiatic*	*Total*	*Per sq. mile*
1870	1,188,207	5,762	48	3	1,194,020	21·5
1930	2,452,677	17,380	660	222	2,470,939	44·1
			All others			
1980	2,839,225	41,700	32,882		2,913,808	51·7
1990	2,683,090	48,090	45,575		2,776,755	49·7
2000	2,748,640	61,853	115,831		2,926,324	52·4

Of the total population in 2000, 1,490,809 were female, 2,192,686 were 18 years old or older and 1,787,432 were urban. In 2000 the Hispanic population was 82,473, up from 32,647 in 1990 (an increase of 152·6%).

The largest cities in the state, with their population in 2003, are: Des Moines (capital), 196,093; Cedar Rapids, 122,542; Davenport, 97,512; Sioux City, 83,876; Waterloo, 67,054; Iowa City, 63,807; Council Bluffs, 58,656; Dubuque, 57,204; Ames, 53,284; West Des Moines, 51,699; Cedar Falls, 36,429; Urbandale, 31,868; Bettendorf, 31,456; Ankeny, 31,144; Marion, 28,756.

SOCIAL STATISTICS

2002 statistics: births, 37,559 (12·8 per 1,000); deaths, 27,978 (9·5 per 1,000); infant mortality, 2001, 5·6 per 1,000 live births; marriages, 2003, 20,371; dissolutions of marriages, 8,285.

CLIMATE

Cedar Rapids, Jan. 17·6°F, July 74·2°F. Annual rainfall 34". Des Moines, Jan. 19·4°F, July 76·6°F. Annual rainfall 33·12". Iowa belongs to the Mid-West climate zone (*see* UNITED STATES: Climate).

CONSTITUTION AND GOVERNMENT

The constitution of 1857 still exists; it has had 46 amendments. The General Assembly comprises a Senate of 50 and a House of Representatives of 100 members, meeting annually for an unlimited session. Senators are elected for four years, half retiring every second year: Representatives for two years. The Governor and Lieut.-Governor are elected for four years.

For the 109th Congress, which convened in Jan. 2005, Iowa sends five members to the House of Representatives. It is represented in the Senate by Chuck Grassley (R. 1981–2011) and Tom Harkin (D. 1985–2009).

Iowa is divided into 99 counties; the capital is Des Moines.

RECENT ELECTIONS

In the 2004 presidential election Bush polled 751,957 votes; Kerry, 741,898; Nader, 5,973.

CURRENT ADMINISTRATION

Governor: Tom Vilsack (D.), 2003–07 (salary: $107,482).
Lieut.-Governor: Sally Pederson (D.), 2003–07 ($76,698).
Secretary of State: Chet Culver (D.), 2003–07 ($87,990).

Government Website: http://www.iowa.gov/state/main/index.html

ECONOMY

Per capita personal income (2002) was $28,141.

Budget. In the fiscal year 2004 net state general fund revenue was $4,684·0m. Total state general fund expenditure was $4,517·5m. (education, $2,782·3m.; human services, $797·3m.; justice, $465·9m.; administration and regulation, $362·9m.; health and human rights, $47·2m.; agriculture and natural resources, $34·2m.; economic development, $19·5m.; transportation, $8·2m.) Outstanding debt, in 2003, $1,561m.

Performance. Gross State Product was $98,232m. in 2002, ranking Iowa 29th in the United States.

ENERGY AND NATURAL RESOURCES

Water. The total area covered by water is approximately 401 sq. miles.

Minerals. Production in 2003: crushed stone, 34·7m. tonnes; sand and gravel, 14·0m. tonnes. The value of domestic non-fuel mineral products in 2003 was $478m.

Agriculture. Iowa is the wealthiest of the agricultural states, partly because nearly the whole area (92%) is arable and included in farms. The total farm area, 2003, is 31·7m. acres. The average farm in 2002 was 352 acres. The average value of buildings and land per acre was, in 2002, $2,005. The number of farms declined in the latter years of the 20th century, from 174,000 in 1960 to 90,000 in 2003.

Farm income (2002), $13,173m.: from crops, $6,757m., and livestock, $5,162m. The net farm income in 2001 was $1,946m. In 2002 production of corn was 1,963m. bu.[1], value $4,359m.; and soybeans, 499m. bu.[1], value $2,766m. In 2003 livestock included: swine, 15·8m.[1]; milch cows, 201,000; all cattle, 3·30m.; sheep and lambs, 255,000. The wool clip yielded 1·36m. lb.

[1]More than any other state.

Forestry. Total forested area was 2·1m. acres in 2002.

INDUSTRY

In 2002 Iowa's 3,718 manufacturing establishments had 222,501 employees, earning $8,049m. Total value added by manufacturing in 2001 was $29,636m.

Labour. In Sept. 2003 services employed 430,200 people; trade, 301,200; manufacturing establishments, 220,700. Iowa had an unemployment rate of 4·6% in Sept. 2003.

COMMUNICATIONS

Roads. In 2003 there were 113,226 miles of streets and highways. There were 2,127,890 licensed drivers and 2,451,048 registered vehicles.

Rail. In 2004 the state had 4,163 miles of track, three Class I, four Class II and 12 Class III railways.

Civil Aviation. Airports numbered 226 in 2004, consisting of 103 publicly owned, 115 privately owned and eight commercial facilities. There were 3,803 registered aircraft and 1,501,546 passenger enplanements in Iowa in 2003.

SOCIAL INSTITUTIONS

Justice. The death penalty was abolished in Iowa in 1965. In 2004 the nine state prisons had 8,611 inmates.

Religion. Chief religious bodies in 2004: Roman Catholics, 529,776 members; United Methodists, 195,877; Evangelical Lutherans in America, 260,832 baptized members; USA Presbyterians, 49,389; United Church of Christ, 38,945.

Education. School attendance is compulsory for 24 consecutive weeks annually during school age (7–16). In 2003–04, 485,011 pupils were attending primary and secondary schools; 37,243 pupils attending non-public schools; classroom teachers numbered 33,688 for public schools with an average salary of $39,432. In 2004 the state spent an average of $6,372 on each elementary and secondary school student.

Leading institutions for higher education enrolment figures (autumn 2004) were:

Founded	*Institution*	*Control*	*Professors*	*Full-time Students*
1843	Clarke College, Dubuque	Independent	83	1,180
1846	Grinnell College, Grinnell	Independent	142	1,485
1847	University of Iowa, Iowa City	State	1,713	29,745
1851	Coe College, Cedar Rapids	Independent	73	1,218
1852	Wartburg College, Waverly	Evangelical Lutheran	104	1,804
1853	Cornell College, Mount Vernon	Independent	85	1154
1854	Upper Iowa University, Fayette	Independent	36	2,758
1858	Iowa State University, Ames	State	1,369	23,783
1859	Luther College, Decorah	Evangelical Lutheran	197	2,497
1876	Univ. of Northern Iowa, Cedar Falls	State	561	11,424
1881	Drake University, Des Moines	Independent	245	2,954
1882	St Ambrose University, Davenport	Roman Catholic	160	2,413
1891	Buena Vista University, Storm Lake	Presbyterian	82	2,775
1894	Morningside College, Sioux City	Methodist	65	806

Health. In 2004 the state had 123 community hospitals (11,924 beds).

Welfare. Iowa has a Civil Rights Act (1939) which makes it a misdemeanour for any place of public accommodation to deprive any person of 'full and equal enjoyment' of the facilities it offers the public.

Supplemental Security Income (SSI) assistance is available for the aged (65 or older), the blind and the disabled. As of June 2004, 3,748 elderly persons were drawing an average of $198·86 per month, 738 blind persons $335·79 per month, and 36,152 disabled persons $372·26 per month. In 2003 temporary assistance to needy families (TANF) was received by on average 20,019 cases monthly representing 52,019 recipients.

CULTURE

There were a total of 80 venues for live performances (2003).

Broadcasting. In 2004 there were 256 radio stations and 24 television stations.

Press. In 2004 there were a total of 326 newspapers.

Tourism. In 2003 there were 16·6m. visitors; value of industry, $4·6bn.

FURTHER READING

Annual Survey of Manufactures. US Department of Commerce
Government Finance. US Department of Commerce
Official Register. Secretary of State. Des Moines. Biennial
Smeal, L., *Iowa Historical and Biographical Index.* New York, 1984

State Government Website: http://www.iowa.gov
State Library of Iowa: Des Moines 50319.

KANSAS

KEY HISTORICAL EVENTS

The area was explored from Mexico in the 16th century, when Spanish travellers found groups of Kansas, Wichita, Osage and Pawnee tribes. The French claimed Kansas in 1682 and they established a valuable fur trade with local tribes in the 18th century. In 1803 the area passed to the USA as part of the Louisiana Purchase and became a base for pioneering trails further west. After 1830 it was 'Indian Territory' and a number of tribes displaced from eastern states were settled there. In 1854 the Kansas Territory was created and opened for white settlement. The early settlers were farmers from Europe or New England, but the Territory's position brought it into contact with southern ideas also. Until 1861 there were frequent outbreaks of violence over the issue of slavery. Slavery had been excluded from the future Territory by the Missouri Compromise of 1820, but the 1854 Kansas-Nebraska Act had affirmed the principle of 'popular sovereignty' to settle the issue, which was then fought out by opposing factions throughout 'Bleeding Kansas'.

Kansas finally entered the Union (as a non-slavery state) in 1861; the part of Colorado which had formed part of the Kansas Territory was then separated from it.

The economy developed through a combination of cattle-ranching and railways. Herds were driven to the railheads and shipped from vast stockyards, or slaughtered and processed in railhead meat-packing plants. Wheat and sorghum also became important once the plains could be ploughed on a large scale.

TERRITORY AND POPULATION

Kansas is bounded north by Nebraska, east by Missouri, with the Missouri River as boundary in the northeast, south by Oklahoma and west by Colorado. Land area, 81,815 sq. miles (211,900 sq. km). Census population, 1 April 2000, 2,688,418, an increase of 8·5% since 1990. July 2004 estimate, 2,735,502.

Population in five federal census years was:

	White	*Black*	*Indian*	*Asiatic*	*Total*	*Per sq. mile*
1870	346,377	17,108	914	—	364,399	4·5
1930	1,811,997	66,344	2,454	204	1,880,999	22·9
			All others			
1980	2,168,221	126,127	69,888		2,364,236	28·8
1990	2,231,986	143,076	102,512		2,477,574	30·3
2000	2,313,944	154,198	220,276		2,688,418	32·9

Of the total population in 2000, 1,359,944 were female, 1,975,425 were 18 years old or older and 1,920,669 were urban. In 1999 the estimated Hispanic population was 188,252, up from 93,671 in 1990 (an increase of 101·0%).

Cities, with 2000 census population: Wichita, 344,284; Overland Park, 149,080; Kansas City, 146,866; Topeka (capital), 122,377; Olathe, 92,962; Lawrence, 80,098.

SOCIAL STATISTICS

Vital statistics 2002: births, 39,412 (14·5 per 1,000 population); deaths, 25,021 (9·2); 2001: infant deaths, 7·4 per 1,000 live births. 2001: marriages, 20,300; divorces, 8,700.

CLIMATE

Dodge City, Jan. 29°F (–1·7°C), July 78°F (25·6°C). Annual rainfall 21" (518 mm). Kansas City, Jan. 30°F (–1·1°C), July 79°F (26·1°C). Annual rainfall 38" (947 mm). Topeka, Jan. 28°F (–2·2°C), July 78°F (25·6°C). Annual rainfall 35" (875 mm). Wichita, Jan. 31°F (–0·6°C), July 81°F (27·2°C). Annual rainfall 31" (777 mm). Kansas belongs to the Mid-West climate zone (*see* UNITED STATES: Climate).

CONSTITUTION AND GOVERNMENT

The year 1861 saw the adoption of the present constitution; it has had 89 amendments. The Legislature includes a Senate of 40 members, elected for four years, and a House of Representatives of 125 members, elected for two years. Sessions are annual.

For the 109th Congress, which convened in Jan. 2005, Kansas sends four members to the House of Representatives. It is represented in the Senate by Pat Roberts (R. 1997–2009) and Sam Brownback (R. 1997–2011).

The capital is Topeka. The state is divided into 105 counties.

RECENT ELECTIONS

In the 2004 presidential election Bush polled 736,456 votes; Kerry, 434,993; Nader, 9,348.

CURRENT ADMINISTRATION

Governor: Kathleen Sebelius (D.), 2003–07 (salary: $101,281).
Lieut.-Governor: John E. Moore (D.), 2003–07 ($28,647).
Secretary of State: Ron Thornburgh (R.), 2003–07 ($78,680).

Government Website: http://www.accesskansas.org

ECONOMY

Per capita income (2002) was $28,838.

Budget. In 2002 total state revenue was $9,694m. Total expenditure was $10,592m. (education, $3,988m.; public welfare, $1,986m.; highways, $1,131m.; health, $504m.; government administration, $502m.) Outstanding debt, in 2002, $2,288m.

Performance. Gross State Product in 2002 was $89,508m., ranking Kansas 31st in the United States.

ENERGY AND NATURAL RESOURCES

Water. The total area covered by water is approximately 459 sq. miles.

Minerals. Important fuel minerals are coal, petroleum and natural gas. Non-fuel minerals, mainly cement, salt and crushed stone, were worth $661m. in 2002.

Agriculture. Kansas is pre-eminently agricultural, but sometimes suffers from lack of rainfall in the west. In 2002 there were 63,000 farms with a total acreage of 47·4m. Average number of acres per farm was 752. Average value of farmland and buildings per acre, in 2002, was $687. Farm income, 2001, from crops, $2,585m.; from livestock and products, $5,536m. Chief crops: wheat, sorghum, maize, hay. The net farm income in 2001 was $958m. Wheat production was 262·98m. bu. in 2002. There is an extensive livestock industry, comprising, in 2000, 6·55m. cattle (only Texas had more), 100,000 sheep, 1·46m. pigs and 1·75m. poultry.

Forestry. The state had a forested area of 1·55m. acres in 2002.

INDUSTRY

In 2001 the state's 3,240 manufacturing establishments had 191,000 employees, earning $7,302m. Total value added by manufacturing in 2001 was $21,008m.

Labour. Total non-agricultural employment, 2001, 1,357,000. Employees by branch, 2001 (in 1,000): services, 358; wholesale and retail trade, 317; government, 249; manufacturing, 206; transportation and public utilities, 89. In 2002 the state unemployment rate was 5·1%.

COMMUNICATIONS

Roads. In 2002 there were 135,038 miles of roads (124,528 miles rural) and 2,336,701 registered motor vehicles.

Rail. There were 5,084 miles of railway as of 31 Dec. 2003.

Civil Aviation. There is an international airport at Wichita. There were 553,656 passenger enplanements statewide in 2000.

SOCIAL INSTITUTIONS

Justice. In June 2002 there were 8,758 federal and state prisoners. The death penalty is authorized for capital murder, but has not been used since 1965.

Religion. The most numerous religious bodies are Roman Catholics, Methodists and Disciples of Christ.

Education. In 1995 there were approximately 463,000 public elementary and secondary pupils enrolled and (1994–95) 30,588 teachers.

Kansas has six state-supported institutions of higher education: Kansas State University, Manhattan (1863); The University of Kansas, Lawrence, founded in 1865; Emporia State University, Emporia; Pittsburg State University, Pittsburg; Fort Hays State University, Hays; and Wichita State University, Wichita. The state also supports a two-year technical school, Kansas College of Technology, at Salina.

Education expenditure by state and local governments in 1997 was $2,874m.

Health. In 2001 there were 133 community hospitals with 11,200 beds. A total of 322,000 patients were admitted during the year.

Welfare. Medicare enrolment in July 2002 totalled 391,782. In 2000 a total of 262,557 people in Kansas received Medicaid. In Dec. 2003 there were 443,706 Old-Age, Survivors, and Disability Insurance (OASDI) beneficiaries. A total of 37,948 people were receiving payments under Temporary Assistance for Needy Families (TANF) in Sept. 2002.

FURTHER READING

Statistical information: Institute for Public Policy and Business Research, Univ. of Kansas, 607 Blake Hall, Lawrence 66045. Publishes *Kansas Statistical Abstract.*

Annual Economic Report of the Governor. Topeka

Drury, J. W., *The Government of Kansas.* Lawrence, Univ. of Kansas, 1970

State Library: Kansas State Library, Topeka.

KENTUCKY

KEY HISTORICAL EVENTS

Lying west of the Appalachians and south of the Ohio River, the area was the meeting place and battleground for the eastern Iroquois and the southern Cherokees. Northern Shawnees also penetrated. The first successful white settlement took place in 1769 when Daniel Boone reached the Bluegrass plains from the eastern, trans-Appalachian, colonies. After 1783 immigration from the east was rapid, settlers travelling by river or crossing the mountains by the Cumberland Gap. The area was originally attached to Virginia but became a separate state in 1792.

Large plantations dependent on slave labour were established, as were small farms worked by white owners. The state became divided on the issue of slavery, although plantation interests (mainly producing tobacco) dominated state government. In the event the state did not secede in 1861, and the majority of citizens supported the Union. Public opinion swung round in support of the south during the difficulties of the reconstruction period.

The eastern mountains became an important coal-mining area, tobacco-growing continued and the Bluegrass plains produced livestock, including especially fine thoroughbred horses.

TERRITORY AND POPULATION

Kentucky is bounded in the north by the Ohio River (forming the boundary with Illinois, Indiana and Ohio), northeast by the Big Sandy River (forming the boundary with West Virginia), east by Virginia, south by Tennessee and west by the Mississippi River (forming the boundary with Missouri). Land area, 39,728 sq. miles (102,895 sq. km). Census population, 2000, 4,041,769, an increase of 9·7% since 1990. July 2004 estimate, 4,145,922.

Population in five census years was:

	White	*Black*	*All others*	*Total*	*Per sq. mile*
1930	2,388,364	226,040	185	2,614,589	65·1
1960	2,820,083	215,949	2,124	3,038,156	76·2
1980	3,379,006	259,477	22,294	3,660,777	92·3
1990	3,391,832	262,907	30,557	3,685,296	92·8
2000	3,640,889	295,994	104,886	4,041,769	101·7

Of the total population in 2000, 2,066,401 were female, 3,046,951 were 18 years old or older and 2,253,800 were urban. Kentucky's Hispanic population was estimated to be 59,939, up 172·4% on the 1990 census figure of 22,005.

The principal cities with census population in 2000 are: Lexington-Fayette, 260,512; Louisville, 256,321; Owensboro, 54,067; Bowling Green, 49,296; Covington, 43,370; Hopkinsville, 30,089; Frankfort (capital), 27,741; Henderson, 27,373; Richmond, 27,152; Jeffersontown, 26,633.

SOCIAL STATISTICS

In 2002: births, 54,233 (13·3 per 1,000 population); deaths, 40,697 (9·9); infant deaths, 2001, 5·9 per 1,000 live births; marriages, 2000, 39,671 (11·4 per 1,000 population); divorces, 21,593 (5·6).

CLIMATE

Kentucky is in the Appalachian Mountains climatic zone (*see* UNITED STATES: Climate). It has a temperate climate. Temperatures are moderate during both winter and summer, precipitation is ample without a pronounced dry season, and winter snowfall amounts are variable. Mean annual temperatures range from 52°F in the northeast to 58°F in the southwest. Annual rainfall averages at about 45". Snowfall ranges from 5 to 10" in the southwest of the state, to 25" in the northeast, and 40" at higher altitudes in the southeast.

CONSTITUTION AND GOVERNMENT

The constitution dates from 1891; there had been three preceding it. The 1891 constitution was promulgated by convention and provides that amendments be submitted to the electorate for ratification. The General Assembly consists of a Senate of 38 members elected for four years, one half retiring every two years, and a House of Representatives of 100 members elected for two years. It has annual sessions. All citizens of 18 or over are qualified as electors. Registered voters, Nov. 2000, 2,556,815.

For the 109th Congress, which convened in Jan. 2005, Kentucky sends six members to the House of Representatives. It is represented in the Senate by Mitch McConnell (R. 1985–2009) and Jim Bunning (R. 1999–2011).

The capital is Frankfort. The state is divided into 120 counties.

RECENT ELECTIONS

In the 2004 presidential election Bush polled 1,069,439 votes; Kerry, 712,733; Nader, 8,856.

CURRENT ADMINISTRATION

Governor: Ernie Fletcher (R.), Dec. 2003–Dec. 2007 (salary: $112,704·96).

Lieut.-Governor: Stephen Pence (R.), Dec. 2003–Dec. 2007 ($95,814·96).

Secretary of State: Trey Grayson (R.), Jan. 2004–Jan. 2008 ($95,814·96).

Government Website: http://kentucky.gov

ECONOMY

Per capita personal income (2002) was $25,657.

Budget. In 2002 total state revenue was $16,073m. Total expenditure was $18,407m. (education, $5,853m.; public welfare, $4,796m.; highways, $1,731m.; government administration, $683m.; health, $530m.) Debt outstanding, in 2002, $9,039m.

Performance. Gross State Product in 2002 was $122,282m., ranking Kentucky 27th in the United States.

ENERGY AND NATURAL RESOURCES

Electricity. In 1999 production was 92,633m. kWh, of which 88,915m. kWh was from coal.

Oil and Gas. Production of crude oil in 2000 was 2·9m. bbls. (of 42 gallons); natural gas, 81,545m. cu. ft.

Water. The total area covered by water is approximately 679 sq. miles.

Minerals. The principal mineral is coal: 139·6m. short tons were mined in 1999, value $3,281m.; crushed stone, 56m. short tons, value $295m.; sand and gravel, 9·6m. short tons, value $33·0m.; clay, 0·9m. tonnes, value $3·8m. Other minerals include fluorspar, ball clay, gemstones, dolomite, cement and lime.

Agriculture. In 2002, 89,000 farms covered an area of 13·6m. acres. The average farm was 153 acres. In 2002 the average value of farmland and buildings per acre was $1,824.

Farm income, 2001, from crops, $1·28bn., and from livestock, $2·27bn. The net farm income in 2001 was $1,230m. The chief crop is tobacco: production, in 2001, 254·6m. lb. Other principal crops include corn (156·2m. bu.), soybeans, wheat, hay, fruit and vegetables, sorghum grain and barley.

Stock-raising is important in Kentucky, which has long been famous for its horses. The livestock in 2001 included 128,000 milch cows, 2·3m. cattle and calves, 21,000 sheep, 5·6m. chickens and 0·45m. swine.

Forestry. In 2002 Kentucky had 12·68m. acres forested land, of which 645,000 acres were national forest.

Fisheries. Cash receipts from aquaculture totalled $1·1m. in 2001.

INDUSTRY

In 2000 the state had 4,209 manufacturing plants and in 2001 there were 293,003 manufacturing employees. The value added by manufacture in 2001 was $31,722m. The leading manufacturing industries (by employment) in 2001 were transportation equipment, industrial machinery, food products, fabricated metal products and electronic equipment.

Labour. In Sept. 2002 the civilian labour force numbered 1,990,531. Of the 1,712,366 employed, 549,210 were engaged in services, 375,795 in trade, transportation and utilities, 293,003 in manufacturing, 40,028 in agriculture and 559,694 in other employment. The unemployment rate in 2001 was 5·6%.

Trade Unions. In 2000, 208,000 (13·6%) workers were union members.

INTERNATIONAL TRADE

Imports and Exports. Exports in 2001 totalled $9·04bn. with manufactured goods accounting for 95% of total exports. Transportation equipment, industrial machinery and chemicals were important manufactured exports. Livestock and coal were major non-manufactured goods exported.

COMMUNICATIONS

Roads. In 2002 there were 78,372 miles of roads comprising 11,889 miles of urban road and 66,483 miles of rural road. There were 3,600,752 registered motor vehicles.

Rail. In 2004 there were 2,760 miles of railway of which 2,299 miles were Class I.

Civil Aviation. There were (1996) 70 publicly used airports and (1992) 2,294 registered aircraft. Commercial airports providing scheduled airline services in Kentucky are located in Erlanger (Covington/Cincinnati area), Louisville, Lexington, Owensboro and Paducah. There were 2,328,894 passenger enplanements statewide in 2000.

Shipping. There is barge traffic on the 1,100 miles of navigable rivers. There are six public river ports, over 30 contract terminal facilities and 150 private terminal operations. Kentucky's waterways have access to the junction of the upper and lower Mississippi, Ohio and Tennessee-Tombigbee navigation corridors.

SOCIAL INSTITUTIONS

Justice. There are 12 adult prisons within the Department of Corrections Adult Institutions and three privately run adult institutions. In June 2002 there were 16,172 prison inmates. The death penalty is authorized for murder and kidnapping. As of Oct. 2004 there were 35 persons (including one female) under sentence of death. The last execution was in 1999.

Religion. The chief religious denominations in 2000 were: Southern Baptists, with 979,994 members, Roman Catholics (406,021), United Methodists (208,720), Christian Churches and Church of Christ (106,638) and Christian (Disciples of Christ) (67,611).

Education. Attendance at school between the ages of five and 16 years (inclusive) is compulsory, the normal term being 175 days. In 2001–02, 40,789 teachers were employed in public elementary and secondary schools. There were 630,436 pupils in public elementary and secondary schools. Public school classroom teachers' salaries (2001–02) averaged $36,688. The average total expenditure per pupil was $6,720.

There were also 4,207 teachers working in private elementary and secondary schools with some 71,812 students in 2001–02.

The state has 28 universities and senior colleges, one junior college and 28 community and technical colleges, with a total enrolment of 187,270 students (autumn 2001). Of these universities and colleges, 36 are state-supported and the remainder are supported privately. The largest of the institutions of higher learning are (autumn 2001): University of Kentucky, with 24,791 students; University of Louisville, 20,394; Western Kentucky University, 16,579; Eastern Kentucky University, 14,697; Northern Kentucky University, 12,548; Murray State University, 9,648; Morehead State University, 9,027; Kentucky State University, 2,314. Five of the several privately endowed colleges of standing are Berea College, Berea; Centre College, Danville; Transylvania University, Lexington; Georgetown College, Georgetown; and Bellarmine College, Louisville.

Health. In 2001 the state had 123 licensed hospitals (18,616 beds). There were 422 licensed long-term care facilities (34,825 beds), 259 family care homes, 126 home health agencies and 1,856 miscellaneous health facilities and laboratories.

Welfare. Medicare enrolment in July 2002 totalled 637,212. In 2000 a total of 770,536 people in Kentucky received Medicaid. In Dec. 2003 there were 768,861 Old-Age, Survivors, and Disability Insurance (OASDI) beneficiaries. A total of 76,843 people were receiving payments under Temporary Assistance for Needy Families (TANF) in Sept. 2002.

CULTURE

The Kentucky Center for the Arts hosts productions by the Kentucky Opera Association, the Louisville Ballet, the Louisville Orchestra and Broadway touring productions.

Tourism. In 1999 tourist expenditure was $8,191·9m., producing over $888m. in tax revenues and supporting 148,781 jobs. The state had (1999) 1,093 hotels and motels, 248 camping grounds and 50 state parks.

FURTHER READING

Kentucky Deskbook of Economic Statistics, Lackey, Brent, (ed.) Kentucky Cabinet for Economic Development, Frankfort

Miller, P. M., *Kentucky Politics and Government: Do We Stand United?* Nebraska Univ. Press, 1994

Ulack, R. (ed.) *Atlas of Kentucky*. The Univ. Press of Kentucky, 1998

LOUISIANA

KEY HISTORICAL EVENTS

Originally the Territory of Choctaw and Caddo tribes, the whole area was claimed for France in 1682. The French founded New Orleans in 1718 and it became the centre of a crown colony in 1731. During the wars which the European powers fought over their American interests, the French ceded the area west of the Mississippi (most of the present state) to Spain in 1762 and the eastern area, north of New Orleans, to Britain in 1763. The British section passed to the USA in 1783, but France bought back the rest from Spain in 1800, including New Orleans and the mouth of the Mississippi. The USA, fearing to be excluded from a strategically important and commercially promising shipping area, persuaded France to sell Louisiana again in 1803. The present states of Missouri, Arkansas, Iowa, North Dakota, South Dakota, Nebraska and Oklahoma were included in the purchase.

The area became the Territory of New Orleans in 1804 and was admitted to the Union as a state in 1812. The economy at first depended on cotton and sugarcane plantations. The population was of French, Spanish and black descent, with a growing number of American settlers. Plantation interests succeeded in achieving secession in 1861, but New Orleans was occupied by the Union in 1862. Planters re-emerged in the late 19th century and imposed rigid segregation of the black population, denying them their new rights.

The state has become mainly urban industrial, with the Mississippi ports growing rapidly. There is petroleum and natural gas, and a strong tourist industry based on the French culture and Caribbean atmosphere of New Orleans.

TERRITORY AND POPULATION

Louisiana is bounded north by Arkansas, east by Mississippi, south by the Gulf of Mexico and west by Texas. Land area, 43,562 sq. miles (112,825 sq. km). Census population, 1 April 2000, 4,468,976, an increase of 5·9% since 1990. July 2004 estimate, 4,515,770.

Population in five census years was:

	White	*Black*	*Indian*	*Asiatic*	*Total*	*Per sq. mile*
1930	1,322,712	776,326	1,536	1,019	2,101,593	46·5
1960	2,211,715	1,039,207	3,587	2,004	3,257,022	72·2
			All others			
1980	2,911,243	1,237,263	55,466		4,205,900	93·5
1990	2,839,138	1,299,281	81,554		4,219,973	96·9
2000	2,856,161	1,451,944	160,871		4,468,976	102·6

Of the total population in 2000, 2,306,073 were female, 3,249,177 were 18 years old or older and 3,245,665 were urban. The Hispanic population was 107,738 in 2000, an increase of 14,671 (15·8%) on the 1990 census figure of 93,067.

The largest cities with their 2000 census population are: New Orleans, 484,674; Baton Rouge, 227,818; Shreveport, 200,145; Lafayette, 100,257; Lake Charles, 71,757; Kenner, 70,517; Bossier City, 56,461; Monroe, 53,107.

SOCIAL STATISTICS

Statistics 2002: live births, 64,872 (14·5 per 1,000 population); deaths, 41,984 (9·4 per 1,000); infant deaths, 2001, 9·8 per 1,000 live births; marriages, 2002, 36,545; divorces, 14,767.

CLIMATE

New Orleans, Jan. 54°F (12·2°C), July 83°F (28·3°C). Annual rainfall 58" (1,458 mm). Louisiana belongs to the Gulf Coast climate zone (*see* UNITED STATES: Climate).

CONSTITUTION AND GOVERNMENT

The present constitution dates from 1974. The Legislature consists of a Senate of 39 members and a House of Representatives of 105 members, both chosen for four years. Sessions are annual; a fiscal session is held in even years.

For the 109th Congress, which convened in Jan. 2005, Louisiana sends seven members to the House of Representatives. It is represented in the Senate by Mary Landrieu (D. 1997–2009) and David Vitter (R. 2005–11).

Louisiana is divided into 64 parishes (corresponding to the counties of other states). The capital is Baton Rouge.

RECENT ELECTIONS

In the 2004 presidential election Bush polled 1,102,169 votes; Kerry, 820,299; Nader, 7,032.

CURRENT ADMINISTRATION

Governor: Kathleen Blanco (D.), 2004–08 (salary: $95,000).
Lieut.-Governor: Mitch Landrieu (D.), 2004–08 ($85,000).
Secretary of State: W. Fox McKeithen (R.), 2004–08 ($85,000).

Government Website: http://www.louisiana.gov

ECONOMY

Per capita personal income (2002) was $25,370.

Budget. In fiscal year 2002–03 total revenue was $16,823·7m. Total expenditure was $17,153·2m. (health and welfare, $6,626·0m.; education, $4,675·0m.; correction, $611·7m.; highways, $323·3m.) Debt outstanding, in 2003, $2,722m.

Performance. Gross State Product in 2002 was $131,584m., ranking Louisiana 24th in the United States.

ENERGY AND NATURAL RESOURCES

Electricity. 50,479m. kWh of electricity were produced in 2002.

Oil and Gas. Louisiana ranks fourth among states of the USA for oil production and second for natural gas production. Production in 2003 of crude oil was 58m. bbls.; and of natural gas, 2,961·4bn. cu. ft.

Water. The area covered by water is approximately 6,085 sq. miles.

Minerals. Principal non-fuel minerals are salt and sand, gravel, and lime. Total non-fuel mineral production in 2003 was $331m.

Agriculture. The state is divided into two parts, the uplands and the alluvial and swamp regions of the coast. A delta occupies about one-third of the total area. Manufacturing is the leading industry, but agriculture is important. The number of farms in 2003 was 27,200 covering 7·85m. acres; the average farm had 289 acres. Average value of farmland per acre, in 2002, was $1,534.

Farm income, 2003, from crops, $1,296m., and from livestock, $697m. The net farm income in 2003 was $719m. Principal crops, 2003 production, were: soybeans, 25·16m. bu.; sugarcane, 12·84m. tons; rice, 26·40m. cwt; corn, 67·00m. bu.; cotton, 1·03m. bales; sweet potatoes, 3·15m. cwt; sorghum, 14·03m. bu.

Forestry. Forestlands cover 48% of the state's area, or 13·8m. acres. Production 2003: sawtimber, 1,266·18m. bd ft; cordwood, 6·74m. standard cords. The economic impact of forestry and forest products industries in Louisiana was $3·7bn. in 2003.

Fisheries. In 2003 Louisiana's commercial fisheries catch for all species totalled 1,189·7m. lb (539,635 tonnes), valued at $294·1m.

INDUSTRY

Louisiana's leading manufacturing activity is the production of chemicals, followed, in order of importance, by the processing of petroleum and coal products, the production of transportation equipment and production of paper products. In 2001 the state's 3,436 manufacturing establishments had 159,000 employees, earning $6,539m. Total value added by manufacturing in 2001 was $22,545m.

Labour. Non-agricultural employment for Aug. 2004 was 1,894,900, including: service industries, 694,800; government, 369,600; wholesale and retail trade, 300,200; manufacturing, 154,700; construction, 116,200; transportation, communications and public utilities, 110,900; finance, insurance and real estate, 101,200; mining, 43,800.

In 2001 the civilian labour force totalled 2,055,100. There were 115,000 persons unemployed, a rate of 5·6% (5·8% preliminary rate for Oct. 2002).

INTERNATIONAL TRADE

In 2003 exports were valued at $18,390·13m. In 1999 foreign investment amounted to $31·8bn.

COMMUNICATIONS

Roads. In 2003 there were 60,937 miles of public roads (46,987 miles rural). In 2003, 3,713,561 motor vehicles were registered.

Rail. In 2003 there were approximately 2,748 miles of main-line track in the state. There is a tramway in New Orleans.

Civil Aviation. In 2004 there were 71 public airports. There were 5,955,868 passenger enplanements statewide in 2000.

Shipping. There are ports at New Orleans, Baton Rouge, St Bernard, Plaquemines and Lake Charles. The Mississippi and other waterways provide 7,500 miles of navigable water.

SOCIAL INSTITUTIONS

Justice. In Sept. 2003 there were 36,612 prisoners in adult correctional institutions and the juvenile offender population totalled 6,067. The death penalty is authorized. There was one execution in 2002 but there have been none since then.

Religion. The Roman Catholic Church is the largest denomination in Louisiana. The leading Protestant Churches are Southern Baptist and Methodist.

Education. School attendance is compulsory between the ages of seven and 15, both inclusive. In 2003 there were 1,505 public schools with 723,252 registered pupils, and 49,371 teachers paid an average salary of $36,433. There are 16 public colleges and universities and ten non-public institutions of higher learning. There are 42 state trade and vocational technical schools, three law schools, three medical schools and a biomedical research centre affiliated with Louisiana's universities.

In 2003–04 there were 210,484 students enrolled at public two- and four-year colleges and universities. Enrolment, 2003–04, in the University of Louisiana System was 83,303 (Lafayette, 16,208; Southeastern, 15,662; Louisiana Tech., 11,960; Northwestern, 10,505; Monroe, 8,592; McNeese, 8,447; Nicholls, 7,260; Grambling, 4,669); Louisiana State University, 62,841 (with campuses at Alexandria, Baton Rouge, Eunice, New Orleans and Shreveport); Southern University System, 15,044. Major private institutions: Tulane University, 9,920; Loyola University, 5,900; Xavier University, 3,994; Dillard University, 1,953.

Health. In 2003 there were 203 hospitals with 24,653 beds.

Welfare. In fiscal year 2003–04 Family Independence Temporary Assistance Program (FITAP) payments to 434,707 recipients totalled $40,056,233. In the fiscal year 2003–04 Food Stamp benefits totalling $735,959,328 were paid to 7,972,477 recipients.

CULTURE

Broadcasting. In 2004 there were 215 radio stations (77 AM; 138 FM) and 48 television stations.

Press. In 2004 there were 309 newspapers in circulation.

Tourism. Tourism is the second most important industry for state income. In 2003 there were over 25m. visitors to the state. Tourism was a $9·4bn. industry in 2003; it provided more than 119,900 jobs and generated in excess of $1·2bn. in tax revenue for federal, state and local governments.

FURTHER READING

1997 Statistical Abstract of Louisiana, 10th Edition, New Orleans, LA: Division of Business and Economic Research, College of Business Administration, Univ. of New Orleans, 1997.
Calhoun, Milburn, (ed.) *Louisiana Almanac 2002–2003 Edition*. Pelican Publishing Co., 2002
Wall, Bennett H., *et al.*, (eds.) *Louisiana: a History, Third Edition*. Harlan Davidson, Inc, 1997
Wilds, J., *et al.*, (eds.) *Louisiana Yesterday and Today: a Historical Guide to the State*. Louisiana State Univ. Press, 1996

State Library: The State Library of Louisiana, Baton Rouge, Louisiana.

MAINE

KEY HISTORICAL EVENTS

Originally occupied by Algonquian-speaking tribes, the Territory was disputed between different groups of British settlers, and between the British and French, throughout the 17th and most of the 18th centuries. After 1652 it was governed as part of Massachusetts, and French claims finally failed in 1763. Most of the early settlers were English and Protestant Irish, with many Quebec French.

The Massachusetts settlers had gained control when the original colonist, Sir Ferdinando Gorges, supported the losing royalist side in the English civil war. Their control was questioned during the English-American war of 1812, when Maine residents claimed that the Massachusetts government did not protect them against British raids. Maine was separated from Massachusetts and entered the Union as a state in 1820.

Maine is a mountainous state and even the coastline is rugged, but the coastal belt is where most settlement has developed. In the 19th century there were manufacturing towns making use of cheap water-power, and the rocky shore supported a shell-fish industry. The latter still flourishes, together with intensive horticulture, producing potatoes and fruit. The other main economic development has been in exploiting the forests for timber, pulp and paper.

The capital is Augusta, a river trading post which was fortified against Indian attacks in 1754, incorporated as a town in 1797 and chosen as capital in 1832.

TERRITORY AND POPULATION

Maine is bounded west, north and east by Canada, southeast by the Atlantic, south and southwest by New Hampshire. Land area, 30,862 sq. miles (79,932 sq. km). Census population, 1 April 2000, 1,274,923, an increase of 3·8% since 1990. July 2004 estimate, 1,317,253.

Population for five census years was:

	White	*Black*	*Indian*	*Asiatic*	*Total*	*Per sq. mile*
1910	739,995	1,363	992	121	742,371	24·8
1950	910,846	1,221	1,522	185	913,774	29·4
			All others			
1980	1,109,850	3,128	12,049		1,125,027	36·3
1990	1,208,360	5,138	14,430		1,227,928	39·8
2000	1,236,014	6,760	32,149		1,274,923	41·3

Of the total population in 2000, 654,614 were female, 973,685 were 18 years old or older and 762,045 were rural (59·8%). Only Vermont has a more rural population. In 2000 the Hispanic population was 9,360, an increase of 37·1% on the 1990 census figure of 6,829. Only North Dakota and Vermont have fewer persons of Hispanic origin in the USA.

The largest city in the state is Portland, with a census population of 64,249 in 2000. Other cities (with population in 2000) are: Lewiston, 35,690; Bangor, 31,473; South Portland, 23,324; Auburn, 23,203; Augusta (capital), 21,819; Brunswick, 21,172; Biddeford, 20,942; Sanford, 20,806.

SOCIAL STATISTICS

Births, 2002, 13,559 (10·5 per 1,000 population—the lowest rate in any US state); deaths, 12,694 (9·8); 2001: infant mortality rate, 6·1 (per 1,000 live births). 2001: marriages, 11,400 (9·0 per 1,000 population); divorces, 4,900 (3·9).

CLIMATE

Average maximum temperatures range from 56·3°F in Waterville to 48·3°F in Caribou, but record high (since *c.* 1950) is 103°F. Average minimum ranges from 36·9°F in Rockland to 28·3°F in Greenville, but record low (also in Greenville) is –42°F. Average annual rainfall ranges from 48·85" in Machias to 36·09" in Houlton. Average annual snowfall ranges from 118·7" in Greenville to 59·7" in Rockland. Maine belongs to the New England climate zone (*see* UNITED STATES: Climate).

CONSTITUTION AND GOVERNMENT

The constitution of 1820 is still in force, but it has been amended 169 times. In 1951, 1965 and 1973 the Legislature approved recodifications of the constitution as arranged by the Chief Justice under special authority.

The Legislature consists of the Senate with 35 members and the House of Representatives with 151 members, both Houses being elected simultaneously for two years. Sessions are annual.

For the 109th Congress, which convened in Jan. 2005, Maine sends two members to the House of Representatives. It is represented in the Senate by Olympia Snowe (R. 1995–2007) and Susan Collins (R. 1997–2009).

The capital is Augusta. The state is divided into 16 counties.

RECENT ELECTIONS

In the 2004 presidential election Kerry polled 396,842 votes; Bush, 330,201; Nader, 8,069.

CURRENT ADMINISTRATION

Governor: John Baldacci (D.), 2003–07 (salary: $70,000).

Senate President: Beth Edmonds (D.).

Secretary of State: Matthew Dunlap (D.), 2005–07 ($81,952).

Government Website: http://www.state.me.us

ECONOMY

Per capita income (2002) was $27,804.

Budget. In 2002 total state revenue was $5,451m. Total expenditure was $6,265m. (public welfare, $1,802m.; education, $1,505m.; highways, $462m.; health, $366m.; government administration, $255m.) Outstanding debt, in 2002, $4,321m.

Performance. Gross State Product was $39,039m. in 2002, ranking Maine 43rd in the United States.

ENERGY AND NATURAL RESOURCES

Water. The total area covered by water is approximately 2,876 sq. miles.

Minerals. Minerals include sand and gravel, stone, lead, clay, copper, peat, silver and zinc. Domestic non-fuel mineral output, 2002, was valued at $106m.

Agriculture. In 2002, 6,700 farms occupied 1·26m. acres; the average farm was 188 acres. Average value of farmland and buildings per acre in 2002 was $1,637. Farm income, 2001: crops, $211m.; livestock and products, $274m. The net farm income in 2001 was $82m. Principal commodities are potatoes, dairy products, chicken eggs and aquaculture.

Forestry. There were 17·70m. acres of forested land in 2002, of which 40,000 acres were national forests. Commercial forest includes pine, spruce and fir. Wood products industries are of great economic importance.

Fisheries. In 2002 the commercial catch was 197·1m. lb, valued at $279·4m.

INDUSTRY

In 2001 the state's 1,866 manufacturing establishments had 77,000 employees, earning $2,705m. Total value added by manufacturing in 2001 was $7,880m.

Labour. Total non-agricultural employment, 2001, 609,000. Employees by branch, 2001 (in 1,000): services, 187; wholesale and retail trade, 151; government, 102; manufacturing, 81; finance, insurance and property, 34. The unemployment rate in 2002 was 4·4%.

COMMUNICATIONS

Roads. In 2002 there were 22,693 miles of roads (20,060 miles rural) and 967,583 registered motor vehicles.

Rail. In 1999 there were 1,516 miles of mainline railway tracks.

Civil Aviation. There are international airports at Portland and Bangor. There were 576,471 passenger enplanements statewide in 2000.

SOCIAL INSTITUTIONS

Justice. In June 2002 there were 1,841 federal and state prisoners. Capital punishment was abolished in 1887.

Religion. The largest religious bodies are Roman Catholics, Baptists and Congregationalists.

Education. Education is free for pupils from five to 21 years of age, and compulsory from seven to 17. In 1994–95 there were 212,322 pupils and 15,398 teachers in public elementary and secondary schools. Education expenditure by state and local government in 1997, $1,494m.

The University of Maine System, created by Maine's state legislature in 1965, consists of seven universities: the University of Maine (founded in 1865); the University of Maine at Augusta, at Farmington, at Fort Kent (1878), at Machias (1909), at Presque Isle (1903); and the University of Southern Maine (1878, campuses at Portland, Gorham and Lewiston-Auburn).

There are several independent universities, including: Bowdoin College, founded in 1794 at Brunswick; Bates College at Lewiston; Colby College at Waterville; Husson College at Bangor; Westbrook College at Westbrook; Unity College at Unity; and the University of New England (formerly St Francis College) at Biddeford.

Health. In 2001 there were 37 community hospitals with 3,800 beds. A total of 149,000 patients were admitted during the year.

Welfare. Medicare enrolment in July 2002 totalled 222,917. In 2000 a total of 191,624 people in Maine received Medicaid. In Dec. 2003 there were 262,533 Old-Age, Survivors, and Disability Insurance (OASDI) beneficiaries. A total of 24,596 people were receiving payments under Temporary Assistance for Needy Families (TANF) in Sept. 2002.

FURTHER READING

Statistical information: Maine Department of Economic and Community Development, State House Station 59, Augusta 04333. Publishes *Maine: a Statistical Summary.*

Palmer, K. T., *et al.*, *Maine Politics and Government.* Univ. of Nebraska Press, 1993

MARYLAND

KEY HISTORICAL EVENTS

The first European visitors found groups of Algonquian-speaking tribes, often under attack by Iroquois from further north. The first white settlement was made by the Calvert family, British Roman Catholics, in 1634. The settlers received some legislative rights in 1638. In 1649 their assembly passed the Act of Toleration, granting freedom of worship to all Christians. A peace treaty was signed with the Iroquois in 1652, after which it was possible for farming settlements to expand north and west. The capital (formerly at St Mary's City) was moved to Annapolis in 1694. Baltimore, which became the state's main city, was founded in 1729.

The first industry was tobacco-growing, which was based on slave-worked plantations. There were also many immigrant British small farmers, tradesmen and indentured servants.

At the close of the War of Independence the treaty of Paris was ratified in Annapolis. Maryland became a state of the Union in 1788. In 1791 the state ceded land for the new federal capital, Washington, and its economy has depended on the capital's proximity ever since. Baltimore also grew as a port and industrial city, attracting much European immigration in the 19th century. Although strong sympathy for the south was expressed, Maryland remained within the Union in the Civil War albeit under the imposition of martial law.

TERRITORY AND POPULATION

Maryland is bounded north by Pennsylvania, east by Delaware and the Atlantic, south by Virginia and West Virginia, with the Potomac River forming most of the boundary, and west by West Virginia. Chesapeake Bay almost cuts off the eastern end of the state from the rest. Land area, 9,774 sq. miles (25,315 sq. km). Census population, 1 April 2000, 5,296,486, an increase since 1990 of 10·8%. July 2004 estimate, 5,558,058.

Population for five federal censuses was:

	White	*Black*	*Indian*	*Asiatic*	*Total*	*Per sq. mile*
1920	1,204,737	244,479	32	400	1,449,661	145·8
1930	1,354,226	276,379	50	857	1,631,526	165·0
1960	2,573,919	518,410	1,538	5,700	3,100,689	314·0
			All others			
1990	3,393,964	1,189,899	197,605		4,781,468	489·2
2000	3,391,308	1,477,411	427,767		5,296,486	541·9

Of the total population in 2000, 2,738,692 were female, 3,940,314 were 18 years old or older and 4,558,668 were urban. In 2000 Maryland's Hispanic population was 227,916, up from 125,102 in 1990 (an increase of 82·2%).

The largest city in the state (containing 12·3% of the population) is Baltimore, with 651,154 (2000 census); Washington, D.C.–Baltimore metropolitan area, 7,608,070 (2000). Maryland residents in the Washington, D.C., metropolitan area total more than 1·8m. Other main population centres (2000 census) are Columbia (88,254); Silver Spring (76,540); Dundalk (62,306); Wheaton-Glenmont (57,694); Ellicott City (56,397); Germantown (55,419); Bethesda (55,277). Incorporated places, 2000: Frederick, 52,767; Gaithersburg, 52,613; Bowie, 50,269; Rockville, 47,388; Hagerstown, 36,687; Annapolis, 35,838; College Park, 24,657; Salisbury, 23,743; Cumberland, 21,518; Greenbelt, 21,456.

SOCIAL STATISTICS

In 2002 births were 73,323 (13·4 per 1,000 population); deaths, 43,970 (8·1 per 1,000); 2001: infant deaths, 8·1 (per 1,000 live births). 2001: marriages, 37,500; divorces, 15,900.

CLIMATE
Baltimore, Jan. 36°F (2·2°C), July 79°F (26·1°C). Annual rainfall 42" (1,066 mm). Maryland belongs to the Atlantic Coast climate zone (*see* UNITED STATES: Climate).

CONSTITUTION AND GOVERNMENT
The present constitution dates from 1867; it has had 125 amendments. Amendments are proposed and considered annually by the General Assembly and must be ratified by the electorate. The General Assembly consists of a Senate of 47, and a House of Delegates of 141 members, both elected for four years, as are the Governor and Lieut.-Governor. Voters are citizens who have the usual residential qualifications.

For the 109th Congress, which convened in Jan. 2005, Maryland sends eight members to the House of Representatives. It is represented in the Senate by Paul Sarbanes (D. 1977–2007) and Barbara Mikulski (D. 1987–2011).

The state capital is Annapolis. The state is divided into 23 counties and Baltimore City.

RECENT ELECTIONS
In the 2004 presidential election Kerry polled 1,334,493 votes; Bush, 1,024,703; Nader, 11,854.

CURRENT ADMINISTRATION
Governor: Robert L. Ehrlich, Jr (R.), 2003–07 (salary: $145,000).
Lieut.-Governor: Michael S. Steele (R.), 2003–07 ($120,833).
Secretary of State: R. Karl Aumann (R.), appointed Jan. 2003 ($84,583).

Government Website: http://www.maryland.gov

ECONOMY
Per capita income (2002) was $36,121.

Budget. In 2002 total state revenue was $20,788m. Total expenditure was $23,317m. (education, $6,892m.; public welfare, $4,626m.; highways, $1,643m.; health, $1,342m.; correction, $1,060m.) Outstanding debt, in 2002, $12,309m.

Performance. Gross State Product in 2002 was $201,879m., ranking Maryland 16th in the United States.

ENERGY AND NATURAL RESOURCES
Electricity. The territory is served by four investor-owned utilities, five municipal systems and four rural co-operatives. 75% of electricity comes from fossil fuels and 25% from nuclear power.

Oil and Gas. Natural gas is produced from one field in Garrett County; 63m. cu. ft (1·78m. cu. metres) in 1998. A second gas field is used for natural gas storage. No oil is produced and there are no major reserves located in Maryland.

Water. The total area covered by water is approximately 2,632 sq. miles. Abundant fresh water resources allow water withdrawals for neighbouring states and the District of Columbia. The state straddles the upper portions of the world's largest freshwater estuary, Chesapeake Bay.

Minerals. Value of non-fuel mineral production, 2002, was $375m. The leading mineral commodities by weight are crushed stone (36·1m. tonnes in 2000) and sand and gravel (25·0m. tonnes in 2000). Stone is the leading mineral commodity by value followed by coal, Portland cement, and sand and gravel. In 2000 output of crushed stone was valued at $136m.; coal output was 4·02m. short tons in 1998, valued at $121m.

Agriculture. In 2002 there were 12,200 farms with an area of 2·1m. acres. The average number of acres per farm was 172. The average value per acre in 2002 was $4,084. In 2003, 1·27m. people were employed in agriculture.

Farm animals, 2002 were: milch cows, 72,800; all cattle, 241,000; swine (2001), 52,000; and sheep, 22,700. As of 2002, chickens (not broilers), 3·17m. Farm income cash receipts, 2001: $1,596m.; from crops, $647m., and from livestock and livestock products, \$949m. The net farm income in 2001 was \$522m. Milk (2002 value \$169·5m.) and broilers (\$440·5m.) are important products.

Forestry. Total forested area was 2·57m. acres in 2002.

Fisheries. In 2002, 53·2m. lb of seafood was landed at a dockside value of \$49m. The total estimated value of the seafood industry was \$700m.

INDUSTRY

In 2001 the state's 3,936 manufacturing establishments had 157,000 employees, earning \$6,792m. Total value added by manufacturing in 2001 was \$18,757m.

Labour. In 1997, 24·1% of the workforce were professional and technical workers, more than any other state in the USA. The workforce is well educated with 32% of the population over age 25 holding a bachelor's or higher degree in 1998; it has the second highest concentration of PhD degrees in the sciences of US states—with 352 per 100,000 of the population. Total non-agricultural employment, 2001, 2,470,000. Employees by branch, 2001 (in 1,000): services, 861; wholesale and retail trade, 554; government, 452; manufacturing, 178. The unemployment rate in 2002 was 4·4%.

COMMUNICATIONS

Roads. In 2002 there were 30,815 miles of roads comprising 14,639 miles of urban road and 16,176 miles of rural road. In 2002 the state highway maintained 5,131 miles of highways. The counties maintained 20,486 miles of highways. There were 3,883,925 registered vehicles.

Rail. Maryland is served by CSX Transportation, Norfolk Southern Railroad as well as by six short-line railroads. Metro lines also serve Maryland in suburban Washington D.C. Amtrak provides passenger service linking Baltimore and BWI Airport to major cities on the Atlantic Coast. MARC commuter rail serves the Baltimore–Washington metropolitan area.

Civil Aviation. There were (1998) 38 public-use airports, and 45 commercial airlines at Baltimore/Washington International Airport (BWI). The airport served 17m. passengers in 1999. A newly opened passenger pier serves the airport's increasing numbers of international customers. Air cargo throughput has grown rapidly to over 350m. tons per annum, with increases planned. There were 8,981,549 passenger enplanements in 2000.

Shipping. In 1997 Baltimore was the 9th largest US seaport in value of imports, and 12th largest in value of exports; in 1996 it ranked 16th in annual tonnage handled. It is located as much as 200 miles further inland than any other Atlantic seaport.

SOCIAL INSTITUTIONS

Justice. Prisons in June 2002 held 24,329 inmates. Maryland's prison system has conducted a work-release programme for selected prisoners since 1963. All institutions have academic and vocational training programmes. There was one execution in 2004, the first since 1998.

Religion. Maryland was the first US state to give religious freedom to all who came within its borders. Present religious affiliations of the population are approximately: Protestant, 32%; Roman Catholic, 24%; Jewish, 10%; remaining 34% is non-related and other faiths.

Education. Education is compulsory from six to 16 years of age. In 1998–99 public schools (including pre-kindergarten through secondary schools) had 828,477 pupils; teachers numbered 65,486; average salary was \$43,081. Expenditure on education, 1998–99, was \$5·9bn., of which the state's contribution was \$2·4bn. Per pupil cost (1998–99) was \$6,821.

There are 54 institutions of higher learning (34 four-year and 20 two-year). The largest is the University System of Maryland (created in 1988), with 125,000 students (autumn 1998), consisting of 11 campuses, two major research institutions, and over 250 learning centres in Europe and the Far East. The USM colleges and universities are: Bowie State University; Coppin State College; Frostburg State

University; Salisbury University; Towson University; the University of Baltimore; and the five campuses of the University of Maryland (Baltimore, Baltimore County, College Park, Eastern Shore and University College). Career and technical education is available through a network of community colleges and in some 200 secondary schools.

Health. In 2000 there were 49 community hospitals with 11,200 beds. A total of 608,000 patients were admitted during the year.

Welfare. Medicare enrolment in July 2002 totalled 663,739. In 2000 a total of 664,576 people in Maryland received Medicaid. In Dec. 2003 there were 751,359 Old-Age, Survivors, and Disability Insurance (OASDI) beneficiaries. A total of 61,886 people were receiving payments under Temporary Assistance for Needy Families (TANF) in Sept. 2002.

CULTURE

Cultural venues include: Frostburg Performing Arts Center, Strathmore Hall Arts Center, and Center Stage. Performing arts institutions include the Baltimore Opera Company, Peabody Music Conservatory and Arena Players.

Broadcasting. There are 15 TV stations, 22 cable television stations, 48 FM radio and 31 AM radio stations.

Tourism. Tourism is one of the state's leading industries. In 1997 tourists spent over $6,500m. Direct employment in tourism (1997) was 94,100.

FURTHER READING

Statistical Information: Maryland Department of Economic and Employment Development, 217 East Redwood St., Baltimore 21202.

DiLisio, J. E., *Maryland.* Boulder, 1982
Rollo, V. F., *Maryland's Constitution and Government.* Maryland Hist. Press, Rev. ed., 1982

State Library: Maryland State Library, Annapolis.

MASSACHUSETTS

KEY HISTORICAL EVENTS

The first European settlement was at Plymouth, when the *Mayflower* landed its company of English religious separatists in 1620. In 1626–30 more colonists arrived, the main body being a large company of English Puritans who founded a Puritan commonwealth. This commonwealth, of about 1,000 colonists led by John Winthrop, became the Massachusetts Bay Colony and was founded under a company charter. Following disagreement between the English government and the colony the charter was withdrawn in 1684, but in 1691 a new charter united a number of settlements under the name of Massachusetts Bay. The colony's government was rigidly theocratic.

Shipbuilding, iron-working and manufacturing were more important than farming from the beginning, the land being poor. The colony was Protestant and of English descent until the War of Independence. The former colony adopted its present constitution in 1780. In the struggle which ended in the separation of the American colonies from the mother country, Massachusetts took the foremost part, and on 6 Feb. 1788 became the 6th state to ratify the US constitution. The state acquired its present boundaries (having previously included Maine) in 1820.

During the 19th century industrialization and immigration from Europe both increased while Catholic Irish and Italian immigrants began to change the population's character. The main inland industry was textile manufacture, the main coastal occupation was whaling; both have now gone. Boston has remained the most important city of New England, attracting a large black population since 1950.

TERRITORY AND POPULATION

Massachusetts is bounded north by Vermont and New Hampshire, east by the Atlantic, south by Connecticut and Rhode Island and west by New York. Land area, 7,840 sq. miles (20,306 sq. km). Census population, 1 April 2000, 6,349,097, an increase of 5·5% since 1990. July 2004 estimate, 6,416,505.

Population at five federal census years was:

	White	*Black*	*Other*	*Total*	*Per sq. mile*
1950	4,611,503	73,171	5,840	4,690,514	598·4
1970	5,477,624	175,817	35,729	5,689,170	725·8
1980	5,362,836	221,279	152,922	5,737,037	732·0
1990	5,405,374	300,130	310,921	6,016,425	767·6
2000	5,367,286	343,454	638,357	6,349,097	809·8

Of the total population in 2000, 3,290,281 were female, 4,849,003 were 18 years old or older and 5,801,367 were urban (91·37%). In 2000 the Hispanic population was 428,729, up from 287,549 in 1990 (an increase of 49·1%).

Population of the largest cities at the 2000 census: Boston, 589,141; Worcester, 172,648; Springfield, 152,082; Lowell, 105,167; Cambridge, 101,355; Brockton, 94,304; New Bedford, 93,768; Fall River, 91,938; Lynn, 89,050; Quincy, 88,025; Newton, 83,829. The Boston–Worcester–Lawrence metropolitan area had a 2000 census population of 5,819,100.

SOCIAL STATISTICS

2002: births, 80,645 (12·5 per 1,000 population); deaths, 56,928 (8·9); 2001: infant deaths, 5·0 per 1,000 live births. 2001: marriages, 40,000; divorces, 14,800.

CLIMATE

Boston, Jan. 28°F (–2·2°C), July 71°F (21·7°C). Annual rainfall 41" (1,036 mm). Massachusetts belongs to the New England climate zone (*see* UNITED STATES: Climate).

CONSTITUTION AND GOVERNMENT

The constitution dates from 1780 and has had 117 amendments. The legislative body, styled the General Court of the Commonwealth of Massachusetts, meets annually, and consists of the Senate with 40 members and the House of Representatives of 160 members, both elected for two years.

For the 109th Congress, which convened in Jan. 2005, Massachusetts sends ten members to the House of Representatives. It is represented in the Senate by Edward Kennedy (D. 1962–2007) and John Kerry (D. 1985–2009).

The capital is Boston. The state has 14 counties.

RECENT ELECTIONS

In the 2004 presidential election Kerry polled 1,803,800 votes; Bush, 1,071,109; Badnarik, 15,022.

CURRENT ADMINISTRATION

Governor: W. Mitt Romney (R.), 2003–07 (salary: $135,000, but not taken).

Lieut.-Governor: Kerry Healey (R.), 2003–07 ($120,000, but not taken).

Secretary of the Commonwealth: William F. Galvin (D.), 2003–07 ($120,000).

Government Website: http://www.mass.gov

ECONOMY

Per capita income (2002) was $39,044, the fourth highest in the country.

Budget. In 2002 total state revenue was $26,885m. Total expenditure was $32,848m. (education, $6,553m.; public welfare, $5,988m.; highways, $2,744m.; health, $1,908m.; government administration, $1,278m.) Outstanding debt, in 2002, $45,216m.

Performance. Gross State Product in 2002 was $288,088m., ranking Massachusetts 12th in the United States.

ENERGY AND NATURAL RESOURCES

Water. The total area covered by water is approximately 1,403 sq. miles.

Minerals. Total domestic non-fuel mineral output in 2002 was valued at $235m., of which most came from sand, gravel, crushed stone and lime.

Agriculture. In 2002 there were approximately 6,000 farms with an average area of 93 acres and a total area of 560,000 acres. Average value per acre in 2002 was $9,234. Farm income in 2001: crops, $273m.; livestock and products, $94m. Principal crops included cranberries and greenhouse products. The net farm income in 2001 was $27m.

Forestry. About 62% of the state is forest. In 2002 State forests covered about 424,000 acres, with total forest land covering 3·13m. acres. Commercially important hardwoods are sugar maple, northern red oak and white ash; softwoods are white pine and hemlock.

Fisheries. In 2002 commercial fishing produced 243·8m. lb of fish with a value of $297·3m.

INDUSTRY

In 2001 the state's 9,015 manufacturing establishments had 390,000 employees, earning $18,907m. Total value added by manufacturing in 2001 was $44,447m.

Labour. Total non-agricultural employment, 2001, 3,335,000. Employees by branch, 2001 (in 1,000): services, 1,228; wholesale and retail trade, 740; government, 429; manufacturing, 424. The state unemployment rate was 5·3% in 2002.

COMMUNICATIONS

Roads. In 2002 there were 35,458 miles of public roads (12,280 miles rural) and 5,406,846 registered motor vehicles.

Rail. In 2000 there were 1,074 miles of mainline railway. There are metro, light rail, tramway and commuter networks in and around Boston.

Civil Aviation. There is an international airport at Boston. There were 11,548,711 passenger enplanements statewide in 2000.

Shipping. The state has three deep-water harbours, the largest of which is Boston. Other ports are Fall River and New Bedford.

SOCIAL INSTITUTIONS

Justice. There were 10,620 federal and state prisoners in June 2002. The death penalty was abolished in 1984.

Religion. The principal religious bodies are the Roman Catholics, Jewish Congregations, Methodists, Episcopalians and Unitarians.

Education. School attendance is compulsory for ages six to 16. In 1994–95 there were 58,893 classroom teachers and 890,240 pupils.

Some leading higher education institutions are:

Year opened	*Name and location of universities and colleges*	*Students 1988*
1636	Harvard University, Cambridge	24,373[1]
1839	Framingham State College	5,697[1]
1839	Westfield State College	4,985[1]
1840	Bridgewater State College	8,955[1]
1852	Tufts University, Medford[2]	8,876
1854	Salem State College	8,081[1]
1861	Mass. Institute of Technology, Cambridge	9,885
1863	University of Massachusetts, Amherst	25,031[1]
1863	Boston College (RC), Chestnut Hill	14,745
1865	Worcester Polytechnic Institute, Worcester	3,821
1869	Boston University, Boston	29,131
1874	Worcester State College	5,212[1]
1894	Fitchburg State College	5,557[1]
1894	University of Massachusetts, Lowell	12,038[1]
1895	University of Massachusetts, Dartmouth	6,963[1]
1898	Northeastern University, Boston[3]	24,027
1899	Simmons College, Boston[4]	3,401[1]
1905	Wentworth Institute of Technology	3,076
1906	Suffolk University	6,445
1917	Bentley College	5,775
1919	Western New England College	4,941
1919	Babson College	3,353
1947	Merrimack College	2,693
1948	Brandeis University, Waltham	4,405
1964	University of Massachusetts, Boston	13,778[1]

[1]1999 figure. [2]Includes Jackson College for women.
[3]Includes Forsyth Dental Center School. [4]For women only.

Health. In 2001 there were 80 community hospitals with 16,500 beds. A total of 767,000 patients were admitted during the year.

Welfare. Medicare enrolment in July 2002 totalled 963,270. In 2000 a total of 1,047,440 people in Massachusetts received Medicaid. In Dec. 2003 there were 1,061,851 Old-Age, Survivors, and Disability Insurance (OASDI) beneficiaries. A total of 115,643 people were receiving payments under Temporary Assistance for Needy Families (TANF) in Sept. 2002.

FURTHER READING

Levitan, D. with Mariner, E. C., *Your Massachusetts Government.* Newton, Mass., 1984

MICHIGAN

KEY HISTORICAL EVENTS

The French were the first European settlers, establishing a fur trade with the local Algonquian Indians in the late 17th century. They founded Sault Ste Marie in 1668 and Detroit in 1701. In 1763 Michigan passed to Britain, along with other French territory east of the Mississippi, and from Britain it passed to the USA in 1783. Britain, however, kept a force at Detroit until 1796, and recaptured Detroit in 1812. Regular American settlement did not begin until later. The Territory of Michigan (1805) had its boundaries extended after 1818 and 1834. It was admitted to the Union as a state (with its present boundaries) in 1837.

During the 19th century there was rapid industrial growth, especially in mining and metalworking. The largest groups of immigrants were British, German, Irish and Dutch. Other significant groups came from Scandinavia, Poland and Italy. Many groups of immigrants came to settle as miners, farmers and industrial workers. The motor industry became dominant, especially in Detroit. Lake Michigan ports shipped bulk cargo, especially iron ore and grain.

Detroit was the capital until 1847, when that function passed to Lansing. Detroit remained, however, an important centre of flour-milling and shipping and, after the First World War, of the motor industry.

TERRITORY AND POPULATION

Michigan is divided into two by Lake Michigan. The northern part is bounded south by the lake and by Wisconsin, west and north by Lake Superior, east by the North Channel of Lake Huron; between the two latter lakes the Canadian border runs through straits at Sault Ste Marie. The southern part is bounded in the west and north by Lake Michigan, east by Lake Huron, Ontario and Lake Erie, south by Ohio and Indiana. Total area is 96,716 sq. miles (250,493 sq. km) of which 56,804 sq. miles (147,122 sq. km) are land and 39,912 sq. miles (103,372 sq. km) water. Census population, 1 April 2000, 9,938,444, an increase of 6·9% since 1990. July 2004 estimate, 10,112,620.

Population of five federal census years was:

	White	*Black*	*Indian*	*Asiatic*	*Total*	*Per sq. mile*
1910	2,785,247	17,115	7,519	292	2,810,173	48·9
1930	4,663,507	69,453	7,080	2,285	4,842,325	84·9
			All others			
1980	7,872,241	1,199,023	190,814		9,262,078	162·6
1990	7,756,086	1,291,706	247,505		9,295,297	160·0
2000	7,966,053	1,412,742	559,649		9,938,444	175·0

Of the total population in 2000, 5,065,349 were female, 7,342,677 were 18 years old or older and 7,419,457 were urban. In 2000 the Hispanic population was 323,877, up from 201,596 in 1990 (an increase of 60·7%).

Populations of the chief cities in 2000 were: Detroit, 951,270; Grand Rapids, 197,800; Warren, 138,247; Flint, 124,943; Sterling Heights, 124,471; Lansing, 119,128; Ann Arbor, 114,024; Livonia, 100,545. The Detroit–Ann Arbor–Flint metropolitan area had a 2000 census population of 5,456,428.

SOCIAL STATISTICS

In 2002 live births were 129,967 (12·9 per 1,000); deaths were 87,795 (8·7 per 1,000); infant deaths, 2001, 8·0 per 1,000 live births; marriages, 2000, 66,326; divorces, 38,932.

CLIMATE

Detroit, Jan. 23·5°F (–5·0°C), July 72°F (22·5°C). Annual rainfall 32" (810 mm). Grand Rapids, Jan. 22°F (–5·5°C), July 71·5°F (22·0°C). Annual rainfall 34" (860 mm). Lansing, Jan. 22°F (–5·5°C), July 70·5°F (21·5°C). Annual rainfall 29" (740 mm). Michigan belongs to the Great Lakes climate zone (*see* UNITED STATES: Climate).

CONSTITUTION AND GOVERNMENT

The present constitution became effective on 1 Jan. 1964. The Senate consists of 38 members, elected for four years, and the House of Representatives of 110 members, elected for two years. Sessions are biennial.

For the 109th Congress, which convened in Jan. 2005, Michigan sends 15 members to the House of Representatives. It is represented in the Senate by Carl Levin (D. 1979–2009) and Debbie Stabenow (D. 2001–07).

The capital is Lansing. The state is organized in 83 counties.

RECENT ELECTIONS

In the 2004 presidential election Kerry polled 2,479,183 votes; Bush, 2,313,746; Nader, 24,035.

CURRENT ADMINISTRATION

Governor: Jennifer Granholm (D.), 2003–07 (salary: $177,000).

Lieut.-Governor: John D. Cherry (D.), 2003–07 ($123,900).

Secretary of State: Terri Lynn Land (R.), 2003–07 ($124,900).

Government Website: http://www.michigan.gov

ECONOMY

Per capita income (2002) was $30,222.

Budget. In the fiscal year ending 2002, total state revenue was $39,476·8m. Total expenditure was $38,720·1m. (community health, $8,525·72m.; family independence, $3,805·68m.; transportation, $3,076·07m.; corrections, $1,682·25m.; education, $995·10m.) Total budget deficit for 2002 was $1·4bn. Total debt outstanding was $21,947m. in 2002.

Performance. New for-profit business incorporations and new limited liability companies for 2001–02 totalled 50,954. In 2001 Michigan's real income per person declined 1·7% compared with a 0·5% national decline. Gross State Product in 2002 was $351,287m., ranking Michigan 9th in the United States.

ENERGY AND NATURAL RESOURCES

Electricity. Electricity sales for 2001 were 102,935m. kWh.

Oil and Gas. Natural gas production in 2001 was 231·8bn. cu. ft; demand was 863·1bn. cu. ft. Production of crude oil averaged 20,000 bbls. per day.

Water. The total area covered by water is approximately 39,895 sq. miles. Total freshwater withdrawn (1995) was 667m. gallons per day; 1,260 gallons per capita.

Minerals. Domestic non-fuel mineral output in 2002 was at an estimated value of $1·58bn. according to the U.S. Geological Survey. Output was mainly iron ore, cement, crushed stone, sand and gravel.

Agriculture. The state, formerly agricultural, is now chiefly industrial. It contained 52,000 farms in 2002, with a total area of 10·4m. acres; the average farm was 200 acres. In 2000, 6,898,000 acres were harvested. Average value per acre in 2002 was $2,667. Principal crops are wheat, corn, oats, sugarbeets, soybeans, hay and dry beans. Principal fruit crops include apples, cherries (tart and sweet), plums and peaches. In 2002 there were 297,000 milch cows, 73,000 beef cows, 3·66m. chickens and 960,000 pigs. Output in 2002 included 77,000 lb of blueberries, 20,160 pots of geraniums and 335,000 cwt of black beans. Farm income in 2001: total $3·47bn.; crops, $1·98bn.; livestock and products, $1·49bn. Net farm income in 2001 fell by 39% to $191m.

Forestry. Forests covered 19·3m. acres in 2002, with 2·7m. acres of national forest. In 1993 about 18·6m. acres was timberland acreage. Three-quarters of the timber volume was hardwoods, principally hard and soft maples, aspen, oak and birch. Christmas trees are another important forest crop. Net annual growth of growing stock and saw timber was 830m. cu. ft and 3·1bn. bd ft respectively in 1993.

Fisheries. In 1997 recreational fishing licences were purchased by 1·4m. residents and 129,000 non-residents. Recreational fishing revenue (1997) was approximately $1·5bn.

INDUSTRY

Manufacturing is important; among principal products are motor vehicles and trucks, machinery, fabricated metals, primary metals, cement, chemicals, furniture, paper, foodstuffs, rubber, plastics and pharmaceuticals. In 2001 Michigan's 15,431 manufacturing establishments had 756,000 employees, earning $33,634m. Total value added by manufacturing in 2001 was $86,262m.

Labour. Total non-agricultural labour force in 2002 was 4,439,500, of which 906,500 were in manufacturing. The unemployment rate in 2002 was 6·2%.

COMMUNICATIONS

Roads. In 2002 there were 122,029 miles of roads (including 9,711 miles of state highways and 89,756 miles of county roads). There were 92,091 miles of rural road and 29,938 miles of urban road. Vehicle registrations in 2002 numbered 8,533,635.

Rail. In 2000 there were 3,950 miles of railway in Michigan and a 3-mile light rail peoplemover in Detroit.

Civil Aviation. There are international airports at Detroit, Flint, Grand Rapids, Kalamazoo, Port Huron, Saginaw and Sault Ste Marie. In 2000 there were 4,359,931 aircraft operations at Michigan's 235 public-use airports and 26 carriers provided passenger service at 19 airports. There were 20,255,728 passenger enplanements statewide in 2000.

Shipping. There are over 100 commercial and recreational ports spanning the state's 3,200 miles of shoreline. In 2000, 39 of these ports served commercial cargoes. The 20 ferry services carried 848,998 passengers and 529,809 vehicles in 68,571 crossings in 2000. Stone, sand, iron ore and coal accounted for 89% of approximately 96m. tonnes of traffic in 1999.

SOCIAL INSTITUTIONS

Justice. A Civil Rights Commission was established, and its powers and duties were implemented by legislation in the extra session of 1963. Statutory enactments guaranteeing civil rights in specific areas date from 1885. The legislature has a unique one-person grand jury system. The Michigan Supreme Court consists of seven non-partisan elected justices. In 2001 there were 2,291 cases filed at the Supreme Court; it disposed of 2,359 cases during the year. In June 2002 there were 49,961 prisoners in state correctional institutions. Capital punishment was officially abolished in 1964 but there has never been an execution in Michigan.

Religion. Roman Catholics make up the largest body and the largest Protestant denominations are: Lutherans, United Methodists, United Presbyterians and Episcopalians.

Education. Education is compulsory for children from six to 16 years of age. Education expenditure by state and local governments in 2000–01 was $215,490,700. In 2000–01 there were 1,720,335 pupils and 76,920 teachers in public elementary and secondary schools.

In 1998 there were 96 institutes of higher education with (autumn 1998) 551,683 students.

Universities and students (autumn 2002):

Founded	*Name*	*Students*
1817	University of Michigan, Ann Arbor	38,972
1959	University of Michigan, Dearborn	10,379
1956	University of Michigan, Flint	6,524
1849	Eastern Michigan University	23,710
1855	Michigan State University	41,114
1884	Ferris State University	11,074

Founded	*Name*	*Students*
1885	Michigan Technological University	6,625
1868	Wayne State University	28,161
1892	Central Michigan University	19,380
1899	Northern Michigan University	8,577
1903	Western Michigan University	28,931
1946	Lake Superior State University	3,077
1957	Oakland University	16,059
1960	Grand Valley State University	19,762
1963	Saginaw Valley State University	8,938

Health. There were, in 2000, 178 Medicare and Medicaid certified hospitals (31,895 beds); 12 psychiatric hospitals (2,547 beds) and five rehabilitation hospitals (315 beds).

Welfare. Old-age assistance is provided for persons 65 years of age or older who have resided in Michigan for one year before application; assets must not exceed various limits. In 1974 federal Supplementary Security Income (SSI) replaced the adults' programme. A monthly average of 69,786 families received $400·09 per month in 2002 through the Family Independence Agency. Medicare enrolment in July 2002 totalled 1,426,169. In 2000 a total of 1,351,650 people in Michigan received Medicaid. In Dec. 2003 there were 1,699,384 Old-Age, Survivors, and Disability Insurance (OASDI) beneficiaries. A total of 185,029 people were receiving payments under Temporary Assistance for Needy Families (TANF) in Sept. 2002.

CULTURE

Tourism. In 1998, 379,000 overseas visitors (1·6% of the market share), excluding Mexico and Canada, visited Michigan.

FURTHER READING

Michigan Manual. Dept of Management and Budget. Lansing. Biennial

Michigan Employment Security Commission. *Michigan Statistical Abstract, 1996.* Univ. of Michigan Press

Browne, W. P. and Verburg, K., *Michigan Politics and Government: Facing Change in a Complex State.* Nebraska Univ. Press, 1995

Dunbar, W. F. and May, G. S., *Michigan: A History of the Wolverine State.* 3rd ed. Grand Rapids, 1995

State Library Services: Library of Michigan, Lansing 48909.

MINNESOTA

KEY HISTORICAL EVENTS

Minnesota remained an Indian territory until the middle of the 19th century, the main groups being Chippewa and Sioux, many of whom are still there. In the 17th century there had been some French exploration, but no permanent settlement. After passing under the nominal control of France, Britain and Spain, the area became part of the Louisiana Purchase and so was sold to the USA in 1803.

Fort Snelling was founded in 1819. Early settlers came from other states, especially New England, to exploit the great forests. Lumbering gave way to homesteading, and the American settlers were joined by Germans, Scandinavians and Poles. Agriculture, mining and forest industries became the mainstays of the economy. Minneapolis, founded as a village in 1856, grew first as a lumber centre, processing the logs floated down the Minnesota River, and then as a centre of flour-milling and grain marketing. St Paul, its twin city across the river, became Territorial capital in 1849 and state capital in 1858. St Paul also stands at the head of navigation on the Mississippi, which rises in Minnesota.

The Territory (1849) included parts of North and South Dakota, but at its admission to the Union in 1858, the state of Minnesota had its present boundaries.

TERRITORY AND POPULATION

Minnesota is bounded north by Canada, east by Lake Superior and Wisconsin, with the Mississippi River forming the boundary in the southeast, south by Iowa, west by South and North Dakota, with the Red River forming the boundary in the northwest. Land area, 79,610 sq. miles (206,189 sq. km). Census population, 1 April 2000, 4,919,479, an increase of 12·4% since 1990. July 2004 estimate, 5,100,958.

Population in five census years was:

	White	*Black*	*Indian*	*Asiatic*	*Total*	*Per sq. mile*
1910	2,059,227	7,084	9,053	344	2,075,708	25·7
1930	2,542,599	9,445	11,077	832	2,563,953	32·0
			All others			
1980	3,935,770	53,344	86,856		4,075,970	51·4
1990	4,130,395	94,944	149,760		4,375,099	55·0
2000	4,400,282	171,731	347,466		4,919,479	61·8

Of the total population in 2000, 2,483,848 were female, 3,632,585 were 18 years old or older and 3,490,059 were urban. In 2000 the Hispanic population was 143,382, up from 53,888 in 1990 (an increase of 116·1%).

The largest cities (with 2000 census population) are Minneapolis (362,618), St Paul (287,151), Duluth (86,918), Rochester (85,806) and Bloomington (85,172). The Minneapolis–St Paul metropolitan area had a 2000 census population of 2,968,806.

SOCIAL STATISTICS

Births in 2002, 68,025 (13·6 per 1,000 population); deaths, 38,510 (7·7); 2001: infant deaths, 5·3 per 1,000 live births. 2001: marriages, 33,000 (6·8 per 1,000 population); divorces, 16,000 (3·3).

CLIMATE

Duluth, Jan. 8°F (–13·3°C), July 63°F (17·2°C). Annual rainfall 29" (719 mm). Minneapolis-St. Paul, Jan. 12°F (–11·1°C), July 71°F (21·7°C). Annual rainfall 26" (656 mm). Minnesota belongs to the Great Lakes climate zone (*see* UNITED STATES: Climate).

CONSTITUTION AND GOVERNMENT

The original constitution dated from 1857; it was extensively amended and given a new structure in 1974. The Legislature consists of a Senate of 67 members, elected for four years, and a House of Representatives of 134 members, elected for two years. It meets for 120 days within each two years.

For the 109th Congress, which convened in Jan. 2005, Minnesota sends eight members to the House of Representatives. It is represented in the Senate by Mark Dayton (D. 2001–07) and Norm Coleman (R. 2003–09).

The capital is St Paul. There are 87 counties.

RECENT ELECTIONS

In the 2004 presidential election Kerry polled 1,445,014 votes; Bush, 1,346,695; Nader, 18,683.

CURRENT ADMINISTRATION

Governor: Tim Pawlenty (R.), 2003–07 (salary: $120,303).

Lieut.-Governor: Carol L. Molnau (R.), 2003–07 ($78,197).

Secretary of State: Mary E. Kiffmeyer (R.), 2003–07 ($90,227).

Government Website: http://www.state.mn.us

ECONOMY

Per capita income (2002) was $33,895.

Budget. In 2002 total state revenue was $22,439m. Total expenditure was $26,693m. (education, $8,820m.; public welfare, $6,741m.; highways, $1,666m.; government administration, $672m.; natural resources, $542m.) Outstanding debt, in 2002, $6,408m.

Performance. In 2002 Gross State Product was $200,061m., ranking Minnesota 17th in the United States.

ENERGY AND NATURAL RESOURCES

Water. The total area covered by water is approximately 7,327 sq. miles.

Minerals. The iron ore and taconite industry is the most important in the USA. Production of usable iron ore in 1996 was 46m. tons, value $1,390m. Other important minerals are sand and gravel, crushed and dimension stone, clays and peat. Total value of mineral production, 2002, $1,090m.

Agriculture. In 2002 there were 79,000 farms with a total area of 28·4m. acres; the average farm was of 359 acres. Average value of land and buildings per acre, 2002, $1,513. Farm income, 2001, from crops, $3,813m.; from livestock and products, $4,288m. The net farm income in 2001 was $696m. Important products: sugarbeet, spring wheat, processing sweet corn, oats, dry milk, cheese, mink, turkeys, wild rice, butter, eggs, flaxseed, milch cows, milk, corn, barley, swine, cattle for market, soybeans, honey, potatoes, rye, chickens, sunflower seed and dry edible beans. In 2001 there were 2·6m. cattle (0·5m. milch cows) and 5·7m. hogs and pigs. In 2002 the wool clip amounted to 986,437 lb of wool from 154,900 sheep.

Forestry. In 2002 Minnesota had 16,680,000 acres of forested land, including 2,625,000 acres of national forest. Forests of commercial timber covered 14·8m. acres, of which 55% was government-owned. The value of forest products in 1994 was $7,500m.—$2,250m. from primary processing, of which $1,687m. was from pulp and paper; and $3,100m. from secondary manufacturing. Logging, pulping, saw-mills and associated industries employed 57,200 in 1995.

INDUSTRY

In 2001 the state's 8,146 manufacturing establishments had 374,000 employees, earning $14,846m. Total value added by manufacturing in 2001 was $38,545m.

Labour. Total non-agricultural employment, 2001, 2,674,000. Employees by branch, 2001 (in 1,000): services, 789; wholesale and retail trade, 633; manufacturing, 423; government, 401; finance, insurance and property, 166. In 2002 the unemployment rate was 4·4%.

COMMUNICATIONS

Roads. In 2002 there were 132,121 miles of roads (116,016 miles rural) and 4,520,314 registered motor vehicles.

Rail. There are three Class I and 16 Class II and smaller railroads operating, with total mileage of 4,650.

Civil Aviation. In 2000 there were 147 airports for public use and 19 public seaplane bases. There were 17,127,205 passenger enplanements statewide in 2000.

SOCIAL INSTITUTIONS

Justice. In June 2002 there were 6,958 federal and state prisoners. There is no death penalty.

Religion. The chief religious bodies are: Lutheran with 1,126,008 members in 1990; Roman Catholic, 1,110,071; Methodist, 142,771. Total membership of all denominations, 2,837,415.

Education. In 1999–2000 there were 853,267 students and 55,639 teachers in public elementary and secondary schools. In 2000–01 there were 1,755 public schools and 65 charter schools. There were 103,043 students enrolled in 564 private schools.

The Minnesota State Colleges and Universities System (created in 1995) is composed of 34 state colleges and universities. In 1999 enrolled students at state colleges numbered 61,491. There are seven universities in the system: St Cloud State University, with 11,962 students in 1999; Minnesota, Mankato, 10,946; Winona, 6,426; Minnesota, Moorhead, 5,987; Bemidji State University, 3,989; Metropolitan State University (in Minneapolis and St Paul), 3,314; Southwest Minnesota State University (in Marshall), 2,669. Minnesota State University's Akita campus in Japan closed in 2003.

The University of Minnesota (founded in 1851) has four campuses at Crookston, Duluth, Morris and Twin Cities.

Health. In 2001 there were 133 community hospitals with 16,500 beds. A total of 586,000 patients were admitted during the year.

Welfare. Medicare enrolment in July 2002 totalled 667,407. In 2000 a total of 559,463 people in Minnesota received Medicaid. In Dec. 2003 there were 765,228 Old-Age, Survivors, and Disability Insurance (OASDI) beneficiaries. A total of 96,800 people were receiving payments under Temporary Assistance for Needy Families (TANF) in Sept. 2002.

CULTURE

Tourism. In 1995 travellers spent about $8,699m. The industry employed about 162,800.

FURTHER READING

Statistical Information: Department of Trade and Economic Development, 500 Metro Square, St Paul 55101. Publishes *Compare Minnesota: an Economic and Statistical Factbook.—Economic Report to the Governor.*

Legislative Manual. Secretary of State. St Paul. Biennial

Minnesota Agriculture Statistics. Dept. of Agric., St Paul. Annual

MISSISSIPPI

KEY HISTORICAL EVENTS

Mississippi was one of the territories claimed by France after the 17th century and ceded to Britain in 1763. The indigenous people were Choctaw and Natchez. French settlers at first traded amicably with them, but in the course of three wars (1716, 1723 and 1729) the French allied with the Choctaw to drive the Natchez out. During hostilities the Natchez massacred the settlers of Fort Rosalie, which the French had founded in 1716 and which was later renamed Natchez.

In 1783 the area became part of the USA except for Natchez which was under Spanish control until 1798. The United States then made it the capital of the Territory of Mississippi. The boundaries of the Territory were extended in 1804 and again in 1812. In 1817 it was divided into two territories, with the western part becoming the state of Mississippi. (The eastern part became the state of Alabama in 1819.) The city of Jackson was laid out in 1822 as the new state capital.

A cotton plantation economy developed, based on black slave labour, and by 1860 the majority of the population was black. Mississippi joined the Confederacy during the Civil War. After defeat and reconstruction there was a return to rigid segregation and denial of black rights. This situation lasted until the 1960s. There was a black majority until the Second World War, when out-migration began to change the pattern. By 1990 about 35% of the population was black, and manufacture (especially clothing and textiles) had become the largest single employer of labour.

TERRITORY AND POPULATION

Mississippi is bounded in the north by Tennessee, east by Alabama, south by the Gulf of Mexico and Louisiana, and west by the Mississippi River forming the boundary with Louisiana and Arkansas. Land area, 46,907 sq. miles (121,489 sq. km). Census population, 1 April 2000, 2,844,658, an increase of 10·5% since 1990. July 2004 estimate, 2,902,966.

Population of five federal census years was:

	White	*Black*	*Indian*	*Asiatic*	*Total*	*Per sq. mile*
1910	786,111	1,009,487	1,253	263	1,797,114	38·8
1930	998,077	1,009,718	1,458	568	2,009,821	42·4
			All others			
1980	1,615,190	887,206	18,242		2,520,638	53·0
1990	1,633,461	915,057	24,698		2,573,216	54·8
2000	1,746,099	1,033,809	63,372		2,844,658	60·6

Of the total population in 2000, 1,373,554 were male, 2,069,471 were 18 years old or older and 1,457,307 were rural (51·2% of the population). In 2000 Mississippi's Hispanic population was estimated to be 39,569, up from 15,998 in 1990 (an increase of 147%).

The largest city (2000 census) is Jackson, 184,256. Others (2000 census) are: Gulfport, 71,127; Biloxi, 50,644; Hattiesburg, 44,779; Greenville, 41,633; Meridian,

39,968; Tupelo, 34,211; Southaven, 28,977; Vicksburg, 26,407; Pascagoula, 26,200; Columbus, 25,944.

SOCIAL STATISTICS

Births occurring in the state, 2002, were 41,518 (14·5 per 1,000 population); deaths, 28,853 (10·0 per 1,000 population); infant deaths, 2001, 10·5 per 1,000 live births; marriages, 2001, 18,605; divorces, 14,198.

CLIMATE

Jackson, Jan. 47°F (8·3°C), July 82°F (27·8°C). Annual rainfall 49" (1,221 mm). Vicksburg, Jan. 48°F (8·9°C), July 81°F (27·2°C). Annual rainfall 52" (1,311 mm). Mississippi belongs to the Central Plains climate zone (*see* UNITED STATES: Climate).

CONSTITUTION AND GOVERNMENT

The present constitution was adopted in 1890 without ratification by the electorate; there were 121 amendments by 2000.

The Legislature consists of a Senate (52 members) and a House of Representatives (122 members), both elected for four years. Electors are all citizens who have resided in the state one year, in the county one year, in the election district six months before the election and have been registered according to law.

For the 109th Congress, which convened in Jan. 2005, Mississippi sends four members to the House of Representatives. It is represented in the Senate by Thad Cochran (R. 1977–2009) and Trent Lott (R. 1989–2007).

The capital is Jackson; there are 82 counties.

RECENT ELECTIONS

In the 2004 presidential election Bush polled 672,660 votes; Kerry, 457,766; Nader, 3,175.

CURRENT ADMINISTRATION

Governor: Haley Barbour (R.), 2004–08 (salary: $122,160).

Lieut.-Governor: Amy Tuck (R.), 2004–08 ($60,000).

Secretary of State: Eric Clark (D.), 2004–08 ($90,000).

Government Website: http://www.mississippi.gov

ECONOMY

Per capita income (2002) was $22,370, the lowest in the country.

Budget. For the fiscal year ending 30 June 2004 general revenue was $13,737m. General expenditures were $13,244m. (education, $3,281m.; public welfare, including public health and health care, $1,146m.; highways, $920m.; police protection, $101m.) Debt outstanding, on 30 June 2004, $3,377m.

Performance. Gross State Product in 2002 was $69,136m. ranking Mississippi 35th in the United States.

ENERGY AND NATURAL RESOURCES

Oil and Gas. Petroleum and natural gas account for about 90% (by value) of mineral production. Output of petroleum, 2003, was 17,412,245 bbls. and of natural gas 164,170,149,000 cu. ft. There are four oil refineries. Taxable value of oil and gas products sold in fiscal year 2003 was $725,088,055.

Minerals. The value of domestic non-fuel mineral production in 2003 was $174m.

Agriculture. Agriculture is the leading industry of the state because of the semi-tropical climate and a rich productive soil. In 2003 farms numbered 42,800 with an area of 11·1m. acres. Average size of farm was 260 acres. This compares with an average farm size of 154 acres in 1962. Average value of farm per acre in 2003 was $1,350.

Cash income from all crops and livestock during 2003 was $3,411,002,000. Cash income from crops was $1,246,444,000, and from livestock and products $2,164,558,000. The chief product is cotton, cash income (2003) $444,445,000 from

1,110,000 acres producing 2,120,000 bales of 480 lb. Soybeans, rice, corn, hay, wheat, oats, sorghum, peanuts, pecans, sweet potatoes, peaches, other vegetables, nursery and forest products continue to contribute.

On 1 Jan. 2005 there were 1·07m. head of cattle and calves on Mississippi farms. In Jan. 2005 milch cows totalled 26,000; beef cows, 564,000; hogs and pigs (2004), 315,000. Of cash income from livestock and products, 2003, $208,136,000 was credited to cattle and calves. Cash income from poultry and eggs, 2003, totalled $1,597,427,000; dairy products, $55,151,000; swine, $42,126,000.

Forestry. In 2002 income from forestry amounted to $1·03bn.; output of pine logs was 1·19bn. bd ft; of hardwood lumber, 426m. bd ft; pulpwood, 5·55m. cords. There were 18·5m. acres of forest (61% of the state's area) in 2002, with 1·1m. acres of national forest area.

Fisheries. Commercial catch, in 2002, totalled 217·1m. lb of fish with a value of $46·1m. Mississippi has the largest aquaculture industry of any state; value, in 2001, was $262·9m. (of which catfish sales accounted for $240·0m.)

INDUSTRY

In 2002 the 2,829 manufacturing establishments had average monthly employment of 188,857 workers, earning $5,731,066,344. The average annual wage was $30,346.

Labour. In 2004 total non-agricultural employment was 1,124,600. Employees by branch, 2004 (in 1,000): services, 473; government, 245; manufacturing, 180; wholesale and retail trade, 175. The unemployment rate in 2004 was 5·7%.

COMMUNICATIONS

Roads. The state as of 1 July 2004 maintained 13,681 miles of highways, of which 13,673 miles were paved. In fiscal year 2004, 2,471,212 passenger vehicles and pick-ups were registered.

Rail. In 2003 the state had 2,584 main-line and short-line miles of railway.

Civil Aviation. There were 79 public airports in 2004, 72 of them general aviation airports. There were 1,166,522 passenger enplanements statewide in 2004.

SOCIAL INSTITUTIONS

Justice. The death penalty is authorized; the last execution was in 2002. As of 1 Feb. 2005 the state prison system had 20,964 inmates.

Religion. In 2003: Southern Baptists in Mississippi, 715,276 members; United Methodists, 190,428. In 2004: Roman Catholics in Jackson Diocese, 50,646; in 2003 Roman Catholics in Biloxi Diocese, 72,158.

Education. Attendance at school is compulsory as laid down in the Education Reform Act of 1982. The public elementary and secondary schools in 2003–04 had 492,557 pupils and 31,357 classroom teachers.

In 2003–04 teachers' average salary was $36,466. The expenditure per pupil in average daily attendance, 2002–03, was $6,402.

There are 21 universities and senior colleges, of which eight are state-supported. In autumn 2004 the University of Mississippi, Oxford had 916 faculty and 14,497 students; Mississippi State University, Starkville, 1,220 faculty and 15,934 students; Mississippi University for Women, Columbus, 183 faculty and 2,231 students; University of Southern Mississippi, Hattiesburg, 865 faculty and 15,253 students; Jackson State University, Jackson, 482 faculty and 8,351 students; Delta State University, Cleveland, 173 faculty and 3,990 students; Alcorn State University, Lorman, 225 faculty and 3,443 students; Mississippi Valley State University, Itta Bena, 135 faculty and 3,621 students. State support for the universities (2004–05) was $325,868,694.

Community and junior colleges had (2003–04) 83,307 full-time equivalent students and 4,083 full-time instructors. The state appropriation for junior colleges, 2003–04, was $157,226,517.

Health. In 2004 the state had 106 acute general hospitals (12,824 beds) listed by the State Department of Health; 14 hospitals with facilities for the care of the mentally ill had 2,341 licensed beds. In addition, one rehabilitation hospital had 124 beds.

Welfare. The Division of Medicaid paid (fiscal year 2004) $2,801,539,621 for medical services, including $639,224,101 for drugs, $614,299,371 for hospital services and $487,265,490 for skilled nursing home care. There were 79,482 persons eligible for Aged Medicaid benefits as of 30 June 2004 and 220,734 persons eligible for Disabled Medicaid benefits. In June 2004, 18,185 families with 30,032 dependent children received $2,566,105 in the Temporary Assistance to Needy Families programme. The average monthly payment was $141·66 per family or $63·42 per recipient.

CULTURE

Tourism. Total receipts in 2004 amounted to $6·1bn.; an estimated 11·4m. overnight tourists visited the state.

FURTHER READING

College of Business and Industry, Mississippi State Univ., Mississippi State 39762. Publishes *Mississippi Statistical Abstract.*

Secretary of State. *Mississippi Official and Statistical Register.* Quadrennial

Mississippi Library Commission: 1221 Ellis Avenue, Jackson, MS 39209–7328.

MISSOURI

KEY HISTORICAL EVENTS

Territory of several Indian groups, including the Missouri, the area was not settled by European immigrants until the 18th century. The French founded Ste Genevieve in 1735, partly as a lead-mining community. St Louis was founded as a fur-trading base in 1764. The area was nominally under Spanish rule from 1770 until 1800 when it passed back to France. In 1803 the USA bought it as part of the Louisiana Purchase.

St Louis was made the capital of the whole Louisiana Territory in 1805, and of a new Missouri Territory in 1812. In that year American immigration increased markedly. The Territory became a state in 1821, but there had been bitter disputes between slave-owning and anti-slavery factions, with the former succeeding in obtaining statehood without the prohibition of slavery required of all other new states north of latitude 36° 30'; this was achieved by the Missouri Compromise of 1820. The Compromise was repealed in 1854 and declared unconstitutional in 1857. During the Civil War the state held to the Union side, although St Louis was placed under martial law.

With the development of steamboat traffic on the Missouri and Mississippi rivers, and the expansion of railways, the state became the transport hub of all western movement. Lead and other mining remained important, as did livestock farming. European settlers came from Germany, Britain and Ireland.

TERRITORY AND POPULATION

Missouri is bounded north by Iowa, east by the Mississippi River forming the boundary with Illinois and Kentucky, south by Arkansas, southeast by Tennessee, southwest by Oklahoma, west by Kansas and Nebraska, with the Missouri River forming the boundary in the northwest. Land area, 68,886 sq. miles (178,414 sq. km).

Census population, 1 April 2000, 5,595,211, an increase since 1990 of 9·3%. July 2004 estimate, 5,754,618.

Population of five federal census years was:

	White	*Black*	*Indian*	*Asiatic*	*Total*	*Per sq. mile*
1930	3,403,876	223,840	578	1,073	3,629,367	52·4
1960	3,922,967	390,853	1,723	3,146	4,319,813	62·5
			All others			
1980	4,345,521	514,276	56,889		4,916,686	71·3
1990	4,486,228	548,208	82,637		5,117,073	74·3
2000	4,748,083	629,391	217,737		5,595,211	81·2

Of the total population in 2000, 2,875,034 were female, 4,167,519 were 18 years old or older and 3,883,442 were urban. In 2000 Missouri's Hispanic population was 118,592, up from 61,702 in 1990 (an increase of 92·2%).

The principal cities at the 2000 census were:

Kansas City	441,545	St Joseph	73,990
St Louis	348,189	Lee's Summit	70,700
Springfield	151,580	St Charles	60,321
Independence	113,288	St Peters	51,381
Columbia	84,531	Florissant	50,497

Metropolitan areas, 2000: St Louis, 2,603,607; Kansas City, 1,776,062.

SOCIAL STATISTICS

Births, 2002, were 75,251 (13·3 per 1,000 population); deaths, 55,940 (9·9). 2001: infant deaths, 7·4 per 1,000 live births. 2001: marriages, 42,200 (7·6 per 1,000 population); divorces, 23,800 (4·3).

CLIMATE

Kansas City, Jan. 30°F (–1·1°C), July 79°F (26·1°C). Annual rainfall 38" (947 mm). St Louis, Jan. 32°F (0°C), July 79°F (26·1°C). Annual rainfall 40" (1,004 mm). Missouri belongs to the Central Plains climate zone (*see* UNITED STATES: Climate).

CONSTITUTION AND GOVERNMENT

A new constitution, the fourth, was adopted on 27 Feb. 1945; it has been revised nine times with over 100 amendments. The General Assembly consists of a Senate of 34 members elected for four years (half for re-election every two years), and a House of Representatives of 163 members elected for two years. The Governor and Lieut.-Governor are elected for four years.

For the 109th Congress, which convened in Jan. 2005, Missouri sends nine members to the House of Representatives. It is represented in the Senate by Christopher Bond (R. 1987–2011) and James Talent (R. 1993–2007).

Jefferson City is the state capital. The state is divided into 114 counties and the city of St Louis.

RECENT ELECTIONS

In the 2004 presidential election Bush polled 1,455,713 votes; Kerry, 1,259,171; Badnarik, 9,831.

CURRENT ADMINISTRATION

Governor: Matt Blunt (R.), 2005–09 (salary: $120,087).

Lieut.-Governor: Peter Kinder (R.), 2005–09 ($77,184).

Secretary of State: Robin Carnahan (D.), 2005–09 ($96,455).

Government Website: http://www.state.mo.us

ECONOMY

Per capita income (2002) was $28,841.

Budget. In 2002 total state revenue was $19,085m. Total expenditure was $20,841m. (education, $6,717m.; public welfare, $5,497m.; highways, $1,871m.; hospitals, $889m.; government administration, $548m.) Outstanding debt, in 2002, $12,693m.

Performance. In 2002 Gross State Product was $187,543m., ranking Missouri 20th in the United States.

ENERGY AND NATURAL RESOURCES

Water. The total area covered by water is approximately 811 sq. miles.

Minerals. The three leading mineral commodities are lead, portland cement and crushed stone. Value of domestic non-fuel mineral production (2002) $1,290m.

Agriculture. In 2002 there were 107,000 farms in Missouri producing crops and livestock on 29·8m. acres; the average farm had 279 acres and was valued at $1,508 per acre. Production of principal crops, 2002: corn, 268·2m. bu.; soybeans, 165·05m. bu.; wheat, 34·9m. bu.; sorghum grain, 16·6m. bu.; oats, 1·29m. bu.; rice, 9·96m. cwt; cotton, 608,280 bales (of 480 lb). Farm income 2001: $4,824m. (from crops, $2,145m.; from livestock and products, $2,679m.). The net farm income in 2001 was $910m.

Forestry. The state had a forested area of 13,992,000 acres in 2002, of which 1,428,000 acres were national forest.

INDUSTRY

In 2001 the state's 7,261 manufacturing establishments had 335,000 employees, earning $11,318m. Total value added by manufacturing in 2001 was $40,284m.

Labour. Total non-agricultural employment, 2001, 2,732,000. Employees by branch, 2001 (in 1,000): services, 787; wholesale and retail trade, 643; government, 428; manufacturing, 379; transportation and public utilities, 175. The unemployment rate was 5·5% in 2002.

COMMUNICATIONS

Roads. In 2002 there were 124,686 miles of roads (107,110 miles rural) and 4,235,031 registered motor vehicles.

Rail. The state has five Class I railways; approximate total mileage, 4,159. There are four Class II and Class III railways (switching, terminal or short-line); total mileage 590 in 2002. There is a light rail line in St Louis.

Civil Aviation. In 1994 there were 114 public airports and 359 private airports. There were 21,165,695 passenger enplanements statewide in 2000.

Shipping. Two major barge lines (1993) operated on about 1,050 miles of navigable waterways including the Missouri and Mississippi Rivers. Boat shipping seasons: Missouri River, April–end Nov.; Mississippi River, all seasons.

SOCIAL INSTITUTIONS

Justice. In June 2002 there were 30,034 federal and state prisoners. The death penalty was reinstated in 1978. There were two executions in 2003 but none in 2004. The Missouri Law Enforcement Assistance Council was created in 1969 for law reform. With reorganization of state government in 1974 the duties of the Council were delegated to the Department of Public Safety. The Department of Corrections was organized as a separate department of State by an Act of the Legislature in 1981.

Religion. Chief religious bodies (1990) are Catholics, with 802,434 members, Southern Baptists (789,183), United Methodists (255,111), Christian Churches (166,412) and Lutherans (142,824). Total membership, all denominations, about 2·3m. in 1990.

Education. School attendance is compulsory for children from seven to 16 years for the full term. In the 1993–94 school year, public schools (kindergarten through grade 12) had 851,086 pupils. Total expenditure for public schools in 1993–94, $3,563,419,000. Salaries for teachers (kindergarten through grade 12), 1993–94, averaged $30,227.

Institutions for higher education include the University of Missouri, founded in 1839 with campuses at Columbia, Rolla, St Louis and Kansas City, with 3,469 accredited teachers and 48,072 students in 1994–95. Washington University at St Louis, founded in 1857, is an independent co-ed university with 11,655 students in 1994–95. St Louis University (1818) is an independent Roman Catholic co-ed university with 10,365 students in 1994–95. 17 state colleges had 129,466 students in 1994–95. Private colleges had (1994–95) 34,548 students. Church-affiliated colleges (1994–95) had 41,420 students. Public junior colleges had 66,853 students. There are about 90 secondary and post-secondary institutions offering vocational courses, and about 294 private career schools. There were 265,186 students in higher education in autumn 1994.

Health. In 2001 there were 117 community hospitals with 19,300 beds. A total of 801,000 patients were admitted during the year.

Welfare. Medicare enrolment in July 2002 totalled 873,816. In 2000 a total of 890,318 people in Missouri received Medicaid. In Dec. 2003 there were 1,033,886 Old-Age, Survivors, and Disability Insurance (OASDI) beneficiaries. A total of 114,175 people were receiving payments under Temporary Assistance for Needy Families (TANF) in Sept. 2002.

CULTURE

Broadcasting. There were 196 commercial radio stations and 29 TV stations in 1995.

Press. There were (1995) 46 daily and 260 weekly newspapers.

FURTHER READING

Statistical information: Business and Public Administration Research Center, Univ. of Missouri, Columbia 65211. Publishes *Statistical Abstract for Missouri.*

Missouri Area Labor Trends. Department of Labor and Industrial Relations, monthly

Missouri Farm Facts. Department of Agriculture, annual

Report of the Public Schools of Missouri. State Board of Education, annual

MONTANA

KEY HISTORICAL EVENTS

Originally the territory of many groups of Indian hunters including the Sioux, Cheyenne and Chippewa, Montana was not settled by American colonists until the 19th century. The area passed to the USA with the Louisiana Purchase of 1803, but the area west of the Rockies was disputed with Britain until 1846. Trappers and fur-traders were the first immigrants, and the fortified trading post at Fort Benton (1846) became the first permanent settlement. Colonization increased when gold was found in 1862. Montana was created a separate Territory (out of Idaho and Dakota Territories) in 1864. In 1866 large-scale grazing of sheep and cattle was allowed, and this provoked violent confrontation with the indigenous people whose hunting lands were invaded. Indian wars led to the defeat of federal forces at Little Bighorn in 1876 and at Big Hole Basin in 1877, but the Indians could not continue the fight and they had been moved to reservations by 1880. Montana became a state in 1889.

Helena, the capital, was founded as a mining town in the 1860s. In the early 20th century there were many European immigrants who settled as farmers or in the mines, especially in copper-mining at Butte.

TERRITORY AND POPULATION

Montana is bounded north by Canada, east by North and South Dakota, south by Wyoming and west by Idaho and the Bitterroot Range of the Rocky Mountains. Land area, 145,552 sq. miles (336,978 sq. km). US Bureau of Indian Affairs (1990) administered 5,574,835 acres, of which 2,663,385 were allotted to tribes. Census population, 1 April 2000, 902,195, an increase of 12·9% since 1990. July 2004 estimate, 926,865.

Population in five census years was:

	White	*Black*	*American Indian*	*Asiatic*	*Total*	*Per sq. mile*
1910	360,580	1,834	10,745	2,870	376,053	2·6
1930	519,898	1,256	14,798	1,239	537,606	3·7
1980	740,148	1,786	37,270	2,503	786,690	5·3
1990	741,111	2,381	47,679	4,259	799,065	5·4
2000	817,229	2,692	56,068	5,161	902,195	6·2

Of the total population in 2000, 452,715 were female, 672,133 were 18 years old or older and 487,878 were urban. Median age, 33·8 years. Households, 306,163. In 2000 Montana's Hispanic population was estimated to be 18,081, up from 12,174 in 1990 (an increase of 48·5%).

The largest cities, 2000, are Billings, 89,847; Missoula, 57,053; Great Falls, 56,690. Others: Butte-Silver Bow, 34,606; Bozeman, 27,509; Helena (capital), 25,780; Kalispell, 14,223; Havre, 9,621; Anaconda-Deer Lodge County, 9,417.

SOCIAL STATISTICS

Births in 2002, 11,049 (12·1 per 1,000 population); deaths, 8,506 (9·4); 2001: infant mortality rate, 6·7 (per 1,000 live births). 2001: marriages, 6,400; divorces, 2,300.

CLIMATE

Helena, Jan. 18°F (–7·8°C), July 69°F (20·6°C). Annual rainfall 13" (325 mm). Montana belongs to the Mountain States climate zone (*see* UNITED STATES: Climate).

CONSTITUTION AND GOVERNMENT

A new constitution came into force on 1 July 1973. The Senate consists of 50 senators, elected for four years, one half at each biennial election. The 100 members of the House of Representatives are elected for two years.

For the 109th Congress, which convened in Jan. 2005, Montana sends one member to the House of Representatives. It is represented in the Senate by Max Baucus (D. 1978–2009) and Conrad Burns (R. 1989–2007).

The capital is Helena. The state is divided into 56 counties.

RECENT ELECTIONS

In the 2004 presidential election Bush polled 266,063 votes; Kerry, 173,710; Nader, 6,168.

CURRENT ADMINISTRATION

Governor: Brian Schweitzer (D.), 2005–09 (salary: $96,462).

Lieut.-Governor: John Bohlinger (R.), 2005–09 ($66,724).

Secretary of State: Brad Johnson (R.), 2005–09 ($76,539).

Government Website: http://www.discoveringmontana.com

ECONOMY

Per capita income (2002) was $24,906.

Budget. In 2002 total state revenue was $4,033m. Total expenditure was $4,265m. (education, $1,289m.; public welfare, $660m.; highways, $453m.; health, $254m.; government administration, $218m.) Outstanding debt, in 2002, $2,752m.

Performance. Gross State Product in 2002 was $23,773m., ranking Montana 48th in the United States.

ENERGY AND NATURAL RESOURCES

Water. The total area covered by water is approximately 1,490 sq. miles.

Minerals. 2002 domestic non-fuel mineral production value was $442m. Principal minerals include copper, gold, platinum-group metals, molybdenum and silver.

Agriculture. In 2002 there were 28,000 farms and ranches with an area of 56·7m. acres. Large-scale farming predominates; in 2002 the average size per farm was 2,025 acres. The average value per acre in 2002 was $386. In 1997 a total of 13,267,000 acres were harvested; including 5,930,000 acres of wheat. The farm population in 2000 was 39,930.

The chief crops are wheat, barley, oats, sugarbeet, hay, potatoes, corn, dry beans and cherries. Farm income, 2001: crops, $657m.; livestock and products, $1,128m. In 2002 there were 2·4m. cattle and calves; value, $1,015m. The net farm income in 2001 was $304m.

Forestry. In 2002 there were 23·3m. acres of forested land with 14·6m. acres in 11 national forests.

INDUSTRY

In 2001 the state's 1,226 manufacturing establishments had 21,000 employees, earning $646m. Total value added by manufacturing in 2001 was $2,091m.

Labour. Total non-agricultural employment, 2001, 392,000. Employees by branch, 2001 (in 1,000): services, 116; wholesale and retail trade, 102; government, 84; manufacturing, 24. In 2002 the unemployment rate was 4·6%.

COMMUNICATIONS

Roads. In 2002 there were a total of 69,502 miles of roads comprising 2,603 miles of urban road and 66,899 miles of rural road. There were 1,056,143 registered motor vehicles.

Rail. In 1999 there were approximately 3,300 route miles of railway in the state.

Civil Aviation. There were 119 public use airports in 1999. There were nine state-owned airports and a further five-state managed. There were 1,062,654 passenger enplanements statewide in 2000.

SOCIAL INSTITUTIONS

Justice. In June 2002 there were 3,515 prison inmates. The death penalty is authorized; the last execution was in 1998.

Religion. The leading religious bodies are Roman Catholic, followed by Lutheran and Methodist.

Education. In 1995 (preliminary) public elementary and secondary schools had 165,000 pupils and (in 1994) 10,079 teachers. Expenditure on public school education by state and local governments in 1997 was $986m.

In 1996 there were 43,000 students enrolled at 26 higher education institutions. The Montana State University System (created in 1994) consists of the Montana State University, at Bozeman (autumn 1992 enrolment: 10,111 students), founded 1893; Montana State University-Billings (3,631); Montana State University-Northern, at Havre (1,973); and Montana State University-Great Falls College of Technology. The University of Montana System comprises the University of Montana, at Missoula, founded in 1893 (10,788); Montana Tech, at Butte (1,881); and the University of Montana-Western, at Dillon (1,106). The University of Great Falls (founded in 1932) had 879 students in autumn 2001.

Health. In 2001 there were 53 community hospitals with 4,500 beds. A total of 103,000 patients were admitted during the year.

Welfare. Medicare enrolment in July 2002 totalled 140,156. In 2000 a total of 103,821 people in Montana received Medicaid. In Dec. 2003 there were 163,659 Old-Age, Survivors, and Disability Insurance (OASDI) beneficiaries. A total of 16,313 people were receiving payments under Temporary Assistance for Needy Families (TANF) in Sept. 2002.

CULTURE

Press. There were 11 daily newspapers and seven Sunday papers in 1997.

FURTHER READING

Statistical information. Census and Economic Information Center, Montana Department of Commerce, 1425 9th Ave., Helena 59620.

Lang, W. L. and Myers, R. C., *Montana, Our Land and People.* Pruett, 1979

NEBRASKA

KEY HISTORICAL EVENTS

The Nebraska region was first reached by Europeans from Mexico under the Spanish general Coronado in 1541. It was ceded by France to Spain in 1763, retroceded to France in 1801, and sold by Napoléon to the USA as part of the Louisiana Purchase in 1803. During the 1840s the Platte River valley became an established trail for thousands of pioneers' wagons heading for Oregon and California. The need to serve and protect the trail led to the creation of Nebraska as a Territory in 1854. In 1862 the Homestead Act opened the area for settlement, but colonization was not very rapid until the Union Pacific Railroad was completed in 1869. The largest city, Omaha, developed as the starting point of the Union Pacific and became one of the largest railway towns in the country.

Nebraska became a state in 1867, with approximately its present boundaries except that it later received small areas from the Dakotas. Many early settlers were from Europe, brought in by railway-company schemes, but from the late 1880s eastern Nebraska suffered catastrophic drought. Crop and stock farming recovered, but crop growing was only established in the west by means of irrigation.

TERRITORY AND POPULATION

Nebraska is bounded in the north by South Dakota, with the Missouri River forming the boundary in the northeast and the boundary with Iowa and Missouri to the east, south by Kansas, southwest by Colorado and west by Wyoming. Land area, 76,872 sq. miles (199,098 sq. km). Census population, 1 April 2000, 1,711,263, an increase of 8·4% since 1990. July 2004 estimate, 1,747,214.

Population in five census years was:

	White	Black	Indian	Asiatic	Total	Per sq. mile
1910	1,180,293	7,689	3,502	730	1,192,214	15·5
1960	1,374,764	29,262	5,545	1,195	1,411,330	18·3
			All others			
1980	1,490,381	48,390	31,054		1,569,825	20·5
1990	1,480,558	57,404	40,423		1,578,385	20·5
2000	1,533,261	68,541	109,461		1,711,263	22·3

Of the total population in 2000, 867,912 were female, 1,261,021 were 18 years old or older and 1,193,725 were urban. In 1999 the estimated Hispanic population of Nebraska was 94,425, up from 36,969 in 1990 (a rise of 155·4%). The largest cities in the state are: Omaha, with a census population, 2000, of 390,007; Lincoln, 225,581; Bellevue, 44,382; Grand Island, 42,940; Kearney, 27,431; Fremont, 25,174; Hastings, 24,064; North Platte, 23,878; Norfolk, 23,516.

The Bureau of Indian Affairs in 1990 administered 64,932 acres, of which 21,742 acres were allotted to tribal control.

SOCIAL STATISTICS

Births, 2002, were 25,383 (14·7 per 1,000 population); deaths, 15,738 (9·1); 2001: infant mortality rate, 6·8 (per 1,000 live births). 2001: marriages, 13,600 (8·1); divorces, 6,200 (3·7).

CLIMATE

Omaha, Jan. 22°F (–5·6°C), July 77°F (25°C). Annual rainfall 29" (721 mm). Nebraska belongs to the High Plains climate zone (*see* UNITED STATES: Climate).

CONSTITUTION AND GOVERNMENT

The present constitution was adopted in 1875; it has been amended 184 times. By an amendment of 1934 Nebraska has a single-chambered legislature (elected for four years) of 49 members elected on a non-party ballot and classed as senators—the only state in the USA to have one. It meets annually.

For the 109th Congress, which convened in Jan. 2005, Nebraska sends three members to the House of Representatives. It is represented in the Senate by Chuck Hagel (R. 1997–2009) and Ben Nelson (D. 2001–07).

The capital is Lincoln. The state has 93 counties.

RECENT ELECTIONS

In the 2004 presidential election Bush polled 512,814 votes; Kerry, 254,328; Nader, 5,698.

CURRENT ADMINISTRATION

Governor: David Heineman (R.), 2005–07 (salary: $85,000).

Lieut.-Governor: Rick Sheehy (R.), 2005–07 ($60,000).

Secretary of State: John Gale (R.), 2003–07 ($65,000).

Government Website: http://www.state.ne.us

ECONOMY

Per capita income (2002) was $29,544.

Budget. In 2002 total state revenue was $6,002m. Total expenditure was $6,537m. (education, $2,191m.; public welfare, $1,661m.; highways, $526m.; health, $364m.; correction, $177m.) Outstanding debt, in 2002, $2,215m.

Performance. Gross State Product was $60,962m. in 2002, ranking Nebraska 37th in the United States.

ENERGY AND NATURAL RESOURCES

Oil and Gas. Petroleum output, 2001: 2·9m. bbls.; natural gas, 1,208m. cu. ft.

Water. The total area covered by water is approximately 481 sq. miles.

Minerals. Output of non-fuel minerals, 1995 (in 1,000 short tons): sand and gravel for construction, 17,637; stone, 7,275; clays, 243. Other minerals include limestone, potash, pumice, slate and shale. Total value of non-fuel mineral output in 2002 was $89m.

Agriculture. Nebraska is one of the most important agricultural states. In 2002 it contained approximately 52,000 farms, with a total area of 46·4m. acres. The average farm was 892 acres and was valued in 2002 at $776 per acre. In 2002 the total acreage harvested was 17·34m. acres.

In 2001 net farm income was $1,610m. Farm income from crops (2001), $3,402m., and from livestock and products, $6,086m. Principal crops were maize, hay, barley, sorghum for grain, soybeans and wheat. Livestock, 2001: cattle, 6·6m.; 2002: pigs, 2·93m.; sheep, 97,400; chickens, 13·7m.; turkeys, 3·5m.

Forestry. The state had a forested area of 947,000 acres in 2002.

INDUSTRY

In 2001 the state's 1,934 manufacturing establishments had 109,000 employees, earning $3,361m. Total value added by manufacturing in 2001 was $11,962m.

Labour. In 2001 non-agricultural employment totalled 909,000. Employees by branch in 2001 (in 1,000): services, 259; wholesale and retail trade, 213; government, 156; manufacturing, 117. In 2002 the unemployment rate was 3·6%.

COMMUNICATIONS

Roads. In 2002 there were 93,171 miles of roads (87,578 miles rural) and 1,655,603 registered motor vehicles.

Rail. In 2002 there were 3,537 miles of railway. There were two Class I operators (2,706 miles), three Class II operators (326 miles) and three Class III operators (505 miles).

Civil Aviation. Publicly owned airports in 1996 numbered 384. There were 2,041,182 passenger enplanements statewide in 2000.

SOCIAL INSTITUTIONS

Justice. A 'Civil Rights Act' revised in 1969 provides that all people are entitled to a full and equal enjoyment of public facilities. In June 2002 there were 4,031 prison inmates. The last execution was in 1997.

Religion. The Roman Catholics had 337,224 members in 1992; United Methodists, 131,665; Evangelical Lutheran Church, 128,014; Lutheran Church-Missouri Synod, 115,204; Presbyterian Church (USA), 36,723.

Education. School attendance is compulsory for children from seven to 16 years of age. Public elementary and secondary schools, in 2001–02, had 285,095 enrolled pupils and 20,808 teachers in 1,250 schools; there were 42,791 non-public pupils. Total enrolment in institutions of higher education, autumn 2000, was 88,532 students in public and 21,518 in independent institutions.

Founded	*Institution*	*Students 2000–01*
1867	Peru State College	2,686
	University of Nebraska (State)	45,183
1869	Lincoln	22,268
1902	Medical Center	2,696
1905	Kearney	6,506
1908	Omaha	13,479
1965	College of Technical Agriculture, Curtis	234
1872	Doane College, Crete (United Church of Christ)	2,135
1878	Creighton University, Omaha (Roman Catholic)	6,237
1882	Hastings College (Presbyterian)	1,130
1883	Midland Lutheran College, Fremont (Lutheran Church of America)	1,025
	Nebraska Methodist College, Omaha (Private)	400
1884	Dana College, Blair (American Lutheran)	583
1887	Nebraska Wesleyan University (Private)	1,699
1888	Clarkson College, Omaha (Private)	400
1890	York College[1] (Private)	497
1891	Union College, Lincoln (Seventh Day Adventist)	788
1894	Concordia University Nebraska, Seward (Lutheran)	1,270
1910	Wayne State College	3,518
1911	Chadron State College	2,686
1923	College of St Mary (Roman Catholic)	947

Founded	*Institution*	*Students 2000–01*
1943	Grace University, Omaha (Mennonite)	578
1945	Nebraska Christian College (Church of Christ)	162
1951	Platte Valley Bible College (Private)	52
1966	Bellevue University (Private)	3,445
1971	Nebraska Community Colleges (Local government)	35,447
	Central Area	7,126
	Metropolitan Area	11,534
	Mid Plains Area	2,607
	Northeast Area	4,520
	Southeast Area	7,396
	Western Area	2,264
1972	Nebraska Indian Community College	170

[1]Two-year college.

Health. In 2001 there were 84 community hospitals with 8,300 beds. A total of 207,000 patients were admitted during the year.

Welfare. Medicare enrolment in July 2002 totalled 255,862. In 2000 a total of 229,038 people in Nebraska received Medicaid. In Dec. 2003 there were 287,891 Old-Age, Survivors, and Disability Insurance (OASDI) beneficiaries. A total of 26,109 people were receiving payments under Temporary Assistance for Needy Families (TANF) in Sept. 2002.

CULTURE

Tourism. In 1995 there were an estimated 16·1m. visits. Travellers and tourists spent over $2,000m.

FURTHER READING

Statistical information: Department of Economic Development, Box 94666, Lincoln 68509.
Nebraska Blue-Book. Legislative Council. Lincoln. Biennial
Olson, J. C., *History of Nebraska.* 3rd ed. Univ. of Nebraska Press, 1997

State Library: State Law Library, State House, Lincoln.

NEVADA

KEY HISTORICAL EVENTS

The area was part of Spanish America until 1821, when it became part of the newly independent state of Mexico. Following a war between Mexico and the USA, Nevada was ceded to the USA as part of California in 1848. Settlement began in 1849, and the area was separated from California and joined with Utah Territory in 1850. In 1859 a rich deposit of silver was found in the Comstock Lode. Virginia City was founded as a mining town and immigration increased rapidly. Nevada Territory was formed in 1861. During the Civil War the Federal government, allegedly in order to obtain the wealth of silver for the Union cause, agreed to admit Nevada to the Union in 1864 as the 36th state. Areas of Arizona and Utah Territories were added to it in 1866–67.

The mining boom lasted until 1882, by which time cattle ranching had become equally important in the valleys where the climate is less arid. Carson City, the capital, developed in association with the nearby mining industry. The largest cities, Las Vegas and Reno, grew most in the 20th century with the building of the Hoover dam, the introduction of legal gambling and of easily obtained divorce.

After 1950 much of the desert area was adopted by the Federal government for weapons testing and other military purposes.

TERRITORY AND POPULATION

Nevada is bounded north by Oregon and Idaho, east by Utah, southeast by Arizona, with the Colorado River forming most of the boundary, south and west by California. Land area, 109,889 sq. miles (284,613 sq. km). In 1999 the federal government owned 83% of the land area.

Census population on 1 April 2000, 1,998,257, an increase of 66·3% since 1990. July 2004 estimate, 2,334,771.

Population in five census years was:

	White	Black	American Indian	All others	Total	Per sq. mile
1910	74,276	513	5,240	1,846	81,875	0·7
1930	84,515	516	4,871	1,156	91,058	0·8
1980	700,360	50,999	13,308	35,841	800,508	7·2
1990	1,012,695	78,771	19,637	90,730	1,201,833	10·9
2000	1,501,886	135,477	26,420	334,474	1,998,257	18·2

Of the total population in 2000, 1,018,051 were male, 1,486,458 were 18 years old or older and 1,828,646 were urban (91·51%, the third highest of the states). In 2000 the Hispanic population was 393,970, up from 124,419 in 1990 (an increase of 216·6%). Nevada was the fastest-growing state in the USA in 2003. Its recent overall population rise has made it the fastest-growing state in the USA every year since 1986.

The largest cities in 2000 were: Las Vegas, 478,434; Reno, 180,480; Henderson, 175,381; North Las Vegas, 115,448; Sparks, 66,346; Carson City (the capital), 52,457.

SOCIAL STATISTICS

Births, 2002, were 32,571 (15·0 per 1,000); deaths, 16,927 (7·8 per 1,000); infant mortality deaths (2001) were 5·7 per 1,000 live births. Marriages (2000), 134,908; divorces, 14,084. Fertility rate, 1998, 2·5 births per woman (the second highest in the USA after Utah).

CLIMATE

Las Vegas, Jan. 57°F (14°C), July 104°F (40°C). Annual rainfall 4·13" (105 mm). Reno, Jan. 45°F (7°C), July 91°F (33°C). Annual rainfall 7·53" (191 mm). Nevada belongs to the Mountain States climate zone (*see* UNITED STATES: Climate).

CONSTITUTION AND GOVERNMENT

The constitution adopted in 1864 is still in force, with 145 amendments as of 2001. The Legislature meets biennially (and in special sessions) and consists of a Senate of 21 members elected for four years, half their number is elected every two years, and an Assembly of 42 members elected for two years. The Governor may be elected for two consecutive four-year terms.

For the 109th Congress, which convened in Jan. 2005, Nevada sends three members to the House of Representatives. It is represented in the Senate by Harry Reid (D. 1987–2011) and John Ensign (R. 2001–07).

The state capital is Carson City. There are 16 counties, 18 incorporated cities and 49 unincorporated communities and one city-county (the Capitol District of Carson City).

RECENT ELECTIONS

In the 2004 presidential election Bush polled 418,690 votes; Kerry, 397,190; Nader, 4,838.

CURRENT ADMINISTRATION

Governor: Kenny C. Guinn (R.), 2003–07 (salary: $117,000).
Lieut.-Governor: Lorraine Hunt (R.), 2003–07 ($50,000).
Secretary of State: Dean Heller (R.), 2003–07 ($80,000).

Government Website: http://www.nv.gov

ECONOMY

Per capita personal income (2002) was $30,169.

Budget. In fiscal year 2002 the total sources of funding totalled $4,987·7m. The tax sources include $655·1m. from Sales and Use Taxes; $589·8m. from Gaming Taxes; $207·5m. from Casino Entertainment Tax; $156·3m. from Insurance Premium Tax; $78·4m. from Business Licence Tax. Total expenditure in 2002 was $4,364m. (education, $999·5m.; human services, $501·6m.; public safety, $210·4m.) Outstanding debt, in 2002, $3,668m.

Performance. Gross State Product in 2002 was $81,182m., ranking Nevada 32nd in the United States.

ENERGY AND NATURAL RESOURCES

Electricity. In 2001 there were 15 geothermal electric plants in ten locations. Total electricity capacity in 1998 was 5·8m. kW. In 1999 total net electrical production was 26·4bn. kWh.

Oil and Gas. In 2001, 571,000 bbls. of crude oil were produced from oil fields located in Nye and Eureka Counties.

Water. The total area covered by water is approximately 761 sq. miles.

Minerals. Nevada led the nation in precious metal production in 2000, producing 76% of gold and 37% of silver. Nevada has been first in silver production since 1987 and first in gold since 1981. In 2000 Nevada produced 267,000 kg of gold and 722,000 kg of silver. Nevada was the only state in 2000 to produce magnesite, lithium minerals, brucite and mercury. Nevada also produces other minerals such as aggregates, clays, copper, diatomite, dolomite, geothermal energy, gypsum, lapidary, lime and limestone. The total value of Nevada's mineral production in 2000 was about $2·7bn.

Agriculture. In 2002 there were an estimated 3,000 farms. Farms averaged 2,267 acres; farms and ranches totalled 6·8m. acres. Average value per acre in 2002 was $446.

In 2001, 45·3% of farm income came from cattle and calves, 14·7% from dairy products, 0·6% from sheep and lambs, and 3·3% from other livestock. Hay production was 22% of all farm income, potatoes 2·4%, vegetables 4·6%, wheat 0·4% and other crops 6·7%. The net farm income in 2001 was $119m.

In 2002 there were 500,000 cattle and 100,000 sheep.

Forestry. Nevada had, in 2002, 10·20m. acres of forested land with 3·23m. acres of national forest.

INDUSTRY

The main industry is the service industry (42·2% of employment in 2000), especially tourism and legalized gambling. In 2000 there were 42,406 persons employed in manufacturing and 88,688 in construction.

Gaming industry gross revenue for 2001 was $9,220m. In 1998 there were 428 non-restricted licensed casinos and 2,700 licences in force. Nevada gets 41% of its tax revenue from the gaming industry.

Labour. In 2000 all industries employed 1,091,970 workers. The service industry employed 247,752; retail trade, 175,730; transportation and public utilities, 61,801; government, 51,920; finance, insurance and real estate, 46,580; manufacturing, 44,380; mining, 10,955. The unemployment rate in 2002 was 5·4%.

COMMUNICATIONS

Roads. In 2001 there were 44,613 miles of roads, of which the state maintained 5,447 miles. Vehicle registrations in 2002 numbered 1,252,879.

Rail. In 2003 there were 1,449 miles of main-line railway. Nevada is served by the Southern Pacific, Union Pacific and Burlington Northern BPH Nevada Railroad railways, and Amtrak passenger service for Las Vegas, Elko, Reno, Caliente, Lovelock, Stateline, Winnemucca and Sparks. Las Vegas has a 4-mile monorail metro system.

Civil Aviation. There were 98 civil airports and 24 heliports in Jan. 1996. During 2001, 43,574,956 passengers arrived at Nevada's airports. McCarran International Airport (Las Vegas) handled 32,647,344 passengers and Reno-Tahoe International Airport handled 4,932,648 passengers.

SOCIAL INSTITUTIONS

Justice. Capital punishment was reintroduced in 1978, and executions began in 1979. There were two executions in 2004. In June 2002 there were 10,426 prison inmates in state or federal correctional institutions.

Religion. Many faiths are represented in Nevada, including Church of Jesus Christ of Latter Day Saints (Mormons), Protestantism, Roman Catholicism, Judaism and Buddhism.

Education. School attendance is compulsory for children from seven to 17 years of age. Numbers of pupils in public schools, 2001–02: pre-kindergarten, 2,147; kindergarten, 26,877; elementary, 177,342; secondary grades 7–9, 87,538; secondary grades 10–12, 60,470; special education, 40,196. Numbers of teachers in public schools, 2001: elementary, 9,870; secondary, 6,070; special education, 2,646; occupational, 198. Numbers of pupils in private schools, 2001–02: kindergartens, 3,109; elementary, 8,281; secondary grades 7–9, 2,892; secondary grades 10–12, 2,056. Number of private school teachers, 1999, 973.

The University of Nevada System comprises the University of Nevada, Las Vegas and Reno, the Nevada State College (at Henderson), the Community College of Southern Nevada (at Las Vegas and Henderson), Great Basin College (at Elko), Truckee Meadows Community College (at Reno) and Western Nevada Community College (at Carson City, Minden and Fallon). In autumn 2002 there were 54,832 students (50,527 in 2001).

Health. In 2001 the state had 24 community hospitals with nine rural hospitals and 15 urban hospitals with 4,059 beds (1·9 per 1,000). In 2000 there were 4,875 physicians and 20,495 full-time and part-time nurses, nursing assistants, aids and orderlies and other hospital personnel.

Welfare. The Nevada Women, Infants and Children (WIC) special nutrition programmes served an average of 39,000 at-risk women, infants and children each month in 2001 and 69,396 people receiving food stamps. In 2000, 5% of the population received public aid. Benefits were paid to 102,162 persons. The average per recipient monthly for TANF (Temporary Assistance for Needy Families) was $124·86.

CULTURE

Tourism. There are 24 State Parks covering 131,861 acres. In 2001, 28,216,174 people visited state and nearby national parks with 49,528,979 tourists coming to Nevada.

FURTHER READING

Statistical information: Budget and Planning Division, Department of Administration, Capitol Complex, Carson City, Nevada 89710. Publishes *Nevada Statistical Abstract* (Biennial).

Bowers, Michael W., *The Stagebrush State: Nevada's History, Government, and Politics.* Univ. of Nevada Press, 1996

Hulse, J. W., *The Nevada Adventure: a History.* 6th ed. Univ. of Nevada Press, 1990.—*The Silver State: Nevada's Heritage Reinterpreted.* Univ. of Nevada Press, 1998

State Government Website: http://www.nv.gov

Nevada State Library: Nevada State Library and Archives, Carson City.

NEW HAMPSHIRE

KEY HISTORICAL EVENTS

The area was part of a grant by the English crown made to John Mason and fellow-colonists, and was first settled in 1623. In 1629 an area between the Merrimack and Piscatagua rivers was called New Hampshire. More settlements followed, and in 1641 they were taken under the jurisdiction of the governor of Massachusetts. New Hampshire became a separate colony in 1679.

After the War of Independence New Hampshire became one of the 13 original states of the Union, ratifying the US constitution in 1788. The state constitution, which dates from 1776, was almost totally rewritten in 1784 and amended again in 1792.

The settlers were Protestants from Britain and Northern Ireland. They developed manufacturing industries, especially shoe-making, textiles and clothing, to which large numbers of French Canadians were attracted after the Civil War.

Portsmouth, originally a fishing settlement, was the colonial capital and is the only seaport. In 1808 the state capital was moved to Concord (having had no permanent home since 1775); Concord produced the Concord Coach which was widely used on the stagecoach routes of the West until at least 1900.

TERRITORY AND POPULATION

New Hampshire is bounded in the north by Canada, east by Maine and the Atlantic, south by Massachusetts and west by Vermont. Land area, 8,968 sq. miles (23,227 sq. km). Census population, 1 April 2000, 1,235,786, an increase of 11·4% since 1990. July 2004 estimate, 1,299,500.

Population at five federal censuses was:

	White	*Black*	*Indian*	*Asiatic*	*Total*	*Per sq. mile*
1910	429,906	564	34	68	430,572	47·7
1960	604,334	1,903	135	549	606,921	65·2
			All others			
1980	910,099	3,990	6,521		920,610	101·9
1990	1,087,433	7,198	14,621		1,109,252	123·7
2000	1,186,851	9,035	39,900		1,235,786	137·8

Of the total population in 2000, 628,099 were female, 926,224 were 18 years old or older and 732,335 were urban. In 2000 the Hispanic population was estimated to be 20,489, up from 11,333 in 1990 (an increase of 80·8%). The largest city in the state is Manchester, with a 2000 census population of 107,006. The capital is Concord, with 40,687. Other main cities and towns (with 2000 populations) are: Nashua, 86,605; Derry, 34,021; Rochester, 28,461; Salem, 28,112; Dover, 26,884; Merrimack, 25,119; Londonderry, 23,236; Hudson, 22,928; Keene, 22,563; Portsmouth, 20,784.

SOCIAL STATISTICS

Births, 2002, were 14,442 (11·3 per 1,000 population); deaths, 9,853 (7·7); 2001: infant mortality rate, 3·8 (per 1,000 live births). 2001: marriages, 10,600; divorces, 6,100.

CLIMATE

New Hampshire is in the New England climate zone (*see* UNITED STATES: Climate). Manchester, Jan. 22°F (–5·6°C), July 70°F (21·1°C). Annual rainfall 40" (1,003 mm).

CONSTITUTION AND GOVERNMENT

While the present constitution dates from 1784, it was extensively revised in 1792 when the state joined the Union. Since 1775 there have been 16 state conventions with 49 amendments adopted to amend the constitution.

The Legislature (called the General Court) consists of a Senate of 24 members, elected for two years, and a House of Representatives, of 400 members, elected for two years. It meets annually. The Governor and five administrative officers called 'Councillors' are also elected for two years.

For the 109th Congress, which convened in Jan. 2005, New Hampshire sends two members to the House of Representatives. It is represented in the Senate by Judd Gregg (R. 1993–2011) and John Sununu (R. 2003–09).

The capital is Concord. The state is divided into ten counties.

RECENT ELECTIONS

In the 2004 presidential election Kerry polled 340,511 votes; Bush, 331,237; Nader, 4,479.

CURRENT ADMINISTRATION

Governor: John Lynch (D.), 2005–07 (salary: $103,000).

Senate President: Thomas R. Eaton (R.), elected Dec. 2002.

Secretary of State: William M. Gardner (D.), first elected by legislature in 1976 ($89,128).

Government Website: http://www.state.nh.us

ECONOMY

Per capita income (2002) was $34,276.

Budget. New Hampshire has no general sales tax or state income tax but does have local property taxes. Other government revenues come from rooms and meals tax, business profits tax, motor vehicle licences, fuel taxes, fishing and hunting licences, state-controlled sales of alcoholic beverages, cigarette and tobacco taxes.

In 2002 total state revenue was $4,636m. Total expenditure was $4,823m. (education, $1,530m.; public welfare, $975m.; highways, $377m.; government administration, $194m.; health, $148m.) Outstanding debt, in 2002, $5,397m.

Performance. Gross State Product in 2002 was $46,448m., ranking New Hampshire 40th in the United States.

ENERGY AND NATURAL RESOURCES

Water. The total area covered by water is approximately 314 sq. miles.

Minerals. Minerals are little worked; they consist mainly of sand and gravel, stone, and clay for building and highway construction. Value of domestic non-fuel mineral production in 2002 was $68m.

Agriculture. In 2002 there were 3,100 farms covering around 410,000 acres; average farm was 132 acres. Average value per acre in 2002, $3,131. Farm income 2001: from crops, $90m.; from livestock and products, $66m. The net farm income in 2001 was $13m.

The chief field crops are hay and vegetables; the chief fruit crop is apples. Livestock, 2002: cattle, 39,900; sheep, 7,423; pigs, 2,718; chickens (including broilers), 204,129.

Forestry. In 2002 the state had a forested area of 4,818,000 acres, of which 717,000 acres were national forest.

Fisheries. 2002 commercial fishing landings amounted to 23·2m. lb worth $16·7m.

INDUSTRY

Principal manufactures: electrical and electronic goods, machinery and metal products. In 2001 the state's 2,249 manufacturing establishments had 96,000 employees, earning $3,819m. Total value added by manufacturing in 2001 was $8,621m.

Labour. Total non-agricultural employment, 2001, 627,000. Employees by branch, 2001 (in 1,000): services, 191; wholesale and retail trade, 165; manufacturing, 104. In 2002 the unemployment rate was 4·7%.

COMMUNICATIONS

Roads. In 2002 there were 15,504 miles of roads (12,505 miles rural) and 1,143,231 registered motor vehicles.

Rail. In 2000 the length of operating railway in the state was 415 miles.

Civil Aviation. In 1997 there were 26 public and 21 private airports. There were 1,520,866 passenger enplanements statewide in 2000.

SOCIAL INSTITUTIONS

Justice. There were 2,476 prison inmates in June 2002. The death penalty was abolished in May 2000—the last execution had been in 1939.

Religion. The Roman Catholic Church is the largest single body. The largest Protestant churches are Congregational, Episcopal, Methodist and United Baptist Convention of N.H.

Education. School attendance is compulsory for children from six to 14 years of age during the whole school term, or to 16 if their district provides a high school. Employed illiterate minors between 16 and 21 years of age must attend evening or special classes, if provided by the district.

In 1995 the public elementary and secondary schools had 209,150 pupils and 12,300 teachers. Public school salaries, 1995, averaged $35,792. An average of $6,449 was spent on education per pupil.

Of the 4-year colleges, the University of New Hampshire (founded in 1866) had 14,538 students in 1998; Southern New Hampshire University (1932, was New Hampshire College), 5,653; Dartmouth College (1769), 5,269; Keene State College (1909), 4,354; Plymouth State University (1871), 3,990. Total enrolment, 1995–96, in the 30 institutions of higher education was 61,128.

Health. In 2001 there were 28 community hospitals with 2,900 beds. A total of 116,000 patients were admitted during the year.

Welfare. Medicare enrolment in July 2002 totalled 175,828. In 2000 a total of 96,935 people in New Hampshire received Medicaid. In Dec. 2003 there were 211,499 Old-Age, Survivors, and Disability Insurance (OASDI) beneficiaries. A total of 14,702 people were receiving payments under Temporary Assistance for Needy Families (TANF) in Sept. 2002.

CULTURE

Broadcasting. Across the state there were 49 radio and six TV stations in 1997.

Press. In 1997 there were 12 daily and eight Sunday newspapers in circulation.

FURTHER READING

Delorme, D. (ed.) *New Hampshire Atlas and Gazetteer.* Freeport, 1983

NEW JERSEY

KEY HISTORICAL EVENTS

Originally the territory of Delaware Indians, the area was first settled by immigrant colonists in the early 17th century, when Dutch and Swedish traders established fortified posts on the Hudson and Delaware Rivers. The Dutch took control but lost it to the English in 1664. In 1676 the English divided the area in two; the eastern portion was assigned to Sir George Carteret and the western granted to Quaker settlers. This division lasted until 1702 when New Jersey was united as a colony of the Crown and placed under the jurisdiction of the governor of New York. It became a separate colony in 1738.

During the War of Independence crucial battles were fought at Trenton, Princeton and Monmouth. New Jersey became the 3rd state of the Union in 1787. Trenton, the state capital since 1790, began as a Quaker settlement and became an iron-working town. Industrial development grew rapidly, there and elsewhere in the state, after the opening of canals and railways in the 1830s. Princeton, also a Quaker settlement, became an important post on the New York road; the college of New Jersey (Princeton University) was transferred there from Newark in 1756.

The need for supplies in the Civil War stimulated industry and New Jersey became a manufacturing state. The growth beyond its borders of New York and Philadelphia, however, produced a pattern of commuting to employment in both centres. By 1980 about 60% of the state's population lived within 30 miles of New York.

TERRITORY AND POPULATION

New Jersey is bounded north by New York, east by the Atlantic with Long Island and New York City to the northeast, south by Delaware Bay and west by Pennsylvania. Land area, 7,417 sq. miles (19,209 sq. km). Census population, 1 April 2000, 8,414,350, an increase of 8·9% since 1990. July 2004 estimate, 8,698,879.

Population at five federal censuses was:

	White	*Black*	*Asiatic*	*Others*	*Total*	*Per sq. mile*
1910	2,445,894	89,760	1,345	168	2,537,167	337·7
1930	3,829,663	208,828	2,630	213	4,041,334	537·3
1980	6,127,467	925,066	103,848	208,442	7,364,823	986·2
1990	6,130,465	1,036,825	272,521	290,377	7,730,188	1,042·0
2000	6,104,705	1,141,821	483,605	684,219	8,414,350	1,134·4

Of the total population in 2000, 4,331,537 were female, 6,326,792 were 18 years old or older and 7,939,087 were urban (94·35%, marginally less than California, the highest). In 2000 the Hispanic population was 1,117,191, up from 739,861 in 1990 (an increase of 51·0%).

Census populations of the largest cities and towns in 2000 were:

Newark	273,546	Edison	97,687	Trenton (capital)	85,403
Jersey City	240,055	Woodbridge	97,203	Camden	79,904
Paterson	149,222	Dover	89,706	Clifton	78,672
Elizabeth	120,568	Hamilton	87,109	Brick	76,119

Cherry Hill	69,965	Bayonne	61,842	Union Township	54,405
East Orange	69,824	Irvington	60,695	Wayne	54,069
Passaic	67,861	Old Bridge	60,456	Franklin	50,903
Union City	67,088	Lakewood	60,352	Parsippany-Troy Hills	50,649
Middletown	66,327	North Bergen	58,092		
Gloucester	64,350	Vineland	56,271	Piscataway	50,482

Largest metropolitan areas (2000) are: Newark, 2,032,989; Bergen–Passaic, 1,373,167; Middlesex–Somerset–Hunterdon, 1,169,641; Monmouth–Ocean, 1,126,217; Jersey City, 608,975.

SOCIAL STATISTICS

2002 (rates per 1,000 population): births, 114,751 (13·4); deaths, 74,009 (8·6); 2001: infant deaths, 6·5 per 1,000 live births. 2001: marriages, 54,100; divorces, 28,500.

CLIMATE

Jersey City, Jan. 31°F (–0·6°C), July 75°F (23·9°C). Annual rainfall 41" (1,025 mm). Trenton, Jan. 32°F (0°C), July 76°F (24·4°C). Annual rainfall 40" (1,003 mm). New Jersey belongs to the Atlantic Coast climate zone (*see* UNITED STATES: Climate).

CONSTITUTION AND GOVERNMENT

The present constitution, ratified by the registered voters on 4 Nov. 1947, has been amended 45 times. There is a 40-member Senate and an 80-member General Assembly. Assembly members serve two years, senators four years, except those elected at the election following each census, who serve for two years. Sessions are held throughout the year.

For the 109th Congress, which convened in Jan. 2005, New Jersey sends 13 members to the House of Representatives. It is represented in the Senate by Frank Lautenberg (D. 1982–2001, 2003–09) and Jon Corzine (D. 2001–07).

The capital is Trenton. The state is divided into 21 counties, which are subdivided into 567 municipalities—cities, towns, boroughs, villages and townships.

RECENT ELECTIONS

In the 2004 presidential election Kerry polled 1,911,430 votes; Bush, 1,670,003; Nader, 19,418.

CURRENT ADMINISTRATION

Governor (acting): Richard J. Codey (D.), 2004–06 (salary: $157,000).

Senate President: Richard J. Codey (D.), elected by Senate in 2004.

Secretary of State: Regena Thomas (D.), appointed Jan. 2002 ($137,165).

Government Website: http://www.state.nj.us

ECONOMY

Per capita income (2002) was $39,567, the third highest in the country.

Budget. In 2002 total state revenue was $32,709m. Total expenditure was $41,988m. (education, $10,244m.; public welfare, $6,703m.; highways, $2,257m.; government administration, $1,359m.; hospitals, $1,343m.) Outstanding debt, in 2002, $32,093m.

Performance. Gross State Product in 2002 was $380,169m., ranking New Jersey 8th in the United States.

ENERGY AND NATURAL RESOURCES

Water. The total area covered by water is approximately 796 sq. miles.

Minerals. In 1992 the chief minerals were stone (17·1m. short tons, value $126m.) and sand and gravel (17·9m. short tons, value $105m.); others are clays, peat and gemstones. New Jersey is a leading producer of greensand marl, magnesium compounds and peat. Total value of domestic non-fuel mineral products, 2002, was $285m.

Agriculture. Livestock raising, market-gardening, fruit-growing, horticulture and forestry are pursued. In 2003 there were 9,900 farms covering a total of 820,000 acres with an average farm size of 83 acres. Average value per acre in 2002 was

$9,245—making it the second most valuable land per acre in the USA, after Connecticut.

Cash receipts from farm marketings, 2003: crops, $658m.; livestock and products, $188m. The net farm income in 2003 was $127m.

Leading crops (2003) are blueberries (value, $45·7m.), tomatoes ($28·0m.), peppers ($25·6m.), peaches ($24·2m.), soybeans ($16·1m.), cranberries ($15·1m.), sweet corn ($12·1m.), corn for grain ($7·1m.). Livestock, 2003: 12,000 milch cows, 46,000 all cattle, 15,300 sheep and lambs and 12,000 swine.

Forestry. Total forested area was 2,132,000 acres in 2002.

Fisheries. 2002 commercial fishing landings amounted to 162·2m. lb worth $112·7m.

INDUSTRY

In 2003 the state's 11,343 manufacturing establishments had 347,822 employees, earning $19,505m. Total value added by manufacturing in 2001 was $50,754m.

Labour. The unemployment rate in Sept. 2004 was 4·8%, the 17th consecutive month in which the rate was below that of the USA.

In Sept. 2001 there were 4,006,900 employees on non-agricultural payrolls; 1,340,000 in services, 934,500 in wholesale and retail trade, 598,700 in government, 438,800 in manufacturing, 266,700 in transportation and public utilities, 158,900 in construction.

COMMUNICATIONS

Roads. In 2004 there were 36,592 miles of public roads and 7,147,853 registered vehicles.

Rail. NJ Transit, the USA's third largest provider of bus, rail and light rail transit, has a fleet of 2,027 buses, 711 trains and 45 light rail vehicles, which serve approximately 725,550 passengers daily on 11 rail lines (848·3 track miles) and 236 bus routes. The state is also served by 13 shortline freight railroads, three Class I rail carriers (Norfolk Southern, CSX and CP Rail) and two statewide terminal railroads (Conrail Shared Assets Carrier and NYS & W Ry) which deliver freight on behalf of Class I rail carriers.

There is a metro link to New York (22 km), a light rail line (7 km) and extensive commuter railways around Newark.

Civil Aviation. There is an international airport at Newark. In total there are an estimated 72,000 jobs in New Jersey that are linked to the general aviation airport system. The annual payroll associated with these jobs is estimated at $2·4bn. The annual value of goods and services purchased by airport tenants, visitors and general aviation-dependent businesses exceeds $4·6bn. There were 15,591,383 passenger enplanements statewide in 2000.

Shipping. In 1999 the maritime industry contributed more than $50bn. to the state economy. The two largest ports are the Port of Newark-Elizabeth and the Port of Camden. The Port of Newark-Elizabeth, the premier port on the Eastern seaboard, employed 229,000 people in 2003.

SOCIAL INSTITUTIONS

Justice. In June 2002 there were 28,054 prison inmates. The death penalty is authorized, but has not been used since 1963.

Religion. In 1994 the Roman Catholic population of New Jersey was 3·25m., and there were 436,000 Jews. Among Protestant sects were United Methodists, 132,000; United Presbyterians (1993), 106,700; Lutherans, 82,200; American Baptists (1992), 66,000; Episcopalians, 64,200.

Education. Elementary instruction is compulsory for all from six to 16 years of age and free to all from five to 20 years of age. 128 school districts with high concentrations of disadvantaged children must offer free pre-school education to three- and four-year olds. In 1999–2000 public elementary schools had 919,665 enrolled pupils and secondary schools had 369,555. Average salary of approximately 90,000 elementary and secondary classroom teachers in public schools in

1999–2000 was $51,571. In 1999–2000 school expenditure totalled $13·7bn.; approximately $10,833 per pupil.

There are 57 universities and colleges in New Jersey. In autumn 2002 public institutions had 289,275 students, including 138,924 in community colleges. Enrolment in autumn 2002: Rutgers, the State University (founded as Queen's College in 1766), had 51,480 students at campuses in Camden, Newark and New Brunswick; The College of New Jersey (1855; formerly Trenton State College), 6,948; Kean University, at Union City (1855), 12,779; Montclair State University (1908), 134,673; Rowan University, at Glassboro (1923), 9,685; William Paterson University, at Wayne (1855), 10,924.

Independent institutions had 72,482 students. Princeton University (founded in 1746) had 6,646 students; Fairleigh Dickinson University, at Teaneck (1941), 10,368; Seton Hall University, at South Orange (1856), 9,596.

Health. In 2001 there were 78 community hospitals with 24,600 beds. A total of 1,084,000 patients were admitted during the year.

Welfare. Medicare enrolment in July 2002 totalled 1,212,966. In 2000 a total of 822,369 people in New Jersey received Medicaid. In Dec. 2003 there were 1,363,838 Old-Age, Survivors, and Disability Insurance (OASDI) beneficiaries. A total of 99,018 people were receiving payments under Temporary Assistance for Needy Families (TANF) in Sept. 2002.

FURTHER READING

Statistical information: New Jersey State Data Center, Department of Labor, CN 388, Trenton 08625. Publishes *New Jersey Statistical Factbook.*

Legislative District Data Book. Bureau of Government Research. Annual

Manual of the Legislature of New Jersey. Trenton. Annual

Cunningham, J. T., *New Jersey: America's Main Road.* Rev. ed. New York, 1976

State Library: 185 W. State Street, Trenton, CN 520, NJ 08625.

NEW MEXICO

KEY HISTORICAL EVENTS

The first European settlement was established in 1598. Until 1771 New Mexico was the Spanish kings' 'Kingdom of New Mexico'. In 1771 it was annexed to the northern province of New Spain. When New Spain won its independence in 1821, it took the name of Republic of Mexico and established New Mexico as its northernmost department. Ceded to the USA in 1848 after war between the USA and Mexico, the area was organized as a Territory in 1850, by which time its population was Spanish and Indian. There was frequent conflict, especially between new settlers and raiding parties of Navajo and Apaches. The Indian war lasted from 1861 until 1866, and from 1864–68 about 8,000 Navajo were imprisoned at Bosque Redondo.

The boundaries were altered several times when land was taken into Texas, Utah, Colorado and lastly (1863) Arizona. New Mexico became a state in 1912.

Settlement proceeded by means of irrigated crop-growing and Mexican-style ranching. During the Second World War the desert areas were brought into use as testing zones for atomic weapons. Mineral extraction also developed, especially after the discovery of uranium and petroleum.

TERRITORY AND POPULATION

New Mexico is bounded north by Colorado, northeast by Oklahoma, east by Texas, south by Texas and Mexico and west by Arizona. Land area, 121,356 sq. miles (316,901 sq. km). Public lands, administered by federal agencies (1975) amounted to 26·7m. acres or 34% of the total area. The Bureau of Indian Affairs held 7·3m. acres; the State of New Mexico held 9·4m. acres; 34·4m. acres were privately owned.

Census population, 1 April 2000, 1,819,046, an increase of 20·1% since 1990. Of the total population in 2000, 924,729 were female, 1,310,472 were 18 years old or older and 1,363,501 were urban. July 2004 estimate, 1,903,289.

The population in five census years was:

	White	Black	American Indian	Asian and Pacific Island	Other	Total	Per sq. mile
1910	304,594	1,628	20,573	506	...	327,301	2·7
1940	492,312	4,672	34,510	324	...	531,818	4·4
1980	977,587	24,020	106,119	6,825	188,343	1,302,894	10·7
1990	1,146,028	30,210	134,355	14,124	190,352	1,515,069	12·5
2000	1,214,253	34,343	173,483	20,758	376,209	1,819,046	15·0

Before 1930 New Mexico was largely a Spanish-speaking state, but after 1945 an influx of population from other states considerably reduced the percentage of persons of Spanish origin or descent. However, in recent years the percentage of the Hispanic population has begun to rise again. In 2000 the Hispanic population was 765,386, up from 579,224 in 1990 (an increase of 32·1%). At 42·1%, New Mexico has the largest percentage of persons of Hispanic origin of any state in the USA.

The largest cities are Albuquerque, with 2000 census population of 448,607; Las Cruces, 74,267; Santa Fe, 62,203; Rio Rancho, 51,765; Roswell, 45,293.

SOCIAL STATISTICS

Statistics 2002: births, 27,753 (15·0 per 1,000 population); deaths, 14,344 (7·7); 2001: infant deaths, 6·4 per 1,000 live births. 2001: marriages, 13,900 (7·9 per 1,000 population); divorces, 9,000 (5·1).

CLIMATE

Santa Fe, Jan. 26·4°F (–3·1°C), July 68·4°F (20°C). Annual rainfall 15·2" (386 mm). New Mexico belongs to the Mountain States climate zone (*see* UNITED STATES: Climate).

CONSTITUTION AND GOVERNMENT

The constitution of 1912 is still in force with 152 amendments. The state Legislature, which meets annually, consists of 42 members of the Senate, elected for four years, and 70 members of the House of Representatives, elected for two years.

For the 109th Congress, which convened in Jan. 2005, New Mexico sends three members to the House of Representatives. It is represented in the Senate by Pete Domenici (R. 1973–2009) and Jeff Bingaman (D. 1983–2007).

The state capital is Santa Fe. The state is divided into 33 counties.

RECENT ELECTIONS

In the 2004 presidential election Bush polled 376,930 votes; Kerry, 370,942; Nader, 4,053.

CURRENT ADMINISTRATION

Governor: Bill Richardson (D.), 2003–06 (salary: $110,000).

Lieut.-Governor: Diane D. Denish (D.), 2003–06 ($85,000).

Secretary of State: Rebecca Vigil-Giron (D.), 2003–06 ($85,000).

Government Website: http://www.state.nm.us

ECONOMY

Per capita income (2002) was $23,908.

Budget. In 2002 total state revenue was $8,746m. Total expenditure was $10,084m. (education, $3,514m.; public welfare, $2,028m.; highways, $938m.; hospitals, $399m.; government administration, $349m.) Outstanding debt, in 2002, $4,493m.

Performance. Gross State Product in 2002 was $53,515m., ranking New Mexico 38th in the United States.

ENERGY AND NATURAL RESOURCES

Oil and Gas. 2001 production: petroleum, 68,967,000 bbls. (of 42 gallons); natural gas, 1,678bn. cu. ft. New Mexico ranks second in the USA behind Texas for natural gas production and also has natural gas reserves second only to Texas. In late 2001, 11,500 persons were employed in the oil and gas industry.

Water. The total area covered by water is approximately 234 sq. miles.

Minerals. New Mexico is one of the largest energy producing states in the USA. Production in 2001: potash, 1,086,410 short tons; copper, 154,580 short tons; coal, 30,525,401 short tons. New Mexico is the country's leading potash producer, accounting for approximately 70% of all potash mined in the USA, and ranked third for copper production in 2001. The value of coal output in 2001 was $584·9m. and of total non-fuel mineral output $651·6m.

Agriculture. New Mexico produces grains, vegetables, hay, livestock, milk, cotton and pecans. In 2002 there were 15,000 farms covering 44·0m. acres; average farm size 2,933 acres. In 2002 average value of farmland and buildings per acre was $234.

2001 cash receipts from crops, $545m., and from livestock products, $1,670m. The net farm income in 2001 was $820m. Principal crops are hay (1·6m. tons from 0·38m. acres), cotton (65m. lb from 0·70m. acres) and chilli (162m. lb from 0·18m. acres). Farm animals in 2001 included 290,000 milch cows, 1·6m. all cattle, 230,000 sheep and 3,000 swine.

Forestry. The state had a forested area of 16,682,000 acres in 2002, of which 8,092,000 acres were national forest.

INDUSTRY

In 2001 the state's 1,585 manufacturing establishments had 37,000 employees, earning $1,299m. Total value added by manufacturing in 2001 was $6,632m.

Labour. Total non-agricultural employment, 2001, 757,000. Employees by branch, 2001 (in 1,000): services, 222; government, 186; wholesale and retail trade, 174; construction, 46. The unemployment rate in 2002 was 5·4%.

COMMUNICATIONS

Roads. In 2002 there were 61,384 miles of roads (54,543 miles rural) and 1,538,284 registered motor vehicles.

Rail. In 1999 there were 2,027 miles of railway in operation.

Civil Aviation. There were 64 public-use airports in Nov. 1995. There were 3,044,305 passenger enplanements statewide in 2000.

SOCIAL INSTITUTIONS

Justice. In June 2002 there were 5,875 prison inmates. The death penalty is authorized and was used in 2001 (one execution) for the first time since 1960.

Since 1949 the denial of employment by reason of race, colour, religion, national origin or ancestry has been forbidden. A law of 1955 prohibits discrimination in public places because of race or colour. An 'equal rights' amendment was added to the constitution in 1972.

Religion. There were (1990) approximately 883,000 Christian Church adherents (421,868 Roman Catholics in 1996).

Education. Elementary education is free, and compulsory between six and 17 years or high-school graduation age. In 1995–96 the 89 school districts had an enrolment of 348,543 students in elementary and secondary schools of which private, parochial and state supported schools had 31,112. In 1994–95 there were 18,500 FTE teachers receiving an average salary of $29,074. Total revenue for public elementary and secondary schools was $1,702m. (1994–95).

In autumn 2002 there were 51,648 students attending public universities and 62,002 students attending community colleges. The state-supported four-year institutes of higher education are (autumn 2002 enrolment):

	Students
University of New Mexico, Albuquerque	24,645
New Mexico State University, Las Cruces	15,621
Eastern New Mexico University, Portales	3,756
New Mexico Highlands University, Las Vegas	3,024
Western New Mexico University, Silver City	2,551
New Mexico Institute of Mining and Technology, Socorro	1,747

Health. In 2001 there were 35 community hospitals with 3,600 beds. A total of 164,000 patients were admitted during the year.

Welfare. Medicare enrolment in July 2002 totalled 243,922. In 2000 a total of 375,585 people in New Mexico received Medicaid. In Dec. 2003 there were 294,669 Old-Age, Survivors, and Disability Insurance (OASDI) beneficiaries. A total of 44,383 people were receiving payments under Temporary Assistance for Needy Families (TANF) in Sept. 2002.

CULTURE

Tourism. In 1995 there were 47,200 travel-generated jobs; total travel expenditure (domestic and international), $3,045·7m.

FURTHER READING

Bureau of Business and Economic Research, Univ. of New Mexico—*Census in New Mexico* (Continuing series. Vols. 1–5, 1992–).—*Economic Census: New Mexico* (Continuing series. Vols. 1–3).—*New Mexico Business*. Monthly; annual review in Jan.–Feb. issue.

Etulain, R., *Contemporary New Mexico, 1940–1990*. Univ. of New Mexico Press, 1994

NEW YORK STATE

KEY HISTORICAL EVENTS

The first European immigrants came in the 17th century, when there were two powerful Indian groups in rivalry: the Iroquois confederacy (Mohawk, Oneida, Onondaga, Cayuga and Seneca) and the Algonquian-speaking Mohegan and Munsee. The Dutch made settlements at Fort Orange (now Albany) in 1624 and at New Amsterdam in 1625, trading with the Indians for furs. In the 1660s there was conflict between the Dutch and the British in the Caribbean; as part of the concluding treaty the British in 1664 received Dutch possessions in the Americas, including New Amsterdam, which they renamed New York.

In 1763 the Treaty of Paris ended war between the British and the French in North America (in which the Iroquois had allied themselves with the British). Settlers of British descent in New England then felt confident enough to expand westward into the area. The climate of northern New York being severe, most settled in the Hudson river valley. After the War of Independence New York became the 11th state of the Union (1778), having first declared itself independent of Britain in 1777.

The economy depended on manufacturing, shipping and other means of distributing goods, and trade. During the 19th century New York became the most important city in the USA. Its manufacturing industries, especially clothing, attracted thousands of European immigrants. Industrial development spread along the Hudson-Mohawk valley, which was made the route of the Erie Canal (1825) linking New York with Buffalo on Lake Erie and thus with the developing farmlands of the middle west.

On 11 Sept. 2001 New York City was attacked by hijackers when two commercial airliners were flown into the World Trade Center. The building was destroyed and 2,749 people died.

TERRITORY AND POPULATION

New York is bounded west and north by Canada with Lake Erie, Lake Ontario and the St Lawrence River forming the boundary; east by Vermont, Massachusetts and Connecticut, southeast by the Atlantic, south by New Jersey and Pennsylvania. Land area, 47,214 sq. miles (122,284 sq. km). Census population, 1 April 2000, 18,976,457, an increase of 5·5% since 1990. July 2004 estimate, 19,227,088.

Population in five census years was:

	White	*Black*	*Indian*	*Asiatic*	*Total*	*Per sq. mile*
1910	8,966,845	134,191	6,046	6,532	9,113,614	191·2
1930	12,143,191	412,814	6,973	15,088	12,588,066	262·6
			All others			
1980	13,961,106	2,401,842	1,194,340		17,557,288	367·0
1990	13,385,255	2,859,055	1,746,145		17,990,455	381·0
2000	12,893,689	3,014,385	3,068,383		18,976,457	401·9

Of the total population in 2000, 9,829,709 were female, 14,286,350 were 18 years old or older and 16,602,582 were urban. In 2000 the Hispanic population was 2,867,583, up from 2,214,026 in 1990 (an increase of 29·5%). California and Texas are the only states with a higher Hispanic population.

The population of New York City, by boroughs, census of 1 April 2000 was: Manhattan, 1,537,195; Bronx, 1,332,650; Brooklyn, 2,465,326; Queens, 2,229,379; Staten Island, 443,728; total, 8,008,278. The New York–Northern New Jersey–Long Island metropolitan area had, in 2000, a population of 21,199,865.

Population of other large cities and incorporated places at the 2000 census was:

Buffalo	292,648	Niagara Falls	55,593	Elmira	30,940
Rochester	219,773	White Plains	53,077	Poughkeepsie	29,871
Yonkers	196,086	Troy	49,170	Ithaca	29,287
Syracuse	147,306	Binghampton	47,380	Auburn	28,574
Albany (capital)	95,658	Freeport	43,783	Newburgh	28,259
New Rochelle	72,182	Valley Stream	36,368	Lindenhurst	27,819
Mount Vernon	68,381	Long Beach	35,462	Watertown	26,705
Schenectady	61,821	Rome	34,950	Glen Cove	26,622
Utica	60,651	North Tonawanda	33,262	Saratoga Springs	26,186
Hempstead	56,554	Jamestown	31,730		

Other large urbanized areas, census 2000; Buffalo–Niagara Falls, 1,170,111; Rochester, 1,098,201; Albany–Schenectady–Troy, 875,583.

SOCIAL STATISTICS

Births in 2002 were 251,415 (13·1 per 1,000 population); deaths, 158,118 (8·3); infant mortality rate, 2001, 5·8 (per 1,000 live births). 2001: marriages, 145,500; divorces, 54,100.

CLIMATE

Albany, Jan. 24°F (–4·4°C), July 73°F (22·8°C). Annual rainfall 34" (855 mm). Buffalo, Jan. 24°F (–4·4°C), July 70°F (21·1°C). Annual rainfall 36" (905 mm). New York, Jan. 30°F (–1·1°C), July 74°F (23·3°C). Annual rainfall 43" (1,087 mm). New York belongs to the Atlantic Coast climate zone (*see* UNITED STATES: Climate).

CONSTITUTION AND GOVERNMENT

New York State has had five constitutions, adopted in 1777, 1821, 1846, 1894 and 1938. The constitution produced by the 1938 convention (which was substantially a modification of the 1894 one), forms the fundamental law of the state (as modified by subsequent amendments). A proposed new constitution in 1967 was rejected by the electorate. In 1997 voters rejected a proposal to hold a new constitutional convention.

The Legislature comprises the Senate, with 62 members, and the Assembly, with 150. All members are elected in even-numbered years for two-year terms. The Legislature meets every year, typically for several days a week from Jan.–June and, if recalled by leaders of the Legislature, at other times during the year. The Governor can also call the Legislature into extraordinary session. The state capital is Albany. For local government the state is divided into 62 counties, five of which constitute the city of New York.

Each of the state's 62 cities is incorporated by charter, under special legislation. The government of New York City is vested in the mayor (Michael Bloomberg), elected for four years, and a city council, whose president and members are elected for four years. The council has a President and 51 members, each elected from a district wholly within the city. The mayor appoints all the heads of departments, except the comptroller (the chief financial officer), who is elected. Each of the five city boroughs (Manhattan, Bronx, Brooklyn, Queens and Staten Island) has a president, elected for four years. Each borough is also a county, although Manhattan borough, as a county, is called New York, Brooklyn is called Kings, and Staten Island is called Richmond.

For the 109th Congress, which convened in Jan. 2005, New York State sends 29 members to the House of Representatives. It is represented in the Senate by Charles Schumer (D. 1999–2011) and Hillary Clinton (D. 2001–07).

RECENT ELECTIONS

In the 2004 presidential election Kerry polled 4,314,280 votes; Bush, 2,962,567; Nader, 99,873.

CURRENT ADMINISTRATION

Governor: George E. Pataki (R.), 2003–07 (salary: $179,000).
Lieut.-Governor: Mary O. Donohue (R.), 2003–07 ($151,500).
Secretary of State: Randy A. Daniels, appointed April 2001 ($120,800).

Government Website: http://www.state.ny.us

ECONOMY

Per capita income (2002) was $35,708.

Budget. In 2002–03 cash receipts from all governmental funds totalled $88,073m. Disbursements from these funds totalled $89,055m. (health and social welfare, $37,601m.; education, $26,734m.; transportation, $5,157m.; public protection, $4,298m.) Outstanding debt in 2003 was $39,415m.

Performance. Gross State Product was $792,058m. in 2002, ranking New York second after California.

Banking and Finance. In 2002 there were 211 financial institutions in New York State insured by the US Federal Deposit Insurance Corporation, with assets worth $1,620bn. They had 4,526 offices with total deposits of $516bn.

ENERGY AND NATURAL RESOURCES

Water. The total area covered by water is approximately 6,766 sq. miles.

Minerals. Principal minerals are: sand and gravel, salt, titanium concentrate, talc, abrasive garnet, wollastonite and emery. Quarry products include trap rock, slate, marble, limestone and sandstone. Value of domestic non-fuel mineral output in 2002, $1,010m.

Agriculture. New York has large agricultural interests. In 2002 it had 37,000 farms, with a total area of 7·6m. acres; average farm was 205 acres. Average value per acre in 2002 was $1,708.

Farm income, 2002, from crops $1,200m. and livestock $1,870m. The net farm income in 2001 was $803m. Dairying is an important type of farming. Field crops comprise maize, winter wheat, oats and hay. New York ranks second in the USA in the production of apples and maple syrup. Other products are grapes, tart cherries, peaches, pears, plums, strawberries, raspberries, cabbages, onions, potatoes and maple sugar. Estimated farm animals, 2003, included 1,450,000 all cattle, 680,000 milch cows, 65,000 sheep and lambs, 73,000 swine and 4·9m. chickens.

Forestry. Total forested area was 18,432,000 acres in 2002, of which 5,000 acres were national forest. There were state parks and recreation areas covering 300,000 acres in 2003.

INDUSTRY

Leading industries are clothing, non-electrical machinery, printing and publishing, electrical equipment, instruments, food and allied products and fabricated metals. In 2002 the state's 22,878 manufacturing establishments had 699,462 employees, earning $31,141m. Total value added by manufacturing in 2001 was $78,484m.

Labour. Total non-agricultural employment, 2002, 8,440,100. Employees by branch, 2001 (in 1,000): services, 3,129; government, 1,403; wholesale and retail trade, 1,239; finance, property and insurance, 736; manufacturing, 699. In 2002 the unemployment rate was 6·1%.

COMMUNICATIONS

Roads. In 2002 there were 114,022 miles of roads (72,560 miles rural). The New York State Thruway extends 559 miles from New York City to Buffalo. The Northway, a 176-mile toll-free highway, is a connecting road from the Thruway at Albany to the Canadian border at Champlain, Quebec.

Motor vehicle registrations in 2002 were 10,455,697. In 2003 there were 1,491 traffic accident fatalities.

Rail. There were in 2000, 2,258 miles of Class I railways. In addition the State had 534 miles of regional railway and 1,068 miles of local railway. New York City has NYCTA and PATH metro systems, and commuter railways run by Metro-North, New Jersey Transit and Long Island Rail Road. Buffalo has a 7-mile metro line.

Civil Aviation. At Jan. 2003 there were 542 aviation facilities in New York State. Of these, 160 were public use airports, 382 were private use airports; two were private use glider ports, six public use heliports, 144 private use heliports, nine public use seaplane bases and ten private use seaplane bases. There were 33,648,816 passenger enplanements statewide in 2003. The busiest airports are New York City's John F. Kennedy International (which handled 31,732,371 passengers in 2003) and LaGuardia (22,482,770 passengers in 2003).

Shipping. The canals of the state, combined in 1918 in what is called the Improved Canal System, have a length of 524 miles, of which the Erie or Barge canal has 340 miles.

SOCIAL INSTITUTIONS

Justice. The State Human Rights Law was approved on 12 March 1945, effective on 1 July 1945. The State Division of Human Rights is charged with the responsibility of enforcing this law. The division may request and utilize the services of all governmental departments and agencies; adopt and promulgate suitable rules and regulations; test, investigate and pass judgment upon complaints alleging discrimination in employment, in places of public accommodation, resort or amusement, education, and in housing, land and commercial space; hold hearings, subpoena witnesses and require the production for examination of papers relating to matters under investigation; grant compensatory damages and require repayment of profits in certain housing cases among other provisions; apply for court injunctions to prevent frustration of orders of the Commissioner.

In Jan. 2004 there were 65,125 federal and state prisoners.

The death penalty is authorized but has not been used since 1963.

Religion. The main religious denominations are Roman Catholics, Jews and Protestant Episcopalians.

Education. Education is compulsory between the ages of seven and 16. In 2001–02 the public elementary and secondary schools had 2,826,620 pupils and 217,210 teachers. There were 493,913 pupils at non-public schools.

The state's educational system, including public and private schools and secondary institutions, universities, colleges, libraries, museums, etc., constitutes (by legislative act) the 'University of the State of New York', which is governed by a Board of Regents consisting of 15 members appointed by the Legislature. Within the framework of this 'University' was established in 1948 a 'State University' (SUNY), which controls 64 colleges and educational centres, 30 of which are locally operated community colleges. The 'State University' is governed by a board of 16 Trustees, appointed by the Governor with the consent and advice of the Senate.

Higher education in the state is conducted in 322 institutions. 1,097,015 students enrolled in autumn 2002. There were 46,399 full-time faculty staff (13,898 at SUNY) in 2001.

Student enrolment (autumn 2002) in higher education in the state included:

Founded	*Name and place*	*Students*
1754	Columbia University, New York City	22,393
1795	Union College, Schenectady and Albany	2,512
1824	Rensselaer Polytechnic Institute, Troy	7,670
1829	Rochester Institute of Technology, Rochester	13,720
1831	New York University, New York City	38,096
1836	Alfred University, Alfred	1,604
1841	Manhattanville College, New York City	2,564
1846	Colgate University, Hamilton	2,837
1846	Fordham University, New York City	14,318
1847	The City University of New York (CUNY), New York City	208,862
1848	University of Rochester, Rochester	8,516
1854	Polytechnic University, New York City	3,032
1856	St Lawrence University, Canton	2,293

Founded	Name and place	Students
1859	Cooper Union for the Advancement of Science and Art, NYC	947
1861	Vassar College, Poughkeepsie	2,472
1863	Manhattan College, New York City	3,207
1865	Cornell University, Ithaca	12,566
1870	Syracuse University, Syracuse	19,301
1870	St John's University, New York City	19,288
1892	Ithaca College, Ithaca	6,431
1906	Pace University, New York City and Westchester	14,095
1926	Long Island University	21,470
1929	Marist College, Poughkeepsie	5,866
1935	Hofstra University, Hempstead	13,412
1948	State University of New York (SUNY)	402,945

Health. In 2001 there were 212 community hospitals with 67,300 beds. Approximately 2,411,000 patients were admitted during 2001.

Welfare. Medicare enrolment in July 2002 totalled 2,746,660. In 2002 an average 3,406,965 people in New York State were Medicaid eligible. In Oct. 2002, 622,068 individuals were recipients of temporary assistance, eligible for one or more programmes including family assistance (326,373), safety net assistance (295,695), supplemental security income (619,128) and food stamps (1,515,884).

CULTURE

Tourism. In 2003 there were a record 37·8m. visitors to New York City (33·0m. domestic and 4·8m. overseas), up from 35·3m. in 2002. Visitor spending in 2002 was $14,100m.

FURTHER READING

Statistical information: Nelson Rockefeller Institute of Government, 411 State St., Albany 12203. Publishes *New York State Statistical Yearbook.*
New York Red Book. Albany. Biennial.
Legislative Manual. Department of State. Biennial.
The Modern New York State Legislature: Redressing the Balance. Albany, Rockefeller Institute, 1991
State Library: The New York State Library, Albany 12230.

NORTH CAROLINA

KEY HISTORICAL EVENTS

The early inhabitants were Cherokees. European settlement was attempted in 1585–87, following an exploratory visit by Sir Walter Raleigh, but this failed. Settlers from Virginia came to the shores of Albemarle Sound after 1650, and in 1663 Charles II chartered a private colony of Carolina. In 1691 the north was put under a deputy governor who ruled from Charleston in the south. The colony was formally separated into North and South Carolina in 1712. In 1729 control was taken from the private proprietors and vested in the Crown, whereupon settlement grew, and the boundary between north and south was finally fixed (1735).

After the War of Independence, North Carolina became one of the original 13 states of the Union. The city of Raleigh was laid out as the new capital. Having been a plantation colony North Carolina continued to develop as a plantation state, growing tobacco with black slave labour. It was also an important source of gold before the western gold-rushes of 1848.

In 1861 at the outset of the Civil War, North Carolina seceded from the Union, but General Sherman occupied the capital unopposed. A military governor was admitted in 1862, and civilian government restored with re-admission to the Union in 1868.

TERRITORY AND POPULATION

North Carolina is bounded north by Virginia, east by the Atlantic, south by South Carolina, southwest by Georgia and west by Tennessee. Land area, 48,711 sq. miles (126,161 sq. km). Census population, 1 April 2000, 8,049,313, an increase of 21·4% since 1990. July 2004 estimate, 8,541,221.

Population in five census years was:

	White	Black	Indian	Asiatic	Total	Per sq. mile
1910	1,500,511	697,843	7,851	82	2,206,287	45·3
1930	2,234,958	918,647	16,579	92	3,170,276	64·5
			All others			
1980	4,453,010	1,316,050	105,369		5,874,429	111·5
1990	5,008,491	1,456,323	163,823		6,628,637	136·1
2000	5,804,656	1,737,545	507,112		8,049,313	165·2

Of the total population in 2000, 4,106,618 were female, 6,085,266 were 18 years old or older and 4,849,482 were urban. In 2000 North Carolina's Hispanic population was 378,963, up from 76,726 in 1990. This represented a rise of 393·9%, the largest increase of any state in the USA over the same period.

The principal cities (with census population in 2000) are: Charlotte, 540,828; Raleigh, 276,093; Greensboro, 223,891; Durham, 187,035; Winston-Salem, 185,776; Fayetteville, 121,015; Cary, 94,536; High Point, 85,839; Wilmington, 75,838.

SOCIAL STATISTICS

Births, 2002, were 117,335 (14·1 per 1,000 population); deaths, 72,027 (8·7); 2001: infant mortality rate, 8·5 (per 1,000 live births). 2001: marriages, 61,100; divorces, 34,900.

CLIMATE

Climate varies sharply with altitude; the warmest area is in the southeast near Southport and Wilmington; the coldest is Mount Mitchell (6,684 ft). Raleigh, Jan. 42°F (5·6°C), July 79°F (26·1°C). Annual rainfall 46" (1,158 mm). North Carolina belongs to the Atlantic Coast climate zone (*see* UNITED STATES: Climate).

CONSTITUTION AND GOVERNMENT

The present constitution dates from 1971 (previous constitution, 1776 and 1868/76); it has had 30 amendments. The General Assembly consists of a Senate of 50 members and a House of Representatives of 120 members; all are elected by districts for two years. It meets in odd-numbered years in Jan.

The Governor and Lieut.-Governor are elected for four years. The Governor may succeed himself but has no veto. There are 18 other executive heads of department, nine elected by the people and nine appointed by the Governor.

For the 109th Congress, which convened in Jan. 2005, North Carolina sends 13 members to the House of Representatives. It is represented in the Senate by Elizabeth Dole (R. 2003–09) and Richard Burr (R. 2005–11).

The capital is Raleigh. There are 100 counties.

RECENT ELECTIONS

In the 2004 presidential election Bush polled 1,961,166 votes; Kerry, 1,525,849; Nader, 1,805.

CURRENT ADMINISTRATION

Governor: Michael F. Easley (D.), 2005–09 (salary: $121,391).
Lieut.-Governor: Beverly Perdue (D.), 2005–09 ($107,136).
Secretary of State: Elaine F. Marshall (D.), 2005–09 ($107,136).

Government Website: http://www.ncgov.com

ECONOMY

Per capita income (2002) was $27,566.

Budget. In 2002 total state revenue was $31,524m. Total expenditure was $33,124m. (education, $11,956m.; public welfare, $6,846m.; highways, $2,629m.; hospitals, $1,289m.; health, $930m.) Outstanding debt, in 2002, $11,128m.

Performance. Gross State Product in 2002 was $300,216m., ranking North Carolina 11th in the United States.

ENERGY AND NATURAL RESOURCES

Water. The total area covered by water is approximately 3,954 sq. miles.

Minerals. Principal minerals are stone, sand and gravel, phosphate rock, feldspar, lithium minerals, olivine, kaolin and talc. North Carolina is a leading producer of bricks, making more than 1bn. bricks a year. Value of domestic non-fuel mineral production in 2002 was $708m.

Agriculture. In 2002 there were 56,000 farms covering 9·1m. acres; average size of farms was 163 acres and average value per acre in 2002 was $3,088.

Farm income, 2001, from crops, $3,087m. and from livestock and products $4,644m. The net farm income in 2001 was $3,201m. Main crop production: flue-cured tobacco, maize, soybeans, peanuts, wheat, sweet potatoes, apples and greenhouse products.

Livestock, 2002: cattle, 848,000; pigs, 9·9m.; chickens, 17·04m.

Forestry. Forests covered 19·3m. acres in 2002, with 1·2m. acres of national forest. Main products are hardwood veneer and hardwood plywood, furniture woods, pulp, paper and lumber.

Fisheries. Commercial fish catch, 2002, had a value of approximately $98·7m. and produced 159·6m. lb. The catch is mainly of blue crab, menhaden, Atlantic croaker, flounder, shark, sea trout, mullet, blue fish and shrimp.

INDUSTRY

The leading industries by employment are textiles, clothing, furniture, electrical machinery and equipment, non-electrical machinery and food processing. In 2001 the state's 10,844 manufacturing establishments had 691,000 employees, earning $21,583m. Total value added by manufacturing in 2001 was $91,184m.

Labour. Total non-agricultural employment, 2001, 3,901,000. Employees by branch, 2001 (in 1,000): services, 1,048; wholesale and retail trade, 890; manufacturing, 734; government, 624. The unemployment rate in 2002 was 6·7%.

COMMUNICATIONS

Roads. In 2002 there were 101,743 miles of roads (77,629 miles rural) and 6,149,474 registered motor vehicles.

Rail. The state in 1999 contained 3,682 miles of railway operating in 91 of the 100 counties. There are 22 Class II and 23 Class III rail companies.

Civil Aviation. In 1999 there were 82 public airports of which 15 are served by major airlines. There were 17,017,001 passenger enplanements statewide in 2000.

Shipping. There are two ocean ports, Wilmington and Morehead City.

SOCIAL INSTITUTIONS

Justice. The death penalty is authorized; there were four executions in 2004. In June 2002 there were 32,755 federal and state prisoners.

Religion. Leading denominations are the Baptists (48·9% of church membership), Methodists (20·7%), Presbyterians (7·7%), Lutherans (3·0%) and Roman Catholics (2·7%). Total estimate of all denominations in 1983 was 2·6m.

Education. School attendance is compulsory between six and 16. In autumn 2002 there were 1,332,140 pupils and 85,557 teachers at public and charter schools; there were 92,890 pupils at 661 independent and religious schools. State and local government expenditure in 1996 was $7,094m.; an average of $5,623 per pupil.

The 16 senior universities are all part of the University of North Carolina system (176,967 students enrolled in autumn 2002). The largest institution is the North Carolina State University (founded 1887), at Raleigh, with 29,637 students in autumn 2002. The University of North Carolina at Chapel Hill (founded in 1789; the first state university to open in America in 1795) had 26,028 students in 2002; East Carolina University (founded in 1907), at Greenville, had 20,577. There were 78,028 students at 37 independent universities and colleges in autumn 2002.

Health. In 2001 there were 111 community hospitals with 23,800 beds. A total of 973,000 patients were admitted during the year.

Welfare. Medicare enrolment in July 2002 totalled 1,178,169. In 2000 a total of 1,208,789 people in North Carolina received Medicaid. In Dec. 2003 there were 1,436,124 Old-Age, Survivors, and Disability Insurance (OASDI) beneficiaries. A total of 86,504 people were receiving payments under Temporary Assistance for Needy Families (TANF) in Sept. 2002.

CULTURE

Tourism. In 2000, 43m. tourists spent $12bn., a 58% increase over 1999.

FURTHER READING

Statistical information: Office of State Planning, 116 West Jones St., Raleigh 27603. Publishes *Statistical Abstract of North Carolina Counties.*
North Carolina Manual. Secretary of State. Raleigh. Biennial
Fleer, J. D., *North Carolina: Government and Population.* Univ. of Nebraska Press, 1995

NORTH DAKOTA

KEY HISTORICAL EVENTS

The original inhabitants were various groups of Plains Indians. French explorers and traders were active among them in the 18th century, often operating from French possessions in Canada. France claimed the area until 1803, when it passed to the USA as part of the Louisiana Purchase, except for the northeastern part which was held by the British until 1818.

Trading with the Indians, mainly for furs, continued until the 1860s, with American traders succeeding the French. In 1861 the Dakota Territory (North and South) was established. In 1862 the Homestead Act was passed (allowing 160 acres of public land free to any family who had worked and lived on it for five years) and this greatly stimulated settlement. Farming settlers came on to the wheat lands in great numbers, many of them from Canada, Norway and Germany.

Bismarck, the capital, began as a crossing-point on the Missouri and was fortified in 1872 to protect workers building the Northern Pacific Railway. There followed a gold-rush nearby, and the town became a service centre for prospectors. In 1889 North and South Dakota were admitted to the Union as separate states, and Bismarck became the Northern capital. The largest city is Fargo which was also a railway town, named after William George Fargo the express-company founder.

The population grew rapidly until 1890 and steadily until 1930 by which time it was about one-third European in parentage. Between 1930 and 1970 there was a steady population drain, increasing whenever farming was affected by the extremes of the continental climate.

TERRITORY AND POPULATION

North Dakota is bounded north by Canada, east by the Red River (forming a boundary with Minnesota), south by South Dakota and west by Montana. Land area, 68,976 sq. miles (178,647 sq. km). The Federal Bureau of Indian Affairs administered (1992) 841,295 acres, of which 214,006 acres were assigned to tribes. Census population, 1 April 2000, 642,200, an increase of 0·5% since 1990. July 2004 estimate, 634,366.

Population at five census years was:

	White	*Black*	*Indian*	*Asiatic*	*Total*	*Per sq. mile*
1910	569,855	617	6,486	98	577,056	8·2
1930	671,851	377	8,617	194	680,845	9·7
			All others			
1980	625,557	2,568	24,692		652,717	9·5
1990	604,142	3,524	31,134		638,800	9·3
2000	593,182	3,916	45,102		642,200	9·3

Of the total population in 2000, 321,676 were female, 481,351 were 18 years old or older and 358,958 were urban. Estimated outward migration, 1980–90, 110 per 1,000 population. Only Vermont has fewer persons of Hispanic origin than North Dakota. In 2000 the Hispanic population was 7,786, up from 4,665 in 1990 (an increase of 66·9%).

The largest cities are Fargo with population, census 2000, of 90,599; Bismarck (capital), 55,532; Grand Forks, 49,321; and Minot, 36,567.

SOCIAL STATISTICS

Births in 2002 were 7,757 (12·2 per 1,000 population); deaths, 5,892 (9·3); 2001: infant mortality rate, 8·8 (per 1,000 live births). 2001: marriages, 4,100; divorces, 1,700.

CLIMATE

Bismarck, Jan. 8°F (–13·3°C), July 71°F (21·1°C). Annual rainfall 16" (402 mm). Fargo, Jan. 6°F (–14·4°C), July 71°F (21·1°C). Annual rainfall 20" (503 mm). North Dakota belongs to the High Plains climate zone (*see* UNITED STATES: Climate).

CONSTITUTION AND GOVERNMENT

The present constitution dates from 1889; it has had 95 amendments. The Legislative Assembly consists of a Senate of 53 members elected for four years, and a House of Representatives of 106 members elected for four years. The Governor and Lieut.-Governor are elected for four years.

For the 109th Congress, which convened in Jan. 2005, North Dakota sends one member to the House of Representatives. It is represented in the Senate by Kent Conrad (D. 1987–2007) and Byron Dorgan (D. 1992–2011).

The capital is Bismarck. The state has 53 organized counties.

RECENT ELECTIONS

In the 2004 presidential election Bush polled 196,651 votes; Kerry, 111,052; Nader, 3,756.

CURRENT ADMINISTRATION

Governor: John Hoeven (R.), Dec. 2004–Dec. 2008 (salary: $87,216).

Lieut.-Governor: Jack Dalrymple (R.), Dec. 2004–Dec. 2008 ($67,708).

Secretary of State: Alvin A. Jaeger (R), 2004–06 ($68,018).

Government Website: http://discovernd.com

ECONOMY

Though the state is still mainly agricultural it is diversifying into high tech and information technology industries. *Per capita* income (2002) was $26,567.

Budget. In 2002 total state revenue was $3,017m. Total expenditure was $3,020m. (education, $943m.; public welfare, $627m.; highways, $377m.; natural resources, $111m.; government administration, $104m.) Outstanding debt, in 2002, $1,673m.

Performance. Gross State Product in 2002 was $19,780m., ranking North Dakota 50th in the United States.

ENERGY AND NATURAL RESOURCES

Oil and Gas. The mineral resources of North Dakota consist chiefly of oil, which was discovered in 1951. Production of crude petroleum in 1996 was 32m. bbls. (value, $629m.); of natural gas, 50bn. cu. ft.

Water. The total area covered by water is approximately 1,710 sq. miles.

Minerals. Output of lignite coal in 1994 was 32m. tons. Total value of domestic non-fuel mineral production, 2002, $39m.

Agriculture. In 2002 there were 30,000 farms (61,963 in 1954) in an area of 39·4m. acres and with an average farm acreage of 1,313. In 2002 the average value of farmland and buildings per acre was $404.

Farm income, 2001, from crops, $2,259m. and from livestock, $720m. The net farm income in 2001 was $587m. Production, 2002: barley, 56·8m. bu.; wheat (durum), 48·9m. bu.; honey, 24m. lb; oats, 12·5m. bu.; flaxseed, 12·2m. bu.; dry edible beans, 10·1m. cwt; sunflower (all), 1,710m. lb. Other important products are all beans, all wheat, and rye.

The state has also an active livestock industry, chiefly cattle raising. Livestock, 2002: cattle, 1·87m.; pigs, 138,800; sheep, 114,000; poultry, 200,400.

Forestry. Forest area, 2002, was 672,000 acres, of which 181,000 acres were national forest.

INDUSTRY

In 2001 the state's 681 manufacturing establishments had 24,000 employees, earning $762m. Total value added by manufacturing in 2001 was $2,669m.

Labour. In 2001 total non-agricultural employment was 330,000. Employees by branch, 2001: services, 94,000; wholesale and retail trade, 82,000; government, 74,000. The unemployment rate in 2002 was 4·0%.

COMMUNICATIONS

Roads. In 2002 there were 86,588 miles of roads (84,753 rural) and 698,424 registered motor vehicles.

Rail. In 2002 there were 3,707 miles of railway.

Civil Aviation. In 1994 there were 100 public airports and 350 private airports. There were 513,669 passenger enplanements statewide in 2000.

Telecommunications. In 1998 there were 32,000 miles of fibre optic cable in the ground.

SOCIAL INSTITUTIONS

Justice. In June 2002 there were 1,168 federal and state prisoners. The Missouri River Correctional Center is a minimum custody institution. There is no death penalty.

Religion. Church membership totalled 484,628 in 1990. The leading religious denominations were: Combined Lutherans, 179,711 members; Roman Catholics, 173,432; Methodists, 23,850; Presbyterians, 11,960.

Education. School attendance is compulsory between the ages of seven and 16, or until the 17th birthday if the eighth grade has not been completed. In 1995–96 the public elementary schools had 81,798 pupils; secondary schools, 36,755 pupils. State expenditure per pupil in elementary and secondary schools, 1997, $5,016. Teachers (4,208 in elementary and 2,208 in secondary schools in 1994) earned an average $25,506 in 1993–94 school year.

The University of North Dakota in Grand Forks, founded in 1883, had 10,392 students in autumn 1998; North Dakota State University in Fargo, 9,688 students (1996). Total enrolment in the 11 public institutions of higher education, autumn 1995, 35,199; in the two private, 2,911.

Health. In 2001 there were 40 community hospitals with 3,700 beds. A total of 92,000 patients were admitted during the year.

Welfare. Medicare enrolment in July 2002 totalled 103,208. In 2000 a total of 60,864 people in North Dakota received Medicaid. In Dec. 2003 there were 114,047 Old-Age, Survivors, and Disability Insurance (OASDI) beneficiaries. A total of 8,505 people were receiving payments under Temporary Assistance for Needy Families (TANF) in Sept. 2002.

CULTURE

Press. There were, in 1997, ten daily and seven Sunday newspapers in circulation.

FURTHER READING

Statistical information: Bureau of Business and Economic Research, Univ. of North Dakota, Grand Forks 58202. Publishes *Statistical Abstract of North Dakota.*
North Dakota Blue Book. Secretary of State. Bismarck
Jelliff, T. B., *North Dakota: A Living Legacy.* Fargo, 1983

OHIO

KEY HISTORICAL EVENTS

The land was inhabited by Delaware, Miami, Shawnee and Wyandot Indians. It was explored by French and British traders in the 18th century and confirmed as part of British North America in 1763. After the War of Independence it became part of the Northwest Territory of the new United States. Former American soldiers of the war came in from New England in 1788 and made the first permanent white settlement at Marietta, at the confluence of the Ohio and Muskingum rivers. In 1803 Ohio was separated from the rest of the Territory and admitted to the Union as the 17th state.

During the early 19th century there was steady immigration from Europe, mainly of Germans, Swiss, Irish and Welsh. Industrial growth began from the processing of local farm, forest and mining products; it increased rapidly with the need to supply the Union armies in the Civil War of 1861–65.

As the industrial cities grew, so immigration began again, with many whites from eastern Europe and the Balkans and blacks from the southern states looking for work in Ohio.

Cleveland, which developed rapidly as a Lake Erie port after the opening of commercial waterways to the interior and the Atlantic coast (1825, 1830 and 1855), became an iron-and-steel town during the Civil War.

TERRITORY AND POPULATION

Ohio is bounded north by Michigan and Lake Erie, east by Pennsylvania, southeast and south by the Ohio River (forming a boundary with West Virginia and Kentucky) and west by Indiana. Land area, 40,948 sq. miles (106,055 sq. km). Census population, 1 April 2000, 11,353,140, an increase of 4·7% since 1990. July 2004 estimate, 11,459,011.

Population at five census years was:

	White	*Black*	*Indian*	*Asiatic*	*Total*	*Per sq. mile*
1910	4,654,897	111,452	127	645	4,767,121	117·0
1930	6,335,173	309,304	435	1,785	6,646,697	161·6
			All others			
1980	9,597,458	1,076,748	123,424		10,797,630	263·2
1990	9,521,756	1,154,826	170,533		10,847,115	264·5
2000	9,645,453	1,301,307	406,380		11,353,140	277·3

Of the total population in 2000, 5,840,878 were female, 8,464,801 were 18 years old or older and 8,782,329 were urban. In 2000 the Hispanic population was 217,123, up from 139,696 in 1990 (an increase of 55·4%).

Census population of chief cities on 1 April 2000 was:

Columbus	711,470	Lorain	68,652	Cleveland Heights	49,458
Cleveland	478,403	Springfield	65,358	Cuyahoga Falls	49,374
Cincinnati	331,285	Hamilton	60,690	Mansfield	49,346
Toledo	313,619	Kettering	57,502	Warren	46,832
Akron	217,074	Lakewood	56,646	Newark	46,279
Dayton	166,179	Elyria	55,953	Strongsville	43,858
Parma	85,655	Euclid	52,717	Fairfield	42,097
Youngstown	82,026	Middletown	51,605	Lima	40,081
Canton	80,806	Mentor	50,278		

Metropolitan areas, 2000 census: Cleveland–Akron, 2,945,831; Cincinnati–Hamilton, 1,979,202; Columbus (the capital), 1,540,157; Dayton–Springfield, 950,558; Toledo, 618,203; Youngstown–Warren, 594,746; Canton–Massillon, 404,934.

SOCIAL STATISTICS

Statistics 2002 (per 1,000 population): births, 148,720 (13·0); deaths, 109,766 (9·6); infant deaths, 2001, 7·7 per 1,000 live births; marriages, 2002, 80,373 (7·7 per 1,000 population in 2000); divorces, 45,955 (4·2 in 2000).

CLIMATE

Average temperatures and rainfall in 2003: Cincinnati, Jan. 25·6°F, July 75·0°F, annual rainfall 46·50"; Cleveland, Jan. 21·2°F, July 72·5°F, annual rainfall 42·50"; Columbus, Jan. 21·0°F, July 71·8°F, annual rainfall 37·11" (2001). Ohio belongs to the Great Lakes climate zone (*see* UNITED STATES: Climate).

CONSTITUTION AND GOVERNMENT

The question of a general revision of the constitution drafted by an elected convention is submitted to the people every 20 years. The constitution of 1851 had 142 amendments by 1994.

The Senate consists of 33 members and the House of Representatives of 99 members. The Senate is elected for four years, half every two years; the House is elected for two years; the Governor, Lieut.-Governor and Secretary of State for four years. Qualified as electors are (with necessary exceptions) all citizens 18 years of age who have the usual residential qualifications.

For the 109th Congress, which convened in Jan. 2005, Ohio sends 18 members to the House of Representatives. It is represented in the Senate by Mike DeWine (R. 1995–2007) and George Voinovich (R. 1999–2011).

The capital (since 1816) is Columbus. Ohio is divided into 88 counties.

RECENT ELECTIONS

In the 2004 presidential election Bush polled 2,859,764 votes; Kerry, 2,741,165; Badnarik, 14,676.

CURRENT ADMINISTRATION

Governor: Bob Taft (R.), 2003–07 (salary: $122,812).

Lieut.-Governor: Bruce Johnson (R.), 2005–07 ($64,375).

Secretary of State: J. Kenneth Blackwell (R.), 2003–07 ($90,725).

Government Website: http://ohio.gov

ECONOMY

Per capita income (2002) was $29,317.

Budget. In 2002–03 general state revenue was $21,749m. General expenditure was $22,429m. (public assistance and medicaid, $8,963m.; education, $6,646m.; justice and public protection, $1,778m.; health and human services, $1,075m.) Debt outstanding was $8,595m. in 2003.

Performance. In 2002 Gross State Product was $388,224m., ranking Ohio 7th in the United States.

ENERGY AND NATURAL RESOURCES

Oil and Gas. In 2003, 5·65m. bbls. of crude oil and 93,640m. cu. ft of gas were produced. In 2003 the value of oil and gas production was $708m.

Water. Lake Erie supplies northern Ohio with its water. The total area covered by water is approximately 3,877 sq. miles, of which Lake Erie covers 3,499 sq. miles.

Minerals. Ohio has extensive mineral resources, of which coal is the most important by value: estimated production (2002) 20,986,495 short tons. Coal production in 2002 was valued at $440,195,284. Production of other minerals (in short tons), 2001: limestone and dolomite, 80,998,236; sand and gravel, 56,829,272; salt, 4,261,545. Total value of non-fuel mineral production in 2002 was $787,872,579.

Agriculture. Ohio is extensively devoted to agriculture. In 2003, 77,600 farms covered 14·6m. acres; average farm value per acre, $2,800. The average size of a farm in 2003 was 188 acres.

Cash income 2001 from total agricultural sector, $4,682m. The net farm income in 2002 was $268m. Estimated crop production 2002–03: corn for grain (478·9m. bu.), soybeans (162·6m. bu.), wheat (68·0m. bu.), oats (3·96m. bu.). In 2003 there were 1·44m. pigs, 1·22m. cattle and 150,000 sheep.

Forestry. Forest area, 2002, 7,855,000 acres. In 2003 there were 74 state parks covering 309,000 acres.

INDUSTRY

In 2002, 17,189 manufacturing establishments employed 829,456 persons, earning $34,319m. The largest industries were manufacturing of transport equipment, fabricated metal products and machinery.

Labour. In 2003, 5,552,000 people were in employment out of a labour force of 5,915,000. Employees by branch, 2001 (in 1,000): services, 1,602; wholesale and retail trade, 1,331; manufacturing, 1,027; government, 794. In 2003 the unemployment rate was 6·1%.

INTERNATIONAL TRADE

Imports and Exports. Ohio exports had a total value of US$29·8bn. in 2003, making it the sixth largest exporting state in the USA.

COMMUNICATIONS

Roads. In 2003 there were 241,973 miles of roads and 12·08m. registered motor vehicles.

Rail. Ohio has about 5,800 miles of railroad track. Cleveland has a 19-mile metro system.

Civil Aviation. In 2003 there were more than 800 airports of varying sizes in the state. There are 165 public use airports and 23 public use heliports. There were 20,799,903 passenger enplanements in 2000.

Shipping. Ohio has more than 700 miles of navigable waterways, with Lake Erie having a 265-mile shoreline. There are nine deep-draft ports in the state. The busiest port is Cleveland, which handles 18m. tons of cargo annually.

SOCIAL INSTITUTIONS

Justice. In 2003 there were 44,000 inmates (92·99% males) in the 32 adult correctional institutions. The death penalty is authorized; there were seven executions in 2004 (three in 2003). There were 204 death-row inmates (203 male) in 2004: 95 were white; 103 black; three Hispanic; and three other.

Religion. Many religious faiths are represented, including (but not limited to) the Baptist, Jewish, Lutheran, Methodist, Muslim, Orthodox, Presbyterian and Roman Catholic.

Education. School attendance during full term is compulsory for children from six to 18 years of age. In 2003–04 public schools had 1,905,570 enrolled pupils. Teachers' salaries (2003–04) averaged $47,652. Estimated expenditure on elementary and secondary schools for 2004 was $7,975m., 39·3% of the total state budget. Total estimated revenue for the co-ordination of higher education in Ohio (controlled by the Board of Regents) was $2·57bn. in fiscal year 2001.

Public colleges and universities had a total enrolment (2002–03) of 461,492 students. Independent colleges and universities enrolled 124,462 students. Estimated annual operating budget for higher education institutions in 1998 was $4·4m. Average annual charge (for undergraduates in 2002–03): $5,755 (state); $18,020 (private).

Main campuses, 1997:

Founded	*Institutions*	*Enrolments*
1804	Ohio University, Athens (State)	19,159
1809	Miami University, Oxford (State)	15,999
1819	University of Cincinnati (State)	27,800
1826	Case Western Reserve University, Cleveland	9,569[1]
1850	University of Dayton (R.C.)	1,709[1]
1870	University of Akron (State)	21,878
1870	Ohio State University, Columbus (State)	48,004
1872	University of Toledo (State)	19,855
1908	Youngstown University (State)	12,050
1910	Bowling Green State University (State)	16,579
1910	Kent State University (State)	20,277
1964	Cleveland State University (State)	15,447
1964	Wright State University (State)	14,292
1986	Shawnee State University, Portsmouth (State)	3,163

[1]Figures for Case Western Reserve University and University of Dayton are for 1994 enrolments.

Health. In 2001 the state had 163 registered community hospitals with 32,981 beds. State facilities for the severely mentally retarded had 12 developmental centres serving 2,000 residents.

Welfare. Public assistance is administered through the Ohio Works First programme (OWF). In 2004 OWF-Combined assistance groups had 193,942 recipients and money payments totalled $316,347,050. OWF-Regular assistance groups had

177,527 recipients with $297,095,852 paid out in 2004. OWF-Unemployed had 16,415 recipients and money payments were $19,251,198 in 2004. Disability Assistance had 13,468 recipients in 2004; and food stamps, 925,584 recipients.

In 2004 Disability Assistance totalled $20,407,767; food stamps in 2004 totalled $981,831,872; and foster care totalled $162,081,492. Optional State Supplement is paid to aged, blind or disabled adults. Free social services are available to those eligible by income or circumstances.

FURTHER READING

Official Roster: Federal, State, County Officers and Department Information. Secretary of State, Columbus. Biennial

Shkurti, W. J. and Bartle, J. (eds.) *Benchmark Ohio.* Ohio State Univ. Press, 1991

OKLAHOMA

KEY HISTORICAL EVENTS

Francisco Coronado led a Spanish expedition in 1541, claiming the land for Spain. There were several Indian groups, but no strong political unit. In 1714 Juchereau de Saint Denis made the first French contact. During the 18th century French fur-traders were active, and France and Spain struggled for control, a struggle which was resolved by the French withdrawal in 1763. France returned briefly in 1800–03, and the territory then passed to the USA as part of the Louisiana Purchase.

In 1828 the Federal government set aside the area of the present state as Indian Territory, that is, a reservation and sanctuary for Indian tribes who had been driven off their lands elsewhere by white settlement. About 70 tribes came, among whom were Creeks, Choctaws and Cherokees from the southeastern states, and Plains Indians.

In 1889 the government took back about 2·5m. acres of the Territory and opened it to white settlement. About 10,000 homesteaders gathered at the site of Oklahoma City on the Santa Fe Railway in the rush to stake their land claims. The settlers' area, and others subsequently opened to settlement, were organized as the Oklahoma Territory in 1890. In 1907 the Oklahoma and Indian Territories were combined and admitted to the Union as a state. Indian reservations were established within the state.

The economy first depended on ranching and farming, with packing stations on the railways. A mining industry grew in the 1870s attracting foreign immigration, mainly from Europe. In 1901 oil was found near Tulsa, and the industry grew rapidly.

TERRITORY AND POPULATION

Oklahoma is bounded north by Kansas, northeast by Missouri, east by Arkansas, south by Texas (the Red River forming part of the boundary) and, at the western extremity of the 'panhandle', by New Mexico and Colorado. Land area, 68,667 sq. miles (177,847 sq. km). Census population, 1 April 2000, 3,450,654, an increase of 9·7% since 1990. July 2004 estimate, 3,523,553.

The population at five federal censuses was:

	White	*Black*	*American Indian*	*Other*	*Total*	*Per sq. mile*
1930	2,130,778	172,198	92,725	339	2,396,040	34·6
1960	2,107,900	153,084	68,689	1,414	2,328,284	33·8
1980	2,597,783	204,658	169,292	53,557	3,025,486	43·2
1990	2,583,512	233,801	252,420	119,723	3,189,456	44·5
2000	2,628,434	260,968	273,230	288,022	3,450,654	50·3

Of the total population in 2000, 1,754,759 were female, 2,558,294 were 18 years old or older and 2,254,563 were urban. The US Bureau of Indian Affairs is responsible for 1,097,004 acres (1990), of which 96,839 acres were allotted to tribes. In 2000 Oklahoma's Hispanic population was 179,304, up from 86,160 in 1990 (an increase of 108·1%).

The most important cities with population, 2000, are Oklahoma City (capital), 506,132; Tulsa, 393,049; Norman, 95,694; Lawton, 92,757; Broken Arrow, 74,859; Edmond, 68,315; Midwest City, 54,088; Enid, 47,045; Moore, 41,138; Stillwater, 39,065; Muskogee, 38,310; Bartlesville, 34,748.

SOCIAL STATISTICS

Births, 2002, 50,387 (14·4 per 1,000 population); deaths, 35,502 (10·2); 2001: infant mortality rate, 7·3 (per 1,000 live births). 2001: marriages, 16,600; divorces, 11,500.

CLIMATE

Oklahoma City, Jan. 34°F (1°C), July 81°F (27°C). Annual rainfall 31·9" (8,113 mm). Tulsa, Jan. 34°F (1°C), July 82°F (28°C). Annual rainfall 33·2" (8,438 mm). Oklahoma belongs to the Central Plains climate zone (*see* UNITED STATES: Climate).

CONSTITUTION AND GOVERNMENT

The constitution, dating from 1907, provides for amendment by initiative petition and legislative referendum; it has had 155 amendments (as of Jan. 1995).

The Legislature consists of a Senate of 48 members, who are elected for four years, and a House of Representatives elected for two years and consisting of 101 members. The Governor and Lieut.-Governor are elected for four-year terms; the Governor can only be elected for two terms in succession. Electors are (with necessary exceptions) all citizens 18 years or older, with the usual qualifications.

For the 109th Congress, which convened in Jan. 2005, Oklahoma sends five members to the House of Representatives. It is represented in the Senate by James Inhofe (R. 1994–2009) and Tom Coburn (R. 2005–11).

The capital is Oklahoma City. The state has 77 counties.

RECENT ELECTIONS

In the 2004 presidential election Bush polled 959,792 votes; Kerry, 503,966.

CURRENT ADMINISTRATION

Governor: Brad Henry (D.), 2003–07 (salary: $110,299).
Lieut.-Governor: Mary Fallin (R.), 2003–07 ($75,530).
Secretary of State: M. Susan Savage (D.), appointed Jan. 2003 ($90,000).

Government Website: http://www.ok.gov

ECONOMY

Per capita income (2002) was $25,136.

Budget. In 2002 total state revenue was $13,134m. Total expenditure was $14,727m. (education, $5,269m.; public welfare, $3,202m.; highways, $1,263m.; correction, $521m.; government administration, $481m.) Outstanding debt, in 2002, $6,477m.

Performance. Gross State Product in 2002 was $95,126m., ranking Oklahoma 30th in the United States.

ENERGY AND NATURAL RESOURCES

Oil and Gas. Production, 1998: crude oil, 78m. bbls.; natural gas, 1,645bn. cu. ft. Oklahoma ranks third in the USA for natural gas production behind Texas and Louisiana. In 2001 there were 201,453 oil and gas wells in production.

Water. The total area covered by water is approximately 1,224 sq. miles.

Minerals. Coal production (2001), 1,714,000 tons. Principal minerals are: crushed stone, cement, sand and gravel, iodine, glass sand, gypsum. Other minerals are helium, clay and sand, zinc, lead, granite, tripoli, bentonite, lime and volcanic ash. Total value of domestic non-fuel minerals produced in 2002 was $462m.

Agriculture. In 2002 the state had 87,000 farms and ranches with a total area of 34m. acres; average size was 391 acres and average value per acre was $699. Area harvested, 2002, 7,705,860 acres. Livestock, 2002: cattle, 5·2m.; sheep and lambs, 80,100; hogs and pigs, 2·25m.

Farm income 2001: crops, $874m.; livestock and products, $3,153m. The net farm income in 2001 was $922m. The major cash grain is winter wheat (value, 2002, $340m.): 102m. bu. of wheat for grain were harvested in 2002. Other crops include barley, oats, rye, grain, corn, soybeans, grain sorghum, cotton, peanuts and peaches. Value of cattle and calves produced, 2002, $2,448m.; racehorses, $63m. (1990).

The Oklahoma Conservation Commission works with 91 conservation districts, universities, state and federal government agencies. The early work of the conservation districts, beginning in 1937, was limited to flood and erosion control: since 1970, they include urban areas also.

Irrigated production has increased in the Oklahoma 'panhandle'. The Ogalala aquifer is the primary source of irrigation water there and in western Oklahoma, a finite source because of its isolation from major sources of recharge. Declining groundwater levels necessitate the most effective irrigation practices.

Forestry. There were 7,665,000 acres of forested land in 2002, with 245,000 acres of national forest. The forest products industry is concentrated in the 118 eastern counties. There are three forest regions: Ozark (oak, hickory); Ouachita highlands (pine, oak); Cross-Timbers (post oak, black jack oak). Southern pine is the chief commercial species, at almost 80% of saw-timber harvested annually. Replanting is essential.

INDUSTRY

In 2001 Oklahoma's 4,025 manufacturing establishments had 163,000 employees, earning $5,509m. Total value added by manufacturing in 2001 was $18,059m.

Labour. Total non-agricultural employment in 2001 was 1,509,000. Employees by branch, 2001 (in 1,000): services, 437; wholesale and retail trade, 343; government, 296; manufacturing, 179. Oklahoma's unemployment rate was 4·5% in 2002.

COMMUNICATIONS

Roads. In 2002 there were 112,531 miles of roads comprising 13,409 miles of urban road and 99,122 miles of rural road. There were 3,070,954 registered motor vehicles.

Rail. In 2000 Oklahoma had 3,591 miles of railway operated by 15 companies.

Civil Aviation. Airports in 1995 numbered 421, of which 127 were publicly owned. Five cities were served by commercial airlines. There were 3,466,415 passenger enplanements statewide in 2000.

Shipping. The McClellan-Kerr Arkansas Navigation System provides access from east central Oklahoma to New Orleans through the Verdigris, Arkansas and Mississippi rivers. In 1991, 63m. tons were shipped inbound and outbound on the Oklahoma Segment. Commodities shipped are mainly chemical fertilizer, farm produce, petroleum products, iron and steel, coal, sand and gravel.

SOCIAL INSTITUTIONS

Justice. There were 23,435 federal and state prisoners in June 2002. In 1990 there were 15 penal institutions, eight community treatment centres and seven probation and parole centres. The death penalty was suspended in 1966 and re-imposed in 1976. There were 14 executions in 2003 and six in 2004. Oklahoma's total of 75 executions between 1997 and 2004 is the third highest in the USA behind Texas and Virginia.

Religion. The chief religious bodies are Baptists, followed by United Methodists, Roman Catholics, Churches of Christ, Assembly of God, Disciples of Christ, Presbyterian, Lutheran, Nazarene and Episcopal.

Education. In 1994–95 there were 609,800 pupils and 39,290 teachers at public elementary and secondary school. The average teacher salary per annum was $28,928. In 1997 total expenditure on the 3,257 schools was $3,033m. There were 177,000 students enrolled at the 45 higher education establishments in 1996.

Institutions of higher education include:

Founded	*Name*	*Place*	*1994 Enrolment*
1890	University of Oklahoma	Norman	21,373
1890	Oklahoma State University	Stillwater	18,290
1890	University of Central Oklahoma	Edmond	16,039
1894	The University of Tulsa	Tulsa	4,579
1897	Northeastern State University	Tahlequah	9,374
1897	Northwestern Oklahoma State University	Alva	1,870
1897	Southwestern Oklahoma State University	Weatherford	5,289

Founded	Name	Place	1994 Enrolment
1908	Cameron University	Lawton	5,863
1909	East Central University	Ada	4,468
1909	Southeastern Oklahoma State University	Durant	4,104
1909	Rogers State College	Claremore	3,404
1950	Oklahoma Christian University of Science and Arts	Oklahoma City	1,505
1969	Rose State College	Midwest City	9,234
1970	Tulsa Junior College	Tulsa	21,055
1972	Oklahoma City Community College	Oklahoma City	11,185

Health. In 2001 there were 108 community hospitals with 11,200 beds. A total of 435,000 patients were admitted during the year.

Welfare. Medicare enrolment in July 2002 totalled 514,542. In 2000 a total of 507,059 people in Oklahoma received Medicaid. In Dec. 2003 there were 613,515 Old-Age, Survivors, and Disability Insurance (OASDI) beneficiaries. A total of 38,327 people were receiving payments under Temporary Assistance for Needy Families (TANF) in Sept. 2002.

CULTURE

Broadcasting. In 1995 there were 172 radio and 25 television broadcasting stations, and 16 cable-TV companies.

Press. There were 49 daily newspapers in 1995 and 190 weeklies in 1990.

Tourism. There are 72 state parks and ten museums and monuments. Tourists spend some $3,000m. annually.

FURTHER READING

Center for Economic and Management Research, Univ. of Oklahoma, 307 West Brooks St., Norman 73019. *Statistical Abstract of Oklahoma.*
Oklahoma Department of Libraries. *Oklahoma Almanac.* Biennial
Morris, J. W., *et al.*, *Historical Atlas of Oklahoma.* 3rd ed. Oklahoma Univ. Press, 1986

State library: Oklahoma Department of Libraries, 200 Northeast 18th Street, Oklahoma City 73105.

OREGON

KEY HISTORICAL EVENTS

The area was divided between many Indian groups including the Chinook, Tillamook, Cayuse and Modoc. In the 18th century English and Spanish visitors tried to establish national claims, based on explorations of the 16th century. The USA also laid claim by right of discovery when an expedition entered the mouth of the Columbia River in 1792.

Oregon was disputed between Britain and the USA. An American fur company established a trading settlement at Astoria in 1811, which the British took in 1812. The Hudson Bay Company were the most active force in Oregon until the 1830s when American pioneers began to migrate westwards along the Oregon Trail. The dispute between Britain and the USA was resolved in 1846 with the boundary fixed at 49°N. lat. Oregon was organized as a Territory in 1848 but with wider boundaries; it became a state with its present boundaries in 1859.

Early settlers were mainly American. They came to farm in the Willamette Valley and to exploit the western forests. Portland developed as a port for ocean-going traffic, although it was 100 miles inland at the confluence of the Willamette and Columbia rivers. Industries followed when the railways came and the rivers were exploited for hydro-electricity. The capital of the Territory from 1851 was Salem, a mission for Indians on the Willamette river; it was confirmed as state capital in 1864. Salem became the processing centre for the farming and market-gardening Willamette Valley.

TERRITORY AND POPULATION

Oregon is bounded in the north by Washington, with the Columbia River forming most of the boundary, east by Idaho, with the Snake River forming most of the boundary, south by Nevada and California and west by the Pacific. Land area, 95,997 sq. miles (248,631 sq. km). The federal government owned (1994) 32,132,581 acres (51·73% of the state area). Census population, 1 April 2000, 3,421,399, an increase of 20·4% since 1990. July 2004 estimate, 3,594,586.

Population at five federal censuses was:

	White	*Black*	*American Indian*	*Asiatic*	*Total*	*Per sq. mile*
1930	938,598	2,234	4,776	8,179	953,786	9·9
1960	1,732,037	18,133	8,026	9,120	1,768,687	18·4
1980	2,490,610	37,060	27,314	34,775	2,633,105	27·3
				All others		
1990	2,636,787	46,178	38,496	120,860	2,842,321	29·6
2000	2,961,623	55,662	45,211	358,903	3,421,399	35·6

Of the total population in 2000, 1,724,849 were female, 2,574,843 were 18 years old or older and 2,694,144 were urban. In 2000 the Hispanic population was 275,314, up from 112,707 in 1990 (an increase of 144·3%).

The US Bureau of Indian Affairs (area headquarters in Portland) administers (1994) 783,227·13 acres, of which 627,615·54 acres are held by the USA in trust for Indian tribes and 138,950·05 acres for individual Indians, and 16,661·54 acres of mineral tracts.

The largest cities (2000 census figures) are: Portland, 529,121; Eugene, 137,893; Salem (the capital), 136,924; Gresham, 90,205; Beaverton, 76,129; Hillsboro, 70,186; Medford, 63,154; Springfield, 52,864; Bend, 52,029. Primary statistical (metropolitan) areas: Portland–Salem, 2,265,223; Eugene-Springfield, 322,959.

SOCIAL STATISTICS

In 2002 births numbered 45,192 (12·8 per 1,000 population); deaths, 31,119 (8·8); 2001: infant mortality rate, 5·4 (per 1,000 live births). 2001: marriages, 26,000; divorces, 16,500.

CLIMATE

Jan. 32°F (0°C), July 66°F (19°C). Annual rainfall 28" (710 mm). Oregon belongs to the Pacific coast climate zone (*see* UNITED STATES: Climate).

CONSTITUTION AND GOVERNMENT

The present constitution dates from 1859; some 250 items in it have been amended. The Legislative Assembly consists of a Senate of 30 members, elected for four years (half their number retiring every two years), and a House of 60 representatives, elected for two years. The Governor is elected for four years. The constitution reserves to the voters the rights of initiative and referendum and recall.

For the 109th Congress, which convened in Jan. 2005, Oregon sends five members to the House of Representatives. It is represented in the Senate by Ron Wyden (D. 1996–2011) and Gordon Smith (R. 1997–2009).

The capital is Salem. There are 36 counties in the state.

RECENT ELECTIONS

In the 2004 presidential election Kerry polled 943,163 votes; Bush, 866,831; Badnarik, 7,260.

CURRENT ADMINISTRATION

Governor: Ted Kulongoski (D.), 2003–07 (salary: $93,600).

Secretary of State: Bill Bradbury (D.), 2005–09 ($72,000).

Government Website: http://www.oregon.gov

ECONOMY

Per capita income (2002) was $28,533.

Budget. In 2002 total state revenue was $14,815m. Total expenditure was $18,029m. (education, $5,208m.; public welfare, $3,856m.; hospitals, $1,190m.; government administration, $902m.; highways, $817m.) Outstanding debt, in 2002, $7,668m.

Performance. Gross State Product was $115,138m. in 2002, ranking Oregon 28th in the United States.

ENERGY AND NATURAL RESOURCES

Water. The total area covered by water is approximately 1,129 sq. miles.

Minerals. Mineral resources include gold, silver, lead, mercury, chromite, sand and gravel, stone, clays, lime, silica, diatomite, expansible shale, scoria, pumice and uranium. There is geothermal potential. Domestic non-fuel mineral production value (2002), $320m.

Agriculture. Oregon, which has an area of 61,557,184 acres, is divided by the Cascade Range into two distinct zones as to climate. West of the Cascade Range there is a good rainfall and almost every variety of crop common to the temperate zone is grown; east of the Range stock-raising and wheat-growing are the principal industries and irrigation is needed for row crops and fruits. In 2002 there were 64,000 hired workers in agriculture.

There were, in 2002, 41,000 farms with an acreage of 17·2m. and an average farm size of 420 acres; most are family-owned corporate farms. Average value per acre (2002), $1,202.

Farm income in 2001: from crops, $2,298m.; from livestock and products, $825m. The net farm income in 2001 was $266m. Principal crops (2003): greenhouse and nursery products ($777·7m.), hay ($365·7m.), grass seed ($291·7m.), wheat ($199·8m.), Christmas trees ($158·0m.), onions ($108·3m.), potatoes ($106·7m.), pears ($72·2m.) and farmforest products.

Livestock, 2002: milch cows, 116,400; cattle and calves, 1·36m.; sheep and lambs, 237,000; swine, 21,000.

Forestry. Oregon had 29,651,000 acres of forest in 2002, with 14,293,000 acres of national forest. Almost half of the state is forested. In 1993, 22·4m. was commercial forest land suitable for timber production; ownership was as follows (acres): US Forestry Service, 13·1m.; US Bureau of Land Management, 2·7m.; other federal, 165,000; State of Oregon, 907,000; other public (city, county), 123,000; private owners, 10·8m., of which the forest industry owned 5·8m., non-industrial private owners, 4·6m., Indians, 399,000. Oregon's commercial forest lands provided a 1992 harvest of 5,742m. bd ft of logs, as well as the benefits of recreation, water, grazing, wildlife and fish. Trees vary from the coastal forest of hemlock and spruce to the state's primary species, Douglas-fir, throughout much of western Oregon. In eastern Oregon, ponderosa pine, lodgepole pine and true firs are found. Here, forestry is often combined with livestock grazing to provide an economic operation. Along the Cascade summit and in the mountains of northeast Oregon, alpine species are found.

Total covered payroll in lumber and wood products industry in 1991 was $1,475m.

Fisheries. Commercial fish and shellfish landings in 2002 was 211·2m. lb and amounted to a value of $68·4m. The most important are: ground fish, shrimp, crab, tuna, salmon.

INDUSTRY

Forest products manufacturing is Oregon's leading industry, followed by high technology. In 2001 the state's 5,587 manufacturing establishments had 198,000 employees, earning $7,981m. Total value added by manufacturing in 2001 was $22,027m.

Labour. Total non-agricultural employment was 1,596,000 in 2001. Employees by branch, 2001 (in 1,000): services, 445; wholesale and retail trade, 391; government, 269; manufacturing, 236. The unemployment rate in 2002 was 7·5%.

COMMUNICATIONS

Roads. There were 66,642 miles of roads in 2002 (55,470 rural) and 3,069,310 registered vehicles.

Rail. In 2001 there were approximately 3,800 total miles of track, including 2,387 route miles. There is a light rail network in Portland.

Civil Aviation. In 1994 there were one public-use and 93 personal-use heliports; 248 personal-use and 101 public-use airports of which 34 were state-owned airports;

and two sea-plane bases, one public-use and one personal-use. There were 7,187,907 passenger enplanements statewide in 2000.

Shipping. Portland is a major seaport for large ocean-going vessels and is 101 miles inland from the mouth of the Columbia River. In 1993 Portland handled 11·7m. short tons of cargo and other Columbia River ports 13·7m. short tons, the main commodities being grain, petroleum and wood products; the ports of Coos Bay and Newport handled 2·7m. short tons of cargo, chiefly logs, lumber and wood products.

SOCIAL INSTITUTIONS

Justice. There are 12 correctional institutions in Oregon. In June 2002 there were 11,812 federal and state prisoners. The sterilization law, originally passed in 1917, was amended in 1967 and abolished in 1993. Some categories of euthanasia were legalized in Dec. 1994.

The death penalty is authorized but there have been no executions since 2001.

Religion. The chief religious bodies are Catholic, Baptist, Lutheran, Methodist, Presbyterian and Latter-day Saints (Mormons).

Education. School attendance is compulsory from seven to 18 years of age if the twelfth year of school has not been completed; those between the ages of 16 and 18 years, if legally employed, may attend part-time or evening schools. Others may be excused under certain circumstances. In 1994–95 the public elementary and secondary schools had 521,000 students and 27,000 teachers; average salary for teachers (1993–94), $37,589. Total expenditure on elementary and secondary education (1997) was $3,769m.

Leading state-supported institutions of higher education (1993–94) included:

	Students
University of Oregon, Eugene	16,680
Oregon Health Sciences University	1,396
Oregon State University, Corvallis	14,131
Portland State University, Portland	14,428
Western Oregon State College, Monmouth	3,871
Southern Oregon State College, Ashland	4,535
Eastern Oregon State College, La Grande	1,931
Oregon Institute of Technology, Klamath Falls	2,444

Enrolment in state colleges and universities, in autumn 1996, was approximately 165,000 students. Largest of the privately endowed universities are Lewis and Clark College, Portland, with 3,132 students (1993–94); University of Portland, 2,700 students; Willamette University, Salem, 2,451 students; Reed College, Portland, 1,277 students; Linfield College, McMinnville, 2,354 students; Marylhurst College, 1,183 students; and George Fox College, 1,557 students. In 1993–94 there were 314,926 students (full-time equivalent) in community colleges.

Health. In 2001 there were 60 community hospitals with 6,700 beds. A total of 335,000 patients were admitted during the year.

Welfare. Medicare enrolment in July 2002 totalled 503,783. In 2000 a total of 542,392 people in Oregon received Medicaid. In Dec. 2003 there were 591,461 Old-Age, Survivors, and Disability Insurance (OASDI) beneficiaries. A total of 40,911 people were receiving payments under Temporary Assistance for Needy Families (TANF) in Sept. 2002.

CULTURE

Broadcasting. In 1996 there were 194 commercial radio stations and 37 educational radio stations. There were 24 commercial television stations and 26 educational television stations. There were also 24 cable companies.

Press. In 1996 there were 21 daily newspapers with a circulation of more than 676,000 and 111 non-daily newspapers.

Tourism. The total income from tourism in 1992 was estimated to be $3,100m.

FURTHER READING

Oregon Blue Book. Issued by the Secretary of State. Salem. Biennial
Conway, F. D. L., *Timber in Oregon: History and Projected Trends.* Oregon State Univ., 1993
Friedman, R., *The Other Side of Oregon.* Caldwell (ID), 1993

McArthur, L. A., *Oregon Geographic Names.* 6th ed., rev. and enlarged. Portland, 1992
Orr, E. L., *et al.*, *Geology of Oregon.* Dubuque (IA), 1992

State Library: The Oregon State Library, Salem.

PENNSYLVANIA

KEY HISTORICAL EVENTS

Pennsylvania was occupied by four powerful tribes in the 17th century: Delaware, Susquehannock, Shawnee and Iroquois. The first white settlers were Swedish, arriving in 1643. The British became dominant in 1664, and in 1681 William Penn, an English Quaker, was given a charter to colonize the area as a sanctuary for his fellow Quakers. Penn's ideal was peaceful co-operation with the Indians and religious toleration within the colony. Several religious groups were attracted to Pennsylvania because of this policy, including Protestant sects from Germany and France. During the 18th century, co-operation with the Indians failed as the settlers pushed into more territory and the Indians resisted.

During the War of Independence the Declaration of Independence was signed in Philadelphia, the main city. Pennsylvania became one of the original 13 states of the Union. In 1812 the state capital was moved to its current location in Harrisburg, which began as a trading post and ferry point on the Susquehanna River in the south-central part of the state. The Mason-Dixon line, the state's southern boundary, became the dividing line between free and slave states during the conflict leading to the Civil War. During the war crucial battles were fought in the state, including the battle of Gettysburg. Industrial growth was rapid after the war. Pittsburgh, founded as a British fort in 1761 during war with the French, had become an iron-making town by 1800 and grew rapidly when canal and railway links opened in the 1830s. The American Federation of Labor was founded in Pittsburgh in 1881, by which time the city was of national importance in producing coal, iron, steel and glass.

At the beginning of the 20th century, industry attracted immigration from Italy and eastern Europe. In farming areas the early sect communities survive, notably Amish and Mennonites. (The Pennsylvania 'Dutch' are of German extraction.)

TERRITORY AND POPULATION

Pennsylvania is bounded north by New York, east by New Jersey, south by Delaware and Maryland, southwest by West Virginia, west by Ohio and northwest by Lake Erie. Land area, 44,817 sq. miles (116,075 sq. km). Census population, 1 April 2000, 12,281,054, an increase of 3·4% since 1990. July 2004 estimate, 12,406,292.

Population at five census years was:

	White	*Black*	*Indian*	*All others*	*Total*	*Per sq. mile*
1910	7,467,713	193,919	1,503	1,976	7,665,111	171·0
1930	9,196,007	431,257	523	3,563	9,631,350	214·8
			All others			
1980	10,652,320	1,046,810	164,765		11,863,895	264·7
1990	10,520,201	1,089,795	271,647		11,881,643	265·1
2000	10,484,203	1,224,612	572,239		12,281,054	274·0

Of the total population in 2000, 6,351,391 were female, 9,358,833 were 18 years old or older and 9,464,101 were urban. In 2000 Pennsylvania's Hispanic population was 394,088, up from 232,262 in 1990 (a rise of 69·7%).

The population of the largest cities and townships, 2000 census, was:

Philadelphia	1,517,550	Upper Darby	81,821	Bethlehem	71,329
Pittsburgh	334,563	Reading	81,207	Lower Merion	59,850
Allentown	106,632	Scranton	76,415	Bensalem	58,434
Erie	103,717				

The Philadelphia–Wilmington–Atlantic City metropolitan area had a 2000 census population of 6,188,463.

SOCIAL STATISTICS

Births, 2002, 142,850 (11·6 per 1,000 population); deaths, 130,223 (10·6); 2001: infant deaths, 7·2 per 1,000 live births. 2001: marriages, 71,400 (6·0 per 1,000 population); divorces, 38,000 (3·2).

CLIMATE

Philadelphia, Jan. 32°F (0°C), July 77°F (25°C). Annual rainfall 40" (1,006 mm). Pittsburgh, Jan. 31°F (–0·6°C), July 74°F (23·3°C). Annual rainfall 37" (914 mm). Pennsylvania belongs to the Appalachian Mountains climate zone (*see* UNITED STATES: Climate).

CONSTITUTION AND GOVERNMENT

The present constitution dates from 1968. The General Assembly consists of a Senate of 50 members chosen for four years, one-half being elected biennially, and a House of Representatives of 203 members chosen for two years. The Governor and Lieut.-Governor are elected for four years. Every citizen 18 years of age, with the usual residential qualifications, may vote. Registered voters in Nov. 1999, 7,460,339.

For the 109th Congress, which convened in Jan. 2005, Pennsylvania sends 19 members to the House of Representatives. It is represented in the Senate by Arlen Specter (R. 1981–2011) and Rick Santorum (R. 1995–2007).

The state capital is Harrisburg. The state is organized in counties (numbering 67), cities, boroughs, townships and school districts.

RECENT ELECTIONS

In the 2004 presidential election Kerry polled 2,938,095 votes; Bush, 2,793,847; Badnarik, 21,185.

CURRENT ADMINISTRATION

Governor: Edward G. Rendell (D.), 2003–07 (salary: $155,572).

Lieut.-Governor: Catherine Baker Knoll (D.), 2003–07 ($130,679).

Secretary of the Commonwealth: Pedro A. Cortés (D.), appointed 2003 ($112,013).

Government Website: http://www.state.pa.us

ECONOMY

Per capita income (2002) was $31,663.

Budget. In 2002 total state revenue was $46,165m. Total expenditure was $55,171m. (public welfare, $15,118m.; education, $13,775m.; highways, $4,566m.; hospitals, $2,234m.; health, $1,917m.) Outstanding debt, in 2002, $20,983m.

Performance. Gross State Product in 2002 was $428,950m., ranking Pennsylvania 6th in the United States.

ENERGY AND NATURAL RESOURCES

Oil and Gas. 1998 production: crude petroleum, 1·98m. bbls.; natural gas, 68,343m. cu. ft.

Water. The total area covered by water is approximately 1,239 sq. miles.

Minerals. Pennsylvania is almost the sole producer of anthracite coal. Production, 1998: industrial minerals (shale, limestone, sandstone, clay, dolomite, sand and gravel), 128,332,415 tons; bituminous coal, 79,544,949 tons; anthracite coal, 7,535,593 tons. Non-fuel mineral production was worth $1,270m. in 2002.

Agriculture. Agriculture, market-gardening, fruit-growing, horticulture and forestry are pursued within the state. In 2002 there were 59,000 farms with a total farm area of 7·7m. acres. Average number of acres per farm in 2002 was 131 and the average value per acre was $3,419. Cash receipts, 2001, from crops, $1,309m., and from livestock and products, $3,146m. The net farm income in 2001 was $969m.

In 2002 Pennsylvania ranked first in the production of mushrooms (459·6m. lb, value $390·3m.). Other production figures include (2001): corn for grain (97m. bu., value $223·2m.); sweet corn (701,000 cwt, value $18·58m.) and tomatoes (537,000 cwt, value $19·65m.). Pennsylvania is also a major fruit producing state. In 2002 apples totalled 370m. lb (value $37·2m.); peaches, 60m. lb (value $19·8m.); and grapes, 53·2m. tons (value $14·9m.). Pennsylvania ranked fourth in milk production in 2002 with 10,780m. lb (6·3% of US milk production). Egg production totalled 6,520m., value $279·3m.; chicken production (excluding broilers) was 29·3m., value

$52·7m.; and production of broilers was 133·2m., value $225·9m. Other products included turkey (9·9m. poults, value $91·1m.) and cheese (374m. lb).

In 2002 there were on farms: 1·63m. cattle and calves, 102,890 sheep, and 1·23m. hogs and swine.

Forestry. Total forested area was 16,905,000 acres in 2002. In 1998 state forest land totalled 2,100,113 acres; state park land, 282,700 acres; state game lands, 1,392,312 acres.

INDUSTRY

In 2001 the state's 16,796 manufacturing establishments had 780,000 employees, earning $29,312m. Total value added by manufacturing in 2001 was $87,984m.

Labour. Total non-agricultural employment, 2001, 5,701,000. Employees by branch, 2001 (in 1,000): services, 1,908; wholesale and retail trade, 1,272; manufacturing, 893; government, 730. The unemployment rate in 2002 was 5·7%.

COMMUNICATIONS

Roads. In 2002 highways and roads in the state (federal, local and state combined) totalled 120,298 miles (85,585 miles rural). Registered motor vehicles numbered 9,524,997.

Rail. In Jan. 1999 there were 70 freight railways operating within the state with a line mileage of 5,379. There are metro, light rail and tramway networks in Philadelphia and Pittsburgh, and commuter networks around Philadelphia.

Civil Aviation. In Jan. 1999 there were 139 public airports, 312 private and eight public heliports, and 349 airports for personal use (includes seaplane bases). There were 20,817,271 passenger enplanements statewide in 2000.

Shipping. Trade at the ports of the Philadelphia area (Chester, Marcus Hook and Philadelphia) for 1998: imports, 50,222,884 short tons of cargo (includes bulk and general cargo); exports, 837,547 short tons of cargo.

SOCIAL INSTITUTIONS

Justice. The death penalty is authorized. The last execution was in 1999. There were 39,275 prisoners in state correctional institutions in June 2002.

Religion. The principal religious bodies in 1990 were the Roman Catholics (3,675,250 members), Protestants (3,615,450) and Jews (282,000 in 1997). The five largest Protestant denominations by adherents were the Evangelical Lutheran Church in America (682,800), the United Methodist Church (678,700), the Presbyterian Church (USA) (388,747), the United Church of Christ (286,500) and the Episcopal Church (140,050).

Education. School attendance is compulsory for children eight to 17 years of age. In 1998–99 there were 1,816,566 pupils and 109,691 teachers in public elementary and secondary schools. The public kindergartens and elementary schools (Grades K-6) had 984,830 pupils and public secondary schools (Grades 7–12) had 831,736 pupils. Non-public elementary schools had 247,466 pupils and non-public secondary had 83,912 pupils. Average salary for public school professional personnel was $49,859; classroom teachers $48,457. In fiscal year 1997–98 state and local government revenues for elementary and secondary schools totalled $13,282m. Total expenditures from all funding sources (state, local, federal government and other financing sources) totalled $13,918m.

Leading senior academic institutions included:

Founded	*Institutions*	*Faculty*[1] *(Autumn 1997)*	*Students*[2] *(Autumn 1998)*
1740	University of Pennsylvania (non-sect.)	6,634	21,729
1787	University of Pittsburgh (all campuses)	6,142	32,292
1832	Lafayette College, Easton (Presbyterian)	264	2,244
1833	Haverford College	121	1,147
1842	Villanova University (R.C.)	1,079	9,952
1846	Bucknell University (Baptist)	285	3,726
1851	St Joseph's University, Philadelphia (R.C.)	474	6,484
1852	California University of Pennsylvania	332	5,800

Founded	Institutions	Faculty[1] (Autumn 1997)	Students[2] (Autumn 1998)
1855	Pennsylvania State University (all campuses)	9,017	75,041
1855	Millersville University of Pennsylvania	440	7,466
1863	LaSalle University, Philadelphia (R.C.)	391	5,384
1864	Swarthmore College	228	1,390
1866	Lehigh University, Bethlehem (non-sect.)	909	6,363
1871	West Chester University of Pennsylvania	711	11,578
1875	Indiana University of Pennsylvania	824	13,790
1878	Duquesne University, Pittsburgh (R.C.)	1,124	9,552
1884	Temple University, Philadelphia	3,697	27,539
1885	Bryn Mawr College	283	1,796
1888	University of Scranton (R.C.)	452	4,711
1891	Drexel University, Philadelphia	1,117	11,646
1900	Carnegie-Mellon University, Pittsburgh	1,235	8,174

[1]Includes full-time and part-time.
[2]Includes undergraduate, graduate and first professional students.

Health. In 2001 there were 205 community hospitals with 42,100 beds. A total of 1,809,000 patients were admitted during the year.

Welfare. Medicare enrolment in July 2002 totalled 2,100,640. In 2000 a total of 1,492,352 people in Pennsylvania received Medicaid. In Dec. 2003 there were 2,386,426 Old-Age, Survivors, and Disability Insurance (OASDI) beneficiaries. A total of 205,220 people were receiving payments under Temporary Assistance for Needy Families (TANF) in Sept. 2002.

CULTURE

Broadcasting. Broadcasting stations in 2000 included 50 television stations and 334 radio stations.

Press. There were (2000) 78 daily and 263 weekly newspapers.

FURTHER READING

Statistical information: Pennsylvania State Data Center, 777 West Harrisburg Pike, Middletown 17057. Publishes *Pennsylvania Statistical Abstract.*

Downey, D. B. and Bremer, F. (eds.) *Guide to the History of Pennsylvania.* London, 1994

RHODE ISLAND

KEY HISTORICAL EVENTS

The earliest white settlement was founded by Roger Williams, an English Puritan who was expelled from Massachusetts because of his dissident religious views and his insistence on the land-rights of the Indians. At Providence he bought land from the Narragansetts and founded a colony there in 1636. A charter was granted in 1663. The colony was governed according to policies of toleration, which attracted Jewish and nonconformist settlers; later there was French Canadian settlement also.

Shipping and fishing developed strongly, especially at Newport and Providence; these two cities were twin capitals until 1900, when the capital was fixed at Providence.

Significant actions took place in Rhode Island during the War of Independence. In 1790 the state accepted the federal constitution and was admitted to the Union.

Early farming development was most successful in dairying and poultry. Early industrialization was mainly in textiles, beginning in the 1790s, and flourishing on abundant water power. Textiles dominated until the industry began to decline after the First World War. British, Irish, Polish, Italian and Portuguese workers settled in the state, working in the mills or in the shipbuilding, shipping, fishing and naval ports. The crowding of a new population into cities led to the abolition of the property qualification for the franchise in 1888.

TERRITORY AND POPULATION

Rhode Island is bounded north and east by Massachusetts, south by the Atlantic and west by Connecticut. Land area, 1,045 sq. miles (2,707 sq. km). Census population, 1 April 2000, 1,048,319, an increase of 4·5% since 1990. July 2004 estimate, 1,080,632.

Population of five census years was:

	White	Black	Indian	Asiatic	Total	Per sq. mile
1910	532,492	9,529	284	305	542,610	508·5
1930	677,026	9,913	318	240	687,497	649·3
			All others			
1980	896,692	27,584	22,878		947,154	903·0
1990	917,375	38,861	4,071	18,325	1,003,164	960·3
2000	891,191	46,908	5,121	24,232	1,048,319	1,003·2

Of the total population in 2000, 554,684 were female, 800,497 were 18 years old or older and 953,146 were urban (90·92%). In 2000 the Hispanic population was 90,820, up from 45,752 in 1990 (an increase of 98·5%).

The chief cities and their population (census, 2000) are Providence, 173,618; Warwick, 85,808; Cranston, 79,269; Pawtucket, 72,958; East Providence, 48,688.

SOCIAL STATISTICS

Births, 2002, were 12,894 (12·1 per 1,000 population); deaths, 10,246 (9·6); 2001: infant mortality rate, 6·8 (per 1,000 live births). 2001: marriages, 8,600; divorces, 3,300.

CLIMATE

Providence, Jan. 28°F (–2·2°C), July 72°F (22·2°C). Annual rainfall 43" (1,079 mm). Rhode Island belongs to the New England climate zone (*see* UNITED STATES: Climate).

CONSTITUTION AND GOVERNMENT

The present constitution dates from 1843; it has had 44 amendments. The General Assembly consists of a Senate of 50 members and a House of Representatives of 100 members, both elected for two years. The Governor and Lieut.-Governor are now elected for four years. Every citizen, 18 years of age, who has resided in the state for 30 days, and is duly registered, is qualified to vote.

For the 109th Congress, which convened in Jan. 2005, Rhode Island sends two members to the House of Representatives. It is represented in the Senate by Jack Reed (D. 1997–2009) and Lincoln Chafee (R. 1999–2007).

The capital is Providence. The state has five counties but no county governments. There are 39 municipalities, each having its own form of local government.

RECENT ELECTIONS

In the 2004 presidential election Kerry polled 259,760 votes; Bush, 169,046; Nader, 4,651.

CURRENT ADMINISTRATION

Governor: Donald L. Carcieri (R.), 2003–07 (salary: $105,194).

Lieut.-Governor: Charles J. Fogerty (D.), 2003–07 ($88,584).

Secretary of State: Matthew A. Brown (D), 2003–07 ($88,584).

Government Website: http://www.ri.gov

ECONOMY

Per capita income (2002) was $31,107.

Budget. In 2002 total state revenue was $4,891m. Total expenditure was $5,767m. (public welfare, $1,690m.; education, $1,344m.; government administration, $260m.; highways, $260m.; health, $182m.) Outstanding debt, in 2002, $5,856m.

Performance. Gross State Product in 2002 was $36,988m., ranking Rhode Island 45th in the United States.

ENERGY AND NATURAL RESOURCES

Water. The total area covered by water is approximately 186 sq. miles.

Minerals. The small non-fuel mineral output—mostly stone, sand and gravel—was valued at $17m. in 2002.

Agriculture. In 2002 there were 700 farms with an area of 60,000 acres. The average size of a farm was 86 acres. In 2002 the average value of land and buildings per acre was $9,225. Farm income 2001: from crops, $40m.; livestock and products, $8m. The net farm income in 2001 was $6m.

Forestry. Total forested area was 385,000 acres in 2002.

Fisheries. In 2002 the commercial catch was 103·7m. lb (mainly lobster and quahog) valued at $64·3m.

INDUSTRY

Manufacturing is the chief source of income and the largest employer. Principal industries are jewellery and silverware, electrical machinery, electronics, plastics, metal products, instruments, chemicals and boat building. In 2001 the state's 2,185 manufacturing establishments had 67,000 employees, earning $2,333m. Total value added by manufacturing in 2001 was $5,877m.

Labour. In 2001 total non-agricultural employment was 479,000. Employees by branch, 2001 (in 1,000): services, 169; wholesale and retail trade, 108; manufacturing, 70. The unemployment rate in 2002 was 5·1%.

COMMUNICATIONS

Roads. In 2002 there were 6,051 miles of roads (4,718 miles urban) and 775,725 registered motor vehicles.

Rail. Amtrak's New York-Boston route runs through the state, serving Providence.

Civil Aviation. In 2000 there were six state-owned airports. Theodore Francis Green airport at Warwick, near Providence, is served by 15 airlines, and handled 5·1m. passengers in 2000 and 37m. lb of freight in 1995. There were 2,554,196 passenger enplanements statewide in 2000.

Shipping. Waterborne freight through the port of Providence (1988) totalled 10·6m. tons.

SOCIAL INSTITUTIONS

Justice. In June 2002 there were 3,694 federal and state prisoners. The death penalty was abolished in 1852, except that it is mandatory in the case of murder committed by a prisoner serving a life sentence.

Religion. Chief religious bodies are Roman Catholic, Protestant Episcopal (baptized persons), Jewish, Baptist, Congregational and Methodist.

Education. In 1996 there were 149,802 pupils in public elementary and secondary schools. There were 219 public elementary schools with 85,691 pupils; about 24,941 pupils were enrolled in private and parochial schools. The 38 public senior and vocational high schools had 64,111 pupils. State and local government expenditure for schools in 1991 totalled $1,212·7m. The total expenditure per pupil in 1995 was $6,634.

There are 11 institutions of higher learning (three public and eight private). The state maintains Rhode Island College, at Providence, with over 350 faculty members, and 8,900 students (2,594 part-time, 1,816 graduates), and the University of Rhode Island, at South Kingstown, with over 650 faculty members and 13,707 students (2,198 part-time, 3,176 graduates). Brown University, at Providence, founded in 1764, is now non-sectarian; in 1996 it had over 500 faculty members and 7,458 students (1,786 part-time or graduate). Providence College, at Providence, founded in 1917 by the Order of Preachers (Dominican), had (1996) 300 faculty members and 5,520 students (1,911 part-time or graduate). The largest of the other colleges are Bryant College, at Smithfield, with over 200 faculty members and 3,310 students (1,100 part-time or graduate), and the Rhode Island School of Design, in Providence, with over 250 faculty members and 1,830 students (170 graduates) in 1996.

Health. In 2001 there were 11 community hospitals with 2,400 beds. A total of 121,000 patients were admitted during the year.

Welfare. Medicare enrolment in July 2002 totalled 172,106. In 2000 a total of 178,859 people in Rhode Island received Medicaid. In Dec. 2003 there were 192,662 Old-Age, Survivors, and Disability Insurance (OASDI) beneficiaries. A total of 37,013 people were receiving payments under Temporary Assistance for Needy Families (TANF) in Sept. 2002.

CULTURE

Broadcasting. There were 24 radio stations, five television stations and eight cable television companies in 1998.

FURTHER READING

Statistical information: Rhode Island Economic Development Corporation, 1 West Exchange Street, Providence, RI 02903. Publishes *Rhode Island Basic Economic Statistics.*
Rhode Island Manual. Prepared by the Secretary of State. Providence
Wright, M. I. and Sullivan, R. J., *Rhode Island Atlas.* Rhode Island Pubs., 1983

State Library: Rhode Island State Library, State House, Providence 02908.

SOUTH CAROLINA

KEY HISTORICAL EVENTS

Originally the territory of Yamasee Indians, the area attracted French and Spanish explorers in the 16th century. There were attempts at settlement on the coast, none of which lasted. Charles I of England made a land grant in 1629, but the first permanent white settlement began at Charles Town in 1670, moving to Charleston in 1680. This was a proprietorial colony including North Carolina until 1712; both passed to the Crown in 1729.

The coastlands developed as plantations worked by slave labour. In the hills there were small farming settlements and many trading posts, dealing with Indian suppliers.

After active campaigns during the War of Independence, South Carolina became one of the original states of the Union in 1788.

In 1793 the cotton gin was invented, enabling the speedy mechanical separation of seed and fibre. This made it possible to grow huge areas of cotton and meet the rapidly growing needs of new textile industries. Plantation farming spread widely, and South Carolina became hostile to the anti-slavery campaign which was strong in northern states. The state first attempted to secede from the Union in 1847, but was not supported by other southern states until 1860, when secession led to civil war.

At that time the population was about 703,000, of whom 413,000 were black. During the reconstruction periods there was some political power for black citizens, but control was back in white hands by 1876. The constitution was amended in 1895 to disenfranchise most black voters, and they remained with hardly any voice in government until the Civil Rights movement of the 1960s. Columbia became the capital in 1786.

TERRITORY AND POPULATION

South Carolina is bounded in the north by North Carolina, east and southeast by the Atlantic, southwest and west by Georgia. Land area, 30,110 sq. miles (77,982 sq. km). Census population, 1 April 2000, 4,012,012, an increase of 15·1% since 1990. July 2004 estimate, 4,198,068.

The population in five census years was:

	White	*Black*	*Indian*	*Asiatic*	*Total*	*Per sq. mile*
1910	679,161	835,843	331	65	1,515,400	49·7
1930	944,049	793,681	959	76	1,738,765	56·8
			All others			
1980	2,150,507	948,623	22,703		3,121,833	100·3
1990	2,406,974	1,039,884	39,845		3,486,703	115·8
2000	2,695,560	1,185,216	131,236		4,012,012	133·2

Of the total population in 2000, 2,063,083 were female, 3,002,371 were 18 years old or older and 2,427,124 were urban. In 2000 the Hispanic population of South Carolina was 95,076, up from 30,551 in 1990 (an increase of 211·2%).

Population estimate of large towns in 1999: Columbia (capital), 111,821; Charleston, 88,596; North Charleston, 81,989; Greenville, 56,873; Rock Hill, 48,474; Mount Pleasant, 44,785.

SOCIAL STATISTICS

Births, 2002, were 54,570 (13·3 per 1,000 population); deaths, 37,736 (9·2); 2001: infant deaths, 8·9 per 1,000 live births. 2001: marriages, 36,800 (9·3); divorces and annulments, 13,800 (3·5).

CLIMATE

Columbia, Jan. 44·7°F (7°C), Aug. 80·2°F (26·9°C). Annual rainfall 49·12" (1,247·6 mm). South Carolina belongs to the Atlantic Coast climate zone (*see* UNITED STATES: Climate).

CONSTITUTION AND GOVERNMENT

The present constitution dates from 1895, when it went into force without ratification by the electorate. The General Assembly consists of a Senate of 46 members, elected for four years, and a House of Representatives of 124 members, elected for two years. It meets annually. The Governor and Lieut.-Governor are elected for four years.

For the 109th Congress, which convened in Jan. 2005, South Carolina sends six members to the House of Representatives. It is represented in the Senate by Lindsey Graham (R. 2003–09) and Jim DeMint (R. 2005–11).

The capital is Columbia. There are 46 counties.

RECENT ELECTIONS

In the 2004 presidential election Bush polled 937,974 votes; Kerry, 661,699; Nader, 5,520.

CURRENT ADMINISTRATION

Governor: Mark Sanford, Jr (R.), 2003–07 (salary: $106,078).

Lieut.-Governor: R. André Bauer (R.), 2003–07 ($46,545).

Secretary of State: Mark Hammond (R.), 2003–07 ($92,007).

Government Website: http://www.myscgov.com

ECONOMY

Per capita income (2002) was $25,395.

Budget. In 2002 total state revenue was $16,997m. Total expenditure was $20,009m. (education, $5,656m.; public welfare, $4,373m.; highways, $1,349m.; hospitals, $905m.; health, $721m.) Outstanding debt, in 2002, $10,116m.

Performance. Gross State Product was $122,354m. in 2002, ranking South Carolina 26th in the United States.

ENERGY AND NATURAL RESOURCES

Water. The total area covered by water is approximately 1,078 sq. miles.

Minerals. Gold is found, though non-metallic minerals are of chief importance: value of non-fuel mineral output in 2002 was $460m., chiefly from cement (Portland), stone and gold. Production of kaolin, vermiculite and scrap mica is also important.

Agriculture. In 2002 there were 24,500 farms covering a farm area of 4·8m. acres. The average farm was of 196 acres. The average value of farmland and buildings per acre was $2,067 in 2002.

Farm income, 2001: from crops $764m., from livestock and products, $882m. The net farm income in 2001 was $684m. Chief crops are tobacco, soybeans, wheat, cotton, peanuts and corn. Production, 2002: cotton, 131,000 bales; peanuts, 19·14m. lb; soybeans, 7·1m. bu.; tobacco, 55·5m. lb; corn, 11·96m. bu.; wheat, 7·03m. bu. Livestock on farms, 2002: 432,300 all cattle, 291,700 swine.

Forestry. The forest industry is important; total forest land (2002), 12·50m. acres. National forests amounted to 596,000 acres.

INDUSTRY

In 2001 the state's 4,430 manufacturing establishments had 326,000 employees, earning $11,289m. Total value added by manufacturing in 2001 was $35,017m.

Labour. In 2001 total non-agricultural employment was 1,835,000. Employees by branch, 2001 (in 1,000): services, 459; wholesale and retail trade, 432; manufacturing, 332; government, 320. The unemployment rate in 2002 was 6·0%.

COMMUNICATIONS

Roads. In 2002 there were 66,194 miles of roads comprising 10,674 miles of urban road and 55,520 miles of rural road; there were 3,202,102 registered motor vehicles. The death rate in traffic accidents stood at 31·9 per 100,000 registered motor vehicles (2000).

Rail. In 2000 the length of railway in the state was 2,470 miles.

Civil Aviation. In 1998 there were 1,450,844 general aviation aircraft operations in South Carolina, 116,542 taxi and commuter aircraft operations, 98,635 air carrier aircraft operations and 89,012 military aircraft operations. There were 2,483,461 passenger enplanements statewide in 2000.

Shipping. The state has three deep-water ports.

SOCIAL INSTITUTIONS

Justice. In June 2002 there were 23,017 federal and state prisoners. The death penalty is authorized. There were four executions in 2004.

Education. In 1995–96 there were 648,677 pupils and 46,073 teachers in public elementary and secondary schools. In 1996–97 the average teaching salary was $32,830.

For higher education the state operates the University of South Carolina (USC), founded at Columbia in 1801, with (autumn 1998), 25,250 enrolled students; USC Aiken, with 3,179 students; USC Spartanburg, with 3,767 students; USC 2-year regional campuses, with 4,484 students; Clemson University, founded in 1889, with 16,685 students; the Citadel, at Charleston, with 4,015 students; Winthrop University, Rock Hill, with 5,591 students; Medical University of S. Carolina, at Charleston, with 2,353 students; S. Carolina State University, at Orangeburg, with 4,795 students; and Francis Marion University, at Florence, with 3,947 students; the College of Charleston has 11,552 students; and Lander University, Greenwood, 2,600. There are 16 technical institutions (60,343).

There are also 387 private kindergartens, elementary and high schools with total enrolment (1996–97) of 49,534 pupils, and 23 private and denominational colleges and four junior colleges with (autumn 1998) enrolments of 29,316 and 1,357 students respectively.

Health. In 2001 there were 62 community hospitals with 11,300 beds. A total of 505,000 patients were admitted during the year.

Welfare. Medicare enrolment in July 2002 totalled 592,039. In 2000 a total of 685,104 people in South Carolina received Medicaid. In Dec. 2003 there were 735,084 Old-Age, Survivors, and Disability Insurance (OASDI) beneficiaries. A total of 49,756 people were receiving payments under Temporary Assistance for Needy Families (TANF) in Sept. 2002.

CULTURE

Press. In 1997 there were 15 daily and 14 Sunday newspapers in circulation.

FURTHER READING

Statistical information: Budget and Control Board, R. C. Dennis Bldg, Columbia 29201. Publishes *South Carolina Statistical Abstract.*

South Carolina Legislative Manual. Columbia. Annual

Edgar, W. B., *South Carolina in the Modern Age.* Univ. of South Carolina Press, 1992

Graham, C. B. and Moore, W. V., *South Carolina Politics and Government.* Univ. of Nebraska Press, 1995

State Library: South Carolina State Library, Columbia.

SOUTH DAKOTA

KEY HISTORICAL EVENTS

The area was part of the hunting grounds of nomadic Dakota (Sioux) Indians. French explorers visited the site of Fort Pierre in 1742–43, and claimed the area for France.

In 1763 the claim fell and, together with French claims to all land west of the Mississippi, passed to Spain. Spain held the Dakotas until defeated by France in the Napoleonic Wars, when France regained the area and sold it to the USA as part of the Louisiana Purchase in 1803.

Fur-traders were active, but there was no settlement until Fort Randall was founded on the Missouri river in 1856. In 1861 North and South Dakota were organized as the Dakota Territory, and the Homestead Act of 1862 stimulated settlement, mainly in the southeast until there was a gold-rush in the Black Hills of the west in 1875–76. Colonization developed as farming communities in the east, miners and ranchers in the west. Livestock farming predominated, attracting European settlers from Scandinavia, Germany and Russia.

In 1889 the North and South were separated and admitted to the Union as states. The capital of South Dakota is Pierre, founded as a railhead in 1880, chosen as a temporary capital and confirmed as permanent capital in 1904. It faces Fort Pierre, the former centre of the fur trade, across the Missouri river. During the 20th century there have been important schemes to exploit the Missouri for power and irrigation.

TERRITORY AND POPULATION

South Dakota is bounded in the north by North Dakota, east by Minnesota, southeast by the Big Sioux River (forming the boundary with Iowa), south by Nebraska (with the Missouri River forming part of the boundary) and west by Wyoming and Montana. Land area, 75,885 sq. miles (196,541 sq. km). Area administered by the Bureau of Indian Affairs, 1985, covered 5m. acres (10% of the state), of which 2·6m. acres were held by tribes. The federal government, 1994, owned 2,698,000 acres.

Census population, 1 April 2000, 754,844, an increase of 8·5% since 1990. July 2004 estimate, 770,883.

Population in five federal censuses was:

	White	*Black*	*American Indian*	*Asiatic*	*Total*	*Per sq. mile*
1910	563,771	817	19,137	163	583,888	7·6
1930	669,453	646	21,833	101	692,849	9·0
			All others			
1980	638,955	2,144	49,079		690,178	9·0
				Asian/ other		
1990	637,515	3,258	50,575	4,656	696,004	9·2
2000	669,404	4,685	62,283	18,472	754,844	9·9

Of the total population in 2000, 380,286 were female, 552,195 were 18 years old or older and 391,427 were urban. In 2000 the Hispanic population was 10,903, up from 5,252 in 1990 (an increase of 107·6%).

Population of the chief cities (census of 2000) was: Sioux Falls, 123,975; Rapid City, 59,607; Aberdeen, 24,658; Watertown, 20,237; Brookings, 18,507; Mitchell, 14,558; Pierre, 13,876; Yankton, 13,528; Huron, 11,893; Vermillion, 9,765; Spearfish, 8,606; Madison, 6,540; Sturgis, 6,442.

SOCIAL STATISTICS

In 2002: births, 10,698 (14·1 per 1,000 population); deaths, 6,898 (9·1); 2001: infant deaths, 7·4 per 1,000 live births. 2001: marriages, 6,700 (9·1 per 1,000 population); divorces, 2,500 (3·4).

CLIMATE

Rapid City, Jan. 25°F (–3·9°C), July 73°F (22·8°C). Annual rainfall 19" (474 mm). Sioux Falls, Jan. 14°F (–10°C), July 73°F (22·8°C). Annual rainfall 25" (625 mm). South Dakota belongs to the High Plains climate zone (*see* UNITED STATES: Climate).

CONSTITUTION AND GOVERNMENT

Voters are all citizens 18 years of age or older. The people reserve the right of the initiative and referendum. The Senate has 35 members, and the House of Representatives 70 members, all elected for two years; the Governor and Lieut.-Governor are elected for four years.

For the 109th Congress, which convened in Jan. 2005, South Dakota sends one member to the House of Representatives. It is represented in the Senate by Tim Johnson (D. 1997–2009) and John Thune (R. 2005–11).

The capital is Pierre. The state is divided into 66 organized counties.

RECENT ELECTIONS

In the 2004 presidential election Bush polled 232,584 votes; Kerry, 149,244; Nader, 4,320.

CURRENT ADMINISTRATION

Governor: Michael Rounds (R.), 2003–07 (salary: $103,221).

Lieut.-Governor: Dennis Daugaard (R.), 2003–07 ($19,140; part-time).

Secretary of State: Chris Nelson (R.), 2003–07 ($70,135).

Government Website: http://www.state.sd.us

ECONOMY

Per capita income (2002) was $26,694.

Budget. In 2002 total state revenue was $2,491m. Total expenditure was $2,772m. (education, $799m.; public welfare, $593m.; highways, $420m.; government administration, $103m.; natural resources, $98m.) Outstanding debt, in 2002, $2,308m.

Performance. Gross State Product in 2002 was $25,003m., ranking South Dakota 47th in the United States.

ENERGY AND NATURAL RESOURCES

Water. The total area covered by water is approximately 1,225 sq. miles.

Minerals. In 1998 there was a major decline in South Dakota's production of gold, although it remained the leading mineral commodity in the state. Production dropped 26% to 389,875 oz, yielding a gross value of $115m. (a drop of 34% in gross value on the previous year). In 1998, 503 companies had active mining licences in South Dakota, with 52 permits covering the mining of non-metallic minerals. Sand and gravel was the major non-metallic industrial mineral commodity with 15·1m. tonnes produced. Other major minerals were: Sioux quartzite (2·8m. tonnes); granite (265,000); pegmatite (17,100). Value of non-fuel mineral production (2002), $186m.

Agriculture. In 2002 there were 32,500 farms with an acreage of 44m. and an average farm size of 1,354 acres. Average value of farmland and buildings per acre in 2002 was $442. Farm income, 2001: crops, $1,852m.; livestock and products, $2,255m. The net farm income in 2001 was $1,218m.

In 2002 South Dakota was a major producer of rye (672,000 bu.), sunflower oil (303·2m. lb) and oats (5·72m. bu.). The other important crops were winter wheat (18·79m. bu.), barley (1·12m. bu.), spring wheat (23·5m. bu.), durum wheat (127,822 bu.), sorghum for grain (2·4m. bu.), corn for grain (295·2m. bu.) and soybeans (126·6m bu.). Total planted area of cropland was 20·32m. acres with 13·5m. being harvested.

The farm livestock in 2002 included 3·9m. cattle; 376,500 sheep and lambs; and 1·38m. hogs. In 2002, 11·5m. lb of honey were produced.

Forestry. South Dakota had 1,619,000 acres of forested land in 2002, of which 979,000 acres were national forest.

INDUSTRY

In 2001 the state's 922 manufacturing establishments had 47,000 employees, earning $1,401m. Total value added by manufacturing in 2001 was $4,558m.

Labour. In 2001 total non-agricultural employment was 379,000, including 102,000 in services, 94,000 in wholesale and retail trade, and 73,000 in government. The state unemployment rate in 2002 was 3·1%, the lowest rate of all the states.

COMMUNICATIONS

Roads. In 2002 there were 83,611 miles of roads comprising 2,136 miles of urban road and 81,475 miles of rural road; there were 813,908 registered vehicles. In 1996 there were 6,979 snowmobiles.

Rail. In 2003 there were 1,839·5 miles of track.

Civil Aviation. In 1996 there were 73 general aviation airports, of which nine were 'air carrier' airports with regular passenger services utilizing turbo-prop or jet aircraft. There were 520,541 passenger enplanements statewide in 2000.

SOCIAL INSTITUTIONS

Justice. In June 2002 there were 2,900 adults in state prisons. The death penalty is authorized, but was last used in 1947.

Religion. The chief religious bodies are: Lutherans, Roman Catholics, Methodists, United Church of Christ, Presbyterians, Baptists and Episcopalians.

Education. Elementary and secondary education are free from six to 21 years of age. Between the ages of six and 16, attendance is compulsory. In 1998–99 there were 131,117 PK-12 public school students at 763 public schools; and, in 1997, 16,792 PK-12 non-public school students at 140 schools.

Teachers' salaries (1998–99) averaged $28,386. Total expenditure on public schools was $646,930,000 ($4,934 per pupil).

Higher education (autumn 1998): the School of Mines at Rapid City, established 1885, had 2,265 students; South Dakota State University at Brookings, 8,635; the University of South Dakota, founded at Vermillion in 1882, 7,317; Northern State University, Aberdeen, 2,873; Black Hills State University at Spearfish, 3,639; Dakota State University at Madison, 1,831. There were 9,287 students at 14 private colleges.

Health. In 2001 there were 50 community hospitals with 4,500 beds. A total of 104,000 patients were admitted during the year.

Welfare. Medicare enrolment in July 2002 totalled 120,720. In 2000 a total of 101,951 people in South Dakota received Medicaid. In Dec. 2003 there were 137,880 Old-Age, Survivors, and Disability Insurance (OASDI) beneficiaries. A total of 6,416 people were receiving payments under Temporary Assistance for Needy Families (TANF) in Sept. 2002.

FURTHER READING

Statistical information: State Data Center, Univ. of South Dakota, Vermillion 57069.

Governor's Budget Report. South Dakota Bureau of Finance and Management. Annual
South Dakota Historical Collections. 1902–82
South Dakota Legislative Manual. Secretary of State, Pierre, S.D. Biennial
Berg, F. M., *South Dakota: Land of Shining Gold.* Hettinger, 1982

State Library: South Dakota State Library, 800 Governor's Drive, Pierre, S.D. 57501–2294.

TENNESSEE

KEY HISTORICAL EVENTS

Bordered on the west by the Mississippi, Tennessee was part of an area inhabited by Cherokee. French, Spanish and British explorers penetrated the area up the Mississippi and traded with the Cherokee in the late 16th and 17th centuries. French claims were abandoned in 1763, colonists from the British colonies of Virginia and Carolina then began to cross the Appalachians westwards, but there was no organized Territory until after the War of Independence. In 1784 there was a short-lived, independent state called Franklin. In 1790 the South West Territory (including Tennessee) was formed, and Tennessee entered the Union as a state in 1796.

The state was active in the war against Britain in 1812. After the American victory, colonization increased and pressure for land mounted. The Cherokee were forcibly removed during the 1830s and taken to Oklahoma, a journey on which many died.

Tennessee was a slave state and seceded from the Union in 1861, although eastern Tennessee was against secession. There were important battles at Shiloh, Chattanooga, Stone River and Nashville. In 1866 Tennessee was re-admitted to the Union.

Nashville, the capital since 1843, Memphis, Knoxville, and Chattanooga all developed as river towns, Memphis becoming an important cotton and timber port.

Growth was greatly accelerated by the creation of the Tennessee Valley Authority in the 1930s, producing power for a manufacturing economy. Industry increased to the extent that, by 1970, the normal southern pattern of emigration and population loss had been reversed.

TERRITORY AND POPULATION

Tennessee is bounded north by Kentucky and Virginia, east by North Carolina, south by Georgia, Alabama and Mississippi and west by the Mississippi River (forming the boundary with Arkansas and Missouri). Land area, 41,217 sq. miles (106,752 sq. km). Census population, 1 April 2000, 5,689,283, an increase of 16·7% since 1990. July 2004 estimate, 5,900,962.

Population in five census years was:

	White	*Black*	*Indian*	*Asiatic*	*Total*	*Per sq. mile*
1910	1,711,432	473,088	216	53	2,184,789	52·4
1930	2,138,644	477,646	161	105	2,616,556	62·4
			All others			
1980	3,835,452	725,942	29,726		4,591,120	111·6
1990	4,048,068	778,035	51,082		4,877,185	115·7
2000	4,563,310	932,809	193,164		5,689,283	138·0

Of the total population in 2000, 2,919,008 were female, 4,290,762 were 18 years old or older and 3,620,018 were urban. In 2000 the Hispanic population of Tennessee was 123,828, up from 32,741 in 1990 (an increase of 278·2%).

The cities, with population (2000) are Memphis, 650,100; Nashville (capital), 569,891; Knoxville, 167,535; Chattanooga, 150,425; Clarksville, 94,879; Johnson City, 55,542; Murfreesboro, 53,996; Jackson, 50,406; Kingsport, 41,335; Oak Ridge, 27,742. Metropolitan Statistical Areas, 2000: Nashville, 1,231,311; Memphis, 1,135,614; Knoxville, 687,249; Johnson City–Kingsport–Bristol, 480,091; Chattanooga, 465,161; Clarksville–Hopkinsville, 207,033; Jackson, 107,377.

SOCIAL STATISTICS

Statistics 2002: births, 77,482 (13·4 per 1,000 population); deaths, 55,606 (9·8); 2001: infant deaths, 8·7 per 1,000 live births. 2001: marriages, 77,700; divorces, 28,800.

CLIMATE

Memphis, Jan. 41°F (5°C), July 82°F (27·8°C). Annual rainfall 49" (1,221 mm). Nashville, Jan. 39°F (3·9°C), July 79°F (26·1°C). Annual rainfall 48" (1,196 mm). Tennessee belongs to the Appalachian Mountains climate zone (*see* UNITED STATES: Climate).

CONSTITUTION AND GOVERNMENT

The state has operated under three constitutions, the last of which was adopted in 1870 and has been since amended 30 times (first in 1953). Voters at an election may authorize the calling of a convention limited to altering or abolishing one or more specified sections of the constitution. The General Assembly consists of a Senate of 33 members and a House of Representatives of 99 members, senators elected for four years and representatives for two years. Qualified as electors are all citizens (usual residential and age (18) qualifications).

For the 109th Congress, which convened in Jan. 2005, Tennessee sends nine members to the House of Representatives. It is represented in the Senate by Bill Frist (R. 1995–2007) and Lamar Alexander (R. 2003–09).

The capital is Nashville. The state is divided into 95 counties.

RECENT ELECTIONS

In the 2004 presidential election Bush polled 1,384,375 votes; Kerry, 1,036,477; Nader, 8,992.

CURRENT ADMINISTRATION

Governor: Phil Bredesen (D.), 2003–07 (salary: $85,000, but not presently taken).

Lieut.-Governor (Senate President): John S. Wilder (D.), 2005–07 ($49,500).

Secretary of State: Riley Darnell (D), 2005–09 ($124,200).

Government Website: http://www.tennessee.gov

ECONOMY

Per capita personal income (2002) was $27,378.

Budget. In 2002 total state revenue was $17,952m. Total expenditure was $20,029m. (public welfare, $6,896m.; education, $6,095m.; highways, $1,534m.; health, $801m.; correction, $530m.) Outstanding debt, in 2002, $3,628m.

Performance. Gross State Product in 2002 was $190,122m., ranking Tennessee 19th in the United States.

ENERGY AND NATURAL RESOURCES

Water. The total area covered by water is approximately 926 sq. miles.

Minerals. Domestic non-fuel mineral production was worth $629m. in 2002.

Agriculture. In 2002, 90,000 farms covered 11·7m. acres. The average farm was of 130 acres. In 2002 the average value of farmland and buildings per acre was $2,405.

Farm income (2001) from crops was $1,034m.; from livestock, $1,127m. The net farm income in 2001 was $511m. Main crops were cotton, tobacco and soybeans.

In 2002 the domestic animals included 84,000 milch cows, 2·2m. all cattle, 23,300 sheep and 230,500 swine.

Forestry. Forests occupied 14·4m. acres in 2002. The forest industry and industries dependent on it employ about 0·04m. workers. Wood products are valued at over $500m. per year. National forest system land (2002) 623,000 acres.

INDUSTRY

The manufacturing industries include iron and steel working, but the most important products are chemicals, including synthetic fibres and allied products, electrical equipment and food. In 2001 the state's 7,013 manufacturing establishments had 449,000 employees, earning $15,237m. Total value added by manufacturing in 2001 was $46,349m.

Labour. In 2001 total non-agricultural employment was 2,712,000. Employees by branch, 2001 (in 1,000): services, 755; wholesale and retail trade, 639; manufacturing, 479; government, 402. The unemployment rate in 2002 was 5·1%.

COMMUNICATIONS

Roads. In 2002 there were 88,287 miles of roads (70,203 miles rural) and 4,776,520 registered motor vehicles.

Rail. The state had (2002) 3,150 miles of track. There is a tramway in Memphis.

Civil Aviation. The state is served by 23 major and regional airlines. In 1997 Tennessee had 83 public airports; there were also 71 heliports and two military air bases. There were 10,490,891 passenger enplanements statewide in 2000. Memphis International handled 2,453,000 tonnes of freight in 2000—the most of any airport in the world.

SOCIAL INSTITUTIONS

Justice. The death penalty is authorized; there has been only one execution (in 2000) since 1976. In June 2002 there were 24,277 prison inmates.

Religion. In 1990 there were 1,086,680 Southern Baptists, 320,724 United Methodists, 199,698 Black Baptists, 168,933 members of the Church of Christ, 137,203 Catholics and followers of various other religions.

Education. School attendance has been compulsory since 1925 and the employment of children under 16 years of age in workshops, factories or mines is illegal.

In 1995–96 there were 1,562 public schools with a net enrolment of 948,217 pupils; 49,627 teachers earned an average salary of $33,646. Total expenditure for operating schools was $4,266m. Tennessee has 49 accredited colleges and universities, 16 two-year colleges and 27 vocational schools. The universities include the University of Tennessee, Knoxville (founded 1794), with 25,337 students in 1996–97; Vanderbilt University, Nashville (1873) with 10,253; Tennessee State University (1912) with 8,643; the University of Tennessee at

Chattanooga (1886) with 8,296; University of Memphis (1912) with 19,271; and Fisk University (1866) with 812.

Health. In 2001 there were 123 community hospitals with 20,600 beds. A total of 751,000 patients were admitted during the year.

Welfare. Medicare enrolment in July 2002 totalled 855,278. In 2000 a total of 1,568,318 people in Tennessee received Medicaid. In Dec. 2003 there were 1,041,360 Old-Age, Survivors, and Disability Insurance (OASDI) beneficiaries. A total of 172,094 people were receiving payments under Temporary Assistance for Needy Families (TANF) in Sept. 2002.

CULTURE

Tourism. In 1994, 29·9m. out-of-state tourists spent $5,900m.

FURTHER READING

Statistical information: Center for Business and Economic Research, Univ. of Tennessee, Knoxville 37996. Publishes *Tennessee Statistical Abstract*

Tennessee Blue Book. Secretary of State, Nashville

Dykeman, W., *Tennessee.* Rev. ed., New York, 1984

State Library: State Library and Archives, Nashville.

TEXAS

KEY HISTORICAL EVENTS

A number of Indian tribes occupied the area before French and Spanish explorers arrived in the 16th century. In 1685 La Salle established a colony at Fort St Louis, but Texas was confirmed as Spanish in 1713. Spanish missions increased during the 18th century with San Antonio (1718) as their headquarters.

In 1820 a Virginian colonist, Moses Austin, obtained permission to begin a settlement in Texas. In 1821 the Spanish empire in the Americas came to an end, and Texas, together with Coahuila, formed a state of the newly independent Mexico. The Mexicans agreed to the Austin venture, and settlers of British and American descent came in.

The settlers became discontented with Mexican government and declared their independence in 1836. Warfare, including the siege of the Alamo fort, ended with the foundation of the independent Republic of Texas, which lasted until 1845. During this period the Texas Rangers were organized as a policing force and border patrol. Texas was annexed to the Union in Dec. 1845, as the Federal government feared its vulnerability to Mexican occupation. This led to war between Mexico and the USA from 1845 to 1848. In 1861 Texas left the Union and joined the southern states in the Civil War, being re-admitted in 1869. Ranching and cotton-growing were the main activities before the discovery of oil in 1901.

TERRITORY AND POPULATION

Texas is bounded north by Oklahoma, northeast by Arkansas, east by Louisiana, southeast by the Gulf of Mexico, south by Mexico and west by New Mexico. Land area, 261,797 sq. miles (678,051 sq. km). Census population, 1 April 2000, 20,851,820, an increase of 22·8% since 1990. July 2004 estimate, 22,490,022.

Population for five census years was:

	White	*Black*	*American Indian*	*Asian*	*Total*	*Per sq. mile*
1910	3,204,848	690,049	702	943	3,896,542	14·8
1930	4,967,172	854,964	1,001	1,578	5,824,715	22·1
			All others			
1980	11,197,663	1,710,250	1,320,470		14,228,383	54·2
				Asian/ other		
1990	12,774,762	2,021,632	65,877	2,124,239	16,986,510	64·9
2000	14,799,505	2,404,566	118,362	3,529,387	20,851,820	79·7

Of the total population in 2000, 10,498,910 were female, 14,965,061 were 18 years old or older, and 17,204,281 were urban. In 2000 the Hispanic population was

6,669,666, up from 4,339,905 in 1990 (an increase of 53·7%). The numerical increase was the second largest in the Hispanic population of any state in the USA, after California. Only New Mexico and California have a greater percentage of Hispanics in the state population.

The largest cities, with census population in 2000, are:

Houston	1,700,672	Garland	187,439	Waco	107,191
Dallas	1,036,309	Irving	166,523	Grand Prairie	103,913
San Antonio	991,861	Amarillo	163,569	Abilene	100,661
El Paso	554,496	Plano	153,624	Wichita Falls	98,356
Austin (capital)	501,637	Laredo	140,688	Midland	95,003
Fort Worth	459,085	Pasadena	127,843	Odessa	92,257
Arlington	277,939	Beaumont	118,289	McAllen	91,184
Corpus Christi	266,958	Brownsville	117,326	Carrollton	90,934
Lubbock	193,194	Mesquite	108,960	San Angelo	87,980

Metropolitan statistical areas, 2000: Dallas–Fort Worth, 5,221,801; Houston–Galveston–Brazoria, 4,669,571; San Antonio, 1,592,383; Austin–San Marcos, 1,249,763.

SOCIAL STATISTICS

Statistics 2002: births, 372,450 (17·1 per 1,000 population); deaths, 155,524 (7·1); infant deaths, 2001, 5·9 per 1,000 live births; marriages, 2001, 194,900 (9·4 per 1,000 population); divorces, 85,400 (4·1).

CLIMATE

Dallas, Jan. 45°F (7·2°C), July 84°F (28·9°C). Annual rainfall 38" (945 mm). El Paso, Jan. 44°F (6·7°C), July 81°F (27·2°C). Annual rainfall 9" (221 mm). Galveston, Jan. 54°F (12·2°C), July 84°F (28·9°C). Annual rainfall 46" (1,159 mm). Houston, Jan. 52°F (11·1°C), July 83°F (28·3°C). Annual rainfall 48" (1,200 mm). Texas belongs to the Central Plains climate zone (*see* UNITED STATES: Climate).

CONSTITUTION AND GOVERNMENT

The present constitution dates from 1876; it has been amended 432 times since. The state legislature consists of the Senate and House of Representatives. The Senate has 31 members elected for four-year terms. Half of the membership is elected every two years. The House has 150 members, elected for two-year terms during polling held in even-numbered years. The legislature meets in regular session for about five months every other year. The session begins in Jan. of odd-numbered years and lasts no more than 140 days (although special sessions can be called by the Governor). The Governor and Lieut.-Governor are elected for four years.

For the 109th Congress, which convened in Jan. 2005, Texas sends 32 members to the House of Representatives. It is represented in the Senate by Kay Hutchison (R. 1993–2007) and John Cornyn (R. 2002–09).

The capital is Austin. The state has 254 counties.

RECENT ELECTIONS

In the 2004 presidential election Bush polled 4,526,917 votes; Kerry, 2,832,704; Badnarik, 38,787.

CURRENT ADMINISTRATION

Governor: Rick Perry (R.), 2003–07 (salary: $115,345).

Lieut.-Governor: David Dewhurst (R.), ($7,200 plus legislature session salary).

Secretary of State: Roger Williams (R.), appointed Nov. 2004 ($117,516).

Government Website: http://www.state.tx.us

ECONOMY

Per capita personal income (2002) was $28,401.

Budget. In 2002 total state revenue was $60,588m. Total expenditure was $70,274m. (education, $25,763m.; public welfare, $15,271m.; highways, $5,219m.; hospitals, $3,238m.; correction, $3,157m.) Outstanding debt, in 2002, $24,008m.

Performance. In 2002 Gross State Product was $773,455m., ranking Texas third after California and New York. From the third quarter of 2001 the Texas economy experienced a sharp decline, with the strongest impact in high technology industries, leading to widespread job losses. A moderate recovery of the state economy began in 2003. The Texas Comptroller of Public Accounts' Index of Leading Economic Indicators grew by 5·3% between March 2003 and March 2004 (the largest percentage increase since June 1994). In addition, the Texas Coincident Index (based on employment, Gross State Product and the unemployment rate) has been improving since 2003, and the regional Consumer Confidence Index increased about 52% between March 2003 and March 2004. Texas is a major oil producer and exporter. With the surge in oil prices in 2004, the state stands to benefit from increases in oil company profitability, royalties and tax revenues.

Banking and Finance. In 2002 there were 715 financial institutions in Texas insured by the US Federal Deposit Insurance Corporation, with assets worth $216,900m. They had 4,980 offices with total deposits of $256,600m.

At Dec. 2003 there were 351 state-chartered banks operating in Texas, with total assets of $121,970m. The largest banks were International Bank of Commerce, Laredo (with assets of $5,294·2m.), Texas State Bank, McAllen ($4,215·6m.), Sterling Bank, Houston ($3,110·1m.), Prosperity Bank, El Campo ($2,395·0m.) and PlainsCapital Bank, Lubbock ($2,061·8m.).

ENERGY AND NATURAL RESOURCES

Oil and Gas. Texas is the leading producer in the USA of both oil and natural gas. In 2001 it produced 23% of the country's oil and 26% of its natural gas. Production, 2001: crude petroleum, 424m. bbls. (value, $9,933m.); natural gas, 6,520bn. cu. ft (value, $26,978m.). Natural gasoline, butane and propane gases are also produced.

Water. The total area covered by water is approximately 5,363 sq. miles.

Minerals. Minerals include helium, crude gypsum, granite and sandstone, salt and cement. Total value of domestic non-fuel mineral products in 2002 was $2,180m.

Agriculture. Texas is one of the most important agricultural states. In 2002 it had 230,000 farms covering 131m. acres; average farm was of 570 acres. Both the number of farms and the total area covered are the highest in the USA. In 2002 land and buildings were valued at $768 per acre. Large-scale commercial farms, highly mechanized, dominate in Texas; farms of 1,000 acres or more in number far exceed that of any other state, but small-scale farming persists. Soil erosion is serious in some parts.

Production: corn, barley, beans, cotton, hay, oats, peanuts, rye, sorghum, soybeans, sunflowers, wheat, oranges, grapefruit, peaches, sweet potatoes. Farm income, 2001, from crops was $4,456m.; from livestock, $9,339m. The net farm income in 2001 was $4,288m. (the largest of any state).

The state has an important livestock industry, leading in the number of all cattle (13·98m.) and sheep (1·03m.); it also had 0·31m. milch cows and 0·95m. swine in 2002.

Forestry. There were 17,149,000 acres of forested land in 2002, with 608,000 acres of national forest.

INDUSTRY

In 2001 the state's 21,370 manufacturing establishments had 948,000 employees, earning $37,288m. Total value added by manufacturing in 2001 was $120,086m.

Labour. Texas has a labour code (adopted 1993) which includes laws concerning protection of labourers, employer-employee relations, employment services and unemployment, and workers' compensation.

In 2001 total non-agricultural employment was 9,513,000. Employees by branch, 2001 (in 1,000): services, 2,751; wholesale and retail trade, 2,266; government, 1,584; manufacturing, 1,058. The unemployment rate in 2002 was 6·3%.

INTERNATIONAL TRADE

Imports and Exports. Exports in 2003 totalled $98·8bn. (an increase of 3·6% from 2002), ranking Texas as the leading US state by export revenue for the second consecutive year. The main export category is computer and electronic products, which accounted for 29% of total exports in 2003. Other major exports are chemicals, non-electrical machinery, transportation equipment, and petroleum and coal products. The leading destinations for exports in 2003 were Mexico (42%), Canada (11%) and China (3%). Asian and Pacific Rim countries accounted for 35% of exports and the European Union (principally the UK) for 2%. Texas is a major producer of agricultural products with exports valued at $2·6bn. in 2003.

COMMUNICATIONS

Roads. In 2002 there were 301,777 miles of roads comprising 83,205 miles of urban road and 218,572 miles of rural road. There were 14,664,328 registered motor vehicles. In 2003 there were 3,675 traffic accident fatalities.

Rail. In 2002 there were almost 12,000 miles of mainline track, the most in any US state. This included 11,377 miles (2000) Class I trackage.

Civil Aviation. There were 60,868,978 passenger enplanements in 2001. In 2002 Texas had 295 public and 1,073 private airports, 429 heliports and 8 stolports. In 2003 a total of 52,465,427 passengers (48,036,422 domestic and 4,429,005 international) embarked and disembarked at Dallas/Fort Worth International airport. It handled 736,023 tons of freight in 2003. The Houston Airport System (HAS) recorded a total of 42,034,978 passengers arriving and departing that year; of these, George Bush Intercontinental airport served 34,151,342 (28,530,960 domestic and 5,620,382 international). HAS cargo shipments in 2003 reached 335,753 tons in 2003.

Shipping. The port of Houston, connected by the Houston Ship Channel (50 miles long) with the Gulf of Mexico, is a large cotton market. Total cargo handled by all ports in 2002 was 442,251,000 tons. There were 834 miles of inland waterways in 2000.

SOCIAL INSTITUTIONS

Justice. In June 2002 there were 158,131 prison inmates. Between 1977 and 2004 Texas was responsible for 336 of the USA's 944 executions (more than three times as many as any other state), although it was not until 1982 that Texas reintroduced the death penalty. In 2004, 23 people were executed in Texas; in 2000, 40 people had been executed, the highest number in a year in any state since the authorities began keeping records in 1930.

Religion. Religious bodies represented include Roman Catholics, Baptists, Methodists, Churches of Christ, Lutherans, Presbyterians and Episcopalians.

Education. School attendance is compulsory from six to 18 years of age.

In the 2001–02 school year there were 7,646 public elementary and secondary schools with 4,163,447 enrolled pupils; there were 282,583 teachers. Total expenditure on public schools in 2000–01 was $26,547m.

In 2003 there were 142 higher education institutions (35 public universities, 38 independent colleges and universities, 50 public community college districts, 4 campuses of the Texas State Technical College System, 3 public Lamar state colleges, 9 public health-related institutions, 1 independent medical school and 2 independent junior colleges). The headcount enrolment in higher education in 2002 was 1,102,504 students, including 455,719 at public universities, 114,082 at independent universities and colleges and 505,212 at public community and state colleges. Enrolment in autumn 2003 was an estimated 1·14m.

Public universities and student enrolment, 2002:

Institutions	*Students*
University of Texas System	153,404
Texas A&M University System	96,729
Texas State University System	57,016
University of Houston System	54,910
Texas Technical University System	36,272
University of North Texas System	30,183
Stephen F. Austin State University, Nacogdoches	11,312
Texas Southern University, Houston	9,739
Midwestern State University, Wichita Falls	6,157

Independent colleges and universities with the largest student enrolments, 2002:

Institutions	*Students*
Baylor University, Waco	14,159
Southern Methodist University, Dallas	10,955
Texas Christian University, Fort Worth	8,074
Wayland Baptist University, Plainview	5,773
University of St Thomas, Houston	5,116
William Marsh Rice University, Houston	4,784
Abilene Christian University, Abilene	4,668
Dallas Baptist University, Dallas	4,417

Health. In 2001 there were 411 community hospitals with 56,300 beds. A total of 2,461,000 patients were admitted during the year.

Welfare. Medicare enrolment in July 2002 totalled 2,338,394. In 2000 a total of 2,602,616 people in Texas received Medicaid. In Dec. 2003 there were 2,792,148 Old-Age, Survivors, and Disability Insurance (OASDI) beneficiaries. A total of 335,178 people were receiving payments under Temporary Assistance for Needy Families (TANF) in Sept. 2002.

CULTURE

Tourism. In 2000 there were 1,169,000 overseas visitors to Texas, generating $705·2m. in tax receipts. In 2002 there were 17,090,000 visitors to state parks and recreation areas, raising $14,860,000 in revenue.

FURTHER READING

Texas Almanac. Dallas. Biennial
Kingston, M., *Texas Almanac's Political History of Texas.* Austin, 1992
Kraemer, R. and Newell, C., *Essentials of Texas Politics.* 5th ed. Austin, 1992
Marten, James, *Texas.* [Bibliography] ABC-Clio, Oxford and Santa Barbara (CA), 1992

Legislative Reference Library: Box 12488, Capitol Station, Austin, Texas 78711-2488.

UTAH

KEY HISTORICAL EVENTS

Spanish Franciscan missionaries explored the area in 1776, finding Shoshoni Indians. Spain laid claim to Utah and designated it part of Spanish Mexico. As such it passed into the hands of the Mexican Republic when Mexico rebelled against Spain and gained independence in 1821.

In 1848, at the conclusion of war between the USA and Mexico, the USA received Utah along with other southwestern territory. Settlers had already arrived in 1847 when the Mormons (the Church of Jesus Christ of Latter-day Saints) arrived, having been driven on by local hostility in Ohio, Missouri and Illinois. Led by Brigham Young, they entered the Great Salt Valley and colonized it. In 1849 they applied for statehood but were refused. In 1850 Utah and Nevada were joined as one Territory. The Mormon community continued to ask for statehood but this was only granted in 1896, after they had renounced polygamy and disbanded their People's Party.

Mining, especially of copper, and livestock farming were the base of the economy. Settlement had to adapt to desert conditions, and the main centres of population were in the narrow belt between the Wasatch Mountains and the Great Salt Lake. Salt Lake City, the capital, was founded in 1847 and laid out according to Joseph Smith's plan for the city of Zion. It was the centre of the Mormons' provisional 'State of Deseret' and Territorial capital from 1856 until 1896, except briefly in 1858 when federal forces occupied it during conflict between territorial and Union governments.

TERRITORY AND POPULATION

Utah is bounded north by Idaho and Wyoming, east by Colorado, south by Arizona and west by Nevada. Land area, 82,144 sq. miles (212,752 sq. km). The Bureau of Indian Affairs in 1990 administered 2,317,604 acres, 2,284,766 acres of which were allotted to Indian tribes.

Census population, 1 April 2000, 2,233,169, an increase of 29·6% since 1990. July 2004 estimate, 2,389,039.

Population at five federal censuses was:

	White	Black	American Indian	Asiatic	Total	Per sq. mile
1910	366,583	1,144	3,123	2,501	373,851	4·5
1930	499,967	1,108	2,869	3,903	507,847	6·2
1980	1,382,550	9,225	19,256	15,076	1,461,037	17·7
1990	1,615,845	11,576	24,283	25,696	1,722,850	21·0
2000	1,992,975	17,657	29,684	37,108	2,233,169	27·2

Of the total population in 2000, 1,119,031 were male, 1,514,471 were 18 years old or older and 1,970,344 were urban. In 2000 the Hispanic population was 201,559, up from 84,597 in 1990 (an increase of 138·3%).

The largest cities are Salt Lake City, with a population (census, 2000) of 181,743; West Valley City, 108,896; Provo, 105,166; Sandy City, 88,418; Orem, 84,324; Ogden, 77,226.

SOCIAL STATISTICS

Births in 2002 were 49,182 (21·2 per 1,000 population—the highest rate in any US state); deaths, 13,116 (5·7); 2001: infant mortality rate, 4·8 (per 1,000 live births). 2001: marriages, 23,200; divorces, 9,700. Fertility rate, 1998, 2·7 births per woman (the highest of any American state).

CLIMATE

Salt Lake City, Jan. 29°F (–1·7°C), July 77°F (25°C). Annual rainfall 16" (401 mm). Utah belongs to the Mountain States climate region (*see* UNITED STATES: Climate).

CONSTITUTION AND GOVERNMENT

Utah adopted its present constitution in 1896 (now with 61 amendments). The Legislature consists of a Senate (in part renewed every two years) of 29 members, elected for four years, and of a House of Representatives of 75 members elected for two years. It sits annually in Jan. The Governor is elected for four years. The constitution provides for the initiative and referendum.

For the 109th Congress, which convened in Jan. 2005, Utah sends three members to the House of Representatives. It is represented in the Senate by Orrin Hatch (R. 1977–2007) and Robert Bennett (R. 1993–2011).

The capital is Salt Lake City. There are 29 counties in the state.

RECENT ELECTIONS

In the 2004 presidential election Bush polled 663,742 votes (71·5% of the vote—Bush's best result); Kerry, 241,199; Nader, 11,305.

CURRENT ADMINISTRATION

Governor: Jon Huntsman, Jr (R.), 2005–09 (salary: $101,600).

Lieut.-Governor: Gary R. Herbert (R.), 2005–09 ($79,000).

Government Website: http://www.utah.gov

ECONOMY

Per capita income (2002) was $24,157.

Budget. In 2002 total state revenue was $8,468m. Total expenditure was $10,107m. (education, $4,327m.; public welfare, $1,581m.; highways, $856m.; hospitals, $494m.; government administration, $463m.) Outstanding debt, in 2002, $4,729m.

Performance. Gross State Product in 2002 was $72,974m., ranking Utah 33rd in the United States.

ENERGY AND NATURAL RESOURCES

Water. The total area covered by water is approximately 2,736 sq. miles.

Minerals. The principal minerals are: copper, gold, magnesium, petroleum, lead, silver and zinc. The state also has natural gas, clays, tungsten, molybdenum, uranium and phosphate rock. The value of domestic non-fuel mineral production in 2002 was $1,240m.

Agriculture. In 2002 Utah had 15,000 farms covering 11·6m. acres. Of the total surface area, 9% is severely eroded and only 9·4% is free from erosion; the balance is moderately eroded. In 2002 about 2·1m. acres were crop land, about 602,300 acres pasture and about 1·1m. acres had irrigation. In 2002 the average farm was of 773 acres and the average value per acre was $756.

Farm income, 2001, from crops, $263m. and from livestock, $853m. The net farm income in 2001 was $395m. The principal crops are: barley, wheat (spring and winter), oats, potatoes, hay (alfalfa, sweet clover and lespedeza) and maize. Livestock, 2002: cattle, 877,000; pigs, 670,000; sheep, 311,000; poultry, 3·4m.

Forestry. Forest area, 2002, was 15,676,000 acres and included 5,605,000 acres of national forest.

INDUSTRY

Leading manufactures by value added are primary metals, ordinances and transport, food, fabricated metals and machinery, and petroleum products. In 2001 Utah's 3,001 manufacturing establishments had 120,000 employees, earning $4,241m. Total value added by manufacturing in 2001 was $11,783m.

Labour. Utah's total non-agricultural employment in 2001 was 1,082,000. Employees by branch, 2001 (in 1,000): services, 315; wholesale and retail trade, 251; government, 190; manufacturing, 127. The unemployment rate in 2002 was 6·1%.

COMMUNICATIONS

Roads. In 2002 there were 42,611 miles of roads (34,637 miles rural) and 1,847,173 registered motor vehicles.

Rail. In 2004 Utah had approximately 1,400 miles of freight railroad track. There was no dedicated passenger rail trackage, although the Utah Transit Authority is preparing a commuter rail service.

Civil Aviation. There is an international airport at Salt Lake City. There were 8,704,131 passenger enplanements statewide in 2000.

SOCIAL INSTITUTIONS

Justice. In June 2002 there were 5,353 prison inmates. The death penalty is authorized; the last execution took place in 1999.

Religion. Latter-day Saints (Mormons) numbered 1,577,000 in 1998. World membership was 9,025,000. The President of the Mormon Church is Gordon B. Hinckley (born 1910). The Roman Catholic church and most Protestant denominations are represented.

Education. School attendance is compulsory for children from six to 18 years of age. There are 40 school districts. Teachers' salaries, 1998–99, averaged $36,030. There were 475,974 pupils and 24,514 teachers in public elementary and secondary schools in the same year. In 1999 education expenditure by state and local government was $2,432·3m.

In autumn 1999 there were 153,884 enrolled in colleges and universities. The University of Utah (1850) (25,788 students in 1999) is in Salt Lake City; the Utah State University (1890) (20,865) is in Logan; Weber State University, Ogden (15,444); Southern Utah University, Cedar City (6,025); The Mormon Church maintains the Brigham Young University at Provo (1875) with 29,217 students. Other colleges include: Westminster College, Salt Lake City (2,250); College of Eastern Utah, Price (2,688); Snow College, Ephraim (4,081); Dixie State College, St George (6,191); Utah Valley State College, Orem (20,062); Salt Lake Community College, Salt Lake City (21,273).

Health. In 2001 there were 42 community hospitals with 4,400 beds. A total of 203,000 patients were admitted during the year.

Welfare. Medicare enrolment in July 2002 totalled 214,881. In 2000 a total of 224,268 people in Utah received Medicaid. In Dec. 2003 there were 256,551

Old-Age, Survivors, and Disability Insurance (OASDI) beneficiaries. A total of 20,494 people were receiving payments under Temporary Assistance for Needy Families (TANF) in Sept. 2002.

FURTHER READING

Statistical information: Bureau of Economic and Business Research, Univ. of Utah, 401 Kendall D. Garff Bldg., Salt Lake City 84112. Publishes *Statistical Abstract of Utah.*
Utah Foundation. *Statistical Review of Government in Utah.* Salt Lake City, 1991

VERMONT

KEY HISTORICAL EVENTS

The original Indian hunting grounds of the Green Mountains and lakes was explored by the Frenchman Samuel de Champlain in 1609 who reached Lake Champlain on the northwest border. The first attempt at permanent settlement was also French, on Isle la Motte in 1666. In 1763 the British gained the area from the French by the Treaty of Paris. The Treaty, which also brought peace with the Indian allies of the French, opened the way for settlement, but in a mountain state transport was slow and difficult. Montpelier, the state capital from 1805, was chartered as a township site in 1781 to command the main pass through the Green Mountains.

During the War of Independence Vermont declared itself an independent state, to avoid being taken over by New Hampshire and New York. In 1791 it became the 14th state of the Union.

Most early settlers were New Englanders of British and Protestant descent. After 1812 a granite-quarrying industry grew around the town of Barre, attracting immigrant workers from Italy and Scandinavia. French Canadians also settled in Winooski. When textile and engineering industries developed in the 19th century these brought more European workers.

Vermont saw the only Civil War action north of Pennsylvania, when a Confederate raiding party attacked from Canada in 1864.

During the 20th century the textile and engineering industries have declined but paper and lumber industries flourish. Settlement is still mainly rural or in small towns, and farming is pastoral.

TERRITORY AND POPULATION

Vermont is bounded in the north by Canada, east by New Hampshire, south by Massachusetts and west by New York. Land area, 9,250 sq. miles (23,957 sq. km). Census population, 1 April 2000, 608,827, an increase of 8·2% since 1990. July 2004 estimate, 621,394.

Population at five census years was:

	White	*Black*	*Indian*	*Asiatic*	*Total*	*Per sq. mile*
1910	354,298	1,621	26	11	355,956	39·0
1930	358,966	568	36	41	359,611	38·8
1980	506,736	1,135	984	1,355	511,456	55·1
1990	555,088	1,951	1,696	3,215[1]	562,758	60·8
2000	589,208	3,063	2,420	5,358[1]	608,827	65·8

[1]Includes Pacific Islander.

Of the total population in 2000, 310,490 were female, 461,304 were 18 years old or older and 376,379 (61·8%) were rural (67·8% in 1990). Vermont still has the highest rural population percentage of any state in the USA. In 2000 the Hispanic population was 5,504, the lowest total of any state. However, this figure represents a rise of 50·3% compared to the 1990 census figure of 3,661. The largest cities are Burlington, with an estimated population (2002) of 38,885; Essex, 18,863; Rutland City, 17,309; Colchester, 17,245.

SOCIAL STATISTICS

Births, 2002, were 6,387 (10·4 per 1,000 population); deaths, 5,075 (8·2); infant deaths, 2001, 5·5 per 1,000 population; marriages, 2002, 6,011; civil unions, 1,707; divorces, 2,653.

CLIMATE

Burlington, Jan. 17°F (–8·3°C), July 70°F (21·1°C). Annual rainfall 33" (820 mm). Vermont belongs to the New England climate zone (*see* UNITED STATES: Climate).

CONSTITUTION AND GOVERNMENT

The constitution was adopted in 1793 and has since been amended. Amendments are proposed by two-thirds vote of the Senate every four years, and must be accepted by two sessions of the legislature; they are then submitted to popular vote. The state Legislature, consisting of a Senate of 30 members and a House of Representatives of 150 members (both elected for two years), meets in Jan. every year. The Governor and Lieut.-Governor are elected for two years. Electors are all citizens who possess certain residential qualifications and have taken the freeman's oath set forth in the constitution.

For the 109th Congress, which convened in Jan. 2005, Vermont sends one member to the House of Representatives. It is represented in the Senate by Patrick Leahy (D. 1975–2011) and Jim Jeffords (R. 1989–2001, ind. 2001–07).

The capital is Montpelier (estimated population of 8,028 in 2002). There are 14 counties and 251 cities, towns and other administrative divisions.

RECENT ELECTIONS

In the 2004 presidential election Kerry polled 184,067 votes; Bush, 121,180; Nader, 4,494.

CURRENT ADMINISTRATION

Governor: James Douglas (R.), 2005–07 (salary: $133,166).

Lieut.-Governor: Brian E. Dubie (R.), 2005–07 ($56,527).

Secretary of State: Deborah L. Markowitz (D.), 2005–07 ($84,439).

Government Website: http://vermont.gov

ECONOMY

Per capita income (2002) was $29,464.

Budget. In fiscal year 2004 total state revenue (prior to budget adjustment) was $3,574m. Major appropriations: education, $1,388m.; human services, $1,280m.; transportation, $354m.; protection, $188m. Outstanding debt in 2003 was $448m.

Performance. Gross State Product was $19,604m. in 2002, ranking Vermont 51st in the United States.

Banking and Finance. In 2003 there were 19 banking institutions domiciled in Vermont, and 16 out-of-state banks operating.

ENERGY AND NATURAL RESOURCES

Water. The total area covered by water is approximately 366 sq. miles. There are 46 utility-owned hydro-sites and 35 independently owned sites providing about 10% of Vermont's energy.

Minerals. Stone, chiefly granite, marble and slate, is the leading mineral produced in Vermont, contributing about 60% of the total value of mineral products. Other products include asbestos, talc, sand and gravel. Value of domestic non-fuel mineral products, 2002, $71m.

Agriculture. Agriculture is the most important industry. In 2002 the state had 6,600 farms covering 1·34m. acres; the average farm was of 203 acres and the average value per acre of land and buildings was $2,051. In 2001 farm income from crops, $67m.; from livestock and products, $490m. The net farm income in 2001 was $136m. The 1,415 dairy farms produced about 2·6bn. lb of milk in 2002. The chief agricultural crops are hay, apples and silage. In 2002 Vermont had 255,000 cattle and calves and 2,000 hogs and pigs.

Forestry. The state is 78% forest, with 17% in public ownership. In 2002 Vermont had 4,618,000 acres of forested land with 337,000 acres of national forest. State-owned forests, parks, fish and game areas (2000), 295,000 acres; municipally owned, 38,500 acres. In 2002 the harvest was 222·4m. bd ft and 171,395 cords of pulpwood.

INDUSTRY

In 2001 the state's 1,180 manufacturing establishments had 48,000 employees, earning $1,825m. Total value added by manufacturing in 2000 was $5,140m.

Labour. In 2003 service industries, including trade, employed 188,760; government, 49,757; manufacturing, 40,697; construction, 14,894. The unemployment rate in 2003 was 3·3%.

COMMUNICATIONS

Roads. In 2002 there were 14,292 miles of roads comprising 1,383 miles of urban road and 12,909 miles of rural road. All motor vehicle registrations totalled 690,091.

Rail. There were, in 2001, 747 miles of railway, 391 miles of which are state owned.

Civil Aviation. There were 17 airports in 2003, of which ten were state operated, two municipally owned and five private. Some are only open in summer. There were 550,050 passenger enplanements statewide in 2003.

Telecommunications. In 2003 there were 12 telephone companies.

SOCIAL INSTITUTIONS

Justice. Prisons and centres had on average, in 2004, 1,875 inmates (including those incarcerated in Virginia for cost-cutting reasons). The death penalty was officially abolished in 1987 but effectively in 1964.

Religion. The principal denominations are Roman Catholic, United Church of Christ, United Methodist, Protestant Episcopal, Baptist and Unitarian–Universalist.

Education. School attendance during the full school term is compulsory for children from seven to 16 years of age, unless they have completed the 10th grade or undergo approved home instruction. In 2003–04 the public elementary and secondary schools had 99,104 pupils and 9,004 teachers. Average teacher's salary was $43,009. State and local governments expenditure on public schools, $944m.

In 2003–04 the University of Vermont (1791), in Burlington, had 10,940 students; Norwich University (1834, founded as the American Literary, Scientific and Military Academy in 1819), had 2,183; St Michael's College (1904), 1,945 (full time undergraduates only); there are four other state colleges and 15 other private schools of higher education.

Health. In 2004 the state had 19 hospitals and health centres.

Welfare. In 2003 Social Services provided approximately $2·4m. to 500 families and 12,600 individuals.

CULTURE

Broadcasting. In 2004 there were 56 radio stations, 11 television stations and 27 cable TV systems.

Press. There were ten dailies and 44 weekly newspapers in 2004.

FURTHER READING

Statistical information: Office of Policy Research and Coordination, Montpelier 05602
Legislative Directory. Secretary of State, Montpelier. Biennial
Vermont Annual Financial Report. Auditor of Accounts, Montpelier. Annual
Vermont Atlas and Gazetteer, Rev. ed., Freeport, 1983
Vermont Year-Book, formerly *Walton's Register.* Chester. Annual

State Library: Vermont Dept. of Libraries, Montpelier.

VIRGINIA

KEY HISTORICAL EVENTS

In 1607 a British colony was founded at Jamestown, on a peninsula in the James River, to grow tobacco. The area was marshy and unhealthy but the colony survived and in 1619 introduced a form of representative government. The tobacco plantations expanded and African slaves were imported. Jamestown was later abandoned, but tobacco-growing continued and spread through the eastern part of the territory.

In 1624 control of the colony passed from the Virginia Company of London to the Crown. Growth was rapid during the 17th and 18th centuries. The movement for American independence was strong in Virginia; George Washington and Thomas Jefferson were both Virginians, and crucial battles of the War of Independence were fought there.

When the Union was formed, Virginia became one of the original states, but with reservations regarding the constitution because of its attachment to slave-owning. In 1831 there was a slave rebellion. The tobacco plantations began to decline, and plantation owners turned to the breeding of slaves. While the eastern plantation lands seceded from the Union in 1861, the small farmers and miners of the western hills refused to secede and remained in the Union as West Virginia.

Richmond, the capital, became the capital of the Confederacy. Much of the Civil War's decisive conflict took place in Virginia, with considerable damage to the economy. After the war the position of the black population was little improved. Blacks remained without political or civil rights until the 1960s.

TERRITORY AND POPULATION

Virginia is bounded northwest by West Virginia, northeast by Maryland and the District of Columbia, east by the Atlantic, south by North Carolina and Tennessee and west by Kentucky. Land area, 39,594 sq. miles (102,548 sq. km). Census population, 1 April 2000, 7,078,515, an increase of 14·4% since 1990. July 2004 estimate, 7,459,827.

Population for five federal census years was:

	White	*Black*	*Indian*	*Asian/Other*	*Total*	*Per sq. mile*
1910	1,389,809	671,096	539	168	2,061,612	51·2
1930	1,770,441	650,165	779	466	2,421,851	60·7
			All others			
1980	4,230,000	1,008,311	108,517		5,346,818	134·7
1990	4,791,739	1,162,994	15,282	217,343	6,187,358	155·9
2000	5,120,110	1,390,293	21,172	546,940	7,078,515	178·8

Of the total population in 2000, 3,606,620 were female, 5,340,253 were 18 years old or older and 5,169,955 were urban. In 2000 the Hispanic population was 329,540, up from 160,288 in 1990 (an increase of 105·6%).

The population (2003 estimates) of the principal cities was: Virginia Beach, 439,467; Norfolk, 241,727; Chesapeake, 210,834; Richmond, 194,729; Arlington CDP, 187,873; Newport News, 181,647; Hampton, 146,878; Alexandria, 128,923.

SOCIAL STATISTICS

In 2002 there were 99,672 births (13·7 per 1,000 population); 57,196 deaths (7·8); infant deaths, 2001, 7·6 per 1,000 live births; 2001: 63,400 marriages (9·0 per 1,000 population) and 30,200 divorces (4·3).

CLIMATE

Average temperatures in Jan. are 41°F in the Tidewater coastal area and 32°F in the Blue Ridge mountains; July averages, 78°F and 68°F respectively. Precipitation averages 36" in the Shenandoah valley and 44" in the south. Snowfall is 5–10" in the Tidewater and 25–30" in the western mountains. Norfolk, Jan. 41°F (5°C), July 79°F (26·1°C). Annual rainfall 46" (1,145 mm). Virginia belongs to the Atlantic Coast climate zone (*see* UNITED STATES: Climate).

CONSTITUTION AND GOVERNMENT

The present constitution became effective in 1971. The General Assembly consists of a Senate of 40 members, elected for four years, and a House of Delegates of 100 members, elected for two years. It sits annually in Jan. The Governor and Lieut.-Governor are elected for four years.

For the 109th Congress, which convened in Jan. 2005, Virginia sends 11 members to the House of Representatives. It is represented in the Senate by John Warner (R. 1979–2009) and George Allen (R. 2001–07).

The state capital is Richmond; the state contains 95 counties and 40 independent cities.

RECENT ELECTIONS

In the 2004 presidential election Bush polled 1,716,959 votes; Kerry, 1,454,742; Badnarik, 11,032.

CURRENT ADMINISTRATION

Governor: Mark R. Warner (D.), 2002–06 (salary: $124,855).

Lieut.-Governor: Timothy M. Kaine (D.), 2002–06 ($36,321).

Secretary of the Commonwealth: Anita A. Rimler (D.), appointed Jan. 2002 ($128,479).

Government Website: http://www.virginia.gov

ECONOMY

Per capita personal income (2002) was $32,676.

Budget. In 2002 total state revenue was $23,577m. Total expenditure was $28,044m. (education, $9,848m.; public welfare, $4,200m.; highways, $2,823m.; hospitals, $1,718m.; correction, $1,243m.) Outstanding debt, in 2002, $13,785m.

Performance. Gross State Product in 2002 was $287,589m., ranking Virginia 13th in the United States.

ENERGY AND NATURAL RESOURCES

Water. The total area covered by water is approximately 2,729 sq. miles.

Minerals. Coal is the most important mineral, with output (2003) of 31,596,000 short tons. Lead and zinc ores, stone, sand and gravel, lime and titanium ore are also produced. Total domestic non-fuel mineral output was valued at $697m. in 2002.

Agriculture. In 2003 there were 47,500 farms with an area of 8·6m. acres; the average farm had 181 acres, and the average value per acre was $2,700. Farm income, 2002, from crops, $718m.; and from livestock and livestock products, $1,642m. The net farm income in 2002 was $504m. The chief crops are tobacco, soybeans, peanuts, winter wheat, maize, tomatoes, apples, potatoes and sweet potatoes. Livestock, 2002: cattle and calves, 1·62m.; milch cows, 115,000; sheep and lambs, 72,000; hogs and pigs, 409,300; turkeys, 20m.; broilers, 266·1m.

Forestry. Forests covered 16,074,000 acres in 2002 (63·4% of the total land area), including 1,626,000 acres of national forest.

Fisheries. Commercial catch (2002) totalled 442·5m. lb of fish, worth $123·3m.

INDUSTRY

The manufacture of cigars and cigarettes, of rayon and allied products, and the building of ships lead in value of products. In 2001 the state's 5,804 manufacturing establishments had 344,000 employees, earning $12,574m. Total value added by manufacturing in 2001 was $53,043m.

Labour. In 2004 Virginia's total non-agricultural employment was 3,595,100. Employees by branch, 2001 (in 1,000): services, 1,155; wholesale and retail trade, 766; government, 631; manufacturing, 372. The unemployment rate in 2002 was 4·1%.

COMMUNICATIONS

Roads. In 2002 there were 70,950 miles of roads (51,759 miles rural) and 6,272,836 registered motor vehicles.

Rail. In 2003 there were 3,399 miles of track including commuter services to Washington, D.C.

Civil Aviation. There are international airports at Norfolk, Dulles, Richmond and Newport News. There were 2,902,086 passenger enplanements statewide in 2000.

SOCIAL INSTITUTIONS

Justice. In June 2003 there were 31,101 prison inmates. The death penalty is authorized. Between 1977 and 2004 there were 95 executions in Virginia, after Texas the most of any state. There were five executions in 2004.

Religion. The principal churches are the Baptist, Methodist, Protestant Episcopal, Roman Catholic and Presbyterian.

Education. Elementary and secondary instruction is free, and for ages 6–17 attendance is compulsory.

In 2000–01 there were 135 school districts. In 2002–03 there were 723,000 pupils in primary schools (55,000 teaching positions) and 422,000 pupils in secondary schools (39,000 teaching positions). Average annual salaries in 2002–03 for elementary teaching positions were $41,839 and for secondary teaching positions $43,850. Total expenditure on education, 2003–04, was $9,454m.

In 2001–02 there were 100 degree-granting education institutions (61 private) including:

Founded	*Name and place of college*	*Staff 1994–95*	*Students 1994*
1693	College of William and Mary, Williamsburg (State)	479	7,547
1749	Washington and Lee University, Lexington	166	1,990
1776	Hampden-Sydney College, Hampden-Sydney (Pres.)	84	970
1819	University of Virginia, Charlottesville (State)	987	21,421
1832	Randolph-Macon College, Ashland (Methodist)	79	1,093
1832	University of Richmond, Richmond (Baptist)	228	4,258
1838	Virginia Commonwealth University, Richmond	777	21,523
1839	Virginia Military Institute Lexington (State)	97	1,179
1865	Virginia Union University, Richmond	83	1,525
1868	Hampton University	303	5,769
1872	Virginia Polytechnic Institute and State University	1,466	25,842
1882	Virginia State University, Petersburg	168	4,007
1908	James Madison University, Harrisonburg	520	11,680
1910	Radford University (State)	394	9,105
1930	Old Dominion University, Norfolk	634	16,490
1956	George Mason University (State)	677	21,774

Health. In 2003 there were 86 community hospitals with 17,241 beds. A total of 746,686 patients were admitted during the year.

Welfare. Medicare enrolment in July 2002 totalled 926,579. In 2000 a total of 627,214 people in Virginia received Medicaid. In Dec. 2003 there were 1,093,695 Old-Age, Survivors, and Disability Insurance (OASDI) beneficiaries. A total of 68,403 people were receiving payments under Temporary Assistance for Needy Families (TANF) in Sept. 2002.

CULTURE

Tourism. Tourists spent over $14bn. in 2002, contributing 4·9% to Gross State Product.

FURTHER READING

Statistical information: Cooper Center for Public Service, Univ. of Virginia, 918 Emmet St. N., Suite 300, Charlottesville 22903-4832. Publishes *Virginia Statistical Abstract.—Population Estimates of Virginia Cities and Counties.*

Rubin, L. D. Jr., *Virginia: a Bicentennial History.* Norris, 1977

Salmon, E. J. and Campbell Jr., E. D. C., *The Hornbook of Virginia History: A Ready-Reference Guide the Old Dominion's People, Places, and Past.* Library of Virginia, Richmond, 1994

State Library: Library of Virginia, Richmond 23219.

WASHINGTON STATE

KEY HISTORICAL EVENTS

The strongest Indian tribes in the 18th century were Chinook, Nez Percé, Salish and Yakima. The area was designated by European colonizers as part of the Oregon Country. Between 1775 and 1800 it had been claimed by explorers for Spain, Britain and the USA; the dispute between the two latter nations was not settled until 1846.

The first small white settlements were Indian missions and fur-trading posts. In the 1840s American settlers began to push westwards along the Oregon Trail, making a speedy solution of the dispute with Britain necessary. When this was achieved the whole area was organized as the Oregon Territory in 1848, and Washington was made a separate Territory in 1853.

Apart from trapping and fishing, the important industry was logging, mainly to supply building timbers to the new settlements of California. After 1870 the westward extension of railways helped to stimulate settlement. Statehood was granted in 1889. The early population was composed mainly of Americans from neighbouring states to the east, and Canadians. Scandinavian immigrants followed. Seattle, the chief city, was laid out in 1853 as a saw-milling town and named after the Indian chief who had ceded the land and befriended the settlers. It grew as a port during the Alaskan and Yukon gold-rushes of the 1890s. The economy thrived on exploiting the Columbia River for hydro-electric power.

TERRITORY AND POPULATION

Washington is bounded north by Canada, east by Idaho, south by Oregon with the Columbia River forming most of the boundary, and west by the Pacific. Land area, 66,544 sq. miles (172,348 sq. km). Lands owned by the federal government, 1993, were 12·7m. acres or 29·8% of the total area. Census population, 1 April 2000, 5,894,121, an increase of 21·1% since 1990. July 2004 estimate, 6,203,788.

Population in five federal census years was:

	White	*Black*	*American Indian*	*Asian/Other*	*Total*	*Per sq. mile*
1910	1,109,111	6,058	10,997	15,824	1,141,990	17·1
1930	1,521,661	6,840	11,253	23,642	1,563,396	23·3
1980	3,779,170	105,574	60,804	186,608	4,132,156	62·1
1990	4,308,937	149,801	81,483	326,471	4,866,692	73·1
2000	4,821,823	190,267	93,301	788,730	5,894,121	88·6

Of the total population in 2000, 2,959,821 were female, 4,380,278 were 18 years old or older and 4,831,106 were urban. In 2000 the Hispanic population was 441,509, up from 214,570 in 1990 (a rise of 105·8%).

There are 27 Indian reservations. Indian reservations in 1990 covered 2,718,516 acres, of which 2,250,731 acres were tribal lands.

Leading cities are Seattle, with a population in 2000 of 563,374; Spokane, 195,629; Tacoma, 193,556; Vancouver, 143,560; Bellevue, 109,569. Others: Everett, 91,488; Federal Way, 83,259; Kent, 79,524; Yakima, 71,845; Bellingham, 67,171; Lakewood, 58,211; Kennewick, 54,693; Shoreline, 53,025; Renton, 50,052. The Seattle–Tacoma–Bremerton metropolitan area had a 2000 census population of 3,554,760.

SOCIAL STATISTICS

Births, 2002, were 79,028 (13·0 per 1,000); deaths, 45,338 (7·5 per 1,000); infant mortality rate, 2001, 5·8 (per 1,000 live births); marriages, 2002, 39,518 (6·5 per 1,000 population); divorces, 27,205 (4·5).

CLIMATE

Seattle, Jan. 40°F (4·4°C), July 63°F (17·2°C). Annual rainfall 34" (848 mm). Spokane, Jan. 27°F (–2·8°C), July 70°F (21·1°C). Annual rainfall 14" (350 mm). Washington belongs to the Pacific Coast climate zone (*see* UNITED STATES: Climate).

CONSTITUTION AND GOVERNMENT

The constitution, adopted in 1889, has had 96 amendments. The Legislature consists of a Senate of 49 members elected for four years, half their number retiring every two years, and a House of Representatives of 98 members, elected for two years. The Governor and Lieut.-Governor are elected for four years.

For the 109th Congress, which convened in Jan. 2005, Washington sends nine members to the House of Representatives. It is represented in the Senate by Patty Murray (D. 1993–2011) and Maria Cantwell (D. 2001–07).

The capital is Olympia. The state contains 39 counties.

RECENT ELECTIONS

In the 2004 presidential election Kerry polled 1,510,201 votes; Bush, 1,304,894; Nader, 23,283.

CURRENT ADMINISTRATION

Governor: Christine Gregoire (D.), 2005–09 (salary: $145,132).
Lieut.-Governor: Brad Owen (D.), 2005–09 ($75,865).
Secretary of State: Sam Reed (R.), 2005–09 ($101,702).

Government Website: http://access.wa.gov

ECONOMY

Per capita personal income (2002) was $32,661.

Budget. In 2002 total state revenue was $23,813m. Total expenditure was $30,378m. (education, $10,298m.; public welfare, $6,174m.; highways, $1,795m.; health, $1,397m.; hospitals, $917m.) Outstanding debt, in 2002, $13,552m.

Performance. In 2002 Gross State Product was $232,940m., ranking Washington 14th in the United States.

ENERGY AND NATURAL RESOURCES

Water. The total area covered by water is approximately 4,055 sq. miles.

Minerals. Mining and quarrying are not as important as forestry, agriculture or manufacturing. Total value of non-fuel mineral production in 2002 was $450m.

Agriculture. Agriculture is constantly growing in value because of more intensive and diversified farming, and because of the 1m.-acre Columbia Basin Irrigation Project.

In 2002 there were 39,000 farms with an acreage of 15·7m.; the average farm was 403 acres. Average value of farmland and buildings per acre in 2002 was $1,486. Apples, milk, wheat, potatoes, and cattle and calves are the top five commodities. In 2002 livestock included 248,700 beef cows, 246,800 milch cows, and 58,500 sheep and lambs. Hogs and pigs as of 2002 totalled 31,000 head.

Farm income, (2001): from crops, $3,464m.; livestock and livestock products, $1,728m. The net farm income in 2001 was $621m.

Forestry. Forests covered 21·8m. acres in 2002, of which 7·9m. acres were national forest. In 2001 timber harvested was an estimated 3,716m. bd ft. Production of wood and bark residues, 2000, was 5,542,000 tons.

Fisheries. Salmon and shellfish are important; total commercial catch, 2002, was 362·0m. lb, and was worth an estimated $142·5m.

INDUSTRY

Principal manufactures are aircraft, pulp and paper, lumber and plywood, aluminium, processed fruit and vegetables. In 2001 the state's 7,565 manufacturing establishments had 316,000 employees, earning $14,458m. Total value added by manufacturing in 2001 was $38,193m.

Labour. In 2001 total non-agricultural employment was 2,698,000. Employees by branch, 2001 (in 1,000): services, 774; wholesale and retail trade, 635; government, 506; manufacturing, 338. The unemployment rate in 2002 was 7·3%.

COMMUNICATIONS

Roads. In 2002 there were 82,181 miles of roads comprising 19,173 miles of urban road and 63,008 miles of rural road. There were 5,336,326 registered motor vehicles.

Rail. In 2000 there were 3,128 route miles.

Civil Aviation. There are international airports at Seattle/Tacoma, Spokane and Boeing Field. There were 15,245,073 passenger enplanements statewide in 2000.

SOCIAL INSTITUTIONS

Justice. In June 2002 there were 15,829 prison inmates. There was one execution in 2001 but none since then.

Religion. Religious faiths represented include the Roman Catholic, United Methodist, Lutheran, Presbyterian and Episcopalian. There were 223,000 Latter-day Saints (Mormons) in 1998.

Education. Education is given free to all children between the ages of five and 21 years, and is compulsory for children from eight to 15 years of age. In Oct. 2003 there were 1,014,142 pupils in public elementary and secondary schools; and 76,845 pupils in private schools. In Oct. 2002 there were 52,888 classroom teachers; average salary, $47,642.

The University of Washington, founded 1861, at Seattle, had, autumn 2002, 39,215 students; and Washington State University at Pullman, founded 1890, for science and agriculture, had 22,184 students. Eastern Washington University had 9,178; Central Washington University, 8,768; The Evergreen State College, 4,318; Western Washington University, 12,493. All counts are state-funded enrolment students. Community colleges had (2002) a total of 191,554 state-funded and excess enrolment students.

Health. In 2001 there were 84 community hospitals with 11,300 beds. A total of 523,000 patients were admitted during the year.

Welfare. Medicare enrolment in July 2002 totalled 759,088. In 2000 a total of 895,279 people in Washington received Medicaid. In Dec. 2003 there were 890,466 Old-Age, Survivors, and Disability Insurance (OASDI) beneficiaries. A total of 130,497 people were receiving payments under Temporary Assistance for Needy Families (TANF) in Sept. 2002.

FURTHER READING

Statistical information: State Office of Financial Management, POB 43113, Olympia 98504-3113. Publishes *Washington State Data Book*

Dodds, G. B., *American North-West: a History of Oregon and Washington.* Arlington (Ill), 1986

WEST VIRGINIA

KEY HISTORICAL EVENTS

In 1861 the state of Virginia seceded from the Union over the issue of slave-owning. The 40 western counties of the state were composed of hilly country, settled by miners and small farmers who were not slave-owners, and these counties ratified an ordinance providing for the creation of a new state that same year. On 20 June 1863 West Virginia became the 35th state of the Union.

The capital, Charleston, was an 18th-century fortified post on the early westward migration routes across the Appalachians. In 1795 local brine wells were tapped and the city grew as a salt town. Coal, oil, natural gas and a variety of salt brines were all found in due course. Huntington, the next largest town, developed as a railway terminus serving the same industrial area, and also providing transport on the Ohio river. Wheeling, the original state capital, was a well established, cosmopolitan city when it hosted the statehood meetings in 1861, located on the major transportation routes of the Ohio River, Baltimore and Ohio Railroad and the National Road.

Three-quarters of the state is forest and settlement has been concentrated in the mineral-bearing Kanawha valley, along the Ohio river and in the industrial Monongahela valley of the north. More than half of the population is still classified as rural. The traditional small firms and small hill-mines, however, support few, and the majority of rural dwellers commute to industrial employment.

TERRITORY AND POPULATION

West Virginia is bounded in the north by Pennsylvania and Maryland, east and south by Virginia, southwest by the Big Sandy River (forming the boundary with Kentucky) and west by the Ohio River (forming the boundary with Ohio). Land area, 24,077 sq. miles (62,359 sq. km). Census population, 1 April 2000, 1,808,344, an increase of 0·8% since 1990. July 2004 estimate, 1,815,354.

Population in five federal census years was:

	White	*Black*	*American Indian*	*Asiatic*	*Total*	*Per sq. mile*
1910	1,156,817	64,173	36	93	1,221,119	50·8
1960	1,770,133	89,378	181	419	1,860,421	77·3
1980	1,874,751	65,051	1,610	5,194	1,949,644	80·3
1990	1,725,523	56,295	2,458	7,459	1,793,477	74·0
2000	1,718,777	57,232	3,606	9,834	1,808,344	75·1

Of the total population in 2000, 929,174 were female, 1,405,951 were 18 years old or older and 975,564 (53·9%) were rural. In 2000 the Hispanic population was 12,279, up from 8,489 in 1990 (an increase of 44·6%).

The 2000 census population of the principal cities was: Charleston, 53,421; Huntington, 51,475. Others: Parkersburg, 33,099; Wheeling, 31,419; Morgantown, 26,809; Weirton, 20,411; Fairmont, 19,097; Beckley, 17,254; Clarksburg, 16,743.

SOCIAL STATISTICS

Statistics 2002: births, 20,712 (11·5 per 1,000 population); deaths, 21,016 (11·7—the highest rate in any US state); 2001: infant deaths, 7·2 per 1,000 live births. 2001: marriages, 14,200 (7·9 per 1,000 population); divorces, 9,300 (5·2). West Virginia is the only state in which the annual number of deaths exceeds births.

CLIMATE

Charleston, Jan. 34°F (1·1°C), July 76°F (24·4°C). Annual rainfall 40" (1,010 mm). West Virginia belongs to the Appalachian Mountains climate zone (*see* UNITED STATES: Climate).

CONSTITUTION AND GOVERNMENT

The present constitution was adopted in 1872; it has had 70 amendments. The Legislature consists of the Senate of 34 members elected for a term of four years, one-half being elected biennially, and the House of Delegates of 100 members, elected biennially. The Governor is elected for four years and may serve one successive term.

For the 109th Congress, which convened in Jan. 2005, West Virginia sends three members to the Houseof Representatives. It is represented in the Senate by Robert Byrd (D. 1959–2007) and Jay Rockefeller (D. 1985–2009).

The state capital is Charleston. There are 55 counties.

RECENT ELECTIONS

In the 2004 presidential election Bush polled 423,778 votes; Kerry, 326,541; Nader, 4,063.

CURRENT ADMINISTRATION

Governor: Joe Manchin, III (D.), 2005–09 (salary: $95,000).

Senate President–Lieut. Governor: Earl Ray Tomblin (D.), 2005–09.

Secretary of State: Betty Ireland (R.), 2005–09 ($70,000).

Government Website: http://www.state.wv.us

ECONOMY

Per capita personal income (2002) was $23,628.

Budget. Total revenues in 2002 were $9,130m. Total expenditures were $9,409m.; major areas of expenditure were: education, $2,495m.; public welfare, $2,136m.; highways, $986m.; government administration, $429m.; health, $210m. Outstanding debt in 2002, $4,537m.

Performance. Gross State Product in 2002 was $45,518m., ranking West Virginia 41st in the United States.

Banking and Finance. There were 56 state banks and 26 national banks with a total of $13,844m. in deposits in 2000. There were also eight federal savings and loans and federal savings banks; total deposits in 1997 were $887m.

ENERGY AND NATURAL RESOURCES

Oil and Gas. Petroleum output (2000), 1,267m. bbls.; natural gas production (2000), 233bn. cu. ft.

Water. The total area covered by water is approximately 145 sq. miles.

Minerals. 38% of the state is underlain with mineable coal; 169·3m. short tons of coal were produced in 2000. Salt, sand and gravel, sandstone and limestone are also produced. The total value of non-fuel mineral production in 2002 was $173m.

Agriculture. In 2002 the state had 20,500 farms with an area of 3·6m. acres; average size of farm was 176 acres, valued at $1,315 per acre. Livestock farming predominates.

Cash income, 2001, from crops was $59m.; from livestock and products, $348m. The net farm income in 2001 was $48m. Main crops harvested: hay (1·31m. tons); all corn (1·3m. bu.); tobacco (1·8m. lb). Area of main crops: hay, 0·61m. acres; corn, 55,000 acres. Apples (90m. lb) and peaches (19·0m. lb) are important fruit crops.

Livestock on farms, 2000, included 400,000 cattle, of which 17,000 were milch cows; sheep, 35,000; hogs, 10,000; chickens, 1·86m. excluding broilers. Production included 91·3m broilers; 20·75m. dozen eggs; 4·1m. turkeys.

Forestry. Forests covered 12,108,000 acres in 2002, with 1,002,000 acres of national forest; 78·5% of the state is woodland.

Fisheries. In 2000, nine state fish hatcheries and one federal fish hatchery sold 363,000 lb trout and stocked 815,000 lb of trout, in addition to 2·4m. fry, 507,162 fingerlings and 5,000 adults of other types of fish.

INDUSTRY

In Oct. 2001, 2,094 manufactures had 76,800 production workers. Leading manufactures are primary and fabricated metals, glass, chemicals, wood products, textiles and apparel, machinery, plastics, speciality chemicals, aerospace, electronics, medical and related technologies and industrial products recycling.

Labour. In Oct. 2001 non-agricultural employment was 741,500 of whom 162,800 were in trade, 142,000 in government and 234,300 in service industries. The state unemployment rate in 2002 was 6·1%.

INTERNATIONAL TRADE

Imports and Exports. The state's major export markets are the EU and Canada, with coal being a major export commodity. West Virginia staffs trade offices in Nagoya, Japan; Taipei, Taiwan; and Munich, Germany.

COMMUNICATIONS

Roads. In 2001 there were 37,370 miles of roads (34,610 miles rural). There were 1,462,983 registered motor vehicles in 2002.

Rail. In 2001 the state had 2,659 miles of railway.

Civil Aviation. There were 37 public airports in 2001. There were 163,825 passenger enplanements statewide in 2000.

Shipping. There are some 420·5 miles of navigable rivers.

Postal Services. In 2001 there were 1,012 postal facilities.

SOCIAL INSTITUTIONS

Justice. The state court system consists of a Supreme Court, 31 circuit courts, and magistrate courts in each county. The Supreme Court of Appeals, exercising original and appellate jurisdiction, has five members elected by the people for 12-year terms. Each circuit court has from one to seven judges (as determined by the Legislature on the basis of population and case-load) chosen by the voters within each circuit for eight-year terms.

There are 11 penal and correctional institutions which had, in Dec. 2001, 3,448 inmates. There were also (Dec. 2001) eight regional jails housing 2,139 county, state and federal inmates, and seven juvenile facilities housing 271 juveniles. Capital punishment was abolished in 1965. The last execution was in 1959.

Religion. Chief denominations in 2001 were: United Methodists (115,062 members), Roman Catholics (97,232), Baptists American (94,000) and Southern (33,000).

Education. Public school education is free for all from five to 21 years of age, and school attendance is compulsory for all between the ages of seven and 16 (school term, 200 days—180–185 days of actual teaching). The public schools are non-sectarian. In 2000–01 public elementary and secondary schools had 285,785 pupils and 24,507 classroom teachers. Average salary of teachers was $35,888. Total 2000–01 education expenditures, including higher education, $2,486m.

Leading institutions of higher education in the autumn of 2000:

Founded		*Full-time students*
1837	Marshall University, Huntington	15,640[1]
1837	West Liberty State College, West Liberty	2,606
1867	Fairmont State College, Fairmont	6,496
1868	West Virginia University, Morgantown	21,987
1872	Concord College, Athens	3,050
1872	Glenville State College, Glenville	2,198
1872	Shepherd College, Shepherdstown	4,703
1891	West Virginia State College, Institute	4,828
1895	West Virginia Univ. Inst. of Technology, Montgomery	2,326
1895	Bluefield State College, Bluefield	2,648
1901	Potomac State College of West Virginia Univ., Keyser	1,111
1961	West Virginia Univ. at Parkersburg, Parkersburg	3,271
1976	School of Osteopathic Medicine, Lewisburg	280

[1]Includes Marshall Univ. Graduate College, South Charleston, founded in 1972.

In addition to the universities and state-supported schools, there are two community colleges (4,911 students in 2000), ten denominational and private institutions of higher education (9,808 students in 1999) and 11 business colleges (2001).

Health. In Dec. 2001 the state had 68 licensed hospitals and 64 licensed personal care homes, 141 skilled-nursing homes and five mental hospitals.

Welfare. The Department of Health Human Resources, originating in the 1930s as the Department of Public Assistance, is both state and federally financed. Medicare enrolment in July 2002 totalled 343,210. In 2000 a total of 335,014 people in West Virginia received Medicaid. In Dec. 2003 there were 405,444 Old-Age, Survivors, and Disability Insurance (OASDI) beneficiaries. A total of 39,527 people were receiving payments under Temporary Assistance for Needy Families (TANF) in Sept. 2002.

CULTURE

Broadcasting. In 2001 there were 156 commercial, 14 college and 14 public radio stations. Television stations numbered 14 commercial and three public.

Press. In 2001 daily newspapers numbered 19, weekly and college newspapers 78.

Tourism. There are 35 state parks, nine state forests, 58 wildlife management areas and two state trails. Visitors are attracted to the area by whitewater rafting, hiking, skiing and biking and the winter outdoor light display at Oglebay Park in Wheeling.

FURTHER READING

West Virginia Blue Book. Legislature, Charleston. Annual, since 1916
Statistical Handbook, 2001. West Virginia Research League, Charleston, 2001
Lewis, R. L. and Hennen, J. C., *West Virginia History: Critical Essays on the Literature.* Kendall/Hunt Publishing, Dubuque, IA, 1993
Rice, O. K., *West Virginia: A History.* 2nd ed. Univ. Press of Kentucky, Lexington, 1994
State Library: Archives and History, Division of Culture and History, Charleston.

WISCONSIN

KEY HISTORICAL EVENTS

The French were the first European explorers of the territory; Jean Nicolet landed at Green Bay in 1634, a mission was founded in 1671 and a permanent settlement at Green Bay followed. In 1763 French claims were surrendered to Britain. In 1783 Britain ceded them to the USA, which designated the Northwest Territory, of which Wisconsin was part. In 1836 a separate Territory of Wisconsin was organized, including the present Iowa, Minnesota and parts of the Dakotas.

Territorial organization was a great stimulus to settlement. In 1836 James Duane Doty founded the town site of Madison and successfully pressed its claim to be the capital of the Territory even before it was inhabited. In 1848 Wisconsin became a state, with its present boundaries.

The city of Milwaukee was founded, on Lake Michigan, when Indian tribes gave up their claims to the land in 1831–33. It grew rapidly as a port and industrial town, attracting Germans in the 1840s, Poles and Italians 50 years later. The Lake Michigan shore was developed as an industrial area; the rest of the south proved suitable for dairy farming; the north, mainly forests and lakes, has remained sparsely settled except for tourist bases.

There are 11 Indian reservations where more than 15,500 of Wisconsin's 47,000 Indians live. Since the Second World War there has been black immigration from the southern states to the industrial lake-shore cities.

TERRITORY AND POPULATION

Wisconsin is bounded north by Lake Superior and the Upper Peninsula of Michigan, east by Lake Michigan, south by Illinois, and west by Iowa and Minnesota, with the Mississippi River forming most of the boundary. Land area, 54,310 sq. miles (140,662 sq. km). Census population, 1 April 2000, 5,363,675, an increase of 9·6% since 1990. July 2004 estimate, 5,509,026.

Population in five census years was:

	White	*Black*	*All others*	*Total*	*Per sq. mile*
1910	2,320,555	2,900	10,405	2,333,860	42·2
1930	2,916,255	10,739	12,012	2,939,006	53·7
1980	4,443,035	182,592	80,015	4,705,642	86·4
1990	4,512,523	244,539	134,707	4,891,769	90·1
2000	4,769,857	304,460	289,358	5,363,675	98·8

Of the total population in 2000, 2,714,634 were female, 3,994,919 were 18 years old or older and 3,663,643 were urban. In 2000 Wisconsin's Hispanic population was 192,921, up from 93,194 in 1990 (an increase of 107·0%).

Population of the large cities, 2000 census, was as follows:

Milwaukee	596,974	Oshkosh	62,916	Fond du Lac	42,203
Madison	208,054	Eau Claire	61,704	Brookfield	38,649
Green Bay	102,313	West Allis	61,254	Wausau	38,426
Kenosha	90,352	Janesville	59,498	New Berlin	38,220
Racine	81,855	La Crosse	51,818	Beloit	35,775
Appleton	70,087	Sheboygan	50,792	Greenfield	35,476
Waukesha	64,825	Wauwatosa	47,271		

Population of largest metropolitan areas, 2000 census: Milwaukee–Racine, 1,689,572; Madison, 426,526; Appleton–Oshkosh–Neenah, 358,365; Duluth–Superior (Minn.–Wis.), 243,815; Green Bay, 226,778.

SOCIAL STATISTICS

Births in 2002 were 68,560 (12·6 per 1,000 population); deaths were 46,981 (8·6); infant deaths, 2001, 7·1 per 1,000 live births. In 2003 there were 34,220 marriages (6·3 per 1,000 population); divorces and annulments, 17,150 (3·1).

CLIMATE

Milwaukee, Jan. 19°F (–7·2°C), July 70°F (21·1°C). Annual rainfall 29" (727 mm). Wisconsin belongs to the Great Lakes climate zone (*see* UNITED STATES: Climate).

CONSTITUTION AND GOVERNMENT

The constitution, which dates from 1848, has 141 amendments. The legislative power is vested in a Senate of 33 members elected for four years, one-half elected alternately, and an Assembly of 99 members all elected simultaneously for two years. The Governor and Lieut.-Governor are elected for four years.

For the 109th Congress, which convened in Jan. 2005, Wisconsin sends eight members to the House of Representatives. It is represented in the Senate by Herbert Kohl (D. 1989–2007) and Russell Feingold (D. 1993–2011).

The capital is Madison. The state has 72 counties.

RECENT ELECTIONS
In the 2004 presidential election Kerry polled 1,489,504 votes; Bush, 1,478,120; Nader, 16,390.

CURRENT ADMINISTRATION
Governor: Jim Doyle (D.), 2003–07 (salary: $131,768).
Lieut.-Governor: Barbara Lawton (D.), 2003–07 ($69,579).
Secretary of State: Douglas LaFollette (D.), 2003–07 ($62,549).

Government Website: http://www.wisconsin.gov

ECONOMY
Per capita personal income in 2002 was $29,996.

Budget. For the year ending 30 June 2004 total state revenue was $41,586m. ($10,739m. from state taxes); total expenditure, $33,894m. (education, $9,660m.; health and human resources, $9,166m.; transportation, $2,346m.; corrections, $989m.; environmental resources, $601m.) Outstanding debt, 30 June 2002, $4,304m.

Performance. Gross State Product in 2002 was $190,650m., ranking Wisconsin 18th in the United States.

Banking and Finance. On 30 Sept. 2004 there were 232 state chartered banks with assets of $68·5bn., and 45 federally chartered banks with $23·7bn. in assets. On 30 Sept. 2004, 19 state chartered savings institutions had $4·2bn. in assets and 20 federally chartered savings institutions had $18·8bn. in assets. As of 30 June 2004 there were 293 state chartered credit unions with $13·5bn. in assets.

ENERGY AND NATURAL RESOURCES
Electricity. 57,241m. kWh of electricity were produced in 2003; and 10,766m. kWh were imported. Fossil fuel plants accounted for 72·3% of state production, nuclear 21·7% and hydropower 3·0%. Coal accounted for 62% of utility energy use in 2003; nuclear fuel, 17%; natural gas, 3%; renewable sources, 2%; and electricity imports, 16%.

Oil and Gas. Petroleum accounted for 29% of the total energy consumed in 2003 and natural gas 22%. Transportation accounted for 83% of petroleum consumption. Natural gas accounted for 51% of residential end use and petroleum 14%. There are no known petroleum or natural gas reserves in Wisconsin.

Water. The total area covered by water is approximately 11,186 sq. miles.

Minerals. Construction sand and gravel, crushed stone, industrial or specialty sand, lime, copper, gold and silver are the chief mineral products. Mineral production in 2000 was valued at over $349m. This value included $140m. for construction sand and gravel, $131m. for crushed stones, $37m. for lime and $32m. for industrial or specialty sand. The value of all other minerals including dimension (building) stone, peat and gemstones was around $9m.

Agriculture. On 1 Jan. 2004 there were 76,500 farms (16,096 dairy herds) with a total acreage of 15·6m. acres and an average size of 204 acres, compared with 142,000 farms with a total acreage of 22·4m. acres and an average of 158 acres in 1959. In 2003 the average value per acre was $2,350. Cash receipts from products sold by Wisconsin farms in 2003, $5·88bn.; $1·78bn. from crops, and $4·10bn. from livestock and livestock products. The net farm income in 2003 was $1,626m.

Dairy farming is important, with 1·25m. milch cows in 2003. Production of cheese accounted for 27% of the USA's total in 2003. Production of the principal field crops in 2003 included: corn for grain, 368m. bu.; corn for silage, 14·1m. tons; oats, 15·4m. bu.; all hay, 4·4m. tons. Other crops of importance: 46·8m. bu. of soybeans, 32·8m. cwt of potatoes, 3·6m. bbls. of cranberries, 96,000 tons of carrots and the processing crops of 687,400 tons of sweet corn, 84,300 tons of green peas, 270,800 tons of snap beans, 36,100 tons of cucumbers for pickles, 13·8m. lb of tart cherries and 989,000 cwt of cabbage.

Wisconsin is also a major producer of mink pelts.

Forestry. Wisconsin had (2002) 15,963,000 acres of forested land. Of 15·7m. acres of timberland (Oct. 1997), national forests covered 1·4m. acres; state forests, 0·7m.; county and municipal forests, 2·3m.; forest industry, 1·1m.; private land, 10·1m.

Growing stock (1996), 18,500m. cu. ft, of which 14,100m. cu. ft is hardwood and 4,400m. cu. ft softwood. Main hardwoods are maple, oak, aspen and basswood; main softwoods are red pine, white pine, northern white cedar and balsam fir. The timber industry employs 99,000, has a payroll of $3,400m. and shipments valued at $19,700m. (1996).

INDUSTRY

Wisconsin has much heavy industry, particularly in the Milwaukee area. Three-fifths of manufacturing employees work on durable goods. Industrial machinery is the major industrial group (17% of all manufacturing employment) followed by fabricated metals, food and kindred products, printing and publishing, paper and allied products, electrical equipment and transportation equipment. Manufacturing establishments in 2002 provided 22% of non-farm wage and salary workers, 22·9% of all earnings. The total number of establishments was 9,846 in 2001; the biggest concentration is in the southeast. In Dec. 2004 manufacturing employed 518,800 people out of a total civilian labour force of 3,112,500.

Labour. The civilian labour force in 2004 was 3,112,500, of whom 2,982,500 were employed. Service enterprises employed 890,000 people, manufacturing 518,800, retail and wholesale 460,300, and government 419,700. Average annual pay per worker (2001) was $31,540 ($35,170 in Milwaukee metropolitan area). Median household income (2003) was $46,269. Women were 48% of the workforce in 2002. Workforce participation rates for people over 16 (2001) were 74% for males and 64% for females. Average weekly earnings ranged from $300 in the retail sector to $750 in manufacturing in 2001. Average unemployment was 5·2% in 2002.

Trade Unions. Labour union membership numbered 414,000 in 2003 and represented 15·9% of the workforce. Union membership was 19·9% of workers in the manufacturing sector in 2002.

COMMUNICATIONS

Roads. The state had, on 1 Jan. 2003, 112,663 miles of public roads. 80% of all roads in the state have a bituminous (or similar) surface. There are 11,753 miles of state and interstate highways and 19,665 miles of county highway roads.

In 2004 there were 5,100,000 registered motor vehicles.

Rail. On 31 Dec. 2002 the state had 5,095 track-miles of railway and 12 railroads that hauled 158m. tons of freight.

Civil Aviation. There were, in 2002, 134 public access airports. There were 4,531,810 passenger enplanements statewide in 2002.

Shipping. Lake Superior and Lake Michigan ports handled 47·8m. tons of freight in 2002; 87% of it at Superior, one of the world's biggest grain ports, and much of the rest at Milwaukee and Green Bay.

SOCIAL INSTITUTIONS

Justice. On 17 Dec. 2004 the state's penal, reformatory and correctional system held 20,839 men and 1,329 women in 19 prisons, 16 community facilities and other institutions for adult offenders, including contract beds in county jails, federal facilities and 128 in a private prison in Minnesota; the probation and parole system was supervising 69,629 adults (56,342 on probation, 13,287 on parole). Parole for new convictions officially ended 31 Dec. 1999 (replaced by 'extended supervision'). Population in the state's five juvenile institutions on 17 Dec. 2004 was 610 males and 46 females; an additional 505 males and 47 females were under field supervision.

The death penalty was abolished in 1853.

Religion. Wisconsin church affiliation, as a percentage of the 2004 population, was estimated at 31% Catholic, 25% Protestant Mainline, 22% Evangelical and 14% unaffiliated.

Education. All children between the ages of six and 18 are required to attend school full-time to the end of the school term in which they become 18 years of age. In 2003–04 the public school grades kindergarten-12 had 853,363 pupils. There were

61,394 (full-time equivalent) teachers in 2002–03. Private schools enrolled 124,248 students grades kindergarten-12. Public pre-schools enrolled 26,668 children, and private 13,604. Children taught in home schools numbered 21,134 in 1999–2000. Public elementary teachers' salaries, 2000–01, averaged $41,403; secondary, $42,175.

In 2002–03 technical colleges had an enrolment of 429,355 and 4,902 (full-time equivalent) teachers, and two Indian tribe community colleges enrolled 1,060 (2003–04). There is a school for the visually handicapped and a school for the deaf.

The University of Wisconsin, established in 1848, was joined by law in 1971 with the Wisconsin State Universities System to become the University of Wisconsin System with 13 degree granting campuses, 13 two-year campuses in the Center System and the University Extension. The system had, in 2002–03, 6,718 full-time professors and instructors. In autumn 2003, 160,703 students enrolled (10,599 at Eau Claire, 5,448 at Green Bay, 8,746 at La Crosse, 40,769 at Madison, 24,875 at Milwaukee, 11,013 at Oshkosh, 5,072 at Parkside, 6,134 at Platteville, 5,799 at River Falls, 8,750 at Stevens Point, 7,708 at Stout, 2,832 at Superior, 10,548 at Whitewater and 12,410 at the Center System freshman-sophomore centres).

UW-Extension enrolled 176,793 students in its continuing education programmes in 2001–02. There are also several independent institutions of higher education: Marquette University (Jesuit), in Milwaukee (11,000 in 2002–03); Cardinal Strich University (Franciscan), with campuses in Milwaukee, Madison and Edina, Minnesota (6,588 in 2002–03); Concordia University Wisconsin (Lutheran), in Mequon (4,541 in 2002–03); and Lawrence University, Appleton (1,325 in 2002–03). There were also 16 higher education colleges, four technical and professional schools and four theological seminaries in 2003. The state's educational and broadcasting service is licensed through the UW Board of Regents.

The total expenditure, 2001–02, for all public education (except capital outlay and debt service) was $12,170·8m. ($2,253 per capita).

Health. In 2002 the state had 128 general medical and surgical hospitals (12,626 beds), 12 psychiatric hospitals (623 beds), one treatment centre for alcohol and drug abuse (24 beds) and one physical rehabilitation hospitals (40 beds). There were two state mental hospitals (541 beds) and two US Veterans' Administration hospitals. Patients in state mental hospitals and institutions for the developmentally disabled averaged 570 in 2003. On 31 Dec. 2003 the state had 403 licensed nursing homes with 36,005 residents and 33 facilities for the developmentally disabled (1,415 residents).

Welfare. In Nov. 2004 there were 136,488 SSI recipients in the state; set monthly payments (2005) are $663 for a single individual, $709 for an eligible individual with an ineligible spouse and $1,001 for an eligible couple. A special payment level of $759 for an individual and $1,346 for a couple may be paid with special approval for SSI recipients who are developmentally disabled or chronically mentally ill, living in a non-medical living arrangement not his or her own home. There is a monthly cash benefit for each child living with an SSI parent of $250 for the first child and $150 for each additional child. All SSI recipients receive state medical assistance coverage and may qualify for food stamps.

Wisconsin completed its conversion to the W-2 (Wisconsin Works) programme on 31 March 1998, ending the 62-year-old Aid to Families with Dependent Children (AFDC) programme. W-2 clients (Nov. 2004) totalled 15,374 with 11,148 receiving cash assistance. W-2 clients must be working, seeking employment or be enrolled in job-training programmes. Recipients are limited to 60 months of financial assistance (consecutive or non-consecutive). Participants are eligible for child care assistance, a state subsidized health plan, job and transportation assistance and food stamps. In Aug. 2004 there were 322,405 (132,313 households) food stamp recipients. Medical Assistance (Medicaid) clients, including low-income, SSI recipients and other disabled, and other elderly totalled 707,869. An additional 94,257 (Aug. 2004) are provided for under BadgerCare, a state-funded medical insurance programme for certain low-income families.

CULTURE

There are two professional opera companies in Wisconsin: the Madison Opera, and the Florentine Opera in Milwaukee.

Broadcasting. In 2003 there were 32 commercial TV stations; eight educational TV stations; 265 commercial radio stations; and 51 non-commercial.

Press. There were 36 daily newspapers in 2003.

Tourism. The tourist-vacation industry ranks among the first three in economic importance with an estimated $11,710m. spent in 2003. The Department of Tourism budgeted $13,665,400 to promote tourism in 2004–05.

FURTHER READING

Wisconsin Blue Book. Wisconsin Legislative Reference Bureau, Madison. Biennial

State Historical Society of Wisconsin: *The History of Wisconsin.* Vol. IV [J. Buenker], Madison, 1999

State Information Agency: Legislative Reference Bureau, One East Main St., Suite 200, Madison, WI 53703-2037. *Chief:* Stephen R. Miller.
Website: http://www.legis.state.wi.us

WYOMING

KEY HISTORICAL EVENTS

The territory was inhabited by Plains Indians (Arapahoes, Sioux and Cheyenne) in the early 19th century. There was some trading between them and white Americans, but very little white settlement. In the 1840s the great western migration routes, the Oregon and the Overland Trails, ran through the territory, Wyoming offering mountain passes accessible to wagons. Once migration became a steady flow it was necessary to protect the route from Indian attack, and forts were built.

In 1867 coal was discovered. In 1868 Wyoming was organized as a separate Territory, and in 1869 the Sioux and Arapaho were confined to reservations. At the same time the route of the Union Pacific Railway was laid out, and working settlements and railway towns grew up in southern Wyoming. Settlement of the north was delayed until after the final defeat of hostile Indians in 1876.

The economy of the settlements at first depended on ranching. Cheyenne had been made Territorial capital in 1869, and also functioned as a railway town moving cattle. Casper, on the site of a fort on the Pony Express route, was also a railway town on the Chicago and North Western. Laramie started as a Union Pacific construction workers' shanty town in 1868. In 1890 oil was discovered at Casper, and Wyoming became a state in the same year. Subsequently, mineral extraction became the leading industry, as natural gas, uranium, bentonite and trona were exploited as well as oil and coal.

TERRITORY AND POPULATION

Wyoming is bounded north by Montana, east by South Dakota and Nebraska, south by Colorado, southwest by Utah and west by Idaho. Land area, 97,100 sq. miles (251,488 sq. km). The Yellowstone National Park occupies about 2·22m. acres; the Grand Teton National Park has 307,000 acres. The federal government in 1986 owned 49,838 sq. miles (50·9% of the total area of the state). The Federal Bureau of Land Management administers 17,546,188 acres.

Census population, 1 April 2000, 493,782, an increase of 8·9% since 1990; July 2004 estimate, 506,529. Wyoming has the smallest population of any of the states of the USA.

Population in five census years was:

	White	*Black*	*American Indian*	*Asiatic*	*Total*	*Per sq. mile*
1910	140,318	2,235	1,486	1,926	145,965	1·5
1930	221,241	1,250	1,845	1,229	225,565	2·3
			All others			
1980	446,488	3,364	19,705		469,557	4·8

	White	*Black*	*American Indian*	*Asian/ Pacific Islands*	*Other*	*Total*	*Per sq. mile*
1990	427,061	3,606	9,479	2,806	10,636	453,588	4·7
2000	454,670	3,722	11,133	3,073	21,184	493,782	5·1

Of the total population in 2000, 248,374 were male, 364,909 were 18 years old or older and 321,344 were urban. At the 2000 census the Hispanic population of Wyoming was 31,669, up from 25,751 in 1990 (an increase of 23%).

The largest towns (with 2000 census population) are Cheyenne, 53,011; Casper, 49,644; Laramie, 27,204; Gillette, 19,646; Rock Springs, 18,708; Sheridan, 15,804; Green River, 11,808.

SOCIAL STATISTICS

Births in 2002 were 6,550 (13·1 per 1,000 population); deaths, 4,174 (8·4); 2001: infant deaths, 5·9 per 1,000 live births. 2001: marriages, 5,000; divorces, 2,900. The abortion rate, at 1·0 for every 1,000 women in 2000, is the lowest of any US state.

CLIMATE

Cheyenne, Jan. 25°F (–3·9°C), July 66°F (18·9°C). Annual rainfall 15" (376 mm). Yellowstone Park, Jan. 18°F (–7·8°C), July 61°F (16·1°C). Annual rainfall 18" (444 mm). Wyoming belongs to the Mountain States climate region (*see* UNITED STATES: Climate).

CONSTITUTION AND GOVERNMENT

The constitution, drafted in 1890, has since had 43 amendments. The Legislature consists of a Senate of 30 members elected for four years, 15 retiring every two years, and a House of Representatives of 60 members elected for two years. It sits annually in Jan. or Feb. The Governor is elected for four years.

For the 109th Congress, which convened in Jan. 2005, Wyoming sends one member to the House of Representatives. It is represented in the Senate by Craig Thomas (R. 1995–2007) and Michael Enzi (R. 1997–2009).

The capital is Cheyenne. The state contains 23 counties.

RECENT ELECTIONS

In the 2004 presidential election Bush polled 167,629 votes; Kerry, 70,776; Nader, 2,741.

CURRENT ADMINISTRATION

Governor: David D. Freudenthal (D.), 2003–07 (salary: $105,000).

Secretary of State: Joseph B. Meyer (R.), 2003–07 ($92,000).

Government Website: http://www.wyoming.gov

ECONOMY

Personal income *per capita* (2002) was $30,494.

Budget. In 2002 total state revenue was $2,770m. Total expenditure was $2,948m. (education, $866m.; public welfare, $374m.; highways, $357m.; natural resources, $160m.; health, $113m.) Outstanding debt, in 2002, $1,298m.

Performance. Gross State Product was $20,285m. in 2002, ranking Wyoming 49th in the United States.

Banking and Finance. In Sept. 2001 there were 20 national and 26 state banks with a total of $6,291m. deposits.

ENERGY AND NATURAL RESOURCES

Oil and Gas. Wyoming is largely an oil-producing state. In 2001 the output of oil was 57m. bbls.; natural gas, 1,070bn. cu. ft.

Water. The total area covered by water is approximately 714 sq. miles.

Minerals. In 2001 the output of coal was 366m. short tons; trona (2000), 17·7m. short tons; uranium (2000), 2·1m. lb. Wyoming is the USA's leading coal producer, accounting for 33% of the country's coal output in 2001. It also has 37% of the country's coal reserves. Total value of non-fuel mineral production, 2002, $1,010m.

Agriculture. Wyoming is semi-arid, and agriculture is carried on by irrigation and dry farming. In 2002 there were 9,200 farms and ranches; total farm area was 34·6m. acres; average size of farm in 2002 was 3,761 acres (the largest of any state). In 2002 the average value of farmland was $290 per acre. In 2000 the farm population numbered 15,150 people.

Total value, 2001, of crops produced, $145m.; of livestock and products, $837m. The net farm income in 2001 was $200m. Crop production in 2000 (1,000 bu.): corn for grain, 8,184; barley, 7,885; wheat, 4,132; oats, 1,485; sugarbeet, 1,156,000 tons. Animals on farms included 1·55m. cattle, 530,000 sheep and 108,000 hogs and pigs. Total egg production in 2000 was 3·6m.

Forestry. The state had a forested area of 10,995,000 acres in 2002, of which 5,858,000 acres were national forest.

INDUSTRY

In 2001 the state's 563 manufacturing establishments had 9,000 employees, earning $321m. In 1999 there were 627 mining establishments. A large portion of the manufacturing in the state is based on natural resources, mainly oil and farm products. Leading industries are food, wood products (except furniture) and machinery (except electrical). The Wyoming Industrial Development Corporation assists in the development of small industries by providing credit.

Labour. In July 2001 the construction industry employed 19,600 wage and salary workers; mining, 19,400; transportation and public utilities, 14,600; manufacturing, 11,400. The total civilian labour force in July 2001 was 276,249, of whom 267,046 were employed; non-agricultural wage and salary employment, 252,400. The unemployment rate was 3·3% in July 2001.

Trade Unions. There were 22,900 working members in trade unions (9·1% of total employment) in 1999.

INTERNATIONAL TRADE

Imports and Exports. In 2000 total export from Wyoming was $502·5m.

COMMUNICATIONS

Roads. In 2002 there were 2,481 miles of urban roads and 24,942 miles of rural roads, the latter including (in miles): federal, 3,217; state, 6,352; county, 14,071. There were 602,935 motor vehicle registrations.

Rail. In 1999, 1,795 miles of Class I railway were operated.

Civil Aviation. There were ten towns with commuter air services and two towns on jet routes in 1995. There were 168,453 passenger enplanements statewide in 2000.

SOCIAL INSTITUTIONS

Justice. In June 2002 there were 1,732 prisoners in state adult correctional institutions. Capital punishment is authorized but has been used only once, in 1992, since the US Supreme Court reinstated the death penalty in 1976.

Religion. Chief religious bodies in 1990 were the Roman Catholic (with 59,565 members), Latter-day Saints (Mormons) (54,000 in 1998) and Protestant churches (110,375).

Education. In 2000–01 public elementary and secondary schools had 89,531 pupils and 6,743 teachers. In 1990–91 enrolment in the parochial elementary and secondary schools was about 3,500. The average expenditure per pupil for 1999–2000 was $8,046. State and local government expenditure in 1999 was $721m.

The University of Wyoming, founded at Laramie in 1887 had, in the academic year 2000–01, 11,743 students. There were seven community colleges in 2000–01 with 12,740 students.

Health. In 2000 the state had 26 general hospitals with 1,631 beds, and 40 registered nursing homes with 3,106 beds.

Welfare. In the fiscal year 2000, $18·2m. was distributed in food stamps; $1·6m. in aid to families with dependent children; and $193m. in Medicaid.

CULTURE

Broadcasting. In 2000 there were 32 AM, 38 FM radio stations and 15 television stations.

Press. In 2000 there were eight daily newspapers.

Tourism. There are over 7m. tourists annually, mainly outdoor enthusiasts. The state has large elk and pronghorn antelope herds, ten fish hatcheries and numerous wild game. In 2000, 6,134,317 people visited the six national areas; 1,925,000 people visited state parks and historic sites. In 1990, 811,183 fishing, game and bird licences were sold. In 2000 there were nine operational ski areas.

FURTHER READING

Statistical information: Department of Administration and Information, 327 E. Emerson Bldg, Cheyenne 82002. Publishes *Wyoming Data Handbook*

Equality State Almanac 2002. Wyoming Department of Administration and Information. Division of Economic Analysis. Cheyenne, WY 82002

Wyoming Official Directory. Secretary of State. Cheyenne, annual

Wyoming Data Handbook. Dept. of Administration and Information. Division of Economic Analysis. Cheyenne, annual

Treadway, T., *Wyoming.* New York, 1982

State Government Website: http://eadiv.state.wy.us

OUTLYING TERRITORIES

The outlying territories of the USA comprise the two Commonwealths of the Northern Mariana Islands and Puerto Rico, a number of unincorporated territories in the Pacific Ocean and one unincorporated territory in the Caribbean Sea.

COMMONWEALTH OF THE NORTHERN MARIANA ISLANDS

KEY HISTORICAL EVENTS

In 1889 Spain ceded Guam (largest and southernmost of the Marianas Islands) to the USA and sold the rest to Germany. Occupied by Japan in 1914, the islands were administered by Japan under a League of Nations mandate until occupied by US forces in Aug. 1944. In 1947 they became part of the US-administered Trust Territory of the Pacific Islands. On 17 June 1975 the electorate adopted a covenant to establish a Commonwealth in association with the USA; this was approved by the US government in April 1976 and came into force on 1 Jan. 1978. In Nov. 1986 the islanders were granted US citizenship. The UN terminated the Trusteeship status on 22 Dec. 1990.

TERRITORY AND POPULATION

The Northern Marianas form a single chain of 16 mountainous islands extending north of Guam for about 560 km, with a total area of 5,050 sq. km (1,950 sq. miles) of which 464 sq. km (179 sq. miles) are dry land, and with a population (2000 census) of 69,221 (female, 37,237).

The areas and populations of the islands are as follows:

Island(s)	*Sq. km*	*1995 Census*	*2000 Census*
Northern Group[1]	171	8	6
Saipan	122	52,698	62,392
Tinian (with Aguijan)	101[2]	2,631	3,540
Rota	83	3,509	3,283

[1]Pagan, Agrihan, Alamagan and nine uninhabited islands. [2]Including uninhabited Aguijan.

In 1980, 55% spoke Chamorro, 11% Woleaian and 13% Filipino languages, but English remains the official language. The largest town is Chalan Kanoa on Saipan.

SOCIAL STATISTICS

In 2002 there were 1,290 births (17·4 per 1,000 population) and 161 deaths (2·2). Infant mortality was 38 per 1,000 live births in 1996.

CONSTITUTION AND GOVERNMENT

The Constitution was approved by a referendum on 6 March 1977 and came into force on 9 Jan. 1978. The legislature comprises a nine-member *Senate*, with three Senators elected from each of the main three islands for a term of four years, and an 18-member *House of Representatives*, elected for a term of two years.

The Commonwealth is administered by a Governor and Lieut.-Governor, elected for four years.

RECENT ELECTIONS

At the elections of 1 Nov. 2003 the Covenant Party won nine seats in the House of Representatives, against the Republican Party which won seven and the Democratic Party which won one seat. One independent was elected. Turn-out was 77·3%.

In the gubernatorial elections of 3 Nov. 2001 Juan Babauta, in tandem with Diego T. Benavente, won 42·8% of votes cast, defeating Benigno Fitial (24·4%), Jesus Camacho Borja (17·5%) and Froilan Cruz Tenorio (11·3%).

CURRENT ADMINISTRATION

Governor: Juan N. Babauta (R.), 2002–06 (salary: $70,000).

Lieut.-Governor: Diego T. Benavente (R.), 2002–06 ($65,000).

Government Website: http://www.gov.mp

ENERGY AND NATURAL RESOURCES

Fisheries. In 2001 total catches were 434,000 lb (197 tonnes), entirely from marine waters.

INDUSTRY

Labour. In 1990 there were 7,476 workers from the indigenous population and 21,188 were foreign workers; 2,699 were unemployed.

INTERNATIONAL TRADE

Imports and Exports. In 1997 imports totalled $836·2m.; in 1999 exports totalled $1,049·0m. Most imports came from other US Pacific territories, Hong Kong and Japan.

COMMUNICATIONS

Roads. There are about 381 km of roads.

Civil Aviation. There are six airports in all. Saipan handled 1,325,000 passengers (1,048,000 on international flights) and 17,900 tonnes of freight in 2000.

Telecommunications. There were 24,000 main telephone lines in 2000, equivalent to 452·5 per 1,000 inhabitants. In 1995 there were 1,200 mobile phone subscribers.

SOCIAL INSTITUTIONS

Religion. The population is predominantly Roman Catholic.

Education. In 2000 there were 679 pupils enrolled in nursery school and pre-school, 946 in kindergarten, 7,884 in elementary school (grades 1–8), 2,750 in high school (grades 9–12) and 1,130 in college or graduate school.

Health. In 1986 there were 23 doctors, four dentists, 103 nursing personnel, two pharmacists and two midwives. In 1988 there was one hospital with 70 beds.

CULTURE

Broadcasting. There were six radio stations, one television station and two cable TV stations on Saipan in 1998. In 1999 there were 10,500 radio and 4,100 television receivers.

Tourism. In 2000 there were 517,000 visitors; spending by tourists in 1998 totalled $647m.

COMMONWEALTH OF PUERTO RICO

KEY HISTORICAL EVENTS

A Spanish dependency since the 16th century, Puerto Rico was ceded to the USA in 1898 after the Spanish defeat in the Spanish-American war. In 1917 US citizenship was conferred and in 1932 there was a name change from Porto Rico to Puerto Rico. In 1952 Puerto Rico was proclaimed a commonwealth with a representative government and a directly elected governor.

TERRITORY AND POPULATION

Puerto Rico is the most easterly of the Greater Antilles and lies between the Dominican Republic and the US Virgin Islands. The total area is 13,791 sq. km (5,325 sq. miles), of which 8,871 sq. km (3,425 sq. miles) are dry land; the population, according to the census of 2000, was 3,808,610, an increase of 8·1% over 1990. The urban population was 3,595,521 in 2000, representing 94·4% (73·3% in 1995) of the total population. Population density was 1,112 per sq. mile in 2000. Of the total population in 2000, 1,975,033 were female. The UN gives a projected population for 2010 of 3·99m.

A law of April 1991 making Spanish the sole official language (which replaced a law of 1902 establishing Spanish and English as joint official languages) was reversed in 1993.

Chief towns, 2002 estimates, are: San Juan, 433,412; Bayamón, 224,670; Carolina, 187,468; Ponce, 186,112; Caguas, 141,693; Arecibo, 101,283; Guaynabo, 101,280.

The Puerto Rican island of Vieques, 10 miles to the east, has an area of 51·7 sq. miles and 9,584 (1999) inhabitants. The island of Culebra, between Puerto Rico and St Thomas, has an area of 10 sq. miles and 1,771 (1999) inhabitants. It has a good harbour.

SOCIAL STATISTICS

2002: births, 52,747 (13·7 per 1,000 population); deaths, 27,924 (7·2); marriages, 28,598; infant mortality rate (2000), 9·7 per 1,000 live births. Annual growth rate, 1995–99, 1·1%. In 2000 the most popular age range for marrying was 20–24 for both males and females. Fertility rate, 1990–95, 2·2 births per woman.

CLIMATE

Warm, sunny winters with hot summers. The north coast experiences more rainfall than the south coast and generally does not have a dry season as rainfall is evenly spread throughout the year. San Juan, Jan. 25°C, July 28°C. Annual rainfall 1,246 mm.

CONSTITUTION AND GOVERNMENT

Puerto Rico has representative government, the franchise being restricted to citizens 18 years of age or over, residence (one year) and such additional qualifications as may be prescribed by the Legislature of Puerto Rico, but no property qualification may be imposed. Puerto Ricans vote in presidential primary elections but not in US general elections. They have one non-voting representative in Washington. The island is given billions of dollars each year in food stamps and other federal aid from Washington and although Puerto Ricans fight in the US army, the island sends its own teams to the Olympic Games. The executive power resides in a Governor, elected directly by the people every four years. 22 heads of departments form the Governor's Council of Secretaries. The legislative functions are vested in a Senate, composed of 28 members, and the House of Representatives, composed of 51 members. Both houses meet annually in Jan. Puerto Rican men are subject to conscription in US services.

A new constitution was drafted by a Puerto Rican Constituent Assembly and approved by the electorate at a referendum on 3 March 1952. It was then submitted to Congress, which struck out Section 20 of Article 11 covering the 'right to work' and the 'right to an adequate standard of living'; the remainder was passed and proclaimed by the Governor on 25 July 1952.

RECENT ELECTIONS

At the gubernatorial election on 2 Nov. 2004 Aníbal Acevedo Vilá (Popular Democratic Party/PPD) won with 48·7% of the vote, ahead of Pedro Rosselló (New Progressive Party /PNP) with 48·5% and Ruben Berrios Martine (Puerto Rican Independence Party/PIP) with 2·7%.

In elections to the Chamber of Representatives on 2 Nov. 2004 the New Progressive Party (PNP) polled 46·3% of the vote and claimed 32 of the 51 seats; the Popular Democratic Party (PPD) 43·1% and 18 seats; Puerto Rican Independence Party (PIP), 9·7% and 1 seat. In the Senate elections of the same day PNP took 17 seats, PPD took 9 seats and PIP took 1.

At a plebiscite on 14 Nov. 1993 on Puerto Rico's future status, 48·6% of votes cast were for Commonwealth (status quo), 46·3% for Statehood (51st State of the USA) and 4·4% for full independence. In a further plebiscite in Dec. 1998, some 52·2% of voters backed the opposition's call for no change, while 46·5% supported statehood. Independence was supported by 2·5%, while free association received 0·3%.

CURRENT ADMINISTRATION

Governor: Aníbal Acevedo Vilá (PPD), 2005–09 (salary: $70,000).

Secretary of State: José Izquierdo Encarnacion (PPD), appointed Feb. 2004.

Government Website (Spanish only): http://www.gobierno.pr

ECONOMY

Budget. Revenues in 2000–01 totalled $11,208m. and expenditures $10,337m. Tax revenues accounted for 57·3% of revenue. Main items of expenditure were education and welfare (both 22·3%) and public safety and protection (15·7%).

Per capita personal income (1996) was $7,882.

Performance. Real GDP growth was 5·6% in 2001. Total GDP in 2001 was $67·9bn.

Banking and Finance. Banks on 30 June 1996 had total deposits of $27,502·2m. Bank loans were $17,940·5m. This includes 15 commercial banks, three government banks and one trust company.

ENERGY AND NATURAL RESOURCES

Environment. Puerto Rico's carbon dioxide emissions from the consumption and flaring of fossil fuels in 2002 were the equivalent of 8·8 tonnes per capita.

Electricity. Installed capacity was 4·4m. kW in 2000. Production in 2000 was about 20·38bn. kWh. Consumption per capita in 2000 was estimated to be 5,254 kWh.

Agriculture. Gross income in agriculture in 1996 was $662·6m., of which $387·2m. consisted of livestock products and $71·2m. traditional crops. Production, 2002 estimates (in 1,000 tonnes): sugarcane, 320; plantains, 82; bananas, 50; oranges, 26; mangoes, 17; pineapples, 15; coffee, 13; pumpkins and squash, 11; tomatoes, 5. Livestock (2002): cattle, 390,000; pigs, 118,000; poultry, 12m.

Forestry. In 1995 the area under forests was 275,000 ha, or 31% of the total land area (down from 287,000 ha in 1990).

Fisheries. The total catch in 2001 was 8,364,000 lb (3,794 tonnes), exclusively from sea fishing.

INDUSTRY

There is some production of cement (1·76m. tonnes in 1999).

Labour. In Sept. 2003 there were 1,208,700 people in employment, including 307,700 people in government, 169,500 in trade, transportation and utilities, 117,800 in manufacturing and 96,200 in professional and business services. 161,100 persons were unemployed in Sept. 2003 (rate of 11·8%).

INTERNATIONAL TRADE

Imports and Exports. In 2001 imports amounted to $27,642m., of which $14,718m. came from the USA; exports were valued at $46,806m., of which $40,981m. went to the USA.

In 1997 main exports (in $1m.) were: chemical products, 10,627·8; machinery (except electrical), 3,490·0; food, 3,386·4. Main imports were: chemical products, 5,416·3; electrical machinery, 2,423·8; transportation equipment, 2,241·2.

Puerto Rico is not permitted to levy taxes on imports.

COMMUNICATIONS

Roads. In 2000 there were 14,871 miles of roads and 2,082,090 registered motor vehicles.

Rail. There are 96 km of railway, although no passenger service.

Civil Aviation. San Juan's Luis Muñoz Marin airport handled 10,350,000 passengers and 239,600 tonnes of freight in 2000.

Shipping. In 1996, 9,931 US and foreign vessels of 81,961,309 gross tons entered and cleared Puerto Rico.

Telecommunications. In 2001 there were 2,540,600 telephone subscribers, or 662·0 for every 1,000 persons. In April 2000 there were 200,000 Internet users. Mobile phone subscribers numbered 169,000 in 1996 and there were 543,000 fax machines in 1995.

SOCIAL INSTITUTIONS

Justice. The Commonwealth judiciary system is headed by a Supreme Court of seven members, appointed by the Governor, and consists of a First Instance Court and an Appellative Court, all appointed by the Governor. The First Instance Court consists of a Superior Tribunal with 78 judges and a municipal Tribunal of 70 judges. The Appellative Court has 33 judges.

The population in penal institutions in Dec. 2002 was 14,725 (378 per 100,000 population).

Religion. In 2001 about 65% of the population were Roman Catholic. In Sept. 2003 there was one cardinal.

Education. Education was made compulsory in 1899. The percentage of literacy in 1990 was 89·4% of those ten years of age or older. Total enrolment in public day schools, 1999, was 613,900. All private schools had a total enrolment of 118,700 pupils in 1999. All instruction below senior high school standard is given in Spanish only.

The University of Puerto Rico, in Río Piedras, seven miles from San Juan, had 62,340 students in 1996. Higher education is also available in the Inter-American University of Puerto Rico (39,319 students in 1996), the Pontifical Catholic University of Puerto Rico (11,786), the Sacred Heart University (5,001) and the Fundación Ana G. Méndez (16,983). Other private colleges and universities had 35,717 students.

Health. There were 72 hospitals in 1994, with a hospital bed provision of 26 per 10,000 population. In 2002 there were 9,511 non-federal physicians.

CULTURE

Broadcasting. In 1995 there were 118 radio and 21 television stations (colour by NTSC). There were 2·8m. radio receivers in 2000 and 530,000 TV receivers in 2001.

Press. In 1996 there were three main newspapers: *El Nuevo Dia* had a daily circulation of 227,661; *El Vocero,* 206,125; *San Juan Star,* 33,353.

Tourism. There were 4,907,800 foreign visitors in 2001. Revenue from tourism amounted to $2,728m. in 2001.

FURTHER READING

Statistical Information: The Area of Economic Research and Social Planning of the Puerto Rico Planning Board publishes: *(a)* annual *Economic Report to the Governor; (b) External Trade Statistics* (annual report); *(c) Reports on national income and balance of payments; (d) SocioEconomic Statistics* (since 1940); *(e) Puerto Rico Monthly Economic Indicators.*

Annual Reports. Governor of Puerto Rico. Washington

Dietz, J. L., *Economic History of Puerto Rico: Institutional Change and Capital Development.* Princeton Univ. Press, 1987

Commonwealth Library: Univ. of Puerto Rico Library, Rio Piedras.

AMERICAN SAMOA

KEY HISTORICAL EVENTS

The Samoan Islands were first visited by Europeans in the 18th century; the first recorded visit was in 1722. On 14 July 1889 a treaty between the USA, Germany and Great Britain proclaimed the Samoan islands neutral territory, under a four-power government consisting of the three treaty powers and the local native government. By the Tripartite Treaty of 7 Nov. 1899, ratified 19 Feb. 1900, Great Britain and Germany renounced in favour of the USA all rights over the islands of the Samoan group east of 171° long. west of Greenwich, the islands to the west of that meridian being assigned to Germany (now the independent state of Samoa). The islands of Tutuila and Aunu'u were ceded to the USA by their High Chiefs on 17 April 1900, and the islands of the Manu'a group on 16 July 1904. Congress accepted the islands under a Joint Resolution approved 20 Feb. 1929. Swain's Island, 210 miles north of the Samoan Islands, was annexed in 1925 and is administered as an integral part of American Samoa.

TERRITORY AND POPULATION

The islands (Tutuila, Aunu'u, Ta'u, Olosega, Ofu and Rose) are approximately 650 miles east-northeast of the Fiji Islands. The total area is 1,511 sq. km (583 sq. miles), of which 200 sq. km (77 sq. miles) are dry land; population (2000 census), 57,291 (29,264 males), nearly all Polynesians or part-Polynesians. Population density was 286 per sq. km in 2000.

In 1995 an estimated 50·3% of the population lived in urban areas. The capital is Pago Pago, which had a population of 14,000 in 1999. The island's three Districts are Eastern (population, 2000, 23,441), Western (32,435) and Manu'a (1,378). There is also Swain's Island, with an area of 1·9 sq. miles and 37 inhabitants (2000), which lies 210 miles to the northwest. Rose Island (uninhabited) is 0·4 sq. mile in area. In 1990 some 85,000 American Samoans lived in the USA.

Samoan and English are spoken.

SOCIAL STATISTICS

In 2002 there were 1,627 births (28·2 per 1,000 population) and 290 deaths (5·0). Infant mortality was 6·4 per 1,000 live births in 2000. Annual growth rate, 2000, 2·0% (1·8% in 1999).

CLIMATE

A tropical maritime climate with a small annual range of temperature and plentiful rainfall. Pago Pago, Jan. 83°F (28·3°C), July 80°F (26·7°C). Annual rainfall 194" (4,850 mm).

CONSTITUTION AND GOVERNMENT

American Samoa is constitutionally an unorganized, unincorporated territory of the USA administered under the Department of the Interior. Its indigenous inhabitants are US nationals and are classified locally as citizens of American Samoa with certain privileges under local laws not granted to non-indigenous persons. Polynesian customs (not inconsistent with US laws) are respected.

Fagatogo is the seat of the government.

The islands are organized in 15 counties grouped in three districts; these counties and districts correspond to the traditional political units. On 25 Feb. 1948 a bicameral legislature was established, at the request of the Samoans, to have advisory legislative functions. With the adoption of the Constitution of 22 April 1960, and the revised Constitution of 1967, the legislature was vested with limited law-making authority. The lower house, or House of Representatives, is composed of 20 members elected by universal adult suffrage and one non-voting member for Swain's Island. The upper house, or Senate, is comprised of 18 members elected, in the traditional Samoan manner, in meetings of the chiefs. The Governor and Lieut.-Governor have been popularly elected since 1978. American Samoa also sends one delegate to the US House of Representatives. The Congressman may participate but not vote on the House floor.

RECENT ELECTIONS

At elections to the Senate and House of Representatives on 5 and 19 Nov. 2002, only non-partisans were elected.

At gubernatorial elections on 2 Nov. 2004 incumbent Togiola Tulafono (Democrat) received 48·4% of votes cast, Afoa Moega Lutu (ind.) 39·4% and Teo Fuavai (ind.) 12·2%. In the run-off held on 16 Nov. 2004 Togiola Tulafono received 55·7% of votes cast and Afoa Moega Lutu 44·3%.

CURRENT ADMINISTRATION

Governor: Togiola Tulafono (D.), Jan. 2005–Jan. 2009 (salary: $50,000).

Lieut.-Governor: Aitofele T. F. Sunia (D.), Jan. 2005–Jan. 2009.

Government Website: http://www.government.as

ECONOMY

Overview. The Economic Development and Planning Office promotes economic expansion and outside investment.

Budget. The chief sources of revenue are annual federal grants from the USA, local revenues from taxes, duties, receipts from commercial operations (enterprise and special revenue funds), utilities, rents and leases, and liquor sales. In 1990–91 revenues were $97m. ($43m. in local revenue and $54m. in grant revenue).

Banking and Finance. The American Samoa branch of the Bank of Hawaii and the American Samoa Bank offer all commercial banking services. The Development Bank of American Samoa, government-owned, is concerned primarily through loans and guarantees with the economic advancement of the Territory.

ENERGY AND NATURAL RESOURCES

Environment. American Samoa's carbon dioxide emissions from the consumption and flaring of fossil fuels in 2002 were the equivalent of 8·3 tonnes per capita.

Electricity. Installed capacity was 35,000 kW in 2000. Production in 2000 was estimated at 133m. kWh. Per capita consumption in 2000 was an estimated 1,956 kWh. All the Manu'a islands have electricity.

Agriculture. Of the 48,640 acres of land area, 11,000 acres are suitable for tropical crops; most commercial farms are in the Tafuna plains and west Tutuila. Principal crops are coconuts, taro, bread-fruit, yams and bananas.

Livestock (2002): pigs, 11,000.

Fisheries. Total catch in 2001 was 8,075,000 lb (3,663 tonnes).

INDUSTRY

Fish canning is important, employing the second largest number of people (after government). Attempts are being made to provide a variety of light industries. Tuna fishing and local inshore fishing are both expanding.

Labour. In 2000 the civilian labour force numbered 17,627, of whom 16,718 were employed. The unemployment rate in 2000 was 5·2%.

INTERNATIONAL TRADE

Imports and Exports. Imports in 2000 totalled $507m. and exports $391m.

Chief exports are canned tuna, watches, pet foods and handicrafts. Chief imports are building materials, fuel oil, food, jewellery, machines and parts, alcoholic beverages and cigarettes.

COMMUNICATIONS

Roads. There are about 150 km of paved roads and 200 km of unpaved roads in all. Motor vehicles in use, 1995, 5,900 (5,300 passenger cars and 600 commercial vehicles).

Civil Aviation. Polynesian Airlines operate daily services between American Samoa (Pago Pago) and Samoa (Apia). Hawaiian Airlines also operates between Pago Pago and Honolulu. Manu'a Air Transport runs local services. There are three airports. There were 24,331 passenger enplanements in 2000.

Shipping. The harbour at Pago Pago, which nearly bisects the island of Tutuila, is the only good harbour for large vessels in American Samoa. By sea there is a twice-monthly service between the Fiji Islands, New Zealand and Australia and regular services between the USA, South Pacific ports, Honolulu and Japan. In 1999 vessels entering totalled 884,000 net registered tons.

Telecommunications. A commercial radiogram service is available to all parts of the world. Commercial phone and telex services are operated to all parts of the world. In Dec. 1997 there were 13,200 main telephone lines in operation and 2,550 mobile phone subscribers.

SOCIAL INSTITUTIONS

Justice. Judicial power is vested firstly in a High Court. The trial division has original jurisdiction of all criminal and civil cases. The probate division has jurisdiction of estates, guardianships, trusts and other matters. The land and title division decides cases relating to disputes involving communal land and Matai title court rules on questions and controversy over family titles. The appellate division hears appeals from trial, land and title and probate divisions as well as having original jurisdiction in selected matters. The appellate court is the court of last resort. Two American judges sit with five Samoan judges permanently. In addition there are temporary judges or assessors who sit occasionally on cases involving Samoan customs. There is also a District Court with limited jurisdiction and there are 69 village courts.

The population in penal institutions in Dec. 2002 was 169 (equivalent to 243 per 100,000 population).

Religion. In 2001 about 41% of the population belonged to the Congregational Church and 19% were Roman Catholics. Methodists and Latter-day Saints (Mormons) are also represented.

Education. Education is compulsory between the ages of six and 18. In 2000 there were 1,557 pupils enrolled in nursery school and pre-school, 1,736 in kindergarten, 11,418 in elementary school (grades 1–8), 4,645 in high school (grades 9–12) and 1,474 in college or graduate school.

Welfare. In Dec. 2001 there were 5,320 beneficiaries including 1,470 survivors, 1,370 retired workers and 1,240 disabled workers. Total payments came to $2m. with average monthly benefits of $442.

CULTURE

Broadcasting. In 1997 there were 57,000 radio sets and in 2000 there were 13,200 TV sets (colour by NTSC).

Tourism. In 2000 there were 44,000 tourist arrivals; receipts totalled $10m. in 1998.

FURTHER READING

Hughes, H. G. A., *Samoa: American Samoa, Western Samoa, Samoans Abroad.* [Bibliography] ABC-Clio, Oxford and Santa Barbara (CA), 1997

GUAM

Guahan

KEY HISTORICAL EVENTS

Magellan is said to have discovered the island in 1521; it was ceded by Spain to the USA by the Treaty of Paris (10 Dec. 1898). The island was captured by the Japanese on 10 Dec. 1941, and retaken by American forces from 21 July 1944. Guam is of great strategic importance; substantial numbers of naval and air force personnel occupy about one-third of the usable land.

TERRITORY AND POPULATION

Guam is the largest and most southern island of the Marianas Archipelago, in 13° 26' N. lat., 144° 45' E. long. Total area, 212 sq. miles (549 sq. km). Hagåtña (previously Agaña), the seat of government, is about 8 miles from the anchorage in

Apra Harbor. The census in 2000 showed a population of 154,805 (79,181 males), of whom 80,737 were born in Guam; density, 282·0 per sq. km. Estimate, 2003, 180,000. In 1995 an estimated 61·7% of the population lived in rural areas. The UN gives a projected population for 2010 of 191,000. The Malay strain is predominant. Chamorro, the native language, and English are the official languages.

SOCIAL STATISTICS

Births, 2002, 3,212; deaths, 638. Birth rate, 2002, 19·9 per 1,000 population; death rate, 4·0 per 1,000 population; infant mortality rate (1997), 8·1 per 1,000 live births. Life expectancy, 1990–95, was 72·2 years for males and 76·0 years for females. Fertility rate, 1990–95, 3·4 births per woman.

CLIMATE

Tropical maritime, with little difference in temperatures over the year. Rainfall is copious at all seasons, but is greatest from July to Oct. Hagåtña, Jan. 81°F (27·2°C), July 81°F (27·2°C). Annual rainfall 93" (2,325 mm).

CONSTITUTION AND GOVERNMENT

Guam's constitutional status is that of an 'unincorporated territory' of the USA. In Aug. 1950 the President transferred the administration of the island from the Navy Department to the Interior Department. The transfer conferred full citizenship on the Guamanians, who had previously been 'nationals' of the USA. There was a referendum on status on 30 Jan. 1982. 38% of eligible voters voted; 48·5% of those favoured Commonwealth status.

The Governor and Lieut.-Governor are elected for four-year terms. The legislature is a 15-member elected Senate; its powers are similar to those of an American state legislature. Guam sends one non-voting delegate (Madeleine Bordallo, D., 2005–07) to the US House of Representatives.

RECENT ELECTIONS

At the election of 5 Nov. 2002 for the Guam Legislature the Democrats won nine seats and the Republicans won six. In gubernatorial elections held on the same day, Republican candidate Felix Camacho won 55·2% of the vote against 44·8% for Democrat Robert Underwood.

CURRENT ADMINISTRATION

Governor: Felix Perez Camacho (R.), 2003–07 (salary: $90,000).

Lieut.-Governor: Kaleo S. Moylan (R.), 2003–07 ($85,000).

Government Website: http://ns.gov.gu/government.html

ECONOMY

Budget. Total revenue (2000) $340m.; expenditure $445m.

Banking and Finance. Banking law makes it possible for foreign banks to operate in Guam. In 2003 there were 12 commercial banks.

ENERGY AND NATURAL RESOURCES

Environment. Guam's carbon dioxide emissions from the consumption and flaring of fossil fuels in 2002 were the equivalent of 13·1 tonnes per capita.

Electricity. Installed capacity was 0·3m. kW in 2000. Production was 830m. kWh in 2000. Consumption per capita in 2000 was estimated at 5,355 kWh.

Water. The total area covered by water is approximately 7 sq. miles. The Navy and Air Force conserve water in reservoirs.

Agriculture. The major products of the island are sweet potatoes, cucumbers, watermelons and beans. In 2001 there were approximately 12,000 acres of arable land and 22,000 acres of permanent cropland. Production (2002 estimates, in 1,000 tonnes): coconuts, 52; copra, 2; watermelons, 2. Livestock (2002) included 1,000 goats and 5,000 pigs. There is an agricultural experimental station at Inarajan.

Fisheries. In 2001 total catches were 613,000 lb (278 tonnes), exclusively from sea fishing.

INDUSTRY

Guam Economic Development Authority controls three industrial estates: Cabras Island (32 acres); Calvo estate at Tamuning (26 acres); Harmon estate (16 acres). Industries include textile manufacture, cement and petroleum distribution, warehousing, printing, plastics and ship-repair. Other main sources of income are construction and tourism.

Labour. In 1990 there were 90,990 persons of employable age, of whom 66,138 were in the workforce (54,186 civilian). 2,042 were unemployed.

INTERNATIONAL TRADE

Guam is the only American territory which has complete 'free trade'; excise duties are levied only upon imports of tobacco, liquid fuel and liquor.

Imports and Exports. In 2002 imports were valued at $389m. and exports at $37m. Main export destinations in 1999 were Japan, 53·9%; Micronesia, 18·6%; Palau, 6·3%.

COMMUNICATIONS

Roads. There are 674 km of all-weather roads. In 1997 there were 79,326 passenger cars and 32,262 commercial vehicles registered.

Civil Aviation. There is an international airport at Tamuning. Seven commercial airlines serve Guam. There were 1,004,354 passenger enplanements in 2000.

Shipping. There is a port at Apra Harbor.

Telecommunications. Overseas telephone and radio dispatch facilities are available. Main telephone lines numbered 112,600 in 2001 (716·3 per 1,000 inhabitants). Mobile phone subscribers numbered 5,600 in 1997. Internet users in 2002 numbered 50,000.

SOCIAL INSTITUTIONS

Justice. The Organic Act established a District Court with jurisdiction in matters arising under both federal and territorial law; the judge is appointed by the President subject to Senate approval. There is also a Supreme Court and a Superior Court; all judges are locally appointed except the Federal District judge. Misdemeanours are under the jurisdiction of the police court. The Spanish law was superseded in 1933 by five civil codes based upon California law.

The population in penal institutions in Dec. 2002 was 542 (334 per 100,000 population).

Religion. About 75% of the Guamanians are Roman Catholics; the other 25% are Baptists, Episcopalians, Bahais, Lutherans, Latter-day Saints (Mormons), Presbyterians, Jehovah's Witnesses and members of the Church of Christ and Seventh Day Adventists.

Education. Education is compulsory from five to 16. Bilingual teaching programmes integrate the Chamorro language and culture into public school courses. Public school enrolment in 2002–03: 2,806 pupils in Head Start and kindergarten, 12,361 in 27 elementary schools (grades 1–5); 7,554 in seven middle schools (grades 6–8); and 9,081 in four high schools (grades 9–12). In 2003 there were about 25 private schools (nine Catholic). The University of Guam is in Mangilao and Guam Community College is in Barrigada.

Health. There is a hospital, eight nutrition centres, a school health programme and an extensive immunization programme. Emphasis is on disease prevention, health education and nutrition.

Welfare. In 1990, $83·2m. was paid in Federal direct payments for individuals, including $1·91m. Medicare, $1·91m. disability insurance and $11·37m. retirement insurance.

CULTURE

Broadcasting. There are four commercial stations, a commercial television station, a public broadcasting station and a cable television station with 24 channels. In 1997 there were 221,000 radio and 106,000 TV sets (colour by NTSC).

Press. There is one daily newspaper, a twice-weekly paper, and four weekly publications (all of which are of military or religious interest only).

Tourism. There were 1,288,000 tourist arrivals in 2000; spending by tourists in 1999 totalled $1·91bn.

FURTHER READING

Report (Annual) of the Governor of Guam to the US Department of Interior
Guam Annual Economic Review. Economic Research Center, Hagåtña

Rogers, R. F., *Destiny's Landfall: a History of Guam*. Hawaii Univ. Press, 1995
Wuerch, W. L. and Ballendorf, D. A., *Historical Dictionary of Guam and Micronesia*. Metuchen, NJ, 1995

VIRGIN ISLANDS OF THE UNITED STATES

KEY HISTORICAL EVENTS

The Virgin Islands of the United States, formerly known as the Danish West Indies, were named and claimed for Spain by Columbus in 1493. They were later settled by Dutch and English planters, invaded by France in the mid-17th century and abandoned by the French *c.* 1700, by which time Danish influence had been established. St Croix was held by the Knights of Malta between two periods of French rule.

The Virgin Islands were purchased by the United States from Denmark for $25m. in a treaty ratified by both nations and proclaimed on 31 March 1917. Their value was wholly strategic, inasmuch as they commanded the Anegada Passage from the Atlantic Ocean to the Caribbean Sea and the approach to the Panama Canal. Although the inhabitants were made US citizens in 1927, the islands are, constitutionally, an 'unincorporated territory'.

TERRITORY AND POPULATION

The Virgin Islands group, lying about 40 miles due east of Puerto Rico, comprises the islands of St Thomas (31 sq. miles), St Croix (83 sq. miles), St John (20 sq. miles) and 65 small islets or cays, mostly uninhabited. The total area is 1,910 sq. km (738 sq. miles), of which 346 sq. km (134 sq. miles) are dry land.

The population according to the 2000 census was 108,612 (females, 56,748); density 811 per sq. mile. Official population estimate for July 2002 was 123,498. 54·1% of the population were rural in 1998.

Population (2000 census) of St Croix, 53,234; St Thomas, 51,181; St John, 4,197. In 2000, 69·8% of the population were native born.

The capital and only city, Charlotte Amalie, on St Thomas, had a population (2000 census) of 11,044. There are two towns on St Croix with 2000 census populations of: Christiansted, 2,637; Frederiksted, 732.

SOCIAL STATISTICS

2002 births, 1,634; deaths, 617. Rates, 2002 (per 1,000 population); birth, 15·0; death, 5·7; infant mortality (1997), 13·0 per 1,000 live births.

CLIMATE

Average temperatures vary from 77°F to 82°F throughout the year; humidity is low. Average annual rainfall, about 45". The islands lie in the hurricane belt; tropical storms with heavy rainfall can occur in late summer.

CONSTITUTION AND GOVERNMENT

The Organic Act of 22 July 1954 gives the US Department of the Interior full jurisdiction; some limited legislative powers are given to a single-chambered legislature, composed of 15 senators elected for two years representing the two legislative districts of St Croix and St Thomas-St John.

The Governor is elected by the residents. Since 1954 there have been four attempts to redraft the Constitution, to provide for greater autonomy. Each has been rejected by the electorate. The latest was defeated in a referendum in Nov. 1981, 50% of the electorate participating.

For administration, there are 14 executive departments, 13 of which are under commissioners and the other, the Department of Justice, under an Attorney-General. The US Department of the Interior appoints a Federal Comptroller of government revenue and expenditure.

The franchise is vested in residents who are citizens of the United States, 18 years of age or over. In 1986 there were 34,183 voters, of whom 26,377 participated in the local elections that year. They do not participate in the US presidential election but they have a non-voting representative in Congress.

The capital is Charlotte Amalie, on St Thomas Island.

RECENT ELECTIONS

Elections for governor held on 5 Nov. 2002 were won by Charles Turnbull, II (Democrat) with 50·5% of the votes, ahead of John DeJongh in second place with 24·4%. The turn-out was 62%. In Senate elections held on 2 Nov. 2004 the Democratic Party of the Virgin Islands won 10 out of 15 seats.

CURRENT ADMINISTRATION

Governor: Charles Turnbull, II (D.), 2003–07 (salary: $80,000).

Lieut.-Governor: Vargrave A. Richards (D.), 2003–07 ($75,000).

US Virgin Islands Parliament: http://www.senate.gov.vi

ECONOMY

Currency. United States currency became legal tender on 1 July 1934.

Budget. Under the 1954 Organic Act finances are provided partly from local revenues—customs, federal income tax, real and personal property tax, trade tax, excise tax, pilotage fees, etc.—and partly from Federal Matching Funds, being the excise taxes collected by the federal government on such Virgin Islands products transported to the mainland as are liable.

Per capita income, 2000, $13,139.

Budget for financial year 1999: revenues, $486·3m.; expenditures, $486·3m.

Banking and Finance. Banks include the Chase Manhattan Bank; the Bank of Nova Scotia; the First Federal Savings and Loan Association of Puerto Rico; the Banco Popular of the Virgin Islands; First Bank of Puerto Rico; the Virgin Islands Community Bank; the Bank of St Croix; Barclays Bank International; Citibank; Banco Popular de Puerto Rico; and FirstBank Virgin Islands.

ENERGY AND NATURAL RESOURCES

Environment. Carbon dioxide emissions from the consumption and flaring of fossil fuels in 2002 were the equivalent of 114·6 tonnes per capita, the second highest in the world.

Electricity. The Virgin Islands Water and Power Authority provides electric power from generating plants on St Croix and St Thomas; St John is served by power cable and emergency generator. Production in 2000 was about 1·09bn. kWh. Per capita consumption in 2000 was an estimated 9,008 kWh. Installed capacity in 2000 was 323,000 kW.

Water. There are six de-salinization plants with maximum daily capacity of 8·7m. gallons of fresh water. Rainwater remains the most reliable source.

The total area covered by water is approximately 37 sq. miles.

Agriculture. Land for fruit, vegetables and animal feed is available on St Croix, and there are tax incentives for development. Sugar has been terminated as a commercial crop and over 4,000 acres of prime land could be utilized for food crops.

Livestock (2002): cattle, 8,000; goats, 4,000; pigs, 3,000; sheep, 3,000.

Fisheries. There is a fishermen's co-operative with a market at Christiansted. There is a shellfish-farming project at Rust-op-Twist, St Croix. The total catch in 2001 was approximately 660,000 lb (300 tonnes).

INDUSTRY

The main occupations on St Thomas are tourism and government service; on St Croix manufacturing is more important. Manufactures include rum (the most valuable product), watches, pharmaceuticals and fragrances. Industries in order of revenue: tourism, refining oil, watch assembly, rum distilling, construction.

Labour. In 2000 the total labour force was 51,042, of whom 7,351 were employed in the arts, entertainment, recreation, accommodation and food services, 6,742 were employed in educational, health and social services, 6,476 in retail trade, 4,931 in public administration and 4,900 in construction. In 2000 there were 4,368 registered unemployed persons, or 5·6% of the workforce.

INTERNATIONAL TRADE

Imports and Exports. Exports, 2001, totalled $4,234·2m. and imports $4,608·7m. The main import is crude petroleum, while the principal exports are petroleum products.

COMMUNICATIONS

Roads. In 1996 the Virgin Islands had 856 km of roads.

Civil Aviation. There is a daily cargo and passenger service between St Thomas and St Croix. Alexander Hamilton Airport on St Croix can take all aircraft except Concorde. Cyril E. King Airport on St Thomas takes 727-class aircraft. There are air connections to mainland USA and other Caribbean islands. There were 658,905 passenger enplanements in 2000.

Shipping. The whole territory has free port status. There is an hourly boat service between St Thomas and St John and a 75-minute catamaran service between St Croix and St Thomas twice or three times a day.

Telecommunications. All three Virgin Islands have a dial telephone system. Telephone subscribers numbered 110,400 in 2002 (1,010·1 per 1,000 population). Direct dialling to Puerto Rico and the mainland, and internationally, is now possible. Worldwide radio telegraph service is also available. In 1998 there were 25,000 mobile phone subscribers. In 2002 there were 30,000 Internet users.

Postal Services. In 1994 there were nine post offices.

SOCIAL INSTITUTIONS

Justice. The population in penal institutions in Dec. 2002 was 647 (522 per 100,000 population).

Religion. At the 2000 census 42% of the population were Baptists, 34% were Roman Catholics and 17% were Episcopalians.

There are places of worship of the Protestant, Roman Catholic and Jewish faiths in St Thomas and St Croix, and Protestant and Roman Catholic churches in St John.

Education. In 2000 there were 32,119 people enrolled in schools, of which 2,484 in nursery and pre-school, 2,230 in kindergarten, 16,858 in elementary school, 7,440 in high school and 3,107 in college or graduate school. In 1997 there were 777 elementary teachers and 782 secondary teachers. In autumn 2003 the University of the Virgin Islands had 2,768 students. The College is part of the United States land-grant network of higher education. The Virgin Islands has the highest proportion of female students in higher education anywhere in the world, at 77% in 1998–99.

Health. In 2002 there were 161 non-federal physicians and in 1985 there were 49 hospital beds per 10,000 inhabitants. The Roy L. Schneider Hospital on St Thomas had 169 beds and over 50 physicians in 2004. The Juan F. Luis Hospital, Christiansted, serves St Croix, with 160 beds in 1994.

Welfare. In 2001 federal direct payments for individuals totalled $233·4m., including: retirement insurance, $72·0m.; housing assistance, $53·4m.; survivors insurance, $20·2m.; disability insurance, $18·0m.; food stamps, $17·6m.

CULTURE

Broadcasting. In 2002 there were 16 radio stations and one public and one commercial TV station. In 1997 there were 107,000 radio receivers and in 2000 there were 64,700 TV receivers (colour by NTSC).

Press. In 1996 there were three dailies with a combined circulation of 42,000, at a rate of 437 per 1,000 inhabitants.

Tourism. Tourism accounts for some 70% of GDP. There were 565,000 foreign tourists in 2000, and 1,616,000 cruise ship arrivals in 1998. Revenue from tourism amounted to $965m. in 2000. 6,800 people were employed in the leisure and hospitality sector in 2003.

St Thomas claims some of the best white-sand beaches in the Caribbean and attracts visitors to its Coral World aquarium. Christiansted, on St Croix, is the old capital of the Danish colony, with well-preserved colonial architecture. St Croix is a major diving destination and has a leatherback turtle nesting beach. St John, the least developed of the islands, is dominated by a thickly forested national park.

FURTHER READING

Moll, V. P., *Virgin Islands.* [Bibliography] ABC-Clio, Oxford and Santa Barbara (CA), 1991

OTHER UNINCORPORATED TERRITORIES

Howland, Baker and Jarvis Islands

Three small Pacific islands, the largest two of which, Howland Island and Baker Island, are 2,600 km southwest of Hawaii. Administered under the US Department of the Interior. Area 2 sq. miles; population (1995) numbered 1,168. There is a National Assembly.

Johnston Atoll

Two small Pacific islands 1,100 km southwest of Hawaii, administered by the US Air Force. Area, under 1 sq. mile; population (1996) totalled 1,200 US military and civilian contractor personnel.

Midway Islands

Two small Pacific islands at the western end of the Hawaiian chain, administered by the US Navy. Area, 2 sq. miles; population (1995) was 453 US military personnel.

Wake Island

Three small Pacific islands 3,700 km west of Hawaii, administered by the US Air Force. Area, 3 sq. miles; population (1995) numbered 302 US military and contract personnel.

Kingman Reef

Small Pacific reef 1,500 km southwest of Hawaii, administered by the US Navy. Area one tenth of a sq. mile; uninhabited.

Navassa Island

Small Caribbean island 48 km west of Haiti, administered by US Coast Guards. Area 2 sq. miles; uninhabited.

Palmyra Atoll

Small atoll 1,500 km southwest of Hawaii, administered by the US Department of the Interior. Area 5 sq. miles; uninhabited.

URUGUAY

República Oriental del Uruguay

Capital: Montevideo
Population projection, 2010: 3·58m.
GDP per capita, 2002: (PPP$) 7,830
HDI/world rank: 0·833/46

KEY HISTORICAL EVENTS

Uruguay was the last colony settled by Spain in the Americas. Part of the Spanish viceroyalty of Rio de la Plata until revolutionaries expelled the Spanish in 1811 and subsequently a province of Brazil, Uruguay declared independence on 25 Aug. 1825. Conflict between two political parties, the *blancos* (conservatives) and the *colorados* (liberals), led, in 1865–70, to the War of the Triple Alliance. In 1903 peace and prosperity were restored under President José Batlle y Ordóñez. Since 1904 Uruguay has been unique in her constitutional innovations, all designed to protect her from dictatorship. A favoured device was the collegiate system of government, in which the two largest political parties were represented.

The early part of the 20th century saw the development of a welfare state in Uruguay which encouraged extensive immigration. In 1919 a new constitution was adopted providing for a *colegiado*—a plural executive based on the Swiss pattern. However, the system was abolished in 1933 and replaced by presidential government, with quadrennial elections. From 1951 to 1966 a collective form of leadership again replaced the presidency. During the 1960s, following a series of strikes and riots, the Army became increasingly influential, repressive measures were adopted and presidential government was restored in 1967. The Tupamaro, Marxist urban guerrillas, sought violent revolution but were finally defeated by the Army in 1972. The return to civilian rule came on 12 Feb. 1985.

TERRITORY AND POPULATION

Uruguay is bounded on the northeast by Brazil, on the southeast by the Atlantic, on the south by the Río de la Plata and on the west by Argentina. The area, including inland waters, is 176,215 sq. km (68,037 sq. miles). The following table shows the area and the population of the 19 departments at census 1996:

Departments	*Sq. km*	*Census 1996*	*Capital*
Artigas	11,928	75,059	Artigas
Canelones	4,536	443,053	Canelones
Cerro-Largo	13,648	82,510	Melo
Colonia	6,106	120,241	Colonia
Durazno	11,643	55,716	Durazno
Flores	5,144	25,030	Trinidad
Florida	10,417	66,503	Florida
Lavalleja	10,016	61,085	Minas
Maldonado	4,793	127,502	Maldonado
Montevideo	530	1,344,839	Montevideo
Paysandú	13,922	111,509	Paysandú
Río Negro	9,282	51,713	Fray Bentos
Rivera	9,370	98,472	Rivera
Rocha	10,551	70,292	Rocha
Salto	14,163	117,597	Salto
San José	4,992	96,664	San José
Soriano	9,008	81,557	Mercedes
Tacuarembó	15,438	84,919	Tacuarembó
Treinta y Tres	9,529	49,502	Treinta y Tres

Total population, census (1996) 3,163,763; population density, 18·0 per sq. km. 2002 population estimate, 3,390,000.

The UN gives a projected population for 2010 of 3·58m.

In 1996 Montevideo (the capital) accounted for 44·5% of the total population. It had a population in 1999 of 1,237,000. Other major cities are Salto (population of

80,323 at 1985 census) and Paysandú (76,191 at 1985 census). Uruguay has the highest percentage of urban population in South America, with 92·1% living in urban areas in 2001.

13% of the population are over 65; 24% are under 15; 63% are between 15 and 64. The official language is Spanish.

SOCIAL STATISTICS

2000: births, 52,720; deaths, 32,456; marriages, 13,888; divorces, 6,822. Rates (per 1,000 population), 2000: birth, 15·9; death, 9·2; marriage, 4·2; divorce, 2·0. Annual population growth rate, 1992–2002, 0·7%. Infant mortality, 2001 (per 1,000 live births), 14. Life expectancy in 2001 was 71·3 years among males and 78·6 years among females. Fertility rate, 2001, 2·3 births per woman.

CLIMATE

A warm temperate climate, with mild winters and warm summers. The wettest months are March to June, but there is really no dry season. Montevideo, Jan. 72°F (22·2°C), July 50°F (10°C). Annual rainfall 38" (950 mm).

CONSTITUTION AND GOVERNMENT

Congress consists of a *Senate* of 31 members and a *Chamber of Deputies* of 99 members, both elected by proportional representation for five-year terms. The electoral system provides that the successful presidential candidate be a member of the party which gains a parliamentary majority. Electors vote for deputies on a first-past-the-post system, and simultaneously vote for a presidential candidate of the same party. The winners of the second vote are credited with the number of votes obtained by their party in the parliamentary elections. Referendums may be called at the instigation of 10,000 signatories.

National Anthem. 'Orientales, la patria o la tumba' ('Easterners, the fatherland or the tomb'); words by F. Acuña de Figueroa, tune by F. J. Deballi.

RECENT ELECTIONS

Elections for the General Assembly were held on 31 Oct. 2004. In elections to the Chamber of Deputies, the Progressive Encounter-Broad Front-New Majority (comprised of the Uruguay Assembly, Frenteamplio Confluence, Current 78, Movement of Popular Participation, Christian-Democratic Party, Communist Party of Uruguay, Party of the Communes, Socialist Party of Uruguay and the Artiguist Tendency) won 53 seats, the National Party (PN) 34, the Colorado Party (PC) 10 and the Independent Party 2. In the Senate election the Progressive Encounter-Broad Front-New Majority (EP-FA-NM) won 17 seats, PN 11 and PC 3.

In the presidential election, also held on 31 Oct. 2004, Tabaré Vázquez (EP-FA-NM) received 50·4% of the vote, Jorge Larrañaga (PN) 34·3% and Guillermo Stirling (Colorado Party) 10·4%. Turn-out was 89·6%.

CURRENT ADMINISTRATION

President: Tabaré Vázquez; b. 1940 (EP-FA-NM; sworn in 1 March 2005).

Vice-President: Rodolfo Nin Novoa.

In March 2005 the government comprised:

Minister of Agriculture, Livestock and Fisheries: José Mujica. *Defence:* Azucena Berrutti. *Education and Culture:* Jorge Brovetto. *Economy:* Danilo Astori. *Foreign Affairs:* Reinaldo Gargano. *Public Health:* María Julia Muñoz. *Housing:* Mariano Arana. *Industry:* Jorge Lepra. *Interior:* José Díaz. *Labour:* Eduardo Bonomi. *Tourism, Sports and Youth:* Héctor Lescano. *Transport:* Víctor Rossi.

Presidency Website (Spanish only): http://www.presidencia.gub.uy

DEFENCE

Defence expenditure totalled US$103m. in 2003 (US$30 per capita), representing 0·9% of GDP.

Army. The Army consists of volunteers who enlist for one–two years service. There are four military regions with divisional headquarters. Strength (2002) 15,200. In addition there are government paramilitary forces numbering 920.

Navy. The Navy includes three ex-French frigates. A naval aviation service 300 strong operates anti-submarine aircraft. Personnel in 2002 totalled 5,700 including 300 naval infantry. The main base is at Montevideo.

Air Force. Organized with US aid, the Air Force had (2002) about 3,000 personnel and 28 combat aircraft.

INTERNATIONAL RELATIONS

Uruguay is a member of the UN, WTO, OAS, Inter-American Development Bank, Mercosur, LAIA, IOM and the Antarctic Treaty.

ECONOMY

In 2002 agriculture contributed 9·4% of GDP, industry 26·8% and services 63·8%.

Overview. Uruguay's economy benefits from a favourable climate for agriculture and substantial hydropower potential. During 1990–98 the economy grew by 3·9% a year on average, above the long-term trend of 2% between 1960–2000. Uruguay is exposed to competition from its neighbours, Brazil and Argentina, where strong rates of growth bolstered export performance. Export performance has also benefited greatly from the creation of Mercosur. In 1999, as a consequence of the devaluation of the Brazilian *real* and the worst drought since 1988, Uruguay's economy shrank by 2·8%. Weak banking regulations and strong links with Argentina left Uruguay exposed to the Argentinian bank-run and the authorities were forced to float the peso in June 2002. GDP contracted by a cumulative 7·5% during 1999–2001 and contracted by a further 10·8% in 2002. The events of 1999–2002 have highlighted macroeconomic and structural weaknesses that leave the economy vulnerable to external shocks, including high trade dependence on the Mercosur region and a weak banking system.

Currency. The unit of currency is the *Uruguayan peso* (UYP), of 100 *centésimos*, which replaced the nuevo peso in March 1993 at 1 Uruguayan peso = 1,000 nuevos pesos. In June 2002 Uruguay allowed the peso to float freely. Foreign exchange reserves were US$1,791m. and gold reserves 8,000 troy oz in May 2002 (1·8m. troy oz in Nov. 1999). Inflation, which had been over 100% in 1990, was 14·0% in 2002. Total money supply in Feb. 2002 was 12,456m. pesos.

Budget. Central government finance (1m. pesos):

	1996	*1997*	*1998*	*1999*	*2000*	*2001*
Revenue	45,535	60,165	70,664	67,197	68,167	62,708
Expenditure	47,914	62,363	72,673	76,079	76,489	77,487

Main components of 2001 revenue: taxes on goods and services, 38·7%; social security contributions, 23·4%; income taxes, 15·2%. Expenditure included: social security and welfare, 56·5%; education, 7·6%; health, 6·6%.

Standard rate of VAT is 23%.

Performance. Uruguay depends heavily on its two large neighbours, Brazil and Argentina. In 1999 Uruguay's economy contracted by 2·8%. In 2000 there was also negative growth, of 1·4%, and the general downturn in the world economy exacerbated by Argentina's crisis caused the economy to contract again in 2001, by 3·4%. In 2002 as Argentina's economic crisis worsened so did the situation in Uruguay, with the economy shrinking by 10·8%. Total GDP in 2003 was US$11·1bn.

Banking and Finance. The Central Bank (*President*, Walter Cancela) was inaugurated on 16 May 1967. It is the bank of issue and supreme regulatory authority. In 2003 there were three other state banks, three principal commercial banks, ten foreign banks and two major credit co-operatives. Savings banks deposits were 1,993,029m. pesos in 1995.

There is a stock exchange in Montevideo.

ENERGY AND NATURAL RESOURCES

Environment. Uruguay's carbon dioxide emissions from the consumption and flaring of fossil fuels in 2002 were the equivalent of 1·3 tonnes per capita. An *Environmental Sustainability Index* compiled for the World Economic Forum meeting in Feb. 2002 ranked Uruguay sixth in the world, with 66·0%. The index measured the ability of countries to maintain favourable environmental conditions and examined various factors including pollution levels and the use or abuse of natural resources.

Electricity. Installed capacity was 2·2m. kW in 2000. Production in 2000 was 7·59bn. kWh, with consumption per capita 2,390 kWh.

Agriculture. Rising investment has helped agriculture, which has given a major boost to the country's economy. Some 41m. acres are devoted to farming, of which 90% to livestock and 10% to crops. Some large *estancias* have been divided up into family farms; the average farm is about 250 acres. In 2001 there were 1·30m. ha of arable land and 40,000 ha of permanent crops. 181,000 ha were irrigated in 2001.

Main crops (in 1,000 tonnes), 2000: rice, 1,175; wheat, 310; barley, 200; sugarcane, 160; oranges, 150; grapes, 140; potatoes, 110; wine, 108; apples, 65; maize, 65; sweet potatoes, 62; tangerines and mandarins, 60; lemons and limes, 48; oats, 45. The country has some 6m. fruit trees, principally peaches, oranges, tangerines and pears.

Livestock, 2000: sheep, 13·03m.; cattle, 10·80m.; horses, 500,000; pigs, 380,000; chickens, 13m.

Livestock products, 2000 (in 1,000 tonnes): beef and veal, 453; lamb and mutton, 51; pork, bacon and ham, 26; poultry meat, 53; milk 1,422; eggs, 37; greasy wool, 55.

Forestry. In 2000 the area under forests was 1·29m. ha (mainly eucalyptus and pine), representing 7·4% of the total land area. In 2001, 5·81m. cu. metres of roundwood were cut.

Fisheries. The total catch in 2001 was 105,034 tonnes, almost entirely marine fish.

INDUSTRY

In 2001 industry accounted for 26·6% of GDP, with manufacturing contributing 16·6%. Industries include meat packing, oil refining, cement manufacture, foodstuffs, beverages, leather and textile manufacture, chemicals, light engineering and transport equipment. Output (in 1,000 tonnes): cement (2001), 674; distillate fuel oil (2000), 624; residual fuel oil (2000), 621; petrol (1999), 325; meat-packing (1991), 1,132,000 head; 9·6bn. cigarettes (2001).

Labour. In 1996 the retirement age was raised from 55 to 60 for women; it remains 60 for men. The labour force in 1996 totalled 1,444,000 (59% males). In 2001, 22·4% of the urban workforce was engaged in wholesale and retail trade/repair of motor vehicles, motorcycles and personal and household goods/hotels and restaurants; 15·5% in manufacturing/electricity, gas and water supply; 9·2% in private households with employed persons; and 9·1% in financial intermediation and real estate, renting and business activities. In 2001 the unemployment rate in urban areas was 15·3%.

INTERNATIONAL TRADE

External debt was US$10,736m. in 2002.

Imports and Exports. Trade in US$1m.:

	1998	*1999*	*2000*	*2001*	*2002*
Imports f.o.b.	3,601·4	3,187·2	3,311·1	2,914·7	1,872·9
Exports f.o.b.	2,829·3	2,290·6	2,383·8	2,139·4	1,933·1

Main imports in 1999: machinery and transport equipment, 31·2%; chemicals, 17·2%; manufactured goods, 15·3%; petroleum, 10·1%; foodstuffs, 8·9%. Main exports in 1999: meat, 17·8%; rice, 8·8%; leather, 7·7%; yarn and textiles, 7·5%; dairy products, 6·9%; road vehicles, 5·6%.

In 1999 the main import suppliers were Argentina (23·9%), Brazil (19·4%), USA (11·3%) and France (4·2%). Leading export destinations were Brazil (24·9%), Argentina (16·5%), USA (6·9%) and Germany (5·0%).

COMMUNICATIONS

Roads. In 1999 it was estimated that there were about 8,983 km of roads, including 2,589 km of national roads and 5,024 km of regional roads. Uruguay has one of the densest road networks in the world. Passenger cars in 1997 numbered 517,000 (153·9 per 1,000 inhabitants). There were 737 fatalities as a result of road accidents in 1997.

Rail. The total railway system open for traffic was (1996) 2,073 km of 1,435 mm gauge. Passenger services, which had been abandoned in 1988, were resumed on a limited basis in 1993. Freight tonne-km in 2000 came to 239m. and passenger-km travelled to 9m.

Civil Aviation. There is an international airport at Montevideo (Carrasco). The national carrier is Pluna. In 2003 it operated domestic services and maintained routes to Asuncion, Buenos Aires, Madrid, Porto Alegre, Rio de Janeiro, Santiago and São Paulo. There were 60 airports in 1996, 45 with paved runways and 15 with unpaved runways. In 1998 Montevideo handled 1,470,000 passengers (1,198,000 on international flights) and 25,500 tonnes of freight. In 1999 scheduled airline traffic of Uruguay-based carriers flew 8·4m. km, carrying 728,000 passengers (all on international flights).

Shipping. In 2002 sea-going shipping totalled 75,000 GRT, including oil tankers 6,000 GRT. In 2000 vessels totalling 5,257,000 NRT entered ports and vessels totalling 19,587,000 NRT cleared. Navigable inland waterways total 1,600 km.

Telecommunications. The telephone system in Montevideo is controlled by the State; small companies operate in the interior. Uruguay had 1,598,500 telephone subscribers in 2002 (472·2 for every 1,000 persons); and there were 370,000 PCs in use in 2001 (110·1 for every 1,000 persons). There were 652,000 mobile phone subscribers in 2002. Internet users numbered 400,000 in 2001.

Postal Services. In 1998 there were 942 post offices.

SOCIAL INSTITUTIONS

Justice. The Supreme Court is elected by Congress; it appoints all other judges. There are six courts of appeal, each with three judges. There are civil and criminal courts. Montevideo has ten courts of first instance, Paysandú and Salto have two each and the other departments have one each. There are approximately 300 lower courts.

The population in penal institutions in Sept. 2003 was 7,100 (209 per 100,000 of national population).

Religion. State and Church are separate, and there is complete religious liberty. In 2001 there were 2·6m. Roman Catholics and 710,000 persons with other beliefs.

Education. Adult literacy in 2001 was 97·6% (male, 97·2%; female, 98·1%). The female literacy rate is the second highest in South America, behind Guyana. Primary education is obligatory; both primary and secondary education are free. In 2003 there were 1,507 pre-primary schools with 3,741 (2000) teachers for 103,619 pupils; 2,396 primary schools with 16,605 teachers for 354,843 pupils and at secondary level there were (2000) 303,883 pupils and 20,778 teachers.

There is one state university, one independent Roman Catholic university and one private institute of technology. In 2000–01 there were 97,541 students and 11,245 academic staff in tertiary education.

In 2000–01 total public expenditure on education came to 2·8% of GNP and represented 11·8% of total government expenditure.

Health. In 1998 there were 11,964 physicians, 3,921 dentists, 2,369 nurses, 1,009 pharmacists and 586 midwives. There were 118 hospitals in 1997 with a provision of 35 beds per 10,000 population.

Welfare. The welfare state dates from the beginning of the 1900s. In 2002 there were 0·5m. recipients of pensions and benefits. A private pension scheme inaugurated in 1996 had 315,000 members at 31 Dec. 1996. State spending on social security has been capped at 15% of GDP.

CULTURE

World Heritage Sites. Uruguay has one site on the UNESCO World Heritage List: the Historic Quarter of the City of Colonia del Sacramento (inscribed on the list in 1995), founded in 1680 by the Portuguese.

Broadcasting. In 2000 there were 2·0m. radio receivers and in 2001 there were 1·8m. television receivers (colour by PAL N). There were 20 TV stations and about 250 radio stations in 2001.

Press. In 1996 there were 36 daily newspapers with a combined circulation of 950,000. There were also 62 non-daily newspapers and periodicals.

Tourism. There were 1·97m. tourists in 2000, mainly from Argentina. Receipts totalled US$652m.

DIPLOMATIC REPRESENTATIVES

Of Uruguay in the United Kingdom (2nd Floor, 140 Brompton Rd, London, SW3 1HY)
Ambassador: Ricardo Varela.

Of the United Kingdom in Uruguay (Calle Marco Bruto 1073, 11300 Montevideo)
Ambassador: John Everard.

Of Uruguay in the USA (1913 I St., NW, Washington, D.C., 20006)
Ambassador: Carlos Gianelli.

Of the USA in Uruguay (Lauro Muller 1776, Montevideo)
Ambassador: Martin J. Silverstein.

Of Uruguay to the United Nations
Ambassador: Alejandro Artuccio.

Of Uruguay to the European Union
Ambassador: Elbio Oscar Rosselli Frieri.

FURTHER READING

González, L. E., *Political Structures and Democracy in Uruguay.* Univ. of Notre Dame Press, 1992

Sosnowski, S. (ed.) *Repression, Exile and Democracy: Uruguayan Culture.* Duke Univ. Press, 1993

National library: Biblioteca Nacional del Uruguay, Guayabo 1793, Montevideo.
Website (Spanish only): http://www.ine.gub.uy/

UZBEKISTAN

Uzbekiston Respublikasy

Capital: Tashkent
Population projection, 2010: 28·84m.
GDP per capita, 2002: (PPP$) 1,670
HDI/world rank: 0·709/107

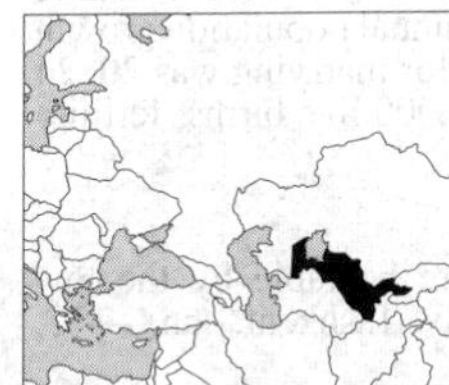

KEY HISTORICAL EVENTS

Descended from nomadic Mongol tribes who settled in Central Asia in the 13th century, the Uzbeks came under Russian control in the late 19th century. In Oct. 1917 the Tashkent Soviet assumed authority. The semi-independent Khanates of Khiva and Bokhara were first (1920) transformed into People's Republics, then (1923–24) into Soviet Socialist Republics, and finally merged in the Uzbek SSR and other republics. On 20 June 1990 the Supreme Soviet adopted a declaration of sovereignty and in Aug. 1991, following an unsuccessful coup, declared independence as the Republic of Uzbekistan. In Dec. 1991 Uzbekistan became a member of the CIS.

Islam Karimov became head of state in 1990 and was elected president in 1991 and again in 2000. In that year Uzbek border guards moved their posts 5 km into a part of neighbouring Kazakhstan. Borders with Russia and Kyrgyzstan still remain undefined, yet the chief cause for concern is the Islamist Movement of Uzbekistan's fight to create an Islamic state in the Fergana Valley. Bomb blasts in Tashkent, one of which almost killed the president in 1999, were blamed on religious extremists and the army suffered losses fighting the IMU in 2000. IMU leader Juma Namangoniy was reportedly killed in Aug. 2002. Nearly 50 people died during a period of bombings and shootings in March 2004, allegedly perpetrated by Islamic militants, and suicide bombers targeted the US and Israeli embassies in Tashkent in July of that year.

TERRITORY AND POPULATION

Uzbekistan is bordered in the north by Kazakhstan, in the east by Kyrgyzstan and Tajikistan, in the south by Afghanistan and in the west by Turkmenistan. Area, 447,400 sq. km (172,741 sq. miles). At the 1989 census the population was 19,810,077 (71·4% Uzbek, 8·4% Russian, 4·7% Tajik, 4·1% Kazakh, 3·2% Tatar and 2·1% Karakalpak). 2002 population estimate, 25,695,000 (12,926,000 females); density, 57·4 per sq. km. In 2001, 63·3% of the population lived in rural areas.

The UN gives a projected population for 2010 of 28·84m.

The areas and populations of the 12 Regions and the Karakalpak Autonomous Republic (Karakalpakstan) are as follows (Uzbek spellings in brackets):

Region	*Area (in sq. km)*	*Population (1994 estimate)*	*Capital*	*Population (1994 estimate)*
Andizhan (Andijon)	4,200	1,899,000	Andizhan	303,000
Bukhara (Bukhoro)	39,400	1,262,000	Bukhara	236,000
Ferghana (Farghona)	7,100	2,338,000	Ferghana	191,000
Dzhizak (Jizzakh)	20,500	831,000	Dzhizak	116,000
Khorezm (Khorazm)	6,300	1,135,000	Urgench (Urganch)	135,000
Namangan	7,900	1,652,000	Namangan	341,000
Navoi (Nawoiy)	110,800	715,000	Nawoiy	115,000
Kashkadar (Qashqadaryo)	28,400	715,000	Karshi (Qarshi)	177,000
Karakalpakstan Autonomous Republic (Qoraqalpoghiston)	164,900	1,343,000	Nukus (Nuqus)	185,000
Samarkand (Samarqand)	16,400	2,322,000	Samarkand	368,000
Syr-Darya (Sirdaryo)	5,100	600,000	Gulistan (Guliston)	57,000[1]
Surkhan-Darya (Surkhondaryo)	20,800	1,437,000	Termez (Termiz)	90,000[1]
Tashkent (Toshkent)	15,600	4,357,000	Tashkent	2,121,000

[1]1991.

The capital is Tashkent (2000 population estimate, 2,133,000); other large towns are Namangan, Samarkand and Andizhan. There are 124 towns, 97 urban settlements and 155 rural districts.

The Roman alphabet (in use 1929–40) was reintroduced in 1994. Arabic script was in use prior to 1929, and Cyrillic, 1940–94.

Uzbek, Russian and Tajik are all spoken.

SOCIAL STATISTICS

2001 births, 512,950; deaths, 132,542; marriages, 170,101; divorces, 15,646. Rates, 2001: birth (per 1,000 population), 20·5; death, 5·3; marriage, 6·8; divorce, 0·6. Life expectancy, 2001, 66·4 years for men and 72·1 for women. Annual population growth rate, 1992–2002, 1·8%. In 1997 the most popular age range for marrying was 20–24 for both males and females. Infant mortality, 2001, 52 per 1,000 live births; fertility rate, 2001, 2·5 births per woman.

CLIMATE

The summers are warm to hot but the heat is made more bearable by the low humidity. The winters are cold but generally dry and sunny. Tashkent, Jan. –1°C, July 25°C. Annual rainfall 14·76" (375 mm).

CONSTITUTION AND GOVERNMENT

A new constitution was adopted on 8 Dec. 1992 stating that Uzbekistan is a pluralist democracy. The constitution restricts the president to standing for two five-year terms. In Jan. 2002 a referendum was held at which 91% of the electorate voted in favour of extending the presidential term from five to seven years. Voters were also in favour of changing from a single-chamber legislature to a bicameral parliament. Uzbekistan switched to a bicameral legislature in Jan. 2005 with the establishment of the 100-member *Senate* (with 16 members selected by the president and 84 elected from the ranks of regional, district and city legislative councils). The lower house is the 120-member (formerly 250-member) *Oliy Majlis* (Supreme Assembly).

RECENT ELECTIONS

Presidential elections were held on 9 Jan. 2000. Incumbent Islam Karimov was elected against a single opponent with 91·9% of the vote. Turn-out was 95%. It was the first presidential election since 1991. Elections were cancelled in 1997 after Karimov's term was extended to 2000 by referendum.

In parliamentary elections held in two rounds on 26 Dec. 2004 and 9 Jan 2005, criticized for electoral abuses, the Liberal-Democratic Party won 41 of the 120 seats, followed by the People's Democratic Party with 28, the Self-Sacrifice National Democratic Party with 18, the Uzbekistan National Revival Democratic Party with 11 and the Justice Social Democratic Party with 10. The remaining seats went to independent candidates. All parties taking part in the election were loyal to President Islam Karimov—opposition parties were barred from participating.

CURRENT ADMINISTRATION

President: Islam Karimov; b. 1938 (sworn in 24 March 1990).

In March 2005 the government comprised:

Prime Minister: Shavkat Mirziyayev; b. 1957 (People's Democratic Party; in office since 11 Dec. 2003).

First Deputy Prime Minister: Rustam Azimov (also *Minister of Economy*). *Deputy Prime Ministers:* Abdukahhor Tukhtaev; Svetlana Inamova; Abdulla Aripov; Oktir Sultanov; Elyor Ganiyev (also *Minister of Foreign Affairs)*; Rustam Kasymov (also *Minister of Higher and Secondary Specialized Education*).

Minister of Agriculture and Water Resources: Sayfiddin Ismoilov. *Internal Affairs:* Zokirjon Almatov. *Defence:* Kodir Ghulomov. *Justice:* Buritosh Mustafayev. *Finance:* Saidahmad Rahimov. *Education:* Turobjon Djuraev. *Culture and Sports:* Alisher Azizkhodjaev. *Health:* Feruz Nazirov. *Labour and Social Protection:* Oqiljon Obidov. *Emergency Situations:* Bakhtiyor Subanov.

Chairman, Oliy Majlis: Erkin Halilov.

Office of the President: http://www.gov.uz

DEFENCE

Conscription is for 18 months. Defence expenditure in 2003 totalled US$2,200 (US$86 per capita), representing 5·0% of GDP. The USA opened a military base in Kyrgyzstan in 2001 to aid the war in Afghanistan against the Taliban.

Army. Personnel, 2002, 40,000. There are, in addition, paramilitary forces totalling 18,000–20,000.

Air Force. Personnel, 2002, 10–15,000. There were 135 combat aircraft in operation (including Su-17s, Su-24s, Su-25s, Su-27s and MiG-29s) and 42 attack helicopters.

INTERNATIONAL RELATIONS

Uzbekistan is a member of the UN, CIS, OSCE, Asian Development Bank, ECO, OIC, Islamic Development Bank and the NATO Partnership for Peace.

ECONOMY

Agriculture accounted for 34·7% of GDP in 2002, industry 21·6% and services 43·7%.

Overview. Agriculture accounts for 35% of GDP and 40% of employment. Uzbekistan is a low-income country with the third lowest GDP per capita in the CIS. The country is rich in natural resources and in 2001 primary commodities (mainly cotton, gold, copper, energy resources and precious stones) accounted for 70% of total exports. Incomes have improved little since independence from the Soviet Union in 1991 and rural poverty is significant. Following independence the government undertook a gradualist transition strategy, with emphasis on self-sufficiency in energy and grains, which led GDP to grow at approximately 4% between 1996–2002. However, the gradualist approach has delayed necessary macroeconomic and structural reforms. According to the World Bank, the combination of high inflation, exchange rate devaluations, low trust in the banking system and restrictions on access to cash resulted in a decline in the monetization of the economy. The government has retained extensive control over foreign exchange, trade, firms and farms. This has limited export growth and discouraged FDI, which has declined steadily since 1997.

Currency. A coupon for a new unit of currency, the *soum* (UKS), was introduced alongside the rouble on 15 Nov. 1993. This was replaced by the *soum* proper at 1 soum = 1,000 coupons on 1 July 1994. In 1994 inflation was 1,568% but has since declined, and was 38·7% in 2002. Exchange controls were abolished on 1 July 1995.

Budget. In 1999 revenues amounted to 611,897m. soums and expenditures to 654,259m. soums. Taxes on income and profits accounted for 30·5% of revenues, VAT 27·3% and excise taxes 22·3%. Social and cultural affairs accounted for 36·7% of expenditures and investments 18·7%.

Performance. Real GDP growth was 3·3% in 2000, 4·1% in 2001 and 3·2% in 2002; total GDP in 2003 was US$9·9bn. Real GDP in 2002 was 6% higher than in 1989. In every other former Soviet republic, GDP was lower in 2002 than it had been in 1989 at the time of the changes which swept through central and eastern Europe.

Banking and Finance. The Central Bank is the bank of issue (*Chairman*, Dr Faizulla Mulladjanov). In 2001 there were 38 commercial banks, of which 16 were privately owned.

ENERGY AND NATURAL RESOURCES

Environment. Irrigation of arid areas has caused the drying up of the Aral Sea. Uzbekistan's carbon dioxide emissions from the consumption and flaring of fossil fuels in 2002 were the equivalent of 4·5 tonnes per capita.

Electricity. Installed capacity was 11·7m. kW in 2000. Production was 46·8bn. kWh in 2000 and consumption per capita 1,944 kWh.

Oil and Gas. Crude oil production was 7·1m. tonnes in 2003; natural gas output in 2002 was 53·8bn. cu. metres. In 2002 there were proven oil reserves of 0·6bn. bbls. and natural gas reserves of 1,870bn. cu. metres.

Minerals. 2·50m. tonnes of lignite and 69,000 tonnes of hard coal were produced in 2000. In 2000, 85 tonnes of gold and 90 tonnes of silver were produced. There are also large reserves of uranium, copper, lead, zinc and tungsten; all uranium mined (1,860 tonnes in 2002) is exported.

Agriculture. Farming is intensive and based on irrigation. In 2001 there were 4·49m. ha of arable land and 0·35m. ha of permanent cropland; 4·28m. ha were irrigated in 2001.

By 1996 some 97% of the 715 state farms were co-operative, private or otherwise owned, and accounted for over 98% of agricultural production.

Cotton is the main crop, accounting for more than 40% of the value of total agricultural production. In 1997 more than 3·6m. tonnes of raw cotton was laid. Fruit, vegetables and rice are also grown; sericulture and the production of astrakhan wool are also important.

Output of main agricultural products (2000, in 1,000 tonnes): seed cotton, 3,006; wheat, 2,787; cottonseed, 1,920; tomatoes, 1,000; cotton lint, 950; cabbages, 882; potatoes, 656; grapes, 625; apples, 480; watermelons, 457; sugarbeets, 380; cucumbers and gherkins, 272.

Livestock, 2000: 5·27m. cattle; 8·92m. sheep; 639,000 goats; 14m. chickens. Animal products, 2000 (in 1,000 tonnes): meat, 536; milk, 3,739; eggs, 69.

Forestry. In 2000 the area under forests was 1·97m. ha, accounting for 4·8% of the total land area. In 2001, 25,000 cu. metres of timber were produced.

Fisheries. The total catch in 2001 was 4,070 tonnes, exclusively freshwater fish.

INDUSTRY

Industrial production increased by 6·5% in 1997 owing to the growth of industrial investment in previous years. The production of consumer goods increased by 11·2%. Major industries include fertilizers, agricultural and textile machinery, aircraft, metallurgy and chemicals. Output, 2001 (in tonnes): cement, 3,700,000; distillate fuel oil (2000), 1,900,000; petrol (2000), 1,709,000; residual fuel oil (2000), 1,700,000; sulphuric acid (2000), 823,000; mineral fertilizer (2000), 800,000; cotton woven fabrics (2000), 360m. sq. metres; footwear (1997), 554,700 pairs; 1,000 tractors (2000); 26,000 TV sets (2000).

Labour. In 1999 a total of 8,885,000 persons were in employment, including: 3,421,000 engaged in agriculture, hunting, forestry and fishing; 1,968,000 in community, social and personal services; 1,142,000 in manufacturing, mining and quarrying, electricity, gas and water; and 734,000 in wholesale and retail trade, restaurants and hotels. In 2000 the unemployment rate was 0·6%. Average monthly salary in 1999 was 8,823 soums. A minimum wage of 6,530 soums a month was imposed on 1 Aug. 2004.

INTERNATIONAL TRADE

In Jan. 1994 an agreement to create a single economic zone was signed with Kazakhstan and Kyrgyzstan. Foreign investors are entitled to a two-year tax holiday and repatriation of hard currency. External debt was US$4,568m. in 2002.

Imports and Exports. In 2002 imports were valued at US$2,712m. and exports at US$2,988m. Principal imports, 1996, were machinery (35% of the total), light industrial goods, food and raw materials; principal exports were cotton (38% of the total), textiles, machinery, chemicals, food and energy products.

The main import sources in 2002 were Russia (20·5%), South Korea (17·4%), Germany (8·9%), Kazakhstan (7·5%) and USA (6·4%). Principal export markets in 2002 were Russia (17·3%), Ukraine (10·2%), Italy (8·3%), Tajikistan (7·8%) and South Korea (7·1%).

COMMUNICATIONS

Roads. Estimated length of roads, 1999, was 81,600 km (87·3% paved).

Rail. The total length of railway in 2000 was 3,645 km of 1,520 mm gauge (432 km electrified). In 2000, 16·3m. passengers and 48·2m. tonnes of freight were carried. There is a metro in Tashkent.

Civil Aviation. The main international airport is in Tashkent (Vostochny). Andizhan, Namangan and Samarkand also have airports. The national carrier is the state-owned Uzbekistan Airways, which in 2003 operated domestic services and flew to Almaty, Amritsar, Ashgabat, Athens, Baku, Bangkok, Beijing, Birmingham, Bishkek, Chelyabinsk, Delhi, Dhaka, Ekaterinburg, Frankfurt, Istanbul, Kazan,

Khabarovsk, Krasnodar, Krasnoyarsk, Kuala Lumpur, Kyiv, London, Mineralnye Vody, Moscow, New York, Novosibirsk, Omsk, Osaka, Paris, Rome, Rostov, St Petersburg, Samara, Seoul, Sharjah, Simferopol, Tel Aviv, Tokyo, Tyumen and Ufa. In 1999 it flew 36·9m. km, carrying 1,657,600 passengers (877,500 on international flights). In 2000 Tashkent handled 1,964,432 passengers (1,165,026 on international flights) and 23,167 tonnes of freight.

Shipping. The total length of inland waterways in 1990 was 1,100 km.

Telecommunications. In 2002 telephone subscribers numbered 1,856,900 (73·4 per 1,000 population), of which 186,900 were mobile phone subscribers. Uzbekistan had 275,000 Internet users in 2002. There were 2,200 fax machines in 1999.

Postal Services. In 1997 there were 3,044 post offices.

SOCIAL INSTITUTIONS

Justice. In 1994, 73,561 crimes were reported, including 1,219 murders and attempted murders. The death penalty is still in force; there were two confirmed executions in 2004. The population in penal institutions in Aug. 2003 was 48,000 (184 per 100,000 of national population).

Religion. The Uzbeks are predominantly Sunni Muslims.

Education. In 1995 there were 1·07m. pre-primary pupils with 96,100 teachers, 1·90m. primary pupils with 92,400 teachers and 3·31m. secondary pupils with 340,200 teachers. There were (1998) 55 higher educational establishments with 272,300 students, and 248 technical colleges with 240,100 students. There are universities and medical schools in Tashkent and Samarkand. Adult literacy rate in 2001 was 99·2% (99·6% among males and 98·9% among females).

Health. In 1995 there were 192 hospitals, with a provision of 84 beds per 10,000 population. There were 74,230 physicians, 5,869 dentists, 243,166 nurses, 746 pharmacists and 16,235 midwives in 1998.

Welfare. In Jan. 1994 there were 1,726,000 old-age pensioners and 1,007,000 other pensioners.

CULTURE

World Heritage Sites. Uzbekistan has four sites on the UNESCO World Heritage List: Itchan Kala (inscribed on the list in 1990); the Historic Centre of Bukhara (1993); the Historic Centre of Shakhrisyabz (2000); and Samarkand—Crossroads of Cultures (2001).

Broadcasting. Broadcasting is under the aegis of the State Teleradio Broadcasting Company. The government-controlled Uzbek Radio transmits two national and several regional programmes, a Radio Moscow relay and a foreign service, Radio Tashkent (Uzbek, Arabic, English, Dari, Farsi, Hindi, Pushtu, Uighur). In 1997 there were 10·8m. radio receivers and in 2001 there were 7·0m. television receivers. Colour transmission is by SECAM H.

Press. In 1996 there were three daily newspapers with a combined circulation of 75,000.

Tourism. There were 332,000 tourists in 2002. Receipts totalled US$68m.

DIPLOMATIC REPRESENTATIVES

Of Uzbekistan in the United Kingdom (41 Holland Park, London, W11 3RP)
Ambassador: Tukhtapulat Riskiev.

Of the United Kingdom in Uzbekistan (Ul. Gulyamova 67, Tashkent 700000)
Ambassador: David Moran.

Of Uzbekistan in the USA (1746 Massachusetts Ave., NW, Washington, D.C., 20036)
Ambassador: Abdulaziz Kamilov.

Of the USA in Uzbekistan (82 Chilanzarskaya, Tashkent)
Ambassador: John Purnell.

Of Uzbekistan to the United Nations
Ambassador: Alisher Vohidov.

Of Uzbekistan to the European Union
Ambassador: Alisher Shaykhov.

FURTHER READING

Bohr, A. (ed.) *Uzbekistan: Politics and Foreign Policy.* The Brookings Institution, Washington (D.C.), 1998

Kalter, J. and Pavaloi, M., *Uzbekistan: Heir to the Silk Road.* Thames & Hudson, London, 1997

Kangas, R. D., *Uzbekistan in the Twentieth Century: Political Development and the Evolution of Power.* New York, 1994

Melvin, N. J., *Uzbekistan: Transition to Authoritarianism on the Silk Road.* Routledge, London, 2000

KARAKALPAK AUTONOMOUS REPUBLIC (KARAKALPAKSTAN)

Area, 164,900 sq. km (63,920 sq. miles); population (Jan. 1994), 1,343,000. Capital, Nukus (1989 census population, 174,000). The Qoraqalpoghs came under Russian rule in the second half of the 19th century. On 11 May 1925 the territory was constituted within the then Kazakh Autonomous Republic (of the Russian Federation) as an Autonomous Region. On 20 March 1932 it became an Autonomous Republic within the Russian Federation, and on 5 Dec. 1936 it became part of the Uzbek SSR. At the 1989 census Qoraqalpoghs were 32·1% of the population, Uzbeks 32·8% and Kazakhs 26·3%.

Its manufactures are in the field of light industry—bricks, leather goods, furniture, canning and wine. In Jan. 1990 cattle numbered 336,000, and sheep and goats 518,100. There were 38 collective and 124 state farms in 1987. The total cultivated area in 1985 was 350,400 ha.

In 1990–91 there were 313,500 pupils at schools, 22,100 students at technical colleges, and 7,800 at Nukus University. There is a branch of the Uzbek Academy of Sciences.

There were 2,600 doctors and 12,800 hospital beds in 1987.

VANUATU

Ripablik blong Vanuatu
(Republic of Vanuatu)

Capital: Vila
Population projection, 2010: 249,000
GDP per capita, 2002: (PPP$) 2,890
HDI/world rank: 0·570/129

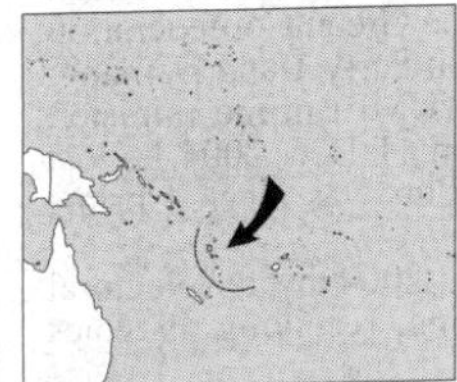

KEY HISTORICAL EVENTS

Vanuatu occupies the group of islands formerly known as the New Hebrides, in the southwestern Pacific Ocean. Captain Bligh and his companions, cast adrift by the *Bounty* mutineers, sailed through part of the island group in 1789. Sandalwood merchants and European missionaries came to the islands in the mid-19th century and were then followed by cotton planters—mostly French and British—in 1868. In response to Australian calls to annexe the islands, Britain and France agreed on joint supervision. Joint sovereignty was held over the indigenous Melanesian people but each nation retained responsibility for its own nationals according to a protocol of 1914. The island group escaped Japanese invasion during the Second World War and became an Allied base. On 30 July 1980 New Hebrides became an independent nation under the name of Vanuatu, meaning 'Our Land Forever'.

TERRITORY AND POPULATION

Vanuatu comprises 80 islands, which lie roughly 800 km west of the Fiji Islands and 400 km northeast of New Caledonia. The estimated land area is 4,706 sq. miles (12,190 sq. km). The larger islands of the group are: (Espiritu) Santo, Malekula, Epi, Pentecost, Aoba, Maewo, Paama, Ambrym, Efate, Erromanga, Tanna and Aneityum. They also claim Matthew and Hunter islands. 67 islands were inhabited in 1990. Population at the 1999 census, 186,678; density, 15·3 per sq. km. 2002 population estimate, 207,000.

The UN gives a projected population for 2010 of 249,000.

In 2001, 77·9% of the population lived in rural areas. Vila (the capital) has a population of 26,000 (1999 estimate), and Luganville 10,000.

40% of the population is under 15 years of age, 57% between the ages of 15 and 64 and 3% 65 or over.

The national language is Bislama (spoken by 82% of the population): English and French are also official languages; about 50,000 speak French.

SOCIAL STATISTICS

Births, 1997, 5,400; deaths, 1,600. Rates per 1,000 population, 1997: birth rate, 29·9; death rate, 8·6. Annual population growth rate, 1992–2002, 2·7%. Life expectancy, 2001, was 67·1 years for males and 70·1 years for females. Infant mortality, 2001, 34 per 1,000 live births; fertility rate, 2001, 4·4 births per woman.

CLIMATE

The climate is tropical, but moderated by oceanic influences and by trade winds from May to Oct. High humidity occasionally occurs and cyclones are possible. Rainfall ranges from 90" (2,250 mm) in the south to 155" (3,875 mm) in the north. Vila, Jan. 80°F (26·7°C), July 72°F (22·2°C). Annual rainfall 84" (2,103 mm).

CONSTITUTION AND GOVERNMENT

Legislative power resides in a 52-member unicameral Parliament elected for a term of four years. The *President* is elected for a five-year term by an electoral college comprising Parliament and the presidents of the 11 regional councils. Executive power is vested in a Council of Ministers, responsible to Parliament, and appointed and led by a Prime Minister who is elected from and by Parliament.

There is also a *Council of Chiefs,* comprising traditional tribal leaders, to advise on matters of custom.

National Anthem. 'Yumi yumi yumi i glat blong talem se, yumi, yumi yumi i man blong Vanuatu' ('We we we are glad to tell, we we we are the people of Vanuatu'); words and tune by F. Vincent.

RECENT ELECTIONS

Parliamentary elections were held on 6 July 2004. The Vanuatu National United Party (NUP) won 10 of 52 seats, the Union of Moderate Parties (UMP) 8, the Party of our Land (VP) 8, ind. 8, the People's Progressive Party 4, the Vanuatu Republican Party (VRP) 4, the Melanesian Progressive Party (MPP) 3, the Green Confederation 3, the National Community Association 2, the People's Action Party 1 and Namangi Aute 1. On 29 July 2004 parliament elected Serge Vohor (UMP) prime minister, with 28 votes, against 24 for Ham Lini (NUP). However, on 11 Dec. 2004 he lost a no-confidence motion and deputy prime minister Ham Lini was elected prime minister.

Kalkot Mataskelekele was elected president on 16 Aug. 2004 by an electoral college after a series of votes in the second round of voting, receiving 49 votes against 7 for Willie David Saul.

CURRENT ADMINISTRATION

President: Kalkot Mataskelekele (since 16 Aug. 2004).

Prime Minister: Ham Lini; b. 1951 (NUP; since 11 Dec. 2004). He put together a multi-party coalition which in March 2005 comprised:

Deputy Prime Minister and Minister of Foreign Affairs: Sato Kilman.

Minister of Internal Affairs: George Wells. *Health:* Morkin Steven. *Education:* Joseph Natuman. *Finance and Economic Management:* Moana Carcasses. *Lands:* Paul Telukluk. *Agriculture, Forestry and Fisheries:* Barak Sope Maautamate. *Comprehensive Reform Programme:* Isabelle Donald. *Ni-Vanuatu Business Development:* Joshua Kalsakau. *Trade, Commerce and Industry:* James Bule. *Public Utilities and Infrastructure:* Maxime Carlot Korman. *Sports and Youth Development:* Arnold Prasad.

Speaker: Sam Dan Avock.

Government Website: http://www.vanuatugovernment.gov.vu

DEFENCE

There is a paramilitary force with about 300 personnel. The Vanuatu Police maritime service operates one inshore patrol craft, and a former motor yacht, both lightly armed. Personnel numbered about 50 in 1996.

INTERNATIONAL RELATIONS

Vanuatu is a member of the UN, the Commonwealth, the Asian Development Bank, the Pacific Community, the Pacific Islands Forum and the International Organization of the Francophonie, and is an ACP member state of the ACP-EU relationship.

ECONOMY

Agriculture accounted for 24·7% of GDP in 1998, industry 12·1% and services 63·2%.

Currency. The unit of currency is the *vatu* (VUV) with no minor unit. There was inflation in 2002 of 2·2%. Foreign exchange reserves in June 2002 were US$34m. Total money supply in June 2002 was 11,254m. vatu.

Budget. Budget revenue and expenditure (in 1m. vatu):

	1995	*1996*	*1997*	*1998*	*1999*
Revenue	6,965	6,352	6,206	6,605	6,753
Expenditure	7,497	7,282	7,023	9,219	7,531

Performance. Vanuatu has been experiencing a recession, with the economy contracting by 2·1% in 2001 and 2·8% in 2002. Total GDP in 2003 was US$0·3bn.

Banking and Finance. The Reserve Bank blong Vanuatu is the central bank and bank of issue. There is also the state-owned National Bank, two development banks and three foreign banks. Commercial banks' assets at 31 Dec. 1988, 20,900m. vatu.

ENERGY AND NATURAL RESOURCES

Environment. Vanuatu's carbon dioxide emissions from the consumption and flaring of fossil fuels in 2002 were the equivalent of 0·4 tonnes per capita.

Electricity. Electrical capacity in 2000 was 12,000 kW. Production in 2000 was about 38m. kWh and consumption per capita an estimated 193 kWh.

Agriculture. About 65% of the labour force are employed in agriculture. In 2001 there were 30,000 ha of arable land and 90,000 ha of permanent crops. The main commercial crops are copra, coconuts, cocoa and coffee. Production (2000 estimates, in 1,000 tonnes): coconuts, 364; copra, 40; bananas, 13; groundnuts, 2. 80% of the population are engaged in subsistence agriculture; yams, taro, cassava, sweet potatoes and bananas are grown for local consumption. A large number of cattle are reared on plantations, and a beef industry is developing.

Livestock (2000): cattle, 152,000; goats, 12,000; pigs, 62,000; horses, 3,000; poultry (1995), 158,000.

Forestry. There were 447,000 ha of forest in 2000 (36·7% of the land area). In 2001, 119,000 cu. metres of roundwood were cut.

Fisheries. The principal catch is tuna, mainly exported to the USA. The total catch in 2001 was an estimated 26,690 tonnes.

INDUSTRY

Principal industries include copra processing, meat canning and fish freezing, a saw-mill, soft drinks factories and a print works. Building materials, furniture, aluminium and cement are also produced.

In 2000 industry accounted for 9·7% of GDP, with manufacturing contributing 3·6% and construction 4·1%.

INTERNATIONAL TRADE

Foreign debt in 2002 amounted to US$84m.

Imports and Exports. In 2001 imports (f.o.b.) amounted to US$77·96m. (US$76·94m. in 2000); exports (f.o.b.) US$19·89m. (US$27·19m. in 2000). Main import suppliers (2000): Australia (28%), Singapore (14%), New Zealand (8%), Japan (4%). Main export destinations (2000): Japan (32%), Belgium (17%), USA (17%), Germany (8%).

The main exports are copra, beef, timber and cocoa.

COMMUNICATIONS

Roads. In 1999 there were 1,070 km of roads, about 260 km paved, mostly on Efate Island and Espiritu Santo. There were estimated to be 4,000 passenger cars and 2,000 commercial vehicles in use in 1996.

Civil Aviation. There is an international airport at Bauerfield Port Vila. In 2003 the state-owned Air Vanuatu flew to Auckland, Brisbane, Honiara, Nadi, Nouméa and Sydney. Domestic services were provided by Vanair, a subsidiary of Air Vanuatu. In 1999 scheduled airline traffic of Vanuatu-based carriers flew 2·6m. km, carrying 86,000 passengers (all on international flights).

Shipping. Sea-going shipping totalled 1·38m. GRT in 2002, including oil tankers 55,000 GRT. Several international shipping lines serve Vanuatu, linking the country with Australia, New Zealand, other Pacific territories, China (Hong Kong), Japan, North America and Europe. The chief ports are Vila and Santo. Small vessels provide frequent inter-island services.

Telecommunications. Services are provided by the Posts and Telecommunications and Radio Departments. There are automatic telephone exchanges at Vila and Santo; rural areas are served by a network of tele-radio stations. In 2002 there were 11,500 telephone subscribers, equivalent to 56·2 per 1,000 population, of which 4,900 were mobile phone subscribers. There were 3,000 PCs in use in 2002 and approximately 600 fax machines in 1995. Vanuatu had 7,000 Internet users in 2002.

External telephone, telegram and telex services are provided by VANITEL, through their satellite earth station at Vila. There are direct circuits to Nouméa, Sydney, Hong Kong and Paris and communications are available on a 24-hour basis to most countries. Air radio facilities are provided. Marine coast station facilities are available at Vila and Santo.

SOCIAL INSTITUTIONS

Justice. A study was begun in 1980 which could lead to unification of the judicial system. The population in penal institutions in 2002 was 96 (46 per 100,000 of national population).

Religion. About two-thirds of the population are Christians, but animist beliefs are still prevalent.

Education. In 2000–01 there were 8,285 pupils with 477 teachers in pre-primary schools. In 2001–02 there were 36,482 pupils with (1999–2000) 1,576 teachers in primary schools and 9,635 pupils with (1999–2000) 381 teachers in secondary schools. Tertiary education is provided at the Vanuatu Technical Institute and the Teachers College, while other technical and commercial training is through regional institutions in the Solomon Islands, the Fiji Islands and Papua New Guinea. The adult literacy rate in 1998 stood at 64%, up from 53% in 1979. In 2000–01 total expenditure on education came to 8·7% of GNP and accounted for 16·9% of total government expenditure.

Health. There were 21 physicians in 1997 and in 1995 there were three dentists, 259 nurses, six pharmacists and 33 midwives. There were 90 hospitals in 1995, with a provision of 32 beds per 10,000 population.

CULTURE

Broadcasting. The government-controlled Radio Vanuatu broadcasts in French, English and Bislama. In 1997 there were 62,000 radio receivers and in 2000 there were 2,300 television sets.

Tourism. In 2000 there were 57,000 visitors to Vanuatu. Receipts totalled US$58m.

DIPLOMATIC REPRESENTATIVES

Of Vanuatu in the United Kingdom
High Commissioner: Vacant.

Of the United Kingdom in Vanuatu (PO Box 567, Port Vila)
High Commissioner: Michael Hill.

Of Vanuatu in the USA
Ambassador: Vacant.

Of the USA in Vanuatu
Ambassador: Robert W. Fitts (resides at Port Moresby, Papua New Guinea).

Of Vanuatu to the United Nations
Ambassador: Vacant.

FURTHER READING

Miles, W. F. S., *Bridging Mental Boundaries in a Postcolonial Microcosm: Identity and Development in Vanuatu.* University of Hawaii Press, 1998

National statistical office: Vanuatu Statistics Office, Private Mail Bag 019, Port Vila.
Website: http://www.vanuatustatistics.gov.vu/

VATICAN CITY STATE

Population estimate, 2000: 900

Stato della Città del Vaticano

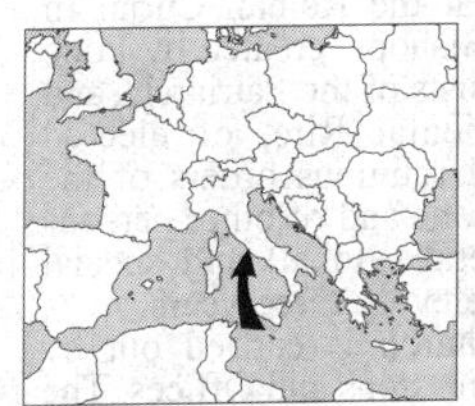

KEY HISTORICAL EVENTS

For many centuries the Popes bore temporal sway over a territory stretching across mid-Italy. In the 19th century the Papal States were incorporated into the Italian Kingdom. On 11 Feb. 1929 a treaty between the Italian Government and the Vatican recognized the sovereignty of the Holy See in the city of the Vatican.

TERRITORY AND POPULATION

The area of Vatican City is 44 ha (108·7 acres). It includes the Piazza di San Pietro (St Peter's Square), which is to remain normally open to the public and subject to the powers of the Italian police. It has its own railway station (for freight only), postal facilities, coins and radio. Twelve buildings in and outside Rome enjoy extra-territorial rights, including the Basilicas of St John Lateran, St Mary Major and St Paul without the Walls, the Pope's summer villa at Castel Gandolfo and a further Vatican radio station on Italian soil. *Radio Vaticana* broadcasts an extensive service in 34 languages from the transmitters in Vatican City and in Italy. The Holy See and the Vatican are not synonymous—the Holy See, referring to the primacy of the Pope, is located in Vatican City.

Vatican City has about 900 inhabitants.

CONSTITUTION AND GOVERNMENT

Vatican City State is governed by a Commission appointed by the Pope. The reason for its existence is to provide an extra-territorial, independent base for the Holy See, the government of the Roman Catholic Church. The Pope exercises sovereignty and has absolute legislative, executive and judicial powers. The judicial power is delegated to a tribunal in the first instance, to the Sacred Roman Rota in appeal and to the Supreme Tribunal of the Signature in final appeal.

The Pope is elected by the College of Cardinals, meeting in secret conclave. The election is by scrutiny and requires a two-thirds majority.

CURRENT ADMINISTRATION

Supreme Pontiff: **Benedict XVI** (Joseph Ratzinger), born at Marktl am Inn, in Bavaria, Germany, 16 April 1927. Archbishop of Munich and Freising 1977–82, created Cardinal in 1977; elected Pope 19 April 2005, inaugurated 24 April 2005. Pope Benedict XVI is only the eighth German to be elected Pope and the first since the 11th century.

Secretary of State: Cardinal Angelo Sodano.

Secretary for Relations with Other States: Archbishop Giovanni Lajolo.

Office of the Sovereign of the Vatican City: http://www.vatican.va

ECONOMY

Currency. Since 1 Jan. 2002 the Vatican City has been using the euro. Italy has agreed that the Vatican City may mint a small part of the total Italian euro coin contingent with their own motifs.

Budget. Revenues in 2001 were US$173·5m. and expenditures US$176·6m.

Performance. Real GDP growth was 1·7% in 2001.

SOCIAL INSTITUTIONS

Justice. In 2002 the Vatican City's legal system hosted 397 civil cases and 608 criminal cases. Most of the offences are committed by outsiders, principally at St Peter's Basilica and the museums.

Roman Catholic Church. As the Vicar of Christ and the Successor of St Peter, the Pope is held to be by divine right the centre of all Catholic unity and exercises universal governance over the Church. He is also the sovereign ruler of Vatican City State. He has for advisers the Sacred College of Cardinals, consisting in March 2005 of 183 cardinals from 66 countries (171 created by Pope John Paul II, including 31 in Sept. 2003), of whom 117 are cardinal electors—those under the age of 80 who may enter into conclave to elect a new Pope. Cardinals, addressed by the title of 'Eminence', are appointed by the Pope from senior ecclesiastics who are either the bishops of important Sees or the heads of departments at the Roman Curia. In addition to the College of Cardinals, there is a Synod of Bishops, created by Pope Paul VI and formally instituted on 15 Sept. 1965. This consists of the Patriarchs and certain Metropolitans of the Catholic Church of Oriental Rite, of elected representatives of the national episcopal conferences and religious orders of the world, of the cardinals in charge of the Roman Congregations and of other persons nominated by the Pope. The Synod meets in both general (global) and special (regional) assemblies. General Synods normally take place every three years.

The central administration of the Roman Catholic Church is carried out by permanent organisms called Congregations, Council, Commissions and Offices. The Congregations are composed of cardinals and diocesan bishops (both appointed for five-year periods), with Consultors and Officials. There are nine Congregations, viz.: Doctrine, Oriental Churches, Bishops, the Sacraments and Divine Worship, Clergy, Religious, Catholic Education, Evangelization of the Peoples and Causes of the Saints. Pontifical Councils have replaced some of the previously designated Secretariats and Prefectures and now represent the Laity, Christian Unity, the Family, Justice and Peace, Cor Unum, Migrants, Health Care Workers, Interpretation of Legislative Texts, Inter-Religious Dialogue, Culture, Preserving the Patrimony of Art and History, and a Commission for Latin America. There are three academies: the Pontifical Academy for Sciences, the Pontifical Academy for Life and the Pontifical Academy for Social Sciences, the latter two instituted by Pope John Paul II.

CULTURE

World Heritage Sites. The Holy See has one site on the UNESCO World Heritage List: Vatican City (inscribed on the list in 1984)—the centre of the Roman Catholic Church, it contains some of the greatest pieces of European art and architecture, including St Peter's Basilica.

DIPLOMATIC REPRESENTATIVES

In its diplomatic relations with foreign countries the Holy See is represented by the Secretariat of State and the Second Section (Relations with States) of the Council for Public Affairs of the Church. It maintains permanent observers to the UN.

Of the Holy See in the United Kingdom (54 Parkside, London, SW19 5NE)
Apostolic Nuncio: Archbishop Faustino Sainz Muñoz.

Of the United Kingdom at the Holy See (91 Via Dei Condotti, 00187 Rome)
Ambassador: Kathryn Colvin.

Of the Holy See in the USA (3339 Massachusetts Ave., NW, Washington, D.C., 20008)
Apostolic Nuncio: Gabriele Montalvo.

Of the USA at the Holy See (Villa Domiziana, Via Delle Terme Deciane 26, 00153 Rome)
Ambassador: Jim Nicholson.

Of the Holy See to the European Union
Apostolic Nuncio: Archbishop Faustino Sainz Muñoz.

FURTHER READING

Reese, T., *Inside the Vatican*. Harvard Univ. Press, 1997

Permanent Observer Mission to the UN: http://www.holyseemission.org

VENEZUELA

República Bolivariana de Venezuela

Capital: Caracas
Population projection, 2010: 28·96m.
GDP per capita, 2002: (PPP$) 5,380
HDI/world rank: 0·778/68

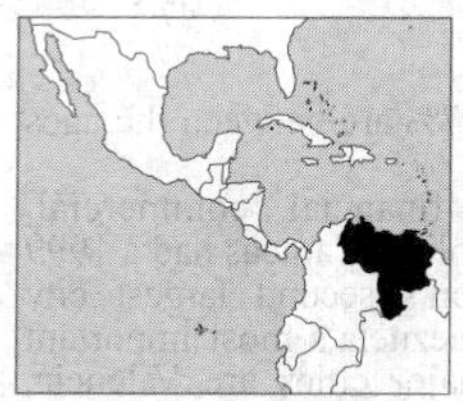

KEY HISTORICAL EVENTS

Columbus sighted Venezuela in 1498 and it was visited by Alonso de Ojeda and Amerigo Vespucci in 1499 who named it Venezuela (Little Venice). It was part of the Spanish colony of New Granada until 1821 when it became independent, at first in union with Colombia and then as an independent republic from 1830. Up to 1945 the country was governed mainly by dictators. In 1945 a three-day revolt against the reactionary government of Gen. Isaias Medina led to constitutional and economic reforms. In 1961 a new constitution provided for a presidential election every five years, a national congress, and state and municipal legislative assemblies. Twenty political parties participated in the 1983 elections. By now the economy was in crisis and corruption linked to drug trafficking was widespread. In Feb. 1992 there were two abortive coups. A state of emergency was declared. In Dec. 1993 Dr Rafael Caldera Rodríguez's election as president reflected disenchantment with the established political parties. He took office in the early stages of a banking crisis which cost 15% of GDP to resolve. Fiscal tightening backed by the IMF brought rapid recovery. Hugo Chávez Frías, who succeeded as president in Feb. 1999, continued with economic reforms and amended the constitution to increase presidential powers. In Dec. 1999 the north coast of Venezuela was hit by devastating floods and mudslides which resulted in approximately 30,000 deaths.

President Chávez was deposed and arrested on 12 April 2002 in a coup following a general strike, but he was back in the presidential palace just 48 hours later.

TERRITORY AND POPULATION

Venezuela is bounded to the north by the Caribbean with a 2,813 km coastline, east by the Atlantic and Guyana, south by Brazil, and southwest and west by Colombia. The area is 916,445 sq. km (353,839 sq. miles) including 72 islands in the Caribbean. Population (1990) census, 19,455,429. Census 2001 (provisional), 23,054,210; density, 25·1 per sq. km. 87·2% of the population lived in urban areas in 2001.

The UN gives a projected population for 2010 of 28·96m.

The official language is Spanish. English is taught as a mandatory second language in high schools.

Area, population and capitals of the 24 states and one federally-controlled area:

State	*Area (sq. km)*	*2001 census population (provisional)*	*Capital*	*Density; inhabitants per sq. km*
Federal District	433	1,836,286	Caracas	4,240·8
Amazonas	180,145	70,464	Puerto Ayacucho	0·4
Anzoátegui	43,300	1,222,225	Barcelona	28·2
Apure	76,500	377,756	San Fernando	4·9
Aragua	7,014	1,449,616	Maracay	206·7
Barinas	35,200	624,508	Barinas	17·7
Bolívar	238,000	1,214,846	Ciudad Bolívar	5·1
Carabobo	4,650	1,932,168	Valencia	415·5
Cojedes	14,800	253,105	San Carlos	17·1
Delta Amacuro	40,200	97,987	Tucupita	2·4
Falcón	24,800	763,188	Coro	30·8
Guárico	64,986	627,086	San Juan de los Morros	9·7
Lara	19,800	1,556,415	Barquisimeto	78·6
Mérida	11,300	715,268	Mérida	63·3
Miranda	7,950	2,330,872	Los Teques	293·2
Monagas	28,900	712,626	Maturín	24·7
Nueva Esparta	1,150	373,851	La Asunción	325·1
Portuguesa	15,200	725,740	Guanare	47·8
Sucre	11,800	786,483	Cumaná	66·7

State	Area (sq. km)	2001 census population (provisional)	Capital	Density; inhabitants per sq. km
Táchira	11,100	992,669	San Cristóbal	89·4
Trujillo	7,400	608,563	Trujillo	82·2
Vargas	1,497	298,109	La Guaira	199·1
Yaracuy	7,100	499,049	San Felipe	70·3
Zulia	63,100	2,983,679	Maracaibo	47·3
Dependencias Federales	120	1,651		

37·3% of all Venezuelans are under 15 years of age, 58·7% are between the ages of 15 and 64, and 4% are over the age of 65.

Caracas, Venezuela's largest city, is the political, financial, commercial, communications and cultural centre of the country. Metropolitan Caracas had a 1999 population estimate of 3,127,000. Maracaibo, the nation's second largest city (estimated 1998 population of 1·7m.), is located near Venezuela's most important petroleum fields and richest agricultural areas. Other major cities are Valencia, Barquisimeto and Ciudad Guayana.

SOCIAL STATISTICS

2001 births, 529,552; deaths, 107,867. 2001 birth rate per 1,000 population, 21·5; death rate, 4·4. Annual population growth rate, 1992–2002, 2·1%. Life expectancy, 2001, was 70·6 years for males and 76·4 years for females. Infant mortality, 2001, 19 per 1,000 live births; fertility rate, 2001, 2·8 births per woman. In 1998 the most popular age for marrying was 20–24 for both men and women.

CLIMATE

The climate ranges from warm temperate to tropical. Temperatures vary little throughout the year and rainfall is plentiful. The dry season is from Dec. to April. The hottest months are July and August. Caracas, Jan. 65°F (18·3°C), July 69°F (20·6°C). Annual rainfall 32" (833 mm). Ciudad Bolívar, Jan. 79°F (26·1°C), July 81°F (27·2°C). Annual rainfall 41" (1,016 mm). Maracaibo, Jan. 81°F (27·2°C), July 85°F (29·4°C). Annual rainfall 23" (577 mm).

CONSTITUTION AND GOVERNMENT

The current constitution was approved in a referendum held on 15 Dec. 1999. Venezuela is a federal republic, comprising 34 federal dependencies, 23 states and one federal district. Executive power is vested in the *President*. The ministers, who together constitute the Council of Ministers, are appointed by the President and head various executive departments. There are 17 ministries and seven officials who also have the rank of Minister of State.

90% of votes cast in a referendum (the first in Venezuela's history) on 25 April 1999 were in favour of the plan to rewrite the constitution proposed by President Chávez. As a result, on 25 July the public was to elect a constitutional assembly to write a new constitution, which was subsequently to be voted on in a national referendum. In Aug. 1999 the constitutional assembly declared a national state of emergency. It subsequently suspended the Supreme Court, turned the elected Congress into little more than a sub-committee, stripping it of all its powers, and assumed many of the responsibilities of government. In Dec. 1999 the President's plan to redraft the constitution was approved by over 70% of voters in a referendum. As a result presidents are able to serve two consecutive six-year-terms instead of terms of five years which cannot be consecutive, the senate is abolished and greater powers are being given to the state and the armed forces. President Chávez has effectively taken over both the executive and the judiciary. The constitution provides for procedures by which the president may reject bills passed by Congress, as well as provisions by which Congress may override such presidential veto acts.

Since the senate was dissolved, Venezuela has become a unicameral legislature, the 165-seat *National Assembly*, with members being elected for five-year terms.

National Anthem. 'Gloria al bravo pueblo' ('Glory to the brave people'); words by Vicente Salias, tune by Juan Landaeta.

RECENT ELECTIONS

Presidential elections were held on 30 July 2000; turn-out was 56%. Incumbent Hugo Chávez Frías (MVR) was elected president against one other candidate with 59% of the vote. In a recall referendum held on 15 Aug. 2004 he was confirmed as president, with 59·3% of the votes cast backing him.

In elections to the Congress, held on 30 July 2000, 165 seats were contested. Movimiento V República (Movement for the Fifth Republic/MVR) won 76 seats, Accion Democrática (Democratic Action/AD) 29, Movimiento al Socialismo (Movement Towards Socialism/MAS) 21, Proyecto Venezuela (Project Venezuela/Proven) 7 and 12 other parties won five seats or fewer.

CURRENT ADMINISTRATION

President: Hugo Chávez Frías; b. 1953 (MVR; sworn in 2 Feb. 1999).

Executive Vice President: José Vicente Rangel.

In March 2005 the government comprised:

Minister of the Interior and Justice: Jesse Chacón. *Foreign Affairs:* Alí Rodríguez Araque. *Finance:* Nelson Merentes. *Communications and Information:* Andrés Izarra. *Defence:* Gen. Jorge García Carneiro. *Infrastructure:* Ramón Carrizález Rengifo. *Agriculture and Lands:* Antonio Albarrán Moreno. *Environment and Natural Resources:* Jacqueline Coromoto Faria Pineda. *Health and Social Development:* Francisco Armada. *Education and Sports:* Aristóbulo Istúriz. *Higher Education:* Samuel Moncada. *Labour:* María Cristina Iglesias. *Light Industry and Commerce:* Edmée Betancourt de García. *Nutrition:* José Rafael Oropeza. *Planning and Development:* Jorge Giordani. *Science and Technology:* Yadira Córdoba. *Tourism:* Wilmar Castro Soteldo. *Basic Industry and Mines:* Víctor Alvarez Rodríguez. *Energy and Petroleum:* Rafael Ramírez.

Government Website: http://www.gobiernoenlinea.ve

DEFENCE

There is selective conscription for 30 months. Defence expenditure totalled US$1,283m. in 2003 (US$50 per capita), representing 1·5% of GDP.

Army. The Army has six infantry divisional headquarters, one cavalry brigade, seven infantry brigades, one airborne brigade, two ranger brigades, one mobile counter guerrilla brigade and one aviation regiment. Equipment includes 81 main battle tanks. Strength (2002) 34,000 (27,000 conscripts). There were estimated to be an additional 8,000 reserves.

A 23,000-strong volunteer National Guard is responsible for internal security.

Navy. The combatant fleet comprises two submarines and six frigates. The Naval Air Arm, 500 strong, operates three combat aircraft and nine armed helicopters. Main bases are at Caracas, Puerto Cabello and Punto Fijo.

Air Force. The Air Force was 7,000 strong in 1999 and had 124 combat aircraft and 31 armed helicopters. There are six combat squadrons. Main aircraft types include CF-5s, Mirage 50s and F-16A/Bs.

INTERNATIONAL RELATIONS

Venezuela is a member of the UN, WTO, OAS, Inter-American Development Bank, LAIA, ACS, OPEC, IOM, WTO, FAO, Interpol, Intelsat, IADB, IAEA, IMO, SELA, UNCTAD, UNESCO, UPU, WHO and the Andean Community.

ECONOMY

In 2002 services accounted for 54·4% of GDP, industry 43·0% and agriculture 2·6%.

Overview. Venezuela's mineral and oil deposits are among the largest in the world and the country supplies 13% of the US oil needs. The oil industry provides for 50% of Venezuela's budget and accounted for 27·4% of GDP and 84·2% of exports in 2000. An overdependence on oil has exposed the economy to variations in oil prices. Almost 60% of the population is below the poverty line. GDP growth has averaged 0·9% per year over the past 20 years, with an annual population growth of 2·5%. This has led to a fall in real income. In recent years there has been increased activity in construction, telecommunications and manufacturing. Monetary policy is tight, although Venezuela has one of the highest inflation rates in South America, reaching 31·2% in 2002. The government controls most prices and interest rates are kept high owing to political uncertainty and a weak banking sector. In Jan. 2003 the unemployment rate was approaching 20%.

Currency. The unit of currency is the *bolívar* (VEB) of 100 *céntimos*. Foreign exchange reserves were US$7,204m. and gold reserves 10·50m. troy oz in June 2002. Exchange controls were abolished in April 1996. The bolívar was devalued by 12·6% in 1998, and in Feb. 2002 it was floated, ending a regime that permitted the bolívar to trade only within a fixed band. However, in Feb. 2003 it was pegged to the dollar. In Feb. 2004 the bolívar was devalued by 16·7%. The inflation rate in 2001 was 12·5%, the lowest in more than 15 years and down from nearly 100% in 1996. There was then a steady rise in inflation, with a rate of 31·2% being recorded in 2002. In 2003 inflation was 27·1%. Total money supply in May 2002 was Bs 7,232·47bn.

Budget. The fiscal year is the calendar year. Revenues and expenditures in Bs 1m.:

	1997	*1998*	*1999*	*2000*	*2001*
Revenue	10,240,962	9,157,084	11,251,838	16,873,493	19,326,543
Expenditure	8,894,305	11,014,036	12,169,972	17,860,230	22,883,815

Performance. In 2001 there was real GDP growth of 2·8%. In 2002, however, the economy shrank by 8·9%. The economy then contracted by a record 29% during the first quarter of 2003. Total GDP in 2003 was US$84·8bn.

Banking and Finance. A law of Dec. 1992 provided for greater autonomy for the Central Bank. Its *President*, currently Gastón Luis Parra Luzardo, is appointed by the President for five-year terms. Since 1993 foreign banks have been allowed a controlling interest in domestic banks. In 2003 there were 24 commercial banks and three foreign banks.

There is a stock exchange in Caracas.

ENERGY AND NATURAL RESOURCES

Environment. Carbon dioxide emissions from the consumption and flaring of fossil fuels in 2002 were the equivalent of 5·7 tonnes per capita.

Electricity. Installed capacity in 2000 was 21·3m. kW; production was 85·21bn. kWh in 2000 and consumption per capita 3,525 kWh.

Oil and Gas. Proven resources of oil were 77·8bn. bbls. in 2002. Venezuela has the highest reserves of oil of any country outside the Middle East. The oil sector was nationalized in 1976, but private and foreign investment have again been permitted since 1992. Crude oil production in 2002 was 151·4m. tonnes. Venezuela is the largest exporter of oil to the USA. Oil provides about 40% of Venezuela's revenues. Natural gas production (2002) 27·3bn. cu. metres. Natural gas reserves in 2002 were 4,190bn. cu. metres, the largest in Latin America.

Minerals. Output (in 1,000 tonnes) in 2001: iron ore, 19,000; limestone (1996), 15,130; coal (2000), 7,885; bauxite, 4,400; aluminium (2000), 569; gold, 9,076 kg. Diamond production in 2001 totalled 52,000 carats.

Agriculture. Coffee, cocoa, sugarcane, maize, rice, wheat, tobacco, cotton, beans and sisal are grown. 50% of farmers are engaged in subsistence agriculture. There were 2·60m. ha of arable land in 2001 and 0·81m. ha of permanent crops. 575,000 ha were irrigated in 2001. There are government price supports and tax incentives.

Production in 2000 in 1,000 tonnes: sugarcane, 6,950; bananas, 1,000; maize, 900; rice, 737; plantains, 551; cassava, 448; potatoes, 352; oranges, 332; sorghum, 320; watermelons, 261; carrots, 239; tomatoes, 188.

Livestock (2000): cattle, 15·80m.; pigs, 4·90m.; goats, 3·60m.; sheep, 781,000; horses, 500,000; chickens, 110m.

Forestry. In 2000 the area under forests was 49·51m. ha, or 56·1% of the total land area. Timber production in 2001 was 4·62m. cu. metres.

Fisheries. In 2001 the total catch was 417,947 tonnes (393,621 tonnes from marine waters).

INDUSTRY

Production (2000, in tonnes): distillate fuel oil, 14·6m.; petrol, 14·6m.; residual fuel oil, 13·7m.; cement (2001), 8·7m.; crude steel (2002), 4·2m.; sugar (2001), 585,000.

Labour. Out of 8,286,800 people in employment in 1997, 2,411,700 were in community, social and personal services, 1,985,500 in wholesale and retail trade, restaurants and hotels, 1,122,400 in manufacturing and 894,000 in agriculture, hunting, fishing and forestry. In Feb. 2000 an estimated 20% of the workforce was unemployed, up from 8·6% in 1991.

In late 2002 and early 2003 a two-month long general strike intended to oust President Chávez ended in failure, instead crippling an already depressed economy.

Trade Unions. The most powerful confederation of trade unions is the CTV (*Confederación de Trabajadores de Venezuela*, formed 1947).

INTERNATIONAL TRADE

The Group of Three free trade pact with Colombia and Mexico came into effect on 1 Jan. 1995. Foreign debt was US$32,563m. in 2002.

Imports and Exports. Trade in US$1m.:

	1998	*1999*	*2000*	*2001*	*2002*
Imports f.o.b.	16,755	14,492	16,592	18,660	13,732
Exports f.o.b.	17,707	20,963	33,194	26,252	26,656

Exports of oil in 2001 were valued at US$19bn., the third highest export revenues after Saudi Arabia and Iran. The main import sources in 2000 were USA (37·8%), Colombia (7·4%), Brazil (5·0%) and Italy (4·4%). The main markets for exports in 2000 were USA (59·6%), Netherlands Antilles (5·6%), Brazil (3·6%) and Colombia (2·8%).

COMMUNICATIONS

Roads. In 1999 there were about 96,155 km of roads, of which 33·6% were paved. There were 1,520,000 passenger cars in use in 1996 (69·3 per 1,000 inhabitants) plus 434,000 trucks and vans. There were 2,900 fatalities as a result of road accidents in 1996.

Rail. Passenger-km travelled in 1995 came to 12m. and freight tonne-km in 2000 to 59m. (railways 336 km—1,435 mm gauge).

There is a metro in Caracas.

Civil Aviation. The main international airport is at Caracas (Simon Bolívar), with some international flights from Maracaibo. Aeropostal Alas de Venezuela is the main Venezuelan carrier. In 1999 scheduled airline traffic of Venezuela-based carriers flew 75·4m. km, carrying 4,690,000 passengers (1,590,000 on international flights).

Shipping. Ocean-going shipping totalled 865,000 GRT in 2002, including oil tankers 376,000 GRT. La Guaira, Maracaibo, Puerto Cabello, Puerto Ordaz and Guanta are the chief ports. In 1995 vessels totalling 21,009,000 NRT entered ports and vessels totalling 8,461,000 NRT cleared. The principal navigable rivers are the Orinoco and its tributaries the Apure and Arauca.

Telecommunications. In 2002 Venezuela had 9,305,300 telephone subscribers (369·2 per 1,000 population) and 1,536,000 PCs were in use (60·9 for every 1,000 persons). Mobile phone subscribers numbered 6,463,600 in 2002 and there were 70,000 fax machines in 1997. The number of Internet users in 2002 was 1,274,400. CANTV, the national telephone company, lost its 50-year monopoly on fixed-line telephony in 2000.

Postal Services. In 1998 there were 407 post offices, or one for every 57,600 persons.

SOCIAL INSTITUTIONS

Justice. A new penal code was implemented on 1 July 1999. The new, US-style system features public trials, verbal arguments, prosecutors, citizen juries and the presumption of innocence, instead of an inquisitorial system inherited from Spain which included secretive trials and long exchanges of written arguments.

In Aug. 1999 the new constitutional assembly declared a judicial emergency, granting itself sweeping new powers to dismiss judges and overhaul the court system. The assembly excluded the Supreme Court and the national Judicial Council from a commission charged with reorganizing the judiciary. President Chávez declared the assembly the supreme power in Venezuela.

The court system is plagued by chronic corruption and an astounding case backlog. Only about 40% of the country's prisoners in 1999 had actually been convicted. In Oct. 1999 over 100 judges accused of corruption were suspended. The population in penal institutions in 2003 was 19,554 (76 per 100,000 population).

Religion. In 2001 there were 22·05m. Roman Catholics. There are four archbishops, one at Caracas, who is Primate of Venezuela, two at Mérida and one at Ciudad Bolívar. There are 19 bishops. In Sept. 2003 there was one cardinal. The remainder of the population follow other religions, notably Protestantism.

Education. In 2001–02 there were 3,506,780 primary school pupils (186,658 teachers in 1997–98) and 1,811,127 secondary school pupils.

In 1995–96 there were in the public sector 16 universities, one polytechnic university and one open (distance) university; and in the private sector, 12 universities, two Roman Catholic universities and one technological university.

Adult literacy was 92·8% in 2001 (male, 93·3%; female, 92·4%).

Health. In 1997 there were 556 hospitals with 17 beds per 10,000 inhabitants. There were 53,818 physicians, 13,000 dentists, 46,305 nurses and 8,751 pharmacists in 1997.

CULTURE

World Heritage Sites. Venezuela has three sites on the UNESCO World Heritage List: Coro and its Port (inscribed on the list in 1993); Canaima National Park (1994); and La Ciudad Universitaria de Caracas (2000).

Broadcasting. There were about 230 radio stations in 1998 and 66 TV stations (colour by NTSC) in 1997. In 2001 there were 4·6m. TV receivers and in 2000 there were 7·1m. radio receivers.

Press. In 1996 there were 86 leading daily newspapers with a circulation of over 4·6m.

Tourism. In 2000 there were 469,000 foreign tourists; spending by tourists in 2000 totalled US$563m.

DIPLOMATIC REPRESENTATIVES

Of Venezuela in the United Kingdom (1 Cromwell Rd, London, SW7 2HW)
Ambassador: Alfredo Toro-Hardy.

Of the United Kingdom in Venezuela (Torre La Castellana, Piso 11, Avenida Principal de La Castellana, Caracas 1061)
Ambassador: Donald Lamont.

Of Venezuela in the USA (1099 30th St., NW, Washington, D.C., 20007)
Ambassador: Bernardo Alvarez-Herrera.

Of the USA in Venezuela (Calle Suapure, con calle F. Colinas de Valle Arriba, Caracas)
Ambassador: William R. Brownfield.

Of Venezuela to the United Nations
Ambassador: Fermín Toro Jiménez.

Of Venezuela to the European Union
Ambassador: Luisa Romero Bermudez.

FURTHER READING

Dirección General de Estadística, Ministerio de Fomento, Boletín Mensual de Estadística.—Anuario Estadístico de Venezuela. Caracas, Annual

Canache, D., *Venezuela: Public Opinion and Protest in a Fragile Democracy.* Univ. of Miami, 2002

McCoy, J., Smith, W. C., Serbin, A. and Stambouli, A., *Venezuelan Democracy Under Stress.* Univ. of Miami, 1995

Naim, M., *Paper Tigers and Minotaurs: the Politics of Venezuela's Economic Reforms.* Washington (D.C.), 1993

Rudolph, D. K. and Rudolph, G. A., *Historical Dictionary of Venezuela.* 2nd ed. Scarecrow Press, Metuchen (NJ), 1995

National statistical office: Oficina Central de Estadística e Informática.

VIETNAM

Công Hòa Xã Hôi Chu Nghĩa
Viêt Nam
(Socialist Republic of Vietnam)

Capital: Hanoi
Population projection, 2010: 89·13m.
GDP per capita, 2002: (PPP$) 2,300
HDI/world rank: 0·691/112

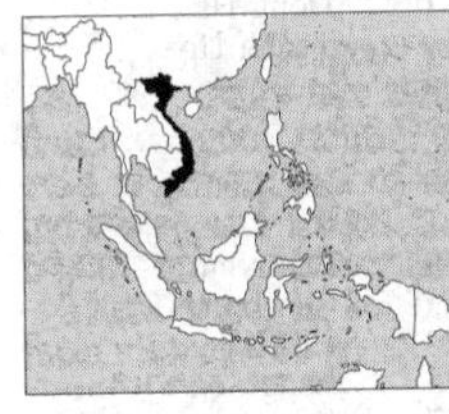

KEY HISTORICAL EVENTS

By the end of the 15th century, the Vietnamese had conquered most of the Kingdom of Champa (now Vietnam's central area) and by the end of the 18th century had acquired Cochin-China (now its southern area). At the end of the 18th century, France helped to establish the Emperor Gia-Long as ruler of a unified Vietnam. Cambodia had become a French protectorate in 1863 and in 1899, after the extension of French protection to Laos in 1893, the Indo Chinese Union was proclaimed.

In 1940 Vietnam was occupied by the Japanese. In Aug. 1945 they allowed the Vietminh movement to seize power, dethrone the Emperor and establish a republic known as Vietnam. On 6 March 1946 France recognized 'the Democratic Republic of Vietnam' as a 'Free State within the Indo-Chinese Federation'. On 19 Dec. Vietminh forces made a surprise attack on Hanoi, the signal for nearly eight years of hostilities. An agreement on the cessation of hostilities was reached on 20 July 1954. The French withdrew and by the Paris Agreement of 29 Dec. 1954 completed the transfer of sovereignty to Vietnam which was divided along the 17th parallel into Communist North Vietnam and the non-Communist South. From 1959 the North promoted insurgency in the south, provoking retaliation from the USA. A full scale guerrilla war developed.

In Paris on 27 Jan. 1973 an agreement was signed ending the war in Vietnam. However, hostilities continued between the North and the South until the latter's defeat in 1975. Between 150,000 and 200,000 South Vietnamese fled the country. The unification of North and South Vietnam into the Socialist Republic of Vietnam finally took place on 2 July 1976. Vietnam invaded Cambodia in Dec. 1978 and China attacked Vietnam in consequence. In 1986 Vietnam implemented economic reforms, gradually shifting to a multi-sectoral market economy under state regulation. On 11 July 1995 Vietnam and the USA normalized relations. On 28 July 1995 Vietnam became a member of the Association of South East Asian Nations (ASEAN) and in the same month signed a trade agreement with the European Union.

TERRITORY AND POPULATION

Vietnam is bounded in the west by Cambodia and Laos, north by China and east and south by the South China Sea. It has a total area of 332,934 sq. km and is divided into eight regions and 60 provinces and a city under central government. Areas and populations:

Province	*Area (sq. km)*	*Census population, 1999*	*Capital*
Dac Lac	19,800	1,776,331	Buon Me Thoat
Gia Lai	16,212	971,920	Play Cu
Kon Tum	9,934	314,042	Kon Tum
Central Highlands	45,946	3,062,293	
An Giang	3,424	2,049,039	Long Xuyen
Bac Lieu	2,485	736,325	Bac Lieu
Ben Tre	2,247	1,296,914	Ben Tre
Ca Mau	5,204	1,117,829	Ca Mau
Can Tho	2,965	1,811,140	Can Tho
Dong Thap	3,276	1,564,977	Sa Dec
Kien Giang	6,243	1,494,433	Rach Gia
Long An	4,338	1,306,202	Tan An
Soc Trang	3,191	1,173,820	Soc Trang

Province	*Area (sq. km)*	*Census population, 1999*	*Capital*
Tien Giang	2,339	1,605,147	My Tho
Tra Vinh	2,369	965,712	Tra Vinh
Vinh Long	1,487	1,010,486	Vinh Long
Mekong River Delta	39,568	16,132,024	
Ha Tinh	6,053	1,269,013	Ha Tinh
Nghe An	16,371	2,858,265	Vinh
Quang Binh	7,948	793,863	Dong Hoi
Quang Tri	4,592	573,331	Dong Ha
Thanh Hoa	11,168	3,467,609	Thanh Hoa
Thua Thien (Hue)	5,010	1,045,134	Hue
North Central Coast	51,142	10,007,215	
Bac Can	4,796	275,250	Bac Can
Bac Giang	3,817	1,492,191	Bac Giang
Bac Ninh	797	941,389	Bac Ninh
Cao Bang	8,445	491,055	Cao Bang
Ha Giang	7,831	602,684	Ha Giang
Lang Son	8,178	704,643	Lang Son
Lao Cai	8,044	594,637	Lao Cai
Phu Tho	3,465	1,261,500	Phu Tho
Quang Ninh	5,938	1,004,461	Ha Long
Thai Nguyen	3,541	1,046,163	Thai Nguyen
Tuyen Quang	5,810	675,110	Tuyen Quang
Vinh Phuc	1,362	1,091,973	Vinh Yen
Yen Bai	6,808	679,684	Yen Bai
North East	68,832	10,860,740	
Ba Ria (Vung Tau)	1,965	800,568	Vung Tau
Binh Duong	2,718	716,427	Thu Dau Mot
Binh Phuoc	6,796	653,644	Dong Xoai
Binh Thuan	7,992	1,047,040	Phan Thiet
Dong Nai	5,864	1,989,541	Bien Hoa
Lam Dong	10,137	996,219	Da Lat
Ninh Thuan	3,427	503,048	Phan Rang
Tay Ninh	4,029	965,420	Tay Ninh
Thanh Pho Ho Chi Minh	2,090	5,037,155	Ho Chi Minh City
North East South	45,018	12,709,062	
Hoa Binh	4,749	757,637	Hoa Binh
Lai Chau	17,133	588,666	Lai Chau
Son La	14,210	881,383	Son La
North West	36,092	2,227,686	
Ha Nam	827	791,618	Phu Ly
Ha Tay	2,169	2,386,770	Ha Dong
Hai Duong	1,661	1,649,779	Hai Duong
Hai Phong	1,508	1,672,992	Hai Phong
Hanoi	921	2,672,122	Hanoi
Hung Yen	889	1,068,705	Hung Yen
Nam Dinh	1,669	1,888,406	Nam Dinh
Ninh Binh	1,399	884,080	Ninh Binh
Thai Binh	1,520	1,785,600	Thai Binh
Red River Delta	12,563	14,800,072	
Binh Dinh	6,076	1,461,046	Quy Nhon
Da Nang	942	684,131	Da Nang
Khanh Hoa	5,257	1,031,262	Nha Trang
Phu Yen	5,278	786,972	Tuy Hoa
Quang Nam	11,043	1,372,424	Tam Ky
Quang Ngai	5,177	1,190,006	Quang Ngai
South Central Coast	33,773	6,525,841	

At the 1999 census the population was 76,324,933 (50·8% female); density, 229 per sq. km. 2002 population estimate; 80,316,000. 75·5% of the population live in rural areas (2001).

The UN gives a projected population for 2010 of 89·13m.

Cities with over 0·2m. inhabitants at the 1989 census: Ho Chi Minh City (3,169,135; 1999 population, 4,549,000), Hanoi (1,088,862), Hai Phong (456,049), Da Nang (370,670), Long Xuyen (217,171), Nha Trang (213,687), Hue (211,085), Can Tho (208,326).

87% of the population are Vietnamese (Kinh). There are also 53 minority groups thinly spread in the extensive mountainous regions. The largest minorities are: Tay, Khmer, Thai, Muong, Nung, Meo, Dao.

The official language is Vietnamese. Chinese, French and Khmer are also spoken.

SOCIAL STATISTICS

Births, 1995, 1,992,000; deaths, 553,000. Rates (1995 per 1,000 population): birth rate, 27·0; death rate, 7·5. Life expectancy, 2001, was 66·3 years for males and 71·0 years for females. Annual population growth rate, 1992–2002, 1·5%. Infant mortality, 2001, 30 per 1,000 live births; fertility rate, 2001, 2·3 births per woman. Vietnam has had one of the largest reductions in its fertility rate of any country in the world over the past 25 years, having had a rate of 5·8 births per woman in 1975. Sanctions are imposed on couples with more than two children. The annual abortion rate, at over 80 per 1,000 women aged 15–44, ranks among the highest in the world. The rate at which Vietnam has reduced poverty, from 58% of the population in 1993 to 29% in 2002, is among the most dramatic of any country in the world. Vietnam has a young population; 60% were born after 1975.

CLIMATE

The humid monsoon climate gives tropical conditions in the south, with a rainy season from May to Oct., and sub-tropical conditions in the north, though real winter conditions can affect the north when polar air blows south over Asia. In general, there is little variation in temperatures over the year. Hanoi, Jan. 62°F (16·7°C), July 84°F (28·9°C). Annual rainfall 72" (1,830 mm).

CONSTITUTION AND GOVERNMENT

The National Assembly unanimously approved a new constitution on 15 April 1992. Under this the Communist Party retains a monopoly of power and the responsibility for guiding the state according to the tenets of Marxism-Leninism and Ho Chi Minh, but with certain curbs on its administrative functions. The powers of the National Assembly are increased. The 498-member *National Assembly* is elected for five-year terms. Candidates may be proposed by the Communist Party or the Fatherland Front (which groups various social organizations), or they may propose themselves as individual Independents. The Assembly convenes three times a year and appoints a prime minister and cabinet. It elects the *President*, the head of state. The latter heads a *State Council* which issues decrees when the National Assembly is not in session.

The ultimate source of political power is the Communist Party of Vietnam, founded in 1930; it had 2·2m. members in 1996.

National Anthem. 'Doàn quân Việt Nam đi chung lòng cúú quóc' ('Soldiers of Vietnam, we are advancing'); words and tune by Van Cao.

RECENT ELECTIONS

In parliamentary elections held on 19 May 2002 Communist Party members won 447 of 498 seats, with 51 seats going to non-party candidates. Turn-out was 99·7%.

CURRENT ADMINISTRATION

President (titular head of state): Tran Duc Luong; b. 1937 (in office since Sept. 1997).

Vice-President: Truong My Hoa.

Full members of the Politburo of the Communist Party of Vietnam: Nong Duc Manh (b. 1940; *Secretary General*); Nguyen Van An; Pham Van Tra; Tran Duc Luong; Truong Tan Sang; Nguyen Tan Dung; Phan Van Khai; Nguyen Phu Trong; Nguyen Minh Triet; Phan Dien; Nguyen Khoa Diem; Truong Quang Duoc; Le Hong Anh; Tran Dinh Hoan.

In March 2005 the government comprised:

Prime Minister: Phan Van Khai; b. 1933 (sworn in 25 Sept. 1997).

Deputy Prime Ministers: Nguyen Tan Dung; Vu Khoan; Pham Gia Khiem.

Minister of Foreign Affairs: Nguyen Dy Nien. *National Defence:* Pham Van Tra. *Public Security:* Le Hong Anh. *Justice:* Uong Chu Luu. *Planning and Investment:* Vo Hong Phuc. *Finance:* Nguyen Sinh Hung. *Trade:* Truong Din Tuyen. *Agriculture and Rural Development (acting):* Cao Duc Phat. *Communications and Transport:* Dao Dinh Binh. *Construction:* Nguyen Hong Quan. *Industries:* Hoang Trung Hai. *Fisheries:* Ta Quang Ngoc. *Labour, War Invalids and Social Affairs:* Nguyen Thi Hang. *Science and Technology:* Hoang Van Phong. *Culture and Information:* Pham Quang Nghi. *Education and Training:* Nguyen Minh Hien. *Public Health:* Tran Thi Trung Chien. *Resources and Environment:* Mai Ai Truc. *Post and Telecommunications:* Do Trung Ta. *Protection and Care of Children:* Le Thi Thu.

Chairman of the National Assembly: Nguyen Van An.

Vietnamese Parliament: http://www.na.gov.vn

DEFENCE

Conscription is for two years (army) or three years (air force and navy). For specialists it is also three years.

In 2003 defence expenditure totalled US$2,901m. (US$36 per capita), representing 7·4% of GDP.

Army. There are eight military regions and two special areas. Strength (2002) was estimated to be 412,000. Paramilitary Local Defence forces number 4m.–5m. and include the Peoples' Self-Defence Force (urban) and the People's Militia (rural).

Navy. The fleet includes six frigates and two diesel submarines. In 2002 personnel was estimated at 42,000 plus an additional Naval Infantry force of 27,000.

Air Force. In 2002 the Air Force had about 30,000 personnel, and 189 combat aircraft and 26 armed helicopters. Equipment in 2002 included Su-22s, Su-27s and MiG-21s.

INTERNATIONAL RELATIONS

Vietnam is a member of the UN, Asian Development Bank, Colombo Plan, APEC, the Mekong Group, ASEAN and the International Organization of the Francophonie.

ECONOMY

Agriculture accounted for 23·0% of GDP in 2002, industry 38·5% and services 38·5%.

Overview. Since the mid-1990s Vietnam has experienced strong growth with a significant reduction of poverty. In 1993, 58% of the population lived in poverty compared to 29% in 2002. Growth averaged 9% between 1993–97 and has recovered after the Asian crisis in 1997. However, GDP per capita still remains low, at under $500. A reform programme (*Doi Moi*) was implemented in 1986, resulting in a boom in foreign investment and increased domestic economic activity. Early liberalization of the agricultural sector was accompanied by more gradual transformation of the role of the state in industry and finance. International integration has increased significantly. Imports have been substantially liberalized over the past decade and the export sector has grown 21% in value terms between 1990–2002, during which time the export to GDP ratio rose from 22% to 50%. Output has grown at more than 5% a year since 2001 and both FDI and private investment have increased. Further economic liberalization was scheduled in the 'Ten Year Socio-Economic Development Strategy 2001–10.'

Currency. The unit of currency is the *dong* (VND). In March 1989 the dong was brought into line with free market rates. The direct use of foreign currency was made illegal in Oct. 1994. Foreign exchange reserves were US$3,888m. in March 2002. Total money supply in May 2002 was 116,936·0bn. dong. There was deflation in both 2000 and 2001, of 1·6% and 0·4% respectively, but inflation in 2002 of 4·0%. Gold reserves were 98,300 troy oz in June 1991.

Budget. Budget revenue and expenditure (in 1bn. dong):

	1997	*1998*	*1999*	*2000*	*2001*[1]
Revenue	62,766	70,822	76,128	88,721	97,750
Expenditure	70,749	73,419	84,817	103,151	117,180

[1]Forecast.

Performance. Real GDP growth was between 8% and 10% each year from 1994 to 1997, but has slowed since then. There was growth of 5·0% in 2001 and 5·8% in 2002. GDP per head, which was US$181 in 1993, had risen to US$368 by 2000. Vietnam's total GDP in 2003 was US$39·2bn.

Banking and Finance. The central bank and bank of issue is the State Bank of Vietnam (founded in 1951; *Governor*, Le Duc Thuy). In 2003 there were four state-owned commercial banks, 37 joint-stock private banks, four joint venture banks, and 50 representative offices and 26 branches of foreign banks. Vietcombank is the foreign trade bank. Foreign direct investment in Vietnam was US$1·45bn. in 2003.

There is a stock exchange in Ho Chi Minh City, which opened in July 2000.

ENERGY AND NATURAL RESOURCES

Environment. Vietnam's carbon dioxide emissions from the consumption and flaring of fossil fuels were the equivalent of 0·7 tonnes per capita in 2002.

Electricity. Total installed capacity of power generation in 2000 was 5·0m. kW. In 2002, 35·56bn. kWh of electricity were produced; in 2000 consumption per capita was 342 kWh. A hydro-electric power station with a capacity of 2m. kW was opened at Hoa-Binh in 1994.

Oil and Gas. Oil reserves in 2002 totalled 600m. bbls. In Aug. 2001 an offshore oil mine containing more than 400m. bbls. of petroleum was discovered. Crude oil production in 2002, 121·9m. bbls. Natural gas reserves in 2002 were 190bn. cu. metres; production in 2000 was 1·39bn. cu. metres. Demarcation, in 1997, allowed for petroleum exploration in the Gulf of Thailand, with each side required to give the other some revenue if an underground reservoir is discovered which straddles the border.

Minerals. Vietnam is endowed with an abundance of mineral resources such as coal (3·5bn. tonnes), bauxite (3bn. tonnes), apatite (1bn. tonnes), iron ore (700m. tonnes), chromate (10m. tonnes), copper (600,000 tonnes) and tin (70,000 tonnes); coal production was estimated at 15·88m. tonnes in 2002. There are also deposits of manganese, titanium, a little gold and marble. 2001 output (in 1,000 tonnes): sand and gravel, 85,100; limestone (1999), 971; salt, 575.

Agriculture. Agriculture employs 70% of the workforce. Ownership of land is vested in the state, but since 1992 farmers may inherit and sell plots allocated on 20-year leases. There were 6·5m. ha of arable land in 2001 and 1·94m. ha of permanent crops. Agricultural production during the period 1990–97 grew on average by 5·2% every year, giving Vietnam the fastest-growing agriculture of any Asian country.

Production in 1,000 tonnes in 2000: rice, 32,554; sugarcane, 15,145; cassava, 2,036; maize, 1,930; sweet potatoes, 1,658; bananas, 1,270; coconuts, 940; coffee, 803; oranges, 427; groundnuts, 353. Vietnam is the second largest coffee producer in the world after Brazil, and one of the world's largest exporters of rice, having doubled its output in the past 15 years.

Livestock, 2000: cattle, 4·14m.; pigs, 20·19m.; buffaloes, 2·90m.; goats, 544,000; chickens, 196m.; ducks, 55m.

Livestock products (2000): meat, 1,968,000 tonnes; eggs, 165,000 tonnes; milk, 72,000 tonnes.

163,000 tractors were in use in 2001 as well as 232,000 harvester-threshers.

Forestry. In 2000 forests covered 9·82m. ha, or 30·2% of the land area. Timber exports were prohibited in 1992. Timber production was 30·80 cu. metres in 2001, nearly all of it for fuel.

Fisheries. Total catch, 2001, approximately 1,491,123 tonnes (89% from sea fishing).

INDUSTRY

Estimated total industrial output in 2002 was 260,202·0bn. dong. In 2002 estimated production (in 1,000 tonnes) was: processed sea produce, 288,701; cement, 19,482; steel, 2,429; fertilizers, 1,176; sugar, 1,074; paper (2003), 800; detergents, 381; beer (2003), 1,049·8m. litres; clothes, 47·6m. items.

Labour. In 1997 the workforce was estimated at 37m. Agriculture, forestry and fishing accounted for 25·4m. people; manufacturing, 3·3m.; trade and restaurants, 3·2m.; public administration and services, 2·2m.; transport and communications, 900,000; finance and insurance, 700,000. A liberal Enterprise Law was adopted in 2000, leading to the creation of over 50,000 new private businesses and more than 1·5m. new jobs during the next three years. Official statistics put unemployment at 7·4% of the workforce in early 2000.

Trade Unions. There are 53 trade union associations.

INTERNATIONAL TRADE

In Feb. 1994 the USA lifted the trade embargo it had imposed in 1975, and in Nov. 2001 a trade agreement with the USA was ratified. The agreement allows Vietnam's exports access to the US market on the same terms as those enjoyed by most other countries. The 1992 constitution regulates joint ventures with western firms; full repatriation of profits and non-nationalization of investments are guaranteed.

Foreign debt was US$13,349m. in 2002.

Imports and Exports. Trade is conducted through the state import-export agencies. Exports in 2002, US$16,706m.; imports, US$17,760m. In 2002 the main exports (by value) were crude oil (20%), textiles and garments (16%), sea produce (12%), footwear (11%) and rice (4%). Other significant exports were electronics, coffee, latex, cashew nuts and coal. Main imports: machinery (19%), petroleum (10%), textiles and garments (9%) and steel (7%). Other significant imports were plastics, vehicles, fertilizers and chemicals.

The main import suppliers in 2000 were Singapore (15·1%), Japan (14·0%), South Korea (11·9%) and China (10·9%). Principal export markets in 2000 were Japan (18·6%), Australia (9·7%), Germany (7·7%) and China (6·6%).

COMMUNICATIONS

Roads. There were about 93,300 km of roads in 1999, of which 25·1% were paved. In 1995 there were 0·31m. four-wheeled vehicles and around 3m. motorcycles.

Rail. There are 3,142 km of single-track line covering seven routes. Rail links with China were reopened in Feb. 1996. In 2000, 9·8m. passengers and 6·1m. tonnes of freight were carried.

Civil Aviation. There are international airports at Hanoi (Noi Bai) and Ho Chi Minh City (Tan Son Nhat) and 13 domestic airports. The national carrier is Vietnam Airlines, which provides domestic services and in 2003 had international flights to Bangkok, Beijing, Dubai, Guangzhou, Hong Kong, Kaohsiung, Kuala Lumpur, Kunming, Manila, Melbourne, Moscow, Osaka, Paris, Phnom Penh, Seoul, Siem Reap, Singapore, Sydney, Taipei, Tokyo and Vientiane. In 1999 it flew 30·7m. km, carrying 2,600,000 passengers (994,300 on international flights). The busiest airport is Ho Chi Minh City, which in 1999 handled 3,378,081 passengers and 69,188 tonnes of freight. Hanoi handled 1,613,973 passengers and 24,567 tonnes of freight in 1999.

Shipping. In 2002 sea-going vessels totalled 1,131,000 GRT, including oil tankers 162,000 GRT. The major ports are Hai Phong, which can handle ships of 10,000 tons, Ho Chi Minh City and Da Nang. There are regular services to Hong Kong, Singapore, Thailand, Cambodia and Japan. There are some 19,500 km of navigable waterways.

Telecommunications. Vietnam Posts and Telecommunications and the military operate telephone systems with the assistance of foreign companies. Telephone subscribers numbered 5,567,100 in 2002 (68·5 per 1,000 persons) and there were 800,000 PCs in use (9·8 for every 1,000 persons). In 2002 there were 1,902,400 mobile phone subscribers and in 1999 fax machines numbered 31,000. Vietnam had 1·5m. Internet users in 2002.

Postal Services. In 1999 there were 3,075 post offices, or one for every 25,200 persons.

SOCIAL INSTITUTIONS

Justice. A new penal code came into force on 1 Jan. 1986 'to complete the work of the 1980 Constitution'. Penalties (including death) are prescribed for opposition to the people's power and for economic crimes. The judicial system comprises the Supreme People's Court, provincial courts and district courts. The president of the Supreme Court is responsible to the National Assembly, as is the Procurator-General, who heads the Supreme People's Office of Supervision and Control.

The death penalty is still in force; there were 64 reported executions in 2004.

The population in penal institutions in 1998 was 55,000 (71 per 100,000 of national population).

Religion. Taoism is the traditional religion but Buddhism is widespread. At a Conference for Buddhist Reunification in Nov. 1981, nine sects adopted a charter for a new Buddhist church under the Council of Sangha. The Hoa Hao sect, associated with Buddhism, claimed 1·7m. adherents in 2001. Caodaism, a synthesis of Christianity, Buddhism and Confucianism founded in 1926, has some 2·8m. followers. In 2001 there were 53·3m. Buddhists and 6·2m. Roman Catholics. In Sept. 2003 there were two cardinals. There is an Archbishopric of Hanoi and 13 bishops. There were two seminaries in 1989.

Education. Adult literacy rate in 2001 was 92·7% (94·5% among males and 90·9% among females). Primary education consists of a ten-year course divided into three levels of four, three and three years respectively. In 2000–01 there were 9,751,434 pupils and 347,833 teachers in primary schools, and 8,321,194 pupils and 309,218 teachers at secondary schools. In 1995–96 there were seven universities, two open (distance) universities and nine specialized universities (agriculture, three; economics, two; technology, three; water resources, one).

Health. In 1998 there were 36,683 physicians, 42,797 nurses and 13,450 midwives. There were 12,500 hospitals in 1994.

CULTURE

World Heritage Sites. Vietnam has five sites on the UNESCO World Heritage List: the Complex of Hue Monuments (inscribed on the list in 1993); Ha Long Bay (1994 and 2000); Hoi An Ancient Town (1999); My Son Sanctuary (1999); and Phong Nha-Ke Bang National Park (2003).

Broadcasting. Broadcasting is controlled by the state Vietnam Radio and Television Committee. There are two national radio programmes from Hanoi and one from Ho Chi Minh City, 14 provincial programmes and an external service, the Voice of Vietnam (11 languages). There is a national and two provincial TV services. There were 8·5m. radio sets in 2000 and 15·1m. TV receivers in 2001 (colour by NTSC, PAL and SECAM).

Press. In 1994 there were some 350 newspaper and periodical titles. There are two national dailies, the Communist Party's *Nhan Dan* ('The People'), circulation, 0·2m., and the Army's *Quan Doi Nhan Dan*, 60,000. There are three major regional dailies with a combined circulation of 155,000. There were ten titles in English, including two dailies, in 1995. 3,043 book titles were published in 1991 totalling 62·4m. copies.

Tourism. There were 2,330,000 foreign tourists in 2001; revenue from tourists in 1998 came to US$86m.

DIPLOMATIC REPRESENTATIVES

Of Vietnam in the United Kingdom (12–14 Victoria Rd, London, W8 5RD)
Ambassador: Trinh Duc Du.

Of the United Kingdom in Vietnam (Central Building, 31 Hai Ba Trung, Hanoi)
Ambassador: Robert Gordon, CMG, OBE.

Of Vietnam in the USA (1233 20th Street, NW, Suite 400, Washington, D.C., 20036)
Ambassador: Chiem Tam Nguyen.

Of the USA in Vietnam (7 Lang Ha, Ba Dinh District, Hanoi)
Ambassador: Michael W. Marine.

Of Vietnam to the United Nations
Ambassador: Le Luong Minh.

Of Vietnam to the European Union
Ambassador: Phan Thuy Thanh.

FURTHER READING

Trade and Tourism Information Centre with the General Statistical Office. *Economy and Trade of Vietnam* [various 5-year periods]

Gilbert, Marc Jason (ed.) *Why the North Won the Vietnam War.* Palgrave Macmillan, Basingstoke, 2002

Harvie, C. and Tran Van Hoa V., *Reforms and Economic Growth.* London, 1997

Karnow, S., *Vietnam: a History.* 2nd ed. London, 1992

Marr, David G., *et al.*, *Vietnam.* [Bibliography] ABC-Clio, Oxford and Santa Barbara (CA), 1992

Morley, J. W. and Nishihara M., *Vietnam Joins the World.* Armonk (NY), 1997

Norlund, I. (ed.) *Vietnam in a Changing World.* London, 1994

National statistical office: General Statistical Office, No. 2 Hoang Van Thu St., Ba Dinh District, Hanoi.

Website: http://www.gso.gov.vn

YEMEN

Jamhuriya al Yamaniya
(Republic of Yemen)

Capital: Sana'a
Commercial capital: Aden
Population projection, 2010: 25·66m.
GDP per capita, 2002: (PPP$) 870
HDI/world rank: 0·482/149

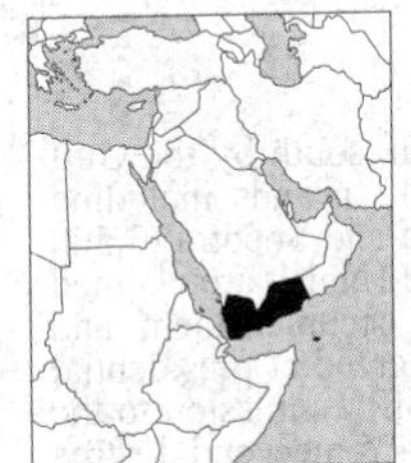

KEY HISTORICAL EVENTS

In the 1st millennium BC the wealth of the kingdom of Saba (or Sheba), in what is now Yemen and southwestern Saudi Arabia, was based on the incense and spice trade and on agriculture. From about 115 BC the Himyarite kingdom absorbed Saba and Hadhramaut (to the east) to claim control of the entire southwest Arabian Peninsula by the 4th century AD. Himyarite dominance came to an end in the 6th century as the forces of Aksum (Ethiopia) invaded in AD 525. Aksumite rule was overthrown in 575 by the Persians, who held power until the advent of Islam in 628.

Yemen became a province of the Muslim caliphate. Thereafter its fortunes reflected the power of the imams (kings and spiritual leaders) of the Zaidi sect, who built the theocratic political structure of Yemen that endured until 1962. Rival dynasties included the Fatimid caliphs of Egypt, who occupied most of Yemen from about 1000 until 1175, and the Ayyubids, who ruled until about 1250. However, central authority had fragmented by the time the Ottoman Turks intervened in Yemen in the first half of the 16th century. They held nominal sovereignty until the end of the First World War when Yemen became independent.

The southern Yemeni port of Aden was a coveted commercial location on the trading routes to the wider East. Britain sought to contain the French threat to communications with British India following Napoléon's conquest of Egypt in 1798 and needed a military and refuelling base in the region. In 1839 the British captured Aden, which was attached administratively to India. The opening of the Suez Canal in 1869 further enhanced Aden's significance.

After the Ottoman evacuation, Imam Yahya sought to expand Yemeni territory. Hostilities with Saudi Arabia (by then under the rule of Ibn Saud) and skirmishes with British forces from Aden led to a 1934 trilateral treaty to fix Yemen's boundaries. Aden meanwhile was made a British crown colony in 1937, and the surrounding region became known as the Aden protectorate.

Opposition to the despotic rule of Imam Yahya led to his assassination in Feb. 1948. His son, Crown Prince Ahmad, succeeded him and put down the insurgents. Ahmad's reign was marked by further repression, renewed friction over the British presence in southern Yemen, and growing pressure in the 1950s to support the Arab nationalist objectives of the Nasser regime in Egypt. Following Ahmad's death his son, Muhammad al-Badr, was deposed a week after his accession in Sept. 1962 by Egyptian-backed revolutionary forces, which took control of the capital, Sana'a, and proclaimed the Yemen Arab Republic (YAR).

In the Aden colony, which had become partially self-governing, a struggle between rival nationalist groups after the British withdrawal in 1967 led to an independent Marxist state, with Aden as the capital. This was renamed the People's Democratic Republic of Yemen (PDRY) in 1970. Mistrust and frequent border clashes between the YAR and the PDRY continued for the next decade, despite an accord in 1972 to merge the two entities. In early 1979 sporadic fighting erupted into full-scale war between North and South Yemen. Arab League mediation brought the hostilities to an end but political disruption in both states delayed a settlement until 1989, when Ali Abdullah Saleh and Ali Salem Albidh agreed a unity constitution. On 22 May 1990 the Republic of Yemen was declared. A five-member Presidential Council assumed power and Saleh was appointed as president for a transitional period. By 1993 relations between the North and South had again deteriorated, Vice-President Albidh having withdrawn to Aden to demand political reforms. Sporadic military clashes escalated into civil war in May 1994. Northern forces prevailed and Aden was captured on 7 July 1994. The former vice-president and other southern leaders went into exile and President Saleh was confirmed in office.

Yemen suffered economic sanctions in the early 1990s for its equivocal response to Iraq's invasion of Kuwait. Its stance exacerbated longstanding border tensions with neighbouring Saudi Arabia. More recent terrorist activity against Western targets in Yemeni territory—a suicide attack on the US naval vessel *USS Cole* in Oct. 2000 and an apparent bomb attack on a French supertanker, the *Limburg*, off the Yemeni coast in Oct. 2002—fuelled concerns that Yemen had become a haven for Islamic extremists. In 1995 Yemen clashed with Eritrea over control of the Hanish Islands in the Red Sea. Following arbitration by an international panel, Yemen assumed control of the main islands in 1998.

TERRITORY AND POPULATION

Yemen is bounded in the north by Saudi Arabia, east by Oman, south by the Gulf of Aden and west by the Red Sea. The territory includes 112 islands including Kamaran (181 sq. km) and Perim (300 sq. km) in the Red Sea and Socotra (3,500 sq. km) in the Gulf of Aden. The islands of Greater and Lesser Hanish are claimed by both Yemen and Eritrea. On 15 Dec. 1995 Eritrean troops occupied them, and Yemen retaliated with aerial bombardments. A ceasefire was agreed at presidential level on 17 Dec. On 20 Dec. the UN resolved to send a good offices mission to the area. In an agreement of 21 May 1996 brokered by France, Yemen and Eritrea renounced the use of force to settle the dispute and agreed to submit it to arbitration. Following a ruling issued by the Permanent Court of Arbitration in the Hague, Yemen assumed control of the main islands in 1998. The area is 555,000 sq. km excluding the desert Empty Quarter (Rub Al-Khahi). A dispute with Saudi Arabia broke out in Dec. 1994 over some 1,500–2,000 km of undemarcated desert boundary. A memorandum of understanding signed on 26 Feb. 1995 reaffirmed the border agreement reached at Taif in 1934, and on 12 June 2000 a 'final and permanent' border treaty between the two countries was signed. An agreement of June 1995 completed the demarcation of the border with Oman.

Census population, 1994: 14,587,807. 2002 estimate: 19·40m.; density, 35 persons per sq. km.

The UN gives a projected population for 2010 of 25·66m.

In 2001, 75·0% of the population lived in rural areas. At the census of 1994 the population was 14,832,673. There were 1,168,199 citizens working abroad, mainly in Saudi Arabia and the United Arab Emirates, not included in the census total. Since 1990 Saudi Arabia has compulsorily repatriated almost all Yemeni workers. In 1994 there were 17 governorates plus the capital city, Sana'a:

	1994 census population		*1994 census population*
Abyan	414,543	Lahej	634,652
Aden	562,162	Mahrah	112,512
Bayd	509,265	Mahwit	403,465
Dhamar	1,050,346	Marib	167,388
Hadhramout	870,025	Sa'adah	486,059
Hajjah	1,262,590	Sana'a (city) } Sana'a }	1,910,286
Hodeida	1,749,944	Shabwah	377,080
Ibb	1,959,313	Ta'iz	2,205,947
Jawf	157,096		

Since the 1994 census two further governorates have been created. Amran was formed from parts of Mahwit, Hajjah and Sana'a governorates. Al-Dhalia was formed from parts of Ibb, Lahej and Ta'iz governorates.

The population of the capital, Sana'a, was 1,231,000 in 1999. The commercial capital is the port of Aden, with a population of (1995) 562,000. Other important towns are Ta'iz, the port of Hodeida, Mukalla, Ibb and Abyan. Sana'a is currently the fastest-growing city in the world, with a population increase of 832·6% in the period 1975–2000 and a projected increase of 128·2% between 2000–15, by when it is expected to have 3·03m. inhabitants.

The national language is Arabic.

SOCIAL STATISTICS

Births, 1995, 724,000; deaths, 168,000. Birth rate, 1995, was 48·2 per 1,000 population; death rate, 11·2. Life expectancy, 2001, was 58·3 years for males and 60·5 years for females. Infant mortality, 2001, 79 per 1,000 live births. Annual population growth rate, 1992–2002, 3·9%; fertility rate, 2001, 7·6 births per woman.

CLIMATE

A desert climate, modified by relief. Sana'a, Jan. 57°F (13·9°C), July 71°F (21·7°C). Aden, Jan. 75°F (24°C), July 90°F (32°C). Annual rainfall 20" (508 mm) in the north, but very low in coastal areas: 1·8" (46 mm).

CONSTITUTION AND GOVERNMENT

Parliament consists of a 301-member *Assembly of Representatives* (*Majlis al-Nuwaab*), elected for a six-year term in single-seat constituencies and, since 2001, a 111-member *Shura Council* (*Majlis al-Shura*), appointed by the president.

On 28 Sept. 1994 the Assembly of Representatives unanimously adopted a new constitution founded on Islamic law. It abolished the former five-member Presidential Council and installed a *President* elected by parliament for a five-year term, subsequently amended to a seven-year term through a referendum held on 20 Feb. 2001. As a result of the same referendum the term for MPs was extended from four to six years.

National Anthem. 'Raddidi Ayyatuha ad Dunya nashidi' ('Repeat, O World, my song'); words by A. Noman, tune by Ayub Tarish.

RECENT ELECTIONS

The *President*, Ali Abdullah Saleh, was elected for his first term in 1990. At the election of 23 Sept. 1999 he was voted in for a third term, claiming 96·3% against the 3·7% of his sole opponent, Najeeb Qahtan Al-Sha'abi. Turn-out was 66%.

Parliamentary elections were held on 27 April 2003, in which the General People's Congress (MSA) gained 238 seats (58·0% of the vote), Yemeni Congregation for Reform (Islah) 46 seats (22·6%), Yemeni Socialist Party 8 seats (3·8%), Nasserite Unionist People's Organization (TWSN) 3 seats (1·9%), the Arab Socialist Rebirth Party (Baath) 2 seats (0·7%) and ind. 4 seats. Turn-out was 76·0%.

CURRENT ADMINISTRATION

President: Ali Abdullah Saleh; b. 1942 (MSA; in office since 1990, re-appointed in 1994 and 1999).

Vice-President: Abd-Rabbu Mansour Hadi.

In March 2005 the government comprised:

Prime Minister: Abd al-Qadir al-Ba Jamal; b. 1946 (MSA; in office since 31 March 2001, re-appointed 10 May 2003).

Deputy Prime Minister and Minister for Finance: Alawi Salih al-Salami. *Deputy Prime Minister and Minister for Planning and International Co-operation:* Ahmed Mohamed Abdallah al-Sufan. *Defence:* Abdullah Ali Elewa. *Foreign Affairs:* Abubakr al-Qirbi. *Oil and Mineral Resources:* Rasheed Ba Raba'a. *Legal Affairs:* Rashad Al-Rassas. *Justice:* Adnan Al-Jefri. *Higher Education and Scientific Research:* Abd al-Wahab al-Raweh. *Labour and Social Affairs:* Abdulkarim al-Arhabi. *Communications and Information Technology:* Abdulmalik Al-Mu'alimi. *Local Administration:* Sadiq Abu Ras. *Fisheries:* Ali Mujawar. *Transport*: Omar Al-Amudi. *Interior:* Rashad Al-Alimi. *Information:* Hussein Al-Awadhi. *Human Rights:* Amatalaeem Al-Suswah. *Youth and Sports:* Abdulrahman Al-Akwa'. *Electricity:* Abdulrahman Turmum. *Agriculture and Irrigation:* Hasan Suwaid. *Trade and Industry:* Khalid Sheikh. *Culture and Tourism:* Khalid Al-Ruwaishan. *Technical and Vocational Training:* Ali Safa'a. *Public Health and Population:* Mohammed Yahia Al-Na'ami. *Education:* Abdulsalam Al-Jufi. *Endowments and Guidance:* Hamoud Ubad. *Water and Environment:* Mohammed Al-Iryani. *Immigrants Affairs:* Abdo Al-Qubati. *Social Security and Civil Service:* Hamoud Al-Sufi.

Speaker: Abdullah Hussain Al-Ahmar.

Government Website: http://www.yemen.gov.ye

DEFENCE

Conscription is for three years. Defence expenditure in 2003 totalled US$798m. (US$42 per capita), representing 7·0% of GDP.

Estimates of the number of small arms in the country are around 70m., equivalent to nearly four firearms for every person, making Yemen arguably the world's most heavily armed country.

Army. Strength (2002) 60,000 with 40,000 reserves. There are paramilitary tribal levies numbering at least 20,000 and a Ministry of Security force of 50,000.

Navy. Navy forces are based at Aden and Hodeida, with other facilities at Mokha, Mukalla and Perim. Personnel in 2002 were estimated at 1,500.

Air Force. The unified Air Forces of the former Arab Republic and People's Democratic Republic are now under one command, although this unity was broken by the attempted secession of the south in 1994 which resulted in heavy fighting between the air forces of Sana'a and Aden. Personnel (2002) about 5,000. There were 76 combat aircraft including F-5Es, Su-20/22s, MiG-21s and MiG-29s.

INTERNATIONAL RELATIONS

Yemen is a member of the UN, the League of Arab States, IOM, OIC and Islamic Development Bank.

With a view to maintaining regional stability the USA supports Yemen and its democracy both in material and moral terms.

ECONOMY

In 2002 agriculture accounted for 11·4% of GDP, industry 41·5% and services 47·1%.

Overview. Yemen's second five-year plan is running from 2001–05. Priorities are economic and structural reform, the improvement in living conditions, increased investment and reduction of unemployment.

Currency. The unit of currency is the *riyal* (YER) of 100 *fils.* During the transitional period to north-south unification the northern *riyal* of 100 *fils* and the southern *dinar* of 1,000 *fils* co-existed. There were three foreign exchange rates operating: an internal clearing rate, an official rate and a commercial rate. In 1996 the official rate was abolished. Total money supply in May 2002 was 262,073m. riyals, gold reserves totalled 50,000 troy oz and foreign exchange reserves were US$3,722m. Inflation was 12·2% in 2002.

Budget. The fiscal year is the calendar year. Total revenues in 2000 were 388,950m. riyals and expenditures 422,250m. riyals. Tax revenue accounted for 90·1% of total revenues in 1999. The main items of expenditure in 1999 were wages and salaries (23·0%), defence (18·1%) and economic development (17·5%).

Performance. Real GDP growth was 3·9% in 2002 (4·6% in 2001); total GDP in 2003 was US$10·8bn.

Banking and Finance. The *Governor* of the Central Bank of Yemen is Ahmed Abdul Rahman Al-Samawi. Total reserves of the Central Bank were 81,089m. riyals in 2002 and there were 446,287m. riyals in deposits.

ENERGY AND NATURAL RESOURCES

Environment. Yemen's carbon dioxide emissions from the consumption and flaring of fossil fuels were the equivalent of 0·5 tonnes per capita in 2002.

Electricity. Installed capacity was 0·8m. kW in 2000. Production in 2000 was 2·96bn. kWh; consumption per capita was 162 kWh.

Oil and Gas. In 2002 there were oil reserves of 4,000m. bbls., mostly near the former north-south border. Crude oil production (2003): 21·4m. tonnes. Natural gas reserves in 2002 were 480bn. cu. metres.

Minerals. In 1998, 147,000 tonnes of salt were produced. Reserves (estimate) 25m. tonnes. In 1999, 103,000 tonnes of gypsum were extracted and 2·55m. cu. metres of stone.

Agriculture. In 2001 there were 1·47m. ha of arable land and 129,000 ha of permanent cropland; 500,000 ha were irrigated in 2001. In the south, agriculture is largely of a subsistence nature, sorghum, sesame and millet being the chief crops, and wheat and barley widely grown at the higher elevations. Cash crops include cotton. Fruit is plentiful in the north.

Estimated production (2000, in 1,000 tonnes): sorghum, 401; tomatoes, 245; potatoes, 213; oranges, 175; grapes, 157; alfalfa, 149 (1992); wheat, 137; melons and watermelons, 119. Livestock in 2000: sheep, 4·76m.; goats, 4·09m.; cattle, 1·28m.; asses, 500,000; camels, 185,000; chickens, 28m. Estimated livestock produce, 2000 (in 1,000 tonnes): meat, 163; milk, 213.

Forestry. There were 449,000 ha of forest in 2000. Timber production in 2001 was 314,000 cu. metres.

Fisheries. Fishing is a major industry. Total catch in 2001 was 142,198 tonnes, exclusively marine fish.

INDUSTRY

Output (in 1,000 tonnes): residual fuel oil (2000), 1,553; cement (2001), 1,493; petrol (2000), 1,081; distillate fuel oil (2000), 837; jet fuels (2000), 343; wheat flour (2000), 338; kerosene (2000), 120. In 2001 industry accounted for 49·2% of GDP, with manufacturing contributing 6·7%.

Labour. Of 3,621,700 persons in employment in 2002, 1,927,700 were engaged in agriculture, hunting and forestry; 394,200 in wholesale and retail trade/repair of motor vehicles, motorcycles and personal and household goods; 358,000 in public administration and defence/compulsory social security; and 238,200 in construction. Unemployment was 18% in 2004.

INTERNATIONAL TRADE

Foreign debt was US$5,290m. in 2002.

Imports and Exports. Trade in US$1m.:

	1998	*1999*	*2000*	*2001*	*2002*
Imports f.o.b.	2,288·8	2,120·5	2,484·4	2,600·4	2,932·0
Exports f.o.b.	1,503·7	2,478·3	3,797·2	3,366·9	3,620·7

Main import suppliers, 1999: United Arab Emirates, 11·7%; Saudi Arabia, 10·2%; USA, 5·5%; Australia, 4·8%. Main export markets, 1999: China, 28·8%; Thailand, 25·5%; South Korea, 14·5%; Singapore, 8·6%.

Oil, cotton and fish are major exports, the largest imports being food and live animals. Oil accounts for more than 80% of exports. A large transhipment and entrepôt trade is centred on Aden, which was made a free trade zone in May 1991.

COMMUNICATIONS

Roads. There were an estimated 67,000 km of roads in 1999, of which 11·5% were paved. In 1996 there were 240,600 passenger cars, 3,400 buses and coaches, and 291,150 goods vehicles. In 1996 there were 7,303 road accidents resulting in 1,267 deaths.

Rail. Passenger-km travelled in 1997 came to 2,492m.

Civil Aviation. There are international airports at Sana'a and Aden. In 2000 Sana'a handled 794,000 passengers (665,000 on international flights) and 13,000 tonnes of freight. The national carrier is Yemenia Yemen Airways, which operates internal services and in 2003 had international flights to Abu Dhabi, Addis Ababa, Amman, Asmara, Bahrain, Beirut, Bombay, Cairo, Damascus, Dar es Salaam, Djibouti, Doha, Dubai, Frankfurt, Jakarta, Jeddah, Khartoum, Kuala Lumpur, London, Marseille, Milan, Moroni, Paris, Riyadh and Rome. In 1999 scheduled airline traffic of Yemen-based carriers flew 14·5m. km, carrying 731,000 passengers (480,000 on international flights).

Shipping. In 2002 sea-going shipping totalled 78,000 GRT, including oil tankers 51,000 GRT. There are ports at Aden, Mokha, Hodeida, Mukalla and Nashtoon. In 1998 vessels totalling 11,210,000 NRT entered ports and vessels totalling 9,851,000 NRT cleared.

Telecommunications. Yemen had 953,300 telephone subscribers in 2002, or 48·9 per 1,000 population, and there were 145,000 PCs in use (7·4 for every 1,000 persons). There were 100,000 Internet users in 2002. Mobile phone subscribers numbered 411,000 in 2002 and there were 2,800 fax machines in 1995.

Postal Services. In 1998 there were 265 post offices.

SOCIAL INSTITUTIONS

Justice. A civil code based on Islamic law was introduced in 1992. The death penalty is still in force; there was one confirmed execution in 2004.

Religion. In 2001 there were some 18·05m. Muslims (mostly Sunnis) and approximately 20,000 followers of other religions.

Education. In 2000–01 there were 7,600 children in pre-primary schools, 2·64m. pupils in primary schools and 1·24m. pupils in general programmes at secondary level. Yemen has the lowest proportion of female pupils enrolled at primary school, at 38% in 2000–01. There are universities at Sana'a (founded 1974) and Aden (1975). The former had 3,520 students and 330 academic staff in 1994–95, the latter 4,800 and 470. The adult literacy rate in 2001 was 47·7% (68·5% among males and 26·9% among females, the biggest difference in literacy rates between the sexes of any country).

In 2000–01 total expenditure on education came to 10·6% of GNP and accounted for 32·8% of total government expenditure.

Health. In 1998 there were 81 hospitals with a provision of 55 beds per 10,000 inhabitants. There were 3,883 physicians and 613 pharmacists in 1998, 245 dentists in 1996, 7,578 nurses in 1995 and 385 midwives in 1994.

CULTURE

World Heritage Sites. There are three sites under Yemeni jurisdiction that appear in the UNESCO World Heritage List. They are (with year entered on the list): the old walled city of Shibam (1982); the old city of Sana'a (1986); and the historic town of Zabid (1993).

Broadcasting. Broadcasting is managed by the government-controlled Yemen Radio and Television Corporation. Programmes are transmitted from Sana'a and Aden. In 2000 there were 1·2m. radio receivers and in 2001 there were 5·3m. TV receivers (colour by PAL).

Press. In 1996 there were three daily newspapers with a circulation of 230,000.

Tourism. There were 73,000 foreign tourists in 2000, bringing revenue of US$76m.

DIPLOMATIC REPRESENTATIVES

Of Yemen in the United Kingdom (57 Cromwell Rd, London, SW7 2ED)
Ambassador: Mutahar Abdullah Alsaeede.

Of the United Kingdom in Yemen (129 Haddah Rd, Sana'a)
Ambassador: Michael Gifford.

Of Yemen in the USA (2600 Virginia Ave., NW, Washington, D.C., 20037)
Ambassador: Abdulwahab Al-Hajjiri.

Of the USA in Yemen (Sa'awan Street, Himyar Zone, Sana'a)
Ambassador: Thomas C. Krajeski.

Of Yemen to the United Nations
Ambassador: Abdullah Al-Saidi.

Of Yemen to the European Union
Ambassador: Jaffer Mohamed Jaffer.

FURTHER READING

Central Statistical Organization. *Statistical Year Book*
Auchterlonie, Paul, *Yemen.* [Bibliography] 2nd ed. ABC-Clio, Oxford and Santa Barbara (CA), 1998
Dresch, Paul, *A History of Modern Yemen.* CUP, 2001
Mackintosh-Smith, T., *Yemen—Travels in Dictionary Land.* London, 1997

National statistical office: Central Statistical Organization, Ministry of Planning and Development

ZAMBIA

Republic of Zambia

Capital: Lusaka
Population projection, 2010: 11·77m.
GDP per capita, 2002: (PPP$) 840
HDI/world rank: 0·389/164

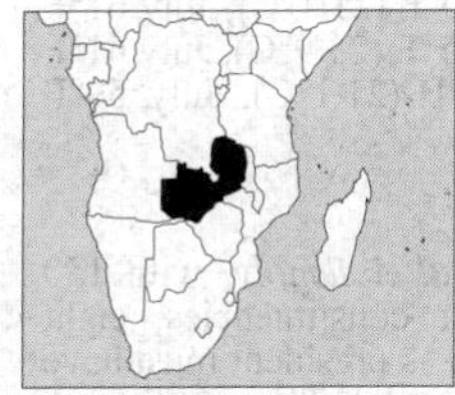

KEY HISTORICAL EVENTS

The majority of the population is of Bantu origin. There are more than 70 different tribes, the most important being the Bemba and the Bgoni in the northeast. One of the more successful of the invading tribes was the Lozi under Lewanika, who obtained the protection of the British government in 1891. In 1900 the British South Africa Company acquired trading and mining rights. From 1911 the territory was known as Northern Rhodesia and in 1924 the Crown took over the administration.

In 1953 the Federation of Rhodesia and Nyasaland, of which Northern Rhodesia was a part, was created. Federation brought economic benefits to Northern Rhodesia but it was from the outset opposed by African leaders. In March 1963 Britain agreed to Northern Rhodesia's right to secede from the Federation. In Jan. 1964 internal self-government was attained. On 24 Oct. Northern Rhodesia became an independent republic within the Commonwealth, changing its name to Zambia. A highly centralized one-party state was created which suffocated the emergent economy. Living standards fell sharply and the production of copper, Zambia's biggest foreign exchange earner, almost halved. In 1991 the Movement for Multiparty Democracy (MMD) was elected on a promise to transform the economy.

TERRITORY AND POPULATION

Zambia is bounded by the Democratic Republic of the Congo in the north, Tanzania in the northeast, Malaŵi in the east, Mozambique in the southeast, Zimbabwe and Namibia in the south, and by Angola in the west. The area is 290,584 sq. miles (752,612 sq. km). Population (2000 census), 9,885,591; population density, 13·1 per sq. km. In 2001, 60·2% of the population were rural.

The UN gives a projected population for 2010 of 11·77m.

The republic is divided into nine provinces. Area, population at the 2000 census and chief towns:

Province	*Area (in sq. km)*	*Population*	*Chief Town*
Central	94,394	1,012,257	Kabwe
Copperbelt	31,328	1,581,221	Ndola
Eastern	69,106	1,306,173	Chipata
Luapula	50,567	775,353	Mansa
Lusaka	21,896	1,391,329	Lusaka
Northern	147,826	1,258,696	Kasama
North-Western	125,827	583,350	Solwezi
Southern	85,283	1,212,124	Livingstone
Western	126,386	765,088	Mongu

The capital is Lusaka, which had a census population in 2000 of 1,084,703. Other major towns (with 2000 census population in 1,000) are: Ndola, 375; Kitwe, 364; Kabwe, 177; Chingola, 147; Mufulira, 122; Luanshya, 116.

The official language is English and the main ethnic groups are the Bemba (34%), Tonga (16%), Nyanja (14%) and Lozi (9%).

SOCIAL STATISTICS

Births, 1995, 351,000; deaths, 149,000. 1995 birth rate per 1,000 population, 43·4; death rate, 18·5. Zambia's life expectancy at birth in 2001 was 33·3 years for males and 33·4 for females (the lowest for females in the world and the lowest overall). Life expectancy has declined dramatically over the last ten years, largely owing to the huge number of people in the country with HIV. Annual population growth rate,

1992–2002, 2·1%. Infant mortality, 2001, 112 per 1,000 live births; fertility rate, 2001, 5·8 births per woman.

CLIMATE

The climate is tropical, but has three seasons. The cool, dry one is from May to Aug., a hot dry one follows until Nov., when the wet season commences. Frosts may occur in some areas in the cool season. Lusaka, Jan. 70°F (21·1°C), July 61°F (16·1°C). Annual rainfall 33" (836 mm). Livingstone, Jan. 75°F (23·9°C), July 61°F (16·1°C). Annual rainfall 27" (673 mm). Ndola, Jan. 70°F (21·1°C), July 59°F (15°C). Annual rainfall 52" (1,293 mm).

CONSTITUTION AND GOVERNMENT

Zambia has a unicameral legislature, the 159-seat *National Assembly*, with 150 members elected for a five-year term in single-member constituencies, eight appointed members and the Speaker. Candidates for election as president must have both parents born in Zambia (this excludes ex-president Kaunda). The constitution was amended in 1996 shortly before the parliamentary and presidential elections. The amendment restricts the president from serving more than two terms of office.

National Anthem. 'Stand and Sing of Zambia'; words collective, tune by M. E. Sontonga.

RECENT ELECTIONS

Parliamentary and presidential elections took place on 27 Dec. 2001. The elections were beset by allegations of vote rigging, prompting investigations from EU monitors. Levy Patrick Mwanawasa, former president Frederick Chiluba's chosen successor, defeated ten other candidates running for the presidency yet only won 28·8% of votes cast.

In the parliamentary elections, Levy Patrick Mwanawasa's party, the Movement for Multiparty Democracy (MMD), gained 69 seats in the 159-seat National Assembly; the United Party for National Development gained 49; the United National Independence Party, 13; the Forum for Democracy and Development, 12; and the Heritage Party, 4. Mwanawasa's inaugural speech was boycotted by all ten opposition parties.

CURRENT ADMINISTRATION

President and Minister of Defence: Levy Patrick Mwanawasa; b. 1948 (MMD; sworn in 2 Jan. 2002).

Vice-President: Lupando Mwape.

In March 2005 the government comprised:

Minister for Agriculture and Co-operatives: Mundia Sikatana. *Commerce, Trade and Industry:* Dipak Patel. *Communication and Transport:* Abel M. Chambeshi. *Community Development and Social Services, and Works and Supply:* Marina Nsingo. *Education:* Andrew Mulenga. *Energy and Water Development:* George Mpombo. *Finance and National Planning:* Peter Magande. *Foreign Affairs:* Ronnie Shikapwaska. *Health:* Brig.-Gen. Dr Brian Chituwo. *Home Affairs:* Kalombo Mwansa. *Information and Broadcasting Services:* Mutale Nalumango. *Labour and Social Security:* Vacant. *Lands:* Judith Kapijimpanga. *Legal Affairs:* George Kunda. *Local Government and Housing:* Sylvia Masebo. *Mines and Mineral Development:* Kaunda Lembalemba. *Science, Technology and Vocational Training:* Bates Namuyamba. *Sport, Youth and Child Development:* Gladys Nyirongo. *Tourism, Environment and Natural Resources:* Patrick Kalifungwa.

Zambian Parliament: http://www.parliament.gov.zm

DEFENCE

In 2003 defence expenditure totalled US$27m. (US$3 per capita), representing 0·6% of GDP.

Army. Strength (2002) 20,000. There are also two paramilitary police units totalling 1,400.

Air Force. In 2002 the Air Force had over 63 combat aircraft including F-6 (Chinese-built MiG-19s) and MiG-21s. Serviceability of most types is reported to be low. Personnel (2002) 1,600.

INTERNATIONAL RELATIONS

Zambia is a member of the UN, WTO, the Commonwealth, SADC, the African Union, African Development Bank, COMESA, IOM and is an ACP member state of the ACP-EU relationship.

During the 1990s Zambia received foreign aid equivalent to approximately US$900 a head, but according to the *World Bank* GNP per head declined from US$390 in 1991 to US$330 in 1999.

ECONOMY

In 2002 agriculture accounted for 22·2% of GDP, industry 26·1% and services 51·7%.

Overview. The Zambian economy is primarily agrarian; the sector employs 85% of the population. The main industries are copper mining and processing, accounting for more than 80% of the country's foreign currency intake. Between 1974–90 the economy experienced negative growth of nearly 5% per year owing to macroeconomic instability, incomplete policy implementation and inefficient state-owned industries. A change of political power in 1990 improved the state of the economy. The government initiated ambitious market-orientated reforms and tried to ameliorate macroeconomic management. The government privatized the copper mines in 2000 and monetary and fiscal policies were tightened. As a result of these reforms, real GDP grew at 3·5% in 2000 and inflation fell to the lowest levels in 20 years. Since 2002 Zambia has been hit by crises in the copper and agriculture sector that have increased food insecurity and decreased growth prospects.

Currency. The unit of currency is the *kwacha* (ZMK) of 100 *ngwee*. Foreign exchange reserves were US$98m. in April 2002. In Dec. 1992 the official and free market exchange rates were merged and the kwacha devalued 29%. Inflation, which was 183·3% in 1993, was down to 22·2% in 2002. Total money supply in May 2002 was 992,836m. kwacha.

Budget. The fiscal year is the calendar year. Revenues in 2001 totalled 2,509bn. kwacha and expenditures 4,212bn. kwacha. Tax revenues accounted for 97·6% of total revenue in 2001; current expenditures accounted for 61·2% of total expenditure.

Performance. Real GDP growth was 4·9% in 2001 and 3·0% in 2002. Total GDP in 2003 was US$4·3bn.

Banking and Finance. The central bank is the Bank of Zambia (*Governor*, Dr Caleb Fundanga). In 2003 there were five commercial banks, six foreign banks and four development banks. The Bank of Zambia monitors and supervises the operations of financial institutions. Banks and building societies are governed by the Banking and Financial Services Act 1994.

There is a stock exchange in Lusaka. Its market capitalization was US$301m. in 1998, a 58% fall from 1997's figure of US$705m.

ENERGY AND NATURAL RESOURCES

Environment. Zambia's carbon dioxide emissions from the consumption and flaring of fossil fuels in 2002 were the equivalent of 0·2 tonnes per capita.

Electricity. Installed capacity in 2000 was 2·3m. kW. Production in 2000 was 7·80bn. kWh; consumption per capita was 562 kWh.

Zambia is a net exporter of hydro-electric power and has huge potential for energy growth. Between Jan. and Sept. 1998 Zambian electricity exports were worth US$3·6m. compared to US$11·9m. in the same period in 1997.

Minerals. Minerals produced (in 1,000 tonnes): copper (2002), 330; cobalt (2000), 4·6; silver (1998), 8,363 kg; gold (2001), 130 kg. Zambia is well-endowed with gemstones, especially emeralds, amethysts, aquamarine, tourmaline and garnets.

Zambia Consolidated Copper Mines, privatized in 2000, is the country's largest employer. In 1990 the government freed the gemstones trade from restrictions. In 2000, 194,000 tonnes of coal were produced.

Agriculture. 70% of the population is dependent on agriculture. There were 5·26m. ha of arable land in 2001 and 20,000 ha of permanent crops. Principal agricultural products (2000 estimates, in 1,000 tonnes): sugarcane, 1,600; maize, 1,260; cassava, 1,020; millet, 71; seed cotton, 62; wheat, 60; groundnuts, 55.

Livestock (2000): cattle, 2·37m.; goats, 1·25m.; pigs, 330,000; sheep, 140,000; chickens, 29m.

Forestry. Forests covered 31·25m. ha in 2000, or 42·0% of the total land area. Timber production in 2001 was 8·05m. cu. metres, most of it for fuel.

Fisheries. Total catch, 2001, approximately 65,000 tonnes (exclusively from inland waters).

INDUSTRY

In 2001 industry accounted for 25·6% of GDP, with manufacturing contributing 11·1%. Industrial production grew by 9·2% in 2001. Zambia's economy is totally dependent upon its mining sector. Other industries include construction, foodstuffs, beverages, chemicals and textiles.

Labour. The labour force totalled 3,454,000 in 1996 (55% males). Around 74% of the economically active population in 1995 were engaged in agriculture, fisheries and forestry. Since 1992 nearly 100,000 jobs have been lost, and fewer than 10% of working-age Zambians work full-time in the formal sector.

Trade Unions. There is a Zambia Congress of Trade Unions.

INTERNATIONAL TRADE

In 2002 foreign debt was US$5,969m.

Imports and Exports. In 2001 exports were valued at US$985m. and imports at US$1,307m.

Exports declined every year from 1997 to 2000 and imports every year from 1997 to 1999, before increasing by 12% in 2000. In 2001 copper provided 55% of all exports (by value). Since 1990 non-copper exports have increased in value from US$50m. to US$450m. The main import sources in 1999 were South Africa (50·3%), Zimbabwe (9·3%), UK (5·9%) and Saudi Arabia (5·7%). Principal export markets were Japan (11·3%), UK (8·5%), India (6·6%) and Thailand (5·7%).

COMMUNICATIONS

Roads. There were, in 2001, 91,440 km of roads, including 4,222 km of highway. 157,000 passenger cars were in use in 1996 (15 per 1,000 inhabitants) and there were 81,000 trucks and vans.

Rail. In 2000 there were 1,273 km of the state-owned Zambia Railways Ltd (ZRL) and, in 1993, 891 km of the Tanzania-Zambia (Tazara) Railway, both on 1,067 mm gauge. ZRL carried 0·8m. passengers in 2000 and 3·4m. tonnes of freight in 1993. Of the 66 locomotives run by Zambia Railways in 1998, 21 were non-operational.

Civil Aviation. The main carrier, Zambia Airways, operates internal flights and in 2003 flew to Harare. Lusaka is the principal international airport. In 2000 Lusaka International handled 441,000 passengers (368,000 on international flights) and 14,700 tonnes of freight. In 1999 scheduled airline traffic of Zambian-based carriers flew 0·8m. km, carrying 42,000 passengers (36,000 on international flights).

Telecommunications. Telephone subscribers numbered 226,800 in 2002, equivalent to 21·2 per 1,000 persons. In 1995 there were direct connections to 16 countries. Telecel (2) Ltd. has been licensed to run a mobile telecommunications service in addition to the Zambia Telecommunications Company (ZAMTEL) since 1996. Mobile phone subscribers numbered 139,100 in 2002 and there were 1,000 fax machines in 1999. Internet services are provided by Zambia Communications

Systems (ZAMNET), a private company of ZAMTEL. There were 80,000 PCs in use (7·5 per 1,000 persons) and 52,400 Internet users in 2002.

Postal Services. In 1998 the Zambia Postal Service (ZAMPOST) operated 164 outlets of which 80% were loss making.

SOCIAL INSTITUTIONS

Justice. The Judiciary consists of the Supreme Court, the High Court and four classes of magistrates' courts; all have civil and criminal jurisdiction.

The Supreme Court hears and determines appeals from the High Court. Its seat is at Lusaka. The High Court exercises the powers vested in the High Court in England, subject to the High Court ordinance of Zambia. Its sessions are held where occasion requires, mostly at Lusaka and Ndola. All criminal cases tried by subordinate courts are subject to revision by the High Court.

The death penalty is authorized, the last execution having taken place in 1997. The population in penal institutions in June 2002 was 13,173 (121 per 100,000 of national population).

Religion. In 1993 the president declared Zambia to be a Christian nation, but freedom of worship is a constitutional right. In 2001 there were 3·89m. Christians. Traditional beliefs are also widespread.

Education. Schooling is for nine years. In April 2002 President Mwanawasa announced the re-introduction of universal free primary education, abolished under former President Chiluba. In 2000–01 there were 1·6m. pupils in primary schools; secondary schools, 283,000 pupils.

There are two universities, three teachers' colleges and one Christian college. In 1998 there were 4,797 university students. The University of Zambia, at Lusaka, was founded in 1965; Copperbelt University, at Kitwe, in 1987. In addition the government sponsored 150 students to be trained abroad.

The adult literacy rate in 2001 was 79·0% (85·8% among males and 72·7% among females).

In 1998–99 total expenditure on education came to 2·5% of GNP and accounted for 17·6% of total government expenditure.

Health. There were 601 physicians and 9,583 nurses in 1995, and 26 dentists, 24 pharmacists and 311 midwives in 1990. There were 42 state, 29 mission and 11 mining company hospitals in 1987, with a total of 15,846 beds and 912 health centres with 7,081 beds.

In the period 1990–98 only 38% of the population had access to safe drinking water.

CULTURE

World Heritage Sites. Zambia shares one site with Zimbabwe on the UNESCO World Heritage List: the Victoria Falls/Mosi-oa-Tunya (inscribed on the list in 1989), waterfalls on the Zambezi River.

Broadcasting. The Zambia National Broadcasting Corporation is an independent statutory body which oversees four radio networks. In 2003 there were three privately-owned radio stations: Radio Phoenix, QFM and Radio Christian Voice. In 2000 there were 1·51m. radio receivers and in 2001 there were 540,000 TV receivers (colour by PAL). Private broadcasting stations were licensed to operate in 1996. One such company was Multi Choice Kaleidoscope (2) Ltd, based in South Africa, which commenced operations in Aug. 1995. By Oct. 1996 the number of subscribers was 6,617.

Press. In 2004 there were two state-owned daily papers, *The Times of Zambia* and the *Zambia Daily Mail*, both with Sunday editions. Privately owned papers include *The Post* (daily), *The National Mirror*, *The Monitor*, *Today*, *The Star* and *Business and Leisure Times*.

Tourism. Tourism-generated earnings from the 574,000 international tourists in 2000 were US$91m. There were a further 102,000 domestic tourists of which the majority were on business. Investment pledges for the industry stood at US$92·2m.

including US$60m. pledged for reconstructing the Livingstone Intercontinental Hotel.

Festivals. The N'cwala ceremony is held in Feb. by the Ngoni people to commemorate their arrival in Zambia in 1835 and the first produce of the year. The Kuomboka, in Feb. or March, is the canoe procession of the Lozi chief and his family from the palace at Leaului down the Zambezi to Limulunga for the rainy season. The National Fishing Competition is held at Lake Tanganyika in March. Likumbi Lya Mize, held at Mize in July, celebrates the Luvale tribe's cultural heritage. The Livingstone Cultural and Arts Festival, held annually in Sept. since 1994, brings together many of Zambia's tribes and their traditional rulers. Independence Day is celebrated on 24 Oct.

DIPLOMATIC REPRESENTATIVES

Of Zambia in the United Kingdom (2 Palace Gate, London, W8 5NG)
High Commissioner: Anderson Kaseba Chibwa.

Of the United Kingdom in Zambia (5210 Independence Ave., 15101 Ridgeway, Lusaka)
High Commissioner: Timothy J. David.

Of Zambia in the USA (2419 Massachusetts Ave., NW, Washington, D.C., 20008)
Ambassador: Inonge Mbikusita-Lewanika.

Of the USA in Zambia (PO Box 31617, Lusaka)
Ambassador: Martin G. Brennan.

Of Zambia to the United Nations
Ambassador: Mwelwa Musambachime.

Of Zambia to the European Union
Ambassador: Irene Mumba Kamanga.

FURTHER READING

Chiluba, F., *Democracy: the Challenge of Change.* Lusaka, 1995

Central Statistical Office. *Monthly Digest of Statistics.*
National statistical office: Central Statistical Office, Lusaka
Website: http://www.zamstats.gov.zm

ZIMBABWE

Republic of Zimbabwe

Capital: Harare
Population projection, 2010: 13·02m.
GDP per capita, 2001: (PPP$) 2,280
HDI/world rank: 0·491/147

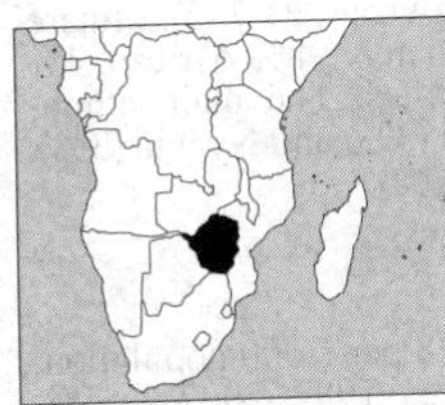

KEY HISTORICAL EVENTS

The territory which now forms Zimbabwe was administered by the British South Africa Company from the beginning of European colonization in 1890 until 1923 when it was granted the status of a self-governing colony. In 1911 it was divided into Southern and Northern Rhodesia (*see* Zambia). In 1953 Southern and Northern Rhodesia were again united, along with Nyasaland, to form the Federation of Rhodesia and Nyasaland. When this federation was dissolved on 31 Dec. 1963 Southern Rhodesia reverted to the status of a self-governing colony within the British Commonwealth.

On 11 Nov. 1965 the white-dominated government issued a unilateral declaration of independence (UDI). The Governor dismissed the prime minister, Ian Smith, and the British government reasserted formal responsibility for Rhodesia; but effective internal government was carried on by the Smith cabinet. From 1–3 Dec. Harold Wilson, the British prime minister, met Smith on board H.M.S. *Tiger* and drafted a 'Working Document' on progress towards legal independence. This statement was rejected by the Smith government. On 2 March 1970 the Smith government declared Rhodesia a republic and adopted a new constitution. On 3 March 1978 Smith signed a constitutional agreement with the internationally-backed nationalist leaders. A draft constitution was published in Jan. 1979 and was accepted by the white electorate in a referendum. Following the Commonwealth Conference held in Lusaka in Aug. 1979, elections took place in March 1980 resulting in a victory for the Zimbabwe African National Union (ZANU). Southern Rhodesia became the Republic of Zimbabwe.

Almost immediately, the question of land redistribution became a hot political issue. In colonial days, Africans had been ejected from the best farming country. All sides recognized the need for reform but were unable to agree on the means of achieving it. In 20 years, 3·5m. ha of land have been taken from white farmers, with the UK footing the £44m. bill for resettlement, but only 70,000 families have benefited. Another 400,000 ha went to senior colleagues in President Mugabe's government. The economy, meanwhile, suffered roaring inflation, unemployment and acute shortages. A policy of land occupation, with black settlers taking over white-owned farms, started in early 2000. Pressures on President Mugabe to restore the rule of law were ignored and violence escalated. Elections took place in June 2000, in which President Mugabe achieved a narrow victory. Violence continued during the months which followed, as support for Mugabe dwindled. In the lead-up to the 2002 presidential election, again won by Mugabe but by dubious means, the opposition leader, Morgan Tsvangirai, was charged with treason. The land reform plan, involving the redistribution of white-owned land to landless black Zimbabweans, continued in 2002 with large numbers of farms seized by war veterans.

TERRITORY AND POPULATION

Zimbabwe is bounded in the north by Zambia, east by Mozambique, south by South Africa and west by Botswana and the Caprivi Strip of Namibia. The area is 150,871 sq. miles (390,757 sq. km). The 1992 census population was 10,401,767 (51·2% female). 2002 census population (provisional), 11,634,663; density, 29·8 per sq. km. In 2001, 64·0% of the population were rural.

The UN gives a projected population for 2010 of 13·02m.

There are eight provinces and two cities, Harare and Bulawayo, with provincial status. Area and population (2002 census, provisional):

	Area (sq. km)	*Population*		*Area (sq. km)*	*Population*
Bulawayo	479	676,787	Manicaland	36,459	1,566,889
Harare	872	1,903,510	Mashonaland Central	28,347	998,265

	Area (sq. km)	Population		Area (sq. km)	Population
Mashonaland East	32,230	1,125,355	Matabeleland North	75,025	701,359
Mashonaland West	57,441	1,222,583	Matebeleland South	54,172	654,879
Masvingo	56,566	1,318,705	Midlands	49,166	1,466,331

Harare, the capital, had a population in 2002 of 1,444,534. Other main cities (with 2002 census populations) were Bulawayo (676,787), Chitungwiza (321,782), Mutare (153,000) and Gweru (137,000). The population is approximately 98% African, 1% mixed and Asian and there are approximately 70,000 whites. The main ethno-linguistic groups are the Shona (71%), Ndebele (16%), Ndau (3%) and Nyanja (3%). Other smaller ones include Kalanga, Manyika, Tonga and Lozi.

The official language is English.

SOCIAL STATISTICS

1995 births, 434,000; deaths, 158,000. Rates, 1995: birth, 38·8 per 1,000 population; death, 14·1 per 1,000. Annual population growth rate, 1992–2002, 1·5%. Zimbabwe's expectation of life at birth in 2001 was 35·5 years for males and 35·4 for females, down from an average of 54 years in 1993. The sharp decline is largely attributed to the huge number of people in the country with HIV. Life expectancy is less than half it would be without AIDS. Researchers predict that by 2008 life expectancy will have dropped to 31 years. Approximately 33% of all adults are infected with HIV. Infant mortality, 2001, 76 per 1,000 live births; fertility rate, 2001, 4·7 births per woman.

CLIMATE

Though situated in the tropics, conditions are remarkably temperate throughout the year because of altitude, and an inland position keeps humidity low. The warmest weather occurs in the three months before the main rainy season, which starts in Nov. and lasts till March. The cool season is from mid-May to mid-Aug. and, though days are mild and sunny, nights are chilly. Harare, Jan. 69°F (20·6°C), July 57°F (13·9°C). Annual rainfall 33" (828 mm). Bulawayo, Jan. 71°F (21·7°C), July 57°F (13·9°C). Annual rainfall 24" (594 mm). Victoria Falls, Jan. 78°F (25·6°C), July 61°F (16·1°C). Annual rainfall 28" (710 mm).

CONSTITUTION AND GOVERNMENT

The Constitution provides for a single-chamber 150-member Parliament (*House of Assembly*), universal suffrage for citizens over the age of 18, an *Executive President* (elected for a six-year term of office by Parliament), an independent judiciary enjoying security of tenure and a Declaration of Rights, derogation from certain of the provisions being permitted, within specified limits, during a state of emergency. The House of Assembly is elected for five-year terms: 120 members are elected by universal suffrage, ten are chiefs elected by all the country's tribal chiefs, 12 are appointed by the President and eight are provincial governors. The constitution can be amended by a two-thirds parliamentary majority.

In a referendum on 12–13 Feb. 2000 on the adoption of a new constitution 697,754 (54·6%) voted against and only 578,210 in favour. Under the new constitution Zimbabwe would have had an Executive President and an Executive Prime Minister sharing power, but many people felt that it would have strengthened President Mugabe's hold on power.

National Anthem. 'Ngaikomborerwe Nyika yeZimbabwe' ('Blessed be the Land of Zimbabwe'); words by Dr Solomon M. Mutswairo; tune by Fred Changundega.

RECENT ELECTIONS

At the parliamentary elections of 31 March 2005 the Zimbabwe African National Union-Patriotic Front (ZANU-PF) gained 78 of the 150 available seats (58·8% of votes cast). The Movement for Democratic Change won 41 seats (37·5%) and one independent gained a seat. 20 seats were appointed by the president and 10 went to *ex-officio* chief members. The opposition refused to accept the result, claiming that the election had been rigged.

Presidential elections were held between 9–11 March 2002. Incumbent Robert Mugabe was re-elected with 56·2% of votes cast, against 42·0% for Morgan

Tsvangirai. There were three other candidates. Observers claimed the elections failed to meet international standards for a democratic poll.

CURRENT ADMINISTRATION

Executive President: Robert G. Mugabe; b. 1924 (ZANU-PF; sworn in on 30 Dec. 1987, having previously been prime minister from 1980 to 1987; re-elected April 1990, March 1996 and again in March 2002).

In March 2005 the council comprised:

First Vice-President: Joseph Msika. *Second Vice-President:* Joyce Mujuru.

Minister of Agriculture and Rural Resettlement: Joseph Made. *Defence:* Sydney Sekeramayi. *Education, Sports and Culture:* Aeneas Chigwedere. *Energy and Power Development:* July Moyo. *Environment and Tourism:* Francis Nhema. *Foreign Affairs:* Stanislaus Mudenge. *Health and Child Welfare:* David Parirenyatwa. *Higher and Tertiary Education, and Finance and Economic Development (acting):* Herbert Murerwa. *Home Affairs:* Kembo Mohadi. *Industry and International Trade:* Samuel Mumbengegwi. *Justice, Legal and Parliamentary Affairs:* Patrick Chinamasa. *Local Government, Public Works and National Housing:* Ignatius Chombo. *Mines and Mining Development:* Amos Midzi. *Public Service, Labour and Social Welfare:* Paul Mangwana. *Rural Resources and Water Development:* Vacant. *Small and Medium Enterprise Development:* Sithembiso Nyoni. *Transport and Communications:* Christopher Mushowe. *Youth Development, Gender Affairs and Employment Creation:* Ambrose Mutinhiri. *Special Affairs Minister responsible for the Land Reform Programme:* John Nkomo. *Special Affairs in the President's Office in Charge of Anti-Corruption and the Anti-Monopolies Programme:* Didymus Mutasa. *Minister without Portfolio:* Elliot Manyika.

Government Website: http://www.zim.gov.zw

DEFENCE

In 2003 military expenditure totalled US$105m. (US$8 per capita), representing 1·7% of GDP.

Army. Strength in 2002 was estimated at 32,000. There were a further 21,800 paramilitary police and a police support unit of 2,300.

Air Force. The Air Force (ZAF) had a strength in 2002 of about 4,000 personnel. The headquarters of the ZAF and the main ZAF stations are in Harare; the second main base is at Gweru, with many secondary airfields throughout the country. There were 54 combat aircraft in 2002, including *Hunters* and F-7s (MiG-21), and 32 armed helicopters.

INTERNATIONAL RELATIONS

Zimbabwe is a member of UN, WTO, the African Union, African Development Bank, COMESA, SADC, IOM and is an ACP member state of the ACP-EU relationship. Following the controversial presidential election of March 2002 Zimbabwe was suspended from the Commonwealth's councils for a year, extended for nine months in March 2003. It withdrew from the Commonwealth in Dec. 2003.

ECONOMY

Agriculture accounted for 17·4% of GDP in 2002, industry 23·8% and services 58·8%.

Robert Mugabe's 25-year rule has left the economy in a desperate state. There is roaring inflation, heavy unemployment and shortages of food and other necessities, culminating in the authorities making an international appeal for food in July 2001. In Feb. 2000 the country ran out of gasoline because it could not pay the import bills.

Overview. The Zimbabwean economy is in crisis. The macroeconomic situation has deteriorated significantly since 1998. Real output dropped by a third between 1998 and 2003. According to the IMF, the economic crisis is attributed to loose fiscal and monetary policies, an overvalued fixed exchange rate, excessive administrative controls and regulations and chronic shortages of goods and foreign exchange. In 2003 inflation was in excess of 400% and in 2002 unemployment climbed to 60%. The effect of these policies has been magnified by collapsing health and education systems, the HIV pandemic, the fast track land reform programme and recurring droughts. The country is experiencing severe shortages in food; two-thirds of the population required food aid in 2002.

Currency. The unit of currency is the *Zimbabwe dollar* (ZWD), divided into 100 *cents*. Gold reserves were 121,000 troy oz in April 2002 and foreign exchange reserves US$72m. The currency was devalued 17% in Jan. 1994 and made fully convertible. Its value dropped by 65% in 1998. It was devalued again in Aug. 2000 by 24%. Whereas at the time of independence the Zimbabwean dollar was on a parity with the US dollar, by 2000 it was worth less than 2 cents. Inflation, which stood at 76·7% in 2001, nearly doubled to 140·0% in 2002 and in 2003 shot up to 431·7%. Total money supply was Z$176,427m. in April 2002.

Budget. Revenues in 2002 totalled Z$300,385m. and expenditures Z$351,321m. Tax revenues accounted for 93·5% of total revenue in 2002; current expenditures accounted for 91·3% of total expenditure.

Performance. Since Zimbabwe's economy began to collapse in 1998 real GDP growth has been negative every year since 1999. The economy contracted by 7·9% in 2000, 2·8% in 2001, 11·1% in 2002 and 9·3% in 2003. Zimbabwe's total GDP in 2002 was US$8·3bn.

Banking and Finance. The Reserve Bank of Zimbabwe is the central bank (established 1965; *Governor*, Gideon Gono). It acts as banker to the government and to the commercial banks, is the note-issuing authority and co-ordinates the application of the government's monetary policy. The Zimbabwe Development Bank, established in 1983 as a development finance institution, is 30·6% government-owned. In 2003 there were seven commercial and four merchant banks. In 1997 there were five registered finance houses, three of which are subsidiaries of commercial banks.

In Aug. 2003 Zimbabwe's banks ran out of banknotes as inflation reached 360%.

There is a stock exchange in Harare.

Weights and Measures. The metric system is in use but the US short ton is also used.

ENERGY AND NATURAL RESOURCES

Environment. Carbon dioxide emissions from the consumption and flaring of fossil fuels were the equivalent of 1·2 tonnes per capita in 2002.

Electricity. Installed capacity was 2·0m. kW in 2000. Production in 2000 was an estimated 7·0bn. kWh. Consumption per capita in 2000 was approximately 959 kWh.

Minerals. The total value of all minerals produced in 2001 was US$39,701·4m. 2001 production: coal, 4·06m. tonnes; asbestos, 136,000 tonnes; nickel (2002), 8,092 tonnes; gold, 18·1 tonnes. Diamond production in 1998 totalled 70,000 carats.

Agriculture. Agriculture is the largest employer, providing jobs for 25% of the workforce. In 2001 there were 3·22m. ha of arable land and 0·13m. ha of permanent crops. 117,000 ha were irrigated in 2001. There were 24,000 tractors in 2001 and 800 harvester-threshers.

A constitutional amendment providing for the compulsory purchase of land for peasant resettlement came into force in March 1992. A provision to seize white-owned farmland for peasant resettlement was part of the government's new draft constitution that was rejected in the referendum of Feb. 2000. Various deadlines were given for white farmers to abandon their property during Aug. and Sept. 2002. The government claims that 300,000 landless black Zimbabweans have been resettled on seized land.

The staple food crop is maize, but 2002 production was less than a third of that in 2000. Tobacco is the most important cash crop. Production, 2000, in 1,000 tonnes: sugarcane, 4,228; maize, 2,108; seed cotton, 327; wheat, 250; tobacco, 228; cottonseed, 199; groundnuts, 191; cassava, 175; soybeans, 144; cotton lint, 128; sorghum, 103; bananas, 80; oranges, 80. In 1996 more than 201,000 tonnes of tobacco were sold, fetching Z$5·8bn. However, the annual crop has been steadily declining since then and in 2003 was only 80,000 tonnes. More than 150,000 people work in the tobacco industry. Tobacco is a highly commercial crop, worth nearly 60 times as much as the same acreage planted with soya or maize.

Livestock (2000): cattle, 5·55m.; sheep, 530,000; pigs, 275,000; goats, 2·79m.; chickens, 16m. Dairy products (2000, in 1,000 tonnes): milk, 310; meat, 177.

Forestry. In 2000 forests covered 19·04m. ha, or 49·2% of the total land area. Timber production in 2001 was 9·11m. cu. metres.

Fisheries. Trout, prawns and bream are farmed to supplement supplies of fish caught in dams and lakes. The catch in 2001 was approximately 13,000 tonnes (all from inland waters).

INDUSTRY

Metal products account for over 20% of industrial output. Important agro-industries include food processing, textiles, furniture and other wood products.

Labour. The labour force in 1996 totalled 5,281,000 (56% males). Unemployment in Jan. 1998 was around 50%.

Trade Unions. There is a Zimbabwe Congress of Trade Unions which has 26 affiliated unions, representing more than 400,000 workers in 1998.

INTERNATIONAL TRADE

Foreign debt was US$4,066m. in 2002. Since 1 Jan. 1995 foreign companies have been permitted to remit 100% of after-tax profits. The Customs Agreement with South Africa was extended in 1982.

Imports and Exports. In 2001 exports totalled US$1,609m.; imports, US$1,779m.

In 1999 main exports were (in US$1m.): tobacco, 648·3; ferrochrome, 127·7; cotton, 109·7; sugar and honey, 102·6; nickel, 75·3. Main imports were: machinery and transport equipment, 748·7; chemicals, 357·0; petroleum, 241·7; foodstuffs, 102·9; yarn and textiles, 89·6; iron and steel, 81·4.

Main import suppliers, 1999: Southern African Customs Union (SACU), 43·2%; UK, 6·7%; Germany, 5·3%; USA, 4·8%; Japan, 4·1%. Main export destinations, 1996: SACU, 16·0%; UK, 9·6%; Germany, 7·9%; Japan, 7·1%; USA, 5·8%.

Trade Fairs. The highlight of the year is the Zimbabwe International Book Fair, held in Harare in Aug.

COMMUNICATIONS

Roads. In 1999 the road network was estimated to cover 18,338 km, of which 47·4% were paved. Number of vehicles, 1996: passenger cars, 323,000; commercial vehicles, 32,000; motorcycles, 362,000. There were 10,382 road accidents involving injury in 2000 with 1,433 fatalities.

Rail. In 1995 the National Railways of Zimbabwe had 2,759 km (1,067 mm gauge) of route ways (313 km electrified). In 1995 the railways carried 1·9m. passengers and in 2000 freight tonne-km came to 3,326m.

Civil Aviation. There are three international airports: Harare (the main airport), Bulawayo and Victoria Falls. Air Zimbabwe, the state-owned national carrier, operates domestic services and in 2003 flew to Blantyre, Johannesburg, Lilongwe, London, Lusaka, Mauritius and Nairobi. In 1999 it flew 11·5m. km, carrying 460,400 passengers (248,200 on international flights). In 1998 Harare handled 1,262,000 passengers (905,000 on international flights).

Shipping. Zimbabwe's outlets to the sea are Maputo and Beira in Mozambique, Dar es Salaam, Tanzania and the South African ports.

Telecommunications. In 2002 Zimbabwe had 640,900 telephone subscribers (55·1 for every 1,000 persons), and 600,000 PCs were in use (51·6 for every 1,000 persons). There were 353,000 mobile phone subscribers in 2002 and 500,000 Internet users. In 1996 there were 4,100 fax machines.

Postal Services. In 1998 there were 296 post offices, or one for every 42,800 persons. A total of 137m. pieces of mail were handled in 1998.

SOCIAL INSTITUTIONS

Justice. The general common law of Zimbabwe is the Roman Dutch law as it applied in the Colony of the Cape of Good Hope on 10 June 1891, as subsequently modified by statute. Provision is made by statute for the application of African customary law by all courts in appropriate cases.

The death penalty is authorized. In 2003 there were four executions.

The Supreme Court consists of the Chief Justice and at least two Supreme Court judges. It is the final court of appeal. It exercises appellate jurisdiction in appeals from the High Court and other courts and tribunals; its only original jurisdiction is that conferred on it by the Constitution to enforce the protective provisions of the Declaration of Rights. The Court's permanent seat is in Harare but it also sits regularly in Bulawayo.

The High Court is also headed by the Chief Justice, supported by the Judge President and an appropriate number of High Court judges. It has full original jurisdiction, in both Civil and Criminal cases, over all persons and all matters in Zimbabwe. The Judge President is in charge of the Court, subject to the directions of the Chief Justice. The Court has permanent seats in both Harare and Bulawayo and sittings are held three times a year in three other principal towns.

Regional courts, established in Harare and Bulawayo but also holding sittings in other centres, exercise a solely criminal jurisdiction which is intermediate between that of the High Court and the Magistrates' courts. Magistrates' courts, established in 20 centres throughout the country, and staffed by full-time professional magistrates, exercise both civil and criminal jurisdiction.

Primary courts consist of village courts and community courts. Village courts are presided over by officers selected for the purpose from the local population, sitting with two assessors. They deal with certain classes of civil cases only and have jurisdiction only where African customary law is applicable. Community courts are presided over by presiding officers in full-time public service who may be assisted by assessors. They have jurisdiction in all civil cases determinable by African customary law and also deal with appeals from village courts. They also have limited criminal jurisdiction in respect of petty offences.

The population in penal institutions in 2002 was approximately 21,000 (160 per 100,000 of national population).

Religion. In 2001, 4·58m. persons were African Christians, 1·40m. Protestants, 1·09m. Roman Catholics and 870,000 followers of other religions. There were also 3·43m. followers of animist beliefs in 2001.

Education. Education is compulsory. 'Manageable' school fees were introduced in 1991; primary education had hitherto been free to all. All instruction is given in English. There are more than 40 private schools. In 2000–01 there were 2,460,669 pupils at primary schools (64,440 teachers) and 844,183 pupils at secondary schools (34,162 teachers). In 2001 the adult literacy rate was 89·3% (93·3% among males and 85·5% among females). Both the overall rate and the rate for males are the highest in Africa. As the crisis in Zimbabwe worsens, so primary school attendance has been declining, from 95% among boys and 90% among girls in 2000 to 67% among boys and 63% among girls in 2003.

There are ten teachers' training colleges, eight of which are in association with the University of Zimbabwe. In addition, there are four special training centres for teacher trainees in the Zimbabwe Integrated National Teacher Education Course. In 1990 there were 17,873 students enrolled at teachers' training colleges, 1,003 students at agricultural colleges and 20,943 students at technical colleges. There are four universities and ten technical colleges.

Health. There were 1,378 government hospitals in 1993. All mission health institutions get 100% government grants-in-aid for recurrent expenditure. In 1995 there were 1,522 physicians, 142 dentists, 14,095 nurses and 3,078 midwives. It is estimated that one in three adults are HIV infected.

Welfare. It is a statutory responsibility of the government in many areas to provide: processing and administration of war pensions and old age pensions; protection of children; administration of remand, probation and correctional institutions; registration and supervision of welfare organizations.

CULTURE

World Heritage Sites. Zimbabwe has four sites on the UNESCO World Heritage List: Mana Pools National Park, Sapi and Chewore Safari Areas (inscribed on the list in 1984); the Great Zimbabwe National Monument (1986); the Khambi Ruins National Monument (1986); and Matobo Hills (2003). It also shares the Victoria Falls with Zambia.

Broadcasting. Zimbabwe Broadcasting Corporation is a statutory body broadcasting a general service in English, Shona, Ndebele, Nyanja, Tonga and Kalanga. There are three national semi-commercial services—Radio 1, 2 and 3, in English, Shona and Ndebele. Radio 4 transmits formal and informal educational programmes. Zimbabwe Television broadcasts on two channels (colour by PAL). In 2001 there were 640,000 TV sets and in 1997 there were 1·14m. radio sets in use.

Press. In 1996 there were two daily newspapers with a combined circulation of 209,000, giving a rate of 19 per 1,000 inhabitants. In Jan. 2002 parliament passed an Access to Information Bill restricting press freedom, making it an offence to report from Zimbabwe unless registered by a state-appointed commission. In Sept. 2003 the independent *Daily News* was shut down for contraventions of the new press law. Zimbabwe's High Court ordered the government to allow its re-opening but the order was ignored.

Tourism. There were 1,868,000 foreign tourists in 2000; spending by tourists totalled US$125m.

Festivals. Of particular importance are Amakhosi Inxusa Festival, a festival of soul, dance and theatre in Bulawayo (March) and the Zimbabwe National Jazz Festival in Harare (Sept.–Nov.).

Libraries. There is a City Library in Harare.

Theatre and Opera. Harare has a Repertory Theatre.

Museums and Galleries. The main attractions are the Queen Victoria Museum and the National Gallery of Zimbabwe.

DIPLOMATIC REPRESENTATIVES

Of Zimbabwe in the United Kingdom (Zimbabwe House, 429 Strand, London, WC2R 0JR)
High Commissioner: Simbarashe Simbanenduku Mumbengegwi.

Of the United Kingdom in Zimbabwe (7th Floor, Corner House, Samora Machel Ave/Leopold Takawira Street, Harare, P.O. Box 4490)
High Commissioner: Sir Brian Donnelly, KBE, CMG.

Of Zimbabwe in the USA (1608 New Hampshire Ave., NW, Washington, D.C., 20009)
Ambassador: Simbi Veke Mubako.

Of the USA in Zimbabwe (172 Herbert Chitepo Ave., Harare)
Ambassador: Christopher W. Dell.

Of Zimbabwe to the United Nations
Ambassador: Boniface Guwa Chidyausiku.

Of Zimbabwe to the European Union
Ambassador: Gift Punungwe.

FURTHER READING

Central Statistical Office. *Monthly Digest of Statistics.*

Hatchard, J., *Individual Freedoms and State Security in the African Context: the Case of Zimbabwe.* Ohio Univ. Press, 1993

Potts, D., *Zimbabwe.* [Bibliography] 2nd ed. ABC-Clio, Oxford and Santa Barbara (CA), 1993

Skålnes, T., *The Politics of Economic Reform in Zimbabwe: Continuity and Change in Development.* London, 1995

Weiss, R., *Zimbabwe and the New Elite.* London, 1994

National statistical office: Central Statistical Office, POB 8063, Causeway, Harare.

ABBREVIATIONS

ACP	African Caribbean Pacific
Adm.	Admiral
Adv.	Advocate
a.i.	ad interim
b.	born
bbls.	barrels
bd	board
bn.	billion (one thousand million)
Brig.	Brigadier
bu.	bushel
Cdr	Commander
CFA	Communauté Financière Africaine
CFP	Comptoirs Français du Pacifique
c.i.f.	cost, insurance, freight
C.-in-C.	Commander-in-Chief
CIS	Commonwealth of Independent States
cu.	cubic
CUP	Cambridge University Press
cwt	hundredweight
D.	Democratic Party
DWT	dead weight tonnes
ECOWAS	Economic Community of West African States
EEA	European Economic Area
EEZ	Exclusive Economic Zone
EMS	European Monetary System
EMU	European Monetary Union
ERM	Exchange Rate Mechanism
f.o.b.	free on board
FDI	foreign direct investment
ft	foot/feet
FTE	full-time equivalent
G8 Group	Canada, France, Germany, Italy, Japan, UK, USA, Russia
GDP	gross domestic product
Gen.	General
GNI	gross national income
GNP	gross national product
GRT	gross registered tonnes
GW	gigawatt
GWh	gigawatt hours
ha	hectare(s)
HDI	Human Development Index
ind.	independent(s)
ICT	information and communication technology
ISO	International Organization for Standardization (domain names)
K	kindergarten
kg	kilogramme(s)
kl	kilolitre(s)

km	kilometre(s)
kW	kilowatt
kWh	kilowatt hours
lat.	latitude
lb	pound(s) (weight)
Lieut.	Lieutenant
long.	longitude
m.	million
Maj.	Major
MW	megawatt
MWh	megawatt hours
n.e.c.	not elsewhere classified
NRT	net registered tonnes
NTSC	National Television System Committee (525 lines 60 fields)
OUP	Oxford University Press
oz	ounce(s)
PAL	Phased Alternate Line (625 lines 50 fields 4·43 MHz sub-carrier)
PAL M	Phased Alternate Line (525 lines 60 PAL 3·58 MHz sub-carrier)
PAL N	Phased Alternate Line (625 lines 50 PAL 3·58 MHz sub-carrier)
PAYE	Pay-As-You-Earn
PPP	Purchasing Power Parity
R.	Republican Party
Rt Hon.	Right Honourable
SADC	Southern African Development Community
SDR	Special Drawing Rights
SECAM H	Sequential Couleur avec Mémoire (625 lines 50 fields Horizontal)
SECAM V	Sequential Couleur avec Mémoire (625 lines 50 fields Vertical)
sq.	square
SSI	Supplemental Security Income
TAFE	technical and further education
TEU	twenty-foot equivalent units
trn.	trillion (one million million)
TV	television
Univ.	University
VAT	value-added tax
v.f.d	value for duty